YEARBOOK OF THE UNITED NATIONS 2003

Volume 57

Yearbook of the United Nations, 2003

Volume 57   Sales No. E.05.I.1

Prepared by the Yearbook Section of the Department of Public Information, United Nations, New York. Although the *Yearbook* is based on official sources, it is not an official record.

Chief Editor: Kathryn Gordon

Senior Editors: Elizabeth Baldwin-Penn, Melody C. Pfeiffer

Editors/Writers: Barbara Christiani, Peter Jackson, Federigo Magherini, John R. Sebesta, Jullyette Ukabiala

Contributing Editors/Writers: Luisa Balacco, Juanita B. Phelan, Nancy Seufert-Barr

Senior Copy Editor: Alison M. Koppelman

Production Coordinator: Rodney Pascual

Editorial Assistants: Jingbo Huang, Lawri Moore, Margaret O'Donnell

Senior Typesetter: Sunita Chabra

Indexer: David Golante

Jacket design by Martin Samaan

YEARBOOK
OF THE UNITED NATIONS 2003

Volume 57

Department of Public Information
United Nations, New York

COPYRIGHT © 2005 UNITED NATIONS
Yearbook of the United Nations, 2003
Vol. 57
ISBN: 92-1-100905-7
ISSN: 0082-8521

UNITED NATIONS PUBLICATIONS
SALES NO. E.05.I.1

Printed in the United States of America

FOREWORD

The year 2003 was one of the most challenging in the history of the United Nations. It began with divisions in the Security Council on how to resolve the Iraq crisis. Despite intense diplomatic efforts, some Member States took the position that the use of force was necessary. The war in Iraq that followed severely tested long-standing principles of collective security and the very resilience of the Organization.

United Nations personnel returned to Iraq in June to provide humanitarian and reconstruction assistance, and to help Iraqis establish post-conflict governance institutions and arrangements. But on 19 August, a savage terrorist attack on the Organization's headquarters in Baghdad resulted in the death of my Special Representative, Sergio Vieira de Mello, and 21 others, and the wounding of many more. The loss of such dear friends and courageous colleagues was a terrible blow to the United Nations, personally and professionally. It also raised fundamental questions about how best to protect our personnel and pursue our work in volatile situations where the United Nations is needed but may also become a target. The Organization continues to mourn our losses and wrestle with these complex questions.

In addition to the controversies and tragedies surrounding the Iraq crisis, many other challenges cast a shadow over the world in 2003, including international terrorism, the risks associated with weapons of mass destruction, a surge in infectious disease—epitomized by the effects of AIDS in Africa—and the long-standing blights of extreme poverty, hunger, environmental degradation, human rights violations and humanitarian emergencies. I told the General Assembly in September that the international system had reached a "fork in the road" in its efforts to meet these challenges. It was against that backdrop of acute concern that, in November, I established a High-level Panel on Threats, Challenges and Change and asked it to assess current threats to global security, and then to make bold yet practicable recommendations for improving the world's ability to face those threats, and for reforming the United Nations itself.

Through its coverage of a difficult year, this volume of the *Yearbook of the United Nations* shows that the achievement of the purposes of our Organization requires a shared consensus about its fundamental goals. While Member States need not agree on all issues, they should, in calculating their national interests, give due weight to the value and importance of a just and stable world order.

KOFI A. ANNAN

Secretary-General of the United Nations
New York, May 2005

Contents

FOREWORD by SECRETARY-GENERAL KOFI A. ANNAN — v

ABOUT THE 2003 EDITION OF THE *YEARBOOK* — xvi

ABBREVIATIONS COMMONLY USED IN THE *YEARBOOK* — xvii

EXPLANATORY NOTE ON DOCUMENTS — xviii

REPORT OF THE SECRETARY-GENERAL ON THE WORK OF THE ORGANIZATION — 3

Part One: *Political and security questions*

I. INTERNATIONAL PEACE AND SECURITY — 47

PROMOTION OF INTERNATIONAL PEACE AND SECURITY, 48: Follow-up to Millennium Summit (2000), 48; Conflict prevention, 49; Peacemaking and peace-building, 57; Political and peace-building missions in 2003, 60; Roster of 2003 political and peace-building offices, 61. THREATS TO INTERNATIONAL PEACE AND SECURITY, 63: International terrorism, 63. PEACEKEEPING OPERATIONS, 71: General aspects of UN peacekeeping, 71; Comprehensive review of peacekeeping, 78; Operations in 2003, 79; Roster of 2003 operations, 80; Financial and administrative aspects of peacekeeping operations, 82. OTHER PEACEKEEPING MATTERS, 99.

II. AFRICA — 102

PROMOTION OF PEACE IN AFRICA, 104. CENTRAL AFRICA AND GREAT LAKES REGION, 107: Democratic Republic of the Congo, 113; Burundi, 145; Rwanda, 154; Central African Republic, 155. WEST AFRICA, 159: Côte d'Ivoire, 165; Liberia, 184; Sierra Leone, 210; Guinea-Bissau, 223. HORN OF AFRICA, 229: Eritrea-Ethiopia, 230; Somalia, 241; Sudan, 256. NORTH AFRICA, 257: Western Sahara, 257; Libyan Arab Jamahiriya, 267. SOUTHERN AFRICA, 269: Angola, 269. OTHER QUESTIONS, 271: Cooperation between the AU and the UN system, 271.

III. AMERICAS — 273

CENTRAL AMERICA, 273: Guatemala, 278. HAITI, 284: Financing of missions, 285. OTHER QUESTIONS, 285: Colombia, 285; Cuba–United States, 285; El Salvador–Honduras, 286.

IV. **ASIAAND THE PACIFIC** 288

AFGHANISTAN, 289: Situation in Afghanistan, 290; Security Council mission, 302; Sanctions, 311. IRAQ, 315: UN Monitoring, Verification and Inspection Commission and IAEA activities, 316; WMD allegations, 322; Military conflict and occupation, 333. IRAQ-KUWAIT, 356: Arms and related sanctions, 361; Oil-for-food programme, 362; UN Compensation Commission and Fund, 369; Other issues, 370. TIMOR-LESTE, 370: Financing of UN operations, 381. OTHER MATTERS, 385: Cambodia, 385; India-Pakistan, 391; Korea question, 391; Papua New Guinea, 392; Solomon Islands, 396; Tajikistan, 396; Turkey, 396; United Arab Emirates-Iran, 396.

V. **EUROPE AND THE MEDITERRANEAN** 397

THE FORMER YUGOSLAVIA, 398: UN operations, 398. BOSNIA AND HERZEGOVINA, 399: Implementation of Peace Agreement, 399; European Union Police Mission in Bosnia and Herzegovina, 409. SERBIA AND MONTENEGRO, 411: Situation in Kosovo, 412. FORMER YUGOSLAV REPUBLIC OF MACEDONIA, 430. GEORGIA, 430: UN Observer Mission in Georgia, 430; Georgia-Russian Federation relations, 443. ARMENIA-AZERBAIJAN, 443. CYPRUS, 445: Good offices mission, 446; UNFICYP, 451. OTHER ISSUES, 455: Strengthening of security and cooperation in the Mediterranean, 455; Stability and development in South-Eastern Europe, 456.

VI. **MIDDLE EAST** 457

PEACE PROCESS, 458: Overall situation, 458; Occupied Palestinian Territory, 459. ISSUES RELATED TO PALESTINE, 496: General aspects, 496; Assistance to Palestinians, 503; UNRWA, 506. PEACEKEEPING OPERATIONS, 516: Lebanon, 516; Syrian Arab Republic, 522.

VII. **DISARMAMENT** 529

UN ROLE IN DISARMAMENT, 529: UN machinery, 529. NUCLEAR DISARMAMENT, 532: Conference on Disarmament, 532; Disarmament Commission, 535; START and other bilateral agreements and unilateral measures, 535; Comprehensive Nuclear-Test-Ban Treaty, 547; Non-Proliferation Treaty, 548; IAEA safeguards, 549; Prohibition of the use of nuclear weapons, 551; Advisory opinion of the International Court of Justice, 552; Radioactive waste, 553; Nuclear-weapon-free zones, 554. BACTERIOLOGICAL (BIOLOGICAL) AND CHEMICAL WEAPONS, 558: Bacteriological (biological) weapons, 558; Chemical weapons, 560. CONVENTIONAL WEAPONS, 562: Programme of Action on illicit trade in small arms, 562; Convention on excessively injurious conventional weapons and Protocols, 565; Practical disarmament, 567; Transparency, 568; Anti-personnel mines, 571. REGIONAL AND OTHER APPROACHES TO DISARMAMENT, 573: Africa, 573; Asia and the Pacific, 575; Europe, 575; Latin America, 577. OTHER DISARMAMENT ISSUES, 579: Terrorism, 579; New types of weapons of mass destruction, 581;

Multilateralism in disarmament and non-proliferation, 581; Prevention of an arms race in outer space, 582; Disarmament and development, 584; Arms limitation and disarmament agreements, 584. STUDIES, INFORMATION AND TRAINING, 585.

VIII. OTHER POLITICAL AND SECURITY QUESTIONS ... 592

GENERAL ASPECTS OF INTERNATIONAL SECURITY, 592: Support for democracies, 592. REGIONAL ASPECTS OF INTERNATIONAL PEACE AND SECURITY, 595: South Atlantic, 595; Indian Ocean, 596. DECOLONIZATION, 597: Decade for the Eradication of Colonialism, 598; Puerto Rico, 608; Territories under review, 609. INFORMATION, 622: UN public information, 622; Information and communications in the context of international security, 639; Role of science and technology in the context of international security and disarmament, 640. PEACEFUL USES OF OUTER SPACE, 641: Implementation of UNISPACE III recommendations, 641; Scientific and Technical Subcommittee, 642; Legal Subcommittee, 645. EFFECTS OF ATOMIC RADIATION, 650.

Part Two: *Human Rights*

I. PROMOTION OF HUMAN RIGHTS ... 655

UN MACHINERY, 655: Commission on Human Rights, 655; Subcommission on the Promotion and Protection of Human Rights, 656; Office of the High Commissioner for Human Rights, 657; Strengthening action to promote human rights, 660. HUMAN RIGHTS INSTRUMENTS, 667: General aspects, 667; Covenant on Civil and Political Rights and Optional Protocols, 669; Covenant on Economic, Social and Cultural Rights, 670; Convention against racial discrimination, 673; Convention against torture, 674; Convention on elimination of discrimination against women and Optional Protocol, 675; Convention on the Rights of the Child, 675; Convention on migrant workers, 676; Convention on genocide, 677. OTHER ACTIVITIES, 677: Follow-up to 1993 World Conference, 677; Advisory services and technical cooperation, 678; Public information and human rights education, 686; Children and a culture of peace, 689; National institutions and regional arrangements, 691; Cooperation with human rights bodies, 694.

II. PROTECTION OF HUMAN RIGHTS ... 695

RACISM AND RACIAL DISCRIMINATION, 695: Third Decade against racism, 695. OTHER FORMS OF INTOLERANCE, 710: Cultural prejudice, 710; Discrimination against minorities, 712; Religious intolerance, 717. CIVIL AND POLITICAL RIGHTS, 720: Right to self-determination, 720; Administration of justice, 724; Right to democracy, 736; Other issues, 739. ECONOMIC, SOCIAL AND CULTURAL RIGHTS, 752: Right to development, 752; Corruption, 764; Extreme poverty, 764; Right to food, 766; Right to adequate housing, 768; Right to education, 770; Environmental and scientific concerns, 771; Right to physical and mental health, 772; Slavery and related issues, 776; Vulnerable groups, 777.

III. HUMAN RIGHTS VIOLATIONS — 808

GENERAL ASPECTS, 808. AFRICA, 808: Burundi, 808; Democratic Republic of the Congo, 809; Liberia, 814; Sierra Leone, 814; Somalia, 814; Sudan, 814; Zimbabwe, 814. AMERICAS, 814: Colombia, 814; Cuba, 815; Haiti, 816. ASIA AND THE PACIFIC, 816: Afghanistan, 816; Cambodia, 816; Democratic People's Republic of Korea, 816; Iran, 817; Iraq, 818; Myanmar, 819; Timor-Leste, 823; Turkmenistan, 823. EUROPE, 824: Belarus, 824; Cyprus, 824; Russian Federation, 824. MIDDLE EAST, 825: Lebanon, 825; Territories occupied by Israel, 825.

Part Three: *Economic and social questions*

I. DEVELOPMENT POLICY AND INTERNATIONAL ECONOMIC COOPERATION — 831

INTERNATIONAL ECONOMIC RELATIONS, 832: Development and international economic cooperation, 832; Sustainable development, 838; Eradication of poverty, 848; Science and technology for development, 854. ECONOMIC AND SOCIAL TRENDS, 862. DEVELOPMENT POLICY AND PUBLIC ADMINISTRATION, 864: Committee for Development Policy, 864; Public administration, 865. DEVELOPING COUNTRIES AND TRANSITION ECONOMIES, 867: Least developed countries, 867; Island developing countries, 871; Landlocked developing countries, 875.

II. OPERATIONAL ACTIVITIES FOR DEVELOPMENT — 879

SYSTEM-WIDE ACTIVITIES, 879. TECHNICAL COOPERATION THROUGH UNDP, 890: UNDP/UNFPA Executive Board, 891; UNDP operational activities, 893; Programme planning and management, 897; Financing, 902. OTHER TECHNICAL COOPERATION, 904: UN activities, 904; UN Fund for International Partnerships, 905; UN Office for Project Services, 906; UN Volunteers, 910; Economic and technical cooperation among developing countries, 910; UN Capital Development Fund, 914.

III. HUMANITARIAN AND SPECIAL ECONOMIC ASSISTANCE — 915

HUMANITARIAN ASSISTANCE, 915: Coordination, 915; Resource mobilization, 922; White Helmets, 922; Mine clearance, 923; Humanitarian activities, 927. SPECIAL ECONOMIC ASSISTANCE, 937: African economic recovery and development, 937; Other economic assistance, 950. DISASTER RELIEF, 954: International cooperation, 955; International Strategy for Disaster Reduction, 957; Disaster assistance, 961.

IV.	**INTERNATIONAL TRADE, FINANCE AND TRANSPORT**	965

INTERNATIONAL TRADE, 965: Trade policy, 972; Trade promotion and facilitation, 974; Commodities, 977. FINANCE, 980: Financial policy, 980; Financing for development, 987; Investment, technology and related financial issues, 990. TRANSPORT, 993: Maritime transport, 993; Transport of dangerous goods, 993. UNCTAD INSTITUTIONAL AND ORGANIZATIONAL QUESTIONS, 995: Preparations for UNCTAD XI, 998; UNCTAD Secretary-General, 998.

V.	**REGIONAL ECONOMIC AND SOCIAL ACTIVITIES**	999

REGIONAL COOPERATION, 999. AFRICA, 1001: Economic trends, 1002; Activities in 2003, 1002. ASIA AND THE PACIFIC, 1007: Economic trends, 1007; Activities in 2003, 1008; Programme and organizational questions, 1014. EUROPE, 1016: Economic trends, 1016; Activities in 2003, 1017; Operational activities, 1020. LATIN AMERICA AND THE CARIBBEAN, 1020: Economic trends, 1020; Activities in 2003, 1020. WESTERN ASIA, 1024: Economic and social trends, 1025; Activities in 2003, 1026; Programme and organizational questions, 1028.

VI.	**ENERGY, NATURAL RESOURCES AND CARTOGRAPHY**	1030

ENERGY AND NATURAL RESOURCES, 1030: Energy, 1030; Natural resources, 1033. CARTOGRAPHY, 1035.

VII.	**ENVIRONMENT AND HUMAN SETTLEMENTS**	1036

ENVIRONMENT, 1036: UN Environment Programme, 1036; International conventions and mechanisms, 1048; Environmental activities, 1055. HUMAN SETTLEMENTS, 1074: Follow-up to the 1996 UN Conference on Human Settlements (Habitat II) and the 2001 General Assembly special session, 1074; UN Human Settlements Programme, 1078; UN Habitat and Human Settlements Foundation, 1084.

VIII.	**POPULATION**	1085

FOLLOW-UP TO THE 1994 CONFERENCE ON POPULATION AND DEVELOPMENT, 1085. UN POPULATION FUND, 1089. OTHER POPULATION ACTIVITIES, 1094.

IX.	**SOCIAL POLICY, CRIME PREVENTION AND HUMAN RESOURCES DEVELOPMENT**	1096

SOCIAL POLICY AND CULTURAL ISSUES, 1096: Social development, 1096; Persons with disabilities, 1105; Cultural development, 1109. CRIME PREVENTION AND CRIMINAL JUSTICE, 1116: Commission on Crime Prevention and Criminal Justice, 1116; Crime prevention programme, 1119; Transnational crime, 1125; Corruption, 1126; Strategies for crime prevention, 1149; UN standards and norms, 1155. HUMAN RESOURCES DEVELOPMENT, 1158: UN research and training institutes, 1160.

X.	WOMEN	1164

FOLLOW-UP TO THE FOURTH WORLD CONFERENCE ON WOMEN AND BEIJING+5, 1164. UN MACHINERY, 1190: Convention on the elimination of discrimination against women, 1190; Commission on the Status of Women, 1192; UN Development Fund for Women (UNIFEM), 1193; International Research and Training Institute (INSTRAW), 1194.

XI.	CHILDREN, YOUTH AND AGEING PERSONS	1202

CHILDREN, 1202: Follow-up to the 2002 General Assembly special session on children, 1202; United Nations Children's Fund, 1203. YOUTH, 1214. AGEING PERSONS, 1218: Follow-up to the Second World Assembly on Ageing (2002), 1218.

XII.	REFUGEES AND DISPLACED PERSONS	1222

OFFICE OF THE UNITED NATIONS HIGH COMMISSIONER FOR REFUGEES, 1222: Programme policy, 1222; Financial and administrative questions, 1227. REFUGEE PROTECTION AND ASSISTANCE, 1229: Protection issues, 1229; Assistance measures, 1230; Regional activities, 1232.

XIII.	HEALTH, FOOD AND NUTRITION	1243

HEALTH, 1243: AIDS prevention and control, 1243; Tobacco, 1251; Roll Back Malaria initiative, 1251; Access to medication, 1253; Follow-up to Millennium Summit, 1255; Road safety, 1257. FOOD AND AGRICULTURE, 1259: Food aid, 1259; Food security, 1260. NUTRITION, 1261.

XIV.	INTERNATIONAL DRUG CONTROL	1262

FOLLOW-UP TO THE TWENTIETH SPECIAL SESSION, 1262. CONVENTIONS, 1267: International Narcotics Control Board, 1270. WORLD DRUG SITUATION, 1271. UN ACTION TO COMBAT DRUG ABUSE, 1279: UN Office on Drugs and Crime, 1279; Commission on Narcotic Drugs, 1282; Strengthening UN mechanisms, 1288.

XV.	STATISTICS	1289

WORK OF STATISTICAL COMMISSION, 1289: Economic statistics, 1290; Demographic and social statistics, 1293; Other statistical activities, 1294.

Part Four: *Legal questions*

I.	INTERNATIONAL COURT OF JUSTICE	1299

Judicial work of the Court, 1299; Other questions, 1309.

II.	**INTERNATIONAL TRIBUNALS**	1310

INTERNATIONAL TRIBUNAL FOR THE FORMER YUGOSLAVIA, 1310: The Chambers, 1310; Ad litem judges, 1315; Office of the Prosecutor, 1316; The Registry, 1317; Financing, 1317. INTERNATIONAL TRIBUNAL FOR RWANDA, 1320: The Chambers, 1320; Office of the Prosecutor, 1325; The Registry, 1325; Financing, 1326. FUNCTIONING OF THE TRIBUNALS, 1329: Office of the Prosecutor, 1329; OIOS report, 1331.

III.	**LEGAL ASPECTS OF INTERNATIONAL POLITICAL RELATIONS**	1332

ESTABLISHMENT OF THE INTERNATIONAL CRIMINAL COURT, 1332. INTERNATIONAL LAW COMMISSION, 1334: International liability, 1336; Unilateral acts of States, 1336; Responsibility of international organizations, 1336; Fragmentation of international law, 1336; Shared natural resources, 1337. INTERNATIONAL STATE RELATIONS AND INTERNATIONAL LAW, 1337: Jurisdictional immunities of States and their property, 1337; International terrorism, 1338; Safety and security of United Nations and associated personnel, 1340. DIPLOMATIC RELATIONS, 1343: Protection of diplomatic and consular missions and representatives, 1343. TREATIES AND AGREEMENTS, 1343.

IV.	**LAW OF THE SEA**	1346

UN CONVENTION ON THE LAW OF THE SEA, 1346: Institutions created by the Convention, 1352; Other developments related to the Convention, 1354; Division for Ocean Affairs and the Law of the Sea, 1362.

V.	**OTHER LEGAL QUESTIONS**	1363

INTERNATIONAL ORGANIZATIONS AND INTERNATIONAL LAW, 1363: Strengthening the role of the United Nations, 1363; UN Programme for the teaching and study of international law, 1369; Host country relations, 1371. INTERNATIONAL LAW, 1374: International bioethics law, 1374. INTERNATIONAL ECONOMIC LAW, 1374: International trade law, 1374.

Part Five: *Institutional, administrative and budgetary questions*

I.	**STRENGTHENING AND RESTRUCTURING OF THE UNITED NATIONS SYSTEM**	1383

PROGRAMME OF REFORM, 1383: General aspects, 1383; Agenda for change, 1384; Implementation of the Millennium Declaration, 1384; Managerial reform and oversight, 1386. INTERGOVERNMENTAL MACHINERY, 1388.

II. UNITED NATIONS FINANCING AND PROGRAMMING — 1393

FINANCIAL SITUATION, 1393. UN BUDGET, 1393: Reforming the process, 1393; Budget for 2002-2003, 1396; Budget for 2004-2005, 1399. CONTRIBUTIONS, 1422: Assessments, 1423. ACCOUNTS AND AUDITING, 1428: Administrative and budgetary coordination, 1429. PROGRAMME PLANNING, 1429: Medium-term plan, 1429; Programme performance, 1430.

III. UNITED NATIONS STAFF — 1431

CONDITIONS OF SERVICE, 1431: International Civil Service Commission, 1431; Remuneration issues, 1433; Other remuneration issues, 1435. OTHER STAFF MATTERS, 1439: Personnel policies, 1439; Joint Staff Pension Fund, 1457; Travel-related matters, 1458; Administration of justice, 1459.

IV. INSTITUTIONAL AND ADMINISTRATIVE MATTERS — 1462

INSTITUTIONAL MACHINERY, 1462: General Assembly, 1462; Security Council, 1465; Economic and Social Council, 1465. COORDINATION, MONITORING AND COOPERATION, 1466: Institutional mechanisms, 1466; Other coordination matters, 1467. THE UN AND OTHER ORGANIZATIONS, 1474: Requests for conversion to UN specialized agency, 1474; Observer status, 1479; Participation of organizations in UN work, 1480. CONFERENCES AND MEETINGS, 1481. UN INFORMATION SYSTEMS, 1492. OTHER MATTERS, 1495: Common services, 1495; UN premises and property, 1500; Security, 1501.

Part Six: *Intergovernmental organizations related to the United Nations*

I.	INTERNATIONAL ATOMIC ENERGY AGENCY (IAEA)	1505
II.	INTERNATIONAL LABOUR ORGANIZATION (ILO)	1508
III.	FOOD AND AGRICULTURE ORGANIZATION OF THE UNITED NATIONS (FAO)	1510
IV.	UNITED NATIONS EDUCATIONAL, SCIENTIFIC AND CULTURAL ORGANIZATION (UNESCO)	1512
V.	WORLD HEALTH ORGANIZATION (WHO)	1514
VI.	WORLD BANK (IBRD AND IDA)	1516
VII.	INTERNATIONAL FINANCE CORPORATION (IFC)	1518
VIII.	INTERNATIONAL MONETARY FUND (IMF)	1520
IX.	INTERNATIONAL CIVIL AVIATION ORGANIZATION (ICAO)	1522

X.	UNIVERSAL POSTAL UNION (UPU)	1524
XI.	INTERNATIONAL TELECOMMUNICATION UNION (ITU)	1525
XII.	WORLD METEOROLOGICAL ORGANIZATION (WMO)	1527
XIII.	INTERNATIONAL MARITIME ORGANIZATION (IMO)	1529
XIV.	WORLD INTELLECTUAL PROPERTY ORGANIZATION (WIPO)	1530
XV.	INTERNATIONAL FUND FOR AGRICULTURAL DEVELOPMENT (IFAD)	1532
XVI.	UNITED NATIONS INDUSTRIAL DEVELOPMENT ORGANIZATION (UNIDO)	1533
XVII.	WORLD TRADE ORGANIZATION (WTO)	1535

Appendices

I.	ROSTER OF THE UNITED NATIONS	1539
II.	CHARTER OF THE UNITED NATIONS AND STATUTE OF THE INTERNATIONAL COURT OF JUSTICE	1541
III.	STRUCTURE OF THE UNITED NATIONS	1556
IV.	AGENDAS OF UNITED NATIONS PRINCIPAL ORGANS IN 2003	1570
V.	UNITED NATIONS INFORMATION CENTRES AND SERVICES	1581

Indexes

USING THE SUBJECT INDEX	1586
SUBJECT INDEX	1587
INDEX OF RESOLUTIONS AND DECISIONS	1625
INDEX OF 2003 SECURITY COUNCIL PRESIDENTIAL STATEMENTS	1629
HOW TO OBTAIN VOLUMES OF THE *YEARBOOK*	1630

About the 2003 edition of the *Yearbook*

This volume of the *YEARBOOK OF THE UNITED NATIONS* continues the tradition of providing the most comprehensive coverage of the activities of the United Nations. It is an indispensable reference tool for the research community, diplomats, government officials and the general public seeking readily available information on the UN system and its related organizations.

Efforts by the Department of Public Information to achieve a more timely publication have resulted in having to rely on provisional documentation and other materials to prepare the relevant articles. Largely, Security Council resolutions and presidential statements, Economic and Social Council resolutions and some other texts in the present volume are provisional.

Structure and scope of articles

The *Yearbook* is subject-oriented and divided into six parts covering political and security questions; human rights issues; economic and social questions; legal questions; institutional, administrative and budgetary questions; and intergovernmental organizations related to the United Nations. Chapters and topical headings present summaries of pertinent UN activities, including those of intergovernmental and expert bodies, major reports, Secretariat activities and, in selected cases, the views of States in written communications.

Activities of United Nations bodies. All resolutions, decisions and other major activities of the principal organs and, on a selective basis, those of subsidiary bodies are either reproduced or summarized in the appropriate chapter. The texts of all resolutions and decisions of substantive nature adopted in 2003 by the General Assembly, the Security Council and the Economic and Social Council are reproduced or summarized under the relevant topic. These texts are preceded by procedural details giving date of adoption, meeting number and vote totals (in favour–against–abstaining) if any; and an indication of their approval by a sessional or subsidiary body prior to final adoption. The texts are followed by details of any recorded or roll-call vote on the resolution/decision as a whole.

Major reports. Most reports of the Secretary-General, in 2003, along with selected reports from other UN sources, such as seminars and working groups, are summarized briefly.

Secretariat activities. The operational activities of the United Nations for development and humanitarian assistance are described under the relevant topics. For major activities financed outside the UN regular budget, selected information is given on contributions and expenditures.

Views of States. Written communications sent to the United Nations by Member States and circulated as documents of the principal organs have been summarized in selected cases, under the relevant topics. Substantive actions by the Security Council have been analysed and brief reviews of the Council's deliberations given, particularly in cases where an issue was taken up but no resolution was adopted.

Related organizations. The *Yearbook* also briefly describes the 2003 activities of the specialized agencies and other related organizations of the UN system.

Multilateral treaties. Information on signatories and parties to multilateral treaties and conventions is taken from *Multilateral Treaties Deposited with the Secretary-General: Status as at 31 December 2003* (ST/LEG/ SER.E/22 (vols. I & II)), Sales No. E.04.V.2.

Terminology

Formal titles of bodies, organizational units, conventions, declarations and officials are given in full on first mention in an article or sequence of articles. They are also used in resolution/decision texts, and in the SUBJECT INDEX under the key word of the title. Short titles may be used in subsequent references.

How to find information in the *Yearbook*

The user may locate information on the United Nations activities contained in this volume by the use of the Table of Contents, the Subject Index, the Index of Resolutions and Decisions and the Index of Security Council presidential statements. The volume also has five appendices: Appendix I comprises a roster of Member States; Appendix II reproduces the Charter of the United Nations, including the Statute of the International Court of Justice; Appendix III gives the structure of the principal organs of the United Nations; Appendix IV provides the agenda for each session of the principal organs in 2003; and Appendix V gives the addresses of the United Nations information centres and services worldwide.

For more information on the United Nations and its activities, visit our Internet site at:

http://www.un.org

ABBREVIATIONS COMMONLY USED IN THE *YEARBOOK*

ACABQ	Advisory Committee on Administrative and Budgetary Questions	OECD	Organisation for Economic Co-operation and Development
AU	African Union	OHCHR	Office of the United Nations High Commissioner for Human Rights
CEB	United Nations System Chief Executives Board for Coordination	OIOS	Office of Internal Oversight Services
CIS	Commonwealth of Independent States	OSCE	Organization for Security and Cooperation in Europe
CPC	Committee for Programme and Coordination	PA	Palestinian Authority
DPKO	Department of Peacekeeping Operations	PLO	Palestine Liberation Organization
DPRK	Democratic People's Republic of Korea	SC	Security Council
DRC	Democratic Republic of the Congo	UN	United Nations
ECA	Economic Commission for Africa	UNAIDS	Joint United Nations Programme on HIV/AIDS
ECE	Economic Commission for Europe	UNAMSIL	United Nations Mission in Sierra Leone
ECLAC	Economic Commission for Latin America and the Caribbean	UNCTAD	United Nations Conference on Trade and Development
ECOWAS	Economic Community of West African States	UNDOF	United Nations Disengagement Observer Force (Golan Heights)
ESCAP	Economic and Social Commission for Asia and the Pacific	UNDP	United Nations Development Programme
ESCWA	Economic and Social Commission for Western Asia	UNEP	United Nations Environment Programme
EU	European Union	UNESCO	United Nations Educational, Scientific and Cultural Organization
FAO	Food and Agriculture Organization of the United Nations	UNFICYP	United Nations Peacekeeping Force in Cyprus
FRY	Federal Republic of Yugoslavia	UNFPA	United Nations Population Fund
FYROM	The former Yugoslav Republic of Macedonia	UN-Habitat	United Nations Human Settlements Programme
GA	General Assembly	UNHCR	Office of the United Nations High Commissioner for Refugees
GDP	gross domestic product	UNIC	United Nations Information Centre
GNP	gross national product	UNICEF	United Nations Children's Fund
HIPC	heavily indebted poor countries	UNIDO	United Nations Industrial Development Organization
IAEA	International Atomic Energy Agency	UNIFIL	United Nations Interim Force in Lebanon
ICAO	International Civil Aviation Organization	UNIKOM	United Nations Iraq-Kuwait Observation Mission
ICJ	International Court of Justice	UNMEE	United Nations Mission in Ethiopia and Eritrea
ICRC	International Committee of the Red Cross	UNMIBH	United Nations Mission in Bosnia and Herzegovina
ICTR	International Criminal Tribunal for Rwanda	UNMIK	United Nations Interim Administration Mission in Kosovo
ICTY	International Tribunal for the Former Yugoslavia	UNMIL	United Nations Mission in Liberia
IDA	International Development Association	UNMISET	United Nations Mission of Support in East Timor
IFAD	International Fund for Agricultural Development	UNMOGIP	United Nations Military Observer Group in India and Pakistan
IFC	International Finance Corporation	UNMOVIC	United Nations Monitoring, Verification and Inspection Commission
ILO	International Labour Organization	UNODC	United Nations Office on Drugs and Crime
IMF	International Monetary Fund	UNOMIG	United Nations Observer Mission in Georgia
IMO	International Maritime Organization	UNOPS	United Nations Office for Project Services
ITC	International Trade Centre (UNCTAD/WTO)	UNRWA	United Nations Relief and Works Agency for Palestine Refugees in the Near East
ITU	International Telecommunication Union	UNTSO	United Nations Truce Supervision Organization
JIU	Joint Inspection Unit	UPU	Universal Postal Union
LDC	least developed country	WFP	World Food Programme
MDGs	Millennium Development Goals	WHO	World Health Organization
MINUGUA	United Nations Verification Mission in Guatemala	WIPO	World Intellectual Property Organization
MINURSO	United Nations Mission for the Referendum in Western Sahara	WMDs	weapons of mass destruction
MONUC	United Nations Organization Mission in the Democratic Republic of the Congo	WMO	World Meteorological Organization
MRU	Mano River Union	WTO	World Trade Organization
NATO	North Atlantic Treaty Organization	YUN	*Yearbook of the United Nations*
NGO	non-governmental organization		
NSGT	Non-Self-Governing Territory		
OAS	Organization of American States		
OCHA	Office for the Coordination of Humanitarian Affairs		
ODA	official development assistance		

EXPLANATORY NOTE ON DOCUMENTS

References in square brackets in each chapter of Parts One to Five of this volume give the symbols of the main documents issued in 2003 on the topic. The following is a guide to the principal document symbols:

A/- refers to documents of the General Assembly, numbered in separate series by session. Thus, A/58/- refers to documents issued for consideration at the fifty-eighth session, beginning with A/58/1. Documents of special and emergency special sessions are identified as A/S- and A/ES-, followed by the session number.

A/C.- refers to documents of the Assembly's Main Committees, e.g. A/C.1/- is a document of the First Committee, A/C.6/-, a document of the Sixth Committee. A/BUR/- refers to documents of the General Committee. A/AC.- documents are those of the Assembly's ad hoc bodies and A/CN.-, of its commissions; e.g. A/AC.105/- identifies documents of the Assembly's Committee on the Peaceful Uses of Outer Space, A/CN.4/-, of its International Law Commission. Assembly resolutions and decisions since the thirty-first (1976) session have been identified by two arabic numerals; the first indicates the session of adoption; the second, the sequential number in the series. Resolutions are numbered consecutively from 1 at each session. Decisions since the fifty-seventh session are numbered consecutively, from 401 for those concerned with elections and appointments, and from 501 for all other decisions. Decisions of special and emergency special sessions are numbered consecutively, from 11 for those concerned with elections and appointments, and from 21 for all other decisions.

E/- refers to documents of the Economic and Social Council, numbered in separate series by year. Thus, E/2003/- refers to documents issued for consideration by the Council at its 2003 sessions, beginning with E/2003/1. E/AC.-, E/C.- and E/CN.-, followed by identifying numbers, refer to documents of the Council's subsidiary ad hoc bodies, committees and commissions. For example, E/CN.5/- refers to documents of the Council's Commission for Social Development, E/C.2/-, to documents of its Committee on Non-Governmental Organizations. E/ICEF/- documents are those of the United Nations Children's Fund (UNICEF). Symbols for the Council's resolutions and decisions, since 1978, consist of two arabic numerals: the first indicates the year of adoption and the second, the sequential number in the series. There are two series: one for resolutions, beginning with 1 (resolution 2003/1); and one for decisions, beginning with 201 (decision 2003/201).

S/- refers to documents of the Security Council. Its resolutions are identified by consecutive numbers followed by the year of adoption in parentheses, beginning with resolution 1(1946).

ST/-, followed by symbols representing the issuing department or office, refers to documents of the United Nations Secretariat.

Documents of certain bodies bear special symbols, including the following:

CD/-	Conference on Disarmament
CERD/-	Committee on the Elimination of Racial Discrimination
DC/-	Disarmament Commission
DP/-	United Nations Development Programme
HS/-	Commission on Human Settlements
ITC/-	International Trade Centre
TD/-	United Nations Conference on Trade and Development
UNEP/-	United Nations Environment Programme

Many documents of the regional commissions bear special symbols, which are sometimes preceded by the following:

E/ECA/-	Economic Commission for Africa
E/ECE/-	Economic Commission for Europe
E/ECLAC/-	Economic Commission for Latin America and the Caribbean
E/ESCAP/-	Economic and Social Commission for Asia and the Pacific
E/ESCWA/-	Economic and Social Commission for Western Asia

"L" in a symbol refers to documents of limited distribution, such as draft resolutions; "CONF." to documents of a conference; "INF." to those of general information. Summary records are designated by "SR.", verbatim records by "PV.", each followed by the meeting number.

United Nations sales publications each carry a sales number with the following components separated by periods: a capital letter indicating the language(s) of the publication; two arabic numerals indicating the year; a Roman numeral indicating the subject category; a capital letter indicating a subdivision of the category, if any; and an arabic numeral indicating the number of the publication within the category. Examples: E.03.II.A.2; E/F/R.03.II.E.7; E.03.X.1.

The public may now access the Official Document System by logging on to: http://documents.un.org.

Report of the Secretary-General

Report of the Secretary-General on the work of the Organization

*Following is the Secretary-General's report on the work of the Organization, dated 28 August 2003, submitted to the fifty-eighth session of the General Assembly. The Assembly took note of it on 9 October (**decision 58/506**). On 23 December, the Assembly decided that the agenda item would remain for consideration during the resumed fifty-eighth (2004) session (**decision 58/565**).*

Introduction

1. This is my seventh annual report on the work of the United Nations. Once again I take stock of what the Organization has done during the past year and how it has responded to the heavy demands upon it. The chapters of this report bear evidence of the ever-increasing number and scope of the tasks that the Organization performs in diverse areas such as peace and security, economic and social development, humanitarian assistance, international law, human rights and the environment. The Organization has made good progress in many areas, but in other important fields it will take more time to achieve its goals.

2. Undoubtedly, in the area of peace and security, it has been a trying year for the United Nations. The war in Iraq severely tested the principle of collective security and the resilience of the Organization. Rarely in its fifty-eight-year history have such dire forecasts been made about the United Nations. The United Nations will emerge strengthened if we make a measured appreciation of what happened, think about the sort of Organization we want in the future, and start making the necessary changes.

3. On 19 August 2003 the United Nations headquarters in Iraq was subjected to a cold-blooded and savage attack. This was the most deliberate and vicious attack against the United Nations in its history. My Special Representative, Sergio Vieira de Mello, and other devoted servants of the United Nations were brutally murdered, and many others were wounded. I would like to pay tribute to all of them for their courage and commitment to the ideals of the United Nations. I wish to express my profound and heartfelt sympathy to their loved ones. Those extremists who killed our colleagues have committed a crime, not only against the United Nations, but against Iraq itself.

4. During the past year the United Nations has been involved in peace operations in many parts of the world, including Afghanistan, Côte d'Ivoire, the Democratic Republic of the Congo, Kosovo, Sierra Leone and Timor-Leste. In Liberia, the multinational force authorized by the Security Council is helping to restore security and stability, and in due course will be replaced by a United Nations peacekeeping force. Peace agreements by themselves, however, mark only the first step in bringing lasting peace and prosperity to war-torn societies. The traumatic rupture of economic, political and social relations between groups and individuals characterizes such societies. Creating or rebuilding civil society is a crucial long-term commitment and is essential to establishing and consolidating democracy. Democratic institutions and principles should be embedded within a self-sustaining civil society. Countries emerging from civil strife must find their own paths to humane governance and national reconciliation, but international assistance will often be necessary.

5. The international community continues to take action to combat international terrorism, especially in view of new attacks in Indonesia, Morocco, the Russian Federation, Saudi Arabia and elsewhere. Human rights must not be sacrificed in the struggle against international terrorism, however. Moreover, while poverty and grievance over injustices are only indirectly related to terrorism, and cannot excuse it, these indirect links must nonetheless be taken into account in strategies aimed at reducing the incidence of terrorist acts. Promoting measures to reduce poverty, address injustices, strengthen good governance and build tolerance are essential to that end, as well as for their own sake. To keep a genuinely

global coalition against terrorism together the world will need to see progress on the other fronts of the struggle for a humane and just world order.

6. Disarmament, including the eradication of weapons of mass destruction, remains a major priority for the international community. Recent developments have underlined the potential threat of weapons of mass destruction falling into the hands of terrorists. The existing global disarmament norms relevant to weapons of mass destruction need to be strengthened and protected against erosion. Disarmament requires multilateral cooperation and can be accomplished only in an atmosphere of trust.

7. While the immediate and urgent challenges of peace and security require sedulous attention, it is also important that they should not divert attention from our work in economic and social development. At present, there is a wide gap between the rhetoric of inclusion and the reality of exclusion. Our efforts for peace will be in vain unless we can begin to bridge this gap by achieving real progress for the poorest countries in the world. Furthermore, our efforts to contain and resolve conflicts should not drain resources from other fights that we are waging around the world to protect refugees and displaced persons, to combat HIV/AIDS and other diseases, and to promote sustainable development.

8. The outbreak of the severe acute respiratory syndrome (SARS) was a sobering reminder of the world's vulnerability to disease and the risks of it spreading rapidly across borders. At the same time, the effective coordinated response demonstrated the value of multilateral cooperation, in this case through the professional and speedy intervention of the World Health Organization.

9. In order to address the broad range of contemporary international problems it is important to forge partnerships and alliances. Governments alone do not have the capacity to find solutions to these problems. We must continue to find greater opportunities for the private sector, non-governmental organizations and civil society, in general, to contribute to the realization of the Organization's goals.

10. The United Nations is not an end in itself. Rather, it is an instrument for achieving common ends. The strength and effectiveness of the Organization depends on the active support of its Member States and their policies. Moreover, achievement of the Organization's purposes requires a shared consensus about its fundamental goals. That does not mean that Member States need to agree on all issues. However, it does mean that they should be ready to use the Organization to achieve mutual objectives and to accommodate different national interests. In calculating their national interests, they should give due weight to the value and importance of a just and stable world order.

Chapter I

Achieving peace and security

11. During the past year, United Nations activities in the area of peace and security continued to focus on the prevention and resolution of conflict and the provision of assistance to societies emerging from conflict. While the United Nations attempted to address a variety of new challenges in this field, issues such as terrorism and the proliferation of weapons of mass destruction remained of great concern. The war in Iraq highlighted how rapidly the security environment in which we now live can evolve, as well as the diversity of perceptions on how global peace and security should be maintained.

12. Increasingly, civil conflicts pose a serious threat to international peace and security. They create situations in which perpetrators of violence act with impunity. In these zones of impunity, the scourges of our time—drug trafficking, arms trafficking, human trafficking, the training of terrorists—flourish. Illicit transboundary networks of finance and trade link these zones, fomenting instability that affects entire regions, or even the international system itself. Decades of development efforts and centuries of social cohesion can thus be undone in a short period of time. The impact on women and girls is particularly severe, as is made clear in my report on women and peace and security submitted to the Security Council in October 2002. The complex nature of present threats to peace and security has led the United Nations system increasingly to focus on thematic issues. Indicative of this is the continuing practice of the Security Council to convene open meetings on questions such as children and armed conflict, women and peace and security, civilians in armed conflict and small arms. This practice has now been expanded to include thematic issues in a regional context, such as small arms and mercenary activities as threats to peace and security in West Africa (18 March 2003) and Africa's food crisis as a threat to peace and security (7 April 2003).

13. The means available to the United Nations for the discharge of its responsibilities in the area of international peace and security vary from preventive diplomacy to peacemaking, peacekeeping and peace-building. In practice, the issues falling within these four areas of action

are integrally related. In Cyprus and Western Sahara, for example, peacemaking and peacekeeping have been taking place side by side for years. Any peace-building effort—Afghanistan is a good example—has a strong component of preventive diplomacy, as applied in the context of a post-conflict situation. The present report contains a special section on Iraq, in acknowledgement of the central place that this question occupied on the agenda of the Organization and in the attention of world public opinion over the year under review.

Iraq

14. On 16 September 2002, the Minister for Foreign Affairs of Iraq informed me that his Government had decided to allow the return of United Nations weapons inspectors without conditions. This followed a series of discussions I had held with the Iraqi side in March, May and July 2002, as well as my appeal in the General Assembly in September 2002, urging Iraq to comply with its obligations under Security Council resolutions. I welcomed the resumption of inspections by the United Nations Monitoring, Verification and Inspection Commission (UNMOVIC) in Iraq in November 2002 that followed the unanimous adoption of Security Council resolution 1441(2002). It was with regret that I noted in the report of 27 January 2003 of the Executive Chairman of UNMOVIC that while Iraq was cooperating on process it did not appear to have come to a genuine acceptance of its obligations.

15. By early March 2003 there were divisions in the Security Council as to how to proceed. I continued to urge united international action, as well as constant and persistent pressure on the leadership of Iraq, through daily exchanges with Council members, the League of Arab States, UNMOVIC and others both in New York and in capitals. By mid-March it was clear, however, that some Member States had taken the position that it was impossible to resolve the crisis without the use of force. On 17 March I informed the Council that I would suspend United Nations activities in Iraq and withdraw all remaining United Nations system personnel the following day.

16. Following the end of major hostilities, which had resulted in the occupation of Iraq by a coalition headed by the United States of America and the United Kingdom of Great Britain and Northern Ireland, and after protracted deliberations, the Security Council adopted, on 22 May 2003, resolution 1483(2003). In paragraph 8 of the resolution the Council requested me to appoint a Special Representative whose responsibilities would include coordinating United Nations activities in Iraq and, in coordination with the Coalition Provisional Authority, assisting the people of Iraq in such areas as humanitarian assistance, reconstruction and development, human rights, legal and judicial reform and the restoration of an internationally recognized, representative Government of Iraq. I proceeded to appoint a Special Representative for an initial period of four months.

17. My Special Representative travelled extensively throughout Iraq and met representatives of a wide and diverse spectrum of Iraqi society. He and his team also established regular contacts with the Administrator and other officials of the Coalition Provisional Authority. I and my Special Representative initiated a dialogue with leaders of countries neighbouring Iraq and the broader international community. In my first report to the Security Council (S/2003/715) I stressed the fundamental principles underlying the activities of the United Nations under resolution 1483 (2003)—including the need to restore sovereignty to the people of Iraq as soon as possible and the need to respect the Iraqi people's right to determine their political future—and our desire to keep foremost in mind the interests of the Iraqi people in our assistance activities. The report provided an initial assessment of the scope of the challenges involved in implementing the mandate conferred by resolution 1483(2003) and indicated those areas in which I consider that the United Nations can play a useful role, on the basis of its expertise and comparative advantage. To this end, I proposed the establishment of a United Nations Assistance Mission for Iraq (UNAMI). On 14 August, the Security Council, by resolution 1500(2003), decided to establish UNAMI for an initial period of 12 months. The Council also welcomed the establishment, on 13 July 2003, of the broadly representative Governing Council of Iraq, as an important step towards the formation of an internationally recognized, representative and sovereign Government of Iraq.

18. The wanton attack on the United Nations headquarters building in Baghdad on 19 August 2003 dealt a severe blow to the Organization's efforts at assisting Iraq's return to normalcy. My Special Representative, Sergio Vieira de Mello, and several international and local staff members lost their lives in this cowardly act, while many more were injured. Their sacrifice will not be in vain. The United Nations will continue helping the Iraqi people to rebuild their country and regain their sovereignty, under leaders of their own choosing. Meanwhile, I shall continue to emphasize that it is vital that the people of Iraq see a clear timetable with a specific sequence of events leading to the full restoration of sovereignty as

soon as possible. This means that the establishment of the Governing Council must be followed by a constitutional process run by Iraqis for Iraqis. To this end, the United Nations will maintain an active role in facilitating and supporting the political process. My new Special Representative will continue to work with the Governing Council and the Coalition Provisional Authority and will pursue further the dialogue with leaders of the countries of the region and beyond.

Conflict prevention and peacemaking

19. A comprehensive exercise is under way to implement my report of 2001 on the prevention of armed conflict. A vital task in this respect is to foster the building of conflict prevention capacities at local and national levels and the elaboration of regional preventive strategies that would integrate political and developmental elements. The United Nations System Chief Executives Board for Coordination chose preventing armed conflict as the main theme of its second regular session of 2002, offering an opportunity to promote greater coherence and coordination in system-wide efforts in the field of structural conflict prevention, at the national, regional and international levels. The resolution recently adopted by the General Assembly on the prevention of armed conflict gives the United Nations a strong mandate not only to continue but to expand and intensify its conflict prevention activities.

20. After almost three years of violence and confrontation, new hope for the resumption of the stalled Middle East peace process has finally emerged. Following the appointment of a Prime Minister of the Palestinian Authority, a road map to a permanent two-State solution to the Israeli-Palestinian conflict was formally presented to the parties on 30 April 2003. This performance-based blueprint, elaborated by the Quartet (the United Nations, the European Union, the Russian Federation and the United States of America) at a series of meetings, includes clear phases, timelines and benchmarks. It aims at achieving progress through parallel and reciprocal steps by the two parties in the political, security, economic, humanitarian and institution-building fields, under an effective international monitoring mechanism. This process should lead to the establishment of an independent, democratic and viable Palestinian State existing side by side in peace and security with Israel and its other neighbours, as affirmed in Security Council resolution 1397(2002). I was particularly encouraged by the outcome of the summit meeting between the parties and the President of the United States of America at Aqaba, Jordan, on 4 June 2003, where the two sides made a firm commitment to implementing the road map.

21. Despite the recent signs of progress, the vicious circle of violence, retaliation and revenge continued during most of the period under review, resulting in further substantial loss of life and destruction. A total collapse of the Palestinian economy was prevented only by the infusion of significant foreign assistance, including through the United Nations Relief and Works Agency for Palestine Refugees in the Near East and other United Nations agencies and programmes. A deteriorating security environment and problems of access hampered the efforts of the United Nations and others to address the growing humanitarian crisis in the Occupied Palestinian Territory, as further detailed in the following chapter.

22. Through my direct contacts and the Quartet mechanism, most recently at the meeting of the Quartet on 22 June 2003 on the shores of the Dead Sea, in Jordan, I remained personally engaged in efforts at achieving peace in the Middle East. The Security Council was kept informed of those efforts and relevant developments in monthly briefings by the Secretariat. The final goal of the road map, and of the entire peace process, remains a comprehensive settlement of the Middle East conflict, including the Syrian-Israeli and Lebanese-Israeli tracks, on the basis of Security Council resolutions 242(1967), 338(1973) and 1397(2002), the Madrid Peace Conference of 1991 and the principle of land for peace, agreements previously reached by the parties, and the peace initiative endorsed by the League of Arab States at its Beirut summit in March 2002.

23. I regret to report that the Cyprus problem, despite the intensive exercise of my good offices, remains unresolved. The lifting of travel restrictions between the north and south of the island in recent months, while welcome, is no substitute for a comprehensive settlement of the core issues. A unique opportunity to achieve a settlement was squandered—a settlement which would have allowed a reunited Cyprus to sign the Treaty of Accession to the European Union on 16 April 2003. With time running out before the Treaty's signature, and with hopes renewed by the election in November 2002 of a Government of Turkey that seemed genuinely disposed to resolving the question, I submitted in November 2002 a draft comprehensive settlement to the two Cypriot leaders. Despite their agreeing to negotiate on the basis of that plan, the negotiations failed to result in an agreement and in April 2003 I closed the office of my Special Adviser. A settlement before the entry into force of the Treaty of

Accession to the European Union—on 1 May 2004—would still allow a reunited Cyprus to accede to the European Union. I do not believe, however, that any purpose would be served by my taking a new initiative unless the parties demonstrate their commitment to a settlement on the basis of the plan. Should such a commitment be forthcoming, I shall resume active efforts to resolve this long-standing dispute. In the meantime, the United Nations Peacekeeping Force in Cyprus continues to monitor the buffer zone across the island.

24. Early in 2003, the Government of Angola and the National Union for the Total Independence of Angola (UNITA) completed the implementation of the political aspects of the 1994 Lusaka Protocol. This led to the dissolution of the United Nations Mission in Angola. The Security Council lifted sanctions against UNITA in December 2002. Responsibility for the remaining activities envisaged by the Security Council was transferred to a strengthened office of the United Nations Resident Coordinator, through which the United Nations Development Programme (UNDP) and other United Nations agencies are supporting communities in the sustainable reintegration of former combatants and internally displaced persons. They are also working to strengthen national capacity on mine action and implement mine-clearing operations; monitor the respect of human rights through a special unit attached to the Resident Coordinator's Office; and strengthen international coordination to assist the Government in organizing a donor conference.

25. In Burundi, the second phase of the transition began in May 2003 with the inauguration of the new President and Vice-President. Facilitation efforts involving the United Nations led to the signing of ceasefire agreements between the Transitional Government and three of the four armed groups, and the establishment of a Joint Ceasefire Commission. In April 2003, the African Union authorized the deployment of the African Mission in Burundi to assist in the implementation of the ceasefire. United Nations agencies are continuing to help the African Union to demobilize and reintegrate combatants in support of the full implementation of the Arusha Agreement. Nonetheless, the continuation of the fighting, most recently in July 2003, points to the urgent need to address all of the outstanding issues in the peace process. I welcome the regional initiatives aimed at implementing a ceasefire.

26. My Representative for Somalia continued to encourage the parties to reach an inclusive and credible agreement at the Somalia National Reconciliation Conference that opened in October 2002 in Kenya, under the auspices of the Intergovernmental Authority on Development (IGAD). By mid-2003, Somali delegates had endorsed the reports of five of the six Reconciliation Committees covering important issues relating to peace-building in Somalia. Still under discussion, before they could move to power-sharing, was a report on the question of a provisional charter for a future transitional Government. I hope that the Somali leaders will build on the Eldoret Declaration of 27 October 2002 and reach a final and inclusive agreement backed by a serious commitment to its implementation.

27. Progress achieved at the IGAD-led peace talks on the Sudan has improved the prospects for lasting peace there. The momentum created by the signing of the Machakos Protocol, in July 2002, if sustained, could lead to a comprehensive agreement soon. My Special Adviser and staff from the Secretariat will continue to support the mediation efforts. In addition, the United Nations Resident Coordinator in the Sudan has prepared an extensive programme to promote economic recovery and thus buttress the peace talks.

28. Faced with a continuing stalemate in Western Sahara, the Security Council requested my Personal Envoy to put forward a political solution that would provide for self-determination of the people of Western Sahara, taking into account concerns expressed by the parties and consulting, as appropriate, others with relevant experience. A plan was accordingly presented to Morocco, the Frente POLISARIO, Algeria and Mauritania in January 2003. In March, Morocco and the Frente POLISARIO expressed their reservations to the plan. Early in July, however, the Frente POLISARIO informed my Personal Envoy of its acceptance of the peace plan. On 9 July, another text of the peace plan, amended to add a third ballot choice in the eventual referendum, providing for self-government or autonomy, was transmitted to the parties. On 31 July, the Security Council unanimously adopted resolution 1495(2003), by which it expressed its support for the peace plan for self-determination of the people of Western Sahara and called upon the parties to work with the United Nations and with each other towards its acceptance and implementation. Meanwhile, the United Nations Mission for the Referendum in Western Sahara continued to monitor the ceasefire between the parties, in effect since September 1991.

29. Since my first meeting in Paris, in September 2002, with the President of Cameroon and the President of Nigeria, my good offices were made available to the two countries as they

negotiated a resolution of their border dispute. At the request of the two heads of State, after our second meeting in November 2002 at Geneva, I established the Cameroon-Nigeria Mixed Commission, chaired by my Special Representative for West Africa, to facilitate a peaceful implementation of the ruling of the International Court of Justice of October 2002 on the land and maritime boundary between Cameroon and Nigeria and help to build confidence between the two countries. The Mixed Commission holds periodic meetings, alternately in Yaoundé and Abuja. Progress has been made with the creation of two subcommissions, one on the demarcation of the land boundary and another on affected populations. The latter subcommission will assess the situation of the populations affected by the Court's ruling and consider modalities relating to the protection of their rights.

30. In Latin America, the United Nations Verification Mission in Guatemala continued to oversee the implementation of the 1996 peace agreements, the timeline for which extends to 2004. Although the Government had pledged to accelerate implementation after a meeting of the Consultative Group in February 2002, the Group concluded at its subsequent meeting in May 2003 that insufficient progress had been made. Increased attacks on human rights defenders and judges, and persistent social unrest, were of particular concern. Conversely, renewed civil society activism in support of the peace agreements allowed some grounds for optimism.

31. I continued to provide my good offices to the search for a peaceful solution to the nearly 40-year-old conflict in Colombia. Despite the rupture in talks between the Government of Colombia and the two major guerrilla groups—the Revolutionary Armed Forces of Colombia and the National Liberation Army—my Special Adviser on Colombia has continued, through regular contacts with the Government, guerrilla groups, civil society and the international community, to assist peacemaking efforts. In addition, the Office of the United Nations High Commissioner for Refugees (UNHCR) has worked with the United Nations country team and my Special Adviser to address the growing problem of displaced persons within the country. The expanding conflict, which is fuelled by funds from the illicit drug trade, constitutes a significant challenge for the United Nations organizations that are working to alleviate its adverse humanitarian effects and address its root causes.

32. Relations between India and Pakistan improved, and it was announced in May 2003 that the two countries would appoint High Commissioners to each other's capitals, restore rail, road and air links, and take other confidence-building measures. I hope that those measures will lead to the resumption of sustained dialogue and to real progress towards a peaceful settlement of the outstanding problems between these two neighbours, including over Jammu and Kashmir.

33. Despite a ceasefire agreement and several rounds of talks between the Government of Nepal and the Communist Party of Nepal (Maoist), the emerging peace process is still fragile. The United Nations remains prepared to provide assistance to strengthen the process, including in the area of human rights. The United Nations system, through the Resident Coordinator and programmes such as UNDP and the United Nations Children's Fund (UNICEF), has reoriented humanitarian, reconstruction and development assistance to better support the peace process.

34. The peace process in Sri Lanka, which had begun to make encouraging progress after the ceasefire of February 2002, suffered a setback in April 2003, when the Liberation Tigers of Tamil Eelam suspended participation in negotiations with the Government of Sri Lanka. I fully support the ongoing efforts by the Governments of Norway and Japan to further the peace process, and hope the talks will resume as soon as possible. The United Nations system, through the Resident Coordinator and in collaboration with the World Bank, will continue to support the process through reconstruction and development activities.

35. The implementation of the Bougainville Peace Agreement of August 2001 between the Bougainville parties and the Government of Papua New Guinea has made significant headway. Following the verification and notification by the United Nations Political Office in Bougainville (UNPOB) of the completion of stage II of the weapons disposal plan at the end of July 2003, the constitutional amendments providing for the establishment of an autonomous Bougainville Government and a referendum on Bougainville's future political status have become operational. While UNPOB is expected to successfully complete its mandate by the end of 2003, the United Nations system and the donor community will need to continue providing assistance to the parties in the implementation of the Agreement.

36. I am gratified to note the continuing cooperation between the United Nations and the Government of Indonesia in support of the latter's pursuit of political, economic and social reforms. I remain convinced that Indonesia's national unity and territorial integrity can best be ensured through respect for democratic norms and the promotion of human rights. Accordingly,

I have called upon all parties to the conflict in Aceh to uphold their obligations to protect civilians in armed conflict and to resume dialogue. I have also been following closely the Indonesian Ad Hoc Human Rights Tribunal for Crimes Committed in East Timor; I firmly believe that the perpetrators of serious human rights violations in 1999 in Timor-Leste (then East Timor) must be brought to justice.

37. I have been paying particular attention to the crisis on the Korean Peninsula that was triggered by an alleged admission in October 2002 by the Democratic People's Republic of Korea that it was carrying out a uranium-enrichment programme. This was followed by the withdrawal of the Democratic People's Republic of Korea from the Treaty on the Non-Proliferation of Nuclear Weapons and by its claim to possess nuclear weapons. A legacy of deep mutual mistrust and hostility between the Democratic People's Republic of Korea and other States, particularly the United States of America, has contributed to continuing tensions in the region. In January 2003, I became concerned that the humanitarian pipeline to the Democratic People's Republic of Korea might dry up. I dispatched my Personal Envoy to the country in January and March 2003 to help prevent a humanitarian disaster and prepare the way for a negotiated settlement. My Envoy had extensive and useful discussions with senior government officials in Pyongyang, as well as in other capitals concerned about developments on the Korean Peninsula. The dangers inherent in the Korean situation cast an ominous cloud over the security and stability of the region. The international consensus that the Korean Peninsula should be free of nuclear weapons and the commitment of all major players to finding a peaceful solution to the crisis allow for guarded optimism that a comprehensive resolution can be achieved. I shall continue to lend my full support to the multilateral diplomatic process launched in April 2003 in Beijing and expanded thereafter.

38. My Special Envoy to Myanmar undertook his ninth and tenth missions to Yangon in November 2002 and June 2003, respectively, to try to facilitate national reconciliation and democratization. My Envoy met the major political actors—leaders of the State Peace and Development Council, officials of the National League for Democracy (NLD) and ethnic minority political parties. The incident of 30 May 2003, which resulted in the detention of many NLD officials, including Daw Aung San Suu Kyi, renewed concerns about progress towards national reconciliation and the eventual transition to democracy. I have urged and will continue to urge the Government of Myanmar to heed the call by the international community, including the countries of the region, and release Daw Aung San Suu Kyi and other NLD leaders without further delay.

Peacekeeping and peace-building

39. Peacekeeping and peace-building are two sides of the same coin, providing as they do assistance to societies emerging from conflict so that they can consolidate their fragile peace. Whether through the dispatch of Blue Helmets or by authorizing the deployment of a multinational force, the United Nations has actively supported the transition from war to peace in many parts of the world. Moreover, through its peace-building efforts, the Organization and the broader United Nations system have provided political, humanitarian and development assistance to meet immediate emergency and reconstruction needs, as well as to establish viable institutions. I am glad to note the successful completion of the United Nations Mission in Bosnia and Herzegovina and the United Nations Mission of Observers in Prevlaka, which demonstrate that the United Nations can complete complex mandates within a realistic time frame.

40. On 4 December 2002, the Security Council authorized a gradual increase in the troop strength of the United Nations Organization Mission in the Democratic Republic of the Congo (MONUC) to 8,700, with a view to contributing to the disarmament, demobilization and repatriation of foreign armed groups. On 17 December, the participants in the inter-Congolese dialogue signed a Global and All-Inclusive Agreement and, on 2 April 2003, the Final Act, formally endorsing that Agreement, the Transitional Constitution and 36 resolutions that had been adopted at an earlier session of the inter-Congolese dialogue, in April 2002, thus paving the way for the formation of a Transitional Government. In May 2003, in view of the progress made at the national level, I presented to the Security Council a comprehensive strategy for the role of MONUC in support of the transition. Despite the political progress, however, fighting continued in the eastern regions of the country; it was especially intense in Ituri and the Kivus, where massacres and widespread human rights violations were committed. In response to the rapid deterioration of security in Ituri, and recognizing the threat it posed to the peace process, the Security Council on 30 May authorized the deployment of an Interim Emergency Multinational Force in Bunia, in the Ituri region. The Force was fielded by the European Union, with France as the lead nation. The deployment of that Force, until 1 September 2003, offered the United Nations and the inter-

national community the opportunity to work in the meantime to strengthen local political institutions and ensure that the humanitarian crisis did not continue to deteriorate. The Transitional Government was formally installed in July 2003, with the swearing-in of the four new Vice-Presidents, the Ministers and the Deputy Ministers. By resolution 1493(2003) of 28 July, acting under Chapter VII of the Charter of the United Nations, the Security Council authorized an increase in the Mission's strength to 10,800.

41. In September 2002, Côte d'Ivoire was plunged into a civil conflict when a group of soldiers, in an attempted coup, simultaneously attacked military installations in Abidjan, Bouaké and Korhogo. While security forces loyal to the Government quickly regained control of Abidjan, the rebels prevailed in the northern half of the country. Mediation efforts by the Economic Community of West African States (ECOWAS) resulted, in October 2002, in a ceasefire agreement monitored by French and ECOWAS forces. In January 2003, the Ivorian parties signed the Linas-Marcoussis Agreement, which called for the creation of a Government of National Reconciliation whose main tasks would be to prepare a timetable for credible and transparent national elections, restructure the defence and security forces and disarm all armed groups. In May 2003, the Security Council authorized the establishment of the United Nations Mission in Côte d'Ivoire (MINUCI), with a mandate to facilitate the implementation of the Linas-Marcoussis Agreement, complementing the operations of the French and ECOWAS forces. The Mission's deployment has proceeded successfully, an initial group of 26 military liaison officers having arrived in Abidjan on 23 June 2003. Throughout the peacemaking process, my Special Representative for West Africa played a critical supporting role in the international efforts that resulted in the Linas-Marcoussis Agreement.

42. The United Nations Mission in Sierra Leone (UNAMSIL) began to implement its drawdown plan, which provides for the total withdrawal of the Mission by the end of 2004, while continuing to assist the Government of Sierra Leone in consolidating peace. The pace of the Mission's drawdown is guided by the ability of the security forces of Sierra Leone to guarantee the security of the country. While the Government took commendable steps to consolidate its authority, its capacity to deliver basic services to the population in the provinces has been limited. The Government has taken measures to restore its control over diamond mining but significant illegal mining persists. The resettlement of internally displaced persons was completed in December 2002, while the repatriation of Sierra Leonean refugees from neighbouring countries continues. UNHCR, UNDP and the World Bank have been working to ensure recovery at the local level, to strengthen the Government's capacity to deliver services and to provide economic alternatives for former combatants and refugees. The Truth and Reconciliation Commission and the Special Court have started functioning and the Security Council has authorized the deployment of 170 civilian police to UNAMSIL to assist in the training of the local police.

43. During the reporting period, the United Nations Peace-building Support Offices in the Central African Republic, Guinea-Bissau and Liberia intensified their efforts to facilitate the promotion of good governance and national reconciliation, the consolidation of democratic processes and the mobilization of international support for the formulation and implementation of reconstruction and development programmes. The respective United Nations country teams have been closely associated with this endeavour. The lack of cooperation on the part of governing parties, however, and the failure by national stakeholders to resolve their major differences on governance issues have seriously hampered the United Nations peace-building efforts, especially in the Central African Republic and Liberia.

44. Regrettably, the situation in Liberia took a dangerous turn as renewed fighting erupted in Monrovia in flagrant violation of a ceasefire agreement signed by the warring parties in Accra on 17 June 2003. In addition to inflicting a severe blow to the promising prospects for the restoration of peace in the country, hostilities led to a humanitarian catastrophe and threatened stability in the entire West African subregion. The United Nations, together with other principal international players, has actively supported the sustained peacemaking efforts of the leaders of ECOWAS. On 28 June 2003, I addressed a letter to the President of the Security Council, with the request that the Council take urgent action to authorize, under Chapter VII of the Charter, the deployment to Liberia of a highly trained and well-equipped multinational force, under the lead of a Member State, to prevent a major humanitarian tragedy and to stabilize the situation in the country. In anticipation of a greater United Nations involvement in these efforts, I appointed a Special Representative for Liberia with the main tasks of coordinating United Nations activities, supporting the emerging transitional arrangements and leading an eventual United Nations peacekeeping operation in that country. On 1 August, the Security Council, by resolution 1497(2003), authorized Member States to estab-

lish a Multinational Force in Liberia and declared its readiness to establish a follow-on, longer-term United Nations stabilization force to relieve the Multinational Force. On 4 August, ECOWAS elements of the Multinational Force started deploying in Liberia with United Nations support. To facilitate the cessation of hostilities and the conclusion of a comprehensive peace agreement, President Charles Taylor relinquished power and left Liberia on 11 August, in keeping with the commitment he had made at the opening of the peace talks in Accra on 4 June. I welcomed the subsequent signing by the Liberian parties, on 18 August, also in Accra, of a comprehensive peace agreement, and called on all concerned to seize this opportunity to work together to restore peace and stability in the country.

45. The United Nations Mission in Ethiopia and Eritrea continued to support the peace process by monitoring the Temporary Security Zone; providing logistical support to the Eritrea-Ethiopia Boundary Commission; and delivering quick-impact projects and coordinating humanitarian assistance in the Temporary Security Zone and adjacent areas. The Mine Action Coordination Centre has continued to coordinate all mine-related activities within the Zone and to clear access routes to boundary pillar sites. It is important that both parties cooperate fully with the Boundary Commission to ensure the demarcation of the border without undue delay. It is equally important for the parties to initiate a political dialogue, in particular to develop mechanisms to resolve residual and future disputes peacefully.

46. In March 2003, just before the United States-led invasion of Iraq from Kuwait, the mandate of the United Nations Iraq-Kuwait Observation Mission (UNIKOM) was suspended and most of its staff evacuated. UNIKOM maintained a small rear headquarters in Kuwait City to provide a peacekeeping presence, undertake political and military liaison functions, and support United Nations humanitarian assistance programmes for Iraq. While much of UNIKOM headquarters at Umm Qasr and other infrastructure were destroyed in the conflict, Camp Khor, on the Kuwaiti side of the border, reopened in May to support humanitarian operations. On 3 July, the Security Council, in resolution 1490(2003), noted that UNIKOM had successfully fulfilled its mandate from 1991 to 2003 and extended it for a final period of three months. The Mission's remaining personnel are preparing for the liquidation of UNIKOM and transferring many of its removable assets to other missions.

47. The United Nations Interim Force in Lebanon continued to monitor the Blue Line between Israel and Lebanon and to liaise with the parties to avert or contain tensions. There were few violent incidents and only minor ground violations of the Line. Frequent Israeli violations of Lebanese airspace, however, drew retaliatory anti-aircraft fire from Hizbollah. I have continued to remind the parties to respect fully the Blue Line. The Lebanese armed forces increased their activity in the south, but the Government of Lebanon has yet to take all necessary steps to restore its full authority there. The Mine Action Coordination Centre coordinated the clearance of over 4 million square metres of mined area in southern Lebanon.

48. The Government of the Democratic Republic of Timor-Leste worked to strengthen its institutions and security, drawing upon the assistance provided by the United Nations Mission of Support in East Timor (UNMISET) and by United Nations agencies. The Government's civil administration and police force progressively assumed greater responsibility for the management of day-to-day affairs in their respective areas. In an important gesture of commitment to human rights principles, the Parliament of Timor-Leste ratified six core human rights treaties and four optional protocols in December 2002. However, in response to rioting in Dili in December 2002 and violent attacks by armed elements in January and February 2003, the Security Council decided to slow the downsizing schedule for the military and police components of UNMISET.

49. In Afghanistan, the security situation has continued to challenge the implementation of the Bonn Agreement of December 2001. Progress has nevertheless been made. All the commissions called for in the Agreement have been formed and have begun their work in their respective areas of human rights, constitutional and judicial reform, and the reorganization of the civil service. The United Nations Assistance Mission in Afghanistan and other United Nations entities have been providing critical support to those commissions. The Transitional Administration adopted concrete measures to extend its control over the country. These included launching a new currency and formulating a national development budget. In May 2003, the Administration secured an agreement with important provincial governors and commanders that called for the centralization of customs revenues and prohibited provincial leaders from simultaneously holding civil and military positions, but those commitments have been only partially implemented. The Transitional Administration has

placed security sector reform at the centre of its agenda. This includes the reform of the Ministry of Defence to make it nationally representative, as a precondition for the implementation of the disarmament, demobilization and reintegration plan. The signing of a declaration on good-neighbourly relations by Afghanistan and neighbouring States on 22 December 2002 was a further step towards the objective of consolidating stability and security in the region.

50. The United Nations Observer Mission in Georgia (UNOMIG) continued to monitor compliance with the ceasefire agreement of 1994. The Group of Friends, under the chairmanship of the United Nations, met at Geneva in February and July 2003, to review progress towards a comprehensive settlement and to consider options for taking the peace process forward. The Georgian and Abkhaz sides took part in the second meeting. My Special Representative, with the support of the Group of Friends, remained in close contact with the parties to build on the momentum generated by those two meetings, as well as the meeting of President Putin and President Shevardnadze in March 2003, particularly in the areas of economic cooperation and the return of refugees and internally displaced persons. My Special Representative also supported efforts to build confidence and advance towards a comprehensive settlement of the conflict, on the basis of the paper entitled "Basic Principles for the Distribution of Competencies between Tbilisi and Sukhumi" and its letter of transmittal. I remain concerned about security in the Kodori Valley, where four UNOMIG personnel were held hostage for six days in June 2003, the sixth such incident since the establishment of the Mission in 1993. None of the perpetrators of those acts, or those responsible for shooting down a helicopter in 2001, have ever been identified and brought to justice.

51. The United Nations Interim Administration Mission in Kosovo (UNMIK) continued to support the establishment of democratic provisional institutions of self-government, as foreseen by the Constitutional Framework for Provisional Self-Government in Kosovo. The gradual transfer of the non-reserved responsibilities listed in chapter 5 of the Constitutional Framework from UNMIK to the provisional institutions continued, at a pace that took into account the capacity of those institutions to assume such responsibilities. The overall authority of UNMIK and the reserved responsibilities listed in chapter 8 of the Constitutional Framework will not be transferred. The Mission, with support from UNDP, maintained efforts to combat organized crime and to create the basis for a viable market economy. It also increased its efforts to foster conditions for minority return and to resolve property right claims by displaced persons. UNMIK continued to seek the resolution of issues that need to be addressed with authorities in Belgrade and encouraged a direct dialogue on practical matters between Belgrade and Pristina.

52. The United Nations Mission in Bosnia and Herzegovina successfully completed its work in December 2002, having established State-level law enforcement institutions and transformed a 40,000 strong wartime militia into a 16,000 strong professional police force. Remaining responsibilities relating to the reform of the police were transferred to the European Union Police Mission. The United Nations Mission of Observers in Prevlaka also completed its tasks in December 2002, having helped to shield this strategically important area from the fighting in the region and to create the space for a political solution to the dispute.

53. Building on last year's efforts to enhance the strategic deployment stocks at Brindisi, the Secretariat this year improved its capacity to deploy staff with the development of a rapid deployment roster for civilian personnel. The Civilian Police Division of the Department of Peacekeeping Operations also established a 100-person roster of dedicated professionals available at short notice. I am most grateful for the cooperation of Member States in this regard. Furthermore, the Division, in collaboration with other United Nations entities, enhanced its capacity to address policing, judicial and corrections matters by establishing a Criminal Law and Judicial Advisory Unit early in 2003.

The United Nations and regional organizations

54. The United Nations continues to work with and rely on regional organizations for the advancement of common goals such as international peace and security, development and respect for human rights. The biennial high-level meetings of the United Nations and regional organizations, a forum inaugurated in 1994, have been instrumental in strengthening cooperation, especially in the areas of conflict prevention and peace-building. In the light of the increasing need for a joint response to challenges to peace and security around the world, I convened the fifth high-level meeting in July 2003, on the theme "New challenges to peace and security, including international terrorism". The conclusions of the meeting, which I intend to make available for wider distribution, confirmed the keen interest of the participants in jointly confronting the new challenges and in meeting more frequently to develop common strategies and policies.

55. During the period under review, the United Nations forged a number of innovative partnerships with regional organizations. For example, as mentioned earlier, the European Union and the United Nations recently combined their efforts in the Democratic Republic of the Congo, where a European Union force was deployed in June 2003 under the authority of the Security Council to keep the peace in the Ituri region. Similarly, in Afghanistan, the North Atlantic Treaty Organization agreed to assume, in August 2003, the leadership of the International Security Assistance Force operating under a Security Council mandate. In the area of development, the signature in April 2003 of a Framework Agreement with the European Commission makes it easier for the United Nations to access Commission funds in the joint pursuit of the Millennium Development Goals.

56. The United Nations also continued to cooperate closely with the African Union and subregional organizations in Africa to assist in the management and resolution of conflicts. The African Chiefs of Defence Staff and the Union's Executive Council, assisted by the United Nations, adopted a number of proposals to enhance Africa's peacekeeping capacity. In addition, my Special Representative for West Africa, with the support of United Nations agencies and the Secretariat, worked closely with ECOWAS to develop an integrated subregional approach to address the challenges facing West African States. At the Security Council's request, I sent a multidisciplinary assessment mission to Central Africa in June 2003 to seek ways for the United Nations to enhance its cooperation with subregional institutions towards achieving sustainable peace. A representative of ECOWAS joined the mission. For its part, UNDP has been developing a comprehensive programme of support for the African Union in building its capacity for conflict management.

57. In Asia, I welcome the increasing contacts and cooperation between the secretariats of the United Nations and the Association of South-East Asian Nations (ASEAN) on matters relating to regional peace and security. In February 2003, the third regional workshop on conflict prevention, conflict resolution and peace-building in South-East Asia was held in Singapore, focusing on ASEAN and United Nations experiences in anticipating and mediating conflicts. In Latin America, I have welcomed and supported, since their inception, the tireless mediation efforts launched by the Secretary-General of the Organization of American States, concerning the situation in Venezuela and that in Haiti. In the Pacific region, I am pleased to note the increased cooperation between the United Nations and the Pacific Islands Forum.

Electoral assistance

58. Electoral assistance is seen by the United Nations as a tool for conflict prevention. A timely and well-executed electoral process which is transparent and inclusive can prevent an increase in tension and violence that could otherwise result from dissatisfaction in the face of real or perceived electoral irregularities. For example, in response to a request from the Palestinian Authority, the United Nations deployed two electoral teams to help establish the Palestinian Central Electoral Commission and to prepare for a voter registration exercise. It did so to enable the Commission to adequately carry out transparent and efficient elections or a referendum when called upon to do so under the road map. This is to ensure that the peace process would not lose momentum for lack of a credible voters register or because of an inadequately prepared Electoral Commission. Moreover, a senior electoral adviser was put in place to counsel the United Nations Special Coordinator for the Middle East Peace Process on the impact of the electoral process on the implementation of the road map.

59. The limited capacity of the Jamaican authorities to properly respond to electoral complaints had given rise to violence in previous elections in Jamaica. To meet the Government's request for assistance in preventing a repetition of violent incidents during the new electoral period, the United Nations focused on enhancing the legal and investigative capacities of the Jamaican electoral authorities and Jamaica's Political Ombudsperson, so as to enable them to deal with electoral appeals and complaints. While the impact of this assistance is difficult to quantify, no deaths were attributed to the parliamentary elections held late in 2002.

60. From September 2002 to July 2003, the United Nations received 32 official requests for electoral assistance. Positive responses were provided to 20 of those requests, nine remain under consideration and three could not be fulfilled.

Terrorism

61. Terrorism continues to pose a major threat to international peace and security. The Counter-Terrorism Committee, established pursuant to Security Council resolution 1373(2001), continued to review reports from Member States on the implementation of relevant measures to suppress and prevent terrorism. It also continued to facilitate the provision to States of the assistance they required to comply with their obliga-

tions under resolution 1373(2001). The United Nations Office on Drugs and Crime launched, in October 2002, the Global Programme against Terrorism, as a framework for its operational activities in this field, and obtained the approval of the General Assembly to strengthen the Terrorism Prevention Branch of the Centre for International Crime Prevention. The Department of Public Information will ensure that the Organization's principled positions and activities relating to terrorism obtain broad coverage.

62. Countering the financing of terrorism has become a principal area of focus for the international community. Assistance to Governments in identifying, tracing and seizing illicit assets increases the ability of States to confront both conventional criminality and terrorism. Assistance provided in this area by the Office on Drugs and Crime includes legislative drafting and capacity-building for investigators, prosecutors and the financial sector, as well as the establishment and strengthening of financial intelligence units—which together form the basis for targeting money-laundering and terrorist financing.

63. While we are vigorously pursuing the struggle against terrorism, it is important to make sure that the dignity of individuals and their fundamental freedoms, as well as democratic practices and the due process of law, are not trampled on. To this end, the Office of the United Nations High Commissioner for Human Rights continues to emphasize the importance of respecting human rights in the context of counter-terrorism efforts and has strengthened contacts between the United Nations human rights bodies and the Counter-Terrorism Committee. In my public pronouncements, I have consistently stressed that there is no trade-off between human rights and security: respecting human rights must be a fundamental element in the fight against terrorism. Promoting values of tolerance and the dialogue among civilizations is also of paramount importance.

Disarmament

64. The year 2003 marks the twenty-fifth anniversary of the convening of the first special session of the General Assembly devoted to disarmament. Yet the body of multilateral disarmament norms has been slowly eroded as a result of weakened international commitment, while the structures set up to deliberate and negotiate further measures remain at a standstill. I am particularly concerned with the prolonged stalemate in the Conference on Disarmament. Lack of agreement on its programme of work has again blocked substantive work, even on issues where there is consensus to begin negotiations. The Conference must be allowed to play its mandated role as the sole multilateral disarmament negotiating body.

65. Developments in 2003 heightened the concern of the world community that nuclear, biological or chemical weapons might be used by State or non-State actors. Universal adherence to, and full and effective compliance with, negotiated multilateral agreements are powerful tools in the battle against the use and proliferation of such weapons. The danger that weapons of mass destruction might fall into the hands of terrorists has been a major global concern. Concerted efforts to promote disarmament, non-proliferation and the security of weapon-related materials are essential for preventing terrorists from obtaining such weapons.

66. I welcomed the entry into force of the Moscow Treaty on Strategic Offensive Reductions between the Russian Federation and the United States of America in June 2003. Further steps to make reductions in strategic nuclear weapons irreversible, transparent and verifiable would greatly strengthen international peace and security. At the second session of the Preparatory Committee for the 2005 Review Conference of the Parties to the Treaty on the Non-Proliferation of Nuclear Weapons, States parties reaffirmed that the Treaty remained the cornerstone of the global non-proliferation regime and the essential foundation for nuclear disarmament. Nevertheless, the decision of the Democratic People's Republic of Korea to withdraw from the Treaty, the first such decision since the Treaty's entry into force 33 years ago, particularly undermined confidence in its effective implementation. While there has been a marked increase in adherence to the Comprehensive Nuclear-Test-Ban Treaty, further efforts are needed to ensure that that Treaty enters into force.

67. The First Biennial Meeting of States to Consider the Implementation of the Programme of Action to Prevent, Combat and Eradicate the Illicit Trade in Small Arms and Light Weapons in All Its Aspects was held in New York in July 2003. After just two years of activity, 99 States were able to present national status reports. I am encouraged by the many initiatives being taken at the national, regional and international levels to stem the illicit trade in these weapons. The Meeting confirmed the need for partnerships at all of those levels, including with civil society, to assist States in implementing the Programme of Action adopted in 2001. The United Nations will continue to do its part to encourage and assist States in their efforts to mitigate the impact on security, development and human rights of the illicit trade in small arms and light weapons.

Sanctions

68. Sanctions remain an important tool in promoting and maintaining international peace and security. Their frequent use in the late 1990s has, however, raised concerns about their effect on civilian populations and their consequences for the humanitarian situation in the targeted country or region. I have been encouraged by progress during the period under review towards refining international sanctions so that they maximize pressure on the intended targets while minimizing adverse effects on the general population and third States. The Security Council now frequently requests assessment reports on the humanitarian implications of current and possible future sanction regimes. The Office for the Coordination of Humanitarian Affairs of the Secretariat has been mandated to carry out such assessments. In addition to the establishment of panels of experts and monitoring mechanisms, improved implementation of targeted sanctions also requires regular, accurate and transparent reporting by States. Such reporting helps sanctions committees to gauge the level of compliance and is useful in identifying technical assistance required by States to improve implementation. I was pleased to note that some of the findings from the Stockholm Process on the Implementation of Targeted Sanctions were reflected in the enhanced reporting requirements contained in Security Council resolution 1455(2003). I wish to encourage further expert discussions on the potential use of targeted measures to prevent or contain conflict.

69. Sanctions were reinforced or expanded against Somalia and Liberia and members of the Taliban and Al-Qa'idah. The Security Council lifted sanctions against UNITA, in view of the end of the war in Angola and the transformation of UNITA into a political party, and decided not to renew prohibitions against the import of rough diamonds from Sierra Leone, given that Government's full participation in the Kimberley Process. The Council also terminated all prohibitions relating to trade with Iraq, except with regard to the supply of arms.

Chapter II

Meeting humanitarian commitments

70. There have been significant improvements and disturbing setbacks in humanitarian affairs over the past year. While long-standing conflicts in Angola, Sierra Leone and the Sudan appear to be moving towards resolution, thus easing the humanitarian situation in those countries, outbreaks of fighting in Côte d'Ivoire, the eastern Democratic Republic of the Congo and Liberia have exacerbated the already devastating human suffering in those areas. Protracted conflicts in Colombia and the Occupied Palestinian Territory continue to give rise to grave concern. Numerous natural disasters have caused much suffering and loss of life, and in some places have wreaked havoc on populations already ravaged by war or infectious diseases such as malaria, tuberculosis and, especially, HIV/AIDS.

71. The United Nations system has sought to respond to the numerous humanitarian crises both equitably and efficiently, placing the principles of humanity, neutrality and impartiality at the core of its efforts. Significant energies have been expended over the year in ensuring a more coherent and strategically coordinated humanitarian response, through further strengthening the consolidated appeals process and partnerships with recipient countries, non-governmental organizations and other international institutions.

The challenge of protecting and assisting refugees and displaced populations

72. Over the past year nascent peace processes in several previously war-torn countries have created opportunities to improve substantially the lives of many returning refugees and internally displaced persons. In Afghanistan, over 2 million refugees and 750,000 internally displaced persons returned home following the fall of the Taliban regime. In Angola, almost 130,000 refugees repatriated spontaneously from neighbouring countries and more than a million internally displaced persons returned to their villages. In Sierra Leone, some 75,000 refugees returned to their homes from Guinea and Liberia and nearly the entire population of internally displaced persons was returned or resettled by December 2002. In Sri Lanka, some 240,000 uprooted people returned to their home areas following the beginning of peace negotiations. The majority of the 170,000 persons from the former Yugoslav Republic of Macedonia who had fled their homes in 2001 were able to return, signifying the end of the emergency.

73. Tragically, millions of refugees around the world remain affected by vicious cycles of conflict and upheaval, with little hope for return. In Africa alone, there were over 3 million persons in such "protracted" refugee situations, including from the Democratic Republic of the Congo, Eritrea, Somalia and the Sudan. In Western Sahara, around 165,000 refugees continued to languish in camps more than a quarter of a century since the dispute began, still waiting for a political solution. Despite progress made in Afghani-

stan, over 1.1 million Afghan refugees remained in the Islamic Republic of Iran and 1.2 million in Pakistan. Overall, the global number of refugees was estimated in early 2003 to be some 10.3 million persons, a decrease of 1.7 million, or 14 per cent, compared with one year earlier. The total population of concern to the Office of the United Nations High Commissioner for Refugees, including refugees, asylum seekers and internally displaced persons, as well as those who returned during the year, increased slightly, from 19.8 million in early 2002 to some 20.5 million in early 2003. Whereas many refugees were able to return home, almost 300,000 additional persons were forced to flee their homes and became refugees in 2002, mainly from Burundi (29,000), the Democratic Republic of the Congo (39,000) and Liberia (105,000). The largest refugee outflows occurred in Africa. In West Africa, the conflicts in Côte d'Ivoire and Liberia led to tragic displacements across the entire subregion and sparked instability in neighbouring countries, while also jeopardizing efforts at consolidating stability in Sierra Leone.

74. Although States have the primary responsibility for the well-being of their citizens, UNHCR has in recent years become more engaged in responding to situations where the protection needs of internally displaced persons mirror those of refugees. Over 6 million internally displaced persons continue to endure suffering and abuse in Burundi, Colombia and the Sudan. In the Democratic Republic of the Congo, optimism over successful peace negotiations was tempered by continuing bloodshed and displacement, in particular in the Ituri region. In Indonesia, the resumption of a military offensive against the separatist movement in Aceh also led to the displacement of thousands of people. There are currently some 370,000 internally displaced persons in the Russian Federation. The work of my Representative on Internally Displaced Persons has contributed significantly to gaining international attention and enhancing the response to the problem of internal displacement. The Guiding Principles on Internal Displacement, which were developed by my Representative and a team of legal experts, provide guidance to all pertinent actors and set forth the rights and guarantees applicable in all relevant phases, that is, during displacement, return, resettlement and reintegration. The Guiding Principles have increasingly been taken into account in the work of regional organizations and have been of assistance in the drafting of legislation on internal displacement in a number of countries. The Internal Displacement Unit of the Office for the Coordination of Humanitarian Affairs has maintained its focus on providing support to specific internal displacement crises, while promoting United Nations system-wide improvements in dealing with such crises. Training workshops and expert advice and guidance provided by the Unit, in collaboration with other humanitarian partners, have for example led to the expression of interest on the part of the authorities of the Sudan in developing a national policy on internally displaced people.

75. The return of refugees and displaced populations presents enormous challenges. Achieving sustainable solutions entails the arduous task of rebuilding shattered economies and finding gainful employment for populations who have known little but war. One approach, referred to as the "4 Rs" (repatriation, reintegration, rehabilitation and reconstruction), brings humanitarian and development actors together in the context of post-conflict situations. In Sierra Leone and Sri Lanka, UNHCR and UNDP have been working to effectively target development and reintegration assistance to areas with high numbers of returnees. Special "4R" collaboration is under way in Afghanistan and Eritrea as well. A United Nations University study emphasizes that the management of refugee movements and protection of displaced people should be an integral part of conflict settlement, peacebuilding and regional security.

76. In developing countries that host refugees, lack of security has remained a major problem. Refugee camps and settlements have been infiltrated by armed elements. The forced recruitment of refugees, especially children—including those previously demobilized—by both government forces and rebel groups have also been of major concern. Such problems were particularly prevalent in the West Africa region over the past year. In Guinea, UNHCR was forced to move some 33,000 refugees from a camp near the Liberian border to a safer location some 250 miles away, following repeated raids by Liberian armed groups.

77. The Office of the United Nations High Commissioner for Refugees, UNICEF and partner agencies have committed considerable resources over the year to improving the protection of refugee women and children. Girls and women have been routinely targeted by campaigns of gender-based violence, including rape, mutilation, prostitution, forced pregnancy and sexual slavery. In response to incidents of sexual and gender-based violence in refugee camps, a series of preventive and remedial measures were put in place, including investigation systems, recourse mechanisms and programmes of victim support. In Guinea, UNHCR and its non-

governmental organization partners promoted the establishment of refugee associations in camps to enhance prevention of and response to sexual and gender-based violence. In Sierra Leone, a sensitization campaign was undertaken by UNICEF in all camps, in the communities surrounding the camps and in four interim care centres. Other measures taken in Sierra Leone included development of a community monitoring system and complaints mechanism in the camps, training of humanitarian workers on sexual abuse and exploitation and training for police in interviewing in cases of sexual abuse, sexual exploitation and domestic violence. UNICEF, the World Food Programme (WFP) and non-governmental organization partners have jointly spearheaded training of United Nations and non-governmental organization staff and partners in preventing and responding to sexual exploitation in six countries in Southern Africa.

78. The period under review has seen new challenges to the protection of refugees, many of them linked to broader developments in the international arena. Security concerns have led to new and stringent checks by States at entry points to their territories, making it increasingly difficult for asylum-seekers to gain access to asylum procedures. Many Governments seem to be succumbing to the temptation of applying discriminatory measures in order to limit the admission of all potential immigrants, including asylum-seekers. Cases of arbitrary detention have also become commonplace in some countries. As a result, public support for the asylum process has been undermined and refugees have faced unfair suspicion, prejudice and xenophobia. Recognizing that States have legitimate security concerns linked to the asylum-migration nexus, UNHCR has been exploring ways to work with Governments on those issues. The year 2002 witnessed the completion of the Global Consultations on International Protection, involving States, intergovernmental organizations, non-governmental organizations, academics, legal practitioners and refugees. As a result of that process, an Agenda for Protection was adopted, reflecting a renewed commitment to address gaps in international protection. UNHCR, as part of its commitment to the process, launched the Convention Plus initiative, the purpose of which is to develop special arrangements that promote durable solutions and fairer burden-sharing.

Delivering humanitarian assistance and the challenge of underfunded emergencies

79. As I mentioned earlier, the consolidated appeals process continued to be strengthened as a strategic planning tool for the United Nations and its partners. During the reporting period, the United Nations and its partners produced 27 consolidated appeals for humanitarian assistance, requesting a total of $5.8 billion from the international community. The overall response to those appeals as at 21 July 2003 stood at 52 per cent. With the funds made available, even if not at the desired level, the United Nations was able to provide food, shelter, medicine and other lifesaving assistance to 45 million victims of conflict, drought and other emergencies.

80. The donor community has generously supported WFP humanitarian operations, providing almost $1.8 billion over the course of 2002. However, not all WFP operations were fully funded and the significant shortfalls compromised assistance efforts in places such as Colombia, Eritrea, the Occupied Palestinian Territory, the Sudan and Tajikistan. In addition, the benefits of food aid can only be fully realized when combined with other programmes. Adequate funding for non-food assistance is therefore critical to ensuring the success of humanitarian action. Such non-food assistance must include support for the restoration of livelihoods, including in sectors such as agriculture. Underfunding of the emergency and early rehabilitation activities of the Food and Agriculture Organization of the United Nations (FAO) jeopardized its ability to assist displaced or other disaster-affected persons in recovering their productive capacity.

81. Health sector programmes in the consolidated appeals remained chronically under-resourced, receiving on average only 10 per cent of the resources requested. Nevertheless, the World Health Organization (WHO) worked to fight a malaria epidemic, meningitis and cholera in Burundi, helped manage a yellow fever epidemic in Guinea and was able to respond to an outbreak of Lassa fever in the refugee camps in Sierra Leone within 48 hours. The severe acute respiratory syndrome (SARS) was the first new disease to emerge in the twenty-first century. When it was first identified by WHO, in February 2003, it was apparent that the disease spread rapidly within hospitals and was being transported by aircraft, that no therapy was effective and that SARS could inflict enormous damage to economies. WHO coordinated global action to identify the cause of SARS, control outbreaks and prevent the disease from becoming established as it moved from country to country. The United Nations Population Fund (UNFPA) was able to provide basic maternity care and HIV prevention for internally displaced people and refugees in a dozen countries. However, because donor support for these reproductive health needs was insufficient and, moreover, concentrated on a

few highly visible emergencies, assistance for many populations facing conflict was inadequate. Adequate attention to health is crucial in dealing with humanitarian emergencies and requires coordinated action and timely provision of the necessary funds by the donors.

82. Underfunding has a particularly direct impact on the lives of children and women. For example, low funding over the past year meant that UNICEF work to provide emergency health assistance in the Republic of the Congo had to focus on high-risk areas and not the entire country. Whereas 1.2 million children should have been vaccinated against measles, only 200,000 were covered, given the low level of resources received. In education, of the 1,700 schools that needed to be re-equipped, only 120 could be covered. In the Democratic People's Republic of Korea, only limited types of medicine could be made available, mainly for the treatment of childhood illnesses.

83. The general shortfall in resources experienced by UNHCR over the year has continued to impede efforts to provide much needed protection and material assistance, in particular in sub-Saharan Africa. At the end of 2002, its overall budget of $829 million was underfunded by some $100 million, which has led in many cases to the scaling back of already reduced assistance and services to more than 4 million refugees and other people of concern to UNHCR, especially in Africa, where the needs are the greatest.

84. Though funding constraints limited the scale of their operations, WHO, UNICEF and their non-governmental partners carried out measles and vitamin A campaigns in Afghanistan, Angola, Burundi, Somalia and elsewhere. Between January 2002 and June 2003, 15.3 million children between six months and 12 years of age were vaccinated against measles and received vitamin A supplements in Afghanistan (93 per cent coverage), preventing an estimated 35,000 child deaths. In Angola, between September 2002 and June 2003, 7.2 million children between nine months and 14 years of age were vaccinated against measles and received vitamin A supplements (95 per cent coverage), averting an estimated 10,000 child deaths. United Nations bodies and their partners also organized successful national immunization days for the eradication of polio in Afghanistan, Liberia, Somalia and the Sudan. Between September 2002 and May 2003, 34 million doses of oral polio vaccine were administered to 6.5 million children under five years of age in Afghanistan, through different rounds of national and subnational immunization days. It is encouraging to note that there has been only one reported case of polio to date this year in Afghanistan.

85. The past year saw a number of important achievements in Afghanistan, allowing for significant economic progress to take place. Higher rainfall in some parts of the country and heavy snowfall resulted in improved harvests, with more people now being able to meet their basic food needs. Significant numbers of Afghans, especially women and children, however, remained vulnerable and continued to rely on food aid. In 2002, WFP fed over 323,700 children in Afghanistan through the back-to-school programme, supported the return and resettlement of 330,000 families and helped to strengthen the civil service through the provision of salary supplements to 251,000 civil servants. Despite marked improvement, however, security continues to be a major constraint on humanitarian action in Afghanistan.

86. In the Democratic People's Republic of Korea, a government assessment of the nutritional status of children made in collaboration with UNICEF and WFP indicated a significant improvement between 1998 and 2002. Food assistance had contributed directly to improving the nutritional status of vulnerable groups, though the needs of those groups remained high. The situation could deteriorate again. WFP was forced to suspend distributions to 3 million beneficiaries as a result of funding shortages at the end of 2002.

87. In Angola, the end of the conflict in April 2002 led to the mass return of internally displaced persons and refugees and the opening up of previously inaccessible areas. The Government estimates that 2.3 million internally displaced persons have returned to their homes, while another 1.4 million remain displaced. WFP has been able to increase the number of people it assists by over 80 per cent, substantially supporting the consolidation of the newly realized peace, and UNICEF has expanded school access.

88. The humanitarian situation continued to worsen in the Democratic Republic of the Congo, in particular its eastern region. Access to the most vulnerable remained the main challenge, driven by lack of security, harassment by the conflicting parties and poor infrastructure. Violence against civilians was rampant, in particular sexual violence against women and girls. UNICEF, together with non-governmental organization partners, provided psychological assistance to almost 1,000 women survivors of sexual violence in South Kivu and strengthened community support networks. UNFPA worked to sensitize military and police leaders to the need to prevent gender violence.

89. In Eritrea and Ethiopia, drought has again sharply increased the number of people in

need of relief assistance. Such assistance is necessary to save lives, prevent mass migration and preserve the assets of farmers and pastoralists. In response to the increasingly alarming situation, in June 2003 I appointed a Special Envoy for the Humanitarian Crisis in the Horn of Africa, who visited Eritrea and Ethiopia in July 2003. While persisting drought conditions and their long-term effects continued to increase the number of people in need of humanitarian assistance in both countries, Ethiopia has been particularly hard hit. Despite generous donor support, which secured almost 100 per cent of funding requirements of the consolidated inter-agency appeal for Ethiopia for 2003, malnutrition levels in many areas of the country continued to increase and, by July 2003, it was determined that an additional 2.3 million people would require assistance until the end of the year, thus bringing the total number of beneficiaries to over 13.1 million.

90. The humanitarian crisis in Southern Africa threatens to be one of the most severe and complex humanitarian disasters of the last decade, the result of a combination of erratic rainfall, poverty, economic decline, inadequate food security policies and high rates of HIV/AIDS infection. During 2002, the number of people at risk of severe food insecurity rose from 12.8 million to 14.4 million. Generous donor support enabled WFP to mobilize capacity rapidly to help millions of people in Lesotho, Malawi, Mozambique, Swaziland, Zambia and Zimbabwe. United Nations entities have been working together in the Regional Inter-Agency Coordination and Support Office to raise awareness and emphasize the need to move beyond the traditional emergency response in order to find durable solutions.

91. My Special Envoy for Humanitarian Needs in Southern Africa has played an important role in raising donor awareness to the unique nature of the crisis, the first major emergency in which high rates of HIV/AIDS infection have played a significant role in exacerbating food insecurity and malnutrition. The HIV/AIDS epidemic has introduced a new complexity into humanitarian crises, which requires rethinking of humanitarian assistance. The lessons learned from the regional response indicate not only that methods for food security analysis, food rations and/or nutrition-related activities should be adjusted, but also that such efforts need to be combined with emergency development action in the social and health sectors.

92. Old and new conflicts in West Africa put considerable strain on humanitarian intervention efforts during the past year and endangered the stability of fragile neighbouring countries. In a worrisome trend, both the escalation of the conflict in Liberia and renewed fighting in Côte d'Ivoire were marked by a blatant disregard for the protection of civilians, increase in recruitment and use of children in armed conflict and contempt for humanitarian work. In an environment without law and order, humanitarian efforts have proved extremely difficult, especially in Liberia, where the escalation of the country's civil war in March 2003 resulted in a humanitarian crisis of immense proportions. Sustained combat in the capital city of Monrovia led to a complete breakdown of law and order, the displacement of about 50 per cent of the city's population and the evacuation of all United Nations international personnel. The arrival of peacekeepers in August 2003, as well as the transitional political arrangements, have provided a new opportunity for humanitarian agencies to assess the situation and resume relief operations for the most vulnerable groups. On 6 August 2003, the United Nations launched a revised consolidated inter-agency appeal for Liberia, requesting $69 million to respond to the increased humanitarian needs. Efforts are under way to strengthen the overall capacity of the humanitarian community to deal effectively with the situation.

93. In Iraq, the Office for the Coordination of Humanitarian Affairs played a key role in the establishment and maintenance of humanitarian coordination mechanisms both prior to and after the onset of the war in March 2003, at the field and headquarters levels. WFP succeeded in dispatching over 1.13 million tons of food commodities into Iraq between April and June 2003. WFP also managed a United Nations joint logistics centre for the Iraq crisis, coordinating the logistics capabilities of humanitarian agencies, and provided common airlift services for the relief operation by managing the United Nations humanitarian air service. WHO led efforts in the health sector through the supply of badly needed drugs and other medical items, public health programmes and rehabilitation of health facilities. UNICEF led the United Nations emergency efforts in the provision of non-food assistance, including critical supplies for child survival, supplemental nutrition and basic education materials, as well as in the provision of emergency water supplies, in collaboration with non-governmental organization partners. UNDP installed generators and rehabilitated electricity facilities that provided power supply for the operation of hospitals, water-pumping stations and sewage-treatment plants.

94. The oil-for-food programme, administered by the Office of the Iraq Programme, has continued to deliver supplies to meet the basic

humanitarian needs of the Iraqi people. Prior to the war, the programme, among other achievements, had succeeded in reducing by half malnutrition rates among children under the age of five. In its resolution 1483(2003), the Security Council stipulated that the programme should be phased out by 21 November 2003. Until that time, the United Nations and its entities and programmes, in coordination with the Coalition Provisional Authority and the emerging Iraqi authorities, will continue to review and prioritize contracts, as well as facilitate the shipment of civilian goods to Iraq from a delivery pipeline valued at some $10 billion. Separately, on 28 March 2003, the United Nations launched a flash appeal for dealing with the Iraq crisis, seeking $2.2 billion. The flash appeal was revised in June 2003, when outstanding requirements of $259 million were presented, reflecting resources already made available by donors and through the oil-for-food programme, as well as new priorities that emerged after the end of major hostilities.

95. The United Nations Development Group has been working, in collaboration with the Office of the Humanitarian Coordinator for Iraq, the World Bank and the International Monetary Fund, under the overall coordination of my Special Representative for Iraq, to identify priorities for Iraq's reconstruction through a joint needs assessment. That exercise is being carried out bearing in mind issues of gender, human rights, environment and capacity-building. The United Nations Development Group has also convened a donor liaison group, consisting of over 50 members who regularly share information on the needs assessment process and on the donor conference on the reconstruction of Iraq scheduled for October 2003.

96. In the Occupied Palestinian Territory, the humanitarian situation has yet to show signs of improvement following the parties' embarking on implementation of the Quartet's road map in June 2003. For most of the past year, the situation has been increasingly desperate and the local population has been facing unprecedented levels of hardship. Closures and curfews have crippled the economy, plunging 1.3 million Palestinians into poverty. Military operations have left over 10,000 homeless. The United Nations Relief and Works Agency for Palestine Refugees in the Near East (UNRWA) has been delivering emergency assistance to over 1 million affected Palestinians, including food aid, shelter reconstruction and employment creation. Heavy restrictions on movement in the Occupied Palestinian Territory have posed serious obstacles to the operations of UNRWA and other international agencies. At the same time, UNRWA received only $37.3 million in funding against an appeal for $94 million to cover emergency operations between January and July 2003. Despite a $37.5 million shortfall in its 2003 regular budget as at 30 June, UNRWA continued to deliver regular education, health and relief and social services to a population of over 4 million registered Palestinian refugees in Jordan, Lebanon, the Syrian Arab Republic, the West Bank and the Gaza Strip. WHO played a key role in coordinating the health sector and in providing technical assistance in key domains, such as nutrition and mental health. It also advocated for access and the right to health of the Palestinian population. The UNDP Programme of Assistance to the Palestinian People provided some emergency assistance, in addition to major employment and technical assistance.

Natural disaster management: responding to emergencies and building capacity

97. Severe floods recurred across Asia between September and November 2002. Serious damage was caused by cyclones in the Pacific region in January 2003. In May 2003, earthquakes occurred in Algeria and Turkey and torrential rains led to the most serious flooding and landslides in Sri Lanka since 1947. Severe and continual rainfall that began in late June 2003 has led to flooding in a number of provinces in China, affecting 130 million people and resulting in the evacuation of more than 3 million from their homes and the death of over 800 persons. Droughts continued to affect large parts of the population in African and Asian countries, compounding very challenging situations also associated with conflicts and lethal epidemics such as HIV/AIDS. From 1 September 2002 to 8 August 2003, the Office for the Coordination of Humanitarian Affairs responded to 75 natural disasters, mobilizing international assistance through appeals and situation reports, providing emergency cash grants, channelling grants from donor Governments and fielding United Nations disaster assessment and coordination missions.

98. The efforts of the United Nations to reduce the impact of natural hazards through mitigating vulnerability and disaster risks have been undermined by limited funding. Humanitarian donors shy away from channelling monies to activities with a longer-term impact, while development donors have not yet fully assumed that responsibility. Nevertheless, advocacy efforts have ensured heightened awareness of the imperative to reduce risk and vulnerability to natural hazards and other technological and environmental disasters in order to achieve sustainable development. The International Strategy for Disaster Reduction, coordinated by its secretariat, has

increasingly been utilized to guide commitment and action by United Nations entities, other international and regional organizations and Governments. The special emphasis on developing subregional and national plans in Africa has been further strengthened by the creation of an International Strategy for Disaster Reduction outreach programme for Africa and by activities undertaken jointly by the secretariat, UNDP, the United Nations Environment Programme (UNEP) and others. Regional consultations have been carried out in Asia, Europe and the South Pacific and are further planned in Africa and the Americas. UNDP has contributed to increased capacity for disaster reduction in 33 countries worldwide, including early warning systems, strengthening of national disaster offices, risk reduction tools and strategies, support to legislative systems and strengthening knowledge networks. Other United Nations entities are also gradually developing substantive disaster reduction programmes and activities within the framework of the International Strategy.

Coordination of assistance and the protection of civilians in armed conflict

99. Effective humanitarian responses require well-managed coordination and rapid resource mobilization. Working through the inter-agency system, the Office for the Coordination of Humanitarian Affairs strives to ensure an adequate response to humanitarian crises by mobilizing resources, promoting access to vulnerable populations and undertaking field coordination. Furthermore, the United Nations system as a whole is committed to ensuring a smooth transition from provision of humanitarian assistance to development activities in post-conflict situations.

100. An example of an effective coordinated approach to a humanitarian crisis was the extensive inter-agency contingency preparations for the Iraq conflict. Well in advance of the outbreak of the war, a regional humanitarian coordination office was established, from which the humanitarian response was planned and coordinated in close collaboration with non-governmental organizations.

101. There has been considerable activity on the part of the Organization over the past year towards mainstreaming protection issues into the policies and decision-making processes of Member States and the United Nations system at large, including in the discussions of the Security Council. In November 2002, in my third report to the Security Council on the protection of civilians in armed conflict, I highlighted three emerging challenges: *(a)* gender-based violence in humanitarian crises and conflict situations; *(b)* the harmful consequences of the commercial exploitation of conflict; and *(c)* the escalating threat of global terrorism.

102. The continuing challenge is to identify and utilize more effective means of implementing the principles and policies that are in place, to mainstream them into the humanitarian work of the United Nations system and to translate them into specific measures in the field. Some important steps have been taken in that regard. For example, United Nations entities in Afghanistan, Burundi and Iraq have used the aide-memoire formulated by the Security Council (S/PRST/2002/6, annex) to put together an active collaborative framework for the protection of civilians that has led to a more coherent inter-agency response. In Iraq, human rights officers deployed with the Office of the Humanitarian Coordinator for Iraq developed a policy framework on human rights protection together with United Nations humanitarian bodies and other international organizations to guide humanitarian assistance. Human rights advisers led inter-agency technical working groups on protection-related issues in Côte d'Ivoire and Iraq. Another significant development has been the inclusion of protection principles in the mandates of certain peacekeeping missions, including the United Nations Organization Mission in the Democratic Republic of the Congo and the Economic Community of West African States and French forces in Côte d'Ivoire.

103. A series of regional workshops on issues of protection of civilians in armed conflict was launched in October 2002. Since that time, workshops have been held in East Asia and the Pacific, Europe, the South Pacific, Southern Africa and West Africa, with additional workshops planned in the coming months in Latin America and South Asia. The workshops aim to examine the nature of humanitarian challenges during complex emergencies within each region and to explore possible means of addressing such challenges from a regional perspective. All these activities are consistent with my call for a "culture of protection" within the international community. The continued commitment of Member States to those issues will be vital in consolidating the positive gains made through our collective efforts to date.

104. Child soldiers continue to be a tragic part of many conflicts. For example, in northern Uganda, an estimated 8,400 children were abducted between June 2002 and May 2003. This is a sharp increase compared with the 12,000 registered child abductions in the 11-year period from 1990 to 2001. Some progress has been made, however, in child soldier disarmament, demobiliza-

tion and reintegration over the year. In Afghanistan, UNICEF has been helping support a child-specific component as part of the Afghanistan New Beginnings Programme, with the aim to disarm, demobilize and reintegrate all under-age soldiers by 2005. Under the leadership of the World Bank, the Multi-Country Demobilization and Reintegration Programme in the greater Great Lakes region of Africa brings together Governments, United Nations entities, regional organizations and the international financial institutions to facilitate the demobilization and reintegration of fighters in seven countries in the subregion. Specific projects for demobilization, disarmament and reintegration of child soldiers in Burundi and the Democratic Republic of the Congo have been developed with UNICEF and are about to be launched.

Chapter III

Cooperating for development

105. Over the past year, the Organization supported Member States in their efforts to achieve the Millennium Development Goals and addressed specific issues emerging from recent major United Nations conferences and summits.

106. I am pleased to report good progress in response to the guidance provided by Member States and in line with my vision for reform of the United Nations. The United Nations system, including the specialized agencies, has continued to strive to achieve greater coherence in their policies and programmes with a view to improving the efficiency and impact of the support they provide at the country level.

Eradicating extreme poverty

107. Extreme poverty is a multidimensional phenomenon with varied causes, including insufficient economic growth and investment, persistent societal inequalities, inadequate social safety nets, a lack of investment in education and health and a shortage of development finance, as well as prevailing international financial and trade relations that leave lower-income countries at a disadvantage. To enhance the process of development, the following elements are critical: new and increased financing for development; cooperation from the private sector; a successful development round of trade negotiations; the alleviation of urban and rural poverty; secure access to food, good health and education; improved governance; opportunities for women living in poverty; and use of new technologies such as information and communications technologies for poverty eradication purposes. The Organization is making every effort to ensure that those issues are addressed at the global, regional and national levels.

108. In its follow-up to the International Conference on Financing for Development, the General Assembly, at its fifty-seventh session, established the high-level dialogue on financing for development, as well as the Financing for Development Office in the Department of Economic and Social Affairs of the Secretariat, which became operational in January 2003. The high-level dialogue will serve as the intergovernmental focal point for the general follow-up to the Conference. The United Nations system, in cooperation with other key stakeholders, including the Bretton Woods institutions and the World Trade Organization (WTO), the private sector and civil society, will undertake activities to help accelerate the process of implementation of the Monterrey Consensus adopted by the Conference.

109. As also envisaged in the Monterrey Consensus, the Economic and Social Council held the first of a new series of high-level meetings in April 2003 with the Bretton Woods institutions and WTO in which ministers of finance and development cooperation, governors of central banks and senior officials from several international organizations participated. The outcome of the meeting, embodied in the summary by the President of the Council (A/58/77-E/2003/62), included a number of recommendations to advance the implementation of the policy commitments in the Monterrey Consensus and to facilitate the discussion process in the high-level dialogue, the first biennial meeting of which is to be held by the General Assembly in October 2003.

110. Economic growth is essential to meet the Millennium Development Goals, in particular the first goal of eradicating extreme poverty. In its *Human Development Report 2003: Millennium Development Goals*, UNDP estimates that an annual GDP growth of 2.9 per cent per year is required between now and 2015 to reach the Millennium Development Goals—about double the present level. This will not be achieved without concurrent growth in the domestic private sector, the key engine of economic growth and employment generation.

111. As a follow-up to the International Conference on Financing for Development and the World Summit on Sustainable Development and as called for by the General Assembly in its resolution 57/265, I launched, in July 2003, in New York, the Commission on the Private Sector and Development. The main purpose of the Commission, which is composed of prominent leaders

from business, the public sector, academia and civil society, is to develop strategic recommendations on how to promote a strong, indigenous private sector in developing countries and to initiate programmes with the highest potential impact in private sector development. The Commission will submit a report to me by the end of 2003 with specific policy recommendations for developing and developed countries, as well as multilateral development agencies. The Commission will seek to highlight successful initiatives already under way in the field of private sector development. Its overall recommendations will also be forwarded for consideration to heads of national and multilateral development agencies, as well as to leaders in the private sector.

112. Increased and more equitable world trade holds forth the prospect of helping nations to combat poverty and hunger and achieve the Millennium Development Goals, including through increased income for small farmers. The Organization, in particular the United Nations Conference on Trade and Development, continues to advocate policies that enhance free and fair trade. The Doha Ministerial Declaration, adopted by the Fourth Ministerial Conference of WTO in November 2001, launched a work programme of trade negotiations to be accomplished by no later than 1 January 2005. By placing development at the heart of multilateral trade negotiations, the Doha Declaration provides a major opportunity as well as a challenge for all stakeholders to fully integrate the concerns and interests of developing countries into the trade negotiations and work programme. The Fifth Ministerial Conference of WTO, to be held at Cancun, Mexico, in September 2003, will take stock of progress in the Doha work programme and provide political guidance and take decisions as necessary. The successful conclusion of the development round of trade negotiations is vital to reviving the world economy. The Fifth Ministerial Conference represents an important milestone on the road to a successful conclusion of the Doha round. I urge Member States to make every effort to ensure a successful outcome of the meeting as well as the success of the round as a whole.

113. Extreme poverty is becoming an increasingly urban phenomenon, with nearly half the world's population now living in cities and 1 billion people in slums. The rate of rural to urban migration in developing countries is increasing at a pace that far exceeds the rate of urbanization as a whole and the phenomenon is having a substantial impact on the food and nutritional security of both producers and consumers in developing countries. At the same time, however, over 60 per cent of the population of low- to middle-income countries live in rural areas and depend on agriculture for their livelihood. Poverty reduction strategies need to take account of both groups in terms of their particular needs. During 2002, Governments launched the Global Campaign for Secure Tenure in collaboration with the United Nations Human Settlements Programme (UN-Habitat) in Brazil, Burkina Faso, Jamaica, Nicaragua, the Philippines and Senegal. The Global Campaign on Urban Governance was launched in Jamaica and the Philippines, where UNDP has supported civic dialogue on critical development questions. The preparations for and launch and follow-up of both campaigns have increased popular awareness of the issues and led to partnerships between civil society and Governments on those issues, leading in many cases to immediate specific policy and legislative outcomes. For example, the Global Campaign on Urban Governance provided input to the review of the Kenya Local Governance Act, drawing on examples of legislation for participatory governance from Bolivia, the Philippines and South Africa. In India, an urban slum improvement policy has been initiated and an urban reform incentive fund has been set up. In Nigeria, a new ministry of housing and urban development has been established and in Namibia a law on flexible land tenure has been drafted with a view to ensuring security of tenure for slum-dwellers.

114. Addressing urban poverty needs to go hand in hand with fighting rural poverty. At its high-level segment, held in July 2003, the Economic and Social Council adopted a ministerial declaration on promoting an integrated approach to rural development in developing countries for poverty eradication and sustainable development. A key message of the declaration was the call for renewed political will to make the global partnership work for rural development. Many countries emphasized the overriding impact of the policies of developed countries on rural development, notably those regarding restricted market access, agricultural producer subsidies and insufficient aid. All recognized that rural development was the responsibility of each country and was predicated on an enabling national environment. The issue of rural poverty is thus back on the international agenda.

115. Economic well-being, nutrition and good health are mutually reinforcing. Eradication of poverty will improve nutrition and health, while poor nutrition and ill health carry adverse economic costs and impede efforts aimed at poverty eradication. The Organization continues to focus on activities that will help improve access to food and ensure good health. FAO is currently assist-

ing countries in revising and updating their food security and agricultural development strategies. As a result, to date, across the regions of the world, over 150 national strategies for food security and agricultural development have been prepared. Governments have officially endorsed some 117 such strategies. The International Fund for Agricultural Development (IFAD) continues to advocate strategies that build on the initiative and capabilities of poor rural producers. Acting as a catalyst, IFAD brings together key stakeholders and mobilizes resources, knowledge and policies to enable the rural poor to overcome poverty. In particular, IFAD projects provide financing and help raise additional resources to increase the access of rural poor people to land, water and other essential resources, to develop rural financial services in support of small enterprises and to encourage sustainable agricultural production, as well as to increase marketing opportunities and access to markets.

116. Food aid will remain an important instrument for hunger reduction, especially in emergency and post-conflict situations. In 2002, WFP provided food aid to 72 million of the world's poorest people. Overall, 77 per cent of WFP resources, or more than $1 billion, was used for activities in the 50 countries identified in the FAO report *State of Food Insecurity in the World 2002* as having the greatest number of hungry people as a proportion of total population.

117. In the area of health, the Global Polio Eradication Initiative, led by UNICEF, WHO, the Centers for Disease Control of the United States and Rotary International, made further strides in 2002. Seven countries were polio-endemic by the end of 2002, down from 10 a year earlier. A record 500 million children received oral polio vaccine in 93 countries; UNICEF purchased and delivered the majority of the vaccines, some 1.3 billion doses. UNICEF and other key stakeholders also supported national and subnational immunization days, reaching more than 200 million children. UNICEF also worked with WHO, Médecins Sans Frontières, the International Committee of the Red Cross and other partners in responding to outbreaks of cholera, meningitis and malaria.

118. An adequate primary education is closely linked to the escape from poverty. In 2003, almost one third of all children in developing countries failed to complete the minimum education requirements for basic literacy and it is estimated that 134 million children in those countries are not in school or have never been to school. Among poor children, the majority of those who have never had access to any formal schooling are girls. Yet girls' education is unquestionably one of the keys to achieving poverty reduction. UNICEF has supported basic education by focusing on a strengthening of the cognitive and psychosocial aspects of early childhood care. This covers the promotion of universal access to and completion of quality basic education, including the development of a healthy, effective and protective learning environment. An important aspect of the support is the promotion of community participation and parents' involvement in schools.

119. Over the past year, the Organization continued to address the challenge of weak institutional structures and inadequate administrative capacity. In 2002, the United Nations Committee of Experts on Public Administration suggested priority areas for Member States to build further capacity in governance and public administration, including in human resource management, knowledge management, management of information and communication technology and the decentralization of administration. To that end, for example, during 2002-2003, the Department of Economic and Social Affairs, in cooperation with UNDP, helped in strengthening municipal and district administration in Rwanda through the preparation of relevant legislation, creation of new management structures and training. The Economic and Social Commission for Western Asia (ESCWA) is building an online database on democracy and good governance practices in the region, including data on the rule of law, human rights and freedom.

120. Promoting the creation of greater economic opportunities for women is critical to the eradication of poverty, since the majority of the people living in poverty, in particular in developing countries, are women. During 2002, the United Nations Development Fund for Women (UNIFEM) collaborated with ESCWA and the Economic and Social Commission for Asia and the Pacific to help national institutions mainstream gender perspectives into statistical systems to better track women's participation in the formal and informal economies. The 2003 Household Income and Expenditure Survey in Mexico is benefiting from that initiative. UNIFEM is also helping to develop strategies to link low-income producers to markets in Burkina Faso, the Democratic People's Republic of Korea, Nigeria, Rwanda, South Asia and the Arab States. Such strategies include facilitating women's access to potential purchasers of their products, through, inter alia, the organization of cooperatives, the use of information and communication technologies—including web sites—for information exchange, and the holding of trading fairs for their products. The second Forum of Women Entre-

preneurs, organized by the Economic Commission for Europe at Geneva in March 2003, exchanged good practices in improving access to financing and information and communication technology for small businesses run by women.

121. In Jordan, a partnership initiated by UNIFEM in 2000 with Cisco Systems, Inc., and the Government of Jordan is yielding positive results in increasing women's ability to access and shape the information and communication technology sector through the development of 10 Cisco networking academies. The project has achieved 63.3 per cent female enrolment in the academies and has produced better information and data on Jordanian women in the information and communication technology sector and greater interest among planners in that area in using such information as a basis for policies and programmes.

122. In 2002, the United Nations Information and Communication Technologies Task Force continued to address policy issues such as the integration of national electronic strategies into overall development and poverty eradication strategies, as well as information and communication technology as an instrument for the advancement and empowerment of women, as emphasized by the Commission on the Status of Women at its forty-seventh session, in March 2003. In 2002, the Task Force undertook a number of initiatives to address different aspects of the ICT for Development agenda. In partnership with UNDP and the United Nations Fund for International Partnerships, the Task Force launched digital diaspora networks for Africa and the Caribbean. Those initiatives aim at creating a network that will link the technological, entrepreneurial, professional and financial resources of members of the diasporas in North America and Europe with their counterparts in Africa and the Caribbean.

123. The Global Virtual University, which I launched in June 2003, a joint initiative of the United Nations University (UNU) and UNEP, is a tangible example of cooperation in building digital bridges to promote human security and prosperity through environmentally sustainable development. The Global Virtual University is an international network of cooperating universities and institutions organized as a branch of UNU with an administrative centre at Arendal, Norway. Its core institutions are UNU, UNEP, the UNEP Global Resource Information Data Centre in Norway (GRID-Arendal) and Agder University College in Norway and it will deliver online courses and programmes on environment and development with a global outreach. Additionally, universities in Ghana, Uganda and South Africa are among its participants.

124. At the regional level, ESCWA is cooperating with the International Labour Organization, the Arab Fund for Economic and Social Development and a number of national non-governmental organizations in implementing the Regional Agenda for Action on Technology, Employment and Poverty Alleviation. That initiative aims at harnessing selected new technologies for employment creation and poverty alleviation with emphasis on economically disadvantaged rural communities. The Agenda includes provision for setting up technology community centres to bring literacy, basic education and vocational training to impoverished communities. The first three of a series of such centres will be launched in Lebanon in September 2003. Others are to follow shortly, both in Lebanon and other member countries. In Africa, technical assistance provided by the Economic Commission for Africa (ECA) is helping strengthen public financial management and build capacity for information and communication technology for development in support of the African Information Society Initiative.

Achieving the Millennium Development Goals

125. In July 2002, the entire United Nations system endorsed a core strategy for supporting the achievement of the Millennium Development Goals. The main elements of that strategy include monitoring progress at the national and global levels, operational support to national priorities, research and advocacy.

126. The United Nations Development Group, the Executive Committee on Economic and Social Affairs and the World Bank are collaborating to monitor progress in the implementation of the United Nations Millennium Declaration (General Assembly resolution 55/2) and to improve the process of reporting and analysing indicators at the national and international levels. My annual report on implementation of the Millennium Development Goals will document progress and shortfalls in attaining the Goals. At the country level, as at June 2003, 37 national Millennium Development Goal reports had been completed, with technical and financial support from UNDP, and I expect that at least an additional 60 will be completed by the end of 2003. The reports are helping to ensure that the Millennium Development Goals become a central part of the development debate throughout societies.

127. In its operational response to the Millennium Development Goals, the United Nations system at the country level has striven to bring its collective expertise together to support the achievement of national goals. It is worth noting

that 117 countries had completed common country assessments and 86 the United Nations Development Assistance Framework by June 2003.

128. The emergence of the World Bank's poverty reduction strategy papers as a critical national tool for focusing expenditures and development assistance on poverty reduction priorities, including the Millennium Development Goals, is providing an opportunity for the United Nations system to further the Goals through its support to national Governments. To date, 30 countries have completed full poverty reduction strategy papers and 48 have completed interim papers.

129. As a contribution to the debate on obstacles to and policies for achieving the Millennium Development Goals, part II of the *World Economic and Social Survey 2003* examines the links between certain macroeconomic policies and poverty, reviewing the relationships between growth-oriented policies and poverty, the impact of trade policies on poverty and the consequences for the urban poor of macroeconomic policy responses to shocks. It analyses the effects of some policies more directly aimed at poverty reduction, such as market-based approaches to land reform and the liberalization and privatization of staple food markets in Africa. It also examines the increase in poverty in the countries with economies in transition since 1990, as well as government and individual reactions. Additionally, under the research pillar, the Millennium Project and its task forces and secretariat collaborated with UNDP in the preparation of the *Human Development Report 2003: Millennium Development Goals*, published in July.

130. In October 2002, I launched the Millennium Development Goal campaign to make the commitments better known throughout the world and to ensure that they are the focus of global action. A Millennium Campaign Unit was established in November 2002 and is assembling a core team of developing and developed country nationals and has started to build networks and partnerships across civil society, parliamentarians, media and other key groups worldwide.

131. The Millennium Campaign team has met with officials from the Organization, parliamentarians, development ministers, religious leaders, media, civil society, non-governmental organizations, trade unions and research institutions. It has established working relationships with parliamentary networks such as the Inter-Parliamentary Union and the Parliamentary Network on the World Bank and has been participating actively in key Parliamentary Network meetings as they begin the process of collaborating on Millennium Development Goal handbooks for parliamentarians. In developing countries, the Campaign is linking and building coalitions for action to encourage Governments to implement pro-poor policies. By means of numerous public speaking engagements, seminars and conferences, including campaign tours through northern Europe and Italy, goal 8 of the Millennium Development Goals, which emphasizes developing global partnerships for development, has taken a central place in many national debates on the Goals. On many occasions, before a variety of audiences, the message has been promoted that action needs to be taken on debt, aid, trade and transfer of technology.

132. Achieving the Millennium Development Goals will require a collective response to the challenges faced by the international community in the area of development. The outcomes of recent major United Nations conferences and summits, in particular, the International Conference on Financing for Development, held at Monterrey, Mexico, in March 2002, the World Summit on Sustainable Development, held at Johannesburg, South Africa, in August 2002, and the Second World Assembly on Ageing, held at Madrid in April 2002, have elaborated upon and added to the commitments made in the Millennium Declaration adopted at the Millennium Summit held at United Nations Headquarters in September 2000. Moreover, at the summit of the Group of Eight in May 2003, the eight heads of State reiterated their support to achieving the Millennium Development Goals and the commitments made at Monterrey. The major challenge continues to be converting those international commitments through cooperation for development into better lives for people around the world. What the conferences and summits have further illustrated is that such implementation needs to be, more than ever before, a multi-stakeholder undertaking involving Governments, civil society, business and others.

Sustainable development

133. The Plan of Implementation adopted at the World Summit on Sustainable Development led to an increased focus on implementation through the adoption of several goals and targets. Those goals and targets were in such areas as water, sanitation, health and energy as well as related to the use and production of chemicals and the maintenance and restoration of fish stocks. The Plan encouraged the development of a 10-year framework of programmes to accelerate the shift towards sustainable consumption and production.

134. Over 200 partnerships for sustainable development were announced as part of the follow-up to the World Summit. Entities of the United Nations system have engaged in many of those partnerships and a significant amount of resources has already been committed for them. I am confident that the partnerships will help to engage key actors in the implementation process.

135. To build on the momentum generated by the World Summit, the Commission on Sustainable Development has reoriented its work to ensure the implementation of the commitments made in Johannesburg. The Organization will fully support the work of the Commission in its activities. The United Nations System Chief Executives Board for Coordination is now finalizing the inter-agency mechanisms for system-wide follow-up to the Summit in such areas as fresh water, sanitation, energy, oceans and coastal areas, and sustainable consumption and production. Those mechanisms will make possible the coordination of policy initiatives by the concerned entities of the United Nations system. At the field level, the Organization is assisting Governments in integrating the outcomes of the Summit into national strategies related to sustainable development. Many member entities of the Executive Committee on Economic and Social Affairs, such as the regional commissions, UNEP, UNDP, UN-Habitat and the Department of Economic and Social Affairs, have made encouraging headway in integrating the operational and normative aspects of the Organization's work in the area of sustainable development through advisory services and technical cooperation. A major objective of such technical cooperation is the creation of national capacity for the implementation of the outcomes of the Summit and previous conferences and summits.

136. In 2002, a secretariat became operational in the Department of Economic and Social Affairs to support the United Nations Forum on Forests, which is recognized in the Johannesburg Plan of Implementation as a key intergovernmental mechanism to facilitate and coordinate the implementation of sustainable forest management worldwide. At its third session, held at Geneva in June 2003, the Forum decided to establish ad hoc expert groups for the protection of forests. Among other issues, those groups will address the finance and transfer of environmentally sound technologies for the preservation of forests.

137. The issue of water and sanitation remained high on the international agenda. In December 2002, the General Assembly declared 2003 International Year of Freshwater. In my message to the Third World Water Forum, held at Kyoto, Shiga and Osaka, Japan, in March 2003, I called for action to secure access to safe drinking water and improve sanitation, especially for the poor and vulnerable. On 22 March 2003, World Water Day, the Organization launched its first *World Water Development Report: Water for People, Water for Life*, the most comprehensive, up-to-date review of the state of the world's water resources.

Africa

138. At its fifty-seventh session, the General Assembly welcomed the New Partnership for Africa's Development (NEPAD), as a programme of the African Union, which should serve as the framework for the international community's support for Africa's development. The Assembly also endorsed my decision to establish the Office of the Special Adviser on Africa in the Secretariat. The main functions of the Office include support for my role in global coordination and advocacy on Africa as well as reporting to the Assembly and the Economic and Social Council in their deliberations on Africa.

139. The Economic Commission for Africa provides support for the implementation of the New Partnership for Africa's Development at the regional level. ECA chairs the annual regional consultation meetings of United Nations entities working in Africa, which is a platform for promoting system-wide coordination and effectiveness in support of the New Partnership. ECA has also been actively involved in developing the codes and standards on economic and corporate governance for the African Peer Review Mechanism. It is also currently undertaking joint technical work with the secretariat of the Organisation for Economic Co-operation and Development aimed at developing an institutional framework for mutual accountability and policy consistency in response to a request from the NEPAD Heads of State and Government Implementation Committee. In 2002, ECA conducted studies, issued reports and organized meetings and workshops on the capacity of the African public sector for effective management and the enhancement of participation of civil society in development and governance processes. ECA technical cooperation is promoting a broad measure of consensus on what constitutes a capable State, a better understanding of governance processes, maintaining governance issues on the agenda of policy makers and assessment of institutional capacity.

140. The United Nations Development Programme developed a strategic framework for supporting the New Partnership for Africa's Development and its secretariat, especially in its promotion of democratic governance, and has

continued to implement the information and communication technology initiatives for Africa of the Tokyo International Conference on African Development aimed at modernizing the communication sector in Africa. The project has so far assisted in the formulation of four national information and communication technology strategies, in Cameroon, Nigeria, the United Republic of Tanzania and Zambia, and the establishment of 36 Cisco networking academies in Africa. Two workshops were held, in Benin and Malaysia, which promoted partnerships between Asian and African private sectors. The workshops enabled 30 African countries to share experience with their Asian counterparts and to identify ways of working closer together in an effort to bolster South-South cooperation.

141. The Department of Economic and Social Affairs, in cooperation with UNDP, supported the Pan-African Conference of Ministers of Public Service, held at Stellenbosch, South Africa, in May 2003, by providing advisory services and technical assistance in capacity-building to improve public administration in Africa. The Fifth Africa Governance Forum, held at Maputo in May 2002, on the theme "Local governance for poverty eradication in Africa" and supported by UNDP, ECA and the Department of Economic and Social Affairs, yielded a set of principles for decentralization and people-centred government. Those principles are expected to reform public sector management and enhance the knowledge and skills of senior civil servants.

142. The United Nations Children's Fund and the African Union will shortly be launching a white paper entitled "The Young Face of NEPAD", in support of giving higher priority to investing in African children for a better future for the continent. Support to African Governments in achieving the objectives of the New Partnership for Africa's Development will be consistent with achieving the Millennium Development Goals, in particular the child and maternal mortality targets. UNICEF thematic work in the areas of HIV/AIDS, girls' education and immunization are also important contributions to progress towards the objectives of the New Partnership. For instance, by the end of 2002, 37 African countries had applied for support from the Global Alliance for Vaccines and Immunization. UNICEF technical staff continue to provide assistance to national counterparts in the poverty reduction strategy papers, the common country assessment and the United Nations Development Assistance Framework processes to help ensure that poverty reduction strategies and debt relief have a positive effect on basic services for children and women that are linked to meeting the developmental objectives of the New Partnership. For example, UNICEF technical staff assisted national counterparts in preparing viable proposals for funding by the Global Alliance for Vaccines and Immunization.

143. The United Nations Population Fund developed and adopted a plan of action for implementation in 2003 that focuses on five objectives of the New Partnership: poverty reduction, health, education, water and sanitation and agriculture. Through its national and regional programmes in Africa, UNFPA is supporting the objectives and activities of the New Partnership through data collection and analysis, provision of reproductive services and capacity-building in the areas of population and development.

144. Food aid continues to be important to Africa. In 2002, WFP provided 2.1 million tons of food aid, or 55 per cent of its total food deliveries, to sub-Saharan Africa and spent 56 per cent of its resources in that region, amounting to $899 million. WFP also purchased more than 590,000 tons of food in sub-Saharan Africa, for a total value of more than $120 million, stimulating local production and markets.

Addressing the needs of the least developed countries, landlocked developing countries and small island developing States

145. Making development more inclusive involves ensuring that particular groups of vulnerable countries, in particular least developed countries, landlocked developing countries and small island developing States, are not left out of the global economy and the development process. During 2002, the Office of the High Representative for the Least Developed Countries, Landlocked Developing Countries and Small Island Developing States continued its efforts to promote mainstreaming of the Brussels Programme of Action for the Least Developed Countries for the Decade 2001-2010 into the work agendas of the various agencies, funds and programmes of the Organization. Other multilateral organizations that have taken similar steps are the African Development Bank, the Asian Development Bank, the Inter-Parliamentary Union and the South Asian Association for Regional Cooperation. I have encouraged the foreign ministers of the least developed countries to establish national arrangements for the implementation, follow-up, monitoring and review of the Brussels Programme of Action.

146. Over the past year, the United Nations Conference on Trade and Development made substantive and operational contributions to the

implementation of the international programmes and initiatives related to least developed countries, landlocked developing countries and small island developing States. UNFPA continued to provide two thirds of its resources to the least developed countries, especially in Africa, for programmes covering reproductive health and rights, with an emphasis on HIV/AIDS prevention and care; gender equality and empowerment of women; and population and development strategies.

147. Major attention has been given to the preparation of the International Ministerial Conference of Landlocked and Transit Developing Countries and Donor Countries and International Financial and Development Institutions on Transit Transport Cooperation, being held in Almaty on 28 and 29 August 2003. This is the first ever United Nations event to address the special needs of landlocked developing countries.

148. Particular attention has been given to the implementation of the Barbados Programme of Action for the Sustainable Development of Small Island Developing States and the Johannesburg Plan of Implementation to enable the Organization to address the developmental challenges of small island developing States arising from their small size, vulnerability to natural disasters, fragile ecosystems and limited or lack of natural resources and freshwater. The Organization is participating actively in the preparations for the International Meeting to Review the Implementation of the Barbados Programme of Action, to be held in Mauritius in 2004.

Battling HIV/AIDS

149. In the past year, the eight co-sponsors and the secretariat of the Joint United Nations Programme on HIV/AIDS (UNAIDS) have been engaged in providing support for the effective implementation of the Declaration of Commitment adopted by the General Assembly at its special session on HIV/AIDS, in 2001. A global consensus has emerged on policies and programmes necessary to fight the disease. UNAIDS has supported efforts to increase global awareness of the disease through education and dissemination of information to the public; to improve access to treatment in areas that are plagued by scarce resources; and to strengthen the capacity of communities with the engagement of civil society in its fight against the disease.

150. Over the past year, HIV/AIDS continued to be a key priority for the Organization's operational activities in development. During 2002, United Nations theme groups on HIV/AIDS have assisted countries to develop multisectoral plans and to integrate HIV/AIDS into development planning instruments. I am pleased to note that, by the end of 2002, a total number of 102 countries had developed national strategic plans for HIV/AIDS.

151. The World Health Organization, with UNICEF and UNAIDS, developed and disseminated strategic information in a number of key areas to support countries in the rational selection and use of HIV medicines. WHO, UNICEF, UNAIDS and Médecins Sans Frontières continue to maintain and provide updated information on prices and sources of HIV medicines in the public domain. That initiative is being expanded to include information on drug registration in countries. UNDP facilitated community conversations in Ethiopia and South Africa on HIV/AIDS to address underlying factors that fuel the epidemic and to strengthen the capacity of communities to initiate and sustain prevention, care and treatment programmes.

152. The World Food Programme, in collaboration with IFAD and FAO, provided food assistance to 34 HIV/AIDS-related projects in over 20 countries worldwide, seeking to ensure that AIDS-affected households received food rations and food baskets adjusted to suit their needs. FAO continued to provide technical assistance to ministries of agriculture to strengthen their capacity to address the agricultural labour shortages created by the HIV/AIDS epidemic and to develop food and nutrition-based interventions to mitigate its effects.

153. UNICEF country offices have demonstrated substantial commitment to achieving the medium-term goals. Growth in expenditure on HIV/AIDS-related activities has more than tripled, from an estimated $30 million in 2000 to $67 million in 2001 and $96 million in 2002, and all 127 country offices supported HIV/AIDS-related activities and/or advocacy in 2002.

154. The United Nations Development Fund for Women is currently working with national AIDS councils in 10 countries to strengthen the councils' capacity to enhance their programmes from a gender perspective. In an effort to support gender-sensitive action worldwide, in February 2003 UNIFEM and UNAIDS launched the first electronic portal on gender and HIV/AIDS.

155. Individuals in refugee situations are often particularly vulnerable to disease. UNHCR and its partners continue to advocate for and accelerate the implementation of HIV/AIDS prevention and care projects in refugee situations. In close collaboration with UNAIDS, UNHCR completed, in February 2002, a Strategic Plan on HIV/AIDS for 2002-2004, which is being implemented in Africa.

156. In the past year, the United Nations Office on Drugs and Crime has initiated comprehensive drug-related HIV/AIDS prevention activities in several countries in Central and Eastern Europe, as well as in Africa, Central Asia, East Asia and the Pacific, Latin America and the Caribbean and South Asia.

157. The Global Fund to Fight AIDS, Tuberculosis and Malaria remains an essential tool of the world community in striving to achieve goal 6 of the Millennium Development Goals, "Combat HIV/AIDS, malaria and other diseases". The commitment of the Fund's Board and secretariat is that it will remain a financing mechanism and not become an operational agency. Success in the field will therefore depend on the active collaboration of the Fund's partners, including Governments, international organizations, the private sector and civil society. The United Nations system is committed to making the Global Fund a success. To date, the Fund has approved proposals, worth $1.5 billion, for activities in 92 countries. Grants to individual countries can represent a significant proportion of the total public spending on health.

Social development

158. The United Nations promotes policies and activities for social development, which focus on achieving a "society for all" that integrates and provides opportunities for specific social groups. The aim is to integrate the particular issues, concerns and interests of those groups into policy-making, so that they become full participants in society and active contributors to national development.

Indigenous issues

159. An example of the Organization's unique role in promoting participation for all is its support for the Permanent Forum on Indigenous Issues. A new secretariat was established within the Department of Economic and Social Affairs in February 2003. The Forum will advise the Economic and Social Council in the areas of development, environment, health, education, culture and human rights.

Ageing and people with disabilities

160. The Madrid International Plan of Action on Ageing, adopted by the Second World Assembly on Ageing in April 2002, formulated objectives and recommendations for action in three priority areas: older persons and development; advancing health and well-being into old age; and ensuring an enabling and supportive environment for older people. Emphasis is placed on building capacity for national implementation of the Madrid International Plan of Action and for incorporating ageing into national policies and international programmes.

161. Follow-up at the regional level includes the adoption by the ECE Ministerial Conference on Ageing, held in Berlin in September 2002, of a Ministerial Declaration and a Regional Implementation Strategy for the Madrid International Plan of Action on Ageing. That Strategy addresses the economic and social concerns related to ageing societies in the region. Governments in the region of Asia and the Pacific adopted the Shanghai Implementation Strategy as a regional guideline for follow-up to the Madrid Plan and the Macao Plan of Action on Ageing for Asia and the Pacific. The Strategy has provided a broad policy framework for Governments in developing national policies on ageing and in encouraging stronger partnership with civil society and older people themselves.

162. The rights of persons with disabilities are currently the focus of work of the Ad Hoc Committee on a Comprehensive and Integral International Convention on the Protection and Promotion of the Rights and Dignity of Persons with Disabilities. The Organization will address issues of concern to people with disabilities worldwide.

Combating illicit drug use and preventing crime

163. The United Nations Office on Drugs and Crime supported alternative income-generating projects aimed at benefiting rural women and children. For example, in Viet Nam, the Office has over the past year been developing a replicable methodology for the substitution of income from opium production among ethnic minority people in Ky Son District. Those activities also contributed to drug demand reduction by strengthening the capacity of national institutions and encouraging community-based development programmes.

164. With the return of large-scale opium production to Afghanistan, resulting in 3,400 tons of opium in 2002, Afghanistan is the source of three quarters of global annual opium production. In 2002, law enforcement measures by the United Nations Office on Drugs and Crime focused on providing support to strengthening law enforcement capacity in neighbouring and transit countries. In the first half of 2003, the Office initiated a package of new law enforcement activities for West and Central Asia worth more than $25 million. That initiative seeks to strengthen capacity for border control, including cross-border cooperation in countries neighbouring Afghanistan, and to support the creation of new drug enforcement units in Kabul and important

Afghan provinces and set up new controls along key Afghan borders.

165. The Office has also introduced a CD-ROM-based training programme for law enforcement training in South-East Asia and Turkey and is involved in setting up law enforcement training centres and national databases on crime and public security in Brazil.

166. During the last year, the United Nations Office on Drugs and Crime managed technical assistance projects to combat corruption and trafficking in persons. Corruption projects in Colombia, Hungary, Nigeria, Romania and South Africa aimed at supporting the development and implementation of national anti-corruption programmes and assisting those countries in strengthening judicial integrity and capacity. Anti-trafficking projects in the Czech Republic, Poland, the Philippines and West Africa aimed at improving the criminal justice response to trafficking in persons, encouraging the implementation of victim support initiatives and assisting with the implementation of the Protocol to Prevent, Suppress and Punish Trafficking in Persons, Especially Women and Children, supplementing the United Nations Convention against Transnational Organized Crime.

Chapter IV

The international legal order and human rights

Human rights development

167. Human rights remain very central to the work of the United Nations. Over the past year I have been encouraged by a growing international consensus concerning the universality of human rights; the efforts by Member States to implement international human rights conventions; international cooperation in building national capacity in human rights; the increasing integration of human rights into activities relating to development, conflict prevention, peacemaking, peacekeeping, peace-building and humanitarian assistance; and the growing strength of the international human rights movement.

168. At the same time, problems in the implementation of human rights continue to be experienced in many parts of the world and gross violations have not ceased. A slowing international economy and inadequacies in governance have lessened the ability of Governments to uphold minimum standards of economic and social rights, as well as of civil and political rights. The Governments of some developed countries show signs of resentment as international human rights conventions are applied to them. At the same time, there is a corresponding disquiet on the part of developing countries in the Commission on Human Rights on the issue of how to deal with allegations of gross violations of human rights levelled at some of them.

169. As the Organization acknowledges such areas of progress and also the challenges that it faces in the field of human rights, it is important to note the large areas of common ground among the membership on such issues and to build on them in enhancing international cooperation for the effective protection of human rights in the future. The number of ratifications of international human rights treaties has continued to increase, consistent with one of the goals of the United Nations Millennium Declaration. Over the past 12 months, five new States have become parties to the International Convention on the Elimination of All Forms of Racial Discrimination; one to the International Covenant on Civil and Political Rights; one to the International Covenant on Economic, Social and Cultural Rights; four to the Convention against Torture and Other Cruel, Inhuman or Degrading Treatment or Punishment; one to the Convention on the Rights of the Child; five to the Convention on the Elimination of All Forms of Discrimination against Women; and three to the International Convention on the Protection of the Rights of All Migrant Workers and Members of Their Families, which entered into force on 1 July 2003. There have also been additional ratifications to the two Optional Protocols to the International Covenant on Civil and Political Rights, the two Optional Protocols to the Convention on the Rights of the Child and the Optional Protocol to the Convention on the Elimination of All Forms of Discrimination against Women. I should like to use this occasion to appeal, once more, to States that have not yet done so to ratify or accede to the fundamental international human rights treaties.

170. The work of the expert bodies established under the human rights treaties continues to be of critical importance. Over the past year the Human Rights Committee, the Committee on Economic, Social and Cultural Rights, the Committee on the Elimination of Racial Discrimination, the Committee on the Rights of the Child and the Committee against Torture have, among them, considered the reports of 112 States parties and adopted five general comments that clarify the meaning of the treaties and offer practical pointers on their implementation. The petitions procedures operating under a number of international human rights treaties offer valuable opportunities to enhance international protection. Over the past year, expert bodies have

adopted well over 100 decisions and views on individual cases, most of which contribute in significant ways to the development of international human rights law. Moreover, a number of practical measures have been taken to improve the methods of work of the treaty bodies and enhance cooperation among them. These include the adoption by the Human Rights Committee and the Committee against Torture of mechanisms to follow up on the adoption of concluding observations.

171. The special rapporteurs and experts appointed by the Commission on Human Rights have continued to perform an indispensable role as front-line protection actors. There are now some 40 such special appointees in action. Over the past year their reports have touched upon numerous human rights themes concerning a total of about 60 situations in different countries. These individual experts, serving in their personal capacity, have issued over 700 urgent appeals to Governments seeking the protection of persons or groups in need. Efforts have continued during the past year to strengthen their methods of operation, including measures to better clarify relations between them and staff of the Office of the United Nations High Commissioner for Human Rights, the introduction of induction sessions and briefing material for new holders of special mandates, better coordination and follow-up to communications with Governments, and increased interaction with strategic partners inside and outside the United Nations system. The interactive dialogue between special procedure mandate-holders and members of the Commission, which has been inspired by the similar exchange taking place within the framework of the Third Committee of the General Assembly, has proved successful and will no doubt be enhanced in coming years. A new Special Procedures Branch has been established within the Office of the High Commissioner to enhance the effectiveness of the special rapporteurs and experts, including helping to develop criteria for appointment, harmonizing operational standards, improving awareness of their activities and providing an adequate level of staff support.

172. In my report of September 2002 entitled "Strengthening of the United Nations: an agenda for further change", I called for intensified efforts to strengthen cooperation within the United Nations system in support of building national capacity in human rights. This is an area where we are seeing important positive developments. Over the past year the Office of the High Commissioner for Human Rights, using mainly voluntary contributions, has assisted some 50 national human rights institutions, as well as regional secretariats serving such institutions. The Office of the High Commissioner has engaged in human rights technical cooperation projects in 32 countries and maintains a field presence in 29 countries. The human rights work of the United Nations thus increasingly emphasizes the importance of effectively functioning national protection systems. To the same end, significant progress has been made in integrating human rights into the development activities of the United Nations system. In May 2003, the second interagency workshop on rights-based approaches to development adopted a number of recommendations for strengthening our activities in that area. At my request, the High Commissioner for Human Rights, in cooperation with the United Nations Development Group and the Executive Committee on Humanitarian Affairs, is preparing a joint plan of action to strengthen human rights–related United Nations action at the country level. The plan, to be adopted in September 2003 and implemented over the next three years, will include specific measures required to improve the capacity of the development and humanitarian agencies of the United Nations to cooperatively assist Member States in their efforts to establish and develop national human rights promotion and protection systems.

173. Human rights violations are often particularly severe in societies undergoing major political, social and economic transformation. A United Nations University study reaffirms the priority of human rights practices in societies in transition, not only because of their intrinsic value, but also because of their multiplier effects on democratization, economic development and conflict resolution.

174. The fifty-ninth session of the Commission on Human Rights, in 2003, included an unprecedented high-level segment, which lasted four days and attracted some 70 dignitaries from around the world. At the same time, more than 40 national human rights institutions participated in the work of the Commission, providing their perspectives, assessments and insights. This has been a significant development in the activity of the Commission. Also, for the first time, national human rights institutions have been invited to participate in the drafting of an international human rights instrument through the work of the Ad Hoc Committee on a Comprehensive and Integral International Convention on the Protection and Promotion of the Rights and Dignity of Persons with Disabilities.

175. Participation in the sessions of the Commission on Human Rights has been impressive by any standard. This past year, in addition to the 53 member States, 100 observer Governments and

some 1,600 representatives of non-governmental organizations attended, together with representatives of regional and subregional organizations and entities of the United Nations system. The Commission has thus evolved into a major forum for partnership between governmental and non-governmental representatives within the United Nations system.

176. The Commission on Human Rights is not without problems, however. There has been public disquiet over the fact that Governments accused of gross violations of human rights are admitted to membership in the Commission. There has been concern about the tone of discussion in the Commission and the fact that it does not address certain situations of grave violations of human rights. These are all important questions that I hope will be seriously addressed by the Bureau of the Commission prior to the next session.

177. At the end of the day, United Nations human rights activities must inspire public trust. Promotional activities without adequate and effective protection will not win that trust—neither of the people at large, nor of the non-governmental organizations and civil society actors on whom we depend so greatly for our human rights work. I should like to take this opportunity to express my appreciation to all those organizations and individuals in the human rights movement who make our human rights work possible, whether it be through research, fact-finding, protection, human rights education or the dissemination of information.

The International Criminal Court

178. Since the Rome Statute of the International Criminal Court entered into force on 1 July 2002, much progress has been made in turning the Court into a functioning judicial institution. The Assembly of States Parties to the Statute held its first session in September 2002 and took important decisions, including the adoption of a number of ancillary instruments necessary for the Court's efficient and effective operation. Notable among these were the Elements of Crimes and the Court's Rules of Procedure and Evidence. At its resumed first session, in February 2003, the Assembly elected the 18 judges of the Court—7 women and 11 men, representing all regions, legal systems and traditions. On 11 March 2003, at an inaugural meeting in The Hague, the 18 judges gave solemn undertakings to perform their duties and exercise their powers honourably, faithfully, impartially and conscientiously. They also elected the Presidency of the Court. In April 2003, at the second resumption of its first session and after several months of consultations, the Assembly took the additional step of electing the Court's first Prosecutor. It also made recommendations on the election of the Registrar. The Prosecutor subsequently gave his solemn undertaking on 16 June 2003 and the judges elected the Registrar on 25 June. With the judges, the Presidency, the Prosecutor and the Registrar in place, the process of electing key officials to constitute the organs of the Court has been completed. In the year ahead, the focus will shift from institution-building to preparing for the Court to exercise its investigative and prosecutorial powers and discharge its judicial functions.

179. The number of States that have ratified or acceded to the Rome Statute has continued to increase steadily. Ninety-one States, from all regions, are now parties to the Statute, compared with 76 this time last year. I am greatly encouraged by this steady increase in support and would appeal to all Member States that have not yet done so to ratify or accede to the Statute and to take the necessary steps to implement its provisions.

180. Pursuant to General Assembly resolution 57/23 of 19 November 2002, the United Nations Secretariat has served as the provisional secretariat of the Assembly of States Parties. The Assembly of States Parties is expected to decide, at its second session, in early September, on the establishment of its own secretariat. I am confident that, in any event, the ties between the United Nations and the Court will endure: the Organization and the Court will be linked by a formal relationship agreement and bonds of history. For over half a century, the United Nations has played a central role in the efforts to establish a permanent international criminal court—an affirmation of the shared conviction that justice and peace are indispensable for human development. The establishment of such a court represents a lasting contribution by the United Nations to the maintenance of international peace and security and to the promotion of the rule of law and respect for human rights and fundamental freedoms around the world.

International Tribunals

International Tribunal for the Former Yugoslavia

181. The International Tribunal for the Former Yugoslavia handed down judgements in two cases during the past year. On 29 November 2002, Trial Chamber II convicted Mitar Vasiljevic, accused of acts against the Muslim population around Višegrad, in Bosnia and Herzegovina, of persecution and murder and sentenced him to 20 years' imprisonment. On 31 March 2003, Trial Chamber I, Section A, convicted Mladen Naletilic and Vinko Martinovic,

for their treatment of Bosnian Muslim civilians and prisoners of war, of crimes against humanity, violations of the laws and customs of war and grave breaches of the Geneva Conventions and sentenced them to 20 and 18 years' imprisonment, respectively. In addition, five accused entered guilty pleas. On 2 October 2002, Biljana Plavšic, formerly active in the Presidency of the Serbian Republic of Bosnia and Herzegovina and later a member of the collective and expanded Presidencies of the Republika Srpska, pleaded guilty to the crime of persecution. In February 2003, the Tribunal sentenced her to 11 years' imprisonment. Subsequently, in May 2003, Momir Nikolic and Dragan Obrenovic, accused of crimes in connection with the fall of Srebrenica, and, in June 2003, Predrag Banovic, accused of crimes at the Keraterm camp, pleaded guilty to the crime of persecution. A further four trials, involving seven accused, are continuing. In July 2003, Darko Mrdja, a former commander of a Bosnian Serb special police unit, pleaded guilty to the crimes of murder and inhumane acts. Meanwhile, in April 2003, the Appeals Chamber rejected the appeals of Zdravko Mucic, a Bosnian Croat, and Hazim Delic and Esad Landzo, both Bosnian Muslims, and confirmed their sentences for murder, torture and inhuman treatment committed while they were staff members at the Celebici prison camp in central Bosnia and Herzegovina. On 31 July 2003, Milomir Stakic, a former leading figure in the Municipality of Prijedor, Bosnia and Herzegovina, where atrocities were committed against non-Serbs, was found guilty of extermination, murder, persecution and deportation.

182. Having received, in July 2002, Security Council endorsement of its completion strategy—that is, to concentrate on trying political, military and paramilitary leaders and to transfer cases involving mid-level accused to national courts for trial—the Tribunal embarked upon implementation of that strategy. In October 2002, it amended its Rules of Procedure and Evidence to provide for the possible referral of certain cases to national courts with jurisdiction over the place where a crime had been committed or a suspect had been arrested. At a more practical level, the Tribunal provided the Office of the High Representative for Bosnia and Herzegovina with advice regarding its project to establish a specialized war crimes chamber in the State Court of Bosnia and Herzegovina, to which the Tribunal could refer certain cases for trial. In February 2003, the Tribunal and the Office of the High Representative signed Joint Conclusions, establishing a basis for a common plan to implement that project. The Tribunal and the High Representative will be taking further steps in that connection in the coming months.

183. In the past year, 11 further accused were transferred to The Hague, bringing the total number of detainees to 50, with 7 more on provisional release. Among those taken into custody were Milan Milutinovic, the former President of Serbia, Vojislav Seselj, the chairman of the Serbian Radical Party and a member of the Serbian parliament, and Jovica Stanisic, Chief of the State Security Service of the Republic of Serbia.

184. On 29 July 2003, I addressed a letter to the President of the Security Council in which I mentioned that I had formed the view, following consultations with members of the Council, that it was now time to split the positions of Prosecutor of the International Tribunal for the Former Yugoslavia and Prosecutor of the International Criminal Tribunal for Rwanda, so that they were occupied by different people. I further indicated in my letter that, as the two Tribunals moved towards implementing their respective completion strategies, it seemed essential and in the interests of efficiency and effectiveness that each Tribunal have its own Prosecutor, who would be able to devote his or her entire energies and attention to the organization, oversight, management and conduct of the outstanding investigations and prosecutions before that Tribunal. By resolution 1503(2003) of 28 August, the Security Council endorsed that suggestion.

International Criminal Tribunal for Rwanda

185. The International Criminal Tribunal for Rwanda has conducted nine trials over the course of the past year, involving a total of 23 accused. In three of those cases, it handed down judgements. On 19 February 2003, Trial Chamber I convicted Gérard Ntakirutimana, a medical doctor, of genocide and crimes against humanity and sentenced him to 25 years' imprisonment. It also found his father, Elizaphan Ntakirutimana, a pastor of the Seventh Day Adventist Church, guilty of aiding and abetting in genocide, sentencing him to 10 years' imprisonment. On 15 May 2003, Trial Chamber I convicted Eliézer Niyitegeka, Minister of Information in Rwanda's Interim Government of 1994, of genocide and crimes against humanity and sentenced him to life imprisonment. On the same day, Trial Chamber III found Laurent Semanza, former *bourgmestre* of Bicumbi Commune, guilty of complicity to commit genocide and crimes against humanity, sentencing him to 25 years' imprisonment. This brings to 11 the total number of judgements that the Tribunal has handed down since trials began in 1997. Four further cases are nearing completion. The Tribunal expects to

have rendered 15 judgements, involving a total of 21 accused, by the end of 2003. Two further trials, involving 10 accused, are currently ongoing and I expect four more, involving another 10 accused, to start later this year.

186. In addition to conducting trials, the three Trial Chambers have supervised pre-trial preparations in 21 cases during the past year, involving 31 accused. The Appeals Chamber, for its part, delivered a judgement on an appeal against conviction—it rejected that appeal and confirmed the original sentence—as well as six decisions on interlocutory appeals and 15 other decisions and orders. The judges also held two plenary meetings at which they considered and adopted a number of changes to the Tribunal's Rules of Procedure and Evidence, which should help to expedite proceedings. Following a decision by the Security Council, in its resolution 1431(2002) of 14 August 2002, to establish a pool of ad litem judges for the Tribunal, so as to further expedite the Tribunal's work, the General Assembly elected 18 such judges on 25 June 2003, each to serve for a four-year term with immediate effect.

187. The Prosecutor has continued investigations and expects to submit indictments against up to 26 additional accused by the end of 2004. The Prosecutor's investigations will then be complete. It is possible that the Tribunal may refer a number of other cases that the Prosecutor has investigated to national courts for trial, including to those of Rwanda. The Registry has undergone changes to strengthen its capacity to support both the Tribunal's other organs and the Defence Counsel. Moreover, a Coordination Council now meets monthly to coordinate the work of the Tribunal's three organs, while a Management Committee meets every fortnight to ensure the best direction of administrative and judicial support from the Registry to the Chambers.

Special Court for Sierra Leone

188. In December 2002, the judges of the Trials and Appeals Chambers of the Special Court for Sierra Leone took their oaths of office in Freetown and elected the President of the Special Court.

189. Over the past year, the Prosecutor and his Office have been investigating crime scenes in Sierra Leone, conducting investigations abroad and interviewing potential witnesses. On 10 March 2003, the Prosecutor announced his first indictments, including those of the commander of the Revolutionary United Front, Foday Sankoh, and of a Minister in the Government of Sierra Leone, Hinga Norman. On 4 June 2003, the Prosecutor announced the indictment of Charles Taylor, President of Liberia. The indictment accuses Mr. Taylor of "bearing the greatest responsibility" for war crimes, crimes against humanity and serious violations of international humanitarian law in Sierra Leone since 30 November 1996. The Court had in fact confirmed Mr. Taylor's indictment three months previously, on 7 March, but had ordered that it remain under seal. To date, the Prosecutor has indicted 12 individuals, 8 of whom are now under arrest. One former Revolutionary United Front commander, Sam Bockarie, was killed in Liberia and the Court is conducting a forensic examination of his remains. The Court is also following up reports that a further indictee, the former leader of the Armed Forces Revolutionary Council, Johnny Paul Koroma, has also been killed in Liberia. In July 2003, Foday Sankoh died while in the custody of the Court awaiting trial.

190. In conjunction with the Management Committee of the Special Court, I have launched several appeals to Member States for funding since March 2003, so as to enable the Court to continue its activities beyond this calendar year. I would take this opportunity to appeal once again to Member States to contribute to the Trust Fund for the Special Court.

Enhancing the rule of law

191. As has been apparent from my previous reports, I have made the strengthening of the international rule of law a priority for the Organization. One of the principal ways in which the United Nations can contribute to that objective is by promoting the full and active participation of States in the international legal order. In that connection, it is gratifying to note the success of the treaty events organized each year since 2000, with a view to encouraging wider participation in the multilateral treaty framework. Last year's event, which took place during the World Summit on Sustainable Development, resulted in the performance by 48 States of a total of 83 treaty actions related to 39 treaties in the field of economic development and environmental protection. I have invited Governments to participate in a treaty event entitled "Focus 2003: multilateral treaties against transnational organized crime and terrorism", to be held during the general debate at the fifty-eighth session of the General Assembly.

192. Many States fail to sign or ratify treaties, however, not because of any lack of political will, but because of a simple shortage of technical expertise necessary for the performance of treaty actions. Some also lack the expertise to enact the necessary laws to implement the treaties that they have signed or ratified or to train the personnel required to apply those laws. In order to address

those needs, I have invited States to inform me of any specific areas in which they might require technical assistance and have adapted the assistance that the Organization currently offers in the light of their responses. The Treaty Section of the Office of Legal Affairs and the United Nations Institute for Training and Research now provide training sessions on treaty law and practice twice a year at Headquarters for government officials, staff members of entities of the United Nations system and representatives of non-governmental organizations. This year, the programme was expanded to the regional level, with a workshop in the Lao People's Democratic Republic in February 2003, and another to follow in Fiji in September 2003. Some 15 other developing countries have requested training sessions in their capitals. I am exploring funding possibilities so that I can respond positively to this demand. More generally, with a view to streamlining the provision of technical legal assistance offered by the United Nations system, I asked all departments, funds, agencies and programmes in March 2002 to review the assistance that they currently offer. One result of that exercise has been the creation of an easily accessible technical legal assistance web site, through which Governments can identify and access the assistance that the Organization makes available. That web site now receives some 5,000 to 6,000 hits every month.

193. Over the past year, the Organization has also taken further steps towards enforcing international law. In December 2002, the General Assembly asked me to resume negotiations to conclude an agreement with the Government of Cambodia on the establishment, with international assistance, of extraordinary chambers within the existing court structure of Cambodia for the prosecution of serious violations of Cambodian law and international law committed during the period of Democratic Kampuchea. Those negotiations resulted in the preparation of a draft agreement between the United Nations and Cambodia, signed at Phnom Penh on 17 March 2003. On 13 May 2003, the General Assembly approved the draft agreement and requested me and the Government of Cambodia to take all the necessary measures for it to enter into force. The Agreement was signed at a ceremony at Phnom Penh on 6 June 2003.

194. Much work lies ahead, both for the United Nations and for Cambodia, before the Agreement can enter into force. The Government of Cambodia will have to submit the Agreement to the relevant national authorities for ratification, take the necessary steps to amend Cambodian law to bring it into line with the Agreement and ensure that the Agreement, once ratified, will apply as law within Cambodia. There is much that the United Nations will have to do also. In particular, I shall have to secure voluntary contributions to fund the assistance that the United Nations is to provide under the Agreement. To that end, I shall soon be launching an appeal to States. First, though, I shall need to form a better picture of the probable requirements of the extraordinary chambers in terms of personnel, equipment, furniture, supplies and other operational needs. I hope to be able to send a planning mission to Phnom Penh for that purpose in September 2003. I am fully conscious of the need to act quickly. Otherwise, as the General Assembly has pointed out, the opportunity of bringing to justice the senior leaders of the Khmer Rouge and those who were most responsible for the terrible atrocities of the Khmer Rouge period may soon be lost. The Cambodian people have waited a long time to see those individuals brought to trial and it is our hope that they will not have to wait much longer.

Legal affairs

195. During the past year, the International Law Commission advanced its work on reservations to treaties by adopting further guidelines on the formulation and communication of reservations and interpretative declarations. It considered several draft articles on diplomatic protection, reviewed progress on the topic of unilateral acts of States and agreed on a conceptual outline for the topic of international liability in case of loss from transboundary harm arising out of hazardous activities. It also appointed special rapporteurs for two of the new topics in its work programme, namely, the responsibility of international organizations and shared natural resources. In the case of the third new topic—fragmentation of international law: difficulties arising out of diversification and expansion of international law—it decided to begin by studying the *lex specialis* rule and the question of self-contained regimes. Meanwhile, the Ad Hoc Committee on Jurisdictional Immunities of States and Their Property succeeded, in February 2003, in resolving all of the outstanding issues regarding the draft articles on the jurisdictional immunities of States and their property that the International Law Commission had adopted in 1991 and recommended that the General Assembly now take a decision on their final form.

196. In July 2003, the United Nations Commission on International Trade Law finalized and adopted its Model Legislative Provisions on Privately Financed Infrastructure Projects and gave preliminary approval to a draft legislative

guide on insolvency law. The Commission highlighted the importance of strengthening its secretariat, within existing resources, so as to help it respond to the increasing demands on it to develop uniform commercial legislation, provide technical legislative assistance, disseminate information on the latest legal developments and coordinate its work with other international organizations.

197. The Sixth Committee of the General Assembly and the Ad Hoc Committee established by General Assembly resolution 51/210 of 17 December 1996 continued their efforts to prepare a draft comprehensive convention on international terrorism and a draft convention for the suppression of acts of nuclear terrorism. Questions of definition and other issues regarding its scope of application, including its relationship with existing and future instruments, stand in the way of adoption of a comprehensive convention, while issues concerning the scope of the draft convention for the suppression of acts of nuclear terrorism have made it difficult to reach agreement on that instrument. Meanwhile, the Ad Hoc Committee on the Scope of Legal Protection under the Convention on the Safety of United Nations and Associated Personnel reconvened in March 2003. A number of important issues concerning measures to enhance the existing legal regime under the Convention still require reflection by States. I intend to remain actively engaged in this important matter.

198. As far as the law of the sea is concerned, several challenges lie ahead: promoting the sustainable development of ocean resources, strengthening implementation of the international legal obligations of flag States and enhancing inter-agency cooperation. In response to concerns regarding inadequate implementation by flag States of international rules and standards for ship safety, pollution prevention, fisheries conservation and labour conditions, I established an Inter-Agency Consultative Group on Flag State Implementation in March 2003 to study the issue. The question of flag State implementation also arose at the fourth meeting of the Open-ended Informal Consultative Process on Oceans and the Law of the Sea, held in June 2003 to consider issues relating to safety of navigation, protection of vulnerable marine ecosystems and inter-agency cooperation and coordination. That meeting also highlighted a number of other issues: transport of hazardous substances; protection of biodiversity on the high seas; the need to take further measures to combat illegal, unreported fishing; the need for more effective inter-agency cooperation and coordination; and establishment of a regular process for global reporting and assessment of the state of the marine environment (Global Marine Assessment). I shall be submitting a report on this last issue to the General Assembly at its fifty-eighth session.

199. During the past year, the Office of Legal Affairs provided advice to various Secretariat units in connection with the formulation of the new Security Council resolutions relating to Iraq, in particular with regard to the operation of the oil-for-food programme. Also of particular note was the role that the Office played in developing and implementing a procedure for the election of the judges and Prosecutor of the International Criminal Court and, in conjunction with the Government of Sierra Leone, implementing the agreement on the establishment of the Special Court for Sierra Leone. Meanwhile, the Office continued to advise the United Nations Interim Administration Mission in Kosovo on the exercise of its legislative and executive authority and to provide advice and support to the Organization's other peacekeeping missions, especially in handling claims and in concluding and implementing arrangements with troop-contributing countries. It also provided advice on a wide range of other issues of concern to the Organization, including procurement, the negotiation of contracts—many involving complex and novel questions, in particular those relating to the capital master plan—and the implementation of personnel reforms.

Chapter V

Enhancing management

Administration and management

200. The delegation of administrative authority to the departments and offices of the Secretariat, with concomitant accountability of programme managers, continues to be strengthened through the implementation of results-based budgeting and management. The development and use of a web-based management performance indicator system, with five indicators—recruitment tracking, status of gender balance, regular budget expenditures, extrabudgetary resource expenditures, and implementation of the recommendations in the audits of the Office of Internal Oversight Services—have provided a management tool for the programme managers and their executive offices across the Secretariat to implement actions within their programme units that will achieve the objectives of the programme.

Common support services

201. The Department of Management and the Department of Peacekeeping Operations have engaged in a partnership with a view to increasing support to peacekeeping missions through the implementation of new arrangements for field procurement. Clearer lines of responsibility and accountability have been established and redundant procedures have been eliminated. Technical and direct procurement support to the peacekeeping missions has included the evaluation of candidates for procurement positions in field missions, and the establishment of training programmes, briefings and a hotline to support peacekeeping procurement staff on any procurement-related matter on a round-the-clock basis.

202. Several common service initiatives, such as the sharing of procurement contracts, the creation of a standardized identity document applicable throughout the Organization and system-wide collective bargaining with international airlines for more favourable fares and conditions are being worked on. Included in these initiatives are organizations that are not a part of the United Nations system, such as the Asian Development Bank, the Organisation for Economic Co-operation and Development, the European Union and Interpol. Such collective endeavours are expected to lead to a greater consistency of practices within the Organization and to yield financial benefits.

Human resources management

203. Since the introduction of the new staff selection system on 1 May 2002 and the revised performance management appraisal system (e-PAS), emphasis has been placed on the institutionalization of these systems, and on improvements to the information technology support tools. The staff selection system has resulted in greater accountability, transparency, a faster recruitment process, and a larger pool of candidates, particularly from developing countries. The revised electronic e-PAS system, which supports discussion between supervisors and staff, has increased compliance and achieved a more measurable appraisal system throughout the Secretariat and in peacekeeping missions. Expanded learning and career support programmes, including mentoring and career resource centres, are strengthening the skills and competencies of staff and managers and contributing to changing the management culture of the Organization. There is a particular focus on Junior Professional staff, including targeted training courses, mentoring and a managed reassignment programme. The flexible working arrangements which came into effect on 1 February 2003, Secretariat-wide, are part of an effort to assist staff to strike a better balance between their professional and personal lives. A priority is the further development and implementation of a Secretariat-wide policy on HIV/AIDS that will enhance awareness and expand access to voluntary counselling and testing, care and treatment.

204. The security of United Nations personnel remains an issue of paramount importance. Regrettably, attacks continued throughout the year under review, but new measures put in place appeared to be having a positive impact. The number of staff members who lost their lives in the service of the Organization during the 12 months prior to August 2003 was the lowest since 1992. All this was changed dramatically by the devastating attack in Baghdad, on 19 August 2003. That shocking incident obliges us to look again at the conditions in which we work and to consider fundamental changes, however sad and painful that may be.

Capital master plan

205. The capital master plan approved in 2002 by the General Assembly authorizes the implementation of the refurbishment of the Headquarters complex and the remaining phases of design development. At the Assembly's request, the possibilities for a financial package from the host country, as well as other contributions from the public and private sectors, are being explored. New York City has offered to construct a new building south of the Headquarters that would serve as alternate accommodation during the renovation and later for the consolidation of United Nations offices currently scattered in the vicinity of the Secretariat. This generous offer is very welcome.

Financial situation

206. The positive financial trends of the last two years are continuing. All three indicators—cash in hand, debt to Member States and amounts unpaid by Member States—continue to improve. One particular trend indicates that there may be problems ahead, however. The number of Member States paying their regular budget contribution in full is slipping from the earlier years when steady progress was made. In fact, in 2002, only 117 Member States paid their regular budget contributions in full, reflecting a serious setback in the progress achieved between 1994, when only 75 Member States paid in full, and 2000, when 141 Member States paid in full. This means that deficits in the regular budget may occur.

Accountability and oversight

207. The Office of Internal Oversight Services is working to strengthen the Organization's integrity and ethics systems through the sponsorship of a United Nations organizational integrity initiative to increase staff awareness and protect the Organization's resources and reputation. The Office is also providing more structured and integrated planning of its oversight assignments through its risk management framework. Under this framework, a risk analysis is made of all the client departments, offices, funds and programmes of the Office of Internal Oversight Services to identify and prioritize those programme and operational areas having a high vulnerability to inefficiencies, fraud, waste and abuse.

Monitoring, evaluation and consulting

208. In the past year, the Office of Internal Oversight Services provided consulting to other departments on changing their work processes and organizational structures with a view to implementing the continuing reform of the Secretariat. Working in close collaboration with four client departments and offices, the Office contributed to ensuring the sustainability and effectiveness of adopted solutions. In response to a request of the General Assembly, a review by the Office of Internal Oversight Services of the Office of the United Nations High Commissioner for Human Rights produced 17 recommendations on streamlining and strengthening its activities and management.

209. An in-depth evaluation of the Division for Ocean Affairs and the Law of the Sea of the Office of Legal Affairs concluded that it had effectively discharged the responsibilities of the Secretary-General under the United Nations Convention on the Law of the Sea. The Office of Internal Oversight Services recommended that the Division actively participate in setting up a new international coordination mechanism requested by the General Assembly to better respond to the growing demand for technical assistance from States parties to the Convention. The Office of Internal Oversight Services made proposals to the Committee for Programme and Coordination for a pilot thematic evaluation intended to provide a systematic review of the activities carried out by several programmes of the Organization sharing common purposes.

Audit management

210. From July 2002 to June 2003, the Internal Audit Division conducted 101 audits, 5 of which resulted in reports to the General Assembly. An audit of United Nations information centres (A/57/747), for example, highlighted the need for an urgent reassessment of the information centre concept in terms of usefulness and continuing relevance. Significant resources were spent on the operations of information centres in developed countries, and the Office of Internal Oversight Services called for a different approach and a reorientation towards developing countries. The Office recommended inter alia that the Department of Public Information reassess and update the goals and strategies of information centres, and the Department has already begun implementing many of the recommendations. Other audits examined the status of recommendations concerning the liquidation of peacekeeping missions (A/57/622), the procurement of goods and services for peacekeeping missions from Governments using letters of assist (A/57/718), and the policies and procedures for recruiting staff for the Department of Peacekeeping Operations (A/57/224).

211. An audit of the International Research and Training Institute for the Advancement of Women examined the sustainability of the Institute, and made a series of recommendations to address its financial and operating difficulties. As recommended by the Office of Internal Oversight Services, the Office of the United Nations High Commissioner for Refugees changed the rules for project agreements with international non-governmental organizations. This has resulted in more reliable financial information and competitive procurement, as well as greater transparency in project staff spending.

Investigations

212. The Investigations Division is exploring ways to deal with the increased volume of allegations of misconduct, mismanagement, abuse of authority and waste of resources, 20 per cent of which were categorized as significant to the Organization in 2002, in part through new partnerships with national law enforcement authorities. For example, in the investigations of refugee smuggling in East Africa and sexual exploitation in West Africa, the Division coordinated ad hoc task forces, which, in addition to investigators, included experts on loan from other agencies or on special service agreements, in areas such as medicine, human rights, child and refugee protection, law and sexual abuse counselling.

213. In close collaboration with the Anti-Fraud Office (OLAF) of the European Commission, the Division recovered $4.2 million that had been misappropriated by a former senior staff member of the United Nations Interim Administration Mission in Kosovo. The investigation led to the successful prosecution of the staff member by the German authorities in June 2003. In an

effort to establish normative standards, the Fourth Conference of International Investigators, hosted by OLAF and held at Brussels in April 2003, unanimously endorsed the guidelines for the conduct of investigations by investigators of international and bilateral organizations which had been drafted and presented by the Division.

Strengthening the Organization

214. The main rationale behind my agenda for further change was to align the activities of the Organization with the priorities agreed upon at the Millennium Summit and the global conferences. During the first half of 2003, major efforts were made to ensure that the programme budget for the biennium 2004-2005 to be presented to the General Assembly reflected this alignment. The proposal which will go before the Assembly later in 2003 includes the reorganization of two major departments, the Department of General Assembly and Conference Management and the Department of Public Information. I also intend to establish a strategic planning capacity in the Department of Economic and Social Affairs, strengthen the management of the Office of the United Nations High Commissioner for Human Rights and increase investment in support to human rights at the national level. Additional investments in staff training and information technology underpin these proposals.

215. There are several areas where the reforms have already taken effect. Efforts to improve the servicing of the General Assembly, through better planning of meetings and related documentation, and work to sharpen the focus of our public information activities are beginning to yield results. The role of the office of the Special Adviser on Africa has been strengthened to ensure a coherent and integrated approach to United Nations deliberations, reports and advocacy in support of Africa and in the follow-up to the New Partnership for Africa's Development.

216. In other instances, work is under way, but not yet complete. For example plans to strengthen actions relating to human rights at the country level, the clarification of roles and responsibilities in the area of technical cooperation, efforts to streamline reporting and publications, and the work of a high-level panel to review the relationship between the Organization and civil society will require additional work. The funds and programmes have made considerable progress in strengthening their country-level impact by developing collaborative programming and budgeting tools for joint programming and pooling of resources. The new programming tools will be introduced in 2003, with the aim of expanding their use to more than 80 country programmes by 2006.

217. The reform package also contained several systemic improvements to the planning and budgeting process. Initial steps have been taken to improve the budget documents themselves, with shorter, more strategic presentations, in particular for peacekeeping operations, and the inclusion of results-based indicators for all programmatic areas. Detailed descriptions of other proposed changes will be contained in other reports submitted to the General Assembly at its fifty-eighth session.

218. Efforts to strengthen the Organization ultimately depend on an able, versatile and well-managed workforce. Improvements to the management of human resources through the new recruitment and placement system are now showing results. Work is in progress to further reduce the barriers to staff mobility both within and between United Nations organizations, particularly in the field. Additional measures will be taken to grant individual programme managers greater decision-making responsibilities.

Chapter VI

Partnerships

Communications

219. Renewed focus and greater clarity of purpose were the twin objectives I mentioned two years ago in initiating a comprehensive review of the work of the Department of Public Information. A new operating model and a new organizational structure for the Department have now been put in place. Activities are now grouped more strategically under three Divisions. A Strategic Communications Division responsible for devising and disseminating information on priority themes, and an Outreach Division, which develops supportive partnerships with civil society, have been established, while the existing News and Media Division has been reorganized to increase its capacity to deliver timely, accurate, objective and balanced news.

220. The key element in the new operating model is the identification of Secretariat departments as departmental "clients" that establish their own communications priorities based on priorities laid down by the General Assembly, which the Department of Public Information then communicates strategically to various target audiences. Once established, these priorities form the basis of issues-driven promotional campaigns, implemented using all the media assets of the Department, including print, radio, televi-

sion and the Internet. Strategic partnerships with the Member States, civil society, the private sector and academic institutions will also serve to disseminate the messages both internationally and, at the local level, through the United Nations information centres. In a clear endorsement of the new strategic direction, the Committee on Information at its twenty-fifth session, in April/May 2003, welcomed the restructuring of the Department of Public Information, including its new operating model and organizational structure.

221. The Department is also engaged in strategic partnerships with entities within the United Nations system. A new communications strategy is being developed for the World Summit on the Information Society, to be held at Geneva in December 2003 in cooperation with the International Telecommunication Union. The Department is also working towards engaging the media as stakeholders in the information society, and emphasizing the role of freedom of speech and the press. In association with the television industry and the Government of Switzerland, the Department is organizing a parallel event at the Summit, the World Electronic Media Forum, which will focus on the role of the electronic media in the information society.

222. As part of an invigorated strategy of outreach to non-State actors, in November 2002 the Department constituted a Civil Society Service in the Outreach Division, charged with integrating all programmes servicing non-governmental organizations, educational institutions and the general public, as well as initiating and fostering partnerships with new entities, including those in the private sector and the media. A new Educational Outreach Section in that Service orients key products, including the flagship publication *UN Chronicle*, the multimedia UN Works programme and the global teaching and learning project, Cyberschoolbus, to the needs of students and teachers the world over.

223. Using new technologies, the Department continues to provide audiences worldwide with instant access to the latest news about the United Nations. On 5 February 2003, the United Nations web site reached a new milestone when it was accessed more than 10 million times in a single 24-hour period. The number of times the site is accessed has grown from more than 11.5 million in 1996 to some 1,695 million hits in 2002, owing in part to the addition of material in all of the official languages. Since September 2002 over 28,000 links have been provided to parliamentary documents on the Official Document System.

224. The United Nations is making increasing use of webcasting—live broadcasting over the Internet of meetings and events. On 7 March, 24,000 users in 66 countries watched the webcast of the Security Council meeting on Iraq live, and many more accessed the images later. An Arabic version of the United Nations News Centre web site has been added to the French and English sites, and sites in the other official languages are now in preparation. A measure of the success of the Centre is the growing number of news outlets and web sites that refer to the United Nations News Service as the source of the material they publish.

225. United Nations Radio has firmly established itself as one of the important traditional multimedia channels for strategically communicating the activities and concerns of the Organization to audiences in all regions of the world. A recent survey offered a conservative estimate that some 133 million people listen to United Nations Radio programmes at least once a week in the six official languages, as well as in Portuguese and Kiswahili. Since April 2003, 10 new official television partners have joined in the dissemination of United Nations Television and have aired about 50 hours of United Nations programming to some 2 billion viewers.

226. The Department of Public Information has undertaken a number of initiatives aimed at strengthening the Organization's public information capacities in its peacekeeping and political missions in the field. Standard operating procedures for field-based public information units are being prepared, in close collaboration with the Department of Peacekeeping Operations. By agreement with the Department of Peacekeeping Operations, a public information expert is now stationed at the United Nations Logistics Base at Brindisi, Italy, to aid in the development of a public information training capacity. A roster of public information personnel for rapid deployment has been established, and a training programme for rapidly deployable field personnel is in preparation. The Department has also organized the dispatch of a senior public information officer to assess the situation on the ground in Côte d'Ivoire and to provide recommendations on local media development, which have been used to guide regional inter-agency efforts to address media issues in that country.

227. In my report entitled "Strengthening of the United Nations: an agenda for further change", I proposed the rationalization of the network of United Nations information centres around regional hubs, starting with the creation of a Western European hub. The Secretariat is implementing a plan for the establishment of the

proposed hub in Western Europe by the beginning of 2004 and, in parallel, is closing nine existing information centres in that region.

228. A noteworthy achievement of the Dag Hammarskjöld Library, launched on 7 February 2003, was the redesigned interface to its main databases, UNBISnet, which is now more powerful and easier to search. Important reference tools, such as the United Nations Documentation Research Guide and the United Nations conferences and observances page, have been updated and on 27 March the UNBIS Thesaurus was launched. It is fully electronic and, like the Documentation Research Guide and the conferences and observances page, is available in all six official languages.

229. A major development for United Nations libraries was the formation in March 2003 of the Steering Committee for the Modernization and Integrated Management of United Nations Libraries, under the leadership of the Department of Public Information. This initiative is intended to create a more modern, efficient and accessible system of library services throughout the Organization.

230. The Cartographic Section of the Department continues to provide valuable technical assistance to the Eritrea-Ethiopia Boundary Commission in its preparation for the demarcation of the international boundary between the two countries, following the successful delimitation of the boundary in April 2002. United Nations cartographers also helped the Cameroon-Nigeria Mixed Commission in developing a work plan for the demarcation of the international boundary between those two countries in February 2003. The Section will, however, be transferred to the Department of Peacekeeping Operations in 2004.

United Nations Fund for International Partnerships

231. Through the successful partnership of the United Nations Fund for International Partnerships (UNFIP) and the United Nations Foundation, $489 million has been programmed, as at 31 December 2002, for 251 projects worldwide in four programme areas, namely, children's health; population and women; environment; and peace, security and human rights. Other multilateral and bilateral donors provided approximately $175 million in additional funding for programmes and projects supported by UNFIP and the Foundation.

232. The projects that comprised the UNFIP children's health programme have contributed to preventing the death of 240,000 children by providing 37 million vaccinations against measles in 2002. These projects have strengthened the national health systems of target countries with continuing training of health-care workers, the promotion of injection safety and the inclusion in the measles campaigns of other health activities, such as vitamin A supplementation, immunization against polio and the distribution of bed nets to prevent malaria. As a result of the $82 million made available in 2002 through the efforts of the Foundation and UNFIP, all but seven countries worldwide are now free of polio.

233. Biodiversity emerged as a central priority of the World Summit on Sustainable Development, which underlined the importance of providing and sustaining the livelihoods of poor rural communities. Funding provided by UNFIP and the Foundation to the United Nations Environment Programme catalysed a major initiative in May 2003, targeted at reversing the decline of coral reefs. In September 2002, UNFIP also facilitated a partnership between the Department of Economic and Social Affairs and the E7—an umbrella organization of nine electric utilities in Japan, Europe and North America—to work together to expand the access to electricity of the poor.

234. The United Nations Fund for International Partnerships also provided advice to the private sector and foundations on partnerships with the United Nations system, including guidance on policies and procedures and suggestions on strategic ways for corporations and foundations to support the Millennium Development Goals. The Fund is also engaged in establishing ties with numerous organizations that aim to raise funds for the causes of the Organization.

Project services

235. In 2002, the United Nations Office for Project Services (UNOPS) acquired a total of $509 million in new business for its project portfolio. Business acquired from UNDP amounted to $334.2 million or 66 per cent, a balance amounting to $174.9 million or 34 per cent coming from other entities within the United Nations system. On the loan portfolio, the International Fund for Agricultural Development entrusted project supervision and loan administration responsibilities to UNOPS for 14 additional projects totalling $225 million in the course of 2002, compared to $328 million in 2001.

236. The United Nations Office for Project Services continued to support the mine action programmes of three major clients—UNDP, the Mine Action Service and the Office of the Iraq Programme—in 18 countries around the world. That role expanded significantly in the course of the year, with increased activities in northern

Iraq, new responsibilities for the existing programme in Afghanistan, and the formulation of new programmes, which are expected to expand, in the Democratic Republic of the Congo and the Sudan.

237. A new form of partnership was initiated in 2002 with the Global Fund to Fight AIDS, Tuberculosis and Malaria. In April 2003, UNOPS was designated by the Fund as one of the four pre-qualified Local Fund Agents, its task being to provide management services and to supervise, on behalf of the Fund, the implementation of nationally executed programmes financed by the Fund. To date, UNOPS has signed agreements with or has been designated to be the Local Fund Agent for China, India, Mongolia, Serbia and Montenegro and Timor-Leste, and negotiations for similar work in other countries are under way. Elsewhere, UNOPS is exploring options to assist the Fund's operations by supporting principal recipients in the implementation of project activities.

238. In May 2003, the Joint United Nations Programme on HIV/AIDS entrusted to UNOPS the implementation of a project entitled "AIDS in Africa: scenarios for the future", developed and funded in partnership with Shell United Kingdom. The project aims at responding to the impact of the HIV/AIDS epidemic in Africa and forming a shared understanding of the problem. Other objectives are to help to activate a broad-based response from all segments of society and to overcome the stigma and discrimination experienced by HIV-positive individuals. The Global Business Development division of Shell International will support the project through technical know-how and contributions to the budget.

239. An example of combining private sector expertise with United Nations goals is the UNDP Human Development Programme in Angola, the execution of which is entrusted to UNOPS and which is supported by the Italian private sector firm Coop, a consortium of over 200 consumer cooperatives. Under the programme, which aims to improve the lives of the children in Angola, 100,000 children were vaccinated and 6,000 children obtained a daily meal, on a budget of $260,715. UNOPS is facilitating the link between Coop and the local economic development agencies created by the Human Development Programme with the objective of bringing Angolan coffee to the Italian market, establishing viable trade relations and creating synergies between development assistance and the private sector. Similar arrangements are being made in the framework of other UNDP-funded projects to be executed by UNOPS in Mozambique and South Africa.

Civil society and business partnerships

240. In my report entitled "Strengthening of the United Nations: an agenda for further change", I highlighted the engagement of civil society as an aspect of the United Nations reform process and announced that I would assemble a group of eminent persons representing a variety of perspectives and experiences to review past and current practices and recommend improvements to make the interaction between civil society and the United Nations more meaningful. In February 2003 I appointed Fernando Enrique Cardoso, former President of Brazil, to chair the High-level Panel on Civil Society, comprising 12 individuals with backgrounds spanning the governmental and non-governmental sectors.

241. The main task of the Panel is to produce a set of practical recommendations on how the Organization's relationship with civil society, and with the private sector and parliaments, could be improved. In particular, the Panel will identify best practices in the Organization and other international organizations with a view to identifying new and better ways of interacting with civil society. The Panel will also examine ways in which the participation of civil society actors from developing countries can be facilitated. At its first meeting, held in New York on 2 and 3 June 2003, the Panel agreed upon a work programme that emphasizes an open, transparent and consultative process. The Panel will submit its final report in April 2004.

242. In the past year the Organization forged several new partnerships. This was an important innovation of the World Summit on Sustainable Development, during which more than 200 partnerships were launched by a wide variety of stakeholders, including various agencies, funds and programmes within the Organization. These partnerships were aimed at implementing sustainable development through various means such as capacity-building, education and improving access to information. The Organization must ensure that the partnerships are successful and help in the effective implementation of the commitments made at the Summit.

243. The Organization continued to strengthen its partnership with the private sector. During the reporting period, the number of companies participating in the Global Compact doubled from approximately 500 to more than 1,000, more than half of which were in developing countries in all regions of the world. At the same time, the Global Compact was launched in 14 countries, bringing to more than 50 the number of countries where the Global Compact has taken root. Moreover, the United Nations Industrial Development Organization (UNIDO) was wel-

comed as an additional member of the Global Compact's core group of agencies, until then consisting of the Office of the United Nations High Commissioner for Human Rights, the International Labour Organization, UNDP and UNEP. The core group of agencies supports the Compact by providing training materials on its principles and supporting outreach activities. UNIDO will be responsible for small and medium-sized enterprises.

244. In January 2003, the Global Compact adopted a new strategic approach to conducting its operations whereby companies are asked to publish a "communication on progress" in their annual or other prominent reports to increase transparency and public accountability. A significant element of this strategic approach is its emphasis on policy dialogues within multi-stakeholder forums to identify and address problems in areas of interest to the international community. During the reporting period, the Global Compact convened policy dialogues on business and sustainable development in 2002; and HIV/AIDS in the workplace and supply chain management and partnerships in 2003, involving participants from business, labour and civil society. These dialogues have resulted in joint initiatives such as the development and application of a business guide to help companies to ensure that their behaviour is not negatively contributing to conflicts; a common set of recommendations on how companies, non-governmental organizations, Governments and intergovernmental organizations can contribute to greater transparency and help to combat corruption; and an initiative on promoting awareness about HIV/AIDS in the workplace. An initiative to encourage sustainable business in the world's least developed countries was launched in Ethiopia, and activities are planned for Angola, Bangladesh, Cambodia and Madagascar. The initiative brings companies together with other stakeholders to identify business opportunities in the least developed countries that will be sustainable and will be designed in ways to help local small and medium-sized enterprises.

245. To enable the Global Compact to accomplish its objective of helping to create a more sustainable and inclusive global economy and to ensure that the Compact's new strategy of "communication on progress" has a significant impact, the Organization must continue to give the Global Compact the creative space it needs to grow.

Conclusion

246. In the perspective of human experience one year is a fleeting moment. It will not be possible for some time to make final judgements on many of the activities of the United Nations. It is clear, nevertheless, that the Organization is contributing to international stability and progress in positive and practical ways, and that it is making a real difference in the lives of individual people around the world.

247. The record of the United Nations activities has also shown that the system is exceedingly flexible. The Organization will need to maintain its capacity to adapt to new challenges and global conditions, while remaining faithful to the purposes and principles of the Charter.

248. Despite its imperfections, the United Nations still embodies the hopes of the peoples of the world for a peaceful and just world. This review of the Organization's work in the past year should contribute to a better understanding of the role which the United Nations plays in global affairs, in particular as an effective instrument of international cooperation.

PART ONE

Political and security questions

Chapter I

International peace and security

The year 2003 was a particularly challenging one for the United Nations in the area of international peace and security. World attention focused on the declaration of war in Iraq and its aftermath, which gave rise to deep divisions in the international community, severely testing the principle of collective security and the resilience of the Organization, and caused questions to be asked regarding the relevance of the United Nations. In December, the General Assembly welcomed the establishment by the Secretary-General of a High-level Panel on Threats, Challenges and Change, the aim of which was to recommend measures for ensuring effective collective action, based on, among other things, a thorough assessment of existing approaches, instruments and mechanisms, including the principal organs of the United Nations.

International terrorism continued to pose a major threat to peace and security. The Security Council held a high-level meeting in January at which it adopted a declaration aimed at reinforcing the international community's mobilization against terrorism. It also examined the work of its Counter-Terrorism Committee throughout the year.

Both the Council and the Assembly continued to focus on the prevention and resolution of conflict and the provision of assistance to countries emerging from conflict. In July, the Assembly emphasized the importance of a comprehensive and coherent strategy for the prevention of conflict and adopted the Secretary-General's recommendations in that regard. In follow-up to that resolution, the Assembly, in September, held an open interactive dialogue on the role of civil society in the prevention of armed conflict. In the context of the international conflict-prevention strategy, the Council and the Assembly strongly supported the adoption of the Kimberley Process Certification Scheme to regulate the sale of rough diamonds. The Council examined its continuing role in the settlement of disputes, and both the Council and the Secretariat held high-level meetings with regional organizations on ways to meet the new challenges to international peace and security. The Council also considered issues relating to the rule of law in post-conflict situations. The Organization maintained 15 political and peace-building missions during 2003.

Efforts to streamline and better manage the Organization's peacekeeping operations included strengthening of the rapid deployment and standby arrangements system and development of a detailed plan for the phased establishment of the strategic deployment stocks system at the United Nations Logistics Base in Brindisi, Italy. The Council considered several peacekeeping-related issues, including gender mainstreaming in all peacekeeping activities and the Secretariat's efforts to develop a coherent policy towards that end, the role of HIV/AIDS and efforts to reduce the risk of peacekeepers contracting or transmitting the disease while on mission, issues related to peacekeeping and the international legal system and the role mine action could play in peacekeeping operations. The safety of UN peacekeepers and associated humanitarian personnel was a priority issue, especially in the light of the bombing of the UN mission in Iraq, in which 22 international and local staff died, including the Secretary-General's Special Representative, and many more were injured. In May, the Assembly decided to donate, as the Secretary-General had done, its portion of the financial award of the Nobel Peace Prize to the United Nations Nobel Peace Prize Memorial Fund, created by the Secretary-General to provide financial assistance for the education of children of UN civilian personnel killed in the line of duty. During the year, the United Nations created one new peacekeeping mission and one mission completed its mandate. At the end of 2003, the number of missions in operation totalled 13, the same as in 2002, and the number of military personnel and civilian police serving under UN command stood at 45,815.

The Special Committee on Peacekeeping Operations, which met in March, made recommendations on procedures for consultations with troop-contributing countries, action to enhance UN peacekeeping capacity and increased cooperation with regional arrangements.

The positive financial position of UN peacekeeping operations continued during the financial period 1 July 2002 to 30 June 2003. As a result of scaled-down activities due to the closure of missions and the creation of only one new mission during that period, expenditure decreased slightly to $2,501 million, compared to a final figure of $2,572 million for the previous financial period. Unpaid assessed contributions also declined to $1.1 billion, compared to $1.2 billion the previous year. The Assembly considered various aspects of peacekeeping financing, including the peacekeeping support account, the financing of the United Nations Logistics Base, the liquidation of closed missions, the Peacekeeping Reserve Fund, proposals for consolidating peacekeeping accounts, the management of peacekeeping trust funds, reimbursement issues, and procurement and inventory management. It also considered a number of personnel issues, including recruitment policies and procedures.

Promotion of international peace and security

Follow-up to Millennium Summit (2000)

In response to General Assembly resolution 57/145 [YUN 2002, p. 41], the Secretary-General submitted a September report [A/58/323] (see also p. 1385) on the implementation of the United Nations Millennium Declaration, adopted at the Millennium Summit in 2000 [YUN 2000, p. 49]. The Secretary-General evaluated progress made or not made in the areas of peace and security, development, and human rights and democracy, and re-examined some of the underlying assumptions of the Declaration, observing that it could no longer be taken for granted that the multilateral institutions were strong enough to cope with all the challenges facing them. He said that, since the Millennium Summit [ibid., p. 47], the international community had had to deal with both new and old threats to international peace and security. However, the climate of cooperation and consensus that was evident following the terrorist attacks in the United States on 11 September 2001 [YUN 2001, p. 60], in terms of the global condemnation, swift adoption of anti-terrorism measures and support for the reconstruction of Afghanistan, was seriously eroded by the war against Iraq (see p. 333). That war exposed deep divisions in the international community and brought to the fore questions of principle and practice that challenged the United Nations and the international community. The Secretary-General stressed that it was vitally important that the international community not allow those differences to persist but to find unity of purpose based on a common security agenda, which should reflect a global consensus on the major threats to peace and security. Such an agenda should strengthen international solidarity based on the shared universal values enshrined in the Charter of the United Nations and not shy away from the need to improve and, where necessary, change the structure and functions of the United Nations and other international institutions. He said that the great strength of the United Nations remained its legitimacy, founded on the principles of international law, for which there was no substitute in the international arena. The conduct of international affairs should, therefore, be in conformity with those principles. The United Nations itself was at a critical juncture, and unless the Security Council regained the confidence of States and of world public opinion, individual States would increasingly resort to their own national perceptions of emerging threats and to their own judgement on how best to address them. To forestall such a development, the United Nations would have to demonstrate its ability to deal effectively with the most difficult issues. In particular, the ability of the Council to garner the widest possible support for its decisions and actions would be enhanced if it was perceived to be broadly representative of the international community and the geopolitical realities of the contemporary world. The Secretary-General hoped, therefore, that Member States would redouble their efforts to reach agreement on the enlargement of the Council.

The Secretary-General also addressed other peace and security issues, such as the need to strengthen and complement existing weapons of mass destruction regimes (see p. 532), the threat posed by small arms and the need for cooperation in tightening export controls and facilitating the identification of sources of illicit weapons (see p. 562), sanctions, terrorism (see p. 63), prevention of violent conflict (see p. 54) and peacekeeping and peace-building.

The collective record of achievement in implementing the commitments of the Millennium Declaration in the area of peace and security was mixed, the Secretary-General concluded. To improve on that record, greater efforts were needed to produce innovative reforms, to be candid in evaluating existing mechanisms and working methods, and to engage in meaningful dialogues on the principles and practices that should guide the Organization in the years ahead. Above all, it was necessary to be intensely aware of the changes in the international security environment. Current challenges to peace and security were global and required complex and collective responses. Legitimacy of action, which might include military action, was essential to ensuring durable solutions to the security needs of the times, and the Charter remained the indispensable basis for legitimate international action. The world looked to the United Nations to address global security threats with the global interest in mind. Therefore, a renewed commitment to work collectively, in accordance with the Charter, was needed. A collective security system built on fairness and consistency would be the best way to meet both old and new challenges.

High-level Panel on Threats, Challenges and Change

The Secretary-General, presenting his annual report on the work of the Organization (see p. 3) to the General Assembly on 23 September [A/58/PV.7], said that events over the preceding 12 months had called into question the shared vision of global solidarity and security expressed in the Millennium Declaration [YUN 2000, p. 49]. He announced his intention to establish a high-level panel of eminent personalities to examine current challenges to peace and security; consider the contribution that collective action could make in addressing those challenges; review the functioning of major UN organs and the relationship between them; and recommend ways of strengthening the United Nations, through reform of its institutions and processes. The panel would focus primarily on threats to peace and security but would also examine other global challenges, insofar as they might influence or connect with those threats. He would ask the panel to report to him before the beginning of the fifty-ninth session of the Assembly in 2004.

By a 3 November letter [A/58/612], the Secretary-General transmitted to the Assembly President the terms of reference of the High-level Panel on Threats, Challenges and Change, to be chaired by Anand Panyarachun, former Prime Minister of Thailand, and comprising eminent persons from Australia, Brazil, China, Egypt, France, Ghana, India, Japan, Norway, Pakistan, the Russian Federation, the United Kingdom, the United Republic of Tanzania, the United States and Uruguay.

GENERAL ASSEMBLY ACTION

On 3 December [meeting 68], the General Assembly adopted **resolution 58/16** [draft: A/58/L.7/Rev.1 & Add.1] without vote [agenda item 60].

Responding to global threats and challenges

The General Assembly,

Recalling its resolutions 55/162 of 14 December 2000, 56/95 of 14 December 2001 and 57/144 of 16 December 2002 on the follow-up to the outcome of the Millennium Summit, and its resolution 57/145 of 16 December 2002,

Guided by the purposes and principles of the Charter of the United Nations,

Reaffirming the coordinating and leading role of the United Nations in establishing a cohesive and effective system for responding to global threats and challenges, and welcoming the ongoing efforts of Member States and the Secretary-General to this end,

Recognizing the importance, in the context of implementing the United Nations Millennium Declaration, of a comprehensive approach aimed at addressing global threats and challenges in accordance with the Charter, international law and relevant international instruments,

Welcoming the report of the Secretary-General on the implementation of the Millennium Declaration and the observations contained therein on ways and means to promote further, with the United Nations lead, a more comprehensive and coherent response to the global threats and challenges of the twenty-first century,

Taking note of the letter dated 3 November 2003 from the Secretary-General to the President of the General Assembly regarding the establishment of the High-level Panel on Threats, Challenges and Change,

1. *Commends* the increased interaction of Member States, the agencies and organizations of the United Nations system and the international and regional organizations cooperating with the United Nations, aimed at countering various global threats and challenges, in particular those posed by international terrorism in all its forms and manifestations, transnational organized crime, regional conflicts, poverty, unsustainable development, illicit drug trafficking, money-laundering, infectious diseases, environmental degradation, natural disasters, complex emergency situations and others;

2. *Expresses its appreciation* to Member States and relevant regional and other organizations for submitting to the Secretary-General their contributions on the issues referred to in paragraphs 1 and 2 of resolution 57/145;

3. *Encourages* the United Nations, its Member States, the agencies and organizations of the United Nations system and other international and regional organizations to continue their efforts towards establishing a comprehensive and effective strategy for responding to global threats and challenges;

4. *Welcomes* the establishment by the Secretary-General of the High-level Panel on Threats, Challenges and Change to make recommendations for the elements of a collective action, and expresses its readiness to consider as a matter of priority at its fifty-ninth session the recommendations of the Secretary-General thereon.

Conflict prevention

On 3 July [meeting 93], the General Assembly, having considered the Secretary-General's 2001 report on the prevention of armed conflict [YUN 2001, p. 48], adopted **resolution 57/337** [draft: A/57/L.79] without vote [agenda item 10].

Prevention of armed conflict

The General Assembly,

Guided by the purposes and principles enshrined in the Charter of the United Nations,

Recalling Chapter VI and Article 2.3 of the Charter of the United Nations,

Recalling also the Declaration on the Granting of Independence to Colonial Countries and Peoples as contained in its resolution 1514(XV) of 14 December 1960,

Recognizing that multilateral cooperation under United Nations auspices could be an effective means to prevent armed conflict and to address its root causes,

Reaffirming its commitment to the principles of the political independence, the sovereign equality and the territorial integrity of all States,

Guided by the Declaration on Principles of International Law concerning Friendly Relations and Cooperation among States in accordance with the Charter of the United Nations, annexed to its resolution 2625(XXV) of 24 October 1970,

Having considered the report of the Secretary-General on the prevention of armed conflict,

Bearing in mind its responsibilities, functions and powers under the Charter of the United Nations, and thus recalling all its relevant resolutions in matters related to the question of the prevention of armed conflict,

Recalling all Security Council resolutions relating to the prevention of armed conflict, and noting all Security Council presidential statements related to this matter,

Recognizing that the prevention of armed conflict and the pacific settlement of disputes could be useful tools for the United Nations in order to build a solid foundation for peace,

Alarmed by the human costs and devastating humanitarian, economic, environmental, political and social consequences of armed conflict, and recognizing the imperatives, including moral, of the prevention of armed conflict and its benefits for peace and development, in particular by addressing the root causes of armed conflict,

Recognizing that peace and development are mutually reinforcing, including in the prevention of armed conflict,

Recognizing also the importance of humanitarian assistance in ensuring an effective transition from conflict to peace and in preventing the recurrence of armed conflict,

Affirming that the fulfilment of the obligation to respect and ensure respect in all circumstances for the provisions of international humanitarian law, particularly the Geneva Convention relative to the Protection of Civilian Persons in Time of War, of 12 August 1949, will enhance the prospects for the peaceful resolution of armed conflict and for the prevention of its occurrence and recurrence,

Affirming also that full respect for all human rights and fundamental freedoms for all is one of the key elements for the prevention of armed conflict,

Recognizing that the root causes of armed conflict are multidimensional in nature, thus requiring a comprehensive and integrated approach to the prevention of armed conflict,

Determined to establish a just and lasting peace all over the world in accordance with the purposes and principles of the Charter of the United Nations, and upholding the sovereign equality of all States, respect for their territorial integrity and political independence, resolution of disputes by peaceful means and in conformity with the principles of justice and international law, the right of self-determination of peoples which remain under colonial domination and foreign occupation, non-interference in the internal affairs of States, respect for human rights and fundamental freedoms, respect for the equal rights of all without distinction as to race, sex, language or religion, and international cooperation in solving international problems of an economic, social, cultural or humanitarian character,

Welcoming the adoption of the Global Agenda for Dialogue among Civilizations, and recognizing the continued inter-religious dialogues and the promotion of religious harmony as contributions to the prevention of armed conflict,

Affirming that the ethnic, cultural and religious identity of minorities, where they exist, must be protected, and that persons belonging to such minorities should be treated equally and enjoy their human rights and fundamental freedoms without discrimination of any kind,

Resolving to take appropriate measures, in accordance with the Charter of the United Nations, combined with the efforts of Member States, to prevent armed conflicts,

1. *Takes note with appreciation* of the report of the Secretary-General on the prevention of armed conflict;

2. *Emphasizes* the importance of a comprehensive and coherent strategy comprising short-term operational and long-term structural measures for the prevention of armed conflict, and recognizes the ten principles outlined in the report of the Secretary-General;

3. *Reaffirms* the primary responsibility of Member States for the prevention of armed conflict, recalls the important role of the United Nations in this regard, and invites Member States, where appropriate, to adopt national strategies, taking into account, inter alia, those ten principles, as well as such elements as multilateral and regional cooperation, mutual benefit, sovereign equality, transparency and confidence-building measures;

4. *Encourages* Member States to utilize regional arrangements or agencies, where available, for the peaceful settlement of their disputes;

5. *Reiterates its call upon* the Member States to settle their disputes by peaceful means as set forth in Chapter VI of the Charter of the United Nations, including by the most effective use of the International Court of Justice;

6. *Resolves* that all Member States strictly adhere to their obligations as laid down in the Charter of the United Nations;

7. *Calls upon* the parties to any dispute, the continuance of which is likely to endanger the maintenance of international peace and security, to seek a solution by negotiation, enquiry, mediation, conciliation, arbitration, judicial settlement, resort to regional agencies or arrangements, or other peaceful means of their own choice in accordance with Article 33 of the Charter of the United Nations;

8. *Reaffirms* the primary responsibility of the Security Council for the maintenance of international peace and security, especially should the parties to such a dispute fail to settle it by the means indicated in paragraph 7 above in accordance with the relevant provisions of the Charter of the United Nations, and also notes in this regard the Manila Declaration on the Peaceful Settlement of International Disputes;

9. *Emphasizes* that the prevention of armed conflict would be promoted by continued cooperation among Member States, the United Nations system, the Bretton Woods institutions and regional and subregional organizations, noting that the private sector and civil society have supporting roles to play;

10. *Reaffirms*, in the context of the prevention of armed conflict, the inadmissibility of the acquisition of territory by force and of acts of colonization, and affirms the need to bring an end to situations of foreign occupation, in accordance with the Charter of the United Nations and international law;

11. *Recognizes* the need for mainstreaming and coordinating the prevention of armed conflict throughout the United Nations system, and calls upon all its relevant organs, organizations and bodies to consider, in accordance with their respective mandates, how they could best include a conflict prevention perspective in their activities, where appropriate, and to inform the General Assembly, pursuant to resolution 55/281 of 1 August 2001, no later than at its fifty-ninth session, of progress achieved in this regard;

12. *Calls upon* Member States and the international community to abide by the resolve of the Millennium Assembly to make the United Nations more effective in maintaining peace and security by giving it the resources and tools it needs for conflict prevention;

13. *Calls* for strengthening the capacity of the United Nations in order to carry out more effectively its responsibilities for the prevention of armed conflict, including relevant peace-building and development activities, and requests the Secretary-General to submit a detailed review of the capacity of the United Nations system in the context of the report on the implementation of the present resolution;

14. *Requests* the Secretary-General to submit a comprehensive report on the implementation of the present resolution, taking into account, inter alia, the views expressed by Member States and the organs, agencies, funds and programmes of the United Nations system in accordance with resolution 55/281, for consideration no later than at its fifty-ninth session;

15. *Decides* to adopt the conclusions and recommendations, based on its consideration of the report of the Secretary-General, as contained in the annex to the present resolution;

16. *Decides also* to include in the provisional agenda of its fifty-ninth session a specific item entitled "Prevention of armed conflict".

Annex

General Assembly conclusions and recommendations on the prevention of armed conflict

The General Assembly

Role of Member States

1. *Calls upon* Member States to achieve the goals embodied in the United Nations Millennium Declaration, including the internationally agreed development goals, as well as the outcomes of the major United Nations conferences and summits;

2. *Calls in this regard upon* Member States and the international community at large to support poverty eradication measures and the development strategies of developing countries;

3. *Urges* developed countries that have not done so to make concrete efforts towards the target of providing 0.7 per cent of their gross national product as official development assistance to developing countries and 0.15 to 0.20 per cent of their gross national product as official development assistance to least developed countries, as reconfirmed at the Third United Nations Conference on the Least Developed Countries, and encourages developing countries to build on progress achieved in ensuring that official development assistance is used effectively to help to achieve development goals and targets;

4. *Encourages* greater transparency in armaments by Member States, as appropriate, including broader and more active participation in the United Nations instruments relating to arms registers and military expenditures, and calls upon them strongly to support confidence-building measures in this area;

5. *Calls upon* Member States to implement the obligations assumed by them as States parties to treaties in such areas as arms control, non-proliferation and disarmament and to strengthen their international verification instruments;

6. *Reaffirms* the resolve of the international community to strive for the elimination of weapons of mass destruction;

7. *Invites* Member States that have not already done so to consider, as appropriate, becoming parties to arms control, non-proliferation and disarmament treaties;

8. *Urges* Member States, as well as relevant United Nations bodies, to take appropriate measures to fully implement the Programme of Action to Prevent, Combat and Eradicate the Illicit Trade in Small Arms and Light Weapons in All Its Aspects;

9. *Urges* Member States which have not already done so to consider ratification, acceptance, approval of or accession to the international human rights and international humanitarian law instruments, and also other international instruments relevant to the prevention of armed conflict;

10. *Calls upon* Member States to comply in good faith with the obligations assumed by them as States parties to international legal instruments relevant to the prevention of armed conflict;

11. *Notes* the entry into force on 1 July 2002 of the Rome Statute of the International Criminal Court and the subsequent establishment of the International Criminal Court;

12. *Stresses* the need to bring to justice the perpetrators of war crimes and crimes against humanity as a significant contribution towards the promotion of a culture of prevention;

13. *Also stresses* the important role that women, in their various capacities, and with their expertise, training and knowledge, can play with regard to the prevention of armed conflict, in all its aspects, and calls for the strengthening of that role in all relevant institutions at the national, regional and international levels;

14. *Urges* Member States to make the most effective use of existing and new procedures and methods for

the peaceful settlement of their disputes, including, as appropriate, arbitration, mediation and other treaty-based arrangements, and the International Court of Justice, to settle their disputes in a peaceful manner and thereby promote the role of international law in international relations;

15. *Emphasizes* the need, at all levels of society and among nations, for strengthening freedom, justice, democracy, tolerance, solidarity, cooperation, pluralism, cultural diversity, dialogue and understanding as important elements for preventing armed conflict;

16. *Encourages* Member States to strengthen national capacities for addressing structural risk factors, as deemed useful by national Governments, with the support, as appropriate, of the international community, including the United Nations system, the Bretton Woods institutions and regional and subregional organizations;

Role of the General Assembly

17. *Expresses its determination* to make more effective use of its powers under Articles 10, 11, 13, 14, 15 and 17 of the Charter of the United Nations for the prevention of armed conflict;

18. *Intends* to make fuller use of Article 96 of the Charter of the United Nations;

19. *Decides* to consider ways of enhancing interaction with the other United Nations organs, especially the Security Council and the Economic and Social Council, and with the Secretary-General in terms of developing and implementing long- and short-term measures and strategies aimed at preventing armed conflict;

Role of the Security Council

20. *Takes note* of the provisions contained in Security Council resolution 1366(2001) of 30 August 2001, in particular the commitment of the Council to take early and effective action to prevent armed conflict;

21. *Encourages* the Security Council to give prompt consideration to early warning or prevention cases brought to its attention by the Secretary-General, and to use appropriate mechanisms, such as the Ad Hoc Working Group on Conflict Prevention and Resolution in Africa, with due regard to relevant regional and subregional dimensions, in accordance with Article 99 of the Charter of the United Nations;

22. *Further encourages* the Security Council to keep under close review situations of potential armed conflict and to consider seriously cases of potential armed conflict brought to its attention by a State or the General Assembly or on the basis of information furnished by the Economic and Social Council;

23. *Recognizes* that the United Nations can continue to play an important role in the prevention of armed conflict by promoting conflict resolution and dispute settlement;

24. *Encourages* the continued strengthening of the process of the peaceful settlement of disputes and efforts to make it more effective;

25. *Notes* the commitment of the Security Council to make wider and effective use of the procedures and means enshrined in the Charter of the United Nations, particularly in Chapter VI, as one of the essential components of its work to promote and maintain international peace and security;

26. *Reaffirms* that the primary responsibility for the maintenance of international peace and security, for which the prevention of armed conflict is important, is conferred upon the Security Council, and reiterates that, under Article 25 of the Charter of the United Nations, the Members of the United Nations have agreed to accept and carry out the decisions of the Security Council in accordance with the Charter;

27. *Recommends* that the Security Council continue to mandate peacekeeping operations and include, as appropriate, peace-building elements therein, in such a way as to generate conditions which, to the maximum extent possible, help to avoid the recurrence of armed conflict;

28. *Encourages* the Security Council to continue to invite the office of the United Nations Emergency Relief Coordinator and other relevant United Nations agencies to brief its members on emergency situations which it deems to represent a threat to international peace and security, and to support the implementation of protection and assistance activities by relevant United Nations agencies in accordance with their respective mandates;

29. *Notes* the willingness of the Security Council to consider, in the context of United Nations peacekeeping operations, preventive deployments with the consent and cooperation of the Member States concerned;

30. *Encourages* the Security Council to give, as appropriate, greater attention to gender perspectives in all its activities aimed at the prevention of armed conflict;

31. *Encourages* the Security Council and the Economic and Social Council to strengthen their mutual cooperation and coordination, in accordance with their respective mandates, for the prevention of armed conflict;

Role of the Economic and Social Council

32. *Supports* the more active involvement of the Economic and Social Council with regard to the prevention of armed conflict, taking into account the relevant recommendations of the Secretary-General and the need to promote socio-economic measures, including economic growth, in support of poverty eradication and development, as a core element of Council strategy in that regard;

33. *Welcomes* Economic and Social Council resolution 2002/1 of 15 July 2002, which envisages the creation of ad hoc advisory groups on African countries emerging from conflicts, as well as Council decision 2002/304 of 25 October 2002, by which the Ad Hoc Advisory Group on Guinea-Bissau was created, requests the Council to present a report on the lessons learned by the ad hoc advisory groups during its substantive session of 2004, and recommends that such endeavours be further strengthened, including through measures that promote more effective responses in cooperation and coordination with the United Nations system as a whole, the Bretton Woods institutions and the World Trade Organization;

Role of the Secretary-General

34. *Welcomes* the intention of the Security Council to engage within the United Nations system in a focused dialogue on what practical measures the United Nations system needs to take to promote greater coher-

ence in its activities aimed at the prevention of armed conflict, and recommends that consideration be given, inter alia, to identifying the proper framework for the elaboration of system-wide coherent and action-oriented strategies within the United Nations system, at Headquarters and in the field, and for rationalizing the funding procedures for the prevention of armed conflict;

35. *Recalls*, in that context, the need to strengthen the capacity of the United Nations for early warning, collection of information and analysis, as referred to in its resolution 47/120 A of 18 December 1992, and notes the relevant conclusions and recommendations endorsed in its resolution 56/225 of 24 December 2001;

36. *Supports* the intention of the Secretary-General to improve the use of means placed at his disposal and within his authority to facilitate the prevention of armed conflict, including through fact-finding missions and confidence-building measures;

Interaction between the United Nations and other international actors in the prevention of armed conflict: role of regional organizations and civil society

Regional organizations

37. *Calls* for the strengthening of cooperation, where appropriate, between the United Nations and regional organizations in the field of prevention of armed conflict, in accordance with their respective mandates, in particular in capacity-building and the coordination of their respective activities, and for that purpose requests the Secretary-General to present concrete proposals for enhancing Secretariat support of those activities within his comprehensive report;

38. *Encourages* the continuation of high-level United Nations/regional organizations meetings, including on the prevention of armed conflict, and requests the Secretary-General to keep the General Assembly informed accordingly;

Civil society

39. *Recognizes* the important supporting role of civil society in the prevention of armed conflict, and invites it to continue to support efforts for the prevention of armed conflict and to pursue practices that foster a climate of peace, help to prevent or mitigate crisis situations and contribute to reconciliation.

Speaking after the adoption of the resolution, the Deputy Secretary-General said that, after two years of hard work, the Assembly had its first substantive resolution on the important issue of armed conflict prevention; she hoped it would become a landmark for UN efforts in that area. The Secretariat was committed to strengthening the capacity of the UN system to carry out more effectively its responsibilities for the prevention of armed conflict. It would submit a detailed review of the UN system capacity in the context of the comprehensive report on the implementation of the resolution that the Assembly had requested in paragraph 14.

Related action. The Security Council, on 30 January, adopted **resolution 1460(2003)** on children and armed conflict (see p. 788). The Council President issued, on 15 December, statement **S/PRST/2003/27** on the protection of civilians in armed conflict (see p. 727).

Role of civil society in conflict prevention

Following the adoption of resolution 57/337 (see p. 50), the President of the General Assembly's fifty-seventh session organized, on 4 September, an open interactive dialogue on the role of civil society in the prevention of armed conflict. The aim of the meeting was to build on the momentum of the resolution in terms of follow-up activities; explore how best to link the work of civil society in conflict prevention with that of Governments and the United Nations; offer substantive content for permanent missions in New York to consider the core issues and respond to the concerns, questions and ideas of Member States; and update Member States about the work of the Global Partnership for the Prevention of Armed Conflict (see below).

In his report on the meeting, transmitted to the Assembly on 12 September [A/57/864], the Assembly President said that civil society organizations provided an array of capabilities and opportunities to supplement the role of Governments and the United Nations in conflict prevention. They could sometimes reach parties on the ground that Governments could not reach, and participants in the dialogue had noted that civil society organizations could also contribute to conflict prevention in the areas of analysis, partnership, sustainability and networks. However, interacting and coordinating with civil society remained a challenge for Governments and the United Nations; how to create strategic linkages among Governments, intergovernmental organizations and civil society to complement each other's work rather than impede or duplicate efforts was not well understood.

The Assembly President noted that, in response to the Secretary-General's 2001 report on the prevention of armed conflict [YUN 2001, p. 48], the Global Partnership for the Prevention of Armed Conflict was established to engage civil society actors from the grass roots to the international level in integrating and mainstreaming conflict prevention, with a view to improving international responses in preventing conflict at all levels. Its goals were: to explore fully the role of civil society in conflict prevention and peacebuilding; to develop a coherent body of research and theory to help the conflict prevention community play its full part in the international debate; to improve interaction between civil society groups, the United Nations, regional organizations and Governments; and to strengthen regional and international networking between conflict prevention actors. Secretariats for the project had been established at the European Centre for Conflict Prevention (Utrecht, Netherlands), with the UN-NGO (non-governmental organization) Conflict Prevention Working Group (New York), and in each region. Regional conferences to produce mutually agreed-upon regional plans of action would be followed by an international conference (New York, June 2005). Among the expected outcomes of the process were: regional publications documenting lessons learned and best practices; regional and international plans of action to guide conflict prevention initiatives; a global network of conflict prevention actors; commitments from Member States to realign existing conflict management mechanisms towards prevention; and support for Member States in their efforts to prevent conflict.

The President stated that the open meeting had shown that, while many questions and concerns existed about the engagement with civil society organizations, there was clear support for exploring and understanding the issues that would strengthen the partnerships among Governments, intergovernmental agencies and civil society in preventing deadly conflicts. Participating Member States recommended that: the Assembly examine its role in the prevention of violent conflict as it related to Article 14 of the Charter, and consider whether such issues should be regularly addressed in the Fourth (Special Political and Decolonization) Committee; the United Nations and Member States support the Global Partnership for the Prevention of Armed Conflict initiative; missions at UN Headquarters appoint a liaison to work with the UN-NGO Conflict Prevention Working Group; UN offices, agencies and programmes link with the Conflict Prevention Working Group and encourage their field offices to liaise with the coordinators of regional conferences; the UN Department of Political Affairs further explore how to establish consultation mechanisms with the Global Partnership in the process of preparing the report to the Assembly's fifty-ninth (2004) session; and Governments continue to support the process financially and other Member States and civil society organizations and foundations aid in the global initiative.

UN role in conflict prevention

Reports of Secretary-General. In a September report [A/58/323] on the implementation of the Millennium Declaration [YUN 2000, p. 49], the Secretary-General said that, as part of its efforts to better understand the current challenges and devise strategies to address them more effectively, the United Nations had to make even greater efforts to prevent the outbreak of violence well before internal tensions and conflicts eroded Governments and economies to the point of collapse. The UN system had been engaged in a comprehensive exercise to implement his 2001 report on the prevention of armed conflict [YUN 2001, p. 48] and to better carry out its obligations, including support of regional, subregional and national efforts to develop preventive strategies. General Assembly **resolution 57/337** (see p. 50) on the prevention of armed conflict gave the United Nations a strong mandate to continue, expand and intensify its conflict prevention activities, and recognized the value of early warning in the prevention of armed conflict. The Secretary-General said that he intended to report more systematically on efforts to strengthen UN capacity in that area in his comprehensive report on conflict prevention, to be submitted in 2004.

He drew attention to the need for effective measures to address the economic incentives that established and maintained war economies, such as the Kimberley Process of diamond certification (see p. 55), and called for further measures against money-laundering. Also, more efforts were needed not only to punish actors involved in war economies but to provide viable economic alternatives.

In response to Assembly resolution 55/281 [YUN 2001, p. 50], the Secretary-General submitted, in September, an interim report on the prevention of armed conflict [A/58/365-S/2003/888], which provided an analytical overview of UN conflict prevention efforts, particularly in the areas of capacity-building, development assistance, human rights, the rule of law, regional dimensions, the role of women, preventive action and terrorism, disarmament, the role of major UN organs and international financial institutions, civil society, the private sector and training.

In elaborating a way forward, the Secretary-General said that, while some progress had been made in improving UN conflict prevention capacity, the Organization had to integrate conflict prevention further into its activities and build a more structured link between political and socio-economic strategies, ensuring that conflict prevention became a deliberate component in planning and coordinating development programmes. There should also be greater coherence and coordination of UN efforts in structural prevention at national, regional and international levels. Moreover, the UN system needed to strengthen its capacity for coordinating all international efforts; make further progress in responding to the political economy of armed conflicts, by exploring the policy aspects of the issues surrounding resource-based intra-State conflicts and the economic agendas of civil war and devising instruments for addressing war economies at all stages of a conflict; and devote greater attention to the potential threats posed by environmental problems, particularly the implications of the scarcity of certain natural resources, including the consideration of ways to build additional capacity to analyse and address potential threats of conflicts emanating from international natural resource disparities. The Secretary-General invited, in the context of resolution 57/337 (see p. 50), Member States, the UN system and its partners, regional organizations, international financial institutions and civil society to prepare for a substantial discussion on the way forward.

Implementation of JIU recommendations. In an August report [A/58/220] on the implementation of the 1995 recommendations [YUN 1995, p. 177], of the Joint Inspection Unit (JIU) on strengthening the UN system capacity for conflict prevention [A/50/853], the Secretary-General indicated that, since the issuance of that report and his comments and those of the Administrative Committee on Coordination thereon [YUN 1997, p. 37], major developments had taken place in conflict prevention and JIU's recommendations had, in many cases, been implemented system-wide.

CEB consideration. The High-level Committee on Programmes of the United Nations System Chief Executives Board for Coordination (CEB), at its sixth session (Rome, Italy, 18-19 September) [CEB/2003/7], emphasized the need for comprehensive system-wide responses to ensure mutual reinforcement in the political, peacekeeping, peace-building and development areas of the system's work and the importance of close interaction with the UN Department of Political Affairs. It also suggested that the UN system would benefit from mechanisms to systematically channel political insights and information accumulated by field staff into the system's situational analysis process.

Conflict diamonds

Kimberley Process. Two meetings of the Kimberley Process, established in 2000 [YUN 2000, p. 76] to stem the flow of rough diamonds used by rebels to finance armed conflict, protect the legitimate diamond industry and achieve the creation and implementation of an international certification scheme for rough diamonds based on national certification schemes, were held in 2002 (Ottawa, Canada, 18-20 March, and Interlaken, Switzerland, 4-5 November). At the Interlaken meeting, Ministers and other heads of delegation adopted the Kimberley Process Certification Scheme, the text of which was annexed to the Interlaken Declaration on the Kimberley Process Certification Scheme for Rough Diamonds. They also committed themselves to the simultaneous launch of the Scheme on 1 January 2003 and reaffirmed their determination to monitor the trade in rough diamonds in order to prevent trade in conflict diamonds. South Africa would chair the Process in the first year of implementation.

On 17 January [S/2003/70], South Africa requested the Security Council to delay its consideration of the draft resolution on the Kimberley Process Certification Scheme (see below) until the Assembly had received the report on the Interlaken Declaration, so as not to pre-empt the debate in the Assembly.

On 29 January [A/57/489], in accordance with Assembly resolution 56/263 [YUN 2002, p. 44], South Africa submitted to the Assembly the final report on the Kimberley Process.

SECURITY COUNCIL ACTION

On 28 January [meeting 4694], the Security Council unanimously adopted **resolution 1459(2003)**. The draft [S/2003/54] was prepared in consultations among Council members.

The Security Council,

Noting with deep concern the linkage between the illicit trade in rough diamonds from certain regions of the world and the fuelling of armed conflicts that affect international peace and security,

Recalling all its relevant resolutions to control the illicit trade in rough diamonds, including resolutions 1173(1998) of 12 June 1998, 1306(2000) of 5 July 2000, 1343(2001) of 7 March 2001, 1385(2001) of 19 December 2001 and 1408(2002) of 6 May 2002,

Highlighting in particular resolution 1295(2000) of 18 April 2000, in which the Council welcomed the proposal that led to the adoption of the Interlaken Declaration of 5 November 2002 on the Kimberley Process Certification Scheme for Rough Diamonds,

Highlighting the importance of conflict prevention through efforts to hinder the fuelling of conflicts by illicit trade in rough diamonds, which is the very nature of the Kimberley Process,

Noting in particular the importance of the major diamond producing, trading, and processing countries participating in the Kimberley Process system of self-regulation,

Expressing its appreciation to the Governments of South Africa, Namibia, Belgium, the Russian Federation, the United Kingdom of Great Britain and Northern Ireland, Angola, Botswana, Canada and Switzerland for hosting meetings of the Kimberley Process,

Noting with appreciation the important contribution made by industry and civil society to the development of the Kimberley Process Certification Scheme,

Noting the decision made at the meeting held in Interlaken, Switzerland, on 5 November 2002 to launch the Kimberley Process Certification Scheme beginning on 1 January 2003,

Welcoming the progress achieved at the Interlaken meeting in developing the Kimberley Process Certification Scheme, including the adoption of the Interlaken Declaration,

1. *Strongly supports* the Kimberley Process Certification Scheme, as well as the ongoing process to refine and implement the regime, adopted at the Interlaken conference as a valuable contribution against trafficking in conflict diamonds, looks forward to its implementation, and strongly encourages the participants to further resolve outstanding issues;

2. *Welcomes* the voluntary system of industry self-regulation, as described in the Interlaken Declaration of 5 November 2002 on the Kimberley Process Certification Scheme for Rough Diamonds;

3. *Stresses* that the widest possible participation in the Kimberley Process Certification Scheme is essential and should be encouraged and facilitated, and urges all Member States to participate actively in the Scheme.

GENERAL ASSEMBLY ACTION

On 15 April [meeting 83], the General Assembly adopted **resolution 57/302** [draft: A/57/L.76/Rev.1 & Add.1] without vote [agenda item 27].

The role of diamonds in fuelling conflict: breaking the link between the illicit transaction of rough diamonds and armed conflict as a contribution to prevention and settlement of conflicts

The General Assembly,

Recognizing that the trade in conflict diamonds is a matter of serious international concern, which can be directly linked to the fuelling of armed conflict, the activities of rebel movements aimed at undermining or overthrowing legitimate Governments, and the illicit traffic in and proliferation of armaments, especially small arms and light weapons,

Recognizing also the devastating impact of conflicts fuelled by the trade in conflict diamonds on the peace, safety and security of people in affected countries, and the systematic and gross human rights violations that have been perpetrated in such conflicts,

Noting the negative impact of such conflicts on regional stability and the obligations placed upon States by the Charter of the United Nations regarding the maintenance of international peace and security,

Recognizing, therefore, that urgent action to curb the trade in conflict diamonds is imperative,

Recognizing also the positive benefits of the legitimate diamond trade to producing countries, and underlining the need for urgent international action to prevent the problem of conflict diamonds from negatively affecting the trade in legitimate diamonds, which makes a critical contribution to the economies of many of the producing, exporting and importing States, especially developing States,

Noting that the vast majority of rough diamonds produced in the world are from legitimate sources,

Recalling the Charter and all the relevant resolutions of the Security Council related to conflict diamonds, and determined to contribute to and support the implementation of the measures provided for in those resolutions,

Recalling also Security Council resolution 1459(2003) of 28 January 2003, in which the Council strongly supported the Kimberley Process Certification Scheme, as well as the ongoing process to refine and implement the regime, as a valuable contribution against trafficking in conflict diamonds,

Recalling further its resolutions 55/56 of 1 December 2000 and 56/263 of 13 March 2002, in which it called for the development of proposals for a simple and workable international certification scheme for rough diamonds, based primarily on national certification schemes and on internationally agreed minimum standards, under the Kimberley Process,

Believing that the introduction of the Kimberley Process Certification Scheme should substantially reduce the opportunity for conflict diamonds to play a role in fuelling armed conflict and should help to protect legitimate trade and ensure the effective implementation of the relevant resolutions on trade in conflict diamonds,

Recalling the objective of ensuring that the Kimberley Process Certification Scheme is simple, effective and pragmatic, that it does not impede the present legitimate trade in diamonds or impose an undue burden on Governments or industry, particularly smaller producers, and that it does not hinder the development of the diamond industry,

Acknowledging the important initiatives already taken to address the problem of conflict diamonds, in particular by the Governments of Angola, the Democratic Republic of the Congo, Guinea and Sierra Leone and by other key producing, exporting and importing countries, and encouraging those Governments to continue the initiatives,

Acknowledging also the continued efforts of regional organizations and other groups of countries to curb conflict diamonds,

Welcoming the important contribution made by the diamond industry, in particular the World Diamond Council, as well as civil society, to assist international efforts to stop the trade in conflict diamonds,

Welcoming also the voluntary self-regulation initiatives for the diamond industry announced by the World Diamond Council, and recognizing that a system of such voluntary self-regulation will contribute, as described in the Interlaken Declaration of 5 November 2002 on the Kimberley Process Certification Scheme for Rough Diamonds, to ensuring the effectiveness of national systems of internal controls for rough diamonds,

Recognizing that the Kimberley Process Certification Scheme will be credible only if all participants have established internal systems of control designed to eliminate the presence of conflict diamonds in the chain of producing, exporting and importing rough diamonds within their own territories, while taking into account that differences in production methods and trading practices, as well as differences in institutional controls thereof, may require different approaches to meet minimum standards,

Welcoming the important contribution of the Kimberley Process, which was initiated by African diamond-producing countries,

Noting with appreciation that the Kimberley Process has pursued its deliberations on an inclusive basis, involving concerned stakeholders, including producing, exporting and importing States, the diamond industry and civil society,

Recognizing that State sovereignty should be fully respected and the principles of equality, mutual benefits and consensus should be adhered to,

Welcoming the Interlaken Declaration, which successfully launched the Kimberley Process Certification Scheme,

1. *Notes with appreciation* the report of the Chair of the Kimberley Process submitted pursuant to resolution 56/263, and congratulates the Governments, and the representatives of the regional economic integration organizations, the organized diamond industry and civil society participating in the Kimberley Process, on having finalized the Kimberley Process Certification Scheme;

2. *Recognizes* that the Kimberley Process Certification Scheme can help to ensure the effective implementation of relevant resolutions of the Security Council containing sanctions on the trade in conflict diamonds, and calls for full implementation of existing Council measures targeting the illicit trade in rough diamonds that play a role in fuelling conflict;

3. *Strongly supports* the Kimberley Process Certification Scheme presented in the form of the document entitled "Kimberley Process Certification Scheme";

4. *Notes* the commitment made at the Kimberley Process ministerial meeting on 5 November 2002 to ensure that measures taken to implement the Kimberley Process Certification Scheme for Rough Diamonds will be consistent with international trade rules;

5. *Welcomes* the decision to implement the Kimberley Process Certification Scheme from 1 January 2003;

6. *Also welcomes* the decision to collate and disseminate relevant statistical data on the production of and international trade in rough diamonds, as a tool for effective implementation;

7. *Stresses* that the widest possible participation in the Kimberley Process Certification Scheme is essential and should be encouraged and facilitated, and urges all Member States to participate actively in the Certification Scheme;

8. *Welcomes* the willingness expressed by the Government of South Africa to chair the Kimberley Process during its first year of implementation;

9. *Requests* the Chair of the Kimberley Process to present to the General Assembly at its fifty-eighth session a report on the implementation of the process;

10. *Decides* to include in the provisional agenda of its fifty-eighth session the item entitled "The role of diamonds in fuelling conflict".

Implementation of 1970 Declaration

The General Assembly, by **decision 58/516** of 8 December, included in the provisional agenda of its fifty-ninth (2004) session the item entitled "Review of the implementation of the Declaration on the Strengthening of International Security" [YUN 1970, p. 105].

Peacemaking and peace-building

Security Council role in settlement of disputes

On 13 May [meeting 4753], the Security Council discussed its role in the pacific settlement of disputes. Addressing the Council, the Secretary-General said that Chapter VI of the UN Charter, which dealt with the pacific settlement of disputes, stood at the heart of the Organization's system of collective security. While the framers of the Charter understood clearly the need for an enforcement mechanism and provided for the use of force against threats to international peace and security, their hopes for a better world lay in the peaceful resolution of armed conflicts. In recent years, the Council had used Chapter VI in various ways, including direct dialogue with the parties to conflict, working more closely with the Economic and Social Council and with regional and subregional organizations to prevent and resolve conflicts in Africa, use of the Secretary-General's good offices and encouraging him to appoint more special representatives and envoys, and fact-finding missions.

Those efforts had achieved mixed results, raising questions as to what had been learned from those experiences and what could be done better. The Secretary-General referred to the recommendations contained in his 2001 report on the prevention of armed conflict [YUN 2001, p. 48], in particular the use of regional prevention mechanisms, more frequent resort to the International Court of Justice and increased reporting by the UN system to the Security Council about serious violations of international law or of human rights, and about potential conflicts arising from ethnic, religious or territorial disputes, or from poverty or other factors. He suggested that the Council could help identify and address root causes early; ensure an integrated approach that would bring together all actors, including civil society; and support other UN organs in their efforts to resolve disputes or address volatile situations. He appealed to the Council to be imaginative, to use its influence and to focus on implementation and action.

SECURITY COUNCIL ACTION

On 13 May [meeting 4753], following consultations among the Security Council members, the President made statement **S/PRST/2003/5** on behalf of the Council:

> The Security Council, guided by the purposes and principles of the Charter of the United Nations, reaffirms its commitment to maintain international peace and security through effective collective measures for the prevention and removal of threats to the peace or other breaches of the peace and to bring

about, by peaceful means and in conformity with the principles of justice and international law, the adjustment or settlement of international disputes or situations which might lead to a breach of the peace.

The Council recognizes that the United Nations and its organs can play an important role in preventing disputes arising between parties, in preventing existing disputes escalating into conflicts and in containing and resolving the conflicts when they occur. The Council recalls, in this regard, the successes of the United Nations in these areas.

The Council recalls that the Charter, particularly Chapter VI, sets forth the means and a framework for the pacific settlement of disputes.

The Council underscores the fact that efforts to strengthen the process of the peaceful settlement of disputes should be continued and made more effective.

The Council reiterates its commitment to make a wider and more effective use of the procedures and means enshrined in the provisions of the Charter regarding the pacific settlement of disputes, particularly Articles 33 to 38 (Chapter VI), as one of the essential components of its work to promote and maintain international peace and security.

The Council decides to continue to keep this item under review.

Cooperation with regional organizations

Security Council public meeting. On 11 April [meeting 4739], the Security Council held a high-level meeting with representatives of regional organizations (the African Union, the League of Arab States, the Organization of American States, the Organization for Security and Cooperation in Europe, the European Union, the Economic Community of West African States) on the theme "The Security Council and regional organizations: facing the new challenges to international peace and security".

In a summary of the discussions, transmitted to the Secretary-General on 25 April [S/2003/506], Mexico reported that the meeting provided an opportunity for sharing experiences regarding specific capacities, instruments for early warning, prevention, management and resolution of conflicts and exchange of information. Among the issues discussed were the need to pay attention to the root causes of instability and threats to peace and security and to find new ways of cooperation and coordination between the United Nations and regional organizations in the maintenance of peace and security. That cooperation should be based on the principle of complementarity so as to make the best use of the comparative advantages of each organization; it should also take place within a flexible framework. There was also a need to develop a comprehensive and integrated approach to conflict prevention, management and resolution.

The meeting proposed: holding a regular high-level dialogue between the Council and regional organizations; improving the exchange of information; establishing a global system to deal with the current challenges and threats to international peace and security; promoting early coordination between the Council and regional organizations before decisions were taken that might involve or affect them; and convening an international conference on international peace, under UN auspices, preceded by regional meetings on the subject.

High-level meeting between the UN and regional organizations. The fifth high-level meeting between the United Nations and regional organizations (New York, 29-30 July) was held under the theme "New challenges to international peace and security, including international terrorism". The 21 participating organizations examined potential threats to international security, such as civil wars and complex emergencies, the proliferation of weapons of mass destruction, international terrorism, gross violations of human rights, genocide, organized crime and other threats, such as environmental degradation and the spread of diseases. As Chairman of the meeting, the Secretary-General transmitted the conclusions in identical letters to the Presidents of the General Assembly and the Security Council on 10 October [A/58/444-S/2003/1022]. He said that the meeting raised important questions relating to the strengthening of cooperation to respond to new challenges and reviewed the follow-up to its previous meetings on cooperation in conflict prevention and peacebuilding [YUN 2001, p. 56]. The meeting also reaffirmed support for multilateralism and international institutions and for the international community to provide effective responses to current challenges to international peace and security. Concern was expressed by many that human rights should not be undermined in counter-terrorism efforts. Participants agreed on a framework for further cooperation in confronting challenges to international peace and security, including international terrorism.

Report of Secretary-General. The Secretary-General, in his report on the work of the Organization [A/58/1], gave examples of United Nations cooperation with regional organizations in the areas of peace and security, development and respect for human rights (see p. 12).

Electoral assistance

In his annual report on the work of the Organization [A/58/1], the Secretary-General stated that, from September 2002 to July 2003, the United Nations received 32 official requests for electoral assistance. Positive responses were provided to 20 of those requests, 9 remained under consideration and 3 could not be fulfilled.

In response to General Assembly resolution 56/159 [YUN 2001, p. 640], the Secretary-General submitted an August report on strengthening the role of the United Nations in enhancing the effectiveness of the principle of periodic and genuine elections and the promotion of democratization [A/58/212]. He said that the Organization provided four categories of electoral assistance: technical assistance; the organization and conduct of elections; observation or monitoring of elections; and participation where elections were expected to play a significant role in the peace-building phase of political negotiations. The last category was a relatively recent development, and experience suggested that it was highly valuable and should be encouraged. The provision of electoral assistance as a component of peace-keeping and peace-building missions had increased. Over the preceding two years, the Electoral Assistance Division had worked with major UN missions in Afghanistan, the Democratic Republic of the Congo and Sierra Leone. That was in part a reflection of the role that elections could play in solidifying peace-building efforts and providing alternative dispute resolution mechanisms that could replace the use of violence.

(For further information on UN electoral assistance, see p. 736.)

Justice and the rule of law

The Secretary-General, in a January report on the implementation of the recommendations of the Special Committee on Peacekeeping Operations [A/57/711], stated that the Executive Committee on Peace and Security Task Force for the Development of Comprehensive Rule-of-Law Strategies for Peace Operations had prepared a detailed report identifying rule-of-law-related expertise available within the UN system for assisting the UN Department of Peacekeeping Operations (DPKO) and field missions; governmental, intergovernmental and non-governmental organizations that might be able to provide such expertise; possible arrangements for UN partners; and guidelines, manuals and handbooks for rule-of-law-related activities developed by the UN system. The Task Force proposals emphasized the need for the United Nations to consult more closely with local actors at the country level and engage them in a meaningful way in devising and undertaking rule-of-law initiatives in peace operations, so as not to impose a rule-of-law strategy on them.

The Special Committee, at its 2003 session [A/57/767], agreed that an essential element to sustained stability in a post-conflict environment was the strengthening and consolidation of local rule-of-law capacity, which should be the focus of attention of UN peacekeeping missions. It welcomed the report of the Executive Committee on Peace and Security Task Force (see above) and asked the Secretariat to report on the implementation of those recommendations in 2004, and to consult with Member States on the means for sharing information on available national rule-of-law resources with the Secretariat.

Security Council consideration. At a ministerial-level meeting on 24 September [meeting 4833] and on 30 September [meeting 4835], the Security Council discussed the issue of justice and the rule of law: the United Nations role. Opening the debate on 24 September, the Council President said that justice and the rule of law were vital for the proper functioning of States and were essential elements in creating and sustaining stable, peaceful and democratic States. The debate was therefore an opportunity to affirm again the central importance of the rule of law and justice in the work of the United Nations, and to ascertain how the international community could better prepare to support States coming out of conflict.

The Secretary-General stated that the Council had a responsibility to promote justice and the rule of law in its efforts to maintain international peace and security and to rebuild shattered societies. Through its many complex operations, the United Nations had learned that people lost faith in a peace process when they did not feel safe from crime, secure in returning to their homes, able to start rebuilding a normal life or confident that the injustices of the past would be addressed. Without credible machinery to enforce the law and resolve disputes, people resorted to violent or illegal means. A comprehensive approach to justice and the rule of law was required that encompassed the entire criminal justice chain and many issues beyond the criminal justice system. UN actions should be based on the Charter, UN standards for human rights and the administration of justice and the principles of international humanitarian law, human rights law, refugee law and criminal law. Local actors should be involved from the start, with the United Nations guiding and reinforcing, and leaving behind strong local institutions when it departed.

As to justice for victims of past crimes, ending the climate of impunity was vital to restoring public confidence and building international support to implement peace agreements. Transitional justice mechanisms had to concentrate not only on individual responsibility for serious crimes, but also on achieving national reconciliation. Criminal justice mechanisms should be tailored to meet the needs of victims and victim societies, with courts being supplemented with mechanisms such as truth and reconciliation commissions if necessary. There should be no amnesty for war crimes, genocide, crimes against humanity or other serious violations of international human rights and humanitarian law, but the rights of the accused should be scrupulously protected.

SECURITY COUNCIL ACTION

On 24 September [meeting 4833], following consultations among Security Council members, the President made statement **S/PRST/2003/15** on behalf of the Council:

> The Security Council met at the ministerial level on 24 September 2003 to consider "Justice and the rule of law: the United Nations role". Ministers expressed their respective views and understandings on, and reaffirmed the vital importance of, these issues, recalling the repeated emphasis given to them in the work of the Council, for example in the context of the protection of civilians in armed conflict, in relation to peacekeeping operations and in connection with international criminal justice.
>
> The statements made on 24 September demonstrated the abundant wealth of relevant experience and expertise that exists within the United Nations system and in the Member States. Ministers considered that it would be appropriate to examine further how to harness and direct this expertise and experience so that it would be more readily accessible to the Council, to the wider United Nations membership and to the international community as a whole, so that the lessons and experience of the past could be, as appropriate, learned and built on. The Council welcomed in particular the offer by the Secretary-General to provide a report which could guide and inform further consideration of these matters.
>
> The Council invites all Members of the United Nations, and other parts of the United Nations system with relevant experience and expertise, to contribute to this process of reflection and analysis on these matters, beginning with the further meeting on this subject which will be convened on 30 September 2003.

During the Council's continued consideration of the issue on 30 September, the Under-Secretary-General for Peacekeeping Operations said that it was time to fundamentally rethink the way in which the United Nations addressed the rule of law in post-conflict societies. The rule of law should figure more prominently from the early stages of peace negotiations, be recognized as a key element of any post-conflict effort, and be reflected by political actors and donors when drafting peace agreements, adopting and interpreting peacekeeping mandates and funding programmes.

Highlighting some of the steps taken over the preceding year to enhance UN rule-of-law capacities, the Under-Secretary-General pointed to the establishment, in February, of the Criminal Law and Judicial Advisory Unit within DPKO's Civilian Police Division. Rule-of-law focal points in 11 UN departments and agencies were conferring regularly on rule-of-law issues that arose in peacekeeping. The Criminal Law and Judicial Advisory Unit was also considering establishing a rule-of-law trust fund to draw upon the resources and expertise of entities outside the UN system to support rule-of-law aspects of peace operations.

On the subject of post-conflict justice, the Under-Secretary-General said that there was much that the Council could do to facilitate UN efforts. The Organization should conduct case-by-case assessments of all mechanisms available. In addition, there should be broader assistance and support to national justice systems. When domestic justice capacities collapsed, the Organization should mandate interim measures, including international support for the establishment of temporary courts, policing capacities and detention facilities, and the provision of provisional codes for criminal law and procedure.

The Under-Secretary-General concluded that there was no single approach to justice and the rule of law, and any strategy adopted should be tailored to the needs and conditions of the host country and have as its primary objective the promotion of national ownership of justice systems and capacity-building.

Political and peace-building missions in 2003

During 2003, 15 UN political and peace-building missions and offices were in operation: 9 in Africa, 1 in the Americas, 4 in Asia and the Pacific and 1 in the Middle East.

In Africa, the United Nations Mission in Angola completed its mandated political tasks and ended on 15 February. The mandate and size of the United Nations Office in Burundi were revised to include assistance to the Joint Ceasefire Commission. The Security Council extended the mandates of the United Nations Peace-building Office in the Central African Republic and of the United Nations Peace-building Support Office in Guinea-Bissau until 31 December 2004. The activities of the United Nations Political Office for Somalia were continued for the 2004-2005 biennium. The mandate of the Office of the Special Representative of the Secretary-General for the Great Lakes Region was extended until 31 December 2004 and that of the United Nations

Peace-building Support Office in Liberia (UNOL) was expanded to include assistance to the Government in addressing capacity needs in the areas of human rights and the conduct of elections. Following further political developments in Liberia, the Secretary-General closed UNOL in September and transferred its functions to the new peacekeeping operation, the United Nations Mission in Liberia. In May, the Council authorized the establishment of the United Nations Mission in Côte d'Ivoire and, in November, extended its mandate to 4 February 2004.

In the Americas, the Organization continued to support the United Nations Verification Mission in Guatemala, whose mandate was extended until 31 December 2003 by General Assembly resolution 57/161 [YUN 2002, p. 247].

In Asia and the Pacific, the mandate of the United Nations Political Office in Bougainville (UNPOB) (Papua New Guinea) was extended for a final period until 31 December 2003; on 23 December, the Council noted the Secretary-General's intention to establish for six months, as of 1 January 2004, a small United Nations Observer Mission in Bougainville to replace UNPOB. The mandate of the United Nations Assistance Mission in Afghanistan, which was extended for a 12-month period ending 28 March 2004, was to fulfil the tasks and responsibilities, including those related to human rights, the rule of law and gender issues, entrusted to the United Nations in the 2001 Bonn Agreement [YUN 2001, p. 263]. The mandate of the United Nations Tajikistan Office of Peace-building was extended to 1 June 2004. The United Nations Command continued to maintain the implementation of the 1953 Armistice Agreement [YUN 1953, p. 136] concerning the Korean peninsula.

During the year, the Council authorized visiting missions by its members to Afghanistan (31 October–8 November) (see p. 302), Central Africa (7-16 June) (see pp. 127 and 149) and West Africa (26 June–5 July) (see p. 163).

(For the financing of UN peace-building missions, see PART FIVE, Chapter II.)

Roster of 2003 political and peace-building offices

UNOB
United Nations Office in Burundi
Established: 25 October 1993.
Mandate: To assist the parties to the peace process with regard to the building of an internal political partnership within the context of the Arusha peace process; extended in 2001 to help in the consolidation of peace and security.

Head of Mission: Berhanu Dinka (Ethiopia).
Strength: 30 international civilian staff (including 3 military advisers), 32 local civilian staff.

MINUGUA
United Nations Verification Mission in Guatemala
Established: 19 September 1994.
Mandate: To verify implementation of the Comprehensive Agreement on Human Rights.
Chief of Mission: Tom Koenigs (Germany).
Strength: 39 international civilian staff, 133 local civilian staff.

UNPOS
United Nations Political Office for Somalia
Established: 15 April 1995.
Mandate: To monitor the situation in Somalia and keep the Security Council informed, particularly about developments affecting the humanitarian and security situation, repatriation of refugees and impacts on neighbouring countries.
Head of Office: Winston A. Tubman (Liberia).
Strength: 5 international civilian staff, 6 local civilian staff.

UNOL
United Nations Peace-building Support Office in Liberia
Established: 1 November 1997.
Ended: 1 October 2003.
Mandate: To act as focal point for peace-building and support reconciliation efforts and the establishment of democratic institutions; revised by the Security Council on 21 April to include support for the implementation of peace agreements, the holding of elections and development of a peace strategy.

Great Lakes region
Office of the Special Representative of the Secretary-General for the Great Lakes Region
Established: 19 December 1997.
Mandate: To monitor developments in the region and their implications for peace and security and contribute to regional efforts in the prevention or peaceful settlement of conflicts.
Special Representative of the Secretary-General: Ibrahima Fall (Senegal).
Strength: 8 international civilian staff, 8 local civilian staff.

UNPOB
United Nations Political Office in Bougainville (Papua New Guinea)
Established: 15 June 1998.
Ended: 31 December 2003.

Mandate: To assist in the promotion of the political process under the Lincoln Agreement.
Head of Office: Noel Sinclair (Guyana).
Strength: 4 international civilian staff, 1 military adviser, 6 local civilian staff.

UNOGBIS

United Nations Peace-building Support Office in Guinea-Bissau
Established: 3 March 1999.
Mandate: To assist in the transition from conflict management to post-conflict peace-building and reconstruction; extended in November 2003 in order to facilitate restoration and consolidation of institutional normality and create conditions conducive to peace and stability and the holding of elections.
Head of Office: David Stephen (United Kingdom).
Strength: 14 international civilian staff, 2 military advisers, 1 civilian police adviser, 13 local civilian staff.

UNSCO

Office of the United Nations Special Coordinator for the Middle East
Established: 1 October 1999.
Mandate: To act as the focal point for the United Nations contribution to the implementation of the peace agreements and to enhance UN assistance.
Special Coordinator and Special Representative: Terje Roed-Larsen (Norway).
Strength: 22 international civilian staff, 19 local civilian staff.

BONUCA

United Nations Peace-building Office in the Central African Republic
Established: 15 February 2000.
Mandate: To support efforts to consolidate peace and national reconstruction and economic recovery.
Head of Office: General Lamine Cissé (Senegal).
Strength: 24 international civilian staff, 5 military advisers, 6 civilian police, 2 UN Volunteers, 32 local civilian staff.

UNTOP

United Nations Tajikistan Office of Peace-building
Established: 1 June 2000.
Mandate: To provide a political framework and leadership for post-conflict peace-building.
Representative of the Secretary-General: Vladimir Sotirov (Bulgaria).

Strength: 10 international civilian staff, including 1 civilian police adviser, 20 local civilian staff.

UNOWA

United Nations Office for West Africa
Established: March 2002.
Mandate: To ensure the strengthening of harmonization and coordination of UN system activities in an integrated regional perspective and development of a partnership with the Economic Community of West African States, other sub-regional organizations and international and national actors, including civil society.
Special Representative of the Secretary-General: Ahmedou Ould-Abdallah (Mauritania).
Strength: 9 international civilian staff, 11 local civilian staff.

UNAMA

United Nations Assistance Mission in Afghanistan
Established: 28 March 2002.
Mandate: To fulfil the tasks and responsibilities entrusted to the United Nations in the Bonn Agreement; promote national reconciliation and rapprochement; manage all UN humanitarian relief, recovery and reconstruction activities; and assist in the promotion of the political process.
Special Representative of the Secretary-General: Lakhdar Brahimi (Algeria).
Strength: 206 international civilian staff, 702 local civilian staff, 8 military advisers, 3 civilian police.

UNMA

United Nations Mission in Angola
Established: 15 August 2002.
Ended: 15 February 2003.

MINUCI

United Nations Mission in Côte d'Ivoire
Established: 13 May 2003.
Mandate: To facilitate implementation by the Ivorian parties of the Linas-Marcoussis Agreement.
Head of Mission: Albert Tévoedjré (Benin).
Authorized strength: 76 military liaison observers.

UNAMI

United Nations Assistance Mission for Iraq
Established: 14 August 2003.
Mandate: To support the Secretary-General in the fulfilment of his mandate under Security Council resolution 1483(2003).
Head of Mission: Ross Mountain (New Zealand).
Authorized strength: 40 international staff.

Threats to international peace and security

International terrorism

High-level meeting of the Security Council: combating terrorism

On 20 January [meeting 4688], the Security Council held a high-level meeting on combating terrorism.

The Secretary-General stated that the ministerial meeting showed the steady determination of the international community to address the scourge of terrorism and was a sign of the importance the world placed on dealing effectively with that global threat. However, the problem required sustained, long-term action to be addressed successfully. In that regard, the United Nations had to set effective international norms, issue a clear message on the unacceptability of violence targeting civilians and deny terrorists the opportunity to commit their appalling crimes. The Council's Counter-Terrorism Committee (CTC) (see p. 66) would continue to have a key role in that area, as would the common efforts to prevent the proliferation of weapons of mass destruction. Greater efforts were needed to ensure universality, verification and full implementation of the key treaties relating to those weapons, tighten national export controls over the items needed to produce them, criminalize the acquisition or use of such weapons by non-State groups and sustain broad, international cooperation by clearly articulating the work of various international, regional and subregional organizations in that effort. The United Nations also had to provide the legal and organizational framework within which the international campaign against terrorism could unfold.

However, questions were being asked about the damage caused by the war on terrorism to the presumption of innocence, human rights, the rule of law and the very fabric of democratic governance. The danger was that, in pursuit of security, crucial liberties were being sacrificed, thereby weakening common security and corroding democratic government from within. Some States were using the fight against terrorism to threaten or justify new military action on long-running disputes, while others combating various forms of unrest or insurgency were finding it tempting to abandon political negotiation for military action.

The Secretary-General called on the United Nations and its Members not to lose sight of the broader international agenda in their fight against terrorism. While there was an urgent and compelling need to prevent acts of terror, there was a no less compelling need to pursue the goals enshrined in the Charter. To the extent that the Organization succeeded in combating poverty, injustice, suffering and war, it was also likely to help end the conditions that served as justification for those who would commit acts of terror.

The CTC Chairman briefed the Council on the Committee's work in fulfilment of resolution 1373(2001) [YUN 2001, p. 61] (see p. 66).

The Council adopted a declaration aimed at reinforcing the international community's mobilization against terrorism (see below).

SECURITY COUNCIL ACTION

On 20 January [meeting 4688], the Security Council unanimously adopted **resolution 1456(2003)**. The draft [S/2003/60] was prepared in consultations among Council members.

The Security Council

Decides to adopt the attached declaration on the issue of combating terrorism.

Annex

The Security Council,

Meeting at the level of Ministers for Foreign Affairs on 20 January 2003, reaffirms that:

(a) Terrorism in all its forms and manifestations constitutes one of the most serious threats to peace and security;

(b) Any acts of terrorism are criminal and unjustifiable, regardless of their motivation, whenever and by whomsoever committed and are to be unequivocally condemned, especially when they indiscriminately target or injure civilians;

(c) There is a serious and growing danger of terrorist access to and use of nuclear, chemical, biological and other potentially deadly materials, and therefore a need to strengthen controls on these materials;

(d) It has become easier, in an increasingly globalized world, for terrorists to exploit sophisticated technology, communications and resources for their criminal objectives;

(e) Measures to detect and stem the flow of finance and funds for terrorist purposes must be urgently strengthened;

(f) Terrorists must also be prevented from making use of other criminal activities such as transnational organized crime, illicit drugs and drug trafficking, money-laundering and illicit arms trafficking;

(g) Since terrorists and their supporters exploit instability and intolerance to justify their criminal acts, the Council is determined to counter this by contributing to the peaceful resolution of disputes and by working to create a climate of mutual tolerance and respect;

(h) Terrorism can only be defeated, in accordance with the Charter of the United Nations and international law, by a sustained comprehensive approach involving the active participation and collaboration of all

States and international and regional organizations, and by redoubled efforts at the national level.

* * *

The Council therefore calls for the following steps to be taken:

1. All States must take urgent action to prevent and suppress all active and passive support to terrorism, and, in particular, comply fully with all relevant resolutions of the Council, in particular resolutions 1373(2001) of 28 September 2001, 1390(2002) of 16 January 2002 and 1455(2003) of 17 January 2003;

2. The Council calls upon States:

(a) To become parties, as a matter of urgency, to all relevant international conventions and protocols relating to terrorism, in particular the International Convention for the Suppression of the Financing of Terrorism of 9 December 1999, and to support all international initiatives taken with that aim, and to make full use of the sources of assistance and guidance which are now becoming available;

(b) To assist each other, to the maximum extent possible, in the prevention, investigation, prosecution and punishment of acts of terrorism, wherever they occur;

(c) To cooperate closely to implement fully the sanctions against terrorists and their associates, in particular Al-Qa'idah and the Taliban and their associates, as reflected in resolutions 1267(1999) of 15 October 1999, 1390(2002) and 1455(2003), to take urgent actions to deny them access to the financial resources they need to carry out their actions, and to cooperate fully with the Monitoring Group established pursuant to resolution 1363(2001);

3. States must bring to justice those who finance, plan, support or commit terrorist acts or provide safe havens, in accordance with international law, in particular on the basis of the principle to extradite or prosecute;

4. The Counter-Terrorism Committee must intensify its efforts to promote the implementation by Member States of all aspects of resolution 1373(2001), in particular by reviewing reports by States and facilitating international assistance and cooperation, and by continuing to operate in a transparent and effective manner, and in that regard the Council:

(a) Stresses the obligation of States to report to the Committee, according to the timetable set by the Committee, calls upon the 13 States that have not yet submitted a first report and on the 56 States that are late in submitting further reports to do so by 31 March, and requests the Committee to report regularly on progress;

(b) Calls upon States to respond promptly and fully to the requests for information, comments and questions of the Committee in full and on time, and instructs the Committee to inform the Council of progress, including any difficulties it encounters;

(c) Requests the Committee, in monitoring the implementation of resolution 1373(2001), to bear in mind all international best practices, codes and standards which are relevant to the implementation of resolution 1373(2001), and underlines its support for the approach of the Committee in constructing a dialogue with each State on further action required to implement fully resolution 1373(2001);

5. States should assist each other to improve their capacity to prevent and fight terrorism, and notes that such cooperation will help to facilitate the full and timely implementation of resolution 1373(2001), and invites the Counter-Terrorism Committee to step up its efforts to facilitate the provision of technical and other assistance by developing targets and priorities for global action;

6. States must ensure that any measures taken to combat terrorism comply with all their obligations under international law, and should adopt such measures in accordance with international law, in particular international human rights, refugee and humanitarian law;

7. International organizations should evaluate ways in which they can enhance the effectiveness of their action against terrorism, including by establishing dialogue and exchanges of information with each other and with other relevant international actors, and directs this appeal in particular to those technical agencies and organizations whose activities relate to the control of the use of or access to nuclear, chemical, biological and other deadly materials; in this context the importance of fully complying with existing legal obligations in the field of disarmament, arms limitation and non-proliferation and, where necessary, strengthening international instruments in this field should be underlined;

8. Regional and subregional organizations should work with the Counter-Terrorism Committee and other international organizations to facilitate sharing of best practice in the fight against terrorism, and to assist their members in fulfilling their obligation to combat terrorism;

9. Those participating in the special meeting of the Counter-Terrorism Committee with international, regional and subregional organizations on 7 March 2003 should use that opportunity to make urgent progress on the matters referred to in the present declaration which involve the work of such organizations;

* * *

The Council also:

10. Emphasizes that continuing international efforts to enhance dialogue and broaden understanding among civilizations, in an effort to prevent the indiscriminate targeting of different religions and cultures, to strengthen further the campaign against terrorism and to address unresolved regional conflicts and the full range of global issues, including development issues, will contribute to international cooperation and collaboration, which by themselves are necessary to sustain the broadest possible fight against terrorism;

11. Reaffirms its strong determination to intensify its fight against terrorism in accordance with its responsibilities under the Charter, takes note of the contributions made during its meeting on 20 January 2003 with a view to enhancing the role of the United Nations in this regard, and invites Member States to make further contributions to this end;

12. Invites the Secretary-General to submit within 28 days a report summarizing any proposals made during its ministerial meeting and any commentary or response to these proposals by any member of the Council;

International peace and security

13. *Encourages* States Members of the United Nations to cooperate in resolving all outstanding issues with a view to the adoption, by consensus, of the draft comprehensive convention on international terrorism and the draft international convention for the suppression of acts of nuclear terrorism;

14. *Decides* to review actions taken towards the realization of the present declaration at further meetings of the Council.

Follow-up to resolution 1456(2003)

Report of Secretary-General. In a February report [S/2003/191 & Add.1], the Secretary-General, in response to resolution 1456(2003) (see p. 63), submitted a summary of proposals made by Council members during its 20 January ministerial meeting as reflected in the provisional verbatim record [S/PV.4688] and written replies from four Council members (Chile, France, Russian Federation, Syrian Arab Republic). The proposals related to international instruments, international cooperation, the role of the international, regional and subregional organizations, assistance and CTC.

CTC action. In a 14 February letter [S/2003/198], the CTC Chairman submitted to the Security Council President a summary of the action in response to the Council's declaration contained in resolution 1456(2003).

Security Council consideration. The Security Council again discussed the question of threats to international peace and security caused by terrorist acts on 20 February [meeting 4710].

2003 terrorist incidents

Colombia

In an 8 February press statement [SG/SM/8599], the Secretary-General expressed his shock at the terrorist attack on a crowded social club in Bogotá, Colombia, on 7 February, and his sympathy for the victims and their families. He strongly condemned the bombing and all other terrorist attacks by any actor in the conflict.

The Security Council, in **resolution 1465 (2003)** (see p. 285) of 13 February, condemned the bomb attack and urged all States to work with and to support Colombia in finding and bringing the perpetrators, organizers and sponsors to justice.

Iraq

On 19 August, 15 UN staff members and seven others were killed, including the Special Representative of the Secretary-General for Iraq, Sergio Vieira de Mello, and well over 100 were wounded in a bomb attack on UN headquarters in Baghdad, Iraq.

In a 20 August statement (**S/PRST/2003/13**) (see p. 347), the Security Council President condemned the terrorist attack and underlined the need to bring the perpetrators to justice.

The Russian Federation, on 19 August [S/2003/822], and Mali, on 22 August [A/58/315-S/2003/845], on behalf of the members of the Human Security Network (Austria, Canada, Chile, Greece, Ireland, Jordan, Mali, Netherlands, Norway, Slovenia, South Africa, Switzerland, Thailand), condemned the 19 August terrorist attack and expressed their condolences to the families of the victims.

In **resolution 1511(2003)** of 16 October (see p. 348), the Council condemned the terrorist bombings of the Embassy of Jordan in Iraq on 7 August, of the United Nations headquarters in Baghdad on 19 August, of Imam Ali Mosque in Najaf on 29 August and of the Embassy of Turkey in Iraq on 14 October, the murder of a Spanish diplomat on 9 October and the assassination of Dr. Akila al-Hashimi, who died on 25 September, and emphasized that those responsible should be brought to justice.

Turkey

On 15 November, two bombs exploded simultaneously in Istanbul, Turkey, near the Neve Shalom and Beth Israel Synagogues. At least 20 people were reported to have been killed and more than 300 wounded, mostly worshippers attending weekly Sabbath services.

On 20 November, 27 persons died and 450 others were wounded as a result of explosions that took place in Istanbul in front of the HSBC Bank Directorate General and 10 minutes later in front of the United Kingdom Consulate. The Consul General was among those killed.

SECURITY COUNCIL ACTION

On 20 November [meeting 4867], the Security Council unanimously adopted **resolution 1516 (2003)**. The draft [S/2003/1106] was prepared in consultations among Council members.

The Security Council,

Reaffirming the purposes and principles of the Charter of the United Nations and its relevant resolutions, in particular its resolution 1373(2001) of 28 September 2001,

Reaffirming also the need to combat by all means, in accordance with the Charter, threats to international peace and security caused by terrorist acts,

1. *Condemns in the strongest terms* the bomb attacks in Istanbul, Turkey, on 15 and 20 November 2003 in which many lives were claimed and people injured, as well as other terrorist acts in various countries, and regards such acts, like any act of terrorism, as a threat to peace and security;

2. *Expresses its deepest sympathy and condolences* to the people and Governments of Turkey and the United Kingdom of Great Britain and Northern Ireland and to the victims of the terrorist attacks and their families;

3. *Urges* all States, in accordance with their obligations under resolution 1373(2001), to cooperate in efforts to find and bring to justice the perpetrators, organizers and sponsors of these terrorist attacks;

4. *Expresses its reinforced determination* to combat all forms of terrorism, in accordance with its responsibilities under the Charter of the United Nations.

Measures to eliminate international terrorism

During 2003, the United Nations pursued action on several fronts to combat and eliminate international terrorism. The General Assembly adopted **resolution 58/48** (see p. 580) on measures to prevent terrorists from acquiring weapons of mass destruction, **resolution 58/81** on measures to eliminate international terrorism (see p. 1339) and **resolution 58/136** on strengthening international cooperation and technical assistance in promoting the implementation of the universal conventions and protocols related to terrorism within the framework of the activities of the Centre for International Crime Prevention of the UN Office on Drugs and Crime (see p. 1149).

The Security Council met five times to consider the work of its Counter-Terrorism Committee and adopted a number of statements (see below).

Communications. In letters dated 12 May [A/58/78-S/2003/541] and 13 May [A/57/812-S/2003/544], respectively, the Libyan Arab Jamahiriya and Cuba responded to the sections relevant to their countries in a 30 April report published by the Office of the Coordinator for Counterterrorism of the United States Government.

On 10 September [S/2003/893], Georgia noted that United States President George W. Bush had, by an 8 August executive order, declared Shamil Basayev, who had assumed responsibility for various terrorist attacks in the Russian Federation, as dangerous for the United States and its citizens. Georgia joined the Russian Federation, the United Kingdom and the United States in requesting that the United Nations include Mr. Basayev in the list of dangerous terrorists.

On 11 September [S/2003/892], Italy, on behalf of the European Union (EU), in a statement to commemorate the 11 September 2001 terrorist attacks in the United States [YUN 2001, p. 60], said that the EU had adopted a wide and significant set of measures and had participated in the activities of international forums aimed at preventing and suppressing terrorism. It had also promoted political dialogue to raise awareness of the need for appropriate and effective domestic and international legislative measures.

On the same date [A/58/361-S/2003/877], and also in commemoration of the 11 September 2001 attacks in the United States, the Russian Federation said that it had adopted and would continue to adopt a firm and uncompromising position in the fight against terrorism.

Counter-Terrorism Committee

In 2003, the Counter-Terrorism Committee (CTC), established by Security Council resolution 1373(2001) [YUN 2001, p. 61], updated the consolidated directory of contact persons in each State, in a number of international/regional organizations and agencies, and in the UN Secretariat, who would provide information or assistance in connection with matters arising under resolution 1373(2001). The revisions were transmitted by the Committee Chairman to the Council President on 28 March [S/2002/1031/Rev.1], 22 July [S/2003/786] and 21 November [S/2003/1121].

The Chairman also submitted CTC's work programmes for the 90-day periods 1 January to 31 March [S/2003/72], 1 April to 30 June [S/2003/387], 1 July to 30 September [S/2003/710] (see p. 68) and 1 October to 31 December [S/2003/995]. The Council considered those reports at meetings held on 4 April, 6 May, 23 July and 16 October under the agenda item "Threats to international peace and security caused by terrorist acts".

In an 8 January note [S/2003/30], the Council President reported that Council members had agreed to elect Ismael Abraão Gaspar Martins (Angola), Adolfo Aguilar Zinser (Mexico) and Sergey Lavrov (Russian Federation) as Vice-Chairmen of CTC with immediate effect. Inocencio Arias (Spain) was elected as the next CTC Chairman. He would take over that position from Sir Jeremy Greenstock (United Kingdom) following the review of CTC's structure and activities, which would take place no later than 4 April.

Security Council consideration (January). The CTC Chairman, reporting to the Council on the Committee's work on 20 January [meeting 4688], said that, for all the progress made by CTC in monitoring and encouraging implementation of resolution 1373(2001), achieving real improvements in practice on the ground everywhere was taking too long. The over 280 reports received from 178 Member States in 15 months showed that the vast majority of Governments had begun to respond to the challenge to prevent and suppress terrorism; parliaments had begun to consider or to adopt new laws and Governments had reviewed the strength of their institutions to fight terrorism, and in some cases had already strengthened them. However, much more remained to be done to raise the bar against terrorism everywhere.

The Chairman suggested that States should begin to work towards the shared goal to further global implementation of resolution 1373(2001). Thirteen States had not yet submitted a report to CTC, 2 had made no contact with it and 11 were working on reports, 3 with outside assistance set up by CTC. The final date for submission of reports was 31 March, after which any non-reporting State would be held to be non-compliant with resolution 1373(2001). States needed to improve their implementation of that resolution, including by becoming party to the 12 conventions and protocols on terrorism [YUN 2001, p. 69].

CTC had not as yet initiated action on paragraph 4 of resolution 1373(2001) on the potential links between terrorism and other forms of international organized crime. However, the structures that the Committee was helping to put in place for counter-terrorism might have a wider value and effectiveness in strengthening the capacity of Governments against international crime of all kinds. There might be advantages also for the Council's work against the proliferation of weapons of mass destruction.

The Council took action on the report of the CTC Chairman in resolution 1456(2003) (see p. 63).

On 31 March [S/2003/404 & Corr.1], the CTC Chairman, recalling that the Council, in resolution 1456(2003), had requested Member States to submit all outstanding first and subsequent reports by 31 March, stated that 351 reports had been received from 188 Member States and five others by that date. The annex to the Chairman's letter indicated that three States had failed to submit a report by the 31 March deadline and had not availed themselves of the Committee's offer of advice and guidance. A total of 41 States had failed to meet the 31 March deadline for the submission of all outstanding second reports and 32 of them were more than three months late. The Chairman suggested that the issue of States' obligation to report to the Committee be considered soon by the Council.

Security Council consideration (April). Reporting to the Council on 4 April [meeting 4734], the CTC Chairman, referring to the Committee's seventh 90-day work programme [S/2003/387], said that the Council should decide what further action to take with respect to the three States that had still not submitted even a preliminary report and the 51 States that had not met the deadline set by CTC for subsequent reports.

For those States that were furthest ahead in their reporting, CTC was moving from examining legislation to establishing the existence of adequate and effectively functioning executive machinery. As it moved into stages B and C—the existence and utilization of government machinery to prevent terrorist activities and bring terrorists to justice—CTC would need to deepen its understanding of what was required of States, and communicate that to Governments. States had to be proactive in their response, setting their own benchmarks or using their regional organizations to do so.

A meeting hosted by the CTC Chairman on 6 March with representatives of some 60 international, regional and subregional organizations with counter-terrorism programmes was important for establishing a global structure. Participants recognized that every organization had its own role and mandate, but agreed that, by working together, they could shorten the journey and add more value to the fight against terrorism. In practical terms, creating a global network meant a better flow of information. The CTC web site would be expanded to host the best information, in a user-friendly format. CTC would further develop the list of contact points, making contacts as simple as possible. The CTC Chairman encouraged all States and international, regional and subregional organizations to use those contact points and the information about what others were doing to develop collective action.

SECURITY COUNCIL ACTION

On 4 April [meeting 4734], following consultations among Security Council members, the President made statement **S/PRST/2003/3** on behalf of the Council:

The Security Council welcomes the briefing by the Chairman of the Counter-Terrorism Committee on the work of the Committee.

The Council recalls the statement by its President of 8 October 2002 (S/PRST/2002/26), which recorded the intention of the Council to review the structure and activities of the Counter-Terrorism Committee no later than 4 April 2003. The Council thanks Sir Jeremy Greenstock, of the United Kingdom of Great Britain and Northern Ireland, for his chairmanship of the Committee during the first 18 months of its work, and confirms the appointment of Mr. Arias, of Spain, as the new Chairman. The Council also confirms the continuation in office of Mr. Gaspar Martins, of Angola, Mr. Aguilar Zinser, of Mexico, and Mr. Lavrov, of the Russian Federation, as Vice-Chairmen of the Committee.

The Council invites the Counter-Terrorism Committee to pursue its agenda as set out in the work programme for the Committee for the seventh 90-day period.

The Council notes that 3 States have not yet submitted a report to the Counter-Terrorism Committee, and that 51 Member States are late in submitting a further report, in contravention of the requirements set out in resolution 1373(2001) of 28 September 2001. It calls upon them urgently to do so, in order to maintain the universality of response which resolution 1373(2001) requires.

The Council invites the Counter-Terrorism Committee to continue reporting on its activities at regular intervals and expresses its intention to review the structure and activities of the Committee no later than 4 October 2003."

Security Council consideration (May). The Prime Minister of Spain, José María Aznar, whose country took over the chairmanship of CTC in April, told the Security Council on 6 May [meeting 4752] that the strategic challenge posed by terrorism required more ambitious collective responses. The Council should strengthen CTC and enhance the means available to it and its capacity for supervision, facilitating assistance to countries, and coordination with other international and regional organizations. Cooperation with disarmament agencies, especially those responsible for weapons of mass destruction, should be a priority. To increase CTC's operational capability and visibility, the Council should consider empowering it to draw up a general list of terrorist organizations, similar to the list kept by the Committee established by resolution 1267(1999) [YUN 1999, p. 265] on Al-Qaida and the Taliban (see p. 312). It was essential to strengthen mechanisms for curbing the proliferation of weapons of mass destruction and the availability of such weapons to terrorist groups. Existing measures to cut off financing to and dismantle financial networks that provided resources to terrorists should also be improved.

Zero tolerance for terrorism should come first in any code of conduct promulgated by the international community, and counter-terrorism assistance should be regularly incorporated into international, bilateral and multilateral cooperation programmes. The World Bank, the International Monetary Fund (IMF) and the Group of Eight major industrialized nations (G-8) should play a particularly relevant role in that area. The Council should elaborate procedures to prevent terrorist groups from using the UN system as a platform for conveying their violent message to the world, and set up an institutional mechanism within the UN framework as a forum for terrorism victims to speak out. It should also address the social factors that terrorist organizations used as excuses, and foster dialogue among civilizations, religions and cultures.

Security Council consideration (July). On 23 July [meeting 4792], the CTC Chairman presented to the Security Council the Committee's 90-day work programme for the period 1 July to 30 September [S/2003/710]. He described the scope of CTC's activity over the preceding year, noting that, as at 30 June 2003, 37 States were parties to the 12 conventions and protocols related to the fight against terrorism [YUN 2001, p. 69], compared to only two in September 2001, and that 385 reports had been received from Member States. However, in the short term, CTC faced two important challenges. The first related to technical assistance to those States that demonstrated genuine political will to fight terrorism but had difficulties implementing resolution 1373(2001) [ibid., p. 61]. The Directory of Counter-Terrorism Information and Sources of Assistance and the Matrix of Assistance were no longer adequate. CTC needed to adopt a more proactive role and ensure that the needs of those States were met, while promoting and coordinating available international assistance towards those priorities it was currently identifying. The second challenge was to tighten the links between CTC and relevant international, regional and subregional organizations. The plan of action adopted at the 6 March meeting with those organizations (see p. 67) had been implemented and had produced good results. The Chairman drew attention to the contacts between CTC and the Organization for the Prohibition of Chemical Weapons, the World Customs Organization, Interpol and the International Atomic Energy Agency, which highlighted the danger represented by terrorist groups having access to weapons of mass destruction or to radioactive, chemical or biological material. The latter threat had not been given sufficient attention and CTC intended to remain seized of the matter.

Security Council consideration (October). The Security Council President, in a 3 October note [S/2003/935], indicated that, in the light of the Council's decision in statement S/PRST/2003/3 (see p. 67) to review CTC structure and activities by 4 October, Council members had agreed that the review would take place during October. CTC Chairman Inocencio Arias would report to the Council on CTC activities.

On 16 October [meeting 4845], the CTC Chairman informed the Council that CTC's rate of review of reports submitted by States had slowed down somewhat compared to previous periods because of the more complex phase of the work. As States moved from stage A (verifying that adequate anti-terrorist legislation was in place) to stage B (actual implementation of those measures), the Committee had taken more time to review reports and draft letters, and had to find a balance between the amount of attention given to States at both stages. For that purpose,

CTC had prepared a working paper on the criteria for the drafting of letters and the need to give attention to all States in line with the principle of equal treatment, while providing flexibility for proper follow-up of States' efforts to implement resolution 1373(2001). By 30 September, CTC had received a total of 419 reports from Member States and others, including 196 initial reports, 102 second reports and 71 third reports. Although all Member States had submitted initial reports, 48 States were late in responding. The Committee agreed that the Chairman would present to the Council, no later than 31 October, a list of States that had not submitted their reports on time at that date.

CTC's work had included, at one of its meetings, consideration of the issue of States becoming parties to the relevant international conventions and protocols relating to terrorism. Its team of experts had presented a report on the status of State participation and of the positive impact of resolution 1373(2001) and of the work of the Committee itself. CTC continued to apply to its working methods the criteria of coordination, transparency and equality of treatment to each case. It was working to ensure a more active approach for collaborating with those States facing difficulties in implementing resolution 1373 (2001). With regard to transparency, the Committee's web page had been completely redesigned to provide for easier and quicker consultation. The English version was fully operative and the French and Spanish would be ready shortly. The web page would also be available soon in Arabic, Chinese and Russian. CTC had strengthened ties with international, regional and subregional organizations, and those working more directly in the fight against terrorism. On 7 October, a second meeting was held with those organizations in Washington, D.C., at which a great deal of information was exchanged. The next meeting was scheduled for March 2004 in Vienna. The Committee would continue, as its main priorities, to follow closely the flow of information exchanges with States, provide technical assistance and ensure adequate coordination of counter-terrorism efforts by international and regional organizations in combating terrorism.

SECURITY COUNCIL ACTION

On 16 October [meeting 4845], following consultations among Security Council members, the President made statement **S/PRST/2003/17** on behalf of the Council:

> The Security Council welcomes the briefing by the Chairman of the Security Council Committee established pursuant to resolution 1373(2001) concerning counter-terrorism (the Counter-Terrorism Committee) on the work of the Committee.
>
> The Council reaffirms that terrorism in all its forms and manifestations constitutes one of the most serious threats to peace and security and that any acts of terrorism are criminal and unjustifiable, regardless of their motivation, whenever and by whomsoever committed.
>
> The Council recalls the statement by its President of 4 April 2003, which recorded the intention of the Council to review the structure and activities of the Counter-Terrorism Committee no later than 4 October 2003. The Council confirms the continuation of the current arrangements for the Bureau of the Committee for a further six months. It invites the Committee to pursue its agenda as set out in the work programme for the Committee for the ninth 90-day period, focusing on practical measures designed to increase the means available to States to combat terrorism, helping States to identify the problems faced by States in implementing resolution 1373(2001) of 20 September 2001, attempting to find solutions to them, working to increase the number of States which are parties to the international conventions and protocols related to counter-terrorism, and deepening its dialogue with international, regional and subregional organizations active in the areas covered by the resolution. The Council invites these organizations to continue to find ways of improving their collective action against terrorism and, where appropriate, to work with donor States to establish suitable programmes.
>
> The Council notes that 48 Member States are late in submitting their reports as called for in resolution 1373(2001). It calls upon them urgently to do so, in order to maintain the universality of response which resolution 1373(2001) requires. By 31 October 2003 the Chairman of the Counter-Terrorism Committee will forward to the Council the list of the States which, at that date, are late in submitting their reports.
>
> The Council invites the Counter-Terrorism Committee to continue reporting on its activities at regular intervals and expresses its intention to review the structure and activities of the Committee no later than 4 April 2004.

Report of CTC Chairman. On 31 October [S/2003/1056 & Corr.2], the CTC Chairman, in accordance with the Committee's ninth 90-day work programme [S/2003/995] and presidential statement S/PRST/2003/17 (see above), presented to the Security Council the list of the 56 States that had failed to meet the 31 October deadline for the submission of outstanding second and third reports on measures they had adopted to implement resolution 1373(2001).

Reports of States. Between January and December, the CTC Chairman transmitted to the Council President reports submitted by Member States on action they had taken or planned to take to implement resolution 1373(2001) and letters from the Committee requesting follow-up information: [S/2003/15-26, S/2003/127-129, S/2003/145-147,

S/2003/179-180, S/2003/258-266, S/2003/267 & Add.1, S/2003/268-280, S/2003/307-308, S/2003/346, S/2003/353-356, S/2003/361, S/2003/383-386, S/2003/388, S/2003/402-403, S/2003/420, S/2003/424-429, S/2003/433-448, S/2003/451 & Corr.1, S/2003/452-464, S/2003/471, S/2003/473-497, S/2003/513, S/2003/521, S/2003/526, S/2003/531-537, S/2003/552, S/2003/568, S/2003/583-598, S/2003/622-628, S/2003/631-634, S/2003/646-651, S/2003/670-671, S/2003/676, S/2003/700-702, S/2003/710, S/2003/719-725, S/2003/729, S/2003/734-748, S/2003/773-776, S/2003/787-790, S/2003/816, S/2003/833, S/2003/837-842, S/2003/852, S/2003/854, S/2003/856, S/2003/860-862, S/2003/868-871, S/2003/894, S/2003/896-897, S/2003/903-906, S/2003/908-912, S/2003/915, S/2003/953-965, S/2003/964-968, S/2003/978-979, S/2003/997-1012, S/2003/1014-1015, S/2003/1018, S/2003/1036-1044, S/2003/1050, S/2003/1057-1065, S/2003/1084-1086, S/2003/1103-1104, S/2003/1117-1119, S/2003/1122-1133, S/2003/1140, S/2003/1150-1156].

CTC conference and support services

The Secretary-General, in his second performance report on the 2002-2003 programme budget [A/58/558], indicated that total estimated CTC conference-servicing requirements for 2002-2003 would amount to $12,425,900, and related support services requirements would total $587,700. Taking into account the amounts already appropriated for the biennium in General Assembly resolution 57/292 [YUN 2002, p. 1375] ($6,531,900 for conference servicing and $364,200 for support services), an additional appropriation of $5,094,100 was required to cover the balance of the requirements for the biennium.

The appropriation was approved in Assembly **resolution 58/267 A** of 23 December (see p. 1397).

The Secretary-General submitted to the General Assembly in December revised estimates under sections of the proposed 2004-2005 programme budget relating to conference and support services for CTC. Because of the extraordinary nature of CTC activities, requirements for those services were not initially included in the 2004-2005 proposed programme budget (see p. 1399). Following the pattern of requests made in the first and second years of the 2002-2003 biennium [YUN 2002, p. 56], resources amounting to $4,843,750 were being requested for 2004 only.

The Advisory Committee on Administrative and Budgetary Questions (ACABQ), in a 3 December report [A/58/7/Add.17] on the Secretary-General's proposals, recommended that the Assembly authorize him to enter into commitments in the amount of $4,193,000 and that any additional appropriations required be dealt with in the context of the first performance report for the 2004-2005 biennium, which should include detailed information on expenditures for 2004.

The Assembly, in **resolution 58/272** (see p. 1417), appropriated $8,193,000 to support CTC's meeting requirements for the 2004-2005 biennium.

Action by Commission on Crime Prevention and Criminal Justice

The Commission on Crime Prevention and Criminal Justice, at its twelfth session (13-22 May) [E/2003/30], recommended to the Economic and Social Council for approval a draft resolution for adoption by the General Assembly entitled "Strengthening international cooperation and technical assistance in promoting the implementation of the universal conventions and protocols related to terrorism within the framework of the activities of the Centre for International Crime Prevention". That resolution was approved by the Council as **resolution 2003/22** and adopted by the Assembly as **resolution 58/136** (see p. 1149).

IAEA action

The General Conference of the International Atomic Energy Agency (IAEA), at its forty-seventh session (Vienna, 15-19 September) (see p. 1505), adopted resolution GC(47)/RES/8 relating to progress on measures to protect against nuclear and radiological terrorism. It called on member States to continue providing political, financial and technical support to improve nuclear and radiological security and prevent nuclear and radiological terrorism, and to support the Nuclear Security Fund.

Action by other organizations to combat terrorism

On 22 January 2003 [S/2003/85], the Secretary-General transmitted to the Security Council President a 6 December 2002 letter from the Secretary General of the North Atlantic Treaty Organization (NATO), in which he communicated the decisions taken at the Prague Summit of Heads of State and Government (21-22 November 2002) relevant to the fight against terrorism. Those decisions included the creation of a NATO Response Force, approval of the Prague Capabilities Commitment to improve and develop new military capabilities for modern warfare in a high-threat environment, and endorsement of a military concept for defence against terrorism.

On 6 June [A/57/826-S/2003/637], France transmitted to the Secretary-General the statement adopted by the G-8 heads of State and Government at their 2003 Summit (Evian, 29 May-3 June) on securing radioactive sources as part of the fight against the proliferation of weapons of mass destruction. Annexed to the statement was the G-8 Action Plan aimed at preventing acts of radiological terrorism.

On 20 November [A/58/608], Lithuania transmitted to the Secretary-General a summary of the seminar, organized in cooperation with the UN Office on Drugs and Crime (Vilnius, 6-7 November), on the theme "Ratification and implementation of the universal anti-terrorism instruments in the Baltic States".

On 3 December [A/58/619], Tajikistan transmitted to the Secretary-General the text of a 27 November statement by the States of the Collective Security Treaty Organization (Armenia, Belarus, Kazakhstan, Kyrgyzstan, Russian Federation, Tajikistan) on their efforts to build a counter-terrorism capacity.

Peacekeeping operations

In 2003, the United Nations continued to manage its peacekeeping operations through implementation of the recommendations contained in the report of the Panel on United Nations Peace Operations (Brahimi report) [YUN 2000, p. 83] and those of the Special Committee on Peacekeeping Operations, whose mandate was to review the whole question of peacekeeping operations in all their aspects. The Special Committee held a general debate on 3 and 4 March, during which it approved a number of recommendations for submission to the General Assembly. It also considered other general issues related to peacekeeping operations and made recommendations for improving their effectiveness.

General aspects of UN peacekeeping

Nobel Peace Prize Memorial Fund

The Secretary-General, on 21 May [A/57/816], submitted to the General Assembly the report requested by the Assembly President on the disposition of the financial award of approximately $1 million of the 2001 Nobel Peace Prize [YUN 2001, p. 46] to the Secretary-General and the United Nations. He referred to his earlier decision to establish the United Nations Peace Prize Memorial Fund for the receipt and administration of the proceeds of the Nobel Peace Prize and to donate his share of that award to the Fund, which would provide financial assistance for the education of children of United Nations civilian personnel killed in the line of duty in the service of peace. It would function as a special account under the Financial Regulations and Rules of the United Nations, and could also receive and administer further contributions.

The Secretary-General believed that it would be appropriate to use the entire award for those who had made the greatest sacrifice by giving their lives for the cause of peace, and was therefore seeking the Assembly's concurrence regarding the disposition of the United Nations portion of the Prize.

By **decision 57/586** of 29 May, the Assembly decided that the United Nations portion of the 2001 Nobel Peace Prize should be donated to the United Nations Nobel Peace Prize Memorial Fund.

Security Council Working Group on Peacekeeping Operations

By a 7 January note [S/2003/12], the Security Council President reported that Council members had agreed that Cristián Maquieira (Chile) would serve as Chairman of the Security Council Working Group on Peacekeeping Operations until 31 December, replacing Wegger Christian Srommen (Norway).

On 18 December [S/2003/1184], the Council President stated that Council members had agreed that the Working Group would continue its work until 31 December 2004.

Standby arrangements and rapid deployment

The Special Committee on Peacekeeping Operations, at its 2003 session (3-4 March) [A/57/767], reiterated the validity of the goal of enhancing UN capacity to deploy peacekeeping operations within 30 days, or 90 days in the case of a complex operation, after the adoption of a mandate, and its belief that, to meet those time frames, the Secretariat should have the capacity to act in a timely manner on the three interdependent aspects of personnel, materiel readiness and funding.

Regarding personnel, the Special Committee encouraged the Secretariat to focus on improving predeployment training and preparations of UN on-call mechanisms, and better cooperation among field units of troop-contributing countries. It welcomed the progress made towards making operational the on-call lists and rosters and the Rapid Deployment Team, and encouraged further training of relevant personnel. In that regard, it noted the upcoming On-Call List Training Course (Hungary, 13-22 May) and the Command Post Exercise (Argentina, June), and asked the Secretariat to share the outcome of those exercises with Member States. The Committee encouraged DPKO to investigate the possibility of a short-term assignment of some of its military officers with the civilian Rapid Deployment Teams and to assist the core planning team deployed in the field during the first phase of a mission. It welcomed the introduction of the civilian police on-call roster, the model police headquarters and corresponding job descriptions as important steps towards preparing for the rapid deployment of civilian police.

In the area of materiel readiness, the Special Committee supported the continuing development of the strategic deployment stocks at the UN Logistics Base (UNLB) at Brindisi, Italy, and the establishment of management mechanisms, policies and procedures to ensure their effective use. Recognizing that many troop-contributing countries faced logistical support problems, the Committee recommended that the United Nations continue to assist countries to overcome shortfalls in contingent-owned equipment or self-sustainability difficulties. The Secretariat should submit the results of its ongoing consideration of ways to overcome equipment shortfalls faced by troop-contributing countries.

In relation to funding, the Special Committee reiterated its request that the Secretariat report before its next session on the difficulties troop-contributing countries faced in complying with rapid deployment requirements and recommend ways of overcoming those difficulties, including the financial aspects. To that end, the Committee requested the creation of a working group to consider the issue, including ways to assure timely reimbursement in the rapid deployment phase.

Concerning strategic lift, the Special Committee welcomed efforts to clarify capabilities regarding specialized enabling resources and strategic lift capabilities, and recommended that DPKO provide Member States with detailed requirements regarding enabling resources. It supported the contracting of private companies to provide the required capabilities. It encouraged the Secretariat to continue to secure firm pledges for strategic lift, and urged those with the means to do so to make such pledges to the United Nations Standby Arrangements System.

Communication. The Secretary-General, in a 4 March letter to the Security Council President [S/2003/284], sought the Council's approval to discontinue the periodic reporting on the progress of the arrangements for standby units and resources, as requested by the Council in statement S/PRST/1994/22 [YUN 1994, p. 118], and to consolidate the reporting on those arrangements in the annual report to the Special Committee. Troop-contributing countries would continue to receive an annual oral briefing on the subject.

On 7 March [S/2003/285], the Council approved the Secretary-General's proposal.

Strategic deployment stocks

In response to General Assembly resolution 56/292 [YUN 2002, p. 64], the Secretary-General submitted a 12 March report on the status of the implementation of the strategic deployment stocks [A/57/751]. He stated that the DPKO Office of Mission Support had developed a detailed project plan for the phased establishment of those critical stocks at UNLB. The plan, which would enable the deployment of a traditional mission headquarters and of traditional and complex missions, took into account the concurrent development of the human resources capacity and the physical infrastructure necessary to receive, inspect and store strategic deployment stocks assets. A phased requisitioning and delivery plan was also developed, based on the use of systems contracts as the procurement strategy to ensure continuity, uniformity and ease of replenishment. Italy, as part of its voluntary contributions in kind to the United Nations, was constructing three warehouses at UNLB. The Office of Mission Support had undertaken a detailed analysis of the property management needs, including the development of a comprehensive inventory management system. In January, DPKO conducted a pilot exercise in rapid deployment at UNLB.

The current strategic deployment stocks holdings at UNLB exceeded $32.5 million in value, including equipment transferred from DPKO's reserve and surplus stocks from peacekeeping operations. As at 20 February, out of the total budget of $141,546,000 approved by the Assembly in resolution 56/292 to meet the requirements of the strategic deployment stocks, expenditures and pre-encumbrances amounted to $115,783,000, including general temporary assistance. The Secretary-General therefore proposed that the validity period in respect of those approved resources be extended to 30 June 2004. The Secretary-General also reported on efforts to improve the procedures for liquidating closed missions.

In an April report [A/57/772/Add.9], ACABQ stated that it had no objection to the Secretary-General's proposal to extend the validity period of resolution 56/292 and recommended that he consolidate the report on the implementation of the strategic deployment stocks with that on UNLB budget and performance.

GENERAL ASSEMBLY ACTION

On 18 June [meeting 90], the General Assembly, on the recommendation of the Fifth (Administrative and Budgetary) Committee [A/57/656/Add.1], adopted **resolution 57/315** without vote [agenda item 126].

Status of the implementation of the strategic deployment stocks

The General Assembly,

Recalling its resolution 56/292 of 27 June 2002 concerning the establishment of the strategic deployment stocks,

Having considered the report of the Secretary-General on the status of the implementation of the strategic deployment stocks and the related report of the Advisory Committee on Administrative and Budgetary Questions,

1. *Takes note* of the report of the Secretary-General;
2. *Endorses* the conclusions and recommendations contained in the report of the Advisory Committee on Administrative and Budgetary Questions, and requests the Secretary-General to ensure their full implementation, subject to the provisions of the present resolution;
3. *Decides* to extend the validity period in respect of the resources approved in its resolution 56/292 to 30 June 2004;
4. *Recalls* paragraph 2 of its resolution 56/292, and requests the Secretary-General to include the procurement statistics in future reports;
5. *Requests* the Secretary-General to continue to submit to it separate reports on the implementation of the strategic deployment stocks and on the budget and performance of the United Nations Logistics Base at Brindisi, Italy, at its fifty-eighth session.

Consultations with troop contributors

The Special Committee on Peacekeeping Operations [A/57/767] reiterated the need for substantive and meaningful consultations and cooperation between the Security Council, the Secretariat and the troop-contributing countries (TCCs). It believed that the meetings and mechanisms established by Council resolution 1353 (2001) [YUN 2001, p. 80] and the Council President's January 2002 note [YUN 2002, p. 65] had improved the consultation process. It recommended that consultative meetings should be more transparent and that all potentially significant actors should be informed beforehand of those meetings.

The Special Committee welcomed the Secretary-General's commitment that cooperation between the Secretariat and TCCs would remain a high priority for the Secretariat in 2003. It urged the Secretariat to consult with TCCs in a timely manner when planning any change in the tasks, rules of engagement, operational concepts or command and control structure affecting personnel, equipment, training and logistics requirements, or a drawdown of troops in any peacekeeping operation. Member States concerned should be fully consulted and provided with a timely account of UN investigations or inquiries into incidents involving possible responsibility on the part of any of their personnel. They should also be involved in the investigation of cases where the loss of or damage to property or death or personal injury was alleged to have been caused by gross negligence or wilful misconduct of nationally contributed personnel or equipment, and therefore a TCC could be seen as liable for such claims. The outcome of the investigation should be made available to the TCC to enable its national authorities to consider questions of legal liability.

The Special Committee recommended that the Secretariat develop additional modalities for information-sharing with TCCs and other personnel contributors. In that regard, it commended DPKO for conducting the first course for TCCs, New York–based military advisers, civilian police advisers and/or officials responsible for peacekeeping issues at permanent missions, and encouraged DPKO to hold the course annually. DPKO was encouraged to make more use of issue-specific workshops and briefings to pursue a focused cooperation with Member States on questions related to peacekeeping, and to consult with them in developing and updating peacekeeping-related guidelines and policy documents. It should provide access for Member States to a comprehensive and up-to-date list of existing and anticipated peacekeeping-related policy papers, guidelines, manuals, standard operating procedures and training materials and to any peacekeeping-related documents, including through the Internet. It recommended that TCCs and DPKO should improve communication relating to pre-deployment visits.

Safety and security

The Special Committee on Peacekeeping Operations [A/57/767], expressing grave concern about the continuing attacks and other acts of violence against UN and associated personnel, stressed that host countries and others should take steps to ensure their safety and security, including a legal regime with no impunity for the perpetrators of such attacks. The Committee urged those States that had not done so to consider becoming parties to the 1994 Convention on the Safety of United Nations and Associated Personnel, adopted by General Assembly resolution 49/59 [YUN 1994, p. 1289] (see p. 1340). It emphasized that status-of-forces and status-of-mission agreements should include specific measures to enhance personnel safety and security, based on the Convention.

The Special Committee stressed the need to expedite consultations to delineate clear lines of responsibility and ensure close coordination between the Office of the United Nations Security Coordinator and DPKO, and requested that the outcome of those consultations be conveyed to Member States. It noted the need to further improve information collection, analysis and dissemination at Headquarters and in the field, and recommended that DPKO's strengthened capacity, especially that of the Situation Centre, be utilized for that purpose.

As the majority of recent incidents involving the death or injury of UN peacekeeping personnel resulted from accidents, the Special Committee welcomed the establishment of a safety council to promote safety awareness, and encouraged Member States to share with the Secretariat relevant information on national safety programmes. The Secretariat should report on its work to formalize a policy on protection from nuclear, biological and chemical threats in the field. The Special Committee noted the progress achieved by DPKO in ensuring the safety of air operations in peacekeeping operations, in particular through the implementation of international aviation standards, rigorous contractual procedures and continuous monitoring of the Department's aviation operations.

The Secretariat should ensure that expeditious, comprehensive, impartial and transparent investigations or inquiries were conducted into incidents leading to loss of life or serious injury among UN peacekeeping personnel and provide TCCs with the results at the earliest stage possible. Early implementation of standard operating procedures to avoid repetition of such accidents should be encouraged, and TCCs of the concerned mission should be provided with information on the actual measures implemented.

Women and peacekeeping

Report of Secretary-General. In response to General Assembly resolution 56/293 [YUN 2002, p. 77], the Secretary-General submitted a February report on gender mainstreaming in peacekeeping activities [A/57/731]. The Assembly had requested the Secretary-General to develop a coherent policy on gender mainstreaming in all of the Organization's peacekeeping activities; the request was related to his proposal for additional resources under the Support Account for the establishment of a senior gender adviser post within DPKO.

The Secretary-General said that peacekeeping missions should identify and address gender-specific problems, such as sexual and gender-based violence against women and girls and prostitution (often combined with trafficking). DPKO's plan of action for gender mainstreaming would build gender perspectives into the work of the different components of peacekeeping operations and determine the most effective means of addressing gender perspectives in the day-to-day work of DPKO both at Headquarters and in the field. Attention to gender perspectives had to be included in all initial assessments and mission statements and plans, so that the needs and priorities of women and men were addressed in the policy frameworks, strategies and programming processes. The development of policies and procedures, codes of conduct, manuals and guidelines had to give adequate consideration to gender perspectives.

In conclusion, the Secretary-General said that work carried out so far on gender mainstreaming in peacekeeping had been financed through voluntary contributions. To ensure that it was systematically and effectively addressed, both at Headquarters and in the field, a full-time, dedicated gender advisory capacity was necessary at Headquarters in the form of a senior gender adviser located in the DPKO Peacekeeping Best Practices Unit, where mainstreaming would be part of the decision-making processes of all peacekeeping activities.

Special Committee consideration. The Special Committee on Peacekeeping Operations [A/57/767], while commending Secretariat efforts to mainstream a gender perspective in DPKO activities, pursuant to Security Council resolution 1325(2000) [YUN 2000, p. 1113] and General Assembly resolution 55/71 [ibid., p. 1107], encouraged the Secretariat to pursue that policy further, including implementation of the recommendations contained in the Secretary-General's 2002 report on women, peace and security [YUN 2002, p. 67].

The Special Committee noted that further action was required to systematically integrate a gender perspective in the mandates of peacekeeping operations and in adequately addressing the specific needs of women in conflict situations. It reiterated its support for the creation of a focal point within DPKO's Peacekeeping Best Practices Unit to support the work of gender offices in field missions and help to mainstream gender issues in all aspects of the Department's work. The Special Committee encouraged Member States to provide the names of qualified candidates, especially women candidates, to serve in high-level positions in peacekeeping activities.

Security Council consideration. On 29 October [meeting 4852], the Security Council considered the issue of women and peace and security. Briefing the Council, the Under-Secretary-General for Peacekeeping Operations, Jean-Marie Guéhenno, described steps taken by DPKO to implement Council resolution 1325(2000), especially in the context of multidimensional peacekeeping operations. DPKO's efforts were focused on five main areas highlighted in the resolution: increasing the number of women in peacekeeping operations; integrating a gender perspective into peacekeeping operations; training in gender awareness and HIV/AIDS issues (see below); strengthening discipline for peacekeeping personnel; and combating trafficking in human beings.

On the issue of gender balance among peacekeeping personnel, DPKO had started, on a pilot basis, to encourage more women applicants by targeting professional women's associations with vacancy announcements. Although women represented one third of Professional staff in the current 15 peacekeeping missions, DPKO intended to be more effective in identifying suitable women candidates for senior positions and in recruiting Professional-level women for missions.

As to gender mainstreaming, a number of practical field manuals were being produced to help demystify the issue, and a gender resource package, a field manual on gender issues for military commanders and one on gender issues in mine action were being developed. The temporary Gender Adviser, based at DPKO headquarters, had already begun to assist in more effectively coordinating efforts on gender issues, in facilitating cross-regional learning, and in identifying some of the main gaps and a comprehensive strategy to move forward. A network of gender focal points would also be established to assist in mainstreaming efforts. The Under-Secretary-General said that he intended to ensure that all future, multidimensional peacekeeping operations included strong gender expertise, in the form of a gender affairs unit that had access to senior-level decision-making in all areas of the mission's work.

As to disciplinary issues, DPKO, following a thorough review of existing policies and procedures, provided all missions in July with an updated set of disciplinary directives covering sexual abuse and exploitation and other types of serious misconduct. Each mission had an active strategy to prevent and respond to those problems and would appoint a senior focal point to receive complaints of misconduct by peacekeeping personnel.

On the issue of trafficking women, DPKO was undertaking a lessons-learned study on anti-trafficking programmes in Bosnia and Herzegovina and the Kosovo province of Yugoslavia, which would help to identify best practices and some lessons learned in tackling the problem.

The Senior Gender Adviser of the United Nations Organization Mission in the Democratic Republic of the Congo also briefed the Council.

Peacekeeping and HIV/AIDS

During the Security Council's consideration on 17 November of HIV/AIDS and international peacekeeping [meeting 4859], at which it was briefed by the Under-Secretary-General for Peacekeeping Operations and the Executive Director of the Joint United Nations Programme on HIV/AIDS (UNAIDS) (see p. 1247), Dr. Peter Piot, the Under-Secretary-General said that, since his last report on the subject [YUN 2001, p. 77], the number of people infected had grown to approximately 42 million. DPKO and UNAIDS were working together on HIV/AIDS and peacekeeping to reduce the risk of peacekeepers contracting or transmitting HIV while on mission. DPKO currently had HIV/AIDS policy advisers, supported by United Nations Volunteers, in four major peacekeeping operations and intended to deploy them in all major peacekeeping missions. HIV/AIDS focal points were established in six missions and others were being identified in the remaining operations. A primary element of DPKO's training strategy was to update and improve training materials. The three publications "Protect yourself, and those you care about, against HIV/AIDS", "HIV prevention and behaviour change in international military populations" and "Policy guidelines on HIV/AIDS prevention and control for United Nations military planners and commanders" were being reviewed and simplified to make them accessible to the broadest possible audience. DPKO had also developed a pre-deployment training module on HIV/AIDS and, with UNAIDS, was distributing HIV/AIDS awareness cards to peacekeepers covering the basic facts about the disease and codes of conduct. Currently available in 10 languages, the goal was for the cards to become a standard feature of a peacekeeper's uniform. Mission training cells for military personnel in eight peacekeeping operations were working closely with the HIV/AIDS policy advisers and focal points to ensure that HIV awareness was included in induction programmes. Similar induction training was conducted for civilian police personnel.

DPKO efforts did not stop at HIV/AIDS awareness and training. To counter behaviour that increased the risk of contracting or transmitting HIV, the Department took a zero tolerance stance regarding sexual abuse and exploitation by peacekeeping personnel. Updated disciplinary directives had been sent to missions, and reporting and investigation mechanisms were being strengthened. DPKO was introducing voluntary confidential counselling and testing capabilities into missions. It had also concluded a memorandum of understanding with the United Nations Population Fund for the provision of reproductive health items to both staff and uniformed personnel in all missions. To measure the impact of its efforts, DPKO was carrying out more systematic mission assessments and was working with UNAIDS to set up monitoring and evaluation systems.

The UNAIDS Executive Director said that UNAIDS had addressed AIDS and security in three ways: it had taken action in conjunction with DPKO in implementing aspects of Council resolution 1308(2000) [YUN 2000, p. 82] relating to peacekeeping forces; it was spearheading a wider response to AIDS among uniformed services; and it was expanding the response to AIDS as a preeminent humanitarian and security challenge. UNAIDS had established an expert panel on HIV testing in UN peacekeeping operations, whose report had informed the formulation of DPKO policy, and was establishing a comprehensive information base for targeting and evaluating HIV activities among peacekeepers.

Despite the progress, major challenges remained, such as a lack of reliable data on the spread of HIV among peacekeepers, the need to back up AIDS responses among peacekeepers by concerted leadership and the challenge of sustainability as peacekeepers were rotated through their missions in relatively short time frames, making it imperative that mission responses were reinforced in the ongoing programmes for uniformed services. UNAIDS was currently working with armed forces to ensure that HIV awareness and prevention took place prior to deployment and was reinforced at demobilization.

The United Kingdom proposed that the Council, on the basis of a progress report by the Secretary-General, hold a further discussion on HIV/AIDS in 2004 to consider strengthening the Council's response to resolution 1308(2000); draw on the experience of UNAIDS, DPKO, civil society groups and others to establish clearly the links between peace, security and HIV/AIDS, with suggestions for action; and ask the Secretary-General to conduct an assessment of both aspects for consideration by the Council in 2005.

The United States told the meeting that, as part of the international partnership against HIV/AIDS in Africa, its Department of Defense had been working with African armed forces to help create policies to deal with HIV/AIDS in a military setting by developing education programmes to reduce the spread of the disease among their personnel. The United States also underwrote the preparation and printing of a UN training booklet on HIV/AIDS awareness and prevention to be used by peacekeeping forces.

Peacekeeping and the international legal system

On 12 June [meeting 4772], at the request of Canada, Jordan, Liechtenstein, New Zealand and Switzerland [S/2003/620], and of Greece, on behalf of the EU [S/2003/639], the Security Council held a public meeting to consider a draft resolution (see p. 77), which sought to renew the request contained in Council resolution 1422(2002) [YUN 2002, p. 70]. By the draft, the Council would again request the International Criminal Court (ICC), consistent with article 16 of the Rome Statute establishing the Court [YUN 1998, p. 1209], to delay for a 12-month period, starting 1 July 2003, investigation or prosecution of any case involving current or former officials from a State not party to the Rome Statute and would express the intention to renew that request each 1 July for as long as might be necessary.

Addressing the Council, the Secretary-General said that article 16 of the Statute was not intended to cover such a sweeping request, but only a specific one relating to a particular situation. He did not believe that request was necessary since it dealt with a hypothetical and highly improbable case. Additionally, people serving in UN peacekeeping missions remained under the jurisdiction of their home States, and any of them accused of committing a crime during a mission were immediately repatriated and dealt with by their country's national courts. Also, no case was admissible in ICC if it had already been or was being investigated or prosecuted by a State that had jurisdiction over it, unless that State was unwilling or unable genuinely to investigate or prosecute. He assumed that the home State of a peacekeeper accused of the kind of crime that fell under ICC jurisdiction would be most anxious to investigate that accusation and prosecute that person, if there was a prima facie case. The case would then not be admissible in ICC.

The adoption of resolution 1422(2002) had given Member States more time to study the Rome Statute and to digest its implications. While the Council might feel it necessary to renew the request for a further 12 months, since the Court was still in its infancy, the Secretary-General hoped that that did not become an annual routine, since it would be interpreted by the world as meaning that the Council wished to claim absolute and permanent immunity for people serving in the operations it established or authorized, undermining not only ICC's authority but also that of the Council and the legitimacy of UN peacekeeping.

Canada appealed to the Council to ensure that the extraordinary situation created by the draft resolution [S/2003/630] did not become permanent. The Rome Statute's array of safeguards and checks and balances screened out any frivolous claims that might be submitted. ICC's principal purpose was to try the perpetrators of heinous crimes, which was the centrepiece in the effort to end impunity for genocide and other mass crimes. Its deterrent character was crucial in sparing future potential victims. ICC's jurisdictional reach was not limitless and its approach was entirely founded in established law. Canada said that it was also concerned about the legitimacy of the action recommended to the Council, which it urged not to renew resolution 1422(2002) indefinitely.

Greece said the EU reiterated its belief that the concerns expressed by the United States about politically motivated prosecutions were unfounded, since those concerns had been met and sufficient safeguards against such prosecutions had been built into the Statute.

New Zealand stated that it saw no need for immunity in principle. There should be no double standard for personnel engaged in UN missions. To put such personnel above the law placed their moral authority and the institution of UN peacekeeping in serious jeopardy. Moreover, the use of the procedure laid down in article 16 of the Rome Statute in a generic resolution, not in response to a particular fact situation and with the intention to renew it on an annual basis, was inconsistent with the terms and purpose of that provision. It also stretched the legitimate limits of the role and responsibility entrusted to the Council under the Charter.

Pakistan, speaking in support of the draft, said that it was unfortunate that the Rome Statute did not provide for reservations by countries, since that might have ensured wider adherence to it. As the largest contributor to UN peacekeeping operations, Pakistan believed that UN peacekeepers should not be exposed to any arbitrary or unilateral action by any national or international body, since that could reduce the incentive for Member States to offer UN peacekeeping forces.

SECURITY COUNCIL ACTION

On 12 June [meeting 4772], the Security Council adopted **resolution 1487(2003)** by vote (12-0-3). The draft [S/2003/630] was prepared in consultations among Council members.

The Security Council,

Noting the entry into force on 1 July 2002 of the Rome Statute of the International Criminal Court, done at Rome on 17 July 1998 (the Rome Statute),

Emphasizing the importance to international peace and security of United Nations operations,

Noting that not all States are parties to the Rome Statute,

Noting also that States parties to the Rome Statute have chosen to accept its jurisdiction in accordance with the Statute, in particular the principle of complementarity,

Noting further that States not party to the Rome Statute will continue to fulfil their responsibilities in their national jurisdictions in relation to international crimes,

Determining that operations established or authorized by the Security Council are deployed to maintain or restore international peace and security,

Determining also that it is in the interest of international peace and security to facilitate the ability of Member States to contribute to operations established or authorized by the Council,

Acting under Chapter VII of the Charter of the United Nations,

1. *Requests*, consistent with the provisions of article 16 of the Rome Statute, that the International Criminal Court, if a case arises involving current or former officials or personnel from a contributing State not a party to the Rome Statute over acts or omissions relating to a United Nations established or authorized operation, shall for a twelve-month period starting 1 July 2003 not commence or proceed with investigation or prosecution of any such case, unless the Security Council decides otherwise;

2. *Expresses the intention* to renew the request set out in paragraph 1 above under the same conditions each 1 July for further twelve-month periods for as long as may be necessary;

3. *Decides* that Member States shall take no action inconsistent with paragraph 1 above and with their international obligations;

4. *Decides* to remain seized of the matter.

VOTE ON RESOLUTION 1487(2003):

In favour: Angola, Bulgaria, Cameroon, Chile, China, Guinea, Mexico, Pakistan, Russian Federation, Spain, United Kingdom, United States.
Against: None.
Abstaining: France, Germany, Syrian Arab Republic.

In a statement after the vote, the United States said that it recognized the difficulty of recruiting troop contributors to UN peacekeeping operations and it was important that Member States not add concern about ICC jurisdiction to that difficulty. It did not agree that the resolution was unnecessary, since even one instance of ICC attempting to exercise jurisdiction over those involved in UN peacekeeping operations would have a seriously damaging impact on future UN operations. ICC was not a UN institution and was vulnerable at every stage of any proceeding to politicization. The Rome Statute provided no adequate check and having confidence in ICC's correct behaviour was not a sufficient safeguard.

France, explaining its abstention, said that the Court's professionalism would be judged on the facts. The recognized quality and competence of its members ensured without doubt the credibility of that international body, which provided the best safeguard against any possible suspicion of a politically motivated Court. The renewal of resolution 1422(2002) risked lending credence to the perception that such exemptions were permanent, which could only weaken the Court and harm its authority.

Germany stated that it did not share the view that ICC was an impediment to peacekeeping. On the contrary, it was a safeguard and, as an institution designed to prevent impunity, it could play an important role in protecting peacekeepers in the execution of their missions.

The Syrian Arab Republic said it did not see any justification for renewing resolution 1422 (2002). The Court was a reality and had become almost universal, since 90 States were party to the Rome Statute and 140 had signed it. Hence, the adoption of resolution 1487(2003) would result in the gradual weakening of the Court's role in persecuting those who had perpetrated the most heinous crimes that came under its jurisdiction.

Comprehensive review of peacekeeping

Special Committee on Peacekeeping Operations

As requested by the General Assembly in resolution 56/225 B [YUN 2002, p. 71], the Special Committee on Peacekeeping Operations continued its comprehensive review of the question of peacekeeping operations in all their aspects [A/57/767]. In response to the Committee's request, the Secretary-General submitted a January report on the implementation of its recommendations [A/57/711].

The Special Committee held an organizational meeting on 3 March and a general debate on 3 and 4 March. It considered guiding principles, definitions and implementation of mandates; cooperation with troop-contributing countries; and enhancing UN peacekeeping capacity, including lessons learned and implementation of best practices, rapid deployment, recruitment and training, gender and peacekeeping, the safety and security of UN and associated personnel, and cooperation with regional arrangements.

The Special Committee welcomed the six issues recommended by the Secretary-General in his January report for particular attention by the Secretariat and Member States in 2003: integrating lessons learned and best practices into operational planning and coordination; developing and implementing comprehensive strategies for challenges faced by complex peacekeeping operations; enhancing rapid deployment capability; strengthening training; minimizing disciplinary problems; and strengthening regional peacekeeping capacities, particularly in Africa. It encouraged the Secretariat to continue collaborating with it in those areas and to communicate with Member States on critical areas and key topics related to the operation and management of peacekeeping operations. The Special Committee requested a briefing by the UN Office of Internal Oversight Services (OIOS) on its evaluation of DPKO's restructuring and an independent review by the Secretariat of the reform process initiated by the report of the Panel on United Nations Peace Operations [YUN 2000, p. 83] for Assembly consideration in 2004.

The Special Committee supported the Secretary-General in ensuring that the Peacekeeping Best Practices Unit played a more prominent role in DPKO's work and encouraged the Department and relevant parts of the UN system to strengthen their dialogue with the Unit. To strengthen best practices, the Special Committee encouraged the Unit to discuss themes of common interest with Member States that had participated in UN peacekeeping missions, develop validation mechanisms for lessons learned and best practices, and make recommendations for applying best practices and implementing lessons learned in the planning and conduct of ongoing and future missions. It endorsed the proposal to develop a field-level lessons-learned network and supported the incorporation of lessons learned in the conduct of all mission tasks.

The Secretariat should further suggest ways to address the Organization's informational and analytical requirements, mainly with respect to peacekeeping operations. The Secretary-General should inform Member States, in his next report to the Committee, on progress made in strengthening relationships between the Secretariat, other UN agencies and the Bretton Woods institutions (the World Bank Group and IMF).

The Special Committee supported the integration of civilian police expertise and other rule-of-law elements in the planning for new missions, and encouraged an increased focus on UN policing issues in peacekeeping operations. Stressing that civilian police and corrections personnel might be required to use enforcement measures, it requested the Secretariat to consider assigning such personnel privileges and immunities equivalent to those of armed military personnel and to report on that issue before the Committee's 2004 session. The Secretariat should also review its policy regarding the recruitment of retired police officers for peacekeeping operations and raising the age-limit for civilian police service.

The Special Committee acknowledged the need for additional research and analysis on the interrelated areas of disarmament, demobilization and reintegration, security sector reform and the strengthening of the rule of law in post-conflict environments, in order to draw lessons for the planning and conduct of current and future peacekeeping operations, and for conceptual clarity and an appraisal of the expertise and capacities within and outside the UN system to ensure operational coherence. It stressed the importance of early planning and coordination of disarmament, demobilization and reintegration components in peacekeeping operations and the provision of resources to accomplish the mandated tasks.

The Special Committee urged the strengthening of cooperation between the United Nations and relevant regional arrangements and agencies to enhance the capabilities of the international community in the maintenance of international peace and security, and encouraged the Secretary-General to take concrete steps towards that end.

GENERAL ASSEMBLY ACTION

On 18 June [meeting 90], the General Assembly, on the recommendation of the Fourth (Special Political and Decolonization) Committee [A/57/522/Add.1], adopted **resolution 57/336** without vote [agenda item 78].

Comprehensive review of the whole question of peacekeeping operations in all their aspects

The General Assembly,

Recalling its resolution 2006(XIX) of 18 February 1965 and all other relevant resolutions,

Recalling in particular its resolutions 56/225 B of 22 May 2002 and 57/129 of 11 December 2002,

Affirming that the efforts of the United Nations in the peaceful settlement of disputes, inter alia, through its peacekeeping operations, are indispensable,

Convinced of the need for the United Nations to continue to improve its capabilities in the field of peacekeeping and to enhance the effective and efficient deployment of its peacekeeping operations,

Considering the contribution that all States Members of the United Nations make to peacekeeping,

Noting the widespread interest in contributing to the work of the Special Committee on Peacekeeping Operations expressed by many Member States, in particular troop-contributing countries,

Bearing in mind the continuous necessity of preserving the efficiency and strengthening the effectiveness of the work of the Special Committee,

1. *Welcomes* the report of the Special Committee on Peacekeeping Operations;
2. *Endorses* the proposals, recommendations and conclusions of the Special Committee, contained in paragraphs 39 to 206 of its report;
3. *Urges* Member States, the Secretariat and relevant organs of the United Nations to take all necessary steps to implement the proposals, recommendations and conclusions of the Special Committee;
4. *Reiterates* that those Member States that become personnel contributors to United Nations peacekeeping operations in years to come or participate in the future in the Special Committee for three consecutive years as observers shall, upon request in writing to the Chairman of the Special Committee, become members at the following session of the Special Committee;
5. *Decides* that the Special Committee, in accordance with its mandate, shall continue its efforts for a comprehensive review of the whole question of peacekeeping operations in all their aspects and shall review the implementation of its previous proposals and consider any new proposals so as to enhance the capacity of the United Nations to fulfil its responsibilities in this field;
6. *Requests* the Special Committee to submit a report on its work to the General Assembly at its fifty-eighth session;
7. *Decides* to include in the provisional agenda of its fifty-eighth session the item entitled "Comprehensive review of the whole question of peacekeeping operations in all their aspects".

By **decision 58/524** of 9 December, the Assembly took note of the report of the Fourth Committee on its consideration of the agenda item "Comprehensive review of the whole question of peacekeeping operations in all their aspects" [A/58/474]. On 23 December, the Assembly decided that that agenda item would remain for consideration during its resumed fifty-eighth (2004) session (**decision 58/565**).

Operations in 2003

On 1 January, 13 UN peacekeeping operations were in place—4 in Africa, 3 in Asia, 3 in Europe and 3 in the Middle East. During the year, 1 mission ended and 1 was launched. The total number in place at the end of the year remained at 13.

Africa

In Africa, the mandate of the United Nations Mission in Sierra Leone (UNAMSIL) was twice extended by the Security Council for six months, the second time from 30 September 2003 to 31 March 2004. In July, the Council approved the Secretary-General's recommendation to draw down the Mission's forces towards a final withdrawal by December 2004. Also in July, the Council extended the mandate of the United Nations Organization Mission in the Democratic Republic of the Congo (MONUC) until 30 July 2004. In May, it had authorized deployment until 1 September 2003 of an Interim Emergency Multinational Force in Bunia, in cooperation with MONUC, and requested the Secretary-General to deploy a reinforced UN presence in Bunia by mid-August. The mandate of the United Nations Mission for the Referendum in Western Sahara

(MINURSO) was extended until 31 January 2004. The Council also extended the mandate of the United Nations Mission in Ethiopia and Eritrea (UNMEE) until 15 March 2004. In September, the Council established the United Nations Mission in Liberia (UNMIL) to, among other things, support implementation of the ceasefire agreement (see p. 188).

In other action, the Council, in August, renewed for six months the authorization given to Member States participating in the forces of the Economic Community of West African States together with the French forces supporting them in Côte d'Ivoire (**resolution 1498(2003)**) (see p. 177).

Asia

In Asia, in the wake of the action of the coalition led by the United States and the United Kingdom in Iraq (see p. 333), the Council, in July, decided that the final mandate of the United Nations Iraq-Kuwait Observation Mission (UNIKOM) would end on 6 October; the demilitarized zone between the two countries would also end on that date. The United Nations Military Observer Group in India and Pakistan (UNMOGIP), established in 1949, remained in place to monitor the ceasefire in Jammu and Kashmir. The Council extended the mandate of the United Nations Mission of Support in East Timor (UNMISET) until 20 May 2004.

In other action, the Council, in October, extended the authorization of the International Security Assistance Force in Afghanistan for a further period of 12 months and expanded its mandate to include support for the Afghan Transitional Authority and its successors in maintaining security in areas outside Kabul and its environs (**resolution 1510(2003)**) (see p. 310). Also in October, it authorized a multinational force under unified command to contribute to the maintenance of security and stability in Iraq (**resolution 1511 (2003)**) (see p. 348).

Europe

In Europe, the Security Council extended the mandate of the United Nations Observer Mission in Georgia (UNOMIG) until 31 January 2004 and endorsed the Secretary-General's recommendation that a civilian police component be added to strengthen its capacity to carry out its mandate. The Council also extended the mandate of the United Nations Peacekeeping Force in Cyprus (UNFICYP) until 15 June 2004. The United Nations Interim Administration Mission in Kosovo (UNMIK), Serbia and Montenegro (formerly the Federal Republic of Yugoslavia), remained in place.

Middle East

Three long-standing operations continued in the Middle East: the United Nations Truce Supervision Organization (UNTSO), which continued to observe the truce in Palestine; the United Nations Interim Force in Lebanon (UNIFIL), whose mandate was extended until 31 January 2004; and the United Nations Disengagement Observer Force (UNDOF), whose mandate was renewed until 30 June 2004.

Roster of 2003 operations

UNTSO
United Nations Truce Supervision Organization
Established: June 1948.
Mandate: To assist in supervising the observance of the truce in Palestine.
Strength as at December 2003: 154 military observers.

UNMOGIP
United Nations Military Observer Group in India and Pakistan
Established: January 1949.
Mandate: To supervise the ceasefire between India and Pakistan in Jammu and Kashmir.
Strength as at December 2003: 44 military observers.

UNFICYP
United Nations Peacekeeping Force in Cyprus
Established: March 1964.
Mandate: To prevent the recurrence of fighting between the two Cypriot communities.
Strength as at December 2003: 1,214 troops, 47 civilian police.

UNDOF
United Nations Disengagement Observer Force
Established: June 1974.
Mandate: To supervise the ceasefire between Israel and the Syrian Arab Republic and the disengagement of Israeli and Syrian forces in the Golan Heights.
Strength as at December 2003: 1,032 troops.

UNIFIL
United Nations Interim Force in Lebanon
Established: March 1978.
Mandate: To restore peace and security and assist the Lebanese Government in ensuring the return of its effective authority in the area.
Strength as at December 2003: 1,991 troops.

UNIKOM
United Nations Iraq-Kuwait Observation Mission
Established: April 1991.
Ended: 6 October 2003.
Mandate: To monitor the demilitarized zone along the border between Iraq and Kuwait.

MINURSO
United Nations Mission for the Referendum in Western Sahara
Established: April 1991.
Mandate: To monitor and verify the implementation of a settlement plan for Western Sahara and assist in the holding of a referendum in the Territory.
Strength as at December 2003: 27 troops, 200 military observers.

UNOMIG
United Nations Observer Mission in Georgia
Established: August 1993.
Mandate: To verify compliance with a ceasefire agreement between the parties to the conflict in Georgia and investigate ceasefire violations; expanded in 1994 to include monitoring the implementation of an agreement on a ceasefire and separation of forces and observing the operation of a multinational peacekeeping force.
Strength as at December 2003: 118 military observers, 10 civilian police.

UNMIK
United Nations Interim Administration Mission in Kosovo
Established: June 1999.
Mandate: To promote, among other things, the establishment of substantial autonomy and self-government in Kosovo, perform basic civilian administrative functions, organize and oversee the development of provisional institutions, facilitate a political process to determine Kosovo's future status, support reconstruction of key infrastructure, maintain civil law and order, protect human rights and assure the return of refugees and displaced persons.
Strength as at December 2003: 3,691 civilian police, 40 military observers.

UNAMSIL
United Nations Mission in Sierra Leone
Established: October 1999.
Mandate: To cooperate with the Government of Sierra Leone and other parties in the implementation of the Peace Agreement signed in Lomé, Togo, on 7 July 1999, including, among other things, to assist in the implementation of the disarmament, demobilization and reintegration plan, monitor adherence to the ceasefire agreement of 18 May 1999 and facilitate the delivery of humanitarian assistance.
Strength as at December 2003: 11,232 troops, 269 military observers, 130 civilian police.

MONUC
United Nations Organization Mission in the Democratic Republic of the Congo
Established: November 1999.
Mandate: To establish contacts with the signatories to the Ceasefire Agreement, provide technical assistance in implementation of the Agreement, provide information on security conditions, plan for the observation of the ceasefire, facilitate the delivery of humanitarian assistance and assist in the protection of human rights.
Strength as at December 2003: 9,981 troops, 553 military observers, 115 civilian police.

UNMEE
United Nations Mission in Ethiopia and Eritrea
Established: July 2000.
Mandate: To establish and put into operation the mechanism for verifying the cessation of hostilities and to assist the Military Coordination Commission in tasks related to demining and in administrative support to its field offices.
Strength as at December 2003: 3,795 troops, 209 military observers.

UNMISET
United Nations Mission of Support in East Timor
Established: May 2002.
Mandate: To provide assistance to the core administrative structures and interim law enforcement and public security of East Timor (renamed Timor-Leste), including assisting in the development of the East Timor Police Service, and contribute to the maintenance of East Timor's external and internal security.
Strength as at December 2003: 1,675 troops, 319 civilian police, 79 military observers.

UNMIL
United Nations Mission in Liberia
Established: 19 September 2003.
Mandate: To support the implementation of the ceasefire agreement and the peace process; protect UN staff and facilities and civilians; support humanitarian and human rights activities; and assist in national security reform, including national police training and formation of a new, restructured military.

Strength as at December 2003: 8,387 troops, 107 military observers, 312 civilian police.

Financial and administrative aspects of peacekeeping operations

Financing

Expenditures for United Nations peacekeeping activities for the period 1 July 2002 to 30 June 2003 totalled $2,501 million, compared to a final figure of $2,572 million for the previous 12-month period. The decrease in expenditure (3 per cent) resulted from scaled-down operations in UNIFIL, UNIKOM, UNAMSIL, UNMIK and the United Nations Transitional Administration in East Timor (UNTAET)/UNMISET, and the completion of the mandate of the United Nations Mission in Bosnia and Herzegovina (UNMIBH), offset by an increase in spending in MONUC.

The overall positive financial position of UN peacekeeping operations was relatively unchanged from the previous year, with increased cash availability in active missions offset by reduced cash in the closed missions (see below). Outstanding unpaid assessments for active peacekeeping operations declined 23 per cent from $662.2 million to $508.3 million. As at 30 June 2003, total unpaid assessments amounted to $1.1 billion, compared to $1.2 billion the previous year. That enabled earlier settlement of debts in active missions to troop-contributing countries. On the other hand, closed missions had reduced cash as funds were used for strategic deployment stocks at UNLB (see p. 72) and $84.4 million was returned to Member States. Available cash for all operations totalled $1,717.4 million, while liabilities came to $1,477.2 million.

Notes of Secretary-General. In accordance with General Assembly resolution 49/233 A [YUN 1994, p. 1338], the Secretary-General submitted to the Assembly's Fifth Committee a February note [A/C.5/57/34] providing information on proposed budgetary requirements for all peacekeeping operations, UNLB and the support account for peacekeeping operations for the period from 1 July 2003 to 30 June 2004 in the amount of $2,186,658,800. That amount was updated in March [A/C.5/57/34/Rev.1] to $2,304,623,700, reflecting revised estimates for the expansion of MONUC, as authorized by Security Council resolution 1445(2002) [YUN 2002, p. 123].

Financial performance and proposed budgets

In February/March [A/57/772], ACABQ considered the financial performance reports for the period 1 July 2001 to 30 June 2002 and the proposed budgets for the period 1 July 2003 to 30 June 2004 of UNOMIG, MINURSO, UNAMSIL, UNFICYP, UNMIK, UNIFIL, UNDOF, UNMEE, UNLB, MONUC, UNTAET and UNMISET. It also considered the Secretary-General's overview report [A/57/723] on the financing of UN peacekeeping operations: budget performance for the period 1 July 2001 to 30 June 2002 and budget for the period 1 July 2003 to 30 June 2004, the report on the financial performance of UNMIBH, including the liaison offices in Belgrade and Zagreb and the United Nations Mission of Observers in Prevlaka from 1 July 2001 to 30 June 2002 [A/57/684], and the report on the financial performance of the support account for peacekeeping operations for the period 1 July 2001 to 30 June 2002 [A/57/725] and the proposed budget of the support account for the period 1 July 2003 to 30 June 2004 [A/57/732].

Expenditures for peacekeeping missions, including UNLB and the support account for peacekeeping operations, for the period ended 30 June 2002 amounted to $2,548.5 million against appropriations of $2,773.3 million gross, leaving an unencumbered balance of $224.8 million. For the preceding period ended 30 June 2001, the unencumbered balance was $258.1 million. ACABQ took those balances into account in its recommendations on budget requirements for 2003/04. UNLB expenditures totalled $9 million against a provision of the same amount, while expenditures against the support account for peacekeeping operations totalled $84.3 million from a provision of $89.7 million. As at 28 February 2003, unliquidated obligations amounted to $221 million.

Commenting on the performance reports, ACABQ noted in a number of missions that substantial resources were regularly retained to meet obligations to vendors, staff and others. It considered that the large amounts of unliquidated obligations and savings regularly realized on prior period obligations indicated a laxity in obligating funds and illustrated weaknesses in budget implementation and monitoring, and requested that those problems be addressed. Noting the numerous budget variances (savings or overexpenditures), with only generic explanations provided, ACABQ recommended that in the future overruns or savings be fully explained, with specific information on the circumstances that led to the savings or overruns in a particular object of expenditure.

Concerning the delegation of financial authority, ACABQ trusted that, when the delegation of authority in budget implementation to chief administrative officers had been effected and monitoring tools were in place at Headquarters and in the field, questions concerning the analysis of budget implementation would be answered promptly.

Having considered results-based budgeting, objective-setting and presentation, ACABQ welcomed the efforts to streamline the budget presentation. However, the results-based budgeting exercise still appeared to be primarily Headquarters-driven and, because it was still relatively new, systematic and more focused training and coaching should be continued to ensure a coherent and comprehensive understanding and commitment to it in all the missions.

ACABQ, referring to the Secretary-General's overview report on the financing of UN peacekeeping (see p. 82), suggested that the report in future should include such cross-cutting issues as air operations, procurement and inventory management. For each mission, the Secretariat should combine in a single document the performance report and the proposed budget.

Acknowledging the Secretary-General's intention that the new results-based budget format would improve decision-making and permit the General Assembly to focus on policy issues rather than details, ACABQ requested that he clearly indicate those policy issues requiring Assembly attention and reinstate the introductory information in the budget document that had been eliminated. Mandate objectives defined in budget documents should be in strict compliance with those established by the Security Council and, except for the support component, the number of expected accomplishments, indicators of achievement and planned outputs should be reduced to facilitate monitoring and reporting.

ACABQ was of the opinion that having a uniform framework comprising three or four components (political, military, civilian police and support) for all missions had led to anomalies in some missions, and considered that it might be appropriate for some missions, depending on their mandate, to have additional ones. The Secretary-General was asked to explain, in the next budget submission, the rationale for the components used to prepare the budgets. The mandate implementation plan should constitute the framework for budget preparation and performance reporting and a clear link should be established in performance reports between the results-based framework and the existing mandate plan. Expected accomplishments, indicators of achievement and planned outputs under each component should be relevant and realistic, and the support component dealing with operational costs should include plans to increase efficiency and productivity. The Committee shared the concerns of the Board of Auditors [A/57/5, vol. II] that not all missions had well-developed tools to measure, monitor and evaluate actual performance against the objectives set out in the proposed results-based programme budgets.

ACABQ, noting the substantial capital expenditure required for communication and information technology projects, recommended that future requirements for new and replacement programmes be based on a comprehensive analysis of the functional requirements of the field missions. A clear time frame for completing such projects should be indicated in the proposed budget submission and the status of their implementation reflected in the performance report. The information provided on the nine information technology systems in DPKO showed a lack of a comprehensive identification of needs and a potential for duplication of databases. The review it had requested of the many databases developed or being developed, with a view to ensuring compatibility and interactiveness, had not been undertaken. ACABQ recommended that the Secretariat, in the context of the 2004/05 peacekeeping budgets, evaluate the cost-benefit and the efficiency and productivity results of the DPKO information technology systems to be implemented by the end of 2003 to ensure that the objectives had been realized and to correct any weaknesses. It reiterated its caution against the tendency to acquire the most up-to-date communication and data-processing equipment, which might not be appropriate to the practical needs of the mission.

GENERAL ASSEMBLY ACTION

On 18 June [meeting 90], the General Assembly, on the recommendation of the Fifth Committee [A/57/656/Add.1], adopted **resolution 57/290 B** without vote [agenda item 126].

Administrative and budgetary aspects of the financing of the United Nations peacekeeping operations

The General Assembly,

Having considered the report of the Secretary-General entitled "Overview of the financing of the United Nations peacekeeping operations: budget performance for the period from 1 July 2001 to 30 June 2002 and budget for the period from 1 July 2003 to 30 June 2004" and the relevant sections of the report of the Advisory Committee on Administrative and Budgetary Questions thereon,

Welcoming the presentation of the overview report,

Results-based budgeting and budget presentation

1. *Recalls* its resolutions 55/231 of 23 December 2000, 56/293 of 27 June 2002 and 57/300 of 20 December 2002;

2. *Welcomes* the continuing efforts of the Secretary-General to implement a results-based budgeting format and the timely presentation of the proposed

peacekeeping budgets for the period from 1 July 2003 to 30 June 2004;

3. *Endorses* the observations and recommendations of the Advisory Committee on Administrative and Budgetary Questions contained in paragraphs 37 to 56 and 134 to 136 of its report, subject to the provisions of the present resolution;

4. *Requests* the Secretary-General to ensure that, in applying results-based budgeting to peacekeeping budgets, the specific characteristics and mandates of each peacekeeping mission are taken fully into account;

5. *Notes* the intention of the Secretary-General, as reflected in paragraph 44 of the report of the Advisory Committee, that the new budget format will improve decision-making, and reaffirms that the peacekeeping budget documents should contain all the information needed for Member States to reach well-informed decisions, including a full justification of the resources requested;

6. *Reiterates* that the format of the budgets should be in accordance with the mandates of the General Assembly;

7. *Requests* the Joint Inspection Unit to submit to the General Assembly at its resumed sixtieth session an evaluation of the implementation of results-based budgeting in peacekeeping operations;

8. *Requests* the Secretary-General to develop further the link between mission objectives and the resources requested in the proposed peacekeeping budgets for the period from 1 July 2004 to 30 June 2005;

9. *Decides* that the performance reports and the proposed budgets for peacekeeping operations and the support account should continue to be presented in separate documents;

Communication and information technology

10. *Notes with concern* the observations of the Advisory Committee on the expansion of information technology programmes in some peacekeeping missions undergoing downsizing of activities and personnel and its caution against an apparent tendency to acquire the most up-to-date communication and data-processing equipment, which might not be appropriate for the practical needs of the missions;

11. *Requests* the Secretary-General to submit to the General Assembly at its fifty-eighth session a comprehensive report on the functional requirements of field missions for communication and information technology, including replacement programmes, disposal of used information technology assets, the status of ongoing and new projects and an evaluation of current policies and practices in terms of their cost-effectiveness, efficiency and productivity benefits;

12. *Also requests* the Secretary-General to ensure that the above-mentioned report is consistent with the direction of the Organization's broader information and communication technology strategy and that it takes into account the observations and recommendations of the Advisory Committee contained in paragraphs 102 to 106 of its report;

Training

13. *Further requests* the Secretary-General to ensure that investments in training are based on need, aimed at improving efficiency and performance and congruent with the career development of staff;

14. *Requests* the Secretary-General, with the assistance of the Office of Internal Oversight Services of the Secretariat, to refine the policy of management on training and training-related travel costs in the Department of Peacekeeping Operations of the Secretariat and in peacekeeping missions, taking into account requirements related to the provision by the United Nations of training for military personnel, civilian police and civilian staff and considering paragraphs 127 to 133 of the report of the Advisory Committee, and to report thereon to the General Assembly at its resumed fifty-eighth session;

Recruitment

15. *Recalls* paragraph 2 of its resolution 57/287 A of 20 December 2002;

16. *Notes with concern* the continuing delays in the recruitment of personnel in the Department of Peacekeeping Operations and its negative impact on peacekeeping missions, in particular those in Africa;

17. *Requests* the Secretary-General to encourage greater use of national staff, as defined in paragraph 80 of the report of the Advisory Committee, whenever possible and cost-effective, and to report thereon to the General Assembly at its resumed fifty-eighth session;

18. *Urges* the Secretary-General to expedite recruitment for field missions, taking into account, as appropriate, the delegation of recruitment authority to field missions and their accountability in that regard, including the use of fair and transparent recruitment procedures and monitoring mechanisms, consistent with the relevant resolutions of the General Assembly, and to report to it thereon at its resumed fifty-eighth session;

19. *Endorses* the observations and recommendations of the Advisory Committee contained in paragraphs 78 and 80 to 85 of its report;

20. *Stresses* that any reclassification of posts should be consistent with the relevant resolutions of the General Assembly and the United Nations Staff Rules and Regulations;

Official travel

21. *Reiterates* that future resource requests for official travel should be adequately justified, including how such travel will help to achieve a measurable result in fulfilling stated objectives;

Procurement and contract management

22. *Requests* the Secretary-General to submit to the General Assembly at its resumed fifty-eighth session a comprehensive report on procurement and contract management for peacekeeping operations containing specific proposals addressing any possible conflict of interest that may arise in this area concerning United Nations staff members associated with the procurement cycle, including the feasibility of establishing a code of ethics, a declaration of independence and provisions to ensure confidentiality of information associated with their functions as United Nations staff members, also taking into account paragraphs 116 to 119 of the report of the Advisory Committee.

On 23 December, the Assembly decided that the item on the administrative and budgetary aspects of the financing of UN peacekeeping operations would remain for consideration at its resumed fifty-eighth (2004) session (**decision 58/565**).

Closed missions

In April [A/57/789], the Secretary-General updated the information, as at 30 June 2002, on the financial position of 10 closed peacekeeping missions for which financial performance reports had already been submitted: the Military Observer Group of the United Nations Verification Mission in Guatemala (MINUGUA); the United Nations Mission in Haiti (UNMIH); the United Nations Observer Group in Central America (ONUCA) and the United Nations Observer Mission in El Salvador (ONUSAL); the United Nations Operation in Mozambique (ONUMOZ); the United Nations Operation in Somalia (UNOSOM); the United Nations Preventive Deployment Force (UNPREDEP); the United Nations Protection Force, the United Nations Confidence Restoration Operation in Croatia, UNPREDEP and the United Nations Peace Forces headquarters (UNPF); the United Nations Support Mission in Haiti (UNSMIH), the United Nations Transition Mission in Haiti (UNTMIH) and the United Nations Civilian Police Mission in Haiti (MIPONUH); the United Nations Transitional Administration for Eastern Slavonia, Baranja and Western Sirmium (UNTAES) and the Civilian Police Support Group; and the United Nations Transitional Authority in Cambodia (UNTAC).

The Secretary-General recommended that, in the light of the overall financial situation of the Organization and the fact that assessed contributions to peacekeeping in the amount of $1.5 billion remained unpaid as at 15 March 2003, the return of cash available for credit to Member States be suspended until the financial position improved in respect of the fund balances of those missions.

In a May report on improving the financial situation of the United Nations [A/57/489/Add.1], the Secretary-General indicated that if, of the $339 million available in the closed missions, $169 million was to be returned to Member States, a balance of only $170 million would remain. He therefore recommended, in view of the projected decrease in peacekeeping cash and as a matter of prudent financial management, that financial regulation 5.5 of the Financial Regulations and Rules in respect of the closed missions be suspended to give the Organization a degree of financial flexibility until its financial situation improved.

Addressing the Fifth Committee on 19 May [A/C.5/57/SR.52], the ACABQ Chairman stated that suspension of financial regulation 5.5 would result in the retention of a revised amount of $168.9 million. ACABQ recommended that more clarification and information be provided in the context of its examination of the report on improving the financial situation of the United Nations and the performance reports of closed missions before a decision was taken on the suspension of the relevant financial regulation.

GENERAL ASSEMBLY ACTION

On 18 June [meeting 90], the General Assembly, on the recommendation of the Fifth Committee [A/57/656/Add.1], adopted **resolution 57/323** without vote [agenda item 126].

Closed peacekeeping missions

The General Assembly

1. *Takes note* of the reports of the Secretary-General on the updated financial position of closed peacekeeping missions as at 30 June 2002, and on the financing of the United Nations Transition Assistance Group, the United Nations Angola Verification Mission and the United Nations Observer Mission in Angola, the United Nations Mission of Observers in Tajikistan, the United Nations Observer Mission in Liberia, the United Nations Observer Mission Uganda-Rwanda and the United Nations Assistance Mission for Rwanda, and the United Nations Mission in the Central African Republic, and the related report of the Advisory Committee on Administrative and Budgetary Questions;

2. *Requests* the Secretary-General to return 50 per cent of the net cash available for credit to Member States as at 30 June 2002, in the amount of 84,446,000 United States dollars, by 30 June 2003, based on the scale applicable to the missions' last assessment;

3. *Decides* to postpone the return of the remaining 50 per cent of the net cash available for credit to Member States, in the amount of 84,446,000 dollars, until 31 March 2004, based on the scale applicable to the missions' last assessment, in respect of the fund balances of the United Nations Mission in Haiti; the United Nations Observer Group in Central America and the United Nations Observer Mission in El Salvador; the United Nations Preventive Deployment Force; the United Nations Protection Force, the United Nations Confidence Restoration Operation in Croatia, the United Nations Preventive Deployment Force and the United Nations Peace Forces headquarters; the United Nations Transitional Administration for Eastern Slavonia, Baranja and Western Sirmium and the Civilian Police Support Group; the United Nations Angola Verification Mission and the United Nations Observer Mission in Angola; the United Nations Observer Mission Uganda-Rwanda and the United Nations Assistance Mission for Rwanda; the United Nations Mission of Observers in Tajikistan; the United Nations Transition Assistance Group; and the United Nations Observer Mission in Liberia in the light of the overall financial situation of the Organization and the fact that assessed contributions to peacekeeping in the amount of 1.4 billion dollars remain unpaid as at 31 March 2003;

4. *Also decides* that the provisions of financial regulation 5.5 of the Financial Regulations and Rules of

the United Nations should be suspended in respect of the liabilities and fund balance of the Military Observer Group of the United Nations Verification Mission in Guatemala; the United Nations Operation in Mozambique; the United Nations Operation in Somalia II; the United Nations Support Mission in Haiti, the United Nations Transition Mission in Haiti and the United Nations Civilian Police Mission in Haiti; the United Nations Transitional Authority in Cambodia; and the United Nations Mission in the Central African Republic in the light of the cash shortage of these missions;

5. *Requests* the Secretary-General to provide an updated report and make proposals for consideration at its resumed fifty-eighth session on how to address the issue of outstanding dues owed to Member States from closed peacekeeping missions that are in net cash deficit;

6. *Takes note* of the reports of the Secretary-General on the disposition of assets of the United Nations Mission of Observers in Tajikistan, the United Nations Assistance Mission for Rwanda and the United Nations Mission in the Central African Republic;

7. *Approves* the donation of assets of the United Nations Assistance Mission for Rwanda with a total inventory value of 12,581,000 dollars and corresponding residual value of 2,401,300 dollars to the Government of Rwanda;

8. *Also approves* the donation of assets of the United Nations Assistance Mission for Rwanda with a total inventory value of 79,200 dollars and corresponding residual value of 53,400 dollars to the medical unit of a Member State;

9. *Decides* to consider at its fifty-eighth session the updated report on the position of closed peacekeeping missions requested in paragraph 5 above under the agenda item entitled "Administrative and budgetary aspects of the financing of the United Nations peacekeeping operations".

Peacekeeping support account

The Secretary-General, in February [A/57/725], submitted the performance report on the budget of the support account for peacekeeping operations for the period 1 July 2001 to 30 June 2002. Expenditures for the period totalled $84,343,000 against an apportionment of $89,749,250, resulting in an unencumbered balance of $5,406,250, which was due mainly to a higher-than-budgeted vacancy rate and underexpenditures in respect of travel, communications and information technology.

Also in February [A/57/732], the Secretary-General submitted the budget for the support account for peacekeeping operations for the period 1 July 2003 to 30 June 2004 in the amount of $115,863,100 gross ($100,318,500 net), which provided for 761 posts.

In April [A/57/776], ACABQ recommended resource reductions totalling $4,371,300 gross ($4,090,800 net) and that the Assembly approve total staffing and non-staffing requirements of $111,491,800 gross ($96,227,700 net) for the period 1 July 2003 to 30 June 2004. It also recommended that miscellaneous income of $3,126,000 for 1 July 2001 to 30 June 2002 be applied to the resources required for the period 1 July 2003 to 30 June 2004 and that the balance ($108,365,800 gross ($93,101,700 net)) be prorated among individual peacekeeping operation budgets for that period.

GENERAL ASSEMBLY ACTION

On 18 June [meeting 90], the General Assembly, on the recommendation of the Fifth Committee [A/57/656/Add.1], adopted **resolution 57/318** without vote [agenda item 126].

Support account for peacekeeping operations

The General Assembly,

Recalling its resolutions 45/258 of 3 May 1991, 47/218 A of 23 December 1992, 48/226 A of 23 December 1993, 56/241 of 24 December 2001 and 56/293 of 27 June 2002, its decisions 48/489 of 8 July 1994, 49/469 of 23 December 1994 and 50/473 of 23 December 1995 and other relevant resolutions of the General Assembly,

Having considered the report of the Secretary-General entitled "Overview of the financing of the United Nations peacekeeping operations: budget performance for the period from 1 July 2001 to 30 June 2002 and budget for the period from 1 July 2003 to 30 June 2004", his report on the financial performance of the support account for peacekeeping operations for the period from 1 July 2001 to 30 June 2002, his report on the budget for the support account for peacekeeping operations for the period from 1 July 2003 to 30 June 2004, and the related reports of the Advisory Committee on Administrative and Budgetary Questions,

Having also considered the reports of the Secretary-General on the experience with resident investigators and on gender mainstreaming in peacekeeping activities, as well as the above-mentioned reports of the Advisory Committee, specifically paragraphs 86 to 95 of the first report with regard to resident investigators and auditors, and paragraph 31 of the second report with regard to gender mainstreaming in peacekeeping activities,

Recognizing the importance of the United Nations being able to respond and deploy rapidly a peacekeeping operation upon adoption of a relevant resolution of the Security Council, within thirty days for traditional peacekeeping operations and ninety days for complex peacekeeping operations,

Recognizing also the need for adequate support during all phases of peacekeeping operations, including the liquidation and termination phases,

Mindful that the level of the support account should broadly correspond to the mandates, number, size and complexity of peacekeeping missions,

1. *Takes note* of the reports of the Secretary-General on the financing of the support account for peacekeeping operations;

2. *Also takes note* of the report of the Secretary-General on the experience with resident investigators;

3. *Further takes note* of the report of the Secretary-General on gender mainstreaming in peacekeeping activities;

4. *Reaffirms* the need for effective and efficient administration and financial management of peacekeeping operations, and urges the Secretary-General to continue to identify measures to increase the productivity and efficiency of the support account;

5. *Affirms* the need for adequate funding for the backstopping of peacekeeping operations, as well as the need for full justification for that funding in support account budget submissions;

6. *Endorses* the conclusions and recommendations contained in the relevant paragraphs of the reports of the Advisory Committee on Administrative and Budgetary Questions, subject to the provisions of the present resolution;

7. *Decides* to maintain, for the period from 1 July 2003 to 30 June 2004, the funding mechanism for the support account used in the current period, from 1 July 2002 to 30 June 2003, as approved in paragraph 3 of its resolution 50/221 B of 7 June 1996;

8. *Reaffirms* the need for the Secretary-General to ensure that delegation of authority to the Department of Peacekeeping Operations of the Secretariat and field missions is in strict compliance with relevant resolutions and decisions and the relevant rules and procedures of the General Assembly on this matter;

9. *Also reaffirms* that any delegation of authority to the Department of Peacekeeping Operations and field missions requires full accountability of programme managers;

10. *Further reaffirms* paragraph 15 of its resolution 56/293, and requests the Secretary-General to submit to the General Assembly at its resumed fifty-eighth session a comprehensive report on measures taken in this regard and the criteria used for recruitment to all support account posts, in particular those in the Department of Peacekeeping Operations, bearing in mind that the system of desirable ranges does not currently apply to support account posts;

11. *Regrets* that the D-2 post for the administration of change management is still vacant, and urges the Secretary-General to fill it as soon as possible;

12. *Requests* the Secretary-General to review the level of the support account on a regular basis, taking into consideration the number, size and complexity of peacekeeping operations;

13. *Requests* the Board of Auditors to carry out a review of the implementation of the recommendations of the Special Committee on Peacekeeping Operations and the Panel on United Nations Peace Operations as approved by the General Assembly, to gauge the effects of management reform measures taken since the approval of the report and to report thereon to the Assembly at its fifty-eighth session;

14. *Decides* to review at its resumed fifty-eighth session the existing posts approved in its resolutions 55/238 of 23 December 2000, 56/241 and 56/293 and in the present resolution in order to consider their justification, taking into account the ongoing evaluation by the Office of Internal Oversight Services of the Secretariat of the impact of the recent restructuring of the Department of Peacekeeping Operations on its performance in the backstopping of peacekeeping operations;

15. *Approves* the establishment of eight posts (2 P-4, 4 P-3 and 2 General Service) for the Investigations Division of the Office of Internal Oversight Services, to be divided evenly between the regional hubs in Vienna and Nairobi, and decides to review these posts and functions in the next support account budget, taking into account the relevant workload and coverage of their activities;

16. *Also approves* the establishment of a P-3 post and general temporary assistance for one General Service post (Other level) in the Executive Office of the Office of Internal Oversight Services;

17. *Further approves* the transfer from peacekeeping operations budgets to the support account budget of 27 resident auditor and assistant posts at the same level as in the budget for the period from 1 July 2002 to 30 June 2003, to be deployed as necessary, bearing in mind that whenever a mission's mandate is adjusted or terminated, the number of audit posts should be adjusted or terminated accordingly;

18. *Decides* that any support account posts that remain vacant and any new posts that are not filled for twelve months from the date of their establishment would require rejustification in the subsequent budget submission, and requests the Secretary-General to report to the General Assembly at its fifty-ninth session on the implementation of this decision;

19. *Requests* the Secretary-General to include in the next support account report details of reclassification upward and reclassification downward, if any, of posts, as well as the breakdown of appointments to posts reclassified upward in the previous two years, as between internal and external candidates, and to provide annual data thereafter;

20. *Decides* that the person recruited to the gender adviser post shall be responsible for all operational support activities and all related activities pertaining to the implementation of individual mandates of various peacekeeping operations in the area of gender mainstreaming, including those activities relating to the field operations of each peacekeeping mission;

21. *Affirms* that the Office of the Special Adviser on Gender Issues and Advancement of Women is the competent authority for gender mainstreaming in the United Nations as a whole and is responsible for the formulation of policy as mandated by the intergovernmental bodies, and in this regard requests the Department of Peacekeeping Operations to establish a viable, effective mechanism for close coordination with the Special Adviser, ensuring that all plans of action on gender mainstreaming in peacekeeping operations are consistent with the existing mandates;

22. *Stresses* that the creation of a gender adviser in the Best Practices Unit of the Department of Peacekeeping Operations does not constitute a precedent to be followed by other departments and should not itself lead to the establishment of a gender unit in the Department, and also stresses the importance of not duplicating functions and capacities that already exist elsewhere in the Secretariat;

23. *Decides* to review the establishment and the level of the post of gender adviser in the context of paragraph 14 above;

24. *Requests* the Secretary-General, through the Office of Internal Oversight Services, to report to the

General Assembly at its resumed fifty-eighth session on the cases processed by the regional investigators;

25. *Decides* to establish, on a trial basis, a P-4 post in the Monitoring, Evaluation and Consulting Division of the Office of Internal Oversight Services to undertake oversight functions with regard to military aspects of peacekeeping operations, and also not to approve the amount covering six months of consultancy services for three experts mentioned in paragraph 70 of the report of the Advisory Committee;

26. *Requests* the Secretary-General to report on the implementation and impact of this decision in the context of his support account budget proposal for the period from 1 July 2005 to 30 June 2006;

27. *Concurs* with the observation of the Advisory Committee in paragraph 51 of its report that the term "inspectorate" or "inspector-general" does not appropriately reflect the intended use of the consultancy funds requested in paragraph 43 of the report of the Secretary-General on the budget for the support account for the period from 1 July 2003 to 30 June 2004 and should not be used;

28. *Requests* the Secretary-General to report on the relationship between the proposals requested in paragraphs 43 and 62 of his report, and decides to review this issue in the context of the consideration of the proposed budget for the support account for the period from 1 July 2005 to 30 June 2006;

29. *Decides* not to approve the resources requested in paragraph 115 of the report of the Secretary-General, and requests the Secretary-General to present a full justification for the establishment of those posts in the context of his next budget submission for the support account for the period from 1 July 2004 to 30 June 2005;

30. *Approves* the Military Division training budget at the level requested by the Secretary-General;

31. *Regrets* that the Secretary-General has not included in his report an annex containing information on the status of implementation of relevant adopted recommendations made by the Advisory Committee and other oversight bodies, as requested in paragraph 17 of its resolution 56/293;

Financial performance report for the period from 1 July 2001 to 30 June 2002

32. *Takes note* of the report of the Secretary-General on the financial performance of the support account for peacekeeping operations for the period from 1 July 2001 to 30 June 2002;

Budget estimates for the period from 1 July 2003 to 30 June 2004

33. *Approves* the support account requirements in the amount of 112,075,800 United States dollars for the period from 1 July 2003 to 30 June 2004, including 702 continuing and 41 new temporary posts and their related post and non-post requirements;

Financing of requirements for the support account for peacekeeping operations

34. *Decides* that requirements for the support account for peacekeeping operations for the period from 1 July 2003 to 30 June 2004 shall be financed as follows:

(a) The unencumbered balance and other income in the total amount of 8,532,250 dollars in respect of the period ended 30 June 2002 to be applied to the resources required for the period from 1 July 2003 to 30 June 2004;

(b) The increase of 517,100 dollars in the estimated staff assessment income in respect of the financial period ended 30 June 2002 to be added to the credits from the amount referred to in subparagraph (a) above;

(c) The amount of 33,250,000 dollars in excess of the authorized level of the Peacekeeping Reserve Fund in respect of the period ended 30 June 2002 to be applied to the resources required for the period from 1 July 2003 to 30 June 2004;

(d) The balance of 70,293,550 dollars to be prorated among the budgets of the active peacekeeping operations for the period from 1 July 2003 to 30 June 2004;

(e) The estimated staff assessment income of 15,320,200 dollars for the period from 1 July 2003 to 30 June 2004 to be set off against the balance referred to in subparagraph (d) above, to be prorated among the individual active peacekeeping operations budgets.

Also on 18 June, by **decision 57/588**, the Assembly deferred until its fifty-eighth session consideration of the ACABQ report on the financial performance report for the period 1 July 2001 to 30 June 2002 and proposed budget for the support account for peacekeeping operations for the period from 1 July 2003 to 30 June 2004.

Peacekeeping Reserve Fund

The Secretary-General reported in April [A/57/798] that the level of the United Nations Peacekeeping Reserve Fund, established by General Assembly resolution 47/217 [YUN 1992, p. 1022] to ensure the rapid deployment of peacekeeping operations, stood at $197,387,000 as at 30 June 2002. Following the transfer of $14,137,000 to the UNLB account to meet requirements for the strategic deployment stocks in accordance with Assembly resolution 56/292 [YUN 2002, p. 64], the amount remaining in the Fund stood at $183,250,000, $33,250,000 above the authorized level of $150,000,000. The Secretary-General recommended that the excess amount be applied to the support account for peacekeeping operations for the period 1 July 2003 to 30 June 2004.

In May [A/C.5/57/SR.52], ACABQ agreed with the Secretary-General's proposal to restore the Fund to its authorized level of $150,000,000.

GENERAL ASSEMBLY ACTION

On 18 June [meeting 90], the General Assembly, on the recommendation of the Fifth Committee [A/57/656/Add.1], adopted **resolution 57/317** without vote [agenda item 126].

Peacekeeping Reserve Fund

The General Assembly,

Having considered the note by the Secretary-General on the Peacekeeping Reserve Fund and the related reports of the Advisory Committee on Administrative and Budgetary Questions,

Recalling its resolution 47/217 of 23 December 1992 on the establishment of the Peacekeeping Reserve Fund and its resolutions 49/233 A of 23 December 1994 and 51/218 E of 17 June 1997,

Recalling also its resolution 57/290 A of 20 December 2002 on the inclusion of Switzerland and Timor-Leste in the Peacekeeping Reserve Fund,

Reaffirming the general principles underlying the financing of United Nations peacekeeping operations, as stated in General Assembly resolutions 1874(S-IV) of 27 June 1963, 3101(XXVIII) of 11 December 1973 and 55/235 of 23 December 2000,

1. *Takes note* of the status of contributions to the Peacekeeping Reserve Fund as at 31 December 2002;

2. *Endorses* the recommendation contained in the report of the Advisory Committee on Administrative and Budgetary Questions, and requests the Secretary-General to ensure its full implementation;

3. *Decides* to apply the amount of 33,250,000 United States dollars, representing the amount in excess of the authorized level of 150 million dollars for the Fund, to the requirements of the support account for peacekeeping operations for the period from 1 July 2003 to 30 June 2004;

4. *Requests* the Secretary-General, consequent upon the full establishment of the strategic deployment stocks and the pre-mandate commitment authority, to review the level of the Fund and to report thereon to the General Assembly at its resumed fifty-eighth session.

Consolidation of peacekeeping accounts

In March [A/57/746], the Secretary-General, in response to the General Assembly request contained in resolution 56/293 [YUN 2002, p. 77] that he report on the feasibility of consolidating the accounts of the different peacekeeping missions, said that it was not possible to implement that request within the framework of current practice for reporting, budgeting and financing of peacekeeping operations and the Financial Regulations and Rules, which treated each peacekeeping mission independently. However, he did outline the possible benefits of consolidation and examined the range of issues that would need to be taken into account.

The potential benefits included greater flexibility in utilizing peacekeeping resources, thus eliminating the need for cross-borrowing between accounts, more consistent and timely reimbursement to troop-contributing Governments, and streamlined legislative and administrative processes for financing, with only one peacekeeping financing resolution to be adopted and one assessment on Member States to be approved.

If consolidation were applied retroactively, outstanding contributions to each operation, under financial regulation 3.5 whereby contributions were applied to the oldest outstanding arrears, would be commingled. If applied prospectively, amounts owed up to the date of consolidation would be mission-specific, while amounts owed thereafter would not. A mechanism for applying subsequent receipts would need to be developed, and financial regulations and rules changed. For accounts of active peacekeeping missions combined prospectively, transitional measures would be required to provide the missions with sufficient cash from the date of consolidation until the receipt of new assessments, and to prioritize the settlement of liabilities.

As at 30 June 2002, 20 closed peacekeeping missions had combined assets of $1,231 million and combined liabilities amounting to $462 million. Of those 20 missions, 12 had sufficient cash to meet all of their respective outstanding liabilities.

The Secretary-General suggested a phased approach to consolidation, with accounts of active peacekeeping missions being consolidated retroactively, with separate accounts maintained for closed missions. Procedures for the appropriation and assessment of resources would need to be revised. The Assembly resolution on the financing of peacekeeping operations, including the support account and UNLB, would contain a single amount to be appropriated and assessed on Member States, with each operation constituting a section, as in the case of the regular budget, and defining the Secretary-General's authority to transfer funds between peacekeeping operations. Assessments would be de-linked from the continuation of Security Council mandates. That approach would streamline the budget approval process, reduce the number of legislative decisions required and assessments to be approved and facilitate planning for Member States. Unencumbered balances, interest and other miscellaneous income would be offset against the next appropriation for peacekeeping. New peacekeeping operations could be financed in accordance with sections IV and XI of resolution 49/233 A [YUN 1994, p. 1338] and resolution 56/292 [YUN 2002, p. 64]. A consolidated summary of the budgetary requirements would serve as the basis for the Assembly to appropriate funds and decide on the financing of peacekeeping operations. Separate annual budget and performance reports would, however, continue to be prepared for each peacekeeping operation, the support account for peacekeeping operations and UNLB. Financial statements for active missions would report on consolidated expenditures compared to the overall appropriation. Final performance reports and annual updates would not be required for those missions since the accounts would be open-ended. However, final performance reports would continue to be submitted in respect of the closed missions, for which separate accounts would be maintained.

ACABQ, in an April report [A/57/772], acknowledged that the approach outlined by the Secretary-General was not compatible with current financial procedures and pointed out that de-linking assessments from Council action on individual mandates might create complications for some Member States which, in accordance with their domestic legal requirements, required Council action before they could pay assessments. The Assembly should provide further guidance on the matter.

GENERAL ASSEMBLY ACTION

On 18 June [meeting 90], the General Assembly, on the recommendation of the Fifth Committee [A/57/656/Add.1], adopted **resolution 57/319** without vote [agenda item 126].

Feasibility of consolidating the accounts of the various peacekeeping operations

The General Assembly,

Recalling paragraph 10 of its resolution 56/293 of 27 June 2002,

Having considered the report of the Secretary-General on the feasibility of consolidating the accounts of the various peacekeeping operations and the related report of the Advisory Committee on Administrative and Budgetary Questions,

1. *Takes note* of the report of the Secretary-General and of the related report of the Advisory Committee on Administrative and Budgetary Questions;

2. *Decides* to defer consideration of this question until the second part of its resumed fifty-eighth session, and requests the Secretary-General to provide a comprehensive report, taking into account the views expressed, questions raised and information requested by Member States at its fifty-seventh session, including a simulation of the options proposed.

Peacekeeping trust funds

ACABQ action. ACABQ, in an April report on the administrative and budgetary aspects of the financing of peacekeeping operations [A/57/772], considered the question of inactive peacekeeping trust funds. It requested the Secretariat to consult with donor Member States on the disposition of the assets of those trust funds and recommended that the Assembly request Member States concerned to respond promptly to the Secretariat on the matter. The Secretary-General should complete the closing of inactive trust funds within a reasonable time.

OIOS report. In November [A/58/613], pursuant to General Assembly resolutions 48/218 B [YUN 1994, p. 1362], 54/244 [YUN 1999, p. 1274] and 57/278 B (see p. 91), the Secretary-General transmitted to the Assembly the report of OIOS on the administration of peacekeeping trust funds. OIOS conducted an audit of 31 trust funds designated by the Office of Programme Planning, Budget and Accounts (OPPBA) as being related to peacekeeping operations, with a combined balance of $170 million as at 30 June 2002, to assess the effectiveness of their administration. Of the funds reviewed, 11 were active, 8 had ceased operations and showed a combined balance of $53,177,000, with no expenditures during the fiscal year ended 30 June 2002, and 5 others related to closed peacekeeping/political missions had a combined total balance of $3,770,000.

OIOS identified a number of common issues that needed to be addressed, including the role of implementing offices and the need for DPKO to support and monitor the designated executing bodies. To improve the management of the trust funds, OIOS recommended that, when the original purpose of a trust fund had been fulfilled or the implementing office had ceased operations, OPPBA should recommend to the donor(s) redirecting the remaining resources and designating a new implementing office, or closing the trust fund and returning the unspent balance to the donor(s). DPKO should issue a standard operating procedures manual for administering peacekeeping trust funds, which should include guidelines for determining advances and progress payments to the executing agencies, and financial reporting formats. DPKO should, in cooperation with OPPBA, develop a mechanism to finance the administrative and management costs of peacekeeping trust funds. To enhance transparency of trust fund utilization, DPKO should establish a web site to publicize information on trust fund activities and fund balances.

All the recommendations were accepted by either OPPBA or DPKO.

Apportionment of costs

In a July report with a later addendum [A/58/157 & Add.1], the Secretary-General described the implementation of General Assembly resolution 55/235 [YUN 2000, p. 102], by which the Assembly adopted a new system of adjustments of the scale of assessments for the regular budget to be used in fixing rates of assessment applicable to Member States for peacekeeping operations, and resolution 55/236 [ibid., p. 104] establishing the criteria for voluntary movements within that system. Annexed to the report were: the list of peacekeeping levels, based on average per capita gross national income of Member States and other factors; and a table showing the initial levels and voluntary and ad hoc movements for 2001-2003, the initial composition of levels and assumed voluntary and ad hoc movements for 2004-2006, and relevant transitional periods, and the respective percentage of rates of assessment for the regular budget payable by each Member State for peacekeeping operations during 2004-2006. In resolution 55/235, the Assembly had, as an ad hoc arrangement, decided on a graduated rate for the share of the Republic of Korea in the costs of peacekeeping operations, ranging from 36 per cent of the regular budget assessment rate on 1 July 2001 and reaching 100 per cent in 2005. On 10 July 2003, the Republic of Korea requested that it be assigned to level D of the system for establishing rates of assessment. The updated composition levels, subject to the Assembly's decision with respect to the placement of the Republic of Korea in 2004-2005, would be used, together with the scale of assessments for 2004-2006, to establish each Member State's peacekeeping rate(s) of assessment.

GENERAL ASSEMBLY ACTION

On 23 December [meeting 79], the General Assembly, on the recommendation of the Fifth Committee [A/58/581], adopted **resolution 58/256** without vote [agenda item 133].

Scale of assessments for the apportionment of the expenses of United Nations peacekeeping operations

The General Assembly,

Recalling its resolutions 55/235 and 55/236 of 23 December 2000,

Recalling also its request to the Secretary-General in its resolution 55/235 to update the composition of the levels of contribution of Member States for peacekeeping operations described therein on a triennial basis, in conjunction with the regular budget scale of assessment reviews, in accordance with the criteria established in the resolution, and to report thereon to the General Assembly,

Having considered the report of the Secretary-General on the implementation of its resolutions 55/235 and 55/236,

1. *Takes note* of the report of the Secretary-General and of the updated composition of levels of contribution for peacekeeping operations for the period 2004 to 2006 contained therein;

2. *Endorses* the updated composition of levels of contribution for peacekeeping operations for the period 2004 to 2006 contained in the addendum to the report of the Secretary-General;

3. *Requests* the Secretary-General to report to the General Assembly at its sixty-first session on the updating of the composition of levels of contribution for peacekeeping operations for the period 2007 to 2009, in accordance with the provisions of resolution 55/235.

Also on 23 December, the Assembly decided that the item on the scale of assessments for the apportionment of expenses of UN peacekeeping operations would remain for consideration at its resumed fifty-eighth (2004) session (**decision 58/565**).

Accounts and auditing

At its resumed fifty-seventh session, the General Assembly considered the financial report and audited financial statements for UN peacekeeping operations for the 12-month period 1 July 2001 to 30 June 2002 [A/57/5, vol. II & Corr.5], the Secretary-General's report on the implementation of the recommendations of the Board of Auditors [A/57/416/Add.2] and the related ACABQ report [A/57/772].

GENERAL ASSEMBLY ACTION

On 18 June [meeting 90], the General Assembly, on the recommendation of the Fifth Committee [A/57/639/Add.1], adopted **resolution 57/278 B** without vote [agenda item 110].

Financial reports and audited financial statements, and reports of the Board of Auditors

The General Assembly,

Having considered the financial report and audited financial statements for the twelve-month period from 1 July 2001 to 30 June 2002 and the report of the Board of Auditors on the United Nations peacekeeping operations, the related section of the report of the Advisory Committee on Administrative and Budgetary Questions and the report of the Secretary-General on the implementation of the recommendations of the Board of Auditors concerning United Nations peacekeeping operations in respect of that period,

1. *Accepts* the audited financial statements of the United Nations peacekeeping operations for the period from 1 July 2001 to 30 June 2002;

2. *Takes note* of the observations and endorses the recommendations of the Board of Auditors contained in its report;

3. *Also takes note* of the observations and endorses the recommendations contained in the report of the Advisory Committee on Administrative and Budgetary Questions related to the report of the Board of Auditors;

4. *Commends* the Board of Auditors for the quality of its report and the streamlined format thereof;

5. *Takes note* of the report of the Secretary-General on the implementation of the recommendations of the Board of Auditors concerning United Nations peacekeeping operations in respect of the financial period ended 30 June 2002;

6. *Requests* the Secretary-General to continue to ensure that internal control in peacekeeping missions is improved with respect to the optimum use of audit resources;

7. *Also requests* the Secretary-General to ensure the full implementation of the recommendations of the Board of Auditors and the related recommendations of the Advisory Committee in a prompt and timely manner;

8. *Further requests* the Secretary-General to submit the report of the Office of Internal Oversight Services

referred to in paragraph 26 of the report of the Board of Auditors to the General Assembly at its fifty-eighth session.

Resident auditors and investigators

Board of Auditors. The Board of Auditors, in its report on the audit of UN peacekeeping operations for the period 1 July 2001 to 30 June 2002 [A/57/5, vol. II & Corr.5], indicated that it had followed up on the action taken by the Internal Audit Division to implement the seven recommendations made in its report for the financial period ended 30 June 2001 [YUN 2002, p. 79]. One recommendation (14 per cent) had been fully implemented and six (86 per cent) were under implementation. The Board recommended that the Internal Audit Division review the standard terms of reference of resident auditors.

ACABQ consideration. ACABQ, in its April report [A/57/772], noting that some 60 per cent of the Board's audit activity was carried out in field offices and peacekeeping missions, said that such fieldwork would be considerably facilitated if the Secretariat and OIOS were to ensure that the internal audit function and the resident audit capacity in peacekeeping missions were operating effectively and efficiently. Having considered the Secretary-General's 2002 report on the experience with resident investigators in peacekeeping operations [YUN 2002, p. 80], the Committee noted that OIOS was pleased with the results of mission-based investigations. However, ACABQ was concerned that the demonstrated growth in cases in the missions might have resulted from an increasing number of administrative management cases referred by mission management to OIOS investigators. Noting the OIOS observation that many peacekeeping cases routinely remained on the inactive list owing to a lack of resources to conduct investigations, ACABQ stated that there was a need to refine further the methodology for determining the cases to be investigated by OIOS, so that cases related to administrative management issues would be investigated and resolved expeditiously by the mission management itself. Based on the information provided to it, ACABQ was unable to assess whether the recommendations of the Board of Auditors on the capacity of the resident auditors to perform structured value-for-money and information and communication technology audits were being implemented or were even implementable.

Reimbursement issues

Equipment

The General Assembly, at its resumed fifty-seventh session, considered the Secretary-General's 2002 reports [YUN 2002, pp. 81-82] on the processing of claims for equipment contributed and self-sustainment undertaken at peacekeeping missions [A/C.5/56/44], on the reform of the procedure for determining reimbursement to Member States for contingent-owned equipment [A/56/939] and on the practical aspects of wet-lease, dry-lease and self-sustainment arrangements [A/57/397].

ACABQ report. ACABQ, in April [A/57/772], considered the report of the Board of Auditors (see above) and the Secretary-General's 2002 reports concerning equipment [YUN 2002, p. 81].

With regard to staff capacity and expertise in the field to manage the contingent-owned equipment system, ACABQ stated that, given the importance of the subject, further progress needed to be made on the matter. It stressed the importance of further review by the Board of Auditors of such issues as memorandums of understanding, pre-deployment inspections, arrival inspections, and verification reports and personnel resources. It noted that memorandums of understanding and status-of-forces agreements had been fraught with problems and delays and expressed concern that the United Nations was often forced to start mission operations without those instruments in place. ACABQ recognized the need to streamline the process for negotiating and approving memorandums of understanding, including reducing the number of steps involved with a view to signing them before deployment. The Secretariat should analyse the experience and make suggestions for possible changes at the next meeting of the Working Group on Reimbursement of Contingent-owned Equipment in 2004.

Noting the discrepancies between equipment negotiated in memorandums of understanding with troop-contributing countries and what was actually deployed, ACABQ recognized the importance of pre-deployment inspections to improve the content of the memorandums of understanding, reduce the possibility of variances in equipment and self-sustainment and improve claims processing. It welcomed the suggestions contained in the Secretary-General's 2002 reports on streamlining the production and processing of verification reports, including electronic submission, and trusted that a reduction in the frequency of reporting requirements would not affect the completion and quality of the reports, and consequent certification and payment of reimbursement for contingent-owned equipment claims. ACABQ recommended that the Secretariat make suggestions to the Working Group on Reimbursement of Contingent-owned Equipment for modifying the current monthly reporting cycle, which was considered too laborious and inefficient, while ensuring that the services contracted for were provided in a timely manner and without compromising the prompt processing of claims and reimbursement.

ACABQ looked forward to the implementation of the plan to process all claims for major equipment contributed and self-sustainment undertaken at peacekeeping operations and suggested that efforts should continue for the early reimbursement of troop costs and amounts held under accounts payable. Those countries that were not in the new contingent-owned equipment arrangement should be encouraged to join, which would end the write-off phenomenon (see below). The Secretariat should prepare a comprehensive working paper, including input data, to facilitate and focus the work of the 2004 meeting of the Working Group on Reimbursement of Contingent-owned Equipment. On the basis of the Working Group's recommendations, the Secretariat should prepare a comprehensive report on the issues that would require legislative action by the General Assembly.

GENERAL ASSEMBLY ACTION

On 18 June [meeting 90], the General Assembly, on the recommendation of the Fifth Committee [A/57/656/Add.1], adopted **resolution 57/314** without vote [agenda item 126].

Management of contingent-owned equipment arrangements

The General Assembly,

Recalling its resolutions 49/233 A of 23 December 1994, 50/222 of 11 April 1996, 51/218 E of 17 June 1997, 54/19 A of 29 October 1999 and 54/19 B of 15 June 2000, 55/238 of 23 December 2000, paragraph 12 of resolution 55/271 of 14 June 2001, and resolutions 55/274 of 14 June 2001 and 56/241 of 24 December 2001,

Recalling also its decision 55/452 of 23 December 2000 to convene the post–Phase V Working Group,

Recalling further its resolution 55/274 of 14 June 2001, in which the Secretary-General was requested to convene in 2004 an open-ended working group of experts, for a period of no less than ten working days, to hold a triennial review of reimbursement rates for contingent-owned equipment and self-sustainment, including medical services,

Having considered the reports of the Secretary-General, on the processing of claims for equipment contributed and self-sustainment undertaken at peacekeeping missions, on the reform of the procedures for determining reimbursement to Member States for contingent-owned equipment and troop costs, and on the practical aspects of wet-lease, dry-lease and self-sustainment arrangements and the section of the report of the Advisory Committee on Administrative and Budgetary Questions on the management of contingent-owned equipment arrangements,

1. *Takes note* of the reports of the Secretary-General;
2. *Also takes note* of the observations and recommendations of the Advisory Committee on Administrative and Budgetary Questions on the management of contingent-owned equipment arrangements, as contained in paragraphs 60 to 76 of its report;
3. *Affirms* the importance of conducting peacekeeping operations with the maximum of efficiency and effectiveness and the need to minimize delays in processing reimbursements to troop- and equipment-contributing countries;
4. *Recognizes* the fact that delay and uncertainty in reimbursements to troop-contributing countries of troop and contingent-owned equipment costs adversely affect the ability of current and potential troop-contributing countries to participate effectively in United Nations peacekeeping operations, and in this context emphasizes the need for all Member States to pay their assessed contributions to all peacekeeping operations in full, on time and without conditions;
5. *Requests* the Secretary-General to submit a comprehensive report, taking into account, inter alia, the observations of the Advisory Committee and based on the experience gained so far, and make suggestions for any modification to the current reporting cycle to the Working Group on Reimbursement of Contingent-owned Equipment at its forthcoming meeting, scheduled for February 2004;
6. *Also requests* the Secretary-General to submit a comprehensive report, on the basis of recommendations of the Working Group, on issues that would require legislative action by the General Assembly at its fifty-ninth session.

Write-off of contingent-owned equipment

Note of Secretary-General. In response to General Assembly decision 56/470 [YUN 2002, p. 81], the Secretary-General submitted an April note [A/57/788] summarizing the status of the processing and settlement of contingent-owned equipment written off at seven liquidated missions. He said that all of the 1,365 cases pending for the 2001-2002 period had been processed. Out of the total reimbursable amount of $34,818,855, $27,561,460 had been paid. Of the remaining amount, $2,348,538 was under certification/placed in accounts payable; $3,861,455 was awaiting the concurrence of five Member States; $1,047,403 was awaiting funding for certification; and $67,727 had been placed in accounts receivable. The Secretariat was requesting Member States to concur with the proposed amounts in order to certify those claims by 30 June 2003.

By **decision 57/590** of 18 June, the Assembly concurred with the Secretariat's request.

Troops

In response to General Assembly resolution 55/274 [YUN 2001, p. 100], the Secretary-General, in April, submitted a report [A/57/774] in which he proposed a new methodology for reimbursement to Governments of troop costs, covering troops and formed police units. The proposed methodology for the review of rates of reimbursement was predicated on direct costs incurred by troop contributors and simplicity of the data collection, and analysis and efficiency in the reimbursement process. The troop-cost components would be maintained, with the addition of post-deployment medical costs and peacekeeping-related training costs. The coverage of the survey would be maintained, with specific guidelines set out in the questionnaire for the number of military personnel on which the response was to be based. Cost information for military observers would be excluded. The items of personal clothing, personal gear and equipment would be modified to reflect the soldier's kit. Medical requirements, excluding those considered as national responsibility or endemic to specific peacekeeping operations, would be revised on the basis of the manual on contingent-owned equipment. Requirements for peacekeeping-related training would be updated on the basis of the proposed DPKO training manual. The proposed methodology would also include criteria for determining the validity of the survey. The Secretary-General proposed that the Assembly consider changing the periodicity of the review to a five-year cycle. The proposed questionnaire, which was annexed to the Secretary-General's report, would reflect the cost components in the new methodology.

In introducing the report in the Fifth Committee [A/C.5/57/SR.52], the UN Controller noted that it had taken into account the views of Member States as reflected in the proposals of the post-Phase V Working Group on reformed procedures for determining reimbursement of contingent-owned equipment [YUN 2001, p. 100], which had failed to agree on a methodology for determining reimbursement. The general principles to be taken into account in the reimbursement of troop costs should be built into the Organization's agreements with troop contributors.

GENERAL ASSEMBLY ACTION

On 18 June [meeting 90], the General Assembly, on the recommendation of the Fifth Committee [A/57/656/Add.1], adopted **resolution 57/321** without vote [agenda item 126].

Review of the rates of reimbursement to the Governments of troop-contributing States

The General Assembly,

Having considered the report of the Secretary-General on the review of the rates of reimbursement to the Governments of troop-contributing States,

1. *Decides* to request the Working Group on reform procedures for determining reimbursement of contingent-owned equipment to consider the proposed methodology contained in the report of the Secretary-General;

2. *Requests* the Working Group to report on the results of its review to the General Assembly at its fifty-ninth session through the Advisory Committee on Administrative and Budgetary Questions.

Management of peacekeeping assets

Liquidation

The General Assembly had before it in June the Secretary-General's 2002 report [YUN 2002, p. 83], by which he transmitted the OIOS update of the status of implementation of its recommendations on mission liquidation activities at the United Nations [A/56/896] and a follow-up review of the status of those recommendations [A/57/622]. It also considered ACABQ's April report [A/57/772], which concluded, from the findings and observations of the Board of Auditors on the liquidation of field missions [A/57/5, vol. II], that numerous problems relating to liquidation had occurred because of the lack of budgeting, finance, accounting, procurement and inventory management skills. ACABQ stressed that staff possessing those skills in missions under liquidation should be given the opportunity to serve in other missions. Recalling its earlier comments on the persistent weaknesses of the mission liquidation process and the lengthy period between the end of a mission and the date of the final performance report, ACABQ remained concerned that all the weaknesses relating to the Secretariat's capacity to handle liquidations and other related tasks had not been fully addressed. Moreover, the expected guidelines for mission liquidation had not been promulgated. The Committee noted some improvements in the liquidation of UNMIBH (see p. 398), but was not convinced that a roster of properly qualified and experienced personnel in mission liquidation was being maintained. ACABQ recommended that the Secretary-General make innovative proposals for using and retaining peacekeeping operation personnel in those areas. However, it stressed that contractual appointments of limited duration to work for peacekeeping operations should not give rise to expectations of offers of career appointments at the United Nations.

By **decision 57/588** of 18 June, the Assembly deferred until its fifty-eighth session consideration of the OIOS 2002 reports.

Field assets control system

In response to General Assembly resolution 56/290 [YUN 2002, p. 83], the Secretary-General submitted a March report on progress in the implementation of the field assets control system (FACS) [A/57/765], covering developments since his previous report in 2001 [YUN 2001, p. 102]. The

Secretary-General said that the Communications and Information Technology Service had decided that FACS should be phased out by mid-2004 and replaced by an upgraded web-based system, Galileo, using structured query language. The new system would include additional data-management, analysis and reporting tools for more effective, reliable and timely information management and enhanced data exchange and reporting. Galileo would be centrally managed and administered from UNLB and UN Headquarters. It would enhance the ability of the Logistics Support Division to effectively monitor property records and allow other field missions to review the property registers of existing missions to maximize the use of the Organization's assets. The web-based system would also enhance real-time reporting and be more intuitive and user-friendly.

The Galileo system, which would be integrated with the Mercury procurement system and the Integrated Management Information System, would be implemented at UNLB in July and at Headquarters in August 2003, and would be deployed in all current missions by March 2004. Once Galileo was fully implemented in all missions, FACS would be decommissioned.

By **decision 57/588** of 18 June, the Assembly deferred to its fifty-eighth (2003) session consideration of the Secretary-General's report on FACS.

Procurement and inventory management

ACABQ, in April [A/57/772], noted that the Board of Auditors, in its report for the financial period ended 30 June 2002 [A/57/5, vol. II], had identified problems in procurement and contract management relating to the issue of a code of ethics for procurement and inadequate training of procurement officers, among other issues. ACABQ found timely and essential the Board's recommendation that the Administration expedite the promulgation and implementation of a code of ethics and declaration of independence by all staff members associated with the procurement cycle. It welcomed the Board's intention to update the audit manual to take account of best practices, and requested the Board to follow up on the implementation of its recommendation on a code of ethics.

With regard to training, ACABQ trusted that the implementation of the Procurement Division's training programme would eliminate the deficiencies identified by the Board. It noted DPKO's intention to conduct a comprehensive review of the acquisition process and requested the Board to follow up on the issues reflected in its report and to include the related information in its next audit report on peacekeeping operations.

As to inventory management, ACABQ was concerned that no progress had been made in achieving efficiency in recording and accounting for inventory and in the work of the Local Property Survey Boards. It stressed that the volume and value of the Organization's inventory in peacekeeping operations demanded that greater attention be paid to proper and effective inventory management, including disposal of obsolete and unusable assets. The Administration should report to the Board of Auditors on the implementation of its recommendations on inventory management and the Board was asked to ascertain whether changes had been made to remedy the inefficiency and other weaknesses it had identified in its current and previous audits.

In **resolution 57/290 B** of 18 June (see p. 83), the Assembly requested the Secretary-General to submit to its resumed fifty-eighth (2004) session a comprehensive report on procurement and contract management for peacekeeping operations.

OIOS report. In January [A/57/718], the Secretary-General, in response to General Assembly resolutions 48/218 B [YUN 1994, p. 1362] and 54/244 [YUN 1999, p. 1274], transmitted the OIOS report on the audit of the procurement of goods and services by DPKO through letters of assist to determine the effectiveness of that procurement method and DPKO's compliance with the relevant Financial Regulations and Rules. A sample of 35 letters of assist valued at $71.4 million was reviewed out of the 274 issued by DPKO valued at $183 million during 2000-2001.

The audit showed that the Procurement Division of the Office of Central Support Services had not revised the guidelines for administering letters of assist, nor had DPKO drawn up a comprehensive list of strictly military goods and services that were unavailable through commercial sources. Letters of assist sometimes included goods and services that could be procured from commercial sources through competitive bidding. DPKO's Finance Management and Support Service had made $11.6 million in payments before the relevant letters of assist were completed and/or signed by the providing Government and had processed claims for goods and services without the required letters of assist. DPKO's selection criteria were also unclear.

To increase transparency and ensure more economical procurement, OIOS recommended that DPKO: ensure that letters of assist were expeditiously prepared and submitted for government signature in order to adequately obligate funds and support payments; promulgate, in consultation with the Procurement Division, revised guidelines for letters of assist that specified the prerequisites for their use, included selection procedures, and required the use of cost-comparison methods; discontinue the use of letters of assist for procuring medical supplies, transferring that responsibility to the Procurement Division, except for supplies provided under memorandums of understanding with Member States; establish, in cooperation with the Procurement Division, a roster of Governments willing to provide goods and services under letters of assist and develop competitive procurement procedures for their award; and ensure that the issuance of letters of assist was based on adequate cost comparison and analysis of competitive offers obtained from the largest possible number of Member States.

OIOS also recommended that the UN Controller review and authorize the payment of claims that were not supported by a duly signed letter of assist after obtaining the necessary justification for such claims from DPKO.

The Assembly, in **resolution 57/287 C** of 15 April (see p. 1387), requested the Secretary-General to ensure that the applicable OIOS recommendations were implemented fully by relevant departments and peacekeeping missions.

UN Logistics Base

The General Assembly, at its resumed fifty-seventh session, considered the financial performance report of the United Nations Logistics Base in Brindisi for the period 1 July 2001 to 30 June 2002 [A/57/671]. Expenditures for the period totalled $8,970,800 gross ($8,149,600 net), resulting in an unencumbered balance of $11,800 gross ($24,800 net). The Assembly was asked to take action on that balance and on the interest income of $289,000, other/miscellaneous income of $156,000 and savings on or cancellation of prior-period obligations of $246,000.

The Assembly also had before it the proposed budget for the period 1 July 2003 to 30 June 2004, amounting to $23,262,900 gross ($22,004,400 net) [A/57/670 & Corr.1], which represented an increase of $8,969,700 gross in total resources in relation to the apportionment for the previous period. The proposed increase reflected an 11.9 per cent rise in civilian personnel costs, a 103.1 per cent increase in operational costs, and a 2.7 per cent increase in staff assessment. The budget provided for the deployment of 37 international and 99 national staff.

Commenting on the performance report for 2001/02, ACABQ, in April [A/57/772/Add.9], requested that information on the technique used and the experience gained in identifying and estimating the cost of each service provided on a reimbursable basis be made available to peacekeeping missions, and that a methodology for reflecting the impact of reimbursable expenditure in the budget estimates be developed and used in the next budget estimate.

Regarding the 2003/04 budget estimates, ACABQ recommended that the current budget presentation be maintained, and that the Secretary-General consolidate the report on the implementation of the strategic deployment stocks with that on the budget and performance of UNLB. It requested a comprehensive examination of the merits of transferring to UNLB post and non-post resources of the support account for peacekeeping operations earmarked for meeting communications and information technology needs and retaining at Headquarters only a few posts for policy and liaison functions. It did not recommend approval of the proposed increases for miscellaneous supplies, services and equipment, training and travel. ACABQ recommended that the unencumbered balance and other income from the previous period be applied to the 2003/04 proposed budget and that the Assembly approve cost estimates of $22,208,100 gross for the period 1 July 2003 to 30 June 2004.

In June [A/C.5/57/38], the Secretary-General submitted to the Fifth Committee a note on the amounts to be apportioned in respect of each peacekeeping mission, including the prorated share of UNLB for the period 1 July 2003 to 30 June 2004.

GENERAL ASSEMBLY ACTION

On 18 June [meeting 90], the General Assembly, on the recommendation of the Fifth Committee [A/57/656/Add.1], adopted **resolution 57/320** without vote [agenda item 126].

Financing of the United Nations Logistics Base at Brindisi, Italy

The General Assembly,

Recalling section XIV of its resolution 49/233 A of 23 December 1994,

Recalling also its decision 50/500 of 17 September 1996 on the financing of the United Nations Logistics Base at Brindisi, Italy, and its subsequent resolutions thereon, the latest of which was resolution 56/289 of 27 June 2002,

Having considered the reports of the Secretary-General on the financing of the United Nations Logistics Base and the related reports of the Advisory Committee on Administrative and Budgetary Questions,

Reiterating the importance of establishing an accurate inventory of assets,

1. *Notes with appreciation* the facilities provided by the Government of Italy to the United Nations Logistics Base at Brindisi, Italy;

2. *Takes note* of the reports of the Secretary-General;

3. *Endorses* the observations and recommendations contained in the report of the Advisory Committee on Administrative and Budgetary Questions;

4. *Requests* the Secretary-General to include in his report on a comprehensive examination of the merits of establishing a global procurement hub for all peacekeeping missions in Brindisi recommended by the Advisory Committee, the merits of relocating to Brindisi all support account post and non-post resources at Headquarters pertaining to the Logistics Division, as well as those related to communications and information technology services related to peacekeeping missions;

5. *Reiterates* the need to implement, as a matter of priority, an effective inventory management standard, especially in respect of peacekeeping operations involving high inventory value;

Financial performance report for the period from 1 July 2001 to 30 June 2002

6. *Takes note* of the report of the Secretary-General on the financial performance of the United Nations Logistics Base for the period from 1 July 2001 to 30 June 2002;

Budget estimates for the period from 1 July 2003 to 30 June 2004

7. *Approves* the cost estimates for the United Nations Logistics Base amounting to 22,208,100 United States dollars for the period from 1 July 2003 to 30 June 2004;

Financing of the cost estimates

8. *Decides* to apply the unencumbered balance and other income in the total amount of 702,800 dollars in respect of the financial period ended 30 June 2002 to the resources required for the period from 1 July 2003 to 30 June 2004;

9. *Decides also* that the increase in the estimated staff assessment income of 13,000 dollars in respect of the financial period ended 30 June 2002 shall be added to the credits from the amount referred to in paragraph 8 above;

10. *Decides further* to prorate the balance of 21,505,300 dollars among the individual active peacekeeping operation budgets to meet the financing requirements of the United Nations Logistics Base for the period from 1 July 2003 to 30 June 2004;

11. *Decides* to set off against the balance referred to in paragraph 10 above the estimated staff assessment income of 1,258,500 dollars for the period from 1 July 2003 to 30 June 2004, to be prorated among the individual active peacekeeping operation budgets;

12. *Decides also* to consider during its fifty-eighth session the question of the financing of the United Nations Logistics Base.

On 23 December, on the basis of a recommendation by the Secretary-General [A/58/596], supported by ACABQ [A/58/609], the Assembly, by **decision 58/557**, approved the transfer of five additional buildings pledged by Italy to UNLB. (See p. 1500 for further details.)

Personnel matters

Mission subsistence allowance

On 23 December [meeting 79], the General Assembly, having considered the 2001 OIOS report [YUN 2001, p. 104] [A/56/648] on the audit of the establishment and management of mission subsistence allowance rates, adopted, on the recommendation of the Fifth Committee [A/58/582], **resolution 58/258** without vote [agenda item 134].

Report of the Office of Internal Oversight Services on the audit of the establishment and management of mission subsistence allowance rates

The General Assembly,

Recalling its resolutions 48/218 B of 29 July 1994 and 54/244 of 23 December 1999,

Having considered the report of the Office of Internal Oversight Services on the audit of the establishment and management of mission subsistence allowance rates,

1. *Takes note* of the report of the Office of Internal Oversight Services on the audit of the establishment and management of mission subsistence allowance rates;

2. *Reaffirms* its resolution 56/246 of 24 December 2001, in particular paragraph 8;

3. *Requests* the Secretary-General to entrust the Office of Internal Oversight Services with the submission of an updated report on the question of mission subsistence allowance rates to the General Assembly at the second part of its resumed fifty-eighth session.

Death and disability benefits

At its resumed fifty-seventh session, the General Assembly considered the Secretary-General's annual reports on the processing of death and disability claims in 2001 [YUN 2002, p. 85] and 2002 [A/C.5/57/37], submitted in response to Assembly decision 54/459 B [YUN 2000, p. 113] and ACABQ recommendations [YUN 2001, p. 105]. He indicated that, during 2002, 82 claims were received, bringing the total number of claims available for processing to 160. Of that number, 126 were processed for a total value of $2,962,236, leaving 34 pending as at 31 December 2002, including 21 for which documentation from troop contributors was lacking. All claims based on the old methodology had been processed. The new methodology was working well and the Claims and Information Management Section had been able to process claims in a timely manner. The Secretary-General suggested that the Assembly might consider whether there was a continuing need for annual reporting outside the framework of the overall claims processing.

ACABQ, in April [A/57/772], recommended that future information on death and disability benefits be included in the overview of the general report on peacekeeping operations.

GENERAL ASSEMBLY ACTION

On 18 June [meeting 90], the General Assembly, on the recommendation of the Fifth Committee [A/57/656/Add.1], adopted **resolution 57/316** without vote [agenda item 126].

Death and disability benefits

The General Assembly,

Having considered the notes by the Secretary-General on death and disability benefits, as well as the related report of the Advisory Committee on Administrative and Budgetary Questions,

1. *Takes note* of the notes by the Secretary-General on death and disability benefits;
2. *Decides* that, in future, information on death and disability benefits shall be included in the overview of the general report on peacekeeping operations.

Recruitment policies and procedures

ACABQ, in April [A/57/772], pointed out that delays and deficiencies continued to plague DPKO recruitment and placement activities. Taking into account the information that upon implementation of the new staff selection system (Galaxy) the targeted time frame for filling vacancies in peacekeeping operations would be reduced from 180 to 95 days, ACABQ recommended that the General Assembly consider establishing a procedure whereby any post that became vacant or any new post that was not filled within 12 months after it became vacant or was approved should be deemed to have lapsed. It encouraged greater use of national staff, whose designation currently included both national professional officers and local staff, wherever feasible and cost-effective. While not objecting to the practice of reassigning national staff from one mission to another, since it could temporarily provide urgently needed skills at short notice, particularly in the start-up phase of new missions, ACABQ cautioned that missions needed to recruit their own staff as quickly as possible. It decided to revert to the matter in the context of its examination of the Secretary-General's report on the future of Field Service officers and to follow up on the review of the Field Service category when considering the peacekeeping budgets in 2004. Noting the considerable underexpenditure for the period 2001/02 in the civilian personnel component of some missions, resulting from the recruitment of international staff below approved grades, ACABQ was of the view that when posts were consistently filled at lower levels in missions with limited duration, the level of the higher graded posts should be reviewed and reclassified accordingly.

In general, ACABQ was of the opinion that missions should have greater authority in the hiring and management of staff. Missions needed to plan and manage more carefully the departure of staff, particularly heads of services, including the preparation of handing-over notes. There should be more collaboration among missions and between the missions and Headquarters on of that issue and on staff mobility between Headquarters and missions.

The Assembly, in **resolution 57/290 B** of 18 June (see p. 83), endorsed ACABQ's observations and recommendations on the recruitment of DPKO personnel.

Field Service category of staff

On 18 June [meeting 90], the General Assembly, having considered the 2001 OIOS report [YUN 2001, p. 106] [A/56/202] on the audit of the policies and procedures of DPKO for the recruitment of international civilian staff for field missions, adopted, on the recommendation of the Fifth Committee [A/57/656/Add.1], **resolution 57/322** without vote [agenda item 126].

Report of the Office of Internal Oversight Services on the audit of the policies and procedures of the Department of Peacekeeping Operations for recruiting international civilian staff for field missions

The General Assembly,

Recalling its resolutions 48/218 B of 29 July 1994 and 54/244 of 23 December 1999,

Having considered the report of the Office of Internal Oversight Services on the audit of the policies and procedures of the Department of Peacekeeping Operations for recruiting international civilian staff for field missions,

1. *Takes note* of the report of the Office of Internal Oversight Services;
2. *Requests* the Secretary-General to conduct, through the Office of Internal Oversight Services, a follow-up audit of the policies and procedures for recruiting international civilian staff for field missions, and to submit a report thereon to the General Assembly for its consideration at its resumed fifty-eighth session.

On 23 December [meeting 79], the Assembly, having considered the 2002 report [YUN 2002, p. 86] [A/57/78] of the Joint Inspection Unit on reforming the Field Service category of staff in UN peace operations, the Secretary-General's comments thereon [A/57/78/Add.1] and those of ACABQ [A/57/434], adopted, on the recommendation of the Fifth Committee [A/58/582], **resolution 58/257** without vote [agenda item 134].

Report of the Joint Inspection Unit on reforming the Field Service category of personnel in United Nations peace operations

The General Assembly,

Having considered the report of the Joint Inspection Unit on reforming the Field Service category of personnel in United Nations peace operations and the note by the Secretary-General transmitting his comments thereon,

Having also considered the report of the Advisory Committee on Administrative and Budgetary Questions,

1. *Takes note* of the report of the Joint Inspection Unit on reforming the Field Service category of personnel in United Nations peace operations and of the comments of the Secretary-General thereon;

2. *Also takes note* of the related observations and recommendations made by the Advisory Committee on Administrative and Budgetary Questions;

3. *Approves* recommendations 1 to 6 contained in the report of the Joint Inspection Unit.

Temporary assignments

In response to General Assembly decision 56/471 [YUN 2002, p. 86], the Secretary-General submitted, in April, a report on assignment of staff in peacekeeping missions [A/57/787]. The report reviewed each category of mission staff eligible for detail or reassignment to, or between, DPKO field missions and outlined the application and selection processes. It also reviewed the related organizational policy and guidelines in the light of relevant administrative instructions and improvements in the Department's internal mechanisms for addressing vacancy and mobility issues in field missions. Since March 2002, vacancy announcements, either generic or specific, had become the normal means of filling vacant posts in field missions; all prospective applicants had access to those announcements through the DPKO web site. Inherent in the wider use of vacancy announcements was a more transparent and competitive process providing enhanced opportunities for career development and mobility of all UN staff, international and locally recruited, in field missions.

To further enhance the integrity of the recruitment and selection process, DPKO had trained all of its mission Placement Officers and Chief Civilian Personnel Officers in competency-based interviewing. In March, it launched the Rapid Deployment Roster to enhance its ability to deploy pre-screened and pre-trained experienced field staff to a new mission within 14 days.

In conclusion, the Secretary-General stated that perhaps the most critical constraint limiting career and mobility of civilian staff in field missions was the recent reduction in the total number of posts in peacekeeping operations. However, the enhanced recruitment, selection and reassignment mechanisms were ensuring that DPKO civilian staff had greater opportunity than at any previous time to pursue and achieve career and mobility goals.

In **decision 57/588** of 18 June, the Assembly deferred until its fifty-eighth session consideration of the Secretary-General's report.

UN Volunteers

By **decision 58/564 A** of 23 December, the General Assembly deferred until its resumed fifty-eighth (2004) session consideration of the Secretary-General's 2001 report [YUN 2001, p. 814] on the participation of United Nations Volunteers in peacekeeping operations.

Conduct and discipline

The Special Committee on Peacekeeping Operations [A/57/767] affirmed the need to ensure that all UN peacekeeping personnel functioned in a manner that preserved the image, credibility, impartiality and integrity of the Organization. The Committee fully supported DPKO's initiatives to prevent misconduct, including the abuse of power and sexual exploitation, and emphasized the need to build greater awareness among UN peacekeepers of their responsibilities, including through improved pre-deployment training; it encouraged the Department to continue to develop training materials to that end.

The Special Committee recommended that common principles and guidelines for accountability be developed and incorporated into the training of UN personnel deployed in peacekeeping missions. It agreed that a single standard of conduct should apply to all peacekeeping personnel and asked the Secretariat, in consultation with troop-contributing countries, to develop a common understanding and agreed procedures for handling cases of alleged violations of the peacekeeping code of conduct. Considering that, in handling such cases, there was the need for agreement on applicable laws, the Committee requested the Secretariat to convene a meeting with Member States in 2003 to discuss ways of meeting the challenges in that area and minimizing misconduct.

The Special Committee emphasized that cases of alleged misconduct should be handled through cooperation between troop-contributing countries concerned and the mission leadership, including with regard to public information, and the need for taking action while respecting national laws. It urged the Secretariat to involve the contributing country concerned from the very outset in an investigation into any case of alleged misconduct, and to make the outcome of the investigation, including all related evidence, available to that country, in order to enable its national judicial authorities to take legal steps.

Other peacekeeping matters

Mine action

Special Committee consideration. The Special Committee on Peacekeeping Operations

[A/57/767], aware of the important role mine action could play in peacekeeping operations, said that mine action activities should be implemented in such a manner that their viable continuity was guaranteed to the maximum degree possible. It welcomed the ongoing "Study of the role of the military in mine action" being conducted at the request of the United Nations by the Geneva International Centre for Humanitarian Demining (GICHD) and hoped that its results would be useful for troop-contributing countries in conducting mine action tasks in peacekeeping operations. The Committee welcomed the rapid response plan in support of the emergency deployment of mine action assets in peacekeeping operations and humanitarian programmes, and encouraged the coordination of mine action training and mine-risk education material and procedures used by troop-contributing countries and relevant UN agenies.

Security Council consideration. On 13 November [meeting 4858], the Security Council considered the importance of mine action for peacekeeping operations. The meeting was addressed by the Under-Secretary-General for Peacekeeping Operations and Martin Dahinden, Director of GICHD.

The Under-Secretary-General said that, since the Council last considered the issue [YUN 1996, p. 42], UN mine action had made remarkable progress. The United Nations Mine Action Service within DPKO, the United Nations Development Programme and the United Nations Children's Fund were the lead actors in undertaking and coordinating mine action initiatives. The Council was going one step further by acknowledging the contribution of mine action to peacekeeping operations and to efforts to maintain international peace and security. The meeting offered an opportunity for the Council to call on a range of actors to undertake specific actions that could greatly enhance mine action in a peacekeeping context. To that end, he raised a number of issues the Council might wish to consider and address. Firstly, although there was a strong normative framework on landmines, an instrument that addressed unexploded ordnance and other explosive remnants of war would greatly facilitate post-conflict clearance efforts. The rights of mine survivors should also be reflected in the proposed international convention on protection and promotion of the rights and dignity of persons with disabilities being discussed in the General Assembly (see p. 1107). Secondly, parties to conflict should be aware of the important confidence-building role that mine action could play, and the United Nations could ensure that special representatives of the Secretary-General, negotiators, moderators and facilitators of peace processes systematically received the United Nations Mine Action Guidelines for Ceasefire and Peace Agreements. The Council could urge parties to conflicts to incorporate mine action into their discussions, whenever relevant. Thirdly, peacekeeping troops could play an important role in mine clearance and, in that regard, the Council should consider calling on troop-contributing countries to train their peacekeeping troops to demine in accordance with the International Mine Action Standards developed by GICHD. Fourthly, peacekeeping missions could collect information on the scope and impact of the landmine and unexploded ordnance problem, and fifthly, mine action could be an important part of disarmament, demobilization and reintegration programmes.

Member States should be encouraged to provide adequate and sustained financial assistance for mine action, thereby alleviating the suffering of populations affected by mines, unexploded ordnance and other explosive remnants of war.

SECURITY COUNCIL ACTION

On 19 November [meeting 4864], following consultations among Security Council members, the President made statement **S/PRST/2003/22** on behalf of the Council:

> The Security Council expresses its grave concern at the harmful and widespread impact of landmines and unexploded ordnance on civilian populations, especially children, and on humanitarian workers and United Nations staff and, in this regard, stresses the vital importance of eliminating the threat of landmines.
>
> The Council recognizes the long-term consequences of landmines and unexploded ordnance for durable peace, security and development.
>
> The Council welcomes the effective coordination of mine action activities within the United Nations system and the important mandate of the United Nations Mine Action Service of the Department of Peacekeeping Operations, in particular its role in ensuring the coordination of mine action throughout the United Nations system and the provision of support to multidimensional peacekeeping operations, as well as the role of the United Nations Development Programme in addressing the problem from a development perspective, and providing technical, management and resource mobilization assistance to Governments of mine-affected States, and the role of the United Nations Children's Fund as the lead agency for mine-risk education. The Council also recognizes the significant contribution to mine action made by States, international and regional organizations and local and international non-governmental organizations.
>
> The Council urges all Member States to respect relevant international law that addresses landmines and unexploded ordnance, and the rights of persons

affected by them, stressing the importance of international technical assistance in helping mine-affected States to harmonize their domestic laws with international obligations.

The Council urges all parties to armed conflicts to abide by their mine-related commitments, to cooperate to the fullest extent possible, with mine-risk education and mine-clearing activities, and to ensure that abandoned stockpiles are adequately guarded or destroyed.

The Council encourages Governments whose countries are affected by the presence of landmines and unexploded ordnance to include a mine action impact assessment in all development planning and to incorporate a strategic plan for mine action in the national development plans and poverty reduction strategies.

The Council recognizes that mine action can play an important role in peace-building and confidence-building in post-conflict situations, and encourages mine-affected States to strengthen cooperation with the United Nations, relevant non-governmental organizations and civil society, where appropriate.

The Council calls upon the Secretary-General to provide information on the scope and humanitarian impact of the mine and unexploded ordnance problem in all relevant country-specific reports to the Council, and expresses its readiness to consider mine action concerns in all of its country-specific deliberations, as appropriate.

The Council notes the importance of ensuring that the provision of technical advice and support for mine action is reflected in the mandates and personnel planning for peacekeeping operations, and expresses its intention to address mine action concerns in the mandates and personnel planning for peacekeeping operations, whenever appropriate.

The Council recognizes the contribution that peacekeeping personnel can make in the areas of mine-risk education and demining, and calls upon troop-contributing countries, where appropriate, to train selected personnel to demine in accordance with the International Mine Action Standards.

The Council recognizes the important role mine action can play in disarmament, demobilization and reintegration efforts by employing former soldiers in mine action programmes and encourages the Secretary-General to consider including mine action in disarmament, demobilization and reintegration initiatives and to reflect such proposals in his reports to the Council, as appropriate.

The Council urges Member States, as appropriate, to provide adequate and sustained financial assistance to support mine action and alleviate the suffering of populations affected by mines and unexploded ordnance, and, whenever possible, to increase their support through further contributions to the Voluntary Trust Fund for Assistance in Mine Action. The Council calls particular attention to the need to address the socio-economic, physical and psychosocial reintegration of landmine survivors, the need to facilitate the orderly return of refugees and internally displaced persons affected by mines and unexploded ordnance, the need to restore land to productive use, and the need to prioritize mine action efforts to enable the risk-free movement of people and goods.

The Council considers that a comprehensive and coordinated approach by Member States, the United Nations and regional and local organizations is required to address the threat and the impact of mines and unexploded ordnance.

To this end, the Council supports the general review made by the General Assembly on this matter since 1993, and invites the Secretary-General to address this subject, as needed, in his reports on the general activities of peacekeeping operations.

Cooperation with regional organizations

The Special Committee on Peacekeeping Operations [A/57/767] urged the strengthening of cooperation between the United Nations and relevant regional arrangements and agencies to enhance the capabilities of the international community in the maintenance of international peace and security. It appreciated the possibility of the practical realization of such cooperation at the regional and subregional levels and encouraged the Secretary-General to take concrete steps towards that end. In that regard, the Committee noted the successful cooperation between the United Nations and a number of subregional arrangements and agencies.

With regard to Africa, the Special Committee welcomed DPKO efforts to work closely with all relevant actors in the continent at the regional, subregional and national levels, in particular for the enhancement of the capabilities of African troop contributors and in capacity-building for regional and subregional organizations. The Committee also welcomed a close relationship among the United Nations, the African Union and subregional organizations, and encouraged those organizations, in close consultation with donors, to discuss the modalities for a suitable focal point or clearing house for activities aimed at strengthening African peacekeeping capacity.

The Committee recommended that the Secretariat study the best cases of cooperation between the United Nations and regional organizations within the context of peacekeeping in order to identify adequate modalities of cooperation and to report the results to the Committee. It also encouraged further use of existing models of cooperation, such as that between the European Union and the Organization for Security and Cooperation in Europe.

Chapter II

Africa

In 2003, Africa continued to be beset by conflicts and political dissension and the United Nations remained involved in the search for solutions. Two regions in particular were the focus of UN attention—the Great Lakes area and West Africa—and although some progress was achieved in peacemaking efforts, the conflicts raised tension and threatened to spread beyond national borders. During the year, the Security Council sent missions to both regions. The Council also examined the causes of conflict in Africa and ways to promote peace and security in order to prevent further hostilities, as did the General Assembly. The Secretary-General also sent a multidisciplinary mission to countries in the Great Lakes region in a renewed effort to move the peace process forward and to investigate the possibility of a comprehensive and integrated approach to peace, security and development. The mission found that the crisis of governance and widespread poverty were the two main underlying causes of conflict in that region.

In the Democratic Republic of the Congo (DRC), fighting between numerous armed militias, whose alliances were constantly shifting, intensified at the beginning of the year, despite signs in late 2002 of progress towards establishing a two-year transitional Government leading up to national elections. The presence of foreign troops in eastern DRC, the site of most of the fighting, further complicated the already tense situation and threatened the stability of the whole region. However, the United Nations, which had increased the size of its mission in the DRC to nearly 11,000 troops, and others continued mediation efforts. In April, participants in the Inter-Congolese Dialogue signed a Final Act endorsing measures to restore peace and national sovereignty, and agreeing to implement the framework for the transitional Government. As the parties agreed, President Joseph Kabila remained in office when a new Government was formed and some foreign troops were withdrawn. A pacification process was begun in eastern DRC, and the parties agreed to a plan for cantonment and demilitarization of their troops. The political institutions of the transitional Government began to function in late 2003, although progress remained slow.

Burundi's Transitional Government witnessed a peaceful transition of power at the level of head of State in 2003. The African Union (AU) deployed a mission to Burundi to oversee the ceasefire agreements and the United Nations Office in Burundi continued to play a role in the peace process, which included agreement by most political parties on defence and security power-sharing.

In Rwanda, which still suffered from the effects of the 1994 genocide, the Government expressed determination to bring peace to the country through reconciliation and by bringing to justice the extremists who carried the greatest responsibility for the genocide. Presidential and parliamentary elections were held, and were, for the most part, orderly. A number of former combatants returned from the DRC during the year.

A coup d'état in the Central African Republic overturned the plans for a national dialogue under President-elect Félix Patassé. Led by General François Bozizé, the new authorities, as part of a transition period, organized a national dialogue that included all political opinions, and stated their intention to hold national elections in late 2004.

Conflicts continued in West Africa, and the concurrent fighting in Côte d'Ivoire, Liberia and Sierra Leone threatened the stability of the whole region, as did the movement of armed militias and individuals between countries to seek refuge, loot and/or serve as mercenaries. The United Nations, the AU, the Economic Community of West African States (ECOWAS) and the European Union (EU) were involved in mediating efforts in those countries and in Guinea-Bissau.

Political factions of Côte d'Ivoire reached an agreement in January, signed at Linas-Marcoussis, France, on a power-sharing mechanism to govern the country, but little progress was made in implementing its terms. The three main rebel movements (the Forces Nouvelles) seized control of the northern half of the country and the Government retained control of the south. In May, the Security Council created the United Nations Mission in Côte d'Ivoire (MINUCI), with an initial strength of 255 troops, to complement and eventually replace the ECOWAS and French forces already serving as peacekeepers. In May, the opposition parties withdrew from the Government of National Reconciliation and fighting resumed; however, the peace process took hold again in December when the two sides agreed to resume disarmament and demobilization of troops, and the opposition rejoined the Government.

In Liberia, rebel movements gained control of nearly two thirds of the country, and elections, originally scheduled for October, were postponed until 2004 due to the resumption of civil war. Although a ceasefire was signed in June by the Government and two rebel groups, it was soon violated and Liberia was plunged into a new cycle of violence. ECOWAS sent a vanguard peacekeeping force to the country in August, which was followed by a multinational force and, on 7 October, by the United Nations Mission in Liberia (UNMIL), which was established by the Security Council with a mandated maximum strength of 15,000 troops. Following the departure of President Charles Taylor from the country, a peace agreement was signed by the Government, two rebel groups, political parties and civil society leaders, providing for a national transitional Government. By the end of the year, some mechanisms for its implementation were set up, but the armed groups had not yet complied with its terms.

Sierra Leone remained relatively calm in 2003 as the Government continued, after 10 years of civil war, to disarm ex-combatants and reintegrate them into society. Having set benchmarks for the withdrawal of the United Nations Mission in Sierra Leone (UNAMSIL) peacekeeping troops, the Security Council approved the Mission's reduction from nearly 16,000 troops to 11,500 by the end of the year. Fighting continued to occur along the Sierra Leone/Liberia border, and fighting in Liberia caused thousands of refugees to flee to Sierra Leone, threatening the security on the Sierra Leonean side of the border. The Government made efforts to reduce tensions internally, in particular by establishing a special court to try war crimes and by regaining control of diamond mining.

Guinea-Bissau's serious political and economic situation deteriorated in 2003. Opposition leaders accused the Government of arbitrary decision-making, restrictions on the media and harassment of political opponents. A non-violent coup d'état, led by the military, overturned the Government in September. An agreement was reached on a transitional Government, which pledged to hold legislative and presidential elections within 6 and 18 months, respectively.

The United Nations continued to mediate in the Eritrea-Ethiopia border dispute and in monitoring the implementation of the 2000 Algiers Agreements on a ceasefire and solving the border issue. Following the completion in 2002 of the border's delimitation, efforts focused in 2003 on demarcation of the border. Both sides were presented with maps of the delimited border and asked for comments. Ethiopia, which had previously accepted the delimitation decision, questioned the boundary, leaving the path for future progress unclear at the end of the year. The situation on the ground remained calm, despite some restrictions on the movement of the United Nations Mission in Ethiopia and Eritrea (UNMEE). Progress was made in the release of the remaining prisoners of war.

The parties to the national reconciliation process in Somalia, begun in 2002 at the Eldoret (Kenya) Conference, continued to participate in discussions on setting up federal governance structures and establishing a ceasefire; the United Nations remained involved in the discussions. Nevertheless, fighting continued in parts of Somalia, especially in Mogadishu and Baidoa, blocking airports and seaports and thus slowing delivery of humanitarian aid.

The United Nations pursued efforts to hold a referendum in Western Sahara, which would give the people the right to decide the fate of the Territory, by electing either independence or integration with Morocco. The decision to hold a referendum was made in 1990 by the Government of Morocco and the Frente Popular para la Liberación de Saguía el-Hamra y de Río de Oro (POLISARIO). In 2003, the Secretary-General's Personal Envoy attempted to break the deadlock over the form of any future Government by proposing a new peace plan. POLISARIO eventually accepted the plan, but Morocco had not given a definitive response by the end of the year. The Identification Commission completed its work on the electronic archiving of the nearly 145,000 individual files of persons who applied to be included on the list of voters. During the year, POLISARIO released 643 Moroccan prisoners of war and continued to hold another 600 in detention.

Angola demonstrated in 2003 that it was firmly on the path of political, social and economic recovery, following the 2002 signing of a memorandum of understanding between the Government and the National Union for the Total Independence of Angola (UNITA). Discussions were held by the two sides in 2003 on the structure of the new Government, and agreement was reached on a basic framework. The Government announced that the next general elections would be held in 2004. The Secretary-General reported that the United Nations Mission in Angola (UNMA) had completed its political mandate, and recommended that the UN Resident Coordinator take over responsibility for UN system activities in Angola.

In the Sudan, the situation improved following the 2002 signing of the Machakos Protocol by the Government and the rebel group, the Sudan People's Liberation Movement/Army (SPLM/A), which provided for autonomy in SPLM/A territory in the south for six years and for holding negotiations on a comprehensive ceasefire. As security improved in 2003, delivery of humanitarian assistance increased; however, armed conflict and ethnic violence continued and natural calamities caused large-scale displacement of people. In September, the Government and SPLM/A signed an agreement on security arrangements, providing for the Sudan to have two armies under separate command and control during the six-year interim period.

The Libyan Arab Jamahiriya announced steps it had taken to comply with 1992 and 1993 Security Council resolutions, which had imposed sanctions against it. Actions taken concerned handing over the Libyan nationals charged with the 1988 bombing of Pan Am flight 103 to the appropriate authorities, payment of compensation to the families of the victims, and acceptance of responsibility for the action of Libyan officials. In September, the Council lifted its sanctions. Libya announced in December that it was halting its programmes for developing weapons of mass destruction.

Promotion of peace in Africa

The General Assembly and the Security Council continued, throughout 2003, to examine the causes of conflict in Africa and ways to promote sustainable peace and development on the continent. In January, Angola took over from Mauritius the chairmanship of the Ad Hoc Working Group on Conflict Prevention and Resolution in Africa; the Council agreed that the Working Group would continue its work until the end of the year. The Working Group reported in December on its consideration of: cooperation between the Security Council and the Economic and Social Council; confidence-building in African regions affected by conflict; enhancing the Security Council's role in prevention and resolution of African conflicts; and enhancing cooperation with the African Union (AU) and subregional organizations.

The Security Council held a meeting in May to consider how Council missions and UN mechanisms could promote peace and security to prevent conflicts in Africa. The Council dispatched two missions to Africa—to Central Africa in June and to West Africa in June/July.

In December, the General Assembly adopted **resolution 58/235** (see p. 106) on implementation of the Secretary-General's 1998 recommendations dealing with the causes of conflict and the promotion of durable peace and sustainable development in Africa.

Appointments. The Secretary-General, on 27 January [S/2003/125], informed the Security Council of his decision to extend until February 2004 the mandate of Ibrahim Gambari as his Adviser for Special Assignments in Africa. Mr. Gambari was participating actively in promoting the peace process in Angola and was advising the Secretary-General on other issues relating to Africa and on the work of the Ad Hoc Open-ended Working Group on the Causes of Conflict and the Promotion of Durable Peace and Sustainable Development in Africa. The Secretary-General also intended to entrust Mr. Gambari with the coordination of the preparation of special reports on Africa in the Secretariat and to place under his responsibility the resources allocated to the Office of the Special Coordinator for Africa and the Least Developed Countries. On 31 January [S/2003/126], the Council took note of the appointment.

The Council, on 7 January [S/2003/11], appointed Ismael Abraão Gaspar Martins, the Permanent Representative of Angola to the United Nations, as Chairman of the Ad Hoc Working Group on Conflict Prevention and Resolution in Africa, established on 1 March 2002 [YUN 2002, p. 93], for a period ending 1 March 2003. On 28 February [S/2003/235], the Council agreed that the Working Group would continue its work until 31 December 2003 and that Mr. Gaspar Martins would continue as Chairman.

Security Council consideration. The Security Council, on 30 May [meeting 4766], discussed "Conflicts in Africa: Security Council missions and United Nations mechanisms to promote peace and security", aimed at exploring how the UN system could promote durable solutions and peace and stability in Africa. As the Council President for May (Pakistan) explained in an August assessment of his presidency [S/2003/826], he had proposed, in a non-paper, that on the eve of Council missions to the Central and West African subregions in June and July, the Council should examine UN involvement with Africa and discuss the efficacy of missions and of other mechanisms for UN engagement with the continent, the imperative of moving from conflict management to conflict prevention and final resolution, the need to find further ways to deepen engagement with Africa, and the desirability of a comprehensive and integrated approach, including cooperation between the main UN organs.

Addressing the Council, the Secretary-General's Adviser for Special Assignments in Africa said that Council missions to Africa were a clear demonstration of engagement with crises and conflicts on the continent. However, they needed to be effective instruments for conflict prevention, management and resolution. Mission locations, timing and expected accomplishments needed to be addressed, and the Council should explore linkages between peace and security, on the one hand, and social and economic development, on the other. He suggested that the Council apply lessons learned from previous missions, by using multidisciplinary UN expert support before and after missions, collaborating actively with regional and subregional organizations, taking regional and global dimensions into account, and planning post-conflict peace-building efforts involving the United Nations, the Bretton Woods institutions (the World Bank Group and the International Monetary Fund) and donor countries. The forthcoming missions to Central Africa (see p. 109) and West Africa (see p. 163) would enable the Council to evaluate the current mandate and resources of the various UN peace operations, to revisit the possibility of convening an international conference on the Great Lakes region, and to assess the capacity of regional organizations to participate in peace operations.

The Chairman of the Ad Hoc Working Group on Conflict Prevention and Resolution in Africa (see p. 104) focused on the need for enhancing the efficiency of the mechanisms currently used by the United Nations in its engagement with Africa, especially the growing role of ad hoc working groups, which, if properly used, could be important tools in promoting peace and dealing with crises. The working groups should cooperate and coordinate with sanctions committees, as sanctions were useful in guaranteeing compliance with internationally accepted norms, leading to the resolution of conflict, as had happened in Angola. The Chairman said the fact that recommendations made by the Ad Hoc Working Group on Conflict Prevention and Resolution in Africa in 2002 [YUN 2002, p. 93] had not been implemented continued to be of great concern and indicated a need to make the recommendations of working groups more implementable and action-friendly.

The Council President for May issued on 11 July [S/2003/705] a summary of the suggestions made during the 30 May meeting on Africa. Among other things, members made general suggestions with regard to the need to take the regional and global dimensions of African conflicts fully into account; the importance of the "partnership" of the Security Council with African regional and subregional organizations and the requirement for greater balance and harmony between regional efforts and Council action; the need for the Council to back up regional initiatives with both political and financial support and to follow up on the implementation of its own decisions and resolutions; and the requirement for African capabilities in the fields of conflict prevention, management and resolution to be strengthened. Specific suggestions were made with regard to: Security Council missions as effective instruments for conflict prevention, management and resolution; conflict prevention measures; addressing the root causes of Africa's conflicts; the illegal exploitation of resources; the proliferation of small arms and light weapons; illegal armed groups from neighbouring countries; sanctions; peacekeeping operations; disarmament, demobilization and reintegration; the humanitarian and human rights dimension; peace and development; other UN mechanisms; intra-United Nations coordination; and new mechanisms.

Working Group. On 22 December [S/2003/1188], the Security Council President transmitted a letter from the Chairman of the Ad Hoc Working Group on Conflict Prevention and Resolution in Africa, established by the Council in 2002 [YUN 2002, p. 93], by which he submitted the report on the Working Group's activities. The Group's work had focused on enhancing cooperation between the Security Council and the Economic and Social Council; promoting confidence-building in African regions affected by conflicts; enhancing the Security Council's role in preventing and resolving conflicts in Africa; and enhancing cooperation with the AU and African subregional organizations.

The Working Group held two joint meetings with the Ad Hoc Advisory Group on Guinea-Bissau, established by the Economic and Social Council by decision 2002/304 [YUN 2002, p. 920], and the Group of Friends of Guinea-Bissau, prior to two Security Council meetings on Guinea-Bissau (see pp. 225 and 227). It also coordinated efforts with the Economic and Social Council Advisory Group on Burundi (see p. 947).

The Working Group participated in preparations for the Security Council mission to the Central African region and to the joint Security Council/Economic and Social Council mission to Guinea-Bissau, both in June.

With regard to conflict prevention and resolution, the Working Group, in April, considered the situation in the Democratic Republic of the Congo (DRC), stressing the need for a firm commitment by the Security Council to prevent the events in the Ituri region from having an adverse impact on the peace process. Following the Council's 20 November public briefing on preparations for convening an international conference on the Great Lakes region (see p. 112), the Working Group met with non-members of the Council to discuss the issue. The Working Group also undertook consultations with the AU and African subregional organizations to enhance cooperation between them and the United Nations in conflict prevention and resolution.

Report of Secretary-General. In response to General Assembly resolution 57/296 [YUN 2002, p. 97], the Secretary-General submitted a report in September [A/58/352] on implementation of the recommendations contained in his 1998 report on the causes of conflict and the promotion of durable peace and sustainable development in Africa [YUN 1998, p. 66]. The September report updated information contained in a 2002 follow-up report on the subject [YUN 2002, p. 95], discussing progress in implementing the recommendations concerning responding to conflict situations by appointing special mediators or special commissions to examine the sources of dispute and recommend solutions; stopping arms proliferation and halting increases in military expenditure; UN peacekeeping in Africa; UN support for African initiatives to resolve disputes; protecting civilians in conflict situations; refugees' security issues; post-conflict reconstruction and development; and providing structural adjustment programmes. It also described action to build durable peace and encourage sustainable development by: promoting good governance; securing respect for human rights and the rule of law; enhancing administrative capacity; creating a positive environment for investment and economic growth; emphasizing social development; investing in human resources; supporting public health priorities; eliminating discrimination against women; restructuring international aid; reducing the debt burden; opening international markets; supporting regional cooperation and integration; and harmonizing international and bilateral initiatives.

Although progress had been made over the review period, it had been slow and uneven. The efforts of African countries and the international community needed to be accelerated in order to implement the recommendations in a timely manner. Among problems encountered were lack of political will, persistent conflicts, weak governance, weak human and institutional capacity for economic management and administration, and limited financial resources to tackle development challenges, particularly reconstruction and rehabilitation in post-conflict countries. In view of the multiplicity of reporting frameworks in which the UN system addressed the issues raised in the Secretary-General's report and the numerous forums in which they were reviewed, it was proposed that the current format for reporting on implementation of the Secretary-General's recommendations be discontinued. Instead, the follow-up and reporting on implementation should be mainstreamed in the existing reports of the Secretary-General and the UN subsidiary bodies.

GENERAL ASSEMBLY ACTION

On 23 December [meeting 78], the General Assembly adopted **resolution 58/235** [draft: A/58/L.56 & Add.1] without vote [agenda item 39 (b)].

Implementation of the recommendations contained in the report of the Secretary-General on the causes of conflict and the promotion of durable peace and sustainable development in Africa

The General Assembly,

Recalling the report of the Open-ended Ad Hoc Working Group on the Causes of Conflict and the Promotion of Durable Peace and Sustainable Development in Africa, and resolutions 53/92 of 7 December 1998, 54/234 of 22 December 1999, 55/217 of 21 December 2000, 55/281 of 1 August 2001, 56/37 of 4 December 2001, 57/296 of 20 December 2002 and 57/337 of 3 July 2003,

Recalling also, in this context, Security Council resolutions 1325(2000) of 31 October 2000 on women and peace and security, and 1366(2001) of 30 August 2001 on the prevention of armed conflicts,

Having considered the updated matrix for 2002 contained in the report of the Secretary-General on the implementation of the recommendations contained in the report of the Secretary-General on the causes of conflict and the promotion of durable peace and sustainable development in Africa,

Recalling its resolution 57/7 of 4 November 2002 on the final review and appraisal of the United Nations New Agenda for the Development of Africa in the 1990s and support for the New Partnership for Africa's Development,

Noting that prevention of conflict must remain the fundamental focus of the work of the United Nations and that peace, security and development, in particular within post-conflict contexts, are inextricably linked,

Noting also that conflict prevention and the consolidation of peace require coordinated, sustained and integrated efforts from the United Nations system and Member States,

Recalling section VII of the United Nations Millennium Declaration, which highlights the special needs of Africa,

Reaffirming that the implementation of the recommendations contained in the report of the Secretary-

General on the causes of conflict and the promotion of durable peace and sustainable development in Africa must remain a priority on the agenda of the United Nations system and of the Member States,

Underscoring the fact that the responsibility for peace and security in Africa, including the capacity to address the root causes of conflict and to resolve conflicts in a peaceful manner, lies primarily with African countries themselves and with regional and subregional structures,

Underscoring also the need to strengthen further the political will to ensure the required political, financial and technical support critical for the effective implementation of the recommendations in all of the areas included in the report of the Secretary-General,

Reaffirming that the General Assembly must continue to play the primary role in monitoring the implementation of the recommendations contained in the report of the Secretary-General and assessing the progress made,

1. *Takes note with appreciation* of the updated matrix for 2002 contained in the report of the Secretary-General on the implementation of the recommendations contained in the report of the Secretary-General on the causes of conflict and the promotion of durable peace and sustainable development in Africa, and the further advances in a wide range of areas made since the last progress report;

2. *Notes with appreciation* that many strides have been made in the prevention and settlement of disputes and that there have been sustained efforts by African regional and subregional initiatives of late to mediate and resolve conflicts;

3. *Requests* Member States to ensure that such initiatives continue to be taken in close consultation and coordination with the United Nations in order to ensure that the United Nations can have a clear role, as appropriate, in the subsequent implementation of such mediated settlements;

4. *Welcomes* the efforts undertaken by African countries towards the establishment of a Peace and Security Council within the African Union, and encourages the States members of the African Union that have not yet ratified the protocol relating to the establishment of the Council to do so;

5. *Encourages* African countries to continue their efforts to develop African capacity to undertake peace-support operations at the regional and subregional levels and the United Nations and donor countries to establish suitable mechanisms to assist African States in developing their capacity to undertake peace-support operations in a coherent and coordinated manner;

6. *Welcomes* the European Union decision to establish a peace facility to support the establishment of the African Peace and Security Mechanism and the implementation of peace initiatives undertaken by the African Union;

7. *Also welcomes* the establishment of the Ad Hoc Working Group on Conflict Prevention and Resolution in Africa of the Security Council and of the Ad Hoc Advisory Group on African Countries Emerging from Conflict, within the framework of the Economic and Social Council;

8. *Notes with concern* that progress in the implementation of the recommendations in the report of the Secretary-General remains slow and uneven;

9. *Notes* that conflict prevention and peace consolidation efforts, in particular efforts to eradicate poverty, promote respect for human rights, strengthen rule-of-law institutions, re-establish transparent and accountable public administration, encourage democratic reform and demobilize, disarm and reintegrate ex-combatants should be supported by Member States and the United Nations system through enhanced coordination, coherence and sustained financial and political support;

10. *Decides* to continue to monitor the implementation of the recommendations contained in the report of the Secretary-General on the causes of conflict and the promotion of durable peace and sustainable development in Africa;

11. *Welcomes* the designation of the Office of the Special Adviser on Africa as a focal point within the Secretariat which should continue to monitor, through the already established interdepartmental task force on Africa affairs, the implementation of the recommendations contained in the report of the Secretary-General on the causes of conflict and the promotion of durable peace and sustainable development in Africa, with special regard being given to preventive action and post-conflict peace consolidation, and make recommendations as to how the implementation of those recommendations could be further enhanced;

12. *Calls upon* Member States to provide financial and technical assistance in a coordinated and sustained way in order to support activities to eradicate poverty, promote respect for human rights, strengthen rule-of-law institutions and promote transparent and accountable public administration;

13. *Encourages* the Secretary-General to explore and recommend suitable arrangements and mechanisms through which Member States could more effectively address the multidisciplinary causes of conflict, including their regional dimensions, and strengthen the coordinated and sustained manner in which they could provide financial and technical assistance in preventive action as well as post-conflict peace-building;

14. *Requests* the Secretary-General to submit to the General Assembly at its fifty-ninth session a report on the implementation of the present resolution, taking into account recent developments related to the cooperation of Africa with the international community on these matters.

The Economic and Social Council, in follow-up to resolution 2002/1 [YUN 2002, p. 919], stressed the need to assess progress made in the implementation of recommendations made by ad hoc advisory groups on African countries emerging from conflict (**resolution 2003/50**) (see p. 947).

Central Africa and Great Lakes region

In 2003, both the Security Council and the Secretary-General sent missions to Central Africa in an effort to move the peace process forward in the countries of the region. In the DRC, the Council encouraged the Congolese parties to put into practice the agreement reached in December 2002 (the All-Inclusive Agreement) on a two-year transition period, to be followed by national elections. Its focus in Burundi was to urge the parties to carry forward with the second phase of the transition under its new President, with assistance from the regional mediators and the African peacekeeping mission. The Secretary-General's multidisciplinary mission determined that the major underlying causes of conflict in the subregion were the crisis of governance and widespread poverty.

The UN Standing Advisory Committee on Security Questions in Central Africa held two sessions in 2003 (see pp. 111 and 573), at which it reviewed the geopolitical and security situation in the subregion, evaluated implementation of its previous decisions and recommendations, and made new recommendations.

The United Nations and the AU began preparations for holding in 2004 an international conference on the Great Lakes region, which would aim to agree on a set of principles to help end the cycle of conflict and ensure peace, security, democracy and good governance and development in that region. The Security Council considered that such a conference would help build on the progress made in the DRC and Burundi peace processes to promote the national reconciliation process in all countries of the region.

Within the region, the DRC faced the most intractable problems, particularly at the beginning of the year when there was an upsurge of violence in the eastern parts of the country. The presence of foreign troops contributed to the confusing situation of warfare among numerous armed militias. The United Nations Organization Mission in the Democratic Republic of the Congo (MONUC) remained in the country to assist in the implementation of the 1999 Lusaka Ceasefire Agreement, among other tasks, and the Security Council increased its size to a maximum of 10,800 troops. During the period of heightened conflict, the United Nations remained involved in mediation efforts, in coordination with others, especially Angola and South Africa. In April, the participants in the Inter-Congolese Dialogue signed a Final Act endorsing a package of agreements on restoring peace and national sovereignty, including the All-Inclusive Agreement of December 2002. As provided for under its terms, Joseph Kabila was sworn in as President when the new transitional Government was formed. The principal political institutions of the transition began to function in late 2003. However, the political parties remained unable to overcome their mutual distrust and progress remained slow.

After 10 years of conflict, developments in Burundi in 2003 followed a mostly positive trajectory towards fulfilling the terms of the 2000 Arusha Agreement on Peace and Reconciliation, by which the signatories outlined plans for a three-year transitional Government and the eventual integration of the Burundi national defence force, with equal numbers of Hutu and Tutsi troops. Although not signed by all the armed groups, much of the Agreement was implemented or was under discussion in 2003. Among the most significant positive developments during the year were the decision by President Buyoya to step down on 1 May under arrangements for the transitional Government, the deployment of an African mission in Burundi to oversee ceasefire agreements, and the signing in November of a comprehensive ceasefire implementation document. The United Nations Office in Burundi remained involved in the peace process, and the Secretary-General enlarged it by adding five specialized staff and other support personnel.

At the time when peace processes in the DRC and Burundi were showing signs of progress, Rwanda was emerging from the shadow of the 1994 genocide and the Government expressed its determination to bring lasting peace to the country and the region, noting that former combatants were returning from the DRC. Presidential and parliamentary elections were held in a mostly orderly manner. As proposed by the AU, the General Assembly decided to designate 7 April 2004 as the International Day of Reflection on the Genocide in Rwanda.

In the Central African Republic, a coup d'état in March, led by General François Bozizé, preempted the expected installation of President-elect Félix Patassé and interrupted plans for a national dialogue. Nevertheless, the new authorities pledged to organize the national dialogue during a transition period leading up to national elections in 2004. An interim Government under the National Transition Council would reportedly include all political parties, including that of former President Patassé. The Central African Economic and Monetary Community sent a multinational force to the country, which was later joined by French forces, to help the new administration restore stability. Held in late 2003 at the Government's initiative, a national dialogue drew up recommendations on a new constitution and electoral procedure.

On 30 October [S/2003/1066], the Secretary-General informed the Security Council that the mandate of his Special Representative for the Great Lakes Region, Ibrahima Fall, would expire on 31 December 2003 and that he intended to extend the mandate until 31 December 2004. He remarked that Mr. Fall had pursued consultations on the international conference on the Great Lakes region (see p. 111) which had led to the launching of the preparatory process of that conference. The Council, on 4 November [S/2003/1067], took note of the intention.

Security Council mission. On 21 May [S/2003/558], the Security Council President informed the Secretary-General of the Council's decision to send a mission to Central Africa in June and of the mission's composition and terms of reference. In the DRC (see p. 127), the mission would emphasize the need to take the peace process forward and would invite the Congolese parties to implement their commitments in the framework of the Inter-Congolese Dialogue. All parties would be pressed to carry out their obligations under relevant Council resolutions, including those to demilitarize Kisangani, ensure the reopening of the Congo River to civilian traffic and provide humanitarian organizations with access to populations in need. The mission would also evaluate the role of MONUC on the basis of the Secretary-General's recommendations on adjusting MONUC's concept.

In Burundi (see p. 149), the mission would express support for the second phase of the transition and the new President, the regional mediators and the African peacekeeping mission, as well as the Implementation Monitoring Committee and the Joint Ceasefire Commission, and would assess the future of the relationship between the United Nations and the African peacekeeping mission.

The mission travelled to the region from 7 to 16 June, visiting Pretoria, South Africa; Luanda, Angola; Kinshasa and Bunia, DRC; Bujumbura, Burundi; Kigali, Rwanda; Dar es Salaam, United Republic of Tanzania; and Entebbe, Uganda. It issued its report on 17 June [S/2003/653]. The mission made recommendations on both the DRC and Burundi (see below under country headings), which were considered by the Council on 25 July.

SECURITY COUNCIL ACTION

On 25 July [meeting 4794], following consultations among Security Council members, the President made statement **S/PRST/2003/12**, which also dealt with the Council's mission to West Africa (see p. 162), on behalf of the Council:

The Security Council welcomes the recommendations made in the reports of its mission to Central Africa undertaken from 7 to 16 June 2003 and its mission to West Africa undertaken from 26 June to 5 July 2003.

The Council endorses the recommendations which fall within its area of responsibility and wishes to see them implemented. It has already taken the relevant recommendations into account in preparing its resolution renewing and strengthening the mandate of the United Nations Organization Mission in the Democratic Republic of the Congo.

Where responsibility for implementation falls to others, the Council looks forward to working in partnership with them, including United Nations agencies and programmes; Governments in Central and West Africa; regional and subregional organizations, notably the Economic Community of West African States; donor countries; non-governmental organizations and civil society. The Council invites them to keep it informed of their efforts at implementation, so that the Council can support them and take any further action necessary.

The Council emphasizes the importance of a subregional approach to issues such as small arms and light weapons, mercenaries, child soldiers and humanitarian access. It stresses that follow-up activity by the United Nations will require close cooperation and coordination throughout the United Nations system. Action in these areas should also involve the appropriate organizations, especially in West Africa.

The Council invites the Secretary-General to follow up those recommendations which lie within his responsibility, and would be grateful for a report on progress by 30 November 2003.

The Council recognizes that resources may be needed to implement its recommendations. Therefore it will continue to encourage donor countries in a position to do so to support such efforts, and to assist regional and subregional organizations in this respect.

The Council intends to review progress in implementing the recommendations in December 2003.

Multidisciplinary mission. The President of the Security Council announced on 17 April [SC/7735] that Council members welcomed the Secretary-General's intention to dispatch a multidisciplinary mission to Central Africa to assess the implementation of a comprehensive, integrated, resolute and concerted approach to peace, security and development in Central Africa, as requested by the Council in presidential statement S/PRST/2002/31 [YUN 2002, p. 101]. The Council welcomed the ongoing consultations between the Secretariat and the Economic Community of Central African States (ECCAS) on the preparations for the mission and the decision to associate ECCAS with the mission. It expressed support for the Secretary-General's proposals to strengthen the coordination between the diverse UN structures in the countries of the subregion and to promote the strengthening of the partnership between the UN system and Central African States.

The Secretary-General dispatched the multidisciplinary mission to the 11 ECCAS member States (Angola, Burundi, Cameroon, the Central African Republic, Chad, the Congo, the DRC, Equatorial Guinea, Gabon, Rwanda, Sao Tome and Principe) from 8 to 22 June. The mission's report was forwarded to the Council on 10 November [S/2003/1077].

The mission observed that the subregion, while rich in a wide variety of natural resources, contained the largest number of countries that ranked lowest in almost all of the human development indices. It was also characterized by the recurrence of armed rebellions and conflicts that had hampered its development for decades; seven of the countries were either in conflict or in post-conflict situations, the most recent outbreaks being the coup d'état in the Central African Republic in March and the attempted coup in Sao Tome and Principe in July. The root causes of the current situation in the subregion could be traced to two main internal sources, namely, the crisis of governance and widespread poverty. The mission's report went on to discuss peace and security issues, the challenges of poverty, humanitarian issues, human rights, HIV/AIDS, the work of subregional institutions and the United Nations in the subregion, and the question of regional integration.

The mission observed that the issues of peace and security lay at the core of the challenges confronting the subregion. While UN offices and missions in Burundi, the Central African Republic and the DRC were focused on country-specific problems of peace consolidation and peacekeeping, there was an urgent need for the United Nations to help implement subregional policies to address cross-cutting challenges, including the promotion of good governance, and to stem the illegal flow of arms, drugs and militia. Because of the close linkage between poverty and conflict, it was essential for the UN system to develop a holistic and integrated approach to the problems of Central Africa, to address conflicts at their core, and to enhance the ability of national, subregional and international actors to be more proactive in identifying and preventing future threats. Cross-border challenges, such as population movements, drugs and small arms trafficking, and transnational movements of mercenaries and militias, should be addressed more vigorously with UN support. Joint activities in border areas, such as health, education and disarmament, demobilization and reintegration programmes, could combat such phenomena. The liberalization of cross-border trade, especially in agricultural products, would help to improve market access and promote relationships between border populations. Policies to promote respect for human rights, the rule of law and the development of inclusive and responsive governance would facilitate peace and stability, as would strengthening institutional capacities of governance at the national, subregional and regional levels and of justice systems to ensure predictability and reliability in the discharge of justice. Human rights protection systems should be strengthened by enhancing national institutional capacity, human rights education, and a mechanism to address the fate of victims of conflicts, including by providing compensation and rehabilitation. Efforts to prevent and fight HIV/AIDS should be intensified and coordinated at the subregional level. Central African subregional institutions, including ECCAS, the Central African Economic and Monetary Community and the Economic Community of the Great Lakes Countries, should integrate the problem of HIV/AIDS into the agenda of peace, security, and political, economic and social issues. The Organisation de coordination pour la lutte contre les endémies en Afrique centrale should ensure the coordination of the subregional monitoring of health issues in order to establish a regional HIV/AIDS strategy, develop a UN assistance programme and integrate HIV/AIDS issues into the concept of peacekeeping operations in the region, specifically in Burundi, the Central African Republic and the DRC, and into the demobilization programmes in Angola, Burundi, the Central African Republic, Chad, the Republic of the Congo and the DRC.

In his letter transmitting the mission's report, the Secretary-General stated that he was in general agreement with the mission's assessment. He had requested a thorough review of UN programmes with a view to enhancing their coherence and effectiveness and would keep the Council informed. Although most Governments in the subregion had expressed their desire for a UN office, the Secretary-General was concerned about the proliferation of offices; there were already a number of UN structures in the subregion, including three offices headed by Special Representatives of the Secretary-General. However, he proposed the appointment of a special envoy to work on political issues with Governments in the subregion and to interface with the UN entities involved in development and humanitarian activities in Central Africa.

The Central African Republic, in a 25 November letter [S/2003/1137], stressed that it supported the establishment of a UN office in the subregion in order to centralize and analyse the activities of UN agencies. That proposal was endorsed by the twentieth ministerial meeting of the member States of the UN Standing Advisory Committee on Security Questions in Central Africa (see below). The Central African Republic remained convinced of the need for such an office despite the Secretary-General's proposal to appoint a special envoy.

Security Council consideration. On 24 November [meeting 4871], the Security Council considered the multidisciplinary mission's report and was briefed by the mission leader, Tuliameni Kalomoh, Assistant Secretary-General for Political Affairs. The mission report stressed the need for the United Nations to help the subregion implement subregional policies and to support efforts directed at addressing cross-cutting challenges, including the promotion of good governance. It emphasized the interlinkages between poverty and conflict and called on the international community to support the ECCAS countries in their efforts to curb the widespread circulation of weapons and gangs of mercenaries in the subregion. It was also important to support the economic stabilization of Central African countries, which were emerging from conflict and embarking on the road to democratic reform.

Advisory Committee on Security Questions. The nineteenth and twentieth ministerial meetings of the United Nations Standing Advisory Committee on Security Questions in Central Africa were held in 2003 (Brazzaville, Congo, 14-17 May [A/57/823-S/2003/610]; Malabo, Equatorial Guinea, 27-31 October [A/58/560-S/2003/1075]). In addition to the member States (Angola, Burundi, Cameroon, Central African Republic, Chad, Congo, DRC, Equatorial Guinea, Gabon, Rwanda, Sao Tome and Principe), representatives of the United Nations and ECCAS participated in the meetings. The nineteenth meeting was preceded by a seminar (12-14 May) on the implementation in Central Africa of the Programme of Action adopted by the 2001 United Nations Conference on the Illicit Trade in Small Arms and Light Weapons in All Its Aspects [YUN 2001, p. 499].

At both meetings, the Committee reviewed the geopolitical and security situation in each Central African country. It took note with satisfaction of the intensification of action by the ECCAS member States within the framework of cooperation in security matters, aimed at lessening tensions, combating insecurity in the border areas, and facilitating exchanges between the various national structures dealing with those questions. It recommended continued cooperation among the security forces of the Central African countries, particularly within the framework of periodic meetings and joint operations. The Committee expressed concern at the persistence of organized crime and insecurity in countries of the subregion, and particularly at the phenomenon of roadblocks. It recommended the intensification of information sharing and the organization of large-scale joint operations to combat the phenomenon. It also called on countries that had not done so to sign and/or ratify the Protocol on the Council for Peace and Security in Central Africa, the Mutual Assistance Pact [YUN 2000, p. 528] and the Non-Aggression Pact between the countries of Central Africa.

The Committee, in May, reiterated its commitment to organize, in cooperation with ECCAS, a military peacekeeping exercise involving the armed forces of its members. It took note of the strengthening of relations between the United Nations and ECCAS since the signing in 2000 of the Memorandum of Cooperation between the two organizations, and noted, in particular, the forthcoming Security Council mission to the region (see p. 109). The Committee also reiterated the need to undertake a study to evaluate the costs and modalities of implementing the early warning mechanism for the region.

The Committee, in October, expressed the view that the outcomes of the UN multidisciplinary mission should include the establishment of a subregional bureau in Central Africa.

The Secretary-General, in response to General Assembly resolution 57/88 [YUN 2002, p. 532], submitted a 22 July report [A/58/177] on the regional confidence-building measures and activities of the Committee at its eighteenth [YUN 2002, p. 99] and nineteenth sessions.

International conference on Great Lakes

In response to a 1997 Security Council request contained in presidential statement S/PRST/1997/22 [YUN 1997, p. 77], the Secretary-General submitted a 17 November report on preparations for an international conference on the Great Lakes region [S/2003/1099]. The Council had called for an international conference on various occasions, starting in 1994 with presidential statement S/PRST/1994/59 concerning Rwanda [YUN 1994, p. 309], and the United Nations had explored the issue with the AU and the core countries (Burundi, DRC, Kenya, Rwanda, Uganda, United Republic of Tanzania). It was stressed that the conference should be action-oriented and focus on specific issues, and that it should be owned by the region. The core countries launched the preparatory process at the meeting of national coordinators (Nairobi, Kenya, 23-24 June), chaired jointly by the United Nations and the AU, which determined the timetable, structure and themes. The purpose of the conference would be to initiate a process that would bring together the leaders of the countries of the Great Lakes region to reach an agreed set of principles (good-neighbourly relations, stability, peace, development, etc.) and launch action to help end the cycle of conflict and ensure durable peace, stability, security, democracy, good governance and development. Participation would also include other stakeholders, including representatives of civil society in the core countries, neighbouring countries and friends of the region, and international development partners. The conference would not be a one-time event but a multi-stage process culminating in two ministerial summits to adopt a declaration of principles and concrete plans of action, which together would constitute the Stability, Security and Development Pact. The preparatory process would involve meetings of national preparatory committees and a regional preparatory committee, and a set of thematic meetings (subregional organizations, women, youth). A self-constituted Group of Friends of the Great Lakes region was being established under Canada's facilitation to work out coordinated ways of providing political, diplomatic, financial and technical support to the conference. Within the UN system, the Special Representative was coordinating with relevant UN agencies, through the inter-agency steering group that he had established in Nairobi. The target date for the first summit was June 2004.

The Secretary-General expressed the view that the stage had been set for the preparations for the conference to proceed. There was a new momentum in the region, as witnessed by the transitional DRC Government, the forward movement of the Burundi peace process and general elections in Rwanda, which made it an opportune time to proceed. To ensure the success of the conference, he urged the core countries to focus on the conference's priorities in order to formulate concrete and feasible policies and activities in the proposed thematic areas. The Secretary-General would seek the political commitment and financial support of the international community.

The Security Council considered the Secretary-General's report on 20 November [meeting 4865]. Addressing the Council, the Secretary-General said that the idea of an international conference had been revived by recent developments, including the adoption, in September, by the countries of the region of the Declaration of Principles on Good-neighbourly Relations and Cooperation. The Special Representative of the Secretary-General for the Great Lakes region, Ibrahima Fall, described the structure of the organizational process for the conference.

SECURITY COUNCIL ACTION

On 20 November [meeting 4865], following consultations among Security Council members, the President made statement **S/PRST/2003/23** on behalf of the Council:

> The Security Council recalls its presidential statement of 24 April 1997 (S/PRST/1997/22) and its other relevant statements and resolutions calling for the holding at an appropriate time of an international conference on peace, security, democracy and development in the Great Lakes region of Africa, with the participation of all Governments of the region of the Great Lakes and Central Africa and all others concerned, to be organized under the aegis of the United Nations and the African Union, with a view to achieving a sustainable peace, security and stability for all countries in the region, in particular through the full normalization of their relations and the establishment of confidence-building measures and mechanisms.
>
> The Council considers that the holding of the proposed conference will help build on the progress made in the Democratic Republic of the Congo and Burundi peace processes to achieve lasting peace and promote the national reconciliation processes in all countries concerned in the region.
>
> The Council welcomes the progress made towards the convening of the proposed conference, expresses satisfaction at the fact that the countries of the region have launched the preparatory process for the conference with the first meeting of their national coordinators, held in Nairobi in June 2003, and considers it now crucial to follow up this initial step with intensified efforts. It takes note with appreciation of the briefing by the Special Representative of the Secretary-General for the Great Lakes region, Mr. Ibrahima Fall, and welcomes the offer made by the Government of Tanzania to host a summit during the year 2004.
>
> The Council encourages the Governments concerned, with the support of their civil societies, their neighbours and development partners, to continue their efforts to bring about a successful conference, based on a regional, all-inclusive and action-oriented approach. It stresses the importance of the participation in this conference of all States concerned, in particular those neighbouring the Democratic Republic of the Congo or Burundi, and encourages the States in the region to reach early agreement on participation in the conference.
>
> The Council emphasizes the relevance to the proposed conference of the Solemn Declaration of the Conference on Security, Stability, Development and Cooperation in Africa adopted by the Organization of African Unity Lomé Summit in July 2000, of the Maputo Decision adopted by the Executive Council of the African Union in July 2003 and of the Declaration of Principles on Good-neighbourly Relations and Cooperation adopted by the Governments of Burundi, the Democratic Republic of the Congo, Rwanda and Uganda in New York on 25 September

2003, as well as of the framework of the New Partnership for Africa's Development.

The Council appeals to the countries of the region and to the international community to provide sustained political and diplomatic support as well as adequate technical and financial assistance so that the conference is well prepared and timely, and so that effective follow-up actions are taken. It commends the active partnership between the United Nations and the African Union in all aspects relating to the preparation of the proposed conference, and welcomes the appointment of Mr. Keli Walubita as Special Envoy of the Chairperson of the African Union Commission for the Great Lakes region.

The Council calls on the countries of the region and the members of the international community to support the efforts of the Special Representative of the Secretary-General for the Great Lakes region and the Special Envoy of the Chairperson of the African Union Commission for the Great Lakes region, expresses its gratitude to the Secretary-General for keeping it informed of developments in the region and requests him to continue to do so on a regular basis.

Democratic Republic of the Congo

In early 2003, the situation in the Democratic Republic of the Congo (DRC) deteriorated, despite positive developments in late 2002 indicating progress in implementing the 1999 Lusaka Ceasefire Agreement [YUN 1999, p. 87], the withdrawal of large numbers of foreign forces from the country [YUN 2002, p. 119] and the signature in December 2002 of the Global and All-Inclusive Agreement on the Transition in the DRC [ibid., p. 125], which provided for a two-year transitional Government followed by national elections. As provided for in that Agreement, President Joseph Kabila remained in office and continued as Supreme Commander of the Armed Forces.

As allegiances among the warring parties shifted, a new scale of violence emerged, characterized by the use of looting, rape and summary execution as tools of warfare. Also, Ugandan troops that had remained in the DRC retook Bunia in March, thereby reinforcing their presence in the eastern region. The situation in eastern DRC, in particular in the Ituri region, was threatening peace and stability throughout the DRC and the Great Lakes region. Against that background, the United Nations continued to press the parties to end hostilities and establish the Ituri Pacification Committee as envisaged in the 2002 Luanda Agreement [ibid., p. 116] between the DRC and Uganda, and the United Nations Organization Mission in the Democratic Republic of the Congo (MONUC) pursued its peacekeeping activities, in particular by assisting in disarmament efforts. With the mediation of South Africa and the Special Envoy of the Secretary-General, the Congolese parties reached agreement in Pretoria on 6 March on transitional arrangements for the DRC Government.

On 2 April in Sun City, South Africa, the participants in the Inter-Congolese Dialogue signed the Final Act of the inter-Congolese political negotiations that had started in October 2001 [YUN 2001, p. 131], thereby endorsing a package of agreements that constituted a comprehensive programme for the restoration of peace and national sovereignty during a two-year transition period. The agreements comprised the 2002 All-Inclusive Agreement, the Transitional Constitution, a 6 March memorandum on military and security issues, and the resolutions adopted in 2002 by the Inter-Congolese Dialogue. The Congolese parties took the first steps towards the establishment of the transitional Government—Joseph Kabila was sworn in as President for that period, amnesty was granted for certain actions relating to war, and the military court was abolished. Ugandan troops began returning home in late April, and some Rwandan combatants were also repatriated. Following the Ugandan withdrawal from Ituri province, hostilities again broke out causing flows of refugees into Uganda. In May, the Security Council authorized the short-term deployment of an interim emergency multinational force in Bunia, Ituri province, in coordination with MONUC, which was already deployed in the town, to help stabilize conditions and to contribute to the security of the civilian population and UN and humanitarian staff. The interim force, sent by the European Union (EU) and replaced in September by MONUC, was able to restore stability to Bunia.

On 30 June, President Kabila announced the formation of the Government of National Unity and Transition, which was made up of all parties participating in the dialogue and was designed to function until elections could be organized and concluded. Welcoming the transitional Government, the Security Council extended MONUC's mandate until 30 July 2004 and authorized an increase in size to 10,800 military personnel.

Under the aegis of the Secretary-General, a meeting of regional heads of State concluded on 25 September with the adoption of the Principles on Good-neighbourly Relations and Cooperation between the DRC and Burundi, Rwanda and Uganda. In that document, the four States, recognizing that the establishment of the DRC Government was essential for the peace and security necessary to ensure good-neighbourly relations, reaffirmed their commitment to: respect the sovereignty, territorial integrity and political independence of one another; prevent the supply of arms and support to armed groups in eastern

DRC; pursue peaceful means to resolve their disputes; and normalize their bilateral relations.

Although the principal political institutions of the transition began to function in late 2003 and several steps were taken towards implementing the All-Inclusive Agreement, progress remained slow and challenges remained. The inability of the transitional leaders to act as a truly unified government and to overcome the atmosphere of distrust remained among major obstacles, as did the continued, though diminished, fighting in eastern DRC.

In January, the Secretary-General extended the mandate of the Panel of Experts on the Illegal Exploitation of Natural Resources and Other Forms of Wealth in the Democratic Republic of the Congo and expanded its role. The Panel reported in October that illegal exploitation remained one of the main sources of funding for groups involved in perpetuating conflict, especially in eastern DRC. The Security Council, in November, condemned the continuing illegal exploitation of natural resources and urged States to take steps to end those activities.

Appointment. On 16 May [S/2003/562], the Secretary-General informed the Security Council that the current Special Representative for the DRC, Amos Namanga Ngongi (Cameroon), would conclude his assignment on 30 June. Consequently, he intended to appoint William Lacy Swing (United States) as his successor, effective 1 July. Mr. Swing had previously served as his Special Representative for Western Sahara. The Council, on 22 May [S/2003/563], took note of the Secretary-General's intention.

Political and military situation

In a 15 January press statement [SC/7634-AFR/543], the Security Council called on all Congolese parties to implement without delay the 2002 All-Inclusive Agreement [YUN 202, p. 125] in order to establish a transitional Government that would lead to elections in the DRC and stressed the need to resolve the key outstanding issues, especially the question of security for all parties in Kinshasa. The Council members expressed deep concern at the resumption of fighting in eastern DRC and instability in the north-east. They urged the parties to abide by the terms of the Gbadolite agreement, signed on 30 December 2002 [ibid.], on the withdrawal of forces in the Beni area, and in particular to cease all military activities there. The members strongly condemned the massacres and systematic violations of human rights perpetrated by the Movement for the Liberation of the Congo (MLC) and the Congolese Rally for Democracy/National (RCD/N) troops in Ituri, stating that Jean-Pierre Bemba, the MLC leader, bore the responsibility for the security of civilian populations in the territory under his control. The members demanded that Mr. Bemba ensure that those massacres and violations ceased immediately and hold the perpetrators accountable. MONUC and the Office of the United Nations High Commissioner for Human Rights (OHCHR) would continue to monitor the situation. The Council stressed the importance of implementation by both Rwanda and the DRC of their commitments under the 2002 Pretoria Agreement [YUN 2002, p. 115] on the withdrawal of Rwandan troops from DRC territory, and encouraged further efforts by MONUC and the Third Party Verification Mechanism to continue to verify implementation of those commitments, in particular the full withdrawal of Rwandan forces and the absence of all forms of support to the foreign armed groups by the Government of the DRC. The Council members expressed concern at reports of continuing sponsorship of proxy groups in the DRC, and called on both sides to cooperate with the verification efforts of MONUC and the Third Party Verification Mechanism.

Communications (January/February). In a 16 January letter [S/2003/52], the DRC thanked the Security Council for the 15 January statement (above). It stated that in north-eastern DRC, particularly in Ituri, adults and children had been murdered and mutilated, and others were victims of cannibalism, among other atrocities. Those intolerable acts were acknowledged by the person chiefly responsible, namely the MLC President, Mr. Bemba. MLC and RCD/N had aimed their attacks in particular at indigenous Pygmies and the Nande ethnic group, which could be qualified as genocide and ethnic cleansing under international law. With a view to ending impunity and ensuring that Mr. Bemba and others responsible for the abuses in Orientale province, particularly in Ituri, were brought to justice, the DRC requested the Council to establish an international criminal court to try all persons alleged to have committed serious violations of international humanitarian law there.

Rwanda, on 16 January [S/2003/63], complained that the DRC had wrongly accused it of failing to withdraw its troops from the DRC, whereas it was the DRC that had not complied with its commitments under the 2002 Pretoria Agreement. Rwanda called on the Council to demand that the DRC respect those commitments, especially the provisions relating to the disarmament and demobilization of the former Rwandan Army forces (ex-FAR) and Interahamwe militiamen responsible for the 1994 genocide of Rwandans [YUN 1994, p. 281]. On 31 January [S/2003/134], the DRC said that a concentration of forces of the Rwandan Patriotic Army had been observed in Kanyabayonga, a DRC town near the Rwandan and Ugandan borders, and that the town might become the point of confrontation between troops from the Rwandan and Ugandan armies in DRC territory. Responding on 4 February [S/2003/149], Rwanda denied the allegations and said that the Rwanda Defence Forces (RDF) had completely withdrawn from the DRC, in conformity with the Pretoria Agreement.

In another letter of 16 January [S/2003/64], the DRC, referring to its complaint in December 2002 [YUN 2002, p. 125] that the Libyan Arab Jamahiriya had been aiding MLC, said that the misunderstanding had been resolved.

Security Council consideration. The Security Council, on 13 February [meeting 4705], considered the situation in the DRC and was briefed by Jean-Marie Guéhenno, Under-Secretary-General for Peacekeeping Operations, who updated the Council on the military situation in the northeast and efforts to achieve a peaceful settlement. He noted that there had been continuous heavy fighting in and around the Ituri region since October 2002, despite the signing of the All-Inclusive Agreement. Following the signing of the Gbadolite ceasefire agreement on 30 December 2002 [YUN 2002, p. 125], MLC began its withdrawal from the Mambasa-Komanda area, which was completed on 3 February. Subsequently, the Union de patriotes congolais (UPC), which was not a signatory to the Gbadolite agreement, had aligned itself with the Goma faction of RCD (RCD-Goma) and took over Komanda, establishing 14 checkpoints. A new Hema-Lendu grouping, the Front for Integration and Peace, opposed UPC and called for the retention of Ugandan forces in Ituri.

MONUC was working to defuse tensions and recommend peace-building mechanisms and to organize a local ceasefire leading up to the convening of the Ituri Pacification Committee (IPC), as stipulated in the 2002 Luanda Agreement [ibid., p. 116]. On 10 February, DRC President Kabila, Ugandan President Yoweri Kaguta Museveni and Angolan President José Eduardo Dos Santos signed an amendment to the Luanda accord, which allowed for a new timetable for the work of the envisaged IPC—composed of two representatives each from MONUC and from the DRC and Uganda Governments and four representatives from the parties represented on the ground in Ituri. IPC was expected to conclude its work on 20 March, and the total withdrawal of Ugandan troops from the DRC would follow (see also p. 120).

Briefing the Council, the United Nations High Commissioner for Human Rights, Sergio Vieira de Mello, said that the impunity with which the Government and other parties to the conflict continued to commit grave violations of human rights represented a major obstacle to lasting peace. The humanitarian situation was deteriorating further because the warring parties were not allowing access by humanitarian workers to impoverished populations, many of whom (estimated at 100,000 persons) had been forced to flee their homes. The economic interests that were at the root of the continued plundering of natural resources and of State revenues were contributing to conditions of anarchy and grave violations of human rights in eastern DRC, as was the rapid deterioration of the economy. In addition, widespread corruption within the judicial system, the armed forces and the police, among others, made public administration ineffective. A mission to Bunia had confirmed gross violations of human rights, and in areas controlled by UPC since August 2002 the human rights situation had also deteriorated significantly. Recent events included persecution on ethnic and tribal grounds, extortion of property, rape, and the forced recruitment of children by military personnel, causing thousands of civilians to flee. The High Commissioner recommended that the Pretoria peace process be based on solid human rights grounds and that effective judicial and national human rights protection systems be created.

Report of Secretary-General (February). The Secretary-General, in response to Security Council resolution 1417(2002) [YUN 2002, p. 112], submitted on 21 February [S/2003/211] his thirteenth report on MONUC and the situation in the DRC, covering developments since his 18 October 2002 report [YUN 2002, p.120]. Despite the signing of the All-Inclusive Agreement, which established the structure of the transitional Government, and the Gbadolite ceasefire agreement, military activities continued. In the Ituri region of eastern DRC, there was widespread insecurity, massive displacement and severely restricted humanitarian access. The neutral Facilitator of the Inter-Congolese Dialogue, Sir Ketumile Masire, was expected to convene the final session of the Dialogue in the coming weeks. At that session, the parties were expected to endorse the All-Inclusive Agreement and adopt the transitional constitution. In the meantime, the Facilitator was consulting with the Congolese parties on preparations for that session, in particular on the formation of a national army, security in Kinshasa and finalization of the draft constitution. The Secretary-General's Special Envoy for the Inter-

Congolese Dialogue, Moustapha Niasse, was pursuing efforts to bring the parties to consensus on those issues.

In January, UPC, which was not covered by the Gbadolite ceasefire agreement, entered into an alliance with RCD-Goma. Throughout that month, MONUC tried to verify allegations of Rwandan troops operating north-east of Bunia and reports of Rwandan material support to UPC; Rwanda denied the presence of any of its troops in the DRC. Throughout the period, the Secretary-General's Special Representative engaged the parties to end hostilities and establish IPC, as envisaged in the 2002 Luanda Agreement. However, fighting continued despite those efforts. On 9 February, the Foreign Ministers of the DRC and Uganda signed an amendment to the Luanda Agreement, allowing for a new timetable for IPC's work. Following the withdrawal of Rwandan troops from North and South Kivu, RCD-Goma territorial control in the area was significantly reduced, leaving a patchwork of unofficial authorities and armed groups. Mayi-Mayi groups appeared to have at least nominal control over large areas, while RCD-Goma control was centred on key towns and cities.

Despite the difficulties in distinguishing between Rwandan and RCD-Goma combatants, MONUC continued to investigate allegations of the presence of foreign troops. There were persistent but unconfirmed reports that RDF was supporting RCD-Goma. Aside from Ugandan troops in Bunia, MONUC found no evidence of formed foreign military units remaining in the DRC.

Despite assurances by President Kabila, MONUC was denied unrestricted access to airports at Kinshasa and Gbadolite and to rail and air transport leaving Lubumbashi. Thus, the Mission had no direct evidence to address suspicions that the DRC continued to support armed groups in the east. On 24 January, MONUC visited Moliro and ascertained that the Congolese Armed Forces (FAC) were occupying that area with up to three battalions and were being allowed access to Lake Tanganyika in violation of the Harare disengagement and redeployment sub-plans, agreed to in 2000 [YUN 2000, p. 137]. In a letter to the DRC Government, MONUC called for FAC to withdraw to the defensive positions outlined in the Harare sub-plans and reiterated in Security Council resolution 1399(2002) [YUN 2002, p. 106].

Under its main operational activity—disarmament, demobilization, repatriation, resettlement or reintegration (DDRRR)—MONUC made efforts to ensure that information on DDRRR reached the rank and file Interahamwe/ex-FAR combatants deep in the forest, in the face of obstruction by hard-line leaders and the de facto authorities. As at 20 February, the total number of Rwandans repatriated by MONUC stood at over 1,000. Working with South Africa in the Third Party Verification Mechanism established pursuant to the 2002 Pretoria Agreement [YUN 2002, p. 115], MONUC also sought to address the situation of the Armée pour la libération de Rwanda (ex-FAR/Interahamwe) leaders apprehended by the DRC Government. Ultimately, 11 of the 19 leaders apprehended in Kinshasa voluntarily agreed to be repatriated and were returned to Rwanda on 22 January. On 15 January, military sector boundaries were redrawn to facilitate DDRRR operations.

At the time of the report, MONUC had trained a total of 161 civilian police officers and had conducted a training programme in criminal law, criminal procedure and human rights for 53 judicial police officers in Kinsangani, among other training activities. MONUC's other operations were in the area of public information, human rights, child protection, mainstreaming gender issues, HIV/AIDS, humanitarian assistance, demining and quick-impact projects.

The Secretary-General, while welcoming the signing of the All-Inclusive Agreement in 2002, said that the Congolese leaders had not taken the steps required to implement it and continued to engage in military confrontation. Despite the declared withdrawal of most of the foreign forces and the commencement of DDRRR, the military situation on the ground, particularly in the Ituri region and the Kivus, continued to be volatile. He warned that prompt inauguration of the transitional Government was critical if the political momentum created by the Pretoria Agreement was not to be lost. He called on all parties to cooperate with his Special Envoy and the neutral Facilitator to resolve the remaining issues, convene expeditiously the final session of the Inter-Congolese Dialogue, ratify the All-Inclusive Agreement and adopt the transitional constitution. MONUC had been hampered by security conditions in its efforts to verify the reports on the presence of foreign forces. The Secretary-General urged the DRC and neighbouring countries to build regional mechanisms to resolve such issues. Equally important for the peace process, he said, was the establishment of IPC. The potentially explosive nature of the military and political situation in the north-east, and the risk that it could draw in military forces from neighbouring States, were sources of major concern. The importance of a political solution to underpin any military disengagement and ceasefire was key.

Since his previous report, MONUC had made progress in the voluntary repatriation of foreign armed groups, with significant numbers returning to Rwanda. The cooperation of the Rwandan authorities and the contribution of South Africa had been crucial in that regard. In that same period, over 100,000 persons in the north-east around Beni had been displaced as a result of military offensives in which horrendous human rights abuses were perpetrated. Some Congolese leaders had been implicated in those abuses and that impunity had to end.

The Special Representative, Amos Namanga Ngongi, and MONUC were in a position to support the transitional arrangements and to coordinate assistance during the transition period. In addition to its observation and peacemaking efforts, MONUC would be able to help create conditions for holding free and fair elections, including in the areas of security sector reform, rule of law and technical assistance for elections. MONUC was currently exploring those areas.

Communications (February/March). In letters of 3 and 7 February [S/2003/136, S/2003/157], Rwanda protested the issuance by MONUC of press releases indicating that reports had been received regarding the presence of Rwandan troops in DRC territory. Rwanda pointed out that MONUC had not verified the presence of Rwandan troops in Ituri or eastern DRC and demanded to know the sources of the information.

On 12 February [S/2003/172], the DRC forwarded the joint communiqué of the consultative summit between Presidents Kabila of the DRC and Museveni of Uganda, signed in Dar es Salaam, United Republic of Tanzania, on 10 February on the complete withdrawal of Ugandan troops from the DRC, the normalization of relations and an amendment to the 2002 Luanda Agreement. The amendment specified a new timetable for establishing IPC. In the communiqué, the two leaders noted with concern the deterioration in the security and humanitarian situation in Ituri. They agreed that IPC would work from 17 February to 20 March, following which Ugandan troops would be totally withdrawn from Ituri. They agreed to establish a standing consultation mechanism that would permit them to monitor developments in Ituri and take action for the maintenance of peace and security. Uganda also transmitted the texts to the Council [S/2003/213].

The DRC, on 19 February [S/2003/199], transmitted the final communiqué of the meeting of ministers to draw up the modalities for the establishment of IPC between the DRC and Uganda (Luanda, Angola, 14 February). A Preparatory Committee would meet in Bunia on 17 February prior to the launching of IPC, scheduled for 25 February. The meeting also resolved issues regarding the timetable, composition and tasks of IPC. The communiqué was signed by Angola, the DRC, Uganda and MONUC.

On 6 March [S/2003/291], the DRC issued a press release on the situation in Ituri, expressing concern over the rising violence, generated by UPC. Demanding implementation of the 2002 Luanda Agreement, it requested the parties to respect international humanitarian law by protecting the lives of civilians. The DRC called on the international community to demand that Rwanda and Uganda protect civilian populations in the territories under their control. Referring to that communication on 11 March [S/2003/303], Rwanda said that its troops had totally withdrawn from the DRC in 2002, and that the situation in Ituri was a creation of the United Nations, the DRC and Uganda. Rwanda called for the withdrawal of Ugandan forces from the DRC and called on the United Nations to demand that Ugandan forces and FAC leave the Ituri region. On 12 March [S/2003/316], Uganda transmitted an 11 March statement by its Minister of Defence on the situation in Ituri. The Minister said that Uganda would deploy adequate forces to stabilize Bunia and its environs, secure roads to Bunia to ensure a supply of food, facilitate the distribution of food and medicine by humanitarian agencies, and make preparations with MONUC to start IPC. Rwanda, on 14 March [S/2003/318], transmitted a government statement alleging that Ugandan forces had overrun Bunia on 6 March and continued to reinforce the Ituri region with heavy armaments. The DRC continued to supply the ex-FAR and Interahamwe, which were a threat to Rwanda's borders, as were the Ugandan troops in eastern DRC.

Report of UN High Commissioner for Human Rights. In response to a request made by the Security Council during its 13 February meeting on the situation in the DRC [meeting 4705], the Council President circulated on 24 February the report of the UN High Commissioner for Human Rights on the human rights situation in the DRC [S/2003/216], covering the period from 18 July 2002 to 30 January 2003. The report, which was based on the joint efforts of OHCHR and MONUC and the High Commissioner's visit to the country from 12 to 15 January, stated that the human rights situation remained grave throughout the DRC, and all parties to the conflict continued to commit gross violations of human rights with impunity. There had been a widespread failure to provide minimum guarantees to the particular needs of the most marginalized and vulnerable people—women, children, the internally displaced and those affected by HIV/AIDS. MONUC, OHCHR and the Special Rapporteur of the Commission on Human Rights on the situation of human rights in the DRC (see p. 810) continued to document massive violations of human rights in the country, especially in areas controlled by RCD-Goma, MLC and UPC. In Government-controlled territory, concerns continued over the administration of justice because of the weakness of the judicial system. The High Commissioner's overall assessment was that the prevailing human rights situation was alarming and a threat to the fragile peace process. Despite the conclusion of the Pretoria and other peace agreements, the ongoing war in the east was causing massive violations of human rights and terrible suffering to thousands of civilians.

The report described some specific atrocities in the territories controlled by the Government and rebels, including arbitrary executions, killings, rape, mutilations, cannibalism, torture, abductions and looting. It also provided information on follow-up action with regard to the May 2002 massacres in Kisangani [YUN 2002, p. 109].

The High Commissioner concluded that there would be a continuing need for the Security Council to exert all possible pressure on the Government and other belligerents and their supporters, notably Rwanda and Uganda, to put an immediate end to the human rights violations and to the culture of impunity. All commanders had to be held responsible for gross violations committed by fighters under their control, and consideration should be given to establishing an international commission of inquiry to investigate violations by all sides. Having ratified the Rome Statute of the International Criminal Court [YUN 1998, p. 1209], the DRC should be pressed to pass the necessary legislation so that those who committed war crimes or crimes against humanity might be prosecuted by the Court, should national jurisdiction be unable to do so. The Truth Commission, to be established pursuant to a resolution adopted by all parties in the 2002 Inter-Congolese Dialogue [YUN 2002, p. 107], would be useful in promoting reconciliation. It could conduct investigations, take testimony from witnesses, victims and perpetrators, and recommend reforms needed to prevent the recurrence of abuses.

Security Council press statements (February/March). On 26 February, the Security Council President issued a press statement [SC/7674] in which Council members expressed their concern at the serious violations of human rights reported by the High Commissioner. They reiterated that there could be no impunity and that each party was responsible for maintaining law and order in the areas under its control. With regard to the Ituri situation, members called on UPC to cooperate with MONUC and humanitarian organizations and to facilitate the implementation of IPC. Regional Governments, in particular the DRC, Rwanda and Uganda, were urged to support the peace process in Ituri, and to refrain from taking or supporting any action that could aggravate the situation. The Congolese parties were urged to implement the 2002 All-Inclusive Agreement and to establish the transitional Government. Full access should be provided to MONUC to enable it to verify the implementation of the Pretoria Agreement. Members condemned the attack against a MONUC helicopter in Bunia and demanded that the perpetrators be brought to justice.

In a 10 March press statement [SC/7684-AFR/577], Council members welcomed the agreement reached on 6 March among Congolese parties in Pretoria on transitional arrangements and stressed the importance of the DRC transitional Government being established as soon as possible. They expressed their concern at the continuation of fighting in Bunia and demanded the immediate cessation of hostilities and that IPC be established immediately. They urged Uganda to abide by its commitment to withdraw its troops by 20 March and demanded that all parties ensure the security of civilian populations and guarantee humanitarian organizations full access to those in need.

SECURITY COUNCIL ACTION (March)

On 20 March [meeting 4723], the Security Council unanimously adopted **resolution 1468(2003)**. The draft [S/2003/334] was prepared in consultations among Council members.

The Security Council,

Recalling its resolutions and the statements by its President regarding the Democratic Republic of the Congo,

Expressing its full support for the efforts of the United Nations High Commissioner for Human Rights and its appreciation of his report on the situation in Ituri, and recalling the previous report on the situation in Kisangani,

Welcoming the thirteenth report of the Secretary-General on the United Nations Organization Mission in the Democratic Republic of the Congo,

Commending the Government of Angola for its efforts in ensuring the implementation by the parties of the Luanda Agreement, which establishes the basis for a settlement in the Ituri area, and expressing its gratitude to the Government of Angola for its readiness to continue these efforts,

Commending the Government of South Africa for its role in cooperation with the Special Envoy of the Secretary-General in helping the Congolese parties to reach an agreement on the transitional arrangements,

Commending the efforts of the Special Envoy of the Secretary-General, the Special Representative of the Secretary-General and their teams for helping to steer the negotiations in Pretoria to a successful conclusion,

Determining that the situation in the Democratic Republic of the Congo continues to pose a threat to international peace and security in the region,

1. *Welcomes* the agreement reached by the Congolese parties, in Pretoria on 6 March 2003, on the transitional arrangements, commends the Congolese parties, whose responsibility it is to implement fully the commitments they have made, for their efforts in settling the outstanding issues, and calls upon them to establish as soon as possible the Transitional Government in the Democratic Republic of the Congo, and stresses that any effort to undermine or delay its establishment would be unacceptable;

2. *Condemns* the massacres and other systematic violations of international humanitarian law and human rights perpetrated in the Democratic Republic of the Congo, in particular sexual violence against women and girls as a tool of warfare and atrocities perpetrated in the Ituri area by troops of the Mouvement de libération du Congo and the Rassemblement congolais pour la démocratie-National, as well as the acts of violence recently perpetrated by the forces of the Union des patriotes congolais, and reiterates that there will be no impunity for such acts and that the perpetrators will be held accountable;

3. *Stresses* that the military officers whose names are mentioned in the report of the United Nations High Commissioner for Human Rights in connection with serious violations of international humanitarian law and human rights should be brought to justice through further investigation and, if it is warranted by that investigation, be held accountable through a credible judicial process;

4. *Calls upon* the Congolese parties, when they are selecting individuals for key posts in the Transitional Government, to take into account the commitment and record of those individuals with regard to respect for international humanitarian law and human rights and the promotion of the well-being of all Congolese;

5. *Strongly encourages* the Congolese parties forming the Transitional Government to establish as soon as possible a truth and reconciliation commission charged with determining responsibility for serious violations of international humanitarian and human rights law, as set forth in the resolutions adopted within the framework of the Inter-Congolese Dialogue held in Sun City, South Africa, in April 2002;

6. *Reiterates* that all parties claiming a role in the future of the Democratic Republic of the Congo must demonstrate their respect for human rights and international humanitarian law, as well as the security and well-being of civilian populations, and emphasizes that the Transitional Government in the Democratic Republic of the Congo will have to restore law and order and respect for human rights and end impunity, across the entire country;

7. *Requests* the Secretary-General to increase the number of personnel in the human rights component of the United Nations Organization Mission in the Democratic Republic of the Congo to assist and enhance, in accordance with its current mandate, the capacity of the Congolese parties to investigate all serious violations of international humanitarian law and human rights perpetrated on the territory of the Democratic Republic of the Congo since the beginning of the conflict in August 1998, and also requests the Secretary-General, in consultation with the High Commissioner, to make recommendations to the Security Council on other ways to help the Transitional Government in the Democratic Republic of the Congo to address the issue of impunity;

8. *Expresses its deep concern* over the heavy fighting in Bunia, demands that all parties to the conflict in Ituri immediately cease the hostilities and that all parties sign an unconditional ceasefire agreement, stresses that they must cooperate with the Mission to set up without further delay the Ituri Pacification Commission, and also stresses that the necessary steps must be taken to restore public order in Bunia, in accordance with the agreements reached among the Congolese parties and within the framework of the Commission;

9. *Requests* the Secretary-General to increase the presence of the Mission in the Ituri area, as security conditions permit, in particular military observers and human rights personnel to monitor developments on the ground, including the use of airfields in the Ituri area, and also requests the Mission to provide further support and assistance to humanitarian efforts, as well as to facilitate the formation of the Ituri Pacification Commission and to assist the work of the Commission as consistent with the current mandate of the Mission, in consultation with all Congolese parties to the conflict;

10. *Encourages* the Mission in its efforts to consult with the relevant parties on possible options for addressing the immediate security situation in the Ituri area, and requests that the Mission keep the Council informed of its efforts in this regard;

11. *Demands* that all Governments in the Great Lakes region immediately cease military and financial support to all parties engaged in armed conflict in the Ituri region, stresses the need for all Congolese parties, including the Government of the Democratic Republic of the Congo, to respect their commitments under the Ceasefire Agreement signed at Lusaka on 10 July 1999, as well as the Kampala plan and the Harare sub-plans for disengagement and redeployment, and reiterates that all foreign troops must be withdrawn from the territory of the Democratic Republic of the Congo;

12. *Calls upon* the Government of Uganda to complete the withdrawal of all its troops without further delay and, in this regard, expresses its concern that the commitment of that Government to withdraw by 20 March 2003 has not been met, and concerned also at the statement of 14 March 2003 issued by the Ministry for Foreign Affairs and Regional Cooperation of Rwanda, calls upon the Government of Rwanda not to return any forces to the territory of the Democratic Republic of the Congo, and stresses that any renewal of the strengthening of a foreign military presence on the territory of the Democratic Republic of the Congo would be unacceptable and would undermine the progress achieved thus far in the peace process;

13. *Expresses its deep concern* at the rising tensions between Rwanda and Uganda and their proxies on the territory of the Democratic Republic of the Congo, and stresses that the Governments of those two countries must take steps to build mutual confidence, must settle their concerns through peaceful means, and without any interference in Congolese affairs, and

must refrain from any action that could undermine the peace process;

14. *Demands* that all parties to the conflict in the Democratic Republic of the Congo, and in particular in Ituri, ensure the security of civilian populations and grant to the Mission and to humanitarian organizations full and unimpeded access to the populations in need;

15. *Reiterates* the demand expressed in its resolution 1460(2003) of 30 January 2003 that all parties to the conflict provide information without delay on steps they have taken to halt the recruitment or use of children in armed conflict, in violation of the international obligations applicable to them, as well as its demands with regard to the protection of children contained in its resolutions 1261(1999) of 25 August 1999, 1314(2000) of 11 August 2000, 1379(2001) of 20 November 2001 and 1460(2003);

16. *Recalls* its demand that full and unimpeded access be granted to the Mission and the Third Party Verification Mechanism so that they could verify the implementation of the Peace Agreement signed at Pretoria on 30 July 2002 and investigate the allegations of the presence of Rwandan troops on the territory of the Democratic Republic of the Congo, as well as allegations of support by the Government of the Democratic Republic of the Congo to the armed groups in the east of the country, reiterates that both would be unacceptable and would undermine the continuation of the peace process, and stresses that any ongoing military activity in the east of the Democratic Republic of the Congo has a detrimental effect on Mission operations of disarmament, demobilization, repatriation, reintegration or resettlement of armed groups;

17. *Requests* that the Mission report as soon as possible to the Council on the results of its investigations referred to in paragraph 16 above;

18. *Expresses its support* to the broad orientations set out by the Secretary-General in paragraph 59 of his last report on the role of the Mission in support of the peace process, and expresses its intention to consider his recommendations in this regard;

19. *Reiterates its full support* for the Mission and the efforts it continues to deploy to help the parties in the Democratic Republic of the Congo and in the region to advance their peace process, and stresses the importance of the Mission moving forward with its phase III deployment, in accordance with resolution 1445(2002) of 4 December 2002;

20. *Decides* to remain actively seized of the matter.

Communications (March/April). Rwanda, in a 25 March letter [S/2003/369] to the Council President, welcomed resolution 1468(2003) and the recent progress made in the Inter-Congolese Dialogue, which brought together participants from numerous factions under the aegis of the neutral Facilitator. It hoped that the United Nations would continue to help Congolese parties overcome the few remaining obstacles, particularly the establishment of the security mechanisms for the transitional Government. It appreciated the Council's concern at the rising tension between Rwanda and Uganda, supported the implementation of the Lusaka [YUN 1999, p. 87] and Pretoria [YUN 2002, p. 115] Agreements through the Dialogue, and called for an immediate withdrawal of Ugandan and Kinshasa forces from Ituri and a deployment of a neutral force in Bunia and at strategic points. The DRC, it said, continued to support the ex-FAR/Interahamwe, enabling them to take over most positions previously held by Rwandan forces, thus posing a threat to Rwanda.

On 8 April [S/2003/413], Uganda transmitted a 3 April statement on resolution 1468(2003), in which it welcomed recent progress by the Congolese parties with regard to transitional arrangements. Uganda shared the Security Council's concern on the situation in Ituri, noting that it would be further aggravated if Ugandan troops were withdrawn without alternative arrangements. Following a ceasefire in Ituri province, which was signed on 18 March in Bunia, with only UPC not signing, IPC was officially inaugurated on 1 April. Uganda was therefore ready to withdraw its troops as soon as alternative security arrangements were put in place. Uganda expressed concern about Rwanda's allegations against it but affirmed that it had no designs to harm Rwanda.

On 9 April [S/2003/415], Rwanda reported to the Security Council that it had observed the massacres of innocent populations on 3 March in parts of eastern DRC controlled by Ugandan forces and their allies. Rwanda disapproved of the mandate for security stewardship in the eastern DRC that the Council had given to Uganda only because its forces were deployed on the ground. It also reaffirmed its rejection of IPC, which was aimed at enabling Kinshasa to reassert its authority in Ituri, as long as the Inter-Congolese Dialogue had not been fully implemented. Rwanda further reaffirmed its view that a quick deployment of a neutral force in eastern DRC, especially in all strategic points held by the Ugandan troops and their allies, would be the best option for solving the crisis. In the meantime, MONUC and the Third Party Verification Mechanism should be enabled to take control of all airfields and ports in eastern DRC, in order to check resupplying and infiltration forces.

On 29 April [S/2003/514], Uganda transmitted a statement issued by the ministerial meeting of Angola, the DRC and Uganda, the signatories of the 2002 Luanda Agreement [YUN 2002, p. 116], with the participation of MONUC (Bunia, 15 April). The delegations expressed satisfaction with the results of IPC. The DRC urged Uganda to communicate its detailed plan of withdrawal, in accordance with the Luanda Agreement, and insisted on the deployment in Ituri of an international force, as well as the National Congolese Police. Uganda provided explanations regarding its presence in Bunia and Ituri and confirmed the strength and location of troops, which would be conveyed to MONUC. It also recalled the presence of elements of Ugandan dissidents deployed in Ituri and reaffirmed its willingness to withdraw all troops by 24 April. It hoped an international force would be deployed in its place, in order to avoid any security vacuum. MONUC indicated that an assessment of the security context of Ituri was being made. The DRC and Uganda reiterated the need for implementation of the security mechanism regarding the western slopes of the Rwenzori Mountains and agreed that experts from both parties would examine modalities at a later date.

Events in Drodro and Mambasa

The Security Council President issued a press statement on 8 April [SC/7722-AFR/599] in which members condemned an offensive launched by RCD-Goma in eastern DRC, and urged it immediately to recall its troops to the agreed positions. Condemning the massacres in the Ituri area and calling for the perpetrators to be brought to justice, members requested the High Commissioner for Human Rights to investigate those events. They called on the Ugandan forces to withdraw from DRC territory without delay and recalled that so long as they were deployed on the ground, those forces had the responsibility to ensure the safety of the civilian population. They further called on all parties to cooperate fully with IPC. Council members demanded the immediate cessation of the fighting and massacres in eastern DRC and called on all Congolese parties to ensure that the transitional Government was established as soon as possible.

On 25 June [S/2003/674], the Secretary-General submitted to the Security Council a MONUC report on incidents that took place in Mambasa in late 2002 and early 2003 and a report of the High Commissioner for Human Rights on the events of 3 April in Drodro, Ituri, which he submitted in response to the request contained in the Council's 8 April press statement (see above). From the testimonies of 503 people, the MONUC special investigation team determined that there was a pattern of looting, killing and violence against women, used as premeditated tools of war by MLC, RCD/N and UPC military forces in October and December 2002. Acts of cannibalism, preceded by corporal mutilations and sectioning of internal body parts, particularly concerning the internal body parts of Pygmies, could be considered to be pure fetishism. The fact of forcing family members to eat body parts of their loved ones could be considered as psychological torture. Most of those violations seemed to have been committed with the aim of taking revenge on the Nande and Pygmy populations perceived as assisting and supporting the RCD-Liberation Movement (ML) authorities.

The team made recommendations aimed at restoring justice and supporting the victims, including: follow-up of rape cases by a female human rights investigator; follow-up of forced disappearance cases; arranging psychological support for victims of rape and eyewitnesses of executions and cannibalism; sending a forensic team to analyse mass graves; providing emergency humanitarian assistance for schools and medical facilities; and providing trauma counselling for children affected by the violations.

In his report on the 3 April events in Drodro, the High Commissioner for Human Rights observed that the human rights situation in Ituri had been deteriorating for nearly five years. The armed conflict that broke out in August 1998 and continuing dissension among the rebel movements and factions, coupled with the interference of neighbouring countries, had exacerbated the situation. As violence increased, the different ethnic groups of the region had organized themselves into militias or armed groups, with the aim, among other things, of influencing the DRC political process. The current cycle of violence began in August 2002, when a UPC faction captured Bunia. In January 2003, after the signing of the All-Inclusive Agreement [YUN 2002, p. 125], a political and military alliance was forged between UPC and RCD-Goma, which led to further deterioration in Bunia. That event, as well as dissent within UPC, led to the establishment of another armed faction, the Front pour l'intégration et la paix en Ituri, which, with support from foreign troops, seized Bunia on 6 March and forced the UPC leader, Thomas Lubanga, and his militias to fall back to Drodro (80 kilometres west of Bunia), where they came under armed attack on 3 April. The report, based on a mission to the area by a special investigation team (18 April–5 May), highlighted the human rights situation in Ituri following the 3 April events in Drodro.

The investigation team determined that about 408 people were summarily executed, including people burned alive. More than 80 others were badly wounded and/or mutilated, about 150 shops were looted and several dozen heads of livestock were stolen. Those events made the already precarious human rights situation throughout Ituri worse. Accounts received by the investigation team indicated that the attacks on Drodro were carried out by Lendu militias; witnesses also reported that some of the attackers wore olive-green mottled military uniforms like those of the Ugandan troops in the region. Further attacks on the vulnerable population of Ituri by Lendu militias took place on 8, 11, 12, 15, 17 and 18 April in various villages, resulting in numerous massacres and atrocities, and thousands of people were left homeless to roam the area, malnourished and without the barest necessities. More recently, following the withdrawal of Ugandan troops and the deployment of the Rapid Reaction Police from Kinshasa, the security situation in Bunia had deteriorated dramatically. Clashes continued between armed militias, and the premises and warehouses of humanitarian agencies were looted, as were private houses. The mostly Hema population was massacred and militia members attacked MONUC, forcing its troops to fire into the air to disperse them. Humanitarian workers were evacuated to Kisangani and Goma and were thereby prevented from assisting the affected population.

In general, the situation in Ituri, in particular in the Drodro area, was extremely threatening to stability in the DRC and the Great Lakes region, and required a response from the international community and the Congolese actors. The events in Drodro occurred during a conflict when various rebel movements were founded—movements backed by neighbouring countries and riven by internal dissension. The proliferation of rival factions and tribal armed groups, which were manipulated and run by a handful of warlords and certain neighbouring countries desirous of protecting their interests or influencing the political process in the DRC, largely explained the unprecedented violence that swept Ituri for months and was responsible for serious human rights violations and a disastrous humanitarian situation.

In the High Commissioner's view, the underlying cause of the situation was a vicious cycle of grave human rights violations and vengeance, buttressed by impunity. He recommended that the future transitional Government establish an appropriate judicial body to try alleged perpetrators of serious human rights violations and breaches of international humanitarian law, and affirmed his readiness to cooperate with the Prosecutor of the International Criminal Court in that regard. The High Commissioner urged the Security Council to strengthen the presence of military observers so that humanitarian organizations and human rights observers could move into Ituri and provide support for national human right institutions and for enhancing the judicial system.

The Security Council considered the report on 7 July [meeting 4784].

Press statements (May). In a 5 May press statement [SC/7749-AFR/613], Security Council members expressed concern on the situation in Ituri. They urged all parties and regional States to support the IPC process and urged Uganda to fulfil its commitment to withdraw its forces from the area. Condemning all harassment of MONUC personnel and the violence that had taken place in the Kivus, they called for an end to support to armed militias and the fuelling of ethnic tensions. They reiterated that the leaders of all warring factions should be personally accountable for human rights violations.

Following a briefing by the Under-Secretary-General for Peacekeeping Operations, Jean-Marie Guéhenno, on the deteriorating situation in Bunia, the Council, on 9 May [SC/7755-AFR/616], issued a press statement condemning attacks against MONUC headquarters in Bunia, where a 700-member guard contingent had been deployed in support of the IPC process. It called on the parties to cease aggression and violence, especially against the civilian population and MONUC.

Letter from Secretary-General (15 May). The Secretary-General, in a 15 May letter to the Security Council President [S/2003/574], expressed concern about the rapidly deteriorating situation in and around Bunia, which had become the site of major violent clashes between Hema- and Lendu-based militia groups, and which had been exacerbated by outside interference. Anticipating further worsening of the situation, he requested the Council to consider urgently his proposal for the rapid deployment to Bunia of a well-trained and well-equipped multinational force, under the leadership of a Member State, to provide security at the airport and other vital installations and to protect the civilian population. The force would be in place for a limited period until a reinforced UN presence could be deployed. All parties, in particular the States involved in the conflict in the DRC, should desist from interference in the affairs of the region. In the face of the current crisis in Ituri, the international community should act decisively to offset the looming humanitarian catastrophe in Bunia and rescue the nascent political process.

Dar es Salaam agreement. On 16 May in Dar es Salaam, the United Republic of Tanzania facilitated a summit between the protagonists in Ituri, all of whom signed a new commitment to restart pacification and proceed with the cantonment of their troops for the purpose of demilitarization. They also supported the Secretary-General's efforts to obtain an international rapid reaction force for Ituri.

SECURITY COUNCIL ACTION (16 May)

On 16 May [meeting 4756], following consultations among Security Council members, the President made statement **S/PRST/2003/6** on behalf of the Council:

> The Security Council condemns the recent killings, violence and other human rights violations and atrocities in Bunia, as well as the attacks against the United Nations Organization Mission in the Democratic Republic of the Congo and the internally displaced persons who have sought refuge at the Mission premises, and reiterates that there will be no impunity for such acts and that the perpetrators will be held accountable. It demands that all hostilities in Ituri cease immediately. The fighting is unacceptable. It threatens the stability of the Ituri area and severely undermines the continuation of the peace process and the establishment of the Transitional National Government.
>
> The Council fully supports the work initiated by the Ituri Pacification Commission, established by the Luanda Agreement of 6 September 2002, under which the Ituri interim administration was formed, encourages donors to provide additional funding and emphasizes that it is up to the various Congolese parties in Ituri to pursue an effective, inclusive political and security mechanism in this framework.
>
> The Council welcomes the Agreement on the Engagement to Relaunch the Ituri Pacification Process, signed in Dar es Salaam on 16 May 2003, and calls upon the parties to implement it fully and without delay.
>
> The Council calls upon all parties in the region to end all support to armed groups and to refrain from any action that might compromise the restoration of peace in Ituri, in particular the work of the Ituri interim administration, and reaffirms its strong commitment to the sovereignty of the Democratic Republic of the Congo over all its territory.
>
> The Council expresses its concern at the deteriorating humanitarian situation in Bunia and demands that all parties grant full and unimpeded access for humanitarian aid and guarantee the safety and security of humanitarian personnel. It also calls upon the donor community to continue to support the humanitarian organizations.
>
> The Council pays tribute to the work that has been achieved by the staff and contingents of the Mission in Ituri, in very difficult conditions, and fully supports them.
>
> The Council welcomes the efforts by the Secretary-General to address the urgent humanitarian and security situation in Bunia, including options for sending an emergency international force, and encourages him to complete consultations to this end as a matter of urgency.
>
> The Council demands that all Congolese parties and regional States involved in the conflict in the Democratic Republic of the Congo refrain from any action that could undermine the possible deployment of an international force, and support the deployment.

Communications (May). Uganda, on 16 May [S/2003/553], discussed developments in eastern DRC. Uganda had completed withdrawal of its forces from Bunia and was therefore no longer responsible for the maintenance of security in Ituri province. Uganda had warned the international community that withdrawal of its forces without deployment of adequate UN forces would create a security vacuum that would lead to renewal of the Lendu-Hema conflict, and indeed the level of deployment of MONUC and the Congolese police deployment had proved inadequate to cope with the situation that arose. Following Uganda's withdrawal, inter-ethic conflict erupted, resulting in an influx of DRC citizens (estimated at 50,000 to 60,000 people), mostly Hema, to Uganda. The resulting humanitarian crisis brought about an urgent need for food, water and shelter for the refugees, for which Uganda appealed to the international community. Uganda also called on the Security Council to expand MONUC's role from peace monitoring to peace enforcement, under Chapter VII of the UN Charter, and to increase MONUC's deployment to fill the security vacuum in Ituri.

By another 16 May letter [S/2003/560], Uganda transmitted a press release following discussions held by its Third Deputy Prime Minister/Minister for Foreign Affairs, James Wapakhabulo, with French Foreign Minister Dominique de Villepin. The French Foreign Minister appreciated the gravity of the situation in north-eastern DRC and the need for a more robust MONUC deployment in Ituri.

Report of Secretary-General (May). In response to Security Council resolution 1417(2002) [YUN 2002, p. 112], the Secretary-General submitted, on 27 May, his second special report on MONUC [S/2003/566 & Corr.1]. The report also covered major developments in the DRC since his report in February (see p. 115). He said that on 2 April in Sun City, the participants in the Inter-Congolese Dialogue signed the Final Act of the inter-Congolese political negotiations that had started in October 2001 [YUN 2001, p. 131], by which they endorsed a package of agreements that constituted a comprehensive programme for the restoration of peace and national sovereignty during a transition period of two years. The agreements comprised the 2002 Global and All-Inclusive Agreement on the Transition in the DRC [YUN 2002, p. 125], the Transitional Constitution, the memorandum of 6 March on military and security issues, and the resolutions adopted in 2002 by the Inter-Congolese Dialogue in Sun City [YUN 2002, p. 107]. Since the signing of the Final Act, the Congolese parties had taken steps towards establishing the transitional Government: Mr. Kabila was sworn in as President for the transitional period on 7 April; amnesty was granted for certain actions relating to war; the military court was abolished; the Follow-up Commission held meetings to prepare for the new institutions;

and the Special Representative, on 10 April, convened the first meeting of the International Committee in Support of the Transition in Kinshasa (comprising representatives of the permanent members of the Security Council and Angola, Belgium, Canada, Gabon, Mozambique, South Africa and Zambia, plus the AU and the EU).

Despite political progress at the national level, hostilities, which were accompanied by widespread and gross violations of human rights, continued in the east, in particular between Lendu-based and Hema-based militias in Ituri, and between RCD-Goma, Mayi-Mayi and other armed groups in North and South Kivu. The root causes of the Ituri conflict, which related to an indigenous power struggle over land and resources, had been exacerbated by the protagonists of the wider conflict in the DRC. As a result of the proliferation of armed groups and their constantly shifting allegiances, the situation in the region had become volatile and unpredictable. UPC engaged in large-scale military operations in four localities in Ituri, resulting in killings, destruction of property and displacement of a large number of people. Since the first major fighting in 1999, the death toll was estimated at more than 60,000. Between 500,000 and 600,000 internally displaced persons—many of whom remained in hiding and could not be accounted for—were dispersed throughout the area, as were almost 100,000 refugees from the Sudan and Uganda.

On 6 March, Ugandan forces recaptured Bunia, which had been under UPC control since August 2002. Subsequently, the Ugandan presence in Ituri was reinforced to over 7,000 troops, who were deployed to strategic locations in the region. Their deployment did not stem the activities of armed militias, however.

In view of rising tensions between Rwanda and Uganda over the increased presence of the latter's forces in the region, the Special Representative proposed a trilateral meeting of the heads of State of the DRC, Rwanda and Uganda, which was held on 9 April in Cape Town, South Africa, and hosted by President Thabo Mbeki. The three leaders confirmed the timetable for Ugandan withdrawal from Ituri, from 24 April to 14 May.

MONUC intensified its consultations with key players in early March, which led to the Governments of the DRC and Uganda and six armed groups (except for UPC, which had lost almost all of its territorial control) reaching a ceasefire agreement that paved the way for convening IPC. The 177 delegates who attended IPC (Bunia, 4-14 April) represented the main communities and groups in Ituri, including UPC. It was agreed to set up an interim administration, which began work on 25 April.

In order to assist in the political process initiated by IPC, MONUC increased its presence in the Bunia area and had 720 troops in place at the time of the report. Their tasks included a presence at the airfield and protection of UN personnel and facilities and sites of IPC meetings. The number of military observer teams in Ituri was also increased. On 26 April, one military observer was killed and another wounded in a landmine accident.

On 25 April, Uganda began withdrawing its troops from Ituri and had completed its withdrawal from Bunia on 6 May. Immediately after the departure of Ugandan troops from Bunia, Hema- and Lendu-based militia groups sought to establish control over the town, resulting in violent clashes and looting, including of UN premises. MONUC was forced to return fire to repel the aggressors. In talks with the Special Representative, President Kabila agreed to deploy troops to Bunia.

RCD-Goma continued to redeploy nearly all its military force away from positions on the disengagement line to conduct offensives in the North and South Kivu and Maniema provinces. Those offensives resulted in serious human rights violations, triggering new waves of population displacement.

The persistent outbreaks of fighting in eastern DRC continued to hamper and delay MONUC operations to disarm, demobilize and repatriate foreign ex-combatants, the main focus of the Mission. MONUC had repatriated more than 1,500 Rwandans, including both combatants and their dependants, since October 2002, while the Office of the United Nations High Commissioner for Refugees (UNHCR) had repatriated 3,021 Rwandan refugees. The voluntary DDRRR programme was hindered by the security situation and by lack of cooperation from the parties concerned. RCD-Goma had not offered its full cooperation and Mayi-Mayi representatives had proved to be unreliable. Nevertheless, MONUC persuaded some combatants to enter the DDRRR process. Progress was also made in reopening the Congo River; the first private commercial traffic allowed by RCD-Goma arrived in Kisangani in February.

MONUC reviewed its deployment strategy to readjust its structure from that based on the 1999 Lusaka Agreement [YUN 1999, p. 87] to one that met the needs of the changing political and military situation. It closed two coordination centres and 22 team sites and redeployed the troops to other priority areas.

The report outlined the responsibilities of the Congolese parties and the role of MONUC during the forthcoming two- to three-year transitional period. First, the transitional Government would have to put in place the transitional institutions and ensure their functioning, and lay the ground for the elected Government that would be established at the end of the transition by preparing for elections and drafting a new Constitution. It would also have to address security and military matters and economic development. The parties would have to observe a number of key benchmarks, including: cessation of hostilities and military support to armed groups; lifting of restrictions on the free movement of people and goods; the liberalization of political activity; the dismantling of armed groups; and taking steps to establish the high command of the national armed forces and to form the initial unit of the integrated police force.

MONUC's priorities would be: to provide political support to the transition by assisting the Congolese parties in implementing their commitments, leading to the holding of elections; to contribute to local conflict resolution and the maintenance of security; to continue DDRRR of foreign armed groups and Congolese combatants; to promote the coordination of international political and donor efforts with regard to the transition; to contribute to confidence-building between the DRC and neighbouring States; and to continue activities in the areas of human rights, humanitarian affairs, child protection and gender affairs. The immediate goals were to help establish the transitional Government; contribute to security in Kinshasa; assist in reconciliation efforts in Ituri; contribute to local-level conflict resolution; and continue DDRRR of armed groups in the Kivus. Given MONUC's new responsibilities, the leadership structure, both civilian and military, would need to be strengthened.

The Secretary-General observed that the DRC, after nearly five years of continuous fighting, found itself at an intersection of peace and war. The definitive and successful conclusion of the Inter-Congolese Dialogue was a crucial milestone that constituted the commitment by the Congolese parties finally to pursue a path of peace and reconciliation. Since the signing of the 1999 Lusaka Ceasefire Agreement, MONUC's primary role had been to facilitate the implementation of that document and supplementary bilateral agreements that provided the framework for addressing the military dimension of the conflict. Despite slow and partial compliance by the parties, there had been some major achievements, including the disengagement of foreign armed forces and their allies to defensive positions, the withdrawal of the majority of foreign troops from the DRC and initial progress in the ad hoc disarmament, demobilization and repatriation of Rwandan armed groups.

MONUC would be required to play a central role in facilitating the transition process and the Mission should be reconfigured and augmented accordingly. The All-Inclusive Agreement and President Kabila had requested the United Nations to deploy a force to participate in the proposed multi-layered confidence-building security system to give confidence to transitional leaders in Kinshasa. The proposed system would comprise the existing Congolese police structures to carry out normal law and order functions; the close protection corps to act as personal bodyguards for political leaders; and a MONUC military contingent of some 740 personnel. Any elements of the Congolese Armed Forces currently deployed in Kinshasa would be garrisoned and monitored by MONUC. A newly formed integrated police unit would be trained to take over security tasks from MONUC. Before the formation of the transitional Government, MONUC would redeploy two guard units, to be assisted by 30 additional military police personnel, to the security zone in the capital. In addition, MONUC civilian police officers would advise, monitor and report on the conduct of the various Congolese entities with security responsibilities. Those arrangements would last from six to nine months and would require 104 security personnel in addition to the MONUC military contingent.

MONUC had already established a Transition Support Unit, which would be supplemented by an electoral assistance cell to plan UN support for elections. The Secretary-General also recommended imposing an arms embargo in Ituri and the Kivus.

As for the MONUC military presence, it would be enhanced by the establishment of the IPC Support Unit, in which all MONUC substantive components would be represented (political affairs, human rights, humanitarian affairs, child protection, public information). MONUC would work closely with the humanitarian and development community in Ituri, which was designing a strategy for that long-inaccessible region. In order to provide protection to UN personnel and assets in Ituri and to establish a framework of security in support of the political process, it was assessed that a brigade-size formation (three battalions with support and totalling up to 3,800 personnel) would be necessary. The current deployment in Bunia of nearly 800 Uruguayan troops was the minimum that was militarily acceptable to establish security for UN operations at the Bunia airfield, protect UN personnel and resources, support the IPC peace process and prepare for follow-on deployments and logistic sustainment. Since the deployment of a large force would take some months, leaving a dangerous interim gap in a volatile area, the Secretary-General called on the Security Council to consider urgently the rapid deployment to Bunia of a highly trained and well-equipped force, under the leadership of a Member State, to provide security at the airport and other vital installations and to protect the civilian population, as a temporary arrangement before the deployment of a reinforced UN presence. Such a deployment—for a limited period—should be authorized under Chapter VII of the UN Charter.

In the Kivus, ongoing military offensives continued to cause widespread suffering and undermine DDRRR activities. The Secretary-General called on RCD-Goma, various Mayi-Mayi groups and other local militias to cease hostilities immediately. MONUC had a role to play in encouraging and assisting local and international partners in conflict resolution in the Kivus by expanding the presence of its civilian personnel and military observers.

DDRRR of foreign armed groups remained an important goal, as that process lay at the heart of the Great Lakes conflict. However, equally important for the transition process in the DRC was the disarmament, demobilization and reintegration of Congolese armed and irregular forces. The Secretary-General proposed that MONUC's mandate be expanded to assist the transitional Government in planning that task.

The Secretary-General stated that the priorities he had outlined would require further resources; he therefore recommended that MONUC's mandate be extended for another year, until 30 June 2004, and that the authorized military strength be increased to 10,800 all ranks. He further recommended that civilian police personnel be increased from 100 to 134 police officers and that other specialized personnel be augmented.

The Secretary-General observed that the peace process could not move forward without the demonstrated commitment of the Congolese leaders and a number of key benchmarks had to be observed by the parties in that regard: immediate cessation of hostilities and of inflammatory rhetoric; lifting of restrictions on the free movement of goods and people; liberalization of political activity; disbandment of armed groups or their transformation into political parties; and taking steps to establish the high command of the integrated national armed forces and to form an initial unit of integrated police. In addition, the Government should be held accountable for the effective management of the natural resources of the DRC.

Press statement (28 May). The President of the Security Council issued a 28 May press statement [SC/7770-AFR/626] in which Council members condemned the recent violence and atrocities committed in the DRC, especially the murder of two MONUC military observers, as well as the looting of humanitarian and medical equipment. They called for full cooperation and restraint by all parties, including neighbouring States, and for them to refrain from arming the belligerents. There was unanimous support in the Council for the Secretary-General's proposal to deploy a multinational force in Bunia.

SECURITY COUNCIL ACTION (30 May and 4 June)

On 30 May [meeting 4764], the Security Council unanimously adopted **resolution 1484(2003)**. The draft [S/2003/578] was prepared in consultations among Council members.

The Security Council,
Recalling its resolutions and the statements by its President on the Democratic Republic of the Congo, in particular the statement of 16 May 2003,

Determined to promote the peace process at the national level, in particular to facilitate the early establishment of an inclusive Transitional Government in the Democratic Republic of the Congo,

Expressing its utmost concern at the fighting and atrocities in Ituri, as well as the gravity of the humanitarian situation in the town of Bunia,

Reaffirming its full support for the political process initiated by the Ituri Pacification Commission, calling for its swift resumption and for the establishment of an effective, inclusive security mechanism within this framework, to complement and support the existing Ituri interim administration,

Recognizing the urgent need for a secure base to allow the full functioning of the institutions of the Ituri interim administration, and recognizing that the Agreement on the Engagement to Relaunch the Ituri Pacification Process, signed in Dar es Salaam on 16 May 2003, reaffirms the commitment of the Ituri parties to the Ituri interim administration, and commits them to join a process of cantonment and demilitarization,

Commending the United Nations Organization Mission in the Democratic Republic of the Congo for its efforts to stabilize the situation in Bunia and to support the political process in Ituri, in particular the effective performance of the Uruguayan contingent deployed there, recognizing the need to support the work of the Mission in the field, and deploring attacks on the Mission and the consequent loss of life,

Taking note of the request of the Secretary-General addressed to the Security Council in his letter dated 15 May 2003, and taking note also of the support for this request expressed in the letter to the Secretary-General from the President of the Democratic Republic of the Congo, and also by the Ituri parties on 16 May 2003 in Dar es Salaam, as well as the support expressed in the letters to the Secretary-General from the President of the Rwandese Republic and from the Minister of State for Foreign Affairs of Uganda, as requested by the Secretary-General, for the deployment of a multinational force in Bunia,

Determining that the situation in the Ituri region, in Bunia in particular, constitutes a threat to the peace process in the Democratic Republic of the Congo and to peace and security in the Great Lakes region,

Acting under Chapter VII of the Charter of the United Nations,

1. *Authorizes* the deployment, until 1 September 2003, of an Interim Emergency Multinational Force in Bunia in close coordination with the United Nations Organization Mission in the Democratic Republic of the Congo, in particular its contingent currently deployed in the town, to contribute to the stabilization of the security conditions and the improvement of the humanitarian situation in Bunia, to ensure the protection of the airport and of the internally displaced persons in the camps in Bunia and, if the situation requires it, to contribute to the safety of the civilian population, United Nations personnel and the humanitarian presence in the town;

2. *Stresses* that this Multinational Force is to be deployed on a strictly temporary basis to allow the Secretary-General to reinforce the presence of the Mission in Bunia, and in this regard authorizes the Secretary-General to deploy, within the overall ceiling authorized for the Mission, a reinforced United Nations presence to Bunia, and requests him to do so by mid-August 2003;

3. *Calls upon* Member States to contribute personnel, equipment and other necessary financial and logistic resources to the Multinational Force, and invites contributing Member States to so inform the leadership of the Force and the Secretary-General;

4. *Authorizes* the Member States participating in the Multinational Force in Bunia to take all necessary measures to fulfil its mandate;

5. *Demands* that all parties to the conflict in Ituri, in particular in Bunia, cease hostilities immediately, and reiterates that international humanitarian law must be respected and that there will be no impunity for violators;

6. *Strongly condemns* the deliberate killing of unarmed personnel of the Mission and staff of humanitarian organizations in Ituri, and demands that the perpetrators be brought to justice;

7. *Demands* that all Congolese parties and all States in the Great Lakes region respect human rights, cooperate with the Multinational Force and with the Mission in the stabilization of the situation in Bunia and provide assistance, as appropriate, that they provide full freedom of movement to the Force and that they refrain from any military activity or from any activity that could further destabilize the situation in Ituri, and in this regard demands also the cessation of all support, in particular weapons and any other military materiel, to the armed groups and militias, and demands further that all Congolese parties and all States in the region actively prevent the supply of such support;

8. *Calls upon* all Member States, in particular those in the Great Lakes region, to provide all necessary support to facilitate the swift deployment in Bunia of the Multinational Force;

9. *Requests* the leadership of the Multinational Force in Bunia to report regularly to the Security Council, through the Secretary-General, on the implementation of its mandate;

10. *Decides* to remain actively seized of the matter.

The Security Council met on 4 June [meeting 4767] with the troop-contributing countries to MONUC and was briefed by Hédi Annabi, Assistant Secretary-General for Peacekeeping Operations. Senegal, in a letter of 1 June [S/2003/602], said that it would participate in the Interim Emergency Multinational Force, pursuant to resolution 1484(2003) (above). On 2 June [S/2003/611], Morocco, as Chairman of the African Group, said that the Group supported the Secretary-General's recommendation on increasing the number of MONUC staff. South Africa, as Chairman of the AU, transmitted on 16 June [S/2003/654] a communiqué issued by the Central Organ of the Mechanism for Conflict Prevention, Management and Resolution (Addis Ababa, 12-13 June), which included a decision on the DRC. Welcoming resolution 1484(2003), the Central Organ recommended that MONUC's mandate be extended to the disarmament of armed groups and demobilization of child soldiers.

Security Council mission

On 17 June [S/2003/653], the Security Council issued a report on its mission to Central Africa from 7 to 16 June (see also p. 149). In the light of the Secretary-General's 27 May report (see p. 123), the mission chose to concentrate, with regard to the DRC, on the urgent questions of the installation of the transitional Government and the creation of a unified national army; the situation in Bunia; the situation in North Kivu; the need for regional countries to exert a positive influence on the situation; and the end of impunity.

The mission registered its expectation with all concerned parties in the DRC that a functioning transitional Government would be set up by 30 June, with a unified national army capable of defending its national borders and population, and a developing economy in control of the country's natural resources. The mission recommended that the Security Council be prepared to pledge its support to the transitional Government and to call on donors to assist in the reconstruction of the country. The installation of the transitional Government and the conclusion of a ceasefire in Burundi (see p. 152) could clear the way for convening an international conference on the Great Lakes region. Having visited Bunia, the mission expressed concern about the possibility of further fighting after the expiration of the mandate of the Interim Emergency Multinational Force on 1 September and suggested a more robust mandate for MONUC in order to avert further conflict and humanitarian catastrophe. The mission emphasized that the parties to the conflict in Ituri should understand that it was in their interest to find a solution to their disputes within the context of IPC, the only legitimate framework that included all the actors in Ituri. The mission heard allegations of the continued supply of arms to the belligerents by outside parties, including foreign parties, and discussed the possibility of imposing an arms embargo on Ituri, as proposed by the Secretary-General.

The mission noted the ongoing fighting in North Kivu, in particular the offensive launched by RCD-Goma. It deplored the impunity that characterized much of the fighting and the accompanying human rights abuses and humanitarian crises in eastern DRC. Noting that some progress had been made in establishing mechanisms to enforce international criminal justice, the mission recommended that consideration be given to practical steps to end impunity in the DRC and Burundi. As to reports of continuing illegal exploitation of natural resources, the mission recommended that the Council act on the recommendations to be made by the Expert Panel in its forthcoming report (see p. 140).

The Security Council considered the mission's report on 18 June [meeting 4775] and the Secretary-General's 27 May report on 26 June [meeting 4780]. At the 18 June meeting, the head of the Council's mission said that both the DRC and Burundi were at a critical juncture in their history. Rwanda said that the DRC Government had maintained its support for the ex-FAR and Interahamwe militias and had spread the rumour that Rwandan Defence Forces had never fully withdrawn from the DRC to justify its reoccupation of South and North Kivu, with the support of the Interahamwe, the ex-FAR, the Mayi-Mayi rebels and RCD-Kisangani/ML. The DRC said that since the signing of the final document on the Inter-Congolese Dialogue, it had taken the necessary steps to install the transitional Government. However, the war hindered the search for a political solution, as did the lack of cooperation demonstrated by certain elements, in particular RCD-Goma, and the negative role that Rwanda played in eastern DRC. The political process undertaken by IPC had stagnated as a result of the renewed hostilities between the Hema and the Lendu in Bunia. The DRC urged the Council to extend and strengthen MONUC's mandate.

Extension of MONUC mandate

On 26 June [meeting 4780], the Security Council unanimously adopted **resolution 1489(2003)**. The draft [S/2003/667] was prepared in consultations among Council members.

The Security Council,

Recalling its resolution 1291(2000) of 24 February 2000 and other relevant resolutions concerning the United Nations Organization Mission in the Democratic Republic of the Congo, especially resolutions 1468(2003) of 20 March 2003 and 1484(2003) of 30 May 2003,

Reaffirming its commitment to the sovereignty, territorial integrity and political independence of the Democratic Republic of the Congo and of all States of the region,

Deeply concerned over the continuation of hostilities in the eastern part of the Democratic Republic of the Congo, in particular in the province of North Kivu,

Taking note of the second special report of the Secretary-General on the United Nations Organization Mission in the Democratic Republic of the Congo, of 27 May 2003, and the recommendations contained therein,

Reaffirming its readiness to support the peace and national reconciliation process, in particular through the United Nations Organization Mission in the Democratic Republic of the Congo, in accordance with resolution 1291(2000),

1. *Decides* to extend the mandate of the United Nations Organization Mission in the Democratic Republic of the Congo until 30 July 2003;

2. *Decides* to remain actively seized of the matter.

Press statement (26 June). On 26 June [SC/7801-AFR/651], the President of the Security Council issued a press statement on the DRC situation, in which Council members expressed their deep concern over the latest developments in the east, particularly in the Kivus. Condemning the recent escalation of fighting, especially the RCD-Goma offensives, which posed a threat to the political process, they called for an immediate cessation of hostilities and complete withdrawal to the previously agreed positions. All Congolese parties, including the Government, were urged to refrain from any new deployments or other provocative actions. Council members urged all parties to comply with all previous agreements and disengagement plans, and with the Acte d'Engagement for the cessation of hostilities in eastern and north-eastern DRC, signed in Bujumbura, Burundi, on 19 June. Expressing concern at the deteriorating humanitarian situation, they reiterated their call on the parties to provide safe access for international humanitarian assistance. They condemned the recent abduction of two MONUC military observers, welcomed their release and demanded that all parties abide by their obligation to provide unhindered access to MONUC to enable it to carry out its mandate.

Installation of transitional Government

On 30 June, President Kabila announced the composition of the Government of National Unity and Transition in the DRC. The President of the Security Council, in a 2 July press statement [SC/7805-AFR/654], said that Council members welcomed the announcement and encouraged the Congolese parties to allow the transitional institutions to begin functioning. They reiterated the terms of their press statement of 26 June (p. 128) and their concern over the latest developments in eastern DRC.

By a 14 July letter [S/2003/712], Italy transmitted to the Secretary-General a statement by the EU Presidency welcoming the formation of the transitional Government. It called on the new Government to take action to achieve the objectives laid down in the 2002 All-Inclusive Agreement [YUN 2002, p. 125], in particular the holding of free and transparent elections and the formation of a restructured and integrated national army.

At a meeting on 7 July [meeting 4784], the Security Council considered the reports from the United Nations High Commissioner for Human Rights and MONUC on the events that had taken place in Drodro and Mambasa [S/2003/674] (see p. 121). The Under-Secretary-General for Peacekeeping Operations, Mr. Guéhenno, reported that the installation of the DRC transitional Government had been delayed due to lack of agreement on the distribution of the military command posts. However, the matter was resolved on 29 June when the parties signed the Second Memorandum on the Army and Security. On 30 June, President Kabila announced the composition of the transitional Government, which would consist of 36 ministers and 25 deputy ministers representing the various components of the Inter-Congolese Dialogue. MONUC was consulting with the parties to ensure that the security concerns of the political leaders, especially MLC and RCD-Goma, were met.

In the Kivus, following the 19 June signing in Bujumbura of the Acte d'Engagement for a cessation of hostilities, the DRC Government, RCD-Kisangani/ML and RCD-Goma, under the mediation of MONUC, established on 26 June the Mission de Vérification Conjointe to verify the withdrawal of RCD-Goma to 15 kilometres south of their positions at Rwese and Kimbulu, as well as the maintenance of the current positions of RCD-Kisangani/ML and the cantonment of FAC troops at Mavivi. MONUC had confirmed that the parties were complying with the initial phase of the ceasefire and withdrawal.

Meanwhile, the situation in Ituri was improving. In Bunia, the security situation was stable and the Interim Emergency Multinational Force (IEMF), with MONUC's cooperation, was patrolling the town, which was declared a weapon-free zone as of 25 June. The two forces were also facilitating the return to town of Lendu inhabitants, and some 6,000 internally displaced persons had returned from camps and outlying areas. The deployment of IEMF in Bunia had begun to change the balance between the warring parties and the legitimate political actors in Ituri.

Reporting to the Council on 18 July [meeting 4790], Mr. Guéhenno said that the security situation in Bunia remained calm but tense following a military operation undertaken by IEMF against UPC on 11 July, in response to its continuing attempt to undermine the weapon-free-zone policy. The operation resulted in some UPC casualties and the confiscation of a large number of weapons. The increased number of returning displaced persons had required reinforced security measures in Bunia, and the humanitarian situation remained a concern. MONUC, with others, was involved in human rights training, recruitment of Iturian police for airport duties, preparing an interim disarmament and reintegration plan for child soldiers, and establishing a trust fund for the Ituri interim administration.

Amos Namanga Ngongi, former Special Representative of the Secretary-General for the DRC, focused on the transitional process and problems encountered since the formation of the transitional Government, such as RCD-Goma's unilateral decision to repartition three military regions. On 15 July, all parties except RCD agreed on the distribution of the military regions among the parties. The formal handover of power between the outgoing and incoming ministers and vice-ministers took place on 15 and 16 July. The establishment of the transitional Government, four years after the signing of the Lusaka Ceasefire Agreement [YUN 1999, p. 87], was a historic milestone.

Addressing the EU decision to deploy IEMF (known as Artemis) to Bunia, the EU Secretary-General, Javier Solana, stated that it was the first EU military operation outside Europe. The multinational force made it possible to stop the massacres there and helped to relaunch the stalled peace process. The rapid deployment of the European multinational force halted the spiral of violence in Ituri and made it possible to relaunch negotiations. The EU was committed to supporting the transition in the DRC until the holding of elections. In that context, Mr. Solana announced that the EU had, on 9 July, adopted a programme of support amounting to 205 million euros.

The EU General Affairs Council issued a 21 July statement [S/2003/772] indicating that, as stipulated in Security Council resolution 1484(2003) (see p. 126) the Artemis military operation would come to an end on 1 September. It asked the Secretary-General to consider certain measures to support the political process under way, including setting up an integrated police unit and support for the electoral process.

SECURITY COUNCIL ACTION (July)

On 28 July [meeting 4797], the Security Council unanimously adopted **resolution 1493(2003)**. The draft [S/2003/757] was prepared in consultations among Council members.

The Security Council,

Recalling its resolutions and the statements by its President concerning the Democratic Republic of the Congo,

Reaffirming its commitment to respect for the sovereignty, territorial integrity and political independence of the Democratic Republic of the Congo and of all the States of the region,

Reaffirming the obligations of all States to refrain from the use of force against the territorial integrity and political independence of any State or in any other manner incompatible with the purposes and principles of the United Nations,

Concerned by the continued illegal exploitation of the natural resources of the Democratic Republic of the Congo, and reaffirming in this regard its commitment to respect for the sovereignty of the Democratic Republic of the Congo over its natural resources,

Welcoming the conclusion of the Global and All-Inclusive Agreement on the Transition in the Democratic Republic of the Congo, signed in Pretoria on 17 December 2002, and the subsequent establishment of the Government of National Unity and Transition,

Deeply concerned by the continuation of hostilities in the eastern part of the Democratic Republic of the Congo, particularly in North and South Kivu and in Ituri, and by the grave violations of human rights and international humanitarian law that accompany them,

Recalling that it is incumbent upon all parties to cooperate in the overall deployment of the United Nations Organization Mission in the Democratic Republic of the Congo,

Renewing its support to the Interim Emergency Multinational Force deployed in Bunia, and stressing the need to ensure effective and timely replacement of the Force, as requested in resolution 1484(2003) of 30 May 2003, to contribute in the best way to the stabilization of Ituri,

Taking note of the second special report of the Secretary-General on the United Nations Organization Mission in the Democratic Republic of the Congo, of 27 May 2003, and of the recommendations contained therein,

Taking note also of the report of the Security Council mission to Central Africa, of 17 June 2003,

Noting that the situation in the Democratic Republic of the Congo continues to constitute a threat to international peace and security in the region,

Acting under Chapter VII of the Charter of the United Nations,

1. *Expresses satisfaction* at the promulgation, on 4 April 2003, of the Transitional Constitution in the Democratic Republic of the Congo and at the formation, announced on 30 June 2003, of the Government of National Unity and Transition, encourages the Congolese parties to take the necessary decisions in order to allow the transitional institutions to begin functioning effectively, and encourages them also in this regard to include representatives of the interim institutions that emerged from the Ituri Pacification Commission in the transitional institutions;

2. *Decides* to extend the mandate of the United Nations Organization Mission in the Democratic Republic of the Congo until 30 July 2004;

3. *Notes with appreciation* the recommendations contained in the second special report of the Secretary-General, and authorizes increasing the military strength of the Mission to 10,800 personnel;

4. *Requests* the Secretary-General to ensure through his Special Representative for the Democratic Republic of the Congo, who convenes the International Committee in support of the Transition, the coordination of all the activities of the United Nations system in the Democratic Republic of the Congo and to facilitate coordination with other national and international actors of activities in support of the transition;

5. *Encourages* the Mission, in coordination with United Nations agencies, donors and non-governmental organizations, to provide assistance during the transition period for the reform of the security forces, the re-establishment of a State based on the rule of law and the preparation and holding of elections, throughout the territory of the Democratic Republic of the Congo, and welcomes in this regard the efforts of the Member States to support the transition and national reconciliation;

6. *Approves* the temporary deployment of Mission personnel intended, during the first months of the establishment of the transitional institutions, to participate in a multi-layer security system in Kinshasa in accordance with paragraphs 35 to 38 of the second special report of the Secretary-General, approves also the reconfiguration of the civilian police component of the Mission as outlined in paragraph 42 of that report, and encourages the Mission to continue to support police development in areas of urgent need;

7. *Encourages* donors to support the establishment of an integrated Congolese police unit and approves the provision by the Mission of the additional assistance that might be needed for its training;

8. *Strongly condemns* the acts of violence systematically perpetrated against civilians, including the massacres, as well as other atrocities and violations of international humanitarian law and human rights, in particular sexual violence against women and girls, stresses the need to bring to justice those responsible, including those at the command level, and urges all parties, including the Government of the Democratic Republic of the Congo, to take all necessary steps to prevent further violations of human rights and international humanitarian law, in particular those committed against civilians;

9. *Reaffirms* the importance of a gender perspective in peacekeeping operations in accordance with resolu-

tion 1325(2000) of 31 October 2000, recalls the need to address violence against women and girls as a tool of warfare, and in this respect encourages the Mission to continue to actively address this issue, and calls upon the Mission to increase the deployment of women as military observers as well as in other capacities;

10. *Reaffirms also* that all Congolese parties have an obligation to respect human rights, international humanitarian law and the security and well-being of the civilian population;

11. *Urges* the Government of National Unity and Transition to ensure that the protection of human rights and the establishment of a State based on the rule of law and of an independent judiciary are among its highest priorities, including the establishment of the necessary institutions as reflected in the Global and All-Inclusive Agreement on the Transition in the Democratic Republic of the Congo, encourages the Secretary-General, through his Special Representative, and the United Nations High Commissioner for Human Rights to coordinate their efforts, in particular to assist the transitional authorities of the Democratic Republic of the Congo in order to put an end to impunity, and encourages also the African Union to play a role in this regard;

12. *States that it is profoundly preoccupied* by the humanitarian situation throughout the country, in particular in the eastern regions, and demands that all parties guarantee the security of the civilian population, thereby enabling the Mission and humanitarian organizations to have total, unrestricted and immediate access to the population groups in need;

13. *Strongly condemns* the continued recruitment and use of children in the hostilities in the Democratic Republic of the Congo, especially in North and South Kivu and in Ituri, and reiterates the request addressed to all parties in Security Council resolution 1460(2003) of 30 January 2003 to provide the Special Representative of the Secretary-General with information on the measures they have taken to put an end to the recruitment and use of children in their armed components, as well as the requests concerning the protection of children set forth in resolution 1261(1999) of 25 August 1999 and subsequent resolutions;

14. *Strongly condemns also* the continuing armed conflict in the eastern part of the Democratic Republic of the Congo, especially the serious ceasefire violations that occurred recently in North and South Kivu, including in particular the offensives by the Rassemblement congolais pour la démocratie-Goma, demands that all parties, in compliance with the Acte d'Engagement for the cessation of hostilities in the eastern and north-eastern Democratic Republic of the Congo, signed in Bujumbura on 19 June 2003, establish without delay or precondition the full cessation of hostilities and withdraw to the positions agreed to in the Kampala plan and the Harare sub-plans for disengagement and redeployment, and that they refrain from any provocative action;

15. *Demands* that all parties desist from any interference with freedom of movement of United Nations personnel, recalls that all parties have the obligation to provide full and unhindered access to the Mission to allow it to carry out its mandate, and asks the Special Representative of the Secretary-General to report any failure to comply with this obligation;

16. *Expresses concern* at the fact that the continuing hostilities in the eastern part of the Democratic Republic of the Congo are seriously compromising Mission action in the process of the disarmament, demobilization, repatriation, reintegration or resettlement of the foreign armed groups referred to in chapter 9.1 of annex A to the Ceasefire Agreement signed at Lusaka on 10 July 1999, urges all parties concerned to cooperate with the Mission, and underscores the importance of making rapid and appreciable progress in that process;

17. *Authorizes* the Mission to assist the Government of National Unity and Transition in disarming and demobilizing those Congolese combatants who may voluntarily decide to enter the disarmament, demobilization and reintegration process within the framework of the Multi-Country Demobilization and Reintegration Programme, pending the establishment of a national disarmament, demobilization and reintegration programme in coordination with the United Nations Development Programme and other agencies concerned;

18. *Demands* that all States, in particular those in the region, including the Democratic Republic of the Congo, ensure that no direct or indirect assistance, especially military or financial assistance, is given to the movements and armed groups present in the Democratic Republic of the Congo;

19. *Demands also* that all parties provide full access to military observers from the Mission, including in ports, airports, airfields, military bases and border crossings, and requests the Secretary-General to deploy military observers from the Mission in North and South Kivu and in Ituri and to report to the Council regularly on the position of the movements and armed groups and on information concerning arms supply and the presence of foreign military, especially by monitoring the use of landing strips in that region;

20. *Decides* that all States, including the Democratic Republic of the Congo, shall, for an initial period of twelve months from the adoption of the present resolution, take the necessary measures to prevent the direct or indirect supply, sale or transfer, from their territories or by their nationals, or using their flag vessels or aircraft, of arms and any related materiel, and the provision of any assistance, advice or training related to military activities, to all foreign and Congolese armed groups and militias operating in the territory of North and South Kivu and of Ituri, and to groups not party to the Global and All-Inclusive Agreement, in the Democratic Republic of the Congo;

21. *Decides also* that the measures imposed by paragraph 20 above shall not apply to:

(*a*) Supplies to the Mission, the Interim Emergency Multinational Force deployed in Bunia and the integrated Congolese national army and police forces;

(*b*) Supplies of non-lethal military equipment intended solely for humanitarian or protective use, and related technical assistance and training as notified in advance to the Secretary-General through his Special Representative;

22. *Decides further* that, at the end of the initial twelve months, the Council will review the situation in the Democratic Republic of the Congo, in particular in the eastern part of the country, with a view to renewing the measures stipulated in paragraph 20 above if no significant progress has been made in the peace pro-

cess, in particular an end to support for armed groups, an effective ceasefire and progress in the disarmament, demobilization, repatriation, reintegration or resettlement by foreign and Congolese armed groups;

23. *Expresses its determination* closely to monitor compliance with the measures laid down in paragraph 20 above and to consider steps that are necessary to ensure the effective monitoring and implementation of those measures, including the possible establishment of a monitoring mechanism;

24. *Urges* the States neighbouring the Democratic Republic of the Congo, particularly Rwanda and Uganda, which have an influence over movements and armed groups operating in the territory of the Democratic Republic of the Congo, to exercise a positive influence on them to settle their disputes by peaceful means and join in the process of national reconciliation;

25. *Authorizes* the Mission to take the necessary measures in the areas of deployment of its armed units, and as it deems it within its capabilities:

(a) To protect United Nations personnel, facilities, installations and equipment;

(b) To ensure the security and freedom of movement of its personnel, including in particular those engaged in missions of observation, verification or disarmament, demobilization, repatriation, reintegration or resettlement;

(c) To protect civilians and humanitarian workers under imminent threat of physical violence;

(d) To contribute to the improvement of the security conditions in which humanitarian assistance is provided;

26. *Also authorizes* the Mission to use all necessary means to fulfil its mandate in the Ituri district and, as it deems it within its capabilities, in North and South Kivu;

27. *Requests* the Secretary-General to deploy in the Ituri district, as soon as possible, the tactical brigade-size force whose concept of operations is set out in paragraphs 48 to 54 of his second special report, including the reinforced presence of the Mission in Bunia, by mid-August 2003 as requested in resolution 1484(2003), particularly with a view to helping to stabilize the security conditions, improving the humanitarian situation, ensuring the protection of airfields and displaced persons living in camps and, if the circumstances warrant it, helping to ensure the security of the civilian population and the personnel of the United Nations and the humanitarian organizations in Bunia and its environs and eventually, as the situation permits, in other parts of Ituri;

28. *Condemns categorically* the illegal exploitation of the natural resources and other sources of wealth of the Democratic Republic of the Congo, and expresses its intention to consider means that could be used to end it, awaits with interest the report to be submitted shortly by the Panel of Experts on such illegal exploitation and on the link that exists between it and the continuation of hostilities, and demands that all parties and interested States offer full cooperation to the Panel;

29. *Encourages* the Governments of the Democratic Republic of the Congo, Rwanda, Uganda and Burundi to take steps to normalize their relations and to cooperate in ensuring mutual security along their common borders, and invites these Governments to conclude good-neighbourly agreements among themselves;

30. *Reaffirms* that an international conference on peace, security, democracy and development in the Great Lakes region of Africa, with the participation of all the Governments of the region and all other parties concerned, should be organized at the appropriate time under the aegis of the United Nations and the African Union, with a view to strengthening stability in the region and working out conditions that will enable everyone to enjoy the right to live peacefully within national borders;

31. *Reiterates its support unreservedly* for the Special Representative of the Secretary-General and for all Mission personnel, and for the efforts they continue to make to assist the parties in the Democratic Republic of the Congo and in the region to advance the peace process;

32. *Decides* to remain actively seized of the matter.

Communication. The Secretary-General, on 14 August [S/2003/821], informed the Security Council President that MONUC's deployment of a brigade-size force to Bunia would be completed by 15 August. The Bangladeshi troops would join the Uruguayan battalion already there, to ensure a smooth transition from IEMF on 1 September. Given the expectation that the situation in Bunia could become volatile during the transition period, the EU and France, as lead nation, had informed the Secretary-General that IEMF would be ready to provide emergency support to MONUC, if required. The Secretary-General recommended that the Council authorize IEMF to provide assistance to MONUC in and around Bunia.

SECURITY COUNCIL ACTION (August)

On 26 August [meeting 4813], the Security Council unanimously adopted **resolution 1501(2003)**. The draft [S/2003/832] was prepared in consultations among Council members.

The Security Council,

Recalling its relevant resolutions and statements by its President on the Democratic Republic of the Congo, in particular resolutions 1484(2003) of 30 May 2003 and 1493(2003) of 28 July 2003,

Reaffirming its commitment to respect for the sovereignty, territorial integrity and political independence of the Democratic Republic of the Congo and all the States of the region,

Deeply concerned by the continuation of hostilities in the eastern part of the Democratic Republic of the Congo, particularly in the district of Ituri as well as in the provinces of North and South Kivu,

Reaffirming its support to the peace process and national reconciliation, in particular through the United Nations Organization Mission in the Democratic Republic of the Congo,

Also reaffirming its support to the Interim Emergency Multinational Force deployed in Bunia in accordance with resolution 1484(2003), and stressing the need to ensure the best conditions for the transfer of authority from the Force to the Mission on 1 September 2003 to contribute in the most efficient way possible to the continuing stabilization of Ituri,

Having taken note of the letter dated 14 August 2003 from the Secretary-General addressed to the Security Council President and of the recommendation contained therein,

Noting that the situation in the Democratic Republic of the Congo continues to constitute a threat to international peace and security in the region,

Acting under Chapter VII of the Charter of the United Nations,

1. *Approves* the recommendation contained in the Secretary-General's letter of 14 August 2003;

2. *Authorizes* the States members of the Interim Emergency Multinational Force, within the limits of the means at the disposal of those elements of the Force which will not yet have left Bunia before 1 September 2003, to provide assistance to the contingent of the United Nations Organization Mission in the Democratic Republic of Congo deployed in the town and its immediate surroundings, if the Mission requests them to do so and if exceptional circumstances demand it, during the period of disengagement of the Force, which should last until 15 September 2003 at the latest;

3. *Decides* to remain actively seized of the matter.

Press statement (3 September). On 3 September, the Council heard a presentation from the Secretariat on the completion of the IEMF mandate, deployed in Bunia in accordance with resolution 1484(2003) (see p. 126), and on the transfer of responsibility to MONUC on 1 September. In a press statement released that day [SC/7862-AFR/695], the President said that Council members welcomed the EU's deployment of that force, which helped to avoid a humanitarian tragedy and was instrumental in stabilizing the situation in Bunia. They expressed concern regarding the continuing hostilities in eastern DRC, in particular in Ituri and the Kivus. Warning all parties against supplying arms and not to engage in further violence, they noted that MONUC had a Chapter VII mandate, on the basis of which it continued to operate.

Principles on good-neighbourly relations

In accordance with Security Council resolution 1493(2003) (see p. 130), the Secretary-General, on 25 September, convened a high-level meeting of heads of State and senior representatives of Burundi, the DRC, Rwanda and Uganda, as well as Angola, Mozambique, South Africa and the United Republic of Tanzania. As he reported in a 7 October letter to the General Assembly and the Council [A/58/428-S/2003/983], he sought to build on the recent positive developments in and around the DRC, including the establishment of the transitional Government. The meeting concluded with the adoption of the Principles on Good-Neighbourly Relations and Cooperation between the DRC and Burundi, Rwanda and Uganda. In that document, the four States, recognizing that the establishment of the Government of National Unity and Transition in the DRC was an essential factor for the peace and security necessary to ensure the development of good-neighbourly relations, reaffirmed their commitment to: respect the sovereignty, territorial integrity and political independence of one another; refrain from interfering in one another's internal affairs; refrain from disrupting the stability, national unity and territorial integrity of one another; prevent the supply of arms and support to armed groups operating in eastern DRC; pursue peaceful means to resolve their disputes; normalize their bilateral relations by re-establishing full diplomatic relations; and cooperate with one another in the political, security, economic, social and cultural fields, in accordance with the principles of sovereign equality and non-intervention and with the aim of promoting peace and development and assuring mutual security along their common borders. The countries decided to pursue bilateral discussions on how to implement those principles.

Communications (October/November). On 6 October [S/2003/950], the DRC referred to Security Council resolution 1304(2000) [YUN 2000, p. 131], in which the Council expressed the view that Uganda and Rwanda should make reparations for loss of life and property damage they had inflicted in Kisangani and requested the Secretary-General to submit an assessment of the damage as a basis for such reparations. Noting the Secretary-General's 2000 report on the interagency assessment mission [ibid., p. 134] he had sent to Kisangani in response to that request, the DRC asked the Council to follow up the report by authorizing the United Nations to establish the cost of the events in Kisangani in June 2000, in order to complete the process of bringing justice to the people of that town.

The DRC informed the Council on 7 October [S/2003/969] of a massacre in Katchele, 70 kilometres north-west of Bunia, in which 23 civilians were killed. The DRC requested the Council to speed up sending MONUC reinforcements to Ituri, to conduct an investigation of the events in Katchele, and to address the issue of impunity that prevailed in Ituri, with a view to compelling warlords who held sway there and their outside supporters to answer for their acts before judicial bodies. On 16 October [S/2003/1017], the DRC said there were indications that Rwanda might be attempting to renew the fighting and called on the Council and the Secretary-General to expand MONUC's deployment to cover the area between Lake Albert and Lake Tanganyika. It urged the Council to apply measures provided for under Chapter VII of the UN Charter against the leaders of Rwanda.

In a 13 October declaration [S/2003/1024], the EU Presidency condemned the renewed massacres in Katchele, which demonstrated the persistence of elements opposing the peace process in the DRC, despite the progress made in recent months. It noted the decision of the International Criminal Court to examine the investigations into the events in Ituri.

On 10 November [S/2003/1076], Rwanda alleged that the illegal supply of arms and ammunition to militia groups in eastern DRC was continuing. In that regard, it referred to the recent crash at Kamina of a cargo aircraft, which delivered arms to both Congolese and foreign armed groups in South Kivu, including ex-FAR/Interahamwe militia. Congolese authorities had prevented MONUC from investigating the matter. It was regrettable that the delivery of weapons occurred less than one month after the goodwill mission of the Minister for Foreign Affairs and Cooperation of Rwanda to Kinshasa. Rwanda also regretted that the DRC had prevented MONUC from carrying out inspection and verification at Kamina.

Press statement (12 November). Having heard a Secretariat briefing on the Ituri situation, particularly the fighting provoked by UPC and other militias on 5 November, which prompted a MONUC response, the Security Council, in a 12 November press statement by the President [SC/7915-AFR/753], condemned the attacks and expressed concern at the continuing hostilities in eastern DRC, particularly in Ituri and the Kivus. The members also condemned the events of October in Katchele. They urged all the parties to ensure respect for human rights and international humanitarian law, to refrain from giving support to armed groups and to cooperate with MONUC.

Report of Secretary-General (November). In his fourteenth report on MONUC, submitted on 17 November [S/2003/1098], the Secretary-General said that despite the advances made in forming the transitional Government in the DRC during the six-month reporting period, fighting and conflict continued in Ituri and eastern DRC, necessitating the full deployment and active engagement of MONUC. In Bunia, approximately 420 civilians had been killed in fighting between Lendu and Hema militias since the departure of Ugandan troops in May. Widespread rape and looting also occurred. In border areas between Uganda and Ituri, MONUC reported 380 cases of human rights abuses, including killings, forced disappearances, mutilations, rape and systematic looting and destruction of property. In view of the increasing threat levels, MONUC military observers were evacuated to Bunia, during which process two observers were killed.

As the situation deteriorated, the Security Council, on 30 May, had authorized, by resolution 1484(2003), the deployment of EU-led IEMF (see p. 126). That force, which began deploying to Bunia in June, restored a measure of security to the town. At its strongest, IEMF numbered just over 1,000 troops in Bunia and 500 support staff in Entebbe, Uganda. From mid-August, with the gradual deployment of the MONUC Ituri brigade (an authorized force of 4,800), the Mission started to take over operational tasks from IEMF, which fully withdrew from the area by 15 September. Agreement was reached among the parties to respect Bunia as a weapon-free zone as from 16 September, following which MONUC began to carry out cordon-and-search operations in Bunia to restore a sense of security in the town and dominate the armed factions. By November, the situation was calm but tense in Bunia, and MONUC began expanding its presence outside the city. With the exception of UPC, the armed groups in Ituri expressed willingness to be incorporated into the new national armed forces. MONUC was making concerted efforts to obtain information from the armed groups on the numbers and locations of their troops.

MONUC intensified its local conflict resolution efforts in the Kivus, Maniema and northern Katanga. Ceasefire agreements were reached between various military groups during October, resulting in the withdrawal of forces in certain local conflicts and increased humanitarian access in South Kivu. MONUC also assisted the transitional Government in implementing a national DDRRR programme, demobilizing child soldiers, normalizing relations with neighbouring States, and monitoring the arms embargo imposed on the Kivus and Ituri.

MONUC played a role in facilitating the political transition and preparing for elections. The transitional Government, established on 30 June, was composed of 36 Ministers and 25 Vice-Ministers from the eight components and entities of the Inter-Congolese Dialogue [YUN 2001, p. 131], who were chosen under the auspices of the Follow-up Commission. That Commission was established on 14 April to address outstanding issues for the installation of the transitional Government. However, two major political parties, the Union pour la démocratie et le progrès social and the Parti Lumumbiste unifié, were not represented in the transitional Government as they did not agree on the process of nominating representatives. On 1 August, the neutral Facilitator of the Inter-Congolese Dialogue, Sir Ketumile Masire, formally handed over to President Kabila the final report of the Dialogue and its 36 resolutions, which were to form the basis of the transitional Government's activities during the two-year period leading to elections. Having completed the tasks assigned to it in the All-Inclusive Agreement, the Follow-up Commission held its final meeting on 18 August and presented its final report to the Council of Ministers on 29 August. The Council of Ministers and four inter-ministerial commissions began to meet regularly and, on 8 August, adopted a comprehensive set of policy goals. On 22 August, the 500-member National Assembly and the 120-member Senate were inaugurated in Kinshasa. The process leading to the installation of the transitional Government was not easy and was supported throughout by the International Committee in Support of the Transition, chaired by the Secretary-General's Special Representative. The presence of all major transitional leaders in Kinshasa owed much to the deployment by MONUC of the "neutral force", which provided security and transportation to those members of the transitional Government who needed it.

A key challenge for the establishment of the transitional Government was how to reach agreement on integrating the armed forces of the belligerents. On 29 June, the Congolese parties signed Memorandum II on the army and security, which provided for the allocation of senior posts in the integrated High Command of the armed forces. That was followed by an agreement to allocate three military regions to the former Government; two each to MLC and RCD-Goma; and one each to RCD-N, RCD-Kisangani/ML and the Mayi-Mayi. After further discussions, President Kabila appointed the Chiefs of Staff of the armed forces and the commanders and deputy commanders of the 10 military regions. However, at that juncture, there was still lack of clarity on the modalities for the integration and restructuring of the armed forces, and effective collaboration at the level of the Chiefs of Staff was lacking.

The All-Inclusive Agreement called for elections to be held within two years of the establishment of the transitional Government. With that in mind, MONUC facilitated meetings of members of the international community in the DRC and established an Electoral Assistance Unit (EAU) to coordinate support. Although the Independent Electoral Commission had not been formally established by law, its members held meetings and EAU was helping the Commission to develop an organizational structure and electoral road map.

MONUC also provided assistance in other areas, such as restoring and strengthening the rule of law by creating institutions and processes; supporting the establishment of an integrated police unit and training a future Congolese national police; investigating human rights abuses, data gathering and analysis, and engaging in capacity-building for Congolese civil society and officials; protecting delivery of humanitarian assistance; protecting children who were victims of the conflict; providing mine clearance; promoting support for women political leaders; informing the public about HIV/AIDS; and enhancing public information capacities.

In general, the Secretary-General found that significant progress had been achieved in the DRC during the reporting period, although considerable work remained to be done on a number of key issues of the peace process. On the positive side, former belligerents were working together in the transitional Government, the process of uniting the formerly divided territory had begun, and peacemaking trends at the local level were encouraging. In addition, the DRC's relations with Rwanda and Uganda had improved. South Africa had played an important role in collaborating with MONUC in the framework of the Third Party Verification Mechanism to help the parties implement the provisions of the All-Inclusive Agreement.

Outstanding challenges included the continuing presence of foreign armed combatants in eastern DRC, which affected the security situation. The recent agreement between the DRC and Rwanda to establish a joint mechanism with MONUC to address DDRRR of Rwandan combatants was a step in the right direction. There continued to be allegations of the presence in the DRC of Rwandan military personnel, which MONUC was investigating. The transitional Government needed to extend State administration throughout the eastern part of the country, integrate the armed forces at the provincial level and extend political and economic benefits to the population of the region, especially in North and South Kivu. The situation in Ituri had been a particular concern, and the EU's deployment of the well-equipped IEMF for a limited period of time helped to stave off an impending humanitarian crisis. Another key concern was the flow of arms into the country, and its link to the illegal exploitation of natural resources. The arms transfers had contributed to the ongoing violence, especially in the east, while the illegal exploitation of resources had robbed the Congolese people of their national wealth (see p. 140). Despite the signs of progress, the tangible benefits of peace had not yet filtered down to the war-weary Congolese population; socio-economic conditions remained dire throughout the country and gross human rights violations continued.

Press statement (11 December). The Security Council was briefed on the situation in the DRC by the Under-Secretary-General for Peacekeeping Operations on 11 December. The Council President issued a press statement [SC/7949-AFR/794], in which Council members welcomed the improvement of bilateral relations between the DRC, Rwanda and Uganda and encouraged them to work on concrete confidence-building measures. Expressing appreciation for the involvement of the AU, and in particular of South Africa and other regional actors, in moving the peace process forward, they took note of the progress made by the transitional Government and urged it to accelerate the implementation of the All-Inclusive Agreement, in particular by the adoption of a national disarmament, demobilization and reintegration programme, and reform of the armed and police forces. The members urged all foreign armed groups to enter DDRRR activities. They stressed the need to adopt legislation establishing the Institutions in Support of Democracy, in particular for enabling the Independent Electoral Commission and the Haute Autorité des Médias to function. They urged all the parties to the conflict, including the DRC Government, to undertake all necessary measures to stop violations of human rights and international humanitarian law and to bring to justice those who had committed, ordered or contributed in any way to such crimes. The members urged the DRC Government and the National Parliament to conduct national consultations on the formation and composition of the Truth and Reconciliation Commission (TRC) and to adopt a revised TRC law, which upheld human rights principles. They called on Member States and international organizations to assist the Government in re-establishing the rule of law throughout the country. They also urged Member States to support the implementation of the arms embargo imposed by Council resolution 1493(2003) (see p. 130) and efforts to end the illegal exploitation of natural resources and their financing (see p. 140). Council members reaffirmed their determination to address that issue and related problems posed by the illicit flow of weapons into the DRC, including by considering the possible establishment of a monitoring mechanism.

Communications (December). On 10 December [S/2003/1164], Rwanda welcomed the return from the DRC of the Commander of the Forces combattantes Abacunguzi, with a total of 100 troops, on 14 November. The event was a step in the DDRRR process, which was a cornerstone of the stabilization of the DRC and the Great Lakes region. At the same time, Rwanda expressed concern about those "génocidaires" who chose to continue with armed conflict from DRC territory. Those hardliners were forcibly preventing the return to Rwanda of many ex-FAR/Interahamwe combatants who were ready to give up arms and follow their former Commander.

The DRC, on 15 December [S/2003/1178], referred to Rwanda's letter and said that the stabilization of the region as a whole would become total when Rwanda ceased to be the centre of tension. The DRC repeated its request that the Security Council set up an international criminal court to prosecute those responsible for serious international humanitarian law violations and human rights abuses committed in DRC territory on or after 28 August 1998. It also requested the Council to require Rwanda to participate in the process of an international conference on the Great Lakes and Central Africa.

Situation at year's end. Although the principal political institutions of the transition began to function in late 2003 and several steps were taken towards the implementation of key provisions of the Global and All-Inclusive Agreement [YUN 2002, p. 125], overall progress remained slow [S/2004/251]. Delays were encountered in setting the legislative agenda; extending State administration; integrating the military; disarmament, demobilization and reintegration; and preparation for elections. Furthermore, tensions within the transitional Government increased. In that connection, President Kabila, on 23 December, sought confirmation by the Supreme Court of his sole legal authority over the appointment of governors and control over military intelligence, a move criticized by some members of the transitional Government as undermining the principles of power sharing.

On 18 December, the transitional Government established an inter-ministerial committee to oversee the planning of a national disarmament, demobilization and reintegration programme, a commission to coordinate and implement the national programme and a Committee for the Management of Demobilization and Reintegration Funds. The World Bank was expected to provide funds for the programme, which was in the planning stages and would involve a role for MONUC.

President Kabila, on 24 November, requested the United Nations to assist in organizing the constitutional referendum and election preparations. Accordingly, MONUC convened an international technical committee on the electoral process, which met weekly under the Mission's chairmanship.

Concerning relations with neighbouring States, the DRC and Rwanda, despite having agreed to confidence-building measures, had not yet set up a joint bilateral commission. Meetings of the joint security commission of the DRC and Uganda were postponed several times.

There was some limited progress in solidifying the political process in Ituri. The meeting on 17 December of the Comité de concertation des groupes armées (CCGA) in Bunia agreed, in principle, to launch a pilot disarmament project. Since then, MONUC, CCGA and the Ituri interim administration continued to verify the Ituri armed groups' designated assembly areas to prepare for disarmament and reintegration. However, armed groups continued to jockey for power and hostile attacks continued.

GENERAL ASSEMBLY ACTION

The General Assembly, on 15 September, decided, at the request of the DRC [A/57/860], to defer consideration of the item entitled "Armed aggression against the Democratic Republic of the Congo" and to include it in the draft agenda of its fifty-eighth session (**decision 57/597**).

In **resolution 58/123** of 17 December, the Assembly took action on special assistance for the economic recovery and reconstruction of the DRC (see p. 944).

MONUC financing

In June, the General Assembly considered a number of reports of the Secretary-General concerning the MONUC budget.

A performance report on the MONUC budget, covering 1 July 2001 to 30 June 2002 [A/57/682], stated that, of the total apportionment of $450 million, $388.8 million was spent, leaving an unexpended balance of $61.2 million (13.6 per cent). The difference was mostly attributable to slow deployment of military contingents and delays in recruiting civilian staff. The Secretary-General recommended that the Assembly: offset the amount of $41 million unassessed during the 2001/02 period against the unencumbered balance of $61.2 million for the period ended 30 June 2002; decide on the treatment of the remaining unencumbered balance of $20.2 million for 1 July 2001 to 30 June 2002; and decide on other miscellaneous income and adjustments for the period ended 30 June 2002 amounting to $23 million.

The MONUC budget for 1 July 2003 to 30 June 2004 [A/57/683 & Add.1] was revised following the Security Council's expansion of the Mission by resolution 1445(2002) [YUN 2002, p. 123]. The revised budget amounted to $636.5 million, inclusive of budgeted voluntary contributions in kind in the amount of $1.7 million, representing an additional $118 million. It provided for the deployment of 7,749 troops, 760 military observers, 100 civilian police, 849 international staff, 1,245 national staff and 341 United Nations Volunteers. The Secretary-General recommended that the Assembly appropriate $634.8 million to maintain the Mission from 1 July 2003 to 30 June 2004, and assess that amount at a monthly rate of $52.9 million, should the Council decide to continue MONUC's mandate.

In a February report [A/57/723], the Secretary-General provided an overview of the financing of UN peacekeeping operations in general, based on budget performance for 1 July 2001 to 30 June 2002 and budgets for 1 July 2003 to 30 June 2004. It stated that MONUC's budget implementation rate for 2001/02 stood at 86 per cent.

In a March progress report on the status of the airfield services contract for MONUC [A/57/756], the Secretary-General stated that final contract negotiations with the recommended vendor of airfield services to replace the existing contract were being undertaken to conclude a contract to commence the services from 1 April. It was planned to use a commercial contractor for services at five sites, with contingent resources being deployed to three others and possibly more airfields as requirements developed.

In its May review of the financial reports and proposed budget [A/57/772/Add.10], the Advisory Committee on Administrative and Budgetary Questions (ACABQ) recommended approval of the Secretary-General's proposals contained in the 2001/02 performance report. Since it was expected that the Council would soon expand MONUC's mandate and that a new budget would be forthcoming, ACABQ recommended that the Assembly appropriate $582 million gross ($572.3 million net), pending the submission of a new budget for 2003/04.

GENERAL ASSEMBLY ACTION (June)

On 18 June [meeting 90], the General Assembly, on the recommendation of the Fifth (Administrative and Budgetary) Committee [A/57/831], adopted **resolution 57/335** without vote [agenda item 151].

Financing of the United Nations Organization Mission in the Democratic Republic of the Congo

The General Assembly,

Having considered the reports of the Secretary-General on the financing of the United Nations Organization Mission in the Democratic Republic of the Congo and the related reports of the Advisory Committee on Administrative and Budgetary Questions,

Recalling Security Council resolutions 1258(1999) of 6 August 1999 and 1279(1999) of 30 November 1999

regarding, respectively, the deployment to the Congo region of military liaison personnel and the establishment of the United Nations Organization Mission in the Democratic Republic of the Congo, and the subsequent resolutions by which the Council extended the mandate of the Mission, the latest of which was resolution 1417(2002) of 14 June 2002,

Recalling also Security Council resolution 1445(2002) of 4 December 2002, by which the Council endorsed the new concept of operation and authorized the expansion of the Mission,

Recalling further its resolution 54/260 A of 7 April 2000, as well as subsequent resolutions on the financing of the Mission, the latest of which was resolution 56/252 C of 27 June 2002,

Reaffirming the general principles underlying the financing of United Nations peacekeeping operations, as stated in General Assembly resolutions 1874(S-IV) of 27 June 1963, 3101(XXVIII) of 11 December 1973 and 55/235 of 23 December 2000,

Noting with appreciation that voluntary contributions have been made to the Mission,

Mindful of the fact that it is essential to provide the Mission with the necessary financial resources to enable it to fulfil its responsibilities under the relevant resolutions of the Security Council,

1. *Takes note* of the status of contributions to the United Nations Organization Mission in the Democratic Republic of the Congo as at 31 March 2003, including the contributions outstanding in the amount of 211.9 million United States dollars, representing some 17 per cent of the total assessed contributions, notes with concern that only twenty-six Member States have paid their assessed contributions in full, and urges all other Member States, in particular those in arrears, to ensure payment of their outstanding assessed contributions;

2. *Expresses its appreciation* to those Member States which have paid their assessed contributions in full, and urges all other Member States to make every possible effort to ensure payment of their assessed contributions to the Mission in full;

3. *Expresses concern* at the financial situation with regard to peacekeeping activities, in particular as regards the reimbursements to troop contributors that bear additional burdens owing to overdue payments by Member States of their assessments;

4. *Also expresses concern* at the delay experienced by the Secretary-General in deploying and providing adequate resources to some recent peacekeeping missions, in particular those in Africa;

5. *Emphasizes* that all future and existing peacekeeping missions shall be given equal and non-discriminatory treatment in respect of financial and administrative arrangements;

6. *Also emphasizes* that all peacekeeping missions shall be provided with adequate resources for the effective and efficient discharge of their respective mandates;

7. *Reiterates its request* to the Secretary-General to make the fullest possible use of facilities and equipment at the United Nations Logistics Base at Brindisi, Italy, in order to minimize the costs of procurement for the Mission;

8. *Takes note* of the progress report of the Secretary-General on the status of the airfield services contract for the Mission, and looks forward to the further review of the subject by the Board of Auditors;

9. *Reaffirms* the relevant provisions of its resolutions 55/232 of 23 December 2000 and 55/247 of 12 April 2001;

10. *Also reaffirms* its resolution 49/233 A of 23 December 1994 and decision 49/478 A of 31 March 1995;

11. *Notes* the intention of the Secretary-General to submit a revised proposed budget for the period from 1 July 2003 to 30 June 2004, reflecting the developments in the Democratic Republic of the Congo and further decisions of the Security Council, to the General Assembly at the main part of its fifty-eighth session;

12. *Endorses* the conclusions and recommendations contained in the report of the Advisory Committee on Administrative and Budgetary Questions, and requests the Secretary-General to ensure their full implementation, with the understanding that the Secretary-General should have adequate resources to address the changing situation on the ground, subject to the provisions of the present resolution;

13. *Requests* the Secretary-General to take all necessary action to ensure that the Mission is administered with maximum efficiency and economy, particularly with regard to air transport;

14. *Also requests* the Secretary-General, in order to reduce the cost of employing General Service staff, to continue efforts to recruit local staff for the Mission against General Service posts, commensurate with the requirements of the Mission;

Financial performance report for the period from 1 July 2001 to 30 June 2002

15. *Takes note* of the report of the Secretary-General on the financial performance of the Mission for the period from July 2001 to 30 June 2002;

16. *Decides* to offset the amount of 41 million dollars, which had been appropriated but not apportioned during the financial period ended 30 June 2001 against the unencumbered balance of 61,173,000 dollars in respect of the financial period ended 30 June 2002;

Budget estimates for the period from 1 July 2003 to 30 June 2004

17. *Decides also* to appropriate to the Special Account for the United Nations Organization Mission in the Democratic Republic of the Congo the amount of 608,228,150 dollars for the period from 1 July 2003 to 30 June 2004, inclusive of 582 million dollars for the maintenance of the Mission, 20,083,850 dollars for the support account for peacekeeping operations and 6,144,300 dollars for the United Nations Logistics Base, pending the submission of the revised proposed budget to the General Assembly;

Financing of the appropriation

18. *Decides further* to apportion among Member States the amount of 608,228,150 dollars at a monthly rate of 50,685,679 dollars, in accordance with the levels set out in resolution 55/235, as adjusted by the General Assembly in its resolutions 55/236 of 23 December 2000, and 57/290 A of 20 December 2002, and taking into account the scale of assessments for 2003, as set out in its resolutions 55/5 B of 23 December 2000 and 57/4 B of 20 December 2002, and for 2004, subject to the decision of the Security Council to extend the man-

date of the Mission, pending the submission of the revised proposed budget to the Assembly;

19. *Decides* that, in accordance with the provisions of its resolution 973(X) of 15 December 1955, there shall be set off against the apportionment among Member States, as provided for in paragraph 18 above, their respective share in the Tax Equalization Fund of 14,599,236 dollars at a monthly rate of 1,216,603 dollars, comprising the estimated staff assessment income of 9,710,736 dollars approved for the Mission, the prorated share of 4,525,200 dollars of the estimated staff assessment income approved for the support account, and the prorated share of 363,300 dollars of the estimated staff assessment income approved for the United Nations Logistics Base;

20. *Decides also* that for Member States that have fulfilled their financial obligations to the Mission, there shall be set off against their apportionment, as provided for in paragraph 18 above, their respective share of the remaining unencumbered balance and other income in the total amount of 43,158,000 dollars in respect of the financial period ended 30 June 2002, in accordance with the levels set out in resolution 55/235, as adjusted by the General Assembly in its resolutions 55/236, and 57/290 A and taking into account the scale of assessments for 2002, as set out in its resolutions 55/5 B and 57/4 B;

21. *Decides further* that for Member States that have not fulfilled their financial obligations to the Mission, their respective share of the remaining unencumbered balance and other income in the total amount of 43,158,000 dollars in respect of the financial period ended 30 June 2002 shall be set off against their outstanding obligations, in accordance with the scheme set out in paragraph 20 above;

22. *Decides* that the decrease of 448,600 dollars in the estimated staff assessment income in respect of the financial period ended 30 June 2002 shall be set off against the credits from the amount referred to in paragraphs 20 and 21 above;

23. *Emphasizes* that no peacekeeping mission shall be financed by borrowing funds from other active peacekeeping missions;

24. *Encourages* the Secretary-General to continue to take additional measures to ensure the safety and security of all personnel under the auspices of the United Nations participating in the Mission;

25. *Invites* voluntary contributions to the Mission in cash and in the form of services and supplies acceptable to the Secretary-General, to be administered, as appropriate, in accordance with the procedure and practices established by the General Assembly;

26. *Decides* to include in the provisional agenda of its fifty-eighth session the item entitled "Financing of the United Nations Organization Mission in the Democratic Republic of the Congo".

Following the Security Council's adoption of resolution 1493(2003) of 28 July (see p. 130), by which MONUC's mandate was extended until 30 July 2004, the Secretary-General submitted to the General Assembly a September report containing MONUC's revised budget for 1 July 2003 to 30 June 2004 [A/58/381]. The total requirements of $677.3 million included budgeted voluntary contributions in kind of $2.27 million. The budget provided for the phased deployment of 10,040 troops, 760 military observers, 182 civilian police, 938 international staff, 1,299 national staff and 419 United Nations Volunteers.

ACABQ reviewed the report and issued its comments in October [A/58/447 & Corr.1]. It found that there had been a continuing and serious trend of overbudgeting for the Mission, that economies of scale should have been achieved as a result of the increase in troop strength, that duplication could be avoided through streamlining, that ratios for vehicles and computer equipment could not be justified and that travel costs could be reduced. Therefore, ACABQ recommended an appropriation of $59 million in addition to the $582 million gross ($572.3 million net) already appropriated by the Assembly in resolution 57/335 (above) for 2003/04, a reduction of $34 million, or 5 per cent. It also recommended that the total amount assessed should not exceed $582 million gross.

GENERAL ASSEMBLY ACTION (December)

On 23 December [meeting 79], the General Assembly, on the recommendation of the Fifth Committee [A/58/583], adopted resolution **58/259 A** without vote [agenda item 138].

Financing of the United Nations Organization Mission in the Democratic Republic of the Congo

The General Assembly,

Having considered the report of the Secretary-General on the financing of the United Nations Organization Mission in the Democratic Republic of the Congo and the related report of the Advisory Committee on Administrative and Budgetary Questions,

Recalling Security Council resolutions 1258(1999) of 6 August 1999 and 1279(1999) of 30 November 1999, regarding, respectively, the deployment to the Congo region of military liaison personnel and the establishment of the United Nations Organization Mission in the Democratic Republic of the Congo, and the subsequent resolutions by which the Council extended the mandate of the Mission, the latest of which was resolution 1493(2003) of 28 July 2003, by which the Council also authorized increasing the military strength of the Mission,

Recalling also its resolution 54/260 A of 7 April 2000, on the financing of the Mission, and its subsequent resolutions thereon, the latest of which was resolution 57/335 of 18 June 2003,

Reaffirming the general principles underlying the financing of United Nations peacekeeping operations, as stated in General Assembly resolutions 1874(S-IV) of 27 June 1963, 3101(XXVIII) of 11 December 1973 and 55/235 of 23 December 2000,

Noting with appreciation that voluntary contributions have been made to the Mission,

Mindful of the fact that it is essential to provide the Mission with the necessary financial resources to enable it to fulfil its responsibilities under the relevant resolutions of the Security Council,

1. *Takes note* of the status of contributions to the United Nations Organization Mission in the Democratic Republic of the Congo as at 31 October 2003, including the contributions outstanding in the amount of 139.7 million United States dollars, representing some 9.1 per cent of the total assessed contributions, notes with concern that only thirty-two Member States have paid their assessed contributions in full, and urges all other Member States, in particular those in arrears, to ensure payment of their outstanding assessed contributions;

2. *Expresses its appreciation* to those Member States which have paid their assessed contributions in full, and urges all other Member States to make every possible effort to ensure payment of their assessed contributions to the Mission in full;

3. *Expresses concern* at the financial situation with regard to peacekeeping activities, in particular as regards the reimbursements to troop contributors that bear additional burdens owing to overdue payments by Member States of their assessments;

4. *Also expresses concern* at the delay experienced by the Secretary-General in deploying some recent peacekeeping missions, in particular those in Africa, and in providing them with adequate resources;

5. *Emphasizes* that all future and existing peacekeeping missions shall be given equal and non-discriminatory treatment in respect of financial and administrative arrangements;

6. *Also emphasizes* that all peacekeeping missions shall be provided with adequate resources for the effective and efficient discharge of their respective mandates;

7. *Reiterates its request* to the Secretary-General to make the fullest possible use of facilities and equipment at the United Nations Logistics Base at Brindisi, Italy, in order to minimize the costs of procurement for the Mission;

8. *Endorses* the conclusions and recommendations contained in the report of the Advisory Committee on Administrative and Budgetary Questions, and requests the Secretary-General to ensure their full implementation;

9. *Requests* the Secretary-General to take all necessary action to ensure that the Mission is administered with a maximum of efficiency and economy, particularly with regard to air transport;

10. *Also requests* the Secretary-General, in order to reduce the cost of employing General Service staff, to continue efforts to recruit local staff for the Mission against General Service posts, commensurate with the requirements of the Mission;

Budget estimates for the period from 1 July 2003 to 30 June 2004

11. *Decides* to appropriate to the Special Account for the United Nations Organization Mission in the Democratic Republic of the Congo the amount of 59,038,300 dollars for the maintenance of the Mission for the period from 1 July 2003 to 30 June 2004, in addition to the amount of 582 million dollars already appropriated and apportioned for the same period under the terms of its resolution 57/335;

12. *Emphasizes* that no peacekeeping mission shall be financed by borrowing funds from other active peacekeeping missions;

13. *Encourages* the Secretary-General to continue to take additional measures to ensure the safety and security of all personnel under the auspices of the United Nations participating in the Mission;

14. *Invites* voluntary contributions to the Mission in cash and in the form of services and supplies acceptable to the Secretary-General, to be administered, as appropriate, in accordance with the procedure and practices established by the General Assembly;

15. *Decides* to keep under review during its fifty-eighth session the item entitled "Financing of the United Nations Organization Mission in the Democratic Republic of the Congo".

Exploitation of natural resources

In January, the Security Council considered the 15 October 2002 report of the Panel of Experts on the Illegal Exploitation of Natural Resources and Other Forms of Wealth of the Democratic Republic of the Congo [YUN 2002, p. 132]. The Panel was established by the Secretary-General, in response to presidential statement S/PRST/2000/20 [YUN 2000, p. 128], to collect information on illegal exploitation and to analyse the links between such exploitation and the conflicts. The report had concluded that the plundering of DRC natural resources was fuelling the conflict. Criminal groups linked to the armies of Rwanda, Uganda and Zimbabwe and the DRC Government had benefited from small conflicts, and had built up a self-financing war economy centred on mineral exploitation. While troop withdrawals had taken place, the countries involved (Rwanda and Zimbabwe) and Ugandan individuals continued to exercise economic control over parts of the DRC.

Following a debate on the issue in late 2002 [YUN 2002, p. 134], the Council took action in January and extended and expanded the mandate of the Panel (below).

SECURITY COUNCIL ACTION (January)

On 24 January [meeting 4691], the Security Council unanimously adopted **resolution 1457 (2003)**. The draft [S/2003/83] was prepared in consultations among Council members.

The Security Council,

Recalling its resolutions 1291(2000) of 24 February 2000, 1304(2000) of 16 June 2000, 1323(2000) of 13 October 2000, 1332(2000) of 14 December 2000, 1341 (2001) of 22 February 2001, 1355(2001) of 15 June 2001, 1376(2001) of 9 November 2001, 1417(2002) of 14 June 2002 and 1445(2002) of 4 December 2002, and the statements by its President of 26 January (S/PRST/2000/2), 2 June (S/PRST/2000/20) and 7 September 2000 (S/PRST/2000/28) and 3 May (S/PRST/2001/13) and 19 December 2001 (S/PRST/2001/39),

Reaffirming the sovereignty, territorial integrity and political independence of the Democratic Republic of the Congo and of all other States in the region,

Reaffirming also the sovereignty of the Democratic Republic of the Congo over its natural resources,

Recalling the letters dated 12 April and 10 November 2001 and 22 May 2002 from the Secretary-General,

Reiterating its commitment to take appropriate action to help to put an end to the plundering of the resources of the Democratic Republic of the Congo, in support of the peace process,

Determining that the situation in the Democratic Republic of the Congo continues to constitute a threat to international peace and stability in the Great Lakes region,

1. *Takes note* of the report of the Panel of Experts on the Illegal Exploitation of Natural Resources and Other Forms of Wealth of the Democratic Republic of the Congo (hereinafter "the Panel"), transmitted by the Secretary-General in his letter dated 15 October 2002;

2. *Strongly condemns* the illegal exploitation of the natural resources of the Democratic Republic of the Congo;

3. *Notes with concern* that the plundering of the natural resources and other forms of wealth of the Democratic Republic of the Congo continues and that it is one of the main elements fuelling the conflict in the region, and in this regard demands that all States concerned take immediate steps to end these illegal activities which are perpetuating the conflict, impeding the economic development of the Democratic Republic of the Congo and exacerbating the suffering of its people;

4. *Reiterates* that the natural resources of the Democratic Republic of the Congo should be exploited transparently, legally and on a fair commercial basis, to benefit the country and its people;

5. *Stresses* that the completion of the withdrawal of all foreign troops from the territory of the Democratic Republic of the Congo as well as the early establishment of an all-inclusive Transitional Government in the country, which will ensure that central government control is reinstated and that viable administrations are empowered to protect and regulate the exploitation activities, are important steps towards ending the plundering of the natural resources of the Democratic Republic of the Congo;

6. *Stresses also* that the possible convening of an international conference on peace, security, democracy and development in the Great Lakes region at the appropriate time could help the States of the region in promoting a sound regional economic integration, to the benefit of all the States in the region;

7. *Notes* the importance of the natural resources and extractive sectors for the future of the Democratic Republic of the Congo, encourages States, international financial institutions and other organizations to assist Governments in the region in their efforts to create appropriate national structures and institutions to control the exploitation of resources, and encourages the Government of the Democratic Republic of the Congo to work closely with the international financial institutions and the donor community to establish Congolese institutional capacity to ensure that these sectors are controlled and operated in a transparent and legitimate way, so that the riches of the Democratic Republic of the Congo can benefit the Congolese people;

8. *Stresses* the importance of following up the independent findings of the Panel regarding the link between the illegal exploitation of the natural resources of the Democratic Republic of the Congo and the continuation of the conflict, stresses the importance of exerting the necessary pressure to put an end to such exploitation, notes that the reports of the Panel to date have made a useful contribution to the peace process in this regard, and therefore requests the Secretary-General to give a new mandate to the Panel for a period of six months, at the end of which the Panel should provide a report to the Security Council;

9. *Stresses also* that the new mandate of the Panel should include:

(a) Further review of relevant data and analysis of information previously gathered by the Panel, as well as any new information, including, specifically, material provided by individuals and entities named in the previous reports of the Panel, in order to verify, reinforce and, where necessary, update the findings of the Panel and/or to clear parties named in its previous reports, with a view to adjusting accordingly the lists attached to those reports;

(b) Information on actions taken by Governments in response to the previous recommendations of the Panel, including information on how capacity-building and reforms in the region are affecting exploitation activities;

(c) An assessment of the actions taken by all those named in the reports in respect of paragraphs 12 and 15 below;

(d) Recommendations on measures that a Transitional Government in the Democratic Republic of the Congo and other Governments in the region could take to develop and enhance their policies, legal framework and administrative capacity to ensure that the resources of the Democratic Republic of the Congo are exploited legally and on a fair commercial basis, to benefit the Congolese people;

10. *Requests* the Chairman of the Panel to brief the Council on any progress towards the cessation of the plundering of the natural resources of the Democratic Republic of the Congo, three months after the resumption of the work of the Panel;

11. *Invites*, in the interests of transparency, individuals, companies and States which have been named in the last report of the Panel to send their reactions, with due regard to commercial confidentiality, to the Secretariat no later than 31 March 2003, and requests the Secretary-General to arrange for the publication of those reactions, upon request by individuals, companies and States named in the report of 8 October 2002, as an attachment to this report, no later than 15 April 2003;

12. *Stresses* the importance of dialogue between the Panel, individuals, companies and States, and requests in this regard that the Panel provide to the individuals, companies and States named, upon request, all information and documentation connecting them to the illegal exploitation of the natural resources of the Democratic Republic of the Congo, and requests the Panel to establish a procedure to provide to Member States, upon request, information previously collected by the Panel to help them to take the necessary investigative action, subject to the duty of the Panel to preserve the safety of its sources, and in accordance with

United Nations established practice, in consultation with the Office of Legal Affairs of the Secretariat;

13. *Emphasizes* the duty of the individuals, companies and States named in the report to respect the confidentiality of the material to be given to them by the Panel so as to ensure that the safety of the sources of the Panel is preserved;

14. *Requests* the Panel to provide information to the Organisation for Economic Co-operation and Development Committee on International Investment and Multinational Enterprises and to the National Contact Points for the Organisation for Economic Co-operation and Development Guidelines for Multinational Enterprises in the States where business enterprises listed in annex III to the last report as being allegedly in contravention of the guidelines of the Organisation for Economic Co-operation and Development are registered, in accordance with United Nations established practice;

15. *Urges* all States, especially those in the region, to conduct their own investigations, including, as appropriate, through judicial means, in order to clarify credibly the findings of the Panel, taking into account the fact that the Panel, which is not a judicial body, does not have the resources to carry out an investigation whereby those findings can be considered as established facts;

16. *Notes with satisfaction*, in this regard, the decision of the Attorney General of the Democratic Republic of the Congo to start a judicial procedure, commends the decision of the Government of the Democratic Republic of the Congo to suspend momentarily the officials named in the reports pending further clarification, and requests the Panel to cooperate fully with the Office of the Attorney General and to provide to that Office information it may need to conduct its investigations, subject to the duty of the Panel to preserve the safety of its sources and in accordance with United Nations established practice, in consultation with the Office of Legal Affairs;

17. *Also notes with satisfaction* the actions taken by other States, including the decision by the Government of Uganda to establish a Judicial Commission of Inquiry, urges all States concerned, and in particular the Governments of Zimbabwe and Rwanda, to cooperate fully with the Panel and to investigate further the accusations made through due judicial process, and stresses the importance of collaboration between the Panel and all investigative bodies;

18. *Encourages* all organizations concerned to consider, as appropriate, the relevant recommendations contained in the reports of the Panel, and in particular encourages the organizations of specialized industries to monitor trade in commodities from conflict areas, in particular the territory of the Democratic Republic of the Congo, and to collect data in this regard, with a view to helping to put an end to the plundering of the natural resources in those areas;

19. *Encourages* the implementation of the decisions taken within the framework of the Inter-Congolese Dialogue, especially its recommendation to establish a special commission to examine the validity of economic and financial agreements in the Democratic Republic of the Congo;

20. *Expresses its full support* to the Panel, and reiterates that all parties and relevant States must extend their full cooperation to the Panel, while ensuring necessary security for the experts;

21. *Decides* to remain actively seized of the matter.

Appointments. Referring to resolution 1457 (2003) (above), the Secretary-General, on 26 February [S/2003/226], informed the Security Council of his intention to reappoint Mahmoud Kassem (Egypt) to continue to chair the Expert Panel, and to appoint four Panel members. A proposal on an additional Panel member would be forthcoming. The reconstituted Panel was expected to reassemble in early March in New York before proceeding to the Great Lakes region.

Responses to Panel's report. The Security Council, in order to give more time to those individuals, companies and States wishing to respond to the Expert Panel's 2002 report, decided on 24 March [S/2003/340] to extend the deadlines set out in resolution 1457(2003) to 31 May for submission, in order for the reactions to be published no later than 20 June. On 20 June [S/2002/1146/Add.1], the Secretary-General submitted to the Council responses received from 58 of the individuals, companies and States named in the Panel's report.

SECURITY COUNCIL ACTION (August)

On 13 August [meeting 4807], the Security Council unanimously adopted **resolution 1499(2003)**. The draft [S/2003/803] was prepared in consultations among Council members.

The Security Council,

Recalling its previous relevant resolutions and statements by its President on the Democratic Republic of the Congo, in particular resolutions 1457(2003) of 24 January 2003 and 1493(2003) of 28 July 2003,

Welcoming recent progress in the political process and the establishment of the transitional Government in the Democratic Republic of the Congo,

Noting with great concern that the plundering of natural resources of the Democratic Republic of the Congo continues, especially in the eastern part of the country, as reported to the Council on 24 July 2003 in an interim briefing by the Chairman of the Panel of Experts on the Illegal Exploitation of Natural Resources and Other Forms of Wealth of the Democratic Republic of the Congo (hereinafter "the Panel"), and stressing that appropriate action should be taken with regard to those responsible for such activities,

Taking note of the efforts of the Panel to establish constructive dialogue with individuals, companies and States named in its report of 8 October 2002,

Welcoming the publication, as an attachment to the report of the Panel, of the reactions of those individuals, companies and States,

Recognizing that exchanging information and attempting to resolve issues will help the transparency of the work of the Panel as well as heighten awareness of the illegal exploitation of natural resources and other forms of wealth of the Democratic Republic of the Congo in the context of the conflict and, in particular, its connection with the illicit trade of small arms and light weapons,

Taking note of the intention of the Panel, in accordance with paragraph 9 of resolution 1457(2003), to remove from the annexes to its report the names of those parties with which it has or will have reached a resolution by the end of its mandate,

Renewing its support to the Panel in its efforts to secure, including through dialogue with parties named in its latest report, particularly with Governments concerned, a clearer picture of activities related to the illegal exploitation of natural resources in the Democratic Republic of the Congo, and to update its findings during the remainder of its mandate period,

1. *Requests* the Secretary-General to extend the mandate of the Panel until 31 October 2003 to enable it to complete the remaining elements of its mandate, at the end of which the Panel will submit a final report to the Council;

2. *Reiterates its demand* that all States concerned take immediate steps to end the illegal exploitation of natural resources and other forms of wealth in the Democratic Republic of the Congo;

3. *Requests* the Panel to provide the necessary information to the Governments concerned, as required in paragraphs 12 and 13 of resolution 1457(2003), with due regard to safety of sources, in order to enable them, if necessary, to take appropriate action according to their national laws and international obligations;

4. *Calls upon* all States to respect the relevant Security Council resolutions in this regard;

5. *Decides* to remain actively seized of the matter.

Report of Expert Panel. In response to resolution 1457(2003) (see p. 140), by which the Security Council requested the Secretary-General to give a new mandate to the Panel of Experts for a period of six months, the Secretary-General, on 23 October [S/2003/1027], submitted to the Council the Panel's final report under that mandate on the illegal exploitation of DRC natural resources and other forms of wealth.

The Panel noted that its October 2002 report [YUN 2002, p. 132] had drawn strong reactions from entities named therein. Of the 157 parties mentioned, responses were received from 119, with whom the Panel met. The Panel grouped the results of its work into five categories: resolved cases, where a solution to the issues that led to the entities being listed was found; provisional resolution, dependent on companies fulfilling commitments after the end of the Panel's mandate; companies, together with their owners, which had been referred to national contact points for updating or further investigation; companies and individuals that had been referred to Governments for further investigation; and parties that did not react to the Panel's report.

The report described the transmission of information for investigations by government authorities in the DRC, Rwanda and Zimbabwe, and noted that the Panel had provided the national contact points of Belgium, Germany and the United Kingdom with information and documentation on a number of individuals and companies under their jurisdiction that were named in the Panel's previous report. The Panel identified States in the region through which goods originating in the DRC might be passing, including Angola, Burundi, the Central African Republic, the Congo, Kenya, Mozambique, Rwanda, Uganda, the United Republic of Tanzania, Zambia and Zimbabwe; and requested them to describe measures they were taking to curb illegal exploitation of the DRC's natural resources. Only Rwanda, Uganda, Zambia and Zimbabwe responded.

During the year since the Panel's previous report, illegal resource exploitation continued to be one of the main sources of funding for groups involved in the conflict, especially in eastern and north-eastern DRC. Such exploitation was characterized by intense competition among the various political and military actors as they sought to maintain or expand their control over territory. The power vacuum caused by the withdrawal of Rwandan and Ugandan armed forces spurred the proliferation of militias, who vied for control over strategic zones where lucrative resources were located and which were formerly held by the foreign forces. The Panel believed that the deteriorating security situation in eastern DRC, which resulted from intensifying armed confrontations among the militias, had a direct impact on the level and nature of resource exploitation, compared to previous years. Overall, the transition of control from foreign forces to the armed groups had led to a temporary reduction in the volume of illegally exploited resources.

From a variety of sources, the Panel determined that much of the recent resource exploitation was concentrated in gold and diamonds, in particular from Ituri, other parts of Orientale province, North and South Kivu and Maniema. Also financed with moneys collected at customs border posts, political and military actors were able to fund their military activities, including the supply of arms. The Panel repeated its earlier assertion that it was difficult to stem or halt illegal exploitation without also tackling the issue of arms trafficking. Accordingly, the focus of the Panel's fieldwork and fact-finding had been on the patterns and trends in arms trafficking and the groups involved. The Panel gathered information on how those groups were adjusting to political developments, especially the establishment of the Government of National Unity. It was clear that they were developing strategies to build and extend their political and economic control in various parts of the DRC. The details on exploitation and arms trafficking had been made available to the Security Council and could be useful for an arms monitoring mechanism, should the Council decide to establish one.

In the absence of a strong, central and democratically elected Government that was in control of its territory, illegal resource exploitation would continue to serve as the fuel for conflicts in the region, to the detriment of the Congolese people. The establishment of the transitional Government was a step in the right direction, but major obstacles continued to be faced. Financial and technical support from the international community was needed to strengthen national capacity to assume control and regulate the exploitation of natural resources. The extension of government authority in problematic areas, accompanied by a reform of the rule-of-law sector and the re-establishment of a criminal justice capacity, was needed to ensure that the Government was in control of its natural resources for the benefit of the population. The most important factor in ensuring the reunification of the national territory would be the integration of the new armed forces. While the transitional partners had reached agreement on the command structure of those forces, actual integration had yet to take place.

Immediate institutional reforms were needed to ensure that the newly elected Government, once in place, could ensure the legal exploitation of natural resources, including: control of the national borders through effective customs administration; strengthening the government auditing function so that it could undertake regular auditing of all government departments and agencies, including in the provinces; and breaking up the large State-owned mineral resource enterprises. Disclosure of revenues earned from natural resources by both private companies and the Government should be implemented in the DRC as a step towards ensuring a more equitable distribution of the national wealth.

Immediate interim measures recommended by the Panel included placing emphasis on stemming and, if possible, halting the flow of illegal arms to the DRC, an area where the international community could play a role, as the Security Council had done by imposing the arms embargo on Ituri and the Kivus in resolution 1493(2003) (see p. 130). In that connection, the Panel suggested that the Council establish a monitoring mechanism, as envisaged in that resolution, to track the full scope of the arms flow supply chain from manufacturer to final beneficiary, including the financing of the process through the illegal exploitation of resources, thus deterring arms trafficking and curbing arms flows. It was also vital to break the dependency link between armed groups carrying out natural resource exploitation and local communities if those activities were to be brought to an end. In that regard, specific quick-impact projects needed to be undertaken to convince people of the advantages of peace: hospitals, clinics and schools needed to be reopened, local policing re-established and jobs created. However, none of those measures could be sustained unless a regional solution was found. The Principles on Good-Neighbourly Relations adopted by the parties on 25 September were a step in that direction. Confidence-building measures were needed to take forward those principles, particularly with regard to tackling the issue of foreign-armed groups in the DRC from Burundi, Rwanda and Uganda, including the ex-FAR/Interahamwe. Also to be addressed was the status of the Banyamulenge and other ethnic groups, such as the Banyarwandans in North and South Kivu.

The Panel observed that its work had spurred Governments, non-governmental organizations (NGOs) and others to pursue their own investigations into the plundering of resources. The Governments of the DRC, Uganda and Belgium had taken such action. In general, the Panel had made valuable contributions to the Security Council's work on peace and security issues. There was, nevertheless, a need to analyse, institutionalize and make available the experiences and lessons learned from investigations mandated by the Council on Afghanistan, Angola, the DRC, Liberia, Sierra Leone and Somalia. The Panel concluded that, to be effective, monitoring activities concerning arms and revenue flows in conflict situations should be institutionalized and cover longer periods. That would require high levels of expertise, flexibility in conducting fieldwork and adequate support of relevant UN bodies and the Secretariat.

Communications (October/November). In late 2003, the Security Council received letters from three Governments reacting to the Expert Panel's October report (see above). Rwanda, on 30 October [S/2003/1048], raised objections to the methodology used by the Panel and said it had been unfairly targeted for condemnation. On 14 November [S/2003/1095], South Africa expressed willingness to investigate allegations against South African–owned or –based entities and individuals, based on credible information. Uganda, on 20 November [S/2003/1116], requested that the report be corrected with regard to the names of two officers of the Uganda People's Defence Forces listed as not responding to the Panel.

SECURITY COUNCIL ACTION (November)

On 19 November [meeting 4863], following consultations among Security Council members, the President made statement **S/PRST/2003/21** on behalf of the Council:

The Security Council,

Takes note of the final report of the Panel of Experts on the Illegal Exploitation of Natural Resources and Other Forms of Wealth in the Democratic Republic of the Congo (the Panel), which concludes its work, and emphasizes the connection, in the context of the continuing conflict, between the illegal exploitation of natural resources and trafficking in raw materials and arms, which the Panel has highlighted;

Condemns the continuing illegal exploitation of natural resources in the Democratic Republic of the Congo, especially in the eastern part of the country, recalls that it has always categorically condemned these activities, which are one of the main elements perpetuating the conflict, and reaffirms the importance of stopping them by exerting, if need be, the necessary pressure on the armed groups, traffickers and all other actors involved;

Urges all States concerned, especially those in the region, to take the appropriate steps to end these illegal activities, by proceeding with their own investigations, on the basis, in particular, of information and documentation accumulated by the Panel during its work and forwarded to Governments, including through judicial means where possible, and, if necessary, to report to the Council;

Reaffirms its determination to closely monitor compliance with the arms embargo imposed in resolution 1493(2003) of 28 July 2003 and expresses its intention to address the problem posed by the illicit flow of weapons into the Democratic Republic of the Congo, including by considering the possible establishment of a monitoring mechanism;

Emphasizes that the prompt re-establishment, by the Government of National Unity and Transition, of State authority throughout the territory, and the establishment of competent administrations to protect and control exploitation activities will constitute decisive elements for ending the plundering of natural resources in the Democratic Republic of the Congo;

Encourages the Government of National Unity and Transition to implement the resolutions adopted in Sun City, South Africa, in April 2002 within the framework of the Inter-Congolese Dialogue;

Encourages States, trade-sector organizations and specialized bodies to monitor the trade in raw materials from the region in order to put an end to the plundering of natural resources in the Democratic Republic of the Congo, particularly within the framework of the Kimberley Process;

Encourages States, the international financial community and the international organizations concerned to provide the aid needed to the Government of National Unity and Transition and to cooperate closely with it in order to support the establishment of national institutions capable of ensuring that the natural resources are exploited transparently to effectively benefit the Congolese people;

Expresses the wish that convening at an appropriate time an international conference on peace, security, democracy and development in the Great Lakes region of Africa will encourage the promotion of regional cooperation to the benefit of all States concerned;

Expresses its intention to continue following closely this situation in the Democratic Republic of the Congo.

Burundi

A number of positive developments took place in Burundi in 2003 as efforts to implement the 2000 Arusha Agreement on Peace and Reconciliation [YUN 2000, p. 146] bore fruit. That Agreement, signed by most political parties but not by some of the main combatant rebel forces, provided a framework for political reform, including the establishment of a three-year transitional Government and the eventual integration of a Burundi national defence force composed of 50 per cent Hutu and 50 per cent Tutsi forces. In late 2002 [YUN 2002, p. 138], ceasefire agreements were signed by the transitional Government of Burundi, established in November 2001 [YUN 2001, p. 148], and three of the four main armed groups. The most significant advances in 2003 were the peaceful transfer of power from the President to the Vice-President on 1 May at the end of the first phase of the three-year transitional period of government; the deployment of the AU African Mission in Burundi and the establishment of the Joint Ceasefire Commission to oversee implementation of the ceasefire agreements; the signing in October and November of the Pretoria Protocols on political, defence and security power-sharing by the transitional Government and the Conseil national pour la défense de la démocratie-Forces pour la défense de la démocratie (CNDD-FDD); and the signing on 16 November of a comprehensive ceasefire implementation document.

The United Nations continued to play a role in the peace process, mainly through the United Nations Office in Burundi (UNOB). Given UNOB's responsibilities, the Secretary-General increased its staff by five specialized staff and the necessary support staff [S/2003/920]. On 29 September [S/2003/921], the Security Council took note of those decisions.

Although the trend in Burundi during 2003 mostly indicated a movement towards a peaceful resolution of the 10-year-old conflict, there was an upsurge of hostilities in April when CNDD-FDD forces attacked Bujumbura and other cities. However, the conflict subsided after the signing of the Pretoria Protocols and, by the end of the year, 95 per cent of the country enjoyed peace. Meanwhile, most main political parties had become part of the peace process and members of the transitional Government, but the Forces nationales de libération remained unwilling to seek a peaceful resolution to the conflict.

The Deputy President of South Africa, Jacob Zuma, continued to act as Facilitator of the Burundi peace process.

Political and military developments

The Secretary-General, on 8 January [S/2003/29], informed the Security Council that the Secretariat was ready in principle to provide the necessary expertise and advice for the planned AU African mission to Burundi provided for in the December 2002 Ceasefire Agreement signed by the transitional Government of Burundi and the CNDD-FDD faction [YUN 2002, p. 139]. The Secretariat had already developed the proposed terms of reference for the chairman of the Joint Ceasefire Commission and was approaching Member States to ascertain their interest in nominating candidates to fill that position. A planning exercise had begun to assist in developing a plan of operations for the proposed African mission.

Meanwhile, the Secretariat awaited additional information from the parties, the Facilitator of the Burundi peace process and/or the Regional Initiative in order to proceed with providing assistance. The information needed included: the relationship of the Joint Ceasefire Commission to the African mission; definition of the objectives and mandate of the African mission; identification of a lead nation for the proposed mission; identification of focal points within all Burundian parties involved to provide information on the number and location of troops, weapons, supply requirements, number of dependants, logistical and communication equipment and transportation needs; identification of special needs in logistical support among potential troop-contributing countries; and agreement on key modalities of cantonment of the armed Burundian elements (location, size, transportation of combatants, availability of locally produced food, availability of water and accessibility). The Secretariat was also awaiting a formal request from the parties regarding the provision of a senior military officer to chair the Joint Ceasefire Commission. The Secretary-General's Special Representative for Burundi, Berhanu Dinka, would take up those and other issues with his regional interlocutors.

The AU Central Organ of the Mechanism for Conflict Prevention, Management and Resolution (Addis Ababa, 14 January), in a decision on Burundi [S/2003/53], expressed satisfaction at the signing of the October 2002 [YUN 2002, p. 138] and the December 2002 [ibid., p. 139] ceasefire agreements, the former between the transitional Government and Jean-Bosco Ndayikengurukiye's faction of CNDD-FDD and Alain Mugabarabona's faction of the Parti pour la libération du peuple hutu-Forces nationales de libération (PALIPEHUTU-FNL), and the latter between the transitional Government and Pierre Nkurunziza's faction of CNDD-FDD. Urging the parties to respect the agreements, the Central Organ expressed concern at recent incidents between the armed forces of Burundi and combatants of CNDD-FDD (Nkurunziza). In particular, it condemned the 12 January ambush of a convoy of vehicles in which several people were killed and many wounded. The Central Organ urged Agathon Rwasa's faction of PALIPEHUTU-FNL to join in the peace process and to end its attacks. It underscored the urgent need to deploy the African mission to supervise the ceasefire and welcomed the initiative of the Interim Chairperson to convene on 15 and 16 January a meeting of experts from the Regional Initiative, the Mediation, the AU Commission and the United Nations to discuss the proposed African mission. The Interim Chairperson was authorized to deploy observers to facilitate communication between the parties, and the United Nations was requested to contribute to the implementation of the ceasefire.

The Central Organ, meeting on 3 February in Addis Ababa at the level of heads of State and Government [S/2003/142], approved the deployment of the African mission and expressed appreciation to South Africa, Ethiopia and Mozambique, which had indicated their willingness to contribute troops. The Central Organ requested South Africa, the Chair of the AU, to lead efforts to deploy the mission in Burundi speedily. It appealed to the international community to provide financial and logistical support for the mission, and to support the deployment of the AU observers to maintain and consolidate the truce between the parties pending the mission's deployment.

Further ceasefire negotiations

President Pierre Buyoya of Burundi and the signatories of the ceasefire agreements of October and December 2002 met in Pretoria and signed joint declarations on 25 and 27 January 2003, respectively, reiterating their commitment to the implementation of the agreements. The transitional Government and CNDD-FDD (Nkurunziza) met again in Pretoria from 9 to 15 February, with a view to reaching agreement on the remaining political and military/security issues, but were unable to make any progress at that time.

The January agreements were welcomed by members of the Security Council in a press statement issued by the Council President on 30 January [SC/7653-AFR/552]. The members also welcomed the decision of Mr. Ndayikengurukiye (PALIPEHUTU-FNL) and Mr. Mugabarabona (CNDD-FDD) to return to Burundi on 10 February and to start cantonment of their troops in mid-February. They reiterated support for the Regional Initiative, South African facilitation and the AU, and commended the AU Central Organ for endorsing the deployment of observers, to be followed immediately by the African mission. The parties to the agreements were urged to refrain from military actions, stop recruitment of fighters and continue negotiations. Council members demanded that PALIPEHUTU-FNL (Agathon Rwasa) immediately cease hostilities and join the peace process, with a view to negotiating a ceasefire agreement. The parties were urged to work towards reform of the security sector and provide the information necessary for a demobilization, disarmament and reintegration plan. All Burundian parties using child soldiers were called on to halt those activities.

In February, the Secretary-General, in response to Security Council statement S/PRST/2002/40 of 18 December 2002 [YUN 2002, p. 140], appointed Colonel El Hadji Alioune Samba (Senegal) as Chairman of the Joint Ceasefire Commission. The Commission operated as a subsidiary organ of the Implementation Monitoring Committee. The Secretary-General informed the Council of the appointment on 29 May [S/2003/920].

Transfer of power

The first 18-month phase of the three-year transition period of the Government of Burundi, as agreed in 2001 [YUN 2001, p. 146], ended on 30 April. After consultations with all Burundian political actors and with the countries of the Regional Peace Initiative on Burundi, the Facilitation and other leaders, President Buyoya announced on 29 March [S/2003/397] that he would step down as planned and hand over power to his Vice-President, Domitien Ndayizeye. On the same day, the Union for National Progress Party (UPRONA) and the Front for Democracy in Burundi concluded an agreement in Pretoria setting out some of the key tasks to be accomplished during the second phase of the transition and the framework for cooperation between them. The Security Council President, in a 3 April press statement [SC/7716-AFR/596], said that Council members welcomed Mr. Buyoya's announcement to yield the presidency on 1 May for the second phase of the transition; they called on the political parties and the Burundian people to continue to settle the issues linked to the restoration of peace through dialogue and consultation.

Both the announcement and the agreement were well received by the general public. The Burundi army expressed support and declared that it had no intention of interfering with the transfer of power and was under the total control of the President, regardless of political affiliations. The majority of political parties expressed support, but the reactions of CNDD-FDD (Nkurunziza), PALIPEHUTU-FNL (Rwasa) and Charles Mukasi, leader of a faction of UPRONA that opposed the Arusha Agreement, were negative. For CNDD-FDD (Nkurunziza), the transfer of power did not have any particular significance before the conclusion of a sustainable ceasefire agreement with it, followed by fair and free elections.

Burundi informed the Security Council of the specific political and security commitments made by the President and Vice-President regarding the conduct of the second phase of the transition period, signed in Pretoria on 28 March [S/2003/394]. Political commitments included: steps towards the passage of the draft law on punishing crimes of genocide, war crimes and crimes against humanity; guaranteeing a balance between the two political-ethnic families—G-7 (Hutu) and G-10 (Tutsi)—particularly at the Executive level; organizing a debate on the electoral system; ensuring the adoption of measures to deal with past acts of genocide, exclusion and impunity; the combating and punishment of terrorism, intimidation or propaganda aimed at dividing citizens along ethnic or political lines; and the establishment of the International Judicial Commission of Inquiry and the International Criminal Tribunal to prosecute and punish crimes of genocide, war crimes and crimes against humanity committed in Burundi between 1 July 1962 and 28 August 2000. In the security area, they pledged to finalize details of the ceasefire, the cantonment process, the integration of rebels in the defence and security forces, the disarmament and demobilization processes, and the reintegration of the demobilized elements; take all steps to obtain a comprehensive and lasting ceasefire, including calling for the political disqualification of PALIPEHUTU-FNL should it persist in following the path of violence; give political and financial support to the national army for security; and maintain a balance between Hutus and Tutsis in the defence and security forces.

In a 16 April press statement [SC/7734-AFR/605], the Council President said that Council members again paid tribute to the upcoming political change in Burundi and encouraged all parties to pursue their efforts in favour of the implementation of the Arusha Agreement in the context of the second period of the transition. They underlined the importance of President Buyoya's commitment to the 1 May handover and recommended that the political leaders of Burundi continue to seek consensus and shared management of public affairs.

Establishment of African mission

The ceasefire agreements of October and December 2002 [YUN 2002, p. 138] called for the deployment of an international peace force and the establishment of the Joint Ceasefire Commission to assist the parties in implementing the agreements. The AU, in February 2003, decided to deploy the African Mission in Burundi (AMIB), and the transitional Government and the AU signed a status-of-forces agreement on 26 March, outlining their commitments and obligations. AU military observers began arriving in Bujumbura in February and were deployed to other towns in March.

On 2 April in Addis Ababa [S/2003/399], the Central Organ of the AU Mechanism for Conflict Prevention, Management and Resolution mandated the deployment of troops for AMIB from Ethiopia, Mozambique and South Africa for a total strength of some 3,500 for an initial period of one year. AMIB would oversee the implementation of the ceasefire agreements; maintain liaison between the parties; facilitate the activities of the Joint Ceasefire Commission and the technical committees for establishing and restructuring the national defence and police forces; secure assembly and disengagement areas; facilitate safe passage for the parties during planned movements to designated assembly areas; provide assistance to the disarmament, demobilization and reintegration process; facilitate the delivery of humanitarian assistance; coordinate mission activities with the UN presence in Burundi; and provide protection for designated returning leaders.

Burundi, on 7 April [S/2003/409], drew the Security Council's attention to the Central Organ's communiqué [S/2003/399], in which it implied that AMIB would eventually be replaced by a UN peacekeeping operation. Burundi stated that a special trust fund should be created to provide financial and logistical support for AMIB.

The twentieth Summit of the Great Lakes Regional Peace Initiative on Burundi (16 November, Dar es Salaam, United Republic of Tanzania) [S/2003/1112] requested the Deputy President of South Africa, Jacob Zuma, as Facilitator of the Burundi peace process, to request the Security Council to deploy a peacekeeping operation to Burundi (see p. 151). The Summit also appealed for urgent direct assistance from the United Nations for the Burundi peace process. Accordingly, Mr. Zuma briefed the Council on 4 December (see p. 153).

By December [S/2003/1146], 2,645 AMIB troops were deployed in Burundi, including 866 from Ethiopia, 228 from Mozambique, 1,508 from South Africa and 43 military observers from Benin, Burkina Faso, Gabon, Mali and Tunisia. Ethiopia was prepared to increase the size of its contingent to 1,300. In June, AMIB established the first cantonment site at Muyange and, by December, some 190 ex-combatants of PALIPEHUTU-FNL (Mugabarabona) and CNDD-FDD (Ndayikengurukiye), including 27 child soldiers, were at the site.

Press statement (16 April). In a 16 April press statement [SC/7734-AFR/605], the President of the Security Council said that Council members paid tribute to the AU for the deployment of observers and encouraged the deployment of AMIB forces without delay. In that connection, they called on the international community to mobilize the necessary funds to allow AMIB's deployment. Members supported the political transition (see p. 147) and welcomed the adoption by the Transitional National Assembly of the law on the punishment of crimes of genocide, war crimes and crimes against humanity.

SECURITY COUNCIL ACTION (May)

On 2 May [meeting 4749], following consultations among Security Council members, the President made statement **S/PRST/2003/4** on behalf of the Council:

> The Security Council congratulates the Burundian parties on a peaceful transition of power in accordance with the Arusha Peace and Reconciliation Agreement for Burundi of 28 August 2000. The transition in presidency represents a major milestone in the implementation of the Agreement.
>
> The Council believes that it is now crucial to follow up this positive development with the implementation of those provisions agreed upon in Arusha, United Republic of Tanzania, that are still outstanding, such as meaningful security-sector and judicial reforms. Resolving such pressing issues, as well as others that are related, is the only way to ensure that the thirty-six-month transitional period is a success.
>
> The Council condemns the attacks carried out on 17 and 25 April 2003 on Bujumbura and other cities by the forces of the Conseil national pour la défense de la démocratie–Front national pour la défense de la démocratie of Mr. Pierre Nkurunziza. The Council takes note of the statement made on 27 April 2003 by the Conseil national pour la défense de la

démocratie-Front national pour la défense de la démocratie that it would refrain from attacking unless attacked, and urges all Burundian parties, in particular the Conseil national pour la défense de la démocratie-Front national pour la défense de la démocratie, to observe the terms of the ceasefire agreements and implement them without delay.

The Council reiterates its demands that the Force nationale de libération of Mr. Agathon Rwasa lay down its arms and immediately enter into a ceasefire with the Government of Burundi, without preconditions. The unwillingness of the Force nationale de libération to date to seek a peaceful resolution of this conflict makes it difficult for the international community to accept the legitimacy of its concerns.

The Council urges all relevant regional parties and actors to continue their efforts to bring about a lasting peace in Burundi and stands ready to consider steps against those who are found to continue to support armed attacks by the Burundian rebels.

The Council also expresses support for the speedy deployment of the African mission in Burundi to facilitate the continuing implementation of the ceasefire agreements. The Council appeals for adequate and sustained international assistance to the mission, while underscoring the importance of providing the donor community with as many details as possible to enable it to make determinations regarding the best way to assist the mission.

The Council urges donors to support the economy of Burundi, to honour the engagements undertaken at the Paris and Geneva Conferences and, within their abilities, to provide as a matter of the utmost urgency budgetary and balance-of-payments support to the Government of Burundi and to contribute generously to the transitional debt relief fund, with continued strong performance on economic reforms by the Government of Burundi.

The Council urges the Burundian parties to take serious, meaningful steps to address human rights and accountability issues. In this regard, the Council welcomes the approval by the Burundian Senate on 23 April 2003 of legislation on genocide, war crimes and crimes against humanity and legislation establishing a truth and reconciliation commission. The Council looks forward to their effective implementation.

The Council reaffirms the vital importance of the Burundian parties themselves taking ownership of the process to address the devastating impact of impunity, as detailed in the Arusha accords. The international community pledges its willingness and readiness to assist in efforts to build up the Burundian capacity for promoting respect for human rights standards and the rule of law.

The Council requests the Secretary-General to continue to support the peace process in Burundi, including the immediate and full implementation of the Ceasefire Agreement signed by the Burundian parties on 2 December 2002.

Press statement (27 May). In a 27 May press statement [SC/7769-AFR/624], Council members welcomed the positive developments in Burundi and encouraged the political actors and armed groups to opt for dialogue and to eschew violence. They supported the proposed regional summit (see p. 151) and urged all Burundian parties to cooperate within the region and with the Facilitation on outstanding issues. Members urged Mr. Rwasa's FNL to cease hostilities, to join the peace process and to start negotiations with the transitional Government. The deployment of AMIB was welcomed, and donor countries were urged to contribute to it. Members commended the International Monetary Fund (IMF) and the World Bank for their decision to release the second tranche of their respective post-conflict programmes for Burundi.

Communication (August). Mozambique, on 13 August [S/2003/814], provided the Security Council with an update on the deployment status of AMIB. The size of the mission was about 3,500 troops, contributed by South Africa (the lead nation), Ethiopia and Mozambique, at an estimated cost of $190 million for the one-year operation. One third of the force had been deployed. The process of cantonment of combatants of CNDD-FDD (Ndayikengurukiye) and PALIPEHUTU-FNL (Mugabarabona) had begun, but the mission faced serious financial and logistical constraints which needed to be addressed.

Security Council mission

The Security Council sent a mission to the Great Lakes region from 7 to 16 June [S/2003/653] (see also p. 127). The mission's objective in Burundi was to demonstrate the Council's support for the second phase of the political transition at a time when the peace process was facing challenges, in particular the need for a cessation of hostilities through a political process and the framework of the 2000 Arusha Agreement [YUN 2000, p. 146], support for AMIB, the mobilization of economic and financial assistance to the country, and the fight against impunity.

All of the mission's interlocutors stressed that the continuation of fighting was the most serious obstacle to the full implementation of the Arusha peace process; they urged the mission to exert pressure on FNL (which had not signed a ceasefire agreement) and FDD (which had signed a ceasefire agreement) to cease hostilities. The mission expressed concern at the very slow pace of ceasefire negotiations between the Government and FDD and FNL, and called on the rebel groups to cease hostilities immediately and join the Arusha process. At the same time, the army would have to exercise restraint and the mission encouraged the Government to make room for the rebel groups in the institutions created by the Arusha Agreement. Both parties assured the mission that they would do their utmost to resolve outstanding issues. The mission encouraged the transitional Government to put in place measures to enable some FDD combatants in the DRC to be repatriated voluntarily to Burundi as a confidence-building measure.

In meetings with AMIB, the mission was told that the preparation of cantonment sites was hampered by the parties' failure to provide their forces' location and troop strength to the Joint Ceasefire Commission. The mission reiterated the Council's support for AMIB on three levels—political, financial and technical.

The mission discussed with the transitional Government and the armed movements the issue of combating impunity and accountability for human rights violations, stressing that those responsible for violations of international humanitarian law would be prosecuted. The Government stressed the importance of establishing an international judiciary commission of inquiry, as provided for in the Arusha Agreement, to help Burundi put an end to impunity and facilitate genuine national reconciliation.

The mission, noting that the Burundi peace process was at a critical juncture, recommended that the Council call on the international financial community to assist AMIB with adequate financial and logistical assistance and on the Secretary-General to provide appropriate expertise. It also saw a need to provide budgetary and economic support to the transitional Government and welcomed the planned September donors' round table, to be organized by UNDP.

Security situation

The security situation, which began to deteriorate in March, culminated in intensive shelling of Bujumbura in April and July by CNDD-FDD (Nkurunziza) and PALIPEHUTU-FNL (Rwasa), respectively [S/2003/1146]. CNDD-FDD (Nkurunziza) also abducted four members of Parliament on 29 June and attacked the cantonment site of Muyange the next day. The attack was repelled by AMIB forces.

The Security Council condemned the April attacks in **S/PRST/2003/4** (see p. 148). In a press statement of 10 July [SC/7813-AFR/659], the President of the Council said that members expressed their deep concern over the latest resumption of hostilities and the deterioration of the humanitarian situation. They condemned the attack launched on Bujumbura since 7 July by PALIPEHUTU-FNL (Rwasa) and called on FNL to end its offensive and to enter into negotiations with the transitional Government without further delay. Members also condemned the abduction of persons and the attack on the Muyange cantonment site by CNDD-FDD (Nkurunziza) and called on that group to stop resorting to violence. They called on all parties to engage in good faith in the search for a peaceful solution through dialogue and to abide by the agreements they had signed. Members urged States in the region to exert their influence on the Burundian rebel groups so that they would cease resorting to violence and join the Arusha Agreement peace process. The proposal to convene a summit of the Regional Initiative to help in the resolution of outstanding issues was welcomed.

The AU, in a communiqué issued by the Central Organ of the Mechanism for Conflict Prevention, Management and Resolution (Addis Ababa, 24 July) [S/2003/760], welcomed the results achieved by AMIB, particularly the cantonment of the combatants of CNDD-FDD (Ndayikengurukiye) and PALIPEHUTU-FNL (Mugabarabona). The Central Organ also welcomed the results of the regional consultative summit on Burundi (Dar es Salaam, 20 July), particularly the commitment by the transitional Government and CNDD-FDD (Nkurunziza) to work towards implementation of the December 2002 ceasefire agreement. The Central Organ urged PALIPEHUTU-FNL (Rwasa) to join the peace process, with a view to concluding a ceasefire agreement and to put an immediate end to its attacks. It expressed concern over the inadequacy of financial and logistical resources that was hampering the completion of AMIB's deployment and appealed to the international community for assistance.

Relative calm returned to Burundi after the July attacks and the release of the abducted Parliament members. Security Council members, in a 14 August press statement [SC/7844-AFR/688], welcomed those developments and again condemned the violence, in particular the atrocities committed against the civilian population and the use of children in warfare. They welcomed the commitments made by the parties concerned during the 20 July summit of the Regional Initiative and encouraged the Burundian parties, in particular FDD (Nkurunziza) and the Governments concerned, especially those of neighbouring States, to abide by those commitments. They expressed the hope that the negotiations taking place would lead to the implementation of a comprehensive agreement in time for the next summit of the Regional Initiative. The Council members reaffirmed their appeal to FNL (Rwasa) to enter into negotiations with the transitional Government, with a view to rejoining the Arusha peace process. They reaffirmed their support for AMIB and appealed to contributors for financial or logistic support. They welcomed the recent contribution of 25 million euros from the EU. Expressing concern at the humanitarian situation,

Council members called on all Burundian parties to facilitate the access of humanitarian agencies to populations in need. The members confirmed the Council's readiness to consider procedures for international assistance to combat impunity. They welcomed Economic and Social Council **resolution 2003/16** establishing the Ad Hoc Advisory Group on Burundi (see p. 947). By **decision 2003/311**, the Council decided on organizational details of the Advisory Group and informed the Security Council of those actions on 25 August [S/2003/836].

The Security Council held a private meeting on 22 September [meeting 4832] to consider the situation in Burundi and heard a statement by President Ndayizeye, among others.

Pretoria Protocols

On 8 October, the transitional Government of President Ndayizeye and Pierre Nkurunziza's CNDD-FDD signed the Pretoria Protocol on political, defence and security power sharing in Burundi [S/2003/971]. Under its terms, CNDD-FDD would have four ministries, including a Minister of State. The number of its representatives in the legislature (National Assembly and Senate) was also determined, as was its representation in governorships of provinces, the diplomatic corps, local government, public enterprises, the new Burundi National Defence Force, police force and gendarmerie. The combatants of CNDD-FDD would move to cantonment areas designated by the Joint Ceasefire Commission under AMIB supervision, and the Burundi Armed Forces would be confined to areas agreed upon by AMIB, with certain elements being exempted.

The outstanding issues—participation of CNDD-FDD in the Senate, temporary immunity, the Forces Technical Agreement, and the transformation of CNDD-FDD (Nkurunziza) into a political party—were resolved at another round of discussions (Pretoria, 30 October–2 November), when the transitional Government and CNDD-FDD (Nkurunziza) signed the second Pretoria Protocol.

The President of the Security Council, in a 9 October press statement [SC/7891-AFR/726], said that Council members welcomed the signing of the first Pretoria Protocol and commended the transitional Government and CNDD-FDD for their commitment to peace, and President Thabo Mbeki and Facilitator Zuma of South Africa and other regional leaders for helping them reach agreement. The Council demanded that FNL join the negotiations without delay.

The EU, in a 13 October statement [S/2003/1025], congratulated the signatories of the Pretoria Protocol. It called on the parties to implement swiftly the agreement's political and military clauses and confirmed its willingness to assist in Burundi's peace and reconstruction process. The EU affirmed its support for the multi-country demobilization and reintegration programme, to which it was the main contributor, and its political and financial support for AMIB. The EU called on Agathon Rwasa's FNL to pursue the path of dialogue.

The President of the Security Council, on behalf of Council members, issued a 6 November press statement [SC/7912-AFR/747] expressing satisfaction with the signing of the supplementary Pretoria Protocol and welcoming efforts made in that regard by President Mbeki and other regional heads of State. The members welcomed the forthcoming regional summit (see below) and emphasized the importance of respecting the timetable for the cessation of hostilities, disengagement, cantonment and quartering in barracks of forces, and the entry of CNDD-FDD into the transitional institutions, as stipulated in the Pretoria Protocol. The members urged PALIPEHUTU-FNL (Rwasa), the last armed rebel group that had not joined the Arusha Agreement peace process, to do so without delay.

The signing of the Pretoria Protocols and the consequent resumption of food delivery to CNDD-FDD (Nkurunziza) combatants in three provinces had a positive impact, with a significant reduction in violence throughout the country.

Regional peace initiative and Global Ceasefire Agreement

The Twentieth Summit of the Great Lakes Regional Peace Initiative on Burundi (Dar es Salaam, 16 November) [S/2003/1112] endorsed the two Pretoria Protocols and called on all Burundian parties to proceed to the preparation of free and fair elections, as agreed in the schedule for the transition. It urged the region and the Facilitation, as guarantors, to continue to monitor the implementation of the agreements. The Summit called on PALIPEHUTU-FNL (Rwasa) to suspend hostilities and to participate in the negotiations with the transitional Government within three months, and mandated the Facilitator to engage that party to begin negotiations with the Government. Transmitting the Summit's communiqué to the Security Council, Burundi drew attention to the request that the Council deploy a peacekeeping operation in Burundi, taking into account the qualitative change that had taken place following the signing of the Pretoria Protocols, which had created a condition of peace and stability in over 95 per cent of Burundi's territory.

The Summit witnessed the signing, on 16 November in Dar es Salaam, of the Global Ceasefire Agreement between the transitional Government of Burundi and CNDD-FDD. By that Agreement, forwarded to the Security Council by Burundi [S/2003/1105], the two sides embraced the agreements and protocols signed since December 2002 and made them part of the 2000 Arusha Agreement. It revoked all earlier conflicting provisions of the Arusha Agreement in relation to CNDD-FDD. The parties appealed to PALIPEHUTU-FNL to join negotiations with the Government as soon as possible, failing which the signatories, the Regional Peace Initiative, the AU and the United Nations would deem it to be an organization inimical to the peace and security of Burundi and would treat it as such.

The EU, in a 19 November statement [S/2003/1136], welcomed the signing of the Global Ceasefire Agreement. At the same time, the EU regretted that fighting was still going on in several provinces of Burundi, especially in rural Bujumbura. It appealed to FNL (Rwasa) to abandon the military option and to the Government to keep the door open for negotiations.

Report of Secretary-General. The Secretary-General reported to the Security Council on 4 December [S/2003/1146] on the situation in Burundi, his first report on that topic since November 2002 [YUN 2002, p. 139]. He described the transfer of power to the transitional Government, the ceasefire negotiations, agreements between the parties and the security situation (above).

In accordance with the Global Ceasefire Agreement, President Ndayizeye formed a new 27-member cabinet on 23 November, including CNDD-FDD leader Pierre Nkurunziza as Minister in charge of good governance and State inspection. Members from his movement subsequently arrived in Bujumbura to take up their new positions in the transitional institutions, including the Joint Ceasefire Commission. PALIPEHUTU-FNL (Rwasa), on the other hand, refused to join the peace process. The territorial area controlled by that movement was, however, limited to the province of Bujumbura Rural, and the movement was weakened since its attacks on Bujumbura in July. Consequently, its ability to hinder the general move towards peace in Burundi was limited. The Secretary-General's Special Representative, Berhanu Dinka, continued efforts to initiate dialogue with that party.

At the time of the report, 27 members representing the transitional Government, CNDD (Léonard Nyangoma), PALIPEHUTU (Etienne Karatasi), FROLINA (Joseph Karumba), CNDD-FDD (Ndayikengurukiye), PALIPEHUTU-FNL (Mugabarabona) and CNDD-FDD (Nkurunziza) were participating in the Joint Ceasefire Commission.

The Implementation Monitoring Committee, chaired by the Special Representative, held five regular sessions and one special session in Bujumbura in 2003. In addition to monitoring ceasefires, the Committee tried to resolve disputes between parties to the Arusha Agreement. It pressed for laws on provisional immunity; punishment for genocide, war crimes and other crimes against humanity; and the establishment of the National Commission for the Rehabilitation of Refugees and *Sinistrés*. It was also working for laws to be enacted on the post-transitional constitution; the electoral code; the mandate, composition, functioning and working conditions of the defence and security forces; and the establishment of a truth and reconciliation commission.

The security situation improved considerably by late 2003, following the signing of the Pretoria Protocols in October and November, and no new clashes were reported between the army and CNDD-FDD (Nkurunziza). However, skirmishes occurred between CNDD-FDD (Nkurunziza) and PALIPEHUTU-FNL (Rwasa) in Bujumbura Rural and Bubanza provinces, leading to the displacement of more than 30,000 people. Assassinations and abductions targeting local administrators around Bujumbura Rural by PALIPEHUTU-FNL (Rwasa) remained a concern.

The socio-economic situation in Burundi deteriorated during 2003. With a high population density and a large population increase, Burundi, classified as a least developed country and a highly indebted poor country, suffered from a shortage of farmland, an illiteracy rate of 52 per cent, a high rate of HIV infection and a life expectancy of 48 years. From 1990 to 2003, Burundi's gross domestic product dropped by 20 per cent. The humanitarian and human rights situation continued to be of serious concern. Humanitarian access remained difficult in some areas, and non-governmental agencies had been the targets of robberies and kidnappings, limiting the distribution of aid, especially for the first nine months of the year. Civilians continued to be the victims of killings, attacks and arbitrary arrests by all factions. Rape and sexual abuses were committed by soldiers and militias of the transitional Government and the armed movements on an unprecedented scale. In the first six months of 2003, more than 800 civilians were reported killed and there were reports of mass graves.

The Secretary-General observed that increased resources had been made available to UNOB for 2003 and the costs related to the ceasefire negotiations continued to be supported by a grant from the United States through the United Nations Trust Fund. However, in order to respond to the increasing needs in peacekeeping-related issues, security sector reform and disarmament, demobilization and reintegration, it would be necessary again to augment the UNOB staff.

The Secretary-General concluded that the transfer of power and the ceasefire negotiations had created a new hope for a democratic and peaceful Burundi, transforming the nature of its politics from one characterized by ethnic-based exclusion to one based on peaceful competition between political alliances. Nevertheless, the socio-economic situation remained a serious concern and could threaten the political gains. Following the request made on 4 December to the Security Council by the Facilitator, Mr. Zuma, for the United Nations to take over from AMIB (see below), the Secretary-General instructed the Secretariat to begin assessing the situation, with a view to making recommendations on the way forward. The transitional period was to end in one year and many challenges lay ahead, including the adoption of a post-transition constitution and electoral code, and the preparations for and conduct of elections.

Security Council consideration. At a Security Council meeting on 4 December [meeting 4876], the Facilitator for the Burundi peace process, Deputy President Zuma of South Africa, requested urgent direct assistance to help consolidate the gains already made, prepare for elections in 11 months' time and place Burundi on the road to lasting peace and stability. Significant developments had taken place in 2003 and the year was ending on a positive note. Progress included the establishment of AMIB, the conclusion of negotiations, the implementation of various agreements and the transformation of the security apparatus. Since the signing of the first Pretoria Protocol between the Government and CNDD-FDD on 8 October, the level of violence had declined, bringing peace to at least 95 per cent of the territory of Burundi. Thus, the Burundi peace process had entered a decisive and irreversible stage. The implementation of all the ceasefire agreements and the Pretoria Protocols had been swift, and change was evident. Those developments had significantly boosted the implementation of the Arusha Agreement, which guided the transitional period; Burundi had successfully completed the first two thirds of the transition period, at the end of which a democratically elected legislature and executive should be in place. Although PALIPEHUTU-FNL (Rwasa) remained outside the peace process, that did not present a major obstacle. The Facilitator had sent a communication to that party in an attempt to include it in the process. Among the goals faced by the Government were the disarmament, demobilization and reintegration of returning combatants and the return of refugees and internally displaced persons. CNDD (Ndayikengurukiye) and PALIPEHUTU-FNL (Mugabarabona) had begun to canton some of their combatants and those of CNDD-FDD (Nkurunziza) were already proceeding to assembly points to be cantoned.

AMIB, which was responsible for the cantonment and disarmament of the combatants prior to demobilization, required immediate financial resources to carry out its mandate and to maintain its force. The continued success of the peace process required more direct UN involvement, in particular by taking over the mission, re-hatting the existing military contingent and deploying a UN peacekeeping operation. A more immediate relief need was the provision of material, logistical and financial support to AMIB pending more UN involvement.

SECURITY COUNCIL ACTION (December)

On 22 December [meeting 4891], following consultations among Security Council members, the President made statement **S/PRST/2003/30** on behalf of the Council:

> The Security Council reaffirms its full support for the peace process of the Arusha for Peace and Reconciliation Agreement for Burundi of 28 August 2000 (the Arusha Agreement), calls on all the Burundian parties to implement their commitments and assures them of its determination to support their efforts in this direction.
>
> The Council welcomes the progress recently made by the Burundian parties, in particular by the signing, at Pretoria, of the protocols of 8 October and 2 November 2003 and by the conclusion, on 16 November 2003 in Dar es Salaam, United Republic of Tanzania, of the Global Ceasefire Agreement between the Transitional Government of Burundi and the Conseil national pour la défense de la démocratie-Forces pour la défense de la démocratie of Mr. Nkurunziza.
>
> The Council welcomes with satisfaction the formation of the new Transitional Government and the participation of the Conseil national pour la défense de la démocratie-Forces pour la défense de la démocratie in the transitional institutions; it again urges the Parti pour la libération du peuple hutu-Forces nationales de libération of Mr. Rwasa, the last rebel group that has not yet joined the peace process of the Arusha Agreement, to do so without further delay.
>
> The Council pays tribute to the efforts of the States of the Regional Initiative and of the Facilitation, in particular South Africa, in favour of peace in Burundi; it expresses its support for the mission of the African Union in Burundi and for its South African, Ethiopian and Mozambican contingents, and calls on donors to give it financial, material and logistical support as soon as possible.

The Council welcomes the recent mission of the Ad Hoc Advisory Group on Burundi of the Economic and Social Council, and calls upon donors and the international financial community to mobilize during the next Forum of Burundi's Partners for Development, scheduled for 13 and 14 January 2004 in Brussels, and to honour fully the pledges made so far.

The Council expresses its concern at the dire humanitarian situation of the population of Burundi and recalls that all parties involved are responsible for the security of the civilian population, which includes facilitating total, unrestricted and immediate access to the population for the humanitarian organizations.

The Council condemns all acts of violence as well as violations of human rights and international humanitarian law, and reaffirms its determination to support Burundian efforts to prevent such acts, based on the rule of law, in order to put an end to impunity.

The Council takes note of the address made by the President of the Republic of Burundi, Mr. Ndayizeye, to the Council on 22 September 2003. It takes note also of the request made by the Deputy President of the Republic of South Africa, Mr. Zuma, on behalf of the States of the Regional Initiative, when he spoke before the Council on 4 December 2003, and which is referred to in paragraph 71 of the latest report of the Secretary-General on the situation in Burundi, of 4 December 2003.

The Council welcomes the decision of the Secretary-General to examine the situation with a view to submitting recommendations to the Council, and requests him in this regard to undertake, as soon as he deems it convenient, the appropriate preparatory work and assessment on how the United Nations might provide the most efficient support for the full implementation of the Arusha agreement.

The Council takes note of the latest report of the Secretary-General on the situation in Burundi; it welcomes the work carried out, in often difficult conditions, by the Special Representative of the Secretary-General and the staff of the United Nations Office in Burundi, and approves the recommendations contained in paragraphs 63 to 65 of the report regarding the renewal of the mandate of the Office.

Rwanda

The presence of Rwandan armed groups in the DRC continued to adversely affect relations between the two countries in the early part of 2003 (see above under "Democratic Republic of the Congo"). During the Security Council mission to Central Africa (7-16 June) [S/2003/653] (see also p. 109), which visited Kigali, the attention of the Rwandan Government was drawn to the disruptions in MONUC's DDRRR operations caused by military offensives by RCD-Goma in North and South Kivu.

Communications. Rwanda, on 19 November [S/2003/113], informed the Security Council that officers and forces of the Forces combattantes Abacunguzi (FOCA), the armed wing of the Democratic Forces for the Liberation of Rwanda, known as the ex-FAR/Interahamwe, had returned peacefully from the DRC on 14 November. The return was an important step in the Government's efforts to unite and reconcile all Rwandan people. The leader of FOCA, Major-General Paul Rwarakabije, and all those who chose to return through peaceful means, would be resettled and integrated into Rwandan society. Those who chose to continue with armed conflict would be dealt with forcefully. Rwanda called on the region and the international community to help bring those extremists to justice.

The EU, in a 13 October statement [S/2003/1023], welcomed Rwanda's parliamentary elections, which represented an important step towards national reconciliation and consolidation of viable democratic institutions. Like the presidential poll on 25 August, the parliamentary elections were conducted in an orderly manner, reflecting the care taken by the Rwandan authorities with Rwanda's political transition. At the same time, the EU noted the comments made by its election observer mission in a 3 October statement concerning the obstacles to opposition activities, such as intimidation, threats and arrests that marked the election campaign, as well as the irregularities discovered at a number of polling stations. The achievement of a political transition in Rwanda came at a time when the peace processes in the DRC and Burundi were showing signs of progress, and the EU reaffirmed its willingness to assist the reconciliation process in the Great Lakes region.

International Day of Reflection on 1994 Genocide

The AU Executive Council, at its second ordinary session (N'Djamena, Chad, 3-6 March) [A/57/775], decided that 7 April 2004, the tenth anniversary of the Rwandan genocide [YUN 1994, p. 282], would be commemorated as a day of remembrance of the victims of that tragedy and reaffirmation of Africa's resolve to prevent and fight genocide on the continent. It recommended that the United Nations and the international community take appropriate steps to commemorate 7 April 2004 as a day of reflection and recommitment against genocide.

GENERAL ASSEMBLY ACTION

On 23 December [meeting 78], the General Assembly adopted **resolution 58/234** [draft: A/58/L.55 & Add.1] without vote [agenda item 39 (b)].

International Day of Reflection on the 1994 Genocide in Rwanda

The General Assembly,

Guided by the Charter of the United Nations and the Universal Declaration of Human Rights,

Recalling its resolution 260 A (III) of 9 December 1948, by which it adopted the Convention on the Prevention and Punishment of the Crime of Genocide, as well as its resolution 53/43 of 2 December 1998, entitled "Fiftieth anniversary of the Convention on the Prevention and Punishment of the Crime of Genocide", and its other resolutions relevant to the issue of genocide,

Recalling also the findings and recommendations of the Independent Inquiry commissioned by the Secretary-General, with the approval of the Security Council, into the actions of the United Nations during the 1994 genocide in Rwanda,

Recalling further Security Council resolution 955 (1994) of 8 November 1994 on the establishment of the International Criminal Tribunal for the Prosecution of Persons Responsible for Genocide and Other Serious Violations of International Humanitarian Law Committed in the Territory of Rwanda and Rwandan Citizens Responsible for Genocide and Other Such Violations Committed in the Territory of Neighbouring States between 1 January and 31 December 1994,

Recalling the report containing the findings and recommendations of the International Panel of Eminent Personalities commissioned by the former Organization of African Unity to investigate the genocide in Rwanda and the surrounding events, entitled "Rwanda: The Preventable Genocide",

Noting with concern that many alleged perpetrators of genocide continue to elude justice,

Recognizing the importance of combating impunity for all violations that constitute the crime of genocide,

Convinced that exposing and holding the perpetrators, including their accomplices, accountable, as well as restoring the dignity of victims through acknowledgement and commemoration of their suffering, would guide societies in the prevention of future violations,

Taking note of the recommendation of the Executive Council of the African Union, at its second ordinary session, held in N'Djamena from 3 to 6 March 2003, that the United Nations and the international community proclaim, in commemoration of the 1994 genocide in Rwanda, an international day of reflection and recommitment to the fight against genocide throughout the world,

Recognizing that April 2004 is the tenth anniversary of the genocide in Rwanda,

1. *Decides* to designate 7 April 2004 as the International Day of Reflection on the Genocide in Rwanda;
2. *Encourages* all Member States, organizations of the United Nations system and other relevant international organizations, as well as civil society organizations, to observe the International Day, including special observances and activities in memory of the victims of the genocide in Rwanda;
3. *Encourages* all Member States, organizations of the United Nations system and other relevant international organizations to consider promoting implementation of the recommendations contained in the report of the Independent Inquiry into the actions of the United Nations during the 1994 genocide in Rwanda;
4. *Calls upon* all States to act in accordance with the Convention on the Prevention and Punishment of the Crime of Genocide so as to ensure that there is no repetition of events of the kind that occurred in Rwanda in 1994.

Financing of UNAMIR and UNOMUR

In a 4 March report [A/57/753] on financing of the United Nations Assistance Mission for Rwanda (UNAMIR), the Secretary-General provided details on the final disposition of the assets of the Mission, which withdrew from Rwanda in 1996 [YUN 1996, p. 62]. The inventory value of the UNAMIR assets as at 31 December 1996 amounted to $64,472,700. Of that amount, 59.5 per cent was transferred to other missions or for temporary storage, 31.4 per cent was disposed of in the mission area, and 9.1 per cent was written off. The Secretary-General proposed that the General Assembly approve the donation of assets with a total inventory value of $12.6 million to the Government of Rwanda and donate assets with a total inventory value of $79,200 to the medical unit of a Member State.

On 17 April [A/57/791], the Secretary-General issued the final performance report of UNAMIR and the United Nations Observer Mission in Uganda-Rwanda (UNOMUR). UNOMUR was established in 1993 [YUN 1993, p. 284] and merged later that year with UNAMIR. The report contained information on income and expenditure, cash position, outstanding liabilities and fund balances, as well as unpaid assessed contributions as at 30 June 2002. In the light of the overall financial situation of the Organization and the fact that, as at 15 March 2003, assessed contributions to peacekeeping in the amount of $1.5 billion remained unpaid, the Secretary-General proposed that the return of cash available for credit to Member States ($45 million) be suspended until the financial situation improved.

Central African Republic

The United Nations Peace-building Support Office in the Central African Republic (BONUCA), established by Security Council presidential statement S/PRST/2000/5 [YUN 2000, p. 162] to take over from the United Nations Mission in the Central African Republic, supported the Government's efforts to return to stability following the attempted takeover in October 2002 by partisans of the former Chief of Staff, General François Bozizé, and an armed rebellion in the northern part of the country. On 15 March 2003, General Bozizé was successful in leading a coup d'état that overturned President-elect Ange Félix Patassé and interrupted preparations for a national dialogue. However, the new authorities pledged to organize a national dialogue during a transition period that would lead to national elections in 2004. Arrangements were made for an interim Government under the National Transition Council (NTC) representing all political opinions, including the party of President Patassé.

The security situation, aggravated by the devastated economy, remained unstable, both before and after the coup d'état, and there were continued reports of human rights abuses. The Central African Economic and Monetary Community (CEMAC) sent in a multinational force, later joined by French forces, to help the new Government restore stability. Positive developments included reintegration of former military and civilian refugees.

At the Government's initiative, the national dialogue was held in late 2003. It made recommendations to the Government on adopting a new constitution, revising the electoral code and establishing a census-based electoral list.

Report of Secretary-General (June). In response to presidential statement S/PRST/2001/25 [YUN 2001, p. 156], the Secretary-General submitted a 20 June report on the situation in the Central African Republic and BONUCA activities [S/2003/661], covering the first six months of 2003. His previous report of 3 January [S/2003/5] covered developments in the second half of 2002 [YUN 2002, p. 144].

The first half of 2003 was marked principally by the 15 March coup d'état led by General Bozizé, which overthrew the regime of President-elect Patassé, thereby interrupting the well-advanced preparations for national dialogue. The coordinators of the dialogue, appointed by Mr. Patassé at the end of December 2002, had met all the parties involved, from both within and outside the country in January and February 2003. The new authorities pledged to organize the national dialogue during the period of transition. The Secretary-General condemned the assumption of power by non-constitutional means in a press release of 17 March [SG/SM/8637-AFR/584], as did the Security Council in a 20 March press statement [SC/7700-AFR/588].

The new authorities stated that the interruption in the democratic process was temporary and was designed to enable favourable conditions for a return to democracy. To that end, they pursued management by consensus for the transition period, with the involvement of every political opinion and other actors of civil society. Elections were scheduled for the second half of 2004, and the Security Council, in a 17 April press statement [SC/7736-AFR/607], expressed the hope that elections would be held as soon as possible. The authorities, however, made the fulfilment of that commitment conditional upon substantial assistance from the international community for restoration of security and improvement of the economic situation.

Meanwhile, institutional arrangements for the transition were in place: a 28-member Government representing all political opinions, including the Mouvement de Libération du Peuple Centrafricain, the party of President Patassé; and NTC, a consultative body that included political actors and civil society organizations. General Bozizé granted amnesty to those responsible for the attempted coup of 28 May 2001 [YUN 2001, p. 154], including ex-President André Kolingba, said to be the instigator of the abortive coup. Soldiers who had participated in that action began to return to the Central African Republic and were reintegrated into the army, and ex-President Kolingba, who had been demoted to private after the attempted coup, was restored to the rank of General. General Bozizé stated that he would not be a candidate in the next presidential elections, thereby bringing relative calm to the transition process.

The security situation continued to be unstable, both before and after the 15 March coup d'état. During the initial days following the coup, Chadian troops were brought in to help end the looting in Bangui and to carry out disarmament operations. Since then, however, lack of security held sway in Bangui, with numerous auto thefts and some acts of armed violence. The situation was little better in the interior of the country where roadblocks were reported on the main highways and weapons proliferated.

The Multinational Force of CEMAC (380 troops), in which the Gabonese and Congolese contingents (139 and 120 men, respectively) were joined by 121 Chadian troops, resumed patrol and monitoring operations in Bangui. The special CEMAC summit (Libreville, Gabon, 3 June) adopted a new mandate for the Force, expanding its duties. The 300 French troops, who arrived the day after the coup d'état and evacuated foreign nationals, provided protection for Bangui airport. Control of the security situation remained the prerequisite for the normal functioning of the State and for the resumption of economic activities, a smooth transition and ensuring the fairness of the elections. Restoring security would require the restructuring of the defence and security forces and systematic disarmament in Bangui and the provinces. The new authorities had begun the reorganization of the military. The BONUCA military team continued its assistance and advisory activities, together with evaluation and disarmament. Its civilian police team continued to monitor the security situation and helped in the return of looted property. It also continued its training activities for the Central African police and gendarmerie.

The Central African economy, which was already extremely fragile because of repeated political-military troubles, collapsed completely after the coup d'état. Owing to the lack of cooperation programmes of any kind with the Bretton Woods institutions (the World Bank Group and IMF), the State had been without budgetary support since January 2001, with the exception of recent Chinese assistance in the amount of $20 million. The new Central African authorities had stated their desire to resume discussions with the Bretton Woods institutions in order to conclude a post-conflict programme. The CEMAC special summit (Brazzaville, Congo, 21 March) also requested those institutions to provide support to the Central African Republic, whose State infrastructure and facilities had been destroyed, with all economic and industrial activity halted. The new Government had made the issue of salaries and pensions its priority, and social tension, which had been simmering for a number of years, was subsiding.

The overall human rights situation deteriorated during the first half of 2003 due to incidents between the rebels and loyalist forces prior to the coup d'état and atrocities committed by the so-called patriotic forces or liberators (composed of Chadians and Central Africans) afterwards. The Government army's recapture in February of then rebel-held towns triggered violations of human rights and humanitarian law—looting, summary executions, rape, forced disappearances, inhuman and cruel treatment, and enrolment of young people. After the coup, there was widespread looting in Bangui by General Bozizé's forces and others, the targets being the residences of former authorities, ministries, diplomatic missions, offices of some UN agencies and residences of UN personnel. The new Government pledged to respect human rights, and a Ministry of Justice, Human Rights and Good Governance was established. BONUCA continued to observe and investigate human rights violations and to assist in national capacity-building in human rights promotion and protection.

Three months after the coup d'état, the overall situation in the Central African Republic was being brought under control with considerable difficulty, said the Secretary-General, and the restoration of security remained the top priority for the new authorities. He urged the international community to provide assistance and promote the conclusion of an agreement on a post-conflict programme between the Central African Republic and the Bretton Woods institutions, once the new Government had announced and implemented the calendar for the transition period. The authorities envisaged a return to constitutional legality in January 2005. If that commitment was honoured, the transition would last 22 months, with a national dialogue in 2003, a constitutional referendum in early 2004, and general elections (presidential, legislative and municipal) in late 2004. On the basis of that calendar, submitted to them by General Bozizé, the CEMAC heads of State, at the special summit (Libreville, 3 June), officially recognized the new regime. The activities of BONUCA would be adjusted in the light of the requirements of the new situation in the country.

Press statements. The Security Council, through its President, issued four press statements on the Central African Republic during 2003.

On 8 January [SC/7626-AFR/541], having been briefed by the Representative of the Secretary-General for the Central African Republic, General Lamine Cissé (Senegal), Council members noted with satisfaction President Patassé's appeal for a national dialogue and welcomed the recent establishment of the national dialogue coordination committee. They encouraged the Central African authorities to create the conditions for a comprehensive and all-inclusive dialogue, and requested the Secretary-General to provide assistance in that regard. Members also welcomed the ongoing deployment of the CEMAC force under Gabon's leadership and with French logistical and financial support.

On 20 March [SC/7700-AFR/588], Council members condemned the 15 March coup d'état and the ensuing violence and pillaging. They invited all the leaders of the Central African Republic to begin a genuine, political, all-inclusive dialogue immediately, in order to restore legality, national cohesion and civil peace and to ensure the restoration of democracy. They reiterated their support for the action of the Secretary-General's Representative as head of BONUCA, and for the efforts of CEMAC and the AU.

On 17 April [SC/7736-AFR/607], having again been briefed by the Secretary-General's Representative, Council members welcomed the political progress in the Central African Republic, the call for a national dialogue and the appointment of a Government of National Unity, including the nomination of a respected Prime Minister. They considered it indispensable that the Central African Republic authorities elaborate a plan for the national dialogue, including a time frame, and hold elections as soon as possible. They invited the donor community to help in the reconstruction of the country.

Council members, on 15 July [SC/7815-AFR/665], following a briefing by the Secretary-General's Representative, noted with satisfaction that the

Central African authorities had opted for a consensual management of the transition period by involving all the political factions and the other actors of civil society. They invited the authorities to fulfil their commitment to organize an inclusive national dialogue and to respect the timetable agreed for the return to constitutional legality, especially the holding of presidential elections before the end of 2004. They expressed concern about the continuing insecurity and human rights violations, and stressed that the restructuring of the security forces, supported by CEMAC, BONUCA and France, and systematic disarmament were essential for restoring security. They insisted on the need for BONUCA to continue its inquiries into human rights violations and to continue to work to strengthen national capacities regarding the rule of law. They called on Member States to provide financial or logistical support to the CEMAC force. Council members would consider convening a public meeting in early 2004 to examine whether constitutional legality had been restored in the Central African Republic.

Communications. On 2 January [S/2003/3], the Libyan Arab Jamahiriya informed the Security Council President that the forces of the Community of Sahel-Saharan States (CEN-SAD) had withdrawn from the Central African Republic and responsibility for ensuring the security of the country had been transferred to the forces of CEMAC. The Libyan Arab Jamahiriya, on 31 January [S/2003/135], described the efforts of the CEN-SAD forces, which had been sent to the Central African Republic in 2002 [YUN 2002, p. 143] at the request of the Government.

The AU Central Organ of the Mechanism for Conflict Prevention, Management and Resolution, at a meeting of heads of State and Government (Addis Ababa, 3 February) [S/2003/142], welcomed the deployment of CEMAC troops in the Central African Republic and requested UN and AU members to provide assistance to the force. It encouraged President Patassé to pursue his efforts to convene a national dialogue. At another meeting held at the ambassadorial level (Addis Ababa, 17 March) [S/2003/344], the Central Organ condemned the 15 March coup d'état and recommended that the Central African Republic be suspended from participating in AU activities until constitutional rule was restored.

Report of Secretary-General (December). On 29 December [S/2003/1209], the Secretary-General reported on the situation in the Central African Republic and BONUCA activities from July to December. That period was marked by three significant events: the activities of NTC; the national dialogue; and General Bozizé's appointment of Célestin Le Roi Gaoumbalet, a retired official of two inter-African banks, as Prime Minister.

Endowed with a consultative status and charged with assisting the head of State and the Government in legislative matters, NTC held its first session from 21 July to 4 September. It recommended that the Government respect the 12 June commitments it had made to the EU on a road map to find a viable strategy to the structural crisis, that the national dialogue be resumed and that the Government be required to explain its actions. Two more NTC sessions were held in late 2003, at which a number of draft ordinances were adopted.

At the Government's initiative, the national dialogue was held from 15 September to 27 October to assess the country's situation and to consider steps for national reconciliation. It adopted recommendations concerning the electoral process, namely the adoption of a new constitution, revision of the electoral code, and a new census-based electoral list. In that regard, the United Nations sent an assessment mission to Bangui (23 November–13 December), which would make recommendations on support that the UN system might provide in the preparations for and the holding of elections. The dialogue also adopted a solemn declaration that declared tribal hatred and division to be crimes against the State and made a commitment to promote national unity, democracy, freedom of press and opinion, justice and good governance.

Security forces in Bangui were strengthened during the reporting period, following rumours of incursions by mercenaries and instances of hold-ups, rape and murder. Abuses were committed by members of the security forces in some cases, which was a major cause for concern. In the interior, the phenomenon of roadblocks continued, especially on the main highways. It was essential for defence and security forces to be supplemented by a CEMAC force, so that they could operate in the interior of the country while helping to restore security to Bangui. The restructuring of the Central African Armed Forces continued. France, with BONUCA assistance, was helping to train the troops. The BONUCA Civilian Police Section was continuing to monitor the security situation and to strengthen the capacities of the police and the gendarmerie (military police). Training had been organized for 120 police officers and 190 gendarmes.

The economic situation remained precarious, with negative economic growth expected for 2003. In an effort to alleviate the State's severe cash-flow problems, talks were held between representatives of the Government and officials of the Bretton Woods institutions (Paris, 30 October–

7 November) on resuming a cooperation programme. The Government also began discussions with the EU on resuming cooperation, which the EU agreed to on a progressive basis, particularly in health, direct support to the population, electoral assistance, good governance and the reform of public finances. The level of budgetary revenue remained very low, with total revenue for 2003 at some 25 per cent below that of 2002. Arrears owed to multilateral and bilateral creditors continued to rise. The new authorities, who froze the salary arrears payable by previous Governments, had been able to make some outstanding salary payments to civil servants, thanks to its partners, including France, China and CEMAC member States, and were thus able to ensure the resumption, somewhat delayed, of the 2003/04 school year.

The human rights situation deteriorated, with reports of rape, theft, abduction, torture and violations of the right to life. Nevertheless, some positive developments were observed, including the acceleration of the reintegration of former military and civilian refugees; the lifting of the curfew that had been in place since 15 March; the strengthening of the process of re-establishing the National Human Rights Commission; the issuance of birth certificates to 97 pygmy children; and the representation of ethnic minorities on NTC and in the national dialogue. The BONUCA human rights section continued to monitor and investigate human rights violations, to conduct its awareness-raising programme, and to strengthen national capacities for the promotion and respect of human rights.

The Secretary-General stated that the overall situation in the Central African Republic was less troubled than it was before the national dialogue, when the atmosphere was charged with suspicion and rumours. However, he was concerned by the re-emergence of acts of rape, hold-ups and violations of the right to life. Only a complete disarmament, supported by the regular payment of salaries to civil servants and State officials, and the restoration of security throughout the country would make it possible to hold credible and transparent elections. He therefore called for strengthening the CEMAC Multinational Force, with a view to restoring security to the country, and for the Government to adopt a new basic law and a revised electoral code, in accordance with the recommendations of the national dialogue. He appealed to the donor community to assist the new authorities in their multisectoral efforts, particularly the restoration of security, in order to ensure the rapid return to constitutional legality through the holding of democratic elections.

Extension of BONUCA mandate

The Secretary-General, on 5 September [S/2003/889], following consultations with the Government of the Central African Republic, proposed an extension of the mandate of the United Nations Peace-building Support Office in the Central African Republic (BONUCA) for an additional year, until 31 December 2004. The extension would enable BONUCA to continue to support the Government's efforts to restore constitutional legality through national dialogue and to strengthen national capacities for the promotion of the rule of law during the transitional period leading up to the general elections, expected to take place in 2004. On 11 September [S/2003/890], the Security Council took note of the proposal.

MINURCA financing

The resumed fifty-seventh session of the General Assembly had before it the Secretary-General's report [A/57/631] on the final disposition of the assets of the United Nations Mission in the Central African Republic (MINURCA), which was withdrawn in 2000 [YUN 2000, p. 161] and replaced by BONUCA. The inventory value of the Mission's assets as at 30 April 2000 amounted to some $12.5 million, 52.5 per cent ($6,545,300) of which had been transferred to other peacekeeping operations or the United Nations Logistics Base at Brindisi, Italy, for temporary storage. The remaining 47.5 per cent related to assets that had been disposed of in the Mission area ($3,058,700) or reported as written off ($2,842,400) or as lost ($20,500). The Secretary-General suggested that the General Assembly take note of the report.

On 17 April [A/57/795], the Secretary-General issued the final performance report of MINURCA, which contained information on income and expenditure, assets, outstanding liabilities and fund balances as at 30 June 2002. The total assessed contributions had been fully appropriated by the General Assembly for the operation of the Mission. The Secretary-General recommended that the provisions of the UN financial regulations be suspended in respect of the liabilities and fund balance of $36,253,000, in the light of the cash shortage of the Mission.

West Africa

West Africa continued to be an area of major and growing concern to the United Nations in 2003. In June, the Security Council sent a mission to the subregion to examine the links between the conflicts in Côte d'Ivoire, Liberia and Sierra Leone and with regard to Guinea-Bissau. The Council, on 18 March, adopted a declaration on the proliferation of small arms and light weapons and mercenary activities, which posed threats to peace and security in West Africa. The concurrent conflicts in Côte d'Ivoire, Liberia and Sierra Leone were further complicated by the movement of armed groups and individuals crossing borders to seek refuge, loot and/or serve as mercenaries. The United Nations, the Economic Community of West African States (ECOWAS), the AU and the EU attempted to mediate with the parties to the various conflicts.

Following an outbreak of fighting in late 2002, the political factions in Côte d'Ivoire reached an agreement in January 2003, signed at Linas-Marcoussis, France, on a mechanism for power sharing. Although some progress was made in implementing its terms, the parties continued to disagree; the three main rebel movements jointly controlled the northern half of the country and the Government retained control of the south. In May, the Security Council responded to the situation by sending in a peacekeeping force, the United Nations Mission in Côte d'Ivoire (MINUCI), to complement the ECOWAS and French forces already serving there. In May, the opposition forces withdrew from the Government of National Reconciliation in protest against some of the President's appointments, and sporadic fighting followed. However, by the end of the year, the stalemate was reversed, and the peace process gained new momentum in December when the two sides met and resumed preparations for the disarmament and demobilization programme. The withdrawal of heavy weapons from the zone between the forces began that month and the opposition announced the end of their suspension of participation in the Government.

In Liberia, fighting between Government forces and two dissident movements was most widespread during the first half of the year, and the rebels gained control of nearly two thirds of the country. Elections, originally scheduled for October, had to be postponed to 2004 due to the lack of security and the resumption of civil war. The United Nations Peace-building Support Office in Liberia (UNOL) spearheaded UN attempts to promote national reconciliation. In June, a ceasefire agreement was signed by the three main opposing parties, but it was soon violated. ECOWAS sent a vanguard peacekeeping force to Liberia in August, which was soon followed by a multinational force and, in September, by the United Nations Mission in Liberia (UNMIL). Following the departure of President Charles Taylor from the country, a Comprehensive Peace Agreement was reached in Accra, Ghana, on 18 August by the Government, two rebel groups, political parties and civil society leaders, which provided for the establishment of a National Transitional Government. By the end of the year, mechanisms for the implementation of the peace process were in place, but the armed groups had not demonstrated full commitment to the peace process.

The situation in Sierra Leone remained relatively stable in 2003, after a decade of civil war that came to an end in 2002 with the completion of the disarmament process and the holding of elections. The security situation improved as the benchmarks set by the Security Council for the reduction of troops of the United Nations Mission in Sierra Leone (UNAMSIL) were met. Under the drawdown plans, the Mission reduced its forces from nearly 16,000 to 11,500 troops. Meanwhile, the Government continued to disarm ex-combatants and reintegrate them into society. Despite the generally positive trends, some areas remained volatile on the Sierra Leone/Liberia border. Fighting in Liberia, which threatened to spill over into Sierra Leone, precipitated an influx of thousands of refugees into Sierra Leone. The Government's efforts to bring peace and reduce tensions internally included setting up a Special Court to try serious crimes linked to the civil war and a Truth and Reconciliation Commission. The Government also reclaimed control of the diamond mining and selling in much of the country by expanding its certificate-of-origin regime, thus bringing in badly needed revenues. In view of that progress, the Security Council did not renew its embargo against Sierra Leonean rough diamonds.

Guinea-Bissau's serious political, economic and social problems, which were monitored by the United Nations Peace-building Support Office in Guinea-Bissau (UNOGBIS), continued to deteriorate throughout most of 2003. Progress towards revising the constitution remained stalled, and opposition leaders accused the Government of arbitrary decision-making, harsh restrictions on the media and harassment of political opponents. Preparations for legislative elections were under way when a non-violent coup d'état, led by the military, overturned the Government of President Kumba Yalá in September. An agreement was quickly reached and a transitional Government was established, led by a transitional President, Henrique Pereira Rosa. The new Government pledged to hold legislative elections within an agreed time limit of six months and to hold presidential elections a year later.

Threats to peace and security

On 18 March [meeting 4720], the Security Council held a workshop on the proliferation of small arms and light weapons and mercenary activities: threats to peace and security in West Africa. Addressing the Council, the Secretary-General said that the uncontrolled proliferation of small arms and light weapons and the use of mercenaries sustained conflict, exacerbated violence, fuelled crime and terrorism, promoted cultures of violence, violated international humanitarian law and impeded political, economic and social development. The easy availability of small arms and light weapons was linked to the rise in the victimization of women and children and with the phenomenon of child soldiers. That link was particularly evident in West Africa, where the conflicts in Liberia, Sierra Leone and, more recently, Côte d'Ivoire had been fuelled by an unregulated trade in small arms, often paid for with the proceeds from the illicit exploitation of natural resources. The flood of arms in the region had been accompanied by—and had facilitated—a rise in mercenaries' activities. That problem was linked, in turn, to the failure to adequately fund and implement disarmament, demobilization and reintegration programmes and the failure to provide enough assistance to countries such as Liberia and Guinea-Bissau in restructuring their armed forces as part of post-conflict peacebuilding arrangements.

One response to the problem was offered by legal instruments and other international agreements, including the 2001 Programme of Action to Prevent, Combat and Eradicate the Illicit Trade in Small Arms and Light Weapons in All Its Aspects [YUN 2001, p. 499] and the 1989 International Convention against the Recruitment, Use, Financing and Training of Mercenaries [YUN 1989, p. 825].

The Security Council had demanded that countries in the Mano River Union (MRU) (Guinea, Liberia, Sierra Leone) cease military support for armed groups in neighbouring countries and refrain from actions that might contribute to the destabilization of the situation on their borders. It had also imposed arms embargoes. The heads of State of ECOWAS agreed to work towards making the region a child-soldier-free zone and had put in place a moratorium on the import, export and manufacture of small arms in the region. To support the moratorium, the United Nations Development Programme (UNDP) had helped the countries involved to strengthen controls at border posts, to establish arms registers, to build up the capacity of national monitoring commissions and to collect and destroy illicit arms. UNAMSIL and UNOL were helping Sierra Leone and Liberia, respectively, to address small arms issues and the full range of post-conflict reconstruction and development tasks. Spillover effects from one country to the next had been common, underscoring the need for regional cooperation and a comprehensive approach.

The Director of UNDP's Programme for Coordination and Assistance for Security and Development (PCASED), who addressed the Council at its invitation, gave a presentation on the Programme's efforts to combat the proliferation of weapons in West Africa, where there were more than 10 million arms. PCASED involved a range of actors—international organizations, States, national organizations, NGOs, media and civil society groups—through national commissions established by States and the national and transnational bodies of civil society. Its mission was to promote the culture of peace, train security forces, establish border controls, create a regional register of light weapons, harmonize laws, collect and destroy weapons, extend the spirit of moratorium to the rest of Africa, mobilize resources and begin a dialogue with arms manufacturers. At that time, 13 of the 15 countries in the West Africa region had national commissions, with Côte d'Ivoire and Liberia being the exceptions. PCASED had assisted Mali and Benin in strengthening border controls and was involved in training the security forces of the 15 participating countries. In West Africa, PCASED had destroyed 38,000 weapons and, with Canada's help, it intended to destroy all government landmine stocks, with demining programmes to follow.

SECURITY COUNCIL ACTION

On 18 March [meeting 4720], the Security Council unanimously adopted **resolution 1467(2003)**. The draft [S/2003/328] was prepared in consultations among Council members.

The Security Council

Decides to adopt the attached declaration on the item entitled "Proliferation of small arms and light weapons and mercenary activities: threats to peace and security in West Africa".

Annex

The Security Council expresses its profound concern at the impact of the proliferation of small arms and light weapons, as well as mercenary activities, on peace and security in West Africa. These contribute to serious violations of human rights and international humanitarian law, which the Council condemns. The Council requests States of the subregion to ensure that relevant measures adopted at the national, regional and international levels to combat these problems are put into effect.

The Council calls upon the States of the subregion to strengthen the measures adopted and to consider other appropriate steps, taking into account the recommendations emanating from this workshop. The Council also emphasizes the need for the States of the subregion to strengthen their cooperation in order to identify individuals and entities that engage illegally in trafficking in small arms and light weapons and provide support for mercenary activities in West Africa.

The Council acknowledges the need to involve national commissions or national committees and other relevant local structures, including civil society, more fully in the practical implementation of the Moratorium on the Importation, Exportation and Manufacture of Small Arms and Light Weapons, adopted by the Economic Community of West African States on 31 October 1998, and of the Programme of Action to Prevent, Combat and Eradicate the Illicit Trade in Small Arms and Light Weapons in All Its Aspects, adopted by the United Nations Conference on the Illicit Trade in Small Arms and Light Weapons in All Its Aspects.

The Council calls upon the States of West Africa to consider the following recommendations that might contribute to the more effective implementation of the Moratorium:

(a) Broadening the Moratorium to include an information-exchange mechanism for all types of small arms procured by members of the Economic Community of West African States as well as for arms transfers by supplier countries;

(b) Enhancement of transparency in armaments, including through the establishment of an Economic Community of West African States register that would record national inventories of small arms and light weapons;

(c) Strengthening national commissions set up to oversee implementation of the Moratorium, in terms of staffing and equipment, and developing national plans of action;

(d) Taking necessary measures to build the capacity of the secretariat of the Economic Community of West African States;

(e) Computerization of aircraft registration lists to ensure better monitoring of airspace, in accordance with the provisions of the Convention on International Civil Aviation, signed at Chicago, United States of America, on 7 December 1944;

(f) Introduction of a standardized end-user certificate for imported weapons.

The Council expresses concern at the serious violations of the arms embargoes in West Africa and calls upon Member States to comply fully with the relevant resolutions of the Council.

The Council expresses its concern at links between mercenary activities, illicit arms trafficking and the violation of arms embargoes, which help to foster and prolong conflicts in West Africa.

The Council emphasizes the need to make peoples and entities of the subregion aware of the danger and the consequences of the illicit trade in small arms and light weapons and of mercenary activities.

The Council encourages all members of the Economic Community of West African States, especially those most affected by the illicit trade in small arms and light weapons, to submit, as did other States, national reports to the Secretary-General on actions undertaken to implement the Programme of Action, in advance of the 2003 biennial review meeting.

The Council appeals to the donor community to assist States of the subregion in implementing and strengthening measures relating to the proliferation of small arms and light weapons and mercenary activities.

The Council calls upon relevant parties to conflicts in West Africa to recognize the importance of activities related to disarmament, demobilization and reintegration in post-conflict situations, and of including such measures in the text of negotiated agreements, as well as specific measures for the collection and disposal of illicit and/or surplus small arms.

The Council calls upon all States in the subregion to cease military support for armed groups in neighbouring countries and to take action to prevent armed individuals and groups using their territory to prepare and launch attacks on neighbouring countries.

The Council calls upon arms-producing and exporting countries that have not yet done so to enact stringent laws, regulations and administrative procedures in order to ensure, through their implementation, more effective control over the transfer to West Africa of small arms by manufacturers, suppliers, brokers, and shipping and transit agents, including a mechanism that would facilitate the identification of illicit arms transfers, as well as careful scrutiny of end-user certificates.

The Council reiterates its call to regional and subregional organizations to develop policies, activities and advocacy for the benefit of war-affected children in their regions. In this regard, the Council welcomes the Accra Declaration and the Plan of Action adopted at the Conference on War-Affected Children in West Africa, held in Accra on 27 and 28 April 2000, and the subsequent establishment of a Child Protection Unit at the secretariat of the Economic Community of West African States.

Security Council mission to West Africa

The Security Council, on 5 May [S/2003/525], informed the Secretary-General that it had decided to send a mission to the West African subregion from 15 to 23 May, and had agreed on the mission's terms of reference. Regarding the region as a whole, it would: demonstrate continuing Council interest in the subregion; encourage more cooperation among countries of the subregion (e.g., MRU and ECOWAS); review the activities of the Office of the Special Representative of the Secretary-General for West Africa; examine the links between the conflicts in Liberia, Côte d'Ivoire and Sierra Leone and their impact on neighbouring countries; assess progress towards the protection of civilians and children affected by armed conflict; and emphasize the need for countries to respect human rights and international humanitarian law.

With regard to Sierra Leone, the mission would: assess the success of UNAMSIL; assess progress in the UNAMSIL drawdown and the ability of the national forces to provide security; assess the transition from peacekeeping to longer-term development; and examine how the Special Court and the Truth and Reconciliation Commission were addressing justice and reconciliation (see p. 213). In Liberia, the mission's mandate was to: urge the Government and rebel groups to engage in ceasefire negotiations and to implement Security Council resolutions; call on the Government to cooperate more with neighbouring countries; assess the Government's response to the Council's proposals for resolving the crisis; and assess the impact of UNOL and the Government's expectations of its new mandate (see p. 185). In Côte d'Ivoire, the mission would: urge all parties to respect the ceasefire and implement the January Linas-Marcoussis Agreement (see p. 166); discuss progress with the UN mission in Côte d'Ivoire; emphasize the need for respect for human rights; and consider security issues in western Côte d'Ivoire (see p. 169). The mission's mandate in respect to Guinea-Bissau was to: urge the Government and President Kumba Yalá to ensure that the forthcoming elections were conducted fairly; and urge the Government to endorse the partnership approach defined by the ad hoc advisory group of the Economic and Social Council (see p. 948).

On 28 May [S/2003/579], Mauritius, as Chairman of the African Group, welcomed the Security Council's decision to send missions to the Great Lakes region (see p. 109) and to West Africa, but expressed concern that the Council was considering excluding Guinea-Bissau from the countries to be visited.

Security Council mission. In its 7 July report on its mission to West Africa [S/2003/688], which it had postponed to 26 June to 5 July, the Security Council stated that it had visited Guinea-Bissau, Nigeria, Ghana, Côte d'Ivoire, Guinea and Sierra Leone. Although the mission was scheduled to visit Liberia, those plans were cancelled due to the conflict there, and it travelled instead to Accra, Ghana, where the parties to the Liberian peace talks, led by ECOWAS, were gathered. In addition to making observations on the subregion as a whole, the mission also made specific observations with regard to Côte d'Ivoire, Guinea-Bissau, Liberia and Sierra Leone (see below under country headings).

The mission took place when the stability of the subregion was particularly precarious. Although Sierra Leone was more stable than it had been at the time of the Council's 2000 mission [YUN 2000, p. 208], the situation in some other countries of the subregion had deteriorated. Côte d'Ivoire, which recently emerged from conflict, was struggling with implementing the Linas-Marcoussis peace agreement (see p. 176); Guinea-Bissau, although apparently peaceful, was at risk of falling back into conflict with postponements of the legislative elections, democratic freedoms threatened, economic regeneration inhibited and the National Assembly's powers usurped; and, most seriously, the conflict had intensified in Liberia, with hundreds of civilians killed even as peace talks were under way. The mission therefore concentrated on supporting efforts to improve the situation in those three countries.

The mission determined that the reasons for instability in West Africa were many, including abject poverty, poor standards of governance and irresponsible leadership in certain countries, illegal exploitation of natural resources and cross-border flows of small arms and mercenaries. An additional major factor was the persistent tendency of certain Governments, in particular Liberia, to exacerbate already existing tensions in neighbouring countries by meddling in domestic disputes and using proxies to undermine Governments. The mission believed that the Security Council, as agreed in resolution 1478(2003) (see p. 203), should consider ways to promote regional compliance by following up its demand that such interference, particularly the provision of weapons to armed groups in neighbouring countries, must cease. The mission called on the international community to step up support for ECOWAS, which was gaining experience in resolving crises, promoting better governance, subregional economic integration, observance of human rights and international humanitarian law and implementation of peace agreements. The mission recommended that the Secretary-General's Special Representative for West Africa, Ahmedou Ould-Abdallah, undertake, in conjunction with the ECOWAS Executive Secretary, a study of ways in which the international community could increase cooperation with, and strengthen the capacity of, ECOWAS. The study should make practical proposals for helping ECOWAS to address subregional problems such as the flows of small arms and mercenaries and the use of child soldiers. In the meantime, the Security Council would benefit from more regular exchanges with the ECOWAS Executive Secretary and invited him to transmit ECOWAS reports to the Council.

A major disadvantage for troop-contributing countries of ECOWAS-led peacekeeping operations was that, unlike UN peacekeeping forces, there was no automatic reimbursement for deployment costs. The mission recommended that the international community give priority to providing timely and adequate funds and materiel for ECOWAS peacekeeping forces. The mission shared the ECOWAS view that a concerted regional approach was needed for stability, and called for additional resources for the new Office of the Special Representative of the Secretary-General for West Africa, based in Dakar, Senegal. It also recommended that an officer from the Special Representative's Office be co-located at ECOWAS headquarters. The mission also recommended that donors consider the funding proposals made by the Economic Commission for Africa (ECA) for strengthening the MRU secretariat and for economic initiatives among MRU countries. Donor assistance, from both the UN system and Member States, was needed for the security sector (expert assistance, training and funding).

The mission was encouraged by the ECOWAS stance regarding the non-recognition of groups taking power by force, as well as insistence on respect for constitutional legality, the rule of law and human rights.

As to the ready availability of weapons, the mission recommended that Member States should take steps to stem arms sales to countries under Security Council embargoes. Council sanctions committees should monitor national efforts to investigate and prosecute sanctions violators. The mission recommended that the United Nations and ECOWAS propose measures to strengthen the 1998 ECOWAS moratorium on small arms and light weapons [YUN 1998, p. 525], as proposed in Council resolution 1467(2003) (see p. 161), through establishing mechanisms for verification and information exchange. Halting mercenaries' activities was another area requiring international action.

Before departing for the subregion, the mission was briefed on the desperate human rights and humanitarian situations there. The mission stressed that the principle of no impunity had to be upheld, and that the Council would consider imposing serious measures against Governments and groups that consistently committed human rights abuses or violated international humanitarian law. It urged the parties to conflict to prosecute those responsible for the recruitment of children, requested the Secretary-General's representatives in the subregion to monitor the protection of children and of women from sexual and other types of violence, called on donors to make further contributions for the protection of refugees, and expressed the hope that the Office of the Special Representative of the Secretary-General for West Africa would undertake collaborative efforts with other UN bodies to devise a practical regional approach to unemployment, which was a perennial source of instability. The issues of peace and security and of sustainable development in Africa should be jointly pursued through strengthened cooperation by the Security Council and the Economic and Social Council.

Security Council action. On 25 July [meeting 4794], the Security Council considered the reports of its missions to Central Africa (see p. 109) and to West Africa (above). In statement **S/PRST/2003/12** (see p. 109) of the same date, the Council endorsed the recommendations contained in the two reports. It looked forward to further collaboration with other organizations, including ECOWAS, and intended to review progress in implementing the recommendations in December.

Report of Secretary-General. In a 5 December report [S/2003/1147], the Secretary-General described progress made in implementing the recommendations of the Security Council mission to West Africa (above). The report highlighted the steps taken or envisaged in implementing the recommendations concerning Côte d'Ivoire, Guinea-Bissau, Liberia and Sierra Leone (see below), and presented a preliminary assessment of practical ways to address cross-border issues.

As to strengthening cooperation with ECOWAS, the Special Representative for West Africa was engaged in consultations with ECOWAS in that regard and a joint UNDP/UN Office for West Africa/European Commission mission would shortly visit ECOWAS headquarters in Abuja, Nigeria, and the four zonal observation and monitoring bureaux in order to undertake an assessment of ECOWAS capacity in early warning, conflict prevention and peace-building, as a key element in preparing the study requested by the Security Council mission. A focal point for ECOWAS matters would be designated within the Office for West Africa. The Special Representative had also been asked to explore with ECOWAS possible areas for cooperation to address the challenges in implementing the moratorium on small arms and light weapons. The Secretary-General expected to submit to the Council a separate report on such cross-border issues as the use of mercenaries and child soldiers and the spread of small arms. He was exploring ways of strengthening the Office for West Africa, reactivating MRU, promoting security sector reform, developing a framework for regional disarmament, demobilization and reintegration, mainstreaming into all UN activities in the subregion the protection of children and women against sexual violence and exploitation, and adopting a regional approach to youth employment.

The Secretary-General observed that the cross-border issues identified by the Council mission to West Africa were at the core of instability in the subregion. The Special Representative would work with UN presences in the subregion and other partners to form a strategy to address those issues, which would include the utilization of the comparative advantages of all the organizations concerned and the possibility of developing cooperative arrangements between them and the UN Office for West Africa.

Côte d'Ivoire

In 2003, political factions in Côte d'Ivoire reached agreement on the creation of a Government of National Reconciliation in the wake of an attempted coup d'état in September 2002 [YUN 2002, p. 180]. The parties signed an agreement in Linas-Marcoussis, France, on 28 January 2003, which established a mechanism for power sharing, defined the tasks of the new Government and called for national elections in 2005. Although some progress was made in fulfilling the terms of the agreement, the parties continued to disagree over power-sharing arrangements, and thus, further implementation of the agreement was delayed. The ministers nominated by the rebel movements did not take up their posts, claiming that their personal security was at risk. In the meantime, both France and ECOWAS maintained peacekeeping forces in Côte d'Ivoire. The three main rebel movements, which formed an umbrella group called the Forces nouvelles, retained control of the northern half of the country and the Government had control of the south.

The Security Council, acting on the Secretary-General's proposal for a peacekeeping force, established on 13 May the United Nations Mission in Côte d'Ivoire (MINUCI) at an initial strength of 255 military and civilian personnel. Its mandate was to facilitate the implementation of the Linas-Marcoussis agreement and complement the operations of the French and ECOWAS forces. A small civilian staff was assigned to support the Special Representative of the Secretary-General on political, legal, electoral, humanitarian and human rights issues, among others.

Further progress was made in the peace process, including the adoption of a plan for disarmament, demobilization and reintegration of forces; the opening of dialogue between the national forces and the Forces nouvelles, resulting in a declaration on 4 July proclaiming the end of the war; the extension of the ceasefire line to western areas not previously covered; and the adoption of an amnesty law. Nevertheless, the Forces nouvelles withdrew from the Government of National Reconciliation in September in protest over the President's appointments of the Ministers of Defence and National Security, and sporadic fighting ensued.

The subsequent stalemate in the peace process led to a deterioration of the situation, in particular in the northern provinces where a state of lawlessness prevailed for several months. In December, President Laurent Gbagbo said that priority should be given to the programme of disarmament, demobilization and reintegration, and, at his initiative, it was agreed to resume preparations for that programme and the situation improved. The withdrawal of heavy weapons from the zone of confidence began on 13 December and was verified by a joint UN-ECOWAS team. On 23 December, the Forces nouvelles announced that the group had decided to end its suspension of participation in the Government.

Appointment. On 7 February [S/2003/168], the Secretary-General informed the Security Council of his decision to appoint Albert Tévoedjré (Benin) as his Special Representative for Côte d'Ivoire. The Council, on 12 February [S/2003/169], took note of his decision.

Human rights situation

Human rights mission

By a 24 January letter [S/2003/90], the Secretary-General transmitted to the Security Council the report of the human rights fact-finding mission to Côte d'Ivoire (23-29 December 2002), led by the Deputy High Commissioner for Human Rights, Bertrand Ramcharan. In statement S/PRST/2002/42 of 20 December 2002 [YUN 2002, p. 181], the Council had welcomed the Secretary-General's decision to dispatch a human rights team to gather precise information about violations of human rights and international humanitarian law.

The mission identified several human rights-related issues that were at the root of the conflict: the difficult process of transition to multiparty democracy after three decades of guided democracy under a one-party State; the essence of nationhood and the contested concept of "ivoirité" (involving the rights of migrants to vote, citizenship, nationality and the right to be elected to high office in Côte d'Ivoire, a prosperous country that had become home to millions of neighbouring nationals); the qualifications to hold the highest office in the land; the right of long-term residents to enjoy their property and possessions in the rural areas and to pass on such property to their heirs; and the right of long-term migrants to become nationals of their adopted country on a basis of equality. A related issue was the new Constitution adopted in 2002, which defined requirements for presidential candidates (a candidate had to be of Ivorian origin with Ivorian parents) and consequently excluded a number of potential candidates.

The recent conflict had given rise to a substantial flow of internally displaced persons, estimated at over 600,000, the vast majority of them women and children. Many migrants wished to return to their countries of origin but their repatriation was made difficult by the numerous combat zones. Almost 72,000 refugees had taken refuge in Côte d'Ivoire, 60,000 of them in the north near the border with Liberia.

The mission stated that the human rights problems in Côte d'Ivoire existed in both the areas under the control of the rebels and those under the control of government forces. It had compiled information dealing with violations of the right to life, detentions and arbitrary arrests, forced disappearances, acts of torture and other inhuman and degrading treatment, treatment of children, acts of incitement to hatred and xenophobia, violations of the freedom of expression and opinion and damage to public and private property.

The mission made a number of recommendations to ensure respect for human rights, including: agreement by all parties on a human rights platform, along with a general ceasefire; investigations into grave breaches of human rights and humanitarian law and no impunity for those breaches; the bringing to justice of members of death squads; a commitment by all parties to the establishment of a truth and reconciliation commission, a national human rights action plan, an independent national commission on human rights and an independent media commission; the establishment of an independent organ to deal with relations between the army and civilians in the context of army reform; a national consensus on a national constitution, and on the law regarding ownership of rural property; an independent assessment of the question of nationality; and an independent review of electoral laws from the point of view of international human rights norms regarding the right of all citizens to participate in politics.

Communication. Côte d'Ivoire, on 5 March [A/57/739-S/2003/338], described the mission's report as based on an ambiguous mandate, lacking rigour in its analysis of the facts, full of inaccuracies and biased. It stated that the mission had sanctioned the argument of force as a fait accompli, to the detriment of the requirements of democracy and human rights.

Further developments

The Secretary-General, in his 26 March report on Côte d'Ivoire [S/2003/374 & Corr.1] (see p. 169), said that since the human rights mission more violations of human rights had taken place, including the looting and destruction of private property during the violent demonstrations that ensued after the signing of the Linas-Marcoussis Agreement (see below) and a resurgence in violence against the media, in particular the attacks on the premises of a newspaper and a radio station. Also, a well-known actor had been abducted and murdered, allegedly by death squads, and 60 villagers were reported to have been killed by Liberian mercenaries.

Côte d'Ivoire, in a letter of 21 May [S/2003/575] to the Security Council, transmitted the statement it made to the Commission on Human Rights, outlining its efforts to promote human rights. It repeated its invitation to the special rapporteurs on discrimination, torture and displaced persons to visit Côte d'Ivoire as soon as the territory was completely liberated.

Peacemaking efforts

A number of organizations and States undertook efforts to support Côte d'Ivoire in restoring peace and security. On 16 January [S/2003/51], Togo forwarded to the Security Council a ceasefire agreement between the Government of Côte d'Ivoire, the Ivorian Popular Movement of the Great West and the Movement for Justice and Peace, signed at Lomé, Togo, on 13 January under the auspices of President Gnassingbé Eyadema of Togo, who was coordinator of the ECOWAS high-level Contact Group on the crisis in Côte d'Ivoire. Those two organizations were thus joining the Patriotic Movement of Côte d'Ivoire, which had already signed a ceasefire agreement in October 2002 [YUN 2002, p. 181]. Under the agreement, the parties agreed to cease hostilities so that a comprehensive peace agreement could be negotiated and to accept the deployment of ECOWAS troops and other personnel in the buffer zone during the ceasefire. They also agreed to ensure freedom of movement of persons and property, and of humanitarian agencies and displaced persons.

The ECOWAS high-level contact group on the crisis in Côte d'Ivoire (Lomé, 20 January) forwarded to the Security Council a communiqué [S/2003/75] in which it urged Ivorians to work hard to strengthen national unity and noted the initiative of the French Government to hold a round table of all the protagonists in the crisis and organize a summit of countries concerned.

Linas-Marcoussis Agreement

At the invitation of the President of France, Jacques Chirac, a round table of 10 Ivorian political groups was held at Linas-Marcoussis, France, from 15 to 23 January. The round table was chaired by the Chairman of the French Constitutional Commission, Pierre Mazeaud, assisted by Judge Keba Mbaye (Senegal) and the former Prime Minister of Côte d'Ivoire, Seydou Diarra, with representatives of the AU, ECOWAS and the United Nations as facilitators. The round table adopted the 23 January Linas-Marcoussis Agreement, which France transmitted to the Security Council on 27 January [S/2003/99], along with the conclusions of the Conference of Heads of State on Côte d'Ivoire (Paris, 25-26 January), which was chaired jointly by the President of France, the AU Chairman and the UN Secretary-General, and attended by the heads of State of concerned African countries and representatives of numerous international organizations.

The round table welcomed the ceasefire made possible and guaranteed by the deployment of ECOWAS forces, supported by French troops, and demanded strict compliance with it. It called for the release of all political prisoners. Stressing the need to restore the authority of the State, it recalled its commitment to democratic accession to and exercise of power. To that end, it agreed that a Government of National Reconciliation would be set up immediately to ensure a return to peace and stability. It would be charged with strengthening the independence of the justice system, restoring the administration and public services and rebuilding the country. The new Government would be led by a consensus Prime Minister appointed by the President, in consultation with other political parties. The Prime Minister, whose mandate would last until the next national elections, scheduled for 2005, would not be eligible to run for office in those elections. The Government would be responsible for restructuring the defence and security forces and for organizing the regrouping and disarmament of all armed groups.

An annex to the Agreement set out a programme for resolving issues that constituted the root causes of instability in Côte d'Ivoire, such as the question of citizenship, the status of foreign nationals, the electoral system, eligibility to run for the presidency, the land tenure regime, incitement to hatred and xenophobia by certain media, the creation of a human rights commission consisting of representatives from all parties, regrouping, disarming and demobilizing and economic recovery and the need for social cohesion.

During the heads of State meeting, President Laurent Gbagbo, in consultation with other Ivorian parties, appointed the former Prime Minister, Seydou Diarra, to head the new Government of National Reconciliation.

The peace agreement provided for the establishment of a committee to follow up on the implementation of the Agreement (the Monitoring Committee). It was composed of representatives of the United Nations, the AU, ECOWAS, the EU, the European Commission, the International Organization of la Francophonie, the Bretton Woods institutions, the Group of Eight industrialized countries, a representative of the troop-contributing countries and France.

Both the Linas-Marcoussis Agreement and the conclusions adopted by the heads of State on 26 January envisaged a UN role in the implementation of the Agreement, including participating in and chairing the Monitoring Committee. The Agreement stipulated that the new Government would seek assistance from ECOWAS, France and the United Nations in guaranteeing the reform and restructuring of the defence and security forces. In their communiqué, the heads of State proposed strengthening the UN presence in Côte d'Ivoire, in particular in security, humanitarian assistance and human rights, as well as the deployment of civilian and military observers, who would help to supervise the implementation of the Linas-Marcoussis Agreement. They also expressed the wish that the Security Council would endorse the peacekeeping operation launched by ECOWAS and France, and authorize that operation to ensure the freedom of movement and security of its personnel, and to guarantee the protection of civilians facing the imminent threat of violence.

Press statement (28 January). In a 28 January press statement [SC/7646-AFR/551], Council members expressed satisfaction with the Linas-Marcoussis Agreement and urged the parties to implement it and to avoid further violence. They welcomed ongoing efforts to deploy the ECOWAS Military Observer Group (ECOMOG) force, under Senegalese command, and appealed to the international community to lend its support. They also expressed appreciation for the efforts of the AU to bring about a settlement and thanked France for its diplomatic efforts and military deployment. They expressed the wish for United Nations support in the implementation of the peace process, and stated their intention to consider promptly the Secretary-General's recommendations to that end.

Communications. ECOWAS, at its twenty-sixth ordinary summit (Dakar, Senegal, 31 January), issued a statement on Côte d'Ivoire [S/2003/141], expressing concern over the persistence of the Ivorian crisis and resolving to support the outcome of the Linas-Marcoussis round table. It was decided that ECOWAS would play the role assigned to it within the Linas-Marcoussis Agreement, and that the ECOWAS Contact Group (Ghana, Guinea-Bissau, Mali, Niger, Nigeria, Senegal, Togo) would continue to monitor and facilitate the application of the Agreement.

The AU Central Organ of the Mechanism for Conflict Prevention, Management and Resolution, at its seventh ordinary session held at the level of heads of State and Government (Addis Ababa, 3 February) [S/2003/142], welcomed the signing of the Linas-Marcoussis Agreement and mandated ECOWAS to continue the initiatives taken by leaders of the region to bring peace to Côte d'Ivoire. It condemned the violations of human rights committed against the civilian populations and urged all the parties to respect human rights and international humanitarian law.

SECURITY COUNCIL ACTION (February)

On 4 February [meeting 4700], the Security Council unanimously adopted **resolution 1464 (2003)**. The draft [S/2003/140] was prepared in consultations among Council members.

The Security Council,

Reaffirming its strong commitment to the sovereignty, independence, territorial integrity and unity of Côte d'Ivoire,

Recalling the importance of the principles of good-neighbourliness, non-interference and regional cooperation,

Recalling also the decision taken by the Economic Community of West African States Summit, held in Accra on 29 September 2002, to deploy a peacekeeping force in Côte d'Ivoire,

Recalling its full support for the efforts of the Economic Community of West African States to promote a peaceful settlement of the conflict, and also appreciating the efforts of the African Union to reach a settlement,

Welcoming the convening, at the invitation of France, of the Round Table of Ivorian political forces, held in Linas-Marcoussis from 15 to 23 January 2003, and the Conference of Heads of State on Côte d'Ivoire, held in Paris on 25 and 26 January 2003,

Welcoming also the statement issued on 31 January 2003 following the twenty-sixth ordinary Summit of the Heads of State and Government of the Economic Community of West African States, held in Dakar, as well as the communiqué issued on 3 February 2003 following the seventh ordinary session of the Central Organ of the Mechanism for Conflict Prevention, Management and Resolution of the African Union, held at the level of heads of State and Government in Addis Ababa,

Noting the existence of challenges to the stability of Côte d'Ivoire, and determining that the situation in Côte d'Ivoire constitutes a threat to international peace and security in the region,

1. *Endorses* the agreement signed by the Ivorian political forces in Linas-Marcoussis, France, on 23 January 2003 ("the Linas-Marcoussis Agreement") and adopted by the Conference of Heads of State on Côte d'Ivoire, and calls upon all Ivorian political forces to implement it fully and without delay;

2. *Notes* the provisions in the Linas-Marcoussis Agreement for the formation of a Government of National Reconciliation, and calls upon all Ivorian political forces to work with the President and the Prime Minister towards the establishment of a balanced and stable Government;

3. *Also notes* the provisions in the Linas-Marcoussis Agreement for the establishment of a Monitoring Committee, calls upon all the members of that Committee to monitor closely compliance with the terms of the Agreement, and urges all parties to cooperate fully with the Committee;

4. *Expresses its gratitude* to the Secretary-General for the vital role he has played in the smooth conduct of these meetings, and encourages him to continue to contribute to a final settlement of the Ivorian crisis;

5. *Requests* the Secretary-General to submit to the Council at the earliest possible date recommendations on how the United Nations could support fully the implementation of the Linas-Marcoussis Agreement, in accordance with the request by the Round Table of Ivorian political forces and by the Conference of Heads of State on Côte d'Ivoire, and declares its readiness to take appropriate measures on the basis of these recommendations;

6. *Welcomes* the intention of the Secretary-General to appoint a Special Representative for Côte d'Ivoire, based in Abidjan, and requests him to do so as soon as possible;

7. *Condemns* violations of human rights and international humanitarian law that have taken place in Côte d'Ivoire since 19 September 2002 and stresses the need to bring to justice those responsible, and urges all parties, including the Government, to take all necessary steps to prevent further violations of human rights and international humanitarian law, in particular against civilians regardless of their origin;

8. *Welcomes* the deployment of forces of the Economic Community of West African States and French troops with a view to contributing to a peaceful solution of the crisis and, in particular, to the implementation of the Linas-Marcoussis Agreement;

9. *Acting* under Chapter VII of the Charter of the United Nations, and in accordance with the proposal contained in paragraph 14 of the conclusions of the Conference of Heads of State on Côte d'Ivoire, authorizes Member States participating in the forces of the Economic Community of West African States in accordance with Chapter VIII of the Charter together with the French forces supporting them to take the necessary steps to guarantee the security and freedom of movement of their personnel and to ensure, without prejudice to the responsibilities of the Government of National Reconciliation, the protection of civilians immediately threatened with physical violence within their zones of operation, using the means available to them, for a period of six months, after which the Council will assess the situation on the basis of the reports referred to in paragraph 10 below and decide whether to renew this authorization;

10. *Requests* the Economic Community of West African States, through the command of its force, and France to report to the Council periodically, through

the Secretary-General, on all aspects of the implementation of their respective mandates;

11. *Calls upon* all States neighbouring Côte d'Ivoire to support the peace process by preventing any action that might undermine the security and territorial integrity of Côte d'Ivoire, particularly the movement of armed groups and mercenaries across their borders and illicit trafficking and proliferation of arms in the region, including small arms and light weapons;

12. *Decides* to remain actively seized of the matter.

Press statement (21 February). In a 21 February press statement [SC/7668-AFR/566], Security Council members expressed satisfaction that the Monitoring Committee of the Linas-Marcoussis Agreement was fully operational, under the chairmanship of the Secretary-General's Special Representative for Côte d'Ivoire. They called on all Ivorian political forces to implement the Agreement without delay and to cooperate with the Monitoring Committee to that end. They encouraged the newly appointed Prime Minister to continue his efforts towards establishing a balanced and stable Government. Members expressed concern at the humanitarian and economic consequences of the Ivorian crisis for the whole region and called on all parties to respect human rights and international humanitarian law for the entire population regardless of its origin. They expressed support for ECOWAS forces and the French forces supporting them and called on Member States to provide financial and logistical support to the ECOWAS forces.

Political developments and renewed fighting

Communication. On 5 March [A/57/754-S/2003/313], Côte d'Ivoire forwarded to the Secretary-General the text of an address by President Gbagbo concerning the Ivorian crisis. The President affirmed that it was never the intention of those who drafted the Linas-Marcoussis Agreement that the national army, gendarmerie and police should be disarmed, nor had he formed a Government, despite the recent claims by certain individuals that they were ministers. He observed that the Linas-Marcoussis Agreement was a compromise text that, in part, contradicted the Constitution of Côte d'Ivoire; it attempted, in places, to edge the presidential regime in the direction of a parliamentary regime. The President intended to retain all the prerogatives assigned to him under the Constitution. In the event of contradiction between the Agreement and the Constitution, he would apply the Constitution; otherwise, he would work for the implementation of the Agreement.

Press statement (14 March). In a 14 March press statement [SC/7691-AFR/582], Security Council members, having been briefed by the Special Representative of the Secretary-General for Côte d'Ivoire, welcomed the first meeting of the Government of National Reconciliation and called on all the parties to participate in subsequent meetings. They called on all parties to implement the Linas-Marcoussis Agreement without delay and on the Government to draw up a timetable for implementation. Council members noted with satisfaction the ECOWAS decision to ensure the safety of all members of the Government of National Reconciliation. They condemned the renewal of fighting in the west of the country and the events that had transpired, in particular in Bangolo. They expressed concern that the fighting had essentially opposed Liberian combatants and called on the parties to desist from using children in the conflict. They also expressed concern at the deplorable humanitarian situation and called on all parties, in particular in the west, to allow relief agencies unimpeded access to civilian populations.

Report of Secretary-General (March). In response to Security Council resolution 1464(2003) (above), the Secretary-General submitted a 26 March report on Côte d'Ivoire [S/2003/374 & Corr.1]. He described the root problems of instability that stemmed from a protracted power struggle following the death of long-term President Félix Houphouët-Boigny in 1993. He stated that the current crisis had erupted in September 2002 with an attempted coup [YUN 2002, p. 180], which began with attacks by soldiers on military installations in the capital, Abidjan, and the second largest city, Bouaké, and in the northern town of Korhogo. While loyalist security forces regained control of Abidjan, rebels retained control of the northern half of the country, and allegations that foreign elements were supporting the rebels prompted harassment of foreigners, including migrant workers from neighbouring countries and refugees from Liberia and Sierra Leone. By the end of September, the rebel forces were operating under the umbrella of a political movement called the Patriotic Movement of Côte d'Ivoire (MPCI), which demanded the resignation of President Gbagbo, the holding of inclusive national elections, a review of the Constitution and an end to the domination by southerners of the country's affairs. The situation was further compounded by the emergence of two new armed groups—the Ivorian Popular Movement of the Great West (MPIGO) and the Movement for Justice and Peace (MJP)—which seized the towns of Danané and Man and demanded the President's resignation. Following a ceasefire agreement between the Government and MPCI in October 2002, ECOWAS, in December, decided to deploy the ECOWAS Peace Force for Côte d'Ivoire (ECOFORCE).

In a fresh initiative, the Foreign Minister of France, Dominique de Villepin, visited Côte d'Ivoire in January 2003 and secured the agreement of all Ivorian political groups to attend a round-table meeting in France. ECOWAS brokered a ceasefire between the Government and MPIGO and MJP, and the signing of the Linas-Marcoussis Agreement on 23 January followed (see p. 167).

The implementation of that Agreement encountered serious obstacles soon after it was signed. Newly appointed Prime Minister Diarra was unable to return immediately to Côte d'Ivoire because a series of often violent demonstrations erupted in Abidjan and other towns to protest the allocation of the Defence and Interior Ministries to rebel movements. Leaders of major political parties also rejected the allocation of those assignments, as did the President. The situation calmed down following an address to the nation by the President (see above).

Efforts by the ECOWAS Contact Group on Côte d'Ivoire to break the impasse on implementing the Agreement culminated in a summit meeting with President Gbagbo in Yamoussoukro on 10 February, attended by the Presidents of Togo, Ghana and Nigeria, the interim Chairman of the AU Commission and the Vice-President of South Africa. Mr. Diarra was installed as Prime Minister on that occasion. The meeting explored alternative arrangements for the allocation of posts in the new Government of National Unity that would be acceptable to all parties. The rebel movements refused to attend on the grounds that they did not wish to renegotiate the understandings already reached. Some progress towards breaking the stalemate was finally made at a meeting of the 10 signatories to the Linas-Marcoussis Agreement, convened by Ghana's President, John Agyekum Kufuor, the ECOWAS Chairman (Accra, 6-8 March), at which they agreed to create a 15-member National Security Council comprising representatives of each of the 10 signatories, as well as the army, the gendarmerie, the police, President Gbagbo and Prime Minister Diarra, to oversee the functioning of the two disputed ministries (Accra II Agreement). They requested the Prime Minister to submit candidates for the two ministries, who would be appointed by consensus, and they reached a new understanding on the allocation of the other cabinet posts. On 10 March, President Gbagbo issued a decree delegating authority to the Prime Minister to implement the work programme set out in the Linas-Marcoussis Agreement, but only for a six-month period. On 11 March, representatives of the rebel movements travelled to Yamoussoukro for talks with the President on the formation of the new Government.

A UN multidisciplinary technical assessment mission, headed by the Assistant Secretary-General for Peacekeeping Operations, Hédi Annabi, visited Côte d'Ivoire from 24 February to 7 March (see p. 183). Several stakeholders expressed the view to the mission that the understandings reached at the Paris summit concerning the power-sharing arrangement that allocated key cabinet posts to the rebel movements were primarily responsible for the impasse. It was widely felt that those understandings, known as the Kléber arrangements, should be separated from the Linas-Marcoussis Agreement, to which all parties had to remain committed. Another obstacle, in the view of many, was the President's reluctance to delegate to the Prime Minister the necessary authority to implement the Agreement. Implementation of other aspects of the Agreement hinged on installation of the Government. There was concern that a prolonged stalemate might lead to renewed hostilities and entrench the current de facto partition of the country. Security and protection of the Prime Minister and his cabinet was also a major concern. The ultimate challenge posed by the crisis was the 2005 elections. The new Government would have to decide how to tackle the issues relating to national identity, citizenship and the status of foreign nationals, the root cause of the crisis. Preparations for elections would be a key area for UN and other assistance.

The military situation in the country had been relatively stable since the ceasefire agreements between the Government and the three rebel movements came into effect. The majority of incidents reported to the assessment mission were more the result of independent action by local rebel commanders than part of any coordinated military action. The ceasefire remained precarious, however, and steps were needed to underpin it with a political settlement. The crisis in Côte d'Ivoire assumed regional dimensions as Liberia and Côte d'Ivoire exchanged accusations about cross-border attacks launched by armed elements from the other's territory. In addition to the two rebel movements operating in western Côte d'Ivoire, there were reports of rogue armed groups, consisting mainly of Liberian elements and some former Sierra Leonean combatants. In addition, both the rebel movements and the government forces were reported to have recruited Liberian nationals.

French forces, numbering approximately 3,900, had been fundamental to maintaining the ceasefire in Côte d'Ivoire. Under arrangements for the deployment of ECOFORCE, French troops would pull back to assume a supporting role in all areas, except in the west where they would maintain their current deployment; they would also continue to provide a quick-reaction capability. ECOFORCE, with contingents from Benin, Ghana, the Niger, Senegal and Togo, was in the process of deploying a 1,300-member task force to monitor the ceasefire and to facilitate the movement of humanitarian agencies; however, logistical constraints were delaying full deployment. ECOWAS recommended that the force be increased to 3,411 troops, including 300 security personnel to protect the new Government. The assessment mission confirmed that no real planning had been done for the programme of disarmament, demobilization, repatriation, resettlement and reintegration of forces, as envisaged in the Linas-Marcoussis Agreement, principally because of the delay in the formation of the Government of National Reconciliation.

The humanitarian situation remained precarious, with population displacements, widespread human rights abuses and a deteriorating social and economic situation. An estimated 800,000 people were internally displaced, and up to 400,000 had fled the country. UNHCR was concerned about Liberian refugees in the country, in the wake of growing hostility against Liberian nationals who were seen as a security threat. There were reports of continuing recruitment of child soldiers. In view of the security situation, UN staff in Côte d'Ivoire were greatly reduced in late 2002, so that only 82 essential staff remained in the country. The Office for the Coordination of Humanitarian Affairs (OCHA), UNHCR, OHCHR, the United Nations Children's Fund (UNICEF), the World Food Programme (WFP), the Food and Agriculture Organization of the United Nations (FAO), the World Health Organization (WHO), UNDP and the International Organization for Migration (IOM) were helping to address the humanitarian consequences of the conflict.

The assessment mission also suggested options for UN action in the military sphere: establishing a military advisory team in the Special Representative's office; deploying a military liaison group that would be co-located with the French and ECOWAS field headquarters; deploying military observers throughout the country; and launching a fully fledged peacekeeping operation. The mission was of the opinion that the United Nations could play a role complementing the operations of the French and ECOWAS forces, and the Secretary-General supported the second option of sending in a military liaison group of 76 personnel, comprising a headquarters team and liaison teams at the location of each of the three rebel movements (MPCI, MPIGO and MJP) and at the main locations of the national army of Côte d'Ivoire (FANCI) and the French and ECOWAS forces. The other options would be reviewed as the situation developed. Civilian activities would include assistance for the electoral process and a human rights component. In the meantime, a civil affairs component in the office of the Special Representative would be set up immediately.

The Secretary-General stated that the Linas-Marcoussis Agreement offered the best chance for the Ivorian people to resolve the conflict peacefully. However, disagreements over power-sharing arrangements had delayed implementation and prolonged the suffering of the population. Although the new Government had met twice, the ministers nominated by the rebel movements had not taken up their posts in protest over their personal security and the responsibility for the fighting in the western part of the country. In the Secretary-General's view, priority should be given to providing security to members of the Government. He expressed concern about the logistical constraints facing the ECOWAS force, and appealed to donors to provide the necessary resources to assist in protecting the new Government. He underlined the need for the international community to pay more attention to the interlinkages of the conflicts in the region. In particular, the interaction between the conflict in Liberia and the developments in Côte d'Ivoire and Sierra Leone called for steps to resolve the Liberian conflict, which was increasingly becoming the source of continuing instability in the wider region. His Special Representative for West Africa would examine the impact of the various aspects of the Côte d'Ivoire crisis on the subregion and explore ways of addressing them. The Special Representative for Côte d'Ivoire, having convened several meetings of the Monitoring Committee, would devise a coordination mechanism for a UN response within Côte d'Ivoire. Once the Government of National Reconciliation was functional, it should develop a work programme for implementing the Linas-Marcoussis Agreement, thus enabling the United Nations and others to determine assistance they could provide to accomplish the key tasks, including the disarmament, demobilization and reintegration of armed groups, preparations for the national elections and reconstruction of the country. In the meantime, the Secretary-General recommended that the Security Council approve his proposed arrangements for UN support to the Ivorian peace process and that a UN mission in Côte d'Ivoire, to be called the Mission des Nations Unies en Côte d'Ivoire (MINUCI), be established for that purpose. That mission would be headed by his Special Representative who would have overall authority for coordinating UN system activities in the country.

In an 11 April addendum [S/2003/374/Add.1] to his report, the Secretary-General said that the financial implications for establishing MINUCI were projected at $26.9 million for a 12-month period. That amount would cover the deployment of 255 military and civilian personnel, consisting of 76 military liaison officers, 85 international and 89 national staff and 5 UN Volunteers, plus related operational costs.

Press statements (March/April). In a 28 March press statement [SC/7714-AFR/592], Security Council members expressed concern about incidents that took place in Daloa on 26 March during a demonstration organized by the "Jeunes Patriotes" and called on the Ivorian authorities to ensure that such incidents did not recur. Members reaffirmed support for the ECOWAS and French forces in their efforts to implement the Linas-Marcoussis Agreement. They condemned the recruitment of mercenaries by any of the parties and requested that an investigation of the violations of human rights in Côte d'Ivoire, in particular the massacres, be conducted. They stressed that neighbouring States should work to prevent the supply of mercenaries who further destabilized Côte d'Ivoire.

On 15 April [SC/7732-AFR/603], Council members welcomed the new decree delegating powers to the Prime Minister and the progressive formation of the Government of National Reconciliation. They expressed concern about recent violations of the ceasefire and the use of mercenaries, other foreign-armed elements and forced recruitment, including recruitment of children, and demanded that all parties refrain from those practices.

Communications (April). On 22 April [S/2003/472], Ghana forwarded to the Security Council the report of the ECOWAS Mission in Côte d'Ivoire (ECOMICI) and the Force Commander's operational review. Working in cooperation with the French force, Operation Unicorn, ECOMICI's mission was to ensure security by separating former belligerents in the centre of the country along the ceasefire line and by providing security for the authorities of the new Government at Yamoussoukro and Abidjan. At its current strength of 1,300 troops, ECOMICI had insufficient human, technical and financial resources, and it was recommended that the force level be raised in phases to 3,205 troops.

President Gbagbo, in an 11 April letter to the Chairman of the Monitoring Committee for the Linas-Marcoussis Agreement, which was transmitted to the Security Council on 22 April [S/2003/470], stated that the rebels were stepping up their attacks on all fronts, and he urged the ECOWAS and French forces to take forceful action against the attackers. On 28 April [S/2003/510], Côte d'Ivoire described the Government's efforts to implement the Linas-Marcoussis Agreement and expressed concern at the lack of interest of the international community with regard to the numerous violations of the Agreement, in particular the ceasefire. Since the crisis began, it said, the Council had not issued any statements condemning the atrocities committed in the occupied areas.

Security Council consideration. On 29 April [meeting 4746], the Security Council considered the situation in Côte d'Ivoire. The Secretary-General said that ECOWAS had found it necessary to increase substantially the size of ECOFORCE, and he appealed to the international community to provide it with the additional financial resources required for the next six months. In order to complement the peacekeeping efforts of ECOWAS and France, he had recommended the establishment of a small UN operation to strengthen the UN role in the Ivorian peace process (see above).

Ghana said that the ECOWAS mandate had been expanded from monitoring the ceasefire to include protecting the new Government, patrolling the borders, demobilizing and disarming the various militias, and creating the conditions to enable the new Government to control the national territory, for which it needed financial assistance. Côte d'Ivoire said that it would abide by all its international commitments. It warned that, despite the Government's efforts, the situation continued to be fragile, particularly in the western part of the country where there were rebels from Liberia and Sierra Leone. On the diplomatic level, the heads of State of Côte d'Ivoire and Liberia met on 27 April in Kara, Togo, and decided on the interposition of forces (Ivorian national forces, and forces from Liberia, ECOFORCE and France) along their joint border.

The Council, in a 29 April communiqué [S/PV.4747], welcomed the action taken by ECOWAS to resolve the Côte d'Ivoire crisis and supported its appeal for logistical and financial support for ECOFORCE.

Establishment of MINUCI

Acting on the Secretary-General's recommendation contained in his 26 March report (see p. 169), the Security Council, on 13 May, established the United Nations Mission in Côte d'Ivoire.

SECURITY COUNCIL ACTION (May)

On 13 May [meeting 4754], the Security Council unanimously adopted **resolution 1479(2003)**. The draft [S/2003/539] was prepared in consultations among Council members.

The Security Council,

Reaffirming its resolution 1464(2003) of 4 February 2003, the statement by its President of 20 December 2002 (S/PRST/2002/42), as well as its resolutions 1460(2003) of 30 January 2003 and 1467(2003) of 18 March 2003,

Reaffirming its strong commitment to the sovereignty, independence, territorial integrity and unity of Côte d'Ivoire, and reaffirming its opposition to any attempts to seize power by unconstitutional means,

Recalling the importance of the principles of good-neighbourliness, non-interference and regional cooperation,

Recalling its full support for the efforts of the Economic Community of West African States and France to promote a peaceful settlement of the conflict, and reiterating its appreciation for the efforts of the African Union to reach a settlement,

Reaffirming its endorsement of the agreement signed by the Ivorian political forces at Linas-Marcoussis, France, on 23 January 2003 ("the Linas-Marcoussis Agreement") and approved by the Conference of Heads of State on Côte d'Ivoire, held in Paris on 25 and 26 January 2003,

Noting with satisfaction the conclusions reached at the meeting held in Accra from 6 to 8 March 2003, under the chairmanship of the President of Ghana, the current presidency of the Economic Community of West African States,

Noting with satisfaction also the appointment of the Government of National Reconciliation and the cabinet meeting of 3 April 2003, attended by all the constituent political groups, in the presence of the Presidents of Ghana, Nigeria and Togo,

Welcoming the report of the Secretary-General of 26 March 2003 and the recommendations contained therein,

Noting the existence of challenges to the stability of Côte d'Ivoire, and determining that the situation in Côte d'Ivoire constitutes a threat to international peace and security in the region,

1. *Reaffirms its strong support* for the Special Representative of the Secretary-General, and approves his full authority for the coordination and conduct of all the activities of the United Nations system in Côte d'Ivoire;

2. *Decides* to establish, for an initial period of six months, a United Nations Mission in Côte d'Ivoire, with a mandate to facilitate the implementation by the Ivorian parties of the Linas-Marcoussis Agreement, and including a military component on the basis of option *(b)* identified in the report of the Secretary-General, complementing the operations of the French forces and the forces of the Economic Community of West African States;

3. *Approves* the establishment of a small staff to support the Special Representative of the Secretary-General on political, legal, civil affairs, civilian police, elections, media and public relations, humanitarian and human rights issues, and the establishment of a military liaison group whose tasks shall include:

   (a) Providing advice to the Special Representative on military matters;

   (b) Monitoring the military situation, including the security of Liberian refugees, and reporting to the Special Representative thereon;

   (c) Establishing liaison with the French and Economic Community of West African States forces for the purpose of advising the Special Representative on military and related developments;

   (d) Establishing also liaison with the Forces armées nationales de Côte d'Ivoire and the Forces nouvelles, in order to build confidence and trust between the armed groups, in cooperation with the French and the forces of the Economic Community of West African States, in particular concerning helicopters and combat aircraft;

   (e) Providing input to forward planning on disengagement, disarmament and demobilization and identifying future tasks, in order to advise the Government of Côte d'Ivoire and support the French and the forces of the Economic Community of West African States;

   (f) Reporting to the Special Representative on the above issues;

4. *Stresses* that the military liaison group should be initially composed of twenty-six military officers and that up to fifty additional officers may be progressively deployed when the Secretary-General determines that there is a need and that security conditions permit;

5. *Requests* that, in addition to the recommendations made in the report of the Secretary-General regarding the organization of the Mission, in particular its reference to the human rights components of the Mission, special attention be given to the gender component within the staff of the Mission and to the situation of women and girls, consistent with resolution 1325(2000) of 31 October 2000;

6. *Renews its appeal* to all Ivorian political forces to implement fully and without delay the Linas-Marcoussis Agreement, and invites the Government of National Reconciliation to this end to develop a timetable for implementing the Linas-Marcoussis Agreement and to communicate this timetable to the Monitoring Committee;

7. *Recalls* the importance of sparing no effort, in keeping with the spirit of the Linas-Marcoussis Agreement, to enable the Government of National Reconciliation fully to exercise its mandate during this transitional period;

8. *Emphasizes again* the need to bring to justice those responsible for the serious violations of human rights and international humanitarian law that have taken place in Côte d'Ivoire since 19 September 2002, and reiterates its demand that all Ivorian parties take all the necessary measures to prevent further violations of human rights and international humanitarian law, particularly against civilian populations whatever their origins;

9. *Stresses* the importance of an early start to the process of disarmament, demobilization and reintegration;

10. *Requests* all Ivorian parties to cooperate with the Mission in the execution of its mandate, to ensure the freedom of movement of its personnel throughout the country and the unimpeded and safe movement of the

personnel of humanitarian agencies, and to support efforts to find safe and durable solutions for refugees and displaced persons;

11. *Requests* the forces of the Economic Community of West African States and the French forces, in the execution of their mandate in accordance with resolution 1464(2003), to continue to work in close consultation with the Special Representative and the Monitoring Committee, and to continue to report to the Council periodically on all aspects of the implementation of their respective mandates;

12. *Welcomes* the complete ceasefire reached on 3 May 2003 between the Forces armées nationales de Côte d'Ivoire and the Forces nouvelles for the entire territory of Côte d'Ivoire, in particular the west, and welcomes the intention of the forces of the Economic Community of West African States and the French forces to lend their full support in the implementation of this ceasefire;

13. *Renews its appeal* to all the States in the region to support the peace process by refraining from any action that might undermine the security and territorial integrity of Côte d'Ivoire, particularly the movement of armed groups and mercenaries across their borders and the illicit trafficking and proliferation in the region of arms, especially small arms and light weapons;

14. *Urges* all Ivorian parties to refrain from any recruitment or use of mercenaries or foreign military units, and expresses its intention to consider possible actions to address this issue;

15. *Demands* that, in accordance with its resolution 1460(2003), all parties to the conflict who are recruiting or using children in violation of the international obligations applicable to them immediately halt such recruitment or use of children;

16. *Emphasizes again* the urgent need to provide logistic and financial support to the forces of the Economic Community of West African States, including through an appropriate trust fund established by the Economic Community of West African States to this effect, and calls upon the member States to provide substantial international aid to meet the emergency humanitarian needs and permit the reconstruction of the country, and in this context stresses that the return of internally displaced persons, particularly to the north of the country, would be important for the process of reconstruction;

17. *Stresses* the importance of the regional dimension of the conflict and its consequences for neighbouring States, and invites the donor community to help the neighbouring States to face the humanitarian and economic consequences of the crisis;

18. *Requests* the Secretary-General to report to the Council every three months on the implementation of the present resolution and to provide monthly updates;

19. *Decides* to remain actively seized of the matter.

Pursuant to resolution 1479(2003) (above), the Secretary-General, on 29 May [S/2003/606], informed the Council of his intention to appoint Brigadier General Abdul Hafiz (Bangladesh) as Chief Military Liaison Officer of MINUCI, effective 4 June. Eighteen countries had agreed to provide military liaison officers for the initial group of 26 officers to be deployed to MINUCI. The Council, on 3 June [S/2003/607], took note of the information.

Press statement (3 June). In a 3 June press statement [SC/7776-AFR/631], the Council expressed satisfaction at the presentation to the National Assembly, by the Prime Minister, of a draft programme for implementing the Linas-Marcoussis Agreement. They also welcomed the start of discussions between FANCI and the Forces nouvelles (comprising MPCI, MPIGO and MJP) on arrangements for disarmament. They called on the parties to continue to take the Linas-Marcoussis process forward, particularly by appointing ministers for defence, the interior and women's affairs. Members welcomed the successful implementation, in particular in the west, of the complete ceasefire reached on 3 May. They expressed concern at the humanitarian situation in Côte d'Ivoire, especially regarding the situation of Liberian refugees who had recently crossed the border into Côte d'Ivoire.

MINUCI financing

In September [A/58/370], the Secretary-General submitted to the General Assembly the budget for MINUCI for 13 May 2003 to 30 June 2004, which amounted to $29,881,700. The budget provided for the phased deployment of 76 military liaison officers, 76 international civilian personnel, including 7 United Nations Volunteers, and 81 national staff. Of the total amount, $1,009,700 was incurred for the period 13 May to 30 June 2003 from the amount of $1,746,200 previously authorized by ACABQ. The total resource requirements for MINUCI for 13 May 2003 to 30 June 2004 were linked to the Mission's objective through a number of results-based frameworks, grouped by components, namely, substantive civilian, military and support. ACABQ, in an October report [A/58/538], commented on the proposed budget. It urged the Mission to re-examine its structure, with a view to consolidating some units and revising grade levels. It recommended approval of $28,872,000 for the Mission for the period from 1 July 2003 to 30 June 2004 and stated that it was for the Assembly to decide whether a special account would be established for MINUCI.

In October [A/58/535], the President of the Security Council informed the Secretary-General that MINUCI was not a peacekeeping operation. Therefore, the Department of Peacekeeping Operations was to administer MINUCI as a special political mission for budgetary and other purposes. In the course of upcoming consultations on the renewal of MINUCI's mandate,

Council members would review its possible designation as a peacekeeping mission and would evaluate possible reinforcement of the UN presence in Côte d'Ivoire. The Secretary-General, taking note of the Council's view on the matter, said that, as the issue also related to the administrative and budgetary aspects of a UN field operation, he would transmit the matter to the Assembly. He also expressed the hope that the Council would reach an early agreement on reinforcing MINUCI. The Secretary-General and the Council President exchanged views on the status of MINUCI in letters transmitted on 29 October [A/C.5/58/12] to the Assembly's Fifth Committee, with the Secretary-General pointing out that the UN Charter assigned to the Assembly the responsibility of apportioning the expenses of the Organization.

In a 17 November note on the MINUCI budget [A/58/598], the Secretary-General reviewed what had transpired in regard to the MINUCI budget and noted that, on 13 November, the Council had extended the Mission's mandate until 4 February 2004. Consequently, he said, should the Assembly decide that the Mission should be financed under the regular budget, resources amounting to $13,865,700 gross ($13,414,500 net) for the period from 13 May to 31 December 2003 would be required for appropriation under the 2002-2003 biennium programme budget.

GENERAL ASSEMBLY ACTION

On 23 December [meeting 79], the General Assembly, on the recommendation of the Fifth Committee [A/58/586], adopted **resolution 58/275** without vote [agenda items 120, 121 & 161].

Financing of the United Nations Mission in Côte d'Ivoire

The General Assembly,

Having considered the report of the Secretary-General on the budget for the United Nations Mission in Côte d'Ivoire for the period from 13 May 2003 to 30 June 2004, the note by the Secretary-General concerning the budget for the United Nations Mission in Côte d'Ivoire and the related report of the Advisory Committee on Administrative and Budgetary Questions,

Having also considered the letter dated 27 October 2003 from the Secretary-General addressed to the President of the General Assembly and the letter dated 29 October 2003 from the President of the General Assembly addressed to the Chairman of the Fifth Committee regarding the United Nations Mission in Côte d'Ivoire,

1. *Reaffirms,* in the context of the decision of the Security Council with respect to the financing of the United Nations Mission in Côte d'Ivoire, the role of the General Assembly, as set out in Article 17 of the Charter of the United Nations, as the organ to consider and approve the budget of the Organization, as well as the apportionment of its expenses among Member States;

2. *Notes* that the financing of the Mission up to now has been provided in accordance with the provisions of General Assembly resolution 49/233 A of 23 December 1994;

3. *Decides*, as a provisional and exceptional measure, to finance the Mission up to the expiration of its current mandate in accordance with the scale of assessments for the apportionment of the expenses of the United Nations under the regular budget;

4. *Decides also* that the issue of the most appropriate funding for the Mission upon the renewal of its mandate should be considered by the General Assembly at the first part of its resumed fifty-eighth session, in the context of established norms and practice;

5. *Requests* the President of the General Assembly to bring to the attention of the President of the Security Council the contents of the present resolution.

Also on 23 December, the Assembly decided that it would consider the agenda item on the financing of MINUCI at its resumed fifty-eighth (2004) session (**decision 58/565**).

Security Council mission to West Africa. In its 7 July report [S/2003/688], the Security Council mission to West Africa (see p. 162) commented and made recommendations on the situation in Côte d'Ivoire. It emphasized to all parties that strict implementation of the Linas-Marcoussis Agreement was the only path acceptable to the international community. The ECOWAS Executive Secretary reported to the mission that there had been significant achievements since the 13 March inauguration of the Government of National Reconciliation. However, strong sentiments and opposition had been expressed by President Gbagbo's party on some issues, especially the question of amnesty for certain Forces nouvelles personnel. The mission also learned that the delay in appointing the ministers of defence and national security was a serious impediment to progress. While recognizing progress in implementing the Agreement, the mission warned that decisive action by President Gbagbo on a number of key issues was essential if a creeping deterioration in the situation was to be avoided. The mission encouraged all parties to take the required steps so that the programme of disarmament, demobilization and reintegration could proceed according to plan. In that connection, it suggested that MINUCI pay attention to the important lessons learned from a similar experience in Sierra Leone. The mission identified a number of areas where government action was needed, including the need to appoint ministers of defence and national security and the assured security of all government ministers. Emphasizing the importance of holding elections in 2005, the mission recommended that, at the appropriate time, the Council should support international involvement in the electoral process. The mission hoped that MINUCI would soon receive its full complement of staffing, especially in crucial areas such as the political and human rights components.

The Council, in presidential statement **S/PRST/2003/12** of 25 July (see p. 109), endorsed the recommendations of the mission.

Implementation of Linas-Marcoussis Agreement

On 4 July, the Defence and Security Forces of Côte d'Ivoire and the Armed Forces of the Forces Nouvelles issued a Joint Declaration stating that the war was ended [S/2003/704]. Noting that the 3 May ceasefire had been observed, the two sides expressed support for the Linas-Marcoussis Agreement and the Accra arrangements, and affirmed that they were subordinate to the President and the Government of National Reconciliation. They recommended that the President appoint the ministers for defence and security, called for an amnesty law, urged an end to the rearmament of forces, and asked the population groups in Côte d'Ivoire to develop tolerance and respect for diversity.

Security Council consideration. Prime Minister Diarra, addressing the Council on 25 July [meeting 4793], described progress in implementing the Agreement and affirmed that ministers had been appointed and were working. He noted that the ceasefire agreement had been extended westward to the border with Liberia, the buffer zone between the two forces had been defined, and the cantonment areas—eight for the National Armed Forces and nine for the Forces nouvelles—had been designated. Relations with neighbouring countries had been normalized. He noted in particular official visits by ministers to Burkina Faso and Mali and by the Foreign Minister of Burkina Faso (see p. 179) and the President of Mali to Côte d'Ivoire. Safe transportation corridors to neighbouring countries had been opened. The Council of Ministers had adopted an amnesty bill which would be considered by the National Assembly on 4 August. The authority of the State had also been strengthened, as had security for political figures. Discussions on the appointment of ministers for defence and internal security were still ongoing. Côte d'Ivoire was seeking assistance from the Council for peacekeeping and from the international community for the reconstruction of the country's economy and infrastructure and for the disarmament, demobilization and reintegration (DDR) programme. That programme, for which a timetable had been drawn up, encompassed amnesty, grouping, disarmament, demobilization, reintegration and restructuring.

SECURITY COUNCIL ACTION (July/August)

On 25 July, following consultations among Security Council members, the President made statement **S/PRST/2003/11** on behalf of the Council:

The Security Council reiterates the need for Ivorian political forces to implement fully and without delay all the provisions of the Linas-Marcoussis Agreement, as well as those of the agreement signed in Accra on 8 March 2003 ("Accra II"), with a view to open, free and transparent elections being held in 2005. The Council takes note with satisfaction of the formation of a Government of National Reconciliation and the progress made, particularly the identification of cantonment areas and the delegation of powers to the Prime Minister, and is looking forward to new progress in accordance with the Linas-Marcoussis Agreement. The Council also welcomes the Joint Declaration of the Defence and Security Forces of Côte d'Ivoire and the Armed Forces of the Forces Nouvelles of 4 July 2003.

The Council emphasizes, however, that much remains to be done to achieve the full implementation of the Linas-Marcoussis Agreement. In this regard, the Council endorses the recommendations of its mission to West Africa. The Council calls upon Ivorian political forces to redouble their efforts in the following areas: voting for the amnesty bill submitted to the National Assembly by the Government, the complete implementation of a "disarmament, demobilization and reintegration" programme, the extension of public services and the authority of the State to areas still under the control of the Forces nouvelles, the appointment of ministers for defence and interior security, the guarantee of equal security for all ministers, the dismantling of militias throughout the country and the termination of the activities of mercenaries and of the purchase of weapons.

The Council renews its support and encouragement to the Special Representative of the Secretary-General for Côte d'Ivoire. It asks him to keep the Council closely informed of developments towards the full implementation of the above objectives. It is pleased that the United Nations Mission in Côte d'Ivoire is now operational and hopes that it will soon be fully staffed, including in such crucial areas as the political and human rights components.

The Council reiterates its full support for the efforts of the Economic Community of West African States and France in contributing to a peaceful solution to the crisis. It welcomes in particular the satisfactory deployment of their peacekeeping forces in the western part of the country to support the implementation of the ceasefire reached on 3 May 2003. The Council calls upon Member States to continue to respond to the appeal made at the donors conference in Paris on 18 July 2003, attended by the Executive Secretary of the Economic Community of West African States and the Special Representative of the Secretary-General, and to provide logistic and financial support to the Economic Community of West African States Mission in Côte d'Ivoire so that it can continue to fulfil its important mandate.

The Council invites donor countries to contribute to the reconstruction of Côte d'Ivoire in compliance with the commitments undertaken at Kléber.

The Council expresses its concern at the continued existence of regional factors of instability, particularly the use of mercenaries and child soldiers, and the spread of small arms and light weapons, which prevent a lasting solution to the crisis in the region. The Council requests the Secretary-General to submit recommendations to the Council as soon as possible on ways to combat such subregional and cross-border problems, focusing in particular on better coordination of United Nations efforts.

The Council is convinced that a lasting solution to the problems of the subregion also requires genuine cooperation among all States concerned, together with confidence-building measures and the personal commitment of heads of State in the subregion.

On 4 August [meeting 4804], the Security Council unanimously adopted **resolution 1498(2003)**. The draft [S/2003/783] was prepared in consultations among Council members.

The Security Council,
Reaffirming its resolutions 1464(2003) of 4 February 2003 and 1479(2003) of 13 May 2003, and the statement by its President of 25 July 2003,
Having considered the report of the Secretary-General,
Reaffirming its strong commitment to the sovereignty, independence, territorial integrity and unity of Côte d'Ivoire,
Reaffirming the importance of the principles of good-neighbourliness, non-interference and regional cooperation,
Stressing the importance of the commitment of the Government of National Reconciliation to redeploy administration throughout the territory of Côte d'Ivoire,
Reaffirming the need to implement the disarmament, demobilization and reintegration programme,
Welcoming the implementation of the United Nations Mission in Côte d'Ivoire, in accordance with its resolution 1479(2003),
Reaffirming its full support for the national reconciliation process in Côte d'Ivoire,
1. *Decides* to renew for a period of six months the authorization given to Member States participating in forces of the Economic Community of West African States together with French forces supporting them;
2. *Requests* the Economic Community of West African States, through the command of its force, and France to report to the Council periodically, through the Secretary-General, on all aspects of the implementation of their respective mandates;
3. *Decides* to remain actively seized of the matter.

Report of Secretary-General (August). In response to Security Council resolution 1479(2003) (see p. 173), the Secretary-General, on 8 August, issued his first report on MINUCI [S/2003/801]. He stated that the security situation in Côte d'Ivoire had improved since his March report (see p. 169). Under the terms of the 3 May ceasefire signed by FANCI and the Forces nouvelles, the French forces and the ECOWAS forces deployed to the western region jointly with FANCI and the Forces nouvelles on 24 May to create a weapons-free zone of confidence, extend the ceasefire line to the border between Côte d'Ivoire and Liberia, and disarm or expel armed Liberian elements from that area. As a result of that deployment, the security situation in the inaccessible western region had significantly improved, resulting in the return of displaced villagers and the resumption of humanitarian activities. FANCI and the Forces nouvelles had established a mechanism for conducting a dialogue on security issues, through which they reached agreement on specific cantonment areas for their respective troops. The two sides, together with the French and ECOWAS forces, set up joint headquarters in Bouaké and Bangolo to facilitate coordination among the quadripartite forces. Another significant development was the 4 July declaration by FANCI and the Forces nouvelles formally proclaiming the end of the war and pledging loyalty to the President (see p. 176).

Remaining negative trends included militias opposing the Linas-Marcoussis Agreement and creating serious security and human rights challenges in the capital, political figures calling for a campaign of civil disobedience against Cabinet ministers affiliated with the Forces nouvelles, uncontrolled elements of the Forces nouvelles maintaining checkpoints along major roads in the north and Liberian elements maintaining a presence in the west. Both FANCI and the Forces nouvelles were reported to be rearming, undermining the confidence between the two sides.

Efforts to implement the Linas-Marcoussis Agreement had yielded mixed results. On the positive side, the Government of National Reconciliation had been installed and was functioning under the leadership of the Prime Minister. On 28 May, the new Government presented its draft programme for implementing the Agreement for consideration by the National Assembly. It included proposals regarding citizenship, national identity and the status of foreign nationals; the electoral system; eligibility for election to the Presidency; land tenure laws; the media; rights and freedoms of the individual; economic recovery and social cohesion; and DDR. It envisaged mechanisms to develop proof of Ivorian nationality, including a national commission on naturalization to review existing laws, study legislation on the identification process in ECOWAS countries and recommend residence permit requirements for ECOWAS nationals and measures to improve the status of foreign nationals.

With respect to the electoral system, the Government planned to restructure the Independent Electoral Commission, introduce legislation on voter identification, review preparation of the voters' register and funding for political parties, and take measures to ensure the independence of the judiciary in adjudicating on electoral disputes. Regarding rights and freedoms of the individual, it was proposed to set up a National Human Rights Commission and establish an international commission to investigate cases of serious violations of human rights and humanitarian law. Legislation on the media and information was foreseen, including on freedom of the press and strengthened media regulatory bodies.

On 9 July, the Government announced a timetable for the DDR programme, in which the cantonment of forces would begin on 31 July and end by 15 August. The commencement of the disarmament component was delayed, however, because the Forces nouvelles linked it to the adoption of an amnesty law and the appointment of the defence and interior ministers. The amnesty law, as Côte d'Ivoire informed the Security Council [S/2003/810], was eventually adopted on 6 August for political acts against the security of the State from September 2000 to September 2002. Other steps towards implementation included the Government's efforts to extend State authority throughout the country and to restore public services in the north and west. The Government also initiated efforts to repair relations and to restore trade links with Burkina Faso and Mali, which had been disrupted during the conflict.

Despite such signs of progress, some members of the ruling party, the Front populaire ivoirien (FPI), still viewed the Agreement as non-workable and in conflict with certain provisions of the national Constitution and were attempting to undermine its implementation.

The Monitoring Committee, which had been meeting on a regular basis, considered grievances from all the political parties.

The group of 26 military liaison officers authorized under Council resolution 1479(2003) (see p. 173) were deployed to MINUCI on 23 June; the pace of further deployment would depend on security conditions.

Persistent violence and lack of security continued to undermine the protection of human rights throughout the country (see p. 165). In March, the Ministry of Human Rights was established. Another positive development was the Government's agreement in principle to visits by the special rapporteurs of the Commission on Human Rights on contemporary forms of racism, racial discrimination, xenophobia and related intolerance, and the promotion and protection of freedom of opinion and expression, as well as by the Special Representative on internally displaced persons. In response to a request by President Gbagbo, the Secretary-General sent a team to Côte d'Ivoire to assess the need for an international commission of inquiry into human rights violations committed during the conflict. Most of the team's interlocutors expressed interest in such a commission. A team of human rights officers, including a gender specialist and child protection officers, had been assigned to MINUCI.

The humanitarian situation remained worrisome. Half a million people, mostly migrant workers from regional countries, had fled Côte d'Ivoire as a result of xenophobia and ethnic tensions. In addition, an estimated 800,000 people were internally displaced. Food security had become noticeably precarious in the north and the west. The United Nations established an Inter-Agency Humanitarian Coordination Committee in February to ensure complementarity of humanitarian operations.

Côte d'Ivoire continued to face a severe economic and social crisis, which also had adverse repercussions for the neighbouring countries of Burkina Faso, Guinea, Mali and the Niger, which depended on Côte d'Ivoire's transport facilities for imports and exports and on remittances from their migrant nationals.

The Secretary-General said that the United Nations stood ready to provide appropriate support in the organization and conduct of the planned elections in Côte d'Ivoire, should the new Government request such support. He warned that peace was not yet at hand. Although the Government was functioning, it remained incomplete and often worked in disharmony, and all parties had yet to demonstrate their full commitment to the Linas-Marcoussis Agreement. The Secretary-General urged the parties to make the concessions necessary to end the impasse over appointments to the vacant ministerial portfolios and to curb the activities of those groups and individuals who sought to undermine the peace process. The presence of the French and ECOWAS forces remained indispensable if the prevailing, albeit fragile, stability was to be sustained. He appealed to Member States to provide the requisite financial assistance to those forces on an urgent basis. The deployment of MINUCI military and civilian personnel continued to make satisfactory progress, and the Mission was engaged in monitoring and liaison activities that complemented the peacekeeping operations of the French and ECOWAS forces. The Secretary-General expressed concern about the existence of armed Liberian elements in western Côte d'Ivoire, which constituted a threat to the efforts to stabilize both countries. He was encouraged about the ECOWAS and Security Council efforts to resolve the conflict in Liberia, which had been the primary source of instability in the subregion. He believed that a peacekeeping operation in Liberia would open up possibilities for addressing cross-cutting regional issues, such as the use of child soldiers and mercenaries, and the exploitation of national resources to fuel conflicts. Pursuant to the request contained in Council presidential statement S/PRST/2003/11 (see p. 176), the Secretary-General had asked his Special Representative for West Africa to conduct a comprehensive study on those issues.

Communications (August-October). Côte d'Ivoire, in a 29 August letter to the Security Council [S/2003/849], said that a plot had been uncovered to destabilize the Government. In a message to the nation, which was annexed to the letter, President Gbagbo said that the plot involved attempts to assassinate senior government members and himself. Rebels had already killed two French servicemen near Lake Kossou. On 19 September [S/2003/913], Côte d'Ivoire forwarded a statement of its President on the first anniversary of the outbreak of the armed rebellion, in which he described efforts to achieve a peaceful transition to democracy and called on the rebels to lay down their weapons.

The EU, in a 22 September statement [S/2003/924], condemned the use of violence in the political process in Côte d'Ivoire. It welcomed the fact that the Government of National Reconciliation was complete and the reopening of the border with Burkina Faso as a prelude to the re-establishment of rail traffic between the two countries. On 27 October [S/2003/1054], the EU condemned the murder in Abidjan of journalist Jean Hélène, and considered it a matter of urgency that the authorities re-establish control over the security forces.

Press statement (3 October). Having been briefed by the Special Representative of the Secretary-General for Côte d'Ivoire, Security Council members issued a 3 October press statement [SC/7886-AFR/719] expressing concern that implementation of the Linas-Marcoussis Agreement had lost momentum and that sporadic violence had erupted. They took particular note of recent events in Bouaké and stressed the importance of re-establishing the authority of the State throughout the territory of Côte d'Ivoire. They urged all Ivorian parties, in particular the Forces nouvelles, to take all necessary measures to restore confidence and called for the full and quick implementation of the Agreement. Members of the Council noted some positive developments in implementing the national reconciliation process, in particular the reopening of the border between Côte d'Ivoire and Burkina Faso and the resumption of rail traffic between the two countries. They also welcomed the fact that all members of the Government of National Reconciliation had been appointed.

Efforts to improve relations between Côte d'Ivoire and Burkina Faso were made during the May visit of the Foreign Minister of Burkina Faso to Abidjan. In a final communiqué [S/2003/564], the two countries outlined steps to secure the border and to restore and renew economic and trade relations.

Report of Secretary-General (November). In his second report on MINUCI [S/2003/1069], the Secretary-General provided an assessment of the implementation of the Linas-Marcoussis Agreement and described MINUCI activities since his previous (August) report (see p. 177). He noted that, following the signing of the Agreement, the peace process in Côte d'Ivoire had made progress until early August. In addition to developments covered in his August report, positive steps included the reopening of road and rail links between the Government-held south and the northern provinces that were still under control of the Forces nouvelles and the release of some 50 prisoners of war by the Government. The Government set up a Commission on National Reunification and made initial efforts, with limited success, to re-establish State authority in areas controlled by the Forces nouvelles.

The protracted impasse over the appointments of the ministers of defence and internal security appeared to have been resolved when, on 12 September, President Gbagbo announced appointments to those posts. However, the Forces nouvelles rejected the appointments and withdrew from the Government on 23 September. In addition, they objected that the President had not allowed the Government and the Prime Minister to exercise the full authority granted to them under the Linas-Marcoussis Agreement. Without the participation of the eight Cabinet ministers from the Forces nouvelles who were boycotting it, the Government was severely handicapped.

The Monitoring Committee on the implementation of the Agreement encouraged the parties to resolve their differences through renewed dialogue. On 26 September, six major political parties issued a memorandum that identified the key issues that needed to be addressed in order to unblock the impasse, including the activities of militias, the ineffective functioning of State institutions due to the "incomplete" delegation of authority to the Prime Minister, and the need for disciplinary procedures involving civil servants to be processed through the Ministry of Labour. President Gbagbo indicated his readiness to convene a forum of all Ivorian political forces to resolve the stalemate. The Council of Ministers, in October, took some decisions to address the concerns of the Forces nouvelles.

Although the ceasefire was continuing to hold, the situation remained tense due to the political stalemate. In the northern provinces controlled by the Forces nouvelles, there was an upsurge of violence by "uncontrolled" armed elements and a situation of lawlessness was emerging. In the Government-controlled south, militia activities were causing concern, and in Abidjan the situation remained unpredictable. In western Côte d'Ivoire, the presence of peacekeeping forces had reduced the activities of the mainly Liberian armed elements. As a result, farming and other economic activities had resumed in some areas. However, there were reports of a residual presence of armed Liberian elements near Toulépleu. Uncontrolled Forces nouvelles combatants were also still harassing the population in some towns; unprovoked fire on a French boat patrol in the Lake Kossou area had resulted in the death of two French soldiers.

The humanitarian situation remained equally worrisome, particularly in the north and west where hundreds of thousands of people lacked basic health care and other public services and tens of thousands of children faced a second consecutive year without schools. Humanitarian organizations had reported high rates of malnutrition in the west. International aid organizations were distributing food, but were not able to fully meet the needs of the vulnerable populations due to the security situation and limited resources. On the human rights front, some progress was made by both sides (FANCI and the Forces nouvelles) in implementing international norms and standards on the protection of children associated with armed groups. However, it was reported that the Forces nouvelles continued to use child soldiers at roadblocks and in other military activities. The economic situation continued to deteriorate, with the growth that Côte d'Ivoire enjoyed in early 2002 completely reversed by the military and political crisis that began in September of that year. The slow pace of implementation of the Linas-Marcoussis Agreement would probably translate into another year of economic contraction.

At the time of the report, the French forces (Licorne) were deployed in the eastern and central sectors of the country to backstop ECOMICI troops (totalling 1,383 troops) that were monitoring the ceasefire line. In the west, the Licorne forces maintained a heavy presence. They had recently deployed in Bouaké, at the request of the Forces nouvelles. ECOMICI troops continued to face severe troop and logistical shortfalls and their operations were plagued by a precarious financial situation. FANCI troops conducted patrols in the Government-controlled south and maintained a heavy presence in Abidjan. The military component of the Forces nouvelles remained a loosely knit outfit led by non-commissioned officers who operated in a semi-autonomous manner. MINUCI's strength stood at 34 UN military liaison officers and 42 more were expected in November and December. Their tasks included liaising with all military forces on the ground, monitoring the security situation, building confidence between the two sides and monitoring the security of Liberian refugees. MINUCI's civilian component was focusing on monitoring the human rights situation and the media, on preparations for the 2005 elections, and on working within the framework of the Monitoring Committee to facilitate the peace process. The public information unit maintained dialogue with the Ivorian media in order to promote the dissemination of accurate and objective information on the Linas-Marcoussis Agreement and the MINUCI mandate.

The Secretary-General observed that, since his August report, the Ivorian peace process had encountered serious difficulties. To keep the peace process on track, differences among the Ivorian political actors over the power-sharing concept envisaged in the Linas-Marcoussis Agreement had to be addressed. The Forces nouvelles and six other signatory parties to the Agreement insisted that the President had not delegated sufficient powers to the Prime Minister and the Government of National Reconciliation as envisaged under the Agreement. The President, however, rejected that interpretation and pointed to the executive powers invested exclusively in the President. Another disagreement was over the restructuring of the defence and security forces, and the related issue of disarmament. The Secretary-General expressed concern that nine months after the signing of the Agreement, some of its key provisions had not been implemented; until they were, the peace process was likely to remain tenuous and the holding of elections would not be possible without the reunification of the country. Once the stalemate was resolved, the United Nations would dispatch an electoral assessment mission to Côte d'Ivoire. The Secretary-General noted that the Security Council was discussing the reinforcement of MINUCI; in the meantime, he recommended that its mandate be renewed for another six months. He noted that, with the recent deployment of a UN peacekeeping operation in Liberia and the consolidation of peace in Sierra Leone (see p. 210), the international community had the opportunity to pursue an effective regional approach to bringing lasting stability to Côte d'Ivoire, Liberia and Sierra Leone.

Communications (November). ECOWAS, having held an 11 November summit meeting on West Africa, issued a press statement, which Ghana transmitted to the Security Council [S/2003/1082]. The heads of State appealed to the Council to increase the strength of ECOMICI and transform it into a UN peacekeeping force.

On 12 November [S/2003/1081], Côte d'Ivoire said that, in considering whether to renew MINUCI's mandate, the Council should reexamine the Mission's very nature. The current status of MINUCI had proved to have limitations for the implementation of the Linas-Marcoussis Agreement: it had no direct mandate to intervene in order to maintain the peace; it complemented the operations carried out by the French and ECOWAS forces, which themselves were limited by their mandate; and its military component was made up of 76 unarmed liaison officers. Maintenance of peace and security was the responsibility of the French (4,000 troops) and ECOWAS (1,383 troops) forces. For Côte d'Ivoire, the only desirable option was for MINUCI to be turned into a UN peacekeeping operation which would include ECOMICI and for the French forces to preserve their current status. In order for MINUCI to be able to carry out such a mission, it would need to expand to at least 10,000 troops.

Extension of MINUCI

On 13 November [meeting 4857], the Security Council unanimously adopted **resolution 1514 (2003)**. The draft [S/2003/1083] was prepared in consultations among Council members.

The Security Council,

Reaffirming its previous resolutions concerning Côte d'Ivoire, in particular its resolution 1479(2003) of 13 May 2003, in which it authorized the establishment of a special political mission in Côte d'Ivoire, as confirmed in the letter dated 13 October 2003 from the President of the Security Council addressed to the Secretary-General, and its resolutions 1464(2003) of 4 February 2003 and 1498(2003) of 4 August 2003,

Having considered the report of the Secretary-General of 4 November 2003,

Reaffirming its strong commitment to the sovereignty, independence, territorial integrity and unity of Côte d'Ivoire, and reaffirming its opposition to any attempts to take power by unconstitutional means,

Reaffirming its endorsement of the agreement signed by the Ivorian political forces at Linas-Marcoussis on 24 January 2003 ("Linas-Marcoussis Agreement") and approved by the Conference of Heads of State on Côte d'Ivoire held in Paris on 25 and 26 January 2003,

Stressing the urgent need for all parties to participate fully in the Government of National Reconciliation so as to enable it to implement fully all the provisions of the Linas-Marcoussis Agreement,

Stressing also the importance of the commitment of the Government of National Reconciliation to resume effective administration throughout Côte d'Ivoire, and reminding all Ivorian parties of their obligation to contribute positively thereto,

Reaffirming the need for the Government of National Reconciliation to commit itself fully and immediately to the disarmament, demobilization and reintegration programme, including the dismantling of militias, and to the restructuring of the armed forces,

Recalling the importance of the principles of good-neighbourliness, non-interference and cooperation in the relations between States of the region,

Further recalling its full support for the efforts of the Economic Community of West African States and France to promote a peaceful settlement of the conflict,

Noting the continued need for the United Nations Mission in Côte d'Ivoire in accordance with its resolution 1479(2003),

Noting with concern the continued existence of challenges to the stability of Côte d'Ivoire and determining that the situation in Côte d'Ivoire continues to constitute a threat to international peace and security in the region,

1. *Decides* that the mandate of the United Nations special political mission in Côte d'Ivoire, the United Nations Mission in Côte d'Ivoire, shall be extended until 4 February 2004;

2. *Requests* the Secretary-General to report to the Security Council by 10 January 2004 on the efforts of the Mission to facilitate peace and stability in Côte d'Ivoire, including how those efforts might be improved and in particular the possible reinforcement of the United Nations presence in Côte d'Ivoire;

3. *Decides* to remain actively seized of the matter.

At the same meeting, following consultations among Council members, the President made statement **S/PRST/2003/20** on behalf of the Council:

The Security Council urges all Ivorian political forces to implement fully, without delay or precondition, all the provisions of the Linas-Marcoussis Agreement as well as those of the agreement reached in Accra on 8 March 2003 ("Accra II"), with a view to open, free and transparent elections being held in Côte d'Ivoire in 2005.

The Council notes with satisfaction the progress made since the statement by its President on 25 July 2003, in particular the appointment of Ministers of the Interior and Defence, the adoption of the amnesty bill by the National Assembly, the reopening of the border with Mali and Burkina Faso and the decisions taken by the Council of Ministers on 16 October to restore public order and reform the statute of Ivorian radio and television.

The Council expresses its serious concern, however, that the implementation of the Linas-Marcoussis Agreement has slowed down. It emphasizes in particular the importance of the entire Government of National Reconciliation meeting as soon as possible in order to implement fully the content of the Linas-Marcoussis Agreement. It reaffirms in this context the urgency of carrying out the cantonment operations of the forces involved, to allow the beginning of disarmament and demobilization, accompanied by measures for reintegration into the regular army or civilian life.

The Council further emphasizes the urgent need to begin reforming land law and electoral rules, restore public services and the authority of the State throughout the territory of Côte d'Ivoire and end the use of mercenaries and the illicit purchase of weapons in violation of national laws.

The Council condemns firmly the grave human rights violations. It further condemns the murder of a French journalist on 21 October in Abidjan. The Security Council calls for a full investigation by the Ivorian authorities of this crime and the punishment of the perpetrators in accordance with the law. It also calls upon them to ensure that organs of the press and groups which sponsor them refrain from encouraging any remark that might incite hatred or violence.

The Council expresses its concern for the grave humanitarian situation in the field. In this context, the Council supports the activities of all United Nations agencies aimed at assisting the Ivorian people.

The Council further condemns the hostile acts against United Nations personnel in Bouaké and Man on 24 and 25 October 2003, and recalls that all the parties are obliged, by resolution 1479(2003) of 13 May 2003, to cooperate with the special political mission established by the Security Council, the United Nations Mission in Côte d'Ivoire, and to ensure freedom of movement of its personnel.

The Council reiterates its full support for the efforts of the Economic Community of West African States, France and the Special Representative of the Secretary-General for Côte d'Ivoire with a view to stabilizing the country and seeking a peaceful settlement of the conflict. The Council welcomes in particular the recent initiatives of the Presidents of the Republic of Ghana and the Federal Republic of Nigeria and the holding of a regional summit in Accra on 11 November 2003 to address security problems in the region.

The Council commends the action of the forces of the Economic Community of West African States and France, and that of the UN Mission in Côte d'Ivoire, and pays tribute to the commitment and dedication shown by their personnel. It also welcomes the efforts of the Office of the Special Representative of the Secretary-General for West Africa and of all United Nations missions in the region to coordinate their action in order to address regional issues in an appropriate manner. It expresses its intention to examine the recommendations by the Secretary-General on ways to facilitate peace and stability in Côte d'Ivoire.

The Security Council continued its discussion of the situation in Côte d'Ivoire on 24 November [meetings 4873 & 4874]. The Secretary-General expressed concern about the current political stalemate created by the withdrawal of the Forces nouvelles from the Government on 23 September. Already, there were signs that the situation in some parts of the northern provinces was degenerating into lawlessness and there was a danger that Côte d'Ivoire could slip back into conflict. In order to jump-start the stalled peace process, the parties had to tackle the fundamental issues behind the deadlock, as he had indicated in his November report. The Secretary-General planned to send an assessment mission to Côte d'Ivoire soon to review the situation on the ground, so that he could make recommendations to the Council that would possibly include reinforcing the UN presence in the country.

The ECOWAS representative spoke of the effect of the crisis on the economy of West Africa as a whole and called for a comprehensive regional approach to the linked crises in Côte d'Ivoire, Liberia and Sierra Leone.

Communications (December). On 3 December [S/2003/1165], Côte d'Ivoire transmitted to the Security Council the text of an address by President Gbagbo to the nation. He announced that the Council of Ministers had begun, on 27 November, to discuss the laws suggested in the Linas-Marcoussis Agreement and affirmed that disarmament had priority among the tasks set by the Agreement. Peace in Côte d'Ivoire was at hand and that would help to safeguard prosperity throughout the subregion.

On 4 December in Yamoussoukro, under the auspices of President Gbagbo, representatives of FANCI and the Forces nouvelles met with the Prime Minister; representatives of MINUCI, ECOMICI and the French forces were also in attendance. In a final communiqué [S/2003/1182], they agreed on the need to do everything possible to create a climate conducive to the resumption of talks in order to restore normalcy and lasting peace. They agreed to: withdraw units from Allangouassou and Bania and all other units stationed in the zone of confidence by 5 December; release all detained soldiers on 7 December; and hold a meeting on 10 December to set a timetable for removing unauthorized checkpoints, establishing administration of the zone of confidence, cantonment of troops, and collecting light arms and heavy weapons.

In a 9 December statement on Côte d'Ivoire [S/2003/1181], the EU welcomed the Yamoussoukro meeting and Mr. Gbagbo's statements on upholding the Linas-Marcoussis Agreement.

SECURITY COUNCIL ACTION (December)

On 4 December [meeting 4875], following consultations among Security Council members, the

President made statement **S/PRST/2003/25** on behalf of the Council:

The Security Council is gravely concerned by attempts on the part of armed elements, observed on 29 and 30 November 2003 by forces of the Economic Community of West African States and France, to cross the ceasefire line, and by the serious consequences that could arise as a result.

The Council reiterates its full support for the forces of the Economic Community of West African States and France and lauds their action to prevent those attempts, in accordance with resolutions 1464 (2003) of 4 February 2003 and 1498(2003) of 4 August 2003,

The Council strongly underscores to all the Ivorian parties their fundamental responsibility to respect the ceasefire in accordance with the Linas-Marcoussis Agreement.

The Council calls upon all the parties to refrain from any act that might compromise respect of the ceasefire and the implementation of the Linas-Marcoussis Agreement, as well as any incitement to such acts.

The Council reiterates the urgent need for all the parties to take all possible measures to accelerate the implementation of the Linas-Marcoussis Agreement. In this context, it once again underscores the importance of having the Forces nouvelles return and participate fully in the Government of National Reconciliation and the full Government meet immediately and taking steps to implement all the provisions of the Linas-Marcoussis Agreement. It also reaffirms the urgent need to conduct operations to canton the forces on the ground, in order to begin disarmament and demobilization, accompanied by measures to facilitate their reintegration into the regular army or into civilian life.

The Council reiterates in this regard its intention to consider the recommendations of the Secretary General on the means of facilitating peace and stability in Côte d'Ivoire.

The Council welcomes the commitments undertaken by President Laurent Gbagbo in his speech on 27 November 2003, in which he reaffirmed his intention to implement without delay the provisions of the Linas-Marcoussis Agreement, and expects the fulfilment of those commitments.

The Council calls upon all parties in Côte d'Ivoire and countries of the region to guarantee the safety and full access of personnel of humanitarian agencies working in the field during the consolidation of the peace process.

Follow-up to Security Council mission. The Secretary-General, in his 5 December progress report [S/2003/1147] on the recommendations of the Security Council mission to West Africa (see p. 163), highlighted the steps taken to implement the recommendations and assessed practical ways to address the cross-border issues identified by the mission.

The Secretary-General estimated that well over 60 per cent of the national territory was under the control of the Forces nouvelles, who precluded the establishment of the central Government's administrative presence, thereby partitioning the country. The extension of administration throughout the national territory had stalled. On 27 October, the President established an operational structure to facilitate the process of redeploying administrators in the country, and 139 administrators took up their posts in western provinces in early November. The Forces nouvelles protested the deployments as tantamount to the use of force.

Prior to the stalemate over the appointment of the ministers of defence and national security, several steps were taken to consolidate peace, including: the creation of zones of confidence along the ceasefire lines; the holding of meetings between miliary commanders of the Forces nouvelles and FANCI; the mounting of joint operations against Liberian armed elements in the west; and the identification of 17 cantonment sites for the DDR process. Preparations for DDR and efforts to disband the various militias and terminate mercenary activities remained hampered by the political stalemate. The Secretary-General warned that, if allowed to continue, the political impasse could dangerously consolidate the de facto partition of Côte d'Ivoire with unpredictable consequences for the country and the subregion. He expressed the hope that Council members would consider the ECOWAS call for an increase in the troop strength of MINUCI and for its transformation into a peacekeeping mission.

Mission to Côte d'Ivoire (December). As requested by the Security Council in resolution 1514(2003) (see p. 181), the Secretary-General dispatched an assessment mission to Côte d'Ivoire, headed by Assistant Secretary-General for Peacekeeping Operations Hédi Annabi, to collect information on MINUCI's efforts to facilitate peace and stability and report on how those efforts could be improved, particularly by possibly reinforcing the UN presence there. The mission visited Côte d'Ivoire from 3 to 11 December and Mr. Annabi also met with the ECOWAS Chairman and the President of Ghana in Accra on 9 December and with senior French officials in Paris on 12 December [S/2004/3]. The mission report noted that the President and the Prime Minister had initiated meetings that yielded important decisions aimed at stabilizing the security situation and reinvigorating the peace process. On 4 December, President Gbagbo chaired a meeting of senior military officers of FANCI and Forces nouvelles, with the participation of Licorne, ECOMICI and MINUCI. The two sides agreed to resume preparations for the cantonment of their forces, the quartering of heavy weapons in designated areas and the implementation of the

DDR programme. They also reaffirmed their commitment to preserving the unity of the country. A follow-up meeting was held in Bouaké on 10 December, at which the two sides decided to begin dismantling their checkpoints and withdrawing heavy weapons from the zone of confidence to specific quartering locations. As a result, the situation improved.

The withdrawal of heavy weapons from the zone of confidence began on 13 December, and a joint ECOMICI/MINUCI team verified the completion of the process between 26 and 29 December. The dismantling of checkpoints was also under way. Also, on 7 December, the Forces nouvelles released 40 FANCI and police personnel who had been held as prisoners of war.

In the political arena, the Prime Minister visited Bouaké on 5 December for consultations to convince the Forces nouvelles to return to the new Government. However, an 11 December shooting incident prompted a decision by the Forces nouvelles to delay their return to the Government. In addition, there appeared to be divisions within the Forces nouvelles over the matter. Nonetheless, on 23 December a Forces nouvelles spokesman announced that the group had decided to end its suspension of participation in the Government. In an effort to address regional aspects of the situation, President Gbagbo met with the Presidents of Burkina Faso (26 November) and of Mali (28 November). The Chairman of the National Transitional Government of Liberia, Charles Gyude Bryant, also held consultations with President Gbagbo in Abidjan on 24 November on the peace processes in the two countries and the repatriation of Liberian refugees and armed elements.

By the end of 2003, ECOMICI troop strength stood at 1,478 and that of the Licorne force stood at some 4,000; MINUCI had 71 military liaison officers.

The assessment mission looked into several proposals for the possible reinforcement of the UN role, taking into account the serious troop and logistical shortfalls faced by ECOMICI. The mission concluded that serious consideration had to be given to the ECOWAS proposal to deploy a UN peacekeeping force in Côte d'Ivoire and to reassign the ECOMICI contingents to that force. The Secretary-General put forward suggestions based on the mission's findings, for the military, civilian, police and judicial, electoral, DDR, human rights, public information and political and civil affairs components of a possibly reinforced UN presence in Côte d'Ivoire. He recommended that, if the Ivorian parties made sufficient progress to ensure that the peace process would become irreversible by 4 February 2004—the date on which the mandates of MINUCI, ECOMICI and Licorne were due to expire—the Security Council should consider authorizing a multidimensional peacekeeping operation. The operation would comprise a military component of 6,240 troops, including 200 military observers and 120 staff officers, and a civilian component, the size of which would be determined based on the recommendations of a small technical team, scheduled to visit Côte d'Ivoire in January 2004.

Liberia

Events in Liberia during 2003 were dominated by the divisions between the Government and the opposing party, the Liberians United for Reconciliation and Democracy (LURD), and later a new dissident movement, the Movement for Democracy in Liberia. The fighting was violent and widespread during the first part of the year and the two rebel movements gained control of nearly two thirds of the country by early May. The concomitant conflicts in neighbouring Côte d'Ivoire and Sierra Leone threatened stability in the subregion. Elections that were originally scheduled for October were postponed until 2004 due to the lack of security. However, conditions improved late in the year following President Charles Taylor's departure from the country and the arrival of a multinational force.

The United Nations Peace-building Support Office in Liberia (UNOL) tried to facilitate the promotion of national reconciliation, good governance and respect for the rule of law and human rights. In April, the Security Council revised UNOL's mandate to focus on assisting the Government to address capacity-building needs in human rights and preparations for elections, as well as on developing a peace-building strategy. Those peace-building efforts were hampered by the inability of the Government and opposition party leaders to resolve their differences over key issues of governance. The Government's policy of exclusion and harassment of political opponents and abuse of human rights undermined efforts to promote reconciliation. That situation, coupled with the lack of reform of the security sector, contributed to the resumption of the civil war.

Mediating efforts yielded some results in midyear. On 17 June, a ceasefire agreement was signed by the three main opposing parties. The agreement was subsequently broken, however, when LURD forces entered Monrovia on several occasions, plunging Liberia into a new cycle of violence. At that point, the Secretary-General proposed a three-phase deployment of international troops to Liberia: first, the deployment of an ECOWAS vanguard force, followed by a reinforced multinational force, which in turn would be relieved by a UN peacekeeping operation. The deployment of the ECOWAS Mission in Liberia (ECOMIL) began in August to support the implementation of the ceasefire agreement.

On 11 August, President Taylor handed over power to Vice-President Moses Blah and left the country. That move, coupled with the arrival of the multinational force in Liberia, made conditions favourable for further progress towards a settlement. On 18 August, the Comprehensive Peace Agreement was reached by Liberia's Government, two rebel groups, political parties and civil society leaders meeting in Accra, Ghana. The Agreement declared an end to the war and provided for the establishment of a National Transitional Government of Liberia, as well as for monitoring mechanisms.

On 19 September, the Council established the United Nations Mission in Liberia (UNMIL) with a strength of up to 15,000 troops, to be accompanied by civilian police and civilian staff. Its main tasks were to observe and monitor the implementation of the ceasefire agreement, to assist in developing cantonment sites and disarming combatants, to monitor disengagement and cantonment, and to facilitate the delivery of humanitarian aid. UNMIL also assumed the functions of UNOL.

The smooth transfer of authority on 14 October from the interim Government led by President Blah to the National Transitional Government of Liberia, led by Chairman Charles Gyude Bryant, augured well for credible future national elections. By the end of the year, the main mechanisms for implementing the peace process were in place, including the National Transitional Government, the National Transitional Legislative Assembly, monitoring committees and a programme for disarmament, demobilization, reintegration and rehabilitation for former combatants. However, skirmishes and serious human rights violations continued, as UNMIL lacked adequate troops and equipment to deploy into the interior of the country, and the armed groups had yet to demonstrate their full commitment to the peace process.

The Security Council, having received a report from its Panel of Experts on Liberia, which determined that Liberia had not complied with demands that it halt support to rebels in Sierra Leone, decided in January to re-establish the Panel. Further reports indicated that Liberia continued to support armed rebel groups in the region, and that the arms, diamond and timber sanctions continued to be violated. In December, however, the Council, taking into consideration the changed circumstances in Liberia, in particular the departure of President Taylor and the formation of the National Transitional Government, revised the sanctions, expressing its readiness to lift those against diamonds and timber once there was evidence that profits from those sources were not used to fuel conflict.

Peace-building efforts

The Secretary-General, on 15 January [S/2003/49], referred to the Security Council's 29 November 2002 letter [YUN 2002, p. 176], in which it outlined the tasks to be implemented by UNOL as part of a revised mandate. As requested by the Council, he had drawn up recommendations for a detailed revised mandate for UNOL, incorporating the Council's additions, and Liberia had been provided with a draft revised mandate for its consideration and agreement. The draft took into account the situation on the ground and Security Council presidential statement S/PRST/2002/36 [ibid.], which outlined a strategy for the peace process. In its initial reaction, the Government said it was studying the revised mandate and that it would respond soon. The Secretary-General informed the Council that he would report Liberia's reaction as soon as it was received.

Press statement (17 January). In a 17 January press statement [SC/7637-AFR/544], Council members expressed regret that Liberia had not responded to the Secretary-General's proposals for a revised UNOL mandate and urged it to do so as soon as possible. They called on the Government and LURD to work together to bring the armed conflict to an end through dialogue, and to create the security conditions necessary for inclusive, peaceful and free legislative and presidential elections, including a ceasefire to guarantee safety for all. They welcomed the outcome of the first meeting of the International Contact Group (Dakar, Senegal, 19 December 2002). Council members expressed concern regarding human rights in Liberia and called on the Government and LURD to ensure that humanitarian aid workers were allowed free access to displaced civilians and refugees. They called on the Government to create the conditions for free, fair and transparent elections and to allow international observers to monitor the electoral process. The Government was urged to build peace in the region, including through restoring relations with its neighbours and the international community.

Report of Secretary-General (February). In response to a Security Council request [YUN 2002, p. 176], the Secretary-General submitted a 26 February report on the situation in Liberia [S/2003/227]. He stated that the main challenge confronting Liberia remained the continuing insurgency mounted by the rebel movement LURD, whose fighters had attacked government forces and seized territory in various parts of the country. In early February, following the capture of the city of Bopolu, LURD fighters reportedly came within 20 miles of the capital, Monrovia, before government troops drove them back more than 50 miles. The situation remained volatile, with the rebels in control of several towns and cities.

The rebel activities coincided with worrisome developments on Liberia's borders with Côte d'Ivoire (see p. 165) and Sierra Leone (see p. 210). The Government of Liberia, which denied allegations of involvement in Côte d'Ivoire's crisis, had moved troops to its eastern border with Côte d'Ivoire to prevent a spillover from fighting there, especially following reports of an armed incursion into the Liberian border town of Gbein, which left two Liberian soldiers dead. Similarly, on the border with Sierra Leone, armed men continued to cross over from Liberia, some of them said to be looting and harassing villages inside Sierra Leone. After LURD seized control of parts of the area bordering Sierra Leone, there was an influx of about 6,000 Liberian refugees. During the same period, about 250 soldiers of the Armed Forces of Liberia fled into Sierra Leone, whose Government was concerned about the possible overstretching of an internment camp that had been constructed to receive a small number of armed elements from Liberia. However, since the inception of joint border patrols by Sierra Leone and UN forces, reports of incursions had declined. On 14 January, Côte d'Ivoire informed the United Nations of the alleged presence in Guiglo, Côte d'Ivoire, of the former Revolutionary United Front commander, Sam Bockarie, who had reportedly participated in the fighting in that region. He was also said to have looted Ivorian villages and sold the stolen goods at the border with Liberia.

Meanwhile, the overall political climate in Liberia remained tense and volatile. The National Peace and Reconciliation Conference, begun in August 2002 and suspended the following month, appeared to have lost the necessary momentum to move the peace process forward. The fact that the reconciliation process did not involve all stakeholders, including exiled politicians, apparently cast doubts on its credibility.

Efforts by ECOWAS to bring the Government and LURD together at the negotiating table included a meeting between ECOWAS parliamentarians, civil society and members of the Inter-Religious Councils of the Mano River Union (MRU) countries (Guinea, Liberia, Sierra Leone) and LURD representatives (Freetown, Sierra Leone, 7-9 February), at which LURD agreed to commit itself to a peaceful resolution of the crisis by the end of the year and to engage in dialogue with the Government.

The difficult internal and subregional situation had severely constrained economic revitalization. With the Government devoting 60 per cent of its budget to the military sector, growth had stalled and unemployment was estimated to be more than 80 per cent. The authorities had taken steps to regulate the mining and marketing of diamonds under the Kimberley Process, and to infuse accountability into its timber and maritime trade.

The Government asserted that, regardless of the prevailing political and security environment, it was determined to go ahead with the legislative and presidential elections scheduled for October. However, a number of obstacles had to be overcome for fair elections to be held on time: a ceasefire with LURD; a reconstituted Elections Commission and the deployment of an international stabilization force for public security. It was argued that the 10-year residency clause contained in the Constitution was a major impediment to holding a fair presidential election, as several opposition candidates who had fled the country would be disqualified. On 2 January, the Elections Commission released the electoral calendar, which provided for the electoral campaign to commence on 20 June and for voting to be held on 14 October.

Concerns over Liberia's human rights situation (see also p. 683) related mainly to the activities of the Anti-Terrorist Unit and the National Police, who were accused of harassing the civilian population in the pursuit of alleged accomplices of LURD rebels. Other concerns were a pervasive culture of impunity, the use of child soldiers by both sides, and the need for human rights education among the civilian population and security agencies. The difficult humanitarian situation was complicated by an estimated 180,000 internally displaced persons in camps and tens of thousands of others squatting in host communities, as well as the ongoing civil conflict in neighbouring Côte d'Ivoire, which forced Liberian refugees to return. In addition, Liberia was hosting 17,000 Sierra Leonean refugees in camps around Monrovia.

The Secretary-General observed that Liberia needed to end the fighting as the first step towards sustainable peace. The subregional dimensions of the Liberian conflict had come to the fore with reports of the involvement of Liberian armed groups on both sides of the fighting in Côte d'Ivoire. The movement of Liberian refugees and incursions by armed groups into

Sierra Leone had also been recorded, rendering that country vulnerable to destabilization.

The conflict in Liberia was one that neither the Government nor LURD was likely to win. The international community should discontinue external military support to LURD, as it had achieved only the massive displacement of innocent civilians, the deaths of thousands of people and the wanton destruction of infrastructure and personal property. If decisive action was not taken to end the tragedy, the Secretary-General warned, a generalized humanitarian and economic crisis could engulf the entire West African region.

The Secretary-General drew the Council's attention to two letters dated 18 February from President Taylor. The first alleged that Guinea had provided military and other support to LURD and the second referred to the sanctions regime imposed on Liberia under Council resolutions 1343(2001) [YUN 2001, p. 181] and 1408(2002) [YUN 2002, p. 169]. The International Contact Group on Liberia, which was scheduled to meet in New York on 28 February, provided the best forum for the international community to engage Liberia and to find a comprehensive solution to the crisis, in addition to addressing the strained relations among the MRU countries. It should also assist Liberia in creating the conditions for the conduct of free and fair elections. The Secretary-General reported that progress had been made in the dialogue between the United Nations and Liberia on a revised mandate for UNOL.

Security Council press statements (March and May). On 5 March [SC/7678-AFR/572], Security Council members, having been briefed by the Representative of the Secretary-General in Liberia, Abou Moussa (Chad), expressed concern at the humanitarian situation in Liberia and called on the Government and LURD to stop human rights abuses and to give unrestricted access to humanitarian organizations. Members welcomed the conclusions of the International Contact Group on Liberia held on 28 February. They encouraged ECOWAS efforts to facilitate ceasefire talks, especially the suggestion that a meeting be held in Mali on 10 March, and urged the Government and LURD to participate constructively. They called on all regional States to refrain from any interference in the affairs of their neighbours, particularly through the movement of arms or mercenaries.

On 5 May [SC/7750-AFR/614], Council members reviewed sanctions against Liberia (see p. 201) and reiterated their concern at the deteriorating security and humanitarian situation in the country and the subregion. They expressed their intention to renew the sanctions and to extend them to include a ban on timber exports.

Revised UNOL mandate

The Secretary-General, on 11 April [S/2003/468], informed the Security Council that Liberia had agreed to the draft revised mandate of UNOL. In finalizing the draft, consideration was given to the capacity-building needs of the Government in human rights and the conduct of elections. Under the new mandate, UNOL would: provide good offices and other services to defuse tensions through promoting national reconciliation and resolution of conflicts; support the Government in implementing any future peace agreements; monitor the political and security situation; enhance respect for human rights, in particular by providing training for security agencies; offer assistance to the authorities and the public for strengthening democratic institutions and the rule of law, including promotion of an independent press; contribute to the preparation of free and fair elections in 2003; promote dialogue between the Government, the United Nations and the international community on peace and security in Liberia; develop a peace-building strategy in which political objectives, programme assistance and human rights considerations were integrated; mobilize national and international political support for such a strategy; provide support to the UN Office in West Africa, in particular pertaining to developments in the MRU subregion as they related to Liberia; and engage in an educational campaign to present UN policies and activities regarding Liberia.

On 21 April [S/2003/469], the Council approved the revised UNOL mandate. In **resolution 1478 (2003)** (see p. 203) of 6 May, the Council welcomed the Government's agreement to the revised mandate and called on all States in the region to participate in all regional peace initiatives, particularly those of ECOWAS, the International Contact Group, MRU and the Rabat Process. It called on Liberia and LURD to enter into ceasefire negotiations under ECOWAS auspices and the mediation of former President Abdulsalami Abubakar of Nigeria.

Report of Secretary-General (June). On 2 June [S/2003/582], the Secretary-General reported on the situation in Liberia in the three months since his previous report (see p. 185), a period that continued to be dominated by the LURD insurgency. Having consolidated its grip on main areas in Lofa County, LURD had reportedly captured other localities, including Tubmanburg, Zwedru and Greenville. It had also launched attacks on other towns, engaging government troops, and on internally displaced persons' camps on the outskirts of Monrovia. In early May, government forces launched an offensive in a bid to retake positions lost to the rebels. Another dissident movement, known as the Movement for Democracy in Liberia (MODEL), surfaced in the south-east, apparently the result of the breaking apart of LURD. Its troops had gained control of the port of Greenville.

In an effort to revitalize the Liberian peace process, the Co-Chairmen of the International Contact Group on Liberia (ICGL), Nana Akufo-Addo, Foreign Minister of Ghana, representing the ECOWAS Chairman, President J. A. Kufuor of Ghana, and Hans Dahlgren, Foreign Minister of Sweden and EU special representative to MRU countries, visited Guinea, Sierra Leone and Liberia on 14 and 15 April. During the visit, President Taylor expressed the readiness of the Liberian Government to negotiate unconditionally on a ceasefire. On 7 April, Abdulsalami Abubakar, former President of Nigeria, was designated by ECOWAS as mediator for the Liberia peace process. LURD had previously accepted the idea of negotiations that would include other stakeholders. On 10 April, Liberia invited the Secretary-General to dispatch a joint UN/AU/ECOWAS needs assessment mission to evaluate the conditions for free and fair elections in Liberia, in accordance with the ICGL recommendation. President Taylor expressed his readiness to hold direct talks with LURD, to be followed by the disarmament of all combatants, including the Anti-Terrorist Unit and government militias.

Meanwhile, Liberia's Elections Commission continued with preparations for the general and presidential elections scheduled for October, although there was a growing sentiment among the public that the requisite conditions did not currently exist, due to the lack of a ceasefire and a stabilization force. Additional problems included logistical and financial obstacles and the need for the Elections Commission to be more neutral and inclusive. Equally important were the issues of voter registration, the delimitation of constituencies and basic civic education. The Chairman of the Commission had concluded that elections as scheduled would be impossible without foreign aid.

The joint UN/AU/ECOWAS needs assessment mission, having visited Liberia from 4 to 9 May, determined that the political, security, military and humanitarian situation was not conducive to the holding of credible elections in October as scheduled. The list of requirements for elections included: providing a secure environment countrywide; restructuring the Elections Commission to ensure independence from the Government and the ruling party; removing major legal impediments to the holding of credible elections; enhancing the operational capabilities of the Commission; and improving communications and interaction between the Commission and political parties, civil society organizations and the media. At a meeting in Brussels on 12 May, ICGL agreed on the immediate steps needed to move the ECOWAS-led peace process forward, namely: a comprehensive political framework for a ceasefire agreement; and preparations for the round-table talks of Liberian parties, scheduled to start in Accra, Ghana, on 4 June, with an agenda, timetable, military planning for the mobilization and deployment of a ceasefire-monitoring mechanism, and benchmarks for attaining peace and stability in Liberia.

The deteriorating security situation had resulted in the inability of humanitarian agencies to provide assistance to 11 of Liberia's 15 counties, or 70 per cent of the country. Government security forces were increasingly unequipped to offer protection to civilians. Armed militiamen continued to attack and loot the camps for displaced persons. All parties continued to commit human rights abuses, and there were reports of extrajudicial killings, torture, rape, deliberate targeting of civilians, abductions, mutilations, the use of civilians for forced labour and forcible recruitment of children.

The Secretary-General stated that the need for a binding ceasefire was the most critical issue and both sides had agreed to hold direct talks and to cooperate with the ECOWAS mediator. They had also agreed that, following a ceasefire, an international force should be deployed to monitor compliance by the parties. The mandate of that force would be defined during the forthcoming peace talks in Accra. In the Secretary-General's view, it was urgent to end the fighting and to deploy a monitoring mechanism once a ceasefire was declared. In addition, the warring parties should be warned that violations of human rights and international humanitarian law should stop; otherwise, violators would be held accountable. He warned that Liberia remained the epicentre of the continuing endemic instability which was affecting the political, humanitarian and security landscape throughout much of West Africa.

Ceasefire agreement

The period of deteriorating security conditions in Liberia was followed on 4 June by President Taylor's announcement that he was prepared to step down no later than the end of his current term. That announcement was welcomed by the Security Council President in an 11 June press statement [SC/7787-AFR/644]. Council members urged all combatants to cease hostilities immediately and agree to a ceasefire and to work together to create a peace process, including a transitional Government. They further demanded that the parties ensure the security and unrestricted access of humanitarian workers.

The AU Central Organ of the Mechanism for Conflict Prevention, Management and Resolution (Addis Ababa, Ethiopia, 12-13 June) [S/2003/654] also urged all the parties to agree to a ceasefire and welcomed the holding of peace talks in Akosombo, Ghana, between the Government, LURD and MODEL, under ECOWAS auspices.

On 17 June in Accra, the Government, LURD and MODEL signed the Agreement on Ceasefire and Cessation of Hostilities [S/2003/657]. Under its terms, an ECOWAS-led Joint Verification Team, with two representatives from each of the parties, plus UN, AU and ICGL representatives, would verify information provided by the parties on the locations of their units, including combat equipment. A Joint Monitoring Committee, chaired by an ECOWAS representative and with representatives from the parties and the United Nations, the AU and ICGL, would supervise and monitor the ceasefire. Talks would commence immediately on a comprehensive peace agreement, to be reached within 30 days, which would include: deployment of an international stabilization force; a disarmament, demobilization and reintegration programme; restructuring of the security forces; human rights concerns; humanitarian issues; socio-economic reforms; reconstruction; creation of a democratic space; formation of a transitional Government; and elections.

The Secretary-General, on 18 June [S/2003/659], informed the Security Council that ECOWAS had requested the United Nations to provide a helicopter for the Joint Verification Team and invited the United Nations to designate two military officers to participate; the United Nations had made arrangements to comply with the request. On 23 June [S/2003/664], the Council took note of the information.

Despite the signing of the ceasefire, the situation in Liberia deteriorated. The Secretary-General, on 28 June [S/2003/678], urged the Council to take action to support the ceasefire agreement and expressed deep concern at the flagrant ceasefire violations, noting that several hundred civilians had been killed in fighting in and around Monrovia and wanton destruction of property and widespread looting had occurred. Approximately a million people, one third of the population of Liberia, were seeking refuge in Monrovia. Virtually all international relief operations had ceased in the capital and most of the country, and a combination of cholera outbreaks and food shortages in an environment of violence, disruption of services and cessation of humanitarian aid threatened to produce a major humanitarian catastrophe. The Secretary-General appealed to ECOWAS to press for observance of the ceasefire agreement and for a comprehensive political arrangement.

The Secretary-General requested the Council to authorize the deployment to Liberia of a highly trained and well-equipped multinational force, under the lead of a Member State, to prevent a major humanitarian tragedy and to stabilize the situation. Such a force would be authorized under Chapter VII of the UN Charter. In the meantime, the Liberian parties should immediately and unconditionally respect the ceasefire, allow the resumption of humanitarian assistance and resume peace talks under ECOWAS auspices. All States, in particular Liberia's neighbours, should desist from any action that might be construed as supporting any party to the conflict.

The Security Council mission to West Africa (26 June-5 July) (see p. 163) had planned to visit Liberia. However, because of the continuing conflict, the mission travelled instead to Accra, where the parties were gathered for peace talks, which were suspended between 27 June and 4 July because of ceasefire violations. In its 7 July report [S/2003/688], the mission noted the delay in deploying the Joint Verification Team, in what appeared to be a tactic to gain time to win military advantage. LURD and MODEL apparently had no common objectives beyond the exclusion from power of President Taylor. ECOWAS hoped to be ready to secure the ceasefire by creating a buffer zone through the deployment of a stabilization force, but it needed financial and logistical assistance from the international community. The ECOWAS Executive Secretary hoped the United States would consider involvement in such a force and that a neutral transitional Government could then be appointed for a period of 18 to 24 months. President Obasanjo of Nigeria informed the mission that the indictment of President Taylor by the Special Court for Sierra Leone had complicated his departure from office, as he was now insisting that the indictment first be rescinded.

The mission recommended that the Security Council urgently consider authorizing an international stabilization force on the basis of current ECOWAS plans, taking account of the ECOWAS appeal for troops and other support from outside the region. Plans for deployment should be drawn up rapidly, since delay would risk renewed breakdowns of the ceasefire. Liberia was likely to require increased UN attention and involvement in the short to medium term. The mission suggested that the Secretary-General appoint a senior representative in Liberia.

The Secretary-General, in an 8 July letter [S/2003/695], described to the Council a number of initiatives he had taken. He had appointed Jacques Paul Klein (United States) as his Special Representative for Liberia to coordinate UN activities in that country. In anticipation of the early deployment of the multinational force and consequent improvement in the security situation, he had instructed his Special Representative to expedite the return to Liberia of all UN agencies providing humanitarian assistance. With a view to advancing developments on the political front, he had sent Ahmedou Ould-Abdallah, Special Representative for West Africa, to Accra to provide UN support, in cooperation with ECOWAS, to the ongoing dialogue among the Liberian parties. He had also requested his Representative in Liberia, Abou Moussa, and the Resident Coordinator, Marc de Bernis, who were evacuated during the fighting, to return to Monrovia and prepare for the return of UN and associated personnel. The Secretary-General expressed the hope for an early establishment of transitional arrangements in Liberia. On 10 July [S/2003/696], the Council took note of the information conveyed by the Secretary-General.

Council members, in a 24 July press statement [SC/7824-AFR/674], expressed concern regarding the continuing deterioration of the security situation and the humanitarian crisis in Liberia. They reiterated that President Taylor had to honour his commitment to leave Liberia so that a transitional Government could be installed and peace restored. They urged LURD to stop its indiscriminate shelling of Monrovia immediately, welcomed the imminent deployment of an ECOWAS vanguard force to Liberia and called on the international community to support ECOWAS efforts.

Both the EU and the AU issued July statements calling for adherence to the ceasefire agreement. The EU Presidency [S/2003/764, S/2003/792] also called on the Liberian parties to sign a comprehensive peace agreement that would end the 13 years of conflict, and stressed the importance of the deployment of an interposition force/international stabilization force and the departure of President Taylor. The AU Central Organ of the Mechanism for Conflict Prevention, Management and Resolution (Addis Ababa, 24 July) [S/2003/760] welcomed the ECOWAS decision to deploy a vanguard force in Monrovia and appealed urgently to the international community to assist ECOWAS and take measures to deploy an international stabilization force.

Establishment of multinational force

The Secretary-General, on 29 July [S/2003/769], informed the Security Council that ECOWAS had indicated its readiness to deploy 1,500 troops to Liberia by mid-August, to serve as a "vanguard force" for the multinational force that he had proposed on 28 June (see p. 189). The vanguard force would comprise two battalions from Nigeria, one of which would be transferred from UNAMSIL, and a third battalion made up of 250 troops each from Ghana, Mali and Senegal. Expressing concern at the dramatic deterioration of the situation following renewed fighting in Monrovia on 18 July, the Secretary-General said it was essential to accelerate the deployment of the vanguard force to pave the way for an early deployment of the multinational force. The United States had announced that it would position appropriate military capabilities off Liberia's coast to support the deployment of the ECOWAS forces.

The deployment of the vanguard force would be the first phase of a three-phase deployment. The deployment of the full multinational force would constitute phase 2, and the establishment of a UN peacekeeping operation would constitute phase 3. Phase 2 troops would arrive immediately after President Taylor's departure. That multinational force would be relieved by a UN peacekeeping operation within the shortest possible time. It would be important for the Security Council to make an early decision on the establishment of such a UN mission, and to authorize a robust mandate in order to ensure that it had a credible deterrence capability. The main objective of the peacekeeping force would be to support implementation of the envisaged peace agreement, culminating in the holding of elections, for which the force would ensure the necessary conditions. An assessment mission would be sent to Liberia to determine the number of troops and other personnel needed. Jacques Klein, the Special Representative, would lead United Nations activities in Liberia. In view of those plans, the mandate of UNOL would have to be terminated and the staff and assets absorbed by the office of the Special Representative.

SECURITY COUNCIL ACTION (August)

On 1 August [meeting 4803], the Security Council adopted **resolution 1497(2003)** by vote (12-0-3). The draft [S/2003/784] was submitted by the United States.

The Security Council,

Deeply concerned over the conflict in Liberia and its effects on the humanitarian situation, including the tragic loss of countless innocent lives, in that country, and its destabilizing effect on the region,

Stressing the need to create a secure environment that enables respect for human rights, including the well-being and rehabilitation of children, protects the well-being of civilians and supports the mission of humanitarian workers,

Reminding the parties of their obligations under the Liberian ceasefire agreement, signed in Accra, 17 June 2003,

Recalling that, in paragraph 4 of its resolution 1343 (2001) of 7 March 2001, the Council demanded that all States take action to prevent armed individuals and groups from using their territory to prepare and commit attacks on neighbouring countries and refrain from any action that might contribute to further destabilization on the borders between Guinea, Liberia and Sierra Leone,

Commending the Economic Community of West African States, in particular its Chairman, President John Kufuor of the Republic of Ghana, for its leadership role in facilitating the achievement of the aforementioned ceasefire agreement, and recognizing the critically important role it has played and necessarily will continue to play in the Liberia peace process, consistent with Chapter VIII of the Charter of the United Nations,

Commending also President Olusegun Obasanjo of the Federal Republic of Nigeria for his efforts to bring peace to Liberia,

Recalling the Secretary-General's request of 28 June 2003 to the Security Council to authorize the deployment of a multinational force to Liberia,

Determining that the situation in Liberia constitutes a threat to international peace and security, to stability in the West African subregion and to the peace process for Liberia,

Acting under Chapter VII of the Charter,

1. *Authorizes* Member States to establish a Multinational Force in Liberia to support the implementation of the ceasefire agreement of 17 June 2003, including establishing conditions for initial stages of disarmament, demobilization and reintegration activities, to help to establish and maintain security in the period after the departure of the current President and the installation of a successor authority, taking into account the agreements to be reached by the Liberian parties, to secure the environment for the delivery of humanitarian assistance and to prepare for the introduction of a longer-term United Nations stabilization force to relieve the Multinational Force;

2. *Declares its readiness* to establish such a follow-on United Nations stabilization force to support the transitional government and to assist in the implementation of a comprehensive peace agreement for Liberia, and requests the Secretary-General to submit to the Council recommendations on the size, structure and mandate of this force, preferably by 15 August 2003, and its subsequent deployment no later than 1 October 2003;

3. *Authorizes* the United Nations Mission in Sierra Leone to extend the necessary logistical support, for a limited period of up to thirty days, to the forward elements of the Economic Community of West African States in the Multinational Force, without prejudicing the operational capability of the Mission with respect to its mandate in Sierra Leone;

4. *Requests* the Secretary-General, pending a decision by the Security Council on the establishment of a United Nations peacekeeping operation in Liberia, to take the necessary steps, including the necessary logistical support to the elements of the Economic Community of West African States in the Multinational Force, and pre-positioning critical logistical and personnel requirements to facilitate the rapid deployment of the envisaged operation;

5. *Authorizes* the Member States participating in the Multinational Force to take all necessary measures to fulfil its mandate;

6. *Calls upon* Member States to contribute personnel, equipment and other resources to the Multinational Force, and stresses that the expenses of the Multinational Force will be borne by the participating Member States and other voluntary contributions;

7. *Decides* that current or former officials or personnel from a contributing State which is not a party to the Rome Statute of the International Criminal Court shall be subject to the exclusive jurisdiction of that contributing State for all alleged acts or omissions arising out of or related to the Multinational Force or the United Nations stabilization force in Liberia, unless such exclusive jurisdiction has been expressly waived by that contributing State;

8. *Decides also* that the measures imposed by paragraphs 5 *(a)* and *(b)* of resolution 1343(2001) shall not apply to supplies of arms and related materiel and technical training and assistance intended solely for support of and use by the Multinational Force;

9. *Demands* that all States in the region refrain from any action that might contribute to instability in Liberia or on the borders between Liberia, Guinea, Sierra Leone and Côte d'Ivoire;

10. *Calls upon* the Liberian parties to cooperate with the Joint Verification Team and Joint Monitoring Commission as established under the ceasefire agreement of 17 June 2003;

11. *Calls upon* all Liberian parties and Member States to cooperate fully with the Multinational Force in the execution of its mandate and to respect the security and freedom of movement of the Multinational Force, as well as to ensure the safe and unimpeded access of international humanitarian personnel to populations in need in Liberia;

12. *Stresses* the urgent need for all Liberian parties who are signatories to the ceasefire agreement of 17 June 2003, in particular the leadership of Liberians United for Reconciliation and Democracy and the Movement for Democracy in Liberia, immediately and scrupulously to uphold the ceasefire agreement, to cease using violent means and to agree as soon as possible to an all-inclusive political framework for a transitional government until such time when free and fair elections can be held, and notes that critical to this endeavour is the fulfilment of the commitment to depart from Liberia made by President Charles Taylor;

13. *Urges* Liberians United for Reconciliation and Democracy and the Movement for Democracy in Liberia to refrain from any attempt to seize power by force, bearing in mind the position of the African Union on unconstitutional changes of government as stated in the 1999 Algiers decision and the 2000 Lomé Decision;

14. *Decides* to review the implementation of the present resolution within thirty days of adoption to consider the report and recommendations of the Secretary-General called for in paragraph 2 above and further steps that might be necessary;

15. *Requests* that the Secretary-General, through his Special Representative, report to the Council periodically on the situation in Liberia in relation to the

implementation of the present resolution, including information on implementation by the Multinational Force of its mandate;

16. *Decides* to remain actively seized of the matter.

VOTE ON RESOLUTION 1497(2003):

In favour: Angola, Bulgaria, Cameroon, Chile, China, Guinea, Pakistan, Russian Federation, Spain, Syrian Arab Republic, United Kingdom, United States.
Against: None.
Abstaining: France, Germany, Mexico.

Comprehensive Peace Agreement

On 18 August in Accra, the Government of Liberia, LURD, MODEL and 18 political parties signed the Comprehensive Peace Agreement, which Ghana forwarded to the Security Council on 27 August [S/2003/850]. Under the terms of the Agreement, the signatories agreed to abide by the 17 June ceasefire agreement (see p. 189) and called on ECOWAS to establish immediately a multinational force to be deployed as an interposition force, the mandate of which was outlined in the Agreement and included a mechanism for monitoring implementation. The parties also agreed on the need for deployment of an international stabilization force in Liberia and requested the United Nations, in collaboration with ECOWAS, the AU and ICGL, to deploy such a force to support the Transitional Government in Liberia and to assist in implementing the Comprehensive Peace Agreement. The force's mandate, which was outlined in the Agreement, included monitoring disengagement and cantonment of forces, collecting weapons at disarmament sites, assisting in the delivery of humanitarian assistance, providing advice to the Transitional Government on forming a new and restructured Liberian army, and protecting civilians and political leaders under imminent threat of violence.

Other articles of the Agreement dealt with: disengagement of forces; a process for the cantonment, disarmament, demobilization, rehabilitation and reintegration of troops; security sector reform, including the disbandment of irregular forces, reforming and restructuring of the Liberian armed forces, and restructuring of the police and other security services; release of prisoners and abductees; human rights issues, including the establishment of a Truth and Reconciliation Commission; providing access for delivery of humanitarian relief; the establishment of a Governance Reform Commission that would ensure transparency and accountability; electoral reform and organization of elections; establishment of an all-inclusive National Transitional Government; post-conflict rehabilitation and reconstruction, including reintegration of refugees and displaced persons, paying special attention to the rehabilitation of vulnerable groups or war victims (children, women, the elderly and the disabled); and a general amnesty for those engaged in military activities during the Liberian civil conflict. The parties called on ECOWAS, the United Nations, the AU and ICGL to use their good offices to ensure that the Peace Agreement was implemented.

Under the Agreement, the National Transitional Government had the responsibility to ensure implementation of the Agreement, including preparation of elections to be held in October 2005. On 21 August, Gyude Bryant, head of the Liberia Action Party, was appointed as Chairman of the National Transitional Government.

Security Council consideration. Addressing the Security Council on 27 August [meeting 4815], the Chairman of ECOWAS, Ghana's Foreign Minister, Nana Akufo-Addo, said that the departure of President Taylor on 11 August for Nigeria had contributed significantly to the conclusion of the Peace Agreement. The ECOWAS interposition force was currently deployed at a strength of 1,696 troops and would increase to about 3,500 by September.

The ECOWAS Executive Secretary, Mohamed Ibn Chambas, said that the issue of armed groups that roamed freely in the MRU area and in western Côte d'Ivoire remained a problem, as did the proliferation of small arms and light weapons in West Africa. He called on the Council to lift its sanctions against Liberia (see p. 201) in order to allow the forthcoming Transitional Government to function effectively.

SECURITY COUNCIL ACTION (August)

On 27 August [meeting 4815], following consultations among Security Council members, the President made statement **S/PRST/2003/14** on behalf of the Council:

The Security Council welcomes the briefing provided by representatives of the Economic Community of West African States, including Mr. Nana Akufo-Addo, Minister for Foreign Affairs of Ghana, Mr. Mamadou Bamba, Minister for Foreign Affairs of Côte d'Ivoire, Mr. François Fall, Minister for Foreign Affairs of Guinea, Mr. Oluyemi Adeniji, Minister for Foreign Affairs of Nigeria, Mr. Papa Louis Fall, Permanent Representative of Senegal to the United Nations, and Mr. Mohamed Ibn Chambas, Executive Secretary of the Economic Community of West African States, on the Comprehensive Peace Agreement reached in Accra on 18 August 2003.

The Council welcomes the Comprehensive Peace Agreement reached by the Government of Liberia, rebel groups, political parties and civil society leaders in Accra on 18 August 2003.

The Council appreciates the efforts of the Economic Community of West African States, particularly those of Mr. John Kufuor, Chairman of that organization and President of the Republic of Ghana,

Mr. Mohamed Ibn Chambas, Executive Secretary, and mediator General Abdulsalami Abubakar, in negotiating this agreement.

The Council remains concerned at the situation in Liberia, particularly the continuing dire humanitarian situation of much of the population. It calls upon all parties to allow full, secure and unimpeded access for humanitarian agencies and personnel.

The Council again stresses the need to create a secure environment that enables respect for human rights, including the well-being and rehabilitation of children, especially child combatants, protects the well-being of civilians and supports the mission of humanitarian workers.

The Council pays tribute to the donors that are supporting the deployment of the Economic Community of West African States' Mission in Liberia, encourages all Member States to provide financial, logistical and material support to the Member States participating in the force led by the Economic Community of West African States, and calls upon the donor community to provide urgent humanitarian assistance to those in need in Liberia.

The Council urges all parties to respect fully the ceasefire and to implement fully all their commitments under the Comprehensive Peace Agreement signed at Accra on 18 August 2003, including through full cooperation with the Economic Community of West African States' Mission in Liberia, the United Nations, the International Contact Group on Liberia, the African Union and the United States of America to establish a Joint Monitoring Committee, which is a critical aspect of the Liberian peace process, as required under the Accra agreement.

The Council reaffirms its readiness, as stated in paragraph 2 of its resolution 1497(2003) of 1 August 2003, to establish a follow-on United Nations stabilization force to support the transitional government and to assist in the implementation of a comprehensive peace agreement for Liberia.

Communications (September). Both the EU [S/2003/859] and the AU [S/2003/876] issued September statements welcoming the Comprehensive Peace Agreement. The EU stressed the importance of completing the deployment of ECOMIL as a vanguard force of the UN stabilization force, in accordance with resolution 1497(2003) (see p. 190). The AU urged the warring factions to observe the 17 June ceasefire agreement.

Report of Secretary-General (September). As requested by the Security Council in resolution 1497(2003) (see p. 190), the Secretary-General submitted an 11 September report on Liberia [S/2003/875], in which he provided the historical background of the Liberian conflict and an account of recent political and military developments. Based on the findings of an August/September assessment mission to Liberia, led by his Special Representative, the Secretary-General presented recommendations for establishing a UN peacekeeping mission (see below).

The Secretary-General noted that the security situation in Liberia continued to improve following the signing of the Comprehensive Peace Agreement, although it was still highly unstable. Government forces were estimated at over 20,000 troops, LURD had a strength of some 5,000 fighters, mainly in western Liberia, and MODEL had a force of 1,500 to 3,000 fighters, operating in the eastern parts of the country. Judicial institutions and the police suffered from problems of corruption and had nearly ceased to function. Of the estimated 250,000 people who had lost their lives in war-related circumstances since 1989, at least half were civilian non-combatants; all sides were responsible for violations of human rights and abuses. The humanitarian situation remained dire; nearly a million Liberians, or a third of the population, were displaced. Large numbers of refugees from Sierra Leone, Côte d'Ivoire and other countries added to the humanitarian woes. The cumulative impact of the conflict had reduced the already declining living standards. Liberia was one of the world's poorest countries, with high illiteracy rates and unemployment, and 75 per cent of the population lived below the poverty line.

Following the deployment of ECOMIL, the UN country team started to return to Monrovia on 11 August. The humanitarian community gave priority to rapid assessments and emergency interventions, particularly in the food, health, nutrition, water and sanitation, education and protection sectors. It was expected that the majority of internally displaced persons would, for the time being, remain in camps and would be dependent on aid for months to come.

One of the greatest challenges in Liberia and the neighbouring countries was the presence of thousands of combatants, including children, of various nationalities. Successful disarmament, demobilization and reintegration (DDR) of those ex-combatants would be crucial to sustainable peace and security. In Liberia alone, there were an estimated 27,000 to 38,000 combatants, many of whom were children. The Secretary-General urged all stakeholders, particularly the National Transitional Government and all other Liberian parties, ECOMIL, the proposed UN peacekeeping operation, all aid agencies and NGO partners, to coordinate efforts to develop an effective DDR programme. Adequate and secure funding would be required for maintaining cantonment sites, supporting ex-combatants and their families during the process, and providing cash and other incentives to encourage them to disarm and demobilize. The UN force should be responsible for disarming and demobilizing the combatants in the cantonment sites. Particular attention should be given to the needs of child combatants, women among the fighting forces, dependants of combatants, camp followers and abductees. Any DDR programme for Liberia should be linked to the ongoing DDR process in Côte d'Ivoire and benefit from lessons learned in Sierra Leone and other peace initiatives in the region and should form part of a strategy aimed at the political and economic recovery of the West African subregion.

The Secretary-General viewed the transfer of power from President Taylor to Vice-President Blah and the signing of the Comprehensive Peace Agreement as a unique window of opportunity to end the suffering and to find a peaceful solution to a conflict that had been the epicenter of instability in the subregion. There remained, however, formidable challenges to lasting peace, and he called on the parties to abide by the terms of the Comprehensive Peace Agreement. The effective functioning of the National Transitional Government would be crucial to its implementation.

Establishment of UNMIL

As envisaged by Security Council resolution 1497(2003) (see p. 190) and the Comprehensive Peace Agreement, the Secretary-General recommended the establishment of a multidimensional UN peacekeeping operation in Liberia, the United Nations Mission in Liberia (UNMIL) [S/2003/875]. On the basis of the findings of the multidisciplinary assessment mission, he proposed a mandate that included supporting the National Transitional Government and the other parties in implementing the Agreement, monitoring the ceasefire, protecting civilians and supporting the safe return of refugees, assisting in the DDR programme and monitoring the human rights situation. The mission would be composed of political, military, civilian police, criminal justice, civil affairs, human rights, gender, child protection, DDR, public information and support components, and would have an electoral component in due course. The Secretary-General described the tasks of each of those components. The mission would also include a mechanism for coordinating its activities with those of the humanitarian and development community and would coordinate closely with ECOWAS and the AU. It would be headed by his Special Representative, who would have overall authority for the Mission and the UN system in Liberia.

The Secretary-General recommended that the Security Council, acting under Chapter VII of the Charter, authorize the deployment of a multidimensional UN peacekeeping operation with adequate resources, and a troop strength of up to 15,000, including 250 military observers, 160 staff officers and up to 875 civilian police officers and an additional five armed formed units, each comprising 120 officers and a significant civilian component and necessary support staff.

On 16 September [S/2003/899], the Secretary-General, noting the planned UN peacekeeping force for Liberia, informed the Council that he intended to close the operations of UNOL as soon as the deployment of the peacekeeping mission was authorized. The major functions performed by UNOL would be transferred to the new UN operation in Liberia.

Security Council consideration. The Security Council considered the proposal for UNMIL at a private meeting on 15 September [meeting 4825] and at an open meeting the next day [meeting 4826]. The Special Representative, Mr. Klein, said that Liberia's massive humanitarian and political crisis called for immediate intervention. The UN force had to be credible, well trained and well equipped, as its tasks were many and arduous.

SECURITY COUNCIL ACTION (September)

On 19 September [meeting 4830], the Security Council unanimously adopted **resolution 1509 (2003).** The draft [S/2003/898] was prepared in consultations among Council members.

The Security Council,
Recalling its resolutions and the statements by its President on Liberia, including its resolution 1497 (2003) of 1 August 2003 and the statement by its President of 27 August 2003, and other relevant resolutions and statements,

Expressing its utmost concern at the dire consequences of the prolonged conflict for the civilian population throughout Liberia, in particular the increase in the number of refugees and internally displaced persons,

Stressing the urgent need for substantial humanitarian assistance to the Liberian population,

Deploring all violations of human rights, particularly atrocities against civilian populations, including widespread sexual violence against women and children,

Expressing its deep concern at the limited access of humanitarian workers to populations in need, including refugees and internally displaced persons, and stressing the need for the continuation of the relief operations of the United Nations and other agencies, as well as the promotion and monitoring of human rights,

Emphasizing the need for all parties to safeguard the welfare and security of humanitarian workers and United Nations personnel in accordance with applicable rules and principles of international law, and recalling in this regard its resolution 1502(2003) of 26 August 2003,

Mindful of the need for accountability for violations of international humanitarian law, and urging the transitional government, once established, to ensure that the protection of human rights and the establishment of a State based on the rule of law and of an independent judiciary are among its highest priorities,

Reiterating its support for the efforts of the Economic Community of West African States, particularly those of Mr. John Kufuor, Chairman of that organization and President of the Republic of Ghana, Mr. Mohammed Ibn Chambas, Executive Secretary, and mediator General Abdulsalami Abubakar, as well as those of President Olusegun Obasanjo of the Federal Republic of Nigeria, to bring peace to Liberia, and recognizing the critically important role that they continue to play in the Liberia peace process,

Welcoming the continued support of the African Union for the leadership role of the Economic Community of West African States in the peace process in Liberia, in particular the appointment of an African Union Special Envoy for Liberia, and further encouraging the African Union to continue to support the peace process through close collaboration and coordination with the Economic Community of West African States and the United Nations,

Commending the rapid and professional deployment to Liberia of the forces of the Economic Community of West African States' Mission in Liberia, pursuant to Council resolution 1497(2003), as well as Member States which have assisted the Economic Community of West African States in its efforts, and stressing the responsibilities of all parties to cooperate with Mission forces in Liberia,

Noting that lasting stability in Liberia will depend on peace in the subregion, and emphasizing the importance of cooperation among the countries of the subregion to this end, as well as the need for coordination of United Nations efforts to contribute to the consolidation of peace and security in the subregion,

Gravely concerned by the use of child soldiers by armed rebel militias, government forces and other militias,

Reaffirming its support, as set out in the statement by its President of 27 August 2003, for the Comprehensive Peace Agreement reached by the Government of Liberia, rebel groups, political parties and civil society leaders in Accra on 18 August 2003 and the Liberian ceasefire agreement signed at Accra on 17 June 2003,

Reaffirming that the primary responsibility for implementing the Comprehensive Peace Agreement and the ceasefire agreement rests with the parties, and urging the parties to move forward with the implementation of those agreements immediately in order to ensure the peaceful formation of a transitional government by 14 October 2003,

Welcoming the resignation and departure from Liberia of former President Charles Taylor on 11 August 2003 and the peaceful transfer of power from Mr. Taylor,

Stressing the importance of the Joint Monitoring Committee, as provided for by the ceasefire agreement of 17 June 2003, to ensuring peace in Liberia, and urging all parties to establish this body as quickly as possible,

Recalling the framework for the establishment of a longer-term United Nations stabilization force to relieve the forces of the Economic Community of West African States' Mission in Liberia, as set out in resolution 1497(2003),

Welcoming the report of the Secretary-General of 11 September 2003 and the recommendations contained therein,

Taking note of the intention of the Secretary-General to terminate the mandate of the United Nations Office in Liberia, as indicated in his letter dated 16 September 2003 addressed to the President of the Security Council,

Taking note also of the intention of the Secretary-General to transfer the major functions performed by the United Nations Office in Liberia to the United Nations Mission in Liberia, together with staff of the Office, as appropriate,

Determining that the situation in Liberia continues to constitute a threat to international peace and security in the region, to stability in the West African subregion and to the peace process for Liberia,

Acting under Chapter VII of the Charter of the United Nations,

1. *Decides* to establish the United Nations Mission in Liberia, the stabilization force called for in resolution 1497(2003), for a period of twelve months, requests the Secretary-General to transfer authority from the forces of the Economic Community of West African States' Mission in Liberia led by the Economic Community of West African States to the United Nations Mission in Liberia on 1 October 2003, and decides that the Mission shall consist of up to 15,000 United Nations military personnel, including up to 250 military observers and 160 staff officers, and up to 1,115 civilian police officers, including formed units to assist in the maintenance of law and order throughout Liberia, and the appropriate civilian component;

2. *Welcomes* the appointment by the Secretary-General of his Special Representative for Liberia to direct the operations of the Mission and coordinate all United Nations activities in Liberia;

3. *Decides* that the Mission shall have the following mandate:

Support for implementation of the ceasefire agreement

(a) To observe and monitor the implementation of the ceasefire agreement and investigate violations of the ceasefire;

(b) To establish and maintain continuous liaison with the field headquarters of military forces of all the parties;

(c) To assist in the development of cantonment sites and to provide security at these sites;

(d) To observe and monitor disengagement and cantonment of military forces of all the parties;

(e) To support the work of the Joint Monitoring Committee;

(f) To develop, as soon as possible, preferably within thirty days of the adoption of the present resolution, in cooperation with the Joint Monitoring Committee, relevant international financial institutions, international development organizations and donor nations, an action plan for the overall implementation of a disarmament, demobilization, reintegration and repatriation programme for all armed parties, with particular attention to the special needs of child combatants and women, and addressing the inclusion of non-Liberian combatants;

(g) To carry out voluntary disarmament and to collect and destroy weapons and ammunition as part of an organized disarmament, demobilization, reintegration and repatriation programme;

(h) To liaise with the Joint Monitoring Committee and to advise on the implementation of its functions under the Comprehensive Peace Agreement and the ceasefire agreement;

(i) To provide security at key government installations, in particular ports, airports and other vital infrastructure;

Protection of United Nations staff, facilities and civilians

(j) To protect United Nations personnel, facilities, installations and equipment, to ensure the security and freedom of movement of its personnel and, without prejudice to the efforts of the government, to protect civilians under imminent threat of physical violence, within its capabilities;

Support for humanitarian and human rights assistance

(k) To facilitate the provision of humanitarian assistance, including by helping to establish the necessary security conditions;

(l) To contribute towards international efforts to promote and protect human rights in Liberia, with particular attention to vulnerable groups, including refugees, returning refugees and internally displaced persons, women, children and demobilized child soldiers, within its capabilities and under acceptable security conditions, in close cooperation with other United Nations agencies, related organizations, governmental organizations and non-governmental organizations;

(m) To ensure an adequate human rights presence, capacity and expertise within the Mission to carry out human rights promotion, protection and monitoring activities;

Support for security reform

(n) To assist the transitional government of Liberia in monitoring and restructuring the police force of Liberia, consistent with democratic policing, to develop a civilian police training programme and to assist otherwise in the training of civilian police, in cooperation with the Economic Community of West African States, international organizations and interested States;

(o) To assist the transitional government in the formation of a new and restructured Liberian military, in cooperation with the Economic Community of West African States, international organizations and interested States;

Support for implementation of the peace process

(p) To assist the transitional government, in conjunction with the Economic Community of West African States and other international partners, in the re-establishment of national authority throughout the country, including the establishment of a functioning administrative structure at both the national and the local levels;

(q) To assist the transitional government, in conjunction with the Economic Community of West African States and other international partners, in developing a strategy to consolidate governmental institutions, including a national legal framework and judicial and correctional institutions;

(r) To assist the transitional government in restoring proper administration of natural resources;

(s) To assist the transitional government, in conjunction with the Economic Community of West African States and other international partners, in preparing for national elections scheduled for no later than the end of 2005;

4. *Demands* that the Liberian parties cease hostilities throughout Liberia and fulfil their obligations under the Comprehensive Peace Agreement and the ceasefire agreement, including cooperation in the formation of the Joint Monitoring Committee as established under the ceasefire agreement;

5. *Calls upon* all parties to cooperate fully in the deployment and operations of the Mission, including by ensuring the safety, security and freedom of movement of United Nations personnel, together with associated personnel, throughout Liberia;

6. *Encourages* the Mission, within its capabilities and areas of deployment, to support the voluntary return of refugees and internally displaced persons;

7. *Requests* the Government of Liberia to conclude a status-of-forces agreement with the Secretary-General within thirty days of the adoption of the present resolution, and notes that, pending the conclusion of such an agreement, the model status-of-forces agreement dated 9 October 1990 shall apply provisionally;

8. *Calls upon* all parties to ensure, in accordance with relevant provisions of international law, the full, safe and unhindered access of relief personnel to all those in need and the delivery of humanitarian assistance, in particular to internally displaced persons and refugees;

9. *Recognizes* the importance of the protection of children in armed conflict, in accordance with its resolution 1379(2001) of 20 November 2001 and related resolutions;

10. *Demands* that all parties cease all use of child soldiers and cease all human rights violations and atrocities against the Liberian population, and stresses the need to bring to justice those responsible;

11. *Reaffirms* the importance of a gender perspective in peacekeeping operations and post-conflict peace-building, in accordance with resolution 1325 (2000) of 31 October 2000, recalls the need to address violence against women and girls as a tool of warfare, and encourages the Mission as well as the Liberian parties actively to address these issues;

12. *Decides* that the measures imposed by paragraphs 5 (a) and (b) of resolution 1343(2001) of 7 March 2001 shall not apply to supplies of arms and related materiel and technical training and assistance intended solely for the support of or use by the Mission;

13. *Reiterates its demand* that all States in the region cease military support for armed groups in neighbouring countries, take action to prevent armed individuals and groups from using their territory to prepare and commit attacks on neighbouring countries and refrain from any actions that might contribute to further destabilization of the situation in the region, and declares its readiness to consider, if necessary, ways of promoting compliance with this demand;

14. *Calls upon* the transitional government to restore fully Liberia's relations with its neighbours and to normalize Liberia's relations with the international community;

15. *Calls upon* the international community to consider how it might help future economic development in Liberia aimed at achieving long-term stability in the country and improving the welfare of its people;

16. *Stresses* the need for an effective public information capacity, including the establishment, as necessary, of United Nations radio stations to promote understanding of the peace process and the role of the Mission among local communities and the parties;

17. *Calls upon* the Liberian parties to engage for the purpose of addressing the question of disarmament, demobilization, reintegration and repatriation on an urgent basis, and urges the parties, in particular the transitional government of Liberia, and the rebel groups Liberians United for Reconciliation and Democracy and the Movement for Democracy in Liberia, to work closely with the Mission, the Joint Monitoring Committee, relevant assistance organizations and donor nations in the implementation of a disarmament, demobilization, reintegration and repatriation programme;

18. *Calls upon* the international donor community to provide assistance for the implementation of a disarmament, demobilization, reintegration and repatriation programme, and sustained international assistance to the peace process, and to contribute to consolidated humanitarian appeals;

19. *Requests* the Secretary-General to provide regular updates, including a formal report every ninety days to the Council, on the progress in the implementation of the Comprehensive Peace Agreement and the present resolution, including the implementation of the mandate of the Mission;

20. *Decides* to remain actively seized of the matter.

The Secretary-General, on 29 September [S/2003/926], informed the Security Council of his intention to appoint Lieutenant General Ishmael Opande (Kenya) as UNMIL Force Commander as of 1 October. On 1 October [S/2003/927], the Council took note of his intention.

In a 9 October press statement [SC/7890-AFR/725], Council members expressed appreciation for the service performed by ECOWAS forces in Liberia and looked forward to a smooth transition from ECOWAS to UNMIL. They welcomed the fact that the new headquarters would be operational by 1 November and that forces would be fully deployed by March 2004. Members expressed concern that former President Taylor was still attempting to influence events in Liberia and noted that any interference from him could threaten the peace agreement. They underscored the importance for Liberia of a programme to demobilize, disarm, reintegrate and repatriate combatants to peace and security and urged all parties to commit to those efforts. They called on all armed groups to respect the ceasefire, to support the Transitional Government and to cooperate in such a programme.

Security Council mission. The Secretary-General reported in December [S/2003/1147] on progress made in implementing the recommendations of the Security Council mission to West Africa (see p. 163). With regard to Liberia, he reported that the ceasefire was generally holding despite sporadic harassment of civilians in some places by all warring parties. A disarmament, demobilization, reintegration and rehabilitation (DDRR) action plan had been completed for 38,000 combatants, including 8,000 child soldiers and 1,000 female combatants. UNMIL had taken over from the ECOMIL force on 1 October. Although Monrovia and its surroundings were secured, UNMIL needed more troops to deploy inside the country so as to stabilize it. Monitoring of the ceasefire had begun, and a number of organizations were working together on improving respect for international humanitarian law and human rights.

In general, the mission found, the early steps taken towards implementing the peace process augured well for the stability of Liberia and for the consolidation of peace in Sierra Leone. However, stabilizing Liberia remained a challenge and was contingent upon the timely mobilization and deployment of the required troops throughout the country, especially as disarmament and demobilization of combatants began.

Report of Secretary-General (December). In accordance with Security Council resolution 1509(2003) (see p. 194), the Secretary-General, on 15 December [S/2003/1175], issued his first progress report on UNMIL.

UNMIL took over peacekeeping responsibilities from ECOMIL on 1 October. All of the approximately 3,600 ECOMIL troops from Benin, the Gambia, Ghana, Guinea-Bissau, Mali, Nigeria, Senegal and Togo were reassigned to UNMIL, switching hats to become UN peacekeepers. Shortly after the takeover, United States ships that had been positioned off the coast since August withdrew from the area. As at 12 December, UNMIL troop strength stood at 5,900 military personnel. More contingents from Bangladesh, Namibia, Pakistan, Sweden and Ukraine, as well as military observers from various Member States, were scheduled to arrive in early 2004, with full deployment expected by the end of February. Delays in finding the necessary troops and equipment, in particular helicopters and signals units, had hampered deployment.

Ceasefire violations were reported in a number of locations. In Monrovia, a violation occurred on 1 October, the day of the handover from ECOMIL to UNMIL, after which UNMIL stepped up its patrols and the ceasefire held there until 7 December, when there were riots by former government soldiers and militias at the launching of the disarmament and demobilization exercise at a cantonment site near the city. Beyond Monrovia and the areas to which UNMIL had deployed, the security situation remained volatile and there was sporadic fighting. Until UNMIL received sufficient troops to deploy to areas affected by clashes, further sporadic fighting, looting and harassment of civilians were likely.

The Joint Monitoring Committee had been a valuable mechanism for monitoring the ceasefire, maintaining dialogue among the armed groups, and facilitating contacts between UNMIL and the ground commanders of those groups. The Committee, comprising representatives of MODEL, LURD and former government forces and chaired by the UNMIL Force Commander, played a key role in the efforts to end the sporadic fighting in the interior of the country. At the first meeting convened by UNMIL on 6 October, the armed groups agreed to declare Monrovia and key areas on the outskirts of the city a "weapon-free zone". Pursuant to that decision, the then interim President, Moses Blah, handed over to UNMIL several tons of arms and ammunition belonging to the former government forces. UNMIL also collected 22 tons of arms and ammunition that had been illegally imported by former President Charles Taylor but were seized by ECOMIL. In addition, some 800 militia personnel loyal to former President Taylor handed over their weapons to UNMIL. In preparation for the cantonment and disarmament of combatants, the Committee was collecting information from the armed groups on the numbers and location of their forces.

UNMIL cooperated with a number of other UN and international organizations on the elaboration of an action plan for DDRR, which would target an estimated 40,000 combatants. The initial phase, which began on 7 December, targeted 1,000 from each of the three armed factions. The plan would involve disarmament, destruction of weapons and interviews for reintegration. Before being discharged from the cantonment sites, each former combatant would receive a stipend for resettlement expenses and would begin a long-term reintegration programme. Special arrangements would be made for child and female combatants. A subregional approach involving foreign combatants in Liberia was being discussed by UNMIL and a number of other UN missions, offices and agencies. A National Commission for DDRR was established to oversee the whole programme and make policy decisions. A Joint Implementation Unit was established to coordinate the implementation of the DDRR process on the ground. By the end of the year, the cantonment facilities for the former government forces were established, but facilities for the LURD and MODEL forces had yet to be prepared.

As requested by the Security Council in resolution 1509(2003), UNMIL civilian police, expected to total 80 by the end of the year, would assist the national police in restructuring and training the force. To that end, a nucleus of the interim police force, comprising 20 police officers, had already received "fast track" training by UNMIL.

The National Transitional Government of Liberia, a key element of the Comprehensive Peace Agreement, was inaugurated on 14 October and power was transferred from the interim Government led by President Moses Blah to the new Government led by Chairman Charles Gyude Bryant. The signatory parties to the Peace Agreement submitted nominations for the 22 Cabinet posts allocated to them under its terms. However, Chairman Bryant rejected the nominations made by LURD for three posts. LURD threatened to pull out of the peace process and to refuse access by UNMIL to areas under its control. Following a series of meetings convened by UNMIL, the three armed groups, on 27 November, renewed their demands for more senior government posts. On 28 November, the Implementation Monitoring Committee, comprising representatives of UNMIL, ECOWAS, the AU, the EU and ICGL, held its first meeting, at which it condemned the attempt by the armed groups to make the attainment of government posts a precondition for their participation in the DDRR programme. It also requested the Joint Monitoring Committee to recommend measures to be taken against parties responsible for continuing violations of the ceasefire agreement, adding that those breaking international humanitarian law would be held accountable for their crimes. The National Transitional Legislative Assembly also began its work, electing officers and establishing its committees. Nine of the 67 seats in that body were not filled at the time of the report.

The UNMIL civil affairs component conducted an assessment of the functional capacities of government ministries and other public administration structures. The preliminary findings indicated that, of the 22 ministries surveyed, only two were working. All the others either were partially functioning or had closed down completely due to looting and non-payment of salaries. The UNMIL mandate envisaged the setting up of judicial and corrections components within the Mission's structure, to include training, advisory and court monitoring programmes. Other UNMIL assistance was planned in the areas of controlling the exploitation of natural resources, electoral planning and public information.

The humanitarian situation in Monrovia was gradually improving. Relief assistance was being delivered to vulnerable groups in and around the capital. Since August, UN agencies and their partners had delivered food assistance to about 380,000 beneficiaries, helped to reduce cholera and prevent fatalities through chlorination of open wells, benefiting 400,000 people, vaccinated 600,000 children against measles, supported basic health-care services in accessible areas, provided protection and assistance to internally displaced persons and refugees, and assisted in the repatriation of Sierra Leonean refugees. Assessment missions by humanitarian agencies, with UNMIL assistance, revealed massive destruction and vandalizing of physical infrastructure and the total collapse of basic social services. UN agencies formulated a consolidated inter-agency appeal aimed at responding to the immediate needs of the Liberian population, in which they requested $137 million to support proposed programmes (see p. 931).

The human rights situation in Liberia remained a major cause for concern. The ongoing skirmishes between the armed factions were accompanied by attacks on civilians, often including deliberate killings, mutilations, rape, torture, arson, abduction and harassment, in addition to extortion, looting and the destruction of property. Reports were received of reprisal attacks and atrocities against ethnic Gio and Mano peoples by Krahn elements associated with MODEL. In collaboration with other organizations, UNMIL was documenting cases of serious violations of human rights and humanitarian law, including information on the perpetrators, victims and eyewitnesses.

In general, the Secretary-General found there had been an encouraging start to the efforts to re-establish security, facilitate the delivery of humanitarian assistance and promote the peace process in Liberia over the previous three months. UNMIL had begun extending its influence beyond the capital through air and ground patrols and had established liaison with the political and military leadership of the three parties. The main mechanisms for the implementation of the peace process were in place. It was essential at that point to expedite the deployment of UNMIL beyond the Monrovia area in order to stabilize the situation in the interior where skirmishes and human rights violations had continued since the signing of the peace agreements. To that end, more specialized support units were needed, in particular helicopter gunships and signals units. Regrettably, the armed groups had yet to demonstrate their full commitment to the peace process, as was apparent from the ongoing skirmishes, violations of human rights and the selfish pursuit of lucrative government posts. The riots that broke out at the beginning of the DDRR process were particularly worrisome.

Liberia remained a main source of instability in neighbouring States, and the conflicts in Sierra Leone and Côte d'Ivoire were linked to the situation there. Subregional challenges needed to be tackled in a coordinated manner.

Later developments. On 25 December, the movement of the first contingent of UNMIL troops outside Monrovia was stopped just outside the capital by LURD elements [S/2004/229]. LURD leaders contended that UNMIL deployment should not take place until a dispute between them and the Chairman of the National Transitional Government over the appointment of 84 assistant ministerial positions had been resolved. However, UNMIL insisted that there should be no linkage between the two issues, and a Pakistani unit was deployed to Klay Junction on 27 December without further hindrance. UNMIL troops subsequently deployed to Gbarnga and Buchanan on 31 December.

The DDRR process at Camp Scheiffelin, on the outskirts of Monrovia, was suspended on 17 December and a review of the operational aspects of the programme was carried out. At that time, 12,664 combatants had been disarmed, registered and given receipts as identification for their participation in the process; 8,686 assorted weapons had been collected.

The civilian police component began its programme of co-location with the Liberian National Police on 15 December. A joint crime prevention patrol programme entitled "Operation Restore Calm" was launched on the same day.

UN agencies and NGOs were in the process of relocating internally displaced persons from irregular shelters in central Monrovia back to their homes in the city or to recognized camps.

Financing of UNOMIL and UNMIL

UNOMIL

In April [A/57/794], the Secretary-General issued the final performance report of the United Nations Observer Mission in Liberia (UNOMIL), whose mandate ended in 1997 [YUN 1997, p. 123]. The report contained information on income and expenditure, assets, outstanding liabilities and fund balances as at 30 June 2002. UNOMIL's assets as at 30 June 2002 comprised $3,576,000 in uncollected assessments and other receivables and net cash available of $12,930,000. In the light of the overall financial situation of the Organization and the fact that as at 15 March 2003 assessed contributions to peacekeeping in the amount of $1.5 billion remained unpaid, the Secretary-General proposed that the return of cash available for credit to Member States be suspended until the financial situation improved.

UNMIL

On 22 September [A/58/233], the Secretary-General requested the inclusion in the agenda of the fifty-eighth (2003) session of the General Assembly of an item on UNMIL financing.

On 29 October [A/58/539], he issued the budget for UNMIL for the period from 1 August 2003 to 30 June 2004, which amounted to $564,614,300, including contributions in kind totalling $120,000. The budget provided for the phased deployment of 14,785 military contingent personnel, 215 military observers, 1,115 civilian police officers, 893 international civilian personnel, including 286 United Nations Volunteers, and 768 national staff. The Secretary-General recommended that the Assembly appropriate the total amount for the operation of the Mission for the 11-month period, inclusive of $47,462,700 previously authorized by ACABQ to meet the initial critical logistical costs and personnel requirements for the period from 1 August to 31 December 2003.

ACABQ reviewed the proposed budget and issued its comments and recommendations in a November report [A/58/591]. It recommended appropriation of the amount of $564,494,300 gross ($559,284,300 net) for the operation of UNMIL for the period from 1 August 2003 to 30 June 2004, inclusive of the $47,462,700 already authorized. It further recommended that the total amount assessed for that period not exceed $450 million at that time.

GENERAL ASSEMBLY ACTION

On 23 December [meeting 79], the General Assembly, on the recommendation of the Fifth Committee [A/58/589], adopted **resolution 58/261 A** without vote [agenda item 165].

Financing of the United Nations Mission in Liberia

The General Assembly,

Having considered the report of the Secretary-General on the financing of the United Nations Mission in Liberia and the related report of the Advisory Committee on Administrative and Budgetary Questions,

Recalling Security Council resolution 1497(2003) of 1 August 2003, by which the Council declared its readiness to establish a United Nations stabilization force to support the transitional government and to assist in the implementation of a comprehensive peace agreement for Liberia,

Recalling also Security Council resolution 1509(2003) of 19 September 2003, by which the Council decided to establish the United Nations Mission in Liberia for a period of twelve months,

Reaffirming the general principles underlying the financing of United Nations peacekeeping operations, as stated in its resolutions 1874(S-IV) of 27 June 1963, 3101(XXVIII) of 11 December 1973 and 55/235 of 23 December 2000,

Noting with appreciation that voluntary contributions have been made to the Mission,

Mindful of the fact that it is essential to provide the Mission with the necessary financial resources to enable it to fulfil its responsibilities under the relevant resolution of the Security Council,

1. *Expresses concern* at the financial situation with regard to peacekeeping activities, in particular as regards the reimbursements to troop contributors that bear additional burdens owing to overdue payments by Member States of their assessments;

2. *Also expresses concern* at the delay experienced by the Secretary-General in deploying some recent peacekeeping missions, in particular those in Africa, and in providing them with adequate resources;

3. *Emphasizes* that all future and existing peacekeeping missions shall be given equal and non-discriminatory treatment in respect of financial and administrative arrangements;

4. *Also emphasizes* that all peacekeeping missions shall be provided with adequate resources for the effective and efficient discharge of their respective mandates;

5. *Requests* the Secretary-General to make the fullest possible use of facilities and equipment at the United Nations Logistics Base at Brindisi, Italy, in order to minimize the costs of procurement for the Mission;

6. *Endorses* the conclusions and recommendations contained in the report of the Advisory Committee on Administrative and Budgetary Questions, and requests the Secretary-General to ensure their full implementation;

7. *Requests* the Secretary-General to take all necessary action to ensure that the Mission is administered with a maximum of efficiency and economy;

8. *Also requests* the Secretary-General, in order to reduce the cost of employing General Service staff, to make efforts to recruit local staff for the Mission against General Service posts, commensurate with the requirements of the Mission;

Budget estimates for the period from 1 August 2003 to 30 June 2004

9. *Authorizes* the Secretary-General to establish a special account for the United Nations Mission in Liberia for the purpose of accounting for income received and expenditure incurred in respect of the Mission;

10. *Decides* to appropriate to the Special Account for the United Nations Mission in Liberia the amount of 564,494,300 United States dollars for the period from 1 August 2003 to 30 June 2004, inclusive of the amount of 47,462,700 dollars previously authorized by the Advisory Committee on Administrative and Budgetary Questions for the operation of the Mission under the terms of section IV of General Assembly resolution 49/233 A of 23 December 1994 for the period from 1 August to 31 December 2003;

Financing of the appropriation

11. *Decides also* to apportion among Member States the amount of 450 million dollars at a monthly rate of 40,909,090 dollars, in accordance with the levels set out in resolution 55/235, as adjusted by the General Assembly in its resolutions 55/236 of 23 December 2000 and 57/290 A of 20 December 2002, and taking

into account the scale of assessments for 2003 as set out in its resolutions 55/5 B of 23 December 2000 and 57/4 B of 20 December 2002 and the scale of assessments for 2004 as set out in its resolution 58/1 B of 23 December 2003;

12. *Decides further* that, in accordance with the provisions of its resolution 973(X) of 15 December 1955, there shall be set off against the apportionment among Member States, as provided for in paragraph 11 above, their respective share in the Tax Equalization Fund of 5,210,000 dollars at a monthly rate of 473,636 dollars, representing the estimated staff assessment income approved for the Mission;

13. *Requests* the Secretary-General to pursue, through collaboration between the United Nations Mission in Liberia, the United Nations Mission in Sierra Leone and the United Nations Mission in Côte d'Ivoire, opportunities for optimizing, where possible, the provision and management of support resources and service delivery to the three missions;

14. *Emphasizes* that no peacekeeping mission shall be financed by borrowing funds from other active peacekeeping missions;

15. *Notes with appreciation* the utilization of the strategic deployment stocks to the Mission at the start-up stage;

16. *Encourages* the Secretary-General to take additional measures to ensure the safety and security of all personnel under the auspices of the United Nations participating in the Mission;

17. *Invites* voluntary contributions to the Mission in cash and in the form of services and supplies acceptable to the Secretary-General, to be administered, as appropriate, in accordance with the procedure and practices established by the General Assembly;

18. *Decides* to keep under review during its fifty-eighth session the item entitled "Financing of the United Nations Mission in Liberia".

Also on 23 December, the Assembly decided that the agenda item on UNMIL financing would remain for consideration during its resumed fifty-eighth (2004) session (**decision 58/565**).

Sanctions

In January, the Security Council considered the October 2002 report [YUN 2002, p. 172] of the Panel of Experts on Liberia, appointed pursuant to Council resolution 1408(2002) [ibid., p. 169]. The Panel was set up to investigate Liberia's compliance with demands made by the Council in resolution 1343(2001) [YUN 2001, p. 181] that sought to end any Liberian military or financial support of the Revolutionary United Front (RUF) of Sierra Leone and other rebel movements, including transfer of arms, military training, provision of communications and logistical assistance, and the import of Sierra Leonean rough diamonds not controlled through the certificate-of-origin regime. The Council had also demanded that Liberia ground all Liberia-registered aircraft until it had updated its aircraft register, as required under international agreements.

SECURITY COUNCIL ACTION (January)

On 28 January [meeting 4693], the Security Council unanimously adopted **resolution 1458 (2003)**. The draft [S/2003/98] was prepared in consultations among Council members.

The Security Council,

Reaffirming its resolution 1408(2002) of 6 May 2002,

Noting that the next six-monthly review by the Security Council of the measures imposed by paragraphs 5 to 7 of resolution 1343(2001) of 7 March 2001, and extended by paragraph 5 of resolution 1408(2002), is scheduled to take place on or before 6 May 2003,

Deeply concerned about the situation in Liberia and neighbouring countries, especially in Côte d'Ivoire,

Recognizing the importance of monitoring the implementation of the provisions of resolutions 1343 (2001) and 1408(2002),

1. *Takes note* of the report of the Panel of Experts on Liberia dated 25 October 2002, submitted pursuant to paragraph 16 of resolution 1408(2002);

2. *Expresses its intention* to continue to give full consideration to the report;

3. *Decides* to re-establish the Panel of Experts appointed pursuant to paragraph 16 of resolution 1408 (2002) for a further period of three months commencing no later than 10 February 2003;

4. *Requests* the Panel of Experts to conduct a follow-up assessment mission to Liberia and neighbouring States, in order to investigate and compile a report on compliance by the Government of Liberia with the demands referred to in paragraph 2 of resolution 1343 (2001) and on any violations of the measures referred to in paragraph 5 of resolution 1408(2002), including any involving rebel movements, to conduct a review of the audits referred to in paragraph 10 of resolution 1408(2002), and to report to the Council through the Security Council Committee established pursuant to paragraph 14 of resolution 1343(2001) (the Committee) no later than 16 April 2003 with the observations and recommendations of the Panel in relation to the tasks set out herein;

5. *Also requests* the Panel of Experts, as far as possible, to bring any relevant information collected in the course of the investigations conducted in accordance with its mandate to the attention of the States concerned for prompt and thorough investigation and, where appropriate, corrective action, and to allow them the right of reply;

6. *Requests* the Secretary-General, upon the adoption of the present resolution and acting in consultation with the Committee, to appoint no more than five experts, with the range of expertise necessary to fulfil the mandate of the Panel referred to in paragraph 4 above, drawing as much as possible and as appropriate on the expertise of the members of the Panel of Experts appointed pursuant to paragraph 16 of resolution 1408(2002), and also requests the Secretary-General to make the necessary financial arrangements to support the work of the Panel;

7. *Urges* all States, relevant United Nations bodies and, as appropriate, other organizations and inter-

ested parties to cooperate fully with the Committee and with the Panel of Experts, including by supplying information on possible violations of the measures imposed by paragraphs 5 to 7 of resolution 1343(2001);

8. *Decides* to remain actively seized of the matter.

In accordance with the Council decision to reestablish the Panel of Experts on Liberia in resolution 1458(2003) (above), the Secretary-General, in letters of 14 February [S/2003/185] and 5 March [S/2003/251], informed the Council of his appointment of five members to the Panel.

The AU Central Organ of the Mechanism for Conflict Prevention, Management and Resolution, at a meeting of heads of State and Government (Addis Ababa, 3 February) [S/2003/142], reiterated its appeal to the Council to reconsider its decision on the sanctions imposed against Liberia.

Report of Secretary-General (April). As requested by the Security Council in resolution 1408(2002) [YUN 2002, p. 169], the Secretary-General issued on 22 April [S/2003/466] his second six-monthly report on whether Liberia had complied with the Council's demands made in that resolution. The report drew on information provided by UNOL, the United Nations Mission in Sierra Leone (UNAMSIL) and ECOWAS. The Government of Liberia claimed that it was in compliance with the Council's demands. With regard to the ban on the importation of uncertified rough diamonds, the Government reiterated that it was still in force. Concerning the export of diamonds, the Government stated that it had set in motion measures to ensure that only diamonds produced in Liberia would be exported with the Kimberley Process certificate of origin. However, mining activities were being carried out by the LURD rebel movement in the diamond-producing areas in the north and the Government could not determine which diamonds had been mined there.

The Government maintained that RUF as a rebel group no longer existed, since it had been transformed into a political party, the Revolutionary United Front Party, and had contested the 2002 elections in Sierra Leone. However, unofficial sources indicated that some RUF elements remained in Liberia. It was also alleged that Sam Bockarie and some RUF elements were engaged in the western front of the Ivorian conflict, with the connivance of the Liberian Government.

Report of Panel (April). On 24 April [S/2003/498] the Panel of Experts on Liberia issued a report, which was submitted to the Security Council. The Panel determined that Liberia's conflict was once more no longer isolated as its refugees and armed fighters had spilled over into its neighbours. Armed youths from Liberia, Sierra Leone, Guinea and, most recently, Côte d'Ivoire, who had become accustomed to a life of conflict, banditry and lawlessness had joined armed groups in Liberia and in western Côte d'Ivoire, posing new risks of a vicious cycle of violence in the subregion. The region was awash with weapons, and several companies that were involved in sanctions-busting by providing arms to Liberia were also delivering weapons to its neighbours, including Côte d'Ivoire. The Panel documented Guinea's support for LURD fighters in Liberia. Guinea was also used as a supply route for arms and supplies. The Panel had some evidence that the Government of Côte d'Ivoire was supporting the newly formed Lima armed militia and the rebel group MODEL.

Internal violence in Liberia had escalated in 2003, causing many humanitarian agencies to withdraw their staff. Poor governance, corruption and insecurity had ensured that there had been no significant investment in years, resulting in 85 per cent unemployment.

President Taylor, in March, openly declared that Liberia would import weapons for self-defence, and the Government provided the Panel with a list of weapons it had procured. The Panel concluded that those weapons were obtained in Serbia in 2002 from the arms manufacturer Zastava, using a false Nigerian end-user certificate. The Panel suspected that preparations were under way for trans-shipments of 50 tons of Serbian military equipment from Belgrade to Liberia via Kinshasa, using an end-user certificate from the DRC. The Panel, noting that Liberia and Guinea continued to violate the arms embargo, said that the basis for the imposition of the sanctions against Liberia needed to be reassessed because violence and conflict were spreading across the region and were generated not only by Liberian forces.

The Government of Liberia and LURD had made the control of diamond-producing areas a key military objective. In the current context, it would be difficult to find an area in Liberia from which rough diamonds could be declared "conflict-free". It was clearly the Government's objective to stamp out the illegal trade in diamonds and a plan was being developed to implement the Kimberley Process Certification Scheme, launched in 2002. Progress had been made in that regard but only an end to the internal conflict could guarantee success.

Government accounting was far from transparent. Revenues over the previous five years had never exceeded $85 million and the Government could be relying increasingly on off-budget income to fund its high defence expenditure. The Panel had documentary evidence of $7.5 million (more than 10 per cent of average annual government revenue) of either questionable or clearly off-budget income, at least some of which was used for defence-related spending. Significant gains were realized by the import/export monopolies organized by the Government.

Among its recommendations, the Panel said that, in the light of the changed situation and escalating hostilities in the region, a new approach by the Security Council to the situation in West Africa was required that must include the input of key regional actors. The financing of armed non-State actors and the funding sources of their foreign sponsors required investigation. To prevent Liberia from further decay, international assistance was required to reorganize its revenue system.

The Panel recommended that: the moratorium on the importation, exportation and manufacturing of small arms in West Africa and its implementation mechanism, the Programme for Coordination and Assistance for Security and Development, should be strengthened through international assistance and technical support, and should become an information exchange mechanism for all types of weapons procured by ECOWAS members; an international mechanism for harmonizing and verifying all end-user certificates for weapons should be established; the Liberian Civil Aviation Authority should cooperate with the modalities of responsibilities, as provided for in the November 2001 letter of agreement between the Flight Information Region and the Approach Control Unit of Robertsfield International Airport [YUN 2001, p. 185], and also register all its aircraft; and, in order to define which areas could be classified "conflict-free" and from where diamonds were fit for export, the services of international mining and geological consultants should be engaged. In addition, the Panel named six individuals against whom financial sanctions should be imposed.

SECURITY COUNCIL ACTION (May)

On 6 May [meeting 4751], the Security Council unanimously adopted **resolution 1478(2003)**. The draft [S/2003/522] was prepared in consultations among Council members.

The Security Council,

Recalling its resolutions 1132(1997) of 8 October 1997, 1171(1998) of 5 June 1998, 1306(2000) of 5 July 2000, 1343(2001) of 7 March 2001, 1385(2001) of 19 December 2001, 1395(2002) of 27 February 2002, 1400(2002) of 28 March 2002, 1408(2002) of 6 May 2002, 1458(2003) of 28 January 2003, 1467(2003) of 18 March 2003 and its other resolutions and the statements by its President on the situation in the region,

Taking note of the report of the Secretary-General of 22 April 2003,

Taking note also of the reports of the Panel of Experts on Liberia dated 25 October 2002 and 24 April 2003 submitted pursuant to paragraph 16 of resolution 1408 (2002) and paragraph 4 of resolution 1458(2003) respectively,

Expressing serious concern at the findings of the Panel of Experts regarding the actions of the Government of Liberia and of Liberians United for Reconciliation and Democracy and other armed rebel groups, including the evidence that the Government of Liberia continues to breach the measures imposed pursuant to resolution 1343(2001), particularly through the acquisition of arms,

Welcoming General Assembly resolution 57/302 of 30 April 2003 and Security Council resolution 1459 (2003) of 28 January 2003, welcoming the launch of the Kimberley Process, on 1 January 2003, and recalling its concern at the role played by the illicit trade in diamonds in the conflict in the region,

Welcoming also the continued efforts of the Economic Community of West African States and the International Contact Group on Liberia to work towards the restoration of peace and stability in the region, particularly the appointment of General Abdulsalami Abubakar, former President of the Federal Republic of Nigeria, as a mediator in the conflict in Liberia,

Noting the positive effects of the Rabat Process on peace and security in the subregion, and encouraging all countries of the Mano River Union to reinvigorate the Process with further meetings and renewed cooperation,

Encouraging civil society initiatives in the region, including those of the Mano River Union Women's Peace Network, to continue their contribution towards regional peace,

Welcoming the summit meeting between the Presidents of the Republic of Liberia and the Republic of Côte d'Ivoire, held in Togo on 26 April 2003, and encouraging them to continue dialogue,

Calling upon all States, and in particular the Government of Liberia, to cooperate fully with the Special Court for Sierra Leone,

Recalling the Economic Community of West African States Moratorium on the Importation, Exportation and Manufacture of Small Arms and Light Weapons in West Africa adopted in Abuja on 31 October 1998, and its extension from 5 July 2001,

Deeply concerned about the deteriorating humanitarian situation and widespread human rights violations in Liberia, and about the serious instability in Liberia and neighbouring countries, including Côte d'Ivoire,

Determining that the active support provided by the Government of Liberia to armed rebel groups in the region, including to rebels in Côte d'Ivoire and former combatants of the Revolutionary United Front who continue to destabilize the region, constitutes a threat to international peace and security in the region,

Acting under Chapter VII of the Charter of the United Nations,

1. *Decides* that the Government of Liberia has not complied fully with the demands set out in resolution 1343(2001);

2. *Notes with concern* that the new aircraft registry updated by the Government of Liberia in response to the demand set out in paragraph 2 *(e)* of resolution 1343(2001) remains inactive;

3. *Stresses* that the demands referred to in paragraph 1 above are intended to help to consolidate and assure peace and stability in Sierra Leone and to build and strengthen peaceful relations among the countries of the region;

4. *Calls upon* all States in the region, and particularly the Government of Liberia, to participate actively in all regional peace initiatives, particularly those of the Economic Community of West African States, the International Contact Group on Liberia, the Mano River Union and the Rabat Process, and expresses its strong support for those initiatives;

5. *Calls upon* the Government of Liberia and Liberians United for Reconciliation and Democracy to enter without delay into bilateral ceasefire negotiations under the auspices of the Economic Community of West African States and the mediation of General Abdulsalami Abubakar, former President of Nigeria;

6. *Stresses* its readiness to grant exemptions from the measures imposed by paragraph 7 *(a)* of resolution 1343(2001) in cases of travel which would assist in the peaceful resolution of the conflict in the subregion;

7. *Welcomes* the agreement of the Government of Liberia to the revised mandate of the United Nations Peace-building Support Office in Liberia, and calls upon the Government to respond constructively to the statement by the President of the Security Council of 13 December 2002 (S/PRST/2002/36);

8. *Calls upon* the Government of Liberia and all parties, particularly Liberians United for Reconciliation and Democracy and other armed rebel groups, to ensure unimpeded and safe movement for the personnel of United Nations humanitarian agencies and non-governmental organizations, to end the use of child soldiers and to prevent sexual violence and torture;

9. *Reiterates its demand* that all States in the region cease military support for armed groups in neighbouring countries, take action to prevent armed individuals and groups using their territory to prepare and commit attacks on neighbouring countries and refrain from any actions that might contribute to further destabilization of the situation in the region, and declares its readiness to consider, if necessary, ways of promoting compliance with this demand;

10. *Decides* that the measures imposed by paragraphs 5 to 7 of resolution 1343(2001) shall remain in force for a further period of twelve months from 0001 hours eastern daylight time on 7 May 2003 and that, before the end of this period, the Council will decide whether the Government of Liberia has complied with the demands referred to in paragraph 1 above, and, accordingly, whether to extend these measures for a further period with the same conditions;

11. *Recalls* that the measures imposed by paragraph 5 of resolution 1343(2001) apply to all sales or supply of arms and related materiel to any recipient in Liberia, including all non-State actors, such as Liberians United for Reconciliation and Democracy;

12. *Decides* that the measures imposed by paragraphs 5 to 7 of resolution 1343(2001) and by paragraph 17 below shall be terminated immediately if the Council, taking into account, inter alia, the reports of the expert panel referred to in paragraph 25 below and the report of the Secretary-General referred to in paragraph 20 below, input from the Economic Community of West African States, any relevant information provided by the Security Council Committee established pursuant to paragraph 14 of resolution 1343(2001) (the Committee) and the Security Council Committee established pursuant to resolution 1132 (1997) and any other relevant information, particularly the conclusions of its forthcoming mission to West Africa, determines that the Government of Liberia has complied with the demands referred to in paragraph 1 above;

13. *Reiterates its call* upon the Government of Liberia to establish an effective certificate-of-origin regime for Liberian rough diamonds that is transparent, internationally verifiable and fully compatible with the Kimberley Process, and to provide the Committee with a detailed description of the proposed regime;

14. *Decides*, notwithstanding paragraph 15 of resolution 1343(2001), that rough diamonds controlled by the Government of Liberia through the certificate-of-origin regime shall be exempt from the measures imposed by paragraph 6 of resolution 1343(2001) when the Committee has reported to the Council, taking into account expert advice obtained through the Secretary-General, that an effective and internationally verifiable regime is ready to become fully operational and to be properly implemented;

15. *Calls again upon* States, relevant international organizations and other bodies in a position to do so to offer assistance to the Government of Liberia and other diamond-exporting countries in West Africa with their certificate-of-origin regimes;

16. *Considers* that the audits commissioned by the Government of Liberia pursuant to paragraph 10 of resolution 1408(2002) do not demonstrate that the revenue derived by the Government of Liberia from the Liberia Ship and Corporate Registry and the Liberian timber industry is used for legitimate social, humanitarian and development purposes, and is not used in violation of resolution 1408(2002);

17. *Decides* that:

(a) All States shall take the necessary measures to prevent, for a period of ten months, the import into their territories of all round logs and timber products originating in Liberia;

(b) These measures shall come into force at 0001 hours eastern daylight time on 7 July 2003, unless the Council decides otherwise;

(c) At the end of this period of ten months, the Council will decide whether the Government of Liberia has complied with the demands referred to in paragraph 1 above and, accordingly, whether to extend these measures for a further period with the same conditions;

18. *Decides also* to consider, by 7 September 2003, how best to minimize any humanitarian or socio-economic impact of the measures imposed by paragraph 17 above, including the possibility of allowing timber exports to resume in order to fund humanitarian programmes, taking into account the recommendations of the expert panel requested in paragraph 25 below and the assessment of the Secretary-General requested in paragraph 19 below;

19. *Requests* the Secretary-General to submit a report to the Council by 7 August 2003 on the possible humanitarian or socio-economic impact of the measures imposed by paragraph 17 above;

20. *Also requests* the Secretary-General to submit a report to the Council by 21 October 2003, and thereafter at six-monthly intervals from that date, drawing on information from all relevant sources, including the United Nations Peace-building Support Office in Liberia, the United Nations Mission in Sierra Leone and the Economic Community of West African States, on whether Liberia has complied with the demands referred to in paragraph 1 above, and calls upon the Government of Liberia to support United Nations efforts to verify all information on compliance which is brought to the notice of the United Nations;

21. *Invites* the Economic Community of West African States to report regularly to the Committee on all activities undertaken by its members pursuant to paragraphs 10 and 17 above and in the implementation of the present resolution, particularly on the implementation of the Economic Community of West African States Moratorium on the Importation, Exportation and Manufacture of Small Arms and Light Weapons in West Africa referred to in the preamble to the present resolution;

22. *Calls upon* States of the subregion to strengthen the measures they have taken to combat the spread of small arms and light weapons and mercenary activities and to improve the effectiveness of the Moratorium, and urges States in a position to do so to provide assistance to the Economic Community of West African States to this end;

23. *Calls upon* all parties to conflicts in the region to include disarmament, demobilization and reintegration provisions in peace agreements;

24. *Requests* the Committee to carry out the tasks set out in the present resolution and to continue with its mandate as set out in paragraphs 14 *(a)* to *(h)* of resolution 1343(2001) and in resolution 1408(2002);

25. *Requests* the Secretary-General to establish, within one month from the date of adoption of the present resolution, in consultation with the Committee, for a period of five months, a Panel of Experts consisting of up to six members, with the range of expertise necessary to fulfil the mandate of the Panel described in the present paragraph, drawing as much as appropriate and as possible on the expertise of the members of the Panel of Experts established pursuant to resolution 1458(2003), to undertake the following tasks:

(a) To conduct a follow-up assessment mission to Liberia and neighbouring States in order to investigate and compile a report on the compliance by Government of Liberia with the demands referred to in paragraph 1 above, and on any violations of the measures referred to in paragraphs 10 and 17 above, including any involving rebel movements;

(b) To investigate whether any revenues of the Government of Liberia are used in violation of the present resolution, with particular emphasis on the effect on the Liberian populace of any possible diversion of funds from civilian purposes;

(c) To assess the possible humanitarian and socioeconomic impact of the measures imposed by paragraph 17 above and to make recommendations to the Council through the Committee by 7 August 2003 on how to minimize any such impact;

(d) To report to the Council through the Committee no later than 7 October 2003 with observations and recommendations, particularly on how to improve the effectiveness of implementing and monitoring the measures referred to in paragraph 5 of resolution 1343(2001), including any recommendations pertinent to paragraphs 28 and 29 below,

and also requests the Secretary-General to provide the necessary resources;

26. *Requests* the Panel of Experts referred to in paragraph 25 above, as far as possible, to bring any relevant information collected in the course of the investigations conducted in accordance with its mandate to the attention of the States concerned for prompt and thorough investigation and, where appropriate, corrective action, and to allow them the right of reply;

27. *Calls upon* all States to take appropriate measures to ensure that individuals and companies within their jurisdiction, in particular those referred to in the reports of the Panels of Experts established pursuant to resolutions 1343(2001), 1395(2002), 1408(2002) and 1458(2003), respectively, act in conformity with United Nations embargoes, in particular those established by resolutions 1171(1998), 1306(2000) and 1343(2001), and, as appropriate, to take the necessary judicial and administrative action to end any illegal activities by those individuals and companies;

28. *Decides* that all States shall take the necessary measures to prevent entry into or transit through their territories of any individuals, including from Liberians United for Reconciliation and Democracy or other armed rebel groups, determined by the Committee, taking account of information provided by the Panel of Experts and other relevant sources, to be in violation of paragraph 5 of resolution 1343(2001), provided that nothing in the present paragraph shall oblige a State to refuse entry into its territory by its own nationals;

29. *Requests* the Committee to establish, maintain and update, taking account of information provided by the Panel of Experts and other relevant sources, a list of air and maritime companies whose aircraft and vessels have been used in violation of paragraph 5 of resolution 1343(2001);

30. *Calls upon* all members of the Economic Community of West African States to cooperate fully with the Panel of Experts in the identification of such aircraft and vessels, and in particular to inform the Panel about any transit on their territory of aircraft and vessels suspected of being used in violation of paragraph 5 of resolution 1343(2001);

31. *Asks* the Government of Liberia to authorize the Approach and Control Unit at Robertsfield International Airport to provide regularly to the Flight Information Region in Conakry statistical data related to aircraft listed pursuant to paragraph 29 above;

32. *Decides* to conduct reviews of the measures referred to in paragraphs 10 and 17 above before 7 November 2003, and every six months thereafter;

33. *Urges* all States, relevant United Nations bodies and, as appropriate, other organizations and all interested parties to cooperate fully with the Committee and with the Panel of Experts referred to in paragraph 25 above, including by supplying information on possible violations of the measures referred to in paragraphs 10 and 17 above;

34. *Decides* to remain actively seized of the matter.

In response to paragraph 25 of resolution 1478(2003) (see p. 203), the Secretary-General, on 5 June [S/2003/618], informed the Security Council of the names of the six members he had appointed to form a Panel of Experts to conduct a follow-up assessment mission to Liberia and neighbouring States, in order to investigate and compile a report on the Liberian Government's compliance with the demands set out in resolution 1343(2001) [YUN 2001, p. 181]; to investigate whether any government revenues were used in violation of resolution 1478(2003); and to assess the possible humanitarian and socio-economic impact of the measures to take effect pursuant to paragraph 17 of that resolution.

Report of Secretary-General (August). In response to Security Council resolution 1478(2003) (see p. 203), the Secretary-General submitted a 5 August report [S/2003/793] on the possible humanitarian and socio-economic impact of the sanctions against timber products originating in Liberia imposed by that resolution. He stated that the Liberian timber industry faced the double constraints of insecurity and sanctions, either of which was sufficient to preclude logging and the export of timber. The timber sanctions on Liberia would have an impact on humanitarian and socio-economic conditions only when the security environment did not already preclude timber export. A newly reconstituted timber sector in Liberia—built on accountability and transparency—could be a driving force for economic growth and sustainable development in the country, but only in the absence of widespread conflict. The current sanctions might permit a breathing period during which the industry could be restructured and alternative sources of revenue such as rubber production or cash crop cultivation could be encouraged. Such diversification would serve to reduce Liberia's dependency on timber and ensure that the timber sector did not re-emerge as a magnet for militia groups and exploitative corporations.

The Secretary-General made several suggestions to mitigate the potential impact of sanctions, including the development of an exemption procedure for specific timber products. Further possible exemptions to the timber ban should be explored in line with recommendations developed as part of the Stockholm Process, the Swedish initiative to enhance the effectiveness of targeted sanctions. They included processes of certification, as in the Kimberley Process, and the listing of approved traders. A mechanism could be established to allow the sale of Liberian timber under externally managed and audited conditions. In addition, specific humanitarian and development programmes could be developed to help mitigate the socio-economic and humanitarian impact of the timber ban. The Council might also consider establishing a long-term monitoring mechanism to review the possible implications of the sanctions regime.

Report of Panel (August). On 7 August [S/2003/779], the Panel of Experts established pursuant to paragraph 25 of Security Council resolution 1478(2003) (see p. 203) submitted its report on the possible humanitarian and socio-economic impact of the timber sanctions against Liberia. The Panel stated that, when the timber sanctions entered into force on 7 July, most timber companies in Liberia had already ceased operations due to the ongoing civil war. Operators feared for the safety of their workers and worried that their equipment would be looted by combatants. Some logging companies removed their equipment from Liberia and abandoned, at least temporarily, their concession, claiming that they had done so once they learned from the Panel that sanctions applied to all exports of forest products. Armed non-State actors had contacted logging operators and NGOs to express their interest in resuming logging to generate revenue. In order to assess their intentions, the Panel had presented the Government of Liberia, LURD and MODEL with a detailed questionnaire relating to the provisions for compliance with the timber sanctions, requesting answers by 15 July. The Panel had received neither answers nor information as to when answers would be forthcoming.

The long-term degradation of the humanitarian and socio-economic conditions that Liberians had endured had to serve as a baseline before any additional burdens imposed on the country could be measured. The most obvious benefit of the timber sanctions was that armed State and non-State actors were deprived of timber revenue. Also, violations of human rights, of rural Liberians in particular, associated with the timber industry would decrease, as would the overharvesting of Liberian forests. The negative impacts associated with the stark reduction of export income and employment might have long-term consequences for the redevelopment of Liberia. However, those negative impacts might currently be overshadowed by the negative effects of the civil war. Rural communities located within the logging concessions did not benefit greatly from the operations, and communities were no better served by social services whether they were inside or outside the concessions.

The Panel recommended that, in order to deprive all combatants of the benefits of war, the Security Council declare a moratorium on all commercial activities in the extractive industries, as had been proposed by the NGO Coalition of

Liberia, to remain in place until peace and stability were restored and good governance was established. Increased emergency aid should be provided to minimize the impact of sanctions while the timber industry was reformed. Over the long term, the Panel said, the United Nations and international donors should help Liberia to reform the timber sector in order to achieve good governance. The Council should encourage Member States, civil society and UN field presences to monitor and report any violations of the timber sanctions, and the Secretary-General should be requested to report quarterly on the implementation of the timber sanctions and their effects on Liberians.

Report of Panel (October). In response to paragraph 25 of Security Council resolution 1478(2003), the Panel of Experts on Liberia submitted an October report [S/2003/937 & Add.1] describing the rapidly changing situation there, with a peace agreement having been signed in August and the National Transitional Government taking power in October. Although levels of violence were declining, until UNMIL forces were deployed throughout the country and DDRR efforts were fully under way, the current proliferation of weapons in the subregion continued to be a threat to peace and stability, not only in Liberia but also in Côte d'Ivoire, Guinea and Sierra Leone. The Panel continued to find evidence of Guinea's support for LURD. After the peace agreement was signed, the Panel witnessed efforts by Guinea to control the presence of LURD forces in the Forest Region (Guinée forestière). The challenge for the international community was to provide adequate support to the Transitional Government while remaining vigilant to the re-emergence of corruption and State-sanctioned violence. Domestic debts resulting from corrupt practices would threaten the economic reconstruction of Liberia, as would the shortage of government revenue.

Despite the ceasefire, on 6 August the Liberian Minister of Defence attempted to receive a shipment of weapons at Robertsfield International Airport; however, the effort was blocked by UN peacekeepers. Other illegal weapons were found in the possession of Liberian government troops. Porous borders and insecurity in neighbouring countries had made the full enforcement of the arms embargo impossible. The restrictions imposed by resolution 1478(2003) on the trafficking of Liberian diamonds had failed to prevent their trade either regionally or internationally. While there had been a recent, steady decline in production, that was the result of internal insecurity and operational constraints imposed by seasonal climatic conditions, rather than the impact of sanctions. Liberian diamonds continued to enter the international market and the internationally accredited certification scheme introduced by neighbouring countries had failed to prevent it. The flow would continue as production increased with improving security and the onset of the dry season. Similarly, there was little evidence of violations of the timber sanctions, as civil war and the rainy season had prevented a resumption of logging since sanctions entered into force on 7 July. The real test would come in November, when conditions would permit logging. The Panel recommended that the sanctions should remain until the industry and the Government had been reformed. As for civil aviation, Liberia had violated the rules of civil aviation since 2000. Its non-compliance with civil aviation regulations continued to endanger air safety in the region, and flight movements in and out of Liberia remained uncoordinated. The new Liberian aircraft registry was still not operational. During its visit to Monrovia, the Panel noted Liberia's lack of human resources and equipment for civil aviation. It also reported that the travel ban was being violated and that no mechanism existed for monitoring the offshore marine activities of Liberia.

Although the immediate effects of the timber ban on the socio-economic and humanitarian situation were not readily apparent, the Panel was of the view that Liberia's economy would surely suffer from the elimination of significantly more than 50 per cent of export income as a result of that action. It pointed out that the National Transitional Government lacked funding to operate properly and to rebuild the necessary institutions to govern.

The Panel recommended that: all Security Council sanctions remain in place; UNMIL monitor the main ports, airports and border crossings to ensure that sanctions were not violated and that all illegal shipments were seized; an independent economic commission of inquiry be formed to protect the new Government from corruption and diversion of government revenues, assist in rebuilding corrupt institutions and conduct investigations of all revenue-producing entities; financial sanctions be imposed on all accounts, assets and property owned and controlled, directly or indirectly, by former President Taylor, to prevent him from further diverting government revenues and to facilitate the repatriation of already diverted funds; and the embargo on Liberian rough diamonds be kept in place until a certification scheme could be implemented and monitored.

Letter of Secretary-General (5 November). The Secretary-General, on 5 November [S/2003/

1071], said that due to the prevailing situation in Liberia, which had necessitated the evacuation of UN personnel, it was not possible to gather the information needed to prepare the third six-monthly report on Liberia's compliance with the Council's demand contained in resolution 1408 (2002) [YUN 2002, p. 169]. It would be necessary to defer submission of that report until early 2004.

Security Council press statement (4 December). Following a review of the measures on Liberia pursuant to resolution 1478(2003), the Security Council President, in a 4 December press statement [SC/7943-AFR/782], stated that there was a general agreement among Council members that the measures should be continued for the time being. The objective of the measures would continue to be to support the peace process in Liberia and to further consolidate peace and stability in the subregion. Bearing in mind the recent positive developments in Liberia, the Council members agreed that there was a need to redefine the legal basis for the sanctions and to evolve appropriate criteria for their eventual lifting.

SECURITY COUNCIL ACTION (December)

On 22 December [meeting 4890], the Security Council unanimously adopted **resolution 1521 (2003)**. The draft [S/2003/1180] was prepared in consultations among Council members.

The Security Council,

Recalling its resolutions and the statements by its President on the situation in Liberia and West Africa,

Taking note of the reports of the Panel of Experts on Liberia of 30 July and 2 October 2003 submitted pursuant to resolution 1478(2003) of 6 May 2003,

Expressing serious concern at the findings of the Panel of Experts that the measures imposed by resolution 1343(2001) of 7 March 2001 continue to be breached, particularly through the acquisition of arms,

Welcoming the Comprehensive Peace Agreement signed by the former Government of Liberia, Liberians United for Reconciliation and Democracy and the Movement for Democracy in Liberia at Accra on 18 August 2003, and the fact that the National Transitional Government of Liberia under Chairman Gyude Bryant took office on 14 October 2003,

Calling upon all States in the region, particularly the National Transitional Government of Liberia, to work together to build lasting regional peace, including through the Economic Community of West African States, the International Contact Group on Liberia, the Mano River Union and the Rabat Process,

Noting with concern, however, that the ceasefire and the Comprehensive Peace Agreement are not yet being universally implemented throughout Liberia and that much of the country remains outside the authority of the National Transitional Government of Liberia, particularly those areas to which the United Nations Mission in Liberia has not yet deployed,

Recognizing the linkage between the illegal exploitation of natural resources such as diamonds and timber, illicit trade in such resources and the proliferation and trafficking of illegal arms as a major source of fuelling and exacerbating conflicts in West Africa, particularly in Liberia,

Determining that the situation in Liberia and the proliferation of arms and armed non-State actors, including mercenaries, in the subregion continue to constitute a threat to international peace and security in West Africa, in particular to the peace process in Liberia,

Acting under Chapter VII of the Charter of the United Nations,

A

Recalling its resolutions 1343(2001), 1408(2002) of 6 May 2002, 1478(2003), 1497(2003) of 1 August 2003 and 1509(2003) of 19 September 2003,

Noting that the changed circumstances in Liberia, in particular the departure of former President Charles Taylor and the formation of the National Transitional Government of Liberia, and progress with the peace process in Sierra Leone, require the determination of the Council for action under Chapter VII of the Charter to be revised to reflect these altered circumstances,

1. *Decides* to terminate the prohibitions imposed by paragraphs 5 to 7 of resolution 1343(2001) and paragraphs 17 and 28 of resolution 1478(2003) and to dissolve the Security Council Committee established pursuant to resolution 1343(2001) concerning Liberia;

B

2. (a) *Decides also* that all States shall take the necessary measures to prevent the sale or supply to Liberia, by their nationals or from their territories or using their flag vessels or aircraft, of arms and related materiel of all types, including weapons and ammunition, military vehicles and equipment, paramilitary equipment and spare parts for the aforementioned, whether or not these originated in their territories;

(b) *Decides further* that all States shall take the necessary measures to prevent any provision to Liberia by their nationals or from their territories of technical training or assistance related to the provision, manufacture, maintenance or use of the items in subparagraph (a) above;

(c) *Reaffirms* that the measures in subparagraphs (a) and (b) above apply to all sales or supply of arms and related materiel destined for any recipient in Liberia, including all non-State actors, such as Liberians United for Reconciliation and Democracy and the Movement for Democracy in Liberia, and to all former and current militias and armed groups;

(d) *Decides* that the measures imposed by subparagraphs (a) and (b) above shall not apply to supplies of arms and related materiel and technical training and assistance intended solely for the support of or use by the United Nations Mission in Liberia;

(e) *Decides also* that the measures imposed by subparagraphs (a) and (b) above shall not apply to supplies of arms and related materiel and technical training and assistance intended solely for the support of or use in an international training and reform programme for the Liberian armed forces and police, as approved in advance by the Committee established pursuant to paragraph 21 below ("the Committee");

(f) *Decides further* that the measures imposed by subparagraphs (a) and (b) above shall not apply to supplies of non-lethal military equipment intended solely for humanitarian or protective use, and related technical assistance or training, as approved in advance by the Committee;

(g) Affirms that the measures imposed by subparagraph *(a)* above do not apply to protective clothing, including flak jackets and military helmets, temporarily exported to Liberia by United Nations personnel, representatives of the media and humanitarian and development workers and associated personnel for their personal use only;

3. *Demands* that all States in West Africa take action to prevent armed individuals and groups from using their territory to prepare and commit attacks on neighbouring countries and refrain from any action that might contribute to further destabilization of the situation in the subregion;

4. *(a) Decides* that all States shall take the necessary measures to prevent the entry into or transit through their territories of all individuals, as designated by the Committee, who constitute a threat to the peace process in Liberia or who are engaged in activities aimed at undermining peace and stability in Liberia and the subregion, including those senior members of the Government of former President Charles Taylor and their spouses and members of Liberia's former armed forces who retain links to former President Charles Taylor, those individuals determined by the Committee to be in violation of paragraph 2 above and any other individuals, or individuals associated with entities, providing financial or military support to armed rebel groups in Liberia or in countries in the region, provided that nothing in the present paragraph shall oblige a State to refuse entry into its territory to its own nationals;

(b) Decides also that the measures in paragraph 4 *(a)* above shall continue to apply to the individuals already designated pursuant to paragraph 7 *(a)* of resolution 1343(2001), pending the designation of individuals by the Committee as required by and in accordance with paragraph 4 *(a)* above;

(c) Decides further that the measures imposed by paragraph 4 *(a)* above shall not apply where the Committee determines that such travel is justified on the grounds of humanitarian need, including religious obligation, or where the Committee concludes that an exemption would otherwise further the objectives of the resolutions of the Council, for the creation of peace, stability and democracy in Liberia and lasting peace in the subregion;

5. *Expresses its readiness* to terminate the measures imposed by paragraphs 2 *(a)* and *(b)* and 4 *(a)* above when the Council determines that the ceasefire in Liberia is being fully respected and maintained, disarmament, demobilization, reintegration, repatriation and restructuring of the security sector have been completed, the provisions of the Comprehensive Peace Agreement are being fully implemented and significant progress has been made in establishing and maintaining stability in Liberia and the subregion;

6. *Decides* that all States shall take the necessary measures to prevent the direct or indirect import of all rough diamonds from Liberia to their territory, whether or not such diamonds originated in Liberia;

7. *Calls upon* the National Transitional Government of Liberia to take urgent steps to establish an effective certificate-of-origin regime for trade in Liberian rough diamonds that is transparent and internationally verifiable with a view to joining the Kimberley Process, and to provide the Committee with a detailed description of the proposed regime;

8. *Expresses its readiness* to terminate the measures referred to in paragraph 6 above when the Committee, taking into account expert advice, decides that Liberia has established a transparent, effective and internationally verifiable certificate-of-origin regime for Liberian rough diamonds;

9. *Encourages* the National Transitional Government of Liberia to take steps to join the Kimberley Process as soon as possible;

10. *Decides* that all States shall take the necessary measures to prevent the import into their territories of all round logs and timber products originating in Liberia;

11. *Urges* the National Transitional Government of Liberia to establish its full authority and control over the timber-producing areas and to take all necessary steps to ensure that government revenues from the Liberian timber industry are not used to fuel conflict or otherwise in violation of the resolutions of the Council but are used for legitimate purposes for the benefit of the Liberian people, including development;

12. *Expresses its readiness* to terminate the measures imposed by paragraph 10 above once the Council determines that the goals in paragraph 11 above have been achieved;

13. *Encourages* the National Transitional Government of Liberia to establish oversight mechanisms for the timber industry that will promote responsible business practices and to establish transparent accounting and auditing mechanisms to ensure that all government revenues, including those from the Liberian International Ship and Corporate Registry, are not used to fuel conflict or otherwise in violation of the resolutions of the Council but are used for legitimate purposes for the benefit of the Liberian people, including development;

14. *Urges* all parties to the Comprehensive Peace Agreement of 18 August 2003 to implement fully their commitments and fulfil their responsibilities in the National Transitional Government of Liberia, and not to hinder the restoration of the Government's authority throughout the country, particularly over natural resources;

15. *Calls upon* States, relevant international organizations and others in a position to do so to offer assistance to the National Transitional Government of Liberia in achieving the objectives in paragraphs 7, 11 and 13 above, including the promotion of responsible and environmentally sustainable business practices in the timber industry, and to offer assistance with the implementation of the Moratorium on the Importation, Exportation and Manufacture of Small Arms and Light Weapons in West Africa adopted by the Economic Community of West African States in Abuja on 31 October 1998;

16. *Encourages* the United Nations and other donors to assist the Liberian civil aviation authorities, including through technical assistance, in improving the professionalism of their staff and their training capabilities and in complying with the standards and practices of the International Civil Aviation Organization;

17. *Takes note* of the establishment by the National Transitional Government of Liberia of a review committee with the task of establishing procedures to fulfil the demands of the Council for the lifting of the measures imposed by the present resolution;

18. *Decides* that the measures in paragraphs 2, 4, 6 and 10 above are established for twelve months from the date of adoption of the present resolution, unless otherwise decided, and that, at the end of this period, the Council shall review the position, assess progress towards the goals in paragraphs 5, 7 and 11 and decide accordingly whether to continue those measures;

19. *Decides also* to review the measures in paragraphs 2, 4, 6 and 10 above by 17 June 2004, to assess progress towards the goals in paragraphs 5, 7 and 11 and to decide accordingly whether to terminate those measures;

20. *Decides further* to keep under regular review the measures imposed by paragraphs 6 and 10 above so as to terminate them as soon as possible once the conditions in paragraphs 7 and 11 above have been met, in order to create revenue for the reconstruction and development of Liberia;

21. *Decides* to establish, in accordance with rule 28 of its provisional rules of procedure, a Committee of the Security Council, consisting of all the members of the Council, to undertake the following tasks:

(a) To monitor the implementation of the measures in paragraphs 2, 4, 6 and 10 above, taking into consideration the reports of the expert panel established pursuant to paragraph 22 below;

(b) To seek from all States, particularly those in the subregion, information about the actions taken by them to implement effectively those measures;

(c) To consider and decide upon requests for the exemptions set out in paragraphs 2 (e) and (f) and 4 (c) above;

(d) To designate the individuals subject to the measures imposed by paragraph 4 above and to update that list regularly;

(e) To make relevant information publicly available through appropriate media, including the list referred to in subparagraph (d) above;

(f) To consider and take appropriate action, within the framework of the present resolution, on pending issues or concerns brought to its attention concerning the measures imposed by resolutions 1343(2001), 1408 (2002) and 1478(2003) while those resolutions were in force;

(g) To report to the Council with its observations and recommendations;

22. *Requests* the Secretary-General to establish, within one month of the date of adoption of the present resolution, in consultation with the Committee, for a period of five months, a Panel of Experts consisting of up to five members, with the range of expertise necessary to fulfil the mandate of the Panel described in the present paragraph, drawing as much as possible on the expertise of the members of the Panel of Experts established pursuant to resolution 1478(2003), to undertake the following tasks:

(a) To conduct a follow-up assessment mission to Liberia and neighbouring States in order to investigate and compile a report on the implementation, and any violations, of the measures referred to in paragraphs 2, 4, 6 and 10 above, including any violations involving rebel movements and neighbouring countries, and including any information relevant to designation by the Committee of the individuals described in paragraph 4 (a) above, and also including the various sources of financing, such as from natural resources, for the illicit trade in arms;

(b) To assess the progress made towards the goals described in paragraphs 5, 7 and 11 above;

(c) To report to the Council, through the Committee, no later than 30 May 2004, with observations and recommendations, including how to minimize any humanitarian and socio-economic impact of the measures imposed by paragraph 10 above;

23. *Welcomes* the readiness of the United Nations Mission in Liberia, within its capabilities and its areas of deployment and without prejudice to its mandate, once it is fully deployed and carrying out its core functions, to assist the Committee established pursuant to paragraph 21 above and the Panel of Experts established pursuant to paragraph 22 above in monitoring the measures in paragraphs 2, 4, 6 and 10 above, and requests the United Nations Mission in Sierra Leone and the United Nations Mission in Côte d'Ivoire, likewise without prejudicing their capacities to carry out their respective mandates, to assist the Committee and the Panel of Experts by passing to the Committee and the Panel any information relevant to the implementation of the measures in paragraphs 2, 4, 6 and 10 above, in the context of enhanced coordination among United Nations missions and offices in West Africa;

24. *Reiterates its call upon* the international donor community to provide assistance for the implementation of a programme of disarmament, demobilization, reintegration and repatriation, and sustained international assistance to the peace process, and to contribute generously to consolidated humanitarian appeals, and further requests the donor community to respond to the immediate financial, administrative and technical needs of the National Transitional Government of Liberia;

25. *Encourages* the National Transitional Government of Liberia to undertake, with the assistance of the United Nations Mission in Liberia, appropriate actions to sensitize the Liberian population to the rationale of the measures in the present resolution, including the criteria for their termination;

26. *Requests* the Secretary-General to submit a report to the Council by 30 May 2004, drawing on information from all relevant sources, including the National Transitional Government of Liberia, the United Nations Mission in Liberia and the Economic Community of West African States, on progress made towards the goals described in paragraphs 5, 7 and 11 above;

27. *Decides* to remain seized of the matter.

Sierra Leone

After a decade of civil war, the situation in Sierra Leone improved markedly in 2003 as further progress was made in implementing the 2000 Agreement on the Ceasefire and Cessation of Hostilities (Abuja Agreement) [YUN 2000, p. 210], the disarmament process was completed and elections were held. Throughout the year, the security situation in Sierra Leone became increasingly stable, facilitating the consolidation of peace and the implementation of the benchmarks set by the Security Council in 2002 for the reduction of troops of the United Nations Mission in Sierra Leone (UNAMSIL). Under those drawdown plans, the Mission continued to reduce its size in four phases. At the beginning of the year, UNAMSIL began the second phase, which envisaged the withdrawal of 3,900 troops from its force of nearly 16,000. Further reductions were linked to benchmarks, including, most importantly, progress in strengthening the capacity of the Sierra Leone police and armed forces to maintain security and stability. The Government's plan to disarm ex-combatants and reintegrate them into society was largely successful and, by the end of the year, nearly 48,000 of the 57,000 registered ex-combatants either were in the resettlement programme or had completed it.

Although the general trend towards stability was positive, some areas on the Liberian border remained volatile and plans by ex-combatants and others to destabilize the Government were uncovered. The joint mechanisms established by UNAMSIL and the Sierra Leone Government to review the security situation met regularly, and the Secretary-General, in a number of 2003 reports, provided assessments of achievement of the benchmarks. Consequently, UNAMSIL continued to reduce its troop strength by stages, as scheduled. At the end of the year, some 11,500 peacekeeping troops remained in the country.

Stability in Sierra Leone was also dependent on peace in the subregion, especially in Liberia where the conflict in the first half of the year threatened to spill over into Sierra Leone. The renewal of fighting in Liberia in early 2003 precipitated an influx of thousands of refugees into Sierra Leone.

The Special Court set up by the Government to try serious crimes committed during the war issued nine indictments, and the Truth and Reconciliation Commission began work by collecting statements.

The Government also made progress in reasserting its control over diamond mining and selling, thereby increasing official exports and bringing new revenue to the country. Sierra Leone reported that its certificate-of-origin regime to control the export of diamonds had been successful in curtailing the use of diamonds to fuel conflict. In the light of the country's efforts to manage and control its diamond industry, the Security Council decided not to renew its embargo against Sierra Leonean rough diamonds.

Appointment. On 28 November [S/2003/1142], the Secretary-General informed the Security Council of his intention to appoint Daudi Ngelautwa Mwakawago (United Republic of Tanzania) as his Special Representative for Sierra Leone, to replace Oluyemi Adeniji (Nigeria). On 3 December [S/2003/1143], the Council took note of the decision.

UNAMSIL activities

Press statement (10 January). The Security Council considered the Secretary-General's December 2002 report on UNAMSIL [YUN 2002, p. 158] in January 2003. In a 10 January press statement [SC/7629-AFR/542], Council members commended him and UNAMSIL for their role in maintaining peace in Sierra Leone and providing a platform for post-conflict reconstruction. They welcomed the progress made by UNAMSIL in its restructuring and the first two phases of its drawdown plans, and encouraged it to continue. They underlined the importance of the Government of Sierra Leone continuing to strengthen the army and police, including through adequate logistical and infrastructural support, so that they could soon assume full responsibility for security. Noting with concern that government control was not yet fully re-established in some regions of Sierra Leone, including the diamond-producing areas, Council members urged the Government to make rapid progress in that regard, including by adopting a policy for the diamond sector.

Members welcomed the progress with reintegration, and hoped that all ex-combatants would have received training by the end of 2003. Sharing the Secretary-General's concerns about the regional security situation, they stressed the need to find a solution to the conflicts in Liberia and Côte d'Ivoire and encouraged States' efforts in helping to find a solution. They reiterated the importance of relaunching the political dialogue among the MRU countries.

The commencement of work by the Special Court was welcomed and members reiterated their full support for the Court and for the Truth and Reconciliation Commission as important elements of the reconciliation process in Sierra Leone.

Communication (March). On 14 March [S/2003/330], Sierra Leone forwarded to the Council an aide-memoire and a letter from President Alhaji Ahmad Tejan Kabbah, in which he reviewed progress achieved in consolidating peace and security and in promoting national recovery. He noted that, despite the end of the rebel war and the holding of elections in 2002 [YUN 2002, p. 153], Sierra Leone continued to face external and internal security threats. In particular, the border area with Liberia was home to dissident groups who served as a recruitment pool for both LURD and the Armed Forces of Liberia. The upsurge in the fighting in Liberia had caused the movement of displaced persons and refugees into Sierra Leone. Internally, there had been recent attacks on the Government by dissident groups. The President therefore urged a cautious approach to the reduction of the number of UNAMSIL troops. He recommended that the Mission not be downsized by any significant number until such time as Sierra Leone could be sure that peace and security in the country was no longer threatened.

Report of Secretary-General (March). On 17 March [S/2003/321 & Corr.1], the Secretary-General, in response to Security Council resolution 1436 (2002) [YUN 2002, p. 157], issued his seventeenth report on UNAMSIL. During the three-month reporting period since his previous report [ibid., p. 158], the overall political and security situation in Sierra Leone had remained generally stable, albeit volatile on the Liberian border. The stability had facilitated the process of gradual peace consolidation and implementation of some of the benchmarks for UNAMSIL's drawdown that the Secretary-General had proposed in September 2002 [ibid., p. 155].

Nevertheless, a number of alarming developments were reported in early 2003. In particular, on 13 January, an armory of the Republic of Sierra Leone Armed Forces (RSLAF) was attacked, unsuccessfully, by a group of former soldiers and some civilians who sought to steal weapons. An investigation of the attack uncovered a plan involving ex-combatants and some serving soldiers aimed at destabilizing State authority and hindering the work of the Special Court (see p. 213). Johnny Paul Koroma, the former Armed Forces Revolutionary Council (AFRC) leader and later a member of Parliament, was implicated in the plot. During an attempt by the police to arrest him, he escaped and remained at large. About 100 other suspects were detained. It was widely believed that ex-combatants who feared indictments were seeking to frustrate the functioning of the Special Court and the Truth and Reconciliation Commission. On 10 March, the Prosecutor of the Special Court announced that indictments had been brought against former Revolutionary United Front (RUF), AFRC, West Side Boys and Civil Defence Force (CDF) leaders, namely, Foday Sankoh, Mr. Koroma, Sam Bockarie, Issa Sesay, Alex Brima, Moris Kallon and Sam Hinga Norman, all of whom, except for Mr. Koroma and Mr. Bockarie, were in custody. Their indictments were for such crimes as murder, rape, extermination, acts of terror, enslavement, looting and burning, sexual slavery, conscription of children into an armed force and attacks on UNAMSIL peacekeepers and humanitarian workers.

In January, some 70 Liberian combatants, believed to be LURD members, crossed into Sierra Leone and attacked a village. RSLAF troops in the area retreated, leaving behind some of their equipment. No progress was made in disbanding all CDF structures despite the Government's agreement to do so.

The implementation of the second phase of the UNAMSIL drawdown plan was expected to be completed in May, when the total force would be reduced to 13,000. A period of review and consolidation would follow. However, planning for phase 3 of the drawdown was already at an advanced stage; it was envisaged that the force would be reduced to about 5,000 by the end of 2004. UNAMSIL expected to implement phase 3 in several steps, each to be followed by an assessment of the prevailing security situation.

The joint mechanisms established by UNAMSIL and the Sierra Leone Government to evaluate the security situation during the drawdown process included an integrated planning group and joint meetings of UNAMSIL and the National Security Coordination Group, which met regularly in early 2003. The Sierra Leone police, at a strength of only 6,053, focused on recruiting and training new cadets with the intention of reaching 9,500 officers by 2005. RSLAF continued to improve its effectiveness through a training and restructuring plan led by the United Kingdom. The intention was to reduce the force from its current strength of 14,000 to about 10,500. Joint UNAMSIL/RSLAF border operations were intensified during the reporting period, which led to improved security around Mandavulahun village, near the Liberian border. However, operations were hindered by the lamentable state of the vehicle fleet and of communications equipment. The situation at the Liberian border continued to pose a threat to the security and stability of Sierra Leone.

Progress was made in consolidating State authority throughout the country. The full deployment of government officials to all districts by March had almost been completed, and the Government planned to devolve powers to the districts in order to promote local governance through decentralization. The Government also made progress with the programme to offer reintegration opportunities to registered ex-combatants. It estimated that 14,700 were awaiting inclusion in the programme. Reintegration of ex-combatants into communities would largely depend on prospects for economic recovery. Restoration of government control over the country's mineral resources, particularly diamond mining, was of critical importance for Sierra Leone's future. Although official exports of diamonds increased to $41 million in 2002 from about $26 million in 2001, illegal diamond mining and trade persisted. The Government, with UNDP assistance, launched an initiative to set up community-based projects in diamond-producing chiefdoms.

UNAMSIL intensified its human rights monitoring and capacity-building activities during the reporting period. It continued to monitor police stations, prisons and the administration of justice and to provide human rights training for the police and RSLAF. It also expanded the training of peacekeepers in the rights and protection of children. The Truth and Reconciliation Commission continued to make progress in recruitment, management and statement-taking despite financial constraints. It opened its new office in Freetown on 17 February. By mid-February, the Commission had collected over 3,500 statements.

The Special Court for Sierra Leone made significant progress in its operations in early 2003, including the announcement of the indictments of seven individuals for war crimes (see p. 212). In January, the Registry of the Special Court opened its permanent site in Freetown. The Witnesses and Victims Support Unit was established and preparations were under way to create a defence support section, which would include both Sierra Leonean and international lawyers.

The renewal of fighting in Liberia precipitated a new influx of refugees into Sierra Leone. As at 4 March, more than 7,800 refugees had been registered crossing into Sierra Leone, but the total number was estimated at more than 9,000. More than 51,000 Sierra Leonean displaced persons returned to their places of origin between December 2002 and January 2003; of those, 13,500 were formally resettled with humanitarian assistance. The UNHCR programme for the repatriation of Sierra Leonean refugees from Guinea, Liberia and other countries in the subregion continued, with some 200,000 having returned from asylum countries.

The Secretary-General commented that recent developments had proved the prudence of pursuing a gradual drawdown of UNAMSIL, consistent with progress made in building up the capacity of the Sierra Leone police and army. Recent challenges to both services had exposed considerable shortcomings, and additional efforts were needed; therefore a cautious approach to the pace of the drawdown was fully justifiable. The Secretary-General recommended that the Council extend UNAMSIL's mandate for a further period of six months.

Press statements (March). The President of the Security Council issued a 14 March press statement [SC/7692-AFR/583] in which Council members noted the Special Court's announcement of indictments against seven individuals charged with crimes against humanity, war crimes and other violations of humanitarian law. Council members welcomed the indictments as the start of a judicial process aimed at bringing to justice those individuals who bore the greatest responsibility for the suffering inflicted on the people of Sierra Leone. They called on other States in the region to support the efforts of the Special Court in combating impunity and addressing accountability for the atrocities that had been committed in Sierra Leone.

In a 21 March press statement [SC/7702-AFR/589], Council members welcomed the role played by UNAMSIL in maintaining stability in Sierra Leone. They agreed that UNAMSIL's rate of withdrawal should take into account the security conditions and the capacity of the Sierra Leone police and army to maintain them, as indicated in the Secretary-General's March report. They invited States to contribute to financing the UN reintegration and civilian police training programmes. The members reiterated their concern at the destabilizing impact of the conflict in Liberia on the subregion, and on Sierra Leone in particular. They called on the Liberian Government and LURD to initiate a direct dialogue with a view to a peaceful settlement of their dispute. The Council members decided to consider a resolution extending UNAMSIL's mandate for another six months.

SECURITY COUNCIL ACTION (March)

On 28 March [meeting 4729], the Security Council unanimously adopted **resolution 1470(2003)**. The draft [S/2003/375] was prepared in consultations among Council members.

The Security Council,

Recalling its resolutions and the statements by its President concerning the situation in Sierra Leone,

Affirming the commitment of all States to respect the sovereignty, political independence and territorial integrity of Sierra Leone,

Expressing its concern at the continuing fragile security situation in the Mano River region, particularly the conflict in Liberia and its consequences for neighbouring States, including Côte d'Ivoire, and at the substantial number of refugees and the humanitarian consequences for the civilian, refugee and internally displaced populations in the region, and emphasizing the importance of cooperation among the countries of the subregion,

Recognizing that the security situation in Sierra Leone remains fragile, and recognizing also the need to strengthen further the capacity and to mobilize the resources of the Sierra Leone police and armed forces to enable them to maintain security and stability independently,

Noting certain recent challenges to security, described in paragraphs 2 to 9 of the report of the Secretary-General of 17 March 2003,

Reiterating the importance of the effective consolidation of State authority throughout Sierra Leone, particularly in the diamond fields, the reintegration of ex-combatants, the voluntary and unhindered return of refugees and internally displaced persons and full respect for human rights and the rule of law, with special attention to the protection of women and children, and stressing continued United Nations support to the Government of Sierra Leone in fulfilling these objectives,

Emphasizing the importance of the Special Court for Sierra Leone and the Truth and Reconciliation Commission in taking effective action on impunity and accountability and in promoting reconciliation,

Emphasizing also the importance of the continuing support of the United Nations Mission in Sierra Leone to the Government of Sierra Leone in the consolidation of peace and stability,

Having considered the report of the Secretary-General,

1. *Decides* that the mandate of the United Nations Mission in Sierra Leone shall be extended for a period of six months from 30 March 2003;

2. *Expresses its appreciation* to those Member States providing troops, civilian police personnel and support elements to the Mission and to those who have made commitments to do so;

3. *Commends* the Mission for the progress made in the adjustments to its size, composition and deployment, as outlined in paragraphs 10 and 11 of the report of the Secretary-General, achieved while continuing to support the Sierra Leonean security forces in maintaining internal security and protecting Sierra Leone's territorial integrity;

4. *Urges* the Mission, guided by an evaluation of the security situation and the capacity and ability of the Sierra Leonean security sector to take responsibility for internal and external security, to complete phase 2 of the plan of the Secretary-General, as planned, and to embark on phase 3 as soon as practicable thereafter;

5. *Requests* the Secretary-General to provide the Council with detailed plans for the remainder of the drawdown once phase 3 is under way, including options for faster and slower withdrawal depending on the security situation and the capacity and ability of the Sierra Leonean security sector to take responsibility for internal and external security;

6. *Expresses concern* at the continuing financial shortfall in the multi-donor trust fund for the disarmament, demobilization and reintegration programme, and urges the Government of Sierra Leone to seek actively the urgently needed additional resources for reintegration;

7. *Emphasizes* that the development of the administrative capacities of the Government of Sierra Leone, particularly an effective and sustainable police force, army, penal system and independent judiciary, is essential to long-term peace and development, and urges the Government of Sierra Leone, with the assistance of donors and the Mission in accordance with its mandate, to accelerate the consolidation of civil authority and public services throughout the country and to strengthen the operational effectiveness and capabilities of the security sector;

8. *Calls upon* States, international organizations and non-governmental organizations to continue to support the national recovery strategy of the Government of Sierra Leone;

9. *Notes* the efforts made by the Government of Sierra Leone towards effective control of the diamond-mining areas, urges the Government of Sierra Leone to consider urgently relevant policy options for more effective regulation and control of diamond-mining activities, and encourages the Government of Sierra Leone to adopt and implement such a policy as soon as possible;

10. *Welcomes* the progress with deployment of United Nations civilian police to the Mission, and urges Member States able to do so to provide qualified civilian police trainers and advisers, and resources, to help the Sierra Leone Police to fulfil its size and capacity targets;

11. *Reiterates its strong support* for the Special Court for Sierra Leone, appeals to States to contribute generously to the Trust Fund for the Special Court, as requested in the letter from the Secretary-General dated 18 March 2003, appeals to existing donors to disburse their pledges rapidly, and urges all States to cooperate fully with the Court;

12. *Welcomes* the launch of the Truth and Reconciliation Commission and the progress made in its activities, and urges donors to commit funds to it generously;

13. *Urges* the Presidents of the Mano River Union member States to resume dialogue and to implement their commitments to building regional peace and security, encourages the Economic Community of West African States, and Morocco, to continue their efforts towards a settlement of the crisis in the Mano River Union region, and expresses its support for the efforts of the International Contact Group on Liberia towards a resolution of the conflict in that country;

14. *Notes with concern* the recent instability on the border between Sierra Leone and Liberia, demands that the armed forces of Liberia and any armed groups refrain from illegal incursions into the territory of Sierra Leone, calls upon all States to comply fully with all relevant resolutions of the Security Council, including the embargo on all deliveries of weapons and military equipment to Liberia, and encourages the Sierra Leonean armed forces, together with the Mission, to maintain intensive patrolling of the border with Liberia;

15. *Encourages* the Government of Sierra Leone to pay special attention to the needs of women and children affected by the war, bearing in mind paragraph 42 of the report of the Secretary-General;

16. *Encourages* the continued support of the Mission, within its capabilities and areas of deployment, for the voluntary return of refugees and displaced persons, and urges all stakeholders to continue to cooperate to this end to fulfil their commitments under the Agreement on the Ceasefire and Cessation of Hostilities, signed in Abuja on 10 November 2000;

17. *Welcomes* the intention of the Secretary-General to keep the security, political, humanitarian and human rights situation in Sierra Leone under close re-

view and to report to the Council, after due consultations with troop-contributing countries and the Government of Sierra Leone, with any additional recommendations;

18. *Decides* to remain actively seized of the matter.

UNAMSIL drawdown

Report of Secretary-General (June). On 23 June [S/2003/663], the Secretary-General issued his eighteenth report on UNAMSIL, which included, as requested by Security Council resolution 1470(2003) (above), plans and options for the remainder of UNAMSIL's drawdown process.

During the reporting period, the security situation remained generally stable, though challenges remained. Unconfirmed reports indicated that Mr. Koroma, who had escaped from arrest, had been recently killed in Liberia where he reportedly had been leading an armed group. Although the Government had undertaken to dismantle CDF by January, the Force continued to exist as an organized group and, in some sectors, operated almost in parallel to the Government's security sector. The influx of a large number of young men to the diamond-mining areas of Kono district and Tongo Fields and the activities of local military youth groups who resented the influx of outsiders also remained a potential source of instability. Youth groups, mainly former combatants, continued to challenge the local authorities.

While the internal situation had improved, external factors contributed to the security risk, particularly the conflict in Liberia, which could have a destabilizing effect on Sierra Leone and the Mano River subregion. Combatants from both sides in the Liberian conflict were seeking refuge in Sierra Leone, giving rise to fears of spillover in the fighting.

In 2002, the Secretary-General had made initial proposals for the drawdown of UNAMSIL [YUN 2002, p. 155], including benchmarks to guide the pace of the process, such as strengthening the capacity of the Sierra Leone police and armed forces, the reintegration of former combatants, consolidating State authority throughout the country and restoring government control over diamond mining. The joint mechanisms established by UNAMSIL and the Government of Sierra Leone to monitor and evaluate the major factors relating to the key security benchmarks continued to meet regularly. UN civilian police continued to assist in training new police officers, and Sierra Leone planned to increase police strength from the current level of about 6,800 to the prewar level of 9,500. Since September 2002, 592 recruits had graduated from training school and another 199 were expected to graduate in July 2003. The deployment of national police was limited by the lack of police infrastructure in the provinces and inadequate transport and communication equipment. Any further delay in expanding the police's capability could result in a security vacuum in areas vacated by UNAMSIL, with serious security risks.

The restructuring of RSLAF continued, with the goal of reducing the force from the current level of 14,000 to 10,500. A third of the RSLAF troops were deployed in the Sierra Leone–Liberia border areas. Since operations lacked the necessary infrastructure and logistics, the army continued to rely on UNAMSIL for some support.

The availability of reintegration opportunities to former combatants had improved, with 5,500 additional ex-combatants having benefited from new projects. Some 9,100 ex-combatants had yet to benefit from reintegration projects. The Government intended to complete the programme by the end of 2003 but lacked sufficient resources. In order to remove small arms and light weapons from general circulation, UNDP was implementing an arms collection programme that would develop new firearms-licensing procedures and a small-arms database.

The deployment of government officials to all districts was completed. However, the capacity of government structures to deliver services in the provinces remained feeble, owing to logistic and infrastructure constraints and lack of qualified personnel. Nationwide district consultations on decentralization and local government reform were completed in April and the Government was seeking opinions on the type of local government structures to be put in place and the type of local elections to be conducted. Progress was also made in the rehabilitation of the judicial sector. Courts resumed sittings in all districts and justices of the peace were assigned to over 20 locations throughout the country.

There was a significant increase in licensed mining activities and in official exports of rough diamonds. More government mining officers and monitors were sent to the mining areas. Although official exports were reported to have reached $25 million between January and May 2003, there was ample evidence that illicit mining persisted in many parts of the country. The Government had yet to put in place a comprehensive legislative framework and a mining policy for better control and regulation of diamond-mining activities. UNAMSIL supported the Government's ground and aerial surveys of mining sites in selected areas.

The drawdown of UNAMSIL was proceeding as planned, with the first two phases having been completed, thus reducing the Mission's troop strength to 13,074 personnel. As requested by the Council in resolution 1470(2003), the Secretariat reviewed the current pace of UNAMSIL's drawdown and developed options for an accelerated and a slower withdrawal, as well as a modified status quo drawdown, taking into account the evolving security situation and Sierra Leone's ability to take responsibility for internal and external security. Under the accelerated plan, all UNAMSIL troops would leave Sierra Leone by June 2004; under the slower plan, UNAMSIL would complete its withdrawal by June 2005; and under the modified status quo plan, withdrawal would be completed by December 2004. The Secretary-General recommended that the Security Council approve the modified status quo option, under which the forthcoming phase 3 of the drawdown plan would be conducted in four stages, with specific reductions by certain dates.

Significant progress was made, with UNAMSIL assistance, in promoting human rights, national reconciliation and justice, and in addressing the needs of children affected by the conflict. The Truth and Reconciliation Commission began public hearings on 14 April, with victims and perpetrators of the civil war telling their stories in public.

Two more indictments were issued by the Special Court and the pre-trial hearings of those in detention began. In June, the Court announced the indictment of President Charles Taylor of Liberia. The case against former RUF leader Foday Sankoh was adjourned sine die to enable him to undergo examinations to establish his mental fitness to stand trial. The body of Sam Bockarie was returned to Sierra Leone for identification by the Court. UNAMSIL continued to provide logistics and security support to the Special Court.

With regard to gender mainstreaming, UNAMSIL's Human Rights Section promoted women's rights with its monitoring and capacity-building activities. Its Gender Specialist monitored and reported human rights abuses against women and girls and promoted women's human rights. The activities of the HIV/AIDS Unit focused on awareness training for the Mission's staff and participation in a UN Theme Group on HIV/AIDS.

The number of refugees entering Sierra Leone from Liberia decreased significantly during the reporting period. An eighth refugee camp was opened in April, increasing the absorption capacity; some 55,000 Liberian refugees were accommodated in camps. There was concern about Liberian combatants infiltrating Sierra Leone among the refugees, and an effort was made to separate those individuals from refugees in order to preserve the humanitarian character of asylum. Repatriation from Liberia was suspended when the security situation there became difficult. An estimated 47,000 Sierra Leonean refugees remained in Guinea, more than half of them in UNHCR camps, and 40,000 were in Liberia.

The Secretary-General reported that the gradual and calibrated approach to the UNAMSIL drawdown was yielding the desired benefits. In particular, the extended presence of the Mission had assured a stable security environment and enabled the Government to make steady progress in consolidating peace and in promoting national reconciliation, justice and national reconstruction. Of the 57,000 disarmed ex-combatants, 48,000 had been reintegrated. The resettlement of internally displaced persons had been completed, and the pace of resettling refugees had accelerated until recent events in Liberia. The conflicts in Liberia and Côte d'Ivoire added to the instability in the subregion as a whole.

Security Council mission (June/July). The Security Council mission to West Africa (26 June–5 July) [S/2003/688] (see p. 163) visited Sierra Leone and recommended that the Government intensify its efforts to develop the capacity of the Sierra Leonean armed forces and police to ensure security after UNAMSIL's departure. It further recommended that: the Government should make a special effort to consolidate its control over the diamond-mining areas by ensuring police deployment there and enforcing the certification regime; the Council should recognize the linkage between establishing peace in Liberia and consolidating stability in Sierra Leone and the MRU subregion, and take that into account when deciding on the best option for UNAMSIL's drawdown; the successful disarmament, demobilization and reintegration (DDR) programme in Sierra Leone should be assessed by the UN system to ensure that lessons were learned, particularly in due course for Liberia; the Council should examine the UNAMSIL experience in peacekeeping, peace-building, humanitarian and development efforts, so that the transition to development could be more effectively managed in other UN operations; the role of women in conflict and peacemaking should also be examined by the Council and the UN system; and the local elections in 2004 should allow as much community representation as possible, and should be monitored by the UN system.

SECURITY COUNCIL ACTION (July)

On 18 July [meeting 4789], the Security Council unanimously adopted **resolution 1492(2003)**. The draft [S/2003/713] was prepared in consultations among Council members.

The Security Council,

Recalling its resolutions and the statements by its President concerning the situation in Sierra Leone,

Recognizing the continuing fragile security situation in the Mano River region, particularly the conflict in Liberia and the need to strengthen further the capacity of the Sierra Leonean police and armed forces to enable them to maintain security and stability independently,

Taking note of the report of the Secretary-General of 23 June 2003, particularly the options for the drawdown of the United Nations Mission in Sierra Leone described in paragraphs 32 to 40 thereof,

1. *Approves* the recommendation of the Secretary-General, set out in paragraph 68 of his report, that the drawdown of the United Nations Mission in Sierra Leone should proceed according to the "modified status quo" option towards withdrawal by December 2004, and welcomes the intention of the Secretary-General to submit additional recommendations to the Council in early 2004 concerning a residual presence of the United Nations;

2. *Decides* to monitor closely the key benchmarks for the drawdown, and requests the Secretary-General to report to the Council at the end of each phase, and at regular intervals, on the progress made with respect to the benchmarks, and to make any necessary recommendations on the planning of subsequent phases of the withdrawal;

3. *Requests* the Secretary-General to proceed accordingly;

4. *Decides* to remain actively seized of the matter.

Report of Secretary-General (September). In response to Security Council resolution 1492 (2003), the Secretary-General, on 5 September, submitted his nineteenth report on UNAMSIL [S/2003/863 & Add.1]. He addressed, in particular, progress made in achieving the benchmarks that would guide the drawdown of the Mission.

The security situation in Sierra Leone remained generally stable and further progress was achieved toward peace consolidation. On 29 July, UNAMSIL troops were put on alert after the death of the former RUF leader, Foday Sankoh, but there was no major public reaction. The stability allowed UNAMSIL to complete the first stage of phase 3 of the drawdown plan, reducing the number of troops to 12,311 by August.

Nevertheless, some problems persisted. The continuing influx of young men to the diamond-mining areas remained a potential source of instability, as did the restiveness of some ex-combatants of CDF, RUF and AFRC/ex-Sierra Leone Army. However, UNAMSIL believed that those problems did not pose immediate internal threats to the country's security. Should the environment remain favourable, the Mission's strength would be gradually reduced to 5,000 by October 2004.

The Secretary-General described progress in implementing specific benchmarks he had outlined in 2002 to guide the UNAMSIL drawdown process: strengthening the capacity of the Sierra Leone police and the armed forces; consolidation of State authority; reintegration of ex-combatants; restoration of government control over diamond mining; and improving human rights, national reconciliation and justice.

By August, the number of Liberian refugees in Sierra Leone camps was reduced by 10 per cent, to 54,298, bringing the total number of confirmed refugees in Sierra Leone to 66,184. Repatriation of Sierra Leonean refugees from Guinea slowed down and was suspended with the onset of heavy rains, while repatriation from Liberia was resumed for a short period before the operation was terminated because of insecurity. The economy of the country also improved, sustained by the dynamic growth of donor-financed imports, large-scale resettlement and reconstruction activities, expansion of land under cultivation, more mining and domestic commerce and increasing investor confidence.

The Secretary-General observed that, with UNAMSIL's continued drawdown, the responsibility for national security in some parts of the country was being shifted to the Government, which was confronted with problems of lack of adequate equipment and infrastructure. Much needed to be done to strengthen the presence of the Sierra Leone police in the areas to be vacated by UNAMSIL, especially in the east. The plan to increase the size of the police force to its pre-war level of 9,500 might be achieved by the end of 2005, a year after UNAMSIL was expected to leave. The Secretary-General urged the Government and its international partners to address the logistical and infrastructure needs of both the police and the army. Given the need to continue the gradual drawdown of UNAMSIL without jeopardizing the security situation in Sierra Leone, he recommended that the Security Council extend its mandate for another six months, until 31 March 2004.

Progress had been made relating to the control of diamond mining. The Secretary-General called for further action, such as establishing a computerized databank on mining licences, a review of incentives for staff of the Ministry of Mineral Resources, and the use of banking channels for all diamond trading transactions.

In other areas, the Secretary-General urged the Government to ensure that the CDF structure was totally dismantled and that the DDR programme was completed on schedule. He also appealed to donors to provide funding in the critical area of the administration of justice and to support the establishment of a national human rights commission.

Recent important developments in Liberia, in particular the Comprehensive Peace Agreement signed in Accra, had given hope that stability would improve. An unregulated return to Sierra Leone of former combatants who might have been involved in the fighting in Liberia would, however, be a matter of serious concern.

SECURITY COUNCIL ACTION (September)

On 19 September [meeting 4829], the Security Council unanimously adopted **resolution 1508 (2003)**. The draft [S/2003/895] was prepared in consultations among Council members.

The Security Council,

Recalling its resolutions and the statements by its President concerning the situation in Sierra Leone,

Affirming the commitment of all States to respect the sovereignty, political independence and territorial integrity of Sierra Leone,

Welcoming the increasingly stable security situation in Sierra Leone, while encouraging further progress towards strengthening the capacity of the Sierra Leone police and armed forces to maintain security and stability independently,

Noting that lasting stability in Sierra Leone will depend on peace in the subregion, especially in Liberia, and emphasizing the importance of cooperation among the countries of the subregion to this end, as well as the need for coordination of United Nations efforts to contribute to the consolidation of peace and security in the subregion,

Reiterating the importance of the effective consolidation of stability and State authority throughout Sierra Leone, particularly in the diamond fields, the reintegration of ex-combatants, the voluntary and unhindered return of refugees and internally displaced persons, and full respect for human rights and the rule of law, paying special attention to the protection of women and children, and stressing continued United Nations support to the Government of Sierra Leone in fulfilling these objectives,

Having considered the report of the Secretary-General,

1. *Decides* that the mandate of the United Nations Mission in Sierra Leone shall be extended for a period of six months from 30 September 2003;

2. *Expresses its appreciation* to those Member States providing troops, civilian police personnel and support elements to the Mission and those who have made commitments to do so;

3. *Commends* the Mission for the progress made to date in the adjustments to its size, composition and deployment, in accordance with Security Council resolutions 1436(2002) of 24 September 2002 and 1492(2003) of 18 July 2003, and welcomes the intention of the Secretary-General to continue with those adjustments, as outlined in paragraph 10 of his report;

4. *Emphasizes* that the development of the administrative capacities of the Government of Sierra Leone, particularly an effective and sustainable police force, army, penal system and independent judiciary, is essential to long-term peace and development, and urges the Government of Sierra Leone, with the assistance of donors and the Mission, in accordance with its mandate, to accelerate the consolidation of civil authority and public services throughout the country and to continue to strengthen the operational effectiveness and capabilities of the security sector;

5. *Urges* the Government of Sierra Leone to continue to strengthen its control over and regulation of diamond mining, including through the High-level Steering Committee, and encourages Member States to volunteer candidates for the post of diamond mining police adviser;

6. *Notes with serious concern* the precarious financial situation of the Special Court for Sierra Leone, reiterates its appeal to States to contribute generously to the Court, as requested in the letter from the Secretary-General dated 18 March 2003, and urges all States to cooperate fully with the Court;

7. *Commends* the Truth and Reconciliation Commission for its work, encourages States to contribute generously to it, and welcomes the intention of the Government of Sierra Leone to establish a Human Rights Commission;

8. *Expresses its strong support* for the efforts of the Economic Community of West African States towards building peace in the subregion, and encourages the Presidents of the member States of the Mano River Union to resume dialogue and to implement their commitments to building regional peace and security;

9. *Welcomes* the deployment of forces of the Economic Community of West African States to Liberia, supported by the Mission, reiterates its demand that armed groups in Liberia refrain from illegal incursions into Sierra Leone, and encourages the Sierra Leonean armed forces, together with the Mission, to maintain intensive patrolling of the border with Liberia;

10. *Encourages* the continued support of the Mission, within its capabilities and areas of deployment, for the voluntary return of refugees and displaced persons;

11. *Welcomes* the intention of the Secretary-General to keep the security, political, humanitarian and human rights situation in Sierra Leone under close review and to report to the Council, after due consultations with troop-contributing countries and the Government of Sierra Leone, with any additional recommendations;

12. *Decides* to remain actively seized of the matter.

Follow-up to Security Council mission. On 5 December [S/2003/1147], the Secretary-General submitted to the Security Council a progress report on the recommendations of the Council mission to West Africa (see p. 163). With regard to Sierra Leone, he observed that the capacity of the army and police had been enhanced, as recommended, particularly that of the police, but further work was needed. For the army, its needs included construction of barracks, improvement of the transport fleet and communications equipment, and acquisition of armed helicopters. For the police, accelerated training of recruits and mid-level officers and construction of essential infrastructure were needed. Tightened control along the borders in the eastern part of the country and political progress in Liberia would contribute to stability in Sierra Leone and in the MRU subregion.

Several lessons had been learned from the UNAMSIL multidimensional peacekeeping operation, including: the importance of keeping open the lines of communication with the warring parties; the usefulness of the two-track approach to dealing with RUF in implementing DDR programmes; the significant role played by the coordination mechanisms; and the importance of the information strategy and administrative support. In an effort to consider the different roles of women in peacemaking and peace-building, UNAMSIL had established a Gender Task Force to support the participation of women in promoting peace and in decision-making, and it intended to facilitate the full participation of women in the forthcoming local elections.

The Government had made progress in reasserting its control over diamonds; official exports had reached $30 million by October 2003. UNAMSIL was continuing to support the Government in the management and governance of diamonds, including in formulating a national resource policy, assisting the police in implementing a strategy for policing diamond mining, jointly patrolling mining areas to help curb illicit mining, and offering public information facilities for sensitization campaigns and assisting the Ministry of Information and Broadcasting in developing programmes in diamond area communities. UNAMSIL would continue to support both the Special Court for Sierra Leone and the Truth and Reconciliation Commission and to seek adequate financial resources to meet their operational requirements.

The Secretary-General concluded that while significant progress had been achieved consolidating peace in Sierra Leone, much remained to be done to ensure that the planned gradual withdrawal of UNAMSIL continued to take into account the Government's ability to assume its primary responsibility for internal and external security, to enhance control over natural resources and to consolidate civil administration throughout the country. In order to address the dilemma related to the drawdown and the still fragile peace, he intended to dispatch an assessment mission to Sierra Leone in early 2004 to evaluate the progress made in accomplishing the benchmarks defined for the withdrawal. In the meantime, it was vital that UNAMSIL continue to monitor the movements of armed elements along Liberia's borders in order to prevent incursions. In response to a Council request that missions in the region develop a contingency plan for preventing cross-border movements of foreign combatants and devise a mechanism to harmonize their activities in areas of mutual concern, UNAMSIL convened a meeting of UN missions in West Africa (Freetown, 14 November), which adopted specific mechanisms for harmonization among the missions.

Report of Secretary-General (December). On 23 December [S/2003/1201], the Secretary-General submitted his twentieth report on UNAMSIL, in which he described progress in implementing phase 3 of the Mission's withdrawal, and assessed the security situation and implementation of the benchmarks.

UNAMSIL had completed the second stage of the four stages of phase 3 and, in December, had begun the third stage, which was expected to be completed in June 2004. The third stage would result in the complete drawdown of UN troops from Sector Centre, its return to Sierra Leone responsibility, reduction of UNAMSIL's troop strength to 10,500 and UNAMSIL's deployment in only two Sectors, East and West. As at 15 December 2003, troop strength stood at 11,528.

The political and security situation in Sierra Leone remained generally stable. UNAMSIL and the Government held regular joint evaluations of the security environment within the framework of the National Security Council Coordinating Group. Local security committees comprising senior members of the national police, the army and the civil service were established to identify security threats and to coordinate responses. UNAMSIL continued to work closely with the security committees and conducted joint exercises with the police and the army. Its intention was to reduce its visibility gradually. The main potential security threat in Sector Centre was the presence of the former CDF, which maintained its structures in some areas. In addition, an internment camp accommodating elements of the former Liberian Armed Forces and of LURD were located in that Sector. The area along the border with Liberia also continued to pose a security challenge. With regard to the diamond-producing areas, UNAMSIL estimated that half of all mining activities were conducted without government licences.

With regard to the key benchmark of strengthening the capacity of the Sierra Leone police and army, UNAMSIL, together with UNDP and other partners, supported the Government's recruitment and training of police; during the year, some 600 recruits joined the force. Training was provided in the areas of family support, criminal intelligence and investigation, drugs, commercial crime, forensics, traffic management, airport security and monitoring of diamond mining. The adjustment of the RSLAF force from 14,000 to 10,500 troops was on track and the effort to address the shortage of barracks was gathering momentum. However, RSLAF still lacked adequate communications equipment and vehicles.

Progress was made in consolidating State authority throughout the country at the provincial and district levels. Advances were also made in extending the judiciary throughout the country, including the rehabilitation and construction of courts and penitentiary facilities, although restoration of the rule of law and speedy dispensation of justice were impeded by resource constraints. Legislation on local government reform and decentralization, in preparation for local elections in May 2004, was drafted for presentation to Parliament. Having been requested by the Government to organize and conduct those elections, the United Nations sent an electoral needs-assessment mission to Sierra Leone in December, which identified needs in logistics, communications, security, public information and establishing an electoral unit.

The Government maintained the date for the completion of the DDR programme at 31 December 2003. It reported that of 56,751 ex-combatants registered for the programme, 32,892 had completed their training and 15,322 were still in programmes. Diamond mining came under tighter government controls, with the number of licences issued reaching 1,800, compared to 900 in June 2002. Official exports of diamonds in 2003 reached $65 million at the end of October.

UNAMSIL continued its human rights monitoring activities, assisted in drafting legislation for a national human rights commission, and supported the Government in strengthening the protection of vulnerable children. The Truth and Reconciliation Commission was granted an extension of its mandate until the end of 2003 and continued its public hearings. The Special Court continued with pre-trial hearings for the nine individuals indicted for war crimes.

There were no significant influxes of refugees into Sierra Leone from Liberia in the latter half of 2003, and the number of Liberians seeking refuge in Sierra Leone was almost unchanged, at about 67,000, of whom 55,600 were accommodated in eight camps, 8,300 in urban areas and 3,100 in the border regions. The repatriation of the 40,000 Sierra Leonean refugees who resided in the subregion recommenced in October with flights from Côte d'Ivoire and Ghana, and by road from Guinea. It was hoped that up to 5,000 Sierra Leoneans would return before the end of 2003. The United Nations Transitional Appeal for Relief and Recovery in Sierra Leone in 2004 was launched in Dublin, Ireland, on 19 November.

Sierra Leone's economic performance maintained a positive trend in 2003; early data indicated that the real gross domestic product target of 6.5 per cent growth was likely to be achieved, largely due to agricultural output, growth in diamond production, a modest increase in manufacturing output and expansion in construction activities.

As mandated by the Security Council, UNAMSIL continued to support UNMIL and maintained contacts with other UN missions in the subregion. Following the inauguration of UNMIL on 1 October (see p. 197), UNAMSIL supported the deployment of the Bangladeshi battalion to Liberia, sent a number of military observers on temporary attachment to UNMIL and assisted in training programmes.

The Secretary-General observed that the stable security situation in Sierra Leone had facilitated the consolidation of peace and the implementation of the drawdown benchmarks. Progress was also made in the gradual handover of responsibility for national security to the Sierra Leone police and RSLAF. However, additional resources were urgently required to continue enhancing the capacity of the security sector so that the armed forces and police could project a credible deterrence profile. The Secretary-General appealed to donors to provide assistance to the Government, particularly in the security sector.

The ongoing efforts to stabilize Liberia were beginning to have a positive impact on the Mano River region. The recent meeting in Freetown of the heads and force commanders of the UN peacekeeping and political missions in West Africa was an important new development. That forum would provide a framework for addressing subregional issues, in particular cross-border problems.

The Secretary-General remained concerned, however, about the numbers of foreign combatants in Liberia and the Liberian internees in Sierra Leone. As the peace process took hold in Liberia, it was expected that the repatriation of those combatants and their reintegration into civilian life would become possible.

UNAMSIL financing

At its resumed fifty-seventh session in 2003, the General Assembly had before it a number of reports of the Secretary-General on UNAMSIL financing. In the performance report on the UNAMSIL budget for 1 July 2001 to 30 June 2002 [A/57/680], the Secretary-General stated that, of the $692 million apportioned, expenditures totalled $617.6 million. The Secretary-General proposed a budget for UNAMSIL for 1 July 2003 to 30 June 2004 [A/57/681] of $520,053,600 gross, providing for the deployment of 12,740 troops, 260 military observers, 170 civilian police advisers, 356 international and 569 national staff, as well as 147 United Nations Volunteers.

Having reviewed those two reports, ACABQ, in May [A/57/772/Add.3], recommended that the Assembly approve a reduction in the UNAMSIL appropriation for the 2001/02 budget from the $717,603,059 provided for in resolution 56/251 A [YUN 2001, p. 175] to $676,603,059, corresponding to the amount actually assessed for the period. It suggested that the unencumbered balance of $33,353,600 resulting from the reduced appropriation should be credited to Member States, as should other income amounting to $23,207,000. ACABQ recommended approval of the Secretary-General's 2003/04 budget proposal and made suggestions for economies.

In a February overview of the financing of UN peacekeeping operations, covering the budget performance for 1 July 2001 to 30 June 2002 and proposed budgets for 1 July 2003 to 30 June 2004 [A/57/723], the Secretary-General stated that the main factors affecting UNAMSIL's budget performance for the 2001/02 period were: savings in the rotation of military personnel; delays in recruiting international civilian staff and UN Volunteers; reduced requirements for prefabricated facilities; and lower transportation costs.

GENERAL ASSEMBLY ACTION (June)

On 18 June [meeting 90], the General Assembly, on the recommendation of the Fifth Committee [A/57/657/Add.1], adopted **resolution 57/291 B** without vote [agenda item 134].

Financing of the United Nations Mission in Sierra Leone

The General Assembly,

Having considered the reports of the Secretary-General on the financing of the United Nations Mission in Sierra Leone and the related reports of the Advisory Committee on Administrative and Budgetary Questions,

Bearing in mind Security Council resolution 1270 (1999) of 22 October 1999 concerning the establishment of the United Nations Mission in Sierra Leone, and the subsequent resolutions by which the Council revised and extended the mandate of the Mission, the latest of which was resolution 1470(2003) of 28 March 2003,

Recalling its resolution 53/29 of 20 November 1998 on the financing of the United Nations Observer Mission in Sierra Leone and subsequent resolutions on the financing of the United Nations Mission in Sierra Leone, the latest of which was resolution 57/291 A of 20 December 2002,

Reaffirming the general principles underlying the financing of United Nations peacekeeping operations, as stated in General Assembly resolutions 1874(S-IV) of 27 June 1963, 3101(XXVIII) of 11 December 1973 and 55/235 of 23 December 2000,

Noting with appreciation that voluntary contributions have been made to the Mission,

Mindful of the fact that it is essential to provide the Mission with the necessary financial resources to enable it to fulfil its responsibilities under the relevant resolutions of the Security Council,

1. *Takes note* of the status of contributions to the United Nations Observer Mission in Sierra Leone and the United Nations Mission in Sierra Leone as at 31 March 2003, including the contributions outstanding in the amount of 170 million United States dollars, representing some 9 per cent of the total assessed contributions, notes with concern that only twenty-seven Member States have paid their assessed contributions in full, and urges all other Member States, in particular those in arrears, to ensure payment of their outstanding assessed contributions;

2. *Expresses its appreciation* to those Member States which have paid their assessed contributions in full, and urges all other Member States to make every possible effort to ensure payment of their assessed contributions to the United Nations Mission in Sierra Leone in full;

3. *Expresses concern* at the financial situation with regard to peacekeeping activities, in particular as regards the reimbursements to troop contributors that bear additional burdens owing to overdue payments by Member States of their assessments;

4. *Also expresses concern* at the delay experienced by the Secretary-General in deploying and providing adequate resources to some recent peacekeeping missions, in particular those in Africa;

5. *Emphasizes* that all future and existing peacekeeping missions shall be given equal and non-discriminatory treatment in respect of financial and administrative arrangements;

6. *Also emphasizes* that all peacekeeping missions shall be provided with adequate resources for the effective and efficient discharge of their respective mandates;

7. *Reiterates its request* to the Secretary-General to make the fullest possible use of facilities and equipment at the United Nations Logistics Base at Brindisi, Italy, in order to minimize the costs of procurement for the Mission;

8. *Endorses* the conclusions and recommendations contained in the report of the Advisory Committee on Administrative and Budgetary Questions, and requests the Secretary-General to ensure their full implementation;

9. *Requests* the Secretary-General to take all necessary action to ensure that the Mission is administered with a maximum of efficiency and economy;

10. *Also requests* the Secretary-General, in order to reduce the cost of employing General Service staff, to continue efforts to recruit local staff for the Mission against General Service posts, commensurate with the requirements of the Mission;

11. *Expresses concern* at the persistent delays in the recruitment and placement of personnel, and requests the Secretary-General to take immediate measures to

redress the situation, and to report thereon to the General Assembly at its fifty-eighth session;

Financial performance report for the period from 1 July 2001 to 30 June 2002

12. *Takes note* of the report of the Secretary-General on the financial performance of the Mission for the period from 1 July 2001 to 30 June 2002;

13. *Decides* to reduce the appropriation authorized for the Mission for the period from 1 July 2001 to 30 June 2002 under the terms of General Assembly resolution 56/251 A of 24 December 2001 from 717,603,059 dollars to 676,603,059 dollars, the amount apportioned among Member States in respect of the same period;

14. *Decides also* to approve the decrease in the estimated staff assessment income for the period from 1 July 2001 to 30 June 2002 from 8,317,778 dollars to 7,989,378 dollars;

Budget estimates for the period from 1 July 2003 to 30 June 2004

15. *Decides further* to appropriate to the Special Account for the United Nations Mission in Sierra Leone the amount of 543,489,900 dollars for the period from 1 July 2003 to 30 June 2004, inclusive of 520,053,600 dollars for the maintenance of the Mission, 17,946,000 dollars for the support account for peacekeeping operations and 5,490,300 dollars for the United Nations Logistics Base;

Financing of the appropriation

16. *Decides* to apportion among Member States the amount of 509,436,300 dollars at a monthly rate of 42,453,025 dollars, in accordance with the levels set out in resolution 55/235, as adjusted by the General Assembly in its resolutions 55/236 of 23 December 2000 and 57/290 A of 20 December 2002, and taking into account the scale of assessments for 2003, as set out in its resolutions 55/5 B of 23 December 2000 and 57/4 B of 20 December 2002, and for 2004, subject to a decision of the Security Council to extend the mandate of the Mission;

17. *Decides also* that, in accordance with the provisions of its resolution 973(X) of 15 December 1955, there shall be set off against the apportionment among Member States, as provided for in paragraph 16 above, their respective share in the Tax Equalization Fund of 10,167,800 dollars at a monthly rate of 847,317 dollars, comprising the estimated staff assessment income of 5.8 million dollars approved for the Mission, the prorated share of 4,043,200 dollars of the estimated staff assessment income approved for the support account and the prorated share of 324,600 dollars of the estimated staff assessment income approved for the United Nations Logistics Base;

18. *Decides further* that for Member States that have fulfilled their financial obligations to the Mission, there shall be set off against their apportionment, as provided for in paragraph 16 above, their respective share of the remaining unencumbered balance and of other income in the total amount of 56,560,600 dollars in respect of the financial period ended 30 June 2002, in accordance with the levels set out in resolution 55/235, as adjusted by the General Assembly in its resolutions 55/236 and 57/290 A, and taking into account the scale of assessments for 2002, as set out in its resolutions 55/5 B and 57/4 B;

19. *Decides* that, for Member States that have not fulfilled their financial obligations to the Mission, there shall be set off against their outstanding obligations their respective share of the remaining unencumbered balance and other income in the total amount of 56,560,600 dollars in respect of the financial period ended 30 June 2002, in accordance with the scheme set out in paragraph 18 above;

20. *Decides also* that the decrease of 510,300 dollars in the estimated staff assessment income in respect of the financial period ended 30 June 2002 shall be set off against the credits from the amount referred to in paragraphs 18 and 19 above, and that the respective shares of Member States therein shall be applied in accordance with the provisions of those paragraphs as appropriate;

21. *Emphasizes* that no peacekeeping mission shall be financed by borrowing funds from other active peacekeeping missions;

22. *Encourages* the Secretary-General to continue to take additional measures to ensure the safety and security of all personnel under the auspices of the United Nations participating in the Mission;

23. *Invites* voluntary contributions to the Mission in cash and in the form of services and supplies acceptable to the Secretary-General, to be administered, as appropriate, in accordance with the procedure and practices established by the General Assembly;

24. *Decides* to include in the provisional agenda of its fifty-eighth session the item entitled "Financing of the United Nations Mission in Sierra Leone".

Sanctions

On 20 May [S/2003/559 & Corr.1], the Chairman of the Security Council Committee established pursuant to resolution 1132(1997) concerning Sierra Leone [YUN 1997, p. 135] forwarded to the Council a letter from Sierra Leone enclosing the fifth review of the certificate-of-origin regime for the export of Sierra Leone diamonds. The review was prepared by the Government in compliance with resolution 1306(2000) [YUN 2000, p. 201], in which the Council had requested Sierra Leone to establish a regime to control the export of its rough diamonds, the profits from which were being used to fuel conflicts. With the end of the rebel war, the completion of the disarmament and demobilization of ex-combatants, and the Government's effort to establish physical control of all alluvial diamond-mining areas and to discourage illicit mining, the certificate-of-origin regime was achieving its primary objective and had made a remarkable contribution to Sierra Leone's post-war development programmes. Although Liberia had not yet established an internationally verifiable certificate-of-origin regime, reports were no longer being received of uncertified Sierra Leonean diamonds transiting through its territory (see p. 201). According to Sierra Leone, the effectiveness of its regime, and that of neighbouring Guinea, had been strengthened by the establishment of the Kimberley Process Certification Scheme [YUN 2000, p. 76]. Sierra Leone's regime was fully compatible with the Kimberley Process. The prospects for its further success depended less on the incidence of illicit mining and smuggling of Sierra Leone diamonds than on adherence by all participants to their responsibilities and obligations under the global Scheme.

Security Council members, in a 5 June press statement [SC/7778-AFR/634] issued by the President on their behalf, said that the UN embargo against the import of rough diamonds from Sierra Leone without a valid certificate of origin, imposed by resolution 1306(2000) and renewed by resolution 1446(2002) [YUN 2002, p. 163], expired on 4 June. In the light of Sierra Leone's increased efforts to control and manage its diamond industry and ensure proper control over diamond-mining areas, and the Government's full participation in the Kimberley Process, members of the Council had agreed not to renew those measures. Council members commended the Government's efforts to strengthen the management of the diamond industry and encouraged the Government to continue those efforts and to work closely with UNAMSIL in ensuring the security of the diamond-mining areas. They agreed that the Council would continue to pay close attention to Sierra Leone's diamond sector because of its importance to the future stability and security of the country.

Guinea-Bissau

Guinea-Bissau continued to be beset by grave political, economic and social problems. The United Nations, through the Secretary-General's Representative and the United Nations Peacebuilding Support Office in Guinea-Bissau (UNOGBIS), monitored internal developments and the situation along its borders. At the beginning of the year, the Secretary-General warned of political and institutional instability that were generating tensions and described a deteriorating situation. Progress towards revising the constitution remained stalled and the National Assembly was not functioning. Opposition leaders accused the Government of President Koumba Yalá of arbitrary decisions, restrictions on media and harassment of political opponents. Subregional organizations and UN bodies became involved in the search for solutions. While internal tensions rose, particularly within the military, the security situation along the borders remained relatively calm.

Preparations for legislative elections were well under way when a military coup took place on 14 September. Three days later, an agreement was reached, providing for the resignation of President Yalá, a provisional Government of civilians, and the soldiers' return to barracks. A Political Transition Charter, which was signed in September by the Military Committee, 23 of the 24 registered political parties and civil society organizations set up a transitional Government and a transitional National Council. The Charter also provided for legislative elections to be held within six months and for presidential elections to take place one year later.

The transitional President, Henrique Perreira Rosa, and the Government pledged to hold elections within the stated time frame. Further work was done to prepare for elections and to restore the judicial system. At the request of President Rosa, the UNOGBIS mandate was extended for one year, until the end of 2004.

Developments and UNOGBIS activities

The economic, social and political problems of Guinea-Bissau, more specifically its post-conflict needs, were studied by the Ad Hoc Advisory Group on Guinea-Bissau, which issued its report in January [E/2003/8] (see p. 948). The Advisory Group, established by Economic and Social Council decision 2002/304 [YUN 2002, p. 920], reported that Guinea-Bissau was a country still emerging from conflict, having halted its civil strife three years earlier. However, the current situation suggested that it was slowly sliding back into conflict. The President of the Economic and Social Council, on 5 February [S/2003/176], drew the attention of the Security Council to the Advisory Group's report. He noted that the Economic and Social Council, in **resolution 2003/1** of 31 January (see p. 948), had welcomed the Advisory Group's recommendations and endorsed the proposed partnership approach. That approach foresaw a compact under which assistance would be provided contingent on political and constitutional measures being taken by the Government and plans of action being drawn up addressing both short- and long-term development needs. The Economic and Social Council President noted with pleasure that Jagdish Koonjul (Mauritius), former Chairman of the Ad Hoc Working Group of the Security Council on Conflict Prevention and Resolution in Africa, had participated in the Advisory Group.

Security Council members, in a 5 March press statement [SC/7677-AFR/571], expressed concern at the political instability in the country. They appealed to the Government to ensure that the forthcoming legislative elections were conducted in a transparent, fair and credible manner. They stressed the need to elect the President and Vice-President of the Supreme Court before the elections and called on the international community to stand ready to send observers and to provide funding. Council members called on ECOWAS to become more strongly involved in the solution of the problems faced by Guinea-Bissau.

Members further expressed concern at the serious economic situation in Guinea-Bissau and called on the Government to take steps to facilitate a constructive dialogue with the international community and to fully endorse the partnership approach defined by the Advisory Group. They welcomed the Secretary-General's decision to assist Guinea-Bissau in holding free and transparent elections and appealed to the donor community to contribute financially to the implementation of the political and economic process in the country. Members expressed concern at the proliferation of small arms in Guinea-Bissau and asked the Government to put an end to it. They were also concerned by information regarding the human rights situation. They expressed their strong support for the Representative of the Secretary-General, David Stephen (United Kingdom), and for UNOGBIS.

Report of Secretary-General (June). The Secretary-General, in response to Security Council resolution 1233(1999) [YUN 1999, p. 140], reported on 9 June [S/2003/621] on developments in Guinea-Bissau and UNOGBIS activities since his previous report of 13 December 2002 [YUN 2002, p. 179]. During that period, he said, the overall situation worsened. Amid political and institutional instability, electoral uncertainty had continued to generate tensions, as the question of the promulgation of the revised constitution remained unresolved. President Yalá continued to argue that, since the National Assembly was not functioning, it was not possible either to make progress on the constitutional issue or to hold elections for President and Vice-President of the Supreme Court of Justice until a new National Assembly had been elected.

The lack of progress in the constitutional and electoral spheres had been mirrored by a general deterioration in the political climate. Opposition leaders continued to accuse the Government of arbitrary executive decisions, restrictions imposed on the media, harassment of political opponents by security officials, the imposition of travel bans on prominent personalities and limitation of access to the media by political parties. Moreover, frequent ministerial changes, notably the President's dismissal of several close associates, raised concerns about the stability and continuity of the Government's activities. Tensions increased when the dismissed Minister of Defence was taken into custody on 30 April in connection with an alleged coup plot. Preparations for the elections, rescheduled for 6 July, were slow and by mid-May none of the benchmarks of the electoral timetable had been met. Opposition parties called for the appointment of a "Government of national unity" until elections were held.

To encourage dialogue between the ruling Partido da Renovação Social and the major opposition parties, UNOGBIS facilitated meetings on 18 March, 1 April and 22 May on the country's future and current issues. It also completed preparations for a six-month countrywide programme of activities to consolidate the process of national reconciliation and to promote the culture of conflict prevention. In preparation for the programme, it assisted the Federation of Women of Guinea-Bissau in launching a plan of action to maximize the participation of women in the political process, including in the elections.

Subregional organizations stepped up efforts to help stabilize the country. On 14 March, the Chairman of the Organization of Portuguese-speaking African States, President dos Santos of Angola, convened an extraordinary summit, attended by President Yalá. In their 14 March communiqué, the heads of State encouraged the authorities of Guinea-Bissau to pursue dialogue and called on the international community to provide technical, logistic and material support for the legislative elections. On 7 April, the ECOWAS Mediation and Security Council met in Abidjan to discuss the security situation in West Africa, including the rising political tensions in Guinea-Bissau. In a press statement, ECOWAS recommended the dispatch to Guinea-Bissau of a delegation of its Council of Elders to assist the Government to strengthen democratic governance and reduce political tensions. The Group of Friends of Guinea-Bissau, the Security Council's Ad Hoc Working Group on Conflict Prevention and Resolution in Africa, and the Economic and Social Council's Ad Hoc Advisory Group on Guinea-Bissau worked together to explore ways to assist the country.

The situation along the border with Senegal remained calm and the security measures put in place two years earlier had been largely successful in preventing incursions into Guinea-Bissau by armed elements of the separatist Movement of Democratic Forces of Casamance (MFDC). In order to promote peace in the subregion, President Yalá offered to host consultations involving MFDC factions at the request of President Wade of Senegal. Internally, there were reported tensions in the armed forces over the non-payment of salaries and desertions. On 9 May, the Chief of Staff of the Armed Forces denounced reports of an imminent coup d'état. The Demobilization, Reinsertion and Reintegration Programme had entered the reintegration phase, which was expected to end in June with the reinsertion of 6,000 ex-combatants. Demining continued to be carried out by two NGOs with support from UNDP. Despite reports of increased criminal activity, the police lacked any quick-reaction capability and training was rudimentary.

The human rights situation had become more fragile, with frequent cases of intimidation of political opponents, sometimes involving physical force, and several prominent personalities had been prevented from travelling abroad. National radio and television broadcasting facilities were monopolized by the ruling party and the private media were subjected to repressive measures. UNOGBIS continued to monitor the human rights situation. Having finally been allowed access to individuals being detained in connection with an alleged coup d'état, UNOGBIS determined that the prisoners were being held in unsatisfactory conditions.

The worsening social and economic situation sharpened political tensions. With accumulated salary arrears owed by the Government reaching $11 million, public dissatisfaction and frustration resulted in periodic strikes by public sector workers, and the Government was forced to pay some workers in rice. Economic assistance was provided by a number of UN agencies.

The Secretary-General concluded that Guinea-Bissau, which had seemed so promising following the end of the 1998-1999 armed conflict and the holding of free and fair general elections, was once again embarked on a downward course. The forthcoming legislative elections were viewed as a crucial test of Guinea-Bissau's young democratic process. The United Nations was providing technical assistance to the National Electoral Commission and would be prepared to coordinate international observation; however, should it be determined that conditions were not conducive for free, fair and credible elections, the Organization could reconsider its assistance. The Secretary-General decided to send another electoral mission to Guinea-Bissau to review the situation.

Security Council consideration. The Security Council, on 19 June [meeting 4776], considered the Secretary-General's June report and was briefed by his Representative for Guinea-Bissau and Head of UNOGBIS, David Stephen. In the context of the approaching elections scheduled for 6 July, Mr. Stephen said that the opposition continued to accuse the Government of restrictions on civil liberties. The caretaker Government continued in office, the National Assembly remained dissolved, and judicial institutions continued to be weak. An electoral needs-assessment mission of the UN Department of Political Affairs, after a visit to the country (5-11 June), noted that it was not technically feasible for the elections to be held on 6 July and urged the authorities to undertake the planned electoral census or revision of the electoral registers with a minimum of delay. Although the President had concurred that the polling date could not be maintained, he had not yet announced publicly that elections would be postponed. Meanwhile, the economic situation remained critical. Among positive developments, the private Radio Bombolom had reopened and continued to function, and the former Minister of Defence and Mr. Yalá's political adviser, who had been detained since April, were provisionally released.

SECURITY COUNCIL ACTION

On 19 June [meeting 4776], following consultations among Security Council members, the President made statement **S/PRST/2003/8** on behalf of the Council:

> The Security Council, recalling its previous statements on Guinea-Bissau, including the statement by its President of 29 November 2000 (S/PRST/2000/37), having considered the report of the Secretary-General on developments in Guinea-Bissau and on the activities of the United Nations Peace-building Support Office in that country, and anticipating the Council mission to Guinea-Bissau, expresses its concern with regard to the fragile political situation in Guinea-Bissau, to the persistent economic and social crisis and to continuing disturbing information regarding the human rights situation. It urges the leaders of the country, and the international community, to work more purposefully together to ensure that the development, humanitarian and peace-building agendas are quickly put back on track.
>
> The Council appeals to the President and the Government of Guinea-Bissau to organize effectively and in a timely manner the forthcoming legislative elections and to ensure that these elections are conducted in a transparent, fair and credible manner, in accordance with the Constitution and the electoral laws. It is the expectation of the Council that neither candidates nor political parties will be subjected to violence and intimidation and that the presence of international observers at these elections will be acceptable to all parties. The Council also expresses the hope that, following the successful conduct of the elections, the Government will embark upon additional concrete measures to show further proof of its commitment to democracy and the rule of law by promulgating the new Constitution and by having the President and Vice-President of the Supreme Court duly elected without further delay.

The Council calls upon the Government of Guinea-Bissau to take the necessary steps to facilitate a constructive dialogue with the international community and the Bretton Woods institutions and to endorse fully the partnership approach defined by the Economic and Social Council Ad Hoc Advisory Group on Guinea-Bissau.

The Council appeals to the donor community to contribute financially to the implementation of the political and economic process in Guinea-Bissau, including necessary support for the legislative elections.

The Council expresses its concern with regard to the situation of human rights and civil liberties and urges the Government of Guinea-Bissau to take the necessary measures in order to improve this situation. It stresses the importance of full respect for freedom of speech and freedom of the press.

The Council acknowledges the importance of the regional dimension in the solution of the problems faced by Guinea-Bissau and, in that regard, calls upon the Economic Community of West African States and the Organization of Portuguese-Speaking African Countries to further strengthen their involvement, and expresses its intention to intensify its cooperation with these organizations.

The Council welcomes the willingness of President Kumba Yalá to host negotiations on the issue of Casamance and appeals to him to continue to co-operate constructively with the Government of Senegal in order to contribute to a solution of this issue.

The Council recognizes and commends the important role played by the Representative of the Secretary-General as well as by the United Nations country team towards helping to consolidate peace, democracy and the rule of law, and expresses its appreciation for their activities.

The Council expresses its full support to the forthcoming mission to Guinea-Bissau, which will be led by the Permanent Representative of Mexico to the United Nations and will be the first part of an overall mission to West Africa, and looks forward to its conclusions and recommendations.

The Council expresses its intention to keep the situation in Guinea-Bissau under regular review.

Advisory Group. The Economic and Social Council's Ad Hoc Advisory Group on Guinea-Bissau, in a supplementary report dated 1 July [E/2003/95] covering its activities since January (see p. 949), noted that it had carried out a joint mission with the Security Council (see below). The Advisory Group concluded that the holding of elections was an urgent priority, and recommended that the Economic and Social Council further appeal to donors to consider funding the elections through contributions to the UNDP Trust Fund. In **resolution 2003/53** of 24 July (see p. 949), the Economic and Social Council reiterated the need to foster a comprehensive approach to Guinea-Bissau's problems in its post-conflict phase, in particular to prepare a long-term programme of support, based on its development priorities.

By a 25 August letter [S/2003/836], the President of the Economic and Social Council informed the Security Council President of the work of the Advisory Group, drawing attention to the supplementary report. He noted the growing working relationship between the two Councils on the situation in Guinea-Bissau, including the joint mission (see below). The Advisory Group's mandate had been extended until 2004.

Security Council mission. The Security Council's mission to West Africa (see p. 163), accompanied by the Economic and Social Council's Ad Hoc Advisory Group on Guinea-Bissau, visited Guinea-Bissau on 27 and 28 June. In its 7 July report [S/2003/688], the mission said that President Yalá had set 12 October as the election date and welcomed international observers, but he made no commitments on restoring democratic freedoms or respecting human rights. The mission stressed the desire of the international community to increase assistance to Guinea-Bissau, but warned that it was contingent on the Government taking the requisite steps to fulfil the partnership approach arrangement.

The overall impression gained by the mission was that Guinea-Bissau was gripped by a deep social, economic, administrative and political crisis. UNOGBIS was increasingly obliged to play a preventive, pre-conflict role. There were concerns that mounting tensions and public discontent could result in popular unrest, perhaps even civil war. While welcoming the President's statement on holding elections, the mission stated that other requirements had to be met, including the revision of electoral registers and ensuring that all parties could campaign freely and had equal access to the media. It recommended that the Security Council monitor progress in the electoral process and in implementing other steps mentioned in presidential statement S/PRST/2003/8. The mission proposed that the Council request the Secretary-General to provide an update by the end of July and regularly thereafter during the electoral period. The mission urged donors to provide financial and technical assistance for electoral preparations, contingent on the Government's creating conditions for credible elections. International electoral observers could play an important role in that respect. The mission recommended that the Security Council continue collaborative initiatives with the Economic and Social Council in the area of peace-building in post-conflict countries.

Security Council press statement (4 August). Having heard a briefing by the Secretary-General's Representative, Security Council members, in a

4 August press statement [SC/7838-AFR/683], welcomed the progress made since the June/July mission to West Africa, especially the announcement by President Yalá of the 12 October date for parliamentary elections, which constituted an important factor for the stability of the country. Council members encouraged President Yalá and his Government to continue working towards holding legislative elections in a transparent, fair and credible manner and commended the international community for having pledged the necessary resources for the organization of the elections. They further noted that the National Electoral Commission had invited international organizations to send observers. In regard to the electoral process, members expressed concern at the delay in voters' registration and appealed to the Government to speed up that process. They also expressed concern at the serious economic situation in the country and appealed for assistance for sustainable development. The Council encouraged the Guinea-Bissau authorities to restore good governance.

Coup d'état

On 14 September, the military staged a coup d'état in Guinea-Bissau, overthrowing President Yalá. In a 15 September press statement [SC/7873], Security Council members condemned the assumption of power through non-constitutional means, especially by threat or the use of force. They called for the speedy restoration of constitutional order and the holding of legislative elections as soon as possible, and called on the parties concerned to ensure the safety and security of all in Guinea-Bissau. Members welcomed the constructive role played by members of ECOWAS to find a peaceful resolution to the crisis.

On 19 September [S/2003/919], Ghana transmitted to the Security Council an ECOWAS communiqué issued following a fact-finding mission to Guinea-Bissau (15-17 September). ECOWAS expressed serious concern about the deepening political crisis and the attempt by the armed forces to remove President Yalá from office. The visiting delegation reminded the leadership of the armed forces about the Algiers Declaration of the Organization of African Unity of 1999 and the ECOWAS protocols on democratic governance, which stipulated that no recognition would be given to any Government that came to power through unconstitutional means or use of force. After discussions with all stakeholders, the following was agreed: the armed forces were not interested in political power and would return to barracks; a transitional Government of national unity composed solely of civilians would be formed through consultations with all stakeholders; President Yalá agreed to step down in the interest of national unity and stability; the transitional Government would be led by a civilian; the transition would be of reasonable duration, at the end of which legislative and presidential elections would be conducted; and ECOWAS would launch an international appeal for support to enable the country to embark on a democratic transition and socio-economic reconstruction.

Also on 19 September [S/2003/923], Italy forwarded an EU statement condemning the coup d'état and the unconstitutional seizure of power. The EU took note of the Military Committee's announcement of its intention to ensure a prompt return to constitutional order and civilian rule. It expressed its commitment to work with the international community to support a quick restoration of constitutional legality, democratic principles and national reconciliation in Guinea-Bissau.

Security Council consideration (September and November). The Security Council, on 29 September [meeting 4834], considered the situation in Guinea-Bissau. It heard a briefing by Tuliameni Kalomoh, Assistant Secretary-General for Political Affairs, who noted that the military officers who staged the coup d'état under the leadership of General Verissimo Correia Seabra had said their action was motivated by the need to re-establish the authority of the State, to rid the public administration of partisanship, to establish a transitional Government to include all political orientations and to create the foundations for elections. Immediately following the coup, ECOWAS had undertaken mediation efforts and, with support from the Community of Portuguese-Speaking Countries, helped reach an agreement on 17 September between President Yalá and the military contingent that staged the coup. Mr. Yalá resigned and a 16-member Ad Hoc Technical Commission, which included representatives of all political parties and of civil society, and religious and traditional leaders, was established to elaborate a transitional charter. The Military Committee nominated Henrique Perreira Rosa, an economist and the former Chairman of the National Electoral Commission in 1994, as transitional President.

On 28 September, agreement was reached on the Political Transitional Charter, which would guide the process of return to constitutional normality. The 56-member National Transition Council would fulfil the role of a parliament. No dates were set for elections, but it was agreed that they would be held within six months (before 28 March 2004), followed by presidential elections within a year of the first round. The urgent task for the international community was to help ensure a successful transition by responding to the economic and budgetary needs of the transitional Government.

The Special Envoy of the Community of Portuguese-Speaking Countries, José Ramos Horta, said that it appeared that the military intervention that brought down Mr. Yalá was welcomed by all of Guinea-Bissau society. He reported that the change occurred without any violence and those involved were motivated by social and economic conditions.

At a private meeting on 18 November [meeting 4860], the Council continued discussions on Guinea-Bissau.

UNOGBIS mandate. The Secretary-General, in an 11 November letter [S/2003/1096], informed the Security Council that President Rosa had requested the extension of the UNOGBIS mandate for one year, until 31 December 2004, to facilitate dialogue among all actors in Guinea-Bissau and to promote national reconciliation during the transition. The Secretary-General proposed that the current mandate be extended for one year and be revised as follows: to support political dialogue, national reconciliation, the rule of law and respect for human rights, and to strengthen democratic institutions; to encourage the Government and other national stakeholders to restore constitutional normality and to create a conducive environment for peace, stability and the holding of free and transparent elections; to assist with elections; to support national efforts aimed at strengthening the country's capacities for conflict prevention and for the peaceful management of differences; to encourage initiatives aimed at maintaining friendly relations between Guinea-Bissau and its neighbours; to encourage the Government to enact the programme of small arms collection and destruction; and to facilitate, in cooperation with the UN country team, the Bretton Woods institutions and others, international political support to address the post-conflict recovery priorities.

The Council, on 14 November [S/2003/1097], took note of the proposal to extend the UNOGBIS mandate and the revised mandate.

Follow-up to Security Council mission. The Secretary-General, in a December progress report [S/2003/1147] on the recommendations of the Security Council mission to West Africa (see p. 163), described the current situation in Guinea-Bissau. The National Election Commission had resumed its work and was expected to finalize the electoral register in November. It had recommended that the legislative elections be held by the end of January 2004, ahead of the 28 March deadline. The Secretary-General welcomed the declared commitment of the newly formed Government to restore legality and hold elections.

With regard to cooperation between the Security Council and the Economic and Social Council in peace-building, the latter's Ad Hoc Advisory Group on Guinea-Bissau, whose mandate had been extended until February 2004, continued to monitor the electoral process and maintained close relations with Guinea-Bissau's major development partners. On 17 November, the Group held a meeting at UN Headquarters with a high-level delegation of the transitional Government, senior UN officials, representatives of the Bretton Woods institutions and donor countries to discuss ways to provide support to the transitional Government. The next day, President Rosa appealed to the Security Council, in a private session, to mobilize urgent assistance for his country. The Secretary-General said it was essential that the international community remain engaged with Guinea-Bissau, including by providing urgent financial and other support to help the authorities follow through on their commitments.

Report of Secretary-General (December). On 5 December [S/2003/1157], the Secretary-General reported on developments in Guinea-Bissau and on UNOGBIS activities, focusing on the efforts of the transitional authorities to implement the transition and on the UNOGBIS contribution in that regard.

After the military coup, the transitional Government, led by a civilian Prime Minister, Artur Sanhá, the National Transitional Council, acting as a parliament, and the transitional President, Mr. Rosa, were sworn in and began to carry out their functions. During the critical time leading up to the transition, UNOGBIS and the Secretary-General's Representative provided good offices and advice to all actors in Guinea-Bissau in order to foster dialogue.

The transitional authorities had taken a number of positive steps towards implementing the Transition Charter. The National Transitional Council approved the appointment of a new Attorney-General, who took office in November, and reinstated Supreme Court judges and other legal officials. It announced that elections for the President and Vice-President of the Supreme Court would be held on 16 December. The Government paid civil service salaries for October and planned to establish a regular payment plan. The State and independent broadcasting and print media were functioning normally. The transitional authorities had made contacts with regional and international partners to engage them in dialogue on possible support for a transition to democracy.

The security situation in Guinea-Bissau had improved, with patrols along the borders having been strengthened. The situation along the border with Senegal remained calm although occasional incidents were reported. In August, Guinea-Bissau sent a contingent of 650 members to join UNMIL. Internally, tensions were reported among the army rank and file over the backlog of salary arrears and poor conditions in the barracks. The reintegration phase of the demobilization, reinsertion and reintegration programme was in progress and was scheduled to end in June 2004. The trust fund for the programme was able to fund only 4,372 beneficiaries, identified as the most vulnerable of a total of 11,300 ex-combatants. Despite the lack of resources and mounting salary arrears, members of the police force were still reporting to work and fulfilling their law and order duties. The transitional Government planned to establish a police training centre, and the UNOGBIS civilian police adviser was assisting in formulating those plans.

UNOGBIS continued to monitor the human rights situation, focusing on civil liberties and dialogue with the authorities. It followed the cases of 10 members of the military detained since December 2002 for allegedly plotting a coup. Former President Yalá remained under house arrest.

The economic and social situation threatened to disrupt the fragile political consensus. Revenue collection had almost collapsed, while expenditure was not controlled or recorded. The non-payment of salaries for most of the year to public sector workers, the inability of the majority of children to attend school, and the high mortality rate fed social tensions. The UN country team worked with other UN and international bodies to deal with those problems. Although the Government intended to draw up a development strategy to be presented to a round-table conference planned for 2004, there was an immediate need for a bridging mechanism to mobilize and coordinate assistance to Guinea-Bissau. The World Bank planned an informal meeting of donors for December and UNDP had established a multi-donor fund to address the most urgent needs of the population.

The Secretary-General observed that the recent removal of the democratically elected President, however reprehensible, should not be seen as a single event interrupting an ongoing democratic process, but as the culmination of an untenable situation during which constitutional norms were repeatedly violated. It was encouraging that the transitional Government had taken some steps in the right direction. It had appealed to the international community for urgent assistance. The crucial task in 2004 would be to help Guinea-Bissau to create a propitious political environment for the peaceful conduct of the transition, as it would be nearing its conclusion in 2005, and in particular for the holding of credible legislative elections by March 2004. In that regard, he hoped that the international community would remain engaged to help ensure that commitments were fulfilled.

Security Council press statement (December). The Security Council considered the Secretary-General's report and was briefed by his Representative during informal consultations on 19 December [SC/7962-AFR/800]. The President then issued a press statement saying that Council members welcomed the positive steps taken recently by the new authorities, especially the announcement of 28 March 2004 as the date for the parliamentary elections. They expressed concern about the critical economic and social situation and renewed their appeal to the international community to provide urgent assistance to Guinea-Bissau. They welcomed the assistance by some countries and organizations, including the contributions to the Emergency Economic Management Fund, established by UNDP, and called on other donors to contribute to it. They also commended the constructive role of the Bretton Woods institutions, the African Development Bank and UNDP.

Members encouraged the AU, ECOWAS and the Community of Portuguese-Speaking Countries to remain actively engaged in Guinea-Bissau. They commended the Ad Hoc Working Group on Conflict Prevention and Resolution in Africa, the Economic and Social Council's Advisory Group on Guinea-Bissau and the Group of Friends of Guinea-Bissau for their role in the follow-up provided to the situation in Guinea-Bissau. They expressed appreciation for the support provided by the UN system for the peace-building process and encouraged it to provide further support.

Horn of Africa

Appointment. The Secretary-General, on 15 January [S/2003/66], informed the Security Council that his Special Adviser, Mohamed Sahnoun (Algeria), had been following developments in the Horn of Africa, especially Somalia and the Sudan, and was providing advice on a possible UN role in negotiating settlements of the conflicts in those countries. Recently, regional peace efforts under the auspices of the Intergovernmental Authority on Development (IGAD) in Somalia (see p. 241) and the Sudan (see p. 256) had been reinvigorated. Significant progress was made in the IGAD-led peace process on the Sudan, resulting in the signing of the Machakos (Kenya) Protocol in July 2002 [YUN 2002, p. 217]. The two sides were expected to resume negotiations in January 2003 on a comprehensive peace agreement, with Mr. Sahnoun representing the Secretary-General. Mr. Sahnoun had also taken part in the IGAD peace initiatives with regard to Somalia and had participated in meetings of the IGAD Partners' Forum in support of the peace processes in both Somalia and the Sudan; he would continue to do so as the pace of negotiations to reach agreements was accelerated.

In view of those undertakings, the Secretary-General had decided to extend the appointment of his Special Adviser until 31 December 2003. The Council, on 20 January [S/2003/67], took note of the decision.

On 14 November [S/2003/1138], the Secretary-General informed the Council that Mr. Sahnoun continued to carry out his functions, especially in Somalia and the Sudan, having led the UN observer delegation at the Sudan peace talks and attended the Somalia National Reconciliation Conference, both in Kenya. He had also represented the Secretary-General at the tenth IGAD summit in Kampala, Uganda, in October. The Secretary-General had decided to extend his appointment until 31 December 2004; on 21 November [S/2003/1139], the Council took note of his decision.

Eritrea-Ethiopia

The United Nations continued to carry out oversight of the implementation of the 2000 Algiers ceasefire and peace agreements between Eritrea and Ethiopia [YUN 2000, p. 180] (known collectively as the Algiers Agreements), including regulating their border dispute, which had led to armed conflict in 1998 and periodic outbreaks of fighting since then. The United Nations Mission in Ethiopia and Eritrea (UNMEE), established in 2000, continued to monitor the border region inside and near the Temporary Security Zone and to support the work of the Boundary Commission, a body set up by the Agreements to determine the border. In 2003, the Commission focused on demarcation of the border, following the completion in 2002 of the border's delimitation. The border area remained generally calm throughout 2003.

In the early months of the year, both sides cooperated with the Boundary Commission and UNMEE, and progress was made in implementing the Algiers Agreements, particularly regarding the release of the remaining prisoners of war. However, progress on the boundary question soon stalled. The Commission submitted maps indicating the delimitation line to both parties and they responded with comments. Despite having previously accepted the delimitation decision, Ethiopia raised issues questioning the boundary as determined by that decision. Eritrea raised issues of a technical nature. Both sides continued to restrict the freedom of movement of UNMEE in areas inside and adjacent to the Temporary Security Zone and both banned direct flights by UN aircraft between Addis Ababa and Asmara. The Secretary-General described the peace process as being at a critical stage and warned that the loss of momentum could have an impact on the longer-term goals of reconstruction and development. Preliminary arrangements were made for placing demarcation pillars along the border. However, the work came to a standstill by the end of the year and the Boundary Commission decided to reduce its activity in the area to a minimum so that it could be resumed, if required.

Implementation of Algiers Agreements

In early 2003, further progress was made in implementing the Algiers Agreements and the parties had generally been cooperating throughout the peace process, according to the Secretary-General [S/2003/257].

Security Council members, having been briefed by Hedi Annabi, Assistant Secretary-General, Department of Peacekeeping Operations, during informal consultations on 7 January, issued a press statement [SC/7625-AFR/539] welcoming the progress made since the Secretary-General's last (December 2002) report [YUN 2002, p. 192]. They urged Ethiopia and Eritrea to continue to extend to UNMEE and the Boundary Commission full cooperation in order to ensure the smooth demarcation of the border. In that regard, members welcomed the seventh report of the Eritrea-Ethiopia Boundary Commission, in particular the schedule for demarcation [ibid., p. 193], and urged the two sides to engage in discussions with the Secretary-General's Special Representative, Legwaila Joseph Legwaila (Botswana), to address any issues that might arise during the demarcation process.

Council members welcomed the release by Ethiopia of all remaining Eritrean prisoners of war in November 2002, under the auspices of the International Committee of the Red Cross (ICRC), as did Eritrea for the Ethiopian prisoners. They called on both parties to resolve all other outstanding issues, including the establishment of a direct high-altitude air corridor between the two capitals.

Members expressed concern about the likely shortfall in the Trust Fund for the Delimitation and Demarcation of the Border once demarcation began. They called on the international community to contribute to the Fund so that the demarcation process could be concluded, in accordance with the Boundary Commission's schedule. Also expressing concern about the looming drought in the two countries and the implications for the peace process, they supported the Secretary-General's appeal for assistance for humanitarian operations through the consolidated appeals process and other mechanisms.

Eritrea, on 6 January [S/2003/8], raised with the Council the Secretary-General's failure to mention, in his December 2002 report, Ethiopia's violation of an order of the Boundary Commission concerning the removal of Ethiopian settlers from the Eritrea territory of Dembe Mengul.

Report of Secretary-General (March). On 6 March [S/2003/257], the Secretary-General submitted a progress report on Ethiopia and Eritrea, updating developments since his December 2002 report [YUN 2002, p. 192] and describing UNMEE activities. As at 26 February, the total strength of UNMEE's military component stood at 4,082 personnel. Annexed to the report was the eighth report of the Eritrea-Ethiopia Boundary Commission.

During the review period, stated the Secretary-General, the situation in the Temporary Security Zone along the joint border and its adjacent areas remained generally calm. UNMEE continued to conduct aerial reconnaissance and ground patrols of the Zone and frequent inspections of militia and police weapon cantonment sites there, and also maintained checkpoints and standing patrols at various strategic locations. The armed forces of both countries cooperated relatively well with UNMEE and no significant changes in military activities were observed. However, local Ethiopian herdsmen and their livestock had been entering grazing land in the Zone's Sector Centre, around Drum Drum and Gafnath Aromo, almost on a daily basis, despite the warnings of UNMEE peacekeepers. Although generally peaceful in nature, the incursions had caused tension and, on 18 December 2002, an Ethiopian herdsman was found shot in the Zone. UNMEE worked to keep the situation calm and met with local authorities to encourage them to be more active in preventing cross-border incidents.

UNMEE continued to experience restrictions on its freedom of movement and denial of access to military authorities by Eritrea, primarily in Sector East, in violation of the model status-of-forces agreement. In Ethiopia, UNMEE personnel passing through the Addis Ababa airport were subjected to immigration formalities in violation of the existing status-of-forces agreement. There had been no progress regarding the establishment of a direct high-altitude flight route for UNMEE aircraft between Asmara and Addis Ababa, compelling UNMEE to have to fly via longer routes at considerable expense and with security implications. The Secretary-General appealed to both parties to resolve that issue.

The Military Coordination Commission held its fifteenth meeting in Nairobi on 29 January, focusing on recent incidents within the Temporary Security Zone and adjacent areas, and on ways to strengthen existing mechanisms for resolving such problems at the local level. The Commission also discussed preparations for demining in support of demarcation of the border.

The Eritrean authorities maintained their position that UNMEE national staff should discharge national service obligations, and some national mission staff had been detained, contravening the model status-of-forces agreement.

In meetings with the Special Representative, Prime Minister Meles Zenawi of Ethiopia expressed concerns regarding the Boundary Commission's demarcation of the border and noted that if those concerns were not addressed, Ethiopia might reject the Commission's demarcation decisions. Mr. Legwaila immediately consulted with the representatives of the Guarantors and Facilitators of the peace process and the group of Friends of UNMEE regarding Ethiopia's position.

At a meeting between the Commission and the parties (London, 8-9 February), a number of matters were discussed that were covered in the Commission's eighth report (see p. 232). Meanwhile, in accordance with its adjusted mandate under resolution 1430(2002) [YUN 2002, p. 189], UNMEE provided support to the Commission in the implementation of the delimitation decision, including through demining activities and providing security for Commission personnel in the field. Landmines and unexploded ordnance constituted a major threat to the population on both sides of the border, as well as to UN personnel. From December 2002 to early February 2003, nine civilians were killed in mine accidents. A recent spate of incidents involving newly laid anti-tank mines in Sector West was of grave concern. Increasingly, UNMEE was focusing on mine action activities associated with the demarcation of the border. In that connection, the Mission consulted with the parties to establish coordination and liaison procedures to facilitate movement for demining operations in support of demarcation.

Progress was made in clearing routes in the Temporary Security Zone, with over 2,000 kilometres of routes having been surveyed or cleared. It was expected that the two countries would provide freedom of movement in the border areas for UNMEE demining efforts for demarcation.

The border areas of Ethiopia and Eritrea were hard hit by the prevailing drought in the region (see also p. 927 and 961). According to humanitarian agencies, malnutrition was rising in both countries and donor response had been slow. Quick-impact projects were an important part of UNMEE's work in the Mission area. Repatriations of civilians by both Ethiopia and Eritrea, under ICRC auspices, had declined. During the reporting period, Ethiopia repatriated 99 persons of Eritrean origin, while Eritrea repatriated 155 persons of Ethiopian origin.

The Secretary-General concluded that, while further progress had been made in implementing the Algiers Agreements, the peace process had reached a critical stage. The parties had generally been cooperating throughout the process; however, it was time for them to translate their commitments into real action, by implementing the April 2002 delimitation decision [YUN 2002, p. 187]. He called on the leaders of both countries to exercise statesmanship and flexibility. Recent démarches made to his Special Representative and to the diplomatic community, together with representations made to the Boundary Commission (see below), could have serious consequences. Issues that arose in the Commission had to be addressed within its proper legal framework, as efforts to reopen fundamental matters already settled through binding arbitration could only be counterproductive. The United Nations was prepared to facilitate the resolution of problems that might arise as a result of the transfer of territorial control, possibly by dispatching a needs-assessment mission and/or mobilizing international assistance. However, such support could be provided only on the basis of an accepted demarcation line.

The Secretary-General noted that although there had been no serious ceasefire violations since the establishment of the Temporary Security Zone, recent cross-border incidents were a source of concern. It was particularly important that both countries begin to sensitize their populations about the demarcation process and its implications. UNMEE, meanwhile, would continue to monitor the situation in the Zone and adjacent areas, and was prepared to assist the parties in normalizing relations. To that end, he recommended that the UNMEE mandate be extended for six months, until 15 September 2003.

Boundary Commission (March). In the eighth report of the Boundary Commission, which was annexed to the Secretary-General's 6 March report, the Commission confirmed that the maps drawn up indicating the demarcation line had been delivered to the two parties for their comments, which, the Commission indicated, were to be of an essentially technical nature. The comments were received in January. Those filed by Eritrea (17 pages) were of a technical nature, while those filed by Ethiopia (141 pages) went far beyond the scope intended. They contained a detailed exposition of views regarding the steps Ethiopia deemed necessary for completing the demarcation. In a number of respects, the comments amounted to an attempt to reopen the substance of the Commission's April 2002 decision on delimitation [YUN 2002, p. 187], notwithstanding Ethiopia's repeated statements of its acceptance of that decision. The main thrust of the Ethiopian comments was that the boundary should be varied so as to take better account of human and physical geography. The Commission had always made it clear that it did not have the power to vary the boundary delimited by the April 2002 decision. In the absence of agreement by both sides on variations to the boundary line, the Commission's ability to ameliorate problems was limited to minor clarifications justified principally by the enlargement of the scale of the maps with which it was working. In addition to seeking variations to the boundary line in terms that appeared to undermine not only the delimitation decision but also the peace process as a whole, Ethiopia had complained that Eritrea had been using the Commission's fieldwork as a cover for an Eritrean military intelligence-collection operation and stated that fieldwork would only be allowed to continue if Eritrea nominated new field liaison officers. Since demarcation could not continue in the absence of field liaison officers of one party, Ethiopia's demand amounted to a prohibition of further fieldwork pending Eritrea's replacement of its officers by others acceptable to Ethiopia. In response to the Commission's requirement that each party appoint two ad hoc field officers in order for demarcation to continue, Eritrea had nominated two officers but Ethiopia had not. The Commission further noted that Ethiopia had not implemented the Commission's order of 17 July 2002 requiring it to withdraw its nationals from Dembe Mengul in Eritrea, after they had returned there with Ethiopian governmental support.

Other issues that remained to be resolved were the preparation of large-scale maps, the marking of boundary pillar sites, arrangements relating to pillar construction and mine clearance and maintenance of cleared areas. The Commission hoped that the Security Council would: confirm that the Commission did not have the authority to vary the delimitation line to meet local needs as asserted by Ethiopia; call on the parties to cooperate with the Commission so that it could fulfil its mandate of expeditiously delimiting and demarcating the boundary; clarify UNMEE's mandate so as to permit accommodation of contractors' personnel within UNMEE encampments; and authorize UNMEE to provide security for Commission personnel.

The Boundary Commission, in a 31 March addendum to the Secretary-General's report [S/2003/257/Add.1], provided observations on its approach to the demarcation phase of its work in the light of certain considerations advanced by the parties in their January comments on the maps indicating the demarcation line. It explained the basis on which the delimitation process was carried out and stated that the next steps were clear: the surveyors would establish locations of the marker pillars and the contractors would construct them. During those operations, the parties had to cooperate with the Commission and the Commission's personnel had to be fully safeguarded. The parties needed to discuss with the chief surveyor the manner in which they would fulfil those undertakings.

Communication. Eritrea, on 11 March [S/2003/305], stated that Ethiopia's efforts to impede the preparatory fieldwork of demarcation ranged from threatening to shoot down the Boundary Commission's helicopter carrying Commission personnel and contractors to refusal to issue appropriate flight permits. Most significantly, Ethiopia refused to accept the delimitation decision of the Commission, in violation of the Algiers Agreements. Those actions were a recipe for conflict and posed a threat to regional peace and security.

SECURITY COUNCIL ACTION (March)

On 14 March [meeting 4719], the Security Council unanimously adopted **resolution 1466(2003)**. The draft [S/2003/312] was prepared in consultations among Council members.

The Security Council,

Reaffirming all its previous resolutions and statements pertaining to the situation between Ethiopia and Eritrea, and the requirements contained therein, including in particular its resolution 1434(2002) of 6 September 2002,

Reaffirming its unwavering support for the peace process and its commitment, including through the role played by the United Nations Mission in Ethiopia and Eritrea in the implementation of its mandate, to the full and expeditious implementation of the comprehensive Peace Agreement signed by the parties on 12 December 2000 and the preceding Agreement on Cessation of Hostilities of 18 June 2000 (hereinafter referred to collectively as "the Algiers Agreements"), the Delimitation Decision of the Boundary Commission of 13 April 2002, embraced by the parties as final and binding in accordance with the Algiers Agreements, including the Orders issued on 17 July 2002, and the ensuing binding Demarcation Directions,

Commending the Governments of Ethiopia and Eritrea on the progress made thus far in the peace process, including the recently concluded release and repatriation of prisoners of war, and calling upon both parties to cooperate with the International Committee of the Red Cross to clarify and to resolve the remaining issues in accordance with the Geneva Conventions of 12 August 1949, and with the commitments made in the Algiers Agreements,

Reiterating the need for both parties to fulfil their obligations under international law, including international humanitarian law, human rights law and refugee law, and to ensure the safety of all personnel of the United Nations, the Boundary Commission, the International Committee of the Red Cross and other humanitarian organizations,

Noting that the peace process is about to enter its crucial phase of demarcation, and emphasizing the importance of ensuring expeditious implementation of the Boundary Decision while maintaining stability in all areas affected by the Decision,

Stressing that only the full implementation of the Algiers Agreements will lead to sustainable peace, which is a crucial precondition to address reconstruction and development needs as well as economic recovery,

Noting with concern the continued violations of the model status-of-forces agreement, which Ethiopia has signed and Eritrea has agreed to respect,

Welcoming the eighth report of the Boundary Commission, noting the concerns expressed therein with regard to full adherence by the parties to the Boundary Decision and demarcation-related decisions of the Commission, and expressing its full support for the work of the Commission and the legal framework within which the Commission is taking its decisions,

Having considered the report of the Secretary-General,

1. *Decides* to extend the mandate of the United Nations Mission in Ethiopia and Eritrea until 15 September 2003 at the troop and military observer levels authorized by its resolution 1320(2000) of 15 September 2000;

2. *Urges* both Ethiopia and Eritrea to continue to assume their responsibilities and fulfil their commitments under the Algiers Agreements, and calls upon them to cooperate fully and promptly with the Boundary Commission to enable it to fulfil the mandate conferred upon it by the parties of expeditiously delimiting and demarcating the boundary, to implement fully the binding Demarcation Directions of the Commission, to abide promptly by all its Orders, including those issued on 17 July 2002, and to take all steps necessary to provide the necessary security on the ground for the staff of the Commission operating in territories under their control;

3. *Expresses concern* regarding recent incidents of incursions across the southern boundary of the Tem-

porary Security Zone and calls upon both parties to ensure an immediate end to such incidents and to cooperate fully with investigations by the Mission in this regard, and expresses further concern about the placement by unknown entities of anti-tank mines in the Temporary Security Zone;

4. *Calls upon* the parties to cooperate fully and expeditiously with the Mission in the implementation of its mandate to ensure the personal security of the staff of the Mission when operating in territories under their control, and to facilitate their work, including by establishing a direct high-altitude flight route for the Mission between Asmara and Addis Ababa, which would relieve the unnecessary additional cost to the Mission;

5. *Demands* that the parties allow the Mission full freedom of movement and remove with immediate effect any and all restrictions on, and impediments to the work of, the Mission and its staff in the discharge of its mandate;

6. *Affirms* the ability of the Mission, within its existing verification mandate, to monitor fulfilment by the parties of their responsibilities with regard to the security of the Boundary Commission staff working in the field;

7. *Notes* the work done by the Mine Action Coordination Centre of the Mission in demining and education on risk related to mines, and urges the parties to pursue efforts on mine clearance;

8. *Urges* the two parties to engage expeditiously in further discussions with the Special Representative of the Secretary-General so that they reach agreement on the timing and modalities of territorial transfer, which could include the establishment by the parties of a mechanism for the resolution of problems in this regard;

9. *Also urges* the two parties to begin to sensitize their populations about the demarcation process and its implications, including the role of the United Nations in support of this process;

10. *Calls upon* the parties to refrain from unilateral troop or population movements, including the establishment of any new settlements in areas near the border, until demarcation and orderly transfer of territorial control has been accomplished, in accordance with article 4, paragraph 16, of the comprehensive Peace Agreement;

11. *Reaffirms* its decision to review frequently the progress made by the parties in the implementation of their commitments pursuant to the Algiers Agreements, including through the Boundary Commission, and to review any implications for the Mission, including with regard to the process of territorial transfers during the demarcation as outlined by the Secretary-General in his report of 10 July 2002;

12. *Encourages* the guarantors, facilitators and witnesses of the Algiers Agreements and the Friends of the United Nations Mission in Ethiopia and Eritrea to intensify further their contacts with the authorities of both countries with a view to contributing to an expeditious demarcation process;

13. *Welcomes* the contributions by Member States to the Trust Fund in Support of the Delimitation and Demarcation of the Ethiopia-Eritrea Border, and calls upon the international community to continue to contribute urgently to the Trust Fund in order to facilitate the conclusion of the demarcation process in accordance with the schedule of the Boundary Commission;

14. *Calls again upon* the parties to increase their efforts to take measures that will build confidence and contribute to the normalization of relations between them, including in particular their political relations and those in the areas listed in paragraph 14 of resolution 1398(2002) of 15 March 2002;

15. *Expresses its concern* at the prevailing drought and worsening humanitarian situation in Ethiopia and Eritrea and the implications this could have for the peace process, and calls upon Member States to continue to provide prompt and generous support for humanitarian operations in Ethiopia and Eritrea;

16. *Invites* the African Union to continue to lend its full support to the peace process;

17. *Expresses its strong support* for the Special Representative of the Secretary-General, Mr. Legwaila Joseph Legwaila, the Force Commander of the Mission, Major General Robert Gordon, the military and civilian personnel of the Mission and the Boundary Commission for their work in support of the peace process;

18. *Decides* to remain actively seized of the matter.

Report of Secretary-General (June). On 23 June [S/2003/665], the Secretary-General issued a progress report on Ethiopia and Eritrea.

In general, the situation in the UNMEE area remained calm during the three-month reporting period and the parties cooperated with the Mission. Both countries maintained a defensive military posture on either side of the Temporary Security Zone, with no observed change in force levels. The number of border incursions by Ethiopian herdsmen entering the Zone to graze their livestock had increased, especially in Sector Centre, and UNMEE raised the matter with Ethiopia because it heightened the risk of conflict. The Mission was investigating three shooting incidents, two in Sector Centre and one in Sector West. Restrictions continued to be imposed on UNMEE freedom of movement in areas adjacent to the Zone. Eritrea had still not signed the status-of-forces agreement with the United Nations and, until it did, the model status-of-forces agreement would continue to be in effect.

The Military Coordination Commission held its sixteenth meeting (Djibouti, 19 March) and both parties agreed to do all in their power to prevent mine placement in the Temporary Security Zone and adjacent areas. They agreed to cooperate in the repatriation or burial of mortal remains in the Zone. At the Commission's seventeenth meeting (Nairobi, 16 June), the parties agreed to an UNMEE proposal on the collection and repatriation of an estimated 164 bodies.

Some progress was made in the demarcation process, but it had not proceeded as quickly as anticipated. Demining activities continued, but the

Temporary Security Zone remained dangerous, and four civilians were killed in mine accidents during the reporting period.

The Secretary-General reiterated that the peace process was at a critical stage. Although the parties, in general, respected the integrity of the Temporary Security Zone, lasting peace could not be built on the basis of temporary arrangements. Lost momentum could prove difficult to regain and could impact on the longer-term goals of reconstruction and development. Specifically, progress was required in two areas—expeditious demarcation of the border and political dialogue between the parties to consolidate the peace process. The absence of political contacts since the negotiation of the Algiers Agreements had hindered the normalization of bilateral relations, a vital element of any peace process.

Claims Commission. The Eritrea-Ethiopia Claims Commission, established under the Algiers Agreements to decide on claims for loss, damage or injury by one Government against the other, and by nationals against the Government of the other party or government-owned entities, issued a report which was annexed to the Secretary-General's June report. An independent body based in The Hague, the Claims Commission received claims in 2001 and held hearings on liability, memorials and counter-memorials in those claims in 2002. Hearings on the parties' prisoner-of-war claims took place over 10 days in December 2002, and the Commission was preparing its awards. In the light of requests from both parties, the Commission, in February 2003, adjusted its schedule of future filings and hearings to take account of requirements resulting from other proceedings involving the parties and of the complexity of the remaining work. The Commission and the parties met informally several times to discuss the means for facilitating the claims process.

Boundary Commission (June). The Boundary Commission, in its ninth report, which was annexed to the Secretary-General's June report, said that Eritrea, on 15 April, had submitted its consolidated comments on the boundary in the area of Tserona and Zalambessa and on the specific provisions of Ethiopia's January comments. Ethiopia's comments were submitted on 2 May. The Commission's work continued with regard to: preparing and revising maps in response to the parties' January comments; marking boundary pillar sites on a sector-by-sector basis, beginning with the Eastern Sector; drafting specifications for pillar emplacement and transmitting them to prospective bidders; preparing field accommodation and facilities for contractors; and exploring the security needs of construction personnel.

In July [S/2003/665/Add.1], the Commission issued a schedule of its activities for the next 12 months.

Boundary Commission decision. The Boundary Commission issued a 7 July decision on the difference concerning the appointment by Eritrea and Ethiopia of field liaison officers for the boundary demarcation process (see p. 232). The Secretary-General transmitted the decision to the Security Council on 18 July [S/2003/752]. The Commission noted that difficulties arose in the initial appointment of the officers, attributable to a lack of specificity in appointment procedures, notably concerning the appointment of currently serving military officers. The Commission decided that field liaison officers would have to be appointed for the remaining demarcation activity under more detailed appointment procedures, and it amended the demarcation directions accordingly.

SECURITY COUNCIL ACTION (July)

On 17 July [meeting 4787], following consultations among Security Council members, the President made statement **S/PRST/2003/10** on behalf of the Council:

> The Security Council, recalling all its resolutions and statements by its President regarding the situation between Ethiopia and Eritrea, as well as the conclusions of the Security Council mission to Eritrea and Ethiopia in 2002, welcomes the progress report of the Secretary-General of 23 June 2003.
>
> The Council reaffirms the commitment of all Member States to the sovereignty, independence and territorial integrity of Ethiopia and Eritrea, and its support for the Delimitation Decision of the Eritrea-Ethiopia Boundary Commission of 13 April 2002.
>
> The Council welcomes the public commitment of both parties to a full and expeditious implementation of the comprehensive Peace Agreement signed in Algiers on 12 December 2000, and reaffirms its commitment to contribute to the completion of the peace process. The Council welcomes the parties' acceptance of the Delimitation Decision of 13 April 2002 as final and binding.
>
> The Council welcomes the fact that the situation in the Temporary Security Zone has remained calm and that the parties have cooperated well with the Special Representative of the Secretary-General and with the United Nations Mission in Ethiopia and Eritrea. The Council reiterates its serious concern about outstanding issues referred to in the report of the Secretary-General, in particular some restrictions on the freedom of movement of the Mission that remain and the continuing absence of a direct high-altitude flight route for aircraft of the Mission between Asmara and Addis Ababa, resulting in additional costs to the Mission.
>
> The Council supports the observation made by the Secretary-General in his progress report that ex-

peditious demarcation of the border is crucial, and expresses concern at the delays so far, particularly given the operational cost of the Mission at a time of growing demands on United Nations peacekeeping. Delays would be contrary to the wish of both parties to achieve lasting peace and stability as manifested in the Algiers Agreement.

The Council urges the parties to provide their full and prompt cooperation to the Boundary Commission for the beginning of demarcation in Sector East and for the initiation of survey work in Sectors Centre and West. The Council calls upon the parties to pursue any matters that may arise in connection with the implementation of the Delimitation Decision of the Boundary Commission within the provisions of the Algiers Agreement.

The Council encourages the parties to continue their cooperation with the Military Coordination Commission in order to resolve military and security coordination issues arising from the activities of the Boundary Commission. The Council welcomes assurances given by both parties regarding the provision of security for the staff of the Boundary Commission and contractors operating in the Temporary Security Zone and adjacent areas during demarcation.

The Council regrets the absence of political contacts between the parties. It believes that political dialogue between the two countries is crucial for the success of the peace process and the consolidation of progress made thus far. The Council calls upon both parties to normalize their relationship through political dialogue, including confidence-building measures such as holding alternating meetings of the Military Coordination Commission in each other's capital.

The Council underlines the readiness of the United Nations to facilitate political dialogue if requested and to offer strong support in addressing the humanitarian and development challenges that would result from the demarcation of the border.

The Council encourages the Mission to continue its local outreach activities in order to provide valuable information about the peace process and mine-awareness programmes to the local population. The Council welcomes the intention of the Mission to continue quick-impact projects, which provide direct assistance to communities in the border regions, and welcomes the recommendation of the Secretary-General contained in paragraph 22 of his report. The Council, expressing appreciation to those Member States that have already provided contributions to the Trust Fund in Support of the Delimitation and Demarcation of the Ethiopia-Eritrea Border and to the Trust Fund to Support the Peace Process in Ethiopia and Eritrea, calls upon Member States in a position to do so to urgently provide further support to these Trust Funds.

The Council is concerned about the serious shortfall of resources received in response to the consolidated appeals to address the humanitarian consequences of the drought in Ethiopia and Eritrea and calls upon Member States and the international community to contribute generously to these appeals.

Report of Secretary-General (September). To his 4 September progress report on Ethiopia and Eritrea [S/2003/858], the Secretary-General annexed the Boundary Commission's tenth report (see below).

During the reporting period, the situation in the Temporary Security Zone and the adjacent areas remained generally calm, and the opposing forces reduced their training and related activities at forward locations on both sides of the Zone. UNMEE, in monitoring the positions of the armed forces of both sides and observing militia and police activities, found that cooperation remained good. However, the number of Ethiopian herdsmen and livestock entering the Zone on a daily basis in Sector Centre had again increased. On a number of occasions, Ethiopian militia fired shots from their territory to signal to the herdsmen the presence of Eritrean militia in the vicinity. In August, several more serious incidents occurred in Sector Centre. Ethiopian militia, on two occasions, pointed their weapons at UNMEE patrols in response to advice not to enter the Zone. At other times, a total of 102 personnel, most of them in Ethiopian army uniforms, entered the Zone and refused to leave when UNMEE protested. In Sector West, livestock rustling increased across the southern boundary of the Zone. With ICRC assistance, UNMEE recovered and repatriated to Ethiopia the mortal remains of 220 fallen soldiers discovered in former battlefields.

The two parties continued to impose restrictions on the Mission's freedom of movement in the Zone and adjacent areas, particularly in Sector Centre. There was no improvement with regard to the difficulties faced by UNMEE personnel entering and exiting the airports in Addis Ababa and Asmara and there were still no direct UN flights between the capitals.

The Military Coordination Commission held its seventeenth and eighteenth meetings (Nairobi, 16 June and 30 July) to discuss demining in support of demarcation; the recovery and repatriation of mortal remains in Sector East; demobilization and restructuring of the armed forces of the two countries; the schedule of the Boundary Commission's activities; security of Commission contractors; and other demarcation issues. Efforts to have the parties hold meetings alternately in the two capitals were not successful.

The Boundary Commission held an internal meeting (New York, 10-11 August) to discuss technical issues relating to the demarcation of the border. The Special Representative attended part of the meeting in order to brief the Commission on UNMEE efforts to support demarcation. He also discussed means of monitoring the parties' provision of security for the Commission's field staff and contractors, in accordance with Security Council resolutions. Meanwhile, the Commission had prepared marked maps of Sector East, showing the line and proposed sites for the boundary pillars. The maps were sent to the parties for comments on 21 August. As the work progressed, UNMEE intensified its demining activities in the border areas, including access routes to possible boundary pillar sites.

The Eritrea-Ethiopia Claims Commission issued its first awards on 1 July. They concerned the treatment of prisoners of war by the two countries during the 1998-2000 conflict. The Commission made 12 findings of liability for violation of international law against Eritrea and eight findings against Ethiopia. The most serious issues of liability against Ethiopia were the failure to provide a proper diet and the delay in repatriation. Those against Eritrea were the refusal to allow ICRC to visit prisoner-of-war camps, failing to protect Ethiopian prisoners of war from being killed at capture and permitting pervasive and continuous physical and mental abuse.

Demining activities continued, but the danger of landmines and unexploded ordnance remained. From early June to mid-August, 14 mine-related incidents occurred in Sectors West and Centre, killing two civilians and injuring 17. Investigations revealed that some of the mines in Sector West were newly planted by unknown perpetrators. From 1 June to 10 August, UNMEE destroyed 62 mines and 821 pieces of unexploded ordnance, and cleared 2.4 million square metres of land and 282.5 kilometres of road. Route verification and road clearance for Sector West were completed in mid-July.

The drought in Ethiopia and Eritrea remained a major concern (see also p. 927 and 961), with more than 13.2 million people in Ethiopia and 2 million in Eritrea in need of relief. In view of the seriousness of the situation, the Secretary-General appointed Martti Ahtisaari in June as his Special Envoy for the Humanitarian Crisis in the Horn of Africa. UNMEE and its implementing partners completed 77 quick-impact projects in the areas of water supply, education and health and sanitation, and 31 additional projects were approved. UNMEE requested Ethiopia to permit access to refugee camps near the Temporary Security Zone, but was turned down. Under ICRC auspices, 213 Ethiopian and six Eritrean civilians were repatriated.

The Secretary-General urged Eritrea and Ethiopia to do their utmost to prevent cross-border incidents before they escalated, and, above all, to proceed with the expeditious demarcation of the border. According to the Boundary Commission's schedule of activities, the first step was the appointment of field liaison officers for the remaining demarcation activities. Eritrea had made those appointments, but until Ethiopia made its appointments and provided the necessary security assurances, it would not be possible for the Commission to begin the field surveys. The Secretary-General again warned that the peace process should not be allowed to lose momentum. The delays in the demarcation process were a source of concern, particularly given the operational cost of UNMEE at a time of growing demands on UN peacekeeping. UNMEE was never meant to be a permanent arrangement. The time might be approaching when the parties would have to be more actively assisted in fulfilling both the letter and the spirit of the Algiers Agreements and concluding the process without further delay. In the meantime, UNMEE had to carry out its mandate, which the Secretary-General recommended should be extended for an additional six months, until 15 March 2004.

Boundary Commission (August). In its tenth report covering 10 June to 29 August, the Boundary Commission stated that the UN Committee on Contracts had approved the selection of contractors for boundary pillar emplacement and the survey of boundary pillars. Once the contracts had been signed, deployment of staff and equipment to the Eastern Sector could begin, with pillar emplacement scheduled to commence shortly thereafter. Preparations for pillar emplacement were continuing in the remaining two sectors. Eritrea had notified the Commission of the appointment of its field liaison officers and had approved the establishment of contractors' accommodation and meal facilities at Barentu. Preparations were continuing for establishing similar facilities in Adigrat and Assab. The Commission had requested the parties to develop procedures for ensuring the security of all demarcation personnel, including arrangements for communication and for facilitating UNMEE's role. Expeditious demarcation of the boundary depended on the cooperation of the two parties, including the granting of prompt approval for flights and site inspections.

SECURITY COUNCIL ACTION (September)

On 12 September [meeting 4822], the Security Council unanimously adopted **resolution 1507 (2003)**. The draft [S/2003/872] was prepared in consultations among Council members.

The Security Council,

Reaffirming all its previous resolutions and the statements by its President pertaining to the situation between Ethiopia and Eritrea, and the requirements contained therein, including in particular resolution

1466(2003) of 14 March 2003 and the statement by its President of 17 July 2003,

Reaffirming its unwavering support for the peace process and its commitment, including through the role played by the United Nations Mission in Ethiopia and Eritrea in the implementation of its mandate, to the full and expeditious implementation of the comprehensive Peace Agreement signed at Algiers by the Governments of Ethiopia and Eritrea (hereinafter referred to as "the parties") on 12 December 2000 and the preceding Agreement on Cessation of Hostilities signed on 18 June 2000 ("the Algiers Agreements"), and the delimitation decision of the Boundary Commission of 13 April 2002, embraced by the parties as final and binding in accordance with the Algiers Agreements,

Noting that the peace process has now entered its crucial phase of demarcation, and emphasizing the importance of ensuring expeditious implementation of the decision of the Boundary Commission while maintaining stability in all areas affected by the decision,

Expressing concern at delays in the demarcation process, particularly given the operational cost of the Mission at a time of growing demands on United Nations peacekeeping,

Expressing concern also at the continuing humanitarian crisis in Ethiopia and Eritrea and the implications that this could have on the peace process, and calling upon Member States to continue to provide prompt and generous support for humanitarian operations in Ethiopia and Eritrea,

Reiterating its urgent demand that the parties allow the Mission full freedom of movement and remove with immediate effect any and all restrictions on, and impediments to the work of, the Mission and its staff in the discharge of their mandate,

Expressing concern regarding the reported increase in incidents of incursions at the local level into the Temporary Security Zone and calling upon both parties to prevent such incidents, and expressing further concern about the increasing number of mine incidents in the Temporary Security Zone, including newly planted mines,

Noting the work done by the Mine Action Coordination Centre of the Mission in demining and education on risk related to mines, and urging the parties to pursue efforts on mine clearance,

Having considered the report of the Secretary-General of 4 September 2003, and fully supporting the observations and recommendations made therein,

1. *Decides* to extend the mandate of the United Nations Mission in Ethiopia and Eritrea until 15 March 2004 at the troop and military observer levels authorized by its resolution 1320(2000) of 15 September 2000;

2. *Calls for* the demarcation of the boundary to begin as scheduled by the Boundary Commission, and further calls upon the parties to create the necessary conditions for demarcation to proceed, including the appointment of field liaison officers;

3. *Urges* the Governments of Ethiopia and Eritrea to assume their responsibilities and to take further concrete steps to fulfil their commitments under the Algiers Agreements;

4. *Calls upon* Ethiopia and Eritrea to cooperate fully and promptly with the Boundary Commission to enable it to fulfil the mandate conferred upon it by the parties of expeditiously demarcating the boundary and to implement fully the Demarcation Directions and Orders of the Commission, and to take all necessary steps to provide the necessary security on the ground for the staff and contractors of the Commission operating in territories under their control, and welcomes assurances given by both parties in this regard;

5. *Urges* the parties to cooperate fully and expeditiously with the Mission in the implementation of its mandate, to ensure the personal security of all Mission staff operating in territories under their control and to facilitate their work, including by establishing a direct high-altitude flight route between Asmara and Addis Ababa to relieve the unnecessary additional cost to the Mission and by lifting all visa restrictions on Mission personnel and mission partners;

6. *Reaffirms* the crucial importance of political dialogue between the two countries for the success of the peace process and the consolidation of progress made so far, welcomes initiatives to facilitate this dialogue, and calls again upon both parties to normalize their relations through political dialogue, including confidence-building measures;

7. *Decides* to follow closely the progress made by the parties in the implementation of their commitments under the Algiers Agreements, including through the Boundary Commission, and to review any implications for the Mission;

8. *Welcomes* the contributions by Member States to the Trust Fund in Support of the Delimitation and Demarcation of the Ethiopia-Eritrea Border, and calls upon the international community to continue to contribute urgently to the Trust Fund in order to facilitate the conclusion of the demarcation process in accordance with the schedule of the Boundary Commission;

9. *Decides* to remain actively seized of the matter.

Communication. The EU Presidency, in a 23 September statement [S/2003/925], expressed concern at delays in the demarcation process and called on the parties to abide by the peace agreements, the Boundary Commission's rulings and Security Council resolution 1507(2003) (above) so as to ensure that the border demarcation began as scheduled. The EU called on both Governments to normalize their relationship through political dialogue in order to ensure the success of the peace process.

Report of Secretary-General (December). On 19 December [S/2003/1186], the Secretary-General issued a progress report on Ethiopia and Eritrea, to which was annexed the eleventh report of the Boundary Commission (see p. 239).

During the reporting period, serious difficulties in the peace process had resulted from delays in implementing the Boundary Commission's decision and inflammatory rhetoric of the parties in that regard. However, the overall situation in the Temporary Security Zone and adjacent areas remained relatively stable. UNMEE reported that cooperation with the parties on the ground remained relatively good, although Eritrea continued to hinder the Mission's freedom of movement. There was an increase in military training exercises in September and October on both sides, in particular in Ethiopia, but those manoeuvres subsided towards the end of the reporting period. The incursions by Ethiopian herdsmen and their livestock into the Zone decreased marginally and incidents of armed Ethiopian militia accompanying them had all but ceased. On 1 November, a shooting incident took place near Fawlina in the Zone's Sector West. Reportedly, a small group of uniformed men fired on two Eritrean militiamen, killing one of them. Another incident occurred on 10 December, when Eritrean militiamen exchanged fire with four Ethiopian soldiers.

Towards the end of the reporting period, UNMEE faced greater restrictions on its movement, particularly on the Eritrean side, and it appeared that Eritrea was hardening its unfounded position that the UNMEE mandate was limited solely to monitoring the Zone and that it had no mandate to monitor the redeployed positions of the armed forces of both parties outside the Zone. UNMEE staff entering and exiting Ethiopia and Eritrea continued to experience difficulties at the airports in Addis Ababa and Asmara, including through the imposition of visa regimes. No direct flights were allowed between the capitals.

The Military Coordination Commission held meetings in Nairobi on 17 September, 5 November and 15 December. While acknowledging difficulties in the peace process at the political level, the two sides stressed their commitment to the Commission process and their intention to ensure military stability on the ground. As at 10 December, the total strength of the UNMEE military component was 4,098. Eritrea had still not signed the status-of-forces agreement, despite repeated requests to do so.

Landmines remained a threat to everyone in the Temporary Security Zone and three children were killed in incidents during the reporting period. UNMEE made further progress in mine-clearing, having destroyed 67 mines and 152 pieces of unexploded ordnance and cleared 830,000 square metres of land and 525 kilometres of road. In addition, UNMEE provided training to 3,610 Eritrean civilians in the Temporary Security Zone.

The drought and consequences of the border war, coupled with the poverty in Eritrea and Ethiopia, remained of major concern to the United Nations and its humanitarian partners. Related issues of concern included malnutrition, displaced persons unable to return to their homes, the repatriation and reintegration of Eritrean refugees from the Sudan, and widespread disease. The General Assembly, in **resolution 58/24** of 5 December (see p. 961), took action on emergency humanitarian assistance to Ethiopia. A total of 82 quick-impact projects had been completed in the Zone and adjacent areas, most of which focused on water, education and health.

In the area of human rights, UNMEE continued to monitor cross-border abductions, detentions and disappearances, most of which were resolved quickly. It monitored camps populated by internally displaced persons, deportees and returnees, and sought to improve conditions for the safe return of Eritrean civilians to five border villages. The number of Eritrean refugees and asylum-seekers at the camp near Shiraro, Ethiopia, continued to grow. In October, the arrival of 300 new refugees brought the total to 6,200, including nearly 4,000 ethnic Kunama who left Eritrea after the war when the Ethiopian forces withdrew from Sector West. UNMEE had not been allowed to visit that camp although the population fell within the Mission's human rights mandate.

In general, the situation between Ethiopia and Eritrea remained difficult, even precarious, at the end of the year. While there were no evident signs of preparations for hostilities by either side, recent inflammatory statements, in particular in Eritrea, had done nothing to advance the peace process. A fundamental requirement for the successful completion of the peace process and normalization of relations between the two sides lay in the expeditious demarcation of their common border. While welcoming Eritrea's continued cooperation with the Boundary Commission, the Secretary-General regretted Ethiopia's failure to extend the necessary cooperation, and he emphasized the importance and mutual benefits that would be derived from normalizing relations. He encouraged any positive initiative undertaken towards political dialogue between the two countries, including that of the AU Chairman.

Boundary Commission (November). In its eleventh report, which was annexed to the Secretary-General's December report (above), the Boundary Commission stated that Eritrea had appointed its field liaison officers, submitted a proposal for security arrangements for the boundary demarcation work and paid its contributions to the Commission's expenses. Although Ethiopia had yet to respond on those matters, it had indicated that it would appoint field liaison officers and give security assurances in relation only to the Eastern Sector and Mareb River section of the boundary. The contractors selected to emplace pillars along the whole boundary would not conclude a contract unless given security assurances. A work programme had been prepared for the field assessment of pillar sites and the parties' liaison representatives had been contacted to discuss the programme, security in the field and the demarcation in the Eastern Sector. On 19 September, the Prime Minister of Ethiopia wrote to the Secretary-General, describing the Commission's decisions on Badme and parts of Sector Centre as illegal, unjust and irresponsible, thus making it clear that Ethiopia's complaint was with the delimitation decision rather than with the demarcation process. At a meeting between the Commission and the parties (The Hague, 19 November), Ethiopia expressed willingness to agree to pillar emplacement in the Eastern Sector, while refusing to permit work in the other two sectors. Eritrea maintained its position that the demarcation of the boundary could not be divided as Ethiopia sought since there was no assurance that Ethiopia would not raise insuperable problems in relation to the demarcation of the remaining sectors of the boundary. The Commission concluded that Ethiopia was presenting its dissatisfaction with the boundary as laid down in the delimitation decision in the form of procedural impediments to the demarcation process, which it was not entitled to interpose. Until the positions of either or both parties were modified, there was nothing more that the Commission could do. For the time being, it would maintain its presence in the area but would reduce its activity to the minimum compatible with its being able to resume it, if and when the parties made it possible.

UNMEE financing

On 5 February [A/57/672], the Secretary-General submitted to the General Assembly the financial performance report on UNMEE for 1 July 2001 to 30 June 2002. The Assembly had apportioned $198,400,000 for the operation of the Mission for that period, of which $185,007,700 was spent, resulting in an unencumbered balance of $13,392,300, a variance of 6.8 per cent.

Having reviewed that report, as well as the Secretary-General's proposed budget for UNMEE for 1 July 2003 to 30 June 2004 [YUN 2002, p. 195], ACABQ issued an 8 April report [A/57/772/Add.8 & Corr.1] containing its comments. It recommended that the unencumbered balance and interest and other income in the amount of $10,547,000 be credited to Member States in a manner to be determined by the Assembly. In view of the persistent underexpenditures experienced by UNMEE, ACABQ recommended that the estimated budget requirement of $198,400,000 be reduced by $10,000,000, or approximately 5 per cent. Accordingly, it recommended that the Assembly appropriate $188,400,000 gross for the period 1 July 2003 to 30 June 2004.

GENERAL ASSEMBLY ACTION

On 18 June [meeting 90], the General Assembly, on the recommendation of the Fifth Committee [A/57/828], adopted **resolution 57/328** without vote [agenda item 130].

Financing of the United Nations Mission in Ethiopia and Eritrea

The General Assembly,

Having considered the reports of the Secretary-General on the financing of the United Nations Mission in Ethiopia and Eritrea and the related reports of the Advisory Committee on Administrative and Budgetary Questions,

Bearing in mind Security Council resolution 1312(2000) of 31 July 2000, by which the Council established the United Nations Mission in Ethiopia and Eritrea, and the subsequent resolutions by which the Council extended the mandate of the Mission, the latest of which was resolution 1466(2003) of 14 March 2003,

Recalling its resolution 55/237 of 23 December 2000 on the financing of the Mission and its subsequent resolutions thereon, the latest of which was resolution 56/250 B of 27 June 2002,

Reaffirming the general principles underlying the financing of United Nations peacekeeping operations, as stated in General Assembly resolutions 1874(S-IV) of 27 June 1963, 3101(XXVIII) of 11 December 1973 and 55/235 of 23 December 2000,

Noting with appreciation that voluntary contributions have been made to the Mission,

Mindful of the fact that it is essential to provide the Mission with the necessary financial resources to enable it to fulfil its responsibilities under the relevant resolutions of the Security Council,

1. *Takes note* of the status of contributions to the United Nations Mission in Ethiopia and Eritrea as at 31 March 2003, including the contributions outstanding in the amount of 30.3 million United States dollars, representing some 6 per cent of the total assessed contributions, notes with concern that only thirty-two Member States have paid their assessed contributions in full, and urges all other Member States, in particular those in arrears, to ensure payment of their outstanding assessed contributions;

2. *Expresses its appreciation* to those Member States which have paid their assessed contributions in full, and urges all other Member States to make every possible effort to ensure payment of their assessed contributions to the Mission in full;

3. *Expresses concern* at the financial situation with regard to peacekeeping activities, in particular as regards the reimbursements to troop contributors that bear additional burdens owing to overdue payments by Member States of their assessments;

4. *Also expresses concern* at the delay experienced by the Secretary-General in deploying and providing adequate resources to some recent peacekeeping missions, in particular those in Africa;

5. *Emphasizes* that all future and existing peacekeeping missions shall be given equal and non-discriminatory treatment in respect of financial and administrative arrangements;

6. *Also emphasizes* that all peacekeeping missions shall be provided with adequate resources for the effective and efficient discharge of their respective mandates;

7. *Reiterates its request* to the Secretary-General to make the fullest possible use of facilities and equipment at the United Nations Logistics Base at Brindisi, Italy, in order to minimize the costs of procurement for the Mission;

8. *Endorses* the conclusions and recommendations contained in the report of the Advisory Committee on Administrative and Budgetary Questions, and requests the Secretary-General to ensure their full implementation;

9. *Requests* the Secretary-General to take all necessary action to ensure that the Mission is administered with a maximum of efficiency and economy;

10. *Also requests* the Secretary-General, in order to reduce the cost of employing General Service staff, to continue efforts to recruit local staff for the Mission against General Service posts, commensurate with the requirements of the Mission;

Financial performance report for the period from 1 July 2001 to 30 June 2002

11. *Takes note* of the report of the Secretary-General on the financial performance of the Mission for the period from 1 July 2001 to 30 June 2002;

Budget estimates for the period from 1 July 2003 to 30 June 2004

12. *Decides* to appropriate to the Special Account for the United Nations Mission in Ethiopia and Eritrea the amount of 196,890,300 dollars for the period from 1 July 2003 to 30 June 2004, inclusive of 188.4 million dollars for the maintenance of the Mission, 6,501,300 dollars for the support account for peacekeeping operations and 1,989,000 dollars for the United Nations Logistics Base;

Financing of the appropriation

13. *Decides also* to apportion among Member States the amount of 196,890,300 dollars at a monthly rate of 16,407,525 dollars, in accordance with the levels set out in resolution 55/235, as adjusted by the General Assembly in its resolutions 55/236 of 23 December 2000 and 57/290 A of 20 December 2002, and taking into account the scale of assessments for 2003, as set out in its resolutions 55/5 B of 23 December 2000 and 57/4 B of 20 December 2002, and for 2004, subject to the decision of the Security Council to extend the mandate of the Mission;

14. *Decides further* that, in accordance with the provisions of its resolution 973(X) of 15 December 1955, there shall be set off against the apportionment among Member States, as provided for in paragraph 13 above, their respective share in the Tax Equalization Fund of 5,482,300 dollars at a monthly rate of 456,858 dollars, comprising the estimated staff assessment income of 3.9 million dollars approved for the Mission, the prorated share of 1,464,700 dollars of the estimated staff assessment income approved for the support account and the prorated share of 117,600 dollars of the estimated staff assessment income approved for the United Nations Logistics Base;

15. *Decides* that for Member States that have fulfilled their financial obligations to the Mission, there shall be set off against their apportionment, as provided for in paragraph 13 above, their respective share of the unencumbered balance and other income in the total amount of 23,939,300 dollars in respect of the financial period ended 30 June 2002, in accordance with the levels set out in resolution 55/235, as adjusted by the General Assembly in its resolutions 55/236 and 57/290 A, and taking into account the scale of assessments for 2002, as set out in its resolutions 55/5 B and 57/4 B;

16. *Decides also* that for Member States that have not fulfilled their financial obligations to the Mission, there shall be set off against their outstanding obligations their respective share of the unencumbered balance and other income in the total amount of 23,939,300 dollars in respect of the financial period ended 30 June 2002, in accordance with the scheme set out in paragraph 15 above;

17. *Decides further* that the decrease of 402,200 dollars in the estimated staff assessment income in respect of the financial period ended 30 June 2002 shall be set off against the credits from the amount referred to in paragraphs 15 and 16 above;

18. *Emphasizes* that no peacekeeping operation shall be financed by borrowing funds from other active peacekeeping operations;

19. *Encourages* the Secretary-General to continue to take additional measures to ensure the safety and security of all personnel under the auspices of the United Nations participating in peacekeeping operations;

20. *Invites* voluntary contributions to the Mission in cash and in the form of services and supplies acceptable to the Secretary-General, to be administered, as appropriate, in accordance with the procedure and practices established by the General Assembly;

21. *Decides* to include in the provisional agenda of its fifty-eighth session the item entitled "Financing of the United Nations Mission in Ethiopia and Eritrea".

On 19 December [A/57/658], the Secretary-General submitted to the Assembly the budget for UNMEE for 1 July 2004 to 30 June 2005, which amounted to $201,460,800 gross. The budget provided for the deployment of 3,980 troops, 220 military observers, 256 international staff, 273 national staff and 82 United Nations Volunteers.

Somalia

During 2003, Somali leaders and their representatives, with the notable exception of those from Somaliland, continued to participate in the deliberations of the Eldoret (Kenya) Conference Process, which, in October 2002, under the auspices of IGAD, had led to the signing of the Declaration on Cessation of Hostilities and the Structures and Principles of the Somalia National Reconciliation Process (the Eldoret Declaration) [YUN 2002, p. 202]. Despite the Eldoret Declaration and the signing in December 2002 by five Mogadishu faction leaders and the Transitional National Government (TNG), set up by the Arta (Djibouti) Conference in 2000 [YUN 2000, p. 215], of agreements on ensuring security in Mogadishu and on reopening the airport and seaport there, fighting continued and those facilities remained blocked in 2003. While parts of Somalia remained unstable, relative stability prevailed in significant portions of the country. The six reconciliation committees of the Somali national reconciliation process continued their work despite disagreements over the representation of those bodies. Some progress was made in mid-2003 with the approval of the reports of five of the committees. Disagreements on federalism and a provisional charter remained the major stumbling block. On 5 July, the Somali Leaders Committee at the Conference reached an accord on a federal system of government, which was adopted by the plenary. However, the TNG President said his Government rejected the agreement, and other Somali leaders also denounced it. The situation was complicated by the 26 August expiration of TNG, as stipulated by the Arta Conference.

The United Nations Political Office for Somalia (UNPOS), led by the Secretary-General's Representative, Winston A. Tubman (Liberia), remained involved in the peace process and humanitarian efforts, and continued to operate from Nairobi.

Conflict and violence within Somalia continued to cause suffering and to hinder humanitarian activities throughout the year; UN activities were curtailed due to the insecurity prevailing in many parts of the country. In December, the General Assembly, in **resolution 58/115** (see p. 928), called on the international community to assist in providing humanitarian relief and in the economic and social rehabilitation of Somalia.

Twice during the year, the Panel of Experts established by the Security Council to investigate violations of the arms embargo against Somalia reported on its findings. It determined that Somalia was subject to ongoing violations of the arms embargo, mainly by a continuous inflow of small quantities of weapons and ammunition from regional countries, which fed the local open arms markets and faction leaders' warehouses. The arms flow had consequences for the security and stability of the region. The Council decided to establish a monitoring group to investigate violations of the arms embargo and to make recommendations on strengthening the ban.

National reconciliation process and security situation

Report of Secretary-General (February). The Secretary-General, in a 26 February report on the situation in Somalia [S/2003/231], submitted in response to the request contained in the Security Council President's statement S/PRST/2001/30 [YUN 2001, p. 210], described developments since his previous report in October 2002 [YUN 2002, p. 201]. He focused on the Somali national reconciliation process at Eldoret, held under IGAD auspices and chaired by Kenya.

During the reporting period, many Somali leaders and their representatives participated in the Eldoret Conference discussions, with the main exception of Somaliland, which refused to join the peace process. Inter- and intra-clan fighting continued to break out in a number of places, particularly in south Mogadishu, Baidoa, Luuq, Kismayo and Qardho district. In Somaliland, security conditions remained generally calm, and local and municipal elections took place in December 2002 without incident. "Presidential" and "parliamentary" elections were scheduled for 15 April and late May 2003, respectively.

The security situation in several areas, particularly in the south, the Mogadishu area and Baidoa, posed serious difficulties for the delivery of humanitarian aid, as did the continued closure of the seaport and airport in Mogadishu. The level of banditry and extortion remained high and the kidnapping of Somalis working for the United Nations and other international aid organizations remained a serious concern. Following attacks on aid workers in October and December 2002, a security assessment was carried out and all UN operations in the area were suspended until 14 January 2003. The provision of humanitarian assistance to a significant proportion of the population, already facing destitution, malnutrition and lack of basic social services, was repeatedly disrupted. Baidoa and Mogadishu remained closed to UN international staff because of fighting. Internally displaced persons continued to live in congested and unsanitary conditions in camps. The United Nations Humanitarian Coordinator launched a two-pronged strategy for addressing the issue of humanitarian access, first, by directly engaging with clan and faction leaders in Eldoret; and, secondly, by approaching representatives of the leaders and civil society, business and religious leaders in the field. Once access was more assured, a coordinated response to the needs of vulnerable communities would be established.

The second phase of the Somali national reconciliation process experienced difficulties due to controversy regarding the number of participants both in the plenary meeting of the Conference and in the six reconciliation committees that would report on specific aspects of the process. The Kenyan Special Envoy and Chairman of the IGAD Technical Committee, Elijah Mwangale, decided on a formula that gave an equal number of seats (84 each) to the four main clans of Somalia and half that number to the minority clans as a group. Membership in the six committees remained unresolved, as did the issue of civil society representation. Bethuel Kiplagat was named Kenya's new Special Envoy on 18 January.

The Foreign Ministers of the front-line States (Djibouti, Ethiopia, Kenya) held consultations on the reconciliation process in Addis Ababa on 2 February. Expressing concern about the violations of the Eldoret Declaration, they established a committee to monitor implementation and take appropriate action. They agreed to establish a mechanism to monitor ceasefire violations, which would consist of representatives of the IGAD Technical Committee and international partners. They welcomed the planned relocation of the Conference venue from Eldoret to Mbagathi, on the outskirts of Nairobi, as a cost-saving measure, and agreed to meet once a month to discuss the process; the first meeting was scheduled for 1 March. On 26 January, the Leaders Committee of the Eldoret Conference called for the representation of Somaliland at the national reconciliation process, a call that was promptly rejected by Somaliland.

The Secretary-General's Representative and staff of UNPOS, located in Nairobi, maintained a permanent presence at the Conference and provided assistance to the IGAD Technical Committee, the Somali parties and civil society groups. The Representative also participated in the meeting of the IGAD Foreign Ministers of the front-line States (Addis Ababa, 2 February). Many UN-affiliated bodies and agencies provided assistance in support of peace and reconciliation in Somalia, including the World Bank, UNDP, the United Nations Development Fund for Women, UNHCR, UNICEF, UNESCO, UNFPA, FAO and WHO.

Efforts by the international community to support the Somali national reconciliation process, launched under IGAD auspices and led by Kenya, included the AU's appointment of a Special Envoy for Somalia and a generous financial contribution from the EU.

The Secretary-General observed that the continued outbreaks of hostilities were motivated by individual rivalries of faction leaders and criminal activities rather than wider issues. It was those with weapons of war who continued to hold the people of Somalia hostage to the cycle of violence. He encouraged the Somali leaders participating in the Conference to cooperate in the IGAD-led endeavour aimed at ending over a decade of conflict in Somalia and the suffering it had caused the Somali people. The work of the six reconciliation committees had continued despite controversy regarding representation at the plenary meetings of the Conference. However, serious hostilities involving the militias and supporters of some of the very leaders who had signed the Eldoret Declaration and the December 2002 agreements had hindered the delivery of essential humanitarian and development assistance. The Mogadishu seaport and airport remained closed and fighting in and around Baidoa had blocked off an essential port of entry for delivering assistance.

While some parts of Somalia remained unstable, relative stability continued to prevail in significant portions of the country. In some of those areas, community-based peace-building activities had evolved with little outside support. Those initiatives presented windows of opportunity for the United Nations, NGOs and donors to help to maintain and build upon the peace and stability that had been achieved. Failure to do so could result in renewed conflict over scarce resources as an impoverished people struggled to survive and rebuild their lives. The Secretary-General welcomed contributions to the Trust Fund for Peace-building in Somalia and the early contributions to the 2003 Consolidated Inter-Agency Appeal for Somalia (see p. 928).

SECURITY COUNCIL ACTION (March)

On 12 March [meeting 4718], following consultations among Security Council members, the President made statement **S/PRST/2003/2** on behalf of the Council:

> The Security Council, recalling its decisions concerning the situation in Somalia, in particular the statements by its President of 28 March (S/PRST/2002/8) and 12 December 2002 (S/PRST/2002/35), and welcoming the report of the Secretary-General of 26 February 2003, reaffirms its commitment to a comprehensive and lasting settlement of the situation in Somalia, and its respect for the sovereignty, territorial integrity, political independence and unity of the country, consistent with the purposes and principles of the Charter of the United Nations.
>
> The Council reiterates its firm support for the Somalia National Reconciliation Process and the ongoing Somalia National Reconciliation Conference in Kenya, launched under the auspices of the Intergovernmental Authority on Development and led by the Government of Kenya. The Council strongly encourages all parties throughout Somalia to participate in the process, which offers a unique opportunity for all Somalis to end the suffering of their people and to restore peace and stability to their country. The Council demands that the Somali par-

ties abide by and implement expeditiously the decisions adopted throughout the process, including the Declaration on Cessation of Hostilities and the Structures and Principles of the Somalia National Reconciliation Process of 27 October 2002 (hereinafter referred to as "the Eldoret Declaration"), as well as the December 2002 agreement reached by five Mogadishu faction leaders and the Transitional National Government regarding the restoration of peace and security in Mogadishu and a subsequent agreement among the five faction leaders which included a commitment to make efforts to reopen the international airport and seaport in Mogadishu, as mentioned in paragraph 26 of the report of the Secretary-General.

The Council commends the Government of Kenya for its crucial role in facilitating the Somalia National Reconciliation Process, and calls upon the Technical Committee of the Intergovernmental Authority comprising the three front-line States (Djibouti, Ethiopia and Kenya) to continue their active role in promoting the Process. The Council welcomes the appointment of Ambassador Bethuel Kiplagat as the Special Envoy of Kenya to the Process. The Council also welcomes the appointment of Mr. Muhammad Ali Foum as the Special Envoy of the African Union for Somalia, the generous financial contribution of the European Union, Norway and the United States of America, and the sustained engagement of their envoys, as well as those of the Partners Forum of the Intergovernmental Authority and the League of Arab States. The Council strongly encourages their continued active and positive role in support of the reconciliation process.

The Council notes that the six reconciliation committees of the Somalia National Reconciliation Process have continued their work despite difficulties faced by the Somali participants regarding representation. The Council urges all parties involved to participate fully in the six reconciliation committees and to resolve the representation issue, and welcomes the establishment of an arbitration committee in this regard. The Council supports the commitment of the Secretary-General to assist in the work of the six reconciliation committees with technical support and relevant expertise.

The Council expresses its strong regret that, even after the signing of the Eldoret Declaration, fighting continued to break out in Somalia, in particular in Mogadishu and Baidoa. The Council condemns all those involved in the fighting and calls for an immediate end to all acts of violence in Somalia. The Council shares the conclusion of the Secretary-General that it is those that have weapons of war who continue to hold the people of Somalia hostage to the cycle of violence. The Council also shares the view of the Secretary-General that these people will be held accountable by the Somali people and the international community for their actions if they persist on the path of confrontation and conflict. In this regard, the Council welcomes the establishment of a mechanism by the front-line States of the Intergovernmental Authority to monitor compliance with the Eldoret Declaration and their intention to consider appropriate measures against all individuals and groups violating the Eldoret Declaration and the December 2002 agreements.

The Council notes with serious concern the continued flow of weapons and ammunition supplies to Somalia, as well as allegations of the role of some of the neighbouring States in breach of the arms embargo established pursuant to resolution 733(1992) of 23 January 1992, and calls upon all States and other actors to comply scrupulously with the arms embargo. The Council welcomes the work of the Panel of Experts established pursuant to resolution 1425(2002) of 22 July 2002, and expresses its intention to give full consideration to and take appropriate action regarding the report of the Panel as a step towards reinforcing the arms embargo and disarmament.

The Council, insisting that persons and entities must not be allowed to take advantage of the situation in Somalia to finance, plan, facilitate, support or commit terrorist acts from the country, emphasizes that efforts to combat terrorism in Somalia are inseparable from the establishment of peace and governance in the country. In this spirit, the Council urges the international community to provide assistance to Somalia for the further and comprehensive implementation of resolution 1373(2001) of 28 September 2001.

The Council expresses serious concern regarding the humanitarian situation in Somalia, in particular that of internally displaced persons, especially in the area of Mogadishu. The Council urges the Somali leaders to live up to their commitments under the Eldoret Declaration, to facilitate the delivery of much-needed humanitarian assistance, to ensure the safety of all international and national aid workers, to provide immediate safe access for all humanitarian personnel, and to support the return and reintegration of refugees. The Council calls upon Member States to respond urgently and generously to the United Nations Consolidated Inter-Agency Appeal for 2003.

The Council notes that, while some parts of Somalia remain unstable, relative stability continues to prevail in significant portions of the country. The Council welcomes the evolution of the community-based peace-building activities and calls for the acceleration of comprehensive peace-building activities. The Council requests the Secretary-General to continue putting in place, in a coherent manner, preparatory activities on the ground for a comprehensive post-conflict peace-building mission in Somalia once security conditions permit, as stipulated in the statement by the President of the Security Council of 28 March 2002, which should take into account combating poverty and strengthening public institutions.

The Council stresses that a comprehensive post-conflict peace-building programme with special emphasis on disarmament, demobilization, rehabilitation and reintegration will be an important contribution towards the restoration of peace and stability in Somalia. The Council welcomes the contribution of Ireland, Italy and Norway to the Trust Fund for Peace-building in Somalia and calls upon other donors to do the same without delay.

The Council commends the work done by the United Nations Country Team, the Red Cross and Red Crescent Movements and non-governmental organizations in support of peace and reconciliation in Somalia. The Council encourages the Secretary-General to continue to support actively the Intergovernmental Authority-sponsored Somalia National Reconciliation Process and to continue to implement and enhance ongoing humanitarian and peace-building activities on the ground.

The Council reiterates its commitment to assist the Somali parties and support the mediation by the Intergovernmental Authority in the implementation of the steps and conclusions for peace, as adopted throughout the Somalia National Reconciliation Process.

Report of Secretary-General (June). On 10 June [S/2003/636], the Secretary-General reported on the situation in Somalia over the preceding four months, focusing on the national reconciliation process at Mbagathi, Kenya, and covering political and security developments, humanitarian conditions and UN development activities.

Kenya's new Special Envoy, Mr. Kiplagat, undertook several initiatives to restructure the reconciliation process: he set up a Somali arbitration committee, with representatives from each major clan, to handle the persistent problems relating to representation at the Conference; and, in order to harmonize the reports of the six reconciliation committees, he set up a technical harmonization committee composed of Somali experts. Those committees were working on draft texts on federalism and a provisional charter; disarmament, demobilization and reintegration; land and property rights; economic recovery, institution-building and resource mobilization; conflict resolution and reconciliation; and regional and international relations. Some members of the Somali Leaders Committee objected to the establishment of the technical harmonization committee, preferring instead to handle the harmonization effort at the political level.

The Kenyan Foreign Minister, on 14 May, launched the plenary of the second phase of the Reconciliation Conference, which was to consider the committees' reports. TNG, represented by its Prime Minister and the Speaker of the Transitional National Assembly, and many other leaders continued to participate in the Conference. Others, based in Mogadishu and Kismayo, were absent for almost two months but returned to Mbagathi for the start of the second phase. On 11 March, a TNG representative accused Ethiopia of amassing troops on its border with Somalia and of crossing the border at several locations. He demanded that Ethiopia be excluded from the IGAD Technical Committee (comprising the front-line States and the IGAD secretariat) that was overseeing the reconciliation process. Ethiopia denied the allegations.

Following the decision of the Foreign Ministers of the front-line States to establish a committee to monitor implementation of the Eldoret Declaration, comprising IGAD, the AU, the United Nations, the European Commission, the League of Arab States and some IGAD Partners Forum member States, the Ceasefire Monitoring Committee, on 4 March, addressed the escalation of hostilities in Somalia, in particular the fighting in the Medina district of Mogadishu and the fighting at Buale in the Juba Valley.

The Secretary-General's Representative and UNPOS continued to actively monitor and support the reconciliation process, while the country team and its partners contributed to peace-building and reconciliation efforts inside Somalia. The Representative met with Somali leaders, IGAD representatives and donors to coordinate support for the process. The United Nations continued to support women's human rights issues at the Conference and provided a gender expert to work with the IGAD mediation team. Two meetings of the Somalia Contact Group were held during the reporting period (New York, 14 March; Nairobi, 27 March), at which progress in the reconciliation process was discussed, as well as the need for increased international support in that process. The Commission on Human Rights extended the mandate of the independent expert on the human rights situation in Somalia for another year (see p. 685).

The TNG President, Abdikassim Salad Hassan, and some faction leaders based in Mogadishu met on 27 March. Citing the lack of progress at the Mbagathi Conference, they affirmed their intention to proceed with efforts to restore security in Mogadishu and to convene a Somali national reconciliation conference inside Somalia. Hussein Aidid and a number of Somali leaders who continued their participation at the Mbagathi Conference denounced the Mogadishu meeting as divisive. He urged the Somali leaders meeting in Mogadishu to proceed to Mbagathi. According to the Prime Minister's Office, the Mogadishu meeting was not intended to be an alternative to the Mbagathi Conference but a way to bring security and stability to the capital. Reports indicated that disagreements had emerged between President Hassan, who remained in Mogadishu, and the Prime Minister and the Speaker of the Transitional National Assembly, who were leading the TNG delegation at Mbagathi. Differences on how the reconciliation process should proceed were also reported among members of the delegation. On 26 May, the Prime Minister returned to Mogadishu for consultations.

After an eight-month recess, the Transitional National Assembly reconvened on 28 April with 165 of the 245 members present. It debated the possibilities of reviewing the Transitional National Charter, with the aim of extending TNG's term of office beyond August 2003, when its three-year term expired.

In Somaliland, "presidential elections" took place on 14 April, and the announced winner was the incumbent, Dahir Riyale Kahin. In Puntland, Colonel Abdullahi Yusuf Ahmed and his opponents participated in a reconciliation conference in Bossasso to end the conflict between his administration and the Puntland Salvation Movement, led by General Ade Muse Hirse. The two sides entered into a power-sharing agreement on 17 May. While the security conditions in Somaliland and Puntland remained calm, the border dispute with regard to Sool and Sanaag districts caused tensions between the two administrations.

Security conditions in southern Somalia remained a serious concern, with no clear local authority in many areas that could control the activities of bandits who extorted money from travellers and merchants and where clan feuds continued to claim lives. In March, humanitarian staff were withdrawn from areas where fighting occurred between the Abgal and Habr Gedir subclans. The security situation also remained difficult in Baidoa, Gedo and Kismayo. Although fighting had subsided in the Buale district, the conflict had claimed numerous lives and led to the displacement of people. The situation in Mogadishu remained dangerous and unpredictable, and access to the city for humanitarian agencies was very limited.

The Somali people continued to struggle with chronic food insecurity, poverty, disease, drought and severely limited educational and employment opportunities. Its human development index remained one of the lowest in the world. About 400,000 Somalis were refugees in neighbouring countries, while up to 370,000 others were internally displaced. In May, the UN country team and its partners reviewed the 2003 Common Humanitarian Action Plan, as well as the international response to the United Nations Consolidated Appeal (see p. 928). They noted that considerable progress had been made in the delivery of humanitarian relief, the reintegration of refugees, the promotion of the rule of law through law enforcement training and judicial reform, and poverty reduction through increased remittance flows and livestock exports. However, at that time, only 24 per cent of the $77.8 million requested through the Appeal had been funded.

Peace-building activities by UN agencies were focused on four strategic operational objectives of the country team: protection and human rights; provision of basic services; HIV/AIDS prevention; and education. Progress in all of those areas was ongoing through multi-agency, multi-sectoral peace-building initiatives focused on the enhancement of skills for Somalis, the provision of basic services and exchanges of technical personnel.

Observing that the Somalia National Reconciliation Conference at Mbagathi was about to enter its final phase, which would entail negotiations on the formation of an all-inclusive Government for Somalia, the Secretary-General stated that the future of the reconciliation process continued to rest largely in Somali hands. The international community could only assist the Somali efforts and commitment to end years of conflict and deprivation. He deplored the frequent violations by the Somali parties of their commitments under the Eldoret Declaration and commended the IGAD efforts to monitor implementation of the Declaration, its appointment of a Coordinator of the Ceasefire Monitoring Committee and the AU decision to dispatch monitors to Somalia. He also expressed concern about the absence of some Somali leaders from the Conference, in some cases for two months, alleging insufficient representation or displeasure with the IGAD efforts. Most of them, however, had returned to the Conference to complete the second phase and to initiate the third and final phase on formation of an all-inclusive Government.

Press statement by Security Council (16 July). Following informal consultations on 16 July, the Security Council President issued a press statement [SC/7816-AFR/668] saying that members reiterated their firm support for the ongoing Somali National Reconciliation Conference at Mbagathi. They took note of recent progress and expressed the hope that the Conference would conclude successfully in the near future. Members noted the efforts of the Ceasefire Monitoring Committee in preparing the monitoring of the implementation of the Eldoret Declaration, and the work of the AU and IGAD fact-finding mission to Somalia. They called on all States to comply with the arms embargo against Somalia (see p. 250). They expressed concern regarding the humanitarian situation in Somalia and urged the Somali parties to assure the delivery of humanitarian assistance.

Communications. On 16 June [S/2003/654], South Africa forwarded to the Security Council a communiqué issued by the AU Central Organ of the Mechanism for Conflict Prevention, Management and Resolution (Addis Ababa, 12-13 June), which included a decision on Somalia. The Central Organ expressed appreciation to the IGAD front-line States for their involvement and welcomed the dispatch of the joint technical IGAD-AU fact-finding mission to Somalia from 22 May to 2 June. It expressed the AU's readiness to play the role expected of it in establishing a mechanism to monitor the cessation of hostilities in Somalia, including the deployment of an AU observer mission there, and requested the Interim Chairperson of the Commission of the AU to undertake the necessary consultations with IGAD and the Somali parties towards the establishment of such a mechanism.

On 10 September [S/2003/876], Mozambique forwarded the decisions of another meeting of the Central Organ (Addis Ababa, 29 August). With regard to Somalia, the Central Organ recalled an earlier appeal to the international community to support the deployment of an international force in Somalia to help facilitate the disarmament, demobilization and reintegration process and requested the Commission Chairperson to study all aspects of such a force. It took note of the outcome of the AU reconnaissance mission to Somalia from 22 to 31 July. It requested the Commission Chairperson to pursue his consultations with the Somali parties, the IGAD Technical Committee and AU members on the deployment of an AU Military Observer Mission in Somalia that would precede the deployment of an international force. The Central Organ urged the Somali parties to demonstrate the political will required to bring the Mbagathi Conference to a successful conclusion.

On 16 July [S/2003/756], Italy submitted to the Council an EU statement on the peace process in Somalia. The Union welcomed the signing on 5 July by Somali leaders in Kenya of a document setting out the principles that would govern the passage from the second to the third phase of the Mbagathi Conference, as well as the four years of the transitional federal Government of the Republic of Somalia (see below). The EU urged those leaders who had been unable to return to Kenya to do so, allowing the Conference to move into the third phase.

Agreement on transitional federal Government

The Secretary-General reported in October [S/2003/987] (see p. 248) that the plenary of the Somalia National Reconciliation Conference had endorsed, by mid-June, the reports prepared by five of the six reconciliation committees, namely those on disarmament, demobilization and reintegration; land and property rights; economic recovery, institution-building and resource mobilization; regional and international relations; and conflict resolution and reconciliation. Disagreements in the committee on federalism and a provisional charter prevented it from concluding its report. The major points of disagreement concerned the length of the transitional period, the members of Parliament and the modality for their selection, the timing of the establishment of a federal system of government and the status of the existing regional and local authorities, in particular Somaliland.

President Mwai Kibaki of Kenya announced the appointment of Mohammed Abdi Affey as Kenya's Ambassador to Somalia. He would assist Mr. Kiplagat, the Kenyan Special Envoy and Chairman of the Conference.

On 5 July, after three weeks of negotiations, the Somali Leaders Committee at the Conference reached an accord that was expected to be part of a draft charter. It was agreed that a federal system of government, to be called the transitional federal Government, would be formed in Somalia during a four-year transitional period. The process of federalism would develop gradually and be completed in two and a half years. The Parliament would comprise 351 members, 12 per cent of whom would be women. The signatories to the Eldoret Declaration and political leaders at the Conference, in consultation with traditional leaders within their respective clan structures, would select the members of Parliament. The transitional federal Government would immediately initiate a dialogue on national unity with Somaliland. The agreement was put before the Conference plenary and adopted by acclamation.

The TNG President, Mr. Hassan, criticized the agreement, claiming that it would divide the country because it would implicitly recognize Somaliland. Stating that his Government would not be party to such a process, he disowned the signatures of the TNG Prime Minister and Speaker of the Transitional National Assembly, whom he had designated to lead the TNG delegation to the Conference. He disagreed with the selection process for members of Parliament and objected to the placing of Arabic, along with English, as one of the two second official languages, instead of placing it on the same level as Somali as one of the two first official languages. Other Somali leaders also denounced the 5 July agreement and declared they had withdrawn from the Conference.

The agreement sharpened the differences between Mr. Hassan on the one hand and his Prime Minister and the Speaker of the Assembly on the other. A session of the Assembly was convened in Mogadishu on 9 August, with 124 of the 245 members in attendance, and it voted for the removal of the Prime Minister and the Speaker. Discussions on the draft charter continued from 5 July until 15 September, and the IGAD Technical Committee worked with the participants to address the concerns raised by some Somali leaders. Mr. Kiplagat circulated a fourth version raising the status of Arabic and affirming the sovereignty and territorial integrity of Somalia. A fifth version removed the call for negotiations with Somaliland. Differences remained on implementation of federalism during the transition. After protracted discussions, a draft charter was adopted on 15 September, but that outcome was rejected by Mr. Hassan and other Somali leaders who had returned to Nairobi. International observers, including the Secretary-General's Representative, tried to find a middle ground between the 5 July agreement and the 15 September decision. On 20 September, Mr. Hassan and the other leaders returned to Mogadishu, stating that the Conference had collapsed and that they would open another reconciliation process in Somalia.

The AU (Maputo, Mozambique, 10-12 July) endorsed the Somali national reconciliation process and undertook to deploy a military observer mission to Somalia to monitor the cessation of hostilities as provided for in the Eldoret Declaration once a comprehensive agreement was reached. Subsequently, an AU/IGAD reconnaissance mission visited Somalia (21-31 July) in an effort to establish mechanisms to support the deployment of some 75 AU monitors. Having encountered difficulties and threats during its visit, the mission concluded that, given the prevailing political and military conditions, more work was needed before military observers could be deployed. It emphasized that the Somali leaders it had consulted were ready to disarm but that for that to happen the assistance of the international community was essential.

Report of Secretary-General (October). In his October report [S/2003/987], the Secretary-General stated that security in the southern parts of Somalia, including Mogadishu, remained precarious. Mounting crime in Mogadishu included frequent abductions, carjackings and civilian deaths. Fierce clashes broke out in Jawhar in July but calm returned in September. Militias clashed in July over control of water in South Mudug, resulting in some 50 people killed. Inter-clan fighting around Baidoa also continued. The lack of local authority and lawlessness made many areas inaccessible to aid workers. Nonetheless, several NGOs and UN agencies continued minimal operations, primarily in the health and education sectors. Puntland authorities agreed that aid workers could visit vulnerable communities in the Sool and Sanaag regions. Those areas, claimed by both Somaliland and Puntland, were visited by the resident and humanitarian coordinator for an assessment. As a result of the combination of food insecurity and poor health conditions, Somalis continued to suffer from malnutrition.

UN agencies were helping authorities in Somalia to improve the administration of justice by developing the rule of law, building their capacity to enforce the law and improving the application of human rights standards. Those programmes had been implemented only in the relatively peaceful area in the north-west, mainly in Somaliland, but plans were being made to expand them to less stable regions in the north-east, centre and south. Activities included the drawing up of training programmes for legal professionals and administrators, helping to draft a statute on establishing a human rights commission, working on establishing legal aid clinics, assessing the rehabilitation needs of court buildings, and building up the capacity of mine action services. On the basis of a child protection study, priority areas to be addressed were identified, including sexual violence, children engaged in exploitative labour, protection of children with disabilities, and minority children. UN agencies and their partners completed assessments of the judiciary system and collated recommendations on ways to improve justice as it affected women. Training was provided to women's organizations for the formation of a women's national human rights advocacy network, the development of advocacy tools and training manuals, the integration of gender and human rights issues into legal systems, and the inclusion of a bill of rights in the future federal and regional charters.

With regard to the refugee situation, UNHCR and other agencies worked with local authorities to assure protection, assistance and durable solutions. From the beginning of 2003, 5,569 people were voluntarily repatriated to Somaliland and Puntland from Djibouti, Ethiopia and Kenya. A UN reintegration programme in north-west Somalia provided new classrooms and furniture for 16 schools. It also carried out projects to repair roads, rehabilitate dams and wells, reconstruct schools and health facilities, and complete a water system to provide clean water to 60,000 people. The World Bank, in addition to its low-income countries under stress initiative, was funding, with the European Commission, the development of a Somali livestock sector strategy. UN agencies continued efforts to improve the standards, procedures and international acceptance of the Somali remittance industry. The strategic framework for the prevention and control of

HIV/AIDS and sexually transmitted infections within Somali populations was finalized, providing a foundation on which to build interventions throughout the country.

The Secretary-General observed that, notwithstanding the progress made at the Mbagathi Conference in approving the reports of the five reconciliation committees, further advances had been slow owing to the differences on the issue of federalism and on the relationship of the future transitional Government with existing regional and local authorities, in particular Somaliland. The situation had been complicated by the expiration on 26 August of the TNG mandate, deriving from the agreement reached in August 2000 at the Somali National Peace Conference held at Arta, Djibouti [YUN 2000, p. 215]. Somali leaders faced the challenge of bridging their differences in order to reach agreement on a viable government.

At the current critical juncture in the reconciliation process, the sustained commitment of the IGAD front-line States, in particular, remained vital for the success of the Conference, the Secretary-General affirmed. Key UN Member States, from within and outside the region, should monitor and support the efforts of Somali leaders and the IGAD Technical Committee to help ensure that the Conference culminated in an inclusive and comprehensive agreement. UNPOS and the UN country team were developing a peace-building plan to be implemented in Somalia once a definitive agreement was reached at the Conference.

Pending an agreement at the Conference and improvement of the security situation that would permit him to propose the establishment of a peace-building office in Somalia and adjustments to the UNPOS mandate, the Secretary-General intended to continue UNPOS activities for the 2004-2005 biennium at the current resource level.

The Secretary-General restated that intention on 10 November [S/2003/1092]; on 13 November [S/2003/1093], the Council took note of the information and intention.

Appointment. The Secretary-General, on 22 October [S/2003/1051], informed the Security Council that the mandate of his Representative for Somalia, Winston A. Tubman, would expire at the end of 2003. Mr. Tubman had been working to advance the peace process through contacts with Somali leaders, civic organizations and the States and organizations concerned, and had provided support to the National Reconciliation Conference that was ongoing in Kenya. The Secretary-General intended to extend his mandate until 31 December 2004. On 28 October [S/2003/1052], the Council took note of the information.

SECURITY COUNCIL ACTION (November)

On 11 November [meeting 4856], following consultations among Security Council members, the President made statement **S/PRST/2003/19** on behalf of the Council:

> The Security Council, recalling its previous decisions concerning the situation in Somalia, in particular the statement by its President of 12 March 2003, and welcoming the report of the Secretary-General of 13 October 2003, reaffirms its commitment to a comprehensive and lasting settlement of the situation in Somalia and its respect for the sovereignty, territorial integrity, political independence and unity of the country, consistent with the purposes and principles of the Charter of the United Nations.
>
> The Council reiterates its firm support for the Somali National Reconciliation Process launched under the auspices of the Intergovernmental Authority on Development and led by Kenya. The Council commends the progress made and acknowledges the challenges ahead.
>
> The Council welcomes the relevant decisions made by the tenth Summit of the Intergovernmental Authority on Development and the first Intergovernmental Authority on Development Ministerial Facilitation Committee meeting on the Somali peace process in October 2003.
>
> The Council urges all Somali leaders to participate constructively in the meeting of leaders planned by the Facilitation Committee in Kenya in November 2003 to bridge their differences and to reach agreements on a viable government and a durable and inclusive solution to the conflict in Somalia.
>
> The Council commends the Government of Kenya for its crucial role in facilitating the Somali National Reconciliation Process, and President Yoweri Museveni of Uganda for joining in the facilitation work, and encourages the Facilitation Committee to work concertedly towards a successful conclusion of the Process.
>
> The Council also commends the support given by the African Union to the Somali National Reconciliation Process, including its participation in the Process and its commitment to deploy a military observer mission to Somalia once a comprehensive agreement is reached.
>
> The Council calls upon the international community to continue its efforts to support the Intergovernmental Authority in its facilitation of the Somali National Reconciliation Process, and calls upon the donor countries to contribute to the Process, the Trust Fund for Peace-building in Somalia and the United Nations Consolidated Inter-Agency Appeal for Somalia.
>
> The Council expresses serious concern regarding the humanitarian situation in Somalia, and calls upon the Somali leaders to facilitate the delivery of much-needed humanitarian assistance and to assure the safety of all international and national aid workers.

The Council welcomes the forthcoming mission of the Security Council Committee established pursuant to resolution 751 (1992) to Somalia and States in the region, from 11 to 21 November 2003, as a step towards giving full effect to the arms embargo. The Council calls upon relevant States and organizations to cooperate with the above-mentioned mission.

The Council reiterates that a comprehensive peace-building programme with special emphasis on disarmament, demobilization, rehabilitation and reintegration will be important to post-conflict Somali.

The Council expresses its readiness to assist the Somali parties and support the Intergovernmental Authority in implementation of the agreements reached in the Somali National Reconciliation Process.

Communication. The EU Presidency, in a 16 December statement [S/2003/1191], welcomed the decision of the IGAD Facilitation Committee to convene a retreat of Somali leaders in order to prepare the third and final phase of the National Reconciliation Conference. It urged all Somali leaders to return to Kenya without delay, with a view to achieving a political settlement for the good of the Somali people.

Further developments. By mid-September, developments at the Somalia National Reconciliation Conference in Mbagathi, which was largely financed by the EU, led to an impasse over the contested adoption of a charter [S/2004/115]. Some leaders, including transitional President Hassan, rejected the adoption and returned to Somalia. On 30 September, a group of them announced the formation of the National Salvation Council consisting of 12 factions under the chairmanship of Musse Sudi. On 7 October, the National Salvation Council signed a memorandum of understanding with the TNG President, in which it acknowledged the TNG's continuance in office. The signatories also announced their intention to convene a new national reconciliation conference separate from the one at Mbagathi.

At the tenth IGAD summit (Kampala, Uganda, 24 October), the heads of State focused on ways to get the national reconciliation process back on track. They decided to expand the membership of the IGAD Technical Committee to include Eritrea, the Sudan and Uganda, in addition to Djibouti, Ethiopia and Kenya, and renamed it the IGAD Facilitation Committee. The AU Special Envoy for Somalia was made a member of the Committee.

The Facilitation Committee, at a ministerial-level meeting (Nairobi, 28 October), agreed that Somali leaders would be invited to a Leaders' Consultation in Kenya on 20 November and that phase three of the Conference would commence only after the successful conclusion of the Consultation. The National Salvation Council and TNG raised several objections to the proposed Consultation, mainly centred on representation. International observers at the Conference, including the Secretary-General's Representative, met with representatives of the TNG and the National Salvation Council in Mogadishu in order to persuade them to participate in the Leaders' Consultation, as well as with leaders of opposing views. Despite its efforts, the Facilitation Committee was obliged to postpone the Leaders' Consultation until 2004 due to the continuing impasse.

The Under-Secretary-General for Political Affairs, Kieran Prendergast, visited the region from 7 to 16 November and held discussions with a wide spectrum of Somali leaders and others involved in the issue of Somali reconciliation to assess the situation and plan for a future UN role in the country.

Following the removal of the Prime Minister and Speaker of the Transitional National Assembly, Mustafa Gududow was elected as the new Speaker on 4 December, and transitional President Hassan appointed Mohamed Abdi Yussuf as the new Prime Minister, who then appointed a cabinet of 37 ministers.

On 21 December, the Somaliland Parliament adopted a resolution asserting Somaliland's authority over the Sool and Sanaag regions, which were also claimed by Puntland. On 27 December, forces loyal to the Puntland administration assumed control of Las-Anod district in the Sool region.

During the last three months of the year, breaches in security in Somaliland, a previously peaceful area, raised serious concerns. In other areas, sporadic inter-clan fighting took place, leaving many dead. Crime and violence in Mogadishu remained a problem and threats of kidnapping and direct attacks on UN and other humanitarian workers continued to be high. Humanitarian deliveries were reduced in most parts of the country.

Arms embargo

Panel of Experts (March). On 25 March [S/2003/223], the Security Council Committee established pursuant to resolution 751(1992) [YUN 1992, p. 202] concerning Somalia transmitted to the Council the report of the Panel of Experts established by resolution 1425(2002) [YUN 2002, p. 206], and mandated to collect independent information on violations of the arms embargo on Somalia and to make recommendations on steps for implementing it. The Panel of Experts found a clear pattern of violation of the arms embargo. Weapons, equipment, training of militia and financial support to Somali factions had been given regularly by neighbouring States and others since the arms embargo was established in 1992. Weapons were also purchased by Somali factions on the international market. Those violations continued, even as the factions and their neighbours were participating in the Somalia National Reconciliation Conference.

The Panel believed that the sanctions regime should be enhanced and implemented with determination. The Somali faction leaders were convinced that they could proceed as usual since they had not seen any real enforcement of the embargo over the preceding 12 years. Those years of conflict had further fragmented Somali society as the fighting increasingly was carried out for the advancement of personal material interests.

The vast majority of the cases investigated by the Panel involved numerous shipments of relatively small amounts of arms and ammunition; the nature of the Somali conflict demanded little more. Fighting in Somalia was normally carried out by small numbers of poorly trained and undisciplined militia members and lasted no more than a few days before ammunition and other supplies were exhausted. Since Somalia was a deeply impoverished country, the faction leaders had to struggle to raise sufficient money to pay their militia members and obtain arms and ammunition. Fighting centred on the control of property or income-generating infrastructure, such as harbours, airports, markets, bridges or road junctions that could be "taxed". Faction leaders had also devised other schemes to raise money, some clearly illegal.

The arms market in Somalia was supplied by both external and internal sources, and arms, cash and ammunition were readily fungible and used to purchase other goods, such as food and khat, the local drug of choice. Ethiopia had played an overt military role in Somalia. It was a major source of weapons for a number of Somali groups and had also invaded and occupied parts of Somalia. After the establishment of the TNG, Ethiopia helped to establish the Somali Reconciliation and Restoration Council, made up of factions hostile to the TNG and its allies. The Ethiopian military provided training and some arms and supplies to all members of the Council. Eritrea had also been a major supplier of arms and ammunition to Somali groups and, at times, Somalia had become a secondary battleground in the war between Eritrea and Ethiopia. Yemen provided a small amount of military assistance to the TNG soon after it was established. According to reliable sources, Djibouti was a trans-shipment point for weapons to Somalia, principally for the TNG. Egypt had acknowledged providing training and uniforms to the TNG police. The TNG also received assistance from Kuwait, the Libyan Arab Jamahiriya, Qatar, Saudi Arabia and the Sudan.

One concern about Somalia was that because of its lack of an effective central Government it could become a haven for international terrorists; so far there was no evidence of that. The continuing lawlessness in Somalia, particularly in the coastal areas, was a threat not only to Somalis but also to the international community. The recent finding that material and explosives used in the terrorist attack of November 2002 in Mombasa, Kenya [YUN 2002, p. 51], were trans-shipped through Somalia to north Kenya was a case in point. The international community could and should do more about security and unsustainable exploitation in Somalia's exclusive economic zone.

The warlords' use of extortion to raise money and the creeping trend to corruption, made possible by the general lawlessness of the country, would be a serious problem over the long term. Piracy and kidnapping were other means by which local militias extorted money from both the international community and the Somalis. The trade in khat was a significant source of revenue for the warlords. The long and remote Somali coast had the potential to accommodate both trade for the north-eastern region of Africa and a wide range of undesirable activities, from unsustainable exploitation of natural resources to arms trafficking, piracy and terrorist operations.

Although the Eldoret Declaration [YUN 2002, p. 202] was signed by all factions attending the Conference and witnessed by the neighbouring countries, most factions continued to fight and import weapons. The Panel therefore recommended that the sanctions be implemented with increased determination. Successful enforcement required an alliance of Governments and Somalis to monitor violations of the arms embargo and deprive violators of any safe haven. The Panel also recommended that all commercial relationships and banking activities that might be linked to arms purchases and the financing of war in Somalia be prevented. It welcomed and encouraged efforts by Somalia's business and civil community and certain segments of non-Somali interest groups to support and participate in actions to strengthen the embargo and the affiliated prohibitions on the financing of arms purchases. Most notably, such support had been expressed in the Declaration of Support by the members of the Dubai-based Somali Business Council and the Somali Intellectuals Association, and in letters from reputable leading currency printing companies.

The Panel believed that an effectively implemented arms embargo could cut the flows of arms to Somalia and concomitantly limit the level of armed conflict. That could contribute to the successful completion of a Somali peace agreement. The embargo had to be enforced to be effective, it warned. Official censure of States that violated the embargo was an important step, but continued vigorous monitoring was also necessary. The Panel also believed that it was important for the Security Council both to renew the Panel's mandate for six months and to implement its recommendations.

The Panel's specific recommendations included that: the United Nations create an Internet-based register of government officials who were authorized to sign end-user certificates for arms exports; a list of individuals deemed to be in violation of the embargo be drawn up so that their funds and assets could be frozen and any international travel banned; a further investigation be carried out of persistent violations of the embargo, including identification of violators and their supporters; and a Somali-based effort be organized to assist in identifying and impeding embargo violators, with the assistance of already deployed military and law-enforcement resources of the Member States.

SECURITY COUNCIL ACTION (April)

On 8 April [meeting 4737], the Security Council unanimously adopted **resolution 1474(2003)**. The draft [S/2003/408] was prepared in consultations among Council members.

The Security Council,

Reaffirming its previous resolutions concerning the situation in Somalia, in particular resolution 733(1992) of 23 January 1992, by which it established an embargo on all deliveries of weapons and military equipment to Somalia (hereinafter referred to as "the arms embargo"), resolution 1407(2002) of 3 May 2002, resolution 1425(2002) of 22 July 2002, and the statements by its President of 28 March (S/PRST/2002/8) and 12 December 2002 (S/PRST/2002/35), and of 12 March 2003 (S/PRST/2003/2),

Noting with regret that the arms embargo has been continuously violated since 1992, including since the signing of the Declaration on Cessation of Hostilities and the Structures and Principles of the Somalia National Reconciliation Process ("the Eldoret Declaration") on 27 October 2002, and expressing concern over the illegal activities linked to the financing of arms purchases and military activities by the violators of the arms embargo in Somalia,

Reiterating its firm support for the Somalia National Reconciliation Process and the ongoing Somalia National Reconciliation Conference, reaffirming the importance of the sovereignty, territorial integrity, political independence and unity of Somalia, consistent with the purposes and principles of the Charter of the United Nations, and commending the efforts of Kenya as the host of the Somalia National Reconciliation Conference sponsored by the Intergovernmental Authority on Development,

Reiterating its insistence that all States, in particular those of the region, should not interfere in the internal affairs of Somalia. Such interference only further destabilizes Somalia, contributes to a climate of fear and impacts adversely on human rights, and could jeopardize the sovereignty, territorial integrity, political independence and unity of Somalia. Stressing that the territory of Somalia should not be used to undermine stability in the subregion,

Reiterating its serious concern over the continued flow of weapons and ammunition supplies to and through Somalia from sources outside the country, in contravention of the arms embargo, which is severely undermining peace and security and the political efforts for national reconciliation in Somalia, and which undermines the commitments made at the Great Lakes and the Horn of Africa Conference on the Proliferation of Small Arms and Light Weapons, held in Nairobi from 12 to 15 March 2000,

Recognizing the importance of improving the implementation and enhancing the monitoring of the arms embargo in Somalia through persistent and vigilant investigation into violations of the arms embargo,

Determining that the situation in Somalia constitutes a threat to international peace and security in the region,

Acting under Chapter VII of the Charter,

1. *Stresses* the obligation of all States and other actors to comply fully with resolution 733(1992), and reaffirms that non-compliance constitutes a violation of the provisions of the Charter;

2. *Welcomes* the report of the Panel of Experts dated 25 March 2003 submitted pursuant to paragraph 11 of resolution 1425(2002), notes with interest the observations and recommendations contained therein, and expresses its intention to give full consideration to the report;

3. *Decides* to re-establish a Panel of Experts for a period of six months commencing no later than three weeks from the date of the adoption of the present resolution, to be based in Nairobi, with the following mandate:

(a) To investigate the violations of the arms embargo covering access to Somalia by land, air and sea, in particular by pursuing any sources that might reveal information related to violations;

(b) To detail information and make specific recommendations in relevant areas of expertise related to violations and measures to give effect to and strengthen the arms embargo in its various aspects;

(c) To carry out field-based research, where possible, in Somalia, States neighbouring Somalia and other States, as appropriate;

(d) To assess the capacity of States in the region to implement fully the arms embargo, including through a review of national customs and border-control regimes;

(e) To focus on the ongoing arms embargo violations, including transfers of ammunition, single-use weapons, and small arms;

(f) To seek to identify those who continue to violate the arms embargo inside and outside Somalia, and their active supporters, and to provide the Security Council Committee established pursuant to resolution 751(1992) of 24 April 1992 (hereinafter referred to as "the Committee") with a draft list for possible future actions;

(g) To explore the possibility of establishing a monitoring mechanism for the implementation of the arms embargo with partners inside and outside Somalia in close cooperation with regional and international organizations, including with the African Union;

(h) To refine the recommendations provided in the report of the Panel of Experts;

4. *Requests* the Secretary-General, upon the adoption of the present resolution and acting in consultation with the Committee, to appoint up to four experts, including the Chairman, drawing as much as possible and as appropriate on the expertise of the members of the Panel of Experts appointed pursuant to resolution 1425(2002), and also requests the Secretary-General to make the necessary financial arrangements to support the work of the Panel;

5. *Also requests* the Secretary-General to ensure that the Panel of Experts comprises, and has access to, sufficient expertise in the areas of armament and the financing thereof, civil aviation, maritime transport and regional affairs, including specialized knowledge of Somalia, in accordance with the resource requirements and administrative and financial arrangements outlined in the report of the Team of Experts pursuant to resolution 1407(2002);

6. *Requests* all Somali and regional parties as well as government officials and other actors contacted outside the region to cooperate fully with the Panel of Experts in the discharge of its mandate, and requests the Panel of Experts to notify the Council immediately, through the Committee, of any lack of cooperation;

7. *Requests* the Panel of Experts to provide a mid term briefing to the Council, through the Committee, and to submit a final report at the end of its mandated period to the Council, through the Committee, for its consideration;

8. *Decides* to send a mission of the Committee, led by the Chairman of the Committee, to the region at the earliest possible stage after the Panel of Experts has resumed its work to demonstrate the determination of the Council to give full effect to the arms embargo;

9. *Calls again upon* all States, in particular those in the region, to provide the Committee with all available information on violations of the arms embargo;

10. *Invites* the neighbouring States to report to the Committee quarterly on their efforts to implement the arms embargo;

11. *Calls upon* regional organizations, in particular the African Union and the League of Arab States, as well as States that have the resources, to assist Somali parties and the States in the region in their efforts to implement fully the arms embargo;

12. *Expresses its determination* to review the situation regarding the implementation of the arms embargo in Somalia on the basis of information provided by the Panel of Experts in its reports;

13. *Decides* to remain actively seized of the matter.

Following a 14 April briefing on the Panel's report by the Chairman of the Committee on the arms embargo, the Council President issued a press statement [SC/7728-AFR/601] in which members welcomed the report, which recommended that all parties inside and outside Somalia be invited to take up their responsibilities in implementing the arms embargo. They expressed concern about the continued flow of weapons and military equipment from sources outside Somalia and called on all Member States to cooperate with the re-established Panel of Experts.

On 10 April [S/2003/423], the TNG of Somalia welcomed the Panel's report, expressed appreciation for the concern expressed on the flow of arms to Somalia and welcomed the extension of the Panel's mandate. It also welcomed the Panel's findings that, among the neighbouring countries of Somalia, Ethiopia and its favourite Somali warlords continued to be the major violators of the arms embargo. The TNG concurred with the Panel's view that the arms embargo should be enforced and sanctions imposed against violators (States or individuals). On the other hand, the TNG refuted the Panel's assertion that the TNG had not fully cooperated with it. The TNG also objected to the Panel's description of police uniforms and equipment as military assistance and the Panel's recommendation for creating regulatory caretaker agencies for Somalia to deal with civil aviation, fiduciary and maritime administration matters.

The Secretary-General, on 30 April [S/2003/515], informed the Council of his appointment of four experts who would form the Panel to investigate violations of the arms embargo. When one member was unable to complete his service, the Secretary-General informed the Council on 28 July [S/2003/770] of his replacement.

On 20 August, following a briefing by the Chairman of the Committee on sanctions against Somalia on the mid-term report of the Panel of Experts, the Council President issued a press statement [SC/7849-AFR/690] in which Council members welcomed the Panel's work so far, which was in support of the Somali national reconciliation process and the ongoing Somali National Reconciliation Conference in Kenya. They reiterated their concern about the persistent flow of weapons and ammunition to Somalia, stressed the responsibility of Member States to implement the arms embargo and reiterated the call on all Somali and regional parties, as well as officials and other actors contacted outside the region, to cooperate with the Panel. Members welcomed the working relationships set up between the Panel and regional and international organizations, in particular the AU and IGAD, and the decision of the Chairman to lead a mission to the region in October. Members emphasized the need for an information campaign to publicize the mission's objectives.

Panel of Experts (November). The Panel of Experts, in accordance with resolution 1474 (2003) (see p. 252), issued a report that was transmitted to the Council by its Committee on sanctions against Somalia on 4 November [S/2003/1035]. The report, based on thorough monitoring over the previous six months, showed a continuous influx of small quantities of weapons and ammunition into Somalia that fed the local open arms markets and faction leaders' warehouses. Major violations of the arms embargo during that period using large vessels or heavy cargo aircraft showed a reduction over previous years, but the constant micro-flow of weapons and ammunition represented hundreds of tons of arms in violation of the embargo.

The Panel also found evidence linking violations of the arms embargo with illicit arms flows to neighbouring countries, piracy in Somali and international waters, and activities of armed groups and extremists beyond Somalia's borders. Weapons shipments destined for Somalia tended to originate in or were routed through Djibouti, Eritrea, Ethiopia, the United Arab Emirates and Yemen. The main entry points were the ports that served Puntland (Boosaaso), Mogadishu (Marha and El Ma'an) and Kismayo, together with airstrips around Mogadishu. The preferred method of sanctions-busting was to transport weapons in a small fishing vessel or concealed in an aircraft's cargo hold. They were then distributed through a long chain of brokers throughout Somalia. Dhows sailing from Yemen to northeast Somalia carried much of the traffic and most shipments went unnoticed and unreported. The bulk of the merchandise was destined for Mogadishu, the hub of the Somali arms trade. About 1,250 flights arrived in Somalia each month, mainly from other States in the region. Their cargo was rarely inspected and regulation of air traffic was limited. Likewise the 1,600-kilometre border between Somalia and Ethiopia was largely unmonitored and traffic passed freely.

Somali faction leaders paid for their arms in a variety of ways, for example, with cash received from foreign sponsors, with the proceeds of taxes and charges levied at ports, airports and roadblocks, with khat, or with counterfeit Somali shillings printed abroad. Transnational terrorists had been able to obtain not only small arms but also portable air defence systems, light anti-tank weapons and explosives. The Panel determined that it remained relatively easy to obtain surface-to-air missiles and import them into Somalia.

The front-line States and regional actors were key external players in Somali affairs. Although they had shown greater respect for the arms embargo over the past six months than in previous years, many persisted in violations and few had taken active measures to curb commercial arms transfers to Somalia. The Panel often found their support for its work lacking, but even where support was provided many lacked the tools to sufficiently monitor exports and/or trans-shipments through their ports, airports, land border crossings, territorial waters and airspace. Many observers attributed reduced arms flows in recent months to the Security Council's monitoring of the embargo. As the Somali peace process entered a critical stage, enforcement of the embargo and robust monitoring could help to reinforce commitment to dialogue, reduce the scope for armed conflict and mitigate its consequences if it happened.

Having discussed the Panel's report, Council members, in a 3 December press statement [SC/7941-AFR/781], said that they had begun to consider a range of measures to improve the effectiveness of the arms embargo. Council members underlined the critical role of the effective enforcement and monitoring of the sanctions regime for the Somalia national peace and reconciliation talks and reiterated the Council's active engagement in the process. They emphasized the need for a united approach and stronger support of the international community for enhanced implementation of the arms embargo and urged the front-line and neighbouring States to comply fully with their obligations under the relevant Council resolutions. They stressed the risks of the continued flow of weapons and ammunition supplies to and through Somalia for stability and security in Africa, and appealed for sustained regional efforts and cooperation to improve the monitoring and implementation of the embargo.

SECURITY COUNCIL ACTION (December)

On 16 December [meeting 4885], the Security Council unanimously adopted **resolution 1519 (2003)**. The draft [S/2003/1177] was prepared in consultations among Council members.

The Security Council,

Reaffirming its previous resolutions concerning the situation in Somalia, in particular resolution 733(1992) of 23 January 1992, by which it established an embargo on all deliveries of weapons and military equipment to Somalia (hereinafter referred to as "the arms embargo"), resolution 1356(2001) of 19 June 2001, resolution 1407(2002) of 3 May 2002, resolution 1425(2002) of 22 July 2002, resolution 1474(2003) of 8 April 2003, and the statements by its President of 12 March and 11 November 2003,

Reiterating its firm support for the Somali National Reconciliation Process and the ongoing Somali National Reconciliation Conference, commending the efforts of Kenya as the host of the Conference sponsored by the Intergovernmental Authority on Development, and reaffirming the importance of the sovereignty, territorial integrity, political independence and unity of Somalia, consistent with the purposes and principles of the Charter of the United Nations,

Reiterating its insistence that States, in particular those of the region, should not interfere in the internal affairs of Somalia—such interference only further destabilizes Somalia, contributes to a climate of fear and impacts adversely on human rights, and could jeopardize the sovereignty, territorial integrity, political independence and unity of Somalia—and stressing that the territory of Somalia should not be used to undermine stability in the subregion,

Reiterating its serious concern over the continued flow of weapons and ammunition supplies to and through Somalia from sources outside the country, in contravention of the arms embargo, bearing in mind that the Somali National Reconciliation Process and the implementation of the arms embargo serve as mutually reinforcing processes,

Having considered the report of the Panel of Experts of 4 November 2003, submitted pursuant to paragraph 7 of resolution 1474(2003),

Welcoming the mission of the Security Council Committee established pursuant to resolution 751(1992) of 24 April 1992 (hereinafter referred to as "the Committee"), led by the Chairman of the Committee, to the States in the region, from 11 to 21 November 2003, as a step towards giving full effect to the arms embargo,

Reiterating the importance of improving the implementation and enhancing the monitoring of the arms embargo in Somalia through persistent and vigilant investigation into violations of the arms embargo, and expressing its determination to hold those violators accountable,

Determining that the situation in Somalia constitutes a threat to international peace and security in the region,

Acting under Chapter VII of the Charter,

1. *Stresses* the obligation of all States and other actors to comply fully with resolution 733(1992) and resolution 1356(2001), and reaffirms that non-compliance constitutes a violation of the provisions of the Charter of the United Nations;

2. *Requests* the Secretary-General to establish a monitoring group (hereinafter referred to as the "Monitoring Group") composed of up to four experts, for a period of six months commencing as soon as possible from the date of adoption of the present resolution, to be based in Nairobi, with the following mandate, which should focus on the ongoing arms embargo violations, including transfers of ammunition, single-use weapons, and small arms:

(a) To investigate the violations of the arms embargo covering access to Somalia by land, air and sea;

(b) To detail information and make specific recommendations in relevant areas of expertise related to violations and measures to give effect to and strengthen the implementation of the arms embargo in its various aspects;

(c) To carry out field-based investigations in Somalia, where possible, and in States neighbouring Somalia and other States, as appropriate;

(d) To assess the progress made by the States in the region to implement fully the arms embargo, including through a review of national customs and border control regimes;

(e) To provide the Committee in its final report with a draft list of those who continue to violate the arms embargo inside and outside Somalia, and their active supporters, with a view to possible future measures by the Council;

(f) To make recommendations based on its investigations and the previous reports of the Panel of Experts appointed pursuant to resolutions 1425(2002) and 1474(2003);

3. *Also requests* the Secretary-General to make the necessary financial arrangements to support the work of the Monitoring Group;

4. *Requests* all Somali and regional parties as well as Government officials and other actors contacted outside the region to cooperate fully with the Monitoring Group in the discharge of its mandate, and requests the Monitoring Group to notify the Security Council immediately, through the Committee, of any lack of cooperation;

5. *Calls upon* all States in the region and regional organizations, in particular the Intergovernmental Authority on Development, the African Union and the League of Arab States, to establish focal points to enhance cooperation with the Monitoring Group and to facilitate information exchange;

6. *Requests* the Monitoring Group to provide a midterm briefing to the Council, through the Committee, and to submit a final report at the end of its mandated period to the Security Council, through the Committee, for its consideration;

7. *Encourages* all States signatories to the Nairobi Declaration on the Problem of the Proliferation of Illicit Small Arms and Light Weapons in the Great Lakes Region and the Horn of Africa to implement quickly the measures required by the Coordinated Agenda for Action as an important means in support of the arms embargo on Somalia;

8. *Calls upon* the neighbouring States to report to the Committee quarterly on their efforts to implement the arms embargo, bearing in mind their crucial role in the implementation of the arms embargo;

9. *Encourages* the donor community, including the Partner Forum Group of the Intergovernmental Authority on Development, to provide technical and material assistance to States in the region, as well as to the regional organizations, in particular the Intergovernmental Authority on Development, the African Union and the League of Arab States, in support of their national and regional capacity for monitoring and implementing the arms embargo, including for monitoring the coastline, land and air boundaries with Somalia;

10. *Encourages* Member States from the region to continue their efforts in enacting legislation or regulations necessary to ensure the effective implementation of the arms embargo;

11. *Expresses its determination* to review the situation regarding the implementation of the arms embargo in Somalia on the basis of information provided by the Monitoring Group in its reports;

12. *Decides* to remain actively seized of the matter.

Security Council Committee. On 31 December, the Chairman of the Security Council Committee established pursuant to resolution 751(1992) [YUN 1992, p. 202] concerning the arms embargo on Somalia submitted its report covering activities in 2003 [S/2003/1216]. The Committee held a number of meetings to discuss the findings of the two reports issued by the Panel of Experts (see p. 254). It sent a mission to the region from 11 to 21 November, which visited Djibouti, Egypt, Eritrea, Ethiopia, Italy, Kenya and Yemen; owing to security considerations, travel to Somalia was not possible

The Committee approved three requests from the United Kingdom to import humanitarian mine-clearance equipment to Somalia and one similar request from UNDP.

During the year, the Committee stepped up its level of engagement. The activities of the Panel of Experts and the Committee's mission to the region were indications of its determination to give full effect to the arms embargo. As in the past, the Committee continued to rely on the cooperation of States and organizations in a position to provide information on violations of the arms embargo.

Sudan

Internal situation

More than two decades of turmoil had taken their toll on the Sudan; the consequence of protracted warfare between government troops based in the north and rebels based in the south. The situation improved following the July 2002 signing of the Machakos (Kenya) Protocol between the Government and the rebel group, the Sudan People's Liberation Movement/Army (SPLM/A) [YUN 2002, p. 217].

With the improved security, delivery of humanitarian assistance increased (see p. 929). Nevertheless, armed conflict and ethnic violence continued to destroy infrastructure, isolate populations, erode coping mechanisms and limit access to markets and resulted in human rights violations. Natural calamities further diverted and drained vital government resources and caused new large-scale displacement of people. The war had resulted in 2 million deaths, and some 4 million people had been displaced. A memorandum of understanding on resumption of peace negotiations, signed on 15 October 2002 by the Government and SPLM/A, provided for the two sides to extend the cessation of hostilities and to facilitate humanitarian access. Further progress on humanitarian access was made under the auspices of the Technical Committee on Humanitarian Assistance, which was chaired by the Secretary-General's Special Envoy for Humanitarian Affairs for the Sudan.

In September, the Government and SPLM/A met in Naivasha, Kenya, and signed an agreement on security arrangements. Under its terms, the Sudan would have two armies under separate command and control during a six-year interim period. The two sides also agreed on a proportional reduction of forces and on establishing joint units under the command of the President.

Communications. The AU Central Organ of the Mechanism for Conflict Prevention, Management and Resolution, at its ninety-second ordinary session (Addis Ababa, 12-13 June), forwarded the decisions adopted to the Security Council on 16 June [S/2003/654], including one on the Sudan. The Central Organ welcomed the progress made in the peace process under the auspices of IGAD, and commended Kenya and its Special Envoy, Lazarus K. Sumbeiywo, for their efforts in facilitating the negotiations between the Sudanese Government and SPLM/A. It appealed to both parties to display the necessary spirit of accommodation so that a lasting solution could be found to the conflict. The Central Organ welcomed the adoption by the parties, during the fifth session of the Political Committee Task Force (Nairobi, 7-21 May), of the Verification and Monitoring Team's Tasking Procedures, within the framework of the addendum of 4 February 2003 to the Memorandum of Understanding on Cessation of Hostilities of 15 October 2002. The Central Organ supported the AU's participation in the work of the Verification and Monitoring Team. It appealed to the international community to provide the necessary resources for post-conflict reconstruction efforts.

In a 15 January statement forwarded to the Council [S/2003/80], the EU Presidency condemned the executions of three persons recently sentenced to death in the Sudan and called on the Government to refrain from further executions and other forms of cruel or inhuman punishment. It stressed that such actions went against the benchmarks applied in the framework of the ongoing dialogue between the EU and the Government of the Sudan.

On 8 August [S/2003/817], the EU Presidency, welcoming the forthcoming resumption, on 10 August, of the IGAD-sponsored peace talks on the Sudan, said that it was time to strike final compromises on the outstanding issues and reach a comprehensive agreement to end the conflict and the sufferings of the civilian population in the Sudan. It called on the parties to work with the IGAD mediators, led by Kenya, with a view to achieving a comprehensive solution, based on strict observance of the rule of law and full respect for human rights and fundamental freedoms. The EU welcomed the extension of the cessation of hostilities and of the addendum on the Verification and Monitoring Team's procedures for a further three months and stood ready to support the monitoring mechanism.

Framework agreement on security

The Government of the Sudan and SPLM/A, on 25 September in Naivasha, Kenya, signed the Framework Agreement on Security Arrangements during the Interim Period, which the Sudan forwarded to the Security Council on 2 October [S/2003/934]. Under its terms, the Sudan would have two armies under separate command and control during the six-year interim period. They agreed on the principles of proportional downsizing of the forces on both sides, following the completion of comprehensive ceasefire arrangements, which would be monitored by international observers. Both sides agreed to contribute troops to serve in joint/integrated units to be deployed by the President.

The EU Presidency, in a 25 September statement [S/2003/948], welcomed the Agreement, which it said augured well for the continuation of negotiations on the remaining outstanding issues. It encouraged the parties to seize the momentum and to reach a final and comprehensive agreement.

SECURITY COUNCIL ACTION

On 10 October [meeting 4839], following consultations among Security Council members, the President made statement **S/PRST/2003/16** on behalf of the Council:

> The Security Council welcomes the agreement on security arrangements reached in Naivasha, Kenya, on 25 September 2003, between the Government of the Sudan and the Sudan People's Liberation Movement/Army. The Council reiterates its welcome for the signing of the Machakos Protocol on 20 July 2002, which represents a viable basis for a resolution of the conflict in the Sudan. The Council looks forward to the successful conclusion of a comprehensive peace agreement, based on the Machakos Protocol. The Council further expresses its appreciation of the key role played by the Intergovernmental Authority on Development, under the leadership of the Kenyan President, the Kenyan Special Envoy, the envoys of the other Intergovernmental Authority member States and the International Observers in the Sudan peace talks.
>
> The Council also welcomes the continuation of the ceasefire and the establishment of the Verification and Monitoring Team, the Joint Military Commission and the Civilian Protection Monitoring Team and encourages Member States in a position to do so to contribute financial and logistical resources.
>
> The Council assures the parties of its readiness to support them in the implementation of the comprehensive peace agreement and requests the Secretary-General, in this connection, to initiate preparatory work, as soon as possible, in consultation with the parties, the Intergovernmental Authority facilitators and the International Observers, on how the United Nations could best fully support the implementation of a comprehensive peace agreement.

Sudan-Uganda

The Defence Minister of the Sudan, Major General Bakri Hassan Saleh, and his Ugandan counterpart, Amama Mbabazi, met in Uganda on 8 and 9 January and issued a communiqué, which Uganda forwarded to the Security Council on 15 January [S/2003/71]. They reviewed cooperation in defence, in particular implementation of existing agreements and protocols. The Ministers agreed that the Sudan People's Armed Forces would deploy in the camps formerly occupied by the Uganda-based Lord's Resistance Army (LRA) as soon as possible. The Sudanese Government reiterated its position against any contacts between its army and the LRA. The two countries agreed to deploy liaison army officers in the joint operations rooms at Gulu, Juba, Arua and Kitgum, on both sides of the joint border.

North Africa

Western Sahara

The United Nations continued its efforts to bring an end to the dispute over the governance of Western Sahara. The Personal Envoy of the Secretary-General attempted to bring the two parties together to reach agreement based on his new proposal. Those parties, Morocco and the Frente Popular para la Liberación de Saguía el-Hamra y de Río de Oro (POLISARIO), had agreed in 1990 to hold a referendum for the people to decide between independence or integration of the Territory with Morocco. Since then, United Nations plans to organize elections had been resisted by both sides. On the ground, the Secretary-General's Special Representative continued to meet with representatives of the parties and neighbouring States. The United Nations Mission for the Referendum in Western Sahara (MINURSO), established by Security Council resolution 690(1991) [YUN 1991, p. 794] to implement the settlement plan approved by the Council in resolution 658(1990) [YUN 1990, p. 920], continued to monitor the ceasefire between Morocco and POLISARIO and to report on developments.

Progress towards a political solution was incremental in 2003, mainly due to the reluctance of Morocco to accept the compromises proposed by the Personal Envoy in the peace plan for self-determination that he submitted to the parties at the beginning of the year. Morocco, however, did not completely reject the negotiating process, and the Security Council, affirming that Morocco needed more time to reflect on the proposal, agreed on five occasions to extend MINURSO's mandate for relatively short periods of time. Under the peace plan, there would be a transition period during which responsibilities would be divided between the parties before the holding of a referendum for self-determination. Unlike earlier plans, it would not require the approval of both sides at every step of implementation. When both sides raised various objections, the Secretary-General concluded that their responses suggested that they lacked the genuine will required to achieve a political solution. Later, POLISARIO indicated its acceptance of the peace plan. At that point, the Secretary-General urged Morocco to seize the opportunity for solving the long-standing dispute; however, by the close of the year, Morocco had not given a definitive response.

The Identification Commission completed its work on the electronic archiving of the nearly 245,000 individual files of persons who applied to be included in the list of voters for the referendum. Those archives were transferred to the United Nations Office at Geneva for safe keeping and, consequently, the MINURSO civilian police component, whose primary mandate was to protect the Commission's records, was withdrawn from the Territory by the end of the year. POLISARIO continued to impose some minor restrictions on the freedom of movement of MINURSO personnel. Both parties cooperated with the Mission on marking and disposing of landmines and unexploded ordnance.

During the year, POLISARIO released 643 Moroccan prisoners of war. More than 600 were still detained by POLISARIO, some of whom had been in detention for more than 20 years. Some progress was made on other confidence-building measures, including an agreement on telephone and personal mail services between some refugee camps in Tindouf, Algeria, and the Territory. However, those steps were not implemented in 2003.

Report of Secretary-General (January). The Secretary-General, in response to Security Council resolution 1429(2002) [YUN 2002, p. 212], submitted a 16 January report on the situation concerning Western Sahara [S/2003/59]. The Council had requested him to report before the end of MINURSO's current mandate (31 January).

Since his previous report of April 2002 [YUN 2002, p. 211], his Special Representative, William Lacy Swing (United States), continued his regular contacts with representatives of the parties and neighbouring States, holding exchanges with representatives of Morocco and POLISARIO in Laayoune (northern sector of Western Sahara) and the Tindouf (western Algeria) area, respectively, in order to keep an open channel of communication with them and to review the situation on the ground. He also visited the capitals of regional countries.

The Identification Commission continued its work in offices in both Laayoune and Tindouf on the electronic archiving of the 244,643 individual files of persons who had applied to be included in the list of voters for the referendum in Western Sahara. Initiated in August 2001, that work had so far resulted in the electronic archiving of some 177,000 files and was expected to be completed in April 2003.

The MINURSO military component, which stood at 211 military observers and troops, continued to monitor the ceasefire between the Royal Moroccan Army and the POLISARIO military forces, which had been in effect since 1991. The MINURSO area of responsibility remained generally calm. The civilian police component of MINURSO continued to provide protection for the files and sensitive materials at the Identification Commission centres at Laayoune and Tindouf. Training activities also continued. MINURSO military observers were deployed across Western Sahara at 10 sites.

The Secretary-General's Personal Envoy, James A. Baker III (United States), had embarked on a visit to the region to present to the parties and neighbouring countries a proposal for a political solution to the conflict over Western Sahara, as requested by the Council in resolution 1429(2002). For almost two decades, the Council and the United Nations had worked diligently to assist the parties to find a solution to the conflict. During that time, every possible option had been presented to them aimed at reaching an agreed solution. The responsibility for a positive culmination of those efforts rested solely with the parties. To give them time to consider the proposal presented by his Personal Envoy, the Secretary-General recommended a technical rollover of MINURSO's mandate for two months, until 31 March 2003. During that period, the United Nations would do all it could to address the humanitarian requirements of the Saharan refugees and to work with ICRC to address the plight of the prisoners of war and persons unaccounted for. He called on the international community to provide the resources necessary for WFP and UNHCR to cover the refugee food requirements. He urged the parties to release all those retained for so long, in contravention of international humanitarian law, and to embark on confidence-building measures to help to alleviate the suffering of the refugees.

Security Council statement. In a 23 January press statement [SC/7640], the Security Council President said that Council members welcomed the Secretary-General's January report (above) and agreed with his observation that the responsibility for a solution rested solely with the parties. They recalled the need to release without further delay all remaining prisoners of war, in compliance with international humanitarian law. They also recalled that Council resolution 1429(2002) called on Morocco and POLISARIO to continue to cooperate with ICRC to resolve the problem of the fate of all those unaccounted for since the beginning of the conflict. Council members expressed concern that confidence-building measures remained stalled and called on the parties to make the necessary compromises to allow person-to-person contact between Saharans on both sides of the berm (defensive sandwall). They agreed to extend MINURSO's mandate to give the parties time to consider the proposal presented to them by the Secretary-General's Personal Envoy.

SECURITY COUNCIL ACTION (January)

On 30 January [meeting 4698], the Security Council unanimously adopted **resolution 1463 (2003)**. The draft [S/2003/116] was prepared in consultations among Council members.

The Security Council,

Reaffirming all its previous resolutions on Western Sahara, in particular resolution 1429(2002) of 30 July 2002,

1. *Decides* to extend the mandate of the United Nations Mission for the Referendum in Western Sahara until 31 March 2003 in order to give the parties time to consider the proposal presented to them by the Personal Envoy of the Secretary-General;

2. *Requests* the Secretary-General to provide a report on the situation by 17 March 2003;

3. *Decides* to remain seized of the matter.

Communication. The Secretary-General, on 19 March [S/2003/341], informed the Security Council of the activities of his Personal Envoy, pursuant to resolution 1463(2003) (above). In January, Mr. Baker had presented his proposal, entitled "Peace plan for self-determination for the people of Western Sahara", to King Mohammed VI of Morocco, to President Abdelaziz Bouteflika of Algeria, to the Secretary-General of POLISARIO, Mohamed Abdelaziz, and to President Maaouya Ould Sid' Ahmed Taya of Mauritania. Council members had received a copy of the proposal in March. When presenting his proposal to the parties, Mr. Baker indicated that their views on it should be made available to him by early March, but not all parties had responded. In order to allow sufficient time to those parties and to the Personal Envoy to assess the responses, the Secretary-General proposed to defer submission of his report to the Council until 19 May. He also proposed that the Council consider authorizing a technical extension of MINURSO's mandate for another two months, until 31 May 2003.

Security Council statement. In a 25 March press statement [SC/7703], Security Council members stated that they intended to extend MINURSO's mandate to 31 May in order to give the Secretary-General's Personal Envoy sufficient time to evaluate the parties' responses to his proposal. They welcomed POLISARIO's recent release of prisoners of war; they recalled, however, that all prisoners of war still in detention should be released without further delay. The members requested the two parties to continue to cooperate with ICRC's efforts to solve the problem of the fate of all persons who had disappeared since the beginning of the conflict. They also expressed concern at the humanitarian situation of persons affected by the ongoing crisis.

SECURITY COUNCIL ACTION (March)

On 25 March [meeting 4725], the Security Council unanimously adopted **resolution 1469(2003)**. The draft [S/2003/360] was prepared in consultations among Council members.

The Security Council,

Reaffirming all its previous resolutions on Western Sahara, in particular resolution 1429(2002) of 30 July 2002,

1. *Decides* to extend the mandate of the United Nations Mission for the Referendum in Western Sahara until 31 May 2003;

2. *Requests* the Secretary-General to provide a report on the situation by 19 May 2003 as proposed by the Secretary-General in his letter dated 19 March 2003 addressed to the President of the Security Council;

3. *Decides* to remain seized of the matter.

Report of Secretary-General (May). In response to resolution 1469(2003) (see above), the Secretary-General submitted a 23 May report on the situation concerning Western Sahara [S/2003/565 & Corr.1]. Annexed to the report were the Personal Envoy's proposal for a peace plan for the self-determination of the people of Western Sahara, as well as the responses of the parties (Morocco, POLISARIO) and the neighbouring States (Algeria, Mauritania).

During the period since his previous (January) report, the Special Representative continued to maintain regular contacts with representatives of the parties and with senior officials of neighbouring countries during visits to Rabat, Tindouf, Algiers and Nouakchott. The Identification Commission completed its work on the electronic archiving of the 244,643 individual files of persons who applied to be included in the list of voters for the referendum in Western Sahara. All files had been scanned, archived and stored on both hard disks and back-up tapes to ensure security of the database. Continuing its monitoring duties, the MINURSO military component, which stood at 229 military observers and troops, reported that the area remained calm. POLISARIO continued to impose some minor limitations on MINURSO's freedom of movement. The Mission cooperated with the parties on the marking and disposal of mines and unexploded ordnance, and also assisted in preparing a regional landmine safety workshop for Western Sahara, to be held in Mauritania in June. Work began on establishing an information system that would consolidate data on mines and unexploded ordnance that MINURSO had collected over the years.

The Special Representative continued to impress upon POLISARIO the need to release all remaining prisoners of war and upon both parties to cooperate with ICRC in determining the fate of persons who were unaccounted for. On 26 February, ICRC repatriated 100 prisoners of war to Morocco. POLISARIO continued to hold 1,160 prisoners of war, some of whom had been in detention for more than 20 years.

Although the parties had agreed in late 2002 on certain confidence-building measures concerning Western Saharan refugees, the two sides expressed divergent views on the selection criteria of family visits between the Tindouf area refugees and their communities of origin in Western Sahara. Efforts to achieve a compromise formula had failed so far, and neither side was willing to reconsider the use of the provisional list of voters as the primary basis for participant selection. The United Nations pursued other confidence-building measures, focusing on activities that were not contested, such as telephone and personal mail services between some Tindouf refugee camps and the Territory, which the two parties approved.

The Secretary-General assessed the progress achieved and problems encountered by his Personal Envoy, summarizing activities since his appointment in 1997. By late 2002, there was still little movement by either side towards a feasible settlement plan to resolve the dispute over Western Sahara; therefore, the Secretary-General and his Personal Envoy presented to the Security Council four options that would not have required the concurrence of the parties [YUN 2002, p. 211]. The Council was not able to agree on any of those options; instead it supported efforts to find a political solution. The Council expressed its readiness to consider any approach providing for self-determination that might be proposed by the Secretary-General and his Personal Envoy. Subsequently, Mr. Baker, assisted by a constitutional expert, drafted a peace plan for self-determination for the people of Western Sahara, which was annexed to the Secretary-General's report. The proposal was presented and explained to the parties and neighbouring countries during his visit to the region from 14 to 17 January 2003.

The Secretary-General believed that the peace plan provided a fair and balanced approach towards a political solution, giving each side some of what it wanted and incorporating elements of previous plans they had agreed on. It envisaged a period of transition during which there would be a division of responsibilities between the parties before the holding of a referendum that would provide the bona fide residents of Western Sahara with an opportunity to decide their future. Unlike the earlier settlement plan, the peace plan did not require the consent of both parties at each and every step of its implementation.

The Secretary-General observed that the proposed plan offered an optimum political solution to the conflict, providing the bona fide residents of Western Sahara, following an appropriate transitional period, the opportunity to determine their own future, which, in turn, would promote peace and stability in the region and would open the way to enhanced exchanges and cooperation between the countries of the Arab Maghreb Union. By combining elements of the framework agreement, favoured by Morocco, and the settlement plan, favoured by POLISARIO, it represented a compromise.

The main objection of Morocco to the peace plan seemed to be that, in the referendum to determine the final status of Western Sahara, one of the ballot choices was independence; however, independence was also one of the two ballot choices under the settlement plan, which Morocco had accepted. It was difficult to envision a political solution that, as required by Security Council resolution 1429(2002) [YUN 2002, p. 212], provided for self-determination but precluded the possibility of independence as one of several ballot questions. The Secretary-General noted that there was one amendment to the peace plan that might assuage the concern of Morocco over the ballot for the referendum. That would be to provide a third ballot choice providing for continuation of the division of authority as set forth in the peace plan, in other words, self-government or autonomy. Morocco had for some time supported the concept of self-government or autonomy as the solution to the conflict over Western Sahara. The Secretary-General and his Personal Envoy proposed that the third ballot question be included on the ballot for the referendum on the peace plan. If none of the three ballot questions obtained a majority of votes, the one receiving the fewest votes would be eliminated and a run-off referendum would be held to allow the voters to choose between the two other possibilities. If the third option, self-government or autonomy, prevailed, the electorate for future elections of the executive and legislative bodies of the Western Sahara Authority would be the bona fide residents of Western Sahara over the age of 18.

POLISARIO's chief objection seemed to be that the peace plan was not the settlement plan. POLISARIO suggested that the parties revert to the implementation of the settlement plan, with two new elements: that the Identification Commission would process all 130,000 appeals, with no requirement that sheikhs participate, and the Commission's decisions would be accepted as final; and that a mechanism would be added to provide for enforcement of the referendum results under Chapter VII of the UN Charter. The Secretary-General observed that even with those two new elements, the settlement plan would still require the parties' consent at every stage of implementation. It was difficult to envision Morocco consenting to POLISARIO proposal as a way of implementing the settlement plan. As far as adding a Chapter VII mechanism to enforce the referendum results, the Secretary-General recalled that, following his report of February 2002 [YUN 2002, p. 210], the Security Council would not choose any of the four options he and his Personal Envoy had proposed because neither party would consent or agree to one of them. It was therefore unlikely that the Council would decide to enforce the referendum result under Chapter VII.

The responses of the parties also contained a number of ostensibly technical objections to the peace plan. In the Secretary-General's view, when taken together, the objections suggested that the parties lacked the genuine will required to achieve a political solution to the conflict. He cautioned that one or both parties might approach the Council to elicit support for a process in which objections and/or changes to the peace plan would be negotiated between them; however, the Secretary-General felt that such an approach would not be conducive to moving forward. He and his Personal Envoy believed that the parties should accept the plan as proposed. Recommending that the Council endorse the peace plan, or fifth option, the Secretary-General said that it combined elements of the draft framework agreement and agreed elements of the settlement plan, and that it was fair and balanced. Following a transitional period of self-government, the proposal offered the bona fide residents of Western Sahara an opportunity to determine their future for themselves.

The Secretary-General stated that he had reluctantly come to the conclusion that unless and until the parties demonstrated their readiness to assume their own responsibilities and make the compromises necessary to reach a successful outcome to the conflict, a fresh initiative to find a solution to the issue was likely to suffer the same fate as earlier ones. He urged the Council to seize the opportunity to address the long-standing issue of Western Sahara by requesting the parties to agree to the peace plan as amended and to work with the United Nations in its implementation. He added that if the parties could not agree on an approach for a political solution and if the Council was not in a position to ask them to take steps that they did not perceive to be in their own interest, despite the fact that it might be in the interest of the population of Western Sahara, the Council might consider whether it would remain actively seized of that political process. In order to give the Council sufficient time to reflect on its decision, the Secretary-General proposed that the MINURSO mandate be extended for two months, until 31 July.

SECURITY COUNCIL ACTION (May, July)

On 30 May [meeting 4765], the Security Council unanimously adopted **resolution 1485(2003)**. The draft [S/2003/577] was prepared in consultations among Council members.

The Security Council,
Recalling all its resolutions on Western Sahara, in particular resolution 1429(2002) of 30 July 2002,
Taking note of the report of the Secretary-General of 23 May 2003,
Commending the work of the Special Representative of the Secretary-General for Western Sahara, includ-

ing his efforts to resolve the pending humanitarian issues related to the conflict and to implement Office of the United Nations High Commissioner for Refugees confidence-building measures,

1. *Decides* to extend the mandate of the United Nations Mission for the Referendum in Western Sahara until 31 July 2003 in order to consider further the report of the Secretary-General;

2. *Decides* to remain seized of the matter.

On 31 July [meeting 4801], the Council unanimously adopted **resolution 1495(2003)**. The draft [S/2003/777] was prepared in consultations among Council members.

The Security Council,

Recalling all its resolutions on the question of Western Sahara, and reaffirming in particular resolution 1429(2002) of 30 July 2002,

Stressing that, in view of the lack of progress in the settlement of the dispute over Western Sahara, a political solution is critically needed,

Concerned that this lack of progress continues to cause suffering to the people of Western Sahara, remains a source of potential instability in the region and obstructs the economic development of the Maghreb region,

Reaffirming its commitment to assist the parties to achieve a just, lasting and mutually acceptable political solution which will provide for the self-determination of the people of Western Sahara in the context of arrangements consistent with the purposes and principles of the Charter of the United Nations, and noting the role and responsibilities of the parties in this respect,

Commending the parties for their continuing commitment to the ceasefire, and welcoming the essential contribution which the United Nations Mission for the Referendum in Western Sahara is making in that regard,

Having considered the report of the Secretary-General of 23 May 2003 and the peace plan for self-determination of the people of Western Sahara presented by his Personal Envoy, as well as the responses of the parties and the neighbouring States,

Acting under Chapter VI of the Charter,

1. *Continues to support strongly* the efforts of the Secretary-General and his Personal Envoy, and similarly supports their peace plan for self-determination of the people of Western Sahara as an optimum political solution on the basis of agreement between the two parties;

2. *Calls upon* the parties to work with the United Nations and with each other towards acceptance and implementation of the peace plan;

3. *Calls upon* all the parties and the States of the region to cooperate fully with the Secretary-General and his Personal Envoy;

4. *Reaffirms its call* upon the Frente Popular para la Liberación de Saguía El-Hamra y de Río de Oro to release without further delay all remaining prisoners of war in compliance with international humanitarian law, and its call upon Morocco and the Frente Popular para la Liberación de Saguía El-Hamra y de Río de Oro to continue to cooperate with the International Committee of the Red Cross to resolve the fate of persons who are unaccounted for since the beginning of the conflict;

5. *Reiterates its call* upon the parties to collaborate with the Office of the United Nations High Commissioner for Refugees in the implementation of confidence-building measures, and continues to urge the international community to provide generous support to the Office of the High Commissioner and the World Food Programme in order to help them to overcome the deteriorating food situation among the refugees;

6. *Decides* to extend the mandate of the United Nations Mission for the Referendum in Western Sahara until 31 October 2003;

7. *Requests* that the Secretary-General submit a report on the situation, before the end of the present mandate, that contains information on progress made in the implementation of the present resolution;

8. *Decides* to remain seized of the matter.

Appointment. The Secretary-General, on 5 August [S/2003/796], informed the Security Council of his intention to appoint Alvaro de Soto (Peru) as his Special Representative for Western Sahara. Mr. de Soto would replace Mr. Swing, who had been appointed as Special Representative for the Democratic Republic of the Congo. The Council took note of his intention on 8 August [S/2003/797].

Report of Secretary-General (October). In response to Security Council resolution 1495(2003) (above), the Secretary-General submitted a 16 October report on the situation concerning Western Sahara [S/2003/1016], covering developments since his May report.

His Personal Envoy had met with a high-level delegation from Morocco (Houston, Texas, United States, 17 September) to discuss the peace plan for self-determination of the people of Western Sahara. The delegation asked for some more time to reflect and consult before giving its final response to resolution 1495(2003), in particular the Council's call on the parties to work with the United Nations and with each other towards acceptance and implementation of the plan.

MINURSO, on 7 October, completed the transfer of all sensitive files of the Identification Commission to the United Nations Office at Geneva for safe storage. The Commission would therefore be reduced and its staff was scheduled to be withdrawn from the Mission by the end of the year. The authorized Commission posts would remain budgeted to the end of the current fiscal year (30 June 2004) to permit the Council to reactivate the Commission quickly should it decide to do so. With the transfer of files, the civilian police component completed its protection duties; accordingly, the remaining police officers were being withdrawn from the Mission, with the budgeted posts retained to the end of the fiscal year.

The MINURSO military component, which stood at 222 military observers and troops, reported that the area of operations remained calm. POLISARIO continued to impose some limitations on the Mission's freedom of movement in areas east of the buffer strip. During the reporting period, MINURSO had marked 56 mines and pieces of unexploded ordnance on both sides of the berm and monitored 31 disposal operations carried out by the Moroccan army. On 1 September, a field containing an unspecified number of grenades was discovered and marked at Bir Lahlou on the eastern side of the berm.

POLISARIO released 243 Moroccan prisoners of war in response to a request from a Member State. On 1 September, those persons were repatriated to Morocco by ICRC. In a 3 September press statement [SC/7863], Security Council members welcomed their release, as did the Secretary-General, who reiterated his call to POLISARIO to expedite the release of all remaining prisoners of war. According to ICRC figures, 914 such prisoners remained, most of whom had been in detention for more than 20 years. Some progress was reported concerning the determination of the fate of unaccounted-for persons, and the Secretary-General urged the two parties to cooperate further with ICRC in that regard. In May, ICRC interviewed four individuals in the Territory who had appeared on a POLISARIO list of unaccounted-for persons, who were subsequently removed from the list.

While the food pipeline for the Western Saharan refugees was relatively stable for some months, WFP foresaw shortages in basic foodstuffs by December if new contributions were not made. Donor interest in the refugee assistance programme remained relatively low.

UNHCR and MINURSO continued to promote a package of confidence-building measures with regard to refugees. On 15 April, UNHCR inaugurated a pilot telephone service between a refugee camp and the Territory; however, the programme was suspended by POLISARIO the next day. In May, Morocco reiterated its agreement to start mail service between the Tindouf refugee camps and the Territory, but requested that further technical discussions on modalities be held before it was started. During those discussions in October, UNHCR informed Algeria that Morocco was proposing that a direct mail service be established between the two national postal services and reminded Algeria that its formal concurrence was needed before the UNHCR-operated telephone service between the refugee camps in Algeria and the Territory could be resumed. The issue of family visits was not on the agenda of the UNHCR talks given the long-standing disagreement between the parties on selection criteria for the participants.

The Secretary-General congratulated the parties on the release of 243 Moroccan prisoners of war, the clarification of the fate of four previously unaccounted-for persons and the agreement on implementing confidence-building measures, all steps towards fostering a positive atmosphere between the parties. He called on the two sides to pursue the confidence-building measures. He also pointed out that Morocco continued to oppose the proposed peace plan, even after it had been adjusted to include a third ballot choice in the referendum, i.e., autonomy for Western Sahara, in addition to the choices of independence or integration with Morocco. Should the parties not be willing to make the necessary compromises on a political solution, the latest initiative would likely meet the same fate as earlier proposals. The acceptance of the peace plan by POLISARIO offered a window of opportunity for solving the long-standing dispute, the Secretary-General said, and he urged Morocco to seize the opportunity and engage in the process by accepting and implementing the plan.

In that context, following his 17 September discussions with the Moroccan delegation, Mr. Baker recommended that Morocco, as it had requested, be given more time to reflect before giving its final response by extending MINURSO's mandate. The Secretary-General agreed with the recommendation and proposed an extension of three months, until 31 January 2004.

Communication. Morocco, in a 21 October letter to the Security Council [S/2003/1028], commented on the Secretary-General's report (above). It claimed that the Secretariat had departed from its neutrality and objectivity by deliberately misinterpreting Council resolution 1495(2003), failing to take into account the content of the resolution, the work done in preparation for its adoption and comments made following its adoption. It was incorrect to infer from that resolution that Morocco was expected to simply sign the Personal Envoy's plan and implement it. Morocco also took issue with the Secretariat's selective presentation and partial interpretation of its objections to the Personal Envoy's proposal. Morocco's reaction concerned the entire architecture of the proposed framework, which was more a product of the settlement plan—a plan Morocco described as unworkable—than of the quest for a third way, or a definitive political solution that would respect Morocco's sovereignty and territorial integrity. All of Morocco's objections were recorded and confirmed in its 10 March observations on the draft peace plan. Since the process of settling the Western Sahara question was at a crucial stage, Morocco called on the Council to assume its responsibilities by putting an end to the dangerous turn that the process had taken. In particular, it called for respecting the terms of resolution 1495(2003).

SECURITY COUNCIL ACTION (October)

On 28 October [meeting 4850], the Security Council unanimously adopted **resolution 1513 (2003)**. The draft [S/2003/1034] was prepared in consultations among Council members.

The Security Council,
Recalling all its previous resolutions on Western Sahara, and reaffirming, in particular, resolution 1495 (2003) of 31 July 2003,
 1. *Decides* to extend the mandate of the United Nations Mission for the Referendum in Western Sahara until 31 January 2004;
 2. *Requests* that the Secretary-General provide a report on the situation before the end of the present mandate;
 3. *Decides* to remain seized of the matter.

Communication. Algeria, on 28 October [S/2003/1045], affirmed its support for the peace plan and for the Council's decision to give Morocco a reprieve to reflect on its final response. It hoped that Morocco would follow POLISARIO's steps and choose to seize the opportunity that was offered.

Further developments. The new Special Representative for Western Sahara, Mr. de Soto, assumed his duties in Laayoune on 29 October and, in November, visited Rabat, Tindouf, Algiers and Nouakchott, where he had introductory meetings with officials of the Governments of Algeria, Mauritania and Morocco and of POLISARIO [S/2004/39]. He was in contact with ICRC officials regarding Moroccan prisoners of war and the fate of persons unaccounted for. With WFP and UNHCR officials, he discussed humanitarian assistance to the refugees in the Tindouf area and other issues.

On 23 December, the Personal Envoy met with a Moroccan delegation to discuss issues pertaining to Morocco's final response to resolution 1495(2003).

The civilian police component of MINURSO completed its mandated duties with the transfer of the Identification Commission files and materials to the United Nations Office at Geneva and was withdrawn from the Mission on 31 December.

On 7 November, POLISARIO announced the release of a further 300 Moroccan prisoners of war, who were repatriated to Morocco under ICRC auspices. That move left 613 such prisoners still in detention.

In November, UNHCR, in consultation with the Special Representative, submitted to Morocco and POLISARIO, and Algeria as the country of asylum, a detailed plan of action defining the modalities for the implementation of the exchange of family visits between the refugee camps in Tindouf and the Territory. In December, the Special Representative and UNHCR staff met in Geneva with POLISARIO representatives to discuss the proposed plan for the exchange of family visits and to seek activation of other confidence-building measures, namely telephone and mail services. POLISARIO reiterated its support for the measures as a package, while accepting that implementation could take place gradually. It expressed readiness to resume the UNHCR telephone service and to start the mail service under the terms proposed by UNHCR, which was, that mail would be collected and distributed by UNHCR on both sides. During discussions in Rabat on 19 December, the Moroccan authorities urged the Special Representative and UNHCR to work for the quick resumption of the telephone service between the camps and the Territory and supported mail service using the Moroccan postal service for the collection and distribution of mail in the Territory. UNHCR stressed the need for its unhindered access to the beneficiaries of the service and assurance of confidentiality of the mail and neutrality in its handling. Following consultations with the parties, UNHCR adjusted its initial plan for implementing confidence-building measures, taking into account the comments of Morocco, POLISARIO and Algeria. A new version of the plan of action for the confidence-building measures was submitted to the parties for their final consideration.

GENERAL ASSEMBLY ACTION

The General Assembly had before it the Secretary-General's July report summarizing developments in Western Sahara from 1 July 2002 to 30 June 2003 [A/58/171].

On 9 December [meeting 72], the Assembly, on the recommendation of the Fourth (Special Political and Decolonization) Committee [A/58/480], adopted **resolution 58/109** without vote [agenda item 19].

Question of Western Sahara

The General Assembly,
Having considered in depth the question of Western Sahara,
Reaffirming the inalienable right of all peoples to self-determination and independence, in accordance with the principles set forth in the Charter of the United Nations and General Assembly resolution 1514(XV) of 14 December 1960 containing the Declaration on the Granting of Independence to Colonial Countries and Peoples,

Recalling its resolution 57/135 of 11 December 2002,

Recalling also all resolutions of the General Assembly and the Security Council on the question of Western Sahara,

Recalling further Security Council resolutions 658 (1990) of 27 June 1990 and 690(1991) of 29 April 1991, by which the Security Council approved the settlement plan for Western Sahara,

Recalling Security Council resolutions 1359(2001) of 29 June 2001 and 1429(2002) of 30 July 2002, as well as resolution 1495(2003) of 31 July 2003, in which the Council expressed its support of the peace plan for self-determination of the people of Western Sahara as an optimum political solution on the basis of agreement between the two parties,

Taking note of the responses of the parties and neighbouring States to the Personal Envoy of the Secretary-General, concerning the peace plan, contained in the report of the Secretary-General of 23 May 2003,

Reaffirming the responsibility of the United Nations towards the people of Western Sahara,

Noting with satisfaction the entry into force of the ceasefire in accordance with the proposal made by the Secretary-General, and stressing the importance it attaches to the maintenance of the ceasefire as an integral part of the settlement plan,

Underlining, in this regard, the validity of the settlement plan, while noting the fundamental differences between the parties in its implementation,

Stressing that the lack of progress in the settlement of the dispute on Western Sahara continues to cause suffering to the people of Western Sahara, remains a source of potential instability in the region and obstructs the economic development of the Maghreb region and that, in view of this, the search for a political solution is critically needed,

Welcoming the efforts of the Secretary-General and his Personal Envoy in search of a mutually acceptable political solution, which will provide for self-determination of the people of Western Sahara,

Having examined the relevant chapter of the report of the Special Committee on the Situation with regard to the Implementation of the Declaration on the Granting of Independence to Colonial Countries and Peoples,

Having also examined the report of the Secretary-General,

1. *Takes note* of the report of the Secretary-General;
2. *Underlines* Security Council resolution 1495 (2003), in which the Council expressed its support of the peace plan for self-determination of the people of Western Sahara as an optimum political solution on the basis of agreement between the two parties;
3. *Continues to support strongly* the efforts of the Secretary-General and his Personal Envoy in order to achieve a mutually acceptable political solution to the dispute over Western Sahara;
4. *Commends* the Secretary-General and his Personal Envoy for their outstanding efforts and the two parties for the spirit of cooperation they have shown in the support they provide for those efforts;
5. *Calls upon* all the parties and the States of the region to cooperate fully with the Secretary-General and his Personal Envoy;
6. *Reaffirms* the responsibility of the United Nations towards the people of Western Sahara;
7. *Calls upon* the parties to cooperate with the International Committee of the Red Cross in its efforts to solve the problem of the fate of the people unaccounted for, and calls upon the parties to abide by their obligations under international humanitarian law to release without further delay all those held since the start of the conflict;
8. *Requests* the Special Committee on the Situation with regard to the Implementation of the Declaration on the Granting of Independence to Colonial Countries and Peoples to continue to consider the situation in Western Sahara and to report thereon to the General Assembly at its fifty-ninth session;
9. *Invites* the Secretary-General to submit to the General Assembly at its fifty-ninth session a report on the implementation of the present resolution.

MINURSO

In 2003, the military component of the United Nations Mission for the Referendum in Western Sahara (MINURSO), which was under the command of Major General Gyorgy Száraz (Hungary), continued its functions of monitoring the ceasefire between the Royal Moroccan Army and the POLISARIO forces that came into effect in 1991 [YUN 1991, p. 796]. It maintained a strength of approximatley 230 troops, its authorized size, throughout the year. The civilian police component, with an authorized strength of 26, was withdrawn at the end of the year, following completion of its mandated duties to protect the Identification Commission's files and documents, as those records were sent to the United Nations Office at Geneva for safe storage.

On 13 February [S/2003/192], the Secretary-General informed the Security Council of his intention to add Croatia, Mongolia and Sri Lanka to the list of countries providing military personnel to MINURSO. The Council took note of the intention on 18 February [S/2003/193].

MINURSO financing

The resumed fifty-seventh session of the General Assembly had before it the performance report on the MINURSO budget for 1 July 2001 to 30 June 2002 [A/57/674]. Expenditures for the year totalled $39,090,500 (gross), against a total apportionment of $48,849,600, leaving an unencumbered balance of $9,759,100. The Secretary-General also submitted the MINURSO budget for 1 July 2003 to 30 June 2004 [A/57/675 & Corr.1], which amounted to $44,239,400, inclusive of budgeted voluntary contributions in kind of $1,776,100.

Having reviewed those reports, ACABQ, in April [A/57/772/Add.2], recommended that $41,529,500 gross ($38,488,500 net) be appropriated for the maintenance of MINURSO for 1 July 2003 to 30 June 2004 and that the amount be assessed at a monthly rate of $3,460,792 gross ($3,207,375 net) should the Security Council decide to extend MINURSO's mandate beyond 31 May 2003.

GENERAL ASSEMBLY ACTION

On 18 June [meeting 90], the General Assembly, on the recommendation of the Fifth Committee [A/57/834], adopted **resolution 57/331** without vote [agenda item 135].

Financing of the United Nations Mission for the Referendum in Western Sahara

The General Assembly,

Having considered the reports of the Secretary-General on the financing of the United Nations Mission for the Referendum in Western Sahara and the related reports of the Advisory Committee on Administrative and Budgetary Questions,

Recalling Security Council resolution 690(1991) of 29 April 1991, by which the Council established the United Nations Mission for the Referendum in Western Sahara, and the subsequent resolutions by which the Council extended the mandate of the Mission, the latest of which was resolution 1485(2003) of 30 May 2003,

Recalling also its resolution 45/266 of 17 May 1991 on the financing of the Mission and its subsequent resolutions and decisions thereon, the latest of which was resolution 56/298 of 27 June 2002,

Reaffirming the general principles underlying the financing of United Nations peacekeeping operations, as stated in General Assembly resolutions 1874(S-IV) of 27 June 1963, 3101(XXVIII) of 11 December 1973 and 55/235 of 23 December 2000,

Noting with appreciation that voluntary contributions have been made to the Mission,

Mindful of the fact that it is essential to provide the Mission with the necessary financial resources to enable it to fulfil its responsibilities under the relevant resolutions of the Security Council,

1. *Takes note* of the status of contributions to the United Nations Mission for the Referendum in Western Sahara as at 31 March 2003, including the contributions outstanding in the amount of 48.1 million United States dollars, representing some 10 per cent of the total assessed contributions, notes with concern that only twenty-three Member States have paid their assessed contributions in full, and urges all other Member States, in particular those in arrears, to ensure payment of their outstanding assessed contributions;

2. *Expresses its appreciation* to those Member States which have paid their assessed contributions in full;

3. *Expresses concern* at the financial situation with regard to peacekeeping activities, in particular as regards the reimbursements to troop contributors that bear additional burdens owing to overdue payments by Member States of their assessments;

4. *Urges* all other Member States to make every possible effort to ensure payment of their assessed contributions to the Mission in full;

5. *Expresses concern* at the delay experienced by the Secretary-General in deploying and providing adequate resources to some recent peacekeeping missions, in particular those in Africa;

6. *Emphasizes* that all future and existing peacekeeping missions shall be given equal and non-discriminatory treatment in respect of financial and administrative arrangements;

7. *Also emphasizes* that all peacekeeping missions shall be provided with adequate resources for the effective and efficient discharge of their respective mandates;

8. *Reiterates its request* to the Secretary-General to make the fullest possible use of facilities and equipment at the United Nations Logistics Base at Brindisi, Italy, in order to minimize the costs of procurement for the Mission;

9. *Endorses* the conclusions and recommendations contained in the report of the Advisory Committee on Administrative and Budgetary Questions, and requests the Secretary-General to ensure their full implementation without prejudice to a future discussion and decision on the proposal to create the post of Deputy Force Commander;

10. *Requests* the Secretary-General to take all necessary action to ensure that the Mission is administered with a maximum of efficiency and economy;

11. *Also requests* the Secretary-General, in order to reduce the cost of employing General Service staff, to continue efforts to recruit local staff for the Mission against General Service posts, commensurate with the requirements of the Mission;

Financial performance report for the period from 1 July 2001 to 30 June 2002

12. *Takes note* of the report of the Secretary-General on the financial performance of the Mission for the period from 1 July 2001 to 30 June 2002;

Budget estimates for the period from 1 July 2003 to 30 June 2004

13. *Decides* to appropriate to the Special Account for the United Nations Mission for the Referendum in Western Sahara the amount of 43,401,000 dollars for the period from 1 July 2003 to 30 June 2004, inclusive of 41,529,500 dollars for the maintenance of the Mission, 1,433,100 dollars for the support account for peacekeeping operations and 438,400 dollars for the United Nations Logistics Base;

Financing of the appropriation

14. *Decides also* to apportion among Member States the amount of 43,401,000 dollars at a monthly rate of 3,616,750 dollars, in accordance with the levels set out in resolution 55/235, as adjusted by the General Assembly in its resolutions 55/236 of 23 December 2000 and 57/290 A of 20 December 2002, and taking into account the scale of assessments for 2003, as set out in its resolutions 55/5 B of 23 December 2000 and 57/4 B of 20 December 2002, and for 2004, subject to a decision of the Security Council to extend the mandate of the Mission;

15. *Decides further* that, in accordance with the provisions of its resolution 973(X) of 15 December 1955, there shall be set off against the apportionment among Member States, as provided for in paragraph 14 above, their respective share in the Tax Equalization Fund of 3,389,800 dollars at a monthly rate of 282,483 dollars, comprising the estimated staff assessment income of 3,041,000 dollars approved for the Mission, the pro-

rated share of 322,900 dollars of the estimated staff assessment income approved for the support account and the prorated share of 25,900 dollars of the estimated staff assessment income approved for the United Nations Logistics Base;

16. *Decides* that for Member States that have fulfilled their financial obligations to the Mission, there shall be set off against their apportionment, as provided for in paragraph 14 above, their respective share of the unencumbered balance and of other income in the total amount of 12,289,500 dollars in respect of the financial period ended 30 June 2002, in accordance with the levels set out in resolution 55/235, as adjusted by the General Assembly in its resolutions 55/236 and 57/290 A, and taking into account the scale of assessments for 2002, as set out in its resolutions 55/5 B and 57/4 B;

17. *Decides also* that for Member States that have not fulfilled their financial obligations to the Mission, there shall be set off against their outstanding obligations their respective share of the unencumbered balance and other income in the total amount of 12,289,500 dollars in respect of the financial period ended 30 June 2002, in accordance with the scheme set out in paragraph 16 above;

18. *Decides further* that the decrease of 817,500 dollars in the estimated staff assessment income in respect of the financial period ended 30 June 2002 shall be set off against the credits from the amount referred to in paragraphs 16 and 17 above;

19. *Emphasizes* that no peacekeeping mission shall be financed by borrowing funds from other active peacekeeping missions;

20. *Encourages* the Secretary-General to continue to take additional measures to ensure the safety and security of all personnel under the auspices of the United Nations participating in the Mission;

21. *Invites* voluntary contributions to the Mission in cash and in the form of services and supplies acceptable to the Secretary-General, to be administered, as appropriate, in accordance with the procedure and practices established by the General Assembly;

22. *Decides* to include in the provisional agenda of its fifty-eighth session the item entitled "Financing of the United Nations Mission for the Referendum in Western Sahara".

Libyan Arab Jamahiriya

In 2003, the Libyan Arab Jamahiriya informed the Security Council of the steps it had taken to comply with Council resolutions adopted in 1992 and 1993, by which the Council had imposed sanctions on Libya because of its failure to cooperate in establishing responsibility for the terrorist attacks against Pan Am flight 103 on 21 December 1988 and Union de transports aériens (UTA) flight 772 on 19 September 1989. The steps taken by Libya related to bringing to justice two suspects charged with the Pan Am flight 103 bombing over Lockerbie, Scotland, payment of compensation to the victims' families, and Libya's acceptance of responsibility for the actions of its officials. The Council decided in September to lift the sanctions, with immediate effect. In December, Libya announced that it was halting its programmes for developing weapons of mass destruction and agreed to sign a number of international treaties on fighting terrorism.

Lockerbie question

The Libyan Arab Jamahiriya, on 20 January [A/57/716, S/2003/82], reacted to the 2 January decision of President George W. Bush of the United States to extend the comprehensive sanctions against Libya for a further year, beginning on 7 January. The sanctions included the freezing of Libyan assets in United States banks, the barring of Libyan students from advanced studies in the United States and a ban on the export to Libya of United States technical equipment. Libya expressed its displeasure at that measure, which it found in contradiction with events, particularly Libya's positive attitude with regard to improving relations between the two countries. Noting that the United States sanctions had been unilaterally applied since 1986, Libya said that Mr. Bush was linking them with the 1988 Pan Am 103 incident (see p. 1300) and with Libya's failure to comply with Security Council resolutions 731 (1992) [YUN 1992, p. 53], 748(1992) [ibid., p. 55] and 883(1993) [YUN 1993, p. 100]. Libya contended that it had complied with those resolutions and trusted that the United States would rescind its coercive measures.

On 15 August [S/2003/818], Libya informed the Council that the remaining issues relating to the fulfilment of all Council resolutions resulting from the Lockerbie incident had been resolved. It had facilitated bringing to justice the two suspects charged with the bombing of Pan Am flight 103 and accepted responsibility for the actions of its officials. It had cooperated with the Scottish investigating authorities before and during the trial and had arranged for payment of appropriate compensation. In addition, Libya was committed to cooperating in the international fight against terrorism.

The United Kingdom and the United States, referring to the Libyan statement in a letter of their own dated 15 August [S/2003/819], noted recent actions by Libya and said they were prepared to lift the measures set forth by the Council in resolutions 748(1992) and 883(1993) once the necessary compensation sums were transferred to the agreed escrow account.

Security Council consideration. On 9 and 12 September [meeting 4820, Parts I & II], the Security Council considered the 15 August letters from Libya and from the United Kingdom and the United States (above) concerning the Lockerbie question. The Council President observed that the bombing of Pan Am flight 103 over Lockerbie was an appalling act of terrorism which cost the lives of 270 people. Following painstaking negotiations, Libya had accepted responsibility and had agreed to pay a substantial sum of compensation to victims' relatives; in addition, it had agreed to cooperate with any further Lockerbie investigation and had renounced terrorism. Those actions opened the possibility of Libya moving back into the international community and of the lifting of sanctions. The President added that the Council needed to act unanimously on the question and that other related issues needed to be resolved; he therefore suggested that the Council adjourn for consultations. The Council voted unanimously in favour of that procedural motion and resumed its discussion on 12 September.

SECURITY COUNCIL ACTION

On 12 September [meeting 4820, Part II], the Security Council adopted **resolution 1506(2003)** by vote (13-0-2). The draft [S/2003/824] was submitted by Bulgaria and the United Kingdom.

The Security Council,

Recalling its resolutions 731(1992) of 21 January 1992, 748(1992) of 31 March 1992, 883(1993) of 11 November 1993 and 1192(1998) of 27 August 1998 relating to the destruction of Pan Am flight 103 over Lockerbie, Scotland, and the destruction of Union de transports aériens flight 772 over Niger,

Recalling also the statement by its President of 8 April 1999,

Welcoming the letter dated 15 August 2003 from the Chargé d'affaires a.i. of the Permanent Mission of the Libyan Arab Jamahiriya to the United Nations addressed to the President of the Security Council recounting steps that the Government of the Libyan Arab Jamahiriya has taken to comply with the abovementioned resolutions, particularly concerning acceptance of responsibility for the actions of Libyan officials, payment of appropriate compensation, renunciation of terrorism and a commitment to cooperating with any further requests for information in connection with the investigation,

Welcoming also the letter dated 15 August 2003 from the Permanent Representatives of the United Kingdom of Great Britain and Northern Ireland and the United States of America to the United Nations addressed to the President of the Security Council,

Acting under Chapter VII of the Charter of the United Nations,

1. *Decides* to lift, with immediate effect, the measures set forth in paragraphs 4 to 6 of its resolution 748(1992) and paragraphs 3 to 7 of its resolution 883(1993);

2. *Decides also* to dissolve the Security Council Committee established pursuant to paragraph 9 of resolution 748(1992);

3. *Decides further* that it has concluded its consideration of the item entitled "Letters dated 20 and 23 December 1991, from France, the United Kingdom of Great Britain and Northern Ireland and the United States of America", and hereby removes this item from the list of matters of which the Council is seized.

VOTE ON RESOLUTION 1506(2003):

In favour: Angola, Bulgaria, Cameroon, Chile, China, Germany, Guinea, Mexico, Pakistan, Russian Federation, Spain, Syrian Arab Republic, United Kingdom.
Against: None.
Abstaining: France, United States.

Following the vote, the United States acknowledged that Libya had addressed the UN requirements related to the Pan Am 103 bombing, accepting responsibility for the actions of its officials and making arrangements for paying compensation. However, the United States continued to have serious concerns about other aspects of Libyan behaviour, including its poor human rights record, its rejection of democratic norms and standards, its irresponsible behaviour in Africa, its history of involvement in terrorism and, in particular, its pursuit of weapons of mass destruction and their delivery.

The United Kingdom said that Libya, by accepting responsibility and agreeing to pay compensation, had met the requirements the Council had placed on it when imposing sanctions. It had also denounced terrorism, and, as a demonstration, had signed the 12 international conventions on the fight against terrorism.

France announced that an agreement had been reached on 11 September between the representatives of the families of those lost on UTA flight 772 and the Qaddafi Foundation. That had allowed France not to oppose the lifting of sanctions.

Communication. On 19 December [A/58/664, S/2003/1196], Libya said that during talks between Libyan, United States and United Kingdom experts concerning Libyan military activities, the Libyan experts briefed their counterparts on Libya's materials, equipment and programmes, such as centrifuges and containers for transporting chemicals that might be used to produce internationally banned weapons. Following those talks, Libya decided to eliminate such materials, equipment and programmes, thus ridding itself of all internationally proscribed weapons. Libya also decided to limit its missile activities to missiles with a range consistent with that agreed under the Missile Technology Control Regime. It would take such steps in a transparent manner that permitted verification, including immediate international monitoring.

Libya affirmed that it considered itself bound by the 1968 Treaty on the Non-Proliferation of Nuclear Weapons [YUN 1968, p. 17], the Agreement on Safeguards of the International Atomic Energy Agency (IAEA) and the 1971 Convention on the Prohibition of the Development, Production and Stockpiling of Bacteriological (Biological) and Toxin Weapons and on Their Destruction [YUN 1971, p. 19] and that it accepted any other commitments, including the Model Protocol Additional to the Safeguards Agreement, approved by the IAEA Board of Governors in 1997 [YUN 1997, p. 486], and the Convention.

Libya believed that the arms race was conducive neither to its own security nor to that of the region and ran counter to its strong desire for a peaceful world. Through its unilateral initiative, Libya wished to encourage all countries to follow its example, starting with those of the Middle East region.

Press statement. In a 23 December press statement [SC/7967], Security Council members took note of Libya's 19 December letter announcing that it would abandon voluntarily its programmes for developing weapons of mass destruction (WMDs). They welcomed Libya's announcement and its recognition of the strength of the international community's concerns over WMD proliferation and its voluntary decision to address those concerns. Council members looked forward to an early implementation of all the commitments made in the announcement, including the subjection to urgent international verification. In that context, they welcomed and encouraged Libya's cooperation with others, including the United Nations and other relevant international bodies, to ensure the verified elimination of all its WMD programmes.

1986 attack against Libya

The General Assembly, by **decision 58/512** of 10 November, deferred consideration of the item "Declaration of the Assembly of Heads of State and Government of the Organization of African Unity on the aerial and naval military attack against the Socialist People's Libyan Arab Jamahiriya by the present United States Administration in April 1986 and included it in the provisional agenda of its fifty-ninth (2004) session.

Southern Africa

Angola

Within a year of the signing of a memorandum of understanding between the Angolan Government and the National Union for the Total Independence of Angola (UNITA), Angola was firmly placed on the path of political, social and economic recovery. For the first time since independence in 1975 [YUN 1975, p. 853], Angolans could live without fear of a recurrent war. The AU Executive Council (Ndjamena, Chad, 3-6 March) [A/57/775] lifted its sanctions against UNITA, as the Security Council had done by resolution 1448(2002) in December 2002 [YUN 2002, p. 232].

During 2003, the Government and UNITA held discussions on the structure of the new Government and agreement was reached on a basic outline. Some other political parties did not support those decisions, however, claiming that the bilateral talks had circumvented them. The Government announced that the next general elections would take place in 2004, but other parties believed that the time frame was insufficient for proper preparations.

The United Nations Mission in Angola (UNMA) continued to assist with the reintegration of ex-combatants, coordination of humanitarian assistance, support for mine action and protection of human rights. The Secretary-General reported that UNMA had completed its political mandate and called for the UN Resident Coordinator to take over the responsibility for UN system activities in Angola at the completion of the UNMA mandate on 15 February.

Political developments

Report of Secretary-General. The Secretary-General, in response to Security Council resolution 1433(2002) [YUN 2002, p. 224], submitted a 7 February report on UNMA [S/2003/158], covering developments in Angola since his previous report of December 2002 [YUN 2002, p. 225] and making recommendations on the future role of the United Nations in that country.

The Secretary-General recalled that UNMA's mandate, as laid out in resolution 1433(2002), by which the Mission was established, was to assist the parties in the consolidation of peace. He reported that there was a consensus between the Government and UNITA that the implementation of the 1994 Lusaka Protocol for the Cessation of Hostilities and the Resolution of Outstanding Military Issues [YUN 1994, p. 346] had been completed. Those two actors, along with other political parties and members of civil society, had since been engaged in identifying the priorities to move the country from a state of armed conflict towards normalcy.

The political commissions of the ruling party, Movimento Popular da Libertação de Angola (MPLA), and UNITA held high-level talks in Luanda from 2 to 5 December 2002 to discuss issues of national interest, in particular a review of the Constitution. They agreed on four main issues, namely, that the President should remain head of State and Government, as well as party leader, the President would appoint provincial Governors on the recommendation of the majority party in each province, the legislature would be unicameral, and a National Council would be established in addition to the legislature, as a consultative body in which "traditional rulers" could participate. Some other political parties did not support those conclusions, however, arguing that the bilateral agreements between MPLA and UNITA had circumvented the Parliament's Constitution Drafting Committee, in which other parties were represented.

President José Eduardo dos Santos appointed the Minister of the Interior, Fernando da Piedade Dias dos Santos, as the new Prime Minister of the Government of Unity and National Reconciliation on 5 December 2002 and the Cabinet was named. Some opposition parties and members of civil society felt that the new Cabinet did not represent sufficient change. The National Assembly approved the $6 billion budget for 2003 that was submitted by the new Government; UNITA abstained in the vote, stating that it had not been consulted beforehand.

The Government indicated that the next general elections would take place in 2004; however, some MPLA and UNITA representatives said the necessary conditions did not yet exist. They proposed postponing the elections by one or two years to allow time to achieve national objectives such as revising the Constitution, elaborating a new electoral law, establishing an independent electoral commission, registering eligible voters and resettling or returning internally displaced persons and ex-combatants. Some representatives from both parties, however, felt that elections should be held as soon as possible. President dos Santos promised to pursue a national consensus on fixing the date for the next general elections.

UNMA activities

UNMA continued to implement its mandated tasks, which included support for the reintegration of ex-combatants, the facilitation and coordination of humanitarian assistance, the provision of technical support for mine action and the protection and promotion of human rights.

The demobilization, resettlement and reintegration of UNITA ex-combatants was one of the Government's main priorities to ensure stability. By the end of January, approximately 90,000 ex-combatants had been registered, and an estimated 15,000 were waiting to move to their designated reception areas from the provinces and neighbouring countries. Owing to operational problems, however, the registration process was halted. Among factors that hindered the demobilization, resettlement and reintegration process was a politicized ex-combatant population, which was not always cooperative with the authorities. A lack of adequate facilities, inaccessible roads, mine infestation and inadequately prepared resettlement areas had added considerably to delays. A further difficulty was that government payments to ex-combatants had been irregular and not universal. About 20 per cent of ex-combatants were still waiting to be included on the payroll. Some communities had expelled resettled ex-combatants, forcing them to return to reception areas. Despite the Government's announced intention to close all reception areas by the end of 2002, only four had been closed by reporting time and 34 were still open. The Government estimated that it could take up to one year to transfer the remaining ex-combatants and their dependants from their current locations to the more than 600 areas designated for resettlement.

UNMA continued to play a coordinating role, including by ensuring that information on ex-combatants gathered by the Angolan Armed Forces during the disarmament phase was shared with the civilian institutions that provided social services. The Technical Group on demobilization, resettlement and reintegration, under the chairmanship of UNMA, integrated and coordinated the activities of the UN system in Angola. It worked with the World Bank, which was preparing to fund a multi-donor resettlement programme to cover the demobilization of some 167,000 and the payment of reintegration benefits to 108,000 ex-combatants.

Although the humanitarian situation in the country had become more stable since late 2002, the need for emergency assistance remained pressing in many parts of Angola. Approximately 1.8 million people, including ex-combatants and their family members, required food assistance to survive, and that number was expected to increase until the April harvest. Mortality rates remained at emergency levels, particularly in remote locations. The onset of seasonal rains and mine incidents had severely affected humanitarian operations.

The end of hostilities had led to major population movements. During 2002, 1.3 million internally displaced persons returned to 500 communities and 85,000 refugees spontaneously returned from neighbouring countries. Basic conditions were in place in 30 per cent of the return sites. According to the Government, 2.8 million people were displaced at the beginning of 2003, and as many as 400,000 refugees remained in neighbouring countries. It was expected that some 1.2 million internally displaced persons, ex-combatants and refugees would return to their areas of origin during 2003. UN assistance was focused on reducing poverty and creating the conditions for sustainable development. Other areas that received UN support included mine action, promotion and protection of human rights, child protection and development activities.

The Secretary-General reported that UNMA had completed its mandated political tasks, as set out in resolution 1433(2002) [YUN 2002, p. 224]. However, the residual tasks foreseen in that resolution, including in the areas of human rights, mine action, reintegration and resettlement of ex-combatants, humanitarian assistance, economic recovery and electoral assistance, required continued attention and support, for which financing was needed. In that context, the Secretary-General requested his Special Representative to consult with Angola and other national and international stakeholders to determine how the United Nations could continue to assist the Government and people in the consolidation of peace in the country. Those discussions took place in Luanda from 18 January to 1 February. As a result, the Secretary-General proposed that the UN Resident Coordinator resume the responsibility for UN activities in the country upon the conclusion of the UNMA mandate on 15 February, including assisting the Government's efforts to implement the residual tasks under resolution 1433(2002). The Office of the Resident Coordinator would be strengthened for that transitional period by adding a unit under his supervision to address the residual tasks, for which additional resources might be required.

The Security Council President, in a 12 February press statement [SC/7660-AFR/562], said that Council members welcomed the steps taken by the Angolan Government towards the full implementation of the Lusaka Protocol. They welcomed the Secretary-General's report on the completion of UNMA on 15 February, and commended his Special Representative in Angola, Ibrahim A. Gambari, for his efforts to bring that phase of the UN involvement in Angola to a conclusion.

Financing of UNAVEM/MONUA

On 17 April, the Secretary-General submitted the final performance report of the United Nations Angola Verification Mission (UNAVEM) and the United Nations Observer Mission in Angola (MONUA). The former's mandate expired in 1997 [YUN 1997, p. 103], when it was transformed into the latter, whose mandate expired in 1999 [YUN 1999, p. 106]. The report contained information on income and expenditure, assets, outstanding liabilities and reserves and fund balances as at 30 June 2002, when net cash (assets less liabilities) for UNAVEM/MONUA totalled $54,658,000. That amount plus uncollected assessments and other receivables in the amount of $60,434,000 brought the fund balance to $115,092,000. The Secretary-General recommended that an amount of $12,458,000 be retained from the balance of appropriations to meet the cost of outstanding government claims. In the light of the overall financial situation of the Organization and the fact that assessed contributions to peacekeeping as at 15 March in the amount of $1.5 billion remained unpaid, he recommended that the return of cash available for credit to Member States be suspended until the financial situation improved.

GENERAL ASSEMBLY ACTION

On 18 June [meeting 90], the General Assembly, on the recommendation of the Fifth Committee [A/57/830], adopted **resolution 57/329** without vote [agenda item 131].

Financing of the United Nations Angola Verification Mission and the United Nations Observer Mission in Angola

The General Assembly,

Having considered the report of the Secretary-General on the financing of the United Nations Angola Verification Mission and the United Nations Observer Mission in Angola and the related report of the Advisory Committee on Administrative and Budgetary Questions,

1. *Authorizes* the Secretary-General to retain an amount of 12,458,000 United States dollars from the balance of appropriations of 72,831,000 dollars to meet the cost of outstanding Government claims;

2. *Decides* to include in the provisional agenda of its fifty-eighth session the item entitled "Financing of the United Nations Angola Verification Mission and the United Nations Observer Mission in Angola".

Other questions

Cooperation between the AU and the UN system

The United Nations and the African Union (AU) continued to cooperate in many areas, especially regarding the conflict situations and threats to peace and security in Africa. The AU forwarded to the United Nations the decisions and statements of its various bodies on African political issues [S/2003/142, A/57/775, S/2003/654, S/2003/760, S/2003/876, A/58/626], including those concerning Angola, Burundi, Côte d'Ivoire, the Central African Republic, the DRC, Liberia, Rwanda, Somalia and the Sudan (see above under relevant country headings). Other decisions or statements concerned the Comoros, Madagascar, Mauritania and Sao Tome and Principe (see below), and the

Comoros

With regard to the Comoros, the AU Central Organ of the Mechanism for Conflict Prevention, Management and Resolution, at a meeting held at the level of heads of State and Government (Addis Ababa, Ethiopia, 3 February) [S/2003/142], took note of the outcome of the ministerial meeting of the countries of the region and the Troika (Mozambique, South Africa, Zambia) (Moroni, Comoros, 28-29 January) and endorsed its recommendations. It called on the Comorian parties to cooperate in implementing those recommendations, in particular the holding of legislative elections according to the timetable proposed by the Follow-up Committee of the Fomboni Agreement of 17 February 2001, in order to complete the process of establishing institutions of the Union of the Comoros, including the National Assembly, Assemblies of the islands and the Constitutional Court.

The Fomboni Agreement (the Framework Agreement for Reconciliation in the Comoros) between the Government and separatist leaders outlined a plan for decentralizing political power in the Comoros. It provided for a new Comorian State with a new Constitution and institutions. The establishment of the new State was accepted by a referendum in December 2001, and an interim Government of transition was established in January 2002.

The AU Executive Council, at its third ordinary session (Maputo, Mozambique, 4-8 July) [A/58/626], expressed concern at the difficulties encountered in implementing the Fomboni Agreement and reiterated that it remained the appropriate framework for resolving the crisis in the Comoros. Taking note of the results of the official visit to South Africa on 20 June of the three Presidents of the autonomous islands of the Comoros, the Executive Council encouraged the Ministerial Committee of the countries of the region and the Troika to pursue their efforts to resolve all outstanding issues in order to pave the way for legislative elections.

Madagascar

The AU Central Organ of the Mechanism for Conflict Prevention, Management and Resolution, held at the level of heads of State and Government (Addis Ababa, 3 February) [S/2003/142], took note of the evolution of the situation in Madagascar and recommended that the AU Assembly recognize Marc Ravalomanana as the legitimate President of Madagascar. It underscored the need for national reconciliation to create conditions for lasting peace and stability and requested the engagement of the Government and the Malagasy parties, including through the convening of a round table to address all outstanding issues related to human rights, the rule of law and the issue of political detainees.

The AU Assembly also adopted a decision on Madagascar at its second ordinary session (Maputo, 10-12 July) [A/58/626]. The Assembly endorsed the Central Organ's decision and decided that Madagascar should resume its seat within the AU. It encouraged the Government to continue its policy of national reconciliation.

Mauritania

The AU Central Organ of the Mechanism for Conflict Prevention, Management and Resolution, at its ninety-second ordinary session (Addis Ababa, 12-13 June) [S/2003/654], condemned the attempted coup d'état that took place in Mauritania on 8 June, which was in flagrant contradiction with the principles of the AU Constitutive Act and with relevant AU declarations and decisions. It expressed satisfaction that constitutional order had been restored and appealed to the people of Mauritania to respect that order and uphold democratic principles.

Sao Tome and Principe

The AU Central Organ of the Mechanism for Conflict Prevention, Management and Resolution, in a communiqué issued after its ninety-third ordinary session (Addis Ababa, 24 July) [S/2003/760], condemned the coup d'état that took place in Sao Tome and Principe on 16 July and welcomed the successful resolution of the crisis through the restoration of constitutional order and the return of the elected President, Fradique de Menezes, thanks to international mediation by representatives of the Economic Community of Central African States (ECCAS), the AU, the Community of Portuguese-speaking Countries and Nigeria. The Central Organ expressed grave concern over the resurgence of coups d'état on the continent.

Chapter III

Americas

In 2003, the United Nations continued its assistance to countries in the Americas region in their efforts to strengthen political stability, security and judicial reform, human rights, demilitarization and the strengthening of civilian power, indigenous rights and socio-economic development. The Organization monitored the political and security situation in Central America, where signs of fragmentation and personalism in political parties had fostered alliances that sought short-term political gain to the detriment of consensus-building around key policy issues.

The United Nations Verification Mission in Guatemala (MINUGUA) continued to fulfil its mandate of verifying compliance with the 1996 peace accords between the Government of Guatemala and the Unidad Revolucionaria Nacional Guatemalteca, and to monitor compliance with the 2000-2004 verification timetable. Implementation of the accords fell short of expectations as progress was overshadowed by a worsening public security situation, persistent corruption, setbacks in the fight against impunity and an ongoing climate of intimidation against justice officials and human rights defenders. However, elections were held successfully in December and the General Assembly extended MINUGUA's mandate for the final time, until 31 December 2004.

In Haiti, despite efforts by the Organization of American States and the Caribbean Community Secretariat, the political and security crisis continued. By late 2003, a newly united opposition movement was calling for the President's resignation. The UN system continued its long-term programme of support for the country.

On 13 February, the Security Council condemned a bomb attack in Bogotá, Colombia, and urged all States to work together and to cooperate with and provide support and assistance to the Colombian authorities in their efforts to find and bring to justice the perpetrators, organizers and sponsors of that terrorist attack. The Council expressed its reinforced determination to combat all forms of terrorism.

In November, the Assembly again called on States to refrain from promulgating laws that imposed economic and trade measures on other States, such as the ongoing United States economic embargo against Cuba.

Central America

In response to General Assembly resolution 57/160 [YUN 2002, p. 241], the Secretary-General submitted an August report on the situation in Central America [A/58/270], focusing in particular on efforts to overcome the aftermath of the conflicts of the 1980s and to build equitable, democratic and peaceful societies. The report also provided information on the work of the UN system on the isthmus since September 2002 and on implementation of the 1996 Guatemala Agreement [YUN 1996, p. 168].

The Secretary-General stated that electoral processes in El Salvador and Guatemala in 2003 had brought key actors in both countries' civil wars closer than ever to executive responsibilities at the national level since the signing of the respective peace agreements. El Salvador's peaceful and orderly municipal and legislative elections on 16 March transformed the party of the former insurgent movement, Frente Farabundo Martí para la Liberación Nacional (FMLN), into the country's leading political force. However, voter absenteeism reached 60 per cent, and organizational and voter-counting problems confirmed the urgent need for electoral reform. Leading up to Guatemala's national elections (9 November and 28 December), a voter registration drive was launched to counter the historically low participation, particularly among indigenous people. However, congress was unable to obtain the two-thirds majority required to approve an Electoral and Political Parties Law that would have expanded opportunities for participation, particularly by members of the Mayan, Xinca and Garífuna indigenous groups. The Supreme Electoral Tribunal and the Supreme Court of Justice upheld the ban on retired General Efraín Ríos Montt registering as a presidential candidate. However, the ban was subsequently overturned by the Constitutional Court. That ruling prompted an outcry by human rights representatives and many sectors of the population and was received with concern by the international community in Guatemala. The retired General, founder of the ruling Frente

Republicano Guatemalteco, was the top military commander at the peak of the civil war, which resulted in the violent deaths of 200,000 people. In a positive step, representatives of the political parties signed on 10 July the Ethical-Political Agreement on the electoral process and a declaration of commitment to the peace agreements.

Efforts to improve the human rights situation in Central America continued to be affected by the lack of sufficient budgetary allocations to the leading national human rights institutions and deficiencies in the way States addressed the pervasive problem of common crime. In Guatemala, a climate of intimidation clouded efforts to enhance the human rights situation and to fight impunity. In March, the Guatemalan Government and the Human Rights Ombudsman's Office reached an agreement to establish the Commission for the Investigation of Illegal Groups and Clandestine Security Apparatuses, with the participation of the United Nations and the Organization of American States (OAS). The Secretary-General was considering recommendations from an exploratory technical mission that he had sent to assess the viability of such a commission and to determine the conditions for possible UN participation. The Ombudsman's Office continued to face challenges but showed encouraging signs of reorganization and strengthening under new leadership. However, the reform process was still hindered by low budgetary allocations and excessive reliance on international cooperation to finance reforms. The common element in the threats and attacks reported in Guatemala had been the lack of results in official investigations; the State's institutional response had been isolated and limited and progress in combating impunity was fragile. The Guatemalan National Civil Police was significantly weakened by lack of resources, and the Government responded to the growing crime problem by resorting to the army for joint operations.

In El Salvador, civil society and its organizations were becoming more mature in the defence, promotion and fulfilment of human rights. The Ombudsman's Office continued to be underfunded and remained isolated from other related State institutions. A new Human Rights Division of the Salvadoran National Civil Police had yet to develop significantly, and the resolution of criminal cases continued to be low. In Honduras, the rate of extrajudicial killings of children remained high and, according to the Public Ministry, there were 74 cases against officials regarding such killings. The proliferation of largely unregistered firearms in the country posed a threat to public security, and an initiative that gave carriers three months to hand over illegal firearms had been met with a lukewarm response. However, the crime rate had decreased as a result of joint police and armed forces operations. The large number of private security companies and the increased participation in citizen security committees had raised concerns about the State's control of such activities. In Nicaragua, the Government had launched an initiative to improve public security, which included investing in crime prevention and working closely with local communities. Also, efforts to modernize the National Police had met with significant success.

In the area of judicial reform and the rule of law, countries in the region had taken important steps to establish a more transparent justice sector. In Honduras and Nicaragua, new criminal procedure codes had introduced significant advances. In El Salvador, on the other hand, the codes still required a full review. However, measures to improve access to prompt and due justice still fell short of expectations, particularly for the indigenous population and the rural poor of the region. Penitentiary system reforms had made little headway and high levels of pre-trial detentions continued to result in overcrowding and lawlessness in prisons. On 5 April, a massacre in a Honduras prison claimed 69 lives, exposing the need for an overhaul of the penitentiary system. In further efforts to strengthen public safety in the region, the Central American countries held the Special Summit on Regional Security (Belize City, 4 September) and the Special Summit on Security (Guatemala City, 17 July).

In the area of good governance, efforts were made to tackle corruption in the region. On 12 December 2002, Nicaragua's National Assembly had stripped former President Arnoldo Alemán, implicated in a $100 million corruption scandal, of his parliamentary immunity; Mr. Alemán was subsequently convicted of money-laundering. Nicaragua also established a multi-donor trust fund to support the fight against corruption, created a Public Ethics Office within the Presidency, advanced the implementation of the Integrated Financial Management System for real-time monitoring of budget execution, began discussing a bill to regulate the transfer of resources from the central budget to the municipalities, and was using foreign financial support to improve the internal audit capacity of its institutions and municipalities. In El Salvador, the Legislative Assembly approved a law reforming the Government's auditing agency, the Court of Accounts. In Honduras, the Comptroller General's Office and the Board of Administrative Integrity were replaced by the Superior Court of Accounts, and the National Congress elected the Court's three members. However, that process was criticized for lack of transparency. The Honduras National Anticorruption Council was limited in its ability to carry out its mandate, owing to the absence of the relevant organic law. In a positive development, Honduras undertook an international audit of the military institute and related companies, which forged a closer relationship between the armed forces and civil society. Guatemala's 2003 budget law came slightly closer than in the previous year to realizing its institutional requirements to carry out the peace agreements but remained insufficient for any significant expansion or improvement in the services required of ministries, secretariats and the other government institutions. New accusations surfaced regarding corruption and influence of drug trafficking and organized crime in Guatemala's governmental spheres; in January, the United States announced that it had decertified Guatemala as a cooperative ally in the fight against illegal drugs.

According to the Economic Commission for Latin America and the Caribbean, the gross domestic product (GDP) of Costa Rica, El Salvador, Guatemala, Honduras and Nicaragua grew by 1.9 per cent, but the per capita GDP fell by 0.46 per cent. The 2003 human development index of the United Nations Development Programme (UNDP), calculated on the basis of life expectancy, adult literacy, level of schooling and per capita GDP, placed the Central American countries, except Costa Rica, in the category of nations with "medium human development"; Costa Rica was classified as a country with "high human development". In January, Central American ministers met with the United States Trade Representative to launch negotiations on the Central America Free Trade Agreement. In addition, talks regarding the Canada–Central America Four Free Trade Agreement, involving Canada, El Salvador, Guatemala, Honduras and Nicaragua, were ongoing. Negotiations on a Central American common customs union continued and a mechanism for trade dispute resolution was approved. On 2 June, in Washington, D.C., delegates of the eight countries involved in the Puebla-Panama Plan—a comprehensive initiative for regional integration and development [YUN 2001, p. 240]—adopted a strategy for the implementation of the Mesoamerican Initiative for Sustainable Development.

The Central American Integration System (SICA) continued to promote regional coordination. The Nineteenth Ministerial Conference on Political Dialogue and Economic Cooperation between the European Union (EU) and SICA (Panama City, 12 May) acknowledged the importance of civil society's participation in strengthening EU–Central America relations, agreed that meetings of the civil society forums in each region should be encouraged, and stated their intention to work on the definition of international forums and mechanisms for consultation on topics such as the peaceful solution of conflicts, the fight against drugs and terrorism. The first round of negotiations of the Political Dialogue and Cooperation Agreement was held in Panama from 13 to 15 May. The OAS Inter-American Committee against Terrorism held its third regular session (San Salvador, El Salvador, 22-24 January), during which the Secretary-General of SICA informed participants of anti-terrorism actions taken by Central American countries. El Salvador ratified the 2002 Inter-American Convention against Terrorism and Nicaragua adhered in June. Costa Rica and Peru signed a letter of understanding relating to the inter-American fight against corruption. The XI Institutionalized Ministerial Meeting between the Rio Group (of Latin American and Caribbean States) and the EU (Athens, Greece, 28 March) discussed EU–Rio Group relations and social cohesion and democratic governance in the new economic environment. The Rio Group, at its XVII Summit of Heads of State and Government (Cuzco, Peru, 23-24 May), adopted the "Cuzco Consensus", a strategic agenda for overcoming poverty and social exclusion and covering democratic governance, cultural identity and external relations, as well as the promotion of a free and fair international trade system. Signatories of the Consensus agreed to hold a special meeting within the framework of the General Assembly's fifty-eighth (2003) session.

Border disputes between Central American countries continued their course in the International Court of Justice (see PART FOUR, Chapter I) and OAS facilitated progress in the Guatemala/Belize boundary dispute. The Secretary-General stated that it was encouraging that bilateral disputes were increasingly finding resolution through established international channels.

The United Nations continued to support the process of peace-building and development in Central America. On 29 May, El Salvador submitted an inventory of the armaments of its armed forces. FMLN, in an 8 July letter to the Secretary-General, confirmed its decision to lift its reservation regarding the permanent character of the armed forces, and its recognition of the role that the armed forces currently fulfilled and the transformation of its doctrine, vision, values and organization. In Guatemala, the United Nations continued to verify compliance with the 1996 Agreement on a Firm and Lasting Peace

[YUN 1996, p. 168]. Progress in implementation of the Agreement fell short of expectations and was insufficient to inject needed momentum into the peace process. Advances were recorded in such areas as legislation against discrimination, the redeployment of military units and the development of a national reparations programme for the victims of human rights violations committed during the armed conflict. However, setbacks occurred in key areas of human rights, demilitarization and the fight against impunity. At the Consultative Group for Guatemala meeting (Guatemala City, 13-14 May), organized by the Inter-American Development Bank, participants agreed that the peace agreements should remain Guatemala's essential road map for development.

UNDP partnered with Central American countries to respond to natural disasters and to ensure continuity after humanitarian relief by putting in place early recovery initiatives. In Guatemala, UNDP's project on an early flood-warning system in the valleys of Madre Vieja River, implemented by the National Coordinator for Disaster Reduction, was helping to reduce risks and sustain human development among highly vulnerable communities. In Honduras, the UN system strengthened its strategic contribution to the development of rural society, and supported risk management, fortification of prevention measures, handling the hydrographic river basins, sustainable rural development, inter-institutional support to the forest sector and decentralization. By March, UNDP, through a capacity-building project in Nicaragua, had trained 86 local authorities and community members in disaster risk management.

The Secretary-General observed that concerted efforts would be required to ensure that all Central American countries and all segments of their populations benefited from new arrangements such as the Central American Free Trade Association and the Puebla-Panama Plan. Only by promoting inclusion at the political, socio-economic and cultural levels would the region achieve peaceful, democratic and just societies, and the United Nations and the international community should continue to accompany the Central American countries in their efforts to reach those goals.

GENERAL ASSEMBLY ACTION

On 23 December [meeting 79], the General Assembly adopted **resolution 58/239** [draft: A/58/L.38 & Add.1] without vote [agenda item 26].

The situation in Central America: progress in fashioning a region of peace, freedom, democracy and development

The General Assembly,

Recalling its relevant resolutions in which it requests the Secretary-General, the United Nations system and the international community to give the Central American peoples the fullest possible support and assistance for the maintenance and strengthening of peace, democracy and sustainable development, as well as the relevant Security Council resolutions,

Reaffirming all its relevant resolutions in which it stresses the importance of international economic, financial and technical cooperation and support, both bilateral and multilateral, aimed at promoting the economic and social development of Central America with a view to supplementing the efforts of the Central American peoples and Governments to consolidate peace and democracy,

Reaffirming also the close link and interaction between peace, democracy and sustainable development, as fundamental and permanent pillars of the political action of the Central American Governments aimed at realizing the legitimate aspirations of the Central American peoples with regard to economic development and social justice,

Recognizing that peace and democracy in Central America are the outcome of a long and arduous process in which obstacles have been encountered but have been overcome through the efforts of the peoples and Governments of the region, with the assistance and cooperation of the United Nations system and the international community,

Commending the efforts of the Central American Governments to continue fulfilling the commitments they have assumed under national, regional and international agreements with a view to strengthening democratic governance in the region by promoting and protecting human rights, implementing social programmes designed to eradicate poverty and eliminate unemployment, improving public safety, strengthening the judiciary, consolidating a modern and transparent public administration and combating corruption,

Taking note of the existence throughout Central America of freely elected Governments, indicating the achievement of political, economic and social changes that are creating a climate conducive to the promotion of economic growth and advancement towards the further development of democratic, just and equitable societies,

Emphasizing, in this context, the importance of the progress made in connection with the Central American Integration System, the Alliance for the Sustainable Development of Central America, the establishment of the regional social policy contained in the Treaty on Central American Social Integration and the Framework Treaty on Democratic Security in Central America, and in other areas,

Noting with satisfaction the progress made in the region in the search for peaceful solutions to existing territorial and border disputes, in accordance with the principles of public international law and the provisions of the Charter of the United Nations,

Recognizing that the slow development of the economies of the area has been aggravated in the past two years by an unfavourable international economic climate, which has had an adverse effect on the efforts of the peoples and Governments of the region to promote sustainable economic development in an efficient manner,

Recognizing with satisfaction the progress made by the Central American region in the promotion and protection of human rights and fundamental freedoms, and the obligation of States to continue guaranteeing their effective enjoyment,

Recognizing the efforts of the region to enhance public safety by taking steps to combat the illicit trade in small arms and light weapons, by arms limitation and control, and by combating transnational organized crime and terrorism,

1. *Takes note* of the report of the Secretary-General on the situation in Central America;

2. *Commends* the efforts of the peoples and Governments of the Central American countries to consolidate peace and democracy and promote sustainable development by implementing the commitments adopted at the meetings and summit meetings held in the region;

3. *Recognizes* the progress made towards the implementation of the peace agreements in the region, and in that context reiterates its special appreciation and congratulations to the people and Government of El Salvador for the successful fulfilment of the commitments set forth in those agreements, and expresses its profound thanks to the Secretary-General for accompanying that process and for the commendable way in which he has carried out his verification work, which is considered to be completed;

4. *Urges* the Government of Guatemala to give renewed impetus to the fulfilment of the commitments contained in the peace agreements, in the context of reprogramming for the period 2001-2004, and to the understanding reached during the fifth meeting of the Consultative Group for Guatemala, organized by the Inter-American Development Bank and held in Guatemala City on 13 and 14 May 2003;

5. *Urges* the Governments of the region to continue to guarantee free, fair and transparent elections with a view to consolidating democracy in Central America;

6. *Commends* the efforts and actions undertaken in the region to combat the scourge of corruption, urges all the States of the area to continue their actions with a view to eradicating that evil, and in that context takes note of the congratulations expressed in the report of the Secretary-General with regard to the work done by the Government of Nicaragua in this field;

7. *Views with satisfaction* the approval of important reforms relating to the conduct of public affairs and judicial matters in Central America, and in that context expresses special satisfaction concerning the progress made in Honduras towards completion of the political transformation process initiated in September 2001, and urges the Central American Governments to redouble their efforts with a view to strengthening those areas even further;

8. *Urges* Member States to continue combining efforts to adapt, strengthen and promote even further the Central American integration process, and appeals to the international community to continue supporting that process in order to contribute to the sustainable development of the region;

9. *Notes with satisfaction* the progress made by the Central American Governments in the peaceful settlement of their territorial and border disputes, and strongly urges them to continue working to resolve outstanding issues in full compliance with the norms of international law and the relevant international decisions and judgements;

10. *Emphasizes* the importance of foreign trade for the development of Central America, and in this context stresses the value of negotiating balanced free-trade agreements between the region and its counterparts outside the region;

11. *Reaffirms* the importance of the Puebla-Panama Plan as a means of promoting the economic and social development of the Mesoamerican region, and recognizes in that connection the progress made in implementing the Plan;

12. *Urges* the Governments of the Central American countries to continue strengthening the institutions responsible for the promotion and protection of human rights and fundamental freedoms, thus helping to ensure their full and effective enjoyment by all the peoples of the region;

13. *Appeals* to the Central American Governments to continue their efforts to combat the illicit trade in small arms and light weapons, promote arms limitation and control and combat transnational organized crime and terrorism by fulfilling the obligations assumed in the relevant international agreements;

14. *Appreciates* the efforts of the Central American countries to strengthen public safety in the area by organizing summit meetings on that issue, such as the Special Summit on Regional Security, held in Belize City on 4 September 2003, and the Special Summit on Security, held in Guatemala City on 17 July 2003;

15. *Welcomes* the efforts made to strengthen civilian police forces and promote the demilitarization of the region, in particular the actions taken in the context of the regional plan to combat organized crime, and emphasizes the need for the international community to continue lending its support to the relevant institutions in the field of public safety;

16. *Takes note with satisfaction* of the intention of the Government of Guatemala to establish a Commission for the Investigation of Illegal Groups and Clandestine Security Apparatuses, and urges the Secretary-General to support that initiative with a view to its prompt implementation;

17. *Appreciates* the initiative of the Government of Nicaragua relating to the programme for arms limitation and control in Central America to achieve a reasonable balance of forces and to foster stability, mutual trust and transparency, which will be implemented in the region in accordance with the established schedule;

18. *Emphasizes* the need for the international community, especially the organs, funds and programmes of the United Nations system and the donor community, to continue their cooperation with and assistance to the Central American countries, including the provision of bilateral and multilateral financial resources, with the aim of supporting the promotion of sustainable development and the consolidation of peace, freedom and democracy in the region;

19. *Requests* the Secretary-General to continue to lend his fullest support to the initiatives and activities

of the Central American Governments, in particular their efforts to consolidate democracy through the promotion of integration and the implementation of a comprehensive sustainable development programme and to submit to the General Assembly a complete consolidated report on the implementation of all the relevant resolutions on Central America at its sixtieth session, under the item entitled "The situation in Central America: progress in fashioning a region of peace, freedom, democracy and development", and decides that, henceforth, the item will be considered every two years.

On 17 December, the Assembly adopted **resolution 58/117** (see p. 950) on international assistance to and cooperation with the Alliance for the Sustainable Development of Central America.

Guatemala

Although progress in Guatemala's peace process fell short of expectations in 2003, peaceful elections took place in December. Advances included the approval of a reparations programme for victims of human rights violations committed during the armed conflict, the partial redeployment of the military in conformity with peacetime needs and the passage of legislation that penalized discrimination, stipulated that public services should be provided in indigenous languages, broadened protection of the rights of children and created civilian service as an alternative to mandatory military service. However, too many governmental initiatives were inconclusive or limited in relation to the magnitude of the problems they sought to address. Advances were overshadowed in the public eye by the worsening public security situation, persistent corruption, obstacles in the fight against impunity and an ongoing climate of intimidation against justice officials and human rights defenders.

The United Nations Verification Mission in Guatemala (MINUGUA) (see below) continued to verify the 1996 Agreement on a Firm and Lasting Peace [YUN 1996, p. 168], signed by the Government of Guatemala and the Unidad Revolucionaria Nacional Guatemalteca (URNG), and monitored compliance with the 2000-2004 verification timetable [YUN 2000, p. 239]. The calendar established in the 1997 Agreement on the Implementation, Compliance and Verification Timetable for the Peace Agreements [YUN 1997, p. 176] for the period 1997-2000, also signed by the Government and URNG, expired in December 2000. Since much of the peace agenda remained outstanding, the Commission to Follow Up the Implementation of the Peace Agreements rescheduled pending commitments in an implementation timetable for 2000-2004, which recognized that the basis of the Timetable Agreement and the peace agreements as a whole remained valid. MINUGUA also embarked on a transition programme to strengthen the capacity of Guatemalan governing and civil institutions to carry forward the peace agenda after the Mission's withdrawal.

In **resolution 58/238** of 23 December, the General Assembly authorized a final renewal of MINUGUA's mandate from 1 January to 31 December 2004 (see p. 283).

MINUGUA

The mandate of MINUGUA, which had been extended to 31 December 2003 by General Assembly resolution 57/161 [YUN 2002, p. 247], included verification of all agreements signed by the Government of Guatemala and URNG, covering human rights, demilitarization and the strengthening of civilian power, indigenous rights, and socio-economic aspects and the agrarian situation. The Mission also verified compliance with the 2000-2004 timetable for the implementation of pending commitments under the peace agreements, and provided good offices, technical assistance and information to the public on its activities and the results of its verification.

Report of Secretary-General. In response to Assembly resolution 57/161, the Secretary-General submitted an August report [A/58/262] covering the state of implementation of the 1996 peace agreements (see p. 280). He also described MINUGUA's transition strategy in preparation for its departure from Guatemala and presented a plan for restructuring the Mission in 2004 as the final stage in the phase-out process leading to its closure.

In view of the fact that a new Government would assume office in January 2004, President Alfonso Portillo had requested in September 2002 that MINUGUA's mandate be extended until the end of 2004.

The Secretary-General noted that implementation of the peace accords since September 2002 had fallen short of expectations and was insufficient to inject new momentum into the peace process. Although progress in specific areas had been verified by the Mission, there were also negative developments, such as the worsening public security situation, persistent corruption, obstacles in the fight against impunity and an ongoing climate of intimidation against justice officials and human rights defenders.

Violence was reported at the start of the election campaign period, and the build-up to the elections, to be held in November and December, was generating tensions at the local level. Electoral authorities had come under increased pressure, especially after a controversial ruling in July by the nation's highest court permitting the presidential candidacy of retired General Efraín Ríos Montt.

The Secretary-General stated that, following the elections, the country's new leaders would face enormous challenges to overcome disunity and provide coherent direction forward. With changes at both national and local levels and the customary enormous staff turnover, it would be no small task to ensure the continuity of the important institutions and programmes that had been developed as part of the peace agreements. The new Government would have a great responsibility in that regard, but civil society and the private sector would also need to play a forceful role and lend their creativity to the building of a stronger and more effective consensus around the peace agenda. The support of the international community and of the United Nations, in particular, would continue to be crucial as new authorities took over and tackled their new functions.

During 2003, MINUGUA focused on building the capacity of partners in Guatemalan institutions to provide oversight and to promote and monitor issues defined in the peace accords. Upon MINUGUA's departure, the Office of the Human Rights Ombudsman would have the national mandate and territorial coverage to investigate complaints and call for State action regarding human rights problems. Support for the Office, pursuant to a memorandum of understanding signed in October 2002, had involved all of the Mission's substantive units and field offices. Major accomplishments in 2003 included country-wide staff training on human rights monitoring and other peace issues, increased joint verification and technical assistance to create computerized information systems. MINUGUA's work with civil society aimed to complement efforts with the Office of the Human Rights Ombudsman and other key State institutions, especially on issues and in regions where the responsible State entities remained weak. That work involved training and providing technical support. Technical assistance had also been provided to local indigenous and women's organizations working in the decentralized structures for participatory planning and oversight, known as Development Councils.

MINUGUA continued to serve as an observer on the Commission to Follow Up the Implementation of the Peace Agreements, participating in discussions to revamp the peace institutions (including the Commission itself) as a step in reinvigorating the peace process. With significant reform and sufficient resources, the Commission could provide general monitoring and oversight of the pending peace agenda and serve as a national advocate for the peace agreements.

In addition to transition efforts with national institutions and organizations, complementary measures had been advanced to ensure specific follow-on by the specialized agencies, funds and programmes of the UN system, as well as by members of the international community. That work would intensify in 2004.

It was envisaged that the Office of the United Nations High Commissioner for Human Rights (OHCHR) would upgrade its current technical assistance project. MINUGUA had been working with OHCHR to implement a joint work plan on indigenous peoples' rights and had assisted in developing plans for OHCHR's future work in Guatemala.

The Mission was also working with the UN country team to develop the new United Nations Development Assistance Framework and to build greater capacity for monitoring and reporting on the implementation of the pending socio-economic commitments contained in the peace agreements. It coordinated efforts to produce a supplement to the annual *Human Development Report* that integrated information from several UN programmes and agencies and presented a joint assessment of the status of the commitments. Follow-up needs established and lessons learned from completed Trust Fund projects on a range of socio-economic, justice, public security and defence issues had been presented to UNDP, which had taken measures to provide greater support and technical assistance to national institutions in those areas. MINUGUA staff were working with the donor community and cooperation agencies to identify priorities that had emerged as a result of the Mission's phase-out process. The Mission also worked closely with the Dialogue Group—composed of major bilateral donors and multilateral development banks—on the implementation of the pending commitments contained in the peace agreements. It would continue to provide information and analysis to the Dialogue Group, given the Group's key role in facilitating direct communication between the international community and Guatemalan political actors on the peace agenda and its potential for channelling cooperation efforts towards consolidation of the peace process after MINUGUA's departure.

Beginning in the third quarter of 2003, the National Transition Volunteers programme, another component of the transition strategy, would train up to 60 Guatemalans, giving priority to indigenous people and to those committed to working in provincial areas, and would integrate them into the Mission's substantive activities, including its verification work. The Mission would then seek formal agreements with the Ombudsman, key human rights and indigenous organizations and other appropriate institutions with the aim of facilitating the volunteers' employment once the Mission had ended.

MINUGUA would continue to verify compliance with the peace agreements in two broad areas—human rights, and demilitarization and the strengthening of civilian power—but with sharply defined priorities, given both budgetary constraints and advances in the transition process. The Office of the Spokesperson, with fewer staff, would continue to play a key role in publicizing peace-process achievements and providing information on the Mission's transition and withdrawal. The Transition Unit, which would also be smaller, would continue to provide strategic advice and monitor benchmarks in the transition process, coordinate follow-on with the Office of the Human Rights Ombudsman and work with the country team and bilateral cooperation agencies to ensure political, technical and financial support for national transition partners. Two thematic advisory units would be maintained in 2004—on human rights and on demilitarization and strengthening civilian power. The advisory units on indigenous rights and on economic policy and rural development would be phased out in 2003 and follow-up mechanisms would be put in place. MINUGUA was seeking support to extend the Programme of Institutional Assistance for Legal Reform into 2004, as its extensive contacts and knowledge of peace accord legislative initiatives would provide significant support to the Mission's political focus, especially work in the new Congress. In addition, it was expected that the National Transition Volunteers programme would be financed by the Trust Fund and implemented directly by the Mission.

The Secretary-General stated that the new Government, to be elected in 2003, together with civil society and the private sector, must work with increased energy and commitment to lead the country into a new period characterized by the rule of law and full human development.

In view of the remaining challenges to the peace process, the Secretary-General recommend that the General Assembly authorize the renewal of MINUGUA's mandate from 1 January to 31 December 2004.

Verification of compliance

In response to General Assembly resolution 57/161 [YUN 2002, p. 247], the Secretary-General in August submitted his eighth report [A/58/267] on the verification of compliance with the agreements signed by the Government of Guatemala and URNG [YUN 1996, p. 168].

The implementation of the commitments entered into by the two parties was governed by the Timetable Agreement [YUN 1997, p. 176], which expired in December 2000. The Commission to Follow Up the Implementation of the Peace Agreements rescheduled pending commitments in an implementation timetable for 2000-2004 [YUN 2000, p. 245].

During the first half of 2003, implementation of the peace accords had lagged and key implementing institutions suffered from inadequate budget resources. The Secretary-General stated that while there had been some advances in the peace accords, the sustainability of the process could be ensured only if Guatemalans assumed full ownership and responsibility to carry it forward.

In March, the Government and the Human Rights Ombudsman agreed to establish an internationally backed investigation into the existence of clandestine groups with the participation of the United Nations and OAS. The Secretary-General sent a technical exploratory mission of independent experts and UN officials to Guatemala to assess the viability of such a commission.

New accusations surfaced regarding corruption and the influence of drug trafficking and organized crime in governmental spheres and, in January, the United States Government decertified Guatemala as a cooperative ally in the fight against illegal drugs. In positive steps, the Government dissolved its anti-narcotics police after members were implicated in corruption and serious human rights violations, and the Attorney General initiated investigations of five former military officers suspected of involvement in illicit activities.

The Government, donors and representatives of civil society and political parties participated in a Consultative Group meeting (Guatemala City, 13-14 May) to evaluate progress in implementing the peace agreements since its 2002 meeting [YUN 2002, p. 244]. Participants agreed that the peace agreements should remain Guatemala's essential road map for development. The President of Guatemala announced that he would introduce legislation to strengthen the Commission to Follow Up the Implementation of the Peace Agreements and the Peace Secretariat of the Presidency so as to ensure the continuation of the peace accords under the next administration. The largest donors expressed continued strong support provided Guatemalans remained committed to moving ahead in the peace process. Following the Consultative Group meeting, the Government presented measures to advance the peace agenda during the remaining months of the Administration, including full demobilization of the Presidential General Staff, passage of a 2004 budget reflecting peace priorities, reductions in the army, initiation of the national reparations programme and the investigation into clandestine groups, as well as the passage of pending legislation, including the land registry law and laws on access to information, on classification and declassification, and on elections and political parties.

The Under-Secretary-General for Political Affairs, Kieran Prendergast, visited Guatemala from 4 to 8 July to review MINUGUA's transition plans. He met with President Portillo and high government officials, electoral authorities and leaders of civil society and underlined the need to intensify national efforts to implement the peace agreements and to hold credible and transparent elections. He emphasized that the rule of law and broader political participation were the keys to Guatemala's future.

MINUGUA's verification activities focused on human rights, the rights and identity of indigenous peoples, demilitarization and the strengthening of civilian power, and socio-economic aspects and the agrarian situation. It took into account the implementation and verification timetable established by the Commission to Follow Up the Implementation of the Peace Agreements, which extended through 2004. It also considered the governmental commitments made at the 2002 Consultative Group meeting for Guatemala [YUN 2002, p. 244].

With the end of the armed conflict, Guatemala's human rights situation improved dramatically, as reflected in reduced levels of such violations as executions, forced disappearances and torture. Political killings were greatly reduced and freedom of the media increased. However, public security deteriorated, impunity persisted, and the climate of intimidation against human rights defenders, social activists and journalists continued. Human rights activists, judges, prosecutors, attorneys, witnesses and forensic anthropologists had also been subject to threats, harassment and violence. A common element in such cases was the lack of results in official investigations and a limited response from justice sector authorities.

In March, in an effort to identify and combat clandestine groups believed to be responsible for such incidents, the Government and the Human Rights Ombudsman, with the support of non-governmental human rights organizations, agreed to create a Commission for the Investigation of Illegal Groups and Clandestine Security Apparatuses and asked the United Nations to support the initiative. Although some justice sector institutions, including the National Civilian Police, received nominal budgetary increases for 2003, the amounts remained insufficient to undertake much-needed expansion and reform plans. In July, the Government inaugurated a National Reparations Commission to create and administer a national reparations programme for victims of Guatemala's 36-year-long armed conflict. The Secretary-General stated that it was important that Congress reverse its earlier refusal to support national reparations and ensure the funding base and institutional stability of payments by enacting the programme into law.

As to the identity and rights of indigenous peoples, Congress, in May, passed a new law that facilitated the use of indigenous languages in official spheres. Legislation that penalized discrimination, including on the basis of gender, was also adopted. However, Guatemala had still not recognized the competence of the UN Committee on the Elimination of Racial Discrimination to receive individual complaints. Also pending was legislation to recognize indigenous people's right to land ownership and indigenous access to radio frequencies and to bilingual education. In addition, the Office for the Defence of Indigenous Women's Rights still lacked a sufficient budget to effectively expand its coverage into the country's interior. There were few advances in promoting access to the justice system by indigenous peoples in their own languages, and educational reforms to reflect linguistic and cultural diversity progressed slowly. In March, President Portillo inaugurated a presidential commission for the elimination of discrimination and racism against indigenous peoples. Its effectiveness would ultimately depend on its ability to generate recommendations and on the Government's willingness to implement them.

Advances in consolidating civilian institutions and reshaping the military continued to be slow, despite progress towards dissolving the Presidential General Staff and redeploying the military according to national defence criteria rather than internal security considerations. Results were mixed on the legislative agenda. Despite discussions between the Government and civil society organizations, laws on access to information and the classification of State information, controls over firearms and munitions, and the regulation of private security firms had yet to be enacted. Congress, however, passed a law establishing a civilian alternative to mandatory military service. In public security, the Government responded to the growing crime problem by involving the army in public security, rather than by strengthening the National Civilian Police. A February 2003 presidential decree established an Advisory Council on Security, composed of prominent citizens, to contribute to the formulation of public security and defence policy. Draft regulations on police discipline, which would help to remove abusive or corrupt officials, were still awaiting approval by the executive branch.

Progress under the Agreement on Social and Economic Aspects and the Agrarian Situation was hindered by inadequate resources for relevant institutions and lack of movement on key legislation in land and rural development, fiscal policy and transparency, decentralization, education, health and housing, and the resettlement of uprooted populations and incorporation of ex-combatants. On the other hand, the Government's continued transfer of funds to the military resulted in a 24 per cent increase in the 2003 budget of the National Defence Ministry and a 95 per cent increase for the Presidential General Staff. On the positive side, the Government agreed to a proposal from civil society organizations to fund a "coffee emergency" plan, including crop diversification and the acquisition of new lands for unemployed peasants, as the depression of coffee prices continued; presented a land registry bill to Congress for action in April; opened discussions on defining a rural development policy with peasant and indigenous groups and members of the private sector; and created a new System for the Decentralization of Educational Management. However, the law on agrarian and environmental jurisdiction remained pending; laws regarding idle lands and territorial taxes recorded no progress; and the Trust Fund for Productive Projects, directed at both the demobilized and the resettled populations, had been awaiting implementation for two years. The Secretary-General urged that national resources be assigned to the Fund. In May, a major EU-funded project in support of the reincorporation of ex-combatants came to a close.

The Secretary-General observed that he was encouraged that Guatemala's main political parties were committed to carrying on with the peace process and by the involvement of civil society organizations and their enthusiasm in framing future work agendas around the agreements' implementation. He stated that, during its remaining months in office, the current Administration should make every effort to implement pending commitments in the peace accords; completely dissolve the Presidential General Staff; accelerate actions against discrimination; reduce military spending and dedicate significantly increased resources to social needs and rule of law institutions in the 2004 budget; adopt in its entirety the list of priority peace legislation prepared by the Commission to Follow Up the Implementation of the Peace Agreements, including the land registry law, the laws on access to information and the classification and declassification of State information and a framework law on civilian intelligence; pass legislation to strengthen the key institutions created by the accords; and begin implementation of the national reparations programme for victims of human rights violations. The Secretary-General indicated that the international community should continue to focus its cooperation on the framework of the peace accords, while national efforts were being strengthened to sustain the process.

On 9 November and 28 December, Guatemala held national elections, which resulted in Oscar José Rafael Berger Perdomo of the Gran Alianza Nacional party being elected President for a four-year term.

Human rights

In November, the Secretary-General transmitted to the General Assembly MINUGUA's fourteenth report [A/58/566] on human rights in Guatemala, which described the Mission's activities from July 2002 to June 2003.

During the reporting period, hopes for improving the human rights situation were dampened by the loss of momentum for the reform of public security and justice institutions. Deterioration of the National Civilian Police and slow modernization of the courts and the Public Prosecutor's Office had undermined key commitments of the peace agreements. There was almost no significant progress in combating impunity or eliminating clandestine groups; human rights defenders and judicial sector officials remained subject to threats, harassment and fatal attacks; and systematic discrimination against indigenous communities continued unabated. Although important advances had been made in promoting human rights since 1997, they might prove to be of limited value without the strengthening of fundamental State institutions.

The Secretary-General stated that it was a cause for concern in Guatemala that, not only were reforms progressing slowly, but the Government and a number of other political and social sectors no longer appeared committed to the changes that were at the heart of the peace process. It was thus urgent for the new Government (2004-2008), with political will, organization and adequate resources, to build on achievements to end impunity and achieve justice for human rights violations; it should adopt a public security strategy that would include the doubling of the police force to 40,000 officers by the end of 2008, the establishment of strong internal professional controls, the dismissal of officers with poor human rights and performance records, comprehensive new recruiting programmes and the strengthening and expansion of the Police Academy. In addition, the prison system required a full overhaul, beginning with the adoption of the prison reform legislation rejected by Congress earlier in the year and implementation of the recommendations of the Commission for the Transformation of the Penal System. Also, the judicial sector must intensify the speed and depth of modernization programmes. The Supreme Court and the Public Prosecutor should fully institutionalize and support the transparent implementation of civil service career structures that had been put in place; the installation of management systems to monitor the flow of cases and performance of every judge and prosecutor should be accelerated; security for judicial sector officials had to be substantially improved; and Constitutional Court magistrates should be selected on the basis of qualifications and merit.

The Supreme Court and the Public Prosecutor should accelerate the full integration of indigenous legal traditions and practices into the formal legal system, dramatically increase the bilingual capacity of the system and educate personnel on indigenous legal customs. Access to justice programmes, particularly the judicial administrative centres and the proposed expansion of the justice of the peace jurisdiction, should be modified to incorporate fully the equity-based, informal and local dispute resolution practices of indigenous communities. The Coordinating Body for Modernization of the Justice Sector, directed by the heads of the Supreme Court, the Office of the Public Prosecutor, the Interior Ministry and the Public Defender Institute, should assume its original purpose of coordinating modernization policies of all the justice sector's actors. What was required was a political commitment by the new Government and Congress to the urgent implementation of those reforms and a significant reallocation of budget resources for the 2004-2008 period to those priorities. Civil society organizations should continue to work to produce independent, non-partisan analyses of the human rights situation, actively engage the State on important issues, and seek cross-sector alliances to advance the strengthening of democratic norms and practices.

Following a request by Guatemala's President, the Secretary-General recommended to the General Assembly that MINUGUA's mandate be extended until the end of 2004.

GENERAL ASSEMBLY ACTION

On 23 December [meeting 79], the General Assembly adopted **resolution 58/238** [draft: A/58/L.30/Rev.1 & Add.1] without vote [agenda item 26].

United Nations Verification Mission in Guatemala

The General Assembly,

Recalling its resolution 57/161 of 16 December 2002, in which it decided to authorize the renewal of the mandate of the United Nations Verification Mission in Guatemala from 1 January to 31 December 2003,

Taking into account the fact that the Government of Guatemala has reaffirmed its commitment to the full implementation of the peace agreements,

Underlining the fact that substantive aspects of the peace agreements have yet to be implemented and that the timetable for implementation and verification established by the Commission to Follow Up the Implementation of the Peace Agreements extends through 2004,

Taking into account the request of the Government of Guatemala for an extension of the mandate of the Mission until the end of 2004, in view of the desirability of maintaining the presence of the Mission during the first year of the new Government, which will take office in January 2004,

Taking into account also the fact that civil society organizations in Guatemala and the international community expressed concerns about potential setbacks to implementation of the peace agreements should the Mission depart Guatemala before a new Government had taken office and demonstrated its commitment to the peace process,

Taking note of the fact that on 10 July 2003, under the auspices of the Organization of American States, representatives of the main political parties of Guatemala signed a declaration expressing support for the peace agreements as State accords that should be incorporated into government plans for the peace process,

Taking into account the eighth report of the Secretary-General on the verification of compliance with the peace agreements,

Taking into account also the fourteenth report of the Mission on human rights,

Taking into account further the report of the Commission for Historical Clarification,

Stressing the positive role played by the Mission in support of the Guatemala peace process, and emphasizing the need for the Mission to continue to enjoy the full support of all parties concerned,

Having considered the report of the Secretary-General on the work of the Mission and the recommendations contained therein,

1. *Welcomes* the eighth report of the Secretary-General on the verification of compliance with the peace agreements;

2. *Also welcomes* the fourteenth report of the United Nations Verification Mission in Guatemala on human rights;

3. *Calls upon* the Government of Guatemala to maintain its commitment to the full implementation of the peace agreements;

4. *Also calls upon* newly elected public officials to act on the commitments made by representatives of the main political parties in July 2003 to support the peace agreements as State accords that should be incorporated into government plans for the peace process;

5. *Takes note* of the recommendations contained in the report of the Secretary-General on the work of the Mission aimed at ensuring that the Mission responds adequately to the demands of the peace process until 31 December 2004, in view of the many outstanding

matters still to be addressed and the need to ensure the commitment of the new Government to the peace agreements;

6. *Notes* that, while in 2003 the Mission verified four broad areas of the peace agreements, in 2004 it will concentrate only on two areas, human rights and demilitarization and the strengthening of civilian power;

7. *Also notes* the results of the meeting of the Consultative Group for Guatemala, held in Guatemala City on 13 and 14 May 2003, at which all participants agreed that the peace agreements should remain Guatemala's essential road map for development;

8. *Further notes* that, while advances were verified in certain areas, such as the passage of legislation against discrimination in its many manifestations, the redeployment of military units and the development of a national reparations programme for the victims of human rights violations committed during the armed conflict, progress in the implementation of the peace agreements in the past year fell short of expectations and was insufficient to inject new momentum into the peace process;

9. *Notes* that the consolidation of the peace-building process remains a significant challenge which will require greater political will, the involvement of all sectors of society and the continued engagement of the international community;

10. *Notes with concern* the climate of intimidation against justice officials, human rights defenders, social activists and journalists;

11. *Takes note* of the agreement reached in March 2003 by the Government of Guatemala and the Human Rights Ombudsman, with the support of civil society, and currently being revised, to create a Commission for the Investigation of Illegal Groups and Clandestine Security Apparatuses;

12. *Welcomes* the agreement signed on 1 December 2003 between the Government of Guatemala and the Office of the United Nations High Commissioner for Human Rights for the establishment of an office of the High Commissioner in Guatemala, with a mandate to monitor the human rights situation in the country and advise the Government on formulating and implementing policies, programmes and measures to promote and protect human rights;

13. *Calls upon* the Government to further reduce military spending and to allocate adequate budgets to those institutions and programmes that are given priority under the peace accords;

14. *Underlines* the importance of implementing fully the Agreement on Identity and Rights of Indigenous Peoples as a key to fighting discrimination and consolidating peace and equality in Guatemala, and highlights the need to implement fully the Agreement on Social and Economic Aspects and Agrarian Situation as a means of addressing the root causes of the armed conflict;

15. *Calls upon* the Government to implement the recommendations of the Commission for Historical Clarification, with a view to promoting national reconciliation, upholding the right to truth and providing redress for the victims of human rights abuses and violence committed during the thirty-six-year conflict;

16. *Invites* the international community, and in particular the specialized agencies, funds and programmes of the United Nations system, to continue to support the consolidation of the peace-building process, with the peace agreements as the framework for their technical and financial assistance programmes and projects, and stresses the continued importance of close cooperation among them in the context of the United Nations Development Assistance Framework for Guatemala;

17. *Urges* the international community to support financially, through existing mechanisms of international cooperation, the strengthening of national capacities to ensure the consolidation of the peace process in Guatemala;

18. *Also urges* the international community to support financially the strengthening of the capacities of the specialized agencies, funds and programmes of the United Nations system, including the future office of the High Commissioner in Guatemala City, as the Mission prepares to intensify its work to ensure specific follow-on by the entities of the United Nations system, as well as by members of the international community, within the framework of a general transition strategy;

19. *Stresses* that, while the Mission has played a key role in promoting the consolidation of peace and the observance of human rights and in verifying compliance with the revised timetable for the implementation of pending commitments under the peace agreements, the long-term success of the peace process depends on the capacities and renewed commitment to the peace agreements of Guatemalan institutions, both of the State and of civil society;

20. *Requests* the United Nations system in Guatemala to continue to monitor and report annually, utilizing the methodology and indicators developed with the Mission, on the implementation of the Agreement on Social and Economic Aspects and Agrarian Situation as part of the national human development report of the United Nations Development Programme;

21. *Decides* to authorize a final renewal of the mandate of the United Nations Verification Mission in Guatemala from 1 January to 31 December 2004;

22. *Requests* the Secretary-General to submit a report on the implementation of the present resolution to the General Assembly at the beginning of its fifty-ninth session, as well as a final report on the work of the Mission before the end of that session, together with the recommendations that he may deem appropriate.

Haiti

During 2003, the political and security crisis in Haiti, which had been ongoing since the contested election of President Jean-Bertrand Aristide in 2000 [YUN 2000, p. 249], deepened. By the end of the year, a newly united opposition movement, comprising political parties, civil society actors and the private sector, was calling for the President's resignation.

Political and security situation

In an April report to the Economic and Social Council on the long-term programme of support for Haiti [E/2003/54] (see also p. 952), the Secretary-General observed that the political crisis in Haiti was continuing despite the efforts of OAS to help the country emerge from the impasse and strengthen its institutions.

On 19 and 20 March, a high-level OAS/Caribbean Community delegation visited Haiti and called on the Government to take specific steps to create a climate conducive to the holding of free and credible local and legislative elections in 2003, while calling on the opposition and civil society to respect their obligations in that regard. In its report to the OAS Permanent Council on 3 April, the delegation took a negative view of developments in Haiti and deplored the fact that the Government and the opposition were continually hurling accusations at each other, thus impeding the electoral process.

In **resolution 2003/46** of 23 July (see p. 952), the Council took action on the Secretary-General's report.

Financing of missions

UNMIH, UNSMIH, UNTMIH, MIPONUH

In an April report [A/57/789], the Secretary-General presented to the General Assembly the updated financial position of closed peacekeeping missions as at 30 June 2002, including the United Nations Mission in Haiti (UNMIH) (mandate ended 30 June 1996 [YUN 1996, p. 174]), the United Nations Support Mission in Haiti (UNSMIH) (mandate ended 31 July 1997 [YUN 1997, p. 188]), the United Nations Transition Mission in Haiti (UNTMIH) (mandate ended 30 November 1997 [ibid., p. 191]) and the United Nations Civilian Police Mission in Haiti (MIPONUH) (mandate ended 15 March 2000 [YUN 2000, p. 249]). The report showed fund balances of $27.2 million for UNMIH and $11.2 million for UNSMIH/UNTMIH/MIPONUH.

The Assembly, in **resolution 57/323** of 18 June (see p. 85), took action on the Secretary-General's report.

Other questions

Colombia

In an 8 February statement [SG/SM/8599], the Secretary-General expressed shock at the terrorist attack on a social club in Bogotá, Colombia, on 7 February. He condemned the bombing and all other terrorist attacks by any actor in the Colombian conflict, and stated that the killing of innocent civilians would deepen the conflict and further undermine Colombia's hopes for the peace it sought and deserved. He extended his profound sympathy to the families of the victims.

SECURITY COUNCIL ACTION

On 13 February [meeting 4706], the Security Council unanimously adopted **resolution 1465 (2003)**. The draft [S/2003/177] was prepared in consultations among Council members.

The Security Council,

Reaffirming the purposes and principles of the Charter of the United Nations and its relevant resolutions, in particular resolution 1373(2001) of 28 September 2001,

Reaffirming also the need to combat by all means, in accordance with the Charter, threats to international peace and security caused by terrorist acts,

1. *Condemns in the strongest terms* the bomb attack in Bogotá on 7 February 2003 in which many lives were lost and people injured, and regards such an act, like any act of terrorism, as a threat to peace and security;

2. *Expresses its deepest sympathy and condolences* to the people and the Government of Colombia and to the victims of the bomb attack and their families;

3. *Urges* all States, in accordance with their obligations under resolution 1373(2001), to work together urgently and to cooperate with and provide support and assistance, as appropriate, to the Colombian authorities in their efforts to find and bring to justice the perpetrators, organizers and sponsors of this terrorist attack;

4. *Expresses its reinforced determination* to combat all forms of terrorism, in accordance with its responsibilities under the Charter.

Cuba–United States

In August [A/58/287], the Secretary-General, in response to General Assembly resolution 57/11 [YUN 2002, p. 252], submitted information received as at 16 July 2003 from 86 States and 19 UN bodies and agencies on the implementation of the resolution, by which the Assembly had called on States to refrain from unilateral application of economic and trade measures against States, and urged them to repeal or invalidate such measures. The preamble to resolution 57/11 had made particular reference to the Helms-Burton Act, promulgated by the United States in 1996, which had strengthened sanctions against Cuba.

GENERAL ASSEMBLY ACTION

On 4 November [meeting 54], the General Assembly adopted **resolution 58/7** [draft: A/58/L.4] by recorded vote (179-3-2) [agenda item 29].

Necessity of ending the economic, commercial and financial embargo imposed by the United States of America against Cuba

The General Assembly,

Determined to encourage strict compliance with the purposes and principles enshrined in the Charter of the United Nations,

Reaffirming, among other principles, the sovereign equality of States, non-intervention and non-interference in their internal affairs and freedom of international trade and navigation, which are also enshrined in many international legal instruments,

Recalling the statements of the heads of State or Government at the Ibero-American Summits concerning the need to eliminate the unilateral application of economic and trade measures by one State against another that affect the free flow of international trade,

Concerned at the continued promulgation and application by Member States of laws and regulations, such as that promulgated on 12 March 1996 known as the "Helms-Burton Act", the extraterritorial effects of which affect the sovereignty of other States, the legitimate interests of entities or persons under their jurisdiction and the freedom of trade and navigation,

Taking note of declarations and resolutions of different intergovernmental forums, bodies and Governments that express the rejection by the international community and public opinion of the promulgation and application of regulations of the kind referred to above,

Recalling its resolutions 47/19 of 24 November 1992, 48/16 of 3 November 1993, 49/9 of 26 October 1994, 50/10 of 2 November 1995, 51/17 of 12 November 1996, 52/10 of 5 November 1997, 53/4 of 14 October 1998, 54/21 of 9 November 1999, 55/20 of 9 November 2000, 56/9 of 27 November 2001 and 57/11 of 12 November 2002,

Concerned that, since the adoption of its resolutions 47/19, 48/16, 49/9, 50/10, 51/17, 52/10, 53/4, 54/21, 55/20, 56/9 and 57/11, further measures of that nature aimed at strengthening and extending the economic, commercial and financial embargo against Cuba continue to be promulgated and applied, and concerned also at the adverse effects of such measures on the Cuban people and on Cuban nationals living in other countries,

1. *Takes note* of the report of the Secretary-General on the implementation of resolution 57/11;

2. *Reiterates its call upon* all States to refrain from promulgating and applying laws and measures of the kind referred to in the preamble to the present resolution in conformity with their obligations under the Charter of the United Nations and international law, which, inter alia, reaffirm the freedom of trade and navigation;

3. *Once again urges* States that have and continue to apply such laws and measures to take the necessary steps to repeal or invalidate them as soon as possible in accordance with their legal regime;

4. *Requests* the Secretary-General, in consultation with the appropriate organs and agencies of the United Nations system, to prepare a report on the implementation of the present resolution in the light of the purposes and principles of the Charter and international law and to submit it to the General Assembly at its fifty-ninth session;

5. *Decides* to include in the provisional agenda of its fifty-ninth session the item entitled "Necessity of ending the economic, commercial and financial embargo imposed by the United States of America against Cuba".

RECORDED VOTE ON RESOLUTION 58/7:

In favour: Afghanistan, Albania, Algeria, Andorra, Angola, Antigua and Barbuda, Argentina, Armenia, Australia, Austria, Azerbaijan, Bahamas, Bahrain, Bangladesh, Barbados, Belarus, Belgium, Belize, Benin, Bhutan, Bolivia, Bosnia and Herzegovina, Botswana, Brazil, Brunei Darussalam, Bulgaria, Burkina Faso, Burundi, Cambodia, Cameroon, Canada, Cape Verde, Central African Republic, Chad, Chile, China, Colombia, Comoros, Congo, Costa Rica, Côte d'Ivoire, Croatia, Cuba, Cyprus, Czech Republic, Democratic People's Republic of Korea, Democratic Republic of the Congo, Denmark, Djibouti, Dominica, Dominican Republic, Ecuador, Egypt, Equatorial Guinea, Eritrea, Estonia, Ethiopia, Fiji, Finland, France, Gabon, Gambia, Georgia, Germany, Ghana, Greece, Grenada, Guatemala, Guinea, Guinea-Bissau, Guyana, Haiti, Honduras, Hungary, Iceland, India, Indonesia, Iran, Ireland, Italy, Jamaica, Japan, Jordan, Kazakhstan, Kenya, Kiribati, Kyrgyzstan, Lao People's Democratic Republic, Latvia, Lebanon, Lesotho, Libyan Arab Jamahiriya, Liechtenstein, Lithuania, Luxembourg, Madagascar, Malawi, Malaysia, Maldives, Mali, Malta, Mauritania, Mauritius, Mexico, Monaco, Mongolia, Mozambique, Myanmar, Namibia, Nauru, Nepal, Netherlands, New Zealand, Niger, Nigeria, Norway, Oman, Pakistan, Panama, Papua New Guinea, Paraguay, Peru, Philippines, Poland, Portugal, Qatar, Republic of Korea, Republic of Moldova, Romania, Russian Federation, Rwanda, Saint Kitts and Nevis, Saint Lucia, Saint Vincent and the Grenadines, Samoa, San Marino, Sao Tome and Principe, Saudi Arabia, Senegal, Serbia and Montenegro, Seychelles, Sierra Leone, Singapore, Slovakia, Slovenia, Solomon Islands, Somalia, South Africa, Spain, Sri Lanka, Sudan, Suriname, Swaziland, Sweden, Switzerland, Syrian Arab Republic, Tajikistan, Thailand, The former Yugoslav Republic of Macedonia, Timor-Leste, Togo, Tonga, Trinidad and Tobago, Tunisia, Turkey, Turkmenistan, Tuvalu, Uganda, Ukraine, United Arab Emirates, United Kingdom, United Republic of Tanzania, Uruguay, Vanuatu, Venezuela, Viet Nam, Yemen, Zambia, Zimbabwe.

Against: Israel, Marshall Islands, United States.

Abstaining: Micronesia, Morocco.

El Salvador–Honduras

On 12 March [S/2003/306], Honduras transmitted to the Security Council President the text of a memorandum from its Acting Minister for Foreign Affairs to the Minister for Foreign Affairs of El Salvador. The memorandum acknowledged receipt of El Salvador's 11 March note concerning the demarcation of the common boundary delimited by the International Court of Justice (ICJ) on 11 September 1992 [YUN 1992, p. 983]. (El Salvador had filed an Application with ICJ for revision of the Judgment in September 2002 [YUN 2002, p. 1272].) Honduras stated that, following agreement to start the demarcation process [ibid., p. 255], reconnaissance visits were initiated in October 2002. The small differences noted prior to that time between the coordinates fixed by the Judgment and the geographical accidents identified were natural and inherent in a delimitation process. (See also p. 1306)

On 8 April [S/2003/430], Honduras transmitted to the Council President the text of a letter to the Pan American Institute of Geography and History, in which Honduras requested the appointment of a technical expert who was not a national or resident of either El Salvador or Honduras to act as third and final arbitrator in resolving technical differences in the 1992 ICJ demarcation Judgment between the two countries. Included in the appendices to the letter were the minutes of the meeting of the Special Demarcation Commission (Metapán, El Salvador, 24-28 February), at which no agreement was reached on the appointment of an arbitrator.

On 20 May [S/2003/561], Honduras transmitted to the Council President a document announcing that OAS, on 30 April, had appointed technical expert John Gates (United States) to assist in resolving the demarcation issue.

Chapter IV
Asia and the Pacific

The year 2003 was a challenging one for the United Nations in the Asia and Pacific region as the war in Iraq severely tested the principle of collective security and the resilience of the Organization.

In Afghanistan, the security situation continued to endanger the peace process. Increased terrorist activity, factional fighting and activities associated with the illegal narcotics trade posed the greatest challenges to stability and socio-economic development. Lack of security in certain parts of the country forced the United Nations to suspend its mission support in four southern provinces. Despite those setbacks, progress continued to be made in implementing the 2001 Bonn Agreement. Constructive events included the beginning of the demobilization, disarmament and reintegration programme, the drafting of a constitution, the commencement of the electoral registration process and the convening of a nationwide constitutional assembly, or Loya Jirga. In May, the Afghan Transitional Authority (TA), led by President Hamid Karzai, secured an agreement with provincial governors and commanders that prohibited provincial leaders from simultaneously holding civil and military positions and called for the centralization of customs revenues; however, those commitments were only partially implemented by the end of the year. The United Nations Assistance Mission in Afghanistan (UNAMA) continued to assist in the implementation of the Bonn Agreement and in reconstruction. The Security Council established an electoral unit within UNAMA to assist the TA with preparations for the holding of national elections, scheduled to take place in 2004. UNAMA's mandate was extended for an additional period of one year. A Council mission visited Afghanistan from 31 October to 7 November to reaffirm its support for the peace process. The Security Council expanded the mandate of the International Security Assistance Force, which continued to assist the TA in the maintenance of security in the capital, Kabul, to allow it to operate in areas outside Kabul and its environs. The North Atlantic Treaty Organization assumed leadership of the Force in August. The Council also adopted new sanctions against Osama bin Laden, the terrorist organization Al-Qaida, the Taliban and their associates. The Secretary-General's Special Representative for Afghanistan, Lakhdar Brahimi, continued to coordinate UN activities in the country.

The war in Iraq, which began on 20 March, severely tested the cohesiveness and purpose of the United Nations. Rarely in its 58-year history had such dire forecasts been made about the Organization. On 19 August, the UN headquarters in Baghdad was subjected to a deliberate and vicious terrorist attack. The Secretary-General's Special Representative for Iraq, Sergio Vieira de Mello, and 21 other persons were killed and many others were wounded. The attack dealt a severe blow to the ability of the United Nations to assist Iraq in the post-war phase. Prior to the commencement of military action, the United Nations Monitoring, Verification and Inspection Commission and the International Atomic Energy Agency carried out extensive inspection activities in Iraq and provided the Security Council with periodic updates on their findings. The Council convened repeatedly at the ministerial level to discuss the situation in Iraq. Three permanent members of the Council strongly opposed the use of force. On 17 March, the Secretary-General suspended UN activities in Iraq and the following day withdrew all UN system personnel. As at 19 March, UN inspectors reported that they had not found any evidence of proscribed weapons of mass destruction in Iraq, though the time available to them was considered insufficient to complete an overall assessment. UN personnel started returning to Iraq in April, following the overthrow of Saddam Hussein's regime by coalition forces, led by the United States. The Coalition Provisional Authority was established by the occupying forces to provide for the provisional administration of Iraq. In July, the Authority established the Governing Council of Iraq, the principal body of the Iraqi interim administration. An escalation of attacks against the United Nations and other foreign organizations, which started in August 2003, led the Secretary-General to temporarily relocate all UN international staff outside the country. Although the United Nations Assistance Mission for Iraq was established in August, its core was set up in Nicosia, Cyprus, due to the deteriorating security situation. In November, the Authority and the Governing Council signed an agreement setting out a political process for the restoration of sovereignty by 30 June 2004, and for the drafting of a new constitution and the holding of national elections. Following the end of major military hostilities, the Security Council lifted civilian sanctions on Iraq. Consequently, the Council's Sanctions Committee and the humanitarian oil-for-food programme were phased out over a period of six months and terminated on 21 November 2003 after 13 years of a comprehensive sanctions regime. The Council established the international Advisory and Monitoring Board, an independent oversight body, to monitor oil sales in Iraq, and established a new committee to continue identifying individuals and entities affiliated with the former Iraqi regime for the purpose of freezing their funds, financial assets and economic resources. The fall of the Hussein regime led to the discovery of mass graves in Iraq and the identification of remains, including those of Kuwaiti missing persons. In March, the mandate of the United Nations Iraq-Kuwait Observation Mission was suspended and most of its staff evacuated. The Mission maintained a small peacekeeping force in Kuwait City to support, among other things, UN humanitarian assistance programmes for Iraq. In July, the Council extended the Mission's mandate for a final three-month period, until 6 October. On 13 December, Saddam Hussein was captured by Coalition forces.

During the year, Timor-Leste continued to establish and strengthen its national institutions with assistance from the United Nations Mission of Support in East Timor (UNMISET) and UN agencies. The Timorese civil administration and police force progressively assumed greater responsibility in their respective areas. However, in response to violent attacks by armed elements in January and February, the Security Council decided to slow down the downsizing schedule for the military and police components of UNMISET. The Mission's mandate was extended for a further year, until 20 May 2004. Relations between Indonesia and Timor-Leste continued to improve, although the two countries did not reach a final agreement on a provisional border line by the target date of 30 November. The ratification of the Timor Sea Treaty between Timor-Leste and Australia paved the way for the exploitation of mineral resources in the Timor Sea and the sharing of revenues, with 90 per cent being awarded to Timor-Leste.

In 2003, the United Nations resumed negotiations with the Government of Cambodia on the establishment of extraordinary chambers within the existing court structure of Cambodia for the prosecution of serious violations of Cambodian law and international law committed during the period of Democratic Kampuchea. Those negotiations resulted in the preparation of a draft agreement between the United Nations and Cambodia, which the General Assembly approved in May, and which was signed on 6 June.

Particular attention was paid to developments in the Democratic People's Republic of Korea, as the country informed the Security Council in January that it was putting into effect its 1993 decision to withdraw from the 1968 Treaty on the Non-Proliferation of Nuclear Weapons. The activities of the United Nations Tajikistan Office of Peace-building were extended for another year, until 1 June 2004, in order to continue to support Tajikistan in its post-conflict peace-building efforts. Among other concerns in the region that were brought to the attention of the United Nations were the deterioration of law and order in Solomon Islands and the situation in Bougainville, Papua New Guinea.

Afghanistan

During 2003, further progress was made in implementing the 2001 Bonn Agreement [YUN 2001, p. 263], which had set in motion Afghanistan's transition from war and instability to peace and democracy. Major steps included the pilot phase of the demobilization, disarmament and reintegration programme, the drafting of a constitution, the beginning of electoral registration and the convening of the Constitutional Loya Jirga (grand council), which was still in session as at 31 December. However, the deterioration in security, brought about by increased terrorist activity, factional fighting, activities associated with the narcotics trade and unchecked criminality, impeded the peace process. The absence of a secure environment led the United Nations to suspend its mission support in four southern provinces. The Afghan Transitional Authority (TA), led by President Hamid Karzai, enacted security reform measures and, in May, through the Afghan National Security Council, forbade the use of private militias and called for the transfer of provincial revenues to the TA.

The United Nations Assistance Mission in Afghanistan (UNAMA), under the leadership of the Secretary-General's Special Representative, Lakhdar Brahimi (Algeria), continued its efforts on behalf of Afghanistan throughout the year, together with its partner organizations. In March, the Security Council extended UNAMA's mandate to provide support for the implementation of the Bonn Agreement for an additional period of one year. The Council also established an electoral unit within UNAMA to assist the TA with preparations for the national elections, scheduled for 2004. Noting the link between drug trafficking and terrorism, the Council further called for coordinated efforts to combat the drug trade in Afghanistan.

A Security Council mission visited Afghanistan in October/November with the primary purpose of reaffirming the international community's support for the peace process and to send a strong signal to the Afghan people that their plight remained high on the Council's agenda. The mission, among other things, called for an end to factional fighting.

In January, the Council also adopted new sanctions measures against Osama bin Laden, Al-Qaida, the Taliban and their associates, including a freeze of financial and economic assets, a travel ban and an arms embargo. In order to clarify its identity and mandate, the Afghanistan Sanctions Committee changed its name to the Security Council Committee established pursuant to resolution 1267(1999) [YUN 1999, p. 265] concerning Al-Qaida and the Taliban and associated individuals and entities. Although the Committee's consolidated list remained a critical tool for implementing all sanctions measures, it was felt that there was a need to further upgrade the list's information quality. The Monitoring Group was reappointed to monitor the implementation of the sanctions measures for a further period of one year.

The International Security Assistance Force (ISAF), a multinational force established by Security Council resolution 1386(2001) [YUN 2001, p. 267], continued to assist the Afghan Government in the maintenance of security in Kabul and its surrounding areas. The North Atlantic Treaty Organization (NATO) assumed lead command for ISAF in August, replacing Germany and the Netherlands. Those two countries had assumed lead command in February 2003 from Turkey. In October, the Council expanded ISAF's mandate to allow it to support the TA in the maintenance of security in areas outside of Kabul and its environs.

The Economic and Social Council, in July, adopted **resolution 2003/43** on the situation of women and girls in Afghanistan (see p. 1175).

Situation in Afghanistan

The situation in Afghanistan in 2003 was described by the Secretary-General in three progress reports to the Security Council and the General Assembly dated 18 March [A/57/762-S/2003/333], 23 July [A/57/850-S/2003/754 & Corr.1] and 30 December [S/2003/1212]. The reports described the status of implementation of the 2001 Bonn Agreement, in particular the work of the TA; political and security issues; humanitarian relief, recovery and reconstruction; developments regarding UN deployment in Afghanistan; and UNAMA's activities and mandate. In a 3 December report to the Assembly [A/58/616], which focused on international assistance for the reconstruction of Afghanistan, the Secretary-General described key political and humanitarian developments from July 2002 to November 2003.

Security Council consideration (January and February). The Security Council discussed the situation in Afghanistan on 31 January [meeting 4699] and 24 February [meeting 4711].

On 31 January, the Council was briefed by the Special Representative of the Secretary-General for Afghanistan, Lakhdar Brahimi, who said that in 2003 Afghanistan would have to strengthen and rebuild the foundations of the State, address the political and security uncertainties and meet the rising expectations of its people. To that end, President Hamid Karzai had been discussing with the United Nations and other partners the need for the Afghan Government to articulate a clear plan of action setting out the main goals for 2003. Broadly, there was a need to focus on three main areas: strengthening the key State institutions; national reconciliation; and reconstruction projects throughout the country. With respect to State institutions, progress had to be made on building the army and training and reform of the police. The drafting and ratification of the new constitution would also be a fundamental State-building exercise. With respect to national reconciliation, the political base supporting the peace process had to be broadened as too many Afghans felt excluded from the Government and the political transformation that Afghanistan was undergoing. As to reconstruction, Afghans had to be presented with clearly identified projects that could build the economy and increase confidence in the Government. Some reports suggested that support for the Taliban was growing in some parts of Afghanistan, a reminder that the peace process was far from secure.

The security situation on the ground during January had been relatively calm, with no outbreak of major, sustained fighting. However, security incidents continued to occur as a result of inter-factional tension and sporadic terrorist activity. Although tensions had been reduced in parts of the country through mediation, the high rate of criminal activity by armed groups in and around the city of Mazar-e-Sharif and attacks against the United States–led coalition forces continued. The Afghan TA continued to implement its agenda for security sector reform. In January, subcommissions for the recruitment of a new national army and for the demobilization and disarmament of former combatants were established. France and the United States, which were providing training for the new army, estimated that by the end of 2003 approximately 7,000 soldiers would have completed the basic training course. Japan had committed significant funding to the Afghan New Beginnings Programme, aimed at registering soldiers and, through a series of benefits and training packages, assisting them in their reintegration into civilian life. The German-led national police training project was providing training for some 1,450 police officers. However, the TA continued to face difficulties in paying police salaries.

In the justice sector, the Afghan Judicial Commission's draft plan for legislative and constitutional reform and the rebuilding of the judicial system was being finalized in consultation with Italy, the lead nation in support of that sector, the UN and its agencies and donors. Progress in establishing the rule of law would continue to be constrained by the depleted pool of experienced lawyers and the limited capacity of the penal system. On 27 January, the Constitutional Drafting Commission, together with UNAMA and the United Nations Development Programme (UNDP), met with donors and interested Member States represented in Kabul to discuss the constitutional process. The Commission was expected to finalize a preliminary draft by March. That draft would be reviewed by the full Constitutional Commission, whose 30 or so members were being selected. From April through early June, the Constitutional Commission was to conduct countrywide public consultations to discern the public's view on key constitutional issues. Taking into account the results of those consultations, the Commission would finalize a draft by late August. The final step would be the convening of a Loya Jirga (grand council), tentatively scheduled for October, to review and adopt the constitution. As for the elections scheduled to take place in June 2004, UNAMA, assisted by the Electoral Assistance Division of the UN Department of Political Affairs, was in the process of assembling an electoral team in Kabul to assist the TA on electoral matters and to help build electoral capacity inside that Government. The Afghan Independent Human Rights Commission had been implementing its work programme with the support of UNAMA, the Office of the United Nations High Commissioner for Human Rights and UNDP. That programme covered capacity-building in the fields of investigations and monitoring, human rights education, promotion of the rights of women and transitional justice.

The United Nations Transitional Assistance Programme for Afghanistan (TAPA) [YUN 2002, p. 900] reflected an agreement between the TA and the UN assistance agencies on relief, recovery and reconstruction programmes and their linkage to national priorities identified by the Afghan Government itself. TAPA aimed to ameliorate the underlying causes of humanitarian needs and to establish the foundation for rehabilitation and long-term development. TAPA's aims included the Mine Action Programme's target to clear high-impact areas of mines and unexploded ordnance within five years and preparations for the national census.

Illegal drug production and trafficking in Afghanistan remained a critical concern, with significant poppy cultivation resuming in 2002 after several years of reduced production. Certain aspects of the drug economy—such as the refining and transportation of drug products—were driven by the opportunity for massive and illicit profit, which, in the past, had been used to nurture a war economy. The TA had launched a poppy eradication programme in conjunction with the governors of the five main drug-producing provinces. Although it was too early to evaluate the effectiveness of that campaign, it was clear that alternative livelihoods in drug-producing areas were needed for the eradication programme to be sustainable over the long term.

On 24 February, the Council was briefed on the latest developments in Afghanistan by Jean-Marie Guéhenno, Under-Secretary-General (USG) for Peacekeeping Operations. Also participating in the meeting were Harald Braun, Special Representative of the German Government for the training of the Afghan police force, at the request of Germany [S/2003/200], and Mutsuyoshi Nishimura, Ambassador of Japan in charge of Afghan Aid Coordination, at the request of Japan [S/2003/209].

The USG said that progress had been made with respect to the implementation of the political transition outlined in the 2001 Bonn Agreement [YUN 2001, p. 263], especially in the drafting of a new constitution. President Karzai's office was preparing a decree that would establish the Constitutional Commission and detail the main elements of the constitutional process. The nine members of the functioning Constitutional Drafting Commission would be made part of the larger Constitutional Commission, to be established in March. A list of almost 80 candidates for possible selection to the Commission had been compiled by President Karzai's office. Public consultations on the constitutional process would take place between April and June throughout the country and among the Afghan diaspora in Iran and Pakistan. Technical assistance from UNAMA, UNDP, bilateral donors and academic sources had been made available to the Drafting Commission and its secretariat. Progress had also been made in the preparations for the elections, scheduled for June 2004. On 15 February, President Karzai sent the Secretary-General a letter formally requesting UNAMA's assistance in organizing the electoral process and coordinating international electoral assistance. The head of UNAMA's electoral section, who had arrived in Kabul, had begun to work on preparations for the elections. A core team of electoral experts was in the process of being deployed to UNAMA. On the Afghan side, President Karzai had identified a number of candidates for membership in the electoral commission, which was expected to be formed in March. Once the commission was established, it would work with UNAMA to create an Afghan electoral authority to manage the electoral process. At the same time, the TA was finalizing its budget for the next financial year, which would begin on 21 March. Afghans were optimistic that the international community would fulfil the commitments it had already made for 2003. The TA looked forward to receiving between $1.7 billion and $2 billion in aid for 2003. However, it was concerned about the slow pace of allocations.

While the Bonn process had averted full-scale fighting between major rival factions, Afghans continued to suffer on a human level from the insecurity created by the conjunction of weak national security institutions and strong local commanders. In eastern Afghanistan, the Government's poppy-eradication campaign continued to face strong opposition from local tribes who did not feel they had been offered sufficient compensation. UN activities had been suspended in four districts in Nargarhar as a result of that tension. Despite a general sense of concern about security conditions across the country, the handover of ISAF command from Turkey to Germany and the Netherlands proceeded smoothly (see p. 308). The challenges of reforming the Afghan security sector were significant: the national army needed to be built, factional armies had to be dissolved, and assistance had to be provided to help ex-combatants reintegrate into civilian life. There was also a need for the creation of a national police force, the re-establishment of the rule of law, the rehabilitation of the justice sector and the countering of the cultivation of and trafficking in illicit drugs. Finally, the bloated and intrusive intelligence structures also needed to be reformed. Security sector reform was all the more urgent because of the need to provide minimal conditions of stability to ensure that the Constitutional Loya Jirga and the national elections were meaningful and credible. The United Nations had established four trust funds for contributions to the police, the justice sector, disarmament, demobilization and reintegration (DDR) of former combatants and the payment of salaries, and the provision of non-lethal equipment to the Afghan national army. While support from the international community was necessary, the political underpinnings of security sector reform had to be strengthened by the deeds and words of the TA.

Mr. Nishimura said that Afghanistan was still replete with weapons and armaments and, despite some notable progress, there was a high level of tension between the armed formations. Nation-building could not succeed under those conditions, nor could national reconciliation be achieved. For the people of Afghanistan, the restoration of peace and the rule of law was their greatest aspiration. There was unanimous agreement among all parties that DDR of soldiers and officers was of the highest priority. However, a new national army and national police force also had to be created to allow the State to exercise the sole enforcement capacity. Counter-narcotics actions and an independent judiciary were likewise necessary. Mindful of those considerations, President Karzai, on 1 December 2002 [YUN 2002, p. 271], had issued a decree outlining principles and conditions with respect to security, the military and DDR. The decree stated that a new Afghanistan National Army (ANA) would be created of not more than 70,000 soldiers. More importantly, the decree stipulated that military formations, armed groups and any other military or paramilitary units that were not a part of ANA would be prohibited. On 11 January 2003, President Karzai took further steps to move ahead with DDR by issuing decrees establishing four government commissions. Nevertheless, it was anticipated that DDR in Afghanistan would be difficult in view of the heavy legacy of factional rivalries. The fact that a new army had to be built in parallel with DDR added to the complexity of the undertaking. Japan had pledged a contribution of $35 million to jump-start the Partnership for Peace Programme, a basic component of the DDR process. Ultimately, the success of DDR would depend on the economic capacity of the country itself and on its ability to generate enough job opportunities to absorb former combatants.

Mr. Braun said that Germany had assumed the lead role in rebuilding the Afghan police force.

Based on an assessment carried out in 2002 by German and Afghan experts and in coordination with other lead nations in the security sector, a three-stage timetable was established. In the first stage, starting with the Bonn process in late 2001 [YUN 2001, p. 263] and running to the Emergency Loya Jirga in June 2002 [YUN 2002, p. 266], the basic structures of the new national police were created in Kabul. The second stage, which was under way and set to last until the 2004 parliamentary elections, comprised the consolidation and expansion of central structures in Kabul and the gradual extension of those structures into the provinces. The third stage would ensure the functionality of federal and provincial police forces and their interlinking with other security structures, in addition to the gradual withdrawal of Germany as a lead nation by the end of 2005. The implementation of the timetable faced some difficulties: the security situation had not significantly improved, with the exception of Kabul, where ISAF guaranteed a reasonably secure environment; regional cooperation in the effort to include all provinces in police training had not been uniformly satisfactory; progress had been difficult in the reconstruction of other security sectors, such as the army and in the fight against illicit drugs; and financing had also been a problem. Notwithstanding those restraining factors, the timetable remained on course. Among other things, the groundwork had been laid for a functioning police force in Kabul; training courses for police officers had begun; the reorganization of the police and of the Ministry of the Interior was making good progress; and the integration of the provinces into the police rebuilding programme had commenced. A strategy for national police reconstruction through 2005 that was synchronized with advances in demobilization and armed forces build-up was being fine-tuned by the Ministry of the Interior. However, much remained to be done before the Bonn process became irreversible and before the Afghan Government could acquire the structures and gain the experience necessary for carrying forward the building process on its own.

Following the open meeting, the Council held a constructive exchange of views [S/PV.4712] with Mr. Braun and the USG for Peacekeeping Operations.

Communications (March). On 4 March [A/57/759-S/2003/332], Malaysia, as Chairman of the Coordinating Bureau of the Non-Aligned Movement, transmitted to the Secretary-General the documents adopted at the Thirteenth Conference of Heads of State or Government of the Non-Aligned Countries (Kuala Lumpur, 20-25 February). In the Final Document, the heads of State or Government expressed concern that terrorist groups in Afghanistan, including former Taliban cadres, were regrouping in the southern and eastern parts of the country.

On 18 March [S/2003/335], Portugal, Spain, the United Kingdom and the United States transmitted to the Security Council President the text of a statement entitled "Commitment to transatlantic solidarity" adopted at the Atlantic Summit (Azores, Portugal, 16 March). The four countries said, among other things, that they were working to bring security to Afghanistan and to root out the terrorists that remained inside Afghan territory. (For further details on the Summit, see p. 332.)

Report of Secretary-General (March). In his 18 March report on the situation in Afghanistan and its implications for international peace and security [A/57/762-S/2003/333], submitted in response to Security Council resolution 1401(2002) [YUN 2002, p. 264] and General Assembly resolutions 57/113 A [ibid., p. 273] and 57/113 B [ibid., p. 900], the Secretary-General summarized the key developments in Afghanistan since his 21 October 2002 report [ibid., p. 269]. He said that progress had been made by the Afghan TA, supported by UNAMA, in implementing the Bonn Agreement. The consolidation of government authority by the TA, in particular through the adoption of a national development budget, the successful completion of a currency reform operation, and the implementation of national programmes to provide clear, tangible economic benefits to the Afghan population had advanced. Progress was also made in key political processes to further the transition towards a multi-ethnic, gender-sensitive and fully representative Afghan Government. They included the Afghan-led constitutional process, by which a draft constitution was to be prepared by March 2003, followed by public consultations and a Constitutional Loya Jirga. Another key process was the preparation of national elections to be held in June 2004. The Electoral Assistance Division of the UN Department of Political Affairs was working with UNAMA to define the modalities for assistance.

Security remained the most serious challenge facing the peace process. Afghans in many parts of the country remained unprotected by legitimate State security structures. Criminal activity by armed groups was particularly evident in the north, east and south, and in many areas confrontation between local commanders continued to contribute to instability, while sporadic acts of terror continued to occur all too frequently. Reports from several sources in the first months of 2003 pointed to increased activity by elements hostile to the Government and to the international community in Afghanistan. It appeared that remnant Taliban groups were trying to reorganize in the south-eastern and eastern border areas. However, some progress was made in security sector reform in January with the creation of four commissions to coordinate the related processes of DDR and the building of the national army. The reorganization and training of ANA troops by France and the United States continued; six ANA battalions had been created with newly trained troops and some ANA units had been deployed on limited operations outside Kabul where they conducted patrols and supported local disarmament efforts. Those deployments, which had been generally well received by local populations, had demonstrated that the new army was developing as a professional and disciplined force. The creation of an effective national army and police depended on the successful reintegration into civilian life of members of non-official military formations. On 22 February, Japan, as lead nation for DDR, hosted a conference in Tokyo to mobilize international support for the process. Contributions and pledges totalling $50.7 million were made. Japan pledged $35 million to UNDP for DDR. Progress was also made in rebuilding the national police force. Discussions were under way on the reorganization of the Ministry of the Interior; the German-led police training programme continued; and the Government had taken steps to ensure the accountability of its police force. The Judicial Commission, entrusted with reforming the justice sector, had identified a set of priorities, which included rehabilitation of court premises and short training programmes for judges and other law officers.

Poppy cultivation and the production of and trafficking in drugs remained a major concern, both nationally and internationally. Afghanistan, once again, was expected to be the largest producer of opium in 2003. Crop eradication, based on a presidential decree, was reportedly taking place in many parts of the country, though verification remained problematic. The success of the eradication campaign would depend upon credible police enforcement and the availability of alternative sources of livelihoods to farmers. The United Kingdom, the lead nation in that sector, was working closely with a core group of government ministries, donors and the United Nations to integrate anti-drug activities and identify alternative livelihood projects.

In Afghanistan in general, the lack of adequate national security and law enforcement capacity and the weakness of the justice system exacerbated human rights violations. Abuses were committed in all parts of the country, most often by forces under the control of regional factions or local commanders. The internally displaced persons situation had stabilized somewhat, though families were still moving from the north in search of assistance. The return of the approximately 480,000 internally displaced persons to their home communities would depend on an improvement in the drought-affected areas, the resolution of land disputes and political developments in the north.

UNAMA had completed the task of assimilating the personnel and equipment of the United Nations Special Mission to Afghanistan and the United Nations Office for the Coordination of Humanitarian Assistance to Afghanistan. The Secretary-General proposed adjustments to UNAMA's structure in a few key areas, the most important of which concerned small additions to the military and police adviser's units, and the establishment of an electoral section headed by a senior expert and supported by an appropriately sized team.

The Secretary-General observed that the TA and the international community, along with UNAMA, could draw satisfaction from a number of significant accomplishments: the timetable of the Bonn Agreement had largely been kept; some 1.5 million refugees and 500,000 internally displaced persons had returned to their homes; a comprehensive national budget had been developed; and no major outbreak of fighting had occurred. At the same time, Afghanistan's peace process remained fragile. Insecurity and the lack of law and order continued to impact negatively on the lives of Afghans, whittling away at the support for the transitional process. Too many Afghans remained dissatisfied at the pace of reconstruction and economic development and far too many remained uncertain as to whether the transitional process was truly national, providing political space and equal opportunities to all Afghans regardless of their political or ethnic affiliation. After 23 years of war, the progress made in 2002 had begun to shore up the fragile foundations of peace, but stability and national reconciliation were by no means firmly consolidated. That goal required progress on a number of fronts in 2003. Key State institutions had to be entrenched and more control over the continuing problem of security and lawlessness had to be achieved. The army and police would be key institutions in that respect and progress in the overall DDR reform effort would help to promote an improved human rights environment, economic development and the Government's ability to enhance its authority and legitimacy. Success in the constitution-drafting process would provide the legal foundations for the institutions of a peaceful, democratic Afghanistan. Specific preparations for elections in 2004 would also have to be advanced in 2003.

Security Council consideration (27 March). On 27 March [meeting 4727], the Security Council discussed the situation in Afghanistan. Assistant Secretary-General for Peacekeeping Operations Hédi Annabi said that UNAMA's focus over the next year would be to continue to assist the TA to consolidate its authority throughout the country and implement national policies that reached the entire nation. That effort would require enhancing administrative capacity, carrying out security sector reform and furthering the political transformation towards representative government. The determination of the Afghan Government to take the leading role in rebuilding its State and the economy was demonstrated during preparations for the 2003 national budget, which was presented to donors at the Afghanistan Development Forum (Kabul, 13-14 March) and at the Afghanistan High-level Strategic Forum (Brussels, Belgium, 17 March). The budget set the role of the State as regulator and guarantor of social well-being and enshrined the principles of geographic equity in the allocation of resources. It provided for some $2.26 billion in expenditure. The TA estimated that it would collect internal revenues of $200 million and donors had pledged $1.87 billion to date, leaving a funding gap of around $191 million in the 2003 budget. At the heart of the budget process was the issue of government ownership and leadership in setting national priorities for the overall reconstruction agenda—in other words, of transforming an ad hoc system that developed during the years of civil war, when non-governmental organizations (NGOs), the United Nations and other international organizations gradually assumed some State functions related to the delivery of services, into one where the State itself had the capacity to exercise its responsibility for national development. The United Nations had supported that transformation, working with and within ministries to build their capacity and coordinating UN programme priorities with national programme priorities. The TA had already taken steps to effect that transformation, in particular through a currency exchange exercise; through staffing changes that better reflected the ethnic composition of the population; and through the establishment of a number of commissions. Despite that progress, a number of challenges remained, in particular the need to strengthen the links between Kabul and the provinces and to augment the capacity of the provincial and local governments. Since the lack of security threatened the peace process at all levels, security sector reform and the fight against illicit drugs were paramount. Meetings were taking place in Kabul on a regular basis to allow the heads of national commissions, the various lead nations and UNAMA to come together to supervise cooperation among themselves on security sector reforms and to push various programmes and processes forward. The reforms had to be coupled with a political transformation process, of which the drafting of a new constitution and preparations for general elections in 2004 were key components. In order to support the elections, and following a February request by President Karzai, the Secretary-General had proposed the establishment of an electoral section within UNAMA. Electoral consultants, who had already been deployed to UNAMA to assist the Government with the election preparation process, had confirmed that the holding of a registration and election would be a very complex exercise. The United Nations envisioned an electoral section within UNAMA that would be able to provide expert advice and technical assistance to the Afghan electoral management body on such issues as voter registration, voter education, the development of political party laws and the development of the electoral system itself. A certain amount of institutional development had to occur and an adequate level of security had to be in place if the elections were to be meaningful and credible. The Afghan Government had to continue to establish the framework for future elections and UNAMA's electoral section had to be established and provided with adequate resources.

SECURITY COUNCIL ACTION (March)

On 28 March [meeting 4730], the Security Council unanimously adopted **resolution 1471(2003)**. The draft [S/2003/380] was prepared in consultations among Council members.

The Security Council,

Reaffirming its previous resolutions on Afghanistan, in particular resolution 1401(2002) of 28 March 2002 establishing the United Nations Assistance Mission in Afghanistan,

Reaffirming its strong commitment to the sovereignty, independence, territorial integrity and national unity of Afghanistan, as well as its endorsement of the Declaration on Good-Neighbourly Relations, signed by the Transitional Administration of Afghanistan and the Governments of the People's Republic of China, the Islamic Republic of Iran, the Islamic Republic of Pakistan, the Republic of Tajikistan, Turkmenistan and the Republic of Uzbekistan, the States neighbouring Afghanistan, in Kabul on 22 December 2002 and its call upon all States to respect and support the implementation of the provisions thereof,

Recognizing the Transitional Administration as the sole legitimate Government of Afghanistan pending democratic elections to be held by June 2004, and reiterating its strong support for the full implementation of the Agreement on Provisional Arrangements in Afghanistan Pending the Re-establishment of Permanent Government Institutions, signed in Bonn, Germany, on 5 December 2001 (the Bonn Agreement), in particular annex II regarding the role of the United Nations during the interim period,

Recognizing also that the United Nations must continue to play its central and impartial role in the international efforts to assist the Afghan people in consolidating peace in Afghanistan and rebuilding their country,

1. *Decides* to extend the mandate of the United Nations Assistance Mission in Afghanistan for an additional period of twelve months from the date of adoption of the present resolution;

2. *Welcomes* the report of the Secretary-General of 18 March 2003 and the recommendations contained therein, endorses the proposal of the Secretary-General that an electoral unit be established within the Mission, and encourages Member States to support the United Nations electoral activities in Afghanistan;

3. *Stresses* that the continued provision of focused recovery and reconstruction assistance can contribute significantly to the implementation of the Bonn Agreement and, to this end, urges bilateral and multilateral donors to coordinate closely with the Special Representative of the Secretary-General and with the Transitional Administration, in particular through the Afghan Consultative Group process;

4. *Stresses also*, in the context of paragraph 3 above, that while humanitarian assistance should be provided wherever there is a need, recovery or reconstruction assistance ought to be provided, through the Transitional Administration, and implemented effectively, where local authorities demonstrate a commitment to maintaining a secure environment, respecting human rights and countering narcotics;

5. *Reaffirms its strong support* for the Special Representative of the Secretary-General and the concept of a fully integrated Mission, and endorses the full authority of the Special Representative, in accordance with its relevant resolutions, over all United Nations activities in Afghanistan;

6. *Requests* the Mission, with the support of the Office of the United Nations High Commissioner for Human Rights, to continue to assist the Afghan Independent Human Rights Commission in the full implementation of the human rights provisions of the Bonn Agreement and the National Human Rights Programme for Afghanistan, in order to support the protection and development of human rights in Afghanistan;

7. *Calls upon* all Afghan parties to cooperate with the Mission in the implementation of its mandate and to ensure the security and freedom of movement of its staff throughout the country;

8. *Requests* the International Security Assistance Force, in implementing its mandate in accordance with resolution 1444(2002) of 27 November 2002, to continue to work in close consultation with the Secretary-General and his Special Representative;

9. *Requests* the Secretary-General to report to the Council every four months on the implementation of the present resolution;

10. *Decides* to remain actively seized of the matter.

Communication (May). On 1 May [A/57/805-S/2003/523], Tajikistan, as chair of the Collective Security Treaty Organization, transmitted to the Secretary-General the 28 April statement of the heads of State of Armenia, Belarus, Kazakhstan, Kyrgyzstan, the Russian Federation and Tajikistan issued at a meeting in Dushanbe. The participants said that there was a need to coordinate and harmonize action by the international community to find a final solution to the Afghan crisis and to bring about post-conflict development in Afghanistan.

Security Council consideration (May). On 6 May [meeting 4750], the Security Council discussed the situation in Afghanistan and heard a briefing on the latest developments by the Special Representative of the Secretary-General for Afghanistan, Mr. Brahimi.

Mr. Brahimi said that although specific aspects of the Bonn Agreement were proceeding, the process as a whole was challenged by the deterioration in the security environment: daily harassment and intimidation; inter-ethnic and inter-factional strife; greater activity on the part of elements linked to the Taliban and to the warlord Gulbuddin Hekmatyar, leader of the Islamic fundamentalist group Hizb-I-Islami; and the drug economy. The process was also challenged by the fact that national security institutions were perceived by many Afghans, perhaps the majority, as not serving the broad national interests of all the people of Afghanistan.

In an important step forward towards meeting the time frame set out in Bonn for convening the Constitutional Loya Jirga, the Constitutional Commission was inaugurated on 26 April. Composed of 35 members, including seven women, the Commission represented the full ethnic, regional and religious diversity of the Afghan people. The previously established Drafting Committee had prepared a preliminary draft constitution; over the summer months, the Commission was to consult the public on their views and aspirations related to the constitution. That would require the members of the Commission to break up into subcommittees that would visit all parts of the country and hold scores of meetings with elders, religious and community leaders, women, intellectuals, traders and ordinary people. The United Nations would support and participate in those activities. On the basis of its findings, the Commission would finalize a draft constitution and present it to the Constitutional Loya Jirga, scheduled for October, for its consideration and ratification. In reference to the elections, the United Nations was in the process of establishing UNAMA's electoral unit, and early planning for national voter registration had begun. In order to plan and effectively fulfil UNAMA's assistance in all phases of the electoral process, the electoral unit would require an element of assured funding through the assessed budget. A complementary budget for voluntary funding had also been prepared. The registration exercise would require the recruitment and training of some 3,000 Afghans who would have to spend time in each of the nearly 400 districts and visit thousands of villages. As in the case with the consultations of the Constitutional Commission, that exercise could be conducted only within a secure environment.

With regard to the drug economy, the TA was in the final stage of completing a 10-year national drug control strategy in an effort to control poppy cultivation.

The rate of assisted refugee returns to Afghanistan increased significantly during April. It was estimated that in 2003, approximately 600,000 Afghans would return from Pakistan, 500,000 from Iran and 100,000 from other countries. In the judicial sector, the Judicial Reform Commission had completed a survey of the state of the judiciary in 10 provinces and major urban centres in the country. With respect to the reform of the public administration, progress, although slow, was picking up, owing in part to the growing role of the Civil Service Commission.

As to the human rights situation, UNAMA was investigating alleged cases of summary executions, rape and other forms of sexual violence, and continuing political intimidation, including against women. Fighting and insecurity had led to renewed displacement of Pashtun families. Security remained the central issue. Rivalries among factions and local commanders, impunity with regard to human rights violations and daily harassment of ordinary Afghan citizens by both commanders and local security forces were all too common. Forces believed to be associated with the Taliban, with Al-Qaida and with the warlord Hekmatyar had stepped up operations against the coalition as well as against Afghan military and non-military targets in the south, the south-east and the east. The threat posed by those elements was driven home by the murder of an International Committee of the Red Cross (ICRC) worker in late March—the first such killing of a foreigner since 1998. As the attacks on NGOs and international organizations became more threatening, the pressure to suspend or withdraw operations increased. ICRC and a number of NGOs were reducing their operations in the south, with immediate consequences for key programmes that provided support to local populations. The United Nations was also reviewing its operations and its security measures. Afghanistan's neighbours played a crucial role in helping to ensure the country's security, especially since hostile elements were reported crossing into Afghanistan over the eastern and southern borders. Pakistan had expressed its readiness to address the problem and had deployed armed forces in the border areas. Insecurity was also exacerbated by continuing factional clashes. The ultimate solution to such problems was the creation of an Afghan security force capable of ensuring peace. President Karzai announced the start date of 22 June for a DDR programme to be carried out by the Afghan New Beginnings Programme, supported by the international community, with Japan and the United Nations in the lead. The planned DDR programme would include those officers and soldiers who were in military formations under the umbrella of the Ministry of Defence, up to a maximum of 100,000 persons. However, before the DDR programme could start, there was a need to reform the Ministry of Defence, the Ministry of the Interior and the intelligence structures. Encouraging progress had been made in the building of a new national army and a national police service, but those efforts and the nationwide DDR programme would be successful only if there was confidence among all Afghans that the new security structures would serve the interests of the whole nation. The senior leaders of the Afghan military met in Kabul on 19 and 20 April to discuss the building of the new army. Their verbal expressions of support for a new multi-ethnic army had to be matched by actions to demobilize their own forces to ensure that the new army would be under civilian control and the only instrument of force remaining in the country. The Special Representative asked the Security Council to consider what international measures were available to help ensure the security needed for the Bonn process to proceed effectively. The expansion of ISAF beyond Kabul and a strengthened Afghan police presence remained part of a potential response to the question of security. However, the United Nations Law and Order Trust Fund for Afghanistan was insufficient to allow the Ministry of the Interior to strengthen the Afghan police. Of the $120 million the Trust Fund expected to cover needs until June 2004, only $11 million had been paid into the Fund and a further $35 million to $40 million had been pledged.

Communications (June). On 3 June [A/57/824-S/2003/619], Iran transmitted to the Secretary-General the documents adopted by the Islamic Conference of Foreign Ministers at its thirtieth session (Tehran, 28-30 May). The Conference, among other things, called on the international community to assist the Afghan TA to curb the planting of opium poppies and the production and trafficking of narcotics and to strengthen the crop substitution programme in Afghanistan.

By a 9 June letter to the Council President [S/2003/641], France transmitted the text of the Paris Statement, issued at the end of the Conference on Drug Routes from Central Asia to Europe (Paris, 21-22 May). The Conference took note of the fight against drugs undertaken by the TA and the international community in Afghanistan. It called on the international community to support the Afghan National Drug Commission and to encourage action aimed at promoting sustainable alternative development.

On 10 June [A/58/94-S/2003/642], the Russian Federation transmitted to the Secretary-General the text of the Declaration of the heads of State of the members of the Shanghai Cooperation Organization (Moscow, 29 May). The members (China, Kazakhstan, Kyrgyzstan, Russia, Tajikistan, Uzbekistan) said that there was a need for the elaboration, under UN auspices, of an international strategy for comprehensive action to counter the threat of illegal drugs from Afghanistan.

Security Council consideration (June). On 17 June [meeting 4774], the Security Council discussed the situation in Afghanistan and was briefed on the latest developments by the USG for Peacekeeping Operations, Mr. Guéhenno, and by the Director-General of the United Nations Office at Vienna and Executive Director of the United Nations Office on Drugs and Crime, Antonio Maria Costa.

Mr. Guéhenno said that some positive progress was made over the preceding month. Most notably, President Karzai took resolute action towards establishing and affirming the Government's authority in the provinces. Also, public consultations on the constitution commenced and planning for the electoral process was in its final stages. However, the security situation remained a serious impediment to progress and was a major risk to the entire process, and the TA's authority beyond Kabul was still too limited. The majority of provincial authorities continued to act with an autonomy that denied the TA the means to implement its national development plan. Yet the population expected the TA to improve the economic situation and the security environment. In a determined effort to assert the authority of his Government, President Karzai summoned 12 of the country's most powerful governors and regional commanders to Kabul on 20 May and threatened to resign if he failed to secure their full cooperation. The persons brought together committed themselves to implementing a 13-point decision of the National Security Council, which sought, among other things, to forbid the recruitment of private militias and military action unauthorized by the central Government, to reaffirm the ban on any individual holding both military and civilian posts and to dissolve some extragovernmental bodies. The National Security Council decision also required that all governors transfer provincial income to the central Government. However, signs that written agreements did not necessarily translate into tangible action were already visible. For example, the governor of Herat province, Ismael Khan, had already signalled his unwillingness to yield any authority to Kabul and had refused to resign one of his posts.

On 7 June, a suicide car bomber detonated a large explosive alongside a German ISAF bus, killing four personnel and one bystander and injuring 29 personnel in the most deadly attack on the international security force in its 18 months of operation. The incident underscored that Kabul was not immune to the security problems of the hinterland. In response to a series of attacks and threats to demining teams, the UN Mine Action Centre was forced to suspend all activities in 10 provinces and along the Kabul-Kandahar road. In effect, one third of the country was inaccessible to the United Nations, which seriously hindered the ability of the Organization and others to carry out reconstruction efforts and to lay the groundwork for the Constitutional Loya Jirga, for the elections and for DDR. Ultimately, national security structures would have to assume responsibility for domestic security, backed by a functioning justice system. Satisfactory progress had been made in the training of the national army and police forces by the lead nations—the United States and Germany, respectively. However, the funding for the forces' salaries was inadequate. The establishment and deployment of three international civilian-military provincial reconstruction teams, with 185 personnel, were assisting in improving security in the provinces. Those teams could provide a platform for supporting security sector reforms and for assisting in the provincial training of police. They could also carry out infrastructure work to support government authority, such as renovating police stations, rebuilding courthouses and constructing barracks for the new Afghan National Army. The commencement of DDR had been made contingent on the implementation of a series of confidence-building measures, signalling that reform of the Ministry of Defence was irreversible.

Mr. Costa said that less than 1 per cent of the land in Afghanistan was devoted to opium poppy cultivation and no more than 6 per cent of its families benefited from the resulting illicit income. The slow progress in re-establishing the rule of law was hurting the TA's ability to reduce the drug economy. In 2003, according to a preliminary survey, opium cultivation appeared to have spread to new areas, while a perceptible decrease had taken place in the traditional provinces. On balance, neither the total surface under cultivation nor the volume of output was likely to change significantly from 2002 levels. However, in the coming years, Afghanistan would continue to be the world's largest opium producer, due to the fact that over the past 20 years, the entire Afghan infrastructure in the countryside had been destroyed, resulting in a war economy in which arms, drugs, smuggling and opium had provided the means of livelihood, savings, credit and the means of exchange for almost one fifth of the economy. About 20 per cent of Afghanistan's gross domestic product was derived from that activity. The drug dealers, among them the remnants of the Taliban and Al-Qaida, had a vested interest in ensuring that the Afghan State remained weak. In pursuing their goals, they were fomenting regional strife and nourishing separatist ambitions and armed conflicts to destabilize the Government. Corruption among State officials was also both a cause and a consequence of narco-trafficking in Afghanistan. However, perhaps the greatest threat had come from the spread of HIV/AIDS because of drug injection. In some of the countries neighbouring Afghanistan, four out of every five new cases of HIV infection had been caused in that way. Unless the problem was brought under control, the risk of a pandemic in the region could not be excluded. In addition, the massive drug trafficking from Afghanistan endangered economic and social stability in the countries located along the trafficking routes, thereby fuelling crime, money-laundering and terrorist activities beyond the Afghan border. The Afghan drug economy could be reconverted to one of peace and growth if the TA was assisted by neighbouring and consumer countries to address the roots of the matter.

The United States said that it was contributing to alternative development, drug treatment and drug reduction programmes and, in addition, was helping to build Afghan national capacities for drug policy-making and enforcement. It expressed concern at the upswing in violence in both Kabul and the provinces. Taliban and Al-Qaida elements appeared to be targeting foreigners, military and civilian, rather than engaging coalition forces.

Afghanistan said that the consolidation of peace, security and stability largely depended on the international community's sustained engagement in providing the necessary assistance for the rehabilitation and reconstruction of Afghanistan's social and economic infrastructure. The success of the DDR process, due to commence by the end of June, was dependent on economic growth and the creation of employment. With respect to narcotics, the Afghan Government had issued two decrees banning the cultivation, production, trafficking and consumption of narcotic drugs. However, the practical success of the implementation of those decrees rested on credible law enforcement and the availability of alternative sources of livelihood for farmers. Supporting the central institutions of Afghanistan in establishing and consolidating effective government control over the opium-producing areas was essential for any drug control strategy. Likewise, other initiatives should focus on re-establishing a sustainable rural economy not only for landowners but also for seasonal labourers and labour forces involved in the opium economy. The TA's drug strategy encompassed programmes for alternative livelihoods, the enhancement of the capacity of law enforcement agencies and the improvement of national legislation. The Afghan Government was committed to eliminating opium production through the implementation of the national long-term drug control strategy by the year 2013.

SECURITY COUNCIL ACTION (June)

On 17 June [meeting 4774], following consultations among Security Council members, the President made statement **S/PRST/2003/7** on behalf of the Council:

The Security Council reaffirms its strong commitment to the sovereignty, independence, territorial integrity and national unity of Afghanistan.

The Council stresses that security remains a serious challenge facing Afghanistan. In particular, the Council expresses its concern over the increased number of attacks against international and local humanitarian personnel, coalition forces, the International Security Assistance Force and Afghan Transitional Administration targets carried out by the Taliban and other rebel elements. In this regard, the Council condemns in the strongest terms the attack against the Force in Kabul on 7 June 2003. The Council also expresses its concern over other security threats, including from illicit drug trafficking. The Council stresses the need to improve the security situation in the provinces and further to extend the authority of the Administration throughout the country. Against this backdrop, the Council underlines the importance of accelerating the comprehensive reform of the security sector of Afghanistan, including the disarmament, demobilization and reintegration of former combatants.

The Council welcomes the establishment and deployment of international civilian-military Provincial Reconstruction Teams in the provinces and encourages States to support further efforts to assist in improving security in the regions.

The Council believes that constructive and mutually supportive bilateral and regional relations between Afghanistan and all States, and in particular its neighbours, based on the principles of mutual respect and non-interference in each other's affairs, are important for stability in Afghanistan. The Council calls upon all States to respect the Declaration on Good-Neighbourly Relations, signed by the Transitional Administration of Afghanistan and the Governments of the People's Republic of China, the Islamic Republic of Iran, the Islamic Republic of Pakistan, the Republic of Tajikistan, Turkmenistan and the Republic of Uzbekistan, the States neighbouring Afghanistan, in Kabul on 22 December 2002 and to support the implementation of the provisions thereof.

The Council reaffirms the principles established in the Political Declaration adopted by the General Assembly at its twentieth special session, inter alia, that action against the world drug problem is a common and shared responsibility requiring an integrated and balanced approach in full conformity with the purposes and principles of the Charter of the United Nations and international law.

The Council recognizes the links between illicit drug trafficking and terrorism as well as other forms of crime, and the challenges posed by these activities inside Afghanistan as well as to transit and neighbouring States and other States affected by the trafficking in drugs from Afghanistan.

The Council expresses its concern at the increasing risk of the spread of HIV/AIDS associated with drug abuse in the region and beyond.

The Council stresses that security will be enhanced by continued coordinated efforts to combat the production of illicit drugs in Afghanistan as well as to interdict narco-trafficking beyond its borders. The Council recognizes that the effort to counter the problem of drugs originating in Afghanistan will be effective only when it is integrated into the wider context of reconstruction and development programmes in the country.

The Council expresses its concern that despite the efforts pursued, the volume of illegal opium production inside Afghanistan in 2002 has returned to former high levels. The Council notes with concern the assessment contained in the Opium Rapid Assessment Survey of the United Nations Office on Drugs and Crime that opium poppy cultivation has been reported in several districts of Afghanistan for the first time. The Council stresses the need to promote the comprehensive international approach, carried out, inter alia, under the auspices of the United Nations and through other international forums, in support of the drugs strategy of the Transitional Administration to eliminate the illicit cultivation of opium poppy. The Council also supports the fight against illicit trafficking in drugs and precursors within Afghanistan and in neighbouring States and countries along trafficking routes, including increased cooperation among them to strengthen anti-narcotic controls to curb the flow of drugs. Extensive efforts have also to be made to reduce the demand for drugs globally in order to contribute to the sustainability of the elimination of illicit cultivation in Afghanistan. The Council welcomes the comprehensive drug strategy for Afghanistan as set out in the drugs strategy of the Transitional Administration and calls for help to be provided within the framework of that strategy. The Council also welcomes the Paris Pact, introduced at the International Conference on Drug Routes from Central Asia to Europe, held in Paris on 21 and 22 May 2003, and thanks the Government of France for convening the Conference.

The Council expresses its support for the commitment by the Transitional Administration to eliminate drug production by the year 2013 and its efforts to implement the decrees prohibiting the cultivation, production and processing of the opium poppy, including illicit drug trafficking and drug abuse.

The Council welcomes the significant contribution by the Office on Drugs and Crime and notes that the work of the Office in Afghanistan is restrained by the lack, in the opium-growing areas of that country, of general stability and security which the international community as a whole should endeavour to ensure. The Council also welcomes projects under way by individual States to counter the threat of drugs in Afghanistan. Most of these projects are long-term, which is vital to eliminate drugs on a sustainable basis. The Council underscores the pressing need to achieve as soon as possible a significant and sustainable decrease in opium production in Afghanistan.

The Council acknowledges the necessity of coordination through the lead nation on this and all other issues in Afghanistan and, in this regard, expresses its gratitude to the United Kingdom of Great Britain and Northern Ireland and Germany for their work on counter-narcotics and police issues, respectively.

The Council recognizes the problems caused to neighbouring countries by the increase in Afghan opium production, as well as the efforts made by them and other countries to interdict illicit drugs.

The Council stresses the need to promote the effective realization of anti-drug projects for Afghanistan. These efforts can be reinforced through promulgation of a comprehensive programme of action in the region and in the States of transit and destination. The Council notes in this regard a major coordinating capacity available through the Office on Drugs and Crime, and calls upon all those concerned to cooperate with the Office in order to adopt harmonized measures in this area. The Council notes the call for all those concerned to adopt compatible and harmonized measures for law enforcement and counter-narcotics efforts through support for implementation of the drugs strategy of the Transitional Administration and the Paris Pact, supported by the G-8 Summit held in Evian, France, on 3 June 2003. The Council urges donor States to work within such a consultative process to maximize the effects of their bilateral and multilateral assistance programmes.

The Council urges the international community, in collaboration with the Office on Drugs and Crime and in accordance with the drugs strategy of the Transitional Administration, to provide assistance to the Administration that addresses, inter alia, certain key areas, including development of alternative livelihoods and markets, improving national institutional capacities, enforcing prohibitions on illicit cultivation and manufacturing and trafficking in drugs, encouraging demand reduction and building up the effective use of intelligence, including aerospace monitoring.

The Council urges the international community, in collaboration with the United Nations Assistance Mission in Afghanistan and the Office on Drugs and Crime, to encourage cooperation among affected countries, specifically in strengthening border controls, in assisting the flow of information between and among appropriate security and law enforcement agencies, in combating groups involved in illicit drug trafficking and related crimes, particularly money-laundering, in carrying out operational interdiction activities and controlled deliveries, in encouraging demand reduction and in coordinating information and intelligence to maximize the effectiveness of all measures taken inside Afghanistan and beyond its borders.

The Council invites the Secretary-General to include in his next report to the Security Council and the General Assembly on the situation in Afghanistan a summary of proposals made during its 4774th meeting, held on 17 June 2003, and any commentary and response to those proposals by any Member State and to submit his relevant recommendations to the Council for its consideration.

The Council decides to remain seized of the matter.

Communication (July). On 9 July [A/58/131-S/2003/703], Kazakhstan transmitted to the Secretary-General the text of the Joint Statement by the heads of State of the members of the Central Asian Cooperation Organization (Almaty, 5 July). The heads of State said that strengthening peace and stability in Afghanistan and establishing good-neighbourly relations with that country were in keeping with the basic interests of the countries of Central Asia. Joint efforts to restore Afghanistan's economy and infrastructure would make a substantial contribution to ensuring regional security and stability.

Report of Secretary-General (July). In a 23 July report [A/57/850-S/2003/754 & Corr.1], the Secretary-General described the continuing efforts by the Afghan TA to implement the Bonn Agreement [YUN 2001, p. 263]. The deteriorating security situation was identified as the main challenge facing the Afghan peace process and the international community was called on to continue its engagement in Afghanistan. The report drew attention to measures taken by the TA to expand its authority throughout the country, the most significant of which was the 20 May decision by the Afghan National Security Council to ban private military personnel and to enforce the collection of provincial revenues. The TA had also made progress in civil service reform through the establishment of the Independent Reforms Commission of Administrative and Civil Services. The constitutional process had progressed with the establishment of the Constitutional Commission, which conducted public consultations throughout the country in June and July. A draft constitution would be made public in September and would be discussed at the Constitutional Loya Jirga, scheduled for October. Preparations for national elections continued. The TA had decided to establish an Interim Afghan Election Commission, which would allow for greater Afghan involvement in the electoral process. The furthering of the political process, together with reconstruction programmes, the improvement in the human rights situation, counter-narcotics programmes, and other aspects of the Bonn process, all depended to a great extent on the security situation. It was noted that security conditions had deteriorated in many parts of the country. Despite progress made in rebuilding the national army and police, much more needed to be done to reform the security sector, and there remained a need for international security assistance beyond Kabul. In view of continuing threats against journalists, the importance of reforming the press law was emphasized. The report also highlighted efforts by the TA and the United Nations to address women's rights, the status of refugee returns, health care and the reconstruction of transportation infrastructure.

The Secretary-General reported that, on 16 April, NATO had stated that it would assume control of ISAF following the completion of the lead command by Germany and the Netherlands in August. NATO command should provide more stability to the Force, particularly by eliminating the need to find a new lead country every six months.

On 17 June, in response to cross-border infiltration of forces opposed to the TA, Afghanistan, Pakistan and the United States established a commission to determine the origin of cross-border attacks and to find mutually agreeable solutions.

UNAMA activities included the establishment of the United Nations Operations Centre in Kabul to assist in the co-location of staff and the bringing together of UN constituent agencies. UNAMA was also conducting a review of its management structure, part of its efforts to enhance the integration of policy coordination between the various components of the Mission and among the members of the UN country team. The Secretary-General proposed that the Military Advisory Unit be enlarged by a further four military liaison officers, bringing the total strength to 12 officers. That would make possible the permanent deployment of one officer to each of the eight regional field offices, and the involvement of the Unit in monitoring DDR at locations across the country in order to build confidence.

The Secretary-General observed that, in spite of considerable obstacles, the implementation of the Bonn Agreement continued to be largely on track. However, the consequences of the civil war were still apparent and strong factional interests were attempting to entrench themselves in the wake of the Taliban's collapse. Therefore, the creation of an environment where the standards of freedom and fairness enunciated in Bonn prevailed remained a major challenge.

On 30 September [S/2003/922], the Council took note of the Secretary-General's intention to increase the Military Advisory Unit to a total strength of 12 officers.

Communication (October). On 3 October [A/58/415-S/2003/952], Iran transmitted to the Secretary-General the final communiqué of the Annual Coordination Meeting of Ministers for Foreign Affairs of the Member States of the Organization of the Islamic Countries (New York, 30 September). In accordance with the Kabul Declaration on Good-Neighbourly Relations of 22 December 2002 [YUN 2002, p. 274], Afghanistan's neighbouring countries reaffirmed their commitment to constructive and supportive bilateral relations based on the principles of territorial integrity, cooperation and non-interference in each other's internal affairs.

Security Council consideration (October). On 24 October [meeting 4848], the Security Council discussed the situation in Afghanistan. The USG for Peacekeeping Operations, Mr. Guéhenno, said that as the final and most important stages of the peace process moved ahead, many of the fundamental and structural causes of insecurity remained unresolved. That was demonstrated in the northern part of the country when, on 9 October, after months of relative calm, the arrest of elements affiliated with Jamiat (an Islamic political party) sparked factional tensions that flared into the worst fighting in the region since the signing of the Bonn Agreement. Sporadic tribal and inter-factional conflicts also contributed to insecurity in the provinces of the south, southeast and east, but the primary source of insecurity remained the risk of terrorist attacks and continued and sizeable cross-border infiltrations by suspected Taliban, Al-Qaida and Hizb-I-Islami elements. In several border districts, the Taliban had been able to establish de facto control over district administration. Attacks by terrorists against government, military and humanitarian personnel were steadily increasing. The trend towards the targeting of civilians who supported the central Government and the peace process indicated that the United Nations itself had to be viewed as a potential target. As a result, the United Nations and the humanitarian community had taken further security precautions, particularly in the south. All UN missions were temporarily suspended in four southern provinces. In Kandahar, armed escorts were required in four districts, and the missions were suspended in another five. Those precautions were restricting reconstruction and the political process, including UNAMA's ability to ensure effective monitoring of the registration of electors for the Constitutional Loya Jirga in the south of the country. Despite serious challenges, the TA had made some progress in addressing the causes of insecurity. In fact, reform of the senior level of the Ministry of Defence had been completed. Although the reform was less sweeping than expected, it marked a step in the right direction to permit the pilot DDR programme to commence. In September, President Karzai postponed the Constitutional Loya Jirga until the end of Ramadan, which fell between the end of November and early December. The revised schedule had provided the Constitutional Commission more time for finalizing the draft constitution. The legal and institutional structures necessary for the national election were gradually being put in place. The registration decree, establishing the guidelines for voter eligibility, was finalized on 9 September and the political parties law, laying out the legal framework for the formation of political parties, was ratified on 12 October.

The Security Council's unanimous adoption on 13 October of **resolution 1510(2003)** (see p. 310), by which it expanded ISAF beyond Kabul, was a welcome and much needed development. Also, Germany's decision to deploy a Provincial Reconstruction Team to Kunduz was a welcome first step, which, it was hoped, would encourage other countries to contribute. The international community had taken steps to improve the overall security situation in Afghanistan with available assets on the ground. A joint coordination cell had been established to improve coordination between the TA, the United Nations, NATO and the coalition in support of the Bonn process. There was also a need for greater donor commitment in order to allow Afghanistan to recover from the near total devastation of its infrastructure and social capital after years of war.

Security Council mission

On 1 October [S/2003/930], the Council President informed the Secretary-General that the Council had decided to send a mission to Afghanistan from 31 October to 7 November 2003, which would be led by Gunter Pleuger (Germany). The mission's objectives would be, among other things, to review the progress achieved so far and to encourage the TA to further strengthen the implementation of the Bonn Agreement; to observe UNAMA's operations, including its role in assisting the TA in preparing for the elections, implementing the constitution and coordinating all UN activities; to observe ISAF's operations; to review the humanitarian and human rights situation; to review the implementation of the Kabul Declaration on Good-Neighbourly Relations of 22 December 2002 [YUN 2002, p. 274]; and to convey a message to regional and factional leaders about the need to reject all violence and to condemn extremism, terrorist and illegal drug activities.

Report of Security Council mission. The report of the Security Council mission to Afghanistan (31 October-7 November) was issued on 11 November [S/2003/1074]. The mission, which was based in Kabul, visited Herat and Mazar-e-Sharif and held extensive discussions on the implementation of the Bonn Agreement [YUN 2001, p. 263] and the implications of Council resolution 1510(2003) (see p. 310) with the TA, regional leaders, UNAMA, UN agencies, ISAF, the coalition forces, the diplomatic community, NGOs and civil society.

In its recommendations, the mission reminded all Afghan parties that had made a commitment to participate in the DDR process that the new national army, police and border police forces were to be responsible for security and law and order in Afghanistan, and all other armed units were to be dissolved. As a first step towards dissolution, the mission recommended that all factional forces be withdrawn from Kabul urgently. The mission drew the international community's attention to the need for enhanced assistance activities in the security sector, particularly with regard to the accelerated training and further deployment of the national police and Afghan national army, and called for further funds for the Law and Order Trust Fund. The TA was urged to take all possible measures to strengthen national unity and reconciliation and to ensure universal participation in the peace process, particularly with regard to the role of women. As a concrete measure, the mission recommended that the TA follow through with the reform of the Ministry of Defence; such reform should be extended to other key institutions. The mission recognized the difficulty of organizing general elections because of insecurity and the risk of disenfranchising a large segment of the population from the political process. It stressed the importance of tackling those issues so that the elections could be held within the time frame provided in the Bonn Agreement. In that regard, the mission noted the transitional provisions of the draft constitution, in particular the definition of a transitional period contained in it, which would include presidential elections followed by parliamentary elections as soon as possible. In order to ensure the necessary financial support and political momentum for peace and stability in Afghanistan, the mission noted with interest President Karzai's wish to convene a follow-up conference to the Bonn process early in 2004, following the conclusion of the Constitutional Loya Jirga. The Secretary-General was invited to study the possibilities for such a conference. The mission called on all Afghanistan's neighbours to fully implement the Kabul Declaration on Good-Neighbourly Relations and to redouble their efforts to help preserve peace and security in Afghanistan, especially in the southern and south-eastern areas. In order to strengthen the central Government and the basic institutions of the State, the mission recommended that the TA initiate a process of national reconciliation directed to all Afghans willing to help rebuild the country irrespective of past events.

Security Council consideration (November). On 11 November [meeting 4855], the Security Council discussed the report of the its mission to Afghanistan. The head of the mission, Mr. Pleuger, reviewed the report's main findings and recommendations, noting that the primary purpose of the mission was to send a signal to the Afghan people that Afghanistan remained high on the Council's agenda and that the international community continued to support the peace process. The mission had also sent a clear message to the local and provincial authorities that it was imperative that they stop factional fighting and cooperate with the central Government. The mission was impressed by the eagerness of the Afghans to stand together and rebuild their country. In particular, and in contrast to other crisis areas, there was, despite the continuing ethnic divisions and factional fighting, an Afghan national identity and there appeared to be no separatist tendencies.

Communication (November). On 21 November [A/58/611-S/2003/1134], India and the Russian Federation transmitted to the Secretary-General the Declaration of the Russian Federation and the Republic of India on Global Challenges and Threats to International Security and Stability, which was adopted during the visit of the Prime Minister of India, Atal Bihari Vajpayee, to the Russian Federation on 12 November. With regard to Afghanistan, both countries expressed support for the TA's work on national reconstruction and for the international community's efforts to bring peace, national reconciliation and economic revival to Afghanistan.

Report of Secretary-General (December). In response to General Assembly resolutions 57/113 A [YUN 2002, p. 273] and 57/113 B [ibid., p. 900], the Secretary-General submitted a 3 December report on the situation in Afghanistan and its implications for international peace and security [A/58/616], covering the period from July 2002 to November 2003. He also reported on emergency international assistance for peace, normalcy and reconstruction of war-stricken Afghanistan (see p. 934). Highlighting the deteriorating security situation throughout the country, the report stated that unchecked criminality, outbreaks of factional fighting and activities surrounding the narcotics trade had all had a negative impact on the Bonn process. During the reporting period, attacks on international and national staff of the assistance community had intensified. The main security threats continued to be terrorist attacks by suspected supporters of Al-Qaida, the Taliban and the warlord Hekmatyar against government forces, the United Nations and the humanitarian community. The attacks had occurred mostly in areas along the border in the south and southeast. It remained essential to create a secure environment in the south of Afghanistan so that reconstruction activities could take place. Equally crucial were the TA's efforts to extend its authority, enhance its administrative capacity and deliver socio-economic benefits on a nationwide scale. Important achievements included the rehabilitation of the national primary education system and one of the largest UN-assisted refugee repatriation efforts in history. The report concluded that the international community had to decide whether to increase its level of involvement in Afghanistan or risk failure. The mandate set in Bonn could be accomplished only if the security situation improved, allowing adequate protection to UN programmes and staff, NGOs and others assisting the Afghan population.

GENERAL ASSEMBLY ACTION

On 5 December [meeting 70], the General Assembly adopted **resolution 58/27 A** [draft: A/58/L.32 & Add.1] without vote [agenda item 28].

The situation in Afghanistan and its implications for international peace and security

The General Assembly,

Recalling its resolution 57/113 A of 6 December 2002 and all its previous relevant resolutions,

Recalling also all relevant Security Council resolutions and statements by the President of the Council on the situation in Afghanistan, in particular resolutions 1267(1999) of 15 October 1999, 1378(2001) of 14 November 2001, 1383(2001) of 6 December 2001, 1390(2002) of 16 January 2002, 1401(2002) of 28 March 2002, 1453(2002) of 24 December 2002 and 1510(2003) of 13 October 2003,

Reaffirming its continued strong commitment to the sovereignty, independence, territorial integrity and national unity of Afghanistan, and respecting its multicultural, multi-ethnic and historical heritage,

Reaffirming its condemnation of all use of Afghan territory for terrorist activities, and welcoming the ongoing successful efforts of the Afghan people and the Operation Enduring Freedom coalition to combat terrorism on their territory,

Convinced that the main responsibility for finding a political solution lies with the Afghan people themselves, expressing in this regard its full support for President Karzai and the Afghan Transitional Administration, and reaffirming its continued support for the implementation of the provisions of the agreement reached among various Afghan groups in Bonn, Germany, on 5 December 2001, including the holding of free and fair elections in 2004,

Convinced also that a political consolidation aimed at the adoption of a pluralistic and democratic constitution and the establishment of a broad-based, multi-ethnic, fully representative and gender-sensitive government, which respects the rule of law, the human rights of all Afghans and the international obligations of Afghanistan and is committed to peace with all countries, can lead to durable peace and reconciliation,

Recognizing the urgent need for the creation of an effective and ethnically balanced Afghan national army, Ministry of Defence and national police force, and acknowledging the importance of the first steps taken in this regard by the Transitional Administration,

Reiterating that a fair and effective justice system that respects international norms and standards, including by ensuring the accountability of perpetrators of violations of human rights, remains of high importance,

Encouraging the Transitional Administration to consider initiating a process of national reconciliation,

Taking note of the positive developments in Afghanistan in the past two years, in particular the return of a large number of refugees and internally displaced persons, the increased Afghan ownership as illustrated by the progress in implementing education and health programmes, the development of a comprehensive national budget, the introduction of the new currency, the publication of a draft text for a constitution, the beginning of the disarmament, demobilization and reintegration process and the reforms thus far in the security sector, and stressing that these processes should be expedited and carried through to completion,

Expressing its appreciation and strong support for the ongoing efforts of the Secretary-General, his Special Representative for Afghanistan and the staff of the United Nations Assistance Mission in Afghanistan to promote peace and stability in Afghanistan, stressing in particular in this regard the highly valuable role that the current Special Representative of the Secretary-General has played throughout the ongoing process,

Reiterating that the United Nations must continue to play its central and impartial role in the international efforts to assist the Afghan people in consolidating peace in Afghanistan and rebuilding their country and its institutions, as well as in efforts to provide humanitarian assistance, provide for rehabilitation and reconstruction and national capacity-building and facilitate the orderly return of refugees,

Recognizing the need for continued strong international commitment to humanitarian assistance and for programmes, under the ownership of the Transitional Administration, of rehabilitation and reconstruction, and noting that visible progress in this regard can further enhance the authority of the Transitional Administration and greatly contribute to the peace process,

Commending the international efforts to help the Transitional Administration to provide a secure environment in Afghanistan, and stressing the need for a coordinated approach across all parts of the security sector and the importance of a national army and police force that are ethnically balanced, professional and accountable to legitimate civilian authorities,

Welcoming, in this regard, the important role played by both the International Security Assistance Force and its respective lead nations in improving security conditions in and around Kabul and other parts of Afghanistan,

Recognizing the need for Afghanistan and its neighbours to work closely together to promote peace, security, stability and mutually beneficial relations, including through trade and investment, and welcoming therefore the signature of the Kabul Declaration on Good-neighbourly Relations on 22 December 2002 and the Declaration on Encouraging Closer Trade, Transit and Investment Cooperation on 22 September 2003,

Noting that, despite improvements in the security sector, the lack of security still remains the most serious challenge facing Afghanistan and Afghans today, expressing its deep concern over a number of recent security incidents in Afghanistan, including the terrorist attacks against United Nations staff, national and international humanitarian personnel and the International Security Assistance Force, noting the necessity of further enhancing the capacity of the Transitional Administration to exercise its authority nationwide, and commending the steps already taken in that regard,

Deeply concerned about the continued increase in the cultivation, production and trafficking of narcotic drugs in Afghanistan, which is undermining stability and security, as well as the political and economic reconstruction of Afghanistan, and has dangerous repercussions in the region and far beyond, and welcoming in this context the commitment of the Transitional Administration to rid Afghanistan of this pernicious production and trade,

Recognizing that the social and economic development of Afghanistan, specifically the development of gainful and sustainable livelihoods in the formal productive sector, is an important condition for the successful implementation of the comprehensive national drug control strategy of the Transitional Administration,

Recognizing also the need for enhanced international cooperation and support to accelerate the implementation of the Afghan national drug control strategy, and looking forward in this regard to the international counter-narcotics conference in Kabul in 2004, to be hosted by the Transitional Administration, the United Nations and the United Kingdom,

1. *Takes note* of the report of the Secretary-General;
2. *Welcomes* the recent Security Council mission to Afghanistan and its report, which contains several positive recommendations;
3. *Stresses* that the fragile situation in Afghanistan poses a continuing risk to peace and stability in the region, and expresses its determination to further assist the efforts of the Transitional Administration to prevent the use of Afghan territory for terrorism;
4. *Reiterates its strong support* for the Transitional Administration in the full implementation of the Bonn Agreement, endorses its priorities, as presented in the National Development Framework and national budget, which are the restoration of the economic infrastructure, the strengthening of the central government, the constitutional process, the building of a national army and police force under civilian control, the verified and fair implementation of disarmament, demobilization and reintegration, demining activities, the rebuilding of the justice system, respect for human rights, and combating illicit drug production and trafficking, and urges the international community to support the efforts in these areas;
5. *Stresses* the importance of strengthening the authority of the Transitional Administration, facilitating security sector reform and reconstruction efforts throughout the country and providing a secure environment for the constitutional process and the preparations for the general elections, and in this regard welcomes the recent expansion of the International Security Assistance Force mandate in accordance with the Bonn Agreement, as well as the progressive establishment of provincial reconstruction teams in various parts of Afghanistan;
6. *Calls upon* all Afghan groups to renounce the use of violence, respect human rights and international humanitarian law, respect the authority of the Transitional Administration and implement fully the provisions of the Bonn Agreement;
7. *Welcomes* the role of the Afghan Independent Human Rights Commission in the promotion and protection of human rights and fundamental freedoms in Afghanistan, including through the provision of expert advice to the Constitutional Commission, and encourages the Transitional Administration and the international community to continue to provide appropriate assistance and support to allow the Afghan Independent Human Rights Commission to fulfil its mandate;
8. *Stresses* the fundamental importance for a peaceful, democratic Afghanistan of the upcoming constitutional Loya Jirga and elections in 2004, in accordance with the time frame set out in the Bonn Agreement for the creation of a representative government, and underscores the need for the broad and open participation of all Afghans, including women, in the political process in a secure environment;
9. *Reiterates* the importance of the full and equal participation of and representation by women in political, civil, economic, cultural and social life throughout the country, calls upon the Transitional Administration to protect and promote the equal rights of men

and women, and notes in this respect the ratification by Afghanistan of the Convention on the Elimination of All Forms of Discrimination against Women on 5 March 2003;

10. *Commends and strongly supports* the important role of the Special Representative of the Secretary-General for Afghanistan and the staff of the United Nations Assistance Mission in Afghanistan in support of efforts of the Transitional Administration to fully implement the Bonn Agreement, and endorses the concept of the Assistance Mission as a fully integrated Mission under the authority of the Special Representative and with a light international footprint;

11. *Calls upon* donor countries to fulfil promptly their assumed commitments made at the International Conference on Reconstruction Assistance to Afghanistan, held in Tokyo on 21 and 22 January 2002, and reiterated in Dubai, United Arab Emirates, on 21 September 2003, invites them to provide additional resources beyond those pledged so far, and also calls upon all Member States to provide humanitarian assistance and to support the Transitional Administration through measures in accordance with the national development budget published by the Transitional Administration;

12. *Calls upon* the international community to support the efforts of the Transitional Administration to coordinate assistance, to formulate a strategy for the long-term development of Afghanistan and to allocate sufficient funds to the Afghanistan Reconstruction Trust Fund;

13. *Calls upon* the signatories of the Kabul Declaration on Good-neighbourly Relations to respect their commitments under the Declaration, and calls upon all other States to respect and support the implementation of its provisions and to promote regional stability;

14. *Welcomes,* in this regard, the signing of the Declaration on Encouraging Closer Trade, Transit and Investment Cooperation as a further sign of the commitment of Afghanistan and its neighbours to closer regional cooperation;

15. *Calls upon* the members of the Tripartite Commission to redouble their efforts to support peace and security in the southern and south-eastern border areas of Afghanistan;

16. *Calls* for continued international assistance to the vast number of Afghan refugees and internally displaced persons to facilitate their safe and orderly return and sustainable reintegration into society so as to contribute to the stability of the entire country;

17. *Welcomes* the efforts of the Transitional Administration to respect fully the international obligations of Afghanistan with regard to narcotic drugs, and calls upon it to strengthen further its efforts to eliminate the annual poppy crop, as well as to efficiently enforce relevant national laws and regulations against narcotic drugs;

18. *Calls upon* the international community to assist the Transitional Administration in the implementation of its comprehensive national drug control strategy, aimed at eliminating illicit poppy cultivation, which continues to constitute a serious threat to the successful political and economic reconstruction of Afghanistan, including through support for increased law enforcement, crop substitution and other alternative livelihood and development programmes and capacity-building for drug control institutions;

19. *Supports* the fight against the illicit trafficking of drugs and precursors within Afghanistan and in neighbouring States and countries along trafficking routes, including increased cooperation among them to strengthen anti-narcotic controls to curb the drug flow, and welcomes the presentation in Moscow on 29 October 2003 of the latest report of the United Nations International Drug Control Programme on drugs in Afghanistan;

20. *Requests* the Secretary-General to report to the General Assembly every four months during its fifty-eighth session on the progress of the United Nations and the efforts of his Special Representative to promote peace in Afghanistan, and to report to the Assembly at its fifty-ninth session on the progress made in the implementation of the present resolution;

21. *Decides* to include in the provisional agenda of its fifty-ninth session the item entitled "The situation in Afghanistan and its implications for international peace and security".

On the same day, the Assembly adopted **resolution 58/27 B** on emergency international assistance for peace, normalcy and reconstruction of war-stricken Afghanistan (see p. 934).

On 23 December, the Assembly decided that the item on the situation in Afghanistan and its implications for international peace and security would remain for consideration at its resumed fifty-eighth (2004) session (**decision 58/565**).

Communications (December). On 16 December [A/58/755-S/2004/277], Liechtenstein transmitted to the Secretary-General the report of an international meeting of experts on the theme "Building security and State in Afghanistan—a critical assessment" (Princeton University, United States, 17-19 October). Participants agreed that in Afghanistan the needs for establishing security and building of State and society were urgent and closely interconnected and that solutions had to be holistic. They urged delivery of immediate international financial assistance to both security and State-building endeavours.

On 22 December [A/58/663], Tajikistan transmitted to the Secretary-General the text of the statement on Afghanistan issued by the Ministers for Foreign Affairs of the member States of the Collective Security Treaty Organization (Bishkek, Kyrgyzstan, 19 November). The Ministers noted the progress achieved by the TA with respect to State-building and the efforts made to combat extremist forces, but noted with concern the growing threat of narcotic drugs emanating from Afghanistan and the unceasing activity of extremist groups. Alongside the need to boost efforts to eradicate terrorism, it was also important to eliminate the social base of terrorism and to revive and rebuild the country's economy.

Report of Secretary-General (December). In response to Security Council resolution 1471 (2003) (see p. 295), the Secretary-General submitted a 30 December report on the situation in Afghanistan and its implications for international peace and security [S/2003/1212]. He stated that the peace process in Afghanistan had reached a critical juncture, two years since the beginning of the implementation of the Bonn Agreement [YUN 2001, p. 263]. A great deal had been accomplished, including the establishment of the TA itself, the return of some 4.2 million children to school, one third of them girls, and the beginning of security sector reform. During the reporting period, the most sensitive and potentially divisive steps of the Bonn process began: the pilot phase of the DDR programme on 24 October, the electoral registration on 1 December and the Constitutional Loya Jirga on 14 December, which was still ongoing. However, fundamental challenges needed to be overcome if the peace process was to become irreversible, in particular the problem of insecurity. The reporting period saw an increase in terrorist activity, factional fighting, activities associated with narcotics trade and unchecked criminality. Attacks on international and national staff of the assistance community and TA officials had been concentrated in the south and south-east regions. A car-bomb attack on UN offices in Kandahar on 13 November was followed three days later by the assassination of an international staff member of the Office of the United Nations High Commissioner for Refugees in Ghazni. In the absence of sufficient forces to provide security, much of the south and south-east of the country had become effectively off limits to UN and TA officials. Lack of access to assistance or State structures risked further alienating the population, which was predominantly Pashtun. In response to the increased threats against the UN and the aid community, President Karzai, on 26 November, established two national task forces, bringing together the Afghan security ministries, ISAF, the coalition forces and the United Nations. One task force was working on short-term measures to ensure the necessary security for the Bonn process and for aid and reconstruction efforts, while the second would work on responses to security threats over the longer term.

Under the Afghan New Beginnings Programme and with financing from Japan and UNDP assistance, the pilot phase of the DDR programme began on 24 October in Kunduz province; it was later extended to Paktia province and Kabul. Hundreds of ex-soldiers and officers had been disarmed and had selected reintegration options, such as agricultural assistance, vocational training and job placement, and demining training. With the aim of establishing a 70,000-strong national army under a 10-year plan, 12 battalions had been trained under the lead of the United States, representing a total force of 6,500. The Ministry of the Interior had begun implementing reforms geared towards the implementation of a five-year plan to develop a national police service of some 50,000 members and a force of 12,000 border guards. It was projected that some 213 higher-ranking and 2,000 lower-ranking officers would be trained by mid-2004. The deployment of newly recruited police officers in three provinces had contributed to stability and public confidence. Yet, at such an early stage of the process, the number of trained police remained too low and ill equipped to provide the full support needed by the central Government in its efforts to establish itself in the provinces. In the justice sector, the civil and criminal codes and other legal frameworks were being reviewed and updated. As part of the efforts to strengthen governance at the provincial level, the justice sector was developing an integrated model of intervention in Paktia province, which combined reconstruction, rehabilitation and refurbishing of judicial and corrections buildings, and training for magistrates, administrative justice personnel, police, corrections staff and defence counsels. The absence of an international commitment to develop a penitentiary system was a significant obstacle to the establishment of institutions for the provision of law and order. The countering of narcotics activities in Afghanistan would continue to face numerous internal obstacles: an environment of rural underdevelopment, the absence of rule of law, the limitations on financial resources for law enforcement and the paucity of alternative livelihoods. Efforts to counter poppy production continued to meet with violent opposition in a number of areas.

On 11 August, control of ISAF was transferred from Germany and the Netherlands to NATO (see p. 308). In addition, three new provincial reconstruction teams were established under coalition command. Communication links had been established between provincial centres and Kabul, and between provincial police stations and the Ministry of the Interior, in an effort to expand the TA's authority across the country. Nevertheless, insecurity continued to be a significant constraint as, beyond Kabul, some factional leaders continued to resist the Government's efforts to install national appointees in the provinces and districts. The TA was working closely with UNAMA, the coalition forces, ISAF and donor Governments to formulate a nationwide stabilization plan aimed at bringing together security improvements, better local governance and reconstruction activities.

The draft constitution was made public on 3 November by the Constitutional Review Commission, the culmination of a drafting process that included a significant national consultation. The draft provided for a strong presidential system of government and a bicameral legislature, codified respect for fundamental rights and called for the nation's laws not to be in contradiction with the religion of Islam. The draft also outlined transitional measures, including those for elections. The Constitutional Loya Jirga, which commenced its deliberations on 14 December and was still ongoing as at 30 December, comprised 502 participants. Ten working committees had been established to review the draft constitution and propose amendments. While debate had been vigorous, delegates had expressed concerns about domineering attitudes expressed by jihadi groups.

The TA had established the institutional framework necessary for the voter registration process; in July it created the Joint Electoral Management Body and the Interim Afghan Electoral Commission to oversee the registration process. Lack of early donor funding caused the start of the electoral registration to be delayed from 15 October to 1 December. In addition, lack of security in certain areas of the country was delaying the deployment of registration teams to remote rural areas.

Some progress had been achieved in regional relations. On 22 September (Dubai, United Arab Emirates), Afghanistan and its neighbours signed the Declaration on Encouraging Closer Trade, Transit and Investment Cooperation Between the Signatory Governments of the Kabul Declaration on Good-Neighbourly Relations [YUN 2002, p. 274], to respect and build on their commitments to support regional political stability and mutual economic well-being. Pakistan had deployed and maintained troops along its border with Afghanistan, in order to deter cross-border infiltration of elements hostile to the Afghan Government. However, there were persistent reports of Taliban leaders operating from inside Pakistan. The tripartite commission formed by Afghanistan, Pakistan and the United States was working to address the issue of cross-border security.

In response to the increased threat of attacks against UN staff and premises, UNAMA and the UN agencies had been reviewing and, where necessary, upgrading security measures at all office compounds and residences. New UNAMA electoral offices were constructed in the eight regional centres in time for the start of the 1 December electoral registration campaign.

The Secretary-General observed that the problem of insecurity remained the main challenge to the successful implementation of the Bonn process. The political elements of that process had been carried forward by concentrating activities in city and regional centres, thereby mitigating threats that predominated in rural areas. The time had come for the international community and the Afghan Government to make the necessary commitments to complete the transition in Afghanistan. President Karzai had discussed with the Security Council mission the possibility of a second international conference and the Special Representative for Afghanistan, Mr. Brahimi, had circulated a non-paper to the TA and diplomatic corps in Kabul. The non-paper acknowledged gains made under the Bonn process, but pointed out that to ensure success further reforms were needed to broaden the representativeness of government, improvements in the security situation had to be made to end the misrule of factions and counter the terrorist threat, and more progress in reconstruction had to be made. The non-paper further argued that donor commitments were needed, beyond the timelines of the Bonn Agreement, to consolidate government authority, entrench the rule of law, counter the threat of the narcotics economy and carry Afghanistan's peace process to the point of irreversibility. The Secretary-General said that one way of addressing the issues raised in that non-paper might be the convening of a new donor conference, in the first months of 2004, to chart the way forward.

International Security Assistance Force

The International Security Assistance Force, a multinational force established by Security Council resolution 1386(2001) [YUN 2001, p. 267], was mandated, among other things, to assist the Afghan Government in the maintenance of security in Kabul and its surrounding areas. Turkey, which had assumed lead nation status for ISAF from the United Kingdom in June 2002, handed over that responsibility to Germany and the Netherlands on 10 February. Those two countries, in turn, handed over ISAF's lead command to NATO on 11 August. The event represented the first operation to be commanded by NATO outside the territory of NATO member States and it brought with it the benefit of continuity of command.

Communications (January/February). During January and February, the Secretary-General received a number of communications from Member States, pledging military personnel, equipment and other resources to ISAF: Hungary [S/2003/78], Belgium [S/2003/159] and Azerbaijan [S/2003/248].

Report of ISAF (February). In response to Security Council resolutions 1386(2001) [YUN 2001, p. 267], 1413(2002) [YUN 2002, p. 276] and 1444 (2002) [ibid., p. 278], Turkey submitted to the Secretary-General a February report [S/2003/210] on ISAF's activities, covering the period from 1 November 2002 to 10 February 2003.

Security circumstances in Kabul continued to improve during the reporting period. The calm and peaceful atmosphere in the capital had consolidated further and no major incident had occurred since the night curfew was lifted, for the first time since 1979, on 3 November 2002. Taking advantage of the improved security in the city, President Karzai asked ISAF to help the local security entities in tackling ordinary crime in some parts of Kabul. ISAF continued to assist the local community through the Civil-Military Cooperation programme, which channelled assistance in the fields of education, health and urban infrastructure through selected quick-impact projects. Arrangements for a smooth transfer of the ISAF command from Turkey to the joint German-Dutch leadership had been completed.

Communication of Secretary-General (April). On 16 April [S/2003/503], the Secretary-General transmitted to the Security Council President a 16 April letter from NATO, which stated that the North Atlantic Council had decided to continue and enhance NATO support to ISAF, beginning in August. As 14 NATO nations already contributed approximately 95 per cent of ISAF's troops, that enhanced support was a logical continuation of NATO efforts to date. The additional support would consist of the following: an in-theatre deployed composite headquarters, including the required communications and logistics support; a force commander from a troop-contributing allied nation; and strategic coordination, command and control exercised by the supreme headquarters of the allied Powers in Europe, with an ISAF operations coordination cell to involve participating nations. The political direction and coordination responsibilities would be undertaken by the North Atlantic Council in close consultation with non-NATO contributors to ISAF. Increased involvement by NATO would be within the context of ISAF's UN mandate and NATO would operate according to Security Council resolutions. ISAF would therefore continue to operate distinct from Operation Enduring Freedom.

On 23 April [S/2003/504], the Council took note of the Secretary-General's communication.

Reports of ISAF (May and August). On 19 May [S/2003/555], Germany and the Netherlands submitted to the Secretary-General a report on ISAF activities from 10 February to 10 May. The joint Germany-Netherlands command said that the security situation in Kabul had remained by and large stable and virtually similar to that in the preceding period. It seemed clear, however, that the increasing instability and rising number of incidents in the southern and south-eastern parts of Afghanistan could converge on the larger Kabul area and pose a threat to ISAF's area of responsibility. Although the TA was in charge of security structures, the international community had assumed specific responsibilities with regard to security sector reform. Key issues in that context were DDR of factional armies, build-up of the Afghan National Army (ANA) and re-establishment of a functional national police. ISAF was contributing to the training of ANA and the national police on a limited scale and stood ready to assist with the DDR process in Kabul if requested by the TA. To achieve safe and secure air lines of communications for its mission, ISAF assisted the TA in the development of Kabul International Airport. In close consultation with UNAMA, ISAF was also monitoring the constitution and election processes as the TA prepared for the convening of the Constitutional Loya Jirga.

On 11 August [S/2003/807], Germany and the Netherlands submitted to the Secretary-General their final report on ISAF, covering the period from 11 May to 11 August, up to the handover of ISAF's command to NATO. The overall security situation remained a point of concern throughout the period. However, although ISAF suffered casualties due to attacks and other incidents, it managed to improve security in and around Kabul. ISAF continued to contribute to the development of Afghan security structures by providing training support to ANA, the police and the border police. Regular contacts with Afghan authorities, the UN Special Representative and the United States military had ensured permanent ISAF input into all major processes related to security.

Communications of Secretary-General (October). On 7 October [S/2003/970], the Secretary-General transmitted to the Security Council President two communications, dated 2 and 6 October, from NATO's Secretary-General, which stated that on 1 October the North Atlantic Council had agreed on a longer-term strategy for NATO in its ISAF role in Afghanistan. The elements of the strategy comprised the political objective of supporting the Bonn process, the desired end state of a self-sustaining, moderate and democratic Afghan government, and benchmarks for a handover strategy.

On 6 October, the NATO Secretary-General transmitted to the Secretary-General information on key issues concerning NATO's possible expansion of the ISAF mission, which had been agreed to by the North Atlantic Council. It was agreed that the expansion of the ISAF mission would strengthen the TA's ability to provide a secure environment for the Afghan population; such expansion would be subject to the adoption of a Security Council resolution providing appropriate authority and the identification and provision of appropriate assets; the Provincial Reconstruction Team (PRT) in Konduz, which Germany had offered to mount, would operate as a pilot project under a new, expanded ISAF Security Council mandate; ISAF, in principle, could expand in a progressive, flexible manner, taking into account the political context, to include other PRTs under an expanded mandate; ISAF, also in principle, could undertake temporary deployment outside Kabul, in support of specific events or processes, such as electoral or DDR-related events; and it was imperative that there be clear command and control arrangements between ISAF, Operation Enduring Freedom and PRTs.

On 13 October [S/2003/986], the Secretary-General transmitted to the Council President a 10 October communication he had received from Afghanistan's Minister for Foreign Affairs. The Minister said that, notwithstanding the considerable progress made in providing security in Kabul and the surrounding areas thanks to the assistance of ISAF, the security situation in various parts of the country remained relatively unstable and was an impediment to further progress in reconstruction and development overall. Afghan authorities welcomed NATO's intention to deploy a pilot project in Kunduz and to undertake deployments outside Kabul in support of specific events or processes subject to a new Security Council mandate. The Afghan Government therefore requested the Council to consider expanding ISAF's mandate.

Expansion of ISAF mandate

On 13 October [meeting 4840], the Security Council unanimously adopted **resolution 1510 (2003)**. The draft [S/2003/984] was prepared in consultations among Council members.

The Security Council,

Reaffirming its previous resolutions on Afghanistan, in particular resolutions 1386(2001) of 20 December 2001, 1413(2002) of 23 May 2002 and 1444(2002) of 27 November 2002,

Reaffirming its strong commitment to the sovereignty, independence, territorial integrity and national unity of Afghanistan,

Reaffirming its resolutions 1368(2001) of 12 September 2001 and 1373(2001) of 28 September 2001, and reiterating its support for international efforts to root out terrorism in accordance with the Charter of the United Nations,

Recognizing that the responsibility for providing security and law and order throughout the country resides with the Afghans themselves, and welcoming the continuing cooperation of the Afghan Transitional Authority with the International Security Assistance Force,

Reaffirming the importance of the Agreement on Provisional Arrangements in Afghanistan Pending the Re-establishment of Permanent Government Institutions, signed in Bonn, Germany, on 5 December 2001 (the Bonn Agreement), and recalling in particular annex I thereto, which, inter alia, provides for the progressive expansion of the Force to other urban centres and other areas beyond Kabul,

Stressing the importance of extending central government authority to all parts of Afghanistan, of comprehensive disarmament, demobilization and reintegration of all armed factions, and of security sector reform, including reconstitution of the new Afghan National Army and Afghan National Police,

Recognizing the constraints upon the full implementation of the Bonn Agreement resulting from concerns about the security situation in parts of Afghanistan,

Noting the letter dated 10 October 2003 from the Minister for Foreign Affairs of Afghanistan requesting the assistance of the Force outside Kabul,

Noting also the letter dated 6 October 2003 from the Secretary-General of the North Atlantic Treaty Organization to the Secretary-General regarding a possible expansion of the mission of the Force,

Determining that the situation in Afghanistan still constitutes a threat to international peace and security,

Determined to ensure the full implementation of the mandate of the Force, in consultation with the Afghan Transitional Authority and its successors,

Acting for these reasons under Chapter VII of the Charter,

1. *Authorizes* expansion of the mandate of the International Security Assistance Force to allow it, as resources permit, to support the Afghan Transitional Authority and its successors in the maintenance of security in areas of Afghanistan outside of Kabul and its environs, so that the Afghan authorities as well as the personnel of the United Nations and other international civilian personnel engaged, in particular, in reconstruction and humanitarian efforts, can operate in a secure environment, and to provide security assistance for the performance of other tasks in support of the Agreement on Provisional Arrangements in Afghanistan Pending the Re-establishment of Permanent Government Institutions (the Bonn Agreement);

2. *Calls upon* the Force to continue to work in close consultation with the Afghan Transitional Authority and its successors and the Special Representative of the Secretary-General as well as with the Operation Enduring Freedom Coalition in the implementation of the mandate of the Force, and to report to the Security

Council on the implementation of the measures set out in paragraph 1 above;

3. *Decides* to extend the authorization of the Force, as defined in resolution 1386(2001) and the present resolution, for a period of twelve months;

4. *Authorizes* the Member States participating in the Force to take all necessary measures to fulfil its mandate;

5. *Requests* the leadership of the Force to provide quarterly reports on the implementation of its mandate to the Security Council through the Secretary-General;

6. *Decides* to remain actively seized of the matter.

Speaking after the vote, France said it considered that ISAF's extension did not entail a commitment of its forces outside Kabul. France did not plan to involve itself in missions beyond those it was already fulfilling.

Later developments. In a later report [S/2004/222] covering ISAF activities in November and December, NATO said that the security situation in Kabul and its environs remained generally calm, but not stable. On 30 December, ISAF took the first step in expanding its supporting role to the TA by taking responsibility for the operations of the German PRT in Konduz. Five attacks on ISAF, which included rockets and improvised explosive devices, took place in December with no fatalities.

Sanctions

The Security Council adopted new measures against Osama bin Laden, Al-Qaida, the Taliban, their associates and associated entities. Those measures included a freeze on financial and economic assets, a travel ban and an arms embargo. They were to be applied by all countries against individuals and entities designated by the Sanctions Committee. The Council also requested the Secretary-General to reappoint five experts to the Monitoring Group to monitor, for a further period of 12 months, the implementation of the sanctions measures.

SECURITY COUNCIL ACTION

On 17 January [meeting 4686], the Security Council unanimously adopted **resolution 1455 (2003)**. The draft [S/2003/48] was prepared in consultations among Council members.

The Security Council,

Recalling its resolutions 1267(1999) of 15 October 1999, 1333(2000) of 19 December 2000, 1363(2001) of 30 July 2001, 1373(2001) of 28 September 2001, 1390 (2002) of 16 January 2002 and 1452(2002) of 20 December 2002,

Underlining the obligation placed upon all Member States to implement, in full, resolution 1373(2001), including with regard to any member of the Taliban and Al-Qaida, and any individuals, groups, undertakings and entities associated with the Taliban and Al-Qaida, who have participated in the financing, planning, facilitating and preparation or perpetration of terrorist acts or in supporting terrorist acts, as well as to facilitate the implementation of counter-terrorism obligations in accordance with relevant Security Council resolutions,

Reaffirming the need to combat by all means, in accordance with the Charter of the United Nations and international law, threats to international peace and security caused by terrorist acts,

Noting that, in giving effect to the measures in paragraph 4 *(b)* of resolution 1267(1999), paragraph 8 *(c)* of resolution 1333(2000) and paragraphs 1 and 2 of resolution 1390(2002), full account is to be taken of the provisions of paragraphs 1 and 2 of resolution 1452 (2002),

Reiterating its condemnation of the Al-Qaida network and other associated terrorist groups for ongoing and multiple criminal terrorist acts, aimed at causing the deaths of innocent civilians, and other victims, and the destruction of property,

Reiterating its unequivocal condemnation of all forms of terrorism and terrorist acts as noted in resolutions 1368(2001) of 12 September 2001, 1438(2002) of 14 October 2002, 1440(2002) of 24 October 2002 and 1450 (2002) of 13 December 2002,

Reaffirming that acts of international terrorism constitute a threat to international peace and security,

Acting under Chapter VII of the Charter,

1. *Decides* to improve the implementation of the measures imposed by paragraph 4 *(b)* of resolution 1267(1999), paragraph 8 *(c)* of resolution 1333(2000) and paragraphs 1 and 2 of resolution 1390(2002);

2. *Also decides* that the measures referred to in paragraph 1 above will be further improved in twelve months, or sooner if necessary;

3. *Stresses* the need for improved coordination and increased exchange of information between the Security Council Committee established pursuant to resolution 1267(1999) (hereinafter referred to as "the Committee") and the Security Council Committee established pursuant to resolution 1373(2001);

4. *Requests* the Committee to communicate to Member States the list referred to in paragraph 2 of resolution 1390(2002) at least every three months, and stresses to all Member States the importance of submitting to the Committee the names of and identifying information, to the extent possible, about members of Al-Qaida and the Taliban and other individuals, groups, undertakings and entities associated with them so that the Committee can consider adding new names and details to its list, unless to do so would compromise investigations or enforcement actions;

5. *Calls upon* all States to continue to take urgent steps to enforce and strengthen through legislative enactments or administrative measures, where appropriate, the measures imposed under domestic laws or regulations against their nationals and other individuals or entities operating in their territory to prevent and punish violations of the measures referred to in paragraph 1 above, and to inform the Committee of the adoption of such measures, and invites States to report the results of all related investigations or enforcement

actions to the Committee, unless to do so would compromise the investigations or enforcement actions;

6. *Also calls upon* all States to submit an updated report to the Committee no later than ninety days from the adoption of the present resolution on all steps taken to implement the measures referred to in paragraph 1 above and all related investigations and enforcement actions, including a comprehensive summary of frozen assets of listed individuals and entities within the territories of Member States, unless to do so would compromise investigations or enforcement actions;

7. *Calls upon* all States, relevant United Nations bodies, and, as appropriate, other organizations and interested parties to cooperate fully with the Committee and with the Monitoring Group referred to in paragraph 8 below, including by supplying such information as may be sought by the Committee pursuant to all pertinent resolutions and by providing all relevant information, to the extent possible, to facilitate proper identification of all listed individuals and entities;

8. *Requests* the Secretary-General, upon adoption of the present resolution and acting in consultation with the Committee, to reappoint five experts, drawing, as much as possible and as appropriate, on the expertise of the members of the Monitoring Group established pursuant to paragraph 4 *(a)* of resolution 1363(2001), to monitor for a further period of twelve months the implementation of the measures referred to in paragraph 1 above and to follow up relevant leads relating to any incomplete implementation of those measures;

9. *Requests* the Chairman of the Committee to report orally at least every ninety days to the Council in detail on the overall work of the Committee and the Monitoring Group, and stipulates that these updates shall include a summary of progress in submitting the reports referred to in paragraph 6 of resolution 1390(2002) and paragraph 6 above;

10. *Requests* the Secretary-General to ensure that the Monitoring Group and the Committee and its Chairman have access to sufficient expertise and resources as and when required to assist in the discharge of their responsibilities;

11. *Requests* the Committee to consider, where and when appropriate, a visit to selected countries by the Chairman of the Committee and/or Committee members to enhance the full and effective implementation of the measures referred to in paragraph 1 above, with a view to encouraging States to implement all relevant Council resolutions;

12. *Requests* the Monitoring Group to submit a detailed work programme within thirty days of the adoption of the present resolution and to assist the Committee in providing guidance for Member States on the format of the reports referred to in paragraph 6 above;

13. *Also requests* the Monitoring Group to submit two written reports to the Committee, the first by 15 June 2003 and the second by 1 November 2003, on implementation of the measures referred to in paragraph 1 above and to brief the Committee when the Committee so requests;

14. *Requests* the Committee, through its Chairman, to provide the Council by 1 August 2003 and by 15 December 2003 with detailed oral assessments of implementation by Member States of the measures referred to in paragraph 1 above based on reports by Member States referred to in paragraph 6 above, paragraph 6 of resolution 1390(2002) and all pertinent parts of reports submitted by Member States under resolution 1373(2001), and in line with transparent criteria to be determined by the Committee and communicated to all Member States, in addition to considering supplementary recommendations by the Monitoring Group, with a view to recommending further measures for consideration by the Council to improve the measures referred to in paragraph 1 above;

15. *Also requests* the Committee, based on its oral assessments, through its Chairman, to the Council referred to in paragraph 14 above, to prepare and circulate a written assessment to the Council of actions taken by States to implement the measures referred to in paragraph 1 above;

16. *Decides* to remain actively seized of the matter.

Sanctions Committee activities

The Security Council Committee established pursuant to resolution 1267(1999) [YUN 1999, p. 265] (the Afghanistan Sanctions Committee) submitted a report [S/2004/281] covering its activities from 1 January to 31 December 2003. During that period, the Committee held 4 formal meetings and 36 informal consultations at the expert level. On 2 September, the Committee agreed to change its name, in order to clarify its identity and mandate, to the Security Council Committee established pursuant to resolution 1267(1999) concerning Al-Qaida and the Taliban and associated individuals and entities (the Al-Qaida and Taliban Sanctions Committee).

On 7 January [S/2003/10], the Security Council, following consultations among its members, elected the Chairman and Vice-Chairmen of the Committee for a term ending 31 December 2003. On 19 June [S/2003/660], the Council agreed to elect Heraldo Muñoz (Chile) as the new Chairman of the Committee, following the departure of his predecessor, Juan Gabriel Valdés (Chile).

The main task before the Committee in 2003 was the objective assessment and evaluation of implementation by States of the arms embargo, the travel ban and the assets freeze imposed by the Council on the individuals and entities on the Committee's consolidated list. Among the Committee's achievements in 2003 were the issuance of a reformatted version of the consolidated list and its approval of the names of 77 individuals and entities for addition to the list. The list represented the Committee's key instrument for the implementation of its mandate and served as the fundamental tool available to States in implementing the sanctions measures. Both the Al-Qaida and the Taliban sections of the list were improved as a result of amendments proposed by Member States. Despite those improvements, further upgrades of the quality of information on the list remained high on the Committee's agenda. Despite the unsatisfactory number of reports submitted by States to the Committee, the reports received did, nevertheless, provide some indication of trends in State compliance. Another avenue available to the Committee was the direct monitoring, in situ, of State implementation. In that regard, the Committee benefited from the two reports submitted by the Monitoring Group (see below). The Committee also gained improved insight of the implementation by States of the sanctions measures through two visits that the Committee's Chairman undertook to selected countries. The task before the Committee remained to evaluate whether States collectively were doing enough to neutralize the Al-Qaida network and the Taliban and to prevent the supporters of those organizations from launching terrorist attacks.

Monitoring Group

The Monitoring Group on Afghanistan, which was established by Security Council resolution 1363(2001) [YUN 2001, p. 270] and reported to the Sanctions Committee, had the mandate of monitoring the implementation of the measures imposed by resolutions 1287(1999) [YUN 1999, p. 265] and 1333(2000) [YUN 2000, p. 273]. To that end, the Group would collate, assess, verify, report and make recommendations on information regarding violations of the measures imposed. Resolution 1363(2001) also called for the establishment of a Sanctions Enforcement Support Team, under the coordination of the Monitoring Group and specialized in customs, border security and counter-terrorism, to be deployed in the States bordering Afghanistan.

Communication of Secretary-General (February). On 3 February [S/2003/143], the Secretary-General informed the Security Council President that he had reappointed the Monitoring Group to monitor for a further period of 12 months, until 17 January 2004, the implementation of the measures referred to in paragraph 1 of Council resolution 1455(2003) (see p. 311) and to follow up relevant leads relating to any incomplete implementation of those measures.

Reports of Monitoring Group (July and December). In response to Security Council resolution 1455(2003) (see p. 311), the Sanctions Committee Chairman transmitted to the Council President two reports, on 7 July [S/2003/669 & Corr.1] and 1 December [S/2003/1070], on the Monitoring Group's activities.

The July report noted that during the reporting period (18 January–31 May 2003) there had been marked successes in the fight against the Al-Qaida network and in the efforts to find and detain key Al-Qaida leaders. The arrest of members of Osama bin Laden's original command team dented the organization's operational capability and provided intelligence concerning the network. That had led to the break-up of cells in a number of countries and the detention of substantial numbers of the network's supporters and operatives. However, Al-Qaida and groups associated with it still posed a threat to international peace and security. They retained strong appeal among Islamic extremist elements around the world and were able to draw on a substantial number of cadres trained in Afghanistan or at training centres elsewhere associated with the Al-Qaida network. There were also indications that the network had been able to reconstitute its level of support. The international community had created new cooperative means and measures to deal with the Al-Qaida financial support network. Numerous countries had adopted new laws, regulations and procedures enabling them to better identify and deter terrorism financing and to take action against those responsible. Despite those successes, the fight against terrorist financing was far from over. Al-Qaida was still able to exploit loopholes and had developed new techniques to acquire, utilize and distribute funds and logistical resources. Substantial funds were still available from the illicit drug trade, through charities and from deep-pocket donors for indoctrination, recruitment and training. Progress against Al-Qaida in those areas would require increased political and economic pressure and the provision of substantial technical assistance and financial aid. Charities and the use of informal transfer mechanisms such as *hawala* continued to pose challenges in the war against terrorist financing. Some steps had been taken in that regard, but a greater effort was still necessary to identify and designate Al-Qaida contributors and those handling their assets. Further success in bringing down Al-Qaida financial networks would require a sustained international effort, along with increased international cooperation, information sharing and coordination.

The Sanctions Committee's consolidated list, which was established by the Security Council to define the individuals and entities that were subject to Council measures, only included a small subset of known Al-Qaida operatives and others associated with the network, including persons trained in terrorism techniques. That had seriously reduced the overall effectiveness of the measures contained in Council resolutions 1390 (2002) [YUN 2002, p. 281] and 1455(2003). The principal value of the travel ban was to serve as a "political statement", intended to make it clear to countries that they should not permit members of the Taliban, Al-Qaida or associated groups to gather or seek refuge in or transit their territories. As a practical matter, few, if any, of the designated Al-Qaida members were likely to seek open entry or transit using their own name and legitimate documents. No instances had been reported to the Committee by countries of designated individuals being stopped or turned back. There had been some reports, however, of countries locating, detaining and extraditing persons suspected of supporting or participating in Al-Qaida terrorist actions. Despite the travel ban, members of Al-Qaida had retained a high degree of mobility and had been able to carry out and contribute to terrorist attacks in several countries around the world. Ostensibly unlisted Al-Qaida members remained free to move from country to country. To date, no attempts by the individuals or entities designated on the comprehensive list to breach or circumvent the arms embargo measures had been discovered or reported by any States to the Committee or the Group. Nonetheless, Al-Qaida, the Taliban and groups associated with them were still able to acquire adequate quantities of weapons and explosives where and when they needed them. That situation was reinforced by reports of a marked increase in the number and the intensity of attacks against coalition forces in Afghanistan. In addition, the activities of groups associated with Al-Qaida in Algeria, Chechnya, Kenya, the Philippines and Saudi Arabia demonstrated that the network was able to acquire all the arms and ammunition it needed for its operations. That fact emphasized the need for greater efforts on the part of all States to interdict the movement of illegal weapons to the Al-Qaida network, particularly those States bordering the above-mentioned areas. The reports submitted to the Group by 51 countries concerning implementation of the sanctions measures demonstrated a wide degree of compliance in adopting and applying the measures imposed under resolution 1455(2003) and previous related resolutions. However, almost half of the reporting States indicated that they had encountered problems with regard to incorporating the comprehensive list within their own regulatory framework. That was due, in large measure, to the absence of required minimum identification data associated with the names.

In the December report, the Group said that Al-Qaida ideology had continued to spread, raising the spectre of further terrorist attacks and further threats to international peace and security. More of those attacks were being perpetrated by suicide bombers and no region had been spared from such terrorist activities. Iraq had become a fertile ground for Al-Qaida, as it was readily accessible to Al-Qaida followers anxious to take up the battle against the coalition forces. Progress was being made, worldwide, by law enforcement agencies and military and security forces in dealing with Al-Qaida and in neutralizing its operatives and supporters. While the UN consolidated list had grown in numbers, it had not kept pace with the actions taken, or the increased intelligence and other information available, concerning Al-Qaida, the Taliban and associated individuals and entities. The list contained a total of 371 names of individuals and entities. That was a small subset of individuals and entities associated with the terrorist network and it reflected a continuing reluctance on the part of many States to provide such names to the Al-Qaida and Taliban Sanctions Committee. In many cases, States had preferred to communicate such information only through bilateral channels.

Important progress had been made towards cutting off Al-Qaida financing. A large part of its funds had been located and frozen, and many key financial managers had been incarcerated. Yet, many Al-Qaida sources of funding had not been uncovered and the network continued to receive funds from charities, deep-pocket donors and business and criminal activities, including the drug trade. Extensive use was still being made of alternative remittance systems, and Al-Qaida had shifted much of its financial activity to areas in Africa, the Middle East and South-East Asia where the authorities lacked the resources to regulate such activity. Controlling charities used for purposes that supported terrorism was proving extremely difficult as the close association of such charities with both religious and humanitarian relief purposes had made government regulation and oversight very sensitive. Even when charities had been designated, it had proved difficult to shut them down. The use of shell companies and offshore trusts to hide the identity of individuals or entities engaged in the financing of terrorism was also a difficult problem. The issue was complicated further by a reluctance on the part of States to freeze tangible assets such as business or property. Another problem pertained to the fact that almost a third of the countries that had submitted the required reports to the Committee had indicated that they had not yet incorporated all the names on the UN consolidated list in their national lists. Only about a half of the States reported that they regularly transmitted updated lists to their border services.

The arms embargo was another area of concern. The Group continued to encounter difficulties in monitoring and reporting on the implementation of the arms embargo as countries were reluctant to provide information concerning the seizure of illegal weapons and explosives believed destined for Al-Qaida, the Taliban and their associates. Several countries in the Middle East were aware that weapons were crossing their borders, but indicated that they had great difficulties in controlling such illegal traffic. The international community had to remain alert also to the increasing availability of man-portable air-defence systems to non-State actors. The scope of Council resolutions and their incomplete implementation appeared unable to stop Al-Qaida, the Taliban and their networks from obtaining whatever weapons they needed. The risk of Al-Qaida's acquiring and using weapons of mass destruction also continued to grow. The terrorist network had already taken the decision to use chemical and biological weapons; the only restraint it faced was the technical complexity of operating them properly and effectively. The possible use of a dirty bomb was also of great concern. The Group concluded that without a tougher and more comprehensive resolution—a resolution that would obligate States to take the mandated measures—the role played by the United Nations in that important battle risked becoming marginalized.

Communication (December). On 22 December [S/2003/1200], Italy transmitted to the Council President an aide-memoire concerning the reactions of the competent Italian authorities to the Monitoring Group's December report.

Iraq

In 2003, the issue of Iraq tested the unity and resilience of the United Nations, and the Organization's staff in Baghdad were the target of a deliberate terrorist bombing. On 20 March, coalition forces, led by the United States, launched a military attack against Iraq without the endorsement of the United Nations and despite a concerted effort at the international level to avert the armed conflict. Following the fall of the Iraqi regime, the Coalition Provisional Authority (the Authority) was established by the occupying forces to provide for, among other things, the interim administration of Iraq. In July, the Authority established the Governing Council of Iraq as its principal body.

Prior to the launching of military action on 20 March, the United Nations Monitoring, Verification and Inspection Commission (UNMOVIC) and the International Atomic Agency (IAEA) carried out inspection activities in Iraq with regard to its compliance with weapons-related obligations and provided the Security Council with periodic updates on their findings. The Secretary-General suspended UN activities in Iraq on 17 March and withdrew all remaining UN system personnel on the following day. As at 19 March, UN inspectors reported that they had not found any evidence of proscribed weapons of mass destruction in Iraq, although the time available to the inspectors was not sufficient to complete an overall review and assessment. UN personnel started to return to Iraq in April, following the end of major hostilities. In May, the Secretary-General appointed Sergio Vieira de Mello as his Special Representative for Iraq, whose responsibilities included coordinating all UN activities in Iraq and working with the occupying forces in rebuilding the country.

On 19 August, the UN headquarters in Baghdad was subjected to a terrorist attack, which killed 22 persons, including the Secretary-General's Special Representative, and wounded more than 150 others. The attack dealt a severe blow to the Organization's efforts to assist Iraq to return to normality.

In view of the escalation in hostile attacks against the United Nations and other foreign organizations and in the light of the overall serious deterioration of the security environment in Iraq, the Secretary-General decided, on 4 November, to temporarily relocate all UN international staff outside the country. However, the UN system continued to manage a broad range of essential assistance activities in all parts of the country, from both within and outside Iraq.

The United Nations Assistance Mission for Iraq was established in August. However, due to deteriorating security conditions, the Secretary-General decided to set up the Mission's core in Nicosia, Cyprus; additional staff were deployed to a small office in Amman, Jordan, and other locations in the region.

The Security Council, in resolution 1511(2003) of 16 October, invited the Governing Council to provide, by 15 December 2003, a timetable and a programme for the drafting of a new constitution for Iraq and for the holding of democratic elections. It also resolved that the United Nations should strengthen and pursue its vital role in Iraq as circumstances permitted and authorized a multinational force to take all necessary measures to contribute to the maintenance of security and stability in Iraq. On 15 November, the Authority and the Governing Council signed an agreement setting out a political process for the restoration of sovereignty by 30 June 2004, and for the drafting of a new constitution and the holding of elections under that constitution.

On 22 May, the Council lifted civilian sanctions against Iraq with the adoption of resolution 1483(2003). Among other things, the resolution's adoption opened the way for the resumption of oil exports, with revenues deposited in a Development Fund for Iraq held by Iraq's Central Bank, and provided for the termination of the Sanctions Committee and the oil-for-food programme by 21 November 2003, transferring responsibility for the administration of any remaining programme activities to the Authority. By resolution 1518(2003) of 24 November, the Council established a new committee to continue identifying individuals and entities affiliated with the former Iraqi regime for the purpose of freezing their funds, financial assets and economic resources.

Work continued on the repatriation or return of all Kuwaiti and third-country nationals from Iraq, and on the return of all Kuwaiti property seized by Iraq during the 1990 invasion and occupation of Kuwait. The fall of Saddam Hussein's regime led to the discovery of mass graves in Iraq and the identification of remains, including those of Kuwaiti missing persons. The Security Council extended the mandate of the Secretary-General's High-level Coordinator, especially in view of the fact that Kuwaiti property, including its national archives, had yet to be returned to Kuwait.

The mandate of the United Nations Iraq-Kuwait Observation Mission (UNIKOM) was terminated on 6 October when the Council also decided to end the demilitarized zone area along the Iraq-Kuwait border.

On 13 December, Coalition forces captured Saddam Hussein, who was hiding at a farmhouse 10 miles south of his hometown of Tikrit.

By **decision 58/514** of 5 December and **decision 58/527** of 17 December, the General Assembly deferred consideration of, respectively, the consequences of the Iraqi occupation of and aggression against Kuwait, and armed Israeli aggression against the Iraqi nuclear installations and its grave consequences for the established international system on the peaceful uses of nuclear energy, the non-proliferation of nuclear weapons and international peace and security. It included both items in the provisional agenda of its fifty-ninth (2004) session.

UN Monitoring, Verification and Inspection Commission and IAEA activities

Iraqi communications (January-March). In communications dated between 1 January and 17 March, Iraq transmitted to the Secretary-General and the Security Council President daily reports on the activities of UNMOVIC and IAEA inspection teams [S/2003/2, S/2003/4, S/2003/13, S/2003/31, S/2003/32, S/2003/33, S/2003/34, S/2003/35, S/2003/37, S/2003/41, S/2003/42, S/2003/43, S/2003/47, S/2003/50, S/2003/56, S/2003/65, S/2003/68, S/2003/69, S/2003/76, S/2003/86, S/2003/87, S/2003/92, S/2003/100, S/2003/104, S/2003/105, S/2003/106, S/2003/121, S/2003/122, S/2003/133, S/2003/137, S/2003/138, S/2003/139, S/2003/144, S/2003/150, S/2003/155, S/2003/160, S/2003/165, S/2003/166, S/2003/167, S/2003/174, S/2003/175, S/2003/181, S/2003/186, S/2003/187, S/2003/188, S/2003/189, S/2003/190, S/2003/205, S/2003/206, S/2003/218, S/2003/219, S/2003/220, S/2003/221, S/2003/228, S/2003/229, S/2003/234, S/2003/236, S/2003/237, S/2003/244, S/2003/245, S/2003/250, S/2003/256, S/2003/286, S/2003/293, S/2003/294, S/2003/295, S/2003/304, S/2003/309, S/2003/315, S/2003/317, S/2003/322, S/2003/323, S/2003/324, S/2003/339].

UNMOVIC

On 18 March, UNMOVIC suspended its weapons inspection activities following the Secretary-General's decision to withdraw all UN staff from Iraq in the light of the imminent outbreak of military conflict. UNMOVIC's Executive Chairman, Hans Blix, and IAEA's Director General, Mohamed ElBaradei, kept the Security Council informed on inspection activities carried out in Iraq until that time. The Commission carried out biological, chemical, missile and multidisciplinary inspections. On 30 June 2003, Mr. Blix ended his assignment. After the 19 August terrorist attack against the UN headquarters in Baghdad, UNMOVIC's inspection-specific equipment was transferred to the Cyprus field office, which assumed the responsibility of the management of the remaining UNMOVIC local staff in Iraq. UNMOVIC had resumed weapons inspection activities in Iraq on 27 November 2002, after a four-year absence.

By a 14 November letter [S/2003/1108], the Secretary-General proposed to the Security Council that Chen Weixiong (China) be appointed to the UNMOVIC College of Commissioners, replacing Li Junhua (China). On 18 November [S/2003/1110], he proposed that Susan F. Burk (United States) be appointed to the College, replacing John Wolf (United States). In two separate replies of 20 November [S/2003/1109], [S/2003/1111], the Council agreed with the Secretary-General's proposals.

Reports of UNMOVIC (February, May, August, November). As called for in Security Council resolution 1284(1999) [YUN 1999, p. 230], UNMOVIC submitted to the Council, through the Secretary-General, four quarterly reports on its activities.

Throughout the year, the Executive Chairman continued his practice of providing monthly briefings to the Council President and kept the Secretary-General informed about UNMOVIC's activities. UNMOVIC staff training courses were held throughout the year.

The February report [S/2003/232] said that the period under review, from 1 December 2002 to 28 February 2003, had been one of intense activity in Iraq due to the resumption of inspections and monitoring in November 2002 [YUN 2002, p. 288]. Since the arrival of the first inspectors in Iraq on 27 November 2002, UNMOVIC had conducted more than 550 inspections covering approximately 350 sites, including 44 new sites. All inspections were performed without notice and access was in virtually all cases provided promptly; in no case had the inspectors seen convincing evidence that the Iraqi side knew in advance of their impending arrival. The inspections took place throughout Iraq at industrial sites, ammunition depots, research centres, universities, presidential sites, mobile laboratories, private houses, missile production facilities, military camps and agricultural sites. At all sites that had been inspected before 1998, re-baselining activities were performed. Those included identification of the function and contents of each building, new or old, at the site. Also included were verification of previously tagged equipment, application of seals and tags, evaluation of locations for the future installation of cameras and other monitors, and the taking of samples and interviews with site personnel. At certain sites, ground-penetrating radar was used to look for underground structures or buried equipment. Inspections were effectively helping to bridge the gap in knowledge that arose due to the absence of inspections between December 1998 and November 2002.

More than 200 chemical and more than 100 biological samples had been collected at different sites. Three quarters of those had been screened using UNMOVIC's own analytical laboratory capabilities at the Baghdad Ongoing Monitoring, Verification and Inspection Centre. The results to date had been consistent with Iraq's 7 December 2002 declaration [YUN 2002, p. 288], submitted in response to Security Council resolution 1441(2002) [ibid., p. 292]. UNMOVIC had identified and started the destruction of approximately 50 litres of mustard declared by Iraq that had been placed under United Nations Special Commission (UNSCOM) supervision in 1998. Towards the end of February 2003, when the rotation of inspectors took place, the number of UNMOVIC personnel in Iraq reached a total of 202 staff, including 84 inspectors. On 19 and 20 January and on 8 and 9 February, the UNMOVIC Executive Chairman and the IAEA Director General, visited Baghdad to discuss relevant inspection and cooperation issues with Iraqi officials. The January meetings were devoted to stocktaking of the inspections that had taken place so far and to resolving certain operational issues. A joint statement, issued upon conclusion of the talks, recorded a number of matters that had been solved and some that remained unsolved, such as flights by U-2 surveillance planes, the conduct of interviews and the enactment of national legislation. At the February meetings, the Iraqi side handed over a number of papers regarding unresolved disarmament issues. However, the papers did not contain any new evidence, nor did they resolve any of the open issues. Following the February meetings, Iraq formally accepted UNMOVIC's use of aerial surveillance platforms and undertook to take the necessary measures to ensure their safety. The first such flight was conducted by a high-altitude U-2 surveillance aircraft on 17 February. During the reporting period, UNMOVIC requested 28 individuals to present themselves for interviews in Baghdad without the presence of observers. At first, none of them agreed. At the January meetings, the Iraqi side committed itself to encouraging persons to accept interviews in private and UNMOVIC started examining the practical modalities for conducting interviews outside Iraq. In February, UNMOVIC directed Iraq to destroy a proscribed missile system and some reconstituted casting chambers that could be used to produce motors for missiles capable of surpassing the 150-kilometre range limit imposed on Iraq by Council resolution 687(1991) [YUN 1991, p. 172]. The destruction process was to commence on 1 March.

The twelfth session of the UNMOVIC College of Commissioners (New York, 24-25 February) discussed, among other things, a draft paper prepared by UNMOVIC outlining clusters of unresolved disarmament issues. UNMOVIC's Executive Chairman observed that, during the reporting period, Iraq could have made greater efforts to find any remaining proscribed items or provide credible evidence showing the absence of such items. The results in terms of disarmament had been very limited and it was hard to understand why a number of measures, which were implemented only in mid-January, could not have been initiated earlier.

The May report [S/2003/580] covered the period from 1 March to 31 May and also provided a wider perspective on UNMOVIC's activities since the resumption of inspections in November 2002. The report noted that on 18 March, UNMOVIC suspended its inspection activities following the

Secretary-General's 17 March decision to withdraw all UN staff from Iraq. Following the armed action against Iraq, which started on 20 March, the Coalition Provisional Authority (the Authority) organized units to identify any Iraqi weapons of mass destruction (WMD) and other proscribed items and to engage in the task of disarming Iraq, which was formerly pursued by UNMOVIC and IAEA. The findings of the relevant units established by the Authority had not been made available to UNMOVIC except through public media reports, nor had the Commission been approached by the Coalition for information or assistance. Between November 2002 and March 2003, UNMOVIC did not find evidence of the continuation or resumption of programmes of WMD or significant quantities of proscribed items from before the adoption of Council resolution 687(1991). A small number of undeclared empty chemical warheads that appeared to have been produced prior to 1990 were uncovered and, together with a few other proscribed items, were destroyed. Some 70 missiles that were determined to exceed the range limits set by the Security Council and associated equipment were destroyed under UNMOVIC supervision before its operations were suspended. Inspections and declarations and documents submitted by Iraq, not least during the period under review, contributed to a better understanding of previous weapons programmes. However, the long list of proscribed items unaccounted for was not shortened either by the inspections or by Iraqi declarations and documentation. From the end of January 2003, the Iraqi side, which until then had been cooperative in terms of process but not equally cooperative in terms of substance, devoted much effort to providing explanations and proposing methods of inquiry into such issues as the production and destruction of anthrax, the VX nerve agent and long-range missiles. Despite those efforts, little progress was made in the solution of outstanding issues during the time of UNMOVIC operations in Iraq.

By the time inspections were suspended, UNMOVIC had performed a number of inspections in order to verify intelligence information that Iraq had mobile units for the production of biological weapons. The Iraqi side denied that any such units existed and provided the Commission with pictures of legitimate vehicles, which they suggested could have been mistaken for mobile units. However, none of the vehicles in those pictures resembled the trucks described by the Coalition. Furthermore, the Commission was not able, before the suspension of inspections, to complete its inquiry into the Iraqi programmes of remotely piloted vehicles and unmanned aerial vehicles, notably to establish whether any of them were designed for the dissemination of chemical or biological weapons or had a longer range than was permitted. UNMOVIC remained ready to resume its inspection activities; the resolutions that guided its work until the armed action would continue to be implemented to the extent that they were still relevant and had not been rendered obsolete by resolution 1483(2003) (see p. 338). It was clear that most of the work performed by the Commission to date relating to the oil-for-food programme would be phased out. From the day of the first resumed inspection on 27 November 2002 until the day of the withdrawal of all UN personnel on 18 March 2003, UNMOVIC conducted 731 inspections, covering 411 sites, 88 of which had not been inspected before. During the first phase of inspections, the focus was on assessing activities and equipment at the sites, determining the changes made since 1998 and identifying existing key personnel. The early inspections provided knowledge about Iraq's programmes and about State companies involved in such activities. The second period, from mid-January to March, was characterized by reinspection of some of the sites with a more investigative approach. The largest effort was expended on industrial and research and development sites, followed by military sites. During the period 1 to 17 March, UNMOVIC made 15 requests for interviews with Iraqi scientists, bringing the total number of requests since January 2003 to 54. During that short period, nine interviews were actually conducted, bringing the total number of interviews in all disciplines to 14. All interviews were conducted under UNMOVIC procedures and format: no witnesses, recording or videotaping were allowed and interviews were conducted in locations selected by UNMOVIC. Information obtained during interviews was found useful and led in some cases to an updating of the assessments contained in UNMOVIC's list of unresolved disarmament issues.

In addition to the portable chemical and biological detectors for in situ direct determination of traces of chemical and biological agents, UNMOVIC had at its disposal advanced geophysical equipment for the search of hidden structures and storage spaces, including ground-penetrating radar; electromagnetic induction soil change mapping; computer and server forensics; and remote drilling and sampling systems for munitions. At the thirteenth session of the College of Commissioners (New York, 28 May), it was agreed that a compendium encompassing the knowledge and experience gained by UNMOVIC and its predecessor over the years would be useful as an objective record. The Executive Chairman observed that even though some of its mandated functions were no longer operable, UNMOVIC continued to be a subsidiary organ of the Security Council until the Council decided otherwise.

The August report [S/2003/844] covered the period from 1 June to 31 August. On 30 June, the UNMOVIC Executive Chairman, Mr. Blix, ended his assignment. The Secretary-General appointed the Deputy Executive Chairman, Demetrius Perricos, as Acting Executive Chairman effective 1 July. Resolution 1483(2003) of 22 May (see p. 338) underlined the intention of the Council to revisit the mandates of UNMOVIC and IAEA as set forth in earlier resolutions. Since that had yet to transpire, UNMOVIC had continued with those parts of its mandate that remained operable, such as developing monitoring and verification projects to adapt to the altered environment in Iraq following the war. The 19 August terrorist attack against the UN headquarters in Baghdad (see p. 346), which included UNMOVIC offices, caused numerous deaths and injuries among international and Iraqi staff. Two UNMOVIC local staff lost their lives in the attack. Given the routine nature of UNMOVIC's activity during the reporting period, the College of Commissioners was not convened in August.

The November report [S/2003/1135], which covered the period from 1 September to 30 November, also provided a historical review of the destruction, removal or rendering harmless of items and materials in connection with Iraq's proscribed biological programme. During the reporting period, no information was available to UNMOVIC on the results of the investigations of the United States–led Iraq Survey Group, other than the statement released to the public on the interim progress report made by the Group to the United States Senate Select Committee on Intelligence. The general impression from that statement was that most of the findings outlined related to complex subjects familiar to UNMOVIC. However, in the absence of access to the full report, UNMOVIC was not in a position to properly assess the information contained in the statement. After the 19 August attack against the UN headquarters in Baghdad, all of UNMOVIC's inspection-specific equipment was transferred to the Cyprus field office, which assumed the responsibility of the management of the remaining UNMOVIC local staff in Baghdad. The fourteenth session of the College of Commissioners (New York, 21 November) recognized the considerable verification experience and expertise of UNMOVIC, as well as its multidisciplinary approach, which it hoped would be given due recognition in any future discussions in the Security Council in the context of revisiting UNMOVIC's mandate.

A later report [S/2004/160] noted that UNMOVIC was continuing to assess material that was in the public domain on the issues pertaining to Iraq's WMD and to compare it against what was known by UNMOVIC about Iraq's various weapons programmes.

IAEA

IAEA report (January). In accordance with Security Council resolution 1441(2002) [YUN 2002, p. 292], IAEA submitted to the Council, through the Secretary-General, a 27 January update [S/2003/95] on its verification activities in Iraq. Since the resumption of inspections on 27 November 2002 [YUN 2002, p. 289], IAEA had conducted 139 inspections at 106 sites, including two presidential sites. The focus of the first phase of inspections was reconnaissance: re-establishment of IAEA's knowledge of Iraq's remaining nuclear capabilities, including confirmation of the locations of major equipment, of nuclear material and significant non-nuclear materials, and of key technical personnel. The first step of the reconnaissance phase was to inspect facilities that were known to have been of significance in the past programme and to confirm that no nuclear activities had been revived at those locations. IAEA also re-inspected several dozen facilities that had been deemed, prior to 1998, capable of supporting the resumption of a nuclear programme. The Agency reported no signs of nuclear activities at any of those facilities.

While IAEA was still continuing with its reconnaissance, the inspectors had initiated the investigative phase, with particular emphasis on Iraq's activities since 1998, focusing on those areas of concern identified by States and by IAEA. Eight sites, all of which had been associated with Iraq's past nuclear activities, were inspected to ascertain whether there had been developments in technical capabilities, organization, structure, facility boundaries or personnel. IAEA observed that, at the majority of those sites, the equipment and laboratories had deteriorated to such a degree that the resumption of nuclear activities would require substantial renovation and no signs of nuclear activity had been found. Several other facilities that had never been inspected by IAEA or by UNSCOM in the past were inspected in response to information that indicated the presence of large industrial capabilities at those locations. None of those facilities had proved to be nuclear-related or to require their declaration by Iraq.

Prior to the withdrawal of IAEA from Iraq in 1998, the Agency had removed from Iraq all nuclear-weapons-usable nuclear material. The remaining stocks of nuclear material were stored under IAEA seal in a storage facility referred to as Location C, just outside the Tuwaitha complex. An inspection of Location C in December 2002 confirmed that the IAEA seals and the inventory of nuclear material remained intact. IAEA had conducted many interviews with Iraqi scientists since the resumption of inspections, some in the form of group interviews. States had expressed concerns about attempts by Iraq to procure high-strength aluminium tubes. Those concerns arose from the fact that high-strength aluminium tubes with appropriate characteristics could be used as components of equipment for the enrichment of uranium. Iraqi officials indicated to IAEA that the tubes had been intended for use in connection with a programme aimed at reverse engineering 81-millimetre rockets. The Agency conducted a series of inspections at sites involved in the production and storage of reverse engineered rockets, held discussions with and interviewed Iraq personnel, took samples of aluminium tubes and had begun a review of the documentation provided by Iraq relating to contracts with private traders. As a result of those efforts, it had been possible to confirm the existence of a programme for producing 81-millimetre rockets. While it would be possible to modify such tubes for the manufacture of centrifuges, they were not directly suitable for such use. In support of the IAEA inspections, Iraqi authorities had provided access to all facilities visited without conditions and without delay. They had also been cooperative in making available additional original documentation. However, those documents did not include any information relevant to questions and concerns outstanding since 1998. The IAEA Director General and the UNMOVIC Executive Chairman visited Baghdad on 19 and 20 January 2003, with a view to encouraging greater transparency and more proactive cooperation on the part of Iraq. IAEA observed that in the first eight weeks of inspections, it had visited all sites identified by it or by States as significant. Although not all of the laboratory results of sample analysis were yet available, no evidence of ongoing prohibited nuclear or nuclear-related activities at those locations had been detected, nor had the inspections revealed signs of new nuclear facilities or direct support to any nuclear activity. However, further verification activities would be necessary before IAEA would be able to provide credible assurance that Iraq had no nuclear weapons programme.

IAEA work programme

In response to Security Council resolution 1284(1999) [YUN 1999, p. 230], the IAEA Director General, on 19 March [S/2003/342], submitted to the Council, though the Secretary-General, the IAEA work programme for the discharge of its mandate. The nature and content of the work programme were based on an understanding of Iraq's past achievements and of its capability to support nuclear or nuclear-related activities. For IAEA to resolve the key issue of whether Iraq had revived or attempted to revive its nuclear weapons programme between 1998 and 2002, a number of key tasks needed to be implemented by Iraq. Although Iraq had initiated work on many of those tasks, it still needed to provide: a complete description of all technical activities related to nuclear weapons components research and development and production, and uranium conversion and enrichment developments; access to all documents; the names and whereabouts of all individuals requested by IAEA, and full access to Iraqi officials for purposes of interviewing; a complete description of the evolution of its industrial infrastructure since 1998; explanations of and documentation on procurement attempts and offers related to the possible development of Iraq's nuclear-related capabilities; and a full description of its post-1998 procurement system. Iraq was also required to enact comprehensive legislation that would secure the enforcement of all prohibitions associated with relevant Council resolutions. Assuming that Iraq would complete those tasks, and barring unforeseen circumstances, IAEA could, within two to three months, provide the Council with an objective assessment of whether Iraq had revived or attempted to revive its nuclear weapons programme. The Agency emphasized that the verification process always had some degree of uncertainty and could not provide absolute guarantees regarding the absence of small-scale nuclear activities. Nevertheless, an intrusive inspection system, such as the one that IAEA was implementing in Iraq, could minimize the risk of prohibited activities going undetected, and deter the revival of a nuclear weapons programme. IAEA monitoring and verification would entail: comprehensive and regular reporting by Iraq on its activities and on its imports and exports; unconditional and immediate access for unannounced inspections at any site deemed necessary by IAEA; the conduct of location-specific and wide-area environmental monitoring; real-time monitoring for the detection of radiation signatures; and the introduction of new technologies and methods of verification. Technical meetings with and interviews of Iraqi personnel would remain a key element of the monitoring and verification regime.

IAEA reports (April and October). In accordance with Security Council resolution 1051(1996) [YUN 1996, p. 218], IAEA submitted to the Council, through the Secretary-General, two consolidated six-monthly reports, on 11 April [S/2003/422] and 10 October [S/2003/993], on the Agency's verification activities in Iraq.

In April, IAEA said that the meetings between its Director General and the UNMOVIC Executive Chairman with Iraqi officials (19-20 January and 9 February) (see also p. 317) permitted the refinement and extension of the practical arrangements for resuming inspections that had been endorsed in resolution 1441(2002) [YUN 2002, p. 292]. Since the first group of inspectors arrived in Iraq on 25 November 2002, IAEA had carried out 237 inspections at some 148 locations, including 27 new locations. More than 1,600 different buildings were inspected. Inspections were undertaken at State-run and private industrial facilities, research centres and universities, either at locations where Iraq's technical capabilities were known to have existed in the past or at new locations suggested by remote monitoring and analysis or identified by other States. IAEA sought to determine what, if anything, had occurred in Iraq since 1998 relevant to the establishment of nuclear capabilities. The vast majority of the inspections were carried out with no prior announcement and a number of them were carried out in cooperation with UNMOVIC. IAEA's activities included a radiometric survey of Iraq's main watercourses, the reinstatement of aerosol sampling and land- and vehicle-based radiometric surveys. The Agency also implemented a programme aimed at understanding Iraq's procurement pattern. Between November 2002 and 17 March 2003, Iraqi authorities provided access to all facilities requested by IAEA, including presidential compounds, private residences and new sites, without conditions or delay. A large number of documents that detailed Iraq's pre-1991 laser enrichment programme were found in the home of a former Iraqi scientist. Iraq provided an updated list of 430 technical staff involved in the Iraqi nuclear programme in the past. IAEA conducted some interviews with individuals and groups in their workplaces, while others were conducted during pre-arranged meetings with scientists and others known to have been involved in the past with the nuclear programme. The Agency was able to interview 17 individuals at locations chosen by it. Some restrictions were imposed on IAEA at the beginning, when interviewees first refused to be interviewed without the presence of an Iraqi observer. Subsequently, two individuals accepted to be interviewed in private but without being taped. Most of those interviews proved to be of help in improving IAEA's understanding of Iraq's nuclear-related capabilities.

As at 17 March 2003, IAEA had not found in Iraq any evidence of the revival of a nuclear programme prohibited under resolutions 687(1991) [YUN 1991, p. 172] and 707(1991) [ibid., p. 188]. However, the time available before inspections were suspended on 17 March was not sufficient to permit IAEA to complete its overall review and assessment. That review would have required further investigation of various types of assets needed for Iraq to develop a nuclear programme and investigation of all the possible processes of nuclear weapon development. The industrial capacity in Iraq had deteriorated substantially over the preceding decade, mainly due to the lack of equipment and of consistent maintenance by Iraq of sophisticated equipment. All previously inspected and tagged critical machine tools were accounted for. At a few inspection sites, new machine tools had been installed, and at a few others machine tools that had been inoperative in 1998 were retrofitted. Many areas of Iraqi expertise seemed to have gone through significant depletion through the years, particularly as a result of the departure of many qualified staff. Less than a third of the group that conducted Iraq's centrifuge enrichment research and development work from 1987 to 1991 remained in the company that succeeded that group. All known procured, indigenously produced and practically recoverable uranium compounds that had not been removed by 1994 had remained in IAEA custody and were stored under IAEA seal. The inspection and verification of the nuclear material subject to IAEA safeguards stored at Location C at Tuwaitha did not uncover any discrepancies. The Agency systematically explored Iraq's nuclear material production capabilities and found no indication of the revival of any facilities destroyed in 1991 that had been related to uranium concentration or conversion. IAEA investigated reports centring on documents provided to it by a number of States that pointed to an agreement between the Niger and Iraq on the sale of uranium to Iraq between 1999 and 2001. Based on its analysis, IAEA concluded, with the concurrence of outside experts, that those documents were in fact forged and the allegations were thus unfounded.

The Agency noted that on 17 March, in consultation with the Security Council President and the Secretary-General, it had withdrawn its staff from Iraq, as part of the decision to withdraw all UN staff, out of concern for their safety and following an advisory of upcoming military action.

As at that date, IAEA found no evidence or plausible indication of the revival of a nuclear weapons programme in Iraq. Nevertheless, that did not mean that IAEA had completed its investigations on whether Iraq had attempted to revive its nuclear programme between 1998 and 2002. Provided that Iraq's cooperation had remained active, and barring unforeseen circumstances, IAEA would have been able to provide the Council with credible assurance regarding the absence of such revival within two to three months of continuing verification activities. However, any such assurance, as with any verification process, would have had a degree of uncertainty. It was for that reason that IAEA would have moved to the implementation of its reinforced ongoing monitoring and verification plan, which was designed to act as an effective deterrent to and insurance against resumption by Iraq of its nuclear weapons programme, while permitting IAEA to continue to look for possible past activities. Though inspections had been halted due to the military action, IAEA's mandate remained valid, and the Agency, as the sole legal authority to verify Iraq's nuclear activities, remained ready to resume its verification activities as soon as conditions permitted.

In October, IAEA reported that it had not been in a position to implement its mandate in Iraq since 17 March. In June, however, following media reports of looting of nuclear and radioactive material at the Tuwaitha complex, the Director General requested that the Agency inspect the nuclear material storage facility near the Tuwaitha complex (see below). Since April, IAEA had analysed the wealth of additional information collected during inspections; consolidated its overall information assets and analysed a variety of new information, including satellite imagery, to update its knowledge of the relevant facilities in Iraq; refined its plan for resumed verification activities; and evaluated lessons learned through its past experience in Iraq. IAEA had also been able, with the support of member States, to continue with some of its investigations outside Iraq, following up inspections and subsequent analysis. Those post-inspections activities had revealed no evidence of the revival of a nuclear weapons programme in Iraq.

In a later report [S/2004/285], the Agency stated that it still had not been in a position to implement its mandate in Iraq during the last months of 2003.

IAEA mission in Tuwaitha

Following extensive media reports of looting of nuclear and radioactive material at the Tuwaitha complex in Iraq, the IAEA Director General requested, and the Authority agreed, that IAEA should conduct an inspection, in order to verify the nuclear material subject to safeguards stored at Location C Nuclear Material Storage Facility near the Tuwaitha complex south of Baghdad. The report on the inspection mission (7-23 June 2003) was submitted to the Security Council on 15 July [S/2003/711].

The nuclear material inspected was in two buildings: building 1 contained a large variety of uranium compounds, while building 2 contained only yellowcake and ammonium diuranate waste. The inspection team found that some safeguards seals applied to the two buildings after the December 2002 inventory verification had been removed, as the team had been informed by the Authority prior to the start of the mission. The inspection team estimated that at least 10 kilograms of uranium compounds could have been dispersed, but that the quantity and type of uranium dispersed were not sensitive from a proliferation point of view.

WMD allegations

Communications (2-24 January). On 2 January [S/2003/7], South Africa, on behalf of the Non-Aligned Movement, called on the Security Council to allow the UNMOVIC Executive Chairman and the IAEA Director General to present their views in an open meeting, thus allowing the rest of the UN membership to receive a first-hand account of their reports.

On 22 January [S/2003/88], Iraq informed the Secretary-General and the Council President that, pursuant to resolution 715(1991) [YUN 1991, p. 194], it had sent its biannual declarations on the sites, equipment and materials subject to monitoring, for the period from July 2002 to January 2003, to the Baghdad Ongoing Monitoring, Verification and Inspection Centre.

On 24 January [S/2003/93], Iraq said that Iraqi scientists who had been contacted to cooperate with UNMOVIC and IAEA requests for private interviews had agreed to do so, but had requested a witness to be present during the interviews.

On the same day [S/2003/94], Iraq said that the declaration submitted by it on 7 December 2002 [YUN 2002, p. 289] to the United Nations, together with the cooperation displayed by Iraqi agencies with the inspection teams since the resumption of inspections in November 2002, proved that Iraq was acting in good faith and was resolved to fulfil its obligations, with the aim of proving that it was not concealing any activity or weapons proscribed by relevant Security Council resolutions. Attestation of those facts should lead the Council to reject American and British threats of aggression directed against Iraq.

On 24 January [S/2003/97], Turkey transmitted to the Secretary-General and the Council President the Joint Declaration of the Regional Initiative on Iraq (Istanbul, 23 January), with the participation of Egypt, Iran, Jordan, Saudi Arabia, the Syrian Arab Republic and Turkey. The participants expressed their common resolve to attain a peaceful solution to the Iraqi issue and stressed that the countries of the region did not wish to live through yet another war and all its devastating consequences. They called on the Iraqi leadership to move irreversibly and sincerely towards assuming its responsibilities in restoring peace and in cooperating with UNMOVIC and IAEA.

Security Council consideration (27 January). On 27 January [meeting 4692], the Security Council invited the Executive Chairman of UNMOVIC, Mr. Blix, and the Director General of IAEA, Mr. ElBaradei, to brief it on the latest developments in Iraq.

Mr. Blix, in reviewing the inspections regime since 1991, said that Iraq appeared not to have come to a genuine acceptance of the disarmament that was demanded of it and that it needed to carry out to win the confidence of the world. However, Iraq had, on the whole, cooperated rather well so far with UNMOVIC on issues pertaining to procedures, mechanisms, infrastructure and practical arrangements. Previewing information contained in his February report (see p. 317), Mr. Blix said that access had been provided to all those sites that UNMOVIC had requested to inspect. Nevertheless, there had been some problems. While UNMOVIC had a U-2 plane at its disposal for aerial surveillance purposes, Iraq had refused to guarantee its safety unless a number of conditions were fulfilled. There had also been a number of incidents and instances of harassment, such as demonstrations in front of UNMOVIC offices and at inspection sites, which were unlikely to occur in Iraq without initiative or encouragement from the authorities. In addition, the December 2002 declaration that Iraq had submitted to the United Nations, which contained a good deal of welcome new material and information, could also have provided supporting evidence regarding the many open disarmament issues. Reports prepared by UNMOVIC experts did not contend that WMD remained in Iraq, nor did they exclude the possibility. They did, however, point to a lack of evidence and to inconsistencies. Regrettably, the declaration did not contain any new evidence that would eliminate unresolved questions. Some of those unresolved questions pertained to whether Iraq had weaponized the nerve agent VX; evidence of the destruction of the biological warfare agent anthrax; and whether Iraq had retained SCUD-type missiles after the 1991 Gulf War [YUN 1991, p. 167]. Though Iraq continued to state that there were no proscribed items in its territory, information provided by Member States indicated the movement and concealment of missiles and chemical weapons and mobile units for biological weapons production. UNMOVIC would follow up any credible leads. It was concerned that Iraq was placing documents in the homes of private individuals, as inspectors had discovered 3,000 pages of documents pertaining to the laser enrichment of uranium inside the private home of a scientist.

Mr. ElBaradei said that IAEA had been engaged since 27 November 2002 in the process of verifying the existence or absence of a nuclear weapon programme in Iraq. An updated progress report on IAEA activities during that period was submitted to the Security Council on 27 January (see p. 319). IAEA had made good progress in its knowledge of Iraq's nuclear capabilities. The investigative inspections focused on areas of concern identified by Member States; facilities identified through satellite images as having been modified or constructed since 1998; and other inspection leads identified independently by IAEA. Iraq's December 2002 declaration was consistent with IAEA's existing understanding of Iraq's pre-1991 nuclear programme. However, it did not provide any new information relevant to certain questions that had been outstanding since 1998, in particular regarding Iraq's progress prior to 1991 related to weapons design and centrifuge development. While those questions did not constitute unresolved disarmament issues, they nevertheless needed further clarification. The inspectors, among other things, had conducted a number of interviews of Iraqi scientists, managers and technicians as a valuable source of information about past and ongoing programmes and activities. IAEA was also investigating reports of Iraqi efforts to import uranium since 1991. IAEA had emphasized to Iraqi officials the need to shift from passive support—responding as needed to inspectors' requests—to proactive support—voluntarily assisting inspectors by providing documentation, people and other evidence that would assist in filling the remaining gaps in IAEA's information. IAEA noted that inspections were time-consuming, but, if successful, they could ensure disarmament through peaceful means. It was worth recalling that in past experience with Iraq, the elimination of its nuclear weapons programme was accomplished mostly through intrusive inspections. The presence of international inspectors in Iraq served as an effective deterrent to, and insurance against, resumption of programmes to develop WMD. IAEA had found no evidence that Iraq had revived its nuclear weapons programme since its elimination in the 1990s. However, IAEA's work was steadily progressing and should be allowed to run its natural course. Barring exceptional circumstances and provided there was sustained, proactive cooperation by Iraq, IAEA should be able within the next few months to provide credible assurance that Iraq had no nuclear programme.

Communications (31 January–4 February). On 31 January [S/2003/131], Iraq responded to some of the comments made by Mr. Blix during his 27 January briefing to the Security Council. Iraq had made every effort to implement Council resolution 1441(2002) [YUN 2002, p. 292] and had supported its December 2002 declaration concerning the unilateral destruction of biological weapons with irrefutable evidence. Iraq emphasized that it had provided unlimited cooperation to both UNMOVIC and IAEA, and had declared all its proscribed programmes and taken the necessary steps to eliminate them. What remained were not WMD programmes, but rather questions about earlier programmes. The allegation that Iraq still had a WMD programme was a politically motivated lie by the United States and its vassals for the purpose of keeping the disarmament file open-ended and providing cover for aggression against Iraq. If the United States had any real, convincing evidence to contradict the Iraqi declarations, it would have presented it. The inspections carried out since November 2002 did not find anything that contradicted Iraq's declarations.

Also on 31 January [S/2003/132], Iraq said that the United States had called for a Security Council meeting on 5 February at which its Secretary of State, Colin Powell, would present what had been dubbed evidence of Iraq's possession of WMD. Iraq requested the United States, through the Secretary-General, to submit its alleged evidence to UNMOVIC or IAEA, so as to enable the two organizations to begin their investigations immediately and inform the Council of the extent to which those allegations were correct.

On 4 February [S/2003/142], South Africa transmitted to the Council President the text of the communiqué issued by the seventh ordinary session of the Central Organ of the Mechanism for Conflict Prevention, Management and Resolution of the African Union, held at the level of heads of State and Government (Addis Ababa, Ethiopia, 3 February). The Central Organ was of the view that a military confrontation in Iraq would be a destabilizing factor for the whole region and would have far-reaching economic and security consequences for all countries of the world, and, particularly, for those of Africa.

Security Council consideration (5 February). On 5 February [meeting 4701], the Security Council considered the situation between Iraq and Kuwait and heard a presentation by the Secretary of State of the United States, Mr. Powell, who said he had asked for the meeting for two purposes: to support the core assessments made by Mr. Blix and Mr. ElBaradei in their 27 January reports to the Council; and to provide the Council with information that the United States had obtained about Iraq's WMD and involvement in terrorism. The material came from a number of sources, including technical, such as intercepted telephone conversations and satellite photos, and from testimony from individuals. The evidence and conclusions pointed to the fact that Saddam Hussein and his regime had made no effort to disarm and were actually concealing their efforts to produce more WMD. According to the Secretary of State, intercepted telephone conversations among Iraqi officials (two tapes of which were played for the Council) and satellite photos (several of which were projected on a screen) proved that Iraq had carried out a policy of evasion and deception that went back 12 years—a policy set at the highest levels of the Iraqi Government. The voluminous December 2002 declaration submitted by Iraq was but an attempt to overwhelm the Security Council with useless information in order to give the false impression that the inspection process was working. According to sources, documents were being moved to avoid detection and hard drives of computers at Iraqi weapons facilities were being replaced. However, WMD were also being moved to keep them from being found by inspectors.

The Secretary of State stressed that his statement was backed by solid sources based on solid intelligence. Iraq was also trying to hide people, as it had not complied with its obligation to allow immediate, unimpeded, unrestricted and private access to all officials and other persons associated with the weapons programme, and it had been reported that Saddam Hussein had directly participated in the effort to prevent interviews by threatening Iraqi scientists with serious consequences. In addition, the Iraqis had never accounted for all the biological agents they admitted they had and, in addition, had never accounted for all the organic material used to make them. They also had not accounted for many of the weapons filled with those agents, such as their R-400 bombs. The United States had first-hand descriptions of biological weapons factories on wheels and on rails. The trucks and train cars were easily moved and were designed to evade detection by inspectors. In a matter of months, they could produce a quantity of biological poison equal to the entire amount that Iraq claimed to have produced in the years prior to the 1991 Gulf War. The United States knew that Iraq had at least seven mobile biological agent factories and the truck-mounted ones had at least two or three trucks each; that meant that the mobile production facilities were very few—perhaps 18 trucks. It had taken the inspectors four years to find out that Iraq was making biological weapons; Mr. Powell asked how long would it take them to find even one of those 18 trucks, without Iraq coming forward as it was supposed to do with information about those kinds of capabilities. The Iraqi regime had also developed ways to disperse lethal biological agents into the water supply and air. Iraq, in fact, had a programme to modify aerial fuel tanks for Mirage jets, allowing the aircraft to spray anthrax. As to chemical weapons, Iraq had embedded key portions of its illicit chemical weapons infrastructure within its legitimate civilian industry. That dual-use infrastructure could turn from clandestine to commercial and then back again. Inspections would be unlikely to turn up anything prohibited, especially if there was any warning that the inspections were coming. The United States estimated that Iraq had a stockpile of between 100 and 500 tons of chemical weapons agent, enough to fill 16,000 battlefield rockets. Saddam Hussein had used chemical weapons against his neighbours and his own people and had recently authorized his field commanders to use them again; he would not be giving out those orders if he did not have the weapons or the intent to use them. Iraq also had a massive clandestine nuclear weapons programme that covered several different techniques to enrich uranium, including electromagnetic isotope separation, gas centrifuge and gas diffusion. Saddam Hussein was so determined to obtain a nuclear bomb that he had made repeated attempts to acquire high-specification aluminium tubes from 11 different countries—even after inspection resumed. United States experts thought that those tubes were intended to serve as rotors in centrifuges used to enrich uranium. Iraq was also developing systems to deliver WMD, in particular ballistic missiles and unmanned aerial vehicles (UAVs). UAVs were well suited for dispensing chemical and biological weapons and there was ample intelligence that Iraq had dedicated much effort to developing and testing spray devices that could be adapted for UAVs.

The Secretary of State also said that there existed a nexus between Iraq and the Al-Qaida terrorist network. In fact, Iraq was harbouring a terrorist network headed by Abu Musab al-Zarqawi, an associate and collaborator of Osama bin Laden, which operated from a camp located in north-eastern Iraq. Although Iraqi officials denied accusations of ties with Al-Qaida, those denials were simply not credible. In 2002, said the Secretary of State, Al-Qaida associates had bragged that the situation in Iraq was "good"—that Baghdad could be transited quickly. Ties between Iraq and Al-Qaida went back to the early and mid-1990s, when President Hussein and bin Laden reached an understanding that Al-Qaida would no longer support activities against Baghdad. From the late 1990s until 2001, the Iraqi Embassy in Pakistan played the role of liaison to the Al-Qaida organization. Although some claimed that those contacts did not amount to much, the Secretary of State said that hatred and ambition were enough to bring Iraq and Al-Qaida together—enough for Al-Qaida to turn to Iraq for help in acquiring expertise on WMD. Saddam Hussein was determined to keep his WMD and determined to make more. The United States would not and could not run the risk that Iraq someday would use those weapons. Leaving Saddam Hussein in possession of those weapons for a few months or years was not an option—not in a post-11 September world. Iraq posed a threat and remained in material breach of Council resolutions. By its failure to seize its one last opportunity to come clean and disarm, Iraq had put itself in deeper material breach and closer to the day when it would face serious consequences for its continued defiance of the Council. The United States Government had an obligation to its citizens—and to the Security Council—to see that resolutions were complied with. The United States wrote resolution 1441(2002) [YUN 2002, p. 292] to try to preserve the peace and to give Iraq one last chance. Iraq was not taking that one last chance. The Council, therefore, could not shrink from its duty and responsibility.

France said that by adopting resolution 1441(2002), the Council had chosen to act through the path of inspections. That policy rested on three fundamental points: a clear objective on which there could be no compromise—the disarmament of Iraq; a method—a rigorous system of inspections that required Iraq's active cooperation and that affirmed the Council's central role at each stage; and finally, a requirement—that of the Council's unity. Important results had already been achieved through the inspections regime, which had enabled UNMOVIC and IAEA to progress in their knowledge of Iraq's capacity. There remained some grey areas in Iraq's cooperation, particularly unresolved questions in the ballistic, chemical and biological domains. Those uncertainties were not acceptable.

There was evidence that Iraq could produce the chemical agents vx and yperite and that it possibly possessed significant stocks of anthrax and botulism toxin. The absence of long-range delivery systems reduced the potential threat of those weapons, but there was disturbing evidence of Iraq's continued determination to acquire ballistic missiles beyond the authorized 150-kilometre range. In the nuclear domain, there was a need to clarify in particular any attempt by Iraq to acquire aluminium tubes. It was a demanding démarche, anchored in resolution 1441(2002), that the Council had to take together. If that path was to fail and lead into a dead end, France ruled out no option, including the recourse to force. For the time being, however, the inspections regime had to be strengthened, since it had not been explored to the end. Use of force could only be a final recourse. With the choice between military intervention and an inspections regime that was inadequate for lack of cooperation on Iraq's part, the Council had to choose to strengthen the means of the inspection. To do that, the Council had to define the requisite tools for increasing the operational capabilities of UNMOVIC and IAEA. France proposed doubling or tripling the number of inspectors, opening up more regional offices, establishing a specialized body to keep under surveillance the sites and areas already inspected, increasing the capabilities for monitoring and collecting information on Iraqi territory and establishing a coordination and information-processing centre that would supply Mr. Blix and Mr. ElBaradei, in real time and in a coordinated way, with all the intelligence resources they might need. With the consent of the inspection teams' leaders, the Council could define a demanding and realistic time frame for moving forward in the assessment and elimination of outstanding issues. That enhanced regime of inspections and monitoring could be complemented by having a permanent UN coordinator for disarmament stationed in Iraq and working under the authority of Mr. Blix and Mr. ElBaradei. Iraq had to cooperate actively, however; it had to comply immediately with the demands of UNMOVIC and IAEA. Before the inspectors' next report, due on 14 February, Iraq would have to promote new elements. It was the Council's moral and political duty first to devote all its energies to Iraq's disarmament in peace and in compliance with the rule of law and justice.

Iraq stated that Mr. Powell's pronouncements on Iraq's possession of WMD were utterly unrelated to the reality on the ground. It noted that, in a 30 January statement to *The New York Times*, Mr. Blix had confirmed that the inspections did not support any of the scenarios alleged by Mr. Powell and he had recently said that UNMOVIC had found no proof of the presence of the mobile laboratories whose existence Mr. Powell alleged. Iraq reminded the Council that WMD programmes could not be easily hidden like an aspirin pill; inspectors had criss-crossed all of Iraq and found no evidence of them. It further referred to a recent statement by a United States official who reported complaints that United States Administration officials had exaggerated reports of WMD in Iraq and of Iraq's presumed relationship with Al-Qaida in order to bolster their case for war.

Communications (10 February). On 10 February [S/2003/164], France, Germany and the Russian Federation transmitted to the Security Council President the text of a joint declaration issued by the three countries on the situation in Iraq, appealing to other Council members to support the declaration. The declaration stated that the common aim of the international community was to disarm Iraq. There was a debate over the means to achieve that. That debate had to continue in the spirit of friendship and respect that characterized the relations of the three countries with the United States. The inspections conducted by UNMOVIC and IAEA had already yielded results. Germany, France and Russia favoured the continuation of inspections and the substantial strengthening of their human and technical capabilities. There was still an alternative to war; the use of force could only be the last resort. It was up to Iraq to face up to its responsibilities in full and to cooperate actively with the inspections regime.

On the same day [S/2003/161], Iraq transmitted to the Secretary-General the text of a television interview with President Hussein by a British former Labour Member of Parliament, Tony Benn, which contained Iraq's position with respect to the elimination of WMD. Among other things, President Hussein said that Iraq had no relationship with Al-Qaida. He also said that if the purpose of the inspectors was to make sure that Iraq was free of nuclear, chemical and biological weapons, then they could do that, for those weapons were not aspirin tablets that a person could hide in his pocket. He repeated that Iraq was free of such weapons.

Security Council consideration (14 and 18-19 February). On 14 February [meeting 4707], the Security Council heard briefings from the UNMOVIC Executive Chairman, Mr. Blix, and the IAEA Director General, Mr. ElBaradei.

Mr. Blix said that through more than 400 inspections covering over 300 sites, UNMOVIC had obtained a good knowledge of the industrial and scientific landscape of Iraq, as well as of its missile capabilities. However, as before, it did not know every cave and corner. Access to sites had been without problems, including to presidential sites and private residences. UNMOVIC had found no WMD nor any related proscribed items, only a small number of empty chemical munitions that should have been declared and destroyed. However, many proscribed weapons and items were not accounted for. UNMOVIC was aware that many governmental intelligence organizations were convinced that proscribed weapons continued to exist in Iraq. Governments had many sources of information that were not available to inspectors. For their part, inspectors had to base their reports only on evidence that they could themselves examine. The December 2002 declaration submitted by Iraq missed the opportunity to provide the fresh material and evidence needed to respond to the unresolved disarmament questions. That was perhaps the most important problem that the international community faced.

Mr. ElBaradei said that IAEA had conducted a total of 177 inspections at 125 locations. Iraq had continued to provide immediate access to all locations. IAEA had carried out, among other things, environmental sampling and radiation detection surveys. In addition, it continued to interview key Iraqi personnel. Iraq had provided further documentation on such issues as the importation of uranium and the attempted procurement of aluminium tubes, which IAEA continued to pursue. In the course of an inspection conducted in connection with the aluminium tube investigation, IAEA inspectors found a number of documents relevant to transactions aimed at the procurement of carbon fibre, a dual-use material used by Iraq in its past clandestine uranium enrichment programme for the manufacture of gas centrifuge rotors. A review of those documents suggested that the carbon fibre sought by Iraq was not intended for enrichment purposes, as the specifications of the material appeared not to be consistent with those needed for manufacturing rotor tubes. To date, IAEA had found no evidence of ongoing prohibited nuclear or non-nuclear activities in Iraq. However, a number of issues were still under investigation and the Agency was not yet in a position to reach a conclusion about them.

France said the option of inspections had not been exhausted and it could provide an effective response to the imperative of disarming Iraq. The use of force would have such heavy consequences for the people, the region and international stability that it should be envisaged only as the last resort. The reports presented by UNMOVIC and IAEA pointed out that the inspections were producing results. There were those who believed that continuing the inspection process would be a kind of delaying tactic aimed at preventing military intervention. That raised the question of the time allotted to Iraq, which was the centre of the debate. According to France, two options were available. The option of war could be seen, on the face of it, to be the swifter, though, after winning the war, peace had to be built. That process would be long and difficult, because it would be necessary to preserve Iraq's unity and to restore stability in a lasting way in a country and a region harshly affected by the intrusion of force. In the light of that perspective, there was the alternative offered by inspections, which enabled the international community to move forward on the path of the peaceful disarmament of Iraq. As to the alleged links between Al-Qaida and the Iraqi regime, France's research and information, gathered with other allies, could not establish those links. Moreover, there was a need to assess the impact that a disputed military action would have on that level. Such an intervention could deepen divisions among societies, among cultures, among peoples—divisions that could nurture terrorism.

The United States said that it was pleased that there had been improvements with respect to the inspection process, but noted that the inspectors still did not have the freedom of access around Iraq that they needed in order to do their job well. What was needed was not more inspections, nor more immediate access, but, instead, immediate, active, unconditional, full cooperation on the part of Iraq. What was needed was for Iraq to disarm. The United States had not seen the level of cooperation on the part of Iraq that was expected, anticipated and hoped for when resolution 1441(2002) was adopted. More inspections and a longer inspection period would not solve the central problem that the international community was facing. That central problem was that Iraq had failed to comply with resolution 1441(2002). The threat of force had to remain. Force should always be the last resort, but the international community could not allow the process to be endlessly strung out, as Iraq was trying to do.

Iraq stressed that it had chosen the path of peace and opted for solutions that would satisfy the international community. It was prepared to assist in making clear the true picture in order to avoid the objections of those who wished to start a war in Iraq.

The Security Council, in a closed meeting on the same day [meeting 4708], had a constructive exchange of views with the UNMOVIC Executive Chairman and the IAEA Director General.

At the request of South Africa, on behalf of the Non-Aligned Movement [S/2003/153], the Security Council, on 18 and 19 February, held an open debate on the situation in Iraq [meeting 4709]. The representative of the League of Arab States (LAS), at the request of the Syrian Arab Republic [S/2003/184], participated in the discussion without the right to vote. The Council had before it a 14 February letter from South Africa [S/2003/183], which informed the Council President that Iraq had accepted South Africa's offer to send to Baghdad a team of government representatives, scientists, engineers and technicians who would share with Iraq their experience in disarmament and in how to eradicate WMD under international supervision based on the South African disarmament programme of the early 1990s.

Addressing the Council, South Africa said that the message that had emanated from the 14 February Council debate was that the inspection process in Iraq was working and that Iraq was showing clear signs of cooperating more proactively with the inspectors. Significantly, the inspectors had also had the opportunity to verify the accuracy of the information that had been provided by several countries. None of that information seemed to justify the abandonment of the inspection process and resorting to serious consequences. The Council had yet to utilize fully the inspection mechanisms of resolution 1441(2002) [YUN 2002, p. 292] that would make for more robust and intrusive inspections. South Africa urged the Council to explore fully practical options to enhance the inspection regime, such as the deployment of additional inspectors, surveillance aircraft and mobile customs teams. Although questions had been raised about how long the inspections should be allowed to continue in Iraq, South Africa recalled that there were no time limitations stipulated for inspections in resolution 1441(2002). As Mr. Blix had stated, the time frame would depend on which task one had in mind: the elimination of WMD and related items or monitoring to verify that no new proscribed activities occurred. Mr. Blix pointed out that monitoring was essential and that it would remain an open-ended and ongoing process until the Council should decide otherwise. South Africa believed that the Council had to redouble its efforts to bring about a peaceful resolution to the situation in Iraq. The United Nations was an organization founded on the need to preserve peace and security. Its credibility and legitimacy could not be undermined by the Iraq issue.

Iraq said that the United States had transformed the issue of inspections from a technical and scientific one into a political one. The United States had requested Iraq to prove that it was free of the alleged WMD, although what had been originally requested was active cooperation with the inspectors. The launching of an attack by the United States and the United Kingdom against Iraq would be proof of the failure of the entire international system. Iraq reaffirmed its commitment to continuing full and active cooperation with UNMOVIC and IAEA.

LAS said that in order to preserve the peace in the Arab region and throughout the world, the international community should reject the option of war and give the inspectors sufficient time to achieve a peaceful settlement of the Iraqi question.

Greece, speaking on behalf of the European Union (EU), said that full and effective disarmament in Iraq should be achieved peacefully. Force should be used only as a last resort. It was for the Iraqi regime to end the crisis by complying with the Council's demands. The EU added that although the UN inspectors should be given the time and resources that the Council believed they needed, inspections could not continue indefinitely in the absence of full Iraqi cooperation. The EU recognized that the unity of the international community, as expressed in resolution 1441(2002), and the military build-up had been essential in obtaining the return of the inspectors. The EU would work with Arab countries and LAS to bring home to Saddam Hussein the extreme danger of miscalculation of the situation and the need for full compliance with resolution 1441(2002).

Communications (19 February–6 March). On 19 February [S/2003/203], Iraq replied to the allegations made in the 5 February statement by the United States Secretary of State to the Security Council. Among other things, Iraq refuted allegations that it had biological weapons factories on wheels and on rails, stating that if the United States had such evidence, it would have submitted it to the inspectors and that UNMOVIC and IAEA were inspecting and monitoring all over Iraq but had found no evidence to confirm the authenticity of those allegations. As to the Jordanian Abu Musab al-Zarqawi, there was no evidence that he had entered Iraq over any border crossing either under his real name or using the aliases that the Jordanian side had indicated to Iraq. According to available information, it appeared that he was in the Al-Bayara region in the north of Iraq, which had not been under central authority since 1991. Terrorist elements were capable of entering and exiting many countries as they used false passports and names; no country could claim itself immune from their infiltration.

On 20 February [S/2003/207], the Libyan Arab Jamahiriya said that the Security Council or the United States should issue a text stating that if Iraq was in possession of WMD and turned them over to the inspectors, there would no longer be any grounds for military preparations. The Council should also adopt a resolution that called for the continuation of the inspectors' work.

Also on 20 February [S/2003/208], El Salvador expressed concern at the failure of Iraq to comply with its clear disarmament obligations. It called on Iraq to cooperate with the inspectors without further delay.

On 24 February [S/2003/214], France, Germany and the Russian Federation transmitted to the Council President a joint memorandum on the situation in Iraq. The three countries said that, while suspicions remained, no evidence had been given that Iraq still possessed WMD or capabilities in that field. Inspections had just reached their full pace and were functioning without hindrance; they had already produced results. While not yet fully satisfactory, Iraqi cooperation was improving. The Council had to step up its efforts to give a real chance to the peaceful settlement of the crisis. In that context, the unity of the Council had to be preserved and the pressure on Iraq had to be increased. Those conditions could be reached through the implementation of the following proposals: a clear programme of action for the inspections; reinforced inspections; and timelines for inspections and assessment. UNMOVIC and IAEA had to submit their programme of work for approval by the Council in accordance with resolution 1284(1999) [YUN 1999, p. 230]. The key remaining tasks had to be defined according to their degree of priority. What was required of Iraq for implementation of each task had to be clearly defined and precise. Further measures to strengthen inspections could include an increase in and diversification of staff and expertise; establishment of mobile units designed in particular to check on trucks; completion of the new system of aerial surveillance; and systematic processing of data provided by that system. The implementation of the inspections programme should be sequenced according to a realistic and rigorous timeline. The inspectors should be asked to submit the programme of work outlining the key substantive tasks for Iraq to accomplish; Chief Inspectors should report to the Council on the implementation of the programme of work every three weeks; a report of UNMOVIC and IAEA assessing the progress made in completing the tasks should be submitted by the inspectors 120 days after the adoption of the programme of work; UNMOVIC and IAEA should report immediately to the Council if and when Iraq interfered with inspections activities; and, at any time, additional Council meetings could be decided, including at a high level. The three countries stressed that to render possible a peaceful solution, inspections should be given the necessary time and resources. However, Iraq had to disarm and cooperate actively with the inspections.

On 28 February [S/2003/238], China and the Russian Federation transmitted to the Secretary-General the texts of the joint communiqués of the Ministers for Foreign Affairs of the two countries (Beijing, 27 February) on the situation on the Korean peninsula and on the Iraq question. The sides favoured a resolution of the Iraqi crisis by political and diplomatic means within the framework of resolution 1441(2002). They stated that the UN inspections had achieved definitive progress and should proceed further.

On 3 March [A/57/743-S/2003/247], Bahrain transmitted to the Secretary-General the Final Declaration of the summit-level fifteenth regular session of the LAS Council (Sharm el-Sheikh, Egypt, 1 March). LAS, among other things, emphasized its categorical rejection of a strike against Iraq or a threat to the security and integrity of any Arab country and underscored the need to resolve the Iraqi crisis peacefully, within the framework of international legitimacy. It also requested that the UN inspection teams be given sufficient time to complete their mission in Iraq. On the same day [S/2003/254], LAS transmitted to the Council President the texts of the resolutions of the fifteenth session of the LAS Council, including that on the Iraq crisis.

On 4 March [A/57/757-S/2003/329], Malaysia, as Chairman of the Coordinating Bureau of the Non-Aligned Movement, transmitted to the Secretary-General the statement concerning Iraq adopted at the Thirteenth Conference of Heads of State or Government of Non-Aligned Countries (Kuala Lumpur, 20-25 February). The heads of State or Government said that war against Iraq would be devastating for the whole region and that it would have far-reaching political, economic and humanitarian consequences for all countries of the world, particularly the States in the region. They reaffirmed their commitment to the principle of non-use of force and called on Iraq to continue to comply with Council resolution 1441(2002).

On 5 March [S/2003/253], France, Germany and the Russian Federation transmitted to the Council President the joint statement by the Ministers for Foreign Affairs of the three countries adopted in Paris that day. They reaffirmed that the disarmament of Iraq could be achieved by peaceful means and that the inspections were producing encouraging results. They emphasized that the inspections should be speeded up, in keeping with the proposals set forth in their 24 February memorandum to the Council (see p. 329). Using that method, the inspectors should submit their work programme without delay, accompanied by regular progress reports to the Council. In those circumstances, the three countries noted that they would not allow a proposed resolution to be adopted that authorized the use of force.

On 6 March [A/57/748-S/2003/288], Qatar transmitted to the Secretary-General the text of a communiqué on Iraq, adopted at the second emergency session of the Islamic Summit (Doha, Qatar, 5 March). The Conference categorically rejected any strike against Iraq and emphasized the need to settle the Iraqi question by peaceful means within the framework of the United Nations. Also on 6 March [A/57/749-S/2003/289], Qatar transmitted to the Secretary-General the text of the statement made by the Emir of Qatar, Sheikh Hamad bin Khalifa Al-Thani, at that session.

Security Council consideration (7 and 11-12 March). At the request of Malaysia, on behalf of the Non-Aligned Movement [S/2003/246], the Security Council held an open meeting on 7 March, at which it heard briefings by UNMOVIC Executive Chairman Mr. Blix and by IAEA Director General Mr. ElBaradei [meeting 4714].

Presenting UNMOVIC's February quarterly report [S/2003/232] (see p. 317), which described three months of inspections, Mr. Blix said that Iraq, which had a highly developed administrative system, should be able to provide more documentary evidence about its proscribed weapons programme. UNMOVIC had not found underground facilities for chemical or biological production or storage. However, it needed to increase its staff in Iraq both for the monitoring of ground transportation and for the inspection of underground facilities. Iraq had started to destroy missiles that were not within the permissible range set by the Council. That process constituted a substantial measure of disarmament, the first since the middle of the 1990s. As at 7 March, 34 missiles, including two combat warheads and one launcher, had been destroyed under UNMOVIC supervision. There was also a significant Iraqi effort under way to clarify a major source of uncertainty as to the quantities of biological and chemical weapons that were unilaterally destroyed in 1991. The Iraqi side had not persisted in attaching conditions to the inspections. However, while the numerous initiatives that were being taken by Iraq with a view to resolving some long-standing open disarmament issues could be seen as active or even proactive, those initiatives, three or four months since the adoption of resolution 1441(2002) [YUN 2002, p. 292], could not be said to constitute immediate cooperation, nor did they necessarily cover all areas of relevance. They were nevertheless welcome, and UNMOVIC was responding to them in the hope of solving outstanding disarmament issues. UNMOVIC was in the process of drafting its work programme (see p. 333), which, among other things, contained a list of key remaining disarmament tasks. Mr. Blix said that the verification and inspection process could not be instant. Even with a proactive Iraqi attitude, it would still take some time to verify sites and items, analyse documents, interview relevant persons and draw conclusions. It would not take years, or weeks, but months.

Mr. ElBaradei said that Iraq's industrial capacity had deteriorated substantially since 1998, a fact of direct relevance to Iraq's capability for resuming a nuclear weapons programme. In recent weeks, Iraq had provided a considerable amount of documentation pertaining to outstanding issues, including Iraq's efforts to procure aluminium tubes, its attempted procurement of magnets and magnet-production capabilities and its reported attempt to import uranium. IAEA had concluded that Iraq's efforts to import aluminium tubes were not likely to have been related to the manufacture of centrifuges and, moreover, it was highly unlikely that Iraq could have achieved the considerable redesign needed to use them in a revived centrifuge programme. IAEA experts had also verified that none of the magnets that Iraq had declared could be used directly for centrifuge magnetic bearings. IAEA would continue to monitor and inspect equipment and material that could be used to make magnets for enrichment centrifuges. With regard to allegations that Iraq had sought to buy uranium from the Niger in recent years, IAEA concluded, after a thorough investigation, that the documents provided by a number of States, which pointed to an agreement between Iraq and the Niger for the sale of uranium, were not authentic and thus the allegations were unfounded. In the area of nuclear weapons, there was no indication of resumed nuclear activities in those buildings that were identified through the use of satellite imagery as having been reconstructed or newly erected since 1998, nor any indication of nuclear-related prohibited activities at any inspected sites. Also, there was no indication that Iraq had attempted to import uranium since 1990. After three months of intrusive inspections, IAEA had found no evidence or plausible indication of the revival of a nuclear-related programme in Iraq.

The United States said that, despite the progress that had been mentioned by Mr. Blix and Mr. ElBaradei, Iraq was still not cooperating. If Iraq genuinely wanted to disarm, the international community would not need to look for mobile biological units or require an extensive programme to search for underground facilities that were known to exist, nor should the inspectors have to search for evidence and proof. UNMOVIC and IAEA reports noted an acceleration of Iraqi initiatives. However, Iraq's small steps were certainly not initiatives as they were not provided willingly and freely by the Iraqis, but had been pulled out by the possibility of military force. The United States expressed pleasure that some missiles were being destroyed but added that evidence showed that the infrastructure to make more missiles remained within Iraq and had not been identified and destroyed. Iraq's intention to keep from turning over all of its WMD had not changed and, thus, it was not cooperating with the international community in the manner intended by resolution 1441(2002). Iraq still had the capability to manufacture chemical and biological weapons and still had tens of thousands of delivery systems, including UAVs. The United States believed that the draft resolution that had been circulated was appropriate and that the Council should soon vote on it.

The Russian Federation said that it had consistently sought to solve the Iraq problem on the basis of international law and of Council resolutions, which was the proper and reliable way. Progress had been achieved in implementing resolution 1441(2002) and Iraq's level of cooperation with the inspectors was very different from the practice under UNSCOM. Russia was firmly in favour of continuing and strengthening inspection activities and of making them more focused.

France said that it was clear that the international community was moving towards the complete elimination of WMD programmes in Iraq. However, Iraq still had to provide information in a timely fashion, so that the inspectors could obtain the most precise knowledge possible about any existing inventories or programmes. There was a need to keep the pressure on Baghdad, while the American and British military presence in the region supported the collective resolve of the international community. That pressure had to be used to achieve the objective of disarmament through inspections. Those inspections could not go on indefinitely and the pace had to be stepped up. However, the military agenda could not dictate the calendar of inspections. France agreed to accelerated timetables, but could not accept an ultimatum as long as the inspectors were reporting progress in terms of cooperation; as that would mean war. To those who believed that war would be the quickest way to disarm Iraq, France replied that it would create divisions and cause wounds that would be long in healing. As a permanent member of the Security Council, France would not allow a resolution to be adopted that authorized the automatic use of force.

China believed that the Council should provide strong support and guidance to the two inspection bodies. It also urged Iraq to strengthen its cooperation. It was not in favour of a new resolution, particularly one authorizing the use of force.

The United Kingdom observed that no Council member had stated that Iraq was fully in compliance with resolution 1441(2002). Iraq had dragged its feet on as many elements of procedural and substantive cooperation as possible. It defied experience to believe that continuing inspections with no firm end date would achieve complete disarmament. The United Kingdom, on behalf of the sponsors of the draft resolution on Iraq (Spain, United Kingdom, United States), would ask the Secretariat to circulate an amendment, specifying a further period beyond the adoption of a resolution for Iraq to take the final opportunity to disarm and bring itself into compliance.

Iraq stated that a possible war of aggression against Iraq had become imminent, regardless of any decision by the Council. The United States and the United Kingdom continued to fabricate facts and evidence suggesting Iraq's possession of WMD; however, they had not managed to convince the international community. Their claims were an attempt to mask their real agenda, which was a complete takeover of Iraq's oil and the political and economic domination of the entire Arab region. The new draft resolution and the most recent amendment did not relate to disarmament; the aim was to drag the Council into taking action that would have detrimental consequences, not only for Iraq, but for the very credibility of the United Nations. War against Iraq would wreak destruction, but would not unearth any WMD as there were no such weapons.

At the request of Malaysia, on behalf of the Non-Aligned Movement [S/2003/283], the Council, on 11 and 12 March, held an open debate on the situation in Iraq [meeting 4717]. LAS, at the request of the Syrian Arab Republic [S/2003/292], and the Organization of the Islamic Conference (OIC), at the request of the Sudan [S/2003/298], participated in the discussion without the right to vote.

Iraq said that Mr. Blix and Mr. ElBaradei had confirmed that inspections had not found any WMD or programmes to produce such weapons inside Iraqi territory. The allegations made by the United States Secretary of State on 5 February were refuted by the facts in the possession of the inspectors following four months of reinforced monitoring. Therefore, none of those allegations had proved to be true. Iraq reconfirmed its decision to rid itself of WMD and its readiness to cooperate with UNMOVIC.

Malaysia welcomed and supported all efforts exerted to avert war against Iraq and called for the persistent continuation of such efforts based on multilateral diplomacy, as opposed to unilateral actions.

Canada said that the division within the Security Council had drawn the focus of the world away from the issue of disarming Iraq and shifted it, instead, onto diplomatic competition, which served no one's interests but Saddam Hussein's. On 18 February, Canada had proposed a set of ideas to bridge that very destructive divide. It suggested that the key remaining disarmament tasks be established and prioritized by the weapons inspectors and that a deadline be established for Iraq to implement them. As Mr. Blix had noted, while cooperation by Iraq had to be immediate and proactive, disarmament and verification could not be instantaneous.

OIC said that the position opposed to war against Iraq enjoyed overwhelming popular support, as highlighted by the many rallies and demonstrations held in hundreds of cities throughout the world and as expressed in many recommendations made by governmental and intergovernmental organizations in many countries. OIC added that the use of military force against Iraq, at that particular moment, when Iraq was cooperating with the Council's demands, was unjustified and represented an assault on the pan-Arab and Islamic world.

Communications (13-18 March). On 13 March [S/2003/311], South Africa said that the deliberations on Iraq would be enhanced if the Security Council received a draft work programme containing the key remaining disarmament tasks from the weapons inspectors.

On 15 March [S/2003/320], Germany transmitted to the Council President the joint declaration by the Ministers for Foreign Affairs of France, Germany and the Russian Federation, adopted on that day. The three countries reaffirmed that nothing justified abandoning the inspections process or resorting to force. Iraq's disarmament had begun, and there was every reason to believe that it could be completed rapidly and in accordance with the rules set out by the Council. Iraq, for its part, had to cooperate actively and unconditionally. The three countries, supported by China, had submitted proposals for achieving disarmament in Iraq by defining key disarmament tasks and establishing a rigorous timetable. UNMOVIC's programme of work was soon to be submitted to the Council (see p. 333). The three countries proposed that the Council meet at the ministerial level to approve key disarmament tasks and establish an implementation timetable that was both demanding and realistic. A peaceful approach was preferred by the Council and supported by the vast majority of the international community.

On 17 March [S/2003/347], the Russian Federation informed the Secretary-General that in connection with the meeting of the leaders of Portugal, Spain, the United Kingdom and the United States held in the Azores, Portugal, on the situation relating to Iraq (see below), it deemed it appropriate to confirm its support for a political settlement of the Iraq problem. The use of force against Iraq was without legal foundation.

By an 18 March letter to the Secretary-General and the Council President [S/2003/325], Iraq noted that the decision by the UN Secretariat to withdraw all UN staff from Iraq, such as in the case of UNIKOM, would make it easier for the United States to wage its aggression against Iraq.

Azores meeting

On 18 March [S/2003/335], Portugal, Spain, the United Kingdom and the United States transmitted to the Council President the texts of two statements adopted by the Atlantic Summit (Azores, 16 March) entitled "A vision for Iraq and the Iraqi people" and "Commitment to transatlantic solidarity". The first statement said that for 12 years, Saddam Hussein had defied the international community. If he refused to cooperate fully with the United Nations, he brought on himself the serious consequences foreseen in resolution 1441(2002). In those circumstances, the four countries would undertake a solemn obligation to help the Iraqi people build a new Iraq at peace with itself and its neighbours. The Iraqi people deserved to be lifted from insecurity and tyranny and freed to determine for themselves the future of their country. The statement also said that the four countries would work to prevent and repair damage done by Hussein's regime to the natural resources of Iraq and pledged to protect them. All Iraqis should share the wealth generated by their national economy. The four countries would seek a swift end to international sanctions and support an international reconstruction programme. They would also fight terrorism in all its forms and Iraq should never again be a haven for terrorists of any kind. In achieving that vision, the four countries planned to work in close partnership with international institutions, including the United Nations. If conflict occurred, the four countries planned to seek the adoption of new Council resolutions that would affirm Iraq's territorial integrity, ensure rapid delivery of humanitarian relief and endorse an appropriate post-conflict administration for Iraq. They would also propose that the Secretary-General be given authority, on an interim basis, to ensure that the humanitarian needs of the Iraqi people continued to be met through the oil-for-food programme. Any military presence, should it be necessary, would be temporary and intended to promote security and the elimination of WMD, the delivery of humanitarian aid and the conditions for the reconstruction of Iraq.

The statement on the commitment to transatlantic solidarity stressed that the four countries would face and overcome terrorism and the spread of WMD. They would not allow differences of the moment to be exploited in ways that brought no solutions.

Military conflict and occupation

On 20 March, coalition forces, led by the United States, commenced military action against Iraq.

Earlier, on 18 March [S/2003/337], the Security Council, taking note of the Secretary-General's decision to suspend, for security reasons, the work of the UN humanitarian personnel in Iraq, stood ready to consider as soon as possible the proposals being prepared by the Secretary-General on how to meet the humanitarian needs of the people of Iraq, taking into account the urgency of the humanitarian situation there.

Security Council consideration (19 March). On 19 March [meeting 4721], the Council was briefed by the Executive Chairman of UNMOVIC, Mr. Blix.

Mr. Blix presented UNMOVIC's draft work programme. He said that during the three and a half months of resumed inspections in Iraq, UNMOVIC had learned a great deal that had been useful for the drafting of its work programme and for the selection of key remaining disarmament tasks. It would have been difficult to draft the work programme without that knowledge and practical experience. Mr. Blix expressed sadness that the inspection work carried out in Iraq did not bring the assurances needed about the absence of WMD or other proscribed items, that no more time was available for inspections and that armed action seemed imminent. He observed that UNMOVIC had withdrawn all its staff from Iraq on the previous day. Mr. Blix noted that the work programme prepared by UNMOVIC inspectors and other resources deployed in Iraq, and submitted to the Council in accordance with resolution 1284(1999) [YUN 1999, p. 230], seemed to have only limited practical relevance considering the situation on the ground. UNMOVIC was a subsidiary organ of the Council. Until the adoption of a new decision by the Council on the role and functions of the Commission, the previous resolutions remained valid to the extent that was practicable. It was evidently for the Council to consider the next steps.

An IAEA representative informed the Council that the IAEA Director General had also transmitted the Agency's work programme, which was self-explanatory.

Germany said that the world was facing an imminent war in Iraq and the Security Council could not remain silent in that situation. The developments of the last few hours had brought the work of the United Nations on the ground to a standstill and those developments were cause for the deepest concern. Mr. Blix's work programme provided clear and convincing guidelines on how to disarm Iraq peacefully within a short space of time and showed that peaceful means had not been exhausted. Germany emphatically rejected the impending war.

France said the Council was meeting just a few hours before the commencement of hostilities. The choice before the Council was between two visions of the world: on one side stood those who thought that they could resolve the world's complexity through swift preventive action, while on the other side stood those who chose resolute action and a long-term approach. In order to ensure collective security, there was a need to take into account the manifold crises and their dimensions, including the cultural and religious ones. France said that the Iraqi problem had allowed the Council to craft an instrument, through the inspection regime, that was unprecedented and could serve as an example. On that basis, an innovative, permanent disarmament body could be established under UN aegis. It also said that an outbreak of force in an unstable area, such as Iraq, could only exacerbate the tensions and fractures on which terrorism fed. However, over and above the differences among countries, there was a need to restore the unity of the international community and to start preparing for the required humanitarian assistance in Iraq. The Secretary-General had already started to mobilize the various UN agencies. France would take part in the collective effort to assist the Iraqi people. Next, it would be necessary to build peace; no single country had the means to build Iraq's future and, above all, no State could claim the necessary legitimacy. The legal and moral authority for such an undertaking could stem only from the United Nations. Two principles had to guide the Council's action: respect for the unity and territorial integrity of Iraq and the preservation of its sovereignty. Similarly, it would be up to the United Nations to establish a framework for Iraq's economic reconstruction.

The United States said that, regrettably, the Council's discussion on UNMOVIC's work programme was incompatible with Iraq's non-compliance with resolution 1441(2002) [YUN 2002, p. 292] and the current reality on the ground. No realistic programme of work or outline of key unresolved issues could be developed pursuant to resolution 1284(1999) [YUN 1999, p. 230] while Iraq failed to cooperate fully, actively and unconditionally, nor could it be developed in the absence of sound information on Iraqi programmes since 1998. Considering a work programme at that particular time was out of touch with the reality that was confronting the international community, as the situation on the ground would change and so would the nature of the remaining disarmament tasks. That said, however, the United States did not exclude the possibility that it may prove useful to return to those documents at some time in the future. In the meantime, the Council would face new challenges related to the future of Iraq. The United States shared the concern for meeting the humanitarian needs of the Iraqi people. Towards that end, it was fielding the Disaster Assistance Response Team, composed of United States civilian humanitarian experts, to the region to assess needs, to liaise with partners and to provide in-field grant-making capacity. It had also pre-positioned millions of dollars worth of food rationing and relief supplies. In addition, the United States had contributed over $60 million to more than a dozen different UN agencies. In recognizing the importance of the oil-for-food programme in order to meet the humanitarian needs of the Iraqi people, the United States was prepared to present in the near future a draft humanitarian resolution that would ensure the continuity of the programme.

The Secretary-General expressed regret that it had not been possible to reach a common position. Whatever the differing views on the Iraqi issue, it was a sad day for the United Nations and the international community; millions of people around the world shared that sense of disappointment and were deeply alarmed by the prospect of imminent war. The plight of the Iraqi people was the Secretary-General's immediate concern. Over the preceding 20 years, Iraqis had been through two major wars, internal uprisings and conflict, and more than a decade of debilitating sanctions. In the short term, the conflict that was clearly about to start could make the situation much worse. Under international law, the responsibility for protecting civilians in conflict fell on the belligerents. In any area under military occupation, responsibility for the welfare of the population fell on the occupying Power. Without in any way assuming or diminishing that ultimate responsibility, the United Nations would do whatever it could to help. The UN humanitarian agencies had for some time been engaged in preparing for that contingency. The United Nations had done its best to assess the possible effects of war, in terms of population displacement and human need, and to position its personnel and equipment accordingly. Of the $123.5 million requested by the United Nations for those preparations, only $45 million had been pledged and only $34 million had been received. The United Nations had also examined the situation caused by the suspension of the activities of the oil-for-food programme and ways that the programme could be adjusted to enable the United Nations to continue providing humanitarian assistance to the Iraqi people during and after hostilities. Such adjustments would require decisions by the Security Council. The Secretary-General expressed the hope that the effort to relieve the suffering of the Iraqi people and to rehabilitate their society after so much destruction might prove to be the task around which the unity of the Council could be rebuilt.

Communications (19-26 March). By a 19 March letter [S/2003/343], the Emir of Qatar, as Chairman of the Ninth Islamic Summit Conference, reaffirmed that the diplomatic and peaceful efforts being made with a view to the elimination of WMD had to be given a chance and rejected the principle of war against Iraq.

Also on 19 March [A/58/68-S/2003/357], Malaysia transmitted to the Secretary-General the statement made that day by the Troika of the Non-Aligned Movement (Cuba, Malaysia, South Africa) on the developments concerning Iraq. The Troika viewed the imminent unilateral military action by the United States and its allies as an illegitimate act of aggression.

On 20 March, in three similar letters to the Council President, Australia [S/2003/352], the United Kingdom [S/2003/350] and the United States [S/2003/351] said that their respective armed forces had engaged in military action in Iraq on that day. The action followed a long history of non-cooperation by Iraq with the United Nations and numerous findings by the Security Council that Iraq had failed to comply with its disarmament obligations. In its resolution 1441(2002) [YUN 2002, p. 292], the Council recognized that Iraq's possession of WMD constituted a threat to international peace and security, that Iraq had failed to disarm and that in consequence Iraq was in material breach of the conditions for the ceasefire at the end of hostilities in 1991 laid down by the Council in resolution 687(1991) [YUN 1991, p. 172]. Military action was undertaken only when it became apparent that there was no other way of achieving compliance by Iraq.

On 20 March [S/2003/348], Russia said that the military action against Iraq was taking place in defiance of world public opinion and in violation of the principles and norms of the UN Charter and international law. Nothing could justify that military action—neither accusations that Iraq was supporting international terrorism, nor the desire to change the political regime in that country, which was in direct contradiction of international law. Political regimes could be determined only by the citizens of the State in question. Iraq posed no threat either to neighbouring States or to other countries or regions of the world, because, especially after a 10-year blockade, it was a weak country, both militarily and economically. It was even less of a danger because international inspectors were working there. Russia called for the early termination of military action and expressed its conviction that the central role in resolving crises around the world, including the situation in Iraq, belonged to the Security Council.

On 24 March [S/2003/364], the Syrian Arab Republic informed the Council President that, on 23 March, British and United States planes bombarded a Syrian civilian bus carrying Syrian workers on their way back to Syria from Iraq. Five Syrian nationals were killed and many others wounded. Syria condemned that action and reserved the right to demand compensation according to relevant international laws.

On the same day [S/2003/365], LAS transmitted to the Council President the text of a resolution entitled "The American/British aggression against fraternal Iraq and its implications for the security and safety of neighbouring Arab States and Arab national security", adopted by the LAS Council during its one hundred and nineteenth regular session (Cairo, Egypt, 22-25 March). LAS, among other things, condemned the American/British aggression against Iraq and called for an immediate and unconditional withdrawal of the invading forces. It affirmed that Arab States had to refrain from joining in any military action against the territorial integrity of Iraq.

Also on 24 March [S/2003/366], Costa Rica transmitted to the Secretary-General a position paper concerning the reconstruction of Iraq following the armed conflict.

In another 24 March letter [S/2003/373], Uganda informed the Council President that it had decided to support the United States–led coalition to disarm Iraq by force and was ready to assist in any way possible.

On 26 March [S/2003/376], Qatar transmitted to the Secretary-General the text of a communiqué issued by the General Secretariat of the Gulf Cooperation Council (GCC) relating to the situation in the Middle East region owing to the confrontation in Iraq. GCC expressed the hope that military operations would be halted as soon as possible and stressed its rejection of any violation of Iraq's territorial integrity.

Security Council consideration (26-27 March). At the request of Iraq, on behalf of LAS, with the reservation of Kuwait [S/2003/362], and Malaysia, on behalf of the Non-Aligned Movement [S/2003/363], the Council, on 26 and 27 March, held an open meeting on the situation in Iraq [meeting 4726]. LAS, at the request of the Syrian Arab Republic [S/2003/370], OIC, at the request of the Sudan [S/2003/371], and the Permanent Observer of Palestine, at his own request [S/2003/372], participated in the discussion without the right to vote.

The Secretary-General said that the Council, which had had Iraq on its agenda for 12 years, had to rediscover its unity of purpose. The war had to be brought to an end as soon as possible, but, while it continued, it was essential to protect the civilian population, the wounded and the prisoners of war, on both sides, and to bring relief to the victims. That obligation was binding on all the belligerents. The Geneva Conventions and all other instruments of international humanitarian law had to be respected. In particular, the 1949 Fourth Geneva Convention, under which those in effective control of any territory were responsible for meeting the humanitarian needs of its population and were required to maintain dialogue and cooperation with international organizations engaged in humanitarian relief, had to be scrupulously respected. The oil-for-food programme had been halted, with a value of some $2.4 billion in supplies, mainly food, in the pipeline. The Council needed to determine how it would adjust the programme to make it possible for those supplies to reach the Iraqi people and to ensure that food, medicine and other essential life-sustaining supplies continued to be provided. The humanitarian effort required in the coming weeks and months was going to be very costly. The United Nations was about to launch a flash appeal to donors, and he urged Member States to respond swiftly and generously. The Council had to determine how it would address the many needs of the Iraqi people, whatever the outcome of the war, and what the United Nations itself might be asked to undertake. A Council mandate was needed for anything beyond strictly humanitarian relief. The Secretary-General said that in the last few months the peoples of the world had showed how much they expected of the United Nations, and of the Security Council in particular. Many of them were bitterly disappointed. Their faith in the United Nations could be restored only if the Council was able to identify and work constructively towards specific goals. He urged the five permanent members, in particular, to show leadership by making a concerted effort to overcome their differences. For his part, the Secretary-General emphasized two guiding principles on which he believed there was no disagreement, and which should guide all the Council's efforts and future decisions on Iraq. The first principle was respect for Iraq's sovereignty, territorial integrity and independence, and the second was respect for the right of the Iraqi people to determine their own political future and control their own natural resources. The Secretary-General appealed to all Member States to begin healing divisions so that the Council could recover its rightful role as the body with primary responsibility for the maintenance of international peace and security.

Iraq said that the American-British full-scale military aggression commenced at dawn on 20 March. The goal of the aggression was the occupation of Iraq and the change of its political regime. The Iraqi armed forces and armed civilian units were fighting fierce battles against that aggression. The international community was well aware that the Council had not authorized the use of force. Both the United States and the United Kingdom confirmed, when resolution 1441(2002) was adopted [YUN 2002, p. 292], that it did not contain a hidden agenda, trigger or automatic use of force. Nevertheless, despite the opposition to war of the majority of Council members, those two countries launched a war against Iraq.

The United Kingdom said that it was aware that Member States, perhaps without exception, found the situation in Iraq deeply disappointing and distasteful, but they could not set aside the universally available evidence that Iraq was repeatedly defying the United Nations in refusing to complete disarmament of its WMD under the terms of successive resolutions. Resolution 1441(2002) was adopted unanimously but not implemented with any rigour by a united Council. Coalition action was therefore under way to enforce Council decisions on complete Iraqi disarmament. Military action was both legitimate and multilateral, as it was authorized under resolutions 678(1990) [YUN 1990, p. 204], 687(1991) [YUN 1991, p. 172] and 1441(2002). A broad coalition of well over 40 States was supporting the action materially or politically. The United Kingdom regretted the differences within the Council that had marked the past few months of discussions on that subject. The time had come to put those aside and to unite to ensure that the United Nations and the international community could act quickly to meet the needs of the Iraqi people during and after military action. The first priority was to ensure that the changing realities on the ground were reflected in the operation of the oil-for-food programme, on which 60 per cent of Iraqis remained dependent. Progress had been made within the Council on a draft resolution that would amend the programme. It was hoped that the outstanding issues could be resolved rapidly so that the Secretary-General could have the necessary authority to maximize the UN role in delivering humanitarian relief. Looking further ahead, there was a need to consider the role that the United Nations could play in building a stable and prosperous Iraq. The United Kingdom was convinced that the United Nations had to take a central role in the future of that country.

Communication (28 March). On 28 March [S/2003/391], Iran informed the Secretary-General that its airspace had been violated and that its territory had been hit by the belligerents in the war against Iraq.

Special Adviser

On 7 April [SG/SM/8660-IK/343], the Secretary-General met with members of the Security Council to inform them that he had appointed Rafeeuddin Ahmed as his Special Adviser on Iraq. Mr. Ahmed would consider possible UN roles in post-war Iraq and their legal, political, operational and resource implications. Any role beyond the coordination of humanitarian activities in Iraq, and other activities mandated by existing resolutions, would first require a new mandate from the Council. The Council members welcomed Mr. Ahmed's appointment.

Iraqi initiatives

On 15 April, near the town of Nasiriyah, up to 100 Iraqis representing every part of the country met to discuss Iraq's future and how best to chart a course towards a democratic representative government. United States officials and coalition representatives also attended. At the end of the session, the Iraqi participants approved a final statement proposing 13 principles for a future Iraqi government. The principles, among other things, stressed that Iraq had to be democratic; the future government should not be based on communal identity; a future government had to be organized as a democratic federal system, but on the basis of countrywide consultation; the rule of law had to be paramount; the Baath party had to be dissolved; and political violence had to be rejected.

On 28 April, over 250 Iraqi representatives, from inside Iraq and from the expatriate and opposition communities, convened in Baghdad to advance the national dialogue among Iraqis regarding composition of an Iraqi interim authority.

Security Council note (5 May). On 5 May [S/2003/524], the Council President circulated a note from the Holy See containing a Statement of Patriarchs and Bishops of Iraq, issued on 29 April. The Statement, among other things, asked that the new Iraqi constitution recognize Christians' religious, social and political rights and envision a legal statute in which each person would be considered according to his or her capacities, without discrimination.

Coalition Provisional Authority

On 8 May [S/2003/538], the United Kingdom and the United States informed the Council President that they continued to act together to ensure the complete disarmament of Iraq of WMD and means of delivery. The Coalition States would abide by their obligations under international law and would ensure that Iraq's oil was protected and used for the benefit of the Iraqi people. In order to meet those objectives and obligations in the post-conflict period, the Coalition, acting under existing command and control arrangements through the Commander of Coalition Forces, had created the Coalition Provisional Authority (the Authority), which included the Office of Reconstruction and Humanitarian Assistance, to exercise powers of government temporarily and, as necessary, to provide security, to allow the delivery of humanitarian aid and to eliminate WMD. The Coalition partners, working through the Authority, would, among other things, provide for security in and for the provisional administration of Iraq by deterring hostilities; maintaining Iraq's territorial integrity and securing its borders; eliminating all of Iraq's WMD; facilitating the orderly and voluntary return of refugees and displaced persons; maintaining civil law and order; eliminating all terrorist infrastructure and resources within Iraq; supporting and coordinating demining activities;

promoting accountability for crimes committed by the previous Iraqi regime; and assuming immediate control of Iraqi institutions responsible for military and security matters. The Coalition was facilitating the efforts of the Iraqi people to take the first steps towards forming a representative government, based on the rule of law, that afforded fundamental freedoms and equal protection and justice to the Iraqi people without regard to ethnicity, religion or gender. According to the Coalition, the United Nations had a vital role to play in providing humanitarian relief, in supporting the reconstruction of Iraq and in helping in the formation of an Iraqi interim authority.

Security Council consideration (22 May). On 22 May [meeting 4762], the Council discussed the response to the humanitarian situation in Iraq (see also p. 936) and heard briefings by the Deputy Secretary-General (DSG), Louise Fréchette, and other UN and intergovernmental organization officials.

The DSG said that the breakdown of essential services and law and order in Iraq had resulted in a range of urgent humanitarian needs. A major humanitarian crisis had been averted, but the civilian population, and children in particular, remained at risk, especially if the security situation did not improve substantially in the near future. UN agencies were at work throughout the country, providing food, water, medicine and other emergency assistance. They had helped repair water and sanitation facilities, assisted in the restoration of electricity and provided relief to internally displaced persons and malnourished children. International UN staff had begun to return to Iraq in April, and more than 300 of them were now deployed, in addition to 3,400 national staff. The overarching priority of virtually all UN assistance efforts was the reactivation of essential public services, including the public distribution system for food. However, the delivery of assistance was made all the more difficult, if not impossible, by the general lack of law and order. Many looted facilities were repaired and restocked only to be looted again. Also, staff movements were limited in many urban areas and people in need could not be reached. The Organization's ability to respond to the urgent needs in Iraq depended greatly on whether the necessary resources would be available. As at 22 May, more than $700 million had been received in response to the UN flash appeal. Moreover, as implementation of resolution 1472(2003) of 28 March on the use of oil-for-food funds to provide aid (see p. 363) continued, the Office of the Iraq Programme and UN agencies had confirmed that nearly $1 billion worth of priority humanitarian supplies could be shipped by 3 June. As UN agencies continued to expand their presence in Iraq, they were conducting comprehensive assessments that would enable the UN system to re-prioritize its response plans. Based on those new assessments, the United Nations would be launching a revised humanitarian appeal in the second half of June.

Lifting of economic sanctions

On 22 May [meeting 4761], the Security Council adopted **resolution 1483(2003)** by vote (14-0). The draft [S/2003/556] was submitted by Spain, the United Kingdom and the United States. The Syrian Arab Republic, which did not participate in the voting, later explained that it would have voted in favour of the resolution had it been granted additional time before the vote, as it had requested on more than one occasion. Syria provided a further explanation to the Council President in writing [S/2003/567].

The Security Council,

Recalling all its relevant resolutions,

Reaffirming the sovereignty and territorial integrity of Iraq,

Reaffirming also the importance of the disarmament of Iraqi weapons of mass destruction and of eventual confirmation of the disarmament of Iraq,

Stressing the right of the Iraqi people freely to determine their own political future and to control their own natural resources, welcoming the commitment of all parties concerned to support the creation of an environment in which they may do so as soon as possible, and expressing resolve that the day when Iraqis govern themselves must come quickly,

Encouraging efforts by the people of Iraq to form a representative Government based on the rule of law that affords equal rights and justice to all Iraqi citizens without regard to ethnicity, religion or gender, and, in this connection, recalling resolution 1325(2000) of 31 October 2000,

Welcoming the first steps of the Iraqi people in this regard, and noting in this connection the Nasiriyah statement of 15 April 2003 and the Baghdad statement of 28 April 2003,

Resolved that the United Nations should play a vital role in humanitarian relief, in the reconstruction of Iraq and in the restoration and establishment of national and local institutions for representative governance,

Taking note of the statement made on 12 April 2003 by the Finance Ministers and Central Bank Governors of the Group of Seven Industrialized Nations in which they recognized the need for a multilateral effort to help to rebuild and develop Iraq and the need for assistance from the International Monetary Fund and the World Bank in these efforts,

Welcoming the resumption of humanitarian assistance and the continuing efforts of the Secretary-General and the specialized agencies to provide food and medicine to the people of Iraq,

Welcoming also the appointment by the Secretary-General of his Special Adviser on Iraq,

Affirming the need for accountability for crimes and atrocities committed by the previous Iraqi regime,

Stressing the need for respect for the archaeological, historical, cultural and religious heritage of Iraq and for the continued protection of archaeological, historical, cultural and religious sites, as well as museums, libraries and monuments,

Noting the letter dated 8 May 2003 from the Permanent Representatives of the United Kingdom of Great Britain and Northern Ireland and the United States of America to the United Nations addressed to the President of the Security Council, and recognizing the specific authorities, responsibilities and obligations under applicable international law of these States as occupying Powers under unified command ("the Authority"),

Noting also that other States that are not occupying Powers are working now, or in the future may work, under the Authority,

Welcoming the willingness of Member States to contribute to stability and security in Iraq by contributing personnel, equipment and other resources under the Authority,

Concerned that many Kuwaitis and third-State nationals have not been accounted for since 2 August 1990,

Determining that the situation in Iraq, although improved, continues to constitute a threat to international peace and security,

Acting under Chapter VII of the Charter of the United Nations,

1. *Appeals* to Member States and concerned organizations to assist the people of Iraq in their efforts to reform their institutions and rebuild their country, and to contribute to conditions of stability and security in Iraq in accordance with the present resolution;

2. *Calls upon* all Member States in a position to do so to respond immediately to the humanitarian appeals of the United Nations and other international organizations for Iraq and to help to meet the humanitarian and other needs of the Iraqi people by providing food, medical supplies, and resources necessary for reconstruction and rehabilitation of Iraq's economic infrastructure;

3. *Appeals* to Member States to deny safe haven to those members of the previous Iraqi regime who are alleged to be responsible for crimes and atrocities and to support actions to bring them to justice;

4. *Calls upon* the Authority, consistent with the Charter of the United Nations and other relevant international law, to promote the welfare of the Iraqi people through the effective administration of the territory, in particular working towards the restoration of conditions of security and stability and the creation of conditions in which the Iraqi people can freely determine their own political future;

5. *Calls upon* all concerned to comply fully with their obligations under international law, in particular the Geneva Conventions of 1949 and the Regulations concerning the Laws and Customs of War on Land, adopted at The Hague on 18 October 1907;

6. *Calls upon* the Authority and relevant organizations and individuals to continue efforts to locate, identify and repatriate all Kuwaiti and third-State nationals or the remains of those present in Iraq on or after 2 August 1990, as well as the Kuwaiti archives, that the

previous Iraqi regime failed to undertake, and in this regard directs the High-Level Coordinator, in consultation with the International Committee of the Red Cross and the Tripartite Commission, and with the appropriate support of the people of Iraq and in coordination with the Authority, to take steps to fulfil his mandate with respect to the fate of Kuwaiti and third-State national missing persons and property;

7. *Decides* that all Member States shall take appropriate steps to facilitate the safe return to Iraqi institutions of Iraqi cultural property and other items of archaeological, historical, cultural, rare scientific and religious importance, illegally removed from the Iraq National Museum, the National Library and other locations in Iraq since the adoption of resolution 661(1990) of 6 August 1990, including by establishing a prohibition on trade in or transfer of such items and items with respect to which reasonable suspicion exists that they have been illegally removed, and calls upon the United Nations Educational, Scientific and Cultural Organization, Interpol and other international organizations, as appropriate, to assist in the implementation of the present paragraph;

8. *Requests* the Secretary-General to appoint a Special Representative for Iraq, whose independent responsibilities shall involve reporting regularly to the Council on his activities pursuant to the present resolution, coordinating activities of the United Nations in post-conflict processes in Iraq, coordinating among United Nations and international agencies engaged in humanitarian assistance and reconstruction activities in Iraq and, in coordination with the Authority, assisting the people of Iraq through:

(a) Coordinating humanitarian and reconstruction assistance by United Nations agencies and between United Nations agencies and non-governmental organizations;

(b) Promoting the safe, orderly and voluntary return of refugees and displaced persons;

(c) Working intensively with the Authority, the people of Iraq and others concerned to advance efforts to restore and establish national and local institutions for representative governance, including by working together to facilitate a process leading to an internationally recognized, representative Government of Iraq;

(d) Facilitating the reconstruction of key infrastructure, in cooperation with other international organizations;

(e) Promoting economic reconstruction and the conditions for sustainable development, including through coordination with national and regional organizations, as appropriate, civil society, donors and the international financial institutions;

(f) Encouraging international efforts to contribute to basic civilian administration functions;

(g) Promoting the protection of human rights;

(h) Encouraging international efforts to rebuild the capacity of the Iraqi civilian police force;

(i) Encouraging international efforts to promote legal and judicial reform;

9. *Supports* the formation, by the people of Iraq with the help of the Authority and working with the Special Representative of the Secretary-General, of an Iraqi interim administration as a transitional administration run by Iraqis until an internationally recognized, representative Government is established by the people of Iraq and assumes the responsibilities of the Authority;

10. *Decides* that, with the exception of prohibitions related to the sale or supply to Iraq of arms and related materiel other than those arms and related materiel required by the Authority to serve the purposes of the present and other related resolutions, all prohibitions related to trade with Iraq and the provision of financial or economic resources to Iraq established pursuant to resolution 661(1990) and subsequent relevant resolutions, including resolution 778(1992) of 2 October 1992, shall no longer apply;

11. *Reaffirms* that Iraq must meet its disarmament obligations, encourages the United Kingdom of Great Britain and Northern Ireland and the United States of America to keep the Council informed of their activities in this regard, and underlines the intention of the Council to revisit the mandates of the United Nations Monitoring, Verification and Inspection Commission and the International Atomic Energy Agency as set forth in resolutions 687(1991) of 3 April 1991, 1284 (1999) of 17 December 1999 and 1441(2002) of 8 November 2002;

12. *Notes* the establishment of a Development Fund for Iraq to be held by the Central Bank of Iraq and to be audited by independent public accountants approved by the International Advisory and Monitoring Board of the Development Fund for Iraq, and looks forward to the early meeting of that Board, whose members shall include duly qualified representatives of the Secretary-General, of the Managing Director of the International Monetary Fund, of the Director-General of the Arab Fund for Social and Economic Development and of the President of the World Bank;

13. *Notes also* that the funds in the Development Fund for Iraq shall be disbursed at the direction of the Authority, in consultation with the Iraqi interim administration, for the purposes set out in paragraph 14 below;

14. *Underlines* the fact that the Development Fund for Iraq shall be used in a transparent manner to meet the humanitarian needs of the Iraqi people, for economic reconstruction and the repair of Iraq's infrastructure, for the continued disarmament of Iraq, for the costs of Iraqi civilian administration and for other purposes benefiting the people of Iraq;

15. *Calls upon* the international financial institutions to assist the people of Iraq in the reconstruction and development of their economy and to facilitate assistance by the broader donor community, and welcomes the readiness of creditors, including those of the Paris Club, to seek a solution to the sovereign debt problems of Iraq;

16. *Requests* that the Secretary-General, in coordination with the Authority, continue the exercise of his responsibilities pursuant to Council resolutions 1472 (2003) of 28 March 2003 and 1476(2003) of 24 April 2003, for a period of six months following the adoption of the present resolution, and terminate within this time period, in the most cost-effective manner, the ongoing operations of the "Oil-for-Food" Programme (the Programme), both at Headquarters level and in the field, transferring responsibility for the administration of any remaining activity under the Programme to the Authority, including by taking the following necessary measures:

(a) To facilitate as soon as possible the shipment and authenticated delivery of priority civilian goods as identified by the Secretary-General and representatives designated by him, in coordination with the Authority and the Iraqi interim administration, under approved and funded contracts previously concluded by the previous Government of Iraq, for the humanitarian relief of the people of Iraq, including, as necessary, negotiating adjustments in the terms or conditions of these contracts and respective letters of credit as set forth in paragraph 4 (d) of resolution 1472(2003);

(b) To review, in the light of changed circumstances, in coordination with the Authority and the Iraqi interim administration, the relative utility of each approved and funded contract with a view to determining whether such contracts contain items required to meet the needs of the people of Iraq both now and during reconstruction, and to postpone action on those contracts determined to be of questionable utility and the respective letters of credit until an internationally recognized, representative Government of Iraq is in a position to make its own determination as to whether such contracts shall be fulfilled;

(c) To provide to the Council within 21 days following the adoption of the present resolution, for the review and consideration of the Council, an estimated operating budget based on funds already set aside in the account established pursuant to paragraph 8 (d) of resolution 986(1995) of 14 April 1995, identifying:

(i) All known and projected costs to the United Nations required to ensure the continued functioning of the activities associated with implementation of the present resolution, including operating and administrative expenses associated with the relevant United Nations agencies and programmes responsible for the implementation of the Programme both at Headquarters and in the field;

(ii) All known and projected costs associated with termination of the Programme;

(iii) All known and projected costs associated with restoring funds of the Government of Iraq that were provided by Member States to the Secretary-General as requested in paragraph 1 of resolution 778(1992);

(iv) All known and projected costs associated with the Special Representative and the qualified representative of the Secretary-General identified to serve on the International Advisory and Monitoring Board, for the six-month time period defined above, following which these costs shall be borne by the United Nations;

(d) To consolidate into a single fund the accounts established pursuant to paragraphs 8 (a) and (b) of resolution 986(1995);

(e) To fulfil all remaining obligations related to the termination of the Programme, including negotiating, in the most cost-effective manner, any necessary settlement payments, which shall be made from the escrow accounts established pursuant to paragraphs 8 (a) and (b) of resolution 986(1995), with those parties that have previously entered into contractual obligations with the Secretary-General under the Programme, and to determine, in coordination with the Authority and the Iraqi interim administration, the future status of contracts undertaken by the United Nations and related agencies under the accounts established pursuant to paragraphs 8 (b) and (d) of resolution 986(1995);

(f) To provide the Council, 30 days prior to the termination of the Programme, with a comprehensive strategy developed in close coordination with the Authority and the Iraqi interim administration that would lead to the delivery of all relevant documentation and the transfer of all operational responsibility of the Programme to the Authority;

17. *Requests also* that the Secretary-General transfer as soon as possible to the Development Fund for Iraq one billion United States dollars from unencumbered funds in the accounts established pursuant to paragraphs 8 (a) and (b) of resolution 986(1995), restore Government of Iraq funds that were provided by Member States to the Secretary-General as requested in paragraph 1 of resolution 778(1992), and decides that, after deducting all relevant United Nations expenses associated with the shipment of authorized contracts and costs to the Programme outlined in paragraph 16 (c) above, including residual obligations, all surplus funds in the escrow accounts established pursuant to paragraphs 8 (a), (b), (d) and (f) of resolution 986(1995) shall be transferred at the earliest possible time to the Development Fund for Iraq;

18. *Decides* to terminate, effective on the adoption of the present resolution, the functions related to the observation and monitoring activities undertaken by the Secretary-General under the Programme, including the monitoring of the export of petroleum and petroleum products from Iraq;

19. *Decides also* to terminate the Security Council Committee established pursuant to paragraph 6 of resolution 661(1990) at the conclusion of the six-month period called for in paragraph 16 above, and decides further that the Committee shall identify individuals and entities referred to in paragraph 23 below;

20. *Decides further* that all export sales of petroleum, petroleum products and natural gas from Iraq following the date of adoption of the present resolution shall be made consistent with prevailing international market best practices, to be audited by independent public accountants reporting to the International Advisory and Monitoring Board referred to in paragraph 12 above in order to ensure transparency, and decides that, except as provided in paragraph 21 below, all proceeds from such sales shall be deposited into the Development Fund for Iraq until such time as an internationally recognized, representative Government of Iraq is properly constituted;

21. *Decides* that 5 per cent of the proceeds referred to in paragraph 20 above shall be deposited into the Compensation Fund established pursuant to resolution 687(1991) and subsequent relevant resolutions and that, unless an internationally recognized, representative Government of Iraq and the Governing Council of the United Nations Compensation Commission, in the exercise of its authority over methods of ensuring that payments are made into the Compensation Fund, decide otherwise, this requirement shall be binding upon a properly constituted, internationally recognized, representative Government of Iraq and any successor thereto;

22. *Notes* the relevance of the establishment of an internationally recognized, representative Government of Iraq and the desirability of prompt completion of

the restructuring of Iraq's debt as referred to in paragraph 15 above, decides that, until 31 December 2007, unless the Council decides otherwise, petroleum, petroleum products and natural gas originating in Iraq shall be immune, until title passes to the initial purchaser, from legal proceedings against them and not be subject to any form of attachment, garnishment or execution, and that all States shall take any steps that may be necessary under their respective domestic legal systems to assure this protection, and that proceeds and obligations arising from sales thereof, as well as the Development Fund for Iraq, shall enjoy privileges and immunities equivalent to those enjoyed by the United Nations except that the above-mentioned privileges and immunities will not apply with respect to any legal proceeding in which recourse to such proceeds or obligations is necessary to satisfy liability for damages assessed in connection with an ecological accident, including an oil spill, that occurs after the date of adoption of the present resolution;

23. *Decides* that all Member States in which there are:

(a) Funds or other financial assets or economic resources of the previous Government of Iraq or its state bodies, corporations, or agencies, located outside Iraq as of the date of adoption of the present resolution; or

(b) Funds or other financial assets or economic resources that have been removed from Iraq or acquired by Saddam Hussein or other senior officials of the former Iraqi regime and their immediate family members, including entities owned or controlled, directly or indirectly, by them or by persons acting on their behalf or at their direction,

shall freeze without delay those funds or other financial assets or economic resources and, unless these funds or other financial assets or economic resources are themselves the subject of a prior judicial, administrative or arbitral lien or judgement, immediately shall cause their transfer to the Development Fund for Iraq, it being understood that, unless otherwise addressed, claims made by private individuals or non-government entities on those transferred funds or other financial assets may be presented to the internationally recognized, representative Government of Iraq; and decides also that all such funds or other financial assets or economic resources shall enjoy the same privileges, immunities, and protections as provided under paragraph 22 above;

24. *Requests* the Secretary-General to report to the Council at regular intervals on the work of his Special Representative with respect to the implementation of the present resolution and on the work of the International Advisory and Monitoring Board, and encourages the United Kingdom of Great Britain and Northern Ireland and the United States of America to inform the Council at regular intervals of their efforts pursuant to the present resolution;

25. *Decides* to review the implementation of the present resolution within twelve months of the adoption thereof and to consider further steps that might be necessary;

26. *Calls upon* Member States and international and regional organizations to contribute to the implementation of the present resolution;

27. *Decides* to remain seized of this matter.

VOTE ON RESOLUTION 1483(2003):

In favour: Angola, Bulgaria, Cameroon, Chile, China, France, Germany, Guinea, Mexico, Pakistan, Russian Federation, Spain, United Kingdom, United States.
Against: None.

Speaking after the vote, the United States said that the lifting of sanctions marked a momentous event for the people of Iraq. The United Nations was to play a vital role in rebuilding Iraq. By recognizing the fluidity of the political situation and that decisions would be made on the ground, the Council had provided a flexible framework under Chapter VII for the Authority, Member States, the United Nations and others in the international community to participate in the administration and reconstruction of Iraq. The resolution affirmed the commitment to the development of an internationally recognized representative Iraqi Government and created a robust mandate for the Secretary-General's Special Representative. The resolution also established a framework for an orderly phase-out of the oil-for-food programme, thereby preserving, for a transitional period, what had become a safety net for the Iraqi people. In addition, it established transparency in all processes and UN participation in monitoring the sale of Iraqi oil resources and expenditures of oil proceeds. In that context, the United States was pleased to announce the creation of the Development Fund for Iraq in the Central Bank of Iraq. The Authority would disburse funds only for the purposes it determined to benefit the Iraqi people. The resolution lifted export restrictions to Iraq, with the exception of trade in arms and related materiel not required by the Authority. Aviation restrictions were also lifted, but Iraq's disarmament obligations remained, and Member States were still barred from assisting Iraq in acquiring WMD and proscribed missile systems or proceeding with civil nuclear activities so long as those restrictions remained in effect. The resolution provided Iraq with adequate time to recover capacity eroded during the sanctions years, yet it preserved its obligations to Kuwait and others who suffered from Saddam Hussein's aggression dating from 1990. It addressed Iraq's sovereign debt, the violations of human rights and international humanitarian law by the previous regime. It also directed Member States to act quickly to seize and return to the Iraqi people money stolen by the Hussein regime.

The Secretary-General said that the international community should be gratified that the Council had come together to chart the way forward in Iraq. The Council had adopted a resolution that spelled out the assistance it expected the United Nations to give to the people of Iraq in coordination with the occupying Powers, which had the responsibility for the effective administration of the territory. The most important task would be to ensure that the Iraqi people were able as soon as possible, through a transparent and impartially managed political process, to form a free and representative Government of their own choice. The Secretary-General would nominate his Special Representative without delay (see below).

Special Representative

On 23 May [S/2003/570], the Secretary-General informed the Security Council President of his intention to appoint as his Special Representative for Iraq, for a period of four months, Sergio Vieira de Mello (Brazil), the UN High Commissioner for Human Rights.

On 27 May [S/2003/571], the Council took note of the Secretary-General's intention.

Communication (3 June). On 3 June [S/2003/612], Iran transmitted to the Secretary-General the Joint Declaration on the regional initiative regarding Iraq, issued by Iraq's neighbouring countries during the thirtieth session of the Islamic Conference of Foreign Ministers (Tehran, 28-30 May). The Foreign Ministers of Bahrain, Egypt, Iran, Jordan, Kuwait, Saudi Arabia, the Syrian Arab Republic and Turkey reiterated the right of the Iraqi people to freely determine their political future and to establish a fully representative and broad-based Government in a safe and peaceful environment. They also emphasized the inalienable right of the Iraqi people to enjoy a decent and comfortable life based on the rule of law, equality and respect for fundamental human rights and freedoms. They underlined the central role of the United Nations in post-war Iraq, especially with regard to the establishment of a representative Government, rehabilitation of local institutions, provision of humanitarian relief and reconstruction, and called for the speedy restoration of full Iraqi sovereignty through the establishment of a legitimate Government and an end to occupation.

Security Council consideration (5 June). On 5 June [meeting 4768], the Council was briefed by the UNMOVIC Executive Chairman, Mr. Blix, on UNMOVIC's report covering 1 March to 31 May [S/2003/580] (see p. 317). He said that for many years neither UNSCOM nor UNMOVIC made significant finds of proscribed weapons, probably because the items were unilaterally destroyed by the Iraqi authorities or else because they were effectively concealed by them. He trusted that in the new environment in Iraq, in which there was full access and cooperation, and in which knowledgeable witnesses should no longer be inhibited from revealing what they knew, it should be possible to establish the truth about those weapons. In resolution 1483(2003) (see p. 338), the Council declared its intention to revisit the mandate of UNMOVIC, and it was aware that UNMOVIC remained ready to resume work in Iraq as an independent verifier or to conduct long-term monitoring, should the Council so decide. Mr. Blix said that his briefing was likely to be his last one and he thanked the Secretary-General and the UN Secretariat for the cooperation they had provided since the creation of UNMOVIC.

The Council President took note of Mr. Blix's intention to retire from his post at the end of June and expressed the Council's gratitude to him for his service.

Communication (10 June). On 10 June [A/58/94-S/2003/642], the Russian Federation transmitted to the Secretary-General the text of the Declaration by the heads of State of the members of the Shanghai Cooperation Organization (Moscow, 29 May) (China, Kazakhstan, Kyrgyzstan, the Russian Federation, Tajikistan, Uzbekistan). The Declaration, among other things, noted that the United Nations should have an important role to play in the reconstruction of Iraq. A precondition for that country's transition to peace and the building of a democratic society was respect for the national interests and sovereign rights of the Iraqi people and concrete and effective aid on the part of the international community.

Report of Secretary-General (July). In response to resolution 1483(2003), the Secretary-General submitted a 17 July report [S/2003/715] on the work of his Special Representative with respect to the implementation of that resolution, provided an initial assessment of the scope of the challenges involved in implementing the mandate conferred by the resolution and recommended an overall approach and structure for the UN presence in Iraq for the remainder of 2003, taking into account the Council's request to terminate the oil-for-food programme in November 2003.

The Secretary-General's Special Representative, Sergio Vieira de Mello, arrived in Baghdad on 2 June and embarked on broad consultations to define the UN role. He had brought Iraqi and Authority representatives together with the United Nations to discuss issues such as the rule of law, past human rights violations and the constitutional process. Contacts had also been initiated with representatives of the diplomatic community in Baghdad and visiting parliamentary delegations. Several common themes ran through the discussions that the Special Representative had with Iraqis of different backgrounds. There was an overwhelming demand for the early restoration of sovereignty and the message was conveyed that democracy could not be imposed from outside. Serious concern was expressed about the process of de-Ba'athification and the dissolution of the Iraqi army. Above all, the Special Representative's contacts expressed deep concern about the precarious, some believed deteriorating, security situation, particularly in Baghdad. Many Iraqis lodged criticism about aspects of the past UN record in Iraq, but they also expressed appreciation for UN humanitarian efforts and stressed the need for the Organization to play an active role, not least in facilitating and supporting the political transition process.

The Special Representative had made efforts to meet with many Iraqi political groups, both the newly emerging and those well established. Their unanimous concern was the urgent need to establish an Iraqi provisional government that could help address some of the immediate practical challenges faced in the country. Iraqis emphasized that they themselves had to conduct the constitutional process and that an Iraqi interim authority should be in place before such a process began. The Special Representative strongly advocated that the Authority devolve real executive authority to a broadly representative and self-selecting Iraqi leadership, including in policy- and decision-making, and in the preparation and execution of a budget. That advice was favourably received by the Authority and, on 13 July, it established the Governing Council, the principal body of the interim administration of Iraq, a move that was welcomed by the Secretary-General. The 25-member Council, which included three women, had a slight Shi'ah majority and an equal representation of Kurds and Sunnis, with additional Christian and Turkmen representation. The Council would name an interim minister for each ministry and would have the right to set policies and take decisions, in cooperation with the Authority, and to designate international representation during the interim period. The Council would also consider appointing a preparatory constitutional commission to recommend a process by which a new constitution would be prepared and approved. According to the Authority, the full restoration of sovereignty would come after the drafting of a new constitution and the holding of national elections. The Special Representative had proposed that voter registration should begin in the near future to demonstrate that tangible steps were being taken to pave the way for elections. To that end, the Secretary-General had instructed the Electoral Assistance Division of the UN Department of Political Affairs to send an assessment mission to Iraq to discuss with relevant Iraqi and Authority counterparts the various possible modalities for electoral registration and the electoral process. The Secretary-General said that the United Nations could make a significant contribution in the constitutional and electoral processes, as its involvement would confer legitimacy and place at the disposal of the Iraqi people the wealth of experience accrued by the United Nations in those fields over the years.

Lack of security and restricted freedom of movement had affected UN activities, particularly humanitarian work, and had the potential to impair reconstruction planning. The work of the UN humanitarian agencies was further impeded by the massive presence of explosive ordnance, mines and unexploded ordnance. So far, UN personnel had seldom been the target of deliberate hostility, with the exception of one incident in the city of Basra on 17 June when a crowd trapped two UN vehicles, apparently not distinguishing the United Nations from the Authority. Both vehicles were eventually released. Shots were fired outside the UN compound at the Canal Hotel in Baghdad on 29 June, causing Coalition forces to go into high alert. On 6 July, a World Food Programme (WFP) office in Mosul and later an empty WFP vehicle were attacked by armed individuals; no WFP staff were hurt in those incidents. However, the international staff presence in Mosul was reduced from 27 to 4. UN contractors and facilities remained vulnerable to criminal activity, both random and organized. For ordinary Iraqis and UN personnel, the principal security threat came from violent crime. Criminals, some of whom were organized and most of whom were armed, continued to take advantage of the easy availability of weapons and the vacuum in rule-of-law institutions. The principal concerns of Iraqis included the lack of personal security and of basic services such as water, electricity and fuel. Some concern had been expressed at the potentially serious implications of the recent dissolution by the Authority of the Iraqi army, which numbered half a million personnel. The United Nations had made available to the Authority its experience and body of best practice in disarmament, demobilization and reintegration. At the Authority's request, a small team of UN experts flew to Baghdad for a week to provide information on lessons learned from previous disarmament programmes run by the Organization.

The Special Representative had also been engaged in a preliminary process of identifying the human rights challenges in Iraq and assessing the resources needed to address them. On 30 June and 1 July, the Special Representative and his team convened the first human rights conference under UN auspices in Baghdad. Organized jointly with the Office of the High Commissioner for Human Rights, the conference brought together Iraqi and international experts, in addition to the Authority, to share perspectives, identify practical measures and develop policy options on justice for past crimes. A central concern raised at the conference was the Authority's actions, especially the treatment and conditions of detention of Iraqi prisoners. The Special Representative had urged the Authority to ensure better treatment of detainees and urged a continued dialogue with the International Committee of the Red Cross (ICRC) on that issue. Vital to the promotion of human rights and respect for the rule of law was the development of civil society, in particular effective and independent human rights and women's rights groups, and free and independent media. To that end, the Special Representative had placed emphasis on training. The United Nations had already been called upon by various sources to train public officials, particularly those involved in the administration of justice. The Special Representative intended to examine the possibility of providing such training, and the possibility of specific programmes to ensure access to justice by vulnerable groups. He also emphasized to all political parties and movements the need to promote the full participation of Iraqi women in the transitional political and constitutional processes.

A number of Governments had informally approached the Special Representative to explore the possibility of deploying international police under UN auspices. Currently, executive law enforcement responsibilities in Iraq were the sole responsibility of the Authority, under resolution 1483(2003). Discussions on that issue between the Special Representative and the Authority had led the Secretary-General to believe that establishing an international police force, under UN auspices, could create a parallel system of law enforcement, which would not be effective for improving law and order. There was scope for UN involvement in the area of civilian policing, in terms of making available its experience in aspects of local police training and development. The UN initial focus would be to provide input into the human rights provisions of the training curricula for the newly recruited Iraqi police, and to provide advice to the Authority and the relevant Iraqi law enforcement institutions, once established, on the development and implementation of independent law enforcement oversight mechanisms. Justice was the focus of the first trilateral meeting (25 June) convened by the United Nations with representatives of the Iraqi judicial community and the Authority. The purpose was to share the UN experience in fostering reform of the judicial system and to provide a forum for promoting dialogue among Iraqis on the issue.

Under international humanitarian law, the Authority bore the primary responsibility for the welfare of the Iraqi people, including the provision of public services. UN agencies had been assisting and would continue to assist the Iraqi people under their standing humanitarian mandates. The UN revised humanitarian appeal for Iraq was launched on 23 June (see also p. 936), specifying requirements for an additional $259 million for the UN system to ensure that it could carry out its activities until the end of 2003. The Special Representative would work to ensure as smooth and integrated a transition as possible from humanitarian and emergency rehabilitation work to economic recovery and reconstruction. To that end, the Secretary-General had designated the Humanitarian Coordinator, Ramiro Lopes da Silva (Portugal), as his Deputy Special Representative and as Resident Coordinator to oversee that process, which entailed, among other things, supervising the winding down, completion and transfer to the Authority of the oil-for-food programme, as prescribed in Council resolution 1483(2003) (see p. 338). The United Nations, in concert with the Authority, had begun to review the applications that had been prioritized and was seeking to verify that the requisite procedures established by the Office of the Iraq Programme had been fully respected and that the process was transparent. All parties were confident that the review of approved and funded applications would be completed prior to the cessation of the programme in November 2003.

UN agencies were in transition from activities launched under the humanitarian appeal on 23 June and progressively moving into reconstruction, recovery and development activities. An informal meeting on reconstruction in Iraq, held in New York on 24 June, helped to further define the framework for the coordination of reconstruction and development efforts.

The Secretary-General said that the focus of UN action in Iraq for the remainder of 2003 would include the following: delivering humanitarian assistance, promoting the safe, orderly and voluntary return of refugees and displaced persons, and conducting emergency rehabilitation; engaging in the facilitation of national dialogue and consensus-building on the political transition process; assisting in the establishment of electoral processes; promoting the protection of human rights; implementing, through UNDP, two concrete projects relating to the emergency rehabilitation of the courts and support for the Judicial Training Centre in Baghdad; establishing an Iraqi media centre; ensuring the orderly phasing out of the oil-for-food programme by 21 November 2003; contributing, through UNDP and international financial institutions, to assessing potential needs for economic reconstruction and sustainable development; sharing UN experiences and lessons learned with Iraqis and the Authority on post-conflict processes in general, as requested; and assisting the Iraqi interim administration to gradually rejoin the international community.

The Secretary-General outlined the structure for the proposed United Nations Assistance Mission for Iraq (UNAMI). In view of the broad range of responsibilities entrusted to the Special Representative, it was envisaged that the staff strength should consist of over 300 civilian staff combined. That figure was inclusive of both substantive and support international and local personnel in Baghdad and each of the regions. The number of international staff would be less than half the total figure, as UNAMI would rely on a skilled Iraqi force. UNAMI's structure envisaged maximum reliance on the existing capacity and structure of the Office of the Humanitarian Coordinator and on the Humanitarian Coordinator himself, whom the Secretary-General concurrently appointed as the Resident Coordinator of the UN country team (of agencies, funds and programmes) and as his Deputy Special Representative for Iraq.

The Secretary-General observed that Iraq could not be treated in isolation from the region. He believed that an inclusive way of working with Iraq's neighbours would need to be found. The Special Representative intended to continue the contacts that the Secretary-General had initiated in Amman, Jordan, during a visit from 21 to 23 June and before long would visit all of Iraq's neighbours.

Security Council consideration (July). On 22 July [meeting 4791], the Council discussed the situation in Iraq and heard a briefing by the Special Representative of the Secretary-General for Iraq, Mr. Vieira de Mello. At the request of Spain [S/2003/750], members of the Governing Council of Iraq participated in the discussion without the right to vote. The Council had before it the Secretary-General's 17 July report.

Introducing the Secretary-General's report, Mr. Vieira de Mello said that the formation in July of Iraq's Governing Council was a significant step forward and a new stage that succeeded the disorienting power vacuum left from the fall of the previous regime. He had visited Iran, Saudi Arabia and the Syrian Arab Republic and had accompanied the Secretary-General to Amman in June, where they had held talks on Iraq and resolution 1483(2003) (see p. 338). He reported that all the regional officials and leaders he met with expressed their desire to see a new Iraq at peace with itself and its neighbours and wished the United Nations to take the lead in achieving that vision.

Security in Iraq remained tenuous. It was imperative that law and order be restored throughout the country as soon as possible as, without them, every area of activity would be impacted for the worse. Iraqis cooperating with the Authority, as well as Iraqi policemen, had been the subject of attacks. In parallel, common law criminality was a major problem. The potential impact of the violence could not be underestimated as it threatened to undermine confidence in the transition and to shake the resolve of Iraqis committed to leading their country though a very delicate period in its history. The UN presence in Iraq remained vulnerable; UN security in Iraq relied significantly on the reputation of the United Nations and its ability to demonstrate its independence. The United Nations was in Iraq to assist the people.

Iraq found itself in a difficult position: a post-conflict situation, but with hostilities occurring every day, awash with weapons and under military occupation. In that context, the protection of human rights was a major concern. The Special Representative had raised with the Authority concerns regarding searches, arrests, the treatment of detainees and the duration of preventive detention. He had also visited the main Iraqi detention complex at Abu Ghraib. The Authority had provided him with responses on action taken to address and resolve those questions.

The Special Representative concluded that, in order to succeed, the Governing Council would need the full support of the international community and of the Iraqi people, whose trust it would need to earn anew each day. It had to be empowered to deliver tangible improvements to the welfare of the population while not becoming the object of criticism. There was also a need for a clear timetable for the earliest restoration of Iraqi sovereignty. Resolution 1483(2003) provided considerable scope for the United Nations to play an effective role in Iraq. It was not a clear mandate, but at the same time the situation in Iraq was exceptional and therefore it required an exceptional approach. The lack of clarity allowed the UN role in Iraq to emerge and develop as the situation on the ground evolved. What the United Nations could not do was replace the Authority, nor should it ever replace the rightful role that Iraqis had to play in shaping the future of their country. What the United Nations could do was to help build consensus among Iraqis and between Iraqis and the Authority.

The head of the delegation of the Governing Council of Iraq, Adnan Pachachi, said that Iraq had rid itself of the tyrannical regime that oppressed the Iraqi people for three decades. A State marked by the intelligence services, mandatory arrests and random executions had ended, never to return. The primary goal of the Governing Council was to shorten the duration of the interim administration period and put together an elected Government under a constitution to be endorsed by the population in free elections. The Governing Council would need to ensure security and stability and to establish institutions that could rebuild the national police and the national army. There was also a need to appoint ministers and to reopen Iraqi embassies abroad. Iraq would require assistance in all areas in order to rebuild its economy, modernize its industrial sector, reform its educational system, improve its sanitation services and provide basic necessities to all its citizens. The United Nations would have a vital role to play in all those areas. In addition, there was a need to re-examine the legislation enacted by the previous regime and to constitute special tribunals in order to bring to justice those who committed criminal acts under that regime.

Communication (31 July). On 31 July [S/2003/782], the United States transmitted to the Council President a letter from the Acting Governor of the Central Bank of Iraq, who said that resolution 1483(2003) (see p. 338) created an obligation for all Member States to identify, freeze and transfer to the Development Fund for Iraq all funds, financial assets or economic resources in their jurisdictions that were established or held by the previous Iraqi Government. Those funds and resources included not only those of the previous Government, but also those of its State bodies, corporations, agencies and entities that had been removed from Iraq or acquired by Saddam Hussein or other senior officials of the former Iraqi regime and their immediate family members. Those funds were urgently needed for humanitarian, reconstruction, civilian administration and other purposes benefiting the people of Iraq.

Establishment of UNAMI

On 14 August [meeting 4808], the Security Council adopted **resolution 1500(2003)** by vote (14-0-1). The draft [S/2003/812] was submitted by Angola, Bulgaria, Cameroon, Chile, Guinea, Spain, the United Kingdom and the United States.

The Security Council,

Recalling all its relevant resolutions, in particular resolution 1483(2003) of 22 May 2003,

Reaffirming the sovereignty and territorial integrity of Iraq,

Reaffirming also the vital role for the United Nations in Iraq which was set out in relevant paragraphs of resolution 1483(2003),

Having considered the report of the Secretary-General of 17 July 2003,

1. *Welcomes* the establishment of the broadly representative Governing Council of Iraq on 13 July 2003, as an important step towards the formation by the people of Iraq of an internationally recognized, representative government that will exercise the sovereignty of Iraq;

2. *Decides* to establish the United Nations Assistance Mission for Iraq to support the Secretary-General in the fulfilment of his mandate under resolution 1483(2003), in accordance with the structure and responsibilities set out in his report of 17 July 2003, for an initial period of twelve months;

3. *Decides* to remain seized of this matter.

VOTE ON RESOLUTION 1500(2003):

In favour: Angola, Bulgaria, Cameroon, Chile, China, France, Germany, Guinea, Mexico, Pakistan, Russian Federation, Spain, United Kingdom, United States.
Against: None.
Abstaining: Syrian Arab Republic.

Speaking after the vote, the United States said the adopted resolution sent a clear signal to those who opposed the political transformation under way in Iraq that they were out of step with world opinion. The resolution endorsed the vital role that the United Nations was playing in Iraq. The United States supported the Secretary-General's request to create UNAMI.

The Syrian Arab Republic said that it had abstained in the vote in keeping with its responsibility as the Arab representative on the Council. All Arab States supported the need to end the occupation of Iraq and to form a legitimate national Iraqi Government, as soon as possible and within a clear time frame. Syria regretted that consultations on the draft resolution did not include the input of rotating members of the Council, including Syria.

Attack on UN headquarters in Baghdad

On 19 August, at approximately 1630 hours local time, a flatbed truck carrying an estimated 1,000 kilograms of high explosives was detonated on the service road adjacent to the south-west corner of the Canal Hotel, UN headquarters in Baghdad. The attack was carefully planned and deliberately targeted the compound's weakest point, with devastating effect. It resulted in the death of 22 persons (15 of them UN staff members) and the wounding of more than 150. The Special Representative for Iraq and UN High Commissioner for Human Rights, Mr. Vieira de

Mello, was among those killed. The attack represented the most deliberate and devastating attack against the United Nations in its history.

In a 19 August press statement [SG/SM/8822-IK/375], the Secretary-General denounced the attack as an inexcusable act of unprovoked and murderous violence against men and women who went to Iraq to help the Iraqi people. In a second press statement [SG/SM/8823-IK/376], issued after the death of Mr. Vieira de Mello was confirmed, he said that the loss of his top envoy for Iraq was a bitter blow for the United Nations and for him personally.

Communications (19-20 August). On 19 August [S/2003/822], the Russian Federation expressed shock at the terrorist act against the UN compound in Baghdad.

On 20 August [S/2003/827], Malaysia, on behalf of the Non-Aligned Movement, condemning the attack, said that such attacks could not break the will of the international community to continue to extend all possible assistance to the Iraqi people to regain their national sovereignty.

SECURITY COUNCIL ACTION (20 August)

On 20 August [meeting 4811], following consultations among Security Council members, the President made statement **S/PRST/2003/13** on behalf of the Council:

> The Security Council unequivocally condemns the terrorist attack that took place on 19 August 2003 against the United Nations headquarters in Baghdad and thereby against the international community as a whole, causing numerous deaths and injuries among international personnel and Iraqi people.
>
> The Council condemns in the strongest terms the perpetrators of that attack and underlines the need to bring them to justice.
>
> The Council pays tribute to and expresses its deepest admiration for all those among the United Nations personnel who have lost their lives or have been injured in the service of the United Nations and of the Iraqi people, including the Special Representative of the Secretary-General, Mr. Sergio Vieira de Mello.
>
> The Council expresses its deepest sympathy and condolences to the victims and their families.
>
> The Council reaffirms the imperative to respect, in all circumstances, the safety and security of United Nations personnel and the need for adequate security measures to be taken in this regard.
>
> The Council reaffirms its determination to assist the Iraqi people to build peace and justice in their country and to determine their own political future by themselves. It welcomes in this regard the determination of the United Nations to continue its operation in Iraq to fulfil its mandate in the service of the Iraqi people, and will not be intimidated by such attacks.

Security Council consideration (21 August). On 21 August [meeting 4812], the Council heard briefings from the representatives of the United States and the United Kingdom on Iraq. Both countries expressed outrage at the attack against the United Nations and extended their deepest sympathies to the victims and their families.

The United States said that the timing of the attack was no accident; it occurred at a critical juncture, when the impact of initial plans and efforts had begun to take positive effect. A secure, democratic and stable Iraq was a threat and a target for those who wished to turn the clock back to the days of tyranny. As a response, the Security Council had to stand together and invigorate its struggle against terrorism. The United States highlighted some markers of progress since the adoption of resolution 1483(2003), the most significant of which was the formation of the Governing Council. The Authority was working to improve economic and security conditions. It had initiated programmes to enable Iraqis to develop a capacity to foil saboteurs who targeted their electrical infrastructure, oil industry and other sectors critical to Iraq's renewal. Tens of thousands of Iraqi police had answered the call to return to work, and recruitment and training were under way to put thousands more on the streets. Nearly 38,000 police officers were deployed throughout the country, some 6,000 in Baghdad. The ultimate goal was to have approximately 65,000 police countrywide. The Authority had also started training a new Iraqi army.

The United Kingdom highlighted progress in the humanitarian, education and health sectors. It also reported on efforts to establish representative governance, especially at the local level, and on human rights reforms.

Appointment of acting Special Representative. On 22 August [S/2003/830], the Secretary-General informed the Council President that, owing to the untimely death of Mr. Vieira de Mello, he had appointed, on an interim basis, Ramiro Lopes da Silva as his acting Special Representative for Iraq.

On the same day [S/2003/831], the Council took note of the Secretary-General's appointment.

Communications (22 August–8 September). On 22 August [A/58/315-S/2003/845], Mali, on behalf of the Human Security Network (Austria, Canada, Chile, Greece, Ireland, Jordan, Mali, Netherlands, Norway, Slovenia, South Africa, Switzerland, Thailand), condemned the 19 August terrorist attacks committed against the United Nations in Baghdad and expressed concern about the increasing number of attacks against the personnel of international organizations in conflict areas.

On 8 September [S/2003/867], Poland informed the Council President that it had decided to dispatch stability forces (both military and an adequate civilian component) and lead a multinational division of stability forces in the central-south sector of Iraq.

General Assembly action. On 15 September, the General Assembly condemned the attack on UN personnel and premises in Baghdad **(resolution 57/338)** (see p. 1452).

Downsizing of UN staff in Iraq

On 25 September [SG/SM/8899-IK/395], the Secretary-General ordered the temporary redeployment of UN international staff in Iraq. International staff members remaining in the country totalled 86, and that number could be expected to diminish even further. Essential humanitarian activities in Iraq would continue, thanks to the efforts of more than 4,000 national staff.

Communication (3 October). On 3 October [A/58/415-S/2003/952], Iran transmitted to the Secretary-General the final communiqué of the Annual Coordination Meeting of Ministers for Foreign Affairs of the member States of OIC (New York, 30 September). The Ministers, among other things, emphasized the responsibility of the occupying Powers to safeguard the civil and religious liberties of the Iraqi people. They also took note of resolution 1483(2003) (see p. 338) and called on member States to support and assist Iraq in its efforts to reactivate economic institutions and infrastructure.

SECURITY COUNCIL ACTION (October)

On 16 October [meeting 4844], the Council unanimously adopted **resolution 1511(2003)**. The draft [S/2003/992] was submitted by Cameroon, Spain, the United Kingdom and the United States.

The Security Council,

Reaffirming its previous resolutions on Iraq, including resolutions 1483(2003) of 22 May 2003 and 1500 (2003) of 14 August 2003, and its resolutions on threats to international peace and security caused by terrorist acts, including resolution 1373(2001) of 28 September 2001, and other relevant resolutions,

Underscoring that the sovereignty of Iraq resides in the State of Iraq, reaffirming the right of the Iraqi people freely to determine their own political future and control their own natural resources, reiterating its resolve that the day when Iraqis govern themselves must come quickly, and recognizing the importance of international support, particularly that of countries in the region, Iraq's neighbours, and regional organizations, in taking forward this process expeditiously,

Recognizing that international support for the restoration of conditions of stability and security is essential to the well-being of the people of Iraq as well as to the ability of all concerned to carry out their work on behalf of the people of Iraq, and welcoming contributions by Member States in this regard under resolution 1483(2003),

Welcoming the decision of the Governing Council of Iraq to form a preparatory constitutional committee to prepare for a constitutional conference that will draft a constitution to embody the aspirations of the Iraqi people, and urging it to complete this process quickly,

Affirming that the terrorist bombings of the Embassy of Jordan on 7 August 2003, of the United Nations headquarters in Baghdad on 19 August 2003, of the Imam Ali Mosque in Najaf on 29 August 2003 and of the Embassy of Turkey on 14 October 2003, and the murder of a Spanish diplomat on 9 October 2003 are attacks on the people of Iraq, the United Nations and the international community, and deploring the assassination of Dr. Akila al-Hashimi, who died on 25 September 2003, as an attack directed against the future of Iraq,

Recalling and reaffirming, in that context, the statement by its President of 20 August 2003 and its resolution 1502(2003) of 26 August 2003,

Determining that the situation in Iraq, although improved, continues to constitute a threat to international peace and security,

Acting under Chapter VII of the Charter of the United Nations,

1. *Reaffirms* the sovereignty and territorial integrity of Iraq, and underscores, in that context, the temporary nature of the exercise by the Coalition Provisional Authority ("the Authority") of the specific responsibilities, authorities and obligations under applicable international law recognized and set forth in resolution 1483(2003), which will cease when an internationally recognized, representative government established by the people of Iraq is sworn in and assumes the responsibilities of the Authority, inter alia, through steps envisaged in paragraphs 4 to 7 and 10 below;

2. *Welcomes* the positive response of the international community, in forums such as the League of Arab States, the Organization of the Islamic Conference, the United Nations General Assembly and the United Nations Educational, Scientific and Cultural Organization, to the establishment of the broadly representative Governing Council of Iraq as an important step towards an internationally recognized, representative government;

3. *Supports* the efforts of the Governing Council to mobilize the people of Iraq, including by the appointment of a cabinet of ministers and a preparatory constitutional committee to lead a process in which the Iraqi people will progressively take control of their own affairs;

4. *Determines* that the Governing Council and its ministers are the principal bodies of the Iraqi interim administration, which, without prejudice to its further evolution, embodies the sovereignty of the State of Iraq during the transitional period until an internationally recognized, representative government is established and assumes the responsibilities of the Authority;

5. *Affirms* that the administration of Iraq will be progressively undertaken by the evolving structures of the Iraqi interim administration;

6. *Calls upon* the Authority, in this context, to return governing responsibilities and authorities to the people of Iraq as soon as practicable, and requests the Authority, in cooperation, as appropriate, with the Governing Council and the Secretary-General, to report to the Security Council on the progress being made;

7. *Invites* the Governing Council to provide to the Security Council for its review, no later than 15 December 2003, in cooperation with the Authority and, as circumstances permit, the Special Representative of the Secretary-General, a timetable and a programme for the drafting of a new constitution for Iraq and for the holding of democratic elections under that constitution;

8. *Resolves* that the United Nations, acting through the Secretary-General, his Special Representative and the United Nations Assistance Mission for Iraq, should strengthen its vital role in Iraq, including by providing humanitarian relief, promoting the economic reconstruction of and conditions for sustainable development in Iraq, and advancing efforts to restore and establish national and local institutions for representative government;

9. *Requests* that, as circumstances permit, the Secretary-General pursue the course of action outlined in paragraphs 98 and 99 of his report of 17 July 2003;

10. *Takes note* of the intention of the Governing Council to hold a constitutional conference and, recognizing that the convening of the conference will be a milestone in the movement to the full exercise of sovereignty, calls for its preparation through national dialogue and consensus-building as soon as practicable, and requests the Special Representative of the Secretary-General, at the time of the convening of the conference or as circumstances permit, to lend the unique expertise of the United Nations to the Iraqi people in this process of political transition, including the establishment of electoral processes;

11. *Requests* the Secretary-General to ensure that the resources of the United Nations and associated organizations are available if requested by the Governing Council and, as circumstances permit, to assist in the furtherance of the programme provided by the Governing Council under paragraph 7 above, and encourages other organizations with expertise in this area to support the Governing Council if requested;

12. *Also requests* the Secretary-General to report to the Security Council on his responsibilities under the present resolution and the development and implementation of a timetable and programme under paragraph 7 above;

13. *Determines* that the provision of security and stability is essential to the successful completion of the political process as outlined in paragraph 7 above and to the ability of the United Nations to contribute effectively to that process and the implementation of resolution 1483(2003), and authorizes a multinational force under unified command to take all necessary measures to contribute to the maintenance of security and stability in Iraq, including for the purpose of ensuring necessary conditions for the implementation of the timetable and programme, as well as to contribute to the security of the United Nations Assistance Mission for Iraq, the Governing Council and other institutions of the Iraqi interim administration, and key humanitarian and economic infrastructure;

14. *Urges* Member States to contribute assistance under this United Nations mandate, including military forces, to the multinational force referred to in paragraph 13 above;

15. *Decides* that it shall review the requirements and mission of the multinational force referred to in paragraph 13 above not later than one year from the date of adoption of the present resolution, and that in any case the mandate of the force shall expire upon the completion of the political process as described in paragraphs 4 to 7 and 10 above, and expresses its readiness to consider on that occasion any future need for the continuation of the multinational force, taking into account the views of an internationally recognized, representative government of Iraq;

16. *Emphasizes* the importance of establishing effective Iraqi police and security forces in maintaining law, order and security and combating terrorism consistent with paragraph 4 of resolution 1483(2003), and calls upon Member States and international and regional organizations to contribute to the training and equipping of Iraqi police and security forces;

17. *Expresses its deep sympathy and condolences* for the personal losses suffered by the Iraqi people and by the United Nations and the families of those United Nations personnel and other innocent victims who were killed or injured in recent tragic attacks;

18. *Unequivocally condemns* the terrorist bombings of the Embassy of Jordan on 7 August 2003, of the United Nations headquarters in Baghdad on 19 August 2003, of the Imam Ali Mosque in Najaf on 29 August 2003 and of the Embassy of Turkey on 14 October 2003, the murder of a Spanish diplomat on 9 October 2003 and the assassination of Dr. Akila al-Hashimi, who died on 25 September 2003, and emphasizes that those responsible must be brought to justice;

19. *Calls upon* Member States to prevent the transit of terrorists to Iraq, arms for terrorists and financing that would support terrorists, and emphasizes the importance of strengthening the cooperation of the countries of the region, particularly neighbours of Iraq, in this regard;

20. *Appeals* to Member States and the international financial institutions to strengthen their efforts to assist the people of Iraq in the reconstruction and development of their economy, and urges those institutions to take immediate steps to provide their full range of loans and other financial assistance to Iraq, working with the Governing Council and appropriate Iraqi ministries;

21. *Urges* Member States and international and regional organizations to support the Iraq reconstruction effort initiated at the United Nations technical consultations of 24 June 2003, including through substantial pledges at the international donors conference to be held in Madrid on 23 and 24 October 2003;

22. *Calls upon* Member States and concerned organizations to help meet the needs of the Iraqi people by providing resources necessary for the rehabilitation and reconstruction of Iraq's economic infrastructure;

23. *Emphasizes* that the International Advisory and Monitoring Board referred to in paragraph 12 of resolution 1483(2003) should be established as a priority, and reiterates that the Development Fund for Iraq

shall be used in a transparent manner as set out in paragraph 14 of resolution 1483(2003);

24. *Reminds* all Member States of their obligations under paragraphs 19 and 23 of resolution 1483(2003), in particular the obligation to immediately cause the transfer of funds, other financial assets and economic resources to the Development Fund for Iraq for the benefit of the Iraqi people;

25. *Requests* that the United States of America, on behalf of the multinational force as outlined in paragraph 13 above, report to the Security Council on the efforts and progress of this force, as appropriate and not less than every six months;

26. *Decides* to remain seized of the matter.

Speaking after the vote, the Secretary-General commended Council members for having reached a significant agreement on what was a particularly important resolution to address the complex situation in Iraq. It was critical to the Iraqi people, the region and the entire international community that the goal of an Iraq at peace with itself and with its neighbours be reached. The Secretary-General said he would do his utmost to implement the mandate established by the Council, bearing in mind the constraints on building up the required capacity and his obligation to care for the safety and security of UN staff. He was grateful to the Council for the flexibility that the new resolution gave him in that respect. Although the United Nations had only a skeletal presence on the ground, the Organization was determined to continue helping the Iraqi people from both inside and outside the country, primarily by providing humanitarian assistance.

International Advisory and Monitoring Board

On 22 October [S/2003/1030], the Secretary-General informed the Council President that he, together with the executive heads of the Arab Fund for Economic and Social Development, the International Monetary Fund and the World Bank, had approved the terms of reference for the establishment of the International Advisory and Monitoring Board (IAMB), as emphasized in resolution 1511(2003) (above). A copy of the Board's terms of reference was attached to the letter. The purpose of IAMB was to promote the objectives set out in Council resolution 1483 (2003) (see p. 338) of ensuring that the Development Fund for Iraq was used in a transparent manner for the purposes set out in paragraph 14 of that resolution and that the export sales of petroleum, petroleum products and natural gas from Iraq were made consistent with prevailing international market best practices. The executive heads intended to make the appointment of their representatives to IAMB forthwith and looked forward to an early IAMB meeting.

Communications (4-21 November). On 4 November [S/2003/1073], Egypt, Iran, Jordan, Kuwait, Saudi Arabia, the Syrian Arab Republic and Turkey transmitted to the Secretary-General and the Council President the text of the final statement of the meeting of the Foreign Ministers of Iraq's neighbouring countries (Damascus, Syria, 1-2 November). The Ministers, among other things, rejected any measure that could lead to the disintegration of Iraq and emphasized the importance of enhancing the UN role in that country. They also expressed their concern about the existence of terrorist groups in Iraq and the threat they represented for neighbouring countries.

On 21 November [A/58/611-S/2003/1134], India and the Russian Federation transmitted to the Secretary-General the text of the Declaration of the Russian Federation and the Republic of India on Global Challenges and Threats to International Security and Stability (Moscow, 12 November). The two countries said that a specific time plan of action should be adopted under the aegis of the United Nations for the speediest restoration of the State sovereignty of Iraq, for the stabilization of the political and humanitarian situation and for ensuring Iraq's economic growth with broad international participation.

Security Council consideration (21 November). On 21 November [meeting 4869], the Council heard briefings by the United States and the United Kingdom on the latest developments in Iraq.

The United States said that violence continued to be directed against the Iraqi people and all those who were trying to assist them in creating a new Iraq. Iraqis were taking on increasing responsibilities for their security every day and were working to rebuild a strong police force and a new army. They also continued to take over administrative responsibilities and to provide for the delivery of basic services. Iraq's ministries were run by Iraqi ministers, appointed by and reporting to the Iraqi Governing Council. The 15 November announcement by the Governing Council of a political process to establish a representative transitional national assembly to assume full sovereign powers in 2004 was a step forward in Iraq's political transition. Under that process, a transitional national assembly would be formed to elect an executive branch, select ministers and serve as a legislative body. By 30 June 2004, that new transitional administration would assume full responsibility for governing Iraq. The Authority would then dissolve, as would the Iraqi Governing Council. The Transitional National Assembly would be formed through caucuses at the provincial level. The selection and structure and powers of the Assembly would be established by a fundamental law, with basic principles of openness and transparency. The delegates to the Assembly should be selected no later than 31 May 2004. The fundamental law would protect freedom of speech and religion and would include a statement of equal rights for all Iraqis. The law would define the relationship between the central Government and provincial authorities and would have an expiration date, by which time a permanent constitution for Iraq was to be drafted and a new Government of Iraq elected. The agreement signed between the Governing Council and the Authority on 15 November established a time line for the direct election of a constitutional convention, no later than 15 March 2005, to draft a permanent constitution for Iraq. The constitution would be ratified through a popular referendum, and a new Iraqi Government would be elected under the terms of the ratified constitution no later than 31 December 2005. Three basic steps—increased assumption by Iraqis for security, creation of the Governing Council, appointment of effective ministers to run Iraqi ministries and continuing transfer of political authority to Iraqis—were part of the Authority's planning for post-Saddam Iraq.

The continued support of the international community in reconstruction efforts was also critical. At a donors conference (Madrid, 23-24 October), the international community pledged over $33 billion in support to Iraq. The Coalition stressed that the United Nations had a vital role to play in Iraq and stood ready to discuss with UN officials appropriate security support, as envisioned under resolution 1511(2003) (see p. 348). Security and stability underpinned all other efforts on the ground. Despite the killings, bombings and other attacks, much of Iraq remained calm. The reality that could not be captured by a television camera was that Iraqis were coming together to expand conditions of security and stability, adding more than 130,000 personnel to the security effort. Over 60,000 police officers were back on the streets and over 12,000 Iraqi border personnel were on duty. The first battalion of the new Iraqi army was formed in October 2003, and by the autumn of 2004 the Iraqi army would have expanded to about 35,000 troops. Notwithstanding those efforts, the United States acknowledged that security conditions in Iraq remained a major preoccupation and that there was a need to deliver a sustainable, improved security situation, particularly in the centre of the country. Over the coming months, the Authority would continue to work with the Governing Council to promote diverse and representative citizen participation within, and among, communities throughout Iraq. The focus would be on increasing financial transparency and accountability and on strengthening the capacity of local administrations to provide municipal services. In June, the Iraqi Survey Group assumed responsibility for searching for and eliminating Iraqi WMD, prohibited missile-delivery systems and related infrastructure. In October, an interim report on the Group's activities detailed numerous violations by Saddam Hussein's regime of its mandated obligations under Council resolutions, including deliberate efforts to conceal from the United Nations equipment and programme activities related to WMD during inspections from November 2002 to March 2003.

The United Kingdom briefed the Council on the main points relating to the provision of basic services, economic and reconstruction issues and human rights and justice.

Constitutional and electoral timetable

On 2 December [S/2003/1169], the Council President acknowledged the receipt of a 24 November letter from the interim President of the Iraqi Governing Council, Jalal Talabani, regarding the timetable agreed upon with the Authority in accordance with paragraph 7 of Council resolution 1511(2003) (see p. 348). The contents of the letter had been brought to the attention of Council members.

On 11 December [S/2003/1170], Iraq requested that its 24 November letter be circulated as a Security Council document. The letter stated that the Governing Council had decided to hold general elections for the establishment of a constitutional convention no later than 15 March 2005. The constitution would then be submitted to the Iraqi people for approval in a referendum. By the end of 2005, elections would be held to elect a new government in accordance with the provisions of the constitution. The Governing Council and the transitional government, to be elected by the end of June 2004, would make the necessary preparations for those elections, which would include conducting a population census, drafting a law containing electoral regulations and adopting laws concerning political parties, the press and meetings. Prior to commencing the constitutional process, the transitional governing council would draft, no later than the end of February 2004, a law concerning the administration of the Iraqi State in accordance with the following principles: respect for human rights and fundamental freedoms, including freedom of religion and equality of all citizens; separation of the three branches of government; introduction of some degree of decentralization in the administration of the governorates, taking into consideration the situation in Iraqi Kurdistan; establishment of the principle of civilian control of the Iraqi armed and security forces; and establishment of a unified federal, democratic and multilateral system that would respect the Islamic identity of the majority of the Iraqi people while ensuring the rights of other religions. The aforementioned law would also provide for the establishment of a provisional legislative body in accordance with procedures that would guarantee broad representation of all segments of Iraqi society. That body, to be established no later than the end of May 2004, would elect a provisional Iraqi government no later than the end of June 2004, at which point the Authority and the Governing Council would be dissolved.

Report of Secretary-General (December). In response to resolution 1483(2003) (see p. 338), the Secretary-General submitted a December report [S/2003/1149] on UN activities and key developments in Iraq since his July report (see p. 342).

The Secretary-General said that, at the beginning of August, the United Nations stood at a critical point with respect to its role and engagement in Iraq. On the one hand, UN agencies, funds and programmes were playing a key role in a variety of sectors, including food and nutrition assistance, the delivery of medical supplies, educational materials and drinking water, and emergency repairs of essential facilities. Thanks in part to UN support for the efforts of the Authority and Iraqi ministries, improvements in the provision of basic services were becoming noticeable. The Authority's efforts to restore Iraqi capacities in the field of law and order were beginning to bear fruit and the formation of the Iraqi Governing Council on 13 July offered the potential to provide a credible and representative Iraqi interlocutor with which the United Nations could develop a comprehensive programme of action. However, major uncertainties remained about the future role of the United Nations. First, the Governing Council and the Authority had not expressed any clear or shared vision on the role to be played by the United Nations in the remainder of the political transition process and other key areas suggested in his 17 July report. Second, on that and other issues, divisions became apparent among Iraqis within and outside the Governing Council. Third, armed attacks against the Coalition forces, Iraqi institutions and other civilian and international targets intensified in sophistication, scale and breadth, precipitating a sharp downturn in the overall security situation. By the time the Security Council, in resolution 1500(2003) of 14 August (see p. 346), authorized the establishment of UNAMI, the situation was already considerably different from that envisaged less than a month earlier, when the Secretary-General outlined the proposed concept of operations for the Mission in his July report.

Responsibility for the 19 August attack against UN headquarters in Baghdad (see p. 346) remained uncertain. Although the Abu-Hafs al-Masri Brigades, a group affiliated with Al-Qaida, among others, claimed responsibility in a message published on the Internet and in Arabic newspapers, the authenticity of the message had not been established. On 21 August, the Secretary-General dispatched to Iraq an investigation team led by the senior security officer of the Office of the United Nations High Commissioner for Human Rights and comprising members of the Office of the United Nations Security Coordinator, the International Tribunal for the Former Yugoslavia and the Office of Internal Oversight Services. They were tasked with determining and recording the events leading up to the explosion and immediately thereafter, assessing the adequacy of preventive measures and making recommendations on required adjustments to enable UN personnel to operate in greater safety in the future. He also instructed the UN Security Coordinator, Tun Myat, to visit Iraq from 23 to 30 August to review the security situation and to make recommendations on what reductions in the number of UN personnel in the country might be required on security grounds. The Security Coordinator, in a 2 September report to the Secretary-General, noted that the overall security situation in Iraq had deteriorated dramatically in August. Iraq had entered a new phase in which all foreign organizations and Iraqis who cooperated with the Authority were potential targets of deliberate and hostile attacks. That type of security threat had not been anticipated. The United Nations had chosen offices in locations that would facilitate contact with and accessibility to Iraqi partners and beneficiaries. The more than 800 international UN personnel deployed throughout the country were thus extremely vulnerable to further attacks. Coalition forces were not in a position to provide dedicated protection to all of them. Hence, the reduction of international personnel, well under way before 2 September, continued after the submission of the Security Coordinator's report. On 5 September, the UN Under-Secretary-General for Political Affairs informed the Security Council in informal consultations of the Secretary-General's decision to withdraw from Iraq all international personnel other than those required for essential humanitarian assistance activities and security and logistics support. On the basis of those criteria, the Secretary-General had decided to reduce the number of international staff in Baghdad from 400 to approximately 50 and in the three northern governorates from 400 to approximately 30, and to vacate the UN offices in Basra, Hilla and Mosul.

On 22 September, the Secretary-General appointed an Independent Panel on the Safety and Security of United Nations Personnel in Iraq. Led by the former President of Finland, Martti Ahtisaari, the Panel was tasked with, among other things, examining the adequacy of UN security, management and practices prior to the attack, the circumstances of the attack itself and the actions taken by various parties in the immediate aftermath. The Panel's report, submitted on 20 October, concluded that there was no place in Iraq without risk and that a new security approach was needed in order to ensure staff security in such a high-risk environment. It also argued that the UN security management system was in need of drastic reform, especially in the light of the new type of threat faced in Iraq and potentially elsewhere. It recommended a separate and independent audit and accountability procedure to review the responsibilities of key individuals in the decision-making processes on security matters prior to the 19 August attack. Accordingly, the Secretary-General established a team on 4 November, headed by Gerald Walzer, former Deputy High Commissioner for Refugees, to determine accountability at all managerial levels at UN Headquarters and in the field with respect to relevant decisions taken prior to the attack. The team was asked to present its findings to the Secretary-General with the least possible delay.

Meanwhile, on 22 September, a second suicide attack was launched against UN headquarters at the Canal Hotel in Baghdad, resulting in the death of one Iraqi policeman and the wounding of others, including two UN national staff. Other attacks directed against civilian foreign organizations, and against Iraqi civilians, coupled with the findings of the Panel led by President Ahtisaari, led the Secretary-General to draw down further the international UN presence in Iraq during the months of September and October; that included the relocation of international programme staff from Baghdad after the 22 September attack. That period of retrenchment culminated with the Secretary-General's decision, on 4 November, to relocate temporarily all international UN staff from Baghdad, pending a comprehensive review of UN operations in Iraq and their security implications, leaving only a small core presence of international personnel in Erbil.

Despite the 19 August attack and the subsequent relocation of UN staff, a substantial number of planned UN activities had continued. That was particularly true with respect to humanitarian relief and emergency rehabilitation efforts, the reconstruction needs assessment process and the termination of the oil-for-food programme. On 23 October, the Secretary-General attended the opening of the international donors conference for the reconstruction of Iraq in Madrid. At the end of the conference, participants announced pledges amounting to more than $33 billion in grants and loans until the end of 2007. In order to help coordinate and channel contributions towards reconstruction and development in Iraq, the United Nations and the World Bank were requested to present terms of reference for an international reconstruction trust fund facility for Iraq. To build on the respective strengths and comparative advantages of both the United Nations and the World Bank, the proposed facility comprised two trust funds. The World Bank trust fund would concentrate mainly on technical assistance and infrastructure support, while the UN-managed trust fund would focus on technical assistance, quick-impact projects and transition activities.

There were significant political developments in Iraq post–19 August, especially with respect to the provisions of resolution 1483(2003). They included the 1 September appointment of interim ministers by the Governing Council and the completion of the preparatory constitutional committee's report; the adoption of resolution 1511 (2003) (see p. 348); and the 15 November agreement reached between the Governing Council and the Authority on the political transition process. With regard to resolution 1511(2003), the Secretary-General was particularly grateful to the sponsors for inserting the caveat "as circumstances permit" with respect to the implementation of the original plans of UNAMI, and in support of the implementation of a timetable and programme for the drafting of a new constitution and the holding of elections, with support from the United Nations "if requested by the Governing Council". In doing so, the Council took into consideration his concerns that the United Nations should not take on responsibilities it could not successfully carry out. For UN engagement to be successful, adequate measures for staff security needed to be in place first. Furthermore, the Secretary-General said that in order for the UN role in the political process to be effective, it needed to be supported by all members of the Governing Council, key Iraqi figures outside the process, the Coalition, key States in the region, a united Security Council and major donor countries.

The 15 November agreement on the political process set out a timetable and programme for drafting a new constitution and holding elections under that constitution (see above). Though the agreement made no specific mention of any role for the United Nations, both the Governing Council and the Authority expressed their desire for the Organization to play an active part in its implementation.

The fact that a sovereign transitional Iraqi Government was envisaged to be established by 30 June 2004 required the United Nations to focus immediately on humanitarian assistance, emergency rehabilitation, technical assistance for ministries related thereto and the initiation of reconstruction programmes. On the political front, it had yet to be established what role, if any, Iraqis and the Authority would like the United Nations to play in the formation of the national assembly by 31 May 2004, how substantive that role might be in relation to the security risks and whether circumstances would permit the Organization to play any such role effectively. The Secretary-General welcomed the holding of regional meetings to encourage and support the political process in Iraq. He established an advisory group on Iraq, composed of neighbouring countries, Egypt and Security Council members. His aim in doing so was to initiate an informal dialogue and to develop a common basis for approaching the situation in Iraq. He also intended to enhance contacts between the United Nations and regional countries and regional organizations with a view to building confidence at three levels: between Iraq and its neighbours, within the region itself and between the region and the larger international community. In the longer term, if the Iraqis requested and as circumstances permitted, the United Nations would make available to the Iraqi people its expertise on the constitutional and electoral processes. However, no determination of electoral assistance by the United Nations could be made without a specific request of the Member States and the launching of a needs assessment mission, as per standard UN practices.

Irrespective of whatever direct contribution the United Nations might make to the political process in the immediate or long term, there was ample potential for it to continue to play an important role in Iraq. The key task was to develop a detailed plan of action that took into consideration the conditions and circumstances required if the United Nations was to play that role effectively both inside and outside the country. To that end, a detailed planning process was initiated at a meeting held in Nicosia, Cyprus, from 11 to 15 November. Representatives of 20 UN departments, agencies, funds and programmes, including the UN agency country team for Iraq, and UNAMI personnel participated. The Nicosia meeting and subsequent meetings at UN Headquarters had resulted in a plan for future UN activities in Iraq in the immediate to medium term, with respect to security, the deployment of UNAMI and criteria for revisions to the UN country strategy for relief, recovery and reconstruction for 2004.

The substantive programmatic review highlighted the fact that the security environment was unlikely to improve and could deteriorate even further; the United Nations would remain a high-value, high-impact target for terrorist activity in Iraq for the foreseeable future. The acting UN Security Coordinator assessed the risk to UN personnel in Iraq as falling in the high to critical category, but considered that, over time, gradual improvements in the security environment, coupled with the full implementation of a range of protective measures, had the potential to reduce the risk to medium to high. Those measures included protection by a highly mobile, responsive armed force on a countrywide basis; preparation and implementation of enhanced Minimum Operating Safety Standards to include security plans and procedures and significant office and residential building upgrades; the establishment of an effective, well-trained and well-equipped security management and coordination structure; training on security matters for staff at all levels; a highly capable and responsive emergency medical support element; protected vehicles; and a comprehensive, far-reaching public information strategy that could effectively explain the role and tasks of the United Nations. In summary, establishing the necessary security conditions would be a time-consuming and expensive process. Under those circumstances, it was difficult to envisage the United Nations operating with a large number of international staff inside Iraq in the near future, unless there was an unexpected and significant improvement in the overall security situation.

It was impossible to forecast if and when circumstances would permit the full deployment of UNAMI in Iraq. The operation would need to build up incrementally, at a pace and scope that could not yet be defined. At the same time, prudent contingency planning was required to enable the United Nations to respond as quickly as possible to requests for assistance from the Iraqi people. Therefore, the Secretary-General decided to commence the incremental process of establishing UNAMI by setting up the core of the

Mission outside Iraq, in Nicosia. Additional UNAMI staff would be deployed to a small office in Amman and other locations in the region. He envisaged an integrated core team of approximately 40 international UNAMI staff in total to be in place by early 2004; that number would be expected to increase to up to 60 international staff once a new Special Representative had been appointed. That core UNAMI team would initially be managed by Ross Mountain, who would serve as acting Special Representative, until such time as a new Special Representative was appointed. The core UNAMI team would lead operational planning efforts for the eventual deployment of UNAMI in Iraq, and also coordinate the activities and provide guidance to UN agencies. The political and human rights officers would meet with Iraqis travelling in the region to discuss with them the political and human rights situation in the country. The UNAMI core team would also lead the articulation and subsequent implementation of a public information strategy through media outlets based in the region and national staff in Iraq.

During the Nicosia consultations, progress was made in working out modalities to implement an integrated approach to the UN relief, recovery and reconstruction activities. The basis for the UN assistance efforts would be a fully integrated UN country team strategy for 2004, which would be finalized by January 2004 and reviewed on a quarterly basis to reflect emerging needs and changing circumstances. The implementation of UN programmes on the ground would be led by an integrated implementation team.

The Secretary-General observed that in order to mitigate the possibility that the insurgency in Iraq would grow over time, various steps had to be taken. First and foremost, there was a need to act on the recognition that the mounting insecurity problem could not be solved through military means alone. A political solution was required, one that would entail making the political transition process more inclusive. That also meant empowering Iraqi institutions to take the decisions that would shape the political and economic future of their country. In order to command widespread support, those institutions needed to function effectively and transparently. Political steps of that kind would make it clearer that the foreign occupation of Iraq was to be short-lived and that it would soon give way to a fully fledged Iraqi Government, hence making it more difficult for insurgents to rally support. Second, the articulation of a national agenda that was seen to be truly representative of all segments of Iraqi society required national reconciliation and unity, not revenge and/or collective punishment. Third, intensified efforts by Coalition forces to demonstrate that they were adhering to international humanitarian law and human rights instruments would make it much more difficult for the insurgents to rally support for their cause. Fourth, it was essential that all those in the international community who were in a position to support the implementation of an Iraqi agenda should do so. The UN would not disengage from Iraq, even though most UN international staff had been temporarily relocated outside the country.

In a later report [S/2004/625], the Secretary-General said that the security environment in Iraq had not improved. On 30 December, the President of the Iraqi Governing Council requested the United Nations to help determine whether elections were feasible by 30 June 2004 and, if not, to identify alternative means of forming an interim Iraqi Government to which sovereignty could be restored. The Secretary-General planned to convene a meeting in January 2004 with representatives of the Governing Council and the Authority to deal with that request. IAMB was constituted in October 2003 and held an organizational session on 5 December in New York when it was agreed that the Secretary-General's representative on the Board, Jean-Pierre Halbwachs, would chair it for a term of no more than one year. The Board oversaw the audits conducted by international accounting firms to ensure that the Development Fund for Iraq was used in a transparent manner for the purposes set out in resolution 1483(2003) and that oil export sales were made consistent with prevailing international market best practices.

Security Council consideration (16 December). On 16 December [meeting 4883], the Council was briefed by the Secretary-General on his December report.

Noting that the Council was meeting three days after the capture by Coalition forces of Saddam Hussein, the Secretary-General said that the capture was not just a symbol of the downfall of the former Iraqi regime, but also an opportunity for a new beginning in the vital task of helping Iraqis to take control of their destiny. The task of restoring the effective exercise of sovereignty to Iraqis, in the form of a provisional Government, was urgent. It was essential that the process leading to the formation of a provisional Government be fully inclusive and transparent. It was also right that Saddam Hussein should be held accountable for past deeds, through a procedure that met the highest international standards of due process. Accounting for the past would be an important part of bringing about national reconciliation. Owing to the persistent security concerns and the temporary relocation of staff outside Iraq, the Organization would need to find creative ways of intensifying its engagement despite diminished capacity on the ground, as explained in the December report. Iraq was likely to remain a difficult environment and the international community should not expect that the end of the occupation and formation of a provisional Government would automatically bring about an end to insecurity, even though that should bring some improvement. There was no panacea; only a credible and inclusive transition offered the best hope of stability and of political mobilization by Iraqis against the violence.

Iraq presented to the Council the timetable set out in the 15 November agreement on political process signed between the Iraqi Governing Council and the Coalition Authority (see p. 354). Iraq stated that Saddam Hussein had to answer to the Iraqi people for his crimes against humanity. At last Iraq could begin the long-overdue healing process of seeking unity and national reconciliation.

The Security Council, in a closed meeting held on the same day [meeting 4884], held a constructive exchange of views with the Minister for Foreign Affairs of Iraq, Hoshya Zebari.

Communication (17 December). On 17 December [S/2003/1190], the EU informed the Secretary-General that it welcomed the capture of Saddam Hussein as a crucial further step towards peace, stability and democracy in Iraq and in the region.

In a later communication [A/58/673-S/2004/7], Kuwait transmitted to the Secretary-General the texts of the closing statement and of the Kuwait Declaration that were adopted by the Supreme Council of the Gulf Cooperation Council at its twenty-fourth session (Kuwait, 21-22 December). The Supreme Council rejected any attempt to dismember Iraq and stressed the importance of a vital role for the United Nations in the country. It also expressed satisfaction with the new direction in United States policy aimed at accelerating the handover of power to Iraqis.

Iraq-Kuwait

POWs, Kuwaiti property and missing persons

Communication (February). On 10 February [S/2003/162], Iraq informed the Secretary-General that on 3 February it had handed over Kuwaiti archives and property to Kuwait.

Reports of Secretary-General (April, June, August, December). Pursuant to Security Council resolution 1284(1999) [YUN 1999, p. 230], the Secretary-General submitted reports in April [S/2003/419], June [S/2003/614], August [S/2003/813] and December [S/2003/1161] on compliance by Iraq with its obligations regarding the repatriation or return of all Kuwaiti and third-country nationals or their remains, and on the return of all Kuwaiti property, including archives, seized by Iraq during its occupation of Kuwait, which began in August 1990 [YUN 1990, p. 189]. The High-level Coordinator for compliance by Iraq with its obligations regarding the return of Kuwaiti nationals and property, Yuli M. Vorontsov (Russian Federation), regularly briefed the Security Council throughout the year.

In April, the Secretary-General observed that some progress had been achieved with the resumption of the meetings of the Technical Subcommittee of the Tripartite Commission, with five being held since the beginning of 2003. However, no concrete results had been achieved. The meetings were interrupted owing to the outbreak of the conflict in Iraq on 20 March. The Subcommittee was established in 1994 to expedite the search for all persons for whom inquiry files had been opened. The Commission, established in 1991 under ICRC auspices, dealt with the questions of persons still unaccounted for, and was made up of representatives of France, Iraq, Kuwait, Saudi Arabia, the United Kingdom and the United States. However, at the end of 1998, Iraq decided not to participate in the Commission's work, arguing that it no longer held captive Kuwaiti prisoners in its territory and, thus, the issue had become one of missing persons, not prisoners of war (POWs). In December 2002, Iraq had expressed its willingness to resume participation in the Technical Subcommittee, and an Iraqi delegation, for the first time since 1998, participated on the sidelines of the Tripartite Commission's meeting.

In his June report, the Secretary-General said that prior to the outbreak of hostilities in Iraq, the then Government of Iraq demonstrated some limited cooperation on the return of Kuwaiti property. However, while some property and some documents were handed over, the Kuwaiti archives, along with Kuwaiti military equipment seized by Iraq, remained largely unreturned. Council resolution 1483(2003) of 22 May (see p. 338) directed the High-level Coordinator to proceed with his duties in fulfilment of his mandate. Lists of Kuwaiti property returned on 22 December 2002 and 3 February 2003 were attached to the report.

In August, the Secretary-General said that the Coalition's discovery of mass graves in Iraq and the subsequent identification of remains, including those of Kuwaiti missing persons, had brought to light the atrocities perpetrated by the previous Iraqi regime. The Tripartite Commission had formulated procedures to exhume and identify the mortal remains of missing Kuwaitis at its Technical Subcommittee meetings. The Secretary-General encouraged continuing collaboration between Iraq and Kuwait within the framework of the Tripartite Commission and ICRC. He said that in the light of the ongoing progress, the Council might wish to consider bringing the High-level Coordinator's mandate to a close with the submission of the December 2003 report on the repatriation and return of all Kuwaitis and third-country nationals or their remains.

In December, the Secretary-General said that after many years of manoeuvring and denial by the previous Iraqi Government, a grim truth was unveiling itself. The discovery of mass graves in Iraq containing the mortal remains of Kuwaitis was a gruesome and devastating development. While hope had not faded that some of the 605 persons in question would be found alive, the prospects for that to happen were diminishing. There was also the possibility that the fate of many individuals would remain unknown for many years to come, if it was ever to emerge. The Secretary-General said that the removal from Kuwait of civilians, their execution in cold blood in remote sites in Iraq, and a decade-long cover-up of the truth constituted a grave violation of human rights and international humanitarian law. Those responsible for the crimes, particularly those who ordered the executions, had to be brought to justice. He regretted that the Kuwaiti archives and military equipment had not been returned to the country. However, the fall of Saddam Hussein's regime and the opening of avenues for direct contact between the parties concerned inspired hope for an early resolution of all outstanding questions. There was room for further progress towards a satisfactory solution of the remaining humanitarian concerns of the State and people of Kuwait, and more time would be needed and more efforts required before those concerns could be settled. Given the fact that not all files relating to the issues of Kuwaiti prisoners and third-country nationals and Kuwaiti properties had been completely closed, Kuwait had called on the United Nations to pursue and resolve those issues and was in favour of extending the High-level Coordinator's mandate. The Secretary-General said that the Council would have to determine whether it would wish the mandate to continue.

In presidential statement S/PRST/2003/28 of 18 December (see below), the Council agreed that the High-level Coordinator's mandate should continue.

SECURITY COUNCIL ACTION

On 18 December [meeting 4887], the Security Council was briefed by the Secretary-General's High-level Coordinator. Following consultations among Council members, the President made statement **S/PRST/2003/28** on behalf of the Council:

The Security Council today heard a briefing from Mr. Yuli Vorontsov, the Secretary-General's High-level Coordinator, on the fourteenth report of the Secretary-General submitted in accordance with paragraph 14 of Council resolution 1284(1999).

The Council expressed its full support towards Mr. Vorontsov and for his tireless efforts on the issues of Kuwaiti and third-country nationals and the return of all Kuwaiti property. The Council agreed that his mandate should continue in accordance with paragraph 14 of resolution 1284(1999) of 17 December 1999.

The Council shared the views expressed by the Secretary-General in his report. The Council has strongly condemned the killing of Kuwaiti and third-country nationals by the previous Iraqi regime in violation of international law, especially the removal from Kuwait of civilian men and women, their execution in cold blood in remote sites in Iraq and a decade-long cover-up of the truth. The Council expressed its strong hope that those responsible for these horrendous crimes would be brought to justice.

The Council expressed its deep condolences to all of the families of the Kuwaiti and third-country nationals and expressed its continuing concern for the plight of the families of those persons whose whereabouts were still unknown.

The Council stressed the importance of the work of the Coalition Provisional Authority, the International Committee of the Red Cross, the Tripartite Commission and its Technical Subcommittee and called upon all parties concerned to continue to work towards a satisfactory solution to all of the outstanding humanitarian aspects covered by Mr. Vorontsov's mandate.

The Council expressed its deep regret that Kuwaiti property, including its national archives, had not yet been returned to Kuwait and encouraged the Coalition Provisional Authority and other parties concerned to continue their commitment to the search for and return of all Kuwaiti properties and archives, in accordance with paragraph 6 of resolution 1483(2003) of 22 May 2003. The Council agreed to continue to keep Mr. Vorontsov's mandate under review and looked forward to receiving his next report.

Later communication. Kuwait transmitted to the Secretary-General the texts of the closing statement and of the Kuwait Declaration that were adopted by the Supreme Council of the Gulf Cooperation Council at its twenty-fourth session (Kuwait, 21-22 December). The Supreme Council applauded the statement made by the Security Council President on 18 December, praised the efforts of ICRC and the Technical

Subcommittee, and appealed to all parties concerned to continue their joint efforts to resolve the outstanding problems related to the repatriation or return of all Kuwaiti and third-country nationals or their remains.

UN Iraq-Kuwait Observation Mission

In March, just before the United States–led invasion of Iraq from Kuwait, the mandate of the United Nations Iraq-Kuwait Observation Mission (UNIKOM) was suspended and most of its staff evacuated. UNIKOM maintained a small rear headquarters in Kuwait City to provide a peacekeeping presence, undertake political and military liaison functions, and support UN humanitarian assistance programmes for Iraq. On 25 March [S/2003/367], Kuwait informed the Security Council President that between 20 and 24 March, Iraq had launched 11 missiles, including a Scud missile, against Kuwait. While much of UNIKOM headquarters at Umm Qasr and other infrastructure were destroyed in the conflict, Camp Khor, on the Kuwaiti side of the border, reopened in May to support humanitarian operations. On 3 July, the Security Council, in resolution 1490 (2003) (see p. 359), noted that UNIKOM had successfully fulfilled its mandate from 1991 to 2003 and extended it for a final period of three months, up to 6 October 2003. Also, on 6 October, the Council decided to end the demilitarized zone (DMZ), an area about 200 to 240 kilometres long and extending 10 kilometres into Iraq and 5 kilometres into Kuwait from the Iraq-Kuwait border.

UNIKOM, established by Security Council resolution 687(1991) [YUN 1991, p. 172], discharged its functions until October in accordance with its terms of reference, as expanded by resolution 806(1993) [YUN 1993, p. 406]. Until March 2003, UNIKOM operations involved surveillance, control, investigation and liaison. Surveillance of the DMZ was based on ground and air patrols and observation points. Control operations included static checkpoints, random checks and maintenance of a mobile reserve force. For operational purposes, the DMZ was divided into northern, southern and maritime sectors, with seven, six and three patrol and observation bases, respectively. Investigation teams were stationed in those sectors and at UNIKOM headquarters. Continued liaison was maintained with Iraqi and Kuwaiti authorities at all levels.

The military observers were responsible for patrol, observation, investigation and liaison activities. The infantry battalion was deployed at Camp Khor, with two companies deployed in Camp Abdally and Camp Sierra in the northern and southern DMZ sectors. The battalion conducted patrols within the sectors and manned checkpoints at border-crossing sites, making random checks in cooperation with Iraqi and Kuwaiti liaison officers. It also provided security for UNIKOM personnel and installations.

UNIKOM maintained headquarters at Umm Qasr in Iraq, liaison offices in Baghdad and Kuwait City and a support centre at Camp Khor.

By a 6 January letter to the Council President [S/2003/27], the Secretary-General proposed to appoint Brigadier General Franciszek Gagor (Poland) as UNIKOM's Force Commander, replacing Major General Miguel Angel Moreno (Argentina).

On 9 January [S/2003/28], the Council took note of the Secretary-General's proposal.

Major General Gagor left the Mission area on 7 July and the Chief of Staff, Brigadier General Upinder Singh Klair (India), was appointed Head of Mission.

Reports of Secretary-General (March, June, October). UNIKOM's activities were described in three reports of the Secretary-General, covering the periods 16 September 2002 to 21 March 2003 [S/2003/393 & Add.1], 22 March to 15 June [S/2003/656] and 16 June to 1 October [S/2003/933].

In the March report, the Secretary-General said that during the period under review, the situation along the border between Iraq and Kuwait became increasingly tense owing to the massive military build-up on the Kuwaiti side of the border. UNIKOM continued to carry out its responsibilities and contributed to the maintenance of stability in the border region until 17 March, when conditions on the ground dictated withdrawal of most of the Mission for security reasons. A small headquarters, consisting of 12 military officers, 20 essential civilian staff and some local staff, remained in Kuwait City. UNIKOM's personnel had been dispersed temporarily and the timing of their return to their assignments would be decided in consultation with the Council. The Secretary-General recommended that the residual peacekeeping presence in Kuwait City be maintained at an appropriate level for a further three months, until 6 July 2003.

In June, the Secretary-General said that the Mission continued to maintain its rear headquarters in Kuwait City to ensure a peacekeeping presence in the UNIKOM area of operations. It undertook high-level military and political liaison duties, retained a capacity to conduct contingency planning for a continued or modified operation, undertook residual tasks for the Mission, such as recovery, reconciliation and disposal of assets, and provided support to other entities of the UN system in the region. Most of UNIKOM's property and premises on the Iraqi side of the DMZ were totally destroyed or stolen during or soon after the military conflict. The Secretary-General said that since the conflict in Iraq had subsided, and following the adoption of Council resolution 1483(2003) (see p. 338), the Council might wish to consider whether the continued presence of UNIKOM in Kuwait with a suspended mandate and in changed circumstances was still desirable. In those altered conditions, he recommended that the residual peacekeeping presence of UNIKOM be maintained for a final three months, until 6 October 2003, when the Mission would be closed. During that period, UNIKOM would scale down its military presence to a minimum, continue to provide support from both the Kheitan Support Centre and Camp Khor to humanitarian assistance operations in Iraq, maintain liaison with Kuwaiti authorities, undertake the reconciliation and liquidation of UNIKOM assets and, most importantly, make appropriate arrangements for handing over its activities in assistance to humanitarian operations to other entities in the area. That would also allow more time for the assessment of the security situation in the Mission's former area of operations, as requested by Kuwait.

In his October report, the Secretary-General said that UNIKOM continued to reduce its staff and finalized preparations for the liquidation of its assets as part of its final mandate period authorized in Council resolution 1490(2003) (see below). It also provided support to humanitarian assistance operations in Iraq and made arrangements for the handover of its facilities to the host country and UN agencies in Kuwait. UNIKOM expected that the technical liquidation of its activities would be completed one month after the closure of the Mission. After the 19 August attack against the UN headquarters in Baghdad, UNIKOM provided urgently needed assets, such as prefabricated accommodations, supplies, water tanks and communications equipment, for the continuation of UN operations in Baghdad. The Secretary-General said that in its last phase, as a residual peacekeeping presence operating in a difficult environment affected by the conflict in Iraq from mid-March until the completion of its mandate on 6 October, UNIKOM proved to be a significant source of support for humanitarian agencies deployed in Iraq and Kuwait.

Communications. In two separate letters addressed to the Secretary-General dated 14 March [S/2003/319] and 16 March [S/2003/327], Iraq said that the UN decision to withdraw UNIKOM observers from their posts along the Iraqi-Kuwaiti border was inconsistent with the Organization's responsibility to maintain peace and security and a violation of relevant Council resolutions.

Security Council consideration (2-3 April). On 2 April, in a closed meeting [meeting 4733], the Council heard a briefing by the UN Assistant Secretary-General for Peacekeeping Operations and had a constructive exchange of views with representatives of the troop-contributing countries to UNIKOM.

On 3 April [S/2003/400], the Council concurred with the Secretary-General's recommendation, expressed in his March report (see above), that a peacekeeping presence be retained at an appropriate level for a further three months, until 6 July 2003.

SECURITY COUNCIL ACTION

On 3 July [meeting 4783], the Security Council unanimously adopted **resolution 1490(2003)**. The draft [S/2003/684] was prepared in consultations among Council members.

The Security Council,

Recalling all its relevant resolutions, including resolutions 687(1991) of 3 April 1991, 689(1991) of 9 April 1991, 806(1993) of 5 February 1993, 833(1993) of 27 May 1993 and 1483(2003) of 22 May 2003,

Taking note of the report of the Secretary-General of 17 June 2003 on the United Nations Iraq-Kuwait Observation Mission,

Reaffirming the commitment of all Member States to the sovereignty and territorial integrity of Iraq and Kuwait,

Recognizing that the continued operation of the Mission and of a demilitarized zone established pursuant to resolution 687(1991) is no longer necessary to protect against threats to international security posed by Iraqi actions against Kuwait,

Expressing its appreciation for the substantial voluntary contributions made to the Mission by the Government of Kuwait,

Commending the superior role played by personnel of the Mission and the Department of Peacekeeping Operations of the Secretariat, and noting that the Mission successfully fulfilled its mandate from 1991 to 2003,

Acting under Chapter VII of the Charter of the United Nations,

1. *Decides* to continue the mandate of the United Nations Iraq-Kuwait Observation Mission for a final period, until 6 October 2003;

2. *Directs* the Secretary-General to negotiate the transfer of non-removable property of the Mission and of those assets that cannot be disposed of otherwise to the States of Kuwait and Iraq, as appropriate;

3. *Decides* to end the demilitarized zone extending 10 kilometres into Iraq and 5 kilometres into Kuwait from the Iraq-Kuwait border at the end of mandate of the Mission on 6 October 2003;

4. *Requests* the Secretary-General to report to the Security Council on the completion of the mandate of the Mission;

5. *Expresses its appreciation* of the decision of the Government of Kuwait to defray, since 1 November 1993, two thirds of the cost of the Mission;

6. *Decides* to remain seized of the matter.

Financing

On 18 June [meeting 90], the General Assembly considered the Secretary-General's reports on UNIKOM's budget for the period from 1 July 2003 to 30 June 2004 [A/57/664 & Corr.1], the performance report on the budget for the period from 1 July 2001 to 30 June 2002 [A/57/665], the overview of the financing of UN peacekeeping operations: budget performance for the period from 1 July 2001 to 30 June 2002 and budget for the period from 1 July 2003 to 30 June 2004 [A/57/723], and the financing of UNIKOM for the period from 1 July 2003 to 30 June 2004 [A/57/811], together with the related reports of the Advisory Committee on Administrative and Budgetary Questions (ACABQ) on the administrative and budgetary aspects of the financing of UN peacekeeping operations [A/57/772] and on the financing of UNIKOM [A/57/813]. On the recommendation of the Fifth (Administrative and Budgetary) Committee [A/57/833], the Assembly adopted **resolution 57/330** without vote [agenda item 132 (a)].

Financing of the United Nations Iraq-Kuwait Observation Mission

The General Assembly,

Having considered the reports of the Secretary-General on the financing of the United Nations Iraq-Kuwait Observation Mission and the related reports of the Advisory Committee on Administrative and Budgetary Questions,

Recalling Security Council resolutions 687(1991) of 3 April 1991 and 689(1991) of 9 April 1991, by which the Council decided to establish the United Nations Iraq-Kuwait Observation Mission and to review the question of its termination or continuation every six months,

Recalling also its resolution 45/260 of 3 May 1991 on the financing of the Observation Mission and its subsequent resolutions and decisions thereon, the latest of which was resolution 56/297 of 27 June 2002,

Reaffirming the general principles underlying the financing of United Nations peacekeeping operations, as stated in General Assembly resolutions 1874(S-IV) of 27 June 1963, 3101(XXVIII) of 11 December 1973 and 55/235 of 23 December 2000,

Expressing its appreciation for the substantial voluntary contributions made to the Observation Mission by the Government of Kuwait and the contributions of other Governments,

Mindful of the fact that it is essential to provide the Observation Mission with the necessary financial resources to enable it to fulfil its responsibilities under the relevant resolutions of the Security Council,

1. *Takes note* of the status of contributions to the United Nations Iraq-Kuwait Observation Mission as at 31 March 2003, including the contributions outstanding in the amount of 10.2 million United States dollars, representing some 3 per cent of the total assessed contributions, notes with concern that only thirty-six Member States have paid their assessed contributions in full, and urges all other Member States, in particular those in arrears, to ensure payment of their outstanding assessed contributions;

2. *Expresses its continued appreciation* of the decision of the Government of Kuwait to defray two thirds of the cost of the Observation Mission, effective 1 November 1993;

3. *Expresses its appreciation* to those Member States which have paid their assessed contributions in full, and urges all other Member States to make every possible effort to ensure payment of their assessed contributions to the Observation Mission in full;

4. *Expresses concern* at the financial situation with regard to peacekeeping activities, in particular as regards the reimbursements to troop contributors that bear additional burdens owing to overdue payments by Member States of their assessments;

5. *Also expresses concern* at the delay experienced by the Secretary-General in deploying and providing adequate resources to some recent peacekeeping missions, in particular those in Africa;

6. *Emphasizes* that all future and existing peacekeeping missions shall be given equal and non-discriminatory treatment in respect of financial and administrative arrangements;

7. *Also emphasizes* that all peacekeeping missions shall be provided with adequate resources for the effective and efficient discharge of their respective mandates;

8. *Reiterates its request* to the Secretary-General to make the fullest possible use of facilities and equipment at the United Nations Logistics Base at Brindisi, Italy, in order to minimize the costs of procurement for the Observation Mission;

9. *Endorses* the recommendation contained in paragraph 5 of the report of the Advisory Committee on Administrative and Budgetary Questions, and requests the Secretary-General to ensure its full implementation;

10. *Requests* the Secretary-General to take all necessary action to ensure that the Observation Mission is administered with maximum efficiency and economy;

11. *Also requests* the Secretary-General, in order to reduce the cost of employing General Service staff, to continue efforts to recruit local staff for the Observation Mission against General Service posts, commensurate with the requirements of the Observation Mission;

Financial performance report for the period from 1 July 2001 to 30 June 2002

12. *Decides* to continue its consideration of the report of the Secretary-General on the financial performance of the Observation Mission for the period from 1 July 2001 to 30 June 2002, and of the treatment of the unencumbered balance and other income in the total amount of 6,443,300 dollars in respect of the financial period ended 30 June 2002, at the main part of its fifty-eighth session;

Budget estimates for the period from 1 July 2003 to 30 June 2004

13. *Takes note* of the report of the Secretary-General on the budget of the Observation Mission and the note by the Secretary-General on the financing of the Ob-

servation Mission for the period from 1 July 2003 to 30 June 2004;

14. *Authorizes* the Secretary-General to enter into commitments in an amount not exceeding 12 million dollars for the period from 1 July to 31 October 2003, to be financed from the accumulated fund balance in the Special Account for the United Nations Iraq-Kuwait Observation Mission;

15. *Emphasizes* that no peacekeeping mission shall be financed by borrowing funds from other active peacekeeping missions;

16. *Encourages* the Secretary-General to continue to take additional measures to ensure the safety and security of all personnel under the auspices of the United Nations participating in the Observation Mission;

17. *Invites* voluntary contributions to the Observation Mission in cash and in the form of services and supplies acceptable to the Secretary-General, to be administered, as appropriate, in accordance with the procedure and practices established by the General Assembly;

18. *Decides* to include in the provisional agenda of its fifty-eighth session, under the item entitled "Financing of the activities arising from Security Council resolution 687(1991)", the sub-item entitled "Financing of the United Nations Iraq-Kuwait Observation Mission".

On 23 December, the Assembly took note of the Secretary-General's note on the financing of UNIKOM for the period from 1 July 2003 to 30 June 2004 [A/58/386] and the related report of ACABQ [A/58/441], and decided to keep under review, during its fifty-eighth (2004) session, the sub-item entitled "Financing of the activities arising from Security Council resolution 687(1991): United Nations Iraq-Kuwait Observation Mission" (**decision 58/559**).

Also on 23 December, the Assembly decided that the item on the financing of activities arising from resolution 687(1991) remained for consideration at the fifty-eighth session (**decision 58/565**).

Arms and related sanctions

Sanctions Committee activities

The Security Council Committee established by resolution 661(1990) [YUN 1990, p. 192] (Sanctions Committee for Iraq) was terminated on 21 November 2003 in accordance with resolution 1483(2003) (see p. 338).

During the year, the Committee issued four reports on the implementation of the arms and related sanctions against Iraq, in accordance with the guidelines approved by Council resolution 700(1991) [YUN 1991, p. 198] for facilitating full international implementation of resolution 687 (1991) [ibid., p. 172]. The reports were transmitted to the Council on 16 January [S/2003/61], 25 April [S/2003/507], 14 July [S/2003/714] and 10 October [S/2003/1032]. All of the reports noted that no State or international organization had consulted the Committee on whether certain items fell within the provisions of paragraph 24 of resolution 687 (1991) and no international organization had reported any relevant information requested under the guidelines. The October report noted that since April 2003, the situation concerning Iraq had undergone fundamental changes and the Council had lifted all prohibitions related to trade with Iraq. However, prohibitions related to the sale or supply to Iraq of arms and related materiel were still in place; hence the Committee had continued to submit its reports and would continued to fulfil its mandate until the termination of its work on 21 November.

Security Council consideration (22 December). On 22 December [meeting 4888], the Security Council heard a presentation by the Chairman of the Sanctions Committee for Iraq who noted that the Committee had been terminated on 21 November, in accordance with Council resolution 1483(2003), after 13 years of a comprehensive sanctions regime. As a subsidiary organ of the Council, the Committee had executed the political decisions of the Council as manifested in relevant Council resolutions. The Committee's mandate comprised two major elements: the implementation and supervision of the sanctions regime against Iraq and the humanitarian oil-for-food programme. Confronted with the interruption of the programme in March due to the military conflict, the Council adopted resolution 1472(2003) (see p. 363), which allowed humanitarian emergency deliveries out of the existing pipeline of approved contracts. The adoption of the resolution on 28 March was the first time that the Council achieved consensus on an issue related to Iraq after months of division. After the war and adoption of resolution 1483(2003) on 22 May, the Committee was tasked to supervise the transitional process leading to the termination of the oil-for-food programme on 21 November and the transfer of all responsibilities from the Office of the Iraq Programme to the Coalition Provisional Authority. The Committee also fulfilled its additional new task pursuant to paragraphs 19 and 23 of resolution 1483(2003) relating to funds or other assets or resources that had been removed from Iraq or acquired by Saddam Hussein or other officials of the former regime (see also p. 362). On 11 June, the Committee adopted guidelines to identify individuals and entities whose financial assets should be transferred to the Development Fund for Iraq; on 26 June, a first list of such individuals was adopted by the

Committee and a list of respective entities followed on 21 November.

Establishment of Security Council Committee pursuant to resolution 1483(2003)

On 24 November [meeting 4872], the Council unanimously adopted **resolution 1518(2003)**. The draft [S/2003/1107] was submitted by Bulgaria, Chile, Guinea, Spain, the United Kingdom and the United States. Council members had before them two press releases from the Sanctions Committee, dated 12 June [SC/7791-IK/365] and 29 July [SC/7831-IK/372], which set the guidelines and definitions for the application of paragraphs 19 and 23 of resolution 1483(2003) (see p. 338).

The Security Council,

Recalling all of its relevant resolutions,

Recalling further its earlier decision in resolution 1483(2003) of 22 May 2003 to terminate the Security Council Committee established by resolution 661 (1990),

Stressing the importance of all Member States fulfilling their obligations under paragraph 10 of resolution 1483(2003),

Determining that the situation in Iraq, although improved, continues to constitute a threat to international peace and security,

Acting under Chapter VII of the Charter of the United Nations,

1. *Decides* to establish, with immediate effect, in accordance with rule 28 of its provisional rules of procedure, a Committee of the Security Council, consisting of all the members of the Council, to continue to identify pursuant to paragraph 19 of resolution 1483(2003) individuals and entities referred to in paragraph 19 of that resolution, including by updating the list of individuals and entities that have already been identified by the Committee established pursuant to paragraph 6 of resolution 661(1990), and to report on its work to the Council;

2. *Decides also* to adopt the guidelines and definitions previously agreed by the Committee established pursuant to paragraph 6 of resolution 661(1990) to implement the provisions of paragraphs 19 and 23 of resolution 1483(2003), and decides that the guidelines and definitions can be amended by the Committee in the light of further considerations;

3. *Decides further* that the mandate of the Committee referred to in paragraph 1 above shall be kept under review, and decides to consider the possible authorization of the additional task of observing fulfilment by Member States of their obligations under paragraph 10 of resolution 1483(2003);

4. *Decides* to remain seized of the matter.

Speaking after the vote, France said that the adopted resolution created a new committee in charge of taking over from the Sanctions Committee pursuant to Council resolution 661(1990), in order to ensure the follow-up of the implementation of freezes and transfers of the financial assets of the Government of Saddam Hussein and of high officials of his regime, as provided for in resolution 1483(2003). It was important to ensure, from a practical and technical standpoint, the continuity of the monitoring of the implementation of those financial sanctions. France stressed that for reasons of principle related to the coherence of the Council's practice in monitoring the implementation of sanctions, and bearing in mind the situation in Iraq, it would seem particularly desirable to broaden the mandate of the new committee as soon as possible to include monitoring the arms embargo.

Oil-for-food programme

In accordance with Security Council resolution 1483(2003) (see p. 338), the oil-for-food programme was phased out over a six-month period and terminated on 21 November 2003. Responsibility for the administration of any remaining programme activities was transferred to the Coalition Provisional Authority. The programme, established by Council resolution 986(1995) [YUN 1995, p. 475], authorized States to import Iraqi petroleum and petroleum products as a temporary measure to finance humanitarian assistance, thereby alleviating the adverse consequences of the sanctions regime on the Iraqi people.

Phase XII

Sanctions Committee report. The Sanctions Committee report for phase XII, 30 May to 4 December 2002, of the oil-for-food programme was transmitted to the Council President on 3 March [S/2003/331]. Issues considered by the Committee included the sale of petroleum and petroleum products, humanitarian supplies to Iraq, and matters relating to oil-indsutry spare parts and equipment for Iraq. The Committee also held formal and informal meetings to discuss various issues related to the humanitarian situation in Iraq and implementation of the oil-for-food programme. The oil overseers continued to advise the Committee on oil-pricing mechanisms, oil contract approvals and amendments, management of revenue objectives and other pertinent questions related to export and monitoring.

As at 31 October 2002, the oil overseers, on behalf of the Committee, had approved 192 oil contracts involving purchasers from 41 countries. The total quantity of oil approved for export under those contracts corresponded to 475 million barrels, with an estimated value of 11.5 billion euros. The contracted amount exceeded the Iraqi export capacity during the phase and the actual volume of oil lifted was expected to be substantially lower. The average rate of Iraqi crude oil exports from the start of the phase until 31 October was only 1.14 million barrels per day, representing about half of the assumed achievable and sustainable export level of 2.1 million barrels per day. Applications received as at 31 October for exports of humanitarian supplies to Iraq under phase XI totalled 1,897, of which 1,418 were approved by the Committee. From the beginning of phase XII until 31 October, 716 applications were received, of which 502 were approved. From the beginning of the programme up to 31 October 2002, 10,063 applications had been approved, with a total value of $22.34 billion. The work of confirmation of goods arrival by the independent inspection agents (Cotecna) continued at five entry points to Iraq. From the beginning of the process to 31 October, the total allocation for oil-industry spare parts and equipment amounted to $4.8 billion. Although the Multinational Interception Force reported a significant reduction in illegal oil exports from Iraq by sea in 2002, oil smuggling continued on a decreasing scale in the Gulf area.

Phase XIII

In accordance with paragraph 1 of Security Council resolution 1447(2002) [YUN 2002, p. 313], the new 180-day extension (phase XIII) of the humanitarian programme established by resolution 986(1995) [YUN 1995, p. 475] began on 5 December 2002. The distribution plan for the new phase was approved by the Secretary-General on 3 January [S/2003/6], on the understanding that its implementation would be governed by resolutions 986(1995), 1281(1999) [YUN 1999, p. 250], 1284 (1999) [ibid., p. 230], 1302(2000) [YUN 2000, p. 307], 1330(2000) [ibid., p. 310], 1360(2001) [YUN 2001, p. 305], 1382(2001) [ibid., p. 308], 1409(2002) [YUN 2002, p. 304], 1447(2002) and 1454(2002) [ibid., p. 307] and by the 1996 Memorandum of Understanding between the UN Secretariat and Iraq [YUN 1996, p. 226], without prejudice to Sanctions Committee procedures. The categorized lists of goods received and amended for the phase XII distribution plan [YUN 2002, p. 313] would constitute the basis for the categorized list for phase XIII. UNMOVIC and IAEA technical experts would provide further assessment following the submission of applications.

Communications (21-28 March). On 21 March [S/2003/358], Iraq condemned the submission by the UN Secretariat of a draft resolution containing changes to be made in the oil-for-food programme.

On 28 March [S/2003/389], Iraq informed the Council President that any discussion of an amendment to the 1996 Memorandum of Understanding between Iraq and the UN Secretariat without Iraq's participation was a violation of Council resolution 986(1995) and brooked no justification whatsoever.

SECURITY COUNCIL ACTION (March)

On 28 March [meeting 4732], the Security Council unanimously adopted **resolution 1472(2003)**. The draft [S/2003/381] was submitted by Angola, Bulgaria, Cameroon, Chile, China, France, Germany, Guinea, Mexico, Pakistan, the Russian Federation, Spain, the United Kingdom and the United States.

The Security Council,

Noting that under the provisions of article 55 of the fourth Geneva Convention relative to the Protection of Civilian Persons in Time of War, of 12 August 1949, to the fullest extent of the means available to it, the occupying Power has the duty of ensuring the food and medical supplies of the population, and should, in particular, bring in the necessary foodstuffs, medical stores and other articles if the resources of the occupied territory are inadequate,

Convinced of the urgent need to continue to provide humanitarian relief to the people of Iraq throughout the country on an equitable basis, and of the need to extend such humanitarian relief measures to the people of Iraq who leave the country as a result of hostilities,

Recalling its relevant resolutions, in particular resolutions 661(1990) of 6 August 1990, 986(1995) of 14 April 1995, 1409(2002) of 14 May 2002 and 1454(2002) of 30 December 2002, as they provide for humanitarian relief to the people of Iraq,

Noting the decision taken by the Secretary-General on 17 March 2003 to withdraw all United Nations and international staff tasked with the implementation of the "Oil-for-Food" Programme (hereinafter "the Programme") established pursuant to resolution 986 (1995),

Stressing the necessity to make every effort to sustain the operation of the present national food basket distribution network,

Stressing also the need for consideration of a further reassessment of the Programme during and after the emergency phase,

Reaffirming the respect for the right of the people of Iraq to determine their own political future and to control their own natural resources,

Reaffirming the commitment of all Member States to the sovereignty and territorial integrity of Iraq,

Acting under Chapter VII of the Charter of the United Nations,

1. *Requests* all parties concerned to abide strictly by their obligations under international law, in particular the Geneva Conventions of 1949 and the Regulations concerning the Laws and Customs of War on Land, adopted at The Hague on 18 October 1907, including those relating to the essential civilian needs of the people of Iraq, both inside and outside Iraq;

2. *Calls upon* the international community also to provide immediate humanitarian assistance to the people of Iraq, both inside and outside Iraq in consultation with relevant States, and in particular to respond immediately to any future humanitarian appeal of the United Nations, and supports the activities of the In-

ternational Committee of the Red Cross and other international humanitarian organizations;

3. *Recognizes* that additionally, in view of the exceptional circumstances prevailing currently in Iraq, on an interim and exceptional basis, technical and temporary adjustments should be made to the Programme so as to ensure the implementation of the approved funded and non-funded contracts concluded by the Government of Iraq for the humanitarian relief of the people of Iraq, including to meet the needs of refugees and internally displaced persons, in accordance with the present resolution;

4. *Authorizes* the Secretary-General and representatives designated by him to undertake as an urgent first step, and with the necessary coordination, the following measures:

(a) To establish alternative locations, both inside and outside Iraq, in consultation with the respective Governments, for the delivery, inspection and authenticated confirmation of humanitarian supplies and equipment provided under the Programme, as well as to redirect shipments of goods to those locations, as necessary;

(b) To review, as a matter of urgency, the approved funded and non-funded contracts concluded by the Government of Iraq to determine the relative priorities of the need for adequate medicine, health supplies, foodstuffs and other materials and supplies for essential civilian needs represented in these contracts, which can be shipped within the period of the present mandate, to proceed with these contracts in accordance with such priorities;

(c) To contact suppliers of these contracts to determine the precise location of contracted goods and, when necessary, to require suppliers to delay, accelerate or divert shipments;

(d) To negotiate and agree upon necessary adjustments in the terms or conditions of these contracts and their respective letters of credit and to implement the measures referred to in paragraphs 4 (a), (b) and (c), notwithstanding distribution plans approved under the Programme;

(e) To negotiate and execute new contracts for essential medical items under the Programme and to authorize issuance of the relevant letters of credit, notwithstanding approved distribution plans, provided that such items cannot be delivered in execution of contracts pursuant to paragraph 4 (b) and subject to the approval of the Security Council Committee established by resolution 661(1990);

(f) To transfer unencumbered funds between the accounts created pursuant to paragraphs 8 (a) and (b) of resolution 986(1995) on an exceptional and reimbursable basis as necessary to ensure the delivery of essential humanitarian supplies to the people of Iraq and to use the funds in the escrow accounts referred to in paragraphs 8 (a) and (b) of resolution 986(1995) to implement the Programme as provided for in the present resolution, irrespective of the phase in which such funds entered the escrow accounts or the phase to which those funds may have been allocated;

(g) To use, subject to procedures to be decided by the Committee prior to the end of the period set out in paragraph 10 below and based on recommendations provided by the Office of the Iraq Programme, funds deposited in the accounts created pursuant to paragraphs 8 (a) and (b) of resolution 986(1995), as necessary and appropriate, to compensate suppliers and shippers for agreed additional shipping, transportation and storage costs incurred as a result of diverting and delaying shipments as directed by him according to the provisions of paragraphs 4 (a), (b) and (c) in order to perform his functions set out in paragraph 4(d);

(h) To meet additional operational and administrative costs resulting from the implementation of the temporarily modified Programme by the funds in the escrow account established pursuant to paragraph 8 (d) of resolution 986(1995) in the same manner as costs arising from those activities set forth in paragraph 8(d) of resolution 986(1995) in order to perform his functions set out in paragraph 4 (d);

(i) To use funds deposited in the escrow accounts established pursuant to paragraphs 8 (a) and (b) of resolution 986(1995) for the purchase of locally produced goods and to meet the local cost for essential civilian needs which have been funded in accordance with the provisions of resolution 986(1995) and related resolutions, including, where appropriate, the costs of milling, transportation and other costs necessary to facilitate the delivery of essential humanitarian supplies to the people of Iraq;

5. *Expresses its readiness* as a second step to authorize the Secretary-General to perform additional functions with the necessary coordination, as soon as the situation permits, as activities of the Programme in Iraq resume;

6. *Expresses its readiness also* to consider making additional funds available, including from the account created pursuant to paragraph 8 (c) of resolution 986(1995), on an exceptional and reimbursable basis, to meet further the humanitarian needs of the people of Iraq;

7. *Decides* that, notwithstanding the provisions of resolution 661(1990) and resolution 687(1991) of 3 April 1991 and for the duration of the present resolution, all applications outside the Programme submitted by the United Nations agencies, programmes and funds, other international organizations and non-governmental organizations for distribution or use in Iraq of emergency humanitarian supplies and equipment, other than medicines, health supplies and foodstuffs, shall be reviewed by the Committee, under a 24-hour no-objection procedure;

8. *Urges* all parties concerned, consistent with the Geneva Conventions and the Hague Regulations, to allow full, unimpeded access by international humanitarian organizations to all people of Iraq in need of assistance, to make available all necessary facilities for their operations and to promote the safety, security and freedom of movement of United Nations and associated personnel and their assets, as well as personnel of humanitarian organizations in Iraq in meeting such needs;

9. *Directs* the Committee to monitor closely the implementation of the provisions of paragraph 4 above and, in that regard, requests the Secretary-General to update the Committee on the measures as they are being taken and to consult with the Committee on prioritization of contracts for shipments of goods, other than foodstuffs, medicines, health and water sanitation related supplies;

10. *Decides* that the provisions contained in paragraph 4 above shall remain in force for a period of 45 days following the date of adoption of the present resolution and may be subject to further renewal by the Council;

11. *Requests* the Secretary-General to take all measures required for the implementation of the present resolution and to report to the Council prior to the termination of the period defined in paragraph 10 above;

12. *Decides* to remain seized of the matter.

Speaking after the vote, the United States said it had full confidence that the Secretary-General and the UN Office of the Iraq Programme would effectively carry out the task of resuming the oil-for-food programme. The United States would facilitate the necessary coordination on the ground in Iraq between coalition authorities and the United Nations and associated relief agency staff, as oil-for-food supplies and other humanitarian assistance arrived and were distributed as circumstances on the ground permitted. It also added that it was gratified that the Council had been able to come together to take that step to meet the immediate humanitarian needs of the Iraqi people.

Communication (31 March). On 31 March [S/2003/396], the Russian Federation said that the adoption of resolution 1472(2003) did not alter the essence of the humanitarian programme, which had been operating for seven years on the basis of Council resolutions and the 1996 Memorandum of Understanding. It merely involved some procedural specifications pertaining to the operation of the programme for the purpose of promptly solving humanitarian problems caused by the war in Iraq. The adoption of the resolution did not mean a legitimization of the military action by the members of the coalition. Under international humanitarian law, the members of the coalition bore responsibility for solving humanitarian problems in the occupied territories.

SECURITY COUNCIL ACTION (April)

On 24 April [meeting 4743], the Council unanimously adopted **resolution 1476(2003)**. The draft [S/2003/465] was prepared in consultations among Council members.

The Security Council,

Recalling its relevant resolutions, in particular resolutions 661(1990) of 6 August 1990, 986(1995) of 14 April 1995, 1409(2002) of 14 May 2002, 1454(2002) of 30 December 2002 and 1472(2003) of 28 March 2003, as they provide for humanitarian relief to the people of Iraq,

Acting under Chapter VII of the Charter of the United Nations,

1. *Decides* that the provisions contained in paragraph 4 of resolution 1472(2003) shall remain in force until 3 June 2003 and may be subject to further renewal by the Council;

2. *Decides* to remain seized of the matter.

Communication. On 24 April [S/2003/499], South Africa, on behalf of South African companies that held contracts under the oil-for-food programme, requested the Council President to provide more information regarding the temporary adjustments that were made to the programme pursuant to resolution 1472(2003) (see p. 363). The request related mainly to goods that were not identified as priority goods, but were already deemed eligible for payment.

Report of Secretary-General (May). In response to resolution 1447(2002), the Secretary-General submitted a 28 May progress report on phase XIII of the oil-for-food programme [S/2003/576]. The report provided information on all implementation aspects up to 23 May 2003.

The Secretary-General observed that since its inception in 1996, the programme had been implemented within the context of a rigorous sanctions regime. It had made a major difference in the daily lives of the Iraqi people, serving as a lifeline to a large segment of the population. As at 20 May, oil proceeds since the start of the programme's implementation totalled approximately $65 billion, of which more than $46 billion had been allocated to the humanitarian programme. A total of $38 billion had been apportioned to the 15 governorates of the centre and south and $8.11 billion to the three northern governorates. More than $28 billion worth of goods had been delivered to Iraq as a whole, including $13 billion for foodstuffs, $2.2 billion for food handling, $2.21 billion for medicines, $1.17 billion for water and sanitation, $2.01 billion for electricity, $2.29 billion for agriculture and irrigation, $1.66 billion for housing, $1.19 billion for transportation and telecommunications, $586 million for education and $1.6 billion for oil-industry spare parts and equipment. In addition, goods to the value of $9.4 billion were in the pipeline for the centre/south and $1.55 million for the three northern governorates. The implementation of programme activities during phase XIII was suspended temporarily due to the military conflict, which necessitated the withdrawal of UN international personnel from Iraq on 17 March. However, some activities continued to be undertaken by the UN national staff, especially with regard to the distribution of food and medical supplies. Despite precarious security conditions, an increasing number of UN international staff began returning to Iraq as of 4 April and resumed implementation of programme activities.

On 22 May, the Security Council, in resolution 1483(2003) (see p. 338), decided that, with the exception of prohibitions related to the sale or supply of arms and related materiel, all prohibitions related to trade with Iraq and the provision of financial or economic resources to Iraq would no longer apply. By the same resolution, the Council also decided to phase out the oil-for-food programme over a period of six months. The Secretary-General would continue to fulfil the responsibilities entrusted to him under resolutions 1472(2003) (see p. 363) and 1476(2003) (see p. 365), in coordination with the Authority, and would terminate within that time period the programme's operations and transfer responsibility for the administration of the remaining activities to the Authority.

Report of Secretary-General (June). Pursuant to paragraph 16 (c) of resolution 1483(2003), the Secretary-General submitted to the Security Council on 11 June a report [S/2003/640] on the estimated operating budget needed to ensure the continued functioning of activities associated with the implementation of that resolution, including the termination of the oil-for-food programme; the projected costs associated with restoring Iraqi government funds that were provided by Member States to the Secretary-General as requested in resolution 778(1992) [YUN 1992, p. 320]; and the projected costs associated with the Secretary-General's Special Representative and the qualified representative to serve on the International Advisory and Monitoring Board (IAMB).

The Secretary-General said that, since the adoption of the resolution, the monitoring and observation tasks deriving from resolution 986(1995) [YUN 1995, p. 475] and the management of letters of credit in respect of oil sales had been discontinued. All substantive operations would be phased out within the six months following the adoption of resolution 1483(2003), including the handover of operational responsibilities and relevant documentation to the Authority/Iraqi interim administration. All UN agencies that supported the implementation of resolution 986(1995) would cease their activities by the end of November 2003. During that period, there would be a need to continue to provide administrative, financial, personnel, information technology, transport, technical, procurement, logistical and warehousing support. After 21 November, a limited number of administrative personnel would remain in Iraq to complete the necessary administrative tasks and close down at the field level; that phase was scheduled to be completed by the end of December 2003. With regard to the administrative tasks at respective agencies' headquarters, it was anticipated that they would be completed by the end of March 2004. A limited number of staff would be required in New York until the end of June 2004.

With regard to letters of credit issued for the purchase of humanitarian supplies for the south/centre of Iraq, since they were irrevocable and non-transferable they would continue to be handled by the United Nations beyond 21 November and would therefore not be transferred to the Authority. As at 11 June, some 3,000 such letters of credit were outstanding, with a value of some $8 billion. The United Nations would retain responsibility for their administration until they were executed or they expired. Collateral for the full value of the letters of credit would be kept by the United Nations. Any balance left after the execution or expiration of such letters of credit would be transferred to the Development Fund for Iraq. For the period after 21 November, the Secretary-General would be making arrangements with the Authority to have the Authority designated as the entity authorized to give authenticated confirmation of the delivery of goods. Assuming that all deliveries were completed by 21 November under outstanding letters of credit, it was anticipated that all letters of credit would have been submitted, authenticated and processed by the end of June 2004; that would allow all financial transactions to be registered in 2004, a final financial statement for the whole operation to be prepared by December 2004 and a final external audit report to be prepared by April 2005.

Given its complexity, it was difficult to evaluate fully, within the time given, the precise costs of effectively terminating the programme and handing over residual activities in an orderly manner. The best estimate for all known and projected costs to ensure the continued functioning of activities associated with the implementation of resolution 1483(2003), both at Headquarters and in the field, including the termination of the oil-for-food programme, were estimated at $106.6 million. Of that amount, $81 million related to the period ending 21 November; the remaining $25.6 million related to liquidation tasks. In addition, there was a need to have a contingency reserve to meet any potential costs that might arise but could not be identified in preparing the estimates. Such a contingency would be established at 15 per cent of the total estimated costs. The known and projected costs associated with restoring the Iraqi government funds that were provided by Member States to the Secretary-General as requested in resolution 778(1992) [YUN 1992, p. 320] were minimal. The restoration of funds to Member States as per paragraph 17 of resolution 1483(2003) was under way. An amount of $404.9 million would be restored, $65.8 million of which would be refunded from balances remaining in the account and the remainder of $339.1 million would be funded from unencumbered funds in the accounts established pursuant to resolution 986(1995).

The costs associated with the Secretary-General's Special Representative and his qualified representative to serve on IAMB should constitute expenses of the Organization rather than be funded from the account established pursuant to resolution 986(1995). No provision had therefore been made in that connection. The balance at the end of May 2003 in that account was estimated at $400 million. After deduction of the estimated operating budget ($106.6 million) and the contingency reserve ($16 million), the surplus available for transfer to the Development Fund for Iraq amounted to $277.4 million. Upon the final closing of the accounts and subsequent to their final audit, any balance remaining from the operational budget and/or the contingency fund would be transferred to the Development Fund for Iraq.

Security Council consideration (28 October). On 28 October [meeting 4851], the Council was briefed by the Executive Director of the Office of the Iraq Programme (OIP), Benon Sevan.

Mr. Sevan said that the United Nations would terminate the oil-for-food programme on 21 November and would continue to facilitate a smooth handover to the Authority, in close cooperation with the relevant Iraqi authorities. In view of the common position taken by the United Nations and the Authority, he saw no alternative to the transfer of assets, ongoing operations and responsibility for the administration of and remaining activity under the programme to the Authority "as is", together with the relevant documentation. Handing over a multi-billion-dollar programme of such complexity and magnitude in a six-month period, as mandated by resolution 1483(2003), would have been difficult even under the best of circumstances. Doing so under conditions of insecurity and reduced on-site staffing capacity required a degree of realism, understanding and pragmatism. Most of the phase-down activities had been undertaken in the three Iraqi northern governorates, where the United Nations was responsible for the implementation of the programme on behalf of the former Government of Iraq. In the north, the handover involved the transfer of projects, assets, inventories and relevant documentation, contracts signed by the United Nations and its agencies with international and national contractors, in addition to an agreement with the Authority on liabilities and calculations concerning ongoing costs of projects after their handover to the Authority. Some $8.1 billion had been allocated to the three northern governorates since the start of the programme's implementation in December 1996 [YUN 1996, p. 225].

With regard to the 15 governorates in the centre and south of Iraq, prior to the war the UN role was limited primarily to monitoring and observing the distribution and utilization of humanitarian supplies provided under the programme. Handover arrangements for the centre and south involved a tripartite review by the United Nations, the Authority and relevant Iraqi authorities of all remaining contracts for humanitarian supplies and equipment submitted under the programme. The review had covered approved and fully-funded contracts, and also those approved but not funded. Adjustments had been made for alternative delivery and authentication sites to enable the delivery of supplies and equipment to Iraq. It was envisaged from the outset that those activities would take place inside Iraq. However, that scenario was undermined by chronic insecurity and, in particular, the 19 August terrorist attack on the UN headquarters in Baghdad. Given the reduction in UN personnel and the late deployment of a handover team by the Authority, the intended joint physical review of all programme assets by the United Nations, the Authority and the local authorities had not been possible. Accordingly, completed and ongoing projects and activities would be transferred to the Authority through dossiers prepared for each project and activity.

As at 27 October, 3,154 approved and funded contracts worth some $6.36 billion had been classified to have relative utility. The number of approved and funded contracts that had not been included in the final review was estimated to be 1,621, with a total value of $1.5 billion. Also, 273 approved but unfunded contracts worth some $700 million had been funded following determination of their relative utility and urgent need. There remained 3,319 approved but unfunded contracts, with a total value of $6.5 billion. Based on the essential needs of the Iraqi people, as identified by the United Nations, the Authority and relevant Iraqi authorities, and following the OIP Executive Director's recommendation, the Sanctions Committee approved, on an exceptional basis, 13 projects for the procurement of items, with a total value of $459 million, not covered by approved and funded or unfunded contracts. As at October, UN agencies and programmes had arranged the delivery of goods worth $1 billion. Some of the goods were still at locations outside Iraq and if they could not be delivered to Iraq by 21 November, arrangements would be made for their transfer to the Authority outside Iraq. A total of $398 million worth of goods was established to be in transit to Iraq when the UN independent inspection agents were withdrawn in mid-March 2003 due to security conditions. A total value of $315 million for such goods had been prioritized and arrangements had been made for the suppliers of the remaining goods to be compensated. The independent inspection agent, Cotecna, was stationed at inspection sites outside Iraq and was authenticating the arrival of goods consistent with arrangements agreed upon between the United Nations, the Authority and the relevant Iraqi authorities. However, due to the fact that Cotecna personnel were not permitted to operate at the port of Umm Qasr, the issuance of authenticated confirmation for goods destined for that port would need to be halted, unless the Authority provided appropriate indemnifications. The Authority had not provided OIP with information regarding contact points within the port or an update concerning any arrangements made to confirm the arrival of goods. Since 10 October, Cotecna had inspected 25 consignments under the revised authentication procedures, with no confirmation of receipt. If that matter was not urgently addressed, the confidence of suppliers in the authentication process could erode, which, in turn, could adversely affect the delivery pipeline. Furthermore, in July, the Authority was provided with details of 21 contracts in connection with which suppliers claimed to have provided services prior to the war, which could not be authenticated due to the withdrawal of Cotecna. Despite repeated reminders, the Authority had only been able to produce a negative response in connection with two of the contracts concerned.

The entire oil-for-food database would be transferred to the Authority on 21 November. The Authority needed to ensure that appropriate arrangements were in place, effective 22 November, for the management of the billions of dollars' worth of supplies and equipment to Iraq from the programme's delivery pipeline and for authenticating the arrival of those goods in order to facilitate payment to suppliers—perhaps through retention of Cotecna's services by the Authority for a limited period after the termination of the programme. Each UN agency and programme had devised individual exit strategies, based on the levels of project implementation and the possible future humanitarian involvement of the organizations concerned under their respective regular programme activities. An agreement had been reached with the Authority for the funding of ongoing projects to be completed after 21 November. Special arrangements would need to be made for goods held or warehoused outside Iraq, largely in neighbouring States. Since the start of the programme in 1996, approximately $65 billion worth of oil was exported; more than $46 billion of that amount was allocated to the programme after deductions for other accounts pursuant to relevant resolutions. Under the programme, more than $30 billion worth of goods had been delivered to Iraq as a whole, including foodstuffs worth $12 billion; food handling worth $2.2 billion; agriculture worth $2.4 billion; medicines worth $2.3 billion; water and sanitation worth $1.3 billion; electricity sector goods worth $2.2 billion; housing worth $1.7 billion; and, for the oil sector, goods worth $1.9 billion.

The United Kingdom said that the Authority and Iraqi ministry officials were engaged in developing an effective transition strategy to ensure the efficient delivery of goods as well as adequate warehousing and inventory management. The Authority would continue to honour its existing commitments to support the fulfilment of all prioritized contracts and was focused on designing a sustainable and predictable goods-authentication system that would pose no problems to suppliers.

Security Council consideration (20 November). On 20 November [meeting 4868], the Secretary-General addressed the Council, stating that it was meeting to mark the completion of one of the largest, most complex and unusual tasks that was ever entrusted to the UN Secretariat—the only humanitarian programme ever to have been funded entirely from resources belonging to the nation it was designed to help. In its nearly seven years of operation, the oil-for-food programme had been required to meet an almost impossible series of challenges, using some $46 billion of Iraqi export earnings on behalf of the Iraqi people. During those years, the programme delivered food rations sufficient to feed all 27 million residents of Iraq. As a result, the malnutrition rate among Iraqi children was reduced by 50 per cent, national vaccination campaigns reduced child mortality from preventable diseases and there had been no reported cases of polio in Iraq for almost three years. Electricity blackouts in Baghdad were reduced under peak summer loads and clean water became more available for personal use. The programme also enabled the overcrowded schools throughout the country to operate in two shifts instead of three. At midnight on 21 November, the United Nations would hand over all the programme's responsibilities, together with the remaining funds and assets—assets ranging from schools to electrical power stations and some $8.2 billion worth of food, medicines and other essential supplies—to the Authority. The actual delivery of those items would continue well into 2004. Any unspent or undisbursed amounts would be transferred to the Development Fund for Iraq after the programme's closure. The Authority was making arrangements to transfer most of the 2,500 Iraqis who had been working for the United Nations in the three northern governorates to posts in the local government. The Secretary-General hoped that their colleagues serving in the centre and south of Iraq, over 800 of them in all, would receive similar consideration. He also said that the United Nations took pride in the fact that it had achieved an orderly handover of such a large and expensive programme on time and in spite of the insecurity in Iraq and the disruptive bomb attack on its headquarters in Baghdad. As the United Nations was closing the oil-for-food programme, it remained determined to continue helping Iraq's long-suffering people.

SECURITY COUNCIL ACTION (November)

On 20 November [meeting 4868], following consultations among Security Council members, the President made statement **S/PRST/2003/24** on behalf of the Council:

The Security Council has heard the statement by the Secretary-General and has considered the briefing by the Executive Director of the Office of the Iraq Programme on the termination on 21 November 2003 of the United Nations humanitarian programme for Iraq ("the Programme") and the transfer of the responsibility for the administration of any remaining activity under the Programme to the Coalition Provisional Authority in Iraq in accordance with Council resolution 1483(2003) of 22 May 2003.

The Council underlines the exceptionally important role of the Programme in providing humanitarian assistance to the people of Iraq under the regime of sanctions imposed by the Council on the previous Government of Iraq. Under this unique programme the value of humanitarian goods delivered to Iraq during the period from December 1996 to March 2003 amounted to about 30 billion United States dollars. Those deliveries made it possible to provide to the Iraqi people essential foods and medicines, as well as to supply various equipment and materials for the key sectors of the Iraqi economy. Purchases under the Programme will in the next few months play a key role in the economic reconstruction of Iraq by providing vital goods in the amount of more than 6 billion United States dollars.

The Council expresses its deep gratitude to the Secretary-General, to the Office of the Iraq Programme, to United Nations personnel who worked on the ground in Iraq and to all other United Nations agencies and structures involved, and applauds their commitment and professionalism. It also thanks the chairmen and members of the Security Council Committee established by resolution 661(1990) for their dedicated efforts to implement the Programme since its inception, and in implementing resolution 1483(2003).

The Council emphasizes the need for continued international efforts aimed at the reconstruction of Iraq and, in this context, takes note with satisfaction of the statements made by the representatives of the United States of America and the United Kingdom of Great Britain and Northern Ireland on the measures which the Coalition Provisional Authority intends to take in order to continue the payment mechanisms and the deliveries under the Programme.

The Council recognizes the important role of the United Nations in coordinating the termination of the Programme, including the transfer at the earliest possible time of all surplus funds in the escrow accounts to the Development Fund for Iraq.

The Council recalls the vital role foreseen for the United Nations in resolutions 1483(2003), 1500 (2003) of 14 August 2003 and 1511(2003) of 16 October 2003, as circumstances permit, inter alia, in the areas of humanitarian assistance, facilitation of economic rehabilitation and reconstruction.

UN Compensation Commission and Fund

The United Nations Compensation Commission, established in 1991 [YUN 1991, p. 195] for the resolution and payment of claims against Iraq for losses and damage resulting from its 1990 invasion and occupation of Kuwait [YUN 1990, p. 189], continued in 2003 to expedite the prompt settlement of claims through the United Nations Compensation Fund, which was established at the same time as the Commission.

Governing Council. The Commission's Governing Council held four sessions in Geneva during the year—the forty-seventh (11-13 March) [S/2003/195], the forty-eighth (24-26 June) [S/2003/755], the forty-ninth (16-18 September) [S/2003/914] and the fiftieth (16-18 December) [S/2003/1205]—at which it considered the reports and recommendations of the Panels of Commissioners appointed to review specific instalments of various categories of claims. The Governing Council also acted on the Executive Secretary's report submitted at each session, which, in addition to providing a summary of the previous period's activities, covered the processing, withdrawal and payment of claims.

Other matters considered by the Council during the year included Iraq's contribution to the Compensation Fund and arrangements for ensuring that payments were made into the Fund; the distribution of payments and transparency; and requests for late filings of claims.

Communication. In a 15 January letter to the Secretary-General [S/2003/57], Iraq drew attention to the fact that the Compensation Commission's practices deprived Iraq of the exercise of its right of self-defence, due to the fact that it was not

Other issues

Iraqi complaints

Iraq submitted several letters to the Secretary-General and the Security Council President on the military build-up and exercises carried out by United States and British armed forces from January to March 2003 near the DMZ between Iraq and Kuwait that was controlled by UNIKOM [S/2003/14, S/2003/107, S/2003/296].

Reaffirming its absolute rejection of the northern and southern air exclusion (no-fly) zones imposed by the United Kingdom and the United States, Iraq reported wanton military attacks by British and United States aircraft against Iraqi civilians and property, and condemned countries that provided the logistic support for those attacks, namely Kuwait and Turkey [S/2003/108].

In a series of letters to the Secretary-General, Iraq detailed violations of its international boundaries committed by British and United States warplanes flying across the DMZ [S/2003/58, S/2003/222]; violations of its territorial waters and provocation by United States naval forces [S/2003/89, S/2003/109, S/2003/123]; and violations of its airspace and international borders [S/2003/230, S/2003/310]. It also reported that during the period from 1 to 31 January 2003, it had found and disposed of 459 items of unexploded ordnance left behind during the 1991 conflict [S/2003/297].

Timor-Leste

During 2003, the United Nations worked to strengthen the newly established democratic institutions in Timor-Leste, which became an independent sovereign State in 2002. The United Nations Mission of Support in East Timor (UNMISET) assisted in developing the Timorese civil administration and police force, which gradually assumed greater responsibility for the management of day-to-day affairs in their respective areas. It also aided Timorese authorities with the investigation and prosecution of serious crimes. Violent attacks by armed elements in January and February 2003 led the Security Council to slow down UNMISET's downsizing, in order to provide greater stability and allow for further development of Timorese police and military institutions. The Council extended UNMISET's mandate for a further year, until 20 May 2004. Despite the remarkable progress achieved towards nationhood, Timor-Leste would continue to need international assistance in certain key areas after the end of UNMISET's mandate.

Relations between Timor-Leste and Indonesia continued to develop and there was significant progress towards determining their joint border and making sustainable arrangements for its management, although the target date of 30 November for finalizing a provisional line for the border was not met. The two countries were also working towards, among other things, resolving residual refugee issues. The ratification of the Timor Sea Treaty between Timor-Leste and Australia, which would enable the exploitation of an offshore oil and gas field, was an important development for Timor-Leste's financial recovery.

The Secretary-General's Special Representative for Timor-Leste and UNMISET's Head, Kamalesh Sharma, briefed the Security Council on UNMISET's activities throughout the year.

UN Mission of Support in East Timor

UNMISET, established under Security Council resolution 1410(2002) [YUN 2002, p. 321], continued to carry out its mandate in Timor-Leste, which included providing assistance to the administrative, law enforcement and public security structures critical to the viability and political stability of Timor-Leste, in addition to contributing to the maintenance of its external and internal security. In the light of the rioting and violent attacks that took place in late 2002 and early 2003, the Security Council decided to slow the downsizing schedule for the military and police components of UNMISET. The Mission's mandate was extended for a further year, until 20 May 2004.

On 14 July [S/2003/716], the Secretary-General informed the Council of his intention to appoint Lieutenant General Khairuddin Mat Yusof (Malaysia) as Force Commander of UNMISET effective 31 August, replacing Major General Huck Gim Tan (Singapore). On 17 July [S/2003/717], the Council took note of the Secretary-General's intention.

Report of Secretary-General (March). Pursuant to Security Council resolution 1410(2002), the Secretary-General submitted a 3 March special report [S/2003/243] on significant changes that had taken place in Timor-Leste since his 6 November 2002 report [YUN 2002, p. 325]. The events suggested the need for a review of the UNMISET downsizing schedule, as envisioned in resolution 1410(2002). Accordingly, he made specific proposals for adjustments to the downsizing plan to allow UNMISET to accomplish its mandated tasks by June 2004 within that changed environment.

The Secretary-General said that since November 2002, there had been a sharp increase in the frequency and magnitude of security-related incidents, which demonstrated the scope of problems that could still emerge and the inadequacy of the means to address them, and they also suggested the need to adjust UNMISET's downsizing plan. The potential for grave civil disturbance became clear when riots erupted in the capital, Dili, on 4 December 2002 [YUN 2002, p. 327]. Further armed attacks took place in January and February 2003. In addition, credible evidence suggested that former militias and armed groups were establishing bases within the country in order to undermine stability. Those who sought to generate unrest could draw upon a largely youthful and unskilled population, which suffered a very high rate of unemployment and had extensive exposure to violence in the past. That situation was exacerbated by elements within the former refugee population located in Indonesia close to the Tactical Coordination Line (TCL)—the informal boundary agreed to by the United Nations Transitional Administration in East Timor (UNTAET) and the Indonesian authorities pending formal demarcation of the border. Former militia elements retained a degree of influence among the approximately 28,000 former refugees remaining in Indonesia and were actively involved in cross-border trade. That threat was likely to remain extant throughout the remainder of the UNMISET mandate and beyond, although supportive actions by the Indonesian military could contribute to containing and mitigating it. The Indonesian Government had indicated that it intended to resettle former East Timorese refugees; voluntary migration to other provinces could significantly improve the security environment. While Indonesia had begun the process, it had been unable to implement it fully due to financial and other constraints.

The 30 June 2003 target date for a finalized agreement on a line that constituted the border remained in effect, but the accomplishment of that objective was not assured. A meeting of a technical group on border demarcation and regulation was scheduled to take place in March. Border delineation, and subsequent demarcation, if decided, were of great importance in terms of removing a potential irritant to future relations between Indonesia and Timor-Leste. At the same time, that issue was not a panacea for all security problems and even a well-defined border would remain porous. Indonesian military authorities had indicated that their policy was not to demilitarize their side of the border, where they would maintain a troop and not a border police presence. The Timor-Leste Government was nonetheless proceeding with plans for police and civilian authorities to assume responsibility for border management.

The deterioration in the security situation suggested that serious deficiencies in Timorese and international capabilities existed and that those deficiencies would be exacerbated if UNMISET continued to follow its downsizing plan. At least a year of further development was required before the Timorese police were in a position to address the more demanding kinds of problems that had emerged since November 2002. Their premature engagement in such activities ran the risk of weakening them and of lowering their public standing. UNMISET's downsizing plans, if followed without change, would further weaken the Mission's real and perceived ability to respond to security challenges. Adjustments were necessary if UNMISET was to maintain security effectively in the short term and prepare the Timorese agencies to assume their full responsibility in the future. At the request of the UN Department of Peacekeeping Operations, former Military Adviser Maurice Baril (Canada) led a review and assessment mission to UNMISET from 15 to 23 January, as the Department's first Inspector-General. The mission's aim was to review UNMISET's capability to implement its mandate and to meet future challenges. The recommendations in the Secretary-General's special report were supported by and drew upon General Baril's findings regarding key areas where sustained or increased capacity was crucial for UNMISET to achieve its mandate.

UNMISET's original downsizing plan was predicated on the assumption that the threat from former militia elements would gradually diminish, that new threats of a similar scale would not emerge and that major civil disturbances would not occur, so that challenges on the ground would be on a scale for which Timor-Leste security agencies could assume an increasing level of responsibility. However, in the evolving security situation, those earlier assumptions were no longer valid. The military component lacked the necessary capacity and mobility to address the threats and had inadequate ability to obtain and process information. If downsizing continued, significantly reduced troop density would not deter the security threat posed by armed bands in rural areas, while the diminished military presence in the westernmost districts would ease the task of criminals or other elements intent on moving illegally across the TCL. At the same time, UNMISET would face still greater obstacles in assisting in the event of large-scale civil disturbance. While planning for Timor-Leste police was being adjusted, the measures proposed to enhance their capacity could produce results only by January 2004 at the earliest.

Adjustments to UNMISET's military strategy and configuration in a number of areas could promote stability and provide the time required for the Timorese security agencies to become operationally ready to assume their tasks. Those adjustments included: establishment within an extended zone adjacent to the TCL of a sufficient military presence to deter and respond to incursions and incidents until such time as the threat was effectively contained and the necessary Timorese capability to meet the threat was operational; maintenance of a security presence in other parts of Timor-Leste to assist the police in ensuring stability; improved ability to use information to assist in the tactical employment of the infantry forces available, in addition to greater coordination and exchange of information with UNMISET police and with Timor-Leste security agencies to improve effectiveness; improved air and land mobility to enable more effective use of forces available and timely response in the event of incidents requiring employment of peacekeeping forces; and promotion of relations with the public and improved public information capability to enhance understanding of the military component's role and to counter potential misinformation campaigns. Those adjustments would be adopted within the context of a simplified, two-phase plan for the military component's deployment until the conclusion of UNMISET's mandate.

During the first phase (March to December 2003), UNMISET would retain primary responsibility for ensuring security, addressing problems that surpassed the capability of Timor-Leste security agencies. A larger military presence would be maintained in an expanded area adjacent to the TCL. A sector headquarters would be maintained in the area to unify the command of forces deployed to limit incursions. Satisfactory progress was being made towards the planned handover of border crossing points in mid-2003 and a specialized Timor-Leste police border patrol unit would be deployed to its positions along the border by the end of June 2003. Those tasks would entail the maintenance of the military deployment at the March 2003 level of 3,870 troops, although the component would be reconfigured to emphasize the proposed adjustments. To ensure that a force of that limited size was capable of timely response, it would be essential for troop-contributing countries to provide the Force Commander with the flexibility required to employ the portion of his force best placed and equipped to undertake the tasks at hand. That phase would be concluded once the relevant Timor-Leste agencies had attained adequate operational capability to respond to threats to internal security, particularly within the border area, and to respond to armed threats elsewhere. The Timor-Leste Government was reviewing plans to enhance the capability of the Timor-Leste police in both areas, while their ability to respond to civil disturbance was also being developed.

In phase two (December 2003 to May 2004), UNMISET's military component would be reconfigured to act as a deterrent and to respond preventively to threats to the security environment. Other efforts would include operations to retain the trust and confidence of the people of Timor-Leste, in addition to close cooperation and information-sharing with Timor-Leste agencies. The military component would include 1,750 troops organized in two response battalions, one of which would be located in the west and the other centred in Dili. During that phase, final preparations would be made for the conclusion of the handover of defence responsibility to the Timor-Leste defence force (Falintil-FDTL) on 20 May 2004. On completion of the mandate, the peacekeeping force would cease operations and concentrate on the orderly extraction of remaining forces in the most expeditious manner possible.

The Timor-Leste Government was reviewing plans to strengthen the capability of its police force, which would offer a means for the Government to respond to major threats to public order without resorting to the use of the military. In that context, the composition and strength of UNMISET's police component and the schedule for its downsizing would be adjusted to enhance its operational capability to address civil disturbances. UNMISET's adjustments would include: inclusion of an international formed police unit for one year, in order to deal with emergencies that exceeded the capacity of the Rapid Intervention Unit; additional training capacity to provide further training to the Timor-Leste police in crowd-control skills and other critical areas, such as forensics, tactical operations and border security; and further emphasis on human rights and the rule of law in UNMISET's development and certification process. UNMISET's downsizing plan should also allow for the retention of a greater monitoring and advisory presence within districts that had been handed over to Timorese authorities. In downsizing, UNMISET would ensure that the handover would take place at a pace that did not jeopardize stability while showing sensitivity to the Government's desire to assume responsibility for security issues as soon as it was feasible. Planning for the gradual transfer of policing authority to Timor-Leste would be adjusted to include safeguards and arrangements for command and control that would allow the military component to play an active role during the final phase of UNMISET's mandate.

The Secretary-General observed that the proposed adjustments to UNMISET's downsizing did not represent a change in the broad concept of operations of UNMISET, in its planned date of withdrawal or in its ultimate goal, which was the creation of a viable Timor-Leste State with an adequate and appropriate security capability. The impact of the adjustments would depend on the full commitment of the Timor-Leste leadership, collaboration with Indonesia and bilateral support. It was likely that further assistance would be required once UNMISET's mandate was terminated. A number of options could be explored by Member States, including the deployment of qualified international police to key advisory positions within the Timor-Leste police through multilateral, regional or bilateral working arrangements with the Government. The Secretary-General said that the initial successful progress that was achieved in Timor-Leste may have led to the development of unrealistic expectations. It was preferable that the international community be reminded, before downsizing progressed beyond a point of no return, of the fragility of what had been achieved so far, despite the fact that Timor-Leste's development towards statehood remained extraordinarily rapid.

Security Council consideration (March). On 10 March [meeting 4715], the Security Council discussed the situation in Timor-Leste, with particular reference to the Secretary-General's March report. The UN Under-Secretary-General (USG) for Peacekeeping Operations, Jean-Marie Guéhenno, introduced the report.

The USG said that the special report was an effort to sound an alarm at a critical time, to indicate to the Council a number of worrisome developments and to recommend, in good time, realistic and prudent adjustments of UNMISET's troop-reduction plans so as to reflect a situation on the ground that had changed and to protect the considerable investments that the international community had made in Timor-Leste. The Secretary-General's recommendations were presented on the premise that it was easier and less expensive to pre-empt a problem than to try to fix one after it had occurred. The cost that was implied would be modest compared to the $1 billion to $2 billion that the international community had spent in Timor-Leste since 2000. The USG also drew attention to a positive development, which was the conclusion of the agreements and legislative processes in Timor-Leste and in Australia that should pave the way for exploitation of mineral resources in the Timor Sea and the sharing of revenues, 90 per cent being awarded to Timor-Leste. The development of those resources was of cardinal importance for Timor-Leste's economic future.

Timor-Leste said it was not surprising that various pro-militia groups from across the border continued to agitate and provoke strife and violence, since the independence struggle was a difficult one that had lasted for decades. The attacks in the border area in January and February reflected a coordinated plan to destroy a nation created with the help of the Security Council and the international community. Timor-Leste wholeheartedly endorsed and supported the reassessment, recommendations and proposals contained in the Secretary-General's March report, as it believed that the adjustments in downsizing would maximize UNMISET's effectiveness. UNMISET's contribution towards the objective of providing a secure and stable environment was significant and had to continue at the required levels while Timorese security forces developed to their full capacities.

Communication (April). On 3 April [S/2003/379], the United Kingdom transmitted to the Council President a 28 March letter from the USG for Peacekeeping Operations addressed to individual members of the Council in connection with UNMISET. The USG said that, at the 10 March Council meeting (see above), Member States had endorsed the broad objective of the recommendations in the Secretary-General's report, namely, to reinforce UNMISET's capability to develop Timor-Leste's police force, while taking the necessary measures to ensure the short-term security and stability that were required for that training to succeed. At the same time, several States sought to review further possible adjustments to UNMISET's military component. Through informal discussions, interested Member States subsequently explored with the UN Secretariat the kind of option that would address some concerns over the security situation in Timor-Leste and that could meet with the support of the Council. Those discussions suggested that such an option would include the retention of two battalions within regions adjoining the TCL, and a more gradual downsizing to 1,750 military peacekeepers in December 2003, and not the full retention of 3,870 military peacekeepers up to that period as was reflected in the Secretary-General's report.

SECURITY COUNCIL ACTION (April)

On 4 April [meeting 4735], the Security Council unanimously adopted **resolution 1473(2003)**. The draft [S/2003/401] was prepared in consultations among Council members.

The Security Council,

Reaffirming its previous resolutions on the situation in Timor-Leste, in particular resolution 1410(2002) of 17 May 2002,

Reiterating its full support for the Special Representative of the Secretary-General and the United Nations Mission of Support in East Timor,

Welcoming the progress that Timor-Leste has achieved with the assistance of the Mission since independence,

Noting the continued existence of challenges to the security and stability of Timor-Leste,

Stressing that improving the overall capabilities of the Timor-Leste police force is a key priority,

Having considered the special report of the Secretary-General on the Mission of 3 March 2003,

Having considered also the letter dated 28 March 2003 from the Under-Secretary-General for Peacekeeping Operations addressed to the members of the Security Council,

1. *Decides* that the composition and strength of the police component of the United Nations Mission of Support in East Timor and the schedule for its downsizing shall be adjusted in line with paragraphs 33 and 35 of the special report of the Secretary-General and shall include the following specific measures:

    (a) The inclusion of an internationally formed unit for one year;

    (b) The provision of additional training capacity in key areas specified in the special report of the Secretary-General;

    (c) Greater emphasis on human rights and rule of law elements;

    (d) The retention of a greater monitoring and advisory presence in districts where policing authority has been handed over to the Timor-Leste police force;

    (e) Follow-up to the recommendations outlined in the report of the joint assessment mission on policing of November 2002;

    (f) Adjustment of planning for the gradual transfer of policing authority to the Timor-Leste police force;

2. *Also decides* that the schedule for the downsizing of the military component of the Mission for the period until December 2003 shall be adjusted in line with the letter dated 28 March 2003 from the Under-Secretary-General for Peacekeeping Operations addressed to the members of the Security Council; and, accordingly, that two battalions shall be retained within regions adjoining the Tactical Coordination Line during this period, together with associated force elements, including mobility; and that the number of military peacekeepers shall be reduced to 1,750 more gradually than was foreseen in resolution 1410(2002);

3. *Requests* the Secretary-General to provide by 20 May 2003 for the approval of the Council a detailed military strategy for the revised schedule for the downsizing of the military component of the Mission;

4. *Also requests* the Secretary-General to keep the Council closely and regularly informed of developments on the ground and the implementation of the revised military and police strategies;

5. *Requests* the Government of Timor-Leste to continue to work closely with the Mission, including in the implementation of the revised police and military strategies;

6. *Decides* to remain seized of the matter.

Report of Secretary-General (April). In response to resolution 1410(2002) [YUN 2002, p. 321], the Secretary-General submitted to the Security Council a 21 April report [S/2003/449] on UNMISET's activities since his November 2002 report [YUN 2002, p. 325]. He also presented a detailed military strategy for UNMISET's revised schedule, as requested in resolution 1473(2003) (above).

He said that the most striking development over the reporting period was the change in the security environment that had taken place in December and January. The search for a solution to those security problems should, however, be viewed in the context of the long-term process of establishing a viable independent State. The strengthening of Timor-Leste's political institutions and a non-political administration, together with the progressive development of a culture of responsible governance and a tradition of pluralistic, democratic debate, were essential for the country's stability and social and economic progress. During the reporting period, the Government of Timor-Leste had emphasized the importance of more open, participatory and accountable governance. Progress had been made in the development of the relationship between Indonesia and Timor-Leste. The new Ambassador of Timor-Leste had assumed his duties in Jakarta in February, and Indonesia had indicated that it would soon establish a formal embassy in Dili. The technical group for demarcation and regulation of the border between Indonesia and Timor-Leste (Dili, 18-20 March) suggested that approximately 80 per cent of the boundary between the countries could be agreed relatively easily after joint field verification. It nonetheless remained uncertain that the two countries would reach agreement by 30 June 2003 on a line that constituted a border, despite their formal commitment to that objective. Timor-Leste had also continued to develop its relationship with other States in the region and beyond. On 6 March, Timor-Leste and Australia concluded the International Unitisation Agreement on the Greater Sunrise field, straddling the Joint Petroleum Development Area in the Timor Gap, on the understanding that the Agreement did not prejudice their positions in the maritime boundary negotiations. On 2 April, the two countries ratified the Timor Sea Treaty (see p. 373).

During the reporting period, it became apparent that further assistance, especially bilateral contributions, would be required to complete the tasks undertaken by UNMISET. The advisers in UNMISET's Civilian Support Group continued to play a crucial role by transferring knowledge and skills to Timor-Leste counterparts, in addition to supporting the functioning of the administration. The Government had filled nearly 15,000 of 16,000 budgeted posts within the administration, which was showing increasing readiness to assume its full responsibilities. UNMISET, in consultation with the Government of Timor-Leste and UNDP, was elaborating a strategic plan that identified areas of need where bilateral support could be required following the withdrawal of the Civilian Support Group. The plan's main purpose was to facilitate the progressive replacement of civilian advisers with bilaterally funded counterparts as required, in order to maintain continuity of training.

The functioning of Timor-Leste's judicial system continued to be hampered by severe shortages of skilled and experienced professional personnel and limited physical infrastructure. That had resulted in delays in the administration of justice, leading to prolonged pre-trial detention and detention without the necessary legal foundation, in addition to overcrowding in the prisons. A comprehensive justice sector support programme was being finalized and the five-member Superior Council of the Magistracy, responsible for the appointment, promotion, discipline and dismissal of judges, was constituted in February. However, that body was not yet operational, since the President of the Court of Appeal had not been sworn in. The Office of the Provedor for Human Rights and Justice, an independent institution provided for in the Constitution, was in the process of being established. UNMISET, through its Serious Crimes Unit, which was set up under UNTAET for the handling of cases of egregious crimes, assisted in the conduct of investigations of serious crimes, though its work had been slower than expected owing to constraints in the justice system. Continuing external assistance would be required after June 2004 to complete investigations, especially since the majority of those accused remained outside of Timor-Leste, including 90 per cent of those accused of crimes against humanity. Through its Human Rights Unit, UNMISET provided support and advice to the Commission for Reception, Truth and Reconciliation, which was conducting community reconciliation procedures and holding community discussions.

Over the reporting period, UNMISET continued to undertake executive policing while supporting the development of the National Police of Timor-Leste (PNTL), which had effectively undertaken the task of routine patrolling in 7 of Timor-Leste's 13 districts. However, further efforts were required for PNTL to play the role in internal security that was envisaged by the country's leadership. PNTL had to be ready to meet the evolving operational challenges posed by civil unrest and an apparent resurgence of activity by armed groups. Resource constraints remained significant but, more fundamentally, management and human resource policies for the force had yet to be developed. As provided for in resolution 1473(2003) (see p. 374), the adjustment of UNMISET's capacity for police training in key areas, greater emphasis on human-rights and rule of law elements, and the retention of a greater monitoring and advisory presence in districts where policing authority had been handed over to PNTL were expected to contribute to enhancing the effectiveness, professionalism, accountability and responsiveness of PNTL. The operational responsibilities of civilian police would be reduced as responsibility for routine policing was handed over; that, in turn, would permit a gradual downsizing of UNMISET's police component, from approximately 625 at the beginning of June 2003 to 325 at the beginning of 2004. Following the attacks of January 2003, the Government had encouraged the formation of village-based security groups to assist the police and military peacekeepers in addressing the threat posed by armed groups.

The military component of UNMISET continued to provide support for the external security and territorial integrity of Timor-Leste, while ensuring the timely handover of responsibilities to Falintil-FDTL and to relevant public administration departments. International military capability remained essential to promote security in the border area, and to provide a short-term response to the threats posed by armed groups, whose tactics, weapons and training exceeded the capacity of any other security force, while the Timorese forces obtained the necessary capability to assume that task. The Secretary-General said that within the capacity provided by UNMISET's revised downsizing schedule, the military component would adopt the following strategy: improve its ability to use information to assist in the tactical employment of the infantry forces available; assist in greater coordination and exchange of information with UNMISET police and with Timor-Leste security agencies to improve effectiveness; promote relations with the public and enhance public understanding of the military component's role; and make more effective use of the forces available and seek a more timely response in the event of incidents requiring employment of peacekeeping forces. The planned configuration of the military component would be adapted in several respects to facilitate that strategy. Rather than withdrawing from the Cova Lima district, forces in Sector West would remain in place as deployed. The tactical headquarters in Sector West would continue to manage day-to-day operations in that sector. Additional flexibility would be facilitated by the assumption of responsibilities at the TCL by the agencies of the Government of Timor-Leste. The military component's public and military information capabilities would be somewhat enhanced through the addition of a number of specialist personnel. The force levels deployed in the central region would remain unchanged until the end of 2003. The implementation of elements of that strategy had already enabled the military component to make some progress in addressing the threat posed by armed groups, as cooperation between the military component and the UN police had led to joint searches for suspected weapons caches, armed groups and suspect individuals. The military component would aim to reach a total of 1,750 by the end of 2003; in the interim, it would be reduced to a total strength of 3,500 by July and to 3,300 by October. When the military component reached a strength of 1,750, it would be structured around two infantry battalions, with responsibility for the western and eastern parts of the country respectively. Development of Falintil-FDTL was making steady progress, with the second of the two planned infantry battalions expected to become operational by the end of 2003. No further handover of defence responsibility for districts was planned until 2004. Border services comprising PNTL border patrol and immigration officers had been trained and were deployed at border crossing points. UNMISET's military component would continue its programme of active patrolling behind the border to deter and resist incursions, while retaining its ability to support PNTL.

The ratification of the Timor Sea Treaty had led to hopes of significant gas and oil revenues in the near future. Timor-Leste remained the poorest country in South-East Asia, with more than 60 per cent of the people living on less than $1 a day. The Government's immediate and longer-term development efforts drew on support provided by UNMISET and by UN agencies, funds and programmes, the World Bank and Member States, in cooperation with civil society and the private sector. Among other things, the UN system was supporting the Transition Support Programme, which focused on poverty reduction, governance, capacity-building, expenditure and policy management, and private sector development.

The Secretary-General observed that much had been achieved since the establishment of UNMISET in May 2002. Building on the foundations laid during UNTAET, the Timorese public administration and police force were assuming increasing levels of responsibility, with growing confidence. Much remained to be done, however, and continued assistance by the international community would be crucial to enable Timor-Leste to confront the political, practical and security challenges that lay ahead. Further bilateral efforts would be necessary alongside and after the contribution of UNMISET, in the civilian administration, justice, police force, and defence and security sectors. The Secretary-General recommended extending UNMISET's mandate for a further year, until 20 May 2004.

Security Council consideration (April). On 28 April [meeting 4744], the Security Council had before it the Secretary-General's April report (above) and heard a briefing on UNMISET by the Special Representative of the Secretary-General for Timor-Leste and Head of Mission, Kamalesh Sharma.

Mr. Sharma said that the strengthening of the police force through a recast strategy involving accretion of capacity and mobility, reinforced training and augmentation of professionalism according to the highest policing standards, on the one hand, and a more gradual drawdown of the peacekeeping forces, on the other, were of critical importance. They would be of enormous assistance in dealing with the risk of civil disorder and the criminal and politically motivated violence in rural areas. A renewed surge of violence could potentially generate a demoralizing psychological apprehension in the population; the initial years of the State were critical in firmly entrenching the confidence both of the Government and of the people that the political, administrative and security order in the State could not be shaken or challenged. The slower drawdown of UNMISET's military component would contribute to reducing the threat posed by armed groups. UNMISET had been mindful to learn the appropriate lessons from the civil riots in Dili and other violence. Those first instances of security threats to the State had provided additional impetus for recasting, planning and augmenting readiness to make such challenges difficult to mount in the future.

The task of developing a professional, dedicated and responsive public administration from ground level was no less a challenge for the new State. The Council had mandated UNMISET to prepare the groundwork for the structure of a national administration over two years, and halfway through that process the progress was satisfactory. It was clear, however, that assistance would be needed in some of the administrative sectors following UNMISET's departure. UNDP's role, which was crucial in advocating the need for further capacity-building support and filling, in parallel, more than 200 development posts, would continue to be central. UNMISET was keeping the civilian support programme under constant review for lessons that were progressively learned and improvements that could be effected. Despite many challenges, the Serious Crimes Unit continued to facilitate the work of the Special Panels for Serious Crimes at the Dili District Court. As at 30 April, investigations had been completed in 9 out of the 10 priority cases of crimes against humanity. Trials were proceeding in those cases where the accused were in Timor-Leste; in many other cases the trials might not commence due to the absence of defendants, a large proportion of whom remained outside Timor-Leste.

The economic situation of the country was slow to improve given the comprehensive legacy of underdevelopment inherited by the new independent State. The path of development and fulfilment of economic and social needs would be long and arduous, and in the foreseeable future the country would have to manage the political and economic pressures created by depressed economic and social indicators and, in particular, joblessness. The majority of people still practised subsistence agriculture, with extremely rudimentary means of production. The economy needed to focus on greater agricultural diversity and quantity of production, creation of professional services and opportunities for self-employment as the basis of the Timorese economy. The ratification of the Timor Sea Treaty between Timor-Leste and Australia, enabling the exploitation of an offshore oil and gas field, was an important development for the public finances of Timor-Leste. Prospects for further revenues would be enhanced through cooperation between the two countries on another identified field. The role played by other UN agencies, funds and programmes would contribute to a smooth transition to a traditional development assistance framework after completion of UNMISET's mandate. Mr. Sharma said that the engagement of the international community in peace-building and institution-building would need to continue.

Timor-Leste said that the violence of December 2002 and the terrorist activities in the border area in January 2003 created some fears about future security. However, the firm and transparent response by the United Nations and the Government of Timor-Leste had provided reassurance and had reasserted confidence and stability.

UNMISET's mission had been and continued to be effective. Much progress had been made in the capacity-building of the Timorese police and military. Timor-Leste fully endorsed the Secretary-General's recommendation that UNMISET's mandate be extended for a further year, until 20 May 2004.

SECURITY COUNCIL ACTION (May)

On 19 May [meeting 4758], the Security Council unanimously adopted **resolution 1480(2003)**. The draft [S/2003/545] was prepared in consultations among Council members.

The Security Council,

Reaffirming its previous resolutions on Timor-Leste, in particular resolutions 1410(2002) of 17 May 2002 and 1473(2003) of 4 April 2003,

Commending the efforts of the people and Government of Timor-Leste and the progress achieved in developing the institutions of an independent State and in promoting a stable, equitable society based on democratic values and respect for human rights,

Commending also the work of the United Nations Mission of Support in East Timor, under the leadership of the Special Representative of the Secretary-General, in assisting the Government of Timor-Leste in developing the nation's infrastructure, public administration, law enforcement and defence capacities, and in planning for the completion of the mandate of the Mission, including through the creation of a mission liquidation task force,

Stressing that improving the overall capabilities of the Timor-Leste police force is a key priority,

Welcoming the continuing progress in developing a positive bilateral relationship between the Governments of Timor-Leste and Indonesia, which is crucial for the future stability of Timor-Leste, and encouraging continued efforts by both Governments to secure agreement on the issue of border demarcation, to promote security in the border area, to facilitate the resettlement of East Timorese remaining in West Timor, and to bring to justice those responsible for serious crimes committed in 1999,

Recognizing the importance of continued efforts to transfer skills and authority from the Mission to the Government of Timor-Leste in a coordinated and structured manner in the run-up to the withdrawal of the Mission, with the aim of helping to ensure the long-term security and stability of Timor-Leste,

Noting the planned end-date for the Mission of 20 May 2004, as indicated in the mandate implementation plan set out in the report of the Secretary-General of 17 April 2002, and in the special report of the Secretary-General of 3 March 2003,

Stressing the need for continued international support for Timor-Leste, and encouraging continued bilateral and multilateral development assistance,

Having considered the report of the Secretary-General of 21 April 2003,

Taking note of the military strategy outlined in paragraphs 38 to 51 of that report,

1. *Decides* to extend the current mandate of the United Nations Mission of Support in East Timor until 20 May 2004;

2. *Decides* to remain actively seized of the matter.

Communication (August). On 6 August [S/2003/802], Italy transmitted to the Secretary-General a statement on Indonesia's Ad Hoc Human Rights Tribunal for Crimes Committed in East Timor issued on that day by the EU Presidency. The EU said that the recently completed trials by the Ad Hoc Tribunal, with the last verdict delivered on 5 August, had failed to deliver justice and did not result in a substantiated account of the violence committed in East Timor in 1999 [YUN 1999, p. 288]. The EU was disappointed that the prosecutors did not submit all the evidence, especially that referred to by UN investigators and the Indonesian National Commission on Human Rights in their reports, suggesting that elements of the military, police and civil government had allegedly funded, trained and abetted local militia groups. In addition, no officials from the United Nations Mission in East Timor (UNAMET), or members of independent observer missions, and only a few victim witnesses from Timor-Leste, were called to testify by the prosecutors. Those deficiencies in the process had jeopardized the credibility of the verdicts, which were disproportionate to the seriousness of the crimes committed. It was of paramount importance that the Indonesian judicial authorities ensure that the appeal process was conducted in a manner consistent with international legal standards and that the appeal judgements were set out in accordance with the principle of transparency.

Report of Secretary-General (October). Pursuant to Security Council resolution 1410(2002) [YUN 2002, p. 321], the Secretary-General submitted an October report [S/2003/944] on UNMISET's activities, covering developments since his April report (see p. 374).

He said that on 28 April, President Xanana Gusmão initiated his "open presidency" programme, which entailed visits to mainly isolated villages to discuss local matters, with a particular focus on security issues. A number of options for local government were under review by the Council of Ministers, any of which would lead to greater decentralization and would bring aspects of government decision-making and resource management closer to communities. The National Parliament concluded its first year of regular legislative activity, including adoption of the national budget. Following assumption of office in May by the President of the Court of Appeal, an additional international judge had been appointed to the Court, permitting it to resume operations in June after a one-and-a-half-year hiatus. At the Joint Ministerial Commission (Dili, 4-6 September), Indonesia and Timor-Leste agreed to finalize agreement on the international land boundary by 30 November, with negotiations on maritime border delimitation to follow thereafter; that new timetable replaced the original deadline of 30 June. The countries also reiterated their intention to encourage resettlement of the Timorese who were still in West Timor away from the area of the border, and to facilitate the return of those refugees who chose to go back to Timor-Leste. Efforts by both countries would also be required to address other aspects of border management, including speedy implementation of the arrangement on traditional border crossings and regulated markets. Timor-Leste was pursuing discussions on maritime boundary delimitation with Australia, which had been identified as the next step subsequent to the entry into force of the Timor Sea Treaty on 2 April.

During the reporting period, significant progress was made towards the major milestones identified in UNMISET's mandate implementation plan. No major security incidents had taken place, though it was clear that it would not be possible for Timor-Leste to achieve self-sufficiency in certain key areas of the mandate by 20 May 2004. Recruitment and training in the area of public administration continued to advance; however, in several areas, including finance, justice, internal administration, infrastructure, the National Parliament and the Office of the President, international assistance would continue to be required for some time to assure that crucial tasks were discharged. The civilian advisers deployed through UNMISET were working to transfer skills, both through on-the-job training and through more formal in-country training programmes. However, progress in preparing the civil administration continued to be undermined by delays in the provision of advisers deployed through bilateral funding. Shortages of qualified personnel and infrastructure had affected the justice sector in particular and generated chronic delays, so that as much as 22 per cent of the prison population comprised individuals in detention under expired warrants. The legislation establishing the Office of the Provedor for Human Rights and Justice was under consideration by the National Parliament. That independent institution, which could be functional by March 2004, could play a key role in supporting good governance and civil rights within Timor-Leste through its advocacy and oversight activities.

Prosecution of serious crimes continued to progress; five additional indictments were filed during the reporting period, including an indictment in the tenth "priority case" of serious crimes, and four convictions were handed down by the Special Panels on Serious Crimes in Dili. UNMISET continued to play a key role in supporting that process through its serious crimes unit, which would be focusing in particular on trials and appeals during the remaining months of the mandate. A number of outstanding questions and issues remained, some of which would not be solved or completed by June 2004.

Over the reporting period, the internal situation in Timor-Leste had been relatively calm despite occasional reports of armed groups and criminal elements in rural areas, smuggling, extortion and robberies and, within urban areas, sporadic violence among martial arts groups and youth gangs. PNTL had continued to develop with UNMISET assistance, although its capacity and resources in a number of key areas remained limited. PNTL assumed responsibility for the management of routine policing in a further six of Timor-Leste's 13 districts, in addition to the six districts where handover had already occurred. UNMISET would retain management responsibility for the Dili district until December 2003. Despite those signs of progress, by the end of UNMISET's mandate, PNTL would continue to lack skills in a number of specialized areas, including investigation, intelligence-gathering and special police operations. More fundamentally, there had been reports of police misconduct, involvement in criminal activities, bribery, excessive use of force and physical assaults of citizens. PNTL's ability to win public confidence would depend on further efforts to strengthen discipline and compliance with internationally accepted standards of policing.

There was no repetition during the reporting period of the kinds of armed attacks that took place in January and February 2003, and overall the situation had remained generally calm. That had been supported by the regular reconnaissance and surveillance activities by UNMISET's military component, drawing on the resources made available through the revised downsizing schedule authorized in Council resolution 1473 (2003) (see p. 374). UNMISET had sought to further institutionalize cooperation on security issues with and among Timorese agencies. Invitations had been extended to PNTL officers and the Timorese armed forces to work together in a joint information centre with international military and police in order to gain further experience in information analysis and planning. The Timorese armed forces would not take on areas of responsibility in addition to the district of Lautem prior to the handover of defence responsibilities to the Government of Timor-Leste, which was planned for 20 May 2004. Development of the Timorese armed forces would continue to depend on donor support through the provision of equipment, training and facilities. UNMISET's military component, which comprised over 3,300 troops as at September 2003, would rapidly reduce in numbers over the coming months, beginning with the withdrawal in October of a battalion currently based in the Oecussi enclave. By the end of 2003, the military component would be reduced to 1,750, with the closure of the tactical headquarters for Sector West.

The area of the TCL remained porous, and illegal hunting, trade and crossings continued, in addition to other criminal activity. Approximately 26,000 former refugees from Timor-Leste remained in West Timor, most of them in the border areas. President Gusmão was engaged in border reconciliation meetings to promote long-term reconciliation among the Timorese. The Indonesian Government was exploring additional means to encourage return and resettlement of the refugees in West Timor, while continuing to assist and encourage voluntary return to Timor-Leste through the provision of registration and transport facilities. UNMISET's military component had supplemented the basic police training of the border patrol unit with additional formal on-the-job training. Some initial progress had been made towards establishing a rapid deployment service, but further steps by the Timorese authorities were needed urgently, including the selection of officers and the provision of necessary equipment. UNMISET continued to foster close and professional ties between Indonesian security agencies and Timorese counterparts to strengthen the foundations for future cooperation and security.

A significant step towards greater prosperity was made in June, with the finalization by the Government of commercial arrangements with Conoco Phillips on Bayu-Undan gas development and the enactment of relevant tax legislation by the Parliament. That development was expected to bring as much as $3 billion to Timor-Leste over approximately 17 years. As a means to address immediate needs for job creation and promote stability, the Government continued to pursue the recovery, employment and stability programme for ex-combatants and communities in Timor-Leste, which was supported by UNDP.

The Secretary-General observed that, since May 2002, when Timor-Leste celebrated its independence, the country had made remarkable progress in laying the foundations for a functioning civil service and police force. However, it was also clear that crucial work remained to be done and that, in a number of areas, requirements would remain outstanding after the conclusion of UNMISET's mandate. It would be essential for the country's stability and development that the leaders of Timor-Leste continue to nurture respect for the rule of law, reach out to civil society and promote political dialogue and discussion, while giving full support to key institutions of democracy—a non-political civil service, a free press and an independent judiciary. In other areas, however, international assistance would continue to be indispensable; it was likely to include further guidance and advice in the areas of civil administration, justice and policing, and human rights training. In that context, the international community should take stock of what had been achieved and consider the best means through which the country's needs could be met after UNMISET's withdrawal.

In the tragic context of the attack that took place in Baghdad, Iraq, on 19 August 2003 (see p. 346), the Secretary-General recalled the remarkable contribution that was made to Timor-Leste by his former Special Representative, Sergio Vieira de Mello. Timor-Leste mourned his loss through national ceremonies that offered an eloquent testimony to the depth of admiration and affection in which he was held as the country's transitional administrator.

Security Council consideration (October). On 15 October [meeting 4843], the Security Council discussed the Secretary-General's October report on UNMISET (above) and was briefed by the Special Representative of the Secretary-General for Timor-Leste, Mr. Sharma.

Mr. Sharma said that while there had been no major security challenges since April 2003, reports persisted of alleged sightings of armed groups by residents in rural areas and of the presence of criminal elements in those areas, particularly in the border districts. There was a risk that such reports might increase as UNMISET's downsizing progressed. Although PNTL had made great progress, it was still a young and inexperienced police service, and it was doubtful that it would be able to respond effectively if tested by major internal security challenges following UNMISET's closure. Operational support and further mentoring and training in specialized and professional police skills would be required on a longer-term basis. Ensuring that police officers maintained human rights standards remained a priority. Timor-Leste's defence force was currently responsible for only one district, thus allowing it to continue to focus on capability development and individual and collective training activities. Given the programme of capability development, the force was not likely to become fully operational at required professional standards at the battalion level until around 2005-2006.

UNMISET's military component continued to downsize according to the revised schedule that was approved in Council resolution 1473(2003) (see p. 374). As they withdrew from border areas, the Timorese agencies, particularly the border patrol unit of PNTL, assumed greater responsibilities for border management. The members of the unit had performed commendably in the preceding few months at all border crossing points that they had taken over from UNMISET, despite the handicaps they faced in terms of logistics, availability of facilities in the remote border areas and equipment. UNMISET was working with the Government of Timor-Leste to address those shortcomings so that the unit could be self-sustaining. The rapid deployment of PNTL, once trained and functional, would provide a response capability to deal with armed criminal groups in rural and border districts. Despite best efforts, however, those units would continue to need advice and support following the end of UNMISET's mandate. Post-UNMISET, international assistance would also be needed to advise and mentor the Timorese security agencies in the various tasks of monitoring and managing the border, including assisting in liaison and thus enhancing cooperation with Indonesian security agencies at the border and providing psychological support to a population not yet prepared for the complete withdrawal of the reassuring international presence.

The evolving relationship between Timor-Leste and Indonesia was a primary asset in the rapid evolution of Timorese nationhood. Both sides were cooperating in the settlement of the border negotiations, residual refugee issues and the continuation of pension payments to former Indonesian civil servants. UNMISET had continued to provide support to the core administrative and judicial structures of the Government and further international support would be required in the post-UNMISET period. The Government, UNMISET and UNDP had completed reviews of the justice and administrative sectors and developed a comprehensive support programme, identifying areas most in need of support from the international community. UNMISET also continued to work closely with the wider UN system of agencies, funds and programmes and international financial institutions, in support of national programmes. It had also contributed, though its Human Rights Unit, to the promotion of human rights by training and advising and through capacity-building in the major institutions of the State. With seven months of its mandate remaining, UNMISET would continue to work with the Government of Timor-Leste to realize all the objectives in the mandate implementation plan. Nevertheless, it was important that the progress that had been achieved so far should not be jeopardized by the absence of adequate support mechanisms, based on assured funding, after the completion of UNMISET's mandate.

Timor-Leste said that the international community had invested huge financial and human resources and know-how in UNMISET, though some resources had not arrived on time. The judicial system, law and order, finance and planning, and defence and security would require substantial assistance and support for some time. It was clear, as the Secretary-General had stated in his October report, that it would not be possible for Timor-Leste to achieve self-sufficiency in certain key areas of the mandate by 20 May 2004. Timor-Leste recommended a credible, strong UN presence in key areas in order to help consolidate stability and security. The President of the General Assembly, Jan Kavan, had visited Timor-Leste in July. Given the fundamental contribution and the crucial role played by the Security Council in the liberation of the country, Timor-Leste invited the Council to send a delegation to visit also.

Later developments. In a later report [S/2004/117], the Secretary-General said that during the last months of 2003, Timor-Leste's National Parliament approved, among other things, a bill on immigration and asylum and one on local governance. The security situation remained generally calm, with occasional demonstrations that did not pose a threat to law and order. Indonesia and Timor-Leste did not meet their target date of 30 November 2003 for the finalization of agreement on a provisional line for the border. The first round of negotiations on the maritime boundary between Timor-Leste and Australia concluded on 14 November. Further talks were scheduled for April 2004. The development of Timor-Leste's public administration had continued to progress. As foreseen, 30 of UNMISET's 100 civil adviser positions were phased out by the end of November 2003. The remaining advisers, who were serving largely in the financial, central management and justice sectors, continued to play a key role in mentoring Timorese counterparts. PNTL assumed responsibility for routine policing throughout the country with the handover of responsibility in Dili district on 10 December. In October, the Border Police Unit assumed responsibility for all junction points along the 259-kilometre TCL. Following the downsizing and restructuring of UNMISET, which was carried out as foreseen in November and December 2003, the military component comprised 1,750 personnel, including 78 military observers and two infantry battalions. The fourth Timor-Leste development partners meeting, which focused on economic recovery issues, was held in Dili from 3 to 5 December 2003.

General Assembly action. By **resolution 58/112** of 17 December, the General Assembly endorsed the recommendation of the Economic and Social Council that Timor-Leste be added to the list of least developed countries (see p. 868).

By **resolution 58/121** of the same date, the Assembly urged assistance for humanitarian relief, rehabilitation and development for Timor-Leste (see p. 953).

Financing of UN operations

During 2003, the General Assembly considered the financing of three UN missions in Timor-Leste—UNTAET, UNMISET and UNAMET. UNTAET was established by Security Council resolution 1272(1999) [YUN 1999, p. 293] to administer East Timor during its transition to independence; its mandate was extended until 20 May 2002, Timor-Leste's date of independence, in accordance with resolution 1392(2002) [YUN 2002, p. 318]. UNMISET was established by Council resolution 1410(2002) [ibid., p. 321] to provide assistance to the administrative, law enforcement and public security structures critical to the viability and political stability of Timor-Leste, in addition to contributing to the maintenance of its external and internal security. UNAMET was established by Council resolution 1246(1999) [YUN 1999, p. 283] to conduct the 1999 popular consultation on East Timor's autonomy [ibid., p. 288]; its mandate ended on 30 November 1999, in accordance with resolution 1262(1999) [ibid., p. 287].

UNTAET and UNMISET

In December 2002 [A/57/666], the Secretary-General submitted to the General Assembly a performance report on the budget of UNTAET and UNMISET for the period from 1 July 2001 to 30 June 2002. Expenditures for the two missions for the period totalled $454,118,000, resulting in an unencumbered balance of $942,000. The Assembly was requested to decide on the treatment of that unencumbered balance and on the treatment of other income and adjustments for the period ended 30 June 2002, amounting to $20,680,000 from interest income ($7,625,000), other/miscellaneous income ($1,642,000) and savings on or cancellation of prior period obligations ($11,413,000).

In February 2003 [A/57/689], the Secretary-General submitted to the Assembly UNMISET's budget for the period from 1 July 2003 to 30 June 2004, which amounted to $188,229,200, inclusive of budgeted voluntary contributions in kind in the amount of $60,000. The budget provided for the maximum monthly average deployment of 106 military observers, 3,764 military contingent members, 650 civilian police, 389 international staff, 732 national staff and 200 UN Volunteers. The Assembly was requested to appropriate $188,169,200 for the maintenance of the Mission from 1 July 2003 to 30 June 2004 and to assess that amount at a monthly rate of $15,680,766, should the Security Council decide to continue the Mission's mandate.

Also in February [A/57/723], the Secretary-General submitted to the Assembly the overview of the financing of UN peacekeeping operations: budget performance for the period from 1 July 2001 to 30 June 2002 and budget for the period from 1 July 2003 to 30 June 2004.

In April [A/57/772/Add.11], ACABQ reviewed the Secretary-General's reports on the budgets of UNTAET and UNMISET for the period from 1 July 2001 to 30 June 2002 and the proposed budget for UNMISET for the period from 1 July 2003 to 30 June 2004 (see above). In connection with the first report on the financing of UNTAET and UNMISET, ACABQ recommended that the unencumbered balance of $942,000 and interest and other income in the amount of $20,680,000 be credited to Member States in a manner to be determined by the Assembly. In connection with the second report on the financing of UNMISET, ACABQ recommended that the estimated budget requirement of $188,169,200 gross be reduced by $3,169,200, or approximately 2 per cent. Accordingly, ACABQ recommended that the Assembly appropriate an amount of $185 million gross ($178,985,600 net), and that the amount be assessed at a monthly rate of $15,416,667 gross ($14,915,467 net) should the Security Council decide to continue the Mission's mandate. However, the reduction did not take into account any future changes in the overall strategy being considered by the Council.

GENERAL ASSEMBLY ACTION (June)

On 18 June [meeting 90], the General Assembly, on the recommendation of the Fifth Committee [A/57/832], adopted **resolution 57/327** without vote [agenda item 129].

Financing of the United Nations Transitional Administration in East Timor and the United Nations Mission of Support in East Timor

The General Assembly,

Having considered the reports of the Secretary-General on the financing of the United Nations Transitional Administration in East Timor and the United Nations Mission of Support in East Timor, and the related reports of the Advisory Committee on Administrative and Budgetary Questions,

Recalling Security Council resolution 1272(1999) of 25 October 1999 regarding the establishment of the United Nations Transitional Administration in East Timor and the subsequent resolutions by which the Council extended the mandate of the Transitional Administration, the latest of which was resolution 1392(2002) of 31 January 2002, by which the mandate was extended until 20 May 2002,

Recalling also its resolution 54/246 A of 23 December 1999 on the financing of the Transitional Administration and its subsequent resolutions thereon, the latest of which was resolution 56/296 of 27 June 2002,

Recalling further Security Council resolution 1410 (2002) of 17 May 2002, by which the Council established the United Nations Mission of Support in East Timor as of 20 May 2002 for an initial period of twelve months, and its subsequent resolution 1480(2003) of 19 May 2003, by which the Council extended the mandate of the Mission until 20 May 2004,

Reaffirming the general principles underlying the financing of United Nations peacekeeping operations, as stated in General Assembly resolutions 1874(S-IV) of 27 June 1963, 3101(XXVIII) of 11 December 1973 and 55/235 of 23 December 2000,

Noting with appreciation that voluntary contributions have been made to the Trust Fund for the United Nations Transitional Administration in East Timor,

Mindful of the fact that it is essential to provide the Mission with the necessary financial resources to enable it to fulfil its responsibilities under the relevant resolutions of the Security Council,

1. *Takes note* of the status of contributions to the United Nations Transitional Administration in East Timor and the United Nations Mission of Support in East Timor as at 31 March 2003, including the contributions outstanding in the amount of 86.1 million United States dollars, representing some 5 per cent of the total assessed contributions, notes with concern that only thirty Member States have paid their assessed contributions in full, and urges all other Member States, in particular those in arrears, to ensure payment of their outstanding assessed contributions;

2. *Expresses its appreciation* to those Member States which have paid their assessed contributions in full, and urges all other Member States to make every possible effort to ensure payment of their assessed contributions to the Transitional Administration and the Mission in full;

3. *Expresses concern* at the financial situation with regard to peacekeeping activities, in particular as regards the reimbursements to troop contributors that bear additional burdens owing to overdue payments by Member States of their assessments;

4. *Also expresses concern* at the delay experienced by the Secretary-General in deploying and providing adequate resources to some recent peacekeeping missions, in particular those in Africa;

5. *Emphasizes* that all future and existing peacekeeping missions shall be given equal and non-discriminatory treatment in respect of financial and administrative arrangements;

6. *Also emphasizes* that all peacekeeping missions shall be provided with adequate resources for the

effective and efficient discharge of their respective mandates;

7. *Reiterates its request* to the Secretary-General to make the fullest possible use of facilities and equipment at the United Nations Logistics Base at Brindisi, Italy, in order to minimize the costs of procurement for the Mission;

8. *Endorses* the conclusions and recommendations contained in the report of the Advisory Committee on Administrative and Budgetary Questions, and requests the Secretary-General to ensure their full implementation;

9. *Requests* the Secretary-General to ensure that the additional resources referred to in paragraph 20 of the report of the Advisory Committee are used to strengthen national judicial capacity consistent with the needs of the people of Timor-Leste and the mandate of the Mission;

Financial performance report for the period from 1 July 2001 to 30 June 2002

10. *Takes note* of the report of the Secretary-General on the financial performance of the Transitional Administration and the Mission for the period from 1 July 2001 to 30 June 2002;

Budget estimates for the period from 1 July 2003 to 30 June 2004

11. *Decides* to appropriate to the Special Account for the United Nations Mission of Support in East Timor the amount of 193,337,100 dollars for the period from 1 July 2003 to 30 June 2004, inclusive of 185 million dollars for the maintenance of the Mission, 6,384,000 dollars for the support account for peacekeeping operations, and 1,953,100 dollars for the United Nations Logistics Base;

Financing of the appropriation

12. *Decides also* to apportion among Member States the amount of 193,337,100 dollars at a monthly rate of 16,111,425 dollars, in accordance with the levels set out in resolution 55/235, as adjusted by the General Assembly in its resolutions 55/236 of 23 December 2000 and 57/290 A of 20 December 2002, and taking into account the scale of assessments for 2003 as set out in its resolutions 55/5 B of 23 December 2000, 57/4 B of 20 December 2002 and for 2004, subject to the decision of the Security Council to extend the mandate of the Mission;

13. *Decides further* that, in accordance with the provisions of its resolution 973(X) of 15 December 1955, there shall be set off against the apportionment among Member States, as provided for in paragraph 12 above, their respective share in the Tax Equalization Fund of 7,568,200 dollars at a monthly rate of 630,683 dollars, comprising the estimated staff assessment income of 6,014,400 dollars approved for the Mission, the prorated share of 1,438,300 dollars of the estimated staff assessment income approved for the support account, and the prorated share of 115,500 dollars of the estimated staff assessment income approved for the United Nations Logistics Base;

14. *Decides* that for Member States that have fulfilled their financial obligations to the Transitional Administration and the Mission, there shall be set off against their apportionment, as provided for in paragraph 12 above, their respective share of the unencumbered balance and of other income in the total amount of 21,622,000 dollars in respect of the financial period ended 30 June 2002, in accordance with the levels set out in resolution 55/235, as adjusted by the General Assembly in its resolutions 55/236 and 57/290 A, and taking into account the scale of assessments for 2002 as set out in its resolutions 55/5 B and 57/4 B;

15. *Decides also* that, for Member States that have not fulfilled their financial obligations to the Transitional Administration and the Mission, there shall be set off against their outstanding obligations their respective share of the unencumbered balance and other income in the total amount of 21,622,000 dollars in respect of the financial period ended 30 June 2002, in accordance with the scheme set out in paragraph 14 above;

16. *Decides further* that the increase of 529,000 dollars in the estimated staff assessment income in respect of the financial period ended 30 June 2002 shall be added to the credits from the amount referred to in paragraphs 14 and 15 above, and that the respective shares of Member States therein shall be applied in accordance with the provisions of those paragraphs as appropriate;

17. *Emphasizes* that no peacekeeping mission shall be financed by borrowing funds from other active peacekeeping missions;

18. *Encourages* the Secretary-General to continue to take additional measures to ensure the safety and security of all personnel under the auspices of the United Nations participating in the Mission;

19. *Invites* voluntary contributions to the Mission in cash and in the form of services and supplies acceptable to the Secretary-General, to be administered, as appropriate, in accordance with the procedure and practices established by the General Assembly;

20. *Decides* to include in the provisional agenda of its fifty-eighth session the item entitled "Financing of the United Nations Transitional Administration in East Timor and the United Nations Mission of Support in East Timor".

In July, the Secretary-General presented to the Assembly the revised budget for UNMISET for the period from 1 July 2003 to 30 June 2004 [A/58/192]. The revised budget incorporated additional requirements for the delay in downsizing the Mission and amounted to $208,887,500 gross ($202,333,200 net), inclusive of budgeted voluntary contributions in kind of $60,000. The revision represented an increase of $23,827,500 gross from the initial approved budget of $185,000,000 and provided for the deployment of a maximum of 3,405 troops, 95 military observers, 550 civilian police, 125 civilian police in formed units, 399 international staff and 928 local staff.

In a September report [A/58/192/Add.1], the Secretary-General provided information on the proposed donation of UNMISET assets to the Government of Timor-Leste, the inventory value of which amounted to some $35.3 million as at 30 June 2003.

In October [A/58/409], ACABQ, having considered the revised budget for UNMISET, recommended that the Assembly appropriate the additional amount of $23,827,500 gross for the period 1 July 2003 to 30 June 2004. It further recommended that the Assembly approve the donation of assets with an inventory value of $35,262,900 and a corresponding residual value of $15,879,900 to Timor-Leste on a free-of-charge basis.

GENERAL ASSEMBLY ACTION (December)

On 23 December [meeting 79], the General Assembly, on the recommendation of the Fifth Committee [A/58/584], adopted **resolution 58/260 A** without vote [agenda item 140].

Financing of the United Nations Mission of Support in East Timor

The General Assembly,

Having considered the reports of the Secretary-General on the financing of the United Nations Mission of Support in East Timor, and the related report of the Advisory Committee on Administrative and Budgetary Questions,

Recalling Security Council resolution 1272(1999) of 25 October 1999 regarding the establishment of the United Nations Transitional Administration in East Timor and the subsequent resolutions by which the Council extended the mandate of the Transitional Administration, the last of which was resolution 1392(2002) of 31 January 2002, by which the mandate was extended until 20 May 2002,

Recalling also Security Council resolution 1410(2002) of 17 May 2002, by which the Council established the United Nations Mission of Support in East Timor as of 20 May 2002 for an initial period of twelve months, and its subsequent resolution 1480(2003) of 19 May 2003, by which the Council extended the mandate of the Mission until 20 May 2004,

Recalling further its resolution 54/246 A of 23 December 1999 on the financing of the United Nations Transitional Administration in East Timor and its subsequent resolutions on the financing of the United Nations Mission of Support in East Timor, the latest of which was resolution 57/327 of 18 June 2003,

Reaffirming the general principles underlying the financing of United Nations peacekeeping operations, as stated in General Assembly resolutions 1874(S-IV) of 27 June 1963, 3101(XXVIII) of 11 December 1973 and 55/235 of 23 December 2000,

Noting with appreciation that voluntary contributions have been made to the Mission and to the Trust Fund for the United Nations Transitional Administration in East Timor,

Mindful of the fact that it is essential to provide the Mission with the necessary financial resources to enable it to fulfil its responsibilities under the relevant resolutions of the Security Council,

1. *Takes note* of the status of contributions to the United Nations Transitional Administration in East Timor and the United Nations Mission of Support in East Timor as at 31 October 2003, including the contributions outstanding in the amount of 65.5 million United States dollars, representing some 4 per cent of the total assessed contributions, notes with concern that only forty-three Member States have paid their assessed contributions in full, and urges all other Member States, in particular those in arrears, to ensure payment of their outstanding assessed contributions;

2. *Expresses its appreciation* to those Member States which have paid their assessed contributions in full, and urges all other Member States to make every possible effort to ensure payment of their assessed contributions to the Transitional Administration and the Mission in full;

3. *Expresses concern* at the financial situation with regard to peacekeeping activities, in particular as regards the reimbursements to troop contributors that bear additional burdens owing to overdue payments by Member States of their assessments;

4. *Also expresses concern* at the delay experienced by the Secretary-General in deploying some recent peacekeeping missions, in particular those in Africa, and in providing them with adequate resources;

5. *Emphasizes* that all future and existing peacekeeping missions shall be given equal and non-discriminatory treatment in respect of financial and administrative arrangements;

6. *Also emphasizes* that all peacekeeping missions shall be provided with adequate resources for the effective and efficient discharge of their respective mandates;

7. *Reiterates its request* to the Secretary-General to make the fullest possible use of facilities and equipment at the United Nations Logistics Base at Brindisi, Italy, in order to minimize the costs of procurement for the Mission;

8. *Endorses* the conclusions and recommendations contained in the report of the Advisory Committee on Administrative and Budgetary Questions, and requests the Secretary-General to ensure their full implementation;

Revised budget estimates for the period from 1 July 2003 to 30 June 2004

9. *Decides* to appropriate to the Special Account for the United Nations Mission of Support in East Timor the amount of 23,827,500 dollars for the maintenance of the Mission for the period from 1 July 2003 to 30 June 2004, in addition to the amount of 193,337,100 dollars already appropriated for the same period under the terms of resolution 57/327;

Financing of the appropriation

10. *Decides also,* taking into account the amount of 193,337,100 dollars previously apportioned under the terms of resolution 57/327, to apportion among Member States the amount of 23,827,500 dollars at a monthly rate of 1,985,625 dollars, in accordance with the levels set out in resolution 55/235, as adjusted by the General Assembly in its resolutions 55/236 of 23 December 2000 and 57/290 A of 20 December 2002, and taking into account the scale of assessments for 2003 as set out in its resolutions 55/5 B of 23 December 2000 and 57/4 B of 20 December 2002 and the scale of assessments for 2004 as set out in its resolution 58/1 B of 23 December 2003, subject to the decision of the Security Council to extend the mandate of the Mission;

11. *Decides further* that, in accordance with the provisions of its resolution 973(X) of 15 December

1955, there shall be set off against the apportionment among Member States, as provided for in paragraph 10 above, their respective share in the Tax Equalization Fund of the amount of 539,900 dollars at a monthly rate of 44,991 dollars, representing the additional estimated staff assessment income approved for the Mission;

Donation of assets to the Government of Timor-Leste

12. *Approves* the donation of the assets of the Mission, with a total inventory value of up to 35,262,900 dollars and corresponding residual value of up to 15,879,900 dollars, to the Government of Timor-Leste;

13. *Emphasizes* that no peacekeeping mission shall be financed by borrowing funds from other active peacekeeping missions;

14. *Encourages* the Secretary-General to continue to take additional measures to ensure the safety and security of all personnel under the auspices of the United Nations participating in the Mission;

15. *Invites* voluntary contributions to the Mission in cash and in the form of services and supplies acceptable to the Secretary-General, to be administered, as appropriate, in accordance with the procedure and practices established by the General Assembly;

16. *Decides* to keep under review during its fifty-eighth session the item entitled "Financing of the United Nations Mission of Support in East Timor".

Also on 23 December, the Assembly decided that the agenda item on financing of UNMISET would remain for consideration at its resumed fifty-eighth (2004) session (**decision 58/565**).

UNAMET

On 15 September, the General Assembly decided to defer consideration of the item on the financing of UNAMET and to include it in the draft agenda of its fifty-eighth session (**decision 57/599**).

Other matters

Cambodia

In a 17 March letter [A/57/758], the Secretary-General, referring to General Assembly resolution 57/228 A [YUN 2002, p. 644], which requested him to resume negotiations to conclude an agreement with the Government of Cambodia on the establishment of Extraordinary Chambers within the court structure of Cambodia for the prosecution of crimes committed during the period of Democratic Kampuchea (1975-1979), informed the Assembly President that his negotiating team had established the text of a draft agreement.

In a 31 March report [A/57/769], the Secretary-General described the steps that he had taken to resume negotiations with the Government of Cambodia and described the draft agreement, which was finalized as a result of the negotiations. The Secretary-General said that, while the text was an improvement over the previously discussed one, doubts might remain as to whether it would ensure the credibility of the Extraordinary Chambers, given the precarious state of the judiciary in Cambodia. He said it would be essential for the United Nations to assist in ensuring that the Chambers functioned in conformity with the agreement and complied with international standards of justice, fairness and due process of law, as set out in the International Covenant on Civil and Political Rights [YUN 1966, p. 423] (see p. 669). The Secretary-General proposed that the United Nations remain engaged in the process of overseeing the implementation of the draft agreement. The report outlined the steps required by the United Nations to conclude the agreement with the Government. Annexed to the report was the draft agreement.

GENERAL ASSEMBLY ACTION

On 13 May [meeting 85], the General Assembly, on the recommendation of the Third (Social, Humanitarian and Cultural) Committee [A/57/806], adopted **resolution 57/228 B** without vote [agenda item 109 (b)].

Khmer Rouge trials

The General Assembly,

Recalling its resolution 57/228 A of 18 December 2002,

Welcoming the efforts of the Secretary-General and the Royal Government of Cambodia to conclude the negotiation of the draft Agreement between the United Nations and the Royal Government of Cambodia concerning the Prosecution under Cambodian Law of Crimes Committed during the Period of Democratic Kampuchea contained in the annex to the present resolution,

Taking note of the report of the Secretary-General,

1. *Approves* the draft Agreement between the United Nations and the Royal Government of Cambodia concerning the Prosecution under Cambodian Law of Crimes Committed during the Period of Democratic Kampuchea contained in the annex to the present resolution;

2. *Urges* the Secretary-General and the Royal Government of Cambodia to take all the measures necessary to allow the draft Agreement referred to in paragraph 1 to enter into force, and to implement it fully after its entry into force;

3. *Decides* that the expenses of the Extraordinary Chambers to be defrayed by the United Nations in accordance with the relevant provisions of the draft Agreement shall be borne by voluntary contributions from the international community as indicated in paragraph 9 of resolution 57/228 A, and appeals to the international community to provide assistance, including financial and personnel support to the Extraordinary Chambers;

4. *Requests* the Secretary-General to report to the General Assembly at its fifty-eighth session on the implementation of the present resolution.

Annex

Draft Agreement between the United Nations and the Royal Government of Cambodia concerning the Prosecution under Cambodian Law of Crimes Committed during the Period of Democratic Kampuchea

Whereas the General Assembly of the United Nations, in its resolution 57/228 A of 18 December 2002, recalled that the serious violations of Cambodian and international humanitarian law during the period of Democratic Kampuchea from 1975 to 1979 continue to be matters of vitally important concern to the international community as a whole,

Whereas in the same resolution the General Assembly recognized the legitimate concern of the Government and the people of Cambodia in the pursuit of justice and national reconciliation, stability, peace and security,

Whereas the Cambodian authorities have requested assistance from the United Nations in bringing to trial senior leaders of Democratic Kampuchea and those who were most responsible for the crimes and serious violations of Cambodian penal law, international humanitarian law and custom, and international conventions recognized by Cambodia, that were committed during the period from 17 April 1975 to 6 January 1979,

Whereas prior to the negotiation of the present Agreement substantial progress had been made by the Secretary-General of the United Nations (hereinafter, "the Secretary-General") and the Royal Government of Cambodia towards the establishment, with international assistance, of Extraordinary Chambers within the existing court structure of Cambodia for the prosecution of crimes committed during the period of Democratic Kampuchea,

Whereas by its resolution 57/228 A, the General Assembly welcomed the promulgation of the Law on the Establishment of the Extraordinary Chambers in the Courts of Cambodia for the Prosecution of Crimes Committed during the Period of Democratic Kampuchea and requested the Secretary-General to resume negotiations, without delay, to conclude an agreement with the Government, based on previous negotiations on the establishment of the Extraordinary Chambers consistent with the provisions of the said resolution, so that the Extraordinary Chambers may begin to function promptly,

Whereas the Secretary-General and the Royal Government of Cambodia have held negotiations on the establishment of the Extraordinary Chambers,

Now therefore the United Nations and the Royal Government of Cambodia have agreed as follows:

Article 1
Purpose

The purpose of the present Agreement is to regulate the cooperation between the United Nations and the Royal Government of Cambodia in bringing to trial senior leaders of Democratic Kampuchea and those who were most responsible for the crimes and serious violations of Cambodian penal law, international humanitarian law and custom, and international conventions recognized by Cambodia, that were committed during the period from 17 April 1975 to 6 January 1979. The Agreement provides, inter alia, the legal basis and the principles and modalities for such cooperation.

Article 2
The Law on the Establishment of Extraordinary Chambers

1. The present Agreement recognizes that the Extraordinary Chambers have subject-matter jurisdiction consistent with that set forth in "the Law on the Establishment of the Extraordinary Chambers in the Courts of Cambodia for the Prosecution of Crimes Committed During the Period of Democratic Kampuchea" (hereinafter: "the Law on the Establishment of the Extraordinary Chambers"), as adopted and amended by the Cambodian Legislature under the Constitution of Cambodia. The present Agreement further recognizes that the Extraordinary Chambers have personal jurisdiction over senior leaders of Democratic Kampuchea and those who were most responsible for the crimes referred to in Article 1 of the Agreement.

2. The present Agreement shall be implemented in Cambodia through the Law on the Establishment of the Extraordinary Chambers as adopted and amended. The Vienna Convention on the Law of Treaties, and in particular its Articles 26 and 27, applies to the Agreement.

3. In case amendments to the Law on the Establishment of the Extraordinary Chambers are deemed necessary, such amendments shall always be preceded by consultations between the parties.

Article 3
Judges

1. Cambodian judges, on the one hand, and judges appointed by the Supreme Council of the Magistracy upon nomination by the Secretary-General of the United Nations (hereinafter: "international judges"), on the other hand, shall serve in each of the two Extraordinary Chambers.

2. The composition of the Chambers shall be as follows:

(a) The Trial Chamber: three Cambodian judges and two international judges;

(b) The Supreme Court Chamber, which shall serve as both appellate chamber and final instance: four Cambodian judges and three international judges.

3. The judges shall be persons of high moral character, impartiality and integrity who possess the qualifications required in their respective countries for appointment to judicial offices. They shall be independent in the performance of their functions and shall not accept or seek instructions from any Government or any other source.

4. In the overall composition of the Chambers due account should be taken of the experience of the judges in criminal law, international law, including international humanitarian law and human rights law.

5. The Secretary-General of the United Nations undertakes to forward a list of not less than seven nominees for international judges from which the Supreme Council of the Magistracy shall appoint five to serve as judges in the two Chambers. Appointment of international judges by the Supreme Council of the Magistracy shall be made only from the list submitted by the Secretary-General.

6. In the event of a vacancy of an international judge, the Supreme Council of the Magistracy shall appoint another international judge from the same list.

7. The judges shall be appointed for the duration of the proceedings.

8. In addition to the international judges sitting in the Chambers and present at every stage of the proceedings, the President of a Chamber may, on a case-by-case basis, designate from the list of nominees submitted by the Secretary-General, one or more alternate judges to be present at each stage of the proceedings, and to replace an international judge if that judge is unable to continue sitting.

Article 4
Decision-making

1. The judges shall attempt to achieve unanimity in their decisions. If this is not possible, the following shall apply:

(a) A decision by the Trial Chamber shall require the affirmative vote of at least four judges;

(b) A decision by the Supreme Court Chamber shall require the affirmative vote of at least five judges.

2. When there is no unanimity, the decision of the Chamber shall contain the views of the majority and the minority.

Article 5
Investigating judges

1. There shall be one Cambodian and one international investigating judge serving as co-investigating judges. They shall be responsible for the conduct of investigations.

2. The co-investigating judges shall be persons of high moral character, impartiality and integrity who possess the qualifications required in their respective countries for appointment to such a judicial office.

3. The co-investigating judges shall be independent in the performance of their functions and shall not accept or seek instructions from any Government or any other source. It is understood, however, that the scope of the investigation is limited to senior leaders of Democratic Kampuchea and those who were most responsible for the crimes and serious violations of Cambodian penal law, international humanitarian law and custom, and international conventions recognized by Cambodia, that were committed during the period from 17 April 1975 to 6 January 1979.

4. The co-investigating judges shall cooperate with a view to arriving at a common approach to the investigation. In case the co-investigating judges are unable to agree whether to proceed with an investigation, the investigation shall proceed unless the judges or one of them requests within thirty days that the difference shall be settled in accordance with Article 7.

5. In addition to the list of nominees provided for in Article 3, paragraph 5, the Secretary-General shall submit a list of two nominees from which the Supreme Council of the Magistracy shall appoint one to serve as an international co-investigating judge, and one as a reserve international co-investigating judge.

6. In case there is a vacancy or a need to fill the post of the international co-investigating judge, the person appointed to fill this post must be the reserve international co-investigating judge.

7. The co-investigating judges shall be appointed for the duration of the proceedings.

Article 6
Prosecutors

1. There shall be one Cambodian prosecutor and one international prosecutor competent to appear in both Chambers, serving as co-prosecutors. They shall be responsible for the conduct of the prosecutions.

2. The co-prosecutors shall be of high moral character, and possess a high level of professional competence and extensive experience in the conduct of investigations and prosecutions of criminal cases.

3. The co-prosecutors shall be independent in the performance of their functions and shall not accept or seek instructions from any Government or any other source. It is understood, however, that the scope of the prosecution is limited to senior leaders of Democratic Kampuchea and those who were most responsible for the crimes and serious violations of Cambodian penal law, international humanitarian law and custom, and international conventions recognized by Cambodia, that were committed during the period from 17 April 1975 to 6 January 1979.

4. The co-prosecutors shall cooperate with a view to arriving at a common approach to the prosecution. In case the prosecutors are unable to agree whether to proceed with a prosecution, the prosecution shall proceed unless the prosecutors or one of them requests within thirty days that the difference shall be settled in accordance with Article 7.

5. The Secretary-General undertakes to forward a list of two nominees from which the Supreme Council of the Magistracy shall select one international co-prosecutor and one reserve international co-prosecutor.

6. In case there is a vacancy or a need to fill the post of the international co-prosecutor, the person appointed to fill this post must be the reserve international co-prosecutor.

7. The co-prosecutors shall be appointed for the duration of the proceedings.

8. Each co-prosecutor shall have one or more deputy prosecutors to assist him or her with prosecutions before the Chambers. Deputy international prosecutors shall be appointed by the international co-prosecutor from a list provided by the Secretary-General.

Article 7
Settlement of differences between the co-investigating judges or the co-prosecutors

1. In case the co-investigating judges or the co-prosecutors have made a request in accordance with Article 5, paragraph 4, or Article 6, paragraph 4, as the case may be, they shall submit written statements of facts and the reasons for their different positions to the Director of the Office of Administration.

2. The difference shall be settled forthwith by a Pre-Trial Chamber of five judges, three appointed by the Supreme Council of the Magistracy, with one as President, and two appointed by the Supreme Council of the Magistracy upon nomination by the Secretary-General. Article 3, paragraph 3, shall apply to the judges.

3. Upon receipt of the statements referred to in paragraph 1, the Director of the Office of Adminis-

tration shall immediately convene the Pre-Trial Chamber and communicate the statements to its members.

4. A decision of the Pre-Trial Chamber, against which there is no appeal, requires the affirmative vote of at least four judges. The decision shall be communicated to the Director of the Office of Administration, who shall publish it and communicate it to the co-investigating judges or the co-prosecutors. They shall immediately proceed in accordance with the decision of the Chamber. If there is no majority, as required for a decision, the investigation or prosecution shall proceed.

Article 8
Office of Administration

1. There shall be an Office of Administration to service the Extraordinary Chambers, the Pre-Trial Chamber, the co-investigating judges and the Prosecutors' Office.

2. There shall be a Cambodian Director of this Office, who shall be appointed by the Royal Government of Cambodia. The Director shall be responsible for the overall management of the Office of Administration, except in matters that are subject to United Nations rules and procedures.

3. There shall be an international Deputy Director of the Office of Administration, who shall be appointed by the Secretary-General. The Deputy Director shall be responsible for the recruitment of all international staff and all administration of the international components of the Extraordinary Chambers, the Pre-Trial Chamber, the co-investigating judges, the Prosecutors' Office and the Office of Administration. The United Nations and the Royal Government of Cambodia agree that, when an international Deputy Director has been appointed by the Secretary-General, the assignment of that person to that position by the Royal Government of Cambodia shall take place forthwith.

4. The Director and the Deputy Director shall cooperate in order to ensure an effective and efficient functioning of the administration.

Article 9
Crimes falling within the jurisdiction of the Extraordinary Chambers

The subject-matter jurisdiction of the Extraordinary Chambers shall be the crime of genocide as defined in the 1948 Convention on the Prevention and Punishment of the Crime of Genocide, crimes against humanity as defined in the 1998 Rome Statute of the International Criminal Court and grave breaches of the 1949 Geneva Conventions and such other crimes as defined in Chapter II of the Law on the Establishment of the Extraordinary Chambers as promulgated on 10 August 2001.

Article 10
Penalties

The maximum penalty for conviction for crimes falling within the jurisdiction of the Extraordinary Chambers shall be life imprisonment.

Article 11
Amnesty

1. The Royal Government of Cambodia shall not request an amnesty or pardon for any persons who may be investigated for or convicted of crimes referred to in the present Agreement.

2. This provision is based upon a declaration by the Royal Government of Cambodia that until now, with regard to matters covered in the law, there has been only one case, dated 14 September 1996, when a pardon was granted to only one person with regard to a 1979 conviction on the charge of genocide. The United Nations and the Royal Government of Cambodia agree that the scope of this pardon is a matter to be decided by the Extraordinary Chambers.

Article 12
Procedure

1. The procedure shall be in accordance with Cambodian law. Where Cambodian law does not deal with a particular matter, or where there is uncertainty regarding the interpretation or application of a relevant rule of Cambodian law, or where there is a question regarding the consistency of such a rule with international standards, guidance may also be sought in procedural rules established at the international level.

2. The Extraordinary Chambers shall exercise their jurisdiction in accordance with international standards of justice, fairness and due process of law, as set out in Articles 14 and 15 of the 1966 International Covenant on Civil and Political Rights, to which Cambodia is a party. In the interest of securing a fair and public hearing and credibility of the procedure, it is understood that representatives of Member States of the United Nations, of the Secretary-General, of the media and of national and international non-governmental organizations will at all times have access to the proceedings before the Extraordinary Chambers. Any exclusion from such proceedings in accordance with the provisions of Article 14 of the Covenant shall only be to the extent strictly necessary in the opinion of the Chamber concerned and where publicity would prejudice the interests of justice.

Article 13
Rights of the accused

1. The rights of the accused enshrined in Articles 14 and 15 of the 1966 International Covenant on Civil and Political Rights shall be respected throughout the trial process. Such rights shall, in particular, include the right: to a fair and public hearing; to be presumed innocent until proved guilty; to engage a counsel of his or her choice; to have adequate time and facilities for the preparation of his or her defence; to have counsel provided if he or she does not have sufficient means to pay for it; and to examine or have examined the witnesses against him or her.

2. The United Nations and the Royal Government of Cambodia agree that the provisions on the right to defence counsel in the Law on the Establishment of Extraordinary Chambers mean that the accused has the right to engage counsel of his or her own choosing as guaranteed by the International Covenant on Civil and Political Rights.

Article 14
Premises

The Royal Government of Cambodia shall provide at its expense the premises for the co-investigating judges, the Prosecutors' Office, the Extraordinary Chambers, the Pre-Trial Chamber and the Office of

Article 15
Cambodian personnel
Salaries and emoluments of Cambodian judges and other Cambodian personnel shall be defrayed by the Royal Government of Cambodia.

Article 16
International personnel
Salaries and emoluments of international judges, the international co-investigating judge, the international co-prosecutor and other personnel recruited by the United Nations shall be defrayed by the United Nations.

Article 17
Financial and other assistance of the United Nations
The United Nations shall be responsible for the following:

(a) Remuneration of the international judges, the international co-investigating judge, the international co-prosecutor, the Deputy Director of the Office of Administration and other international personnel;

(b) Costs for utilities and services as agreed separately between the United Nations and the Royal Government of Cambodia;

(c) Remuneration of defence counsel;

(d) Witnesses' travel from within Cambodia and from abroad;

(e) Safety and security arrangements as agreed separately between the United Nations and the Government;

(f) Such other limited assistance as may be necessary to ensure the smooth functioning of the investigation, the prosecution and the Extraordinary Chambers.

Article 18
Inviolability of archives and documents
The archives of the co-investigating judges, the co-prosecutors, the Extraordinary Chambers, the Pre-Trial Chamber and the Office of Administration, and in general all documents and materials made available, belonging to or used by them, wherever located in Cambodia and by whomsoever held, shall be inviolable for the duration of the proceedings.

Article 19
Privileges and immunities of international judges, the international co-investigating judge, the international co-prosecutor and the Deputy Director of the Office of Administration

1. The international judges, the international co-investigating judge, the international co-prosecutor and the Deputy Director of the Office of Administration, together with their families forming part of their household, shall enjoy the privileges and immunities, exemptions and facilities accorded to diplomatic agents in accordance with the 1961 Vienna Convention on Diplomatic Relations. They shall, in particular, enjoy:

(a) Personal inviolability, including immunity from arrest or detention;

(b) Immunity from criminal, civil and administrative jurisdiction in conformity with the Vienna Convention;

(c) Inviolability for all papers and documents;

(d) Exemption from immigration restrictions and alien registration;

(e) The same immunities and facilities in respect of their personal baggage as are accorded to diplomatic agents.

2. The international judges, the international co-investigating judge, the international co-prosecutor and the Deputy Director of the Office of Administration shall enjoy exemption from taxation in Cambodia on their salaries, emoluments and allowances.

Article 20
Privileges and immunities of Cambodian and international personnel

1. Cambodian judges, the Cambodian co-investigating judge, the Cambodian co-prosecutor and other Cambodian personnel shall be accorded immunity from legal process in respect of words spoken or written and all acts performed by them in their official capacity under the present Agreement. Such immunity shall continue to be accorded after termination of employment with the co-investigating judges, the co-prosecutors, the Extraordinary Chambers, the Pre-Trial Chamber and the Office of Administration.

2. International personnel shall be accorded:

(a) Immunity from legal process in respect of words spoken or written and all acts performed by them in their official capacity under the present Agreement. Such immunity shall continue to be accorded after termination of employment with the co-investigating judges, the co-prosecutors, the Extraordinary Chambers, the Pre-Trial Chamber and the Office of Administration;

(b) Immunity from taxation on salaries, allowances and emoluments paid to them by the United Nations;

(c) Immunity from immigration restrictions;

(d) The right to import free of duties and taxes, except for payment for services, their furniture and effects at the time of first taking up their official duties in Cambodia.

3. The United Nations and the Royal Government of Cambodia agree that the immunity granted by the Law on the Establishment of the Extraordinary Chambers in respect of words spoken or written and all acts performed by them in their official capacity under the present Agreement will apply also after the persons have left the service of the co-investigating judges, the co-prosecutors, the Extraordinary Chambers, the Pre-Trial Chamber and the Office of Administration.

Article 21
Counsel

1. The counsel of a suspect or an accused who has been admitted as such by the Extraordinary Chambers shall not be subjected by the Royal Government of Cambodia to any measure which may affect the free and independent exercise of his or her functions under the present Agreement.

2. In particular, the counsel shall be accorded:

(a) Immunity from personal arrest or detention and from seizure of personal baggage;

(b) Inviolability of all documents relating to the exercise of his or her functions as a counsel of a suspect or accused;

(c) Immunity from criminal or civil jurisdiction in respect of words spoken or written and acts performed by them in their official capacity as counsel. Such immunity shall continue to be accorded to them after termination of their functions as a counsel of a suspect or accused.

3. Any counsel, whether of Cambodian or non-Cambodian nationality, engaged by or assigned to a suspect or an accused shall, in the defence of his or her client, act in accordance with the present Agreement, the Cambodian Law on the Statutes of the Bar and recognized standards and ethics of the legal profession.

Article 22
Witnesses and experts

Witnesses and experts appearing on a summons or a request of the judges, the co-investigating judges, or the co-prosecutors shall not be prosecuted, detained or subjected to any other restriction on their liberty by the Cambodian authorities. They shall not be subjected by the authorities to any measure which may affect the free and independent exercise of their functions.

Article 23
Protection of victims and witnesses

The co-investigating judges, the co-prosecutors and the Extraordinary Chambers shall provide for the protection of victims and witnesses. Such protection measures shall include, but shall not be limited to, the conduct of *in camera* proceedings and the protection of the identity of a victim or witness.

Article 24
Security, safety and protection of persons referred to in the present Agreement

The Royal Government of Cambodia shall take all effective and adequate actions which may be required to ensure the security, safety and protection of persons referred to in the present Agreement. The United Nations and the Government agree that the Government is responsible for the security of all accused, irrespective of whether they appear voluntarily before the Extraordinary Chambers or whether they are under arrest.

Article 25
Obligation to assist the co-investigating judges, the co-prosecutors and the Extraordinary Chambers

The Royal Government of Cambodia shall comply without undue delay with any request for assistance by the co-investigating judges, the co-prosecutors and the Extraordinary Chambers or an order issued by any of them, including, but not limited to:

(a) Identification and location of persons;

(b) Service of documents;

(c) Arrest or detention of persons;

(d) Transfer of an indictee to the Extraordinary Chambers.

Article 26
Languages

1. The official language of the Extraordinary Chambers and the Pre-Trial Chamber is Khmer.

2. The official working languages of the Extraordinary Chambers and the Pre-Trial Chamber shall be Khmer, English and French.

3. Translations of public documents and interpretation at public hearings into Russian may be provided by the Royal Government of Cambodia at its discretion and expense on condition that such services do not hinder the proceedings before the Extraordinary Chambers.

Article 27
Practical arrangements

1. With a view to achieving efficiency and cost-effectiveness in the operation of the Extraordinary Chambers, a phased-in approach shall be adopted for their establishment in accordance with the chronological order of the legal process.

2. In the first phase of the operation of the Extraordinary Chambers, the judges, the co-investigating judges and the co-prosecutors will be appointed along with investigative and prosecutorial staff, and the process of investigations and prosecutions shall be initiated.

3. The trial process of those already in custody shall proceed simultaneously with the investigation of other persons responsible for crimes falling within the jurisdiction of the Extraordinary Chambers.

4. With the completion of the investigation of persons suspected of having committed the crimes falling within the jurisdiction of the Extraordinary Chambers, arrest warrants shall be issued and submitted to the Royal Government of Cambodia to effectuate the arrest.

5. With the arrest by the Royal Government of Cambodia of indicted persons situated in its territory, the Extraordinary Chambers shall be fully operational, provided that the judges of the Supreme Court Chamber shall serve when seized with a matter. The judges of the Pre-Trial Chamber shall serve only if and when their services are needed.

Article 28
Withdrawal of cooperation

Should the Royal Government of Cambodia change the structure or organization of the Extraordinary Chambers or otherwise cause them to function in a manner that does not conform with the terms of the present Agreement, the United Nations reserves the right to cease to provide assistance, financial or otherwise, pursuant to the present Agreement.

Article 29
Settlement of disputes

Any dispute between the parties concerning the interpretation or application of the present Agreement shall be settled by negotiation, or by any other mutually agreed upon mode of settlement.

Article 30
Approval

To be binding on the parties, the present Agreement must be approved by the General Assembly of the United Nations and ratified by Cambodia. The Royal Government of Cambodia will make its best endeavours to obtain this ratification by the earliest possible date.

Article 31
Application within Cambodia

The present Agreement shall apply as law within the Kingdom of Cambodia following its ratification in accordance with the relevant provisions of the internal law of the Kingdom of Cambodia regarding competence to conclude treaties.

Article 32
Entry into force

The present Agreement shall enter into force on the day after both parties have notified each other in writing that the legal requirements for entry into force have been complied with.

Done at [place] on [day, month] 2003 in two copies in the English language.

For the United Nations   For the Royal Government of Cambodia

In a 3 December report [A/58/617], the Secretary-General stated that the Agreement had been signed by the United Nations and the Government of Cambodia and was awaiting ratification through the Cambodian legislative process. In the meantime, a UN technical team would visit Cambodia to prepare a draft concept of operation, gather more precise cost parameters for an overall budget for the Chambers and ascertain the availability of facilities and utilities. A more substantive report would be submitted based on the team's findings. In conclusion, the Secretary-General expressed concern at the delays in the implementation of the Agreement and called on the Government to ensure that its ratification was accorded priority.

India-Pakistan

On 19 August, Pakistan addressed identical letters [A/58/298-S/2003/823] to the Presidents of the General Assembly and the Security Council, raising issues relating to peace and security in South Asia, in the context of India-Pakistan relations and the Jammu and Kashmir dispute. Although earlier in the year the two countries had taken steps to reduce tensions by restoring diplomatic relations at the level of High Commissioners (Ambassadors) and resuming transportation links, there had not been movement in resolving the outstanding differences between the two countries, especially over Jammu and Kashmir. Pakistan believed that the international community should urgently call on India to respond positively to Pakistan's proposals to revive the bilateral dialogue, install an effective ceasefire along the Line of Control in Kashmir, halt threatening statements and propaganda, stop its repression in Kashmir, reduce military deployments in the disputed State and evolve confidence-building measures with Pakistan to reduce the risk of accidental or deliberate conflict.

The final communiqué of the annual coordination meeting of the Ministers for Foreign Affairs of the States members of the Organization of the Islamic Conference (New York, 30 September) [A/58/415-S/2003/952] welcomed the measures taken by India and Pakistan to normalize their bilateral relations and urged India to enter into meaningful and result-oriented dialogue with Pakistan.

Korea question

On 24 January [S/2003/91], the Democratic People's Republic of Korea (DPRK) transmitted to the President of the Security Council three statements. A letter from the DPRK Foreign Minister informed the Council of the Government's decision to put into effect its withdrawal from the 1968 Treaty on the Non-Proliferation of Nuclear Weapons (NPT), adopted by the General Assembly in resolution 2373(XXII) [YUN 1968, p. 17], as the Government had decided in 1993 [YUN 1993, p. 356]. The DPRK explained it would revoke the "suspension" on the withdrawal, which would come into effect. A statement issued by the Government on 10 January said that the United States had instigated the International Atomic Energy Agency (IAEA) to adopt a 6 January resolution demanding that the DPRK scrap its nuclear programme. Although it had pulled out of NPT, the DPRK had no intention of producing nuclear weapons. If the United States dropped its hostile policy towards it, the DPRK might allow a separate verification by the United States. The DPRK also forwarded a report of 21 January by the Korean Central News Agency on the circumstances and historical background of the DPRK's withdrawal from NPT.

On 26 June [S/2003/673], the DPRK transmitted to the Council President a statement by its Foreign Minister, which noted that one permanent member of the Council had sought to bring before it the nuclear issue on the Korean peninsula. The DPRK expressed its wish for bilateral, tripartite or multilateral talks with concerned parties and attached priority to the DPRK–United States bilateral talks. It stated that the Council should avoid giving any impression that it might apply double standards in the application of international instruments.

The DPRK, on 1 July [S/2003/681], forwarded to the Council a statement by the DPRK Chief of the Panmunjom Mission of the Korean People's Army, in which he stated that the United States was reinforcing its presence in the Republic of Korea. Its preparations for attack on the DPRK were in their final stage under the new strategy of "pre-emptive strike" instead of the previous "deterrence" strategy.

By a 28 July letter [S/2003/768], the DPRK transmitted a memorandum of the Panmunjom Mission of the DPRK Army on the occasion of the fiftieth anniversary of the signing of the 1953 Korean Armistice Agreement [YUN 1953, p. 136]. The memorandum reviewed events on the Korean peninsula since the Agreement was signed, in particular the "hostile" policy against the DPRK adopted by the United States, and said that the United States had brought about nuclear threat and danger of war on the peninsula by having violated key provisions of the Agreement.

The Libyan Arab Jamahiriya, in a 20 February letter to the Secretary-General and the Council [S/2003/224], transmitted an initiative of Colonel Muammar Qaddafi on resolution of the Korean crisis through peaceful reunification on the peninsula.

India and the Russian Federation, on 21 November [A/58/611-S/2003/1134], transmitted to the Council and the General Assembly a joint declaration adopted during the visit of the Prime Minister of India, Atal Bihari Vajpayee, to the Russian Federation on 12 November. The two countries expressed support for efforts to pursue a peaceful solution to the nuclear problem on the Korean peninsula and to ensure its denuclearized status, including continuing six-way talks in Beijing, finding a mutually acceptable solution and further developing inter-Korean dialogue and cooperation.

Papua New Guinea

Significant progress was made in 2003 in UN efforts to resolve the conflict in the Papua New Guinea province of Bougainville, as implementation of the 2001 Bougainville Peace Agreement, concluded between the Government of Papua New Guinea and the Bougainville parties, entered its final stage. That Agreement, which had established the framework for a peace process, including a permanent ceasefire, as provided for in the 1998 Lincoln Agreement [YUN 1998, p. 319] and its annex, the Arawa Agreement [ibid.], covered issues of autonomy, the holding of a referendum and agreements on weapons disposal. The parties to the Peace Agreement completed phase II of the weapons disposal plan and reached agreement on the final disposal of the weapons collected, which allowed the United Nations Political Office in Bougainville (UNPOB) to carry out the necessary certification and verification. That set the stage for the next steps to be taken, particularly the entry into force of constitutional amendments to the Papua New Guinea constitution, which would lead to the drafting and presentation of a constitution for Bougainville, the delegation of police powers and expediting consultations on the functions of the interim provincial government and arrangements for elections. However, significant challenges remained, prompting the Secretary-General, in December, to accede to Papua New Guinea's request to maintain a UN presence on the island. The new mission, the United Nations Observer Mission in Papua New Guinea (UNOMB), would, among other functions, monitor the constitutional process leading to the adoption of a Bougainville constitution and verify and certify compliance by the parties with the weapons disposal plan. The Mission would work with UNDP, which would lead international reconstruction and rehabilitation efforts.

UNPOB activities

Report of Secretary-General. In March [S/2003/345], the Secretary-General, as requested by the Security Council in 2002 [YUN 2002, p. 332], reported on the activities of UNPOB, including the remaining challenges and UNPOB's exit strategy. He stated that, following the 17 February adoption of an Action Plan for the Completion of Weapons Collection by political and former combatant leaders, 80.2 per cent of Bougainville had reached stage II of the weapons disposal plan under the Bougainville Peace Agreement and two districts had completely disarmed. Some 7.4 per cent of weapons had been destroyed ahead of the formal launch of stage III. Since the start of the Action Plan, the parties had re-contained one trunk of stolen weapons, held one stage I containment ceremony and scheduled more stage II containment ceremonies across the island. The parties to the peace process, the Bougainville Resistance Force (BRF) and the Bougainville Revolutionary Army (BRA), had scheduled separate discussions on the final fate of the collected weapons and were expected to reach a unified position on the matter. However, a major obstacle to completing weapons disposal was the continued non-involvement of Francis Ona and his Me'ekamui Defence Force (MDF) in the peace process, despite appeals by the parties to the Bougainville Peace Agreement. In the meantime, UNPOB was seeking ways to facilitate and expedite the completion of the stage II weapons collection in the shortest possible time.

On 1 February, the Bougainville Constitutional Commission released a draft constitution for Bougainville for island-wide consultations. On the basis of feedback, a second draft had been prepared and would be examined by the Joint Assembly of the Bougainville Interim Provincial

Government and the Bougainville People's Congress. The draft would be returned to the Constitutional Commission following review by the bipartisan Ministerial Committee and the National Executive Council of the Government of Papua New Guinea. The text was expected to be finalized by the end of April and submitted for adoption to a Bougainville Constituent Assembly, which would be established on completion of stage II of weapons disposal. It was hoped that elections could then be held before the end of the year.

The Government of Papua New Guinea continued to demonstrate its commitment to implementing the Bougainville Peace Agreement. Following confidence-building cabinet-level visits to the island, the Government and the Bougainville parties signed a memorandum of understanding establishing a mechanism for consultations between them on all aspects of the autonomy arrangements, including the transfer of powers, functions and resources, and the settlement of disputes. An indication of the growing confidence between the two sides was the national Government's withdrawal on 26 March of its Defence Force from Bougainville, well ahead of schedule.

The regional Peace Monitoring Group, which had made a valuable contribution to the peace process since 1998 [YUN 1998, p. 319], including the provision of logistical support to weapons collection and meetings of the Peace Process Consultative Committee, informed the parties of its intention to cease all operations on 30 June and to withdraw thereafter. UNPOB was working to ensure that, by that date, weapons disposal would be so far advanced that it would no longer require that level of support. However, since the process was unlikely to be completed by that date, UNPOB was of the view that the parties should review the weapons disposal process and, if necessary, replace the Peace Monitoring Group with an alternative arrangement.

The Secretary-General indicated that, in accordance with its mandate, once UNPOB had verified that stage II of the weapons disposal plan had been completed, the constitutional amendments would enter into force, paving the way for the election of an autonomous Bougainville government by the end of 2003 and the closure of UNPOB. UNPOB was looking to UNDP and other UN agencies to take the lead in facilitating the reintegration and rehabilitation of former combatants and the restoration of community services and infrastructure. Consultations were being held with UNDP aimed at ensuring its valuable contribution to post-conflict peace-building, including the improvement of governance. To further solidify peace in Bougainville, the Secretary-General appealed to the donor community to continue its assistance to the island following the expected departure of UNPOB at the end of 2003.

Security Council consideration (March). On 28 March [S/PV.4728], the Assistant Secretary-General for Political Affairs, Danilo Türk, updated the Security Council on developments in Bougainville. He informed the Council, which had before it the Secretary-General's report, that implementation of the Plan of Action for the Completion of Weapons Collection seemed to be proceeding well. Additional weapons had been retrieved and three new stage II containments had taken place. As a result of direct contacts with persons responsible for previous break-ins into the containers, it was expected that weapons removed would soon be returned. In several other districts, former combatants, acting on UNPOB's behalf, had been promoting reconciliation, settling issues and thus creating an atmosphere conducive to the containment of more weapons. The Assistant Secretary-General said that, after a decade of suffering, the people of Bougainville were working diligently to achieve a better future, giving confidence that, despite the remaining obstacles and political spoilers, particularly Mr. Ona, the Bougainville Peace Agreement could be fully implemented before the end of the year, allowing UNPOB to withdraw.

The Papua New Guinea representative told the Council that, with the active cooperation of ex-combatants, the break-ins and removal of weapons from containers that caused much concern in 2002 appeared to have ended and the national Government was cooperating with the police in providing financial and other support for efforts to provide security. The process was slow but UNPOB and the Peace Monitoring Group had been working hard to keep it moving ahead, as had the leaders of BRA and BRF. The Constitutional Commission had prepared a second draft of the proposed constitution, which was soon to be presented to the national Government. The Government had also appointed a high-level bipartisan National Committee to advise on its response to the Commission's proposals. The Defence Force was expected to complete its withdrawal from Bougainville under the agreed weapons disposal plan at about the same time. The establishment of the Interim Joint Supervisory Body was another initiative taken well before any legal requirement, and the two sides had already begun to cooperate in managing the implementation of the agreed autonomy arrangements. The national Government was making some $1.5 million available in 2003 and 2004 as an establishment grant to assist the autonomous Bougainville government in meeting start-up expenses. Reform in the public sector was proceeding in readiness for the establishment of the autonomous government, with the assistance of the international community. As with the deadline set for the end of the UN mission [YUN 2002, p. 332], the challenge posed by the planned withdrawal of the Peace Monitoring Group at the end of June was how to make the utmost use of its presence and conclude weapons disposal before the Group left. Its withdrawal would also leave a void for UNPOB, especially as far as communications, transport and technical support for weapons disposal were concerned. The Government believed that the stage III meeting to decide on the final fate of weapons should be brought forward.

The New Zealand representative said that it had noted UNPOB's intention to certify substantial compliance on the basis of affirmation from village and district communities in Bougainville that they were satisfied that the weapons in their areas had been contained and that the communities felt safe. UNPOB should formally declare that criterion without further delay and move quickly to certify that former combatants were in substantial compliance with stage II of weapons disposal as set out in the Bougainville Peace Agreement. There was currently a range of views on what the final fate of the weapons should be; New Zealand held the view that all weapons should be destroyed so that safety and security were not compromised by the return of weapons into the hands of those with criminal intent.

Completion of weapons disposal phase

Security Council consideration (August). The Head of UNPOB, Noel Sinclair, briefed the Security Council on 6 August [S/PV.4805]. He said that some dramatic steps had been taken since the last briefing to the Council, the most significant of which was the completion of stage II of weapons disposal, as required by the Bougainville Peace Agreement. Following an island-wide process of consultations to determine how the people of Bougainville felt as a result of what had been achieved, UNPOB informed the Peace Process Consultative Committee of its judgement that stage II of weapons disposal had come to an end and that the weapons disposal plan had served its purpose. On 30 July, UNPOB made that verification and certification to the national Government, which so advised the Governor General. It was expected that the Organic Law on Peace-Building in Bougainville would become fully operational shortly, setting the stage for the next steps to be taken, including the holding of elections for a Bougainville autonomous government. Consultations were taking place on those issues and a budget was being prepared for the funding of constitutional and electoral activities, including meetings of the Bougainville Constitutional Commission and of a constituent assembly.

Meanwhile, the process of weapons collection continued, and UNPOB was pushing ahead with its Operation Continuing Vigilance and Final Phase programmes. As to the final fate of the collected weapons, the national Government and BRF had indicated a preference for their destruction, while BRA preferred secure storage. UNPOB had been requested to preside over a consultation of the parties to seek a unified position on the question at the end of August. In the remaining months of its mandate, UNPOB would continue to ensure that the peace process kept moving forward. It was happy to have the support of the newly established Bougainville Transition Team, the successor to the Peace Monitoring Group, which completed its mission on 30 June. As responsibility for providing continuing international support for Bougainville peace consolidation efforts would devolve on UNDP, consultations were going on with a view to developing a joint approach for a smooth transition.

Mr. Sinclair observed that, with the completion of stage II of the weapons disposal plan, the parties had begun to talk seriously among themselves about stage III, for which a deadline of the middle of December had been set. The parties were also working to advance the autonomy aspects of the Peace Agreement, most importantly the finalization of a constitution and the holding of elections.

End of UNPOB and establishment of UNOMB

Security Council consideration (December). The Security Council, on 15 December [S/PV.4881], was briefed by the Assistant Secretary-General for Political Affairs on the situation in Bougainville. He reported that, as a result of the completion of stage II of the weapons disposal programme, BRA and BRF had put more than 1,900 pieces of weapons into 16 secured containers and 68 trunks, with a key being held by the relevant commander and UNPOB pending a final decision on the fate of those weapons. The achievement of that important benchmark allowed the national Government to enact the constitutional amendment and the Organic Law on Peace-Building in Bougainville, which expedited consultations among the parties on the constitution, the delegation of police powers, functions of the interim provincial government and arrangements for elections.

As to the constitutional process, the Papua New Guinea Attorney-General presented his comments on the second draft of the Bougainville constitution in October and differences relating to the consistency between the second draft and the Papua New Guinea constitution were being resolved. On 5 December, the Papua New Guinea cabinet, the National Executive Council, reaffirmed its commitment to honour the Bougainville Peace Agreement and to implement corresponding laws. It was expected that the Bougainville constitution would be adopted during the first quarter of 2004 and endorsed by the national Government by midyear.

Regarding phase III of weapons disposal, BRA and BRF adopted a 30 November resolution declaring that the final fate of the contained weapons should be their destruction, to take place upon the finalization of the essential components of the peace process: the coming into force of the Bougainville constitution, the resolution of outstanding issues with MDF and reconciliation between MDF, and BRA and BRF. That unified position on weapons destruction would facilitate the meeting of the Peace Process Consultative Committee (16-17 December), at which the national Government and Bougainville leaders were expected to meet or modify some of the conditions enunciated by the Bougainville factions, thereby facilitating the adoption of the stage III decision on the final fate of the weapons. UNPOB had prepared a statement on the administrative and technical issues that needed to be addressed before the process of destruction could begin and was grateful for the offers of technical support pledged by regional partners to facilitate the process.

On the issue of police powers, the National Executive Council decided to delegate police powers and functions to the Bougainville interim provincial government, with the formal handover scheduled for 16 or 17 December. Meanwhile, arrangements were being finalized for further strengthening Bougainville's law and justice capacity through the deployment of 30 Bougainville police from the mainland and the recruitment of the first 50 to 100 Bougainvillean cadets for training. No progress was made on the so-called "no go zone", the area controlled by Francis Ona, who continued to refuse to contain MDF's weapons—a decision that could affect implementation of the BRA/BRF decision on the destruction of their weapons. Mr. Ona's supporters also maintained roadblocks to prevent the delivery of government services and development assistance to the zone.

Recalling the deadline set by the Council for the closure and withdrawal of UNPOB, the Assistant Secretary-General said that the peace process would not be completed by 31 December 2003 and the United Nations shared the view of Papua New Guinea, as expressed in its letter of 11 December to the Secretary-General, and of the Bougainville parties, that a UN presence in Bougainville was still required, albeit a downsized presence, given the maturity of the peace process and the limited tasks remaining. Moreover, since the Bougainville Transitional Team was scheduled to withdraw by the end of the year also, a continued UN political presence would contribute to building confidence among the parties in the peace process and give the autonomous government to be established a fair chance of starting out in an environment that provided a reasonable prospect for the continued strengthening of peace, security and stability on the island. The proposed successor mission, the United Nations Observer Mission in Bougainville (UNOMB), to be established for six months starting in January 2004, would have as its functions: chairing the Peace Process Consultative Committee, reporting on security and the subsequent destruction of contained weapons, monitoring the constitutional process leading to adoption of the Bougainville constitution, verifying and certifying substantial compliance by the parties with the weapons disposal plan, and performing other good offices as appropriate. Given that limited role, the UNPOB staff would be reduced from six to a head of mission, one political adviser and two support staff, and consultations were taking place on sharing office space with UNDP in Buka and Arawa, which would result in substantial savings in both instances. The new mission would continue to work with UNDP and other UN bodies on practical aspects of peacebuilding in Bougainville. UNDP was working on the second phase of its rehabilitation programme for Bougainville, which would include assistance in agriculture and capacity-building.

Communication. The Secretary-General, on 19 December [S/2003/1198], informed the Council President of his intention to establish, with the Council's concurrence, a small follow-on UN observer mission in Bougainville (UNOMB) for a period of six months, with the functions as outlined by the Assistant Secretary-General (above). On 23 December [S/2003/1199], the Council President informed the Secretary-General that Council members had taken note of his intention to establish UNOMB, and of the functions and staffing structure outlined.

Solomon Islands

Fiji, on behalf of the Pacific Islands Forum Group, transmitted to the Security Council President the Outcomes Statement of the Pacific Forum Foreign Affairs Ministers Meeting (Sydney, Australia, 30 June) [S/2003/753], which outlined the response of Forum members to a request from Solomon Islands for regional assistance in restoring peace and security. The Ministers agreed that the deterioration of law and order had undermined the country's stability and the situation called for a concerted regional response. In that regard, they welcomed an assistance package proposed by Australia.

On 31 July [S/2003/799], Solomon Islands forwarded documents relating to the Australia-led Regional Assistance Mission, which was deployed to Solomon Islands to restore law and order and economic recovery: a Solomon Islands government policy statement on Australia's offer of assistance; the Facilitation International Assistance Act 2003, adopted by Solomon Islands on 17 July to make provisions for assistance to restore law and order; and an Agreement between Australia, Fiji, New Zealand, Papua New Guinea, Samoa, Solomon Islands and Tonga regarding the operations and status of the police and armed forces and other personnel deployed to Solomon Islands.

Tajikistan

The Secretary-General, on 8 May [S/2003/542], informed the Security Council of his intention to continue the activities of the United Nations Tajikistan Office of Peace-building (UNTOP) for another year, until 1 June 2004, in view of its role and the country's need for continuing support in its post-conflict peace-building efforts. The Council took note of his intention on 13 May [S/2003/543].

UNTOP was established in 2000 [YUN 2000, p. 315] following the withdrawal of the United Nations Mission of Observers in Tajikistan (UNMOT). The Office continued to focus its activities during the year on the consolidation of peace and national reconciliation, promotion of the rule of law, strengthening of democratic institutions and support for national capacity-building in the area of human rights. The Secretary-General reported that during the preceding year, UNTOP continued a series of Political Discussion Club meetings, attended by a number of national and local government and military officials, and representatives of the business community, civil society and the media, which focused on issues of national reconciliation, good governance, economic reform, improvement of the electoral system, democratization of society and promotion of human rights. UNTOP played an important role in strengthening the rule of law in Tajikistan and continued its support for the social integration of ex-combatants and demobilized contractual soldiers through assistance for vocational training for 270 ex-combatants.

UNMOT financing

On 17 April [A/57/792], the Secretary-General issued the final performance report of the United Nations Mission of Observers in Tajikistan (UNMOT), whose mandate expired in 2000 [YUN 2000, p. 314]. As at 30 June 2002, the total fund balance was $8,903,000. Uncollected assessments and other receivables totalled $1,552,000. The Secretary-General recommended that the General Assembly suspend the return of cash available for credit to Member States in the light of the Organization's overall financial situation and the fact that, as at 15 March 2003, assessed contributions to peacekeeping in the amount of $1.5 billion remained unpaid.

Turkey

On 15 November, a suicide bomb attack against two synagogues in Istanbul, Turkey, killed 25 people. Five days later, double bomb attacks on the British consulate and the HSBC bank headquarters in Istanbul left many more dead and injured.

On 20 November, the Security Council, in **resolution 1516(2003)** (see p. 65), condemned the bomb attacks in Istanbul and other terrorist acts in various countries.

United Arab Emirates–Iran

Greater Tunb, Lesser Tunb and Abu Musa

The United Arab Emirates, in an 11 March letter to the Secretary-General [S/2003/302], requested that the Security Council retain on its agenda for 2003 the item entitled "Letter dated 3 December 1971 from the Permanent Representatives of Algeria, Iraq, the Libyan Arab Republic and the People's Democratic Republic of Yemen to the United Nations addressed to the Secretary-General (S/10409)", concerning Iran's occupation of three islands belonging to the United Arab Emirates, namely Greater Tunb, Lesser Tunb and Abu Musa, until a settlement of the related conflict was achieved by peaceful means through direct negotiation or through recourse to the International Court of Justice.

Chapter V
Europe and the Mediterranean

In 2003, the countries in post-conflict situations in Europe and the Mediterranean continued their slow and difficult progress towards the restoration of peace and stability by consolidating the progress made so far in re-establishing their governance institutions and social and economic infrastructure, especially in Bosnia and Herzegovina and the Serbia and Montenegro province of Kosovo. However, many political issues and situations remained unresolved. In Bosnia and Herzegovina, through the efforts of the international community, currently led by the European Union (EU), a number of reforms were undertaken, particularly in the areas of the rule of law, refugee return and economic development, in accordance with European standards. The country thus moved one step closer to full integration into Europe through meeting the requirements of the EU Stabilization and Association Process and the North Atlantic Treaty Organization Partnership for Peace. In the Kosovo province of the Federal Republic of Yugoslavia (renamed Serbia and Montenegro on 4 February), the United Nations continued to assist in efforts to build a modern, European, multi-ethnic society through the United Nations Interim Administration Mission in Kosovo (UNMIK). Further progress was made in establishing the Provisional Institutions of Self-Government and in transferring authority to those institutions. By the end of the year, UNMIK had completed the transfer of all the competences under chapter V of the Constitutional Framework for Provisional Self-Government and had instituted a mechanism for involving Kosovo authorities in those competences reserved to the Special Representative, without prejudice to his authority. The Special Representative and the Security Council monitored progress made towards the fulfilment of the benchmarks for determining when the political process of deciding Kosovo's future status could begin. Advances were also made in normalizing relations between the two capitals, Belgrade and Pristina, when, on 14 October, dialogue was launched between them on matters of practical interest. That progress was marred, however, by several incidents of violence and crimes against minorities, which were condemned by the Council in December.

Efforts intensified to advance the Georgian/Abkhaz peace process. Senior officials of the Group of Friends of the Secretary-General (France, Germany, Russian Federation, United Kingdom, United States) met twice in Geneva in an effort to overcome the political impasse and get the two parties to begin discussions of the 2001 Basic Principles for the Distribution of Competences between Tbilisi (Georgia's Government) and Sukhumi (the Abkhaz leadership) [YUN 2001, p. 386], which were intended to serve as a basis for substantial negotiations over the status of Abkhazia as a sovereign entity within the State of Georgia. That initiative was given a further boost by a March meeting between the Presidents of Georgia and the Russian Federation and a high-level meeting of the parties in July, which agreed to create working groups to address the issues of the return of refugees and internally displaced persons to the Gali district, the reopening of railway traffic between Sochi and Tbilisi and energy projects. Unfortunately, no progress was made with regard to the core political issue, as the Abkhaz side maintained its refusal to discuss the 2001 Basic Principles document. That process was further stalled by the complex political situation on both sides of the ceasefire line and events that led to the resignation of Georgia's President, Eduard Shevardnadze, in November.

No progress was made towards a settlement of the conflict between Armenia and Azerbaijan over the Nagorny Karabakh region in Azerbaijan.

In the Mediterranean, the situation in Cyprus was marked by hope and disappointment. The direct talks initiated in 2002, which aimed to resolve the Cyprus question and lead to a reunited country, resumed, but stalled once again due to the wide differences between the two leaders. To further accommodate those differences, the Secretary-General, on 26 February, again revised his comprehensive settlement proposal "Basis for Agreement on a Comprehensive Settlement of the Cyprus Problem", which required the two sides to commit themselves to finalizing negotiations by the end of February and to submit the plan for approval to separate simultaneous referendums on 30 March. In meetings with the Secretary-General in March in The Hague, the two leaders failed to reach agreement and the process came to an end. While the Secretary-General's plan remained on the table, he did not propose taking any new initiative until there was evidence that the political will existed for a successful outcome.

The former Yugoslavia

UN operations

In 2003, the United Nations maintained only one peacekeeping mission in the territories of the former Yugoslavia. Through the United Nations Interim Administration Mission in Kosovo (UNMIK), it continued efforts to restore peace and stability to the province of Kosovo in Serbia and Montenegro (formerly the Federal Republic of Yugoslavia).

Financing and liquidation of closed peacekeeping operations

The financing of the United Nations Protection Force (UNPROFOR), which ended in 1999, the United Nations Confidence Restoration Operation in Croatia (UNCRO), which ended in 1996, the United Nations Preventive Deployment Force (UNPREDEP), which ended in 1999—known collectively as the United Nations Peace Forces (UNPF)—and UNPF headquarters (UNPF-HQ) was treated in the Secretary-General's April report on the updated financial position of closed peacekeeping missions as at 30 June 2002 [A/57/789] (see p. 85).

UNMIBH

In April [A/57/773], the Advisory Committee on Administrative and Budgetary Questions (ACABQ) submitted its comments and recommendations on the 2002 performance report [YUN 2002, p. 365] on the budget for the United Nations Mission in Bosnia and Herzegovina (UNMIBH), which ended on 31 December 2002, for the period from 1 July 2001 to 30 June 2002 [A/57/684]. ACABQ recommended that the unencumbered balance of $9,281,400, and the amount of $5,739,000 resulting from other income and adjustments, for that period be credited to Member States in a manner to be decided by the General Assembly.

GENERAL ASSEMBLY ACTION

On 18 June [meeting 90], the General Assembly, on the recommendation of the Fifth (Administrative and Budgetary) Committee [A/57/643/Add.1], adopted **resolution 57/334** without vote [agenda item 147].

Financing of the United Nations Mission in Bosnia and Herzegovina

The General Assembly,

Having considered the report of the Secretary-General on the financial performance of the United Nations Mission in Bosnia and Herzegovina for the period from 1 July 2001 to 30 June 2002, his report containing an overview of the financing of the United Nations peacekeeping operations and the related reports of the Advisory Committee on Administrative and Budgetary Questions,

Recalling Security Council resolution 1035(1995) of 21 December 1995 regarding the establishment of the United Nations Mission in Bosnia and Herzegovina and the subsequent resolutions by which the Council extended the mandate of the Mission, the latest of which was resolution 1423(2002) of 12 July 2002, by which the Council extended the mandate of the Mission until 31 December 2002,

Recalling also Security Council resolution 1437(2002) of 11 October 2002, in which the Council authorized the United Nations military observers to continue to monitor the demilitarization of the Prevlaka peninsula until 15 December 2002,

Recalling further its decision 50/481 of 11 April 1996 on the financing of the Mission and its subsequent resolutions and decisions thereon, the latest of which was decision 57/559 of 20 December 2002,

Reaffirming the general principles underlying the financing of United Nations peacekeeping operations, as stated in General Assembly resolutions 1874(S-IV) of 27 June 1963, 3101(XXVIII) of 11 December 1973 and 55/235 of 23 December 2000,

Noting with appreciation that voluntary contributions have been made to the Mission,

Mindful of the fact that it is essential to provide the Mission with the necessary financial resources to enable it to meet its outstanding liabilities,

1. *Takes note* of the status of contributions to the United Nations Mission in Bosnia and Herzegovina as at 31 March 2003, including the contributions outstanding in the amount of 59 million United States dollars, representing some 6 per cent of the total assessed contributions, notes with concern that only thirty-three Member States have paid their assessed contributions in full, and urges all other Member States, in particular those in arrears, to ensure payment of their outstanding assessed contributions;

2. *Expresses its appreciation* to those Member States which have paid their assessed contributions in full, and urges all other Member States to make every possible effort to ensure payment of their assessed contributions to the Mission in full;

3. *Expresses concern* at the delay experienced by the Secretary-General in deploying and providing adequate resources to some recent peacekeeping missions, in particular those in Africa;

4. *Emphasizes* that all future and existing peacekeeping missions shall be given equal and non-discriminatory treatment in respect of financial and administrative arrangements;

5. *Also emphasizes* that all peacekeeping missions shall be provided with adequate resources for the effective and efficient discharge of their respective mandates;

6. *Endorses* the conclusions and recommendations contained in the report of the Advisory Committee on Administrative and Budgetary Questions, and requests the Secretary-General to ensure their full implementation;

7. *Takes note* of the report of the Secretary-General on the financial performance of the Mission for the period from 1 July 2001 to 30 June 2002;

8. *Decides* that Member States that have fulfilled their financial obligations to the Mission shall be credited their respective share of the unencumbered balance and other income in the total amount of 15,020,400 dollars in respect of the financial period ended 30 June 2002, in accordance with the levels set out in its resolution 55/235, as adjusted by the General Assembly in its resolutions 55/236 of 23 December 2000 and 57/290 A of 20 December 2002, and taking into account the scale of assessments for 2002, as set out in its resolutions 55/5 B of 23 December 2000 and 57/4 B of 20 December 2002;

9. *Decides also* that for Member States that have not fulfilled their financial obligations to the Mission, their respective share of the unencumbered balance and other income in the total amount of 15,020,400 dollars in respect of the financial period ended 30 June 2002 shall be set off against their outstanding obligations, in accordance with the scheme set out in paragraph 8 above;

10. *Decides further* that the increase of 1,092,400 dollars in the estimated staff assessment income in respect of the financial period ended 30 June 2002 shall be added to the credits from the amount referred to in paragraphs 8 and 9 above, and that the respective shares of Member States therein shall be applied in accordance with the provisions of those paragraphs, as appropriate;

11. *Emphasizes* that no peacekeeping mission shall be financed by borrowing funds from other active peacekeeping missions;

12. *Decides* to include in the provisional agenda of its fifty-eighth session the item entitled "Financing of the United Nations Mission in Bosnia and Herzegovina".

Bosnia and Herzegovina

In 2003, the international community continued to assist the two entities comprising the Republic of Bosnia and Herzegovina (the Federation of Bosnia and Herzegovina (where mainly Bosnian Muslims (Bosniacs) and Bosnian Croats resided) and Republika Srpska (where mostly Bosnian Serbs resided)) in implementing the 1995 General Framework Agreement for Peace in Bosnia and Herzegovina and the annexes thereto (the Peace Agreement) [YUN 1995, p. 544]. Those efforts were directed by the EU, following the conclusion and withdrawal of the United Nations Mission in Bosnia and Herzegovina (UNMIBH) in December 2002 [YUN 2002, p. 359], and were accomplished through the activities of the Office of the High Representative for the implementation of the Peace Agreement, who was responsible for the Agreement's civilian aspects [YUN 1996, p. 293], and the European Union Police Mission in Bosnia and Herzegovina (EUPM), launched on 1 January 2003 to ensure follow-on to UNMIBH. The North Atlantic Treaty Organization (NATO) continued to execute its responsibilities for the Agreement's military aspects, while the Peace Implementation Council (PIC) and its Steering Board continued to oversee and facilitate the Agreement's implementation.

The High Representative reported on the progress made in the Agreement's implementation process and related political developments during the year in the context of his Mission Implementation Plan, which set out a number of core tasks to be accomplished. Bosnia and Herzegovina undertook a number of reforms, particularly in the areas of the rule of law, refugee return and economic development, in accordance with European standards, allowing it to move one step closer to full integration into Europe through the EU Stabilization and Association Process and NATO's Partnership for Peace requirements.

Implementation of Peace Agreement

Civilian aspects

The civilian aspects of the 1995 Peace Agreement entailed a wide range of activities, including humanitarian aid, infrastructure rehabilitation, establishment of political and constitutional institutions, promoting respect for human rights and the holding of free and fair elections. The High Representative for the Implementation of the Peace Agreement, who chaired the PIC Steering Board and other key implementation bodies, was the final authority with regard to implementing the civilian aspects of the Peace Agreement [ibid., p. 547]. The reports on the activities of EUPM were submitted by the EU Secretary-General and High Representative for the Common Foreign and Security Policy, Javier Solana, to the Security Council President through the UN Secretary-General.

Office of High Representative

Reports of High Representative. The High Representative, Lord Paddy Ashdown (United Kingdom), reported to the Council through the Secretary-General on the peace implementation process covering the periods from 12 October 2002 to 31 August 2003 [S/2003/918] and from 1 September to 31 December [S/2004/126] (for details on the reports' specific topics, see below).

SECURITY COUNCIL ACTION

On 11 July [meeting 4786], the Security Council, having considered the High Representative's report [S/2002/1176] of 16 October 2002 [YUN 2002, p. 348], unanimously adopted **resolution 1491 (2003)**. The draft [S/2003/697] was prepared in consultations among Council members.

The Security Council,

Recalling all its relevant resolutions concerning the conflicts in the former Yugoslavia and relevant statements by its President, including resolutions 1031 (1995) of 15 December 1995, 1088(1996) of 12 December 1996 and 1423(2002) of 12 July 2002,

Reaffirming its commitment to the political settlement of the conflicts in the former Yugoslavia, preserving the sovereignty and territorial integrity of all States there within their internationally recognized borders,

Emphasizing its full support for the continued role in Bosnia and Herzegovina of the High Representative for the Implementation of the Peace Agreement on Bosnia and Herzegovina,

Underlining its commitment to support the implementation of the General Framework Agreement for Peace in Bosnia and Herzegovina and the annexes thereto (collectively the "Peace Agreement"), as well as the relevant decisions of the Peace Implementation Council,

Emphasizing its appreciation to the High Representative, the Commander and personnel of the multinational Stabilization Force, the Organization for Security and Cooperation in Europe, and the personnel of other international organizations and agencies in Bosnia and Herzegovina for their contributions to the implementation of the Peace Agreement,

Emphasizing that a comprehensive and coordinated return of refugees and displaced persons throughout the region continues to be crucial to lasting peace,

Recalling the declarations of the ministerial meetings of the Peace Implementation Council,

Taking note of the reports of the High Representative, including his latest report of 16 October 2002,

Determining that the situation in the region continues to constitute a threat to international peace and security,

Determined to promote the peaceful resolution of the conflicts in accordance with the purposes and principles of the Charter of the United Nations,

Recalling the relevant principles contained in the Convention on the Safety of United Nations and Associated Personnel of 9 December 1994 and the statement by its President of 9 February 2000 (S/PRST/2000/4),

Welcoming and encouraging efforts by the United Nations to sensitize peacekeeping personnel in the prevention and control of HIV/AIDS and other communicable diseases in all its peacekeeping operations,

Acting under Chapter VII of the Charter,

I

1. *Reaffirms once again its support* for the General Framework Agreement for Peace in Bosnia and Herzegovina and the annexes thereto (collectively the "Peace Agreement"), as well as for the Dayton Agreement on Implementing the Federation of Bosnia and Herzegovina of 10 November 1995, calls upon the parties to comply strictly with their obligations under those Agreements, and expresses its intention to keep the implementation of the Peace Agreement, and the situation in Bosnia and Herzegovina, under review;

2. *Reiterates* that the primary responsibility for the further successful implementation of the Peace Agreement lies with the authorities in Bosnia and Herzegovina themselves and that the continued willingness of the international community and major donors to assume the political, military and economic burden of implementation and reconstruction efforts will be determined by the compliance and active participation by all the authorities in Bosnia and Herzegovina in implementing the Peace Agreement and rebuilding a civil society, in particular in full cooperation with the International Tribunal for the Prosecution of Persons Responsible for Serious Violations of International Humanitarian Law Committed in the Territory of the Former Yugoslavia since 1991, in strengthening joint institutions which foster the building of a fully functioning self-sustaining State able to integrate itself into the European structures, and in facilitating returns of refugees and displaced persons;

3. *Reminds* the parties once again that, in accordance with the Peace Agreement, they have committed themselves to cooperate fully with all entities involved in the implementation of this peace settlement, as described in the Peace Agreement, or which are otherwise authorized by the Security Council, including the International Tribunal for the Former Yugoslavia, as it carries out its responsibilities for dispensing justice impartially, and underlines that full cooperation by States and entities with the Tribunal includes, inter alia, the surrender for trial of all persons indicted by the Tribunal and the provision of information to assist in Tribunal investigations;

4. *Emphasizes its full support* for the continued role of the High Representative for the Implementation of the Peace Agreement on Bosnia and Herzegovina in monitoring the implementation of the Peace Agreement and giving guidance to and coordinating the activities of the civilian organizations and agencies involved in assisting the parties to implement the Peace Agreement, and reaffirms that the High Representative is the final authority in theatre regarding the interpretation of annex 10 on civilian implementation of the Peace Agreement and that in case of dispute he may give his interpretation and make recommendations, and make binding decisions as he judges necessary on issues as elaborated by the Peace Implementation Council in Bonn on 9 and 10 December 1997;

5. *Expresses its support* for the declarations of the ministerial meetings of the Peace Implementation Council;

6. *Recognizes* that the parties have authorized the multinational force referred to in paragraph 10 below to take such actions as required, including the use of necessary force, to ensure compliance with annex 1-A of the Peace Agreement;

7. *Reaffirms its intention* to keep the situation in Bosnia and Herzegovina under close review, taking into account the reports submitted pursuant to paragraphs 18 and 20 below, and any recommendations those reports might include, and its readiness to consider the imposition of measures if any party fails significantly to meet its obligations under the Peace Agreement;

II

8. *Pays tribute* to those Member States which participated in the multinational Stabilization Force established in accordance with its resolution 1088(1996), and welcomes their willingness to assist the parties to the Peace Agreement by continuing to deploy a multinational stabilization force;

9. *Notes* the support of the parties to the Peace Agreement for the continuation of the Force, set out in the declaration of the ministerial meeting of the Peace Implementation Council in Madrid on 16 December 1998;

10. *Authorizes* the Member States acting through or in cooperation with the organization referred to in annex 1-A of the Peace Agreement to continue for a further planned period of twelve months the Force as established in accordance with its resolution 1088(1996) under unified command and control in order to fulfil the role specified in annexes 1-A and 2 of the Peace Agreement, and expresses its intention to review the situation with a view to extending this authorization further, as necessary, in the light of developments in the implementation of the Peace Agreement and the situation in Bosnia and Herzegovina;

11. *Also authorizes* the Member States acting under paragraph 10 above to take all necessary measures to effect the implementation of and to ensure compliance with annex 1-A of the Peace Agreement, stresses that the parties shall continue to be held equally responsible for compliance with that annex and shall be equally subject to such enforcement action by the Force as may be necessary to ensure implementation of that annex and the protection of the Force, and takes note that the parties have consented to the Force taking such measures;

12. *Authorizes* Member States to take all necessary measures, at the request of the Force, either in defence of the Force or to assist the Force in carrying out its mission, and recognizes the right of the Force to take all necessary measures to defend itself from attack or threat of attack;

13. *Authorizes* the Member States acting under paragraph 10 above, in accordance with annex 1-A of the Peace Agreement, to take all necessary measures to ensure compliance with the rules and procedures established by the Commander of the Force, governing command and control of airspace over Bosnia and Herzegovina with respect to all civilian and military air traffic;

14. *Requests* the authorities in Bosnia and Herzegovina to cooperate with the Commander of the Force to ensure the effective management of the airports of Bosnia and Herzegovina, in the light of the responsibilities conferred on the Force by annex 1-A of the Peace Agreement with regard to the airspace of Bosnia and Herzegovina;

15. *Demands* that the parties respect the security and freedom of movement of the Force and other international personnel;

16. *Invites* all States, in particular those in the region, to continue to provide appropriate support and facilities, including transit facilities, for the Member States acting under paragraph 10 above;

17. *Recalls* all the agreements concerning the status of forces as referred to in appendix B to annex 1-A of the Peace Agreement, and reminds the parties of their obligation to continue to comply therewith;

18. *Requests* the Member States acting through or in cooperation with the organization referred to in annex 1-A of the Peace Agreement to continue to report to the Security Council, through the appropriate channels and at least at monthly intervals;

***

19. *Welcomes* the deployment by the European Union of its Police Mission to Bosnia and Herzegovina since 1 January 2003;

20. *Requests* the Secretary-General to continue to submit to the Council reports from the High Representative, in accordance with annex 10 of the Peace Agreement and the conclusions of the Peace Implementation Conference held in London on 4 and 5 December 1996, and later Peace Implementation Conferences, on the implementation of the Peace Agreement and in particular on compliance by the parties with their commitments under that Agreement;

21. *Decides* to remain seized of the matter.

Mission implementation plan

The High Representative, in his September report [S/2003/918], said that the mission implementation plan of his Office, drawn up in 2002 [YUN 2002, p. 359] and introduced in January 2003, had six core tasks: entrenching the rule of law; ensuring that extreme nationalists, war criminals and their organized criminal networks could not reverse peace implementation; reforming the economy; strengthening the capacity of governing institutions, especially at the State level; establishing State-level civilian command and control over the armed forces, reforming the security sector and paving the way for integration into the Euro-Atlantic framework; and promoting the sustainable return of refugees and displaced persons. Each task was divided into several subprogrammes, with departments within the Office responsible for defining and implementing the steps needed to achieve each goal.

A formal report on and assessment of the plan's first year of implementation was submitted in December to the PIC Steering Board for endorsement, said the High Representative in his later report [S/2004/126]. In the light of progress made, the core tasks were reduced from six to four: rule of law; economic reform; capacity strengthening of institutions; and establishing State-level civilian command and control of the armed forces. Each subprogramme of the updated plan identified a transition point for completing or handing over to a lead domestic authority. Overlaps with the priority goals set by the European Commission in its feasibility study and NATO in its Partnership for Peace requirements (see p. 402) were clarified.

Civil affairs

Communication. On 16 January [S/2003/81], the EU Presidency issued a statement welcoming the formation of the Council of Ministers of Bosnia and Herzegovina for a four-year term of office, under the terms of the election law. It pledged to work closely with the new State Government, which should be genuinely committed to reform to move closer to the EU. In that context, a feasibility study by the European Commission would be the next step. The EU urged the new State Government to carry out all the reforms necessary for the EU's Stabilization and Association Process so that the country could move from stabilization to association. For that purpose, it had to speed up adoption of European rule-of-law standards, the functioning of State institutions, the fight against organized crime, the sustainable return of refugees and internally displaced persons, full cooperation with the International Tribunal for the Former Yugoslavia (ICTY) and establishment of State-level civilian command and control over the armed forces.

Reports of High Representative. The High Representative, in his September report [S/2003/918], said that, following the October 2002 elections [YUN 2002, p. 349], the State-level Council of Ministers, led by Prime Minister Adnan Terzic, was in place. However, the administration was hampered by the constitutional dysfunction of the Council (the Prime Minister could not appoint or remove ministers) and the lack of capacity and support within the Council's institutions, resulting in limited legislative activity and the slow restructuring of ministries and bodies. The entity governments faced similar problems. In the Federation, the government of Canton 7 was not finalized until the end of June, while Herzegovina-Neretva Canton was the last self-governing unit in the entire country to put its elected government in place. In the divided city of Mostar, a commission, composed solely of local representatives, was established in the spring to explore options for a permanent statute for the city; by the beginning of August, it had achieved limited results. However, in Republika Srpska, major processes, such as the Independent Tax Commission, the Defence Reform Commission and the Intelligence Commission, were functioning smoothly.

The Defence Reform Commission, established by the High Representative on 9 May as part of efforts to correct the systematic weaknesses exposed by the scandal involving the illegal export of arms to Iraq by the Republika Srpska State-owned company, Orao, was mandated to propose reforms, principally to the command and control of the Bosnia and Herzegovina armed forces. The entity defence laws and constitutions were also amended to ensure that a similar scandal did not arise again. The resignation of Mirko Sarovic as a member of the Bosnia and Herzegovina Presidency on 4 April, in the wake of that scandal, was a step towards establishing political accountability in the country.

In other developments, the Expert Commission on Intelligence Reform was launched at the end of May to make proposals for setting up a single intelligence structure. In that regard, the necessary legislative changes and other legal instruments in line with European democratic principles and practices were to be in place by mid-September. The terms of reference for the Secretary-General of the Standing Committee on Military Matters (SCMM) had been agreed upon and he had been invited to attend meetings of the Council of Ministers. The Committee's secretariat was to expand to allow it to operate as a fledgling ministry, coordinating with other ministries and acting on behalf of the State in matters of defence.

In a later report [S/2004/126], the High Representative said that the period from 1 September to 31 December was marked by political clashes between the Government and the opposition, coupled with growing tensions in the ruling coalition, dominated by the three national parties. Relations between the Party of Democratic Action (SDA) and the Nationalist Croat Democratic Party (HDZ) (the two main governing parties in the Federation) remained strained, thus sustaining parallelism along ethnic lines. Increasing political rivalry within the SDA leadership, in part triggered by the death of its founder and first President of Bosnia and Herzegovina, Alija Izetbegovic, had a particular impact on the Government of the Federation. Meanwhile, opposition parties from both entities were attempting to consolidate forces in advance of the October 2004 municipal elections, including through the signature of a joint platform, taking advantage of the country's continuing economic difficulties, and a common desire for early general elections.

In November, the European Commission, in its feasibility study on Bosnia and Herzegovina, said that it hoped to be able to recommend the opening of negotiations on a Stabilization and Association Agreement in 2004, on condition that the country made significant progress in a number of priority areas. In December, NATO issued clear benchmarks for the country's entry into the Partnership for Peace programme.

In December, two key institutions on defence and taxation, with Statewide competences, were established by the Bosnia and Herzegovina Parliament. The Defence Law gave the Bosnia and Herzegovina Presidency command and control of the armed forces across the country and established a Ministry of Defence for Bosnia and Herzegovina, while the Law on Indirect Taxation established the Statewide Indirect Taxation Authority (see p. 406).

On 15 September, following the failure of the Mostar City Council Commission to produce a new statute for the city, the High Representative established a Commission, chaired by Norbert Winterstein (Germany), to draft a permanent statute for the city. The Commission included members nominated by the Bosnia and Herzegovina political parties represented in the City Council, in addition to several local and international experts. Although agreement was reached on the majority of the items in the text of the new statute, two crucial questions—the system of elections and the status of the existing municipalities—prevented a final agreement from being reached. The Croat-dominated parties (led by HDZ) disagreed with the election system, while the Bosniac side (led by SDA) objected to the abolition of the municipalities. The Chairman proposed a compromise solution, by which an election system would be established that precluded domination of one group of people over another in the City Council, thereby protecting minority rights. The Office of the High Representative concurred with him that abolition of the municipalities was essential to unifying the city and preventing the continuation of the parallel structures that had divided Mostar along ethnic lines. In December, the High Representative asked the Commission to further explore ways to develop a permanent statute for Mostar by the end of January 2004, not ruling out the possibility of amendments to the Chairman's proposal. The interlocutors, including PIC members, agreed with the strategy of consultations and with the idea that, should the talks fail to produce a solution agreeable to the parties by the end of January, the High Representative would impose a new statute for Mostar.

The once-disputed Brcko district also moved forward in the latter part of the year, particularly in regard to judicial reform and property repossession. The Brcko Assembly adopted a long-awaited but controversial Election Law, enabling the Brcko Supervisor to schedule the District's first local elections, to be held together with the Bosnia and Herzegovina municipal elections planned for October 2004.

In the areas of security and defence, the Law on Defence (see above) was adopted, as recommended by the Defence Reform Commission. The Commission also made recommendations for a common law on the army of the Federation and the introduction of parliamentary democratic control over the armed forces, the downsizing of the defence establishment for economic reasons, and an explicit commitment by Bosnia and Herzegovina to achieving NATO membership. On 4 December, the North Atlantic Treaty Council noted that the passage of the Defence Law proved Bosnia and Herzegovina to be a credible candidate for the Partnership for Peace and emphasized that it looked forward to welcoming it into the Partnership once the conditions set by the Alliance had been met. In other developments, the Joint Defence and Steering Committee of Bosnia and Herzegovina's Parliamentary Assembly became operational, manifesting the principle of parliamentary oversight. The Presidency was urged to appoint key State-level positions quickly so that the Minister of Defence and Deputies would be in post by mid-February 2004. Preparations for the transition of the SCMM secretariat into a Ministry of Defence were initiated and progress was made towards its restructuring.

At the end of August, the expert Commission on Intelligence Reform finalized the draft law on the intelligence and security agency, which envisaged the creation of a single intelligence agency. In mid-September, the draft law was submitted to the Council of Ministers, which was reluctant to consider it. On 18 December, the High Representative submitted the draft law directly to the Bosnia and Herzegovina Parliamentary Assembly for adoption by 1 March 2004.

Srebrenica

The High Representative reported in September [S/2003/918] that phase I of construction on the Potocari burial site, identified in 2000 [YUN 2000, p. 353] as the location of a cemetery and memorial for the victims of the July 1995 Srebrenica massacre [YUN 1995, p. 529], was completed at the end of January for the burials of up to 1,000 individuals. Phase II, which had started, involved the provision of grave sites for some 9,000 additional individuals and the construction of the Musala Mutual Crypt, with garden, service facilities and parking. The burials of the first 600 identified individuals took place on 31 March, and a further 400 were buried on 11 July.

On 25 March, at the request of surviving family members and following consultations with Republika Srpska authorities, the High Representative issued a decision transferring the ownership of the nearby Battery Factory site, proposed in 2002 to be added to the memorial site [YUN 2002, p. 347], to the Foundation of the Srebrenica-Potocari Memorial and Cemetery, and establishing a commission to determine the compensation to be paid by Republika Srpska to the Factory's current owners and users. The Foundation, in consultation with the families of victims, would determine the future use of the Battery Factory site. The Foundation raised some 3.5 million euros, which allowed work to begin at the site. The Human Rights Chamber, on 7 March, ordered the Republika Srpska Government to pay 2 million convertible marka (KM) by 7 September to the Foundation and another 500,000 KM each year for the next four years. Since families opposed such a decision, the Foundation's Executive Board agreed to proceed with its fund-raising activities and to consult families on how to use the funds to be paid by Republika Srpska. An additional 1.5 million euros was still needed to complete the project.

In his later report [S/2004/126], the High Representative stated that the opening ceremony of the Srebrenica-Potocari Memorial and Cemetery was held on 20 September, with former United States President William J. Clinton as the guest of honour. In conjunction with the ceremony, 107 identified individuals were buried at the site. On 28 October, the Executive Board of the Foundation appointed Beriz Belkic, a former member of the State Presidency, as co-chairman with Amor Masovic, head of the Federal Commission for Missing Persons and Exhumations, replacing the High Representative. On 6 December, the Executive Board appointed Mersed Smajlovic as Director of the Service of the Foundation, taking over from the Office of the High Representative, which continued to support and coordinate tasks until the end of 2003. In September, the Republika Srpska Government made its initial payment of 2 million KM (1 million euros) to the Foundation to compensate families of persons missing since the 1995 massacre.

On 8 September, Republika Srpska submitted a report to the Human Rights Chamber purporting to disclose information about the deceased and their whereabouts, but which still failed to provide sufficient information concerning the events that occurred during the 1995 massacre. At the urging of the High Representative, Republika Srpska, on 15 December, established the Srebrenica Commission to investigate and report on missing persons, among other duties. He indicated to the Republika Srpska President and Prime Minister on 19 December that the Commission should complete its task and publish its final report by 14 April 2004 and warned against any attempts to obstruct its work. He confirmed the nomination of Gordon Bacon as the Commission's chief of staff and Smail Cekic as its representative to the survivor community. Two international observers would also be part of the Commission. On 25 December, the Government of Republika Srpska appointed seven members to the Commission.

Judicial reform

The High Representative reported in September [S/2003/918] that further progress had been made in judicial reform, which was a priority of the programme of justice and jobs through reform outlined in 2002 [YUN 2002, p. 348]. Implementation of the streamlined court system had started, with meetings held with the Ministers of Justice and courts visited to assess budget, space, renovation and equipment needs. On 1 November 2002, the High Representative imposed amendments to the laws establishing judicial training centres to make them operational and to begin the training of judges and prosecutors throughout Bosnia and Herzegovina. In December 2002, the High Judicial and Prosecutorial Councils (HJPCs) adopted two training programmes on criminal procedure for judges and prosecutors and established 13 disciplinary panels to hear complaints against incumbent judges and prosecutors. During the reporting period, 166 complaints were received and 23 judges submitted their resignations; 10 of them had been previously suspended by the High Representative.

On 16 January 2003, the Bosnia and Herzegovina HJPC appointed eight members to the Criminal Division of the State Court and a Chief Prosecutor and three assistants to the Prosecutor's Office. The Bosnia and Herzegovina Criminal Procedure Code, imposed on 24 January, entered into force on 1 March, together with the Criminal Code; it represented a significant advance in the process of reforming the criminal justice system and rendering the Court of Bosnia and Herzegovina operative. The Rule of Law Pillar of the Office of the High Representative worked closely with the Prosecutor to resolve issues related to the new codes and to find additional resources to support the work of his Office. On 27 January, the newly appointed judges and prosecutors took their oaths of office and the Court of Bosnia and Herzegovina officially occupied its newly renovated temporary facilities. International judges and prosecutors were currently being recruited to serve in the special criminal panels of the Court and the special division of the Prosecutor's Office.

A new Anti-Crime and Corruption Unit (formerly the Serious Crimes Unit) was created to provide the Office of the High Representative with broad support capabilities for the local prosecution, investigation and analysis of systemic organized crime and corruption. The Unit was guiding two major criminal investigation task forces, providing specialized support capacities, such as forensic audit work or specialized experts as court witnesses, and assisting in the assessment of cases to be transferred to the Prosecutor's Office as part of the implementation of the new Criminal Code and Criminal Procedure Code.

On 7 March, legal amendments were imposed in both entities to permit their banking agencies to freeze bank accounts of persons and firms providing financial support to persons impeding or obstructing implementation of the Peace Agreement. On 7 July, a further set of decisions was issued, freezing the bank accounts of several more individuals on suspicion of providing material support to Radovan Karadzic, who had been indicted by ICTY [YUN 1995, p. 1314].

The Rule of Law Pillar continued to discuss with the Organization for Security and Cooperation in Europe (OSCE) and the Council of Europe the future of the Human Rights Chamber. In consultation with local officials, they devised a plan for processing the large backlog of pending cases of alleged human rights violations and to provide for future cases to be handled by other Bosnia and Herzegovina institutions. The plan was discussed with the Constitutional Court and the Human Rights Chamber to identify issues to be resolved during its implementation, and was presented to PIC in June.

In his later report [S/2004/126], the High Representative noted that PIC had endorsed the "road map" developed by the Rule of Law Pillar, the Constitutional Court, the Human Rights Chamber, Bosnia and Herzegovina officials at both the State and entity levels, and international organizations for transferring the mandate and some of the staff of the Human Rights Chamber to the Constitutional Court. An agreement to deal with the backlog of cases pending before the Human Rights Chamber and to redirect additional cases to the Constitutional Court was signed on 25 September.

In October, the Office of the High Representative worked with parliamentary leaders and Federation officials to secure the adoption by the Federation Parliament of the Civil Procedure Code, and the establishment of the State Information and Protection Agency. The draft laws relating to the Agency, which were awaiting parliamentary consideration, included an amendment to establish a State-level law enforcement agency, a law on police officials that would establish professional standards and procedures for all State-level law enforcement agencies, and laws on the prevention of money-laundering and witness protection.

The number of international judges serving on the special panel of the State Court of Bosnia and Herzegovina rose to five, while four international prosecutors were serving in the special department of the Prosecutor's Office. Amendments to the laws relating to the State Court and the Prosecutor's Office were enacted in October to remove the limits on the number of international judges and prosecutors in those bodies.

The Criminal Institutions and Prosecutorial Reform Unit continued to assist the ministries in both entities to address problems relating to court and prosecutorial restructuring, especially in developing rules for the operations of the special department of the Prosecutor's Office and the Special Chamber of the Court. The Unit presented a policy paper on the establishment of a civil asset forfeiture programme to PIC and drafted a proposed money-laundering law.

Negotiations among the Office of the High Representative, the Independent Judicial Council and Bosnia and Herzegovina officials resulted in a proposed agreement on creating a single, State-level HJPC. A draft law, which was submitted for parliamentary approval, provided for a representative and multi-ethnic HJPC, which would appoint and discipline judges and prosecutors, and regulate and supervise the administrative and budgetary affairs of the judiciary. The Independent Judicial Council developed a transition plan to phase out its own operations by the beginning of April 2004 and to shift them to the secretariat of the permanent national HJPC. The Office of the High Representative continued to advocate a single HJPC, in the face of substantial opposition from the Republika Srpska Government, as a critical step towards developing a strong and independent judiciary, free of political interference. In the meantime, Bosnia's current HJPCs, with the Independent Judicial Council acting as their secretariat, made steady progress in the reselection process for judges and prosecutors and in verifying all remaining applications. The HJPCs appointed 347 judges and prosecutors to 15 courts and six prosecutors' offices. At the end of 2003, approximately 550 appointments remained to be made before the 31 March 2004 deadline for establishing a single State-level HJPC. During the reporting period, 776 new complaints were received against judges and prosecutors. The HJPCs conducted several disciplinary proceedings.

The Office of the High Representative, through the Independent Judicial Council, continued to oversee the complete restructuring of the court system in Bosnia and Herzegovina. That process, scheduled for completion by April 2004, would significantly reduce the total number of judges (by 28 per cent), generate considerable savings (approximately 3.6 million euros annually) and involve 22 court mergers, 2 of which were successfully completed in the fourth quarter of 2003. Early in December, the final drafts of the entity laws on courts, which would harmonize the court structure of the entities to achieve uniformity throughout the country, were completed and sent to the Ministers of Justice to be submitted for parliamentary approval. The law on courts for the Federation would replace the 10 existing cantonal laws on courts. The minor offence court restructuring project to assess the entire system and provide recommendations for its future streamlining issued its preliminary report in December.

Economic reform and reconstruction

In September [S/2003/918], the High Representative reported that 13 decisions were issued on 21 October 2002 to help promote growth in Bosnia and Herzegovina through reforms in banking, statistics land registry, communications and other areas. To dismantle barriers to business growth and job creation, the Bulldozer Initiative was launched on 12 November 2002 to help businesses remove roadblocks and cut red tape. In December 2002, the Bulldozer Committee identified 50 such economic roadblocks, along with their respective legal solutions, which were presented to the State and entity authorities during the first quarter of 2003. Implementation committees coordinated by local business associations were set up to ensure proper reform implementation and follow-up. All 50 pieces of legislation were adopted by 4 June, and the domestic authorities assumed complete responsibility for the next phase of the project.

Other progress included the establishment in February 2003 of the Indirect Tax Policy Commission to promote a single customs service for Bosnia and Herzegovina and the adoption of a single State-level value added tax. On 1 July, the Commission agreed on a framework law to establish the Indirect Tax Authority (ITA), which would provide for the unification of the customs administrations in Bosnia and Herzegovina, ITA working methods and authority, and its Governing Board. That legislation was awaiting endorsement by the Council of Ministers and parliamentary approval. A number of other laws were passed, including a State-level veterinary law, a Federation forestry law and a law on telecommunications. Efforts were also made to implement the State Electricity Law.

In transportation, the State Licensing Commission commenced licensing of international and inter-entity bus services under the Law on International and Inter-entity Road Transportation. A draft of a new State law on the railways of Bosnia and Herzegovina was prepared for presentation to the Council of Ministers, which provided for State-level regulation of all railway operations. A new post of Minister of Communications and Transport was established under the new Council of Ministers structure.

In his later report [S/2004/126], the High Representative indicated that the second stage of the Bulldozer Initiative had begun; the Bulldozer Committee had identified an additional 50 economic roadblocks and discussed legal solutions to those impediments. The Office of the High Representative continued efforts to transfer the competency for the privatization of strategic enterprises from the canton to the Federation privatization agency, and to establish a single information point (web site) for privatization opportunities. Of the 15 enterprises scheduled for sale by tender by the end of 2003, 14 had been published, among which was the Holiday Inn Hotel in Sarajevo.

To capitalize on the momentum of the economic reforms, the Office identified several objectives for the next six months: full implementation of the indirect tax reforms without delay; creation of a single business registration system; and the drawing up of a comprehensive trade policy that promoted exports. Other priorities included the creation of and improvements to institutions and services supporting local businesses, such as the Foreign Investment Promotion Agency and the Standardization Institute; implementation of the domestic debt package; and acceleration of the privatization process by strengthening entity privatization agencies. On 29 December, the Parliament of Bosnia and Herzegovina adopted the Law on the Indirect Taxation System, which abolished the entity customs administrations and installed a unified Indirect Taxation Authority for the country.

The Office also oversaw an agreement on an internal debt plan for Bosnia and Herzegovina, which removed a major obstacle to investment and job creation. The State, entity and Brcko authorities agreed to settle outstanding financial claims held by citizens against the various governments, involving a combination of cash payments and bonds.

The audits of the three public telecommunications companies revealed patterns of mismanagement and incompetence. Laws on public enterprises, investment of public funds and public procurement were drafted to institutionalize management oversight and modern accounting standards. The Council of Ministers adopted laws establishing the Electricity Transmission

Company and the Independent System Operator, which were still awaiting parliamentary approval. Progress was made towards finalizing the legal framework in the utilities sector. In December, the Parliament adopted the Law on Civil Aviation, which was expected to come into force soon.

Public administration reform

In his September report [S/2003/918], the High Representative stated that the State Civil Service Agency had become fully operational on 23 January. Republika Srpska was setting up a similar agency with international technical and financial support, while the Federation of Bosnia and Herzegovina adopted legislation to set up its agency in May. The Office of the High Representative was working with the United Nations Development Programme (UNDP) to ensure that the Civil Service Agency was properly funded and staffed. Meanwhile, politically motivated replacements of members of governing boards of various public bodies and appointments to civil service positions were still taking place.

In his later report [S/2004/126], the High Representative said that, on 1 September, the public administration reform process was further strengthened by the appointment of a National Coordinator at the Ministry of Justice responsible for managing and overseeing the reform agenda; the reform process was presented to the PIC Steering Board in March 2003, including the development of a more efficient and affordable public administration, as a prerequisite for European integration. The Office of the High Representative was involved in the recruitment of the first Director of the Federation Civil Service Agency, and continued to supervise the final phase of the reform process, including the staffing and establishment of the Agency, and the full implementation of the legislation at the entity, cantonal and municipal levels. UNDP had pledged additional financial and technical support, but more funds were required.

Refugees

At the end of 2003, the Office of the United Nations High Commissioner for Refugees (UNHCR) reported that the total number of registered returns to and within Bosnia and Herzegovina had risen to nearly 1 million people, including some 430,000 so-called minority returns. Approximately 350,000 refugees and displaced persons, as estimated by the Bosnia and Herzegovina Ministry for Human Rights and Refugees, still had not returned to their pre-war homes, although many among them still wanted to do so.

The High Representative noted in September [S/2003/918] that, on 30 January, PIC endorsed the strategy under annex VII of the Peace Agreement, drawn up by the Bosnia and Herzegovina authorities, UNHCR and his Office, to ensure continued progress in refugee returns. In addition to facilitating some 500,000 additional returns over the next four years, the strategy provided for the building of additional domestic capacity to take over eventually from international organizations, and called for the closure of the Reconstruction and Return Task Force of the Office of the High Representative by the end of 2003. Property law implementation progressed, reaching a country-wide repossession rate of 67 per cent. However, large urban centres, such as Sarajevo and Banja Luka, lagged behind entity averages of 71 and 61 per cent in the Federation and Republika Srpska, respectively. The current focus was on ensuring adequate budgeting for alternative accommodation in connection with the approximately 40,000 remaining property claims in the entities.

In his later report [S/2004/126], the High Representative said that there had been substantial completion of the property laws implementation, as indicated by a countrywide property repossession rate of over 90 per cent, with likely finalization in all Bosnia and Herzegovina municipalities early in 2004. While there were no major internal obstacles to achieving that goal, problems remained with those refugees in Bosnia and Herzegovina who were still unable to repossess property in their countries of origin and who continued to occupy the pre-war homes of Bosnia and Herzegovina citizens, including more than 20,000 Croatian Serbs. The High Representative welcomed recent commitments by Croatia to address that problem. The Office of the High Representative continued to transfer the responsibilities of the Commission for Real Property Claims to domestic authorities, including transferring the Commission's databases and records, putting in place entity legislation for the takeover of undecided claims, and identifying the body for reviewing the Commission's decisions. However, the Framework Agreement for realizing those activities was not signed, calling into question the actual transfer of the Commission's responsibilities and also some basic rights of the people of Bosnia and Herzegovina.

In preparation for the closure of the Refugee and Return Task Force on 31 December and the transfer of its annex VII responsibilities to the Bosnia and Herzegovina Ministry for Human Rights and Refugees authorities, the Office of the High Representative introduced a number of key legislative reforms, including amendments to the State law on refugees from and displaced persons in Bosnia and Herzegovina. The amendments, adopted by the Bosnia and Herzegovina Parliament on 30 September, identified the Ministry for Human Rights and Refugees as the main policy-making and supervisory body for annex VII issues; established four regional centres (Banja Luka, Mostar, Sarajevo, Tuzla); strengthened the role of the Bosnia and Herzegovina Commission for Refugees and Displaced Persons as the main coordinating body between the State, entities and Brcko District; and established the Return Fund as a State-level institution responsible for the financial realization of return and reconstruction projects. After 31 December, the Office would retain a small annex VII Verification Unit to monitor the process and advise its domestic partners.

Significant progress was also made on sustainability, including putting in place a legal framework to ensure returnees' unbiased access to socio-economic facilities and opportunities. The Office continued developing information campaigns to inform returnees about the applicable laws and their rights under those laws, especially access to health care and reconnection to utility networks. It also developed a media programme and information booklet on agricultural production as a means of income to assist returnees, and was identifying alternative sources of funding for the ongoing return process.

Human rights

The High Representative, in September [S/2003/918], reported that, following discussions between ICTY and the Ministries of Justice, prosecutors of both entities and the State, and consultations with OSCE and the Council of Europe, recommendations for the domestic trial of war crimes in a special panel of the Court of Bosnia and Herzegovina were presented to and approved by the PIC Steering Board of Political Directors on 12 June. The decision called for the establishment of a War Crimes Chamber within the Court of Bosnia and Herzegovina and a war crimes department within the State Prosecutor's Office. The High Representative would establish and co-chair with Bosnia and Herzegovina authorities a Multi-Agency Implementation Task Force to coordinate implementation of the project.

In his later report [S/2004/126], the High Representative indicated that he had established that Task Force, which developed a detailed management plan. The working groups initiated by the Task Force general secretariat to address issues related to the establishment of the Chamber, such as legislation, witness protection and case review, met with all relevant national and international agencies. At its inaugural session on 5 December, members of the Joint Executive Board of the Implementation Task Force committed themselves to establishing the War Crimes Chamber and participating in the multi-agency working groups. The Office of the High Representative, EUPM and OSCE formed a group to monitor cases cleared by the ICTY "rules of the road" process of the 1996 Rome Agreement [YUN 1996, p. 1187] and returned to local law enforcement and prosecutorial agencies. The group would ensure that the cases were appropriately investigated and prosecuted after clearance by ICTY.

At a donors conference on 30 October, 15.7 million euros in pledges were made of the estimated 38 million euros needed for the operations of the War Crimes Chamber for the first two years.

The Security Council, in **resolution 1503 (2003)** of 28 August (see p. 1330), noted that the establishment of the War Crimes Chamber was a prerequisite to achieving the objectives of ICTY completion strategies (see below) and called on the donor community to support the High Representative in creating the special chamber within the Court of Bosnia and Herzegovina.

Security Council consideration (October). During the Security Council's consideration of the situation in Bosnia and Herzegovina on 8 October [meeting 4837], the ICTY President, Judge Theodor Meron, said that the Sarajevo War Crimes Chamber would serve as a prerequisite for the success of ICTY's completion strategy—its plan for completing its mission within the time frame indicated by the Council in presidential statement S/PRST/2002/21 [YUN 2002, p. 1281]. Within that overall strategy, the establishment of an orderly process for transferring certain cases from ICTY to a judicial institution of an emerging Bosnian Government would play a vital role. The Chamber would contribute directly to the realization of the Office of the High Representative's mission implementation plan (see p. 401), contribute to the overall efforts of the Office to establish a firm foundation for the rule of law in the national institutions of Bosnia and Herzegovina, and ensure that the prosecution of war criminals took place in Bosnia and Herzegovina efficiently and fairly and in accordance with internationally recognized standards of due process.

Media issues

The High Representative reported in September [S/2003/918] that, on 31 December 2002, he had closed his Office's Media Development Department. He summarized the achievements made in implementing PIC directives regarding the media, and said that he would continue monitoring media developments and assisting where necessary. The mandate of the broadcasting agent in his Office expired on 30 June 2003 and the High Representative was working to ensure that Bosnia and Herzegovina authorities established a sustainable mechanism for financing the Communication Regulatory Agency to ensure its continued independence and the maintenance of European media standards. His Office was working also with the European Commission to monitor the adoption of legislation conforming to those standards. He had been encouraging Bosnia and Herzegovina authorities to take steps to ensure the long-term viability of a financially and editorially independent and integrated Statewide public broadcasting system sharing a common infrastructure.

Relations with other countries

A significant step was reached in Bosnia and Herzegovina/Croatia relations in January when Croatia ratified the provisionally applied agreement on the determination of border crossings of 6 April 2001. The Bosnia and Herzegovina presidency and Croatian President Stjepan Mesic agreed to complete pending procedures and negotiations regarding border issues and dual citizenship. In February, they initiated a draft agreement on the local border zone regime and the three annexes to the Co-location Treaty of 17 June 2002, which were awaiting the signature of their Foreign Ministers.

Bosnia and Herzegovina and Serbia and Montenegro (formerly the Federal Republic of Yugoslavia) ratified the October 2002 agreement on dual citizenship, which entered into force in both countries in December 2003. Also, heads of delegations to the commissions dealing with border issues initialled draft agreements on the local border zone regime and on a simplified regime to be applied in a zone in the eastern part of Bosnia and Herzegovina enmeshed in the territory of Serbia and Montenegro.

Progress was made towards reconciliation between Bosnia and Herzegovina, Croatia and Serbia and Montenegro. On 10 September, Serbia and Montenegro President Svetozar Marovic publicly apologized to Croatian President Mesic, during his trip to Belgrade, for atrocities committed against Croatian citizens during the war, which broke out in the former Yugoslavia in 1991 [YUN 1991, p. 214], and to the people of Bosnia and Herzegovina on 13 November during the Inter-State Cooperation Council meeting. On 2 October, the three countries signed the Protocol on the Three-Point Border between the countries, establishing two points where their borders met and proclaiming that those borders could not be changed. Bosnia and Herzegovina simplified the movement of people among the three countries by signing bilateral agreements separately with Croatia and with Serbia and Montenegro.

European Union Police Mission in Bosnia and Herzegovina

Reports of EU Secretary-General. As requested by the Security Council in presidential statement S/PRST/2002/33 [YUN 2002, p. 363], the EU Secretary-General and High Representative for Common Foreign and Security Policy submitted two reports on the activities of the EU Police Mission (EUPM) covering the periods 1 January to 30 June [S/2003/732] and 1 July to 31 December [S/2004/106]. As at 31 December, the Mission comprised 861 personnel, including 471 civilian police officers, 58 international civilians and 322 national staff. Participants from all 15 EU member States and 18 non-EU contributing States were co-located with their Bosnia and Herzegovina counterparts in 47 locations.

In the first report, the EU Secretary-General said that EUPM began operations on 1 January upon the completion of the UNMIBH International Police Task Force (IPTF) mandate [YUN 2002, p. 362]. The transition from IPTF to EUPM concluded on 30 June when the UN liquidation team terminated its mission. EUPM's mandate was to establish sustainable policing arrangements under Bosnia and Herzegovina ownership, in accordance with European and international practice. Its goals were to preserve the levels of institutional and professional proficiency achieved during IPTF's mission, enhance police managerial and operational capacities, strengthen police professionalism at senior levels and within ministries, and monitor the exercise of political control over the police. EUPM was supported by the European Commission's institution-building programmme. It launched seven programmes: crime police; criminal justice; internal affairs; police administration; public order and security; the State Border Service (SBS); and the State Information and Protection Agency (SIPA). Its operational priorities were returnee security and the fight against organized crime; another focus was the development of State-level institutions. While SBS had been established at all border points, SIPA had yet to become operational. EUPM was working with the Office of the High Representative to set up the Agency and to expand its powers to include investigative capacities.

The most significant challenge to EUPM was the repeated attempts to call into question the IPTF police certification process [YUN 2002, p. 353]. The UN Under-Secretary-General for Peacekeeping Operations, at the request of the EU Secretary-General, issued on 28 May a clear statement on the final and binding nature of the Bosnia and Herzegovina police certification process. EUPM remained firm that the certification process concluded with the end of the IPTF mission and its decisions on certification were binding; it refused to reopen cases or accept appeals against those decisions.

In his later report [S/2004/106], the EU Secretary-General said that, as noted in a recent European Commission feasibility study on Bosnia and Herzegovina's preparedness to negotiate a Stabilization and Association Agreement with the EU, policing in the country had improved, as had management capacity and understanding and cooperation between police services and other enforcement agencies. In November, for the first time, a joint operation was conducted by the Federation, Republika Srpska and the Brcko District Police. SBS had also improved its operational cooperation with local police forces, and inter-cantonal coordination was much enhanced. The Bosnia and Herzegovina Police Steering Board, comprising the heads of SIPA and SBS, the Police Director of the two entities, the Brcko Chief of Police and the EUPM Police Head of Mission, was established with the aim of advancing the changes required to improve the effectiveness and efficiency of the police under local ownership and to promote synergies, coordination and cooperation between the different police forces.

Implementation of two EUPM projects on major and organized crime, and on the fight and intervention against human trafficking had produced improved police and SBS performance in tackling car theft, drug seizures and human trafficking. The local police forces' ability to fight organized crime had improved, but their capacity to fight it in a coherent and coordinated way was still limited, especially since their structure and size were financially and operationally inefficient.

One of the major challenges during the last quarter of 2003 was political interference in the police in the Federation, which prompted the holding of a press conference on 29 October by the High Representative and the EUPM Police Head of Mission, during which they drew attention to the issue. Their engagement, together with the involvement of senior Bosnia and Herzegovina and Federation officials, helped to stem the problem. EUPM remained vigilant and would continue to work towards the eradication of undue political influence or interference in policing. Challenges to and attempts to overturn the IPTF certification process continued, with some local courts declaring the dismissal of former police officers null and void because the Ministry of the Interior did not apply domestic legislation. The UN Department of Peacekeeping Operations, the Office of the High Representative, the UN representative in Bosnia and Herzegovina and EUPM agreed that UN Headquarters would examine the specifics of the issue before coming to a final assessment on how to deal with it.

Military aspects

Stabilization Force

Under the command of NATO, the multinational Stabilization Force (SFOR), also known as Operation Joint Guard, continued in 2003 to oversee the implementation of the military aspects of the 1995 Peace Agreement. Its activities from 1 December 2002 to 31 December 2003 were recorded in 11 reports [S/2003/103, S/2003/377, S/2003/512, S/2003/615, S/2003/679, S/2003/780, S/2003/851, S/2003/928, S/2003/1159, S/2004/34, S/2004/97], submitted by the NATO Secretary-General through the UN Secretary-General to the Security Council, in accordance with Council resolution 1088(1996) [YUN 1996, p. 310].

SFOR's strength decreased during the year from 12,500 troops in December 2002 to just over 11,400 in December 2003. The Council, by **resolution 1491(2003)** of 11 July (see p. 400), authorized the continuation of SFOR for a further period of 12 months.

During the year, SFOR continued to contribute to the maintenance of a safe and secure environment in Bosnia and Herzegovina, monitor compliance by the entity armed forces, conduct inspections and monitor consolidation of weapons storage sites, support international organizations and the Federation authorities in collecting weapons and ammunition (Operation Harvest), and monitor possible terrorist-related threats. It also conducted searches for war crime indictees, detaining Naser Oric on 10 April, Miloslav Deronjic in July and Enes Sakrak in August. On 15 October, SFOR launched a large-scale operation to support some 100 ICTY representatives searching for evidence to help prosecute war crime indictees held in the Detention Unit.

In April, President Dragan Cavic of Republika Srpska requested SFOR assistance in conducting a weapons amnesty similar to Operation Harvest in his entity. SFOR acknowledged the proposals from both entities for a national campaign and recommended that an operation be initiated by the tri-presidency and conducted through the Bosnia and Herzegovina chain of command, with monitoring by SFOR.

On 22 April, at a meeting hosted by SFOR, the Federation Minister of Defence and the Chiefs of General Staff of the Federation and Republika Srpska armies discussed the restructuring of the armed forces of Bosnia and Herzegovina to bring them under effective civilian control, as mandated by the High Representative (see p. 401). In July, the Defence Reform Commission was working on proposed legislative changes and the Joint Military Commission was helping the armed forces to prepare detailed restructuring plans. In June, representatives of the Federation and Republika Srpska agreed to form a national-level Joint Armed Forces Headquarters. On 21 August, the Republika Srpska Army (VRS) announced plans to close 32 accommodation sites and reduce the number of ammunition depots from 19 to 8. The Government of Bosnia and Herzegovina completed a review of its conscription policy and announced plans to reduce the period of military service from six to five months; a further reduction to four months was being considered. On 28 November, the Republika Srpska National Assembly passed eight amendments to the Constitution related to defence reform. The jurisdiction over the command of VRS was transferred from the entity President to the tri-presidency of Bosnia and Herzegovina and the right to declare war was transferred from the Assembly to the State level. On 11 December, the Assembly agreed on a draft defence reform law establishing the subordination of the military to the civilian authority of Bosnia and Herzegovina. That action created the legal basis to integrate the Bosnian Ministry of Defence into the structure of an overall Bosnia and Herzegovina military command, conforming to NATO's Partnership for Peace requirement of establishing a supreme command under the civilian control of the Bosnia and Herzegovina tri-presidency.

Serbia and Montenegro

In 2003, the United Nations continued to assist the authorities and people of the Kosovo province of the Federal Republic of Yugoslavia (FRY) (renamed Serbia and Montenegro on 4 February) in their efforts to build a modern, European, multi-ethnic society. The United Nations Interim Administration Mission in Kosovo (UNMIK) co-operated with the Kosovo authorities in establishing the Provisional Institutions of Self-Government, mainly the Kosovo Assembly and the Kosovo Government, and in transferring authority to those institutions, in accordance with the 2001 Constitutional Framework for Provisional Self-Government [YUN 2001, p. 352]. By the end of the year, UNMIK had completed the transfer of all the competences under chapter V of the Constitutional Framework and had instituted a mechanism for involving Kosovo authorities in the competences reserved to the Special Representative of the Secretary-General under chapter VIII, without prejudice to his authority.

The Special Representative and the Security Council monitored the progress made towards the fulfilment of the benchmarks established by the Special Representative in 2002 [YUN 2002, p. 369], as part of the "standards before status" policy [ibid., p. 372] for determining when the political process of deciding Kosovo's future status could begin. In that regard, a mechanism to review the progress of the Provisional Institutions in meeting those benchmarks was established, involving quarterly reviews and leading to a comprehensive review in 2005. To facilitate that process, the Special Representative and the Kosovo Prime Minister launched the "standards for Kosovo" document, setting out in clear and detailed terms the goals Kosovo had to reach. The Council, in December, welcomed the launch of the review mechanism and supported the "standards for Kosovo" document. Progress was made in reaching the objectives of one of the most challenging benchmarks, normalization of relations with Belgrade. On 14 October, dialogue on matters of practical interest between the two capitals, Belgrade and Pristina, was launched, although not with the full representation expected. Minority returns increased, reaching a total of 3,629; some were returning to areas where it would have been previously impossible. However, violence and crimes against minorities continued and were condemned by Council members in a number of press statements. Progress continued in meeting the other benchmarks: economic reconstruction was strengthened as Kosovo established its economic legislative framework; the privatization process was set in motion; and efforts continued to put a functioning and representative justice and rule-of-law system in place by consolidating Kosovo's law enforcement and judiciary structures. However, progress in other areas was hindered by Belgrade's support for parallel administrative structures in Kosovo, inadequate minority representation in Kosovo's institutions at both the central and municipal levels, the politicization of the civil service, and the overstepping of competences by the Provisional Institutions of Self-Government.

New union of Serbia and Montenegro. In accordance with the constitutional arrangement signed by the leaders of the FRY constituent Republics of Serbia and Montenegro in 2002 [YUN 2002, p. 383], the constitutional charter for the new union of Serbia and Montenegro was adopted by the legislature of each Republic in January 2003 and adopted and proclaimed by the FRY parliament on 4 February. On that date FRY ceased to exist and was succeeded by Serbia and Montenegro.

Situation in Kosovo

The United Nations continued to work towards the full implementation of Security Council resolution 1244(1999) [YUN 1999, p. 353], which set out the modalities for a political solution to the crisis in the Serbia and Montenegro province of Kosovo, and of resolutions 1160(1998) [YUN 1998, p. 369], 1199(1998) [ibid., p. 377], 1203(1998) [ibid., p. 382] and 1239(1999) [YUN 1999, p. 349]. The civilian aspects of resolution 1244(1999) were being implemented by UNMIK and the military aspects by the international security presence (KFOR).

Appointment of Special Representative. UNMIK was headed by the Special Representative of the Secretary-General. On 24 July, the Secretary-General appointed Harri Holkeri (Finland) to replace Michael Steiner (Germany) in that position [S/2003/761]. The Security Council took note of the appointment on 28 July [S/2003/762].

Establishment and transfer of authority to provisional institutions of self-government

In 2003, the United Nations, through UNMIK, continued to assist the Kosovo authorities in establishing the Provisional Institutions of Self-Government (the Kosovo Assembly and the Kosovo Government) and transferring authority from UNMIK to those institutions, in accordance with the Constitutional Framework for Provisional Self-Government adopted in 2001 [YUN 2001, p. 352].

Report of Secretary-General (January). In a January report on UNMIK [S/2003/113], the Secretary-General said that progress in transferring executive functions from international staff to Kosovo civil servants varied between the ministries, depending on their organizational structure and ability to recruit and retain qualified staff. Senior staff appointments were delayed, owing to, among other things, difficulties in identifying suitable candidates willing to accept a comparatively low salary and the politicization of senior civil servant posts. Nearly 50 per cent of senior Kosovo civil servant posts remained unfilled, requiring international staff to remain in line functions in some ministries. The level of minority community representation in most of the central bodies averaged less than 6 per cent, while minority community employment in the civil service at the municipal level averaged 12 per cent. The highest representation in municipal structures was in the Gnjilane region, where four out of five mixed municipalities reflected an acceptable level (12 per cent) of minority employment; the lowest was in the Pec region.

The transfer of responsibilities was also hindered by the lack of appropriate rules and procedures and non-adherence to existing rules, including rules of executive business of the Government, office procedure for the ministries, rules for delegation of financial and administrative powers, pay rules and accounting guidelines. UNMIK had drafted provisional rules for some of those areas and encouraged the relevant ministries to draft the rules within their purview.

Government meetings and Assembly sessions towards the end of 2002 were characterized by an increasing desire to encroach on the powers reserved for the Special Representative, such as the power to set budgetary parameters. On 15 January 2003, in the face of adverse public reaction to an income tax increase, the Government issued a statement distancing itself from the increase, which it had previously agreed to in the Economic and Fiscal Council in mid-October 2002. It called for the postponement of the implementation of the relevant regulation (UNMIK regulation 2002/4) until the Law on Financial Management and Accountability was promulgated and recommended the continuation of 2002 taxation levels until that time. In an extraordinary session on 24 January 2003, the Economic and Fiscal Council endorsed a revised scale of personal income tax rates presented by the Government and agreed to by the World Bank and the International Monetary Fund.

Despite a stated commitment by the Provisional Institutions, particularly the Government, to fulfilling the benchmarks (referred to as "standards before status" policy) for Kosovo's future status [YUN 2002, p. 369], some Kosovo Albanian Cabinet members publicly distanced themselves from them. Despite consultations on the benchmarks, the Provisional Institutions remained reluctant to engage. Moreover, several of the New Year messages of leading Kosovo Albanian politicians called for independence in 2003. On the other hand, the majority of Kosovo Serb leaders endorsed the "standards before status" approach and took a firm stance that status should not be negotiated before the standards had been reached. However, in January 2003, the Prime Minister of Serbia called for final status negotiations to begin during the year.

The beginning of 2003 saw renewed tensions among the Kosovo Albanian coalition partners, specifically between the Democratic League of Kosovo, on the one hand, and the Democratic Party of Kosovo and the Alliance for the Future of Kosovo, on the other.

The Assembly, with the assistance of the Institution-Building Pillar's Assembly Support Initiative, formed the rudimentary structures needed for a functioning parliament. On 9 January, the Assembly adopted its rules of procedure, which UNMIK was currently reviewing to ensure compliance with the Constitutional Framework. It had become apparent that 18 committees for a 120-member Assembly was a cumbersome structure and that the work of the committees would benefit from technical expertise and public hearings. It was also difficult for the representatives of the smaller minority groups to participate adequately in committee work, thus limiting their participation in the legislative process in some areas. UNMIK initiated the formal monitoring of Assembly proceedings to ensure compliance with the Constitutional Framework and the provisional rules of procedure, with particular emphasis on respect for the rights of communities, and to make recommendations for corrective action.

Security Council consideration (February). The Secretary-General's Special Representative for Kosovo and Head of UNMIK, Michael Steiner, briefed the Security Council on 6 February [meeting 4702], during its consideration of the Secretary-General's January report on UNMIK (see p. 412). He noted that much had been accomplished in the preceding 12 months. To achieve further progress, UNMIK intended to focus in 2003 on: standards; the three priorities of jobs, security and real multi-ethnicity; the transfer of power; the establishment of direct dialogue between Pristina and Belgrade; and preparation for European integration. Within that strategy, UNMIK would concentrate on the standards required for a decent life in Kosovo, including intensifying its fight against organized crime, corruption and politically motivated violence, with the participation of the Kosovo Police Service. Unemployment continued to be the number-one concern, but the creation of jobs depended on being able to create an appropriate investment climate. With the cooperation of the Government, the Special Representative undertook to develop the legal system, institutions and basis for property rights to generate investor confidence and to open an office to speed up registration and legal requirements to facilitate business investment.

The Special Representative was concerned about ethnically defined interest politics on the part of Kosovo Albanians, Kosovo Serbs and Belgrade. Parallel structures could not be allowed to operate. While the entire Mitrovica region had been brought under international control [YUN 2002, p. 374], Belgrade continued to support structures that operated on a mono-ethnic basis and to focus exclusively on Kosovo's Serb population. By the same token, the majority Albanian community had failed to take ownership of the interests of the Kosovo Serb community and other minorities. Kosovo had to prove that it was creating a multi-ethnic society where every Kosovan, regardless of ethnic origin, could live in security and dignity.

As to the transfer of power, the Special Representative indicated his readiness to hand over all competences legally permissible to the Provisional Institutions of Self-Government by the end of 2003. However, they had to make progress in meeting the benchmarks for Kosovo's future, established in 2002 [YUN 2002, p. 369], and to demonstrate their ability to handle added responsibilities and accomplish things. The municipalities had had over two years of running local affairs; UNMIK would soon be able to fully hand over executive responsibilities to the most successful municipalities and withdraw into a monitoring and oversight function. At the central level, UNMIK was reviewing the effectiveness of the handover of real responsibility in the transferred areas to identify, with the Provisional Institutions, all other areas that could be transferred in 2003. Less than one year had passed since the Government was set up and effective checks and balances between the executive, the legislative, the judiciary and the media were still lacking. In addition, minority protection was still weak throughout the institutions.

The Special Representative said that it was time to lay the groundwork for the political process leading towards finally resolving Kosovo's status. Dialogue between Pristina and Belgrade on issues of mutual interest was necessary and would facilitate the political dialogue at a later stage.

Noting the EU intention to outline a more energetic policy towards the Balkans, the Special Representative said that any engagement by the international community should be matched by an equal engagement of local partners in fulfilling the standards of a functioning democratic society.

SECURITY COUNCIL ACTION

On 6 February [meeting 4703], following consultations among Security Council members, the President made statement **S/PRST/2003/1** on behalf of the Council:

The Security Council reaffirms its continued commitment to the full and effective implementation of its resolution 1244(1999) of 10 June 1999. The Council notes the transformation of the Federal Republic of Yugoslavia into Serbia and Montenegro and, in this context, reaffirms that resolution 1244(1999) remains fully valid in all its aspects. Resolution 1244(1999) continues to be the basis of the policy of the international community on Kosovo.

The Council further reaffirms its commitment to the objective of a multi-ethnic and democratic Kosovo and calls upon all communities to work towards this goal and actively participate in the public institutions as well as the decision-making process, and integrate into society. It condemns all attempts to establish and maintain structures and institutions as well as initiatives that are inconsistent with resolution 1244(1999) and the Constitutional Framework for Provisional Self-Government in Kosovo. The Council calls for the authority of the United Nations Interim Administration Mission in Kosovo to be respected throughout Kosovo, and welcomes the establishment of the authority of the Mission in the northern part of Mitrovica. It encourages the establishment of direct dialogue between Pristina and Belgrade on issues of practical importance to both sides.

The Council condemns the violence within the Kosovo Albanian community, as well as the violence against the Kosovo Serb community. It urges local institutions and leaders to exert influence on the climate for the rule of law by condemning all violence and actively supporting the efforts of the police and the judiciary. It underlines the responsibility of the majority to make the minority communities feel that Kosovo is their home too, and that the laws apply equally to everyone. The minority community representatives must join and work within the institutions to benefit from them. The Council stresses that all communities must make renewed efforts to inject momentum into improving inter-ethnic dialogue and promoting the reconciliation process, not least through full cooperation with the International Tribunal for the Prosecution of Persons Responsible for Serious Violations of International Humanitarian Law Committed in the Territory of the Former Yugoslavia since 1991.

The Council welcomes the report of the Secretary-General on the activities of the Mission and recent developments in Kosovo and the briefing of the Special Representative of the Secretary-General on the status of implementation of the benchmarks for Kosovo. The Council reiterates its full support for the "standards before status" policy with postulated targets in the eight key areas: functioning of democratic institutions, the rule of law, freedom of movement, the return of refugees and internally displaced persons, the economy, property rights, dialogue with Belgrade, and the Kosovo Protection Corps. The Council welcomes the presentation of a detailed plan for its implementation that will provide the appropriate baseline against which progress can be measured, as discussed with the Special Representative of the Secretary-General during the Security Council mission in December 2002. The fulfilment of these targets is essential to commencing a political process designed to determine the future of Kosovo, in accordance with resolution 1244 (1999). The Council strongly rejects unilateral initiatives which may jeopardize stability and the normalization process not only in Kosovo but also in the entire region. It urges all political leaders in Kosovo and in the region to shoulder responsibility for democratization, peace and stability in the region by rejecting all initiatives contravening resolution 1244 (1999). The Council rejects any attempts to exploit the question of the future of Kosovo for other political ends.

The Council welcomes the progress made in 2002, as outlined in the report of the Secretary-General. It supports the continued efforts of the Special Representative of the Secretary-General, including in such priority areas as revitalizing the economy through investment, combating crime and illegal trafficking, and building a multi-ethnic society, while ensuring conditions for the sustainable return of refugees and internally displaced persons.

The Council welcomes the intention of the Special Representative of the Secretary-General to transfer remaining competencies to the provisional institutions of self-government by the end of the year, except those reserved for the Special Representative of the Secretary-General under resolution 1244(1999). It calls upon the Kosovo provisional institutions of self-government as well as all Kosovars to take on their responsibilities and genuinely cooperate for this transfer to be successful.

The Council reiterates its full support for the Special Representative of the Secretary-General and urges Kosovo's leaders once again to work in close cooperation with the Mission and the Kosovo Force for a better future for Kosovo and stability in the region.

Report of Secretary-General (April). The Secretary-General reported on 14 April [S/2003/421] that Kosovo still had some way to go in establishing representative and functioning institutions. During the first three months of 2003, the Kosovo Provisional Government took 36 policy decisions, of which 16 involved legislation. Ten draft laws were submitted to the Kosovo Assembly for review, four of which were adopted. Ad hoc inter-ministerial committees were formed on war damages, missing persons, the review of personal income tax, the levelling of public sector wages, and the transfer of responsibilities.

Although regular weekly meetings of the Kosovo Assembly continued to take place, they were affected by boycotts by both Kosovo Albanian and Kosovo Serb parties. The three major Kosovo Albanian parties and the non-Serb minorities signed a joint statement, presented to the

Assembly, stating that the declaration of independence would be dealt with at a later meeting. At its 3 April meeting, the Assembly adopted the position that the Provisional Institutions should implement a law on higher education, which it had adopted in 2002 [YUN 2002, p. 372], even though it had not been promulgated by the Special Representative. The Special Representative issued a determination stating that the Assembly's position on that subject was without legal effect, which was supported by the Security Council in a 14 April press statement [SC/7729].

The Senior Public Appointments Committee completed the recruitment of 80 per cent of senior civil servants, including the first female Permanent Secretary, through competitive examinations. At the central level, the recruitment process complied with the Civil Service Law and minority requirements were met in setting up selection panels. However, there was a perception by civil servants that their career depended on political allegiance more than on professional skills, leading to an alignment of civil servants along party lines. The recruitment of minority representatives at the central level progressed, averaging some 13 per cent by the end of March, compared to less than 6 per cent at the beginning of the year. At the management levels, minority employment reached some 19 per cent overall. However, minority employment in most of the public and socially owned enterprises remained unsatisfactory, with less than 1 per cent employed in most public enterprises. Institutional mechanisms in support of minority participation in the civil service at the central level were further strengthened through legislation and administrative support, such as the outreach programme initiated by the Office of the Prime Minister, which resulted in a ninefold increase in minority applications, the establishment of gender/equal opportunity focal points within ministries, and a range of legal mechanisms, such as appeal procedures and fair and transparent recruitment, announced in a government administrative directive.

At the municipal level, the Gnjilane region had the best record in achieving employment goals, with three municipalities having acceptable levels of minority representation. The functioning of inter-ethnic municipal administrations varied considerably. In Kamenica, Gnjilane, Novo Brdo (all in the Gnjilane region) and Kosovo Polje (Pristina region), the municipalities' joint administrations functioned at a reasonable level. Kosovo Serbs had not taken up municipal positions in Vitina municipality (Gnjilane region), owing to several security incidents. Positions reserved for them in Lipljan municipality (Pristina region) remained vacant, as no suitable candidate had applied. Two unions of Kosovo Serb-majority municipalities were formed, the first in northern Mitrovica and the second in eastern Kosovo. UNMIK did not recognize either union as a legitimate structure, as they were based on mono-ethnicity. The UNMIK administration in Mitrovica made progress in establishing its administrative structure and in providing administration and public services in the northern part of Mitrovica city.

Much remained to be done to foster responsible and professional media. Some of the local press continued to publish inflammatory and sensational reports and to present inaccurate or provocative information. The Temporary Media Commissioner was working to ensure that retractions were issued and to enforce temporary print and broadcast codes of conduct in the absence of self-regulatory mechanisms.

The assassination of the Prime Minister of Serbia, Zoran Djindjic, which was condemned by Council members in a 12 March press statement [SC/7688], and provocative statements by Belgrade officials on the future status of Kosovo had a negative impact on the political situation in Kosovo, as did provocative statements by Kosovo Albanian leaders on Kosovo's final status. To initiate a dialogue on practical matters between the authorities in Belgrade and those of the Provisional Institutions, the Special Representative, on 2 March, invited a ministerial delegation from Belgrade for talks on a proposed agenda. However, leading Kosovo Albanian politicians reneged on their initial support for the initiative, citing preconditions for dialogue, including the need for further progress in the transfer process and the approval of a joint platform by the Kosovo Assembly. Similarly, the Belgrade authorities requested the inclusion of additional agenda items and expressed their unwillingness to participate. The process was postponed following the assassination of Prime Minister Djindjic.

Security Council consideration (April and June). The Assistant Secretary-General for Peacekeeping Operations, Hédi Annabi, briefing the Security Council on 23 April [meeting 4742], said that a significant step in the transfer to the Kosovo Provisional Institutions of Self-Government of responsibilities under the Constitutional Framework was the establishment of a joint Transfer Council, comprising UNMIK and Provisional Institutions representatives, to oversee, coordinate and manage the process. At its first meeting on 8 April, the Transfer Council established working groups on finance, recruitment and logistics; technical assistance; and monitoring and intervention. The Assistant Secretary-General said that the pace of the transfer of responsibilities would depend on the capacity of the Provisional Institutions to assume the relevant responsibilities. He noted the increasing attempts to undercut resolution 1244 (1999) [YUN 1999, p. 353] and the Constitutional Framework, especially the Kosovo Government's recent challenge of the Special Representative's reserved powers in the Transfer Council by asking for the creation of new ministries to exercise authority over reserved areas and attempts by the Kosovo Assembly to implement a law on higher education (see p. 415). UNMIK was concerned that the Assembly had not acted on four laws, including the education law, returned to it for remedial action. The Assistant Secretary-General warned that, should the Assembly not amend those laws, the Special Representative would be forced to promulgate them, after the necessary adjustments were made.

He said that radical action and pronouncements by all sides had increased since the beginning of the year. Voices of moderation were weak or muted, making the promotion of dialogue across political and ethnic lines difficult, both with regard to Kosovars and between Belgrade and the Provisional Institutions of Self-Government. UNMIK had sought to balance the competing demands of the leaders and people of Kosovo, with a view to preventing extremism, and would continue to encourage dialogue and multi-ethnicity and facilitate the acceptance and achievement of the benchmarks for Kosovo's future status [YUN 2002, p. 369].

In a further briefing to the Council on 10 June [meeting 4770], the Assistant Secretary-General said that four years into UNMIK's mandate, there had been significant progress in Kosovo, but challenges were still being faced with regard to freedom of movement, meaningful minority participation, returns, the institutional development of local bodies and dialogue between Belgrade and Pristina. Following the emergency phase, the focus had been on political and institutional development. The guiding principles for the current phase were the benchmarks set out by the Special Representative and the policy of "standards before status". Political pressure on UNMIK had increased significantly, with attempts to challenge its role under resolution 1244(1999) and the Constitutional Framework. The Provisional Institutions, particularly the Kosovo Assembly, had overstepped their competences and Belgrade, by lending support to parallel structures, supported the boycott of UNMIK policy and programmes. Unilateral calls from Kosovo Albanians, Kosovo Serbs and Belgrade for mutually exclusive solutions for Kosovo's future continued and had not contributed to reconciliation and inter-ethnic dialogue. In addition, organized criminal groups and extremist elements were increasing their intrusions into political life.

Report of Secretary-General (June). In a 26 June report on UNMIK [S/2003/675], the Secretary-General said that the Transfer Council, at its second meeting on 28 May, agreed to the transfer of 19 non-reserved competences, with a further 17 to be transferred as soon as the Provisional Institutions were ready to assume them. It agreed to return eight competences to its three working groups for further consideration. Kosovo Serb representatives did not participate in either meeting of the Transfer Council.

Between 1 April and 16 June, the Government of Kosovo took 27 policy decisions, including 12 related to legislation. That was a slight increase in the average number of decisions taken each month relative to the first three months of 2003 and a significant increase in the proportion of those having legal implications. As the decision-making process became more inclusive and transparent, there was a higher degree of ownership by Kosovo civil servants of that process. Inter-ministerial communication and coordination improved with the setting up of two inter-ministerial working groups on gender equality and disabilities. A Commission for Cooperation with ICTY was also established.

The Kosovo Assembly, in nine plenary meetings held since 1 April, with all political groups attending, made progress in adopting and forwarding legislation to the Special Representative for promulgation, including the four laws (on external trade, telecommunications, higher education, and public financial management and accountability), which had been returned to it for revision (see above). The Government undertook to implement all the laws, including those with changes introduced by UNMIK. The Assembly adopted six other laws, including one on immovable property taxes, a subject outside its area of competence. In a special procedure, the Assembly agreed to the Provisional Criminal Code and the Provisional Criminal Procedure Code, which, as reserved competences, would be issued as UNMIK Regulations. On 15 May, it endorsed a controversial resolution on the liberation war of the people of Kosovo for freedom and independence, which the Special Representative declared to be divisive and contrary to the spirit of resolution 1244(1999). In addition, on 24 April, the Assembly endorsed an initiative that instructed an "appropriate body" to draft a law on elections, even though election matters were outside its competence. The Assembly's functional committees met regularly, but there continued to be a lack of effective minority community participation in the legislative process.

In contrast to the Kosovo Assembly, policy-making and legislative development in the municipal assemblies were slow, as almost all of them were still hiring municipal civil servants and setting up municipal committees. Only four municipalities currently had an adequate number of functioning committees, and in about one third of them politicization of the civil service recruitment process continued. In two municipalities, the budget had still not been approved, and in three there was political gridlock because of the refusal of the major Kosovo Albanian parties to cooperate with each other. Meanwhile, the functioning of mixed Kosovo Serb–Kosovo Albanian municipal administrations varied considerably.

The administrative development of some Provisional Institutions and municipalities remained hampered by the continued operation of Belgrade-supported parallel administrative structures in some parts of Kosovo, especially in the health and education sectors. UNMIK was developing a comprehensive action plan to address that issue. In northern Mitrovica, UNMIK had appointed an eight-member Advisory Board, consisting of six Kosovo Serbs, one Kosovo Albanian and one Bosniac, to help communicate the concerns of residents in that region (primarily Kosovo Serbs) to the UNMIK administration. However, at its first meeting on 30 May, Kosovo Serb representatives objected to the Board's composition, while the Kosovo Albanian Municipal President expressed his reservations regarding the Board's establishment and functions.

Overall, minority representation in the Kosovo ministries was estimated to be about 10 per cent, but fell to only 1.3 per cent at management levels. The affirmative action plan "Community Proportional Representation", approved in principle in 2002 [YUN 2002, p. 372] by the Special Representative and the Office of the Prime Minister, had still not been implemented.

Civic education continued in all Albanian-language lower secondary schools, but with an outdated curriculum. The Ministry of Education, Science and Technology was developing new civics curricula, to be introduced in schools in September. It was also proceeding with measures to eliminate inflammatory and/or emotive material from some Albanian-language history textbooks.

Security Council consideration (July). On 3 July [meeting 4782], the Security Council was briefed by outgoing Special Representative Michael Steiner, who reviewed Kosovo's progress in meeting the benchmark standards for its future.

He noted that, although not perfect, the Provisional Institutions of Self-Government were functioning and improving and an orderly process was in place for completing the transfer of non-reserved responsibilities to the Kosovo Government by the end of the year. As to the rule of law, a multi-ethnic judiciary and a police force of 5,407 officers had been built from scratch. Crime had dropped significantly, UNMIK had demonstrated zero tolerance for corruption, notorious criminals had been convicted and major trials were ongoing. With regard to the economy, unemployment was running at 57 per cent. However, the groundwork had been laid for a sustainable economy for the future, the euro provided monetary stability and an effective banking system had been established successfully. Kosovo had a balanced budget that relied on revenue collection, a legal framework was in place to protect investment and foster a market economy, and a privatization process had been launched. Regarding multi-ethnicity and returns, some 7,000 displaced persons had returned, a number that was still too small. However, the Framework for Returns was in place. Multi-ethnicity had been improving gradually, although a lot more work was required for Kosovo to become a truly multi-ethnic society. The slowness of returns and integration remained the most serious shortcoming.

Direct dialogue between Pristina and Belgrade, which had long been elusive, was brought on track (see p. 418) at the EU-Western Balkans Summit (Thessaloniki, Greece, 21 June).

Report of Secretary-General (October). The Secretary-General reported in October [S/2003/996] that, in accordance with the 28 May decision of the Transfer Council (see p. 416), 19 non-reserved responsibilities under chapter 5 of the Constitutional Framework had been transferred, 17 had been identified for such action and the remaining eight were expected to be completely transferred by the end of 2003. However, the Provisional Institutions had called for the transfer also of the Special Representative's reserved responsibilities under chapter 8. In that context, and in accordance with resolution 1244(1999) and the Constitutional Framework, the Prime Minister of Kosovo presented to the Special Representative proposals for closer cooperation between UNMIK and the Provisional Institutions, and for their involvement in those reserved areas. Some proposals had been accepted or were being given positive consideration, and mechanisms were being developed to gradually increase the responsibilities of the Provisional Institutions. A benchmark implementation plan was also being developed, with time lines and success criteria in line with the "standards before status" formula, while assigning clear responsibility for lead institutions in particular areas. In that context, UNMIK had produced a mission performance management plan to guide coordinated Mission action.

The Government introduced a quarterly planning and reporting cycle to allow ministers to identify their policy aims and report on progress made in those areas. Inter-ministerial coordination and governmental planning had also profited from the establishment of three new working groups on the issues of trafficking, the Government's annual legislative work programme for the period from October 2003 to October 2004 and land management. The Government approved five draft laws, which were forwarded to the Kosovo Assembly, and agreed on a general policy direction for nine others.

As public sector wage levels in Kosovo continued to cause concern, the Government instituted a recruitment freeze from 1 July to the end of the year in order to fund a 20 per cent increase in civil servant salaries in the health and education sectors. The freeze did not apply to minorities. Generally, reports indicated that recruitment procedures under the Kosovo Civil Service Law and subsequent instructions were not being followed and the service was experiencing increasing politicization, which it was hoped would be countered by the establishment of the Independent Oversight Board in November. The functioning of the Assembly improved, as did its working relationship with the Government. Several of its committees were also reaching out to the public, conducting public hearings and field visits. UNMIK and the Assembly set up a joint working group to remove obstacles to UNMIK's recognition of the Assembly's revised rules of procedure. On 10 July, the Assembly issued a declaration acknowledging the right to return of internally displaced persons from all communities.

Steps were taken to improve the effectiveness and responsiveness of municipal administrations. Political gridlocks that had affected the operations of some municipal assemblies had been resolved and fair share financing from municipal budgets improved slightly. Six municipalities had achieved the minimum level of fair share financing in all three budget lines (municipal administration, health and education), four had done so in two of them and 12 had done so in one budget line. Five had not achieved the minimum required allocation in even one budget line; UNMIK and the Ministry of Finance and Economy called on them to submit expenditure plans ensuring the minimum required percentage allocation for the 2003 fiscal year and stating that executive action would be taken, including the imposition of fiscal sanctions, should those expenditure plans still be unsatisfactory.

Minority employment in the civil service at the central and municipal levels remained unsatisfactory. The Ministry of Public Services had not issued an administrative instruction outlining affirmative action provisions and the outreach programme initiated by the Office of the Prime Minister had not resulted in a significant increase in the number of minority staff, who allegedly opted for the higher remuneration and longer-term job security offered by parallel structures operating in Kosovo. The representation of women at the professional level in the public sector improved and a senior position of Municipal Gender Officer was established in all 30 municipalities. The Assembly's Gender Equality Commission was to consider a draft law on gender equality.

Direct dialogue between Belgrade and Pristina

In his October report on UNMIK [S/2003/996], the Secretary-General informed the Security Council that direct dialogue between Belgrade and Pristina on matters of mutual interest was launched on 14 October in Vienna, with the participation of the President of Kosovo and the Assembly Speaker, and the Prime Minister and Deputy Prime Minister of the Republic of Serbia. Working groups of experts were to continue discussions in key areas of the agenda, notably energy, missing persons, returns and transport and communications. Meanwhile, working-level cooperation between the two capitals continued through the mediation of UNMIK officials. Cooperation had been fruitful in the areas of police, security and justice, including the return of 43 mortal remains to Kosovo.

Security Council consideration. On 30 October [meeting 4853], during consideration of the Secretary-General's October report on UNMIK, the new Special Representative, Harri Holkeri, told the Council that organizing the direct dialogue between Pristina and Belgrade had proved to be a challenging and strenuous effort. Kosovo's Prime Minister, Bajram Rexhepi, had consistently hinged the Government's participation in the dialogue on the consensual approval of the main coalition parties or a consensus of the Assembly, while some Kosovo Albanian political leaders made their participation in any talks conditional on changes in the governmental responsibilities and structures, as well as the establishment of new ministries, including in reserved areas. Stressing that there could be no linkage between the dialogue process and enhancement of the responsibilities and structures of the Provisional Institutions, the Special Representative said that such bargaining was not acceptable. Dialogue was one of the standards approved by the Security Council in presidential statement S/PRST/2002/11 [YUN 2002, p. 369]. Failure of the Government and the coalition parties to accept responsibility for contributing to the achievement of that particular benchmark resulted in only two out of three institutional leaders (Ibrahim Rugova, President of Kosovo, and Nexhat Daci, President of the Kosovo Assembly) participating in the launching of the 14 October talks in Vienna. It was regrettable that the Government's absence prevented a multi-ethnic representation from Pristina at that meeting. Although the Belgrade and Pristina delegation members did not interact, they did listen to each other and, in certain areas, their comments provided encouraging signals that progress could be made. The international community's representatives emphasized that, as one of the eight benchmarks [ibid.] to be fulfilled before talks on final status or future status could begin, the Government had to decide promptly to engage in the technical talks and determine how best it could contribute to the process. The four working groups with multi-ethnic representation on the Kosovo side should be promptly established and begin technical talks in Belgrade and Pristina at the expert level. The Special Representative appealed to the Council and to the international community to continue support for the dialogue process.

Assessment of other developments

The Special Representative, in assessing progress in other areas, told the Security Council on 30 October [meeting 4853] that, while efforts to continue direct talks between Belgrade and Pristina were ongoing, the Provisional Institutions of Self-Government and UNMIK were focused on a joint plan for implementing the eight benchmarks [YUN 2002, p. 369] by developing achievable goals within agreed time frames. The joint plan should offer clarity both to the people of Kosovo and to the international community on implementation of the standards and the evaluation of progress.

Meanwhile, UNMIK was nearing completion of the agreed transfer of competences in non-reserved areas to the Provisional Institutions based on the Constitutional Framework. It was necessary to ensure that the Provisional Institutions were in a position to absorb the new responsibilities and to carry them out with the necessary technical competence and political fairness. At the same time, Kosovo's leaders were increasingly demanding that UNMIK also transfer competences in reserved areas, but that was outside the Special Representative's mandate and would require Council action. However, the Special Representative expressed his commitment to working with the Government to enhance its effectiveness in a true spirit of partnership, and his readiness to consider establishing new structures for that purpose, in conformity with resolution 1244(1999) [YUN 1999, p. 353] and the Constitutional Framework.

Kosovo's democratic institutions, at both the central and municipal levels, continued to develop and were gradually improving their administrative skills and effectiveness. UNMIK would receive, in mid-November, the Council of Europe mission's recommendations on decentralization in Kosovo, which should form a good basis for bringing democratic local government closer to the people and increasing its efficiency. The process of decentralization was likely to be complex and lengthy and would depend on the ability of local representatives to take on additional responsibilities.

It was of very serious concern that the Belgrade authorities continued to strengthen parallel structures in Kosovo, as evidenced by the recent unilateral appointment by the Coordination Centre for Kosovo of so-called regional and municipal coordinators, the functioning of parallel courts and the issuance of international arrest warrants against Kosovo residents. Belgrade should work with Kosovo structures and replace the unacceptable policy with a commitment to truly multi-ethnic organs of government in Kosovo. Failure to change course would impede the development of genuine multi-ethnicity in Kosovo.

The short- to medium-term outlook for Kosovo was uncertain, but the strong desire of its people to live in a peaceful, stable, lawful society was clear. Infighting and jockeying for position among politicians in advance of elections in Kosovo and Serbia proper would continue to hamper implementation of UNMIK's mandate. The public was growing increasingly frustrated with the Government's apparent inability to tackle matters affecting its well-being, such as the continued high levels of unemployment, while the Provisional Institutions of Self-Government were constantly blaming all deficiencies on their lack of authority to deal with those matters. Tensions caused by Belgrade's continued support of parallel structures and the possibility of a renewal of ethnically motivated violence, which would continue to keep many internally displaced persons from returning to Kosovo, challenged the Council to maintain a firm commit-

Review mechanism for "standards before status" benchmarks

On 5 November, a mechanism to review the progress of the Provisional Institutions of Self-Government towards meeting the benchmarks [YUN 2002, p. 369] in the "standards before status" policy [ibid., p. 372] was launched [S/2004/71]. The mechanism envisaged quarterly reviews of progress towards meeting the benchmarks and, depending on those assessments, a first comprehensive review of progress in mid-2005. Initiation of the political process to determine Kosovo's future status would depend on the outcome of that review. The review mechanism gave new momentum to the "standards before status" policy and refocused the work of the Provisional Institutions on meeting the benchmarks contained in the eight areas covered by that policy—functioning democratic institutions; rule of law; freedom of movement; returns and integration; economy; property rights; dialogue with Belgrade; and the Kosovo Protection Corps.

On 10 December, the Special Representative and the Kosovo Prime Minister launched the "standards for Kosovo" document, which elaborated on the original standards paper [YUN 2002, p. 372] and set out in clear and detailed terms the standards that Kosovo had to reach, in full compliance with resolution 1244(1999) [YUN 1999, p. 353], the Constitutional Framework and the original standards/benchmarks statement, endorsed by the Security Council in presidential statement S/PRST/2002/11 [YUN 2002, p. 369], adhering to the primacy of the regulations promulgated by UNMIK and subsidiary instruments thereunder as the law applicable in Kosovo. The document was prepared by the Special Representative, in consultation with the Provisional Institutions, all major political parties in Kosovo, including Kosovo Serb Coalition Return, and political parties representing other smaller ethnic groups, such as Turks, Ashkali, Roma, Egyptians and Bosniacs, as well as with Belgrade. However, the document was unacceptable to Belgrade because, in its view, the consultations were insufficient and the document itself undermined resolution 1244 (1999). The Kosovo Serb leadership also distanced itself from it, as did some Kosovo Albanian leaders.

Following the launch of the "standards for Kosovo" document, and under the auspices of a steering group co-chaired by the Special Representative and the Kosovo Prime Minister, UNMIK and the Provisional Institutions convened meetings of five working groups covering the eight sets of standards. The groups would prepare an implementation work plan, setting out the policies and specific, measurable steps to be taken by the Provisional Institutions to reach the standards, including a timetable for implementing those policies and steps. The groups comprised representatives from UNMIK and the Provisional Institutions. Kosovo Serb representatives had not participated in them.

SECURITY COUNCIL ACTION

On 12 December [meeting 4880], following consultations among Security Council members, the President made statement **S/PRST/2003/26** on behalf of the Council:

> The Security Council welcomes the launching of a review mechanism, under the auspices of the Special Representative of the Secretary-General, as presented on 5 November 2003 in Pristina and Belgrade, on the initiative of the Contact Group (France, Germany, Italy, the Russian Federation, the United Kingdom of Great Britain and Northern Ireland and the United States of America, with representatives from the European Union), giving new momentum to the implementation of the 'standards before status' policy that was designed for Kosovo, Serbia and Montenegro, and endorsed by the Council in application of its resolution 1244(1999) of 10 June 1999.
>
> The Council recalls the eight standards, namely, functioning democratic institutions, rule of law, freedom of movement, returns and reintegration, economy, property rights, dialogue with Belgrade, and the Kosovo Protection Corps. The Council in this respect urges the Provisional Institutions of Self-Government to participate fully and constructively in the working groups within the framework of the direct dialogue with Belgrade on practical issues of mutual interest to demonstrate their commitment to the process.
>
> The Council supports the 'standards for Kosovo' document presented on 10 December 2003. The Council awaits an implementation plan, to be finalized by the Special Representative of the Secretary-General in his continuing consultation with the Provisional Institutions of Self-Government, and other relevant parties as appropriate, and submitted to the Council. The plan should serve as a basis for the assessment of the progress of the Provisional Institutions of Self-Government in meeting the standards.
>
> The Council takes note of the fact that the Special Representative of the Secretary-General, within his authority as set out in resolution 1244(1999), inter alia, in the context of the review mechanism, will continue to consult closely with interested parties, in particular the Contact Group. The Council reaffirms its intention to continue to consider the regular reports of the Secretary-General, including an assessment by the Special Representative, as to the progress of the Provisional Institutions of Self-Government towards meeting the standards. The Council takes note of the fact that the Contact Group

intends to make a substantive contribution to the regular reviews and to submit its assessments to the Special Representative.

The Council supports the prospect of a comprehensive review of the progress of the Provisional Institutions of Self-Government in meeting the standards. The Council notes that, depending on progress made as assessed during the periodical review, a first opportunity for such a comprehensive review should occur around mid-2005. Reaffirming the 'standards before status' policy, the Council stresses that further advancement towards a process to determine the future status of Kosovo in accordance with resolution 1244(1999) will depend on the positive outcome of this comprehensive review. The Council reiterates the primacy of the regulations promulgated by the Special Representative of the Secretary-General and subsidiary instruments as the law applicable in Kosovo.

The Council reaffirms its full support to the Special Representative of the Secretary-General, Mr. Harri Holkeri, and calls upon the Provisional Institutions of Self-Government of Kosovo and all concerned to cooperate fully with him.

Kosovo's future status

Security Council consideration. The Under-Secretary-General for Peacekeeping Operations, briefing the Security Council on 17 December [meeting 4886], said that further advancement leading to a determination of Kosovo's future status would depend on the positive outcome of the 2005 comprehensive review of progress towards meeting the eight standards set out in the policy of "standards before status". If the Provisional Institutions did not fulfil those standards by that time, they would be given a further period to work on meeting them, during which the periodic reviews would continue, leading up to the next general review. There was no deadline and the future status process would not start automatically on the review date. A prerequisite for any discussion on Kosovo's future status remained the achievement of those standards. At the same time, achieving them would lead to a qualitative change in Kosovo, which was an essential precondition to advance democracy and a multi-ethnic society in Kosovo.

The Under-Secretary-General noted that the introduction to the "standards for Kosovo" document (see p. 420), which included a reference to full compliance with resolution 1244(1999) [YUN 1999, p. 353], the Constitutional Framework and other applicable law and the original standards and benchmarks statement, had been omitted due to opposition by Kosovo Albanian leaders to the term "applicable law". The Special Representative was working to ensure that the introduction was incorporated in the document at a later stage.

The Under Secretary-General also reported that direct dialogue between Belgrade and Pristina (see p. 418) had not moved forward since its launching on 14 October, partly because of the failure of the Kosovo Government, for political reasons, to endorse the process publicly, even though it continued preparatory work, and the Serbian parliamentary election campaign, which made the Coordination Centre for Kosovo unwilling to discuss preparations for the dialogue.

The Serbia and Montenegro representative, addressing the Council, raised a number of concerns regarding the "standards for Kosovo" document, which, he said, failed to define the standards in a way that would open up prospects for creating a multi-ethnic society in Kosovo and Metohija. He said that UNMIK had rejected the proposals, among others, to make the unconditional and progressive return of refugees and displaced persons a key standard, to require full protection of cultural heritage and to list measures for reforming the Kosovo Protection Corps. Serbia and Montenegro considered the last-minute deletion of the introductory paragraph unjustifiable, since the references contained therein formed the basis for that important document.

Functioning of democratic institutions

Reporting on developments in Kosovo between 1 October and 31 December [S/2004/71], the Secretary-General said that the announcement of the "standards for Kosovo" document (see p. 420) and, in particular, the launch of the review process for standards implementation led to a renewed atmosphere of cooperation between UNMIK and the Kosovo Government, except in the areas of privatization (see p. 427) and direct dialogue with Belgrade.

UNMIK completed the transfer of chapter 5 responsibilities of the Constitutional Framework to the Provisional Institutions at the end of 2003. It undertook to involve the Provisional Institutions in an advisory and consultative capacity in the chapter 8 areas reserved for the Special Representative, without affecting his powers and responsibilities. As part of that process, UNMIK was reviewing the Government's proposal to create a number of offices within the Office of the Prime Minister responsible for internal coordination and liaison with UNMIK. To further improve coordination between UNMIK and the Provisional Institutions, the Special Representative had a Government Liaison Officer within his Office.

Political appointees throughout the Government had begun to take a more active role in executive functions and responsibilities. While that resulted in moving legislation and policy decisions forward, it blurred the division of responsibilities between political appointees and civil servants, who were increasingly subjected to political pressure.

During the last quarter of 2003, 20 legal initiatives and eight draft laws were approved by the Government. With EU assistance, a Standardization Unit was set up in the Office of the Prime Minister to check all laws for compatibility with EU law and the Constitutional Framework. An inter-ministerial Working Group on the Legislative Strategy for 2004 identified 117 laws to be drafted before the end of the current administration's term in late 2004. The functioning of the Kosovo Assembly in the preparation of legislation had improved. The public hearings held by the Assembly on the draft laws on gender equality, anti-discrimination and health were indicative of increased transparency in its work. However, in some instances, the Assembly had reverted to adopting declarations and decisions in areas outside its responsibility, as it did on 22 December when it passed a declaration calling for the abolition of the right of Kosovo Serbs to vote in the 28 December Serbian parliamentary elections. Recent Assembly plenary sessions were also marked by procedural violations and inconsistencies in the counting of votes. A working group was established in October to propose amendments to the Constitutional Framework. If supported by two thirds of the Assembly, the Special Representative would decide on their acceptability and compatibility with Security Council resolution 1244(1999) [YUN 1999, p. 353] and the Constitutional Framework.

The modest positive trend in the functioning of the municipalities continued. For the first time, all of Kosovo's municipal assemblies completed their budgetary processes before the promulgation of the 2004 budget, allowing the municipal administrations to access funds earlier. The functioning of joint Kosovo Serb–Kosovo Albanian municipal administrations also improved slightly, particularly in the Gnjilane region, despite the fact that UNMIK Municipal Representatives had to intervene to suspend some decisions, particularly those relating to the misuse of public funds and attempted misappropriation of land, and to ensure compliance with the rule of law. As a result, the municipalities' actions within the scope of their responsibilities under UNMIK Regulation 2000/45 on local self-government in Kosovo improved. The mandatory municipal committees were functioning better, since their mandate and role had been clarified by UNMIK. With regard to the 2003 municipal budget, fair-share financing results at the end of September showed that there was further incremental improvement in minority spending. Following political gridlock affecting the functioning of some municipalities earlier in 2003, most municipalities were active in the field of local law-making. However, minorities still had very little impact on their decision-making process; the involvement of committees and civil society in the drafting process remained rare, and municipal regulations were not properly implemented and enforced. Translation of official documents in many municipalities remained unsatisfactory and relied on UNMIK initiatives and resources. The Council of Europe Decentralization Mission officially released its report entitled "Reform of Local Self-Government and Public Administration in Kosovo—Final Recommendations". The initial reaction of some local leaders was cautious and critical. The report was currently being reviewed by UNMIK and the Provisional Institutions. In Mitrovica, the UNMIK Administration continued to implement infrastructure projects and service delivery programmes, but Belgrade-supported parallel structures in the northern part of the city continued to exist. Those structures also hampered the work of other municipalities. The Serbia and Montenegro Coordination Centre for Kosovo, whose activities had increased during the reporting period, appeared better organized and funded, executing projects and becoming more committed to providing the Kosovo Serb community with social and administrative services. The Centre wanted to formalize the status of its offices in Kosovo, but declined to provide information on the exact function and responsibilities of each office, as required by UNMIK.

Despite a slight improvement, minority employment at the central and municipal levels remained unsatisfactory. The recent hiring freeze in the Kosovo civil service (see p. 418), except for minority communities, had led to an increase of some 1.5 per cent in the number of minority civil servants, but that was still well below target levels for all of the Provisional Institutions. The record of the Provisional Institutions in placing women in high-level and managerial positions was also poor.

The Government had still not forwarded to the Assembly a draft law on the Independent Media Commission. In the meantime, the Temporary Media Commissioner ensured that the Kosovo media conformed to international standards. As part of that task, the Commissioner issued a revised policy on radio and television licensing, which allowed for limited exceptions to the current licensing moratorium, especially for areas currently underserved by local media and applications for multi-ethnic stations. A contract signed between the public broadcaster, Radio-

Television Kosovo (RTK), and the Kosovo Electricity Company in November established a public broadcasting fee collection system to provide some 57 per cent of RTK's total operating budget.

UNMIK began to prepare for the 2004 Kosovo-wide Assembly elections, with the establishment of the operational arm of the Central Election Commission, whose secretariat would be independent from but supported by the Provisional Institutions. OSCE would retain control over sensitive aspects of the election operation, including the management of the voters list, the operation of the central count and results centre and supervision of the by-mail voter programme. The Elections Working Group continued to meet to formulate recommendations to the Special Representative on the regulatory framework for the 2004 elections, to be presented by the end of January 2004.

UN Interim Administration Mission in Kosovo (UNMIK)

The United Nations Interim Administration Mission in Kosovo, established in June 1999 [YUN 1999, p. 357] to facilitate a political process to determine Kosovo's political future, comprised five components referred to as pillars: interim administration (led by the United Nations); institution-building (led by OSCE); economic reconstruction (led by the EU); humanitarian affairs (led by UNHCR); and police and justice (led by the United Nations). UNMIK was headed by the Special Representative of the Secretary-General. Harri Holkeri replaced Michael Steiner as Special Representative on 13 August (see p. 412).

UNMIK continued to implement its downsizing strategy in line with the approved budget for fiscal year July 2003 to June 2004 (**resolution 57/326**) (see p. 428).

On 1 July, the United Nations Liaison Office in Belgrade and the UNMIK Liaison Office in Belgrade were merged, becoming the United Nations Office in Belgrade, which retained the reporting and liaison functions of both offices.

Sectoral developments

Kosovo minority communities

Minority returns increased during 2003, reaching a total of 3,629 persons, including 1,487 Kosovo Serbs, 1,387 Roma/Ashkali/Egyptians, 377 Bosniacs, 133 Gorani and 245 Kosovo Albanians. While security and freedom of movement remained problematic, returns were occurring in many areas where it would have been previously impossible, including the first Kosovo Serb returns to southern Mitrovica. A key development affecting the return process was the marked increase in the engagement in, and support for, returns and minority integration among senior-level representatives of the Provisional Institutions of Self-Government. In July, Kosovo Albanian and non-Serb minority leaders signed an "open letter" encouraging displaced persons to return, and Kosovo authorities took steps to follow up on that commitment. On 10 July, the President and the leader of the Democratic Party of Kosovo travelled to Urosevac (Gnjilane region) to encourage future returns to the town, while the Kosovo Assembly, in a special session, adopted a resolution supporting returns. The Prime Minister travelled to a returns site in Bica (Pec region) following a shooting incident involving Kosovo Serbs from that village. There were also signs of increasing engagement by Kosovo society generally in support of a more secure environment for all the people of Kosovo. Municipal authorities continued their engagement in the returns process through the municipal working groups formed in 29 of the 30 municipalities. They were constructively engaged in most locations where return projects were being implemented or envisaged, with the notable exception of Pec. The Kosovo Police Service was increasingly engaged in the returns process, participating in most "go and see" visits, inter-ethnic dialogue initiatives and the staffing of police offices in mixed communities. UNMIK initiated a "lessons learned" process to evaluate the results of the current returns season and further develop the 2004 returns strategy (see p. 424). A central feature of the process was to enhance the local component in returns by vesting additional responsibility in local authorities where the political will existed or could be fostered.

UNMIK continued to support the implementation of community-based projects with a wide array of initiatives throughout Kosovo, aimed at fostering inter-ethnic dialogue and cooperation between receiving communities and returnees. Some 20 projects in all four regions had enabled local non-governmental organizations (NGOs) and citizens' initiatives to develop cooperative efforts. Particular emphasis was placed on engaging the municipal-level representatives to ensure their longer-term sustainability. The Government approved a draft anti-discrimination law on 17 September, which complied with EU anti-discrimination regulations and would provide vulnerable groups with effective legal remedies and sanctions against any form of discrimination in the public or private sector.

The 7 million euros allocated by the Kosovo Government from the 2002 Kosovo Consolidated Budget surplus to support returns was directed to a broad range of returns initiatives throughout Kosovo, with 5 million euros used to fill funding gaps in projects endorsed by municipal working groups and included on the Returns Coordination Group's list of priority projects. The remaining 2 million euros was allocated to 39 municipal projects across 21 municipalities that contributed positively to returns.

The 2004 Strategy for Sustainable Returns, launched in December, provided information on funding needs amounting to 38.5 million euros. The Strategy included expanded participation of the Provisional Institutions and internally displaced persons in the return process and an improved information flow to those internally displaced. It also addressed property-related obstacles to return.

Efforts to encourage integration within the educational system continued to encounter substantial resistance from all sides. At midyear, there were 42 mixed or shared schools, although only eight of them taught both Kosovo Serb and Kosovo Albanian children (five in Gnjilane, two in Lipljan and one in Orahovac). All 39 Turkish-language and Bosniac-language schools offered the Albanian language as a subject for Bosnian and Turkish students, but no schools in the Kosovo Serb or Roma communities did so, while schools in the Kosovo Albanian communities did not offer classes in the Serbian language. To address concerns regarding the content of textbooks, a Council on Curriculum and Textbooks was established to ensure that textbooks prescribed in Kosovo schools were non-discriminatory, free from prejudices and did not offend any ethnic community.

Minority community members remained unable to use their own language and alphabet freely throughout Kosovo, including in the Provisional Institutions, municipalities and other public bodies. The translation of official municipal publications into all required languages occurred on a regular basis in only seven municipalities. Official signs were reportedly bilingual in only six municipalities and only partly bilingual in 13, although the Serbian language on those signs was usually blacked out. In 14 municipalities there was zero compliance with the requirement to post bilingual signs.

Access to public services and public utilities throughout Kosovo was still problematic. The Kosovo Electric Company continued to disconnect service to minorities for unpaid debts accumulated by previous illegal occupants. Public enterprises still failed to employ a fair proportion of minorities and remained essentially mono-ethnic.

Judicial system and rule of law

In 2003, progress continued in the prosecution of serious criminal acts, such as war crimes, terrorism and organized crime. Three war crimes trials were completed, with sentences ranging from 3 to 17 years imprisonment. On 27 October, police arrested five Kosovo Albanian males for war crimes committed against other Kosovo Albanians in 1999. The Kosovo Organized Crime Bureau continued to develop its operational and investigative capabilities. An organized crime unit comprising local Kosovo Police Service (KPS) officers was established to work in coordination with and under the supervision of the Crime Bureau. UNMIK continued to successfully address prostitution and human trafficking and its Trafficking and Prostitution Investigation Unit, consisting of UNMIK police and KPS officers, uncovered numerous cases of trafficking, made a number of arrests and closed down many establishments. With UNMIK's acquisition of an electronic surveillance capability, drug seizures and investigations relating to corruption, white-collar fraud, organized crime and terrorism increased. UNMIK also established an Investigation Task Force, comprising representatives from the UN Office of Internal Oversight Services, the EU Anti-fraud Office and the Financial Investigation Unit, to initiate, conduct and coordinate administrative investigations to identify fraud and corruption involving UNMIK, the Provisional Institutions, independent bodies and offices established under the Constitutional Framework, publicly owned enterprises, other entities operating with public assets and any other institution or entity performing activities funded in whole or in part from the Kosovo Consolidated Budget.

UNMIK continued to pursue a regional approach to combating organized crime. On 31 October, it signed a memorandum of understanding on police cooperation with Montenegro, adding to the existing protocols with the Republic of Serbia, the Republic of Albania and the former Yugoslav Republic of Macedonia.

By the end of the year, KPS numbered 5,704 serving officers, including 846 women and 880 minorities. Four additional police stations were placed under its command, bringing the total number of such stations to 10. As the number of KPS officers and its capacity increased, UNMIK further downsized the international civilian police component to a strength of 3,689.

Efforts to increase minority participation in Kosovo's justice system continued with the appointment on 4 December of 26 new Kosovo judges and prosecutors, including six judges and one prosecutor from the Kosovo Serb community. The total number of Kosovo judges increased to 316, 90 per cent of whom were Kosovo Albanians, 5 per cent Kosovo Serbs and 5 per cent from other ethnic groups. Of the 53 prosecutors, some 10 per cent (including 4 per cent Kosovo Serbs) were from minority ethnic groups. Women comprised 25 per cent of judges and 17 per cent of prosecutors. A Municipal Court department and a minor offences court became operational in the Kosovo Serb majority area of Strpce (Gnjilane region), a Court Liaison Office opened in Gracanica (Pristina region) and more were being opened in Novo Brdo (Gnjilane region) and Gorazdevac (Pec region) to increase access to justice for Kosovo Serbs. However, Belgrade had yet to implement the joint declaration signed in July 2002 [YUN 2002, p. 378] on the preservation of pensions and other benefits to facilitate the integration of Kosovo Serbs into the Kosovo judicial and prosecutorial system. Owing to continuing support by the Serbian Government, parallel judicial structures still existed in Leposavic, Zubin Potok and Zvecan (Mitrovica region) and Strpce (Gnjilane region), despite the opening of UNMIK courts in those areas.

Following a riot at Dubrava Prison, Kosovo's largest correctional facility, on 4 September, during which five inmates died and 16 were injured, an independent Commission of Inquiry, comprising local and international members, was established to examine the causes of the riot and make recommendations. In its findings, submitted on 4 November, the Dubrava Commission made wide-ranging recommendations relating to security, living conditions, training and service conditions for correctional staff, funding mechanisms and incident management, which were being addressed. Although prison officials had managed to improve conditions, the situation at Dubrava and other prison facilities remained tense owing to crowded conditions throughout the penal system.

The Kosovo Correctional Service increased its staff to 1,416 (84.9 per cent Kosovo Albanians, 11.2 per cent Kosovo Serbs, 3.8 per cent non-Serbian minorities).

Security situation

Although crime rates continued to decrease in 2003, incidents of violence and crimes against minorities were a cause of concern. On 12 April, an explosion caused serious damage to a railway bridge in northern Kosovo, killing two individuals, one of whom was a Kosovo Protection Corps (KPC) officer, who were purportedly involved in planting the bomb. An ethnic Albanian extremist group claimed responsibility for the attack. On 17 April, the Special Representative issued an administrative direction defining that group as a terrorist organization. Three Kosovo Serb residents in the Obilic municipality (Pristina region) were murdered on 4 June. UNMIK established a Special Police Squad to investigate the crime, working with advisers from both Kosovo Serb and Albanian communities. In the same area, the Kosovo Serb former deputy mayor of Klokot was shot dead on 19 May and two elderly Kosovo Serbs were assaulted.

In a 6 June press statement [SC/7781], the Security Council President said that Council members strongly condemned the Obilic murders and supported the efforts of the Special Representative to investigate the incident and bring the perpetrators to justice. They underscored that such acts undermined the efforts of the international community to foster ethnic reconciliation in Kosovo, and towards building a multi-ethnic and tolerant society and conditions for the safe return of refugees and internally displaced persons.

On 13 August, two Kosovo Serb youths were killed and four injured in a shooting incident in the village of Gorazdevac near Pec. On 18 August, a Kosovo Serb male died of gunshot wounds received on 11 August, and another was seriously injured on 26 August in a shooting incident at the Bica returns site near Klina (Pec region). On 31 August, four Kosovo Serbs were injured and one killed in an explosive attack in the village of Cernica (Gnjilane region). Those violent incidents had further heightened the feelings of insecurity among Kosovo Serbs and led other minorities to keep a low profile. UNMIK police took measures to enhance security in minority areas and other sensitive locations. In three critical areas—the northern part of Mitrovica, Pec town and Pristina town—mobile reserve units conducted random vehicle checkpoints, and patrols targeted high-crime areas.

There was an increase in violent crime against UNMIK law enforcement personnel and property. On 3 August, an UNMIK international police officer was murdered in a sniper attack in the northern part of Kosovo and, on 6 September, an off-duty KPS officer was murdered near Djakovica (Pec region). Another KPS officer was shot at but not injured in Pristina on 10 September, but his companion was killed. Council members, in an 8 August press statement issued by the President [SC/7840], condemned the killing of the UNMIK police officer and appealed to all concerned to cooperate fully with UNMIK and KFOR to identify the perpetrators and bring them to justice.

Security Council consideration. The Council President issued a press statement on 14 August [SC/7845], in which Council members condemned the violence in Kosovo in the strongest terms and extended their condolences to the families affected. They expressed deep concern that four years after the conflict such brutal incidents continued to occur and demanded that no effort be spared to arrest the perpetrators and bring them to justice. Council members recalled that the Provisional Institutions of Self-Government had committed themselves to interethnic reconciliation. They welcomed the arrival of the new Special Representative of the Secretary-General, Harri Holkeri, in Kosovo and stressed that his presence there was much needed.

On 18 August [meeting 4809], the Security Council considered Serbia and Montenegro's request of 14 August [S/2003/815] that the Council discuss urgently the latest developments in Kosovo and Metohija, especially the 13 August terrorist attack in Gorazdevac (see p. 425). Serbia and Montenegro said that those attacks, which occurred as the new Special Representative arrived in Kosovo and Metohija, were aimed at further destabilizing the situation in the province and represented a serious challenge to UNMIK and KFOR authority.

Addressing the Council, Serbia's Deputy Prime Minister, Nebojsa Covic, said that the killings were part of a pattern of activity by a determined Albanian minority seeking to drive all Serbs from Kosovo and Metohija, and to discourage refugees and internally displaced persons from returning. They were also sending a message to the new Special Representative that any of his decisions that did not meet their expectations would result in fresh violence and in the destabilization of the situation. Mr. Covic claimed that UNMIK and KFOR had not done as much as they could, and the international community had to recognize that the actions of Albanian extremist and terrorist groups represented the main threat to the stabilization of Kosovo and Metohija and to the region as a whole. Measures had to be taken that would lead to the full and consistent implementation of resolution 1244(1999) [YUN 1999, p. 353], major progress in the return of internally displaced persons, and security and freedom of movement for all ethnic communities. In that regard, he outlined some urgent steps that were needed to normalize the situation in Kosovo and Metohija: building a multi-ethnic and tolerant community with a solid economic foundation and functioning provisional democratic institutions; equitable implementation of resolution 1244(1999); maintaining the international security forces at least at the current level; full protection by KFOR and UNMIK of the administrative line between central Serbia and Kosovo and Metohija; investigation of ethnically motivated crimes by international law enforcement officials and bringing perpetrators to justice; full protection of witnesses by KFOR and UNMIK; the thorough and energetic disarmament of all citizens of Kosovo and Metohija; the placing of the Albanian National Army on the list of terrorist organizations; investigation of KPC, leading to its abolishment; indictment of perpetrators of war crimes by ICTY and their extradition to The Hague; closer cooperation between the security forces in Kosovo and Metohija with those in the region, and with those of Serbia and Montenegro in particular; the urging of Albanian political leaders to implement their formal support for returns, the democratization of society, the rule of law and inter-ethnic reconciliation; and holding liable officials of the international presence in Kosovo and Metohija who did not fully carry out those measures.

The United Kingdom said that every effort should be made to track down and bring to justice those responsible for the recent series of violent incidents. It welcomed the initiative of the Special Representative in setting up an inquiry and the prompt action of KFOR in deploying 300 men as a strengthened and visible presence. It therefore rejected Mr. Covic's statement about the inertia of the international community as unfounded and unfair. The international community had made clear its rejection of ethnic cleansing in Kosovo, was committed to justice and determined to succeed.

Economic reconstruction and development

Kosovo's economy continued to grow, although the projected rate of 4.5 per cent annual growth for 2003 was lower than in previous years, mainly due to the withdrawal of international donors. The estimated gross domestic product for 2003 was 1.34 billion euros, compared to 1.99 billion euros in 2002, or approximately 700 euros per capita. Growing exports and declining imports contributed to an improved trade balance for 2003 from the 2002 deficit of 1.7 billion euros, but was still grossly negative. Unemployment remained high at between 50 and 60 per cent, with the number of officially registered unemployed numbering 276,000 in July.

Total revenue collected by Customs in 2003 amounted to 424.1 million euros, some 63 million euros over target. On 18 February, the administrative and operational responsibilities for the Tax Administration were formally transferred to the Kosovo Ministry of Finance and Economy. In July, the Ministry outlined proposals to reform and amend Kosovo's tax policy during 2004, including reducing the value added tax threshold from 50,000 to 30,000 euros, transforming the current wage tax into a fully comprehensive personal income tax and absorbing the presumptive tax into the profit tax. A new law on tax administration and procedures was to be drafted. The Government and the Assembly agreed on a draft Customs Code and the Government approved laws on internal trade and on tourism and hotelier activities.

Kosovo continued to make progress in developing its economic legislative framework. The Assembly passed a law on bankruptcy on 13 March, which was promulgated by the Special Representative on 15 April. Laws on public financial management and accountability, on external trade and on telecommunications were promulgated on 12 May, following adjustments to bring them into conformity with resolution 1244(1999) [YUN 1999, p. 353] and the Constitutional Framework. In drafting new legislative acts and revising existing ones, particular attention was given to compatibility with EU standards. A major instrument in that regard was the Stabilization and Association Process Tracking Mechanism of the European Commission, a technical working group designed to support Kosovo in its EU-compatible structural reforms through policy advice and guidance.

On 15 February, the Board of the Kosovo Trust Agency (KTA) adopted its operational policies and procedures, and approved the first six socially owned enterprises for privatization. Preparatory work was completed for a majority of the 480 socially owned enterprises that fell within KTA's purview, in preparation for their privatization or liquidation. As the privatization process entered its operational phase, the Special Representative promulgated, on 9 May, Regulation No. 2003/13 on the Transformation of the Right of Use to Socially Owned Immovable Property (referred to as the "land use" regulation), converting land use rights held by those enterprises into 99-year leaseholds. The Special Chamber of the Supreme Court, which became operational on 16 June, would adjudicate claims submitted by persons who believed that their rights had been violated by the privatization process. By October, the first six privatization tenders were in the final phase of the process. A second group of 18 socially owned enterprises was tendered on 2 July and a third group of 24 on 10 September.

The Office of Auditor General was established and local auditors were being recruited and trained. Audits were carried out in a number of publicly owned enterprises during the year, including the Kosovo Electricity Company (KEK), the Post and Telecommunications Company, UNMIK Railways, Pristina Airport and the major publicly owned utilities in the water, waste and irrigation sectors. The audits revealed shortcomings in accounting, corporate governance and human resources. KTA was following up on the audit recommendations, while the Investigation Task Force would follow up on cases of suspected fraud and misappropriations of resources. External audits and additional examinations by the Banking and Payments Authority of Kosovo were being carried out annually for all banks.

The energy situation remained a significant problem, as less than 40 per cent of the electricity supplied was paid for by customers, making it difficult for KEK to maintain a constant power supply. That, in turn, was a major deterrent to foreign investment and inhibited economic development.

OIOS report. In response to General Assembly resolutions 48/218 B [YUN 1994, p. 1362] and 54/244 [YUN 1999, p. 1274], the Secretary-General, by a 13 November note [A/58/592], transmitted the report of the Office of Internal Oversight Services (OIOS) on the results of its investigation into the fraudulent diversion of $4.3 million by a senior staff member of the UNMIK economic reconstruction pillar (pillar IV), administered by the EU. The investigation, conducted in cooperation with the European Anti-Fraud Office of the European Commission, examined reports alleging significant acts of fraud in excess of $4.3 million by Jo Hans Dieter Trutschler. The investigation established that Mr. Trutschler had caused the public electric company in Serbia to transfer $4.3 million derived from the sale of electricity on the power grid of the former Yugoslavia, and due to KEK, to a bank account under his control in Gibraltar and subsequently to his offshore account in Belize to evade recovery of the funds after they were discovered missing. OIOS confirmed that Mr. Trutschler had obtained a further amount of 220,000 euros of UNMIK funds through the submission of false invoices, and had fraudulently made use of an academic title and provided false information about his academic, professional and personal achievements on recruitment. In July 2002, the case was referred to the authorities in Germany, the country of his citizenship, where he was convicted and sentenced to a prison term of three years and six months. Most of the funds had been recovered. OIOS concluded that the employment of Mr. Trutschler without background or reference checks was a significant and alarming breakdown in human resources–related due diligence, which was mitigated neither by exigency nor by the fact that the European Agency for Reconstruction, not UNMIK, financed the contract. More alarming was the lack of management oversight, which allowed the abuses to occur and Mr. Trutschler to avoid being made to account for the failures in the execution of his responsibilities.

OIOS made a number of recommendations to correct the situation and prevent further acts of that nature, including that UNMIK's reconstruction pillar should devise standard written administrative and management procedures for personnel and financial functions, and UNMIK management should urgently review the operations of pillar IV to ensure that proper management and supervisory controls were enacted.

Financing

On 18 June [meeting 90], the General Assembly, having considered the financial performance report for UNMIK for the period 1 July 2001 to 30 June 2002 [YUN 2002, p. 382], the proposed budget for the period 1 July 2003 to 30 June 2004 [ibid.] and the comments and recommendations of ACABQ thereon [A/57/772/Add.5], adopted, on the recommendation of the Fifth Committee [A/57/827], **resolution 57/326** without vote [agenda item 128].

Financing of the United Nations Interim Administration Mission in Kosovo

The General Assembly,

Having considered the reports of the Secretary-General on the financing of the United Nations Interim Administration Mission in Kosovo and the related reports of the Advisory Committee on Administrative and Budgetary Questions,

Recalling Security Council resolution 1244(1999) of 10 June 1999 regarding the establishment of the United Nations Interim Administration Mission in Kosovo,

Recalling also its resolution 53/241 of 28 July 1999 on the financing of the Mission and its subsequent resolutions thereon, the latest of which was resolution 56/295 of 27 June 2002,

Acknowledging the complexity of the Mission,

Reaffirming the general principles underlying the financing of United Nations peacekeeping operations as stated in its resolutions 1874(S-IV) of 27 June 1963, 3101(XXVIII) of 11 December 1973 and 55/235 of 23 December 2000,

Mindful of the fact that it is essential to provide the Mission with the necessary financial resources to enable it to fulfil its responsibilities under the relevant resolution of the Security Council,

1. *Takes note* of the status of contributions to the United Nations Interim Administration Mission in Kosovo as at 31 March 2003, including the contributions outstanding in the amount of 105.2 million United States dollars, representing some 7 per cent of the total assessed contributions, notes with concern that only thirty-three Member States have paid their assessed contributions in full, and urges all other Member States, in particular those in arrears, to ensure payment of their outstanding assessed contributions;

2. *Expresses its appreciation* to those Member States which have paid their assessed contributions in full, and urges all other Member States to make every possible effort to ensure payment of their assessed contributions to the Mission in full;

3. *Expresses concern* at the financial situation with regard to peacekeeping activities, in particular as regards the reimbursements to troop contributors that bear additional burdens owing to overdue payments by Member States of their assessments;

4. *Also expresses concern* at the delay experienced by the Secretary-General in deploying and providing adequate resources to some recent peacekeeping missions, in particular those in Africa;

5. *Emphasizes* that all future and existing peacekeeping missions shall be given equal and non-discriminatory treatment in respect of financial and administrative arrangements;

6. *Also emphasizes* that all peacekeeping missions shall be provided with adequate resources for the effective and efficient discharge of their respective mandates;

7. *Reiterates its request* to the Secretary-General to make the fullest possible use of facilities and equipment at the United Nations Logistics Base at Brindisi, Italy, in order to minimize the costs of procurement for the Mission;

8. *Endorses* the conclusions and recommendations contained in the report of the Advisory Committee on Administrative and Budgetary Questions, and requests the Secretary-General to ensure their full implementation;

9. *Requests* the Secretary-General to take all necessary action to ensure that the Mission is administered with a maximum of efficiency and economy;

10. *Also requests* the Secretary-General, in order to reduce the cost of employing General Service staff, to continue efforts to recruit local staff for the Mission against General Service posts, commensurate with the requirements of the Mission;

Financial performance report for the period from 1 July 2001 to 30 June 2002

11. *Takes note* of the report of the Secretary-General on the financial performance of the Mission for the period from 1 July 2001 to 30 June 2002;

Budget estimates for the period from 1 July 2003 to 30 June 2004

12. *Decides* to appropriate to the Special Account for the United Nations Interim Administration Mission in Kosovo the amount of 329,737,100 dollars for the period from 1 July 2003 to 30 June 2004, inclusive of 315,518,200 dollars for the maintenance of the Mission, 10,887,900 dollars for the support account for peacekeeping operations and 3,331,000 dollars for the United Nations Logistics Base;

Financing of the appropriation

13. *Decides also* to apportion among Member States the amount of 329,737,100 dollars at a monthly rate of 27,478,092 dollars, in accordance with the levels set out in resolution 55/235, as adjusted by the General Assembly in its resolutions 55/236 of 23 December 2000 and 57/290 A of 20 December 2002, and taking into account the scale of assessments for 2003, as set out in its resolutions 55/5 B of 23 December 2000 and 57/4 B of 20 December 2002, and for 2004;

14. *Decides further* that, in accordance with the provisions of its resolution 973(X) of 15 December 1955, there shall be set off against the apportionment among Member States, as provided for in paragraph 13 above, their respective share in the Tax Equalization Fund of

22,354,400 dollars at a monthly rate of 1,862,867 dollars, comprising the estimated staff assessment income of 19,704,400 dollars approved for the Mission, the prorated share of 2,453,100 dollars of the estimated staff assessment income approved for the support account, and the prorated share of 196,900 dollars of the estimated staff assessment income approved for the United Nations Logistics Base;

15. *Decides* that for Member States that have fulfilled their financial obligations to the Mission, there shall be set off against their apportionment, as provided for in paragraph 13 above, their respective share of the unencumbered balance and other income in the total amount of 63,626,000 dollars in respect of the financial period ended 30 June 2002, in accordance with the levels set out in resolution 55/235, as adjusted by the General Assembly in its resolutions 55/236 and 57/290 A, and taking into account the scale of assessments for 2002 as set out in its resolutions 55/5 B and 57/4 B;

16. *Decides also* that for Member States that have not fulfilled their financial obligations to the Mission, there shall be set off against their outstanding obligations their respective share of the unencumbered balance and other income in the total amount of 63,626,000 dollars in respect of the financial period ended 30 June 2002 in accordance with the scheme set out in paragraph 15 above;

17. *Decides further* that the decrease of 506,200 dollars in the estimated staff assessment income in respect of the financial period ended 30 June 2002 shall be set off against the credits from the amount referred to in paragraphs 15 and 16 above;

18. *Emphasizes* that no peacekeeping mission shall be financed by borrowing funds from other active peacekeeping missions;

19. *Encourages* the Secretary-General to continue to take additional measures to ensure the safety and security of all personnel under the auspices of the United Nations participating in the Mission;

20. *Invites* voluntary contributions to the Mission in cash and in the form of services and supplies acceptable to the Secretary-General, to be administered, as appropriate, in accordance with the procedure and practices established by the General Assembly;

21. *Decides* to include in the provisional agenda of its fifty-eighth session the item entitled "Financing of the United Nations Interim Administration Mission in Kosovo".

In December, the Secretary-General submitted the performance report [A/58/634] for UNMIK for the period 1 July 2002 to 30 June 2003 and the proposed budget [A/58/638] for the period 1 July 2004 to 30 June 2005.

International security presence (KFOR)

During the year, the Secretary-General submitted to the Security Council, in accordance with resolution 1244(1999) [YUN 1999, p. 353], reports on the activities of the international security presence in Kosovo (KFOR), also known as Operation Joint Guard, covering the periods 1 December 2002 to 31 May 2003 [S/2003/130, S/2003/301, S/2003/378, S/2003/511, S/2003/616, S/2003/682], 1 July to 31 August [S/2003/855, S/2003/931] and 1 to 31 October [S/2003/1141]. A later report covered activities from 1 to 31 December [S/2004/98]. As at 31 December, the force, which operated under NATO leadership, comprised 19,168 troops.

KFOR continued to conduct intelligence-based surveillance operations and patrols throughout the province to stop illegal activities and weapons smuggling, and to minimize the risk of terrorist activity. The largest seizure of weapons occurred in March, when 150 assorted weapons, 198 grenades and mines and 102,290 rounds of ammunition were confiscated, including 97,500 rounds on the Beli Drim River, the largest in a single operation since 1999.

KFOR continued to monitor the border areas with Albania and the former Yugoslav Republic of Macedonia for persons attempting to enter Kosovo illegally. It also began to support UNMIK in its efforts to increase security measures at the Administrative Boundary Line bordering the Presevo Valley in Serbia, following reports that extremists in the Kosovska Kamenica and Gnjilane areas were about to move towards Bujanovac and Presevo.

KFOR continued to provide assistance on request to international organizations and NGOs working throughout Kosovo, and to provide security assistance in support of UNMIK police operations. The KFOR Commander and the Special Representative co-chaired the Civil Protection Development Group, established to engage the international community and KPC as partners in the development of KPC.

Relations with Serbia and Montenegro

During 2003, contacts between UNMIK and Serbia and Montenegro continued within the framework of the UNMIK–Serbia and Montenegro High-Ranking Working Group. However, a planned meeting of the Group did not take place owing to preconditions set by Belgrade. As a result, the protocol on the recognition of Kosovo licence plates was not signed.

While efforts continued to establish political dialogue between Belgrade and Pristina (see p. 418), limited working-level contacts took place in the area of transport and communications, as did regular working contacts with regard to the return of internally displaced persons. The second meeting of the Working Group on Cultural Issues took place in May and made progress on preservation of cultural heritage and the return of documentation. Constructive working-level cooperation between the two sides continued in police cooperation, cross-boundary repatriation of human remains and exchange of experts and expertise on missing persons. The Kosovo Ministry of Labour and Social Welfare held regular monthly meetings with counterparts in Belgrade, leading to the transfer of more than 50 mentally disabled adults and children to their original homes.

Former Yugoslav Republic of Macedonia

Relations with Greece

Pursuant to the 13 September 1995 Interim Accord on the normalization of relations between the former Yugoslav Republic of Macedonia (FYROM) and Greece [YUN 1995, p. 599], representatives of both countries met three times during 2003 (24 April, 6 June and 27 August), under the auspices of the Secretary-General. The countries exchanged views in the context of article 5 of the Accord, which provided for the continuation of negotiations with a view to reaching agreement on their differences, as described in Security Council resolutions 817(1993) [YUN 1993, p. 208] and 845(1993) [ibid., p. 209], concerning the name of the State of FYROM. They decided to meet again at a date to be agreed upon.

Georgia

In 2003, efforts intensified to advance the Georgian/Abkhaz peace process, which had stalled when the two parties failed to begin discussions of the 2001 Basic Principles for the Distribution of Competences between Tbilisi (Georgia's Government) and Sukhumi (the Abkhaz leadership) [YUN 2001, p. 386], which were intended to serve as a basis for substantive negotiations over the status of Abkhazia as a sovereign entity within the State of Georgia. Senior officials of the Group of Friends of the Secretary-General (France, Germany, Russian Federation, United Kingdom, United States) met twice in Geneva in an effort to overcome the political impasse. They recommended that the Georgian and Abkhaz sides work in parallel on economic issues, the return of internally displaced persons and refugees, and political and security issues, with the help of task forces on each of the issues. That initiative was given a further boost by the March meeting between the Presidents of Georgia and the Russian Federation, and a high-level meeting of the parties in July, chaired by the Special Representative of the Secretary-General, and with the participation of the Group of Friends. The two leaders agreed to create working groups to address the issues of the return of refugees and internally displaced persons to the Gali district, the reopening of railway traffic between Sochi and Tbilisi and energy projects. They also agreed that the opening of the railway would proceed in parallel with the return of refugees and displaced persons. Unfortunately, although there was some advance on those issues, no progress was made with regard to the core political issue as the Abkhaz side maintained its refusal to discuss the document on Basic Principles for the Distribution of Competences between Tbilisi and Sukhumi. That process was further delayed by the complex political situation on both sides of the ceasefire line and the events that led to the resignation of Georgia's President, Eduard Shevardnadze, in November. The situation on the ground deteriorated in October, especially in the Gali district, which further hindered any progress in the return of refugees and displaced persons.

UN Observer Mission in Georgia

The United Nations Observer Mission in Georgia (UNOMIG), established by Security Council resolution 858(1993) [YUN 1993, p. 509], continued to monitor and verify compliance with the 1994 Agreement on a Ceasefire and Separation of Forces (Moscow Agreement) [YUN 1994, p. 583] and to fulfil other tasks as mandated by Council resolution 937(1994) [ibid., p. 584]. The Mission operated in close collaboration with the collective peacekeeping forces of the Commonwealth of Independent States (CIS) that had been in the zone of conflict, at the request of the parties, since 1994 [ibid., p. 583]. The Council extended the Mission's mandate twice during the year, the first time until 31 July 2003 (see p. 431) and the second until 31 January 2004 (see p. 435). The Council also added a civilian police component of 20 officers to the Mission to strengthen its capacity to fulfil its mandate.

UNOMIG's main headquarters was located in Sukhumi (Abkhazia, Georgia), with some administrative headquarters in Pitsunda, a liaison office in the Georgian capital of Tbilisi, and team bases and a sector headquarters in each of the Gali and Zugdidi sectors. A team base in the Kodori Valley was manned by observers operating from Sukhumi. As at December 2003, UNOMIG had a strength of 118 military observers and 10 civilian police officers.

Heidi Tagliavini (Switzerland) continued as the Secretary-General's Special Representative for Georgia and Head of UNOMIG. She was assisted by Major General Kazi Ashfaq Ahmed (Bangladesh), UNOMIG's Chief Military Observer.

Political aspects of the conflict

Report of Secretary-General (January). The Secretary-General, in a 13 January report [S/2003/39] describing the situation in Abkhazia, Georgia, and UNOMIG operations there since his October 2002 report [YUN 2002, p. 389], observed that, after a year of strenuous efforts by the Special Representative and the Group of Friends, the two sides had not moved any closer to the start of negotiations based on the document "Basic Principles for the Distribution of Competences between Tbilisi and Sukhumi" and its transmittal letter [YUN 2001, p. 386]. Indeed, the tone of the parties had hardened, there was a deep mistrust between them and they showed little willingness to make the substantive compromises necessary for a meaningful peace process. The Abkhaz side, in particular, refused even to enter into discussions on the principles on which negotiations should be based. In an effort to overcome the current impasse, the Secretary-General intended to invite senior representatives of the Group of Friends to an informal brainstorming session on the way ahead (see p. 433). The Secretary-General stated that the resumption of Coordinating Council meetings, the last of which was held in January 2001 [YUN 2001, p. 378], was essential for further progress to be made in the peace process and, in particular, to turn the recommendations of its working groups into firm commitments. A prompt convening of the Council's next session would also make it possible for a timely decision to be made on convening the fourth conference on confidence-building, which had not met since March 2001 [ibid., p. 377].

On the question of the return of internally displaced persons, no progress was made in the implementation of the 1994 quadripartite agreement on the voluntary return of refugees and displaced persons [YUN 1994, p. 581]. In that regard, the recommendations of the November 2000 joint assessment mission to the Gali district [YUN 2000, p. 397] should be implemented. On the specific issue of strengthening law enforcement institutions, the Secretary-General noted that an assessment mission agreed to in 2002 [YUN 2002, p. 393] had been conducted, and welcomed the full cooperation of the two sides as a positive sign of their willingness to improve the situation for returnees and internally displaced persons.

As UNOMIG's presence remained essential for maintaining stability in the conflict zone and for pursuing the process towards a political settlement of the conflict, the Secretary-General recommended a further extension of its mandate until 31 July 2003.

SECURITY COUNCIL ACTION

On 30 January [meeting 4697], the Security Council unanimously adopted **resolution 1462 (2003)**. The draft [S/2003/102] was prepared in consultations among Council members.

The Security Council,

Recalling all its relevant resolutions, in particular resolution 1427(2002) of 29 July 2002,

Having considered the report of the Secretary-General of 13 January 2003,

Recalling the conclusions of the summits of the Organization for Security and Cooperation in Europe held in Lisbon in December 1996 and in Istanbul on 18 and 19 November 1999, regarding the situation in Abkhazia, Georgia,

Recalling also the relevant principles contained in the Convention on the Safety of United Nations and Associated Personnel of 9 December 1994,

Recalling further its condemnation of the shooting down of a helicopter of the United Nations Observer Mission in Georgia on 8 October 2001, which resulted in the death of the nine people on board, and deploring the fact that the perpetrators of that attack have still not been identified,

Stressing that the continued lack of progress on key issues of a comprehensive settlement of the conflict in Abkhazia, Georgia, is unacceptable,

Welcoming the important contributions made by the Mission and the collective peacekeeping force of the Commonwealth of Independent States in stabilizing the situation in the zone of conflict, and stressing its attachment to the close cooperation existing between them in the performance of their respective mandates,

1. *Welcomes* the report of the Secretary-General of 13 January 2003;

2. *Reaffirms* the commitment of all Member States to the sovereignty, independence and territorial integrity of Georgia within its internationally recognized borders, and the necessity to define the status of Abkhazia within the State of Georgia in strict accordance with these principles;

3. *Commends and strongly supports* the sustained efforts of the Secretary-General and his Special Representative, with the assistance of the Russian Federation in its capacity as facilitator, as well as of the Group of Friends of the Secretary-General and the Organization for Security and Cooperation in Europe, to promote the stabilization of the situation and the achievement of a comprehensive political settlement, which must include a settlement of the political status of Abkhazia within the State of Georgia;

4. *Reiterates, in particular, its support* for the document on "Basic Principles for the Distribution of Competences between Tbilisi and Sukhumi" and for its letter of transmittal, finalized by, and with the full support of, all members of the Group of Friends of the Secretary-General;

5. *Regrets* the lack of progress on the initiation of political status negotiations, and recalls once again that the purpose of those documents is to facilitate meaningful negotiations between the parties, under the leadership of the United Nations, on the status of Abkhazia within the State of Georgia and is not an attempt to impose or dictate any specific solution to the parties;

6. *Underlines further* the fact that the process of negotiation leading to a lasting political settlement acceptable to both sides will require concessions from both sides;

7. *Deeply regrets*, in particular, the repeated refusal of the Abkhaz side to agree to a discussion on the substance of that document, again strongly urges the Abkhaz side to receive the document and its letter of transmittal, urges both parties thereafter to give them full and open consideration, and to engage in constructive negotiations on their substance, and urges those having influence with the parties to promote this outcome;

8. *Welcomes*, in that regard, the intention of the Secretary-General to invite senior representatives of the Group of Friends to an informal brainstorming session on the way ahead;

9. *Calls upon* the parties to spare no efforts to overcome their ongoing mutual mistrust;

10. *Condemns* any violations of the provisions of the Agreement on a Ceasefire and Separation of Forces signed in Moscow on 14 May 1994;

11. *Welcomes* the decrease of tensions in the Kodori Valley and the intention reaffirmed by the parties to resolve the situation peacefully, recalls its strong support for the protocol signed by the two sides on 2 April 2002 regarding the situation in the Kodori Valley, calls upon both sides, and in particular the Georgian side, to continue to fully implement this protocol, and recognizes the legitimate security concerns of the civilian populations in the area, calls upon the political leaders in Tbilisi and Sukhumi to observe security agreements, and calls upon both sides to spare no efforts to agree on a mutually acceptable arrangement for security of the population in, and in the vicinity of, the Kodori Valley;

12. *Calls upon* the Georgian side to continue to improve security for joint patrols of the United Nations Observer Mission in Georgia and the collective peacekeeping force of the Commonwealth of Independent States in the Kodori Valley to enable them to monitor the situation independently and regularly;

13. *Strongly urges* the parties to ensure the necessary revitalization of the peace process in all its major aspects, to resume their work in the Coordinating Council and its relevant mechanisms, to build on the results of the third meeting on confidence-building measures between the Georgian and Abkhaz sides, held in Yalta, Ukraine, on 15 and 16 March 2001, to implement the proposals agreed on that occasion in a purposeful and cooperative manner, and to consider holding a fourth conference on confidence-building measures;

14. *Stresses* the urgent need for progress on the question of refugees and internally displaced persons, calls upon both sides to display a genuine commitment to make returns the focus of special attention and to undertake this task in close coordination with the Mission, reaffirms the unacceptability of the demographic changes resulting from the conflict, reaffirms also the inalienable right of all refugees and internally displaced persons affected by the conflict to return to their homes in secure and dignified conditions, in accordance with international law and as set out in the Quadripartite Agreement on the Voluntary Return of Refugees and Displaced Persons of 4 April 1994 and the Yalta Declaration, recalls that the Abkhaz side bears a particular responsibility to protect the returnees and to facilitate the return of the remaining displaced population, and requests further measures to be undertaken, inter alia, by the United Nations Development Programme, the Office of the United Nations High Commissioner for Refugees and the Office for the Coordination of Humanitarian Affairs of the Secretariat to create conditions conducive to the return of refugees and internally displaced persons, including through quick-impact projects, to develop their skills and to increase their self-reliance, with full respect for their inalienable right to return to their homes in secure and dignified conditions;

15. *Once again urges* the parties to implement the recommendations of the joint assessment mission to the Gali district, carried out under the aegis of the United Nations, welcomes the recent visit of a United Nations police assessment team to the Gali and Zugdidi sectors, looks forward to its recommendations, and calls in particular upon the Abkhaz side to improve law enforcement involving the local population and to address the lack of instruction in their mother tongue for the ethnic Georgian population;

16. *Calls upon* both parties publicly to dissociate themselves from militant rhetoric and demonstrations of support for military options and for the activities of illegal armed groups, and encourages the Georgian side in particular to continue its efforts to put an end to the activities of illegal armed groups;

17. *Welcomes* the additional safeguards for helicopter flights instituted in response to the shooting down of a helicopter of the Mission on 8 October 2001, calls once again upon the parties to take all necessary steps to identify those responsible for the incident, to bring them to justice and to inform the Special Representative on the implementation of these steps;

18. *Underlines* the fact that it is the primary responsibility of both sides to provide appropriate security and to ensure the freedom of movement of the Mission, the collective peacekeeping force and other international personnel;

19. *Welcomes* the constant review by the Mission of its security arrangements in order to ensure the highest possible level of security for its staff;

20. *Decides* to extend the mandate of the Mission for a new period terminating on 31 July 2003, and to review further that mandate unless a decision on the presence of the collective peacekeeping force is taken by 15 February 2003;

21. *Requests* the Secretary-General to continue to keep the Security Council regularly informed and to report three months from the date of the adoption of the present resolution on the situation in Abkhazia, Georgia;

22. *Decides* to remain actively seized of the matter.

Communication. In a 30 January letter to the Security Council President [S/2003/117], Georgia reiterated its unwavering commitment to the "Basic Principles for the Distribution of Competences between Tbilisi and Sukhumi" and explained the challenges that the situation in Abkhazia, Georgia, posed, setting them as a benchmark against which the responses of those involved in the peace process, especially the Russian Federation, were to be measured.

Georgia deplored the relatively new Security Council practice of linking the renewal of UNOMIG's mandate to that of the CIS peacekeeping forces. In fact, UNOMIG's operational capabilities were limited to merely reporting on events in the conflict zone and cast doubt on the leading role of the United Nations in the peace process. The current status quo was unacceptable and untenable, and decisive actions were needed to bring the peace process on track, including consideration of the possibility of resorting to measures under Chapter VII of the Charter, which provided for the use of armed intervention. It was high time the Council took a genuine lead in the peace process, including the launching of effective UN peacekeeping operations parallel to meaningful political negotiations on the basis of the paper on the distribution of constitutional competences, and ensured the return of displaced persons to Abkhazia, Georgia.

Report of Secretary-General (April). In a 9 April report on the situation in Abkhazia, Georgia [S/2003/412], the Secretary-General stated that, at his invitation, senior representatives of the Group of Friends convened, under the chairmanship of the Under-Secretary-General for Peacekeeping Operations, and with the participation of the Special Representative, for an informal brainstorming session (Geneva, 19-20 February) on the way ahead in the Georgian-Abkhaz peace process. The Group recommended that the Georgian and Abkhaz sides work in parallel on economic issues, the return of internally displaced persons and refugees, and political and security issues, and that three task forces be established for that purpose, with the participation of representatives of the parties, the Group of Friends and external experts under UN chairmanship. They would assess the progress on each of the issues in June and, depending on their evaluation, the Group would pursue further steps, including the possibility of convening a fourth conference on confidence-building measures to address all aspects of the peace process, including the substance of the three task forces and other projects aimed at rebuilding confidence between the sides.

On 3 March, for the first time in approximately four years, the Group of Friends was received at the ambassadorial level by the Abkhaz de facto authorities in Sukhumi. They conveyed the recommendations resulting from the Geneva session, presented the international community's position and listened to the Abkhaz viewpoint. The Abkhaz side raised a number of objections to the Group's recommendations, in particular the inclusion of the political aspect in the third task force. It maintained its refusal to discuss the status issue and rejection of the paper on competences as a basis for substantive negotiations as, in its view, Abkhazia's status had long been determined. While the Abkhaz side had not formulated its final position with regard to the Geneva recommendations, the Georgian side took a cautiously positive stance towards them, declaring its readiness to work towards their implementation. Meanwhile, UNOMIG continued preparatory work for launching the task forces once final approval had been received from both sides. At the same time, the Coordinating Council remained suspended, with neither the Council itself nor its three working groups being able to convene.

The period was also marked by increased high-level bilateral activity between the Russian Federation and Georgia. During the informal summit of CIS heads of State (Kyiv, Ukraine, 28-29 January), Russian Federation President Vladimir Putin and Georgian President Eduard Shevardnadze discussed the re-establishment of the railway link between Sochi and Tbilisi and the return of internally displaced persons and refugees. At a later meeting (Sochi, 6-7 March), the two Presidents agreed to create working groups to address those two issues and the question of energy projects, including the modernization of the hydroelectric power station, Inguri-GES. It was understood that the opening of the railway would proceed in parallel with the return of the refugees and internally displaced persons. The Abkhaz de facto Prime Minister, Gennadi Gagulia, took part in some of the deliberations in Sochi.

In February, the Secretary-General's Special Representative for Georgia briefed OSCE and EU officials on the situation in the country. Subsequently, an ad hoc delegation of the European Parliament (24-28 February), the OSCE High Commissioner on National Minorities, Rolf Ekéus (25-27 March), and OSCE Permanent Representatives (27 March–1 April) visited Georgia, including Abkhazia, to meet with Georgian government officials and the Abkhaz de facto authorities and to familiarize themselves with the situation in the area. In Sukhumi, Mr. Ekéus raised the issue of the language of instruction in schools in the Gali district and discussed the situation of persons belonging to national and ethnic minorities in the region.

On 18 March, the Abkhaz de facto Parliament adopted a proposal, addressed to the Council of Federation and the State Duma of the Russian Federation, calling for the establishment of associated relations between Abkhazia and the Russian Federation. The Georgian authorities objected, stressing that it would be a violation of international legal norms.

Communications. Georgia, in a 16 May letter to the Security Council President [S/2003/547], said that the Geneva high-level brainstorming session and the Sochi meeting between the Russian Federation and Georgian Presidents gave new impetus to the peace process in Abkhazia, Georgia; implementation of the Geneva session recommendations could and should play an indispensable role in a reinvigorated and strengthened UN-led peace process. Georgia appealed to the Group of Friends and the Special Representative to intensify efforts to make the best use of opportunities opened by the Geneva session, as a way to provide for greater and more active involvement of the Council in the peace process.

On 22 May [S/2003/569], Georgia transmitted to the Council President a 19 May statement of its National Security Council, in which it expressed concern over attempts to implement separately the part of the agreements reached at Sochi between the Georgian and Russian Federation Presidents (see p. 433) relating to the restoration of railway communication between the two countries, but not fulfilling, or fulfilling only partially, the agreement on the parallel return of refugees and forcibly displaced persons. The National Security Council declared the partial selective implementation of the Sochi agreements to be unacceptable, and the unilateral restoration of railway communication without Georgia's agreement and before the start of the process of the organized and safe return of the expelled population to be illegal. It reserved the right to demand appropriate explanations and to take adequate measures.

Report of Secretary-General (July). On 21 July [S/2003/751], the Secretary-General reported that his Special Representative was continuing efforts to build upon the positive momentum begun at the February brainstorming session of the Group of Friends (see p. 433). She met with representatives of the Group in New York in May, and consulted with Valery Loshchinin, President Putin's Special Representative for the Georgian-Abkhaz conflict, in Tbilisi in April and in Moscow in June and July. She also met with Rudolf Perina, the United States Special Negotiator for Eurasian Conflicts, in New York in May. The senior representatives of the Group of Friends agreed to meet again in Geneva in July. The Georgian and Abkhaz sides accepted invitations to participate in a part of that meeting.

Of the three sets of issues identified as key in advancing the peace process at the Geneva brainstorming session (see p. 433), work on two of them—economic cooperation and refugee return—was actively pursued by the Russian Federation and Georgia within the framework of the agreements reached by the two Presidents in Sochi. Three bilateral working groups were established and UNOMIG provided expertise to them, while representatives of the UNHCR Tbilisi office attended working group meetings on the return of refugees and internally displaced persons. The Abkhaz side participated in the consultations on energy issues and was briefed about the outcome of the other working groups. The Georgian side stressed the need to proceed in parallel on railway restoration and refugee return and highlighted that the activities of all three bilateral working groups and their outcomes would best be discussed within the framework of the Geneva brainstorming session recommendations.

While the parties moved ahead on economic cooperation and refugee return, little notable progress was made on political and security matters, including the future status of Abkhazia within the State of Georgia, and the question of security guarantees. The Special Representative explored with the two sides the possibility of launching consultations on those topics. Following consultations with the Russian Federation on the Abkhaz readiness to participate in a meeting on security guarantees within the framework of the Geneva recommendations, and with the Georgian side and representatives of the Group of Friends, the Special Representative was able to convene such a meeting on 15 July, during which views were exchanged on the issue and on procedural questions. As the Abkhaz side had expressed its willingness to resume participation in the Coordinating Council, the Special Representative consulted with both sides to identify an opportune time for resuming the Council's work.

Those efforts took place against the background of internal developments affecting both the Abkhaz and Georgian sides. On 7 April, the Abkhaz de facto government, headed by Gennadi Gagulia, resigned, and was succeeded on 22 April by Raul Khadzhimba, the former de facto Minister of Defence. The Georgian side continued to be sharply critical of the ongoing campaign by the Abkhaz side to acquire Russian citizenship, the functioning of the Sochi-Sukhumi railway and the flow of private, mainly Russian, investment to the area. The Abkhaz side, for its part, was disturbed by statements of some Georgian politicians that the military option for resolving the conflict had not been completely ruled out.

The Secretary-General, while expressing strong support for the enhanced cooperation between the two sides, regretted that the core political issue of the future status of Abkhazia within the State of Georgia still had not been addressed. He recommended a further extension of UNOMIG's mandate until 31 January 2004, with the addition of a civilian police component of 20 officers to strengthen its capacity to carry out its mandate and, in particular, to contribute to the creation of conditions conducive to the safe and dignified return of internally displaced persons and refugees.

Security Council consideration (July). The Security Council held two meetings on 30 July: the first [meeting 4799], held in private, considered the agenda item "The situation in Georgia" and the second [meeting 4800] considered the Secretary-General's 21 July report on the situation in Abkhazia, Georgia (see p. 434). At the end of the private meeting, the Council issued an official communiqué [S/PV.4799], indicating that it was briefed during that session by the Secretary-General's Special Representative and had a constructive exchange of views with her and with the representative of Georgia.

SECURITY COUNCIL ACTION

On 30 July [meeting 4800], the Security Council unanimously adopted **resolution 1494(2003).** The draft [S/2003/771] was prepared in consultations among Council members.

The Security Council,

Recalling all its relevant resolutions, in particular resolution 1462(2003) of 30 January 2003,

Having considered the report of the Secretary-General of 21 July 2003,

Recalling the conclusions of the summits of the Organization for Security and Cooperation in Europe held in Lisbon in December 1996 and in Istanbul on 18 and 19 November 1999, regarding the situation in Abkhazia, Georgia,

Recalling also the relevant principles contained in the Convention on the Safety of United Nations and Associated Personnel of 9 December 1994,

Deploring that the perpetrators of the shooting down of a helicopter of the United Nations Observer Mission in Georgia on 8 October 2001, which resulted in the death of the nine people on board, have still not been identified,

Stressing that the continued lack of progress on key issues of a comprehensive settlement of the conflict in Abkhazia, Georgia, is unacceptable,

Welcoming, however, the positive momentum given to the United Nations-led peace process by the two high-level meetings of the Group of Friends of the Secretary-General in Geneva and the subsequent meeting of the Presidents of Georgia and the Russian Federation in Sochi, Russian Federation,

Welcoming also the important contributions made by the Mission and the collective peacekeeping force of the Commonwealth of Independent States in stabilizing the situation in the zone of conflict, and stressing its attachment to the close cooperation existing between them in the performance of their respective mandates,

1. *Welcomes* the report of the Secretary-General of 21 July 2003;
2. *Reaffirms* the commitment of all Member States to the sovereignty, independence and territorial integrity of Georgia within its internationally recognized borders, and the necessity to define the status of Abkhazia within the State of Georgia in strict accordance with these principles;
3. *Commends and strongly supports* the sustained efforts of the Secretary-General and his Special Representative, with the assistance of the Russian Federation in its capacity as facilitator, as well as of the Group of Friends of the Secretary-General and the Organization for Security and Cooperation in Europe, to promote the stabilization of the situation and the achievement of a comprehensive political settlement, which must include a settlement of the political status of Abkhazia within the State of Georgia;
4. *Stresses, in particular, its strong support* for the document on "Basic Principles for the Distribution of Competences between Tbilisi and Sukhumi" and for its letter of transmittal, finalized by, and with the full support of, all members of the Group of Friends of the Secretary-General;
5. *Deeply regrets* the continued refusal of the Abkhaz side to agree to a discussion on the substance of that document, again strongly urges the Abkhaz side to receive the document and its letter of transmittal, urges both parties thereafter to give them full and open consideration, and to engage in constructive negotiations on their substance, and urges those having influence with the parties to promote this outcome;
6. *Regrets* the lack of progress on the initiation of political status negotiations, and recalls once again that the purpose of those documents is to facilitate meaningful negotiations between the parties, under the leadership of the United Nations, on the status of Abkhazia within the State of Georgia, and is not an attempt to impose or dictate any specific solution to the parties;
7. *Underlines further* the fact that the process of negotiation leading to a lasting political settlement acceptable to both sides will require concessions from both sides;
8. *Welcomes* the convening of two meetings of senior representatives of the Group of Friends of the Secretary-General in Geneva, and particularly welcomes the participation in a positive spirit of representatives of the two parties at the second meeting;
9. *Welcomes also* the identification at the first Geneva meeting of three sets of issues as key to advancing the peace process (economic cooperation, the return of internally displaced persons and refugees, and political and security matters) and the following work on the substance of those issues, including in bilateral working groups by the Russian Federation and Georgia as

agreed by the two Presidents at their meeting in Sochi on 6 and 7 March 2003, and also at the initial high-level meeting of the parties on 15 July 2003, chaired by the Special Representative of the Secretary-General and with the participation of the Group of Friends of the Secretary-General;

10. *Welcomes further* the commitment of the parties to continue their dialogue on economic cooperation, refugee returns and political and security matters regularly and in a structured manner and their agreement to join the Group of Friends of the Secretary-General again towards the end of the year to review progress and explore future steps, and encourages them to act upon that commitment;

11. *Calls upon* the parties to spare no efforts to overcome their ongoing mutual mistrust;

12. *Calls again upon* the parties to ensure the necessary revitalization of the peace process in all its major aspects, including their work in the Coordinating Council and its relevant mechanisms, to build on the results of the third meeting on confidence-building measures between the Georgian and Abkhaz sides, held in Yalta, Ukraine, on 15 and 16 March 2001, to implement the proposals agreed on that occasion in a purposeful and cooperative manner, and to consider holding a fourth conference on confidence-building measures;

13. *Reminds* all concerned to refrain from any action that might impede the peace process;

14. *Stresses* the urgent need for progress on the question of refugees and internally displaced persons, calls upon both sides to display a genuine commitment to make returns the focus of special attention and to undertake this task in close coordination with the United Nations Observer Mission in Georgia and in consultation with the Office of the United Nations High Commissioner for Refugees and the Group of Friends of the Secretary-General, recalls the understanding reached in Sochi by Georgia and the Russian Federation that the reopening of the Sochi-Tbilisi railway will be undertaken in parallel with the return of refugees and displaced persons, starting in the Gali district, reaffirms the unacceptability of the demographic changes resulting from the conflict, and reaffirms also the inalienable right of all refugees and internally displaced persons affected by the conflict to return to their homes in secure and dignified conditions, in accordance with international law and as set out in the Quadripartite Agreement on the Voluntary Return of Refugees and Displaced Persons of 4 April 1994 and the Yalta Declaration;

15. *Recalls* that the Abkhaz side bears a particular responsibility to protect the returnees and to facilitate the return of the remaining displaced population, and requests further measures to be undertaken, inter alia, by the United Nations Development Programme, the Office of the United Nations High Commissioner for Refugees and the Office for the Coordination of Humanitarian Affairs of the Secretariat to create conditions conducive to the return of refugees and internally displaced persons, including through quick-impact projects, to develop their skills and to increase their self-reliance, with full respect for their inalienable right to return to their homes in secure and dignified conditions;

16. *Welcomes* the positive consideration given by the parties to the recommendations of the joint assessment mission to the Gali district, urges them once again to implement those recommendations, and in particular calls upon the Abkhaz side to agree to the opening as soon as possible of the Gali branch of the human rights office in Sukhumi and to provide security conditions for its unhindered functioning;

17. *Endorses* the recommendations of the Secretary-General in his report of 21 July 2003 that a civilian police component of twenty officers be added to the Mission to strengthen its capacity to carry out its mandate and in particular contribute to the creation of conditions conducive to the safe and dignified return of internally displaced persons and refugees, and welcomes the commitment of the parties to implement the recommendations of the security assessment mission of October to December 2002;

18. *Calls in particular upon* the Abkhaz side to improve law enforcement involving the local population and to address the lack of instruction in their mother tongue for the ethnic Georgian population;

19. *Condemns* any violations of the provisions of the Agreement on a Ceasefire and Separation of Forces signed in Moscow on 14 May 1994;

20. *Calls upon* both parties publicly to dissociate themselves from militant rhetoric and demonstrations of support for military options and for the activities of illegal armed groups, and encourages the Georgian side in particular to continue its efforts to put an end to the activities of illegal armed groups;

21. *Welcomes* the relative calm in the Kodori Valley and the intention reaffirmed by the parties to resolve the situation peacefully, recalls its strong support for the protocol signed by the two sides on 2 April 2002 regarding the situation in the Kodori Valley, calls upon both sides, and in particular the Georgian side, to continue to fully implement this protocol, and recognizes the legitimate security concerns of the civilian populations in the area, calls upon the political leaders in Tbilisi and Sukhumi to observe security agreements, and calls upon both sides to spare no efforts to agree on a mutually acceptable arrangement for security of the population in, and in the vicinity of, the Kodori Valley;

22. *Strongly condemns*, however, the abduction of four Mission personnel on 5 June 2003, which is the sixth hostage-taking since the establishment of the Mission, deeply deplores that none of the perpetrators have ever been identified or brought to justice, and supports the call of the Secretary-General that this impunity must end;

23. *Welcomes* the additional safeguards for helicopter flights instituted in response to the shooting down of a helicopter of the Mission on 8 October 2001, calls once again upon the parties to take all necessary steps to identify those responsible for the incident, to bring them to justice, and to inform the Special Representative of the Secretary-General on the implementation of these steps;

24. *Calls upon* the Georgian side to continue to improve security for joint patrols of the Mission and the collective peacekeeping force of the Commonwealth of Independent States in the Kodori Valley to enable them to monitor the situation independently and regularly;

25. *Underlines* the fact that it is the primary responsibility of both sides to provide appropriate security and to ensure the freedom of movement of the Mission, the collective peacekeeping force and other international personnel;

26. *Welcomes* the constant review by the Mission of its security arrangements in order to ensure the highest possible level of security for its staff;

27. *Decides* to extend the mandate of the Mission for a new period terminating on 31 January 2004, subject to a review, as appropriate, of its mandate by the Council in the event of changes in the mandate of the collective peacekeeping force;

28. *Requests* the Secretary-General to continue to keep the Council regularly informed and to report three months from the date of the adoption of the present resolution on the situation in Abkhazia, Georgia;

29. *Decides* to remain actively seized of the matter.

Report of Secretary-General (October). In a 17 October report [S/2003/1019], the Secretary-General said that, in order to move the peace process forward, his Special Representative maintained a regular dialogue with the two sides and with representatives of the Group of Friends, both in Tbilisi and in their respective capitals. At the end of July, she held separate meetings in Geneva and New York with representatives of each of the countries constituting the Group of Friends. She also met with UNOMIG troop-contributing countries in New York and, in early October, she had consultations in Moscow with the Russian President's Special Representative for the Georgian-Abkhaz conflict.

The Group of Friends, at its second meeting (Geneva, 21-22 July) to review progress in economic cooperation, return of refugees and internally displaced persons and political and security matters, expressed support for the substantive work being done on those issues, including the preparations for the deployment of the UNOMIG civilian police component and the further exploration of security guarantees. Among other proposals, the Group recommended that the Special Representative explore with the two sides how administrative arrangements in the Gali district could be made more conducive to the sustainable return of refugees and internally displaced persons. The meeting was attended for the first time by representatives of the Georgian and Abkhaz sides, which greatly enhanced the Group's understanding of the concerns vital to both parties. In that regard, the Georgian side stressed the need for measures to support and promote the process of return to the Gali district, in particular in the areas of security, human rights protection and language of instruction, as outlined in the 2000 joint assessment mission [YUN 2000, p. 397], the 2001 Yalta Declaration and Programme of Action [YUN 2001, p. 377] and the 2002 security assessment mission [YUN 2002, p. 393]. It noted, in particular, the importance of opening a Gali branch of the United Nations Human Rights Office in Abkhazia, Georgia, and advocated, as a long-term measure, a joint interim administration in the Gali district under international supervision. For its part, the Abkhaz side stressed its security concerns and the need for a mechanism to ensure the non-resumption of hostilities. It expressed its willingness to address constructively humanitarian questions related to refugee return and to consider the opening of a Gali branch of the UN Human Rights Office, as well as involvement by UNHCR in the registration of returnees, provided that those issues were not politicized. The Abkhaz representatives also expressed general support for the 2001 Yalta decisions and the recommendations of both the joint assessment mission and the security assessment mission.

Both sides were committed to further cooperation and agreed to join the Group of Friends again to review progress and explore future steps. As both sides reacted positively to the suggestion of a joint visit to a post-conflict situation to study best practices, UNOMIG made arrangements for such a visit to Bosnia and Herzegovina and the Kosovo province of Serbia and Montenegro in mid-October (see p. 439).

However, despite those signs of positive engagement, the Abkhaz side remained negatively disposed towards including the core political issue of the conflict in any negotiation framework, referring to its unilateral declaration of independence of 1999 [YUN 1999, p. 383], prompting the Georgian Parliament to adopt a resolution on 16 July calling for peace enforcement measures under Chapter VII of the UN Charter (see p. 433).

The Special Representative, in consultation with the two sides and Tbilisi-based representatives of the Group of Friends, continued preparations for a second meeting on security guarantees as a follow-up to the dialogue launched in July (see p. 434). On 8 October, she convened a high-level extraordinary meeting on security matters to address the deteriorating situation in the Gali district (see p. 440).

At the second meeting of the Georgian-Russian bilateral working group on the return of refugees and internally displaced persons (Tbilisi, 31 July), held pursuant to the March Sochi agreements between the Russian and Georgian Presidents, the Georgian side continued to insist on the establishment of a joint interim administration in the Gali district under international supervision, while the Russian side emphasized that such a proposal would not be acceptable to the Abkhaz side, which was not currently participating in the working group.

UNOMIG's efforts were affected by events in both Sukhumi and Tbilisi. On 30 September, the Abkhaz side celebrated the tenth anniversary of the takeover of Sukhumi as "independence day", while Tbilisi marked the day as one of mourning for the victims of the 1992/93 armed confrontation [YUN 1992, p. 391]. During the reporting period, the Georgian side continued to protest against the organized campaign by the Abkhaz to acquire Russian citizenship; the reopening of a Sochi-Sukhumi maritime connection (see below) and the Sochi-Sukhumi railway; the flow of private, mainly Russian, investment; and the signing by the Abkhaz side of cooperation agreements with administrative units of the Russian Federation in September. The Abkhaz side continued to be disturbed by the militant rhetoric of some Georgian politicians implying that a military solution to the conflict was not excluded.

At their summit meeting on 19 September, the CIS heads of State reaffirmed their commitment not to support secessionist regimes nor to engage in economic operations or in official contacts with the Abkhaz side without the consent of the Georgian authorities.

Communications. Georgia, in identical letters of 1 August [A/58/855, S/2003/791] addressed to the General Assembly and Security Council Presidents, complained about the Sukhumi-Sochi-Sukhumi sea voyage made on 26 July by the steamer *Vega-I* and the failure of the Russian Federation to inform it of the vessel's movements. Georgia noted that there were plans to organize regular maritime service between Sochi and Sukhumi, in violation of Georgia's legislation and its 31 January 1996 decree [YUN 1996, p. 352] on the closure of the Sukhumi seaport and port facilities, the maritime area and the section of the State border lying within Abkhazia, Georgia, to all international transport. Georgia considered the Russian action as part of the continued policy of support for the separatist regime in Abkhazia, Georgia, and demanded that the offending ship be detained pending appropriate reaction from its side.

Georgia, in an 11 November letter [S/2003/1080], shared with the Security Council its views on what remained to be done, beyond the positive elements achieved during the year, so that real progress in the peace process could be achieved. It referred to the Council's unwillingness to endorse the 2001 Basic Principles on the Distribution of Competences between Tbilisi and Sukhumi [YUN 2001, p. 386], which would have given the Council the collective authority of all its members; the unilateral actions of one Council member, which were detrimental to the peace process; the continued refusal of the Abkhaz side to allow the opening of the human rights office in the Gali district; the prohibition of teaching in the native Georgian language; the continued functioning of so-called customs and border authorities of the Abkhaz separatist regime; the illegal searches, detentions and interrogations of the civilian Georgian population in the Zugdidi region by CIS peacekeepers; and the illegal operation of the Russian military base in Gudauta, Abkhazia, despite Russia's commitment to shut it down.

Further report of Secretary-General. In a later report [S/2004/26], the Secretary-General described developments in Georgia during the remainder of the year. He said that, since the 2 November parliamentary elections, developments in Georgian domestic politics had led to increased instability in the country. Following the resignation of President Eduard Shevardnadze on 23 November, the Secretary-General assured Georgia's Interim President, Nino Burjanadze, of UN support and continued engagement in the Georgian-Abkhaz peace process. To prevent that process from stalling or backsliding in the light of the volatile political situation, the Special Representative remained in close contact with the two sides and with representatives of the Group of Friends, both in Tbilisi and in their respective capitals, including separate consultations with the Russian Federation President's Special Representative for the Georgian-Abkhaz conflict, the German Special Envoy for Russia, the Caucasus and Central Asia, Norbert Baas, in Moscow and Berlin, respectively, and with the United States Special Negotiator for Eurasian Conflicts, Rudolf Perina.

The Under-Secretary-General for Peacekeeping Operations, Jean-Marie Guéhenno, with the Special Representative, held talks with the Georgian and Abkhaz leaders in Tbilisi and Sukhumi (20-24 November), during which he impressed upon the sides the importance of further compliance with the 1994 Moscow Agreement [YUN 1994, p. 583], regular dialogue and continued practical cooperation, in particular on security matters and issues of return. On 24 November, he confirmed, in a meeting with Georgia's Interim President, the continued commitment of the United Nations to facilitating a lasting settlement with full respect for Georgia's sovereignty and territorial integrity.

UNOMIG pursued its mandated activities, despite the complex and politically volatile environment resulting from the change of leadership in Tbilisi and the pre-positioning of political forces in Sukhumi in anticipation of the 2004 elections for the de facto presidency. Following President Shevardnadze's resignation, the Abkhaz side expressed apprehension that the instability in Tbilisi could spill over to its territory or that the new leadership would adopt a harder line vis-à-vis the conflict settlement. At the same time, it expressed a keen interest in the stabilization of the situation in Tbilisi and a continuation of the negotiation process after a new president and government were in place. The Georgian side strongly criticized the invitation for simultaneous visits to Moscow by high-level Abkhaz and South Ossetian de facto officials and the head of the Autonomous Republic of Adjara at the end of November without prior consultation or coordination with the leaders of Georgia. It protested statements made by some Abkhaz de facto officials about enhanced military preparedness and continued to be sharply critical of the visa-free travel regime to the Russian Federation for Abkhaz residents, the organized campaign by the Abkhaz to acquire Russian citizenship and further Abkhaz efforts to establish associated relations with the Russian Federation. In view of those political developments, it was agreed that the next brainstorming session of the Group of Friends would be held in early 2004.

The Special Representative stepped up efforts to convene the second meeting on security guarantees, but failed to do so as the Abkhaz side refused to engage in a dialogue with the Georgian side until after the presidential elections to be held in January 2004. The planned review meeting on the implementation of the Gali protocol of 8 October (see p. 440), scheduled for December, was postponed for similar reasons.

Meanwhile, UNOMIG continued to prepare the ground for the sustainable return of refugees and internally displaced persons, initially to the Gali district. In cooperation with UNHCR, it further elaborated its draft concept paper on return, on the basis of feedback received from both sides, in preparation for a subsequent session of the Sochi working group on that issue. In line with the recommendations of the second meeting of the Group of Friends (see p. 437), the Special Representative led a joint Georgian-Abkhaz ministerial-level visit to Bosnia and Herzegovina and to the Kosovo province of Serbia and Montenegro to study best practices of UN-led operations in post-conflict situations, in particular policing and refugee return, and to witness the ongoing efforts towards multi-ethnic reconciliation. Both sides positively assessed the UN role in those processes and the results achieved so far, and expressed particular interest in having their police officers trained at the OSCE-led Kosovo Police Service School. UNOMIG completed its initial analysis of ways to transpose some of the lessons learned from specific post-conflict problems in the Balkans to the Georgian-Abkhaz peace process.

Communication. In a 24 November statement [S/2003/1158], the EU noted with satisfaction the peaceful outcome of the political crisis in Georgia and looked forward to working with the new political leaders. It attached the highest importance to Georgia's sovereignty and territorial integrity and declared that positive developments in Georgia might contribute to peace and stability in the whole of the South Caucasus. It stood ready to assist Georgia in the preparation and conduct of the announced elections.

Situation on the ground

Kodori Valley

In the Kodori Valley, the upper part of which was controlled by Georgia and the lower part by the de facto Abkhaz authorities, seven joint UNOMIG/CIS patrols conducted between January and March, in compliance with the 2 April 2002 protocol on security measures [YUN 2002, p. 390], observed no changes in the armed presence or activities in the upper Kodori Valley. During the 11 to 14 February patrol, the upper Kodori Valley Administration proposed a confidence-building meeting with the de facto Abkhaz authorities, who received the proposal positively. The UNOMIG Chief Military Observer was trying to arrange such a meeting. During the 25 to 28 February patrol, an unidentified jet aircraft was heard circling over the upper Kodori Valley, triggering concerns among local residents over possible bombing raids. The most serious incident occurred on 5 June when two UNOMIG military observers, one medic and a Georgian interpreter, were taken hostage by an armed group during a routine patrol in the upper Kodori Valley. They were released unharmed on 11 June following negotiations between the Georgian authorities and the hostage takers. UNOMIG patrols in the area were subsequently suspended, pending a full review of the Mission's operational procedures and the introduction of more robust security measures.

The Abkhaz de facto authorities repeated their allegations that the Kodori Valley was being used to harbour a large military force and might become a staging ground for Georgian operations into Abkhazia later in the year; the Georgian side reiterated that the armed presence in the Valley was for defensive and border control purposes only. The Abkhaz side maintained their demand that a CIS peacekeeping force checkpoint be established in the upper Kodori Valley. In an effort to establish additional confidence-building mechanisms between the two sides in the Kodori Valley, UNOMIG facilitated the establishment of a direct telephone link between the Abkhaz authorities and the senior Georgian authorities there.

Gali and Zugdidi sectors

In the Gali and Zugdidi sectors, where UNOMIG continued daily ground patrols, the overall situation was assessed as generally calm but unstable. Local Abkhaz law enforcement agencies increased patrolling in the city of Gali and the lower Gali area to combat and apprehend criminals, but with little success. The number of criminally motivated incidents, including robberies, kidnappings, murders and explosions, increased in the Gali sector. A 15-member armed group, which committed several armed robberies in the upper Gali area, was believed to be responsible for the armed attack and robbery of a UNOMIG patrol on 24 January, north of Gumurishi. On 14 February, two buses travelling between Zugdidi and Gali were hijacked and robbed, and an Abkhaz militia officer was shot dead in the town of Gali as he tried to prevent a robbery. On the night of 22 to 23 February, a relative of the Georgian Deputy Chairman of Parliament was abducted and executed on the outskirts of Gali. Law enforcement officials struggled to address the continuing high level of criminal activity in the Gali sector. In that regard, Abkhaz law enforcement agencies conducted stop-and-search operations in the upper and lower Gali regions, the most intensive of which was launched on the eve of Georgia's Independence Day, 26 May, to address reports of the presence of illegal armed groups. The increase of UNOMIG patrols helped to limit the impact of the search operations on the local population. On 4 August, four Abkhaz de facto customs officers were killed and three others wounded close to the ceasefire line in the Gali district. A month later, Abkhaz de facto customs officers were accused of beating a number of residents of Tagiloni. The de facto Abkhaz authorities promised to take disciplinary action once those responsible had been identified.

In early October, the security environment deteriorated significantly, with the killing of 10 persons over an eight-day period. On 8 October, the Special Representative convened a high-level extraordinary meeting on security matters, with the participation of the two sides and the CIS peacekeeping force, to address the deteriorating security situation in the zone of conflict, particularly in the Gali district. A protocol was signed providing for, among other things, cooperation between the sides and immediate measures to stop all criminal activities; exchange of information on such crimes; a commitment to ensure that perpetrators would be brought to justice; and cooperation by the two sides with UNOMIG's incoming civilian police component (see above). The two sides agreed to meet in December to review the efficiency of existing security mechanisms. Implementation of the protocol was monitored at the weekly quadripartite meetings. To improve security further, UNOMIG increased its patrolling, with the deployment to the Gali sector of six additional military observers from other parts of the mission area. Although the security situation improved by mid-October, there were further periods of instability and six more killings were reported.

The report of the 2002 security assessment mission to the Gali and Zugdidi sectors [YUN 2002, p. 393] contained recommendations for assisting law enforcement agencies in both districts to perform their duties more professionally and effectively, including provision for training and equipment, strengthening human rights activities, increased recruitment of local residents into law enforcement structures, improving cooperation between law enforcement agencies on both sides of the ceasefire line and economic rehabilitation. The mission was of the view that implementation of its recommendations should be monitored by UNOMIG. The Special Representative would consult with all sides to obtain their consent for the implementation of the recommendations.

As a follow-up to the 2002 security assessment mission, the UNDP Bureau for Crisis Prevention and Recovery, in collaboration with UNHCR, the United Nations Children's Fund, the United Nations Volunteers programme and UNOMIG, led a mission to the Gali region and the adjoining conflict-affected areas of Ochamchira and Tkvarcheli districts (30 November–17 December) to assess the feasibility of a sustainable recovery process for the local population and potential returnees and to identify further actions to improve the overall security conditions and ensure sustainable return. In particular, the mission examined the social and economic rehabilitation needs and the modalities and priorities for implementation of the 2002 security mission's recommendations. It also reviewed the level of damage to the local economic and social infrastructure, rehabilitation needs in agriculture and economics, shelter and infrastructure, health and education, and institutional strengthening, and examined the feasibility of a phased holistic and area-based rehabilitation approach. The mission noted that possible rehabilitation programme efforts should contribute to the achievement of an adequate security environment and vice versa.

In the Zugdidi sector, a relatively low level of criminal activity continued, involving killings, shooting incidents, explosions and abductions, robberies and car thefts. Several peaceful demonstrations took place to protest the living conditions of displaced persons, but attempts by the local authorities to improve the situation were largely ineffective. The blocking of the main bridge over the Inguri River by internally displaced persons, which began on 6 January to protest, among other things, the extension of the CIS peacekeeping mandate, the resumption of the Sochi-Sukhumi rail link and the continued granting of Russian citizenship and passports to residents of Abkhazia, ended on 18 February, but not before several explosive devices were discovered. Frequent demonstrations and acts of civil disobedience posed a challenge for local law enforcement in the Zugdidi sector, hindering implementation of UNOMIG's mandated tasks. Further blockades of the bridge over the Inguri River took place on 1 and 5 June; the exit road of UNOMIG logistics headquarters in Zugdidi was also blocked by local residents. The quadripartite joint fact-finding group continued to investigate violent incidents, but its work was hampered by lack of continuity and poor handling of evidence, and the slow completion of investigations. Eight cases were currently under investigation.

As in the Gali sector, the number of violent and criminal acts increased in the Zugdidi sector during the latter part of the year, though the number of killings was well below that recorded in the Gali sector. On 4 December, some 65 internally displaced persons staged a peaceful protest outside the Zugdidi sector headquarters. Opposition groups also staged low-key demonstrations outside government buildings throughout November to protest the official results of the parliamentary elections.

Communication. On 29 June [S/2003/680], Georgia drew the Security Council's attention to a 25 June incident at a Russian checkpoint in the security zone in Abkhazia, Georgia, in which illegal Abkhaz formations opened mortar fire at civilians, killing two and wounding one. Another Georgian civilian was killed 10 days earlier by the "death squad" of the illegal formations, whose aim was to terrorize Georgians living in the Gali district and deter the return of internally displaced persons and refugees. Those incidents attested to the urgent need to launch the United Nations peacekeeping operation and to the need for reinforced security arrangements to secure the safe return of internally displaced persons and refugees. Georgia called on the Council to take immediate measures to avert the escalation of the situation, put an end to the killing of civilians and address the issue of their protection in the zone of conflict.

Humanitarian situation and human rights

International agencies and NGOs continued activities to alleviate acute food and medical needs and restore basic facilities. However, their work continued to be hampered by restrictions on border crossings between Abkhazia, Georgia, and the Russian Federation at the Psou River. The level of criminality in the zone of conflict also negatively affected humanitarian relief efforts.

UNHCR continued to focus on the rehabilitation of communal educational infrastructures. In addition to the 73 schools rehabilitated in 2001-2002, the Office was in the process of assisting in the rehabilitation of 10 more school buildings. By the end of the year, it had completed repairs on 7 of them, including 6 in the Gali district, benefiting more than 14,000 children. UNOMIG provided timely and targeted assistance to improve living conditions for internally displaced persons, with the completion of 16 quick-impact projects. UNHCR provided food and non-food assistance to more than 270 vulnerable and elderly persons in Sukhumi. The European Community Humanitarian Office, with an additional allocation of 2.2 million euros, continued programmes for enhancing the food security of vulnerable families on both sides of the ceasefire line. The International Committee of the Red Cross and the Spanish NGO, Acción Contra el Hambre, were to implement a World Food Programme "food for work" project, aimed at community mobilization and improvement of food security for some 13,550 vulnerable families through the rehabilitation of agricultural potential. The Swiss Agency for Development and Cooperation funded a project to improve the quality of housing and the United Nations Development Fund for Women continued to work with local NGOs to promote the roles, responsibilities and rights of women.

The human rights situation in Abkhazia, Georgia, showed no sign of improvement. Basic human rights continued to be infringed upon and the de facto law enforcement agencies lacked the capacity to curb criminality, including kidnappings and murder, and effectively protect its citizens. The United Nations Human Rights Office in Abkhazia, Georgia, monitored pre-trial detention facilities, provided advisory services and carried out small field projects to promote international human rights standards, including several projects on education and the media. It noted with concern that children in the Gali district still did not have access to education in their mother tongue.

The human rights situation deteriorated further in August in the wake of the killing of Abkhaz de facto customs officers near the cease-fire line on 4 August (see p. 440) and the subsequent beating of local residents in the same area a month later. Additional reports of assault or harassment of local residents by uniformed Abkhaz personnel in the Gali district were also recorded. Although the United Nations Human Rights Office in Sukhumi had stepped up its presence in the Gali district, the absence of a full-time presence continued to hamper efforts to raise awareness of and adherence to human rights principles.

Financing

The Secretary-General submitted to the General Assembly the UNOMIG financial performance report for the period 1 July 2001 to 30 June 2002 [A/57/676], the proposed budget for the period 1 July 2003 to 30 June 2004 [A/57/677] and the related ACABQ report [A/57/772/Add.1].

On 18 June [meeting 90], the Assembly, on the recommendation of the Fifth Committee [A/57/835], adopted **resolution 57/333** without vote [agenda item 143].

Financing of the United Nations Observer Mission in Georgia

The General Assembly,

Having considered the reports of the Secretary-General on the financing of the United Nations Observer Mission in Georgia and the related reports of the Advisory Committee on Administrative and Budgetary Questions,

Recalling Security Council resolution 854(1993) of 6 August 1993, by which the Council approved the deployment of an advance team of up to ten United Nations military observers for a period of three months and the incorporation of the advance team into a United Nations observer mission if such a mission was formally established by the Council,

Recalling also Security Council resolution 858(1993) of 24 August 1993, by which the Council decided to establish the United Nations Observer Mission in Georgia, and the subsequent resolutions by which the Council extended the mandate of the Observer Mission, the latest of which was resolution 1462(2003) of 30 January 2003,

Recalling further its decision 48/475 A of 23 December 1993 on the financing of the Observer Mission and its subsequent resolutions and decisions thereon, the latest of which was resolution 56/503 of 27 June 2002,

Reaffirming the general principles underlying the financing of United Nations peacekeeping operations, as stated in General Assembly resolutions 1874(S-IV) of 27 June 1963, 3101(XXVIII) of 11 December 1973 and 55/235 of 23 December 2000,

Mindful of the fact that it is essential to provide the Observer Mission with the necessary financial resources to enable it to fulfil its responsibilities under the relevant resolutions of the Security Council,

1. *Takes note* of the status of contributions to the United Nations Observer Mission in Georgia as at 31 March 2003, including the contributions outstanding in the amount of 16.4 million United States dollars, representing some 9 per cent of the total assessed contributions, notes with concern that only twenty-two Member States have paid their assessed contributions in full, and urges all other Member States, in particular those in arrears, to ensure payment of their outstanding assessed contributions;

2. *Expresses its appreciation* to those Member States which have paid their assessed contributions in full, and urges all other Member States to make every possible effort to ensure payment of their assessed contributions to the Observer Mission in full;

3. *Expresses concern* at the delay experienced by the Secretary-General in deploying and providing adequate resources to some recent peacekeeping missions, in particular those in Africa;

4. *Emphasizes* that all future and existing peacekeeping missions shall be given equal and non-discriminatory treatment in respect of financial and administrative arrangements;

5. *Also emphasizes* that all peacekeeping missions shall be provided with adequate resources for the effective and efficient discharge of their respective mandates;

6. *Reiterates its request* to the Secretary-General to make the fullest possible use of facilities and equipment at the United Nations Logistics Base at Brindisi, Italy, in order to minimize the costs of procurement for the Observer Mission;

7. *Endorses* the conclusions and recommendations contained in the report of the Advisory Committee on Administrative and Budgetary Questions, and requests the Secretary-General to ensure their full implementation;

8. *Requests* the Secretary-General to take all necessary action to ensure that the Observer Mission is administered with a maximum of efficiency and economy, with particular regard to air transport;

9. *Also requests* the Secretary-General, in order to reduce the cost of employing General Service staff, to continue efforts to recruit local staff for the Observer Mission against General Service posts, commensurate with the requirements of the Mission;

Financial performance report for the period from 1 July 2001 to 30 June 2002

10. *Takes note* of the report of the Secretary-General on the financial performance of the Observer Mission for the period from 1 July 2001 to 30 June 2002;

Budget estimates for the period from 1 July 2003 to 30 June 2004

11. *Decides* to appropriate to the Special Account for the United Nations Observer Mission in Georgia the amount of 32,092,900 dollars for the period from 1 July 2003 to 30 June 2004, inclusive of 30,709,000 dollars for the maintenance of the Observer Mission, 1,059,700 dollars for the support account for peace-

keeping operations and 324,200 dollars for the United Nations Logistics Base;

Financing of the appropriation

12. *Decides also* to apportion among Member States the amount of 32,092,900 dollars at a monthly rate of 2,674,408 dollars, in accordance with the levels set out in resolution 55/235, as adjusted by the General Assembly in its resolutions 55/236 of 23 December 2000 and 57/290 A of 20 December 2002, and taking into account the scale of assessments for 2003, as set out in its resolutions 55/5 B of 23 December 2000 and 57/4 B of 20 December 2002, and for 2004, subject to the decision of the Security Council to extend the mandate of the Mission;

13. *Decides further* that, in accordance with the provisions of its resolution 973(X) of 15 December 1955, there shall be set off against the apportionment among Member States, as provided for in paragraph 12 above, their respective share in the Tax Equalization Fund of 2,218,100 dollars at a monthly rate of 184,841 dollars, comprising the estimated staff assessment income of 1,960,200 dollars approved for the Mission, the prorated share of 238,700 dollars of the estimated staff assessment income approved for the support account, and the prorated share of 19,200 dollars of the estimated staff assessment income approved for the United Nations Logistics Base;

14. *Decides* that for Member States that have fulfilled their financial obligations to the Observer Mission, there shall be set off against their apportionment, as provided for in paragraph 12 above, their respective share of the unencumbered balance and other income in the total amount of 2,687,000 dollars in respect of the financial period ended 30 June 2002, in accordance with the levels set out in resolution 55/235, as adjusted by the General Assembly in its resolutions 55/236 and 57/290 A, and taking into account the scale of assessments for 2002, as set out in its resolutions 55/5 B and 57/4 B;

15. *Decides also* that for Member States that have not fulfilled their financial obligations to the Observer Mission, there shall be set off against their outstanding obligations their respective share of the unencumbered balance and other income in the total amount of 2,687,000 dollars in respect of the financial period ended 30 June 2002, in accordance with the scheme set out in paragraph 14 above;

16. *Decides further* that the increase of 137,200 dollars in the estimated staff assessment income in respect of the financial period ended 30 June 2002 shall be added to the credits from the amount referred to in paragraphs 14 and 15 above, and that the respective shares of Member States therein shall be applied in accordance with the provisions of those paragraphs, as appropriate;

17. *Emphasizes* that no peacekeeping mission shall be financed by borrowing funds from other active peacekeeping missions;

18. *Encourages* the Secretary-General to continue to take additional measures to ensure the safety and security of all personnel under the auspices of the United Nations participating in the Observer Mission;

19. *Invites* voluntary contributions to the Observer Mission in cash and in the form of services and supplies acceptable to the Secretary-General to be administered, as appropriate, in accordance with the procedure and practices established by the General Assembly;

20. *Decides* to include in the provisional agenda of its fifty-eighth session the item entitled "Financing of the United Nations Observer Mission in Georgia".

On 18 December, the Secretary-General submitted the UNOMIG financial performance report for the period 1 July 2002 to 30 June 2003 [A/58/639] and the budget for the maintenance of UNOMIG for the period 1 July 2004 to 30 June 2005 [A/58/640].

Georgia–Russian Federation relations

Georgia, in a 9 July letter to the Security Council President [S/2003/694], expressed concern at the 4 July statement of the self-styled "president of South Ossetia", E. Kokoity, made in Nalchik, Karbardino-Balkaria, Russian Federation, appealing to the Russian President to admit South Ossetia to membership in the Russian Federation. The statement was accompanied by provocative comments by officials of the Russian Federation State Duma and the President of the Russian Federation Republic of Karbardino-Balkaria, Valeri Kokov, in support of that appeal. Georgia considered all those actions to be an attempt to infringe upon its territorial integrity and counter to the fundamental principles of relationships between Georgia and the Russian Federation.

In an 11 December letter to the Council President [S/2003/1167], Georgia protested the unilateral introduction by the Russian Federation of a simplified entry and departure procedure for residents of Georgia's Autonomous Republic of Adjaria. According to Georgia's Ministry of Foreign Affairs, the implementation of the simplified visa regime with one of its regions, without preliminary agreement with the leaders of Georgia, was a blatant violation of international law and the political ethics of relations between sovereign States and contradicted the Russian Federation's repeatedly stated good-neighbourly policy.

Armenia and Azerbaijan

In 2003, the positions of Armenia and Azerbaijan remained unchanged with regard to the armed conflict between them, which had erupted in 1992 [YUN 1992, p. 388] over the Nagorny Karabakh region in Azerbaijan. The Minsk Group of OSCE (France, Russian Federation,

United States) continued its efforts to mediate the conflict. Both sides addressed communications to the Organization during the year regarding relations between them. Nagorny Karabakh's communications were transmitted by Armenia.

Communications. On 26 February [A/57/742-S/2003/233], Armenia transmitted to the Secretary-General the text of a memorandum entitled "Facts relating to the anti-Armenian pogroms in Sumgait (Azerbaijan) in February 1988". According to Armenia, over three days in February 1988, the entire territory of the city of a quarter of a million people became the arena for widespread, unrestrained pogroms against the Armenian population. Dozens were killed, a significant number of whom had been burned alive, after being beaten and tortured, and hundreds were wounded, many of them left disabled for life. Women and young girls were raped, more than 200 homes wrecked and looted, scores of cars set on fire or smashed up and dozens of workshops, shops, kiosks and other social facilities smashed and plundered. Thousands of people became refugees. The events of Sumgait were a natural consequence of the atmosphere of total lawlessness, spurred on by Azerbaijani leaders. Subsequent events in Azerbaijan demonstrated that the Sumgait approach to the settlement of ethnic scores would be the chosen method. In May 1988, on the initiative of the Shusha district party committee, the process of deporting Armenians from Shusha commenced and the last Armenians were driven out of Shusha in September. In November, pogroms were being waged throughout Azerbaijan. There was no response, either political or legal, to any of those actions and an atmosphere of total impunity prevailed. Armenia claimed that the Sumgait events were organized with a view to hushing up and concealing the Nagorny Karabkh problem. The organizers and perpetrators of the Sumgait atrocities had to be punished. The world had to know the truth about the cruelty and barbarity of the Azerbaijani authorities and those responsible for that notorious crime.

On 4 March [S/2003/249], Azerbaijan transmitted to the Secretary-General an appeal from the Khojaly refugees addressed to the United Nations, the Council of Europe and OSCE, to bring to world attention the truth of the February 1992 Khojaly genocide perpetrated by Armenian armed units in the Nagorny Karabakh region of Azerbaijan and to ensure that that bloody crime was given a legal and political assessment. A previous appeal was submitted in 2002 [YUN 2002, p. 397]. The Khojaly refugees appealed to all peace-loving peoples and international organizations not to remain indifferent and unconcerned about their suffering and grief as a result of Armenian aggression. They were certain that the world community would condemn Armenia's military aggression against Azerbaijan and assist in ensuring Azerbaijan's territorial integrity, bringing about the return of more than 1 million refugees and displaced persons and achieving a peaceful settlement of the Nagorny Karabakh conflict.

In a 28 March memorandum [S/2003/392] addressed to the Secretary-General, Armenia accused Azerbaijan of falsifying for 11 years the accounts of the Khojaly events and provided a series of accounts by Azerbaijanis themselves to prove that the deaths of Khojaly civilians were the result of a power struggle in Azerbaijan.

In identical letters of 2 May [S/2003/528] addressed to the Secretary-General and the Council President, Azerbaijan, recalling the action taken by the Security Council in resolutions 822(1993) [YUN 1993, p. 502], 853(1993) [ibid.], 874(1993) [ibid., p. 504] and 884(1993) [ibid., p. 505], and by the General Assembly in resolution 48/114 [ibid., p. 1086], in response to the armed seizure of Azerbaijani territories by Armenia, noted that, 10 years later, none of those resolutions had been implemented by Armenia. The Council had consigned the problem to oblivion and turned a blind eye to the occupation and ethnic cleansings, allowing the aggressor to have a sense of impunity and to continue to commit unlawful acts. Armenia had tried to realize its territorial claims on Nagorny Karabakh and achieve a forceful solution of the conflict on the basis of fait accompli, which was unacceptable to Azerbaijan.

On 11 July [S/2003/706], Azerbaijan again drew the Council's attention to Armenia's non-compliance with its resolutions on the conflict between the two countries and emphasized that the absence of appropriate reaction from the international community would encourage continued illegal action by the aggressor. It appealed to the Secretary-General and to the Chairman-in-Office of the OSCE Minsk Conference, in accordance with the requests contained in the Council's 1993 resolutions (see above), to report to the Council on all aspects of the situation on the ground and on its development. Azerbaijan expected the Council to take decisive action to put an end to Armenia's criminal aggressive actions in occupied Azerbaijani territory.

Responding to the accusations contained in Azerbaijan's 2 May and 11 July letters, Armenia, on 28 July [S/2003/765], accused Azerbaijan of violating Council resolutions by not pursuing, as requested by the Council, negotiations within the framework of the OCSE Minsk Group and through direct contacts. The refusal to negotiate directly with the elected representatives of Nagorny Karabakh was one of the main impediments to resolving the conflict. It was unacceptable and alarming that Azerbaijani officials were openly contemplating abandoning the negotiating process in favour of a military solution of the conflict. Armenia called on the Azerbaijani side to occupy themselves constructively with the peace process rather than resorting to rhetoric.

On 12 November [A/58/594-S/2003/1090], Azerbaijan said that in view of Armenia's non-compliance with the Council's 1993 resolutions and the United Nations, and of the Council's failure to compel enforcement, it was submitting a report prepared by its Ministry of Foreign Affairs on some of the results and consequences of the Armenian aggression against Azerbaijan and recent developments in the occupied Azerbaijani territories. The report, annexed to its letter, described socio-economic damage caused by the aggression, damage to the environment and natural resources, cultural property damage, illegal activities in the occupied territories, and crimes committed and violations of the ceasefire by Armenia.

Cyprus

In 2003, hopes for achieving a comprehensive settlement of the Cyprus question were dashed as the direct talks initiated in 2002 stalled once again, despite the continued efforts of the Secretary-General's Special Adviser and the personal involvement of the Secretary-General himself. To further accommodate the positions of the two sides, the Secretary-General, on 26 February, again revised his comprehensive settlement proposal "Basis for Agreement on a Comprehensive Settlement of the Cyprus Problem". The revised plan required the two sides to commit themselves to finalizing negotiations, with UN assistance, by the end of February and to submit the plan for approval to separate simultaneous referendums on 30 March. In meetings with the Secretary-General in March in The Hague, Netherlands, it became clear that it would be impossible to reach agreement on conducting such referendums and the process came to an end. Consequently, the Secretary-General took the position that, while his plan remained on the table, he did not propose taking a new initiative without solid reason to believe that the political will existed for a successful outcome.

The Security Council met twice in April to consider the Secretary-General's report on his mission of good offices. It gave its full support to the Secretary-General's plan as a basis for further negotiations.

The United Nations Peacekeeping Force in Cyprus (UNFICYP) continued to assist in the restoration of normal conditions and in humanitarian functions. The Council twice extended UNFICYP's mandate, the second time until June 2004.

By **decision 57/596** of 15 September, the General Assembly deferred consideration of the agenda item "Question of Cyprus" and included it in the draft agenda of its fifty-eighth (2003) session.

Incidents

Communications. Throughout 2003, the Secretary-General received letters from the Government of Cyprus and from the Turkish Cypriot authorities containing charges and counter-charges, protests and accusations, and explanations of position regarding the question of Cyprus. The letters from the "Turkish Republic of Northern Cyprus" were transmitted by Turkey.

In communications dated between 15 January and 26 December, Cyprus reported violations of its national airspace and unauthorized intrusions into Nicosia's flight information region by Turkish military aircraft, while those from the "Representative of the Turkish Republic of Northern Cyprus" claimed, in refutation, the existence of two independent states in Cyprus and that the flights took place within the sovereign airspace of the "Turkish Republic of Northern Cyprus" [A/57/709-S/2003/55, A/57/764-S/2003/349, A/57/781-S/2003/411, A/57/843-S/2003/687, A/57/859-S/2003/828, A/58/195-S/2003/781, A/58/340-S/2003/857, A/58/433-S/2003/991, A/58/621-S/2003/1163, A/58/665-S/2003/1203].

In other communications, Cyprus, on 9 October [A/58/429-S/2003/982] and on 17 November [A/58/603-S/2003/1101], complained about attempts by the Turkish Cypriot authorities to silence voices in the Turkish Cypriot community that were in favour of a solution to the Cyprus problem and peaceful coexistence of the two communities in a reunited Cyprus. The "Turkish Republic of Northern Cyprus" refuted those claims in letters of 27 October [A/58/541-S/2003/ 1049] and 10 December [A/58/628-S/2003/1179].

The "Turkish Republic of Northern Cyprus" drew attention to the statement made by the Greek Cypriot leader at the fifty-eighth session of the General Assembly on 25 September [A/58/PV.11], which, it said, contained baseless allegations against it, and outlined its own position on several questions raised in that statement, including the reasons for the failure of the direct talks on the future of Cyprus [A/58/438-S/2003/1013].

Good offices mission

Resumption of direct talks

Direct talks between the President of Cyprus, Glafkos Clerides, and the Turkish Cypriot leader, Rauf R. Denktash, on the Secretary-General's settlement plan "Basis for Agreement on a Comprehensive Settlement of the Cyprus Problem" [YUN 2002, p. 400], as revised in December 2002 [ibid.], resumed on 15 January 2003 in Nicosia, in the presence of the Secretary-General's Special Adviser on Cyprus, Alvaro de Soto, in accordance with the three-track negotiation process proposed by the Secretary-General in 2002 [ibid.]. The Secretary-General reported that, during those negotiations, Mr. Denktash sought changes to the plan, some of which would have radically altered key concepts. As a result, little substantive progress was made in the talks. However, Mr. Clerides did indicate to Mr. Denktash that should they not be able to agree on the changes by the end of February, the date set for the completion of negotiations, he would be prepared to sign the plan as it stood.

In parallel with the direct talks, the second track of the negotiations moved forward, as Greece and Turkey met (Ankara, 21 February) to address security issues related to the plan. Those talks did not produce agreement or progress either. Some reasonable results were achieved, however, under the third track of the negotiations as the technical committees agreed to by the two leaders in October 2002 [YUN 2002, p. 400] began to meet after a delay of three months. The committees reached agreement on some important issues, producing a large number of draft laws for consideration and finalization, and a list of treaties and instruments for consideration, but issues of principle made real progress difficult.

The leaders authorized the United Nations to conduct a flag and anthem competition for a united Cyprus, to be included in the plan and put to a referendum, and to prepare a list of names of potential transitional Supreme Court judges for their consideration. However, the leaders did not respond to the Special Adviser's repeated requests to react to the list of judges submitted or appoint committee members to select a flag and anthem (despite the massive public response to the competitions).

The negotiations were briefly interrupted by Presidential elections on 16 February, in which Tassos Papadopoulos was elected to succeed Mr. Clerides as President of Cyprus. Mr. Papadopoulos, while indicating the continuity of Mr. Clerides's policy, raised a number of concerns regarding the workability and implementation of the Secretary-General's plan.

The Secretary-General visited Greece, Turkey and Cyprus during the last week of February. On 26 February, he formally presented a third and final version of his plan "Basis for a Comprehensive Settlement of the Cyprus Problem", which contained further refinements, particularly regarding the basic requirements of the Turkish side, while meeting a number of Greek Cypriot concerns so as to maintain overall balance. The Secretary-General also filled in the remaining gaps in the core parts of the plan, particularly those relating to security, on which Greece and Turkey had been unable to agree.

The Secretary-General met jointly with Messrs. Clerides, Denktash and Papadopoulos on 27 February and proposed that the plan be submitted to simultaneous referendums on 30 March. In that regard, he recommended that they sign a "Commitment to submit the Foundation Agreement to separate simultaneous referenda in order to achieve a Comprehensive Settlement of the Cyprus Problem". He invited them to The Hague, Netherlands, on 10 March, at which time they would inform him whether they were prepared to sign a commitment. The Secretary-General also proposed that the work of the technical committees should continue until the week before the referendums to finalize outstanding technical aspects.

In a 28 February press release [SG/SM/8618], the Secretary-General reported that Messrs. Denktash and Papadopoulos had accepted his invitation to meet in The Hague on 10 March, by which date he had asked them to complete all necessary internal consultations and processes so that a response regarding the commitment to submit the Foundation Agreement to referendums would be definitive. The Secretary-General said he was convinced that Greece, Turkey and the two parties on the island of Cyprus understood that the holding of referenda on 30 March was the key to the signing by a reunited Cyprus of the Treaty of Accession to the EU on 16 April. Noting that a settlement would benefit all the people of Cyprus, the region and the world, he urged the parties not to miss that unique opportunity. He believed that the settlement plan was fair and balanced, based on compromise.

The Hague consultations

During the meeting in The Hague (10-11 March), which was also attended by representatives of the guarantor States (Greece, Turkey, United Kingdom), Mr. Papadopoulos indicated his readiness to commit to putting the plan to referendum. However, before the referendum was held he wanted to ensure that the gaps in the plan regarding federal legislation and constituent state constitutions were filled. He underlined the importance of agreement and commitment by Greece and Turkey to the security provisions in the plan and claimed that considerably more time was needed than was available for a proper public campaign on the referendum. He said that he would not reopen discussion on the substantive provisions of the plan if the other side was prepared to do likewise.

For his part, Mr. Denktash said that he was not prepared to agree to putting the plan to referendum as he had fundamental objections to it on basic points. Further negotiations were likely to be successful only if they began from a new starting point and if the parties agreed on basic principles. He added that Turkey was, in any case, not in a position to sign the statement requested of the guarantors concerning underwriting the principles of the agreement. Turkey confirmed its inability to make the commitment required of the guarantors, citing previously unmentioned constitutional reasons. Mr. Papadopoulos insisted that that commitment was necessary before any referendum could be held.

To salvage the process, the Secretary-General, with the guarantor States, proposed extending the deadline for finalizing negotiations to 28 March, and taking a decision at that time on the holding of separate simultaneous referendums on 6 April. Mr. Denktash refused, making it impossible to achieve a comprehensive settlement before the signature of the accession treaty to the EU by Cyprus on 16 April. Accordingly, the Secretary-General announced that the process had come to an end, while making it clear, however, that his plan remained on the table, ready for the Greek Cypriots and the Turkish Cypriots to carry forward if they could summon the will to do so.

In an 11 March press statement [SG/SM/8630], the Secretary-General said that, although the two leaders had expressed their willingness to continue the talks, the commitment to do so was not there. He had therefore asked his Special Adviser to proceed to New York to prepare a detailed report to the Security Council. The Secretary-General also announced that the Office of the Special Adviser would be closed in the coming weeks. He wanted the people of Cyprus to know that he had not given up on them and was ready to assist whenever there was a clear and realistic prospect, with the backing of Greece and Turkey, of finalizing negotiations.

Secretary-General's assessment of the negotiations

In his 1 April report on his mission of good offices in Cyprus [S/2003/398], covering the period since his last report in 1999 [YUN 1999, p. 388], the Secretary-General gave a thematic and analytical assessment of the process of negotiations, including the position of the parties during the proximity and direct talks, an explanation of his plan, observations on the reasons for the failure and a look to the future.

The Secretary-General said that, during the proximity and direct talks, the parties were far apart on all main issues. Prime Minister Clerides favoured a single State of Cyprus, comprising two politically equal communities in a bicommunal and bi-zonal federation with a single sovereignty and international personality and a single citizenship. The Turkish Cypriot leader, Mr. Denktash, favoured a Confederation of Cyprus founded by two pre-existing sovereign states, which would have a single international legal personality but would be sovereign only to the extent that sovereignty was given to it by the founding states. During the direct talks, Mr. Denktash abandoned the term "confederation" in favour of a "new Partnership State of Cyprus", but the overall concept remained the same. The dispute was, therefore, whether there would be one preexisting state that would continue in existence and federalize itself under a new Constitution, or two pre-existing states that would establish a new confederal or partnership structure.

That difference in overall vision was matched by major differences on all core issues. On governance, the Greek Cypriots proposed a freestanding federal government, based on a federal constitution, with representation determined primarily by population ratios but with effective participation of both communities in decision-making. The Turkish Cypriots, emphasizing the need to prevent domination and maintain their separate status and identity, proposed instead channels of cooperation and coordination between the institutions of two separate but juxtaposed states, with numerical equality and consensus decision-making. The basis would be an international treaty with international arbitration in the case of disputes.

On security, the Greek Cypriot side favoured a completely demilitarized island, with all foreign troops (and "settlers") withdrawing and a United Nations–mandated international force to keep the peace, while the Turkish Cypriot side favoured the extension of the rights of the guarantor Powers (Greece and Turkey) and the stationing by them of large troop contingents in the respective constituent states.

On territory, the Greek Cypriot side took the position that a substantial territorial adjustment was necessary and justified, given the disproportionate amount of territory and coastline currently controlled by the Turkish Cypriots and Turkey, and the need for displaced persons to be able to return to their homes under Greek Cypriot administration. The Turkish Cypriot side ruled out any substantial transfer of territory, proposing only minor adjustments along the buffer zone. The Greek Cypriots wished to see a settlement based on freedom of movement, freedom of settlement and the right of displaced persons to return to their homes, while the Turkish Cypriots argued that the distrust between the two sides, the need for security, the realities on the island, the numerical and economic disparities between both sides, and the principle of bi-zonality meant that property claims should be liquidated by a global exchange and compensation scheme and that freedom of movement and residence should be strictly controlled.

Explaining his plan, the Secretary-General said that it was not a framework, but a truly comprehensive proposal, including all necessary legal instruments and leaving nothing to be negotiated subsequently. It was in the form of a covering document, to be signed by the leaders and accompanied by signatures of representatives of the guarantor States, to which was appended a Foundation Agreement, comprising main articles and a series of detailed annexes, including a Constitution. The plan foresaw that upon the entry into force of the Foundation Agreement, the leaders of the two sides would become co-Presidents of the United Cyprus Republic and, within 40 days, Greek Cypriots and Turkish Cypriots would elect the assemblies of their constituent states, which would in turn delegate 24 members each to a transitional unicameral federal Parliament. The other institutions of State would be gradually put in place over a two-and-a-half year period. Territorial adjustment and solutions to property issues would also be implemented very gradually over two to five years, depending on the circumstances.

The Secretary-General concluded that there had been many missed opportunities over the years in the United Nations good offices efforts on Cyprus, for which both sides bore a share of the blame. In the case of the latest failure, he believed that Mr. Denktash, the Turkish Cypriot leader, bore prime responsibility by putting emphasis on overall conceptual issues and his own legal interpretation of the Cyprus problem. Mr. Denktash generally declined to engage in negotiation on the basis of give and take, which complicated the efforts to accommodate not only the legitimate concerns of principle but also the concrete and practical interests of the Turkish Cypriots. He also seemed to perceive EU accession and the EU's strong preference for welcoming a united Cyprus not as an opportunity to achieve a favourable settlement but as a trap and a threat. Despite his earlier willingness to let his people decide the issue, and notwithstanding the considerable efforts to accommodate the interests of the Turkish Cypriots at the Hague meeting, Mr. Denktash rejected the appeal to send the plan to a referendum. He wanted the negotiation to revert to square one for an open-ended discussion of principles, and refused to contemplate a work programme. Faced with Mr. Denktash's adamant opposition to considering credible ways to achieve a settlement before 16 April, the Secretary-General had no alternative but to terminate the process.

Mr. Clerides had approached the proximity talks with considerable hesitation because of the terms in which it was couched at the insistence of Mr. Denktash. He was uncomfortable with the proximity format and the somewhat hypothetical exercises that format entailed. In the direct talks, however, he sought to find ways to address the interests and concerns of the Turkish Cypriot side in exchange for reciprocity in satisfying the basic aims of the Greek Cypriots. While there were points on which he was not prepared to compromise, Mr. Clerides showed a willingness to circumvent ideological barriers and solve problems in a practical way. Throughout the process, he showed a capacity to accept his side's share of responsibility for the bitter experiences of the past.

Both the Turkish Cypriot leadership and many Turkish interlocutors were convinced, however, that having been accepted by the international community as the Government of Cyprus, and with EU accession seemingly guaranteed, the Greek Cypriots had no serious interest in reaching a settlement with the Turkish Cypriots. They were convinced that Greek Cypriots continued to see Cyprus as a Greek island and were not ready to accept the Turkish Cypriots as equal partners, not having been prepared by their leaders for the far-reaching compromises that a settlement would entail. While people on both sides promoted reconciliation and compromise, there remained, among Greek Cypriots in particular, a general reluctance to accept that the ultimate choice was not between a compromise along the lines of the plan that had been put forward and a better one, but between that and no settlement at all. There was little effort by the Greek Cypriot leadership to explain to the public that that was the case.

Mr. Papadopoulos, although thrown into the leadership of the Greek Cypriot side at a very late stage, continued the policy of his predecessor. While expressing misgivings concerning the proposed plan, he vowed to refrain from requesting substantive alterations and to seek improvements to make it workable. He did not attach great importance to achieving a settlement in time for a united Cyprus to sign the Treaty of Accession to the EU on 16 April, since, in his view, the door to a settlement would still remain open. He also laid down stringent conditions for submitting the plan to referendum, which would have made it difficult to complete the laws and treaties to be attached to the settlement in time. Turkey raised difficulties of a constitutional nature concerning Mr. Papadopoulos's insistence that the guarantor States should sign the commitment foreseen in the plan before it was submitted to referendum. Mr. Papadopoulos also argued that one or two months were required between the completion of the negotiations and the holding of the referendums; that would have exceeded the time frame and prevented the signature of the EU Treaty of Accession by a reunited Cyprus. Mr. Denktash's rejection of the request to submit the plan to referendum made it pointless to press Mr. Papadopoulos on those issues.

The role of Greece and Turkey, both as guarantors and as motherlands, was crucial to reaching a settlement, for both legal and political reasons. The Secretary-General said that he was pleased to have counted on the strong support of Greece throughout the effort.

One of the obstacles to solving the Cyprus problem was the perception on both sides that it was a zero-sum game: one side's gain was the other side's loss. The Secretary-General was convinced that, had it been accepted, his proposal would have created a win-win situation. It was in the interests of all, Greek Cypriots, Turkish Cypriots, Greece and Turkey, that there should be a settlement of the Cyprus problem.

As to the way forward, the Secretary-General stated that he did not intend to take a new initiative, unless and until he was given solid reason to believe that the political will existed for a successful outcome, and he did not believe that such an opportunity would occur any time soon. A solution could be achieved if there was an unequivocally stated preparedness on the part of both leaders, backed at the highest political level in both motherlands, to commit themselves to finalizing the plan (without reopening its basic principles or essential trade-offs) by a specific date with United Nations assistance, and to put it to separate simultaneous referendums on a date soon thereafter.

Security Council consideration. The Security Council met on 10 [meeting 4738] and 14 April [meeting 4740] to consider the Secretary-General's report on his mission of good offices (see p. 447). At the 10 April meeting, his Special Adviser told the Council that the failure to achieve a solution was due to failings of political will rather than to the absence of favourable conditions. A unique opportunity had been missed, thereby denying Greek Cypriots and Turkish Cypriots the opportunity to vote to reunite Cyprus. The Secretary-General's plan, though not perfect, represented the best effort by the United Nations to generate a balanced and truly comprehensive proposal that resolved all issues, and a fair and honourable settlement that met the core interests and aspirations of both sides, based on a three-and-a-half-year process. The onus was on the parties and the motherlands to demonstrate the political will to solve the problem on the basis of the plan.

He noted that, since the failure of the talks, the two leaders appeared to be in agreement in their continued support for the Secretary-General's good offices mission (see p. 446). However, while Mr. Papadopoulos had called on Mr. Denktash to accept the Secretary-General's plan as the basis for a further negotiating process, Mr. Denktash had proposed instead that the leaders discuss amendments to the plan before putting it to a referendum, contrary to the Secretary-General's position that future negotiations not reopen the basic principles or key trade-offs in the plan.

SECURITY COUNCIL ACTION

On 14 April [meeting 4740], the Security Council unanimously adopted **resolution 1475(2003)**. The draft [S/2003/418] was submitted by Bulgaria, France, Germany, Spain, the United Kingdom and the United States.

The Security Council,

Reaffirming all its resolutions on Cyprus, in particular resolution 1250(1999) of 29 June 1999, aimed at achieving agreement on a comprehensive Cyprus settlement,

Reiterating its strong interest in achieving an overall political settlement on Cyprus which takes full consideration of relevant Security Council resolutions and treaties,

Welcoming the report of the Secretary-General of 1 April 2003 on his mission of good offices in Cyprus,

1. *Commends* the extraordinary effort made by the Secretary-General and his Special Adviser and his team since 1999 in pursuance of his mission of good offices and within the framework of Security Council resolution 1250(1999);

2. *Also commends* the Secretary-General for taking the initiative to present to the parties a comprehensive settlement plan aimed at bridging the gaps between them, drawing upon the talks that began in December 1999 under United Nations auspices and, following

negotiations, to revise that plan on 10 December 2002 and 26 February 2003;

3. *Regrets* that, as described in the report of the Secretary-General, due to the negative approach of the Turkish Cypriot leader, culminating in the position taken at the meeting held in The Hague on 10 and 11 March 2003, it was not possible to reach agreement to put the plan to simultaneous referenda as suggested by the Secretary-General, and thus, that the Turkish Cypriots and the Greek Cypriots have been denied the opportunity to decide for themselves on a plan that would have permitted the reunification of Cyprus and as a consequence it will not be possible to achieve a comprehensive settlement before 16 April 2003;

4. *Gives its full support* to the Secretary-General's carefully balanced plan of 26 February 2003 as a unique basis for further negotiations, and calls upon all concerned to negotiate within the framework of the Secretary-General's good offices, using the plan to reach a comprehensive settlement as set forth in paragraphs 144 to 151 of the report of the Secretary-General;

5. *Stresses its full support* for the mission of good offices of the Secretary-General as entrusted to him in resolution 1250(1999), and requests the Secretary-General to continue to make available his good offices for Cyprus as outlined in his report;

6. *Decides* to remain actively seized of the matter.

The Russian Federation, speaking after the vote, expressed support for the efforts of the Secretary-General and his Special Adviser. It believed, taking into account the well-known concerns of both sides regarding individual elements of the plan, that it would be possible to adjust the plan, which would help in reaching compromise solutions.

Further developments

On 3 April [A/57/777-S/2003/406], Turkey transmitted to the Secretary-General the text of a letter from Mr. Denktash to Mr. Papadopoulos. The Turkish Cypriot leader said that, following the re-evaluation of and responses given to the Secretary-General's proposals, he had become convinced that the deep crisis of confidence between the two sides had been overlooked. He therefore proposed that the two leaders discuss his suggestions for initiating a working relationship between the two parties, which should enhance the prospects for a mutually acceptable settlement. His ideas included: transferring the fenced area of Varosha south of Dhimoktrathias street, including the area extending to the UN buffer zone, to Greek Cypriot control, to be opened for resettlement; lifting all restrictions on overseas trade, transport, travel and cultural and sporting activities in both parts of Cyprus, including those imposed by Greece and Turkey; facilitating freedom of movement between the two sides and lifting restrictions on the movement of tourists; normalizing the flow of goods between the two parts of the island; lifting by the Turkish Cypriot side of measures imposed in July 2000 [YUN 2000, p. 404] regarding UNFICYP's movements; and establishing a bilateral reconciliation committee to promote understanding, tolerance, mutual respect and bilateral contacts and projects between the two parties. He also expressed his readiness to discuss the core issues of the comprehensive settlement and matters related to EU membership, with the objective of reaching a mutually satisfactory conclusion.

The Special Adviser reported to the Council during its 10 April session [meeting 4738] (see p. 449)) that Mr. Papadopoulos's response was that, in his view, the stalemate was caused not by a crisis of confidence but by Mr. Denktash and Turkey not accepting the Secretary-General's plan as the basis for negotiating a final settlement. Mr. Papadopoulos remained committed, even after 16 April, to finding a solution "within the parameters of the Annan plan" and called on Mr. Denktash to accept that plan as the basis for further negotiations.

In a 4 April letter [A/57/778-S/2003/407], transmitted to the Secretary-General by Turkey on the same date, Mr. Denktash said that he had engaged in good faith in the negotiation of the Secretary-General's suggestions and had put forward ideas for improving them. He reminded Mr. Papadopoulos of his own reservations regarding the Secretary-General's plan and the strict conditions the Greek Cypriot side had insisted on for submitting that plan to referendum. Mr. Denktash recalled his proposal made in The Hague that the two leaders discuss their respective amendments to the plan and, if agreed, put the plan to referendum. He stated that the core issues could only be tackled in the framework of such a process. Mr. Denktash said that his proposals were still on the table and encouraged Mr. Papadopoulos to look at them from a new perspective.

Mr. Denktash, in an 11 July letter, transmitted to the Secretary-General by Turkey on 14 July [A/57/849-S/2003/708], said that, following the Greek Cypriot side's refusal of his confidence-building measures package (see above), the Turkish Cypriot side had unilaterally facilitated the free movement of peoples between the two sides, to which both the Turkish Cypriot people and the Greek Cypriot people had reacted positively. In view of those encouraging results, Mr. Denktash was seeking the Secretary-General's support, within the context of the confidence-building measures proposed by his predecessor as Secretary-General in 1992 [YUN 1992, p. 269], but which were not concluded, to re-open Nicosia

International Airport to serve both sides, on the basis of the final 1993-1994 United Nations confidence-building proposals [YUN 1994, p. 598]. Mr. Denktash said that the Government of Turkey had confirmed its intention, if the confidence-building package was implemented, to open Turkish seaports and airports and airspace to Greek Cypriot ships and aeroplanes and to develop reciprocal trade relations. He asked the Secretary-General to use his good offices in moving the proposal forward. In any case, it was high time that the restrictions and embargo weighing so heavily on the Turkish Cypriot people, especially with regard to overseas travel, tourism, trade and exports/imports, were lifted. Mr. Denktash also confirmed, in a 24 July letter [A/57/852-S/2003/759] transmitted by Turkey, that the military authorities of the "Turkish Republic of Northern Cyprus" were prepared to discuss with UNFICYP demining in Nicosia and its close vicinity.

In a 31 July response [A/57/853-S/2003/785] to Mr. Denktash's 11 July letter, Mr. Papadopoulos pointed out to the Secretary-General that Mr. Denktash's explanation that a crisis of confidence was responsible for the stalemate in The Hague talks was unfounded, as evidenced by the interaction witnessed recently between Greek Cypriots and Turkish Cypriots following the partial lifting of restrictions on freedom of movement, which showed that what was really lacking was a comprehensive settlement to the Cyprus problem. He said that, after the deadlock at The Hague, Mr. Denktash had consistently tried to eliminate every prospect for resuming the talks on the basis of the Secretary-General's plan and to disorient international and Turkish Cypriot public opinion about who was to blame for the failure of the talks and the current stalemate. The Greek Cypriot leader noted that the 1993-1994 discussions on confidence-building measures had deadlocked solely due to Mr. Denktash's insistence on promoting the acknowledgement of his secessionist entity. Mr. Papadopoulos said that the best hope for proceeding forward was through the resumption of negotiations; he repeated his readiness to engage in substantive negotiations on the basis of the Secretary-General's plan. However, for any resumption of the talks to be meaningful, both communities should indicate their acceptance of that plan.

On 16 April, Cyprus signed the Treaty of Accession to the EU in Athens, Greece, and ratified it in July, paving the way for the country to become an EU member when the Treaty entered into force on 1 May 2004. In accordance with the decision of the European Council (Copenhagen, Denmark, 12-13 December 2002) that, in the absence of a settlement, the application of the acquis of the northern part of the island would be suspended until the Council decided otherwise, the Council invited the European Commission to consider ways of promoting the economic development of the northern part of Cyprus and bringing it closer to the Union; that programme was launched in June 2003.

In December, parliamentary elections took place in the northern part of Cyprus, bringing to the fore a new Turkish Cypriot leadership.

Statement of Secretary-General. The Spokesman for the Secretary-General, in a 15 December statement [SC/SM/9082], said that the Secretary-General had seen the reports of the Turkish Cypriot voting. It appeared that it might take some time for a new political dispensation to be established. However, he restated his position that his plan for a comprehensive settlement remained on the table but he did not intend to take a new initiative without solid reason to believe that the political will for a successful outcome existed. The Secretary-General hoped that the Turkish Cypriot side would soon be in a position to make the necessary commitment so that a reunited Cyprus might accede to the EU on 1 May 2004.

Statement of Council President. In an 18 December press statement [SC/7961], the Security Council President said that Council members welcomed the fact that the majority of Turkish Cypriots had expressed their desire for a solution to the Cyprus problem and for accession to the EU, a result that was all the more noteworthy given the pressures they faced to support the status quo. Council members hoped that all parties in northern Cyprus and all other concerned parties would honour the desire of the majority of Turkish Cypriots. Council members reiterated their full support for the Secretary-General's good offices and urged the Turkish Cypriot leadership and all parties concerned to strongly support the Secretary-General's efforts. They called for an immediate resumption of talks on the basis of his proposals.

UNFICYP

The United Nations Peacekeeping Force in Cyprus, established by Security Council resolution 186(1964) [YUN 1964, p. 165], continued in 2003 to monitor the ceasefire lines between the Turkish and Turkish Cypriot forces on the northern side and the Cypriot National Guard on the southern side of the island; to maintain the military status quo and prevent a recurrence of fighting; and to undertake humanitarian and economic activities. In the absence of a formal ceasefire agreement, UNFICYP's task was to judge whether changes in military positions constituted violations of the military status quo, as recorded by the Force in 1974.

UNFICYP, under the overall authority of the Acting Special Representative and Chief of Mission, Zbigniew Wlosowicz (Poland), continued to keep the area between the ceasefire lines, known as the buffer zone, under constant surveillance through a system of observation posts and through air, vehicle and foot patrols.

During 2003, Alvaro de Soto continued as the Secretary-General's Special Adviser on Cyprus.

As at 31 December, UNFICYP, under the command of Major General Herbert Joaquin Figoli Almandos (Uruguay), who succeeded Lieutenant-General Jin Ha Hwang (Republic of Korea) on 25 December [S/2003/1214, S/2003/1215], comprised 1,214 troops and 47 civilian police.

Activities

Report of Secretary-General (May). The Secretary-General, in his 27 May report covering developments and UNFICYP activities from 16 November 2002 to 20 May 2003 [S/2003/572], said that the military situation along both ceasefire lines remained calm and air violations of the UN buffer zone decreased. The restrictions imposed on UNFICYP's movement in 2000 [YUN 2000, p. 404] by the Turkish Cypriot authorities were slightly eased on 9 May, allowing it to use the newly established crossing point at Ayios Dometios/Metehan. UNFICYP was also allowed limited use of the Pergamos and Strovilia crossing points for military personnel from Sector 4 only and use of the Ledra crossing point for official purposes only. Restrictions on UNFICYP's movement along the Famagusta-Dherinia road continued. There was no change in the violation of the status quo in the village of Strovilia, where the Turkish Cypriot authorities were using a Greek Cypriot house for manning the newly established crossing point there. Crossings of the maritime security lines (the seaward extension of the median line of the buffer zone), both the western and the eastern, continued.

Normal conditions were restored on 23 April with the opening by the Turkish Cypriot authorities, for the first time in almost three decades, of the Ledra and Pergamos crossing points to the public for visits in both directions. Another checkpoint was opened near Strovilia on 26 April, allowing some 140,000 Greek Cypriots and 34,000 Turkish Cypriots to cross in both directions. On 10 May, both sides established an additional crossing point at Ayios Dometios/Metehan in Nicosia. The United Nations Civilian Police (UNCIVPOL) had to be assisted by some 100 UNFICYP soldiers in ensuring safe and orderly passage within the buffer zone until the crossing arrangements were clarified and the number of crossings stabilized. There was also a significant increase in the number of incidents requiring UNFICYP's involvement outside the buffer zone since the crossings began. As a result of its additional responsibilities, UNFICYP's requirements were reviewed and it was determined that up to 34 additional UNCIVPOL officers would be needed. UNFICYP would review and adjust its capabilities and new requirements as the need arose.

On 30 April, a set of governmental measures was announced, including: free movement of Turkish Cypriots and their goods and vehicles throughout the island; the establishment of telecommunications links to the north and to Turkey; employment opportunities for Turkish Cypriots in the south; the establishment of a bicommunal committee for humanitarian and other related issues; encouragement of contracting and subcontracting to Turkish Cypriots; issuance of identity cards, travel documents, birth certificates and other official documents; and the establishment of an office for Turkish Cypriot affairs. On 9 May, a set of Turkish Cypriot measures was announced, including offering scholarships for Greek Cypriot students to study at the tertiary educational institutions in the north and a proposal for improved telephone communications facilities and normalization of trade with the south.

UNFICYP facilitated a number of bicommunal events, such as a blood sample collection drive, a youth festival, monthly gatherings of politicians, and an international women's day celebration. It continued to perform its mandated humanitarian tasks in support of the Greek Cypriot and Maronite minorities living in the island's north and Turkish Cypriots in the south. In February, UNFICYP secured an agreement from the north for Greek Cypriots and Maronites to vote in the elections held in the south. Its support for civilian activities in the buffer zone continued.

The Secretary-General said that it was important for UNFICYP to be adequately equipped to meet its increased workload and to respond in a timely manner to developments. He therefore recommended that UNCIVPOL be complemented by 34 officers and that the Security Council extend UNFICYP's mandate until 15 December 2003.

SECURITY COUNCIL ACTION

On 11 June [meeting 4771], the Security Council unanimously adopted **resolution 1486(2003)**. The draft [S/2003/635] was prepared in consultations among Council members.

The Security Council,

Welcoming the report of the Secretary-General of 27 May 2003 on the United Nations operation in Cyprus, and in particular the call to the parties to assess and address the humanitarian issue of missing persons with due urgency and seriousness,

Noting that the Government of Cyprus has agreed that, in view of the prevailing conditions in the island, it is necessary to keep the United Nations Peacekeeping Force in Cyprus beyond 15 June 2003,

Welcoming and encouraging efforts by the United Nations to sensitize peacekeeping personnel in the prevention and control of HIV/AIDS and other communicable diseases in all its peacekeeping operations,

1. *Reaffirms* all its relevant resolutions on Cyprus, and in particular resolution 1251(1999) of 29 June 1999 and subsequent resolutions;
2. *Decides* to extend the mandate of the United Nations Peacekeeping Force in Cyprus for a further period, ending on 15 December 2003;
3. *Endorses* the increase of the civilian police component of the Force by no more than thirty-four officers in order to meet the increased workload resulting from the welcome partial easing of restrictions on island-wide freedom of movement, which has been met by goodwill from Greek and Turkish Cypriots;
4. *Notes* the limited steps taken by the Turkish Cypriot side to ease some of the restrictions imposed on 30 June 2000 on the operations of the Force, but urges the Turkish Cypriot side and the Turkish forces to rescind all remaining restrictions on the Force;
5. *Expresses concern* at the recent further violations by the Turkish Cypriot side and Turkish forces at Strovilia, and urges them to restore the military status quo which existed there prior to 30 June 2000;
6. *Requests* the Secretary-General to submit a report by 1 December 2003 on the implementation of the present resolution;
7. *Decides* to remain seized of the matter.

Report of Secretary-General (November). On 12 November [S/2003/1078], the Secretary-General reported that the military situation along the ceasefire lines remained unchanged. However, there was an increase in the number of forward moves by Turkish forces into the buffer zone, as well as more incidents of verbal abuse, threats, stone-throwing, and cocking and pointing of weapons by both the Cypriot National Guard and Turkish forces. The number of air violations by both sides increased. In July and August, UNFICYP observed an increase in the activity of Turkish forces/Turkish Cypriot security forces in the fenced-in area of Varosha. At the same time, Turkish forces delayed UNFICYP's routine maintenance tasks and continued to restrict its patrols to a northern sector of the fence line, static observation posts and a short patrol route inside Varosha.

As at 2 November, 2 million crossings by Greek Cypriots and Turkish Cypriots had taken place at the Ledra, Ayios Dometios/Metehan, Pergamos and Strovila crossing points since their opening on 23 April (see p. 452). UNFICYP continued to assist in ensuring safe and orderly crossings. The arrival of additional officers helped to reinforce the civilian presence on the ground and to improve the response time in cases of incidents requiring their assistance.

The Secretary-General said that in the absence of a comprehensive settlement, UNFICYP's presence on the island continued to be necessary, and he recommended that the Council extend its mandate until 15 June 2004.

SECURITY COUNCIL ACTION

On 24 November [meeting 4870], the Security Council unanimously adopted **resolution 1517 (2003)**. The draft [S/2003/1114] was prepared in consultations among Council members.

The Security Council,

Welcoming the report of the Secretary-General of 12 November 2003 on the United Nations operation in Cyprus, and in particular the call to the parties to assess and address the humanitarian issue of missing persons with due urgency and seriousness,

Noting that the Government of Cyprus has agreed that in view of the prevailing conditions in the island, it is necessary to keep the United Nations Peacekeeping Force in Cyprus beyond 15 December 2003,

Welcoming and encouraging efforts by the United Nations to sensitize peacekeeping personnel in the prevention and control of HIV/AIDS and other communicable diseases in all its peacekeeping operations,

1. *Reaffirms* all its relevant resolutions on Cyprus, in particular resolution 1251(1999) of 29 June 1999 and subsequent resolutions;
2. *Decides* to extend the mandate of the United Nations Peacekeeping Force in Cyprus for a further period, ending 15 June 2004;
3. *Urges* the Turkish Cypriot side and the Turkish forces to rescind all remaining restrictions on the Force;
4. *Expresses its concern* at the further continuing violations by the Turkish Cypriot side and Turkish forces at Strovilia and urges them to restore the military status quo which existed there prior to 30 June 2000;
5. *Requests* the Secretary-General to submit a report by 1 June 2004 on the implementation of the present resolution;
6. *Decides* to remain seized of the matter.

Financing

On 18 June [meeting 90], the General Assembly, having considered the Secretary-General's report on UNFICYP's financial performance for the period 1 July 2001 to 30 June 2002 [A/57/667], the proposed budget for UNFICYP's maintenance for the period 1 July 2003 to 30 June 2004 [A/57/687 & Corr.1] and ACABQ's comments and recommendations [A/57/772/Add.4 & Corr.1], adopted, on the recommendation of the Fifth Committee [A/57/838], **resolution 57/332** without vote [agenda item 142].

Financing of the United Nations Peacekeeping Force in Cyprus

The General Assembly,

Having considered the reports of the Secretary-General on the financing of the United Nations Peacekeeping Force in Cyprus and the related reports of the Advisory Committee on Administrative and Budgetary Questions,

Recalling Security Council resolution 186(1964) of 4 March 1964, regarding the establishment of the United Nations Peacekeeping Force in Cyprus, and the subsequent resolutions by which the Council extended the mandate of the Force, the latest of which was resolution 1486(2003) of 11 June 2003,

Recalling also its resolution 47/236 of 14 September 1993 on the financing of the Force for the period beginning 16 June 1993 and its subsequent resolutions and decisions thereon, the latest of which was resolution 56/502 of 27 June 2002,

Reaffirming the general principles underlying the financing of United Nations peacekeeping operations as stated in General Assembly resolutions 1874(S-IV) of 27 June 1963, 3101(XXVIII) of 11 December 1973 and 55/235 of 23 December 2000,

Noting with appreciation that voluntary contributions have been made to the Force by certain Governments,

Noting that voluntary contributions were insufficient to cover all the costs of the Force, including those incurred by troop-contributing Governments prior to 16 June 1993, and regretting the absence of an adequate response to appeals for voluntary contributions, including that contained in the letter dated 17 May 1994 from the Secretary-General to all Member States,

Mindful of the fact that it is essential to provide the Force with the necessary financial resources to enable it to fulfil its responsibilities under the relevant resolutions of the Security Council,

1. *Takes note* of the status of contributions to the United Nations Peacekeeping Force in Cyprus as at 31 March 2003, including the contributions outstanding in the amount of 20.2 million United States dollars, representing some 9 per cent of the total assessed contributions, notes with concern that only thirty-one Member States have paid their assessed contributions in full, and urges all other Member States, in particular those in arrears, to ensure payment of their outstanding assessed contributions;

2. *Expresses concern* at the financial situation with regard to peacekeeping activities, in particular as regards the reimbursements to troop contributors that bear additional burdens owing to overdue payment by Member States of their assessments;

3. *Expresses its appreciation* to those Member States that have paid their assessed contributions in full, and urges all other Member States to make every possible effort to ensure payment of their assessed contributions to the Force in full;

4. *Expresses concern* at the delay experienced by the Secretary-General in deploying and providing adequate resources to some recent peacekeeping missions, in particular those in Africa;

5. *Emphasizes* that all future and existing peacekeeping missions shall be given equal and non-discriminatory treatment in respect of financial and administrative arrangements;

6. *Also emphasizes* that all peacekeeping missions shall be provided with adequate resources for the effective and efficient discharge of their respective mandates;

7. *Reiterates its request* to the Secretary-General to make the fullest possible use of facilities and equipment at the United Nations Logistics Base at Brindisi, Italy, in order to minimize the costs of procurement for the Force;

8. *Endorses* the conclusions and recommendations contained in the report of the Advisory Committee on Administrative and Budgetary Questions, and requests the Secretary-General to ensure their full implementation;

9. *Requests* the Secretary-General to take all necessary action to ensure that the Force is administered with a maximum of efficiency and economy;

10. *Also requests* the Secretary-General, in order to reduce the cost of employing General Service staff, to continue efforts to recruit local staff for the Force against General Service posts, commensurate with the requirements of the Force;

Financial performance report for the period from 1 July 2001 to 30 June 2002

11. *Takes note* of the report of the Secretary-General on the financial performance of the Force for the period from 1 July 2001 to 30 June 2002;

Budget estimates for the period from 1 July 2003 to 30 June 2004

12. *Decides* to appropriate to the Special Account for the United Nations Peacekeeping Force in Cyprus the amount of 45,772,600 dollars for the period from 1 July 2003 to 30 June 2004, inclusive of 43,798,800 dollars for the maintenance of the Force, 1,511,400 dollars for the support account for peacekeeping operations and 462,400 dollars for the United Nations Logistics Base;

Financing of the appropriation

13. *Notes with appreciation* that a one-third share of the net appropriation, equivalent to 14,567,500 dollars, will be funded through voluntary contributions from the Government of Cyprus and the amount of 6.5 million dollars from the Government of Greece;

14. *Decides* to apportion among Member States the amount of 24,705,100 dollars at a monthly rate of 2,058,758 dollars, in accordance with the levels set out in resolution 55/235, as adjusted by the General Assembly in its resolutions 55/236 of 23 December 2000 and 57/290 A of 20 December 2002, and taking into account the scale of assessments for 2003, as set out in its resolutions 55/5 B of 23 December 2000 and 57/4 B of 20 December 2002, and for 2004, subject to the decision of the Security Council to extend the mandate of the Force;

15. *Decides also* that, in accordance with the provisions of its resolution 973(X) of 15 December 1955, there shall be set off against the apportionment among Member States, as provided for in paragraph 14 above, their respective share in the Tax Equalization Fund of 2,070,100 dollars at a monthly rate of 172,508 dollars, comprising the estimated staff assessment income of 1,702,300 dollars approved for the Force, the prorated share of 340,500 dollars of the estimated staff assessment income approved for the support account and

the prorated share of 27,300 dollars of the estimated staff assessment income approved for the United Nations Logistics Base;

16. *Decides further* that, taking into account the unencumbered balance and other income in the total amount of 5,381,600 dollars for the financial period ended 30 June 2002, for Member States that have fulfilled their financial obligations to the Force, there shall be set off against their apportionment, as provided for in paragraph 14 above, their respective share of the unencumbered balance and other income in the amount of 2,747,000 dollars in respect of the financial period ended 30 June 2002, in accordance with the levels set out in resolution 55/235, as adjusted by the General Assembly in its resolutions 55/236 and 57/290 A, and taking into account the scale of assessments for 2002, as set out in its resolutions 55/5 B and 57/4 B;

17. *Decides* that for Member States that have not fulfilled their financial obligations to the Force, there shall be set off against their outstanding obligations their respective share of the unencumbered balance and other income in the amount of 2,747,000 dollars in respect of the financial period ended 30 June 2002, in accordance with the scheme set out in paragraph 16 above;

18. *Decides also* that the decrease of 38,000 dollars in the estimated staff assessment income in respect of the financial period ended 30 June 2002 shall be set off against the credits from the amount of 2,747,000 dollars referred to in paragraphs 16 and 17 above, and that the respective shares of Member States therein shall be applied in accordance with the provisions of those paragraphs, as appropriate;

19. *Decides further*, taking into account its voluntary contribution for the financial period ended 30 June 2002, that one third of the net unencumbered balance and other income in the amount of 1,781,200 dollars in respect of the financial period ended 30 June 2002 shall be returned to the Government of Cyprus;

20. *Decides*, taking into account its voluntary contribution for the financial period ended 30 June 2002, that the prorated share of the net unencumbered balance and other income in the amount of 853,400 dollars in respect of the financial period ended 30 June 2002 shall be returned to the Government of Greece;

21. *Decides also* to continue to maintain as separate the account established for the Force for the period prior to 16 June 1993, invites Member States to make voluntary contributions to that account, and requests the Secretary-General to continue his efforts in appealing for voluntary contributions to the account;

22. *Emphasizes* that no peacekeeping mission shall be financed by borrowing funds from other active peacekeeping missions;

23. *Encourages* the Secretary-General to continue to take additional measures to ensure the safety and security of all personnel under the auspices of the United Nations participating in the Force;

24. *Invites* voluntary contributions to the Force in cash and in the form of services and supplies acceptable to the Secretary-General, to be administered, as appropriate, in accordance with the procedure and practices established by the General Assembly;

25. *Decides* to include in the provisional agenda of its fifty-eighth session the item entitled "Financing of the United Nations Peacekeeping Force in Cyprus".

In December, the Secretary-General submitted the proposed budget for UNFICYP's maintenance for the period 1 July 2004 to 30 June 2005 [A/58/644 & Corr.1].

Other issues

Strengthening of security and cooperation in the Mediterranean

In response to General Assembly resolution 57/99 [YUN 2002, p. 410], the Secretary-General submitted a July report with later addenda [A/58/132 & Adds.1,2], containing replies received from Algeria, Italy, Jordan, Mexico, Slovenia and Venezuela, and from the Holy See and the Organization for Security and Cooperation in Europe, to his 7 March note verbale requesting the views of all States and intergovernmental organizations on ways to strengthen security and cooperation in the Mediterranean region.

GENERAL ASSEMBLY ACTION

On 8 December [meeting 71], the General Assembly, on the recommendation of the First (Disarmament and International Security) Committee [A/58/467], adopted **resolution 58/70** without vote [agenda item 78].

Strengthening of security and cooperation in the Mediterranean region

The General Assembly,

Recalling its previous resolutions on the subject, including resolution 57/99 of 22 November 2002,

Reaffirming the primary role of the Mediterranean countries in strengthening and promoting peace, security and cooperation in the Mediterranean region,

Bearing in mind all the previous declarations and commitments, as well as all the initiatives taken by the riparian countries at the recent summits, ministerial meetings and various forums concerning the question of the Mediterranean region,

Recognizing the indivisible character of security in the Mediterranean and that the enhancement of cooperation among Mediterranean countries with a view to promoting the economic and social development of all peoples of the region will contribute significantly to stability, peace and security in the region,

Recognizing also the efforts made so far and the determination of the Mediterranean countries to intensify the process of dialogue and consultations with a view to resolving the problems existing in the Mediterranean region and to eliminating the causes of tension and the consequent threat to peace and security, and their growing awareness of the need for further joint efforts to strengthen economic, social, cultural and environmental cooperation in the region,

Recognizing further that prospects for closer Euro-Mediterranean cooperation in all spheres can be enhanced by positive developments worldwide, in particular in Europe, in the Maghreb and in the Middle East,

Reaffirming the responsibility of all States to contribute to the stability and prosperity of the Mediterranean region and their commitment to respecting the purposes and principles of the Charter of the United Nations as well as the provisions of the Declaration on Principles of International Law concerning Friendly Relations and Cooperation among States in accordance with the Charter of the United Nations,

Noting the peace negotiations in the Middle East, which should be of a comprehensive nature and represent an appropriate framework for the peaceful settlement of contentious issues in the region,

Expressing its concern at the persistent tension and continuing military activities in parts of the Mediterranean that hinder efforts to strengthen security and cooperation in the region,

Taking note of the report of the Secretary-General,

1. *Reaffirms* that security in the Mediterranean is closely linked to European security as well as to international peace and security;

2. *Expresses its satisfaction* at the continuing efforts by Mediterranean countries to contribute actively to the elimination of all causes of tension in the region and to the promotion of just and lasting solutions to the persistent problems of the region through peaceful means, thus ensuring the withdrawal of foreign forces of occupation and respecting the sovereignty, independence and territorial integrity of all countries of the Mediterranean and the right of peoples to self-determination, and therefore calls for full adherence to the principles of non-interference, non-intervention, non-use of force or threat of use of force and the inadmissibility of the acquisition of territory by force, in accordance with the Charter of the United Nations and the relevant resolutions of the United Nations;

3. *Commends* the Mediterranean countries for their efforts in meeting common challenges through coordinated overall responses, based on a spirit of multilateral partnership, towards the general objective of turning the Mediterranean basin into an area of dialogue, exchanges and cooperation, guaranteeing peace, stability and prosperity, encourages them to strengthen such efforts through, inter alia, a lasting multilateral and action-oriented cooperative dialogue among States of the region, and recognizes the role of the United Nations in promoting regional and international peace and security;

4. *Recognizes* that the elimination of the economic and social disparities in levels of development and other obstacles as well as respect and greater understanding among cultures in the Mediterranean area will contribute to enhancing peace, security and cooperation among Mediterranean countries through the existing forums;

5. *Calls upon* all States of the Mediterranean region that have not yet done so to adhere to all the multilaterally negotiated legal instruments related to the field of disarmament and non-proliferation, thus creating the necessary conditions for strengthening peace and cooperation in the region;

6. *Encourages* all States of the region to favour the necessary conditions for strengthening the confidence-building measures among them by promoting genuine openness and transparency on all military matters, by participating, inter alia, in the United Nations system for the standardized reporting of military expenditures and by providing accurate data and information to the United Nations Register of Conventional Arms;

7. *Encourages* the Mediterranean countries to strengthen further their cooperation in combating terrorism in all its forms and manifestations, taking into account the relevant resolutions of the United Nations, and in combating international crime and illicit arms transfers and illicit drug production, consumption and trafficking, which pose a serious threat to peace, security and stability in the region and therefore to the improvement of the current political, economic and social situation and which jeopardize friendly relations among States, hinder the development of international cooperation and result in the destruction of human rights, fundamental freedoms and the democratic basis of pluralistic society;

8. *Requests* the Secretary-General to submit a report on means to strengthen security and cooperation in the Mediterranean region;

9. *Decides* to include in the provisional agenda of its fifty-ninth session the item entitled "Strengthening of security and cooperation in the Mediterranean region".

Stability and development in South-Eastern Europe

On 10 April [A/57/784-S/2003/417], Serbia and Montenegro transmitted to the Secretary-General the text of the Belgrade Declaration, adopted at the Sixth Meeting of the Heads of State and Government of the South-East Europe Cooperation Process (Belgrade, 9 April), in which they reiterated their commitment to the basic principles and objectives of the Charter on Good-Neighbourly Relations, Stability, Security and Cooperation in South-East Europe [YUN 2000, p. 412] and all other documents adopted within the South-East Europe Cooperation Process.

Chapter VI

Middle East

In 2003, the Middle East situation was marked by both hope and disappointment as the international community set in motion a process for a settlement of the Israeli-Palestinian conflict, only to be thwarted by the intensification of the Palestinian intifada (uprising) and the defensive countermeasures adopted by Israel, stalling the political process and creating an unprecedented humanitarian and socio-economic crisis in the Occupied Palestinian Territory.

The Quartet, a coordinating mechanism for international peace efforts, comprising the Russian Federation, the United States, the European Union and the United Nations, continued its efforts to mediate a ceasefire and to revive the peace process. It formally presented to both parties at Aqaba, Jordan, on 30 April, its plan for restarting peace negotiations, the so-called "road map", which aimed to achieve progress through parallel and reciprocal steps by the two parties in the political, security, economic, humanitarian and institution-building areas, under an international monitoring system, reaching a permanent status solution by 2005. On 19 November, the Security Council endorsed the road map. In keeping with the terms of the road map, the Palestinian Authority (PA) initiated the reform of its institutions, including the creation of the post of Prime Minister, and Israel took measures to improve the lives of the Palestinian population. The two sides undertook to restart negotiations based on the road map. Also, a number of Palestinian groups declared a ceasefire in June. Those measures led to a significant reduction in the violence and a marked improvement in the security situation. A June summit meeting held at Aqaba, organized at the initiative of United States President George W. Bush, and attended by Israeli Prime Minister Ariel Sharon and Palestinian Prime Minister Mahmoud Abbas, gave new impetus to the implementation of the road map and fostered new hopes about a peace settlement. Those hopes were dashed by the outbreak of a renewed cycle of violence in August, with a heavy loss of civilian lives on both sides. The already critical situation was made worse by the continued expansion of Israeli settlements, Israel's accelerated construction of a separation barrier to deter terrorist activities, with large parts of it cutting into Palestinian territory, with serious economic consequences for over 200,000 Palestinians, and the September decision of the Israeli Security Cabinet to "remove" PA President Yasser Arafat, who remained under siege at his headquarters.

Concerned about the deteriorating situation in the region, the Security Council convened on a monthly basis during the year, and at times even more frequently, to discuss the situation in the Middle East, including the Palestinian question. On 16 September, a draft resolution, by which the Council would have called on Israel to desist from any act of deportation and cease any threat to the safety of President Arafat, was not adopted due to the negative vote of a permanent Council member, nor was a 14 October draft resolution on the legality of the Israeli separation barrier in the Occupied Palestinian Territory.

The General Assembly, at its resumed tenth emergency special session, convened in September, October and December to discuss the item "Illegal Israeli actions in Occupied East Jerusalem and the rest of the Occupied Palestinian Territory", adopted three resolutions: one calling on Israel to desist from any act of deportation and cease any threat to the safety of President Arafat; another demanding that Israel stop and reverse the construction of the barrier and asking the Secretary-General to report on Israel's compliance with the resolution; and the third requesting the International Court of Justice to render an advisory opinion on the legal consequences arising from the construction of the barrier. In November, the Secretary-General reported that Israel was not in compliance with the Assembly's demands.

In southern Lebanon, Israeli forces and their main Lebanese opponents, the paramilitary group, Hizbullah, continued to face each other along the "Blue Line", the provisional border drawn by the United Nations following the withdrawal of Israeli troops from south Lebanon in June 2000. An initial period of relative calm was replaced in the second half of the year by an escalation of violence in the Shab'a farmland area, which also strained relations between Israel and the Syrian Arab Republic.

Tensions escalated further in early October 2003, when, in retaliation for a suicide bombing attack carried out by the paramilitary group

Islamic Jihad in the city of Haifa, the Israeli air force bombed a target inside Syrian territory. The Security Council convened in emergency session to discuss the attack, though no action was taken on a draft resolution submitted by Syria.

The mandates of the United Nations Interim Force in Lebanon and of the United Nations Disengagement Observer Force in the Golan Heights were extended twice during the year, and the United Nations Truce Supervision Organization continued to assist both peacekeeping operations in their tasks.

The United Nations Relief and Works Agency for Palestine Refugees in the Near East continued to provide education and health and social services to nearly 4 million Palestinian refugees living both in and outside camps in the West Bank and the Gaza Strip, as well as in Jordan, Lebanon and Syria. An emergency appeal was launched in June 2003 to provide food, health services, shelter and short-term emergency employment opportunities for refugees.

During the year, the Special Committee to Investigate Israeli Practices Affecting the Human Rights of the Palestinian People and Other Arabs of the Occupied Territories reported to the Assembly on the situation in the West Bank, including East Jerusalem, the Gaza Strip and the Golan Heights. The Committee on the Exercise of the Inalienable Rights of the Palestinian People continued to mobilize international support for the Palestinians.

By **decision 58/527** of 17 December, the General Assembly deferred consideration of the agenda item "Armed Israeli aggression against the Iraqi nuclear installations and its grave consequences for the established international system concerning the peaceful use of nuclear energy, the non-proliferation of nuclear weapons and international peace and security" and included it in the provisional agenda of its fifty-ninth (2004) session. The item had been inscribed yearly on the Assembly's agenda since 1981, following the bombing by Israel of a nuclear research centre near Baghdad [YUN 1981, p. 275].

Peace process

Overall situation

In his October report on the peaceful settlement of the question of Palestine [A/58/416-S/2003/947] (see also p. 496), the Secretary-General observed that the first half of 2003 witnessed the emergence of hope for a turning point in the Israeli-Palestinian conflict. For the first time since September 2000, both parties, with the active assistance of the Quartet (the Russian Federation, the United States, the European Union and the United Nations), committed themselves to serious negotiations to halt the violence and reach a peaceful settlement. However, renewed violence in the latter half of August 2003 signalled the breakdown of the ceasefire declared by Palestinian groups in June (see p. 468) and a reversal in progress. In the renewed cycle of violence and counter-violence, suicide bombings by Palestinian militant groups and targeted assassinations of members of those groups by Israel resumed. Consequently, the implementation of the road map for resolving the conflict, formally submitted to the parties on 30 April (see p. 464), was frozen and some steps had actually been reversed.

The performance-based and goal-driven road map presented clear phases, time lines, target dates and benchmarks aimed at the progression by the two parties, through reciprocal steps in the political, security, economic, humanitarian and institution-building fields under the auspices of the Quartet, towards resolving the Israeli-Palestinian conflict and ending the occupation. A settlement would lead to the emergence of an independent, democratic and viable Palestinian State living side by side in peace and security with Israel and its other neighbours. At the beginning of June, at the Aqaba Peace Summit (see p. 465), organized by the United States President, George W. Bush, and hosted by Jordan, Israeli Prime Minister Ariel Sharon and Palestinian Prime Minister Mahmoud Abbas committed themselves to begin implementing the road map. On 22 June, the Quartet principals, meeting in Amman, Jordan, reviewed the steps needed to begin that implementation. They called on the Palestinian Authority (PA) to make all possible efforts to halt the activities of groups and individuals planning and conducting terror attacks against Israelis and called on Israel, while recognizing its right to self-defence, to respect international humanitarian law and to exert maximum efforts to avoid civilian casualties among the Palestinians. They also pointed out that steps had to be taken to improve the humanitarian situation and normalize the daily lives of the Palestinian people. Steps taken by the parties to start implementation of the road map included the withdrawal of Israeli forces from parts of the Gaza Strip and Bethlehem and the declaration of a ceasefire by various Palestinian groups, which was arranged with the active involvement of Egypt. President Bush deployed Ambassador John Wolf to lead the informal monitoring structure of the road map's phase one commitments (see p. 464) on the ground, in full cooperation with other Quartet members.

In other developments, with the help of the international community, notable progress was achieved in reforming the PA. The United Kingdom hosted the Quartet's Task Force on Palestinian Reform in London on 20 February (see p. 461), which welcomed Israel's decision to resume monthly transfers of Palestinian tax revenues and the considerable progress made by the PA in its reform efforts, especially in the fiscal sector. On 18 March, President Yasser Arafat approved a bill of amendments to the PA Basic Law to create the post and define the powers of Prime Minister. On 29 April, the Palestinian Legislative Council confirmed Prime Minister Abbas and his new cabinet in office. In September, Ahmed Qurei was nominated to replace Mr. Abbas, following his resignation. Throughout that period, Israel persisted in its efforts to confine PA President Arafat to his headquarters in the West Bank. On 11 September, the Israeli security cabinet agreed in principle on the removal of Mr. Arafat from the West Bank and Gaza Strip, a decision which the Secretary-General strongly urged the Israeli security cabinet to reconsider, since, in his opinion, the action proposed would be dangerous and counterproductive given the instability in the region.

Throughout 2003, the situation in the Middle East remained the subject of extensive consultations and debates in the Security Council. The UN Secretariat continued to provide regular informal briefings to the Council on the latest developments in the region. The Secretary-General stressed his strong belief that the principle of parallelism, on which the road map was based, had to be maintained, since previous attempts had failed because of their reliance on sequentialism. A crucial role for the international community was to assist the parties to address security, economic, humanitarian and political issues at the same time.

Occupied Palestinian Territory

Communications (2-16 January). On 2 January [A/ES-10/210-S/2003/1], the Permanent Observer of Palestine to the United Nations informed the Secretary-General and the Security Council President that Israel continued to wage its military campaign throughout the Occupied Palestinian Territory. Since 26 December 2002, Israeli forces had killed 15 Palestinian civilians and raided a number of refugee camps.

On 6 January [A/57/703-S/2003/9], Israel informed the Secretary-General that on 5 January two Palestinian suicide bombers, in coordinated attacks, blew themselves up in Tel Aviv, killing 23 civilians and wounding more than 100 others; it was one of the bloodiest attacks carried out since September 2000.

Israel, in a 16 January letter [A/57/710-S/2003/62] to the Secretary-General, detailed further Palestinian attacks against Israeli civilians and security forces that took place between 12 and 16 January.

Security Council consideration (16 January). The Security Council met on 16 January [meeting 4685] to discuss the situation in the Middle East, including the Palestinian question.

The Under-Secretary-General (USG) for Political Affairs, Kieran Prendergast, said that the Quartet, in December 2002 [YUN 2002, p. 441], had finalized the road map, which would realize the creation of two States—Israel and Palestine—living side by side in peace and security, and had agreed to present it to the parties following the Israeli general elections, scheduled to be held on 28 January. The road map set out a three-phase plan for achieving a negotiated settlement of the Israeli-Palestinian conflict, as part of an effort to achieve a just, lasting and comprehensive peace in the Middle East (see p. 464 for details).

With regard to the 5 January attack carried out in Tel Aviv (see above), the PA had condemned it and pledged to bring to justice those involved in its planning. The United Nations expected the PA to do everything in its power to fulfil that promise and called on all Palestinian groups to end such attacks. It also supported the efforts of Egypt and others to broker an end to them. The Secretary-General had also repeatedly emphasized that Israel had to act in compliance with international humanitarian law, for, almost on a daily basis, Palestinian civilians were killed and injured by Israel Defence Forces (IDF). As the occupying Power, Israel had particular responsibilities for protecting civilians, which were clearly defined in the 1949 Geneva Convention relative to the Protection of Civilian Persons in Time of War (Fourth Geneva Convention), and it should review its rules of engagement to ensure that Palestinian civilian deaths were investigated and that those guilty of misconduct were prosecuted. The Secretary-General was still awaiting a written account from Israel of the outcome of its investigation into the death of Iain Hook in November 2002 [YUN 2002, p. 440], a staff member of the United Nations Relief and Works Agency for Palestine Refugees in the Near East (UNRWA). The USG said that Israel also had to stop carrying out extrajudicial killings (targeted assassinations) and home demolitions, which the Israeli cabinet had announced would, on the contrary, be intensified following the suicide attacks in Tel Aviv.

The USG also also noted that there had been no appreciable improvement in the humanitarian situation in the Occupied Palestinian Territory. In addition to curfews, Israel had imposed new travel and other restrictions on Palestinians, which exacerbated the humanitarian crisis. The international community responded to the humanitarian aid emergency. The World Food Programme extended its emergency food assistance, the World Bank announced a programme expanding support for emergency social services to the Palestinians and UNRWA continued to provide food assistance to more than a million refugees. On account of the dire circumstances, it was important that Israel honoured its commitment to transfer monthly tax revenues owed to the PA and developed a schedule for remitting the hundreds of millions of dollars in arrears. Israel's announcement that it might reconsider its commitment on that issue was consequently very troubling.

The USG also expressed concern about Israel's construction of a security barrier in the West Bank, which would adversely affect thousands of Palestinians living in its vicinity. Communities were already being cut off from their agricultural lands and from health and education services in the West Bank, and the town of Qalqilya would be almost completely enveloped by the barrier. While he acknowledged Israel's need to defend itself against infiltration, it had to ensure that its security measures were not taken at the expense of the Palestinian civilian population.

Communications (21 January–10 February). In a series of letters dated between 21 January and 6 February [A/ES-10/211-S/2003/74, A/ES-10/212-S/2003/101, A/ES-10/213-S/2003/119, A/ES-10/215-S/2003/154], the Permanent Observer of Palestine informed the Secretary-General and the Council President that Israel continued to wage a military campaign against the Palestinian people. In particular, IDF's incursion on 26 January in Gaza City caused many civilian deaths and extensive property destruction.

Israel, in letters dated 27 January [A/57/719-S/2003/110] and 10 February [A/57/729-S/2003/171], detailed Palestinian terrorist attacks against IDF, which wounded a number of soldiers, in addition to missile attacks against Israeli towns and villages.

On 30 January [A/ES-10/214-S/2003/120], the Chairman of the Committee on the Exercise of the Inalienable Rights of the Palestinian People (Committee on Palestinian Rights) said that the situation in the Occupied Palestinian Territory continued to deteriorate. One disturbing aspect concerned IDF closure, on 15 January, of Hebron University and Palestine Polytechnic University as a measure aimed at fighting terrorists and suicide bombers. The Committee viewed that closure as an illegal act of collective punishment, which deprived thousands of Palestinians of their right to education. The closures also added to the mistrust and suspicion between the two peoples and further exacerbated an already dangerous situation on the ground.

Security Council consideration (13 February). The Security Council, on 13 February [meeting 4704], discussed the situation in the Middle East, including the Palestinian question.

The USG for Political Affairs said that parliamentary elections were held in Israel on 28 January, resulting in a substantial increase in seats for the Likud party, led by Prime Minister Ariel Sharon. Meanwhile, the violence between Israelis and Palestinians continued unabated, causing further loss of life and destruction. Since 16 January, 65 Palestinians and 7 Israelis had been killed, bringing the death toll since the outbreak of the second intifada in September 2000 to more than 2,300 Palestinians and nearly 700 Israelis. On 25 January, after a number of rockets were fired by Palestinians on Israeli communities inside the Gaza Strip, IDF entered Gaza City in their biggest operation in that region since September 2000. The incursion left 13 Palestinians dead and scores injured. Egypt, through meetings it had hosted in Cairo, tried to encourage talks among Palestinian groups on adopting a ceasefire. At the same time, stringent closures and curfews continued to cause economic conditions in the West Bank and Gaza Strip to deteriorate and to hamper the work of the international donor community.

The Palestinian reform process continued to progress with active international support. The London conference on Palestinian reform, held on 14 January would be followed by a series of follow-up meetings in London between 18 and 20 February, including a meeting of Quartet envoys, a donor Ad Hoc Liaison Committee meeting on international assistance to the Palestinian people, and meetings of the Task Force on Palestinian Reform. The UN Special Coordinator for the Middle East Peace Process and Personal Representative of the Secretary-General to the PA, Terje Roed-Larsen, together with the ambassadors of the EU and the Russian Federation, met on 11 February with Chairman Arafat to discuss the upcoming London meetings and called on him to take bold and immediate steps to support and facilitate institutional and security reforms prior to those meetings.

Communications (18 February–19 March). In letters dated between 18 February and 17 March [A/ES-10/216-S/2003/194, A/ES-10/217-S/2003/201, A/ES-

10/219-S/2003/217, A/ES-10/220-S/2003/239, A/ES-10/221-S/2003/287, A/ES-10/222-S/2003/326], the Permanent Observer of Palestine informed the Secretary-General and the Council President of the killing and wounding of Palestinians by IDF, Israeli raids against civilian areas and the destruction of Palestinian homes; lists of the names of those killed and injured were annexed to the letters. Particular attention was devoted to Israeli military assaults in the Gaza Strip, especially in Gaza City. Refugee camps were also attacked, causing the death of many civilians.

Israel, in letters to the Secretary-General dated between 25 February and 10 March [A/57/741-S/2003/225, A/57/745-S/2003/252, A/57/750-S/2003/299], detailed Palestinian attacks against Israeli civilians and IDF. On 5 March, a Palestinian terrorist bombing in the city of Haifa killed at least 15 people and wounded more than 40 others. Between 6 and 9 March, Palestinians launched rocket attacks against southern Israeli towns and villages, including the Negev town of Sderot. Israeli security forces thwarted numerous other attacks.

On 20 February [A/ES-10/218-S/2003/202], the Chairman of the Committee on Palestinian Rights expressed concern over an IDF plan to evict Palestinian residents and seize land in northern Bethlehem in order to construct a separation wall. The wall would cause major disruption of the city's economic activity and restrict the freedom of movement of Palestinians. He called on the Secretary-General to use his good offices to prevent the planned division of the city and to stop implementation of the separation plan.

The Council of the League of Arab States (LAS), in the Final Declaration of its fifteenth regular session (Sharm el-Sheikh, Egypt, 1 March), transmitted to the Secretary-General by Bahrain and to the Council President by the LAS Permanent Observer to the United Nations on 3 March [A/57/743-S/2003/247, S/2003/254], decided, among other things, to provide as at 1 April financial support for the PA's budget for six months, renewable automatically under arrangements established at its 2002 Beirut Summit [YUN 2002, p. 419] as long as the Israeli aggression continued.

The Islamic Summit, at its second emergency session (Doha, Qatar, 5 March) [A/57/748-S/2003/288], in a declaration on Palestine transmitted to the Secretary-General on 6 March, called on the international community, particularly the Quartet, to take action, among other things, to stop Israeli aggression against the Palestinian people and Palestinian cities, including the construction of the separation wall, halt Israeli settlement action in the Occupied Palestinian Territory, ensure international protection of the Palestinian people and resume negotiations. The statement of the Emir of Qatar [A/57/749-S/2003/289] to the special session, in his capacity as Chairman of the ninth Islamic Summit Conference, and his letter [S/2003/343] conveying the results of the Conference to the Secretary-General were transmitted on 6 and 19 March, respectively.

On 4 March [A/57/759-S/2003/332], Malaysia transmitted the documents adopted at the Thirteenth Conference of Heads of State or Government of the Non-Aligned Movement (Kuala Lumpur, 20-25 February), including a statement on Palestine. The heads of State or Government expressed their support for the efforts of the Quartet and encouraged it to proceed speedily with the implementation of the road map, which had been delayed. In that regard, they stressed the need for consultation between the Movement and the Quartet.

On 18 March, Portugal, Spain, the United Kingdom and the United States transmitted to the Council President a statement on Iraq (see p. 332) and a "Commitment to transatlantic solidarity" adopted at the Atlantic Summit (Azores, Portugal, 16 March) [S/2003/335]. Among other things, they reaffirmed a vision of a Middle East peace, with two States, Israel and Palestine, living side by side in peace and security. The leaders welcomed the fact that the road map would soon be delivered to the Palestinians and Israelis and that a Palestinian Prime Minister with sufficient authority to put an end to terrorism and consolidate reforms would be appointed. They looked to the parties to work together constructively.

Task Force on Palestinian Reform

The fourth meeting of the Quartet Task Force on Palestinian Reform, established in 2002 [YUN 2002, p. 432] to develop and implement a comprehensive action plan for reform, was held in London on 19 and 20 February to review the status of Palestinian civil reform efforts (see also p. 503). Those efforts were also reviewed with Israeli and Palestinian representatives.

The Task Force, in a statement issued on 20 February, recognized that the continued terror and violence, restrictions on the movement of persons and goods, deterioration of the humanitarian situation and destruction of local infrastructure and facilities significantly hindered reforms. However, the Task Force welcomed the progress in several areas of civil reform, in particular in fiscal transparency and accountability and the development of the public institutions and laws needed to promote a market economy. It welcomed the Palestinian decision to appoint a Prime Minister and underscored the importance of that position being credible and fully empowered. It commended the commitment of the PA Ministerial Reform Committee and the establishment of a Reform Coordination Support Unit.

The Task Force noted that the 1 February approval by the Palestinian Legislative Council of the 2003 budget was a considerable accomplishment and looked forward to early implementation of the further reform measures announced by the Finance Minister on 31 December 2002 before the Legislative Council. The Task Force also noted the considerable progress made in public administration and civil service reform and looked forward to the early implementation of a detailed action plan in that area. Reforms in some areas, such as the judiciary, were much slower due to counterproductive steps by the Palestinian leadership. The Task Force emphasized the need to comply fully with the recently passed Basic and Judiciary Laws.

The Task Force welcomed the Israeli Government's decision to resume monthly transfers of Palestinian tax revenues and to begin clearing the arrearages. It was paramount that the revenue transfers and return of arrearages continued on a regular basis.

Other developments

Security Council consideration (19 March). The Security Council, on 19 March [meeting 4722], discussed the situation in the Middle East, including the Palestinian question.

The Special Coordinator for the Middle East Peace Process and Personal Representative of the Secretary-General, Mr. Roed-Larsen, said that, for the first time since 2000, there was a real opportunity not only to begin rebuilding the shattered Israeli and Palestinian relationship, but also to start implementing a process that could lead to peace and security in the region. To achieve that, the parties needed to get back to the negotiating table, and for that to happen three critical decisions had to be taken in parallel by the key actors in the process: the PA had to make fundamental decisions on reform in order to re-establish itself as a credible partner for Israel and the international community; the Quartet had to introduce the road map, as agreed in its final draft in 2002 [YUN 2002, p. 441]; and Israel had to sit down at the negotiating table and take immediate and serious steps to prevent harm to Palestinian civilians and to alleviate the widespread suffering caused by its security measures.

The decision on 18 March by the Palestinian Legislative Council and President Arafat to amend the PA Basic Law to create the post of a credible and empowered Prime Minister provided an opportunity to begin building a partnership of negotiations. Mahmoud Abbas was nominated to the new post. The amendments gave the Prime Minister a number of powers which had been held previously by the PA President, including appointing or removing cabinet ministers and supervising the work of PA ministries, especially the Ministry of the Interior. Other key areas of reform were discussed at the February meeting of the Quartet's Task Force on Palestinian Reform (see pp. 461 and 503), which agreed that the PA had made impressive progress in implementing reforms under difficult circumstances. Although the Task Force remained very critical of the lack of progress in the judicial sector, there was general consensus that financial accountability and market economy reforms continued to progress at a rapid pace.

The announcement by the United States President that the Quartet would present the road map to the parties as soon as a credible and empowered Palestinian Prime Minister was confirmed was an important step forward. Under the road map and under the auspices of the Quartet, progress would be monitored and assessed on the basis of the parties' compliance with specific performance benchmarks. The Israelis and the Palestinians had to implement in parallel a number of reciprocal obligations for implementation of the road map to be effective. The PA had to declare an unequivocal end to violence and terrorism and undertake efforts on the ground to prevent attacks on Israelis. At the same time, Israel had to end actions that undermined trust, such as proactive security operations, attacks on civilians, and confiscation and demolition of Palestinian homes and property. Israel also had to dismantle settlement outposts erected since March 2001 and, consistent with the Mitchell report [YUN 2001, p. 409], freeze all settlement activity. A second and critical feature of the road map was its clearly defined final destination. In accordance with Council resolution 1397(2002) [YUN 2002, p. 418], the final negotiated settlement would result in the emergence of an independent, democratic and viable Palestinian State living side by side in peace and security with Israel and its other neighbours. The settlement would resolve the Palestinian-Israeli conflict and end the occupation that began in 1967—a vital element of international efforts to promote comprehensive peace in the region.

Turning to the security and humanitarian situations, the Special Coordinator said that the new Palestinian Government had to do everything within its power to curb terrorism and all forms of violence and threats. Since the last briefing to the Council in February (see p. 460), 162 people had lost their lives: 135 Palestinians and 27 Israelis. The PA security forces had to take action to confront those who murdered civilians in acts that could not be seen as political or justified by any means. Unless the PA exercised its monopoly on the use of force, it would have failed in its authority and leadership. During the past month, IDF conducted intensive operations in a number of Palestinian cities and refugee camps throughout the West Bank and Gaza Strip. Those operations caused high numbers of civilian casualties, particularly in Gaza, and reports indicated that IDF used excessive and at times indiscriminate force. The physical insecurity was also creating serious economic insecurity. The construction by Israel of the separation barrier in the West Bank, coupled with severe movement restrictions, had denied many communities access to their land and sources of livelihood. At the Ad Hoc Liaison Committee meeting of all major donors (London, 18 February), participants expressed their conviction that support to the PA remained the best short-term vehicle for addressing the dire economic and humanitarian situation. They also stressed that Israel had to do more to reduce the burden of security restrictions on civilians and facilitate the provision of international assistance to communities in need. More broadly, donors stressed the urgent need to re-establish a tripartite effort involving Palestinians, Israelis and the international community, working in partnership to address those problems, along with the security and political issues that had spawned them.

Communications (31 March–9 April). On 31 March [A/57/770-S/2003/395], Israel informed the Secretary-General that on the previous day a Palestinian suicide bomber wounded 58 people at a cafe in the city of Netanya.

In two letters dated 4 April [A/ES-10/223-S/2003/405] and 9 April [A/ES-10/224-S/2003/416], the Permanent Observer of Palestine informed the Secretary-General and the Council President that Israel continued to wage its military campaign against the Palestinian people. In particular, IDF continued to launch attacks in the Gaza Strip.

On 7 April [A/57/780-S/2003/410], Qatar transmitted to the Secretary-General the text of a statement made by the Emir of Qatar at the Forum on Islamic-Christian Dialogue (Doha, 7 April), in which he stated that the use of religious doctrines for political aims and the labelling of an entire nation based on the behaviour of a handful of extremists or ignorant people were the main obstacles to cooperation between the two faiths.

Security Council consideration (16 April). The Security Council, on 16 April [meeting 4741], discussed the situation in the Middle East, including the Palestinian question.

The Assistant Secretary-General (ASG) for Political Affairs, Danilo Türk, said that, since the last briefing on 19 March (see p. 462), the attention of the international community had been focused on the war in Iraq (see p. 333). At the same time, there was a growing realization of the urgent need to address the Middle East conflict. The Quartet would present the road map to Israel and the PA following the confirmation by the Palestinian Legislative Council of the appointment of Prime Minister Abbas. The crucial period of implementation would then begin and the parties, with the help of the Quartet, would have to take the necessary steps to end the cycle of violence. The international community should be prepared to stay the course charted by the road map. Implementation would not be easy but its goal was too important for the parties to be deterred by early difficulties. Some of those obstacles were apparent. Some 64 Palestinians and 5 Israelis had been killed since 19 March. On 30 March, a suicide bomber struck in the Israeli city of Netanya (see above). Also in March, 103 Palestinians were killed, the highest monthly death toll in the preceding 12 months. The socio-economic situation in the West Bank continued to deteriorate and no amount of donor assistance would alleviate the crisis in the Occupied Palestinian Territory. The economy needed to operate normally and for that to happen Israel would have to change its security approach by removing internal roadblocks and lifting curfews. However, the damage done to Palestinian society would likely be more difficult to reverse, as over half of the children of the Gaza Strip were suffering from acute post-traumatic stress disorder, due to exposure to violence and destruction. Similar pain and trauma had also been inflicted on Israelis, especially children. The continued construction of the separation barrier in the West Bank might constrain the delivery of basic social services to Palestinian populations and inhibit commercial exchanges if there were not sufficient access points. The placement of the barrier inside the West Bank could also have a negative impact on the Quartet's efforts, through the road map, to establish a viable Palestinian State.

Those conditions highlighted the challenges facing the new Palestinian Prime Minister, who would have to build on the progress achieved in reforming the PA, especially bringing the judicial sector up to par with the financial sector, restoring law and order and bringing to justice those involved in carrying out terrorist acts. He would have to provide the Palestinian people with a transparent and effective Government and the

Israelis with the partner in peace. The Prime Minister would receive the active support of the international community, in particular the Quartet. Israel also had an important part to play in ensuring the success of the new Palestinian Government, particularly by helping to facilitate the reform process and acting to minimize the effects of its security measures. The terrorism that had beset Israel presented it with enormous challenges, but such steps could help empower the PA and its Prime Minister to take action against terrorists. Prime Minister Sharon's recent statements in support of a peace process, including his acknowledgement of the "painful concessions" Israel might need to make, were welcomed. The path ahead charted by the Quartet represented the only realistic hope for ending the current cycle of violence and counter-violence.

Communications (25 April–19 May). In letters dated between 25 April and 6 May [A/57/799-S/2003/502, A/57/804-S/2003/517, A/57/807-S/2003/527], Israel detailed a number of Palestinian attacks against Israeli civilians. The attacks included the detonation of explosives by Palestinian suicide bombers, such as the one on 24 April in the town of Kfar Saba, which wounded 14 Israelis, and the one on 30 April in Tel Aviv, which killed three civilians and wounded 60 others.

By a 1 May letter [A/ES-10/225-S/2003/518], the Permanent Observer of Palestine said that Israel, in a span of less than 24 hours, had killed at least 21 Palestinians, including 15 during an attack by IDF on the densely populated Shijaiyah neighbourhood of Gaza City.

In letters dated 12 and 19 May [A/57/810-S/2003/540, A/57/815-S/2003/557], Israel detailed Palestinian attacks against Israeli civilians and IDF. Five suicide bombing attacks occurred between 17 and 19 May, including one on 18 May inside a bus in Jerusalem, which resulted in the death of seven civilians and wounded 20 others, and another one on 19 May in the city of Afula, which killed three Israelis and wounded 47 others.

By a 16 May letter [A/ES-10/226-S/2003/548], the Permanent Observer of Palestine said that, since 1 May, IDF had killed 34 Palestinian civilians and wounded many others.

Road map

On 30 April, the "performance-based road map to a permanent two-State solution to the Israeli-Palestinian conflict", as affirmed in Security Council resolution 1397(2002) [YUN 2002, p. 418], was presented by the Quartet to the Israeli Government and the PA. The text of the road map, transmitted by the Secretary-General to the Council President on 7 May [S/2003/529], outlined a goal-driven plan, with clear phases, time lines, target dates and benchmarks aimed at progress through reciprocal steps by the two parties in the political, security, economic, humanitarian and institution-building fields, under the auspices of the Quartet. The final goal was a comprehensive settlement of the Israeli-Palestinian conflict by 2005, consistent with a 24 June 2002 statement [YUN 2002, p. 431] by United States President George W. Bush, in which he called for two democratic States living side by side in peace and security.

A two-State solution would be achieved only through an end to violence and terrorism, with a Palestinian leadership acting decisively against terror and willing to build a practising democracy based on tolerance and liberty, and through Israel's readiness to do what was necessary for a democratic Palestinian State to be established, and a clear, unambiguous acceptance by both parties of the goal of a negotiated settlement. The Quartet would assist and facilitate implementation of the plan, including direct discussions between the parties as required. The initiative was a vital element of international efforts to promote a comprehensive peace on all tracks, including the Syrian-Israeli and Lebanese-Israeli tracks. The Quartet would meet regularly at senior levels to evaluate the parties' performance on implementation of the plan.

The road map was divided into three phases. Phase I, which was to be implemented by the end of May 2003, focused on ending terror and violence, normalizing Palestinian life and building Palestinian institutions. During that phase, the Palestinians had to call for and undertake an unconditional cessation of violence against Israelis anywhere. Likewise, Israel had to call for and undertake an unconditional cessation of violence against Palestinians everywhere. Both sides had to resume security cooperation to end violence, terrorism and incitement through restructured and effective Palestinian security services. The PA had to undertake political reform in preparation for statehood, including drafting a Palestinian constitution, and free, fair and open elections on the basis of those measures. Israel had to take all necessary steps to normalize Palestinian life, withdraw from Palestinian areas occupied from 28 September 2000, and freeze all settlement activity, consistent with the Mitchell report [YUN 2001, p. 409]. In phase II, from June to December 2003, efforts would focus on creating an independent Palestinian State with provisional borders and attributes of sovereignty, based on the new constitution, as a way station to a permanent status settlement. Its goals would be to further build on and sustain the goals outlined in phase I: ratification of a democratic Palestinian constitution, formal establishment of the office of Prime Minister and consolidation of political reform. The objectives of phase III, (2004-2005), were consolidation of reform and stabilization of Palestinian institutions, sustained Palestinian security performance and Israeli-Palestinian negotiations aimed at a permanent status agreement in 2005. The Quartet would convene a second international conference in 2004 to endorse agreement on an independent Palestinian State, leading to a final status solution in 2005, including borders, Jerusalem, refugees, settlements, and progress towards a comprehensive Middle East settlement between Israel and Lebanon and Israel and the Syrian Arab Republic soon after.

On 30 April [S/2003/519], the Russian Federation, in a statement issued by its Ministry of Foreign Affairs regarding the official release of the road map, said that the agreed approach of the Quartet, which had presented the road map that day to Israel and the PA (see p. 464), was the best path towards peace, the point of departure for Palestinian-Israeli negotiations and a framework programme of action.

On 1 May [S/2003/520], the Russian Federation welcomed the approval by the Palestinian Legislative Council of the cabinet of Prime Minister Abbas, thus removing the existing obstacles impeding implementation of the road map for a Middle East settlement.

Security Council consideration (19 May). The Security Council, on 19 May [meeting 4757], discussed the situation in the Middle East, including the Palestinian question.

The Special Coordinator for the Middle East Peace Process and Personal Representative of the Secretary-General said that the success of the road map, and, consequently, of the new tentative peace process, would depend on the good faith and performance of the parties, key regional actors and the determination of the international community. The obstacles to peace in the region were numerous, especially since 79 Palestinians and 16 Israelis had been killed since the last briefing to the Council on 16 April (see p. 463). The PA had to bring to justice those involved in planning and carrying out suicide bombing attacks against Israelis. It needed assistance to rebuild and refocus its security forces, and Israel needed to support the new Palestinian Government in that regard so as to allow it to increase security for Palestinians and prevent terror attacks on Israelis. Reciprocal confidence-building measures were essential in order to create legitimacy and popular support for Prime Minister Abbas's anti-terror policies. Under the first phase of the road map, Israel was required to take no actions undermining trust, including attacks on civilians or confiscation and/or demolition of Palestinian homes. However, only hours after the presentation of the road map, IDF operations in Gaza City resulted in the death of at least 13 Palestinians and injury to many more, in addition to the destruction of Palestinian property. The Special Coordinator said that, while taking into consideration Israel's right to self-defence, Israel had to abandon the use of excessive force in densely populated areas. He also pointed out that illegal armed elements in Palestinian areas were responsible for violence that affected Palestinian civilians by basing themselves in civilian areas, and noted that Prime Minister Abbas had made the disarming of such groups one of his Government's goals.

At the same time, the humanitarian and socio-economic conditions in the West Bank and Gaza Strip continued to deteriorate, due mainly to movement restrictions imposed by IDF. The situation in Gaza was exacerbated by a draconian closure regime recently instituted by Israeli authorities that had resulted in the closing of Gaza to all but those with diplomatic passports. Holders of valid UN laissez-passer and service visas for Israel were also barred from entering or leaving Gaza, with the result that a significant number of UN staff were stuck on either side of the boundary and unable to carry out their work. The United Nations would be unable to carry out its operations in Gaza if the closure situation continued. The humanitarian situation also significantly complicated the task ahead for Prime Minister Abbas. Nevertheless, he had made substantial progress in implementing the first phase of the road map, such as action towards a draft constitution for Palestinian statehood and the establishment of an independent Palestinian election commission. The fate and credibility of his Government would depend on a radical and credible change of policy in the security sector, an area in which the PA had failed over the past two years. Israel, on the other hand, had yet to endorse the road map and commit to its implementation. Prime Minister Abbas's work would be aided by Egypt's planned renewed attempt to induce all Palestinian groups to agree to a ceasefire.

Aqaba Peace Summit

At the initiative of the United States President, and hosted by King Abdullah of Jordan, the Middle East Peace Summit was held in Aqaba, Jordan, on 4 June. Both Israeli Prime Minister Sharon and Palestinian Prime Minister Abbas attended the meeting. It was preceded on 3 June by a meeting in Sharm el-Sheikh, which was attended by the United States President, King Abdullah, Egyptian President Hosni Mubarak,

King Hamad of Bahrain, Crown Prince Abdullah of Saudi Arabia and Prime Minister Abbas.

In his statement following the meeting, Prime Minister Sharon said that Israel supported the United States President's vision of two States—Israel and a Palestinian State—living side by side in peace and security and welcomed the opportunity to resume direct negotiations according to the road map, as adopted by the Israeli Government, to achieve that vision. It was not in Israel's interest to govern the Palestinians, but for the Palestinians to govern themselves in their own State. A democratic Palestinian State fully at peace with Israel would promote the long-term security and well-being of all Israelis. However, there could be no peace without the abandonment and elimination of terrorism, violence and incitement. Israel would work with the Palestinians to fight terrorism and would seek to restore normal Palestinian life, improve the humanitarian situation, rebuild trust and promote progress. Israel understood the importance of territorial contiguity in the West Bank for a viable Palestinian State and would begin to remove any unauthorized outposts. It accepted the principle that no unilateral actions by any party could prejudge the outcome of negotiations.

Prime Minister Abbas said that the PA had accepted the road map without any reservations and, like Israel, was prepared to meet its responsibilities. He stressed that there could be no military solution to the conflict and thus reaffirmed the Palestinians' renunciation of terror against Israelis anywhere. Such methods were inconsistent with Palestinian religious and moral traditions and were obstacles to the achievement of an independent, sovereign Palestinian State. The PA would exert all of its efforts to end the militarization of the intifada and establish a democratic Palestinian State based on the rule of law, with a single political authority and weapons only in the hands of official law enforcement officers.

United States President Bush said that pledges made by Prime Minister Sharon were meaningful signs of respect for the rights of the Palestinians and their hope for a viable, democratic, peaceful Palestinian State. The efforts pledged by Prime Minister Abbas demonstrated his leadership and commitment to building a better future for the Palestinian people. However, the two leaders alone could not bring about peace. It required the support of other nations in the region. In that regard, Arab leaders, at the meeting in Sharm el-Sheikh the previous day, promised to cut off assistance and the flow of money and weapons to terrorist groups and to help Prime Minister Abbas rid Palestinian areas of terrorism.

The United States would strive to see that the commitments made by both sides were fulfilled and would provide training and support for a new, restructured Palestinian security service. It would also place a mission on the ground, led by Ambassador John Wolf, to help the parties move towards peace, monitor their progress and state clearly who was fulfilling their responsibilities. President Bush had also asked Secretary of State Colin Powell and National Security Adviser Condoleezza Rice to give the matter the highest priority.

The Secretary-General, in a statement [SG/SM/8736] issued by his Spokesman, welcomed the impetus given to the Middle East peace process by the Aqaba Summit and believed that the statements made by Prime Ministers Sharon and Abbas opened the way for both parties to implement the Quartet's road map. The Secretary-General pledged through his personal efforts, together with the Quartet partners, to continue to assist the parties.

Further developments

Communications (3-13 June). By a 3 June letter to the Secretary-General [A/57/824-S/2003/619], Iran transmitted the texts of the final communiqué, the Tehran Declaration and the resolutions adopted by the Islamic Conference of Foreign Ministers at its thirtieth session (Tehran, Iran, 28-30 May). The Conference adopted eight resolutions on Palestinian affairs, with a focus on the Arab-Israeli conflict and Al-Quds Al-Sharif (Jerusalem), and on an Islamic boycott of Israel.

The Permanent Observer of Palestine, in two communications dated 10 and 12 June [A/ES-10/227-S/2003/638, A/ES-10/228-S/2003/643], informed the Secretary-General and the Council President that IDF had carried out three extrajudicial executions, using helicopter gunship missiles, killing at least 19 Palestinians and wounding many more.

On 13 June [A/57/839-S/2003/645], Israel informed the Secretary-General that, since the convening of the Middle East Peace Summit at Aqaba (see above), a new wave of Palestinian attacks had killed 25 Israelis. On 11 June alone, 16 Israelis were killed and 112 wounded in Jerusalem. Israel stated that on 23 May it had agreed to accept the steps set out in the road map (see p. 464), indicating the desire of the people of Israel to renew direct negotiations, and had already started to implement the commitments it made at the Summit, by releasing Palestinian detainees, dismantling unauthorized outposts and easing security restrictions. The PA, on the other hand, had yet to take a single step towards fulfilling its obligations to dismantle the terrorist infrastructure which it continued to sustain. By refusing to take real steps to confront terrorism, the Palestinian side was endangering any prospect for peace and compelling Israel to continue to take self-defence measures. Israel hoped that the new Palestinian leadership would prove its seriousness about ending violence, including confronting and eradicating terrorist organizations, such as Hamas.

Security Council consideration (13 June). The Security Council, on 13 June [meeting 4773], discussed the situation in the Middle East, including the Palestinian question.

The Under-Secretary-General for Political Affairs, Mr. Prendergast, said that President Bush's initiative to hold the Aqaba Summit gave an important impetus to the renewal of the peace process. However, the Summit was followed by a sharp rise in violence, re-igniting the familiar spiral of violence, counter-violence and revenge. The situation had reached a crossroads where either the promise of peace or a resumption of violence would define the course of the political process in the months ahead. Not unexpectedly, Prime Ministers Sharon and Abbas had each met resistance at home to the commitments they made at Aqaba. In the circumstances, the international community had to help the parties to remain on track and provide active support throughout the road map implementation process.

The circulation of Palestinians within the West Bank had been reduced since the suicide bomb attack in Afula on 19 May (see p. 464), while the movement of West Bank residents with permits to Jerusalem had been completely halted since 2 June. The movement of international personnel and goods into the Gaza Strip remained subject to a stringent Israeli security closure regime. Representatives of the United Nations and the broader international community had met on 27 and 29 May with the Israeli Government to discuss the movement restrictions imposed by IDF, particularly on the Gaza Strip (see p. 465), which continued to have a detrimental effect on their efforts to provide humanitarian assistance. The renewal of the closure regime, after assurances by the Israeli authorities that the situation would improve, was worrying. The United Nations would continue efforts to resolve the issue at the local level. However, the security of staff and goods remained a serious concern.

Communication (20 June). In a 20 June letter [A/57/842-S/2003/662], Israel detailed Palestinian attacks against Israelis, which included suicide bombers and rocket attacks. Israel reiterated that, since the Aqaba Summit, and in accordance with its acceptance of the steps set out in the road map, it had released Palestinian detainees, dismantled unauthorized outposts, eased security restrictions and held security meetings with the Palestinian leadership. Failure on the part of the PA to take real and genuine steps to eliminate terrorism would prevent any progress in the peace process.

Quartet meeting (22 June)

Representatives of the Quartet—the UN Secretary-General, the Russian Foreign Minister, the Greek Foreign Minister, the United States Secretary of State, the High Representative for European Common Foreign and Security Policy and the European Commissioner for External Affairs—met at the Dead Sea in Jordan on 22 June to review developments since their last meeting [YUN 2002, p. 441]. In a statement issued following the meeting [S/2003/672], which was transmitted to the Security Council President by the Secretary-General on 25 June, the representatives welcomed the appointment of Prime Minister Abbas and the acceptance by Israel and the PA of the road map. They endorsed the results of the Red Sea Summit meetings (see p. 465) and pledged to support Prime Ministers Abbas and Sharon in carrying out the commitments made at those meetings. They also welcomed the decision by the United States President to place a mission on the ground to help the parties to move towards peace (see p. 466), and shared his expectation that both parties would meet their obligations in full.

The Quartet condemned the terror attacks against Israeli citizens carried out by Palestinian military groups and called on the Palestinian authorities to take all possible steps to halt immediately the activities of those groups. It supported immediate Palestinian action to restructure and consolidate under Prime Minister Abbas all security services and called on both sides to reach agreement as soon as possible on workable security arrangements. It expressed concern over Israeli military action that resulted in the killing of innocent Palestinians and other civilians, and, while recognizing Israel's right to self-defence, the Quartet called on the Israeli Government to respect international humanitarian law and to exert maximum efforts to avoid such civilian casualties, as well as to ease the plight of the Palestinian people by facilitating movement of people and goods, in addition to access by international humanitarian organizations. Recalling its position that settlement activity had to stop, the Quartet welcomed Prime Minister Sharon's undertaking at Aqaba (see p. 465) and the first steps taken by Israel on the ground to remove unauthorized outposts. The

Quartet reaffirmed its commitment to a just, comprehensive and lasting settlement of the Arab-Israeli conflict, including progress towards peace between Israel and Syria and Israel and Lebanon.

In comments made after the meeting, the Secretary-General said that in keeping with the approach laid out in the road map, the principle of parallelism should be maintained. Security, humanitarian and political issues had to be addressed at the same time. The Secretary-General called on Israel not to use disproportionate force in civilian areas, carry out house demolitions or engage in extrajudicial killings, for unless Palestinians felt that positive change in their daily lives, including ending movement restrictions, freezing settlement activities and re-establishing economic activity, there would not be sufficient public support to sustain peace. Simultaneously, the PA had to spare no effort to bring to an end all acts of terror against Israelis anywhere. Terror was counterproductive to the ultimate goals of ending occupation, establishing a Palestinian State, and the universal recognition of the State of Israel and the State of Palestine.

The Russian Minister for Foreign Affairs, in a 22 June statement regarding the outcome of the Quartet meeting, transmitted to the Secretary-General on 24 June [S/2003/666], said that the situation remained tense and the latest outbreak of violence testified to the fact that the forces opposed to a settlement had not abandoned their attempts to defeat the implementation of the road map. Everything possible, therefore, should be done to prevent a new cycle of confrontation and preserve the opportunity for resolving the crisis. The Russian Minister said that it was time to develop a programme for resuming the negotiating process on the Syrian and Lebanese tracks, as it could ensure greater stability in moving the road map forward.

Developments between 27 June and 19 August

Communications (27 June–10 July). On 27 June [A/ES-10/229-S/2003/677], the Permanent Observer of Palestine said IDF, on that day, had carried out a military attack on a civilian neighbourhood in Gaza City, killing four men and wounding more than 15 other Palestinians.

On 10 July [A/57/846-S/2003/699], Israel detailed Palestinian shooting and mortar attacks against Israeli civilians, which resulted in the death of two Israelis.

Security Council consideration (17 July). The Security Council, on 17 July [meeting 4788], discussed the situation in the Middle East, including the Palestinian question.

The Special Coordinator for the Middle East Peace Process and Personal Representative of the Secretary-General, Mr. Roed-Larsen, said that, since the last Council briefing on 13 June (see p. 467), the revived peace process based on the road map had made encouraging progress. Israelis and Palestinians were meeting regularly and working together at all levels, which had resulted in greater mobility for Palestinians in the Gaza Strip and Bethlehem and in greater security for Israelis. IDF had withdrawn from parts of Gaza and Bethlehem, enabling the PA to re-establish control over those areas. Announced on 30 June, a ceasefire that suspended attacks on Israelis was reached among Palestinian groups and was largely being honoured. The ceasefire was achieved through the efforts of the Palestinian leadership and with the support of Egypt. Regular meetings were occurring between the Palestinian and Israeli Prime Ministers, and both sides met frequently at the ministerial level to discuss such issues as security, prisoners, incitement, economic development, investment and health. Though the challenges to the peace process remained numerous, there had been a sharp decrease in violent attacks and incitement during the reporting period. IDF had largely ceased security activities in those areas in which the PA had re-established its authority. In addition, with the announcement of the Palestinian ceasefire, IDF had refrained from extrajudicial killings. The humanitarian situation had seen little improvement, despite the decrease in violent clashes following the declaration of a ceasefire by Palestinian groups. The withdrawal of IDF from parts of the Gaza Strip had been accompanied by some easing of restrictions on the movement of Palestinian workers and commodities. The movement of humanitarian agencies in entering and leaving the Gaza Strip had improved. However, closures, curfews and checkpoints had not been relaxed significantly in the West Bank and the construction of the separation barrier was continuing. In order to further the peace process, Prime Minister Sharon had to demonstrate to the Israeli people that participation in the road map process would lead to an end to violence and terror. Prime Minister Abbas had to continue to carry out the reform and consolidation of the Palestinian security forces, and in order to do so he needed the active support of Mr. Arafat, who was the Chairman of the Palestine Liberation Organization (PLO) and President of the PA.

Communications (17 July–12 August). On 17 July [A/ES-10/230-S/2003/730], the Chairman of the Committee on Palestinian Rights reported that IDF had ordered the closure of the Palestine Polytechnic University for an additional month. The

University had been closed by IDF since January 2003 (see p. 460).

On 12 August [A/57/858-S/2003/809], Israel said that on that day Palestinian suicide bombers killed two Israelis and wounded 13 others in two separate attacks. Israel said that it held the Palestinian leadership fully responsible for its failure to suppress the campaign of terror, and only when terrorism and incitement were fully and finally rejected would the peace process advance.

Security Council consideration (19 August). The Security Council, on 19 August [meeting 4810], discussed the situation in the Middle East, including the Palestinian question.

The ASG for Political Affairs, Mr. Türk, said that the situation in the Middle East remained fragile. However, the overall level of violence in the Israeli-Palestinian conflict, compared to previous months, had dropped considerably, even though lives continued to be lost. Despite setbacks, progress continued in the implementation of some areas of the road map. Since the PA resumed security responsibility in July for the Gaza Strip and Bethlehem, violence in those areas had significantly decreased. However, six weeks into the 30 June ceasefire, the parties had been unable to agree on the conditions under which the PA would resume security responsibility in the remaining seven West Bank Palestinian cities. Both parties needed to deepen their commitment to security cooperation, as it was at the heart of further progress.

Israel's settlement policy was one of the key challenges to the fulfilment of the road map's goal of a two-State solution. Israel had to recognize that that policy, as well as the construction of the separation barrier and its route in the West Bank, undermined the possibility of a future viable and contiguous Palestinian State. According to an Israeli monitoring group, some 60 settlement outposts were established between March 2001 and June 2003. Since the last briefing, new settlement expansion plans were being discussed by the Israeli Government, which had approved new bypass roads in three locations in the West Bank. On 31 July, the Israeli Defence Ministry approved the issuance of a tender to build new housing units at the Neveh Dekalim settlement in the Gaza Strip, in addition to significant expansion of the lands surrounding the Morag settlement. The building of the separation wall and the continued presence of settlement outposts had caused many Palestinians to question Israel's intent in the peace process.

There had been a marked improvement in July in the humanitarian situation in the Occupied Palestinian Territory, although the situation remained dire. The movement of UN staff into and within Gaza had eased considerably and fewer access incidents had been reported by international organizations. IDF removed several key roadblocks in July, although some of them were replaced by manned checkpoints. However, most villages and towns continued to experience severe access problems. In fulfilment of Prime Minister Sharon's commitments made at the Aqaba Summit (see p. 465), Israel had released over 400 Palestinian prisoners as at 18 August; over 6,000 more remained in Israeli detention centres.

Escalation of violence

Communications (25 August–11 September). In a series of communications dated between 25 August and 10 September [A/ES-10/231-S/2003/834, A/ES-10/232-S/2003/843, A/ES-10/233-S/2003/848, A/ES-10/234-S/2003/853, A/ES-10/235-S/2003/865, A/ES-10/236-S/2003/874], the Permanent Observer of Palestine informed the Secretary-General and the Council President of the killing, including extrajudicial executions, and imprisonment of Palestinians by Israeli forces, and submitted lists of those killed and injured. On 21 August, IDF killed Ismail Abu Shanab, a political leader of Hamas; destroyed large areas of farmland in the Gaza Strip on 28 August; dropped a 550-pound bomb in Gaza City on 6 September in an attempt to kill the spiritual leader of Hamas, Sheikh Ahmed Yassin, which wounded 15 Palestinians; and dropped another bomb in Gaza City on 10 September, which killed two Palestinians and wounded 20 others.

On 10 September [A/57/862-S/2003/873], Israel informed the Secretary-General and the Council President of two terrorist attacks on 9 September by Palestinian suicide bombers, one of whom attacked a cafe in Jerusalem, killing at least seven civilians and wounding 40 others, while the other carried out an attack near a bus depot in Rishon Letzion in central Israel, killing seven Israelis and wounding 30 others. Those attacks were preceded by other acts of terrorism, including the one on 19 August by a Palestinian suicide bomber who detonated a bomb inside a bus in Jerusalem, killing 22 people and wounding 135. Israel expected the new Palestinian leadership to put an absolute end to terrorism by working to fulfil their obligations, which consisted of, among other things, completely dismantling terrorist networks, confiscating and destroying illegal weapons, and bringing terrorists to justice. In the light of the continuing rejection by the Palestinian leadership of those obligations, Israel was compelled to take the necessary measures to defend its citizens, while making every effort to minimize harm to innocent civilians.

On 11 September [S/2003/892], the European Union (EU) Presidency, in a statement condemning the 9 September attack, said that the resurgence of terrorist attacks was obstructing the international community's efforts to restore peace and was damaging the cause of the Palestinian people. In the context of the global fight against terrorism, the EU had decided (Riva del Garda, Spain, 5-6 September) to place the political branch of Hamas on the European list of terrorist organizations. Noting the resignation of Palestinian Prime Minister Abbas, it urged the new Prime Minister, Ahmed Qurei, to continue on the same path. It called on the PA to reorganize its security forces, re-establish public order and undertake visible efforts to dismantle the terrorist organizations. At the same time, it called on Israel, among other actions, to withdraw its army from the autonomous areas, put an end to targeted killings, and relieve the Palestinian people of roadblocks and other restrictions.

Security Council consideration (12-16 September). On 12 September, the Council met at the request of the Non-Aligned Movement caucus and the Arab Group to discuss the situation in the Middle East, and in particular Israel's decision in principle to expel Chairman Arafat. In a press statement [SC/7871] issued by its President, the Council expressed the view that such action would be unhelpful and should not be implemented. It also condemned the violence and urged both parties to act with maximum restraint.

At the request of the Sudan, on behalf of the Arab Group [S/2003/880], the Security Council, on 15 September [meeting 4824], considered the situation in the Middle East, including the Palestinian question. With the Council's consent, the President invited, among others, Israel, Syria [S/2003/887] and the Permanent Observer of Palestine [S/2003/886], at their request, to participate in the deliberations. The Special Coordinator for the Middle East Peace Process and Personal Representative of the Secretary-General said that, since the last Council briefing on 19 August (see p. 469), the Israeli-Palestinian peace process had stalled. The cycle of terror attacks and extrajudicial killings had broken the Palestinian ceasefire, bringing the process to a standstill. A combination of violence and slow implementation of the road map peace plan had brought the region to a potential turning point. Once again, the parties and the international community were confronted with the question whether the parties would recommit themselves to peace or whether the debilitating conflict would grind on. Without a major change in the situation on the ground, further deterioration would be inevitable. Since 19 August, violence had increased. On that day, a suicide bombing in Jerusalem killed 23 people, after IDF had carried out two military operations that resulted in the death of four Palestinians. Israel responded by declaring all-out war against Hamas and other terrorist elements in the Occupied Palestinian Territory, including a stepped-up campaign of attempted extrajudicial killings of Hamas leaders. After two more suicide bombings on 9 September, the Israeli Government announced that it had decided in principle to remove PA President Arafat "in a manner and at a time of its choosing".

The Special Coordinator said that the implementation of the road map never effectively began, as neither party actively addressed the core concerns of the other side. For Israelis, that concern was security and freedom from terrorist attacks. The PA failed again to grasp control of the security situation, and while the unilateral ceasefire declared by Palestinian militant groups was a useful step, other steps such as the consolidation of security forces and security reforms could have been taken. For Palestinians, the core concern was an assurance that the peace process would lead to the end of the occupation and the establishment of a viable, independent Palestinian State on the basis of the 1967 borders. The settlement activity and continued construction of the separation barrier caused Palestinians to wonder whether that goal was achievable. In addition, Israel had never fully endorsed the road map. Thus, the two key issues in the peace process were terrorism and occupation and real action had to be taken to end both. The very limited approach to implementing the road map never effectively tackled either issue. A core concept of the road map, the principle of parallelism, or reciprocal steps by both sides in all fields, was not emphasized during the preceding four months of half-hearted implementation of the road map, leading to the single issue of the Israelis' security from terrorism becoming its sole focus. As a result, violent groups were allowed to set the pace and the agenda for the process. The principle of parallelism should, therefore, be reasserted by taking steps to end both terrorism and occupation and regain control of the process.

Despite the setbacks, the Quartet needed to redouble its efforts. Its principals had agreed to meet in late September to address all relevant issues, including devising ways of putting the peace process back on track. Palestinian Prime Minister Abbas had resigned and the new nominee, Ahmed Qurei, had not been able to take up the reins of power. The rapid appointment and confirmation of a credible and fully empowered Prime Minister was an essential step in order for the PA to disarm militant groups and establish law and order. For its part, Israel had to make significant concessions, for without them neither the peace process nor any peace-minded Palestinian leader would be credible in the eyes of the Palestinian people.

Given the current situation, the Special Coordinator said that it might be appropriate to speed up the road map process. Bold steps in the areas of settlements and security, and involving increased activity by the international community, might be necessary to jump-start a resumption of the process.

The Permanent Observer of Palestine said that Israel's threats reached a new level with its decision to remove President Arafat and to request the Israeli army to draw up a plan for his expulsion. Mr. Sharon and his Government represented a threat to the stability of the region, for they did not seek a permanent settlement but only long-term transitional arrangements. Mr. Sharon's vision was the imposition of a number of walled and separate enclaves, confining the Palestinians to less than half of the West Bank and to slightly more than half of the Gaza Strip. The Israeli Government had not accepted the road map, only the "steps" in the plan, and had attached 14 reservations, which effectively undermined most of it. The essential problem was Israel's policy of settlement building, its refusal to end the occupation of Palestinian land and its failure to accept an independent and sovereign Palestinian State with East Jerusalem as its capital. Without a change in that policy, there would be no peace process and no implementation of the road map. The revival of the road map would require new and serious implementation, with both sides facing up to their responsibilities. The Council could play an important role in that respect, by providing strong support to the road map and officially ordering the two sides to comply with its provisions and to implement them. The Quartet, with the help of the Council, should build the agreed-upon monitoring mechanism and have a real international presence, perhaps even international troops.

Israel said that it had come to the conclusion that Mr. Arafat had not been truthful about his intentions. His continuing rejection of Israel's right to exist and his support of terrorists and their tactics had brought suffering to the region and denied the promise of peace to Israelis and Palestinians alike. In addition, he had undermined the road map at every step of the way. In fact, he actively sought to prevent the Palestinian Prime Minister from fulfilling the Palestinian obligations under the road map and had sabotaged attempts to establish a new and different leadership in the PA. Mr. Arafat had refused to allow the consolidation of security forces under the control of an empowered minister for internal security, who would have worked towards the dismantling of the terrorist infrastructure. In so doing, he had undermined former Prime Minister Abbas, forcing him to resign. Mr. Arafat had kept terrorist groups like the Tanzim under his direct control and prevented efforts to introduce accountability in the PA's finances, so that money could continue to be funnelled into his private accounts. The decision by the Israeli cabinet to remove him merely stated the obvious, namely, that Mr. Arafat was an obstacle to peace. Israel hoped that a new and different Palestinian leadership would be ready to implement its obligations to fight terrorism. If that did happen, the new Palestinian leadership would find in Israel a willing partner ready to make painful compromises.

The Russian Federation expressed concern about Israel's decision to expel Mr. Arafat, for such a step would erase any prospects for a peaceful settlement of the conflict. Russia condemned terrorism in all its forms and called on both sides to act with the utmost responsibility. Russia stressed that the road map provided the only chance of finding a way out of the crisis.

The United States said that, while all parties had responsibilities in bringing peace to the Middle East, ending terrorism had to be the highest priority. Those responsible for targeting civilians and obstructing the Quartet's efforts and Palestinian prospects for an independent State were known groups: Hamas, the Palestinian Islamic Jihad and the Al-Aqsa Martyrs Brigade. The Council had to take a clear stand against those terrorist groups and call for decisive action against them. Any Council resolution on the Middle East that the United States would support had to contain a robust condemnation of the acts of those Palestinian terrorist groups, and call for the dismantling of their support infrastructure, wherever located, consistent with Council resolution 1373(2001) [YUN 2001, p. 61]. The next Palestinian Prime Minister had to have real political authority to act against terrorist organizations, in addition to control over all the security organizations within the PA. For its part, Israel had to move forward and fulfil its obligations and commitments under the road map. The United States did not support either the elimination of Mr. Arafat or his forced exile and, accordingly, had cautioned Israel against that.

On 16 September [meeting 4828], the Council resumed discussion of the situation in the Middle East, including the Palestinian question. It had before it a draft resolution [S/2003/891] submitted by Pakistan, South Africa, the Sudan and the Syrian Arab Republic, by which the Council would have reiterated its demand for the complete cessation of all acts of violence, including terrorism, demanded that Israel desist from any act of deportation and cease any threat to the safety of the PA President, and expressed full support for the Quartet and called for increased efforts to ensure implementation of the road map. The draft resolution was not adopted, owing to the negative vote of the United States, a permanent member of the Council.

Speaking after the vote, the United States said that the draft resolution was flawed, as it failed to include a robust condemnation of acts of terrorism, an explicit condemnation of Palestinian terrorist groups, and a call for the dismantlement of infrastructure that supported those terror operations wherever located. The United States, along with Quartet partners, would continue to work towards the implementation of President Bush's vision of a two-State solution to the conflict, as set forth in the road map.

The Syrian Arab Republic said that the United States veto of the draft resolution would only further complicate an already complex situation in the Middle East and would have a negative impact on the general situation in the region.

The Permanent Observer of Palestine regretted that the United States had accepted Israeli positions almost completely and to such an extent that it did not permit it to play an unbiased role in the Arab-Israeli conflict or to act as an honest sponsor of the peace process.

Israel said that the draft resolution was lopsided. It did not focus on terrorism that killed innocent people or on the legal responsibility of the Palestinian leadership to dismantle the terrorist infrastructure. Instead, it focused its criticism on the victims of terrorism and on the response to terrorists rather than on terrorism itself. To advance the cause of peace, both sides needed to commit themselves to resolving the dispute through dialogue in an atmosphere free from terrorism, violence and incitement.

Emergency special session

In accordance with General Assembly resolution ES-10/11 [YUN 2002, p. 435] and at the request of the Sudan [A/ES-10/237], on behalf of the Arab Group and LAS, as well as the request of Malaysia, in its capacity as Chairman of the Coordinating Bureau of the Non-Aligned Movement [A/ES-10/238], the tenth emergency special session of the Assembly resumed on 19 September to discuss "Illegal Israeli actions in Occupied East Jerusalem and the rest of the Occupied Palestinian Territory". The session was first convened in April 1997 [YUN 1997, p. 394] and resumed in July and November of that year, as well as in March 1998 [YUN 1998, p. 425], February 1999 [YUN 1999, p. 402], October 2000 [YUN 2000, p. 421], December 2001 [YUN 2001, p. 414], May 2002 [YUN 2002, p. 428] and resumed in August of that year [ibid., p. 435].

GENERAL ASSEMBLY ACTION

On 19 September [meeting 20], the General Assembly adopted **resolution ES-10/12** [draft: A/ES-10/L.12 & Add.1, as orally amended] by recorded vote (133-4-15) [agenda item 5].

Illegal Israeli actions in Occupied East Jerusalem and the rest of the Occupied Palestinian Territory

The General Assembly,

Recalling the previous resolutions adopted at its tenth emergency special session,

Recalling also Security Council resolutions 242(1967) of 22 November 1967, 338(1973) of 22 October 1973, 1397(2002) of 12 March 2002, 1402(2002) of 30 March 2002, 1403(2002) of 4 April 2002, 1405(2002) of 19 April 2002 and 1435(2002) of 24 September 2002,

Reiterating its grave concern at the tragic and violent events that have taken place since September 2000 which have caused enormous suffering and many innocent victims throughout the Occupied Palestinian Territory, including East Jerusalem, and in Israel,

Condemning the suicide bombings and their recent intensification, and recalling in that regard that in the framework of the road map, the Palestinian Authority has to take all necessary measures to end violence and terror,

Deploring the extrajudicial killings and their recent escalation, and underlining that they are a violation of international law and international humanitarian law and compromise the efforts to relaunch the peace process and must be stopped,

Reaffirming the illegality of the deportation of any Palestinian by Israel, the occupying Power, and affirming its opposition to any such deportation,

Reiterating the need for respect, in all circumstances, of international humanitarian law, including the Geneva Convention relative to the Protection of Civilian Persons in Time of War of 12 August 1949,

1. *Reiterates its demand* for the complete cessation of all acts of violence, including all acts of terrorism, provocation, incitement and destruction;

2. *Demands* that Israel, the occupying Power, desist from any act of deportation and cease any threat to the safety of the elected President of the Palestinian Authority;

3. *Expresses its full support* for the efforts of the Quartet, and demands that the two sides fully implement their obligations in accordance with the road map, and emphasizes in this context the importance of the forthcoming meeting of the Quartet in New York;

4. *Decides* to adjourn the tenth emergency special session temporarily and to authorize the current President of the General Assembly to resume its meeting upon request from Member States.

RECORDED VOTE ON RESOLUTION ES-10/12:

In favour: Albania, Algeria, Andorra, Angola, Antigua and Barbuda, Argentina, Armenia, Austria, Azerbaijan, Bahrain, Bangladesh, Barbados, Belarus, Belgium, Belize, Benin, Bolivia, Bosnia and Herzegovina,

Botswana, Brazil, Brunei Darussalam, Bulgaria, Burkina Faso, Cambodia, Cape Verde, Chad, Chile, China, Congo, Côte d'Ivoire, Croatia, Cuba, Cyprus, Czech Republic, Democratic People's Republic of Korea, Denmark, Djibouti, Dominica, Ecuador, Egypt, Estonia, Ethiopia, Finland, France, Gambia, Germany, Greece, Grenada, Guinea, Guyana, Haiti, Hungary, Iceland, India, Indonesia, Iran, Ireland, Italy, Jamaica, Japan, Jordan, Kazakhstan, Kuwait, Lao People's Democratic Republic, Latvia, Lebanon, Lesotho, Libyan Arab Jamahiriya, Liechtenstein, Lithuania, Luxembourg, Malaysia, Maldives, Mali, Malta, Mauritania, Mauritius, Mexico, Monaco, Morocco, Mozambique, Myanmar, Namibia, Nepal, Netherlands, New Zealand, Nigeria, Norway, Oman, Pakistan, Panama, Philippines, Poland, Portugal, Qatar, Republic of Korea, Romania, Russian Federation, Saint Lucia, Saint Vincent and the Grenadines, Samoa, San Marino, Saudi Arabia, Senegal, Serbia and Montenegro, Sierra Leone, Singapore, Slovakia, Slovenia, South Africa, Spain, Sri Lanka, Sudan, Suriname, Swaziland, Sweden, Switzerland, Syrian Arab Republic, Thailand, The former Yugoslav Republic of Macedonia, Togo, Trinidad and Tobago, Tunisia, Turkey, Uganda, Ukraine, United Arab Emirates, United Kingdom, United Republic of Tanzania, Uruguay, Venezuela, Viet Nam, Yemen.

Against: Israel, Marshall Islands, Micronesia, United States.

Abstaining: Australia, Cameroon, Canada, Colombia, Fiji, Guatemala, Honduras, Kenya, Nauru, Nicaragua, Papua New Guinea, Paraguay, Peru, Tonga, Tuvalu.

The Permanent Observer of Palestine, speaking before the vote, said that threats by Israel against the Palestinian people and its leadership reached an unprecedented level on 11 September, with the decision by the Israeli security cabinet to remove and expel President Arafat from his land and country, proving once again the intentions of Mr. Sharon's Government to attack the PA and to destroy the Palestinians' socio-economic conditions. Any implementation of those threats would be considered a terrorist act that would lead to the end of the PA and the demise of the peace process. Israel had carried out a military campaign against the Palestinians for almost three years, during which its military forces had committed war crimes. At the same time, Israel was trying to depict all that had happened and was happening in the region as a battle against terrorism. The PA had been very clear in its condemnation of actions committed by Palestinian groups in contravention of international law, specifically the suicide bombings that had targeted Israeli civilians. The main issue of contention remained Israel's occupation of Palestinian land, the settler population and Israel's rejection of the Palestinian right to national independence. If the occupation and Israeli violence continued, Palestinian violence would also go on. The road map should be revived and implemented in a real and honest way.

Israel said that the Assembly was convening to consider an initiative that relapsed into the familiar preoccupation with one-sided resolutions that had contributed little to the security and peace of Israelis and Palestinians. The Security Council had just rejected a draft resolution (see p. 472) that would have defended a man (Mr. Arafat) who had devoted all of his energies to scuttling a long list of peace efforts. Like so many other resolutions presented by the Palestinian side, the draft resolution imagined an alternate reality where acts of terrorism garnered merely a passing mention. By focusing criticism on the response to terrorism and not on terrorism itself, the draft resolution was devoid of moral substance. The first clauses of the road map demanded the dismantling of Palestinian terrorist organizations. The failure of the Palestinian leadership to live up to that obligation should take a prominent role in any balanced assessment of the obstacles to peace. Israel continued to hold out hope for a new Palestinian leadership that would live up to its obligations, for it was committed to resolving the conflict through dialogue and to making compromises so as to realize the vision of two States living side by side in mutual dignity and security.

The Russian Federation said that the emergency special session was taking place against the backdrop of the tragic situation in the Palestinian territories. Despite diplomatic efforts, Palestinian and Israeli relations had been plunged into a vicious cycle of violence, including terrorism and acts of retribution. Russia called on the PA to undertake immediate measures to stop terrorist actions, and on Israel to implement its obligations under the road map. The Council's lack of readiness to adopt a resolution in connection with the exacerbation of Palestinian-Israeli confrontation reaffirmed the need for more active international efforts aimed at solving the crisis.

The United States said that the draft resolutions that had been considered that week by the Council and the Assembly were flawed in their lack of balance, because they singled out Israel and ignored those groups whose aim it was to sabotage the road map.

Quartet meeting (26 September)

The Quartet, meeting in New York on 26 September, issued a statement [S/2003/951], transmitted to the Security Council President by the Secretary-General on 6 October, in which it viewed with concern the stalled implementation of the road map. It reminded both parties of the need to take into account the long-term consequences of their actions and their obligation to make rapid progress towards full implementation of the road map. Condemning the terror attacks of August and September (see p. 469) carried out by Palestinian groups, they called on Palestinians to take immediate, decisive steps against those groups, and on all States to end harbouring and supporting any groups or individuals using terror and violence to advance their goals. The Quartet also affirmed that the PA security services had to be consolidated under the clear control of an empowered Prime Minister and Interior Minister, and made the sole armed authority in the West Bank and Gaza. The PA should ensure that its rebuilt security apparatus began effective operations to confront terror and dismantle terrorist capabilities and infrastructure. The Quartet called on Israel to take no action that undermined trust, including deportations, confiscation and/or demolition of Palestinian homes and property and destruction of Palestinian institutions, and to ease the humanitarian and economic plight of the Palestinians. It also called for a halt to settlement activity and expressed concern over the proposed and actual route of Israel's West Bank barrier, which could prejudice the final borders of a future Palestinian State.

Construction of separation barrier

Communications (1-13 October). On 1 October [A/58/399-S/2003/929], the Permanent Observer of Palestine said that Israel continued to plan and erect a separation wall in the Occupied Palestinian Territory. The first stage, approximately 150 kilometres in length, had already been built, beginning in the northern areas of the West Bank. The wall, which consisted of a complex system of concrete barriers, trenches, electric fences and barbed wire, cut deep inside Palestinian territory, at some points as deep as 6 kilometres. That construction had involved the destruction of extensive tracts of fertile Palestinian farmland, the separation of villages and cities, and the destruction of the livelihood of thousands of Palestinians, who were being cut off from their land, work, schools and institutions and even from each other. As the course of the wall expanded southward, parts of it were being built in and around East Jerusalem. The Israeli cabinet had approved plans for the construction of the wall's central section, which would go even deeper into Palestinian land and would begin with a segment at least 22 kilometres from the 1967 line. The Permanent Observer called on the Security Council to address that grave matter and bring a halt to the illegal actions.

On 2 October [A/58/420], Malaysia transmitted to the Secretary-General a declaration and statement on Palestine adopted by the Ministers for Foreign Affairs of the Non-Aligned Movement (New York, 26 September), expressing support for the idea that the General Assembly, during its fifty-eighth (2003) session, should focus on the expansionist Israeli wall, which had confiscated and destroyed Palestinian land and isolated Palestinian cities, towns and villages. They also supported the proposal for a comprehensive Council resolution in line with the road map, which would set forth positions on the components of a final settlement of the conflict.

By a 3 October letter [A/58/411-S/2003/938], the Permanent Observer of Palestine said that, on the previous day, the Israeli Government had publicized its intention to build another 600 settlement housing units in the Occupied Palestinian Territory, a decision that should be viewed in the context of the building of the wall on Palestinian land.

On the same day [A/58/415-S/2003/952], Iran transmitted to the Secretary-General the final communiqué of the Annual Coordination Meeting of Ministers for Foreign Affairs of the Member States of the Organization of the Islamic Conference (OIC) (New York, 30 September), in which they condemned, among other things, the construction of the separation wall and the expansion of Israeli settlements in the Occupied Palestinian Territory.

On 6 October [S/2003/981], Italy, on behalf of the EU, condemned the 4 October Palestinian suicide bombing in Haifa, which killed 21 Israelis and wounded at least 60 others (see p. 523).

On 10 October [A/ES-10/239-S/2003/985] and 13 October [A/ES-10/241-S/2003/990], the Permanent Observer of Palestine informed the Secretary-General and the Council President that Israeli forces continued to carry out their military campaign against the Palestinian people and the PA. On 10 October, IDF carried out a raid inside the Rafah refugee camp in the Gaza Strip, which caused the death of seven Palestinians and injured 50 others. At least 120 homes were reported destroyed inside the camp.

Security Council consideration (14 October). At the request of the Syrian Arab Republic, on behalf of the Arab Group and LAS [S/2003/973], supported by Malaysia [S/2003/974] and Iran [S/2003/977], on behalf of the Non-Aligned Movement and OIC, respectively, the Security Council, on 14 October [meetings 4841 and 4842], discussed the situation in the Middle East, including the Palestinian question. Those countries had requested that the Council discuss, in particular, the construction by Israel of a separation wall in the Occupied Palestinian Territory and Israeli settlement activity. With the Council's consent, the President invited, among others, Israel, the Permanent Observer of Palestine [S/2003/988], the Permanent Observer of LAS [S/2003/975] and the Deputy Permanent Observer of OIC [S/2003/989], at their request, to participate in the discussion.

The Permanent Observer of Palestine said that, with the continuing extension of the separation wall, Israel would have effectively transferred large numbers of Palestinians, confined the others in several walled enclaves with secondary walls inside them, effectively destroying the possibility of the existence of an independent, sovereign State of Palestine and the potential for achieving a political settlement of the Israeli-Palestinian conflict. The construction of the wall and the confiscation of Palestinian land had partially or completely separated those civilians from their land and water resources. Severe restrictions had been placed on the movement of Palestinians, including the complete walling of the city of Qalqilya and the control of entry and exit of the city through one gate for its 40,000 inhabitants. In East Jerusalem, Israel had built a separation wall up to 8 kilometres long and similar plans were in store for Bethlehem. The construction of the wall was illegal and violated the UN Charter, the Fourth Geneva Convention and relevant Security Council resolutions.

The construction of the wall complemented Israeli settlement activities. Israel had transferred more than 400,000 settlers to the Occupied Palestinian Territory, placing them in more than 200 settlements built on more than 8 per cent of Palestinian land, in addition to the land in their vicinity and the additional land they attempted to control. It had established a separate infrastructure and a complete network of roads for those settlers, enabling them to exploit Palestinian natural resources. With the building of the wall, Israel was attempting to annex the Palestinian land on which half of those settlers were living, while leaving enough room for the expansion of the rest of the settlements. Settlements and the wall had to be stopped in order to rescue the potential for achieving peace and a final settlement based on the existence of two States.

Israel said that the Assembly had gathered for yet another meeting to censure Israel for its measures to prevent terrorism, rather than to address the terrorism itself. Israel had decided to construct a security fence with great reluctance because of three factors, the most important of which was Yasser Arafat and the PA. Mr. Arafat had proved that he was incapable of and uninterested in making peace with Israel and unwilling to do so. He had chosen a partnership with Palestinian terrorist groups rather than with Israel, thereby flouting Council resolutions, the road map and undertakings in peace agreements between the two sides, which required the PA to dismantle terrorist infrastructure, prevent terrorism and incitement and bring those responsible to justice. In fact, he prevented the emergence of a Palestinian leadership that would do something other than sponsor terrorism or tolerate the smuggling of weapons into the hands of terrorist groups. The occasional half-hearted condemnations of terrorist activities by the Palestinian leadership were just a tactic. In short, had there been any concerted action by the Palestinian leadership to confront and prevent the terrorists, the security fence might not have been necessary.

The fence was also constructed because there were no other options available. In a situation where terrorists were operating with impunity in the heart of civilian centres, there was no perfect way for Israel to obstruct them without having an impact on the lives of the Palestinians among whom they were hiding. The construction of the security fence, therefore, was one of the most effective non-violent methods of preventing the passage of terrorists and their armaments from Palestinian terrorist areas to civilian areas in Israel. That had been the case in the Gaza Strip, where, since the construction of a similar fence, under an Israeli-Palestinian agreement of 1994 [YUN 1994, p. 616], not a single terrorist had succeeded in penetrating into Israel from Gaza. Likewise, in those areas of the West Bank where a fence had been constructed, a reduction in terrorist attacks was already evident. The construction of the fence would also enable Israel to reduce its involvement in the daily lives of Palestinians. The net effect of the construction of the fence would be a reduction in terrorism and an overall improvement in the quality of life for both the Israelis and the Palestinians. Israel would also be able to significantly reduce the presence of its forces in Palestinian areas, further diminish the necessity for defensive action within Palestinian cities, including the removal of roadblocks and checkpoints, and help create an atmosphere conducive to peaceful negotiations. The fence was a crucial measure in taking terrorism out of the equation.

In determining the route of the fence, Israel had sought to create a barrier between those areas from which the terrorists originated and those that they sought to target. Constructing the fence along the so-called Green Line, as suggested by some, would create far greater humanitarian problems, arbitrarily dividing villages and separating others from access to water and other basic services on a large scale. Israel had taken into consideration humanitarian and environmental concerns, for the rights and interests of local populations had to be weighed against the rights of civilians to protection from terrorism. Local Palestinian residents had been engaged and consulted throughout that process, with a view to providing individual solutions and ensuring access to schools, health resources and other facilities. Dozens of agricultural gates had been established along the route of the fence to enable farmers to continue cultivating their lands. Any private land used in building the fence was requisitioned for military purposes, in full conformity with international humanitarian law and local laws. Compensation matching the properties' value was provided, as well as for the full value of crop yield as long as the property was needed. Israel refuted the allegations that the fence was an act of de facto annexation and an attempt to prejudice final-status negotiations, for the fence had no political significance as it did not annex territories to the State of Israel nor did it change the status of the land, its ownership or the legal status of the residents in those areas. Israel was ready, at great cost, to adjust or dismantle the fence if so required as part of a political settlement. The fence was a response to Palestinian terror, designed not to establish a border, but to create a terror-free environment in which a border could be agreed through negotiations.

The Syrian Arab Republic said that Israel's statement was part of a campaign to distort reality and mislead international public opinion. Israel failed to mention that the wall had been built on the remains of Palestinian territories and under the logic of sheer force. By building the wall, Israel was in fact annexing vast expanses of the territories of the West Bank. Its aim was to put an end to the peace process and any real chance of implementing it.

The United Kingdom said that it had consistently condemned the intolerable suicide bombings that Israel had suffered, but stressed that the separation wall undermined the trust between the parties that was necessary for negotiations, had a negative impact on the daily lives of Palestinians and called into question the two-State solution. Facts on the ground created by Israeli settlement activity also threatened the viability of a Palestinian State and made the possibility of a negotiated settlement more difficult to reach.

The United States said that ending terrorism had to be the highest priority. Any Council resolution concerning the Middle East had to take into account the security situation, including the devastating suicide attacks that Israelis had had to endure over the last three years. The United States views on the construction of the Israeli fence had been made clear by its National Security Adviser, Condoleezza Rice, who had said that the fence was not really consistent with the United States view of what the Middle East would one day have to look like: two States living side by side in peace. It was extremely important, if the fence was going to be built, that it should not intrude on the lives of Palestinians and that it should not look as if it was trying to prejudge the outcome of a peace agreement. The United States had urged Israel to consider carefully the consequences of its actions. However, a Council resolution focused on the fence did not further the goals of peace and security in the region. The United States urged both sides to avoid actions that exacerbated the situation.

Following discussion on the agenda item [meeting 4842], the Security Council voted (10-1-4) on a draft resolution [S/2003/980] submitted by Guinea, Malaysia, Pakistan and the Syrian Arab Republic. The draft resolution was not adopted owing to the negative vote of the United States, a permanent member of the Council.

Resumed emergency special session (October)

In accordance with General Assembly resolution ES-10/12 (see p. 472) and at the request of the Syrian Arab Republic [A/ES-10/242], on behalf of the Arab Group and LAS, of Malaysia [A/ES-10/243], in its capacity as Chairman of the Coordinating Bureau of the Non-Aligned Movement, and of Iran [A/ES-10/244], in its capacity as Chairman of the OIC Group at the United Nations, the tenth emergency special session of the Assembly resumed on 20 and 21 October. The Assembly had before it two draft resolutions [A/ES-10/L.13 and A/ES-10/L.14] on illegal Israeli actions in Occupied East Jerusalem and the rest of the Occupied Palestinian Territory.

The Permanent Observer of Palestine said that, on 14 October, the Security Council had failed to exercise its primary responsibility for the maintenance of international peace and security because of the exercise of veto by one of its permanent members, which prevented it from adopting a binding resolution declaring the separation wall illegal and from demanding that Israel cease its construction and dismantle the existing parts. The practical result of the veto was that the construction of the wall would continue with catastrophic consequences, unless the Assembly and the Council did something about it. The September report [E/CN.4/2004/6] (see p. 488) of the Special Rapporteur of the Commission on Human Rights on the situation of human rights in the Occupied Palestinian Territory highlighted the fact that the wall did not follow the Green Line, the de facto boundary between Israel and Palestine, but incorporated substantial areas of the West Bank into Israel, affecting over 210,000 Palestinians by its construction. Israel could build walls on its own land along the armistice line, which, while not being conducive to coexistence between the two sides, would not be illegal.

Israel had used the security pretext in the past to justify its illegal settlement activities throughout the territories occupied since 1967 and was currently doing that again with anti-terrorism measures. Israel should not be allowed to exploit the battle against international terrorism and its own civilian casualties as a cover for its illegal policies and measures and for the continuation of its settlements, expansionism and obstruction of peace. To save hope and peace in the region, the Assembly had to formulate a unanimous international position against the wall, one that would help terminate its construction. It could also request an advisory opinion of the International Court of Justice (ICJ) on Israel's obligations regarding the wall, the cessation of its construction and the dismantling of its existing parts.

Israel said the only reason why the Security Council did not adopt the draft resolution on 14 October was because its sponsors had refused to negotiate a fair and balanced text that would have properly referred to Palestinian responsibilities to end support and encouragement of terrorism. Israel added that the Palestinian side had become all too confident in its ability to abuse the Assembly and push through one-sided resolutions, full of acrimony and blame. It turned to the Assembly each and every time to rubber-stamp what it failed to garner in the Council, and was currently relying on the Assembly to approve the exploitation of yet another UN organ in an ill-conceived and manipulative request for an advisory opinion. That request would not enhance the prospects for peace in the region, for it involved outstanding political issues that the parties had themselves agreed to resolve through negotiations. It could only undermine, complicate and further delay efforts to resolve the dispute. The request was another attempt by the Palestinians to divert attention from the one thing that continued to prevent a peaceful settlement and that had necessitated Israeli security measures, including the fence itself: the continuing refusal by the Palestinians to fight terrorism. In seeking to politicize the Court and to bring an issue that was the subject of dispute before the Court in its advisory capacity risked causing serious harm to the reputation, independence and authority of the UN's principal judicial organ.

The United States said that it opposed the call for an ICJ advisory opinion—a move that would only complicate the international community's efforts to realize a two-State solution.

On 21 October, with the consent of the sponsors of the two draft resolutions before the Assembly, Italy, on behalf of the EU, submitted a compromise replacement draft resolution (see below).

GENERAL ASSEMBLY ACTION

On 21 October [meeting 22], the General Assembly adopted **resolution ES-10/13** [draft: A/ES-10/L.15, as orally corrected] by recorded vote (144-4-12) [agenda item 5].

Illegal Israeli actions in Occupied East Jerusalem and the rest of the Occupied Palestinian Territory

The General Assembly,

Recalling its relevant resolutions, including resolutions of the tenth emergency special session,

Recalling also Security Council resolutions 242(1967) of 22 November 1967, 267(1969) of 3 July 1969, 298(1971) of 25 September 1971, 446(1979) of 22 March 1979, 452(1979) of 20 July 1979, 465(1980) of 1 March 1980, 476(1980) of 30 June 1980, 478(1980) of 20 August 1980, 904(1994) of 18 March 1994, 1073(1996) of 28 September 1996 and 1397(2002) of 12 March 2002,

Reaffirming the principle of the inadmissibility of the acquisition of territory by force,

Reaffirming also its vision of a region where two States, Israel and Palestine, live side by side within secure and recognized borders,

Condemning all acts of violence, terrorism and destruction,

Condemning in particular the suicide bombings and their recent intensification with the attack in Haifa,

Condemning the bomb attack in the Gaza Strip, which resulted in the death of three American security officers,

Deploring the extrajudicial killings and their recent intensification, in particular the attack on 20 October 2003 in Gaza,

Stressing the urgency of ending the current violent situation on the ground, the need to end the occupation that began in 1967, and the need to achieve peace based on the vision of two States mentioned above,

Particularly concerned that the route marked out for the wall under construction by Israel, the occupying Power, in the Occupied Palestinian Territory, including in and around East Jerusalem, could prejudge future negotiations and make the two-State solution physically impossible to implement and would cause further humanitarian hardship to the Palestinians,

Reiterating its call upon Israel, the occupying Power, to fully and effectively respect the Geneva Convention relative to the Protection of Civilian Persons in Time of War of 12 August 1949,

Reiterating its opposition to settlement activities in the Occupied Territories and to any activities involving the confiscation of land, disruption of the livelihood of protected persons and the de facto annexation of land,

1. *Demands* that Israel stop and reverse the construction of the wall in the Occupied Palestinian Territory, including in and around East Jerusalem, which is in departure of the Armistice Line of 1949 and is in contradiction to relevant provisions of international law;

2. *Calls upon* both parties to fulfil their obligations under relevant provisions of the road map, the Palestinian Authority to undertake visible efforts on the ground to arrest, disrupt and restrain individuals and groups conducting and planning violent attacks, and the Government of Israel to take no actions undermining trust, including deportations and attacks on civilians and extrajudicial killings;

3. *Requests* the Secretary-General to report on compliance with the present resolution periodically, with the first report on compliance with paragraph 1 above

to be submitted within one month and upon receipt of which further actions should be considered, if necessary, within the United Nations system;

4. *Decides* to adjourn the tenth emergency special session temporarily and to authorize the current President of the General Assembly to resume its meeting upon request from Member States.

RECORDED VOTE ON RESOLUTION ES-10/13

In favour: Albania, Algeria, Andorra, Angola, Antigua and Barbuda, Argentina, Armenia, Austria, Azerbaijan, Bahamas, Bahrain, Bangladesh, Barbados, Belarus, Belgium, Belize, Benin, Bosnia and Herzegovina, Botswana, Brazil, Brunei Darussalam, Bulgaria, Burkina Faso, Cambodia, Cameroon, Canada, Cape Verde, Chile, China, Colombia, Comoros, Costa Rica, Côte d'Ivoire, Croatia, Cuba, Cyprus, Czech Republic, Democratic People's Republic of Korea, Denmark, Djibouti, Dominica, Egypt, Eritrea, Estonia, Ethiopia, Finland, France, Gabon, Gambia, Germany, Ghana, Greece, Grenada, Guatemala, Guinea, Guinea-Bissau, Guyana, Hungary, Iceland, India, Indonesia, Iran, Ireland, Italy, Jamaica, Japan, Jordan, Kazakhstan, Kenya, Kuwait, Kyrgyzstan, Lao People's Democratic Republic, Latvia, Lebanon, Lesotho, Libyan Arab Jamahiriya, Liechtenstein, Lithuania, Luxembourg, Malaysia, Maldives, Mali, Malta, Mauritania, Mauritius, Mexico, Monaco, Mongolia, Morocco, Mozambique, Myanmar, Namibia, Nepal, Netherlands, New Zealand, Niger, Nigeria, Norway, Oman, Pakistan, Panama, Paraguay, Peru, Philippines, Poland, Portugal, Qatar, Republic of Korea, Romania, Russian Federation, Saint Lucia, San Marino, Saudi Arabia, Senegal, Serbia and Montenegro, Sierra Leone, Singapore, Slovakia, Slovenia, Somalia, South Africa, Spain, Sri Lanka, Sudan, Suriname, Swaziland, Sweden, Switzerland, Syrian Arab Republic, Thailand, The former Yugoslav Republic of Macedonia, Togo, Trinidad and Tobago, Tunisia, Turkey, Ukraine, United Arab Emirates, United Kingdom, United Republic of Tanzania, Venezuela, Viet Nam, Yemen, Zambia, Zimbabwe.

Against: Israel, Marshall Islands, Micronesia, United States.

Abstaining: Australia, Burundi, Dominican Republic, Ecuador, Honduras, Malawi, Nauru, Nicaragua, Papua New Guinea, Rwanda, Tuvalu, Uruguay.

Communications (21 October–11 November). On 21 October [A/ES-10/246-S/2003/1029], the Permanent Observer of Palestine informed the Secretary-General and the Security Council President that on 20 October IDF carried out air strikes in Gaza City, killing at least 10 Palestinians and wounding at least 90 other civilians.

On 22 October [A/ES-10/247-S/2003/1031], the Permanent Observer of Palestine said that Israel had declared its intention to continue building the separation wall in the Occupied Palestinian Territory, including East Jerusalem.

On 4 November [S/2003/1072], the Permanent Observer of LAS informed the Council President that the Head of the Auditing Bureau and Governor of the Islamic Development Bank in Palestine reported that the total losses and damage inflicted on the Palestinian people by Israel during the past three years had amounted to $17,262,500,000.

On 11 November [S/2003/1079], the Secretary-General of LAS transmitted to the Council President a written plea from the Palestinian residents of the city of Qalqilya, which described the developments that were taking place in that city as a consequence of the construction of the Israeli separation wall. According to the plea, the 42,000 inhabitants were blocked on all four sides of the city, with only a single entrance controlled by IDF.

Compliance with resolution ES-10/13

In November [A/ES-10/248], the Secretary-General submitted a report pursuant to General Assembly resolution ES-10/13 (see p. 477), which required that he report on compliance with its request in paragraph 1 that Israel "stop and reverse the construction of the wall in the Occupied Palestinian Territory, including in and around East Jerusalem". The report, which focused on the period from 14 April 2002, when the Israeli Government decided to build the barrier, to 20 November 2003, examined the route of the barrier and its economic and social impact. Annexed to the report were summaries of the legal positions of the Government of Israel and the PLO.

The Secretary-General stated that Israel was not in compliance with the Assembly's request, as UN field monitoring had shown ongoing construction in the Occupied Palestinian Territory along the north-east boundary of the West Bank and East Jerusalem; levelling of land for a section in the north-west of the West Bank; ongoing issuance of land requisition orders; and release of the first official map showing the planned route of the barrier and declaration of intent to complete it by 2005. The Secretary-General noted that, on 1 October 2003, after nearly a year of construction on various sections, the Israeli Government approved a full barrier route, which, according to the plan, would form one continuous line stretching 720 kilometres along the West Bank. The planned route, if constructed, would deviate up to 22 kilometres in places from the Green Line. Based on the Israeli Ministry of Defence's official map, approximately 975 square kilometres, or 16.6 per cent of the entire West Bank, would lie between the barrier and the Green Line, the home to about 17,000 Palestinians in the West Bank and 220,000 in East Jerusalem. The barrier complex consisted of a fence with electronic sensors designed to alert IDF of infiltration attempts; a ditch (up to 4 metres deep); an asphalt two-lane patrol road; a trace road (a strip of sand smoothed to detect footprints) parallel to the fence; and a stack of six coils of barbed wire marking the complex's perimeter. Various observation systems were being installed along the barrier. Concrete walls covered about 8.5 kilometres of the approximately 180 kilometres of the barrier completed or under construction. Those parts of the barrier were generally found where Palestinian population centres shared common boundaries with Israel, such as the towns of Qalqilya and parts of Jerusalem. Phase A of the barrier, which ran 123 kilometres from the Salem checkpoint north of Jenin to the settlement of Elkana in the central West Bank, was completed in July, although work continued in some parts. Much of Phase A construction, which deviated from the Green Line, incorporated Israeli settlements. Phase B was planned to run 45 kilometres east from the Salem checkpoint along the northern part of the Green Line to the Jordan Valley and was scheduled for completion in December. The existing barrier and planned route around Jerusalem was also beyond the Green Line. Completed sections included two parts totalling 19.5 kilometres that flanked Jerusalem and a 1.5-kilometre concrete wall in an eastern Jerusalem neighbourhood.

The barrier appeared likely to further deepen the fragmentation of the West Bank created by the closure system of checkpoints and blockades imposed by Israel after the outbreak of hostilities in September/October 2000 that restricted the movement of Palestinian people and goods and caused serious socio-economic harm. The construction of the barrier had increased such damage in communities along its route, primarily through the loss of, or severely limited access to, land, jobs and markets. Palestinians living in enclaves were facing some of the harshest consequences of the barrier's construction. Towns such as Qalqilya had only one entry and exit point controlled by IDF, which resulted in the isolation of the town from all its agricultural land.

The Secretary-General observed that the scope of construction and the amount of occupied West Bank land that was requisitioned for the barrier's route or that would end up between the barrier and the Green Line were of serious concern and had implications for the future. In the midst of the road map process, when each party should be making good-faith confidence-building gestures, the barrier's construction could not be seen as anything but a deeply counterproductive act. The placing of most of the structure on occupied Palestinian land could impair future negotiations. The Secretary-General acknowledged and recognized Israel's right and duty to protect its people against terrorist attacks. That duty, however, should not be carried out in a way that could damage the longer-term prospects of peace by making the creation of a viable and contiguous Palestinian State more difficult.

Resumed emergency special session (December)

Following a request [A/ES-10/249] from Kuwait, as Chairman of the Arab Group and on behalf of LAS, the General Assembly resumed its tenth emergency special session on 8 December. Support for the request to resume the session was voiced by Malaysia on behalf of the Non-Aligned Movement [A/ES-10/251]. The Assembly had before it the Secretary-General's November report (see p. 478).

Kuwait said that the draft resolution before the Assembly showed in clear terms the legal implication of the construction of the wall, reaffirmed the applicability of the Fourth Geneva Convention and its Additional Protocol to the Occupied Palestinian Territory, including East Jerusalem, and the need to end the conflict on the basis of the establishment of two States according to the 1949 Armistice Line, and underlined the fact that, with the passage of time, conditions on the ground would become more difficult because of the construction of the wall. It also called on ICJ to render an advisory opinion on what were the legal consequences arising from the construction of the wall in the Occupied Palestinian Territory, including in and around East Jerusalem—as described in the Secretary-General's report—bearing in mind the rules and principles of international law and relevant Security Council and General Assembly resolutions.

The Permanent Observer of Palestine said that Israel, as observed by the Secretary-General in his report, was not in compliance with Assembly resolution ES-10/13 and therefore further actions had to be taken. In the absence of any specific practical measures to compel Israel to stop building the wall and to dismantle the existing parts, there was a need to affirm, at a minimum, the legal aspects of the matter, such as the illegality of the wall and its non-recognition by the UN system. If Israel continued building the wall, it would be the end of the road map and resolution 1515(2003) (see p. 483) endorsing it. The Security Council had to react in the form of a comprehensive resolution, in which the form of a final settlement would be defined, while calling on the parties to negotiate the details.

Israel stated that it did not deny that, in exercising its right to self-defence against terrorism, it had to act within the limits of international law, but it rejected attempts to apply that law selectively to misrepresent the nature and purpose of the security fence and to ignore the context in which its actions were taken. Israel reiterated that the security fence was a temporary, proven, necessary and non-violent measure adopted in accordance with international and local laws to defend the people of Israel from a continuing terrorist campaign. As long as the Palestinian leadership continued to flout its obligations to fight terrorism, there was simply no alternative to the fence. Israel was ready to dismantle or alter the fence's route in accordance with any political settlement reached. That route was determined not by politics, but by a balance between security, humanitarianism and topographical considerations. The fence was not an obstacle to a two-State solution nor to the creation of a contiguous and viable Palestinian State. Prompted by a clearly one-sided resolution, the Secretary-General's November report lacked fairness, balance and perspective. The silence of the report on the threat posed by Palestinian terrorism and the complicity of the Palestinian leadership was incomprehensible, given that the fence was a response to that threat. The question of whether Israel's defensive measures were permissible depended on whether they were proportionate to the threat faced by Israel and its citizens. The draft resolution presented for adoption was a politically biased text, rife with supposed legal conclusions, which made a mockery of ICJ and threatened to undermine its status.

Italy, speaking on behalf of the EU, said that it shared the concerns expressed by the Secretary-General in his report (see p. 478) and supported his observations. However, it believed that the proposed request for an advisory opinion from ICJ would not help the efforts of the two parties to relaunch a political dialogue and was therefore inappropriate. The EU stressed that the Palestinian leadership had to concretely demonstrate its determination in the fight against extremist violence in compliance with the road map, while Israel, in exercising its right of self-defence, had to respect international law, in particular human rights and international humanitarian law.

The United States said the Assembly's emergency special session did not contribute to the shared goal of implementing the road map. The path to peace was the Quartet plan for a permanent two-State solution to the conflict. Involving ICJ in that conflict could delay that solution and negatively impact the road map implementation. Furthermore, referral of that issue to ICJ risked politicizing the Court. The United States policy on Israel's fence was clear and consistent, for it opposed any activity by either party that prejudged final status negotiations. However, the Assembly's meeting and the draft resolution undermined rather than encouraged direct negotiations between the parties to resolve their differences.

GENERAL ASSEMBLY ACTION

On 8 December [meeting 23], the General Assembly adopted **resolution ES-10/14** [draft: A/ES-10/L.16] by recorded vote (90-8-74) [agenda item 5].

Illegal Israeli actions in Occupied East Jerusalem and the rest of the Occupied Palestinian Territory

The General Assembly,

Reaffirming its resolution ES-10/13 of 21 October 2003,

Guided by the principles of the Charter of the United Nations,

Aware of the established principle of international law on the inadmissibility of the acquisition of territory by force,

Aware also that developing friendly relations among nations based on respect for the principle of equal rights and self-determination of peoples is among the purposes and principles of the Charter of the United Nations,

Recalling relevant General Assembly resolutions, including resolution 181(II) of 29 November 1947, which partitioned mandated Palestine into two States, one Arab and one Jewish,

Recalling also the resolutions of the tenth emergency special session of the General Assembly,

Recalling further relevant Security Council resolutions, including resolutions 242(1967) of 22 November 1967, 338(1973) of 22 October 1973, 267(1969) of 3 July 1969, 298(1971) of 25 September 1971, 446(1979) of 22 March 1979, 452(1979) of 20 July 1979, 465(1980) of 1 March 1980, 476(1980) of 30 June 1980, 478(1980) of 20 August 1980, 904(1994) of 18 March 1994, 1073(1996) of 28 September 1996, 1397(2002) of 12 March 2002 and 1515(2003) of 19 November 2003,

Reaffirming the applicability of the Fourth Geneva Convention as well as Additional Protocol I to the Geneva Conventions to the Occupied Palestinian Territory, including East Jerusalem,

Recalling the Regulations annexed to the Hague Convention Respecting the Laws and Customs of War on Land of 1907,

Welcoming the convening of the Conference of High Contracting Parties to the Fourth Geneva Convention on measures to enforce the Convention in the Occupied Palestinian Territory, including Jerusalem, at Geneva on 15 July 1999,

Expressing its support for the declaration adopted by the reconvened Conference of High Contracting Parties to the Fourth Geneva Convention at Geneva on 5 December 2001,

Recalling in particular relevant United Nations resolutions affirming that Israeli settlements in the Occupied Palestinian Territory, including East Jerusalem, are illegal and an obstacle to peace and to economic and social development as well as those demanding the complete cessation of settlement activities,

Recalling relevant United Nations resolutions affirming that actions taken by Israel, the occupying Power, to change the status and demographic composition of Occupied East Jerusalem have no legal validity and are null and void,

Noting the agreements reached between the Government of Israel and the Palestine Liberation Organization in the context of the Middle East peace process,

Gravely concerned at the commencement and continuation of construction by Israel, the occupying Power, of a wall in the Occupied Palestinian Territory, including in and around East Jerusalem, which is in departure from the Armistice Line of 1949 (Green Line) and which has involved the confiscation and destruction of Palestinian land and resources, the disruption of the lives of thousands of protected civilians and the de facto annexation of large areas of territory, and underlining the unanimous opposition by the international community to the construction of that wall,

Gravely concerned also at the even more devastating impact of the projected parts of the wall on the Palestinian civilian population and on the prospects for solving the Palestinian-Israeli conflict and establishing peace in the region,

Welcoming the report of 8 September 2003 of the Special Rapporteur of the Commission on Human Rights on the situation of human rights in the Palestinian territories occupied by Israel since 1967, in particular the section regarding the wall,

Affirming the necessity of ending the conflict on the basis of the two-State solution of Israel and Palestine living side by side in peace and security based on the Armistice Line of 1949, in accordance with relevant Security Council and General Assembly resolutions,

Having received with appreciation the report of the Secretary-General, submitted in accordance with resolution ES-10/13,

Bearing in mind that the passage of time further compounds the difficulties on the ground, as Israel, the occupying Power, continues to refuse to comply with international law vis-à-vis its construction of the above-mentioned wall, with all its detrimental implications and consequences,

Decides, in accordance with Article 96 of the Charter of the United Nations, to request the International Court of Justice, pursuant to Article 65 of the Statute of the Court, to urgently render an advisory opinion on the following question:

What are the legal consequences arising from the construction of the wall being built by Israel, the occupying Power, in the Occupied Palestinian Territory, including in and around East Jerusalem, as described in the report of the Secretary-General, considering the rules and principles of international law, including the Fourth Geneva Convention of 1949, and relevant Security Council and General Assembly resolutions?

RECORDED VOTE ON RESOLUTION ES-10/14:

In favour: Algeria, Antigua and Barbuda, Argentina, Armenia, Azerbaijan, Bahamas, Bahrain, Bangladesh, Barbados, Belarus, Belize, Benin, Bhutan, Botswana, Brazil, Brunei Darussalam, Burkina Faso, Cambodia, Cape Verde, Central African Republic, Chad, China, Comoros, Côte d'Ivoire, Cuba, Democratic People's Republic of Korea, Djibouti, Egypt, Gambia, Ghana, Grenada, Guinea, Guinea-Bissau, Guyana, Haiti, India, Indonesia, Iran, Jamaica, Jordan, Kazakhstan, Kenya, Kuwait, Kyrgyzstan, Lao People's Democratic Republic, Lebanon, Lesotho, Libyan Arab Jamahiriya, Malaysia, Maldives, Mali, Mauritania, Mauritius, Mexico, Mongolia, Morocco, Mozambique, Myanmar, Namibia, Nepal, Niger, Nigeria, Oman, Pakistan, Panama, Qatar, Saint Lucia, Saint Vincent and the Grenadines, Saudi Arabia, Senegal, Sierra Leone, Somalia, South Africa, Sri Lanka, Sudan, Suriname, Swaziland, Syrian Arab Republic, Timor-Leste, Togo, Trinidad and Tobago, Tunisia, Turkey, Turkmenistan, United Arab Emirates, United Republic of Tanzania, Viet Nam, Yemen, Zambia, Zimbabwe.

Against: Australia, Ethiopia, Israel, Marshall Islands, Micronesia, Nauru, Palau, United States.

Abstaining: Albania, Andorra, Austria, Belgium, Bolivia, Bosnia and Herzegovina, Bulgaria, Burundi, Cameroon, Canada, Chile, Colombia, Costa Rica, Croatia, Cyprus, Czech Republic, Denmark, Dominican Republic, Ecuador, Estonia, Fiji, Finland, France, Georgia, Germany, Greece, Guatemala, Honduras, Hungary, Iceland, Ireland, Italy, Japan, Latvia, Liechtenstein, Lithuania, Luxembourg, Malta, Monaco, Netherlands, New Zealand, Nicaragua, Norway, Papua New Guinea, Paraguay, Peru, Philippines, Poland, Portugal, Republic of Korea, Republic of Moldova, Romania, Russian Federation, Samoa, San Marino, Serbia and Montenegro, Singapore, Slovakia, Slovenia, Solomon Islands, Spain, Sweden, Switzerland, Tajikistan, Thailand, The former Yugoslav Republic of Macedonia, Tonga, Uganda, Ukraine, United Kingdom, Uruguay, Uzbekistan, Vanuatu, Venezuela.

Speaking after the vote, Israel said that over half of the UN Member States did not vote for the resolution, which it regarded as a moral victory. Most of the world's enlightened democracies had chosen to not support the resolution, while about 90 other States, mostly tyrannical dictatorships, corrupt and human rights–defying regimes, supported it.

Also on 8 December, the Assembly adopted **decision ES-10/22** [draft: A/ES-10/L.17 & Add.1] by recorded vote (111-7-55) [agenda item 5].

Illegal Israeli actions in Occupied East Jerusalem and the rest of the Occupied Palestinian Territory

At its 23rd plenary meeting, on 8 December 2003, the General Assembly decided to adjourn the tenth emergency special session temporarily and to authorize the current President of the General Assembly to resume its meetings upon request from Member States.

RECORDED VOTE ON DECISION ES-10/22:

In favour: Afghanistan, Algeria, Antigua and Barbuda, Argentina, Armenia, Azerbaijan, Bahamas, Bahrain, Bangladesh, Barbados, Belarus, Belize, Benin, Bhutan, Bolivia, Botswana, Brazil, Brunei Darussalam, Burkina Faso, Cambodia, Cape Verde, Central African Republic, Chad, Chile, China, Comoros, Congo, Costa Rica, Côte d'Ivoire, Cuba, Cyprus, Democratic People's Republic of Korea, Djibouti, Ecuador, Egypt, Ethiopia, Gabon, Gambia, Ghana, Grenada, Guatemala, Guinea, Guinea-Bissau, Guyana, Haiti, India, Indonesia, Iran, Jamaica, Japan, Jordan, Kazakhstan, Kenya, Kuwait, Kyrgyzstan, Lao People's Democratic Republic, Lebanon, Lesotho, Libyan Arab Jamahiriya, Malaysia, Maldives, Mali, Mauritania, Mauritius, Mexico, Mongolia, Morocco, Mozambique, Myanmar, Namibia, Nepal, Niger, Nigeria, Oman, Pakistan, Panama, Paraguay, Peru, Philippines, Qatar, Russian Federation, Saint Lucia, Saint Vincent and the Grenadines, Saudi Arabia, Senegal, Sierra Leone, Singapore, Somalia, South Africa, Sri Lanka, Sudan, Suriname, Swaziland, Syrian Arab Republic, Tajikistan, Thailand, Togo, Trinidad and Tobago, Tunisia, Turkey, Turkmenistan, Uganda, United Arab Emirates, United Republic of Tanzania, Uruguay, Uzbekistan, Venezuela, Viet Nam, Yemen, Zambia, Zimbabwe.

Against: Australia, Israel, Marshall Islands, Micronesia, Nauru, Palau, United States.

Abstaining: Albania, Andorra, Austria, Belgium, Bosnia and Herzegovina, Bulgaria, Burundi, Canada, Colombia, Croatia, Czech Republic, Denmark, Dominican Republic, Estonia, Fiji, Finland, France, Georgia, Germany, Greece, Honduras, Hungary, Iceland, Ireland, Italy, Latvia, Liechtenstein, Lithuania, Luxembourg, Malta, Monaco, Netherlands, New Zealand, Nicaragua, Norway, Papua New Guinea, Poland, Portugal, Republic of Korea, Republic of Moldova, Romania, Samoa, San Marino, Serbia and Montenegro, Slovakia, Slovenia, Solomon Islands, Spain, Sweden, Switzerland, The former Yugoslav Republic of Macedonia, Tonga, Ukraine, United Kingdom, Vanuatu.

Communications (10-11 December). On 10 December [A/ES-10/253], South Africa, on behalf of the African Group, said that Israel used the forum of the General Assembly to make derogatory and offensive remarks specifically directed at the sponsors of the draft resolution, the majority of which were African Group members.

On 11 December [A/ES-10/252-S/2003/1168], the Permanent Observer of Palestine said that on that day, IDF carried out a raid inside the Rafah refugee camp, which killed at least six Palestinians and wounded 17 others. The raid followed other attacks carried out by IDF in and around the city of Ramallah during the previous week, which resulted in the death of four Palestinians.

Follow-up to resolution ES-10/14

On 19 December, further to the request by the Assembly for an advisory opinion on the question of the legal consequences of the construction of the wall in the Occupied Palestinian Territory, ICJ made an Order fixing 30 January 2004 as the time limit within which UN Member States could submit written statements on the question. It also decided that Palestine could submit to the Court a written statement on the question within the above time limit. The Court fixed 23 February 2004 as the date for the opening of the oral hearings. (For further information, see p. 1309.)

Communications (23-26 December). On 23 December [A/ES-10/254-S/2003/1202] and on 26 December [A/ES-10/255-S/2003/1206], the Permanent Observer of Palestine detailed Israeli attacks against Palestinians. IDF carried out an attack on the Rafah refugee camp on 23 December, killing eight Palestinians and wounding at least 40 others. On 25 December, IDF carried out an extrajudicial execution in the Gaza Strip, killing five Palestinians and wounding 14 others.

In a later communication [A/58/673-S/2004/7], Kuwait transmitted to the Secretary-General the texts of the closing statements and the Kuwait Declaration, adopted by the Supreme Council of the Gulf Cooperation Council at its twenty-fourth session (Kuwait, 21-22 December). The Council, among other things, took note of a speech made by Prime Minister Sharon indicating Israel's determination to take unilateral action to implement its so-called "disengagement plan", thereby rejecting any negotiations with the Palestinian side. It also expressed concern about the separation fence, which was viewed as designed to seize more Palestinian land and to abort the road map.

Further developments in the peace process

Security Council consideration (21 October). On 21 October [meeting 4846], the Security Council discussed the situation in the Middle East, including the Palestinian question.

The USG for Political Affairs said that the Council was meeting at a low point. It was urgent to re-establish momentum towards a lasting and comprehensive peace in the Middle East. Since the previous briefing on 15 September (see p. 470), there had been an escalation of violence that had crossed formerly respected lines, principles and borders. Events in the past month included a suicide bomb in Haifa (see p. 523); the first Israeli air strike into the Syrian Arab Republic in 30 years (see p. 522); serious and fatal violations of the Blue Line; Israeli incursions into Rafah in the Gaza Strip; increasingly tight closures in the West Bank and Gaza Strip that had exacerbated the already dire humanitarian conditions of the Palestinians; and a terrorist attack on a United Stated diplomatic convoy that killed three American security officers. During the preceding three days alone, 21 Palestinians and three Israeli soldiers were killed. The parties were unable to return to the negotiating table on their own and there was a need for the international community, and the Quartet in particular, to assist them along the road map to peace. If Israelis and Palestinians were to re-engage with the negotiation process, they had to be in a position to send to the negotiating table representatives who could commit to credible confidence-building measures. Noteworthy were the PA's efforts to appoint a new Prime Minister, who should be empowered and to whom, together with the Minister of the Interior, the consolidated Palestinian security force should report. Israel, for its part, had to reverse its policy of settlement expansion, implement a settlement freeze and halt the construction of the security barrier and remove those sections already constructed in order to address Palestinian concerns about the viability of a future Palestinian State. A rare positive note amid the general gloom was the track-two effort, led by Israeli and Palestinian civil society leaders Yossi Beilin and Yasser Abed Rabbo and others, referred to as the Geneva Accord, which led Israelis and Palestinians through a process of imagining a future final status settlement that detailed possible solutions based on the same goals as those of the road map: a two-State solution and the end of the occupation. Though the Secretariat had yet to see the text of that plan, the United Nations welcomed any initiative that brought Israelis and Palestinians together to discuss their common future.

Security Council consideration (19 November). On 19 November [meeting 4861], the Security Council again discussed the situation in the Middle East, including the Palestinian question.

The USG for Political Affairs said that, though the situation on the ground had been relatively quiet, the period since his briefing of 21 October (see above) was marked by inaction. The Israeli Government had waited for the PA to form an empowered Government and for terrorism to end, while the PA had waited for Israel to halt military operations and take steps to ease the closures, for the international community to lead the parties towards peace, and for its own political wrangling to end. The international community had waited also for the parties to make progress on their own, despite evidence of their inability to make peace without international intervention. Progress towards Middle East peace could not just be contingent on the actions expected of others. Even if Israelis and Palestinians were not at the negotiating table, there was much they could do to meet their road map obligations. Ahmed Qurei, whose appointment as Prime Minister was confirmed during the preceding week by the Palestinian Legislative Council, should take immediate steps to establish law and order, control violence and start operations to confront those who engaged in terror. Such steps would begin to address Israel's security concerns and build the confidence necessary to develop a partnership for peace. The United Nations would assist Mr. Qurei and his Government to implement the road map and pursue the path to peace.

The humanitarian situation continued to worsen, largely caused by Israeli security measures. The Israeli Government had given multiple assurances that donor activity and humanitarian aid would be fully facilitated. However, those assurances contrasted with the facts on the ground. In the absence of significant improvement of the conditions under which the international community operated, many donors were reviewing the basis on which their operations in the West Bank and Gaza could continue. The USG called on Israel to live up to its assurances and do all it could to facilitate humanitarian and emergency aid efforts.

The USG concluded that inertia, excuses and conditionality in Middle East peacemaking had to end. Advantage should be taken of the current conditions to make progress. The Geneva Accord (see p. 482) and the July 2002 Ayalon-Nusseibeh statement of principles (the "People's Voice") underlined the glaring vacuum in Middle East peacemaking.

SECURITY COUNCIL ACTION

On 19 November [meeting 4862], the Security Council unanimously adopted **resolution 1515 (2003)**. The draft [S/2003/1100] was submitted by Bulgaria, Chile, China, France, Germany, Guinea, Mexico, the Russian Federation, Spain and the United Kingdom. With the Council's consent, the President invited Israel and the Permanent Observer of Palestine [S/2003/1102], at their request, to participate in the meeting.

The Security Council,

Recalling all its previous relevant resolutions, in particular resolutions 242(1967) of 22 November 1967, 338(1973)of 22 October 1973, 1397(2002) of 12 March 2002, and the Madrid principles,

Expressing its grave concern at the continuation of the tragic and violent events in the Middle East,

Reiterating its demand for an immediate cessation of all acts of violence, including all acts of terrorism, provocation, incitement and destruction,

Reaffirming its vision of a region where two States, Israel and Palestine, live side by side within secure and recognized borders,

Emphasizing the need to achieve a comprehensive, just and lasting peace in the Middle East, including the Israeli-Syrian and Israeli-Lebanese tracks,

Welcoming and encouraging the diplomatic efforts of the international Quartet and others,

1. *Endorses* the Quartet performance-based road map to a permanent two-State solution to the Israeli-Palestinian conflict;

2. *Calls upon* the parties to fulfil their obligations under the road map in cooperation with the Quartet and to achieve the vision of two States living side by side in peace and security;

3. *Decides* to remain seized of the matter.

Security Council consideration (12 December). On 12 December [meeting 4879], the Security Council discussed the situation in the Middle East, including the Palestinian question.

The Special Coordinator for the Middle East Peace Process and Personal Representative of the Secretary-General, Mr. Roed-Larsen, said that, with no major terror attacks by Palestinians and a marked decline in Israeli military operations, there was a narrow window of opportunity, one in which the parties needed to take positive steps to put the peace process back on track. A number of factors were behind the opening of that window. The new Palestinian Prime Minister, Mr. Qurei, who had a long history of negotiating with Israel, had reiterated since assuming office in November the PA's full commitment to the road map and expressed a willingness to resume talks with Israeli authorities. Israeli Prime Minister Sharon had also made clear his desire to meet with his Palestinian counterpart and restart the peace process, based on the Quartet's road map. The Egyptian Government continued efforts to secure a new ceasefire, working with the PA and a variety of Palestinian groups. Civil society initiatives, such as the Geneva Accord and the People's Voice, showed that Israelis and Palestinians could work together to bridge their differences, and the Council's endorsement of the road map deepened the international community's support of the peace process.

The only viable route towards a renewal of the peace process was a step-by-step approach assisted by bold confidence-building measures, particularly bilateral negotiations based on the road map and facilitated by the international community. To that end, the Special Coordinator met with his Quartet counterparts in Rome, Italy, on 10 December, after a high-level donor meeting (see p. 484). The Quartet reaffirmed that it would assist the nascent bilateral efforts and guide the parties in their implementation of the road map. The issue was how to spark that process. To do so, each of the parties would need to address the core concerns of the other side, and both parties and the international community would have to overcome the fundamental dilemmas facing them. For Israelis, the closure system in the Occupied Palestinian Territory was a catch-22 situation that developed as a response to terrorist attacks. If those closures were eased, the potential for new terrorist attacks would rise, but if they persisted, the living conditions of the Palestinians would only deteriorate. For Palestinians, the crisis was more than the hardship they were enduring; it was a struggle for their identity and national aspirations. The donor community also faced a dilemma, in that the more than $1 billion provided annually, while helping to alleviate the suffering of the Palestinian people, in some eyes also helped to subsidize an Israeli occupation that increased the hardship for the average Palestinian. The peace process could proceed if those core issues and dilemmas were recognized and accepted as a reality by all interested parties, and addressed in parallel, not sequentially or with preconditions.

Since the last briefing to the Council, on 19 November (see p. 482), 27 people had lost their lives to the conflict—24 Palestinians and three Israelis, a relatively low number compared to previous periods. The overall death toll since September 2000 was 2,969 Palestinians and 863 Israelis. There had not been a completed suicide bombing since 4 October, due in part to attempts being thwarted by Israeli security forces. In Rome, the main donors that provided support to the PA met in the Ad Hoc Liaison Committee for the Coordination of International Assistance to Palestinians to review their assistance programmes. New proposals for assisting the Palestinian people included a possible new performance-based trust fund to help alleviate the estimated $650 million shortfall in the PA budget and a proposed new tripartite framework for the donors, the PA and Israel to work together in a spirit of cooperation. Donors voiced concerns that the humanitarian crisis had forced them to redirect funding from development to emergency relief. That in turn was often hampered by Israeli security actions. Many donors would require a renewed peace process in order to sustain their levels of support. Those humanitarian and other concerns were exacerbated by the continuing construction of the barrier in the West Bank.

Jerusalem

East Jerusalem, where most of the city's Arab inhabitants lived, remained one of the most sensitive issues in the Middle East peace process and a focal point of concern for the United Nations in 2003.

Committee on Palestinian Rights. In its annual report [A/58/35], the Committee on the Exercise of the Inalienable Rights of the Palestinian People (Committee on Palestinian Rights) said that Israel had stepped up the construction of a separation wall in the West Bank. In August, the Israeli authorities issued land expropriation orders for the "Jerusalem envelope" barrier, which could leave thousands of Palestinians isolated on the Israeli side. In September, Israel provided $112 million to complete the separation barrier in the Jerusalem area, and, on 1 October, it approved the construction of the second phase of the wall, running from Elkana to Jerusalem, where a separate network of barriers was being built. The Committee stressed that the wall could prejudice the outcome of future permanent status negotiations and inhibit the establishment of a contiguous Palestinian State.

Transfer of diplomatic missions

Report of Secretary-General. On 13 August [A/58/278], the Secretary-General reported that eight Member States, including Israel, had replied to his request for information on steps taken or envisaged to implement General Assembly resolution 57/111 [YUN 2002, p. 444], which addressed the transfer by some States of their diplomatic missions to Jerusalem in violation of Security Council resolution 478(1980) [YUN 1980, p. 426] and called on them to abide by the relevant UN resolutions. Israel viewed those resolutions as unbalanced and said that they threatened to prejudge the outcome of the Middle East peace process. They undermined the principle that a lasting peace in the region was possible only through direct bilateral negotiations. The Syrian Arab Republic said that the resolution determined that all legislative and administrative measures enacted by Israel concerning Jerusalem were null and void and had to be rescinded forthwith.

GENERAL ASSEMBLY ACTION

On 3 December [meeting 68], the General Assembly adopted **resolution 58/22** [draft: A/58/L.27 & Add.1] by recorded vote (155-8-7) [agenda item 37].

Jerusalem

The General Assembly,

Recalling its resolution 181(II) of 29 November 1947, in particular its provisions regarding the City of Jerusalem,

Recalling also its resolution 36/120 E of 10 December 1981 and all subsequent resolutions, including resolution 56/31 of 3 December 2001, in which it, inter alia, determined that all legislative and administrative measures and actions taken by Israel, the occupying Power, which have altered or purported to alter the character and status of the Holy City of Jerusalem, in particular the so-called "Basic Law" on Jerusalem and the proclamation of Jerusalem as the capital of Israel, were null and void and must be rescinded forthwith,

Recalling further Security Council resolutions relevant to Jerusalem, including resolution 478(1980) of 20 August 1980, in which the Council, inter alia, decided not to recognize the "Basic Law" and called upon those States which had established diplomatic missions in Jerusalem to withdraw such missions from the Holy City,

Expressing its grave concern at any action taken by any body, governmental or non-governmental, in violation of the above-mentioned resolutions,

Reaffirming that the international community, through the United Nations, has a legitimate interest in the question of the City of Jerusalem and the protection of the unique spiritual, religious and cultural dimension of the city, as foreseen in relevant United Nations resolutions on this matter,

Having considered the report of the Secretary-General,

1. *Reiterates its determination* that any actions taken by Israel to impose its laws, jurisdiction and administration on the Holy City of Jerusalem are illegal and therefore null and void and have no validity whatsoever;

2. *Deplores* the transfer by some States of their diplomatic missions to Jerusalem in violation of Security Council resolution 478(1980), and calls once more upon those States to abide by the provisions of the relevant United Nations resolutions, in conformity with the Charter of the United Nations;

3. *Stresses* that a comprehensive, just and lasting solution to the question of the City of Jerusalem should take into account the legitimate concerns of both the Palestinian and Israeli sides and should include internationally guaranteed provisions to ensure the freedom of religion and of conscience of its inhabitants, as well as permanent, free and unhindered access to the holy places by the people of all religions and nationalities;

4. *Requests* the Secretary-General to report to the General Assembly at its fifty-ninth session on the implementation of the present resolution.

RECORDED VOTE ON RESOLUTION 58/22:

In favour: Afghanistan, Algeria, Andorra, Antigua and Barbuda, Argentina, Armenia, Australia, Austria, Azerbaijan, Bahamas, Bahrain, Bangladesh, Barbados, Belarus, Belgium, Belize, Bolivia, Bosnia and Herzegovina, Botswana, Brazil, Brunei Darussalam, Bulgaria, Burkina Faso, Burundi, Cambodia, Canada, Cape Verde, Central African Republic, Chile, China, Colombia, Comoros, Congo, Côte d'Ivoire, Croatia, Cuba, Cyprus, Czech Republic, Democratic People's Republic of Korea, Denmark, Djibouti, Dominican Republic, Ecuador, Egypt, Eritrea, Estonia, Ethiopia, Fiji, Finland, France, Gabon, Georgia, Germany, Ghana, Greece, Grenada, Guinea, Guinea-Bissau, Guyana, Haiti, Hungary, Iceland, India, Indonesia, Iran, Ireland, Italy, Jamaica, Japan, Jordan, Kazakhstan, Kenya, Kuwait, Kyrgyzstan, Lao People's Democratic Republic, Latvia, Lebanon, Lesotho, Libyan Arab Jamahiriya, Liechtenstein, Lithuania, Luxembourg, Madagascar, Malaysia, Maldives, Mali, Malta, Mauritania, Mauritius, Mexico, Monaco, Mongolia, Morocco, Mozambique, Myanmar, Namibia, Nepal, Netherlands, New Zealand, Niger, Nigeria, Norway, Oman, Pakistan, Panama, Paraguay, Peru, Philippines, Poland, Portugal, Qatar, Republic of Korea, Republic of Moldova, Romania, Russian Federation, Saint Lucia, Saint Vincent and the Grenadines, Samoa, San Marino, Saudi Arabia, Senegal, Serbia and Montenegro, Seychelles, Sierra Leone, Singapore, Slovakia, Slovenia, Somalia, South Africa, Spain, Sri Lanka, Sudan, Suriname, Swaziland, Sweden, Switzerland, Syrian Arab Republic, Tajikistan, Thailand, The former Yugoslav Republic of Macedonia, Togo, Trinidad and Tobago, Tunisia, Turkey, Turkmenistan, Ukraine, United Arab Emirates, United Kingdom, United Republic of Tanzania, Uruguay, Venezuela, Viet Nam, Yemen, Zambia, Zimbabwe.

Against: Costa Rica, Israel, Marshall Islands, Micronesia, Nauru, Palau, Uganda, United States.

Abstaining: El Salvador, Guatemala, Honduras, Nicaragua, Rwanda, Solomon Islands, Tonga.

Economic and social situation

A June report on the economic and social repercussions of the Israeli occupation on the living conditions of Palestinians in the occupied territory, including Jerusalem, and of the Arab population in the occupied Syrian Golan [A/58/75-E/2003/21] was prepared by the Economic and Social Commission for Western Asia (ESCWA), in accordance with Economic and Social Council resolution 2002/31 [YUN 2002, p. 446] and General Assembly resolution 57/269 [ibid., p. 447]; it covered developments since the last ESCWA report [ibid., p. 445].

The report noted that the occupation of Palestinian territory by Israel continued to have a serious detrimental effect on all aspects of the living conditions of the Palestinian people. IDF continued to resort to excessive use of force, arbitrary detentions, house demolitions, increasingly severe mobility restrictions and closure policies, in addition to the confiscation and bulldozing of Palestinian agricultural land. The Palestinian economy accumulated losses and unemployment increased threefold, while two thirds of the population was living below the poverty line. Women and children bore a special and enduring burden resulting from the occupation. In particular, Palestinian children faced exposure to mounting violence, and their access to educational opportunities and health facilities had been reduced to extremely low levels. Educational levels were consistently declining, as were nutritional standards and public health conditions.

Israeli settlements in the Occupied Palestinian Territory remained one of the principal issues fuelling the conflict. The geographic distribution of Israeli settlements severely restricted the growth of Palestinian communities and was an obstacle to their economic and social development. Israel contended that the expansion of settlements was a function of the existing population's natural growth. Successive Israeli Governments had strongly encouraged migration from Israel to the settlements by offering financial benefits and incentives. The annual increase of 11 to 12 per cent in settler numbers far exceeded the 2 per cent population growth inside Israel. A critical factor affecting Palestinian life was the allotment of land resources for settlement. Though planning maps remained largely inaccessible to the public, available data indicated that Israeli authorities had allotted 41.9 per cent of all the West Bank to settlements as building, planning and development zones. The Israeli-occupied Syrian Golan Heights continued to witness settlement expansion beyond the 33 settlements already in place. Social services such as schooling, higher education and medical facilities remained insufficient for the Arab population.

ECONOMIC AND SOCIAL COUNCIL ACTION

On 24 July [meeting 48], the Economic and Social Council adopted **resolution 2003/59** [draft: E/2003/L.26] by recorded vote (48-2-3) [agenda item 11].

Economic and social repercussions of the Israeli occupation on the living conditions of the Palestinian people in the Occupied Palestinian Territory, including Jerusalem, and the Arab population in the occupied Syrian Golan

The Economic and Social Council,

Recalling General Assembly resolution 57/269 of 20 December 2002,

Recalling also its resolution 2002/31 of 25 July 2002,

Guided by the principles of the Charter of the United Nations affirming the inadmissibility of the acquisition of territory by force, and recalling relevant Security Council resolutions, including resolutions 242(1967) of 22 November 1967, 465(1980) of 1 March 1980 and 497(1981) of 17 December 1981,

Reaffirming the applicability of the Geneva Convention relative to the Protection of Civilian Persons in Time of War, of 12 August 1949, to the Occupied Palestinian Territory, including East Jerusalem, and other Arab territories occupied by Israel since 1967,

Stressing the importance of the revival of the Middle East peace process on the basis of Security Council resolutions 242(1967), 338(1973) of 22 October 1973, 425(1978) of 19 March 1978 and 1397(2002) of 12 March 2002, and the principle of land for peace as well as compliance with the agreements reached between the Government of Israel and the Palestine Liberation Organization, the representative of the Palestinian people,

Reaffirming the principle of the permanent sovereignty of peoples under foreign occupation over their natural resources,

Convinced that the Israeli occupation impedes efforts to achieve sustainable development and a sound economic environment in the Occupied Palestinian Territory, including East Jerusalem, and the occupied Syrian Golan,

Gravely concerned about the deterioration of the economic and living conditions of the Palestinian people in the Occupied Palestinian Territory, including East Jerusalem, and of the Arab population of the occupied Syrian Golan and the exploitation by Israel, the occupying Power, of their natural resources,

Expressing grave concern over the continuation of the recent tragic and violent events since September 2000 that have led to many deaths and injuries,

Aware of the important work being done by the United Nations and the specialized agencies in support of the economic and social development of the Palestinian people,

Conscious of the urgent need for the reconstruction and development of the economic and social infrastructure of the Occupied Palestinian Territory, including East Jerusalem, as well as the urgent need to address the humanitarian crisis facing the Palestinian people,

Welcoming the acceptance of the Quartet road map for peace, presented by the Secretary-General, the United States of America, the Russian Federation and the European Union, as well as the Summit at Aqaba, Jordan, and stressing the importance of prompt and full implementation in good faith by the two sides of the road map and further steps to reduce the level of violence,

1. *Stresses* the need to preserve the territorial integrity of all of the Occupied Palestinian Territory and to guarantee the freedom of movement of persons and goods in the Territory, including the removal of restrictions on going into and from East Jerusalem, and the freedom of movement to and from the outside world;

2. *Also stresses* the vital importance of the construction and operation of the seaport in Gaza and safe passage to the economic and social development of the Palestinian people;

3. *Demands* the complete cessation of all acts of violence, including all acts of terror, provocation, incitement and destruction;

4. *Calls upon* Israel, the occupying Power, to end its occupation of Palestinian cities and other populated centres, to end all kinds of closures and to cease destruction of homes and economic facilities and agricultural fields;

5. *Reaffirms* the inalienable right of the Palestinian people and the Arab population of the occupied Syrian Golan to all their natural and economic resources, and calls upon Israel, the occupying Power, not to exploit, endanger or cause loss or depletion of these resources;

6. *Also reaffirms* that Israeli settlements in the Occupied Palestinian Territory, including East Jerusalem, and the occupied Syrian Golan, are illegal and an obstacle to economic and social development;

7. *Stresses* the importance of the work of the organizations and agencies of the United Nations and of the United Nations Special Coordinator for the Middle East Peace Process and Personal Representative of the Secretary-General to the Palestine Liberation Organization and the Palestinian Authority;

8. *Urges* Member States to encourage private foreign investment in the Occupied Palestinian Territory, including East Jerusalem, in infrastructure, job-creation projects and social development in order to alleviate the hardship of the Palestinian people and improve living conditions;

9. *Requests* the Secretary-General to submit to the General Assembly at its fifty-ninth session, through the Economic and Social Council, a report on the implementation of the present resolution and to continue to include, in the report of the United Nations Special Coordinator, an update on the living conditions of the Palestinian people, in collaboration with relevant United Nations agencies;

10. *Decides* to include the item entitled "Economic and social repercussions of the Israeli occupation on the living conditions of the Palestinian people in the

Occupied Palestinian Territory, including East Jerusalem, and the Arab population in the occupied Syrian Golan" in the agenda of its substantive session of 2004.

RECORDED VOTE ON RESOLUTION 2003/59:

In favour: Andorra, Argentina, Azerbaijan, Benin, Bhutan, Brazil, Burundi, Chile, China, Congo, Cuba, Ecuador, Egypt, Ethiopia, Finland, France, Germany, Ghana, Greece, Hungary, India, Iran, Ireland, Italy, Jamaica, Japan, Kenya, Libyan Arab Jamahiriya, Malaysia, Mozambique, Nepal, Netherlands, Nigeria, Pakistan, Peru, Portugal, Qatar, Republic of Korea, Romania, Russian Federation, Saudi Arabia, Senegal, South Africa, Sweden, Uganda, Ukraine, United Kingdom, Zimbabwe.
Against: Georgia, United States.
Abstaining: Australia, Guatemala, Nicaragua.

On the same date, the Council took note of the note by the Secretary-General transmitting the report prepared by ESCWA on the economic and social repercussions of the Israeli occupation on the living conditions of the Palestinian people in the Occupied Palestinian Territory, including Jerusalem, and of the Arab population in the occupied Syrian Golan (**decision 2003/292**).

GENERAL ASSEMBLY ACTION

On 23 December [meeting 78], the General Assembly, on the recommendation of the Second (Economic and Financial) Committee [A/58/493], adopted **resolution 58/229** by recorded vote (157-4-10) [agenda item 103].

Permanent sovereignty of the Palestinian people in the Occupied Palestinian Territory, including East Jerusalem, and of the Arab population in the occupied Syrian Golan over their natural resources

The General Assembly,

Recalling its resolution 57/269 of 20 December 2002, and taking note of Economic and Social Council resolution 2003/59 of 24 July 2003,

Reaffirming the principle of the permanent sovereignty of peoples under foreign occupation over their natural resources,

Guided by the principles of the Charter of the United Nations, affirming the inadmissibility of the acquisition of territory by force, and recalling relevant Security Council resolutions, including resolutions 242(1967) of 22 November 1967, 465(1980) of 1 March 1980 and 497(1981) of 17 December 1981,

Reaffirming the applicability of the Geneva Convention relative to the Protection of Civilian Persons in Time of War, of 12 August 1949, to the Occupied Palestinian Territory, including East Jerusalem, and other Arab territories occupied by Israel since 1967,

Expressing its concern at the exploitation by Israel, the occupying Power, of the natural resources of the Occupied Palestinian Territory, including East Jerusalem, and other Arab territories occupied by Israel since 1967,

Expressing its concern also at the extensive destruction by Israel, the occupying Power, of agricultural land and orchards in the Occupied Palestinian Territory during the recent period, including the uprooting of a vast number of olive trees,

Aware of the detrimental impact of the Israeli settlements on Palestinian and other Arab natural resources, especially the confiscation of land and the forced diversion of water resources, and of the dire economic and social consequences in this regard,

Aware also of the detrimental impact on Palestinian natural resources of the wall being constructed by Israel inside the Occupied Palestinian Territory, including in and around East Jerusalem, and of its grave effect on the economic and social conditions of the Palestinian people,

Reaffirming the need for the immediate resumption of negotiations within the Middle East peace process, on the basis of Security Council resolutions 242(1967), 338(1973) of 22 October 1973, 425(1978) of 19 March 1978 and 1397(2002) of 12 March 2002, the principle of land for peace and the Quartet performance-based road map to a permanent two-State solution to the Israeli-Palestinian conflict, as endorsed by the Security Council in its resolution 1515(2003) of 19 November 2003, and for the achievement of a final settlement on all tracks,

Recalling the need to end all acts of violence, including acts of terror, provocation, incitement and destruction,

Taking note of the note by the Secretary-General transmitting the report prepared by the Economic and Social Commission for Western Asia on the economic and social repercussions of the Israeli occupation on the living conditions of the Palestinian people in the Occupied Palestinian Territory, including Jerusalem, and of the Arab population in the occupied Syrian Golan,

1. *Reaffirms* the inalienable rights of the Palestinian people and the population of the occupied Syrian Golan over their natural resources, including land and water;

2. *Calls upon* Israel, the occupying Power, not to exploit, cause loss or depletion of or endanger the natural resources in the Occupied Palestinian Territory, including East Jerusalem, and in the occupied Syrian Golan;

3. *Recognizes* the right of the Palestinian people to claim restitution as a result of any exploitation, loss or depletion of, or danger to, their natural resources, and expresses the hope that this issue will be dealt with in the framework of the final status negotiations between the Palestinian and Israeli sides;

4. *Requests* the Secretary-General to report to it at its fifty-ninth session on the implementation of the present resolution, and decides to include in the provisional agenda of its fifty-ninth session the item entitled "Permanent sovereignty of the Palestinian people in the Occupied Palestinian Territory, including East Jerusalem, and of the Arab population in the occupied Syrian Golan over their natural resources".

RECORDED VOTE ON RESOLUTION 58/229:

In favour: Afghanistan, Albania, Algeria, Andorra, Angola, Antigua and Barbuda, Argentina, Armenia, Austria, Azerbaijan, Bahamas, Bahrain, Bangladesh, Barbados, Belarus, Belgium, Belize, Benin, Bhutan, Bolivia, Bosnia and Herzegovina, Botswana, Brazil, Brunei Darussalam, Bulgaria, Burkina Faso, Burundi, Cambodia, Canada, Cape Verde, Central African Republic, Chile, China, Colombia, Comoros, Congo, Côte d'Ivoire, Croatia, Cuba, Cyprus, Czech Republic, Democratic People's Republic of Korea, Denmark, Djibouti, Dominica, Ecuador, Egypt, Eritrea, Estonia, Ethiopia, Fiji, Finland, France, Gabon, Germany, Ghana, Greece, Grenada, Guatemala, Guinea, Guinea-Bissau, Guyana, Haiti, Hungary, Iceland, India, Indonesia, Iran, Ireland, Italy, Jamaica, Japan, Jordan, Kazakhstan, Kenya, Kuwait, Kyrgyzstan, Lao People's Democratic Republic, Latvia, Lebanon, Lesotho, Libyan Arab Jamahiriya, Liechtenstein, Lithuania, Luxembourg, Madagascar, Malaysia, Maldives, Mali, Malta, Mauritania, Mauritius, Mexico, Monaco, Mongolia, Morocco, Mozambique, Myanmar, Namibia, Nepal, Netherlands, New Zealand, Niger, Nigeria, Norway, Oman, Pakistan, Panama, Paraguay, Peru, Philippines, Portugal, Qatar, Republic of Korea, Republic of Moldova, Romania, Russian Federation, Saint Lucia, Saint Vincent and the Grenadines, Samoa, San Marino, Saudi Arabia, Serbia and Montenegro, Seychelles, Singapore, Slovakia, Slovenia, Somalia, South Africa, Spain, Sri Lanka, Sudan, Suriname, Swaziland, Sweden, Switzerland, Syrian Arab Republic, Tajikistan, Thailand, The former Yugoslav Republic of Macedonia, Timor-Leste, Togo, Trinidad and Tobago, Tunisia, Turkey, Turkmenistan, Uganda, Ukraine, United Arab Emirates, United Kingdom, United Republic of Tanzania, Uruguay, Venezuela, Viet Nam, Yemen, Zambia, Zimbabwe.

Against: Israel, Marshall Islands, Micronesia, United States.

Abstaining: Australia, Cameroon, Costa Rica, Dominican Republic, Honduras, Nauru, Nicaragua, Papua New Guinea, Solomon Islands, Tonga.

Other aspects

Special Committee on Israeli Practices. In response to General Assembly resolution 57/124 [YUN 2002, p. 450], the Special Committee to Investigate Israeli Practices Affecting the Human Rights of the Palestinian People and Other Arabs of the Occupied Territories, in August, reported for the thirty-fifth time to the General Assembly on events and the human rights situation in the territories it considered occupied—the Golan Heights, the West Bank, including East Jerusalem, and the Gaza Strip [A/58/311]. The report contained information obtained from, among others, non-governmental organizations (NGOs), including Palestinian and Israeli NGOs; testimony from persons from the occupied territories; and communications and reports from regional Governments, organizations and individuals. As in the past, the Committee received no response from Israel to its request for cooperation and was unable to obtain access to the occupied territories, which had been the case since 1968, when the Committee was established [YUN 1968, p. 556].

The Committee's review of the human rights situation in the occupied territories focused on the right of self-determination; the right to liberty of movement; the right to an adequate standard of living, including adequate food, clothing and housing; the right to just and favourable conditions of work; the right to education; the right to health; the right to liberty and security of person; the rights to freedom of opinion and of association; and the right to life. The Committee stated that the human rights situation had drastically deteriorated since Israel's military incursions; despite some hopes generated by the official presentation and launching of the road map in April 2003 (see p. 464), the construction by Israel of a separation wall was perceived by the Palestinians as an annexation of parts of their homeland.

The Special Committee observed that the increased military occupation of the Palestinian territory and its related curfews, road closures and multiplication of checkpoints made the life of the Palestinians and other Arabs unbearable. The legitimate security arguments used by Israel could not overlook the fact that many human rights were being ignored in non-combat situations. The Occupied Palestinian Territory and the Gaza Strip were on the verge of a major humanitarian collapse, with 60 per cent of the Palestinians living below the poverty line, given their inability to go to work and earn a living and their increased dependency on foreign food assistance.

The Special Committee visited the Syrian Arab Republic and reported on the Israeli-occupied Syrian Golan Heights (for details, see p. 523).

Report of Secretary-General. On 15 July [A/58/156], the Secretary-General informed the General Assembly that Israel had not replied to his June request for information on steps taken or envisaged to implement Assembly resolution 57/127 [YUN 2002, p. 448], demanding that Israel, among other things, cease all practices and actions that violated the human rights of the Palestinian people, and condemning all acts of terror, provocation, incitement and destruction, especially the excessive use of force by Israeli forces against Palestinian civilians.

Commission on Human Rights. In an 8 September report [E/CN.4/2004/6], the Special Rapporteur of the Commission on Human Rights, John Dugard (South Africa), described the situation of human rights in the Palestinian territories occupied by Israel since 1967. The Special Rapporteur observed that the occupation continued to result in the widespread violation of human rights, affecting both civil and socio-economic rights, and of international humanitarian law. Israel's justification for those actions was that they were necessary in the interests of its own national security. The lawfulness of Israel's response was to be measured in accordance with the principle of proportionality. The Special Rapporteur found it difficult to accept that the excessive use of force that disregarded the distinction between civilians and combatants, the creation of a humanitarian crisis by restrictions on the mobility of goods and people, the killing of children, the destruction of property and territorial expansion could be justified as a proportionate response to the violence and threats to which Israel was subjected. The construction of a separation wall and the continued expansion of settlements raised serious doubts about the good faith of Israel's justification in the name of security (for details, see p. 826).

GENERAL ASSEMBLY ACTION

On 9 December [meeting 72], following consideration of the Special Committee's annual report and five reports of the Secretary-General on specific aspects of the situation in the occupied territories [A/58/155, A/58/156, A/58/263, A/58/264, A/58/310], the General Assembly, on the recommendation of the Fourth (Special Political and Decolonization) Committee [A/58/473 & Corr.1], adopted **resolution 58/99** by recorded vote (150-6-19) [agenda item 84].

Israeli practices affecting the human rights of the Palestinian people in the Occupied Palestinian Territory, including East Jerusalem

The General Assembly,

Recalling its relevant resolutions, including those adopted at its tenth emergency special session, and the resolutions of the Commission on Human Rights,

Bearing in mind the relevant resolutions of the Security Council,

Having considered the report of the Special Committee to Investigate Israeli Practices Affecting the Human Rights of the Palestinian People and Other Arabs of the Occupied Territories and the reports of the Secretary-General,

Taking note of the report of the Human Rights Inquiry Commission established by the Commission on Human Rights and the report of the Special Rapporteur of the Commission on Human Rights on the situation of human rights in the Palestinian territories occupied by Israel since 1967,

Aware of the responsibility of the international community to promote human rights and ensure respect for international law,

Reaffirming the principle of the inadmissibility of the acquisition of territory by force,

Reaffirming also the applicability of the Geneva Convention relative to the Protection of Civilian Persons in Time of War, of 12 August 1949, to the Occupied Palestinian Territory, including East Jerusalem, and other Arab territories occupied by Israel since 1967,

Reaffirming further the obligation of the States parties to the Fourth Geneva Convention under articles 146, 147 and 148 with regard to penal sanctions, grave breaches and responsibilities of the High Contracting Parties,

Stressing the need for full compliance with the Israeli-Palestinian agreements reached within the context of the Middle East peace process and the implementation of the Quartet road map to a permanent two-State solution to the Israeli-Palestinian conflict,

Concerned about the continuing systematic violation of the human rights of the Palestinian people by Israel, the occupying Power, including the use of collective punishment, the reoccupation and closure of areas, the confiscation of land, the establishment and expansion of settlements, the construction of a wall inside the Occupied Palestinian Territory in departure from the Armistice Line of 1949, the destruction of property and all other actions by it designed to change the legal status, geographical nature and demographic composition of the Occupied Palestinian Territory, including East Jerusalem,

Gravely concerned about the tragic events that have occurred since 28 September 2000 and that have led to thousands of deaths and injuries among Palestinian civilians,

Gravely concerned also about the use of suicide bombing attacks against Israeli civilians resulting in extensive loss of life and injury,

Expressing deep concern about the extensive destruction caused by the Israeli occupying forces, including the destruction of homes and properties, of religious, cultural and historical sites, of vital infrastructure and institutions of the Palestinian Authority, and of agricultural land throughout Palestinian cities, towns, villages and refugee camps,

Also expressing deep concern about the Israeli policy of closure and the severe restrictions, including curfews, imposed on the movement of persons and goods, including medical and humanitarian personnel and goods, throughout the Occupied Palestinian Territory, including East Jerusalem, and the consequent impact on the socio-economic situation of the Palestinian people, which has resulted in a dire humanitarian crisis,

Expressing concern that thousands of Palestinians continue to be held in Israeli prisons or detention centres, and also expressing concern about the ill-treatment and harassment of any Palestinian prisoners and all reports of torture,

Convinced of the need for an international presence to monitor the situation, to contribute to ending the violence and protecting the Palestinian civilians and to help the parties to implement agreements reached, and, in this regard, recalls the positive contribution of the Temporary International Presence in Hebron,

Stressing the necessity for the full implementation of all relevant Security Council resolutions,

1. *Determines* that all measures and actions taken by Israel, the occupying Power, in the Occupied Palestinian Territory, including East Jerusalem, in violation of the relevant provisions of the Geneva Convention relative to the Protection of Civilian Persons in Time of War, of 12 August 1949, and contrary to the relevant resolutions of the Security Council, are illegal and have no validity;

2. *Demands* that Israel, the occupying Power, comply fully with the provisions of the Fourth Geneva Convention of 1949 and cease immediately all measures and actions taken in violation of the Convention, including the extrajudicial executions;

3. *Condemns* all acts of violence, including all acts of terror, provocation, incitement and destruction, especially the excessive use of force by Israeli forces against Palestinian civilians, resulting in extensive loss of life, vast numbers of injuries and massive destruction;

4. *Also condemns* the events that have occurred in the Jenin refugee camp in April 2002, including the loss of life, injury, destruction and displacement inflicted on many of its civilian inhabitants;

5. *Demands* that Israel, the occupying Power, cease all practices and actions that violate the human rights of the Palestinian people;

6. *Stresses* the need to preserve the territorial integrity of all the Occupied Palestinian Territory and to guarantee the freedom of movement of persons and goods within the Palestinian territory, including the removal of restrictions on movement into and from

East Jerusalem, and the freedom of movement to and from the outside world;

7. *Requests* the Secretary-General to report to the General Assembly at its fifty-ninth session on the implementation of the present resolution.

RECORDED VOTE ON RESOLUTION 58/99:

In favour: Afghanistan, Algeria, Andorra, Angola, Antigua and Barbuda, Argentina, Armenia, Austria, Azerbaijan, Bahamas, Bahrain, Bangladesh, Barbados, Belarus, Belgium, Belize, Benin, Bhutan, Bolivia, Bosnia and Herzegovina, Botswana, Brazil, Brunei Darussalam, Bulgaria, Burkina Faso, Burundi, Cambodia, Canada, Cape Verde, Chile, China, Colombia, Comoros, Côte d'Ivoire, Croatia, Cuba, Cyprus, Democratic People's Republic of Korea, Denmark, Djibouti, Ecuador, Egypt, Equatorial Guinea, Eritrea, Estonia, Ethiopia, Fiji, Finland, France, Gabon, Gambia, Ghana, Greece, Grenada, Guinea, Guinea-Bissau, Guyana, Haiti, Hungary, Iceland, India, Indonesia, Iran, Ireland, Italy, Jamaica, Japan, Jordan, Kazakhstan, Kenya, Kuwait, Kyrgyzstan, Lao People's Democratic Republic, Latvia, Lebanon, Lesotho, Libyan Arab Jamahiriya, Liechtenstein, Lithuania, Luxembourg, Madagascar, Malaysia, Maldives, Mali, Malta, Mauritania, Mauritius, Mexico, Monaco, Mongolia, Morocco, Mozambique, Myanmar, Namibia, Nepal, Netherlands, New Zealand, Niger, Nigeria, Norway, Oman, Pakistan, Panama, Paraguay, Philippines, Poland, Portugal, Qatar, Republic of Korea, Republic of Moldova, Romania, Russian Federation, Saint Lucia, Saint Vincent and the Grenadines, Samoa, San Marino, Saudi Arabia, Senegal, Serbia and Montenegro, Seychelles, Singapore, Slovakia, Slovenia, South Africa, Spain, Sri Lanka, Sudan, Suriname, Swaziland, Sweden, Switzerland, Syrian Arab Republic, Tajikistan, Thailand, The former Yugoslav Republic of Macedonia, Timor-Leste, Togo, Trinidad and Tobago, Tunisia, Turkey, Turkmenistan, Ukraine, United Arab Emirates, United Republic of Tanzania, Uruguay, Venezuela, Viet Nam, Yemen, Zambia, Zimbabwe.

Against: Israel, Marshall Islands, Micronesia, Nauru, Palau, United States.

Abstaining: Albania, Australia, Cameroon, Costa Rica, Czech Republic, Dominican Republic, El Salvador, Georgia, Germany, Guatemala, Honduras, Nicaragua, Papua New Guinea, Peru, Rwanda, Solomon Islands, Tonga, Tuvalu, United Kingdom.

By **resolution 58/163** of 22 December, the Assembly reaffirmed the right of the Palestinian people to self-determination, including their right to a State, and urged all States and UN specialized agencies and organizations to continue to support the Palestinian people in their quest for self-determination (see p. 721).

Work of Special Committee

In an August report [A/58/310], the Secretary-General stated that all necessary facilities were provided to the Special Committee on Israeli Practices, as requested in General Assembly resolution 57/124 [YUN 2002, p. 450]. Arrangements were made for it to meet in June, and a field mission was carried out to Egypt, Jordan and the Syrian Arab Republic from 13 to 24 June. Due to the restrictions imposed on the elaboration of Assembly reports, the Special Committee gave up the submitting of periodic reports during the period under review. The UN Department of Public Information continued to provide press coverage of Special Committee meetings and to disseminate information materials on its activities.

GENERAL ASSEMBLY ACTION

On 9 December [meeting 72], the General Assembly, on the recommendation of the Fourth Committee [A/58/473 & Corr.1], adopted **resolution 58/96** by recorded vote (87-7-78) [agenda item 84].

Work of the Special Committee to Investigate Israeli Practices Affecting the Human Rights of the Palestinian People and Other Arabs of the Occupied Territories

The General Assembly,

Guided by the purposes and principles of the Charter of the United Nations,

Guided also by international humanitarian law, in particular the Geneva Convention relative to the Protection of Civilian Persons in Time of War, of 12 August 1949, as well as international standards of human rights, in particular the Universal Declaration of Human Rights and the International Covenants on Human Rights,

Recalling its relevant resolutions, including resolutions 2443(XXIII) of 19 December 1968 and 57/124 of 11 December 2002, and the relevant resolutions of the Commission on Human Rights,

Recalling also relevant resolutions of the Security Council,

Convinced that occupation itself represents a gross and grave violation of human rights,

Gravely concerned about the continuation of the tragic events that have taken place since 28 September 2000, including the excessive use of force by the Israeli occupying forces against Palestinian civilians, resulting in thousands of deaths and injuries,

Having considered the report of the Special Committee to Investigate Israeli Practices Affecting the Human Rights of the Palestinian People and Other Arabs of the Occupied Territories and the relevant reports of the Secretary-General,

Recalling the Declaration of Principles on Interim Self-Government Arrangements of 13 September 1993 and the subsequent implementation agreements between the Palestinian and Israeli sides,

Expressing the hope that the Israeli occupation will be brought to an early end and that therefore the violation of the human rights of the Palestinian people will cease,

1. *Commends* the Special Committee to Investigate Israeli Practices Affecting the Human Rights of the Palestinian People and Other Arabs of the Occupied Territories for its efforts in performing the tasks assigned to it by the General Assembly and for its impartiality;

2. *Reiterates its demand* that Israel, the occupying Power, cooperate with the Special Committee in implementing its mandate;

3. *Deplores* those policies and practices of Israel that violate the human rights of the Palestinian people and other Arabs of the occupied territories, as reflected in the report of the Special Committee covering the reporting period;

4. *Expresses grave concern* about the situation in the Occupied Palestinian Territory, including East Jerusalem, since 28 September 2000, as a result of Israeli practices and measures, and especially condemns the excessive and indiscriminate use of force against the civilian population, including extrajudicial executions, which has resulted in more than 2,600 Palestinian deaths and tens of thousands of injuries;

5. *Requests* the Special Committee, pending complete termination of the Israeli occupation, to continue to investigate Israeli policies and practices in the Occupied Palestinian Territory, including East Jerusalem, and other Arab territories occupied by Israel since 1967, especially Israeli violations of the Geneva Convention relative to the Protection of Civilian Persons in Time of War, of 12 August 1949, and to consult, as appropriate, with the International Committee of the Red Cross according to its regulations in order to ensure that the welfare and human rights of the peoples of the occupied territories are safeguarded and to report to the Secretary-General as soon as possible and whenever the need arises thereafter;

6. *Also requests* the Special Committee to submit regularly to the Secretary-General periodic reports on the current situation in the Occupied Palestinian Territory, including East Jerusalem;

7. *Further requests* the Special Committee to continue to investigate the treatment of prisoners and detainees in the Occupied Palestinian Territory, including East Jerusalem, and other Arab territories occupied by Israel since 1967;

8. *Requests* the Secretary-General:

(a) To provide the Special Committee with all necessary facilities, including those required for its visits to the occupied territories, so that it may investigate Israeli policies and practices referred to in the present resolution;

(b) To continue to make available such additional staff as may be necessary to assist the Special Committee in the performance of its tasks;

(c) To circulate regularly to Member States the periodic reports mentioned in paragraph 6 above;

(d) To ensure the widest circulation of the reports of the Special Committee and of information regarding its activities and findings, by all means available, through the Department of Public Information of the Secretariat and, where necessary, to reprint those reports of the Special Committee that are no longer available;

(e) To report to the General Assembly at its fifty-ninth session on the tasks entrusted to him in the present resolution;

9. *Decides* to include in the provisional agenda of its fifty-ninth session the item entitled "Report of the Special Committee to Investigate Israeli Practices Affecting the Human Rights of the Palestinian People and Other Arabs of the Occupied Territories".

RECORDED VOTE ON RESOLUTION 58/96:

In favour: Afghanistan, Algeria, Angola, Armenia, Azerbaijan, Bahrain, Bangladesh, Belarus, Belize, Benin, Bolivia, Botswana, Brazil, Brunei Darussalam, Burkina Faso, Cambodia, Cape Verde, Chile, China, Colombia, Comoros, Côte d'Ivoire, Cuba, Democratic People's Republic of Korea, Djibouti, Ecuador, Egypt, Gabon, Gambia, Ghana, Grenada, Guinea, Guinea-Bissau, Guyana, Haiti, India, Indonesia, Iran, Jordan, Kenya, Kuwait, Lao People's Democratic Republic, Lebanon, Lesotho, Libyan Arab Jamahiriya, Madagascar, Malaysia, Maldives, Mali, Malta, Mauritania, Mauritius, Morocco, Mozambique, Myanmar, Namibia, Nepal, Niger, Nigeria, Oman, Pakistan, Panama, Paraguay, Philippines, Qatar, Saint Lucia, Saudi Arabia, Senegal, Singapore, South Africa, Sri Lanka, Sudan, Suriname, Swaziland, Syrian Arab Republic, Togo, Trinidad and Tobago, Tunisia, Turkey, Turkmenistan, United Arab Emirates, United Republic of Tanzania, Venezuela, Viet Nam, Yemen, Zambia, Zimbabwe.

Against: Australia, Israel, Marshall Islands, Micronesia, Nauru, Palau, United States.

Abstaining: Albania, Andorra, Antigua and Barbuda, Argentina, Austria, Bahamas, Belgium, Bhutan, Bosnia and Herzegovina, Bulgaria, Burundi, Cameroon, Canada, Costa Rica, Croatia, Cyprus, Czech Republic, Denmark, Dominican Republic, El Salvador, Equatorial Guinea, Estonia, Ethiopia, Fiji, Finland, France, Georgia, Germany, Greece, Guatemala, Honduras, Hungary, Iceland, Ireland, Italy, Jamaica, Japan, Kazakhstan, Kyrgyzstan, Latvia, Liechtenstein, Lithuania, Luxembourg, Mexico, Monaco, Mongolia, Netherlands, New Zealand, Nicaragua, Norway, Papua New Guinea, Peru, Poland, Portugal, Republic of Korea, Republic of Moldova, Romania, Russian Federation, Rwanda, Saint Vincent and the Grenadines, Samoa, San Marino, Serbia and Montenegro, Slovakia, Slovenia, Solomon Islands, Spain, Sweden, Switzerland, Tajikistan, Thailand, The former Yugoslav Republic of Macedonia, Tonga, Tuvalu, Ukraine, United Kingdom, Uruguay, Uzbekistan.

Fourth Geneva Convention

Report of Secretary-General. In July [A/58/155], the Secretary-General informed the General Assembly that Israel had not replied to his June request for information on steps taken or envisaged to implement Assembly resolution 57/125 [YUN 2002, p. 451] demanding that Israel accept the de jure applicability of the Fourth Geneva Convention in the Occupied Palestinian Territory, including East Jerusalem, and that it comply scrupulously with its provisions. The Secretary-General noted that he had drawn the attention of all States parties to the Convention to paragraph 3 of resolution 57/125 calling on them to exert all efforts to ensure respect by Israel for the Convention's provisions, and to paragraph 6 of resolution 57/128 [ibid., p. 482] calling on States not to recognize any legislative or administrative measures and actions taken by Israel in the occupied Syrian Golan.

The High Contracting Parties to the Fourth Geneva Convention had reaffirmed the applicability of the Convention to the Occupied Palestinian Territory at meetings in 1999 [YUN 1999, p. 415] and in 2001 [YUN 2001, p. 425].

GENERAL ASSEMBLY ACTION

On 9 December [meeting 72], the General Assembly, on the recommendation of the Fourth Committee [A/58/473 & Corr.1], adopted **resolution 58/97** by recorded vote (164-6-4) [agenda item 84].

Applicability of the Geneva Convention relative to the Protection of Civilian Persons in Time of War, of 12 August 1949, to the Occupied Palestinian Territory, including East Jerusalem, and the other occupied Arab territories

The General Assembly,

Recalling its relevant resolutions,

Bearing in mind the relevant resolutions of the Security Council,

Recalling the Regulations annexed to the Hague Convention IV of 1907, the Geneva Convention relative to the Protection of Civilian Persons in Time of War, of 12 August 1949, and relevant provisions of customary law, including those codified in Additional Protocol 1 to the four Geneva Conventions,

Having considered the report of the Special Committee to Investigate Israeli Practices Affecting the Human Rights of the Palestinian People and Other Arabs of the Occupied Territories and the relevant reports of the Secretary-General,

Considering that the promotion of respect for the obligations arising from the Charter of the United Nations and other instruments and rules of international law is among the basic purposes and principles of the United Nations,

Noting the convening of the meeting of experts of High Contracting Parties to the Geneva Convention relative to the Protection of Civilian Persons in Time of War, of 12 August 1949, at Geneva from 27 to 29 October 1998, at the initiative of the Government of Switzerland in its capacity as the depositary of the Convention, concerning problems of application of the Convention in general and, in particular, in occupied territories,

Noting also the convening for the first time, on 15 July 1999, of the Conference of High Contracting Parties to the Fourth Geneva Convention, as recommended by the General Assembly in its resolution ES-10/6 of 9 February 1999, on measures to enforce the Convention in the Occupied Palestinian Territory, including East Jerusalem, and to ensure respect thereof in accordance with article 1 common to the four Geneva Conventions, and aware of the statement adopted by the Conference,

Welcoming the reconvening of the Conference of High Contracting Parties to the Fourth Geneva Convention on 5 December 2001 in Geneva and stressing the importance of the Declaration adopted by the Conference, and underlining the need for the parties to follow up the implementation of the Declaration,

Welcoming and encouraging the initiatives by States parties to the Convention, both individually and collectively, according to article 1 common to the four Geneva Conventions, aimed at ensuring respect for the Convention,

Stressing that Israel, the occupying Power, should comply strictly with its obligations under international law, including international humanitarian law,

1. *Reaffirms* that the Geneva Convention relative to the Protection of Civilian Persons in Time of War, of 12 August 1949, is applicable to the Occupied Palestinian Territory, including East Jerusalem, and other Arab territories occupied by Israel since 1967;

2. *Demands* that Israel accept the de jure applicability of the Convention in the Occupied Palestinian Territory, including East Jerusalem, and other Arab territories occupied by Israel since 1967, and that it comply scrupulously with the provisions of the Convention;

3. *Calls upon* all High Contracting Parties to the Convention, in accordance with article 1 common to the four Geneva Conventions, to continue to exert all efforts to ensure respect for its provisions by Israel, the occupying Power, in the Occupied Palestinian Territory, including East Jerusalem, and other Arab territories occupied by Israel since 1967;

4. *Reiterates* the need for speedy implementation of the relevant recommendations contained in its resolutions of the tenth emergency special session with regard to ensuring respect by Israel, the occupying Power, for the provisions of the Convention;

5. *Requests* the Secretary-General to report to the General Assembly at its fifty-ninth session on the implementation of the present resolution.

RECORDED VOTE ON RESOLUTION 58/97:

In favour: Afghanistan, Albania, Algeria, Andorra, Angola, Antigua and Barbuda, Argentina, Armenia, Australia, Austria, Azerbaijan, Bahamas, Bahrain, Bangladesh, Barbados, Belarus, Belgium, Belize, Benin, Bolivia, Bosnia and Herzegovina, Botswana, Brazil, Brunei Darussalam, Bulgaria, Burkina Faso, Burundi, Cambodia, Canada, Cape Verde, Chile, China, Colombia, Comoros, Costa Rica, Côte d'Ivoire, Croatia, Cuba, Cyprus, Czech Republic, Democratic People's Republic of Korea, Denmark, Djibouti, Dominican Republic, Ecuador, Egypt, El Salvador, Equatorial Guinea, Eritrea, Estonia, Ethiopia, Fiji, Finland, France, Gabon, Gambia, Georgia, Germany, Ghana, Greece, Grenada, Guatemala, Guinea, Guinea-Bissau, Guyana, Haiti, Hungary, Iceland, India, Indonesia, Iran, Ireland, Italy, Jamaica, Japan, Jordan, Kazakhstan, Kenya, Kuwait, Kyrgyzstan, Lao People's Democratic Republic, Latvia, Lebanon, Lesotho, Libyan Arab Jamahiriya, Liechtenstein, Lithuania, Luxembourg, Madagascar, Malaysia, Maldives, Mali, Malta, Mauritania, Mauritius, Mexico, Monaco, Mongolia, Morocco, Mozambique, Myanmar, Namibia, Nepal, Netherlands, New Zealand, Nicaragua, Niger, Nigeria, Norway, Oman, Pakistan, Panama, Paraguay, Peru, Philippines, Poland, Portugal, Qatar, Republic of Korea, Republic of Moldova, Romania, Russian Federation, Saint Lucia, Saint Vincent and the Grenadines, Samoa, San Marino, Saudi Arabia, Senegal, Serbia and Montenegro, Seychelles, Singapore, Slovakia, Slovenia, Solomon Islands, South Africa, Spain, Sri Lanka, Sudan, Suriname, Swaziland, Sweden, Switzerland, Syrian Arab Republic, Tajikistan, Thailand, The former Yugoslav Republic of Macedonia, Timor-Leste, Togo, Tonga, Trinidad and Tobago, Tunisia, Turkey, Turkmenistan, Tuvalu, Ukraine, United Arab Emirates, United Kingdom, United Republic of Tanzania, Uruguay, Venezuela, Viet Nam, Yemen, Zambia, Zimbabwe.

Against: Israel, Marshall Islands, Micronesia, Nauru, Palau, United States.

Abstaining: Cameroon, Honduras, Papua New Guinea, Rwanda.

Israeli settlements

Report of Secretary-General. On 8 August [A/58/263], the Secretary-General informed the General Assembly that Israel had not replied to his June request for information on steps taken or envisaged to implement the relevant provisions of resolution 57/126 [YUN 2002, p. 443], demanding that Israel, among other things, cease all construction of new settlements in the Occupied Palestinian Territory, including Jerusalem.

GENERAL ASSEMBLY ACTION

On 9 December [meeting 72], the General Assembly, on the recommendation of the Fourth Committee [A/58/473 & Corr.1], adopted **resolution 58/98** by recorded vote (156-6-13) [agenda item 84].

Israeli settlements in the Occupied Palestinian Territory, including East Jerusalem, and the occupied Syrian Golan

The General Assembly,

Guided by the principles of the Charter of the United Nations, and affirming the inadmissibility of the acquisition of territory by force,

Recalling its relevant resolutions, including those adopted at its tenth emergency special session, as well as relevant Security Council resolutions, including resolutions 242(1967) of 22 November 1967, 446(1979) of 22 March 1979, 465(1980) of 1 March 1980, 476(1980) of 30 June 1980, 478(1980) of 20 August 1980, 497(1981) of 17 December 1981 and 904(1994) of 18 March 1994,

Reaffirming the applicability of the Geneva Convention relative to the Protection of Civilian Persons in Time of War, of 12 August 1949, to the Occupied Palestinian Territory, including East Jerusalem, and to the occupied Syrian Golan,

Taking note of the report of the Special Rapporteur of the Commission on Human Rights on the situation of human rights in the Palestinian territories occupied by Israel since 1967,

Recalling the Declaration of Principles on Interim Self-Government Arrangements of 13 September 1993 and the subsequent implementation agreements between the Palestinian and Israeli sides,

Welcoming the presentation by the Quartet to the parties of the road map to a permanent two-State solution to the Israeli-Palestinian conflict, and noting its call for a freeze on all settlement activity,

Aware that Israeli settlement activities have involved, inter alia, the transfer of nationals of the occupying Power into the occupied territories, the confiscation of land, the exploitation of natural resources and other illegal actions against the Palestinian civilian population,

Bearing in mind the detrimental impact of Israeli settlement policies, decisions and activities on efforts to achieve peace in the Middle East,

Expressing grave concern about the continuation by Israel of settlement activities in violation of international humanitarian law, relevant United Nations resolutions and the agreements reached between the parties, including the construction and expansion of the settlements in Jabal Abu-Ghneim and Ras Al-Amud in and around Occupied East Jerusalem,

Expressing grave concern also about the construction by Israel of a wall inside the Occupied Palestinian Territory, including in and around East Jerusalem, and expressing its concern in particular about the route of the wall in departure from the Armistice Line of 1949, which could prejudge future negotiations and make the two-State solution physically impossible to implement and would cause the Palestinian people further humanitarian hardship,

Reiterating its opposition to settlement activities in the Occupied Palestinian Territory, including East Jerusalem, and to any activities involving the confiscation of land, the disruption of the livelihood of protected persons and the de facto annexation of land,

Recalling the need to end all acts of violence, including acts of terror, provocation, incitement and destruction,

Gravely concerned about the dangerous situation resulting from actions taken by the illegal armed Israeli settlers in the occupied territory, as illustrated in the recent period,

Taking note of the relevant reports of the Secretary-General,

1. *Reaffirms* that Israeli settlements in the Palestinian territory, including East Jerusalem, and in the occupied Syrian Golan are illegal and an obstacle to peace and economic and social development;

2. *Calls upon* Israel to accept the de jure applicability of the Geneva Convention relative to the Protection of Civilian Persons in Time of War, of 12 August 1949, to the Occupied Palestinian Territory, including East Jerusalem, and to the occupied Syrian Golan and to abide scrupulously by the provisions of the Convention, in particular article 49;

3. *Reiterates its demand* for the complete cessation of all Israeli settlement activities in the Occupied Palestinian Territory, including East Jerusalem, and in the occupied Syrian Golan;

4. *Demands* that Israel stop and reverse the construction of the wall in the Occupied Palestinian Territory, including in and around East Jerusalem, which is in departure from the Armistice Line of 1949 and is in contradiction to relevant provisions of international law;

5. *Stresses* the need for full implementation of Security Council resolution 904(1994), in which, among other things, the Council called upon Israel, the occupying Power, to continue to take and implement measures, including confiscation of arms, with the aim of preventing illegal acts of violence by Israeli settlers, and called for measures to be taken to guarantee the safety and protection of the Palestinian civilians in the occupied territory;

6. *Reiterates its calls* for the prevention of all acts of violence by Israeli settlers, particularly in the light of recent developments;

7. *Requests* the Secretary-General to report to the General Assembly at its fifty-ninth session on the implementation of the present resolution.

RECORDED VOTE ON RESOLUTION 58/98:

In favour: Afghanistan, Albania, Algeria, Andorra, Angola, Antigua and Barbuda, Argentina, Armenia, Austria, Azerbaijan, Bahamas, Bahrain, Bangladesh, Barbados, Belarus, Belgium, Belize, Benin, Bhutan, Bolivia, Bosnia and Herzegovina, Botswana, Brazil, Brunei Darussalam, Bulgaria, Burkina Faso, Burundi, Cambodia, Canada, Cape Verde, Chile, China, Colombia, Comoros, Côte d'Ivoire, Croatia, Cuba, Cyprus, Czech Republic, Democratic People's Republic of Korea, Denmark, Djibouti, Ecuador, Egypt, Equatorial Guinea, Eritrea, Estonia, Ethiopia, Fiji, Finland, France, Gabon, Gambia, Georgia, Germany, Ghana, Greece, Grenada, Guinea, Guinea-Bissau, Guyana, Haiti, Hungary, Iceland, India, Indonesia, Iran, Ireland, Italy, Jamaica, Japan, Jordan, Kazakhstan, Kenya, Kuwait, Kyrgyzstan, Lao People's Democratic Republic, Latvia, Lebanon, Lesotho, Libyan Arab Jamahiriya, Liechtenstein, Lithuania, Luxembourg, Madagascar, Malaysia, Maldives, Mali, Malta, Mauritania, Mauritius, Mexico, Monaco, Mongolia, Morocco, Mozambique, Myanmar, Namibia, Nepal, Netherlands, New Zealand, Niger, Nigeria, Norway, Oman, Pakistan, Panama, Paraguay, Peru, Philippines, Poland, Portugal, Qatar, Republic of Korea, Republic of Moldova, Romania, Russian Federation, Saint Lucia, Saint Vincent and the Grenadines, Samoa, San Marino, Saudi Arabia, Senegal, Serbia and Montenegro, Seychelles, Singapore, Slovakia, Slovenia, South Africa, Spain, Sri Lanka, Sudan, Suriname, Swaziland, Sweden, Switzerland, Syrian Arab Republic, Tajikistan, Thailand, The former Yugoslav Republic of Macedonia, Timor-Leste, Togo, Trinidad and Tobago, Tunisia, Turkey, Turkmenistan, Ukraine, United Arab Emirates, United Kingdom, United Republic of Tanzania, Uruguay, Venezuela, Viet Nam, Yemen, Zambia, Zimbabwe.

Against: Israel, Marshall Islands, Micronesia, Nauru, Palau, United States.

Abstaining: Australia, Cameroon, Costa Rica, Dominican Republic, El Salvador, Guatemala, Honduras, Nicaragua, Papua New Guinea, Rwanda, Solomon Islands, Tonga, Tuvalu.

Palestinian women

The Secretary-General, in a report [E/CN.6/2003/3] to the Commission on the Status of Women, reviewed, in response to Economic and Social Council resolution 2002/25 [YUN 2002, p. 453], the situation of Palestinian women and assistance provided by UN organizations from September 2001 to September 2002. He said that during the period under review, the situation in the Occupied Palestinian Territory was characterized by continued violence, which left hundreds of civilians dead and thousands of Palestinians, including women and children, wounded. Women were injured near or inside their homes or when attempting to cross checkpoints. They had also assumed the major responsibility as caregivers to the injured.

The expansion of Israeli settlements, the demolition of Palestinian homes, the destruction of land and the building of bypass roads in the occupied territory continued to create difficulties for the Palestinians, especially for women who carried household responsibilities. Lack of domestic economic activity had led to an almost 20 per cent contraction of employment. That decline had affected women's participation in the labour force, which had remained persistently low. Women had also been severely affected by the decline in the agriculture sector as they played a major role in agriculture production for the household economy, while loss of land, or of access to land, deprived them of a vital source of income. The conflict had an impact on the nutritional and health status of women and children, as border closures, curfews and checkpoints affected access to high-protein food and, in particular, to infant formula and powdered milk. The adverse impact of closures and prolonged curfews on Palestinian villages restricted the access of civilians, especially women, to life-saving services such as emergency obstetric care. The crisis affected the psychosocial well-being of Palestinians, particularly women and young people.

While the situation in the Occupied Palestinian Territory had made it difficult for international organizations to provide direct assistance to Palestinian women, the UN system continued to respond to their needs. In its 2002-2005 medium-term plan and its 2002-2003 programme of work and priorities [YUN 2002, p. 1020], ESCWA gave special attention to the socio-economic situation of Palestinian women. Likewise, the United Nations Development Programme continued to provide support and services to women-owned household economy projects. The United Nations Development Fund for Women launched and continued to support a regional resource network of women's small and microenterprises in the Gaza Strip, and UNRWA, among other things, granted almost 3,000 loans, valued at $1.36 million, to women through its microfinance and microenterprise programme. It also provided maternal and child health care and family planning services as an integral part of its primary health care. The International Labour Organization developed several projects aimed at strengthening women's security and employability in the West Bank and Gaza Strip and women's participation in Palestinian trade unions. The World Bank, among other things, implemented its emergency services support project in order to improve the availability of basic services in the health sector. The World Food Programme (WFP) provided assistance to thousands of non-refugee vulnerable Palestinians who had no reliable source of income. Women were the primary recipients of WFP's food aid in the Palestinian territories. They also participated in WFP's food-for-work schemes in the West Bank and Gaza Strip.

The Secretary-General observed that the situation of Palestinian women was inextricably linked to overall developments in the region and to progress in the peace process. There existed, however, important differences in the way that women and men, respectively, were affected by the socio-economic and political situation, particularly in such areas as basic social services, economic opportunities and means of livelihood, which required particular attention in terms of data collection and analysis, in addition to remedial action. Further opportunities should be sought to highlight the impact of the crisis on women so that targeted action could be taken to mitigate their specific condition. Continued support by UN system entities was critical to secure benefits for Palestinian women in the occupied territories and in the refugee camps. As the conflict exacerbated existing hardships and created new difficulties, continued assistance needed to focus on such areas as women's employment and economic empowerment, education, health, social welfare and violence against women. Further efforts had to be undertaken to identify and address gender perspectives in all international assistance programmes, in addition to implementing projects specifically targeted to women.

ECONOMIC AND SOCIAL COUNCIL ACTION

On 22 July [meeting 44], the Economic and Social Council, on the recommendation of the Commission on the Status of Women [E/2003/27], adopted **resolution 2003/42** by recorded vote (42-2-4) [agenda item 14 (a)].

Situation of and assistance to Palestinian women

The Economic and Social Council,

Having considered with appreciation the report of the Secretary-General,

Recalling the Nairobi Forward-looking Strategies for the Advancement of Women, in particular paragraph 260 concerning Palestinian women and children, the Beijing Platform for Action adopted at the Fourth World Conference on Women and the outcome of the twenty-third special session of the General Assembly entitled "Women 2000: gender equality, development and peace for the twenty-first century",

Recalling also its resolution 2002/25 of 24 July 2002 and other relevant United Nations resolutions,

Recalling further the Declaration on the Elimination of Violence against Women as it concerns the protection of civilian populations,

Expressing the urgent need for the resumption of negotiations within the Middle East peace process on its agreed basis and towards the speedy achievement of a final settlement between the Palestinian and Israeli sides,

Concerned about the grave deterioration of the situation of Palestinian women in the Occupied Palestinian Territory, including East Jerusalem, and about the severe consequences of continuous illegal Israeli settlement activities as well as the harsh economic conditions and other severe consequences of the continuing Israeli attacks and sieges on Palestinian cities, towns, villages and refugee camps, which has resulted in the dire humanitarian crisis being faced by Palestinian women and their families,

Expressing its condemnation of all acts of violence, including all acts of terror, provocation, incitement and destruction, especially the excessive use of force against Palestinian civilians, many of them women and children, resulting in injury and loss of human life,

1. *Calls upon* the concerned parties, as well as the international community, to exert all the necessary efforts to ensure the immediate resumption of the peace process on its agreed basis, taking into account the common ground already gained, and calls for measures for tangible improvement of the difficult situation on the ground and the living conditions faced by Palestinian women and their families;

2. *Reaffirms* that the Israeli occupation remains a major obstacle for Palestinian women with regard to their advancement, self-reliance and integration in the development planning of their society;

3. *Demands* that Israel, the occupying Power, comply fully with the provisions and principles of the Universal Declaration of Human Rights, the Regulations annexed to The Hague Convention IV of 18 October 1907 and the Geneva Convention relative to the Protection of Civilian Persons in Time of War of 12 August 1949, in order to protect the rights of Palestinian women and their families;

4. *Calls upon* Israel to facilitate the return of all refugees and displaced Palestinian women and children to their homes and properties, in compliance with the relevant United Nations resolutions;

5. *Calls upon* the international community to continue to provide urgently needed assistance and services in an effort to alleviate the dire humanitarian crisis being faced by Palestinian women and their families and to help in the reconstruction of relevant Palestinian institutions;

6. *Requests* the Commission on the Status of Women to continue to monitor and take action with regard to the implementation of the Nairobi Forward-looking Strategies for the Advancement of Women, in particular paragraph 260 concerning Palestinian women and children, the Beijing Platform for Action and the outcome of the special session of the General Assembly, entitled "Women 2000: gender equality, development and peace for the twenty-first century";

7. *Requests* the Secretary-General to continue to review the situation and to assist Palestinian women by all available means, including those laid out in his report, and to submit to the Commission on the Status of Women at its forty-eighth session a report, including information provided by the Economic and Social Commission for Western Asia, on the progress made in the implementation of the present resolution.

RECORDED VOTE ON RESOLUTION 2003/42:

In favour: Andorra, Argentina, Benin, Bhutan, Brazil, Burundi, Chile, China, Congo, Cuba, Egypt, Ethiopia, Finland, France, Ghana, Greece, Hungary, India, Iran, Iceland, Italy, Jamaica, Japan, Libyan Arab Jamahiriya, Malaysia, Mozambique, Nepal, Netherlands, Nigeria, Pakistan, Portugal, Qatar, Republic of Korea, Romania, Russian Federation, Saudi Arabia, Senegal, South Africa, Sweden, Uganda, Ukraine, United Kingdom.

Against: Georgia, United States.

Abstaining: Australia, Germany, Nicaragua, Peru.

Palestinian children

On 22 December [meeting 77], the General Assembly, on the recommendation of the Third (Social, Humanitarian and Cultural) Committee [A/58/504], adopted **resolution 58/155** by recorded vote (106-5-65) [agenda item 113].

Situation of and assistance to Palestinian children

The General Assembly,

Recalling the Convention on the Rights of the Child,

Recalling also the World Declaration on the Survival, Protection and Development of Children and the Plan of Action for Implementing the World Declaration on the Survival, Protection and Development of Children in the 1990s, adopted by the World Summit for Children, held in New York on 29 and 30 September 1990,

Recalling further the Declaration and Plan of Action adopted by the General Assembly at its twenty-seventh special session,

Concerned that the Palestinian children under Israeli occupation remain deprived of many basic rights under the Convention,

Concerned also about the continued grave deterioration of the situation of Palestinian children in the Occupied Palestinian Territory, including East Jerusalem, and about the severe consequences of the continuing Israeli assaults and sieges on Palestinian cities, towns, villages and refugee camps, resulting in the dire humanitarian crisis,

Emphasizing the importance of the safety and well-being of all children in the whole Middle East region,

Expressing its condemnation of all acts of violence, resulting in extensive loss of human life and injuries, including among Palestinian children,

Deeply concerned about the severe consequences, including psychological consequences, of the Israeli military actions for the present and future well-being of Palestinian children,

1. *Stresses* the urgent need for Palestinian children to live a normal life free from foreign occupation, destruction and fear in their own State;

2. *Demands,* in the meanwhile, that Israel, the occupying Power, respect relevant provisions of the Convention on the Rights of the Child and comply fully with the provisions of the Geneva Convention relative to the Protection of Civilian Persons in Time of War, of 12 August 1949, in order to ensure the well-being and protection of Palestinian children and their families;

3. *Calls upon* the international community to provide urgently needed assistance and services in an effort to alleviate the dire humanitarian crisis being faced by Palestinian children and their families and to help in the reconstruction of relevant Palestinian institutions.

RECORDED VOTE ON RESOLUTION 58/155:

In favour: Afghanistan, Algeria, Antigua and Barbuda, Argentina, Armenia, Azerbaijan, Bahamas, Bahrain, Bangladesh, Barbados, Belarus, Belize, Benin, Bhutan, Bolivia, Bosnia and Herzegovina, Botswana, Brazil, Brunei Darussalam, Burkina Faso, Cambodia, Cape Verde, Chile, China, Comoros, Congo, Côte d'Ivoire, Cuba, Democratic People's Republic of Korea, Democratic Republic of the Congo, Djibouti, Dominica, Ecuador, Egypt, Eritrea, Ethiopia, Fiji, Gabon, Gambia, Ghana, Grenada, Guinea, Guinea-Bissau, Guyana, Haiti, India, Indonesia, Iran, Jamaica, Jordan, Kazakhstan, Kenya, Kuwait, Kyrgyzstan, Lao People's Democratic Republic, Lebanon, Lesotho, Libyan Arab Jamahiriya, Madagascar, Malawi, Malaysia, Maldives, Mali, Mauritania, Mauritius, Mexico, Mongolia, Morocco, Mozambique, Myanmar, Namibia, Nepal, Niger, Nigeria, Oman, Pakistan, Panama, Paraguay, Philippines, Qatar, Russian Federation, Saint Lucia, Saint Vincent and the Grenadines, Saudi Arabia, Senegal, Seychelles, Sierra Leone, Singapore, Somalia, South Africa, Sri Lanka, Sudan, Syrian Arab Republic, Thailand, Togo, Tunisia, Turkey, Turkmenistan, Uganda, United Arab Emirates, United Republic of Tanzania, Venezuela, Viet Nam, Yemen, Zambia, Zimbabwe.

Against: Israel, Marshall Islands, Micronesia, Palau, United States.

Abstaining: Albania, Andorra, Australia, Austria, Belgium, Bulgaria, Cameroon, Canada, Central African Republic, Colombia, Costa Rica, Croatia, Cyprus, Czech Republic, Denmark, Dominican Republic, El Salvador, Estonia, Finland, France, Georgia, Germany, Greece, Guatemala, Honduras, Hungary, Iceland, Ireland, Italy, Japan, Latvia, Liechtenstein, Lithuania, Luxembourg, Malta, Monaco, Nauru, Netherlands, New Zealand, Norway, Papua New Guinea, Peru, Poland, Portugal, Republic of Korea, Republic of Moldova, Romania, Rwanda, Samoa, San Marino, Serbia and Montenegro, Slovakia, Slovenia, Solomon Islands, Spain, Suriname, Sweden, Switzerland, The former Yugoslav Republic of Macedonia, Tonga, Tuvalu, Ukraine, United Kingdom, Uruguay, Uzbekistan.

Issues related to Palestine

General aspects

The General Assembly continued to consider the question of Palestine in 2003. Having discussed the annual report of the Committee on the Exercise of the Inalienable Rights of the Palestinian People (Committee on Palestinian Rights) [A/58/35], the Assembly adopted four resolutions, reaffirming, among other things, the necessity of achieving a peaceful settlement of the Palestine question—the core of the Arab-Israeli conflict—and stressing the need for the realization of the inalienable rights of the Palestinians, primarily the right to self-determination, for Israeli withdrawal from the Palestinian territory occupied since 1967 and for resolving the problem of the Palestine refugees. The Assembly called on the Secretariat to continue its activities to promote and raise awareness of Palestinian rights.

In observance of the International Day of Solidarity with the Palestinian People, celebrated annually on 29 November in accordance with Assembly resolution 32/40 B [YUN 1977, p. 304], the Committee held a solemn meeting and other activities on 1 December. In cooperation with the Permanent Observer Mission of Palestine, the Committee presented an exhibit entitled "Palestine: Reflections of Resilience and Hope".

Report of Secretary-General. In an October report on the peaceful settlement of the question of Palestine [A/58/416-S/2003/947], submitted in response to Assembly resolution 57/110 [YUN 2002, p. 455], the Secretary-General made observations on the Middle East peace process. By notes verbales of 16 and 19 June, the Secretary-General had sought the positions of Egypt, Israel, Jordan, Lebanon, the Syrian Arab Republic and the PLO regarding steps taken by them to implement the resolution. As at 17 September, Israel, Jordan, Syria and the PLO had responded.

Israel said that it viewed the resolution as unbalanced and an undue interference in the Israeli-Palestinian bilateral negotiations. The ongoing violence was a result of the Palestinian decision to abandon negotiations and to pursue goals through violence and terrorism. The approach of the resolution sought to dictate the outcome of the negotiation process and rewarded violence when the Palestinian side should be compelled to renounce violence and return to peaceful dialogue.

Jordan stated that it was committed to achieving a comprehensive, just and lasting peace in the Middle East on the basis of UN resolutions in implementation of the principle of land for security and recognition. Jordan had worked to create conditions conducive to the resumption of negotiations between the two sides, participated in the finalization of the road map and was working on its implementation after acceptance of it by both sides at the June Aqaba Summit. Jordan was convinced that the 30 June declaration of a truce by Palestinian groups (see p. 468) was a positive development and that all parties had to consolidate it by abiding by their obligations under the road map. Furthermore, Jordan had stressed the role of the United Nations and of the international community in bringing about a comprehensive peace in the region.

Syria affirmed that Israeli settlements in the territory occupied since 1967 and actions aimed at changing the status of Jerusalem represented obstacles to the conclusion of a peaceful settlement of the question of Palestine and that successive Israeli Governments had had no political will to conclude a lasting peace in the region based on UN resolutions.

The Permanent Observer of Palestine said that the resolution had been adopted by an overwhelming majority of Member States, reaffirming long-established convictions and positions of the international community on the issue. It was regrettable that Israel had chosen to vote against the resolution and had continued illegal actions and measures against the Palestinian people. In addition, Israel had yet to comply with any of its obligations under the road map, for, among other things, it continued its settlement activities, including the building of a separation wall that isolated many Palestinian communities from one another, destroying their means of livelihood. The situation on the ground had calmed down as a result of the efforts made by the Palestinian Government to secure assurances from all Palestinian groups to a ceasefire agreement.

The Secretary-General said that, since September 2000, more than 2,800 Palestinians and more than 800 Israelis had been killed, while thousands had been injured. The overwhelming majority of casualties in Israel resulted from terrorist attacks by various Palestinian militant groups. Bombs had been set off in cafes and restaurants and attacks carried out against public transport, including school buses, creating a climate of fear and constant watchfulness. A large number of Palestinian civilian casualties had resulted from Israeli Defence Forces (IDF) operations, including incursions, pre-emptive strikes and targeted assassinations of suspected militants in Palestinian areas. The use of heavy weaponry in densely populated Palestinian areas had been of particular concern. Since the declaration of a ceasefire and redeployment at the end of June, there had been a marked decline in violence. The Secretary-General said that he had repeatedly stressed the obligation of the PA to assume full security responsibility in the areas under its control, and had urged Israel to refrain from the excessive and disproportionate use of deadly force in civilian areas.

Israel continued its policy of demolishing houses as a reaction to security incidents. From 1 January to 21 August, 158 homes of Palestinians who had carried out attacks against Israel or who were suspected of involvement in or of planning future attacks were destroyed. The confiscation of land and the levelling of agricultural land continued unabated, particularly in border areas, around settlements and settler roads and in connection with the construction of the separation wall. Continued Israeli settlement construction and the building of a separation wall were two key challenges to the fulfilment of the road map's goal of the two-State solution. Over time, they had made the creation of a viable and contiguous Palestinian State more difficult. Despite the obligation set out in phase I of the road map to dismantle settlement outposts and to freeze all settlement expansion, the Israeli Government had not taken decisive action in that direction.

The humanitarian and economic situation of the Palestinian people continued to deteriorate, a direct result of the impact of the policy of systematic closures and curfews on Palestinian social and economic life. According to the World Bank, two thirds of the population of the West Bank and Gaza Strip lived on less than $2 per day, and gross national income per capita had fallen to nearly half of its 2001 level. More than half of the workforce was unemployed and more than half of the population was receiving some form of donor-financed food assistance. The limited steps taken by Israel to lift closures, curfews and other restrictions were not sufficient to significantly ease the economic deterioration in the Occupied Palestinian Territory. The humanitarian situation had also worsened because of the unprecedented movement restrictions imposed on UN and NGO personnel, limiting their access into and out of the Gaza Strip.

The Secretary-General said that he would continue to press for the implementation of the road map, which he believed provided the best opportunity to move forward in the peace process. He called on the international community to provide the resources for UN programmes to address the deteriorating economic and humanitarian situation of the Palestinian people, and especially to UNRWA so that it could continue to deliver the necessary services to the Palestinian refugees.

GENERAL ASSEMBLY ACTION

On 3 December [meeting 68], the General Assembly adopted **resolution 58/21** [draft: A/58/L.26/Rev.1 & Add.1] by recorded vote (160-6-5) [agenda item 38].

Peaceful settlement of the question of Palestine
The General Assembly,

Recalling its relevant resolutions, including those adopted at the tenth emergency special session,

Recalling also the relevant Security Council resolutions, including resolutions 242(1967) of 22 November 1967, 338(1973) of 22 October 1973, 1397(2002) of 12 March 2002 and 1515(2003) of 19 November 2003,

Welcoming the affirmation by the Security Council of the vision of a region where two States, Israel and Palestine, live side by side within secure and recognized borders,

Noting that it has been fifty-six years since the adoption of resolution 181(II) of 29 November 1947 and thirty-six years since the occupation of Palestinian territory, including East Jerusalem, in 1967,

Having considered the report of the Secretary-General submitted pursuant to the request made in its resolution 57/110 of 3 December 2002,

Reaffirming the permanent responsibility of the United Nations with regard to the question of Palestine until the question is resolved in all its aspects,

Convinced that achieving a final and peaceful settlement of the question of Palestine, the core of the Arab-Israeli conflict, is imperative for the attainment of a comprehensive and lasting peace and stability in the Middle East,

Aware that the principle of equal rights and self-determination of peoples is among the purposes and principles enshrined in the Charter of the United Nations,

Affirming the principle of the inadmissibility of the acquisition of territory by war,

Reaffirming the illegality of the Israeli settlements in the territory occupied since 1967 and of Israeli actions aimed at changing the status of Jerusalem, and affirming that the construction by Israel of a wall inside the Occupied Palestinian Territory, including in and around East Jerusalem, is in contravention of relevant provisions of international law,

Affirming once again the right of all States in the region to live in peace within secure and internationally recognized borders,

Recalling the mutual recognition between the Government of the State of Israel and the Palestine Liberation Organization, the representative of the Palestinian people, and the existing agreements concluded between the two sides, and the need for full compliance with those agreements,

Welcoming the endorsement by the Security Council, in resolution 1515(2003), of the Quartet performance-based road map to a permanent two-State solution to the Israeli-Palestinian conflict, and stressing the need for its implementation and compliance with its provisions,

Noting with satisfaction the establishment of the Palestinian Authority, and recognizing the urgent need to rebuild, reform and strengthen its damaged institutions,

Welcoming the positive contribution of the United Nations Special Coordinator for the Middle East Peace Process and Personal Representative of the Secretary-General to the Palestine Liberation Organization and the Palestinian Authority to the peace process, including in the framework of the activities of the Quartet,

Welcoming also the convening of international donor meetings, as well as the establishment of international mechanisms to provide assistance to the Palestinian people,

Expressing its grave concern over the tragic events in the Occupied Palestinian Territory, including East Jerusalem, since 28 September 2000 and the continued deterioration of the situation, including the rising number of deaths and injuries, mostly among Palestinian civilians, the deepening humanitarian crisis facing the Palestinian people and the widespread destruction of Palestinian property and infrastructure, both private and public, including many institutions of the Palestinian Authority,

Expressing its grave concern also over the repeated incursions into Palestinian-controlled areas and the reoccupation of many Palestinian population centres by the Israeli occupying forces,

Emphasizing the importance of the safety and well-being of all civilians in the whole Middle East region, and condemning all acts of violence and terror against civilians on both sides, including the suicide bombings and extrajudicial executions,

Gravely concerned over the increased suffering and casualties on both the Palestinian and Israeli sides, the loss of confidence on both sides and the dire situation facing the Middle East peace process,

Aware of the urgent need for revitalized and active international involvement to support both parties in overcoming the current dangerous impasse in the peace process,

Affirming the urgent need for the parties to cooperate with all international efforts, including the efforts of the Quartet, to end the current tragic situation and to resume negotiations towards a final peace settlement,

Welcoming recent initiatives and efforts undertaken by civil society in pursuit of a peaceful settlement of the question of Palestine,

1. *Reaffirms* the necessity of achieving a peaceful settlement of the question of Palestine, the core of the Arab-Israeli conflict, in all its aspects and of intensifying all efforts towards that end;

2. *Also reaffirms* its full support for the Middle East peace process, which began in Madrid, and the existing agreements between the Israeli and Palestinian sides, stresses the necessity for the establishment of a comprehensive, just and lasting peace in the Middle East, and welcomes in this regard the efforts of the Quartet;

3. *Welcomes* the Arab Peace Initiative adopted by the Council of the League of Arab States at its fourteenth session, held in Beirut on 27 and 28 March 2002;

4. *Calls upon* both parties to fulfil their obligations in implementation of the road map by taking parallel and reciprocal steps in this regard, and stresses the importance and urgency of establishing a credible and effective third-party monitoring mechanism including all members of the Quartet;

5. *Stresses* the necessity for a commitment to the vision of the two-State solution and the principle of land for peace, and the implementation of Security Council resolutions 242(1967), 338(1973), 1397(2002) and 1515(2003);

6. *Also stresses* the need for a speedy end to the reoccupation of Palestinian population centres and for the complete cessation of all acts of violence, including military attacks, destruction and acts of terror;

7. *Calls upon* the concerned parties, the Quartet and other interested parties to exert all efforts and undertake initiatives necessary to halt the deterioration of the situation and to reverse all measures taken on the ground since 28 September 2000, and to ensure a successful and speedy resumption of the peace process and the conclusion of a final peaceful settlement;

8. *Stresses* the need for:

(a) The withdrawal of Israel from the Palestinian territory occupied since 1967;

(b) The realization of the inalienable rights of the Palestinian people, primarily the right to self-determination and the right to their independent State;

9. *Also stresses* the need for resolving the problem of the Palestine refugees in conformity with its resolution 194(III) of 11 December 1948;

10. *Urges* Member States to expedite the provision of economic, humanitarian and technical assistance to the Palestinian people and the Palestinian Authority during this critical period to help to alleviate the suffering of the Palestinian people, rebuild the Palestinian economy and infrastructure and support the restructuring and reform of Palestinian institutions;

11. *Requests* the Secretary-General to continue his efforts with the parties concerned, and in consultation with the Security Council, towards the attainment of a peaceful settlement of the question of Palestine and

the promotion of peace in the region and to submit to the General Assembly at its fifty-ninth session a report on these efforts and on developments on this matter.

RECORDED VOTE ON RESOLUTION 58/21:

In favour: Afghanistan, Albania, Algeria, Andorra, Antigua and Barbuda, Argentina, Armenia, Austria, Azerbaijan, Bahamas, Bahrain, Bangladesh, Barbados, Belarus, Belgium, Belize, Bolivia, Bosnia and Herzegovina, Botswana, Brazil, Brunei Darussalam, Bulgaria, Burkina Faso, Burundi, Cambodia, Canada, Cape Verde, Central African Republic, Chile, China, Colombia, Comoros, Congo, Costa Rica, Côte d'Ivoire, Croatia, Cuba, Cyprus, Czech Republic, Democratic People's Republic of Korea, Denmark, Djibouti, Dominican Republic, Ecuador, Egypt, El Salvador, Eritrea, Estonia, Ethiopia, Fiji, Finland, France, Gabon, Germany, Ghana, Greece, Grenada, Guatemala, Guinea, Guinea-Bissau, Guyana, Haiti, Hungary, Iceland, India, Indonesia, Iran, Ireland, Italy, Jamaica, Japan, Jordan, Kazakhstan, Kenya, Kuwait, Kyrgyzstan, Lao People's Democratic Republic, Latvia, Lebanon, Lesotho, Libyan Arab Jamahiriya, Liechtenstein, Lithuania, Luxembourg, Madagascar, Malawi, Malaysia, Maldives, Mali, Malta, Mauritania, Mauritius, Mexico, Monaco, Mongolia, Morocco, Mozambique, Myanmar, Namibia, Nepal, Netherlands, New Zealand, Nicaragua, Niger, Nigeria, Norway, Oman, Pakistan, Panama, Paraguay, Peru, Philippines, Poland, Portugal, Qatar, Republic of Korea, Republic of Moldova, Romania, Russian Federation, Saint Lucia, Saint Vincent and the Grenadines, Samoa, San Marino, Saudi Arabia, Senegal, Serbia and Montenegro, Seychelles, Sierra Leone, Singapore, Slovakia, Slovenia, Solomon Islands, Somalia, South Africa, Spain, Sri Lanka, Sudan, Suriname, Swaziland, Sweden, Switzerland, Syrian Arab Republic, Tajikistan, Thailand, The former Yugoslav Republic of Macedonia, Timor-Leste, Togo, Trinidad and Tobago, Tunisia, Turkey, Ukraine, United Arab Emirates, United Kingdom, United Republic of Tanzania, Uruguay, Venezuela, Viet Nam, Yemen, Zambia, Zimbabwe.

Against: Israel, Marshall Islands, Micronesia, Palau, Uganda, United States.

Abstaining: Australia, Honduras, Nauru, Rwanda, Tonga.

Speaking before the vote, Israel said that the draft resolution went against the agreements already achieved between the parties and undermined the peace process it professed to support. As with other Assembly resolutions on Arab-Israeli issues, it pretended that Israel had responsibilities with no rights and that Palestinians had rights but no responsibilities. In addition, the draft resolution sought to predetermine issues that had to be resolved through negotiations and undermined the integrity and the foundations of the peace process.

Speaking after the vote, the United Kingdom said that it voted in favour of the resolution because it supported the need to find a just and peaceful solution to the Israeli-Palestine conflict, even though it regretted that the resolution was not better balanced. The United Kingdom condemned terrorism and stressed that both sides had obligations to fulfil in order to make progress on the road map.

By **decision 58/565** of 23 December, the Assembly decided that the agenda items entitled "Question of Palestine" and "The situation in the Middle East" would remain for consideration during its resumed fifty-eighth (2004) session.

Committee on Palestinian Rights

As mandated by General Assembly resolution 57/107 [YUN 2002, p. 458], the Committee on the Exercise of the Inalienable Rights of the Palestinian People continued to review the situation relating to the Palestine question, reported on it and made suggestions to the Assembly and the Security Council.

The Committee continued to follow the Palestine-related activities of intergovernmental bodies, such as the African Union and the Non-Aligned Movement, and, through its Chairman, participated in high-level meetings of those bodies. In September, the Committee's Bureau held consultations with EU representatives as part of the continuing effort to build a constructive relationship on issues of common concern. Throughout the year, the Committee held a number of international events, including the United Nations International Meeting in Support of Middle East Peace (Kyiv, Ukraine, 13-14 May); a Public Forum in Support of Middle East Peace (Kyiv, 15 May); the United Nations Seminar on Assistance to the Palestinian People (Geneva, 15-16 July); and the United Nations International Conference of Civil Society in Support of the Palestinian People (New York, 4-5 September).

In its annual report to the Assembly [A/58/35] covering the period from 11 October 2002 to 9 October 2003, the Committee welcomed the presentation of the road map, but expressed concern that, while the PA had accepted it without reservations, Israel had not fully endorsed it, putting forward a series of conditions for its acceptance that threatened to render most of the plan ineffective. During the year, IDF conducted regular military raids in the Occupied Palestinian Territory, reoccupied Palestinian cities, imposed closures and curfews and used disproportionate and indiscriminate force in civilian areas. The army operations were often backed by heavy armour, helicopters and fighter jets. IDF also continued to carry out extrajudicial executions of Palestinians and imposed restrictions on the movement of PA President Arafat, who had been confined to his headquarters in Ramallah. The situation with respect to Palestinian prisoners remained unresolved; an estimated 6,500 prisoners, including children, remained in Israeli detention facilities.

Israel continued its territorial expansion through the illegal construction of settlements and outposts, road networks and the demolition of Palestinian homes and property. The removal of some outposts by Israel, as required by the road map, was quickly followed by the construction of new ones by settlers; consequently there was no real improvement in the situation concerning the outposts. At the same time, Israel had stepped up the construction of a barrier in the West Bank.

Overall, the humanitarian situation in the Occupied Palestinian Territory remained dire.

The most significant impediment to recovery of the Palestinian economy and improvement in the humanitarian situation was the closure regime, which forced many Palestinians to use long detours to reach their jobs, medical facilities or schools. Although the movement of people and goods was eased in some areas, frequent incursions by IDF into Palestinian areas, the re-establishment of roadblocks and the imposition of curfews continued to stifle the Palestinian livelihood. Even though security responsibilities were transferred to the PA in the Gaza Strip, Palestinians were still unable to move around freely. Such restrictions, combined with Israeli military operations, had virtually paralysed the Palestinian economic life. Constant water shortages and the deteriorating hygiene situation affected health and living conditions of thousands of families. The problem had become even more acute with the construction of the separation barrier, for its route limited Palestinian access to water wells.

The Committee, in its conclusions and recommendations, expressed concern about the lack of serious headway in the political process and, consequently, the absence of any tangible improvement in the security area. The initial positive steps aimed at creating confidence between the parties had collapsed, stalling the political process. The Committee remained hopeful that the situation could be redressed through the efforts of the Quartet, its individual members and other regional and international players. It emphasized that the United Nations should maintain its responsibility with respect to all aspects of the question of Palestine until it was resolved in a satisfactory manner, in conformity with relevant UN resolutions, in accordance with international legitimacy and until the inalienable rights of the Palestinian people were fully realized.

The Committee intended to continue promoting support for the road map. It stressed its opposition to the construction by Israel of the barrier in the occupied West Bank and in areas close to East Jerusalem, which had devastating immediate and long-term implications for the livelihood of the Palestinian people and endangered international efforts aimed at resolving the conflict. The Committee called on the Security Council and the General Assembly to attach the necessary importance to that issue, with a view to stopping its construction and the de facto annexation of Palestinian land. In its programme of work for the following year, the Committee would address such issues as the status of the peace process and the implementation of the road map, the security situation, the construction of the separation barrier and its implications, the humanitarian and socio-economic situation and the further involvement of civil society.

GENERAL ASSEMBLY ACTION

On 3 December [meeting 68], the General Assembly adopted **resolution 58/18** [draft: A/58/L.23 & Add.1] by recorded vote (97-7-60) [agenda item 38].

Committee on the Exercise of the Inalienable Rights of the Palestinian People

The General Assembly,

Recalling its resolutions 181(II) of 29 November 1947, 194(III) of 11 December 1948, 3236(XXIX) of 22 November 1974, 3375(XXX) and 3376(XXX) of 10 November 1975, 31/20 of 24 November 1976 and all subsequent relevant resolutions, including those adopted by the General Assembly at its emergency special sessions and resolution 57/107 of 3 December 2002,

Having considered the report of the Committee on the Exercise of the Inalienable Rights of the Palestinian People,

Recalling the mutual recognition between the Government of the State of Israel and the Palestine Liberation Organization, the representative of the Palestinian people, as well as the existing agreements between the two sides and the need for full compliance with those agreements,

Welcoming the official presentation by the Quartet of the performance-based road map to a permanent two-State solution to the Israeli-Palestinian conflict,

Reaffirming that the United Nations has a permanent responsibility towards the question of Palestine until the question is resolved in all its aspects in a satisfactory manner in accordance with international legitimacy,

1. *Expresses its appreciation* to the Committee on the Exercise of the Inalienable Rights of the Palestinian People for its efforts in performing the tasks assigned to it by the General Assembly, and takes note of its annual report, including the conclusions and recommendations contained in chapter VII thereof;

2. *Requests* the Committee to continue to exert all efforts to promote the realization of the inalienable rights of the Palestinian people, to support the Middle East peace process and to mobilize international support for and assistance to the Palestinian people, and authorizes the Committee to make such adjustments in its approved programme of work as it may consider appropriate and necessary in the light of developments and to report thereon to the General Assembly at its fifty-ninth session and thereafter;

3. *Also requests* the Committee to continue to keep under review the situation relating to the question of Palestine and to report and make suggestions to the General Assembly, the Security Council or the Secretary-General, as appropriate;

4. *Further requests* the Committee to continue to extend its cooperation and support to Palestinian and other civil society organizations in order to mobilize international solidarity and support for the achievement by the Palestinian people of its inalienable rights and for a peaceful settlement of the question of Palestine, and to involve additional civil society organizations in its work;

5. *Requests* the United Nations Conciliation Commission for Palestine, established under General Assembly resolution 194(III), and other United Nations bodies and entities working on various aspects of the question of Palestine to continue to cooperate fully with the Committee and to make available to it, at its request, the relevant information and documentation which they have at their disposal;

6. *Invites* all Governments and organizations to extend their cooperation to the Committee in the performance of its tasks;

7. *Requests* the Secretary-General to circulate the report of the Committee to all competent bodies of the United Nations, and urges them to take the necessary action, as appropriate;

8. *Also requests* the Secretary-General to continue to provide the Committee with all necessary facilities for the performance of its tasks.

RECORDED VOTE ON RESOLUTION 58/18:

In favour: Afghanistan, Algeria, Antigua and Barbuda, Armenia, Azerbaijan, Bahamas, Bahrain, Bangladesh, Barbados, Belarus, Belize, Bolivia, Botswana, Brazil, Brunei Darussalam, Burkina Faso, Burundi, Cambodia, Cape Verde, Central African Republic, Chile, China, Colombia, Comoros, Côte d'Ivoire, Cuba, Cyprus, Democratic People's Republic of Korea, Djibouti, Ecuador, Egypt, Eritrea, Ethiopia, Fiji, Gabon, Grenada, Guinea, Guinea-Bissau, Guyana, Haiti, India, Indonesia, Iran, Jamaica, Jordan, Kenya, Kuwait, Lao People's Democratic Republic, Lebanon, Lesotho, Libyan Arab Jamahiriya, Madagascar, Malaysia, Maldives, Mali, Malta, Mauritania, Mauritius, Mexico, Morocco, Mozambique, Myanmar, Namibia, Nepal, Niger, Nigeria, Oman, Pakistan, Panama, Paraguay, Philippines, Qatar, Saint Lucia, Saudi Arabia, Senegal, Seychelles, Sierra Leone, Singapore, Somalia, Sri Lanka, Sudan, Suriname, Swaziland, Syrian Arab Republic, Timor-Leste, Togo, Trinidad and Tobago, Tunisia, Turkey, Uganda, Ukraine, United Republic of Tanzania, Venezuela, Viet Nam, Yemen, Zambia, Zimbabwe.

Against: Australia, Israel, Marshall Islands, Micronesia, Nauru, Palau, United States.

Abstaining: Albania, Andorra, Argentina, Austria, Belgium, Bosnia and Herzegovina, Bulgaria, Canada, Costa Rica, Croatia, Czech Republic, Denmark, Dominican Republic, El Salvador, Estonia, Finland, France, Germany, Greece, Guatemala, Honduras, Hungary, Iceland, Ireland, Italy, Japan, Kazakhstan, Kyrgyzstan, Latvia, Liechtenstein, Lithuania, Luxembourg, Monaco, Netherlands, New Zealand, Nicaragua, Norway, Peru, Poland, Portugal, Republic of Korea, Republic of Moldova, Romania, Russian Federation, Rwanda, Samoa, San Marino, Serbia and Montenegro, Slovakia, Slovenia, Spain, Sweden, Switzerland, Tajikistan, Thailand, The former Yugoslav Republic of Macedonia, Tonga, United Kingdom, Uruguay, Uzbekistan.

Division for Palestinian Rights

Under the guidance of the Committee on Palestinian Rights, the Division for Palestinian Rights of the UN Secretariat continued to research, monitor, prepare studies, and collect and disseminate information on all issues related to the Palestine question. The Division responded to requests for information and issued the following publications: a monthly bulletin covering action by the United Nations and intergovernmental organizations concerned with the issue of Palestine; a monthly chronology of events relating to the question of Palestine, based on media reports and other sources; reports of meetings organized under the auspices of the Committee; a special bulletin on the observance of the International Day of Solidarity with the Palestinian People (29 November); periodic reviews of developments relating to Middle East peace efforts; and an annual compilation of relevant General Assembly and Security Council action.

The Committee, in its annual report [A/58/35], stressed that the Division should continue its programme of publications and other informational activities, including further development of the electronic United Nations Information System on the Question of Palestine (UNISPAL) documents collection. It requested that the training programme for PA staff be continued.

GENERAL ASSEMBLY ACTION

On 3 December [meeting 68], the General Assembly adopted **resolution 58/19** [draft: A/58/L.24 & Add.1] by recorded vote (98-6-63) [agenda item 38].

Division for Palestinian Rights of the Secretariat

The General Assembly,

Having considered the report of the Committee on the Exercise of the Inalienable Rights of the Palestinian People,

Taking note in particular of the relevant information contained in chapter V.B of that report,

Recalling its resolution 32/40 B of 2 December 1977 and all subsequent relevant resolutions, including resolution 57/108 of 3 December 2002,

1. *Notes with appreciation* the action taken by the Secretary-General in compliance with its resolution 57/108;

2. *Considers* that the Division for Palestinian Rights of the Secretariat continues to make a useful and constructive contribution;

3. *Requests* the Secretary-General to continue to provide the Division with the necessary resources and to ensure that it continues to carry out its work as detailed in the relevant earlier resolutions, in consultation with the Committee on the Exercise of the Inalienable Rights of the Palestinian People and under its guidance, including, in particular, the organization of meetings and conferences in various regions with the participation of all sectors of the international community, the further development and expansion of the documents collection of the United Nations Information System on the Question of Palestine, the preparation and widest possible dissemination of publications and information materials on various aspects of the question of Palestine and the provision of the annual training programme for staff of the Palestinian Authority;

4. *Also requests* the Secretary-General to ensure the continued cooperation of the Department of Public Information and other units of the Secretariat in enabling the Division to perform its tasks and in covering adequately the various aspects of the question of Palestine;

5. *Invites* all Governments and organizations to extend their cooperation to the Division in the performance of its tasks;

6. *Requests* the Committee and the Division, as part of the observance of the International Day of Solidarity with the Palestinian People on 29 November, to continue to organize an annual exhibit on Palestinian rights in cooperation with the Permanent Observer Mission of Palestine to the United Nations, and encourages Member States to continue to give the widest

support and publicity to the observance of the Day of Solidarity.

RECORDED VOTE ON RESOLUTION 58/19:

In favour: Afghanistan, Algeria, Antigua and Barbuda, Azerbaijan, Bahamas, Bahrain, Bangladesh, Barbados, Belarus, Belize, Bolivia, Botswana, Brazil, Brunei Darussalam, Burkina Faso, Burundi, Cambodia, Cape Verde, Central African Republic, Chile, China, Colombia, Comoros, Congo, Côte d'Ivoire, Cuba, Cyprus, Democratic People's Republic of Korea, Djibouti, Ecuador, Egypt, Eritrea, Ethiopia, Gabon, Ghana, Grenada, Guinea, Guinea-Bissau, Guyana, Haiti, India, Indonesia, Iran, Jamaica, Jordan, Kenya, Kuwait, Lao People's Democratic Republic, Lebanon, Lesotho, Libyan Arab Jamahiriya, Madagascar, Malaysia, Maldives, Mali, Malta, Mauritania, Mauritius, Mexico, Morocco, Mozambique, Myanmar, Namibia, Nepal, Niger, Nigeria, Oman, Pakistan, Panama, Paraguay, Philippines, Qatar, Saint Lucia, Saudi Arabia, Senegal, Seychelles, Sierra Leone, Singapore, Somalia, South Africa, Sri Lanka, Sudan, Suriname, Swaziland, Syrian Arab Republic, Togo, Trinidad and Tobago, Tunisia, Turkey, Uganda, United Arab Emirates, United Republic of Tanzania, Uruguay, Venezuela, Viet Nam, Yemen, Zambia, Zimbabwe.

Against: Israel, Marshall Islands, Micronesia, Nauru, Palau, United States.

Abstaining: Albania, Andorra, Argentina, Armenia, Australia, Austria, Belgium, Bosnia and Herzegovina, Bulgaria, Canada, Costa Rica, Croatia, Czech Republic, Denmark, Dominican Republic, El Salvador, Estonia, Fiji, Finland, France, Germany, Greece, Guatemala, Honduras, Hungary, Iceland, Ireland, Italy, Japan, Kazakhstan, Latvia, Liechtenstein, Lithuania, Luxembourg, Malawi, Monaco, Netherlands, New Zealand, Nicaragua, Norway, Peru, Poland, Portugal, Republic of Korea, Republic of Moldova, Romania, Russian Federation, Rwanda, Samoa, San Marino, Serbia and Montenegro, Slovakia, Slovenia, Spain, Sweden, Switzerland, Tajikistan, Thailand, The former Yugoslav Republic of Macedonia, Tonga, Ukraine, United Kingdom, Uzbekistan.

Special information programme

As requested in General Assembly resolution 57/109 [YUN 2002, p. 460], the UN Department of Public Information (DPI) in 2003 continued its special information programme on the question of Palestine, which included the organization of its annual training programme for Palestinian broadcasters and journalists, and the launching, in January, of the Arabic version of the United Nations News Centre web site (*www.un.org/news*). The Radio Section provided extensive coverage of various aspects of the question in its daily live broadcasts in all six UN official languages. The updated permanent exhibit "The United Nations and the Question of Palestine" was on display in the General Assembly Hall. The quarterly *UN Chronicle* continued to cover the Palestine question and reported on relevant UN action. DPI's Video Section produced a *World Chronicle* programme entitled "Palestine Refugees: Present and Future Challenges".

DPI, in cooperation with the Foundation of the Three Cultures of the Mediterranean, organized an international media seminar on peace in the Middle East (Seville, Spain, 21-22 October). With the overall theme "Towards a two-State solution", the seminar provided an opportunity for media representatives and international experts to discuss the status of the road map; the role of culture, literature and education in facilitating a dialogue for peace; and the media's coverage of the conflict.

As in previous years, the United Nations information centres (UNICs) and other UN offices carried out activities in connection with the International Day of Solidarity with the Palestinian People. Throughout the year, many UNICs dealt with the Palestine question and organized related outreach activities.

GENERAL ASSEMBLY ACTION

On 3 December [meeting 68], the General Assembly adopted **resolution 58/20** [draft: A/58/L.25 & Add.1] by recorded vote (159-6-6) [agenda item 38].

Special information programme on the question of Palestine of the Department of Public Information of the Secretariat

The General Assembly,

Having considered the report of the Committee on the Exercise of the Inalienable Rights of the Palestinian People,

Taking note in particular of the information contained in chapter VI of that report,

Recalling its resolution 57/109 of 3 December 2002,

Convinced that the worldwide dissemination of accurate and comprehensive information and the role of civil society organizations and institutions remain of vital importance in heightening awareness of and support for the inalienable rights of the Palestinian people,

Recalling the mutual recognition between the Government of the State of Israel and the Palestine Liberation Organization, the representative of the Palestinian people, as well as the existing agreements concluded between the two sides and the need for full compliance with those agreements,

Welcoming the official presentation by the Quartet of the road map to a permanent two-State solution to the Israeli-Palestinian conflict,

1. *Notes with appreciation* the action taken by the Department of Public Information of the Secretariat in compliance with resolution 56/35 of 3 December 2001;

2. *Considers* that the special information programme on the question of Palestine of the Department is very useful in raising the awareness of the international community concerning the question of Palestine and the situation in the Middle East and that the programme is contributing effectively to an atmosphere conducive to dialogue and supportive of the peace process;

3. *Requests* the Department, in full cooperation and coordination with the Committee on the Exercise of the Inalienable Rights of the Palestinian People, to continue, with the necessary flexibility as may be required by developments affecting the question of Palestine, its special information programme for the biennium 2004-2005, in particular:

(*a*) To disseminate information on all the activities of the United Nations system relating to the question of Palestine, including reports on the work carried out by the relevant United Nations entities;

(*b*) To continue to issue and update publications on the various aspects of the question of Palestine in all fields, including materials concerning the recent developments in that regard, in particular the prospects for peace;

(*c*) To expand its collection of audio-visual material on the question of Palestine and to continue the production and preservation of such material and the updating of the exhibit in the Secretariat;

(d) To organize and promote fact-finding news missions for journalists to the area, including the territory under the jurisdiction of the Palestinian Authority and the Occupied Territory;

(e) To organize international, regional and national seminars or encounters for journalists, aiming in particular at sensitizing public opinion to the question of Palestine;

(f) To continue to provide assistance to the Palestinian people in the field of media development, in particular to strengthen the training programme for Palestinian broadcasters and journalists initiated in 1995.

RECORDED VOTE ON RESOLUTION 58/20:

In favour: Afghanistan, Albania, Algeria, Andorra, Antigua and Barbuda, Argentina, Armenia, Austria, Azerbaijan, Bahamas, Bahrain, Bangladesh, Barbados, Belarus, Belgium, Belize, Bolivia, Bosnia and Herzegovina, Botswana, Brazil, Brunei Darussalam, Bulgaria, Burkina Faso, Burundi, Cambodia, Canada, Cape Verde, Central African Republic, Chile, China, Colombia, Comoros, Congo, Costa Rica, Côte d'Ivoire, Croatia, Cuba, Cyprus, Czech Republic, Democratic People's Republic of Korea, Denmark, Djibouti, Dominican Republic, Ecuador, Egypt, El Salvador, Eritrea, Estonia, Ethiopia, Fiji, Finland, France, Gabon, Germany, Ghana, Greece, Grenada, Guatemala, Guinea, Guinea-Bissau, Guyana, Haiti, Hungary, Iceland, India, Indonesia, Iran, Ireland, Italy, Jamaica, Japan, Jordan, Kazakhstan, Kenya, Kuwait, Kyrgyzstan, Lao People's Democratic Republic, Latvia, Lebanon, Lesotho, Libyan Arab Jamahiriya, Liechtenstein, Lithuania, Luxembourg, Madagascar, Malawi, Malaysia, Maldives, Mali, Malta, Mauritania, Mauritius, Mexico, Monaco, Mongolia, Morocco, Mozambique, Myanmar, Namibia, Nepal, Netherlands, New Zealand, Nicaragua, Niger, Nigeria, Norway, Oman, Pakistan, Panama, Paraguay, Peru, Philippines, Poland, Portugal, Qatar, Republic of Korea, Republic of Moldova, Romania, Russian Federation, Saint Lucia, Saint Vincent and the Grenadines, Samoa, San Marino, Saudi Arabia, Senegal, Serbia and Montenegro, Seychelles, Sierra Leone, Singapore, Slovakia, Slovenia, Somalia, South Africa, Spain, Sri Lanka, Sudan, Suriname, Swaziland, Sweden, Switzerland, Syrian Arab Republic, Tajikistan, Thailand, The former Yugoslav Republic of Macedonia, Timor-Leste, Togo, Trinidad and Tobago, Tunisia, Turkey, Ukraine, United Arab Emirates, United Kingdom, United Republic of Tanzania, Uruguay, Venezuela, Viet Nam, Yemen, Zambia, Zimbabwe.

Against: Israel, Marshall Islands, Micronesia, Nauru, Palau, United States.

Abstaining: Australia, Honduras, Rwanda, Tonga, Uganda, Uzbekistan.

Assistance to Palestinians

UN activities

In response to General Assembly resolution 57/147 [YUN 2002, p. 462], the Secretary-General submitted a May report [A/58/88-E/2003/84 & Corr.1] describing UN and other assistance to the Palestinian people between June 2002 and May 2003.

During the reporting period, the cycle of violence between Israelis and Palestinians continued, with hundreds of victims on both sides. Tight internal and external closures, widespread curfews, incursions and other measures taken by IDF led to a further deterioration of economic indicators and to an increase in poverty and unemployment levels among Palestinians. The PA's capacity was diminished just as needs increased. The UN system continued to work to maintain Palestinian capacities to provide essential services, to repair damage to infrastructure and to meet urgent needs. The United Nations Development Programme (UNDP) continued its technical assistance and infrastructure support and played an important role in the PA's reform efforts, especially in the establishment of the Palestinian Central Elections Commission. Other UN agencies continued to carry out technical assistance projects and programmes. However, the planning, management and implementation of those projects were hampered by restrictions placed on UN staff, notably locally recruited Palestinian staff, a deteriorating security environment and problems of access, often requiring the rescheduling of programme activities and a shift in emphasis from development to emergency activity.

Overall donor commitments increased by 57 per cent during the period under review. However, while emergency and budgetary assistance increased, development assistance declined by 70 per cent. International community support focused on the PA's institutional reform efforts, direct support to the PA budget and mitigating the impact of the economic and social crisis.

The Quartet's Task Force on Palestinian Reform, established in 2002 [YUN 2002, p. 432], continued to monitor and support implementation of Palestinian civil reforms and guided the international donor community in its support for the Palestinian reform agenda. At its meeting in London on 20 February 2003, the Task Force recognized that the conflict, continued restrictions on freedom of movement of persons and goods, deterioration of the humanitarian situation and destruction of local infrastructure and facilities constituted a significant hindrance to reforms. Noting the difficult security situation, it welcomed the considerable progress made in several areas of Palestinian civil reform, in particular the implementation of higher standards of fiscal transparency and accountability, as well as work towards development of the public institutions and laws needed to promote a market economy. It also welcomed Israel's decision to resume monthly transfers of Palestinian tax revenues, which permitted the Palestinian Ministry of Finance to submit a fully financed budget for 2003. The Task Force commended efforts to develop appropriate legislation and to coordinate economic policy with Palestinian business leaders, but noted that progress in some areas, such as judicial reform, had been much slower. While acknowledging Israel's legitimate security concerns, there was consensus in the Task Force that mobility restrictions constituted a major impediment to reform, slowing progress and undermining the credibility of the reform process in many areas.

The Secretary-General observed that the humanitarian and socio-economic crisis in the Occupied Palestinian Territory had reached unprecedented levels. The Palestinians' capacity to manage their own affairs had been dramatically reduced, making them dependent on budgetary, technical and humanitarian aid. The challenge ahead was how to meet urgent needs without undermining the prospects for a viable Palestinian State. The PA's depleted administrative, financial and service delivery capacities had to be restored, while efforts continued to meet emergency requirements. Both parties had to make every effort to facilitate the work of UN agencies and partners. The Secretary-General called especially on Israel to lift restrictions, revive the economy, restore Palestinian livelihood and facilitate the work of the assistance community, and on the international community to provide the resources for the assistance programmes to the Palestinian people.

The Economic and Social Council, on 24 July, took note of the Secretary-General's report (**decision 2003/273**).

UNCTAD assistance to Palestinians

At its fiftieth session (Geneva, 6-17 October) [A/58/15], the Trade and Development Board of the United Nations Conference on Trade and Development (UNCTAD) took note of the report on UNCTAD assistance to the Palestinian people [TD/B/50/4] and of the statements made by delegations during deliberations on that item. UNCTAD intensified its programme of assistance to the Palestinian people in close cooperation with the PA, focusing on building capacities for effective economic policy-making and management and strengthening the enabling environment for the private sector. Its technical cooperation was directed at trade policies and strategies, trade facilitation and logistics, finance and development, and enterprise, investment and competition policy. Despite the intensification of the conflict, which interrupted the development process and rendered the provision of technical assistance increasingly difficult, UNCTAD was able to make concrete progress in its technical assistance programmes. It contributed to an initiative to support the Palestinian olive oil industry through international trade and targeted markets, and provided advisory services, observations, a mission and reports on several areas of economic policy and trade, including proposals for "Israeli economic facilitation measures" submitted by the PA as part of confidence-building measures and a World Bank study on long-term policy options for the Palestinian economy.

GENERAL ASSEMBLY ACTION

On 17 December [meeting 75], the General Assembly adopted **resolution 58/113** [draft: A/58/L.33/Rev.1 & Add.1] by recorded vote (170-0-2) [agenda item 40 (e)].

Assistance to the Palestinian people

The General Assembly,

Recalling its resolution 57/147 of 16 December 2002, as well as previous resolutions on the question,

Recalling also the signing of the Declaration of Principles on Interim Self-Government Arrangements in Washington, D.C., on 13 September 1993, by the Government of the State of Israel and the Palestine Liberation Organization, the representative of the Palestinian people, and the subsequent implementation agreements concluded by the two sides,

Gravely concerned at the deterioration in the living conditions of the Palestinian people throughout the occupied territory, which constitutes a mounting humanitarian crisis,

Conscious of the urgent need for improvement in the economic and social infrastructure of the occupied territory,

Aware that development is difficult under occupation and is best promoted in circumstances of peace and stability,

Noting the great economic and social challenges facing the Palestinian people and their leadership,

Conscious of the urgent necessity for international assistance to the Palestinian people, taking into account the Palestinian priorities,

Welcoming the results of the Conference to Support Middle East Peace, convened in Washington, D.C., on 1 October 1993, the establishment of the Ad Hoc Liaison Committee and the work being done by the World Bank as its secretariat and the establishment of the Consultative Group, as well as all follow-up meetings and international mechanisms established to provide assistance to the Palestinian people,

Welcoming also the work of the Joint Liaison Committee, which provides a forum in which economic policy and practical matters related to donor assistance are discussed with the Palestinian Authority,

Stressing the continued importance of the work of the Ad Hoc Liaison Committee in the coordination of assistance to the Palestinian people,

Noting the convening of the Ad Hoc Liaison Committee meetings, held in London on 18 and 19 February 2003 and in Rome on 10 December 2003, to review the state of the Palestinian economy,

Stressing the need for the full engagement of the United Nations in the process of building Palestinian institutions and in providing broad assistance to the Palestinian people, and welcoming in this regard the support to the Palestinian Authority by the Task Force on Palestinian Reform established by the Quartet in 2002,

Noting, in this regard, the active participation of the United Nations Special Coordinator for the Middle East Peace Process and Personal Representative of the Secretary-General to the Palestine Liberation Organization and the Palestinian Authority in the activities of the Special Envoys of the Quartet,

Welcoming the endorsement by the Security Council, in its resolution 1515(2003) of 19 November 2003, of the performance-based road map to a permanent two-State solution to the Israeli-Palestinian conflict, and stressing the need for its implementation and compliance with its provisions,

Having considered the report of the Secretary-General,

Expressing grave concern at the continuation of the recent tragic and violent events that have led to many deaths and injuries,

1. *Takes note* of the report of the Secretary-General;
2. *Also takes note* of the report of the Personal Humanitarian Envoy of the Secretary-General on the humanitarian conditions and needs of the Palestinian people;
3. *Expresses its appreciation* to the Secretary-General for his rapid response and efforts regarding assistance to the Palestinian people;
4. *Also expresses its appreciation* to the Member States, United Nations bodies and intergovernmental, regional and non-governmental organizations that have provided and continue to provide assistance to the Palestinian people;
5. *Stresses* the importance of the work of the United Nations Special Coordinator for the Middle East Peace Process and Personal Representative of the Secretary-General to the Palestine Liberation Organization and the Palestinian Authority and of the steps taken under the auspices of the Secretary-General to ensure the achievement of a coordinated mechanism for United Nations activities throughout the occupied territories;
6. *Urges* Member States, international financial institutions of the United Nations system, intergovernmental and non-governmental organizations and regional and interregional organizations to extend, as rapidly and as generously as possible, economic and social assistance to the Palestinian people, in close cooperation with the Palestine Liberation Organization and through official Palestinian institutions;
7. *Calls upon* relevant organizations and agencies of the United Nations system to intensify their assistance in response to the urgent needs of the Palestinian people in accordance with Palestinian priorities set forth by the Palestinian Authority;
8. *Urges* Member States to open their markets to exports of Palestinian products on the most favourable terms, consistent with appropriate trading rules, and to implement fully existing trade and cooperation agreements;
9. *Calls upon* the international donor community to expedite the delivery of pledged assistance to the Palestinian people to meet their urgent needs;
10. *Stresses*, in this context, the importance of ensuring the free passage of aid to the Palestinian people and the free movement of persons and goods;
11. *Urges* the international donor community, United Nations agencies and organizations and non-governmental organizations to extend as rapidly as possible emergency economic and humanitarian assistance to the Palestinian people to counter the impact of the current crisis;
12. *Stresses* the need to implement the Paris Protocol on Economic Relations of 29 April 1994, fifth annex to the Israeli-Palestinian Interim Agreement on the West Bank and the Gaza Strip, signed in Washington, D.C., on 28 September 1995, in particular with regard to the full and prompt clearance of Palestinian indirect tax revenues, and welcomes the progress made in this regard;
13. *Suggests* the convening in 2004 of a United Nations-sponsored seminar on assistance to the Palestinian people;
14. *Requests* the Secretary-General to submit a report to the General Assembly at its fifty-ninth session, through the Economic and Social Council, on the implementation of the present resolution, containing:

(a) An assessment of the assistance actually received by the Palestinian people;

(b) An assessment of the needs still unmet and specific proposals for responding effectively to them;

15. *Decides* to include in the provisional agenda of its fifty-ninth session the sub-item entitled "Assistance to the Palestinian people".

RECORDED VOTE ON RESOLUTION 58/113:

In favour: Afghanistan, Albania, Algeria, Andorra, Angola, Antigua and Barbuda, Argentina, Armenia, Australia, Austria, Azerbaijan, Bahamas, Bahrain, Bangladesh, Belarus, Belgium, Belize, Bolivia, Bosnia and Herzegovina, Botswana, Brazil, Brunei Darussalam, Bulgaria, Burundi, Cambodia, Canada, Central African Republic, Chile, China, Colombia, Comoros, Congo, Costa Rica, Côte d'Ivoire, Croatia, Cuba, Cyprus, Czech Republic, Democratic People's Republic of Korea, Democratic Republic of the Congo, Denmark, Djibouti, Dominica, Dominican Republic, Ecuador, Egypt, El Salvador, Eritrea, Estonia, Ethiopia, Fiji, Finland, France, Gabon, Gambia, Georgia, Germany, Ghana, Greece, Grenada, Guatemala, Guinea, Guyana, Honduras, Hungary, Iceland, India, Indonesia, Iran, Ireland, Italy, Jamaica, Japan, Jordan, Kazakhstan, Kuwait, Kyrgyzstan, Lao People's Democratic Republic, Latvia, Lebanon, Lesotho, Libyan Arab Jamahiriya, Liechtenstein, Lithuania, Luxembourg, Madagascar, Malaysia, Maldives, Mali, Malta, Marshall Islands, Mauritania, Mauritius, Mexico, Micronesia, Monaco, Mongolia, Morocco, Mozambique, Myanmar, Namibia, Nauru, Nepal, Netherlands, New Zealand, Nicaragua, Niger, Nigeria, Norway, Oman, Pakistan, Palau, Panama, Papua New Guinea, Paraguay, Peru, Philippines, Poland, Portugal, Qatar, Republic of Korea, Republic of Moldova, Romania, Russian Federation, Rwanda, Saint Lucia, San Marino, Saudi Arabia, Senegal, Serbia and Montenegro, Sierra Leone, Singapore, Slovakia, Slovenia, Solomon Islands, Somalia, South Africa, Spain, Sri Lanka, Sudan, Suriname, Swaziland, Sweden, Switzerland, Syrian Arab Republic, Tajikistan, Thailand, The former Yugoslav Republic of Macedonia, Timor-Leste, Togo, Tonga, Trinidad and Tobago, Tunisia, Turkey, Turkmenistan, Tuvalu, Uganda, Ukraine, United Arab Emirates, United Kingdom, United Republic of Tanzania, United States, Uruguay, Uzbekistan, Vanuatu, Venezuela, Viet Nam, Yemen, Zambia, Zimbabwe.

Against: None.

Abstaining: Israel, Kenya.

Speaking before the vote, Israel said that it shared the concern of the international community over the deterioration in the humanitarian situation in the Middle East and that it had done its utmost to cooperate with international actors in an effort to facilitate their humanitarian work aimed at improving the Palestinians' living conditions in the West Bank and Gaza Strip. However, Palestinian terrorists had viewed measures intended to increase freedom of movement as opportunities to infiltrate Israeli cities, and had used the immunity granted to medical and humanitarian vehicles to smuggle weapons and explosives. It was therefore disingenuous to suggest that Israeli policies were the source of the hardships facing the Palestinian people. If the international community was serious about alleviating the Palestinian humanitarian plight, the single most important thing it could do was to insist that the Palestinian leadership end its campaign of violence, terror and incitement. Unlike previous years, Israel would abstain on the resolution because it included new language unrelated to humanitarian assistance to the Palestinian people, including reference to Security Council resolution 1515(2003) (see p. 483). It expressed regret that the Assembly session had been used to further a partisan and political agenda, and had denied Israel the opportunity to present for a vote a draft resolution on the welfare of Israeli children, after adopting a similar draft resolution on Palestinian children.

Speaking after the vote, the Observer of Palestine said that he regretted the fact that Israel chose to break away from the consensus on the resolution and to depart from the only positive tradition regarding the Middle East which had been in effect for 10 years. Israel took that stand because of an added paragraph that welcomed the unanimous adoption of Council resolution 1515(2003) and, in its statement before the vote, tried to convince the international community that it had no responsibility for the humanitarian tragedy being endured by the Palestinian people.

UNRWA

In 2003, the United Nations Relief and Works Agency for Palestine Refugees in the Near East continued to provide vital education, health and relief and social services to an ever-growing refugee population, despite a severe budget deficit and cash flow crisis.

As at 30 June, 4.08 million refugees were registered with UNRWA, an increase of 2.7 per cent over the 2002 figure of 3.97 million. The largest refugee population was registered in Jordan (42.1 per cent of the Agency-wide total), followed by the Gaza Strip (22.2 per cent), the West Bank (16 per cent), the Syrian Arab Republic (10 per cent) and Lebanon (9.6 per cent). Of the registered population, 51 per cent were 18 years of age or under.

In his annual report on the work of the Agency from 1 July 2002 to 30 June 2003 [A/58/13 & Corr.1], the UNRWA Commissioner-General said that UNRWA was actively involved in the UN contingency planning efforts before the conflict in Iraq erupted (see p. 333) and had followed developments closely as they affected tens of thousands of Palestinians living in Iraq, many of them Palestine refugees. The Agency, among other things, participated in delivering emergency assistance to Palestinian families fleeing the conflict and temporarily accommodated them in tented camps on the Jordanian-Iraqi border. The Agency was also forced to relocate non-essential staff and their dependants between March and April 2003.

During the reporting period, the conditions of strife in the Occupied Palestinian Territory persisted. Suicide bombings inside Israel continued, causing heavy loss of life, while the reoccupation by IDF of almost all of the West Bank and Gaza Strip and ensuing large-scale military operations caused heavy loss of life and widespread damage to and destruction of Palestinian property. The incidence of large-scale military incursions into refugee camps, in particular in the Gaza Strip, increased significantly. The severe economic downturn in the Palestinian economy since September 2000 intensified, as closures and other measures kept large numbers of Palestinians unemployed. At the end of 2002, real gross national income had shrunk by 38 per cent from its 1999 level, while real per capita income fell by 46 per cent during the same period. As a result, approximately 60 per cent of the Palestinian population was living below the poverty line.

The environment in which UNRWA carried out its operations in the Occupied Palestinian Territory continued to affect negatively its ability to deliver services. Israeli military operations in the West Bank and the Gaza Strip and internal closures led to severe disruption in the delivery of UNRWA humanitarian supplies to distribution centres. Moreover, six UNRWA staff members were killed during the reporting period and 64 others were detained by the Israeli authorities. IDF also destroyed some UNRWA installations, such as schools, training centres and health-care facilities. Some UNRWA school buildings were taken over by IDF and used as bases and detention centres. Instances in which Palestinian militants entered UNRWA premises were also reported. The Agency took immediate steps to effect their removal from the installations and protested to the PA.

The Agency put into place an extensive emergency assistance programme for refugees affected by the strife in the Occupied Palestinian Territory, providing temporary accommodation and emergency assistance to refugees when their shelters were destroyed. It also launched several housing projects to afford the refugees new dwellings which conformed to standards of minimum human decency. In the West Bank, after a year of heavy destruction caused by Israeli military operations, UNRWA expanded its shelter rehabilitation and rehousing programmes, including the reconstruction of the destroyed area in the Jenin camp. To facilitate UNRWA's activities under its emergency programme, the Operational Support Officers programme was expanded in the West Bank and reintroduced in the Gaza Strip. The programme played a crucial role in facilitating the delivery of humanitarian goods and safe passage of UNRWA staff through checkpoints, and enhanced the implementation of Agency programmes in accordance with UN norms. During the reporting period, emergency programme appeals were launched for 2002 ($172.8 million) and for the first half of 2003 ($93.7 million). By the end of 2002, only $96.8 million had been pledged towards that year's appeals, and only 40 per cent ($37.3 million) of the appeal for the first half of 2003. It was clear that other crises had to some extent diverted the attention of traditional donors from the Palestinian issue. In addition, the Agency feared that the construction of a separation barrier by Israel inside the West Bank, when completed, would impoverish and isolate thousands of refugee families and would constitute a new and formidable obstacle to the delivery of UNRWA services to refugees in its vicinity.

UNRWA's internal reforms during the reporting period focused, among other things, on improving the efficiency and effectiveness of its resource management, the cultivation of an open management culture, the strengthening of strategic planning capabilities, and expansion and improvement in the Agency's relations with donor countries, host countries and other UN agencies and programmes.

Advisory Commission. By a 25 September letter to the Commissioner-General, which was included in his annual report [A/58/13 & Corr.1], the Chairperson of the Advisory Commission of UNRWA noted with concern the continuing deteriorating political, economic and social situation in the region and the humanitarian crisis in the Occupied Palestinian Territory. The crisis was evidenced primarily by rising levels of malnutrition among children, high levels of poverty and unemployment, deteriorating health conditions, and the displacement of an increasing number of Palestinians following the destruction of their homes. He noted that the Agency had launched appeals totalling $196.6 million for 2003, though the response of the international community to those appeals had been slow, with only $76.8 million pledged as at mid-September. In addition, it was noted that, against planned regular budget expenditure of $315.1 million during 2003, pledges of only $293.3 million had been received as at the end of August.

Report of Conciliation Commission. The United Nations Conciliation Commission for Palestine, in its fifty-seventh report covering the period from 1 September 2002 to 31 August 2003 [A/58/256], submitted in response to General Assembly resolution 57/117 [YUN 2002, p. 466], noted its August 2002 report [ibid., p. 471] and observed that it had nothing new to report since its submission.

Communication. In a 6 November response [A/58/557] to the Commissioner-General's report (see p. 506), Israel said that its officials had been continuously available to meet and coordinate matters with UNRWA officials regarding both general and practical issues arising out of UNRWA operations. Israel remained committed to its obligations to facilitate UNRWA humanitarian activities and would continue to explore pragmatic solutions to facilitate such activity. There was, however, little recognition by UNRWA in its report that the conditions under which it operated had been determined by the continuing violence in the region. That violence necessitated self-defence actions, including military operations. In addition, terrorist organizations used and exploited UNRWA installations as hideouts and places of refuge. While recognizing that UNRWA was not responsible for security in refugee camps, Israel did expect the organization to draw greater attention to the violent actions taking place in those camps. At least 16 Palestinian employees of UNRWA were in custody; the alleged crimes included involvement in a variety of security-related crimes, such as membership in terrorist organizations, and armed attacks against Israeli targets.

Projects

During the reporting period, project funding enabled UNRWA to complete, among other things, the construction of eight schools and the rehabilitation of shelters and health centres. In recognition of the fact that project funding had taken on an increasing financial and programmatic importance over the years, and in order to establish a more targeted fund-raising approach, UNRWA established Agency-wide project priorities that formed the basis for the projects component of its biennium budget. UNRWA received pledges in the amount of $20.5 million towards its project budget, of which $9.9 million was allocated to the health sector, $4.1 million to education, $3.9 million to the relief and social services sector and $2.6 million to other projects. The Peace Implementation Programme, established in 1993 [YUN 1993, p. 569] to fund extrabudgetary activities within the Agency's major service areas, was merged under the projects budget following the adoption of the 2000-2001 programme-based biennium budget [YUN 2000, p. 450].

Lebanon appeal

Most of the over 389,000 registered Palestine refugees in Lebanon continued to face deplorable living conditions and depended almost entirely on UNRWA for basic services. By the end of June 2003, the Agency had received the $11 million pledged under the special emergency appeal, launched in 1997 to support essential health, education, relief and social services activities for Palestine refugees in Lebanon, and had expended $9.1 million of that amount. During the reporting period, UNRWA completed the mechanization of a solid waste collection and disposal system project and offered short-term vocational courses.

Emergency appeals

UNRWA continued its programme of emergency assistance, focusing on food aid, emergency employment creation, shelter repair and rebuilding, cash assistance, health and education. In December 2002, UNRWA launched a $93.7 million appeal to cover emergency needs for the period January to June 2003. The appeal was developed under the Humanitarian Action Plan prepared by the United Nations Technical Assessment Mission which visited the region following the visit by the Secretary-General's Personal Humanitarian Envoy, Catherine Bertini, to the area [YUN 2002, p. 455]. As at 30 June, confirmed pledges amounted to $38.4 million. Another appeal totalling $102.9 million covering the period July to December 2003 was launched in June.

By the end of June 2003, UNRWA had provided 41,000 Palestine refugees in the West Bank and the Gaza Strip with short-term emergency employment, and more than 250,000 people had benefited from short-term jobs managed directly by the Agency. Many more benefited from work opportunities created through private sector construction projects contracted by UNRWA.

Major service areas

UNRWA continued to provide educational, health, and relief and social services to, and carried out microfinance and microenterprise activities for, Palestine refugees throughout the occupied territories.

The Agency's education programme, its largest activity, operated 651 schools providing basic and preparatory education to approximately 490,000 pupils, as well as five secondary schools in Lebanon, eight vocational training centres and three teacher training colleges. It continued to be supported by the United Nations Educational, Scientific and Cultural Organization (UNESCO), which funded senior managerial and technical posts within UNRWA and provided it with technical assistance and general guidance. As the Agency's schools followed the national curricula of the host countries, it was required to implement all improvements and enhancements to the curriculum introduced by the host country authorities, but had been struggling to keep pace with those enhancements because of its precarious financial situation. The Agency's university scholarship programme was being discontinued due to financial constraints, a decision which in time would affect UNRWA's capacity to attract trained medical staff to its health centres. Financial constraints had also hampered the modernization of the curriculum and the infrastructure of the Agency's vocational training centres. Despite the financial challenges, UNRWA's Education Department continued to reform and improve its internal processes within the framework of its five-year development plan, in addition to projects such as the initiative in computer information technology. In the reporting period, UNRWA continued to introduce limited secondary schooling in Lebanon, as a result of continued access restrictions for Palestine refugees to the Lebanese public education system. In the West Bank and Gaza Strip, because operations were severely hampered by the ongoing crisis, UNRWA's emergency programme included remedial and compensatory education for approximately 40,000 pupils.

Technical supervision of UNRWA's health programme was provided by the World Health Organization (WHO), which also supplied the services of senior management staff and short-term consultants, technical literature and publications. The Agency focused on sustaining adequate levels of investment in primary health care, enhancing institutional capacity-building and developing its human resources. Management reforms implemented led to the introduction of new health information, hospital management and drug supply management systems. UNRWA's health services continued to face abnormally high workloads, and studies also warned of breakdowns in preventive services to women and children. UNRWA incurred additional expenditure following the breakdown of cost-sharing arrangements in the West Bank regarding secondary care, while in Lebanon the Agency strengthened its cooperation with the Palestinian Red Crescent Society, providing cost-effective secondary health care to refugees unable to afford the cost of private hospitalization. UNRWA also continued its environmental health services in refugee camps, introducing and/or improving sewerage disposal, storm water drainage and the provision of safe drinking water. Major projects were under way in the Syrian Arab Republic and Lebanon for construction of water and sewerage systems in various refugee camps.

UNRWA's relief and social services programme addressed the needs of the most vulnerable among the refugee population and applied a community development (self-help) approach in fostering community-based organizations with a focus on women, children and youth, and physically/mentally challenged refugees. The Agency's special hardship programme was in increasing demand due to the difficult socio-economic situation in Jordan, continuing restrictions on the employment of Palestine refugees in Lebanon, and the crisis in the Occupied Palestinian Territory. The number of refugees in households that met the programme's eligibility criteria—no male adult medically fit to earn an income and no other identifiable means of financial support above a defined threshold—increased by 1.6 per cent, from 229,404 in June 2002 to 233,044 in June 2003. The trends in the programme pointed to a feminization of poverty among the refugees, as the incidence of female-headed households increased. Shelter rehabilitation continued according to the availability of extrabudgetary funding, as the state of the General Fund did not allow such activities to be funded from the Agency's regular budget. During the reporting period, the provision of land by the host authority enabled UNRWA to launch rehousing projects in Gaza, following large-scale destruction of refugee shelters.

The Agency continued to promote income-generation activities within the context of its relief and social services programme and as a commercial, self-sustaining and market-oriented microfinance and microenterprise programme. The latter programme expanded its operations into Jordan and the Syrian Arab Republic, providing almost 9,000 loans worth $6.01 million, with women entrepreneurs receiving 43 per cent of the loans. On account of the decline in economic conditions in the Occupied Palestinian Territory, the programme was unable to maintain its normal state of financial self-sufficiency for the second year in a row. By June 2003, the lending outreach in Gaza increased to 1,141 loans valued at $806,175, compared to 923 in the previous period valued at $655,276, but was still less than the 1,304 loans amounting to $1.46 million in September 2000.

GENERAL ASSEMBLY ACTION

On 9 December [meeting 72], the General Assembly, on the recommendation of the Fourth Committee [A/58/472], adopted **resolution 58/91** by recorded vote (167-1-8) [agenda item 83].

Assistance to Palestine refugees

The General Assembly,

Recalling its resolution 194(III) of 11 December 1948 and all its subsequent resolutions on the question, including resolution 57/117 of 11 December 2002,

Recalling also its resolution 302(IV) of 8 December 1949, by which, inter alia, it established the United Nations Relief and Works Agency for Palestine Refugees in the Near East,

Recalling further relevant Security Council resolutions,

Aware of the fact that the Palestine refugees have, for more than five decades, lost their homes, lands and means of livelihood,

Affirming the imperative of resolving the problem of the Palestine refugees for the achievement of justice and for the achievement of lasting peace in the region,

Acknowledging the essential role that the United Nations Relief and Works Agency for Palestine Refugees in the Near East has played for more than fifty-three years since its establishment in ameliorating the plight of the Palestine refugees in the fields of education, health and relief and social services,

Taking note of the report of the Commissioner-General of the United Nations Relief and Works Agency for Palestine Refugees in the Near East covering the period from 1 July 2002 to 30 June 2003,

Aware of the continuing needs of Palestine refugees throughout all the fields of operation, namely Jordan, Lebanon, the Syrian Arab Republic, and the Occupied Palestinian Territory,

Expressing grave concern at the especially difficult situation of the Palestine refugees under occupation, including with regard to their safety, well-being and living conditions, and the continuous deterioration of those conditions during the recent period,

Noting the signing of the Declaration of Principles on Interim Self-Government Arrangements on 13 September 1993 by the Government of Israel and the Palestine Liberation Organization and the subsequent implementation agreements,

Aware that the Multilateral Working Group on Refugees of the Middle East peace process has an important role to play in the peace process,

1. *Notes with regret* that repatriation or compensation of the refugees, as provided for in paragraph 11 of its resolution 194(III), has not yet been effected and that, therefore, the situation of the Palestine refugees continues to be a matter of concern;

2. *Also notes with regret* that the United Nations Conciliation Commission for Palestine has been unable to find a means of achieving progress in the implementation of paragraph 11 of General Assembly resolution 194(III), and requests the Commission to exert continued efforts towards the implementation of that paragraph and to report to the Assembly as appropriate, but no later than 1 September 2004;

3. *Affirms* the necessity for the continuation of the work of the United Nations Relief and Works Agency for Palestine Refugees in the Near East and the importance of its operation and services for the well-being of the Palestine refugees and for the stability of the region, pending the resolution of the question of the Palestine refugees;

4. *Calls upon* all donors to continue to make the most generous efforts possible to meet the anticipated needs of the Agency, including those mentioned in recent emergency appeals.

RECORDED VOTE ON RESOLUTION 58/91:

In favour: Afghanistan, Albania, Algeria, Andorra, Angola, Antigua and Barbuda, Argentina, Armenia, Australia, Austria, Azerbaijan, Bahamas, Bahrain, Bangladesh, Barbados, Belarus, Belgium, Belize, Benin, Bhutan, Bolivia, Bosnia and Herzegovina, Botswana, Brazil, Brunei Darussalam, Bulgaria, Burkina Faso, Burundi, Cambodia, Canada, Cape Verde, Central African Republic, Chile, China, Colombia, Comoros, Costa Rica, Côte d'Ivoire, Croatia, Cuba, Cyprus, Czech Republic, Democratic People's Republic of Korea, Denmark, Djibouti, Dominican Republic, Ecuador, Egypt, El Salvador, Equatorial Guinea, Eritrea, Estonia, Ethiopia, Fiji, Finland, France, Gabon, Gambia, Georgia, Germany, Ghana, Greece, Grenada, Guatemala, Guinea, Guinea-Bissau, Guyana, Haiti, Hungary, Iceland, India, Indonesia, Iran, Ireland, Italy, Jamaica, Japan, Jordan, Kazakhstan, Kenya, Kuwait, Kyrgyzstan, Lao People's Democratic Republic, Latvia, Lebanon, Lesotho, Libyan Arab Jamahiriya, Liechtenstein, Lithuania, Luxembourg, Madagascar, Malaysia, Maldives, Mali, Malta, Mauritania, Mauritius, Mexico, Monaco, Mongolia, Morocco, Mozambique, Myanmar, Namibia, Nauru, Nepal, Netherlands, New Zealand, Nicaragua, Niger, Nigeria, Norway, Oman, Pakistan, Panama, Paraguay, Peru, Philippines, Poland, Portugal, Qatar, Republic of Korea, Republic of Moldova, Romania, Russian Federation, Rwanda, Saint Lucia, Saint Vincent and the Grenadines, Samoa, San Marino, Saudi Arabia, Senegal, Serbia and Montenegro, Seychelles, Singapore, Slovakia, Slovenia, Solomon Islands, South Africa, Spain, Sri Lanka, Sudan, Suriname, Swaziland, Sweden, Switzerland, Syrian Arab Republic, Tajikistan, Thailand, The former Yugoslav Republic of Macedonia, Timor-Leste, Togo, Tonga, Trinidad and Tobago, Tunisia, Turkey, Turkmenistan, Ukraine, United Arab Emirates, United Kingdom, United Republic of Tanzania, Uruguay, Venezuela, Viet Nam, Yemen, Zambia, Zimbabwe.

Against: Israel.

Abstaining: Cameroon, Honduras, Marshall Islands, Micronesia, Palau, Papua New Guinea, Tuvalu, United States.

The Assembly, also on 9 December [meeting 72] and on the Fourth Committee's recommendation [A/58/472], adopted **resolution 58/93** by recorded vote (162-5-8) [agenda item 83].

Operations of the United Nations Relief and Works Agency for Palestine Refugees in the Near East

The General Assembly,

Recalling its resolutions 194(III) of 11 December 1948, 212(III) of 19 November 1948, 302(IV) of 8 December 1949 and all subsequent related resolutions, including resolution 57/121 of 11 December 2002,

Recalling also the relevant Security Council resolutions,

Having considered the report of the Commissioner-General of the United Nations Relief and Works Agency for Palestine Refugees in the Near East covering the period from 1 July 2002 to 30 June 2003,

Taking note of the letter dated 25 September 2003 from the Chairperson of the Advisory Commission of the United Nations Relief and Works Agency for Palestine Refugees in the Near East addressed to the Commissioner-General,

Deeply concerned about the continuing critical financial situation of the Agency and its effect on the continuing provision of necessary Agency services to the Palestine refugees, including its emergency-related programmes and its development programmes,

Recalling Articles 100, 104 and 105 of the Charter of the United Nations and the Convention on the Privileges and Immunities of the United Nations,

Affirming the applicability of the Geneva Convention relative to the Protection of Civilian Persons in Time of War, of 12 August 1949, to the Palestinian territory occupied since 1967, including East Jerusalem,

Aware of the continuing needs of Palestine refugees throughout the Occupied Palestinian Territory and in the other fields of operation, namely, in Jordan, Lebanon and the Syrian Arab Republic,

Also aware of the valuable work done by the refugee affairs officers of the Agency in providing protection to the Palestinian people, in particular Palestine refugees,

Gravely concerned about the increased suffering of the Palestine refugees, including the loss of life, injury and destruction and damage to their shelters and properties, during the ongoing crisis in the Occupied Palestinian Territory, including East Jerusalem,

Expressing grave concern about the continuing impact of the events that occurred in the Jenin refugee camp in April 2002, including the loss of life, injury, destruction and displacement inflicted on many of its civilian inhabitants,

Aware of the extraordinary efforts being undertaken by the Agency for the repair and rebuilding of thousands of destroyed and damaged refugee shelters,

Gravely concerned about the safety of the Agency's staff and about the damage caused to facilities of the Agency as a result of Israeli military operations during the reporting period,

Deploring the killing of six Agency staff members by the Israeli occupying forces during the reporting period,

Expressing deep concern about the continuing policies of closure and severe restrictions, including the curfews, that have been imposed on the movement of persons and goods throughout the Occupied Palestinian Territory, including East Jerusalem, and which have had a grave impact on the socio-economic situation of the Palestine refugees and have greatly contributed to the dire humanitarian crisis facing the Palestinian people,

Deeply concerned about the continuing restrictions on the freedom of movement of the Agency staff, vehicles and goods, including the harassment of personnel, which adversely affect the ability of the Agency to provide its services, including its education, health and relief and social services,

Recalling the signing, on 13 September 1993, of the Declaration of Principles on Interim Self-Government Arrangements by the Government of Israel and the Palestine Liberation Organization and the subsequent implementation agreements,

Aware of the agreement between the Agency and the Government of Israel,

Aware also of the establishment of a working relationship between the Advisory Commission of the Agency and the Palestine Liberation Organization in accordance with General Assembly decision 48/417 of 10 December 1993,

Taking note of the agreement reached on 24 June 1994, embodied in an exchange of letters between the Agency and the Palestine Liberation Organization,

1. *Expresses its appreciation* to the Commissioner-General of the United Nations Relief and Works Agency for Palestine Refugees in the Near East, as well as to all of the staff of the Agency, for their tireless efforts and valuable work, particularly in the light of the increasingly difficult conditions throughout the past year;

2. *Also expresses its appreciation* to the Advisory Commission of the Agency, and requests it to continue its efforts and to keep the General Assembly informed of its activities, including the full implementation of decision 48/417;

3. *Takes note with appreciation* of the report of the Working Group on the Financing of the United Nations Relief and Works Agency for Palestine Refugees in the Near East, for its efforts to assist in ensuring the financial security of the Agency, and requests the Secretary-General to provide the necessary services and assistance to the Working Group for the conduct of its work;

4. *Commends* the continuing efforts of the Commissioner-General to increase the budgetary transparency and efficiency of the Agency, as reflected in the Agency's programme budget for the biennium 2004-2005;

5. *Acknowledges* the support of the host Governments for the Agency in the discharge of its duties;

6. *Takes note* of the functioning of the headquarters of the Agency in Gaza City on the basis of the Headquarters Agreement between the Agency and the Palestinian Authority;

7. *Calls upon* Israel, the occupying Power, to comply fully with the provisions of the Geneva Convention relative to the Protection of Civilian Persons in Time of War, of 12 August 1949;

8. *Also calls upon* Israel to abide by Articles 100, 104 and 105 of the Charter of the United Nations and the Convention on the Privileges and Immunities of the United Nations with regard to the safety of the personnel of the Agency, the protection of its institutions and the safeguarding of the security of its facilities in the Occupied Palestinian Territory, including East Jerusalem;

9. *Urges* the Government of Israel to compensate the Agency for damage to its property and facilities resulting from actions by the Israeli side, particularly during the reporting period;

10. *Calls upon* Israel particularly to cease obstructing the movement of the personnel, vehicles and supplies of the Agency and to cease the levying of extra fees and charges, which have a detrimental effect on the Agency's operations;

11. *Requests* the Commissioner-General to proceed with the issuance of identification cards for Palestine refugees and their descendants in the Occupied Palestinian Territory;

12. *Affirms* that the functioning of the Agency remains essential in all fields of operation;

13. *Notes* the success of the Agency's microfinance and microenterprise programme, and calls upon the Agency, in close cooperation with the relevant agencies, to continue to contribute towards the development of the economic and social stability of the Palestine refugees;

14. *Reiterates its request* to the Commissioner-General to proceed with the modernization of the archives of the Agency through the Palestine Refugee Records Project, and to indicate progress in his report to the General Assembly at its fifty-ninth session;

15. *Reiterates its previous appeals* to all States, specialized agencies and non-governmental organizations to continue and to augment the special allocations for grants and scholarships for higher education to Palestine refugees in addition to their contributions to the regular budget of the Agency and to contribute towards the establishment of vocational training centres for Palestine refugees, and requests the Agency to act as the recipient and trustee for the special allocations for grants and scholarships;

16. *Urges* all States, specialized agencies and non-governmental organizations to continue and to increase their contributions to the Agency so as to ease the ongoing financial constraints, exacerbated by the current humanitarian situation on the ground, and to support the Agency's valuable work in assistance to the Palestine refugees.

RECORDED VOTE ON RESOLUTION 58/93:

In favour: Afghanistan, Albania, Algeria, Andorra, Angola, Antigua and Barbuda, Argentina, Armenia, Australia, Austria, Azerbaijan, Bahamas, Bahrain, Bangladesh, Barbados, Belarus, Belgium, Belize, Benin, Bhutan, Bolivia, Bosnia and Herzegovina, Botswana, Brazil, Brunei Darussalam, Bulgaria, Burkina Faso, Cambodia, Canada, Cape Verde, Chile, China, Colombia, Comoros, Côte d'Ivoire, Croatia, Cuba, Cyprus, Czech Republic, Democratic People's Republic of Korea, Denmark, Djibouti, Dominican Republic, Ecuador, Egypt, Equatorial Guinea, Eritrea, Estonia, Ethiopia, Fiji, Finland, France, Gabon, Gambia, Georgia, Germany, Ghana, Greece, Grenada, Guatemala, Guinea, Guinea-Bissau, Guyana, Haiti, Hungary, Iceland, India, Indonesia, Iran, Ireland, Italy, Jamaica, Japan, Jordan, Kazakhstan, Kenya, Kuwait, Kyrgyzstan, Lao People's Democratic Republic, Latvia, Lebanon, Lesotho, Libyan Arab Jamahiriya, Liechtenstein, Lithuania, Luxembourg, Madagascar, Malaysia, Maldives, Mali, Malta, Mauritania, Mauritius, Mexico, Monaco, Mongolia, Morocco, Mozambique, Myanmar, Namibia, Nauru, Nepal, Netherlands, New Zealand, Niger, Nigeria, Norway, Oman, Pakistan, Panama, Paraguay, Peru, Philippines, Poland, Portugal, Qatar, Republic of Korea, Republic of Moldova, Romania, Russian Federation, Saint Lucia, Saint Vincent and the Grenadines, Samoa, San Marino, Saudi Arabia, Senegal, Serbia and Montenegro, Seychelles, Singapore, Slovakia, Slovenia, Solomon Islands, South Africa, Spain, Sri Lanka, Sudan, Suriname, Swaziland, Sweden, Switzerland, Syrian Arab Republic, Tajikistan, Thailand, The former Yugoslav Republic of Macedonia, Timor-Leste, Togo, Tonga, Trinidad and Tobago, Tunisia, Turkey, Turkmenistan, Tuvalu, Ukraine, United Arab Emirates, United Kingdom, United Republic of Tanzania, Uruguay, Venezuela, Viet Nam, Yemen, Zambia, Zimbabwe.

Against: Israel, Marshall Islands, Micronesia, Palau, United States.

Abstaining: Burundi, Cameroon, Costa Rica, El Salvador, Honduras, Nicaragua, Papua New Guinea, Rwanda.

On 23 December, the Assembly decided that the agenda item on UNRWA would remain for consideration at its resumed fifty-eighth (2004) session (**decision 58/565**).

UNRWA financing

UNRWA ended 2002 with a positive working balance of $18.7 million, despite the decreased level of donor contributions ($282.4 million in 2001 and $275.8 million in 2002). It also achieved a relatively favourable financial result due to the depreciation of the United States dollar against other currencies; the Agency made $13 million in exchange rate gains in 2002, compared to a loss of $3.5 million in 2001. The Agency's total working capital stood at $18.7 million as at 31 December 2002.

The Agency's cash flow position remained critical owing to repeated funding shortfalls in previous years. As at mid-2003, expected cash expenditure in the regular programme was $315.1 million, as against expected cash income of $290.8 million. As at 31 December 2002, outstanding cash pledges under all accounts amounted to $5.1 million, of which $4.9 million pertained to the regular budget and $0.2 million to the emergency appeal. In addition, UNRWA had not yet been fully reimbursed by the PA in respect of payments made against value added tax (VAT) and related charges, although the Agency had made some progress in that regard. As at 30 June 2003, UNRWA had received from the PA a reimbursement of VAT charges of approximately $7.7 million.

The Commissioner-General said that the Agency's 2004-2005 budget [A/58/13/Add.1], developed on the results-based format, was a programme-based budget structured around UNRWA's mandated service-providing role and programme plans. It was derived from a biennial programme of work specifying objectives, expected accomplishments, planned activities and key performance indicators to measure the performance of each programme; the budget preparation was guided by planning assumptions rather than budget ceilings. The Agency's budget requirements for 2004-2005 were estimated at $805 million.

Working Group. The Working Group on the Financing of UNRWA held three meetings in 2003, on 10 September and 17 and 20 October. In its report to the General Assembly [A/58/450], the Working Group said that, by the end of September, UNRWA faced the prospect of a funding gap in its 2003 regular cash budget of $8.3 million. Income for 2003 was expected to be $306.8 million, against a net cash expenditure of $315.1 million. Furthermore, of the $303.8 million in income expected for the regular budget in 2003, $279.4 million was received by the end of September, with $24.4 million still outstanding. The Working Group expressed concern about the increasing shortfalls in funding for UNRWA's 2002-2003 emergency appeals. Against a total request of $172.8 million for emergency appeals during 2002, the Agency had received $95.9 million in pledges, and $82.9 million against a total request of $196.6 million for emergency appeals in 2003. The shortfalls in emergency appeal contributions had curtailed UNRWA's humanitarian activities, among others, its food distribution and emergency employment generation programmes.

The Working Group said that the austerity measures adopted in the previous years and continuing funding shortfalls had affected the Agency's ability to expand its programmes at a rate commensurate with the growth in the refugee population and, in some cases, had necessitated curtailments of programme activities. The Working Group appealed to the international community to do its utmost to meet the target of $103 million for the emergency appeal issued in June. The services provided by UNRWA had to be viewed as the minimum required to enable the refugees to lead productive lives. Any further reduction in those services not only would deprive them of the minimum level of support, but could have a destabilizing effect on the entire region.

GENERAL ASSEMBLY ACTION

On 9 December [meeting 72], the General Assembly, on the recommendation of the Fourth Committee [A/58/472], adopted **resolution 58/95** by recorded vote (133-0-35) [agenda item 83].

Assistance to Palestine refugees and support for the United Nations Relief and Works Agency for Palestine Refugees in the Near East

The General Assembly,

Recalling its resolutions 212(III) of 19 November 1948, on assistance to Palestine refugees, and 302(IV) of 8 December 1949, by which, inter alia, it established the United Nations Relief and Works Agency for Palestine Refugees in the Near East,

Recalling also all its subsequent resolutions on the question, including resolution 56/52 of 10 December 2001,

Recalling further relevant Security Council resolutions,

Acknowledging the essential role that the Agency has played for more than fifty years since its establishment in ameliorating the plight of the Palestine refugees in the fields of education, health and relief and social services,

Aware of the continuing needs of Palestine refugees throughout all the fields of operation, namely the West Bank and the Gaza Strip, Jordan, Lebanon and the Syrian Arab Republic,

Gravely concerned about the increased suffering of the Palestine refugees, including the loss of life, injury and destruction and damage to refugee shelters and properties, as well as the safety of the staff and the damage to the facilities of the Agency,

Regretting the death of six Agency staff members during the reporting period,

Deeply concerned about the continuing restrictions on the freedom of movement of the Agency's staff, vehicles and goods, which adversely affect the ability of the Agency to provide its services, including its educational, health and relief and social services,

Stressing the necessity for compliance with Articles 100, 104 and 105 of the Charter of the United Nations and the Convention on the Privileges and Immunities of the United Nations with regard to the safety of the personnel of the Agency, the protection of its institutions and the safeguarding of the security of its facilities, including throughout the occupied territories,

Stressing also the need for respect of international humanitarian law,

Emphasizing the obligations of all parties in accordance with the Geneva Convention relative to the Protection of Civilian Persons in Time of War, of 12 August 1949,

Having considered the report of the Commissioner-General of the United Nations Relief and Works Agency for Palestine Refugees in the Near East covering the period from 1 July 2002 to 30 June 2003, the report of the Working Group on the Financing of the United Nations Relief and Works Agency for Palestine Refugees in the Near East, the letter dated 25 September 2003 from the Chairperson of the Advisory Commission of the United Nations Relief and Works Agency for Palestine Refugees in the Near East addressed to the Commissioner-General, and the report of the United Nations Conciliation Commission for Palestine for the period from 1 September 2002 to 31 August 2003,

Deeply concerned about the continuing financial situation of the Agency, which has affected and affects the continuing provision of necessary Agency services to Palestine refugees, including the emergency-related and humanitarian programmes,

1. *Affirms* the necessity for the continuation of the work of the United Nations Relief and Works Agency for Palestine Refugees in the Near East and the importance of its operation and services for the well-being of the Palestine refugees and for the stability of the region, pending the resolution of the question of the Palestine refugees;

2. *Calls upon* all States to make the most generous efforts possible to meet the anticipated needs of the Agency, including those mentioned in recent emergency appeals, and to support the Agency's valuable work in providing assistance to the Palestine refugees;

3. *Takes note with approval* of the report of the Working Group on the Financing of the United Nations Relief and Works Agency for Palestine Refugees in the Near East, for its efforts to assist in ensuring the financial security of the Agency, and requests the Secretary-General to provide the necessary services and assistance to the Working Group for the conduct of its work;

4. *Endorses* the efforts of the Commissioner-General of the United Nations Relief and Works Agency for Palestine Refugees in the Near East to continue to provide humanitarian assistance, as far as practicable, on an emergency basis and as a temporary measure, to persons in the area who are currently displaced and in serious need of continuing assistance as a result of the June 1967 and subsequent hostilities;

5. *Strongly appeals* to all Governments and to organizations and individuals to contribute generously to the Agency and to the other intergovernmental and non-governmental organizations concerned for the above-mentioned purposes;

6. *Reiterates its previous appeals* to all States, specialized agencies and non-governmental organizations to continue and to augment the special allocations for grants and scholarships to Palestine refugees, in addition to their contributions to the regular budget of the Agency;

7. *Appeals* to all States, specialized agencies and other international bodies to extend assistance for higher education to Palestine refugee students and to contribute towards the establishment of vocational training centres for Palestine refugees, and requests the Agency to act as the recipient and trustee for the special allocations for grants and scholarships;

8. *Expresses its appreciation* to the Commissioner-General of the Agency, as well as to all of the staff of the Agency, for their tireless efforts and valuable work, particularly in the light of the increasingly difficult conditions throughout the past year;

9. *Also expresses its appreciation* to the Advisory Commission of the Agency, and requests it to continue its efforts and to keep the General Assembly informed of its activities, including the full implementation of Assembly decision 48/417 of 10 December 1993;

10. *Commends* the efforts of the Commissioner-General to increase the budgetary transparency and efficiency of the Agency, as well as the support of the host Governments for the Agency in the discharge of its duties;

11. *Calls upon* all relevant parties to take effective measures to ensure the safety of the personnel of the Agency, the protection of its institutions and the safeguarding of the security of its facilities;

12. *Notes* the success of the Agency's microfinance and enterprise programmes, and calls upon the Agency, in close cooperation with the relevant agencies, to continue to contribute towards the development of the economic and social stability of the Palestine refugees.

RECORDED VOTE ON RESOLUTION 58/95:

In favour: Afghanistan, Albania, Algeria, Andorra, Angola, Antigua and Barbuda, Argentina, Armenia, Australia, Austria, Bahamas, Bangladesh, Barbados, Belarus, Belgium, Benin, Bhutan, Bolivia, Bosnia and Herzegovina, Botswana, Brazil, Bulgaria, Cambodia, Cameroon, Canada, Cape Verde, Central African Republic, Chile, Colombia, Costa Rica, Côte d'Ivoire, Croatia, Cyprus, Czech Republic, Democratic People's Republic of Korea, Denmark, Dominican Republic, Ecuador, Egypt, El Salvador, Equatorial Guinea, Eritrea, Estonia, Ethiopia, Fiji, Finland, France, Gabon, Georgia, Germany, Ghana, Greece, Grenada, Guatemala, Guinea, Guinea-Bissau, Guyana, Haiti, Hungary, Iceland, Indonesia, Iran, Ireland, Israel, Italy, Jamaica, Japan, Kazakhstan, Lao People's Democratic Republic, Latvia, Lesotho, Liechtenstein, Lithuania, Luxembourg, Madagascar, Maldives, Mali, Malta, Marshall Islands, Mexico, Micronesia, Monaco, Mongolia, Mozambique, Namibia, Nepal, Netherlands, New Zealand, Nicaragua, Niger, Nigeria, Norway, Palau, Panama, Papua New Guinea, Paraguay, Peru, Philippines, Poland, Portugal, Republic of Korea, Republic of Moldova, Romania, Russian Federation, Rwanda, Saint Kitts and Nevis, Saint Vincent and the Grenadines, Samoa, San Marino, Senegal, Serbia and Montenegro, Singapore, Slovakia, Slovenia, Solomon Islands, Spain, Sri Lanka, Swaziland, Sweden, Switzerland, Tajikistan, Thailand, The former Yugoslav Republic of Macedonia, Timor-Leste, Tonga, Trinidad and Tobago, Ukraine, United Kingdom, United States, Uruguay, Venezuela, Zambia, Zimbabwe.

Against: None.

Abstaining: Bahrain, Belize, Brunei Darussalam, Burkina Faso, Burundi, China, Comoros, Cuba, India, Jordan, Kenya, Kuwait, Lebanon, Libyan Arab Jamahiriya, Malaysia, Mauritania, Mauritius, Morocco, Myanmar, Nauru, Oman, Pakistan, Qatar, Saint Lucia, Saudi Arabia, South Africa, Sudan, Suriname, Syrian Arab Republic, Tunisia, Turkey, Tuvalu, United Arab Emirates, United Republic of Tanzania, Yemen.

Displaced persons

In a July report [A/58/119] on compliance with General Assembly resolution 57/119 [YUN 2002, p. 469], which called for accelerated return of all persons displaced as a result of the June 1967 and subsequent hostilities to their homes or former places of residence in the territories occupied by Israel since 1967, the Secretary-General said that, since UNRWA was not involved in arrangements for the return of either refugees or displaced persons not registered with it, the Agency's information was based on requests by returning registered refugees for the transfer of their entitlements to their areas of return. Displaced refugees known by UNRWA to have returned to the West Bank and Gaza Strip since 1967 totalled about 23,900. As far as UNRWA knew, between 1 July 2002 and 30 June 2003, 879 registered refugees had returned to the West Bank and 154 to Gaza. Some of those refugees might not have been displaced since 1967, but were possibly family members of a displaced registered refugee.

GENERAL ASSEMBLY ACTION

On 9 December [meeting 72], the General Assembly, on the recommendation of the Fourth Committee [A/58/472], adopted **resolution 58/92** by recorded vote (168-5-3) [agenda item 83].

Persons displaced as a result of the June 1967 and subsequent hostilities

The General Assembly,

Recalling its resolutions 2252(ES-V) of 4 July 1967, 2341 B (XXII) of 19 December 1967 and all subsequent related resolutions,

Recalling also Security Council resolutions 237(1967) of 14 June 1967 and 259(1968) of 27 September 1968,

Taking note of the report of the Secretary-General submitted in pursuance of its resolution 57/119 of 11 December 2002,

Taking note also of the report of the Commissioner-General of the United Nations Relief and Works Agency for Palestine Refugees in the Near East covering the period from 1 July 2002 to 30 June 2003,

Concerned about the continuing human suffering resulting from the June 1967 and subsequent hostilities,

Taking note of the relevant provisions of the Declaration of Principles on Interim Self-Government Arrangements of 1993 with regard to the modalities for the admission of persons displaced in 1967, and concerned that the process agreed upon has not yet been effected,

1. *Reaffirms* the right of all persons displaced as a result of the June 1967 and subsequent hostilities to return to their homes or former places of residence in the territories occupied by Israel since 1967;
2. *Expresses deep concern* that the mechanism agreed upon by the parties in article XII of the Declaration of Principles on Interim Self-Government Arrangements of 1993 on the return of displaced persons has not been effected, and stresses the necessity for an accelerated return of displaced persons;
3. *Endorses*, in the meanwhile, the efforts of the Commissioner-General of the United Nations Relief and Works Agency for Palestine Refugees in the Near East to continue to provide humanitarian assistance, as far as practicable, on an emergency basis and as a temporary measure, to persons in the area who are currently displaced and in serious need of continuing assistance as a result of the June 1967 and subsequent hostilities;
4. *Strongly appeals* to all Governments and to organizations and individuals to contribute generously to the Agency and to the other intergovernmental and non-governmental organizations concerned for the above-mentioned purposes;
5. *Requests* the Secretary-General, after consulting with the Commissioner-General, to report to the General Assembly before its fifty-ninth session on the progress made with regard to the implementation of the present resolution.

RECORDED VOTE ON RESOLUTION 58/92:

In favour: Afghanistan, Albania, Algeria, Andorra, Angola, Antigua and Barbuda, Argentina, Armenia, Australia, Austria, Azerbaijan, Bahamas, Bahrain, Bangladesh, Barbados, Belarus, Belgium, Belize, Benin, Bhutan, Bolivia, Bosnia and Herzegovina, Botswana, Brazil, Brunei Darussalam, Bulgaria, Burkina Faso, Burundi, Cambodia, Cameroon, Canada, Cape Verde, Central African Republic, Chile, China, Colombia, Comoros, Costa Rica, Côte d'Ivoire, Croatia, Cuba, Cyprus, Czech Republic, Democratic People's Republic of Korea, Denmark, Djibouti, Dominican Republic, Ecuador, Egypt, El Salvador, Equatorial Guinea, Eritrea, Estonia, Ethiopia, Fiji, Finland, France, Gabon, Gambia, Georgia, Germany, Ghana, Greece, Grenada, Guatemala, Guinea, Guinea-Bissau, Guyana, Haiti, Hungary, Iceland, India, Indonesia, Iran, Ireland, Italy, Jamaica, Japan, Jordan, Kazakhstan, Kenya, Kuwait, Kyrgyzstan, Lao People's Democratic Republic, Latvia, Lebanon, Lesotho, Libyan Arab Jamahiriya, Liechtenstein, Lithuania, Luxembourg, Madagascar, Malaysia, Maldives, Mali, Malta, Mauritania, Mauritius, Mexico, Monaco, Mongolia, Morocco, Mozambique, Myanmar, Namibia, Nauru, Nepal, Netherlands, New Zealand, Nicaragua, Niger, Nigeria, Norway, Oman, Pakistan, Panama, Paraguay, Peru, Philippines, Poland, Portugal, Qatar, Republic of Korea, Republic of Moldova, Romania, Russian Federation, Saint Lucia, Saint Vincent and the Grenadines, Samoa, San Marino, Saudi Arabia, Senegal, Serbia and Montenegro, Seychelles, Singapore, Slovakia, Slovenia, Solomon Islands, South Africa, Spain, Sri Lanka, Sudan, Suriname, Swaziland, Sweden, Switzerland, Syrian Arab Republic, Tajikistan, Thailand, The former Yugoslav Republic of Macedonia, Timor-Leste, Togo, Tonga, Trinidad and Tobago, Tunisia, Turkey, Turkmenistan, Tuvalu, Ukraine, United Arab Emirates, United Kingdom, United Republic of Tanzania, Uruguay, Venezuela, Viet Nam, Yemen, Zambia, Zimbabwe.

Against: Israel, Marshall Islands, Micronesia, Palau, United States.

Abstaining: Honduras, Papua New Guinea, Rwanda.

Property rights

In response to General Assembly resolution 57/122 [YUN 2002, p. 472], the Secretary-General submitted an August report [A/58/206] on steps taken to protect and administer Arab property, assets and property rights in Israel, and establish a fund for income derived therefrom, on behalf of the rightful owners. He indicated that he had transmitted the resolution to Israel and all other Member States, requesting information on any steps taken or envisaged to implement it.

In a 1 July reply, reproduced in the report, Israel stated that its position on the resolutions on Palestine refugees had been set forth in successive annual replies, the latest of which had been included in the Secretary-General's 2002 report on the subject [YUN 2002, p. 471]. Israel regretted that the resolutions continued to be rife with irrelevant politicized rhetoric that detracted from important efforts at hand. Israel fully supported UNRWA's humanitarian mission and believed that the Agency contributed to the alleviation of the suffering of the Palestinian refugees. However, on several occasions, UNRWA had issued anti-Israeli statements that ignored the right and duty of Israel to defend its citizens from the campaign of terror being waged against them for close to three years.

GENERAL ASSEMBLY ACTION

On 9 December [meeting 72], the General Assembly, on the recommendation of the Fourth Committee [A/58/472], adopted **resolution 58/94** by recorded vote (164-5-4) [agenda item 83].

Palestine refugees' properties and their revenues

The General Assembly,

Recalling its resolutions 194(III) of 11 December 1948, 36/146 C of 16 December 1981 and all its subsequent resolutions on the question,

Taking note of the report of the Secretary-General submitted in pursuance of its resolution 57/122 of 11 December 2002,

Taking note also of the report of the United Nations Conciliation Commission for Palestine for the period from 1 September 2002 to 31 August 2003,

Recalling that the Universal Declaration of Human Rights and the principles of international law uphold the principle that no one shall be arbitrarily deprived of his or her property,

Recalling in particular its resolution 394(V) of 14 December 1950, in which it directed the Conciliation Commission, in consultation with the parties concerned, to prescribe measures for the protection of the rights, property and interests of the Palestine refugees,

Noting the completion of the programme of identification and evaluation of Arab property, as announced by the Conciliation Commission in its twenty-second progress report, and the fact that the Land Office had a schedule of Arab owners and file of documents defining the location, area and other particulars of Arab property,

Expressing its appreciation for the work done to preserve and modernize the existing records, including the land records, of the Conciliation Commission and the importance of such records for a just resolution of the plight of the Palestine refugees in conformity with General Assembly resolution 194(III),

Recalling that, in the framework of the Middle East peace process, the Palestine Liberation Organization and the Government of Israel agreed, in the Declaration of Principles on Interim Self-Government Arrangements of 13 September 1993, to commence negotiations on permanent status issues, including the important issue of the refugees,

1. *Reaffirms* that the Palestine refugees are entitled to their property and to the income derived therefrom, in conformity with the principles of equity and justice;

2. *Requests* the Secretary-General to take all appropriate steps, in consultation with the United Nations Conciliation Commission for Palestine, for the protection of Arab property, assets and property rights in Israel;

3. *Calls once again upon* Israel to render all facilities and assistance to the Secretary-General in the implementation of the present resolution;

4. *Calls upon* all the parties concerned to provide the Secretary-General with any pertinent information in their possession concerning Arab property, assets and property rights in Israel that would assist him in the implementation of the present resolution;

5. *Urges* the Palestinian and Israeli sides, as agreed between them, to deal with the important issue of Palestine refugees' properties and their revenues in the framework of the final status negotiations of the Middle East peace process;

6. *Requests* the Secretary-General to report to the General Assembly at its fifty-ninth session on the implementation of the present resolution.

RECORDED VOTE ON RESOLUTION 58/94:

In favour: Afghanistan, Albania, Algeria, Andorra, Angola, Antigua and Barbuda, Argentina, Armenia, Australia, Austria, Azerbaijan, Bahamas, Bahrain, Bangladesh, Barbados, Belarus, Belgium, Belize, Benin, Bhutan, Bolivia, Bosnia and Herzegovina, Botswana, Brazil, Brunei Darussalam, Bulgaria, Burkina Faso, Cambodia, Canada, Cape Verde, Chile, China, Colombia, Comoros, Costa Rica, Côte d'Ivoire, Croatia, Cuba, Cyprus, Czech Republic, Democratic People's Republic of Korea, Denmark, Djibouti, Dominican Republic, Ecuador, Egypt, El Salvador, Equatorial Guinea, Eritrea, Estonia, Ethiopia, Fiji, Finland, France, Gabon, Gambia, Georgia, Germany, Ghana, Greece, Grenada, Guatemala, Guinea, Guinea-Bissau, Guyana, Haiti, Hungary, Iceland, India, Indonesia, Iran, Ireland, Italy, Jamaica, Japan, Jordan, Kazakhstan, Kenya, Kuwait, Kyrgyzstan, Lao People's Democratic Republic, Latvia, Lebanon, Lesotho, Libyan Arab Jamahiriya, Liechtenstein, Lithuania, Luxembourg, Madagascar, Malaysia, Maldives, Mali, Malta, Mauritania, Mauritius, Mexico, Monaco, Mongolia, Morocco, Mozambique, Myanmar, Namibia, Nepal, Netherlands, New Zealand, Nicaragua, Niger, Nigeria, Norway, Oman, Pakistan, Panama, Paraguay, Peru, Philippines, Poland, Portugal, Qatar, Republic of Korea, Republic of Moldova, Romania, Russian Federation, Saint Lucia, Saint Vincent and the Grenadines, Samoa, San Marino, Saudi Arabia, Senegal, Serbia and Montenegro, Seychelles, Singapore, Slovakia, Slovenia, Solomon Islands, South Africa, Spain, Sri Lanka, Sudan, Suriname, Swaziland, Sweden, Switzerland, Syrian Arab Republic, Tajikistan, Thailand, The former Yugoslav Republic of Macedonia, Timor-Leste, Togo, Tonga, Trinidad and Tobago, Tunisia, Turkey, Turkmenistan, Tuvalu, Ukraine, United Arab Emirates, United Kingdom, United Republic of Tanzania, Uruguay, Venezuela, Viet Nam, Yemen, Zambia, Zimbabwe.

Against: Israel, Marshall Islands, Micronesia, Palau, United States.

Abstaining: Cameroon, Honduras, Papua New Guinea, Rwanda.

Education, training and scholarships

In a September report [A/58/339], the Secretary-General transmitted responses to the General Assembly's appeal in resolution 57/120 [YUN 2002, p. 470] for States, specialized agencies and NGOs to augment special allocations for scholarships and grants to Palestine refugees, for which UNRWA acted as recipient and trustee.

In 2002/03, Japan awarded 12 fellowships to Palestine refugees employed by UNRWA as vocational staff at the eight vocational training centres in the Agency's area of operations. During the 2002/03 academic year, owing to the cancellation in 1999 of the portion of the university scholarship fund for secondary school graduates financed from UNRWA's General Fund budget and the fact that financing was not forthcoming from donors to fund the subprogramme, UNRWA's Education Department used funds already available from contributions from Japan and Switzerland to finance the studies of some students until their graduation. WHO provided 15 fellowships/study tours for qualified Palestinian candidates in 2002/03 and UNESCO granted 10 scholarships during the 2001-2002 biennium. Through the Scholarship Fund for Palestine Refugee Women in Lebanon, financed by the International Development Research Centre, 90 students were enrolled in specializations at Lebanese universities in 2002/03. Other financing was pledged or received from private individuals and foundations.

Proposed University of Jerusalem "Al-Quds"

In response to General Assembly resolution 57/123 [YUN 2002, p. 471], the Secretary-General submitted an August report on the proposal to establish a university for Palestine refugees in Jerusalem [A/58/205]. First mentioned by the Assembly in resolution 35/13 B [YUN 1980, p. 443], the issue had been the subject of annual reports by the Secretary-General.

To assist in the feasibility study and at the Secretary-General's request, the Rector of the United Nations University again asked expert Mihaly Simai to visit the area and meet with Israeli officials. In response to the Secretary-General's note verbale of 13 June, Israel, in a 26 June reply, stated that it had consistently voted against the resolution on the proposed university and that its position remained unchanged. It charged that the resolution's sponsors sought to exploit higher education for political purposes extraneous to genuine academic pursuit. Accordingly, Israel was of the opinion that the proposed visit would serve no useful purpose. The Secretary-General reported that it had not been possible to complete the study as planned.

In response to the Secretary-General's note verbale to Member States of 19 June concerning the implementation of Assembly resolutions 57/117 to 57/123 [YUN 2002, pp. 466-472], the Syrian Arab Republic, in a 3 July reply, expressed concern with the occupying Power's continued rejection of UN resolutions, its failure to cooperate with the international community and its obstruction of implementation of the UNRWA proposal regarding the need to establish the University of Jerusalem "Al-Quds".

Peacekeeping operations

In 2003, the United Nations Truce Supervision Organization (UNTSO), originally set up to monitor the ceasefire called for by the Security Council in resolution S/801 of 29 May 1948 [YUN 1947-48, p. 427] in newly partitioned Palestine, continued its work. UNTSO's unarmed military observers fulfilled changing mandates—from supervising the original four armistice agreements between Israel and its neighbours (Egypt, Jordan, Lebanon, Syrian Arab Republic) to observing and monitoring other ceasefires, as well as performing a number of additional tasks. During the year, UNTSO personnel worked with the two remaining UN peacekeeping forces in the Middle East—the United Nations Disengagement Observer Force (UNDOF) in the Golan Heights and the United Nations Interim Force in Lebanon (UNIFIL).

Lebanon

The relative calm that marked the first half of 2003 was replaced in the second half by a renewed escalation of violence in the Shab'a farmlands area on the Lebanese-Israeli border. The paramilitary group Hizbullah carried out attacks against positions of the Israel Defence Forces (IDF) in the farmlands and targets inside Israel, and IDF continued to carry out attacks within Lebanon. The Shab'a farmlands had been a source of contention since the withdrawal of Israeli forces from Lebanon in June 2000 [YUN 2000, p. 465]. According to the Lebanese Government, Israel's withdrawal from southern Lebanon was incomplete, as Israeli forces continued to occupy the Shab'a farms, while Israel held the view that the area was occupied Syrian territory and thus within the purview of Security Council resolution 242(1967) [YUN 1967, p. 257] on the Israeli-Syrian conflict, and not resolution 425 (1978) [YUN 1978, p. 312], which dealt with Israel's withdrawal from Lebanon. However, Lebanon and the Syrian Arab Republic maintained that the Shab'a farmlands were inside Lebanese territory.

In their monthly briefings to the Security Council on the Palestinian question, including East Jerusalem, the Special Coordinator for the Middle East Peace Process and Personal Representative of the Secretary-General, Terje Roed-Larsen, and the Under-Secretary-General for Political Affairs, Kieran Prendergast, also reported on developments in southern Lebanon.

Staffan de Mistura continued to act as the Secretary-General's Personal Representative for Southern Lebanon, responsible for coordinating UN activities in the area.

Communications. In a series of communications received throughout the year [A/57/713-S/2003/73, A/57/722-S/2003/148, A/57/755-S/2003/314, A/57-782-S/2003/414, A/57/844-S/2003/698, A/57/856-S/2003/804, A/58/405-S/2003/932, A/58/418-S/2003/966, A/58/442-S/2003/1020, A/58/443-S/2003/1021, A/58/551-S/2003/1068, A/58/624-S/2003/1166, A/58/668-S/2003/1220], Lebanon detailed Israel's violations of the Blue Line, the provisional border drawn by the United Nations following the withdrawal of Israeli troops from southern Lebanon in June 2000, and consequently, of Lebanese sovereignty and territorial integrity.

In communications throughout 2003 [A/57/717-S/2003/96, A/57/820-S/2003/603, A/57/851-S/2003/758, A/58/425-S/2003/976], Israel reported attacks carried out by Hizbullah against Israeli military and civilian targets across the Blue Line. Israel also alleged that Hizbullah was supported by the Governments of Iran, Lebanon and the Syrian Arab Republic.

By a 12 February letter [A/57/730-S/2003/178], the Syrian Arab Republic refuted Israel's allegations, stating that the Lebanese national resistance emerged as a response to Israel's policy of occupation.

UNIFIL

In 2003, the United Nations Interim Force in Lebanon continued to discharge its mandate by observing, monitoring and reporting on developments in its area of operation. The Security Council twice extended UNIFIL's mandate in 2003, in January and in July, each time for a six-month period.

UNIFIL, established by Council resolution 425(1978) following Israel's invasion of Lebanon [YUN 1978, p. 296], was originally entrusted with confirming the withdrawal of Israeli forces, restoring international peace and security, and assisting Lebanon in regaining authority in southern Lebanon. Following a second invasion of Lebanon in 1982 [YUN 1982, p. 428], the Council, in resolution 511(1982) [ibid., p. 450], authorized the Force to carry out the additional task of providing protection and humanitarian assistance to the local population. With the withdrawal of IDF from Lebanon in June 2000 [YUN 2000, p. 465], UNIFIL's operational role changed. A reinforcement was initiated to enable UNIFIL to monitor Israel's withdrawal, which included extending its operations into those territories previously occupied by IDF [ibid.]. In 2001, having fulfilled those responsibilities, UNIFIL began a reconfiguration and redeployment phase [YUN 2001, p. 453], which was completed in December 2002 [YUN 2002, p. 478].

The Force headquarters, based in Naqoura, provided command and control, and liaison with Lebanon and Israel, UNDOF, UNTSO and a number of NGOs.

Composition and deployment

As at 31 December 2003, UNIFIL comprised 2,000 troops from France (202), Ghana (650), India (650), Ireland (7), Italy (53), Poland (238) and Ukraine (200). The Force was assisted in its tasks by 52 UNTSO military observers. It employed 415 civilian staff, of whom 119 were recruited internationally and 296 locally. Major General Lalit Mohan Tewari (India) continued as Force Commander.

Since UNIFIL's establishment, 244 members had lost their lives: 78 as a result of firings or bomb explosions, 104 in accidents and 62 from other causes.

Activities

Report of Secretary-General (January). In a report on developments from 13 July 2002 to 14 January 2003 in the UNIFIL area of operations [S/2003/38], the Secretary-General said that the situation on the ground was one of general stability, despite some incidents in the Shab'a farms area and attacks across the Blue Line. UNIFIL completed its reconfiguration and redeployment in December 2002 and had stabilized at a strength of about 2,000 troops.

The Secretary-General observed that UNIFIL would continue to discharge its mandate by observing, monitoring and reporting on developments in its area of operations, liaising with parties to maintain peace and security. The Lebanese Government had further demonstrated its capacity to exercise its authority effectively throughout southern Lebanon, strengthening administrative structures and extending the reach of the Lebanese Army. The Secretary-General recommended that the Force's mandate be extended for another six months, until 31 July 2003.

Communication. By a 9 January letter [S/2003/36] to the Secretary-General, Lebanon requested that UNIFIL's mandate, due to expire at the end of the month, be extended for a further six-month period, especially in the light of Israel's violations of Lebanese sovereignty.

SECURITY COUNCIL ACTION (January)

On 30 January [meeting 4696], the Security Council unanimously adopted **resolution 1461(2003)**. The draft [S/2003/111] was submitted by France.

The Security Council,

Recalling all its resolutions on Lebanon, in particular resolutions 425(1978) and 426(1978) of 19 March 1978 and 1428(2002) of 30 July 2002 as well as the statements by its President on the situation in Lebanon, in particular the statement of 18 June 2000 (S/PRST/2000/21),

Recalling also the letter dated 18 May 2001 from the President of the Security Council addressed to the Secretary-General,

Recalling further the conclusion of the Secretary-General that, as of 16 June 2000, Israel had withdrawn its forces from Lebanon in accordance with resolution 425(1978) and met the requirements defined in the report of the Secretary-General of 22 May 2000, as well as the conclusion of the Secretary-General that the United Nations Interim Force in Lebanon had essentially completed two of the three parts of its mandate, focusing now on the remaining task of restoring international peace and security,

Emphasizing the interim nature of the Force,

Recalling its resolution 1308(2000) of 17 July 2000,

Recalling also its resolution 1325(2000) of 31 October 2000,

Recalling further the relevant principles contained in the Convention on the Safety of United Nations and Associated Personnel of 9 December 1994,

Responding to the request of the Government of Lebanon, as stated in the letter dated 9 January 2003 from the Chargé d'affaires a.i. of the Permanent Mission of Lebanon to the United Nations addressed to the Secretary-General,

1. *Endorses* the report of the Secretary-General of 14 January 2003 on the United Nations Interim Force in Lebanon, and in particular its recommendation to renew the mandate of the Force for a further period of six months;

2. *Decides* to extend the present mandate until 31 July 2003;

3. *Takes note* of the completion of the reconfiguration of the Force as outlined in paragraph 26 of the report of the Secretary-General and in accordance with the letter dated 18 May 2001 from the President of the Security Council addressed to the Secretary-General;

4. *Reiterates its strong support* for the territorial integrity, sovereignty and political independence of Lebanon within its internationally recognized boundaries;

5. *Commends* the Government of Lebanon for taking steps to ensure the restoration of its effective authority throughout the south, including the deployment of Lebanese armed forces, and calls upon it to continue to extend these measures and to do its utmost to ensure a calm environment throughout the south;

6. *Calls upon* the parties to ensure that the Force is accorded full freedom of movement in the discharge of its mandate throughout its area of operation as outlined in the report of the Secretary-General;

7. *Reiterates its call* upon the parties to continue to fulfil the commitments they have given to respect fully the withdrawal line identified by the United Nations, as set out in the report of the Secretary-General of 16 June 2000, to exercise the utmost restraint and to cooperate fully with the United Nations and the Force;

8. *Condemns* all acts of violence, expresses great concern about the serious breaches and the air, sea and land violations of the withdrawal line, and urges the parties to put an end to these violations and to abide scrupulously by their obligation to respect the safety of the personnel of the Force and other United Nations personnel;

9. *Supports* the continued efforts of the Force to maintain the ceasefire along the withdrawal line through mobile patrols and observation from fixed positions and through close contacts with the parties to correct violations, resolve incidents and prevent the escalation thereof;

10. *Welcomes* the continued contribution of the Force to operational demining, encourages further assistance in mine action by the United Nations to the Government of Lebanon in support of both the continued development of its national mine action capacity and emergency demining activities in the south, commends donor countries for supporting these efforts through financial and in-kind contributions and encourages further international contributions, takes note of the communication to the Government of Lebanon and the Force of maps and information on the location of mines, and stresses the necessity to provide the Government of Lebanon and the Force with any additional maps and records on the location of mines;

11. *Requests* the Secretary-General to continue consultations with the Government of Lebanon and other parties directly concerned on the implementation of the present resolution and to report thereon to the Council before the end of the present mandate as well as on the activities of the Force and the tasks presently carried out by the United Nations Truce Supervision Organization;

12. *Looks forward* to the early fulfilment of the mandate of the Force;

13. *Stresses* the importance of, and the need to achieve, a comprehensive, just and lasting peace in the Middle East, based on all its relevant resolutions, including resolutions 242(1967) of 22 November 1967 and 338(1973) of 22 October 1973.

Report of Secretary-General (July). In response to Security Council resolution 1461(2003) (see p. 517), the Secretary-General submitted a July report on UNIFIL covering 15 January to 23 July [S/2003/728]. He said that the situation on the ground remained generally quiet but tense through a reporting period marked by regional conflict. The most significant sources of tension were the persistent Israeli violations of Lebanese airspace and instances of Hizbullah anti-aircraft fire directed across the Blue Line towards Israeli villages. A ceasefire breach in the Shab'a farms area occurred on 21 January when Hizbullah fired 56 mortar rounds at an IDF position. Israeli forces retaliated with artillery and mortar fire and two aerial bombs directed at the area from which the Hizbullah fire had emanated. One Lebanese civilian was killed and at least two others injured by IDF fire.

The Lebanese Joint Security Forces and the Lebanese Army continued to operate in the areas vacated by Israel; their activities increased, with a more visible presence, including along the Blue Line. The Lebanese Government maintained its position that, so long as there was no comprehensive peace with Israel, the Lebanese armed forces would not be deployed along the Blue Line. Hizbullah maintained a visible presence near the line and reinforced some positions, but its interference with the freedom of movement of UNIFIL staff during the reporting period was negligible. Official local governing structures were extending their authority throughout the south at a steady pace. Communications, infrastructure, health and welfare systems and postal services continued their slow progress towards integration with the rest of the country.

UNIFIL provided assistance to the civilian population in the form of medical care, water projects, equipment or services for schools and orphanages, and supplies of social services to the needy. In southern Lebanon, collaboration between the United Nations, the Lebanese Government and various donors had led to dramatic progress in demining efforts, and advocacy efforts began emphasizing socio-economic needs to rehabilitate formerly mine-affected areas. The Secretary-General's Personal Representative continued to collaborate with UNDP and the World Bank to facilitate funding for and implementation of development projects.

The Secretary-General observed that almost six months had passed since the January incidents across the Blue Line, the longest period of relative calm since Israel withdrew from Lebanon in 2000 after 22 years of occupation. However, despite encouraging trends, tensions between Israel and Lebanon remained high and the relative calm along the Blue Line was an uneasy one. The Secretary-General called on both parties to respect fully the withdrawal line identified by the United Nations and to refrain from any action that could destabilize the situation on the ground. As the Lebanese Government demonstrated its capacity to increase its authority throughout southern Lebanon, the relative improvement in terms of security in that area coupled with the achievements in demining pointed to the need for an increased focus on the economic development of the area.

Communication. By a 2 July letter to the Secretary-General [S/2003/685], Lebanon requested that UNIFIL's mandate be extended for a further six months, as a reaffirmation of the international community's commitment to the restoration of Lebanon's sovereignty over its entire territory.

SECURITY COUNCIL ACTION (July)

The Security Council, in a closed meeting on 25 July [meeting 4795], exchanged views with UNIFIL troop-contributing countries and heard a briefing from the Director of the Asia and Middle East Division of the Department of Peacekeeping Operations.

On 31 July [meeting 4802], the Council unanimously adopted **resolution 1496(2003)**. The draft [S/2003/778] was submitted by France.

The Security Council,

Recalling all its resolutions on Lebanon, in particular resolutions 425(1978) and 426(1978) of 19 March 1978 and 1461(2003) of 30 January 2003, as well as the statements by its President on the situation in Lebanon, in particular the statement of 18 June 2000 (S/PRST/2000/21),

Recalling also the letter dated 18 May 2001 from the President of the Security Council addressed to the Secretary-General,

Recalling further the conclusion of the Secretary-General that, as of 16 June 2000, Israel had withdrawn its forces from Lebanon in accordance with resolution 425(1978) and met the requirements defined in the report of the Secretary-General of 22 May 2000, as well as the conclusion of the Secretary-General that the United Nations Interim Force in Lebanon had essentially completed two of the three parts of its mandate, focusing now on the remaining task of restoring international peace and security,

Emphasizing the interim nature of the Force,

Recalling its resolution 1308(2000) of 17 July 2000,

Recalling also its resolution 1325(2000) of 31 October 2000,

Recalling further the relevant principles contained in the Convention on the Safety of United Nations and Associated Personnel of 9 December 1994,

Responding to the request of the Government of Lebanon, as stated in the letter dated 2 July 2003 from the Chargé d'affaires a.i. of the Permanent Mission of Lebanon to the United Nations addressed to the Secretary-General,

1. *Endorses* the report of the Secretary-General of 23 July 2003 on the United Nations Interim Force in Lebanon, and in particular its recommendation to renew the mandate of the Force for a further period of six months;

2. *Decides* to extend the present mandate until 31 January 2004;

3. *Reiterates its strong support* for the territorial integrity, sovereignty and political independence of Lebanon within its internationally recognized boundaries;

4. *Welcomes* the steps already taken by the Government of Lebanon to ensure the return of its effective authority throughout the south, including the deployment of Lebanese armed forces, and calls upon it to continue to extend these measures and to do its utmost to ensure a calm environment throughout the south;

5. *Calls upon* the parties to ensure that the Force is accorded full freedom of movement in the discharge of its mandate throughout its area of operation as outlined in the report of the Secretary-General;

6. *Reiterates its call* upon the parties to continue to fulfil the commitments they have given to respect fully the withdrawal line identified by the United Nations, as set out in the report of the Secretary-General of 16 June 2000, to exercise utmost restraint and to cooperate fully with the United Nations and the Force;

7. *Condemns* all acts of violence, expresses great concern about the serious breaches and the air, sea and land violations of the withdrawal line, and urges the parties to put an end to these violations and to abide scrupulously by their obligation to respect the safety of the personnel of the Force and other United Nations personnel;

8. *Supports* the continued efforts of the Force to maintain the ceasefire along the withdrawal line through mobile patrols and observation from fixed positions and through close contacts with the parties to correct violations, resolve incidents and prevent the escalation thereof;

9. *Welcomes* the continued contribution of the Force to operational demining, applauds the progress in demining efforts noted by the Secretary-General in his report, encourages further assistance in mine action by the United Nations to the Government of Lebanon in support of both the continued development of its national mine action capacity and emergency demining activities in the south, commends donor countries for supporting these efforts through financial and in-kind contributions and encourages further international contributions, takes note of the communication to the Government of Lebanon and the Force

of maps and information on the location of mines, and stresses the necessity to provide the Government of Lebanon and the Force with any additional maps and records on the location of mines;

10. *Requests* the Secretary-General to continue consultations with the Government of Lebanon and other parties directly concerned on the implementation of the present resolution and to report thereon to the Council before the end of the present mandate, as well as on the activities of the Force and the tasks presently carried out by the United Nations Truce Supervision Organization;

11. *Looks forward* to the early fulfilment of the mandate of the Force;

12. *Stresses* the importance of, and the need to achieve, a comprehensive, just and lasting peace in the Middle East, based on all its relevant resolutions, including its resolutions 242(1967) of 22 November 1967 and 338(1973) of 22 October 1973.

Further developments. In a report on developments during the second half of 2003 [S/2004/50], the Secretary-General said that the situation in UNIFIL's area of operation was marked by numerous incidents threatening the fragile stability of southern Lebanon. The relative calm that had prevailed in the first half of the year gave way to renewed exchanges of fire in the Shab'a farms area. Air strikes and shooting incidents across the Blue Line resulted in the death of three Israelis, two soldiers and one civilian, and three Lebanese civilians. The persistent Israeli violations of Lebanese airspace and several instances of Hizbullah anti-aircraft fire directed towards Israeli villages contributed to the tension. Roadside explosive devices found on four occasions along the Blue Line adjacent to the IDF patrol route further strained relations between the parties. The Lebanese Joint Security Forces and the Lebanese Army continued to operate in the areas vacated by Israel in 2000. Their strength and activity remained the same, apart from a more visible presence in the first half of October, when regional and local tensions were heightened. Hizbullah maintained its visible presence near the border line through its network of mobile and fixed positions, as Lebanese armed forces were not deployed along the withdrawal line.

UNIFIL continued to provide assistance to the civilian population and cooperated on humanitarian matters with Lebanese authorities, UN agencies, the International Committee of the Red Cross (ICRC) and other organizations operating in Lebanon. The presence of a large number of minefields in UNIFIL's area of operation, which were largely concentrated along the Blue Line as other sectors had been cleared of mines, remained a matter of serious concern. Approximately 4.8 million square metres of land had been cleared of mines in other parts of southern Lebanon. The Secretary-General's Personal Representative and UNDP continued to coordinate international assistance to the Lebanese Government in the framework of the International Support Group for Mine Action.

The Secretary-General said that the situation along the Blue Line was susceptible to volatile regional developments. That underscored the need to achieve a comprehensive, just and lasting peace in the Middle East, based on all the relevant Security Council resolutions.

Financing

Reports of Secretary-General and ACABQ. In June, the General Assembly considered the performance report on UNIFIL's budget for the period 1 July 2001 to 30 June 2002 [A/57/662 & Corr.1]. Total expenditures for the period amounted to $131,112,200, compared with a total apportionment of $136,816,100, resulting in an unencumbered balance of $5,703,900.

The Assembly also had before it UNIFIL's proposed budget for the period from 1 July 2003 to 30 June 2004 in the amount of $91,752,400 [A/57/663] and the overview of the financing of UN peacekeeping operations: budget performance for the period from 1 July 2001 to 30 June 2002 and budget for the period from 1 July 2003 to 30 June 2004 [A/57/723]. Also considered were the comments and recommendations of the Advisory Committee on Administrative and Budgetary Questions (ACABQ) [A/57/772/Add.6].

GENERAL ASSEMBLY ACTION

On 18 June [meeting 90], the General Assembly, on the recommendation of the Fifth (Administrative and Budgetary) Committee [A/57/829], adopted **resolution 57/325** by recorded vote (135-2) [agenda item 127 *(b)*].

Financing of the United Nations Interim Force in Lebanon

The General Assembly,

Having considered the reports of the Secretary-General on the financing of the United Nations Interim Force in Lebanon and the related reports of the Advisory Committee on Administrative and Budgetary Questions,

Recalling Security Council resolution 425(1978) of 19 March 1978 regarding the establishment of the United Nations Interim Force in Lebanon, and the subsequent resolutions by which the Council extended the mandate of the Force, the latest of which was resolution 1461(2003) of 30 January 2003,

Recalling also its resolution S-8/2 of 21 April 1978 on the financing of the Force and its subsequent resolutions thereon, the latest of which was resolution 56/214 B of 27 June 2002,

Reaffirming its resolutions 51/233 of 13 June 1997, 52/237 of 26 June 1998, 53/227 of 8 June 1999, 54/267 of 15 June 2000, 55/180 A of 19 December 2000,

55/180 B of 14 June 2001, 56/214 A of 21 December 2001 and 56/214 B,

Reaffirming also the general principles underlying the financing of United Nations peacekeeping operations, as stated in General Assembly resolutions 1874 (S-IV) of 27 June 1963, 3101(XXVIII) of 11 December 1973 and 55/235 of 23 December 2000,

Noting with appreciation that voluntary contributions have been made to the Force,

Mindful of the fact that it is essential to provide the Force with the necessary financial resources to enable it to fulfil its responsibilities under the relevant resolutions of the Security Council,

1. *Takes note* of the status of contributions to the United Nations Interim Force in Lebanon as at 31 March 2003, including the contributions outstanding in the amount of 108.3 million United States dollars, representing some 4 per cent of the total assessed contributions, notes with concern that only twenty-three Member States have paid their assessed contributions in full, and urges all other Member States, in particular those in arrears, to ensure payment of their outstanding assessed contributions;

2. *Expresses its appreciation* to those Member States which have paid their assessed contributions in full, and urges all other Member States to make every possible effort to ensure payment of their assessed contributions to the Force in full;

3. *Expresses its deep concern* that Israel did not comply with General Assembly resolutions 51/233, 52/237, 53/227, 54/267, 55/180 A, 55/180 B, 56/214 A and 56/214 B;

4. *Stresses once again* that Israel should strictly abide by General Assembly resolutions 51/233, 52/237, 53/227, 54/267, 55/180 A, 55/180 B, 56/214 A and 56/214 B;

5. *Expresses concern* at the financial situation with regard to peacekeeping activities, in particular as regards the reimbursements to troop contributors that bear additional burdens owing to overdue payments by Member States of their assessments;

6. *Takes note* of the fact that indemnities have been paid to staff working on fixed-term contracts without a clear or detailed legislative basis, and requests the Secretary-General to ensure that similar cases do not occur in the future without previous specific authorization by the General Assembly;

7. *Expresses concern* at the delay experienced by the Secretary-General in deploying and providing adequate resources to some recent peacekeeping missions, in particular those in Africa;

8. *Emphasizes* that all future and existing peacekeeping missions shall be given equal and non-discriminatory treatment in respect of financial and administrative arrangements;

9. *Also emphasizes* that all peacekeeping missions shall be provided with adequate resources for the effective and efficient discharge of their respective mandates;

10. *Reiterates its request* to the Secretary-General to make the fullest possible use of facilities and equipment at the United Nations Logistics Base at Brindisi, Italy, in order to minimize the costs of procurement for the Force;

11. *Endorses* the conclusions and recommendations contained in the report of the Advisory Committee on Administrative and Budgetary Questions, and requests the Secretary-General to ensure their full implementation without prejudice to a future discussion and decision on the proposal to create the post of Deputy Force Commander;

12. *Requests* the Secretary-General to take all necessary action to ensure that the Force is administered with a maximum of efficiency and economy;

13. *Also requests* the Secretary-General, in order to reduce the cost of employing General Service staff, to continue efforts to recruit local staff for the Force against General Service posts, commensurate with the requirements of the Force;

14. *Reiterates its request* to the Secretary-General to take the measures necessary to ensure the full implementation of paragraph 8 of its resolution 51/233, paragraph 5 of its resolution 52/237, paragraph 11 of its resolution 53/227, paragraph 14 of its resolution 54/267, paragraph 14 of its resolution 55/180 A, paragraph 15 of its resolution 55/180 B, paragraph 13 of its resolution 56/214 A and paragraph 13 of its resolution 56/214 B, stresses once again that Israel shall pay the amount of 1,117,005 dollars resulting from the incident at Qana on 18 April 1996, and requests the Secretary-General to report on this matter to the General Assembly at its resumed fifty-eighth session;

Financial performance report for the period from 1 July 2001 to 30 June 2002

15. *Takes note* of the report of the Secretary-General on the financial performance of the Force for the period from 1 July 2001 to 30 June 2002;

Budget estimates for the period from 1 July 2003 to 30 June 2004

16. *Decides* to appropriate to the Special Account for the United Nations Interim Force in Lebanon the amount of 94,055,900 dollars for the period from 1 July 2003 to 30 June 2004, inclusive of 90 million dollars for the maintenance of the Force, 3,105,700 dollars for the support account for peacekeeping operations and 950,200 dollars for the United Nations Logistics Base;

Financing of the appropriation

17. *Also decides* to apportion among Member States the amount of 94,055,900 dollars at a monthly rate of 7,837,992 dollars, in accordance with the levels set out in resolution 55/235, as adjusted by the General Assembly in its resolutions 55/236 of 23 December 2000 and 57/290 A of 20 December 2002, and taking into account the scale of assessments for 2003 as set out in its resolutions 55/5 B of 23 December 2000 and 57/4 B of 20 December 2002, and for 2004, subject to a decision of the Security Council to extend the mandate of the Force;

18. *Further decides* that, in accordance with the provisions of its resolution 973(X) of 15 December 1955, there shall be set off against the apportionment among Member States, as provided for in paragraph 17 above, their respective share in the Tax Equalization Fund of 4,555,000 dollars at a monthly rate of 379,583 dollars, comprising the estimated staff assessment income of 3,799,100 dollars approved for the Force, the prorated share of 699,700 dollars of the estimated staff assessment income approved for the support account and the prorated share of 56,200 dollars of the estimated staff assessment income approved for the United Nations Logistics Base;

19. *Decides* that for Member States that have fulfilled their financial obligations to the Force, there shall be set off against their apportionment, as provided for in paragraph 17 above, their respective share of the unencumbered balance and other income in the total amount of 20,861,900 dollars in respect of the financial period ended 30 June 2002, in accordance with the levels set out in resolution 55/235, as adjusted by the General Assembly in its resolutions 55/236 and 57/290 A, and taking into account the scale of assessments for 2002, as set out in its resolutions 55/5 B and 57/4 B;

20. *Also decides* that, for Member States that have not fulfilled their financial obligations to the Force, their respective share of the unencumbered balance and other income in the total amount of 20,861,900 dollars in respect of the financial period ended 30 June 2002 shall be set off against their outstanding obligations in accordance with the scheme set out in paragraph 19 above;

21. *Further decides* that the increase of 398,800 dollars in the estimated staff assessment income in respect of the financial period ended 30 June 2002 shall be added to the credits from the amount referred to in paragraphs 19 and 20 above and that the respective shares of Member States therein shall be applied in accordance with the provisions of those paragraphs, as appropriate;

22. *Emphasizes* that no peacekeeping mission shall be financed by borrowing funds from other active peacekeeping missions;

23. *Encourages* the Secretary-General to continue to take additional measures to ensure the safety and security of all personnel under the auspices of the United Nations participating in the Force;

24. *Invites* voluntary contributions to the Force in cash and in the form of services and supplies acceptable to the Secretary-General, to be administered, as appropriate, in accordance with the procedure and practices established by the General Assembly;

25. *Decides* to include in the provisional agenda of its fifty-eighth session, under the item entitled "Financing of the United Nations peacekeeping forces in the Middle East", the sub-item entitled "United Nations Interim Force in Lebanon".

RECORDED VOTE ON RESOLUTION 57/325:

In favour: Albania, Algeria, Andorra, Antigua and Barbuda, Argentina, Armenia, Australia, Austria, Azerbaijan, Bahamas, Bahrain, Bangladesh, Barbados, Belarus, Belgium, Belize, Benin, Bhutan, Bolivia, Botswana, Brazil, Brunei Darussalam, Bulgaria, Burkina Faso, Canada, Cape Verde, Chile, China, Colombia, Congo, Costa Rica, Croatia, Cuba, Cyprus, Czech Republic, Democratic People's Republic of Korea, Denmark, Dominica, Dominican Republic, Egypt, Ethiopia, Fiji, Finland, France, Gabon, Gambia, Germany, Ghana, Greece, Grenada, Guatemala, Guinea, Guyana, Hungary, Iceland, India, Indonesia, Ireland, Italy, Jamaica, Japan, Jordan, Kazakhstan, Kenya, Kuwait, Lao People's Democratic Republic, Latvia, Lebanon, Lesotho, Libyan Arab Jamahiriya, Liechtenstein, Lithuania, Luxembourg, Malaysia, Mali, Malta, Mauritania, Mexico, Monaco, Mongolia, Morocco, Mozambique, Myanmar, Nepal, Netherlands, New Zealand, Nicaragua, Nigeria, Oman, Pakistan, Panama, Paraguay, Peru, Philippines, Poland, Qatar, Republic of Korea, Republic of Moldova, Romania, Russian Federation, Saint Lucia, Saudi Arabia, Senegal, Serbia and Montenegro, Sierra Leone, Singapore, Slovakia, Slovenia, Somalia, South Africa, Spain, Sri Lanka, Sudan, Sweden, Switzerland, Syrian Arab Republic, Thailand, The former Yugoslav Republic of Macedonia, Timor-Leste, Togo, Tonga, Trinidad and Tobago, Tunisia, Turkey, Uganda, Ukraine, United Arab Emirates, United Kingdom, United Republic of Tanzania, Uruguay, Venezuela, Viet Nam, Yemen, Zambia, Zimbabwe

Against: Israel, United States.

Subsequently, the delegations of Maldives, Mauritius and Portugal informed the Secretariat that they had intended to vote in favour.

The Assembly and the Committee each had adopted the fourth preambular paragraph and operative paragraphs 3, 4 and 14 by a single recorded vote of 85 to 2, with 45 abstentions, and 80 to 2, with 47 abstentions, respectively.

Syrian Arab Republic

In 2003, the General Assembly again called for Israel's withdrawal from the Golan Heights in the Syrian Arab Republic, which it had occupied since 1967. The area was effectively annexed by Israel when it extended its laws, jurisdiction and administration to the territory towards the end of 1981 [YUN 1981, p. 309].

Tension escalated in the region on 5 October, when, in retaliation to a suicide bombing attack carried out by Islamic Jihad in Haifa, Israeli military forces bombed a site inside Syrian territory. The Security Council convened on that same day in an emergency session to discuss the Israeli raid; no action was taken on a draft resolution submitted by Syria, though the Council decided to continue discussion of the subject in informal consultations.

Israeli policies and measures affecting the human rights of the population in the Golan Heights and other occupied territories were monitored by the Special Committee to Investigate Israeli Practices Affecting the Human Rights of the Palestinian People and Other Arabs of the Occupied Territories (Committee on Israeli Practices) and were the subject of resolutions adopted by the Commission on Human Rights (see PART TWO, Chapter III) and the Assembly.

Escalation of tension

Communications. On 5 October [S/2003/940], the Syrian Arab Republic informed the Secretary-General and the Security Council President that, on that day, the Israeli air force violated Syrian and Lebanese airspace and launched a missile attack in the village of Ain Al Sahib, north-west of the capital, Damascus, causing material damage. Syria invited the Council to convene an emergency meeting to consider the Israeli aggression.

Also on 5 October [S/2003/949], the League of Arab States (LAS) issued a statement, in which it declared that Israel's targeting of a civilian site in Syrian territory was a serious escalation that threatened regional security and a further defiance of all international charters and treaties and principles of international law. It called on the Council to bring an immediate and decisive end to Israeli occupation practices against the Palestinians and against Syria and Lebanon.

Security Council consideration (5 October). At the request of the Syrian Arab Republic [S/2003/939] and Lebanon [S/2003/943], the Security Council, on 5 October [meeting 4836], met to discuss the violations of Syrian and Lebanese airspace committed that day by the Israeli air force and the missile attack carried out by the latter against a civilian site situated inside Syrian territory. With the Council's consent, the President invited, among others, Israel and the Permanent Observers of LAS [S/2003/941] and Palestine [S/2003/942], at their request, to participate in the discussion without the right to vote.

Syria said that the act of aggression that Israel committed that day was part of the Israeli Government's strategic policy to escalate tension in the Middle East. Syria had exercised maximum self-restraint and had turned to the Council in order to condemn Israel's action. In that regard, it had officially submitted the text of a draft resolution that responded to the Israeli challenge, in accordance with the principles of the UN Charter.

Israel said that on 4 October a suicide bomber killed 19 Israelis and wounded at least 60 others inside a restaurant in the city of Haifa. According to Israel, Islamic Jihad, a terrorist organization that operated from PA territory, with its headquarters in Damascus, claimed responsibility for the attack. The attack in Haifa was the latest of over 40 atrocities committed by Islamic Jihad in the past few years. Among the many terrorist groups that operated and benefited from the auspices of Syria were Islamic Jihad, Hams, Hizbullah and the Popular Front for the Liberation of Palestine. Safe harbour and training facilities were provided throughout Syria for those terrorist organizations, both in separate facilities and in Syrian army bases. The Ein Saheb base, which was targeted on that day by Israel's measured defensive operation, was just one of those facilities sponsored by Syria and Iran. Recruits at camps such as Ein Saheb were taught how to assemble bombs, conduct kidnapping, prepare suicide belts and establish terrorist cells. Syria facilitated and directed acts of terrorism by coordination and briefings via phone and Internet and by calling activists to Damascus for consultations. Using the Syrian and Palestinian banking systems, Iran sustained a systematic money transfer system and large sums had been transferred to Islamic Jihad. Council resolution 1373(2001) [YUN 2001, p. 61] made clear that States were obligated to prevent acts of terrorism and refrain from any form of financing, support or toleration of terrorist groups. Israel's response to the suicide bombings against a terrorist training facility in Syria was a clear act of self-defence.

The United States called on all sides to avoid heightening the tension in the Middle East and to think carefully about the consequences of their actions. It also called on Syria to stop harbouring and supporting the groups that perpetrated terrorist acts such as the one that occurred in Haifa on 4 October.

Lebanon said that Israel's violations of relevant UN resolutions and of international agreements were the cause of the pain and turbulence throughout the Middle East. Israel's actions would only further fuel the cycle of violence. Lebanon hoped that the Council would condemn Israel's aggression against a Syrian village.

Following the meeting, in accordance with the understanding reached in prior consultations, the Council President invited the members to continue discussion of the subject in informal consultations.

Committee on Israeli Practices. In its annual report [A/58/311], the Committee on Israeli Practices stated that it had visited Damascus and Quneitra province, which bordered the occupied area, where it met with Syrian authorities and received information from witnesses with personal knowledge of the occupied Syrian Arab Golan. Syrian government officials emphasized that the situation of human rights in the occupied Syrian Golan had further deteriorated and that Israel was still pursuing its policy of occupation. In addition, the Israeli Government was offering compensation and favourable loans to encourage additional settlers to move into the occupied Golan during the next 10 years. At the same time, Israeli authorities continued to confiscate a large portion of land. Syrian villagers were also compelled to buy allocated water supplies at a higher price than those paid by Jewish settlers. Life in general was becoming increasingly difficult for the 500,000 Syrian Arabs, many of whom were refugees from the occupied Golan. For the first time, several checkpoints had been set up on the border separating Syria from the occupied Syrian Golan, which was perceived by the Syrians as a provocative measure since there was hardly any population movement from both sides of the borders.

Reports of Secretary-General. On 8 August [A/58/264], the Secretary-General reported that no reply had been received from Israel to his June request for information on steps taken or envisaged to implement General Assembly resolution 57/128 [YUN 2002, p. 482], which called on Israel to desist from changing the physical character, demographic composition, institutional structure and legal status of the Golan, and from its repressive measures against the population.

By a 13 August report [A/58/278], the Secretary-General transmitted replies received from eight Member States, including Israel, in response to his request for information on steps taken or envisaged to implement Assembly resolution 57/112 [YUN 2002, p. 481], which dealt with Israeli policies in the Syrian territory occupied since 1967, and resolution 57/111 [ibid., p. 444], on the transfer by some States of their diplomatic missions to Jerusalem (see p. 484).

GENERAL ASSEMBLY ACTION

On 3 December [meeting 68], the General Assembly adopted **resolution 58/23** [draft: A/58/L.28 & Add.1] by recorded vote (104-5-61) [agenda item 37].

The Syrian Golan

The General Assembly,

Having considered the item entitled "The situation in the Middle East",

Taking note of the report of the Secretary-General,

Recalling Security Council resolution 497(1981) of 17 December 1981,

Reaffirming the fundamental principle of the inadmissibility of the acquisition of territory by force, in accordance with international law and the Charter of the United Nations,

Reaffirming once more the applicability of the Geneva Convention relative to the Protection of Civilian Persons in Time of War, of 12 August 1949, to the occupied Syrian Golan,

Deeply concerned that Israel has not withdrawn from the Syrian Golan, which has been under occupation since 1967, contrary to the relevant Security Council and General Assembly resolutions,

Stressing the illegality of the Israeli settlement construction and other activities in the occupied Syrian Golan since 1967,

Noting with satisfaction the convening in Madrid on 30 October 1991 of the Peace Conference on the Middle East, on the basis of Security Council resolutions 242(1967) of 22 November 1967, 338(1973) of 22 October 1973 and 425(1978) of 19 March 1978 and the formula of land for peace,

Expressing grave concern over the halt in the peace process on the Syrian track, and expressing the hope that peace talks will soon resume from the point they had reached,

1. *Declares* that Israel has failed so far to comply with Security Council resolution 497(1981);

2. *Also declares* that the Israeli decision of 14 December 1981 to impose its laws, jurisdiction and administration on the occupied Syrian Golan is null and void and has no validity whatsoever, as confirmed by the Security Council in its resolution 497(1981), and calls upon Israel to rescind it;

3. *Reaffirms its determination* that all relevant provisions of the Regulations annexed to the Hague Convention of 1907, and the Geneva Convention relative to the Protection of Civilian Persons in Time of War, continue to apply to the Syrian territory occupied by Israel since 1967, and calls upon the parties thereto to respect and ensure respect for their obligations under those instruments in all circumstances;

4. *Determines once more* that the continued occupation of the Syrian Golan and its de facto annexation constitute a stumbling block in the way of achieving a just, comprehensive and lasting peace in the region;

5. *Calls upon* Israel to resume the talks on the Syrian and Lebanese tracks and to respect the commitments and undertakings reached during the previous talks;

6. *Demands once more* that Israel withdraw from all the occupied Syrian Golan to the line of 4 June 1967 in implementation of the relevant Security Council resolutions;

7. *Calls upon* all the parties concerned, the co-sponsors of the peace process and the entire international community to exert all the necessary efforts to ensure the resumption of the peace process and its success by implementing Security Council resolutions 242(1967) and 338(1973);

8. *Requests* the Secretary-General to report to the General Assembly at its fifty-ninth session on the implementation of the present resolution.

RECORDED VOTE ON RESOLUTION 58/23:

In favour: Afghanistan, Algeria, Antigua and Barbuda, Argentina, Armenia, Azerbaijan, Bahamas, Bahrain, Bangladesh, Barbados, Belarus, Belize, Bolivia, Botswana, Brazil, Brunei Darussalam, Burkina Faso, Burundi, Cambodia, Cape Verde, Chile, China, Colombia, Comoros, Congo, Côte d'Ivoire, Cuba, Cyprus, Djibouti, Ecuador, Egypt, Eritrea, Ethiopia, Fiji, Gabon, Ghana, Grenada, Guinea, Guinea-Bissau, Guyana, Haiti, India, Indonesia, Iran, Jamaica, Jordan, Kenya, Kuwait, Kyrgyzstan, Lao People's Democratic Republic, Lebanon, Lesotho, Libyan Arab Jamahiriya, Madagascar, Malaysia, Maldives, Mali, Mauritania, Mauritius, Mexico, Mongolia, Morocco, Mozambique, Myanmar, Namibia, Nepal, Niger, Nigeria, Oman, Pakistan, Panama, Paraguay, Philippines, Qatar, Russian Federation, Saint Lucia, Saint Vincent and the Grenadines, Saudi Arabia, Senegal, Seychelles, Sierra Leone, Singapore, Somalia, South Africa, Sri Lanka, Sudan, Suriname, Swaziland, Syrian Arab Republic, Tajikistan, Thailand, Timor-Leste, Togo, Trinidad and Tobago, Tunisia, Turkey, Turkmenistan, United Arab Emirates, United Republic of Tanzania, Venezuela, Viet Nam, Yemen, Zambia, Zimbabwe.

Against: Israel, Marshall Islands, Micronesia, Palau, United States.

Abstaining: Albania, Andorra, Australia, Austria, Belgium, Bosnia and Herzegovina, Bulgaria, Canada, Costa Rica, Croatia, Czech Republic, Denmark, Dominican Republic, El Salvador, Estonia, Finland, France, Georgia, Germany, Greece, Guatemala, Honduras, Hungary, Iceland, Ireland, Italy, Japan, Kazakhstan, Latvia, Liechtenstein, Lithuania, Luxembourg, Malta, Monaco, Nauru, Netherlands, New Zealand, Nicaragua, Norway, Peru, Poland, Portugal, Republic of Korea, Republic of Moldova, Romania, Rwanda, Samoa, San Marino, Serbia and Montenegro, Slovakia, Slovenia, Solomon Islands, Spain, Sweden, Switzerland, The former Yugoslav Republic of Macedonia, Tonga, Uganda, Ukraine, United Kingdom, Uruguay.

On 9 December [meeting 72], the Assembly, under the agenda item on the report of the Committee on Israeli Practices and on the Fourth Committee's recommendation [A/58/473 & Corr.1], adopted **resolution 58/100** by recorded vote (163-1-11) [agenda item 84].

The occupied Syrian Golan

The General Assembly,

Having considered the report of the Special Committee to Investigate Israeli Practices Affecting the Human Rights of the Palestinian People and Other Arabs of the Occupied Territories,

Deeply concerned that the Syrian Golan, occupied since 1967, has been under continued Israeli military occupation,

Recalling Security Council resolution 497(1981) of 17 December 1981,

Recalling also its previous relevant resolutions, the last of which was resolution 57/128 of 11 December 2002,

Having considered the report of the Secretary-General submitted in pursuance of resolution 57/128,

Recalling its previous relevant resolutions in which, inter alia, it called upon Israel to put an end to its occupation of the Arab territories,

Reaffirming once more the illegality of the decision of 14 December 1981 taken by Israel to impose its laws, jurisdiction and administration on the occupied Syrian Golan, which has resulted in the effective annexation of that territory,

Reaffirming that the acquisition of territory by force is inadmissible under international law, including the Charter of the United Nations,

Reaffirming also the applicability of the Geneva Convention relative to the Protection of Civilian Persons in Time of War, of 12 August 1949, to the occupied Syrian Golan,

Bearing in mind Security Council resolution 237 (1967) of 14 June 1967,

Welcoming the convening at Madrid of the Peace Conference on the Middle East on the basis of Security Council resolutions 242(1967) of 22 November 1967 and 338(1973) of 22 October 1973 aimed at the realization of a just, comprehensive and lasting peace, and expressing grave concern about the stalling of the peace process on all tracks,

1. *Calls upon* Israel, the occupying Power, to comply with the relevant resolutions on the occupied Syrian Golan, in particular Security Council resolution 497 (1981), in which the Council, inter alia, decided that the Israeli decision to impose its laws, jurisdiction and administration on the occupied Syrian Golan was null and void and without international legal effect, and demanded that Israel, the occupying Power, rescind forthwith its decision;

2. *Also calls upon* Israel to desist from changing the physical character, demographic composition, institutional structure and legal status of the occupied Syrian Golan and in particular to desist from the establishment of settlements;

3. *Determines* that all legislative and administrative measures and actions taken or to be taken by Israel, the occupying Power, that purport to alter the character and legal status of the occupied Syrian Golan are null and void, constitute a flagrant violation of international law and of the Geneva Convention relative to the Protection of Civilian Persons in Time of War, of 12 August 1949, and have no legal effect;

4. *Calls upon* Israel to desist from imposing Israeli citizenship and Israeli identity cards on the Syrian citizens in the occupied Syrian Golan and from its repressive measures against the population of the occupied Syrian Golan;

5. *Deplores* the violations by Israel of the Geneva Convention relative to the Protection of Civilian Persons in Time of War, of 12 August 1949;

6. *Calls once again upon* Member States not to recognize any of the legislative or administrative measures and actions referred to above;

7. *Requests* the Secretary-General to report to the General Assembly at its fifty-ninth session on the implementation of the present resolution.

RECORDED VOTE ON RESOLUTION 58/100:

In favour: Afghanistan, Albania, Algeria, Andorra, Angola, Antigua and Barbuda, Argentina, Armenia, Australia, Austria, Azerbaijan, Bahamas, Bahrain, Bangladesh, Barbados, Belarus, Belgium, Belize, Benin, Bhutan, Bolivia, Bosnia and Herzegovina, Botswana, Brazil, Brunei Darussalam, Bulgaria, Burkina Faso, Burundi, Cambodia, Canada, Cape Verde, Chile, China, Colombia, Comoros, Costa Rica, Côte d'Ivoire, Croatia, Cuba, Cyprus, Czech Republic, Democratic People's Republic of Korea, Denmark, Djibouti, Dominican Republic, Ecuador, Egypt, El Salvador, Eritrea, Estonia, Ethiopia, Fiji, Finland, France, Gabon, Gambia, Georgia, Germany, Ghana, Greece, Grenada, Guatemala, Guinea, Guinea-Bissau, Guyana, Haiti, Hungary, Iceland, India, Indonesia, Iran, Ireland, Italy, Jamaica, Japan, Jordan, Kazakhstan, Kenya, Kuwait, Kyrgyzstan, Lao People's Democratic Republic, Latvia, Lebanon, Lesotho, Libyan Arab Jamahiriya, Liechtenstein, Lithuania, Luxembourg, Madagascar, Malaysia, Maldives, Mali, Malta, Mauritania, Mauritius, Mexico, Monaco, Mongolia, Morocco, Mozambique, Myanmar, Namibia, Nepal, Netherlands, New Zealand, Nicaragua, Niger, Nigeria, Norway, Oman, Pakistan, Panama, Papua New Guinea, Paraguay, Peru, Philippines, Poland, Portugal, Qatar, Republic of Korea, Republic of Moldova, Romania, Russian Federation, Saint Lucia, Saint Vincent and the Grenadines, Samoa, San Marino, Saudi Arabia, Senegal, Serbia and Montenegro, Seychelles, Singapore, Slovakia, Slovenia, Somalia, South Africa, Spain, Sri Lanka, Sudan, Suriname, Swaziland, Sweden, Switzerland, Syrian Arab Republic, Tajikistan, Thailand, The former Yugoslav Republic of Macedonia, Timor-Leste, Togo, Trinidad and Tobago, Tunisia, Turkey, Turkmenistan, Ukraine, United Arab Emirates, United Kingdom, United Republic of Tanzania, Uruguay, Venezuela, Viet Nam, Yemen, Zambia, Zimbabwe.

Against: Israel.

Abstaining: Cameroon, Equatorial Guinea, Honduras, Marshall Islands, Micronesia, Nauru, Palau, Rwanda, Tonga, Tuvalu, United States.

UNDOF

The mandate of the United Nations Disengagement Observer Force, established by Security Council resolution 350(1974) [YUN 1974, p. 205] to supervise the observance of the ceasefire between Israel and the Syrian Arab Republic in the Golan Heights and ensure the separation of their forces, was renewed twice in 2003, in June and December, each time for a six-month period.

UNDOF maintained an area of separation, which was some 80 kilometres long and varied in width between approximately 10 kilometres in the centre to less than 1 kilometre in the extreme south. The area of separation was inhabited and policed by the Syrian authorities, and no military forces other than UNDOF were permitted within it.

As at 30 November, UNDOF comprised 1,046 troops from Austria (365), Canada (188), Japan (45), Poland (353) and Slovakia (95). It was assisted by 78 UNTSO military observers. The Secretary-General appointed Major General Franciszek Gagor (Poland) as Force Commander from 13 August [S/2003/726] to succeed Major General Bo Wranker (Sweden), who completed his tour of duty on 12 August. The Security Council took note of the Secretary-General's intention on 18 July [S/2003/727].

Reports of Secretary-General. The Secretary-General reported to the Security Council on UNDOF activities between 6 December 2002 and 18 June 2003 [S/2003/655] and between 19 June and 9 December 2003 [S/2003/1148]. Both reports noted that the UNDOF area of operation remained calm, except in the Shab'a farms area (see

p. 520). The ceasefire in the Israel-Syria sector remained generally quiet, with the exception of a 5 October Israeli air strike on a target north-west of Damascus (see p. 522). UNDOF continued in 2003 to supervise the area of separation between Israeli and Syrian troops in the Golan Heights, to ensure that no military forces of either party were deployed there, by means of fixed positions and patrols. The Force, accompanied by liaison officers from the party concerned, carried out fortnightly inspections of equipment and force levels in the area of limitation. As in the past, both sides denied inspection teams access to some of their positions and imposed restrictions on the Force's freedom of movement. Mines, especially in the area of separation, continued to pose a threat to UNDOF personnel and local inhabitants. The Force supported the United Nations Children's Fund in mine-awareness activities.

UNDOF assisted ICRC with facilities for mail and the passage of persons through the area of separation. Within the means available, medical treatment was provided to the local population on request.

The Secretary-General observed that tension in the Israel-Syria sector had been high since the Israeli air strike of 5 October. The overall situation in the Middle East was also very tense and was likely to remain so, unless and until a comprehensive settlement covering all aspects of the problem could be reached. He hoped that determined efforts would be made by all concerned to tackle the problem, with a view to arriving at a just and durable peace settlement, as called for by Security Council resolution 338(1973) [YUN 1973, p. 213]. Stating that he considered the Force's continued presence in the area to be essential, the Secretary-General, with the agreement of both Israel and Syria, recommended that UNDOF's mandate be extended until 31 December 2003 in the first instance and until 30 June 2004 in the second.

SECURITY COUNCIL ACTION

On 23 June [meeting 4778], the Security Council held a closed meeting and had a constructive exchange of views with UNDOF troop-contributing countries.

On 26 June [meeting 4779], the Council unanimously adopted **resolution 1488(2003)**. The draft [S/2003/668] was prepared in consultations among Council members.

The Security Council,

Having considered the report of the Secretary-General of 18 June 2003 on the United Nations Disengagement Observer Force, and reaffirming its resolution 1308(2000) of 17 July 2000,

1. *Calls upon* the parties concerned to implement immediately Security Council resolution 338(1973) of 22 October 1973;
2. *Decides* to renew the mandate of the United Nations Disengagement Observer Force for a period of six months, that is, until 31 December 2003;
3. *Requests* the Secretary-General to submit, at the end of this period, a report on the developments in the situation and the measures taken to implement resolution 338(1973).

On 11 December, the Council, in a closed meeting [meeting 4878], had an exchange of views with UNDOF troop-contributing countries and heard a briefing from the Director of the Asia and Middle East Division of the Department of Peacekeeping Operations.

On 22 December [meeting 4889], the Council unanimously adopted **resolution 1520(2003)**. The draft [S/2003/1176] was prepared during consultations among Council members.

The Security Council,

Having considered the report of the Secretary-General of 9 December 2003 on the United Nations Disengagement Observer Force, and reaffirming its resolution 1308(2000) of 17 July 2000,

1. *Calls upon* the parties concerned to implement immediately its resolution 338(1973) of 22 October 1973;
2. *Decides* to renew the mandate of the United Nations Disengagement Observer Force for a period of six months, that is, until 30 June 2004;
3. *Requests* the Secretary-General to submit, at the end of this period, a report on the developments in the situation and the measures taken to implement resolution 338(1973).

After the adoption of each resolution, the President, following consultations among Council members, made identical statements **S/PRST/2003/9** [meeting 4779] on 26 June and **S/PRST/2003/29** [meeting 4889] on 22 December, on behalf of the Council:

In connection with the resolution just adopted on the renewal of the mandate of the United Nations Disengagement Observer Force, I have been authorized to make the following complementary statement on behalf of the Security Council:

As is known, the report of the Secretary-General on the United Nations Disengagement Observer Force states in paragraph 11: "The situation in the Middle East is very tense and is likely to remain so unless and until a comprehensive settlement covering all aspects of the Middle East problem can be reached". That statement of the Secretary-General reflects the view of the Security Council.

Financing

Reports of Secretary-General and ACABQ. On 18 December 2002, the Secretary-General presented a performance report on UNDOF's budget for the period from 1 July 2001 to 30 June 2002

[A/57/668]. Expenditures totalled $34,422,900 gross ($33,464,700 net), resulting in an unencumbered balance of $113,400. On 19 December, he submitted UNDOF's budget for the period from 1 July 2003 to 30 June 2004 [A/57/688], totalling $40,212,900 gross ($39,192,400 net). On 6 February 2003, he also submitted an overview report on the financing of UN peacekeeping operations: budget performance for the period from 1 July 2001 to 30 June 2002 and budget for the period from 1 July 2003 to 30 June 2004 [A/57/723].

ACABQ's comments and recommendations on the two December reports were contained in an April report to the Assembly [A/57/772/Add.7].

GENERAL ASSEMBLY ACTION

On 18 June [meeting 90], the General Assembly, on the recommendation of the Fifth Committee [A/57/837], adopted **resolution 57/324** without vote [agenda item 127 (a)].

Financing of the United Nations Disengagement Observer Force

The General Assembly,

Having considered the reports of the Secretary-General on the financing of the United Nations Disengagement Observer Force and the related reports of the Advisory Committee on Administrative and Budgetary Questions,

Recalling Security Council resolution 350(1974) of 31 May 1974 regarding the establishment of the United Nations Disengagement Observer Force and the subsequent resolutions by which the Council extended the mandate of the Force, the latest of which was resolution 1451(2002) of 17 December 2002,

Recalling also its resolution 3211 B (XXIX) of 29 November 1974 on the financing of the United Nations Emergency Force and of the United Nations Disengagement Observer Force, and its subsequent resolutions thereon, the latest of which was resolution 56/294 of 27 June 2002,

Reaffirming the general principles underlying the financing of United Nations peacekeeping operations, as stated in General Assembly resolutions 1874(S-IV) of 27 June 1963, 3101(XXVIII) of 11 December 1973 and 55/235 of 23 December 2000,

Mindful of the fact that it is essential to provide the Force with the necessary financial resources to enable it to fulfil its responsibilities under the relevant resolutions of the Security Council,

1. *Takes note* of the status of contributions to the United Nations Disengagement Observer Force as at 31 March 2003, including the contributions outstanding in the amount of 25.7 million United States dollars, representing some 2 per cent of the total assessed contributions, notes with concern that only thirty-three Member States have paid their assessed contributions in full, and urges all other Member States, in particular those in arrears, to ensure payment of their outstanding assessed contributions;

2. *Expresses its appreciation* to those Member States which have paid their assessed contributions in full;

3. *Expresses concern* at the financial situation with regard to peacekeeping activities, in particular as regards the reimbursements to troop contributors that bear additional burdens owing to overdue payments by Member States of their assessments;

4. *Urges* all Member States to make every possible effort to ensure payment of their assessed contributions to the Force in full;

5. *Expresses concern* at the delay experienced by the Secretary-General in deploying and providing adequate resources to some recent peacekeeping missions, in particular those in Africa;

6. *Emphasizes* that all future and existing peacekeeping missions shall be given equal and non-discriminatory treatment in respect of financial and administrative arrangements;

7. *Also emphasizes* that all peacekeeping missions shall be provided with adequate resources for the effective and efficient discharge of their respective mandates;

8. *Reiterates its request* to the Secretary-General to make the fullest possible use of facilities and equipment at the United Nations Logistics Base at Brindisi, Italy, in order to minimize the costs of procurement for the Force;

9. *Takes note* of the observation contained in paragraph 20 of the report of the Advisory Committee on Administrative and Budgetary Questions and endorses the remaining conclusions and recommendations, and requests the Secretary-General to ensure their full implementation, without prejudice to a future discussion and decision on the proposal to create the post of Deputy Force Commander, subject to the provisions of the present resolution;

10. *Authorizes* the Secretary-General to fill the three general staff posts referred to in paragraph 22 of the report of the Advisory Committee for a period not to exceed one year, and invites the Secretary-General to resubmit with full justification this request in connection with the budget request for the period from 1 July 2004 to 30 June 2005;

11. *Invites* the Secretary-General to resubmit with full justification his request concerning the proposed upgrade of the Chief Administrative Officer in connection with the budget proposal for the period from 1 July 2004 to 30 June 2005;

12. *Decides* to eliminate the vacant Field Service driver position in the Office of the Force Commander;

13. *Requests* the Secretary-General to take all necessary action to ensure that the Force is administered with a maximum of efficiency and economy;

14. *Also requests* the Secretary-General, in order to reduce the cost of employing General Service staff, to continue efforts to recruit local staff for the Force against General Service posts, commensurate with the requirements of the Force;

15. *Notes with appreciation* the implementation of paragraph 10 of its resolution 56/294 through making allowance for difficulties resulting from the relocation of the headquarters of the Force from Damascus to Camp Faouar;

16. *Welcomes* the Secretary-General's observation in paragraph 17 of his report that all outstanding issues have been satisfactorily resolved, and in this regard recognizes the need for continuing dialogue between staff and management, consistent with the existing mechanisms in all peacekeeping missions;

17. *Requests* the Secretary-General to ensure that the modernization programme should fully respect the relevant mandates of the United Nations Disengagement Observer Force and the United Nations Truce Supervision Organization;

Financial performance report for the period from 1 July 2001 to 30 June 2002

18. *Takes note* of the report of the Secretary-General on the financial performance of the Force for the period from 1 July 2001 to 30 June 2002;

Budget estimates for the period from 1 July 2003 to 30 June 2004

19. *Decides* to appropriate to the Special Account for the United Nations Disengagement Observer Force the amount of 41,812,200 dollars for the period from 1 July 2003 to 30 June 2004, inclusive of 40,009,200 dollars for the maintenance of the Force, 1,380,600 dollars for the support account for peacekeeping operations, and 422,400 dollars for the United Nations Logistics Base;

Financing of the appropriation

20. *Decides also* to apportion among Member States the amount of 41,812,200 dollars at a monthly rate of 3,484,350 dollars, in accordance with the levels set out in resolution 55/235, as adjusted by the General Assembly in its resolutions 55/236 of 23 December 2000 and 57/290 A of 20 December 2002, and taking into account the scale of assessments for 2003, as set out in its resolutions 55/5 B of 23 December 2000 and 57/4 B of 20 December 2002, and for 2004, subject to a decision of the Security Council to extend the mandate of the Force;

21. *Decides further* that, in accordance with the provisions of its resolution 973(X) of 15 December 1955, there shall be set off against the apportionment among Member States, as provided for in paragraph 20 above, their respective share in the Tax Equalization Fund of 1,318,100 dollars at a monthly rate of 109,842 dollars, comprising the estimated staff assessment income of 982,100 dollars approved for the Force, the prorated share of 311,000 dollars of the estimated staff assessment income approved for the support account, and the prorated share of 25,000 dollars of the estimated staff assessment income approved for the United Nations Logistics Base;

22. *Decides* that for Member States that have fulfilled their financial obligations to the Force, there shall be set off against their apportionment, as provided for in paragraph 20 above, their respective share of the unencumbered balance and other income in the total amount of 2,488,400 dollars in respect of the financial period ended 30 June 2002, in accordance with the levels set out in resolution 55/235, as adjusted by the General Assembly in its resolutions 55/236 and 57/290 A, and taking into account the scale of assessments for 2002, as set out in its resolutions 55/5 B and 57/4 B;

23. *Decides also* that for Member States that have not fulfilled their financial obligations to the Force, their respective share of the unencumbered balance and other income in the total amount of 2,488,400 dollars in respect of the financial period ended 30 June 2002 shall be set off against their outstanding obligations in accordance with the scheme set out in paragraph 22 above;

24. *Decides further* that the increase of 200,800 dollars in the estimated staff assessment income in respect of the financial period ended 30 June 2002 shall be added to the credits from the amount referred to in paragraphs 22 and 23 above, and that the respective shares of Member States therein shall be applied in accordance with the provisions of those paragraphs as appropriate;

25. *Emphasizes* that no peacekeeping mission shall be financed by borrowing funds from other active peacekeeping missions;

26. *Encourages* the Secretary-General to continue to take additional measures to ensure the safety and security of all personnel under the auspices of the United Nations participating in the Force;

27. *Invites* voluntary contributions to the Force in cash and in the form of services and supplies acceptable to the Secretary-General, to be administered, as appropriate, in accordance with the procedure and practices established by the General Assembly;

28. *Decides* to include in the provisional agenda of its fifty-eighth session, under the item entitled "Financing of the United Nations peacekeeping forces in the Middle East", the sub-item entitled "United Nations Disengagement Observer Force".

Chapter VII

Disarmament

In 2003, despite continuing differences among Member States on many disarmament issues, progress was made in addressing problems relating to small arms and light weapons, and in promoting transparency in armaments.

The Conference on Disarmament did not reach consensus on a comprehensive programme of work, which made it unable, for the fifth consecutive year, to take action on its agenda items. Marked disagreements among Member States also prevented the Disarmament Commission from adopting concrete proposals on substantive issues.

Member States, UN bodies and regional and subregional organizations pressed forward with measures and activities to implement the Programme of Action adopted by the 2001 UN Conference on the Illicit Trade in Small Arms and Light Weapons in All Its Aspects, including through weapons collection and destruction and other practical disarmament measures. The first biennial meeting of States on the implementation process reviewed experiences in coping with related problems. The Group of Governmental Experts established to address the issue of tracing illicit stockpiles of the weapons concluded that it was desirable to develop an international instrument to enable States to identify and trace them in a timely and reliable manner. The General Assembly established an open-ended working group to begin negotiations on the instrument and decided to convene, in 2006, a UN conference to review progress made in implementing the Programme of Action.

In April and May, the First Review Conference of the States parties to the Convention on the Prohibition of the Development, Stockpiling and Use of Chemical Weapons and on Their Destruction reviewed the Convention's operation and considered its role in enhancing international peace and security, as well as measures to ensure its universality. In November, the first of three scheduled annual meetings of States parties to the Convention on the Prohibition of the Development, Production and Stockpiling of Bacteriological (Biological) and Toxin Weapons and on Their Destruction considered the adoption of national measures to implement the prohibitions set forth in the Convention and national mechanisms to establish and maintain the security and oversight of pathogenic micro-organisms and toxins. A November meeting of the States parties to the 1980 Convention on Prohibitions or Restrictions on the Use of Certain Conventional Weapons Which May Be Deemed to Be Excessively Injurious or to Have Indiscriminate Effects adopted a new legally binding instrument, Protocol V, on Explosive Remnants of War and related weapons, which would be annexed to the Convention.

In August, the Group of Governmental Experts on the continuing operation and further development of the UN Register of Conventional Arms recommended a number of measures to enhance its effectiveness and global relevance. The Secretary-General established a Group of Governmental Experts mandated to undertake the second review since 1981 of the relationship between disarmament and development, for consideration in 2004.

In June, the 2002 Strategic Offensive Reductions Treaty (SORT) between the United States and the Russian Federation entered into force. SORT, also known as the Moscow Treaty, established a new strategic framework for further reductions of the parties' strategic offensive weapons.

UN role in disarmament

UN machinery

Disarmament issues before the United Nations were considered mainly through the General Assembly and its First (Disarmament and International Security) Committee, the Disarmament Commission (a deliberative body) and the Conference on Disarmament (a multilateral negotiating forum, which met in Geneva).

The Department for Disarmament Affairs of the UN Secretariat continued to support the work of Member States and treaty bodies, to service the Advisory Board on Disarmament Matters and to administer the UN disarmament fellowship programme.

General Assembly issues

Fourth special session devoted to disarmament

The General Assembly had decided, by resolution 51/45 C [YUN 1996, p. 447], to convene the fourth special session of the Assembly devoted to disarmament in 1999, subject to the emergence of a consensus on its agenda and objectives, which had not been achieved.

In 2002, the Assembly, in resolution 57/61 [YUN 2002, p. 487], established an open-ended working group to consider, on the basis of consensus, the objectives and agenda of the special session and to make substantive recommendations thereon.

Working group activities. The Open-ended Working Group to consider the objectives and agenda of the fourth special session of the General Assembly devoted to disarmament held three sessions (New York, 10-14 March, 19-23 May and 23-27 June) [A/57/848] and conducted informal consultations during an intersessional period. The Group, in accordance with its mandate, also considered the possible establishment of a preparatory committee for the special session. The Chairman, in an effort to facilitate agreement, prepared a working paper [A/AC.268/2003/WP.3] containing salient points from various proposals and views put forth by the Non-Aligned Movement, the European Union (EU) and other delegations. As the Group was unable to reach consensus on any of the agenda items, on 27 June it adopted its report to the Assembly, which was limited to procedural questions. The Group underlined the need to refer back to the Assembly for consideration the session's objectives and agenda.

On 15 September, the Assembly took note of the Group's report (**decision 57/592**).

On 8 December, the Assembly, taking further note of the Group's report and of the requests made for Member States to continue consultations, decided to include in the provisional agenda of its fifty-ninth (2004) session the item entitled "Convening of the fourth special session of the General Assembly devoted to disarmament" (**decision 58/521**).

Disarmament Commission

In 2003, the Disarmament Commission, composed of all UN Member States, held six plenary meetings (New York, 31 March–17 April) [A/58/42] and an organizational meeting on 6 November [A/59/42], at which the Commission considered the agenda items "Ways and means to achieve nuclear disarmament" (see p. 535) and "Practical confidence-building measures in the field of conventional arms" (see p. 567). The Commission did not reach consensus on concrete proposals regarding either of the two items. The Commission decided that its next substantive session would be held in April 2004 and requested its Chairman to undertake informal consultations as to the agenda items to be considered. Although the Chairman held 35 such consultations with various groups of States and delegations, a lack of consensus persisted.

GENERAL ASSEMBLY ACTION

On 8 December [meeting 71], the General Assembly, on the recommendation of the First Committee [A/58/464], adopted **resolution 58/67** without vote [agenda item 75 (c)].

Report of the Disarmament Commission

The General Assembly,

Having considered the report of the Disarmament Commission,

Recalling its resolutions 47/54 A of 9 December 1992, 47/54 G of 8 April 1993, 48/77 A of 16 December 1993, 49/77 A of 15 December 1994, 50/72 D of 12 December 1995, 51/47 B of 10 December 1996, 52/40 B of 9 December 1997, 53/79 A of 4 December 1998, 54/56 A of 1 December 1999, 55/35 C of 20 November 2000, 56/26 A of 29 November 2001 and 57/95 of 22 November 2002,

Considering the role that the Disarmament Commission has been called upon to play and the contribution that it should make in examining and submitting recommendations on various problems in the field of disarmament and in the promotion of the implementation of the relevant decisions adopted by the General Assembly at its tenth special session,

Bearing in mind its decision 52/492 of 8 September 1998,

1. *Takes note* of the report of the Disarmament Commission;
2. *Reaffirms* the importance of further enhancing the dialogue and cooperation among the First Committee, the Disarmament Commission and the Conference on Disarmament;
3. *Also reaffirms* the role of the Disarmament Commission as the specialized, deliberative body within the United Nations multilateral disarmament machinery that allows for in-depth deliberations on specific disarmament issues, leading to the submission of concrete recommendations on those issues;
4. *Requests* the Disarmament Commission to continue its work in accordance with its mandate, as set forth in paragraph 118 of the Final Document of the Tenth Special Session of the General Assembly, and with paragraph 3 of Assembly resolution 37/78 H of 9 December 1982, and to that end to make every effort to achieve specific recommendations on the items on its agenda, taking into account the adopted "Ways and means to enhance the functioning of the Disarmament Commission";
5. *Recommends* that the Disarmament Commission consider the following items at its 2004 substantive session:

(a) [To be determined];

(b) [To be determined];

6. *Requests* the Disarmament Commission to meet for a period not exceeding three weeks during 2004, namely, from 5 to 23 April, and to submit a substantive report to the General Assembly at its fifty-ninth session;

7. *Requests* the Secretary-General to transmit to the Disarmament Commission the annual report of the Conference on Disarmament, together with all the official records of the fifty-eighth session of the General Assembly relating to disarmament matters, and to render all assistance that the Commission may require for implementing the present resolution;

8. *Also requests* the Secretary-General to ensure full provision to the Disarmament Commission and its subsidiary bodies of interpretation and translation facilities in the official languages and to assign, as a matter of priority, all the necessary resources and services, including verbatim records, to that end;

9. *Decides* to include in the provisional agenda of its fifty-ninth session the item entitled "Report of the Disarmament Commission".

Conference on Disarmament

The Conference on Disarmament, a multilateral negotiating body, held a three-part session in Geneva in 2003 (20 January–28 March, 12 May–27 June and 28 July–10 September) [A/58/27].

The Conference again considered the cessation of the nuclear arms race and nuclear disarmament; prevention of nuclear war; prevention of an arms race in outer space; effective international arrangements to assure non-nuclear-weapon States against the use or threat of use of nuclear weapons; new types of weapons of mass destruction (WMDs) and new systems of such weapons; radiological weapons; a comprehensive programme of disarmament; and transparency in armaments.

During the session, successive Presidents of the Conference conducted consultations, with a view to reaching consensus on the programme of work. However, the Conference did not agree on a programme of work and did not establish or re-establish any mechanism to deal with the agenda items. In an effort to break the impasse that had undermined progress in the Conference for many years, five former Presidents (Algeria, Belgium, Chile, Colombia, Sweden), whose previous joint proposal [YUN 2002, p. 489] was not agreed upon, introduced in 2003 another cross-group proposal ("A-5 proposal") on the work programme [CD/1693/Rev.1]. The proposal included a presidential declaration by which the Conference would have decided to establish a programme of work and required Member States to build on converging points that could lead to international instruments acceptable to all. The proposal envisaged the establishment of ad hoc committees on negative security assurances, nuclear disarmament, a treaty banning the production of fissile material for nuclear weapons or other nuclear explosive devices and prevention of an arms race in outer space. It also envisaged the appointment of three special coordinators to deal with new types of WMDs and new systems of such weapons, a comprehensive programme of disarmament and transparency in armaments. Although many delegations expressed support for the proposal, the consensus sought remained elusive for the fifth consecutive year. Thus, the Conference concluded its 2003 session without reaching agreement on a programme of work. It decided to hold its 2004 session between January and September, and requested its current President and the incoming President to hold consultations during the intersessional period and to make recommendations, taking into account relevant proposals, views and discussions.

GENERAL ASSEMBLY ACTION

On 8 December [meeting 71], the General Assembly, on the recommendation of the First Committee [A/58/464], adopted **resolution 58/66** without vote [agenda item 75 *(d)*].

Report of the Conference on Disarmament

The General Assembly,

Having considered the report of the Conference on Disarmament,

Convinced that the Conference on Disarmament, as the single multilateral disarmament negotiating forum of the international community, has the primary role in substantive negotiations on priority questions of disarmament,

Recognizing the need to conduct multilateral negotiations with the aim of reaching agreement on concrete issues,

Recalling, in this respect, that the Conference has a number of urgent and important issues for negotiation,

Taking note of active discussions held on the programme of work during the 2003 session of the Conference, as duly reflected in the report and the records of the plenary meetings,

Taking note also of significant contributions made during the 2003 session to promote substantive discussions on issues on the agenda in the plenary meetings, as well as of discussions held on other issues that could also be relevant to the current international security environment,

Stressing the urgent need for the Conference to commence substantive work on its agreed agenda items at this juncture,

1. *Reaffirms* the role of the Conference on Disarmament as the single multilateral disarmament negotiating forum of the international community;

2. *Urges* the Conference to fulfil that role in the light of the evolving international situation, with a view to making early substantive progress on priority items on its agenda;

3. *Welcomes* the strong collective interest of the Conference in commencing substantive work as soon as possible during its 2004 session;

4. *Also welcomes* the decision of the Conference to request its current President and the incoming President to conduct consultations during the inter-sessional period and, if possible, to make recommendations, taking into account all relevant proposals, including that contained in CD/1693/Rev.1, views presented and discussions held, and to endeavour to keep the membership of the Conference informed, as appropriate, of their consultations, as expressed in paragraph 38 of its report;

5. *Requests* all States members of the Conference to cooperate with the current President and successive Presidents in their efforts to guide the Conference to the early commencement of substantive work in its 2004 session;

6. *Requests* the Secretary-General to continue to ensure the provision to the Conference of adequate administrative, substantive and conference support services;

7. *Requests* the Conference to submit a report on its work to the General Assembly at its fifty-ninth session;

8. *Decides* to include in the provisional agenda of its fifty-ninth session the item entitled "Report of the Conference on Disarmament".

Multilateral disarmament agreements

As at 31 December 2003, the following numbers of States had become parties to the multilateral agreements listed below (in chronological order, with the years in which they were initially signed or opened for signature).

(Geneva) Protocol for the Prohibition of the Use in War of Asphyxiating, Poisonous or Other Gases, and of Bacteriological Methods of Warfare (1925): 133 parties

The Antarctic Treaty (1959): 45 parties

Treaty Banning Nuclear Weapon Tests in the Atmosphere, in Outer Space and under Water (1963): 124 parties

Treaty on Principles Governing the Activities of States in the Exploration and Use of Outer Space, including the Moon and Other Celestial Bodies (1967) [YUN 1966, p. 41, GA res. 2222(XXI), annex]: 98 parties

Treaty for the Prohibition of Nuclear Weapons in Latin America and the Caribbean (Treaty of Tlatelolco) (1967): 39 parties

Treaty on the Non-Proliferation of Nuclear Weapons (1968) [YUN 1968, p. 17, GA res. 2373(XXII), annex]: 189 parties

Treaty on the Prohibition of the Emplacement of Nuclear Weapons and Other Weapons of Mass Destruction on the Seabed and the Ocean Floor and in the Subsoil Thereof (1971) [YUN 1970, p. 18, GA res. 2660(XXV), annex]: 92 parties

Convention on the Prohibition of the Development, Production and Stockpiling of Bacteriological (Biological) and Toxin Weapons and on Their Destruction (1972) [YUN 1971, p. 19, GA res. 2826 (XXVI), annex]: 151 parties

Convention on the Prohibition of Military or Any Other Hostile Use of Environmental Modification Techniques (1977) [YUN 1976, p. 45, GA res. 31/72, annex]: 69 parties

Agreement Governing the Activities of States on the Moon and Other Celestial Bodies (1979) [YUN 1979, p. 111, GA res. 34/68, annex]: 10 parties

Convention on Prohibitions or Restrictions on the Use of Certain Conventional Weapons Which May Be Deemed to Be Excessively Injurious or to Have Indiscriminate Effects (1981): 93 parties

South Pacific Nuclear Free Zone Treaty (Treaty of Rarotonga) (1985): 17 parties

Treaty on Conventional Armed Forces in Europe (CFE Treaty) (1990): 30 parties

Treaty on Open Skies (1992): 30 parties

Convention on the Prohibition of the Development, Production, Stockpiling and Use of Chemical Weapons and on Their Destruction (1993): 158 parties

Treaty on the South-East Asia Nuclear-Weapon-Free Zone (Bangkok Treaty) (1995): 10 parties

African Nuclear-Weapon-Free Zone Treaty (Pelindaba Treaty) (1996): 22 parties

Comprehensive Nuclear-Test-Ban Treaty (1996): 108 parties

Inter-American Convention against the Illicit Manufacturing of and Trafficking in Firearms, Ammunition, Explosives, and Other Related Materials (1997): 21 parties

Convention on the Prohibition of the Use, Stockpiling, Production and Transfer of Anti-personnel Mines and on Their Destruction (Mine-Ban Convention, formerly known as Ottawa Convention) (1997): 141 parties

Inter-American Convention on Transparency in Conventional Weapons Acquisitions (1999): 8 parties

Agreement on Adaptation of the CFE Treaty (1999): 2 parties

[*The United Nations Disarmament Yearbook*, vol. 28: *2003*, Sales No. E.04.IX.1]

Nuclear disarmament

Conference on Disarmament

In 2003, owing to the continuing impasse over its programme of work, the Conference on Disarmament was not able to establish any subsidiary body to deal with nuclear disarmament, despite the fact that the idea of setting up such a body, as suggested in the proposal put forth by five former Presidents [CD/1693/Rev.1], remained uncontested. Consequently, the question of nuclear disarmament was addressed by delegations during plenary meetings, with frequent references to the Final Document of the 2000 Review Conference of the Parties to the Treaty on the Non-Proliferation of Nuclear Weapons (NPT) [YUN 2000, p. 487], particularly the 13 practical steps for systematic and progressive efforts towards nuclear disarmament. Many Western countries emphasized that negotiations on the fissile material cut-off treaty (see below), together with an early entry into force of the Comprehensive Nuclear-Test-Ban Treaty (see p. 547), constituted the next essential steps in nuclear disarmament and non-proliferation. Non-aligned countries, on the other hand, emphasized that they attached the highest priority to nuclear disarmament.

Fissile material

Persisting difficulties in reaching agreement on a comprehensive programme of work (see p. 531) prevented the Conference on Disarmament from establishing an ad hoc committee on the prohibition of the production of fissile material for nuclear weapons and other nuclear explosive devices. As a result, the issue was discussed only in plenary meetings. Western countries had intensified efforts to stimulate substantive discussion on the item and, in that context, the Netherlands organized informal meetings on banning the production of fissile material for nuclear weapons and other nuclear explosive devices on 4 April [CD/1705] and on 26 September [CD/1719], both in Geneva, while Japan submitted an August working paper on the item [CD/1714].

GENERAL ASSEMBLY ACTION

On 8 December [meeting 71], the General Assembly, on the recommendation of the First Committee [A/58/462], adopted **resolution 58/57** without vote [agenda item 73].

The Conference on Disarmament decision (CD/1547) of 11 August 1998 to establish, under item 1 of its agenda entitled "Cessation of the nuclear arms race and nuclear disarmament", an ad hoc committee to negotiate, on the basis of the report of the Special Coordinator (CD/1299) and the mandate contained therein, a non-discriminatory, multilateral and internationally and effectively verifiable treaty banning the production of fissile material for nuclear weapons or other nuclear explosive devices

The General Assembly,

Recalling its resolutions 48/75 L of 16 December 1993, 53/77 I of 4 December 1998, 55/33 Y of 20 November 2000, 56/24 J of 29 November 2001 and 57/80 of 22 November 2002,

Convinced that a non-discriminatory, multilateral and internationally and effectively verifiable treaty banning the production of fissile material for nuclear weapons or other nuclear explosive devices would be a significant contribution to nuclear disarmament and nuclear non-proliferation,

Recalling the 1998 report of the Conference on Disarmament, in which, inter alia, the Conference recorded that, in proceeding to take a decision on this matter, that decision was without prejudice to any further decisions on the establishment of further subsidiary bodies under agenda item 1 and that intensive consultations would be pursued to seek the views of the members of the Conference on Disarmament on appropriate methods and approaches for dealing with agenda item 1, taking into consideration all proposals and views in that respect,

1. *Recalls* the decision of the Conference on Disarmament to establish, under item 1 of its agenda entitled "Cessation of the nuclear arms race and nuclear disarmament", an ad hoc committee which shall negotiate, on the basis of the report of the Special Coordinator and the mandate contained therein, a non-discriminatory, multilateral and internationally and effectively verifiable treaty banning the production of fissile material for nuclear weapons or other nuclear explosive devices;

2. *Urges* the Conference on Disarmament to agree on a programme of work that includes the immediate commencement of negotiations on such a treaty.

Security assurances

The Conference on Disarmament addressed the issue of security assurances for non-nuclear-weapon States against the use or threat of use of nuclear weapons in the framework of overall discussions on the agenda and programme of work. During plenary meetings, delegations reaffirmed or further elaborated their respective positions on the item.

Communication. The Thirteenth Conference of Heads of State or Government of the Non-Aligned Countries (Kuala Lumpur, Malaysia, 20-25 February) [A/57/759-S/2003/332] said that, pending the total elimination of nuclear weapons, it would pursue, as a matter of priority, the conclusion of a universal, unconditional and legally binding instrument on security assurances to non-nuclear-weapon States.

GENERAL ASSEMBLY ACTION

On 8 December [meeting 71], the General Assembly, on the recommendation of the First Committee [A/58/460], adopted **resolution 58/35** by recorded vote (119-0-58) [agenda item 71].

Conclusion of effective international arrangements to assure non-nuclear-weapon States against the use or threat of use of nuclear weapons

The General Assembly,

Bearing in mind the need to allay the legitimate concern of the States of the world with regard to ensuring lasting security for their peoples,

Convinced that nuclear weapons pose the greatest threat to mankind and to the survival of civilization,

Welcoming the progress achieved in recent years in both nuclear and conventional disarmament,

Noting that, despite recent progress in the field of nuclear disarmament, further efforts are necessary towards the achievement of general and complete disarmament under effective international control,

Convinced that nuclear disarmament and the complete elimination of nuclear weapons are essential to remove the danger of nuclear war,

Determined to abide strictly by the relevant provisions of the Charter of the United Nations on the non-use of force or threat of force,

Recognizing that the independence, territorial integrity and sovereignty of non-nuclear-weapon States need to be safeguarded against the use or threat of use of force, including the use or threat of use of nuclear weapons,

Considering that, until nuclear disarmament is achieved on a universal basis, it is imperative for the international community to develop effective measures and arrangements to ensure the security of non-nuclear-weapon States against the use or threat of use of nuclear weapons from any quarter,

Recognizing that effective measures and arrangements to assure non-nuclear-weapon States against the use or threat of use of nuclear weapons can contribute positively to the prevention of the spread of nuclear weapons,

Bearing in mind paragraph 59 of the Final Document of the Tenth Special Session of the General Assembly, the first special session devoted to disarmament, in which it urged the nuclear-weapon States to pursue efforts to conclude, as appropriate, effective arrangements to assure non-nuclear-weapon States against the use or threat of use of nuclear weapons, and desirous of promoting the implementation of the relevant provisions of the Final Document,

Recalling the relevant parts of the special report of the Committee on Disarmament submitted to the General Assembly at its twelfth special session, the second special session devoted to disarmament, and of the special report of the Conference on Disarmament submitted to the Assembly at its fifteenth special session, the third special session devoted to disarmament, as well as the report of the Conference on its 1992 session,

Recalling also paragraph 12 of the Declaration of the 1980s as the Second Disarmament Decade, contained in the annex to its resolution 35/46 of 3 December 1980, which states, inter alia, that all efforts should be exerted by the Committee on Disarmament urgently to negotiate with a view to reaching agreement on effective international arrangements to assure non-nuclear-weapon States against the use or threat of use of nuclear weapons,

Noting the in-depth negotiations undertaken in the Conference on Disarmament and its Ad Hoc Committee on Effective International Arrangements to Assure Non-Nuclear-Weapon States against the Use or Threat of Use of Nuclear Weapons, with a view to reaching agreement on this question,

Taking note of the proposals submitted under the item in the Conference on Disarmament, including the drafts of an international convention,

Taking note also of the relevant decision of the Thirteenth Conference of Heads of State or Government of Non-Aligned Countries, held in Kuala Lumpur from 20 to 25 February 2003, as well as the relevant recommendations of the Organization of the Islamic Conference,

Taking note further of the unilateral declarations made by all the nuclear-weapon States on their policies of non-use or non-threat of use of nuclear weapons against the non-nuclear-weapon States,

Noting the support expressed in the Conference on Disarmament and in the General Assembly for the elaboration of an international convention to assure non-nuclear-weapon States against the use or threat of use of nuclear weapons, as well as the difficulties pointed out in evolving a common approach acceptable to all,

Taking note of Security Council resolution 984(1995) of 11 April 1995 and the views expressed on it,

Recalling its relevant resolutions adopted in previous years, in particular resolutions 45/54 of 4 December 1990, 46/32 of 6 December 1991, 47/50 of 9 December 1992, 48/73 of 16 December 1993, 49/73 of 15 December 1994, 50/68 of 12 December 1995, 51/43 of 10 December 1996, 52/36 of 9 December 1997, 53/75 of 4 December 1998, 54/52 of 1 December 1999, 55/31 of 20 November 2000, 56/22 of 29 November 2001 and 57/56 of 22 November 2002,

1. *Reaffirms* the urgent need to reach an early agreement on effective international arrangements to assure non-nuclear-weapon States against the use or threat of use of nuclear weapons;

2. *Notes with satisfaction* that in the Conference on Disarmament there is no objection, in principle, to the idea of an international convention to assure non-nuclear-weapon States against the use or threat of use of nuclear weapons, although the difficulties with regard to evolving a common approach acceptable to all have also been pointed out;

3. *Appeals* to all States, especially the nuclear-weapon States, to work actively towards an early agreement on a common approach and, in particular, on a common formula that could be included in an international instrument of a legally binding character;

4. *Recommends* that further intensive efforts be devoted to the search for such a common approach or common formula and that the various alternative approaches, including, in particular, those considered in the Conference on Disarmament, be explored further in order to overcome the difficulties;

5. *Also recommends* that the Conference on Disarmament actively continue intensive negotiations with a view to reaching early agreement and concluding effective international arrangements to assure the non-nuclear-weapon States against the use or threat of use of nuclear weapons, taking into account the widespread support for the conclusion of an international convention and giving consideration to any other proposals designed to secure the same objective;

6. *Decides* to include in the provisional agenda of its fifty-ninth session the item entitled "Conclusion of effective international arrangements to assure non-nuclear-weapon States against the use or threat of use of nuclear weapons".

RECORDED VOTE ON RESOLUTION 58/35:

In favour: Afghanistan, Algeria, Angola, Antigua and Barbuda, Azerbaijan, Bahamas, Bahrain, Bangladesh, Barbados, Belize, Benin, Bhutan, Botswana, Brazil, Brunei Darussalam, Burkina Faso, Burundi, Cambodia, Cameroon, Cape Verde, Central African Republic, Chile, China, Colombia, Comoros, Congo, Costa Rica, Côte d'Ivoire, Cuba, Democratic People's Republic of Korea, Djibouti, Dominican Republic, Ecuador, Egypt, El Salvador, Eritrea, Ethiopia, Fiji, Gabon, Gambia, Ghana, Grenada, Guatemala, Guinea, Guinea-Bissau, Guyana, Haiti, India, Indonesia, Iran, Jamaica, Japan, Jordan, Kazakhstan, Kenya, Kuwait, Kyrgyzstan, Lao People's Democratic Republic, Lebanon, Lesotho, Libyan Arab Jamahiriya, Madagascar, Malawi, Malaysia, Maldives, Mali, Mauritania, Mauritius, Mexico, Mongolia, Morocco, Mozambique, Myanmar, Namibia, Nauru, Nepal, Nicaragua, Niger, Nigeria, Oman, Pakistan, Panama, Papua New Guinea, Paraguay, Peru, Philippines, Qatar, Rwanda, Saint Lucia, Samoa, Saudi Arabia, Senegal, Seychelles, Singapore, Somalia, Sri Lanka, Sudan, Suriname, Swaziland, Syrian Arab Republic, Thailand, Timor-Leste, Togo, Tonga, Trinidad and Tobago, Tunisia, Turkmenistan, Uganda, Ukraine, United Arab Emirates, United Republic of Tanzania, Uruguay, Uzbekistan, Vanuatu, Venezuela, Viet Nam, Yemen, Zambia, Zimbabwe.

Against: None.

Abstaining: Albania, Andorra, Argentina, Armenia, Australia, Austria, Belarus, Belgium, Bolivia, Bosnia and Herzegovina, Bulgaria, Canada, Croatia, Cyprus, Czech Republic, Denmark, Estonia, Finland, France, Georgia, Germany, Greece, Honduras, Hungary, Iceland, Ireland, Israel, Italy, Latvia, Liechtenstein, Lithuania, Luxembourg, Malta, Micronesia, Monaco, Netherlands, New Zealand, Norway, Poland, Portugal, Republic of Korea, Republic of Moldova, Romania, Russian Federation, Saint Vincent and the Grenadines, San Marino, Serbia and Montenegro, Slovakia, Slovenia, South Africa, Spain, Sweden, Switzerland, Tajikistan, The former Yugoslav Republic of Macedonia, Turkey, United Kingdom, United States.

Disarmament Commission

In April [A/58/42], Working Group I of the Disarmament Commission considered its Chairman's working paper on ways and means to achieve nuclear disarmament. Based on comments and ideas presented on the paper, the Chairman prepared further papers and a proposal, on which the Group did not achieve consensus. The proposal, which was annexed to the Commission's report, addressed the importance of nuclear disarmament and the interrelationship between nuclear disarmament and international peace, security and stability; achievements and current developments in nuclear disarmament; and mechanisms dealing with nuclear disarmament and the role of the United Nations.

START and other bilateral agreements and unilateral measures

On 1 June, the 2002 Strategic Offensive Reductions Treaty (SORT) [YUN 2002, p. 493] between the Russian Federation and the United States entered into force following the completion of the ratification procedures. SORT, also known as the Moscow Treaty, established a new framework for further reductions of their strategic offensive weapons following the completion of reductions agreed upon under the 1991 Treaty on the Reduction and Limitation of Strategic Offensive Arms (START I). SORT committed the parties to reducing the level of their deployed strategic nuclear warheads to between 1,700 and 2,200 by 31 December 2012, which superseded their agreement for reductions to between 3,000 and 3,500 under the 1993 START II process [YUN 1993, p. 117]. In a 1 June joint statement on the new strategic relationship embodied in SORT (Saint Petersburg, Russian Federation) [A/58/91-S/2003/617], Presidents George W. Bush of the United States and Vladimir V. Putin of the Russian Federation pledged to intensify efforts to confront the global threats of terrorism and the proliferation of weapons of mass destruction (WMDs) and their means of delivery, declared their intention to advance concrete joint projects in the field of missile defence and reaffirmed their commitment on issues relating to space exploration.

Reports of Secretary-General. Pursuant to General Assembly resolutions 57/59 [YUN 2002, p. 495], 57/79 [ibid., p. 500] and 57/84 [ibid., p. 502], the Secretary-General, in a July report [A/58/162], assessed progress made towards a nuclear-weapon-free world. Noting that 2003 marked the twenty-fifth anniversary of the Assembly's tenth special session, the first devoted to disarmament [YUN 1978, p. 17], the Secretary-General observed that WMDs, particularly nuclear weapons, remained a grave concern and that the implementation of disarmament and non-proliferation measures continued to pose a major challenge to international peace and security. Regarding efforts being made to reduce existing nuclear arsenals and to strengthen the nuclear non-proliferation regime, the Secretary-General said there had been some progress through measures taken by nuclear-weapon States. Despite the progress made, he added, further steps were required to advance the process of nuclear disarmament agreements and non-proliferation. Existing arms limitation and disarmament agreements needed to be reinforced by ensuring effective implementation of their provisions and universality. The Secretary-General suggested that efforts intensify towards the full implementation of the recommendations to significantly reduce the risk of nuclear war put forth in 2001 by the Advisory Board on Disarmament Matters [YUN 2001, p. 474]. As to the proposal to convene an international conference to identify ways of eliminating nuclear danger, contained in the Millennium Declaration [YUN 2000, p. 49], the Secretary-General stated that consultations with Member States demonstrated that the time had not yet come for consideration of interim measures for convening such a conference. However, pursuant to Assembly resolution 57/84, he would continue to encourage Member States to create the conditions that would facilitate international consensus to hold the conference.

In a September report [A/58/323] on progress made to implement the goals contained in the Millennium Declaration (see also p. 48) relating to international security and disarmament, the Secretary-General addressed the need to strengthen and complement existing WMD regimes, the threat posed by small arms and the importance of cooperation in tightening export controls and facilitating the identification of sources of illicit weapons.

Communications. France and the Russian Federation adopted the French-Russian declaration on strategic issues (Paris, 10 February) [CD/1700], which expressed their determination to strengthen cooperation in combating the growing threat posed by the proliferation of WMDs and their means of delivery, and reaffirmed their commitment to the Group of Eight (G-8) major industrialized countries' Global Partnership Against the Spread of Weapons and Materials of Mass Destruction, launched in 2002 [YUN 2002, p. 494].

The heads of State or Government of non-aligned countries, at their Thirteenth Conference (Kuala Lumpur, Malaysia, 20-25 February) [A/57/759-S/2003/332], expressed concern at the slow pace of progress towards nuclear disarmament and called for an international conference to draw up an agreement on a phased programme for the total elimination of nuclear weapons.

On 31 May, President Bush, during a State visit to Poland, announced the proliferation security initiative, designed by the United States and a number of its close allies to reinforce the fight against WMD proliferation, including through agreements to search planes and ships carrying suspect cargo and the seizure of illegal weapons or missile technologies.

The G-8 major industrialized countries (Evian, France, 1-3 June) [CD/1708] adopted a declaration recognizing the proliferation of WMDs and their means of delivery, together with the spread of international terrorism, as the pre-eminent threat to international peace and security: a global challenge demanding a multifaceted solution. They called for the effective control of the transfer of materials, technology and expertise that might facilitate the development or use of WMDs, and reviewed the implementation status of their 2002 initiative: the Global Partnership Against the Spread of Weapons and Materials of Mass Destruction [YUN 2002, p. 494].

Similar declarations on the non-proliferation of WMDs were made by the European Council (Thessaloniki, Greece, 20 June) [CD/1711], and by the Asia-Europe Meeting (Bali, Indonesia, 23-24 July) [CD/1712], an informal forum for dialogue and cooperation between the 15 European Union (EU) member States and 10 Asian countries (Brunei, China, Indonesia, Japan, Malaysia, Philippines, Singapore, South Korea, Thailand, Viet Nam).

The Foreign Ministers of the New Agenda Coalition countries (Brazil, Egypt, Ireland, Mexico, New Zealand, South Africa, Sweden) (New York, 23 September) [A/58/406] reviewed nuclear disarmament developments relating to their joint initiative, "Towards a nuclear-weapon-free world: the need for a new agenda", launched in 1998 [YUN 1998, p. 496].

The EU adopted an official strategy against the proliferation of WMDs (Brussels, Belgium, 12-13 December) [CD/1724], conceived to prevent, deter, halt and possibly eliminate proliferation programmes of concern worldwide. It was termed a "living action plan", subject to regular revision and updating every six months.

On 19 December [A/58/664], the Libyan Arab Jamahiriya stated that it had satisfied all its obligations under treaties and conventions relating to the elimination of all types of WMDs.

GENERAL ASSEMBLY ACTION

On 8 December [meeting 71], the General Assembly, on the recommendation of the First Committee [A/58/462], adopted five resolutions and one decision related to nuclear disarmament. The Assembly adopted **resolution 58/47** by recorded vote (114-47-17) [agenda item 73 (x)].

Reducing nuclear danger

The General Assembly,

Bearing in mind that the use of nuclear weapons poses the most serious threat to mankind and to the survival of civilization,

Reaffirming that any use or threat of use of nuclear weapons would constitute a violation of the Charter of the United Nations,

Convinced that the proliferation of nuclear weapons in all its aspects would seriously enhance the danger of nuclear war,

Convinced also that nuclear disarmament and the complete elimination of nuclear weapons are essential to remove the danger of nuclear war,

Considering that, until nuclear weapons cease to exist, it is imperative on the part of the nuclear-weapon States to adopt measures that assure non-nuclear-weapon States against the use or threat of use of nuclear weapons,

Considering also that the hair-trigger alert of nuclear weapons carries unacceptable risks of unintentional or accidental use of nuclear weapons, which would have catastrophic consequences for all mankind,

Emphasizing the imperative need to adopt measures to avoid accidental, unauthorized or unexplained incidents arising from computer anomaly or other technical malfunctions,

Conscious that limited steps relating to detargeting have been taken by the nuclear-weapon States and that further practical, realistic and mutually reinforcing steps are necessary to contribute to the improvement in the international climate for negotiations leading to the elimination of nuclear weapons,

Mindful that reduction of tensions brought about by a change in nuclear doctrines would positively impact on international peace and security and improve the conditions for the further reduction and the elimination of nuclear weapons,

Reiterating the highest priority accorded to nuclear disarmament in the Final Document of the Tenth Special Session of the General Assembly and by the international community,

Recalling that in the advisory opinion of the International Court of Justice on the *Legality of the Threat or Use of Nuclear Weapons* it is stated that there exists an obligation for all States to pursue in good faith and bring to a conclusion negotiations leading to nuclear disarmament in all its aspects under strict and effective international control,

Recalling also the call in the United Nations Millennium Declaration to seek to eliminate the dangers posed by weapons of mass destruction and the resolve to strive for the elimination of weapons of mass destruction, particularly nuclear weapons, including the possibility of convening an international conference to identify ways of eliminating nuclear dangers,

1. *Calls* for a review of nuclear doctrines and, in this context, immediate and urgent steps to reduce the risks of unintentional and accidental use of nuclear weapons;

2. *Requests* the five nuclear-weapon States to take measures towards the implementation of paragraph 1 above;

3. *Calls upon* Member States to take the necessary measures to prevent the proliferation of nuclear weapons in all its aspects and to promote nuclear disarmament, with the objective of eliminating nuclear weapons;

4. *Takes note* of the report of the Secretary-General submitted pursuant to paragraph 5 of General Assembly resolution 57/84 of 22 November 2002;

5. *Requests* the Secretary-General to intensify efforts and support initiatives that would contribute towards the full implementation of the seven recommendations identified in the report of the Advisory Board on Disarmament Matters that would significantly reduce the risk of nuclear war, and also to continue to encourage Member States to endeavour to create conditions that would allow the emergence of an international consensus to hold an international conference as proposed in the United Nations Millennium Declaration, to identify ways of eliminating nuclear dangers, and to report thereon to the General Assembly at its fifty-ninth session;

6. *Decides* to include in the provisional agenda of its fifty-ninth session the item entitled "Reducing nuclear danger".

RECORDED VOTE ON RESOLUTION 58/47:

In favour: Afghanistan, Algeria, Angola, Antigua and Barbuda, Bahamas, Bahrain, Bangladesh, Barbados, Belize, Benin, Bhutan, Bolivia, Botswana, Brunei Darussalam, Burkina Faso, Burundi, Cambodia, Cameroon, Cape Verde, Central African Republic, Chile, Colombia, Comoros, Congo, Costa Rica, Côte d'Ivoire, Cuba, Democratic People's Republic of Korea, Djibouti, Dominican Republic, Ecuador, Egypt, El Salvador, Eritrea, Ethiopia, Fiji, Gabon, Gambia, Ghana, Grenada, Guatemala, Guinea, Guinea-Bissau, Guyana, Haiti, Honduras, India, Indonesia, Iran, Jamaica, Jordan, Kenya, Kuwait, Lao People's Democratic Republic, Lebanon, Lesotho, Libyan Arab Jamahiriya, Madagascar, Malawi, Malaysia, Maldives, Mali, Mauritania, Mauritius, Mexico, Mongolia, Morocco, Mozambique, Myanmar, Namibia, Nauru, Nepal, Nicaragua, Niger, Nigeria, Oman, Pakistan, Panama, Papua New Guinea, Peru, Philippines, Qatar, Saint Lucia, Saint Vincent and the Grenadines, Samoa, Saudi Arabia, Senegal, Sierra Leone, Singapore, Solomon Islands, Somalia, South Africa, Sri Lanka, Sudan, Suriname, Swaziland, Syrian Arab Republic, Thailand, Timor-Leste, Togo, Tonga, Trinidad and Tobago, Tunisia, Turkmenistan, Uganda, United Arab Emirates, United Republic of Tanzania, Uruguay, Vanuatu, Venezuela, Viet Nam, Yemen, Zambia, Zimbabwe.

Against: Albania, Andorra, Australia, Austria, Belgium, Bosnia and Herzegovina, Bulgaria, Canada, Croatia, Cyprus, Czech Republic, Denmark, Estonia, Finland, France, Germany, Greece, Hungary, Iceland, Ireland, Italy, Latvia, Liechtenstein, Lithuania, Luxembourg, Malta, Marshall Islands, Micronesia, Monaco, Netherlands, New Zealand, Norway, Poland, Portugal, Romania, Russian Federation, San Marino, Serbia and Montenegro, Slovakia, Slovenia, Spain, Sweden, Switzerland, The former Yugoslav Republic of Macedonia, Turkey, United Kingdom, United States.

Abstaining: Argentina, Armenia, Azerbaijan, Belarus, Brazil, China, Georgia, Israel, Japan, Kazakhstan, Kyrgyzstan, Paraguay, Republic of Korea, Republic of Moldova, Tajikistan, Ukraine, Uzbekistan.

The Assembly adopted **resolution 58/50** by recorded vote (128-4-43) [agenda item 73 *(c)*].

Reduction of non-strategic nuclear weapons

The General Assembly,

Recalling its resolutions 55/33 D of 20 November 2000 and 57/58 and 57/59 of 22 November 2002,

Stressing the unequivocal undertaking by the nuclear-weapon States, in the Final Document of the 2000 Review Conference of the Parties to the Treaty on the Non-Proliferation of Nuclear Weapons, to accomplish the total elimination of their nuclear arsenals leading to nuclear disarmament, to which all States parties to the Treaty are committed under its article VI,

Recognizing that disarmament and non-proliferation are essential for the maintenance of international peace and security,

Reaffirming the necessity of strict compliance at all times and in all circumstances by all parties with their obligations under the Treaty on the Non-Proliferation of Nuclear Weapons and the necessity of upholding their commitments in the decisions and final documents agreed at the 1995 and 2000 Review Conferences,

Noting the advisory opinion of the International Court of Justice on the *Legality of the Threat or Use of Nuclear Weapons*, issued at The Hague on 8 July 1996,

Reiterating the responsibility of the nuclear-weapon States for transparent, verifiable and irreversible reductions in nuclear weapons leading to nuclear disarmament,

Stressing the commitment made in the Final Document of the 2000 Review Conference to the further reduction of non-strategic nuclear weapons,

Convinced that the further reduction of non-strategic nuclear weapons constitutes an integral part of the nuclear-arms reduction and disarmament process,

Concerned about the threat posed by non-strategic nuclear weapons due to their portability and proximity to areas of conflict, and thus about the risk of proliferation and of use,

Concerned also about emerging approaches to the broader role of nuclear weapons as part of security strategies, including the possible development of new types of low-yield non-strategic nuclear weapons,

Taking into consideration the lack of transparency and of formal agreements with regard to non-strategic nuclear weapons,

Emphasizing that further reductions of non-strategic nuclear weapons should be accorded a higher priority, as an important step towards the elimination of nuclear weapons, and be carried out in a comprehensive manner,

1. *Agrees* that further reductions in and elimination of non-strategic nuclear weapons should be based on unilateral initiatives and included as an integral part of the nuclear-arms reduction and disarmament process;

2. *Also agrees* that reductions of non-strategic nuclear weapons should be carried out in a transparent, verifiable and irreversible manner;

3. *Further agrees* on the importance of preserving, reaffirming and implementing the 1991 and 1992 presidential nuclear initiatives of the United States of America and the Union of Soviet Socialist Republics/Russian Federation on non-strategic nuclear weapons;

4. *Calls upon* the Russian Federation and the United States of America to formalize their presidential nuclear initiatives into legal instruments and to initiate negotiations on further reductions of such weapons;

5. *Stresses* the importance of the enhancement of special security and physical protection measures for the transport and storage of non-strategic nuclear weapons, their components and related materials through, inter alia, the placing of such weapons in physically secure central storage sites, with a view to their removal and subsequent elimination by the nuclear-weapon States as a part of the nuclear disarmament process to which they are committed under the Treaty on the Non-Proliferation of Nuclear Weapons, and calls upon all nuclear-weapon States in possession of such weapons to take the necessary steps in this regard;

6. *Calls* for further confidence-building and transparency measures to reduce the threats posed by non-strategic nuclear weapons;

7. *Also calls* for concrete agreed measures to reduce further the operational status of non-strategic nuclear weapons systems so as to reduce the risk of use of non-strategic nuclear weapons;

8. *Stresses* the need for an undertaking by the nuclear-weapon States that possess such weapons not to increase the number or types of weapons deployed and not to develop new types of these weapons or rationalizations for their use;

9. *Calls* for the prohibition of those types of non-strategic nuclear weapons that have already been removed from the arsenals of some nuclear-weapon States and the development of transparency mechanisms for the verification of the elimination of these weapons;

10. *Decides* to include in the provisional agenda of its sixtieth session the item entitled "Reduction of non-strategic nuclear weapons".

RECORDED VOTE ON RESOLUTION 58/50:

In favour: Algeria, Andorra, Angola, Antigua and Barbuda, Argentina, Austria, Azerbaijan, Bahamas, Bahrain, Bangladesh, Barbados, Belize, Benin, Bhutan, Bolivia, Botswana, Brazil, Brunei Darussalam, Burkina Faso, Burundi, Cambodia, Cameroon, Cape Verde, Central African Republic, Chile, Colombia, Comoros, Congo, Costa Rica, Côte d'Ivoire, Cuba, Cyprus, Democratic People's Republic of Korea, Djibouti, Dominican Republic, Ecuador, Egypt, El Salvador, Eritrea, Ethiopia, Fiji, Finland, Gabon, Gambia, Ghana, Grenada, Guatemala, Guinea, Guinea-Bissau, Guyana, Haiti, Honduras, Indonesia, Iran, Ireland, Jamaica, Jordan, Kazakhstan, Kenya, Kuwait, Lao People's Democratic Republic, Lebanon, Lesotho, Libyan Arab Jamahiriya, Liechtenstein, Madagascar, Malawi, Malaysia, Maldives, Mali, Malta, Mauritania, Mauritius, Mexico, Mongolia, Morocco, Mozambique, Myanmar, Namibia, Nauru, Nepal, New Zealand, Nicaragua, Niger, Nigeria, Oman, Panama, Papua New Guinea, Paraguay, Peru, Philippines, Qatar, Rwanda, Saint Lucia, Saint Vincent and the Grenadines, Samoa, San Marino, Saudi Arabia, Senegal, Seychelles, Sierra Leone, Singapore, Somalia, South Africa, Sri Lanka, Sudan, Suriname, Swaziland, Sweden, Syrian Arab Republic, Thailand, Timor-Leste, Togo, Tonga, Trinidad and Tobago, Tunisia, Turkmenistan, Uganda, Ukraine, United Arab Emirates, United Republic of Tanzania, Uruguay, Vanuatu, Venezuela, Viet Nam, Yemen, Zambia, Zimbabwe.

Against: France, Russian Federation, United Kingdom, United States.

Abstaining: Albania, Armenia, Australia, Belarus, Belgium, Bosnia and Herzegovina, Bulgaria, Canada, Croatia, Czech Republic, Denmark, Estonia, Georgia, Germany, Greece, Hungary, Iceland, India, Israel, Italy, Japan, Kyrgyzstan, Latvia, Lithuania, Luxembourg, Micronesia, Netherlands, Norway, Pakistan, Poland, Portugal, Republic of Korea, Republic of Moldova, Romania, Serbia and Montenegro, Slovakia, Slovenia, Spain, Switzerland, Tajikistan, The former Yugoslav Republic of Macedonia, Turkey, Uzbekistan.

The Assembly adopted **resolution 58/51** by recorded vote (133-6-38) [agenda item 73 *(d)*].

**Towards a nuclear-weapon-free world:
a new agenda**

The General Assembly,

Recalling its resolutions 53/77 Y of 4 December 1998, 54/54 G of 1 December 1999, 55/33 C of 20 November 2000 and 57/59 of 22 November 2002,

Convinced that the existence of nuclear weapons is a threat to the survival of humanity and that the only real guarantee against the use or threat of use of these weapons is their complete elimination and the assurance that they will never be used or produced again,

Convinced also that the retention of nuclear weapons carries the inherent risk of proliferation of those weapons and their falling into the hands of non-State actors,

Reaffirming that nuclear non-proliferation and nuclear disarmament are equally important and mutually reinforcing processes requiring continuous irreversible progress on both fronts,

Declaring that the participation of the international community as a whole is central to the maintenance and enhancement of international peace and stability, and that international security is a collective concern requiring collective engagement,

Declaring also that internationally negotiated treaties in the field of disarmament have made a fundamental contribution to international peace and security, and that unilateral and bilateral nuclear disarmament measures complement the treaty-based multilateral approach towards nuclear disarmament,

Noting the advisory opinion of the International Court of Justice on the *Legality of the Threat or Use of Nuclear Weapons,* issued at The Hague on 8 July 1996,

Declaring that any presumption of the indefinite possession of nuclear weapons by the nuclear-weapon States is incompatible with the integrity and sustainability of the nuclear non-proliferation regime and with the broader goal of the maintenance of international peace and security,

Declaring that each article of the Treaty on the Non-Proliferation of Nuclear Weapons is binding on the States parties at all times and in all circumstances and that it is imperative that all States parties be held fully accountable with respect to the strict compliance with their obligations under the Treaty, and that the undertakings therein on nuclear disarmament have been given and implementation of them remains imperative,

Expressing its deep concern at the limited progress made to date in implementing the thirteen steps on nuclear disarmament, and determined to implement these thirteen practical steps, to which all States parties agreed at the 2000 Review Conference of the Parties to the Treaty on the Non-Proliferation of Nuclear Weapons,

Expressing its deep concern at the continued failure of the Conference on Disarmament to deal with nuclear disarmament and to resume negotiations on a non-discriminatory, multilateral and internationally and effectively verifiable treaty banning the production of fissile material for nuclear weapons and other devices, taking into consideration both nuclear disarmament and nuclear non-proliferation objectives,

Expressing grave concern that the Comprehensive Nuclear-Test-Ban Treaty has not yet entered into force,

Stressing the importance of regular reporting in promoting confidence in the Treaty on the Non-Proliferation of Nuclear Weapons,

Noting the successful completion in September 2002 of the first phase of the Trilateral Initiative, involving the International Atomic Energy Agency, the Russian Federation and the United States of America, which aims to enable the placement of excess nuclear materials from dismantled weapons under international safeguards,

Convinced that the further reduction of non-strategic nuclear weapons constitutes an integral part of the nuclear arms reduction and disarmament process,

Noting that, despite bilateral agreements, there is no sign of engagement of all of the five nuclear-weapon States in the multilateral process leading to the total elimination of nuclear weapons,

Declaring that it is essential that the fundamental principles of transparency, verification and irreversibility apply to all nuclear disarmament measures,

Expressing its deep concern at the continued retention of the nuclear-weapons option by those three States, India, Israel and Pakistan, that have not yet acceded to the Treaty on the Non-Proliferation of Nuclear Weapons and that operate unsafeguarded nuclear facilities, in particular given the effects of regional volatility on international security, and, in this context, the continued regional tensions and deteriorating security situation in South Asia and the Middle East,

Expressing also its deep concern at the announcement by the Democratic People's Republic of Korea to withdraw from the Treaty on the Non-Proliferation of Nuclear Weapons and at its decision to restart the Yongbyon nuclear reactor without International Atomic Energy Agency safeguards,

Expressing concern that the development of missile defences could impact negatively on nuclear disarmament and non-proliferation and lead to a new arms race on earth and in outer space,

Stressing that no actions be taken that would lead to the weaponization of outer space,

Expressing its deep concern about emerging approaches to the broader role of nuclear weapons as part of security strategies, including rationalizations for the use, and the possible development, of new types of nuclear weapons,

Welcoming further the progress in the development of nuclear-weapon-free zones,

Recalling the United Nations Millennium Declaration, in which the heads of State and Government resolved to strive for the elimination of weapons of mass destruction, in particular nuclear weapons, and to keep all options open for achieving this aim, including the possibility of convening an international conference to identify ways of eliminating nuclear dangers,

Taking into consideration the unequivocal undertaking by the nuclear-weapon States, in the Final Document of the 2000 Review Conference of the Parties to the Treaty on the Non-Proliferation of Nuclear Weapons, to accomplish the total elimination of their nuclear arsenals leading to nuclear disarmament, to which all the States parties to the Treaty are committed under article VI of the Treaty,

1. *Reaffirms* that any possibility that nuclear weapons could be used represents a continued risk for humanity;

2. *Calls upon* all States to refrain from any action that could lead to a new nuclear-arms race or that could impact negatively on nuclear disarmament and non-proliferation;

3. *Calls upon* all States to fulfil all their obligations under international treaties and international law in the field of nuclear disarmament and non-proliferation;

4. *Calls upon* all States parties to pursue, with determination, the full and effective implementation of the agreements reached at the 2000 Review Conference of the Parties to the Treaty on the Non-Proliferation of Nuclear Weapons, the outcome of which provides the requisite plan to achieve nuclear disarmament;

5. *Agrees* on the importance and urgency of signatures and ratifications required to achieve the early entry into force of the Comprehensive Nuclear-Test-Ban Treaty;

6. *Calls* for the upholding and maintenance of the moratorium on nuclear-weapon-test explosions or any other nuclear explosions pending the entry into force of the Comprehensive Nuclear-Test-Ban Treaty;

7. *Underlines* the urgency of the entry into force of the Comprehensive Nuclear-Test-Ban Treaty in the context of the progress achieved in implementing the international monitoring system;

8. *Calls upon* the nuclear-weapon States to implement the commitments made in the Treaty on the Non-Proliferation of Nuclear Weapons, as well as in other nuclear disarmament or reductions agreements or initiatives, and to apply the principle of irreversibility by destroying their nuclear warheads and avoid keeping them in a state that lends itself to their possible redeployment;

9. *Acknowledges* that the reductions in the number of deployed strategic nuclear warheads envisaged by the Treaty on Strategic Offensive Reductions ("the Moscow Treaty") represent a positive first step, and calls on the United States of America and the Russian Federation to make the Treaty verifiable, irreversible and transparent and to address non-operational warheads, thus making it an effective nuclear disarmament measure;

10. *Agrees* that the further reduction of non-strategic nuclear weapons should be accorded a higher priority as an important step towards the elimination of nuclear weapons and be carried out in a comprehensive manner, including:

(a) Further reductions in and elimination of non-strategic nuclear weapons based on unilateral initiatives and as an integral part of the nuclear-arms reduction and disarmament process;

(b) The implementation of reductions in a transparent, verifiable and irreversible manner;

(c) The preservation, reaffirmation and implementation of the 1991 and 1992 presidential nuclear initiatives of the United States of America and the Union of Soviet Socialist Republics/Russian Federation on non-strategic nuclear weapons;

(d) The formalization by the Russian Federation and the United States of America of their presidential nuclear initiatives into legal instruments and the initiation of negotiations on further reductions of such weapons;

(e) The enhancement of special security and physical protection measures for the transport and storage of non-strategic nuclear weapons, their components and related materials through, inter alia, the placing of such weapons in physically secure central storage sites with a view to their removal and subsequent elimination by the nuclear-weapon States as a part of the nuclear disarmament process to which they are committed under the Treaty on the Non-Proliferation of Nuclear Weapons, as well as the necessary steps to be taken by all nuclear-weapon States in possession of such weapons in this regard;

(f) The achievement of further confidence-building and transparency measures to reduce the threats posed by non-strategic nuclear weapons;

(g) The achievement of concrete agreed measures to reduce further the operational status of non-strategic nuclear weapons systems so as to reduce the risk of use of non-strategic nuclear weapons;

(h) The undertaking by the nuclear-weapon States that possess these weapons not to increase the number or types of weapons deployed and not to develop new types of these weapons or rationalizations for their use;

(i) The prohibition of those types of non-strategic nuclear weapons that have already been removed from the arsenals of some nuclear-weapon States and the development of transparency mechanisms for the verification of the elimination of these weapons;

11. *Calls upon* the nuclear-weapon States to increase their transparency and accountability with regard to their nuclear weapons arsenals and their implementation of disarmament measures;

12. *Agrees* that the Conference on Disarmament should establish, without delay, an appropriate ad hoc committee to deal with nuclear disarmament;

13. *Agrees* that the Conference on Disarmament should resume negotiations on a non-discriminatory, multilateral and internationally and effectively verifiable treaty banning the production of fissile material for nuclear weapons or other nuclear explosive devices, taking into consideration both nuclear disarmament and nuclear non-proliferation objectives;

14. *Agrees* that the Conference on Disarmament should complete the examination and updating of the mandate on the prevention of an arms race in outer space in all its aspects, as contained in its decision of 13 February 1992, and re-establish an ad hoc committee as early as possible;

15. *Calls upon* the nuclear-weapon States to undertake the necessary steps towards the seamless integration of all five nuclear-weapon States into a process leading to the total elimination of nuclear weapons;

16. *Notes* that the third and, as appropriate, fourth meetings of the Preparatory Committee for the 2005 Review Conference of the Parties to the Treaty on the Non-Proliferation of Nuclear Weapons, taking into account the deliberations and results of the previous sessions, should make every effort to produce a report containing recommendations to the Review Conference;

17. *Stresses* the importance of regular reporting in promoting confidence in the Treaty on the Non-Proliferation of Nuclear Weapons;

18. *Calls upon* the nuclear-weapon States to respect fully their existing commitments with regard to security assurances pending the conclusion of multilaterally negotiated legally binding security assurances for all non-nuclear-weapon States parties;

19. *Notes* the proposals on security assurances that have been submitted to the States parties to the Treaty on the Non-Proliferation of Nuclear Weapons, and calls upon the Preparatory Committee for the 2005 Review Conference to allow time to thoroughly consider the matter of security assurances at its third meeting so as to make recommendations to the Review Conference on how to take the matter forward;

20. *Calls upon* those three States, India, Israel and Pakistan, which are not yet parties to the Treaty on the Non-Proliferation of Nuclear Weapons and which operate unsafeguarded nuclear facilities, to accede to the Treaty as non-nuclear-weapon States promptly and without condition, to bring into force the required comprehensive safeguards agreements, together with additional protocols, consistent with the Model Protocol Additional to the Agreement(s) between State(s) and the International Atomic Energy Agency for the Application of Safeguards approved by the Board of Governors of the International Atomic Energy Agency on 15 May 1997, for ensuring nuclear non-proliferation and to reverse clearly and urgently any policies to pursue any nuclear weapons development or deployment and refrain from any action that could undermine regional and international peace and security and the efforts of the international community towards nuclear disarmament and the prevention of nuclear weapons proliferation;

21. *Reaffirms the conviction* that the establishment of internationally recognized nuclear-weapon-free zones on the basis of arrangements freely arrived at among the States of the regions concerned enhances global and regional peace and security, strengthens the nuclear non-proliferation regime and contributes towards realizing the objective of nuclear disarmament;

22. *Expresses concern* at tensions in the Middle East and South Asia, and renews support for the establishment of a Middle East zone free of nuclear weapons and other weapons of mass destruction and of a nuclear-weapon-free zone in South Asia;

23. *Calls upon* those States that have not yet done so to conclude full-scope safeguards agreements with the International Atomic Energy Agency and to conclude additional protocols to their safeguards agreements on the basis of the Model Protocol;

24. *Calls upon* the Democratic People's Republic of Korea to reconsider its recent announcements, with a view to being in full compliance with the provisions of the Treaty on the Non-Proliferation of Nuclear Weapons, and in this connection supports all diplo-

matic efforts for an early, peaceful resolution of the situation and for the establishment of an area free of nuclear weapons on the Korean peninsula;

25. *Stresses* that the International Atomic Energy Agency must be able to verify and ensure that nuclear facilities of the States parties to the Treaty on the Non-Proliferation of Nuclear Weapons are being used for peaceful purposes only, and calls on States to cooperate fully and immediately with the Agency in resolving issues arising from the implementation of their respective obligations towards it;

26. *Calls upon* the Russian Federation and the United States of America to approach the International Atomic Energy Agency to carry out the verification requirements set forth in the Plutonium Management and Disposition Agreement signed by the two States on the basis of the model legal framework that has been agreed on and that is now available to be used in new verification agreements between the Agency and each of the two States;

27. *Calls upon* all nuclear-weapon States to make arrangements for the placing, as soon as practicable, of their fissile material no longer required for military purposes under International Atomic Energy Agency or other relevant international verification and to make arrangements for the disposition of such material for peaceful purposes in order to ensure that such material remains permanently outside military programmes;

28. *Affirms* that a nuclear-weapon-free world will ultimately require the underpinning of a universal and multilaterally negotiated legally binding instrument or a framework encompassing a mutually reinforcing set of instruments;

29. *Acknowledges* the report of the Secretary-General on the implementation of resolution 57/59, and requests him to prepare a report, within existing resources, on the implementation of the present resolution;

30. *Decides* to include in the provisional agenda of its fifty-ninth session an item entitled "Towards a nuclear-weapon-free world: a new agenda", and to review the implementation of the present resolution at that session.

RECORDED VOTE ON RESOLUTION 58/51:

In favour: Afghanistan, Algeria, Andorra, Angola, Antigua and Barbuda, Argentina, Armenia, Austria, Azerbaijan, Bahamas, Bahrain, Bangladesh, Barbados, Belize, Benin, Bolivia, Botswana, Brazil, Brunei Darussalam, Burkina Faso, Burundi, Cambodia, Cameroon, Canada, Cape Verde, Central African Republic, Chile, China, Colombia, Comoros, Congo, Costa Rica, Côte d'Ivoire, Cuba, Cyprus, Djibouti, Dominican Republic, Ecuador, Egypt, El Salvador, Eritrea, Ethiopia, Fiji, Finland, Gabon, Gambia, Ghana, Grenada, Guatemala, Guinea, Guinea-Bissau, Guyana, Haiti, Honduras, Indonesia, Iran, Ireland, Jamaica, Jordan, Kazakhstan, Kenya, Kuwait, Kyrgyzstan, Lebanon, Lesotho, Libyan Arab Jamahiriya, Liechtenstein, Madagascar, Malawi, Malaysia, Maldives, Mali, Malta, Mauritania, Mauritius, Mexico, Mongolia, Morocco, Mozambique, Myanmar, Namibia, Nauru, Nepal, New Zealand, Nicaragua, Niger, Nigeria, Oman, Panama, Papua New Guinea, Paraguay, Peru, Philippines, Qatar, Rwanda, Saint Lucia, Saint Vincent and the Grenadines, Samoa, San Marino, Saudi Arabia, Senegal, Seychelles, Sierra Leone, Singapore, Solomon Islands, Somalia, South Africa, Sri Lanka, Sudan, Suriname, Swaziland, Sweden, Syrian Arab Republic, Tajikistan, Thailand, Timor-Leste, Togo, Tonga, Trinidad and Tobago, Tunisia, Turkmenistan, Uganda, Ukraine, United Arab Emirates, United Republic of Tanzania, Uruguay, Uzbekistan, Vanuatu, Venezuela, Viet Nam, Yemen, Zambia, Zimbabwe.

Against: France, India, Israel, Pakistan, United Kingdom, United States.

Abstaining: Albania, Australia, Belarus, Belgium, Bhutan, Bosnia and Herzegovina, Bulgaria, Croatia, Czech Republic, Democratic People's Republic of Korea, Denmark, Estonia, Georgia, Germany, Greece, Hungary, Iceland, Italy, Japan, Latvia, Lithuania, Luxembourg, Micronesia, Netherlands, Norway, Poland, Portugal, Republic of Korea, Republic of Moldova, Romania, Russian Federation, Serbia and Montenegro, Slovakia, Slovenia, Spain, Switzerland, The former Yugoslav Republic of Macedonia, Turkey.

The First Committee adopted the twentieth preambular paragraph by a separate recorded vote of 117 to 6, with 39 abstentions; the Assembly retained it by a recorded vote of 128 to 6, with 41 abstentions.

The Assembly adopted **resolution 58/56** by recorded vote (112-45-20) [agenda item 73 *(t)*].

Nuclear disarmament

The General Assembly,

Recalling its resolution 49/75 E of 15 December 1994 on a step-by-step reduction of the nuclear threat, and its resolutions 50/70 P of 12 December 1995, 51/45 O of 10 December 1996, 52/38 L of 9 December 1997, 53/77 X of 4 December 1998, 54/54 P of 1 December 1999, 55/33 T of 20 November 2000, 56/24 R of 29 November 2001 and 57/79 of 22 November 2002 on nuclear disarmament,

Reaffirming the commitment of the international community to the goal of the total elimination of nuclear weapons and the establishment of a nuclear-weapon-free world,

Bearing in mind that the Convention on the Prohibition of the Development, Production and Stockpiling of Bacteriological (Biological) and Toxin Weapons and on Their Destruction of 1972 and the Convention on the Prohibition of the Development, Production, Stockpiling and Use of Chemical Weapons and on Their Destruction of 1993 have already established legal regimes on the complete prohibition of biological and chemical weapons, respectively, and determined to achieve a nuclear weapons convention on the prohibition of the development, testing, production, stockpiling, loan, transfer, use and threat of use of nuclear weapons and on their destruction, and to conclude such an international convention at an early date,

Recognizing that there now exist conditions for the establishment of a world free of nuclear weapons, and stressing the need to take concrete practical steps towards achieving this goal,

Bearing in mind paragraph 50 of the Final Document of the Tenth Special Session of the General Assembly, the first special session devoted to disarmament, calling for the urgent negotiation of agreements for the cessation of the qualitative improvement and development of nuclear-weapon systems, and for a comprehensive and phased programme with agreed time frames, wherever feasible, for the progressive and balanced reduction of nuclear weapons and their means of delivery, leading to their ultimate and complete elimination at the earliest possible time,

Reaffirming the conviction of the States parties to the Treaty on the Non-Proliferation of Nuclear Weapons that the Treaty is a cornerstone of nuclear non-proliferation and nuclear disarmament and the importance of the decision on strengthening the review process for the Treaty, the decision on principles and objectives for nuclear non-proliferation and disarmament, the decision on the extension of the Treaty and the resolution on the Middle East, adopted by the

1995 Review and Extension Conference of the Parties to the Treaty on the Non-Proliferation of Nuclear Weapons,

Stressing the importance of the thirteen steps for the systematic and progressive efforts to achieve the objective of nuclear disarmament leading to the total elimination of nuclear weapons, as agreed to by the States parties in the Final Document of the 2000 Review Conference of the Parties to the Treaty on the Non-Proliferation of Nuclear Weapons,

Reiterating the highest priority accorded to nuclear disarmament in the Final Document of the Tenth Special Session of the General Assembly and by the international community,

Noting with appreciation the entry into force of the Treaty on the Reduction and Limitation of Strategic Offensive Arms (START I), to which Belarus, Kazakhstan, the Russian Federation, Ukraine and the United States of America are States parties,

Reiterating its call for an early entry into force of the Comprehensive Nuclear-Test-Ban Treaty,

Noting with appreciation the entry into force of the Treaty on Strategic Offensive Reductions ("the Moscow Treaty") between the United States of America and the Russian Federation as a significant step towards reducing their deployed strategic nuclear weapons, while calling for further irreversible deep cuts in their nuclear arsenals,

Noting with appreciation also the unilateral measures taken by the nuclear-weapon States for nuclear arms limitation, and encouraging them to take further such measures,

Recognizing the complementarity of bilateral, plurilateral and multilateral negotiations on nuclear disarmament, and that bilateral negotiations can never replace multilateral negotiations in this respect,

Noting the support expressed in the Conference on Disarmament and in the General Assembly for the elaboration of an international convention to assure non-nuclear-weapon States against the use or threat of use of nuclear weapons, and the multilateral efforts in the Conference on Disarmament to reach agreement on such an international convention at an early date,

Recalling the advisory opinion of the International Court of Justice on the *Legality of the Threat or Use of Nuclear Weapons*, issued on 8 July 1996, and welcoming the unanimous reaffirmation by all Judges of the Court that there exists an obligation for all States to pursue in good faith and bring to a conclusion negotiations leading to nuclear disarmament in all its aspects under strict and effective international control,

Mindful of paragraph 74 and other relevant recommendations in the Final Document of the Thirteenth Conference of Heads of State or Government of Non-Aligned Countries, held at Kuala Lumpur from 20 to 25 February 2003, calling upon the Conference on Disarmament to establish, as soon as possible and as the highest priority, an ad hoc committee on nuclear disarmament and to commence negotiations on a phased programme for the complete elimination of nuclear weapons with a specified framework of time,

Recalling paragraph 11 of the declaration of the Meeting of the Ministers for Foreign Affairs of the Non-Aligned Movement, held in New York on 26 September 2003,

Bearing in mind the principles and guidelines on the establishment of nuclear-weapon-free zones, adopted by the Disarmament Commission at its substantive session of 1999,

Recalling the United Nations Millennium Declaration, in which heads of State and Government resolve to strive for the elimination of weapons of mass destruction, in particular nuclear weapons, and to keep all options open for achieving this aim, including the possibility of convening an international conference to identify ways of eliminating nuclear dangers,

Reaffirming that, in accordance with the Charter of the United Nations, States should refrain from the use or the threat of use of nuclear weapons in settling their disputes in international relations,

Seized of the danger of the use of weapons of mass destruction, particularly nuclear weapons, in terrorist acts and the urgent need for concerted international efforts to control and overcome it,

1. *Recognizes* that, in view of recent political developments, the time is now opportune for all the nuclear-weapon States to take effective disarmament measures with a view to achieving the elimination of these weapons;

2. *Reaffirms* that nuclear disarmament and nuclear non-proliferation are substantively interrelated and mutually reinforcing, that the two processes must go hand in hand and that there is a genuine need for a systematic and progressive process of nuclear disarmament;

3. *Welcomes and encourages* the efforts to establish new nuclear-weapon-free zones in different parts of the world on the basis of agreements or arrangements freely arrived at among the States of the regions concerned, which is an effective measure for limiting the further spread of nuclear weapons geographically and contributes to the cause of nuclear disarmament;

4. *Recognizes* that there is a genuine need to diminish the role of nuclear weapons in strategic doctrines and security policies to minimize the risk that these weapons will ever be used and to facilitate the process of their total elimination;

5. *Urges* the nuclear-weapon States to stop immediately the qualitative improvement, development, production and stockpiling of nuclear warheads and their delivery systems;

6. *Also urges* the nuclear-weapon States, as an interim measure, to de-alert and deactivate immediately their nuclear weapons and to take other concrete measures to reduce further the operational status of their nuclear-weapon systems;

7. *Reiterates its call* upon the nuclear-weapon States to undertake the step-by-step reduction of the nuclear threat and to carry out effective nuclear disarmament measures with a view to achieving the total elimination of these weapons;

8. *Calls upon* the nuclear-weapon States, pending the achievement of the total elimination of nuclear weapons, to agree on an internationally and legally binding instrument on a joint undertaking not to be the first to use nuclear weapons, and calls upon all States to conclude an internationally and legally binding instrument on security assurances of non-use and non-threat of use of nuclear weapons against non-nuclear-weapon States;

9. *Urges* the nuclear-weapon States to commence plurilateral negotiations among themselves at an appropriate stage on further deep reductions of nuclear weapons as an effective measure of nuclear disarmament;

10. *Underlines* the importance of applying the principle of irreversibility to the process of nuclear disarmament, nuclear and other related arms control and reduction measures;

11. *Underscores* the importance of the unequivocal undertaking by the nuclear-weapon States, in the Final Document of the Review Conference of the Parties to the Treaty on the Non-Proliferation of Nuclear Weapons, held in New York from 24 April to 19 May 2000, to accomplish the total elimination of their nuclear arsenals leading to nuclear disarmament, to which all States parties are committed under article VI of the Treaty, and the reaffirmation by the States parties that the total elimination of nuclear weapons is the only absolute guarantee against the use or threat of use of nuclear weapons;

12. *Calls* for the full and effective implementation of the thirteen steps for nuclear disarmament contained in the Final Document of the 2000 Review Conference of the Parties to the Treaty on the Non-Proliferation of Nuclear Weapons;

13. *Urges* the nuclear-weapon States to carry out further reductions of non-strategic nuclear weapons, based on unilateral initiatives and as an integral part of the nuclear arms reduction and disarmament process;

14. *Calls* for the immediate commencement of negotiations in the Conference on Disarmament on a non-discriminatory, multilateral and internationally and effectively verifiable treaty banning the production of fissile material for nuclear weapons or other nuclear explosive devices on the basis of the report of the Special Coordinator and the mandate contained therein;

15. *Urges* the Conference on Disarmament to agree on a programme of work which includes the immediate commencement of negotiations on such a treaty with a view to their conclusion within five years;

16. *Calls* for the conclusion of an international legal instrument or instruments on adequate security assurances to non-nuclear-weapon States;

17. *Also calls* for the early entry into force and strict observance of the Comprehensive Nuclear-Test-Ban Treaty;

18. *Expresses its regret* that the Conference on Disarmament was unable to establish an ad hoc committee on nuclear disarmament at its 2003 session, as called for in General Assembly resolution 57/79;

19. *Reiterates its call* upon the Conference on Disarmament to establish, on a priority basis, an ad hoc committee to deal with nuclear disarmament early in 2004 and to commence negotiations on a phased programme of nuclear disarmament leading to the eventual total elimination of nuclear weapons;

20. *Calls* for the convening of an international conference on nuclear disarmament in all its aspects at an early date to identify and deal with concrete measures of nuclear disarmament;

21. *Requests* the Secretary-General to submit to the General Assembly at its fifty-ninth session a report on the implementation of the present resolution;

22. *Decides* to include in the provisional agenda of its fifty-ninth session the item entitled "Nuclear disarmament".

RECORDED VOTE ON RESOLUTION 58/56:

In favour: Afghanistan, Algeria, Angola, Antigua and Barbuda, Bahamas, Bahrain, Bangladesh, Barbados, Belize, Benin, Bhutan, Bolivia, Botswana, Brazil, Brunei Darussalam, Burkina Faso, Burundi, Cambodia, Cameroon, Cape Verde, Central African Republic, Chile, China, Colombia, Comoros, Congo, Costa Rica, Côte d'Ivoire, Cuba, Democratic People's Republic of Korea, Djibouti, Dominican Republic, Ecuador, Egypt, El Salvador, Eritrea, Ethiopia, Fiji, Gabon, Gambia, Ghana, Grenada, Guatemala, Guinea, Guinea-Bissau, Guyana, Haiti, Honduras, Indonesia, Iran, Jamaica, Jordan, Kenya, Kuwait, Lao People's Democratic Republic, Lebanon, Lesotho, Libyan Arab Jamahiriya, Madagascar, Malawi, Malaysia, Maldives, Mali, Mauritania, Mexico, Mongolia, Morocco, Mozambique, Myanmar, Nauru, Nepal, New Zealand, Nicaragua, Niger, Nigeria, Oman, Panama, Papua New Guinea, Paraguay, Peru, Philippines, Qatar, Saint Lucia, Saint Vincent and the Grenadines, Samoa, Saudi Arabia, Senegal, Singapore, Solomon Islands, Somalia, South Africa, Sri Lanka, Sudan, Suriname, Swaziland, Syrian Arab Republic, Thailand, Timor-Leste, Togo, Tonga, Trinidad and Tobago, Tunisia, Uganda, United Arab Emirates, United Republic of Tanzania, Uruguay, Vanuatu, Venezuela, Viet Nam, Yemen, Zambia, Zimbabwe.

Against: Albania, Andorra, Australia, Austria, Belgium, Bosnia and Herzegovina, Bulgaria, Canada, Croatia, Cyprus, Czech Republic, Denmark, Estonia, Finland, France, Germany, Greece, Hungary, Iceland, Israel, Italy, Latvia, Liechtenstein, Lithuania, Luxembourg, Malta, Marshall Islands, Micronesia, Monaco, Netherlands, Norway, Poland, Portugal, Romania, San Marino, Serbia and Montenegro, Sierra Leone, Slovakia, Slovenia, Spain, Switzerland, The former Yugoslav Republic of Macedonia, Turkey, United Kingdom, United States.

Abstaining: Argentina, Armenia, Azerbaijan, Belarus, Georgia, India, Ireland, Japan, Kazakhstan, Kyrgyzstan, Mauritius, Pakistan, Republic of Korea, Republic of Moldova, Russian Federation, Rwanda, Sweden, Tajikistan, Ukraine, Uzbekistan.

The Assembly adopted **resolution 58/59** by recorded vote (164-2-14) [agenda item 73].

A path to the total elimination of nuclear weapons

The General Assembly,

Recalling its resolutions 49/75 H of 15 December 1994, 50/70 C of 12 December 1995, 51/45 G of 10 December 1996, 52/38 K of 9 December 1997, 53/77 U of 4 December 1998, 54/54 D of 1 December 1999, 55/33 R of 20 November 2000, 56/24 N of 29 November 2001 and 57/78 of 22 November 2002,

Recognizing that the enhancement of international peace and security and the promotion of nuclear disarmament mutually complement and strengthen each other,

Expressing deep concern regarding the growing dangers posed by the proliferation of weapons of mass destruction,

Convinced that every effort should be made to avoid nuclear devastation,

Reaffirming the crucial importance of the Treaty on the Non-Proliferation of Nuclear Weapons as the cornerstone of the international regime for nuclear non-proliferation and as an essential foundation for the pursuit of nuclear disarmament, and welcoming accession by Timor-Leste to the Treaty,

Bearing in mind that challenges to the Treaty and to the nuclear non-proliferation regime have further increased the necessity of full compliance and that the Treaty can fulfil its role only if there is confidence in compliance by all States parties,

Recognizing the progress made by the nuclear-weapon States in the reduction of their nuclear weapons unilaterally or through their negotiations, including the recent entry into force of the Treaty on Strategic Offensive Reductions ("the Moscow Treaty") by the United States of America and the Russian Federation, which should serve as a step for further nuclear disarmament, and the efforts for nuclear disarmament and non-proliferation by the international community,

Reaffirming the conviction that further advancement in nuclear disarmament will contribute to consolidating the international regime for nuclear non-proliferation, ensuring international peace and security,

Welcoming the continuation of a moratorium on nuclear-weapon-test explosions or any other nuclear explosions since the last nuclear tests,

Welcoming also the successful adoption of the Final Document of the 2000 Review Conference of the Parties to the Treaty on the Non-Proliferation of Nuclear Weapons, and stressing the importance of implementing its conclusions,

Welcoming further the constructive discussions at the second session, held from 28 April to 9 May 2003, of the Preparatory Committee for the Review Conference of the Parties to the Treaty on the Non-Proliferation of Nuclear Weapons to be held in 2005,

Welcoming the successful convening of a series of seminars and conferences aiming at further reinforcement of International Atomic Energy Agency safeguards, including the International Conference on Wider Adherence to Strengthened International Atomic Energy Agency Safeguards, held in Tokyo on 9 and 10 December 2002, and sharing the hope that, by making utmost use of the outcomes from the foregoing seminars and conferences, the International Atomic Energy Agency safeguards system will be further strengthened, by means of universalization of safeguards agreements and the additional protocols,

Encouraging the Russian Federation and the United States of America to continue their intensive consultations in accordance with the Joint Declaration on the New Strategic Relationship between the two States,

Welcoming the Final Declaration of the third Conference on Facilitating the Entry into Force of the Comprehensive Nuclear-Test-Ban Treaty, convened in Vienna from 3 to 5 September 2003 in accordance with article XIV of the Treaty,

Recognizing the importance of preventing terrorists from acquiring or developing nuclear weapons or related materials, radioactive materials, equipment and technology and underlining the role of the International Atomic Energy Agency in this regard,

Stressing the importance of education on disarmament and non-proliferation for future generations, and welcoming the recommendations contained in the report of the Secretary-General on the United Nations study on disarmament and non-proliferation education, submitted to the General Assembly at its fifty-seventh session,

1. *Reaffirms* the importance of achieving the universality of the Treaty on the Non-Proliferation of Nuclear Weapons, and calls upon States not parties to the Treaty to accede to it as non-nuclear-weapon States without delay and without conditions;

2. *Also reaffirms* the importance for all States parties to the Treaty on the Non-Proliferation of Nuclear Weapons to fulfil their obligations under the Treaty;

3. *Stresses* the central importance of the following practical steps for the systematic and progressive efforts to implement article VI of the Treaty on the Non-Proliferation of Nuclear Weapons, and paragraphs 3 and 4 *(c)* of the decision on principles and objectives for nuclear non-proliferation and disarmament of the 1995 Review and Extension Conference of the Parties to the Treaty:

(a) The importance and urgency of signatures and ratifications, without delay and without conditions and in accordance with constitutional processes, to achieve the early entry into force of the Comprehensive Nuclear-Test-Ban Treaty as well as a moratorium on nuclear-weapon-test explosions or any other nuclear explosions pending the entry into force of that Treaty;

(b) The establishment of an ad hoc committee in the Conference on Disarmament as early as possible during its 2004 session to negotiate a non-discriminatory, multilateral and internationally and effectively verifiable treaty banning the production of fissile material for nuclear weapons or other nuclear explosive devices, in accordance with the report of the Special Coordinator of 1995 and the mandate contained therein, taking into consideration both nuclear disarmament and non-proliferation objectives, with a view to its conclusion within five years and, pending its entry into force, a moratorium on the production of fissile material for nuclear weapons;

(c) The establishment of an appropriate subsidiary body with a mandate to deal with nuclear disarmament in the Conference on Disarmament as early as possible during its 2004 session in the context of establishing a programme of work;

(d) The inclusion of the principle of irreversibility to apply to nuclear disarmament, nuclear and other related arms control and reduction measures;

(e) An unequivocal undertaking by the nuclear-weapon States, as agreed at the 2000 Review Conference of the Parties to the Treaty on the Non-Proliferation of Nuclear Weapons, to accomplish the total elimination of their nuclear arsenals, leading to nuclear disarmament, to which all States parties to the Treaty are committed under article VI of the Treaty;

(f) Deep reductions by the Russian Federation and the United States of America in their strategic offensive arsenals, while placing great importance on the existing multilateral treaties, with a view to maintaining and strengthening strategic stability and international security;

(g) Steps by all the nuclear-weapon States leading to nuclear disarmament in a way that promotes international stability, and based on the principle of undiminished security for all:

(i) Further efforts by all the nuclear-weapon States to continue to reduce their nuclear arsenals unilaterally;

(ii) Increased transparency by the nuclear-weapon States with regard to their nuclear weapons capabilities and the implementation of agreements pursuant to article VI of the Treaty and as voluntary confidence-building measures to support further progress on nuclear disarmament;

(iii) The further reduction of non-strategic nuclear weapons, based on unilateral initiatives and as an integral part of the nuclear arms reduction and disarmament process;

(iv) Concrete agreed measures to reduce further the operational status of nuclear weapons systems;

(v) A diminishing role for nuclear weapons in security policies to minimize the risk that these weapons will ever be used and to facilitate the process of their total elimination;

(vi) The engagement, as soon as appropriate, of all the nuclear-weapon States in the process leading to the total elimination of their nuclear weapons;

(h) Reaffirmation that the ultimate objective of the efforts of States in the disarmament process is general and complete disarmament under effective international control;

4. *Recognizes* that the realization of a world free of nuclear weapons will require further steps, including deeper reductions by all the nuclear-weapon States in the process of working towards achieving their elimination;

5. *Invites* the nuclear-weapon States to keep the Members of the United Nations duly informed of the progress or efforts made towards nuclear disarmament;

6. *Emphasizes* the importance of a successful Review Conference of the Parties to the Treaty on the Non-Proliferation of Nuclear Weapons in 2005, as the third session of the Preparatory Committee will be convened in 2004;

7. *Welcomes* the ongoing efforts in the dismantlement of nuclear weapons, notes the importance of the safe and effective management of the resultant fissile materials, and calls for arrangements by all the nuclear-weapon States to place, as soon as practicable, fissile material designated by each of them as no longer required for military purposes under International Atomic Energy Agency or other relevant international verification and arrangements for the disposition of such material for peaceful purposes to ensure that such material remains permanently outside of military programmes;

8. *Stresses* the importance of further development of the verification capabilities, including International Atomic Energy Agency safeguards, that will be required to provide assurance of compliance with nuclear disarmament agreements for the achievement and maintenance of a nuclear-weapon-free world;

9. *Calls upon* all States to redouble their efforts to prevent and curb the proliferation of nuclear and other weapons of mass destruction, confirming and strengthening, if necessary, their policies not to transfer equipment, materials or technology that could contribute to the proliferation of those weapons, while ensuring that such policies are consistent with the obligations of States under the Treaty on the Non-Proliferation of Nuclear Weapons;

10. *Also calls upon* all States to maintain the highest possible standards of security, safe custody, effective control and physical protection of all materials that could contribute to the proliferation of nuclear and other weapons of mass destruction in order, inter alia, to prevent those materials from falling into the hands of terrorists;

11. *Welcomes* the adoption of resolution GC(47)/RES/11 on 19 September 2003 by the General Conference of the International Atomic Energy Agency, in which it is recommended that States members of the Agency continue to consider implementing the elements of the plan of action outlined in resolution GC(44)/RES/19, adopted on 22 September 2000 by the General Conference of the Agency, and in the Agency's updated plan of action of April 2003, with the aim of facilitating the entry into force of comprehensive safeguards agreements and additional protocols, and calls for the early and full implementation of that resolution;

12. *Encourages* the constructive role played by civil society in promoting nuclear non-proliferation and nuclear disarmament.

RECORDED VOTE ON RESOLUTION 58/59:

In favour: Afghanistan, Albania, Algeria, Andorra, Angola, Antigua and Barbuda, Argentina, Armenia, Australia, Austria, Azerbaijan, Bahamas, Bahrain, Bangladesh, Barbados, Belarus, Belgium, Belize, Benin, Bolivia, Bosnia and Herzegovina, Botswana, Brunei Darussalam, Bulgaria, Burkina Faso, Burundi, Cambodia, Cameroon, Canada, Cape Verde, Central African Republic, Chile, Colombia, Comoros, Congo, Costa Rica, Côte d'Ivoire, Croatia, Cyprus, Czech Republic, Denmark, Djibouti, Dominican Republic, Ecuador, El Salvador, Eritrea, Estonia, Ethiopia, Fiji, Finland, France, Gabon, Gambia, Georgia, Germany, Ghana, Greece, Grenada, Guatemala, Guinea, Guinea-Bissau, Guyana, Haiti, Honduras, Hungary, Iceland, Indonesia, Iran, Italy, Jamaica, Japan, Jordan, Kazakhstan, Kenya, Kuwait, Kyrgyzstan, Lao People's Democratic Republic, Latvia, Lebanon, Lesotho, Libyan Arab Jamahiriya, Liechtenstein, Lithuania, Luxembourg, Madagascar, Malawi, Malaysia, Maldives, Mali, Malta, Marshall Islands, Mauritania, Mauritius, Micronesia, Monaco, Mongolia, Morocco, Mozambique, Namibia, Nauru, Nepal, Netherlands, Nicaragua, Niger, Nigeria, Norway, Oman, Panama, Papua New Guinea, Paraguay, Peru, Philippines, Poland, Portugal, Qatar, Republic of Korea, Republic of Moldova, Romania, Russian Federation, Rwanda, Saint Lucia, Saint Vincent and the Grenadines, Samoa, San Marino, Saudi Arabia, Senegal, Serbia and Montenegro, Seychelles, Sierra Leone, Singapore, Slovakia, Slovenia, Solomon Islands, Somalia, Spain, Sri Lanka, Sudan, Suriname, Swaziland, Switzerland, Syrian Arab Republic, Tajikistan, Thailand, The former Yugoslav Republic of Macedonia, Timor-Leste, Togo, Tonga, Trinidad and Tobago, Tunisia, Turkey, Turkmenistan, Uganda, Ukraine, United Arab Emirates, United Kingdom, United Republic of Tanzania, Uruguay, Uzbekistan, Vanuatu, Venezuela, Viet Nam, Yemen, Zambia, Zimbabwe.

Against: India, United States.

Abstaining: Bhutan, Brazil, China, Cuba, Democratic People's Republic of Korea, Egypt, Ireland, Israel, Mexico, Myanmar, New Zealand, Pakistan, South Africa, Sweden.

The Assembly adopted **decision 58/517** [agenda item 73 (z)].

United Nations conference to identify ways of eliminating nuclear dangers in the context of nuclear disarmament

At its 71st plenary meeting, on 8 December 2003, the General Assembly, by a recorded vote of 133 to 6, with 38 abstentions, and on the recommendation of the First Committee, recalling its resolution 57/69 of 22 November 2002, decided to include in the provisional agenda of its fifty-ninth session the item entitled "United Nations conference to identify ways of eliminating nuclear dangers in the context of nuclear disarmament".

RECORDED VOTE ON DECISION 58/517:

In favour: Afghanistan, Algeria, Angola, Antigua and Barbuda, Argentina, Armenia, Bahamas, Bahrain, Bangladesh, Barbados, Belarus, Belize, Benin, Bhutan, Bolivia, Botswana, Brazil, Brunei Darussalam, Burkina Faso, Burundi, Cambodia, Cameroon, Cape Verde, Central African Republic, Chile, China, Colombia, Comoros, Congo, Costa Rica, Côte d'Ivoire, Cuba, Cyprus, Democratic People's Republic of Korea, Djibouti, Dominican Republic, Ecuador, Egypt, El Salvador, Eritrea, Ethiopia, Fiji, Gabon, Gambia, Ghana, Grenada, Guatemala, Guinea, Guinea-Bissau, Guyana, Haiti, Honduras, India, Indonesia, Iran, Ireland, Jamaica, Japan, Jordan, Kenya, Kuwait, Kyrgyzstan, Lao People's Democratic Republic, Lebanon, Lesotho, Libyan Arab Jamahiriya, Madagascar, Malawi, Malaysia, Maldives, Mali, Marshall Islands, Mauritania, Mauritius, Mexico, Micronesia, Mongolia, Morocco, Mozambique, Myanmar, Namibia, Nauru, Nepal, New Zealand, Nicaragua, Niger, Nigeria, Oman, Pakistan, Panama, Papua New Guinea, Paraguay, Peru, Philippines, Qatar, Russian Federation, Rwanda, Saint Lucia, Saint Vincent and the Grenadines, Samoa, Saudi Arabia, Senegal, Seychelles, Sierra Leone, Singapore, Solomon Islands, Somalia, South Africa, Sri Lanka, Sudan, Suriname, Swaziland, Sweden, Syrian Arab Republic, Tajikistan, Thailand, Timor-Leste,

Togo, Tonga, Trinidad and Tobago, Tunisia, Turkmenistan, Uganda, United Arab Emirates, United Republic of Tanzania, Uruguay, Uzbekistan, Vanuatu, Venezuela, Viet Nam, Yemen, Zambia, Zimbabwe.

Against: France, Israel, Monaco, Poland, United Kingdom, United States.

Abstaining: Albania, Andorra, Australia, Austria, Azerbaijan, Belgium, Bosnia and Herzegovina, Bulgaria, Canada, Croatia, Czech Republic, Denmark, Estonia, Finland, Georgia, Greece, Hungary, Iceland, Italy, Latvia, Liechtenstein, Lithuania, Luxembourg, Malta, Netherlands, Norway, Portugal, Republic of Korea, Republic of Moldova, Romania, San Marino, Serbia and Montenegro, Slovakia, Slovenia, Spain, Switzerland, The former Yugoslav Republic of Macedonia, Turkey.

ABM Treaty and other missile issues

In 2003, Member States continued to express concern over the United States unilateral withdrawal, effective 2002 [YUN 2002, p. 504], from the Treaty on the Limitation of Anti-Ballistic Missile Systems (ABM Treaty). Delegates at the second session of the Preparatory Committee for the 2005 Review Conference of NPT (see p. 549) maintained that the withdrawal brought an additional element of uncertainty to international security, impacted negatively on strategic stability and would have negative consequences for nuclear disarmament and non-proliferation.

Other missile-related issues, particularly the proliferation of long-range ballistic missiles and United States efforts to build a missile defence system [YUN 1999, p. 469], remained an area of concern. On 20 May, the United States, in a statement on its national policy on ballistic missiles, announced plans to begin deploying its missile defence capabilities in 2004, as a starting point for fielding improved and expanded versions of such systems at a later stage. In response to perceived threats in the region, Australia announced, on 4 December, that it had in principle decided to join the United States missile defence system, and, on 19 December, the Government of Japan announced that it would build a missile defence system based on technology from the United States. In June, Defence Ministers of North Atlantic Treaty Organization (NATO) member States announced that the organization had secured funding for a new missile defence feasibility study, to be launched in October to examine alternatives for protecting NATO territory and forces from missile threats, determine the best mix of systems and capabilities to obtain a NATO missile defence and recommend options for system elements that were consistent with NATO and national missile defence capabilities. The subscribing States to the international code of conduct against ballistic missile proliferation, also known as the Hague code of conduct, adopted in 2002 [YUN 2002, p. 504], held their first (Vienna, 24-25 June) and second (New York, 2-3 October) regular meetings [A/58/595-S/2003/1091]. In June, they discussed, among other things, the exchange of annual declarations on national ballistic missile and space launch vehicle policies and pre-launch notifications. In October, they discussed the standardization and qualitative improvement of the annual declarations and pre-launch notifications of ballistic missiles and space launch vehicles. The subscribing States held an outreach seminar (New York, 1 October), aimed at strengthening the profile of the code by reaching out to non-subscribing States, the media, interested non-governmental organizations (NGOs) and other external parties. At year's end, subscribing States numbered 109. In December, the Libyan Arab Jamahiriya declared its agreement to restrict the range of its missiles to no more than 300 kilometres, in line with standards agreed upon under the Missile Technology Control Regime.

Report of Secretary-General. In response to General Assembly resolution 57/71 [YUN 2002, p. 505], the Secretary-General, in a July report with later addenda [A/58/117 & Add.1,2], presented the views of 10 Member States on the issue of missiles in all its aspects.

Communication. In January [CD/1690], the Russian Federation stated that the abandonment of the principles of the ABM Treaty, from which the United States had withdrawn unilaterally, could only lead to a weakening of strategic stability, a new arms race, including the proliferation of WMDs and their missile delivery systems, and the diversion of resources from efforts to combat real present-day challenges and threats, particularly international terrorism.

GENERAL ASSEMBLY ACTION

On 8 December [meeting 71], the General Assembly, on the recommendation of the First Committee [A/58/462], adopted **resolution 58/37** by recorded vote (113-3-57) [agenda item 73 *(m)*].

Missiles

The General Assembly,

Recalling its resolutions 54/54 F of 1 December 1999, 55/33 A of 20 November 2000, 56/24 B of 29 November 2001 and 57/71 of 22 November 2002,

Reaffirming the role of the United Nations in the field of arms regulation and disarmament and the commitment of Member States to take concrete steps to strengthen that role,

Realizing the need to promote regional and international peace and security in a world free from the scourge of war and the burden of armaments,

Convinced of the need for a comprehensive approach towards missiles, in a balanced and non-discriminatory manner, as a contribution to international peace and security,

Bearing in mind that the security concerns of Member States at the international and regional levels should be taken into consideration in addressing the issue of missiles,

Underlining the complexities involved in considering the issue of missiles in the conventional context,

Expressing its support for the international efforts against the development and proliferation of all weapons of mass destruction,

Considering that the Secretary-General, in response to resolution 55/33 A, with the assistance of a Panel of Governmental Experts, submitted a report for the consideration of the General Assembly at its fifty-seventh session on the issue of missiles in all its aspects,

Welcoming the report of the Secretary-General on the issue of missiles in all its aspects,

1. *Takes note* of the report of the Secretary-General containing the replies from Member States on the report on the issue of missiles in all its aspects, submitted pursuant to resolution 57/71;

2. *Requests* the Secretary-General further to seek the views of Member States on the report on the issue of missiles in all its aspects and to submit a report to the General Assembly at its fifty-ninth session;

3. *Also requests* the Secretary-General, with the assistance of a Panel of Governmental Experts, to be established in 2004 on the basis of equitable geographical distribution, to explore further the issue of missiles in all its aspects and to submit a report for consideration by the General Assembly at its fifty-ninth session;

4. *Decides* to include in the provisional agenda of its fifty-ninth session the item entitled "Missiles".

RECORDED VOTE ON RESOLUTION 58/37:

In favour: Afghanistan, Algeria, Antigua and Barbuda, Bahamas, Bahrain, Bangladesh, Barbados, Belarus, Belize, Benin, Bhutan, Botswana, Brazil, Brunei Darussalam, Burkina Faso, Cambodia, Cameroon, Cape Verde, Central African Republic, Chile, China, Colombia, Comoros, Congo, Costa Rica, Côte d'Ivoire, Cuba, Djibouti, Dominican Republic, Ecuador, Egypt, El Salvador, Eritrea, Ethiopia, Fiji, Gabon, Ghana, Grenada, Guatemala, Guinea, Guinea-Bissau, Guyana, Haiti, Honduras, India, Indonesia, Iran, Ireland, Jamaica, Jordan, Kazakhstan, Kenya, Kuwait, Kyrgyzstan, Lao People's Democratic Republic, Lebanon, Lesotho, Libyan Arab Jamahiriya, Madagascar, Malawi, Malaysia, Maldives, Mali, Mauritania, Mauritius, Mexico, Mongolia, Morocco, Mozambique, Myanmar, Namibia, Nauru, Nepal, Nicaragua, Niger, Nigeria, Oman, Pakistan, Panama, Papua New Guinea, Peru, Philippines, Qatar, Russian Federation, Saint Lucia, Saudi Arabia, Senegal, Somalia, South Africa, Sri Lanka, Sudan, Suriname, Swaziland, Sweden, Syrian Arab Republic, Tajikistan, Thailand, Timor-Leste, Togo, Tonga, Trinidad and Tobago, Tunisia, Turkmenistan, Uganda, Ukraine, United Arab Emirates, United Republic of Tanzania, Vanuatu, Venezuela, Viet Nam, Yemen, Zambia, Zimbabwe.

Against: Israel, Micronesia, United States.

Abstaining: Albania, Andorra, Argentina, Armenia, Australia, Austria, Azerbaijan, Belgium, Bolivia, Bosnia and Herzegovina, Bulgaria, Canada, Croatia, Cyprus, Czech Republic, Denmark, Estonia, Finland, France, Georgia, Germany, Greece, Hungary, Iceland, Italy, Japan, Latvia, Liechtenstein, Lithuania, Luxembourg, Malta, Marshall Islands, Monaco, Netherlands, New Zealand, Norway, Paraguay, Poland, Portugal, Republic of Korea, Republic of Moldova, Romania, Rwanda, Saint Vincent and the Grenadines, Samoa, San Marino, Serbia and Montenegro, Singapore, Slovakia, Slovenia, Spain, Switzerland, The former Yugoslav Republic of Macedonia, Turkey, United Kingdom, Uruguay, Uzbekistan.

Comprehensive Nuclear-Test-Ban Treaty

Status

As at 31 December 2003, 170 States had signed the 1996 Comprehensive Nuclear-Test-Ban Treaty (CTBT), adopted by General Assembly resolution 50/245 [YUN 1996, p. 454], and 108 had ratified it. During the year, instruments of ratification were deposited by Afghanistan, Albania, Algeria, Côte d'Ivoire, Cyprus, Eritrea, Honduras, Kuwait, Kyrgyzstan, Mauritania and Oman. In accordance with article XIV, CTBT was to enter into force 180 days after the 44 States possessing nuclear reactors, listed in annex 2 of the Treaty, had deposited their instruments of ratification. By year's end, 32 of those States had ratified the Treaty.

Conference on facilitating entry into force

The third Conference on Facilitating the Entry into Force of CTBT (Vienna, 3-5 September) [CTBT-Art.XIV/2003/5] was convened in accordance with article XIV of the Treaty, which stipulated that if the Treaty had not entered into force three years from the date it had opened for signature [YUN 1996, p. 452], the depositary should convene a conference at the request of a majority of ratifying States to consider and decide by consensus measures to facilitate an early entry into force. The first such Conference took place in 1999 [YUN 1999, p. 471], and the second, in 2001 [YUN 2001, p. 482].

On 5 September, the Conference adopted a Final Declaration and measures to promote the Treaty's entry into force. Participants called on States that had not done so to sign and ratify the Treaty promptly, particularly those whose ratification was needed to enable the Treaty to take effect. They agreed to select one of the ratifying States as coordinator, to be assisted by a special representative, to promote cooperation and further signatures and ratifications, and recommended that ratifying States consider establishing a trust fund, financed through voluntary contributions, to support an outreach programme to promote the Treaty. They further recommended that the provisional technical secretariat of the Preparatory Commission for the Comprehensive Nuclear-Test-Ban-Treaty Organization (CTBTO) (see p. 548) continue to provide States with legal assistance regarding the ratification process and implementation measures, and asked it to act as a focal point where information about the activities of ratifying and signatory States could be collected, in order to promote the Treaty's entry into force.

GENERAL ASSEMBLY ACTION

On 8 December [meeting 71], the General Assembly, on the recommendation of the First Committee [A/58/468], adopted **resolution 58/71** by recorded vote (173-1-4) [agenda item 79].

Comprehensive Nuclear-Test-Ban Treaty

The General Assembly,

Reiterating that the cessation of nuclear-weapon test explosions or any other nuclear explosions constitutes an effective nuclear disarmament and non-proliferation measure,

Recalling that the Comprehensive Nuclear-Test-Ban Treaty, adopted by its resolution 50/245 of 10 September 1996, was opened for signature on 24 September 1996,

Stressing that a universal and effectively verifiable Comprehensive Nuclear-Test-Ban Treaty constitutes a fundamental instrument in the field of disarmament and nuclear non-proliferation,

Encouraged by the signing of the Treaty by one hundred and sixty-nine States, including forty-one of the forty-four needed for its entry into force, and welcoming the ratification of one hundred and seven States, including thirty-two of the forty-four needed for its entry into force, among which there are three nuclear-weapon States,

Recalling its resolution 57/100 of 22 November 2002,

Welcoming the Final Declaration of the third Conference on Facilitating the Entry into Force of the Comprehensive Nuclear-Test-Ban Treaty, held at Vienna from 3 to 5 September 2003, pursuant to article XIV of the Treaty,

1. *Stresses* the importance and urgency of signature and ratification, without delay and without conditions and in accordance with constitutional processes, to achieve the earliest entry into force of the Comprehensive Nuclear-Test-Ban Treaty;

2. *Welcomes* the contributions by the States signatories to the work of the Preparatory Commission for the Comprehensive Nuclear-Test-Ban Treaty Organization, in particular to its efforts to ensure that the Treaty's verification regime will be capable of meeting the verification requirements of the Treaty upon its entry into force, in accordance with article IV of the Treaty;

3. *Urges* States to maintain their moratoriums on nuclear-weapons test explosions or any other nuclear explosions, pending the entry into force of the Treaty;

4. *Urges* all States that have not yet signed the Treaty to sign and ratify it as soon as possible and to refrain from acts that would defeat its object and purpose in the meanwhile;

5. *Urges* all States that have signed but not yet ratified the Treaty, in particular those whose ratification is needed for its entry into force, to accelerate their ratification processes with a view to their earliest successful conclusion;

6. *Urges* all States to remain seized of the issue at the highest political level;

7. *Decides* to include in the provisional agenda of its fifty-ninth session the item entitled "Comprehensive Nuclear-Test-Ban Treaty".

RECORDED VOTE ON RESOLUTION 58/71:

In favour: Afghanistan, Albania, Algeria, Andorra, Angola, Antigua and Barbuda, Argentina, Armenia, Australia, Austria, Azerbaijan, Bahamas, Bahrain, Bangladesh, Barbados, Belarus, Belgium, Belize, Benin, Bhutan, Bolivia, Bosnia and Herzegovina, Botswana, Brazil, Brunei Darussalam, Bulgaria, Burkina Faso, Burundi, Cambodia, Cameroon, Canada, Cape Verde, Central African Republic, Chile, China, Comoros, Congo, Costa Rica, Côte d'Ivoire, Croatia, Cuba, Cyprus, Czech Republic, Denmark, Djibouti, Dominican Republic, Ecuador, Egypt, El Salvador, Eritrea, Estonia, Ethiopia, Fiji, Finland, France, Gabon, Gambia, Georgia, Germany, Ghana, Greece, Grenada, Guatemala, Guinea, Guinea-Bissau, Guyana, Haiti, Honduras, Hungary, Iceland, Indonesia, Iran, Ireland, Israel, Italy, Jamaica, Japan, Jordan, Kazakhstan, Kenya, Kuwait, Kyrgyzstan, Lao People's Democratic Republic, Latvia, Lesotho, Libyan Arab Jamahiriya, Liechtenstein, Lithuania, Luxembourg, Madagascar, Malawi, Malaysia, Maldives, Mali, Malta, Marshall Islands, Mauritania, Mexico, Micronesia, Monaco, Mongolia, Morocco, Mozambique, Myanmar, Namibia, Nauru, Nepal, Netherlands, New Zealand, Nicaragua, Niger, Nigeria, Norway, Oman, Pakistan, Panama, Papua New Guinea, Paraguay, Peru, Philippines, Poland, Portugal, Qatar, Republic of Korea, Republic of Moldova, Romania, Russian Federation, Rwanda, Saint Lucia, Saint Vincent and the Grenadines, Samoa, San Marino, Saudi Arabia, Senegal, Serbia and Montenegro, Seychelles, Sierra Leone, Singapore, Slovakia, Slovenia, Solomon Islands, Somalia, South Africa, Spain, Sri Lanka, Sudan, Suriname, Swaziland, Sweden, Switzerland, Tajikistan, Thailand, The former Yugoslav Republic of Macedonia, Timor-Leste, Togo, Tonga, Trinidad and Tobago, Tunisia, Turkey, Turkmenistan, Uganda, Ukraine, United Arab Emirates, United Kingdom, United Republic of Tanzania, Uruguay, Uzbekistan, Vanuatu, Venezuela, Viet Nam, Yemen, Zambia, Zimbabwe.

Against: United States.

Abstaining: Colombia, India, Mauritius, Syrian Arab Republic.

Preparatory Commission for the CTBT Organization

The Preparatory Commission for the Comprehensive Nuclear-Test-Ban Treaty Organization, established in 1996 [YUN 1996, p. 452], continued to develop the Treaty's verification regime. Steady progress was made in establishing the International Monitoring System (IMS) [YUN 1999, p. 472], the global network of 337 facilities in 90 countries designed to track and detect nuclear explosions prohibited by CTBT via a global satellite communication system, and to transmit relevant information to the International Data Centre (IDC) in Vienna. During the year, 12 additional facilities were certified, bringing the total to 67. Site surveys were completed for 91 per cent of IMS stations, of which 52 per cent substantially met specifications. Some 70 secure signatory accounts (one for each requesting signatory State) had been established, with over 490 users authorized to access IMS data and IDC products. The development of the draft on-site inspections operational manual remained a priority task for the Commission's provisional technical secretariat.

The Preparatory Commission held its twentieth (24-25 June) [CTBT/PC-20/1] and twenty-first (10-13 November) [CTBT/PC-21/1] sessions, both in Vienna, to consider the reports of its working groups and to discuss organizational, budgetary and other matters. The Commission adopted its 2004 programme budget, totalling $95 million, of which $45 million was earmarked for the IMS network. The remainder would be used to develop IDC, the global communications infrastructure, and procedures and guidelines for on-site inspection and evaluation once the Treaty entered into force.

Note by Secretary-General. In September [A/58/385], the Secretary-General informed the General Assembly of the availability of the report of the Commission's Executive Secretary covering 2002.

Non-Proliferation Treaty

Status

As at 31 December, the number of States party to the 1968 Treaty on the Non-Proliferation of Nuclear Weapons (NPT), adopted by the General

Assembly in resolution 2373(XXII) [YUN 1968, p. 17], stood at 188. In 2003, the Democratic People's Republic of Korea (DPRK) withdrew from the Treaty (see p. 391) and Timor-Leste acceded to it. NPT entered into force on 5 March 1970.

2005 review conference

Quinquennial review conferences, as called for under article VIII, paragraph 3, of the Treaty, were held in 1975 [YUN 1975, p. 27], 1980 [YUN 1980, p. 51], 1985 [YUN 1985, p. 56], 1990 [YUN 1990, p. 50], 1995 [YUN 1995, p. 189] and 2000 [YUN 2000, p. 487].

As decided by the NPT parties in 2002 [YUN 2002, p. 507], the Preparatory Committee for the 2005 Review Conference held its second session (Geneva, 28 April–9 May) [NPT/CONF.2005/PC.II/50] to consider the implementation of the Treaty's provisions relating to non-proliferation of nuclear weapons, disarmament and international peace and security; safeguards and nuclear-weapon-free zones; and the right of States parties to research, produce and use nuclear energy for peaceful purposes. Also discussed were the decision on the principles and objectives for nuclear non-proliferation and the resolution on the Middle East, both adopted at the 1995 Review Conference, the final document of the 2000 Review Conference and the safety and security of peaceful nuclear programmes. Documents before the Committee included a note by the Secretariat on the estimated cost of the 2005 Review Conference [NPT/CONF.2005/PC.II/1]; a statement by the Agency for the Prohibition of Nuclear Weapons in Latin America and the Caribbean regarding its work [NPT/CONF.2005/PC.II/3/Rev.1]; a report by CTBTO updating the work of its Preparatory Commission (see p. 548) [NPT/CONF.2005/PC.II/4]; a joint statement by the Russian Federation and the United States on SORT (see p. 535) [NPT/CONF.2005/PC.II/21]; reports by the New Agenda Coalition (see p. 536 et seq.) [NPT/CONF.2005/PC.II/16] and by 25 other States on implementation of NPT and of the 1995 decision [NPT/CONF.2005/PC.II/2, 5, 7, 8, 10 & Corr.1, 13, 14, 17, 18, 19, 22, 23, 24, 25, 26, 27, 28, 29, 32, 33, 34, 37, 39, 41, 42]; reports by 14 States on steps they had taken to promote the establishment of the Middle East as a zone free of nuclear weapons [NPT/CONF.2005/PC.II/6, 9, 12, 15, 20, 30, 31, 35, 36, 43, 44, 46, 47, 48]; and numerous working papers. The Committee's third session was scheduled to take place from 26 April to 7 May 2004.

Communication. A ministerial declaration by the Foreign Ministers of the New Agenda Coalition countries (Brazil, Egypt, Ireland, Mexico, New Zealand, South Africa, Sweden) (New York, 23 September) [A/C.1/58/4] expressed concern at the lack of progress in implementing the 13 practical steps on nuclear disarmament to which all NPT States parties agreed at the 2000 Review Conference [YUN 2000, p. 487].

IAEA safeguards

As at 31 December, the Model Protocol Additional to Safeguards Agreements strengthening the safeguards regime of the International Atomic Energy Agency (IAEA), approved by the IAEA Board of Governors in 1997 [YUN 1997, p. 486], had been signed by 79 States, including the five nuclear-weapon States, and the European Atomic Energy Community, and was in force or being provisionally applied in 38 States.

The IAEA General Conference [GC(47)/RES/11], as in previous years, requested concerned States and other parties to safeguards agreements that had not done so to sign the additional protocols promptly. Encouraging those that had signed the protocols to bring them into force, the Conference advocated cooperation among member States to facilitate exchange of equipment, material and scientific and technological information for implementing those protocols. It commended member States that had implemented elements of a plan of action outlined in a 2000 resolution of the Conference [YUN 2000, p. 505] and recommended that other member States consider doing the same to facilitate the entry into force of comprehensive safeguards agreements and additional protocols.

On 17 March, IAEA inspectors in Iraq withdrew upon notice from the United States Government that coalition forces were about to begin hostilities. Agency inspectors returned to Iraq in June to re-verify the nuclear material subject to safeguards following reports of looting at a nuclear storage facility south of Baghdad. They found that, although some uranium compounds could have been dispersed, neither the quantity nor the material involved was sensitive from a proliferation perspective, as was confirmed by the General Conference [GC(47)/DEC/12]. (See also p. 319.)

IAEA was not able to verify that the DPRK had declared all the nuclear material subject to Agency safeguards, nor could it provide any assurance of its diversion given that the DPRK had prevented IAEA inspectors from carrying out any verification activities within the country in 2003. On 19 September [GC(47)/RES/12], the General Conference, deploring the DPRK's continuing unwillingness to accept the dialogue proposed by IAEA, urged it to reconsider its actions, to dismantle completely any nuclear weapons programme promptly and to accept comprehensive IAEA safeguards.

During the year, IAEA took action regarding the implementation of NPT safeguards agreements in Iran and the Libyan Arab Jamahiriya.

On 12 September [GOV/2003/69], the Board of Governors, referring to Iran's failure to meet its safeguards obligations with respect to the reporting of nuclear material, facilities and activities, decided it was essential and urgent that Iran remedy that failure and cooperate to ensure verification of its compliance. In November [GOV/2003/81], the Board noted that Iran had taken specific actions as requested, welcomed its decision to voluntarily suspend all enrichment-related and reprocessing activities, and requested it to adhere to that decision.

Following Libya's revelation that it had been engaged in an undeclared development of uranium enrichment capability and had obtained nuclear weapon design documents, IAEA conducted verification activities to ascertain the extent of the country's programme. However, on 19 December [A/58/664-SC/2003/1196], Libya announced its decision to eliminate all materials, equipment and programmes relevant to the production of internationally proscribed weapons, including nuclear weapons, and agreed to pursue with IAEA a policy of full transparency and active cooperation.

Note by Secretary-General. In August [A/58/312], the Secretary-General informed the General Assembly of the availability of the forty-seventh report of IAEA [GC(47)/2] for 2002.

Communications. On 17 January [CD/1696], Peru transmitted the text of a communiqué issued by countries of the Permanent Body for Political Consultation and Coordination (Rio Group) (Argentina, Bolivia, Brazil, Chile, Colombia, Ecuador, Mexico, Panama, Paraguay, Peru, Uruguay, Venezuela), which regretted the DPRK's decision to withdraw from NPT and the IAEA safeguards system (see p. 549).

On 14 February [A/57/733-S/2003/182], the Secretary-General conveyed to the Presidents of the General Assembly and of the Security Council the text of a 12 February resolution of the IAEA Board of Governors, which declared that the DPRK was in further non-compliance with its obligations under its safeguards agreement pursuant to NPT.

On 8 October [A/58/431], Cuba announced that it had signed, in September, the comprehensive safeguards agreement with IAEA and the Additional Protocol thereto, in order to expedite the fulfilment of its obligations as a State party to NPT and to the Treaty for the Prohibition of Nuclear Weapons in Latin America and the Caribbean (Treaty of Tlatelolco) (see p. 555).

Middle East

In 2003, the General Assembly (see below) and the IAEA General Conference [GC(47)/RES/13] took action regarding the risk of nuclear proliferation in the Middle East. While the Assembly once again called on the non-party in the region to place all its nuclear facilities under IAEA safeguards, IAEA continued to emphasize the need for States in the region to accept the application of full-scope Agency safeguards to all their nuclear activities.

Pursuant to Assembly resolution 57/97 [YUN 2002, p. 508], the Secretary-General reported in October [A/58/137 (Part II)] that, apart from the IAEA resolution on the application of IAEA safeguards in the Middle East, which was annexed to his report, he had not received any additional information since 2002.

GENERAL ASSEMBLY ACTION

On 8 December [meeting 71], the General Assembly, on the recommendation of the First Committee [A/58/465], adopted **resolution 58/68** by recorded vote (162-4-10) [agenda item 76].

The risk of nuclear proliferation in the Middle East

The General Assembly,

Bearing in mind its relevant resolutions,

Taking note of the relevant resolutions adopted by the General Conference of the International Atomic Energy Agency, the latest of which is resolution GC(47)/RES/13, adopted on 19 September 2003,

Cognizant that the proliferation of nuclear weapons in the region of the Middle East would pose a serious threat to international peace and security,

Mindful of the immediate need for placing all nuclear facilities in the region of the Middle East under full-scope safeguards of the International Atomic Energy Agency,

Recalling the decision on principles and objectives for nuclear non-proliferation and disarmament adopted by the 1995 Review and Extension Conference of the Parties to the Treaty on the Non-Proliferation of Nuclear Weapons on 11 May 1995, in which the Conference urged universal adherence to the Treaty as an urgent priority and called upon all States not yet parties to the Treaty to accede to it at the earliest date, particularly those States that operate unsafeguarded nuclear facilities,

Recognizing with satisfaction that, in the Final Document of the 2000 Review Conference of the Parties to the Treaty on the Non-Proliferation of Nuclear Weapons, the Conference undertook to make determined efforts towards the achievement of the goal of universality of the Treaty on the Non-Proliferation of Nuclear Weapons, called upon those remaining States not parties to the Treaty to accede to it, thereby accepting an international legally binding commitment not to acquire nuclear weapons or nuclear explosive devices and to accept International Atomic Energy Agency safeguards on all their nuclear activities, and underlined the necessity of universal adherence to the Treaty and of strict compliance by all parties with their obligations under the Treaty,

Recalling the resolution on the Middle East adopted by the 1995 Review and Extension Conference of the Parties to the Treaty on the Non-Proliferation of Nuclear Weapons on 11 May 1995, in which the Conference noted with concern the continued existence in the Middle East of unsafeguarded nuclear facilities, reaffirmed the importance of the early realization of universal adherence to the Treaty and called upon all States in the Middle East that had not yet done so, without exception, to accede to the Treaty as soon as possible and to place all their nuclear facilities under full-scope International Atomic Energy Agency safeguards,

Noting that Israel remains the only State in the Middle East that has not yet become party to the Treaty on the Non-Proliferation of Nuclear Weapons,

Concerned about the threats posed by the proliferation of nuclear weapons to the security and stability of the Middle East region,

Stressing the importance of taking confidence-building measures, in particular the establishment of a nuclear-weapon-free zone in the Middle East, in order to enhance peace and security in the region and to consolidate the global non-proliferation regime,

Emphasizing the need for all parties directly concerned to consider seriously taking the practical and urgent steps required for the implementation of the proposal to establish a nuclear-weapon-free zone in the region of the Middle East in accordance with the relevant resolutions of the General Assembly and, as a means of promoting this objective, inviting the countries concerned to adhere to the Treaty on the Non-Proliferation of Nuclear Weapons and, pending the establishment of the zone, to agree to place all their nuclear activities under International Atomic Energy Agency safeguards,

Noting that one hundred and sixty-nine States have signed the Comprehensive Nuclear-Test-Ban Treaty, including a number of States in the region,

1. *Welcomes* the conclusions on the Middle East of the 2000 Review Conference of the Parties to the Treaty on the Non-Proliferation of Nuclear Weapons;

2. *Reaffirms* the importance of Israel's accession to the Treaty on the Non-Proliferation of Nuclear Weapons and placement of all its nuclear facilities under comprehensive International Atomic Energy Agency safeguards, in realizing the goal of universal adherence to the Treaty in the Middle East;

3. *Calls upon* that State to accede to the Treaty on the Non-Proliferation of Nuclear Weapons without further delay and not to develop, produce, test or otherwise acquire nuclear weapons, and to renounce possession of nuclear weapons, and to place all its unsafeguarded nuclear facilities under full-scope International Atomic Energy Agency safeguards as an important confidence-building measure among all States of the region and as a step towards enhancing peace and security;

4. *Requests* the Secretary-General to report to the General Assembly at its fifty-ninth session on the implementation of the present resolution;

5. *Decides* to include in the provisional agenda of its fifty-ninth session the item entitled "The risk of nuclear proliferation in the Middle East".

RECORDED VOTE ON RESOLUTION 58/68:

In favour: Afghanistan, Albania, Algeria, Andorra, Angola, Antigua and Barbuda, Argentina, Armenia, Austria, Azerbaijan, Bahamas, Bahrain, Bangladesh, Barbados, Belarus, Belgium, Belize, Benin, Bhutan, Bolivia, Bosnia and Herzegovina, Botswana, Brazil, Brunei Darussalam, Bulgaria, Burkina Faso, Cambodia, Cape Verde, Central African Republic, Chile, China, Colombia, Comoros, Congo, Costa Rica, Côte d'Ivoire, Croatia, Cuba, Cyprus, Czech Republic, Democratic People's Republic of Korea, Denmark, Djibouti, Dominican Republic, Ecuador, Egypt, El Salvador, Eritrea, Estonia, Fiji, Finland, France, Gabon, Gambia, Georgia, Germany, Ghana, Greece, Grenada, Guatemala, Guinea, Guyana, Haiti, Honduras, Hungary, Iceland, Indonesia, Iran, Ireland, Italy, Jamaica, Japan, Jordan, Kazakhstan, Kenya, Kuwait, Kyrgyzstan, Lao People's Democratic Republic, Latvia, Lebanon, Lesotho, Libyan Arab Jamahiriya, Liechtenstein, Lithuania, Luxembourg, Madagascar, Malawi, Malaysia, Maldives, Mali, Malta, Mauritania, Mauritius, Mexico, Monaco, Mongolia, Morocco, Mozambique, Myanmar, Namibia, Nauru, Nepal, Netherlands, New Zealand, Nicaragua, Niger, Nigeria, Norway, Oman, Pakistan, Panama, Paraguay, Peru, Philippines, Poland, Portugal, Qatar, Republic of Korea, Republic of Moldova, Romania, Russian Federation, Saint Lucia, Saint Vincent and the Grenadines, Samoa, San Marino, Saudi Arabia, Senegal, Serbia and Montenegro, Seychelles, Sierra Leone, Singapore, Slovakia, Slovenia, Solomon Islands, Somalia, South Africa, Spain, Sri Lanka, Sudan, Swaziland, Sweden, Switzerland, Syrian Arab Republic, Tajikistan, Thailand, The former Yugoslav Republic of Macedonia, Timor-Leste, Togo, Tunisia, Turkey, Turkmenistan, Uganda, Ukraine, United Arab Emirates, United Kingdom, United Republic of Tanzania, Uruguay, Venezuela, Viet Nam, Yemen, Zambia, Zimbabwe.

Against: Israel, Marshall Islands, Micronesia, United States.

Abstaining: Australia, Cameroon, Canada, Ethiopia, India, Papua New Guinea, Rwanda, Tonga, Trinidad and Tobago, Vanuatu.

The First Committee adopted the sixth preambular paragraph by a separate recorded vote of 142 to 2, with 11 abstentions. The Assembly retained the paragraph by a recorded vote of 162 to 2, with 10 abstentions.

Prohibition of the use of nuclear weapons

In 2003, the Conference on Disarmament was unable to undertake negotiations on a convention on the prohibition of the use of nuclear weapons, as called for in General Assembly resolution 57/94 [YUN 2002, p. 509].

GENERAL ASSEMBLY ACTION

On 8 December [meeting 71], the General Assembly, on the recommendation of the First Committee [A/58/463], adopted **resolution 58/64** by recorded vote (118-46-13) [agenda item 74 *(f)*].

Convention on the Prohibition of the Use of Nuclear Weapons

The General Assembly,

Convinced that the use of nuclear weapons poses the most serious threat to the survival of mankind,

Bearing in mind the advisory opinion of the International Court of Justice of 8 July 1996 on the *Legality of the Threat or Use of Nuclear Weapons*,

Convinced that a multilateral, universal and binding agreement prohibiting the use or threat of use of nuclear weapons would contribute to the elimination of the nuclear threat and to the climate for negotiations leading to the ultimate elimination of nuclear weapons, thereby strengthening international peace and security,

Conscious that some steps taken by the Russian Federation and the United States of America towards a reduction of their nuclear weapons and the improvement in the international climate can contribute towards the goal of the complete elimination of nuclear weapons,

Recalling that, in paragraph 58 of the Final Document of the Tenth Special Session of the General

Assembly, whose twenty-fifth anniversary is being marked this year, it is stated that all States should actively participate in efforts to bring about conditions in international relations among States in which a code of peaceful conduct of nations in international affairs could be agreed upon and that would preclude the use or threat of use of nuclear weapons,

Reaffirming that any use of nuclear weapons would be a violation of the Charter of the United Nations and a crime against humanity, as declared in its resolutions 1653(XVI) of 24 November 1961, 33/71 B of 14 December 1978, 34/83 G of 11 December 1979, 35/152 D of 12 December 1980 and 36/92 I of 9 December 1981,

Determined to achieve an international convention prohibiting the development, production, stockpiling and use of nuclear weapons, leading to their ultimate destruction,

Stressing that an international convention on the prohibition of the use of nuclear weapons would be an important step in a phased programme towards the complete elimination of nuclear weapons, with a specified framework of time,

Noting with regret that the Conference on Disarmament, during its 2003 session, was unable to undertake negotiations on this subject as called for in General Assembly resolution 57/94 of 22 November 2002,

1. *Reiterates its request* to the Conference on Disarmament to commence negotiations in order to reach agreement on an international convention prohibiting the use or threat of use of nuclear weapons under any circumstances;

2. *Requests* the Conference on Disarmament to report to the General Assembly on the results of those negotiations.

RECORDED VOTE ON RESOLUTION 58/64:

In favour: Afghanistan, Algeria, Angola, Antigua and Barbuda, Bahamas, Bahrain, Bangladesh, Barbados, Belarus, Belize, Benin, Bhutan, Bolivia, Botswana, Brazil, Brunei Darussalam, Burkina Faso, Burundi, Cambodia, Cameroon, Cape Verde, Central African Republic, Chile, China, Colombia, Comoros, Congo, Costa Rica, Côte d'Ivoire, Cuba, Democratic People's Republic of Korea, Djibouti, Dominican Republic, Ecuador, Egypt, El Salvador, Eritrea, Ethiopia, Fiji, Gabon, Gambia, Ghana, Grenada, Guatemala, Guinea, Guinea-Bissau, Guyana, Haiti, Honduras, India, Indonesia, Iran, Jamaica, Jordan, Kenya, Kuwait, Lao People's Democratic Republic, Lebanon, Lesotho, Libyan Arab Jamahiriya, Madagascar, Malawi, Malaysia, Maldives, Mali, Mauritania, Mauritius, Mexico, Mongolia, Morocco, Mozambique, Myanmar, Namibia, Nauru, Nepal, Nicaragua, Niger, Nigeria, Oman, Pakistan, Panama, Papua New Guinea, Paraguay, Peru, Philippines, Qatar, Rwanda, Saint Lucia, Saint Vincent and the Grenadines, Samoa, Saudi Arabia, Senegal, Sierra Leone, Singapore, Somalia, South Africa, Sri Lanka, Sudan, Suriname, Swaziland, Syrian Arab Republic, Thailand, Timor-Leste, Togo, Tonga, Trinidad and Tobago, Tunisia, Turkmenistan, Uganda, United Arab Emirates, United Republic of Tanzania, Uruguay, Vanuatu, Venezuela, Viet Nam, Yemen, Zambia, Zimbabwe.

Against: Andorra, Australia, Austria, Belgium, Bosnia and Herzegovina, Bulgaria, Canada, Croatia, Cyprus, Czech Republic, Denmark, Estonia, Finland, France, Germany, Greece, Hungary, Iceland, Ireland, Israel, Italy, Latvia, Liechtenstein, Lithuania, Luxembourg, Malta, Marshall Islands, Micronesia, Monaco, Netherlands, New Zealand, Norway, Poland, Portugal, Romania, San Marino, Serbia and Montenegro, Slovakia, Slovenia, Spain, Sweden, Switzerland, The former Yugoslav Republic of Macedonia, Turkey, United Kingdom, United States.

Abstaining: Argentina, Armenia, Azerbaijan, Georgia, Japan, Kazakhstan, Kyrgyzstan, Republic of Korea, Republic of Moldova, Russian Federation, Tajikistan, Ukraine, Uzbekistan.

Advisory opinion of the International Court of Justice

Pursuant to General Assembly resolution 57/85 [YUN 2002, p. 510] on the advisory opinion of the International Court of Justice that the threat or use of nuclear weapons was contrary to the UN Charter [YUN 1996, p. 461], the Secretary-General presented information received from five States (Antigua and Barbuda, Cuba, Malaysia, Mexico, Venezuela) on measures they had taken to implement the resolution and towards nuclear disarmament [A/58/162 & Add.1].

GENERAL ASSEMBLY ACTION

On 8 December [meeting 71], the General Assembly, on the recommendation of the First Committee [A/58/462], adopted **resolution 58/46** by recorded vote (124-29-22) [agenda item 73 (y)].

Follow-up to the advisory opinion of the International Court of Justice on the *Legality of the Threat or Use of Nuclear Weapons*

The General Assembly,

Recalling its resolutions 49/75 K of 15 December 1994, 51/45 M of 10 December 1996, 52/38 O of 9 December 1997, 53/77 W of 4 December 1998, 54/54 Q of 1 December 1999, 55/33 X of 20 November 2000, 56/24 S of 29 November 2001 and 57/85 of 22 November 2002,

Convinced that the continuing existence of nuclear weapons poses a threat to all humanity and that their use would have catastrophic consequences for all life on Earth, and recognizing that the only defence against a nuclear catastrophe is the total elimination of nuclear weapons and the certainty that they will never be produced again,

Reaffirming the commitment of the international community to the goal of the total elimination of nuclear weapons and the creation of a nuclear-weapon-free world,

Mindful of the solemn obligations of States parties, undertaken in article VI of the Treaty on the Non-Proliferation of Nuclear Weapons, particularly to pursue negotiations in good faith on effective measures relating to cessation of the nuclear-arms race at an early date and to nuclear disarmament,

Recalling the principles and objectives for nuclear non-proliferation and disarmament adopted at the 1995 Review and Extension Conference of the Parties to the Treaty on the Non-Proliferation of Nuclear Weapons,

Emphasizing the unequivocal undertaking by the nuclear-weapon States to accomplish the total elimination of their nuclear arsenals leading to nuclear disarmament, adopted at the 2000 Review Conference of the Parties to the Treaty on the Non-Proliferation of Nuclear Weapons,

Recalling the adoption of the Comprehensive Nuclear-Test-Ban Treaty in its resolution 50/245 of 10 September 1996, and expressing its satisfaction at the increasing number of States that have signed and ratified the Treaty,

Recognizing with satisfaction that the Antarctic Treaty and the treaties of Tlatelolco, Rarotonga, Bangkok and Pelindaba are gradually freeing the entire southern hemisphere and adjacent areas covered by those treaties from nuclear weapons,

Stressing the importance of strengthening all existing nuclear-related disarmament, arms control and reduction measures,

Recognizing the need for a multilaterally negotiated and legally binding instrument to assure non-nuclear-weapon States against the threat or use of nuclear weapons,

Reaffirming the central role of the Conference on Disarmament as the single multilateral disarmament negotiating forum, and regretting the lack of progress in disarmament negotiations, particularly nuclear disarmament, in the Conference during its 2003 session,

Emphasizing the need for the Conference on Disarmament to commence negotiations on a phased programme for the complete elimination of nuclear weapons with a specified framework of time,

Expressing its deep concern at the lack of progress in the implementation of the thirteen steps to implement article VI of the Treaty on the Non-Proliferation of Nuclear Weapons agreed to at the 2000 Review Conference of the Parties to the Treaty on the Non-Proliferation of Nuclear Weapons,

Desiring to achieve the objective of a legally binding prohibition of the development, production, testing, deployment, stockpiling, threat or use of nuclear weapons and their destruction under effective international control,

Recalling the advisory opinion of the International Court of Justice on the *Legality of the Threat or Use of Nuclear Weapons*, issued on 8 July 1996,

Taking note of the relevant portions of the report of the Secretary-General relating to the implementation of resolution 57/85,

1. *Underlines once again* the unanimous conclusion of the International Court of Justice that there exists an obligation to pursue in good faith and bring to a conclusion negotiations leading to nuclear disarmament in all its aspects under strict and effective international control;

2. *Calls once again upon* all States immediately to fulfil that obligation by commencing multilateral negotiations leading to an early conclusion of a nuclear weapons convention prohibiting the development, production, testing, deployment, stockpiling, transfer, threat or use of nuclear weapons and providing for their elimination;

3. *Requests* all States to inform the Secretary-General of the efforts and measures they have taken on the implementation of the present resolution and nuclear disarmament, and requests the Secretary-General to apprise the General Assembly of that information at its fifty-ninth session;

4. *Decides* to include in the provisional agenda of its fifty-ninth session the item entitled "Follow-up to the advisory opinion of the International Court of Justice on the *Legality of the Threat or Use of Nuclear Weapons*".

RECORDED VOTE ON RESOLUTION 58/46:

In favour: Algeria, Angola, Antigua and Barbuda, Argentina, Bahamas, Bahrain, Bangladesh, Barbados, Belize, Benin, Bhutan, Bolivia, Botswana, Brazil, Brunei Darussalam, Burkina Faso, Burundi, Cambodia, Cameroon, Cape Verde, Central African Republic, Chile, China, Colombia, Comoros, Congo, Costa Rica, Côte d'Ivoire, Cuba, Democratic People's Republic of Korea, Djibouti, Dominican Republic, Ecuador, Egypt, El Salvador, Eritrea, Ethiopia, Fiji, Gabon, Gambia, Ghana, Grenada, Guatemala, Guinea, Guinea-Bissau, Guyana, Haiti, Honduras, India, Indonesia, Iran, Ireland, Jamaica, Jordan, Kenya, Kuwait, Kyrgyzstan, Lao People's Democratic Republic, Lebanon, Lesotho, Libyan Arab Jamahiriya, Madagascar, Malawi, Malaysia, Maldives, Mali, Malta, Mauritania, Mauritius, Mexico, Mongolia, Morocco, Mozambique, Myanmar, Namibia, Nauru, Nepal, New Zealand, Nicaragua, Niger, Nigeria, Oman, Pakistan, Panama, Papua New Guinea, Paraguay, Peru, Philippines, Qatar, Saint Lucia, Saint Vincent and the Grenadines, Samoa, San Marino, Saudi Arabia, Senegal, Seychelles, Singapore, Solomon Islands, Somalia, South Africa, Sri Lanka, Sudan, Suriname, Swaziland, Sweden, Syrian Arab Republic, Thailand, Timor-Leste, Togo, Tonga, Trinidad and Tobago, Tunisia, Turkmenistan, Uganda, Ukraine, United Arab Emirates, United Republic of Tanzania, Uruguay, Vanuatu, Venezuela, Viet Nam, Yemen, Zambia, Zimbabwe.

Against: Albania, Belgium, Bulgaria, Czech Republic, Denmark, France, Germany, Greece, Hungary, Iceland, Israel, Italy, Latvia, Lithuania, Luxembourg, Marshall Islands, Monaco, Netherlands, Norway, Poland, Portugal, Romania, Russian Federation, Slovakia, Slovenia, Spain, Turkey, United Kingdom, United States.

Abstaining: Andorra, Armenia, Australia, Austria, Azerbaijan, Belarus, Bosnia and Herzegovina, Canada, Croatia, Cyprus, Estonia, Finland, Georgia, Japan, Kazakhstan, Liechtenstein, Republic of Korea, Republic of Moldova, Serbia and Montenegro, Switzerland, The former Yugoslav Republic of Macedonia, Uzbekistan.

The First Committee adopted paragraph 1 by a recorded vote of 140 to 4, with 5 abstentions. The Assembly retained the paragraph by a recorded vote of 165 to 4, with 3 abstentions.

Radioactive waste

In September [GC(47)/RES/7], the IAEA General Conference requested the Agency to develop an action plan addressing the safety of the transport of radioactive material based on the findings of the IAEA International Conference on the Safety of Transport of Radioactive Material (Vienna, 7-11 July). It urged member States that did not have national regulatory documents governing the transport of radioactive materials by sea to adopt them.

The first Review Meeting of the Contracting Parties (Vienna, 3-14 November) to the Joint Convention on the Safety of Spent Fuel Management and on the Safety of Radioactive Waste Managment [YUN 1997, p. 487], which entered into force in 2001 [YUN 2001, p. 487], reviewed States parties national reports and discussed, among other issues, the need for all countries to have in place a long-term strategy for managing spent fuel and radioactive waste.

GENERAL ASSEMBLY ACTION

On 8 December [meeting 71], the General Assembly, on the recommendation of the First Committee [A/58/462], adopted **resolution 58/40** without vote [agenda item 73 *(b)*].

Prohibition of the dumping of radioactive wastes

The General Assembly,

Bearing in mind resolutions CM/Res.1153(XLVIII) of 1988 and CM/Res.1225(L) of 1989, adopted by the Council of Ministers of the Organization of African Unity, concerning the dumping of nuclear and industrial wastes in Africa,

Welcoming resolution GC(XXXIV)/RES/530 establishing a Code of Practice on the International Transboundary Movement of Radioactive Waste, adopted on 21 September 1990 by the General Conference of the International Atomic Energy Agency at its thirty-fourth regular session,

Taking note of the commitment by the participants in the Summit on Nuclear Safety and Security, held in Moscow on 19 and 20 April 1996, to ban the dumping at sea of radioactive wastes,

Considering its resolution 2602 C (XXIV) of 16 December 1969, in which it requested the Conference of the Committee on Disarmament,[a] inter alia, to consider effective methods of control against the use of radiological methods of warfare,

Aware of the potential hazards underlying any use of radioactive wastes that would constitute radiological warfare and its implications for regional and international security, in particular for the security of developing countries,

Recalling all its resolutions on the matter since its forty-third session in 1988, including its resolution 51/45 J of 10 December 1996,

Also recalling resolution GC(45)/RES/10 adopted by consensus on 21 September 2001 by the General Conference of the International Atomic Energy Agency at its forty-fifth regular session, in which States shipping radioactive materials are invited to provide, as appropriate, assurances to concerned States, upon their request, that the national regulations of the shipping State take into account the Agency's transport regulations and to provide them with relevant information relating to the shipment of such materials; the information provided should in no case be contradictory to the measures of physical security and safety,

Welcoming the adoption at Vienna, on 5 September 1997, of the Joint Convention on the Safety of Spent Fuel Management and on the Safety of Radioactive Waste Management, as recommended by the participants at the Summit on Nuclear Safety and Security,

Noting with satisfaction that the Joint Convention on the Safety of Spent Fuel Management and on the Safety of Radioactive Waste Management entered into force on 18 June 2001,

Noting that the first Review Meeting of the Contracting Parties to the Joint Convention on the Safety of Spent Fuel Management and on the Safety of Radioactive Waste Management was convened in Vienna from 3 to 14 November 2003,

Desirous of promoting the implementation of paragraph 76 of the Final Document of the Tenth Special Session of the General Assembly, the first special session devoted to disarmament,

1. *Takes note* of the part of the report of the Conference on Disarmament relating to a future convention on the prohibition of radiological weapons;

2. *Expresses grave concern* regarding any use of nuclear wastes that would constitute radiological warfare and have grave implications for the national security of all States;

3. *Calls upon* all States to take appropriate measures with a view to preventing any dumping of nuclear or radioactive wastes that would infringe upon the sovereignty of States;

4. *Requests* the Conference on Disarmament to take into account, in the negotiations for a convention on the prohibition of radiological weapons, radioactive wastes as part of the scope of such a convention;

5. *Also requests* the Conference on Disarmament to intensify efforts towards an early conclusion of such a convention and to include in its report to the General Assembly at its sixtieth session the progress recorded in the negotiations on this subject;

6. *Takes note* of resolution CM/Res.1356(LIV) of 1991, adopted by the Council of Ministers of the Organization of African Unity, on the Bamako Convention on the Ban on the Import of Hazardous Wastes into Africa and on the Control of Their Transboundary Movements within Africa;

7. *Expresses the hope* that the effective implementation of the International Atomic Energy Agency Code of Practice on the International Transboundary Movement of Radioactive Waste will enhance the protection of all States from the dumping of radioactive wastes on their territories;

8. *Appeals* to all Member States that have not yet taken the necessary steps to become party to the Joint Convention on the Safety of Spent Fuel Management and on the Safety of Radioactive Waste Management to do so as soon as possible;

9. *Decides* to include in the provisional agenda of its sixtieth session the item entitled "Prohibition of the dumping of radioactive wastes".

[a]The Conference of the Committee on Disarmament became the Committee on Disarmament as from the tenth special session of the General Assembly. The Committee on Disarmament was redesignated the Conference on Disarmament as from 7 February 1984.

Nuclear-weapon-free zones

Africa

As at 31 December, 22 States had ratified the African Nuclear-Weapon-Free Zone Treaty (Treaty of Pelindaba) [YUN 1995, p. 203], which was opened for signature in 1996 [YUN 1996, p. 486]. China, France and the United Kingdom had ratified Protocols I and II thereto, and France had also ratified Protocol III. The Russian Federation and the United States had signed Protocols I and II. The Treaty had 55 signatories.

GENERAL ASSEMBLY ACTION

On 8 December [meeting 71], the General Assembly, on the recommendation of the First Committee [A/58/454], adopted **resolution 58/30** without vote [agenda item 65].

African Nuclear-Weapon-Free Zone Treaty (Treaty of Pelindaba)

The General Assembly,

Recalling its resolutions 51/53 of 10 December 1996 and 56/17 of 29 November 2001 and all its other relevant resolutions, as well as those of the Organization of African Unity,

Recalling also the signing of the African Nuclear-Weapon-Free Zone Treaty (Treaty of Pelindaba) at Cairo on 11 April 1996,

Recalling further the Cairo Declaration adopted on that occasion, which emphasized that nuclear-weapon-free zones, especially in regions of tension, such as the Middle East, enhance global and regional peace and security,

Taking note of the statement made by the President of the Security Council on behalf of the members of the Council on 12 April 1996, affirming that the signature of the African Nuclear-Weapon-Free Zone Treaty constituted an important contribution by the African countries to the maintenance of international peace and security,

Considering that the establishment of nuclear-weapon-free zones, especially in the Middle East, would enhance the security of Africa and the viability of the African nuclear-weapon-free zone,

1. *Calls upon* African States that have not yet done so to sign and ratify the African Nuclear-Weapon-Free Zone Treaty (Treaty of Pelindaba) as soon as possible so that it may enter into force without delay;

2. *Expresses its appreciation* to the nuclear-weapon States that have signed the Protocols that concern them, and calls upon those that have not yet ratified the Protocols concerning them to do so as soon as possible;

3. *Calls upon* the States contemplated in Protocol III to the Treaty that have not yet done so to take all necessary measures to ensure the speedy application of the Treaty to territories for which they are, de jure or de facto, internationally responsible and that lie within the limits of the geographical zone established in the Treaty;

4. *Calls upon* the African States parties to the Treaty on the Non-Proliferation of Nuclear Weapons that have not yet done so to conclude comprehensive safeguards agreements with the International Atomic Energy Agency pursuant to the Treaty, thereby satisfying the requirements of article 9 *(b)* of and annex II to the Treaty of Pelindaba when it enters into force, and to conclude additional protocols to their safeguards agreements on the basis of the Model Protocol approved by the Board of Governors of the Agency on 15 May 1997;

5. *Expresses its gratitude* to the Secretary-General, the Chairman of the Commission of the African Union and the Director General of the International Atomic Energy Agency for the diligence with which they have rendered effective assistance to the signatories to the Treaty;

6. *Decides* to include in the provisional agenda of its sixtieth session the item entitled "African Nuclear-Weapon-Free Zone Treaty".

Asia

Central Asia

In 2003, the five Central Asian States (Kazakhstan, Kyrgyzstan, Tajikistan, Turkmenistan, Uzbekistan) continued consultations with the five nuclear-weapon States on the draft text of a treaty for a nuclear-weapon-free zone in Central Asia. Four of the nuclear five had submitted their comments on the draft earlier in the year, and the United Nations Regional Centre for Peace and Disarmament in Asia and the Pacific (see p. 588), in collaboration with IAEA, organized several meetings to help the regional States examine those comments. The process resulted in a proposal for a revised treaty text.

On 8 December, the General Assembly decided to include in the provisional agenda of its fifty-ninth (2004) session the item entitled "Establishment of a nuclear-weapon-free zone in Central Asia" (**decision 58/518**).

Mongolia

In a report to the NPT Preparatory Committee (see p. 549), Mongolia described its nuclear-weapon-free status as a reaffirmation of its commitment to the goals of nuclear non-proliferation and highlighted ongoing efforts to institutionalize that status at the international level [NPT/CONF.2005/PC.II/40].

South-East Asia

In 2003, the States parties to the Treaty on the South-East Asia Nuclear-Weapon-Free Zone (Bangkok Treaty) continued to focus on establishing an institutional framework to implement the Treaty. Consultations with nuclear-weapon States on the Treaty's Protocols, with a view to securing their accession, also continued within the organizational framework of the Association of Southeast Asian Nations (ASEAN). Some progress was made, as China and ASEAN countries reached agreements on the Protocols. With no new ratifications, the number of States that had ratified the Treaty remained at 10.

Latin America and the Caribbean

The eighteenth regular session of the General Conference of the Agency for the Prohibition of Nuclear Weapons in Latin America and the Caribbean (OPANAL) (Havana, Cuba, 5-6 November) [A/58/622] adopted the Havana Declaration, which committed OPANAL members to promoting the convening of a conference of States parties and signatories that had established nuclear-weapon-free zones and to strengthening the integrity of the statute of denuclearization provided for in the Treaty for the Prohibition of Nuclear Weapons in Latin America and the Caribbean (Treaty of Tlatelolco) [YUN 1967, p. 13].

GENERAL ASSEMBLY ACTION

On 8 December [meeting 71], the General Assembly, on the recommendation of the First Committee [A/58/455], adopted **resolution 58/31** (as orally amended) without vote [agenda item 66].

Consolidation of the regime established by the Treaty for the Prohibition of Nuclear Weapons in Latin America and the Caribbean (Treaty of Tlatelolco)

The General Assembly,

Recalling that the Treaty for the Prohibition of Nuclear Weapons in Latin America and the Caribbean (Treaty of Tlatelolco) was opened for signature at Mexico City on 14 February 1967,

Recalling also that, in its preamble, the Treaty of Tlatelolco states that military denuclearized zones are not an end in themselves but rather a means for achieving general and complete disarmament at a later stage,

Recalling further that, in its resolution 2286(XXII) of 5 December 1967, it welcomed with special satisfaction the Treaty of Tlatelolco as an event of historic significance in the efforts to prevent the proliferation of nuclear weapons and to promote international peace and security,

Recalling that in 1990, 1991 and 1992 the General Conference of the Agency for the Prohibition of Nuclear Weapons in Latin America and the Caribbean approved and opened for signature a set of amendments to the Treaty of Tlatelolco, with the aim of enabling the full entry into force of that instrument,

Highlighting that, with the ratification of Cuba, the Treaty of Tlatelolco is now in force for thirty-three sovereign States of the region, thereby consolidating the first nuclear-weapon-free zone established in a densely populated region,

Noting with satisfaction the interest that the Agency for the Prohibition of Nuclear Weapons in Latin America and the Caribbean has manifested to promote mechanisms of cooperation and consultation in other nuclear-weapon-free zones,

Reaffirming the importance of strengthening the Agency as the appropriate legal and political forum for ensuring cooperation with the agencies of other nuclear-weapon-free zones,

1. *Welcomes* the fact that the Treaty for the Prohibition of Nuclear Weapons in Latin America and the Caribbean (Treaty of Tlatelolco) is now in force for the sovereign States of the region, and that this fact was officially acknowledged by the General Conference of the Agency for the Prohibition of Nuclear Weapons in Latin America and the Caribbean at its eighteenth session, held at Havana on 5 and 6 November 2003, and takes note of the results of the aforementioned session of the General Conference, including the adoption of the Havana Declaration;

2. *Urges* the countries of the region that have not yet done so to deposit their instruments of ratification of the amendments to the Treaty of Tlatelolco approved by the General Conference of the Agency in its resolutions 267(E-V), 268(XII) and 290(E-VII);

3. *Decides* to include in the provisional agenda of its sixtieth session the item entitled "Consolidation of the regime established by the Treaty for the Prohibition of Nuclear Weapons in Latin America and the Caribbean (Treaty of Tlatelolco)".

Middle East

In response to General Assembly resolution 57/55 on the establishment of a nuclear-weapon-free zone in the Middle East [YUN 2002, p. 514], the Secretary-General, in a July report with later addendum [A/58/137 (Part I) & Add.1 & Add.1/Corr.1], reported on the resolution's implementation. He said he was encouraged by new developments, including the presentation of the road map: an international plan for peace in the Middle East developed by the Quartet—the coordinating mechanism for international peace efforts in the region, comprising the Russian Federation, the United States, the EU and the United Nations [YUN 2002, p. 423] (see pp. 467 and 473). The Secretary-General hoped that recent developments in the region would have a positive influence towards securing a stable environment that would facilitate the establishment of the zone. The report included the views of Egypt, Israel, Italy (on behalf of the EU), Mexico and Venezuela.

In September, the IAEA General Conference, in a resolution on the Middle East [GC(47)/RES/13], called on all parties directly concerned to take the steps required for the implementation of the proposal for a mutually and effectively verifiable nuclear-weapon-free zone in the region.

GENERAL ASSEMBLY ACTION

On 8 December [meeting 71], the General Assembly, on the recommendation of the First Committee [A/58/459], adopted **resolution 58/34** without vote [agenda item 70].

Establishment of a nuclear-weapon-free zone in the region of the Middle East

The General Assembly,

Recalling its resolutions 3263(XXIX) of 9 December 1974, 3474(XXX) of 11 December 1975, 31/71 of 10 December 1976, 32/82 of 12 December 1977, 33/64 of 14 December 1978, 34/77 of 11 December 1979, 35/147 of 12 December 1980, 36/87 A and B of 9 December 1981, 37/75 of 9 December 1982, 38/64 of 15 December 1983, 39/54 of 12 December 1984, 40/82 of 12 December 1985, 41/48 of 3 December 1986, 42/28 of 30 November 1987, 43/65 of 7 December 1988, 44/108 of 15 December 1989, 45/52 of 4 December 1990, 46/30 of 6 December 1991, 47/48 of 9 December 1992, 48/71 of 16 December 1993, 49/71 of 15 December 1994, 50/66 of 12 December 1995, 51/41 of 10 December 1996, 52/34 of 9 December 1997, 53/74 of 4 December 1998, 54/51 of 1 December 1999, 55/30 of 20 November 2000, 56/21 of 29 November 2001 and 57/55 of 22 November 2002 on the establishment of a nuclear-weapon-free zone in the region of the Middle East,

Recalling also the recommendations for the establishment of such a zone in the Middle East consistent with paragraphs 60 to 63, and in particular paragraph 63 *(d)*, of the Final Document of the Tenth Special Session of the General Assembly,

Emphasizing the basic provisions of the above-mentioned resolutions, which call upon all parties directly concerned to consider taking the practical and urgent steps required for the implementation of the proposal to establish a nuclear-weapon-free zone in the region of the Middle East and, pending and during the establishment of such a zone, to declare solemnly that they will refrain, on a reciprocal basis, from producing, acquiring or in any other way possessing nuclear weapons and nuclear explosive devices and from permitting the stationing of nuclear weapons on their territory by any third party, to agree to place their nuclear facilities under International Atomic Energy Agency safeguards and to declare their support for the establishment of the zone and to deposit such declarations with the Security Council for consideration, as appropriate,

Reaffirming the inalienable right of all States to acquire and develop nuclear energy for peaceful purposes,

Emphasizing the need for appropriate measures on the question of the prohibition of military attacks on nuclear facilities,

Bearing in mind the consensus reached by the General Assembly since its thirty-fifth session that the establishment of a nuclear-weapon-free zone in the Middle East would greatly enhance international peace and security,

Desirous of building on that consensus so that substantial progress can be made towards establishing a nuclear-weapon-free zone in the Middle East,

Welcoming all initiatives leading to general and complete disarmament, including in the region of the Middle East, and in particular on the establishment therein of a zone free of weapons of mass destruction, including nuclear weapons,

Noting the peace negotiations in the Middle East, which should be of a comprehensive nature and represent an appropriate framework for the peaceful settlement of contentious issues in the region,

Recognizing the importance of credible regional security, including the establishment of a mutually verifiable nuclear-weapon-free zone,

Emphasizing the essential role of the United Nations in the establishment of a mutually verifiable nuclear-weapon-free zone,

Having examined the report of the Secretary-General on the implementation of resolution 57/55,

1. *Urges* all parties directly concerned to consider seriously taking the practical and urgent steps required for the implementation of the proposal to establish a nuclear-weapon-free zone in the region of the Middle East in accordance with the relevant resolutions of the General Assembly, and, as a means of promoting this objective, invites the countries concerned to adhere to the Treaty on the Non-Proliferation of Nuclear Weapons;

2. *Calls upon* all countries of the region that have not done so, pending the establishment of the zone, to agree to place all their nuclear activities under International Atomic Energy Agency safeguards;

3. *Takes note* of resolution GC(46)/RES/16, adopted on 20 September 2002 by the General Conference of the International Atomic Energy Agency at its forty-sixth regular session, concerning the application of Agency safeguards in the Middle East;

4. *Notes* the importance of the ongoing bilateral Middle East peace negotiations and the activities of the multilateral Working Group on Arms Control and Regional Security in promoting mutual confidence and security in the Middle East, including the establishment of a nuclear-weapon-free zone;

5. *Invites* all countries of the region, pending the establishment of a nuclear-weapon-free zone in the region of the Middle East, to declare their support for establishing such a zone, consistent with paragraph 63 *(d)* of the Final Document of the Tenth Special Session of the General Assembly, and to deposit those declarations with the Security Council;

6. *Also invites* those countries, pending the establishment of the zone, not to develop, produce, test or otherwise acquire nuclear weapons or permit the stationing on their territories, or territories under their control, of nuclear weapons or nuclear explosive devices;

7. *Invites* the nuclear-weapon States and all other States to render their assistance in the establishment of the zone and at the same time to refrain from any action that runs counter to both the letter and the spirit of the present resolution;

8. *Takes note* of the report of the Secretary-General;

9. *Invites* all parties to consider the appropriate means that may contribute towards the goal of general and complete disarmament and the establishment of a zone free of weapons of mass destruction in the region of the Middle East;

10. *Requests* the Secretary-General to continue to pursue consultations with the States of the region and other concerned States, in accordance with paragraph 7 of resolution 46/30 and taking into account the evolving situation in the region, and to seek from those States their views on the measures outlined in chapters III and IV of the study annexed to his report of 10 October 1990 or other relevant measures, in order to move towards the establishment of a nuclear-weapon-free zone in the Middle East;

11. *Also requests* the Secretary-General to submit to the General Assembly at its fifty-ninth session a report on the implementation of the present resolution;

12. *Decides* to include in the provisional agenda of its fifty-ninth session the item entitled "Establishment of a nuclear-weapon-free zone in the region of the Middle East".

South Pacific

In 2003, the number of States that had ratified the 1985 South Pacific Nuclear Free Zone Treaty (Treaty of Rarotonga) [YUN 1985, p. 58] remained at 17. China and the Russian Federation had ratified Protocols 2 and 3, and France and the United Kingdom had ratified all three Protocols.

Under Protocol 1, the States internationally responsible for territories situated within the zone would undertake to apply the relevant prohibitions of the Treaty to those territories; under Protocol 2, the five nuclear-weapon States would provide security assurances to parties or territories within the same zone; and under Protocol 3, the five would not carry out nuclear tests in the zone.

Southern hemisphere and adjacent areas

On 8 December [meeting 71], the General Assembly, on the recommendation of the First Committee [A/58/462], adopted **resolution 58/49** by recorded vote (168-3-8) [agenda item 73 *(o)*].

Nuclear-weapon-free southern hemisphere and adjacent areas

The General Assembly,

Recalling its resolutions 51/45 B of 10 December 1996, 52/38 N of 9 December 1997, 53/77 Q of 4 December 1998, 54/54 L of 1 December 1999, 55/33 I of 20 November 2000, 56/24 G of 29 November 2001 and 57/73 of 22 November 2002,

Welcoming the adoption by the Disarmament Commission at its 1999 substantive session of a text entitled

"Establishment of nuclear-weapon-free zones on the basis of arrangements freely arrived at among the States of the region concerned",

Determined to pursue the total elimination of nuclear weapons,

Determined also to continue to contribute to the prevention of the proliferation of nuclear weapons in all its aspects and to the process of general and complete disarmament under strict and effective international control, in particular in the field of nuclear weapons and other weapons of mass destruction, with a view to strengthening international peace and security, in accordance with the purposes and principles of the Charter of the United Nations,

Recalling the provisions on nuclear-weapon-free zones of the Final Document of the Tenth Special Session of the General Assembly, the first special session devoted to disarmament,

Stressing the importance of the treaties of Tlatelolco, Rarotonga, Bangkok and Pelindaba establishing nuclear-weapon-free zones, as well as the Antarctic Treaty, to, inter alia, achieve a world entirely free of nuclear weapons,

Underlining the value of enhancing cooperation among the nuclear-weapon-free-zone treaty members by means of mechanisms such as joint meetings of States parties, signatories and observers to those treaties,

Recalling the applicable principles and rules of international law relating to the freedom of the high seas and the rights of passage through maritime space, including those of the United Nations Convention on the Law of the Sea,

1. *Welcomes* the continued contribution that the Antarctic Treaty and the treaties of Tlatelolco, Rarotonga, Bangkok and Pelindaba are making towards freeing the southern hemisphere and adjacent areas covered by those treaties from nuclear weapons;

2. *Also welcomes* the ratification by all original parties of the Treaty of Rarotonga, and calls upon eligible States to adhere to the treaty and the protocols thereto;

3. *Further welcomes* the efforts towards the completion of the ratification process of the Treaty of Pelindaba, and calls upon the States of the region that have not yet done so to sign and ratify the treaty, with the aim of its early entry into force;

4. *Calls upon* all concerned States to continue to work together in order to facilitate adherence to the protocols to nuclear-weapon-free-zone treaties by all relevant States that have not yet done so;

5. *Welcomes* the steps taken to conclude further nuclear-weapon-free-zone treaties on the basis of arrangements freely arrived at among the States of the region concerned, and calls upon all States to consider all relevant proposals, including those reflected in its resolutions on the establishment of nuclear-weapon-free zones in the Middle East and South Asia;

6. *Affirms its conviction* of the important role of nuclear-weapon-free zones in strengthening the nuclear non-proliferation regime and in extending the areas of the world that are nuclear-weapon-free, and, with particular reference to the responsibilities of the nuclear-weapon States, calls upon all States to support the process of nuclear disarmament and to work for the total elimination of all nuclear weapons;

7. *Calls upon* the States parties and signatories to the treaties of Tlatelolco, Rarotonga, Bangkok and Pelindaba, in order to pursue the common goals envisaged in those treaties and to promote the nuclear-weapon-free status of the southern hemisphere and adjacent areas, to explore and implement further ways and means of cooperation among themselves and their treaty agencies;

8. *Welcomes* the vigorous efforts being made among States parties and signatories to those treaties to promote their common objectives, and considers that an international conference of States parties and signatories to the nuclear-weapon-free-zone treaties might be held to support the common goals envisaged in those treaties;

9. *Encourages* the competent authorities of the nuclear-weapon-free-zone treaties to provide assistance to the States parties and signatories to those treaties so as to facilitate the accomplishment of these goals;

10. *Decides* to include in the provisional agenda of its fifty-ninth session the item entitled "Nuclear-weapon-free southern hemisphere and adjacent areas".

RECORDED VOTE ON RESOLUTION 58/49:

In favour: Afghanistan, Albania, Algeria, Andorra, Angola, Antigua and Barbuda, Argentina, Armenia, Australia, Austria, Azerbaijan, Bahamas, Bahrain, Bangladesh, Barbados, Belarus, Belgium, Belize, Benin, Bolivia, Bosnia and Herzegovina, Botswana, Brazil, Brunei Darussalam, Bulgaria, Burkina Faso, Burundi, Cambodia, Cameroon, Canada, Cape Verde, Central African Republic, Chile, China, Colombia, Comoros, Congo, Costa Rica, Côte d'Ivoire, Croatia, Cuba, Cyprus, Czech Republic, Democratic People's Republic of Korea, Denmark, Djibouti, Dominican Republic, Ecuador, Egypt, El Salvador, Eritrea, Estonia, Ethiopia, Fiji, Finland, Gabon, Gambia, Germany, Ghana, Greece, Grenada, Guatemala, Guinea, Guinea-Bissau, Guyana, Haiti, Honduras, Hungary, Iceland, Indonesia, Iran, Ireland, Italy, Jamaica, Japan, Jordan, Kazakhstan, Kenya, Kuwait, Kyrgyzstan, Lao People's Democratic Republic, Latvia, Lebanon, Lesotho, Libyan Arab Jamahiriya, Liechtenstein, Lithuania, Luxembourg, Madagascar, Malawi, Malaysia, Maldives, Mali, Malta, Mauritania, Mauritius, Mexico, Mongolia, Morocco, Mozambique, Myanmar, Namibia, Nauru, Nepal, Netherlands, New Zealand, Nicaragua, Niger, Nigeria, Norway, Oman, Pakistan, Panama, Papua New Guinea, Paraguay, Peru, Philippines, Poland, Portugal, Qatar, Republic of Korea, Republic of Moldova, Romania, Rwanda, Saint Lucia, Saint Vincent and the Grenadines, Samoa, San Marino, Saudi Arabia, Senegal, Serbia and Montenegro, Seychelles, Sierra Leone, Singapore, Slovakia, Slovenia, Solomon Islands, Somalia, South Africa, Sri Lanka, Sudan, Suriname, Swaziland, Sweden, Switzerland, Syrian Arab Republic, Tajikistan, Thailand, The former Yugoslav Republic of Macedonia, Timor-Leste, Togo, Tonga, Trinidad and Tobago, Tunisia, Turkey, Turkmenistan, Uganda, Ukraine, United Arab Emirates, United Republic of Tanzania, Uruguay, Uzbekistan, Vanuatu, Venezuela, Viet Nam, Yemen, Zambia, Zimbabwe.

Against: France, United Kingdom, United States.

Abstaining: Bhutan, Georgia, India, Israel, Marshall Islands, Micronesia, Russian Federation, Spain.

The First Committee adopted paragraph 5 and its last three words, "and South Asia", by separate recorded votes of 145 to 1, with 11 abstentions, and 142 to 2, with 11 abstentions, respectively. The Assembly retained paragraph 5 and its last three words by recorded votes of 163 to 2, with 9 abstentions, and 159 to 3, with 9 abstentions, respectively.

Bacteriological (biological) and chemical weapons

Bacteriological (biological) weapons

The potential use of chemical and biological weapons and related materials and technology by terrorists continued to be of concern to the international community. Calls were made for further strengthening of the Convention on the Prohibition of the Development, Production and Stockpiling of Bacteriological (Biological) and Toxin Weapons and on Their Destruction (BWC) and the Convention on the Prohibition of the Development, Stockpiling and Use of Chemical Weapons and on Their Destruction, and for efforts by States parties to implement national measures that would respond to those calls.

Meeting of States parties

As decided in 2002 [YUN 2002, p. 516] by the Fifth Review Conference of the States parties to BWC, adopted by the General Assembly in resolution 2826(XXVI) [YUN 1971, p. 19], the first of three annual meetings of States parties to the Convention was convened (Geneva, 10-14 November) [BWC/MSP/2003/4 (vols. I & II)]. Working sessions focused on national measures to implement the prohibitions set forth in the Convention, national mechanisms to establish and maintain the security and oversight of pathogenic micro-organisms and toxins, enforcement, biosecurity evaluation and the implementation of biosecurity procedures, identification and licensing/registration, and efforts by relevant international organizations. The States parties noted that, notwithstanding the differing legal and constitutional arrangements among them, they had all adopted similar basic approaches and shared common principles. They agreed on the value of reviewing, enacting or updating national legal measures to ensure effective implementation of the Convention's prohibitions and enhance the security of pathogens and toxins; the positive effect of cooperation between States parties with differing legal and constitutional arrangements; the need for those in a position to do so to consider assisting others in framing and/or expanding their legislation and controls in the fields of national implementation and biosecurity; and the need for comprehensive and concrete national measures to secure pathogen collections and the control of their use for peaceful purposes. Participants considered a number of working papers submitted by States parties, of which a list was annexed to the meeting's report, as were statements, presentations and other contributions from delegations. Participants also drew on a CD-ROM-based repository of information, prepared by the Secretariat, which contained a listing of relevant national implementation measures adopted by many States parties and other relevant information that was updated in the course of the meeting. The States parties decided that their next meeting would be held in Geneva from 6 to 10 December 2004.

Expert meeting. In accordance with a decision of the Fifth Review Conference [YUN 2002, p. 516], the meeting of States parties (see above) was preceded by a preparatory expert meeting (Geneva, 18-29 August) [BWC/MSP.2003/MX/4 (Parts I & II)], which discussed issues relevant to the agenda items of the meeting of States parties. The expert meeting heard national statements and thematic presentations from delegates. On 29 August, the meeting adopted its report, to which was annexed a list of the working papers, presentations and other contributions that the experts had considered.

GENERAL ASSEMBLY ACTION

On 8 December [meeting 71], the General Assembly, on the recommendation of the First Committee [A/58/469], adopted **resolution 58/72** without vote [agenda item 80].

Convention on the Prohibition of the Development, Production and Stockpiling of Bacteriological (Biological) and Toxin Weapons and on Their Destruction

The General Assembly,

Recalling its previous resolutions relating to the complete and effective prohibition of bacteriological (biological) and toxin weapons and to their destruction,

Noting with satisfaction that there are one hundred and fifty States parties to the Convention on the Prohibition of the Development, Production and Stockpiling of Bacteriological (Biological) and Toxin Weapons and on Their Destruction, including all of the permanent members of the Security Council,

Bearing in mind its call upon all States parties to the Convention to participate in the implementation of the recommendations of the Review Conferences, including the exchange of information and data agreed to in the Final Declaration of the Third Review Conference of the Parties to the Convention on the Prohibition of the Development, Production and Stockpiling of Bacteriological (Biological) and Toxin Weapons and on Their Destruction, and to provide such information and data in conformity with standardized procedure to the Secretary-General on an annual basis and no later than 15 April,

Welcoming the reaffirmation made in the Final Declaration of the Fourth Review Conference that under all circumstances the use of bacteriological (biological) and toxin weapons and their development, production and stockpiling are effectively prohibited under article I of the Convention,

Recalling the decision reached at the Fifth Review Conference to hold three annual meetings of the States parties of one week duration each year commencing in 2003 until the Sixth Review Conference and to hold a two-week meeting of experts to prepare for each meeting of the States parties,

1. *Notes with satisfaction* the increase in the number of States parties to the Convention on the Prohibition of the Development, Production and Stockpiling of Bacteriological (Biological) and Toxin Weapons and on Their Destruction, reaffirms the call upon all signa-

tory States that have not yet ratified the Convention to do so without delay, and calls upon those States that have not signed the Convention to become parties thereto at an early date, thus contributing to the achievement of universal adherence to the Convention;

2. *Welcomes* the information and data provided to date, and reiterates its call upon all States parties to the Convention to participate in the exchange of information and data agreed to in the Final Declaration of the Third Review Conference of the Parties to the Convention;

3. *Recalls* the decision reached at the Fifth Review Conference, and calls upon the States parties to the Convention to participate in its implementation;

4. *Requests* the Secretary-General to continue to render the necessary assistance to the depositary Governments of the Convention and to provide such services as may be required for the implementation of the decisions and recommendations of the Review Conferences, including all necessary assistance to the annual meetings of the States parties and the meetings of experts;

5. *Decides* to include in the provisional agenda of its fifty-ninth session the item entitled "Convention on the Prohibition of the Development, Production and Stockpiling of Bacteriological (Biological) and Toxin Weapons and on Their Destruction".

Chemical weapons

Chemical weapons convention

In 2003, Afghanistan, Cape Verde, Guatemala and Kyrgyzstan ratified the Convention on the Prohibition of the Development, Production, Stockpiling and Use of Chemical Weapons and on Their Destruction (CWC); Andorra, Belize, Palau, Timor-Leste and Tonga acceded to the Convention and Sao Tome and Principe accepted it. At year's end, the total number of States parties stood at 158, with 165 signatories. CWC was adopted by the Conference on Disarmament in 1992 [YUN 1992, p. 65] and entered into force in 1997 [YUN 1997, p. 499].

The second special session of the Conference of the States Parties to the Convention (The Hague, Netherlands, 30 April) [C-SS-2/3] adopted a decision [C-SS-2/Dec.1] on the staff tenure policy of the Organization for the Prohibition of Chemical Weapons (OPCW) (see p. 561).

The eighth session of the Conference of the States Parties to the Convention (The Hague, 20-24 October) [C-8/7] considered, among other issues, the status of the Convention's implementation, fostering international cooperation for peaceful purposes in the field of chemical activities, agreements on the privileges and immunities of OPCW, ensuring the Convention's universality, and administrative and budgetary matters. The Conference adopted decisions on the extension of deadlines for destruction of category 1 chemical weapons stockpiles; understandings regarding declarations under article VI of the Convention relating to activities not prohibited; and administrative, financial and oversight matters, including OPCW's programme and budget for 2004 and other issues relevant to its work. The Conference approved procedures for revising the technical specifications for approved equipment and a plan of action regarding the implementation of obligations assumed under article VII of the Convention. It decided to hold its ninth session in November/December 2004.

Review Conference

The First Review Conference of the States Parties to the Convention (The Hague, 28 April-9 May) [RC-1/5] reviewed the Convention's operation since its entry into force. The Conference considered the role of the Convention in enhancing international peace and security, measures to ensure its universality, implementation of its provisions, including general obligations and verification provisions, chemical weapons and chemical weapons production facilities, activities not prohibited under CWC, national implementation measures, assistance and protection against chemical weapons, economic and technological development, the protection of confidential information and the functioning of OPCW. On 9 May, the Conference adopted its report, which contained its agreed assessment of those issues. It adopted a Political Declaration [RC-1/3] and recommended that the OPCW Executive Council develop and implement an action plan to further encourage adherence to the Convention. Regarding the impact of science and technology on prohibited activities, the Conference noted that, although definitions contained in the Convention relating to chemical weapons and their production facilities adequately covered relevant developments, science was rapidly advancing and new chemicals might need to be assessed within the context of the schedules of chemicals set out in the Convention. The Conference also addressed the importance of effective verification of chemical weapons stockpiles and recommended that the Council intensify its study of how to further optimize the OPCW verification system, with a view to providing recommendations that could possibly take effect in 2004.

GENERAL ASSEMBLY ACTION

On 8 December [meeting 71], the General Assembly, on the recommendation of the First Committee [A/58/462], adopted **resolution 58/52** without vote [agenda item 73 *(v)*].

Implementation of the Convention on the Prohibition of the Development, Production, Stockpiling and Use of Chemical Weapons and on Their Destruction

The General Assembly,

Recalling its previous resolutions on the subject of chemical weapons, in particular resolution 57/82 of 22 November 2002, adopted without a vote, in which it noted with appreciation the ongoing work to achieve the objective and purpose of the Convention on the Prohibition of the Development, Production, Stockpiling and Use of Chemical Weapons and on Their Destruction,

Determined to achieve the effective prohibition of the development, production, acquisition, transfer, stockpiling and use of chemical weapons and their destruction,

Noting with satisfaction that since the adoption of resolution 57/82, eleven additional States have ratified the Convention or acceded to it, bringing the total number of States parties to the Convention to one hundred and fifty-eight,

1. *Emphasizes* that the universality of the Convention on the Prohibition of the Development, Production, Stockpiling and Use of Chemical Weapons and on Their Destruction is fundamental to the achievement of its objective and purpose;

2. *Underlines* that the Convention and its implementation contribute to enhancing international peace and security, and emphasizes that its full, universal and effective implementation will contribute further to that purpose by excluding completely, for the sake of all humankind, the possibility of the use of chemical weapons;

3. *Stresses* that the full and effective implementation of all provisions of the Convention is in itself an important contribution to the efforts of the United Nations in the global fight against terrorism in all its forms and manifestations;

4. *Emphasizes* the necessity of universal adherence to the Convention, and calls upon all States that have not yet done so to become parties to the Convention without delay;

5. *Notes with appreciation* the outcome of the First Special Session of the Conference of the States Parties to Review the Operation of the Chemical Weapons Convention, convened in The Hague from 28 April to 9 May 2003, and the Political Declaration, in which the States parties reaffirm their commitment to achieving the objective and purpose of the Convention;

6. *Stresses* the importance to the Convention that all possessors of chemical weapons, chemical weapons production facilities or chemical weapons development facilities, including previously declared possessor States, should be among the States parties to the Convention, and welcomes progress to that end;

7. *Notes* that the effective application of the verification system builds confidence in compliance with the Convention by States parties;

8. *Stresses* the importance of the Organization for the Prohibition of Chemical Weapons in verifying compliance with the provisions of the Convention as well as in promoting the timely and efficient accomplishment of all its objectives;

9. *Urges* all States parties to the Convention to meet in full and on time their obligations under the Convention and to support the Organization for the Prohibition of Chemical Weapons in its implementation activities;

10. *Notes* the undertaking of the States parties to foster international cooperation for peaceful purposes in the field of chemical activities of the States parties and the importance of that cooperation and its contribution to the promotion of the Convention as a whole;

11. *Notes with appreciation* the ongoing work of the Organization for the Prohibition of Chemical Weapons to achieve the objective and purpose of the Convention, to ensure the full implementation of its provisions, including those for international verification of compliance with it, and to provide a forum for consultation and cooperation among States parties;

12. *Welcomes* the cooperation between the United Nations and the Organization for the Prohibition of Chemical Weapons within the framework of the Relationship Agreement between the United Nations and the Organization, in accordance with the provisions of the Convention;

13. *Decides* to include in the provisional agenda of its fifty-ninth session the item entitled "Implementation of the Convention on the Prohibition of the Development, Production, Stockpiling and Use of Chemical Weapons and on Their Destruction".

Organization for the Prohibition of Chemical Weapons

In 2003, OPCW continued efforts to achieve the objective and purpose of CWC. Between the Convention's entry into force in 1997 and 31 July 2003, OPCW inventoried and verified the non-diversion of over 8 million chemical munitions and bulk agent, of which it monitored the destruction of over 22 per cent. No fewer than 70,000 metric tonnes of chemical agent, otherwise classified as exceedingly lethal weapons, had been secured, of which 11 per cent was verifiably destroyed, while over two thirds of former production facilities for those weapons had been destroyed or converted to peaceful purposes.

The OPCW Executive Council, at its thirty-second (18-21 March), thirty-third (24-26 June), thirty-fourth (23-26 September) and thirty-fifth (2-5 December) sessions, addressed issues relating to deadlines for the destruction of chemical weapons stockpiles, the conversion to peaceful purposes of related production facilities, the optimization of verification activities, the agenda of the First Review Conference of the States Parties (see p. 560) and administrative and financial questions. The Council adopted decisions on the list of new validated data for inclusion in the OPCW central analytical database and privileges and immunities agreements between OPCW and Bosnia and Herzegovina, Burundi, Cyprus and Slovakia.

Conventional weapons

Programme of Action on illicit trade in small arms

Expert meeting. Pursuant to General Assembly resolution 56/24 V [YUN 2001, p. 503], the Secretary-General, in July [A/58/138], transmitted the report of the Group of Governmental Experts he had appointed to examine the feasibility of developing an international instrument to help identify and trace illicit small arms and light weapons, which completed its work during the year. The 30-member Group, at its second (Geneva, 24-28 March) and final (New York, 2-6 June) sessions, considered the nature and scope of the problem posed by the weapons and a variety of issues relating to the definition and other aspects of tracing, including the questions of marking, record-keeping and cooperation. The Group concluded that it was desirable to develop an international instrument to help clarify, develop and strengthen standards and practices with regard to marking and record-keeping on those weapons. The proposed instrument would also help to foster and promote international cooperation in tracing activities, enhance existing international and regional agreements to prevent, combat and eradicate those weapons, and strengthen States' commitments on the issue. The Group recommended that the Assembly take a decision at its fifty-eighth (2003) session to negotiate, under UN auspices, the international instrument.

The Assembly, in **resolution 58/241** of 23 December (see p. 564), decided to establish an open-ended working group to negotiate the proposed instrument.

Biennial Meeting of States. In response to General Assembly resolution 57/72 [YUN 2002, p. 523], the First Biennial Meeting of States to Consider the Implementation of the Programme of Action to Prevent, Combat and Eradicate the Illicit Trade in Small Arms and Light Weapons in All Its Aspects [YUN 2001, p. 499] was convened (New York, 7-11 July) [A/CONF.192/BMS/2003/1]. The Meeting, which was facilitated by the voluntary submission of national reports by over 80 Member States, held thematic discussions on implementation, international cooperation and assistance issues. Annexed to the Meeting's report was the Chairperson's summary of the discussions. The Meeting had before it national reports regarding efforts to implement the Programme of Action [A/CONF.192/BMS/2003/CRP.1-98]; a list of initiatives undertaken at the regional and sub-regional levels to address the illicit trade in small arms and light weapons [A/CONF.192/BMS/2003/CRP.99]; and the report of the Group of Governmental Experts to study the feasibility of developing an international instrument to help identify and trace such weapons (see above).

Reports of Secretary-General. Pursuant to General Assembly resolutions 57/70 [YUN 2002, p. 522] and 57/72 [ibid., p. 523], the Secretary-General, in an August report [A/58/207] covering the period from July 2002 to July 2003, summarized national, subregional and regional activities undertaken in Africa, in response to States' requests for UN assistance in curbing the illicit trade in small arms and to collect and dispose of them. He also described other activities undertaken by the UN system and by States to implement the Programme of Action. The Secretary-General concluded that, during the period under review, Member States, international and regional organizations and civil society had remained strongly committed to implementing the Programme of Action, and had used the First Biennial Meeting of States (see above) to consolidate existing partnerships and to forge new ones around programmes focusing on concrete action. The UN system, through the Coordinating Action on Small Arms mechanism, relevant departments, agencies and funds, and with the support of interested partners, was determined to continue to play its role in global efforts to prevent, combat and eradicate the illicit trade in small arms and light weapons. Annexed to the report were the views of nine States on further steps they had taken to enhance international cooperation in preventing, combating and eradicating brokering in those weapons.

In a September report [A/58/323] on progress towards implementing the UN Millennium Declaration, as set out in Assembly resolution 55/2 [YUN 2000, p. 49], the Secretary-General said small arms, which were readily available at very low cost, even in the most remote corners of the world, were continuing to be used to kill millions of people. However, with the cooperation of all countries, it should be possible to tighten export controls and facilitate the identification of the sources of illicit weapons through the use of markings.

In response to presidential statement S/PRST/2002/30 [YUN 2002, p. 521], the Secretary-General, in a December report [S/2003/1217], described initiatives undertaken to implement the recommendations contained in his 2002 report regarding the Security Council's contribution to dealing with the illicit trade in small arms and light weapons in situations under its consideration [YUN 2002, p. 521]. He stated that significant progress had been achieved in implementing the recommendations on tracing illicit weapons; disarmament, demobilization and reintegration in post-conflict situations; control of the export and transit of small arms and light weapons; and transparency in armaments. Efforts were being made to implement recommendations on the Interpol Weapons and Explosives Tracking System, the small arms advisory service and links between illicit weapons and illicit exploitation of natural and other resources. Considering further recommendations, he noted that the issue of end-user certificates and illicit brokering activities had emerged as areas of common efforts by the Council and the Assembly. Although progress on the enforcement of Council resolutions and sanctions and on coercive measures against Member States that deliberately violated arms embargoes depended on the political will of Member States, further efforts by the Council were required to stimulate Member States to fulfil their obligations and to assist them in strengthening their capacity to address the issue. The implementation of the recommendation on the use of arms embargoes presented a mixed picture, for while some of those embargoes were employed to consolidate the peace process in certain conflict situations, the restriction on ammunition supply to areas of instability required more attention and vigorous action in order to achieve the desired objectives. The recommendation on the need to finance disarmament, demobilization and reintegration programmes through the assessed budgets for peacekeeping remained an issue of concern, as voluntary funding available for relevant activities, particularly at the early stages, was often very limited.

GENERAL ASSEMBLY ACTION

On 8 December [meeting 71], the General Assembly, on the recommendation of the First Committee [A/58/462], adopted **resolution 58/58** without vote [agenda item 73].

Assistance to States for curbing the illicit traffic in small arms and collecting them

The General Assembly,

Considering that the illicit proliferation and circulation of and traffic in small arms impede development, constitute a threat to populations and to national and regional security and are a factor contributing to the destabilization of States,

Deeply disturbed by the magnitude of the illicit proliferation and circulation of and traffic in small arms in the States of the Sahelo-Saharan subregion,

Noting with satisfaction the conclusions of the United Nations advisory missions dispatched by the Secretary-General to the affected countries of the subregion to study the most appropriate way of halting the illicit circulation of small arms and collecting them,

Welcoming the designation of the Department for Disarmament Affairs of the Secretariat as a centre for the coordination of all activities of United Nations bodies concerned with small arms,

Congratulating the Secretary-General for his report on the causes of conflict and the promotion of durable peace and sustainable development in Africa, and bearing in mind the statement on small arms made by the President of the Security Council on 24 September 1999,

Welcoming the recommendations resulting from the meetings of the States of the subregion held at Banjul, Algiers, Bamako, Yamoussoukro and Niamey to establish close regional cooperation with a view to strengthening security,

Welcoming also the decision taken by the Economic Community of West African States to renew the Declaration of a Moratorium on the Importation, Exportation and Manufacture of Small Arms and Light Weapons in West Africa, adopted by the heads of State and Government of the Community at Abuja on 31 October 1998,

Recalling the Algiers Declaration adopted by the Assembly of Heads of State and Government of the Organization of African Unity at its thirty-fifth ordinary session, held at Algiers from 12 to 14 July 1999,

Emphasizing the need to advance efforts towards wider cooperation and better coordination in the struggle against the illicit proliferation of small arms through the common understanding reached at the meeting on small arms held at Oslo on 13 and 14 July 1998 and the Brussels Call for Action adopted by the International Conference on Sustainable Disarmament for Sustainable Development, held at Brussels on 12 and 13 October 1998,

Bearing in mind the Bamako Declaration on an African Common Position on the Illicit Proliferation, Circulation and Trafficking of Small Arms and Light Weapons, adopted at Bamako on 1 December 2000,

Recalling the millennium report of the Secretary-General,

Welcoming the Programme of Action to Prevent, Combat and Eradicate the Illicit Trade in Small Arms and Light Weapons in All Its Aspects, adopted by the United Nations Conference on the Illicit Trade in Small Arms and Light Weapons in All Its Aspects, and calling for its expeditious implementation,

Recognizing the important role that the organizations of civil society play in detection, prevention and raising public awareness, in efforts to curb the illicit traffic in small arms,

1. *Notes with satisfaction* the Declaration of the Ministerial Conference on Security, Stability, Development and Cooperation in Africa, held at Abuja on 8 and 9 May 2000, and encourages the Secretary-General to pursue his efforts in the context of the implementation of General Assembly resolution 49/75 G of 15 December 1994 and the recommendations of the United Nations advisory missions, aimed at curbing the illicit circulation of small arms and collecting such arms in the affected States that so request, with the support of the United Nations Regional Centre for Peace and Disarmament in Africa and in close cooperation with the African Union;

2. *Welcomes* the decision of the Economic Community of West African States to renew the Declaration of a Moratorium on the Importation, Exportation and Manufacture of Small Arms and Light Weapons in West Africa for a three-year period, until October 2004, and encourages the international community to support the implementation of the moratorium;

3. *Encourages* the establishment in the countries of the Sahelo-Saharan subregion of national commissions to combat the illicit proliferation of small arms, and invites the international community to lend its support wherever possible to ensure the smooth functioning of the commissions;

4. *Also encourages* the involvement of organizations and associations of civil society in the efforts of the national commissions to combat the illicit traffic in small arms and their participation in the implementation of the moratorium on the importation, exportation and manufacture of small arms and light weapons in West Africa as well as in the implementation of the Programme of Action to Prevent, Combat and Eradicate the Illicit Trade in Small Arms and Light Weapons in All Its Aspects;

5. *Further encourages* cooperation among State organs, international organizations and civil society in combating the illicit traffic in small arms and supporting operations to collect the said arms in the subregions;

6. *Calls upon* the international community to provide technical and financial support to strengthen the capacity of civil organizations to take action to combat the illicit trade in small arms;

7. *Takes note* of the conclusions of the meeting of Ministers for Foreign Affairs of the Economic Community of West African States, held at Bamako on 24 and 25 March 1999, on the modalities for the implementation of the Programme for Coordination and Assistance for Security and Development, and welcomes the adoption by the meeting of a plan of action;

8. *Takes note also* of the conclusions of the African Conference on the Implementation of the United Nations Programme of Action on Small Arms: Needs and Partnerships, held at Pretoria from 18 to 21 March 2002;

9. *Invites* the Secretary-General and those States and organizations that are in a position to do so to provide assistance to States for curbing the illicit traffic in small arms and collecting them;

10. *Requests* the Secretary-General to continue to consider the matter and to report to it at its fifty-ninth session on the implementation of the present resolution;

11. *Decides* to include in the provisional agenda of its fifty-ninth session the item entitled "Assistance to States for curbing the illicit traffic in small arms and collecting them".

On 23 December [meeting 79], the Assembly, also on the recommendation of the First Committee [A/58/462], adopted **resolution 58/241** without vote [agenda item 73 (n)].

The illicit trade in small arms and light weapons in all its aspects

The General Assembly,

Reaffirming its resolution 57/72 of 22 November 2002,

Recalling its resolutions 50/70 B of 12 December 1995, 52/38 J of 9 December 1997, 53/77 E and 53/77 T of 4 December 1998, 54/54 R of 1 December 1999, 54/54 V of 15 December 1999, 55/33 Q of 20 November 2000 and 56/24 V of 24 December 2001,

Emphasizing the importance of early and full implementation of the Programme of Action to Prevent, Combat and Eradicate the Illicit Trade in Small Arms and Light Weapons in All Its Aspects, adopted by the United Nations Conference on the Illicit Trade in Small Arms and Light Weapons in All Its Aspects,

Welcoming the adoption by consensus of the report of the First Biennial Meeting of States to Consider the Implementation of the Programme of Action to Prevent, Combat and Eradicate the Illicit Trade in Small Arms and Light Weapons in All Its Aspects, held in New York from 7 to 11 July 2003,

Welcoming also the efforts by Member States to submit, on a voluntary basis, national reports on their implementation of the Programme of Action,

Noting with satisfaction regional efforts being undertaken in support of the implementation of the Programme of Action,

Taking note of the report of the Secretary-General on the implementation of resolution 57/72,

Welcoming the report on the feasibility of developing an international instrument to enable States to identify and trace, in a timely and reliable manner, illicit small arms and light weapons, prepared by the Group of Governmental Experts established pursuant to resolution 56/24 V,

Conscious of its decision to convene a conference, no later than 2006, to review progress made in the implementation of the Programme of Action, the date and venue to be decided by the General Assembly at its fifty-eighth session,

1. *Decides* to convene a United Nations conference to review progress made in the implementation of the Programme of Action to Prevent, Combat and Eradicate the Illicit Trade in Small Arms and Light Weapons in All Its Aspects in New York for a period of two weeks between June and July 2006;

2. *Also decides* that a session of the preparatory committee for the conference is to be held in New York for a period of two weeks in January 2006, and that, if necessary, a subsequent session may be held;

3. *Further decides* to convene in 2005 the second biennial meeting of States as stipulated in the Programme of Action to consider the national, regional and global implementation of the Programme of Action;

4. *Determines* that it is feasible to develop an international instrument to enable States to identify and trace, in a timely and reliable manner, illicit small arms and light weapons;

5. *Notes* that the character of the international instrument will be determined in the course of negotiations;

6. *Also notes* that the international instrument should be complementary to, and not inconsistent with, the existing commitments of States under relevant international instruments;

7. *Further notes* that the international instrument should take into account the national security and legal interests of States;

8. *Decides* to establish an open-ended working group, to meet in three sessions of two weeks each, to negotiate an international instrument to enable States to identify and trace, in a timely and reliable manner, illicit small arms and light weapons;

9. *Also decides* that the open-ended working group shall hold an organizational session in New York on 3 and 4 February 2004 in order to set the dates for its substantive sessions;

10. *Requests* the Secretary-General to provide the open-ended working group with the assistance and services that may be required for the discharge of its tasks;

11. *Also requests* the Secretary-General to hold broad-based consultations, within available financial resources and with any other assistance provided by Member States in a position to do so, with all Member States, interested regional and subregional organizations, international agencies and experts in the field, on further steps to enhance international cooperation in preventing, combating and eradicating illicit brokering in small arms and light weapons, taking into consideration the views of States provided to the Secretary-General, and requests the Secretary-General to report to the General Assembly at its fifty-ninth session on the outcome of his consultations;

12. *Continues to encourage* all initiatives to mobilize resources and expertise to promote the implementation of the Programme of Action and to provide assistance to States in its implementation;

13. *Requests* the Secretary-General to continue to collate and circulate data and information provided by States on a voluntary basis, including national reports, on the implementation by those States of the Programme of Action, and encourages Member States to submit such reports;

14. *Also requests* the Secretary-General to report to the General Assembly at its fifty-ninth session on the implementation of the present resolution;

15. *Decides* to include in the provisional agenda of its fifty-ninth session the item entitled "The illicit trade in small arms and light weapons in all its aspects".

(For regional initiatives regarding implementation of the Programme of Action, see pp. 573-579.)

Convention on excessively injurious conventional weapons and Protocols

In response to General Assembly resolution 57/98 [YUN 2002, p. 525], the Secretary-General reported on the status, as at 10 July [A/58/163], of the 1980 Convention on Prohibitions or Restrictions on the Use of Certain Conventional Weapons Which May Be Deemed to Be Excessively Injurious or to Have Indiscriminate Effects and its annexed Protocols [YUN 1980, p. 76] on Non-Detectable Fragments (Protocol I); on Prohibitions or Restrictions on the Use of Mines, Booby Traps and Other Devices, as amended on 3 May 1996 (Protocol II) [YUN 1996, p. 484]; and on Prohibitions or Restrictions on the Use of Incendiary Weapons (Protocol III); as well as the 1995 Protocol on Blinding Laser Weapons (Protocol IV) [YUN 1995, p. 221], which took effect on 30 July 1998 [YUN 1998, p. 530].

The accessions of Burkina Faso and Honduras and the acceptance of Chile brought the number of States parties to 93 as at 31 December.

The Group of Governmental Experts established by the Second Review Conference of the States Parties to the Convention [YUN 2001, p. 504] to consider the issues of explosive remnants of war, mines other than anti-personnel mines, small-calibre weapons and ammunition, and promotion of compliance with the Convention and its annexed Protocols, held its fourth (10-14 March) [CCW/GGE/IV/2], fifth (16-27 June) [CCW/GGE/V/3] and sixth (17-24 November) [CCW/GGE/VI/2] sessions, all in Geneva. The Group discussed issues relating to the weapons under consideration and working papers and presentations from delegations, international organizations and other experts. On 24 November, the Group endorsed the recommendations of its working groups on explosive remnants of war and on mines other than anti-personnel mines, which were annexed to the report on its sixth session, as was the text of a proposed protocol on explosive remnants of war, which the Group recommended for adoption by the Meeting of the States Parties to the Convention (see below). The Group agreed that intersessional work of five weeks would be undertaken in three sessions during 2004, on dates to be decided by the Meeting of States Parties, which was scheduled to be held in conjunction with the Sixth (2004) Annual Conference of the States Parties to Amended Protocol II.

The Fifth Annual Conference of the States Parties to Amended Protocol II (Geneva, 26 November) [CCW/AP.II/CONF.5/2] reviewed the operation and status of amended Protocol II, considered other major related issues and examined national reports received from 50 States parties. The Conference adopted a final document containing conclusions and recommendations, and an appeal to States that had not done so to accede to amended Protocol II as soon as possible. It recommended that the Secretary-General, as depositary, and the President of the Conference exercise their authority to achieve the goal of universality of the Protocol and called on the High Contracting Parties to promote wider adherence. The Sixth Annual Conference was scheduled to take place in 2004, on dates to be decided by the Meeting of the States Parties (see below).

As decided by the Meeting of the States Parties in 2002 [YUN 2002, p. 525], the States parties met

(Geneva, 27-28 November) [CCW/MSP/2003/3] to consider the work of the Group of Governmental Experts (see p. 565). As recommended by the Experts, the Meeting decided to adopt a new legally binding instrument—a protocol on explosive remnants of war, which would be annexed to the Convention. The Meeting also decided that the Group of Governmental Experts should continue its work in 2004 in three sessions scheduled for March, July and November, and approved new mandates for its working groups. The working group on explosive remnants of war was mandated to continue to consider the implementation of existing principles of international humanitarian law and possible preventive measures aimed at improving the design of certain types of munitions, including sub-munitions, with a view to minimizing the humanitarian risk of those munitions becoming explosive remnants of war. The working group on mines other than anti-personnel mines was charged to consider all proposals on that category of mines, with the aim of making appropriate recommendations for consideration in 2004. The Meeting decided that the Sixth Annual Conference of the States Parties would be held in November 2004 in Geneva, and that its Chairman-designate should undertake consultations during the intersessional period on possible options to promote compliance with the Convention and its annexed Protocols.

GENERAL ASSEMBLY ACTION

On 8 December [meeting 71], the General Assembly, on the recommendation of the First Committee [A/58/466], adopted **resolution 58/69** without vote [agenda item 77].

Convention on Prohibitions or Restrictions on the Use of Certain Conventional Weapons Which May Be Deemed to Be Excessively Injurious or to Have Indiscriminate Effects

The General Assembly,

Recalling its resolution 57/98 of 22 November 2002 and previous resolutions referring to the Convention on Prohibitions or Restrictions on the Use of Certain Conventional Weapons Which May Be Deemed to Be Excessively Injurious or to Have Indiscriminate Effects,

Recalling with satisfaction the adoption, on 10 October 1980, of the Convention, together with the Protocol on Non-Detectable Fragments (Protocol I), the Protocol on Prohibitions or Restrictions on the Use of Mines, Booby Traps and Other Devices (Protocol II) and the Protocol on Prohibitions or Restrictions on the Use of Incendiary Weapons (Protocol III), which entered into force on 2 December 1983,

Also recalling with satisfaction the adoption by the First Review Conference of the States Parties to the Convention on Prohibitions or Restrictions on the Use of Certain Conventional Weapons Which May Be Deemed to Be Excessively Injurious or to Have Indiscriminate Effects, on 13 October 1995 of the Protocol on Blinding Laser Weapons (Protocol IV), and on 3 May 1996 of the amended Protocol on Prohibitions or Restrictions on the Use of Mines, Booby Traps and Other Devices (Protocol II), which entered into force on 30 July 1998 and 3 December 1998 respectively,

Welcoming the results of the Second Review Conference of the States Parties to the Convention on Prohibitions or Restrictions on the Use of Certain Conventional Weapons Which May Be Deemed to Be Excessively Injurious or to Have Indiscriminate Effects, and commending the efforts of the President of the Conference,

Recalling with satisfaction the decision by the Second Review Conference, on 21 December 2001, to extend the scope of the Convention and the Protocols thereto to include armed conflicts of a non-international character,

Recalling the decision by the Second Review Conference to commission follow-up work under the oversight of the Chairman-designate of a meeting of States parties to the Convention and in this context the decision to establish an open-ended group of governmental experts with two separate coordinators on explosive remnants of war and on mines other than anti-personnel mines,

Welcoming the additional ratifications and acceptances of or accessions to the Convention and to amended Protocol II and Protocol IV, as well as accessions to the amendment of article I of the Convention, as adopted in 2001,

Recalling the role played by the International Committee of the Red Cross in the elaboration of the Convention and the Protocols thereto,

Noting that the rules of procedure of the First Annual Conference of States Parties to Amended Protocol II provide for the invitation of States not parties to the Protocol, the International Committee of the Red Cross and interested non-governmental organizations to take part in the Conference,

Welcoming the particular efforts of various international, non-governmental and other organizations in raising awareness of the humanitarian consequences of explosive remnants of war,

Welcoming also the results of the Fourth Annual Conference of States Parties to Amended Protocol II, held at Geneva on 11 December 2002,

1. *Calls upon* all States that have not yet done so to take all measures to become parties, as soon as possible, to the Convention on Prohibitions or Restrictions on the Use of Certain Conventional Weapons Which May Be Deemed to Be Excessively Injurious or to Have Indiscriminate Effects and the Protocols thereto, as amended, as well as the amendment of article I extending the scope of the Convention, with a view to achieving the widest possible adherence to these instruments at an early date, and calls upon successor States to take appropriate measures so that ultimately adherence to these instruments will be universal;

2. *Calls upon* all States parties to the Convention that have not yet done so to express their consent to be bound by the Protocols to the Convention;

3. *Calls upon* all States parties to the Convention that have not yet done so to notify the depositary at an early date of their consent to be bound by the amendment extending the scope of the Convention and the

Protocols thereto to include armed conflicts of a non-international character;

4. *Notes* the decision of the Meeting of the States Parties to the Convention held on 12 and 13 December 2002 that the Working Group on Explosive Remnants of War would continue its work in 2003 with the mandate to negotiate an instrument on post-conflict remedial measures of a generic nature that would reduce the risks of explosive remnants of war and to explore and determine whether these negotiations could successfully address preventive generic measures for improving the reliability of munitions and, separate from these negotiations, to continue to consider the implementation of existing principles of international humanitarian law and to further study, on an open-ended basis, possible preventive measures aimed at improving the design of certain specific types of munitions, including sub-munitions, with a view to minimizing the humanitarian risk of these munitions' becoming explosive remnants of war;

5. *Also notes* the decision of the Meeting of the States Parties to the Convention that the Working Group on Mines Other Than Anti-Personnel Mines would continue its work in 2003 with the mandate to explore the issue of mines other than anti-personnel mines, and consider the most appropriate way to reduce the risks posed by the irresponsible use of mines other than anti-personnel mines, including the possibility of concluding a negotiating mandate for a new instrument and other appropriate measures, taking into account the issues specified in the decision;

6. *Further notes* the decision of the Meeting of the States Parties to the Convention that the Chairman-designate should continue to undertake consultations during the intersessional period on possible options to promote compliance with the Convention and the Protocols thereto, taking into account proposals put forward;

7. *Expresses support* for the work conducted by the Group of Governmental Experts, and encourages the Chairman-designate and the Group to conduct work expeditiously with a view to submitting a possible proposal for an instrument on explosive remnants of war to States parties for consideration at their meeting on 27 and 28 November 2003 and with a view to submitting to the States parties' reports on mines other than anti-personnel mines and on compliance;

8. *Requests* the Secretary-General to render the necessary assistance and to provide such services, including summary records, as may be required for the Meeting of States Parties to the Convention to be held on 27 and 28 November 2003, as well as for any possible continuation of work after the Meeting, should the States parties deem it appropriate;

9. *Also requests* the Secretary-General, in his capacity as depositary of the Convention and the Protocols thereto, to continue to inform the General Assembly periodically, by electronic means, of ratifications and acceptances of and accessions to the Convention and the Protocols thereto;

10. *Decides* to include in the provisional agenda of its fifty-ninth session the item entitled "Convention on Prohibitions or Restrictions on the Use of Certain Conventional Weapons Which May Be Deemed to Be Excessively Injurious or to Have Indiscriminate Effects".

Practical disarmament

The group of interested States, established in 1998 [YUN 1998, p. 531] to examine and support concrete projects of practical disarmament, met three times during 2003 to address practical disarmament measures in Kenya, Mozambique and Slovenia, and to continue its consideration of the disarmament education project conceived jointly by the Department for Disarmament Affairs (DDA) and the Hague Appeal for Peace, an NGO. In so doing, the group accorded priority attention to the provisions of the Programme of Action adopted by the UN Conference on small arms [YUN 2001, p. 499]. The group also reassessed its purpose and operation after five years of activities and would continue to do so in the light of the conclusions of the first biennial meeting of States, held to consider efforts to implement the Programme of Action (see p. 562), in order to better position itself to assist Member States to implement the Programme of Action.

Disarmament Commission action. In 2003 [A/58/42], the Disarmament Commission allocated to Working Group II the item entitled "Practical confidence-building measures (CBMs) in the field of conventional arms". Based on intersessional informal consultations, the Chairman submitted a working paper, which the Group adopted as a basis for discussion, during which many delegations put forth proposals on the item. Subsequently, the Chairman submitted four revised versions of his working paper, on which the Group was unable to achieve consensus. The paper discussed the scope of CBMs, the significance of the purposes and principles of the UN Charter within the context of CBMs, the status of existing CBMs in the field of conventional arms and the way forward in addressing the subject, including measures to strengthen and improve confidence among States.

Report of Secretary-General. Pursuant to General Assembly resolution 57/81 [YUN 2002, p. 526], the Secretary-General, in August [A/58/207], presented an overview of the activities of States, including the group of interested States and regional and subregional organizations, regarding practical disarmament measures during the period from July 2002 to July 2003. The report focused on efforts to implement the Programme of Action, and concluded that Member States, international and regional organizations and civil society had remained strongly committed to doing so.

On 8 December, the Assembly took note of the Secretary-General's report and, taking into consideration the work of the group of interested States (see above), deferred consideration of the item entitled "Consolidation of peace through practical disarmament measures" until its fifty-ninth (2004) session and decided to consider it biennially in the future; the Assembly included the item in the provisional agenda of its 2004 session (**decision 58/519**).

Transparency

Conference on Disarmament. In 2003, the issue of transparency in armaments was considered during plenary meetings of the Conference on Disarmament [A/58/27], within the context of discussions on how to achieve consensus on a comprehensive programme of work. A joint proposal on the item put forth by five former Presidents of the Conference (see p. 531) had envisaged, among other things, the appointment of a special coordinator to seek the views of Conference members on the most appropriate way to deal with transparency in armaments. However, owing to the persisting lack of agreement over the programme of work, the Conference did not establish or re-establish any mechanism to deal with the subject.

UN Register of Conventional Arms

In response to General Assembly resolution 57/75 [YUN 2002, p. 528], the Secretary-General submitted the eleventh annual report on the United Nations Register of Conventional Arms [A/58/203 & Corr.1,2 & Add.1], established in 1992 [YUN 1992, p. 75] to promote enhanced levels of transparency on arms transfers.

The report presented information provided by 119 Governments on imports and exports in 2002 in the seven categories of conventional arms (battle tanks, armoured combat vehicles, large-calibre artillery systems, attack helicopters, combat aircraft, warships and missiles and missile launchers). Governments also provided information on procurement from national production and military holdings, on the continuing operation of the Register and its further development and on transparency measures related to weapons of mass destruction. The report indicated a slight reduction in the number of submissions compared with the previous year.

In response to the Assembly's request in resolution 57/75 that the Secretary-General implement the recommendations contained in the 2000 report of the Group of Governmental Experts on the continuing operation and further development of the Register [YUN 2000, p. 524], the report outlined regional activities undertaken by the Secretariat during the year, through DDA, in collaboration with Governments and regional organizations, to enhance familiarity and greater participation in the Register.

Group of Governmental Experts. In response to resolution 57/75, the Secretary-General transmitted an August report [A/58/274] on the continuing operation of the Register and its further development, prepared by the Group of Governmental Experts he had appointed and which had concluded its work in three sessions held between March and August (New York). The report summarized periodic reviews of the Register undertaken since its establishment, analysed available data on reporting, including reporting patterns among regions, assessed the Register's operation and examined in some detail issues related to its further development, including the expansion of its scope and technical adjustments to the seven categories of arms covered. The Group concluded that, although the Register had made significant progress since its inception and had entered a period of increased participation, renewed efforts were required to ensure regular reporting and progress towards universal participation, as well as continued attention to its further development and increased relevance. Wide variations in the level of participation among and within some regions called for targeted regional and subregional efforts to encourage wider participation. The Group's recommendations, designed to enhance the effectiveness of the Register, included technical adjustments to two of the seven categories of conventional arms covered. In that context, it proposed the lowering of the reporting threshold for artillery pieces from 100- to 75-millimetre-calibre systems, including man-portable air-defence systems in the category of missiles and missile launchers. The Group addressed a number of other recommendations to Member States towards achieving the shared goals of the instrument and proposed that the General Assembly consider providing additional resources to strengthen the Secretariat's role in that regard. In December, the Assembly endorsed the report and the Group's recommendations and decided to adapt the Register's scope in conformity with the Group's recommendations (see below).

GENERAL ASSEMBLY ACTION

On 8 December [meeting 71], the General Assembly, on the recommendation of the First Committee [A/58/462], adopted **resolution 58/54** by recorded vote (150-0-27) [agenda item 73 (q)].

Transparency in armaments

The General Assembly,

Recalling its resolutions 46/36 L of 9 December 1991, 47/52 L of 15 December 1992, 48/75 E of 16 December 1993, 49/75 C of 15 December 1994, 50/70 D of 12 December 1995, 51/45 H of 10 December 1996, 52/38 R of 9 December 1997, 53/77 V of 4 December

1998, 54/54 O of 1 December 1999, 55/33 U of 20 November 2000, 56/24 Q of 29 November 2001 and 57/75 of 22 November 2002 entitled "Transparency in armaments",

Continuing to take the view that an enhanced level of transparency in armaments contributes greatly to confidence-building and security among States and that the establishment of the United Nations Register of Conventional Arms constitutes an important step forward in the promotion of transparency in military matters,

Welcoming the consolidated report of the Secretary-General on the Register, which includes the returns of Member States for 2002,

Welcoming also the response of Member States to the request contained in paragraphs 9 and 10 of resolution 46/36 L to provide data on their imports and exports of arms, as well as available background information regarding their military holdings, procurement through national production and relevant policies,

Stressing that the continuing operation of the Register and its further development should be reviewed in order to secure a Register that is capable of attracting the widest possible participation,

1. *Reaffirms its determination* to ensure the effective operation of the United Nations Register of Conventional Arms, as provided for in paragraphs 7 to 10 of resolution 46/36 L;

2. *Endorses* the report of the Secretary-General on the continuing operation of the Register and its further development and the recommendations ensuing from the consensus report of the 2003 group of governmental experts contained therein;

3. *Decides* to adapt the scope of the Register in conformity with the recommendations contained in the 2003 report of the Secretary-General;

4. *Calls upon* Member States, with a view to achieving universal participation, to provide the Secretary-General by 31 May annually with the requested data and information for the Register, including nil reports if appropriate, on the basis of resolutions 46/36 L and 47/52 L, the recommendations contained in paragraph 64 of the 1997 report of the Secretary-General on the continuing operation of the Register and its further development, the recommendations contained in paragraph 94 of the 2000 report of the Secretary-General and the appendices and annexes thereto as well as the 2003 report of the Secretary-General;

5. *Invites* Member States in a position to do so, pending further development of the Register, to provide additional information on procurement from national production and military holdings and to make use of the "Remarks" column in the standardized reporting form to provide additional information such as types or models;

6. *Reaffirms its decision*, with a view to further development of the Register, to keep the scope of and participation in the Register under review;

7. *Recalls*, to that end, its request to Member States to provide the Secretary-General with their views on the continuing operation of the Register and its further development and on transparency measures related to weapons of mass destruction;

8. *Requests* the Secretary-General to implement the recommendations contained in his 2003 report on the continuing operation of the Register and its further development and to ensure that sufficient resources are made available for the Secretariat to operate and maintain the Register;

9. *Reiterates its call upon* all Member States to cooperate at the regional and subregional levels, taking fully into account the specific conditions prevailing in the region or subregion, with a view to enhancing and coordinating international efforts aimed at increased openness and transparency in armaments;

10. *Requests* the Secretary-General to report to the General Assembly at its fifty-ninth session on progress made in implementing the present resolution.

RECORDED VOTE ON RESOLUTION 58/54:

In favour: Afghanistan, Albania, Andorra, Angola, Antigua and Barbuda, Argentina, Armenia, Australia, Austria, Azerbaijan, Bahamas, Bangladesh, Barbados, Belgium, Belize, Benin, Bhutan, Bolivia, Bosnia and Herzegovina, Botswana, Brazil, Brunei Darussalam, Bulgaria, Burkina Faso, Burundi, Cambodia, Cameroon, Canada, Cape Verde, Central African Republic, Chile, Colombia, Congo, Costa Rica, Croatia, Cyprus, Czech Republic, Denmark, Dominican Republic, Ecuador, El Salvador, Eritrea, Estonia, Ethiopia, Fiji, Finland, France, Gabon, Gambia, Georgia, Germany, Ghana, Greece, Grenada, Guatemala, Guinea, Guinea-Bissau, Guyana, Haiti, Honduras, Hungary, Iceland, India, Indonesia, Ireland, Israel, Italy, Jamaica, Japan, Kazakhstan, Kenya, Kyrgyzstan, Lao People's Democratic Republic, Latvia, Lesotho, Liechtenstein, Lithuania, Luxembourg, Madagascar, Malawi, Malaysia, Maldives, Mali, Malta, Marshall Islands, Mauritius, Mexico, Micronesia, Monaco, Mongolia, Mozambique, Namibia, Nauru, Nepal, Netherlands, New Zealand, Nicaragua, Niger, Nigeria, Norway, Pakistan, Panama, Papua New Guinea, Paraguay, Peru, Philippines, Poland, Portugal, Republic of Korea, Republic of Moldova, Romania, Russian Federation, Saint Lucia, Saint Vincent and the Grenadines, Samoa, San Marino, Senegal, Serbia and Montenegro, Seychelles, Sierra Leone, Singapore, Slovakia, Slovenia, Solomon Islands, South Africa, Spain, Sri Lanka, Suriname, Swaziland, Sweden, Switzerland, Tajikistan, Thailand, The former Yugoslav Republic of Macedonia, Timor-Leste, Togo, Tonga, Trinidad and Tobago, Turkey, Turkmenistan, Uganda, Ukraine, United Kingdom, United Republic of Tanzania, United States, Uruguay, Uzbekistan, Venezuela, Zambia, Zimbabwe.

Against: None.

Abstaining: Algeria, Bahrain, China, Comoros, Côte d'Ivoire, Cuba, Democratic People's Republic of Korea, Djibouti, Egypt, Iran, Jordan, Kuwait, Lebanon, Libyan Arab Jamahiriya, Mauritania, Morocco, Myanmar, Oman, Qatar, Rwanda, Saudi Arabia, Somalia, Sudan, Syrian Arab Republic, Tunisia, United Arab Emirates, Yemen.

The First Committee adopted by separate recorded votes paragraph 2 (138 to none, with 22 abstentions); paragraph 3, together with the last nine words of paragraph 4 ("as well as the 2003 report of the Secretary-General") and paragraph 8 (138 to none, with 22 abstentions); and paragraph 4 (137 to none, with 22 abstentions). The Assembly retained those paragraphs by separate recorded votes of 153 to none, with 23 abstentions; 152 to none, with 22 abstentions; and 152 to none, with 22 abstentions, respectively.

Also on 8 December [meeting 71], the Assembly, on the recommendation of the First Committee [A/58/462], adopted **resolution 58/42** without vote [agenda item 73 *(i)*].

National legislation on transfer of arms, military equipment and dual-use goods and technology

The General Assembly,

Recognizing that disarmament, arms control and non-proliferation are essential for the maintenance of international peace and security,

Recalling that effective national control of the transfer of arms, military equipment and dual-use goods and technology, including those transfers that could contribute to proliferation activities, is an important tool for achieving those objectives,

Recalling also that the States parties to the international disarmament and non-proliferation treaties have undertaken to facilitate the fullest possible exchange of materials, equipment and technological information for peaceful purposes, in accordance with the provisions of those treaties,

Considering that the exchange of national legislation, regulations and procedures on the transfer of arms, military equipment and dual-use goods and technology contributes to mutual understanding and confidence among Member States,

Convinced that such an exchange would be beneficial to Member States that are in the process of developing such legislation,

Reaffirming the inherent right of individual or collective self-defence in accordance with Article 51 of the Charter of the United Nations,

1. *Invites* Member States that are in a position to do so to enact or improve national legislation, regulations and procedures to exercise effective control over the transfer of arms, military equipment and dual-use goods and technology, while ensuring that such legislation, regulations and procedures are consistent with the obligations of States parties under international treaties;

2. *Encourages* Member States to provide, on a voluntary basis, information to the Secretary-General on their national legislation, regulations and procedures on the transfer of arms, military equipment and dual-use goods and technology, as well as the changes therein, and requests the Secretary-General to make this information accessible to Member States;

3. *Decides* to include in the provisional agenda of its fifty-ninth session the item entitled "National legislation on transfer of arms, military equipment and dual-use goods and technology".

Transparency of military expenditures

In response to General Assembly resolution 56/14 [YUN 2001, p. 508], the Secretary-General, in August, presented reports from 75 Member States on military expenditures for the latest fiscal year for which data were available [A/58/202 & Add.1,2]. The reporting instrument was that recommended by the Assembly in resolution 35/142 B [YUN 1980, p. 88].

The report noted that DDA, in cooperation with Canada, Germany, Japan and the Netherlands, organized regional workshops on transparency in armaments devoted to the Register of Conventional Arms and the standardized instrument for reporting military expenditures. It also published a booklet devoted to the standardized instrument, which contained basic information regarding global participation in the instrument since 1981.

GENERAL ASSEMBLY ACTION

On 8 December [meeting 71], the General Assembly, on the recommendation of the First Committee [A/58/451], adopted **resolution 58/28** (as orally amended) without vote [agenda item 62 (b)].

Objective information on military matters, including transparency of military expenditures

The General Assembly,

Recalling its resolutions 53/72 of 4 December 1998, 54/43 of 1 December 1999 and 56/14 of 29 November 2001 on objective information on military matters, including transparency of military expenditures,

Also recalling its resolution 35/142 B of 12 December 1980, which introduced the United Nations system for the standardized reporting of military expenditures, and its resolutions 48/62 of 16 December 1993, 49/66 of 15 December 1994, 51/38 of 10 December 1996 and 52/32 of 9 December 1997, calling upon all Member States to participate in it, and its resolution 47/54 B of 9 December 1992, endorsing the guidelines and recommendations for objective information on military matters and inviting Member States to provide the Secretary-General with relevant information regarding their implementation,

Noting that since then, national reports on military expenditures and on the guidelines and recommendations for objective information on military matters have been submitted by a number of Member States belonging to different geographic regions,

Convinced that the improvement of international relations forms a sound basis for promoting further openness and transparency in all military matters,

Also convinced that transparency in military matters is an essential element for building a climate of trust and confidence between States worldwide and that a better flow of objective information on military matters can help to relieve international tension and is therefore an important contribution to conflict prevention,

Noting the role of the standardized reporting system, as instituted through its resolution 35/142 B, as an important instrument to enhance transparency in military matters,

Conscious that the value of the standardized reporting system would be enhanced by a broader participation of Member States,

Welcoming, therefore, the report of the Secretary-General on ways and means to implement the guidelines and recommendations for objective information on military matters, including, in particular, how to strengthen and broaden participation in the standardized reporting system,

Recalling that the guidelines and recommendations for objective information on military matters recommended certain areas for further consideration, such as the improvement of the standardized reporting system,

Noting the efforts of several regional organizations to promote transparency of military expenditures, including standardized annual exchanges of relevant information among their member States,

1. *Calls upon* Member States to report annually, by 30 April, to the Secretary-General their military expenditures for the latest fiscal year for which data are available, using, preferably and to the extent possible, the reporting instrument as recommended in its resolution 35/142 B or, as appropriate, any other format developed in conjunction with similar reporting on

military expenditures to other international or regional organizations, and, in the same context, encourages Member States to submit nil returns, if appropriate;

2. *Recommends* the guidelines and recommendations for objective information on military matters to all Member States for implementation, fully taking into account specific political, military and other conditions prevailing in a region, on the basis of initiatives and with the agreement of the States of the region concerned;

3. *Encourages* relevant international bodies and regional organizations to promote transparency of military expenditures and to enhance complementarity among reporting systems, taking into account the particular characteristics of each region, and to consider the possibility of an exchange of information with the United Nations;

4. *Takes note* of the report of the Secretary-General on objective information on military matters, including transparency of military expenditures;

5. *Requests* the Secretary-General, within available resources:

(a) To continue the practice of sending an annual note verbale to Member States requesting the submission of data to the United Nations system for the standardized reporting of military expenditures, together with the reporting format and related instructions, and to publish in a timely fashion in appropriate United Nations media the due date for transmitting data on military expenditures;

(b) To circulate annually the reports on military expenditures as received from Member States;

(c) To continue consultations with relevant international bodies, within existing resources, with a view to ascertaining requirements for adjusting the present instrument, with a view to encouraging wider participation, and to make recommendations, based on the outcome of those consultations and taking into account the views of Member States, on necessary changes to the content and structure of the standardized reporting system;

(d) To encourage relevant international bodies and organizations to promote transparency of military expenditures and to consult with those bodies and organizations with emphasis on examining possibilities for enhancing complementarity among international and regional reporting systems and for exchanging related information between those bodies and the United Nations;

(e) To encourage the United Nations regional centres for peace and disarmament in Africa, in Asia and the Pacific, and in Latin America and the Caribbean to assist Member States in their regions in enhancing their knowledge of the standardized reporting system;

(f) To promote international and regional/subregional symposiums and training seminars to explain the purpose of the standardized reporting system and to give relevant technical instructions;

(g) To report on experiences gained during such symposiums and training seminars;

6. *Encourages* Member States:

(a) To inform the Secretary-General about possible problems with the standardized reporting system and their reasons for not submitting the requested data;

(b) To continue to provide the Secretary-General, in time for deliberation by the General Assembly at its sixtieth session, with their views and suggestions on ways and means to strengthen and broaden participation in the standardized reporting system, including necessary changes to its content and structure;

7. *Decides* to include in the provisional agenda of its sixtieth session the item entitled "Objective information on military matters, including transparency of military expenditures".

Verification

In response to General Assembly resolution 56/15 [YUN 2001, p. 509], the Secretary-General submitted a July report [A/58/128] updating developments since 2001 on verification measures. The report contained the views of two Member States (Bolivia, Mexico) on the recommendations contained in the expert study on verification in all its aspects, including the UN role in verification [YUN 1995, p. 233].

On 8 December, the Assembly decided to include in the provisional agenda of its fifty-ninth (2004) session the item entitled "Verification in all its aspects, including the role of the United Nations in the field of verification" (**decision 58/515**).

Anti-personnel mines

1997 Convention

The number of States parties to the Convention on the Prohibition of the Use, Stockpiling, Production and Transfer of Anti-personnel Mines and on Their Destruction (Mine-Ban Convention), which was adopted in 1997 [YUN 1997, p. 503] and entered into force in 1999 [YUN 1999, p. 498], totalled 141 as at 31 December. During the year, 11 States ratified or acceded to the Convention.

The Fifth Meeting of the States Parties to the Convention (Bangkok, Thailand, 15-19 September) [APLC/MSP.5/2003/5], convened pursuant to General Assembly resolution 57/74 [YUN 2002, p. 530], reviewed the Convention's general status and operation; victim assistance and socio-economic reintegration; mine clearance; mine-risk education and related technologies; the destruction of stockpiled anti-personnel mines; and the development of technologies to clear anti-personnel mines. The Meeting noted that over 110 States parties no longer stockpiled anti-personnel mines, considerable areas of mined land had been cleared over the past year, casualty rates had been reduced in several of the world's most mine-affected areas and more and better efforts were being made to assist landmine victims. However, the States parties acknowledged that challenges remained in achieving the Convention's humanitarian aims and expressed determination to sharpen their focus on areas most directly related to those aims. The Meeting endorsed the final reports of the Standing Committees (Geneva, February and May), as annexed to its report, and agreed to hold the Convention's First Review Conference in Nairobi, Kenya, from 29 November to 3 December 2004, with preparatory meetings in February and June 2004. It welcomed the President's action programme, also annexed to the report, as a practical means of focusing the collective efforts of States parties and other relevant actors on achieving the Convention's humanitarian aims in the period leading up to the Conference.

The Meeting adopted the Bangkok Declaration, in which States reaffirmed their commitment to the total eradication of anti-personnel mines, called on Governments and people to join in meeting the challenges of mine action and urged non-State actors to embrace the international norm established by the Convention.

GENERAL ASSEMBLY ACTION

On 8 December [meeting 71], the General Assembly, on the recommendation of the First Committee [A/58/462], adopted **resolution 58/53** by recorded vote (153-0-23) [agenda item 73 (p)].

Implementation of the Convention on the Prohibition of the Use, Stockpiling, Production and Transfer of Anti-personnel Mines and on Their Destruction

The General Assembly,

Recalling its resolutions 54/54 B of 1 December 1999, 55/33 V of 20 November 2000, 56/24 M of 29 November 2001 and 57/74 of 22 November 2002,

Reaffirming its determination to put an end to the suffering and casualties caused by anti-personnel mines, which kill or maim hundreds of people every week, mostly innocent and defenceless civilians and especially children, obstruct economic development and reconstruction, inhibit the repatriation of refugees and internally displaced persons, and have other severe consequences for years after emplacement,

Believing it necessary to do the utmost to contribute in an efficient and coordinated manner to facing the challenge of removing anti-personnel mines placed throughout the world, and to assure their destruction,

Wishing to do the utmost in ensuring assistance for the care and rehabilitation, including the social and economic reintegration, of mine victims,

Welcoming the entry into force, on 1 March 1999, of the Convention on the Prohibition of the Use, Stockpiling, Production and Transfer of Anti-personnel Mines and on Their Destruction, and noting with satisfaction the work undertaken to implement the Convention and the substantial progress made towards addressing the global landmine problem,

Recalling the First Meeting of States Parties to the Convention, held at Maputo from 3 to 7 May 1999, and the reaffirmation made in the Maputo Declaration of a commitment to the total eradication of anti-personnel mines,

Recalling also the Second Meeting of States Parties to the Convention, held at Geneva from 11 to 15 September 2000, and the Declaration of the Second Meeting of States Parties, reaffirming the commitment to implement completely and fully all provisions of the Convention,

Recalling further the Third Meeting of States Parties to the Convention, held at Managua from 18 to 21 September 2001, and the Declaration of the Third Meeting of States Parties, reaffirming the unwavering commitment both to the total eradication of anti-personnel mines and to addressing the insidious and inhumane effects of those weapons,

Recalling the Fourth Meeting of States Parties to the Convention, held at Geneva from 16 to 20 September 2002, and the Declaration of the Fourth Meeting of States Parties reaffirming the commitment of the States parties to intensify further their efforts in those areas most directly related to the core humanitarian objectives of the Convention,

Recalling also the Fifth Meeting of States Parties to the Convention, held at Bangkok from 15 to 19 September 2003, and the Declaration of the Fifth Meeting of States Parties committing the States parties, one year before their First Review Conference, to pursue, with renewed vigour, efforts to clear mined areas, assist victims, destroy stockpiled anti-personnel mines and promote universal adherence to the Convention,

Noting with satisfaction that additional States have ratified or acceded to the Convention, bringing the total number of States that have formally accepted the obligations of the Convention to one hundred and forty-one,

Emphasizing the desirability of attracting the adherence of all States to the Convention, and determined to work strenuously towards the promotion of its universalization,

Noting with regret that anti-personnel mines continue to be used in conflicts around the world, causing human suffering and impeding post-conflict development,

1. *Invites* all States that did not sign the Convention on the Prohibition of the Use, Stockpiling, Production and Transfer of Anti-personnel Mines and on Their Destruction to accede to it without delay;

2. *Urges* all States that signed but have not ratified the Convention to ratify it without delay;

3. *Stresses* the importance of the full and effective implementation of, and compliance with, the Convention;

4. *Urges* all States parties to provide the Secretary-General with complete and timely information as required under article 7 of the Convention, in order to promote transparency and compliance with the Convention;

5. *Invites* all States that have not ratified the Convention or acceded to it to provide, on a voluntary basis, information to make global mine action efforts more effective;

6. *Renews its call upon* all States and other relevant parties to work together to promote, support and advance the care, rehabilitation and social and economic reintegration of mine victims, mine risk education programmes, and the removal of anti-personnel mines placed throughout the world and the assurance of their destruction;

7. *Invites and encourages* all interested States, the United Nations, other relevant international organizations or institutions, regional organizations, the International Committee of the Red Cross and relevant non-governmental organizations to participate in the programme of intersessional work established at the First Meeting of States Parties to the Convention and further developed at subsequent Meetings of the States parties;

8. *Requests* the Secretary-General, in accordance with article 12, paragraph 1, of the Convention, to undertake the preparations necessary to convene the Convention's First Review Conference, at Nairobi from 29 November to 3 December 2004;

9. *Also requests* the Secretary-General, on behalf of States parties and in accordance with article 12, paragraph 3, of the Convention, to invite States not parties to the Convention, as well as the United Nations, other relevant international organizations or institutions, regional organizations, the International Committee of the Red Cross and relevant non-governmental organizations to attend the First Review Conference as observers, and urges participation at the highest possible level in a high-level segment to be held at the end of the Review Conference;

10. *Decides* to include in the provisional agenda of its fifty-ninth session the item entitled "Implementation of the Convention on the Prohibition of the Use, Stockpiling, Production and Transfer of Antipersonnel Mines and on Their Destruction".

RECORDED VOTE ON RESOLUTION 58/53:

In favour: Afghanistan, Albania, Algeria, Andorra, Angola, Antigua and Barbuda, Argentina, Armenia, Australia, Austria, Bahamas, Bahrain, Bangladesh, Barbados, Belarus, Belgium, Belize, Benin, Bhutan, Bolivia, Bosnia and Herzegovina, Botswana, Brazil, Brunei Darussalam, Bulgaria, Burkina Faso, Burundi, Cambodia, Cameroon, Canada, Cape Verde, Central African Republic, Chile, Colombia, Comoros, Congo, Costa Rica, Côte d'Ivoire, Croatia, Cyprus, Czech Republic, Denmark, Djibouti, Dominican Republic, Ecuador, El Salvador, Eritrea, Estonia, Ethiopia, Fiji, Finland, France, Gabon, Gambia, Georgia, Germany, Ghana, Greece, Grenada, Guatemala, Guinea, Guinea-Bissau, Guyana, Haiti, Honduras, Hungary, Iceland, Indonesia, Ireland, Italy, Jamaica, Japan, Jordan, Kenya, Latvia, Lesotho, Liechtenstein, Lithuania, Luxembourg, Madagascar, Malawi, Malaysia, Maldives, Mali, Malta, Mauritania, Mauritius, Mexico, Monaco, Mongolia, Mozambique, Namibia, Nauru, Nepal, Netherlands, New Zealand, Nicaragua, Niger, Nigeria, Norway, Oman, Panama, Papua New Guinea, Paraguay, Peru, Philippines, Poland, Portugal, Qatar, Republic of Moldova, Romania, Rwanda, Saint Lucia, Saint Vincent and the Grenadines, Samoa, San Marino, Senegal, Serbia and Montenegro, Seychelles, Sierra Leone, Singapore, Slovakia, Slovenia, Solomon Islands, Somalia, South Africa, Spain, Sri Lanka, Sudan, Suriname, Swaziland, Sweden, Switzerland, Thailand, The former Yugoslav Republic of Macedonia, Timor-Leste, Togo, Tonga, Trinidad and Tobago, Tunisia, Turkey, Turkmenistan, Uganda, Ukraine, United Arab Emirates, United Kingdom, United Republic of Tanzania, Uruguay, Vanuatu, Venezuela, Yemen, Zambia, Zimbabwe.

Against: None.

Abstaining: Azerbaijan, China, Cuba, Egypt, India, Iran, Israel, Kazakhstan, Kyrgyzstan, Lebanon, Libyan Arab Jamahiriya, Marshall Islands, Micronesia, Morocco, Myanmar, Pakistan, Republic of Korea, Russian Federation, Syrian Arab Republic, Tajikistan, United States, Uzbekistan, Viet Nam.

Regional and other approaches to disarmament

Report of Secretary-General. Pursuant to General Assembly resolution 57/77 [YUN 2002, p. 537], the Secretary-General, in July [A/58/130], presented the views of one State (Colombia) regarding conventional arms control at the regional and subregional levels.

Africa

In 2003, African States maintained efforts to implement the Programme of Action adopted by the 2001 UN Conference on small arms [YUN 2001, p. 499]. A regional framework in that regard continued to be provided by the Moratorium on the Importation, Exportation and Manufacture of Small Arms and Light Weapons in West Africa, adopted by the Economic Community of West African States in 1998 [YUN 1998, p. 537] and renewed in 2001 [YUN 2001, p. 511]. During the year, an extensive disarmament campaign across the region resulted in the destruction of a great number of small arms and light weapons. Eleven States had established national commissions on small arms and light weapons, although some were not fully operational. The Moratorium's implementation was also facilitated by a number of other factors and by disarmament initiatives launched by the Programme for Coordination and Assistance for Security and Development, established by the United Nations Development Programme (UNDP) to address security challenges that were linked to small arms proliferation. Efforts were under way to harmonize legislation in the region, enhance border patrols and establish efficient national registration and relevant arms control schemes.

Member States of the Southern African Development Community continued efforts to promote the ratification of the Community's 2001 Protocol on the Control of Firearms, Ammunition and Other Related Materials, which outlined minimum standards for national legislation and committed regional states to harmonize firearms control legislation.

Standing Advisory Committee

In response to General Assembly resolution 57/88 [YUN 2002, p. 532], the Secretary-General, in July [A/58/177], described the activities of the Standing Advisory Committee on Security Questions in Central Africa. He observed that, although the Committee continued to play a vital role in promoting peace and security in the region, much remained to be done in order to establish conditions for lasting peace, disarmament and development. It was incumbent on Committee members to strive to become the driving force in that regard, but continuing international support was imperative.

At its eighteenth (Bangui, Central African Republic, 26-30 August 2002) and nineteenth (Brazzaville, Congo, 14-17 May 2003) [A/57/823-S/2003/610] ministerial meetings, the Committee reviewed the geopolitical and security situation of its member States, as well as progress made in implementing its previous decisions and recommendations. It organized a subregional seminar on the implementation in Central Africa of the 2001 Programme of Action on small arms, adopting a two-year programme of activities at the national and subregional levels, which addressed priority areas such as the establishment of national commissions or structures to coordinate national policies to combat the proliferation of small arms and light weapons, and their collection and destruction.

In November, Equatorial Guinea transmitted the report of the Committee's twentieth ministerial meeting (Malabo, 27-31 October) [A/58/560-S/2003/1075]. The Committee continued to consider its member States' geopolitical and security situation, security cooperation among them and its previous recommendations and decisions. It also considered the activities of other relevant subregional organizations and adopted its 2003-2004 work programme.

GENERAL ASSEMBLY ACTION

On 8 December [meeting 71], the General Assembly, on the recommendation of the First Committee [A/58/463], adopted **resolution 58/65** without vote [agenda item 74 (b)].

Regional confidence-building measures: activities of the United Nations Standing Advisory Committee on Security Questions in Central Africa

The General Assembly,

Bearing in mind the purposes and principles of the United Nations and its primary responsibility for the maintenance of international peace and security in accordance with the Charter of the United Nations,

Recalling its resolutions 43/78 H and 43/85 of 7 December 1988, 44/21 of 15 November 1989, 45/58 M of 4 December 1990, 46/37 B of 6 December 1991, 47/53 F of 15 December 1992, 48/76 A of 16 December 1993, 49/76 C of 15 December 1994, 50/71 B of 12 December 1995, 51/46 C of 10 December 1996, 52/39 B of 9 December 1997, 53/78 A of 4 December 1998, 54/55 A of 1 December 1999, 55/34 B of 20 November 2000, 56/25 A of 29 November 2001 and 57/88 of 22 November 2002,

Considering the importance and effectiveness of confidence-building measures taken at the initiative and with the participation of all States concerned and taking into account the specific characteristics of each region, since such measures can contribute to regional stability and to international peace and security,

Convinced that the resources released by disarmament, including regional disarmament, can be devoted to economic and social development and to the protection of the environment for the benefit of all peoples, in particular those of the developing countries,

Recalling the guidelines for general and complete disarmament adopted at its tenth special session, the first special session devoted to disarmament,

Convinced that development can be achieved only in a climate of peace, security and mutual confidence both within and among States,

Bearing in mind the establishment by the Secretary-General on 28 May 1992 of the United Nations Standing Advisory Committee on Security Questions in Central Africa, the purpose of which is to encourage arms limitation, disarmament, non-proliferation and development in the subregion,

Recalling the Brazzaville Declaration on Cooperation for Peace and Security in Central Africa, the Bata Declaration for the Promotion of Lasting Democracy, Peace and Development in Central Africa, and the Yaoundé Declaration on Peace, Security and Stability in Central Africa,

Bearing in mind resolutions 1196(1998) and 1197(1998), adopted by the Security Council on 16 and 18 September 1998 respectively, following its consideration of the report of the Secretary-General on the causes of conflict and the promotion of durable peace and sustainable development in Africa,

Emphasizing the need to strengthen the capacity for conflict prevention and peacekeeping in Africa,

Recalling the decision of the fourth ministerial meeting of the Standing Advisory Committee in favour of establishing, under the auspices of the United Nations High Commissioner for Human Rights, a subregional centre for human rights and democracy in Central Africa at Yaoundé,

1. *Takes note* of the report of the Secretary-General on regional confidence-building measures, which deals with the activities of the United Nations Standing Advisory Committee on Security Questions in Central Africa in the period since the adoption by the General Assembly of resolution 57/88;

2. *Reaffirms its support* for efforts aimed at promoting confidence-building measures at the regional and subregional levels in order to ease tensions and conflicts in Central Africa and to further peace, stability and sustainable development in the subregion;

3. *Also reaffirms its support* for the programme of work of the Standing Advisory Committee adopted at the organizational meeting of the Committee, held at Yaoundé from 27 to 31 July 1992;

4. *Notes with satisfaction* the progress made by the States members of the Standing Advisory Committee in implementing the programme of activities for the period 2002-2003, in particular by:

(a) Holding a seminar on the implementation in the Central African region of the Programme of Action to Prevent, Combat and Eradicate the Illicit Trade in Small Arms and Light Weapons in All Its Aspects at Brazzaville from 12 to 14 May 2003;

(b) Holding the nineteenth ministerial meeting of the Standing Advisory Committee at Brazzaville from 14 to 17 May 2003;

(c) Holding the "Biyongho 2003" military peacekeeping exercise at Franceville, Gabon, from 21 to 28 July 2003;

(d) Holding the twentieth ministerial meeting of the Standing Advisory Committee at Malabo from 27 to 31 October 2003;

5. *Emphasizes* the importance of providing the States members of the Standing Advisory Committee with the essential support they need to carry out the full programme of activities which they adopted at their ministerial meetings;

6. *Welcomes* the creation of a mechanism for the promotion, maintenance and consolidation of peace and security in Central Africa, to be known as the Council for Peace and Security in Central Africa, by the Conference of Heads of State and Government of the member countries of the Economic Community of Central African States, held at Yaoundé on 25 February 1999, and requests the Secretary-General to give his full support to the effective realization of that important mechanism;

7. *Emphasizes* the need to make the early warning mechanism in Central Africa operational so that it will serve, on the one hand, as an instrument for analysing and monitoring political situations in the States members of the Standing Advisory Committee with a view to preventing the outbreak of future armed conflicts and, on the other hand, as a technical body through which the member States will carry out the programme of work of the Committee, adopted at its organizational meeting held at Yaoundé in 1992, and requests the Secretary-General to provide it with the assistance necessary for it to function properly;

8. *Requests* the Secretary-General and the United Nations High Commissioner for Human Rights to continue to provide their full assistance for the proper functioning of the Subregional Centre for Human Rights and Democracy in Central Africa;

9. *Requests* the Secretary-General, pursuant to Security Council resolution 1197(1998), to provide the States members of the Standing Advisory Committee with the necessary support for the implementation and smooth functioning of the Council for Peace and Security in Central Africa and the early warning mechanism;

10. *Also requests* the Secretary-General to support the establishment of a network of parliamentarians with a view to the creation of a subregional parliament in Central Africa;

11. *Requests* the Secretary-General and the United Nations High Commissioner for Refugees to continue to provide increased assistance to the countries of Central Africa for coping with the problems of refugees and displaced persons in their territories;

12. *Thanks* the Secretary-General for having established the Trust Fund for the United Nations Standing Advisory Committee on Security Questions in Central Africa;

13. *Appeals* to Member States and to governmental and non-governmental organizations to make additional voluntary contributions to the Trust Fund for the implementation of the programme of work of the Standing Advisory Committee;

14. *Thanks* the Secretary-General for sending a multidisciplinary assessment mission to the Central African region from 8 to 22 June 2003 for the purposes of identifying priority needs and challenges confronting the subregion, in particular focusing on issues of peace, security, economic development, humanitarian questions, human rights and HIV/AIDS;

15. *Requests* the Secretary-General to continue to provide the States members of the Standing Advisory Committee with assistance to ensure that they are able to carry on their efforts;

16. *Also requests* the Secretary-General to submit to the General Assembly at its fifty-ninth session a report on the implementation of the present resolution;

17. *Decides* to include in the provisional agenda of its fifty-ninth session the item entitled "Regional confidence-building measures: activities of the United Nations Standing Advisory Committee on Security Questions in Central Africa".

Asia and the Pacific

In 2003, regional security and stability issues in Asia and the Pacific continued to be addressed by the Association of Southeast Asian Nations, its Regional Forum (ARF) and the six-member Shanghai Cooperation Organization (SCO) (China, Kazakhstan, Kyrgyzstan, Russian Federation, Tajikistan, Uzbekistan), founded in 2001 as a multilateral platform for strengthening regional peace, security and stability. At a seminar (Bali, Indonesia, February), organized by DDA in collaboration with Japan and Indonesia, regional States exchanged views on key issues relating to the implementation of the 2001 Programme of Action on small arms. Also in February in Bali, a meeting focused on transparency of armaments, aimed at encouraging the further participation of the regional States in the UN Register of Conventional Arms (see p. 568) and in the standardized instrument for reporting military expenditures (see p. 570). In March, ARF organized, in collaboration with other regional bodies, a workshop on counter-terrorism measures. In May, the heads of State of SCO countries adopted a declaration (Moscow, 29 May) [A/58/94-S/2003/642], highlighting the organization's potential in maintaining regional and global peace and stability. The Pacific Island Forum (Auckland, New Zealand, 12-19 August) considered issues relating to the collective security of its members, such as weapons control legislation, the shipment of radioactive materials and the status of the South Pacific Nuclear Free Zone Treaty (see p. 557). Asian Senior-level Talks on Non-Proliferation (Tokyo, Japan, 13 November) considered ways to prevent the non-proliferation of weapons of mass destruction (WMDs), their delivery systems and related materials and technology.

Europe

During the year, regional security and disarmament issues of concern to European countries related mainly to small arms and to the proliferation of WMDs. In addressing those issues, the Organization for Security and Cooperation in Europe (OSCE) urged its member States to focus on the illicit trafficking and uncontrolled spread of conventional weaponry, including small arms and light weapons, the proliferation of WMDs and the danger of criminals and terrorist organizations gaining access to them. Following a March decision of the OSCE Permanent Council, which encouraged assistance and expert advice to its participating States in dealing with small arms-related problems in post-conflict situations, the organization's Forum for Security Cooperation helped Belarus destroy its surplus inventory of those weapons. Also in March, OSCE collaborated with the International Organization for Migration to initiate a disarmament, demobilization and reintegration programme in Bosnia and Herzegovina. Further collaboration between DDA, OSCE and Slovenia facilitated the convening of a conference on the illicit trade in small arms and light weapons in all its aspects in South-Eastern Europe (Brdo pri Kranju, Slovenia, 11-12 March). On 27 May, a NATO partnership for peace project in Ukraine culminated in the destruction of some 400,000 of an estimated 7 million anti-personnel landmines in the country. NATO's Verification Coordinating Committee, the organization's main decision-making body on matters relating to conventional arms control implementation and verification coordination, at its annual seminar (Brussels, Belgium, 26-28 May), addressed the practical aspects of the ongoing implementation of the 1990 Treaty on Conventional Armed Forces in Europe (CFE Treaty) [YUN 1990, p. 79]. On 23 July, the OSCE Forum for Security Cooperation, taking into account the concern expressed by its participating States regarding the potential access of terrorist groups to man-portable air-defence systems, urged participating States to propose projects for tackling the issue; the OSCE Forum continued to monitor and enhance the implementation of the related OSCE Code of Conduct on Politico-Military Aspects for Security. Also on 23 July, the EU adopted a common position on the control of arms brokering, aimed at preventing the circumvention of UN, EU or OSCE embargoes on arms exports. On 29 July, the EU and NATO announced a common vision for the future of the Western Balkans in an agreement: "Framework for an Enhanced NATO-EU Dialogue and a Concerted Approach on Security and Stability in the Western Balkans", which covered areas relating to the enhancement of security and stability. A weapons for development project initiated by DDA and UNDP in Albania's Gramsh district continued to encourage the local community to collect and voluntarily dispose of surrendered weapons in exchange for UN-sponsored development projects. The EU continued to implement its 1998 Code of Conduct for Arms Exports [YUN 1998, p. 540] and, in November, agreed on a "User's Guide" clarifying members' responsibilities in sharing information on denials, and, on 17 November, it updated the Common Military List of Equipment covered by the Code. In follow-up action to a commitment to develop a coherent EU strategy to address the threat of proliferation, EU member States (Brussels, 12 December) adopted a security strategy to enable them to deal better with global threats and challenges and to address the proliferation of WMDs. The 1999 Stability Pact for South-Eastern Europe [YUN 1999, p. 397] continued efforts to promote stability in the subregion; its Working Table III, dedicated to addressing security issues, advocated enhanced regional cooperation in tackling multiple challenges in the area of security sector reform and encouraged the regional States to improve their technical standards on issues relating to small arms and light weapons. During the year, the Regional Arms Control Verification and Implementation Assistance Centre (a Stability Pact project) organized regional seminars on disarmament and security issues, and, in cooperation with NATO, conducted training courses to enable designated individuals to serve as inspectors and/or escorts, in accordance with the verification regime of the General Framework Agreement for Peace in Bosnia and Herzegovina [YUN 1995, p. 544]. The South-Eastern Europe Clearing House for the Control of Small Arms and Light Weapons, established in 2002 [YUN 2002, p. 534], became operational and focused on the provision of immediate assistance to initiatives relating to small arms and light weapons. The Clearing House conducted five projects on the physical destruction of weapons and ammunitions in Bulgaria and in Serbia and Montenegro. Overall, about 41,000 weapons and over 813,777 rounds of small arms ammunition were destroyed.

GENERAL ASSEMBLY ACTION

On 8 December [meeting 71], the General Assembly, on the recommendation of the First Committee [A/58/462], adopted **resolution 58/55** without vote [agenda item 73].

Promotion at the regional level in the Organization for Security and Cooperation in Europe of the United Nations programme of action on the illicit trade in small arms and light weapons in all its aspects

The General Assembly,

Recalling its resolutions 50/70 B of 12 December 1995, 52/38 J of 9 December 1997, 53/77 T of 4 December 1998, 54/54 R of 1 December 1999, 54/54 V of 15 December 1999 and 55/33 Q of 20 November 2000,

Also recalling the Programme of Action to Prevent, Combat and Eradicate the Illicit Trade in Small Arms and Light Weapons in All Its Aspects adopted on 20 July 2001, which encourages in particular regional organizations to take initiatives to promote its implementation,

Welcoming the results of the First Biennial Meeting of States to Consider the Implementation of the Programme of Action to Prevent, Combat and Eradicate the Illicit Trade in Small Arms and Light Weapons in All Its Aspects, held in New York from 7 to 11 July 2003,

Convinced of the importance of national, regional and international measures to combat trafficking and illicit trade in small arms, including those measures that could be adapted to regional approaches,

Acknowledging the capacity of the Organization for Security and Cooperation in Europe, as a regional arrangement under Chapter VIII of the Charter of the United Nations, to provide a substantial contribution at the regional level to the process in the United Nations on combating the illicit trade in small arms and light weapons in all its aspects, taking into account regional particularities,

Taking note of the adoption on 24 November 2000 of the Organization for Security and Cooperation in Europe document on small arms and light weapons,

Also taking note of the work done so far within the framework of the Organization for Security and Cooperation in Europe to develop best practice guides related to the control of small arms and light weapons, and acknowledging that a handbook compiling these best practice guides could also be useful to other Member States in their efforts to implement the United Nations programme of action with a view to combating the illicit trade in small arms and light weapons,

1. *Reaffirms* the importance of measures to prevent, combat and eradicate the illicit trade in small arms and light weapons in all its aspects, including ongoing efforts at the regional and subregional levels;

2. *Commends* the progress that has already been made in this regard by organizations in various regions and subregions and, in this context, the progress made so far in drawing up best practice guides to prevent, combat and eliminate the illicit trade in small arms and light weapons among Organization for Security and Cooperation in Europe participating States, and the hope expressed in it to see this process rapidly come to a positive conclusion;

3. *Invites* all Member States that have not yet done so to examine the possibility of developing and adopting regional and subregional measures, as appropriate, to combat the illicit trade in small arms and light weapons in all its aspects and contributing to international peace and security.

Latin America

The General Assembly of the Organization of American States (OAS) (Santiago, Chile, 8-10 June) adopted resolutions relating to peace, arms control and disarmament, which focused in particular on the vision of the hemisphere as an anti-personnel landmine-free zone, consolidation of the regime established by the Treaty for the Prohibition of Nuclear Weapons in Latin America and the Caribbean (Treaty of Tlatelolco) (see p. 555), inter-American support for the Comprehensive Nuclear-Test-Ban Treaty and the development of an inter-American strategy to combat threats to cybersecurity. In October, the OAS Special Conference on Security (Mexico City, 27-28 October) adopted a declaration on security in the Americas, which highlighted new security threats and challenges. It also reaffirmed regional States' commitment to strengthen hemispheric peace through conflict prevention and peaceful settlement of disputes, to arms control, disarmament and the non-proliferation of all categories of WMDs, and to the full implementation by all States parties of the Biological and Chemical Weapons Conventions (see p. 558).

GENERAL ASSEMBLY ACTION

On 8 December [meeting 71], the General Assembly, on the recommendation of the First Committee [A/58/462], adopted **resolution 58/38** without vote [agenda item 73 *(r)*].

Regional disarmament

The General Assembly,

Recalling its resolutions 45/58 P of 4 December 1990, 46/36 I of 6 December 1991, 47/52 J of 9 December 1992, 48/75 I of 16 December 1993, 49/75 N of 15 December 1994, 50/70 K of 12 December 1995, 51/45 K of 10 December 1996, 52/38 P of 9 December 1997, 53/77 O of 4 December 1998, 54/54 N of 1 December 1999, 55/33 O of 20 November 2000, 56/24 H of 29 November 2001 and 57/76 of 22 November 2002 on regional disarmament,

Believing that the efforts of the international community to move towards the ideal of general and complete disarmament are guided by the inherent human desire for genuine peace and security, the elimination of the danger of war and the release of economic, intellectual and other resources for peaceful pursuits,

Affirming the abiding commitment of all States to the purposes and principles enshrined in the Charter of the United Nations in the conduct of their international relations,

Noting that essential guidelines for progress towards general and complete disarmament were adopted at the tenth special session of the General Assembly,

Taking note of the guidelines and recommendations for regional approaches to disarmament within the context of global security adopted by the Disarmament Commission at its 1993 substantive session,

Welcoming the prospects of genuine progress in the field of disarmament engendered in recent years as a result of negotiations between the two super-Powers,

Taking note of the recent proposals for disarmament at the regional and subregional levels,

Recognizing the importance of confidence-building measures for regional and international peace and security,

Convinced that endeavours by countries to promote regional disarmament, taking into account the specific characteristics of each region and in accordance with the principle of undiminished security at the lowest level of armaments, would enhance the security of all States and would thus contribute to international peace and security by reducing the risk of regional conflicts,

1. *Stresses* that sustained efforts are needed, within the framework of the Conference on Disarmament and under the umbrella of the United Nations, to make progress on the entire range of disarmament issues;

2. *Affirms* that global and regional approaches to disarmament complement each other and should therefore be pursued simultaneously to promote regional and international peace and security;

3. *Calls upon* States to conclude agreements, wherever possible, for nuclear non-proliferation, disarmament and confidence-building measures at the regional and subregional levels;

4. *Welcomes* the initiatives towards disarmament, nuclear non-proliferation and security undertaken by some countries at the regional and subregional levels;

5. *Supports and encourages* efforts aimed at promoting confidence-building measures at the regional and subregional levels to ease regional tensions and to further disarmament and nuclear non-proliferation measures at the regional and subregional levels;

6. *Decides* to include in the provisional agenda of its fifty-ninth session the item entitled "Regional disarmament".

On 8 December [meeting 71], the Assembly, also on the recommendation of the First Committee [A/58/462], adopted **resolution 58/39** by recorded vote (172-1-1) [agenda item 73 (s)].

Conventional arms control at the regional and subregional levels

The General Assembly,

Recalling its resolutions 48/75 J of 16 December 1993, 49/75 O of 15 December 1994, 50/70 L of 12 December 1995, 51/45 Q of 10 December 1996, 52/38 Q of 9 December 1997, 53/77 P of 4 December 1998, 54/54 M of 1 December 1999, 55/33 P of 20 November 2000, 56/24 I of 29 November 2001 and 57/77 of 22 November 2002,

Recognizing the crucial role of conventional arms control in promoting regional and international peace and security,

Convinced that conventional arms control needs to be pursued primarily in the regional and subregional contexts since most threats to peace and security in the post-cold-war era arise mainly among States located in the same region or subregion,

Aware that the preservation of a balance in the defence capabilities of States at the lowest level of armaments would contribute to peace and stability and should be a prime objective of conventional arms control,

Desirous of promoting agreements to strengthen regional peace and security at the lowest possible level of armaments and military forces,

Noting with particular interest the initiatives taken in this regard in different regions of the world, in particular the commencement of consultations among a number of Latin American countries and the proposals for conventional arms control made in the context of South Asia, and recognizing, in the context of this subject, the relevance and value of the Treaty on Conventional Armed Forces in Europe, which is a cornerstone of European security,

Believing that militarily significant States and States with larger military capabilities have a special responsibility in promoting such agreements for regional security,

Believing also that an important objective of conventional arms control in regions of tension should be to prevent the possibility of military attack launched by surprise and to avoid aggression,

1. *Decides* to give urgent consideration to the issues involved in conventional arms control at the regional and subregional levels;

2. *Requests* the Conference on Disarmament to consider the formulation of principles that can serve as a framework for regional agreements on conventional arms control, and looks forward to a report of the Conference on this subject;

3. *Requests* the Secretary-General, in the meantime, to seek the views of Member States on the subject and to submit a report to the General Assembly at its fifty-ninth session;

4. *Decides* to include in the provisional agenda of its fifty-ninth session the item entitled "Conventional arms control at the regional and subregional levels".

RECORDED VOTE ON RESOLUTION 58/39:

In favour: Afghanistan, Albania, Algeria, Andorra, Angola, Antigua and Barbuda, Argentina, Armenia, Australia, Austria, Azerbaijan, Bahamas, Bahrain, Bangladesh, Barbados, Belarus, Belgium, Belize, Benin, Bolivia, Bosnia and Herzegovina, Botswana, Brazil, Brunei Darussalam, Bulgaria, Burkina Faso, Burundi, Cambodia, Cameroon, Canada, Cape Verde, Central African Republic, Chile, China, Colombia, Comoros, Congo, Costa Rica, Côte d'Ivoire, Croatia, Cyprus, Czech Republic, Denmark, Djibouti, Dominican Republic, Ecuador, Egypt, El Salvador, Eritrea, Estonia, Ethiopia, Fiji, Finland, France, Gabon, Gambia, Georgia, Germany, Ghana, Greece, Grenada, Guatemala, Guinea, Guinea-Bissau, Guyana, Haiti, Honduras, Hungary, Iceland, Indonesia, Iran, Ireland, Israel, Italy, Jamaica, Japan, Jordan, Kazakhstan, Kenya, Kuwait, Kyrgyzstan, Latvia, Lebanon, Lesotho, Libyan Arab Jamahiriya, Liechtenstein, Lithuania, Luxembourg, Madagascar, Malawi, Malaysia, Maldives, Mali, Malta, Marshall Islands, Mauritania, Mauritius, Mexico, Micronesia, Monaco, Mongolia, Morocco, Mozambique, Myanmar, Namibia, Nauru, Nepal, Netherlands, New Zealand, Nicaragua, Niger, Nigeria, Norway, Oman, Pakistan, Panama, Papua New Guinea, Paraguay, Peru, Philippines, Poland, Portugal, Qatar, Republic of Korea, Republic of Moldova, Romania, Russian Federation, Rwanda, Saint Lucia, Saint Vincent and the Grenadines, Samoa, San Marino, Saudi Arabia, Senegal, Serbia and Montenegro, Seychelles, Singapore, Slovakia, Slovenia, Somalia, South Africa, Spain, Sri Lanka, Sudan, Suriname, Swaziland, Sweden, Switzerland, Syrian Arab Republic, Tajikistan, Thailand, The former Yugoslav Republic of Macedonia, Timor-Leste, Togo, Tonga, Trinidad and Tobago, Tunisia, Turkey, Turkmenistan, Uganda, Ukraine, United Arab Emirates, United Kingdom, United Republic of Tanzania, United States, Uruguay, Uzbekistan, Vanuatu, Venezuela, Yemen, Zambia, Zimbabwe.

Against: India.

Abstaining: Bhutan.

Also on 8 December [meeting 71], on the recommendation of the First Committee [A/58/462], the Assembly adopted **resolution 58/43** by recorded vote (73-48-46) [agenda item 73].

Confidence-building measures in the regional and subregional context

The General Assembly,

Guided by the purposes and principles enshrined in the Charter of the United Nations,

Recalling its resolution 57/337 of 3 July 2003 entitled "Prevention of armed conflict", in which it calls upon Member States to settle their disputes by peaceful means, as set out in Chapter VI of the Charter, inter alia, by any procedures adopted by the parties, including the most effective use of the International Court of Justice,

Recalling also the Security Council resolutions relating to the prevention of armed conflict, and noting all Security Council presidential statements relating to this matter,

Considering the importance and effectiveness of confidence-building measures taken at the initiative and with the participation of all States concerned and taking into account the specific characteristics of each region, since such measures can contribute to regional stability,

Convinced that resources released by disarmament, including regional disarmament, can be devoted to economic and social development and to the protection of the environment for the benefit of all peoples, in particular those of the developing countries,

Recognizing the need for meaningful dialogue among States concerned in the regions of tension to avert conflict,

Welcoming the peace processes already initiated by States concerned to resolve their disputes through peaceful means bilaterally or through mediation, inter alia, by third parties, regional organizations or the United Nations,

Recognizing that States in some regions have already taken steps towards confidence-building measures at the bilateral, subregional and regional levels in the political and military fields, including arms control and disarmament, and noting that such confidence-building measures have improved peace and security in those regions and contributed to progress in the socio-economic conditions of their people,

Concerned that the continuation of disputes among States, particularly in the absence of an effective mechanism to resolve them through peaceful means, may contribute to the arms race and endanger the maintenance of international peace and security and the efforts of the international community to promote arms control and disarmament,

1. *Calls upon* Member States to refrain from the use or threat of use of force in accordance with the purposes and principles of the Charter of the United Nations;

2. *Reaffirms its commitment* to the peaceful settlement of disputes under Chapter VI of the Charter, in particular Article 33, which provides for a solution by negotiation, enquiry, mediation, conciliation, arbitration, judicial settlement, resort to regional agencies or arrangements or other peaceful means chosen by the parties;

3. *Calls upon* Member States that have not already done so to open consultations and dialogue in the regions of tension without preconditions;

4. *Urges* States to comply strictly with all bilateral, regional and international agreements, including arms control and disarmament agreements, to which they are party;

5. *Also urges*, in the context of confidence-building measures, the maintenance of military balance between States in the regions of tension consistent with the principle of undiminished security at the lowest level of armaments;

6. *Encourages* the promotion of unilateral, bilateral and regional confidence-building measures to avoid conflict and prevent the unintended and accidental outbreak of hostilities;

7. *Requests* the Secretary-General to seek the views of Member States with a view to exploring possibilities of furthering efforts towards confidence-building measures in the regional and subregional context, particularly in the regions of tension;

8. *Also requests* the Secretary-General to report on the subject to the General Assembly at its fifty-ninth session;

9. *Decides* to include in the provisional agenda of its fifty-ninth session an item entitled "Confidence-building measures in the regional and subregional context".

RECORDED VOTE ON RESOLUTION 58/43:

In favour: Algeria, Antigua and Barbuda, Azerbaijan, Bahrain, Bangladesh, Bolivia, Botswana, Brazil, Brunei Darussalam, Burkina Faso, Cameroon, Cape Verde, Central African Republic, China, Comoros, Congo, Côte d'Ivoire, Cuba, Djibouti, Ecuador, Egypt, Eritrea, Gabon, Gambia, Grenada, Guinea, Guinea-Bissau, Guyana, Haiti, Indonesia, Iran, Jamaica, Jordan, Kenya, Kuwait, Lebanon, Lesotho, Libyan Arab Jamahiriya, Malawi, Malaysia, Mali, Mauritania, Mexico, Morocco, Mozambique, Namibia, Nicaragua, Niger, Oman, Pakistan, Paraguay, Philippines, Qatar, Saint Lucia, Saudi Arabia, Senegal, Singapore, Somalia, Sudan, Suriname, Syrian Arab Republic, Thailand, Togo, Trinidad and Tobago, Tunisia, Turkey, Turkmenistan, Uganda, United Arab Emirates, Venezuela, Yemen, Zambia, Zimbabwe.

Against: Albania, Andorra, Austria, Belgium, Bhutan, Bulgaria, Croatia, Cyprus, Czech Republic, Denmark, Estonia, Finland, France, Georgia, Germany, Greece, Hungary, Iceland, India, Ireland, Israel, Italy, Latvia, Liechtenstein, Lithuania, Luxembourg, Malta, Marshall Islands, Mauritius, Micronesia, Monaco, Netherlands, Norway, Poland, Portugal, Romania, San Marino, Serbia and Montenegro, Slovakia, Slovenia, Spain, Sri Lanka, Sweden, Switzerland, The former Yugoslav Republic of Macedonia, Timor-Leste, United Kingdom, United States.

Abstaining: Angola, Argentina, Armenia, Australia, Bahamas, Barbados, Belarus, Belize, Benin, Bosnia and Herzegovina, Burundi, Cambodia, Canada, Chile, Colombia, Costa Rica, Dominican Republic, Ethiopia, Fiji, Ghana, Guatemala, Honduras, Japan, Kazakhstan, Kyrgyzstan, Madagascar, Mongolia, Nepal, New Zealand, Nigeria, Panama, Papua New Guinea, Peru, Republic of Korea, Republic of Moldova, Russian Federation, Rwanda, Saint Vincent and the Grenadines, Samoa, South Africa, Swaziland, Tajikistan, Ukraine, United Republic of Tanzania, Uruguay, Uzbekistan.

Other disarmament issues

Terrorism

In 2003, terrorist attacks worldwide enhanced the sense of urgency to international efforts under way to accord high priority to concerted multilateral action in tackling the terrorism threat. In January, the Security Council adopted a declaration on combating terrorism (see p. 63), in which it called on States to take urgent action to prevent and suppress all forms of support for terrorism, bring to justice those who supported it and cooperate in resolving outstanding issues. Work continued by the Ad Hoc Committee established in General Assembly resolution 51/210 [YUN 1996, p. 1208] to elaborate international conventions for the suppression of terrorist bombings and of nuclear terrorism. The Counter-

Terrorism Committee, established pursuant to Council resolution 1373(2001) [YUN 2001, p. 61], convened special meetings with international, regional and subregional organizations, and with technical agencies, with a view to building a common structure to deal effectively with terrorism and to help enhance Member States' capacity to combat terrorist acts (see p. 66). The Assembly urged Member States to adopt or strengthen national measures to prevent terrorists from acquiring WMDs (see below).

IAEA continued work on its action plan for nuclear security to further enhance the capacity of Member States and of the Agency to respond effectively to acts of terrorism involving nuclear and other radioactive materials. In September [GC(47)/RES/8], the IAEA General Conference, in a resolution on protection measures against nuclear and radiological terrorism, appealed to States that had not done so to accede to the 1979 Convention on the Physical Protection of Nuclear Material [YUN 1979, p. 1239]. The Conference had before it a report of the Director General [GC(47)/17] on nuclear security: measures to protect against nuclear terrorism, which discussed activities taken by IAEA against the illicit trafficking of nuclear and other radioactive materials.

During the year, the United Nations considered ways to implement the recommendations of the Policy Working Group on the United Nations and Terrorism [YUN 2002, p. 538] established by the Secretary-General to propose steps that should be taken in combating terrorism, of which four related to disarmament.

Report of Secretary-General. Pursuant to General Assembly resolution 57/83 [YUN 2002, p. 539], the Secretary-General, in an August report with a later addendum [A/58/208 & Add.1], presented the views of Member States, international organizations, specialized agencies and UN bodies and organs on measures they had taken to prevent terrorists from acquiring WMDs.

Communication. The heads of State or Government of the Non-Aligned Movement (Kuala Lumpur, Malaysia, 20-25 February) [A/57/759-S/2003/332] stressed that the most effective way of preventing terrorists from acquiring WMDs was through their total elimination. They urged member States to take or strengthen national measures to prevent terrorists from acquiring WMDs, their means of delivery and materials and technologies related to their manufacture.

GENERAL ASSEMBLY ACTION

On 8 December [meeting 71], the General Assembly, on the recommendation of the First Committee [A/58/462], adopted **resolution 58/48** without vote [agenda item 73 (w)].

Measures to prevent terrorists from acquiring weapons of mass destruction

The General Assembly,

Recalling its resolution 57/83 of 22 November 2002,

Recognizing the determination of the international community to combat terrorism, as evident in relevant General Assembly and Security Council resolutions,

Deeply concerned by the growing risk of linkages between terrorism and weapons of mass destruction, and in particular by the fact that terrorists may seek to acquire weapons of mass destruction,

Noting the support expressed in the Final Document of the Thirteenth Conference of Heads of State or Government of Non-Aligned Countries, which was held in Kuala Lumpur from 20 to 25 February 2003, for measures to prevent terrorists from acquiring weapons of mass destruction,

Noting also that the Group of Eight, the European Union, the Regional Forum of the Association of Southeast Asian Nations and others have taken into account in their deliberations the dangers posed by the acquisition by terrorists of weapons of mass destruction, and the need for international cooperation in combating it,

Acknowledging the consideration of issues relating to terrorism and weapons of mass destruction by the Advisory Board on Disarmament Matters,

Taking note of resolution GC(47)/RES/8, adopted on 19 September 2003 by the General Conference of the International Atomic Energy Agency at its forty-seventh regular session, and the setting up of an Advisory Group on Security in the Agency to advise the Director General on the Agency's activities relating to nuclear security,

Taking note also of the report of the Policy Working Group on the United Nations and Terrorism,

Taking note further of the report of the Secretary-General, submitted pursuant to paragraphs 2 and 4 of resolution 57/83,

Mindful of the urgent need for addressing, within the United Nations framework and through international cooperation, this threat to humanity,

Emphasizing that progress is urgently needed in the area of disarmament and non-proliferation in order to help to maintain international peace and security and to contribute to global efforts against terrorism,

1. *Calls upon* all Member States to support international efforts to prevent terrorists from acquiring weapons of mass destruction and their means of delivery;

2. *Urges* all Member States to take and strengthen national measures, as appropriate, to prevent terrorists from acquiring weapons of mass destruction, their means of delivery and materials and technologies related to their manufacture, and invites them to inform the Secretary-General, on a voluntary basis, of the measures taken in this regard;

3. *Encourages* cooperation among and between Member States and relevant regional and international organizations for strengthening national capacities in this regard;

4. *Requests* the Secretary-General to compile a report on measures already taken by international organizations on issues relating to the linkage between the fight against terrorism and the proliferation of weapons of mass destruction, to seek the views of

Member States on additional relevant measures for tackling the global threat posed by the acquisition by terrorists of weapons of mass destruction, and to report to the General Assembly at its fifty-ninth session;

5. *Decides* to include in the provisional agenda of its fifty-ninth session the item entitled "Measures to prevent terrorists from acquiring weapons of mass destruction".

New types of weapons of mass destruction

In 2003, the Conference on Disarmament [A/58/27] was unable to establish an ad hoc committee to address the item on "New types of weapons of mass destruction and new systems of such weapons; radiological weapons" owing to the continuing lack of consensus over an overall programme of work. Consequently, delegations considered the issue in plenary meetings, during which they reaffirmed or further elaborated their respective positions.

Multilateralism in disarmament and non-proliferation

Pursuant to General Assembly resolution 57/63 [YUN 2002, p. 536], the Secretary-General, in a July report with a later addendum [A/58/176 & Add.1], presented replies received from six Governments regarding the promotion of multilateralism in the area of disarmament and non-proliferation.

GENERAL ASSEMBLY ACTION

On 8 December [meeting 71], the General Assembly, on the recommendation of the First Committee [A/58/462], adopted **resolution 58/44** by recorded vote (118-12-46) [agenda item 73 (*f*)].

Promotion of multilateralism in the area of disarmament and non-proliferation

The General Assembly,

Determined to foster strict respect for the purposes and principles enshrined in the Charter of the United Nations,

Recalling its resolution 56/24 T of 29 November 2001 on multilateral cooperation in the area of disarmament and non-proliferation and global efforts against terrorism and other relevant resolutions, as well as its resolution 57/63 of 22 November 2002 on promotion of multilateralism in the area of disarmament and non-proliferation,

Recalling also the purpose of the United Nations to maintain international peace and security and, to that end, to take effective collective measures for the prevention and removal of threats to the peace and for the suppression of acts of aggression or other breaches of the peace, and to bring about by peaceful means, and in conformity with the principles of justice and international law, adjustment or settlement of international disputes or situations which might lead to a breach of the peace, as enshrined in the Charter,

Recalling further the United Nations Millennium Declaration, which states, inter alia, that the responsibility for managing worldwide economic and social development, as well as threats to international peace and security, must be shared among the nations of the world and should be exercised multilaterally and that, as the most universal and most representative organization in the world, the United Nations must play the central role,

Convinced that in the globalization era and with the information revolution, arms regulation, non-proliferation and disarmament problems are more than ever the concern of all countries in the world, which are affected in one way or another by these problems and, therefore, should have the possibility to participate in the negotiations that arise to tackle them,

Bearing in mind the existence of a broad structure of disarmament and arms regulation agreements resulting from non-discriminatory and transparent multilateral negotiations with the participation of a large number of countries, regardless of their size and power,

Aware of the need to advance further in the field of arms regulation, non-proliferation and disarmament on the basis of universal, multilateral, non-discriminatory and transparent negotiations with the goal of reaching general and complete disarmament under strict international control,

Recognizing the complementarity of bilateral, plurilateral and multilateral negotiations on disarmament,

Recognizing also that the proliferation and development of weapons of mass destruction, including nuclear weapons, are among the most immediate threats to international peace and security which need to be dealt with, with the highest priority,

Considering that the multilateral disarmament agreements provide the mechanism for States parties to consult one another and to cooperate in solving any problems which may arise in relation to the objective of, or in the application of, the provisions of the agreements and that such consultations and cooperation may also be undertaken through appropriate international procedures within the framework of the United Nations and in accordance with the Charter,

Stressing that international cooperation, the peaceful settlement of disputes, dialogue and confidence-building measures would contribute essentially to the creation of multilateral and bilateral friendly relations among peoples and nations,

Being concerned at the continuous erosion of multilateralism in the field of arms regulation, non-proliferation and disarmament, and recognizing that a resort to unilateral actions by Member States in resolving their security concerns would jeopardize international peace and security and undermine confidence in the international security system as well as the foundations of the United Nations itself,

Reaffirming the absolute validity of multilateral diplomacy in the field of disarmament, and determined to promote multilateralism as an essential way to develop arms regulation and disarmament negotiations,

1. *Reaffirms* multilateralism as the core principle in negotiations in the area of disarmament and non-proliferation with a view to maintaining and strengthening universal norms and enlarging their scope;

2. *Also reaffirms* multilateralism as the core principle in resolving disarmament and non-proliferation concerns;

3. *Urges* the participation of all interested States in multilateral negotiations on arms regulation, non-proliferation and disarmament in a non-discriminatory and transparent manner;

4. *Underlines* the importance of preserving the existing agreements on arms regulation and disarmament, which constitute an expression of the results of international cooperation and multilateral negotiations in response to the challenges facing mankind;

5. *Calls once again upon* all Member States to renew and fulfil their individual and collective commitments to multilateral cooperation as an important means of pursuing and achieving their common objectives in the area of disarmament and non-proliferation;

6. *Requests* the States parties to the relevant instruments on weapons of mass destruction to consult and cooperate among themselves in resolving their concerns with regard to cases of non-compliance as well as on implementation, in accordance with the procedures defined in those instruments, and to refrain from resorting or threatening to resort to unilateral actions or directing unverified non-compliance accusations against one another to resolve their concerns;

7. *Takes note* of the report of the Secretary-General containing the replies of Member States on the promotion of multilateralism in the area of disarmament and non-proliferation, submitted pursuant to resolution 57/63;

8. *Requests* the Secretary-General to seek the views of Member States on the issue of the promotion of multilateralism in the area of disarmament and non-proliferation and to submit a report thereon to the General Assembly at its fifty-ninth session;

9. *Decides* to include in the provisional agenda of its fifty-ninth session the item entitled "Promotion of multilateralism in the area of disarmament and non-proliferation".

RECORDED VOTE ON RESOLUTION 58/44:

In favour: Algeria, Angola, Antigua and Barbuda, Azerbaijan, Bahamas, Bahrain, Bangladesh, Barbados, Belarus, Belize, Benin, Bhutan, Bolivia, Botswana, Brazil, Brunei Darussalam, Burkina Faso, Burundi, Cambodia, Cameroon, Cape Verde, Central African Republic, Chile, China, Colombia, Comoros, Congo, Costa Rica, Côte d'Ivoire, Cuba, Democratic People's Republic of Korea, Djibouti, Dominican Republic, Ecuador, Egypt, El Salvador, Eritrea, Ethiopia, Fiji, Gabon, Gambia, Ghana, Grenada, Guatemala, Guinea, Guinea-Bissau, Guyana, Haiti, Honduras, India, Indonesia, Iran, Jamaica, Jordan, Kazakhstan, Kenya, Kuwait, Kyrgyzstan, Lao People's Democratic Republic, Lebanon, Lesotho, Libyan Arab Jamahiriya, Madagascar, Malawi, Malaysia, Maldives, Mali, Mauritania, Mauritius, Mexico, Mongolia, Morocco, Mozambique, Myanmar, Namibia, Nepal, Nicaragua, Niger, Nigeria, Oman, Pakistan, Panama, Papua New Guinea, Paraguay, Peru, Philippines, Qatar, Russian Federation, Rwanda, Saint Lucia, Saudi Arabia, Senegal, Seychelles, Singapore, Somalia, South Africa, Sri Lanka, Sudan, Suriname, Swaziland, Syrian Arab Republic, Tajikistan, Thailand, Timor-Leste, Togo, Trinidad and Tobago, Tunisia, Turkmenistan, Uganda, United Arab Emirates, United Republic of Tanzania, Uruguay, Vanuatu, Venezuela, Viet Nam, Yemen, Zambia, Zimbabwe.

Against: Albania, Bulgaria, Israel, Italy, Latvia, Marshall Islands, Micronesia, Poland, Portugal, Spain, United Kingdom, United States.

Abstaining: Andorra, Argentina, Armenia, Australia, Austria, Belgium, Bosnia and Herzegovina, Canada, Croatia, Cyprus, Czech Republic, Denmark, Estonia, Finland, France, Georgia, Germany, Greece, Hungary, Iceland, Ireland, Japan, Liechtenstein, Lithuania, Luxembourg, Malta, Monaco, Nauru, Netherlands, New Zealand, Norway, Republic of Korea, Republic of Moldova, Romania, Saint Vincent and the Grenadines, Samoa, San Marino, Serbia and Montenegro, Slovakia, Slovenia, Solomon Islands, Sweden, Switzerland, The former Yugoslav Republic of Macedonia, Turkey, Ukraine.

Prevention of an arms race in outer space

In 2003, despite the efforts made to harmonize views on a mandate for an ad hoc committee on the prevention of an arms race in outer space, the Conference on Disarmament was unable to reach consensus on the mandate and, consequently, did not establish any subsidiary body to deal with the item. China and the Russian Federation, building on their 2002 joint working paper [YUN 2002, p. 540], held consultations and meetings among delegations on the issue. Delegations also discussed the item during plenary meetings and submitted amendments to the draft mandate contained in the joint proposal on a work programme put forth by five former Presidents (see p. 531). In the end, the continuing lack of consensus prevented the Conference from undertaking any substantive work on the item. Russia circulated an 11 June communication [CD/1710] regarding the development of an initiative to promote openness and to build confidence in the domain of outer space activities. Annexed to it was a schedule of spacecraft launches for June 2003 under Russian, international cooperation and commercial programmes.

GENERAL ASSEMBLY ACTION

On 8 December [meeting 71], the General Assembly, on the recommendation of the First Committee [A/58/461], adopted **resolution 58/36** by recorded vote (174-0-4) [agenda item 72].

Prevention of an arms race in outer space

The General Assembly,

Recognizing the common interest of all mankind in the exploration and use of outer space for peaceful purposes,

Reaffirming the will of all States that the exploration and use of outer space, including the Moon and other celestial bodies, shall be for peaceful purposes and shall be carried out for the benefit and in the interest of all countries, irrespective of their degree of economic or scientific development,

Reaffirming also the provisions of articles III and IV of the Treaty on Principles Governing the Activities of States in the Exploration and Use of Outer Space, including the Moon and Other Celestial Bodies,

Recalling the obligation of all States to observe the provisions of the Charter of the United Nations regarding the use or threat of use of force in their international relations, including in their space activities,

Reaffirming paragraph 80 of the Final Document of the Tenth Special Session of the General Assembly, in which it is stated that in order to prevent an arms race in outer space, further measures should be taken and appropriate international negotiations held in accordance with the spirit of the Treaty,

Recalling its previous resolutions on this issue, and taking note of the proposals submitted to the General Assembly at its tenth special session and at its regular sessions, and of the recommendations made to the competent organs of the United Nations and to the Conference on Disarmament,

Recognizing that prevention of an arms race in outer space would avert a grave danger for international peace and security,

Emphasizing the paramount importance of strict compliance with existing arms limitation and disarmament agreements relevant to outer space, including bilateral agreements, and with the existing legal regime concerning the use of outer space,

Considering that wide participation in the legal regime applicable to outer space could contribute to enhancing its effectiveness,

Noting that the Ad Hoc Committee on the Prevention of an Arms Race in Outer Space, taking into account its previous efforts since its establishment in 1985 and seeking to enhance its functioning in qualitative terms, continued the examination and identification of various issues, existing agreements and existing proposals, as well as future initiatives relevant to the prevention of an arms race in outer space, and that this contributed to a better understanding of a number of problems and to a clearer perception of the various positions,

Noting also that there were no objections in principle in the Conference on Disarmament to the re-establishment of the Ad Hoc Committee, subject to re-examination of the mandate contained in the decision of the Conference on Disarmament of 13 February 1992,

Emphasizing the mutually complementary nature of bilateral and multilateral efforts in the field of preventing an arms race in outer space, and hoping that concrete results will emerge from those efforts as soon as possible,

Convinced that further measures should be examined in the search for effective and verifiable bilateral and multilateral agreements in order to prevent an arms race in outer space, including the weaponization of outer space,

Stressing that the growing use of outer space increases the need for greater transparency and better information on the part of the international community,

Recalling, in this context, its previous resolutions, in particular resolutions 45/55 B of 4 December 1990, 47/51 of 9 December 1992 and 48/74 A of 16 December 1993, in which, inter alia, it reaffirmed the importance of confidence-building measures as a means conducive to ensuring the attainment of the objective of the prevention of an arms race in outer space,

Conscious of the benefits of confidence- and security-building measures in the military field,

Recognizing that negotiations for the conclusion of an international agreement or agreements to prevent an arms race in outer space remain a priority task of the Ad Hoc Committee and that the concrete proposals on confidence-building measures could form an integral part of such agreements,

1. *Reaffirms* the importance and urgency of preventing an arms race in outer space and the readiness of all States to contribute to that common objective, in conformity with the provisions of the Treaty on Principles Governing the Activities of States in the Exploration and Use of Outer Space, including the Moon and Other Celestial Bodies;

2. *Reaffirms its recognition*, as stated in the report of the Ad Hoc Committee on the Prevention of an Arms Race in Outer Space, that the legal regime applicable to outer space does not in and of itself guarantee the prevention of an arms race in outer space, that the regime plays a significant role in the prevention of an arms race in that environment, that there is a need to consolidate and reinforce that regime and enhance its effectiveness and that it is important to comply strictly with existing agreements, both bilateral and multilateral;

3. *Emphasizes* the necessity of further measures with appropriate and effective provisions for verification to prevent an arms race in outer space;

4. *Calls upon* all States, in particular those with major space capabilities, to contribute actively to the objective of the peaceful use of outer space and of the prevention of an arms race in outer space and to refrain from actions contrary to that objective and to the relevant existing treaties in the interest of maintaining international peace and security and promoting international cooperation;

5. *Reiterates* that the Conference on Disarmament, as the single multilateral disarmament negotiating forum, has the primary role in the negotiation of a multilateral agreement or agreements, as appropriate, on the prevention of an arms race in outer space in all its aspects;

6. *Invites* the Conference on Disarmament to complete the examination and updating of the mandate contained in its decision of 13 February 1992 and to establish an ad hoc committee as early as possible during its 2004 session;

7. *Recognizes*, in this respect, the growing convergence of views on the elaboration of measures designed to strengthen transparency, confidence and security in the peaceful uses of outer space;

8. *Urges* States conducting activities in outer space, as well as States interested in conducting such activities, to keep the Conference on Disarmament informed of the progress of bilateral and multilateral negotiations on the matter, if any, so as to facilitate its work;

9. *Decides* to include in the provisional agenda of its fifty-ninth session the item entitled "Prevention of an arms race in outer space".

RECORDED VOTE ON RESOLUTION 58/36:

In favour: Afghanistan, Albania, Algeria, Andorra, Angola, Antigua and Barbuda, Argentina, Armenia, Australia, Austria, Azerbaijan, Bahamas, Bahrain, Bangladesh, Barbados, Belarus, Belgium, Belize, Benin, Bhutan, Bolivia, Bosnia and Herzegovina, Botswana, Brazil, Brunei Darussalam, Bulgaria, Burkina Faso, Burundi, Cambodia, Cameroon, Canada, Cape Verde, Central African Republic, Chile, China, Colombia, Comoros, Congo, Costa Rica, Côte d'Ivoire, Croatia, Cuba, Cyprus, Czech Republic, Democratic People's Republic of Korea, Denmark, Djibouti, Dominican Republic, Ecuador, Egypt, El Salvador, Eritrea, Estonia, Ethiopia, Fiji, Finland, France, Gabon, Gambia, Georgia, Germany, Ghana, Greece, Grenada, Guatemala, Guinea, Guinea-Bissau, Guyana, Haiti, Honduras, Hungary, Iceland, India, Indonesia, Iran, Ireland, Italy, Jamaica, Japan, Jordan, Kazakhstan, Kenya, Kuwait, Kyrgyzstan, Lao People's Democratic Republic, Latvia, Lebanon, Lesotho, Libyan Arab Jamahiriya, Liechtenstein, Lithuania, Luxembourg, Madagascar, Malawi, Malaysia, Maldives, Mali, Malta, Mauritania, Mauritius, Mexico, Monaco, Mongolia, Morocco, Mozambique, Myanmar, Namibia, Nauru, Nepal, Netherlands, New Zealand, Nicaragua, Niger, Nigeria, Norway, Oman, Pakistan, Panama, Papua New Guinea, Paraguay, Peru, Philippines, Poland, Portugal, Qatar, Republic of Korea, Republic of Moldova, Romania, Russian Federation, Rwanda, Saint Lucia, Saint Vincent and the Grenadines, Samoa, San Marino, Saudi Arabia, Senegal, Serbia and Montenegro, Seychelles, Singapore, Slovakia, Slovenia, Somalia, South Africa, Spain, Sri Lanka, Sudan, Suriname, Swaziland, Sweden, Switzer-

land, Syrian Arab Republic, Tajikistan, Thailand, The former Yugoslav Republic of Macedonia, Timor-Leste, Togo, Tonga, Trinidad and Tobago, Tunisia, Turkey, Turkmenistan, Uganda, Ukraine, United Arab Emirates, United Kingdom, United Republic of Tanzania, Uruguay, Uzbekistan, Vanuatu, Venezuela, Viet Nam, Yemen, Zambia, Zimbabwe.
Against: None.
Abstaining: Israel, Marshall Islands, Micronesia, United States.

Disarmament and development

The controversy regarding the question of the relationship between disarmament and development continued during the year. While the vast majority of Member States, mostly non-aligned countries, maintained support for the implementation of the action programme adopted by the 1987 International Conference that examined the relationship in all its aspects [YUN 1987, p. 82], a number of other States, including the EU member States and the United States, continued to argue that there was no automatic link between the two concepts.

Expert group. Pursuant to General Assembly resolution 57/65 [YUN 2002, p. 542], the Secretary-General established a Group of Governmental Experts, drawn from 16 countries, to review the relationship between disarmament and development. At its first session (Geneva, 17-21 November), the Group assessed the implementation of the 1987 action programme and a number of issues relating to the current international context, and agreed on a draft outline for its future work. Its second and third sessions were scheduled to take place in New York in March and May 2004. A previous review by governmental experts was undertaken between 1978 [YUN 1978, p. 30] and 1981 [YUN 1981, p. 96].

GENERAL ASSEMBLY ACTION

On 8 December, the General Assembly, on the recommendation of the First Committee [A/58/462], adopted **decision 58/520** by recorded vote [agenda item 73 *(h)*].

Relationship between disarmament and development

At its 71st plenary meeting, on 8 December 2003, the General Assembly, by a recorded vote of 177 to 1, with 2 abstentions, and on the recommendation of the First Committee, decided, pursuant to its resolution 57/65 of 22 November 2002, to include in the provisional agenda of its fifty-ninth session the item entitled "Relationship between disarmament and development".

RECORDED VOTE ON DECISION 58/520:

In favour: Afghanistan, Albania, Algeria, Andorra, Angola, Antigua and Barbuda, Argentina, Armenia, Australia, Austria, Azerbaijan, Bahamas, Bahrain, Bangladesh, Barbados, Belarus, Belgium, Belize, Benin, Bhutan, Bolivia, Bosnia and Herzegovina, Botswana, Brazil, Brunei Darussalam, Bulgaria, Burkina Faso, Burundi, Cambodia, Cameroon, Canada, Cape Verde, Central African Republic, Chile, China, Colombia, Comoros, Congo, Costa Rica, Côte d'Ivoire, Croatia, Cuba, Cyprus, Czech Republic, Democratic People's Republic of Korea, Denmark, Djibouti, Dominican Republic, Ecuador, Egypt, El Salvador, Eritrea, Estonia, Ethiopia, Fiji, Finland, France, Gabon, Gambia, Georgia, Germany, Ghana, Greece, Grenada, Guatemala, Guinea, Guinea-Bissau, Guyana, Haiti, Honduras, Hungary, Iceland, India, Indonesia, Iran, Ireland, Italy, Jamaica, Japan, Jordan, Kazakhstan, Kenya, Kuwait, Kyrgyzstan, Lao People's Democratic Republic, Latvia, Lebanon, Lesotho, Libyan Arab Jamahiriya, Liechtenstein, Lithuania, Luxembourg, Madagascar, Malawi, Malaysia, Maldives, Mali, Malta, Marshall Islands, Mauritania, Mauritius, Mexico, Micronesia, Monaco, Mongolia, Morocco, Mozambique, Myanmar, Namibia, Nauru, Nepal, Netherlands, New Zealand, Nicaragua, Niger, Nigeria, Norway, Oman, Pakistan, Panama, Papua New Guinea, Paraguay, Peru, Philippines, Poland, Portugal, Qatar, Republic of Korea, Republic of Moldova, Romania, Russian Federation, Saint Lucia, Saint Vincent and the Grenadines, Samoa, San Marino, Saudi Arabia, Senegal, Serbia and Montenegro, Seychelles, Sierra Leone, Singapore, Slovakia, Slovenia, Solomon Islands, Somalia, South Africa, Spain, Sri Lanka, Sudan, Suriname, Swaziland, Sweden, Switzerland, Syrian Arab Republic, Tajikistan, Thailand, The former Yugoslav Republic of Macedonia, Timor-Leste, Togo, Tonga, Trinidad and Tobago, Tunisia, Turkey, Turkmenistan, Uganda, Ukraine, United Arab Emirates, United Kingdom, United Republic of Tanzania, Uruguay, Uzbekistan, Vanuatu, Venezuela, Viet Nam, Yemen, Zambia, Zimbabwe.
Against: United States.
Abstaining: Israel, Rwanda.

Arms limitation and disarmament agreements

Pursuant to General Assembly resolution 57/64 [YUN 2002, p. 543], the Secretary-General submitted a July report with later addendum [A/58/129 & Add.1], containing information from six Member States on measures they had taken to ensure the application of scientific and technological progress in the context of international security, disarmament and related areas, without detriment to the environment or to its effective contribution to attaining sustainable development.

GENERAL ASSEMBLY ACTION

On 8 December [meeting 71], the General Assembly, on the recommendation of the First Committee [A/58/462], adopted **resolution 58/45** by recorded vote (173-1-4) [agenda item 73 *(g)*].

Observance of environmental norms in the drafting and implementation of agreements on disarmament and arms control

The General Assembly,

Recalling its resolutions 50/70 M of 12 December 1995, 51/45 E of 10 December 1996, 52/38 E of 9 December 1997, 53/77 J of 4 December 1998, 54/54 S of 1 December 1999, 55/33 K of 20 November 2000, 56/24 F of 29 November 2001 and 57/64 of 22 November 2002,

Emphasizing the importance of the observance of environmental norms in the preparation and implementation of disarmament and arms limitation agreements,

Recognizing that it is necessary to take duly into account the agreements adopted at the United Nations Conference on Environment and Development, as well as prior relevant agreements, in the drafting and implementation of agreements on disarmament and arms limitation,

Taking note of the report of the Secretary-General,

Mindful of the detrimental environmental effects of the use of nuclear weapons,

1. *Reaffirms* that international disarmament forums should take fully into account the relevant environmental norms in negotiating treaties and agreements on disarmament and arms limitation and that all States, through their actions, should contribute fully to ensuring compliance with the aforementioned norms in the implementation of treaties and conventions to which they are parties;

2. *Calls upon* States to adopt unilateral, bilateral, regional and multilateral measures so as to contribute to ensuring the application of scientific and technological progress in the framework of international security, disarmament and other related spheres, without detriment to the environment or to its effective contribution to attaining sustainable development;

3. *Welcomes* the information provided by Member States on the implementation of the measures they have adopted to promote the objectives envisaged in the present resolution;

4. *Invites* all Member States to communicate to the Secretary-General information on the measures they have adopted to promote the objectives envisaged in the present resolution, and requests the Secretary-General to submit a report containing this information to the General Assembly at its fifty-ninth session;

5. *Decides* to include in the provisional agenda of its fifty-ninth session the item entitled "Observance of environmental norms in the drafting and implementation of agreements on disarmament and arms control".

RECORDED VOTE ON RESOLUTION 58/45:

In favour: Afghanistan, Albania, Algeria, Andorra, Angola, Antigua and Barbuda, Argentina, Armenia, Australia, Austria, Azerbaijan, Bahamas, Bahrain, Bangladesh, Barbados, Belarus, Belgium, Belize, Benin, Bhutan, Bolivia, Bosnia and Herzegovina, Botswana, Brazil, Brunei Darussalam, Bulgaria, Burkina Faso, Burundi, Cambodia, Cameroon, Canada, Cape Verde, Central African Republic, Chile, China, Colombia, Comoros, Congo, Costa Rica, Côte d'Ivoire, Croatia, Cuba, Cyprus, Czech Republic, Democratic People's Republic of Korea, Denmark, Djibouti, Dominican Republic, Ecuador, Egypt, El Salvador, Eritrea, Estonia, Ethiopia, Fiji, Finland, Gabon, Gambia, Georgia, Germany, Ghana, Greece, Grenada, Guatemala, Guinea, Guinea-Bissau, Guyana, Haiti, Honduras, Hungary, Iceland, India, Indonesia, Iran, Ireland, Italy, Jamaica, Japan, Jordan, Kazakhstan, Kenya, Kuwait, Kyrgyzstan, Lao People's Democratic Republic, Latvia, Lebanon, Lesotho, Libyan Arab Jamahiriya, Liechtenstein, Lithuania, Luxembourg, Madagascar, Malawi, Malaysia, Maldives, Mali, Malta, Mauritania, Mauritius, Mexico, Monaco, Mongolia, Morocco, Mozambique, Myanmar, Namibia, Nauru, Nepal, Netherlands, New Zealand, Nicaragua, Niger, Nigeria, Norway, Oman, Pakistan, Panama, Papua New Guinea, Paraguay, Peru, Philippines, Poland, Portugal, Qatar, Republic of Korea, Republic of Moldova, Romania, Russian Federation, Rwanda, Saint Lucia, Saint Vincent and the Grenadines, Samoa, San Marino, Saudi Arabia, Senegal, Serbia and Montenegro, Seychelles, Singapore, Slovakia, Slovenia, Solomon Islands, Somalia, South Africa, Spain, Sri Lanka, Sudan, Suriname, Swaziland, Sweden, Switzerland, Syrian Arab Republic, Tajikistan, Thailand, The former Yugoslav Republic of Macedonia, Timor-Leste, Togo, Tonga, Trinidad and Tobago, Tunisia, Turkey, Turkmenistan, Uganda, Ukraine, United Arab Emirates, United Republic of Tanzania, Uruguay, Uzbekistan, Vanuatu, Venezuela, Viet Nam, Yemen, Zambia, Zimbabwe.

Against: United States.

Abstaining: France, Israel, Micronesia, United Kingdom.

Studies, information and training

Disarmament studies programme

The Group of Governmental Experts on the identification and tracing of illicit small arms and light weapons completed and submitted its report [A/58/138] (see p. 562), as did the Group of Governmental Experts on the continuing operation of the UN Register of Conventional Arms [A/58/274] (see p. 568). During the year, the recommendations contained in the study on disarmament and non-proliferation education, completed in 2002 [YUN 2002, p. 544], began to be implemented by Member States, UN system organizations, civil society, NGOs and the media. In that context, the Department for Disarmament Affairs (DDA) and the Hague Appeal for Peace, an NGO, inaugurated a two-year project on small arms, peace and disarmament education in four countries, across four continents. The Group of Governmental Experts established by the Secretary-General to reappraise the relationship between disarmament and development in the current international context met during the year (see p. 584).

In 2003, the General Assembly, in **resolution 58/37** (see p. 546), requested the Secretary-General, with the assistance of a panel of governmental experts, to explore further the issue of missiles in all its aspects, for consideration in 2004.

Disarmament Information Programme

During the year, priority issues for the Disarmament Information Programme of DDA included WMDs; conventional weapons, particularly small arms and light weapons, and the transparency mechanism of the Register of Conventional Arms; the relationship between disarmament and development; and disarmament and non-proliferation education. The Programme was implemented through public speaking engagements, media campaigns, print and electronic publications, web-site access, symposiums, panel discussions and exhibits. DDA collaborated closely with the UN Department of Public Information to address the information needs of the first biennial meeting of States to consider the implementation of the Programme of Action adopted by the UN Conference on small arms [YUN 2001, p. 499] (see p. 562). The Programme continued to broaden its cooperation with civil society by integrating NGOs and research institutes into DDA's work and improving existing relationships.

Advisory Board on Disarmament Matters

The Advisory Board on Disarmament Matters, which advised the Secretary-General on the disarmament studies programme and implementation of the Disarmament Information Programme and served as the Board of Trustees of the United Nations Institute for Disarmament Research (UNIDIR) (see p. 586), held its fortieth and forty-first sessions (New York, 5-7 February; Geneva, 16-18 July) [A/58/316]. The Board deliberated on compliance, verification and enforcement of multilateral disarmament treaties; disarmament and human security; disarmament and development; rising military expenditure; a review of the functioning and effectiveness of the Board; and open-source data for promoting disarmament and non-proliferation. It recommended that the United Nations identify the best way to preserve the expertise and knowledge of the United Nations Monitoring, Verification and Inspection Commission (see p. 316), with a view to maintaining the Organization's readiness to address future non-compliance cases. The Board also recommended, among other things, the convening of a group of experts to examine and establish due procedures for the Security Council in dealing more effectively with non-compliance cases, and a more comprehensive examination of the relationship between disarmament and development. It agreed on the need for a new disarmament paradigm promoting new perceptions of security, particularly human security, measures aimed at improving its functioning and effectiveness, and practical steps for maximizing the use of potential open-source data, such as satellite technology for disarmament purposes.

UN Institute for Disarmament Research

The Secretary-General transmitted to the General Assembly the report of the UNIDIR Director covering the period from August 2002 to July 2003, as well as the report of the UNIDIR Board of Trustees on the proposed 2003-2004 programme of work and budget [A/58/259]. The Institute's research activities continued to focus on global security, regional security and human security. The report highlighted UNIDIR's range of research activities worldwide, including conferences, seminars and discussion meetings, as well as its networking initiatives with specialized agencies and UN system organizations and institutions. During the reporting period, UNIDIR produced a number of publications, which were listed on its web site.

The Board of Trustees recommended a subvention of $227,600 from the UN regular budget for 2004, which the Assembly approved on 23 December (**resolution 58/272**, section III) (see p. 1417).

Disarmament fellowship, training and advisory services

In 2003, 30 fellows participated in the UN disarmament fellowship, training and advisory services programme, which began in Geneva on 1 September and terminated in New York on 5 November. The programme comprised study sessions in Geneva and New York and study visits to intergovernmental organizations working in the area of disarmament, and to Germany, Japan, The Hague and Vienna.

Regional centres for peace and disarmament

On 8 December [meeting 71], the General Assembly, on the recommendation of the First Committee [A/58/463], adopted **resolution 58/63** without vote [agenda item 74 (a)].

United Nations regional centres for peace and disarmament

The General Assembly,

Recalling its resolution 57/87 of 22 November 2002 regarding the maintenance and revitalization of the three United Nations regional centres for peace and disarmament,

Recalling also the reports of the Secretary-General on the United Nations Regional Centre for Peace and Disarmament in Africa, the United Nations Regional Centre for Peace and Disarmament in Asia and the Pacific and the United Nations Regional Centre for Peace, Disarmament and Development in Latin America and the Caribbean,

Reaffirming its decision, taken in 1982 at its twelfth special session, to establish the United Nations Disarmament Information Programme, the purpose of which is to inform, educate and generate public understanding and support for the objectives of the United Nations in the field of arms control and disarmament,

Bearing in mind its resolutions 40/151 G of 16 December 1985, 41/60 J of 3 December 1986, 42/39 D of 30 November 1987 and 44/117 F of 15 December 1989 on the regional centres for peace and disarmament in Nepal, Peru and Togo,

Recognizing that the changes that have taken place in the world have created new opportunities as well as posed new challenges for the pursuit of disarmament, and, in this regard, bearing in mind that the regional centres for peace and disarmament can contribute substantially to understanding and cooperation among States in each particular region in the areas of peace, disarmament and development,

Noting that in paragraph 146 of the Final Document of the Twelfth Conference of Heads of State or Government of the Non-Aligned Countries, held at Durban, South Africa, from 29 August to 3 September 1998, the heads of State or Government welcomed the decision adopted by the General Assembly on maintaining and revitalizing the three regional centres for peace and disarmament in Nepal, Peru and Togo,

1. *Reiterates* the importance of the United Nations activities at the regional level to increase the stability and security of its Member States, which could be promoted in a substantive manner by the maintenance and revitalization of the three regional centres for peace and disarmament;

2. *Reaffirms* that, in order to achieve positive results, it is useful for the three regional centres to carry out dissemination and educational programmes that promote regional peace and security and that are

aimed at changing basic attitudes with respect to peace and security and disarmament so as to support the achievement of the principles and purposes of the United Nations;

3. *Appeals* to Member States in each region and those that are able to do so, as well as to international governmental and non-governmental organizations and foundations, to make voluntary contributions to the regional centres in their respective regions to strengthen their activities and initiatives;

4. *Emphasizes* the importance of the activities of the regional branch of the Department for Disarmament Affairs of the Secretariat;

5. *Requests* the Secretary-General to provide all necessary support, within existing resources, to the regional centres in carrying out their programmes of activities;

6. *Decides* to include in the provisional agenda of its fifty-ninth session the item entitled "United Nations regional centres for peace and disarmament".

Africa

Pursuant to General Assembly resolution 57/91 [YUN 2002, p. 548], the Secretary-General described the activities of the United Nations Regional Centre for Peace and Disarmament in Africa [A/58/139], covering the period from July 2002 to June 2003. The Centre was established in Lomé, Togo, in 1986 [YUN 1986, p. 85].

During the reporting period, the Centre focused on support for peace processes and related initiatives in Africa; disarmament and arms control; information, research and publication; and advocacy and resource mobilization. The Centre also initiated activities in cooperation with regional and subregional organizations and Member States to promote effective implementation of the Programme of Action adopted by the UN Conference on the Illicit Trade in Small Arms and Light Weapons in All Its Aspects [YUN 2001, p. 499], the 1997 Bamako Declaration on small arms and light weapons [YUN 1997, p. 515], the 1998 Moratorium on the Importation, Exportation and Manufacture of Small Arms and Light Weapons in West Africa of the Economic Community of West African States [YUN 1998, p. 537] and the 2001 Declaration concerning Firearms, Ammunition and Other Related Materials, adopted by the Southern African Development Community member States [YUN 2001, p. 511]. The Centre collaborated with the Lions Clubs International, an NGO, to organize a conference (Lomé, 24 January) entitled "Rethinking African culture for the promotion of sustainable peace and security on the continent", which considered the relationship between culture and peaceful conflict resolution in the region. The Centre, on 14 February, assisted the Government of Togo in the destruction of over 600,000 rounds of ammunition seized from gunrunners along the Togo-Ghana border. Within the collaborative framework it had established with the African Strategic and Peace Research Group, the Centre provided support for a round table (Minna, Nigeria, 27 February–2 March) on multi-track approaches to early response to crises in Africa. In April, it helped the Niger State College of Education (Nigeria) to finalize the curriculum for the professional diploma in peace and sustainable development. Within the framework of the activities of the UN Standing Advisory Committee on Security Questions in Central Africa (see p. 573), the Centre helped to elaborate a working document on priority areas for implementing the 2001 Programme of Action on small arms, which was adopted by the Committee in May, and, in September, it organized a workshop on the control of small arms in Central Africa. On 1 October, it launched the Small Arms Transparency and Control Regime in Africa, a three-year programme funded by Sweden and Finland to encourage African States to promote transparency by providing data on their manufacture and stockpiling of small arms and light weapons. Other activities included the training of messengers of peace from Zambia and the Democratic Republic of the Congo, a regional consultation on training for peace in West Africa, and participation in an exploratory mission to Côte d'Ivoire. In the Mano River Union countries (Guinea, Liberia, Sierra Leone), the Centre joined the Economic Commission for Africa for a data collection mission aimed at improving understanding of the magnitude and scope of the illicit trafficking in weapons at the common borders of the three countries.

GENERAL ASSEMBLY ACTION

On 8 December [meeting 71], the General Assembly, on the recommendation of the First Committee [A/58/463], adopted **resolution 58/61** without vote [agenda item 74 (d)].

United Nations Regional Centre for Peace and Disarmament in Africa

The General Assembly,

Mindful of the provisions of Article 11, paragraph 1, of the Charter of the United Nations stipulating that a function of the General Assembly is to consider the general principles of cooperation in the maintenance of international peace and security, including the principles governing disarmament and arms limitation,

Recalling its resolutions 40/151 G of 16 December 1985, 41/60 D of 3 December 1986, 42/39 J of 30 November 1987 and 43/76 D of 7 December 1988 on the United Nations Regional Centre for Peace and Disarmament in Africa, and its resolutions 46/36 F of 6 December 1991 and 47/52 G of 9 December 1992 on regional disarmament, including confidence-building measures,

Recalling also its resolutions 48/76 E of 16 December 1993, 49/76 D of 15 December 1994, 50/71 C of 12 December 1995, 51/46 E of 10 December 1996, 52/220 of 22 December 1997, 53/78 C of 4 December 1998, 54/55 B of 1 December 1999, 55/34 D of 20 November 2000, 56/25 D of 29 November 2001 and 57/91 of 22 November 2002,

Aware of the widespread support for the revitalization of the Regional Centre and the important role that the Centre can play in the present context in promoting confidence-building and arms-limitation measures at the regional level, thereby promoting progress in the area of sustainable development,

Taking note of the report of the Secretary-General that the Centre has received an increasing number of requests from Member States in the African region for substantive support for several peace initiatives and conflict resolution activities in the region,

Taking note also of the report by the Secretary-General that very limited financial contributions were made to the Centre despite continued fund-raising efforts,

Concerned that the continued financial difficulties faced by the Centre have impaired its ability to realize its full potential and to fulfil its mandate adequately,

Bearing in mind the efforts undertaken in the framework of the revitalization of the activities of the Regional Centre for the mobilization of the resources necessary for its operational costs,

Taking into account the need to establish close cooperation between the Regional Centre and the Mechanism for Conflict Prevention, Management and Resolution of the African Union, in conformity with the decision adopted by the Assembly of Heads of State and Government of the Organization of African Unity at its thirty-fifth ordinary session, held at Algiers from 12 to 14 July 1999,

Welcoming the adoption by consensus of the report of the United Nations First Biennial Meeting of States to Consider the Implementation of the Programme of Action to Prevent, Combat and Eradicate the Illicit Trade in Small Arms and Light Weapons in All Its Aspects, held in New York from 7 to 11 July 2003,

1. *Commends* the activities which the United Nations Regional Centre for Peace and Disarmament in Africa is continuing to carry out, in particular in support of the efforts made by the African States in the areas of peace and security;

2. *Reaffirms its strong support* for the revitalization of the Regional Centre, and emphasizes the need to provide it with the necessary resources to enable it to strengthen its activities and carry out its programmes;

3. *Appeals once again* to all States, as well as to international governmental and non-governmental organizations and foundations, to make voluntary contributions in order to strengthen the programmes and activities of the Regional Centre and facilitate their implementation;

4. *Requests* the Secretary-General to continue to provide the necessary support to the Regional Centre for better achievements and results;

5. *Also requests* the Secretary-General to facilitate close cooperation between the Regional Centre and the African Union, in particular in the area of peace, security and development, and to continue to assist the Director of the Regional Centre in his efforts to stabilize the financial situation of the Centre and revitalize its activities;

6. *Appeals in particular* to the Regional Centre, in cooperation with the African Union, regional and subregional organizations and the African States, to take steps to promote the consistent implementation of the Programme of Action to Prevent, Combat and Eradicate the Illicit Trade in Small Arms and Light Weapons in All Its Aspects;

7. *Requests* the Secretary-General to report to the General Assembly at its fifty-ninth session on the implementation of the present resolution;

8. *Decides* to include in the provisional agenda of its fifty-ninth session the item entitled "United Nations Regional Centre for Peace and Disarmament in Africa".

Asia and the Pacific

As requested by the General Assembly in resolution 57/92 [YUN 2002, p. 550], the Secretary-General reported in July on the activities of the United Nations Regional Centre for Peace and Disarmament in Asia and the Pacific from August 2002 to July 2003 [A/58/190]. The Centre was inaugurated in Kathmandu, Nepal, in 1989 [YUN 1989, p. 88].

During the period under review, the Centre focused on issues relating to nuclear-weapon-free zones and on organizing disarmament-related regional meetings. The Centre continued to assist the five Central Asian States in drafting a treaty on the establishment of a nuclear-weapon-free zone in Central Asia by organizing an expert group meeting and consultations among the regional States and between them and the five nuclear-weapon States. Similarly, in continuing efforts to assist Mongolia in taking measures to consolidate and strengthen its international security and nuclear-weapon-free status, the Centre organized, in January, an informal consultation among relevant UN bodies. In February, the Centre, in cooperation with Indonesia and Japan, organized a regional seminar (Bali, Indonesia, 10-11 February), which addressed the issue of small arms and light weapons from a regional perspective, explored how to implement the Programme of Action adopted by the 2001 UN Conference on those weapons [YUN 2001, p. 499] and helped the regional States prepare for the first biennial meeting of States (see p. 562) on the implementation of the outcome of the Conference. The Centre also hosted, in cooperation with Indonesia and DDA, a UN workshop on transparency in armaments (Bali, 14-15 February), intended to promote greater participation in the UN Register of Conventional Arms (see p. 568) and in the standardized instrument for military expenditure reporting. The Centre provided support to the United Nations Association of Japan in organizing the ninth Kanazawa symposium (Kanazawa, 10-12 June) on security and stability in North-East Asia and restoring confidence. It convened a UN conference (Osaka, Japan, 19-22 August) on arms control, disarmament and their future, which considered, among other matters, the current international security situation, WMDs and ways of fostering a culture of peace. In a further effort to address non-proliferation issues, the Centre, in cooperation with the Republic of Korea, organized a conference on disarmament and non-proliferation (Jeju Island, 3-5 December). The Centre, in a bid to promote further cooperation and interaction in the region, improved its contacts with academic institutions, foundations and regional and sub-regional organizations, such as the Council for Security Cooperation in the Asia Pacific and the Association of Southeast Asian Nations, and with disarmament-related international organizations, including IAEA, the Organization for the Prohibition of Chemical Weapons (see p. 561) and the Comprehensive Nuclear-Test-Ban Treaty Organization (see p. 547).

Owing to the lack of extrabudgetary resources, the Centre continued to operate from UN Headquarters, as consultations on its relocation continued with the host country. In that regard, a reminder was sent to the Government of Nepal regarding a draft host country agreement and a draft memorandum of understanding previously forwarded to it.

GENERAL ASSEMBLY ACTION

On 8 December [meeting 71], the General Assembly, on the recommendation of the First Committee [A/58/463], adopted **resolution 58/62** without vote [agenda item 74 (e)].

United Nations Regional Centre for Peace and Disarmament in Asia and the Pacific

The General Assembly,

Recalling its resolutions 42/39 D of 30 November 1987 and 44/117 F of 15 December 1989, by which it established the United Nations Regional Centre for Peace and Disarmament in Asia and renamed it the United Nations Regional Centre for Peace and Disarmament in Asia and the Pacific, with headquarters in Kathmandu and with the mandate of providing, on request, substantive support for the initiatives and other activities mutually agreed upon by the Member States of the Asia-Pacific region for the implementation of measures for peace and disarmament, through appropriate utilization of available resources,

Welcoming the report of the Secretary-General, in which he expresses his belief that the mandate of the Regional Centre remains valid and that the Centre has been a useful instrument for fostering a climate of cooperation for peace and disarmament in the region,

Noting that trends in the post-cold-war era have emphasized the function of the Regional Centre in assisting Member States as they deal with new security concerns and disarmament issues emerging in the region,

Commending the useful activities carried out by the Regional Centre in encouraging regional and sub-regional dialogue for the enhancement of openness, transparency and confidence-building, as well as the promotion of disarmament and security through the organization of regional meetings, which has come to be widely known within the Asia-Pacific region as the "Kathmandu process",

Expressing its appreciation to the Regional Centre for its organization of meetings and conferences in the region, held in Samarkand, Uzbekistan, from 25 to 27 September 2002, on Jeju Island, Republic of Korea, from 3 to 5 December 2002, in Bali, Indonesia, on 10 and 11 February 2003 and on 14 and 15 February 2003, in Kanazawa, Japan, from 10 to 12 June 2003 and in Osaka, Japan, from 19 to 22 August 2003,

Welcoming the idea of the possible creation of an educational and training programme for peace and disarmament in Asia and the Pacific for young people with different backgrounds, to be financed from voluntary contributions,

Noting the important role of the Regional Centre in assisting region-specific initiatives of Member States, including its continued assistance in finalizing a treaty related to the establishment of a nuclear-weapon-free zone in Central Asia, as well as to Mongolia's international security and nuclear-weapon-free status, including the organization of an informal consultation among relevant United Nations bodies in January 2003 to discuss the status of implementation of the non-nuclear aspects of Mongolia's status,

Appreciating highly the overall support that Nepal has extended as the host nation of the headquarters of the Regional Centre,

1. *Reaffirms its strong support* for the forthcoming operation and further strengthening of the United Nations Regional Centre for Peace and Disarmament in Asia and the Pacific;

2. *Underlines* the importance of the Kathmandu process as a powerful vehicle for the development of the practice of region-wide security and disarmament dialogue;

3. *Expresses its appreciation* for the continuing political support and voluntary financial contributions to the Regional Centre, which are essential for its continued operation;

4. *Appeals* to Member States, in particular those within the Asia-Pacific region, as well as to international governmental and non-governmental organizations and foundations, to make voluntary contributions, the only resources of the Regional Centre, to strengthen the programme of activities of the Centre and the implementation thereof;

5. *Requests* the Secretary-General, taking note of paragraph 6 of General Assembly resolution 49/76 D of 15 December 1994, to provide the Regional Centre with the necessary support, within existing resources, in carrying out its programme of activities;

6. *Urges* the Secretary-General to ensure the physical operation of the Regional Centre from Kathmandu within six months of the date of signature of the host country agreement and to enable the Centre to function effectively;

7. *Requests* the Secretary-General to report to the General Assembly at its fifty-ninth session on the implementation of the present resolution;

8. *Decides* to include in the provisional agenda of its fifty-ninth session the item entitled "United Nations Regional Centre for Peace and Disarmament in Asia and the Pacific".

Latin America and the Caribbean

As requested by the General Assembly in resolution 57/89 [YUN 2002, p. 551], the Secretary-General reported in July on the activities of the United Nations Regional Centre for Peace, Disarmament and Development in Latin America and the Caribbean from July 2002 to June 2003 [A/58/122]. The Centre was inaugurated in Lima, Peru, in 1987 [YUN 1987, p. 88].

The Centre's activities were related to firearms, ammunition and explosives; anti-personnel mines; disarmament and development; conventional, nuclear and chemical weapons; and information dissemination. It also promoted existing firearms agreements and undertook cooperative activities with regional States, UN agencies, international organizations and NGOs on practical disarmament activities, including the destruction of firearms, ammunition and explosives and the improvement of stockpile management practices; support to disarmament-related processes, such as the regime established by the Treaty for the Prohibition of Nuclear Weapons in Latin America and the Caribbean (Treaty of Tlatelolco) (see p. 555); new disarmament, demobilization and reintegration initiatives; and confidence- and security-building measures.

During the reporting period, the Centre continued to consolidate its Regional Clearing-House Programme on Firearms, Ammunition and Explosives, which served as a platform for assisting States to implement the Inter-American Convention against the Illicit Manufacturing of and Trafficking in Firearms, Ammunition, Explosives, and Other Related Materials [YUN 1997, p. 519] and relevant regional arrangements, as well as the Programme of Action adopted by the 2001 UN Conference on small arms [YUN 2001, p. 499]. The Centre continued to develop its Small Arms and Light Weapons Administration System, which would provide information on all its activities and those of its partners regarding projects related to the Clearing-House Programme, relevant documentation, points of contact and other activities concerning firearms, ammunition and explosives; the system was scheduled to be launched later in the year. The Centre's potential to help strengthen the nuclear-weapon-free zone regime in Latin America and the Caribbean (Treaty of Tlatelolco) increased markedly following an April memorandum of understanding between DDA and the Agency for the Prohibition of Nuclear Weapons in Latin America and the Caribbean, designed to facilitate formal cooperation between the Agency and the Centre. In May, the Centre provided technical assistance to UNDP to develop a proposal for a project on strengthening mechanisms for the control of firearms in El Salvador. The Centre organized, in May and June, a series of meetings, which considered and approved a manual for training NGOs in Latin America and the Caribbean on the use of firearms, with the first training course scheduled for later in the year in El Salvador. As part of its efforts to assist Latin American and Caribbean States to implement the 2001 UN Programme of Action on small arms, the Centre held a series of technical meetings, which ended in June, aimed at training 800 police, customs, intelligence and armed forces officials to serve as instructors on the legal trade and illegal trafficking in firearms, ammunition and related issues. The Centre continued to promote the implementation of the Mine-Ban Convention in Latin America and the Caribbean and, in that context, provided support to an OAS conference (Lima, 14-15 August) aimed at making the hemisphere free of anti-personnel landmines.

GENERAL ASSEMBLY ACTION

On 8 December [meeting 71], the General Assembly, on the recommendation of the First Committee [A/58/463], adopted **resolution 58/60** (as orally amended) without vote [agenda item 74 (c)].

United Nations Regional Centre for Peace, Disarmament and Development in Latin America and the Caribbean

The General Assembly,

Recalling its resolutions 41/60 J of 3 December 1986, 42/39 K of 30 November 1987 and 43/76 H of 7 December 1988 on the United Nations Regional Centre for Peace, Disarmament and Development in Latin America and the Caribbean, with headquarters in Lima,

Recalling also its resolutions 46/37 F of 9 December 1991, 48/76 E of 16 December 1993, 49/76 D of 15 December 1994, 50/71 C of 12 December 1995, 52/220 of 22 December 1997, 53/78 F of 4 December 1998, 54/55 F of 1 December 1999, 55/34 E of 20 November 2000, 56/25 E of 29 November 2001 and 57/89 of 22 November 2002,

Underlining the revitalization of the Regional Centre, the efforts made by the Government of Peru and other countries to that end, as well as the important work done by the Director of the Centre,

Recognizing that the Regional Centre has continued to act as an instrument for the implementation of regional initiatives and has intensified its contribution to the coordination of United Nations efforts towards peace and security,

Welcoming the report of the Secretary-General, which concludes that the Regional Centre also acts as a facilitator for the implementation of regional initiatives by identifying regional security needs and new areas of cooperation with States and organizations in the region, by providing more in-depth information on firearms matters, including training for the law enforcement community and non-governmental organizations on such matters, and by promoting the dissemination of information on security issues among diplomats, the military, non-governmental organizations and civil society,

Welcoming also that the report stresses that the Regional Centre has initiated a new level of activity in the important area of disarmament and development, and encouraging the Centre to further develop this activity,

Noting that security and disarmament issues have always been recognized as significant topics in Latin America and the Caribbean, the first inhabited region in the world to be declared a nuclear-weapon-free zone,

Welcoming the fact that the Treaty for the Prohibition of Nuclear Weapons in Latin America and the Caribbean (Treaty of Tlatelolco) is now in force for the sovereign States of the region, and that this fact was officially acknowledged by the General Conference of the Agency for the Prohibition of Nuclear Weapons in Latin America and the Caribbean, at its eighteenth session, held at Havana on 5 and 6 November 2003,

Bearing in mind the important role that the Regional Centre can play in promoting confidence-building measures, arms control and limitation, disarmament and development at the regional level,

Also bearing in mind the importance of information, research, education and training for peace, disarmament and development in order to achieve understanding and cooperation among States,

Recognizing the need to provide the three United Nations regional centres for peace and disarmament with sufficient financial resources and cooperation for the planning and implementation of their programmes of activities,

1. *Reiterates its strong support* for the role of the United Nations Regional Centre for Peace, Disarmament and Development in Latin America and the Caribbean in the promotion of United Nations activities at the regional level to strengthen peace, stability, security and development among its member States;

2. *Expresses its satisfaction and congratulates* the Regional Centre for the expansion of the vast range of activities carried out last year in the field of peace, disarmament and development, and requests the Regional Centre to take into account the proposals to be submitted by the countries of the region in promoting confidence-building measures, arms control and limitation, transparency, disarmament and development at the regional level;

3. *Expresses its appreciation* for the political support and financial contributions to the Regional Centre, which are essential for its continued operation;

4. *Invites* all States of the region to continue to take part in the activities of the Regional Centre, proposing items for inclusion in its programme, making greater and better use of the Centre's potential to meet the current challenges facing the international community and with a view to fulfilling the aims of the Charter of the United Nations in the field of peace, disarmament and development;

5. *Recognizes* that the Regional Centre has an important role in the promotion and development of regional initiatives agreed upon by the countries of Latin America and the Caribbean in the field of weapons of mass destruction, in particular nuclear weapons, conventional arms, including small arms and light weapons, as well as the relationship between disarmament and development;

6. *Welcomes* the establishment of the Group of Governmental Experts on the relationship between disarmament and development pursuant to General Assembly resolution 57/65 of 22 November 2002, whose report, to be submitted to the General Assembly at its fifty-ninth session, will be of utmost interest for the role the Regional Centre plays in promoting those issues in the region in pursuit of its mandate to promote economic and social development related to peace and disarmament;

7. *Highlights* the conclusion of the Secretary-General that the Regional Centre has demonstrated, in a concrete manner, the role of the Organization as a regional catalyst for peace and disarmament in assisting countries in the region to advance the cause of peace, disarmament and development in Latin America and the Caribbean;

8. *Appeals* to Member States, in particular those within the Latin American and Caribbean region, as well as to international governmental and non-governmental organizations and foundations, to make and increase voluntary contributions to strengthen the Regional Centre, its programme of activities and the implementation thereof;

9. *Requests* the Secretary-General to provide the Regional Centre with all necessary support, within existing resources, so that it may carry out its programme of activities in accordance with its mandate;

10. *Also requests* the Secretary-General to report to the General Assembly at its fifty-ninth session on the implementation of the present resolution;

11. *Decides* to include in the provisional agenda of its fifty-ninth session the item entitled "United Nations Regional Centre for Peace, Disarmament and Development in Latin America and the Caribbean".

Chapter VIII

Other political and security questions

The United Nations continued in 2003 to consider political and security questions relating to the Organization's efforts to support democratization worldwide, the promotion of decolonization, public information activities and the peaceful uses of outer space.

The Fifth International Conference of New or Restored Democracies, held in Ulaanbaatar, Mongolia, in September, adopted the Ulaanbaatar Declaration and Plan of Action, which outlined benchmark principles for democratic Government, committed participating Member States to strengthening democracy at the national, regional and international levels, and made recommendations for strengthening the Conference's Follow-up Mechanism.

The Special Committee on the Situation with regard to the Implementation of the Declaration on the Granting of Independence to Colonial Countries and Peoples continued to review progress in implementing the 1960 Declaration, particularly the exercise of self-determination by the remaining Non-Self-Governing Territories. The General Assembly requested the Special Committee to continue to seek suitable means for the immediate and full implementation of the Declaration and to carry out actions approved by the Assembly regarding the International Decade for the Eradication of Colonialism (1990-2000) and the Second International Decade (2001-2010).

The Committee on Information continued its comprehensive review of the management and operation of the Department of Public Information (DPI), based on a number of reports submitted by the Secretary-General. In that regard, as part of a continuing process of departmental reform, a new operating model for DPI and a new organizational structure were instituted, comprising a Strategic Communications Division, a News and Media Division and an Outreach Division. The rationalization of the network of United Nations information centres around regional hubs was initiated with the creation of a Western European hub. The Department continued to develop and enhance the UN web site in all official languages. To improve the management of UN libraries, the Steering Committee for the Modernization and Integrated Management of United Nations Libraries was established in January, with the objective of developing policies and coordinating operations among all UN libraries.

In a December resolution on developments in information and telecommunications, the Assembly called on Member States to promote the consideration of existing and potential threats in the field of information security. Regarding the role of science and technology in the context of international security, the Assembly, in another December resolution, encouraged UN bodies to contribute, within existing mandates, to promoting the application of science and technology for peaceful purposes.

Action teams established in 2001 to implement the recommendations of the Third (1999) United Nations Conference on the Exploration and Peaceful Uses of Outer Space (UNISPACE III) reported on progress in their work; five of the teams completed their mandates. In December, the Assembly decided to review in 2004 progress in the implementation of the UNISPACE III recommendations.

In January, the United Nations Scientific Committee on the Effects of Atomic Radiation held its fifty-first session, which had been postponed from 2002 due to a budget shortfall.

General aspects of international security

Support for democracies

UN system activities

Report of Secretary-General. In response to General Assembly resolutions 56/96 [YUN 2001, p. 526] and 56/269 [YUN 2002, p. 553], the Secretary-General submitted a September report [A/58/392] outlining UN system support of Governments' efforts to promote and consolidate new or restored democracies, particularly its activities in democratization and governance, and describing the outcome of the Fifth International Conference of New or Restored Democracies (see p. 593).

The Secretary-General stated that strengthening democracy worldwide was a recent priority of the United Nations, and he had emphasized the need to focus increasingly on ways to promote better governance. Over the preceding decade, the Organization had increased its support for new and restored democracies in Africa, Asia, Eastern Europe and Latin America, many of which were countries emerging from civil war and conflict. The promotion of democracy was also one of the Organization's main goals for the twenty-first century. Its democracy assistance was multifaceted and included State and institutional reform, with specific emphasis on free and fair elections (see p. 58) and respect for international law and human rights principles, the development of a vibrant civil society based on free speech and organization, and a political culture that encouraged public debate and participation, especially at the local level. Many of its activities and programmes focused on providing legal, technical and financial assistance and advice, monitoring and observation services, and civic education and training. The Organization had also published a number of studies and held several conferences and workshops on democratization and good governance.

The Secretary-General observed that the Ulaanbaatar Conference (see below) provided new momentum to pursue the emerging democratization agenda of the United Nations, and the Conference's Follow-up Mechanism would assume a key role in the Organization's future work.

The Secretary-General stated that, despite the assistance the UN system had provided to new or restored democracies, much more needed to be done to make its work more integrated and effective and to improve the focus and coherence of its democratization activities. At the international level, a more coherent approach to democratization was needed, requiring a global dialogue on common challenges and practices of governance in the twenty-first century. International cooperation should also be strengthened, along with the tools to carry out work in that field. The Secretary-General was pleased that, irrespective of recent conflicting views on promoting democracy, the concept of advocating and consolidating democracy had remained strong and viable. He was more convinced than ever that the United Nations had to remain on course on promoting democracy globally, regionally and nationally, and a full debate on the UN role in that undertaking in the twenty-first century would be desirable.

Communication. Ukraine transmitted a 29 January statement [A/58/62-S/2003/156] on the signing of the Treaty on the Ukraine-Russian State Border, to be a road map for further cooperation between the two States, and requested that it be considered under the item on the promotion and consolidation of new and restored democracies.

Fifth International Conference

The Fifth International Conference of New or Restored Democracies (Ulaanbaatar, Mongolia, 10-12 September), organized and hosted by Mongolia in collaboration with the United Nations, had as its theme "Democracy, good governance and civil society". A record number of States (119) participated in the Conference, which was preceded by a Parliamentary Forum, organized jointly by the Parliament of Mongolia and the Inter-Parliamentary Union, and an interactive civil society forum.

The Conference discussed globalization and its impact on democracy, international terrorism and crime; poverty, unemployment and social exclusions as threats to democracy and increased support from donors and international financial institutions to developing countries to support democracy and the achievement of the Millennium Development Goals [YUN 2000, p. 51]; the importance of a vibrant, active civil society and the necessity of government support to its varied elements, and the interdependence of democracy, human rights and peace; the decline of trust in authorities, particularly in older democracies; electoral systems and "the winner takes all" policy as a source for tension and risks for long-term political stability; the media as an important watchdog for democratic practices; and unilateralism as a threat to democracy. The Conference concluded with the adoption of the Ulaanbaatar Declaration and Plan of Action [A/58/387]. Qatar offered to host the sixth international conference in Doha in 2006.

In the Declaration, participants undertook to dedicate their efforts to helping new and restored democracies to consolidate and deepen democracy. They endorsed a series of principles regarding democratic societies, namely, that such societies were just and responsible; were inclusive and participatory; promoted and protected the rights and freedoms of all their members; were open and transparent; functioned under agreed rules of law and accountability, regardless of possible challenges; and showed solidarity towards others. Participants also agreed to work towards implementing those principles, in accordance with international, regional and national plans of action.

The Ulaanbaatar Plan of Action would guide the work of the Conference President and Bureau in the years leading to the sixth conference, and committed participating States to strengthening democracy at the national, regional and international levels.

At the national level, the Plan called on countries to draw up, in collaboration with citizens and civil society, a national plan for strengthening democracy that was consistent with the Ulaanbaatar Declaration; prepare, prior to the sixth conference, "country information notes" outlining the prospects of advancing and deepening democracy; and develop national democratic indicator databases to monitor progress. Countries were also to give special attention to the issues of participation and representation, sustainable development and eradication of poverty, the protection of human rights, open and transparent government, and the rule of law and accountability.

To strengthen regional collaboration in democratic development, countries were to draw up a plan of action for regions through regional intergovernmental organizations, in collaboration with Governments and civil society, and adopt regional declarations or charters focusing on collaboration for the promotion and support of democracy, among other actions.

At the international level, the Plan recommended that the General Assembly strengthen the Follow-up Mechanism by ensuring that: it was responsible for implementing the Plan of Action; the Conference President or Bureau represented the Conference at international forums; and the Follow-up Mechanism coordinated with the international civil society forum follow-up mechanism. The Conference President should establish, with UN assistance, a working group to examine the Conference's conclusions and the proposals submitted to and interventions made at the Conference, with the aim of improving the Conference's effectiveness and efficiency and establishing a programme of work for future conferences. The President or the Bureau were to initiate discussions with the Chair of the Community of Democracies to exchange views on ways of bringing the two movements closer together.

Follow-up Mechanism

The Secretary-General, in his report on UN support to promote and consolidate new or restored democracies [A/58/392], said that the follow-up action had not been as effective as anticipated and needed substantive and logistic strengthening. He noted that, 15 years since the first conference, there was serious talk of institutionalizing the follow-up and monitoring progress achieved between conferences. The follow-up could take place through country information notes and/or democracy indicators, as mentioned in the Plan of Action. The Fifth Conference had set up an ambitious follow-up plan to implement its recommendations, and the Follow-up Mechanism, originally established at the Third Conference in 1997 [YUN 1997, p. 530] and which was to convene in New York, would assume a key role in the conferences's future work.

The current arrangement through the United Nations Development Programme (UNDP), which gave substantive and logistical support for each conference through its resident coordinator, the relevant host country team and the regional bureau at headquarters, and the UN Department of Political Affairs, provided continuity and support for the Follow-up Mechanism and the General Assembly's deliberations, and could be maintained on an interim basis. However, if the conference were to be institutionalized, a new support structure would be needed.

The Secretary-General, noting the measures recommended by the Fifth Conference for strengthening the Follow-up Mechanism (see above), suggested that the Assembly, at its fifty-eighth (2003) session, support those measures.

GENERAL ASSEMBLY ACTION

On 17 November [meeting 62], the General Assembly adopted **resolution 58/13** [draft: A/58/L.15 & Add.1, orally revised] without vote [agenda item 20].

Support by the United Nations system of the efforts of Governments to promote and consolidate new or restored democracies

The General Assembly,

Bearing in mind the indissoluble links between the principles embodied in the Universal Declaration of Human Rights and the foundations of any democratic society,

Recalling its resolutions 49/30 of 7 December 1994, 50/133 of 20 December 1995, 51/31 of 6 December 1996, 52/18 of 21 November 1997, 53/31 of 23 November 1998, 54/36 of 29 November 1999, 55/43 of 27 November 2000, 56/96 of 14 December 2001 and 56/269 of 27 March 2002,

Recalling also the United Nations Millennium Declaration adopted by heads of State and Government on 8 September 2000, in particular paragraphs 6 and 24 thereof,

Recalling further the declarations and plans of action of the five international conferences of new or restored democracies adopted in Manila in 1988, Managua in 1994, Bucharest in 1997, Cotonou in 2000 and Ulaanbaatar in 2003,

Recalling that the Fifth International Conference of New or Restored Democracies, which was held in Ulaanbaatar from 10 to 12 September 2003, focused on democracy, good governance and civil society,

Considering the major changes taking place on the international scene and the aspirations of all peoples for an international order based on the principles enshrined in the Charter of the United Nations, including the promotion and encouragement of respect for human rights and fundamental freedoms for all and other important principles, such as respect for the equal rights and self-determination of peoples, peace, democracy, justice, equality, the rule of law, pluralism, development, better standards of living and solidarity,

Expressing its deep appreciation to the Government of Mongolia for the successful organization of the Fifth International Conference,

Bearing in mind that the activities of the United Nations carried out in support of the efforts of Governments to promote and consolidate democracy are undertaken in accordance with the Charter and only at the specific request of the Member States concerned,

Taking note with satisfaction of the seminars, workshops and conferences on democratization and good governance convened in 2002 and 2003, as well as those held under the auspices of the Fifth International Conference,

Taking note of the views expressed by Member States in the debate on this question at its fifty-sixth to fifty-eighth sessions,

Bearing in mind that democracy, development and respect for all human rights and fundamental freedoms are interdependent and mutually reinforcing and that democracy is based on the freely expressed will of the people to determine their own political, economic, social and cultural systems and on their full participation in all aspects of their lives,

Noting that a considerable number of societies have recently undertaken significant efforts to achieve their social, political and economic goals through democratization, good governance practices and the reform of their economies, pursuits that are deserving of the support and recognition of the international community,

Expressing its deep appreciation for the support provided by Member States, the United Nations system and other intergovernmental organizations to the Government of Mongolia for the holding of the Fifth International Conference,

Taking note of the conclusions of the parliamentarians' forum held in Ulaanbaatar on 11 September 2003 and the contribution of the ensuing parliamentary declaration to the proceedings of the Fifth International Conference,

Welcoming the holding of an international civil society forum within the framework of the Fifth International Conference,

Having considered the report of the Secretary-General and its focus on the Ulaanbaatar Declaration and Plan of Action: Democracy, Good Governance and Civil Society, adopted on 12 September 2003 at the Fifth International Conference,

1. *Takes note with appreciation* of the report of the Secretary-General;
2. *Welcomes* the Ulaanbaatar Declaration and Plan of Action: Democracy, Good Governance and Civil Society, adopted at the Fifth International Conference of New or Restored Democracies;
3. *Encourages* Member States, the relevant organizations of the United Nations system, other intergovernmental organizations, national parliaments, including in collaboration with the Inter-Parliamentary Union and other parliamentary organizations, and non-governmental organizations to contribute actively to the follow-up to the Fifth International Conference and to make additional efforts to identify possible steps in support of the efforts of Governments to promote and consolidate new or restored democracies, including those set out in the Ulaanbaatar Declaration and Plan of Action;
4. *Recognizes* that the United Nations has an important role to play in providing timely, appropriate and coherent support to the efforts of Governments to achieve democratization and good governance within the context of their development efforts;
5. *Encourages* the Secretary-General to continue to improve the capacity of the Organization to respond effectively to the requests of Member States by providing coherent and adequate support for their efforts to achieve the goals of good governance and democratization;
6. *Stresses* that the activities of the Organization must be undertaken in accordance with the Charter of the United Nations;
7. *Commends* the Secretary-General, and through him the United Nations system, for the activities undertaken at the request of Governments to support efforts to consolidate democracy and good governance, and requests him to continue those activities;
8. *Requests* the Secretary-General to examine options for strengthening the support provided by the United Nations system for the efforts of Member States to consolidate democracy and good governance, including the provision of support to the President of the Fifth International Conference in his efforts to make the Conference and its follow-up more effective and efficient;
9. *Also requests* the Secretary-General to submit a report to the General Assembly at its sixtieth session on the implementation of the present resolution;
10. *Decides* to include in the provisional agenda of its sixtieth session the item entitled "Support by the United Nations system of the efforts of Governments to promote and consolidate new or restored democracies".

Regional aspects of international peace and security

South Atlantic

As requested in General Assembly resolution 56/7 [YUN 2001, p. 527], the Secretary-General submitted an August report on the zone of peace and cooperation of the South Atlantic [A/58/265], declared in 1986 to promote cooperation among States of the region in the political, economic, scientific, technical, cultural and other fields [YUN 1986, p. 369]. The Secretary-General stated that, as at 8 August, three Governments (Argentina, Mexico, Sudan) had responded to his request for views on the implementation of the declaration's objectives. Five UN bodies had also responded.

GENERAL ASSEMBLY ACTION

On 5 November [meeting 56], the General Assembly adopted **resolution 58/10** [draft: A/58/L.12 & Add.1] without vote [agenda item 27].

Zone of peace and cooperation of the South Atlantic

The General Assembly,

Recalling its resolution 41/11 of 27 October 1986, in which it solemnly declared the Atlantic Ocean, in the region between Africa and South America, a zone of peace and cooperation of the South Atlantic,

Recalling also its subsequent resolutions on the matter, including resolution 45/36 of 27 November 1990, in which it reaffirmed the determination of the States of the zone to enhance and accelerate their cooperation in the political, economic, scientific, cultural and other spheres,

Reaffirming the importance of the purposes and objectives of the zone of peace and cooperation of the South Atlantic as a basis for the promotion of cooperation among the countries of the region,

Reaffirming also that the questions of peace and security and those of development are interrelated and inseparable and that cooperation for peace and development among States of the region will promote the objectives of the zone of peace and cooperation of the South Atlantic,

Recalling the agreement reached at the third meeting of the States members of the zone, held in Brasilia on 21 and 22 September 1994, to encourage democracy and political pluralism and, in accordance with the Vienna Declaration and Programme of Action, adopted by the World Conference on Human Rights on 25 June 1993, to promote and defend all human rights and fundamental freedoms and to cooperate towards the achievement of these goals,

Aware of the importance that the States of the zone attach to the protection of the environment of the region, and recognizing the threat that pollution from any source poses to the marine and coastal environment, its ecological balance and its resources,

Welcoming the adoption of the Programme of Action to Prevent, Combat and Eradicate the Illicit Trade in Small Arms and Light Weapons in All Its Aspects at the United Nations Conference on the Illicit Trade in Small Arms and Light Weapons in All Its Aspects, held in New York from 9 to 20 July 2001,

Taking note with appreciation of the report of the Secretary-General, submitted in accordance with resolution 56/7 of 21 November 2001,

1. *Calls upon* all States to cooperate in the promotion of the objectives established in the declaration of the zone of peace and cooperation of the South Atlantic and to refrain from any action inconsistent with those objectives and with the Charter of the United Nations and relevant resolutions of the Organization, in particular actions that may create or aggravate situations of tension and potential conflict in the region;

2. *Notes with satisfaction* the full entry into force of the Treaty for the Prohibition of Nuclear Weapons in Latin America and the Caribbean (Treaty of Tlatelolco), and also notes with satisfaction the progress towards the full entry into force of the African Nuclear-Weapon-Free Zone Treaty (Treaty of Pelindaba);

3. *Encourages* all States, in particular the members of the zone of peace and cooperation of the South Atlantic, to cooperate in promoting and strengthening global, regional, subregional and national initiatives to prevent, combat and eradicate the illicit trade in small arms and light weapons;

4. *Commends* regional efforts being undertaken by States members of the zone in support of the implementation of the Programme of Action to Prevent, Combat and Eradicate the Illicit Trade in Small Arms and Light Weapons in All Its Aspects, and calls upon them to keep up their efforts in this regard;

5. *Affirms* the importance of the South Atlantic to global maritime and commercial transactions, and its determination to preserve the region for all peaceful purposes and activities protected by international law, in particular the United Nations Convention on the Law of the Sea;

6. *Views with concern* the increase in drug trafficking and related crimes, including drug abuse, and calls upon the international community and the States members of the zone to promote regional and international cooperation to combat all aspects of the problem of drugs and related offences;

7. *Recognizes,* in the light of the number, magnitude and complexity of natural disasters and other emergencies, the need to continue to strengthen the coordination of humanitarian assistance by States members of the zone, so as to ensure a timely and effective response;

8. *Welcomes* the offer by Benin to host the sixth meeting of the States members of the zone;

9. *Requests* the relevant organizations, organs and bodies of the United Nations system to render all appropriate assistance that States members of the zone may seek in their joint efforts to implement the declaration of the zone of peace and cooperation of the South Atlantic;

10. *Requests* the Secretary-General to keep the implementation of resolution 41/11 and subsequent resolutions on the matter under review and to submit a report to the General Assembly at its sixtieth session, taking into account, inter alia, the views expressed by Member States;

11. *Decides* to include in the provisional agenda of its sixtieth session the item entitled "Zone of peace and cooperation of the South Atlantic".

Indian Ocean

In 2003, the Ad Hoc Committee on the Indian Ocean (New York, 8 July) [A/58/29] continued to consider approaches for achieving the goals of the 1971 Declaration of the Indian Ocean as a Zone of Peace, adopted by the General Assembly in resolution 2832(XXVI) [YUN 1971, p. 34].

Pursuant to Assembly resolution 56/16 [YUN 2001, p. 529], the Chairman of the Committee, following informal consultations with Committee members, concluded that the objectives of the 1971 Declaration remained valid. However, in view of the complexities and difficulties involved in the implementation of the Declaration, further time would be needed before any discussion could begin on practical measures to ensure peace and stability in the Indian Ocean, and the Assembly should give more time and allow the

Chairman to continue his consultations. Three permanent members of the Security Council (France, United Kingdom, United States) continued their non-participation in the Committee's work. The Committee remained convinced that the participation of all permanent Council members and the major maritime users of the Indian Ocean in its work would assist the progress of a mutually beneficial dialogue aimed at developing conditions of peace, security and stability in the region.

The Committee reaffirmed the conclusions of its 1994 [YUN 1994, p. 155], 1995 [YUN 1995, p. 182] and 1996 [YUN 1996, p. 512] sessions and re-emphasized the need to foster consensual, step-by-step approaches. The Chairman was requested to continue informal consultations and report to the Assembly at its sixtieth (2005) session.

GENERAL ASSEMBLY ACTION

On 8 December [meeting 71], the General Assembly, on the recommendation of the First (Disarmament and International Security) Committee [A/58/453], adopted **resolution 58/29** by recorded vote (130-3-42) [agenda item 64].

Implementation of the Declaration of the Indian Ocean as a Zone of Peace

The General Assembly,

Recalling the Declaration of the Indian Ocean as a Zone of Peace, contained in its resolution 2832(XXVI) of 16 December 1971, and recalling also its resolutions 54/47 of 1 December 1999 and 56/16 of 29 November 2001 and other relevant resolutions,

Recalling also the report of the Meeting of the Littoral and Hinterland States of the Indian Ocean held in July 1979,

Recalling further paragraph 102 of the Final Document of the Thirteenth Conference of Heads of State or Government of Non-Aligned Countries, held at Kuala Lumpur, from 20 to 25 February 2003, in which it was noted, inter alia, that the Chairperson of the Ad Hoc Committee on the Indian Ocean would continue his informal consultations on the future work of the Committee,

Emphasizing the need to foster consensual approaches that are conducive to the pursuit of such endeavours,

Noting the initiatives taken by countries of the region to promote cooperation, in particular economic cooperation, in the Indian Ocean area and the possible contribution of such initiatives to overall objectives of a zone of peace,

Convinced that the participation of all permanent members of the Security Council and the major maritime users of the Indian Ocean in the work of the Ad Hoc Committee is important and would assist the progress of a mutually beneficial dialogue to develop conditions of peace, security and stability in the Indian Ocean region,

Considering that greater efforts and more time are required to develop a focused discussion on practical measures to ensure conditions of peace, security and stability in the Indian Ocean region,

Having considered the report of the Ad Hoc Committee on the Indian Ocean,

1. *Takes note* of the report of the Ad Hoc Committee on the Indian Ocean;
2. *Reiterates its conviction* that the participation of all permanent members of the Security Council and the major maritime users of the Indian Ocean in the work of the Ad Hoc Committee is important and would greatly facilitate the development of a mutually beneficial dialogue to advance peace, security and stability in the Indian Ocean region;
3. *Requests* the Chairman of the Ad Hoc Committee to continue his informal consultations with the members of the Committee and to report through the Committee to the General Assembly at its sixtieth session;
4. *Requests* the Secretary-General to continue to render, within existing resources, all necessary assistance to the Ad Hoc Committee, including the provision of summary records;
5. *Decides* to include in the provisional agenda of its sixtieth session the item entitled "Implementation of the Declaration of the Indian Ocean as a Zone of Peace".

RECORDED VOTE ON RESOLUTION 58/29:

In favour: Afghanistan, Algeria, Antigua and Barbuda, Argentina, Armenia, Australia, Azerbaijan, Bahamas, Bahrain, Bangladesh, Barbados, Belarus, Belize, Bhutan, Bolivia, Botswana, Brazil, Brunei Darussalam, Burkina Faso, Burundi, Cambodia, Cameroon, Cape Verde, Central African Republic, Chile, China, Colombia, Comoros, Congo, Costa Rica, Côte d'Ivoire, Cuba, Democratic People's Republic of Korea, Djibouti, Dominican Republic, Ecuador, Egypt, El Salvador, Eritrea, Ethiopia, Fiji, Gabon, Gambia, Ghana, Grenada, Guatemala, Guinea, Guinea-Bissau, Guyana, Haiti, Honduras, India, Indonesia, Iran, Jamaica, Japan, Jordan, Kazakhstan, Kenya, Kuwait, Kyrgyzstan, Lao People's Democratic Republic, Lebanon, Lesotho, Libyan Arab Jamahiriya, Madagascar, Malawi, Malaysia, Maldives, Mali, Marshall Islands, Mauritania, Mauritius, Mexico, Mongolia, Morocco, Mozambique, Myanmar, Namibia, Nauru, Nepal, New Zealand, Nicaragua, Niger, Nigeria, Oman, Pakistan, Panama, Papua New Guinea, Paraguay, Peru, Philippines, Portugal, Qatar, Republic of Korea, Russian Federation, Rwanda, Saint Lucia, Saint Vincent and the Grenadines, Samoa, Saudi Arabia, Senegal, Seychelles, Singapore, Somalia, South Africa, Sri Lanka, Sudan, Suriname, Swaziland, Syrian Arab Republic, Tajikistan, Thailand, Timor-Leste, Togo, Tonga, Trinidad and Tobago, Tunisia, Turkmenistan, Uganda, Ukraine, United Arab Emirates, United Republic of Tanzania, Uruguay, Uzbekistan, Vanuatu, Venezuela, Viet Nam, Yemen, Zambia.

Against: France, United Kingdom, United States.

Abstaining: Albania, Andorra, Austria, Belgium, Bosnia and Herzegovina, Bulgaria, Canada, Croatia, Cyprus, Czech Republic, Denmark, Estonia, Finland, Georgia, Germany, Greece, Hungary, Iceland, Ireland, Israel, Italy, Latvia, Liechtenstein, Lithuania, Luxembourg, Malta, Micronesia, Monaco, Netherlands, Norway, Poland, Republic of Moldova, Romania, San Marino, Serbia and Montenegro, Slovakia, Slovenia, Spain, Sweden, Switzerland, The former Yugoslav Republic of Macedonia, Turkey.

Decolonization

The General Assembly's Special Committee on the Situation with regard to the Implementation of the Declaration on the Granting of Independence to Colonial Countries and Peoples (Special Committee on decolonization) held its annual session in New York in two parts—12 February and 11 April (first part); and 2, 4, 9, 12, 16, 18 and 23 June (second part). It considered various aspects of the implementation of the 1960 Declaration, adopted by the Assembly in resolution 1514(XV) [YUN 1960, p. 49], including general decolonization issues and the situation of individual Non-Self-Governing Territories (NSGTs). In accordance with Assembly resolution 57/140 [YUN 2002, p. 557], the Special Committee transmitted to the Assembly the report on its 2003 activities [A/58/23].

Decade for the Eradication of Colonialism

Caribbean regional seminar

As part of its efforts to implement the plan of action for the Second International Decade for the Eradication of Colonialism (2001-2010) [YUN 2001, p. 530], declared by the General Assembly in resolution 55/146 [YUN 2000, p. 548], the Special Committee on decolonization [A/58/23] organized a Caribbean regional seminar (The Valley, Anguilla, 20-22 May) to assess the situation in NSGTs. It was the first such seminar to be held in an NSGT.

Participants reaffirmed the Special Committee's role as the primary vehicle for fostering the decolonization process and expediting the goals of the Second Decade. The Seminar recommended that the Special Committee continue to participate actively in monitoring the evolution of NSGTs towards self-determination and play a catalytic role in the search for a specific solution for each of the remaining NSGTs, in accordance with the freely expressed wishes of the peoples concerned and in conformity with the UN Charter, Assembly resolutions 1514(XV) and 1541(XV) [YUN 1960, p. 509] on the transmission of information called for under Article 73 e of the Charter, and other relevant UN resolutions and decisions. It noted the proposal by the Special Committee Chairman to expedite a work programme with specified time frames, based on a case-by-case approach, in order to complete the decolonization process by the end of the Second Decade, and recommended that the Special Committee implement the programme, in consultation and coordination with the peoples of the NSGTs in which there were no pending sovereignty disputes and with the administering Powers concerned.

Noting the call by all elected representatives of the United Kingdom's NSGTs for greater devolution of powers from the governors to locally elected representatives, seminar participants recommended that the United Kingdom and representatives of the Territories further discuss the issue. It recommended that the Special Committee consult, in the immediate future, with the United Kingdom on the application of its policy of constitutional modernization in NSGTs under its administration in the context of resolution 1541(XV), and discuss with it, in consultation with the representatives of the NSGTs concerned, which Territories in the region would achieve full self-government in the near future and, accordingly, be subject to "de-listing".

The seminar reaffirmed the right of the peoples of NSGTs to be informed about the full range of available self-determination options and their implications, and urged the United Kingdom to include the examination of those options in its discussions with the Territories. It recommended that the Special Committee conduct studies on the implications of those options for Bermuda and Caribbean NSGTs and welcomed the possibility of assistance in that regard from UNDP. The seminar also recommended that UNDP provide capacity-building and institutional development assistance for all Caribbean NSGTs that were reviewing their self-determination options.

Participants welcomed the presence at the seminar of a senior-level representative of the United Kingdom and looked forward to further engagement and cooperation between the Special Committee and that country. They regretted the absence of the other administering Power in the region.

GENERAL ASSEMBLY ACTION

On 9 December [meeting 72], the General Assembly adopted **resolution 58/111** [draft: A/58/L.21] by recorded vote (154-2-8) [agenda item 19].

Implementation of the Declaration on the Granting of Independence to Colonial Countries and Peoples

The General Assembly,

Having examined the report of the Special Committee on the Situation with regard to the Implementation of the Declaration on the Granting of Independence to Colonial Countries and Peoples,

Recalling its resolution 1514(XV) of 14 December 1960, containing the Declaration on the Granting of Independence to Colonial Countries and Peoples, and all its subsequent resolutions concerning the implementation of the Declaration, most recently resolution 57/140 of 11 December 2002, as well as the relevant resolutions of the Security Council,

Bearing in mind the declaration of the period 2001-2010 as the Second International Decade for the Eradication of Colonialism, and the need to examine ways to ascertain the wishes of the peoples of the Non-Self-Governing Territories on the basis of resolution 1514(XV) and other relevant resolutions on decolonization,

Recognizing that the eradication of colonialism has been one of the priorities of the Organization and continues to be one of its priorities for the decade that began in 2001,

Reconfirming the need to take measures to eliminate colonialism before 2010, as called for in its resolution 55/146 of 8 December 2000,

Reiterating its conviction of the need for the eradication of colonialism, as well as of racial discrimination and violations of basic human rights,

Noting with satisfaction the achievements of the Special Committee in contributing to the effective and complete implementation of the Declaration and other relevant resolutions of the United Nations on decolonization,

Stressing the importance of the participation of the administering Powers in the work of the Special Committee,

Noting with concern that the non-participation of certain administering Powers has adversely affected the implementation of the mandate and work of the Special Committee,

Noting with satisfaction the cooperation and active participation of some administering Powers in the work of the Special Committee,

Noting that the other administering Powers have now agreed to work informally with the Special Committee,

Taking note of the consultations and agreements between the parties concerned in some Non-Self-Governing Territories and the action taken by the Secretary-General in relation to certain Non-Self-Governing Territories,

Aware of the pressing need of newly independent and emerging States for assistance from the United Nations and its system of organizations in the economic, social and other fields,

Aware also of the pressing need of many of the remaining Non-Self-Governing Territories, many of which are small island Territories, for economic, social and other assistance from the United Nations and the organizations of its system,

Taking special note of the fact that, for the first time in a Non-Self-Governing Territory, the Special Committee held a Caribbean regional seminar on advancing the decolonization process in the Caribbean and Bermuda in Anguilla from 20 to 22 May 2003,

1. *Reaffirms* its resolution 1514(XV) and all other resolutions and decisions on decolonization, including its resolution 55/146, in which it declares the period 2001-2010 the Second International Decade for the Eradication of Colonialism, and calls upon the administering Powers, in accordance with those resolutions, to take all necessary steps to enable the peoples of the Non-Self-Governing Territories concerned to exercise fully as soon as possible their right to self-determination, including independence;

2. *Reaffirms once again* that the existence of colonialism in any form or manifestation, including economic exploitation, is incompatible with the Charter of the United Nations, the Declaration on the Granting of Independence to Colonial Countries and Peoples and the Universal Declaration of Human Rights;

3. *Reaffirms its determination* to continue to take all steps necessary to bring about the complete and speedy eradication of colonialism and the faithful observance by all States of the relevant provisions of the Charter, the Declaration on the Granting of Independence to Colonial Countries and Peoples and the Universal Declaration of Human Rights;

4. *Affirms once again its support* for the aspirations of the peoples under colonial rule to exercise their right to self-determination, including independence, in accordance with relevant resolutions of the United Nations on decolonization;

5. *Approves* the report of the Special Committee on the Situation with regard to the Implementation of the Declaration on the Granting of Independence to Colonial Countries and Peoples covering its work during 2003, including the programme of work envisaged for 2004;

6. *Calls upon* the administering Powers to cooperate fully with the Special Committee to finalize before the end of 2004 a constructive programme of work on a case-by-case basis for the Non-Self-Governing Territories to facilitate the implementation of the mandate of the Special Committee and the relevant resolutions on decolonization, including resolutions on specific Territories;

7. *Welcomes* the ongoing consultations between the Special Committee and New Zealand, as administering Power for Tokelau, with the participation of representatives of the people of Tokelau, with a view to advancing the programme of work on the question of Tokelau;

8. *Requests* the Special Committee to continue to seek suitable means for the immediate and full implementation of the Declaration and to carry out the actions approved by the General Assembly regarding the International Decade for the Eradication of Colonialism and the Second International Decade in all Territories that have not yet exercised their right to self-determination, including independence, and in particular:

(*a*) To formulate specific proposals to bring about an end to colonialism and to report thereon to the General Assembly at its fifty-ninth session;

(*b*) To continue to examine the implementation by Member States of resolution 1514(XV) and other relevant resolutions on decolonization;

(*c*) To continue to examine the political, economic and social situation in the Non-Self-Governing Territories, and to recommend, as appropriate, to the General Assembly the most suitable steps to be taken to enable the populations of those Territories to exercise their right to self-determination, including independence, in accordance with relevant resolutions on decolonization, including resolutions on specific Territories;

(*d*) To finalize before the end of 2004 a constructive programme of work on a case-by-case basis for the Non-Self-Governing Territories to facilitate the implementation of the mandate of the Special Committee and the relevant resolutions on decolonization, including resolutions on specific Territories;

(*e*) To continue to dispatch visiting missions to the Non-Self-Governing Territories in accordance with relevant resolutions on decolonization, including resolutions on specific Territories;

(*f*) To conduct seminars, as appropriate, for the purpose of receiving and disseminating information on the work of the Special Committee, and to facilitate participation by the peoples of the Non-Self-Governing Territories in those seminars;

(*g*) To take all necessary steps to enlist worldwide support among Governments, as well as national and international organizations, for the achievement of the objectives of the Declaration and the implementation of the relevant resolutions of the United Nations;

(h) To observe annually the Week of Solidarity with the Peoples of Non-Self-Governing Territories;

9. *Calls upon* all States, in particular the administering Powers, as well as the specialized agencies and other organizations of the United Nations system, to give effect within their respective spheres of competence to the recommendations of the Special Committee for the implementation of the Declaration and other relevant resolutions of the United Nations;

10. *Calls upon* the administering Powers to ensure that the economic activities in the Non-Self-Governing Territories under their administration do not adversely affect the interests of the peoples but instead promote development, and to assist them in the exercise of their right to self-determination;

11. *Urges* the administering Powers concerned to take effective measures to safeguard and guarantee the inalienable rights of the peoples of the Non-Self-Governing Territories to their natural resources, including land, and to establish and maintain control over the future development of those resources, and requests the administering Powers to take all necessary steps to protect the property rights of the peoples of those Territories;

12. *Urges* all States, directly and through their action in the specialized agencies and other organizations of the United Nations system, to provide moral and material assistance to the peoples of the Non-Self-Governing Territories, and requests that the administering Powers take steps to enlist and make effective use of all possible assistance, on both a bilateral and a multilateral basis, in the strengthening of the economies of those Territories;

13. *Reaffirms* that the United Nations visiting missions to the Territories are an effective means of ascertaining the situation in the Territories, as well as the wishes and aspirations of their inhabitants, and calls upon the administering Powers to continue to cooperate with the Special Committee in the discharge of its mandate and to facilitate visiting missions to the Territories;

14. *Calls upon* the administering Powers that have not participated formally in the work of the Special Committee to do so at its session in 2004;

15. *Requests* the Secretary-General, the specialized agencies and other organizations of the United Nations system to provide economic, social and other assistance to the Non-Self-Governing Territories and to continue to do so, as appropriate, after they exercise their right to self-determination, including independence;

16. *Requests* the Secretary-General to provide the Special Committee with the facilities and services required for the implementation of the present resolution, as well as of the other resolutions and decisions on decolonization adopted by the General Assembly and the Special Committee.

RECORDED VOTE ON RESOLUTION 58/111:

In favour: Algeria, Andorra, Angola, Antigua and Barbuda, Argentina, Armenia, Australia, Austria, Bahrain, Bangladesh, Barbados, Belarus, Belize, Benin, Bhutan, Bolivia, Bosnia and Herzegovina, Botswana, Brazil, Brunei Darussalam, Bulgaria, Burkina Faso, Burundi, Cambodia, Cameroon, Canada, Cape Verde, Central African Republic, Chile, China, Colombia, Comoros, Costa Rica, Côte d'Ivoire, Croatia, Cuba, Cyprus, Czech Republic, Democratic People's Republic of Korea, Denmark, Djibouti, Dominican Republic, Ecuador, Egypt, El Salvador, Equatorial Guinea, Eritrea, Ethiopia, Fiji, France, Gambia, Ghana, Greece, Grenada, Guatemala, Guinea, Guyana, Haiti, Honduras, Hungary, Iceland, India, Indonesia, Iran, Ireland, Italy, Jamaica, Japan, Jordan, Kazakhstan, Kenya, Kuwait, Kyrgyzstan, Lao People's Democratic Republic, Latvia, Lebanon, Lesotho, Libyan Arab Jamahiriya, Liechtenstein, Lithuania, Luxembourg, Madagascar, Malaysia, Maldives, Mali, Malta, Mauritania, Mauritius, Mexico, Monaco, Mongolia, Morocco, Mozambique, Myanmar, Namibia, Nauru, Nepal, Netherlands, New Zealand, Nicaragua, Niger, Nigeria, Norway, Oman, Pakistan, Panama, Papua New Guinea, Paraguay, Peru, Philippines, Poland, Qatar, Republic of Korea, Republic of Moldova, Romania, Russian Federation, Saint Kitts and Nevis, Saint Lucia, Saint Vincent and the Grenadines, Samoa, San Marino, Saudi Arabia, Senegal, Serbia and Montenegro, Singapore, Slovakia, Slovenia, Somalia, South Africa, Spain, Sri Lanka, Sudan, Suriname, Sweden, Switzerland, Syrian Arab Republic, Tajikistan, Thailand, The former Yugoslav Republic of Macedonia, Timor-Leste, Togo, Tonga, Trinidad and Tobago, Turkey, Turkmenistan, Tuvalu, Ukraine, United Arab Emirates, United Republic of Tanzania, Venezuela, Viet Nam, Yemen, Zambia, Zimbabwe.

Against: United Kingdom, United States.

Abstaining: Albania, Belgium, Estonia, Finland, Georgia, Germany, Israel, Micronesia.

Speaking after the vote, the United Kingdom said that it continued to find some elements of the text unacceptable. However, it remained committed to modernizing its relationship with its overseas Territories, taking into account the views of the peoples of those Territories, and to furthering the process of informal dialogue with the Special Committee on decolonization.

Implementation by international organizations

In a March report [A/58/66], the Secretary-General stated that he had brought General Assembly resolution 57/133 [YUN 2002, p. 561] to the attention of the specialized agencies and other international institutions associated with the United Nations and invited them to submit information regarding their implementation of activities in support of NSGTs. Replies received from six agencies or institutions were summarized in an April report of the Economic and Social Council President on consultations held with the Chairman of the Special Committee on decolonization [E/2003/47]. According to the information provided, a number of specialized agencies and organizations continued to extend programmes of assistance to NSGTs from within their own budgetary resources, in addition to their respective contributions as executing agencies of projects funded by UNDP.

ECONOMIC AND SOCIAL COUNCIL ACTION

On 24 July [meeting 47], the Economic and Social Council adopted **resolution 2003/51** [draft: E/2003/L.33] by recorded vote (32-0-20) [agenda item 9].

Implementation of the Declaration on the Granting of Independence to Colonial Countries and Peoples by the specialized agencies and the international institutions associated with the United Nations

The Economic and Social Council,

Having examined the report of the Secretary-General and the report of the President of the Economic and Social Council containing the information submitted by the specialized agencies and the international institutions associated with the United Nations on their activities with regard to the implementation of the Declaration on the Granting of Independence to Colonial Countries and Peoples,

Having heard the statement by the representative of the Special Committee on the Situation with regard to the Implementation of the Declaration on the Granting of Independence to Colonial Countries and Peoples,

Recalling General Assembly resolutions 1514(XV) of 14 December 1960 and 1541(XV) of 15 December 1960, the resolutions of the Special Committee and other relevant resolutions and decisions, including in particular Economic and Social Council resolution 2002/30 of 25 July 2002,

Bearing in mind the relevant provisions of the final documents of the successive Conferences of Heads of State or Government of Non-Aligned Countries and of the resolutions adopted by the Assembly of Heads of State and Government of the Organization of African Unity, now the African Union, the South Pacific Forum, now the Pacific Islands Forum, and the Caribbean Community,

Conscious of the need to facilitate the implementation of the Declaration,

Welcoming the participation, in the capacity of observer, of those Non-Self-Governing Territories that are associate members of the regional commissions in United Nations world conferences in the economic and social sphere, subject to the rules of procedure of the General Assembly and in accordance with relevant United Nations resolutions and decisions, including resolutions and decisions of the Assembly and the Special Committee on specific Territories, as well as in the World Summit on Sustainable Development, held in Johannesburg, South Africa, from 26 August to 4 September 2002,

Noting that the large majority of the remaining Non-Self-Governing Territories are small island Territories,

Welcoming the assistance extended to Non-Self-Governing Territories by certain specialized agencies and other organizations of the United Nations system, in particular the United Nations Development Programme,

Stressing that, because the development options of the small island Non-Self-Governing Territories are limited, there are special challenges to planning for and implementing sustainable development and that those Territories will be constrained in meeting the challenges without the continued cooperation and assistance of the specialized agencies and other organizations of the United Nations system,

Stressing also the importance of securing the necessary resources for funding expanded assistance programmes for the peoples concerned and the need to enlist the support of all major funding institutions within the United Nations system in that regard,

Reaffirming the mandates of the specialized agencies and other organizations of the United Nations system to take all the appropriate measures, within their respective spheres of competence, to ensure the full implementation of resolution 1514(XV) and other relevant resolutions,

Expressing its appreciation to the African Union, the Pacific Islands Forum, the Caribbean Community and other regional organizations for the continued cooperation and assistance they have extended to the specialized agencies and other organizations of the United Nations system in this regard,

Expressing its conviction that closer contacts and consultations between and among the specialized agencies and other organizations of the United Nations system and regional organizations help to facilitate the effective formulation of programmes of assistance to the peoples concerned,

Mindful of the imperative need to keep under continuous review the activities of the specialized agencies and other organizations of the United Nations system in the implementation of the various United Nations decisions relating to decolonization,

Bearing in mind the extremely fragile economies of the small island Non-Self-Governing Territories and their vulnerability to natural disasters, such as hurricanes, cyclones and sea-level rise, and recalling the relevant resolutions of the General Assembly,

Recalling General Assembly resolution 57/140 of 11 December 2002, entitled "Implementation of the Declaration on the Granting of Independence to Colonial Countries and Peoples",

1. *Takes note* of the report of the President of the Economic and Social Council containing the information submitted by the specialized agencies and the international institutions associated with the United Nations on their activities with regard to the implementation of the Declaration on the Granting of Independence to Colonial Countries and Peoples, and endorses the observations and suggestions arising therefrom;

2. *Also takes note* of the report of the Secretary-General;

3. *Recommends* that all States intensify their efforts in the specialized agencies and other organizations of the United Nations system to ensure the full and effective implementation of the Declaration, contained in resolution 1514(XV), and other relevant resolutions of the United Nations;

4. *Reaffirms* that the specialized agencies and other organizations and institutions of the United Nations system should continue to be guided by the relevant resolutions of the United Nations in their efforts to contribute to the implementation of the Declaration and all other relevant General Assembly resolutions;

5. *Also reaffirms* that the recognition by the General Assembly, the Security Council and other United Nations organs of the legitimacy of the aspirations of the peoples of the Non-Self-Governing Territories to exercise their right to self-determination entails, as a corollary, the extension of all appropriate assistance to those peoples;

6. *Expresses its appreciation* to those specialized agencies and other organizations of the United Nations system that have continued to cooperate with the United Nations and the regional and subregional organizations in the implementation of resolution 1514(XV) and other relevant resolutions of the United Nations, and requests all the specialized agencies and other organizations of the United Nations system to

implement the relevant provisions of those resolutions;

7. *Requests* the specialized agencies and other organizations of the United Nations system and international and regional organizations to examine and review conditions in each Territory so as to take appropriate measures to accelerate progress in the economic and social sectors of the Territories;

8. *Requests* the specialized agencies and the international institutions associated with the United Nations and regional organizations to strengthen existing measures of support and to formulate appropriate programmes of assistance to the remaining Non-Self-Governing Territories, within the framework of their respective mandates, in order to accelerate progress in the economic and social sectors of those Territories;

9. *Recommends* that the executive heads of the specialized agencies and other organizations of the United Nations system formulate, with the active cooperation of the regional organizations concerned, concrete proposals for the full implementation of the relevant resolutions of the United Nations and submit the proposals to their governing and legislative organs;

10. *Also recommends* that the specialized agencies and other organizations of the United Nations system continue to review, at the regular meetings of their governing bodies, the implementation of resolution 1514(XV) and other relevant resolutions of the United Nations;

11. *Welcomes* the continuing initiative exercised by the United Nations Development Programme in maintaining close liaison among the specialized agencies and other organizations of the United Nations system and in providing assistance to the peoples of the Non-Self-Governing Territories;

12. *Encourages* Non-Self-Governing Territories to take steps to establish and/or strengthen disaster preparedness and management institutions and policies;

13. *Requests* the administering Powers concerned to facilitate, when appropriate, the participation of appointed and elected representatives of Non-Self-Governing Territories in the meetings and conferences on specific Territories held by the specialized agencies and other organizations of the United Nations system, in accordance with relevant United Nations resolutions and decisions, including resolutions and decisions of the General Assembly and the Special Committee on the Situation with regard to the Implementation of the Declaration on the Granting of Independence to Colonial Countries and Peoples, so that the Territories may benefit from the related activities of those agencies and organizations;

14. *Recommends* that all Governments intensify their efforts in the specialized agencies and other organizations of the United Nations system of which they are members to accord priority to the question of providing assistance to the peoples of the Non-Self-Governing Territories;

15. *Draws the attention* of the Special Committee to the present resolution and to the discussion held on the subject at the substantive session of 2003 of the Council;

16. *Welcomes* the adoption by the Economic Commission for Latin America and the Caribbean of resolution 574(XXVII) of 16 May 1998 calling for the necessary mechanisms for its associate members, including small island Non-Self-Governing Territories, to participate in the special sessions of the General Assembly, subject to the rules of procedure of the Assembly, to review and assess the implementation of the plans of action of those United Nations world conferences in which the Territories originally participated in the capacity of observer, and in the work of the Council and its subsidiary bodies;

17. *Requests* the President of the Economic and Social Council to continue to maintain close contact on these matters with the Chairman of the Special Committee and to report thereon to the Council;

18. *Requests* the Secretary-General to follow the implementation of the present resolution, paying particular attention to cooperation and integration arrangements for maximizing the efficiency of the assistance activities undertaken by various organizations of the United Nations system, and to report thereon to the Council at its substantive session of 2004;

19. *Decides* to keep these questions under continuous review.

RECORDED VOTE ON RESOLUTION 2003/51:

In favour: Argentina, Benin, Bhutan, Brazil, Burundi, Chile, China, Congo, Cuba, Ecuador, Egypt, El Salvador, Ethiopia, Ghana, Guatemala, India, Iran, Jamaica, Kenya, Libyan Arab Jamahiriya, Malaysia, Mozambique, Nepal, Nicaragua, Nigeria, Pakistan, Peru, Saudi Arabia, Senegal, South Africa, Uganda, Zimbabwe.

Against: None.

Abstaining: Andorra, Australia, Azerbaijan, Finland, France, Georgia, Germany, Greece, Hungary, Ireland, Italy, Japan, Netherlands, Portugal, Republic of Korea, Russian Federation, Sweden, Ukraine, United Kingdom, United States.

GENERAL ASSEMBLY ACTION

On 9 December [meeting 72], the General Assembly, on the recommendation of the Fourth (Special Political and Decolonization) Committee [A/58/478], adopted **resolution 58/104** by recorded vote (116-0-55) [agenda items 89 & 12].

Implementation of the Declaration on the Granting of Independence to Colonial Countries and Peoples by the specialized agencies and the international institutions associated with the United Nations

The General Assembly,

Having considered the item entitled "Implementation of the Declaration on the Granting of Independence to Colonial Countries and Peoples by the specialized agencies and the international institutions associated with the United Nations",

Having also considered the report of the Secretary-General on the item,

Having examined the chapter of the report of the Special Committee on the Situation with regard to the Implementation of the Declaration on the Granting of Independence to Colonial Countries and Peoples relating to the item,

Recalling its resolutions 1514(XV) of 14 December 1960 and 1541(XV) of 15 December 1960 and the resolutions of the Special Committee, as well as other relevant resolutions and decisions, including in particular Economic and Social Council resolution 2002/30 of 25 July 2002,

Bearing in mind the relevant provisions of the final documents of the successive Conferences of Heads of State or Government of Non-Aligned Countries and of the resolutions adopted by the Assembly of Heads of State and Government of the African Union, the Pacific Islands Forum and the Caribbean Community,

Conscious of the need to facilitate the implementation of the Declaration on the Granting of Independence to Colonial Countries and Peoples, contained in resolution 1514(XV),

Noting that the large majority of the remaining Non-Self-Governing Territories are small island Territories,

Welcoming the assistance extended to Non-Self-Governing Territories by certain specialized agencies and other organizations of the United Nations system, in particular the United Nations Development Programme,

Also welcoming the current participation in the capacity of observers of those Non-Self-Governing Territories that are associate members of regional commissions in the world conferences in the economic and social sphere, subject to the rules of procedure of the General Assembly and in accordance with relevant United Nations resolutions and decisions, including resolutions and decisions of the Assembly and the Special Committee on specific Territories,

Noting that only some specialized agencies and other organizations of the United Nations system have been involved in providing assistance to Non-Self-Governing Territories,

Stressing that, because the development options of the small island Non-Self-Governing Territories are limited, there are special challenges to planning for and implementing sustainable development and that those Territories will be constrained in meeting the challenges without the continuing cooperation and assistance of the specialized agencies and other organizations of the United Nations system,

Stressing also the importance of securing the necessary resources for funding expanded programmes of assistance for the peoples concerned and the need to enlist the support of all major funding institutions within the United Nations system in that regard,

Reaffirming the mandates of the specialized agencies and other organizations of the United Nations system to take all appropriate measures, within their respective spheres of competence, to ensure the full implementation of General Assembly resolution 1514(XV) and other relevant resolutions,

Expressing its appreciation to the African Union, the Pacific Islands Forum, the Caribbean Community and other regional organizations for the continued cooperation and assistance they have extended to the specialized agencies and other organizations of the United Nations system in this regard,

Expressing its conviction that closer contacts and consultations between and among the specialized agencies and other organizations of the United Nations system and regional organizations help to facilitate the effective formulation of programmes of assistance to the peoples concerned,

Mindful of the imperative need to keep under continuous review the activities of the specialized agencies and other organizations of the United Nations system in the implementation of the various United Nations decisions relating to decolonization,

Bearing in mind the extremely fragile economies of the small island Non-Self-Governing Territories and their vulnerability to natural disasters, such as hurricanes, cyclones and sea-level rise, and recalling the relevant resolutions of the General Assembly,

Recalling General Assembly resolution 57/133 of 11 December 2002 on the implementation of the Declaration by the specialized agencies and the international institutions associated with the United Nations,

1. *Takes note* of the report of the Secretary-General;

2. *Recommends* that all States intensify their efforts in the specialized agencies and other organizations of the United Nations system to ensure the full and effective implementation of the Declaration on the Granting of Independence to Colonial Countries and Peoples, contained in General Assembly resolution 1514(XV), and other relevant resolutions of the United Nations;

3. *Reaffirms* that the specialized agencies and other organizations and institutions of the United Nations system should continue to be guided by the relevant resolutions of the United Nations in their efforts to contribute to the implementation of the Declaration and all other relevant General Assembly resolutions;

4. *Reaffirms also* that the recognition by the General Assembly, the Security Council and other United Nations organs of the legitimacy of the aspirations of the peoples of the Non-Self-Governing Territories to exercise their right to self-determination entails, as a corollary, the extension of all appropriate assistance to those peoples;

5. *Expresses its appreciation* to those specialized agencies and other organizations of the United Nations system that have continued to cooperate with the United Nations and the regional and subregional organizations in the implementation of General Assembly resolution 1514(XV) and other relevant resolutions of the United Nations, and requests all the specialized agencies and other organizations of the United Nations system to implement the relevant provisions of those resolutions;

6. *Requests* the specialized agencies and other organizations of the United Nations system and international and regional organizations to examine and review conditions in each Territory so as to take appropriate measures to accelerate progress in the economic and social sectors of the Territories;

7. *Urges* those specialized agencies and organizations of the United Nations system that have not yet provided assistance to Non-Self-Governing Territories to do so as soon as possible;

8. *Requests* the specialized agencies and other organizations and institutions of the United Nations system and regional organizations to strengthen existing measures of support and formulate appropriate programmes of assistance to the remaining Non-Self-Governing Territories, within the framework of their respective mandates, in order to accelerate progress in the economic and social sectors of those Territories;

9. *Requests* the specialized agencies and other organizations of the United Nations system concerned to provide information on:

(*a*) Environmental problems facing the Non-Self-Governing Territories;

(*b*) The impact of natural disasters, such as hurricanes and volcanic eruptions, and other environmental problems, such as beach and coastal erosion and droughts, on those Territories;

(c) Ways and means to assist the Territories to fight drug trafficking, money-laundering and other illegal and criminal activities;

(d) The illegal exploitation of the marine resources of the Territories and the need to utilize those resources for the benefit of the peoples of the Territories;

10. *Recommends* that the executive heads of the specialized agencies and other organizations of the United Nations system formulate, with the active cooperation of the regional organizations concerned, concrete proposals for the full implementation of the relevant resolutions of the United Nations and submit the proposals to their governing and legislative organs;

11. *Also recommends* that the specialized agencies and other organizations of the United Nations system continue to review at the regular meetings of their governing bodies the implementation of General Assembly resolution 1514(XV) and other relevant resolutions of the United Nations;

12. *Welcomes* the continuing initiative exercised by the United Nations Development Programme in maintaining close liaison among the specialized agencies and other organizations of the United Nations system and in providing assistance to the peoples of the Non-Self-Governing Territories;

13. *Encourages* the Non-Self-Governing Territories to take steps to establish and/or strengthen disaster preparedness and management institutions and policies;

14. *Requests* the administering Powers concerned to facilitate, when appropriate, the participation of appointed and elected representatives of Non-Self-Governing Territories in the relevant meetings and conferences of the specialized agencies and other organizations of the United Nations system, in accordance with relevant United Nations resolutions and decisions, including resolutions and decisions of the General Assembly and the Special Committee on the Situation with regard to the Implementation of the Declaration on the Granting of Independence to Colonial Countries and Peoples on specific Territories, so that the Territories may benefit from the related activities of those agencies and organizations;

15. *Recommends* that all Governments intensify their efforts in the specialized agencies and other organizations of the United Nations system of which they are members to accord priority to the question of providing assistance to the peoples of the Non-Self-Governing Territories;

16. *Requests* the Secretary-General to continue to assist the specialized agencies and other organizations of the United Nations system in working out appropriate measures for implementing the relevant resolutions of the United Nations and to prepare for submission to the relevant bodies, with the assistance of those agencies and organizations, a report on the action taken in implementation of the relevant resolutions, including the present resolution, since the circulation of his previous report;

17. *Commends* the Economic and Social Council for its debate and resolution on this question, and requests it to continue to consider, in consultation with the Special Committee, appropriate measures for the coordination of the policies and activities of the specialized agencies and other organizations of the United Nations system in implementing the relevant resolutions of the General Assembly;

18. *Requests* the specialized agencies to report periodically to the Secretary-General on the implementation of the present resolution;

19. *Requests* the Secretary-General to transmit the present resolution to the governing bodies of the appropriate specialized agencies and international institutions associated with the United Nations so that those bodies may take the necessary measures to implement the resolution, and also requests the Secretary-General to report to the General Assembly at its fifty-ninth session on the implementation of the present resolution;

20. *Requests* the Special Committee to continue to examine the question and to report thereon to the General Assembly at its fifty-ninth session.

RECORDED VOTE ON RESOLUTION 58/104:

In favour: Afghanistan, Algeria, Angola, Antigua and Barbuda, Argentina, Australia, Bahamas, Bahrain, Bangladesh, Barbados, Belarus, Belize, Benin, Bhutan, Bolivia, Botswana, Brazil, Brunei Darussalam, Burkina Faso, Burundi, Cambodia, Cameroon, Cape Verde, Central African Republic, Chile, China, Colombia, Comoros, Costa Rica, Côte d'Ivoire, Cuba, Democratic People's Republic of Korea, Djibouti, Dominican Republic, Ecuador, Egypt, El Salvador, Equatorial Guinea, Eritrea, Ethiopia, Fiji, Gambia, Ghana, Grenada, Guatemala, Guinea, Guinea-Bissau, Guyana, Haiti, Honduras, India, Indonesia, Iran, Jamaica, Jordan, Kenya, Kuwait, Lao People's Democratic Republic, Lebanon, Lesotho, Libyan Arab Jamahiriya, Madagascar, Malaysia, Maldives, Mali, Mauritania, Mauritius, Mexico, Mongolia, Morocco, Mozambique, Myanmar, Namibia, Nauru, Nepal, New Zealand, Nicaragua, Niger, Nigeria, Oman, Pakistan, Panama, Papua New Guinea, Paraguay, Peru, Philippines, Qatar, Saint Kitts and Nevis, Saint Lucia, Saint Vincent and the Grenadines, Samoa, Saudi Arabia, Senegal, Seychelles, Singapore, South Africa, Sri Lanka, Sudan, Suriname, Swaziland, Syrian Arab Republic, Thailand, Timor-Leste, Togo, Tonga, Trinidad and Tobago, Tunisia, Tuvalu, United Arab Emirates, United Republic of Tanzania, Uruguay, Venezuela, Viet Nam, Yemen, Zambia, Zimbabwe.

Against: None.

Abstaining: Albania, Andorra, Armenia, Austria, Azerbaijan, Belgium, Bosnia and Herzegovina, Bulgaria, Canada, Croatia, Cyprus, Czech Republic, Denmark, Estonia, Finland, France, Georgia, Germany, Greece, Hungary, Iceland, Ireland, Israel, Italy, Japan, Kazakhstan, Kyrgyzstan, Latvia, Liechtenstein, Lithuania, Luxembourg, Malta, Micronesia, Monaco, Netherlands, Norway, Poland, Portugal, Republic of Korea, Republic of Moldova, Romania, Russian Federation, San Marino, Serbia and Montenegro, Slovakia, Slovenia, Spain, Sweden, Switzerland, Tajikistan, The former Yugoslav Republic of Macedonia, Turkey, Ukraine, United Kingdom, United States.

Military activities and arrangements in colonial countries

In accordance with General Assembly decision 57/525 [YUN 2002, p. 564], Secretariat working papers on Bermuda [A/AC.109/2003/13], Guam [A/AC.109/2003/15] and the United States Virgin Islands [A/AC.109/2003/1] contained information on, among other subjects, military activities and arrangements by the administering Powers in those Territories.

Economic and other activities affecting the interests of NSGTs

The Special Committee on decolonization continued consideration of economic and other activities affecting the interests of the peoples of NSGTs. It had before it Secretariat working papers containing information on, among other things, economic conditions, with particular reference to foreign economic activities, in American Samoa [A/AC.109/2003/12], Anguilla [A/AC.109/2003/11], Bermuda [A/AC.109/2003/13], the British Virgin Islands [A/AC.109/2003/5], the Cayman Islands [A/AC.109/2003/9], Guam [A/AC.109/2003/15], Montserrat [A/AC.109/2003/2], the Turks and Caicos Islands [A/AC.109/2003/8] and the United States Virgin Islands [A/AC.109/2003/1].

GENERAL ASSEMBLY ACTION

On 9 December [meeting 72], the General Assembly, on the recommendation of the Fourth Committee [A/58/477], adopted **resolution 58/103** by recorded vote (164-2-3) [agenda item 88].

Economic and other activities which affect the interests of the peoples of the Non-Self-Governing Territories

The General Assembly,

Having considered the item entitled "Economic and other activities which affect the interests of the peoples of the Non-Self-Governing Territories",

Having examined the chapter of the report of the Special Committee on the Situation with regard to the Implementation of the Declaration on the Granting of Independence to Colonial Countries and Peoples relating to the item,

Recalling its resolution 1514(XV) of 14 December 1960, as well as all other relevant Assembly resolutions including, in particular, resolutions 46/181 of 19 December 1991 and 55/146 of 8 December 2000,

Reaffirming the solemn obligation of the administering Powers under the Charter of the United Nations to promote the political, economic, social and educational advancement of the inhabitants of the Territories under their administration and to protect the human and natural resources of those Territories against abuses,

Reaffirming also that any economic or other activity that has a negative impact on the interests of the peoples of the Non-Self-Governing Territories and on the exercise of their right to self-determination in conformity with the Charter of the United Nations and General Assembly resolution 1514(XV) is contrary to the purposes and principles of the Charter,

Reaffirming further that the natural resources are the heritage of the peoples of the Non-Self-Governing Territories, including the indigenous populations,

Aware of the special circumstances of the geographical location, size and economic conditions of each Territory, and bearing in mind the need to promote the economic stability, diversification and strengthening of the economy of each Territory,

Conscious of the particular vulnerability of the small Territories to natural disasters and environmental degradation,

Conscious also that foreign economic investment, when undertaken in collaboration with the peoples of the Non-Self-Governing Territories and in accordance with their wishes, could make a valid contribution to the socio-economic development of the Territories and also to the exercise of their right to self-determination,

Concerned about any activities aimed at exploiting the natural and human resources of the Non-Self-Governing Territories to the detriment of the interests of the inhabitants of those Territories,

Bearing in mind the relevant provisions of the final documents of the successive Conferences of Heads of State or Government of Non-Aligned Countries and of the resolutions adopted by the Assembly of Heads of State and Government of the African Union, the Pacific Islands Forum and the Caribbean Community,

1. *Reaffirms* the right of peoples of Non-Self-Governing Territories to self-determination in conformity with the Charter of the United Nations and with General Assembly resolution 1514(XV), containing the Declaration on the Granting of Independence to Colonial Countries and Peoples, as well as their right to the enjoyment of their natural resources and their right to dispose of those resources in their best interest;

2. *Affirms* the value of foreign economic investment undertaken in collaboration with the peoples of the Non-Self-Governing Territories and in accordance with their wishes in order to make a valid contribution to the socio-economic development of the Territories;

3. *Reaffirms* the responsibility of the administering Powers under the Charter of the United Nations to promote the political, economic, social and educational advancement of the Non-Self-Governing Territories, and reaffirms the legitimate rights of their peoples over their natural resources;

4. *Reaffirms its concern* about any activities aimed at the exploitation of the natural resources that are the heritage of the peoples of the Non-Self-Governing Territories, including the indigenous populations, in the Caribbean, the Pacific and other regions, and of their human resources, to the detriment of their interests, and in such a way as to deprive them of their right to dispose of those resources;

5. *Affirms* the need to avoid any economic and other activities that adversely affect the interests of the peoples of the Non-Self-Governing Territories;

6. *Calls once again upon* all Governments that have not yet done so to take, in accordance with the relevant provisions of General Assembly resolution 2621(XXV) of 12 October 1970, legislative, administrative or other measures in respect of their nationals and the bodies corporate under their jurisdiction that own and operate enterprises in the Non-Self-Governing Territories that are detrimental to the interests of the inhabitants of those Territories, in order to put an end to such enterprises;

7. *Reiterates* that the damaging exploitation and plundering of the marine and other natural resources of the Non-Self-Governing Territories, in violation of the relevant resolutions of the United Nations, are a threat to the integrity and prosperity of those Territories;

8. *Invites* all Governments and organizations of the United Nations system to take all possible measures to ensure that the permanent sovereignty of the peoples of the Non-Self-Governing Territories over their natural resources is fully respected and safeguarded in accordance with the relevant resolutions of the United Nations on decolonization;

9. *Urges* the administering Powers concerned to take effective measures to safeguard and guarantee

the inalienable right of the peoples of the Non-Self-Governing Territories to their natural resources and to establish and maintain control over the future development of those resources, and requests the administering Powers to take all necessary steps to protect the property rights of the peoples of those Territories in accordance with the relevant resolutions of the United Nations on decolonization;

10. *Calls upon* the administering Powers concerned to ensure that no discriminatory working conditions prevail in the Territories under their administration and to promote in each Territory a fair system of wages applicable to all the inhabitants without any discrimination;

11. *Requests* the Secretary-General to continue, through all means at his disposal, to inform world public opinion of any activity that affects the exercise of the right of the peoples of the Non-Self-Governing Territories to self-determination in conformity with the Charter of the United Nations and General Assembly resolution 1514(XV);

12. *Appeals* to the mass media, trade unions and non-governmental organizations, as well as individuals, to continue their efforts to promote the economic well-being of the peoples of the Non-Self-Governing Territories;

13. *Decides* to follow the situation in the Non-Self-Governing Territories so as to ensure that all economic activities in those Territories are aimed at strengthening and diversifying their economies in the interest of their peoples, including the indigenous populations, and at promoting the economic and financial viability of those Territories;

14. *Requests* the Special Committee on the Situation with regard to the Implementation of the Declaration on the Granting of Independence to Colonial Countries and Peoples to continue to examine this question and to report thereon to the General Assembly at its fifty-ninth session.

RECORDED VOTE ON RESOLUTION 58/103:

In favour: Afghanistan, Albania, Algeria, Andorra, Angola, Antigua and Barbuda, Argentina, Armenia, Australia, Austria, Bahamas, Bahrain, Bangladesh, Barbados, Belarus, Belgium, Belize, Benin, Bhutan, Bolivia, Bosnia and Herzegovina, Botswana, Brazil, Brunei Darussalam, Bulgaria, Burkina Faso, Burundi, Cambodia, Cameroon, Canada, Cape Verde, Central African Republic, Chile, China, Colombia, Comoros, Costa Rica, Croatia, Cuba, Cyprus, Czech Republic, Democratic People's Republic of Korea, Denmark, Djibouti, Dominican Republic, Ecuador, Egypt, El Salvador, Equatorial Guinea, Eritrea, Estonia, Ethiopia, Fiji, Finland, Gambia, Georgia, Germany, Ghana, Greece, Grenada, Guatemala, Guinea, Guinea-Bissau, Guyana, Haiti, Honduras, Hungary, Iceland, India, Indonesia, Iran, Ireland, Italy, Jamaica, Japan, Jordan, Kazakhstan, Kenya, Kuwait, Kyrgyzstan, Lao People's Democratic Republic, Latvia, Lebanon, Lesotho, Libyan Arab Jamahiriya, Liechtenstein, Lithuania, Luxembourg, Madagascar, Malaysia, Maldives, Mali, Malta, Mauritania, Mauritius, Mexico, Mongolia, Morocco, Mozambique, Myanmar, Namibia, Nauru, Nepal, Netherlands, New Zealand, Nicaragua, Niger, Nigeria, Norway, Oman, Pakistan, Panama, Papua New Guinea, Paraguay, Peru, Philippines, Poland, Portugal, Qatar, Republic of Korea, Republic of Moldova, Romania, Russian Federation, Saint Kitts and Nevis, Saint Lucia, Saint Vincent and the Grenadines, Samoa, San Marino, Saudi Arabia, Senegal, Serbia and Montenegro, Seychelles, Singapore, Slovakia, Slovenia, South Africa, Spain, Sri Lanka, Sudan, Suriname, Swaziland, Sweden, Switzerland, Syrian Arab Republic, Tajikistan, Thailand, The former Yugoslav Republic of Macedonia, Timor-Leste, Togo, Tonga, Trinidad and Tobago, Tunisia, Turkey, Turkmenistan, Tuvalu, Ukraine, United Arab Emirates, United Republic of Tanzania, Uruguay, Venezuela, Viet Nam, Yemen, Zambia, Zimbabwe.

Against: Israel, United States.

Abstaining: France, Micronesia, United Kingdom.

Dissemination of information

The Special Committee on decolonization held consultations in June with representatives of the UN Departments of Political Affairs and of Public Information (DPI) on the dissemination of information on decolonization. It also considered a report of the Secretary-General on DPI activities on the topic from June 2002 to May 2003 [A/AC.109/2003/18].

GENERAL ASSEMBLY ACTION

On 9 December [meeting 72], the General Assembly, on the recommendation of the Special Committee on decolonization [A/58/23], adopted **resolution 58/110** by recorded vote (162-3) [agenda item 19].

Dissemination of information on decolonization

The General Assembly,

Having examined the chapter of the report of the Special Committee on the Situation with regard to the Implementation of the Declaration on the Granting of Independence to Colonial Countries and Peoples relating to the dissemination of information on decolonization and publicity for the work of the United Nations in the field of decolonization,

Recalling its resolution 1514(XV) of 14 December 1960, containing the Declaration on the Granting of Independence to Colonial Countries and Peoples, and other resolutions and decisions of the United Nations concerning the dissemination of information on decolonization, in particular resolution 57/139 of 11 December 2002,

Recognizing the need for flexible, practical and innovative approaches towards reviewing the options of self-determination for the peoples of Non-Self-Governing Territories with a view to achieving the goals of the Second International Decade for the Eradication of Colonialism,

Reiterating the importance of dissemination of information as an instrument for furthering the aims of the Declaration, and mindful of the role of world public opinion in effectively assisting the peoples of Non-Self-Governing Territories to achieve self-determination,

Recognizing the role played by the administering Powers in transmitting information to the Secretary-General in accordance with the terms of Article 73 *e* of the Charter of the United Nations,

Aware of the role of non-governmental organizations in the dissemination of information on decolonization,

1. *Approves* the activities in the field of dissemination of information on decolonization undertaken by the Department of Public Information and the Department of Political Affairs of the Secretariat in accordance with the relevant resolutions of the United Nations on decolonization;

2. *Considers it important* to continue its efforts to ensure the widest possible dissemination of information on decolonization, with particular emphasis on the options of self-determination available for the peoples of Non-Self-Governing Territories;

3. *Requests* the Department of Political Affairs and the Department of Public Information to take into ac-

count the suggestions of the Special Committee on the Situation with regard to the Implementation of the Declaration on the Granting of Independence to Colonial Countries and Peoples to continue their efforts to take measures through all the media available, including publications, radio and television, as well as the Internet, to give publicity to the work of the United Nations in the field of decolonization and, inter alia:

(a) To continue to collect, prepare and disseminate, particularly to the Territories, basic material on the issue of self-determination of the peoples of Non-Self-Governing Territories;

(b) To seek the full cooperation of the administering Powers in the discharge of the tasks referred to above;

(c) To maintain a working relationship with the appropriate regional and intergovernmental organizations, particularly in the Pacific and Caribbean regions, by holding periodic consultations and exchanging information;

(d) To encourage the involvement of non-governmental organizations in the dissemination of information on decolonization;

(e) To report to the Special Committee on measures taken in the implementation of the present resolution;

4. *Requests* all States, including the administering Powers, to continue to extend their cooperation in the dissemination of information referred to in paragraph 2 above;

5. *Requests* the Special Committee to follow the implementation of the present resolution and to report thereon to the General Assembly at its fifty-ninth session.

RECORDED VOTE ON RESOLUTION 58/110:

In favour: Albania, Algeria, Andorra, Angola, Antigua and Barbuda, Argentina, Armenia, Australia, Austria, Bahrain, Bangladesh, Barbados, Belarus, Belgium, Belize, Benin, Bhutan, Bolivia, Bosnia and Herzegovina, Botswana, Brazil, Brunei Darussalam, Bulgaria, Burkina Faso, Cambodia, Cameroon, Canada, Cape Verde, Central African Republic, Chile, China, Colombia, Comoros, Costa Rica, Côte d'Ivoire, Croatia, Cuba, Cyprus, Czech Republic, Democratic People's Republic of Korea, Denmark, Djibouti, Dominican Republic, Ecuador, Egypt, El Salvador, Equatorial Guinea, Eritrea, Estonia, Ethiopia, Fiji, Finland, France, Gambia, Georgia, Germany, Ghana, Greece, Grenada, Guatemala, Guinea, Guinea-Bissau, Guyana, Haiti, Honduras, Hungary, Iceland, India, Indonesia, Iran, Ireland, Italy, Jamaica, Japan, Jordan, Kazakhstan, Kenya, Kuwait, Kyrgyzstan, Lao People's Democratic Republic, Latvia, Lebanon, Lesotho, Libyan Arab Jamahiriya, Liechtenstein, Lithuania, Luxembourg, Madagascar, Malaysia, Maldives, Mali, Malta, Mauritania, Mauritius, Mexico, Monaco, Mongolia, Morocco, Mozambique, Myanmar, Namibia, Nauru, Nepal, Netherlands, New Zealand, Nicaragua, Niger, Nigeria, Norway, Oman, Pakistan, Panama, Papua New Guinea, Paraguay, Peru, Philippines, Poland, Portugal, Qatar, Republic of Korea, Republic of Moldova, Romania, Russian Federation, Saint Kitts and Nevis, Saint Lucia, Saint Vincent and the Grenadines, Samoa, San Marino, Saudi Arabia, Senegal, Serbia and Montenegro, Singapore, Slovakia, Slovenia, Somalia, South Africa, Spain, Sri Lanka, Sudan, Suriname, Sweden, Switzerland, Syrian Arab Republic, Tajikistan, Thailand, The former Yugoslav Republic of Macedonia, Timor-Leste, Togo, Tonga, Trinidad and Tobago, Tunisia, Turkey, Turkmenistan, Tuvalu, Ukraine, United Arab Emirates, United Republic of Tanzania, Venezuela, Viet Nam, Yemen, Zambia, Zimbabwe.

Against: Israel, United Kingdom, United States.

Speaking after the vote, the United Kingdom stated that it continued to view the obligation the text placed on the Secretariat to publicize decolonization issues as an unwarranted drain on scarce UN resources.

Information on Territories

In response to General Assembly resolution 57/131 [YUN 2002, p. 567], the Secretary-General submitted an April report [A/58/69] indicating the dates of transmittal of information on economic, social and educational conditions in NSGTs for the years 2001-2004, under Article 73 *e* of the Charter of the United Nations.

GENERAL ASSEMBLY ACTION

On 9 December [meeting 72], the General Assembly, on the recommendation of the Fourth Committee [A/58/476], adopted **resolution 58/102** by recorded vote (163-0-6) [agenda item 87].

Information from Non-Self-Governing Territories transmitted under Article 73 *e* of the Charter of the United Nations

The General Assembly,

Recalling its resolution 1970(XVIII) of 16 December 1963, in which it requested the Special Committee on the Situation with regard to the Implementation of the Declaration on the Granting of Independence to Colonial Countries and Peoples to study the information transmitted to the Secretary-General in accordance with Article 73 *e* of the Charter of the United Nations and to take such information fully into account in examining the situation with regard to the implementation of the Declaration, contained in General Assembly resolution 1514(XV) of 14 December 1960,

Recalling also its resolution 57/131 of 11 December 2002, in which it requested the Special Committee to continue to discharge the functions entrusted to it under resolution 1970(XVIII),

Stressing the importance of timely transmission by the administering Powers of adequate information under Article 73 *e* of the Charter, in particular in relation to the preparation by the Secretariat of the working papers on the Territories concerned,

Having examined the report of the Secretary-General,

1. *Reaffirms* that, in the absence of a decision by the General Assembly itself that a Non-Self-Governing Territory has attained a full measure of self-government in terms of Chapter XI of the Charter of the United Nations, the administering Power concerned should continue to transmit information under Article 73 *e* of the Charter with respect to that Territory;

2. *Requests* the administering Powers concerned to transmit or continue to transmit to the Secretary-General the information prescribed in Article 73 *e* of the Charter, as well as the fullest possible information on political and constitutional developments in the Territories concerned, within a maximum period of six months following the expiration of the administrative year in those Territories;

3. *Requests* the Secretary-General to continue to ensure that adequate information is drawn from all available published sources in connection with the preparation of the working papers relating to the Territories concerned;

4. *Requests* the Special Committee on the Situation with regard to the Implementation of the Declaration

on the Granting of Independence to Colonial Countries and Peoples to continue to discharge the functions entrusted to it under General Assembly resolution 1970(XVIII), in accordance with established procedures.

RECORDED VOTE ON RESOLUTION 58/102:

In favour: Afghanistan, Albania, Algeria, Andorra, Antigua and Barbuda, Argentina, Armenia, Australia, Austria, Bahamas, Bahrain, Bangladesh, Barbados, Belarus, Belgium, Belize, Benin, Bhutan, Bolivia, Bosnia and Herzegovina, Botswana, Brazil, Brunei Darussalam, Bulgaria, Burkina Faso, Burundi, Cambodia, Cameroon, Canada, Cape Verde, Central African Republic, Chile, China, Colombia, Comoros, Costa Rica, Côte d'Ivoire, Croatia, Cuba, Cyprus, Czech Republic, Democratic People's Republic of Korea, Denmark, Djibouti, Dominican Republic, Ecuador, Egypt, El Salvador, Equatorial Guinea, Eritrea, Estonia, Ethiopia, Fiji, Finland, Gambia, Georgia, Germany, Ghana, Greece, Grenada, Guatemala, Guinea, Guinea-Bissau, Guyana, Haiti, Honduras, Hungary, Iceland, India, Indonesia, Iran, Ireland, Italy, Jamaica, Japan, Jordan, Kazakhstan, Kenya, Kuwait, Kyrgyzstan, Lao People's Democratic Republic, Latvia, Lebanon, Lesotho, Libyan Arab Jamahiriya, Liechtenstein, Lithuania, Luxembourg, Madagascar, Malaysia, Maldives, Mali, Malta, Mauritania, Mauritius, Mexico, Mongolia, Morocco, Mozambique, Myanmar, Namibia, Nauru, Nepal, Netherlands, New Zealand, Nicaragua, Niger, Nigeria, Norway, Oman, Pakistan, Panama, Papua New Guinea, Paraguay, Peru, Philippines, Poland, Portugal, Qatar, Republic of Korea, Republic of Moldova, Romania, Russian Federation, Saint Kitts and Nevis, Saint Lucia, Saint Vincent and the Grenadines, Samoa, San Marino, Saudi Arabia, Senegal, Serbia and Montenegro, Singapore, Slovakia, Slovenia, South Africa, Spain, Sri Lanka, Sudan, Suriname, Swaziland, Sweden, Switzerland, Syrian Arab Republic, Tajikistan, Thailand, The former Yugoslav Republic of Macedonia, Timor-Leste, Togo, Tonga, Trinidad and Tobago, Tunisia, Turkey, Turkmenistan, Tuvalu, Ukraine, United Arab Emirates, United Republic of Tanzania, Uruguay, Venezuela, Viet Nam, Yemen, Zambia, Zimbabwe.

Against: None.

Abstaining: Angola, France, Israel, Micronesia, United Kingdom, United States.

Study and training

In response to General Assembly resolution 57/134 [YUN 2002, p. 568], the Secretary-General reported on offers of study and training scholarships for inhabitants of NSGTs during the period 11 June 2002 to 1 April 2003 by the following Member States: Antigua and Barbuda, Argentina, Mexico, Sweden and the United Kingdom [A/58/71]. Fifty-six Member States and one non-member State had made such offers over the years.

GENERAL ASSEMBLY ACTION

On 9 December [meeting 72], the General Assembly, on the recommendation of the Fourth Committee [A/58/479], adopted **resolution 58/105** without vote [agenda item 90].

Offers by Member States of study and training facilities for inhabitants of Non-Self-Governing Territories

The General Assembly,

Recalling its resolution 57/134 of 11 December 2002,

Having examined the report of the Secretary-General on offers by Member States of study and training facilities for inhabitants of Non-Self-Governing Territories, prepared pursuant to its resolution 845(IX) of 22 November 1954,

Conscious of the importance of promoting the educational advancement of the inhabitants of Non-Self-Governing Territories,

Strongly convinced that the continuation and expansion of offers of scholarships is essential in order to meet the increasing need of students from Non-Self-Governing Territories for educational and training assistance, and considering that students in those Territories should be encouraged to avail themselves of such offers,

1. *Takes note* of the report of the Secretary-General;

2. *Expresses its appreciation* to those Member States that have made scholarships available to the inhabitants of Non-Self-Governing Territories;

3. *Invites* all States to make or continue to make generous offers of study and training facilities to the inhabitants of those Territories that have not yet attained self-government or independence and, wherever possible, to provide travel funds to prospective students;

4. *Urges* the administering Powers to take effective measures to ensure the widespread and continuous dissemination in the Territories under their administration of information relating to offers of study and training facilities made by States and to provide all the necessary facilities to enable students to avail themselves of such offers;

5. *Requests* the Secretary-General to report to the General Assembly at its fifty-ninth session on the implementation of the present resolution;

6. *Draws the attention* of the Special Committee on the Situation with regard to the Implementation of the Declaration on the Granting of Independence to Colonial Countries and Peoples to the present resolution.

Visiting missions

In June, the Special Committee on decolonization considered the question of sending visiting missions to NSGTs [A/58/23]. It adopted a resolution in which it stressed the need to dispatch periodic visiting missions to facilitate the full implementation of the 1960 Declaration on decolonization, called on administering Powers to receive those missions in the Territories under their administration, and asked its Chairman to enter into consultations with the administering Power of Guam to facilitate a mission to that Territory.

The Committee recommended to the General Assembly for adoption draft resolutions on 11 small NSGTs (see p. 616) and on Tokelau (see p. 613). In its draft resolutions, the Committee endorsed a number of conclusions and recommendations concerning the sending of visiting missions to the Territories.

Puerto Rico

In accordance with the Special Committee's 2002 resolution concerning the self-determination and independence of Puerto Rico [YUN 2002, p. 568], the Committee's Rapporteur, in a May report [A/AC.109/2003/L.3], provided information on

Puerto Rico, including recent political, military and economic developments and UN action.

Following its usual practice, the Committee acceded to requests for hearings from representatives of a number of organizations, who presented their views on 9 June [A/58/23]. The Committee adopted a resolution without vote, by which it reaffirmed the inalienable right of the people of Puerto Rico to self-determination and independence; called on the United States to assume its responsibility of expediting a process to allow the Puerto Rican people to exercise that right; urged the United States to return the island of Vieques to the people of Puerto Rico; and requested the Rapporteur to report in 2004 on the resolution's implementation.

Territories under review

Falkland Islands (Malvinas)

The Special Committee on decolonization considered the question of the Falkland Islands (Malvinas) on 16 June [A/58/23], when it examined a Secretariat working paper on constitutional and political developments, mine clearance, and economic and social conditions in that Territory [A/AC.109/2003/17]. The Special Committee adopted a resolution [A/AC.109/2003/24] requesting Argentina and the United Kingdom to consolidate the current process of dialogue and cooperation through the resumption of negotiations in order to find, as soon as possible, a peaceful solution to the sovereignty dispute.

Argentina, in a 3 January letter [A/57/704], transmitted to the Secretary-General a press release recalling its objective to recover full sovereignty over the Malvinas Islands, South Georgia and the South Sandwich Islands and surrounding maritime areas through peaceful means; reaffirmed its conviction that the resumption of negotiations on the sovereignty issue would contribute to the establishment of a framework conducive to achieving a fair and lasting solution to the dispute; and stated that it was acting in the belief that interim understandings reached with the United Kingdom under the formula for safeguarding sovereignty rights in the South Atlantic were also contributing to the search for a solution. The United Kingdom responded on the same date [A/57/708], stating that it had no doubt about its sovereignty over the Falkland Islands, South Georgia and the South Sandwich Islands and rejecting as unfounded Argentina's claim to sovereignty.

Addressing the General Assembly during the general debate on 25 September [A/58/PV.11], Argentina's President, Néstor Carlos Kirchner, stated that his country was fully willing to negotiate in order to settle conclusively the sovereignty dispute, and urged the United Kingdom to resume bilateral negotiations. In exercise of its right of reply, the United Kingdom, in a 25 September statement [A/58/408], welcomed Argentina's resolve, which it shared, to engage in positive bilateral exchanges of practical cooperation in the South Atlantic. However, while such exchanges contributed further to the mutual understanding embodied in the 1999 Anglo-Argentine joint statement [YUN 1999, p. 536], nothing in that statement compromised the United Kingdom's position on sovereignty. On 16 June, elected representatives of the Islands again asked the Special Committee to recognize that they, like any other people, were entitled to exercise the right of self-determination and reiterated that the people of the Falkland Islands did not wish to change the status of the islands. The United Kingdom remained committed to the right of the people of the Falkland Islands to determine their own future, and there would be no change in the island's sovereignty unless the islanders wished it. It was confident that its relationship with Argentina would develop and believed that cooperation between the two countries on matters of mutual interest would enable them to manage their differences, while assisting in the development of confidence and trust in the South Atlantic.

Argentina, in an 11 November letter to the Assembly President [A/58/602], pointed out that the persons from the Malvinas Islands who participated in the 16 June meeting of the Special Committee on decolonization did so as petitioners, without the representative status claimed by the United Kingdom in its statement and rejected by Argentina. With respect to the United Kingdom's reference to self-determination, Argentina reaffirmed the need to apply the principle of territorial integrity to the special and particular colonial situation under the item on the question of the Malvinas Islands; it cited Assembly resolution 2065(XX) [YUN 1965, p. 578], which called on both countries to resume bilateral negotiations with a view to finding a just, peaceful and definitive solution to the sovereignty dispute, bearing in mind the interests of the islands' population. Argentina clarified that, in addition to the 1999 joint statement, other provisional understandings with the United Kingdom relating to sovereignty safeguarded Argentina's position in the dispute over the Territories, and that those understandings, in addition to resolving some practical problems in the South Atlantic, were conducive to the renewal of bilateral negotiations on sovereignty.

In a 20 October letter to the Secretary-General [A/58/527], Argentina reiterated its rejection of the 1999 "White Paper on Partnership for Peace and Prosperity: Britain and the Overseas Territories" [YUN 2001, p. 542] and the designation of the Malvinas, South Georgia and the South Sandwich Islands as British Overseas Territories, as well as any unilateral changes in the situation while the sovereignty dispute was unresolved. The letter recalled several Assembly resolutions recognizing the existence of a sovereignty dispute regarding those Territories and recommending that it be resolved through bilateral negotiations. Argentina reaffirmed its sovereignty over the islands and surrounding maritime spaces, which were an integral part of its national territory.

By **decision 58/511** of 5 November, the Assembly deferred consideration of the item on the Falkland Islands (Malvinas) and included it in the provisional agenda of its fifty-ninth (2004) session.

Gibraltar

The Special Committee on decolonization took up consideration of the question of Gibraltar on 4 June [A/58/23]. Before it was a Secretariat working paper describing political developments and economic and social conditions in the Territory, and setting forth the positions of the United Kingdom (the administering Power), Gibraltar and Spain concerning Gibraltar's future status [A/AC.109/2003/3].

On 12 July 2002, British Foreign Secretary Jack Straw had announced before the House of Commons that, within the context of the Anglo-Spanish negotiations on Gibraltar, the United Kingdom and Spain were in broad agreement on principles that should underpin a lasting settlement, including that Britain and Spain should share sovereignty over the Territory, which should retain its British traditions and its institutions, including its Government, House of Assembly, courts and police service, as well as the right to British nationality. It would gain the right to Spanish nationality. Gibraltar could choose to participate fully in the European Union (EU) single market and other EU arrangements. If a comprehensive settlement was reached by all parties based on those principles, the whole package would be put to the people of Gibraltar to decide in a referendum.

Gibraltar's Chief Minister Peter Caruana, speaking before the Fourth Committee on 3 October 2002, condemned the Foreign Secretary's formal statement regarding shared sovereignty with Spain. He explained that he had declined an invitation to participate in the Anglo-Spanish negotiations because he would not have had an equal say or been given assurances of not being excluded from agreements reached between Spain and the United Kingdom, and his presence would have been used to flesh out details of a predetermined agreement on joint sovereignty. He urged the Committee to refer the case to the International Court of Justice for an advisory opinion, amend its annual draft decision on Gibraltar, which continued to favour Spain and the United Kingdom, in order to give the people of Gibraltar an equal and separate voice in the dialogue, and affirm the primacy of the wishes of the people of Gibraltar and the principle of self-determination.

On 4 October 2002, the United Kingdom representative said that the agreement on co-sovereignty was a historic one and questioned the purpose of the referendum being organized by Gibraltar since no proposal for such a vote had been put forward. He made it clear that it was the British Government's responsibility, in consultation with Gibraltar, to oversee the organization and timing of any referendum once a comprehensive settlement with Spain had been reached.

In a 7 November 2002 referendum held by the Government of Gibraltar on the issue of Anglo-Spanish joint sovereignty, 98.97 per cent of voters rejected the concept. On 8 November 2002, the British Minister for Europe stated that the United Kingdom had always made clear that there would be no change in Gibraltar's sovereignty without the consent of the people in a referendum, and there were no such proposals on the table. Spain's Vice-President, its Minister for Foreign Affairs and its Permanent Representative to the United Nations, among other officials, stated that the 7 November referendum had no legal validity and stressed the importance of continuing the Anglo-Spanish negotiations.

In his 2003 New Year message, Gibraltar's Chief Minister said that Gibraltar remained willing to negotiate in a structured, reasonable, open-agenda dialogue with no predetermined outcome, but dialogue should not be confused with sovereignty transfer negotiations. He proposed that formal negotiations with the United Kingdom should begin in 2003 on the constitutional reform proposals made in 2002 [YUN 2002, p. 570].

A later Secretariat working paper [A/AC.109/2004/7] reported that, on 15 July 2003, the Foreign Affairs Committee of the British House of Commons recommended that the Foreign and Commonwealth Office withdraw its joint sovereignty proposal and proceed with establishing normal and cooperative relations between Gibraltar and Spain. In September, the Secretary of State for

Foreign and Commonwealth Affairs responded that the British Government fully agreed that normal and cooperative relations between Spain and Gibraltar were highly desirable, and it would continue to press the Spanish Government to that end, but its position regarding the issue of joint sovereignty remained the same (see p. 610).

The Chief Minister of Gibraltar said that the Gibraltar Parliament had unanimously adopted a resolution asking the Special Committee to visit Gibraltar, and he urged the Fourth Committee to ask the Special Committee to do so. With respect to the principle of sharing sovereignty between Spain and the United Kingdom, the Chief Minister reaffirmed that it was unacceptable to the people of Gibraltar, who saw it as a way to perpetuate the colonization of their Territory by two Powers instead of one.

Spain's representative replied that Gibraltar, by inviting the Special Committee to send a visiting mission to the Territory and launching a petition of support for the mission, was attempting to garner support for its opposition to the principle of territorial integrity traditionally recognized by the United Nations and international law. Stressing its opposition to such a mission, Spain declared that in cases related to sovereignty, the sending of a visiting mission of the Special Committee had to be approved by both the administering Power and the other party to the dispute.

Joint talks between Spain and the United Kingdom on Gibraltar were not held in 2003, but Gibraltar's Chief Minister, in a speech during Gibraltar's National Day (10 September), warned Spain and the United Kingdom that if they restarted the joint sovereignty negotiations, Gibraltar would restart its political campaign to oppose them, adding that no Government of Gibraltar had ever been, or would ever be, willing to negotiate the transfer of any part of Gibraltar's sovereignty to Spain.

On 22 December, Gibraltar's Chief Minister submitted the 2002 constitutional reform proposals formally to the British Secretary for Foreign and Commonwealth Affairs and suggested that the two sides meet informally to discuss the proposals and the way forward. The Secretary of State acknowledged the importance of the proposals and said they would receive careful consideration; he would meet the Chief Minister soon for an initial discussion and was looking forward to discussing them in due course, with a view to the further development of a modern and appropriate relationship with Gibraltar.

After hearing statements by the Deputy Chief Minister of Gibraltar, the Leader of the Opposition in Gibraltar and the representative of Spain, the Special Committee decided to continue consideration of the question in 2004.

GENERAL ASSEMBLY ACTION

In December, the General Assembly, on the recommendation of the Fourth Committee [A/58/480], adopted **decision 58/526** without vote [agenda item 19].

Question of Gibraltar

At its 72nd plenary meeting, on 9 December 2003, the General Assembly, on the recommendation of the Special Political and Decolonization Committee (Fourth Committee), adopted the following text:

"The General Assembly, recalling its decision 57/526 of 11 December 2002, and recalling at the same time that the statement agreed to by the Governments of Spain and the United Kingdom of Great Britain and Northern Ireland at Brussels on 27 November 1984 stipulates, inter alia, the following:

'The establishment of a negotiating process aimed at overcoming all the differences between them over Gibraltar and at promoting cooperation on a mutually beneficial basis on economic, cultural, touristic, aviation, military and environmental matters. Both sides accept that the issues of sovereignty will be discussed in that process. The British Government will fully maintain its commitment to honour the wishes of the people of Gibraltar as set out in the preamble of the 1969 Constitution',

takes note of the fact that, as part of this process, the Ministers for Foreign Affairs of Spain and the United Kingdom of Great Britain and Northern Ireland hold annual meetings alternately in each country, the most recent of which were held in Barcelona on 20 November 2001 and in London on 4 February 2002, and urges both Governments to continue their negotiations with the object of reaching a definitive solution to the problem of Gibraltar in the light of relevant resolutions of the General Assembly and in the spirit of the Charter of the United Nations."

New Caledonia

In accordance with the 1998 Nouméa Accord on New Caledonia's future status [YUN 1998, p. 574], the transfer of power from France (the administering Power) continued in 2003. The Special Committee on decolonization considered the question of the Territory on 12 June [A/58/23]. Before it was a Secretariat working paper describing the political situation and economic data and developments in the Territory [A/AC.109/2003/7].

A later Secretariat working paper [A/AC.109/2004/11] reported that, according to France, the institutions created under the Nouméa Accord continued to function properly throughout 2003, and the Territory's pro-independence (Front de libération nationale kanak socialiste (FLNKS)) and pro-integration (formerly Rassemblement pour la Calédonie dans la République and still usually referred to as RPCR) political parties continued to be committed to the Accord's implementation. During the year, the Institut de formation des personnels administratifs and the Office des postes et télécommunications were transferred and steps were taken to finalize the transfer of services for labour inspection, foreign trade, primary education, mining and energy.

In spite of considerable institutional and administrative advances, progress continued to be hindered by friction between the pro-integration and pro-independence parties, owing to differing interpretations of the concept of collegiality in Government, and other sensitive issues, including voter eligibility and mining initiatives. According to France, the New Caledonian political scenario was more calm and less bipolar in 2003. However, according to the Economist Intelligence Unit, a provider of country, industry and management analysis, discontent among the indigenous Kanak population over the pace of the implementation of the Nouméa Accord was expected to fuel political tensions, and there was growing concern among FLNKS members about its lack of representation in the Government. The July visit of French President Jacques Chirac further increased tensions between the pro- and anti-independence parties. President Chirac stressed France's role as a partner in the transfer of further jurisdictions to New Caledonia and pledged that France would fully implement and respect the Nouméa Accord and help to develop further education, environment, regional cooperation and metallurgical projects.

Prior to President Chirac's visit, the committee of Nouméa Accord signatories, including the French Minister for Overseas Territories and representatives of RPCR and FLNKS, met in June in Kone, New Caledonia. According to France, the parties affirmed in a joint declaration that the institutions created by the Accord were working well and that the transfer of powers was continuing. The committee members reaffirmed their intentions to meet frequently and to follow closely the implementation of the Accord and ongoing reforms.

In September, a visiting French parliamentary delegation also concluded that implementation of the Nouméa Accord was proceeding well. However, the Kanak community argued that the reforms outlined in the Accord were being implemented too slowly, especially those relating to voters' residency requirements [YUN 1999, p. 538], which remained unsettled pending the scheduling of a joint session of the French National Assembly and the Senate to ratify a constitutional amendment on the issue; President Chirac promised a resolution of the question by 2007. A long-delayed FLNKS congress was to be held in December, during which its two main constituent parties, the Union calédonienne and Palika, hoped to resolve their disputes and draw up a common platform for the May 2004 provincial elections. FLNKS had been leaderless since 2001 [YUN 2001, p. 544], a situation that was expected to continue until after the elections. The ongoing instability could jeopardize the Nouméa Accord process, and the dissolution of FLNKS could not be ruled out.

The inter-ethnic strain between Kanaks and settlers from the French territory of Wallis and Futuna continued to cause tension. After a long-standing dispute over the housing of people from Wallis and Futuna on disputed land near Nouméa, the last 30 Wallisian families were moved from the area under police guard in September, prompting claims of ethnic cleansing by Didier Leroux, leader of the Opposition Alliance Party. The Wallisians were expected to seek compensation from France. Nevertheless, the Kanak and Wallisian communities signed an accord in December stipulating that the principle of dialogue on all decisions taken by New Caledonia could affect its inhabitants from Wallis and Futuna.

In September, the Customary Senate, considered the institutional guarantor of Kanak identity, with a rotating presidency, selected a new chief, Gabriel Poadae. Mr. Poadae promised to focus on indigenous rights to New Caledonia's nickel resources, the teaching of indigenous languages in schools and the mapping of traditional lands.

On 12 June, the Special Committee adopted a resolution on the question of New Caledonia [A/AC.109/2003/23], deciding to keep under continuous review the Nouméa Accord process and to report to the General Assembly in 2004.

GENERAL ASSEMBLY ACTION

On 9 December [meeting 72], the General Assembly, on the recommendation of the Fourth Committee [A/58/480], adopted **resolution 58/106** without vote [agenda item 19].

Question of New Caledonia

The General Assembly,

Having considered the question of New Caledonia,

Having examined the chapter of the report of the Special Committee on the Situation with regard to the Implementation of the Declaration on the Granting of Independence to Colonial Countries and Peoples relating to New Caledonia,

Reaffirming the right of peoples to self-determination as enshrined in the Charter of the United Nations,

Recalling its resolutions 1514(XV) of 14 December 1960 and 1541(XV) of 15 December 1960,

Noting the importance of the positive measures being pursued in New Caledonia by the French authorities, in cooperation with all sectors of the population, to promote political, economic and social development in the Territory, including measures in the area of environmental protection and action with respect to drug abuse and trafficking, in order to provide a framework for its peaceful progress to self-determination,

Noting also, in this context, the importance of equitable economic and social development, as well as continued dialogue among the parties involved in New Caledonia in the preparation of the act of self-determination of New Caledonia,

Noting with satisfaction the intensification of contacts between New Caledonia and neighbouring countries of the South Pacific region,

1. *Welcomes* the significant developments that have taken place in New Caledonia as exemplified by the signing of the Nouméa Accord of 5 May 1998 by the representatives of New Caledonia and the Government of France;

2. *Urges* all the parties involved, in the interest of all the people of New Caledonia, to maintain, in the framework of the Nouméa Accord, their dialogue in a spirit of harmony;

3. *Notes* the relevant provisions of the Nouméa Accord aimed at taking more broadly into account the Kanak identity in the political and social organization of New Caledonia, and also those provisions of the Accord relating to control of immigration and protection of local employment;

4. *Also notes* the relevant provisions of the Nouméa Accord to the effect that New Caledonia may become a member or associate member of certain international organizations, such as international organizations in the Pacific region, the United Nations, the United National Educational, Scientific and Cultural Organization and the International Labour Organization, according to their regulations;

5. *Further notes* the agreement between the signatories of the Nouméa Accord that the progress made in the emancipation process shall be brought to the attention of the United Nations;

6. *Welcomes* the fact that the administering Power invited to New Caledonia, at the time the new institutions were established, a mission of information which comprised representatives of countries of the Pacific region;

7. *Calls upon* the administering Power to transmit information regarding the political, economic and social situation of New Caledonia to the Secretary-General;

8. *Invites* all the parties involved to continue promoting a framework for the peaceful progress of the Territory towards an act of self-determination in which all options are open and which would safeguard the rights of all New Caledonians according to the letter and the spirit of the Nouméa Accord, which is based on the principle that it is for the populations of New Caledonia to choose how to control their destiny;

9. *Welcomes* measures that have been taken to strengthen and diversify the New Caledonian economy in all fields, and encourages further such measures in accordance with the spirit of the Matignon and Nouméa Accords;

10. *Also welcomes* the importance attached by the parties to the Matignon and Nouméa Accords to greater progress in housing, employment, training, education and health care in New Caledonia;

11. *Acknowledges* the contribution of the Melanesian Cultural Centre to the protection of the indigenous culture of New Caledonia;

12. *Notes* the positive initiatives aimed at protecting the natural environment of New Caledonia, notably the "Zonéco" operation designed to map and evaluate marine resources within the economic zone of New Caledonia;

13. *Acknowledges* the close links between New Caledonia and the peoples of the South Pacific and the positive actions being taken by the French and territorial authorities to facilitate the further development of those links, including the development of closer relations with the countries members of the Pacific Islands Forum;

14. *Welcomes,* in this regard, the accession by New Caledonia to the status of observer in the Pacific Islands Forum, continuing high-level visits to New Caledonia by delegations from countries of the Pacific region and high-level visits by delegations from New Caledonia to countries members of the Pacific Islands Forum;

15. *Decides* to keep under continuous review the process unfolding in New Caledonia as a result of the signing of the Nouméa Accord;

16. *Requests* the Special Committee on the Situation with regard to the Implementation of the Declaration on the Granting of Independence to Colonial Countries and Peoples to continue to examine the question of the Non-Self-Governing Territory of New Caledonia and to report thereon to the General Assembly at its fifty-ninth session.

Tokelau

On 23 June, the Special Committee on decolonization considered the question of Tokelau (the three small atolls of Nukunonu, Fakaofo and Atafu in the South Pacific), administered by New Zealand [A/58/23]. Before it was a Secretariat working paper covering constitutional and political developments and economic and social conditions in the Territory, and setting out the positions of New Zealand and Tokelau on the Territory's future status [A/AC.109/2003/10].

A later Secretariat working paper [A/AC.109/2004/8] reported that, in January, Fakaofo's Faipule (the representative of each village/atoll), Kolouei O'Brien, was installed as *Ulu-o-Tokelau* (titular head of the Territory), a position that was rotated annually among the three Faipule.

Following a review of representation within the General Fono (Tokelau's national representative body) at the October meeting of its Special Committee on the Constitution and by a November meeting of the General Fono, it was decided that existing arrangements would be maintained for the time being. The October meeting endorsed the General Fono's current powers and decided to appoint an independent Chairperson of the General Fono on an annual rotation. The General Fono took a number of decisions relating to Tokelau's legislative framework, passed new laws on issues such as dangerous goods, criminal proceedings, business incorporation rules, biosecurity and health regulations, land ownership, and the role of Law Commissioners, and enacted rules concerning Tokelau's observance of international human rights norms and standards. It also renamed the Council of Faipule the Council for Ongoing Government and expanded its membership to include the Pulenuku (mayor) from each of the villages.

In June, the General Fono agreed that the three Village Councils should assume full responsibility for all public services on their atolls by 30 June 2004. The decision stemmed from an earlier agreement on the Modern House of Tokelau approach [YUN 1998, p. 575], whereby the traditional Council of Elders on each atoll should serve as the foundation for a future governance structure. The Territory's New Zealand-appointed Administrator was asked to review Tokelau's public services to ensure that they were suitably equipped to handle their new responsibilities, and a Commission of Inquiry, conducted in September/October towards that end, issued a report containing recommendations relating to the future shape and functioning of Tokelau's public.

The General Fono also agreed that the activities previously undertaken under the Modern House project aimed at strengthening governance systems, boosting capability and enhancing development would henceforth be mainstreamed and run under the overall annual budget and planning process. From 1 July and beginning with the 2003/04 budget, Tokelau would be responsible for its full budget, including the budgetary support grant and development assistance provided by New Zealand.

Also in June, following a series of consultations, the General Fono agreed on the Principles of Partnership statement, drafted in 2002 [YUN 2002, p. 574] and subsequently approved by New Zealand; a formal signing ceremony was held in Tokelau in November, in the presence of New Zealand's Governor-General. The Partnership agreement provided the medium- to long-term context for carrying forward work on Tokelau's constitutional and other developments and addressed the management of the partnership, self-determination for Tokelau, its language and culture, New Zealand citizenship, shared values, economic and administrative assistance, coordination of services to the Territory, defence and security, foreign affairs, and the Tokelauan community in New Zealand. New Zealand also approved an administrative assistance scheme for Tokelau, whereby all New Zealand government agencies would provide assistance to Tokelau within their spheres of responsibility. The Tokelau Unit in Wellington would act as liaison and coordination point for the scheme; activities were already under way in health, education and fisheries.

In November, following consultations conducted by the Tokelau public service on all three atolls, the General Fono adopted a draft paper which brought together the main elements expected in the eventual Tokelauan Constitution. The paper, recommended by the Special Committee on the Constitution, drew upon customary practice, the written rules of the General Fono and parts of New Zealand law. The draft paper would be further developed as new governance structures were determined, and would form part of the dialogue between Tokelau and New Zealand on the Territory's future political status.

Also in November, based on a recommendation of the Special Committee on the Constitution, after extensive consultations held in each atoll, the General Fono formally endorsed, by consensus and with the support of the Village Councils, self-government in free association with New Zealand. The meeting of the Special Committee on the Constitution was greatly assisted by funding from UNDP.

Speaking before the Special Committee on decolonization, the Administrator of Tokelau said that, during the previous year, Tokelau had made significant advances in its political evolution and in the management of its national and regional interests. The Principles of Partnership agreement, which would be put before the New Zealand Cabinet, committed New Zealand to the ongoing provision of economic and technical support and outlined the way in which the two partners would work together for Tokelau's benefit. A constitutional conference would be held later in the year to discuss Tokelau's future political development.

At a 7 October meeting of the Fourth Committee, New Zealand noted that the Joint Statement on the Principles of Partnership, a political rather than legal document, was intended to give Tokelau some certainty and confidence as it worked towards self-determination. An early requirement was to develop information material on the three options available to NSGTs. New Zealand, with the cooperation of UNDP, would be working towards that goal, and Tokelau had organized a series of constitutional workshops.

At a 23 June meeting of the Special Committee on decolonization, the *Ulu-o-Tokelau* stated that, at the current stage, Tokelau needed practical details of the implications of an act of self-determination, and he hoped that New Zealand and the Special Committee would listen to Tokelau's views with regard to the pace of the process of exercising that right. The *Ulu* said that Tokelau was grateful to New Zealand for its efforts to express formally the principles underpinning the unique relationship between the two countries, and that the Principles of Partnership provided a firm foundation for Tokelau's ongoing development. The aim of current village consultations on constitutional developments was to assist the Council of Faipule to set an agenda for the upcoming September constitutional conference, and options for self-determination and governance arrangements would be part of the agenda. Devolution of authority to villages and traditional institutions was key to Tokelau's future.

GENERAL ASSEMBLY ACTION

On 9 December [meeting 72], the General Assembly, on the recommendation of the Fourth Committee [A/58/480], adopted **resolution 58/107** without vote [agenda item 19].

Question of Tokelau

The General Assembly,

Having considered the question of Tokelau,

Having examined the chapter of the report of the Special Committee on the Situation with regard to the Implementation of the Declaration on the Granting of Independence to Colonial Countries and Peoples relating to Tokelau,

Recalling the solemn declaration on the future status of Tokelau, contained in the 1994 "Voice of Tokelau", which stated that an act of self-determination in Tokelau was under active consideration, together with the constitution of a self-governing Tokelau, and that the then preference of Tokelau was for a status of free association with New Zealand,

Recalling also its resolution 1514(XV) of 14 December 1960, containing the Declaration on the Granting of Independence to Colonial Countries and Peoples, and all resolutions and decisions of the United Nations relating to Non-Self-Governing Territories, in particular General Assembly resolution 57/137 of 11 December 2002,

Recalling further the emphasis placed in the solemn declaration on the terms of Tokelau's special relationship with New Zealand, including the expectation that the form of help that Tokelau could continue to expect from New Zealand in promoting the well-being of its people, besides its external interests, would be clearly established within the framework of that relationship,

Noting with appreciation the continuing exemplary cooperation of New Zealand as the administering Power with regard to the work of the Special Committee relating to Tokelau and its readiness to permit access by United Nations visiting missions to the Territory,

Noting also with appreciation the collaborative contribution to the development of Tokelau by New Zealand and the specialized agencies and other organizations of the United Nations system, in particular the United Nations Development Programme and the World Health Organization,

Recalling the dispatch in August 2002 of a United Nations Mission to Tokelau, at the invitation of the Government of New Zealand and the representatives of Tokelau,

Recalling also the report of the United Nations Mission to Tokelau, 2002,

Noting that, as a small island Territory, Tokelau exemplifies the situation of most remaining Non-Self-Governing Territories,

Noting also that, as a case study pointing to successful cooperation for decolonization, Tokelau has wider significance for the United Nations as it seeks to complete its work in decolonization,

1. *Notes* that Tokelau remains firmly committed to the development of self-government and to an act of self-determination that would result in Tokelau assuming a status in accordance with the options on future status for Non-Self-Governing Territories contained in principle VI of the annex to General Assembly resolution 1541(XV) of 15 December 1960;

2. *Also notes* the desire of Tokelau to move at its own pace towards an act of self-determination;

3. *Further notes* the inauguration in 1999 of a national Government based on village elections by universal adult suffrage;

4. *Acknowledges* Tokelau's goal to return authority to its traditional leadership, and its wish to provide that leadership with the necessary support to carry out its functions in the contemporary world;

5. *Acknowledges also* the progress made towards that goal under the Modern House of Tokelau project, and welcomes the decision taken by the General Fono in June 2003 to set a target date of 30 June 2004 for the transfer to each Taupulega (Village Council) of full responsibility for the management of all its public services;

6. *Acknowledges further* Tokelau's initiative in devising a strategic economic development plan for the period 2002-2004 to advance its capacity for self-government;

7. *Notes* that, consistent with the expressed desires of past traditional leaders and the principles of the Modern House of Tokelau, Tokelau has established a local public service employer;

8. *Welcomes* the continuing dialogue with the administering Power and the Territory with a view to the development of a programme of work for Tokelau in accordance with General Assembly resolution 55/147 of 8 December 2000;

9. *Acknowledges* the continuing support that New Zealand has committed to the Modern House of Tokelau project in 2002-2003, and the cooperation of the United Nations Development Programme in aligning its programmes under the project;

10. *Notes* that the Constitution of a self-governing Tokelau will continue to develop as a part and as a con-

sequence of the building of the Modern House of Tokelau, and that both have national and international importance for Tokelau;

11. *Acknowledges* Tokelau's need for continued reassurance, given the cultural adjustments that are taking place with the strengthening of its capacity for self-government and, since local resources cannot adequately cover the material side of self-determination, the ongoing responsibility of Tokelau's external partners to assist Tokelau in balancing its desire to be self-reliant to the greatest extent possible with its need for external assistance;

12. *Notes* the special challenge inherent in the situation of Tokelau, among the smallest of the small Territories, and that a Territory's exercise of its inalienable right to self-determination may be brought closer, as in the case of Tokelau, by the meeting of that challenge in innovative ways;

13. *Acknowledges* the desire of the partners to reaffirm their commitment to each other, and welcomes the agreement reached in Wellington on 19 June 2003 on the text of an agreement on the principles underpinning the relationship for which the formal approval of the Government of New Zealand is being sought;

14. *Welcomes* the assurance of the Government of New Zealand that it will meet its obligations to the United Nations with respect to Tokelau and abide by the freely expressed wishes of the people of Tokelau with regard to their future status;

15. *Also welcomes* the cooperative attitude of the other States and Territories in the region towards Tokelau, its economic and political aspirations and its increasing participation in regional and international affairs;

16. *Further welcomes* Tokelau's associate membership in the United Nations Educational, Scientific and Cultural Organization and its recent accession to associate membership in the Forum Fisheries Agency;

17. *Reaffirms its approval* of the report of the United Nations Mission to Tokelau, 2002;

18. *Notes* that a study to review the options for Tokelau's future self-determination is recommended in the report, and further notes the willingness expressed by the United Nations Development Programme to assist in this regard upon request from Tokelau;

19. *Calls upon* New Zealand and Tokelau to consider developing an information programme to apprise the population of Tokelau of the nature of self-determination, including the three options of integration, free association and independence, so that it may be better prepared to face a future decision on this matter, and welcomes the invitation extended to the Chairman of the Special Committee on the Situation with regard to the Implementation of the Declaration on the Granting of Independence to Colonial Countries and Peoples to attend the constitutional convention to be held in Tokelau;

20. *Calls upon* the administering Power and United Nations agencies to continue to provide assistance to Tokelau as it further develops its economy and governance structures in the context of its ongoing constitutional evolution;

21. *Requests* the Special Committee to continue to examine the question of the Non-Self-Governing Territory of Tokelau and to report thereon to the General Assembly at its fifty-ninth session.

Western Sahara

The Special Committee on decolonization considered the question of Western Sahara on 9 June [A/58/23]. A Secretariat working paper [A/AC.109/2003/14] detailed the Secretary-General's good offices with the parties concerned and action taken by the General Assembly and Security Council (see p. 257). The Special Committee transmitted the relevant documentation to the Assembly's fifty-eighth (2003) session to facilitate the Fourth Committee's consideration of the question. The Secretary-General's report was submitted to the Assembly in July [A/58/171].

Island Territories

In June, the Special Committee on decolonization [A/58/23] considered working papers on American Samoa [A/AC.109/2003/12], Anguilla [A/AC.109/2003/11], Bermuda [A/AC.109/2003/13], the British Virgin Islands [A/AC.109/2003/5], the Cayman Islands [A/AC.109/2003/9], Guam [A/AC.109/2003/15], Montserrat [A/AC.109/2003/2], Pitcairn [A/AC.109/2003/16], Saint Helena [A/AC.109/2003/4], the Turks and Caicos Islands [A/AC.109/2003/8] and the United States Virgin Islands [A/AC.109/2003/1], describing political developments and economic and social conditions in each of those 11 island Territories. On 23 June, the Committee approved a two-part consolidated draft resolution for adoption by the General Assembly (see below).

GENERAL ASSEMBLY ACTION

On 9 December [meeting 72], the General Assembly, on the recommendation of the Fourth Committee [A/58/480], adopted **resolutions 58/108 A** and **B** without vote [agenda item 19].

Questions of American Samoa, Anguilla, Bermuda, the British Virgin Islands, the Cayman Islands, Guam, Montserrat, Pitcairn, Saint Helena, the Turks and Caicos Islands and the United States Virgin Islands

A

General

The General Assembly,

Having considered the questions of the Non-Self-Governing Territories of American Samoa, Anguilla, Bermuda, the British Virgin Islands, the Cayman Islands, Guam, Montserrat, Pitcairn, Saint Helena, the Turks and Caicos Islands and the United States Virgin Islands, hereinafter referred to as "the Territories",

Having examined the relevant chapter of the report of the Special Committee on the Situation with regard to the Implementation of the Declaration on the Granting of Independence to Colonial Countries and Peoples,

Recalling its resolution 1514(XV) of 14 December 1960, containing the Declaration on the Granting of Independence to Colonial Countries and Peoples, and all resolutions and decisions of the United Nations relating to those Territories, including, in particular, the resolutions adopted by the General Assembly at its fifty-seventh session on the individual Territories covered by the present resolution,

Recognizing that in the decolonization process there is no alternative to the principle of self-determination as enunciated by the General Assembly in its resolutions 1514(XV), 1541(XV) and other resolutions,

Recognizing also that all available options for self-determination of the Territories are valid as long as they are in accordance with the freely expressed wishes of the peoples concerned and in conformity with the clearly defined principles contained in resolutions 1514(XV), 1541(XV) and other resolutions of the General Assembly,

Recalling its resolution 1541(XV) of 15 December 1960, containing the principles that should guide Member States in determining whether or not an obligation exists to transmit the information called for under Article 73 *e* of the Charter of the United Nations,

Expressing its concern that more than forty years after the adoption of the Declaration there still remains a number of Non-Self-Governing Territories,

Conscious of the importance of continuing effective implementation of the Declaration, taking into account the target set by the United Nations to eradicate colonialism by 2010 and the plan of action for the Second International Decade for the Eradication of Colonialism,

Recognizing that the specific characteristics and the sentiments of the peoples of the Territories require flexible, practical and innovative approaches to the options of self-determination, without any prejudice to territorial size, geographical location, size of population or natural resources,

Welcoming the stated position of the Government of the United Kingdom that it continues to take seriously its obligations under the Charter to develop self-government in the dependent Territories and, in cooperation with the locally elected Governments, to ensure that their constitutional frameworks continue to meet the wishes of the people, and the emphasis that it is ultimately for the peoples of the Territories to decide their future status,

Welcoming also the stated position of the Government of the United States of America that it supports fully the principles of decolonization and takes seriously its obligations under the Charter to promote to the utmost the well-being of the inhabitants of the Territories under United States administration,

Noting the constitutional developments in some Non-Self-Governing Territories about which the Special Committee has received information,

Aware of the usefulness both to the Territories and to the Special Committee of the participation of elected and appointed representatives of the Territories in the work of the Special Committee,

Convinced that the wishes and aspirations of the peoples of the Territories should continue to guide the development of their future political status and that referendums, free and fair elections and other forms of popular consultation play an important role in ascertaining the wishes and aspirations of the people,

Convinced also that any negotiations to determine the status of a Territory must take place with the active involvement and participation of the people of that Territory, and that the views of the peoples of the Non-Self-Governing Territories in respect of their right to self-determination should be ascertained under the supervision of the United Nations, on a case-by-case basis,

Mindful that United Nations visiting missions provide an effective means of ascertaining the situation in the Territories, that some Territories have not received a United Nations visiting mission for a long time and that no visiting missions have been sent to some of the Territories, and considering the possibility of sending further visiting missions to the Territories at an appropriate time and in consultation with the administering Powers,

Mindful also that, in order for the Special Committee to enhance its understanding of the political status of the peoples of the Territories and to fulfil its mandate effectively, it is important for it to be apprised by the administering Powers and to receive information from other appropriate sources, including the representatives of the Territories, concerning the wishes and aspirations of the peoples of the Territories,

Recognizing the need for the Special Committee to embark actively on a public awareness campaign aimed at assisting the peoples of the Territories in gaining an understanding of the options of self-determination,

Mindful, in this connection, that the holding of regional seminars in the Caribbean and Pacific regions and at Headquarters and other venues, with the active participation of representatives of the Non-Self-Governing Territories, provides a helpful means for the Special Committee to fulfil its mandate, and that the regional nature of the seminars, which alternate between the Caribbean and the Pacific, is a crucial element in their success, while recognizing the need for reviewing the role of those seminars in the context of a United Nations programme for ascertaining the political status of the Territories,

Mindful also that, by holding a Caribbean regional seminar at The Valley, Anguilla, from 20 to 22 May 2003, the Special Committee was able to hear the views of the representatives of the Territories and Member States as well as organizations and experts in the region, in order to review the political, economic and social conditions in the Territories,

Aware of the special circumstances of the geographical location and economic conditions of each Territory, and bearing in mind the necessity of promoting economic stability and diversifying and strengthening further the economies of the respective Territories as a matter of priority,

Conscious of the particular vulnerability of the Territories to natural disasters and environmental degradation and, in this connection, bearing in mind the programmes of action of the United Nations Conference on Environment and Development, the World Conference on Natural Disaster Reduction, the Global Conference on the Sustainable Development of Small Island Developing States, the International Conference on Population and Development, the United Nations Conference on Human Settlements (Habitat II), the

World Summit on Sustainable Development and other relevant world conferences,

Noting with appreciation the contribution to the development of some Territories by specialized agencies and other organizations of the United Nations system, in particular the United Nations Development Programme, and regional institutions such as the Caribbean Development Bank, the Caribbean Community, the Organization of Eastern Caribbean States, the Pacific Islands Forum and the agencies of the Council of Regional Organizations in the Pacific,

Noting that some territorial Governments have made efforts towards achieving the highest standards of financial supervision,

Concerned that in 2002 economic growth slowed in many Non-Self-Governing Territories, in particular in the tourism and construction sectors,

Recalling the ongoing efforts of the Special Committee in carrying out a critical review of its work with the aim of making appropriate and constructive recommendations and decisions to attain its objectives in accordance with its mandate,

1. *Reaffirms* the inalienable right of the peoples of the Territories to self-determination, in conformity with the Charter of the United Nations and with General Assembly resolution 1514(XV), containing the Declaration on the Granting of Independence to Colonial Countries and Peoples;

2. *Reaffirms also* that, in the process of decolonization, there is no alternative to the principle of self-determination, which is also a fundamental human right;

3. *Reaffirms further* that it is ultimately for the peoples of the Territories themselves to determine freely their future political status in accordance with the relevant provisions of the Charter, the Declaration and the relevant resolutions of the General Assembly, and in that connection calls upon the administering Powers, in cooperation with the territorial Governments, to facilitate programmes of political education in the Territories in order to foster an awareness among the people of their right to self-determination in conformity with the legitimate political status options, based on the principles clearly defined in General Assembly resolution 1541(XV);

4. *Requests* the administering Powers to transmit to the Secretary-General information called for under Article 73 *e* of the Charter and other updated information and reports, including reports on the wishes and aspirations of the peoples of the Territories regarding their future political status as expressed in fair and free referendums and other forms of popular consultation, as well as the results of any informed and democratic processes consistent with practice under the Charter that indicate the clear and freely expressed wish of the people to change the existing status of the Territories;

5. *Stresses* the importance for it to be apprised of the views and wishes of the peoples of the Territories and to enhance its understanding of their conditions;

6. *Reaffirms* that United Nations visiting missions to the Territories at an appropriate time and in consultation with the administering Powers are an effective means of ascertaining the situation in the Territories, and requests the administering Powers and the elected representatives of the peoples of the Territories to facilitate the work of the Special Committee on the Situation with regard to the Implementation of the Declaration on the Granting of Independence to Colonial Countries and Peoples in this regard;

7. *Reaffirms also* the responsibility of the administering Powers under the Charter to promote the economic and social development and to preserve the cultural identity of the Territories, and recommends that priority continue to be given, in consultation with the territorial Governments concerned, to the strengthening and diversification of their respective economies;

8. *Requests* the Territories and the administering Powers to take all necessary measures to protect and conserve the environment of the Territories against any environmental degradation, and once again requests the specialized agencies concerned to continue to monitor environmental conditions in those Territories;

9. *Calls upon* the administering Powers, in cooperation with the respective territorial Governments, to continue to take all necessary measures to counter problems related to drug trafficking, money-laundering and other offences;

10. *Notes* the cooperative efforts of some Non-Self-Governing Territories to address the problem of illegal drugs, with a focus on demand reduction, education, treatment and legal issues;

11. *Notes with concern* that the plan of action for the first International Decade for the Eradication of Colonialism was not fully implemented by 2000, and stresses the importance of implementing the plan of action for the Second International Decade, in particular by expediting the application of the work programme for the decolonization of each Non-Self-Governing Territory, on a case-by-case basis;

12. *Invites* the administering Powers to participate fully in the work of the Special Committee and to enter into constructive dialogue with the Special Committee before the fifty-ninth session of the General Assembly in order to implement the provisions of Article 73 *e* of the Charter and the Declaration on the Granting of Independence to Colonial Countries and Peoples for the period 2001-2010;

13. *Urges* Member States to contribute to the efforts of the United Nations to usher in a world free of colonialism within the Second International Decade for the Eradication of Colonialism, and calls upon them to continue to give their full support to the Special Committee in its endeavours towards that noble goal;

14. *Urges also* the specialized agencies and other organizations of the United Nations system to initiate or to continue to take all necessary measures to accelerate progress in the economic and social life of the Territories, and calls for closer cooperation between the Special Committee and the Economic and Social Council in furtherance of the provision of assistance to the Territories;

15. *Notes* that some Non-Self-Governing Territories have expressed concern at the procedure followed by one administering Power, contrary to the wishes of the Territories themselves, namely, of amending or enacting legislation for the Territories through Orders in Council, in order to apply to the Territories the international treaty obligations of the administering Power;

16. *Takes note* of statements made by the elected representatives of the Territories concerned and other appropriate authorities emphasizing their willingness to cooperate in all international efforts aimed at preventing abuse of the international financial system and to promote regulatory environments with highly selective licensing procedures, robust supervisory practices and well-established anti-money-laundering regimes;

17. *Requests* the Secretary-General to report to the General Assembly on the implementation of decolonization resolutions since the declaration of the Second International Decade for the Eradication of Colonialism;

18. *Requests* the Special Committee to continue to examine the question of the small Territories and to report thereon to the General Assembly at its fifty-ninth session with recommendations on appropriate ways to assist the peoples of the Territories in exercising their right to self-determination.

B
Individual Territories

The General Assembly,
Referring to resolution A above,

I
American Samoa

Taking note of the report by the administering Power that most American Samoan leaders express satisfaction with the Territory's present relationship with the United States of America, as reflected in statements made by those leaders in the regional seminars held in Havana, Cuba, and Nadi, Fiji, in 2001 and 2002, respectively,

Noting that the Government of the Territory continues to have financial, budgetary and internal control problems, but that it has recently taken steps to increase revenues and decrease government expenditures,

Noting also that the Territory, similar to isolated communities with limited funds, continues to experience a lack of adequate medical and other infrastructural facilities,

Aware of the efforts of the Government of the Territory to control and reduce expenditures, while continuing its programme of expanding and diversifying the local economy,

Concerned that massive flooding and mudslides in May 2003 resulted in loss of life and damage initially estimated by the territorial Government at more than 50 million United States dollars, and taking note of the official request by the Territory for recovery assistance from the administering Power,

1. *Notes* that the Department of the Interior of the United States of America provides that the Secretary of the Interior has administrative jurisdiction over American Samoa;

2. *Calls upon* the administering Power to continue to assist the territorial Government in the economic and social development of the Territory, including measures to rebuild financial management capabilities and strengthen other governmental functions of the Government of the Territory, and welcomes the assistance from the administering Power to the Territory in its recovery efforts following the recent floods;

3. *Welcomes* the invitation extended to the Special Committee by the Governor of American Samoa to send a visiting mission to the Territory, and calls upon the administering Power to facilitate such a mission;

II
Anguilla

Noting the continuation of the conduct of the constitutional and electoral reform review process in the Territory,

Welcoming the holding of the 2003 Caribbean regional seminar in Anguilla, the first time that the seminar has been held in a Non-Self-Governing Territory,

Noting the desire of the territorial Government and the people of Anguilla for a visiting mission by the Special Committee,

Aware of the efforts of the Government of Anguilla to continue to develop the Territory as a viable offshore centre and well-regulated financial centre for investors, by enacting modern company and trust laws, as well as partnership and insurance legislation, and computerizing the company registry system,

Noting the need for continued cooperation between the administering Power and the territorial Government in tackling the problems of drug trafficking and money-laundering,

1. *Welcomes* the emphasis placed in the initial stages of the constitutional and electoral reform review process on participation, information and education and the support provided by the United Nations Development Programme and the United Kingdom Government fund for good government;

2. *Welcomes also* the cooperation of the territorial Government of Anguilla and the United Kingdom in holding the 2003 Caribbean regional seminar in Anguilla, and notes that the staging of the seminar in a Non-Self-Governing Territory for the first time as well as a town hall meeting between the people of Anguilla and the Special Committee during the seminar contributed to its success;

3. *Calls upon* the administering Power and all States, organizations and United Nations agencies to continue to assist the Territory in social and economic development;

III
Bermuda

Noting the results of the independence referendum held on 16 August 1995, and conscious of the different viewpoints of the political parties of the Territory on the future status of the Territory,

1. *Calls upon* the administering Power to continue to work with the Territory for its socio-economic development;

2. *Welcomes* the agreement reached in June 2002 between the United States of America, the United Kingdom and the Territory formally transferring the former military base lands to the territorial Government, and the provision of financial resources to address some of the environmental problems;

3. *Welcomes also* the convening in the Territory in March 2003 of an international conference on conservation in overseas territories and other small island States, which included governmental and non-governmental organizations to address issues of common concern;

IV
British Virgin Islands

Taking note of the steps currently being taken to review the Constitution with the aim of modernizing it,

Noting that the Territory continues to emerge as one of the world's leading offshore financial centres, and that the financial services sector is becoming the cornerstone of the Government's recurrent budget,

Noting also the need for continued cooperation between the administering Power and the territorial Government in countering drug trafficking and money-laundering,

Noting further that the Territory commemorated its annual British Virgin Islands–United States Virgin Islands Friendship Day on 31 May 2003 in Charlotte Amalie, St. Thomas,

Requests the administering Power, the specialized agencies and other organizations of the United Nations system and all financial institutions to continue to provide the Territory with assistance for socio-economic development and the development of human resources, bearing in mind the vulnerability of the Territory to external factors;

V
Cayman Islands

Noting the formation for the first time of a political party in the Territory and the subsequent emergence of a party system in the Territory,

Taking note of the constitutional review process being undertaken by the territorial Government in consultation with the administering Power,

Noting the actions taken by the territorial Government to promote increased participation by the local population in the decision-making process in the economic and social sectors in the Cayman Islands,

Aware that the Territory has one of the highest per capita incomes in the region, a stable political climate and has emerged as one of the world's leading offshore financial centres with virtually no unemployment,

Noting with concern the vulnerability of the Territory to drug trafficking, money-laundering and related activities, and noting the measures taken by the authorities to deal with those problems,

Noting the approval by the Cayman Islands Legislative Assembly of the Territory's Vision 2008 Development Plan, which aims to promote development that is consistent with the aims and values of Caymanian society,

1. *Welcomes* the completion of the report of the Constitutional Review Commission, which conducted an extensive review of the current Constitution, and the recommended changes, following public discussions with community groups and individuals, pursuant to the recommendations of the administering Power as stated in its White Paper entitled "Partnership for Progress and Prosperity: Britain and the Overseas Territories";

2. *Requests* the administering Power, the specialized agencies and other organizations of the United Nations system to continue to provide the territorial Government with all required expertise to enable it to achieve its socio-economic aims;

3. *Requests* the administering Power, in consultation with the territorial Government, to continue to facilitate the expansion of the current programme of securing employment for the local population, in particular at the decision-making level;

VI
Guam

Recalling that, in a referendum held in 1987, the registered and eligible voters of Guam endorsed a draft Guam Commonwealth Act that would establish a new framework for relations between the Territory and the administering Power, providing for a greater measure of internal self-government for Guam and recognition of the right of the Chamorro people of Guam to self-determination for the Territory,

Recalling also the requests by the elected representatives and non-governmental organizations of the Territory that Guam not be removed from the list of the Non-Self-Governing Territories with which the Special Committee is concerned, pending the self-determination of the Chamorro people and taking into account their legitimate rights and interests,

Aware that negotiations between the administering Power and the territorial Government on the draft Guam Commonwealth Act are no longer continuing and that Guam has established the process for a self-determination vote by the eligible Chamorro voters,

Cognizant that the administering Power continues to implement its programme of transferring surplus federal land to the Government of Guam,

Noting that the people of the Territory have called for reform in the programme of the administering Power with respect to the thorough, unconditional and expeditious transfer of land property to the people of Guam,

Conscious that immigration into Guam has resulted in the indigenous Chamorros becoming a minority in their homeland,

Aware of the potential for diversifying and developing the economy of Guam through commercial fishing and agriculture and other viable activities,

Recalling the dispatch in 1979 of a United Nations visiting mission to the Territory, and noting the recommendation of the 1996 Pacific regional seminar for sending a visiting mission to Guam,

Taking note with interest of the statements made and the information on the political and economic situation in Guam provided by the representatives of the Territory at the 5th meeting of the Fourth Committee on 3 October 2002,

Concerned that the 2001 census figures in the Territory show that 23 per cent of the population lives in poverty,

1. *Calls upon* the administering Power to take into consideration the expressed will of the Chamorro people as supported by Guam voters in the plebiscite of 1987 and as provided for in Guam law, encourages the administering Power and the territorial Government of Guam to enter into negotiations on the matter, and requests the administering Power to inform the Secretary-General of progress to that end;

2. *Requests* the administering Power to continue to assist the elected territorial Government in achieving its political, economic and social goals;

3. *Also requests* the administering Power, in cooperation with the territorial Government, to continue

to transfer land to the original landowners of the Territory;

4. *Further requests* the administering Power to continue to recognize and respect the political rights and the cultural and ethnic identity of the Chamorro people of Guam, and to take all necessary measures to respond to the concerns of the territorial Government with regard to the question of immigration;

5. *Requests* the administering Power to cooperate in establishing programmes specifically intended to promote the sustainable development of economic activities and enterprises, noting the special role of the Chamorro people in the development of Guam;

6. *Also requests* the administering Power to continue to support appropriate measures by the territorial Government aimed at promoting growth in commercial fishing and agricultural and other viable activities;

7. *Calls upon* the administering Power to facilitate a visiting mission to Guam as requested by the territorial Government;

VII

Montserrat

Taking note with interest of the statements made and the information on the political and economic situation in Montserrat provided by the Chief Minister of the Territory to the Caribbean regional seminar, held at The Valley, Anguilla, from 20 to 22 May 2003,

Noting with concern the dire consequences of the volcanic eruption, which led to the evacuation of three quarters of the Territory's population to safe areas of the island and to areas outside the Territory, in particular Antigua and Barbuda and the United Kingdom, and which continues to have enduring consequences upon the economy of the island,

Welcoming the continued assistance provided to the Territory by States members of the Caribbean Community, in particular Antigua and Barbuda, which has offered safe refuge and access to educational and health facilities, as well as employment for thousands who have left the Territory,

Noting the continuing efforts of the administering Power to deal with the consequences of the volcanic eruption,

Noting with concern that a number of the inhabitants of the Territory continue to live in shelters because of volcanic activity,

Noting that the Chief Minister of Montserrat assumed the chairmanship of the Organization of Eastern Caribbean States in May 2003,

1. *Calls upon* the administering Power, the specialized agencies and other organizations of the United Nations system, as well as regional and other organizations, to continue to provide assistance to the Territory in alleviating the consequences of the volcanic eruption;

2. *Takes note* of the completion of the report of the Constitutional Review Commission prepared after extensive consultations with Montserratians both in the Territory and abroad and the consensus that, while Montserratians reserve the right to future self-determination, independence is not a priority given the present socio-economic status of the Territory;

VIII

Pitcairn

Taking into account the unique nature of Pitcairn in terms of population and area,

Welcoming the participation of a representative of the Mayor of Pitcairn in the Caribbean regional seminar at The Valley, Anguilla, from 20 to 22 May 2003, and taking note of the concerns expressed by him with regard to the ongoing court case in the Territory,

Requests the administering Power to continue its assistance for the improvement of the economic, social, educational and other conditions of the population of the Territory and to continue its discussions with the representatives of Pitcairn on how best to support its economic security;

IX

Saint Helena

Taking into account the unique character of Saint Helena, its population and its natural resources,

Aware of the efforts of the administering Power and the territorial authorities to improve the socio-economic conditions of the population of Saint Helena, in particular as regards food production, continuing high unemployment and limited transport and communications,

Noting with concern the problem of unemployment on the island and the joint action of the administering Power and the territorial Government to deal with it,

1. *Welcomes* the acceptance by the administering Power of the majority of the proposals for constitutional change made by the territorial Government;

2. *Requests* the administering Power and relevant international organizations to continue to support the efforts of the territorial Government to address the socio-economic development challenges, including the high unemployment and the limited transport and communications problems;

X

Turks and Caicos Islands

Noting that the People's Democratic Movement was elected to a third consecutive term in the Legislative Council elections held in March 2003,

Also noting the efforts by the Government of the Territory to strengthen financial management in the public sector, including efforts to increase revenue,

Noting with concern the vulnerability of the Territory to drug trafficking and related activities, as well as its problems caused by illegal immigration, and noting the need for continued cooperation between the administering Power and the territorial Government in countering drug trafficking and money-laundering,

Noting that the Chief Minister was elected as the chairman of the newly established Overseas Countries and Territories Association of Europe,

1. *Welcomes* the establishment of the Constitutional Review Commission, which embarked on a public education programme on the Constitution, ascertained the views of the population and made recommendations to the administering Power on changes which may be envisaged, pursuant to the recommendations as stated in its White Paper entitled "Partnership for Progress and Prosperity: Britain and the Overseas Territories";

2. *Calls upon* the administering Power and the relevant regional and international organizations to continue to provide assistance for the improvement of the economic, social, educational and other conditions of the population of the Territory;

3. *Calls upon* the administering Power and the territorial Government to continue to cooperate to counter problems related to money-laundering, smuggling of funds and other related crimes, as well as drug trafficking;

XI
United States Virgin Islands

Taking note with interest of the statements made and the information provided by the representative of the Governor of the Territory to the Caribbean regional seminar, held at The Valley, Anguilla, from 20 to 22 May 2003,

Noting the continuing interest of the territorial Government in seeking associate membership in the Organization of Eastern Caribbean States and observer status in the Caribbean Community and the current request by the Territory to the administering Power for the delegation of authority to proceed,

Noting also the expressed interest of the territorial Government to be included in regional programmes of the United Nations Development Programme,

Noting further the necessity of further diversifying the economy of the Territory,

Noting the efforts of the Government of the Territory to promote the Territory as an offshore financial services centre,

Recalling that the Territory has not received a United Nations visiting mission since 1977, and bearing in mind the formal request of the Territory for such a mission in 1993 to assist the Territory in its political education process and to observe the Territory's only referendum on political status options in its history,

Noting that the Territory commemorated its annual British Virgin Islands–United States Virgin Islands Friendship Day on 31 May 2003 in Charlotte Amalie, St. Thomas,

1. *Requests* the administering Power to continue to assist the territorial Government in achieving its political, economic and social goals;

2. *Once again requests* the administering Power to facilitate the participation of the Territory, as appropriate, in various organizations, in particular the Organization of Eastern Caribbean States, the Caribbean Community and the Association of Caribbean States;

3. *Calls* for the inclusion of the Territory in regional programmes of the United Nations Development Programme, consistent with the participation of other Non-Self-Governing Territories;

4. *Notes* the economic difficulties being experienced by the territorial Government and the fiscal austerity measures being implemented, and others proposed, to relieve the Territory's cash flow shortage, and calls upon the administering Power to continue to provide every assistance required by the Territory to further alleviate the difficult economic situation, including, inter alia, the provision of debt relief and loans;

5. *Notes with interest* the entering into force in 2001 of the joint memorandum of cooperation on the exchange of artefacts between the Territory and Denmark, the Territory's former administering Power, as a companion agreement to the 1999 memorandum for the repatriation of archival material from the Danish colonial period, consistent with the Durban Declaration and Programme of Action, adopted by the World Conference against Racism, Racial Discrimination, Xenophobia and Related Intolerance on 8 September 2001, and once again requests the United Nations Educational, Scientific and Cultural Organization, under its records and archives management programme, to assist the Territory in carrying out its archival and artefacts initiative;

6. *Notes* the position of the territorial Government, including its articulation in resolution 1609 of 9 April 2001 of the 24th Legislature of the United States Virgin Islands, opposing the assumption by the administering Power of submerged land in territorial waters, having regard to relevant resolutions of the General Assembly on the ownership and control of natural resources, including marine resources, by the people of the Non-Self-Governing Territories, and its calls for the return of those marine resources to the people of the Territory;

7. *Notes with concern* that the 2000 census figures for the Territory indicate that 32.5 per cent of the population is living in poverty.

Information

UN public information

The General Assembly's Committee on Information, at its twenty-fifth session (New York, 28 April–9 May) [A/58/21], continued to consider UN public information policies and activities and to evaluate and follow up efforts made and progress achieved in information and communications. The major report before the Committee dealt with the reorientation of UN activities in the field of public information and communications. Other reports covered programmatic aspects of the proposed 2004-2005 programme budget for the Department of Public Information (DPI), implementation of the pilot project on the development of an international radio broadcasting capacity for the United Nations, modernization and integrated management of UN libraries, the 2002 activities of the United Nations Communications Group (UNCG) [YUN 2002, p. 589], and the structure and operations of the UN information centres (UNICs).

Those reports and the Secretary-General's report on questions relating to information [A/58/175] are discussed in the relevant sections below.

By **decision 58/525** of 9 December, the Assembly increased the Committee's membership from 99 to 102.

GENERAL ASSEMBLY ACTION

On 9 December [meeting 72], the General Assembly, on the recommendation of the Fourth Committee [A/58/475], adopted **resolution 58/101 A** without vote [agenda item 86].

Information in the service of humanity

The General Assembly,

Taking note of the comprehensive and important report of the Committee on Information,

Also taking note of the report of the Secretary-General on questions relating to information,

Urges all countries, organizations of the United Nations system as a whole and all others concerned, reaffirming their commitment to the principles of the Charter of the United Nations and to the principles of freedom of the press and freedom of information, as well as to those of the independence, pluralism and diversity of the media, deeply concerned by the disparities existing between developed and developing countries and the consequences of every kind arising from those disparities that affect the capability of the public, private or other media and individuals in developing countries to disseminate information and communicate their views and their cultural and ethical values through endogenous cultural production, as well as to ensure the diversity of sources and their free access to information, and recognizing the call in this context for what in the United Nations and at various international forums has been termed "a new world information and communication order, seen as an evolving and continuous process":

(*a*) To cooperate and interact with a view to reducing existing disparities in information flows at all levels by increasing assistance for the development of communication infrastructures and capabilities in developing countries, with due regard for their needs and the priorities attached to such areas by those countries, and in order to enable them and the public, private or other media in developing countries to develop their own information and communication policies freely and independently and increase the participation of media and individuals in the communication process, and to ensure a free flow of information at all levels;

(*b*) To ensure for journalists the free and effective performance of their professional tasks and condemn resolutely all attacks against them;

(*c*) To provide support for the continuation and strengthening of practical training programmes for broadcasters and journalists from public, private and other media in developing countries;

(*d*) To enhance regional efforts and cooperation among developing countries, as well as cooperation between developed and developing countries, to strengthen communication capacities and to improve the media infrastructure and communication technology in the developing countries, especially in the areas of training and dissemination of information;

(*e*) To aim at, in addition to bilateral cooperation, providing all possible support and assistance to the developing countries and their media, public, private or other, with due regard to their interests and needs in the field of information and to action already adopted within the United Nations system, including:

(i) The development of the human and technical resources that are indispensable for the improvement of information and communication systems in developing countries and support for the continuation and strengthening of practical training programmes, such as those already operating under both public and private auspices throughout the developing world;

(ii) The creation of conditions that will enable developing countries and their media, public, private or other, to have, by using their national and regional resources, the communication technology suited to their national needs, as well as the necessary programme material, especially for radio and television broadcasting;

(iii) Assistance in establishing and promoting telecommunication links at the subregional, regional and interregional levels, especially among developing countries;

(iv) The facilitation, as appropriate, of access by the developing countries to advanced communication technology available on the open market;

(*f*) To provide full support for the International Programme for the Development of Communication of the United Nations Educational, Scientific and Cultural Organization, which should support both public and private media.

Also on 9 December [meeting 72] and on the recommendation of the Fourth Committee [A/58/475, orally revised], the Assembly adopted **resolution 58/101 B** without vote [agenda item 86].

United Nations public information policies and activities

The General Assembly,

Reiterating its decision to consolidate the role of the Committee on Information as its main subsidiary body mandated to make recommendations to it relating to the work of the Department of Public Information of the Secretariat,

Concurring, with the view of the Secretary-General that the fundamental premise underlying the reorientation efforts of the Department of Public Information remains General Assembly resolution 13(I) of 13 February 1946, establishing the Department, which states in paragraph 2 of annex I that "the activities of the Department should be so organized and directed as to promote to the greatest possible extent an informed understanding of the work and purposes of the United Nations among the peoples of the world",

Concurring also with the view of the Secretary-General that the contents of public information and communications should be placed at the heart of the strategic management of the United Nations and that a culture of communications should permeate all levels of the Organization, as a means of fully informing the peoples of the world of the aims and activities of the United Nations, in accordance with the purposes and principles enshrined in the Charter of the United Nations, in order to create broad-based global support for the United Nations,

Stressing that the primary mission of the Department of Public Information is to provide, through its outreach activities, accurate, impartial, comprehensive and timely information to the public on the tasks and responsibilities of the United Nations in order to strengthen international support for the activities of the Organization with the greatest transparency,

Noting that the comprehensive review of the work of the Department of Public Information, requested by the General Assembly in its resolution 56/253 of 24 December 2001, and the implementation of its first phase, described in the report of the Secretary-General on reorientation of United Nations activities in the field of public information and communications to the Committee on Information at its twenty-fourth session, as well as the report of the Secretary-General entitled "Strengthening of the United Nations: an agenda for further change", and its resolution 57/300 of 20 December 2002, as they apply to the Department of Public Information, provide an opportunity to take further steps to rationalize the work of the Department in order to enhance its efficiency and effectiveness, and to maximize the use of its resources,

Expressing its concern that the gap in the information and communication technologies between the developed and the developing countries has continued to widen and that vast segments of the population in developing countries are not benefiting from the present information and technology revolution, and, in this regard, underlining the necessity of rectifying the imbalances of the global information and technology revolution in order to make it more just, equitable and effective,

Recognizing that developments in the information and communication technology revolution open vast new opportunities for economic growth and social development and can play an important role in the eradication of poverty in developing countries, and, at the same time, emphasizing that it also poses challenges and risks and could lead to the further widening of disparities between and within countries,

Recalling its resolution 56/262 of 15 February 2002 on multilingualism, and emphasizing the importance of making appropriate use of the official languages of the United Nations in the activities of the Department of Public Information, aiming to eliminate the disparity between the use of English and the other five official languages,

Welcoming Saudi Arabia to membership in the Committee on Information,

I

Introduction

1. *Reaffirms* its resolution 13(I), in which it established the Department of Public Information, and all other relevant General Assembly resolutions related to the activities of the Department;

2. *Calls upon* the Secretary-General, in respect of the public information policies and activities of the United Nations, to continue to implement fully the recommendations contained in paragraph 2 of its resolution 48/44 B of 10 December 1993 and other mandates as established by the General Assembly;

3. *Emphasizes* the importance of the medium-term plan for the period 2002-2005 as a guideline that sets out the overall orientation of the public information programme for the Organization's goals through effective communication;

4. *Reaffirms* that the United Nations remains the indispensable foundation of a peaceful and just world and that its voice must be heard in a clear and effective manner, and emphasizes the essential role of the Department of Public Information in this context;

5. *Welcomes* the proposals of the Secretary-General to improve the effective and targeted delivery of public information activities, including the restructuring of the Department of Public Information, in accordance with the relevant resolutions and decisions of the General Assembly;

6. *Reaffirms* the central role of the Committee on Information in United Nations public information policies and activities, including the restructuring process of the Department of Public Information, and the prioritization of its activities, and welcomes the continued constructive interaction between the Department and the members of the Committee;

7. *Calls upon* Member States to ensure, to the extent possible, that recommendations relating to the programme of the Department of Public Information originate and are considered in the Committee on Information;

8. *Requests* the Department of Public Information, following the priorities laid down by the General Assembly in the medium-term plan and using the United Nations Millennium Declaration as its guide, to pay particular attention to such major issues as the eradication of poverty, conflict prevention, sustainable development, human rights, the human immunodeficiency virus/acquired immunodeficiency syndrome (HIV/AIDS) epidemic, combating terrorism in all its forms and manifestations and the needs of the African continent;

9. *Also requests* the Department of Public Information to pay attention to all major issues addressed in the United Nations Millennium Declaration and the Millennium Development Goals in carrying out its activities;

10. *Concurs* with the Secretary-General on the need to enhance the technological infrastructure of the Department of Public Information in order to widen its outreach and improve the United Nations web site;

11. *Recognizes* the important work carried out by the United Nations Educational, Scientific and Cultural Organization and its collaboration with news agencies and broadcasting organizations in developing countries in disseminating information on priority issues, and encourages a continued collaboration between the Department of Public Information and the United Nations Educational, Scientific and Cultural Organization in the promotion of culture and in the fields of education and communication;

II

General activities of the Department of Public Information

12. *Welcomes* the steps taken towards the restructuring of the Department of Public Information, as described in the report of the Secretary-General on the reorientation of United Nations activities in the field of public information and communications, and encourages the Secretary-General to continue the reorientation exercise and efforts to improve the efficiency and productivity of the Department, including wide-ranging and possibly new innovative proposals, taking into account broad principles and directions contained

in the present resolution, and to report thereon to the Committee on Information at its twenty-sixth session;

13. *Reaffirms* that the Department of Public Information is the focal point for information policies of the United Nations and the primary news centre for information about the United Nations, its activities and those of the Secretary-General, and encourages a closer integration of functions between the Department and those offices providing spokesman services for the Secretary-General;

14. *Welcomes* the progress achieved since the commencement of the reorientation exercise in enhancing the performance and effectiveness of the Department of Public Information in accordance with the mandates established by the General Assembly and the recommendations of the Committee on Information, also welcomes, in this regard, its decision to implement an annual programme impact review, making self-evaluation a part of the daily work of all programme managers with a view to institutionalizing performance management, and requests the Secretary-General to transmit the report on the Department's annual programme impact review to the Committee on Information at its successive sessions;

15. *Requests* the Secretary-General, in the context of the reorientation process, to continue to exert all efforts to ensure that publications and other information services of the Secretariat, including the United Nations web site and the United Nations News Service, contain comprehensive, objective and equitable information about the issues before the Organization and that they maintain editorial independence, impartiality, accuracy and full consistency with resolutions and decisions of the General Assembly;

16. *Reiterates* that all printed materials of the Department of Public Information, in accordance with existing mandates, should not duplicate other publications of the United Nations system and should be produced in a cost-effective manner;

17. *Welcomes* the efforts of the Department of Public Information to reconstitute the Publications Board, in accordance with existing legislative mandates;

18. *Urges* the Department of Public Information to continue to exhibit transparency to the greatest extent possible, so as to increase awareness of the impact of its programmes and activities;

19. *Emphasizes* that, through its reorientation, the Department of Public Information should maintain and improve its activities in the areas of special interest to developing countries and, where appropriate, other countries with special needs, including countries in transition, and that such reorientation contributes to bridging the existing gap between the developing and the developed countries in the crucial field of public information and communications;

20. *Encourages* the Secretary-General to strengthen the coordination between the Department of Public Information and other departments of the Secretariat, including the designation of focal points to work with substantive departments to identify target audiences and develop information programmes and media strategies for priority issues, and emphasizes that public information capacities and activities in other departments should function under the guidance of the Department;

21. *Welcomes* the initiatives that have been taken by the Department of Public Information to strengthen the public information system of the United Nations, and, in this regard, stresses the importance of a coherent and results-oriented approach being taken by the United Nations, the specialized agencies and the programmes and funds of the United Nations system involved in public information activities as well as the provision of resources for their implementation, and that feedback from Member States on the relevance and effectiveness of its programme delivery should be taken into account;

22. *Also welcomes* the report of the Secretary-General on the activities of the United Nations Communications Group in 2002, commends the Department of Public Information on its active and constructive participation in the Group, in particular its efforts to promote inter-agency coordination in the field of public information, encourages the Department to continue to play a key role in the newly established Group, takes note of the efforts being undertaken by the Group to develop further several key initiatives, and requests the Secretary-General to report to the Committee on Information at successive sessions on the activities of the Group;

23. *Appreciates* the continued efforts of the Department of Public Information in issuing daily press releases, and requests the Department to continue providing this invaluable service to both Member States and representatives of the media, while considering possible means of improving their production process and streamlining their format, structure and length, keeping in mind the views of Member States and the fact that other departments may be providing similar or overlapping services in this regard;

24. *Acknowledges* the mission statement proposed in the report of the Secretary-General, which is intended to include all activities of the Department, and which reads as follows: "The Department of Public Information's mission is to help fulfil the substantive purposes of the United Nations by strategically communicating the activities and concerns of the Organization to achieve the greatest public impact";

25. *Welcomes* the new operating model of the Department of Public Information as described in the report of the Secretary-General which, inter alia, recognizes that content generation emanates from the other departments and offices of the Secretariat and organizations of the United Nations system, while content coordination and refinement as well as content presentation and distribution are the responsibility of the Department, working in close cooperation with the media, Member States and civil society partners;

26. *Requests* that during the deliberations on the item entitled "Questions relating to information" in the Special Political and Decolonization Committee (Fourth Committee) during the successive regular sessions of the General Assembly, an informal interaction between the Secretariat and members of the Committee should take place after the presentation by the Under-Secretary-General for Communications and Public Information on the substance of that oral briefing, within existing resources;

Multilingualism and public information

27. *Welcomes* the ongoing efforts of the Department of Public Information to enhance multilingualism in its activities and encourages the Department to continue its endeavours in this regard;

28. *Emphasizes* the importance of ensuring the full, equitable treatment of all the official languages of the United Nations in all activities of the Department of Public Information, and stresses the importance of fully implementing its resolution 52/214 of 22 December 1997, in section C of which it requested the Secretary-General to ensure that the texts of all new public documents in all six official languages, and information materials of the United Nations, are made available daily through the United Nations web site and are accessible to Member States without delay;

29. *Reaffirms* its request to the Secretary-General to ensure that the Department of Public Information has appropriate staffing capacity in all official languages of the United Nations to undertake all its activities;

30. *Reminds* the Secretary-General of the need to include in future programme budget proposals for the Department of Public Information the importance of using all six official languages in its activities;

Bridging the digital divide

31. *Recalls* the decision, endorsed in its resolution 56/183 of 21 December 2001, to convene the World Summit on the Information Society in Geneva in December 2003 and in Tunis in 2005, welcomes the initiatives undertaken by the Department of Public Information for this Summit, encourages States, relevant United Nations bodies and entities, other intergovernmental institutions and civil society to continue to actively participate in this process, and reaffirms the importance of the active involvement and support of the Department in raising global awareness of the Summit and its main objectives;

32. *Commends* the Secretary-General for the establishment of the United Nations Information Technology Service, the Health InterNetwork and the Information and Communications Technology Task Force with a view to bridging the digital divide and as a response to the continuing gulf between developed and developing countries, welcomes the contribution of the Department of Public Information in publicizing the efforts of the Secretary-General to close the digital divide as a means of spurring economic growth and as a response to the continuing gulf between developed and developing countries, and, in this context, requests the Department to further enhance its role;

III

New programmatic priorities for the Department of Public Information

33. *Takes note* of the report of the Secretary-General on programmatic aspects of the proposed programme budget for 2004-2005 for the Department of Public Information, and welcomes the new subprogramme structure that includes: strategic communications services, news services, library services and outreach services;

34. *Acknowledges* that the Department of Public Information, with the assistance of the Office of Internal Oversight Services of the Secretariat, is currently in the process of formulating methodologies and conducting a systematic evaluation of the impact, efficiency and cost-effectiveness of the activities of the Department over a three-year period, as requested by the General Assembly in its resolution 57/300, and requests the Secretary-General to report on the progress made to the Committee on Information at its twenty-sixth session;

35. *Reaffirms* that the Department of Public Information must prioritize its work programme while respecting existing mandates and in line with rule 5.6 of the Regulations and Rules Governing Programme Planning, the Programme Aspects of the Budget, the Monitoring of Implementation and the Methods of Evaluation, to focus its message and concentrate its efforts better and, as a function of performance management, to match its programmes with the needs of its target audiences, on the basis of improved feedback and evaluation mechanisms;

36. *Underlines* the need for the proposed indicators of achievement and expected accomplishments, which for the first time form part of the programme budget, to be clearly defined, measurable and able to contribute to a meaningful evaluation of activities;

United Nations information centres

37. *Stresses* that the United Nations information centres and information components or regional hubs, as applicable, should play a significant role in disseminating information about the work of the Organization to the peoples of the world, including in the areas outlined in the United Nations Millennium Declaration, and emphasizes that the information centres, or regional hubs, as applicable, as the "field voice" of the Department of Public Information, should promote public awareness of and mobilize support for the work of the United Nations at the local level, bearing in mind that information in the local languages has the strongest impact on the local populations;

38. *Takes note* of the note by the Secretary-General transmitting the report of the Office of Internal Oversight Services on the review of the structure and operations of United Nations information centres, and requests the Secretary-General to submit further detailed information to the Committee on Information at its twenty-sixth session;

39. *Welcomes* the ongoing efforts of the Department of Public Information to review the allocation of both staff and financial resources to United Nations information centres with a view to possibly transferring resources from information centres in developed countries to United Nations information activities in developing countries, emphasizing the needs of the least developed countries, and to any other activities of high priority, such as multilingualism on the United Nations web site and evaluation of services, in consultation with concerned Member States;

40. *Reaffirms* paragraph 15 of its resolution 57/300, in which it took note of the proposal of the Secretary-General contained in action 8 of his report, to rationalize the network of United Nations information centres around regional hubs, where appropriate, in consultation with concerned Member States, starting with the creation of a Western European hub, followed by a similar approach in other high-cost developed countries, and requests the Secretary-General to submit a progress report on the implementation of the proposal with the objective of applying this initiative in

other regions, in consultation with Member States, where this initiative will strengthen the flow and exchange of information in developing countries;

41. *Encourages* the efforts by some United Nations information centres to develop their own web pages in local languages, also encourages the Department of Public Information to provide resources and technical facilities, in particular to those information centres whose web pages are not yet operational and to develop web pages in the respective local languages of their host countries, and further encourages host countries to respond to the needs of the information centres;

42. *Recalls* the appeal made by the Secretary-General to the host countries of United Nations information centres to facilitate the work of the centres in their countries by providing rent-free or rent-subsidized premises, while taking into account the economic condition of the host countries and bearing in mind that such support should not be a substitute for the full allocation of financial resources for the information centres in the context of the programme budget of the United Nations;

43. *Notes* the continuing support of the Department of Public Information in the consolidation of the United Nations field presence in a single United Nations house, and requests the Secretary-General to report in detail on the progress made to the Committee on Information at its twenty-sixth session;

IV

Strategic communications services

44. *Acknowledges* that the strategic communications services, to be implemented by the newly created Strategic Communications Division, will be responsible for devising and disseminating United Nations messages by developing communications strategies, in close collaboration with the substantive departments, United Nations funds and programmes and the specialized agencies of the United Nations, in full compliance with the legislative mandates;

Promotional campaigns

45. *Recognizes* that promotional campaigns aimed at supporting special sessions and international conferences of the United Nations are part of the core responsibility of the Department of Public Information, and welcomes the efforts of the Department to examine creative ways in which it can organize and implement these campaigns in partnership with the substantive departments concerned, using the United Nations Millennium Declaration as its guide;

46. *Supports* the efforts of the Department of Public Information, while ensuring respect for the priorities established by the General Assembly, to also focus its promotional campaigns on the major issues identified by the Secretary-General;

47. *Appreciates* the work of the Department of Public Information in promoting, through its campaigns, issues of importance to the international community, such as sustainable development, children, HIV/AIDS, malaria and other diseases and decolonization, as well as the dialogue among civilizations, culture of peace and tolerance and the consequences of the Chernobyl disaster, and encourages the Department, in cooperation with the countries concerned and with the relevant organizations and bodies of the United Nations system, to continue to take appropriate measures to enhance world public awareness of these and other important global issues;

48. *Encourages* the Department of Public Information to continue to work within the United Nations Communications Group to coordinate the implementation of communication strategies with the heads of information of the agencies, funds and programmes of the United Nations system;

49. *Stresses* the need for the renewed emphasis in support of Africa's development, in particular by the Department of Public Information, in order to promote awareness in the international community of the nature of the critical economic and social situation in Africa and of the priorities of the New Partnership for Africa's Development;

Role of the Department of Public Information in United Nations peacekeeping

50. *Commends* the efforts of the Secretary-General to strengthen the public information capacity of the Department of Public Information for the establishment and functioning of the information components of peacekeeping operations and of political and peacebuilding missions of the United Nations, including its promotional efforts and other information support activities, and requests the Secretariat to continue to ensure the involvement of the Department from the planning stage of future operations through interdepartmental consultations and coordination with other departments of the Secretariat, in particular with the Department of Peacekeeping Operations;

51. *Stresses* the importance of enhancing the public information capacity of the Department of Public Information in the field of peacekeeping operations and its role in the selection process of spokespersons for United Nations peacekeeping operations or missions, and, in this regard, encourages the Department to second spokespersons who have the necessary skills to fulfil the tasks of the operations or missions, taking into account the equitable geographical distribution in accordance with Chapter XV, Article 101, paragraph 3, of the Charter of the United Nations, and to consider views expressed, especially by host countries, when appropriate, in this regard;

52. *Requests* the Secretary-General to continue to report to the Committee on Information on the role of the Department of Public Information in United Nations peacekeeping at its successive sessions;

53. *Welcomes* the transfer of the functions of the Cartographic Section from the Department of Public Information to the Department of Peacekeeping Operations, since the outputs of the Section are more closely aligned to the needs and activities of that Department;

V

News services

54. *Stresses* that the central objective of the news services, implemented by the News and Media Division, is the timely delivery of accurate, objective and balanced news and information emanating from the United Nations system in all four mass media—print, radio, television and Internet—to the media and other audiences worldwide with the overall emphasis on multilingualism;

Traditional means of communication

55. *Also stresses* that radio remains one of the most cost-effective and far-reaching traditional media available to the Department of Public Information and an important instrument in United Nations activities, including development and peacekeeping, with a view to achieving a broad client base around the world;

56. *Notes with satisfaction* the success of the pilot project on the development of an international radio broadcasting capacity for the United Nations, and endorses the proposal of the Secretary-General that the pilot project be made an integral part of the activities of the Department;

57. *Requests* the Secretary-General to pay full attention to the parity of the six official languages in expanding the international radio broadcasting capacity;

58. *Notes* the efforts being made by the Department of Public Information to disseminate programmes directly to broadcasting stations all over the world in the six official languages, with the addition of Portuguese, as well as in other languages, where possible, and, in this regard, stresses the need for impartiality and objectivity concerning information activities of the United Nations;

59. *Encourages* the Department of Public Information to continue building partnerships with local, national and regional broadcasters to extend the United Nations message to all the corners of the world;

60. *Emphasizes* that United Nations Radio and Television should take full advantage of the technological infrastructure made available in recent years, including satellite platforms, information and communication technologies and the Internet, and requests the Secretary-General, as a part of the reorientation of the Department of Public Information, to consider a global strategy for broadcasting, taking into account existing technologies;

United Nations web site

61. *Reiterates its appreciation* for the efforts of the Department of Public Information in creating a high-quality, user-friendly and cost-effective web site, noting that this is especially noteworthy considering the scope of the undertaking, the budget constraints within the United Nations and the remarkably rapid expansion of the World Wide Web, reaffirms that the web site remains a very useful tool for media, non-governmental organizations, educational institutions, Member States and the general public, and welcomes the creation of the United Nations web site on terrorism;

62. *Encourages* the Department of Public Information to continue to take the necessary measures in order to ensure accessibility to the United Nations web site by persons with disabilities, including visual and hearing disabilities, and asks the Department to report to the Committee on Information at its twenty-sixth session on its efforts in this regard;

63. *Notes with concern* that the multilingual development and enrichment of the United Nations web site has been slower than expected, because of a lack of resources, among other factors, and that content-providing offices have not, in general, been making their materials available on the United Nations web site in all six official languages;

64. *Stresses* the need to adopt a decision on the multilingual development, maintenance and enrichment of the United Nations web site, considering, inter alia, the possibility of organizational restructuring towards separate language units for each of the six official languages within the Department of Public Information, in order to achieve full parity among the official languages of the United Nations;

65. *Reaffirms* its request to the Secretary-General to ensure, until such a decision has been taken and implemented, to the extent possible and while maintaining an up-to-date and accurate web site, the equitable distribution of financial and human resources within the Department of Public Information allocated to the United Nations web site among all official languages on a continuous basis, and to make every possible effort to ensure also that all materials contained on the web site that do not change and do not need regular maintenance are made available in all six official languages;

66. *Also reaffirms* the need to achieve full parity among the six official languages on the United Nations web site, and, in this regard, takes note of the proposal of the Secretary-General, as contained in paragraph 33 of his report on the continued development, maintenance and enrichment of the United Nations web site in the six official languages, to translate all English materials and databases posted on the United Nations web site by the respective content-providing offices of the Secretariat into all official languages, and requests the Secretary-General to report to the Committee on Information at its twenty-sixth session on the most practical, efficient and cost-effective means of implementing this proposal;

67. *Requests* the Secretary-General to include in his report to the Committee on Information at its twenty-sixth session proposals relating to the designation of a date by which all supporting arrangements would be in place for the implementation of this concept, after which date parity would continue, as well as proposals relating to the exemption from translation of specific items on the United Nations web site;

68. *Stresses* the importance of access for the public to the United Nations Treaty Collection and United Nations parliamentary documentation;

69. *Encourages* the Secretary-General, through the Department of Public Information, to continue to take full advantage of recent developments in information technology, including the Internet, in order to improve, in a cost-effective manner, the expeditious dissemination of information on the United Nations, in accordance with the priorities established by the General Assembly and taking into account the linguistic diversity of the Organization;

70. *Welcomes* the establishment of the United Nations News Centre in Arabic, and looks forward to the implementation of the United Nations News Centre in the remaining official languages by the end of 2003, with a view to achieving language parity on the United Nations web site;

71. *Also welcomes* the proposal of the Secretary-General to provide free, public access to the Official Document System of the United Nations through a linkage with the Organization's web site for consideration in the context of the proposed programme budget for 2004-2005, and requests the Secretary-General

to report to the Committee on Information at its twenty-sixth session in this regard;

72. *Commends* the Information Technology Services Division of the Office of Central Support Services of the Secretariat on its efforts to ensure that the required technological infrastructure is in place to accommodate the imminent linkage of the Official Document System to the United Nations web site, and also commends the Department of Public Information for addressing issues of content management relating to that System;

73. *Notes* that the integration of the Official Document System with the United Nations web site will significantly enhance the multilingual nature of the site and will lead to efficiencies throughout all Secretariat departments through the elimination of duplicate formatting and duplicate posting of documents on the site;

74. *Welcomes* the electronic mail-based United Nations News Service, distributed worldwide through e-mail by the Department of Public Information, and requests the Department to provide this service in all official languages, ensuring that news-breaking stories and news alerts are accurate, impartial and free of bias;

75. *Takes note* of the report of the Secretary-General on the efforts of the High-Level Committee on Management to establish a United Nations portal, an interagency search facility encompassing the public web sites of all United Nations system organizations, a description of which is contained in annex II to the report of the Secretary-General;

76. *Calls upon* the Department of Public Information to encourage all United Nations system entities to participate in the United Nations system search pilot project, and requests the Secretary-General to report to the Committee on Information at its twenty-sixth session on the activities of the High-Level Committee on Management in this regard;

VI

Library services

77. *Notes* that the Dag Hammarskjöld Library is part of the Outreach Division of the Department of Public Information, also notes the continuing efforts of the Secretary-General to make the Library a virtual library with world outreach, reiterates the need to maintain the provision of hard copies to Member States, subject to the relevant provisions of its resolution 57/283 B of 15 April 2003, and further notes the efforts of the Secretary-General to enrich, on a multilingual basis, the stock of books and journals in the Library, including publications on peace and security and development-related issues, in order to ensure that the Library continues to be a broadly accessible resource for information about the United Nations and its activities;

78. *Welcomes* the creation of the Steering Committee on the Modernization and Integrated Management of United Nations Libraries, which is to develop and implement a strategy to achieve a more modern, efficient and accessible system within the United Nations, requests the Secretary-General, in guiding the work of the Steering Committee, to take into account the specificity and comparative advantage of each member library while ensuring an integrated, coherent and coordinated approach on United Nations libraries management and policy, and also requests the Secretary-General to report on the work of the Steering Committee to the Committee on Information at its twenty-sixth session;

79. *Recognizes* the importance of the depository libraries in disseminating information and knowledge about United Nations activities, and, in this connection, urges the Dag Hammarskjöld Library, in its capacity as the focal point, to take the initiatives necessary to strengthen such libraries by providing regional training and other assistance;

80. *Notes* the holding of training courses, conducted by the Dag Hammarskjöld Library for the representatives of Member States and Secretariat staff on the use of Cyberseek, web search, the Intranet, United Nations documentation, United Nations Info Quest and the Official Document System of the United Nations;

81. *Recalls* paragraph 44 of its resolution 56/64 B of 24 December 2001, in which it welcomed the role of the Department of Public Information in fostering increased collaboration among libraries of the United Nations system, particularly in establishing one central system-wide online catalogue that would allow for the searching of the bibliographic records of all print holdings of all United Nations system libraries; commends the International Computing Centre for developing the United Nations System Shared Cataloguing and Public Access System, which provides a single point of access to library catalogues, indexes and abstract databases, library holdings, links to full-text resources, and archives; also commends the Department for its role in the development of the United Nations Shared Cataloguing and Public Access System; requests the Department to encourage all United Nations system organizations to participate in the System; and requests the Secretary-General to report to the Committee on Information at its twenty-sixth session in this regard;

82. *Looks forward* to the in-depth review of the library activities requested in paragraph 34 of its resolution 56/253, and requests that such a review be presented as soon as possible, and no later than at the twenty-sixth session of the Committee on Information;

83. *Takes note* of the report of the Secretary-General on modernization and integrated management of United Nations libraries, and looks forward to further information and proposals as requested in paragraph 14 of its resolution 57/300, to be submitted to the relevant United Nations bodies, including the Committee on Information at its twenty-sixth session;

VII

Outreach services

84. *Acknowledges* that the outreach services, which are to be implemented by the Outreach Division of the Department of Public Information, will work towards promoting awareness of the role and work of the United Nations on priority issues;

85. *Notes* the importance of the continued implementation by the Department of Public Information of the ongoing programme for broadcasters and journalists from developing countries and countries in transition, as mandated by the General Assembly, and encourages the Department to consider how best to

maximize the benefits derived from the programme by reviewing, inter alia, its duration and the number of its participants;

86. *Recognizes* the need for the Department of Public Information to increase its outreach services in all regions, and reiterates the need to include, in the reorientation of United Nations activities in the field of public information and communications, an analysis of the present reach and scope of the activities of the Department, identifying the widest possible spectrum of audiences and geographical areas that are not covered adequately and that may require special attention, including the appropriate means of communication and bearing in mind local language requirements;

87. *Congratulates* the United Nations Correspondents Association for its Dag Hammarskjöld Memorial Scholarship Fund, which sponsors journalists from developing countries to come to the United Nations Headquarters and report on the activities during the General Assembly, and urges donors to extend financial support to the Fund so that it may increase the number of such scholarships to journalists in this context;

VIII
Final remarks

88. *Requests* the Secretary-General to report to the Committee on Information at its twenty-sixth session and to the General Assembly at its fifty-ninth session on the activities of the Department of Public Information and on the implementation of the recommendations contained in the present resolution;

89. *Requests* the Committee on Information to report to the General Assembly at its fifty-ninth session;

90. *Decides* to include in the provisional agenda of its fifty-ninth session the item entitled "Questions relating to information".

Reorientation of information and communications activities

In response to General Assembly resolution 57/130 B [YUN 2002, p. 590], the Secretary-General submitted a March report to the Committee on Information [A/AC.198/2003/2] on progress in repositioning DPI to meet the UN communications challenges with renewed focus and greater clarity of purpose. It built on a previous reorientation report [YUN 2002, p. 584], which outlined the findings of a comprehensive review of DPI's management and operations and possible strategic actions to be taken as a result. The March report also detailed, in response to resolution 57/300 [ibid., p. 1353], the next phase of departmental reform and set out steps to be taken to implement the actions contained in the Secretary-General's 2002 report on strengthening the United Nations: an agenda for further change, as they applied to DPI [ibid., p. 585].

To clarify its goals and purposes and enhance its effectiveness and efficiency, DPI formulated a new mission statement which affirmed that its mission was "to help fulfil the substantive purposes of the United Nations by strategically communicating the activities and concerns of the Organization to achieve the greatest public impact". Its core message, in line with the Millennium Declaration adopted by Assembly resolution 55/2 [YUN 2000, p. 49], would focus on poverty eradication, conflict prevention, sustainable development, human rights, HIV/AIDS, the battle against international terrorism and the needs of Africa. To fulfil its mission, DPI would continue to disseminate the UN message, taking into account the needs of its target audiences, through traditional means, including print materials, radio and television, and the Internet on the UN web site and associated sites. Resource levels allocated to each function would be readjusted as part of a continuing review process.

The Secretary-General approved a new operating model for DPI, based on a clear conception of the Department's role and an elaboration of its functions, emphasizing the communications needs of the United Nations, while also providing expected services to Member States. The model recognized that, while content emanated from other Secretariat departments and offices and UN system organizations, content coordination, refinement, presentation and distribution were DPI's responsibility, in cooperation with the media, Member States and civil society. A new organizational structure for DPI based on that model, which included a Strategic Communications Division, a News and Media Division and an Outreach Division, was put into effect on 1 November 2002. The Office of the Spokesman for the Secretary-General remained administratively within and worked closely with DPI, but continued to report directly to the Executive Office of the Secretary-General. The former Public Affairs Division was abolished and its functions divided between the new Strategic Communications and Outreach Divisions.

The Strategic Communications Division would devise and disseminate UN messages centred around priority themes, and ensure that communication was placed at the heart of strategic management of the United Nations. The Division included the Information Centres Service, which managed the administrative, programme and dissemination functions of the global UNIC network, a Committee Liaison Unit, which included the secretariats of the Committee on Information and UNCG, and a Communications Campaign Service, which served client offices through focal points in its four sections: development; Palestine, decolonization and human rights; peace and security; and Africa. The new Africa Section was devoted to promoting Africa's development and would include the quarterly magazine *Africa Recovery*, published in English and French, as one of its outputs. Information and operational support for the information component of field missions would continue as a core function of the Peace and Security Section.

Thematic promotional campaigns would be implemented using all the Department's assets, including its multimedia outlets, outreach to civil society, private sector partnerships and, at the local level, UNICs. A new issue-driven communications strategy for each department, rather than one that was event-driven, was being developed to promote UN work, building on the success of the global conferences campaigns.

The central objective of the News and Media Division was the real-time delivery of accurate, objective and balanced news and information to the media and other audiences worldwide in the context of the Internet-driven 24-hour news cycle, through the immediate dissemination in print, radio, television and the Internet, of news emanating from the UN system. The creation of an Internet Service, comprising the News Services and the Website Sections, had greatly facilitated the new approach. The new United Nations News Service, part of the United Nations News Centre on the web site, delivered news throughout the day to 10,000 subscribers in 130 countries; an Arabic version of the News Centre was launched in January and work was under way on similar sites in other official languages. Developments in the production and dissemination of the Division's products were complemented by partnerships with broadcasters and other promotional activities.

DPI was placing new emphasis on its relations with clients and partners external to the United Nations through the Outreach Division, which combined much of the former Library and Information Resources Division with the functions previously carried out by the Public Liaison Service of the Public Affairs Division. Its Civil Society Service brought together under one umbrella the new Educational Outreach Section, "The UN Works" programme, partnerships with the private sector, ongoing programmes such as those for non-governmental organization (NGOs), and special programmes and observances, exhibits, guided tours and other services to the public. The Educational Outreach Section was strengthening relationships with the academic community by working closely with the Group Programmes Unit and the NGO Section, among other measures. DPI would widen the reach of its publications through an energized and constantly updated web site, and by placing their contents as syndicated features in publications around the world, with the assistance of UNICs.

As a first step in the implementation of the Secretary-General's 2002 reform proposals [YUN 2002, p. 585], a Steering Committee for the Modernization and Integrated Management of United Nations Libraries was established to improve the provision of UN library services (see p. 634). As to his proposals regarding UN publications, the Executive Committees would be called on to plan and coordinate all publications within their respective thematic areas [YUN 1997, p. 1389] in order to reduce their number and improve the coherence, focus and scheduling among the Organization's many publications. DPI also planned to reconstitute the Publications Board within the Outreach Division as a standard-setting body with appropriate membership and terms of reference. The functions formerly performed by the Production and Coordination Unit had been eliminated or were being handled elsewhere. The Secretary-General's proposal to transfer the Cartographic Section from DPI to the Department of Peacekeeping Operations would be reflected in the context of the proposed 2004-2005 programme budget.

DPI was preparing to implement his proposal to rationalize the network of UNICs around regional hubs, starting with the creation of a Western European hub. The new operating concept aimed to achieve a more equitable distribution of resources to information centres in all regions and to redeploy resources to other high-priority activities, including advancing multilingualism on the UN web site and the systematic evaluation of the impact of major product and service lines, in accordance with results-based management. (For more information on the regionalization of UNICs, see p. 637.)

Regarding performance management, DPI was formulating methodologies and planned to conduct a systematic evaluation of the impact, efficiency and cost-effectiveness of its activities over a three-year period, with assistance from the Office of Internal Oversight Services (OIOS), as requested by the Assembly in resolution 57/300 [YUN 2002, p. 1353]. It had also introduced an annual programme impact review, with a view to institutionalizing performance management, and, in that context, agreed to be an OIOS pilot as it looked to update and promote monitoring and self-evaluation.

The report also provided information on the UN web site, which was dealt with in a separate report of the Secretary-General [A/58/217] (see p. 637).

Annexed to the report were guidelines and criteria for the regionalization of UNICs and information concerning the Official Document System and the UN web site portal, as requested by the General Assembly in resolution 57/130 B [YUN 2002, p. 590].

Agenda for further change

In response to General Assembly resolution 57/300 [YUN 2002, p. 1353], the Secretary-General, in a September report [A/58/351] on the status of implementation of reform measures described in his 2002 report on strengthening the United Nations: an agenda for further change [YUN 2002, p. 585], provided information on, among other subjects, enhancing public information and streamlining publications. The Secretary-General discussed the restructuring of DPI, the new evaluation process, the regionalization of UNICs and libraries management.

Updating the information provided in his March report to the Committee on Information (see p. 630), the Secretary-General said that results from the first annual programme impact review (see p. 631), which DPI was developing with OIOS, would be reported to the Committee on Information in 2004. By the end of 2003, the Department would have a set of preliminary performance measures in place, along with baseline data relating to departmental goals, following which a two-step process for assessing impact would be undertaken. Since the exercise would require resources and expertise not currently available to DPI, the involvement of external partners was anticipated. Training to support DPI's new operating model was under way. Most programme managers had been trained in evaluation techniques, and staff at all levels were undergoing training in measuring the impact and effectiveness of products and activities.

DPI was working on an action plan, in consultation with Member States, to ensure a seamless transition from the model of UNICs at the national level to a regional model. The regional hub in Western Europe, to be created by 31 December, would be located in Brussels, Belgium (see p. 637). The Committee on Information would consider, in 2004, a progress report on the regional hub proposal, with the objective of applying the initiative in other regions.

The Steering Committee for the Modernization and Integrated Management of United Nations Libraries, established in January, was tasked with developing policies and coordinating operations among all UN libraries (see p. 634). It planned to complete by late 2003 the establishment of a multilingual UN libraries research gateway on the Internet, the creation of a master list of core areas of specialization at UN Libraries worldwide and the full incorporation of the Economic and Social Commission for Asia and the Pacific in the Shared Indexing Programme.

The Publications Board was reconstituted as a standard-setting body in February, and its main mandate was to review and determine the policies governing the preparation, distribution and sale of printed and electronic publications, and to draft new and revised administrative instructions to implement publications policy. As a follow-up to resolution 57/300, a separate working group was established to examine the feasibility and cost of online publications delivery, supplemented by a print-on-demand capability. As an integral part of the preparation of the biennial budget, all publications programmes proposed by Secretariat entities were channelled through the relevant Executive Committees, each of which was responsible for reviewing plans for publication, ensuring coherence, avoiding duplication and establishing clear priorities regarding what was to be published. During the previous year, the Executive Committee on Economic and Social Affairs pioneered an exercise, which would continue annually, to coordinate its members' publication programmes. Overall, there had been an 18 per cent decrease in recurrent publications and a 23 per cent decrease in non-recurrent publications during the period 2002/03 to 2004/05. Budget data indicated that 192 publications and reports had been discontinued.

UN international radio broadcasting capacity

The Committee on Information considered a March report of the Secretary-General [A/AC.198/2003/4], submitted pursuant to General Assembly resolutions 56/64 B [YUN 2001, p. 559] and 57/130 B [YUN 2002, p. 590], on the implementation of the pilot project to develop an international radio broadcasting capacity for the United Nations, which was launched in 2000 [YUN 2000, p. 574]. The Secretary-General stated that DPI commissioned an independent, in-depth survey on the estimated worldwide audience for UN Radio programmes in the six official UN languages, plus Portuguese. Representing a snapshot of listenership as at November 2002, and carried out with the active participation of 180 partner stations, the survey estimated conservatively that more than 133 million people listened to UN Radio at least once a week. That figure did not include affiliate radio stations of partner broadcasters, nor stations transmitting by short wave or satellite. Such extensive outreach was achieved with the relatively small investment of the additional $2.4 million provided to DPI by Member States per biennium. Many of the participating partner stations were major national broadcasters, a clear indication of worldwide interest in UN Radio broadcasts. The daily UN Radio feeds provided a valuable service, supplying material not available from other news sources. UN Radio also provided a range and depth of coverage, including regional focus and regional voices, and, as the public voice of the United Nations, it spoke with unique authority. However, technological factors, particularly the continuing heavy dependence on transmitting programmes through the telephone, were a constraint on the further fulfilment of the potential of UN Radio. Efforts by the international community to help bridge the digital divide, specifically by increasing broadcasters' access to satellite and Internet technology, would help to overcome such limitations. The report described the methodology of the survey and included a breakdown of results by language and region.

To ensure the further expansion of UN Radio outreach, building partnerships with local, regional and national broadcasters worldwide continued to be a priority for DPI. UN Radio was also building a higher profile on the Internet through active cooperation with the United Nations News Centre, and the expansion of the News Centre into more of the official languages would increase the synergy between the two. The expansion of the UN Radio's client base would continue to be central to DPI's efforts to increase the interest of news organizations and the media. In that regard, renewed efforts would be directed towards Asia, where there was great potential. As part of its promotional efforts, DPI was exploring a number of possible initiatives, including coordinated telemarketing to cultivate new clients; an electronic newsletter with updated information on the Department's radio programming and its radio station partners; and more regular participation of broadcasters in relevant major international meetings and conferences. An important element of the strategy was expanding the number of partners in developed countries. Work was under way on the new integrated and automated news-gathering and production capacity, which would considerably strengthen the capacity to provide broadcasters with material more rapidly and flexibly. The planned modernization and upgrading of the UN International Broadcasting Centre with digital technology would also greatly facilitate the dissemination of the radio programmes to client stations. Continued efforts by Member States to close the digital divide were directly relevant to DPI's efforts to improve and expand its radio services.

The report concluded that radio remained the most potent means of communication for the United Nations, particularly in developing countries. A firm mandate from Member States to continue the international broadcasting capacity would ensure that radio continued to contribute, cost-effectively, to DPI's overall goal of generating understanding about the United Nations.

DPI activities

In response to General Assembly resolution 57/130 B [YUN 2002, p. 590], the Secretary-General submitted a July report on questions relating to information [A/58/175], covering DPI's activities from July 2002 to July 2003 and the implementation of the resolution's recommendations. It also described progress in the implementation of the proposal for the regionalization of UNICs, as requested in resolution 57/300 [YUN 2002, p. 1353].

The report provided further details on the restructuring of DPI, which was aligned to a new proposed four-part subprogramme under the 2004-2005 programme budget: subprogramme 1, communications services (Strategic Communications Division); subprogramme 2, news services (News and Media Division and the Office of the Spokesman for the Secretary-General; subprogramme 3, library services (the Dag Hammarskjöld Library of the Outreach Division); and subprogramme 4, outreach services (the Outreach Division). The programmatic aspects of the 2004-2005 programme budget for DPI under Section 28, public information, were submitted in a March report of the Secretary-General [A/AC.198/2003/3] to the Committee on Information. (See p. 1399 for more information on the proposed 2004-2005 budget.)

As a result of the reform of DPI's structure and operating methods, its message was more focused, its target audience better identified, its resources prioritized and certain outputs that were no longer useful or needed improvement identified. To maximize its capacity to deliver messages globally, the Department was developing synergies between the new technology and traditional means of communication.

To address the challenges it faced in connection with the Iraq crisis in 2002 [YUN 2002, p. 285], DPI established a system-wide, inter-agency communications task force to ensure coordination of UN information gathering and to develop a joint communications strategy that would provide the UN system with a rapid public information response to the rapidly changing situation. Once conflict began in 2003 (see p. 333), DPI changed its focus, producing messages on the protection of Iraqi civilians, meeting their humanitarian needs, and preserving Iraqi sovereignty and territorial integrity. The current focus was on postwar rebuilding.

DPI remained fully engaged in thematic communications campaigns, using all assets at its disposal, including its multimedia outlets, civil society outreach, private sector partnerships and UNICs. It devised issue-driven communications strategies in connection with several major international conferences and global observances, and it coordinated promotional campaigns through the United Nations Communications Group (see p. 638). A long-standing but growing area of activity was DPI's support for the information components of peacekeeping and peace-building and other political missions (see PART I, Chapter I). In February, it participated in a multidisciplinary assessment mission to Côte d'Ivoire, resulting in recommendations on the public information component of the new UN mission as the crisis unfolded there (see p. 183).

DPI continued to strengthen the coordination and management of the UN web site and to offer guidance to other content providers, both inside and outside the Secretariat, in support of their Internet activities. Since September 2002, over 28,000 documents in the six official UN languages had been directly linked to the Official Document System (ODS), and it was expected that all ODS documents would be made freely accessible to the public by 2004. The Department continued to develop its in-house capability for live and on-demand webcasting, which was emerging as a cost-effective communication and information tool with global outreach. The UN News Centre portal was significantly enhanced as the major gateway on the UN web site to daily UN system news and information. An Arabic-language version was launched in January, and similar sites in the remaining three official languages (Chinese, Russian, Spanish) were to be operational by the third quarter of 2003, substantially advancing DPI's goal of language parity on the UN web site. The e-mail service launched in 2002 [YUN 2002, p. 586] to bring news directly to the desks of redisseminators in the media, civil society and academia was expanded to include service in Arabic and French.

The live radio project was firmly established as one of the important multimedia channels for strategically communicating UN activities and concerns to large audiences worldwide. In view of its proven successful and cost-effective global outreach, DPI requested that the project be made permanent and was seeking regular budget funding at the current level for the 2004-2005 biennium. United Nations Television continued to produce and distribute high-quality, in-house video coverage of meetings, press conferences and special events at Headquarters. DPI expanded considerably its formal partnerships with major television broadcasters around the world.

The *UN Chronicle* continued to enhance its online editions in English and French. The English online edition established its home page as an educational outreach portal, featuring web-exclusive articles and providing Internet links and other educational resources on the work of the United Nations. The Department's educational outreach efforts were further enhanced through the UN Chronicle Feature Service, which, with the help of UNICs, redisseminated print articles from eminent contributors to select newspapers and magazines worldwide. The Cyberschoolbus, the web site for children and teachers, continued to develop new educational materials on a wide range of issues, and significant progress was made in translating its materials from English to Chinese, Russian and Spanish.

DPI continued to provide an intensive information programme for NGOs, particularly those associated with the Department and those having consultative status with the United Nations through the Economic and Social Council. Reflecting its rigorous evaluation and review programme, DPI associated 30 new NGOs and disassociated 80 organizations that no longer met the criteria for association, bringing the total number of associated NGOs to 1,375.

The General Assembly, in **resolution 58/270** of 23 December (see p. 1399), asked the Secretary-General, with the assistance of OIOS, to conduct a systematic evaluation of the impact, efficiency and cost-effectiveness of all DPI activities and report to the Assembly, through the Committee on Information and the Fifth (Administrative and Budgetary) Committee, in 2004.

Library services

The Dag Hammarskjöld Library continued to improve its web site in the six official languages to provide access to electronic information, as well as materials in hard copy, and to offer training programmes to mission personnel, Secretariat staff and depository libraries. As at May 2003, there were 405 UN depository libraries, 45 of which were visited and inspected by UN staff. In addition to oversight and training, the Library was increasingly emphasizing outreach to and by the depository libraries. It encouraged them to publicize their document collections and UN themes, and provided promotional materials to assist them; as from 1 June 2002, 10 depository libraries had held events in various countries.

The Library's web page was also expanded, increasing the availability of materials in the six official languages. It reorganized its two major Internet-based services, UNBISNET and the UNBIS Thesaurus. The new UNBISNET provided for easier searching of the Library's bibliographic databases and, with UNBISNET's new features, the Library was able to establish direct links from the indexed record to the full text of more than 13,500 documents in ODS in all languages of issuance. The UNBIS Thesaurus was officially launched in March in the six official languages. The Library provided official users with access to a variety of external electronic services, including the *Economist Intelligence Unit, Factiva, Oxford Analytica* and *SourceOECD*, most acquired at concessional prices through the United Nations System Electronic Information Acquisitions Consortium. It continued to make progress in the retrospective digitization of parliamentary documentation, and efforts were made to complete the language parity of documentation already digitized in English and uploaded to ODS. The Library also assisted various Secretariat departments in converting their materials to electronic format.

The General Assembly, in **resolution 58/270** of 23 December (see p. 1399), requested the Secretary-General to review, through OIOS, the operation and management of UN libraries, so as to assess their staffing requirements in the light of technological advances in the delivery of information, and to report to the Assembly in 2004.

Steering Committee

As requested by the General Assembly in resolution 57/300 [YUN 2002, p. 1353], the Secretary-General reported in March [A/AC.198/2003/5] on the implementation of the measures he had proposed for improving the management of UN libraries in his 2002 report on strengthening the United Nations: an agenda for further change [YUN 2002, p. 585]. Arising out of a meeting between the Deputy Secretary-General, the Under-Secretaries-General for Communications and Public Information and for Management, representatives of the UN Offices at Geneva, Nairobi and Vienna, the regional commissions and the United Nations University, the Steering Committee for the Modernization and Integrated Management of United Nations Libraries was established in January. Its mandate was to facilitate interdependency, foster initiatives to create a dynamic, synergistic and fully functional network of library services throughout the United Nations and encourage a shift from a culture of "ownership" to one of access in order to expand cooperative strategies for collection development and resource-sharing, and develop new ones.

Chaired by the Director of DPI's Outreach Division and comprising representatives of each UN Office, the Steering Committee would meet quarterly to set priorities and policies. It would report to the Deputy Secretary-General through the Under-Secretary-General for Communications and Public Information. The work of the Committee would concentrate on: inter-library management initiatives promoting collaborative and coordinated activities, products and services; optimization of financial resources; sharing best practices and lessons learned; expanded technical assistance programmes for the small, field and depository libraries; archival storage; digitization; bibliographic control of UN documentation; production of multilingual web pages and portals; collaborative reference services; database management and maintenance; strategies for marketing library outputs and services; staff training and development; and staff mobility. The Committee would also play a leading role in ensuring that all libraries of the Organization brought their specialized expertise in information management to bear in the development of all UN knowledge-sharing initiatives.

The report concluded that the Steering Committee's primary aim would be to provide instantaneous, electronic access to a seamlessly integrated, coordinated and interdependent global repository of intellectual resources for users worldwide. It would work to leverage existing investments in human, financial, technological and information resources in the UN system of library services and to blend traditional library functions with advanced technologies. Through coordinated management, it was expected that economies and efficiencies would be achieved and services optimized to strengthen UN outreach.

The Committee met on 20 March, 16-18 June and 25 September. It adopted a work plan focused on bibliographic control of UN documents; collaborative reference services; collections/resource-sharing; hardware, software and web content; public relations; and small and field libraries.

UN information centres

The United Nations information centres (UNICs), services and offices continued to provide a local voice to the global messages of the United Nations on priority themes. With the adoption of the new operating model for DPI and the resulting integration of the Information Centres Service into the new Strategic Communications Division (see p. 630), the network of DPI's field communications outposts became an integral part of the planning and implementation of strategic outreach on priority issues. As a follow-up to an OIOS review of the structure and operations of UNICs (see p. 636), all centres, services and offices were asked to develop, with guidance and coordination from Headquarters, annual work plans for 2003 and to implement them in cooperation with local partners, including Governments, local authorities, the media, educational institutions, NGOs and the private sector. UNICs often took the lead in coordinating the strategic communications initiatives of the UN country team, thereby promoting a unified image of the United Nations at the local level. Such initiatives included activities aimed at promoting the Millennium Development Goals [YUN 2000, p. 51], issues before the World Summit on Sustainable Development [YUN 2002, p. 821] and the International Year of Freshwater (2003) (see p. 1033). In developing countries, UNICs assisted individual members of the country team in promoting their special observances, providing public information support for visits by their senior officials and organizing the local launches of their flagship reports, in addition to their regular tasks. The centres relied increasingly on modern communications technology to strengthen their outreach. DPI continued to provide training and technical assistance to UNICs to enable them to establish their own presence on the Internet. The centres continued to train local media professionals in the use of UN information resources on the Internet and extended the programme to include NGOs, educators and students, among others.

OIOS report. In March, the Secretary-General transmitted a report to the General Assembly on the OIOS review of the structure and operations of UNICs [A/57/747 & Corr.1]. The audit, conducted at the DPI offices in New York and at UNICs in Bogotá, Colombia; Rio de Janeiro, Brazil; Mexico City; Port of Spain, Trinidad and Tobago; and Rome, Italy, assessed the adequacy and cost-effectiveness of the services provided by UNICs in implementation of DPI's legislative mandates, taking into consideration evolving global and regional information needs, and examined whether the resources were rationally and equitably allocated, efficiently used and accounted for properly. Although the tools and data needed to measure performance were inadequate in some instances, OIOS was able to develop sufficient evidence to conclude that an overall public information strategy needed to be formulated and coordinated. The audit showed that DPI needed to re-examine the broad mandates, goals and strategies of the operation to take account of regional information needs and changing regional and global circumstances, and to reassess urgently the UNIC concept in terms of impact, usefulness and continued relevance with regard to operational effectiveness and resource allocations. The review found that logistical and financial constraints prevented some centres from achieving adequate coverage throughout a country or region. Moreover, overlap and duplication hindered closer cooperation with other UN entities in a country or region, and there was no policy for UNICs to charge for services provided to those entities.

The absence of a requirement for UNICs to submit annual plans to DPI for review and approval was a serious shortcoming, which, in some cases, resulted in the ad hoc coverage of mandates and an imbalance in programme activities. The monthly report providing statistics on UNIC activities, the major tool for evaluating performance and impact, was submitted by only one third of the centres on a regular basis at the time of the audit. The criteria used for assessing UNIC performance were also insufficient.

Other findings of the audit related to filling posts allocated to the Information Centres Service; rent and rent-related expenses of UNIC premises; equitable resource allocation to individual UNICs; the relevance of UNIC reference libraries; and the role of National Information Officers. Additional findings and recommendations were detailed in an internal audit report submitted to DPI.

OIOS recommended that DPI undertake an in-depth evaluation of the implementation of the UNIC operation mandate, update relevant goals, objectives and strategies, and apply appropriate measures to achieve them, taking into account regional information needs and changing regional and global circumstances. In implementing the updated goals, objectives and strategies, DPI should identify and secure adequate resources, including travel funds, and assess opportunities for reducing duplication of activities between UNICs and other UN entities in a country or region. OIOS also recommended that DPI: assess the nature and extent of services provided by UNICs to other UN entities and develop a policy and issue guidelines for charging for services rendered to and for sharing costs with such entities; require all UNICs to prepare and submit for review and approval an annual plan of activities for the forthcoming year and review each plan to ensure adequate mandate coverage and cost-effectiveness; and submit to the General Assembly, through the Secretary-General, a proposal requesting that the continued operation of UNICs and the establishment of new centres be conditional on the concerned Member States providing rent-free premises or a subsidy for rent and maintenance costs. Other recommendations dealt with monitoring UNIC activities; reviewing UNIC reporting requirements; establishing performance criteria for assessing UNIC activities; formulating a programme of Information Officer visits to UNICs; establishing criteria for allocating funds and posts to UNICs and for determining the staffing level of the head of centre; determining the optimum staffing levels of each

UNIC; monitoring UNIC library visitor numbers; and establishing an additional grade level for the National Information Officer position.

The Secretary-General, in his transmittal note, said that he concurred with the thrust of the recommendations, which would streamline and revitalize the operation of UNICs and optimize the benefit of UN financial and human resource investment in that activity. He was pleased to note that DPI was already taking steps to address the issues highlighted in the report through the implementation of the recommendations contained therein.

Regionalization of UN information centres

As requested by the General Assembly in resolution 57/300 [YUN 2002, p. 1353], the Secretary-General, in his report on questions related to information [A/58/175], described the implementation of his 2002 proposal for the rationalization of the network of UNICs around regional hubs, beginning with the creation of a Western European hub [YUN 2002, p. 585].

On 14 January, the Deputy Secretary-General and the Under-Secretary-General for Communications and Public Information met with the EU Presidency to discuss the implementation of that proposal. The Under-Secretary-General also held consultations with EU member States as a group on 8 April in New York and on 9 July with the group of the Council on the United Nations in Brussels; bilateral discussions were also held with concerned UN Member States. On 10 June, the Secretary-General decided to proceed with the implementation phase of the plan for Western Europe, which would entail the closure by 31 December of the nine centres located in Athens, Greece; Bonn, Germany; Brussels; Copenhagen, Denmark; Lisbon, Portugal; London; Madrid, Spain; Paris and Rome, and the establishment of a regional UNIC on 1 January 2004. He, in principle, accepted Belgium's offer to locate the regional hub in rent-free premises in Brussels, subject to the conclusion of a satisfactory agreement between Belgium and the Secretariat.

The Western European hub would articulate its information programmes in the 15 EU member States around a common list of UN priorities, which would be conveyed strategically through key intermediaries for maximum impact. That approach would lend coherence to UN messages in the region and contribute to influencing European public opinion in support of the United Nations. Resources released would be redistributed to UN information activities in developing countries and to other high-priority activities, including advancing multilingualism on the UN web site and evaluating the impact of DPI's major products and services. DPI was developing an action plan to ensure a seamless transition from country-based UNICs to the new regional model and the smooth transfer of the accrued experience, country-specific knowledge, institutional memory, and existing partnerships and contacts to the hub. The Department would develop a strong triangular relationship between the hub and the UN Information Services in Geneva and Vienna, which would continue to serve Switzerland and Austria, respectively, to strengthen DPI's overall information capacity in Western Europe. In particular, advantage would be taken of the large accredited press corps at the UN Office at Geneva and the proximity of the UN Office in Vienna to some acceding EU States.

The Secretary-General proposed consulting with concerned Member States on further regionalization, using criteria provided in his report on the reorientation of UN activities in the field of public information and communications [A/AC.198/2003/2] and the views of the members of the Committee on Information to guide the application of the "hub" approach in other regions, taking into account the special circumstances prevailing in developing countries. The Secretary-General would submit to the Committee in 2004 a further progress report on the implementation of the regionalization proposal and the possible establishment of other regional UNICs.

Development of UN web site

In response to General Assembly decision 57/579 [YUN 2002, p. 589], the Secretary-General submitted an August report on progress in the implementation of his 2002 proposal [ibid., p. 588] for strengthening DPI within the existing capacity to support and enhance the UN web site in all official languages [A/58/217]. He said that, as the UN web site continued to grow in popularity, it had become a very cost-effective medium for the worldwide dissemination of information on UN activities at a continually decreasing cost per unit, and the number of developing country users had increased due to improved connectivity to the site. The recent linkage of ODS for parliamentary documentation to the web site was an important step towards the goal of parity among the official languages on the site and had significantly boosted the number of documents available in each language. DPI was implementing other innovative approaches towards achieving multilingualism within existing resources. The Committee on Information, at its twenty-fifth (2003) session [A/58/21], endorsed the Secretary-General's proposal to redeploy some of the resources freed up by consolidating UNICs in Europe into a regional hub (see above), to enhance, among other areas, the language capacity of the Website Section. The possibility of redeploying some resources to other UNICs working in the respective languages to carry out portions of the work on the multilingual web site, such as translations, routine updating and maintenance, had been examined. DPI intended to test the viability of the concept in a pilot exercise at one duty station, depending on the availability of resources, and, if successful, would consider expanding it to others.

Another key component for strengthening language parity on the web site was the expansion of the United Nations News Centre, currently available in Arabic, English, French and Russian, into all official languages by mid-September. DPI was using the worldwide academic community to expand its language capacity through agreements with universities to provide translation of material in a particular language at no cost to the United Nations. It was also encouraging and assisting other Secretariat departments to increase the availability of their materials in all official languages. A number of departments had requested increased provisions in their 2004-2005 budget to help meet that goal. A thorough analysis of the web site would be conducted with the assistance of pro bono services, with the aim of formulating realistic proposals for redesigning, restructuring and refocusing the web site, including the multilingual aspects, together with the necessary hardware and connectivity requirements and the time frame for implementation.

The re-engineered ODS, using the Lotus Notes multilingual capability, could be accessed from the UN web site and was incorporated into other specialized UN system web sites. Those improvements were mandatory prerequisites for making ODS freely available. However, changing from the current subscription-based service to free access would result in a significant increase in the number of users, a load that the current ODS infrastructure would not be able to handle; it would have to be upgraded. Resources for the required upgrading had been requested in the 2004-2005 biennial budget and, if approved by the General Assembly, would allow implementation of free ODS access in late 2004.

Enhancing the UN web site in the official UN languages would be carried out in phases. In the first phase, three posts were to be made available to institutionalize the language capacity in the Website Section, so that all official languages had one regular language assistant. In the second phase, in the context of the 2004-2005 budget, seven posts would be redeployed to the Section, thus strengthening the language capacity dedicated to the web site. Identification of resources for implementing the remaining elements of the proposals was ongoing.

The report concluded that the realignment of priorities with regard to the web site, as envisaged in the report of the Secretary-General on the reorientation of UN public information and communications activities [A/AC.198/2003/2] (see p. 637), would increase synergies and boost the team approach, thereby reducing compartmentalization to the extent possible, and position UN Internet capacity to take advantage of evolving technology. The ultimate objective was a technologically sound, continually updated, intuitive and user-friendly web site that was available to users in their choice of language.

ACABQ report. In a September report [A/58/7/Add.1 & Corr.1], the Advisory Committee on Administrative and Budgetary Questions (ACABQ) took note of the Secretary-General's August report (above). The Committee referred to its comments in its first report on the proposed 2004-2005 programme budget [A/58/7], emphasizing the importance of continued efforts to achieve parity among languages on the web site and supporting the redeployment of resources to that end.

By **decision 58/562** of 23 December, the General Assembly took note of the Secretary-General's August report and ACABQ's related report (above).

In **resolution 58/270** of the same date (see p. 1399), the Assembly requested the Secretary-General to continue to strengthen the UN web site through further redeployment to the required language posts and report in 2004.

UN Communications Group

The United Nations Communications Group (UNCG), which replaced the Joint United Nations Information Committee in 2002 [YUN 2002, p. 589], at its second annual session (New York, 23-24 June), discussed the role and effectiveness of the United Nations in the light of the crisis in Iraq (see p. 333), and considered options for meaningful and effective public information campaigns at a time of declining credibility for the Organization and growing uncertainty about its future role in that region. The Group identified several elements it considered vital in formulating future public information campaigns and concluded that the United Nations remained the principle multilateral voice. Its communicators should remind the world of the role and responsibility of Member States within the multilateral framework; while UN communicators could not replace Governments making decisions, they could influence the climate in which those deci-

Other political and security questions

sions were made. They also had to speak in a common language and tell the UN story in the most effective manner; UNCG was a key platform for developing that voice. UNCG agreed that the use of UN field experts, including local and national staff members, in public information campaigns should be encouraged, and local staff should be trained and prepared for media outreach. Launches of major UN reports should be used as opportunities for engaging the media in the issues involved. Statistical information, such as that offered in periodic reports on the Millennium Development Goals (MDGs) [YUN 2000, p. 51], should be used to tell the UN story, and use of the Internet as a communications tool within and outside the UN system should be maximized.

In order to involve the UN information services in the overall MDG campaign, UNCG decided to set up a task force, led by DPI, focusing on communications strategies and their implementation. The Group endorsed guidelines for designating UN Goodwill Ambassadors and agreed to recognize and make better use of local celebrities in promoting UN issues. It created a task force, headed by UNDP, to explore ways of involving international pollsters and mobilizing resources for using global opinion surveys as communication tools. The Group recommended that members enhance their financial support for the Non-Governmental Liaison Service and requested the High-level Committee on Programmes of the United Nations System Chief Executives Board for Coordination to strengthen the Service's financial standing.

Information and communications in the context of international security

In response to General Assembly resolution 57/53 [YUN 2002, p. 597], the Secretary-General, in a September report [A/58/373], transmitted the views of seven Member States on the general appreciation of the issues of information security; the definition of basic notions related to information security, including unauthorized interference with or misuse of information and telecommunication systems and information resources; and the context of relevant international concepts aimed at strengthening the security of global information and telecommunication systems.

GENERAL ASSEMBLY ACTION

On 8 December [meeting 71], the General Assembly, on the recommendation of the First Committee [A/58/457], adopted **resolution 58/32** without vote [agenda item 68].

Developments in the field of information and telecommunications in the context of international security

The General Assembly,

Recalling its resolutions 53/70 of 4 December 1998, 54/49 of 1 December 1999, 55/28 of 20 November 2000, 56/19 of 29 November 2001 and 57/53 of 22 November 2002,

Recalling also its resolutions on the role of science and technology in the context of international security, in which, inter alia, it recognized that scientific and technological developments could have both civilian and military applications and that progress in science and technology for civilian applications needed to be maintained and encouraged,

Noting that considerable progress has been achieved in developing and applying the latest information technologies and means of telecommunication,

Affirming that it sees in this process the broadest positive opportunities for the further development of civilization, the expansion of opportunities for cooperation for the common good of all States, the enhancement of the creative potential of humankind and additional improvements in the circulation of information in the global community,

Recalling, in this connection, the approaches and principles outlined at the Information Society and Development Conference, held in Midrand, South Africa, from 13 to 15 May 1996,

Bearing in mind the results of the Ministerial Conference on Terrorism, held in Paris on 30 July 1996, and the recommendations that it made,

Noting that the dissemination and use of information technologies and means affect the interests of the entire international community and that optimum effectiveness is enhanced by broad international cooperation,

Expressing its concern that these technologies and means can potentially be used for purposes that are inconsistent with the objectives of maintaining international stability and security and may adversely affect the integrity of the infrastructure of States to the detriment of their security in both civil and military fields,

Considering that it is necessary to prevent the use of information resources or technologies for criminal or terrorist purposes,

Noting the contribution of those Member States that have submitted their assessments on issues of information security to the Secretary-General pursuant to paragraphs 1 to 3 of resolutions 53/70, 54/49, 55/28, 56/19 and 57/53,

Taking note of the reports of the Secretary-General containing those assessments,

Welcoming the initiative taken by the Secretariat and the United Nations Institute for Disarmament Research in convening an international meeting of experts in Geneva in August 1999 on developments in the field of information and telecommunications in the context of international security, as well as its results,

Considering that the assessments of the Member States contained in the reports of the Secretary-General and the international meeting of experts have contributed to a better understanding of the substance of issues of international information security and related notions,

Confirming the request to the Secretary-General contained in paragraph 4 of its resolutions 56/19 and 57/53,

1. *Calls upon* Member States to promote further at multilateral levels the consideration of existing and potential threats in the field of information security, as well as possible measures to limit the threats emerging in this field, consistent with the need to preserve the free flow of information;

2. *Considers* that the purpose of such measures could be served through the examination of relevant international concepts aimed at strengthening the security of global information and telecommunications systems;

3. *Invites* all Member States to continue to inform the Secretary-General of their views and assessments on the following questions:

(a) General appreciation of the issues of information security;

(b) Definition of basic notions related to information security, including unauthorized interference with or misuse of information and telecommunications systems and information resources;

(c) The content of the concepts mentioned in paragraph 2 of the present resolution;

4. *Requests* the Secretary-General to consider existing and potential threats in the sphere of information security and possible cooperative measures to address them, and to conduct a study on the concepts referred to in paragraph 2 of the present resolution, with the assistance of a group of governmental experts, to be established in 2004, appointed by him on the basis of equitable geographical distribution and with the help of Member States in a position to render such assistance, and to submit a report on the outcome of the study to the General Assembly at its sixtieth session;

5. *Decides* to include in the provisional agenda of its fifty-ninth session the item entitled "Developments in the field of information and telecommunications in the context of international security".

Cybersecurity and protection of information infrastructures

In **resolution 58/199** of 23 December (see p. 861), the General Assembly took note of elements for protecting critical information infrastructures, which were set out in an annex to the resolution.

Role of science and technology in the context of international security and disarmament

On 8 December [meeting 71], the General Assembly, on the recommendation of the First Committee [A/58/458], adopted **resolution 58/33** by recorded vote (106-49-19) [agenda item 69].

Role of science and technology in the context of international security and disarmament

The General Assembly,

Recognizing that scientific and technological developments can have both civilian and military applications and that progress in science and technology for civilian applications needs to be maintained and encouraged,

Concerned that military applications of scientific and technological developments can contribute significantly to the improvement and upgrading of advanced weapons systems and, in particular, weapons of mass destruction,

Aware of the need to follow closely the scientific and technological developments that may have a negative impact on international security and disarmament, and to channel scientific and technological developments for beneficial purposes,

Cognizant that international transfers of dual-use as well as high-technology products, services and know-how for peaceful purposes are important for the economic and social development of States,

Also cognizant of the need to regulate such transfers of dual-use goods and technologies and high technology with military applications through multilaterally negotiated, universally applicable, non-discriminatory guidelines,

Expressing its concern about the growing proliferation of ad hoc and exclusive export control regimes and arrangements for dual-use goods and technologies, which tend to impede the economic and social development of developing countries,

Recalling that in the Final Document of the Thirteenth Conference of Heads of State or Government of Non-Aligned Countries, held in Kuala Lumpur from 20 to 25 February 2003, it was again noted with concern that undue restrictions on exports to developing countries of material, equipment and technology for peaceful purposes persisted,

Emphasizing that internationally negotiated guidelines for the transfer of high technology with military applications should take into account the legitimate defence requirements of all States and the requirements for the maintenance of international peace and security, while ensuring that access to high-technology products and services and know-how for peaceful purposes is not denied,

1. *Affirms* that scientific and technological progress should be used for the benefit of all mankind to promote the sustainable economic and social development of all States and to safeguard international security, and that international cooperation in the use of science and technology through the transfer and exchange of technological know-how for peaceful purposes should be promoted;

2. *Invites* Member States to undertake additional efforts to apply science and technology for disarmament-related purposes and to make disarmament-related technologies available to interested States;

3. *Urges* Member States to undertake multilateral negotiations with the participation of all interested States in order to establish universally acceptable, non-discriminatory guidelines for international transfers of dual-use goods and technologies and high technology with military applications;

4. *Encourages* United Nations bodies to contribute, within existing mandates, to promoting the application of science and technology for peaceful purposes;

5. *Decides* to include in the provisional agenda of its fifty-ninth session the item entitled "Role of science and technology in the context of international security and disarmament".

RECORDED VOTE ON RESOLUTION 58/33:

In favour: Afghanistan, Algeria, Angola, Antigua and Barbuda, Bahamas, Bahrain, Bangladesh, Barbados, Belize, Bhutan, Bolivia, Botswana, Brunei Darussalam, Burkina Faso, Burundi, Cambodia, Cameroon, Cape Verde, Central African Republic, Chile, China, Colombia, Comoros, Congo, Costa Rica, Côte d'Ivoire, Cuba, Democratic People's Republic of Korea, Djibouti, Dominican Republic, Ecuador, Egypt, El Salvador, Eritrea, Ethiopia, Fiji, Gabon, Gambia, Ghana, Grenada, Guatemala, Guinea, Guinea-Bissau, Guyana, Haiti, Honduras, India, Indonesia, Iran, Jamaica, Jordan, Kenya, Kuwait, Lao People's Democratic Republic, Lebanon, Lesotho, Libyan Arab Jamahiriya, Madagascar, Malawi, Malaysia, Maldives, Mali, Mauritania, Mauritius, Mexico, Mongolia, Morocco, Mozambique, Myanmar, Namibia, Nauru, Nepal, Nicaragua, Nigeria, Oman, Pakistan, Panama, Papua New Guinea, Peru, Philippines, Qatar, Saint Lucia, Saudi Arabia, Senegal, Singapore, Somalia, Sri Lanka, Sudan, Suriname, Swaziland, Syrian Arab Republic, Tajikistan, Thailand, Timor-Leste, Togo, Trinidad and Tobago, Tunisia, Turkmenistan, Uganda, United Arab Emirates, United Republic of Tanzania, Venezuela, Viet Nam, Yemen, Zambia, Zimbabwe.

Against: Albania, Andorra, Australia, Austria, Belgium, Bosnia and Herzegovina, Bulgaria, Canada, Croatia, Cyprus, Czech Republic, Denmark, Estonia, Finland, France, Georgia, Germany, Greece, Hungary, Iceland, Ireland, Israel, Italy, Latvia, Liechtenstein, Lithuania, Luxembourg, Malta, Micronesia, Monaco, Netherlands, New Zealand, Norway, Poland, Portugal, Republic of Korea, Republic of Moldova, Romania, San Marino, Serbia and Montenegro, Slovakia, Slovenia, Spain, Sweden, Switzerland, The former Yugoslav Republic of Macedonia, Turkey, United Kingdom, United States.

Abstaining: Argentina, Armenia, Azerbaijan, Belarus, Brazil, Japan, Kazakhstan, Kyrgyzstan, Paraguay, Russian Federation, Rwanda, Saint Vincent and the Grenadines, Samoa, South Africa, Tonga, Ukraine, Uruguay, Uzbekistan, Vanuatu.

Peaceful uses of outer space

The Committee on the Peaceful Uses of Outer Space (Committee on Outer Space), at its forty-sixth session (Vienna, 11-20 June) [A/58/20], discussed ways and means to maintain outer space for peaceful purposes, the spin-off benefits of space technology, and space and society. It examined the implementation of the recommendations of the Third (1999) United Nations Conference on the Exploration and Peaceful Uses of Outer Space (UNISPACE III) [YUN 1999, p. 556], and reviewed the work of its two subcommittees, one dealing with scientific and technical issues and the other with legal questions.

Implementation of UNISPACE III recommendations

In response to General Assembly resolution 57/116 [YUN 2002, p. 602], the Committee on Outer Space reconvened the working group established in 2002 [YUN 2002, p. 598] to prepare a report to enable the Assembly, in accordance with its resolution 54/68 [YUN 1999, p. 557], to review and appraise, in 2004, the implementation of the recommendations of UNISPACE III and to consider further action and initiatives.

The working group had before it a compilation of input [A/AC.105/L.247] from the action teams established by the Committee in 2001 [YUN 2001, p. 568] (see below). It noted the progress made by the teams and agreed that they should submit updates or revised input on further progress made. It agreed on criteria for selecting recommendations for inclusion in the report to the Assembly.

The working group also considered a compilation of contributions from UN system entities, intergovernmental organizations and NGOs having permanent observer status with the Committee on Outer Space and space-related regional entities that had been invited to provide input for the report to the Assembly. It noted that some action teams had taken into account relevant input from those organizations in developing recommendations, and encouraged interaction between the action teams and those organizations with initiatives, programmes or projects that could benefit their work. A December Secretariat note [A/AC.105/819] contained information on the activities of four international organizations that had contributed to the implementation of the UNISPACE III recommendations.

The working group finalized an indicative, preliminary draft outline of the report to the Assembly and agreed to hold informal consultations during the 2004 sessions of the Scientific and Technical and Legal Subcommittees to advance the preparation of the draft report. It recommended that the Committee on Outer Space, at its forty-seventh (2004) session, reconvene the working group and allocate sufficient time for it to finalize the report for endorsement by the Committee.

In accordance with resolution 57/116, the Scientific and Technical Subcommittee, at its fortieth session (see p. 642), reconvened its Working Group of the Whole to consider, among other issues, the implementation of the UNISPACE III recommendations, including the progress of the action teams. Before the Working Group was an updated report of the Secretary-General on the implementation of the recommendations in tabular form [A/AC.105/C.1/L.262], as recommended by the Subcommittee in 2002 [YUN 2002, p. 599]. The Working Group established an action team on improving knowledge-sharing through the promotion of universal access to space-based communication services. Based on a template circulated to the action teams by the Working Group for the submission of reports and recommendations, input from the 11 action teams was annexed to a May Secretariat note [A/AC.105/L.247]. The Working Group agreed that the results of the 2000 Millennium Summit [YUN 2000, p. 47], the 2002 World Summit on Sustainable Development [YUN 2002, p. 821] and the first phase of the World Summit on the Information Society in 2003 (see p. 857) should be taken into account in the preparation of the report to the Assembly and that the recommendations or actions resulting from those conferences should be correlated with specific UNISPACE III recommendations. Appended to the Subcommittee's report were guidelines circulated to UN entities, organizations with observer status with the Committee on Outer Space and regional entities on inputs from them that would best assist the Committee's working group in preparing its report. The Working Group of the Whole agreed that inputs to be provided in accordance with the guidelines should be submitted by the beginning of May.

The Committee on Outer Space, at its June session, endorsed the recommendations of its Working Group. It noted that all action teams had reported on their work, including the submission of the final reports of the Action Team on Sustainable Development [A/AC.105/C.1/L.264] to the Scientific and Technical Subcommittee and of the Action Team on New and Innovative Sources of Funding [A/AC.105/L.246] to the Committee. During the year, final reports were also submitted by the Action Teams on Weather and Climate Forecasting [A/AC.105/C.1/L.269], on Disaster Management [A/AC.105/C.1/L.273] and on Global Navigation Satellite Systems [A/AC.105/C.1/L.274]. The Committee noted that the low level of feedback and participation by some action team members could be related to the lack of capacity and institutionalized mechanisms and a shortage of resources and expertise in gathering information and data exchange among national institutions. Some action teams had divided tasks and responsibilities among members based on their capacities and capabilities; that method of work had proved to be beneficial and could be followed by some action teams.

Report of Secretary-General. In response to General Assembly resolution 57/116 [YUN 2002, p. 602], the Secretary-General submitted a July report [A/58/174] on action taken by the Committee on Outer Space and its subsidiary bodies to implement the UNISPACE III recommendations, implementation of the plan of action of the Office for Outer Space Affairs, and action taken to further enhance inter-agency coordination and cooperation.

GENERAL ASSEMBLY ACTION

On 9 December [meeting 72], the General Assembly, on the recommendation of the Fourth Committee [A/58/471], adopted **resolution 58/90** without vote [agenda item 82].

Review of the implementation of the recommendations of the Third United Nations Conference on the Exploration and Peaceful Uses of Outer Space

The General Assembly,

Recalling its resolutions 54/68 of 6 December 1999, 55/122 of 8 December 2000, 56/51 of 10 December 2001 and 57/116 of 11 December 2002, concerning the review and appraisal by the General Assembly at its fifty-ninth session of the implementation of the recommendations of the Third United Nations Conference on the Exploration and Peaceful Uses of Outer Space (UNISPACE III), held at Vienna from 19 to 30 July 1999,

Taking note with satisfaction of the work of the Committee on the Peaceful Uses of Outer Space and its subsidiary bodies, in particular the action teams established by the Committee at its forty-fourth and forty-fifth sessions under the voluntary leadership of Member States, to implement the recommendations of UNISPACE III,

Noting the progress made by the Committee through its Working Group in preparing a report for submission to the General Assembly for the review, in accordance with paragraph 31 of Assembly resolution 55/122,

1. *Decides* to conduct the review of the progress made in the implementation of the recommendations of the Third United Nations Conference on the Exploration and Peaceful Uses of Outer Space (UNISPACE III) in plenary meeting(s) at its fifty-ninth session, under a separate agenda item entitled "Review of the implementation of the recommendations of the Third United Nations Conference on the Exploration and Peaceful Uses of Outer Space";

2. *Requests* the Committee on the Peaceful Uses of Outer Space to submit its report on the review of the implementation of the recommendations of UNISPACE III to the General Assembly at its fifty-ninth session in plenary meeting(s);

3. *Decides* that the plenary meeting(s) for the review shall be held in October 2004;

4. *Invites* Member States to participate in the plenary meeting(s) at the ministerial level or at the highest level possible.

Scientific and Technical Subcommittee

The Scientific and Technical Subcommittee of the Committee on Outer Space, at its fortieth session (Vienna, 17-28 February) [A/AC.105/804], considered the United Nations Programme on Space Applications and the implementation of the UNISPACE III recommendations. It also dealt with matters relating to remote sensing of the Earth by satellite, including applications for developing countries and monitoring of the Earth's environment; the use of nuclear power sources in outer space; mechanisms for strengthening inter-agency cooperation and increasing the use of space applications and services within and among UN system entities; implementation of an integrated, space-based global natural disaster management system; space debris; the examination of the physical nature and technical attributes of the geostationary orbit and its utilization and applications; the mobilization of financial resources to develop capacity in space science and technology applications; and the use of space

UN Programme on Space Applications

The United Nations Programme on Space Applications, as mandated by General Assembly resolution 37/90 [YUN 1982, p. 163], continued to assist developing countries and countries with economies in transition to establish or strengthen their capacity in space science and technology through long-term training fellowships, technical advisory services, regional and international training courses and conferences, and to promote cooperation between developed and developing countries.

The United Nations Expert on Space Applications [A/AC.105/815] stated that Programme efforts to develop indigenous capability continued to focus on the establishment and operation of regional centres for space science and technology education in developing countries. Under the Programme's priority area of space technology and disaster management, which aimed at supporting developing countries to use space technology to deal with disasters successfully, a European regional workshop was held in Romania. The Programme was implementing the natural resource management and environmental monitoring priority theme to support developing countries in incorporating space-based solutions for solving environmental monitoring and natural resource management issues, focusing on workshops and expert meetings to define regional plans of action and pilot projects. The Programme also promoted the use of enabling technologies, including global navigation satellite systems for social and economic benefits, and the use of space science and technology and their applications to support sustainable development. The Office for Outer Space Affairs was accepted as a cooperating body to the International Charter on Space and Major Disasters, enabling the UN system to have access to the Charter as an authorized user. Beginning on 1 July, the Office set up a permanent hotline through which UN agencies could request data through the International Charter to respond to emergency situations.

The Programme held 13 workshops, training courses and conferences in 2003; the European Space Agency continued to support the long-term fellowship programme for in-depth training. Various technical advisory services for activities promoting regional cooperation continued to be provided.

Following its consideration of the January 2003 report of the Expert on Space Applications [A/AC.105/790 & Corr.1], which described activities in 2002, those scheduled for 2003 and those planned for 2004, the Subcommittee continued to express concern over the Programme's limited financial resources and appealed to Member States for voluntary contributions. It noted that, while some progress had been made in bringing the benefits of the use of space applications for sustainable economic and social development and for the protection of the environment to the awareness of high-level decision makers, more needed to be done.

The General Assembly, in **resolution 58/89** (see p. 646), endorsed the Programme on Space Applications for 2004, as proposed by the Expert.

Cooperation

The Inter-Agency Meeting on Outer Space Activities, at its twenty-third session (Vienna, 22-24 January) [A/AC.105/791 & Corr.1], discussed the coordination of plans and programmes in the practical application of space technology and related areas and the space-related outcomes of the 2002 World Summit on Sustainable Development [YUN 2002, p. 821]. It also reviewed electronic information networking in the UN system and the implementation of the UNISPACE III recommendations.

The Meeting noted that the UN-affiliated regional centres for space science and technology education complemented training programmes offered by other UN entities and should be supported, and that participating entities were making efforts to ensure that contributions of space technology would be considered at the World Summit on the Information Society (see p. 857). It considered a proposal for sharing space-related educational activities or events among UN entities, through participation in or co-sponsoring events organized by other agencies. It agreed that the Office for Outer Space Affairs should request focal points of UN entities for the Inter-Agency Meeting to provide information on their education activities or events for posting on its web site.

The Meeting agreed to hold, in conjunction with its annual session, an open informal session, and that its agenda should focus on a particular topic or topics to be chosen in advance. Noting the desire of participating UN entities to keep the Scientific and Technical Subcommittee informed about their ongoing space activities, the Meeting agreed to invite the Subcommittee to consider requesting annual reports from UN entities on specific themes. It approved a revised version of the Secretary-General's report on the coordination of outer space activities within the UN system: programme of work for 2003 and 2004 and future years [A/AC.105/792], and adopted a revised structure for the preparation of the 2004-2005 report, which was annexed to its report.

The Meeting noted that recommendations in the Plan of Implementation of the 2002 World Summit on Sustainable Development made specific reference to space technologies, and it invited participants to report on the status of their organizations' plans for Summit follow-up. The Meeting considered a preliminary list of actions recommended in the Plan of Implementation with direct or potential relevance to space science and technology and their applications and actions to address cross-cutting issues, and agreed that UN entities should complete the list with their planned space-related initiatives and programmes in response to the recommendations. Members of the Committee on Outer Space should also consider completing the list, which could serve as a comprehensive survey of the space community's response to the Summit's outcomes. The Office for Outer Space Affairs should circulate the list electronically to the focal points of UN system entities, which would be reviewed in 2004 to ensure the harmonized and balanced presentation of all relevant initiatives and programmes within the UN system.

Regarding the implementation of UNISPACE III recommendations, the Meeting noted the significant progress achieved by the Integrated Global Observing Strategy (IGOS)-Partnership in implementing IGOS by, among other actions, preparing reports on selected IGOS themes and implementing recommendations contained in those reports. It agreed that UN entities should be provided with further guidelines on inputs from them that would best assist the working group of the Committee on Outer Space in preparing its 2004 report to the General Assembly on UNISPACE III implementation and noted that the Office for Outer Space Affairs would work with the chairman to develop such guidelines (see p. 641).

Scientific and technical issues

In 2003, the Scientific and Technical Subcommittee [A/AC.105/804] continued to emphasize the importance of the provision of non-discriminatory access to state-of-the-art remote sensing data and to derived information at reasonable cost and in a timely manner; capacity-building, in particular to meet the needs of developing countries; and remote sensing systems to support key development activities. It also emphasized that international cooperation in the use of remote sensing satellites should be encouraged and actively promoted. It noted that all new achievements in Earth observation contributing to sustainable development, including agriculture, health and human security, should be applied in the interests of all States, taking into account the needs of developing countries.

The Subcommittee adopted the 2003-2006 multi-year work plan on the use of nuclear power sources in outer space, which was annexed to the Subcommittee's report. In accordance with resolution 57/116 [YUN 2002, p. 602], it reconvened its Working Group on the Use of Nuclear Power Sources in Outer Space, endorsed the Working Group's report, which was annexed to the Subcommittee's report, and agreed that the Working Group should be requested to continue its work until 2004. It endorsed the recommendation of the Inter-Agency Meeting on Outer Space Activities to hold an open informal session in conjunction with the annual Meeting, and invited UN entities to submit annual reports to the Subcommittee on specific themes. The Subcommittee also invited member States of the Committee on Outer Space to complete the preliminary draft list of actions recommended in the Plan of Implementation of the World Summit on Sustainable Development [YUN 2002, p. 821] with direct or potential relevance to space science and technology.

The Subcommittee reviewed possible global operational structures to handle natural disaster management, making maximum use of existing and planned space systems. It noted that achieving a global management infrastructure for natural disasters would require the use of a "system engineering" approach, which could tie existing satellite missions to various scientific models of natural phenomena and to support systems to enhance decision-making during natural disasters. It also noted that several objectives foreseen in its work plan on the implementation of an integrated, space-based global natural disaster management system for 2001 and 2002, including the examination of existing satellite and data distribution systems, had been addressed by a number of States.

In accordance with its multi-year work plan on space debris [YUN 2001, p. 570], the Subcommittee began its review of the proposals on space debris mitigation presented by the Inter-Agency Space Debris Coordination Committee (IADC), including means of endorsing their utilization. It requested member States of the Committee on Outer Space to study the proposals and provide their comments to the Office for Outer Space Affairs before the Subcommittee's 2004 session. The Subcommittee agreed that member States should pay more attention to the problem of collisions of space objects, including those with nuclear power sources on board, with space debris and to other aspects of space debris; member

States and international organizations should make available the results of national research on space debris, including information on minimizing its creation.

The Committee on Outer Space [A/58/20] agreed that it was important that States making use of nuclear power sources conducted their activities in full accordance with the 1992 Principles Relevant to the Use of Nuclear Power Sources in Outer Space [YUN 1992, p. 116].

The Committee endorsed the proposals of the Inter-Agency Meeting on Outer Space Activities to strengthen inter-agency cooperation in the use of outer space within the UN system (see p. 643).

The Committee stressed the importance of operational access to global satellite databases for dealing with natural disasters, especially in developing countries, and the need to identify and close gaps in the coverage of remote sensing satellites so that reliable information could be provided to all disaster-affected areas. It requested the Office for Outer Space Affairs to convene a one-day workshop for industry during its forty-seventh (2004) session, inviting all major communications satellite operators to present their systems' capabilities and views on how they could be used during natural disasters.

The Committee requested its members to study the IADC proposals on space debris mitigation (see above) and to provide their comments to the Office for Outer Space Affairs before the Subcommittee's 2004 session. A Secretariat note [A/AC.105/820] contained replies received from three member States.

In response to the Subcommittee's request that Member States and regional space agencies report on national research concerning the safety of space objects with nuclear power sources, the Secretariat submitted replies received from 11 States and one agency on the subject [A/AC.105/789/Add.1 & A/AC.105/817].

Other related documents submitted to the Scientific and Technical Subcommittee were two Secretariat notes [A/AC.105/788 & A/AC.105/816] containing information received from 24 Member States on their space activities.

Legal Subcommittee

The Legal Subcommittee, at its forty-second session (Vienna, 24 March–4 April) [A/AC.105/805], established, in accordance with General Assembly resolution 57/116 [YUN 2002, p. 602], a working group to examine the preliminary draft protocol on matters specific to space assets to the Convention on International Interests in Mobile Equipment, which was opened for signature in 2001 [YUN 2001, p. 570]. The working group also considered the possibility of the United Nations serving as supervisory authority under the preliminary draft protocol and the relationship between the terms of the draft protocol and the rights and obligations under the legal regime applicable to outer space. Before it was a Secretariat report on the subject [A/AC.105/C.2/L.238]. The working group noted that, under article 17 of the preliminary draft protocol, supervisory authority would be designated at a diplomatic conference to adopt a space assets protocol to the Convention, and that the International Institute for the Unification of Private Law had approached the United Nations as a possible supervisory authority. It also noted that the General Assembly would decide on whether the United Nations would assume those functions. In that event, the working group recommended that no funds should be used from the UN regular budget for that purpose and all costs incurred would be recovered by start-up funding and user fees.

In accordance with Assembly resolution 57/116, the Subcommittee reconvened its working group established in 2002 [YUN 2002, p. 601] on the status and application of the five UN treaties on outer space. The treaties in question were: the 1966 Treaty on Principles Governing the Activities of States in the Exploration and Use of Outer Space, including the Moon and Other Celestial Bodies, adopted by the Assembly in resolution 2222(XXI) [YUN 1966, p. 41]; the 1967 Agreement on the Rescue of Astronauts, the Return of Astronauts and the Return of Objects Launched into Outer Space, adopted in resolution 2345(XXII) [YUN 1967, p. 33]; the 1971 Convention on International Liability for Damage Caused by Space Objects, contained in resolution 2777(XXVI) [YUN 1971, p. 52]; the 1974 Convention on Registration of Objects Launched into Outer Space, contained in resolution 3235(XXIX) [YUN 1974, p. 63]; and the 1979 Agreement Governing the Activities of States on the Moon and Other Celestial Bodies, contained in resolution 34/68 [YUN 1979, p. 111]. The working group suggested that the Secretary-General write letters to ministers for foreign affairs of States that had not become parties to the UN treaties on outer space and international organizations that had not declared their acceptance of those treaties, which should include a list of those treaties, a table on the status of their implementation, and information summarizing the benefits and responsibilities of participation, in particular for non-space-faring and developing countries. A model for such a letter and accompanying information material would be developed by the working group in 2004. Efforts by the Subcommittee to increase the level of participation in those treaties could include initiatives such as regional and global meetings to raise public awareness about them.

The working group had before it three proposals on matters relating to its mandate that had been informally announced: a proposal by the United States for a new agenda item on registration practice; a proposal by France for a new agenda item on space debris; and a draft resolution for adoption by the General Assembly on the legal concept of the "launching State", contained in a working paper [A/AC.105/C.2/L.242 & Add.1] submitted by Germany. The working group recommended that the merits and substance of that draft resolution be further considered by the Committee on Outer Space at its 2003 session.

The working group agreed that the Office for Outer Space Affairs should compile a directory of institutions teaching space law. It recommended that those institutions participate in an electronic network of institutions teaching international and national space law, and the UN-affiliated regional centres for space science and technology education should include a basic course in space law in their curricula.

The Subcommittee re-established its working group on the definition and delimitation of outer space, which agreed to request the Secretariat to prepare for consideration at its 2004 session an analytical summary of the replies received from Member States to the questionnaire on possible legal issues with regard to aerospace objects, with a view to taking a decision on the need to continue consideration of the questionnaire. Delegations were urged to respond by 31 August to ensure that their replies were included in the summary.

The Committee on Outer Space, at its forty-sixth session [A/58/20], agreed that the treaties on outer space had established a framework that had encouraged the exploration of outer space benefiting both space-faring and non-space-faring States and the Legal Subcommittee should undertake activities that supported the continued vitality of that legal framework. The Committee also agreed that the Subcommittee should consider at its 2004 session the revised text [A/AC.105/L.249] of the draft resolution on the application of the legal concept of the "launching State", and that the UN-affiliated regional centres for space science and technology education should include a basic course on space law in their curricula. It agreed to transmit the report of the Group of Experts on the Ethics of Outer Space [A/AC.105/C.2/L.240/Rev.1] to the Director-General of the United Nations Educational, Scientific and Cultural Organization (UNESCO), with the request that UNESCO keep the Committee and its subcommittees informed about UNESCO's outer space activities.

GENERAL ASSEMBLY ACTION

On 9 December [meeting 72], the General Assembly, on the recommendation of the Fourth Committee [A/58/471], adopted **resolution 58/89** without vote [agenda item 82].

International cooperation in the peaceful uses of outer space

The General Assembly,

Recalling its resolutions 51/122 of 13 December 1996, 54/68 of 6 December 1999 and 57/116 of 11 December 2002,

Deeply convinced of the common interest of mankind in promoting and expanding the exploration and use of outer space, as the province of all mankind, for peaceful purposes and in continuing efforts to extend to all States the benefits derived therefrom, and also of the importance of international cooperation in this field, for which the United Nations should continue to provide a focal point,

Reaffirming the importance of international cooperation in developing the rule of law, including the relevant norms of space law and their important role in international cooperation for the exploration and use of outer space for peaceful purposes, and of the widest possible adherence to international treaties that promote the peaceful uses of outer space in order to meet emerging new challenges, especially for developing countries,

Seriously concerned about the possibility of an arms race in outer space, and bearing in mind the importance of article IV of the Treaty on Principles Governing the Activities of States in the Exploration and Use of Outer Space, including the Moon and Other Celestial Bodies,

Recognizing that all States, in particular those with major space capabilities, should contribute actively to the goal of preventing an arms race in outer space as an essential condition for the promotion and strengthening of international cooperation in the exploration and use of outer space for peaceful purposes,

Considering that space debris is an issue of concern to all nations,

Noting the progress achieved in the further development of peaceful space exploration and applications as well as in various national and cooperative space projects, which contributes to international cooperation, and the importance of further developing the legal framework to strengthen international cooperation in this field,

Convinced of the importance of the recommendations in the resolution entitled "The Space Millennium: Vienna Declaration on Space and Human Development", adopted by the Third United Nations Conference on the Exploration and Peaceful Uses of Outer Space (UNISPACE III), held at Vienna from 19 to 30 July 1999, and the need to promote the use of space technology towards implementing the United Nations Millennium Declaration,

Taking note of the report of the Secretary-General on the implementation of the recommendations of UNISPACE III,

Convinced that the use of space science and technology and their applications, in such areas as telemedicine, tele-education and Earth observation, contribute to achieving the objectives of the global conferences of the United Nations that address various aspects of economic, social and cultural development, inter alia, poverty eradication,

Having considered the report of the Committee on the Peaceful Uses of Outer Space on the work of its forty-sixth session,

1. *Endorses* the report of the Committee on the Peaceful Uses of Outer Space on the work of its forty-sixth session;

2. *Urges* States that have not yet become parties to the international treaties governing the uses of outer space to give consideration to ratifying or acceding to those treaties as well as incorporating them in their national legislation;

3. *Notes* that, at its forty-second session, the Legal Subcommittee of the Committee on the Peaceful Uses of Outer Space continued its work, as mandated by the General Assembly in its resolution 57/116;

4. *Endorses* the recommendation of the Committee that the Legal Subcommittee, at its forty-third session, taking into account the concerns of all countries, in particular those of developing countries:

(a) Consider the following as regular agenda items:
 (i) General exchange of views;
 (ii) Status and application of the five United Nations treaties on outer space;
 (iii) Information on the activities of international organizations relating to space law;
 (iv) Matters relating to:
  a. The definition and delimitation of outer space;
  b. The character and utilization of the geostationary orbit, including consideration of ways and means to ensure the rational and equitable use of the geostationary orbit without prejudice to the role of the International Telecommunication Union;

(b) Consider the following single issues/items for discussion:
 (i) Review and possible revision of the Principles Relevant to the Use of Nuclear Power Sources in Outer Space;
 (ii) Examination of the preliminary draft protocol on matters specific to space assets to the Convention on International Interests in Mobile Equipment, opened for signature at Cape Town, South Africa, on 16 November 2001:
  a. Considerations relating to the possibility of the United Nations serving as supervisory authority under the preliminary draft protocol;
  b. Considerations relating to the relationship between the terms of the preliminary draft protocol and the rights and obligations of States under the legal regime applicable to outer space;
 (iii) Contributions by the Legal Subcommittee to the Committee for the preparation of its report to the General Assembly for its review of the progress made in the implementation of the recommendations of the Third United Nations Conference on the Exploration and Peaceful Uses of Outer Space (UNISPACE III);

(c) Consider the practice of States and international organizations in registering space objects in accordance with the work plan adopted by the Committee;

5. *Notes* that the Legal Subcommittee, at its forty-third session, will submit its proposals to the Committee for new items to be considered by the Subcommittee at its forty-fourth session, in 2005;

6. *Notes also* that, in the context of paragraph 4 (a) (ii) above, the Legal Subcommittee will reconvene its Working Group with the terms of reference as agreed upon by the Legal Subcommittee, to meet for three years, from 2002 to 2004;

7. *Notes further* that, in the context of paragraph 4 (a) (iii) above, the Group of Experts on the Ethics of Outer Space, invited by the Committee at its forty-fourth session to identify which aspects of the report of the World Commission on the Ethics of Scientific Knowledge and Technology of the United Nations Educational, Scientific and Cultural Organization might need to be studied by the Committee and to draft a report, in consultation with other international organizations and in close liaison with the World Commission, presented its report to the Legal Subcommittee, and agrees that the report should be transmitted to the United Nations Educational, Scientific and Cultural Organization with the request that it keep the Committee and its subcommittees informed about its activities relating to outer space;

8. *Notes* that, in the context of paragraph 4 (a) (iv) above, the Legal Subcommittee will reconvene its Working Group on the item only to consider matters relating to the definition and delimitation of outer space;

9. *Agrees* that the Legal Subcommittee should reconvene its Working Group to consider the questions reflected in paragraphs 4 (b) (ii) a. and b. above separately;

10. *Notes with satisfaction* that, in accordance with paragraph 13 of General Assembly resolution 57/116, the Government of Austria continued to convene and facilitate intersessional informal consultations on the composition of the bureaux of the Committee and its subsidiary bodies for the third term, and that consensus agreement was reached, before the forty-sixth session of the Committee, on the extension of the term of office of the current bureau of the Committee and the future composition of the bureaux of the Committee and its subsidiary bodies;

11. *Endorses* the agreement reached by the Committee on the extension of the term of office of the current bureau of the Committee and future composition of the bureaux of the Committee and its subsidiary bodies, on the basis of the measures relating to the working methods of the Committee and its subsidiary bodies, which were endorsed by the General Assembly in its resolution 52/56 of 10 December 1997, and notes that, in accordance with paragraph 14 of General Assembly resolution 57/116, the Committee conducted the election of its officers at its forty-sixth session;

12. *Agrees* that the Committee and its subcommittees, at the beginning of their sessions in 2004, should conduct the election of the officers agreed upon by the Committee at its forty-sixth session;

13. *Also agrees* that, in accordance with the measures relating to the future composition of the bureaux of the Committee and its subsidiary bodies indicated in paragraph 11 above, the Committee at its forty-seventh session, in 2004, should reach agreement on all the officers of the bureaux of the Committee and its subsid-

iary bodies for the next term and that, for this purpose, the Committee should include in the agenda of its forty-seventh session an item on the composition of the bureaux of the Committee and its subsidiary bodies for the period 2006-2007;

14. *Urges* each of the five regional groups to ensure that agreement within the group on the officer to be determined for the period 2006-2007 is reached before the forty-seventh session of the Committee;

15. *Notes* that the Scientific and Technical Subcommittee, at its fortieth session, continued its work as mandated by the General Assembly in its resolution 57/116;

16. *Endorses* the recommendation of the Committee that the Scientific and Technical Subcommittee, at its forty-first session, taking into account the concerns of all countries, in particular those of developing countries:

(a) Consider the following items:
(i) General exchange of views and introduction to reports submitted on national activities;
(ii) United Nations Programme on Space Applications;
(iii) Implementation of the recommendations of UNISPACE III;
(iv) Matters relating to remote-sensing of the Earth by satellite, including applications for developing countries and monitoring of the Earth's environment;

(b) Consider the following items in accordance with the work plans adopted by the Committee:
(i) Space debris;
(ii) Use of nuclear power sources in outer space;
(iii) Space-system-based telemedicine;

(c) Consider the following single issues/items for discussion:
(i) Examination of the physical nature and technical attributes of the geostationary orbit and its utilization and applications, including, inter alia, in the field of space communications, as well as other questions relating to developments in space communications, taking particular account of the needs and interests of developing countries;
(ii) Implementation of an integrated, space-based global natural disaster management system;
(iii) Solar-terrestrial physics;

17. *Notes* that the Scientific and Technical Subcommittee at its forty-first session will submit its proposal to the Committee for a draft provisional agenda for the forty-second session of the Subcommittee, in 2005;

18. *Endorses* the recommendation of the Committee that the symposium to strengthen the partnership with industry should be organized during the first week of the forty-first session of the Scientific and Technical Subcommittee and should address small satellite applications in agriculture, health and human security;

19. *Agrees* that, in the context of paragraphs 16 (a) (ii) and (iii) and 17 above, the Scientific and Technical Subcommittee at its forty-first session should reconvene the Working Group of the Whole;

20. *Also agrees* that, in the context of paragraph 16 (b) (i) above, the Scientific and Technical Subcommittee, at its forty-first session, could establish a working group to consider comments from member States of the Committee on the proposals on debris mitigation presented by the Inter-Agency Space Debris Coordination Committee to the Subcommittee at its fortieth session;

21. *Further agrees* that, in the context of paragraph 16 (b) (ii) above, the Scientific and Technical Subcommittee at its forty-first session should reconvene its Working Group on the Use of Nuclear Power Sources in Outer Space;

22. *Endorses* the United Nations Programme on Space Applications for 2004, as proposed to the Committee by the Expert on Space Applications;

23. *Notes with satisfaction* that, in accordance with paragraph 30 of General Assembly resolution 50/27 of 6 December 1995, the African regional centres for space science and technology education, in the French language and in the English language, located in Morocco and Nigeria, respectively, and the Centre for Space Science and Technology Education in Asia and the Pacific continued their education programmes in 2003, that the Regional Centre for Space Science and Technology Education for Latin America and the Caribbean became affiliated to the United Nations and began its education programme, and that the United Nations Programme on Space Applications is providing technical support to the Government of Jordan for the establishment of the regional centre for space science and technology education for Western Asia;

24. *Also notes with satisfaction* the success of the Fourth Space Conference of the Americas, held at Cartagena de Indias, Colombia, from 14 to 17 May 2002, which adopted the Declaration of Cartagena de Indias and the Plan of Action, and notes the desire of Member States in the Latin American and Caribbean region to institutionalize the Space Conference of the Americas;

25. *Welcomes* the memorandum of understanding between the Office for Outer Space Affairs of the Secretariat and the Pro Tempore Secretariat of the Fourth Space Conference of the Americas, under which the parties demonstrated their intention to collaborate in promoting and implementing joint activities, and invites the Pro Tempore Secretariat to inform the Committee of the work accomplished;

26. *Urges* all Governments, entities of the United Nations system as well as intergovernmental and non-governmental entities conducting space-related activities to take the necessary action for the effective implementation of the recommendations of UNISPACE III, in particular its resolution entitled "The Space Millennium: Vienna Declaration on Space and Human Development", bearing in mind the need to promote the use of space technology towards implementing the United Nations Millennium Declaration;

27. *Agrees* that, in accordance with paragraph 30 of General Assembly resolution 55/122 of 8 December 2000, the Committee should include in the agenda of its forty-seventh session an item on the implementation of the recommendations of UNISPACE III;

28. *Notes with satisfaction* the work conducted by the twelve action teams that the Committee had established at its forty-fourth and forty-sixth sessions under the voluntary leadership of Member States to implement the recommendations of UNISPACE III, and urges Member States to provide full support to the action teams in conducting their work;

29. *Also notes with satisfaction* that the Committee made further progress in the preparation of its report under the agenda item on the implementation of the recommendations of UNISPACE III for submission to the General Assembly, in order for the Assembly to review and appraise, at its fifty-ninth session, in 2004, in accordance with paragraph 16 of its resolution 54/68, the implementation of the outcome of UNISPACE III and to consider further actions and initiatives, and agrees that, in this context, the Working Group established by the Committee to prepare the abovementioned report should be reconvened at the forty-seventh session of the Committee to complete its work;

30. *Notes* that in order to advance the preparation of the report of the Committee, mentioned in paragraph 29 above, the Working Group of the Committee could hold informal consultations during the forty-first session of the Scientific and Technical Subcommittee as well as the forty-third session of the Legal Subcommittee;

31. *Urges* all Member States to contribute to the Trust Fund for the United Nations Programme on Space Applications to support activities to implement the recommendations of UNISPACE III, in particular the priority project proposals as recommended by the Committee at its forty-third session;

32. *Recommends* that more attention be paid and political support be provided to all matters relating to the protection and the preservation of the outer space environment, especially those potentially affecting the Earth's environment;

33. *Considers* that it is essential that Member States pay more attention to the problem of collisions of space objects, including those with nuclear power sources, with space debris, and other aspects of space debris, calls for the continuation of national research on this question, for the development of improved technology for the monitoring of space debris and for the compilation and dissemination of data on space debris, also considers that, to the extent possible, information thereon should be provided to the Scientific and Technical Subcommittee, and agrees that international cooperation is needed to expand appropriate and affordable strategies to minimize the impact of space debris on future space missions;

34. *Urges* all States, in particular those with major space capabilities, to contribute actively to the goal of preventing an arms race in outer space as an essential condition for the promotion of international cooperation in the exploration and use of outer space for peaceful purposes;

35. *Emphasizes* the need to increase the benefits of space technology and its applications and to contribute to an orderly growth of space activities favourable to sustained economic growth and sustainable development in all countries, including mitigation of the consequences of disasters, in particular in the developing countries;

36. *Notes* that space science and technology and their applications could make important contributions to economic, social and cultural development and welfare as indicated in the resolution entitled "The Space Millennium: Vienna Declaration on Space and Human Development", and notes also that the International Fair on Air and Space to be held at Santiago de Chile early in 2004 will address in an international conference the question "Space and water: towards sustainable development and human security";

37. *Agrees* that the benefits of space technology and its applications should be prominently brought to the attention of conferences organized within the United Nations system to address global issues relating to social, economic and cultural development and that the use of space technology should be promoted towards achieving the objectives of those conferences and implementing the United Nations Millennium Declaration;

38. *Notes with satisfaction* the increased efforts of the Committee and its Scientific and Technical Subcommittee as well as the Office for Outer Space Affairs and the Inter-Agency Meeting on Outer Space Activities to promote the use of space science and technology and their applications in carrying out actions recommended in the Plan of Implementation of the World Summit on Sustainable Development ("Johannesburg Plan of Implementation");

39. *Urges* entities of the United Nations system, particularly those participating in the Inter-Agency Meeting on Outer Space Activities, to examine, in cooperation with the Committee, how space science and technology and their applications could contribute to implementing the United Nations Millennium Declaration, particularly in the areas relating to, inter alia, food security and increasing opportunities for education;

40. *Invites* the Inter-Agency Meeting on Outer Space Activities to continue to contribute to the work of the Committee and to report to the Committee and its Scientific and Technical Subcommittee on the work conducted at its annual session;

41. *Requests* the Committee to continue to consider, as a matter of priority, ways and means of maintaining outer space for peaceful purposes and to report thereon to the General Assembly at its fifty-ninth session, and agrees that during its consideration of the matter, the Committee could consider ways to promote regional and interregional cooperation based on experiences stemming from the Space Conference of the Americas and the role space technology could play in the implementation of recommendations emerging from the World Summit on Sustainable Development;

42. *Agrees* that the Committee should continue to consider a report on the activities of the International Satellite System for Search and Rescue as a part of its consideration of the United Nations Programme on Space Applications under the agenda item entitled "Report of the Scientific and Technical Subcommittee", and invites Member States to report on their activities regarding the System;

43. *Notes* that in connection with the consideration of the implementation of an integrated, space-based global natural disaster management system, under the agenda item entitled "Report of the Scientific and Technical Subcommittee", during the forty-seventh session of the Committee, a one-day workshop for industry would be organized with the participation of Member States and communications satellite operators to discuss how satellite-based communications could be used during natural disasters;

44. *Requests* the Committee to continue to consider, at its forty-seventh session, its agenda item entitled

"Spin-off benefits of space technology: review of current status";

45. *Also requests* the Committee to continue to consider, at its forty-seventh session, its agenda item entitled "Space and society", and agrees that a special theme for the focus of discussions for the period 2004-2006 should be "Space and education", in accordance with the work plan adopted by the Committee;

46. *Agrees* that a new item entitled "Space and water" should be included in the agenda of the Committee at its forty-seventh session, and urges entities of the United Nations system and invites other intergovernmental entities dealing with issues relating to the use and management of water resources as well as space agencies to contribute to the work of the Committee in this field;

47. *Welcomes* the continued interest of the Libyan Arab Jamahiriya in becoming a member of the Committee, and, to this end, requests that constructive consultations be conducted as soon as possible within the Committee as well as among regional groups, taking into account the principle of equitable geographical distribution, with a view to reaching a positive and final decision on the membership of the Libyan Arab Jamahiriya at the fifty-ninth session of the General Assembly;

48. *Requests* the Committee to consider ways to improve participation by member States and entities with observer status in its work, with a view to agreeing on specific recommendations in that regard at its forty-eighth session;

49. *Endorses* the decision of the Committee to grant permanent observer status to the Regional Centre for Remote Sensing of the North African States and the International Institute for Applied Systems Analysis;

50. *Invites* the Committee to expand the scope of international cooperation relating to the social, economic, ethical and human dimension in space science and technology applications;

51. *Requests* entities of the United Nations system and other international organizations to continue and, where appropriate, to enhance their cooperation with the Committee and to provide it with reports on the issues dealt with in the work of the Committee and its subsidiary bodies;

52. *Requests* the Committee to consider and identify new mechanisms of international cooperation in the peaceful uses of outer space to strengthen multilateralism, in accordance with the preamble to the present resolution, and to submit a report to the General Assembly at its fifty-ninth session, including its views on which subjects should be studied in the future.

Effects of atomic radiation

At its fifty-first session (Vienna, 27-31 January) [A/58/46], the United Nations Scientific Committee on the Effects of Atomic Radiation advanced the programme of work established in 2001 [YUN 2001, p. 574]. It considered new information relevant to assessing sources of radiation, exposures from those sources and the resulting effects. The Committee reviewed Secretariat documents on exposures of workers and the public to various sources of radiation; sources-to-effects assessment for radon in homes and workplaces; radioecology; epigenetic effects of exposure to ionizing radiation; health effects due to radiation from the 1986 Chernobyl accident [YUN 1986, p. 584], for which the Committee had established official collaboration with scientists in Belarus, the Russian Federation and Ukraine; evaluation of new epidemiological studies of radiation and cancer; epidemiological evaluation and dose response of diseases other than cancer that might be related to radiation exposure; medical radiation exposures; the health effects of radiation; and the sources of ionizing radiation exposure.

The Committee's fifty-first session, which had been rescheduled from 2002 due to a budget shortfall [YUN 2002, p. 606], was made possible by combining non-post funds for both years of the 2002-2003 biennium. The report stated that the programme initiated at the session could not survive the loss of another annual meeting, and it was imperative that a solution to the Committee's budgetary crisis be found. In anticipation that adequate funds for the Committee to hold annual meetings would be restored for the 2004-2005 and subsequent bienniums, in accordance with resolution 57/115 [YUN 2002, p. 606], the Committee decided to hold its fifty-second session in Vienna from 26 to 30 April 2004.

GENERAL ASSEMBLY ACTION

On 9 December [meeting 72], the General Assembly, on the recommendation of the Fourth Committee [A/58/470], adopted **resolution 58/88** without vote [agenda item 81].

Effects of atomic radiation

The General Assembly,

Recalling its resolution 913(X) of 3 December 1955, by which it established the United Nations Scientific Committee on the Effects of Atomic Radiation, and its subsequent resolutions on the subject, including resolution 57/115 of 11 December 2002, in which, inter alia, it requested the Scientific Committee to continue its work,

Taking note with appreciation of the work of the Scientific Committee,

Reaffirming the desirability of the Scientific Committee continuing its work,

Concerned about the potentially harmful effects on present and future generations resulting from the levels of radiation to which mankind and the environment are exposed,

Noting the views expressed by Member States at its fifty-eighth session with regard to the work of the Scientific Committee,

Noting with satisfaction that some Member States have expressed particular interest in becoming members of the Scientific Committee, and expressing its intention to consider the issue further at its next session,

Conscious of the continuing need to examine and compile information about atomic and ionizing radiation and to analyse its effects on mankind and the environment,

1. *Commends* the United Nations Scientific Committee on the Effects of Atomic Radiation for the valuable contribution it has been making in the course of the past forty-eight years, since its inception, to wider knowledge and understanding of the levels, effects and risks of ionizing radiation, and for fulfilling its original mandate with scientific authority and independence of judgement;

2. *Reaffirms* the decision to maintain the present functions and independent role of the Scientific Committee;

3. *Requests* the Scientific Committee to continue its work, including its important activities to increase knowledge of the levels, effects and risks of ionizing radiation from all sources, and invites the Scientific Committee to submit its programme of work to the General Assembly;

4. *Endorses* the intentions and plans of the Scientific Committee for its future activities of scientific review and assessment on behalf of the General Assembly;

5. *Requests* the Scientific Committee to continue at its next session the review of the important problems in the field of ionizing radiation and to report thereon to the General Assembly at its fifty-ninth session;

6. *Requests* the United Nations Environment Programme to continue providing support for the effective conduct of the work of the Scientific Committee and for the dissemination of its findings to the General Assembly, the scientific community and the public;

7. *Expresses its appreciation* for the assistance rendered to the Scientific Committee by Member States, the specialized agencies, the International Atomic Energy Agency and non-governmental organizations, and invites them to increase their cooperation in this field;

8. *Invites* the Scientific Committee to continue its consultations with scientists and experts from interested Member States in the process of preparing its future scientific reports;

9. *Welcomes*, in this context, the readiness of Member States to provide the Scientific Committee with relevant information on the effects of ionizing radiation in affected areas, and invites the Scientific Committee to analyse and give due consideration to such information, particularly in the light of its own findings;

10. *Invites* Member States, the organizations of the United Nations system and non-governmental organizations concerned to provide further relevant data about doses, effects and risks from various sources of radiation, which would greatly help in the preparation of future reports of the Scientific Committee to the General Assembly;

11. *Urges* the United Nations Environment Programme to review and strengthen the present funding of the Scientific Committee, pursuant to paragraph 11 of resolution 57/115, so that the Committee can discharge the responsibilities and mandate entrusted to it by the General Assembly;

12. *Emphasizes* the need for the Scientific Committee to hold regular sessions on an annual basis so that its report can reflect the latest developments and findings in the field of ionizing radiation and thereby provide updated information for dissemination among all States.

PART TWO

Human rights

Chapter I

Promotion of human rights

In 2003, human rights were promoted through legally binding instruments and the Commission on Human Rights and its subsidiary body, the Subcommission on the Promotion and Protection of Human Rights. The Office of the United Nations High Commissioner for Human Rights continued its human rights coordination and implementation activities, and provided advisory services and technical cooperation.

The International Convention on the Protection of the Rights of All Migrant Workers and Members of Their Families, adopted by the General Assembly in 1990, entered into force on 1 July, following the deposit of the twentieth instrument of ratification or accession. The First Meeting of the States Parties to the Convention (New York, 11 December) met to elect the members of the Convention's monitoring body, the Committee on the Protection of the Rights of All Migrant Workers and Members of Their Families. Other monitoring bodies of human rights instruments promoted civil, political, economic, social and cultural rights, and aimed to eliminate racial discrimination and discrimination against women, to protect children and to end the practice of torture and other cruel, inhuman or degrading treatment or punishment.

On Human Rights Day, 10 December, the Assembly marked the tenth anniversary of the Vienna Declaration and Programme of Action, adopted at the 1993 World Conference on Human Rights, and the fifty-fifth anniversary of the Universal Declaration of Human Rights.

In view of the fact that human rights education was a long-term process, the High Commissioner presented guidelines for the development of a second decade to follow on from the United Nations Decade for Human Rights Education (1995-2004).

Sergio Vieira de Mello, whose four-year term of office as High Commissioner for Human Rights began on 12 September 2002, died in Baghdad in a terrorist attack on UN headquarters on 19 August, while serving as the Secretary-General's Special Representative for Iraq for a four-month assignment, which began on 1 June (see p. 346).

UN machinery

Commission on Human Rights

The Commission on Human Rights held its fifty-ninth session in Geneva from 17 March to 24 April [E/2003/23], during which it adopted 86 resolutions and 18 decisions. It recommended one draft resolution and 34 draft decisions for adoption by the Economic and Social Council. The Council took note of the Commission's report on 24 July (**decision 2003/310**).

In response to a 2000 Commission decision on enhancing the Commission's effectiveness [YUN 2000, p. 595], the Commission Chairperson convened a one-day informal meeting on 30 September to facilitate exchange of information in preparation for the General Assembly's fifty-eighth (2003) session [E/CN.4/IM/2003/1]. In a September note [E/CN.4/IM/2003/2], the Secretariat summarized the post-sessional meetings and activities of the Commission's Expanded Bureau.

Organization of work
Notes by Secretariat. The Commission considered a note by the Secretariat [E/CN.4/2003/12 & Corr.1] containing statistical data on its 2002 session to assist with the organization of the Commission's work in 2003.

A March note by the Secretariat transmitted a report by the United Nations Development Programme (UNDP) [E/CN.4/2003/128], the first of a series that UNDP intended to submit to every Commission session to inform the international community about its human rights activities.

A further Secretariat note [E/CN.4/2004/115] stated that, on 31 October, the President of the Economic and Social Council, in a letter to the 2003 Commission Chairperson, which was annexed to the note, drew attention to the policy recommendations adopted by the Council at its 2003 substantive session for consideration by its subsidiary bodies.

Commission action. On 17 March [dec. 2003/101], the Commission endorsed the recommendations of its Expanded Bureau regarding the reform of its working methods [E/CN.4/2003/118 & Corr.1]. The recommendations dealt with the duration of the Commission's annual session; the periodicity of the consideration of agenda items and sub-items; documentation for annual consideration; organization of work during the annual session; the role of the Expanded Bureau; the holding of special debates; participation of dignitaries in the annual session; establishment and programming of intersessional working groups; and organization and programming of parallel events, activities and meetings during annual sessions. Related issues were the need to narrow the gap between the end of the session of the Subcommission on the Promotion and Protection of Human Rights and the Commission's session (see below), and better utilization of the special procedures activity, including dialogue with Governments. A March note by the Secretariat [E/CN.4/2003/132], referring to one of the recommendations, stated that a compilation of executive summaries of all available reports was available on the web site of the Office of the High Commissioner for Human Rights (OHCHR).

On 25 April [dec. 2003/116], the Commission authorized its Bureau to consider steps that could be recommended to the Expanded Bureau of its 2004 session to improve the organization of the Commission's work based on decision 2003/101.

On 17 March [dec. 2003/102], the Commission invited special representatives, special rapporteurs, chairpersons and chairpersons/rapporteurs of various working groups, and experts to participate in its meetings.

On 25 April [dec. 2003/114], the Commission recommended to the Economic and Social Council that it authorize eight additional meetings for the Commission's sixtieth (2004) session and requested the Chairperson of the session to organize the session's work within the time normally allotted so that the additional meetings would be utilized only if necessary. The Council approved the Commission's decision on 23 July (**decision 2003/269**).

Also on 25 April [dec. 2003/115], the Commission decided that its first meeting would be held on the third Monday in January to elect its officers and that its 2004 session would take place from 15 March to 23 April. The Council endorsed the Commission's decision on 23 July (**decision 2003/270**).

ECONOMIC AND SOCIAL COUNCIL ACTION

In July, the Economic and Social Council, on the recommendation of the Commission on Human Rights [E/2003/23], adopted **decision 2003/269** by recorded vote (43-3-8) [agenda item 14 (g)].

Organization of work of the sixtieth session of the Commission on Human Rights

At its 46th plenary meeting, on 23 July 2003, the Economic and Social Council took note of Commission on Human Rights decision 2003/114 of 25 April 2003, and authorized eight fully serviced additional meetings, including summary records, in accordance with rules 29 and 31 of the rules of procedure of the functional commissions of the Council, for the Commission's sixtieth session.

The Council approved the Commission's decision to request the Chairperson of the sixtieth session of the Commission to make every effort to organize the work of the session within the time normally allotted so that the additional meetings authorized by the Council might be utilized only if they proved to be absolutely necessary.

RECORDED VOTE ON DECISION 2003/269:

In favour: Andorra, Argentina, Azerbaijan, Benin, Bhutan, Brazil, Burundi, Chile, Congo, Cuba, Ecuador, Egypt, El Salvador, Ethiopia, Finland, France, Georgia, Germany, Ghana, Greece, Guatemala, Hungary, India, Ireland, Italy, Jamaica, Japan, Libyan Arab Jamahiriya, Netherlands, Nicaragua, Nigeria, Peru, Portugal, Qatar, Republic of Korea, Romania, Russian Federation, Saudi Arabia, Senegal, South Africa, Sweden, Ukraine, Zimbabwe.

Against: Australia, United Kingdom, United States.

Abstaining: China, Iran, Kenya, Malaysia, Mozambique, Nepal, Pakistan, Uganda.

Thematic procedures

Pursuant to a 2002 Commission resolution [YUN 2002, p. 613], the Secretary-General prepared a list of thematic and country-specific procedures and other Commission mechanisms [E/CN.4/2003/1/Add.1] and submitted a March report [E/CN.4/2003/108] containing references to the conclusions and recommendations of thematic special rapporteurs and working groups.

The tenth meeting of special rapporteurs/representatives, independent experts and chairpersons of working groups of the special procedures of the Commission and of the advisory services programme was held in June [E/CN.4/2004/4] (see p. 678).

Subcommission on the Promotion and Protection of Human Rights

The Subcommission on the Promotion and Protection of Human Rights, at its fifty-fifth session (Geneva, 28 July–15 August) [E/CN.4/2004/2], adopted 30 resolutions and 17 decisions, and recommended one draft resolution and 14 draft decisions for adoption by the Commission.

On 13 August [dec. 2003/112], the Subcommission approved the composition of its working groups for 2004. On the same date [dec. 2003/103], it postponed action on a draft text on preparing a working paper on its work methods for report preparation and on the organization of its work so as to ensure full consideration of reports by Subcommission and national delegation members [dec. 2003/103].

Report of OHCHR. In response to a 2002 Commission request [YUN 2002, p. 613], OHCHR submitted a report [E/CN.4/2003/95] on ways to address issues raised by the Subcommission regarding possible early action by the Commission on Subcommission draft proposals requiring the Commission's approval and which presented possible options for narrowing the gap between the end of the Subcommission's session and the Commission's actions on Subcommission proposals: changing the dates of the Subcommission's session; early action by the Commission at its informal meeting in September; or action by the Commission at its January (election) meeting.

Report of Subcommission Chairperson. The Commission had before it a report [E/CN.4/2003/94] of the Subcommission's 2002 Chairperson, Paulo Sérgio Pinheiro (Brazil), which reviewed various aspects of the Subcommission's work, such as its methods and innovative approaches, in view of the 2001 ban [YUN 2001, p. 580] on the Subcommission's adoption of country-specific resolutions.

Commission action. On 24 April [res. 2003/59], the Commission decided that the Subcommission could best assist it by providing it with independent expert studies and working papers by its members or their alternates; recommendations based on the studies; and studies, research and expert advice at the Commission's request. It recommended that the Subcommission continue the innovations carried out in 2001 [YUN 2001, p. 580], which were confirmed at its 2002 session [YUN 2002, p. 613], by having annual closed meetings with the Commission's Expanded Bureau; streamlining its agenda; holding closed meetings on its working rules, procedures and timetables; drafting as many of its resolutions as possible in closed session; and using a "question and answer" format and expert panel discussions. The Commission also recommended that the Subcommission improve its work methods by focusing on its primary role as advisory body to the Commission; giving attention to studies recommended by the Commission or proposals suggested by treaty bodies or other UN human rights bodies; respecting the highest standards of impartiality and expertise, and avoiding acts that would affect confidence in its members' independence; facilitating participation of non-governmental organizations (NGOs); considering studies and working papers by special rapporteurs and its members before sending them to the Commission; taking steps to accomplish its work within a three-week session; making proposals to the Commission on how it might assist the Subcommission in improving its work and vice versa; focusing on human rights questions relating to its mandate; avoiding duplication of its work with that of other bodies and mechanisms; and giving appropriate regard to legal opinions addressed to it. The Commission requested States to consider certain criteria when nominating and electing Subcommission members and alternates.

The Secretary-General was asked to support the Subcommission by making documentation available in good time before each session in the UN official languages and assisting it in requests for information from Governments, intergovernmental organizations and NGOs. The Commission recommended that the Subcommission Chairperson or representative attend the meeting of special rapporteurs/representatives, experts and chairpersons of working groups of the special procedures of the Commission (see p. 678) and the meeting of chairpersons of treaty bodies (see p. 669) to facilitate coordination between the Subcommission and other relevant UN bodies and procedures. The Chairperson of the Subcommission's 2003 session was asked to report in 2004 on how recent enhancements of the Subcommission had worked in practice.

Note by Secretary-General. A June note by the Secretary-General [E/CN.4/Sub.2/2003/25] reviewed developments between 1 June 2002 and 1 June 2003 in areas with which the Subcommission had been concerned.

Office of the High Commissioner for Human Rights

Reports of High Commissioner. The United Nations High Commissioner for Human Rights, Sergio Vieira de Mello (Brazil), in his first annual report to the Commission [E/CN.4/2003/14], said that although the international community had developed a solid body of international human rights norms and humanitarian law, there was widespread failure in the concrete protection of human rights. He summarized some of the contemporary challenges to human rights protection and called for domestic action and international cooperation to prevent gross human rights violations, the integration of human rights in peacemaking, peacekeeping, peace-building, development and humanitarian operations, and the application of a rights-based approach in all spheres of operation—trade, finance, development and security. The High Commissioner supported the Secretary-General's plan to strengthen the special procedures system and improve OHCHR management [YUN 2002, p. 614].

The Acting High Commissioner, on behalf of the High Commissioner who was serving as the Secretary-General's Special Representative for Iraq for four months beginning 1 June, submitted a June report to the Economic and Social Council [E/2003/73]. The report focused on the human rights dimension of the Millennium Development Goals (MDGs) [YUN 2000, p. 51]; poverty reduction; health; HIV/AIDS; education; food; housing; disability; trafficking in persons; and globalization and trade. He concluded that applying an approach that integrated human rights in development, humanitarian and conflict-resolution schemes, and political, economic and cultural life, led to empowering people, ensuring their participation in decision-making and implementation. OHCHR had opened its programme to the areas of development and humanitarian work; conflict prevention and resolution and peace-building; the rule of law, democracy and good governance; and economic and social life.

The Acting High Commissioner submitted the High Commissioner's report to the General Assembly [A/58/36], following the High Commissioner's death in Baghdad in a terrorist attack on UN headquarters on 19 August (see p. 346). The report described OHCHR activities on the application of the human rights treaties; human rights and peace; human rights and development; human rights and justice; human rights and conflicts; gross violations of human rights; and new challenges, such as terrorism, bioethics and the role of the private sector in upholding human rights. The Assembly took note of the report on 22 December (**decision 58/541**).

Enhancing the functioning of OHCHR

Note of OHCHR. In a February note [E/CN.4/2003/124], submitted in response to General Assembly resolution 57/300 [YUN 2002, p. 1353], OHCHR presented recommendations on enhancing the effectiveness of the human rights special procedures in order to rationalize their work.

Commission action. On 25 April [dec. 2003/113], by a recorded vote of 28 to 24, with 1 abstention, the Commission requested the High Commissioner to ensure more effective coordination among OHCHR branches to preclude overlapping and/or duplication; to ensure that communications received or urgent appeals issued under the special procedures system were forwarded to the country concerned with written authorization from the special rapporteurs, independent experts or working groups; to discontinue the practice of transmitting ex officio monthly lists of communications and their contents to other UN organs/bodies, unless express authorization to that effect had been granted by the Commission or the Economic and Social Council; and to report to the Commission in 2004. The Commission's decision was overridden by Council **resolution 2003/58** (below).

In 2003, the Special Procedures Branch was established within OHCHR to provide strengthened support to the special procedures.

ECONOMIC AND SOCIAL COUNCIL ACTION

On 24 July [meeting 48], the Economic and Social Council adopted **resolution 2003/58** [draft: E/2003/L.37, as orally amended] by recorded vote (27-26-1) [agenda item 14 (g)].

Enhancement of the functioning of the Office of the United Nations High Commissioner for Human Rights in regard to the operation of the mechanisms of the Commission on Human Rights

The Economic and Social Council,

Reaffirming that the Office of the High Commissioner for Human Rights should continue to ensure effective coordination between its various branches in order to avoid any overlapping among all the mechanisms mandated by and/or reporting to the Commission on Human Rights, as referred to in the report of the intersessional open-ended Working Group on Enhancing the Effectiveness of the Mechanisms of the Commission on Human Rights,

Taking note of decision 47/102 of the Commission on the Status of Women, in which the Commission requested the Secretary-General to prepare a report on the future work of the Working Group on Communications on the Status of Women for its consideration,

1. *Decides* to postpone any decision on the transmission of communications and their contents between the functional commissions of the Economic and Social Council until the Commission on the Status of Women concludes its consideration of the report of the Secretary-General regarding the future work of the Working Group on Communications on the Status of Women and, in the meantime, to continue with present practice, as set out, notably, in its resolution 1983/27 of 26 May 1983;

2. *Confirms* that communications and urgent appeals are to be forwarded to the concerned States under the authorization of the special mechanism mandate-holders;

3. *Decides* that the present decision overrides Commission on Human Rights decision 2003/113 of 25 April 2003.

RECORDED VOTE ON RESOLUTION 2003/58:

In favour: Andorra, Argentina, Australia, Brazil, Chile, Ecuador, El Salvador, Finland, France, Georgia, Germany, Greece, Guatemala, Hungary, Ireland, Italy, Japan, Netherlands, Nicaragua, Peru, Portugal, Republic of Korea, Romania, Sweden, Ukraine, United Kingdom, United States.
Against: Azerbaijan, Bhutan, Burundi, China, Congo, Cuba, Egypt, Ethiopia, Ghana, India, Iran, Jamaica, Kenya, Libyan Arab Jamahiriya, Malaysia, Mozambique, Nepal, Nigeria, Pakistan, Qatar, Russian Federation, Saudi Arabia, Senegal, South Africa, Uganda, Zimbabwe.
Abstaining: Benin.

Management review

On 18 June [meeting 90], the General Assembly, having considered the 2002 management review of OHCHR [A/57/488], undertaken by the UN Office of Internal Oversight Services (OIOS) [YUN 2002, p. 615] and on the recommendation of the

Fifth (Administrative and Budgetary) Committee [A/57/604/Add.2], adopted **resolution 57/313** without vote [agenda item 122].

Management review of the Office of the United Nations High Commissioner for Human Rights

The General Assembly,

Recalling its resolutions 48/218 B of 29 July 1994 and 54/244 of 23 December 1999, and all its other relevant resolutions,

Recalling also its resolutions 56/253 of 24 December 2001 and 57/300 of 20 December 2002,

Recalling further its decision 55/488 of 7 September 2001,

Having considered the report of the Office of Internal Oversight Services on the management review of the Office of the United Nations High Commissioner for Human Rights,

1. *Takes note* of the report of the Office of Internal Oversight Services;

2. *Requests* the Secretary-General to report to the General Assembly at its fifty-eighth session on measures pertaining to the administration and management of the Office of the United Nations High Commissioner for Human Rights, taking into account the report of the Office of Internal Oversight Services, as appropriate, and the report of the United Nations High Commissioner for Human Rights requested by the Secretary-General in action 5 of his report entitled "Strengthening of the United Nations: an agenda for further change";

3. *Decides* to revert at its fifty-eighth session to the issue of the administration and management of the Office of the High Commissioner, in the context of its consideration of the proposed programme budget for the biennium 2004-2005, as well as to the issues relevant to the functioning of the Office addressed in resolution 57/300, in particular paragraphs 6, 8, 9 and 10, in the context of the procedures it establishes for consideration of the progress report of the Secretary-General on the implementation of the reform measures considered in that resolution.

Report of Secretary-General. In response to General Assembly resolution 57/313 (above), the Secretary-General, in a November report [A/58/569], described progress in implementing the 2002 OIOS recommendations [YUN 2002, p. 615] on the administration and management of OHCHR and indicated resources required for the Office in the 2004-2005 programme budget. At midyear, OIOS considered 3 of the 17 recommendations implemented and closed, and others were in the process of implementation. The report summarized resources proposed for 2004-2005 relating to costs for developing and implementing a plan to strengthen human rights–related UN actions at the country level, for consultations with treaty bodies on new streamlined reporting procedures, for reviewing the special procedures and for developing a plan to strengthen management. A proposed OHCHR organizational structure and post distribution for 2004-2005 were included.

In response to Assembly resolution 57/300 on reform measures [YUN 2002, p. 1353], the Secretary-General said that OHCHR was taking action to increase support for national human rights capacity-building, enhance implementation of human rights treaties and improve the system of special procedures.

ACABQ report. The Advisory Committee on Administrative and Budgetary Questions (ACABQ), in a November report [A/58/7/Add.12], reviewed the Secretary-General's report and made recommendations on the new posts proposed for OHCHR for 2004-2005.

The Assembly, by **resolution 58/272** of 23 December, took note of the reports of the Secretary-General and ACABQ (see p. 1417).

Composition of staff

Report of High Commissioner. In response to a 2002 Commission resolution [YUN 2002, p. 615], the High Commissioner submitted a report on the composition of OHCHR staff by nationality, grade and gender as at 1 December 2002 [E/CN.4/2003/111]. Also pursuant to that resolution, OHCHR had established the Advisory Panel on Personnel Issues, developed job descriptions, advertised temporary vacancies and circulated openings on its web site. The High Commissioner had recommended that the UN Office of Human Resources Management (OHRM) establish a human rights occupational group. In May 2001, OHRM had organized a specialized competitive human rights examination.

Commission action. On 25 April [res. 2003/74], by a recorded vote of 32 to 14, with 7 abstentions, the Commission expressed regret that one region (Western European and other States) accounted for more than half of the OHCHR posts and for more posts than the other four regional groups combined, and that there had been a decrease in the posts subject to geographical distribution and an increase in the staff not subject to geographical distribution. It considered it necessary to take immediate action to change that situation in favour of a more equitable distribution of staff; particular attention should be paid to recruiting personnel from unrepresented and underrepresented Member States, particularly from developing countries. The High Commissioner was requested to ensure that new personnel had a command of at least one of the working languages of the Secretariat and that the use of another of the six official languages was duly encouraged; to ensure that Junior Professional Officers were not given sensitive political assignments where their impartiality might be questioned; and to report in 2004. Annexed to the Commission's resolution was tabular information on the geographical distribution of OHCHR staff from 2000 to 2003.

Annual Appeal 2003

During the year, paid contributions to the 2003 Annual Appeal amounted to $47.4 million, up from $40.2 million in 2002. The voluntary contributions were received from 59 Governments, one foundation and various associations and individuals.

Strengthening action to promote human rights

In response to General Assembly resolutions 56/153 [YUN 2001, p. 582] and 57/203 [YUN 2002, p. 616], the Secretary-General, in a July report with later addenda [A/58/185 & Add.1,2], submitted the proposals of three Member States to strengthen UN action in human rights through the promotion of international cooperation based on the principles of non-selectivity, impartiality and objectivity.

GENERAL ASSEMBLY ACTION

On 22 December [meeting 77], the General Assembly, on the recommendation of the Third (Social, Humanitarian and Cultural) Committee [A/58/508/Add.2], adopted **resolution 58/168** without vote [agenda item 117 (b)].

Strengthening United Nations action in the field of human rights through the promotion of international cooperation and the importance of non-selectivity, impartiality and objectivity

The General Assembly,

Bearing in mind that among the purposes of the United Nations are those of developing friendly relations among nations based on respect for the principle of equal rights and self-determination of peoples and taking other appropriate measures to strengthen universal peace, as well as achieving international cooperation in solving international problems of an economic, social, cultural or humanitarian character and in promoting and encouraging respect for human rights and fundamental freedoms for all without distinction as to race, sex, language or religion,

Desirous of achieving further progress in international cooperation in promoting and encouraging respect for human rights and fundamental freedoms,

Considering that such international cooperation should be based on the principles embodied in international law, especially the Charter of the United Nations, as well as the Universal Declaration of Human Rights, the International Covenants on Human Rights and other relevant instruments,

Deeply convinced that United Nations action in this field should be based not only on a profound understanding of the broad range of problems existing in all societies but also on full respect for the political, economic and social realities of each of them, in strict compliance with the purposes and principles of the Charter and for the basic purpose of promoting and encouraging respect for human rights and fundamental freedoms through international cooperation,

Recalling its previous resolutions in this regard,

Reaffirming the importance of ensuring the universality, objectivity and non-selectivity of the consideration of human rights issues, as affirmed in the Vienna Declaration and Programme of Action adopted by the World Conference on Human Rights on 25 June 1993,

Affirming the importance of the objectivity, independence and discretion of the special rapporteurs and representatives on thematic issues and on countries, as well as of the members of the working groups, in carrying out their mandates,

Underlining the obligation that Governments have to promote and protect human rights and to carry out the responsibilities that they have undertaken under international law, especially the Charter, as well as various international instruments in the field of human rights,

1. *Reiterates* that, by virtue of the principle of equal rights and self-determination of peoples enshrined in the Charter of the United Nations, all peoples have the right freely to determine, without external interference, their political status and to pursue their economic, social and cultural development, and that every State has the duty to respect that right within the provisions of the Charter, including respect for territorial integrity;

2. *Reaffirms* that it is a purpose of the United Nations and the task of all Member States, in cooperation with the Organization, to promote and encourage respect for human rights and fundamental freedoms and to remain vigilant with regard to violations of human rights wherever they occur;

3. *Calls upon* all Member States to base their activities for the promotion and protection of human rights, including the development of further international cooperation in this field, on the Charter of the United Nations, the Universal Declaration of Human Rights, the International Covenant on Economic, Social and Cultural Rights, the International Covenant on Civil and Political Rights and other relevant international instruments, and to refrain from activities that are inconsistent with that international framework;

4. *Considers* that international cooperation in this field should make an effective and practical contribution to the urgent task of preventing mass and flagrant violations of human rights and fundamental freedoms for all and to the strengthening of international peace and security;

5. *Reaffirms* that the promotion, protection and full realization of all human rights and fundamental freedoms, as a legitimate concern of the world community, should be guided by the principles of non-selectivity, impartiality and objectivity and should not be used for political ends;

6. *Requests* all human rights bodies within the United Nations system, as well as the special rapporteurs and representatives, independent experts and working groups, to take duly into account the contents of the present resolution in carrying out their mandates;

7. *Expresses its conviction* that an unbiased and fair approach to human rights issues contributes to the promotion of international cooperation as well as to

the effective promotion, protection and realization of human rights and fundamental freedoms;

8. *Stresses*, in this context, the continuing need for impartial and objective information on the political, economic and social situations and events of all countries;

9. *Invites* Member States to consider adopting, as appropriate, within the framework of their respective legal systems and in accordance with their obligations under international law, especially the Charter, and international human rights instruments, the measures that they may deem appropriate to achieve further progress in international cooperation in promoting and encouraging respect for human rights and fundamental freedoms;

10. *Requests* the Commission on Human Rights to take duly into account the present resolution and to consider further proposals for the strengthening of United Nations action in the field of human rights through the promotion of international cooperation and the importance of non-selectivity, impartiality and objectivity;

11. *Takes note* of the report of the Secretary-General, and requests the Secretary-General to invite Member States to present practical proposals and ideas that would contribute to the strengthening of United Nations action in the field of human rights, through the promotion of international cooperation based on the principles of non-selectivity, impartiality and objectivity, and to submit a comprehensive report on this question to the General Assembly at its fifty-ninth session;

12. *Decides* to consider this matter at its fifty-ninth session under the item entitled "Human rights questions".

Also on 22 December, the Assembly took note of a series of documents submitted under the item on human rights questions (**decision 58/536**). On 23 December, the Assembly decided that the item on human rights questions, including alternative approaches for improving the effective enjoyment of human rights and fundamental freedoms, would remain for consideration during its resumed fifty-eighth (2004) session (**decision 58/565**).

International cooperation in the field of human rights

On 24 April [res. 2003/60], the Commission called on Member States, specialized agencies and intergovernmental organizations to continue to carry out a constructive dialogue and consultations to enhance the understanding and the promotion and protection of all human rights and fundamental freedoms, and encouraged NGOs to contribute to that endeavour. It invited States and relevant UN human rights mechanisms and procedures to pay attention to the importance of mutual cooperation, understanding and dialogue in ensuring human rights promotion and protection.

GENERAL ASSEMBLY ACTION

On 22 December [meeting 77], the General Assembly, on the recommendation of the Third Committee [A/58/508/Add.2], adopted **resolution 58/170** without vote [agenda item 117 *(b)*].

Enhancement of international cooperation in the field of human rights

The General Assembly,

Reaffirming its commitment to promoting international cooperation, as set forth in the Charter of the United Nations, in particular Article 1, paragraph 3, as well as relevant provisions of the Vienna Declaration and Programme of Action, adopted by the World Conference on Human Rights on 25 June 1993, for enhancing genuine cooperation among Member States in the field of human rights,

Recalling its adoption of the United Nations Millennium Declaration on 8 September 2000 and its resolution 57/224 of 18 December 2002, and taking note of Commission on Human Rights resolution 2003/60 of 24 April 2003 on the enhancement of international cooperation in the field of human rights,

Recalling also the World Conference against Racism, Racial Discrimination, Xenophobia and Related Intolerance, held at Durban, South Africa, from 31 August to 8 September 2001, and its role in the enhancement of international cooperation in the field of human rights,

Recognizing that the enhancement of international cooperation in the field of human rights is essential for the full achievement of the purposes of the United Nations, including the effective promotion and protection of all human rights,

Reaffirming that dialogue among religions, cultures and civilizations in the field of human rights could contribute greatly to the enhancement of international cooperation in this field, and recalling its decision to proclaim 2001 the United Nations Year of Dialogue among Civilizations, as well as its resolution 56/6 of 9 November 2001, entitled "Global Agenda for Dialogue among Civilizations",

Emphasizing the need for further progress in the promotion and encouragement of respect for human rights and fundamental freedoms through, inter alia, international cooperation,

Underlining the fact that mutual understanding, dialogue, cooperation, transparency and confidence-building are important elements in all the activities for the promotion and protection of human rights,

Recalling the adoption of resolution 2000/22 of 18 August 2000, on the promotion of dialogue on human rights issues, by the Subcommission on the Promotion and Protection of Human Rights at its fifty-second session,

1. *Reaffirms* that it is one of the purposes of the United Nations and the responsibility of all Member States to promote, protect and encourage respect for human rights and fundamental freedoms through, inter alia, international cooperation;

2. *Recognizes* that, in addition to their separate responsibilities to their individual societies, States have a collective responsibility to uphold the principles of human dignity, equality and equity at the global level;

3. *Reaffirms* that dialogue among cultures and civilizations facilitates the promotion of a culture of tolerance and respect for diversity, and welcomes in this regard the holding of conferences and meetings at the national, regional and international levels on dialogue among civilizations;

4. *Urges* all actors on the international scene to build an international order based on inclusion, justice, equality and equity, human dignity, mutual understanding and promotion of and respect for cultural diversity and universal human rights, and to reject all doctrines of exclusion based on racism, racial discrimination, xenophobia and related intolerance;

5. *Reaffirms* the importance of the enhancement of international cooperation for the promotion and protection of human rights and for the achievement of the objectives of the fight against racism, racial discrimination, xenophobia and related intolerance;

6. *Considers* that international cooperation in this field, in conformity with the purposes and principles set out in the Charter of the United Nations and international law, should make an effective and practical contribution to the urgent task of preventing violations of human rights and fundamental freedoms;

7. *Reaffirms* that the promotion, protection and full realization of all human rights and fundamental freedoms should be guided by the principles of universality, non-selectivity, objectivity and transparency, in a manner consistent with the purposes and principles set out in the Charter;

8. *Calls upon* Member States, specialized agencies and intergovernmental organizations to continue to carry out a constructive dialogue and consultations for the enhancement of understanding and the promotion and protection of all human rights and fundamental freedoms, and encourages non-governmental organizations to contribute actively to this endeavour;

9. *Invites* States and relevant United Nations human rights mechanisms and procedures to continue to pay attention to the importance of mutual cooperation, understanding and dialogue in ensuring the promotion and protection of all human rights;

10. *Decides* to continue its consideration of this question at its fifty-ninth session.

On the same date [meeting 77], the Assembly, also on the recommendation of the Third Committee [A/58/508/Add.2], adopted **resolution 58/188** by recorded vote (106-55-19) [agenda item 117 (b)].

Respect for the purposes and principles contained in the Charter of the United Nations to achieve international cooperation in promoting and encouraging respect for human rights and for fundamental freedoms and in solving international problems of a humanitarian character

The General Assembly,

Recalling that, in accordance with Article 56 of the Charter of the United Nations, all Member States have pledged themselves to take joint and separate action in cooperation with the Organization for the achievement of the purposes set forth in Article 55, including universal respect for and observance of human rights and fundamental freedoms for all without distinction as to race, sex, language or religion,

Recalling also the Preamble to the Charter, in particular the determination to reaffirm faith in fundamental human rights, in the dignity and worth of the human person and in the equal rights of men and women and of nations large and small,

Reaffirming that the promotion and protection of all human rights and fundamental freedoms must be considered a priority objective of the United Nations in accordance with its purposes and principles, in particular the purpose of international cooperation, and that, within the framework of these purposes and principles, the promotion and protection of all human rights is a legitimate concern of the international community,

Considering the major changes taking place on the international scene and the aspirations of all peoples to an international order based on the principles enshrined in the Charter, including promoting and encouraging respect for human rights and fundamental freedoms for all and respect for the principle of equal rights and self-determination of peoples, peace, democracy, justice, equality, the rule of law, pluralism, development, better standards of living and solidarity,

Recognizing that the international community should devise ways and means to remove current obstacles and meet the challenges to the full realization of all human rights and to prevent the continuation of human rights violations resulting therefrom throughout the world, and should continue to pay attention to the importance of mutual cooperation, understanding and dialogue in ensuring the promotion and protection of all human rights,

Reaffirming that the enhancement of international cooperation in the field of human rights is essential for the full achievement of the purposes of the United Nations and that human rights and fundamental freedoms are the birthright of all human beings, the promotion and protection of such rights and freedoms being the first responsibility of Governments,

Reaffirming also that all human rights are universal, indivisible, interdependent and interrelated and that the international community must treat human rights globally in a fair and equal manner, on the same footing and with the same emphasis,

Reaffirming further the various Articles of the Charter setting out the respective powers and functions of the General Assembly, the Security Council and the Economic and Social Council, as the paramount framework for the achievement of the purposes of the United Nations,

Reaffirming the commitment of all States to fulfil their obligations under other important instruments of international law, in particular those of international human rights and humanitarian law,

Taking into account that, in accordance with Article 103 of the Charter, in the event of a conflict between the obligations of the Members of the United Nations under the Charter and their obligations under any other international agreement, their obligations under the Charter shall prevail,

Recalling all its previous resolutions on the question, including its resolution 57/217 of 18 December 2002,

1. *Reiterates* the solemn commitment of all States to enhance international cooperation in the field of human rights and in the solution to international problems of a humanitarian character in full compliance with the Charter of the United Nations, inter alia, by the strict observance of all the purposes and principles set forth in Articles 1 and 2 thereof;

2. *Stresses* the vital role of the work of United Nations and regional arrangements, acting consistently with the purposes and principles enshrined in the Charter, in promoting and encouraging respect for human

rights and fundamental freedoms, as well as in solving international problems of a humanitarian character, and affirms that all States, in these activities, must fully comply with the principles set forth in Article 2 of the Charter, in particular respecting the sovereign equality of all States and refraining from the threat or use of force against the territorial integrity or political independence of any State, or acting in any other manner inconsistent with the purposes of the United Nations;

3. *Reaffirms* that the United Nations shall promote universal respect for and observance of human rights and fundamental freedoms for all without distinction as to race, sex, language or religion;

4. *Calls upon* all States to cooperate fully, through constructive dialogue, to ensure the promotion and protection of all human rights for all and in promoting peaceful solutions to international problems of a humanitarian character and, in their actions towards that purpose, to comply strictly with the principles and norms of international law, inter alia, by fully respecting international human rights and humanitarian law;

5. *Requests* the Secretary-General to bring the present resolution to the attention of Member States, organs, bodies and other components of the United Nations system, and intergovernmental and non-governmental organizations, and to disseminate it as widely as possible;

6. *Decides* to consider this question at its fifty-ninth session under the item entitled "Human rights questions".

RECORDED VOTE ON RESOLUTION 58/188:

In favour: Algeria, Angola, Antigua and Barbuda, Azerbaijan, Bahamas, Bahrain, Bangladesh, Barbados, Belarus, Belize, Benin, Bhutan, Bolivia, Botswana, Brunei Darussalam, Burkina Faso, Burundi, Cambodia, Cameroon, Cape Verde, Central African Republic, China, Colombia, Comoros, Congo, Costa Rica, Côte d'Ivoire, Cuba, Democratic People's Republic of Korea, Democratic Republic of the Congo, Djibouti, Dominica, Dominican Republic, Ecuador, Egypt, El Salvador, Eritrea, Ethiopia, Gabon, Gambia, Ghana, Grenada, Guinea, Guinea-Bissau, Guyana, Haiti, India, Indonesia, Iran, Jamaica, Jordan, Kazakhstan, Kenya, Kuwait, Kyrgyzstan, Lao People's Democratic Republic, Lebanon, Lesotho, Libyan Arab Jamahiriya, Madagascar, Malawi, Malaysia, Maldives, Mali, Mauritania, Mauritius, Mexico, Mongolia, Morocco, Mozambique, Myanmar, Namibia, Nepal, Nicaragua, Niger, Nigeria, Oman, Pakistan, Panama, Qatar, Russian Federation, Rwanda, Saint Lucia, Saudi Arabia, Senegal, Sierra Leone, Somalia, South Africa, Sri Lanka, Sudan, Suriname, Syrian Arab Republic, Tajikistan, Timor-Leste, Togo, Trinidad and Tobago, Tunisia, Turkmenistan, Uganda, United Arab Emirates, United Republic of Tanzania, Venezuela, Viet Nam, Yemen, Zambia, Zimbabwe.

Against: Albania, Andorra, Armenia, Australia, Austria, Belgium, Bosnia and Herzegovina, Bulgaria, Canada, Croatia, Cyprus, Czech Republic, Denmark, Estonia, Finland, France, Georgia, Germany, Greece, Hungary, Iceland, Ireland, Israel, Italy, Japan, Latvia, Liechtenstein, Lithuania, Luxembourg, Malta, Marshall Islands, Micronesia, Monaco, Netherlands, New Zealand, Norway, Palau, Poland, Portugal, Republic of Korea, Republic of Moldova, Romania, Samoa, San Marino, Serbia and Montenegro, Slovakia, Slovenia, Spain, Sweden, Switzerland, The former Yugoslav Republic of Macedonia, Turkey, Ukraine, United Kingdom, United States.

Abstaining: Argentina, Brazil, Chile, Fiji, Guatemala, Honduras, Nauru, Papua New Guinea, Paraguay, Peru, Philippines, Saint Vincent and the Grenadines, Singapore, Solomon Islands, Thailand, Tonga, Tuvalu, Uruguay, Uzbekistan.

Right to promote and protect human rights

Human rights defenders

Reports of Special Representative. In a January report [E/CN.4/2003/104], the Secretary-General's Special Representative on human rights defenders, Hina Jilani (Pakistan), described her activities, analysed evolving trends in violations and difficulties faced by human rights defenders, considered ways to strengthen implementation of the 1998 Declaration on the Right and Responsibility of Individuals, Groups and Organs of Society to Promote and Protect Universally Recognized Human Rights and Fundamental Freedoms, adopted by the General Assembly in resolution 53/144 [YUN 1998, p. 608], and described the types of violations committed in specific countries. The Special Representative identified priorities for a strategic approach to the situation and role of human rights defenders, including the protection of human rights defenders, strengthening the role of the media, increasing the responsibilities of local government, implementation of the 1998 Declaration in the context of democratization and of the MDGs, the special role of the UN country team for mainstreaming human rights, regional actions, and support from the special procedures and treaty bodies. A February addendum to the report [E/CN.4/2003/104/Add.1] summarized communications sent to and received from Governments, including urgent appeals and allegation letters, and presented guidelines for submitting allegations to the Special Representative.

The Special Representative visited the former Yugoslav Republic of Macedonia (27-30 January) to assess the role and situation of human rights defenders in the country [E/CN.4/2004/94/Add.2]. Defenders were active in addressing such issues as democratization; development; citizen participation; organization and monitoring of elections; human rights education and training; investigation of allegations of torture, illegal arrest and detention; monitoring and investigation of corruption; identifying discrimination; improving access to education; increasing literacy; support to minority languages and culture; trafficking in women and children; violence against women; promoting the rights of women, children and minorities; disarmament, demining and demobilization; labour rights and employment; and access to public services. While defenders reported considerable progress over the past decade, an analysis of the capacity of defenders in terms of their coordination, funding, integrity, training and overall sustainability suggested that the human rights community was still an emergent one. The Special Representative noted that very few defenders operated outside human rights organizations, and a majority needed greater knowledge of international human rights standards, and skills and expertise in developing human rights strategies. There had been a number of attacks on defenders because of their ethnicity and/or because they were perceived as advocating for human rights of a particular ethnic group.

The Special Representative concluded that the current capacity of human rights defenders was insufficient to meet the human rights challenges in the country, the opportunities available for them to influence human rights were limited and an enabling environment was not fully developed. She recommended that the Government adopt and implement legislation to enact the 1998 Declaration, report regularly to UN treaty bodies and involve civil society in the preparation and follow-up of reports, accord tax-exempt status to human rights organizations, grant defenders access to information required for their work, set up a mechanism through which the Government would respond to human rights concerns raised by human rights defenders, secure the independence of the judiciary, strengthen the police forces to ensure their respect for human rights and encourage action by the Ombudsman's Office to take up concerns raised by defenders. Human rights defenders were urged to take note of defenders' responsibilities under the 1998 Declaration; define strategies; ensure transparency; strengthen monitoring, reporting and protection activities; increase opportunities for training on human rights standards; develop domestic fund-raising strategies; inform the public of human rights issues and strengthen public participation; and strengthen cooperation with UN and regional human rights bodies. Recommendations to international donors were to verify the capacity and legitimacy of civil society organizations; define a collective strategy; provide core funding to organizations; and strengthen support for human rights NGOs. The UN country team was asked to contribute to the implementation of the 1998 Declaration and strengthen contacts with civil society organizations.

The Special Representative visited Thailand (19-27 May) [E/CN.4/2004/94/Add.1], where she noted a widely praised Constitution, which was constrained by weaknesses in implementation. She welcomed the work of the National Human Rights Commission (NHRC) but regretted the limited action by Government or Parliament in response to its concerns. The most common issues addressed by human rights defenders were economic and social rights, often in the context of national economic development plans and policies, including the right to land ownership of hill tribes communities; the right to livelihood of small farming and fishing communities threatened by industrial projects; environmental rights; labour rights for migrant workers; trafficking in people; the right to health; human rights in the context of HIV/AIDS; strengthening of the education system; respect for children's rights to participate in decisions affecting them; and discrimination against persons with disabilities. Although Thailand had a vibrant human rights community, there were limitations on that capacity, such as public statements by government officials denigrating NGOs, efforts to control NGO funding, restrictions on freedom of association, and alleged surveillance and harassment of some NGOs through State security mechanisms. The Special Representative considered that the law was applied selectively against defenders. Defenders feared that police powers had been abused at the local level to target defenders raising human rights concerns. The Special Representative expressed concern at the numerous cases of alleged or attempted murder of defenders and described cases involving hill tribes leaders and labour rights activists. Defenders within the NGO community, journalists, Thai and foreign defenders, academics, community activists and others expressed a widespread sense of insecurity.

The Special Representative recommended that the Government signal stronger political support for NHRC; consider ways in which the Ministry of Social Development and Human Security could consult with defenders in developing its definition of human security, use the 1998 Declaration as an integral component of its policies, and collaborate with the UN country team and OHCHR to build its programmes and capacity; ensure a more stable legal and political environment for human rights defenders; hold consultations with human rights defenders and organizations; give greater opportunities for defenders representing hill tribes, landless farmers and migrant workers to find solutions to their human rights concerns; review and consider withdrawing prosecutions against defenders; and ensure the prompt investigation of reported violations against defenders. The Parliament should facilitate constitutional human rights guarantees and fundamental freedoms; involve civil society in developing new legislation; act on the reports, concerns and recommendations of NHRC; and scrutinize more closely government actions that impacted human rights. Recommendations for human rights defenders were to maintain transparency in their activities and promote peaceful means for the assertion of rights, use peaceful advocacy to highlight laws that obstructed the work of human rights defenders, and enhance their security. The UN country team and the OHCHR Asia regional representative should support the Government in implementing the 1998 Declaration; strengthen collaboration with NGOs and other human rights defenders; and establish contacts with the Senate Committee for People's Participation to identify areas of cooperation for strengthening the legal framework for human rights.

A September note by the Secretary-General [A/58/380] transmitted the Special Representative's annual report, as requested in General Assembly resolution 57/209 [YUN 2002, p. 620], which addressed the related concerns of the use of security legislation against human rights defenders and the role and situation of human rights defenders in emergencies. General trends indicated a significant increase in the use of security legislation, including in counter-terrorism policies and actions, to limit the possibilities for defenders to conduct human rights work. The Special Representative drew attention to, among other issues, violations of defenders' rights to freedom of association, expression and access to information, and gave examples of the arbitrary arrest and detention, prosecution, conviction and sentencing of defenders, all under security legislation provisions. The restrictions on defenders were justified as measures to improve security and support counter-terrorism, while in many cases the actual objective was to conceal human rights abuses that defenders would have revealed, or to punish defenders for their work and to discourage others from continuing it. Regarding emergency situations, the Special Representative described situations when work to monitor and protect human rights was most urgent and defenders were prevented by some State and non-State actors from having access to victims of violations or places where violations occurred. She expressed deep concern that in those situations, the defenders were targeted and were increasingly victims of killings, torture, arrest, detention and other acts.

Recommendations to States included ensuring that security legislation was not applied against human rights defenders as a means to prevent their work, applying transparency when defenders were arrested, detained and/or prosecuted under security legislation, upholding the provisions of the 1998 Declaration and protecting human rights defenders under national laws. The United Nations was asked to provide support to human rights defenders and OHCHR to consider publishing guidelines indicating the human rights standards that should be referred to and protected by domestic security laws. Regional organizations should pay attention to deteriorating situations of defenders in emergencies within the region and those having a human rights mandate should establish a human rights defenders capacity. Defenders should ensure that their work met the standard of responsibility required by the 1998 Declaration, provide input during the drafting of security legislation, monitor the implementation of existing legislation and promote the Declaration.

The Assembly took note of the report on 22 December (**decision 58/538**).

Communication. In January [E/CN.4/2003/G/35], Guatemala presented its views on the Special Representative's report on her visit to the country [YUN 2002, p. 620], stating that the report was balanced and well documented. Guatemala offered its comments to provide more insight into the facts presented in the report and to seek ways to overcome the problems that it raised.

Commission action. On 24 April [res. 2003/64], the Commission, condemning human rights violations against human rights defenders, called on States to promote and give full effect to the 1998 Declaration and to ensure the protection of defenders. It decided to extend the Special Representative's mandate for an additional three years and asked her to continue to report to the General Assembly and the Commission. The Economic and Social Council approved, on 23 July, the Commission's decision and request to the Special Representative (**decision 2003/255**).

GENERAL ASSEMBLY ACTION

On 22 December [meeting 77], the General Assembly, on the recommendation of the Third Committee [A/58/508/Add.2], adopted **resolution 58/178** without vote [agenda item 117 (b)].

Declaration on the Right and Responsibility of Individuals, Groups and Organs of Society to Promote and Protect Universally Recognized Human Rights and Fundamental Freedoms

The General Assembly,

Recalling its resolution 53/144 of 9 December 1998, by which it adopted by consensus the Declaration on the Right and Responsibility of Individuals, Groups and Organs of Society to Promote and Protect Universally Recognized Human Rights and Fundamental Freedoms, annexed to that resolution,

Reiterating the importance of the Declaration, and stressing the importance of its wide dissemination,

Recalling all previous resolutions on this subject, in particular its resolution 57/209 of 18 December 2002 and Commission on Human Rights resolution 2003/64 of 24 April 2003,

Noting with deep concern that, in many countries, persons and organizations engaged in promoting and defending human rights and fundamental freedoms are facing threats, harassment and insecurity as a result of those activities,

Gravely concerned by the human rights violations committed against persons engaged in promoting and defending human rights and fundamental freedoms around the world,

Recalling that human rights defenders are entitled to equal protection of the law, and deeply concerned about any abuse of civil or criminal proceedings against them because of their activities for the promotion and protection of human rights and fundamental freedoms,

Concerned by the considerable number of communications received by the Special Representative of the Secretary-General on human rights defenders that, together with the reports submitted by some of the special procedure mechanisms, indicate the serious nature of the risks faced by human rights defenders, in particular those active at the local and community levels, and the severe consequences for women human rights defenders and defenders of rights of persons belonging to minorities,

Noting with deep concern that, in a number of countries in all regions of the world, impunity for threats, attacks and acts of intimidation against human rights defenders persists and that this has a negative impact on their work and safety,

Emphasizing the important role that individuals, non-governmental organizations and groups play in the promotion and protection of human rights and fundamental freedoms, including in combating impunity and in promoting, strengthening and preserving democracy,

Recalling that, under the International Covenant on Civil and Political Rights, certain rights are recognized as non-derogable, and emphasizing that derogation from other rights and freedoms can take place only under strict observance of the agreed conditions and procedures identified under article 4 of the Covenant,

Gravely concerned that, in some instances, national security and counter-terrorism legislation and other measures have been misused to target human rights defenders or have hindered their work and safety in a manner contrary to international law,

Acknowledging the significant work conducted by the Special Representative of the Secretary-General during the first three years of her mandate,

Welcoming the cooperation between the Special Representative and other special procedures of the Commission on Human Rights,

Welcoming also regional initiatives for the promotion and protection of human rights and the cooperation between international and regional mechanisms for the protection of human rights defenders, and encouraging further development in this regard,

Recalling that the primary responsibility for promoting and protecting human rights rests with the State, and noting with deep concern that the activities of some non-State actors pose a major threat to the security of human rights defenders,

Emphasizing the need for strong and effective measures for the protection of human rights defenders,

1. *Calls upon* all States to promote and give full effect to the Declaration on the Right and Responsibility of Individuals, Groups and Organs of Society to Promote and Protect Universally Recognized Human Rights and Fundamental Freedoms, including by taking, as appropriate, practical steps to that end;

2. *Welcomes* the reports of the Special Representative of the Secretary-General on human rights defenders and her contribution to the effective promotion of the Declaration and the improvement of the protection of human rights defenders worldwide;

3. *Encourages* all States to ensure and maintain an environment conducive to the work of human rights defenders;

4. *Condemns* all human rights violations committed against persons engaged in promoting and defending human rights and fundamental freedoms around the world, and urges States to take all appropriate action, consistent with the Declaration and all other relevant human rights instruments, to eliminate such human rights violations;

5. *Calls upon* all States to take all necessary measures to ensure the protection of human rights defenders, at both the local and the national levels;

6. *Urges* States to ensure that any measures to combat terrorism and preserve national security comply with their obligations under international law, in particular under international human rights law, and do not hinder the work and safety of human rights defenders;

7. *Emphasizes* the importance of combating impunity, and in this regard urges States to take appropriate measures to address the question of impunity for threats, attacks and acts of intimidation against human rights defenders;

8. *Urges* all Governments to cooperate with and assist the Special Representative in the performance of her tasks and to furnish all information in the fulfilment of her mandate upon request;

9. *Calls upon* Governments to give serious consideration to responding favourably to the requests of the Special Representative to visit their countries, and urges them to enter into a constructive dialogue with the Special Representative with respect to the follow-up to her recommendations, so as to enable her to fulfil her mandate even more effectively;

10. *Urges* those Governments that have not yet responded to the communications transmitted to them by the Special Representative to answer without further delay;

11. *Invites* Governments to consider translating the Declaration into national languages, and encourages them to disseminate it widely;

12. *Requests* all concerned United Nations agencies and organizations, within their mandates, to provide all possible assistance and support to the Special Representative in the implementation of her programme of activities;

13. *Invites* relevant United Nations bodies, including at the country level, within their mandates and working in cooperation with States, to give due consideration to the Declaration and to the reports of the Special Representative, and requests the Office of the United Nations High Commissioner for Human Rights to draw the attention of all relevant United Nations bodies, including at the country level, to the reports of the Special Representative;

14. *Requests* the Secretary-General to provide the Special Representative with all necessary human, material and financial resources in order to enable her to continue to carry out her mandate effectively, including through country visits;

15. *Decides* to consider this question at its fifty-ninth session under the item entitled "Human rights questions".

Human rights and human responsibilities

In response to Economic and Social Council decision 2002/277 [YUN 2002, p. 622], Special Rapporteur Miguel Alfonso Martínez (Cuba) submitted, in March, his final report on human rights and human responsibilities [E/CN.4/2003/105]. He pointed out that the responsibilities in question were not those dictated by law, but those that corresponded to social ethics and human solidarity. While the view of the essential linkage between those rights and responsibilities had not been generally accepted in human rights forums, the Special Rapporteur concluded that they were key to each other's realization. He asserted that every right was linked to some obligation or an ethical responsibility and that compliance with the latter prevented violations of the former. The Special Rapporteur discussed the duties that existed between States, such as the duty to contribute to compliance by every State with its obligation to promote, realize and protect the rights and liberties recognized for every person under its jurisdiction. The Special Rapporteur suggested that UN human rights bodies should be tasked to create a new standard on the matter, and that the Commission should consider the issue in future. Annexed to the report was a draft declaration on human social responsibilities for adoption by the Council.

Other aspects

Good governance

Report of High Commissioner. In response to a 2002 Commission request [YUN 2002, p. 622], the High Commissioner, in a January report [E/CN.4/2003/103], summarized examples of activities, submitted by Member States, international governmental organizations and NGOs, that had been effective in strengthening good governance practices for the promotion of human rights at the national level. He concluded that the information submitted reflected a broad understanding of the concept of good governance as well as its relevance for the promotion of human rights at the national level. It also indicated a growing interest and awareness of the importance of good governance for the realization of the broad range of human rights and sustainable development. The High Commissioner said the convening of a seminar on practical approaches and activities that had been effective in strengthening good governance practices for the promotion of human rights at the national level, as called for by the Commission in 2002, had been postponed owing to financial constraints.

Commission action. On 24 April [res. 2003/65], the Commission welcomed the High Commissioner's commitment, using extrabudgetary funding and working jointly with UNDP, to convene a seminar, prior to the Commission's 2005 session, on practical approaches and activities that had been effective in strengthening good governance practices for the promotion of human rights at the national level. It requested him to invite States, national human rights institutions, relevant UN bodies, other international bodies and NGOs to attend the seminar and to report to the Commission. It also asked him to compile indicative ideas and practices arising from the seminar and the material provided by States, intergovernmental organizations and NGOs that could be consulted by interested States.

Human rights instruments

General aspects

In 2003, seven UN human rights instruments were in force that required monitoring of their implementation by expert bodies. The instruments and their treaty bodies were: the 1965 International Convention on the Elimination of All Forms of Racial Discrimination [YUN 1965, p. 440, GA res. 2106 A (XX)] (Committee on the Elimination of Racial Discrimination); the 1966 International Covenant on Civil and Political Rights and the Optional Protocol thereto [YUN 1966, p. 423, GA res. 2200 A (XXI)] and the Second Optional Protocol, aiming at the abolition of the death penalty [YUN 1989, p. 484, GA res. 44/128] (Human Rights Committee); the 1966 International Covenant on Economic, Social and Cultural Rights [YUN 1966, p. 419, GA res. 2200 A (XXI)] (Committee on Economic, Social and Cultural Rights); the 1979 Convention on the Elimination of All Forms of Discrimination against Women [YUN 1979, p. 895, GA res. 34/180] and Optional Protocol [YUN 1999, p. 1100, GA res. 54/4] (Committee on the Elimination of Discrimination against Women); the 1984 Convention against Torture and Other Cruel, Inhuman or Degrading Treatment or Punishment [YUN 1984, p. 813, GA res. 39/46] and 2002 Optional Protocol [YUN 2002, p. 631, GA res. 57/199] (Committee against Torture); the 1989 Convention on the Rights of the Child [YUN 1989, p. 560, GA res. 44/25] and Optional Protocols on the involvement of children in armed conflict and on the sale of children, child prostitution and child pornography [YUN 2000, pp. 616 & 618, GA res. 54/263] (Committee on the Rights of the Child); and the 1990 International Convention on the Protection of the Rights of All Migrant Workers and Members of Their Families [YUN 1990, p. 594, GA res. 45/158] (Committee on the Protection of the Rights of All Migrant Workers and Members of Their Families).

Working paper. As requested by the Subcommission in 2002 [YUN 2002, p. 623], Emmanuel Decaux (France) submitted a June working paper on the effective universality of international human rights treaties [E/CN.4/Sub.2/2003/37]. The paper reviewed efforts to encourage the universal acceptance of human rights instruments carried out since the 1993 World Conference on Human Rights [YUN 1993, p. 908]. It presented data gathered by OHCHR on the number of ratifications to the seven main human rights treaty instruments from January 1993 to June 2003. The current total of 955 ratifications, 10 years after the 1993 World Conference, reflected a marked deceleration and a shortfall of over 200 ratifications compared with the target of universal ratification for the six selected instruments for which monitoring bodies existed. The report noted that almost two thirds (130) of the 209 non-ratifications were concentrated in some 30 States, which it listed. It suggested that the status of the instruments or the system of reservations to treaties were legal issues that should be regrouped under the agenda item on the administration of justice, the rule of law and democracy, which would be more logical in that the concept of the rule of law implied a reference both to the domestic order and to respect for international law. The future study should seek to: clarify the issues raised by the effective universality of human rights treaties, including to refine the concept of universal treaties or treaties of universal scope from the standpoint of public international law; draw up an inventory of the relevant treaties and assess the machinery for monitoring commitments and encouraging ratification; take into account relevant experience in other treaty monitoring systems; and consider the most effective modalities that would allow a constructive dialogue with States concerning legal, political, social or other difficulties encountered in the ratification, entry into force, interpretation and application of the treaties in question, with a view to seeking effective universality.

Subcommission action. On 14 August [res. 2003/25], the Subcommission decided to appoint Mr. Decaux Special Rapporteur to undertake a study on the universal implementation of international human rights treaties and asked him to submit a preliminary report in 2004, an interim report in 2005 and a final report in 2006. It decided that the reports would be considered under the agenda item on the administration of justice, the rule of law and democracy. The Secretary-General was asked to assist the Special Rapporteur.

Human rights treaty body system

Note by OHCHR. Pursuant to General Assembly resolution 57/300 [YUN 2002, p. 1353] and in the light of the Secretary-General's report on strengthening the United Nations [ibid., p. 614], OHCHR, in a February note [E/CN.4/2003/126], described action it had taken to facilitate a review by States parties and the respective treaty bodies on the reporting procedures of the treaty bodies with a view to developing a more coordinated approach and streamlining the reporting requirements.

In June [HRI/GEN/4/Rev.3], OHCHR published an outline of the recent reporting history of States parties to the treaties as at 2 June 2003.

Notes by Secretariat. An April note by the Secretariat [HRI/GEN/3/Rev.1] contained a compilation of the rules of procedure adopted by the main treaty bodies, as requested in General Assembly resolution 55/90 [YUN 2000, p. 607].

A May note [HRI/GEN/1/Rev.6] presented a compilation of general comments and general recommendations adopted by the Committee on Economic, Social and Cultural Rights, the Human Rights Committee, the Committee on the Elimination of Racial Discrimination (CERD), the Committee on the Elimination of Discrimination against Women, the Committee against Torture and the Committee on the Rights of the Child.

Expert meeting. A meeting of experts (Malbun, Liechtenstein, 4-7 May) [A/58/123] on the theme of treaty body reform, organized by OHCHR and Liechtenstein, considered the harmonization of reporting guidelines to govern the technical and formal elements of reports, the submission of a single report satisfying States parties' reporting obligations under all treaties to which they were a party, an expanded core document to avoid repetition and overlap, focused periodic reports, thematic or modular (a common document for all treaty bodies to which specific reports under each treaty would be attached) reporting, periodicity of reporting on human rights treaties, and capacity-building aimed at implementation of treaty obligations and follow-up to recommendations of treaty bodies. The report of the meeting was submitted to the second inter-committee meeting of the human rights treaty bodies and the fifteenth meeting of chairpersons of human rights treaty bodies (see below).

Inter-committee meeting. The second inter-committee meeting of human rights treaty bodies (Geneva, 18-20 June) [A/58/350, annex I] reached agreement and made recommendations on the need to enhance consistency in the examination of reports by all treaty bodies; the State party report as the basis for consideration of implementation of treaties; the role of national human rights institutions in the human rights reporting process; capacity-building to improve national reporting; joint or parallel general comments/recommendations reached by treaty bodies; the dissemination of concluding observations/comments; strengthening the human rights treaty body system; procedures to follow up on treaty body recommendations; and procedures to examine the human rights situation in a State party whose reports were long overdue and that had not responded to reminders. The inter-committee meeting had before it a Secretariat background document on methods of work relating to the State reporting process [HRI/ICM/2003/3 & Add.1].

Meeting of chairpersons. The fifteenth meeting of chairpersons of human rights treaty bodies (Geneva, 23-27 June) [A/58/350] considered recommendations of the fourteenth meeting [YUN 2002, p. 622] and reviewed developments relating to the work of the treaty bodies. The fifth joint meeting was held with the participants of the tenth meeting of special rapporteurs/representatives, independent experts and chairpersons of working groups of the special procedures of the Commission and of the advisory services programme (see p. 678). The chairpersons adopted recommendations relating to proposals to strengthen the human rights treaty body system; the provision by treaty bodies of lists of issues and questions prior to the examination of States parties' reports; the inter-committee meeting in 2004 to examine draft guidelines for the expanded core document and to focus on technical and organizational issues; cooperation with the Commission, the Subcommission and special rapporteurs; the accuracy of UN press releases; and honorariums for the treaty body experts of all committees. The meeting considered a review of recent developments relating to the work of treaty bodies issued in June by the Secretariat [HRI/MC/2003/2]. The General Assembly took note of the meeting's report on 22 December (**decision 58/537**).

Reservations to human rights treaties

As requested by the Subcommission in 2001 [YUN 2001, p. 589], Françoise Hampson (United Kingdom) issued, in August, an expanded report on reservations to human rights treaties [E/CN.4/Sub.2/2003/WP.2], in which she concluded that States were free to formulate a reservation to a human rights treaty, where the reservation was not prohibited by the treaty, on condition that the reservation was not incompatible with the treaty's purposes; States could not formulate a reservation incompatible with the purposes of a treaty and other States could not accept such a reservation; a human rights treaty body had the jurisdiction to determine the validity of a reservation; and where a human rights treaty body reached the conclusion that a reservation was incompatible with a treaty's purpose, the reserving State had the option to withdraw or modify the reservation so as to make it compatible with the treaty or denounce the treaty. She proposed encouraging human rights treaty bodies to continue to enter into a dialogue with the reserving State, with a view to changing the incompatible reservation as to make it compatible with the treaty. She recommended forwarding the expanded working paper to CERD, other treaty bodies and the Special Rapporteur of the International Law Commission.

Universal Declaration of Human Rights

In accordance with General Assembly decision 57/534 [YUN 2002, p. 625], human rights prizes were awarded in 2003 to mark the fifty-fifth anniversary of the Universal Declaration of Human Rights, adopted by Assembly resolution 217 A (III) [YUN 1948-49, p. 535]. The United Nations, on the occasion of Human Rights Day (10 December), awarded prizes to Enriqueta Estela Barnes de Carlotto (Argentina), President of the Association of Plaza de Mayo Grandmothers; Deng Pufang (China), founder and Director of the China Disabled Persons Federation; Shulamith Koenig (United States), Executive Director of the People's Movement for Human Rights; and two ground-breaking organizations—Family Protection Project Management Team (Jordan) and the Mano River Women's Peace Network (West Africa). A special posthumous award was given to Sergio Vieira de Mello, the late High Commissioner. The prizes were awarded every five years for outstanding promotion and protection of civil liberties and fundamental freedoms.

Covenant on Civil and Political Rights and Optional Protocols

Accessions and ratifications

As at 31 December 2003, parties to the International Covenant on Civil and Political Rights and the Optional Protocol thereto, adopted by the General Assembly in resolution 2200 A (XXI) [YUN 1966, p. 423], numbered 151 and 104, respectively. During the year, Timor-Leste and Turkey became parties to the Covenant.

The Second Optional Protocol, aiming at the abolition of the death penalty, adopted by the Assembly in resolution 44/128 [YUN 1989, p. 484], was acceded to by Paraguay and Timor-Leste, bringing the total number of States parties to 51 as at 31 December.

The Secretary-General reported on the status of the Covenant and its Optional Protocols as at 1 August [A/58/307] and 1 December [E/CN.4/2004/85].

Implementation

Monitoring body. The Human Rights Committee, established under article 28 of the Covenant, held three sessions in 2003: its seventy-seventh from 17 March to 4 April, its seventy-eighth from 14 July to 8 August, which included an additional week for the plenary and was devoted to the consideration of communications under the Optional Protocol, so as to reduce the backlog of pending cases [A/58/40, vol. I], and its seventy-ninth from 20 October to 7 November [A/59/40, vol. I], all in Geneva. The General Assembly took note of the Committee's report on its seventy-seventh and seventy-eighth sessions on 22 December (**decision 58/537**).

In 2003, the Committee considered reports from 11 States—El Salvador, Estonia, Israel, Latvia, Luxembourg, Mali, the Philippines, Portugal, the Russian Federation, Slovakia and Sri Lanka—under article 40. In the absence of a report, the Committee made public final concluding observations on country situations in Equatorial Guinea and the Gambia. It adopted views on communications from individuals claiming that their rights under the Covenant had been violated, and decided that other such communications were inadmissible. Those views and decisions were annexed to the Committee's reports [A/58/40, vol. II; A/59/40, vol. II].

Colombia notified other States parties, through the intermediary of the Secretary-General, on 12 February, of the second extension of a declaration of internal disturbance issued in 2002 [YUN 2002, p. 626]. Serbia and Montenegro notified other States parties of the adoption, by the Acting President on 12 March, of a decision and order declaring a state of emergency for the territory of the State, following the assassination of Serbian Prime Minister Zoran Djindjic (see p. 415); the state of emergency was terminated on 23 April. Peru notified other States parties of the declaration of a state of emergency for a period of 30 days, with effect from 29 May; by notifications of 30 September and 1 December, Peru stated that it had extended the state of emergency in different provinces and parts of the country.

Covenant on Economic, Social and Cultural Rights

Accessions and ratifications

As at 31 December 2003, there were 148 parties to the International Covenant on Economic, Social and Cultural Rights, adopted by the General Assembly in resolution 2200 A (XXI) [YUN 1966, p. 419]. Timor-Leste and Turkey became parties during the year. The Secretary-General reported on the status of the Covenant as at 1 July [A/58/307] and 1 December [E/CN.4/2004/85].

Draft optional protocol

Report of independent expert. The independent expert on the question of a draft optional protocol to the Covenant, Hatem Kotrane (Tunisia), in a January report [E/CN.4/2003/53 & Corr.1,2], focused on issues raised in a 2002 Commission resolution [YUN 2002, p. 627] relating to the nature and scope of States parties' obligations under the Covenant, the justiciability of economic, social and cultural rights, a complaint mechanism under the Covenant and complementarity between different mechanisms. He recommended that the Commission adopt a resolution confirming its decision [YUN 2002, p. 627] to establish an open-ended working group to consider options regarding the elaboration of an optional protocol.

Commission action. On 22 April [res. 2003/18], the Commission, taking note of Economic and Social Council decision 2002/254 [YUN 2002, p. 627], which endorsed the Commission's decision [ibid.] to establish the working group, requested the group to meet for 10 working days prior to the Commission's 2004 session. It asked OHCHR to make available for the group's session the comments and views of States, intergovernmental organizations and NGOs regarding the issues raised by the expert (above). Special Rapporteurs whose mandates related to the realization of economic, social and cultural rights were asked to share their views on an optional protocol and to make recommendations to the working group. The group was requested to report in 2004 and to make recommendations on its course of action regarding the draft optional protocol.

ECONOMIC AND SOCIAL COUNCIL ACTION

In July, the Economic and Social Council, on the recommendation of the Commission on Human Rights [E/2003/23], adopted **decision 2003/242** by recorded vote (51-2-1) [agenda item 14 (g)].

Question of the realization in all countries of the economic, social and cultural rights contained in the Universal Declaration of Human Rights and in the International Covenant on Economic, Social and Cultural Rights, and study of special problems which the developing countries face in their efforts to achieve these human rights

At its 46th plenary meeting, on 23 July 2003, the Economic and Social Council, recalling its decision 2002/254 of 25 July 2002, in which the Council endorsed the decision of the Commission on Human Rights to establish, at its fifty-ninth session, an open-ended working group of the Commission with a view to considering options regarding the elaboration of an optional protocol to the International Covenant on Economic, Social and Cultural Rights, and taking note of Commission resolution 2003/18 of 22 April 2003, endorsed the Commission's request that the working group should meet for a period of ten working days, prior to the sixtieth session of the Commission, with a view to considering options regarding the elaboration of an optional protocol to the Covenant, in the light, inter alia, of the report of the Committee on Economic, Social and Cultural Rights to the Commission on a draft optional protocol for the consideration of communications in relation to the Covenant, comments and views submitted by States, intergovernmental organizations, including United Nations specialized agencies, and non-governmental organizations, and the reports of the independent expert to examine the question of a draft optional protocol to the Covenant.

Subcommission action. On 13 August [res. 2003/19], the Subcommission urged the Commission in 2004 to mandate the open-ended working group to proceed with drafting the text of an optional protocol. It urged the group to draft an optional protocol that was comprehensive in scope and provided that communications might be initiated by individual and collective victims; further, the instrument should be conceptualized as both a complaint mechanism and an inquiry procedure and should preclude State party reservations.

Implementation

Monitoring body. The Committee on Economic, Social and Cultural Rights held its thirtieth (5-23 May) and thirty-first (10-28 November) sessions, both in Geneva [E/2004/22]. Its pre-sessional working group held meetings in Geneva from 1 to 5 December to identify issues to be discussed with reporting States.

On 24 July, the Economic and Social Council took note of the Committee's report on its twenty-eighth and twenty-ninth sessions, held in 2002 [YUN 2002, p. 627] (**decision 2003/310**).

In 2003, the Committee examined reports under articles 16 and 17 of the Covenant submitted by Brazil, the Democratic People's Republic of Korea, Guatemala, Iceland, Israel, Luxembourg, New Zealand, the Republic of Moldova, the Russian Federation and Yemen.

On 24 November, the Committee held a day of general discussion on the right to work, as provided for in article 6 of the Covenant. The discussion was intended to lay the groundwork for the elaboration of a general comment on the right to work.

The Committee asked OHCHR to consider organizing, in 2005, a workshop on follow-up action to its concluding observations for the States parties to the Covenant from the Asian region.

Commission action. On 22 April [res. 2003/18], the Commission encouraged the Committee to continue efforts to promote, protect and fully realize the rights enshrined in the Covenant, at the national and international levels.

GENERAL ASSEMBLY ACTION

On 22 December [meeting 77], the General Assembly, on the recommendation of the Third Committee [A/58/508/Add.1 & Corr.1], adopted **resolution 58/165** without vote [agenda item 117 (a)].

International Covenants on Human Rights

The General Assembly,

Recalling its resolution 56/144 of 19 December 2001 and Commission on Human Rights resolution 2002/78 of 25 April 2002,

Mindful that the International Covenants on Human Rights constitute the first all-embracing and legally binding international treaties in the field of human rights and, together with the Universal Declaration of Human Rights, form the core of the International Bill of Human Rights,

Taking note of the report of the Secretary-General on the status of the International Covenant on Economic, Social and Cultural Rights, the International Covenant on Civil and Political Rights and the Optional Protocols to the International Covenant on Civil and Political Rights,

Recalling the International Covenant on Economic, Social and Cultural Rights and the International Covenant on Civil and Political Rights, and reaffirming that all human rights and fundamental freedoms are universal, indivisible, interdependent and interrelated and that the promotion and protection of one category of rights should never exempt or excuse States from the promotion and protection of the other rights,

Recognizing the important role of the Human Rights Committee and the Committee on Economic, Social and Cultural Rights in examining the progress made by States parties in fulfilling the obligations undertaken in the International Covenants on Human Rights and the Optional Protocols to the International Covenant on Civil and Political Rights and in providing recommendations to States parties on their implementation,

Considering that the effective functioning of the Human Rights Committee and the Committee on Economic, Social and Cultural Rights is indispensable for the full and effective implementation of the International Covenants on Human Rights,

Recognizing the importance of regional human rights instruments and monitoring mechanisms in complementing the universal system of promotion and protection of human rights,

1. *Reaffirms* the importance of the International Covenants on Human Rights as major components of international efforts to promote universal respect for

and observance of human rights and fundamental freedoms;

2. *Welcomes once again* the initiative of the Secretary-General at the Millennium Assembly of the United Nations to invite heads of State and Government to sign, ratify or accede to the International Covenants on Human Rights, and expresses its appreciation to those States that have done so;

3. *Strongly appeals* to all States that have not yet done so to become parties to the International Covenant on Economic, Social and Cultural Rights and the International Covenant on Civil and Political Rights, as well as to consider as a matter of priority acceding to the Optional Protocols to the International Covenant on Civil and Political Rights and making the declaration provided for in article 41 of the Covenant;

4. *Invites* the United Nations High Commissioner for Human Rights to intensify systematic efforts to encourage States to become parties to the International Covenants on Human Rights and, through the programme of advisory services in the field of human rights, to assist such States, at their request, in ratifying or acceding to the Covenants and to the Optional Protocols to the International Covenant on Civil and Political Rights with a view to achieving universal adherence;

5. *Emphasizes* the importance of the strictest compliance by States parties with their obligations under the International Covenant on Economic, Social and Cultural Rights and the International Covenant on Civil and Political Rights and, where applicable, the Optional Protocols to the International Covenant on Civil and Political Rights;

6. *Also emphasizes* that States must ensure that any measure to combat terrorism complies with their obligations under relevant international law, including their obligations under the International Covenants on Human Rights;

7. *Stresses* the importance of avoiding the erosion of human rights by derogation, and underlines the necessity of strict observance of the agreed conditions and procedures for derogation under article 4 of the International Covenant on Civil and Political Rights, bearing in mind the need for States parties to provide the fullest possible information during states of emergency so that the justification for the appropriateness of measures taken in those circumstances can be assessed, and in this regard particularly takes note of General Comment No. 29 adopted by the Human Rights Committee;

8. *Encourages* States parties to consider limiting the extent of any reservations that they lodge to the International Covenants on Human Rights, to formulate any reservations as precisely and narrowly as possible and to ensure that no reservation is incompatible with the object and purpose of the relevant treaty;

9. *Also encourages* States parties to review regularly any reservations made in respect of the provisions of the International Covenants on Human Rights and the Optional Protocols to the International Covenant on Civil and Political Rights with a view to withdrawing them;

10. *Welcomes* the annual reports of the Human Rights Committee submitted to the General Assembly at its fifty-seventh and fifty-eighth sessions, and takes note of the General Comments adopted by the Committee;

11. *Also welcomes* the reports of the Committee on Economic, Social and Cultural Rights on its twenty-fifth, twenty-sixth and twenty-seventh sessions and on its twenty-eighth and twenty-ninth sessions, and takes note of the General Comments adopted by the Committee;

12. *Urges* States parties to fulfil their reporting obligations under article 40 of the International Covenant on Civil and Political Rights on time and to attend and participate in the consideration of the reports by the Human Rights Committee when so requested, and in this regard takes note of General Comment No. 30 adopted by the Committee;

13. *Also urges* States parties to fulfil their reporting obligations under article 16 of the International Covenant on Economic, Social and Cultural Rights on time and to attend and participate in the consideration of the reports by the Committee on Economic, Social and Cultural Rights when so requested;

14. *Further urges* States parties to make use in their reports of gender-disaggregated data, and stresses the importance of taking fully into account a gender perspective in the implementation of the International Covenants on Human Rights at the national level, including in the national reports of States parties and in the work of the Human Rights Committee and of the Committee on Economic, Social and Cultural Rights;

15. *Strongly encourages* States parties that have not yet submitted core documents to the Office of the United Nations High Commissioner for Human Rights to do so, and invites all States parties regularly to review and update their core documents;

16. *Urges* States parties to take duly into account, in implementing the provisions of the International Covenants on Human Rights, the recommendations and observations made during the consideration of their reports by the Human Rights Committee and by the Committee on Economic, Social and Cultural Rights, as well as the views adopted by the Human Rights Committee under the first Optional Protocol to the International Covenant on Civil and Political Rights;

17. *Invites* States parties to give particular attention to the dissemination at the national level of their reports submitted to the Human Rights Committee and the Committee on Economic, Social and Cultural Rights, the summary records relating to the examination of those reports by the Committees and the recommendations and observations made by the Committees after the examination of those reports;

18. *Urges* all States to publish the texts of the International Covenant on Economic, Social and Cultural Rights, the International Covenant on Civil and Political Rights and the Optional Protocols to the International Covenant on Civil and Political Rights in as many local languages as possible and to distribute them and make them known as widely as possible in their territories;

19. *Urges* each State party to translate, publish and make available as widely as possible in its territory by appropriate means the full text of the concluding observations on its reports to the Human Rights Committee and the Committee on Economic, Social and Cultural Rights;

20. *Reiterates* that States parties should take into account, in their nomination of members to the Human Rights Committee and the Committee on Economic, Social and Cultural Rights, that the Committees shall be composed of persons of high moral character and recognized competence in the field of human rights, consideration being given to the usefulness of the participation of some persons having legal experience, as well as to equal representation of women and men, and that members serve in their personal capacity, and also reiterates that, in the elections of the Committees, consideration shall be given to equitable geographical distribution of membership and to the representation of the different forms of civilization and of the principal legal systems;

21. *Invites* the Human Rights Committee and the Committee on Economic, Social and Cultural Rights, when considering the reports of States parties, to continue to identify specific needs that might be addressed by United Nations departments, funds and programmes and the specialized agencies, including through the advisory services and technical assistance programme of the Office of the United Nations High Commissioner for Human Rights;

22. *Stresses* the need for improved coordination among relevant United Nations mechanisms and bodies in supporting States parties, upon their request, in implementing the International Covenants on Human Rights and the Optional Protocols to the International Covenant on Civil and Political Rights, and encourages continued efforts in this direction;

23. *Welcomes* the meeting held by the Human Rights Committee and States parties in October 2002 and the meeting held by the Committee on Economic, Social and Cultural Rights and States parties in May 2003 to exchange ideas on how to render the working methods of the Committees more efficient, and encourages all States parties to continue to contribute to the dialogue with practical and concrete proposals and ideas on ways to improve the effective functioning of the Committees;

24. *Also welcomes* the continuing efforts of the Human Rights Committee and the Committee on Economic, Social and Cultural Rights to strive for uniform standards in the implementation of the provisions of the International Covenants on Human Rights, and appeals to other bodies dealing with similar human rights questions to respect those uniform standards, as expressed in the general comments of the Committees;

25. *Notes* the need for further consideration of the issue of justiciability of the rights set forth in the International Covenant on Economic, Social and Cultural Rights and for further efforts towards developing indicators and benchmarks to measure progress in the national implementation by States parties of the rights protected by the Covenant;

26. *Takes note with interest* of the establishment by the Commission on Human Rights at its fifty-ninth session of an open-ended working group with a view to considering options regarding the elaboration of an optional protocol to the International Covenant on Economic, Social and Cultural Rights and making specific recommendations on its course of action concerning the question of such an optional protocol, and encourages all parties to participate actively in the first session of the working group;

27. *Encourages* the specialized agencies that have not yet done so to submit their reports on the progress made in achieving the observance of the provisions of the International Covenant on Economic, Social and Cultural Rights, in accordance with article 18 of the Covenant, and expresses its appreciation to those that have done so;

28. *Encourages* the Secretary-General to continue to assist States parties to the International Covenants on Human Rights in the preparation of their reports, including by convening seminars or workshops at the national level for the training of government officials engaged in the preparation of such reports and by exploring other possibilities available under the programme of advisory services in the field of human rights;

29. *Requests* the Secretary-General to ensure that the Office of the United Nations High Commissioner for Human Rights effectively assists the Human Rights Committee and the Committee on Economic, Social and Cultural Rights in the implementation of their respective mandates by providing, inter alia, adequate Secretariat staff resources and conference and other relevant support services;

30. *Welcomes* the initiative of the Secretary-General, taking into account the suggestions of the Human Rights Committee, to take determined steps, in particular through the Department of Public Information of the Secretariat, to give more publicity to the work of that Committee and of the Committee on Economic, Social and Cultural Rights;

31. *Requests* the Secretary-General to submit to the General Assembly at its sixtieth session, under the item entitled "Human rights questions", a report on the status of the International Covenant on Economic, Social and Cultural Rights, the International Covenant on Civil and Political Rights and the Optional Protocols to the International Covenant on Civil and Political Rights, including all reservations and declarations.

Convention against racial discrimination

Accessions and ratifications

As at 31 December, the number of parties to the International Convention on the Elimination of All Forms of Racial Discrimination, adopted by the General Assembly in resolution 2106 A (XX) [YUN 1965, p. 440], increased to 169, with ratification by Paraguay and accession by Oman, Thailand and Timor-Leste.

On 23 April [res. 2003/30], by a recorded vote of 38 to 1, with 13 abstentions, the Commission urged States that had not done so to accede to or ratify the Convention, make the declaration provided for in article 14 (see p. 674) and ratify the amendment to article 8 on CERD financing (see p. 674).

The Assembly, on 22 December, urged States that had not become parties to ratify or accede to the Convention with a view to achieving universal ratification by 2005 (**resolution 58/160**) (p. 699).

Implementation

Monitoring body. The Committee on the Elimination of Racial Discrimination (CERD), established under article 8 of the Convention, held its sixty-second and sixty-third sessions, both in Geneva, from 3 to 31 March and from 4 to 22 August, respectively [A/58/18].

The Committee considered reports submitted by Albania, Bolivia, Cape Verde, Côte d'Ivoire, the Czech Republic, Ecuador, Fiji, Finland, Ghana, Iran, Latvia, Morocco, Norway, Poland, the Republic of Korea, the Russian Federation, Saint Vincent and the Grenadines, Saudi Arabia, Slovenia, Tunisia, Uganda and the United Kingdom. The Committee reviewed the Convention's implementation by Malawi based on a variety of material at its disposal and by Papua New Guinea. It decided that, in the absence of any indication of compliance on the part of Papua New Guinea, it would consider the State party's implementation in 2004.

Under article 14 of the Convention, CERD considered communications from individuals or groups of individuals claiming violation by a State party of their rights enumerated in the Convention. Forty-three States parties had recognized CERD's competence to do so (Algeria, Australia, Austria, Azerbaijan, Belgium, Brazil, Bulgaria, Chile, Costa Rica, Cyprus, Czech Republic, Denmark, Ecuador, Finland, France, Germany, Hungary, Iceland, Ireland, Italy, Luxembourg, Malta, Mexico, Monaco, Netherlands, Norway, Peru, Poland, Portugal, Republic of Korea, Romania, Russian Federation, Senegal, Serbia and Montenegro, Slovakia, Slovenia, South Africa, Spain, Sweden, Switzerland, the former Yugoslav Republic of Macedonia, Ukraine, Uruguay).

Pursuant to article 15, the Committee was empowered to consider petitions, reports and other information relating to Trust and Non-Self-Governing Territories. It noted additional information contained in the working papers on Bermuda and the United States Virgin Islands on two cases of racial discrimination in the two Territories; and information on the United Kingdom's plans to introduce a human rights chapter in the constitutions of the British Virgin Islands, the Cayman Islands and St. Helena. The Committee noted, as it had in the past, the difficulty in fulfilling its functions because the documents did not include petitions and contained scant information directly related to the Convention's principles and objectives.

CERD considered follow-up to the World Conference against Racism, Racial Discrimination, Xenophobia and Related Intolerance [YUN 2001, p. 615] and the Third Decade to Combat Racism and Racial Discrimination (1993-2003) (see p. 696), proclaimed by the General Assembly in resolution 48/91 [YUN 1993, p. 853].

A 10 March statement of the Committee, drawing the attention of the international community to the devastating effects of any resort to war, called on the Security Council and the international community to find a peaceful solution to the current crisis of compliance with the international legal order that was binding upon all. On 13 August [dec. 3(63)], the Committee, noting that, as at that date, only 37 States parties had ratified the amendment to article 8 regarding the financing of CERD [YUN 1992, p. 714], decided to address an urgent appeal to all States parties to ratify the amendment. The Secretary-General was requested to bring the Committee's decision to the attention of all States parties. In a 14 August decision [dec. 2(63)], CERD expressed concern about Israel's Temporary Suspension Order of May 2002, enacted into law as the Nationality and Entry into Israel Law (Temporary Order) on 31 July 2003, which suspended the possibility of family reunification, subject to limited and discretionary exceptions. The Nationality and Entry into Israel Law of 31 July raised serious issues under the Convention and should be revoked by Israel, which should reconsider its policy with a view to facilitating family unification on a non-discriminatory basis. CERD, on 21 August [dec. 1(63)], taking note of information it had received on the human rights situation in the Lao People's Democratic Republic, urged the State party to halt immediately acts of violence against members of the Hmong population, called on it to ensure they had freedom of movement and access to adequate food and medical care, requested it to release the Hmong assistants who contributed to a report of two foreign journalists on the Hmong situation, given that the journalists had been released, and called on the authorities to submit a special report on those matters and measures to prevent racial discrimination. The Secretary-General was asked to draw the attention of UN bodies to the human rights situation in the country and to request them to take appropriate measures, including the dispatch of a mission.

On 22 December, the General Assembly took note of the Committee's report (**decision 58/535**).

Convention against torture

Accessions and ratifications

As at 31 December, 134 States were parties to the 1984 Convention against Torture and Other

Cruel, Inhuman or Degrading Treatment or Punishment, adopted by the General Assembly in resolution 39/46 [YUN 1984, p. 813]. The Congo and Timor-Leste acceded to the Convention during the year. The Optional Protocol to the Convention, which was adopted in resolution 57/199 [YUN 2002, p. 631] and opened for signature on 4 February, had 21 signatories and three States parties (Albania, Malta, United Kingdom). The Protocol would enter into force 30 days following the deposit of the twentieth instrument of ratification or accession. As at 10 December, 50 parties had made the required declarations under articles 21 and 22 (under which a party recognized the competence of the Committee against Torture to receive and consider communications to the effect that a party claimed that another was not fulfilling its obligations under the Convention, and to receive communications from or on behalf of individuals who claimed to be victims of a violation of the Convention by a State party) and four had made the declaration only under article 21, bringing the total of declarations under that article to 54; five parties had made the declaration only under article 22, bringing the total of declarations under that article to 55. Amendments to articles 17 and 18, adopted in 1992 [YUN 1992, p. 735], had been accepted by 25 parties at year's end.

On 23 April [res. 2003/32], the Commission urged States to become parties to the Convention and to limit the extent of their reservations. All ratifying or acceding States were invited to make the declarations provided for in articles 21 and 22 and to consider withdrawing their reservations to article 20.

The Secretary-General reported on the status of the Convention, its Optional Protocol and declarations provided for in articles 21 and 22 as at 22 August [A/58/326] and 10 December [E/CN.4/2004/52]. On 22 December, the Assembly took note of the former report (**decision 58/537**).

Implementation

Monitoring body. The Committee against Torture, established as a monitoring body under the Convention, held its thirtieth and thirty-first sessions in Geneva from 28 April to 16 May [A/58/44] and from 10 to 21 November [A/59/44], respectively. Under article 19, it considered reports submitted by Azerbaijan, Belgium, Cambodia, Cameroon, Colombia, Iceland, Latvia, Lithuania, Morocco, the Republic of Moldova, Slovenia, Turkey and Yemen.

In accordance with article 20, the Committee studied reliable information it received that contained well-founded indications that torture was systematically practised in a State party. Under those provisions, the Committee, after consultations with the State party concerned, decided to include in its April/May report a summary account of the results of proceedings, begun in 1998, in connection with Mexico. Under article 22, the Committee considered communications submitted by individuals who claimed that their rights, as enumerated in the Convention, had been violated by a State party and who had exhausted all available domestic remedies.

A working group met (24-25 April) to discuss matters relating to the adoption of the Optional Protocol to the Convention, contained in General Assembly resolution 57/199 [YUN 2002, p. 631], and adopted a statement and guidelines regarding general issues, the composition and meetings of the Subcommittee on Prevention—the Protocol's future supervisory body—and areas of coordination between the Committee and the Subcommittee.

Convention on elimination of discrimination against women and Optional Protocol

(For details on the status of the Convention and on the Optional Protocol, see p. 1190.)

Convention on the Rights of the Child

Accessions and ratifications

As at 31 December, the number of States parties to the 1989 Convention on the Rights of the Child, adopted by the General Assembly in resolution 44/25 [YUN 1989, p. 560], rose to 192 with the accession of Timor-Leste. Sixty-seven States were parties to the Optional Protocol to the Convention on the involvement of children in armed conflict, adopted by the Assembly in resolution 54/263 [YUN 2000, p. 615], with ratification during the year by Belize, Bosnia and Herzegovina, Chile, Costa Rica, France, Greece, Kazakhstan, Lesotho, Lithuania, Norway, the Philippines, Portugal, Serbia and Montenegro, Sweden, Tunisia, the United Kingdom, Uruguay and Venezuela, and accession by Afghanistan, Kyrgyzstan and the Syrian Arab Republic. The Optional Protocol to the Convention on the sale of children, child prostitution and child pornography, also adopted by resolution 54/263, had 69 States parties, with ratification in 2003 by Argentina, Belize, Bolivia, Chile, Colombia, Denmark, France, Lesotho, Mongolia, Paraguay, Portugal, Senegal, the former Yugoslav Republic of Macedonia, Ukraine and Uruguay, and accession by Botswana, Equatorial Guinea, Kyrgyzstan, Mozambique, South Africa, the Syrian Arab Republic, Timor-Leste and the United Republic of Tanzania.

The Secretary-General reported on the status of the Convention and Optional Protocols as at 2 July [A/58/282], 20 November [E/CN.4/2003/76] and 12 December [E/CN.4/2004/67].

In accordance with an amendment to the Convention, approved by the Assembly in resolution 50/155 [YUN 1995, p. 706] and which entered into force in 2002 [YUN 2002, p. 638], the membership of the Committee on the Rights of the Child (CRC) was expanded from 10 to 18. New Committee members were elected at the Ninth Meeting of States parties (New York, 10 February). As at 31 December 2003, the amendment had been accepted by 137 States parties.

On 25 April [res. 2003/86], the Commission urged States that had not done so to sign and ratify or accede to the Convention and the Optional Protocols, and to strengthen cooperation with CRC. The Secretary-General was requested to report on the Convention's status in 2004.

On 22 December, the Assembly urged States that had not done so to sign and ratify or accede to the Convention and the Optional Protocols, and called on them to ensure that the rights set forth in the Convention were respected without discrimination (**resolution 58/157**) (see p. 781).

Implementation

In 2003, CRC held its thirty-second (13-31 January) [CRC/C/124], thirty-third (19 May-6 June) [CRC/C/132] and thirty-fourth (15 September-3 October) [CRC/C/133] sessions, all in Geneva. Each session was preceded by a working group meeting to review State party reports and identify the main questions to be discussed with representatives of the reporting States. The sessions also considered technical assistance and international cooperation.

Under article 44 of the Convention, CRC considered initial or periodic reports submitted by Bangladesh, Brunei Darussalam, Canada, Cyprus, the Czech Republic, Eritrea, Estonia, Georgia, Haiti, Iceland, Italy, Jamaica, Kazakhstan, the Libyan Arab Jamahiriya, Madagascar, Morocco, New Zealand, Pakistan, the Republic of Korea, Romania, San Marino, Singapore, Solomon Islands, Sri Lanka, the Syrian Arab Republic, Viet Nam and Zambia.

The Committee adopted general comments on HIV/AIDS and the rights of children (30 January); on adolescent health and development in the context of the Convention (5 June); and on general measures of implementation for the Convention (3 October).

On 19 September, the Committee held a day of general discussion on the rights of indigenous children.

OHCHR convened a workshop (Damascus, Syrian Arab Republic, 17-19 December) on the implementation of the concluding observations of CRC.

Convention on migrant workers

Accessions and ratifications

The International Convention on the Protection of the Rights of All Migrant Workers and Members of Their Families, adopted by the General Assembly in resolution 45/158 [YUN 1990, p. 594], entered into force on 1 July, following the deposit of the twentieth instrument of ratification or accession. As at 31 December, there were 24 States parties to the Convention, with ratification during the year by Burkina Faso, El Salvador and Guatemala, and accession by Kyrgyzstan and Mali.

The Secretary-General reported on the status of the Convention as at 10 June [A/58/221] and 15 December [E/CN.4/2004/73].

On 23 April [res. 2003/48], the Commission called on States that had not done so to sign and ratify or accede to the Convention. It asked the Secretary-General to convene the initial meeting of States parties to the Convention and to make provisions for the establishment of the Committee on the Protection of the Rights of All Migrant Workers and Members of Their Families (see p. 677). He was also asked to assist the active promotion of the Convention, through the World Public Information Campaign (see p. 686) and the programme of advisory services and technical cooperation (see p. 678); and to report in 2004 on the Convention's status and on efforts made by the Secretariat to promote the Convention and protect migrant workers' rights.

GENERAL ASSEMBLY ACTION

On 22 December [meeting 77], the General Assembly, on the recommendation of the Third Committee [A/58/508/Add.1 & Corr.1], adopted **resolution 58/166** without vote [agenda item 117 (a)].

International Convention on the Protection of the Rights of All Migrant Workers and Members of Their Families

The General Assembly,

Guided by the basic instruments regarding the international protection of human rights, in particular the Universal Declaration of Human Rights, the International Covenants on Human Rights, the International Convention on the Elimination of All Forms of Racial Discrimination, the Convention on the Elimination of All Forms of Discrimination against Women and the Convention on the Rights of the Child, and reaffirming the obligation of States to promote and protect human rights and fundamental freedoms,

Bearing in mind the principles and norms established within the framework of the International Labour Organization and the importance of the work done in connection with migrant workers and members of their families in other specialized agencies and in various organs of the United Nations,

Recalling that, despite the existence of an already established body of principles and norms, there is an urgent need to make further efforts worldwide to improve the situation and to guarantee respect for the human rights and dignity of all migrant workers and members of their families,

Conscious of the marked increase in migratory movements that has occurred, especially in certain parts of the world,

Deeply concerned at the grave situation of vulnerability of migrant workers and members of their families,

Considering that, in the Vienna Declaration and Programme of Action adopted by the World Conference on Human Rights on 25 June 1993, all States are urged to guarantee the protection of the human rights of all migrant workers and members of their families,

Underlining the importance of the creation and promotion of conditions to foster greater harmony and tolerance between migrant workers and the rest of the society of the State in which they reside, with the aim of eliminating the growing manifestations of racism and xenophobia directed against migrant workers by individuals or groups in segments of many societies,

Recalling its resolution 45/158 of 18 December 1990, by which it adopted and opened for signature, ratification and accession the International Convention on the Protection of the Rights of All Migrant Workers and Members of Their Families,

Bearing in mind that, in the Vienna Declaration and Programme of Action, States are invited to consider the possibility of signing and ratifying the Convention at the earliest possible time,

1. *Acknowledges with appreciation* the entry into force of the International Convention on the Protection of the Rights of All Migrant Workers and Members of Their Families on 1 July 2003;

2. *Expresses its deep concern* at the growing manifestations of racism, xenophobia and other forms of discrimination and inhuman or degrading treatment directed against migrant workers in various parts of the world;

3. *Welcomes* the signature or ratification of or accession to the Convention by some States, and takes note of the report of the Secretary-General on the status of the Convention;

4. *Calls once again upon* all Member States that have not yet ratified the Convention to consider urgently signing and ratifying or acceding to it;

5. *Takes note* of the arrangements for the initial meeting of States parties to the Convention, held on 11 December 2003;

6. *Requests* the Secretary-General to make all necessary provisions for the timely establishment of the Committee on the Protection of the Rights of All Migrant Workers and Members of Their Families, referred to in article 72 of the Convention;

7. *Calls upon* States parties to the Convention to submit in a timely manner their first periodic report, as requested in article 73 of the Convention;

8. *Requests* the Secretary-General to provide all the facilities and assistance necessary for the promotion of the Convention through the World Public Information Campaign on Human Rights and the programme of advisory services in the field of human rights;

9. *Welcomes* the increasing activities of the global campaign for the entry into force of the Convention, and invites the organizations and bodies of the United Nations system and intergovernmental and non-governmental organizations to intensify further their efforts with a view to disseminating information on and promoting understanding of the importance of the Convention;

10. *Also welcomes* the work of the Special Rapporteur of the Commission on Human Rights on the human rights of migrants in relation to the Convention, and encourages her to persevere in that endeavour;

11. *Requests* the Secretary-General to submit an updated report on the status of the Convention to the General Assembly at its fifty-ninth session;

12. *Decides* to consider the report of the Secretary-General at its fifty-ninth session under the sub-item entitled "Implementation of human rights instruments".

Implementation

The first Meeting of the States Parties to the Convention (New York, 11 December) [CMW/SP/2] considered the curricula vitae of nominations for membership to the Committee on the Protection of the Rights of All Migrant Workers and Members of Their Families and procedural issues regarding the Committee [CMW/SP/3].

Convention on genocide

As at 31 December, 135 States were parties to the 1948 Convention on the Prevention and Punishment of the Crime of Genocide, adopted by the General Assembly in resolution 260 A (III) [YUN 1948-49, p. 959]. During the year, the Sudan acceded to the Convention.

Commission action. On 24 April [res. 2003/66], the Commission invited States that had not ratified or acceded to the Convention to do so and, where necessary, to enact national legislation in conformity with the Convention's provisions. The Secretariat and relevant UN organs and agencies were asked to disseminate the Convention widely.

Other activities

Follow-up to 1993 World Conference

Report of High Commissioner. In a February report [E/CN.4/2003/14] on follow-up to the World Conference on Human Rights [YUN 1993, p. 908], the High Commissioner presented the pressing challenges of protection, advancing human dignity, equality and security, and encouraging human rights protection through the rule of law. He said human rights must be integrated in efforts towards conflict prevention, peacemaking, peacekeeping, peace-building, development and humanitarian operations.

Annual meeting. In August, the High Commissioner transmitted the report of the tenth meeting of special rapporteurs/representatives, experts and chairpersons of working groups of the Commission's special procedures and advisory services programme (Geneva, 23-27 June) [E/CN.4/2004/4]. Participants discussed measures to enhance effectiveness in accordance with the Secretary-General's reform agenda (see p. 1383), the challenges that the current international climate and the fight against terrorism posed for human rights promotion and protection, globalization and ways of improving cooperation with the Commission, human rights treaty bodies and NGOs. They recommended that efforts be made to improve links between their mandates and the Secretariat, particularly with the Secretary-General, and to improve cooperation with UN country teams. It was felt that more needed to be done by all partners to disseminate information about the work of special rapporteurs. The participants issued a joint statement voicing their concern at the multiplication of policies, legislation and practices adopted by many countries in the name of the fight against terrorism, which negatively affected the enjoyment of human rights.

Tenth anniversary

On the occasion of the tenth anniversary of the adoption of the 1993 Vienna Declaration and Programme of Action at the World Conference on Human Rights, the Foreign Minister of Austria and the High Commissioner, in cooperation with the United Nations Office on Drugs and Crime, convened an international symposium on the role of judges in the promotion and protection of human rights (Vienna, 24 November) [E/CN.4/2004/G/26].

On 10 December, Human Rights Day, the General Assembly held a plenary meeting [A/58/PV.73] to commemorate the tenth anniversary of the Vienna Declaration and the fifty-fifth anniversary of the Universal Declaration of Human Rights, adopted by Assembly resolution 217 A (III) [YUN 1948-49, p. 535]. During the meeting, the Assembly awarded the UN prizes in the field of human rights for 2003 to four individuals and two organizations that had made outstanding contributions to the promotion and protection of human rights and fundamental freedoms. (See p. 669 for the recipients' names.)

The Assembly, on 22 December, took note of the Third Committee's report [A/58/508/Add.4] on the implementation of and follow-up to the Vienna Declaration and Programme of Action (**decision 58/540**). The Assembly decided, on 23 December, that the item "Comprehensive implementation of and follow-up to the Vienna Declaration and Programme of Action" would remain for consideration at its resumed fifty-eighth (2004) session (**decision 58/565**).

Advisory services and technical cooperation

A report of the Secretary-General [E/CN.4/2004/99] described the OHCHR technical cooperation programme, which supported countries in promoting and protecting human rights, at their request, by providing assistance for incorporating international human rights standards in national laws, policies and practices or by strengthening national capacities to implement the standards and ensure respect for human rights and the rule of law. The programme offered assistance for constitutional and legislative reform, the administration of justice, national parliaments, national human rights institutions, national plans of action, human rights education and awareness raising, and treaty reporting. As at November, there were 37 ongoing projects.

During the year, OHCHR had technical cooperation offices in Azerbaijan, Croatia, El Salvador, Guatemala, Mexico, Solomon Islands, Somalia, the Sudan and the former Yugoslav Republic of Macedonia, as well as Palestine; OHCHR field presences, combining a monitoring and a technical cooperation mandate, were operating in Bosnia and Herzegovina, Burundi, Cambodia, Colombia, the Democratic Republic of the Congo and Serbia and Montenegro; support to UN peace missions was provided to Afghanistan, Angola, the Central African Republic, Côte d'Ivoire, Georgia (Abkhazia), Guinea-Bissau, Iraq, Liberia, Sierra Leone, Tajikistan and Timor-Leste; and human rights advisers were deployed in Mongolia, Nepal and Sri Lanka. The Assisting Communities Together (ACT) project, jointly carried out with UNDP, aimed to provide financial support to human rights initiatives taken by NGOs. OHCHR, in partnership with UNDP, launched in October the fourth phase of the ACT project, expected to be completed by the end of 2004, during which some 150 activities would be supported.

Technical cooperation activities were funded mainly by the United Nations Voluntary Fund for Technical Cooperation in the Field of Human

Rights and partly from the UN regular budget. The Fund's Board of Trustees, at its nineteenth (28-30 July) and twentieth (20-22 November) sessions, reviewed the programme's regional activities, discussed thematic issues, methodologies and procedures, and examined financial and administrative matters. In November, the Board held a one-day joint meeting with the heads of OHCHR field presences. Expenditures rose from $8.8 million in the 2000-2001 biennium to $19.3 million in 2002-2003. The dramatic rise was made possible by the balance carried over from previous years and not by a parallel increase in contributions, which amounted to only $15.7 million for the biennium. During 2003, a very limited carry-over and late arrival of contributions seriously affected the implementation of the programme in the first quarter of the year and obliged OHCHR to suspend all new projects. The Fund's income in 2002-2003 amounted to $27.3 million for 2003; as at 30 November, commitments totalled $21.8 million, leaving a balance of $5.5 million.

OHCHR undertook a global review of the programme to improve future interventions with a view to a more strategic approach to the programme. The authors of the review made several recommendations. A synthesis report of the review entitled "From development of human rights to managing human rights development" was available on the Internet.

Afghanistan

Commission action. On 25 April [res. 2003/77], the Commission, welcoming positive human rights developments in Afghanistan, noted with concern reports of violence perpetrated by Afghan elements against certain ethnic groups, internally displaced persons and refugees, as well as cases of arbitrary detention and attacks against women and girls. It requested the Secretary-General to ensure that the post of senior gender adviser in the United Nations Assistance Mission in Afghanistan was filled immediately and on a permanent basis. He was also asked to appoint an independent expert for one year to develop advisory services to ensure human rights protection and the promotion of the rule of law, and to receive information about and report on the human rights situation in the country. That request was approved by the Economic and Social Council on 23 July (**decision 2003/257**). The independent expert was requested to report to the General Assembly and the Commission. The Special Rapporteur on violence against women was asked to review the situation of women and girls in Afghanistan (see p. 779) and to report to those bodies.

Note by Secretary-General. In an August note [A/58/334], the Secretary-General said the independent expert had not been appointed. The Assembly took note of the Secretary-General's note on 22 December (**decision 58/539**).

(For details of the visit to Afghanistan by the Special Rapporteur on the right to adequate housing and of the report by the Special Rapporteur on violence against women, its causes and consequences, see pp. 768 and 779, respectively.)

Cambodia

Commission action. On 25 April [res. 2003/79], the Commission, noting with concern the continued problems related to the rule of law and the functioning of the judiciary in Cambodia, urged the Government to expedite legal and judicial reform and to ensure the independence, impartiality and effectiveness of the judicial system. It also urged the Government to tackle the problems related to land, to work towards free and fair general elections in July 2003, to investigate past incidents of intimidation, violence and killings, and reports of vote-buying, and to prosecute those responsible. Expressing concern about the continued human rights violations, including torture, excessive pre-trial detention, violation of labour rights and forced evictions, as well as political violence, it urged the Government to prevent the violations and racial violence against ethnic groups, and to combat all forms of discrimination. The Commission welcomed efforts to improve the status of women, impede the spread of HIV/AIDS, remove landmines and reduce small arms, draft a penal code, a code on criminal procedures, a civil code and a code on civil procedures, and increase judges' and prosecutors' salaries. The Commission requested the Secretary-General to report in 2004.

Reports of Special Representative. An August note of the Secretary-General [A/58/317] transmitted the report of his Special Representative for human rights in Cambodia, Peter Leuprecht (Austria), based on his visits to the country (25 February-4 March; 30 June-8 July). He said that on 27 July, Cambodia held its third National Assembly elections, which marked an important step in efforts to establish a multiparty democracy. There was a significant improvement in the technical aspects of election administration, the month-long campaign period allowed for more freedom of political expression and polling was conducted peacefully. However, the establishment of a level playing field for all political parties and a transparent electoral process encountered obstacles. Prior to the official campaign period, arbitrary restrictions were placed on freedoms of assembly and expression, and there was considerable intimidation, which continued throughout the campaign. In confronting electoral fraud, vote-buying, intimidation and violence, the National Election Committee failed to impose fines and other sanctions. Law enforcement remained a continuing problem, as did land issues, which remained a source of conflict and of human rights violations. Many difficulties persisted in the delivery of the right to housing, such as forced evictions and the lack of adequate shelter for displaced Cambodians. An agreement was signed in Phnom Penh on 6 June between the United Nations and the Government regarding the prosecution under Cambodian law of crimes committed during the period of Democratic Kampuchea. The Special Representative recommended measures to the Government to improve the justice sector and accountability, the administration of criminal justice and land issues.

During a further visit to Cambodia (27 November–6 December) [E/CN.4/2004/105], the Special Representative focused on the general political climate in the wake of the elections and on the political deadlock that followed, and the impact of natural resources policies and practices on human rights. The problems of continuing restrictions on freedoms of expression, assembly and association; corruption; a weak judiciary; and impunity remained. Mob violence continued and possibly increased. Imprisonment remained the routine punishment for most crimes, even very minor ones. Poor prison facilities and inadequate food and clean water represented a significant threat to the health of inmates. Access to prisoners by lawyers, human rights groups and NGOs was difficult. Detainees were frequently subjected to excessive pre-trial detention, were convicted without legal representation and were denied the right to appeal. The Government's policy of granting large-scale agricultural and forestry concessions to private interests in a non-transparent manner continued to represent a serious threat to the rural poor. High spending on health care was one of the main reasons for impoverishment and debt accumulation. The Special Representative made recommendations regarding the conduct of future elections, legal and judicial reform, mob killings, prison sentencing and conditions, land and forestry issues, health care, policies towards economic development and poverty reduction, and access to information about human rights, land rights, contract procedures and the law in general.

OHCHR/Cambodia

Reports of the Secretary-General covered the role and achievements of OHCHR in assisting the Government and people of Cambodia in human rights promotion and protection from January to July [A/58/268] and from July to December [E/CN.4/2004/104].

In connection with the National Assembly elections of 27 July, OHCHR/Cambodia provided technical assistance to the Government in drafting electoral laws and regulations; protection activities associated with human rights violations in the context of the elections; and information to the Government and the international community on the political climate and electoral matters. It worked with local NGOs conducting election-related human rights monitoring and assisted in the preparation of public reports issued by the Special Representative. The Office embarked on a study to identify the effects of large-scale agricultural plantations on the human rights of populations living within or close to their boundaries, and the extent to which they had contributed to the development and well-being of the Cambodian people. It continued to contribute to the legislative process and efforts to advance judicial reform, was active in implementing education and advisory services programmes, cooperated with and supported NGOs, and participated in UN and donor coordinating mechanisms relevant to human rights and rule-of-law issues.

In October and November, an external evaluation of the Office was undertaken to assess the impact and relevance of its programmes, major human rights protection and promotion issues, possible developments as a result of the National Assembly election and the complementarity of the Office's programme with other UN activities. The evaluation concluded that the Office represented a positive commitment of the international community to Cambodia, and that its continued existence was essential for fostering respect for human rights.

GENERAL ASSEMBLY ACTION

On 22 December [meeting 77], the General Assembly, on the recommendation of the Third Committee [A/58/508/Add.2], adopted **resolution 58/191** without vote [agenda item 117 (b)].

Situation of human rights in Cambodia

The General Assembly,

Recalling its resolutions 57/225 and 57/228 A of 18 December 2002 and 57/228 B of 13 May 2003, Commission on Human Rights resolution 2003/79 of 25 April 2003 and previous relevant resolutions,

Recalling also the decision of the Commission on Human Rights, in its resolution 2003/79, to request a report to the Commission at its sixtieth session on the role and achievements of the Office of the United Nations High Commissioner for Human Rights in assisting the Government and the people of Cambodia, and to continue its consideration of the situation of human rights in Cambodia at its sixtieth session,

Recognizing that the tragic history of Cambodia requires special measures to ensure the protection of the human rights of all people in Cambodia and the non-return to the policies and practices of the past, as stipulated in the Agreement on a Comprehensive Political Settlement of the Cambodia Conflict, signed in Paris on 23 October 1991,

I

Support of and cooperation with the United Nations

1. *Requests* the Secretary-General, through his Special Representative for human rights in Cambodia, in collaboration with the office in Cambodia of the United Nations High Commissioner for Human Rights, to assist the Government of Cambodia in ensuring the protection of the human rights of all people in Cambodia and to ensure adequate resources for the continued functioning of the operational presence of the office and to enable the Special Representative to continue to fulfil his tasks expeditiously;

2. *Welcomes* the report of the Secretary-General on the role and achievements of the Office of the United Nations High Commissioner for Human Rights in assisting the Government and the people of Cambodia in the promotion and protection of human rights, the report of the Special Representative of the Secretary-General for human rights in Cambodia and the use of the United Nations Trust Fund for a Human Rights Education Programme in Cambodia to finance the programme of activities of the office in Cambodia, and invites the international community to consider contributing to the Trust Fund;

3. *Encourages* the Government of Cambodia to continue to cooperate with the office and other agencies of the United Nations system in their joint efforts to promote human rights and to implement in full their obligations under international human rights treaties and instruments;

II

The role of non-governmental organizations

Commends the vital role played by non-governmental organizations in Cambodia, inter alia, in human rights education and training and in the development of civil society, and encourages the Government of Cambodia to continue to ensure the protection of those human rights organizations and their members and to continue to work closely and cooperatively with them;

III

Administrative, legislative and judicial reform

1. *Welcomes* the progress achieved by the Government of Cambodia in the administration of national elections in July 2003, inter alia, in a generally free and peaceful atmosphere and in improved access for political parties to the public service media, and urges the Government to investigate fully incidents of intimidation, violence, killings and vote-buying, to prosecute those responsible, to strengthen the enforcement capacity and independence of the National Election Committee and to build on the improvements achieved so as to further consolidate the process of democratization;

2. *Notes with concern* the continued problems relating to the rule of law and the functioning of the judiciary resulting from, inter alia, corruption and interference by the executive with the independence of the judiciary, urges the Government of Cambodia, as a matter of priority, to expedite the implementation of legal and judicial reform, including finalization without further delay of the adoption of the laws and codes that are essential components of the basic legal framework, in particular a law on the organization and functioning of adjudicate courts, and to ensure the independence, impartiality and effectiveness of the Supreme Council of the Magistracy and of the judicial system as a whole;

3. *Welcomes* the drafts of the civil code, code of civil procedure, penal code, code of criminal procedure, anti-corruption law, law on the status of judges and prosecutors (statute of magistracy), draft law to amend the Law on the Organization and Functioning of the Supreme Council of the Magistracy, strategy for legal and judicial reform and action plan for its implementation, urges the Government of Cambodia to continue to enhance the training of judges and lawyers through the Royal School for Training Judges and Prosecutors and the Centre for Lawyer Training and Legal Professional Improvement of the Bar Association of the Kingdom of Cambodia, and encourages the Government to provide access to justice for all and establish a legal aid scheme appropriate for Cambodia;

4. *Also welcomes* the adoption of the Sub-Decree on Land Concessions for Social Purposes, and urges the Government of Cambodia to strengthen its efforts to tackle the problems related to land rights by, inter alia, adopting the sub-decrees on land concessions for economic purposes and on procedures for the reduction of and specific exemptions from the land concessions that exceed 10,000 hectares, enhancing transparency and giving high priority to the land management and administration reform project, and to continue to undertake a review of land concession contracts and their implementation, and notes with concern the remaining problems of land-grabbing, forced evictions and further displacement;

5. *Encourages* further efforts by the Government of Cambodia to implement expeditiously and effectively its reform programme, including the Governance Action Plan and police and military reforms, inter alia, the demobilization programme;

6. *Welcomes* the progress made by the Government of Cambodia to eradicate anti-personnel landmines and to reduce the number of small arms in Cambodia, and encourages the continuing efforts of the Government and the international community to tackle these issues;

7. *Expresses serious concern* about the fact that the situation of impunity still exists in Cambodia, recognizes efforts and actions by the Government of Cambodia to prosecute perpetrators of violations, and calls upon the Government, as a matter of critical priority, to increase its efforts to investigate urgently and to prosecute, in accordance with due process of law and international human rights standards, all those who have perpetrated serious crimes, including violations of human rights;

8. *Notes with serious concern* the prison conditions in Cambodia, notes with interest some important efforts to improve the prison system, recommends the continuation of international assistance to improve the material conditions of detention, and calls upon the Government of Cambodia to take further measures to

improve the conditions of detention, including reviewing sentencing policy and developing non-custodial options as an alternative to imprisonment, to prevent any form of torture, to provide proper food and health care to prisoners and detainees, to meet the special needs of women and children and to restore access to prisons and inmates for lawyers, family members and human rights organizations in accordance with relevant regulations in force;

IV
Human rights violations and violence

1. *Expresses grave concern* about the continued violations of human rights, including torture, excessive pre-trial detention, violation of labour rights, forced evictions and political violence, including the killings of political activists, involvement by police and military personnel in violence and the apparent lack of protection from mob killings, notes that some progress has been made by the Government of Cambodia in addressing these issues, and urges the Government to take all necessary measures to prevent such violations, including to consider establishing a board of inquiry on the issue of mob killings;

2. *Urges* the Government of Cambodia to take all steps to combat discrimination in all its manifestations and prevent violence against members of any racial or ethnic group and to protect the human rights and fundamental freedoms of all persons, as well as to meet its obligations as a party to the International Convention on the Elimination of All Forms of Racial Discrimination, inter alia, by seeking technical assistance;

V
Khmer Rouge Tribunal

1. *Reaffirms* that the most serious human rights violations in Cambodia in recent history have been committed by the Khmer Rouge, and acknowledges that the final collapse of the Khmer Rouge and the continued efforts of the Government of Cambodia have provided the basis for the restoration of peace and stability with the aim of achieving national reconciliation in Cambodia and the investigation and prosecution of senior leaders of Democratic Kampuchea and those who were most responsible for the crimes and serious violations of Cambodian penal law, international humanitarian law and custom and international conventions recognized by Cambodia that were committed during the period from 17 April 1975 to 6 January 1979;

2. *Welcomes* the Agreement reached on 6 June 2003 between the United Nations and the Government of Cambodia to set up Extraordinary Chambers exercising their jurisdiction in accordance with international standards of justice, fairness and due process as set out in article 12 of the Agreement, urges the Secretary-General and the Government of Cambodia to take all the measures necessary for the early establishment of the Extraordinary Chambers, and appeals to the international community to provide assistance, including financial and personnel support to the Extraordinary Chambers, in accordance with General Assembly resolution 57/228 B;

VI
Protection of women and children

1. *Welcomes* the efforts and progress made to improve the status of women, including on the draft law on prevention of domestic violence and protection of victims of domestic violence, and urges the Government of Cambodia to take further measures to combat violence against women in all its forms, inter alia, sexual violence, and to take all steps to meet its obligations as a party to the Convention on the Elimination of All Forms of Discrimination against Women, inter alia, by seeking technical assistance;

2. *Commends* the Government of Cambodia for its efforts to impede the spread of HIV/AIDS, and encourages it to continue to focus on the problem;

3. *Welcomes* the series of efforts made by the Government of Cambodia to combat human trafficking, including on the draft anti-trafficking law, while noting with serious concern the growth of human trafficking and sexual exploitation of women and children internationally, and requests the Government and the international community to strengthen their concerted efforts to address these problems comprehensively;

4. *Notes with serious concern* the problem of child labour in its worst forms, calls upon the Government of Cambodia to take immediate and effective measures to protect children from economic exploitation and from performing any work that is likely to be hazardous, to interfere with their education or to be harmful to their health, safety or morals, by enforcing Cambodian laws on child labour, the existing labour law and anti-trafficking law provisions on behalf of children, and by prosecuting those who violate these laws, invites the International Labour Organization to continue to extend the necessary assistance in this regard, and encourages the Government to consider ratifying the International Labour Organization Convention concerning the Prohibition and Immediate Action for the Elimination of the Worst Forms of Child Labour, 1999 (Convention No. 182);

5. *Welcomes* the increased budget allocation in the areas of education and health, and encourages their timely disbursement and the efforts of the Government of Cambodia to improve further the health conditions of children and their access to education, to promote free and accessible birth registration and to establish a juvenile justice system;

VII
Conclusion

Invites the international community to assist the Government of Cambodia in its efforts to implement the present resolution.

(For information on the Khmer Rouge trials, see p. 385.)

Chad

On 2 April [dec. 2003/104], the Commission decided to discontinue consideration of the human rights situation in Chad under the confidential procedure governed by Economic and Social Council resolution 1503(XLVIII) [YUN 1970, p. 530] and revised by Council resolution 2000/3 [YUN 2000, p. 596], and to consider the matter under the Commission's public procedure.

On 25 April [res. 2003/81], the Commission asked the High Commissioner, in consultation with the Government of Chad, to develop a programme of human rights technical assistance and advisory services.

Haiti

Commission action. On 25 April [E/2003/23], the Commission Chairperson expressed the Commission's deep concern about the deteriorating human rights situation in Haiti and invited the Haitian authorities and the international community to press forward with their initiatives to promote democracy. The Commission urged the Government to continue and to step up efforts to combat impunity, to strengthen the rule of law, to safeguard democratic pluralism, to ensure the independence of the judiciary and to protect political leaders, journalists, trade union activists and human rights defenders. It strongly urged the application of the measures identified by a high-level delegation of the group of friendly countries during its visit on 19 and 20 March. OHCHR was requested to expand its activities by setting up an office in the country.

Report of independent expert. Independent expert Louis Joinet (France) visited Haiti (9-15 April and 23 October-5 November) [E/CN.4/2004/108] where he focused on the effects of impunity on the human rights situation, the shortcomings of the police force and the malfunctioning of the justice system, the steady deterioration of the systems of popular organizations and the need for further cooperation in technical assistance and human rights, including the establishment of an OHCHR branch office. In addition to recommending such an office, the expert proposed reforms in the justice system and in the police force, finalization of the statute and regulations of the Institute of Forensic Medicine, and strengthening cooperation with NGOs.

Liberia

On 2 April [dec. 2003/105], the Commission decided to discontinue consideration of the human rights situation in Liberia under the confidential procedure governed by Economic and Social Council resolution 1503(XLVIII) [YUN 1970, p. 530] and revised by Council resolution 2000/3 [YUN 2000, p. 596], and to consider the matter under the Commission's public procedure. It recommended the appointment of an independent expert and that the Council make public the independent expert's report. The Government was invited to ensure the functioning of its human rights mechanisms and to improve respect for human rights. The Council, on 23 July, took note of the decision and endorsed the recommendation to make public the expert's report (**decision 2003/263**).

On 25 April [res. 2003/82], the Commission decided to appoint an independent expert for a three-year period, a decision endorsed by the Council on 23 July (**decision 2003/260**). The Commission asked the expert to visit Liberia and to report in 2004. In July, Charlotte Abaka (Ghana) was reappointed independent expert.

Report of High Commissioner. In an August report to the Commission [E/CN.4/2004/5], the High Commissioner said that since January the armed conflict in Liberia had intensified (see p. 184). Both government and rebel troops were committing human rights abuses and violating international humanitarian law. Violations included denial of the right to life, arbitrary and summary executions, torture, enforced and involuntary disappearances, violence against women, violations of children's rights, forced recruitment, displacement and the denial of humanitarian access. The poor security situation, restricted access and limited UN presence had made direct monitoring of the human rights situation impossible. Information had been obtained predominantly through interviews with refugees and internally displaced persons. The High Commissioner said a human rights assessment mission should be deployed and a UN presence re-established when the security situation permitted. National institutions should be established to address human rights violations and to respond to challenges in human rights promotion and protection. In the long term, direct monitoring of the situation of displaced persons in camps, through the UN presence and the UNDP protection strategy, should be expanded.

Reports of independent expert. In September [E/CN.4/2004/8], the Secretariat, as suggested by the Commission [dec. 2003/105] and endorsed by the Council (**decision 2003/263**), made public a confidential report of the expert covering the human rights situation in Liberia based on her visit to the country (16-21 December 2002). According to the information she received, the Government had done little to prevent human rights violations and had not brought the perpetrators to justice. Concerns about the independence and impartiality of the judiciary were also reported. Serious human rights violations, including restrictions on freedom of expression, arbitrary arrests and detention, torture and ill-treatment, occurred. An estimated 14,000 child soldiers had reportedly participated in the Liberian civil war from 1990 to 1997, and the practice had re-emerged since the outbreak of the current conflict in 1999. The instability in the country had resulted in a protracted humanitarian crisis in which nearly one quarter of the population was dependent on humanitarian aid. The expert concluded that a comprehensive solution should be sought addressing all aspects and root causes of the conflict, taking into consideration the overall situation in the Mano River region, and made a series of recommendations for human rights promotion and protection in Liberia.

In a later report [E/CN.4/2004/113], the expert stated that the conflict intensified as from January and was accompanied by increased human rights abuses, including the denial of the fundamental right to life, extrajudicial and arbitrary executions, torture, violence against women, rape, forced recruitment and denial of humanitarian access. The expert described peace initiatives, including the signing in August of the Comprehensive Peace Agreement by the Liberian parties and the institution of the National Transitional Government (see p. 192). She made recommendations regarding the protection of civilians; the establishment of an independent national commission on human rights, a truth and reconciliation commission and an independent electoral commission; disarmament, demobilization and reintegration; the mobilization of resources to assist the National Transitional Government to implement relief and recovery programmes; and the security situation.

Sierra Leone

Commission action. On 25 April [res. 2003/80], the Commission, welcoming the work of the Special Court for Sierra Leone, the Truth and Reconciliation Commission, the National Commission on Disarmament, Demobilization and Reintegration, and the National Commission for War-Affected Children, and steps taken by the Government and civil society to build the human rights infrastructure in the country, expressed deep concern about the number of girls and women held against their will by former combatants, continuing reports of trafficking and illegal supply of small arms and related material, reports of the use of children in diamond-mining activities and the humanitarian situation caused by ongoing violence in border regions. It requested: the High Commissioner and the international community to continue to assist the Government to maintain the Truth and Reconciliation Commission, and to cooperate with the Special Court; the international community to participate in strengthening the judicial system and in establishing a national human rights commission; the Secretary-General to facilitate the activities of the Special Court (see p. 213); the High Commissioner and the international community to make further assistance available to the Special Court and the Truth and Reconciliation Commission; and the High Commissioner to report to the General Assembly in 2003 and to the Commission in 2004. On 23 July, the Economic and Social Council endorsed the Commission's request to the High Commission to submit reports (**decision 2003/259**).

Reports of High Commissioner. A September report of the High Commissioner [A/58/379], covering events through early August, stated that the human rights situation in Sierra Leone had improved significantly. Government authority had been re-established nationwide, the judicial system and courts were gradually being restored, and magistrate courts and police formations had almost reached the pre-war levels of deployment. Progress in the implementation of the peace process had been complemented by efforts to address war-related violations of human rights and international humanitarian law. The Truth and Reconciliation Commission was in the final phase of its operational period, and the Special Court had issued a series of indictments. Despite the progress, structural deficiencies linked to the recent history of abuses and violations stymied the emergence of a society based on the rule of law. Human rights challenges included addressing impunity for past abuses and preventing and addressing ongoing violations while building local capacities to protect and promote human rights.

The General Assembly took note of the report on 22 December (**decision 58/539**).

In a later report [E/CN.4/2004/106], the High Commissioner noted that the consolidation of the human rights situation in the area of civil and political rights continued to be a source of encouragement. However, some problems remained, such as the 14 death sentences passed in 2003 and the continuing illegal detention of some 90 members of the Revolutionary United Front and the West Side Boys (see p. 212), who were arrested in 2000. Remarkable progress in the implementation of the peace process had been accompanied by parallel accomplishments in the area of transitional justice. On 10 March, the Special Court issued its first set of indictments against seven persons accused of war crimes, crimes against humanity and other violations of international law. Attacks against civilians by any of the former parties to the conflict had ceased to be an issue. Child abuse remained widespread, female genital mutilation was still widely practised and sexual violence against girls and women was frequently unreported. Progress in terms of economic, social and cultural rights remained bleak, with high rates of child malnourishment, maternal mortality, illiteracy and poverty. The High Commissioner described the activities of the Human Rights Section of the United Nations Mission in Sierra Leone (UNAMSIL) in monitoring the courts, police stations and prisons; training activities; capacity-building, technical cooperation and advocacy; and technical support to the Government in preparation for the establishment of a national human rights commission. The High Commissioner called for a post-UNAMSIL residual UN presence with a substantial human rights component for monitoring human rights and providing technical cooperation and advisory services.

Somalia

Commission action. On 25 April [res. 2003/78], the Commission welcomed the conclusion of the first phase of the Somali national reconciliation process which ended in the signing of the Eldoret Declaration (see p. 241), the efforts of the Intergovernmental Authority on Development Technical Committee and the consultations of the front-line States on the reconciliation process (Addis Ababa, Ethiopia, 2 February), and the establishment of a contact group for Somalia in Nairobi and in New York. It condemned widespread violations and abuses of human rights and humanitarian law, as well as violations by the parties of their commitments. The Commission asked the High Commissioner to provide for the translation of its resolution into the Somali language for distribution within the country. The Commission decided to extend the independent expert's mandate for a further year, and to request him, with UN assistance, to report in 2004. The Economic and Social Council endorsed the Commission's decision on 23 July (**decision 2003/258**).

Report of independent expert. Independent expert Ghanim Alnajjar (Kuwait) visited Somalia and Kenya (24 August–4 September) [E/CN.4/2004/103], including Puntland (Bosasso) and Somaliland (Hargeisa), as well as Kismayo, Somalia, and Nairobi, Kenya.

The expert said that the right to life continued to be violated on an extensive scale, particularly in the south, caused mainly by killings in faction-based or inter-clan fighting, as well as casualties from mine explosions, widespread banditry and other criminal activity. Factors that affected the legal framework of Somalia, one of the poorest countries in the world, were untrained staff, low salaries, lack of basic equipment, training and reference materials, gender inequity and lack of harmonization among secular, customary and Islamic laws. Gender-based violence was a problem, despite a widespread culture of denial, and the practice of female genital mutilation was estimated to affect 98 per cent of the female population. Children were exposed to traumatic events caused by conflict, and the average age of enlistment in militia activities was 12 years old. The practice of *asiwalid*, whereby parents sent their disobedient children to be kept in prison until they ordered their release, continued to prevail.

Progress was made in restoring freedom of the press and a wider participation by women in politics. An estimated 35,000 refugees from Kenya, Ethiopia and Djibouti began returning to Somalia in 2003 and needed humanitarian assistance. In Somaliland, a law had been drafted for the establishment of an independent national human rights commission and a new police station was under construction. In Puntland, officials reported that all political prisoners had been released and the crime level was low. The police force needed rehabilitation, the lack of women's participation in politics was problematic and food security was impaired by drought. The Kismayo police force lacked transport, communications equipment, uniforms and other basic supplies, and its members were not paid and had not received training for the last 13 years. The judiciary of Kismayo informed the expert that it practised Islamic law; while it also applied Somali law, it did not have copies of the laws and relied on memory. The area lacked clean water, schools and health services.

The expert made a number of recommendations. He called on the international community to consider development activity to support advances made in the rule of law and related fronts. The Secretary-General and the Security Council were called on to establish a committee of independent experts to examine allegations of past massive human rights violations and crimes against humanity committed in Somalia, and to report on options to address those issues. The international community was urged to follow up on the peace process to ensure that human rights were integrated in institutions and frameworks. The expert recommended the establishment of an OHCHR office in Somaliland.

Timor-Leste

A report of the High Commissioner [E/CN.4/2004/107] said that in 2003 progress was slow in establishing an effective and accountable justice system in Timor-Leste. Serious functional problems with the judicial system continued to resonate in the police and prison services. The tendency of prosecutors, judges and investigating judges to divert cases from the formal justice system to local dispute resolution methods continued, and there had been instances of political interference in the judicial process. Prison infrastructure was poor, at times placing health and safety at risk. The police force needed institutional strengthening, particularly regarding the mainstreaming of respect for human rights standards. Reports were received weekly of police misconduct amounting to human rights violations. Psychological and physical violence against women and the girl child remained a serious problem. Child abuse by family members and teachers was reported and there was no specialized juvenile justice system. The Office of the United Nations High Commissioner for Refugees estimated that in 1999 between 1,200 and 2,000 children were separated from their families and placed in orphanages. As at November 2003, some 584 East Timorese children remained separated from their parents. OHCHR and the United Nations Children's Fund sent a joint letter to the Governments of Indonesia and Timor-Leste to highlight the plight of those children.

A new technical cooperation project between OHCHR and the United Nations Mission of Support in East Timor covering a two-year period started in June. Programme activities focused on the incorporation of international human rights standards in national laws and policies; on building or strengthening national institutions to promote and protect human rights and democracy under the rule of law; on the formulation of national plans of action for human rights promotion and protection; on human rights education and training; and on promoting a human rights culture. In 2003, activities included support to the Commission for Reception, Truth and Reconciliation (CAVR), human rights training of the police, support to the Government in reporting to treaty bodies and support to civil society. During the March to November period, CAVR held three national public hearings—on women and conflict, forced displacement and famine, and massacres. The Serious Crimes Unit, which was responsible for the investigation and prosecution of all serious crimes between 1 January and 25 October 1999 [YUN 1999, p. 707], focused on the prosecution of 10 priority cases relating to specific incidents and five cases that showed a widespread pattern of serious crime. Some 79 indictments were filed, including indictments relating to the 10 priority cases. About 367 individuals were charged, of whom 308 were alleged to have committed crimes against humanity. The Unit estimated that 280 of those indicted were in Indonesia.

The High Commissioner outlined technical cooperation plans for 2004. Among his recommendations, he called for: the Government to address gaps in legislation to ensure its conformity with international human rights treaties to which the Government was a party; the enforcement of codes of conduct for lawyers and judicial officers; support by the international community to fight corruption; improvements in the police force; legislation, policy measures and programmes to prevent violence against women; and strengthening ways of reviewing the ad hoc human rights trials as well as the serious crimes process.

Public information and human rights education

Public information

Report of Secretary-General. In a January report [E/CN.4/2003/99], the Secretary-General described public information activities in the area of human rights, including the World Public Information Campaign on Human Rights, launched by the General Assembly in resolution 43/128 [YUN 1988, p. 539] and carried out by the High Commissioner and the UN Department of Public Information (DPI).

The OHCHR publications programme issued fact sheets, training and educational material, special issue papers, and reference and promotional material. The Office continued to expand the content of its web site in order to reach a wider audience and to strengthen its capacity to communicate the human rights message through liaison with the media. OHCHR external relations programmes included briefings, exhibitions and human rights observances, an internship programme, and training courses and other technical cooperation activities.

DPI continued to initiate and coordinate activities within the context of the World Public Information Campaign and the United Nations Decade for Human Rights Education (1995-2004) (see p. 687). Activities were also carried out to publicize the Third Decade to Combat Racism and Racial Discrimination (1993-2003) (see p. 695), the International Decade of the World's Indigenous People (1995-2004) (see p. 800) and the United Nations Decade for the Eradication of Poverty (1997-2006) (see p. 848). DPI carried out human rights information programmes, covered UN human rights activities, issued press releases, updated and maintained a human rights web site, published and disseminated human rights publications, aired radio and television broadcasts, and organized the observance of special days. The report presented an overview of the activities of the United Nations Information Service in Geneva, as well as those of the UN information centres and services and UN offices.

Commission action. On 24 April [res. 2003/62], the Commission requested the Secretary-

General to take advantage of the collaboration of international and regional intergovernmental organizations and NGOs to implement the World Campaign and the Decade for Human Rights Education; to make available resources to allow OHCHR and DPI to implement fully their respective programmes in regard to human rights; and to report in 2005.

Report of High Commissioner. By an August note [A/58/318], the Secretary-General transmitted a report of the High Commissioner on human rights education, including the Decade for Human Rights Education and the human rights public information activities of OHCHR and DPI. The demand for OHCHR publications had increased considerably, with the Office distributing more than 74,000 copies of human rights publications and adding to the number of publications available on its web site. Plans were being made to make the web site available in the six official languages and several web pages had been designed to improve accessibility for persons with disabilities. DPI's activities were part of an overall communications strategy to promote the work of OHCHR through publications, the distribution of press kits, magazines, television, photo and radio activities, and briefings.

Human rights education

Reports of High Commissioner. A January report of the High Commissioner [E/CN.4/2003/100] summarized activities undertaken by the UN system, NGOs and Member States to implement the Plan of Action of the United Nations Decade for Human Rights Education (1995-2004), which was proclaimed by the General Assembly in resolution 49/184 [YUN 1994, p. 1039]. The report, requested by the Commission in 2002 [YUN 2002, p. 647], covered the period from mid-July to mid-November 2002.

A February report of the High Commissioner [E/CN.4/2003/101] contained an outline of possible action to follow up the Decade. Input received by OHCHR affirmed the importance of continuing the Decade framework, considering that human rights education was a long-term process, and the High Commissioner presented guidelines for a second decade. The High Commissioner proposed the establishment of a fund for human rights education, the creation of an intergovernmental or a joint governmental/nongovernmental committee to monitor human rights education, expanded use of existing human rights mechanisms and enhancing the contribution of intergovernmental organizations. Recommendations were made for the subregional, regional, national and local levels, and all levels were urged to support the training of educators and trainers, set priorities for specific target groups, particularly those in need of human rights education, and develop indicators to measure the impact of human rights education activities and evaluation systems.

By an August note [A/58/318], the Secretary-General transmitted a report of the High Commissioner on the United Nations Decade for Human Rights Education and the human rights public information activities of OHCHR and DPI (see above). The High Commissioner summarized the activities of the UN system and Member States to implement the Plan of Action. The report highlighted the need for Governments to fulfil the commitments made at the international level to develop national strategies for human rights education that were comprehensive and participatory, with priority given to sustainable approaches. It recommended the development, implementation and evaluation of national strategies. Regional and international organizations and institutions should continue to support national initiatives by facilitating the sharing of information and materials, and by creating and strengthening networks, the training of trainers and related activities.

Commission action. On 25 April [res. 2003/70], the Commission urged States to implement further the Plan of Action and to intensify efforts in the area of education, including human rights education. It requested OHCHR to implement and expand the Assisting Communities Together (ACT) project and to consider other ways to support human rights education activities. All relevant Commission mechanisms were requested to include human rights education in their reports and as an agenda item of their annual meetings. OHCHR was requested to report to the Commission in 2004 on the establishment by the Secretary-General of a voluntary fund for human rights education, to be administered by OHCHR, and on the achievements and shortcomings of the Decade.

Subcommission action. On 13 August [res. 2003/5], the Subcommission recommended that human rights treaty bodies (see p. 668), when examining States parties' reports, devote attention to human rights education and include the subject in the agenda of the annual meeting of the chairpersons of the treaty bodies. It recommended that the High Commissioner, jointly with the United Nations Educational, Scientific and Cultural Organization (UNESCO) and in consultation with Member States, encourage Governments to organize meetings, workshops and other activities at the regional and international levels on the achievements and shortcomings of the Decade, to be coordinated by OHCHR.

OHCHR was requested to make available to the Subcommission the High Commissioner's February report (see p. 687).

GENERAL ASSEMBLY ACTION

On 22 December [meeting 77], the General Assembly, on the recommendation of the Third Committee [A/58/508/Add.2], adopted **resolution 58/181** without vote [agenda item 117 (b)].

United Nations Decade for Human Rights Education, 1995-2004

The General Assembly,

Guided by the fundamental and universal principles enshrined in the Charter of the United Nations and the Universal Declaration of Human Rights,

Reaffirming article 26 of the Universal Declaration, which states that "education shall be directed to the full development of the human personality and to the strengthening of respect for human rights and fundamental freedoms", and recalling the provisions of other relevant international human rights instruments that reflect the aims of the article,

Recalling the relevant resolutions adopted by the General Assembly and the Commission on Human Rights concerning the United Nations Decade for Human Rights Education, 1995-2004,

Believing that human rights education constitutes an important vehicle for the elimination of gender-based discrimination and for ensuring equal opportunities through the promotion and protection of the human rights of women,

Convinced that human rights education should constitute a comprehensive, lifelong process by which all people learn respect for the dignity of others and the means and methods of ensuring that respect in all societies,

Convinced also that every woman, man and child, in order to realize their full human potential, must be made aware of all their human rights and fundamental freedoms and the corresponding responsibility of States,

Recognizing that human rights education is essential to the realization of human rights and fundamental freedoms and that carefully designed training, dissemination and information programmes can have a catalytic effect on national, regional and international initiatives to promote and protect human rights and prevent human rights violations,

Convinced that human rights education contributes to a holistic concept of development consistent with the dignity of people of all ages, which contributes to the promotion of the rights of those in the most vulnerable segments of society, such as children, young persons, older persons, indigenous people, minorities, the rural and urban poor, migrant workers, refugees, persons with HIV/AIDS and disabled persons,

Convinced also that the effectiveness of existing human rights education and public information activities would be enhanced by better coordination and cooperation at the national, regional and international levels,

Recognizing the invaluable, creative and active role that non-governmental and community-based organizations play in the promotion and protection of human rights by disseminating information and engaging in human rights education, especially at the grass-roots level,

Aware of the potential role of the private sector in human rights education through financial support for governmental and non-governmental activities as well as their own creative and effective initiatives,

Noting with appreciation the efforts undertaken thus far by the Office of the United Nations High Commissioner for Human Rights to implement the Plan of Action for the United Nations Decade for Human Rights Education, 1995-2004, and to increase information-sharing in the area of human rights education,

Welcoming other United Nations public information activities in the field of human rights,

Noting Commission on Human Rights resolution 2003/70 of 25 April 2003, in which the Commission requested the Office of the High Commissioner, jointly with the United Nations Educational, Scientific and Cultural Organization, to report on the achievements and shortcomings of the current United Nations Decade for Human Rights Education,

1. *Notes with appreciation* the report of the United Nations High Commissioner for Human Rights on education and public information activities in the field of human rights;

2. *Welcomes* the steps taken by Governments and intergovernmental and non-governmental organizations to implement the Plan of Action for the United Nations Decade for Human Rights Education, 1995-2004, and to develop public information activities in the field of human rights;

3. *Urges* all Governments to promote the development of comprehensive, participatory and sustainable national strategies for human rights education and to establish and strengthen in their education policies knowledge of human rights, in both its theoretical dimensions and its practical applications;

4. *Also urges* all Governments to intensify their efforts to contribute to the implementation of the Plan of Action and, in particular, to implement the suggestions in relevant resolutions adopted by the General Assembly and the Commission on Human Rights regarding possible activities to be included in national strategies for human rights education;

5. *Encourages* Governments to support further, through voluntary contributions, the education and public information efforts undertaken by the Office of the High Commissioner within the framework of the Plan of Action;

6. *Encourages* the Office of the High Commissioner to continue to support national capacities for human rights education and information through its technical cooperation programme in the field of human rights;

7. *Urges* the Department of Public Information of the Secretariat to continue to utilize United Nations information centres for the timely dissemination of basic information, reference and audio-visual materials on human rights and fundamental freedoms;

8. *Requests* the High Commissioner to continue to coordinate and harmonize human rights education and information strategies and the implementation of the Plan of Action and the World Public Information Campaign on Human Rights within the United Nations system, in cooperation with, inter alia, the United Nations Educational, Scientific and Cultural

Organization and the Department of Public Information, and to ensure maximum effectiveness and efficiency in the collection, use, processing, management and distribution of human rights information and educational materials, including through electronic means;

9. *Encourages* all relevant organs, bodies and agencies of the United Nations system to provide training in human rights for all United Nations personnel and officials;

10. *Encourages* the human rights treaty bodies, within their mandates, when examining reports of States parties, to consider the activities of States parties in the area of human rights education;

11. *Encourages* all relevant mechanisms of the Commission on Human Rights to include systematically in their reports a specific section on human rights education, as relevant to their mandate, as well as to include human rights education as an item on the agenda of their annual meetings, with a view to strengthening their contribution to human rights education;

12. *Calls upon* international, regional and national non-governmental organizations and intergovernmental organizations to develop human rights education programmes in implementing the Plan of Action;

13. *Welcomes* initiatives to include civil society, non-governmental organizations, children and youth in national delegations to United Nations meetings as an important component of human rights education;

14. *Encourages* Governments, regional organizations and intergovernmental and non-governmental organizations to seek the cooperation of the private sector, development, trade and financial institutions and the media in developing human rights education strategies;

15. *Encourages* regional organizations to develop strategies for the wider distribution of materials on human rights education in all relevant languages and to maximize the participation of national entities in regional programmes on human rights education;

16. *Requests* the High Commissioner to bring the present resolution to the attention of all members of the international community and of intergovernmental and non-governmental organizations concerned with human rights education and public information;

17. *Decides* to dedicate a plenary meeting during the fifty-ninth session of the General Assembly on the occasion of Human Rights Day, 10 December 2004, structured as an interactive dialogue to review the achievements of the United Nations Decade for Human Rights Education, 1995-2004, and to discuss possible future activities for the enhancement of human rights education.

Children and a culture of peace

In response to General Assembly resolution 57/6 [YUN 2002, p. 651] on the International Decade for a Culture of Peace and Non-Violence for the Children of the World (2001-2010), proclaimed in Assembly resolution 53/25 [YUN 1998, p. 639], the Secretary-General transmitted, in July [A/58/182], a report of the UNESCO Director-General covering implementation of the Programme of Action on a Culture of Peace, adopted in Assembly resolution 53/243 B [YUN 1999, p. 594]. The report was a preparatory contribution to the Secretary-General's report, to be submitted in 2005, on the observance of the Decade and on the implementation of the Declaration on a Culture of Peace, adopted in Assembly resolution 53/243 A [ibid., p. 593], and the Programme of Action.

The report presented examples of activities carried out by UNESCO, as the lead agency for the Decade, with the participation of other UN bodies, Governments and civil society, and included actions to foster a culture of peace through education, promote sustainable economic and social development, promote respect for all human rights, ensure equality between women and men, foster democratic participation, advance understanding, tolerance and solidarity, support participatory communication and the free flow of information, and promote international peace and security. The report reviewed the role of civil society, and communication and networking arrangements among actors for a culture of peace. The Director-General asked Member States to develop further their activities to promote a culture of peace and non-violence, and to inform UNESCO of those activities through their national focal points for the Decade. Civil society should be encouraged to complement Member States' initiatives. UNESCO was urged to strengthen its efforts to coordinate activities implemented by the actors of the culture of peace network.

GENERAL ASSEMBLY ACTION

On 10 November [meeting 59], the General Assembly adopted **resolution 58/11** [draft: A/58/L.14 & Add.1] without vote [agenda item 44].

International Decade for a Culture of Peace and Non-Violence for the Children of the World, 2001-2010

The General Assembly,

Bearing in mind the Charter of the United Nations, including the purposes and principles contained therein, and especially the dedication to saving succeeding generations from the scourge of war,

Recalling the Constitution of the United Nations Educational, Scientific and Cultural Organization, which states that, "since wars begin in the minds of men, it is in the minds of men that the defences of peace must be constructed",

Recalling also its previous resolutions on a culture of peace, in particular resolution 52/15 of 20 November 1997 proclaiming 2000 the International Year for the Culture of Peace, resolution 53/25 of 10 November 1998 proclaiming the period 2001-2010 the International Decade for a Culture of Peace and Non-Violence for the Children of the World, resolution 56/5 of 5 November 2001 and resolution 57/6 of 4 November 2002,

Reaffirming the Declaration and Programme of Action on a Culture of Peace, recognizing that they serve, inter alia, as the basis for the observance of the Decade, and convinced that the effective and successful observance of the Decade throughout the world will promote a culture of peace and non-violence that benefits humanity, in particular future generations,

Recalling the United Nations Millennium Declaration, which calls for the active promotion of a culture of peace,

Taking note of Commission on Human Rights resolution 2000/66 of 26 April 2000, entitled "Towards a culture of peace",

Taking note also of the report of the Secretary-General on the International Decade for a Culture of Peace and Non-Violence for the Children of the World, including paragraph 28 thereof, which indicates that each of the ten years of the Decade will be marked with a different priority theme related to the Programme of Action,

Noting the relevance of the World Summit on Sustainable Development, held in Johannesburg, South Africa, from 26 August to 4 September 2002, the International Conference on Financing for Development, held in Monterrey, Mexico, from 18 to 22 March 2002, the special session of the General Assembly on children, held in New York from 8 to 10 May 2002, the World Conference against Racism, Racial Discrimination, Xenophobia and Related Intolerance, held in Durban, South Africa, from 31 August to 7 September 2001, and the United Nations Decade for Human Rights Education, 1995-2004, for the International Decade for a Culture of Peace and Non-Violence for the Children of the World, 2001-2010, as well as the need to implement, as appropriate, the relevant decisions agreed upon therein,

Recognizing that all efforts made by the United Nations system in general and the international community at large for peacekeeping, peace-building, the prevention of conflicts, disarmament, sustainable development, the promotion of human dignity and human rights, democracy, the rule of law, good governance and gender equality at the national and international levels contribute greatly to the culture of peace,

Noting that its resolution 57/337 of 3 July 2003 on the prevention of armed conflict could contribute to the further promotion of a culture of peace,

Taking into account the "Manifesto 2000" initiative of the United Nations Educational, Scientific and Cultural Organization promoting a culture of peace, which has so far received over seventy-five million signatures of endorsement throughout the world,

Taking note with appreciation of the report of the Director-General of the United Nations Educational, Scientific and Cultural Organization on the implementation of General Assembly resolution 57/6,

1. *Reiterates* that the objective of the International Decade for a Culture of Peace and Non-Violence for the Children of the World, 2001-2010, is to strengthen further the global movement for a culture of peace following the observance of the International Year for the Culture of Peace in 2000;

2. *Invites* Member States to continue to place greater emphasis on and expand their activities promoting a culture of peace and non-violence, in particular during the Decade, at the national, regional and international levels and to ensure that peace and non-violence are fostered at all levels;

3. *Commends* the United Nations Educational, Scientific and Cultural Organization for recognizing the promotion of a culture of peace as the expression of its fundamental mandate, and encourages it, as the lead agency for the Decade, to strengthen further the activities it has undertaken for promoting a culture of peace, including the dissemination of the Declaration and Programme of Action on a Culture of Peace and related materials in various languages across the world;

4. *Also commends* the relevant United Nations bodies, in particular the United Nations Children's Fund, the United Nations Development Fund for Women and the University for Peace, for their activities in further promoting a culture of peace and non-violence, including the promotion of peace education and activities related to specific areas identified in the Programme of Action on a Culture of Peace, and encourages them to continue and further strengthen and expand their efforts;

5. *Encourages* the appropriate authorities to provide education, in children's schools, that includes lessons in mutual understanding, tolerance, active citizenship, human rights and the promotion of a culture of peace;

6. *Encourages* civil society, including non-governmental organizations, to strengthen its efforts in furtherance of the objectives of the Decade, inter alia, by adopting its own programme of activities to complement the initiatives of Member States, the organizations of the United Nations system and other international and regional organizations;

7. *Encourages* the involvement of the mass media in education for a culture of peace and non-violence, with particular regard to children and young people, including through the planned expansion of the Culture of Peace News Network as a global network of Internet sites in many languages;

8. *Welcomes* the efforts made by the United Nations Educational, Scientific and Cultural Organization to continue the communication and networking arrangements established during the International Year for providing an instant update of developments related to the observance of the Decade;

9. *Invites* Member States to observe 21 September each year as the International Day of Peace, as a day of global ceasefire and non-violence, in accordance with General Assembly resolution 55/282 of 7 September 2001;

10. *Invites* Member States as well as civil society, including non-governmental organizations, to provide information to the Secretary-General on the observance of the Decade and the activities undertaken to promote a culture of peace and non-violence;

11. *Emphasizes* the significance of the plenary meetings on the item planned for its sixtieth session, and in that regard encourages participation at a high level, and decides to consider, at an appropriate time, the possibility of organizing those meetings as close as possible to the general debate;

12. *Requests* the Secretary-General to submit to the General Assembly at its fifty-ninth session a report on the implementation of the present resolution;

13. *Decides* to include in the provisional agenda of its fifty-ninth session the item entitled "Culture of peace".

National institutions and regional arrangements

National institutions for human rights promotion and protection

Commission action. On 25 April [res. 2003/76], the Commission welcomed the decisions of a growing number of States to establish national institutions for human rights promotion and protection, and called on OHCHR to continue to strengthen its coordinating role in the establishment and strengthening of those institutions and to allocate resources for such work. It also welcomed the role of the International Coordinating Committee of National Institutions for the Promotion and Protection of Human Rights, for which OHCHR acted as the secretariat, in assessing conformity with the principles relating to the status of national institutions for the promotion and protection of human rights (Paris Principles), adopted in General Assembly resolution 48/134 [YUN 1993, p. 899]. The Secretary-General was requested to provide assistance to the meetings of the Coordinating Committee and for international and regional meetings of national institutions, and to report in 2004.

Reports of Secretary-General. As requested by the General Assembly in resolution 56/158 [YUN 2001, p. 611], the Secretary-General, in an August report [A/58/261] covering July 2001 to July 2003, described the activities of OHCHR in the area of national institutions for human rights promotion and protection.

During the reporting period, at the request of Governments, OHCHR provided advice or assistance regarding the establishment of national institutions to Afghanistan, Armenia, Azerbaijan, Côte d'Ivoire, Fiji, Germany, Ireland, Jordan, Kazakhstan, Mongolia, Nepal, Nigeria, Palestine, the Republic of Korea, Rwanda, Serbia and Montenegro, Sierra Leone, Sri Lanka, the Sudan, Switzerland, Thailand, the former Yugoslav Republic of Macedonia, Timor-Leste and the United Kingdom. The Office provided advice or support to several established national human rights institutions, including the 43 national institutions fully accredited by the International Coordinating Committee, newly established institutions (Jordan, Republic of Korea, Thailand) and other institutions. Support was given in 2003 to regional initiatives, including the second General Assembly of the Network of National Human Rights Institutions of the Americas (San José, Costa Rica, March); a training workshop on the implementation of human rights instruments in Southern Africa (Mbabane, Swaziland, 9-13 June); and the eleventh Workshop on Regional Cooperation for the Promotion and Protection of Human Rights in the Asian and Pacific Region (see p. 694). The report described cooperation between human rights treaty bodies and national institutions; cooperation between OHCHR, UN agencies and programmes, and international and regional organizations; and various thematic issues addressed by national human rights institutions, such as economic, social and cultural rights, racism and racial discrimination, the rights of the child, the rights of persons with disabilities, the prevention of torture, reproductive rights and HIV/AIDS.

A later report of the Secretary-General [E/CN.4/2004/101], covering November 2002 to 19 December 2003, stated that advisory missions were undertaken to Afghanistan, Jordan, Norway, Slovenia and Sri Lanka and to the Occupied Palestinian Territories. Support was given to regional bodies such as the Network of National Human Rights Institutions of the Americas for a workshop on security and human rights (Cartagena, Colombia, 2-3 September), the Seventh Annual Congress of the Ibero-American Federation of Ombudsmen (Panama City, 18-21 November) and the Asia Pacific Forum of National Human Rights Institutions (Sri Lanka, 8-12 November). OHCHR established closer links with the Office of the Human Rights Commissioner of the Council of Europe, which was the focal point for the Council's work on national institutions, including consultations with the Council in September and a joint mission to Slovenia in October. The report described cooperation between human rights treaty bodies, special mechanisms of the Commission and national institutions; cooperation between OHCHR, UN agencies and programmes, and international and regional organizations; and thematic issues addressed by national human rights institutions, such as economic, social and cultural rights, racism and racial discrimination, the administration of justice, the rights of persons with disabilities, the prevention of torture, reproductive rights and HIV/AIDS.

Annexed to the report were the conclusions of discussions held on 13 and 14 November by chairs, members and representatives of 22 national human rights institutions from Africa, Asia and the Pacific, Europe and Latin America, hosted by the Danish Institute for Human Rights and OHCHR. Participants highlighted the centrality and importance of implementing the Paris Principles and their reference to the quasi-jurisdictional powers of national institutions.

Topics discussed included the relationship between national human rights institutions and the judiciary, judicial enforcement mechanisms and national institutions, direct powers of intervention and national institutions, the complaints-handling powers of national institutions and case-handling systems. Also annexed to the report were the conclusions of discussions held by the Chair of the International Coordinating Committee, chairs, members and senior representatives of 13 of its members, NGO representatives and OHCHR during a round table on the Paris Principles (Geneva, 10-11 December). The round table was held to commemorate the tenth anniversary of the adoption of the Principles by the General Assembly in resolution 48/134.

GENERAL ASSEMBLY ACTION

On 22 December [meeting 77], the General Assembly, on the recommendation of the Third Committee [A/58/508/Add.2], adopted **resolution 58/175** without vote [agenda item 117 (b)].

National institutions for the promotion and protection of human rights

The General Assembly,

Recalling its resolutions and those of the Commission on Human Rights concerning national institutions for the promotion and protection of human rights,

Welcoming the rapidly growing interest throughout the world in the creation and strengthening of independent, pluralistic national institutions for the promotion and protection of human rights,

Convinced of the important role that such national institutions play and will continue to play in promoting and protecting human rights and fundamental freedoms and in developing and enhancing public awareness of those rights and freedoms,

Recognizing that the United Nations has played an important role and should continue to play a more important role in assisting the development of national institutions,

Recalling the Vienna Declaration and Programme of Action adopted by the World Conference on Human Rights on 25 June 1993, which reaffirmed the important and constructive role played by national human rights institutions, in particular in their advisory capacity to the competent authorities and their role in remedying human rights violations, in disseminating information on human rights and in education in human rights,

Recalling also the Beijing Platform for Action, in which Governments were urged to create or strengthen independent national institutions for the promotion and protection of human rights, including the human rights of women,

Noting the diverse approaches adopted throughout the world for the promotion and protection of human rights at the national level, emphasizing the universality, indivisibility and interdependence of all human rights, and emphasizing and recognizing the value of such approaches in promoting universal respect for and observance of human rights and fundamental freedoms,

Recalling the programme of action adopted by national institutions for the promotion and protection of human rights, meeting in Vienna from 14 to 16 June 1993 during the World Conference on Human Rights, in which it was recommended that United Nations activities and programmes should be reinforced to meet the requests for assistance from States wishing to establish or strengthen their national institutions for the promotion and protection of human rights,

Noting the valuable role played and contributions made by national institutions in United Nations meetings dealing with human rights and the importance of their continued appropriate participation,

Welcoming the strengthening in all regions of regional cooperation among national human rights institutions and between national human rights institutions and other regional human rights forums,

Noting with appreciation the existence of the regional human rights networks in Europe and Africa, the continuing work of the Network of National Institutions for the Promotion and Protection of Human Rights in the Americas and the work of the Asia Pacific Forum of National Human Rights Institutions,

Welcoming the strengthening of international cooperation among national human rights institutions, including through the International Coordinating Committee of National Institutions,

1. *Welcomes* the report of the Secretary-General;

2. *Reaffirms* the importance of the development of effective, independent and pluralistic national institutions for the promotion and protection of human rights, in keeping with the principles relating to the status of national institutions for the promotion and protection of human rights ("the Paris Principles"), contained in the annex to resolution 48/134 of 20 December 1993;

3. *Reiterates*, on the tenth anniversary of their recognition by the General Assembly, the continued importance of the Paris Principles, recognizes the value of further strengthening their application, where appropriate, and encourages States, national institutions and other interested parties to consider ways to achieve this;

4. *Recognizes* that, in accordance with the Vienna Declaration and Programme of Action, it is the right of each State to choose the framework for national institutions that is best suited to its particular needs at the national level in order to promote human rights in accordance with international human rights standards;

5. *Encourages* Member States to establish or, where they already exist, to strengthen national institutions for the promotion and protection of human rights, as outlined in the Vienna Declaration and Programme of Action;

6. *Welcomes* the growing number of States establishing or considering the establishment of national institutions for the promotion and protection of human rights;

7. *Encourages* national institutions for the promotion and protection of human rights established by Member States to continue to play an active role in preventing and combating all violations of human rights as enumerated in the Vienna Declaration and Programme of Action and relevant international instruments;

8. *Notes with satisfaction* the efforts of those States that have provided their national institutions with more autonomy and independence, including by giving them an investigative role or enhancing such a role,

and encourages other Governments to consider taking similar steps;

9. *Reaffirms* the role of national institutions, where they exist, as appropriate agencies, inter alia, for the dissemination of human rights materials and other public information activities, including those of the United Nations, in particular in the context of the United Nations Decade for Human Rights Education, 1995-2004;

10. *Urges* the Secretary-General to continue to give high priority to requests from Member States for assistance in the establishment and strengthening of national human rights institutions as part of the United Nations Programme of Advisory Services and Technical Assistance in the Field of Human Rights;

11. *Commends* the high priority given by the Office of the United Nations High Commissioner for Human Rights to work on national institutions, encourages the High Commissioner, in view of the expanded activities relating to national institutions, to ensure that appropriate arrangements are made and budgetary resources provided to continue and further extend activities in support of national human rights institutions, and invites Governments to contribute additional funds to the United Nations Voluntary Fund for Technical Cooperation in the Field of Human Rights for that purpose;

12. *Welcomes* the establishment of a national institutions web site as an important vehicle for the delivery of information to national institutions and for sharing best practice, and further notes with satisfaction the intention of the Office of the United Nations High Commissioner for Human Rights to publish a compendium of national legislation relevant to national institutions;

13. *Notes with appreciation* the increasingly active and important role of the International Coordinating Committee of National Institutions, as recognized in Commission on Human Rights resolution 1994/54 of 4 March 1994, in close cooperation with the Office of the United Nations High Commissioner for Human Rights, in assisting Governments and national institutions, when requested, to follow up on relevant resolutions and recommendations concerning the strengthening of national institutions;

14. *Also notes with appreciation* the holding of regular meetings of the International Coordinating Committee and the arrangements for the participation of national human rights institutions in the annual sessions of the Commission on Human Rights;

15. *Requests* the Secretary-General to continue to provide the necessary assistance for holding meetings of the International Coordinating Committee during the sessions of the Commission on Human Rights, in cooperation with the Office of the United Nations High Commissioner for Human Rights;

16. *Welcomes* the continuation of the practice of national institutions convening regional meetings in some regions, and its initiation in others, and encourages national institutions, in cooperation with the United Nations High Commissioner for Human Rights, to organize similar events with Governments and non-governmental organizations in their own regions;

17. *Requests* the Secretary-General to continue to provide, including from the Voluntary Fund for Technical Cooperation, the necessary assistance for holding international and regional meetings of national institutions;

18. *Recognizes* the important and constructive role that non-governmental organizations may play, in cooperation with national institutions, for better promotion and protection of human rights;

19. *Expresses its appreciation* to those Governments that have contributed additional resources for the purpose of the establishment and strengthening of national human rights institutions;

20. *Encourages* all Member States to take appropriate steps to promote the exchange of information and experience concerning the establishment and effective operation of national institutions;

21. *Encourages* all United Nations entities, funds and agencies to work in close cooperation with national institutions in the promotion and protection of human rights;

22. *Requests* the Secretary-General to report to the General Assembly at its sixtieth session on the implementation of the present resolution.

Regional arrangements

Report of Secretary-General. A February report of the Secretary-General [E/CN.4/2003/107 & Corr.1] described assistance provided by OHCHR to regional activities of national human rights institutions. Among those activities, the Office facilitated a training workshop on human rights mainstreaming for Eastern and Central Africa UN country teams (Addis Ababa, 27-29 January) and, also in January, organized a workshop to bring together government representatives of the five Portuguese-speaking countries in Africa and human rights NGOs. The first activity under the regional project on human rights and human development in the Arab States, supported by UNDP and OHCHR and implemented by the Arab Organization for Human Rights, "Human rights and media", took place (Cairo, Egypt, January).

Commission action. On 25 April [res. 2003/75], the Commission requested the Secretary-General to strengthen exchanges between the United Nations and regional human rights intergovernmental organizations and to make resources available to OHCHR to promote regional arrangements. It asked him to report to the General Assembly in 2004 and to the Commission in 2005. The Commission asked OHCHR to continue to pay special attention to the most appropriate ways of assisting countries, at their request.

Africa

In 2003, the Subregional Centre for Human Rights and Democracy in Central Africa, based in Yaoundé, Cameroon, organized a subregional training workshop on military law (Libreville, Gabon, January), training sessions for officials of the Congolese Ministry of Justice and members of the legal clinic (Brazzaville, January) and training courses for students, members of human rights organizations and UN staff, and provided technical support to national institutions [A/57/823-S/2003/610]. The Centre also organized seminars on the media, human rights and democracy (Malabo, Equatorial Guinea, 20-22 May) and on the role of civil society in Central Africa in the promotion and protection of the human rights of vulnerable groups (Ndjamena, Chad, 22-24 July) [A/58/560-S/2003/1075].

GENERAL ASSEMBLY ACTION

On 22 December [meeting 77], the General Assembly, on the recommendation of the Third Committee [A/58/508/Add.2], adopted **resolution 58/176** without vote [agenda item 117 (b)].

Subregional Centre for Human Rights and Democracy in Central Africa

The General Assembly,

Recalling its resolution 55/105 of 4 December 2000 concerning regional arrangements for the promotion and protection of human rights,

Recalling also its resolutions 55/34 B of 20 November 2000 and 55/233 of 23 December 2000 and section III of its resolution 55/234 of 23 December 2000,

Recalling further that the World Conference on Human Rights recommended that more resources be made available for the strengthening of regional arrangements for the promotion and protection of human rights under the programme of technical cooperation in the field of human rights of the Office of the United Nations High Commissioner for Human Rights,

Recalling the report of the United Nations High Commissioner for Human Rights,

Taking note of the holding of the twentieth ministerial meeting of the United Nations Standing Advisory Committee on Security Questions in Central Africa, in Malabo, from 27 to 31 October 2003,

1. *Welcomes* the activities of the Subregional Centre for Human Rights and Democracy in Central Africa at Yaoundé;
2. *Notes with satisfaction* the support provided for the establishment of the Centre by the host country;
3. *Requests* the Secretary-General and the United Nations High Commissioner for Human Rights to continue to provide their full assistance for the proper functioning of the Centre;
4. *Requests* the Secretary-General to submit to the General Assembly at its fifty-ninth session a report on the implementation of the present resolution.

Asia and the Pacific

Commission action. On 25 April [res. 2003/73], the Commission endorsed the conclusions of the eleventh Workshop on Regional Cooperation for the Promotion and Protection of Human Rights in the Asian and Pacific Region (see below) and requested the Secretary-General to submit a report to the Commission in 2004 on the conclusions of the twelfth workshop.

Report of Secretary-General. A March report of the Secretary-General [E/CN.4/2003/109] contained the conclusions of the eleventh Workshop on Regional Cooperation for the Promotion and Protection of Human Rights in the Asian and Pacific Region (Islamabad, Pakistan, 25-27 February), which formulated the 2002-2004 Programme of Action for the Asia-Pacific Framework for Regional Cooperation for the Promotion and Protection of Human Rights. The Workshop reviewed progress made since the tenth Workshop [YUN 2002, p. 654] and noted new draft guidelines on poverty reduction strategies issued by OHCHR, the launch of the OHCHR Handbook on National Human Rights Action Plans and the activities conducted under the areas identified in the Tehran Framework for Technical Cooperation [YUN 1998, p. 641].

Cooperation with human rights bodies

Report of Secretary-General. A February report of the Secretary-General [E/CN.4/2003/34] described situations in which private individuals or NGO members had allegedly been intimidated or suffered reprisals for having cooperated with UN human rights bodies regarding human rights violations.

Commission action. On 16 April [res. 2003/9], the Commission urged Governments to refrain from all acts of intimidation against: persons who sought to cooperate or had cooperated with representatives of UN human rights bodies, or who had provided testimony or information to them; persons who availed themselves of UN procedures and those who had provided legal assistance to them for that purpose; those who submitted communications under procedures established by human rights instruments; and relatives of victims of human rights violations. It requested representatives of UN human rights bodies and treaty bodies monitoring human rights to help prevent such intimidation and to include in their reports allegations of intimidation or reprisal and of hampering access to UN human rights procedures, as well as an account of the action taken. The Secretary-General was asked to draw the Commission's resolution to the attention of UN human rights treaty bodies and to report in 2004.

Chapter II

Protection of human rights

In 2003, the protection of human rights—civil and political, as well as economic, social and cultural—remained a major focus of UN activities. During the year, follow-up activities continued to be undertaken to implement the Durban Declaration and Programme of Action (DDPA), adopted at the 2001 World Conference against Racism, Racial Discrimination, Xenophobia and Related Intolerance, including the first meeting of the Intergovernmental Working Group established by the Economic and Social Council to make recommendations for effective implementation of DDPA and the first meeting of the five independent eminent experts appointed by the Secretary-General to follow up the implementation process. The General Assembly closed the Third Decade to Combat Racism and Racial Discrimination (1993-2003) and emphasized the implementation of DDPA as a solid foundation for a broad-based consensus for further action to eliminate racism.

On 30 January, the Security Council considered a list of parties to armed conflict that reportedly recruited child soldiers, which constituted a significant advance in efforts to apply international norms and standards for protecting children affected by armed conflict. In related action, in December, the Council considered a 10-point action plan to protect civilians in situations of armed conflict.

In 2003, the Commission on Human Rights and its subsidiary body, the Subcommission on the Promotion and Protection of Human Rights, established new mandates for an independent expert concerned with the question of violence against children, and for special rapporteurs on issues dealing with human rights and the human genome and with corruption and its impact on the full enjoyment of human rights.

Special rapporteurs, special representatives and independent experts of the Commission and the Subcommission examined, among other issues, contemporary forms of racism; the rights of migrants; freedom of religion or belief; mercenary activity; the independence of the judiciary; extralegal executions; allegations of torture; impunity; freedom of expression; human rights and terrorism; the prevention of human rights violations committed with small arms and light weapons; the right to development; globalization and its impact on human rights; the effects of structural adjustment programmes and foreign debt on human rights; the question of human rights and extreme poverty; the right to food; the right to adequate housing; the right to education; illicit practices related to toxic and dangerous products and wastes; violence against women; the right to physical and mental health; the sale of children, child prostitution and child pornography; children affected by armed conflict; internally displaced persons; and the human rights and fundamental freedoms of indigenous people.

Working groups considered problems of racial discrimination affecting people of African descent, recommendations for the effective implementation of DDPA and complementary standards to strengthen related international instruments, discrimination against minorities, arbitrary detention, enforced or involuntary disappearances, the right to development, bioethics, contemporary forms of slavery and the rights of indigenous peoples.

Racism and racial discrimination

Third Decade against racism

The General Assembly, in resolution 48/91 [YUN 1993, p. 853], had proclaimed the Third Decade to Combat Racism and Racial Discrimination (1993-2003) and adopted the Decade's Programme of Action, which was revised in Assembly resolution 49/146 [YUN 1994, p. 988]. Up until 1998, the Third Decade's goals and objectives were the same as those of the first Decade, which the Assembly had adopted in resolution 3057 (XXVIII) [YUN 1973, p. 523]. In 2001, however, related activities were reorganized to focus on the World Conference against Racism, Racial Discrimination, Xenophobia and Related Intolerance [YUN 2001, p. 615].

The Assembly, by resolution 58/160 of 22 December (see p. 699), decided to close the Decade.

Implementation of Programme of Action

Report of High Commissioner. Pursuant to General Assembly resolution 57/195 [YUN 2002, p. 662] and to a 2002 Commission on Human Rights request [ibid., p. 661], the High Commissioner, in a February report [E/CN.4/2003/19], summarized all Third Decade activities, including international seminars, national and regional initiatives, UN system-wide consultations and other measures to strengthen the coordination of relevant programmes, and research, studies and publications. Although some activities requested by the Programme of Action were yet to be implemented, the final document of the 2001 World Conference against Racism, Racial Discrimination, Xenophobia and Related Intolerance forged the path for future action.

In a March addendum to the report [E/CN.4/2003/19/Add.1], the High Commissioner summarized the last activity held under the Third Decade—a workshop convened jointly by the Office of the United Nations High Commissioner for Human Rights (OHCHR) and the United Nations Educational, Scientific and Cultural Organization (UNESCO) (Paris, 19-20 February). The workshop aimed to develop for publication educational materials for teachers, students and other opinion leaders on combating racism and racial discrimination in its contemporary forms and fostering tolerance. Discussions were based on background papers presented by 10 experts, which analysed the problems of racism and racial discrimination in relation to education; health; HIV/AIDS; contemporary forms of slavery; employment; migration; the administration of justice; the media; gender dimension; and the 1965 International Convention on the Elimination of All Forms of Racial Discrimination, adopted by the Assembly in resolution 2106 A (XX) [YUN 1965, p. 440]. The papers would form the basis for chapters in the publication.

Commission action. On 23 April [E/2003/23 (res. 2003/30)], the Commission on Human Rights, by a recorded vote of 38 to 1, with 13 abstentions, noting with concern that the objectives of the Programme of Action for the Third Decade had largely not been achieved, recommended that the General Assembly, in future activities to combat racism, emphasize the implementation of the Durban Declaration and Programme of Action (DDPA) adopted by the 2001 World Conference. It further recommended that the Assembly, after considering the Secretary-General's analytical report on the extent of implementation of the Third Decade's Programme of Action (see below), consider the Decade's closure.

By **decision 2003/246** of 23 July (see p. 698), the Economic and Social Council endorsed the Commission's recommendations.

Report of Secretary-General. Pursuant to General Assembly resolution 57/195 [YUN 2002, p. 662], the Secretary-General, in a May analytical report on the extent of implementation of the Third Decade's Programme of Action [A/58/80-E/2003/71], drew attention to the High Commissioner's February and March reports (see above).

On 24 July, the Economic and Social Council took note of the Secretary-General's report (**decision 2003/310**).

By **resolution 58/160** (see p. 699), the Assembly, after considering the Secretary-General's report, decided to close the Third Decade and to emphasize the implementation of DDPA for further actions and initiatives to eliminate racism.

Follow-up to 2001 World Conference

Working Group on people of African descent. The Working Group of Experts on People of African Descent, established by the Commission in 2002 [YUN 2002, p. 661] to consider problems of racial discrimination affecting people of African descent, in accordance with DDPA, held its first (25-29 November 2002) and second (3-7 February 2003) sessions [E/CN.4/2003/21] as well as its third session (29 September–10 October) [E/CN.4/2004/21], all in Geneva.

Discussions at the Group's first and second sessions formed the basis of a set of conclusions, including the Group's view that it's work was linked to UNESCO's project "The Slave Route" and to related International Labour Organization (ILO) conventions. It believed that DDPA provided a good framework for understanding the issues of racial discrimination facing people of African descent. The Group asserted that, although people of African descent shared similarities, they represented a diverse community in different continents, with different issues, needs and expectations, and those variations should be acknowledged and studied further. The Group proposed recommendations to the Commission regarding the study, to be conducted with OHCHR assistance, of problems of racial discrimination faced by people of African descent in the diaspora; the drafting of measures to ensure their full access to the justice system; measures to eliminate racial profiling against them; the development of short-, medium- and long-term proposals to eliminate discrimination against people of African descent, including proposals for a mechanism to monitor and promote all their human rights; and the full and equal participation of relevant non-governmental organizations (NGOs) in the Group's work. The Group recommended the study of the political, economic and social status of people of African descent; the eradication of poverty, marginalization, social exclusion and development; health and HIV/AIDS; racial profiling; the administration of justice; the gender dimension of racial discrimination; discrimination against children; the protection and management of ancestral lands and traditional rights; and access to education and information technology.

At its third session, the Group made further recommendations to the Commission regarding the administration of justice, the media and access to education. It decided that its future work should include cooperation with UN bodies, consultations, regional round tables and thematic seminars.

Report of High Commissioner. Pursuant to General Assembly resolution 56/266 [YUN 2002, p. 659], the High Commissioner, in a February report on the implementation of and follow-up to the 2001 World Conference [E/CN.4/2003/18], described the activities of States, human rights treaty bodies, special procedures and other Commission mechanisms, UN agencies, international and regional organizations, national human rights institutions and NGOs to implement DDPA.

Intergovernmental Working Group. The Intergovernmental Working Group established by Economic and Social Council decision 2002/270 [YUN 2002, p. 661] to make recommendations for effective implementation of DDPA and to prepare complementary standards to strengthen relevant international instruments held its first session (Geneva, 21-31 January and 21 March) [E/CN.4/2003/20]. The Group examined DDPA on a chapter-by-chapter basis and, on 21 March, adopted recommendations calling on States to formulate and implement policies and action plans to combat racism, racial discrimination, xenophobia and related intolerance, including their gender-based manifestations. The Group invited OHCHR to appoint, in cooperation with intergovernmental organizations, the International Olympic Committee and sports federations, goodwill ambassadors to educate youth on sport practised without discrimination. Similar goodwill ambassadors should be appointed in all regions drawn from the field of culture to promote respect for human rights and a culture of tolerance, and to assist OHCHR to raise funds for programmes to combat racial discrimination. Regarding complementary standards, the Group agreed that a thorough assessment of existing international standards and instruments to combat racism was needed, and invited the Committee on the Elimination of Racial Discrimination (CERD) and other human rights treaty bodies to contribute towards that end. OHCHR was requested to prepare an analytical report on existing standards, identifying possible areas where complementary standards might be needed. The Group decided to consider, at its next session, the implementation of DDPA, a thematic analysis of the implementation process from the perspective of victims and reports on existing complementary standards. It would also discuss poverty and education.

Commission action. On 24 March [dec. 2003/103], the Commission revised its agenda by making the item entitled "Comprehensive implementation of and follow-up to the Durban Declaration and Programme of Action" a sub-item of the item entitled "Racism, racial discrimination, xenophobia and all forms of discrimination".

On 23 April [res. 2003/30], the Commission called for the implementation of the recommendations of the Intergovernmental Working Group (see above) by all stakeholders. OHCHR was requested to submit to the Group an analytical report assessing the effectiveness of current regional and international instruments to combat racism and identifying possible areas where complementary standards might be needed, in order to assist the Group in fulfilling its mandate. It decided that the Group should convene its future sessions for an initial period of three years, and requested it to convene its second session of 10 working days and to focus on poverty, education and complementary standards, as decided in its recommendations, and to report in 2004.

The Commission decided to readjust the terms of reference of the independent eminent experts (see p. 698) as follows: to follow the implementation of DDPA provisions, in cooperation with OHCHR; assist the High Commissioner in preparing his annual progress report to the Commission and the General Assembly; and to assist the High Commissioner in assessing and evaluating existing international standards and instruments to combat racism, with a view to preparing complementary standards. The Commission, revising parts of its resolution 2002/68 [YUN 2002, p. 661], decided to entrust the Working Group on people of African descent (see p. 696) with additional mandates, including to make proposals on the elimination of racial discrimination against Africans and people of African descent worldwide, and to address all issues concerning their well-being contained in DDPA. It decided that the experts should convene future sessions for an initial period of three years and requested them to convene their second session of 10 working days and to report in 2004.

ECONOMIC AND SOCIAL COUNCIL ACTION

In July, the Economic and Social Council, on the recommendation of the Commission on Human Rights [E/2003/23], adopted, as orally amended, **decision 2003/246** by recorded vote (37-1-16) [agenda item 14 (g)].

World Conference against Racism, Racial Discrimination, Xenophobia and Related Intolerance and the comprehensive implementation of and follow-up to the Durban Declaration and Programme of Action

At its 46th plenary meeting, on 23 July 2003, the Economic and Social Council took note of Commission on Human Rights resolution 2003/30 of 23 April 2003, and endorsed the Commission's decision:

(a) To request the Intergovernmental Working Group to make recommendations with a view to the effective implementation of the Durban Declaration and Programme of Action and to prepare complementary international standards to strengthen and update international instruments against racism, racial discrimination, xenophobia and related intolerance in all their aspects, to convene its upcoming sessions for an initial period of three years, while encouraging it to work effectively to fulfil its mandate, to convene its second session of ten working days, focusing on areas decided upon in its recommendations, namely, poverty, education and complementary standards, and to report on progress in this regard at the sixtieth session of the Commission;

(b) That the working group of experts on people of African descent should convene its future sessions for an initial period of three years, while encouraging it to work effectively towards the fulfilment of its mandate, and also the Commission's decision to request the working group to convene its second session of ten working days and to report to the Commission at its sixtieth session on progress towards the fulfilment of the mandate of the working group.

The Council also endorsed the Commission's recommendations that the General Assembly, after considering the analytical report of the Secretary-General on the extent of implementation of the Programme of Action for the Third Decade to Combat Racism and Racial Discrimination, to be submitted pursuant to Assembly resolution 57/195 of 18 December 2002, consider the closure of the Third Decade.

The Council also endorsed the Commission's recommendation that the General Assembly, in the coming decade of activities to combat racism, racial discrimination, xenophobia and related intolerance, place emphasis on the concrete implementation of the Durban Declaration and Programme of Action on the basis of a broad-based consensus on the importance of the anti-discrimination struggle worldwide.

The Council also endorsed the Commission's request that the Secretary-General provide the Special Rapporteur on contemporary forms of racism, racial discrimination, xenophobia and related intolerance with all the necessary human and financial assistance to carry out his mandate efficiently, effectively and expeditiously and to enable him to submit an interim report to the General Assembly at its fifty-eighth session.

RECORDED VOTE ON DECISION 2003/246:

In favour: Argentina, Azerbaijan, Benin, Bhutan, Brazil, Burundi, Chile, China, Congo, Cuba, Ecuador, Egypt, El Salvador, Ethiopia, Georgia, Ghana, Guatemala, India, Iran, Jamaica, Japan, Kenya, Libyan Arab Jamahiriya, Malaysia, Mozambique, Nepal, Nicaragua, Nigeria, Pakistan, Peru, Qatar, Russian Federation, Saudi Arabia, Senegal, South Africa, Uganda, Zimbabwe.

Against: United States.

Abstaining: Andorra, Australia, Finland, France, Germany, Greece, Hungary, Ireland, Italy, Netherlands, Portugal, Republic of Korea, Romania, Sweden, Ukraine, United Kingdom.

CERD action. In March and August [A/58/18], the Committee on the Elimination of Racial Discrimination (CERD), at its sixty-second and sixty-third sessions, considered follow-up to the World Conference, particularly with regard to the work of the Intergovernmental Working Group on the effective implementation of DDPA (see p. 697). The Committee decided to request that it be duly represented in the Group's meetings, considering that the International Convention on the Elimination of All Forms of Racial Discrimination, adopted by the General Assembly in resolution 2106 A (XX) [YUN 1965, p. 440], for which the Committee served as a monitoring body, was the main international legal instrument in the struggle against racial discrimination. (For more on CERD, see p. 674.)

Further report of High Commissioner. An August note of the Secretary-General [A/58/324] transmitted a report of the High Commissioner summarizing activities taken by States, UN bodies, specialized agencies, international organizations and NGOs in follow-up to the World Conference, as requested in General Assembly resolution 56/266 [YUN 2002, p. 659].

By **decision 58/535** of 22 December, the Assembly took note of the High Commissioner's report.

Report of independent experts. A Secretariat note [E/CN.4/2004/112] transmitted the views of the five independent eminent experts appointed by the Secretary-General to follow up the implementation of DDPA provisions, pursuant to General Assembly resolutions 56/266 and 57/195 [YUN 2002, p. 662]. In accordance with Commission resolution 2003/30 (see p. 696), the experts were also mandated to assist the High Commissioner in preparing annual progress reports to the Commission and the Assembly, and in assessing and evaluating existing international standards and instruments to combat racism, with a view to preparing complementary standards.

At their first meeting (Geneva, 16-18 September), the experts identified access to education, access to justice and awareness-raising as priority areas and underlined the importance of the principle of non-discrimination in combating terrorism. Poverty eradication was vital in the effort to eliminate all forms of discrimination. The experts recommended the development of a "racial equality index" to measure existing racial inequalities. The experts indicated that a study on updating international standards would facilitate their consideration of the issue.

Regional seminars. As part of follow-up activities to the World Conference, OHCHR, in collaboration with the Government of Uruguay, organized a workshop on the adoption and implementation of policies of affirmative action for people of African descent of the Latin American and Caribbean region (Montevideo, 7-9 May) [E/CN.4/2004/17/Add.3], which recommended positive actions and strategies as a means to overcome inequalities.

Other regional activities included expert seminars for Eastern European (Prague, 24-26 September) [E/CN.4/2004/17/Add.1] and Western European States (Brussels, 10-12 December) [E/CN.4/2004/17/Add.2], organized by OHCHR, in collaboration with the Governments of the Czech Republic and of Belgium, respectively. The seminars exchanged views on ways to move forward on DDPA implementation and adopted conclusions and recommendations.

Communication. On 22 January [E/CN.4/2003/G/36], Brazil described its efforts to implement proposals agreed upon at the World Conference.

GENERAL ASSEMBLY ACTION

On 22 December [meeting 77], the General Assembly, on the recommendation of the Third (Social, Humanitarian and Cultural) Committee [A/58/506], adopted **resolution 58/160** by recorded vote (174-2-2) [agenda item 115].

Global efforts for the total elimination of racism, racial discrimination, xenophobia and related intolerance and the comprehensive implementation of and follow-up to the Durban Declaration and Programme of Action

The General Assembly,

Recalling its resolution 56/266 of 27 March 2002, in which it endorsed the Durban Declaration and Programme of Action, adopted by the World Conference against Racism, Racial Discrimination, Xenophobia and Related Intolerance, held at Durban, South Africa, from 31 August to 8 September 2001, as constituting a solid foundation for further action and initiatives towards the total elimination of the scourge of racism,

Recalling also its resolution 57/195 of 18 December 2002, in which it outlined the important roles and responsibilities of the various organs of the United Nations and other stakeholders at the international, regional and national levels, including, in particular, the Commission on Human Rights,

Taking note of Commission on Human Rights resolutions 2002/68 of 25 April 2002 and 2003/30 of 23 April 2003,

Stressing that the Vienna Declaration and Programme of Action, adopted by the World Conference on Human Rights on 25 June 1993, attaches importance to the elimination of racism, racial discrimination, xenophobia and other forms of intolerance,

Recognizing that racism, racial discrimination, xenophobia and related intolerance occur on the grounds of race, colour, descent or national or ethnic origin and that victims can suffer multiple or aggravated forms of discrimination based on other related grounds such as sex, language, religion, political and other opinion, social origin, property, birth and other status,

Reiterating that all human beings are born free and equal in dignity and rights and have the potential to contribute constructively to the development and well-being of their societies, and that any doctrine of racial superiority is scientifically false, morally condemnable, socially unjust and dangerous and must be rejected, together with theories that attempt to determine the existence of separate human races,

Reaffirming its commitment to a global drive for the total elimination of racism, racial discrimination, xenophobia and related intolerance,

Reaffirming that universal adherence to and full implementation of the International Convention on the Elimination of All Forms of Racial Discrimination are of paramount importance for the promotion of equality and non-discrimination in the world,

Convinced that racism, racial discrimination, xenophobia and related intolerance reveal themselves in a differentiated manner for women and girls and may be among the factors leading to a deterioration in their living conditions, poverty, violence, multiple forms of discrimination and the limitation or denial of their human rights, and recognizing the need to integrate a gender perspective into relevant policies, strategies and programmes of action against racism, racial discrimination, xenophobia and related intolerance in order to address multiple forms of discrimination,

Reaffirming its firm determination and its commitment to eradicate totally and unconditionally racism and racial discrimination, and its conviction that racism and racial discrimination constitute a negation of the purposes and principles of the Charter of the United Nations and the Universal Declaration of Human Rights,

Recognizing that the successful implementation of the Durban Programme of Action requires political will, international cooperation and adequate funding at the national, regional and international levels,

Deeply concerned that, despite continuing efforts, racism, racial discrimination, xenophobia and related intolerance and acts of violence persist and even grow in magnitude, incessantly adopting new forms, including tendencies to establish policies based on racial, religious, ethnic, cultural and national superiority or exclusivity,

Alarmed, in particular, at the increase in racist violence and xenophobic ideas in many parts of the world, in political circles, in the sphere of public opinion and in society at large, inter alia, as a result of the resurgent activities of associations established on the basis of racist and xenophobic platforms and charters, and the persistent use of those platforms and charters to promote or incite racist ideologies,

Underlining the importance of urgently eliminating continuing and violent trends involving racism and racial discrimination, and conscious that any form of impunity for crimes motivated by racist and xenophobic attitudes plays a role in weakening the rule of law and democracy, tends to encourage the recurrence of such crimes and requires resolute action and cooperation for its eradication,

Recognizing that States should implement and enforce appropriate and effective legislative, judicial, regulatory and administrative measures to prevent and protect against acts of racism, racial discrimination, xenophobia and related intolerance, thereby contributing to the prevention of human rights violations,

Emphasizing that poverty, underdevelopment, marginalization, social exclusion and economic disparities are closely associated with racism, racial discrimination, xenophobia and related intolerance and contribute to the persistence of racist attitudes and practices, which in turn generate more poverty,

Deeply concerned about the misuse, by those advocating racism and racial discrimination, of new communication technologies, including the Internet, to disseminate their repugnant views,

Noting that the use of such technologies can also contribute to combating racism, racial discrimination, xenophobia and related intolerance,

Noting also developments that have occurred within the framework of the Commission on Human Rights through its intersessional working groups and other mechanisms created for the effective implementation of the Durban Declaration and Programme of Action, in particular the work of the group of independent eminent experts, the Working Group of Experts on People of African Descent and the Intergovernmental Working Group on the Effective Implementation of the Durban Declaration and Programme of Action,

Welcoming all the regional initiatives being undertaken to implement the Durban commitments, and in this context expressing its appreciation to the Governments of Mexico, Kenya and the Czech Republic for hosting the regional expert seminars with a view to the implementation of the Durban Declaration and Programme of Action within their respective regions, and encouraging other regions to take the necessary action in this regard,

I
Basic general principles

1. *Acknowledges* that no derogation from the prohibition of racial discrimination, genocide, the crime of apartheid or slavery is permitted, as defined in the obligations under the relevant human rights instruments;

2. *Expresses its profound concern about and its unequivocal condemnation* of all forms of racism and racial discrimination, including related acts of racially motivated violence, xenophobia and intolerance, as well as propaganda activities and organizations that attempt to justify or promote racism, racial discrimination, xenophobia and related intolerance in any form;

3. *Affirms* that racism and racial discrimination, and xenophobia and related intolerance, where they amount to racism and racial discrimination, constitute serious violations of and obstacles to the full enjoyment of all human rights;

4. *Stresses* that States and international organizations have a responsibility to ensure that measures taken in the struggle against terrorism do not discriminate in purpose or effect on grounds of race, colour, descent or national or ethnic origin, and urges all States to rescind or refrain from all forms of racial profiling;

5. *Recognizes* that States should implement and enforce appropriate and effective legislative, judicial, regulatory and administrative measures to prevent and protect against acts of racism, racial discrimination, xenophobia and related intolerance, thereby contributing to the prevention of human rights violations;

6. *Emphasizes* that it is the responsibility of States to adopt effective measures to combat criminal acts motivated by racism, racial discrimination, xenophobia and related intolerance, including measures to ensure that such motivations are considered an aggravating factor for the purposes of sentencing, to prevent those crimes from going unpunished and to ensure the rule of law;

7. *Urges* all States to review and, where necessary, revise their immigration laws, policies and practices so that they are free of racial discrimination and compatible with their obligations under international human rights instruments;

8. *Condemns* the misuse of print, audio-visual and electronic media and new communication technologies, including the Internet, to incite violence motivated by racial hatred, and calls upon States to take all necessary measures to combat this form of racism in accordance with the commitments that they have undertaken under the Durban Declaration and Programme of Action, in particular paragraph 147 of the Programme of Action, in accordance with existing international and regional standards of freedom of expression and taking all necessary measures to guarantee the right to freedom of opinion and expression;

9. *Condemns also* political platforms and organizations based on racism, xenophobia or doctrines of racial superiority and related discrimination, as well as legislation and practices based on racism, racial discrimination, xenophobia and related intolerance as incompatible with democracy and transparent and accountable governance;

10. *Encourages* all States to include in their educational curricula and social programmes at all levels, as appropriate, knowledge of and tolerance and respect for foreign cultures, peoples and countries;

11. *Stresses* the responsibility of States to mainstream a gender perspective in the design and development of prevention, education and protection measures aimed at the eradication of racism, racial discrimination, xenophobia and related intolerance at all levels, to ensure that they effectively target the distinct situations of women and men;

12. *Expresses its concern* at the increasing incidents of racism in various sporting events;

13. *Notes with appreciation* the efforts being made by some sporting governing bodies to combat racism, and encourages other such bodies to take similar actions;

II
International Convention on the Elimination of All Forms of Racial Discrimination

14. *Urges* States that have not yet done so to consider ratifying or acceding to the international human rights instruments that combat racism, racial discrimination, xenophobia and related intolerance, in particular to accede to the International Convention on the Elimination of All Forms of Racial Discrimination as a matter of urgency, with a view to achieving universal ratification by 2005, and to consider making the declaration envisaged under article 14 thereof, to comply with their reporting obligations, to publish and act upon the concluding observations of the Committee on the Elimination of Racial Discrimination, to withdraw reservations contrary to the object and purpose of the

Convention and to consider withdrawing other reservations;

15. *Invites* States parties to the Convention to ratify the amendment to article 8 of the Convention, on the financing of the Committee on the Elimination of Racial Discrimination, and calls for adequate additional resources from the United Nations regular budget to enable the Committee to discharge its mandate fully;

16. *Urges* all States parties to the Convention to intensify their efforts to implement the obligations that they have accepted under article 4 of the Convention, with due regard to the principles of the Universal Declaration of Human Rights and article 5 of the Convention;

17. *Notes* that the Committee on the Elimination of Racial Discrimination holds that the prohibition of the dissemination of ideas based on racial superiority or racial hatred is compatible with the right to freedom of opinion and expression as outlined in article 19 of the Universal Declaration of Human Rights and in article 5 of the Convention;

18. *Welcomes* the emphasis placed by the Committee on the Elimination of Racial Discrimination on the importance of follow-up to the World Conference against Racism, Racial Discrimination, Xenophobia and Related Intolerance and the measures recommended to strengthen the implementation of the Convention as well as the functioning of the Committee;

III
Comprehensive implementation of and follow-up to the Durban Declaration and Programme of Action

19. *Emphasizes* that the basic responsibility for effectively combating racism, racial discrimination, xenophobia and related intolerance lies with States, and to this end stresses that States have the primary responsibility to ensure full and effective implementation of all commitments and recommendations contained in the Durban Declaration and Programme of Action;

20. *Also emphasizes*, in that context, the fundamental and complementary role of national human rights institutions, regional bodies and centres and civil society, working jointly with States towards the achievement of the objectives of the Durban Declaration and Programme of Action;

21. *Calls upon* States to elaborate action plans, in consultation with national human rights institutions, other institutions created by law to combat racism, and civil society, and to provide the United Nations High Commissioner for Human Rights with such action plans and other relevant materials on measures taken to implement the provisions of the Durban Declaration and Programme of Action;

22. *Calls upon* all States to formulate and implement without delay, at the national, regional and international levels, policies and plans of action to combat racism, racial discrimination, xenophobia and related intolerance, including their gender-based manifestations;

23. *Urges* States to support the activities of existing regional bodies and centres that combat racism, racial discrimination, xenophobia and related intolerance in their respective regions, and recommends the establishment of such bodies or centres in all regions where they do not exist;

24. *Recognizes* the fundamental role of civil society in the fight against racism, racial discrimination, xenophobia and related intolerance, in particular in assisting States to develop regulations and strategies, in taking measures and action against such forms of discrimination and through follow-up implementation;

25. *Emphasizes* that, in accordance with the Durban Declaration and Programme of Action, States have a shared responsibility, at the international level and within the framework of the United Nations system, to determine modalities for the overall review of the implementation of the Declaration and Programme of Action;

26. *Stresses and reaffirms* its role as the highest intergovernmental mechanism for the formulation and appraisal of policy on matters related to the economic, social and related fields, in accordance with Chapter IX of the Charter of the United Nations, including in the comprehensive implementation of and follow-up to the goals and targets set at all the major United Nations conferences, summits and special sessions;

27. *Acknowledges* that the outcome of the World Conference against Racism, Racial Discrimination, Xenophobia and Related Intolerance is on an equal footing with the outcomes of all the major United Nations conferences, summits and special sessions in the human rights and social fields;

28. *Invites* all relevant organs, organizations and bodies of the United Nations system to become involved in the follow-up to the World Conference against Racism, Racial Discrimination, Xenophobia and Related Intolerance, and invites specialized agencies and related organizations of the United Nations system to strengthen and adjust, within their respective mandates, their activities, programmes and medium-term strategies to take into account the follow-up to the Conference;

29. *Invites* all human rights treaty-monitoring bodies and all mechanisms and subsidiary bodies of the Commission on Human Rights to consider the relevant provisions of the Durban Declaration and Programme of Action in the discharge of their respective mandates;

30. *Reaffirms* that the Economic and Social Council shall oversee the system-wide coordination of the implementation of the Durban Declaration and Programme of Action;

31. *Takes note* of the recommendations adopted by consensus by the Intergovernmental Working Group on the Effective Implementation of the Durban Declaration and Programme of Action at its first session, on 21 March 2003;

32. *Notes* that the Working Group will continue its future sessions on the basis of the thematic approach adopted during its first session, and notes with appreciation that to this end the next session of the Working Group, which the representative of Chile has expressed interest in chairing, will analyse the themes relating to poverty eradication and education;

33. *Also notes* the convening of the sessions of the Working Group of Experts on People of African Descent, the renewal of its mandate and the adjustments effected thereto;

34. *Welcomes* the inaugural session of the group of independent eminent experts, held at Geneva from 16

to 18 September 2003, with the participation of representatives of Member States, the United Nations system and civil society, takes note of its substantive outcome, and in this context requests the United Nations High Commissioner for Human Rights to examine the possibility of the development of a racial equality index, as proposed by the group of independent eminent experts, and to report thereon to the Commission on Human Rights;

35. *Acknowledges with appreciation* the entry into force of the International Convention on the Protection of the Rights of All Migrant Workers and Members of Their Families on 1 July 2003, and invites all States that have not yet done so to consider acceding to that important instrument;

36. *Notes with satisfaction* the progress made during the first and second sessions of the Ad Hoc Committee on a Comprehensive and Integral International Convention on the Protection and Promotion of the Rights and Dignity of Persons with Disabilities, held in New York from 29 July to 9 August 2002 and from 16 to 27 June 2003;

37. *Notes with appreciation* the first and second sessions of the Permanent Forum on Indigenous Issues, held in New York from 13 to 24 May 2002 and from 12 to 23 May 2003;

38. *Stresses* the need to ensure adequate financial and human resources, including through the regular budget of the United Nations, for the Office of the United Nations High Commissioner for Human Rights to carry out its responsibilities efficiently in the implementation of the Durban Declaration and Programme of Action;

39. *Encourages* improvements in the current efforts of the Anti-Discrimination Unit of the Office of the High Commissioner in providing strong leadership and greater support to the mechanisms created by the Commission on Human Rights to follow up the implementation of the Durban Declaration and Programme of Action;

IV

Implementation of the Programme of Action for the Third Decade to Combat Racism and Racial Discrimination and coordination of activities

40. *Notes with great concern* that, despite the many efforts of the international community, the objectives of the Programme of Action for the Third Decade to Combat Racism and Racial Discrimination have largely not been achieved, welcomes, therefore, the adoption of the Durban Declaration and Programme of Action, and calls for its full implementation at the national, regional and international levels;

41. *Decides*, after considering the report of the Secretary-General on the extent of the implementation of the Programme of Action for the Third Decade, to close the Third Decade;

42. *Decides also*, as part of the activities to combat racism, racial discrimination, xenophobia and related intolerance, to place emphasis on the concrete implementation of the Durban Declaration and Programme of Action as a solid foundation for a broad-based consensus for further actions and initiatives towards the total elimination of the scourge of racism;

V

Special Rapporteur of the Commission on Human Rights on contemporary forms of racism, racial discrimination, xenophobia and related intolerance and follow-up to his visits

43. *Expresses its full support and appreciation* for the work of the Special Rapporteur of the Commission on Human Rights on contemporary forms of racism, racial discrimination, xenophobia and related intolerance, and encourages its continuation;

44. *Reiterates its call* to all Member States, intergovernmental organizations, relevant organizations of the United Nations and non-governmental organizations to cooperate fully with the Special Rapporteur;

45. *Requests* the Special Rapporteur to continue his exchange of views with Member States and relevant mechanisms and treaty bodies within the United Nations system in order to enhance further their effectiveness and mutual cooperation;

46. *Recognizes with deep concern* the increase in anti-Semitism, Christianophobia and Islamophobia in various parts of the world, as well as the emergence of racial and violent movements based on racism and discriminatory ideas directed against Arab, Christian, Jewish and Muslim communities, communities of people of African descent, communities of people of Asian descent and other communities;

47. *Requests* the Special Rapporteur to collect information from all concerned, to respond effectively to reliable information that becomes available to him, to follow up on communications and country visits and to seek the views and comments of Governments and reflect them, as appropriate, in his reports;

48. *Calls upon* States to cooperate with the Special Rapporteur and to give serious consideration to his requests to visit their countries so as to enable him to fulfil his mandate fully and effectively;

49. *Encourages* closer collaboration between the Special Rapporteur and the Office of the United Nations High Commissioner for Human Rights, in particular the Anti-Discrimination Unit;

50. *Urges* the United Nations High Commissioner for Human Rights to provide States, at their request, with advisory services and technical assistance to enable them to implement fully the recommendations of the Special Rapporteur;

51. *Requests* the Secretary-General to provide the Special Rapporteur with all the necessary human and financial assistance to carry out his mandate efficiently, effectively and expeditiously and to enable him to submit an interim report to the General Assembly at its fifty-ninth session;

52. *Takes note with appreciation* of the recommendations contained in the interim report of the Special Rapporteur, and encourages the continuation of his work;

53. *Urges* Member States to consider implementing the recommendations contained in the reports of the Special Rapporteur, and invites other relevant stakeholders to implement those recommendations;

54. *Calls upon* the Special Rapporteur, in carrying out his mandate, to pay special attention to the increasing frequency of incidents of racism at various sporting events;

VI
General

55. *Requests* the Secretary-General to submit a report on the implementation of the present resolution to the General Assembly at its fifty-ninth session;

56. *Decides* to remain seized of this important matter at its fifty-ninth session under the item entitled "Elimination of racism and racial discrimination".

RECORDED VOTE ON RESOLUTION 58/160:

In favour: Afghanistan, Albania, Algeria, Andorra, Angola, Antigua and Barbuda, Argentina, Armenia, Austria, Azerbaijan, Bahamas, Bahrain, Bangladesh, Barbados, Belarus, Belgium, Belize, Benin, Bhutan, Bolivia, Bosnia and Herzegovina, Botswana, Brazil, Brunei Darussalam, Bulgaria, Burkina Faso, Cambodia, Cameroon, Cape Verde, Central African Republic, Chile, China, Colombia, Comoros, Congo, Costa Rica, Cote d'Ivoire, Croatia, Cuba, Cyprus, Czech Republic, Democratic People's Republic of Korea, Democratic Republic of the Congo, Denmark, Djibouti, Dominica, Dominican Republic, Ecuador, Egypt, El Salvador, Eritrea, Estonia, Ethiopia, Fiji, Finland, France, Gabon, Gambia, Georgia, Germany, Ghana, Greece, Grenada, Guatemala, Guinea, Guinea-Bissau, Guyana, Haiti, Honduras, Hungary, Iceland, India, Indonesia, Iran, Ireland, Italy, Jamaica, Japan, Jordan, Kazakhstan, Kenya, Kuwait, Kyrgyzstan, Lao People's Democratic Republic, Latvia, Lebanon, Lesotho, Libyan Arab Jamahiriya, Liechtenstein, Lithuania, Luxembourg, Madagascar, Malawi, Malaysia, Maldives, Mali, Malta, Marshall Islands, Mauritania, Mauritius, Mexico, Micronesia, Monaco, Mongolia, Morocco, Mozambique, Myanmar, Namibia, Nauru, Nepal, Netherlands, New Zealand, Nicaragua, Niger, Nigeria, Norway, Oman, Pakistan, Panama, Papua New Guinea, Paraguay, Peru, Philippines, Poland, Portugal, Qatar, Republic of Korea, Republic of Moldova, Romania, Russian Federation, Rwanda, Saint Lucia, Saint Vincent and the Grenadines, Samoa, San Marino, Saudi Arabia, Senegal, Serbia and Montenegro, Seychelles, Sierra Leone, Singapore, Slovakia, Slovenia, Solomon Islands, South Africa, Spain, Sri Lanka, Sudan, Suriname, Sweden, Switzerland, Syrian Arab Republic, Tajikistan, Thailand, The former Yugoslav Republic of Macedonia, Timor-Leste, Togo, Tonga, Trinidad and Tobago, Tunisia, Turkey, Turkmenistan, Tuvalu, Uganda, Ukraine, United Arab Emirates, United Kingdom, United Republic of Tanzania, Uruguay, Venezuela, Viet Nam, Yemen, Zambia, Zimbabwe.

Against: Israel, United States.

Abstaining: Australia, Canada.

The Third Committee adopted paragraph 31 by a recorded vote of 105 to 40, with 8 abstentions. The Assembly retained the paragraph by a recorded vote of 115 to 44, with 13 abstentions.

Contemporary forms of racism

Reports of Special Rapporteur. In January [E/CN.4/2003/24], the Special Rapporteur on contemporary forms of racism, racial discrimination, xenophobia and related intolerance, Doudou Diène (Senegal), highlighted activities he had undertaken since his appointment in 2002 [YUN 2002, p. 670], with a view to starting a process of consensus-building in efforts to combat racism. He described serious allegations of racial discrimination and xenophobia that came to his attention in Côte d'Ivoire and Guyana, racial discrimination against the Roma/Gypsies/Sinti/Travellers, as well as measures taken by European States to deal with the problem, and ongoing manifestations of anti-Semitism. The Special Rapporteur examined allegations of discrimination in Germany, Greece, Guyana, the Russian Federation, Spain and the United Kingdom, of which summaries, communicated to the Governments concerned, and the replies thereto, were annexed to the report. To counter the resurgence of racial discrimination, in both its conventional and insidious new forms, the Special Rapporteur proposed, in the light of DDPA, a dual strategy emphasizing the legal and political issue of ratifying and implementing relevant international instruments, and the intellectual and ethical question of promoting better understanding of the culture of discrimination. He recommended a series of actions to the Commission.

In response to a 2002 Commission request [YUN 2002, p. 682], the Special Rapporteur submitted a January preliminary report [E/CN.4/2003/23], which examined the situation of Muslim and Arab peoples in various parts of the world, with special reference to physical assaults and attacks against their places of worship, cultural centres, businesses and properties in the aftermath of the 2001 terrorist attacks in the United States [YUN 2001, p. 60]. The Special Rapporteur noted that in the aftermath of the attacks, despite efforts by public institutions and political figures to forestall a drift towards xenophobia and racism, displays of intolerance towards people originating from the Near East, the Middle East and South-East Asia became more frequent. He warned that there was a serious risk that the situation of Muslims and Arabs since the attacks might lead to a long-term and far-reaching disruption of the international order if not dealt with urgently, in accordance with international law. He recommended that the Commission accord high priority to ways of dealing with terrorism; it should, in that context, pursue a legal strategy to implement relevant international instruments and an intellectual strategy to root out the culture and ideology of discrimination, xenophobia and intolerance. For that purpose, the Commission should promote the idea of combating racism through DDPA implementation, encourage States to take preventive measures to guarantee religious and cultural rights, keep the matter under review and request the Special Rapporteur to prepare in 2004 a more complete report on the topic.

The United States, in a 21 March response [E/CN.4/2003/G/48] to the Special Rapporteur's report, stated that, following the 2001 terrorist attacks [YUN 2001, p. 60], there was an increase in hate crimes against Arabs, Muslims and Sikhs (mistaken for Muslims) residing in the United States. The rate of those offences dropped within a few weeks until mid-January 2002, when it almost returned to the rate prevailing before the attacks. The United States highlighted its commitment to non-discrimination and efforts to combat biased attacks against Muslims and Arabs.

The Special Rapporteur visited Guyana and Trinidad and Tobago (14-25 July) [E/CN.4/2004/18/Add.1], where he undertook a comparative study of race relations, given the countries' similar historical heritage of slavery and colonialism and demographic composition. In Guyana, he noted that, although the country's Constitution outlawed discrimination, ethnic polarization had festered among Guyanese of African, Amerindian and Indian descent, who accounted for 35 per cent, 7 per cent and 49 per cent, respectively, of Guyana's estimated population of 765,000. The division was mostly reflected in the ethnic composition of the political parties and in the structure of State mechanisms, particularly the public sector, army and police, with severe economic, social and cultural consequences. The Special Rapporteur said the Guyanese authorities had informed him of their determination to break with the legacy of ethnic polarization through political reforms; the President and the leader of the opposition had signed a joint communiqué pledging to ensure democracy, peace and development in Guyana, and had signed a follow-up agreement. The Special Rapporteur urged the implementation of the reforms contained in the joint communiqué and follow-up initiatives. Dialogue and consensus in the democratic process should include the Amerindian community, which could help end the Afro- and Indo-Guyanese face-off that was a major cause of polarization, and initiation of a new order of democratic pluralism would end the relative neglect of the Amerindians.

In Trinidad and Tobago, the Special Rapporteur found a similar multi-ethnic population and society divided by conflict among communities and racial discrimination, but which faced less ethnic polarization compared to Guyana. Racial animosity, which broke out in the heat of political campaigns, did not take on alarming proportions as in Guyana because the tension was mostly tempered by the fact that the two dominant communities—the Indo-Trinidadians and Afro-Trinidadians—were not completely homogeneous. The periodic exploitation of race in political campaigns was offset by the people's strong desire to live together. Thus, Trinidad and Tobago enjoyed a distinct multicultural vitality in individual contacts and religious practices, and the political class, regardless of party, bore the responsibility to use that multicultural potential to achieve democratic, social and economic ends, said the Special Rapporteur. He proposed measures to facilitate progress towards a political commitment and democratic consensus, and made proposals to combat discrimination.

Commission action. On 14 April [res. 2003/4], by a recorded vote of 32 to 14, with 7 abstentions, the Commission requested the Special Rapporteur to examine the situation of Muslim and Arab peoples in various parts of the world in the aftermath of the events of 11 September 2001 and to submit a progress report in 2004. By a recorded vote of 38 to 1, with 13 abstentions, the Commission, on 23 April [res. 2003/30], welcoming the Special Rapporteur's reports, urged Member States to consider implementing his recommendations. The Special Rapporteur was requested to continue his exchange of views with Member States, relevant mechanisms and UN system treaty bodies. The Secretary-General was requested to assist him and to enable him to submit an interim report to the General Assembly at its fifty-eighth (2003) session.

Further reports of Special Rapporteur. Pursuant to General Assembly resolution 57/195 [YUN 2002, p. 662], the Secretary-General, in August [A/58/313], transmitted an interim report of the Special Rapporteur on the fight against racism, racial discrimination, xenophobia and related intolerance. The report, which summarized the Special Rapporteur's activities during the year, drew the Assembly's attention to the persistence of racist propaganda on the Internet, the upsurge of racism in sports and anti-Semitism and Islamophobia. The Special Rapporteur described action taken or planned by Governments and other entities, and recommended that the Assembly alert Member States to the need for legislative and judicial action, as well as measures in the areas of information and education, to ensure that the legitimate struggle against terrorism did not breed new forms of discrimination.

At the invitation of the Government, the Special Rapporteur visited Canada (15-26 September) [E/CN.4/2004/18/Add.2], where an estimated population of 31 million comprised over 200 ethnic groups. The Special Rapporteur found that, although the country supported its diversity with a multifaceted, multicultural policy, democratic institutions, human rights protection and numerous federal and provincial programmes, racial discrimination persisted. The main victims were aboriginal peoples and those of African and Caribbean descent, who numbered 1.3 million and 662,200, respectively. Members of both communities reportedly suffered discrimination with regard to their rights to land and ancestral homes, and to education, housing and health facilities, as well as in the criminal justice system. There were also reports of discrimination against the Chinese, Jewish, Muslim and Arab communities. The Special Rapporteur recommended that the Government enhance credibility and trust in its commitment to combat racism and discrimination by recognizing that such practices persisted despite its efforts to counter them. He proposed a national programme structured around a legal and intellectual strategy, based on DDPA, to fight racial discrimination.

In Colombia (27 September–11 October) [E/CN.4/2004/18/Add.3], the Special Rapporteur evaluated, against the background of the 1996 visit of his predecessor [YUN 1997, p. 631], progress achieved in improving the situation of Afro-Colombian and indigenous communities, who accounted for 27 per cent (12 million) and 2 per cent (875,516), respectively, of the country's estimated total population of 44 million. He also examined the situation of the Roma, who also suffered marked discrimination. Despite the adoption of laws and the establishment of promising institutions, the situation of indigenous, Afro-Colombian and Roma communities remained precarious. The Special Rapporteur, noting that the proposal of his predecessor that the Government adopt a general act on racism and racial discrimination had not been implemented, recommended adopting such an act prohibiting racial discrimination and establishing a national commission towards that end, with a view to promoting democratic and interactive multiculturalism. Other recommendations emphasized the importance of a lasting solution to the conflict in Colombia and respect for human rights (see p. 814); a national programme to combat racism, based on DDPA; ending the precarious economic and social situation of the vulnerable communities; addressing the situation of displaced persons; an intellectual and ethical strategy for eradicating discriminatory cultures and attitudes; and improving the status of parts of the indigenous population living on the island of San Andrés.

(For the Assembly's action regarding the Special Rapporteur, see p. 699.)

Racism and democracy

Report of High Commissioner. In response to a 2002 Commission request [YUN 2002, p. 672], the High Commissioner, in a January report and later addendum [E/CN.4/2003/62 & Add.1], summarized replies received from Governments, UN agencies, regional organizations and national institutions to OHCHR's request for information on the incompatibility between democracy and racism, especially regarding the issue of political parties with racist platforms and actions to counter such trends.

Commission action. On 23 April [res. 2003/41], the Commission invited its mechanisms and treaty bodies, particularly the Special Rapporteur on contemporary forms of racism, to pay attention to human rights violations stemming from racism and xenophobia. The Special Rapporteur was invited to update the April 2001 study on political platforms which promoted or incited racial discrimination [YUN 2001, p. 617] and to report in 2004.

GENERAL ASSEMBLY ACTION

On 22 December [meeting 77], the General Assembly, on the recommendation of the Third Committee [A/58/506], adopted **resolution 58/159** without vote [agenda item 115].

The incompatibility between democracy and racism

The General Assembly,

Guided by the Universal Declaration of Human Rights, the Charter of the United Nations, the International Covenants on Human Rights and the International Convention on the Elimination of All Forms of Racial Discrimination,

Recalling the commitment reached in the Vienna Declaration and Programme of Action, adopted by the World Conference on Human Rights on 25 June 1993, concerning the elimination of racism, racial discrimination, xenophobia and related intolerance,

Recalling also the Durban Declaration and Programme of Action, adopted by the World Conference against Racism, Racial Discrimination, Xenophobia and Related Intolerance on 8 September 2001,

Taking note of Commission on Human Rights resolution 2003/41 of 23 April 2003,

Mindful of the responsibility of Governments to ensure such equality as is established in the relevant international and regional human rights instruments, inter alia, the Universal Declaration of Human Rights, the International Covenants on Human Rights and the International Convention on the Elimination of All Forms of Racial Discrimination,

Reaffirming that acts of racial violence and discrimination do not constitute legitimate expressions of opinion, but rather are offences,

Alarmed by the rise of racism, racial discrimination, xenophobia and related intolerance in political circles, in the sphere of public opinion and in society at large,

Recognizing the fundamental role of education and other active policies in the promotion of tolerance and respect for others and in the construction of pluralistic and inclusive societies,

1. *Condemns* political platforms and organizations based on racism, xenophobia or doctrines of racial superiority and related discrimination, as well as legislation and practices based on racism, racial discrimination, xenophobia and related intolerance as incompatible with democracy and transparent and accountable governance;

2. *Affirms* that racism, racial discrimination, xenophobia and related intolerance condoned by governmental policies violate human rights and may endanger friendly relations among peoples, cooperation among nations, international peace and security and the harmony of persons living side by side within one and the same State;

3. *Affirms also* that any form of impunity condoned by public authorities for crimes motivated by racist and xenophobic attitudes plays a role in weakening the rule of law and democracy and tends to encourage the recurrence of such acts;

4. *Condemns* the persistence and resurgence of neo-Nazism, neo-fascism and violent nationalist ideologies based on racial or national prejudice, and states that these phenomena can never be justified in any instance or in any circumstances;

5. *Recognizes with deep concern* the increase in anti-Semitism and Islamophobia in various parts of the world, as well as the emergence of racial and violent movements based on racism and discriminatory ideas against Arab, Jewish and Muslim communities, as well as communities of people of African descent, communities of people of Asian descent and other communities;

6. *Emphasizes* that the elimination of all forms of discrimination, especially gender, ethnic and racial discrimination, as well as diverse forms of intolerance, the promotion and protection of the human rights of persons of indigenous origin and members of indigenous communities and migrants, and respect for ethnic, cultural and religious diversity contribute to strengthening and promoting democracy and political participation;

7. *Urges* States to reinforce their commitment to promote tolerance and human rights and to fight against racism, racial discrimination, xenophobia and related intolerance as a way to strengthen democracy, the rule of law and transparent and accountable governance, and in that regard recommends measures such as introducing or reinforcing human rights education in schools and in institutions of higher education;

8. *Also urges* States to ensure that their political and legal systems reflect the multicultural diversity within their societies and, where necessary, to improve democratic institutions so that they are more fully participatory and avoid marginalization and exclusion of, and discrimination against, specific sectors of society;

9. *Underlines* the key role that political leaders and political parties can and ought to play in strengthening and promoting democracy by combating racism, racial discrimination, xenophobia and related intolerance, and encourages political parties to take concrete steps to promote solidarity, tolerance and respect, inter alia, by developing voluntary codes of conduct, including internal disciplinary measures for violations thereof, so their members refrain from public statements and actions that encourage or incite racism, racial discrimination, xenophobia and related intolerance;

10. *Invites* the Inter-Parliamentary Union and other relevant inter-parliamentary organizations to encourage debate in, and action by, parliaments on various measures, including laws and policies, to combat racism, racial discrimination, xenophobia and related intolerance;

11. *Invites* the mechanisms of the Commission on Human Rights and the treaty bodies to continue to pay particular attention to violations of human rights stemming from the rise of racism and xenophobia in political circles and in society at large, with due consideration to a gender perspective, especially as regards their incompatibility with democracy;

12. *Takes note* of the report of the United Nations High Commissioner for Human Rights on the incompatibility between democracy and racism;

13. *Also takes note* of the outcome of the expert seminar on the interdependence between democracy and human rights, held by the Office of the United Nations High Commissioner for Human Rights at Geneva on 25 and 26 November 2002;

14. *Invites* the Special Rapporteur of the Commission on Human Rights on contemporary forms of racism, racial discrimination, xenophobia and related intolerance to submit to the General Assembly the study on the issue of political platforms that promote or incite racial discrimination, as requested by the Commission in its resolution 2003/41, and updated and expanded as appropriate;

15. *Decides* to continue consideration of the matter at its fifty-ninth session under the item entitled "Elimination of racism and racial discrimination".

Protection of migrants

Report of Special Rapporteur. The Special Rapporteur on the human rights of migrants, Gabriela Rodríguez Pizarro (Costa Rica), in a report covering her 2002 activities [E/CN.4/2003/85], analysed the situation of migrants deprived of their liberty, based on responses to a questionnaire she had circulated and on her personal observations. She reviewed fundamental international human rights obligations in the context of national legislation and practices, and discussed migration management and conditions of detention. The Special Rapporteur concluded that migrants were particularly vulnerable to the deprivation of liberty, noting a tendency among States to criminalize violations of immigration regulations and to punish migrants severely to discourage irregular migration. Victims of trafficking and smuggling were criminalized, detained and deported for offences committed as inevitable consequences of the violations they themselves had suffered. Often, there were no specific provisions for the detention of children and other vulnerable groups, resulting in their detention in conditions that violated their basic human rights. The Special Rapporteur recommended that infractions of immigration laws not be considered criminal offences under national legislation, and that Governments consider abolishing administrative detention and take other measures to ensure respect for the human rights of migrants deprived of their liberty.

An addendum to the report [E/CN.4/2003/85/Add.1 & Corr.1] summarized communications the Special Rapporteur had sent to 26 Governments and responses thereto, regarding individual cases of alleged violations of migrants' human rights and general situations concerning their rights in specific countries.

Commission action. On 23 April [res. 2003/46], the Commission asked the Special Rapporteur to report to the General Assembly in 2003 and to the Commission in 2004. The Secretary-General was asked to assist her.

Report of Secretary-General. Pursuant to General Assembly resolution 57/218 [YUN 2002, p. 674], the Secretary-General, in a July report [A/58/121], summarized information received from 11 States on legal provisions, programmes, campaigns and policies they had established to protect migrants. The Secretary-General was encouraged by the increasing bilateral and regional dialogues, and cooperation between the United Nations and migration organizations. He welcomed the 1 July entry into force of the 1990 International Convention on the Protection of the Rights of All Migrant Workers and Members of Their Families, adopted in Assembly resolution 45/158 [YUN 1990, p. 594] (see p. 676). Member States that had not done so were urged to adhere to the Convention, to also consider ratifying the 2000 United Nations Convention against Transnational Organized Crime and the Protocols thereto on smuggling and trafficking in persons, adopted in Assembly resolution 55/25 [YUN 2000, p. 1048], and to include aspects relating to migrants in national plans of action towards DDPA implementation.

On 22 December, the Assembly took note of the Secretary-General's report (**decision 58/538**).

Further reports of Special Rapporteur. In response to General Assembly resolution 57/218 [YUN 2002, p. 674] and to Commission resolution 2003/46 (see p. 706), the Secretary-General, in August [A/58/275], transmitted a report of the Special Rapporteur, which described her activities and the situation of migrants' human rights. The Special Rapporteur observed that the strengthening of security policies and the tendency to consider migration a State security issue threatened migrants' rights. Rather than consider migration only as a national security matter, the Special Rapporteur recommended that the ministries of foreign affairs, health, education, social welfare and labour, as well as civil society, be involved in developing related national policies. Increased international cooperation and dialogue for the development of human rights–informed migration policies and comprehensive, coordinated and harmonized systems of migration management were necessary to combat irregular migration, smuggling, trafficking and violations of migrants' human rights. Efforts should be made to develop guidelines and tools to assess migration policies in the framework of existing international human rights norms.

On 22 December, the Assembly took note of the Special Rapporteur's report (**decision 58/538**).

At the invitation of the Government, the Special Rapporteur visited Spain (15-27 September) [E/CN.4/2004/76/Add.2], where she highlighted Spain's transformation, in a period of two decades, from a country of origin of migrants to one of transit and destination. The Special Rapporteur noted that, as at 30 June, migrants with a residence permit in the country numbered 1.4 million, of whom 35 per cent were of European origin, 30 per cent from Latin America and 27 per cent from Africa, of whom the great majority were Moroccans. She noted with concern a large number of illegal migrants totalling some 600,000, owing mainly to clandestine entry, facilitated by criminal networks and aggravated by difficulties in carrying out expulsions, as well as procedural delays. She observed that, although Spain was making efforts to adapt its legislation and policy aimed at curbing illegal migration and to comply with commitments made within the European Union (EU), irregular migration had not decreased, as migrants resorted to far more dangerous means of entering Spain through the criminal networks. The Special Rapporteur recommended measures to the Government to ensure the effective protection of immigrants' human rights.

In Morocco (19-31 October) [E/CN.4/2004/76/Add.3], the Special Rapporteur examined migration from the legislative, institutional/political and operational perspectives, and described migrants' vulnerabilities and the circumstances that exposed them to risks and abuse. Noting that over 2.5 million Moroccans lived overseas, of whom 85 per cent were in Europe, the Special Rapporteur observed that the phenomenon had been encouraged by the demand for labour abroad and the desire for family reunification or the forming of new families. An estimated 1 million Moroccans were living illegally abroad. The country had also become a country of transit for significant migration flows from sub-Saharan African countries to Europe. While expressing satisfaction with the Government's efforts to protect the rights of its nationals abroad, the Special Rapporteur was concerned about the situation regarding the rights of Moroccan irregular migrants and about conditions for sub-Saharans in Morocco. In her recommendations, the Special Rapporteur emphasized the need to manage migration flows within the framework of socio-economic development and encouraged the EU to increase its contribution in that regard, to continue its dialogue with Morocco and to base their partnership on cooperation strategies aimed at combating illegal migration through technical assistance and joint development programmes.

Communications. In January [E/CN.4/2003/G/44] and March [E/CN.4/2003/G/55], Mexico presented its comments on issues raised in the Special Rapporteur's report on her visits to the common border between Mexico and the United

States and to Mexico itself, respectively [YUN 2002, p. 673].

GENERAL ASSEMBLY ACTION

On 22 December [meeting 77], the General Assembly, on the recommendation of the Third Committee [A/58/508/Add.2], adopted **resolution 58/190** without vote [agenda item 117 (b)].

Protection of migrants

The General Assembly,

Recalling its resolution 57/218 of 18 December 2002,

Reaffirming that the Universal Declaration of Human Rights proclaims that all human beings are born free and equal in dignity and rights and that everyone is entitled to all the rights and freedoms set out therein, without distinction of any kind, in particular as to race, colour or national origin,

Reaffirming also the provisions concerning migrants adopted by the World Conference on Human Rights, the International Conference on Population and Development, the World Summit for Social Development and the Fourth World Conference on Women,

Welcoming the provisions on the human rights of migrants contained in the Durban Declaration and Programme of Action, adopted by the World Conference against Racism, Racial Discrimination, Xenophobia and Related Intolerance on 8 September 2001, and expressing its satisfaction at the important recommendations made for the development of international and national strategies for the protection of migrants and for the design of migration policies that fully respect the human rights of migrants,

Recalling its resolution 40/144 of 13 December 1985, by which it approved the Declaration on the Human Rights of Individuals Who are not Nationals of the Country in which They Live,

Recognizing the positive contributions that migrants frequently make, including through their eventual integration into their host society,

Bearing in mind the situation of vulnerability in which migrants and their families frequently find themselves, owing, inter alia, to their absence from their States of origin and to the difficulties they encounter because of differences of language, custom and culture, as well as the economic and social difficulties and obstacles to the return to their States of origin of migrants who are non-documented or in an irregular situation,

Bearing in mind also the need for a focused and consistent approach towards migrants as a specific vulnerable group, in particular migrant women and children,

Deeply concerned about the manifestations of violence, racism, xenophobia and other forms of discrimination and inhuman and degrading treatment against migrants, especially women and children, in different parts of the world,

Underlining the importance of the creation of conditions that foster greater harmony between migrants and the rest of the society of the States in which they reside, with the aim of eliminating the growing manifestations of racism and xenophobia perpetrated in segments of many societies by individuals or groups against migrants,

Taking note of Advisory Opinion OC-16/99, issued by the Inter-American Court of Human Rights on 1 October 1999, on The Right to Information on Consular Assistance in the Framework of the Guarantees of the Due Process of Law, in the case of foreign nationals detained by the authorities of a receiving State,

Taking note also of Advisory Opinion OC-18/03, issued by the Inter-American Court of Human Rights on 17 September 2003, on the juridical situation and rights of undocumented migrants,

Encouraged by the increasing interest of the international community in the effective and full protection of the human rights of all migrants, and underlining the need to make further efforts to ensure respect for the human rights and fundamental freedoms of all migrants,

Taking note of the decision of the International Labour Organization to have a general discussion on migrant workers, based on an integrated approach, at the International Labour Conference to be held in Geneva in June 2004,

1. *Welcomes* the renewed commitment made in the United Nations Millennium Declaration to take measures to ensure respect for and protection of the human rights of migrants, migrant workers and their families, to eliminate the increasing acts of racism and xenophobia in many societies and to promote greater harmony and tolerance in all societies;

2. *Requests* all Member States, in conformity with their respective constitutional systems, effectively to promote and protect the human rights of all migrants, in conformity with the Universal Declaration of Human Rights and the international instruments to which they are party, which may include the International Covenants on Human Rights, the Convention against Torture and Other Cruel, Inhuman or Degrading Treatment or Punishment, the International Convention on the Elimination of All Forms of Racial Discrimination, the International Convention on the Protection of the Rights of All Migrant Workers and Members of Their Families, the Convention on the Elimination of All Forms of Discrimination against Women, the Convention on the Rights of the Child and other applicable international human rights instruments;

3. *Calls upon* States to promote and protect fully the human rights of migrants, as contained in the Durban Declaration and Programme of Action;

4. *Acknowledges with satisfaction* the entry into force of the International Convention on the Protection of the Rights of All Migrant Workers and Members of Their Families, and the forthcoming entry into force of the Protocol to Prevent, Suppress and Punish Trafficking in Persons, Especially Women and Children, supplementing the United Nations Convention against Transnational Organized Crime, and of the Protocol against the Smuggling of Migrants by Land, Sea and Air, supplementing the United Nations Convention against Transnational Organized Crime;

5. *Strongly condemns* the manifestations and acts of racism, racial discrimination, xenophobia and related intolerance against migrants and the stereotypes often applied to them, and urges States to apply the existing laws when xenophobic or intolerant acts or manifestations or expressions against migrants occur, in order to

eradicate impunity for those who commit xenophobic and racist acts;

6. *Strongly condemns also* all forms of racial discrimination and xenophobia with regard to access to employment, vocational training, housing, schooling, health services and social services, as well as services intended for use by the public, and welcomes the active role played by governmental and non-governmental organizations in combating racism and assisting individual victims of racist acts, including migrant victims;

7. *Requests* all States, in conformity with national legislation and applicable international legal instruments to which they are party, firmly to prosecute violations of labour law with regard to the conditions of work of migrant workers, including those related to, inter alia, their remuneration and the conditions of health and safety at work;

8. *Calls upon* all States to consider reviewing and, where necessary, revising immigration policies, with a view to eliminating all practices which victimize migrants and their families, and to provide specialized training for policy-making, law enforcement, immigration and other concerned government officials, including in cooperation with non-governmental organizations and civil society, thus underlining the importance of effective action to create conditions that foster greater harmony and tolerance within societies;

9. *Reiterates* the need for all States parties to protect fully the universally recognized human rights of migrants, especially women and children, regardless of their legal status, and to treat them humanely, in particular with regard to assistance and protection;

10. *Reaffirms emphatically* the duty of States parties to the Vienna Convention on Consular Relations of 1963 to ensure full respect for and observance of the Convention, in particular with regard to the right of foreign nationals, regardless of their immigration status, to communicate with a consular official of their own State in the case of detention, and the obligation of the State in whose territory the detention occurs to inform the foreign national of that right;

11. *Reaffirms* the responsibility of Governments to safeguard and protect the rights of migrants against illegal or violent acts, in particular acts of racial discrimination and crimes perpetrated with racist or xenophobic motivation by individuals or groups, and urges them to reinforce measures in this regard;

12. *Urges* all States to adopt effective measures to put an end to the arbitrary arrest and detention of migrants, including by individuals or groups;

13. *Encourages* Member States that have not yet done so to enact domestic criminal legislation to combat the international trafficking of migrants, which should take into account, in particular, trafficking that endangers the lives of migrants or includes different forms of servitude or exploitation, such as any form of debt bondage or sexual or labour exploitation, and to strengthen international cooperation to combat such trafficking;

14. *Calls upon* States, when enacting national security legislation measures, to observe national legislation and applicable international legal instruments to which they are party, in order to respect the human rights of migrants;

15. *Encourages* States to consider participating in international and regional dialogues on migration that include countries of origin and destination, as well as countries of transit, and invites them to consider negotiating bilateral and regional agreements on migrant workers within the framework of applicable human rights law and designing and implementing programmes with States of other regions to protect the rights of migrants;

16. *Encourages* all Governments to remove obstacles that may prevent the safe, unrestricted and expeditious transfer of earnings, assets and pensions of migrants to their country of origin or to any other countries, in conformity with applicable legislation, and to consider, as appropriate, measures to solve other problems that may impede such transfers;

17. *Welcomes* immigration programmes, adopted by some countries, that allow migrants to integrate fully into the host countries, facilitate family reunification and promote a harmonious and tolerant environment, and encourages States to consider the possibility of adopting these types of programmes;

18. *Calls upon* all States to protect the human rights of migrant children, in particular unaccompanied migrant children, ensuring that the best interests of the children and the importance of reuniting them with their parents, when possible and appropriate, are the paramount consideration, and encourages the relevant United Nations bodies, within the framework of their respective mandates, to pay special attention to the conditions of migrant children in all States and, where necessary, to put forward recommendations for strengthening their protection;

19. *Requests* States to adopt concrete measures to prevent the violation of the human rights of migrants while in transit, including in ports and airports and at borders and migration checkpoints, to train public officials who work in those facilities and in border areas to treat migrants and their families respectfully and in accordance with the law, and to prosecute, in conformity with applicable law, any act of violation of the human rights of migrants and their families, such as arbitrary detention, torture and violations of the right to life, including extrajudicial executions, during their transit from their country of origin to the country of destination and vice versa, including their transit through national borders;

20. *Calls upon* States to facilitate family reunification in an expeditious and effective manner, with due regard to applicable laws, as such reunification has a positive effect on the integration of migrants;

21. *Encourages* States of origin to promote and protect the human rights of those families of migrant workers which remain in the countries of origin, paying particular attention to children and adolescents whose parents have emigrated, and encourages international organizations to consider supporting States in this regard;

22. *Encourages* States, in cooperation with non-governmental organizations, to undertake information campaigns aimed at clarifying opportunities, limitations and rights in the event of migration, so as to enable everyone, in particular women, to make informed decisions, and to prevent them from becoming victims of trafficking and utilizing dangerous means of access that put their lives and physical integrity at risk;

23. *Welcomes* the proclamation of 18 December as International Migrants Day and the invitation to Member States and intergovernmental and non-governmental organizations to observe it through, inter alia, the dissemination of information on the human rights and fundamental freedoms of migrants and on their economic, social and cultural contributions to their host and home countries, the sharing of experience and the design of actions to ensure their protection;

24. *Urges* States to consider ratifying, accepting, approving or acceding to the United Nations Convention against Transnational Organized Crime and the Protocols thereto, namely, the Protocol to Prevent, Suppress and Punish Trafficking in Persons, Especially Women and Children and the Protocol against the Smuggling of Migrants by Land, Sea and Air, and to implement fully those instruments;

25. *Takes note* of the interim report of the Special Rapporteur of the Commission on Human Rights on the human rights of migrants, and requests her to continue taking into account the recommendations contained in the Durban Declaration and Programme of Action in the performance of her mandate, tasks and duties;

26. *Requests* all Governments to cooperate fully with the Special Rapporteur in the performance of the tasks and duties mandated, to furnish all information requested and to react promptly to her urgent appeals;

27. *Requests* the Secretary-General to submit to the General Assembly at its fifty-ninth session a report on the implementation of the present resolution under the sub-item entitled "Human rights questions, including alternative approaches for improving the effective enjoyment of human rights and fundamental freedoms", and requests the Special Rapporteur to submit to the Assembly at its fifty-ninth session an interim report on the fulfilment of her mandate.

Other forms of intolerance

Cultural prejudice

Report of High Commissioner (January). In response to a 2002 Commission request to the High Commissioner to consult States, intergovernmental organizations and NGOs on the possibility of appointing a special rapporteur to implement the Commission's 2002 resolution on the promotion of cultural rights [YUN 2002, p. 677], the High Commissioner, in a January report [E/CN.4/2003/51], stated that no new information had been received since the Secretary-General's 2002 report summarizing the views of Governments and the UN system on human rights and cultural diversity [YUN 2002, p. 677].

Commission action. On 22 April [res. 2003/26], the Commission, reaffirming that cultural rights were an integral part of human rights, recognized that States had the responsibility to promote the full enjoyment of cultural rights and to enhance respect for different cultural identities. States, intergovernmental organizations and NGOs were called on to implement the Commission's resolution, and the High Commissioner was asked to consult with them on the possibility of appointing a special rapporteur, whose mandate would be the comprehensive implementation of the resolution, and to report on the results in 2004.

Report of Secretary-General. In response to General Assembly resolution 57/204 [YUN 2002, p. 677], the Secretary-General, in an August report [A/58/309], summarized the views expressed by Member States, UN entities, intergovernmental organizations and NGOs on human rights and cultural diversity.

Report of High Commissioner (December). In response to a 2002 Commission request [YUN 2002, p. 677] and to Commission resolution 2003/26 (see above), the High Commissioner, in a December report with later addendum [E/CN.4/2004/41 & Corr.1 & Add.1], summarized replies received from 11 Governments and two UN system agencies on steps they had taken to promote the full enjoyment of cultural rights.

GENERAL ASSEMBLY ACTION

On 22 December [meeting 77], the General Assembly, on the recommendation of the Third Committee [A/58/508/Add.2], adopted **resolution 58/167** without vote [agenda item 117 (b)].

Human rights and cultural diversity

The General Assembly,

Recalling the Universal Declaration of Human Rights, the International Covenant on Economic, Social and Cultural Rights and the International Covenant on Civil and Political Rights, as well as other pertinent human rights instruments,

Recalling also its resolutions 54/160 of 17 December 1999, 55/91 of 4 December 2000 and 57/204 of 18 December 2002, and recalling further its resolutions 54/113 of 10 December 1999 and 55/23 of 13 November 2000 on the United Nations Year of Dialogue among Civilizations,

Noting that numerous instruments within the United Nations system promote cultural diversity, as well as the conservation and development of culture, in particular the Declaration of the Principles of International Culture Cooperation proclaimed on 4 November 1966 by the General Conference of the United Nations Educational, Scientific and Cultural Organization at its fourteenth session,

Taking note of the report of the Secretary-General,

Welcoming the adoption of the Global Agenda for Dialogue among Civilizations by its resolution 56/6 of 9 November 2001,

Welcoming also the contribution of the World Conference against Racism, Racial Discrimination, Xenophobia and Related Intolerance, held at Durban,

South Africa, from 31 August to 8 September 2001, to the promotion of respect for cultural diversity,

Welcoming further the Universal Declaration on Cultural Diversity of the United Nations Educational, Scientific and Cultural Organization, together with its Action Plan, adopted on 2 November 2001 by the General Conference of the United Nations Educational, Scientific and Cultural Organization at its thirty-first session, in which member States invited the United Nations system and other intergovernmental and non-governmental organizations concerned to cooperate with the United Nations Educational, Scientific and Cultural Organization in the promotion of the principles set forth in the Declaration and its Action Plan with a view to enhancing the synergy of actions in favour of cultural diversity,

Reaffirming that all human rights are universal, indivisible, interdependent and interrelated and that the international community must treat human rights globally in a fair and equal manner, on the same footing and with the same emphasis, and that, while the significance of national and regional particularities and various historical, cultural and religious backgrounds must be borne in mind, it is the duty of States, regardless of their political, economic and cultural systems, to promote and protect all human rights and fundamental freedoms,

Recognizing that cultural diversity and the pursuit of cultural development by all peoples and nations are a source of mutual enrichment for the cultural life of humankind,

Taking into account that a culture of peace actively fosters non-violence and respect for human rights and strengthens solidarity among peoples and nations and dialogue between cultures,

Recognizing that all cultures and civilizations share a common set of universal values,

Recognizing also that the promotion of the rights of indigenous people and their cultures and traditions will contribute to the respect for and observance of cultural diversity among all peoples and nations,

Considering that tolerance of cultural, ethnic, religious and linguistic diversities, as well as dialogue among and within civilizations, is essential for peace, understanding and friendship among individuals and people of different cultures and nations of the world, while manifestations of cultural prejudice, intolerance and xenophobia towards different cultures and religions generate hatred and violence among peoples and nations throughout the world,

Recognizing in each culture a dignity and value that deserve recognition, respect and preservation, and convinced that, in their rich variety and diversity, and in the reciprocal influences that they exert on one another, all cultures form part of the common heritage belonging to all humankind,

Convinced that the promotion of cultural pluralism and tolerance towards and dialogue among various cultures and civilizations would contribute to the efforts of all peoples and nations to enrich their cultures and traditions by engaging in a mutually beneficial exchange of knowledge and intellectual, moral and material achievements,

1. *Affirms* the importance for all peoples and nations to hold, develop and preserve their cultural heritage and traditions in a national and international atmosphere of peace, tolerance and mutual respect;

2. *Welcomes* the adoption of the United Nations Millennium Declaration of 8 September 2000, in which Member States consider, inter alia, that tolerance is one of the fundamental values essential to international relations in the twenty-first century and that it should include the active promotion of a culture of peace and dialogue among civilizations, with human beings respecting one another in all their diversity of belief, culture and language, neither fearing nor repressing differences within and between societies but cherishing them as a precious asset of humanity;

3. *Recognizes* the right of everyone to take part in cultural life and to enjoy the benefits of scientific progress and its applications;

4. *Affirms* that the international community should strive to respond to the challenges and opportunities posed by globalization in a manner that ensures respect for the cultural diversity of all;

5. *Expresses its determination* to prevent and mitigate cultural homogenization in the context of globalization, through increased intercultural exchange guided by the promotion and protection of cultural diversity;

6. *Affirms* that intercultural dialogue essentially enriches the common understanding of human rights and that the benefits to be derived from the encouragement and development of international contacts and cooperation in the cultural fields are important;

7. *Welcomes* the recognition at the World Conference against Racism, Racial Discrimination, Xenophobia and Related Intolerance of the necessity of respecting and maximizing the benefits of diversity within and among all nations in working together to build a harmonious and productive future by putting into practice and promoting values and principles such as justice, equality and non-discrimination, democracy, fairness and friendship, tolerance and respect within and among communities and nations, in particular through public information and educational programmes to raise awareness and understanding of the benefits of cultural diversity, including programmes in which the public authorities work in partnership with international and non-governmental organizations and other sectors of civil society;

8. *Recognizes* that respect for cultural diversity and the cultural rights of all enhances cultural pluralism, contributing to a wider exchange of knowledge and understanding of cultural background, advancing the application and enjoyment of universally accepted human rights throughout the world and fostering stable, friendly relations among peoples and nations worldwide;

9. *Emphasizes* that the promotion of cultural pluralism and tolerance at the national, regional and international levels is important for enhancing respect for cultural rights and cultural diversity;

10. *Also emphasizes* that tolerance and respect for diversity facilitate the universal promotion and protection of human rights, including gender equality and the enjoyment of all human rights by all, and underlines the fact that tolerance and respect for cultural diversity and the universal promotion and protection of human rights are mutually supportive;

11. *Urges* all actors on the international scene to build an international order based on inclusion, jus-

tice, equality and equity, human dignity, mutual understanding and promotion of and respect for cultural diversity and universal human rights, and to reject all doctrines of exclusion based on racism, racial discrimination, xenophobia and related intolerance;

12. *Urges* States to ensure that their political and legal systems reflect the multicultural diversity within their societies and, where necessary, to improve democratic institutions so that they are more fully participatory and avoid marginalization and exclusion of, and discrimination against, specific sectors of society;

13. *Calls upon* States, international organizations and United Nations agencies, and invites civil society, including non-governmental organizations, to recognize and promote respect for cultural diversity for the purpose of advancing the objectives of peace, development and universally accepted human rights;

14. *Requests* the Secretary-General, in the light of the present resolution, to prepare a report on human rights and cultural diversity, taking into account the views of Member States, relevant United Nations agencies and non-governmental organizations, as well as the considerations in the present resolution regarding the recognition and importance of cultural diversity among all peoples and nations in the world, and to submit the report to the General Assembly at its sixtieth session;

15. *Decides* to continue consideration of this question at its sixtieth session under the sub-item entitled "Human rights questions, including alternative approaches for improving the effective enjoyment of human rights and fundamental freedoms".

Discrimination against minorities

Report of Secretary-General (January). In response to a 2002 Commission request [YUN 2002, p. 679], the Secretary-General, in a January report [E/CN.4/2003/82], described activities carried out by the High Commissioner to promote the implementation of the 1992 Declaration on the Rights of Persons Belonging to National or Ethnic, Religious and Linguistic Minorities, adopted by the General Assembly in resolution 47/135 [YUN 1992, p. 722]. The report summarized international and regional approaches to minority protection and OHCHR expertise to assist Governments in situations involving minorities. The views of the Special Rapporteur on freedom of religion or belief regarding religious minorities were presented (see p. 717).

Report of High Commissioner. In response to a 2002 Commission request [YUN 2002, p. 679], a February report of the High Commissioner [E/CN.4/2003/87] analysed information on minority rights presented in the reports of special procedures, human rights treaty bodies and the Working Group on Minorities, particularly regarding conflict prevention. The analysis revealed many problems faced by minorities, which, if unresolved, might lead to tensions and conflicts. Those problems were mostly caused by the non-recognition of elements of minorities' identities, including their language, religion or history. One of the routes to minority-related conflict prevention was to address the legitimate claims of minorities and reduce inequalities between groups.

Commission action. On 23 April [res. 2003/50], the Commission called on States to facilitate the participation of NGO and minority representatives in the Working Group on Minorities (see below) and asked the High Commissioner to seek voluntary contributions in that regard. The High Commissioner was also asked to promote the implementation of the 1992 Declaration in order to improve the cooperation of UN programmes and agencies regarding minority rights, to invite Governments and relevant intergovernmental organizations and NGOs to submit their views on how best to protect minorities' rights, to examine existing mechanisms and to report in 2004. The Secretary-General was asked to assist the Working Group to provide, at the request of Governments, qualified expertise for situations involving minorities, and to report in 2004.

Working Group activities. The five-member Working Group on Minorities, at its ninth session (Geneva, 12-16 May) [E/CN.4/Sub.2/2003/19], reviewed the promotion of the 1992 Declaration, examined possible solutions to problems involving minorities, including the promotion of mutual understanding between and among minorities and Governments, and recommended measures to promote and protect minority rights. The Group also discussed its future role.

The Group had before it working papers, including "Towards a set of regional guidelines or codes of practice on the implementation of the Declaration" [E/CN.4/Sub.2/AC.5/2003/WP.1], a "Statement of principles on minority and group rights in South Asia" [E/CN.4/Sub.2/AC.5/2003/WP.2], the report of the seminar on minority rights: cultural diversity and development, held in Thailand [YUN 2002, p. 679], and "Possible new United Nations mechanisms for the protection and promotion of the rights of minorities" [E/CN.4/Sub.2/AC.5/2003/WP.3]. It considered, among other subjects, specific minority situations, national measures frequently called for by minorities and responses by Governments.

In its decisions and recommendations, the Group addressed ways to strengthen dialogue between minorities and Governments in order to better implement its mandate. It decided to consider in 2004 effective enforcement mechanisms and remedies, and to concentrate on the following themes: the relationship and differences between self-determination and autonomy, on which José Bengoa (Chile) was asked to prepare a paper; minorities and development and an examination of approaches by international development agencies to minority issues, regarding which the Minority Rights Group International (London) was asked to prepare a paper; identifying gaps in the international protection of minorities, with Asbjørn Eide (Norway) asked to prepare a synthesis of the discussion on the issue at the Group's current session, to be submitted to the High Commissioner for possible use in drafting a report to the Commission in 2004; strengthening international standards for protecting minority rights, with Vladimir Kartashkin (Russian Federation) asked to formulate, in cooperation with other Working Group members, suggestions on the possible contents of an additional protocol to the 1966 International Covenant on Civil and Political Rights (see p. 669) and remedies for violations thereof; and the role of national institutions in protecting minority rights, with OHCHR asked to provide information on relevant guidelines and practices of those institutions in relation to minority issues. The Working Group encouraged the holding of regional or subregional seminars and welcomed suggestions that such seminars be held in Central, South and East Asia, in the Americas and in Western and Central Africa, and recommended that they discuss regional codes of conduct or guidelines based on universal norms and international minority rights standards. The Group also recommended cooperation with the Council of Europe in organizing a seminar on the Roma, and that the Subcommission on the Promotion and Protection of Human Rights prepare draft decisions on the establishment of a voluntary fund to support the participation of minority representatives and experts in the Group's meetings and on the proclamation of an international year for minorities, to be followed by a decade, for consideration by the Commission in 2004. The African Commission on Human and Peoples' Rights was invited to provide information to the Group on the mandate and activities of the recently established African Commission Working Group on Indigenous Peoples/Communities. OHCHR was asked to organize training on universal and regional standards and mechanisms in order to strengthen minority representatives' cooperation with human rights procedures; prepare pamphlets for inclusion in the *United Nations Guide for Minorities* on regional conflict-prevention initiatives and development matters; provide for the Group's members to participate in regional human rights meetings, with a view to fostering cooperation with such mechanisms, and to report on progress made; consider ways of ensuring that papers submitted to the Group were made available, including on the UN Offical Document System and web site; and to convene a two-day workshop in 2004 to mark the Group's tenth session and to discuss proposals for strengthening the promotion and protection of minority rights. Further measures were recommended to Governments, international, regional and national development agencies and UN entities.

Progress report. In response to a 2002 Subcommission request [YUN 2002, p. 680], Mr. Eide submitted a June progress report [E/CN.4/Sub.2/2003/21], updating his 1993 study on peaceful and constructive approaches to situations involving minorities [YUN 1993, p. 869]. The report focused on setting the stage for a discussion of guidelines for the application of the 1992 Declaration and, in that context, reviewed the framework for minority protection under international law. It concluded that many minority concerns could be met through the responsible application and protection of universal human rights, and minorities should be protected from discrimination in their enjoyment of the rights set out in the Universal Declaration of Human Rights, adopted by the General Assembly in resolution 217 A (III) [YUN 1948-49, p. 535] (see p. 669).

Report of Secretary-General (August). Pursuant to General Assembly resolution 56/162 [YUN 2001, p. 624], the Secretary-General, in an August report [A/58/255], described expert assistance regarding minority issues made available to Governments, including on dispute prevention and resolution. The report also provided information on cooperation among UN bodies and regional organizations, the participation of NGOs and minorities, particularly from developing countries, in the Working Group on Minorities (see p. 712), and good practices in the areas of education and the effective participation of minorities in decision-making processes. The Secretary-General observed that the protection of minority rights had received increased international attention. OHCHR and the Working Group were pursuing regional approaches to minority issues, strengthening international cooperation to better protect minority rights and enhancing international, regional and national systems of minority protection so as to reduce tensions and prevent conflict. The focus in that regard was the effective participation of minorities in public life and in social and economic development.

Subcommission action. On 13 August [E/CN.4/2004/2 (res. 2003/23)], the Subcommission endorsed the Working Group's recommendations. Welcoming the Group's proposal for a two-day meeting prior to its 2004 session, the Sucbcommission recommended that minority experts, members of national human rights institutions, and representatives of regional mechanisms and of other intergovernmental organizations, such as the United Nations Development Programme and the World Bank, be invited to provide information on their policies concerning minority situations and on the incorporation of such concerns in their country programmes. Mr. Eide was asked to submit in 2004 the final report updating his 1993 study. OHCHR was asked to organize training workshops at the national level on the implementation of minority rights. It was also asked, when inviting Governments to submit their views on the protection of minority rights, to request them to provide the names of experts with a view to facilitating their participation in regional and international meetings, and to detail information about recent cases relating to minority rights. The Office was urged to reflect in its 2004 report to the Commission, the discussions within the Working Group on the possible establishment of a special procedure on minority issues. The Commission was requested to ask OHCHR to seek information from Governments on the national or ethnic, religious and linguistic minorities recognized within their countries, on whether the principle of self-identification was recognized in law or practice and on the measures in place for protecting the identity of minorities, and to transmit that information to the Working Group. The Subcommission recommended the proclamation of an international year for the world's minorities, to be followed by a decade, to advance the implementation of the 1992 Declaration, and the establishment of a voluntary fund to facilitate the participation of minority representatives in the Working Group; it decided to prepare draft decisions on both proposals for the Commission's consideration in 2004.

Also on 13 August [dec. 2003/111], the Subcommission adopted a draft decision requesting the Commission to endorse its recommendation to establish a voluntary fund.

GENERAL ASSEMBLY ACTION

On 22 December [meeting 77], the General Assembly, on the recommendation of the Third Committee [A/58/508/Add.2], adopted **resolution 58/182** without vote [agenda item 117 (b)].

Effective promotion of the Declaration on the Rights of Persons Belonging to National or Ethnic, Religious and Linguistic Minorities

The General Assembly,

Recalling its resolution 47/135 of 18 December 1992, as well as its subsequent resolutions on the Declaration on the Rights of Persons Belonging to National or Ethnic, Religious and Linguistic Minorities,

Considering that the promotion and protection of the rights of persons belonging to national or ethnic, religious and linguistic minorities contributes to political and social stability and peace and enriches the cultural diversity and heritage of society as a whole in the States in which such persons live,

Concerned by the frequency and severity of disputes and conflicts concerning minorities and their often tragic consequences, and concerned also that persons belonging to minorities are particularly vulnerable to displacement,

Recognizing that the effective promotion and protection of the rights of persons belonging to minorities is a fundamental part of the promotion and protection of human rights, and acknowledging that measures in this area can also contribute significantly to conflict prevention,

Emphasizing the role that national institutions can play in early warning for problems regarding minority situations,

Emphasizing also the importance of human rights education as an effective tool to promote an inclusive society and understanding of and tolerance towards and among persons belonging to minorities,

Acknowledging that the United Nations has an important role to play regarding the protection of minorities by, inter alia, taking due account of and giving effect to the Declaration,

Noting that the Working Group on Minorities of the Subcommission on the Promotion and Protection of Human Rights held its eighth and ninth sessions from 27 to 31 May 2002 and 12 to 16 May 2003, respectively,

1. *Takes note* of the report of the Secretary-General;
2. *Recognizes* that respect for human rights and the promotion of understanding and tolerance by Governments as well as between and among minorities are central to the promotion and protection of the rights of persons belonging to minorities;
3. *Reaffirms* the obligation of States to ensure that persons belonging to minorities may exercise fully and effectively all human rights and fundamental freedoms without any discrimination and in full equality before the law, in accordance with the Declaration on the Rights of Persons Belonging to National or Ethnic, Religious and Linguistic Minorities, and as emphasized at the World Conference against Racism, Racial Discrimination, Xenophobia and Related Intolerance, held at Durban, South Africa, from 31 August to 8 September 2001;
4. *Encourages* States, in their follow-up to the World Conference, to include aspects relating to minorities in their national plans of action and, in this context, to take forms of multiple discrimination fully into account;
5. *Urges* States and the international community to promote and protect the rights of persons belonging to national or ethnic, religious and linguistic minorities, as set out in the Declaration, including through the provision of adequate education and the facilitation of their participation in all aspects of the political, economic, social, religious and cultural life of society and in the economic progress and development of their country, and to apply a gender perspective while doing so;
6. *Calls upon* States to give special attention to the promotion and protection of the human rights of children belonging to minorities, taking into account that girls and boys may face different types of risks;

7. *Urges* States to take, as appropriate, all necessary constitutional, legislative, administrative and other measures to promote and give effect to the Declaration, and appeals to States to cooperate bilaterally and multilaterally, in accordance with the Declaration, in order to promote and protect the rights of persons belonging to national or ethnic, religious and linguistic minorities;

8. *Calls upon* States to take all appropriate measures to protect the cultural and religious sites of national or ethnic, religious and linguistic minorities;

9. *Calls upon* the Secretary-General to make available, at the request of Governments concerned, qualified expertise on minority issues, including the prevention and resolution of disputes, to assist in existing or potential situations involving minorities;

10. *Calls upon* the United Nations High Commissioner for Human Rights to promote, within his mandate, the implementation of the Declaration, to continue to engage in a dialogue with Governments for that purpose and to disseminate widely the *United Nations Guide for Minorities*;

11. *Requests* the High Commissioner to continue his efforts to improve the coordination and cooperation among United Nations programmes and agencies on activities related to the promotion and protection of the rights of persons belonging to minorities and to take the work of relevant regional organizations active in the field of human rights into account in his endeavours;

12. *Welcomes* the inter-agency consultation of the High Commissioner with United Nations programmes and agencies on minority issues, and calls upon those programmes and agencies to contribute actively to this process;

13. *Invites* the human rights treaty bodies, when considering reports submitted by States parties, as well as the reports of special representatives, special rapporteurs and working groups of the Commission on Human Rights, to continue to give attention, within their respective mandates, to situations and rights of persons belonging to national or ethnic, religious and linguistic minorities;

14. *Encourages* intergovernmental and non-governmental organizations to continue to contribute to the promotion and protection of the rights of persons belonging to national or ethnic, religious and linguistic minorities;

15. *Calls upon* the Working Group on Minorities of the Subcommission on the Promotion and Protection of Human Rights to implement fully its mandate with the involvement of a wide range of participants, inter alia, by recommending, on the basis of its findings, further measures, as appropriate, for the promotion and protection of the rights of persons belonging to national or ethnic, religious and linguistic minorities;

16. *Invites* the High Commissioner to seek voluntary contributions to facilitate the effective participation, including through training seminars, in the work of the Working Group on Minorities of representatives of non-governmental organizations and persons belonging to minorities, in particular those from developing countries;

17. *Requests* the Secretary-General to report to the General Assembly at its sixtieth session on the implementation of the present resolution and to continue to include examples of good practices in the field of education and of the effective participation of minorities in decision-making processes;

18. *Decides* to continue consideration of this question at its sixtieth session under the item entitled "Human rights questions".

Discrimination based on work and descent

Working paper. In response to a 2002 Subcommission request [YUN 2002, p. 680], Mr. Eide and Yozo Yokota (Japan) submitted, in June, an expanded working paper on discrimination based on work and descent [E/CN.4/Sub.2/2003/24], which supplemented a 2001 working paper [YUN 2001, p. 625]. The current paper identified communities other than those traditionally referred to as "castes" in South Asia, which continued to suffer discrimination based on work and descent. Among the affected communities were endogamous groups in West and North-East Africa, such as the Dime people and the Watta; the Somali *sab* groups; the *akhdam* of Yemen; African and Japanese diaspora communities; and the Roma/Sinti/Travellers in Eastern Europe. The report analysed the main similarities regarding the causes of marginalization affecting the diverse communities, and concluded that discrimination based on work and descent was more widespread than might have been envisaged, and required much closer examination and attention by national Governments and the international human rights system. It recommended that the Subcommission mandate a further working paper on outstanding issues and/or a study for the possible drafting of principles and guidelines for eliminating discrimination based on work or descent; invite UNESCO, the United Nations Research Institute for Social Development and other UN agencies to undertake a more comprehensive review of the phenomenon; and propose the convening of a seminar to provide a basis for drafting the proposed principles and guidelines.

Subcommission action. On 13 August [res. 2003/22], the Subcommission called on States to formulate and implement promptly enhanced policies and action plans to eliminate discrimination based on work and descent. The Subcommission decided to entrust Messrs. Eide and Yokota with the task of preparing, without financial implications, a further working paper for submission in 2004.

Rights of non-citizens

Report of Special Rapporteur. In accordance with a 2000 Subcommission request [YUN 2000, p. 657], the Special Rapporteur on the rights of non-citizens, David Weissbrodt (United States), submitted, in May, his final report on a comprehensive study of the rights of non-citizens [E/CN.4/Sub.2/2003/23]. The report, which built on a 1999 working paper [YUN 1999, p. 611], a 2001 preliminary report [YUN 2001, p. 625] and a 2002 progress report [YUN 2002, p. 680], summarized relevant international law and jurisprudence pertaining to the rights of non-citizens and focused on the narrow exceptions to the rule that States might not discriminate against them. The report also identified some of the problems facing noncitizens. The Special Rapporteur concluded that the continued discriminatory treatment of non-citizens demonstrated the need for clear, comprehensive standards governing their rights, and for States' implementation of the standards and more effective monitoring of compliance. States should pursue universal ratification and implementation of the principal human rights treaties, particularly the International Convention on the Protection of the Rights of All Migrant Workers and Members of Their Families (see p. 676). The Special Rapporteur recommended that the Subcommission continue his mandate. It should authorize the Special Rapporteur to cooperate with the Committee on the Elimination of Racial Discrimination (CERD) in preparing a revised general recommendation on the issue. He added that his reports on the topic should be compiled into a single report, published in all UN official languages and distributed widely.

Addenda to the Special Rapporteur's report, also issued in May, updated international standards and jurisprudence of treaty-monitoring bodies relevant to the rights of non-citizens [E/CN.4/Sub.2/2003/23/Add.1]; updated information on the rights of non-citizens within regional human rights bodies, including the European Court of Human Rights and the Inter-American Commission on Human Rights [E/CN.4/Sub.2/2003/23/Add.2]; presented examples of the human rights problems faced by non-citizens [E/CN.4/Sub.2/2003/23/Add.3]; and summarized comments received from 22 Member States [E/CN.4/Sub.2/2003/23/Add.4] in response to a questionnaire disseminated by the Special Rapporteur, pursuant to a 2002 Commission request [YUN 2002, p. 680].

Subcommission action. On 13 August [res. 2003/21], the Subcommission decided to transmit the Special Rapporteur's final report (see above) to the Commission, Governments, ILO, IOM, the United Nations High Commissioner for Refugees, CERD, other human rights treaty bodies (see p. 667), the International Committee of the Red Cross (ICRC) and relevant UN entities, and asked him to cooperate with CERD on a revised general recommendation on the rights of non-citizens. Cooperation was encouraged among the Commission, Subcommission, human rights treaty bodies, the Special Rapporteur on migrants and other relevant bodies within and outside the UN system in safeguarding the rights of non-citizens and in preparing the studies and working papers authorized by the Subcommission.

Also on 13 August [dec. 2003/110], the Subcommission decided to submit a draft decision to the Commission requesting the Special Rapporteur to compile and update all his reports, addenda and questionnaire replies into a single report, and recommending to the Economic and Social Council a draft decision requesting publication of the consolidated report in all UN official languages and wide distribution.

Regulation of citizenship by successor States

Note by Secretariat. A July note of the Secretariat [E/CN.4/Sub.2/2003/33] informed the Subcommission that Vladimir Kartashkin (Russian Federation) would make an oral presentation on the regulation of citizenship by successor States, in lieu of the working paper requested in a 2002 Subcommission decision [YUN 2002, p. 681].

On 6 August [E/CN.4/Sub.2/2003/SR.11], Mr. Kartashkin, in a statement before the Subcommission, noted that in the light of the adoption by the International Law Commission (ILC) of the final draft articles on the nationality of natural persons in relation to the succession of States [YUN 1999, p. 1230] and of General Assembly resolution 55/153 [YUN 2000, p. 1242], in which the Assembly took note of the draft articles and decided to include the item in the provisional agenda of its fifty-ninth (2004) session, he believed it inappropriate to duplicate the work of ILC and the Assembly by preparing the working paper.

Rights of women married to foreigners

In response to a 2002 Subcommission request [YUN 2002, p. 681], Mr. Kartashkin, in a June working paper [E/CN.4/Sub.2/2003/34], analysed international instruments that formulated principles and rules relating to the nationality of women married to foreigners. He noted that in many countries, women who married foreigners still faced discrimination, since marriage with foreigners involved the loss and change of their nationality and entailed an infringement of their civil, political, social and economic rights. Problems relating to the rights of women married to foreigners did not always receive due attention in international forums and, owing to globalization, marriage between nationals of different States was growing. Recommendations included the adoption of non-discriminatory regulations regarding the nationality of women married to foreigners and rules that guaranteed their equality with men. The Committee on the Elimination of Discrimination against Women (CEDAW) (see p. 1190) should request participating States to provide information on measures taken to guarantee the rights of women married to foreigners and, based on the information received, CEDAW should consider drafting a recommendation on the issue.

Non-discrimination

Note by Secretariat. A July note [E/CN.4/Sub.2/2003/15] by the Secretariat informed the Subcommission that Fried van Hoof (Netherlands), owing to health reasons, would be unable to submit the working paper on non-discrimination requested by the Subcommission in 2002 [YUN 2002, p. 681].

Subcommission action. On 13 August [res. 2003/12], the Subcommission requested Emmanuel Decaux (France) to prepare, without financial implications, a working paper on non-discrimination as enshrined in article 2, paragraph 2, of the International Covenant on Economic, Social and Cultural Rights (see p. 670), regarding the exercise of the rights enunciated in the Covenant without discrimination as to race, colour, sex, language, religion, political or other opinion, national or social origin, property, birth or other status. It asked him to take into account other relevant studies of the Subcommission, to enable it to take a decision in 2004 on the feasibility of a study on the subject.

Religious intolerance

Report of Special Rapporteur. In January [E/CN.4/2003/66], the Special Rapporteur on freedom of religion or belief, Abdelfattah Amor (Tunisia), summarized 37 communications, including two urgent appeals, he had sent to 24 States, and the replies received from seven States, regarding incidents and governmental action inconsistent with the provisions of the 1981 Declaration on the Elimination of All Forms of Intolerance and of Discrimination Based on Religion or Belief, adopted in General Assembly resolution 36/55 [YUN 1981, p. 881]. In the context of prevention activities, the Special Rapporteur pointed to the situation of freedom of religion or belief following the 2001 terrorist attacks in the United States [YUN 2001, p. 60]; follow-up action to the International Consultative Conference on School Education in relation to Freedom of Religion and Belief, Tolerance and Non-discrimination (Madrid Conference) [ibid., p. 627]; and initiatives regarding interreligious dialogue. He concluded that an analysis of communications under the 1981 Declaration revealed violations of the principles of non-discrimination and tolerance regarding the freedom of thought, conscience, religion or belief, and of freedom to dispose of religious property. Once again, there was a rise in intolerance and discrimination against religious minorities and women in situations of extreme risk, and an increase in religious extremism affecting all religions. The Special Rapporteur advocated education and interreligious dialogue as vital pillars to prevent violations resulting from religious extremism. Studies should be made of the issue of sects and religious extremism and an in-depth examination of the situation in the aftermath of the terrorist attacks should be undertaken.

Report of High Commissioner. In response to a 2002 Commission request [YUN 2002, p. 682], the High Commissioner submitted a January report [E/CN.4/2003/17] on combating defamation of religions as a means to promote human rights, social harmony and religious and cultural diversity. The report reviewed initiatives and activities of UN intergovernmental bodies, human rights procedures and mechanisms, OHCHR and the specialized agencies. The High Commissioner noted that, as stated in the 2001 UNESCO Universal Declaration on Cultural Diversity [YUN 2001, p. 1409], the defence of cultural diversity implied a commitment to human rights and fundamental freedoms. Thus, human rights were the cornerstone of a common humanity that built on the common values of tolerance, respect and dignity.

Commission action. On 14 April [res. 2003/4], the Commission, by a recorded vote of 32 to 14, with 7 abstentions, called on the High Commissioner to promote and include human rights aspects in the dialogue among civilizations, by integrating them into topical seminars and special debates on the positive contributions of cultures and religious and cultural diversity, to hold joint conferences with other international organizations to promote understanding of the universality of human rights and their implementation, and to report in 2004.

On 24 April [res. 2003/54], by a recorded vote of 51 to none, with 2 abstentions, the Commission asked the Special Rapporteur to submit an interim report to the General Assembly at its fifty-eighth (2003) session and to report to the Commission in 2004. The Secretary-General was asked to assist him.

The Economic and Social Council, on 23 July, endorsed the Commission's requests to the Special Rapporteur (**decision 2003/252**).

Further reports of Special Rapporteur. Pursuant to General Assembly resolution 57/208 [YUN 2002, p. 683], the Secretary-General, by an August note [A/58/296], transmitted the interim report of the Special Rapporteur, which summarized 41 communications sent to 33 States and the replies of five States. The Special Rapporteur reviewed his country visits and follow-up since his 1993 appointment and his activities regarding follow-up to the International Consultative Conference on School Education in relation to Freedom of Religion and Belief, Tolerance and Non-discrimination [YUN 2001, p. 627]. He concluded that the communications and replies contained in the report indicated that nearly two years after 11 September 2001, the events of that day impacted profoundly on the exercise of human rights, particularly the right to freedom of religion or belief. In many cases, States had used the pretext of security in response to terrorist threats to limit the exercise of that right. The Special Rapporteur hoped that, in addressing genuine security problems, States would respect their fundamental obligations regarding civil and political rights, and emphasized that action in the area of education and culture was a prerequisite to combat extremism and intolerance.

At the invitation of the Government, the Special Rapporteur visited Georgia (31 August–7 September) [E/CN.4/2004/63/Add.1], particularly the capital, Tbilisi, where the great majority of religious activities in the country occurred, and where most of the religious communities were based. He focused on the status and importance of the Georgian Orthodox Church, to which 70 per cent of the country's estimated population of 5.5 million belonged, and on the situation of non-Orthodox religious minorities and government policy on freedom of religion, especially regarding incidents of intolerance and religious violence that had occurred in recent years. The Special Rapporteur said the main concern was the frequency and extent of the persecution of many religious minorities in the country. Noting that acts of violence and religious intolerance, which appeared to have begun in 1999 or earlier, had grown more serious and diverse, the Special Rapporteur called on the Government to investigate such incidents, subject those responsible to due process and ensure that alleged victims were able to set forth their grievances without hindrance. The authorities should ensure that the practical application of the constitutional agreement and other relations between the Church and the State did not give rise to confusion between their powers that might affect the rights of religious minorities. He proposed action against messages that aroused religious hatred, and against religious intolerance in the education system.

In Romania (7-13 September) [E/CN.4/2004/63/Add.2], the Special Rapporteur focused mainly on the status of the Romanian Orthodox Church, to which some 19 million persons belonged, comprising 86.7 per cent of an estimated total population of 22 million, and on the situation of religious minorities, government policy regarding freedom of religion or belief and the return of religious property. He encouraged the Government to abolish Romanian law that distinguished between religions that were recognized and those that were not, and recommended that all religious minorities be consulted about a new draft law before its approval. As to the restitution of confiscated property, the Special Rapporteur, although he believed that the issue concerned situations that did not necessarily violate the right to freedom of religion or belief, asked the Government to speed up and complete the restitution process as soon as possible and to end its policy of non-involvement in related dispute-settlement arrangements. Regarding speeches and other means of conveying messages of religious intolerance and hatred in the press, in politics and in schools, the Special Rapporteur encouraged the authorities to be more proactive in identifying related incidents, and to punish and stop such behaviour. Education, he pointed out, was one of the main tools for combating intolerance.

GENERAL ASSEMBLY ACTION

On 22 December [meeting 77], the General Assembly, on the recommendation of the Third Committee [A/58/508/Add.2], adopted **resolution 58/184** by recorded vote (179-0-1) [agenda item 117 (b)].

Elimination of all forms of religious intolerance

The General Assembly,

Recalling that all States have pledged themselves, under the Charter of the United Nations, to promote and encourage universal respect for and observance of human rights and fundamental freedoms for all without distinction as to race, sex, language or religion,

Reaffirming that discrimination against human beings on the grounds of religion or belief constitutes an affront to human dignity and a disavowal of the principles of the Charter,

Recalling article 18 of the Universal Declaration of Human Rights, article 18 of the International Covenant on Civil and Political Rights and paragraph 4 of the United Nations Millennium Declaration,

Reaffirming its resolution 36/55 of 25 November 1981, by which it proclaimed the Declaration on the Elimination of All Forms of Intolerance and of Discrimination Based on Religion or Belief,

Noting the provisions of the Durban Declaration and Programme of Action adopted by the World Conference against Racism, Racial Discrimination, Xenophobia and Related Intolerance, held in Durban, South Africa, from 31 August to 8 September 2001, aimed at combating religious intolerance,

Emphasizing that the right to freedom of thought, conscience, religion and belief is far-reaching and profound and that it encompasses freedom of thought on all matters, personal conviction and the commitment to religion or belief, whether manifested individually or in community with others, and in public or in private,

Reaffirming the call, made ten years ago in Vienna at the World Conference on Human Rights, for all Governments to take all appropriate measures in compliance with their international obligations and with due regard to their respective legal systems to counter intolerance and related violence based on religion or belief, including practices of discrimination against women and the desecration of religious sites, recognizing that every individual has the right to freedom of thought, conscience, expression and religion,

Underlining the important role of education in the promotion of tolerance, which involves the acceptance of and respect for diversity, and underlining also that education, in particular at school, should contribute in a meaningful way to promoting tolerance and the elimination of discrimination based on religion or belief,

Alarmed that serious instances of intolerance and discrimination on the grounds of religion or belief, including acts of violence, intimidation and coercion motivated by religious intolerance, continue to occur in many parts of the world and threaten the full enjoyment of human rights and fundamental freedoms,

Profoundly concerned at acts and situations of violence and discrimination resulting from religious intolerance that affect many women,

Deeply concerned at the overall rise in intolerance and discrimination on the grounds of religion or belief, including restrictive legislation, administrative regulations and discriminatory registration and the arbitrary application of these and other measures,

Recognizing that such intolerance and discrimination frequently manifests itself through acts of violence against religious minorities in all parts of the world,

Believing that further intensified efforts are therefore required to promote and protect the right to freedom of thought, conscience, religion or belief and to eliminate all forms of hatred, intolerance and discrimination based on religion or belief, as emphasized also at the World Conference against Racism, Racial Discrimination, Xenophobia and Related Intolerance,

1. *Reaffirms* that freedom of thought, conscience, religion or belief is a human right derived from the inherent dignity of the human person and guaranteed to all without discrimination;

2. *Urges* States to ensure that their constitutional and legal systems provide effective guarantees of freedom of thought, conscience, religion or belief, including the provision of effective remedies in cases where the right to freedom of thought, conscience, religion or belief is violated;

3. *Also urges* States to ensure, in particular, that no one within their jurisdiction is, because of their religion or belief, deprived of the right to life, liberty and security of person, the right to freedom of expression, the right not to be subjected to torture or other cruel, inhuman or degrading treatment or punishment and the right not to be arbitrarily arrested or detained, and to protect their physical integrity and bring to justice all perpetrators of violations of these rights;

4. *Further urges* States, in conformity with international standards of human rights, to take all necessary action to combat hatred, intolerance and acts of violence, intimidation and coercion motivated by intolerance based on religion or belief, with particular regard to persons belonging to religious minorities;

5. *Urges* States to devote particular attention to combating all practices motivated by religion or belief which lead, directly or indirectly, to human rights violations and to discrimination against women;

6. *Emphasizes* that, as underlined by the Human Rights Committee, restrictions on the freedom to manifest religion or belief are permitted only if those limitations that are prescribed by law are necessary to protect public safety, order, health or morals, or the fundamental rights and freedoms of others, and are applied in a manner that does not vitiate the right to freedom of thought, conscience and religion;

7. *Urges* States to ensure that all public officials and civil servants, including members of law enforcement bodies, the military and educators, in the course of their official duties, respect different religions and beliefs and do not discriminate on the grounds of religion or belief and to ensure that all necessary and appropriate education or training is provided;

8. *Calls upon* all States to recognize, as provided in the Declaration on the Elimination of All Forms of Intolerance and of Discrimination Based on Religion or Belief, the right of all persons to worship or assemble in connection with a religion or belief and to establish and maintain places for those purposes;

9. *Expresses its grave concern* at all attacks upon religious places, sites and shrines, and calls upon all States, in accordance with their national legislation and in conformity with international human rights standards, to exert their utmost efforts to ensure that such places, sites and shrines are fully respected and protected and to take additional measures in cases where they are vulnerable to desecration or destruction;

10. *Recognizes* that legislation alone is not enough to prevent violations of human rights, including the right to freedom of religion or belief, and that the exercise of tolerance and non-discrimination by persons and groups is necessary for the full realization of the aims of the Declaration, and in this regard invites States, religious bodies and civil society to undertake dialogue at all levels to promote greater tolerance, respect and understanding of freedom of religion or belief and to encourage and promote, through the educational system and by other means, understanding, tolerance and respect in matters relating to freedom of religion or belief;

11. *Emphasizes* the importance of a continued and strengthened dialogue among religions or beliefs, including as encompassed in the dialogue among civilizations, to promote greater tolerance, respect and mutual understanding;

12. *Takes note with appreciation* of the interim report of the Special Rapporteur of the Commission on Human Rights on freedom of religion or belief, and encourages his continued efforts to examine incidents and governmental actions in all parts of the world that are incompatible with the provisions of the Declaration and to recommend remedial measures as appropriate;

13. *Urges* all States to cooperate fully with the Special Rapporteur, including by considering favourably his requests to visit their countries so as to enable him to fulfil his mandate even more effectively, welcomes the initiatives of States to collaborate with the Special Rapporteur, and encourages civil society to continue its active collaboration with him;

14. *Urges* States to make all appropriate efforts to encourage those engaged in education to cultivate respect for all religions or beliefs, thereby promoting mutual understanding and tolerance;

15. *Encourages* Governments, when seeking the assistance of the United Nations Programme of Advisory Services and Technical Assistance in the Field of Human Rights, to consider, where appropriate, including requests for assistance in the field of the promotion and protection of the right to freedom of thought, conscience, religion or belief;

16. *Welcomes and encourages* the continuing efforts of non-governmental organizations and religious bodies and groups to promote the implementation and dissemination of the Declaration, and further encourages their work in relation to promoting freedom of religion or belief and in highlighting cases of religious intolerance, discrimination and persecution;

17. *Requests* the Commission on Human Rights to continue its consideration of measures to implement the Declaration;

18. *Requests* the Secretary-General to ensure that the Special Rapporteur receives the necessary resources to enable him to discharge his mandate fully;

19. *Decides* to consider the question of the elimination of all forms of religious intolerance at its fifty-ninth session under the item entitled "Human rights questions", and requests the Special Rapporteur to submit an interim report to the General Assembly on the item.

RECORDED VOTE ON RESOLUTION 58/184:

In favour: Afghanistan, Albania, Algeria, Andorra, Angola, Antigua and Barbuda, Argentina, Armenia, Australia, Austria, Azerbaijan, Bahamas, Bahrain, Bangladesh, Barbados, Belarus, Belgium, Belize, Benin, Bhutan, Bolivia, Bosnia and Herzegovina, Botswana, Brazil, Brunei Darussalam, Bulgaria, Burkina Faso, Burundi, Cambodia, Cameroon, Canada, Cape Verde, Central African Republic, Chile, China, Colombia, Comoros, Congo, Costa Rica, Côte d'Ivoire, Croatia, Cuba, Cyprus, Czech Republic, Democratic People's Republic of Korea, Democratic Republic of the Congo, Denmark, Djibouti, Dominica, Dominican Republic, Ecuador, Egypt, El Salvador, Eritrea, Estonia, Ethiopia, Fiji, Finland, France, Gabon, Gambia, Georgia, Germany, Ghana, Greece, Grenada, Guatemala, Guinea, Guinea-Bissau, Guyana, Haiti, Honduras, Hungary, Iceland, India, Indonesia, Iran, Ireland, Italy, Jamaica, Japan, Jordan, Kazakhstan, Kenya, Kuwait, Kyrgyzstan, Lao People's Democratic Republic, Latvia, Lebanon, Lesotho, Libyan Arab Jamahiriya, Liechtenstein, Lithuania, Luxembourg, Madagascar, Malawi, Malaysia, Maldives, Mali, Malta, Marshall Islands, Mauritania, Mauritius, Mexico, Micronesia, Monaco, Mongolia, Morocco, Mozambique, Myanmar, Namibia, Nepal, Netherlands, New Zealand, Nicaragua, Niger, Nigeria, Norway, Oman, Pakistan, Palau, Panama, Papua New Guinea, Paraguay, Peru, Philippines, Poland, Portugal, Qatar, Republic of Korea, Republic of Moldova, Romania, Russian Federation, Rwanda, Saint Lucia, Saint Vincent and the Grenadines, Samoa, San Marino, Saudi Arabia, Senegal, Serbia and Montenegro, Seychelles, Sierra Leone, Singapore, Slovakia, Slovenia, Solomon Islands, Somalia, South Africa, Spain, Sri Lanka, Sudan, Suriname, Sweden, Switzerland, Syrian Arab Republic, Tajikistan, Thailand, The former Yugoslav Republic of Macedonia, Timor-Leste, Togo, Trinidad and Tobago, Tunisia, Turkey, Turkmenistan, Tuvalu, Uganda, Ukraine, United Arab Emirates, United Kingdom, United Republic of Tanzania, United States, Uruguay, Uzbekistan, Venezuela, Viet Nam, Yemen, Zambia, Zimbabwe.

Against: None.

Abstaining: Israel.

(For information on the situation of Muslim and Arab peoples in the aftermath of the events of 11 September 2001, see p. 703.)

Civil and political rights

Right to self-determination

Report of Secretary-General. In response to General Assembly resolution 57/197 [YUN 2002, p. 685], the Secretary-General, in July [A/58/180], summarized the views of one Member State on the right of peoples to self-determination, and provided an account of the Commission's consideration of the topic and related issues during the year.

GENERAL ASSEMBLY ACTION

On 22 December [meeting 77], the General Assembly, on the recommendation of the Third Committee [A/58/507], adopted **resolution 58/161** by recorded vote (109-3-61) [agenda item 116].

Universal realization of the right of peoples to self-determination

The General Assembly,

Reaffirming the importance, for the effective guarantee and observance of human rights, of the universal realization of the right of peoples to self-determination enshrined in the Charter of the United Nations and embodied in the International Covenants on Human Rights, as well as in the Declaration on the Granting of Independence to Colonial Countries and Peoples contained in General Assembly resolution 1514(XV) of 14 December 1960,

Welcoming the progressive exercise of the right to self-determination by peoples under colonial, foreign or alien occupation and their emergence into sovereign statehood and independence,

Deeply concerned at the continuation of acts or threats of foreign military intervention and occupation that are threatening to suppress, or have already suppressed, the right to self-determination of peoples and nations,

Expressing grave concern that, as a consequence of the persistence of such actions, millions of people have been and are being uprooted from their homes as refugees and displaced persons, and emphasizing the urgent need for concerted international action to alleviate their condition,

Recalling the relevant resolutions regarding the violation of the right of peoples to self-determination and other human rights as a result of foreign military intervention, aggression and occupation, adopted by the Commission on Human Rights at its fifty-ninth and previous sessions,

Reaffirming its previous resolutions on the universal realization of the right of peoples to self-determination, including resolution 57/197 of 18 December 2002,

Reaffirming also its resolution 55/2 of 8 September 2000, containing the United Nations Millennium Declaration, which, inter alia, upholds the right to self-determination of peoples under colonial domination and foreign occupation,

Taking note of the report of the Secretary-General on the right of peoples to self-determination,

1. *Reaffirms* that the universal realization of the right of all peoples, including those under colonial, foreign and alien domination, to self-determination is a fundamental condition for the effective guarantee and observance of human rights and for the preservation and promotion of such rights;

2. *Declares its firm opposition* to acts of foreign military intervention, aggression and occupation, since these have resulted in the suppression of the right of peoples to self-determination and other human rights in certain parts of the world;

3. *Calls upon* those States responsible to cease immediately their military intervention in and occupation of foreign countries and territories and all acts of repression, discrimination, exploitation and maltreatment, in particular the brutal and inhuman methods reportedly employed for the execution of those acts against the peoples concerned;

4. *Deplores* the plight of millions of refugees and displaced persons who have been uprooted as a result of the aforementioned acts, and reaffirms their right to return to their homes voluntarily in safety and honour;

5. *Requests* the Commission on Human Rights to continue to give special attention to the violation of human rights, especially the right to self-determination, resulting from foreign military intervention, aggression or occupation;

6. *Requests* the Secretary-General to report on this question to the General Assembly at its fifty-ninth session under the item entitled "Right of peoples to self-determination".

RECORDED VOTE ON RESOLUTION 58/161:

In favour: Albania, Algeria, Angola, Antigua and Barbuda, Argentina, Armenia, Australia, Austria, Azerbaijan, Bahamas, Bahrain, Bangladesh, Barbados, Belize, Benin, Bolivia, Bosnia and Herzegovina, Botswana, Brazil, Brunei Darussalam, Bulgaria, Burkina Faso, Cambodia, Cameroon, Canada, Central African Republic, Chile, China, Congo, Costa Rica, Côte d'Ivoire, Croatia, Cuba, Democratic People's Republic of Korea, Democratic Republic of the Congo, Djibouti, Dominica, Dominican Republic, Ecuador, Egypt, El Salvador, Eritrea, Ethiopia, Gabon, Ghana, Grenada, Guatemala, Guinea, Guinea-Bissau, Haiti, Honduras, Iran, Ireland, Jamaica, Japan, Jordan, Kazakhstan, Kenya, Kuwait, Kyrgyzstan, Lao People's Democratic Republic, Lebanon, Lesotho, Libyan Arab Jamahiriya, Madagascar, Malaysia, Mali, Mauritania, Mexico, Mongolia, Morocco, Mozambique, Myanmar, New Zealand, Nicaragua, Niger, Nigeria, Oman, Pakistan, Panama, Papua New Guinea, Paraguay, Peru, Philippines, Portugal, Qatar, Republic of Korea, Saint Lucia, Saint Vincent and the Grenadines, Samoa, Saudi Arabia, Sierra Leone, Singapore, Solomon Islands, South Africa, Sudan, Syrian Arab Republic, Thailand, Togo, Tunisia, Turkey, Turkmenistan, United Arab Emirates, Uruguay, Venezuela, Viet Nam, Yemen, Zambia, Zimbabwe.

Against: Bhutan, India, Mauritius.

Abstaining: Andorra, Belarus, Belgium, Burundi, Colombia, Comoros, Cyprus, Czech Republic, Denmark, Estonia, Fiji, Finland, France, Georgia, Germany, Greece, Guyana, Hungary, Iceland, Indonesia, Israel, Italy, Latvia, Liechtenstein, Lithuania, Luxembourg, Malawi, Maldives, Malta, Marshall Islands, Micronesia, Monaco, Namibia, Nauru, Netherlands, Norway, Palau, Poland, Republic of Moldova, Romania, Russian Federation, Rwanda, San Marino, Senegal, Serbia and Montenegro, Slovakia, Spain, Sri Lanka, Suriname, Sweden, Switzerland, Tajikistan, The former Yugoslav Republic of Macedonia, Tonga, Trinidad and Tobago, Tuvalu, Uganda, Ukraine, United Kingdom, United Republic of Tanzania, United States.

Rights of Palestinians

By a recorded vote of 51 to 1, with 1 abstention, the Commission, on 14 April [res. 2003/3], reaffirming the right of the Palestinian people to self-determination, requested the Secretary-General to transmit its resolution to Israel and all other Governments, to disseminate it as widely as possible, and to make available to the Commission before its 2004 session information pertaining to its implementation by the Government of Israel.

The Commission had before it a report of the Secretary-General [E/CN.4/2003/15], stating that he had received no reply from Israel to his request for information regarding the implementation of the Commission's 2002 resolution on the situation in occupied Palestine [YUN 2002, p. 685]. The United Nations Department of Public Information (DPI) had undertaken activities to implement the Commission's resolution, by revising and updating the departmental publication: *The question of Palestine and the United Nations,* and through news coverage programmes, dissemination of press releases and related public information services.

GENERAL ASSEMBLY ACTION

On 22 December [meeting 77], the General Assembly, on the recommendation of the Third Committee [A/58/507], adopted **resolution 58/163** by recorded vote (169-5) [agenda item 116].

The right of the Palestinian people to self-determination

The General Assembly,

Aware that the development of friendly relations among nations, based on respect for the principle of equal rights and self-determination of peoples, is among the purposes and principles of the United Nations, as defined in the Charter,

Recalling the International Covenants on Human Rights, the Universal Declaration of Human Rights, the Declaration on the Granting of Independence to Colonial Countries and Peoples and the Vienna Declaration and Programme of Action adopted at the World Conference on Human Rights on 25 June 1993,

Recalling also the Declaration on the Occasion of the Fiftieth Anniversary of the United Nations,

Recalling further the United Nations Millennium Declaration,

Expressing the urgent need for the resumption of negotiations within the Middle East peace process on its agreed basis and for the speedy achievement of a final settlement between the Palestinian and Israeli sides,

Affirming the right of all States in the region to live in peace within secure and internationally recognized borders,

1. *Reaffirms* the right of the Palestinian people to self-determination, including the right to their independent State of Palestine;

2. *Urges* all States and the specialized agencies and organizations of the United Nations system to continue to support and assist the Palestinian people in the early realization of their right to self-determination.

RECORDED VOTE ON RESOLUTION 58/163:

In favour: Afghanistan, Albania, Algeria, Andorra, Angola, Antigua and Barbuda, Argentina, Armenia, Australia, Austria, Azerbaijan, Bahamas, Bahrain, Bangladesh, Barbados, Belarus, Belgium, Belize, Benin, Bhutan, Bolivia, Bosnia and Herzegovina, Botswana, Brazil, Brunei Darussalam, Bulgaria, Burkina Faso, Burundi, Cambodia, Cameroon, Canada, Cape Verde, Central African Republic, Chile, China, Colombia, Comoros, Congo, Costa Rica, Côte d'Ivoire, Croatia, Cuba, Cyprus, Czech Republic, Democratic People's Republic of Korea, Democratic Republic of the Congo, Denmark, Djibouti, Dominica, Dominican Republic, Ecuador, Egypt, El Salvador, Eritrea, Estonia, Ethiopia, Finland, France, Gambia, Georgia, Germany, Ghana, Greece, Grenada, Guatemala, Guinea, Guinea-Bissau, Guyana, Haiti, Honduras, Hungary, Iceland, India, Indonesia, Iran, Ireland, Italy, Jamaica, Japan, Jordan, Kazakhstan, Kenya, Kuwait, Kyrgyzstan, Lao People's Democratic Republic, Latvia, Lebanon, Lesotho, Libyan Arab Jamahiriya, Liechtenstein, Lithuania, Luxembourg, Madagascar, Malawi, Malaysia, Maldives, Mali, Malta, Mauritania, Mauritius, Mexico, Monaco, Mongolia, Morocco, Mozambique, Myanmar, Namibia, Nauru, Nepal, Netherlands, New Zealand, Nicaragua, Niger, Nigeria, Norway, Oman, Pakistan, Panama, Papua New Guinea, Paraguay, Peru, Philippines, Poland, Portugal, Qatar, Republic of Korea, Republic of Moldova, Romania, Russian Federation, Rwanda, Saint Lucia, Saint Vincent and the Grenadines, Samoa, San Marino, Saudi Arabia, Senegal, Serbia and Montenegro, Seychelles, Sierra Leone, Singapore, Slovakia, Slovenia, Solomon Islands, South Africa, Spain, Sri Lanka, Sudan, Sweden, Switzerland, Syrian Arab Republic, Thailand, The former Yugoslav Republic of Macedonia, Timor-Leste, Togo, Trinidad and Tobago, Tunisia, Turkey, Turkmenistan, Uganda, Ukraine, United Arab Emirates, United Kingdom, United Republic of Tanzania, Uruguay, Venezuela, Viet Nam, Yemen, Zambia, Zimbabwe.

Against: Israel, Marshall Islands, Micronesia, Palau, United States.

Western Sahara

On 14 April [res. 2003/1], the Commission urged Morocco and the Frente Popular para la Liberación de Saguia el-Hamra y de Río de Oro to cooperate with the Secretary-General and his Personal Envoy, with a view to reaching a mutually acceptable political solution to their dispute. It reaffirmed support for further efforts of the Secretary-General, in cooperation with the African Union, for a UN-supervised referendum on self-determination of the people of Western Sahara (see p. 616). The parties were further called on to cooperate with ICRC to solve the problem of the fate of people unaccounted for and to abide by their obligation under international humanitarian law to release all those being held.

Mercenaries

Reports of Special Rapporteur. In response to a 2002 Commission resolution [YUN 2002, p. 687], the Special Rapporteur on the question of the use of mercenaries, Enrique Bernales Ballesteros (Peru), submitted a report [E/CN.4/2003/16] on the implementation of the resolution. He summarized replies received from States in response to his request for information on mercenary activities, described progress towards a legal definition of a mercenary and reviewed the current status of mercenary operations, focusing on the role of mercenaries in African conflicts and the relationship between terrorism and mercenary activities. Mercenary operations had increased, and recent studies and statements attributable to some government spokespersons had suggested the possible legalization of mercenary activities, by allowing and formalizing the recruitment and use of mercenaries by private security and military consultancy companies. Terrorist groups and organizations, with their shifting operational links to mercenaries, remained active. The Special Rapporteur recommended that the Commission reaffirm its condemnation of mercenary activities as something incompatible with the purposes and principles of the United Nations and human rights, call on States to reject the practice and ensure that domestic law prohibited and punished it, and pay particular attention to the recent concentration of mercenaries in Africa, especially West Africa. He further recommended that the Commission invite States not parties to the 1989 International Convention against the Recruitment, Use, Financing and Training of Mercenaries (see p. 723) to ratify or accede to the Convention.

In response to General Assembly resolution 57/196 [YUN 2002, p. 687], the Secretary-General transmitted in July a report of the Special Rapporteur [A/58/115], which addressed the definition of mercenaries and made suggestions regarding the international adoption of a new definition. The Special Rapporteur noted that the gaps in the legal provisions on mercenaries rendered the international community, particularly the smallest countries, defenceless in the face of mercenary activities. The legal definition proposed by the Special Rapporteur, which was annexed to the report, reflected the multi-purpose criminal characteristics of mercenary activity, linking it to participation in armed conflicts, attacks against the self-determination of peoples, trafficking in persons and in arms/ammunition and drugs, and terrorism. He recommended that the Assembly: prohibit all activities that encouraged the presence of mercenaries, and suggest that the Commission extend the mandate on mercenary activities; circulate among States parties to the 1989 Convention the proposed new legal definition of mercenary, which would replace articles 1, 2 and 3 of the Convention, and suggest that they study it and adopt a position thereon; and arrange for the distribution of the proposed definition to enable the Special Rapporteur to gather additional comments and observations towards the review and acceptance of amendments to the Convention. Other aspects of the report dealt with the Special Rapporteur's activities and the status of the Convention.

Commission action. On 14 April [res. 2003/2], the Commission, by a recorded vote of 37 to 9, with 7 abstentions, called on States that had not done so to sign or ratify the Convention. The Commission requested OHCHR to publicize the adverse effects of mercenary activities and to render advisory services to affected States. The Special Rapporteur was asked to report in 2004, and the High Commissioner to assist him.

1989 International Convention

As at 31 December, 25 States had become parties to the 1989 International Convention against the Recruitment, Use, Financing and Training of Mercenaries, adopted by the General Assembly in resolution 44/34 [YUN 1989, p. 825], with Guinea acceding in 2003. The Convention entered into force in 2001 [YUN 2001, p. 632].

GENERAL ASSEMBLY ACTION

On 22 December [meeting 77], the General Assembly, on the recommendation of the Third Committee [A/58/507], adopted **resolution 58/162** by recorded vote (125-26-29) [agenda item 116].

Use of mercenaries as a means of violating human rights and impeding the exercise of the right of peoples to self-determination

The General Assembly,

Recalling its resolution 57/196 of 18 December 2002, and taking note of Commission on Human Rights resolution 2003/2 of 14 April 2003,

Recalling also all of its relevant resolutions, in which, inter alia, it condemned any State that permitted or tolerated the recruitment, financing, training, assembly, transit and use of mercenaries with the objective of overthrowing the Governments of States Members of the United Nations, especially those of developing countries, or of fighting against national liberation movements, and recalling further the relevant resolutions and international instruments adopted by the Security Council, the Economic and Social Council and the Organization of African Unity, inter alia, the Organization of African Unity Convention for the elimination of mercenarism in Africa,

Reaffirming the purposes and principles enshrined in the Charter of the United Nations concerning the strict observance of the principles of sovereign equality, political independence, the territorial integrity of States, the self-determination of peoples, the non-use of force or of the threat of use of force in international relations and non-interference in affairs within the domestic jurisdiction of States,

Reaffirming also that, by virtue of the principle of self-determination, all peoples have the right freely to determine their political status and to pursue their economic, social and cultural development, and that every State has the duty to respect this right in accordance with the provisions of the Charter,

Reaffirming further the Declaration on Principles of International Law concerning Friendly Relations and Cooperation among States in accordance with the Charter of the United Nations,

Alarmed and concerned at the danger that the activities of mercenaries constitute to peace and security in developing countries, in particular in Africa and in small States,

Deeply concerned at the loss of life, the substantial damage to property and the negative effects on the policy and economies of affected countries resulting from criminal mercenary activities,

Convinced that, notwithstanding the way in which they are used or the form that they take to acquire some semblance of legitimacy, mercenaries or mercenary-related activities are a threat to peace, security and the self-determination of peoples and an obstacle to the enjoyment of human rights by peoples,

1. *Welcomes* the report of the Special Rapporteur of the Commission on Human Rights on the question of the use of mercenaries as a means of impeding the exercise of the right of peoples to self-determination;

2. *Reaffirms* that the use of mercenaries and their recruitment, financing and training are causes for grave concern to all States and violate the purposes and principles enshrined in the Charter of the United Nations;

3. *Recognizes* that armed conflict, terrorism, arms trafficking and covert operations by third Powers, inter alia, encourage the demand for mercenaries on the global market;

4. *Urges* all States to take the necessary steps and to exercise the utmost vigilance against the menace posed by the activities of mercenaries and to take legislative measures to ensure that their territories and other territories under their control, as well as their nationals, are not used for the recruitment, assembly, financing, training and transit of mercenaries for the planning of activities designed to impede the right of peoples to self-determination, to destabilize or overthrow the Government of any State or to dismember or impair, totally or in part, the territorial integrity or political unity of sovereign and independent States conducting themselves in compliance with the right of peoples to self-determination;

5. *Requests* all States to exercise the utmost vigilance against any kind of recruitment, training, hiring or financing of mercenaries by private companies offering international military consultancy and security services, as well as to impose a specific ban on such companies intervening in armed conflicts or actions to destabilize constitutional regimes;

6. *Welcomes* the entry into force of the International Convention against the Recruitment, Use, Financing and Training of Mercenaries, and calls upon all States that have not yet done so to consider taking the necessary action to accede to or ratify the Convention;

7. *Welcomes also* the cooperation extended by those countries that have received visits from the Special Rapporteur;

8. *Welcomes further* the adoption by some States of national legislation that restricts the recruitment, assembly, financing, training and transit of mercenaries;

9. *Calls upon* States to investigate the possibility of mercenary involvement whenever and wherever criminal acts of a terrorist nature occur and to bring to trial those found responsible or to consider their extradition, if so requested, in accordance with domestic law and applicable bilateral or international treaties;

10. *Welcomes* the organization, in Geneva from 13 to 17 May 2002, in compliance with General Assembly resolution 56/232 of 24 December 2001, of the second meeting of experts on traditional and new forms of mercenary activities as a means of violating human rights and impeding the exercise of the right of peoples to self-determination, and takes note of its conclusions;

11. *Takes note with appreciation* of the proposal for an enhanced legal definition of mercenaries contained

in the report of the Special Rapporteur, and requests the Secretary-General to circulate it to the Member States and to seek their views in order to include them in the report of the Special Rapporteur to the General Assembly at its fifty-ninth session;

12. *Requests* the Office of the United Nations High Commissioner for Human Rights, as a matter of priority, to publicize the adverse effects of the activities of mercenaries on the right of peoples to self-determination and, when requested and where necessary, to render advisory services to States that are affected by those activities;

13. *Requests* the Special Rapporteur to continue to take into account, in the discharge of his mandate, the fact that mercenary activities continue to occur in many parts of the world and are taking on new forms, manifestations and modalities;

14. *Recommends* that the Commission on Human Rights renew the mandate of the Special Rapporteur for a period of three years;

15. *Urges* all States to cooperate fully with the Special Rapporteur in the fulfilment of his mandate;

16. *Requests* the Secretary-General and the United Nations High Commissioner for Human Rights to provide the Special Rapporteur with all the necessary assistance and support for the fulfilment of his mandate, both professional and financial, including through the promotion of cooperation between the Special Rapporteur and other components of the United Nations system that deal with countering mercenary-related activities;

17. *Requests* the Special Rapporteur to consult States and intergovernmental and non-governmental organizations in the implementation of the present resolution and to report, with specific recommendations, to the General Assembly at its fifty-ninth session his findings on the use of mercenaries to undermine the right of peoples to self-determination;

18. *Decides* to consider at its fifty-ninth session the question of the use of mercenaries as a means of violating human rights and impeding the exercise of the right of peoples to self-determination under the item entitled "Right of peoples to self-determination".

RECORDED VOTE ON RESOLUTION 58/162:

In favour: Afghanistan, Algeria, Angola, Antigua and Barbuda, Argentina, Armenia, Azerbaijan, Bahamas, Bahrain, Bangladesh, Barbados, Belarus, Belize, Benin, Bhutan, Bolivia, Botswana, Brazil, Brunei Darussalam, Burkina Faso, Burundi, Cambodia, Cameroon, Cape Verde, Central African Republic, Chile, China, Colombia, Comoros, Congo, Costa Rica, Côte d'Ivoire, Cuba, Democratic People's Republic of Korea, Democratic Republic of the Congo, Djibouti, Dominica, Dominican Republic, Ecuador, Egypt, El Salvador, Eritrea, Ethiopia, Fiji, Gabon, Gambia, Ghana, Grenada, Guatemala, Guinea, Guinea-Bissau, Guyana, Haiti, Honduras, India, Indonesia, Iran, Jamaica, Jordan, Kenya, Kuwait, Kyrgyzstan, Lao People's Democratic Republic, Lebanon, Lesotho, Libyan Arab Jamahiriya, Madagascar, Malawi, Malaysia, Maldives, Mali, Marshall Islands, Mauritania, Mauritius, Mexico, Mongolia, Morocco, Mozambique, Myanmar, Namibia, Nepal, Nicaragua, Niger, Nigeria, Oman, Pakistan, Panama, Papua New Guinea, Paraguay, Peru, Philippines, Qatar, Russian Federation, Rwanda, Saint Lucia, Saint Vincent and the Grenadines, Samoa, Saudi Arabia, Senegal, Seychelles, Sierra Leone, Singapore, Solomon Islands, South Africa, Sri Lanka, Sudan, Suriname, Syrian Arab Republic, Thailand, Timor-Leste, Togo, Trinidad and Tobago, Tunisia, Turkmenistan, Tuvalu, Uganda, Ukraine, United Arab Emirates, United Republic of Tanzania, Uruguay, Venezuela, Viet Nam, Yemen, Zambia, Zimbabwe.

Against: Albania, Belgium, Bosnia and Herzegovina, Bulgaria, Canada, Czech Republic, Denmark, Estonia, Finland, France, Germany, Hungary, Iceland, Israel, Italy, Japan, Lithuania, Luxembourg, Micronesia, Monaco, Netherlands, Norway, Poland, Sweden, United Kingdom, United States.

Abstaining: Andorra, Australia, Austria, Croatia, Cyprus, Georgia, Greece, Ireland, Kazakhstan, Latvia, Liechtenstein, Malta, Nauru, New Zealand, Palau, Portugal, Republic of Korea, Republic of Moldova, Romania, San Marino, Serbia and Montenegro, Slovakia, Slovenia, Spain, Switzerland, The former Yugoslav Republic of Macedonia, Tonga, Turkey, Uzbekistan.

Administration of justice

Commission action. On 23 April [dec. 2003/108], the Commission decided to approve the Subcommission's 2002 decision [YUN 2002, p. 689] to appoint Leïla Zerrougui (Algeria) as Special Rapporteur to conduct a detailed study of discrimination in the criminal justice system, its request that she submit a preliminary report in 2003, a progress report in 2004 and a final report in 2005, and its request to the Secretary-General to assist her.

On 23 July, the Economic and Social Council endorsed the Commission's decision and approved its request to the Secretary-General (**decision 2003/265**).

Working group activities. Established by the Subcommission on 28 July [dec. 2003/101], the five-member sessional working group on the administration of justice met on 28 and 30 July and 7 August [E/CN.4/Sub.2/2003/6]. The group discussed the imposition of the death penalty; the privatization of prisons; current trends in international penal justice; the domestic implementation in practice of the obligation to provide domestic remedies; mechanisms of truth and reconciliation; and witnesses and rules of evidence, including medical secrecy, problems in prosecuting rape and sexual assault cases, especially the problem of gender discrimination, and the need for guidelines on the criminalization, investigation and prosecution of acts of serious sexual violence during armed conflict against civilians and provision of remedies.

The group considered a working paper on the problem of evidence in cases of sexual abuse [E/CN.4/Sub.2/2003/WG.1/CRP.1], prepared by Lalaina Rakotoarisoa (Madagascar), and proposed that she prepare an expanded background paper examining procedural and evidential barriers that impacted on victims of sexual abuse.

Pursuant to a 2002 Subcommission request [YUN 2002, p. 689], the group had before it a preliminary report on a study of discrimination in the criminal justice system [E/CN.4/Sub.2/2003/3], submitted by Ms. Zerrougui, which clarified the general approach and conceptual framework of the study, and proposed, for the Subcommission's consideration, a work plan culminating in the elaboration of conclusions and recommendations, including guidelines, to guarantee vulnerable persons the right to non-discrimination and respect for their basic rights in the criminal justice system. In accordance with a further request of the Subcommission [YUN 2002, p. 690], the group had before it a June report on the administration of justice through military tribunals [E/CN.4/Sub.2/2003/4], submitted by Mr. Decaux, which updated a previous report on the subject considered in 2002 [YUN 2002, p. 689]. The author analysed the special jurisdictions of military tribunals and of the judicial guarantees in the concept of an independent and impartial tribunal. He concluded that the administration of justice through military tribunals was being gradually "demilitarized" through a process that limited their jurisdiction and strengthened guarantees of a fair trial, with a view to making the tribunals an integral part of the general judicial system. He made recommendations regarding the competence of military courts to try civilians, trial of persons accused of serious human rights violations, limitations on military secrecy, guarantees of habeas corpus, the right to an independent and impartial tribunal, publicity of hearings, strengthening the rights of the defence, victims' access to proceedings, recourse procedures in ordinary courts, the principle of due obedience, conscientious objection to military service, the trial of children and minors under 18 years, and the death penalty.

Subcommission action. On 13 August [res. 2003/7], the Subcommission, concerned that historically discriminatory practices might sometimes lead to disproportionate numbers of the poor and minorities in a criminal justice system, urged States to examine their treatment of convicted persons after they had served their punishment. It requested the sessional working group to examine the question and suggest types of information that could be collected to understand better the extent of discrimination against convicted persons who had served their sentences and the relevant international human rights standards applicable in such situations.

Also on 13 August [res. 2003/8], the Subcommission asked Mr. Decaux to continue to develop principles governing the administration of justice through military tribunals and to submit an updated report in 2004.

In further action on 13 August [dec. 2003/107], the Subcommission asked Ms. Rakotoarisoa to prepare, without financial implications, an expanded working paper on the difficulties of establishing guilt and/or responsibility with regard to crimes of sexual violence and to submit it in 2004.

On the same date [dec. 2003/104], the Subcommission asked working group member Florizelle O'Connor (Jamaica) to prepare, without financial implications, a working paper on women in prison and to submit it in 2004.

GENERAL ASSEMBLY ACTION

On 22 December [meeting 77], the General Assembly, on the recommendation of the Third Committee [A/58/508/Add.2], adopted **resolution 58/183** without vote [agenda item 117 (b)].

Human rights in the administration of justice

The General Assembly,

Bearing in mind the principles embodied in articles 3, 5, 8, 9 and 10 of the Universal Declaration of Human Rights and the relevant provisions of the International Covenant on Civil and Political Rights and the Optional Protocols thereto, in particular article 6 of the Covenant, which states, inter alia, that no one shall be arbitrarily deprived of his life and prohibits the imposition of the death penalty for crimes committed by persons below 18 years of age, and article 10, which provides that all persons deprived of their liberty shall be treated with humanity and with respect for the inherent dignity of the human person,

Bearing in mind also the relevant provisions of the Convention against Torture and Other Cruel, Inhuman or Degrading Treatment or Punishment, the International Convention on the Elimination of All Forms of Racial Discrimination, in particular the right to equal treatment before tribunals and all other organs administering justice, the Convention on the Rights of the Child, in particular article 37, according to which every child deprived of liberty shall be treated in a manner that takes into account the needs of persons of his or her age, and the Convention on the Elimination of All Forms of Discrimination against Women, in particular the obligation to treat men and women equally in all stages of procedures in courts and tribunals,

Calling attention to the numerous international standards in the field of the administration of justice,

Convinced that the independence and impartiality of the judiciary are essential prerequisites for the protection of human rights and for ensuring that there is no discrimination in the administration of justice and should therefore be respected in all circumstances,

Emphasizing that the right to access to justice, as contained in applicable international human rights instruments, forms an important basis for strengthening the rule of law through the administration of justice,

Mindful of the importance of ensuring respect for the rule of law and human rights in the administration of justice, in particular in post-conflict situations, as a crucial contribution to building peace and justice and ending impunity,

Recalling the Guidelines for Action on Children in the Criminal Justice System and the establishment and subsequent meetings of the coordination panel on technical advice and assistance in juvenile justice,

Calling attention to the relevant provisions of the Vienna Declaration on Crime and Justice: Meeting the Challenges of the Twenty-first Century, and of the plans of action for its implementation and follow-up,

Recalling its resolution 56/161 of 19 December 2001, as well as Commission on Human Rights resolution 2002/47 of 23 April 2002 and Economic and Social Council resolution 2003/30 of 22 July 2003, entitled "United Nations standards and norms in crime prevention and criminal justice",

1. *Reaffirms* the importance of the full and effective implementation of all United Nations standards on human rights in the administration of justice;

2. *Reiterates its call* to all Member States to spare no effort in providing for effective legislative and other mechanisms and procedures, as well as adequate resources, to ensure the full implementation of those standards;

3. *Affirms* that States must ensure that any measure taken to combat terrorism, including in the administration of justice, complies with their obligations under international law, in particular international human rights, refugee and humanitarian law;

4. *Invites* Governments to provide training, including anti-racist, multicultural and gender-sensitive training, in human rights in the administration of justice, including juvenile justice, to all judges, lawyers, prosecutors, social workers, immigration and police officers and other professionals concerned, including personnel deployed in international field presences;

5. *Invites* States to make use of technical assistance offered by the relevant United Nations programmes in order to strengthen national capacities and infrastructures in the field of the administration of justice;

6. *Appeals* to Governments to include in their national development plans the administration of justice as an integral part of the development process and to allocate adequate resources for the provision of legal-aid services with a view to promoting and protecting human rights, and invites the international community to respond favourably to requests for financial and technical assistance for the enhancement and strengthening of the administration of justice;

7. *Encourages* the regional commissions, the specialized agencies, United Nations institutes active in the areas of human rights and crime prevention and criminal justice, and other relevant parts of the United Nations system, as well as intergovernmental and non-governmental organizations, including national professional associations concerned with promoting United Nations standards in this field, and other segments of civil society, including the media, to continue to develop their activities in promoting human rights in the administration of justice;

8. *Takes note with interest* of the debates held in the Security Council on the agenda item entitled "Justice and the Rule of Law: the United Nations role";

9. *Invites* the Commission on Human Rights and the Commission on Crime Prevention and Criminal Justice, as well as the Office of the United Nations High Commissioner for Human Rights and the crime programme of the United Nations Office on Drugs and Crime, to closely coordinate their activities relating to the administration of justice;

10. *Calls upon* mechanisms of the Commission on Human Rights and its subsidiary bodies, including special rapporteurs, special representatives and working groups, to continue to give special attention to questions relating to the effective promotion and protection of human rights in the administration of justice, including juvenile justice, and to provide, where appropriate, specific recommendations in this regard, including proposals for advisory services and technical assistance measures;

11. *Calls upon* the United Nations High Commissioner for Human Rights to reinforce, within his mandate, his activities relating to national capacity-building in the field of the administration of justice, in particular in post-conflict situations;

12. *Encourages* the Office of the High Commissioner to continue organizing training courses and other relevant activities aimed at enhancing the promotion and protection of human rights in the field of the administration of justice, and welcomes the publication of the Manual on Human Rights for Judges, Prosecutors and Lawyers within the framework of the United Nations Decade for Human Rights Education, 1995-2004;

13. *Welcomes* the increased attention paid to the issue of juvenile justice by the High Commissioner and the United Nations Children's Fund, in particular through technical assistance activities, and, taking into account the fact that international cooperation to promote juvenile justice reform has become a priority within the United Nations system, encourages the further activities of the High Commissioner and the United Nations Children's Fund, within their mandates, in this regard;

14. *Calls upon* the coordination panel on technical advice and assistance in juvenile justice to further increase cooperation among the partners involved, to share information and to pool their capacities and interests in order to increase the effectiveness of programme implementation;

15. *Invites* Governments, relevant international and regional bodies, national human rights institutions and non-governmental organizations to devote increased attention to the issue of women in prison, including the children of women in prison, with a view to identifying the key problems and ways in which they can be addressed, and notes the proposal of the Sub-commission on the Promotion and Protection of Human Rights to prepare a working paper on this question;

16. *Underlines* the importance of rebuilding and strengthening structures for the administration of justice and respect for the rule of law and human rights in post-conflict situations, and requests the Secretary-General to ensure system-wide coordination and coherence of programmes and activities of the relevant parts of the United Nations system in the field of the administration of justice in post-conflict situations, including assistance provided through United Nations field presences;

17. *Stresses* the special need for national capacity-building in the field of the administration of justice, in particular through reform of the judiciary, the police and the penal system, as well as juvenile justice reform, in order to establish and maintain stable societies and the rule of law in post-conflict situations, and in this context welcomes the role of the Office of the High Commissioner in supporting the establishment and functioning of transitional justice mechanisms in post-conflict situations;

18. *Decides* to consider the question of human rights in the administration of justice at its sixtieth session under the item entitled "Human rights questions".

Compensation for victims

Commission action. On 23 April [res. 2003/34], the Commission asked the Secretary-General to circulate to Member States, intergovernmental organizations and NGOs the draft text of the basic principles and guidelines on the right to restitution, compensation and rehabilitation for victims of grave violations of human rights and humanitarian law [YUN 2000, p. 665], and to request them to send their comments to OHCHR. Taking note of the 2002 consultative meeting held to finalize the text [YUN 2002, p. 690], the Commission asked the High Commissioner to hold a second consultative meeting (see below), with a view to finalizing the text; to consider, if appropriate, options for the adoption of those principles and guidelines; and to report in 2004. The Chairperson-Rapporteur of the 2002 consultative meeting was asked to prepare, in consultation with independent experts Theo van Boven (Netherlands) and Cherif Bassiouni (Egypt/United States), a revised version of the text and to conduct informal consultations with interested parties.

Consultative meeting. In accordance with Commission resolution 2003/34 (see above), OHCHR, in cooperation with Chile, convened the second international consultation (Geneva, 20, 21 and 23 October) [E/CN.4/2004/57] to finalize the draft basic principles and guidelines. Participants considered a revised text and a proposal put forward by the Chairperson-Rapporteur following informal consultations, which were appended to the meeting's report. Subsequently, the Chairperson-Rapporteur summarized the main issues addressed and announced that he planned to convene an additional one-day informal consultation prior to the Commission's 2004 session, in order to give delegations more time to examine the proposal and revised text, and to submit their written comments and suggestions.

State of siege or emergency

As requested by the Commission in 1998 [YUN 1998, p. 664], OHCHR submitted, in June [E/CN.4/Sub.2/2003/39], a list of States in which a state of emergency had been proclaimed before June 2001 and continued thereafter, as well as states of emergency proclaimed between June 2001 and May 2003.

Civilians in armed conflict

On 15 December [meeting 4882], the Security Council discussed the protection of civilians in armed conflict. Its President made statement **S/PRST/2003/27** on behalf of the Council:

> The Security Council recalls its resolutions 1265 (1999) of 17 September 1999 and 1296(2000) of 19 April 2000 on the protection of civilians in armed conflict, as well as the statements by its President of 12 February 1999 (S/PRST/1999/6) and 15 March (S/PRST/2002/6) and 20 December 2002 (S/PRST/2002/41), and reaffirms the need to keep the protection of civilians in armed conflict as an important item on the Council's agenda.
>
> The Council also reaffirms its concern at the suffering inflicted upon and hardships borne by civilians during armed conflict and recognizes the consequent impact that this has on durable peace, reconciliation and development. The Council strongly condemns all attacks and acts of violence directed against civilians or other persons protected under international law, in particular international humanitarian law, in situations of armed conflict, including attacks and acts of violence against women, children, refugees, internally displaced persons and other vulnerable groups. The Council reaffirms the need for parties to armed conflict to take all possible measures to ensure the safety, security and freedom of movement of United Nations and associated personnel as well as personnel of international humanitarian organizations in accordance with applicable international law and recognizes that secure humanitarian access and the swift re-establishment of the rule of law, justice and reconciliation are essential components for an effective transition from conflict to peace. The Council reiterates its call to all parties to armed conflict to comply fully with the provisions of the Charter of the United Nations and with the rules and principles of international law, in particular international humanitarian, human rights and refugee law, and to implement fully the relevant decisions of the Council. The Council recalls the obligations of States to respect and to ensure respect for international humanitarian law, including the four Geneva Conventions of 12 August 1949, and emphasizes the responsibility of States to end impunity and to prosecute those responsible for genocide, war crimes, crimes against humanity and serious violations of humanitarian law. The Council also notes with interest the proposal presented by the Under-Secretary-General for Humanitarian Affairs at the 9 December open meeting of the Council for a "10-point action plan" on the protection of civilians in armed conflict, and looks forward to further discussions and consultations on this issue.
>
> Recalling that on 15 March 2002 the Council adopted the aide-memoire annexed to the statement by its President as a means to facilitate its consideration of issues pertaining to protection of civilians, and recalling further that in the statement by its President of 20 December 2002 the Council expressed its willingness to update the aide-memoire annually in order to reflect emerging trends in the protection of civilians in armed conflict. The Council adopts the updated aide-memoire contained in the annex to the present statement by its President. The Council reiterates the importance of the aide-memoire as a practical tool that provides a basis for improved analysis and diagnosis of key protection issues during deliberations on peacekeeping mandates, and stresses the need to implement the approaches set out therein on a more regular and consistent basis, taking into account the particular circumstances of each conflict situation, and undertakes to remain actively seized of the matter.

Annex

Protection of civilians in armed conflict

Aide-memoire for the consideration of issues pertaining to the protection of civilians during the Security Council's deliberation of peacekeeping mandates

Protection of civilians in armed conflict is at the core of the work of the Security Council for peace and security. On 15 March 2002, the Council adopted an aide-memoire as a practical guide for its consideration of protection issues and agreed to review and update its contents periodically. The present document provides the first update of this important operational tool, adopted as an annex to the statement by the President of the Security Council of 15 December 2003.

In a letter dated 21 June 2001 from the President of the Security Council addressed to the Secretary-General, the members of the Council welcomed the report of the Secretary-General of 30 March 2001 on the protection of civilians in armed conflict, and were of the view that further advice of the Secretary-General would be useful in the Council's consideration of the issues contained in the report.

In order to facilitate due consideration, whenever appropriate, of issues pertaining to the protection of civilians in its deliberations on the establishment, change, or close of peacekeeping operations, the members of the Council suggested that an aide-memoire listing those issues that are relevant in this regard should be drafted in close cooperation with the Council.

The present aide-memoire is the result of an interactive consultation between the Council and the Secretariat, and comprises the experiences of a wide range of agencies within the United Nations, including the Inter-Agency Standing Committee. The document is based on the Council's previous consideration of these issues, including resolutions 1265(1999) of 17 September 1999 and 1296(2000) of 19 April 2000. It highlights primary objectives for Council action, offers specific issues for consideration in meeting those objectives, and lists previous Council resolutions and presidential statements that make reference to such concerns.

Bearing in mind that each peacekeeping mandate has to be designed on a case-by-case basis, the document is not intended as a blueprint. The relevance and practicality of each issue described has to be considered and adapted to the specific conditions in each situation. As highlighted in the report of the Secretary-General entitled "No exit without strategy", the Council should reach agreement on clear and achievable mandates for peace operations based on a common understanding of the conflict. In this respect, mobilization, from the outset, of necessary funding and adequate resources needs to be an integrated part of the Council's overall consideration.

Most frequently civilians are caught in circumstances of dire need where a peacekeeping operation has not been established. Such situations may require the Council's urgent attention. The present aide-memoire may therefore also provide guidance in circumstances where the Council may wish to consider action outside the scope of a peacekeeping operation.

As a practical tool, the aide-memoire is without prejudice to the provisions of Council resolutions and other decisions by the Council. The document is regularly reviewed and updated to reflect the latest concerns pertaining to the protection of civilians in armed conflict, including new trends and measures to address them.

Primary objectives	*Issues for consideration*	*Precedents*
Security for displaced persons and host communities		
1. To prioritize and support the immediate protection needs of displaced persons and civilians in host communities.	Measures to enhance security for displaced persons, support the location of camps in secure areas, and facilitate return under safe and dignified conditions. Measures to enhance security for civilians who remain in their communities and for host communities living in or around areas where refugees or internally displaced persons take shelter. Provision of appropriate and rapid international assistance.	Resolutions 1509(2003), paras. 3 *(j)* and *(l)* and 6, 1508(2003), para. 10, 1493(2003), para. 27, 1484(2003), para. 1, 1479(2003), para. 10, 1470(2003), para. 16, 1427(2002), para. 12, 1419(2002), para. 11, 1393(2002), para. 11, 1355(2001), para. 14, 1346(2001), paras. 7-9, 1319(2000), para. 1, 1296(2000), paras. 12 and 14, 1286(2000), para. 12, 1270(1999), para. 19, 1244(1999), paras. 9 *(c)*, 11 *(k)* and 18 and 1208(1998), paras. 4 and 12.
2. To prioritize and support the maintenance of the humanitarian and civilian character of camps and settlements for displaced persons.	Provision of external and internal security (screening procedures to separate armed elements from civilians; demobilization and disarmament measures; technical assistance and training by international civilian police and/or military observers; location of camps at a significant distance from international border and risk zones; regional and subregional arrangements). Cooperation with host State in provision of security measures, including through technical assistance and training. Deployment of multidisciplinary assessment and security evaluation teams. Regional approach to massive population displacement, including appropriate security arrangements.	

Protection of human rights

Primary objectives	Issues for consideration	Precedents
Access to vulnerable populations		
To facilitate safe and unimpeded access to vulnerable populations as the fundamental prerequisite for humanitarian assistance and protection.	Appropriate security arrangements (role of multinational force; safe corridors; protected areas; armed escorts). Engagement in sustained dialogue with all parties to the armed conflict. Facilitation of the delivery of humanitarian assistance. Compliance with obligations under relevant international humanitarian, human rights and refugee law. Counter-terrorism measures (legislation, training, enforcement, regional and international cooperation) in full compliance with all obligations under international law, in particular international human rights, refugee and humanitarian law.	Resolutions 1509(2003), paras. 3 *(j)*, 5 and 8, 1502(2003), paras. 4 and 5 *(b)*, 1494(2003), para. 25, 1493(2003), paras. 12, 15 and 25, 1479(2003), para. 10, 1456(2003), annex, para. 6, 1445(2002), para. 14, 1419(2002), para. 12, 1417(2002), para. 7, 1405(2002), para. 1, 1379(2001), paras. 4 and 5, 1378(2001), para. 2, 1314(2000), paras. 7 and 14, 1296(2000), paras. 8, 10, 12 and 15, 1286(2000), paras. 9 and 10, 1279(1999), paras. 5 *(e)* and 7, 1272(1999), paras. 2 *(d)*, 10 and 11, 1270(1999), paras. 8 *(d)* and *(g)*, 13, 14 and 22, 1265(1999), paras. 7, 8 and 10, 1264(1999), para. 2, 1244(1999), para. 9 *(h)*, and presidential statement S/PRST/2000/4.
Safety and security of humanitarian and associated personnel		
To ensure the safety and security of humanitarian, United Nations and associated personnel.	Respect by all parties to the conflict for the impartiality and neutrality of humanitarian operations. Support for a safe and secure working environment for humanitarian personnel.	Resolutions 1509(2003), paras. 3 *(j)* and 5, 1502(2003), paras. 1, 3, 4, 5 *(a)-(c)* and 6, 1494(2003), paras. 25 and 26, 1493(2003), para. 25, 1445(2002), para. 14, 1417(2002), para. 7, 1378(2001), paras. 2 and 5, 1319(2000), para. 1, 1296(2000), para. 12, 1286(2000), para. 9, 1272(1999), para. 10, 1270(1999), paras. 8 *(d)*, 13 and 14, 1265(1999), paras. 7-10, 1244(1999), para. 9 *(h)*, and presidential statement S/PRST/2000/4.
Security and the rule of law		
To strengthen the capacity of local police and judicial systems to physically protect civilians and enforce law and order.	Deployment of qualified and well-trained international civilian police as a component of peacekeeping operations to enhance the capacity of the United Nations and to assist the host State with law enforcement. Technical assistance for local police, judiciary and penitentiaries (mentoring; legislative drafting; integration of international personnel). Reconstruction and rehabilitation of institutional infrastructure (salaries; buildings; communications). Mechanisms for monitoring and reporting of alleged violations of humanitarian, human rights and criminal law.	Resolutions 1509(2003), para. 3 *(n)*, 1493(2003), para. 7, 1401(2002), para. 4, 1400(2002), para. 7, 1378(2001), paras. 3 and 4, 1315(2000), para. 4, 1272(1999), para. 2 *(a)-(c)* and *(e)*, 3 *(a)* and 13, 1270(1999), para. 23, 1265(1999), para. 15, and 1244(1999) para. 9 *(d)* and 11 *(i)* and *(j)*.
Disarmament, demobilization, reintegration and rehabilitation		
To facilitate the stabilization and rehabilitation of communities.	Programmes for disarmament and demobilization of combatants, including special measures for women, children and dependants (amnesties; weapons buy-back; economic and development incentives). Programmes for reintegration and rehabilitation of ex-combatants within their communities, including special measures for women and children (community service; counselling services; appropriate education/skills training; family reunification; employment opportunities). Encouragement of full participation of armed groups in disarmament, demobilization, reintegration and rehabilitation programmes. Measures to address the regional dimensions affecting disarmament, demobilization, reintegration and rehabilitation programmes.	Resolutions 1509(2003), paras. 3 *(f)* and *(g)*, 17 and 18, 1479(2003), paras. 3 *(f)* and 9, 1460(2003), para. 13, 1445(2002), paras. 4-6, 1417(2002), para. 9, 1400(2002), para. 6, 1379(2001), paras. 11 *(c)*, *(d)* and *(f)* and 12 *(a)*, 1376(2001), para. 12, 1366(2001), para. 16, 1325(2000), paras. 8 *(a)* and 13, 1318(2000), annex, sect. V, 1296(2000), para. 16, 1270(1999), paras. 3, 4, 8 *(b)* and *(c)*, 9 and 20, 1265(1999), para. 12, 1261(1999), para. 15, and presidential statements S/PRST/2000/10 and S/PRST/1999/28.

Primary objectives	Issues for consideration	Precedents
Small arms and mine action		
To facilitate a secure environment for vulnerable populations and humanitarian personnel.	Mine-action (coordination centres; land-mine clearance; mine-awareness training; victim assistance).	Resolutions 1479(2003), para. 13, 1460(2003), para. 7, 1433(2002), para. 3 *(b)* (ii), 1379(2001), paras. 6 and 9 *(d)*, 1318(2000), annex, sect. VI, first para., 1314(2000), para. 8, 1296(2000), paras. 10 and 20, 1286(2000), para. 12, 1265(1999), para. 17, 1261(1999), paras. 14 and 17 *(a)*, 1244(1999), para. 9 *(e)*, and presidential statement S/PRST/1999/28.
	Measures to control and reduce the illicit traffic in small arms and light weapons (voluntary moratoria; arms embargoes; sanctions; regional and subregional approaches).	
	Involvement of ex-combatants and local communities, in particular women, in the collection and destruction of small arms and light weapons and in demining and other mine-action activities.	
Effects on and contribution of women		
1. To address the specific needs of women for assistance and protection.	Special measures to protect women and girls from gender-based discrimination and violence, rape and other forms of sexual violence (access to legal redress, crisis centres, shelters, health care, counselling and other assistance programmes; monitoring and reporting mechanisms).	Resolutions 1509(2003), para. 11, 1493(2003), para. 9, 1479(2003), para. 5, 1460(2003), para. 10, 1436(2002), para. 15, 1400(2002), para. 14, 1379(2001), para. 4, 1325(2000), paras. 1, 4, 5, 8 *(a)*, 10, 13 and 15, 1314(2000), paras. 13 and 16 *(e)*, 1296(2000), paras. 9 and 10, and presidential statement S/PRST/2001/31.
	Implementation of measures for reporting on and prevention of sexual abuse and exploitation of civilians by humanitarian workers and peacekeepers.	
	Mainstreaming of a gender perspective, including the integration of gender advisers in peace operations.	
2. To strengthen the role of women as constructive actors in developing and implementing appropriate responses to protecting civilians.	Expansion of the representation, role and contribution of women in United Nations field-based operations (among military observers, civilian police and humanitarian and human rights personnel).	
	Increased and more equitable participation of women at all decision-making levels (political processes; organization and management of refugee and internally displaced-persons camps; design and distribution of assistance; local governance; education; rehabilitation policies).	
Effects on children		
To address the specific needs of children for assistance and protection.	Prevention of and putting an end to the recruitment of child soldiers in violation of international law.	Resolutions 1509(2003), paras. 9 and 10, 1493(2003), para. 13, 1479(2003), para. 15, 1460(2003), paras. 3, 9, 10, 12 and 13, 1436(2002), para. 15, 1400(2002), para. 14, 1379(2001), paras. 2, 4, 8 *(e)*, 10 *(c)*, 11 *(c)*, *(d)* and *(f)* and 12 *(a)*, 1314(2000), paras. 11-14, 16 and 17, 1296(2000), paras. 9 and 10, 1270(1999), para. 18, 1261(1999), paras. 2, 8, 13, 15 and 17 *(a)*, and presidential statement S/PRST/1998/18.
	Initiatives, where appropriate, to secure access to war-affected children (days of immunization; temporary ceasefires; days of tranquillity).	
	Negotiated release of children abducted in situations of armed conflict.	
	Effective measures to disarm, demobilize, reintegrate and rehabilitate children recruited or used in hostilities.	
	Specific provisions for the protection of children, including where appropriate, the integration of child protection advisers in peace operations.	
	Implementation of measures for reporting on, and prevention of, sexual abuse and exploitation of civilians by humanitarian workers and peacekeepers.	
	Family reunification of separated children.	
	Monitoring and reporting on the situation of children.	
Justice and reconciliation		
1. To put an end to impunity for those responsible for serious violations of international humanitarian, human rights and criminal law.	Establishment and use of effective arrangements for investigating and prosecuting serious violations of humanitarian and criminal law at the local and/or international level (from the outset of the operation).	Resolutions 1509(2003), para. 10, 1479(2003), para. 8, 1436(2002), paras. 11 and 15, 1400(2002), para. 5, 1398(2002), para. 14, 1379(2001), para. 9 *(a)*, 1325(2000), para. 11, 1319(2000), paras. 2 and 3, 1318(2000), annex, sect. VI, third para., 1315(2000), paras. 1-3 and 8, 1314(2000), paras. 2 and 9, 1272(1999), para. 16, 1270(1999), para. 17, 1265(1999), paras. 4 and 6, 1261(1999), para. 3, 955(1994), paras. 1 and 2 and 827(1993), paras. 2 and 4.
	Cooperation of States for the apprehension and surrender of alleged perpetrators.	
	Technical assistance to strengthen local capacities for apprehension, investigation, and prosecution of alleged perpetrators.	
	Exclusion of genocide, crimes against humanity and war crimes from amnesty provisions.	

Protection of human rights

Primary objectives	Issues for consideration	Precedents
	Referral of situations, where possible and appropriate, to international courts and tribunals.	
2. To build confidence and enhance stability within the host State by promoting truth and reconciliation.	Requests for troop-contributing States to investigate and prosecute, when appropriate, their peacekeepers and security personnel suspected of violating criminal law while in a host State.	
	Appropriate locally adapted mechanisms for truth and reconciliation (technical assistance; funding; amnesties for lower-level perpetrators; just reinstallation of civilians within communities).	
	Measures for restitution and reparations (trust funds; property commissions).	

Training of security and peacekeeping forces

Primary objectives	Issues for consideration	Precedents
To ensure adequate sensitization of multinational forces to issues pertaining to the protection of civilians.	Appropriate training in humanitarian and human rights law, civil-military coordination, codes of conduct, negotiation and communication skills, child protection and child rights, gender and cultural sensitization, and the prevention of HIV/AIDS and other communicable diseases.	Resolutions 1460(2003), para. 9, 1445(2002), para. 18, 1379(2001), para. 10 (b), 1325(2000), para. 6, 1318(2000), annex, sect. III, second para., 1308(2000), para. 3, 1296(2000), para. 19, 1270(1999), para. 15, 1265(1999), para. 14, and presidential statements S/PRST/2001/31, S/PRST/2001/16 and S/PRST/1998/18.

Media and information

Primary objectives	Issues for consideration	Precedents
1. To counter occurrences of speech used to incite violence.	Establishment of media-monitoring mechanisms to ensure effective monitoring, reporting and documenting of any incidents, origins and contents that incite "hate media".	Resolutions 1509(2003), para. 16, 1417(2002), paras. 4 and 5, 1353(2001), annex I, sect. B, paras. 10 and 11 and 1296(2000), paras. 17 and 18.
	Responsive steps to media broadcasts inciting genocide, crimes against humanity and/or serious violations of international humanitarian law, including, as a last resort, consideration of closing down such media broadcasts.	
2. To promote and support accurate management of information on the conflict.	Technical assistance to draft and enforce anti–hate speech legislation.	
	Establishment of media coordination centres to facilitate accurate and reliable information management on, and awareness of, the conflict.	
	Establishment and assistance of local and international media and information outlets in support of peace operations.	

Natural resources and armed conflict

Primary objectives	Issues for consideration	Precedents
To address the impact of natural resource exploitation on the protection of civilians.	Investigation of the linkages between illicit trade in natural resources and the conduct of the conflict.	Resolutions 1509(2003), para. 3 (r), 1493(2003), para. 28, 1460(2003), para. 16 (b), 1436(2002), para. 8, 1417(2002), para. 15, 1379(2001), paras. 6 and 9 (d), 1376(2001), para. 8, 1318(2000), annex, sect. VI, second para., 1314(2000), para. 8 and 1306(2000), paras. 1, 2, 9 and 19 (a).
	Measures to address the direct or indirect import of natural resources where proceeds are used to fuel conflict (sanctions; regional and subregional approaches).	
	Measures against corporate actors, individuals and entities involved in illicit trade of natural resources in violation of relevant Security Council resolutions and the Charter of the United Nations (legislation; penalties for dealers; certification and registration systems; embargoes).	

Humanitarian impact of sanctions

Primary objectives	Issues for consideration	Precedents
To minimize unintended adverse side effects of sanctions on the civilian population.	Humanitarian exemptions in sanction regimes.	Resolutions 1478(2003), paras. 18 and 19, 1409(2002), paras. 4-6, 1408(2002), para. 16, 1379(2001), para. 7, 1343(2001), paras. 5 (a)-(d), 6, 7 (a) and (b) and 13 (a), 1333(2000), paras. 5 (a)-(c), 7, 8 (a)-(c), 10-12, 14, 15 (d) and 23, 1325(2000), para. 14, 1314(2000), para. 15, 1298(2000), paras. 6-8 and 16, 1296(2000), para. 21, 1267(1999), para. 4, 1265(1999), para. 16, and presidential statement S/PRST/1999/28.
	Targeted sanctions (sanctions limited in scope and targeted at specific individuals, groups, or activities).	
	Relevant assessment and review of the humanitarian impact of sanctions, and the behaviour of those targeted by the sanctions.	

Index of resolutions*

1509(2003) on the situation in Liberia
1508(2003) on the situation in Sierra Leone
1502(2003) on the protection of United Nations personnel, associated personnel and humanitarian personnel in conflict zones
1494(2003) on the situation in Georgia
1493(2003) on the situation concerning the Democratic Republic of the Congo
1484(2003) on the situation concerning the Democratic Republic of the Congo
1479(2003) on the situation in Côte d'Ivoire
1478(2003) on the situation in Liberia
1470(2003) on the situation in Sierra Leone
1460(2003) on children and armed conflict
1456(2003) on the high-level meeting of the Security Council: combating terrorism
1445(2002) on the situation concerning the Democratic Republic of the Congo
1436(2002) on the situation in Sierra Leone
1433(2002) on the situation in Angola
1427(2002) on the situation in Georgia
1419(2002) on the situation in Afghanistan
1417(2002) on the situation concerning the Democratic Republic of the Congo
1409(2002) on the situation between Iraq and Kuwait
1408(2002) on the situation in Liberia
1405(2002) on the situation in the Middle East, including the Palestine question
1401(2002) on the situation in Afghanistan
1400(2002) on the situation in Sierra Leone
1393(2002) on the situation in Georgia
1379(2001) on children and armed conflict
1378(2001) on the situation in Afghanistan
1376(2001) on the situation concerning the Democratic Republic of the Congo
1366(2001) on the role of the Security Council in the prevention of armed conflicts
1355(2001) on the situation concerning the Democratic Republic of the Congo
1353(2001) on strengthening cooperation with troop-contributing countries
1346(2001) on the situation in Sierra Leone
1343(2001) on the situation in Liberia
1333(2000) on the situation in Afghanistan
1327(2000) on ensuring an effective role of the Security Council in the maintenance of international peace and security
1325(2000) on women and peace and security
1319(2000) on the situation in East Timor
1318(2000) on ensuring an effective role for the Security Council in the maintenance of international peace and security, particularly in Africa
1315(2000) on the situation in Sierra Leone
1314(2000) on children and armed conflict
1308(2000) on the responsibility of the Security Council in the maintenance of international peace and security: HIV/AIDS and international peacekeeping operations
1306(2000) on the situation in Sierra Leone
1298(2000) on the situation between Eritrea and Ethiopia
1296(2000) on the protection of civilians in armed conflict
1286(2000) on the situation in Burundi
1279(1999) on the situation concerning the Democratic Republic of the Congo
1272(1999) on the situation in East Timor
1270(1999) on the situation in Sierra Leone
1267(1999) on the situation in Afghanistan
1265(1999) on the protection of civilians in armed conflict
1264(1999) on the situation in East Timor
1261(1999) on children and armed conflict
1244(1999) on Security Council resolutions 1160(1998), 1199(1998), 1203(1998) and 1239(1999)
1208(1998) on the situation in Africa
955(1994) on the situation concerning Rwanda
827(1993) on the establishment of an international tribunal for the prosecution of persons responsible for serious violations in international humanitarian law committed in the territory of the former Yugoslavia
824(1993) on the situation in the Republic of Bosnia and Herzegovina

*The Security Council also recognized the relevance of General Assembly resolutions 46/182 of 19 December 1991 and 55/2 of 8 September 2000 in the broader context of the protection of civilians and the root causes of conflicts.

Index of presidential statements

S/PRST/2002/41 on the protection of civilians in armed conflict
S/PRST/2002/6 on the protection of civilians in armed conflict
S/PRST/2001/31 on women and peace and security
S/PRST/2001/16 on the responsibility of the Security Council in the maintenance of international peace and security: HIV/AIDS and international peacekeeping operations
S/PRST/2000/10 on maintaining peace and security and post-conflict peace-building

S/PRST/2000/4 on the protection of United Nations personnel, associated personnel and humanitarian personnel in conflict zones
S/PRST/1999/28 on small arms
S/PRST/1998/18 on children and armed conflict

(For Security Council action regarding the situation of children in armed conflict, see p. 788.)

Arbitrary detention

Commission action. On 23 April [res. 2003/31], the Commission decided to extend for three years the mandate of the Working Group and asked it to report in 2004. The Secretary-General was asked to assist Governments, special rapporteurs and working groups to ensure the promotion and observance of guarantees relating to states of emergency embodied in international instruments, and to assist the Group.

On 23 July, the Economic and Social Council endorsed the Commission's decision to extend the Working Group's mandate for three years **(decision 2003/247)**.

Working Group activities. The Working Group on Arbitrary Detention held its thirty-sixth (5-9 May), thirty-seventh (1-5 September) and thirty-eighth (19-28 November) sessions, all in Geneva [E/CN.4/2004/3]. During the year, the Group adopted 26 opinions regarding 151 persons in 12 countries; the text of the opinions were contained in a separate report [E/CN.4/2004/3/Add.1]. The Group also transmitted 157 urgent appeals to 47 Governments regarding 812 individuals, of which 147 appeals were issued jointly by the Group and thematic or geographical special rapporteurs. In 33 cases, the Governments concerned informed the Group that they had taken measures to remedy the situation of the detainees.

The Group examined the question of protecting human rights and fundamental freedoms in the context of the fight against terrorism and other issues, including discrimination, the deprivation of liberty of vulnerable persons, pre-trial detention and the deprivation of liberty linked to the use of the Internet. It drew the Commission's attention to the fact that, since the events of 11 September 2001 [YUN 2001, p. 60], it had received many communications about the arbitrary character of detention in many countries where inquiries into terrorist acts had been carried out. Bearing in mind the rising importance of the Internet and other modern information media, the Group expressed concern that some States unduly interfered with the use of the Internet through the application of criminal law sanctions. It considered that the question of arbitrary detention with regard to the use of the Internet deserved more extensive study.

Two Working Group members visited Iran at the invitation of the Government (15-27 February) [E/CN.4/2004/3/Add.2 & Corr.1], where they analysed the prospects for reform of the administration of justice, particularly with regard to detention pending trial and visiting rights, and reform of the public prosecution service and criminal procedure. Among the causes of situations of arbitrary detention were: the shortcomings of due process, the abuse of solitary confinement, special clerical courts, sentences disproportionate to the seriousness of the offence, non-respect for procedural formalities as a guarantee against arbitrary detention and the removal of prosecutors between 1995 and 2002, which affected the exercise of the right to due process. The Group, while acknowledging that the visit was conducted transparently and without hindrance, noted that follow-up exchanges with the authorities regarding specific individuals or incidents had not been encouraging. It also indicated that the persecution of the press had increased. The Group made recommendations regarding the reduction of the proliferation of judicial decision-making bodies, the practice of solitary confinement, the situation of prisoners of conscience, the right to due process and imprisonment for debt.

In Argentina (22 September–2 October) [E/CN.4/2004/3/Add.3], the Group recommended that the Government review its legislation and practices regarding pre-trial detention at both the federal and provincial levels; address overcrowding in prisons and at police stations; avoid detaining children and foreigners under immigration laws; guarantee detainees the right to communicate freely with their attorney; monitor the behaviour of police officers; ensure an effective judicial remedy in situations of arrest for a minor offence and for detained foreigners; pay particular attention to compliance with the Convention on the Rights of the Child (see p. 675) with regard to the arrest and detention of juveniles; and study the practice of detaining social protesters, bearing in mind that the protests emanated from jobs lost owing to the country's recession.

Communications. In March [E/CN.4/2003/G/53], Mexico transmitted its comments on the report of the Working Group following the Group's 2002 visit to the country [YUN 2002, p. 698].

On 2 April [E/CN.4/2003/G/72], the United States, in response to a 2002 opinion of the Working Group [YUN 2002, p. 698] relating to the detention of two persons, stated that the Group's findings were based on unsubstantiated and false facts, and on a misunderstanding of its laws.

Also on 2 April [E/CN.4/2003/G/73], the United States stated that it disagreed with the Group's conclusions [YUN 2002, p. 698] regarding persons detained at the Naval Base at Guantánamo Bay, Cuba.

Impunity

Report of Secretary-General. In response to a 2002 Commission request [YUN 2002, p. 699], the Secretary-General, in a January report [E/CN.4/2003/97], summarized replies received from Governments, intergovernmental organizations and NGOs regarding steps they had taken to combat impunity for human rights violations and on remedies available to victims. He concluded that there was broad agreement that there should be no impunity for human rights violations, war crimes, crimes against humanity and genocide. Information provided by Member States highlighted the importance of pursuing prosecutions, finding and publicizing the truth, assisting and protecting victims, witnesses and others involved in the proceedings, and providing reparation and remedies to victims.

Commission action. On 25 April [res. 2003/72], the Commission asked the Secretary-General to obtain information from States on steps taken to combat impunity for human rights violations and on remedies available to victims; to commission an independent study on best practices to assist States in strengthening their domestic capacity in that regard, taking into account the application of the 1997 set of principles for the promotion and protection of human rights through action to combat impunity [YUN 1997, p. 655], as well as comments received pursuant to the resolution; and to report in 2004.

Working paper. On 6 August [E/CN.4/Sub.2/2003/SR.12], Françoise Hampson (United Kingdom) described progress made in preparing a working paper on the scope of activities and accountability of armed forces, UN civilian police, international civil servants and experts taking part in peace support operations, entrusted to her by the Subcommission in 2002 [YUN 2002, p. 699].

Subcommission action. On 13 August [res. 2003/10], the Subcommission, convinced that ratification of the Rome Statute of the International Criminal Court [YUN 1998, p. 1209], which entered into force in 2002 [YUN 2002, p. 1298], by the largest number of States would constitute an important guarantee in combating impunity, welcomed the Court's establishment following the election of its judges, representatives of all continents and legal systems, and the appointment of its prosecutor. It urged all States to ratify the Statute as soon as possible and to ensure its implementation.

Independence of the judicial system

Report of Special Rapporteur. In January, the Special Rapporteur on the independence of judges and lawyers, Dato' Param Cumaraswamy (Malaysia), submitted a report covering his activities in 2002 [E/CN.4/2003/65]. He transmitted 24 interventions to 20 Governments, three interventions jointly with other special rapporteurs to three States and 13 urgent appeals to nine States. Replies were received from 13 countries to the interventions and from 13 countries to the urgent appeals. To avoid duplication of work, the Special Rapporteur joined other special rapporteurs and working groups to transmit 46 additional urgent appeals to 22 countries. An addendum to the report [E/CN.4/2003/65/Add.1] contained summaries of the urgent appeals and interventions, and replies thereto. Annexed to the January report were the Bangalore Principles of Judicial Conduct, designed to promote judicial integrity and accountability around the world, which were adopted by a round-table meeting of Chief Justices (The Hague, Netherlands, 25-26 November 2002). The Special Rapporteur observed that the independence of the judicial system and of the legal profession continued to be threatened in many parts of the world, and accountability had become a source of concern owing to increasing allegations of judicial corruption. Since the terrorist attacks of 11 September 2001 [YUN 2001, p. 60], the principles of due process, including the right to a fair public hearing by independent and impartial tribunals, were in jeopardy in some countries, among them, well-developed States that previously supported those values. The Special Rapporteur recommended greater monitoring of the implementation of the United Nations Basic Principles on the Independence of the Judiciary, adopted in 1985 by the Seventh UN Congress on the Prevention of Crime and the Treatment of Offenders [YUN 1985, pp. 738 & 757], as well as the Guidelines on the Role of Prosecutors and the Basic Principles on the Role of Lawyers, both adopted in 1990 by the Eighth UN Congress [YUN 1990, p. 697]. Addressing the impact of terrorism on the principles of due process, the Special Rapporteur urged the Commission to remind Member States of their obligations under international law, and to address issues of concern in Swaziland, Zimbabwe, countries in transition in Eastern and Central Europe and Asia, particularly Timor-Leste and Afghanistan, and the United Kingdom and the United States.

Commission action. By a recorded vote of 31 to 1, with 21 abstentions, the Commission, on 23 April [res. 2003/39], called on States that used military courts to try criminal offenders to ensure that the courts were an integral part of the general judicial system and employed established legal proceedings. The Special Rapporteur was asked to report in 2004.

Also on 23 April [res. 2003/43], the Commission asked the High Commissioner to continue to provide technical assistance to train judges and lawyers. It decided to extend the Special Rapporteur's mandate for a further three years and asked him to report in 2004, and asked the Secretary-General to assist him.

The Economic and Social Council endorsed the Commission's requests on 23 July (**decision 2003/250**).

Communication. On 3 March [E/CN.4/2003/G/46], Italy responded to the Special Rapporteur's report on his visit to the country [YUN 2002, p. 700], regarding the independence of Italian magistrates.

Capital punishment

Note by Secretariat. A January note [E/CN.4/2003/106/Add.1] of the Secretariat stated that information received as at 20 January from Member States regarding the death penalty, pursuant to a 2002 Commission resolution [YUN 2002, p. 701], were summarized in the Secretary-General's report (see below).

Report of Secretary-General. In response to a 2002 Commission request [YUN 2002, p. 701], the Secretary-General, in January [E/CN.4/2003/106], supplemented information in his sixth quinquennial report [YUN 2000, p. 672] on capital punishment and implementation of the safeguards guaranteeing protection of the rights of those facing the death penalty, covering the period from January 2001 to December 2002. The report summarized information received from 15 countries relating to the use of capital punishment, changes in law and practice concerning the death penalty and implementation of the safeguards, with special attention to the imposition of the death penalty against persons younger than 18 years of age at the time of the offence. Additional information was provided by five intergovernmental organizations and NGOs. During the reporting period, two countries abolished the death penalty for all crimes, two abolished it for ordinary crimes, one limited its use, eight acceded to or ratified instruments that abolished it, four established a moratorium on executions and one reintroduced the death penalty. Overall, at least 5,265 persons were sentenced to death in 68 countries, and 3,048 people were executed in 31 countries during 2001. Nonetheless, the Secretary-General concluded that the trend towards abolition continued, given that the number of completely abolitionist countries increased from 76 to 77, while abolitionist countries for ordinary crimes increased from 11 to 15. The number of retentionist countries remained at 71 and de facto abolitionist countries numbered 33. An increasing number of countries ratified international instruments abolishing the death penalty. During the reporting period, Amnesty International reported three executions of juvenile offenders in three countries. The report highlighted initiatives by the Commission and its mechanisms regarding relevant international developments and the implementation of safeguards.

Commission action. By a recorded vote of 24 to 18, with 10 abstentions, the Commission, on 24 April [res. 2003/67], called on States parties to the International Covenant on Civil and Political Rights that had not done so to consider acceding to or ratifying the Second Optional Protocol thereto on the death penalty (see p. 669). Among other measures, States that maintained the death penalty were urged not to impose it for crimes committed by persons below 18 years of age and to exclude pregnant women and mothers with dependent infants; to restrict the number of offences for which the penalty might be imposed; to establish a moratorium on executions; and to provide the Secretary-General and relevant UN bodies with information relating to the use of capital punishment and the observance of the safeguards guaranteeing the rights of those facing the death penalty, as contained in Economic and Social Council resolution 1984/50 [YUN 1984, p. 709]. The Secretary-General was asked to submit annually a supplement to his quinquennial report, paying attention to the imposition of the death penalty against persons under 18 years of age at the time of the offence.

Communication. In April [E/CN.4/2003/G/84], Saudi Arabia, also on behalf of 62 other States, dissociated itself from the Commission's resolution.

Subcommission action. On 13 August [res. 2003/11], the Subcommission urged States not to transfer persons to the jurisdiction of other States which still imposed the death penalty unless there was a guarantee that the penalty would neither be sought nor applied; not to transfer persons to States where they might be held without trial or subjected to an unfair trial; to ensure that no person was transferred outside the context of extradition; and to ensure that all persons had the possibility to challenge in courts any proposed transfer to the jurisdiction of another State.

Forensic science

On 23 April [res. 2003/33], the Commission, welcoming the publication by OHCHR of the *Istanbul Protocol: Manual on the Effective Investigation and Documentation of Torture and Other Cruel, Inhuman or Degrading Treatment or Punishment* (Professional Training Series, No. 8) [Sales No. E.01.XIV.1], and the establishment by the Office of a consolidated database of forensic experts, asked the High Commissioner to update the database continuously. It recommended that OHCHR encourage forensic experts to produce additional manuals on examinations of living persons and asked it to report in 2005. The Commission further recommended that the Secretary-General establish procedures to evaluate the use of forensic experts and the results of those efforts, and asked him to provide resources to fund OHCHR activities in implementing the Commission's current resolution, including a revision of the *Manual on the Effective Prevention and Investigation of Extralegal, Arbitrary and Summary Executions* [Sales No. E.91.IV.1].

Right to democracy

Report of High Commissioner. The Commission had before it a report of the High Commissioner [E/CN.4/2003/64], submitted pursuant to a 2002 Commission request [YUN 2002, p. 701], which summarized the views of one UN body, one specialized agency, one regional organization and two national institutions on the role they played in promoting and consolidating democracy.

Commission action. By a recorded vote of 36 to none, with 17 abstentions, the Commission, on 23 April [res. 2003/36], called on OHCHR to pay increased attention to the promotion and consolidation of democracy by the UN system, intergovernmental organizations and NGOs; to coordinate efforts with relevant UN bodies to collect and analyse data; to invite the views of regional, subregional and other organizations and arrangements on the role they played in promoting and consolidating democracy; and to report in 2004. It asked the Office to compile documents or texts adopted and used by various intergovernmental, international, regional and subregional organizations aimed at promoting and consolidating democracy, and to report in 2005, and to organize a second expert seminar in 2004 on the interdependence between democracy and human rights, and to report on the seminar's conclusions in 2005.

Note by Secretariat. A July note [E/CN.4/Sub.2/2003/7] by the Secretariat stated that Manuel Rodríguez Cuadros (Peru) would submit in 2004 an expanded working paper on measures to promote and consolidate democracy, pursuant to a 2002 Subcommission request [YUN 2002, p. 702].

Subcommission action. On 13 August [dec. 2003/106], the Subcommission decided to request Mr. Rodríguez Cuadros to prepare, without financial implications, the final version of his 2002 working paper [YUN 2002, p. 702] for consideration in 2004.

Report of Secretary-General. A September report [A/58/323] of the Secretary-General evaluated progress made in fulfilling the commitments contained in the Millennium Declaration [YUN 2000, p. 49] (see also p. 48). Regarding human rights and democracy, in many countries the transition to democracy had been accompanied by serious social and economic problems, while in some others resistance to democracy was strong, even though the majority of the people desired change. Although primarily home-grown, the international community could respond to democratization processes in post-conflict situations, and also provide electoral assistance.

Electoral processes

Commission action. By a recorded vote of 29 to 12, with 12 abstentions, the Commission, on 23 April [res. 2003/35], urged States to foster a democracy that guaranteed all citizens participation in government. The Secretary-General and the High Commissioner were asked to bring the Commission's resolution to the attention of Member States, UN organs, intergovernmental organizations and NGOs, and to disseminate it widely.

Report of Secretary-General. In response to General Assembly resolution 56/159 [YUN 2001, p. 640], the Secretary-General, in an August report [A/58/212] covering UN electoral activities undertaken since his 2001 report on the subject [YUN 2001, p. 640], stated that the United Nations had received 52 requests for electoral assistance from Member States, of which 26 were for technical assistance. Major electoral missions, in Afghanistan, East Timor and Sierra Leone were supported, while advance planning began for a future electoral mission in the Democratic Republic of the Congo. Coordination and support were provided in five countries, and in several cases more than one request for assistance was submitted by the same Member State. Technical assistance continued to be the most widely requested form of assistance for electoral processes such as registration, training for polling officers, civic education and advisory support for national election administrations.

GENERAL ASSEMBLY ACTION

On 22 December [meeting 77], the General Assembly, on the recommendation of the Third Committee [A/58/508/Add.2], adopted **resolution 58/180** by recorded vote (169-0-8) [agenda item 117 (b)].

Strengthening the role of the United Nations in enhancing the effectiveness of the principle of periodic and genuine elections and the promotion of democratization

The General Assembly,

Recalling its previous resolutions on the subject, in particular resolution 56/159 of 19 December 2001,

Reaffirming that United Nations electoral assistance and support for the promotion of democratization are provided only at the specific request of the Member State concerned,

Noting with satisfaction that increasing numbers of Member States are using elections as a peaceful means of discerning the will of the people, which builds confidence in representative governance and contributes to greater national peace and stability,

Recalling the Universal Declaration of Human Rights, adopted on 10 December 1948, in particular the principle that the will of the people, as expressed through periodic and genuine elections, shall be the basis of government authority, as well as the right freely to choose representatives through periodic and genuine elections, which shall be by universal and equal suffrage and held by secret vote or by equivalent free voting procedures,

Noting with interest Commission on Human Rights resolution 2003/36 of 23 April 2003,

Recognizing the need for strengthening democratic processes, electoral institutions and national capacity-building, including the capacity to administer fair elections, increase citizen participation and provide civic education in requesting countries in order to consolidate and regularize the achievements of previous elections and support subsequent elections,

Welcoming the support provided by States to the electoral assistance activities of the United Nations, inter alia, through the provision of electoral experts, including electoral commission staff, and observers, as well as through contributions to the United Nations Trust Fund for Electoral Observation,

Welcoming also the contributions made by international and regional organizations and also by non-governmental organizations to enhancing the effectiveness of the principle of periodic and genuine elections and the promotion of democratization,

Having considered the report of the Secretary-General on United Nations activities aimed at enhancing the effectiveness of the principle of periodic and genuine elections and the promotion of democratization,

1. *Welcomes* the report of the Secretary-General;

2. *Commends* the electoral assistance provided upon request to Member States by the United Nations, and requests that such assistance continue on a case-by-case basis in accordance with the evolving needs of requesting countries to develop, improve and refine their electoral institutions and processes, recognizing that the fundamental responsibility of organizing free and fair elections lies with Governments;

3. *Requests* the Electoral Assistance Division of the Department of Political Affairs of the Secretariat, in its role as coordinator of United Nations electoral assistance, to continue to inform Member States regularly about the requests received and the nature of any assistance provided;

4. *Requests* that the United Nations continue its efforts to ensure, before undertaking to provide electoral assistance to a requesting State, that there is adequate time to organize and carry out an effective mission for providing such assistance, including the provision of long-term technical cooperation, that conditions exist to allow a free and fair election and that the mission's results will be reported comprehensively and consistently;

5. *Recommends* that, throughout the time span of the entire electoral process, including before and after elections, as appropriate, based on needs assessment missions, the United Nations continue to provide technical advice and other assistance to requesting States and electoral institutions in order to help to strengthen their democratic processes;

6. *Notes with appreciation* additional efforts being made to enhance cooperation with other international, governmental and non-governmental organizations in order to facilitate more comprehensive and needs-specific responses to requests for electoral assistance, and encourages those organizations to share knowledge and experience in order to promote best practices in the assistance they provide and in the reporting they make on electoral processes, and expresses its appreciation to those Member States, regional organizations and non-governmental organizations that have provided observers or technical experts in support of United Nations electoral assistance efforts;

7. *Recalls* the establishment by the Secretary-General of the United Nations Trust Fund for Electoral Observation, and calls upon Member States to consider contributing to the Fund;

8. *Encourages* the Secretary-General, through the Electoral Assistance Division, to continue responding to the evolving nature of requests for assistance and the growing need for specific types of medium-term expert assistance aimed at supporting and strengthening the existing capacity of the requesting Government, in particular through enhancing the capacity of national electoral institutions;

9. *Requests* the Secretary-General to provide the Electoral Assistance Division with adequate human and financial resources to allow it to carry out its mandate, and to continue to ensure that the Office of the United Nations High Commissioner for Human Rights is able to respond, within its mandate and in close coordination with the Division, to the numerous and increasingly complex and comprehensive requests from Member States for advisory services;

10. *Notes with satisfaction* the comprehensive coordination between the Electoral Assistance Division and the United Nations Development Programme, and encourages further engagement of the Office of the United Nations High Commissioner for Human Rights in this context;

11. *Requests* the United Nations Development Programme to continue its governance assistance programmes in cooperation with other relevant organizations, in particular those that strengthen democratic

institutions and linkages between civil society and Governments;

12. *Reiterates* the importance of reinforced coordination within and outside the United Nations system in this regard;

13. *Requests* the Secretary-General to report to the General Assembly at its sixtieth session on the implementation of the present resolution, in particular on the status of requests from Member States for electoral assistance, and on his efforts to enhance support by the Organization for the democratization process in Member States.

RECORDED VOTE ON RESOLUTION 58/180:

In favour: Afghanistan, Albania, Algeria, Andorra, Angola, Antigua and Barbuda, Argentina, Armenia, Australia, Austria, Azerbaijan, Bahamas, Bahrain, Bangladesh, Barbados, Belarus, Belgium, Belize, Benin, Bhutan, Bolivia, Bosnia and Herzegovina, Botswana, Brazil, Bulgaria, Burkina Faso, Burundi, Cambodia, Cameroon, Canada, Cape Verde, Central African Republic, Chile, Colombia, Comoros, Congo, Costa Rica, Côte d'Ivoire, Croatia, Cyprus, Czech Republic, Democratic Republic of the Congo, Denmark, Djibouti, Dominica, Dominican Republic, Ecuador, Egypt, El Salvador, Eritrea, Estonia, Ethiopia, Fiji, Finland, France, Gabon, Gambia, Georgia, Germany, Ghana, Greece, Grenada, Guatemala, Guinea, Guinea-Bissau, Guyana, Haiti, Honduras, Hungary, Iceland, India, Indonesia, Iran, Ireland, Israel, Italy, Jamaica, Japan, Jordan, Kazakhstan, Kenya, Kuwait, Kyrgyzstan, Latvia, Lebanon, Lesotho, Liechtenstein, Lithuania, Luxembourg, Madagascar, Malawi, Malaysia, Maldives, Mali, Malta, Marshall Islands, Mauritania, Mauritius, Mexico, Micronesia, Monaco, Mongolia, Morocco, Mozambique, Namibia, Nauru, Nepal, Netherlands, New Zealand, Nicaragua, Niger, Nigeria, Norway, Oman, Pakistan, Palau, Panama, Papua New Guinea, Paraguay, Peru, Philippines, Poland, Portugal, Qatar, Republic of Korea, Republic of Moldova, Romania, Russian Federation, Rwanda, Saint Lucia, Saint Vincent and the Grenadines, Samoa, San Marino, Senegal, Serbia and Montenegro, Seychelles, Sierra Leone, Singapore, Slovakia, Slovenia, Solomon Islands, Somalia, South Africa, Spain, Sri Lanka, Sudan, Suriname, Sweden, Switzerland, Tajikistan, Thailand, The former Yugoslav Republic of Macedonia, Timor-Leste, Togo, Trinidad and Tobago, Tunisia, Turkey, Tuvalu, Uganda, Ukraine, United Kingdom, United Republic of Tanzania, United States, Uruguay, Uzbekistan, Venezuela, Yemen, Zambia, Zimbabwe.

Against: None.

Abstaining: Brunei Darussalam, China, Cuba, Democratic People's Republic of Korea, Libyan Arab Jamahiriya, Myanmar, Syrian Arab Republic, Viet Nam.

Also on 22 December [meeting 77], the Assembly, on the recommendation of the Third Committee [A/58/508/Add.2], adopted **resolution 58/189** by recorded vote (111-10-55) [agenda item 117 *(b)*].

Respect for the principles of national sovereignty and diversity of democratic systems in electoral processes as an important element for the promotion and protection of human rights

The General Assembly,

Reaffirming the purpose of the United Nations to develop friendly relations among nations based on respect for the principle of equal rights and self-determination of peoples and to take other appropriate measures to strengthen universal peace,

Recalling its resolution 1514(XV) of 14 December 1960, containing the Declaration on the Granting of Independence to Colonial Countries and Peoples,

Recalling also its resolution 2625(XXV) of 24 October 1970, by which it approved the Declaration on Principles of International Law concerning Friendly Relations and Cooperation among States in accordance with the Charter of the United Nations,

Reaffirming the right to self-determination, by virtue of which all peoples can freely determine their political status and freely pursue their economic, social and cultural development,

Recognizing that the principles enshrined in Article 2 of the Charter of the United Nations, in particular respect for national sovereignty, should be respected in the holding of elections,

Recognizing also the richness and diversity of democratic political systems and models of free and fair electoral processes in the world, based on national and regional particularities and various backgrounds,

Stressing the responsibility of States in ensuring ways and means to facilitate full and effective popular participation in their electoral processes,

Recognizing the contribution made by the United Nations of electoral assistance provided to numerous States upon their request,

Reaffirming the solemn commitment of all States to fulfil their obligations to promote universal respect for, and observance and protection of, all human rights and fundamental freedoms for all in accordance with the Charter, other instruments relating to human rights, and international law,

Welcoming the commitment of all Member States, expressed in the United Nations Millennium Declaration, to work collectively for more inclusive political processes allowing genuine participation by all citizens in all countries,

1. *Reaffirms* that all peoples have the right to self-determination, by virtue of which they freely determine their political status and freely pursue their economic, social and cultural development, and that every State has the duty to respect that right, in accordance with the provisions of the Charter of the United Nations;

2. *Reiterates* that periodic, fair and free elections are important elements for the promotion and protection of human rights;

3. *Reaffirms* the right of peoples to determine methods and to establish institutions regarding electoral processes and, consequently, that there is no single model of democracy or of democratic institutions and that States should ensure all the necessary mechanisms and means to facilitate full and effective popular participation in those processes;

4. *Reaffirms also* that free development of the national electoral process in each State should be fully honoured in a manner that fully respects the principles established in the Charter and in the Declaration on Principles of International Law concerning Friendly Relations and Cooperation among States in accordance with the Charter of the United Nations;

5. *Calls upon* all States to refrain from financing political parties or other organizations in any other State in a way that is contrary to the principles of the Charter and that undermines the legitimacy of its electoral processes;

6. *Condemns* any act of armed aggression or threat or use of force against peoples, their elected Governments or their legitimate leaders;

7. *Reaffirms* that the will of the people shall be the basis of the authority of government and that this will shall be expressed in periodic and genuine elections, which shall be by universal and equal suffrage and shall be held by secret vote or by equivalent free voting procedures.

RECORDED VOTE ON RESOLUTION 58/189:

In favour: Algeria, Angola, Antigua and Barbuda, Azerbaijan, Bahamas, Bahrain, Bangladesh, Barbados, Belarus, Belize, Benin, Bhutan, Bolivia,

Brazil, Brunei Darussalam, Burkina Faso, Burundi, Cambodia, Cameroon, Cape Verde, Central African Republic, China, Colombia, Comoros, Congo, Côte d'Ivoire, Cuba, Democratic People's Republic of Korea, Democratic Republic of the Congo, Djibouti, Dominica, Dominican Republic, Ecuador, Egypt, El Salvador, Eritrea, Ethiopia, Fiji, Gabon, Gambia, Ghana, Grenada, Guinea, Guinea-Bissau, Guyana, Haiti, Honduras, Indonesia, Iran, Jamaica, Japan, Jordan, Kazakhstan, Kenya, Kuwait, Lao People's Democratic Republic, Lebanon, Lesotho, Libyan Arab Jamahiriya, Madagascar, Malawi, Malaysia, Maldives, Mali, Marshall Islands, Mauritania, Mauritius, Mongolia, Morocco, Mozambique, Myanmar, Namibia, Nicaragua, Niger, Nigeria, Oman, Pakistan, Panama, Paraguay, Peru, Philippines, Qatar, Russian Federation, Rwanda, Saint Lucia, Saint Vincent and the Grenadines, Senegal, Seychelles, Sierra Leone, Singapore, Solomon Islands, Somalia, South Africa, Sri Lanka, Suriname, Syrian Arab Republic, Thailand, Timor-Leste, Togo, Trinidad and Tobago, Tunisia, Turkmenistan, Uganda, United Arab Emirates, United Republic of Tanzania, Uruguay, Venezuela, Viet Nam, Yemen, Zambia, Zimbabwe.

Against: Argentina, Australia, Canada, Chile, Israel, New Zealand, Norway, Sudan, Switzerland, United States.

Abstaining: Albania, Andorra, Armenia, Austria, Belgium, Bosnia and Herzegovina, Botswana, Bulgaria, Costa Rica, Croatia, Cyprus, Czech Republic, Denmark, Estonia, Finland, France, Georgia, Germany, Greece, Guatemala, Hungary, Iceland, India, Ireland, Italy, Kyrgyzstan, Latvia, Liechtenstein, Lithuania, Luxembourg, Malta, Mexico, Monaco, Nauru, Nepal, Netherlands, Papua New Guinea, Poland, Portugal, Republic of Korea, Republic of Moldova, Romania, Samoa, San Marino, Serbia and Montenegro, Slovakia, Slovenia, Spain, Sweden, The former Yugoslav Republic of Macedonia, Turkey, Tuvalu, Ukraine, United Kingdom, Uzbekistan.

Other issues

Extralegal executions

Reports of Special Rapporteur. In a January report with a later addendum [E/CN.4/2003/3 & Corr.1 & Add.1 & Add.1/Corr.1], the Special Rapporteur on extrajudicial, summary or arbitrary executions, Asma Jahangir (Pakistan), updated developments since her last report [YUN 2002, p. 705]. Between 2 December 2001 and 1 December 2002, she transmitted 56 communications containing allegations of violations of the right to life of a large number of individuals and groups to 42 countries and the Palestinian Authority (PA). In more than 29 of those cases, she intervened jointly with other special rapporteurs. In addition, she transmitted 188 urgent appeals, 128 of them jointly with other Commission mechanisms, to prevent imminent loss of life on behalf of several thousand persons and several groups in 54 States and the PA. The report summarized the cases transmitted and the replies received. The Special Rapporteur said that during the reporting period the situation with regard to extrajudicial, summary and arbitrary executions had not improved. An issue of serious concern was resorting to extrajudicial killings in order to fight terrorism. There were growing reports of extrajudicial killings of journalists, and human rights defenders, lawyers, students, trade union officials and judges were increasingly targeted. Special forces, intelligence services and military personnel accused of killings often enjoyed impunity and were rarely held accountable. Stating that the recommendations in her 2002 reports to the Commission and the General Assembly [YUN 2002, p. 705] remained valid, the Special Rapporteur further recommended a greater focus on preventive actions to ensure that violence did not escalate or turn into armed conflict; a stronger system of response to early warnings; and addressing past suspected crimes against humanity in Afghanistan. Other recommendations were made regarding journalists at risk, the use of the military for internal security, respect for relevant safeguards and restrictions when imposing the death penalty, and ending impunity for those who killed women in the name of honour.

The Special Rapporteur visited Jamaica (17-27 February) [E/CN.4/2004/7/Add.2 & Corr.1] following reports over the years of alleged extrajudicial executions by Jamaican security and police forces, and information she received that international standards on safeguards and restrictions relating to the imposition of capital punishment had not always been observed. She described the international human rights legal framework as it related to Jamaica, provided a historical, social and economic overview of the country, and statistics regarding incidents of alleged extrajudicial executions over the past few years. Individual cases were summarized and the issue of capital punishment was examined. The Special Rapporteur concluded that extrajudicial executions of civilians by the police, and possibly by the Jamaica Defence Force, had taken place, and although the figures provided by various sources, including the Government, were not consistent, they were high enough to cause concern. There was a tendency, across the board, to cover up suspected cases of extrajudicial killings. The Special Rapporteur recommended, among other measures, that the Government streamline the criminal justice system to grant complainants access to all legal remedies and to ensure an acceptable level of accountability on the part of the security forces. The authorities should condemn the misuse of force by the security forces, not protect those accused of extrajudicial executions, and refrain from imposing capital punishment on minors or mentally ill persons.

The Special Rapporteur visited Brazil (16 September-8 October) [E/CN.4/2004/7/Add.3], where she investigated alleged violations of the right to life, including extrajudicial executions by the police and death in custody. Numerous accounts of extrajudicial killings by the police, which she had gathered from a variety of sources, were summarized in an appendix to the report. Some 521 civilians were reportedly killed in confrontations with the police in greater Rio de Janeiro alone during the first five months of 2003. The

Special Rapporteur, while aware of government efforts to improve the criminal legal system for preventing extrajudicial, summary or arbitrary executions, concluded that the measures adopted were inadequate. She recommended that all proposed legislative or administrative reforms address both prevention and accountability of extrajudicial or summary executions, and the Government ensure that persons in danger of such executions were protected. The Special Rapporteur proposed that the Special Rapporteur on the independence of judges and lawyers undertake a mission to Brazil.

Commission action. By a recorded vote of 37 to none, with 16 abstentions, the Commission, on 24 April [res. 2003/53], encouraged the Special Rapporteur to continue to collect information, respond effectively to reliable information that came before her, follow up on communications and country visits, seek the views of Governments and continue to draw the High Commissioner's attention to situations of serious concern or where early action might prevent further deterioration. The Secretary-General was asked to provide the Special Rapporteur with adequate resources, to continue to use his best endeavours in cases where the minimum standard of legal safeguards provided for by the International Covenant on Civil and Political Rights (see p. 669) appeared not to be respected, and to ensure that personnel specialized in human rights and humanitarian law formed part of UN missions.

Communications. On 21 March [E/CN.4/2003/G/57], Singapore, referring to its reply to the Special Rapporteur's urgent appeal [E/CN.4/2003/3/Add.1], listed the reasons why it felt that she had transgressed her mandate.

In April [E/CN.4/2003/G/78], Honduras, referring to the Special Rapporteur's report on her 2001 visit to the country [YUN 2002, p. 705], transmitted a report of its Standing Committee for the Protection of the Physical and Moral Integrity of the Child.

On 14 April [E/CN.4/2003/G/80], the United States transmitted its response to the Special Rapporteur's communication [E/CN.4/2003/3] regarding an incident in Yemen in 2002. It presented reasons why the Commission and Special Rapporteur lacked the competence to address the issue, which arose under the law of armed conflict.

Disappearance of persons

Draft instrument. Pursuant to a 2002 Commission request [YUN 2002, p. 709], the intersessional open-ended working group established to prepare a draft legally binding instrument for the protection of all persons from enforced disappearance held its first meeting (Geneva, 6-17 January) [E/CN.4/2003/71]. After considering the report of the independent expert charged with examining the existing international criminal and human rights framework on the issue [YUN 2002, p. 709], the group discussed the draft's provisions, including the definition of enforced disappearance, offences and penalties, protection against impunity, domestic prosecution and international cooperation, prevention, victims' rights and the children of disappeared persons. The group concluded that, in order to ensure further progress within a reasonable time, it should meet before the Commission's 2004 session.

Commission action. On 23 April [res. 2003/38], the Commission urged Governments to cooperate with the Working Group on Enforced or Involuntary Disappearances and invited States to provide it with information on prevention measures and in giving effect to the 1992 Declaration on the Protection of All Persons from Enforced Disappearance, adopted by the General Assembly in resolution 47/133 [YUN 1992, p. 744]. The Working Group was asked to report in 2004 and the Secretary-General was asked to assist it, to provide resources to update the database on cases of enforced disappearance and to inform the Commission of steps taken to disseminate and promote the Declaration. The Commission asked the intersessional working group (see above) to meet for 10 working days before the Commission's 2004 session and to report at that session. On 23 July, the Economic and Social Council authorized the group to meet and endorsed the request for a report in 2004 (**decision 2003/249**). The group's Chairperson-Rapporteur was asked to hold informal consultations and the High Commissioner to invite experts to participate in the group's activities.

Working Group activities. The five-member Working Group on Enforced or Involuntary Disappearances held three sessions in 2003: its sixty-ninth (22-25 April), seventieth (11-15 August) and seventy-first (10-19 November), all in Geneva [E/CN.4/2004/58]. In addition to its original mandate, which was to act as a channel of communication between families of disappeared persons and the Governments concerned, with a view to ensuring that sufficiently documented individual cases were investigated, the Working Group monitored States' compliance with the 1992 Declaration. Cases under active consideration by the Group totalled 41,934, while countries with outstanding cases of alleged disappearance numbered 79. During the period under review, up to 19 November, the last day of its seventy-first session, the Group transmitted 234 new cases of disappearances to 22 States, 43 of which allegedly occurred in 2003. It also sent urgent action appeals to 10 countries in respect of 43 cases and clarified 837 cases. The Group's report summarized information concerning disappearances received from 53 countries.

Torture and cruel treatment

Reports of Special Rapporteur. In response to a 2002 Commission request [YUN 2002, p. 712], the Special Rapporteur on torture, Theo van Boven (Netherlands), described his activities from 1 December 2001 to 15 December 2002 [E/CN.4/2003/68]. He sent 109 letters to 65 countries regarding the alleged torture of individuals, 68 letters reminding Governments of cases transmitted in previous years and 294 urgent appeals to 82 Governments on behalf of individuals who, it was feared, might be subjected to torture and other forms of ill-treatment. Replies were received from 72 Governments. A summary of the communications sent by the Special Rapporteur and of the replies received were summarized in an addendum to the report [E/CN.4/2003/68/Add.1]. The Special Rapporteur revised recommendations put forth by his predecessor [YUN 2001, p. 644] and asked States that had not done so to accede to relevant international instruments, including the 1984 Convention against Torture and Other Cruel, Inhuman or Degrading Treatment or Punishment, annexed to General Assembly resolution 39/46 [YUN 1984, p. 813] (see p. 674). He recommended that States define torture as a crime of the utmost gravity in national legislation, abolish corporal punishment, investigate complaints of torture, ensure that victims obtained redress and adequate compensation, and prohibit the expulsion or extradition of a person to another State where there were substantial grounds to believe they would be in danger of being tortured.

As requested by the Commission [YUN 2002, p. 712], the Special Rapporteur, in January [E/CN.4/2003/69], submitted a preliminary study on the trade in and production of equipment specifically designed to inflict torture or other cruel, inhuman or degrading treatment, with a view to finding the best ways to prohibit it and combat its proliferation. The Special Rapporteur said that certain kinds of equipment, such as handcuffs and kinetic and chemical devices, the use of which was recognized as legitimate in certain circumstances, were allegedly being misused or intentionally used to inflict torture. Numerous other types of equipment, including stun devices and bar fetters, breached the prohibition of torture. The Special Rapporteur found that the trade in such equipment was a phenomenon that involved countries in every region. He believed that States' enactment of legal and other measures to stop the production and trade of the equipment was part of their obligation to prevent acts of torture under the 1984 Convention, and that it was necessary to keep the study ongoing. He drew the Commission's attention to the European Commission's proposal for a regulation on trade in certain equipment and products and to Amnesty International's recommendations to Governments and companies, both of which were annexed to his report.

The Special Rapporteur reported [E/CN.4/2004/56/Add.3] on follow-up to recommendations made regarding visits to Azerbaijan [YUN 2000, p. 682], Brazil [ibid., p. 681], Chile [YUN 1995, p. 756], Mexico [YUN 1997, p. 666], Romania [YUN 1999, p. 636], Turkey [YUN 1998, p. 681] and Uzbekistan [YUN 2002, p. 712].

Communication. In March [E/CN.4/2003/G/67], Uzbekistan, referring to the Special Rapporteur's report on his 2002 visit to the country [YUN 2002, p. 712], presented a number of proposals and remarks to reflect more fully and objectively the outcome of the visit, update data on some regulations of the country's criminal legislation and explain the reasons for a misunderstanding that occurred during the visit.

Commission action. On 23 April [res. 2003/32], the Commission urged States to become parties to the Convention against Torture and Other Cruel, Inhuman or Degrading Treatment or Punishment. Governments were called on to eliminate the practice, to provide redress and to prevent and prohibit the production, trade, export and use of equipment specifically designed to inflict torture. States and NGOs were called on to provide information requested by the Special Rapporteur and to combat the equipment's proliferation; he was asked to report on the phenomenon. He was also asked to submit an interim report to the General Assembly in 2003 and a full report to the Commission in 2004.

Further reports of Special Rapporteur. Pursuant to General Assembly resolution 57/200 [YUN 2002, p. 713] and to Commission resolution 2003/32 (see above), the Secretary-General, in July, transmitted an interim report of the Special Rapporteur [A/58/120]. As follow-up to his 2002 report to the Assembly [YUN 2002, p. 712], which had addressed the prohibition of torture and other forms of ill-treatment in the context of anti-terrorism measures, the Special Rapporteur drew attention to recent conclusions and recommendations on the topic issued by international and regional human rights monitoring bodies. He summarized information contained in his study on trade in and production of equipment that was specifically designed to inflict torture or other cruel, inhuman or degrading treatment (see p. 741). Regarding reparation for victims of torture, he drew attention to an initiative of Redress Trust, a London-based human rights/legal organization, which indicated that laws were inadequate and/or lacking in most of the 30 countries studied and, even when present, were rarely implemented. He noted renewed efforts to underscore the need for justice in that regard, through a review of the draft basic principles and guidelines on the right to a remedy and reparation for victims of violations of human rights and humanitarian law (see p. 727). Annexed to the report were a statement issued jointly by the Commission's mechanisms on torture and OHCHR on the occasion of the UN International Day in Support of Victims of Torture, observed on 26 June, and a joint statement by the special rapporteurs/representatives, experts and chairpersons of the working groups of the special procedures of the Commission on 30 June.

The Special Rapporteur visited Spain (5-10 October) [E/CN.4/2004/56/Add.2], where he focused on investigating allegations of torture or ill-treatment of detainees held on terrorism charges, studying various safeguards for protecting the detainees and identifying possible approaches on how to fight terrorism while respecting human rights. He found that a recurring factor with negative implications for human rights was acts and threats of terrorism, mainly by Euskadi Ta Askatasuna, (ETA) which had victimized hundreds of people and spread fear among many more. The Government's denial of allegations of torture and ill-treatment was countered by credible sources. While denouncing terrorist acts, the Special Rapporteur emphasized that counter-terrorism laws should conform with international human rights law, and recommended that the highest authorities officially and publicly prohibit torture and draw up a plan to prevent it; abrogate incommunicado detention, which seemed to encourage acts of torture; ensure detainees the rights of access to a lawyer, to a doctor of their choice and to have relatives informed of their arrest and place of detention; ensure that reports of torture or ill-treatment were investigated promptly and effectively; and ensure that torture victims obtained redress and adequate reparation.

Voluntary fund for torture victims

Commission action. On 23 April [res. 2003/32], the Commission appealed to Governments, organizations and individuals to contribute annually to the United Nations Voluntary Fund for Victims of Torture and, if possible, to increase their contributions. It called on the Fund's Board of Trustees to report in 2004 on an independent evaluation of the Fund's functioning, to be initiated before the Commission's next session. The Secretary-General was asked to continue to include the Fund among the programmes receiving donations at the annual UN Pledging Conference for Development Activities and to ensure adequate staffing and technical facilities for UN bodies and mechanisms dealing with torture.

On 23 July, the Economic and Social Council endorsed the Commission's request for an independent evaluation (**decision 2003/248**).

Reports of Secretary-General. In response to a 2002 Commission request [YUN 2002, p. 713], the Secretary-General submitted a February report [E/CN.4/2003/61], which supplemented and updated information contained in his previous report on the operation of the Fund [YUN 2002, p. 713].

In his annual report to the General Assembly on the status of the Fund, submitted in August [A/58/284], the Secretary-General stated that contributions received between 12 May 2002 and 28 May 2003 totalled $7,332,981 from 39 countries, two NGOs and seven private individuals. The Board of Trustees held its twenty-second session in Geneva (12-28 May). The total available for new grants to assist victims of torture amounted to some $7 million, against requests amounting to $13 million. In addition, some $50,000 was available for emergency grants before the Board's next annual session. During the year, new grants were allocated to 186 projects in 68 countries that provided psychological, medical, social, legal and economic assistance to victims of torture and members of their families. In accordance with Commission resolution 2003/32 (see p. 741), OHCHR initiated an independent evaluation of the Fund, including the lessons and best practices learned from its activities, with a view to further enhancing its effectiveness. The Secretary-General urged Governments, organizations and individuals in a position to do so to contribute to the Fund yearly, to enable it to meet the increasing demand for assistance.

In a December report [E/CN.4/2004/53], the Secretary-General stated that additional contributions received as at 1 December 2003 amounted to $202,365.

GENERAL ASSEMBLY ACTION

On 22 December [meeting 77], the General Assembly, on the recommendation of the Third Committee [A/58/508/Add.1], adopted **resolution 58/164** without vote [agenda item 117 (a)].

Torture and other cruel, inhuman or degrading treatment or punishment

The General Assembly,

Recalling article 5 of the Universal Declaration of Human Rights, article 7 of the International Covenant on Civil and Political Rights, the Declaration on the Protection of All Persons from Being Subjected to Torture and Other Cruel, Inhuman or Degrading Treatment or Punishment and its resolution 39/46 of 10 December 1984, by which it adopted and opened for signature, ratification and accession the Convention against Torture and Other Cruel, Inhuman or Degrading Treatment or Punishment,

Recalling also that freedom from torture and other cruel, inhuman or degrading treatment or punishment is a non-derogable right that must be protected under all circumstances, including in times of internal or international disturbance or armed conflict, and that the prohibition of torture is explicitly affirmed in all relevant international instruments,

Recalling further all previous resolutions or decisions on torture and other cruel, inhuman or degrading treatment or punishment of the General Assembly, the Economic and Social Council and the Commission on Human Rights, in particular Assembly resolution 57/200 of 18 December 2002 and Commission resolution 2003/32 of 23 April 2003,

Recalling the recommendation contained in the Vienna Declaration and Programme of Action adopted by the World Conference on Human Rights on 25 June 1993 that high priority should be given to providing the necessary resources to assist victims of torture and effective remedies for their physical, psychological and social rehabilitation, inter alia, through additional contributions to the United Nations Voluntary Fund for Victims of Torture,

Noting with satisfaction the existence of a considerable international network of centres for the rehabilitation of victims of torture, which plays an important role in providing assistance to victims of torture, and the collaboration of the Fund with the centres,

Commending the persistent efforts by non-governmental organizations to combat torture and to alleviate the suffering of victims of torture,

Mindful of its proclamation, in its resolution 52/149 of 12 December 1997, of 26 June as the United Nations International Day in Support of Victims of Torture,

1. *Condemns* all forms of torture, including through intimidation, as described in article 1 of the Convention against Torture and Other Cruel, Inhuman or Degrading Treatment or Punishment;

2. *Urges* all Governments to promote the full implementation of the Vienna Declaration and Programme of Action adopted by the World Conference on Human Rights on 25 June 1993, and stresses in particular that all allegations of torture or other cruel, inhuman or degrading treatment or punishment should be promptly and impartially examined by the competent national authority, that those who encourage, order, tolerate or perpetrate acts of torture must be held responsible and severely punished, including the officials in charge of the place of detention where the prohibited act is found to have been committed, and that national legal systems should ensure that the victims of such acts obtain redress, are awarded fair and adequate compensation and receive appropriate social and medical rehabilitation, and encourages the development of rehabilitation centres for victims of torture;

3. *Takes note* of the Principles on the Effective Investigation and Documentation of Torture and Other Cruel, Inhuman or Degrading Treatment or Punishment annexed to its resolution 55/89 of 4 December 2000 as a useful tool in efforts to combat torture;

4. *Urges* Governments to take effective measures to provide redress and to prevent torture and other cruel, inhuman or degrading treatment or punishment, including their gender-based manifestations;

5. *Stresses* that, under article 4 of the Convention, torture must be made an offence under domestic criminal law, and emphasizes that acts of torture are serious violations of international humanitarian law and that the perpetrators are liable to prosecution and punishment;

6. *Notes with appreciation* that one hundred and thirty-four States have become parties to the Convention, and urges all States that have not yet done so to become parties to the Convention as a matter of priority;

7. *Invites* all States ratifying or acceding to the Convention and those States that are parties to the Convention and have not yet done so to consider joining the States parties that have already made the declarations provided for in articles 21 and 22 of the Convention and to consider the possibility of withdrawing their reservations to article 20;

8. *Urges* all States parties to the Convention to notify the Secretary-General of their acceptance of the amendments to articles 17 and 18 of the Convention as soon as possible;

9. *Urges* States parties to comply strictly with their obligations under the Convention, including, in view of the high number of reports not submitted, their obligation to submit reports in accordance with article 19 of the Convention, and invites States parties to incorporate a gender perspective and information concerning children and juveniles when submitting reports to the Committee against Torture;

10. *Emphasizes* the obligation of States parties under article 10 of the Convention to ensure education and training for personnel who may be involved in the custody, interrogation or treatment of any individual subjected to any form of arrest, detention or imprisonment;

11. *Stresses*, in this context, that States must not punish personnel referred to in paragraph 10 above for not obeying orders to commit or conceal acts amounting to torture or other cruel, inhuman or degrading treatment or punishment;

12. *Calls upon* States parties to consider signing and ratifying the Optional Protocol to the Convention against Torture and Other Cruel, Inhuman or Degrading Treatment or Punishment, adopted by the General Assembly in its resolution 57/199 of 18 December 2002, which provides further measures for use in the fight against and the prevention of torture, and notes in this context that ratifications by twenty States parties are required for the Optional Protocol to enter into force, and that twenty-one States have already signed the Protocol and two States have ratified it;

13. *Calls upon* all Governments to take appropriate effective legislative, administrative, judicial or other measures to prevent and prohibit the production, trade, export and use of equipment that is specifically designed to inflict torture or other cruel, inhuman or degrading treatment;

14. *Welcomes* the work of the Committee against Torture and the report of the Committee, submitted in accordance with article 24 of the Convention;

15. *Calls upon* the United Nations High Commissioner for Human Rights, in conformity with his mandate established in General Assembly resolution 48/141 of 20 December 1993, to continue to provide, at the request of Governments, advisory services for the preparation of national reports to the Committee and for the prevention of torture, as well as technical assistance in the development, production and distribution of teaching material for this purpose;

16. *Urges* States parties to take fully into account the conclusions and recommendations made by the Committee after its consideration of their reports;

17. *Notes with appreciation* the interim report of the Special Rapporteur of the Commission on Human Rights on the question of torture, describing the overall trends and developments with regard to his mandate, and encourages the Special Rapporteur to continue to include in his recommendations proposals on the prevention and investigation of torture;

18. *Invites* the Special Rapporteur to continue to examine questions of torture and other cruel, inhuman or degrading treatment or punishment directed against women, and conditions conducive to such torture, and to make appropriate recommendations for the prevention and redress of gender-specific forms of torture, including rape or any other form of sexual violence, and to exchange views with the Special Rapporteur of the Commission on Human Rights on violence against women, its causes and consequences, with the aim of enhancing further their effectiveness and mutual cooperation;

19. *Also invites* the Special Rapporteur to continue to consider questions relating to the torture of children and conditions conducive to such torture and other cruel, inhuman or degrading treatment or punishment and to make appropriate recommendations for the prevention of such torture;

20. *Calls upon* all Governments to cooperate with and assist the Special Rapporteur in the performance of his task, to supply all necessary information requested by the Special Rapporteur, to respond appropriately and expeditiously to his urgent appeals and to give serious consideration to requests by the Special Rapporteur to visit their countries, and urges them to enter into a constructive dialogue with the Special Rapporteur in following up his recommendations;

21. *Reiterates* the need for the Special Rapporteur to be able to respond effectively, in particular to urgent appeals, to credible and reliable information that comes before him, and invites the Special Rapporteur to continue to seek the views and comments of all concerned, in particular Member States;

22. *Requests* the Special Rapporteur to continue to consider including in his report information on the follow-up by Governments to his recommendations, visits and communications, including progress made and problems encountered;

23. *Stresses* the need for the continued regular exchange of views among the Committee against Torture, the Special Rapporteur and other relevant United Nations mechanisms and bodies, as well as for the pursuance of cooperation with relevant United Nations programmes, notably the United Nations Crime Prevention and Criminal Justice Programme, with a view to enhancing further their effectiveness and cooperation on issues relating to torture, inter alia, by improving their coordination;

24. *Expresses its gratitude and appreciation* to the Governments, organizations and individuals that have already contributed to the United Nations Voluntary Fund for Victims of Torture;

25. *Stresses* the importance of the work of the Board of Trustees of the Fund, and appeals to all Governments and organizations to contribute annually to the Fund, preferably by 1 March before the annual meeting of the Board, if possible with a substantial increase in the level of contributions, so that consideration may be given to the ever-increasing demand for assistance;

26. *Requests* the Secretary-General to transmit to all Governments the appeals of the General Assembly for contributions to the Fund and to continue to include the Fund on an annual basis among the programmes for which funds are pledged at the United Nations Pledging Conference for Development Activities;

27. *Also requests* the Secretary-General to assist the Board of Trustees of the Fund in its appeal for contributions and in its efforts to make better known the existence of the Fund and the financial means currently available to it, as well as in its assessment of the global need for international funding of rehabilitation services for victims of torture and, in this effort, to make use of all existing possibilities, including the preparation, production and dissemination of information materials;

28. *Further requests* the Secretary-General to ensure, within the overall budgetary framework of the United Nations, the provision of adequate staff and facilities for the bodies and mechanisms involved in combating torture and assisting victims of torture, commensurate with the strong support expressed by Member States for combating torture and assisting victims of torture;

29. *Invites* donor countries and recipient countries to consider including in their bilateral programmes and projects relating to the training of armed forces, security forces, prison and police personnel and health-care personnel matters relating to the protection of human rights and the prevention of torture, while bearing in mind a gender perspective;

30. *Requests* the Secretary-General to submit to the Commission on Human Rights at its sixtieth session and to the General Assembly at its fifty-ninth session a report on the status of the Convention and a report on the operations of the Fund;

31. *Calls upon* all Governments, the Office of the United Nations High Commissioner for Human Rights and other United Nations bodies and agencies, as well as relevant intergovernmental and non-governmental organizations, to commemorate, on 26 June, the United Nations International Day in Support of Victims of Torture;

32. *Decides* to consider at its fifty-ninth session the reports of the Secretary-General, including the report on the United Nations Voluntary Fund for Victims of Torture, the report of the Committee against Torture and the interim report of the Special Rapporteur of the Commission on Human Rights on the question of torture.

Freedom of expression

Reports of Special Rapporteur. In accordance with a 2002 Commission request [YUN 2002, p. 716], the Special Rapporteur on the promotion and protection of the right to freedom of opinion and expression, Ambeyi Ligabo (Kenya), described his 2002 activities [E/CN.4/2003/67]. He had sent allegation letters to 109 countries, on behalf of numerous individuals whose right to the freedom of opinion and expression was reportedly threatened or violated. The texts of the communications he had sent and replies received from Governments were summarized in a separate report [E/CN.4/2003/67/Add.1]. As requested by the Commission, the Special Rapporteur also discussed access to information for the purposes of education on and prevention of HIV/AIDS, and the right to freedom of opinion and expression in the context of counter-terrorism measures.

The Special Rapporteur concluded that, although violations of the right might occur in all countries, democratic institutions offered more guarantees for its protection. He expressed concern that journalists suffered attacks, including killings, which were often perpetrated with impunity, and was of the view that an in-depth study on the security of journalists was necessary, particularly in situations of armed conflict. Regarding HIV/AIDS, he believed that respect for and protection of freedom of opinion and expression had a direct impact on the effectiveness of education and information policies, programmes and campaigns for preventing the disease. As to counter-terrorism activities, the Special Rapporteur recommended that, in considering measures restricting human rights, particularly the freedom of opinion and expression, attention should be paid to the provisions of article 4 (1) of the 1966 International Covenant on Civil and Political Rights, adopted by the General Assembly in resolution 2200 A (XXI) [YUN 1966, p. 423] (see p. 669), concerning the latitude of measures that States might take during a public emergency. The Special Rapporteur encouraged ongoing efforts, particularly within the United Nations, to develop a universally valid definition of terrorism and terrorist acts to help the human rights monitoring of measures adopted to combat terrorism, as well as technical assistance to States when adopting such measures.

During the Special Rapporteur's visit to Iran (4-10 November) [E/CN.4/2004/62/Add.2], he found that, although some constituent elements of the freedom of opinion and expression were recognized in the Constitution, there were no provisions that specifically protected it as the right to hold opinions without interference. Other laws also contained clauses that restricted the right. Persons and institutions mostly affected were the print media, journalists and intellectuals, students, lawyers, parliamentarians and persons involved in political activities. Over the past years, the situation regarding the right seemed to have deteriorated. Although he found a strong desire for reform among civil society and at the highest levels of Government, there were impediments to reform, particularly owing to the control exercised by unelected institutions and bodies that had no accountability. He urged the authorities to review the relevant laws and bring them into line with international human rights norms and standards, and pointed to an urgent need to define more clearly the contents of Islamic principles in law. The Special Rapporteur endorsed the findings of members of the Working Group on Arbitrary Detention, who had visited Iran (see p. 733), regarding human rights violations, and called on the authorities to grant a complete amnesty to all prisoners prosecuted or convicted for related offences. He believed that a visit to the country by the Special Rapporteurs on torture (see p. 741) and on the independence of judges and lawyers (see p. 734) would be useful.

Commission action. On 23 April [res. 2003/42], the Commission called on States to ensure respect and support for all persons who exercised the right to freedom of opinion and expression and related rights, and that relevant national legislation complied with their international human rights obligations; to promote and protect those rights in the media; to investigate threats and acts of violence against journalists; and to refrain from using counter-terrorism as a pretext to restrict freedom of expression. The Special Rapporteur was invited to draw the High Commissioner's attention to situations of particularly serious concern; pay particular attention, in cooperation with the Special Rapporteur on violence against women (see p. 777), to the situation of women; consider approaches taken to access to information with a view to sharing best practices; provide his views on the advantages and challenges of new information technologies; seek the views of Governments and others concerned; seek to participate in the World Summit on the Information Society (see p. 857); and report in 2004, including on the issue of security and protection of media professionals. The Secretary-General was asked to assist him.

Terrorism

Report of Secretary-General. Pursuant to General Assembly resolution 57/219 [YUN 2002, p. 717], the Secretary-General, in a March report on protecting human rights and fundamental freedoms while countering terrorism [E/CN.4/2003/120], described action taken by UN bodies and entities, including the Security Council (see p. 63), the High Commissioner, the Secretary-General's Policy Working Group on the United Nations and Terrorism, and UN human rights mechanisms and special procedures. The dialogue that had been established between the Council's Counter-Terrorism Committee and OHCHR would be further built upon, as would the dialogue initiated within the UN system and with regional and non-governmental partners and Member States, in order to better implement resolution 57/219.

Commission action. By a recorded vote of 30 to 12, with 11 abstentions, the Commission, on 23 April [res. 2003/37], urged relevant human rights mechanisms to address the consequences of the acts, methods and practices of terrorist groups, and asked OHCHR to respond to requests from interested Governments for assistance and advice on ensuring full compliance with international human rights standards when undertaking measures to combat terrorism. The Secretary-General was asked to seek the views of Member States on the implications of terrorism for the full enjoyment of all human rights and on how the needs of victims of terrorism might be addressed, including through the possible establishment of a voluntary fund. The Commission asked the Special Rapporteur to give attention to the questions raised in the resolution and endorsed the Subcommission's 2002 request [YUN 2002, p. 717] to the Secretary-General to assist her.

On 25 April [res. 2003/68], the Commission asked the High Commissioner to examine the question of the protection of human rights and fundamental freedoms while countering terrorism, to make recommendations to States, to provide them with assistance and advice upon their request, and to report to the General Assembly in 2003 and to the Commission in 2004.

On 23 July, the Economic and Social Council approved the Commission's request to the High Commissioner (**decision 2003/256**).

Further reports of Secretary-General. In accordance with General Assembly resolution 57/219 [YUN 2002, p. 717], the Secretary-General, in August [A/58/266], reviewed comments received from Governments, international organizations and NGOs in response to a request of the High Commissioner seeking their views on the protection of human rights while countering terrorism. The report also described action taken in that regard by UN bodies and entities. Areas of concern in the protection of human rights while countering terrorism included the rights to life, to freedom from torture and cruel, inhuman or degrading treatment or punishment, and to a fair trial; conditions and treatment in detention; the principle of legality, according to which criminal conduct should be defined before an offence could be committed, and with sufficient precision so as to prevent arbitrary enforcement; pre-trial detention; access to counsel; freedom of thought, conscience and religion; freedom of expression and assembly; freedom from discrimination; the treatment of non-nationals, including asylum-seekers; and states of emergency. The Secretary-General pointed to the urgent need for States to act against terrorism, with respect for human rights as an essential part of an effective counter-terrorism strategy, not an impediment to it. OHCHR had compiled a digest of universal and regional jurisprudence on protecting human rights while countering terrorism, and States should consider availing themselves of the technical assistance the Office was willing to provide to help them fully integrate human rights protection into measures against terrorism.

In October [A/58/533], the Secretary-General, in response to Assembly resolution 56/160 [YUN 2001, p. 649], summarized the views of two Member States on the implications of terrorism for the full enjoyment of human rights and fundamental freedoms, and on the possible establishment of a voluntary fund for the victims of terrorism.

Report of Special Rapporteur. In response to a 2002 Subcommission request [YUN 2002, p. 717], the Special Rapporteur on terrorism and human rights, Kalliopi K. Koufa (Greece), submitted, in August, a progress report [E/CN.4/Sub.2/2003/WP.1], in which she presented preliminary comments and updated information relating to the scope of the study on non-State terrorism since she submitted her first progress report [YUN 2001, p. 648]. Addenda to the report reviewed and updated information regarding international anti-terrorist activities and initiatives undertaken at the global and regional levels [E/CN.4/Sub.2/2003/WP.1/Add.1] since her 2002 report [YUN 2002, p. 717], and summarized the views of Governments, intergovernmental organizations, NGOs and UN special procedures between May 2002 and May 2003 [E/CN.4/Sub.2/2003/WP.1/Add.2].

Subcommission action. On 13 August [res. 2003/6], the Subcommission, having considered the Special Rapporteur's additional progress report (see above), requested its translation into the UN official languages and publication as an official document. OHCHR was asked to ensure its distribution at the Commission's 2004 session, and the Secretary-General to ensure that the report and addenda could be accessed by those seeking information on the Web and to transmit it to Governments, specialized agencies and concerned intergovernmental organizations and

NGOs, with the request that they submit to the Special Rapporteur comments, information and data relating to the study on terrorism and human rights. He was also requested to make available to the Special Rapporteur all the collected information and to assist her to finalize her study. The Special Rapporteur was asked to submit her final report in 2004.

Also on 13 August [res. 2003/15], the Subcommission decided, with a view to rationalizing its work on terrorism, to rename sub-item 6 (c) "New priorities, in particular terrorism and counter-terrorism", in order to study the compatibility of counter-terrorism measures with international human rights standards, emphasizing their impact on the most vulnerable groups, with a view to elaborating detailed guidelines. The Subcommission appointed Ms. Koufa as coordinator, with a mandate to gather the necessary documentation, and asked Governments, intergovernmental organizations, national institutions for the promotion and protection of human rights, experts and NGOs to provide it and the coordinator with pertinent information.

GENERAL ASSEMBLY ACTION

On 22 December [meeting 77], the General Assembly, on the recommendation of the Third Committee [A/58/508/Add.2], adopted **resolution 58/174** by recorded vote (120-42-18) [agenda item 117 (b)].

Human rights and terrorism

The General Assembly,

Guided by the Charter of the United Nations, the Universal Declaration of Human Rights, the Declaration on Principles of International Law concerning Friendly Relations and Cooperation among States in accordance with the Charter of the United Nations and the International Covenants on Human Rights,

Recalling the Declaration on the Occasion of the Fiftieth Anniversary of the United Nations, as well as the Declaration on Measures to Eliminate International Terrorism,

Recalling also the Vienna Declaration and Programme of Action adopted by the World Conference on Human Rights on 25 June 1993, in which the Conference reaffirmed that the acts, methods and practices of terrorism in all its forms and manifestations, as well as its linkage in some countries to drug trafficking, are activities aimed at the destruction of human rights, fundamental freedoms and democracy, threatening territorial integrity and the security of States and destabilizing legitimately constituted Governments, and that the international community should take the necessary steps to enhance cooperation to prevent and combat terrorism,

Recalling further the United Nations Millennium Declaration adopted by the General Assembly,

Recalling, in this regard, the reference in the report of the Secretary-General on the implementation of the Millennium Declaration to the fact that terrorism itself is a violation of human rights and must be combated as such and that efforts at combating it must be pursued, however, in full compliance with established international norms,

Recalling also its resolutions 48/122 of 20 December 1993, 49/185 of 23 December 1994, 50/186 of 22 December 1995, 52/133 of 12 December 1997, 54/109 and 54/110 of 9 December 1999, 54/164 of 17 December 1999, 55/158 of 12 December 2000, 56/160 of 19 December 2001 and 57/219 and 57/220 of 18 December 2002,

Recalling in particular that, in its resolution 52/133, it requested the Secretary-General to seek the views of Member States on the implications of terrorism in all its forms and manifestations for the full enjoyment of human rights and fundamental freedoms,

Recalling previous resolutions of the Commission on Human Rights,

Bearing in mind all other relevant General Assembly resolutions,

Bearing in mind also relevant Security Council resolutions,

Aware that, at the dawn of the twenty-first century, the world is witness to historic and far-reaching transformations, in the course of which forces of aggressive nationalism and religious and ethnic extremism continue to produce fresh challenges,

Alarmed that acts of terrorism in all its forms and manifestations aimed at the destruction of human rights have continued despite national and international efforts,

Bearing in mind that the right to life is the basic human right, without which a human being can exercise no other right,

Bearing in mind also that terrorism creates an environment that destroys the right of people to live in freedom from fear,

Reiterating that all States have an obligation to promote and protect all human rights and fundamental freedoms and to ensure effective implementation of their obligations under international law,

Seriously concerned about the gross violations of human rights perpetrated by terrorist groups,

Expressing its deepest sympathy and condolences to all the victims of terrorism and their families,

Alarmed in particular at the possibility that terrorist groups may exploit new technologies to facilitate acts of terrorism, which may cause massive damage, including huge loss of human life,

Emphasizing the need to intensify the fight against terrorism at the national level, to enhance effective international cooperation in combating terrorism in conformity with international law, including relevant State obligations under international human rights and international humanitarian law, and to strengthen the role of the United Nations in this respect,

Emphasizing also that States shall deny safe haven to those who finance, plan, support or commit terrorist acts or provide safe havens,

Reaffirming that all measures to counter terrorism must be in strict conformity with international law, including international human rights standards and obligations,

Mindful of the need to protect the human rights of and guarantees for the individual in accordance with the relevant human rights principles and instruments, in particular the right to life,

Noting the growing consciousness within the international community of the negative effects of terrorism in all its forms and manifestations on the full enjoyment of human rights and fundamental freedoms and on the establishment of the rule of law and democratic freedoms as enshrined in the Charter of the United Nations and the International Covenants on Human Rights,

Noting also the developments that have occurred since its fifty-sixth session, on addressing the issue of human rights and terrorism at the national, regional and international levels,

1. *Reiterates its unequivocal condemnation* of the acts, methods and practices of terrorism in all its forms and manifestations as activities aimed at the destruction of human rights, fundamental freedoms and democracy, threatening the territorial integrity and security of States, destabilizing legitimately constituted Governments, undermining pluralistic civil society and having adverse consequences for the economic and social development of States;

2. *Strongly condemns* the violations of the right to life, liberty and security;

3. *Profoundly deplores* the increasing number of innocent persons, including women, children and the elderly, killed, massacred and maimed by terrorists in indiscriminate and random acts of violence and terror, which cannot be justified in any circumstances;

4. *Expresses its solidarity* with the victims of terrorism;

5. *Reaffirms* the decision of the heads of State and Government, as contained in the United Nations Millennium Declaration, to take concerted action against international terrorism and to accede as soon as possible to all the relevant regional and international conventions;

6. *Urges* the international community to enhance cooperation at the regional and international levels in the fight against terrorism in all its forms and manifestations, in accordance with relevant international instruments, including those relating to human rights, with the aim of its eradication;

7. *Calls upon* States to take all necessary and effective measures, in accordance with relevant provisions of international law, including international human rights standards, to prevent, combat and eliminate terrorism in all its forms and manifestations, wherever and by whomever it is committed, and also calls upon States to strengthen, where appropriate, their legislation to combat terrorism in all its forms and manifestations;

8. *Urges* all States to deny safe haven to terrorists;

9. *Calls upon* States to take appropriate measures, in conformity with relevant provisions of national and international law, including international human rights standards, before granting refugee status, for the purpose of ensuring that an asylum-seeker has not planned, facilitated or participated in the commission of terrorist acts, including assassinations, and in this context urges those States that have granted refugee status or asylum to persons involved in or claiming to have committed acts of terrorism to review those situations;

10. *Condemns* the incitement to ethnic hatred, violence and terrorism;

11. *Stresses* that every person, regardless of nationality, race, sex, religion or any other distinction, has a right to protection from terrorism and terrorist acts;

12. *Expresses concern* about the growing connection between terrorist groups and other criminal organizations engaged in the illegal traffic in arms and drugs at the national and international levels, as well as the consequent commission of serious crimes such as murder, extortion, kidnapping, assault, the taking of hostages and robbery, and requests the relevant United Nations bodies to continue to give special attention to this question;

13. *Welcomes* the report of the Secretary-General on human rights and terrorism, and requests him to continue to seek the views of Member States on the implications of terrorism in all its forms and manifestations for the full enjoyment of all human rights and fundamental freedoms and on the possible establishment of a voluntary fund for the victims of terrorism, as well as on ways and means to rehabilitate the victims of terrorism and to reintegrate them into society, with a view to incorporating his findings in his report to the General Assembly;

14. *Decides* to consider this question at its sixtieth session under the item entitled "Human rights questions".

RECORDED VOTE ON RESOLUTION 58/174:

In favour: Afghanistan, Algeria, Angola, Antigua and Barbuda, Azerbaijan, Bahamas, Bahrain, Bangladesh, Barbados, Belarus, Belize, Benin, Bhutan, Brunei Darussalam, Burkina Faso, Cambodia, Cameroon, Cape Verde, Central African Republic, China, Colombia, Comoros, Congo, Costa Rica, Côte d'Ivoire, Cuba, Democratic People's Republic of Korea, Democratic Republic of the Congo, Djibouti, Dominica, Dominican Republic, Ecuador, Egypt, El Salvador, Eritrea, Ethiopia, Gabon, Gambia, Georgia, Ghana, Grenada, Guatemala, Guinea, Guinea-Bissau, Guyana, Haiti, Honduras, India, Indonesia, Iran, Jamaica, Jordan, Kazakhstan, Kenya, Kuwait, Kyrgyzstan, Lao People's Democratic Republic, Lebanon, Lesotho, Libyan Arab Jamahiriya, Madagascar, Malawi, Malaysia, Maldives, Mali, Mauritania, Mauritius, Mexico, Mongolia, Morocco, Mozambique, Myanmar, Namibia, Nepal, Nicaragua, Niger, Nigeria, Oman, Pakistan, Panama, Paraguay, Peru, Philippines, Qatar, Russian Federation, Rwanda, Saint Lucia, Saint Vincent and the Grenadines, Samoa, Saudi Arabia, Senegal, Seychelles, Sierra Leone, Singapore, Solomon Islands, Somalia, South Africa, Sri Lanka, Sudan, Suriname, Tajikistan, Thailand, Timor-Leste, Togo, Tonga, Tunisia, Turkey, Turkmenistan, Tuvalu, Uganda, Ukraine, United Arab Emirates, United Republic of Tanzania, Uruguay, Uzbekistan, Venezuela, Viet Nam, Yemen, Zambia, Zimbabwe.

Against: Albania, Australia, Austria, Belgium, Bosnia and Herzegovina, Bulgaria, Canada, Croatia, Czech Republic, Denmark, Estonia, Finland, France, Germany, Greece, Hungary, Iceland, Ireland, Italy, Latvia, Liechtenstein, Lithuania, Luxembourg, Malta, Marshall Islands, Micronesia, Monaco, Netherlands, Norway, Palau, Poland, Portugal, Republic of Korea, Romania, Serbia and Montenegro, Slovakia, Slovenia, Sweden, Switzerland, The former Yugoslav Republic of Macedonia, United Kingdom, United States.

Abstaining: Andorra, Argentina, Armenia, Bolivia, Botswana, Brazil, Chile, Cyprus, Fiji, Israel, Japan, Nauru, New Zealand, Papua New Guinea, Republic of Moldova, San Marino, Spain, Syrian Arab Republic.

Also on 22 December [meeting 77], the Assembly, on the recommendation of the Third Committee [A/58/508/Add.2], adopted **resolution 58/187** by recorded vote (181-0-1) [agenda item 117 *(b)*].

Protection of human rights and fundamental freedoms while countering terrorism

The General Assembly,

Reaffirming the purposes and principles of the Charter of the United Nations,

Reaffirming also the fundamental importance, including in response to terrorism and the fear of terrorism, of respecting all human rights and fundamental freedoms and the rule of law,

Recalling that States are under the obligation to protect all human rights and fundamental freedoms of all persons,

Recognizing that the respect for human rights, the respect for democracy and the respect for the rule of law are interrelated and mutually reinforcing,

Recalling its resolution 57/219 of 18 December 2002 and Commission on Human Rights resolution 2003/68 of 25 April 2003,

Recalling also its resolution 48/141 of 20 December 1993 and, inter alia, the responsibility of the United Nations High Commissioner for Human Rights to promote and protect the effective enjoyment of all human rights,

Reiterating paragraph 17 of section I of the Vienna Declaration and Programme of Action, adopted by the World Conference on Human Rights on 25 June 1993, which states that acts, methods and practices of terrorism in all its forms and manifestations are activities aimed at the destruction of human rights, fundamental freedoms and democracy, threatening territorial integrity, security of States and destabilizing legitimately constituted Governments, and that the international community should take the necessary steps to enhance cooperation to prevent and combat terrorism,

Noting its resolution 56/160 of 19 December 2001, and noting also Commission on Human Rights resolution 2003/37 of 23 April 2003 on human rights and terrorism,

Noting also the declaration on the issue of combating terrorism contained in the annex to Security Council resolution 1456(2003) of 20 January 2003, in particular the statement that States must ensure that any measures taken to combat terrorism comply with all their obligations under international law and should adopt such measures in accordance with international law, in particular international human rights, refugee and humanitarian law,

Recalling the relevant resolutions of the General Assembly and the Security Council,

Noting the declarations, statements and recommendations by a number of human rights treaty monitoring bodies and special procedures on the question of the compatibility of counter-terrorism measures with human rights obligations,

Reaffirming its unequivocal condemnation of all acts, methods and practices of terrorism, in all their forms and manifestations, wherever and by whomsoever committed, regardless of their motivation, as criminal and unjustifiable, and renewing its commitment to strengthen international cooperation to prevent and combat terrorism,

Stressing that everyone is entitled to all the rights and freedoms recognized in the Universal Declaration of Human Rights without distinction of any kind, including on the grounds of race, colour, sex, language, religion, political or other opinion, national or social origin, property, birth or other status,

Recalling that, in accordance with article 4 of the International Covenant on Civil and Political Rights, certain rights are recognized as non-derogable in any circumstances and that any measures derogating from the provisions of the Covenant must be in accordance with that article in all cases, and underlining the exceptional and temporary nature of any such derogations, as stated in General Comment No. 29, on states of emergency, adopted by the Human Rights Committee on 24 July 2001,

1. *Reaffirms* that States must ensure that any measure taken to combat terrorism complies with their obligations under international law, in particular international human rights, refugee and humanitarian law;

2. *Calls upon* States to raise awareness about the importance of these obligations among national authorities involved in combating terrorism;

3. *Takes note* of the report of the Secretary-General submitted pursuant to General Assembly resolution 57/219, and welcomes its conclusions on the necessity of ensuring respect for human rights in the international fight to eliminate terrorism and on the important role that the United Nations has in promoting the maintenance of international peace and security and in achieving international cooperation for the promotion and protection of human rights and fundamental freedoms for all;

4. *Takes note with interest* of the report of the Secretary-General on the protection of human rights and fundamental freedoms while countering terrorism, and welcomes the various initiatives to strengthen the protection of human rights in the context of counter-terrorism adopted by the United Nations and regional intergovernmental bodies as well as by States;

5. *Welcomes* the publication of the "Digest of Jurisprudence of the United Nations and Regional Organizations on the Protection of Human Rights while Countering Terrorism", and requests the United Nations High Commissioner for Human Rights to update and publish it periodically;

6. *Also welcomes* the ongoing dialogue established in the context of the fight against terrorism between the Security Council and its Counter-Terrorism Committee and the relevant bodies for the promotion and protection of human rights, and encourages the Security Council and its Counter-Terrorism Committee to continue to develop the cooperation with relevant human rights bodies, in particular with the Office of the United Nations High Commissioner for Human Rights, giving due regard to the promotion and protection of human rights in the ongoing work pursuant to relevant Security Council resolutions relating to terrorism;

7. *Requests* all relevant special procedures and mechanisms of the Commission on Human Rights, as well as the United Nations human rights treaty bodies, to consider, within their mandates, the protection of human rights and fundamental freedoms in the context of measures to combat terrorism and to coordinate their efforts, as appropriate, in order to promote a consistent approach on this subject;

8. *Encourages* States, while countering terrorism, to take into account relevant United Nations resolutions and decisions on human rights, and encourages them to consider the recommendations of the special procedures and mechanisms of the Commission on Human Rights and the relevant comments and views of United Nations human rights treaty bodies;

9. *Requests* the High Commissioner, making use of existing mechanisms, to continue:

(a) To examine the question of the protection of human rights and fundamental freedoms while countering terrorism, taking into account reliable information from all sources;

(b) To make general recommendations concerning the obligation of States to promote and protect human rights and fundamental freedoms while taking actions to counter terrorism;

(c) To provide assistance and advice to States, upon their request, on the protection of human rights and fundamental freedoms while countering terrorism, as well as to relevant United Nations bodies;

10. *Also requests* the High Commissioner, taking into account the views of States, to submit a study on the extent to which the human rights special procedures and treaty monitoring bodies are able, within their existing mandates, to address the compatibility of national counter-terrorism measures with international human rights obligations in their work, for consideration by States in strengthening the promotion and protection of human rights and fundamental freedoms while countering terrorism, with regard to the international human rights institutional mechanisms;

11. *Further requests* the High Commissioner to submit the requested study to the General Assembly at its fifty-ninth session, with an interim report to the Commission on Human Rights at its sixtieth session;

12. *Requests* the Secretary-General to submit a report on the implementation of the present resolution to the Commission on Human Rights at its sixtieth session and to the General Assembly at its fifty-ninth session.

RECORDED VOTE ON RESOLUTION 58/187:

In favour: Afghanistan, Albania, Algeria, Andorra, Angola, Antigua and Barbuda, Argentina, Armenia, Australia, Austria, Azerbaijan, Bahamas, Bahrain, Bangladesh, Barbados, Belarus, Belgium, Belize, Benin, Bhutan, Bolivia, Bosnia and Herzegovina, Botswana, Brazil, Brunei Darussalam, Bulgaria, Burkina Faso, Burundi, Cambodia, Cameroon, Canada, Cape Verde, Central African Republic, Chile, China, Colombia, Comoros, Congo, Costa Rica, Côte d'Ivoire, Croatia, Cuba, Cyprus, Czech Republic, Democratic People's Republic of Korea, Democratic Republic of the Congo, Denmark, Djibouti, Dominica, Dominican Republic, Ecuador, Egypt, El Salvador, Eritrea, Estonia, Ethiopia, Fiji, Finland, France, Gabon, Gambia, Georgia, Germany, Ghana, Greece, Grenada, Guatemala, Guinea, Guinea-Bissau, Guyana, Haiti, Honduras, Hungary, Iceland, Indonesia, Iran, Ireland, Israel, Italy, Jamaica, Japan, Jordan, Kazakhstan, Kenya, Kuwait, Kyrgyzstan, Lao People's Democratic Republic, Latvia, Lebanon, Lesotho, Libyan Arab Jamahiriya, Liechtenstein, Lithuania, Luxembourg, Madagascar, Malawi, Malaysia, Maldives, Mali, Malta, Marshall Islands, Mauritania, Mauritius, Mexico, Micronesia, Monaco, Mongolia, Morocco, Mozambique, Myanmar, Namibia, Nauru, Nepal, Netherlands, New Zealand, Nicaragua, Niger, Nigeria, Norway, Oman, Pakistan, Palau, Panama, Papua New Guinea, Paraguay, Peru, Philippines, Poland, Portugal, Qatar, Republic of Korea, Republic of Moldova, Romania, Russian Federation, Rwanda, Saint Lucia, Saint Vincent and the Grenadines, Samoa, San Marino, Saudi Arabia, Senegal, Serbia and Montenegro, Seychelles, Sierra Leone, Singapore, Slovakia, Slovenia, Solomon Islands, Somalia, South Africa, Spain, Sri Lanka, Sudan, Suriname, Sweden, Switzerland, Syrian Arab Republic, Tajikistan, Thailand, The former Yugoslav Republic of Macedonia, Timor-Leste, Togo, Tonga, Trinidad and Tobago, Tunisia, Turkey, Turkmenistan, Tuvalu, Uganda, Ukraine, United Arab Emirates, United Kingdom, United Republic of Tanzania, United States, Uruguay, Uzbekistan, Venezuela, Viet Nam, Yemen, Zambia, Zimbabwe.

Against: None.

Abstaining: India.

The Committee retained paragraphs 10 and 11 by a recorded vote of 136 to 1, with 15 abstentions. The Assembly retained the paragraphs by a recorded vote of 160 to 1, with 12 abstentions.

Hostage-taking

On 23 April [res. 2003/40], the Commission, condemning all acts of hostage-taking, demanded the immediate and unconditional release of all hostages. It called on States to prevent, combat and punish hostage-taking and urged thematic rapporteurs and working groups to address the consequences of such acts in their reports.

Peace and security

By a recorded vote of 33 to 16, with 4 abstentions, the Commission, on 24 April [res. 2003/61], affirming that States should promote international peace and security, urged them to respect and put into practice the principles and purposes of the UN Charter in their relations with other States.

GENERAL ASSEMBLY ACTION

On 22 December [meeting 77], the General Assembly, on the recommendation of the Third Committee [A/58/508/Add.2], adopted **resolution 58/192** by recorded vote (119-50-9) [agenda item 117 (b)].

Promotion of peace as a vital requirement for the full enjoyment of all human rights by all

The General Assembly,

Recalling its resolution 57/216 of 18 December 2002,

Recalling also Commission on Human Rights resolution 2003/61 of 24 April 2003, entitled "Promotion of peace as a vital requirement for the full enjoyment of all human rights by all",

Recalling further its resolution 39/11 of 12 November 1984, entitled "Declaration on the Right of Peoples to Peace", and the United Nations Millennium Declaration,

Bearing in mind the fundamental principles of international law set forth in the Charter of the United Nations,

Underlining, in accordance with the purposes and principles of the United Nations, its full and active support for the United Nations and for the enhancement of its role and effectiveness in strengthening international peace, security and justice and in promoting the solution of international problems, as well as the development of friendly relations and cooperation among States,

Reaffirming the obligation of all States to settle their international disputes by peaceful means in such a manner that international peace and security and justice are not endangered,

Emphasizing its objective of promoting better relations among all States and contributing to setting up conditions in which their people can live in true and lasting peace, free from any threat to or attempt against their security,

Reaffirming the obligation of all States to refrain in their international relations from the threat or use of force against the territorial integrity or political independence of any State, or in any other manner inconsistent with the purposes of the United Nations,

Reaffirming also its commitment to peace, security and justice and the continuing development of friendly relations and cooperation among States,

Rejecting the use of violence in pursuit of political aims, and stressing that only peaceful political solutions can ensure a stable and democratic future for all people around the world,

Reaffirming the importance of ensuring respect for the principles of the sovereignty, territorial integrity and political independence of States and non-intervention in matters that are essentially within the domestic jurisdiction of any State, in accordance with the Charter and international law,

Reaffirming also that all peoples have the right to self-determination, by virtue of which they freely determine their political status and freely pursue their economic, social and cultural development,

Reaffirming further the Declaration on Principles of International Law concerning Friendly Relations and Cooperation among States in accordance with the Charter of the United Nations,

Underlining that the subjection of peoples to alien subjugation, domination and exploitation constitutes a denial of fundamental rights, is contrary to the Charter and is an impediment to the promotion of world peace and cooperation,

Recalling that everyone is entitled to a social and international order in which the rights and freedoms set forth in the Universal Declaration of Human Rights can be fully realized,

Convinced of the aim of creating conditions of stability and well-being, which are necessary for peaceful and friendly relations among nations based on respect for the principles of equal rights and self-determination of peoples,

Convinced also that life without war is the primary international prerequisite for the material well-being, development and progress of countries and for the full implementation of the rights and fundamental human freedoms proclaimed by the United Nations,

1. *Stresses* that peace is a vital requirement for the promotion and protection of all human rights for all;

2. *Solemnly declares* that the preservation and promotion of peace constitute a fundamental obligation of each State;

3. *Emphasizes* that the preservation and promotion of peace demand that the policies of States be directed towards the elimination of the threat of war, particularly nuclear war, the renunciation of the use or threat of use of force in international relations and the settlement of international disputes by peaceful means on the basis of the Charter of the United Nations;

4. *Affirms* that all States should promote the establishment, maintenance and strengthening of international peace and security and an international system based on respect for the principles enshrined in the Charter and the promotion of all human rights and fundamental freedoms, including the right to development and the right of peoples to self-determination;

5. *Urges* all States to respect and to put into practice the purposes and principles of the Charter in their relations with other States, irrespective of their political, economic or social system and of their size, geographical location or level of economic development;

6. *Decides* to continue consideration of the question of the promotion of the right of peoples to peace at its sixtieth session under the item entitled "Human rights questions".

RECORDED VOTE ON RESOLUTION 58/192:

In favour: Afghanistan, Algeria, Angola, Antigua and Barbuda, Armenia, Azerbaijan, Bahamas, Bahrain, Bangladesh, Barbados, Belarus, Belize, Benin, Bhutan, Bolivia, Botswana, Brazil, Brunei Darussalam, Burkina Faso, Burundi, Cambodia, Cameroon, Cape Verde, Central African Republic, China, Colombia, Comoros, Congo, Costa Rica, Côte d'Ivoire, Cuba, Democratic People's Republic of Korea, Democratic Republic of the Congo, Djibouti, Dominica, Dominican Republic, Ecuador, Egypt, El Salvador, Eritrea, Ethiopia, Fiji, Gabon, Gambia, Ghana, Grenada, Guinea, Guinea-Bissau, Guyana, Haiti, Honduras, Indonesia, Iran, Jamaica, Jordan, Kazakhstan, Kenya, Kuwait, Kyrgyzstan, Lao People's Democratic Republic, Lebanon, Lesotho, Libyan Arab Jamahiriya, Madagascar, Malawi, Malaysia, Maldives, Mali, Mauritania, Mauritius, Mexico, Mongolia, Morocco, Mozambique, Myanmar, Namibia, Nepal, Nicaragua, Niger, Nigeria, Oman, Pakistan, Panama, Papua New Guinea, Paraguay, Peru, Philippines, Qatar, Russian Federation, Rwanda, Saint Lucia, Saint Vincent and the Grenadines, Saudi Arabia, Senegal, Seychelles, Sierra Leone, Solomon Islands, Somalia, South Africa, Sri Lanka, Sudan, Suriname, Syrian Arab Republic, Tajikistan, Thailand, Togo, Trinidad and Tobago, Tunisia, Turkmenistan, Tuvalu, Uganda, United Arab Emirates, United Republic of Tanzania, Uruguay, Venezuela, Viet Nam, Yemen, Zambia, Zimbabwe.

Against: Albania, Andorra, Australia, Austria, Belgium, Bosnia and Herzegovina, Bulgaria, Canada, Croatia, Cyprus, Czech Republic, Denmark, Estonia, Finland, France, Georgia, Germany, Greece, Hungary, Iceland, Ireland, Israel, Italy, Japan, Latvia, Liechtenstein, Lithuania, Luxembourg, Malta, Monaco, Netherlands, New Zealand, Norway, Poland, Portugal, Republic of Korea, Republic of Moldova, Romania, San Marino, Serbia and Montenegro, Slovakia, Slovenia, Spain, Sweden, Switzerland, The former Yugoslav Republic of Macedonia, Turkey, Ukraine, United Kingdom, United States.

Abstaining: Argentina, Chile, Guatemala, India, Marshall Islands, Nauru, Samoa, Singapore, Timor-Leste.

Weapons of mass destruction

In accordance with a 2002 Subcommission request [YUN 2002, p. 720], Yeung Kam Yeung Sik Yuen (Mauritius) submitted, in June, an updated working paper [E/CN.4/Sub.2/2003/35] regarding a possible study on the real and potential dangers to the enjoyment of human rights posed by the testing, production, storage, transfer, trafficking or use of weapons of mass destruction or with indiscriminate effect, or of a nature to cause superfluous injury. He reviewed his 2002 working paper [YUN 2002, p. 720], focusing on aspects regarding humanitarian law, and presented new information on depleted uranium weapons, nuclear weapons, cluster bombs, other weapons (anthrax, fuel-air bombs, landmines) and new weapons. He concluded that all the weapons reviewed should be universally banned for all States and that those who employed them should assume their duties relative to compensation, clean-up and warning. There was a pressing need to know what weapons were used and where in Afghanistan, Iraq and other conflict areas in order to assess damage and provide medical assistance to affected persons, in conformity with the right to health. The Subcommission could join in the appeal of other UN entities for disclosure; call for a new environmental assessment of Afghanistan that would more closely examine the effects from weaponry used after the terrorist attacks of 11 September 2001 [YUN 2001, p. 60]; and call for an in-depth study of the nature of newer weapons, their ill effects and potential misuse. Owing to rapid developments, the Subcommission might consider requesting the High Commissioner to prepare a paper for its 2004 session on progress achieved on those issues.

Small arms

Commission action. On 25 April [dec. 2003/112], the Commission decided to endorse the Subcommission's 2002 appointment [YUN 2002, p. 720] of Barbara Frey (United States) as Special Rapporteur with the task of preparing a comprehensive study on the prevention of human rights violations committed with small arms and light weapons; its request to her to submit a preliminary report in 2003, a progress report in 2004 and a final report in 2005; and its request to the Secretary-General to assist her.

On 23 July, the Commission's decision was endorsed by the Economic and Social Council (**decision 2003/268**).

Report of Special Rapporteur. In response to a 2002 Subcommission request [YUN 2002, p. 720], the Special Rapporteur on the prevention of human rights violations committed with small arms and light weapons, Ms. Frey, submitted a June preliminary report [E/CN.4/Sub.2/2003/29], which developed the broad parameters for the legal and practical issues involved and analysed the role of international human rights laws and procedures in preventing the violations. Arms were used to foment a range of human rights abuses and more guns were getting into more hands with fewer restraints. The most visible impact of small arms on human rights was the human carnage, including half a million people killed yearly in war, homicides, accidents and suicides. The report discussed the misuse of small arms by State agents, such as police and military officials, and by armed individuals and groups, as well as the transfer of those arms to commit serious violations of international human rights and humanitarian law. It recommended measures to reduce the demand for small arms and the spiralling violence that occurred in heavily armed communities, and to prevent their misuse and transfer. It further proposed that States adopt national laws regarding small arms and incorporate into those laws the United Nations Basic Principles on the Use of Force and Firearms by Law Enforcement Officials [YUN 1990, p. 701].

Subcommission action. On 13 August [dec. 2003/105], the Subcommission requested the Secretary-General to transmit a questionnaire developed by the Special Rapporteur to Governments, national human rights institutions and NGOs to solicit information required in connection with her study so that she might take them into account in preparing her 2004 progress report.

Economic, social and cultural rights

Right to development

Reports of High Commissioner. In response to a 1998 Commission request [YUN 1998, p. 683], the High Commissioner submitted a [E/CN.4/2003/7], which described OHCHR activities taken to implement the right to development and provided information regarding the implementation of relevant General Assembly and Commission resolutions, as well as inter-agency coordination within the UN system to implement Commission resolutions.

In response to General Assembly resolution 57/223 [YUN 2002, p. 722], the Secretary-General, in a February note by the Secretariat [E/CN.4/2003/125], drew attention to the High Commissioner's report.

A further report of the High Commissioner on the importance and application of the principle of equity [E/CN.4/2003/25], submitted pursuant to a 2002 Commission request [YUN 2002, p. 722], examined the various ways and contexts in which "equity" was used and referred to, and the views of Member States, international organizations, programmes and funds. It concluded that, although none of the human rights instruments adopted under UN auspices contained a definition of equity, there were references to it in those instruments and in the general comments/recommendations adopted by treaty monitoring bodies. It appeared more frequently in the decisions of the main UN human rights bodies and in Commission and Subcommission reports. It was also often referred to in global conferences and was particularly mentioned in the UN Millennium Declaration [YUN 2000, p. 49].

Report of independent expert. In accordance with 2001 [YUN 2001, p. 657] and 2002 [YUN 2002, p. 722] Commission requests, the independent expert on the right to development, Arjun Sengupta (India), submitted a preliminary study [E/CN.4/2003/WG.18/2] to the Working Group on the Right to Development (see p. 753) on the implications of international economic issues for realization of the right. He summarized the imperatives of the right, and examined the main characteristics of the globalized world and their relationship with possible indicators of rights-based development. The expert discussed international assistance and trade liberalization, the extent to which they had met developing countries' requirements, and the possible implications of integrative policies that those countries might follow towards poverty reduction and the realization of the right to development. The expert concluded that the process of globalization and integration into the world economy had not improved developing countries' enjoyment of the right because appropriate policies had rarely been adopted. He recommended that the policies be aimed at the realization of a rights-based approach to development and summarized barriers that needed to be overcome, especially regarding merchandise trade in textiles and clothing and in agriculture. It was also necessary to examine the functioning of the World Trade Organization (WTO) and other trade arrangements, "safeguards" of special and preferential treatment of poor countries and the dispute-settlement mechanism, with a view to enabling trade liberalization policies to realize a rights-based process of development. For that purpose, a group of professionals and experts from WTO and the Commission should be established. The expert suggested that he present a position paper to move the discussion towards concrete proposals for action.

Working Group activities. The open-ended Working Group on the Right to Development, at its fourth session (Geneva, 3-14 February) [E/CN.4/2003/26 & Corr.1], considered the High Commissioner's report and the independent expert's study (see p. 752) and the expert's 2002 report on the proposed development compact [YUN 2002, p. 721]. It asked the High Commissioner to bring its conclusions to the attention of major international institutions, to consider supplementing future reports with additional analyses of the issues covered, to ensure that OHCHR representatives participated in the Group's future deliberations, to strengthen the technical assistance programme and to prioritize the right to development. The Chairperson-Rapporteur recommended that OHCHR consider collecting good practices related to the implementation of the right in development programmes and policies, including specific initiatives such as those aimed at combating HIV/AIDS, and that the Office undertake analytical studies of the role that national human rights institutions could play in creating and implementing development partnerships. The Group indicated the need for further clarification of a number of aspects of the proposed development compact. The Chairperson-Rapporteur suggested that the expert pursue further the feasibility of implementing the proposal in consultation with bilateral donors, multilateral agencies and other stakeholders. As to the expert's preliminary study, the Group asked him to provide further analysis at its 2004 session on the impact of such topics as international trade, access to technology, good governance and equity at the international level, and the debt burden on the right to development. Regarding existing development instruments and mechanisms, the Group discussed the World Bank/International Monetary Fund (IMF) poverty reduction strategy papers, the common country assessment, the United Nations Development Assistance Framework, the New Partnership for Africa's Development (NEPAD) and South-South cooperation as potential mechanisms for the advancement of the right. It encouraged OHCHR, international agencies and financial institutions to integrate all human rights in those and other existing development instruments and mechanisms, to use them to promote the right and to report to the Group in 2004. The expert and OHCHR were encouraged to develop, in cooperation with international agencies and financial institutions, country-specific studies in developed and developing countries, examining in an integrated manner national and international aspects and the role of all stakeholders in the right in those countries. Stressing that NEPAD could provide a suitable framework for implementing the right, the Group expected the expert and OHCHR to present information to it in that regard in 2004 and hoped that the NEPAD secretariat would participate in the discussions. Following the Group's discussion of the question of holding an expert seminar on crucial aspects of the right, the Chairperson-Rapporteur stated that the Commission should facilitate such a seminar. The Group scheduled for its 2004 session the discussion of a suitable and permanent follow-up mechanism, and recommended the extension of its mandate for an additional year.

Commission action. By a recorded vote of 47 to 3, with 3 abstentions, the Commission, on 25 April [res. 2003/83], asked the Subcommission to prepare a concept document, for consideration in 2005, proposing options for the implementation of the right to development and their feasibility, including an international binding legal standard, guidelines on the implementation of the right and principles for development partnership, based on the 1986 Declaration on the Right to Development, annexed to General Assembly resolution 41/128 [YUN 1986, p. 717]. It asked the Subcommission to take into account the outcomes of all major UN and global meetings in the economic and social areas, as well as the Group's 2002 conclusions [YUN 2002, p. 721]. OHCHR was asked to assist the Subcommission, and the High Commissioner to convene a two-day high-level seminar prior to the Group's 2004 session and within its 10 working days, to review and identify effective strategies for mainstreaming the right in the policies and operational activities of the major international organizations/institutions, and as a way of contributing to the Subcommission's work on the proposed concept document. The expert was asked to collaborate with the Subcommission in preparing the document and, in consultation with relevant UN agencies and the Bretton Woods institutions (the World Bank Group and IMF), to deepen his study on the elements contained in his preliminary study on the impact of international economic and financial issues on the right's enjoyment and to report in 2004. The Commission renewed the Working Group's mandate for a further year and asked it to convene its fifth session before the Commission's 2004 session to consider the outcome of the seminar and further initiatives.

ECONOMIC AND SOCIAL COUNCIL ACTION

On 23 July, the Economic and Social Council, on the recommendation of the Commission on Human Rights [E/2003/23], adopted **decision 2003/261** by recorded vote (51-3) [agenda item 14 (g)].

The right to development

At its 46th plenary meeting, on 23 July 2003, the Economic and Social Council took note of Commission on Human Rights resolution 2003/83 of 25 April 2003, and decided to endorse the decision of the Commission to renew the mandate of the Working Group on the Right to Development for one year and to convene its fifth session before the sixtieth session of the Commission, for a period of ten working days.

RECORDED VOTE ON DECISION 2003/261:

In favour: Andorra, Argentina, Azerbaijan, Benin, Bhutan, Brazil, Burundi, Chile, China, Congo, Cuba, Ecuador, Egypt, El Salvador, Ethiopia, Finland, France, Georgia, Germany, Ghana, Greece, Guatemala, Hungary, India, Iran, Ireland, Italy, Jamaica, Kenya, Libyan Arab Jamahiriya, Malaysia, Mozambique, Nepal, Netherlands, Nicaragua, Nigeria, Pakistan, Peru, Portugal, Qatar, Republic of Korea, Romania, Russian Federation, Saudi Arabia, Senegal, South Africa, Sweden, Uganda, Ukraine, United Kingdom, Zimbabwe.

Against: Australia, Japan, United States.

Note by Secretariat. In May [E/CN.4/Sub.2/2003/8], the Secretariat, referring to a 1999 Subcommission request to the Secretary-General [YUN 1999, p. 652], noted that, as at 21 May 2003, no reply had been received from UN bodies and agencies regarding steps taken to promote international cooperation for the realization of the right to development in the context of the United Nations Decade for the Eradication of Poverty (1997-2006) (see p. 848). However, the Secretary-General drew the Subcommission's attention to the High Commissioner's report (see p. 752) containing information on OHCHR activities relating to the right's implementation, and to the General Assembly's request to him in resolution 57/223 [YUN 2002, p. 722].

Report of Secretary-General. In accordance with General Assembly resolution 57/223, the Secretary-General submitted an August report with later addendum on the right to development [A/58/276 & Add.1] based on information received from seven Governments and from seven UN specialized agencies, departments and programmes, and other international organizations.

On 22 December, the Assembly took note of the report (**decision 58/538**).

Subcommission action. On 14 August [dec. 2003/116], the Subcommission requested Florizelle O'Connor (Jamaica) to prepare, without financial implications, for consideration in 2004, a working paper identifying and analysing possible alternatives to enable the Subcommission to respond fully and effectively to the request contained in Commission resolution 2003/83 (see p. 753).

Also on 14 August [dec. 2003/115], the Subcommission, referring to a 2002 Commission request [YUN 2002, p. 722], asked Rui Baltazar Dos Santos Alves (Mozambique) to prepare, without financial implications, a working paper on human rights and international solidarity as a component of efforts of developing countries to realize the right to development, for consideration in 2004.

GENERAL ASSEMBLY ACTION

On 22 December [meeting 77], the General Assembly, on the recommendation of the Third Committee [A/58/508/Add.2], adopted **resolution 58/172** by recorded vote (173-3-5) [agenda item 117 (b)].

The right to development

The General Assembly,

Guided by the Charter of the United Nations, which expresses, in particular, the determination to promote social progress and better standards of life in larger freedom, as well as to employ international mechanisms for the promotion of the economic and social advancement of all peoples,

Reaffirming the objective of making the right to development a reality for everyone, as set out in the United Nations Millennium Declaration, adopted by the General Assembly on 8 September 2000,

Stressing the need for undertaking urgent measures to implement the goals and targets set at all the major United Nations conferences and summits and their review processes, which are paramount in the process of the realization of the right to development,

Taking note of the outcome of the Fourth Ministerial Conference of the World Trade Organization, held in Doha from 9 to 14 November 2001,

Recalling that the Declaration on the Right to Development, adopted by the General Assembly in its resolution 41/128 of 4 December 1986, confirmed that the right to development is an inalienable human right and that equality of opportunity for development is a prerogative both of nations and of individuals who make up nations, and the individual as the central subject and beneficiary of development,

Stressing that the Vienna Declaration and Programme of Action reaffirmed the right to development as a universal and inalienable right and an integral part of fundamental human rights, and the individual as the central subject and beneficiary of development,

Recalling all its previous resolutions and those of the Commission on Human Rights on the right to development, in particular Commission resolution 1998/72 of 22 April 1998, on the urgent need to make further progress towards the realization of the right to development as set out in the Declaration on the Right to Development,

Welcoming its adoption of the United Nations Convention against Corruption on 31 October 2003,

Recalling the high-level plenary meetings of the General Assembly held on 22 September 2003 devoted to the follow-up to the outcome of its twenty-sixth special session and the implementation of the Declaration of Commitment on HIV/AIDS,

Recalling also the Thirteenth Conference of Heads of State or Government of the Non-Aligned Movement, held in Kuala Lumpur from 20 to 25 February 2003,

Reiterating its continuing support for the New Partnership for Africa's Development as a development framework for Africa,

Recognizing that historical injustices have undeniably contributed to the poverty, underdevelopment, marginalization, social exclusion, economic disparity, instability and insecurity that affect many people in different parts of the world, in particular in developing countries,

Stressing that poverty eradication is one of the critical elements in the promotion and realization of the right to development and that poverty is a multifaceted problem that requires a multifaceted and integrated approach in addressing economic, political, social, environmental and institutional dimensions at all levels, especially in the context of the millennium development goal of halving, by 2015, the proportion of the world's people whose income is less than one dollar a day and the proportion of people who suffer from hunger,

Expressing regret that the Working Group on the Right to Development, at its fourth session, did not reach a conclusion, in particular on the implementation of the conclusions of the third session of the Working Group, while aware of the views and observations of the Chairperson-Rapporteur,

1. *Endorses* the conclusions of the third session of the Working Group on the Right to Development, as adopted by the Commission on Human Rights in its resolution 2002/69 of 25 April 2002, which constitute a solid foundation for further initiatives towards the promotion and the realization of the right to development;

2. *Requests* the Working Group at its fifth session to revisit and build upon the conclusions of its third session in order to constructively and effectively fulfil its mandate, bearing in mind that the Working Group did not reach a conclusion at its fourth session;

3. *Stresses* the importance of the core principles contained in the conclusions of the third session of the Working Group, congruent with the purpose of international human rights instruments, such as equality, non-discrimination, accountability, participation and international cooperation, as critical to mainstreaming the right to development at the international level, and underlines the importance of the principles of equity and transparency;

4. *Reaffirms* the commitment to implement the goals and targets set out in all the outcome documents of the major United Nations conferences and summits and their review processes, in particular those relating to the realization of the right to development, recognizing that the realization of the right to development is critical to achieving the objectives, goals and targets set in those outcome documents;

5. *Reaffirms also* that the realization of the right to development is essential to the implementation of the Vienna Declaration and Programme of Action, which regards all human rights as universal, indivisible, interdependent and interrelated, places the human person at the centre of development and recognizes that, while development facilitates the enjoyment of all human rights, the lack of development may not be invoked to justify the abridgement of internationally recognized human rights;

6. *Stresses* that the basic responsibility for the promotion and protection of all human rights lies with the State, and reaffirms that States have the primary responsibility for their own economic and social development and that the role of national policies and development strategies cannot be overemphasized;

7. *Reaffirms* that States have the primary responsibility for the creation of national and international conditions favourable to the realization of the right to development and their commitment to cooperating with each other to that end;

8. *Reaffirms also* the need for an international environment that is conducive to the realization of the right to development;

9. *Stresses* the need to strive for greater acceptance, operationalization and realization of the right to development at the international and national levels, and calls upon States to institute the measures required for the implementation of the right to development as a fundamental human right;

10. *Emphasizes* the critical importance of identifying and analysing obstacles impeding the full realization of the right to development at both the national and the international levels;

11. *Affirms* that, while globalization offers both opportunities and challenges, the process of globalization remains deficient in achieving the objectives of integrating all countries into a globalized world, and stresses the need for policies and measures at the national and global levels to respond to the challenges and opportunities of globalization if this process is to be made fully inclusive and equitable;

12. *Recognizes* that, despite continuous efforts on the part of the international community, the gap between developed and developing countries remains unacceptably wide, that developing countries continue to face difficulties in participating in the globalization process and that many risk being marginalized and effectively excluded from its benefits;

13. *Reaffirms* the commitment, and urges developed countries that have not yet done so, to make

concrete efforts towards meeting the targets of 0.7 per cent of their gross national product for official development assistance to developing countries and 0.15 to 0.2 per cent of their gross national product to least developed countries, and encourages developing countries to build on the progress achieved in ensuring that official development assistance is used effectively to help to meet development goals and targets;

14. *Recognizes* the need to address market access for developing countries, including in respect of agriculture, services and non-agricultural products, in particular those of interest to developing countries;

15. *Considers* that a desirable pace of meaningful trade liberalization, including in areas under negotiation; implementation of commitments on implementation-related issues and concerns; review of special and differential-treatment provisions, with a view to strengthening them and making them more precise, effective and operational; avoidance of new forms of protectionism; and capacity-building and technical assistance for developing countries are important issues in making progress towards the effective implementation of the right to development;

16. *Underlines* the fact that the international community is far from meeting the target set in the United Nations Millennium Declaration of halving the number of people living in poverty by 2015, and emphasizes the principle of international cooperation, including partnership and commitment, between developed and developing countries towards achieving the goal;

17. *Recognizes* the important link between the international economic, commercial and financial spheres and the realization of the right to development, stresses, in this regard, the need to broaden the base of decision-making at the international level on issues of development concern and to fill organizational gaps, as well as strengthen the United Nations system and other multilateral institutions, and also stresses the need to broaden and strengthen the participation of developing countries and economies in transition in international economic decision-making and norm-setting;

18. *Recognizes also* that good governance and the rule of law at the national level assist all States in the promotion and protection of human rights, including the right to development, and agrees on the value of the ongoing efforts being made by States to identify and strengthen good governance practices, including transparent, responsible, accountable and participatory government, that are responsive and appropriate to their needs and aspirations, including in the context of agreed partnership approaches to development, capacity-building and technical assistance;

19. *Recognizes further* the important role and the rights of women and the application of a gender perspective as a cross-cutting issue in the process of realizing the right to development, and notes in particular the positive relationship between women's education and their equal participation in the civil, cultural, economic, political and social activities of the community and the promotion of the right to development;

20. *Stresses* the need for the integration of the rights of children, girls and boys alike, in all policies and programmes, and for ensuring the protection and promotion of those rights, especially in areas relating to health, education and the full development of their capacities;

21. *Stresses also* that further and additional measures must be taken at the national and international levels to fight HIV/AIDS and other communicable diseases, taking into account ongoing efforts and programmes, and reiterates the need for international assistance in this regard;

22. *Recognizes* the need for strong partnerships with civil society organizations and the private sector in pursuit of poverty eradication and development, as well as for good corporate governance;

23. *Emphasizes* the urgent need for taking concrete measures to fight against all forms of corruption at the national and international levels, to prevent, detect and deter in a more effective manner international transfers of illicitly acquired assets and to strengthen international cooperation in asset recovery, stresses the importance of a genuine political commitment on the part of all Governments through a firm legal framework, and in this context urges States to sign and ratify the United Nations Convention against Corruption as soon as possible;

24. *Looks forward* to the consideration by the Commission on Human Rights at its sixty-first session of the concept document to be prepared by the Subcommission on the Promotion and Protection of Human Rights establishing options for the implementation of the right to development and their feasibility;

25. *Emphasizes* the need to strengthen further the activities of the Office of the United Nations High Commissioner for Human Rights in the promotion and realization of the right to development, including ensuring effective use of the financial and human resources necessary to fulfil its mandate and better servicing of and support for the Working Group on the Right to Development;

26. *Requests* the Secretary-General to ensure that the Office of the High Commissioner effectively assists in implementing the recommendations contained in the conclusions of the third session of the Working Group on the Right to Development, and to ensure also the meaningful participation and contribution of all relevant United Nations agencies, funds and programmes, the specialized agencies and international organizations in the next session of the Working Group;

27. *Calls upon* the United Nations agencies, funds and programmes, as well as the specialized agencies, to mainstream the right to development in their operational programmes and objectives, and stresses the need for the international financial and multilateral trading systems to mainstream the right to development in their policies and objectives;

28. *Requests* the Secretary-General to bring the present resolution to the attention of Member States, United Nations organs and bodies, specialized agencies, funds and programmes, international development and financial institutions, in particular the Bretton Woods institutions, and non-governmental organizations;

29. *Also requests* the Secretary-General to submit a report to the General Assembly at its fifty-ninth session and an interim report to the Commission on Human Rights at its sixtieth session on the implementation of the present resolution, including efforts

undertaken at the national, regional and international levels in the promotion and realization of the right to development.

RECORDED VOTE ON RESOLUTION 58/172:

In favour: Afghanistan, Albania, Algeria, Andorra, Angola, Antigua and Barbuda, Argentina, Armenia, Austria, Azerbaijan, Bahamas, Bahrain, Bangladesh, Barbados, Belarus, Belgium, Belize, Benin, Bhutan, Bolivia, Bosnia and Herzegovina, Botswana, Brazil, Brunei Darussalam, Bulgaria, Burkina Faso, Burundi, Cambodia, Cameroon, Cape Verde, Central African Republic, Chile, China, Colombia, Comoros, Congo, Costa Rica, Côte d'Ivoire, Croatia, Cuba, Cyprus, Czech Republic, Democratic People's Republic of Korea, Democratic Republic of the Congo, Denmark, Djibouti, Dominica, Dominican Republic, Ecuador, Egypt, El Salvador, Eritrea, Estonia, Ethiopia, Fiji, Finland, France, Gabon, Gambia, Germany, Ghana, Greece, Grenada, Guatemala, Guinea, Guinea-Bissau, Guyana, Haiti, Honduras, Hungary, Iceland, India, Indonesia, Iran, Ireland, Italy, Jamaica, Jordan, Kazakhstan, Kenya, Kuwait, Kyrgyzstan, Lao People's Democratic Republic, Latvia, Lebanon, Lesotho, Libyan Arab Jamahiriya, Liechtenstein, Lithuania, Luxembourg, Madagascar, Malawi, Malaysia, Maldives, Mali, Malta, Marshall Islands, Mauritania, Mauritius, Mexico, Monaco, Mongolia, Morocco, Mozambique, Myanmar, Namibia, Nauru, Nepal, Netherlands, New Zealand, Nicaragua, Niger, Nigeria, Norway, Oman, Pakistan, Panama, Papua New Guinea, Paraguay, Peru, Philippines, Poland, Portugal, Qatar, Republic of Korea, Republic of Moldova, Romania, Russian Federation, Rwanda, Saint Lucia, Saint Vincent and the Grenadines, Samoa, San Marino, Saudi Arabia, Senegal, Serbia and Montenegro, Seychelles, Sierra Leone, Singapore, Slovakia, Slovenia, Solomon Islands, Somalia, South Africa, Spain, Sri Lanka, Sudan, Suriname, Switzerland, Syrian Arab Republic, Tajikistan, Thailand, The former Yugoslav Republic of Macedonia, Timor-Leste, Togo, Tonga, Trinidad and Tobago, Tunisia, Turkey, Turkmenistan, Tuvalu, Uganda, Ukraine, United Arab Emirates, United Kingdom, United Republic of Tanzania, Uruguay, Uzbekistan, Venezuela, Viet Nam, Yemen, Zambia, Zimbabwe.

Against: Israel, Palau, United States.

Abstaining: Australia, Canada, Georgia, Japan, Sweden.

Democratic and equitable international order

By a recorded vote of 31 to 15, with 7 abstentions, the Commission, on 24 April [res. 2003/63], urged States to continue efforts to establish a democratic and equitable international order. The Commission asked human rights treaty bodies, OHCHR and Commission and Subcommission mechanisms to contribute to the implementation of its resolution. The Secretary-General was asked to bring the resolution to the attention of Member States, UN organs and bodies, intergovernmental organizations and NGOs and to disseminate it widely.

Globalization

Report of High Commissioner. The Commission had before it a report of the High Commissioner [E/CN.4/2003/49], submitted in response to a 2002 Commission request [YUN 2002, p. 725], which described activities integrating the theme of globalization in regional arrangements for the promotion and protection of human rights, covering Latin America and the Caribbean and the Asia-Pacific region.

Note by Secretariat. A February note of the Secretariat [E/CN.4/2003/50], referring to a 2002 Commission request for a study on the principle of non-discrimination in the context of globalization [YUN 2002, p. 725], stated that OHCHR held consultations with the United Nations Conference on Trade and Development, WTO, the World Intellectual Property Organization, the Food and Agriculture Organization of the United Nations (FAO), academics and other experts. The Office prepared a draft report, which was shared with those organizations and experts for review. Following further discussion, the final report would be submitted in 2004.

Commission action. By a recorded vote of 38 to 15, the Commission, on 22 April [res. 2003/23], reaffirmed the commitment to create an environment conducive to development and to the elimination of poverty through good governance, transparency in the financial, monetary and trading systems and the commitment to an open, equitable, rule-based, predictable and non-discriminatory multilateral trading and financial system. The High Commissioner was asked to bring his 2002 report [YUN 2002, p. 725] to the attention of WTO and the World Commission on the Social Dimension of Globalization, launched by ILO with the aim of building a consensus on a model of globalization that reduced poverty and insecurity and increased opportunities for all. Referring to the Secretariat's note (see above), the Commission asked the High Commissioner to focus on the need to clarify the human rights principle of non-discrimination relative to WTO's trade rules, especially as they applied to the WTO Agreement on Agriculture.

Report of Special Rapporteurs. In a final report [E/CN.4/Sub.2/2003/14], the Special Rapporteurs on globalization and its impact on human rights, Joseph Oloka-Onyango (Uganda) and Deepika Udagama (Sri Lanka), updated developments since their 2001 report [YUN 2001, p. 663]. They reviewed areas for future study and action by the Subcommission, considered the manner in which the events of 11 September 2001 [ibid., p. 60] had reshaped many concerns in the debate about globalization, and summarized the implications of the continued drive towards increased trade liberalization at WTO and the current state of discussions about and within multilateral lending institutions. The Special Rapporteurs, noting that the processes of globalization would grow in magnitude in terms of the exercise and protection of human rights, recommended that the Subcommission remain seized of the issue and maintain oversight of the major institutional actors and of the manner in which the varied processes of globalization developed. Annexed to the report was a proposal of issues key to the extension of the dialogue between the Subcommission and the main actors involved in the globalization process, which drew attention to the human rights obligations of the latter.

Report of Secretary-General. In response to General Assembly resolution 57/205 [YUN 2002,

p. 726], the Secretary-General, in an August report [A/58/257], submitted the views of one Government on globalization and its impact on human rights.

Subcommission action. On 15 August [dec. 2003/117], the Subcommission decided to transmit to the Commission the Special Rapporteurs' preliminary report [YUN 2000, p. 696], progress report [YUN 2001, p. 663] and final report (see p. 757), with a request that they be published in the UN official languages.

GENERAL ASSEMBLY ACTION

On 22 December [meeting 77], the General Assembly, on the recommendation of the Third Committee [A/58/508/Add.2], adopted **resolution 58/193** by recorded vote (123-51-4) [agenda item 117 (b)].

Globalization and its impact on the full enjoyment of all human rights

The General Assembly,

Guided by the purposes and principles of the Charter of the United Nations, and expressing in particular the need to achieve international cooperation in promoting and encouraging respect for human rights and fundamental freedoms for all without distinction,

Recalling the Universal Declaration of Human Rights, as well as the Vienna Declaration and Programme of Action adopted by the World Conference on Human Rights on 25 June 1993,

Recalling also the International Covenant on Civil and Political Rights and the International Covenant on Economic, Social and Cultural Rights,

Recalling further the Declaration on the Right to Development adopted by the General Assembly in its resolution 41/128 of 4 December 1986,

Recalling the United Nations Millennium Declaration and the outcome documents of the twenty-third and twenty-fourth special sessions of the General Assembly, held, respectively, in New York from 5 to 10 June 2000 and in Geneva from 26 June to 1 July 2000,

Recalling also its resolutions 57/204 and 57/205 of 18 December 2002,

Recalling further Commission on Human Rights resolution 2003/23 of 22 April 2003 on globalization and its impact on the full enjoyment of human rights,

Recognizing that all human rights are universal, indivisible, interdependent and interrelated and that the international community must treat human rights globally in a fair and equal manner, on the same footing and with the same emphasis,

Realizing that globalization affects all countries differently and makes them more exposed to external developments, positive as well as negative, inter alia, in the field of human rights,

Realizing also that globalization is not merely an economic process, but that it also has social, political, environmental, cultural and legal dimensions, which have an impact on the full enjoyment of all human rights,

Realizing further the need to undertake a thorough, independent and comprehensive assessment of the social, environmental and cultural impact of globalization on societies,

Recognizing in each culture a dignity and value that deserve recognition, respect and preservation, and convinced that, in their rich variety and diversity and in the reciprocal influences that they exert on one another, all cultures form part of the common heritage belonging to all humankind, and aware that the risk of a global monoculture poses more of a threat if the developing world remains poor and marginalized,

Recognizing also that multilateral mechanisms have a unique role to play in meeting the challenges and opportunities presented by globalization,

Expressing concern at the negative impact of international financial turbulence on social and economic development and on the full enjoyment of all human rights,

Deeply concerned that the widening gap between the developed and the developing countries, and within countries, has contributed, inter alia, to deepening poverty and has adversely affected the full enjoyment of all human rights, in particular in developing countries,

Noting that human beings strive for a world that is respectful of human rights and cultural diversity and that, in this regard, they work to ensure that all activities, including those affected by globalization, are consistent with those aims,

1. *Recognizes* that, while globalization, by its impact on, inter alia, the role of the State, may affect human rights, the promotion and protection of all human rights is first and foremost the responsibility of the State;

2. *Reaffirms* that narrowing the gap between rich and poor, both within and between countries, is an explicit goal at the national and international levels, as part of the effort to create an enabling environment for the full enjoyment of all human rights;

3. *Reaffirms also* the commitment to creating an environment at both the national and the global level that is conducive to development and to the elimination of poverty through, inter alia, good governance within each country and at the international level, transparency in the financial, monetary and trading systems and commitment to an open, equitable, rule-based, predictable and non-discriminatory multilateral trading and financial system;

4. *Recognizes* that, while globalization offers great opportunities, the fact that its benefits are very unevenly shared and its costs unevenly distributed represents an aspect of the process that affects the full enjoyment of all human rights, in particular in developing countries;

5. *Welcomes* the report of the United Nations High Commissioner for Human Rights on globalization and its impact on the full enjoyment of human rights, which focuses on the liberalization of agricultural trade and its impact on the realization of the right to development, including the right to food, and takes note of the conclusions and recommendations contained therein;

6. *Calls upon* Member States, relevant agencies of the United Nations system, intergovernmental organizations and civil society to promote equitable and environmentally sustainable economic growth for managing globalization, so that poverty is systematically

reduced and the international development targets are achieved;

7. *Recognizes* that only through broad and sustained efforts, including policies and measures at the global level to create a shared future based upon our common humanity in all its diversity, can globalization be made fully inclusive and equitable and have a human face, thus contributing to the full enjoyment of all human rights;

8. *Underlines* the urgent need to establish an equitable, transparent and democratic international system in which poor people and countries have a more effective voice;

9. *Affirms* that globalization is a complex process of structural transformation, with numerous interdisciplinary aspects, which has an impact on the enjoyment of civil, political, economic, social and cultural rights, including the right to development;

10. *Affirms also* that the international community should strive to respond to the challenges and opportunities posed by globalization in a manner that ensures respect for the cultural diversity of all;

11. *Underlines*, therefore, the need to continue to analyse the consequences of globalization for the full enjoyment of all human rights;

12. *Takes note* of the report of the Secretary-General, and requests the Secretary-General to seek further the views of Member States and relevant agencies of the United Nations system and to submit a substantive report on this subject to the General Assembly at its fifty-ninth session.

RECORDED VOTE ON RESOLUTION 58/193:

In favour: Afghanistan, Algeria, Angola, Antigua and Barbuda, Argentina, Armenia, Azerbaijan, Bahamas, Bahrain, Bangladesh, Barbados, Belarus, Belize, Benin, Bhutan, Bolivia, Botswana, Brunei Darussalam, Burkina Faso, Burundi, Cambodia, Cameroon, Cape Verde, Central African Republic, China, Colombia, Comoros, Congo, Costa Rica, Côte d'Ivoire, Cuba, Democratic People's Republic of Korea, Democratic Republic of the Congo, Djibouti, Dominica, Dominican Republic, Ecuador, Egypt, El Salvador, Eritrea, Ethiopia, Fiji, Gabon, Gambia, Ghana, Grenada, Guinea, Guinea-Bissau, Guyana, Haiti, Honduras, India, Indonesia, Iran, Jamaica, Jordan, Kazakhstan, Kenya, Kuwait, Kyrgyzstan, Lao People's Democratic Republic, Lebanon, Lesotho, Libyan Arab Jamahiriya, Madagascar, Malawi, Malaysia, Maldives, Mali, Mauritania, Mauritius, Mexico, Mongolia, Morocco, Mozambique, Myanmar, Namibia, Nauru, Nepal, Nicaragua, Niger, Nigeria, Oman, Pakistan, Panama, Papua New Guinea, Paraguay, Peru, Philippines, Qatar, Russian Federation, Rwanda, Saint Lucia, Saint Vincent and the Grenadines, Samoa, Saudi Arabia, Senegal, Sierra Leone, Solomon Islands, Somalia, South Africa, Sri Lanka, Sudan, Suriname, Syrian Arab Republic, Tajikistan, Thailand, Timor-Leste, Togo, Tonga, Trinidad and Tobago, Tunisia, Turkmenistan, Tuvalu, Uganda, United Arab Emirates, United Republic of Tanzania, Uruguay, Venezuela, Viet Nam, Yemen, Zambia, Zimbabwe.

Against: Albania, Andorra, Australia, Austria, Belgium, Bosnia and Herzegovina, Bulgaria, Canada, Croatia, Cyprus, Czech Republic, Denmark, Estonia, Finland, France, Georgia, Germany, Greece, Hungary, Iceland, Ireland, Israel, Italy, Japan, Latvia, Liechtenstein, Lithuania, Luxembourg, Malta, Monaco, Netherlands, New Zealand, Norway, Palau, Poland, Portugal, Republic of Korea, Republic of Moldova, Romania, San Marino, Serbia and Montenegro, Slovakia, Slovenia, Spain, Sweden, Switzerland, The former Yugoslav Republic of Macedonia, Turkey, Ukraine, United Kingdom, United States.

Abstaining: Brazil, Chile, Guatemala, Singapore.

Liberalization of trade in services

In response to a 2002 Subcommission request [YUN 2002, p. 728], the High Commissioner, in a July report [E/CN.4/Sub.2/2003/9] on the relationship between human rights and investment and on trade concerns that were directly related to investment, examined the liberalization of investment through investment agreements and reviewed areas of those agreements relevant to human rights promotion and protection. The report considered the need to allow flexibility to enable States to respect, protect and fulfil human rights through appropriate regulation. Areas for action included the incorporation of human rights promotion and protection among the objectives of investment agreements, promoting investors' obligations alongside their rights, fostering international cooperation as part of investment liberalization, advancing human rights in the context of privatization, increasing dialogue on human rights and trade, and undertaking human rights assessments of investment liberalization.

Structural adjustment policies

Note by Secretariat. The Commission had before it a note by the Secretariat [E/CN.4/2003/57] referring to Economic and Social Council decision 2002/57 [YUN 2002, p. 728], which stated that the fourth session of the open-ended working group on structural adjustment programmes (SAPs), scheduled for November 2002 in Geneva, had been postponed as the working group's Chairman-designate needed more time to consult with regional groups.

Reports of independent expert. The Commission considered a report [E/CN.4/2003/10 & Corr.1] of the independent expert on the effects of structural adjustment policies and foreign debt on human rights, Bernards Mudho (Kenya), which examined debt reduction and poverty alleviation and described the ambiguities arising from the implementation of SAPs and the inadequacy of debt relief alone to realize the human rights dimension of poverty, as illustrated by a case study of Bolivia. The expert observed that, although the effects of foreign debt and SAPs on the full enjoyment of human rights varied in scope and severity in heavily indebted poor countries (HIPCs) and least developed countries (LDCs), there was common ground that heavy foreign borrowing by developing countries in the 1970s and 1980s, supposedly to finance large-scale development projects, led to unsustainably high levels of debt by those countries. Consequently, both borrowers and lenders were jointly responsible for the current untenable levels of foreign debt incurred by HIPCs and LDCs. The expert recommended a series of actions by the Commission, including establishing a reporting mechanism to monitor accomplishments, problems and lessons learned in promoting and protecting human rights with regard to implementing the Millennium Development Goals [YUN 2000, p. 51] (see also p. 48).

The expert visited Uganda (26-30 May) [E/CN.4/2004/47/Add.1] to examine the effects of foreign debt and policies adopted to deal with them, and to initiate dialogue in efforts to secure economic and social rights. He accorded particular attention to the situation of HIV/AIDS in the country. The expert said that, although Uganda had made impressive strides in the human development of its people, it still faced significant challenges, in terms of ensuring gender parity in secondary education, combating infant and maternal mortality, reducing malaria and improving environmental sanitation while maintaining the necessary macroeconomic stability and debt sustainability. The expert suggested that more expanded and explicit linkages be made between the country's development goals and human rights and, towards that end, recommended that the Government and its development partners, while encouraging increased support by donors, explore ways to reduce dependence on external resources and the adverse implications for poverty reduction and the realization of human rights.

Commission action. By a recorded vote of 29 to 14, with 10 abstentions, the Commission, on 22 April [res. 2003/21], affirmed that the exercise of the basic rights of the people of debtor countries to food, housing, clothing, employment, education, health services and a healthy environment could not be subordinated to the implementation of structural adjustment policies, growth programmes and economic reforms arising from the debt problem. It decided to renew the independent expert's mandate for three years and asked him to submit an analytical report annually on the implementation of the current resolution; the Secretary-General was asked to assist him. The High Commissioner was asked to pay attention to the problem of the debt burden of developing countries.

ECONOMIC AND SOCIAL COUNCIL ACTION

On 23 July, the Economic and Social Council, on the recommendation of the Commission on Human Rights [E/2003/23], adopted **decision 2003/243** by recorded vote (31-17-5) [agenda item 14 (g)].

Effects of structural adjustment policies and foreign debt on the full enjoyment of all human rights, particularly economic, social and cultural rights

At its 46th plenary meeting, on 23 July 2003, the Economic and Social Council took note of Commission on Human Rights resolution 2003/21 of 22 April 2003, and approved the Commission's decision to renew the mandate of the independent expert on the effects of structural adjustment policies and foreign debt on the full enjoyment of human rights, particularly economic, social and cultural rights, for three years and to request him to submit an analytical report to the Commission on an annual basis on the implementation of Commission resolution 2003/21, paying particular attention to the effects of the burden of foreign debt and the policies adopted to face them on the capacity of the Governments of developing countries to adopt policies and programmes for the enjoyment of economic, social and cultural rights, as well as to recommend measures and actions that could be taken to alleviate such effects, especially in the poorest and heavily indebted countries.

The Council also approved the Commission's request to the Secretary-General to provide the independent expert with all necessary assistance, in particular the staff and resources required to carry out his functions.

RECORDED VOTE ON DECISION 2003/243:
In favour: Benin, Bhutan, Brazil, Burundi, Chile, China, Congo, Cuba, Ecuador, Egypt, El Salvador, Ethiopia, Ghana, Guatemala, India, Iran, Jamaica, Kenya, Libyan Arab Jamahiriya, Malaysia, Mozambique, Nepal, Nicaragua, Nigeria, Pakistan, Qatar, Russian Federation, Senegal, South Africa, Uganda, Zimbabwe.
Against: Andorra, Australia, Finland, France, Germany, Greece, Hungary, Ireland, Italy, Japan, Netherlands, Portugal, Republic of Korea, Romania, Sweden, United Kingdom, United States.
Abstaining: Argentina, Georgia, Peru, Saudi Arabia, Ukraine.

Adverse effects of debt

On 13 August [dec. 2003/109], the Subcommission asked El-Hadji Guissé (Senegal) to prepare, without financial implications, a working paper on the effects of debt on human rights, for submission in 2004.

Social Forum

Commission action. By a recorded vote of 36 to 1, with 16 abstentions, the Commission, on 22 April [dec. 2003/107], taking note of a 2002 Subcommission resolution [YUN 2002, p. 729], recommended that the Economic and Social Council authorize the holding of the Social Forum, an annual pre-sessional forum on economic, social and cultural rights, for two days and on dates that would permit the attendance of 10 Subcommission members. The Council was asked to provide the facilities for the preparation and servicing of the event.

ECONOMIC AND SOCIAL COUNCIL ACTION

On 23 July, the Economic and Social Council, on the recommendation of the Commission on Human Rights [E/2003/23], adopted **decision 2003/264** by recorded vote (34-2-18) [agenda item 14 (g)].

The Social Forum

At its 46th plenary meeting, on 23 July 2003, the Economic and Social Council took note of Commission on Human Rights decision 2003/107 of 22 April 2003, and authorized the Subcommission on the Promotion and Protection of Human Rights to convene in Geneva an annual intersessional forum on economic, social and cultural rights, to be known as the "Social Forum", for two days on dates that would permit the possible participation of ten members of the Subcommission, to be appointed by the regional groups of the Subcommission, and also authorized the provision of all the necessary facilities for the preparation and servicing of the event.

RECORDED VOTE ON DECISION 2003/264:

In favour: Argentina, Azerbaijan, Benin, Bhutan, Brazil, Burundi, Chile, China, Congo, Cuba, Ecuador, Egypt, El Salvador, Ethiopia, Ghana, Guatemala, India, Iran, Jamaica, Kenya, Libyan Arab Jamahiriya, Malaysia, Mozambique, Nepal, Nicaragua, Nigeria, Pakistan, Peru, Qatar, Russian Federation, Senegal, South Africa, Uganda, Zimbabwe.

Against: Australia, United States.

Abstaining: Andorra, Finland, France, Georgia, Germany, Greece, Hungary, Ireland, Italy, Japan, Netherlands, Portugal, Republic of Korea, Romania, Saudi Arabia, Sweden, Ukraine, United Kingdom.

Note by Secretariat. A June note by the Secretariat [E/CN.4/Sub.2/2003/16] provided information regarding the Forum's next session, as requested by the Commission and authorized by the Economic and Social Council (see p. 760). Annexed to the note was a memorandum prepared by José Bengoa (Chile), which summarized the Forum's goals and the key aspects of its 2002 session [YUN 2002, p. 729], and stated that the Subcommission, in consultation with the Secretariat, would decide on a suitable date for its next session, bearing in mind the need for proper preparation. The memorandum contained proposals on the Forum's organization and work, policies to be adopted, campaigns to be conducted relative to the Forum's objectives, and a proposal on the rights of rural communities and peasants.

Subcommission action. On 13 August [res. 2003/14], the Subcommission decided that the Social Forum would meet in Geneva on 20 and 21 May 2004, and recommended that it address themes relating to civil, political, economic, social and cultural rights; the relationship between poverty, extreme poverty and human rights; income distribution; basic resources; the impact of trade, finance and economic policies on vulnerable groups; multilateral and bilateral international development cooperation; follow-up to world conferences and summits; and social and economic indicators. The Subcommission decided that the 2004 session would have as its overall theme "Rural poverty, development and the rights of peasants and other rural communities", and asked Mr. Bengoa to prepare a working paper on the topic and related matters. OHCHR was requested to seek effective means of ensuring consultation with the most vulnerable on the theme. UN bodies and specialized agencies, functional commissions of the Economic and Social Council, regional commissions, international financial institutions, the Committee on Economic, Social and Cultural Rights, special rapporteurs and independent experts, NGOs, scholars, trade unions and workers' associations were invited to participate in and to submit studies to the Forum. The Forum was invited to submit in 2004 a separate report on its discussions, in addition to recommendations, including draft resolutions. The Commission was requested to establish a voluntary fund to facilitate the participation of grass-roots groups and similar disadvantaged organizations in the Forum, and the Secretary-General to disseminate information about the Forum, invite relevant individuals and organizations to the Forum, prepare two videoconferences before the Forum and take measures to ensure its success.

Transnational corporations

Working group activities. The working group on the working methods and activities of transnational corporations (TNCs), at its fifth session (Geneva, 29-31 July) [E/CN.4/Sub.2/2003/13], continued to work towards a binding instrument. The group had before it an updated version of the draft norms on the responsibilities of TNCs and other business enterprises [E/CN.4/Sub.2/2003/12], which took into account related comments considered in an earlier intersessional meeting, as well as the commentary thereto [E/CN.4/Sub.2/2003/38]. The group, in response to a 2002 Subcommission request [YUN 2002, p. 730], had disseminated various versions of the draft and encouraged Governments, international organizations, NGOs, TNCs, other business enterprises, unions and other interested parties to provide suggestions, observations or recommendations.

At its July meeting, the group considered proposed amendments to the draft norms and commentary and, on 31 July, adopted revisions to both [E/CN.4/Sub.2/2003/12/Rev.1, E/CN.4/Sub.2/2003/38/Rev.1 & Corr.1], which were submitted to the Subcommission. The group considered the impact of TNCs on the enjoyment of civil, cultural, economic, political and social rights, and recommendations for its future work regarding the effects of TNC activities on human rights, including the rights to development and to a healthy environment.

Subcommission action. On 28 July [dec. 2003/102], the Subcommission decided to establish a sessional working group to examine the working methods and activities of TNCs (see above).

On 13 August [res. 2003/16], the Subcommission approved the revised draft norms on the responsibilities of TNCs and other business enterprises with regard to human rights submitted by the working group [E/CN.4/Sub.2/2003/12/Rev.2] and decided to transmit them to the Commission for consideration and adoption. It recommended that the Commission invite Governments, UN bodies, specialized agencies, NGOs and other interested parties to submit to the Commission and Subcommission in 2005 comments on the draft norms and commentary [E/CN.4/Sub.2/2003/38/Rev.2], and to consider establishing an open-ended working group to review both. The working group was asked to receive information from Governments, NGOs, business enterprises, individuals and other sources regarding the possible negative impact of the activities of TNCs and other business enterprises on human rights, and particularly affecting the implementation of the norms, to invite comments thereon from TNCs and other business enterprises concerned, and to study the information submitted and transmit its comments and recommendations to the appropriate TNCs or other businesses, Governments and relevant NGOs. The Subcommission recommended that the group continue its discussions, in accordance with its mandate, and particularly pursue efforts to explore possible mechanisms for implementing the norms, such as the continuation of the 1998 working document on the impact of TNCs on the realization of economic, social and cultural rights [YUN 1998, p. 688], prepared by Mr. Guissé. The Subcommission asked the Secretary-General to provide the group with the services required to complete its work, and the Working Group on Indigenous Populations (see p. 798) to gather the views of indigenous peoples, organizations and communities, as well as other interested parties, to supplement the commentary on the norms and/or to draft a new set of principles that would include further references to indigenous concerns and rights with regard to TNCs and other business enterprises.

Coercive economic measures

Commission action. By a recorded vote of 36 to 14, with 2 abstentions, the Commission, on 22 April [res. 2003/17], requested the open-ended working group established to monitor and review progress made in the promotion and implementation of the right to development (see p. 753) to consider the question of human rights and the negative impact of unilateral coercive measures. The Commission decided to consider the negative impact of such measures in its work regarding the implementation of the right to development. It asked the High Commissioner to give urgent consideration to its resolution, and the Secretary-General to bring the resolution to the attention of States, to seek their views on the implications and negative effects of those measures and to report in 2004.

Note by Secretariat. The Commission had before it a Secretariat note [E/CN.4/2003/47], which stated that, in accordance with a 2002 Commission resolution [YUN 2002, p. 730], the Secretary-General had brought the resolution to the attention of all Member States. As at 10 December 2002, no information had been received from States regarding the implications and negative effects of unilateral coercive measures.

Report of Secretary-General. Pursuant to General Assembly resolution 57/222 [YUN 2002, p. 730], the Secretary-General, in an August report [A/58/279], stated that, as at 13 August, no information had been received from Member States regarding the effects of unilateral coercive measures.

On 22 December, the Assembly took note of the Secretary-General's report (**decision 58/538**).

GENERAL ASSEMBLY ACTION

On 22 December [meeting 77], the General Assembly, on the recommendation of the Third Committee [A/58/508/Add.2], adopted **resolution 58/171** by recorded vote (125-53) [agenda item 117 (b)].

Human rights and unilateral coercive measures

The General Assembly,

Recalling all its previous resolutions, the most recent of which was resolution 57/222 of 18 December 2002, and Commission on Human Rights resolution 2003/17 of 22 April 2003,

Reaffirming the pertinent principles and provisions contained in the Charter of Economic Rights and Duties of States proclaimed by the General Assembly in its resolution 3281(XXIX) of 12 December 1974, in particular article 32 thereof, in which it declared that no State may use or encourage the use of economic, political or any other type of measures to coerce another State in order to obtain from it the subordination of the exercise of its sovereign rights,

Taking note of the report of the Secretary-General, submitted pursuant to Commission on Human Rights resolution 1999/21 of 23 April 1999, and the reports of the Secretary-General on the implementation of resolutions 52/120 of 12 December 1997 and 55/110 of 4 December 2000,

Recognizing the universal, indivisible, interdependent and interrelated character of all human rights, and, in this regard, reaffirming the right to development as an integral part of all human rights,

Recalling that the World Conference on Human Rights, held at Vienna from 14 to 25 June 1993, called upon States to refrain from any unilateral coercive measure not in accordance with international law and the Charter of the United Nations that creates obstacles to trade relations among States and impedes the full realization of all human rights,

Bearing in mind all the references to this question in the Copenhagen Declaration on Social Development, adopted by the World Summit for Social Development on 12 March 1995, the Beijing Declaration and Platform for Action, adopted by the Fourth World Conference on Women on 15 September 1995, the Istanbul Declaration on Human Settlements and the Habitat Agenda, adopted by the second United Nations Conference on Human Settlements (Habitat II) on 14 June 1996, and their five-year reviews,

Expressing its concern about the negative impact of unilateral coercive measures on international relations, trade, investment and cooperation,

Expressing its grave concern that, in some countries, the situation of children is adversely affected by unilateral coercive measures not in accordance with international law and the Charter that create obstacles to trade relations among States, impede the full realization of social and economic development and hinder the well-being of the population in the affected countries, with particular consequences for women and children, including adolescents,

Deeply concerned that, despite the recommendations adopted on this question by the General Assembly and recent major United Nations conferences, and contrary to general international law and the Charter, unilateral coercive measures continue to be promulgated and implemented with all their negative implications for the social-humanitarian activities and economic and social development of developing countries, including their extraterritorial effects, thereby creating additional obstacles to the full enjoyment of all human rights by peoples and individuals under the jurisdiction of other States,

Bearing in mind all the extraterritorial effects of any unilateral legislative, administrative and economic measures, policies and practices of a coercive nature against the development process and the enhancement of human rights in developing countries, which create obstacles to the full realization of all human rights,

Noting the continuing efforts of the open-ended Working Group on the Right to Development of the Commission on Human Rights, and reaffirming in particular its criteria, according to which unilateral coercive measures are one of the obstacles to the implementation of the Declaration on the Right to Development,

1. *Urges* all States to refrain from adopting or implementing any unilateral measures not in accordance with international law and the Charter of the United Nations, in particular those of a coercive nature with all their extraterritorial effects, which create obstacles to trade relations among States, thus impeding the full realization of the rights set forth in the Universal Declaration of Human Rights and other international human rights instruments, in particular the right of individuals and peoples to development;

2. *Also urges* all States to take steps to avoid and to refrain from adopting any unilateral measures not in accordance with international law and the Charter that impede the full achievement of economic and social development by the population of the affected countries, in particular children and women, that hinder their well-being and that create obstacles to the full enjoyment of their human rights, including the right of everyone to a standard of living adequate for their health and well-being and their right to food, medical care and the necessary social services, as well as to ensure that food and medicine are not used as tools for political pressure;

3. *Invites* all States to consider adopting administrative or legislative measures, as appropriate, to counteract the extraterritorial applications or effects of unilateral coercive measures;

4. *Rejects* unilateral coercive measures with all their extraterritorial effects as tools for political or economic pressure against any country, in particular against developing countries, because of their negative effects on the realization of all the human rights of vast sectors of their populations, in particular children, women and the elderly;

5. *Calls upon* Member States that have initiated such measures to commit themselves to their obligations and responsibilities arising from the international human rights instruments to which they are party by revoking such measures at the earliest time possible;

6. *Reaffirms*, in this context, the right of all peoples to self-determination, by virtue of which they freely determine their political status and freely pursue their economic, social and cultural development;

7. *Urges* the Commission on Human Rights to take fully into account the negative impact of unilateral coercive measures, including the enactment of national laws and their extraterritorial application, in its task concerning the implementation of the right to development;

8. *Requests* the United Nations High Commissioner for Human Rights, in discharging his functions relating to the promotion, realization and protection of the right to development and bearing in mind the continuing impact of unilateral coercive measures on the population of developing countries, to give priority to the present resolution in his annual report to the General Assembly;

9. *Requests* the Secretary-General to bring the present resolution to the attention of all Member States, to continue to collect their views and information on the implications and negative effects of unilateral coercive measures on their populations and to submit an analytical report thereon to the General Assembly at its fifty-ninth session, highlighting the practical and preventive measures in this respect;

10. *Decides* to examine this question on a priority basis at its fifty-ninth session under the sub-item entitled "Human rights questions, including alternative approaches for improving the effective enjoyment of human rights and fundamental freedoms".

RECORDED VOTE ON RESOLUTION 58/171:

In favour: Algeria, Angola, Antigua and Barbuda, Argentina, Armenia, Azerbaijan, Bahamas, Bahrain, Bangladesh, Barbados, Belarus, Belize, Benin, Bhutan, Bolivia, Botswana, Brazil, Brunei Darussalam, Burkina Faso, Burundi, Cambodia, Cameroon, Cape Verde, Central African Republic, Chile, China, Colombia, Comoros, Congo, Costa Rica, Côte d'Ivoire, Cuba, Democratic People's Republic of Korea, Democratic Republic of the Congo, Djibouti, Dominica, Dominican Republic, Ecuador, Egypt, El Salvador, Eritrea, Ethiopia, Fiji, Gabon, Gambia, Ghana, Grenada, Guatemala, Guinea, Guinea-Bissau, Guyana, Haiti, Honduras, India, Indonesia, Iran, Jamaica, Jordan, Kazakhstan, Kenya, Kuwait, Kyrgyzstan, Lao People's Democratic Republic, Lebanon, Lesotho, Libyan Arab Jamahiriya, Madagascar, Malawi, Malaysia, Mali, Mauritania, Mauritius, Mexico, Mongolia, Morocco, Mozambique, Myanmar, Namibia, Nauru, Nepal, Nicaragua, Niger, Nigeria, Oman, Pakistan, Panama, Papua New Guinea, Paraguay, Peru, Philippines, Qatar, Russian Federation, Rwanda, Saint Lucia, Saint Vincent and the Grenadines, Samoa, Saudi Arabia, Senegal, Sierra Leone, Singapore, Somalia, South Africa, Sri Lanka, Sudan, Suriname, Syrian Arab Republic, Tajikistan, Thailand, Timor-Leste, Togo, Tonga, Trinidad and Tobago, Tunisia, Turkmenistan, Tuvalu, Uganda, United Arab Emirates, United Republic of Tanzania, Uruguay, Uzbekistan, Venezuela, Viet Nam, Yemen, Zambia, Zimbabwe.

Against: Albania, Andorra, Australia, Austria, Belgium, Bosnia and Herzegovina, Bulgaria, Canada, Croatia, Cyprus, Czech Republic, Denmark, Estonia, Finland, France, Georgia, Germany, Greece, Hungary, Iceland, Ireland, Israel, Italy, Japan, Latvia, Liechtenstein, Lithuania, Luxembourg, Malta, Marshall Islands, Micronesia, Monaco, Netherlands, New Zealand, Norway, Palau, Poland, Portugal, Republic of Korea, Republic of

Moldova, Romania, San Marino, Serbia and Montenegro, Slovakia, Slovenia, Spain, Sweden, Switzerland, The former Yugoslav Republic of Macedonia, Turkey, Ukraine, United Kingdom, United States.

Corruption

Working paper. In response to a 2002 Subcommission request [YUN 2002, p. 732], Christy Mbonu (Nigeria) submitted a May working paper on the impact of corruption on the realization and enjoyment of all human rights [E/CN.4/Sub.2/2003/18]. Economically, corruption led to inefficient resource allocation, increased investment costs and lowered investors' confidence, promoted inequalities and inefficiency in the private sector and compromised the quality of related services. The report described the various forms and causes of corruption, and its impact on individuals and institutions. It summarized national, regional and international initiatives against the phenomenon, and observed that, despite past remedies, the problem was worsening and should be accorded priority. Recommendations included undertaking a study to help promote transparency, accountability and good governance in Member States.

Subcommission action. On 13 August [res. 2003/2], the Subcommission decided to appoint Ms. Mbonu as Special Rapporteur with the task of preparing a comprehensive study on corruption and its impact on the full enjoyment of human rights, particularly economic, social and cultural rights, and asked her to submit a preliminary report in 2004, a progress report in 2005 and a final report in 2006. The Secretary-General was asked to assist her.

Also on 13 August [res. 2003/20], the Subcommission recommended that the proposed international convention against corruption (see p. 1126) should provide for strong measures to criminalize corrupt practices and prevent the transfer of illicit funds, and for the seizure, confiscation and repatriation of such funds to countries of origin.

Extreme poverty

Reports of independent expert. In accordance with a 2002 Commission request [YUN 2002, p. 732], the independent expert on the question of human rights and extreme poverty, Anne-Marie Lizin (Belgium), submitted a January report [E/CN.4/2003/52] indicating the various themes she intended to explore in a report to be submitted in 2004. She continued to analyse good practices by States, NGOs and local authorities in taking account of the needs of the poorest, examined the link between extreme poverty, migration and trafficking in human beings, and reviewed and reaffirmed the validity of key recommendations contained in her previous report [YUN 2002, p. 732]. She summarized her ongoing dialogue with international financial institutions. Evidence of action to reduce poverty remained mixed, despite some positive developments, such as States' increasing willingness to tackle the issue, successes in countries like China and the multiplication of poverty-reduction programmes presented to donors. However, the situation was deteriorating in Argentina, Mongolia, the Republic of Moldova, Southern Africa and in various other countries where the State fabric continued to unravel. The expert recommended poverty reduction measures relating specifically to the nature of the State and its capacity to protect and establish respect for the rights of its citizens. The expert hoped that States would respond to a related questionnaire she intended to send to them, which was annexed to the report.

The expert visited Yemen (2-5 October) [E/CN.4/2004/43/Add.1], where impoverishment had worsened as a result of conflicts in the region and some 42 per cent of the people lived below the poverty line. Since the events of 11 September 2001 [YUN 2001, p. 60], port activity had slumped, the oil sector had difficulties, unemployment had risen and revenue from tourism had declined. The expert recommended that the Government pursue its efforts to promote recognition of women's rights; re-establish an independent national human rights institution; assign priority to combating illiteracy among women and to reducing the birth rate; ratify relevant international instruments; continue to strengthen the role of local authorities in dealing with the problem; and further develop the civil registration programme in the Ministry of the Interior. She recommended a series of actions for UN agencies in the field and other lenders, and called on the Secretary-General to ensure that Yemen's efforts were made known to UN institutions. International NGOs should continue to support Yemeni voluntary organizations, particularly those dealing with persons with disabilities and women's rights.

In the Sudan (18-23 November), the expert observed how the Government took advantage of the peace process, initiated to resolve many years of civil war (see p. 256), to begin preparing an interim poverty reduction strategy, geared to cut military spending in order to increase the welfare budget. She said a lack of statistics made the task difficult and that decentralized budgets of the federated States did not permit real spending on education or health to be measured. The expert studied the system for collecting and distributing *zakat*—a donation proportionate to one's wealth, collected and distributed to the poor as money or food under Muslim culture—and made suggestions that would enable the Sudan to draw up a proper map of the poorest segment of its population benefiting from the donation, in line with the poverty reduction strategy being prepared. The expert recommended a series of actions by the Sudanese authorities to further strengthen the status of women and to expand the role of the savings and social development banks in the area of microcredit.

The expert visited Washington, D.C. (30 November–5 December), where, with IMF officials, she highlighted factors that complemented the monetary and trade policies of interest to the Fund, such as social safety nets, improved performance by relevant institutions, including the judiciary, and incentives to prevent corruption. Following parallel talks with the World Bank, the expert described the differences between the Bank and IMF. She recommended enhancing the Bank's human rights unit and advocated the integration of human rights into the poverty and social impact analyses and assessments carried out by international financial institutions; closer relations between officials of international financial institutions and of UN human rights bodies; and the implementation of a new generation of more comprehensive and participatory poverty reduction strategies.

Commission action. On 22 April [res. 2003/24], the Commission urged States, intergovernmental organizations and NGOs to continue to take into account, in activities carried out under the United Nations Decade for the Eradication of Poverty (1997-2006), proclaimed by the General Assembly in resolution 50/107 [YUN 1995, p. 844] (see p. 848), the links between human rights and extreme poverty, and efforts to empower people living in poverty to participate in decision-making processes regarding policies affecting them. The United Nations was called on to strengthen poverty eradication as a priority throughout the system. The ad hoc working group, appointed by the Subcommission in 2001 [YUN 2001, p. 668] to prepare a study to contribute to the drafting of an international declaration on extreme poverty and human rights (see below), was encouraged to adopt an approach based on the universality, indivisibility, interdependence and interrelation of all human rights.

Report of High Commissioner. In June [E/2003/73], the High Commissioner stated that OHCHR had developed draft guidelines on a human rights approach to poverty reduction strategies, to guide development practitioners on how to integrate human rights into national poverty reduction strategies and illustrate how attention to human rights could reinforce each of the Millennium Development Goals [YUN 2000, p. 51]. The draft guidelines, which included a set of operational guidelines for a number of specific human rights, would be piloted through substantive consultations and field testing during 2003-2004.

International declaration

Working paper. In response to a 2002 Subcommission request [YUN 2002, p. 733], Mr. Bengoa, coordinator of the ad hoc working group appointed to work towards a draft international declaration on extreme poverty and human rights, submitted, in June, a preliminary working paper [E/CN.4/Sub.2/2003/17] on the need to develop guiding principles on the implementation of existing human rights norms and standards in the context of the fight against extreme poverty. He proposed broad consultations on the basis of a conceptual framework and collaboration with actors involved in poverty reduction; a review of the ad hoc group's work programme; and the submission of an interim joint working paper to the Subcommission in 2004 on the need to develop guiding principles.

Subcommission action. On 13 August [res. 2003/13], the Subcommission approved the underlying principles of the conceptual framework set out in the working paper (see above). It requested Iulia-Antoanelle Motoc (Romania), Emmanuel Decaux (France), Yozo Yokota (Japan), El-Hadji Guissé (Senegal) and Mr. Bengoa to prepare, without financial implications, a joint working paper on the need to develop guiding principles on the implementation of existing human rights norms and standards in the context of the fight against extreme poverty, and to submit a progress report in 2004 and a final report in 2005. They were also asked to work towards a specific instrument that did not overlap with existing treaties, to consider specifically situations of poverty in various parts of the world, as well as the policies of the World Bank, WTO, IMF and other international bodies for fighting poverty, to adopt an approach towards extreme poverty that strengthened bonds of solidarity and social inclusion mechanisms, and to present conclusions and recommendations on the draft declaration on extreme poverty and human rights. The Secretariat was asked to assist in the study, while Governments, regional specialized bodies in Asia, Africa, Europe and Latin America and international agencies were asked to provide information for the study.

Right to food

Reports of Special Rapporteur. Pursuant to a 2002 Commission request [YUN 2002, p. 735], the Special Rapporteur on the right to food, Jean Ziegler (Switzerland), in a January report [E/CN.4/2003/54], focused on two new initiatives to protect the right at the international level. The first, a development arising from the World Food Summit + 5 [YUN 2002, p. 1225], was the establishment by Governments of voluntary guidelines on the right, under the auspices of FAO, which strengthened hope in the fight against hunger. The second was the adoption of a new general comment No. 15 on the right to water by the Committee on Economic, Social and Cultural Rights [YUN 2002, p. 628], which greatly improved the legal framework for protecting the right. The Special Rapporteur discussed concrete examples of the relationship between the rights to water and to food in Bangladesh, Brazil and the Niger, and presented appeals he had made regarding allegations in three countries to which he had received no reply. At the World Food Summit + 5, it became clear that little action had been taken to meet the goal of halving the number of hunger victims by 2015, set at the 1996 World Food Summit [YUN 1996, p. 1129]. The Special Rapporteur recommended the development of voluntary guidelines on the right to food, based on the legal interpretation of the right contained in general comment No. 12 of the Committee on Economic, Social and Cultural Rights [YUN 1999, p. 575]; the wide dissemination of general comment No. 15 on the right to water; and government action to meet the 1996 commitment to halve the number of hunger victims by 2015, to enshrine the right to food in a national law, to develop a national strategy to realize the right and to combat hunger and malnutrition in their territory.

The Special Rapporteur visited the Occupied Palestinian Territories (3-12 July) [E/CN.4/2004/10/Add.2] to gain a greater understanding of the emerging food crisis there. He travelled to the West Bank and Gaza Strip, home to some 3.5 million Palestinians, where he reported that the area was on the verge of a humanitarian catastrophe owing to harsh military measures by Israeli forces since the outbreak of the second intifada in September 2000 [YUN 2000, p. 416]. Malnutrition levels among Palestinians had increased rapidly and affected over 22 per cent of children under five, of whom an estimated 16 per cent suffered acute anaemia, with potential permanent effects on their physical and mental development. Food consumption had fallen by 25-30 per cent per capita, owing largely to job losses and curfews, and the situation was exacerbated by an economic crisis. The Special Rapporteur recommended that the Israeli Government respect its de jure obligations under international human rights and humanitarian law and end restrictions on humanitarian access and the regime of closures and curfews, ease measures that restricted the people's access to food and prevented the destruction of their land and other resources, monitor violations of the right to food and implement his current recommendations, and, among other measures, end the occupation, since most of the violations of the right stemmed from it.

Commission action. By a recorded vote of 51 to 1, with 1 abstention, on 22 April [res. 2003/25], the Commission decided to extend the Special Rapporteur's mandate for a further three years, encouraged him to continue mainstreaming a gender perspective in his work and asked him to report to the General Assembly in 2003 and to the Commission in 2004. The High Commissioner was asked to assist him, while Governments, UN agencies, funds and programmes, treaty bodies and NGOS were invited to cooperate with him by submitting suggestions on ways to realize the right to food.

ECONOMIC AND SOCIAL COUNCIL ACTION

On 23 July, the Economic and Social Council, on the recommendation of the Commission on Human Rights [E/2003/23], adopted **decision 2003/244** by recorded vote (52-1-1) [agenda item 14 (g)].

The right to food

At its 46th plenary meeting, on 23 July 2003, the Economic and Social Council took note of Commission on Human Rights resolution 2003/25 of 22 April 2003, and endorsed the Commission's decision to extend the mandate of the Special Rapporteur on the right to food for a further three years and to request the Special Rapporteur to submit a report to the General Assembly at its fifty-eighth session and to the Commission at its sixtieth session on the implementation of resolution 2003/25.

RECORDED VOTE ON DECISION 2003/244:

In favour: Andorra, Argentina, Azerbaijan, Benin, Bhutan, Brazil, Burundi, Chile, China, Congo, Cuba, Ecuador, Egypt, El Salvador, Ethiopia, Finland, France, Georgia, Germany, Ghana, Greece, Guatemala, Hungary, India, Iran, Ireland, Italy, Jamaica, Japan, Kenya, Libyan Arab Jamahiriya, Malaysia, Mozambique, Nepal, Netherlands, Nicaragua, Nigeria, Pakistan, Peru, Portugal, Qatar, Republic of Korea, Romania, Russian Federation, Saudi Arabia, Senegal, South Africa, Sweden, Uganda, Ukraine, United Kingdom, Zimbabwe.
Against: United States.
Abstaining: Australia.

Subcommission action. On 13 August [res. 2003/9], the Subcommission recommended convening in early 2004 the fourth expert consultation on the right to food, proposed by the Commission [YUN 2001, p. 669], drawing on the findings of the earlier consultations held in 1997 and 1998 [YUN 1998, p. 693], and in 2001 [YUN 2001, p. 669], and on the lessons learned from national seminars on the subject. It appealed to the High Commissioner to continue to seek funds to facilitate the fourth consultation, and to donor countries to express their interest in funding it.

Further report of Special Rapporteur. Pursuant to General Assembly resolution 57/226 [YUN 2002, p. 736], the Secretary-General, in August [A/58/330], transmitted a report of the Special Rapporteur, which discussed two new thematic issues—gender and TNC activities—as they related to the right to food. Gender discrimination persisted in a variety of forms that had a profound impact on women's right to food, as did the activities of TNCs. He recommended that Governments address discrimination against women, particularly where it contributed to the malnutrition of women and girls; improve the enforcement of existing legislation to protect women; and regulate TNCs and their activities in the food system and implement the human rights norms relating to their responsibilities. He advocated judicial and administrative remedies for violations of the right.

Communications. On 18 September [E/CN.4/2004/G/9], Israel claimed that an unedited copy of the Special Rapporteur's report on his visit (see p. 766) had been made available to a journalist before it was given to the Israeli authorities. It requested that steps be taken to ensure that such disregard for procedure did not recur.

On 23 October [E/CN.4/2004/G/13], the Permanent Observer of Palestine, referring to Israel's communication (see above), questioned how Israel could evaluate the Special Rapporteur's work as Israel had never cooperated with or respected the United Nations.

GENERAL ASSEMBLY ACTION

On 22 December [meeting 77], the General Assembly, on the recommendation of the Third Committee [A/58/508/Add.2], adopted **resolution 58/186** by recorded vote (176-1-2) [agenda item 117 (b)].

The right to food

The General Assembly,

Recalling its resolution 57/226 of 18 December 2002, as well as all Commission on Human Rights resolutions in this regard, in particular resolution 2003/25 of 22 April 2003,

Recalling also the Universal Declaration of Human Rights, which provides that everyone has the right to a standard of living adequate for her or his health and well-being, including food,

Recalling further the provisions of the International Covenant on Economic, Social and Cultural Rights, in which the fundamental right of every person to be free from hunger is recognized,

Recalling the Universal Declaration on the Eradication of Hunger and Malnutrition, as well as the United Nations Millennium Declaration,

Bearing in mind the Rome Declaration on World Food Security and the World Food Summit Plan of Action,

Bearing in mind also the Declaration of the World Food Summit: five years later, adopted in Rome on 13 June 2002,

Reaffirming that all human rights are universal, indivisible, interdependent and interrelated,

Recognizing that the problems of hunger and food insecurity have global dimensions and that they are likely to persist and even to increase dramatically in some regions unless urgent, determined and concerted action is taken, given the anticipated increase in the world's population and the stress on natural resources,

Reaffirming that a peaceful, stable and enabling political, social and economic environment, at both the national and the international levels, is the essential foundation that will enable States to give adequate priority to food security and poverty eradication,

Reiterating, as in the Rome Declaration and the Declaration of the World Food Summit: five years later, that food should not be used as an instrument of political or economic pressure, and reaffirming in this regard the importance of international cooperation and solidarity, as well as the necessity of refraining from unilateral measures that are not in accordance with international law and the Charter of the United Nations and that endanger food security,

Convinced that each State must adopt a strategy consistent with its resources and capacities to achieve its individual goals in implementing the recommendations contained in the Rome Declaration and the World Food Summit Plan of Action and, at the same time, cooperate regionally and internationally in order to organize collective solutions to global issues of food security in a world of increasingly interlinked institutions, societies and economies where coordinated efforts and shared responsibilities are essential,

Stressing the importance of reversing the continuing decline of official development assistance devoted to agriculture, both in real terms and as a share of total official development assistance,

1. *Reaffirms* that hunger constitutes an outrage and a violation of human dignity and therefore requires the adoption of urgent measures at the national, regional and international levels for its elimination;

2. *Also reaffirms* the right of everyone to have access to safe and nutritious food, consistent with the right to adequate food and the fundamental right of everyone to be free from hunger, so as to be able to fully develop and maintain their physical and mental capacities;

3. *Considers it intolerable* that there are around 840 million undernourished people in the world, that every seven seconds a child under the age of 10 dies, directly or indirectly, of hunger somewhere in the world and that more than 2 billion people worldwide suffer from "hidden hunger" or micronutrient malnutrition;

4. *Expresses its concern* that women are disproportionately affected by hunger, food insecurity and poverty, in part as a result of gender inequality, that in many countries, girls are twice as likely as boys to die from malnutrition and preventable childhood dis-

eases, and that it is estimated that almost twice as many women suffer from malnutrition as men;

5. *Encourages* all States to take steps with a view to achieving progressively the full realization of the right to food, including steps to promote the conditions for everyone to be free from hunger and, as soon as possible, to enjoy fully the right to food, and to create and adopt national plans to combat hunger;

6. *Also encourages* all States to take action to address discrimination against women, particularly where it contributes to the malnutrition of women and girls, including measures to ensure the realization of the right to food, and ensuring that women have equal access to resources, including income, land and water, to enable them to feed themselves;

7. *Stresses* the need to make efforts to mobilize and optimize the allocation and utilization of technical and financial resources from all sources, including external debt relief for developing countries, and to reinforce national actions to implement sustainable food security policies;

8. *Invites once again* all international financial and developmental institutions, as well as the relevant United Nations agencies and funds, to give priority to and provide the necessary funding to realize the aim of halving by 2015 the proportion of people who suffer from hunger, as well as the right to food as set out in the Rome Declaration on World Food Security and the United Nations Millennium Declaration;

9. *Urges* States to give adequate priority in their development strategies and expenditures to the realization of the right to food;

10. *Takes note with appreciation* of the interim report of the Special Rapporteur of the Commission on Human Rights on the right to food, and commends the Special Rapporteur for his valuable work in the promotion of the right to food;

11. *Supports* the realization of the mandate of the Special Rapporteur as extended by the Commission on Human Rights in its resolution 2003/25;

12. *Expresses its appreciation* to the Special Rapporteur for his effective contribution to the medium-term review of the implementation of the Rome Declaration on World Food Security and the World Food Summit Plan of Action through the submission to the United Nations High Commissioner for Human Rights of his recommendations on all aspects of the right to food, and his participation in and contribution to the proceedings of that event;

13. *Encourages* the Special Rapporteur to mainstream a gender perspective in the activities relating to his mandate;

14. *Requests* the Secretary-General and the High Commissioner to provide all the necessary human and financial resources for the effective fulfilment of the mandate of the Special Rapporteur;

15. *Welcomes* the work already done by the Committee on Economic, Social and Cultural Rights in promoting the right to adequate food, in particular its general comment No. 12 (1999) on the right to adequate food (article 11 of the International Covenant on Economic, Social and Cultural Rights), in which the Committee affirmed, inter alia, that the right to adequate food is indivisibly linked to the inherent dignity of the human person and is indispensable for the fulfilment of other human rights enshrined in the International Bill of Human Rights, and is also inseparable from social justice, requiring the adoption of appropriate economic, environmental and social policies, at both the national and the international levels, oriented to the eradication of poverty and the fulfilment of all human rights for all;

16. *Also welcomes* the work of the Intergovernmental Working Group mandated by the Council of the Food and Agriculture Organization of the United Nations to elaborate, in a period of two years, a set of voluntary guidelines to support the efforts of Member States to achieve the progressive realization of the right to adequate food in the context of national food security;

17. *Further welcomes* the continued cooperation of the High Commissioner, the Committee on Economic, Social and Cultural Rights and the Special Rapporteur, and encourages them to continue their cooperation in this regard;

18. *Requests* the Special Rapporteur to submit a comprehensive report to the Commission on Human Rights at its sixtieth session and an interim report to the General Assembly at its fifty-ninth session on the implementation of the present resolution;

19. *Invites* Governments, relevant United Nations agencies, funds and programmes, treaty bodies and non-governmental organizations to cooperate fully with the Special Rapporteur in the fulfilment of his mandate, inter alia, through the submission of comments and suggestions on ways and means of realizing the right to food;

20. *Decides* to continue the consideration of this matter at its fifty-ninth session under the item entitled "Human rights questions".

RECORDED VOTE ON RESOLUTION 58/186:

In favour: Afghanistan, Albania, Algeria, Andorra, Angola, Antigua and Barbuda, Argentina, Armenia, Australia, Austria, Azerbaijan, Bahamas, Bahrain, Bangladesh, Barbados, Belarus, Belgium, Belize, Benin, Bhutan, Bolivia, Bosnia and Herzegovina, Botswana, Brazil, Brunei Darussalam, Bulgaria, Burkina Faso, Burundi, Cambodia, Cameroon, Canada, Cape Verde, Central African Republic, Chile, China, Colombia, Comoros, Congo, Costa Rica, Côte d'Ivoire, Croatia, Cuba, Cyprus, Czech Republic, Democratic People's Republic of Korea, Democratic Republic of the Congo, Denmark, Djibouti, Dominica, Dominican Republic, Ecuador, Egypt, El Salvador, Eritrea, Estonia, Ethiopia, Fiji, Finland, France, Gabon, Gambia, Georgia, Germany, Ghana, Greece, Grenada, Guatemala, Guinea, Guinea-Bissau, Guyana, Haiti, Honduras, Hungary, Iceland, India, Indonesia, Iran, Ireland, Italy, Jamaica, Japan, Jordan, Kazakhstan, Kenya, Kuwait, Kyrgyzstan, Lao People's Democratic Republic, Latvia, Lebanon, Lesotho, Libyan Arab Jamahiriya, Liechtenstein, Lithuania, Luxembourg, Madagascar, Malawi, Malaysia, Maldives, Mali, Malta, Mauritania, Mauritius, Mexico, Monaco, Mongolia, Morocco, Mozambique, Myanmar, Namibia, Nauru, Nepal, Netherlands, New Zealand, Nicaragua, Niger, Nigeria, Norway, Oman, Pakistan, Panama, Papua New Guinea, Paraguay, Peru, Philippines, Poland, Portugal, Qatar, Republic of Korea, Republic of Moldova, Romania, Russian Federation, Rwanda, Saint Lucia, Saint Vincent and the Grenadines, Samoa, San Marino, Saudi Arabia, Senegal, Serbia and Montenegro, Seychelles, Sierra Leone, Singapore, Slovakia, Slovenia, Solomon Islands, Somalia, South Africa, Spain, Sri Lanka, Sudan, Suriname, Sweden, Switzerland, Syrian Arab Republic, Tajikistan, Thailand, The former Yugoslav Republic of Macedonia, Timor-Leste, Togo, Tonga, Trinidad and Tobago, Tunisia, Turkey, Turkmenistan, Uganda, Ukraine, United Arab Emirates, United Kingdom, United Republic of Tanzania, Uruguay, Uzbekistan, Venezuela, Viet Nam, Yemen, Zambia, Zimbabwe.

Against: United States.

Abstaining: Israel, Marshall Islands.

Right to adequate housing

Reports of Special Rapporteur. The Special Rapporteur on the right to adequate housing,

Miloon Kothari (India), in a March report [E/CN.4/2003/5], highlighted emerging issues relating to water and sanitation as essential elements for the realization of the right, the need for further research on innovative local responses to globalization in urban and rural development, the development of rights-based indicators and assessment tools for monitoring the Millennium Development Goals and other relevant outcomes of major UN conferences and summits, and the rights of persons with disabilities. The Special Rapporteur recommended a series of actions to the Commission, including that it request him to seek, receive and respond to information on all aspects of the realization of the right, focus on issues relating to water, sanitation and disability, and report to the General Assembly and relevant mechanisms of the Economic and Social Council, and ask OHCHR to organize, in collaboration with relevant treaty bodies, an expert group meeting to further develop policy guidelines for preventing discrimination and segregation in housing and civic services, and to develop, jointly with the United Nations Programme on Human Settlements (UN-Habitat) and civil society, criteria for and a database on good practices regarding housing rights. He further recommended that the Commission address additional measures to UN-Habitat, States, UN agencies, intergovernmental organizations and the Commission on Sustainable Development (see p. 842).

The Special Rapporteur visited Peru (3-15 March) [E/CN.4/2004/48/Add.1] to examine the status of the realization of the right to adequate housing and other related rights, with particular attention to gender equality and non-discrimination, and to identify practical solutions and best practices. Impediments to securing the right were the lack of title, security of tenure and of civic services, particularly water and sanitation; houses built in areas vulnerable to floods, earthquakes and landslides; land collapse from mining activities; eviction; the pollution of natural resources; and the impact of privatization and globalization on the housing and living conditions of the poor. Challenges in the country's housing sector needed to be tackled from a human rights perspective and should address issues relating to housing, water, sanitation, electricity and protection from eviction, according priority to women and vulnerable groups. A series of further measures outlined policy recommendations for the Government and other concerned parties.

Key issues in Afghanistan (31 August-13 September) [E/CN.4/2004/48/Add.2] related to land occupation, the destruction of houses and land, sanitation facilities, water resources and livelihood, inadequate housing for many of the over 2 million returning refugees repatriated from neighbouring countries and for a large number of internally displaced persons, forced evictions without compensation or alternative arrangements, and land speculation that made housing and land inaccessible to many people. The Special Rapporteur recommended measures to be taken by the Transitional Government and other stakeholders to establish a workable framework to address the issue, based on a combined humanitarian, human rights and sustainable development approach.

Commission action. On 22 April [res. 2003/27], the Commission decided to renew the Special Rapporteur's mandate for a three-year period and requested him to report in 2004. The High Commissioner was asked to support cooperation between the Special Rapporteur and other Commission mechanisms and relevant UN bodies. The Secretary-General was asked to assist him. The Commission requested OHCHR and UN-Habitat to strengthen their cooperation, to continue developing the joint United Nations Housing Rights Programme and to explore further possibilities to support the Special Rapporteur.

On 23 July (**decision 2003/245**), the Economic and Social Council endorsed the Commission's decision to renew the Special Rapporteur's mandate and its request to him to report.

Subcommission action. On 13 August [res. 2003/17], the Subcommission asked the High Commissioner to accord attention to the practice of forced eviction and urged the Commission to invite States to consider the comprehensive human rights guidelines on development-based displacement, as contained in the report of the 1997 expert seminar on the practice of forced evictions [YUN 1997, p. 676], with a view to approving the guidelines in 2005.

Communication. On 14 March [E/CN.4/2003/G/52], Mexico transmitted its comments on the report of the Special Rapporteur on his 2002 visit to the country [YUN 2002, p. 739].

Women's right to property and adequate housing

Report of Special Rapporteur. In response to a 2002 Commission request [YUN 2002, p. 739], the Special Rapporteur on the right to adequate housing (see above) submitted a March study [E/CN.4/2003/55] on women's equal ownership of, access to and control over land and equal rights to own property and to adequate housing, which analysed national and international legal provisions for the rights and highlighted existing gaps. It concluded that a considerable difference existed between the recognition of women's right to housing in international and national laws and the reality of large-scale denial in the implementation or non-implementation of those laws. The Special Rapporteur requested more detailed responses to a questionnaire he had circulated to States, as well as information on good practices to enable him to make a more comprehensive analysis and to identify practical solutions. He asked the Commission to recommend that OHCHR and UN-Habitat hold additional regional consultations, request UN agencies to intensify their work in the area, ask OHCHR, in collaboration with the United Nations Development Fund for Women and UN-Habitat, to organize an expert seminar, and expand the study's mandate to include women's rights to land, property and inheritance.

Commission action. On 22 April [res. 2003/22], the Commission encouraged Governments to increase access to land and housing for women living in poverty. OHCHR, the Office of the United Nations High Commissioner for Refugees and other relevant international organizations were asked to address discrimination against women with respect to land, property and adequate housing. The Secretary-General was invited to encourage UN entities to take further initiatives that promoted women's equal ownership of, access to and control over land and their equal rights to own property and to adequate housing, and to allocate further resources to study the impact of complex emergency situations. The Special Rapporteur was asked to submit a study in 2005, and States were invited to respond to the questionnaire he had prepared.

Right to education

Reports of Special Rapporteur. The Special Rapporteur on the right to education, Katarina Tomasevski (Croatia), in a January report [E/CN.4/2003/9], summarized trends in the realization of education as a civil, cultural, economic political and social right, and addressed the importance of strengthening related human rights safeguards. She proposed action to clarify and simplify the legal framework of the right to education, highlight key principles and core standards, and identify the most important quantitative and qualitative data concerning the right as a civil, cultural, economic, political and social right. Additional areas covered related to commitments to free primary education, integrating human rights in global funding strategies, rights-based law reform, the rights of the child, delineating public and private law, the potential and limitations of quantitative data, benchmarks for the quality of education, a multifaceted right to education, eliminating obstacles to teaching and promoting rights-based learning. She recommended an assessment of the conformity of World Bank policy and practice in education lending with the international human rights obligations of borrowers.

In China (10-19 September) [E/CN.4/2004/45/Add.1], the Special Rapporteur found that the country's law did not conform to the international legal framework defining the right to education. Provisions of the Convention on the Rights of the Child (see p. 675) regarding parental freedom to choose education for their children were not recognized in domestic law. Also, in China's Constitution and legislation, although the term "the right to education" was used abundantly, education was defined as an individual duty, and, contrary to China's international human rights obligations, religious education remained prohibited. The country's goal of eliminating illiteracy and attaining nine years of compulsory education by the end of its ninth five-year plan (1996-2000) was not accomplished. Obstacles were linked to poor budgetary allocations, poverty and increasing tuition costs, a free market in education and limited access owing to gender, migration and disability. The Special Rapporteur recommended a review of Chinese law using the yardstick of international human rights law; affirmation of China's international obligation to ensure free education; monitoring school attendance; elimination of the practice of permitting schoolchildren to work; increasing the budgetary allocation for education to cover the costs of compulsory schooling; and raising teachers' status, including guarantees of their freedom of association.

In Colombia (1-10 October) [E/CN.4/2004/45/Add.2], the Special Rapporteur learned of a large number of cases of violation of the right to education and of human rights in education. She noted that Colombian law did not recognize adults' right to education, despite the international obligations Colombia had undertaken in that regard, and in most cases there was a lack of available and accessible schooling for children of school age. Other problems were related to a dysfunctional system that permitted both private and public schools, as well as free and fee-paying ones, which created confusion, exorbitant tuition, a history of exclusions based on all the discriminatory criteria currently prohibited, and violence against teachers, which had resulted in many deaths. The Special Rapporteur recommended that the Government commit itself to protecting economic, social and cultural rights, reaffirm its obligation to ensure free education for all children of compulsory school age, take measures against the problems undermining the educational system and ensure the full realization of the right to education. She proposed studies on the impact of an education revolution on the right and on the nature and extent of discrimination in education, and increased budget spending on education.

Commission action. On 22 April [res. 2003/19], the Commission urged States to submit information on best practices to eliminate discrimination in education. The Special Rapporteur was asked to report in 2004 and the Secretary-General was asked to assist her.

Communications. On 18 March [E/CN.4/2003/G/45], Turkey alleged that the Special Rapporteur's January report misrepresented facts regarding efforts to follow up on her 2002 visit to the country [YUN 2002, p. 740]. It claimed that, contrary to what the Special Rapporteur reported, she enjoyed the Government's full cooperation.

On 10 December [E/CN.4/2004/G/16], China, referring to the Special Rapporteur's report on her visit to the country (see p. 770), stated that she had made groundless comments and accusations regarding the Government's efforts to protect human rights and realize the right to education based on information from overseas sources. It requested the Special Rapporteur to revise her report accordingly.

Environmental and scientific concerns

Toxic wastes

Reports of Special Rapporteur. In January [E/CN.4/2003/56], the Special Rapporteur on the adverse effects of the illicit movement and dumping of toxic and dangerous products and wastes on the enjoyment of human rights, Fatma-Zohra Ouhachi-Vesely (Algeria), described her activities and presented replies received from five Governments and a number of intergovernmental organizations and NGOs in response to a communication she had circulated pursuant to a 2002 Commission request [YUN 2002, p. 741]. She also summarized communications concerning six new cases involving 11 countries brought to her attention, and an additional communication updating one case mentioned in her previous reports. Reaffirming the validity of the findings in her previous reports, the Special Rapporteur drew the Commission's attention to the conclusions and recommendations relating to her 2002 visits to Canada and the United States [YUN 2002, p. 741] and underlined a new trend regarding the export of hazardous electronic waste from developed countries to Asian States. According to a variety of sources, those wastes were being processed in operations that were extremely harmful to human health and the environment, with severe implications for human rights. The problem posed by pesticides, particularly persistent organic pollutants, remained very serious and the majority of the incidents reported related to that issue. The Special Rapporteur intended to present in 2004 a report on the last three years of her mandate.

The Special Rapporteur visited the United Kingdom (27 May–6 June) [E/CN.4/2004/46/Add.2] where in England and Wales alone about 5 million tonnes of toxic and dangerous waste were produced yearly, and some 750,000 consignment notes pertaining to 500,000 shipments of those materials were processed annually. Issues of concern were the lack of transparency regarding waste, claims by NGOs regarding limitations and difficulties, particularly with respect to information and the costs of waste management, and the fact that, other than the restrictions arising from the 1998 Convention on the Prior Informed Consent Procedure for Certain Hazardous Chemicals and Pesticides in International Trade (Rotterdam Convention) [YUN 1998, p. 997], there was currently no ban on the export of chemical products that had been restricted or prohibited in the United Kingdom. She recommended that the Government introduce a ban and complement its promotion of voluntary initiatives by implementing legally binding minimum standards for corporate behaviour and transparency, including regarding corporate activities abroad, and advocated strengthening the enforcement of legislation and more dissuasive civil and criminal sanctions against those who broke the law. The Special Rapporteur pointed out that the scope and validity of her findings and conclusions were limited by the fact that many of the country's central regulations or legislation in areas of concern were under review, being drafted or in the process of implementation. Consequently, parts of her observations and recommendations were based on draft or future legislation rather than practice.

Commission action. By a recorded vote of 38 to 13, with 2 abstentions, the Commission, on 22 April [res. 2003/20], requested Governments of developed countries and international financial institutions to provide financial assistance for the implementation of the Programme of Action adopted at the First Continental Conference for Africa on the Environmentally Sound Management of Unwanted Stocks of Hazardous Wastes and Their Prevention [YUN 2001, p. 972]. The Special Rapporteur was asked to study existing problems of and solutions to illicit trafficking, particularly in developing countries, and to report in 2004. The Secretary-General was asked to assist her.

Environmental protection and sustainable development

On 25 April [res. 2003/71], the Commission, welcoming actions taken by States that assisted in promoting environmental protection and sustainable development, asked the High Commissioner and the United Nations Environment Programme to coordinate their efforts in capacity-building activities for the judiciary. The Secretary-General was asked to report in 2004 on the consideration being given by States to the possible relationship between the environment and human rights.

Disappearance of States for environmental reasons

On 14 August [res. 2003/24], the Subcommission, noting environmental changes which reduced significantly the surface area of States, with serious social, economic and cultural consequences, recommended a decision to the Commission on the implications of the phenomenon.

Right to physical and mental health

Report of Special Rapporteur. In accordance with Economic and Social Council decision 2002/259 [YUN 2002, p. 742], the Special Rapporteur on the right to the highest attainable standard of physical and mental health, Paul Hunt (New Zealand), submitted a February preliminary report [E/CN.4/2003/58], in which he proposed to examine poverty reduction strategies, neglected diseases, impact assessments, relevant WTO agreements, mental health and the role of health professionals. He said he attached particular importance to the identification of good practices, some of which he hoped to set out in subsequent reports.

Commission action. By a recorded vote of 39 to 1, with 13 abstentions, the Commission, on 22 April [res. 2003/28], asked the High Commissioner to solicit proposals from Governments, NGOs and UN bodies and specialized agencies, particularly the World Health Organization (WHO), for possible measures and activities to be carried out during the proposed United Nations Year for Violence Prevention (see Economic and Social Council action below), and to submit a compilation thereof in 2004. OHCHR, WHO and other UN bodies and specialized agencies were invited to organize an international expert consultation on violence prevention and human rights, with the aim of developing guidelines on violence, based on human rights instruments. Special rapporteurs were invited to report on the issue of violence prevention and to make recommendations in 2004. The Commission asked the Special Rapporteur to pay particular attention to the linkages between poverty reduction strategies and the right to health, and between the realization of that right and aspects of discrimination and stigma, and to the identification of best practices. He was also asked to pursue his analysis of neglected diseases and the role of health impact assessments, to report annually to the Commission and to submit an interim report to the General Assembly. The High Commissioner was asked to assist him.

ECONOMIC AND SOCIAL COUNCIL ACTION

On 23 July [meeting 45], the Economic and Social Council, on the recommendation of the Commission on Human Rights [E/2003/23], adopted **resolution 2003/45** by recorded vote (33-1-17) [agenda item 14 (g)].

The right of everyone to the enjoyment of the highest attainable standard of physical and mental health

The Economic and Social Council,

Taking note of Commission on Human Rights resolution 2003/28 of 22 April 2003, in which the Commission highlighted the importance of enhancing the international community's response to violence by strengthening prevention efforts at the national level and through international cooperation,

1. *Recommends* that the General Assembly declare 2007 the United Nations Year for Violence Prevention;
2. *Requests* the Commission on Human Rights to submit to the Council a draft programme of action for the Year.

RECORDED VOTE ON RESOLUTION 2003/45:

In favour: Argentina, Benin, Bhutan, Brazil, Burundi, Chile, China, Congo, Cuba, Ecuador, Egypt, Ethiopia, Ghana, Guatemala, Iran, Jamaica, Japan, Kenya, Libyan Arab Jamahiriya, Malaysia, Mozambique, Nepal, Nicaragua, Nigeria, Pakistan, Peru, Qatar, Republic of Korea, Russian Federation, Saudi Arabia, South Africa, Uganda, Zimbabwe.
Against: United States.
Abstaining: Andorra, Australia, Finland, France, Georgia, Germany, Greece, Hungary, India, Ireland, Italy, Netherlands, Portugal, Romania, Sweden, Ukraine, United Kingdom.

Further reports of Special Rapporteur. The Special Rapporteur undertook a mission to WTO (Geneva, 16-23 July and 27-28 August) [E/CN.4/2004/49/Add.1] to enhance the quality of dialogue between the human rights right to health and trade communities. He outlined the sources and scope of the right in relation to trade, explored analytical frameworks to deepen understanding of key issues and considered a number of specific trade agreements and other relevant questions, including the Agreement on Trade-Related Aspects of Intellectual Property Rights and neglected diseases, the General Agreement on Trade in Services, impact assessments, gender and trade, technical assistance, the Trade Policy Review Mechanism and acceding countries. The Special Rapporteur was concerned that pressure in trade negotiations, particularly by stronger trading partners over smaller acceding countries, might lead to unsustainable commitments to trade liberalization that, in practice, diminished States' capacity to realize the right to health. He recommended deepening the dialogue between the human rights and trade communities and supporting it by research on issues such as the relationship between international human rights law and trade law. He proposed a series of measures to the Commission, special rapporteurs, human rights treaty bodies, WTO member States, international organizations and civil society.

Pursuant to Economic and Social Council resolution 2003/45 (see p. 772), the Secretary-General, in October [A/58/427], transmitted the Special Rapporteur's interim report, which addressed relevant conceptual issues, such as the consideration of what constituted a right-to-health indicator and an overview of good practices for the right. He also discussed the obstacles that HIV/AIDS and neglected diseases, such as leprosy, posed to the realization of the right. The Special Rapporteur concluded that some components of a right to health strategy demanded new concepts and tools and suggested that human rights indicators could help States and others recognize when national and international policy adjustments were needed, and proposed the establishment of a right to health approach to the elimination of leprosy, and the adoption of an optional protocol to the International Covenant on Economic, Social and Cultural Rights (see p. 670) to help ensure that those living in poverty received attention and provide both a complaints and an enquiry procedure.

The Special Rapporteur visited Mozambique (15-19 December) [E/CN.4/2004/49/Add.2], but stated that his report on the mission could not be prepared and shared with the Government prior to the deadline for submitting reports to the Commission. Therefore, he would submit a written report on the visit in 2005 and an oral report in 2004.

GENERAL ASSEMBLY ACTION

On 22 December [meeting 77], the General Assembly, on the recommendation of the Third Committee [A/58/508/Add.2], adopted **resolution 58/173** by recorded vote (174-2-4) [agenda item 117 (b)].

The right of everyone to the enjoyment of the highest attainable standard of physical and mental health

The General Assembly,

Reaffirming the Universal Declaration of Human Rights, the International Covenant on Economic, Social and Cultural Rights, the International Convention on the Elimination of All Forms of Racial Discrimination, the Convention on the Elimination of All Forms of Discrimination against Women and the Convention on the Rights of the Child,

Reaffirming also that the right of everyone to the enjoyment of the highest attainable standard of physical and mental health is a human right, and that such right derives from the inherent dignity of the human person,

Recalling that, according to the Constitution of the World Health Organization, health is a state of complete physical, mental and social well-being and not merely the absence of disease or infirmity,

Recognizing the need to progressively achieve the full realization of the right of everyone to the enjoyment of the highest attainable standard of physical and mental health,

Recalling the relevant provisions of declarations and programmes of action adopted by the major United Nations conferences, summits and special sessions and at their follow-up meetings, in particular the four health-related development goals contained in the United Nations Millennium Declaration,

Noting Commission on Human Rights resolution 2003/28 of 22 April 2003 and all previous resolutions adopted by the Commission concerning the realization of the right of everyone to the enjoyment of the highest attainable standard of physical and mental health,

Welcoming the adoption of the World Health Organization Framework Convention on Tobacco Control by the fifty-sixth World Health Assembly, on 21 May 2003,

Recognizing the important contribution of all regional and subregional intergovernmental initiatives regarding HIV/AIDS, including those aimed at strengthening horizontal technical cooperation and encouraging best practices,

Aware that for millions of people throughout the world the full realization of the right of everyone to the enjoyment of the highest attainable standard of physical and mental health still remains a distant goal and that, in many cases, especially for those living in poverty, this goal is becoming increasingly remote,

Recognizing the need for States, in cooperation with international organizations and civil society, including non-governmental organizations and the private sector, to create favourable conditions at the national, regional and international levels to ensure the full and effective realization of the right of everyone to the enjoyment of the highest attainable standard of physical and mental health,

Recognizing also, in this regard, the important role of civil society, including non-governmental organizations, and in particular that of people living with HIV/AIDS, in the fight against this pandemic,

Recognizing further the indispensable role that health professionals play in the promotion and protection of the right of everyone to the enjoyment of the highest attainable standard of physical and mental health,

Welcoming the initiatives by the Secretary-General and relevant United Nations bodies and programmes, including the World Health Organization and the Joint United Nations Programme on HIV/AIDS, as well as public-private partnership initiatives, such as the Global Fund to Fight AIDS, Tuberculosis and Malaria, which contribute to improvements in addressing health issues worldwide, including in developing countries, while noting that further progress should be achieved in this regard, including in the mobilization of resources,

Concerned about the interrelationships between poverty and the realization of the right of everyone to the enjoyment of the highest attainable standard of physical and mental health, and in particular about the fact that ill health can be both a cause and a consequence of poverty,

Considering that sexual and reproductive health are integral elements of the right of everyone to the enjoyment of the highest attainable standard of physical and mental health,

Recalling the Declaration on the Agreement on Trade-Related Aspects of Intellectual Property Rights (TRIPS Agreement) and Public Health adopted at the Fourth World Trade Organization Ministerial Conference in Doha in November 2001, and welcoming the World Trade Organization General Council decision of 30 August 2003 on the implementation of paragraph 6 of the Declaration,

1. *Urges* States to take steps, individually and through international assistance and cooperation, especially economic and technical, to the maximum extent of their available resources, with a view to achieving progressively, by all appropriate means, the full realization of the right of everyone to the enjoyment of the highest attainable standard of physical and mental health, including, in particular, the adoption of legislative measures;

2. *Calls upon* the international community to continue to assist the developing countries in promoting the full realization of the right of everyone to the enjoyment of the highest attainable standard of physical and mental health, including through financial and technical support as well as training of personnel, while recognizing that the primary responsibility for promoting and protecting all human rights rests with States;

3. *Calls upon* States to guarantee that the right of everyone to the enjoyment of the highest attainable standard of physical and mental health will be exercised without discrimination of any kind;

4. *Reaffirms* that the achievement of the highest attainable level of health is a most important worldwide social goal, the realization of which requires action on the part of many other social and economic sectors in addition to the health sector;

5. *Affirms* that good governance at all levels, sound economic policies and solid democratic institutions responsive to the needs of the people are also key to the full realization of the right of everyone to the enjoyment of the highest attainable standard of physical and mental health;

6. *Calls upon* States to pay special attention to the situation of vulnerable groups, including by the adoption of positive measures, in order to safeguard the full realization of the right of everyone to the enjoyment of the highest attainable standard of physical and mental health;

7. *Also calls upon* States to place a gender perspective at the centre of all policies and programmes affecting women's health;

8. *Further calls upon* States to protect and promote sexual and reproductive health as integral elements of the right of everyone to the enjoyment of the highest attainable standard of physical and mental health;

9. *Invites* States to consider signing and ratifying the World Health Organization Framework Convention on Tobacco Control;

10. *Takes note with interest* of the interim report of the Special Rapporteur on the right of everyone to the enjoyment of the highest attainable standard of physical and mental health;

11. *Also takes note with interest* of the approach proposed by the Special Rapporteur to encompass the responsibilities of States at all levels in his future work on how to evaluate the progressive realization of the right of everyone to the highest attainable standard of physical and mental health, and of his efforts to apply this approach to specialized areas of health care, such as essential medicines, sexual and reproductive health, HIV/AIDS, children's health and water and sanitation;

12. *Welcomes* the special attention given by the Special Rapporteur to the identification of good practices for the effective implementation of the right of everyone to the highest attainable standard of physical and mental health;

13. *Recognizes* the need for further international cooperation and research to promote the development of new drugs, vaccines and diagnostic tools for diseases causing a heavy burden in developing countries, and stresses the need to support developing countries in their efforts in this regard, taking into account that the failure of market forces to address such diseases has a direct negative impact on the progressive realization in these countries of the right of everyone to the highest attainable standard of physical and mental health;

14. *Requests* the United Nations High Commissioner for Human Rights to provide the necessary resources for the effective fulfilment of the mandate of the Special Rapporteur from within existing resources;

15. *Calls upon* Governments to cooperate fully with the Special Rapporteur in the implementation of his mandate, to provide all information requested and to respond promptly to his communications;

16. *Notes* the request of the Commission on Human Rights to the Special Rapporteur to submit annually a report to the Commission and an interim report to the General Assembly on the activities performed under his mandate;

17. *Requests* the Commission on Human Rights to continue consideration of this matter at its sixtieth session under the same agenda item.

RECORDED VOTE ON RESOLUTION 58/173:

In favour: Afghanistan, Albania, Algeria, Andorra, Angola, Antigua and Barbuda, Argentina, Armenia, Austria, Azerbaijan, Bahamas, Bahrain, Bangladesh, Barbados, Belarus, Belgium, Belize, Benin, Bhutan, Bolivia, Bosnia and Herzegovina, Botswana, Brazil, Brunei Darussalam, Bulgaria, Burkina Faso, Burundi, Cambodia, Cameroon, Canada, Cape Verde, Central African Republic, Chile, China, Comoros, Congo, Costa Rica, Côte d'Ivoire, Croatia, Cuba, Cyprus, Democratic People's Republic of Korea, Democratic Republic of the Congo, Denmark, Djibouti, Dominica, Dominican Republic, Ecuador, Egypt, El Salvador, Eritrea, Estonia, Ethiopia, Fiji, Finland, France, Gabon, Gambia, Georgia, Germany, Ghana, Greece, Grenada, Guatemala, Guinea, Guinea-Bissau, Guyana, Haiti, Honduras, Hungary, Iceland, India, Indonesia, Iran, Ireland, Israel, Italy, Jamaica, Japan, Jordan, Kazakhstan, Kenya, Kuwait, Kyrgyzstan, Lao People's Democratic Republic, Latvia, Lebanon, Lesotho, Libyan Arab Jamahiriya, Liechtenstein, Lithuania, Luxembourg, Madagascar, Malawi, Malaysia, Maldives, Mali, Malta, Mauritania, Mauritius, Mexico, Micronesia, Monaco, Mongolia, Morocco, Mozambique, Myanmar, Namibia, Nauru, Nepal, Netherlands, New Zealand, Nicaragua, Niger, Nigeria, Norway, Oman, Pakistan, Panama, Papua New Guinea, Paraguay, Peru, Philippines, Poland, Portugal, Qatar, Republic of Korea, Republic of Moldova, Romania, Russian Federation, Rwanda, Saint Lucia, Saint Vincent and the Grenadines, Samoa, San Marino, Saudi Arabia, Senegal, Serbia and Montenegro, Seychelles, Sierra Leone, Singapore, Slovakia, Slovenia,

Solomon Islands, Somalia, South Africa, Spain, Sri Lanka, Sudan, Suriname, Switzerland, Syrian Arab Republic, Tajikistan, Thailand, The former Yugoslav Republic of Macedonia, Timor-Leste, Togo, Tonga, Trinidad and Tobago, Tunisia, Turkey, Turkmenistan, Tuvalu, Uganda, Ukraine, United Arab Emirates, United Republic of Tanzania, Uruguay, Uzbekistan, Venezuela, Viet Nam, Yemen, Zambia, Zimbabwe.
Against: Marshall Islands, United States.
Abstaining: Australia, Czech Republic, Sweden, United Kingdom.

Water and sanitation services

Report of Special Rapporteur. In response to 2002 Commission and Subcommission requests [YUN 2002, p. 743], the Special Rapporteur on the right to adequate water and sanitation, El Hadji Guissé, submitted an August progress report [E/CN.4/Sub.2/2003/WP.3] on a study on the relationship between the enjoyment of economic, social and cultural rights and the promotion of the realization of the right to drinking water supply and sanitation. He noted that the right to clean water impacted other human rights, including the rights to peace, self-determination, development, a healthy environment, health, adequate housing and education. Problems relating to water were universal and, in addressing them, collaboration among all nations was essential. The obligation of States to cooperate in that regard was enshrined in the UN Charter and in a number of international instruments.

Subcommission action. On 13 August [res. 2003/1], the Subcommission asked the Secretary-General to invite Governments, UN bodies and specialized agencies and interested NGOs to provide the Special Rapporteur with information for the preparation of his final report, and to assist him.

Bioethics

Report of Secretary-General. In response to a 2001 Commission request [YUN 2001, p. 674], the Secretary-General, in a February report with later addendum [E/CN.4/2003/98 & Add.1], summarized information received from five Governments, two specialized agencies and the secretariat of the Convention on Biological Diversity (see p. 1051) regarding the coordination of activities and thinking on bioethics.

Commission action. On 25 April [res. 2003/69], the Commission invited the High Commissioner to participate in the discussion on questions relating to human rights and bioethics and Governments that had not done so to consider establishing ethics committees, in conjunction with UNESCO's International Bioethics Committee, to assess the ethical, social and human rights questions raised by biomedical research regarding humans and to inform the Secretary-General of action taken. It asked the Subcommission to consider the contribution it could make to the Committee regarding the follow-up to the 1997 Universal Declaration on the Human Genome and Human Rights [YUN 1997, p. 1530] and to report in 2005. The Secretary-General was asked to report in 2005 based on those contributions.

Working paper. In response to a 2002 Subcommission decision [YUN 2002, p. 743], Iulia-Antoanella Motoc (Romania) submitted, in July, an expanded working paper [E/CN.4/Sub.2/2003/36] on the question of bioethics and human rights, which outlined the main questions to be analysed in a future study: the human genome as the common heritage of mankind; manipulation of the human genome and human rights; discrimination and the human genome; and intellectual property rights and human rights. She advocated the development of an international framework, taking into account public and private research in the field. A proposal to organize a world summit on the future of the human species, to protect the integrity of the human species and to prevent the market and its industries, businesses and self-serving scientists from deciding the future of humanity, was worthy of consideration.

Subcommission action. On 13 August [res. 2003/4], the Subcommission decided to appoint Ms. Motoc as Special Rapporteur to undertake a study on human rights and the human genome based on her working paper and asked her to submit a preliminary report to the Subcommission in 2004 and a final report to the Commission in 2005. The Secretary-General was asked to assist her.

Genetic privacy

Pursuant to Economic and Social Council resolution 2001/39 [YUN 2001, p. 675], the Secretary-General submitted a June report with later addendum [E/2003/91 & Add.1], which summarized information received from two Member States and UN system entities regarding genetic privacy and non-discrimination. The Secretary-General said there was a need to ensure non-discrimination on genetic grounds, and to assist countries, particularly developing countries, in taking advantage of genetics, biotechnologies and other related scientific progress in their development process, with due respect for human rights. He said the Council might wish to be kept informed of developments regarding the draft international declaration on human genetic data and to continue considering the implications relating to ethical, legal, medical and employment issues, as well as other aspects of social life, and to advocate for assistance to countries to deal better with those issues.

On 22 July, the Council decided to postpone consideration of the question of genetic privacy and non-discrimination to 2004, to allow for a thorough review of the matter and its implications on ethical, legal, medical, employment-related and other aspects of social life, on the basis of the Secretary-General's report, among other things (**decision 2003/232**).

Slavery and related issues

Working group activities. The five-member Working Group on Contemporary Forms of Slavery, at its twenty-eighth session (Geneva, 16-20 June) [E/CN.4/Sub.2/2003/31], reviewed developments in contemporary forms of slavery and measures to prevent and repress all its forms, including the consideration of corruption and international debt as promoting factors of the phenomenon. It considered as a matter of priority contemporary forms of slavery related to and generated by discrimination, particularly gender discrimination, such as forced and child marriage and the sale of wives. Other issues examined related to the activities of the United Nations Voluntary Trust Fund on Contemporary Forms of Slavery (see p. 777), forced labour, the status of slavery conventions, migrant and domestic workers, especially women, bonded labour and debt bondage, child labour, trafficking in persons and the exploitation of the prostitution of others, including children, the activities of the Special Rapporteurs on the sale of children, child prostitution and child pornography and on violence against women (see pp. 777 & 787), the activities of certain religious and other sects, traffic in children's organs and tissues, and slavery-like practices in armed conflict. The Group concluded that serious forms of slavery still existed and that new insidious forms were emerging. It made recommendations on the issues it considered during the session and decided to focus on the question of forced labour in 2004 and to consider as a priority issue in 2005 the assessment of its activities, in commemoration of the thirtieth anniversary of its establishment.

Documents considered by the Group included May notes by the Secretary-General [E/CN.4/Sub.2/AC.2/2003/2, E/CN.4/Sub.2/AC.2/2003/3] updating the status of the slavery conventions (1956 Supplementary Convention on the Abolition of Slavery, the Slave Trade and Institutions and Practices Similar to Slavery [YUN 1956, p. 228] and 1949 Convention for the Suppression of the Traffic in Persons and of the Exploitation of the Prostitution of Others, adopted by the General Assembly in resolution 317(IV) [YUN 1948-49, p. 613]) and a May report of the Secretary-General [E/CN.4/Sub.2/AC.2/2003/4] containing information submitted by Governments and a specialized agency on measures they had taken to prevent and repress all forms of slavery.

Subcommission action. On 13 August [res. 2003/3], the Subcommission addressed contemporary forms of slavery related to and generated by discrimination, particularly gender discrimination; traffic in persons and exploitation of the prostitution of others; sexual exploitation of children and the activities of the Special Rapporteur on the sale of children, child prostitution and child pornography; bonded labour and child labour; migrant workers; forced labour; corruption in the perpetuation of slavery and slavery-like practices; and the misuse of the Internet for the purpose of sexual exploitation.

The Subcommission recommended that the General Assembly consider declaring a UN year against trafficking in persons, especially women, youth and children. It requested the Secretary-General to ask States to continue to inform the Group of measures adopted to implement the 1992 Programme of Action for the Prevention of the Sale of Children, Child Prostitution and Child Pornography (see below) and on measures adopted to implement the 1993 Programme of Action for the Elimination of the Exploitation of Child Labour [YUN 1993, p. 965], and to report to the Subcommission and the Commission in 2004. The Group was asked to consider in 2004 the issue of forced labour, and ILO to consider organizing, in cooperation with the Group, consultations on the topic.

1992 Programme of Action

In response to a 1998 Subcommission request [YUN 1998, p. 697], a May report of the Secretary-General [E/CN.4/Sub.2/2003/26] summarized the activities of six Governments and two NGOs to implement the 1992 Programme of Action for the Prevention of the Sale of Children, Child Prostitution and Child Pornography [YUN 1992, p. 814].

Sexual exploitation during armed conflict

Report of High Commissioner. The High Commissioner, in a June report [E/CN.4/Sub.2/2003/27], supplemented information contained in a previous report [YUN 2002, p. 744] regarding steps taken by human rights mechanisms, the Commission, UN field offices, the International Tribunal for the Former Yugoslavia (ICTY) and the International Criminal Tribunal for Rwanda (ICTR) to address the problem of systematic rape, sexual slavery and slavery-like practices during armed conflicts. The High Commissioner said that, despite legal advances, such as ICTY verdicts and the provisions of the Rome Statute of the International Criminal Court (see p. 1332), women continued to face widespread sexual gender-based violence during conflicts. Human rights mechanisms should continue to strengthen their consideration of all gender-based human rights violations, and, to assist them, the international community should provide relevant information on the issue. To end impunity for such crimes, political will and concerted action were required from the international community, Governments and non-governmental actors.

Subcommission action. On 13 August [dec. 2003/108], the Subcommission, in follow-up to a 1998 report on systematic rape, sexual slavery and slavery-like practices during armed conflict [YUN 1998, p. 698], requested Françoise Hampson (United Kingdom) to prepare, without financial implications, a working paper on the criminalization, investigation and prosecution of acts of serious sexual violence occurring in the context of an armed conflict or committed as part of a widespread or systematic attack directed against any civilian population, for consideration in 2004.

On 14 August [res. 2003/26], the Subcommission encouraged States to provide effective criminal penalties and compensation for unremedied violations in order to end impunity regarding sexual violence during armed conflicts. The High Commissioner was asked to report in 2004.

Fund on slavery

Reports of Secretary-General. In February [E/CN.4/2003/83/Add.1], August [A/58/306] and December [E/CN.4/2004/78], the Secretary-General reported on the status of the United Nations Voluntary Trust Fund on Contemporary Forms of Slavery.

The Fund's Board of Trustees, at its eighth session (Geneva, 20-24 January), recommended 28 project grants, amounting to $130,920, and eight travel grants, amounting to $21,995, to enable NGO representatives to participate in the deliberations of the Working Group on Contemporary Forms of Slavery (see p. 776). The Board estimated that in order to fulfil its mandate satisfactorily, the Fund would need at least $300,000 before its ninth session, scheduled for January 2004. The High Commissioner, in October, launched an appeal for that amount. The Secretary-General reported that contributions available to the Fund as at 18 November 2003 stood at $45,394.

On 22 December, the General Assembly took note of the Secretary-General's August report (**decision 58/537**).

Subcommission action. On 14 August [res. 2003/27], the Subcommission urged Governments, NGOs and other private or public entities to contribute to the Fund.

Vulnerable groups

Women

In a September report [A/58/323] on progress made to implement the UN Millennium Declaration, as set out in General Assembly resolution 55/2 [YUN 2000, p. 49] (see also p. 48), the Secretary-General noted that, despite increased global awareness of issues affecting women's rights, little progress had been made at the country level and, in many cases, the rights that had been achieved were threatened. Rape and sexual violence continued to be used as weapons of war and women continued to be excluded from almost all peace negotiations. Also of grave concern was the increasing and widespread practice of trafficking in women and girls, one of the fastest-growing aspects of organized crime. Highlighting women's underrepresentation in decision-making at all levels of government, the Secretary-General noted that specific support was needed to ensure women's effective participation.

Violence against women

Note of Secretary-General. Pursuant to General Assembly resolution 50/166 [YUN 1995, p. 1188], the Secretary-General submitted, in January, to the Commission on Human Rights and to the Commission on the Status of Women the report of the United Nations Development Fund for Women regarding the Fund's activities to eliminate violence against women [E/CN.6/2003/11-E/CN.4/2003/121] (see p. 1193).

Report of Special Rapporteur. The Special Rapporteur on violence against women, its causes and consequences, Radhika Coomaraswamy (Sri Lanka), in a January final report to the Commission [E/CN.4/2003/75 & Corr.1], reviewed developments at the international, regional and national levels aimed at eliminating the violence since the 1994 creation of her mandate [YUN 1994, p. 1122], in order to present her successor with information necessary to assess future developments. She described how the international community had considered the violence with regard to situations of armed conflict, family violence, sexual violence/rape, sexual harassment, trafficking, and religious extremism and harmful traditional practices. In the course of the preceding decade, the greatest achievements to eradicate the violence were awareness-raising and standard-setting, said the Special Rapporteur. The development of jurisprudence and the prosecution of perpetrators through international, regional and national courts were important steps in the fight against impunity for gender-based crimes. However, very little had changed in the lives of most women, and statistics continued to show high rates of violence and abuse, mostly resulting in impunity for the perpetrators. The Special Rapporteur suggested that her successor focus on how to protect women's rights effectively and equal access to justice for women who had suffered violence. Measures at the national and international levels highlighted the need to address the root causes of violence, including women's poor economic, social and political status, which constrained knowledge of their rights and access to options and resources; equal access to the criminal justice system; and impunity for gender-based violence.

Addenda to the report detailed country-by-country developments from 1994 to 2003 [E/CN.4/2003/75/Add.1], to which Bhutan provided additional information [E/CN.4/2004/G/3], and a summary of recent communications she had sent to 29 Governments and the PA regarding specific allegations and replies received [E/CN.4/2003/75/Add.2 & Corr.1].

Commission action. On 23 April [res. 2003/45], the Commission decided that the Special Rapporteur's mandate should be renewed for a three-year period and asked her to report annually and to respond effectively to reliable information that came before her. The Secretary-General was asked to assist her and to ensure that her reports were brought to the attention of the Commission on the Status of Women (see p. 1192) in 2004 and of the Committee on the Elimination of Discrimination against Women (see p. 1190).

On 23 July, the Economic and Social Council endorsed the Commission's decision to renew the Special Rapporteur's mandate and its request to the Secretary-General to assist her (**decision 2003/251**).

In August, Yakin Ertürk (Turkey) was appointed Special Rapporteur.

On 22 December, the General Assembly, in **resolution 58/185** (see p. 1172), requested the Secretary-General to conduct an in-depth study on all forms and manifestations of violence against women, as identified in the Beijing Declaration and Platform for Action adopted at the Fourth World Conference on Women [YUN 1995, p. 1170] and the outcome of the Assembly's twenty-third special session on women [YUN 2000, p. 1082].

Women migrant workers

On 23 April [res. 2003/46], the Commission requested States to promote the human rights and fundamental freedoms of migrants, particularly women and children, and to prosecute violations of labour law with regard to migrant workers' conditions of work.

On 22 December, the General Assembly, in **resolution 58/143**, urged concerned Governments, particularly those of the countries of origin and destination, to strengthen further their national efforts to protect and promote the rights and welfare of women migrant workers (see also p. 1172).

Traditional practices affecting the health of women and girls

Report of Special Rapporteur. In response to a 2002 Subcommission request [YUN 2002, p. 746], the Special Rapporteur on traditional practices affecting the health of women and the girl child, Halima Warzazi (Morocco), in a July report [E/CN.4/Sub.2/2003/30], reviewed national legislative measures and programmes and recent regional initiatives to combat female genital mutilation. Major initiatives were a conference on zero tolerance for the practice (Addis Ababa, Ethiopia, 4-6 February), held by the Inter-African Committee on Traditional Practices Affecting the Health of Women and Children, which adopted a joint programme of action aimed at eradicating the practice by 2010, and a consultation of experts from the African and Arab regions (Cairo, Egypt, 21-23 June), held within the context of a campaign launched and financed by the EU. The Special Rapporteur recommended that the Subcommission follow up on the implementation of the agenda for action drawn up by the Addis Ababa conference, and proposed a study on the problems of host countries resulting from harmful practices imported by communities in their territory. The Special Rapporteur suggested that she prepare a questionnaire for Governments to identify all practices aimed at maintaining women in a situation of inferiority, dependence and submission, and an evaluation to assess progress made to combat female genital mutilation.

Subcommission action. On 14 August [res. 2003/28], the Subcommission called on the General Assembly to declare 6 February the international day on the elimination of female genital mutilation and all other harmful traditional practices affecting the health of women and girls. Governments were called on to give attention to the implementation of the 1994 Plan of Action for the Elimination of Harmful Traditional Practices [YUN 1994, p. 1123], and the Secretary-General was requested to invite them to submit information on the situation regarding harmful practices in their countries. The Subcommission proposed that three seminars be held in Africa, Asia and Europe to review progress achieved and to explore ways of overcoming the obstacles encountered in implementing the Plan of Action, and asked the High Commissioner to help raise funds to organize the seminars. It decided to renew for a further three-years the Special Rapporteur's mandate, requested her to submit an updated report in 2004 and recommended that the Commission approve its decision and request. The Commission was invited to consider the possibility of appointing a special rapporteur on harmful traditional practices affecting the health of women and girls. (See also p. 1174.)

Women in Afghanistan

Commission action. On 25 April [res. 2003/77], the Commission called on the Afghan Transitional Authority to investigate allegations of human rights violations, particularly against women and girls. It asked the Secretary-General to ensure that the post of senior gender adviser in the United Nations Assistance Mission in Afghanistan (see p. 289) was filled immediately and on a permanent basis, in order to mainstream a gender perspective in its activities. The Special Rapporteur on violence against women, its causes and consequences was invited to continue to review the situation of women and girls in Afghanistan and to report to the General Assembly and the Commission.

Report of Special Rapporteur. In accordance with Commission resolution 2003/77 (see above), the Secretary-General, in October [A/58/421], transmitted a report of Yakin Ertürk, the Special Rapporteur on violence against women, its causes and consequences, which reviewed new developments regarding the opportunities for and continuing vulnerabilities of women and girls in Afghanistan. The most significant development was the March ratification by the Afghan Transitional Authority, without reservation, of the 1979 Convention on the Elimination of All Forms of Discrimination against Women, adopted by the General Assembly in resolution 34/180 [YUN 1979, p. 895] (see also p. 1190). Also encouraging was that, despite many obstacles, large numbers of women sought to participate in public consultations on the drafting of the country's new constitution. On the negative side, the Special Rapporteur said persisting political instability posed a continuing challenge to the Transitional Authority and the international community, and for the promotion of women's and girls' human rights and their protection from multiple forms of violence and abuse. Outside Kabul, in particular, women's security was threatened by the presence and influence of local commanders who reportedly committed acts of extortion, looting, harassment, kidnapping and sexual abuse of women with impunity. The Special Rapporteur made recommendations to the Afghan Transitional Authority regarding non-discrimination on the basis of gender, ethnicity and religion; strict adherence to obligations under human rights instruments and international humanitarian law; support to the Ministry of Women's Affairs; action to ensure that harmful practices and rituals that violated women's human rights were eliminated; and strategies involving legislative and educational reforms and awareness-raising. She recommended that the international community provide long-term assistance for the social and economic reconstruction and rehabilitation of Afghan society, and for ensuring sustainable change for women. (See also p. 1175.)

On 22 December, the Assembly took note of the Special Rapporteur's report (**decision 58/539**).

The girl child

On 25 April [res. 2003/86], the Commission called on States to take measures, including legal reforms, to ensure girls' enjoyment of human rights and fundamental freedoms, and to eliminate discrimination and all forms of violence against them.

(See also p. 1185.)

Mainstreaming women's rights

Reports of Secretary-General. Pursuant to a 2002 Commission request [YUN 2002, p. 748], the Secretary-General, in a January report [E/CN.4/2003/72], described measures to integrate gender perspectives into the UN system, taken by Commission mechanisms and procedures, human rights treaty bodies and OHCHR. Although there had been progress in improving the integration of gender and women's rights issues into the UN human rights system, it was uneven. The Commission might wish to reiterate the importance of the relevant provisions of the Beijing Platform for Action adopted at the Fourth World Conference on Women [YUN 1995, p. 1170] and of its resolutions, and to invite the Secretary-General to bring gender trends in the membership of treaty bodies to the attention of States parties when inviting their nominations for the election of members. In addition, gender balance and gender expertise in the designation of experts by the Commission required further attention. More specific references to gender analysis should be included in designing and assessing all Commission mandates, particularly those concerning special procedures.

A further report [E/CN.4/2003/73-E/CN.6/2003/5] of the Secretary-General presented the joint work plan of the UN Division for the Advancement of Women and OHCHR for 2003. The two bodies would continue to cooperate on the work of treaty bodies in training activities on reporting under international human rights instruments, in the creation of multimedia training packages on international human rights instruments, in the preparation of reports on similar issues to be submitted to intergovernmental bodies, in disseminating relevant information and within the framework of inter-agency mechanisms, including with regard to activities related to the implementation of Security Council resolution 1325 (2000) [YUN 2000, p. 1113] on women, peace and security. Their web sites would be improved further and they would share information on and coordinate planned technical cooperation activities. The Division would update the 1998 study on integrating a gender perspective into the work of human rights treaty bodies [YUN 1998, p. 611] and continue to provide targeted input for the work of extra-conventional human rights mechanisms, particularly the Commission's Special Rapporteurs on the elimination of violence against women, the human rights of migrants, the sale of children, child prostitution and child pornography, and the right to adequate housing, as well as the Secretary-General's Special Representative on the situation of human rights defenders.

Commission action. On 23 April [res. 2003/44], the Commission requested special procedures and other Commission and Subcommission mechanisms and human rights treaty bodies to integrate a gender perspective into the implementation of their mandates and to include in their reports information on and analysis of women's and girls' human rights. It invited the Secretary-General to bring the current resolution to the attention of the World Summit on the Information Society (see p. 857) in order to stress the need for integrating a gender perspective into the outcome of the Summit, and requested him to report in 2004. The Commission decided to integrate a gender perspective into all its agenda items.

Trafficking in women and girls

As requested by the Commission in 2002 [YUN 2002, p. 748], the Secretary-General, in a January report [E/CN.4/2003/74], described activities taken by UN bodies, specialized agencies and other international organizations to combat trafficking in women and girls. Noting that in many parts of the world trafficking was perceived as a criminal law matter rather than a human rights issue, the Secretary-General pointed out that trafficked persons were victims of serious human rights violations and that it was important that human rights promoters took up the issue fully. Human rights were the common frame that should underpin anti-trafficking efforts. The Recommended Principles and Guidelines on Human Rights and Human Trafficking [YUN 2002, p. 748] contributed to the identification of the basic principles on which that common frame should be built.

Children

On 25 April [res. 2003/86], the Commission called on States to ensure children's registration immediately after birth; to respect children's rights and to preserve their identity; and to ensure children's right to know and be cared for by their parents and not be separated from their parents against their will, except when competent authorities determined that it was in the child's best interests. Among other things, States were also called on to support and participate in global poverty eradication efforts and to promote the rights of the child in that context; ensure children's right, without discrimination, to health; support and rehabilitate children and their families affected by HIV/AIDS and ensure the prevention of HIV infections; promote children's right to education and ensure they did not suffer discrimination; protect the rights of children with disabilities, and those of migrant children, street children, and refugee and internally displaced children; ensure that children were not deprived of their liberty except as a last resort and protect those deprived of their liberty from torture and other cruel, inhuman or degrading treatment or punishment; and eliminate child labour. The Commission requested the independent expert on violence against children (see below) to conduct a study on the topic as soon as possible, in collaboration with OHCHR, UNICEF and WHO, and asked Member States, UN bodies and intergovernmental organizations to support the study; NGOs were asked to contribute to it and the Secretary-General to submit a progress report in 2004 and a final report in 2005. The Secretary-General was requested to submit a further report on the problems addressed in the Commission's current resolution in 2004. Human rights mechanisms, particularly special rapporteurs and working groups, were asked to pay attention to the special situation of violence against children.

(Other aspects of the Commission's resolution—child labour, the prevention and eradication of the sale of children, child prostitution and child pornography, and the protection of children affected by armed conflict—are covered below.)

In response to a 2002 Commission request [YUN 2002, p. 748], Paulo Sérgio Pinheiro (Brazil) was appointed independent expert to conduct a study on violence against children, pursuant to General Assembly resolution 56/138 [YUN 2001, p. 681].

GENERAL ASSEMBLY ACTION

On 22 December [meeting 77], the General Assembly, on the recommendation of the Third Committee [A/58/504], adopted **resolution 58/157** by recorded vote (179-1) [agenda item 113].

Rights of the child

The General Assembly,

Recalling its previous resolutions on the rights of the child, the most recent of which is resolution 57/190 of 18 December 2002, as well as Commission on Human Rights resolution 2003/86 of 25 April 2003,

Emphasizing that the Convention on the Rights of the Child must constitute the standard in the promotion and protection of the rights of the child, and bearing in mind the importance of the Optional Protocols to the Convention on the Rights of the Child on the involvement of children in armed conflict and on the sale of children, child prostitution and child pornography, as well as other relevant human rights instruments,

Reaffirming that the general principles of, inter alia, the best interests of the child, non-discrimination, participation and survival and development provide the framework for all actions concerning children, including adolescents,

Reaffirming also the World Declaration on the Survival, Protection and Development of Children and the Plan of Action for Implementing the World Declaration on the Survival, Protection and Development of Children in the 1990s adopted by the World Summit for Children, held in New York on 29 and 30 September 1990, and the Vienna Declaration and Programme of Action adopted by the World Conference on Human Rights, held in Vienna from 14 to 25 June 1993,

Reaffirming further the United Nations Millennium Declaration and the Declaration of Commitment on HIV/AIDS,

Reaffirming the outcome document of the special session of the General Assembly on children, entitled "A world fit for children", and the commitments contained therein to promote and protect the rights of each child, every human being below the age of 18 years, including adolescents, and the integration of child rights issues into the outcome documents of all major United Nations conferences, special sessions and summits,

Reaffirming also the essential roles of the General Assembly, the Economic and Social Council and the Commission on Human Rights in promoting and protecting the rights and welfare of children, and noting the importance of the debates held by the Security Council on children and armed conflict, of Council resolutions 1379(2001) of 20 November 2001 and 1460(2003) of 30 January 2003 and of the undertaking by the Council to give special attention to the protection, welfare and rights of children in armed conflict when taking action aimed at maintaining peace and security, including provisions for the protection of children in the mandates of peacekeeping operations, as well as the inclusion of child protection advisers in these operations,

Welcoming the reports of the Secretary-General on the status of the Convention on the Rights of the Child and on progress achieved in realizing the commitments set out in the document entitled "A world fit for children", and the report of the Special Representative of the Secretary-General for Children and Armed Conflict,

Welcoming also the work of the Committee on the Rights of the Child in examining the progress made by States parties to the Convention in implementing the obligations undertaken in the Convention and in providing recommendations to States parties on the implementation of the Convention and, in cooperation with the Office of the United Nations High Commissioner for Human Rights, in enhancing awareness of the principles and provisions of the Convention,

Welcoming further the increase in the membership of the Committee on the Rights of the Child from ten to eighteen,

Welcoming the appointment by the Secretary-General of the independent expert for the United Nations study on violence against children,

Profoundly concerned that the situation of children in many parts of the world remains critical as a result of the persistence of poverty, social inequality, inadequate social and economic conditions in an increasingly globalized economic environment, pandemics, in particular HIV/AIDS, malaria and tuberculosis, environmental damage, natural disasters, armed conflict, displacement, exploitation, illiteracy, hunger, intolerance, discrimination, gender inequality, disability and inadequate legal protection, and convinced that urgent and effective national and international action is called for,

Bearing in mind the International Decade for a Culture of Peace and Non-Violence for the Children of the World, 2001-2010, and recalling the Declaration and Programme of Action on a Culture of Peace, which serve as the basis for the Decade,

Recognizing that the family is the basic unit of society and as such should be strengthened, that it is entitled to receive comprehensive protection and support, that the primary responsibility for the protection, upbringing and development of children rests with the family and that all institutions of society should respect the rights of the child and secure his or her well-being and render appropriate assistance to parents, families, legal guardians and other caregivers so that children can grow and develop in a safe and stable environment and in an atmosphere of happiness, love and understanding, bearing in mind that in different cultural, social and political systems, various forms of family exist,

Recognizing also that partnership among Governments, international organizations and relevant organs and organizations of the United Nations system, in particular the United Nations Children's Fund, and all actors of civil society, including non-governmental organizations, as well as the private sector, is important for the realization of the rights of the child,

Underlining the need for mainstreaming a gender perspective in all policies and programmes relating to children,

Implementation of the Convention on the Rights of the Child and the Optional Protocols thereto on the involvement of children in armed conflict and on the sale of children, child prostitution and child pornography

1. *Urges* States that have not yet done so to sign and ratify or accede to the Convention on the Rights of the Child as a matter of priority, and urges States parties to implement it fully, while stressing that the implementation of the Convention and the achievement of the goals of the World Summit for Children and the special session of the General Assembly on children are mutually reinforcing;

2. *Expresses its concern* about the great number of reservations to the Convention, and urges States parties to withdraw reservations incompatible with the object and purpose of the Convention and to consider reviewing other reservations with a view to withdrawing them;

3. *Urges* States that have not yet done so to consider signing and ratifying or acceding to the Optional Protocols to the Convention on the Rights of the Child on the involvement of children in armed conflict and on the sale of children, child prostitution and child pornography, and urges States parties to implement them fully;

4. *Calls upon* States parties to ensure that the rights set forth in the Convention are respected without discrimination of any kind and that the best interest of the child is a primary consideration in all actions concerning children, to recognize the child's inherent right to life and to ensure the child's survival and development to the maximum extent possible and to ensure also that the child is able to express his or her views freely in all matters affecting him or her and that these views are listened to and given due weight in accordance with his or her age and maturity;

5. *Urges* States parties to take all appropriate measures for the implementation of the rights recognized in the Convention, bearing in mind article 4 of the Convention, by:

(*a*) Putting in place effective national legislation, policies and action plans and by strengthening relevant governmental structures for children, including, where appropriate, ministers in charge of child issues and independent commissioners for the rights of the child;

(*b*) Ensuring adequate and systematic training in the rights of the child for professional groups working with and for children, including specialized judges, law enforcement officials, lawyers, social workers, medical doctors, health professionals and teachers, and coordination among various governmental bodies involved in children's rights, and encourages States and relevant bodies and organizations of the United Nations system to continue to promote education and training in this regard;

6. *Calls upon* States parties:

(*a*) To ensure that the members of the Committee on the Rights of the Child are of high moral standing and recognized competence in the field covered by the Convention, and serve in their personal capacity, consideration being given to equitable geographical distribution as well as to the principal legal systems;

(*b*) To strengthen their cooperation with the Committee and to comply in a timely manner with their reporting obligations under the Convention and the Optional Protocols thereto, in accordance with the guidelines elaborated by the Committee, as well as to take into account the recommendations made by the Committee in the implementation of the provisions of the Convention;

7. *Calls upon* all States and relevant actors concerned to continue to cooperate with the special rapporteurs and special representatives of the United Nations system in the implementation of their mandates, requests the Secretary-General to provide them with appropriate staff and facilities from the United Nations regular budget, when this is in accordance with their respective mandates, invites States to continue to make voluntary contributions, where appropriate, and urges all relevant parts of the United Nations system to provide them with comprehensive reporting to make possible the full discharge of their mandates;

8. *Calls upon* all States to end impunity for perpetrators of crimes committed against children, recognizing in this regard the contribution of the establishment of the International Criminal Court as a way to prevent violations of human rights and international humanitarian law, in particular when children are victims of serious crimes, including the crime of genocide, crimes against humanity and war crimes, and to bring perpetrators of such crimes to justice, and not to grant amnesties for these crimes;

9. *Encourages* all States:

(*a*) To strengthen their national statistical capacities and to use statistics disaggregated, inter alia, by age, gender and other relevant factors that may lead to disparities and other statistical indicators at the national, subregional, regional and international levels to develop and assess social policies and programmes so that economic and social resources are used efficiently and effectively for the full realization of the rights of the child;

(*b*) To strengthen their partnership with United Nations organs, within their respective mandates, the Bretton Woods institutions and other multilateral agencies, as well as other relevant actors;

10. *Requests* all relevant organs of the United Nations system, the Office of the United Nations High Commissioner for Human Rights and United Nations mechanisms regularly and systematically to incorporate a strong child rights perspective throughout all activities in the fulfilment of their mandates, as well as to ensure that their staff is trained in child protection matters, and calls upon States to cooperate closely with them;

11. *Encourages* Governments and relevant United Nations bodies, as well as relevant non-governmental organizations and child rights advocates, to continue to contribute, as appropriate, to the web-based database launched by the United Nations Children's Fund in order to continue the provision of information on laws, structures, policies and processes adopted at the national level to translate the Convention into practice, and in this regard commends that body for its work to disseminate lessons learned in the implementation of the Convention;

Promoting and protecting the rights of children and non-discrimination against children, including children in particularly difficult situations

Identity, family relations and birth registration

12. *Calls upon* all States to intensify efforts to ensure the registration of all children immediately after birth, including through the consideration of simplified, expeditious and effective procedures;

13. *Also calls upon* all States to undertake to respect the right of the child to preserve his or her identity, including nationality, name and family relations as recognized by law, without unlawful interference and, where a child is illegally deprived of some or all of the elements of his or her identity, to provide appropriate assistance and protection with a view to speedily re-establishing his or her identity;

14. *Urges* all States to ensure, as far as possible, the right of the child to know and be cared for by his or her parents;

15. *Calls upon* States to guarantee, to the extent consistent with each State's obligations, the right of a child whose parents reside in different States to maintain, on a regular basis, save in exceptional circumstances, personal relations and direct contact with both parents by providing means of access and visitation in both States and by respecting the principle that both parents have common responsibilities for the upbringing and development of their children;

16. *Urges* all States to ensure that a child shall not be separated from his or her parents against their will, except when the competent authorities, subject to judicial review, determine, in accordance with applicable law and procedures, that such separation is necessary in the best interest of the child, and, where alternative care is necessary, to promote family and community-based care in preference to placement in institutions, recognizing that such determination may be necessary in a particular case, such as one involving abuse or neglect of the child by the parents or one in which the parents are living separately and a decision must be made as to the child's place of residence;

17. *Calls upon* States to take all necessary measures to ensure that the best interest of the child is the primary consideration in the adoption of children and to take all necessary measures to prevent and combat illegal adoptions and adoptions that do not follow the normal procedures;

18. *Also calls upon* States to take all necessary measures to address the problem of children growing up without parents, in particular orphaned children and children who are victims of family and social violence, neglect and abuse;

19. *Urges* States to address cases of international kidnapping of children by one of the parents;

Poverty

20. *Reaffirms* that investments in children and the realization of their rights are among the most effective ways to eradicate poverty;

21. *Calls upon* States and the international community to cooperate, support and participate in the global efforts for poverty eradication at the global, regional and country levels, recognizing that strengthened availability and effective allocation of resources are required at all of these levels, in order to ensure that all the development and poverty eradication goals, as set out in the United Nations Millennium Declaration, are realized within their time framework, and to promote the enjoyment of the rights of the child;

Health

22. *Calls upon* all States to take all appropriate measures to develop sustainable health systems and social services and to ensure access to such systems and services without discrimination and to pay particular attention to adequate food and nutrition to prevent disease and malnutrition, to prenatal and post-natal health care, to the special needs of adolescents, to reproductive and sexual health and to threats from substance abuse and violence, in particular to all vulnerable groups, and calls upon all States parties to take all necessary measures to ensure the right of all children, without discrimination, to the enjoyment of the highest attainable standard of health;

23. *Urges* all States to assign priority to activities and programmes aimed at preventing the abuse of narcotic drugs, psychotropic substances and inhalants as well as preventing other addictions, in particular addiction to alcohol and tobacco, among children and young people, especially those in vulnerable situations, and to counter the use of children and young people in the illicit production of and trafficking in narcotic drugs and psychotropic substances;

24. *Calls upon* all States to give support and rehabilitation to children and their families affected by HIV/AIDS and to involve children and their caregivers, as well as the private sector, to ensure the effective prevention of HIV infections through correct information and access to voluntary and confidential care, treatment and testing, including pharmaceutical products and medical technologies, affordable to all, giving due importance to the prevention of mother-to-child transmission of the virus;

Education

25. *Also calls upon* all States:

(a) To recognize the right to education on the basis of equal opportunity by making primary education compulsory and available free to all, without discrimination, by ensuring that all children, including girls, children in need of special protection, children with disabilities, indigenous children, children belonging to minorities and children from different ethnic origins, have access without discrimination to education of good quality, as well as by making secondary education generally available and accessible to all, in particular by the progressive introduction of free education, bearing in mind that special measures to ensure equal access, including affirmative action, contribute to achieving equal opportunity and combating exclusion, and to ensure that the education of the child is carried out and States parties develop and implement programmes for the education of the child in accordance with articles 28 and 29 of the Convention;

(b) To develop national plans of action, or to strengthen existing ones, in order to achieve the objectives of Education for All so as to ensure that all boys and girls complete a full course of primary schooling, and reaffirms the coordinating role of the United Nations Educational, Scientific and Cultural Organization in this regard;

(c) To design and implement programmes to provide social services and support to pregnant adolescents and adolescent mothers, in particular to enable them to continue and complete their education;

(d) To promote an educational setting that eliminates all barriers that impede the schooling of pregnant adolescents and adolescent mothers;

(e) To take all appropriate measures to prevent racism and discriminatory and xenophobic attitudes and behaviour through education, keeping in mind the important role that children play in changing those practices;

(f) To ensure that children, from an early age, benefit from education and from participation in activities that develop respect for human rights and emphasize the practice of non-violence, with the aim of instilling in them the values and goals of a culture of peace, and invites States to develop national strategies for human rights education that are comprehensive, participatory and effective;

(g) To ensure that education programmes and materials reflect fully the promotion and protection of human rights and values of peace, tolerance and gender equality, using every opportunity presented by the International Decade for a Culture of Peace and Non-Violence for the Children of the World, 2001-2010;

(h) To harness the rapidly evolving information and communication technologies to support education at an affordable cost, including open and distance education, while reducing inequality in access and quality;

26. *Urges* States:

(a) To take measures to protect students from violence, injury or abuse, including sexual abuse and intimidation or maltreatment in schools, to establish complaint mechanisms that are age-appropriate and accessible to children and to undertake thorough and prompt investigations of all acts of violence and discrimination;

(b) To take measures to eliminate the use of corporal punishment in schools;

Freedom from violence

27. *Calls upon* States to take all appropriate measures to prevent and protect children from all forms of violence, including physical, mental and sexual violence, torture, child abuse, abuse by police, other law enforcement authorities and employees and officials in detention centres or welfare institutions, including orphanages, and domestic violence;

28. *Also calls upon* States to investigate and submit cases of torture and other forms of violence against children to the competent authorities for the purpose of prosecution and to impose appropriate disciplinary or penal sanctions against those responsible for such practices;

29. *Requests* all relevant human rights mechanisms, in particular special rapporteurs and working groups, within their mandates, to pay attention to the special situations of violence against children, reflecting their experiences in the field;

Non-discrimination

30. *Calls upon* all States to ensure that children are entitled to their civil, political, economic, social and cultural rights without discrimination of any kind;

31. *Notes with concern* the large number of children, particularly girls, among the victims of racism, racial discrimination, xenophobia and related intolerance, and stresses the need to incorporate special measures, in accordance with the principle of the best interests of the child and respect for his or her views, in programmes to combat racism, racial discrimination, xenophobia and related intolerance, in order to give priority attention to the rights and the situation of children who are victims of these practices, and calls upon States to provide special support and ensure equal access to services for those children;

32. *Calls upon* all States in which ethnic, religious or linguistic minorities or persons of indigenous origin exist not to deny to a child belonging to such a minority or an indigenous child the right, in community with other members of his or her group, to enjoy his or her own culture, to profess and practise his or her own religion or to use his or her own language;

The girl child

33. *Calls upon* all States to take all necessary measures, including legal reforms where appropriate:

(a) To ensure the full and equal enjoyment by girls of all human rights and fundamental freedoms, to take effective actions against violations of those rights and freedoms and to base programmes and policies on the rights of the child, taking into account the special situation of girls;

(b) To eliminate all forms of discrimination against girls and all forms of violence, including female infanticide and prenatal sex selection, rape, sexual abuse and harmful traditional or customary practices, including female genital mutilation, the root causes of son preference, marriages without free and full consent of the intending spouses, early marriages and forced sterilization, by enacting and enforcing legislation and, where appropriate, formulating comprehensive, multidisciplinary and coordinated national plans, programmes or strategies protecting girls;

Children with disabilities

34. *Also calls upon* all States to take necessary measures to ensure the full and equal enjoyment of all human rights and fundamental freedoms by children with disabilities in both the public and the private spheres, including access to good quality education and health care and protection from violence, abuse and neglect, and to develop and, where it already exists, to enforce legislation to prohibit discrimination against them to ensure their dignity, promote their self-reliance and facilitate their active participation and integration in the community, taking into account the particularly difficult situation of children with disabilities living in poverty;

35. *Encourages* the Ad Hoc Committee on a Comprehensive and Integral International Convention on the Protection and Promotion of the Rights and Dignity of Persons with Disabilities to consider the issue of children with disabilities in its deliberations;

Migrant children

36. *Calls upon* all States to ensure, for migrant children, the enjoyment of all human rights as well as access to health care, social services and education of good quality and to ensure that migrant children, and especially those who are unaccompanied, in particular victims of violence and exploitation, receive special protection and assistance;

Children working and/or living on the street

37. *Also calls upon* all States to prevent violations of the rights of children working and/or living on the street, including discrimination, arbitrary detention and extrajudicial, arbitrary and summary executions, torture, all kinds of violence and exploitation, and to bring the perpetrators to justice, to adopt and implement policies for the protection, social and psychosocial rehabilitation and reintegration of these children and to adopt economic, social and educational strategies to address the problems of children working and/or living on the street;

Refugee and internally displaced children

38. *Further calls upon* all States to protect refugee, asylum-seeking and internally displaced children, in particular those who are unaccompanied, who are particularly exposed to risks in connection with armed conflict, such as recruitment, sexual violence and exploitation, to pay particular attention to programmes for voluntary repatriation and, wherever possible, local integration and resettlement, to give priority to family tracing and reunification and, where appropriate, to cooperate with international humanitarian and refugee organizations, including by facilitating their work;

Child labour

39. *Calls upon* all States to translate into concrete action their commitment to the progressive and effective elimination of child labour that is likely to be hazardous to or interfere with the child's education or to be harmful to the child's health or physical, mental, spiritual, moral or social development, to eliminate immediately the worst forms of child labour, to promote education as a key strategy in this regard, including the creation of vocational training and apprenticeship programmes and the integration of working children into the formal education system, and to examine and devise economic policies, where necessary, in cooperation with the international community, that address factors contributing to these forms of child labour;

40. *Urges* all States that have not yet done so to consider ratifying the Convention concerning Minimum Age for Admission to Employment, 1973 (Convention No. 138) and the Convention concerning the Prohibition and Immediate Action for the Elimination of the Worst Forms of Child Labour, 1999 (Convention No. 182) of the International Labour Organization, and calls upon States parties to those instruments to implement them fully and to comply in a timely manner with their reporting obligations;

Children alleged to have infringed or recognized as having infringed penal law

41. *Calls upon*:

(a) All States, in particular States in which the death penalty has not been abolished, to comply with their obligations as assumed under relevant provisions of international human rights instruments, including, in particular, articles 37 and 40 of the Convention on the Rights of the Child and articles 6 and 14 of the International Covenant on Civil and Political Rights, keeping in mind the safeguards guaranteeing protection of the rights of those facing the death penalty and guarantees set out in Economic and Social Council resolutions 1984/50 of 25 May 1984 and 1989/64 of 24 May 1989, and calls upon those States to abolish by law, as soon as possible, the death penalty for those below the age of 18 years at the time of the commission of the offence;

(b) All States to protect children deprived of their liberty from torture and other cruel, inhuman or degrading treatment or punishment;

(c) All States to take appropriate steps to ensure compliance with the principle that depriving children of their liberty should be used only as a measure of last resort and for the shortest appropriate period of time, in particular before trial, and to ensure that, if they are arrested, detained or imprisoned, children are provided with adequate legal assistance and are separated from adults, to the greatest extent feasible, unless it is considered in their best interest not to do so, and also to take appropriate steps to ensure that no child in detention is sentenced to forced labour or corporal punishment or deprived of access to and provision of health-care services, hygiene and environmental sanitation, education, basic instruction and vocational training, taking into consideration the special needs of children with disabilities in detention, in accordance with their obligations under the Convention;

Recovery and social reintegration

42. *Encourages* States to cooperate, including through bilateral and multilateral technical cooperation and financial assistance, in the implementation of their obligations under the Convention, including in the prevention of any activity contrary to the rights of the child and in the rehabilitation and social integration of the victims, such assistance and cooperation to be undertaken in consultation among concerned States and relevant international organizations as well as other relevant actors;

Prevention and eradication of the sale of children, child prostitution and child pornography

43. *Calls upon* all States:

(a) To take all appropriate national, bilateral and multilateral measures, inter alia, to develop national laws and allocate resources for the development of long-term policies, programmes and practices and to collect comprehensive data, disaggregated by age, gender and other relevant factors, to facilitate the participation of child victims of sexual exploitation in the development of strategies, taking into account their age and maturity, and to ensure the effective implementation of relevant international instruments concerning the prevention and the combating of trafficking and sale of children for any purpose or in any form, including the transfer of the organs of the child for profit, child prostitution and child pornography, and encourages all actors of civil society, the private sector and the media to cooperate in efforts to this end;

(b) To increase cooperation at all levels to prevent and dismantle networks trafficking in children;

(c) To consider ratifying or acceding to the Protocol to Prevent, Suppress and Punish Trafficking in Persons, Especially Women and Children, supplementing the United Nations Convention against Transnational Organized Crime;

(d) To criminalize and effectively penalize all forms of sexual exploitation and sexual abuse of children, including within the family or for commercial purposes, child pornography and child prostitution, child sex tourism, the sale of children and their organs, and the use of the Internet for these purposes, while ensuring that, in the treatment by the criminal justice system of children who are victims, the best interests of the child shall be a primary consideration, and to take effective measures against the criminalization of children who are victims of exploitation and effective measures to ensure the prosecution of offenders, whether local or foreign, by the competent national authorities, either in the country where the crime was committed, or in the country of which the offender is a national or resident, or in the country of which the victim is a national, or on any other basis permitted under domestic law in accordance with due process of law;

(e) In cases of the sale of children, child prostitution and child pornography, to address effectively the needs of victims, including their physical and psychological recovery and full reintegration into their family and society;

(f) To combat the existence of a market that encourages such criminal practices against children, including through the adoption, effective application and enforcement of preventive, rehabilitative and punitive measures targeting customers or individuals who sexually exploit or sexually abuse children, as well as by ensuring public awareness;

(g) To afford one another the greatest measure of assistance in connection with investigations or criminal or extradition proceedings brought in respect of the offences set forth in article 3, paragraph 1, of the Optional Protocol to the Convention on the Rights of the Child on the sale of children, child prostitution and child pornography, including assistance in obtaining evidence at their disposal for the proceedings;

(h) To contribute to the elimination of the sale of children, child prostitution and child pornography by adopting a holistic approach, addressing the contributing factors, including underdevelopment, poverty, economic disparities, inequitable socio-economic structures, dysfunctional families, lack of education, urban-rural migration, gender discrimination, irresponsible adult sexual behaviour, harmful traditional practices, armed conflicts and trafficking in children;

Children in armed conflict

44. *Recognizes* the inclusion in the Rome Statute of the International Criminal Court, as a war crime, of crimes involving sexual violence and crimes of conscripting or enlisting children under the age of 15 years or using them to participate actively in hostilities in both international and non-international armed conflicts;

45. *Urges* all States and all other parties to armed conflicts to end the recruitment and use of children in situations of armed conflict contrary to international law and to ensure their demobilization, effective disarmament and rehabilitation, physical and psychological recovery and reintegration into society;

46. *Urges* all States:

(a) When ratifying the Optional Protocol to the Convention on the Rights of the Child on the involvement of children in armed conflict, to raise the minimum age for voluntary recruitment of persons into their national armed forces from that set out in article 38, paragraph 3, of the Convention, bearing in mind that under the Convention persons below the age of 18 years are entitled to special protection, and to adopt safeguards to ensure that such recruitment is not forced or coerced;

(b) To protect children affected by armed conflict, in particular to protect them from acts that constitute violations of international humanitarian law and human rights law and to ensure that they receive timely, effective and unhindered humanitarian assistance as well as support for physical and psychological recovery;

47. *Emphasizes* the importance of giving systematic consideration to the rights, special needs and particular vulnerability of the girl child during conflicts and in post-conflict situations;

48. *Regrets* the fact that the report on a comprehensive assessment of the United Nations response to the issue of children affected by armed conflict, requested in resolution 57/190, has not yet been submitted, and reiterates its request to the Secretary-General to submit his report for consideration as soon as possible;

Follow-up

49. *Urges* those States that have not yet done so to complete a national action plan as soon as possible incorporating the goals agreed at the special session of the General Assembly on children, as reflected in its outcome document entitled "A world fit for children", and to place those goals within the framework of the Convention on the Rights of the Child;

50. *Decides*:

(a) To request the Secretary-General to prepare an updated report on progress achieved in realizing the commitments set out in the document entitled "A world fit for children", with a view to identifying problems and constraints and making recommendations on the action needed to achieve further progress, and to submit his report to the General Assembly at its fifty-ninth session;

(b) To request the Secretary-General to submit to the General Assembly at its fifty-ninth session a report on the rights of the child containing information on the status of the Convention and the problems addressed in the present resolution;

(c) To request the Special Representative of the Secretary-General for Children and Armed Conflict to continue to submit to the General Assembly, the Security Council and the Commission on Human Rights reports containing relevant information on the situation of children affected by armed conflict, taking into account the outcome document adopted by the General Assembly at its special session on children and bearing in mind existing mandates and reports of relevant bodies;

(d) To request the independent expert for the United Nations study on violence against children to conduct the study as soon as possible, invites Member States, United Nations bodies and organizations, including the Committee on the Rights of the Child, as well as other relevant intergovernmental organizations, to provide substantive and, where appropriate, financial support, including through voluntary contributions, for the effective conduct of the study, invites non-governmental organizations to contribute to the study, taking into account the recommendations of the Committee made following the general discussions on violence against children held in September 2000 and 2001, and encourages the independent expert to also seek the participation of children in the study, taking into account their age and maturity;

(e) To invite the independent expert for the United Nations study on violence against children to present an oral progress report on the study to the General Assembly at its fifty-ninth session;

(f) To request the Secretary-General to ensure the provision of appropriate staff and facilities from the United Nations regular budget for the effective and expeditious performance of the functions of the Committee, and invites the Committee to continue to enhance its constructive dialogue with the States parties to the Convention and its transparent and effective functioning;

(g) To continue its consideration of this question at its fifty-ninth session under the item entitled "Promotion and protection of the rights of children".

RECORDED VOTE ON RESOLUTION 58/157:

In favour: Afghanistan, Albania, Algeria, Andorra, Angola, Antigua and Barbuda, Argentina, Armenia, Australia, Austria, Azerbaijan, Bahamas, Bahrain, Bangladesh, Barbados, Belarus, Belgium, Belize, Benin, Bhutan, Bolivia, Bosnia and Herzegovina, Botswana, Brazil, Brunei Darussalam, Bulgaria, Burkina Faso, Burundi, Cambodia, Cameroon, Canada, Cape Verde, Central African Republic, Chile, China, Colombia, Comoros, Congo, Costa Rica, Côte d'Ivoire, Croatia, Cuba, Cyprus, Czech Republic, Democratic People's Republic of Korea, Democratic Republic of the Congo, Denmark, Djibouti, Dominica, Dominican Republic, Ecuador, Egypt, El Salvador, Eritrea, Estonia, Ethiopia, Fiji, Finland, France, Gabon, Gambia, Georgia, Germany, Ghana, Greece, Grenada, Guatemala, Guinea, Guinea-Bissau, Guyana, Haiti, Honduras, Hungary, Iceland, India, Indonesia, Iran, Ireland, Israel, Italy, Jamaica, Japan, Jordan, Kazakhstan, Kenya, Kuwait, Kyrgyzstan, Lao People's Democratic Republic, Latvia, Lebanon, Lesotho, Libyan Arab Jamahiriya, Liechtenstein, Lithuania, Luxembourg, Madagascar, Malawi, Malaysia, Maldives, Mali, Malta, Marshall Islands, Mauritania, Mauritius, Mexico, Micronesia, Monaco, Mongolia, Morocco, Mozambique, Myanmar, Namibia, Nauru, Nepal, Netherlands, New Zealand, Nicaragua, Niger, Nigeria, Norway, Oman, Pakistan, Panama, Papua New Guinea, Paraguay, Peru, Philippines, Poland, Portugal, Qatar, Republic of Korea, Republic of Moldova, Romania, Russian Federation, Rwanda, Saint Lucia, Saint Vincent and the Grenadines, Samoa, San Marino, Saudi Arabia, Senegal, Serbia and Montenegro, Seychelles, Sierra Leone, Singapore, Slovakia, Slovenia, Solomon Islands, South Africa, Spain, Sri Lanka, Sudan, Suriname, Sweden, Switzerland, Syrian Arab Republic, Tajikistan, Thailand, The former Yugoslav Republic of Macedonia, Timor-Leste, Togo, Tonga, Trinidad and Tobago, Tunisia, Turkey, Turkmenistan, Tuvalu, Uganda, Ukraine, United Arab Emirates, United Kingdom, United Republic of Tanzania, Uruguay, Uzbekistan, Venezuela, Viet Nam, Yemen, Zambia, Zimbabwe.

Against: United States.

The Third Committee adopted, by separate recorded votes, paragraph 26 (b) and the words "corporal punishment" in paragraph 41 (c) by 117 to 10, with 23 abstentions, and 123 to 6, with 24 abstentions, respectively. The Assembly retained the paragraph and the words by recorded votes of 135 to 8, with 27 abstentions, and 129 to 4, with 31 abstentions, respectively.

Sale of children, child prostitution and child pornography

Reports of Special Rapporteur. In response to a 2002 Commission request [YUN 2002, p. 757], the Special Rapporteur on the sale of children, child prostitution and child pornography, Juan Miguel Petit (Uruguay), submitted a January report [E/CN.4/2003/79] on the legal consequences of the problem, particularly the criminalization of child victims and recent national policy and legislative developments addressing those concerns. The report was based on 97 responses to the Special Rapporteur's request for information from Governments, international organizations and NGOs, of which 53 were summarized in the report. The report summarized communications sent to five Governments concerning individual or country-specific complaints, of which two were sent jointly with the Special Rapporteur on violence against women (see p. 777) and one with the Working Group on Arbitrary Detention (see p. 733). The Special Rapporteur also focused on illegal or coercive adoption practices and the relationship between HIV/AIDS and sexual exploitation. He stated that, although criminal liability for crimes against children was being strengthened, the treatment of child victims, especially when they were placed in protective custody, continued to have a punitive effect. He pointed to a continuing lack of data concerning the nature and extent of the sale of children, child prostitution and child pornography, noting that in many countries those offences were not criminalized. There was an alarming lack of child rights training for law enforcement officials and members of the judiciary, even in some developed countries. The Special Rapporteur recommended giving special protection to child victims of sexual exploitation, penalizing those who sexually abused or exploited children, or who profited from such crimes, and making accessible to children education, information and services to enable them to make informed choices about their future sexual behaviour.

An October report [E/CN.4/2004/9/Add.1] of the Special Rapporteur, which focused on the sale of children in the context of trafficking and child prostitution, and on child pornography and its links with domestic child sexual abuse, supplemented the conclusions and recommendations contained in his report on his 2002 visit to France [YUN 2002, p. 757].

The Special Rapporteur visited Brazil (3-14 November) [E/CN.4/2004/9/Add.2], where he focused on child sexual exploitation, which was linked to social problems such as poverty, social exclusion, child labour, gender discrimination and violence. The victims were predominantly female and adolescent Afro-Brazilians, of whom the most targeted were between 15 and 17 years old. The Government's commitment to fight child sexual exploitation was strong. However, filtering related policies and programmes to the grass-roots level posed a major difficulty, as did the ineffectiveness of the Statute for the Child and Adolescent (ECA), designed as the framework for protecting children's rights. The Special Rapporteur recommended as a priority measure steps towards the full implementation of ECA, as well as combating impunity through the reform of the police and judiciary; promoting the role of public defenders in protecting children's rights; reforming juvenile detention centres; extending assistance programmes to cover sexually exploited children; addressing the root causes of sexual exploitation by strengthening social programmes aimed at reducing poverty and social inequalities in ways that were relevant to children's rights; and focusing on education.

Commission action. On 25 April [res. 2003/86], the Commission called on States to take measures to prevent and combat the trafficking and sale of children and to criminalize and penalize all forms of sexual exploitation and abuse of children, child pornography and child prostitution, child sex tourism, the sale of children and their organs and the use of the Internet for those purposes. The Special Rapporteur was asked to report in 2004.

Child labour

On 25 April [res. 2003/86], the Commission called on States to eliminate child labour that was hazardous, interfered with a child's education or was harmful to the child's health, and to promote education as a key strategy. It also called on them to consider ratifying and implementing ILO Convention No. 182 concerning the prohibition and elimination of the worst forms of child labour (Worst Forms of Child Labour Convention), adopted in 1999 [YUN 1999, p. 1388], and Convention No. 138 concerning the minimum, age for employment (Minimum Age Convention), adopted in 1973 [YUN 1973, p. 885].

Children and armed conflict

On 30 January [meeting 4695], the Security Council unanimously adopted **resolution 1460 (2003)**. The draft [S/2003/112] was prepared in consultations with Council members.

The Security Council,

Reaffirming its resolutions 1261(1999) of 25 August 1999, 1314(2000) of 11 August 2000 and 1379(2001) of 20 November 2001, which provide a comprehensive framework for addressing the protection of children affected by armed conflict,

Recalling its resolutions 1265(1999) of 17 September 1999, 1296(2000) of 19 April 2000, 1306(2000) of 5 July 2000, 1308(2000) of 17 July 2000, and 1325(2000) of 31 October 2000, as well as all statements by its President on children and armed conflict, and taking note of the report of the Secretary-General of 16 October 2002 on women, peace and security,

Reiterating its primary responsibility for the maintenance of international peace and security and, in this connection, its commitment to address the widespread impact of armed conflict on children,

Underlining the need for all parties concerned to comply with the provisions of the Charter of the United Nations and international law, in particular those regarding children,

Emphasizing the responsibilities of States to end impunity and to prosecute those responsible for genocide, crimes against humanity, war crimes and other egregious crimes perpetrated against children,

Underlining the importance of the full, safe and unhindered access of humanitarian personnel and goods and the delivery of humanitarian assistance to all children affected by armed conflict,

Welcoming the entry into force on 12 February 2002 of the Optional Protocol to the Convention on the Rights of the Child on the involvement of children in armed conflict,

Noting the fact that the conscription or enlistment of children under the age of 15 into the national armed forces or using them to participate actively in hostilities is classified as a war crime by the Rome Statute of the International Criminal Court, which recently entered into force,

Having considered the report of the Secretary-General of 26 November 2002 on the implementation of, inter alia, its resolution 1379(2001),

1. *Supports* the call of the Secretary-General for "an era of application" of international norms and standards for the protection of children affected by armed conflict;

2. *Encourages* the agencies, funds and programmes of the United Nations, within their respective mandates, to strengthen their cooperation and their coordination when addressing the protection of children in armed conflict;

3. *Calls upon* all parties to armed conflict who are recruiting or using children in violation of the international obligations applicable to them to halt immediately such recruitment or use of children;

4. *Expresses its intention* to enter into dialogue, as appropriate, or to support the Secretary-General in entering into dialogue with parties to armed conflict in violation of the international obligations applicable to them on the recruitment or use of children in armed conflict, in order to develop clear and time-bound action plans to end this practice;

5. *Notes with concern* the list annexed to the report of the Secretary-General, and calls upon the parties identified in this list to provide information on steps they have taken to halt their recruitment or use of children in armed conflict in violation of the international obligations applicable to them to the Special Representative of the Secretary-General for Children and Armed Conflict, bearing in mind the provisions of paragraph 9 of its resolution 1379(2001);

6. *Expresses, accordingly, its intention* to consider taking appropriate steps further to address this issue, in accordance with the Charter of the United Nations and its resolution 1379(2001), if it deems that insufficient progress has been made upon the review of the next report of the Secretary-General;

7. *Urges* Member States, in accordance with the Programme of Action to Prevent, Combat and Eradicate the Illicit Trade in Small Arms and Light Weapons in All Its Aspects, to take effective action through, inter alia, conflict resolution and the development and implementation of national legislation, in a manner

which is consistent with existing responsibilities of States under relevant international law, to control the illicit trade of small arms to parties in armed conflict that do not respect fully the relevant provisions of applicable international law relating to the rights and protection of children in armed conflict;

8. *Calls upon* States to respect fully the relevant provisions of applicable international humanitarian law relating to the rights and protection of children in armed conflict, in particular the four Geneva Conventions of 12 August 1949, inter alia, the Geneva Convention relative to the Protection of Civilian Persons in Time of War;

9. *Reiterates its determination* to continue to include specific provisions for the protection of children in the mandates of United Nations peacekeeping operations, including provisions recommending child protection advisers on a case-by-case basis and training for United Nations and associated personnel on child protection and child rights;

10. *Notes with concern* all the cases of sexual exploitation and abuse of women and children, especially girls, in humanitarian crisis, including those cases involving humanitarian workers and peacekeepers, and requests contributing countries to incorporate the six core principles of the Inter-Agency Standing Committee on Emergencies into pertinent codes of conduct for peacekeeping personnel and to develop appropriate disciplinary and accountability mechanisms;

11. *Requests* the agencies, funds and programmes of the United Nations, with support from contributing countries, to implement HIV/AIDS education and offer HIV testing and counselling services for all United Nations peacekeepers, police and humanitarian personnel;

12. *Calls upon* all concerned parties to ensure that the protection, rights and well-being of children are integrated into the peace processes, peace agreements and the post-conflict recovery and reconstruction phases;

13. *Calls upon* Member States and international organizations to ensure that children affected by armed conflict are involved in all disarmament, demobilization and reintegration processes, taking into account the specific needs and capacities of girls, and that the duration of these processes is sufficient for a successful transition to normal life, with a particular emphasis on education, including the monitoring, through, inter alia, schools, of children demobilized in order to prevent re-recruitment;

14. *Calls upon* parties involved in armed conflict to abide by the concrete commitments they have made to the Special Representative of the Secretary-General for Children and Armed Conflict and to cooperate fully with the United Nations system in the implementation of their commitments;

15. *Requests* the Secretary-General to ensure that, in all his reports to the Council on country-specific situations, the protection of children in armed conflict is included as a specific aspect of the report;

16. *Also requests* the Secretary-General to submit a report by 31 October 2003 on the implementation of the present resolution and of its resolution 1379(2001) which would include, inter alia:

(a) Progress made by the parties listed in the annex to his report in ending the recruitment or use of children in armed conflict in violation of international obligations applicable to them, taking into account the parties to other armed conflicts that recruit or use children which are mentioned in the report in accordance with paragraph 16 of resolution 1379(2001);

(b) An assessment of violations of rights and abuses of children in armed conflict, including in the context of illicit exploitation and trafficking of natural resources and of illicit trafficking of small arms in conflict zones;

(c) Specific proposals on ways to ensure monitoring and reporting in a more effective and efficient way within the existing United Nations system on the application of the international norms and standards for the protection of children in situations of armed conflict in all its various aspects;

(d) Best practices on integrating the specific needs of children in armed conflict into disarmament, demobilization, rehabilitation and reintegration programmes, including an assessment of child protection advisers in peacekeeping and peace-building support operations, and on negotiations aimed at ending the recruitment or use of children in armed conflict in violation of international obligations applicable to the parties concerned;

17. *Decides* to remain actively seized of this matter.

Report of Special Representative. In accordance with General Assembly resolution 51/77 [YUN 1996, p. 665], the Secretary-General's Special Representative for Children and Armed Conflict, Olara A. Otunnu (Côte d'Ivoire), in a March report [E/CN.4/2003/77], outlined progress and new developments regarding the situation of children affected by armed conflict. He described the activities of his Office relating to impunity and to bring to justice violators of children's rights in conflict situations, the engagement of youth in tackling the issue, the work of the Inter-Agency Working Group on the Incorporation of Child Protection in United Nations Peacemaking, Peacekeeping and Peace-building Processes and of the Inter-Agency Standing Committee Task Force on Prevention of Sexual Exploitation, deployment of child protection advisers, the impact on children of the illicit commercial exploitation of natural resources in conflict zones, the activities of relevant regional and subregional organizations and arrangements, field missions, and the work of the Committee on the Rights of the Child on Guinea-Bissau and of the Commission. The Special Representative urged the UN system to consider the issue of war-affected children as a cross-cutting theme in agendas and to coordinate efforts in that regard.

Commission action. On 25 April [res. 2003/86], the Commission called on States to end the use of children in armed conflicts and, together with parties to armed conflict, to respect international humanitarian law. It asked States, UN bodies and agencies and regional organizations to integrate the rights of the child in all activities in conflict and post-conflict situations and to support national and international mine-action efforts.

Further reports of Special Representative. In response to General Assembly resolution 57/190 [YUN 2002, p. 749], the Secretary-General, in August, transmitted a report of the Special Representative [A/58/328 & Corr.1], which further reviewed progress achieved since his appointment by Assembly resolution 52/107 [YUN 1997, p. 687] and proposed a course of action for the next three years. He said that, although the international community possessed unprecedented means and collective influence that could be brought to bear on parties in conflict to ensure the observance of relevant standards, children continued to be abused and brutalized worldwide on a massive and horrendous scale. The most pressing challenge facing the international community was to galvanize and unify that collective influence into a coherent and concerted project to serve as an effective regime of protection for war-affected children. For that purpose, the Special Representative proposed an agenda for action, which encompassed two interrelated tasks: the first was to ensure that the initiatives and gains made over the past several years were consolidated and institutionalized, and the second involved the imperative of embarking on the era of application. Specific measures relating to the proposed agenda were outlined in the report.

In a 20 October statement to the Third Committee [A/C.3/58/SR.18], the Special Representative, reflecting on the extension of his mandate, further reviewed the progress achieved by his Office and the constraints it had faced.

Report of Secretary-General. Pursuant to Security Council resolution 1460(2003) (see p. 788), the Secretary-General, in a November report [A/58/546-S/2003/1053 & Corr.1, 2], described advances made to protect children affected by armed conflict. He made proposals for systematic monitoring, reporting and action. In order to deepen and sustain progress made, and to strengthen the foundation of the "era of application", the Secretary-General recommended the incorporation of children's issues into all peace negotiations, accords and post-conflict programmes; the inclusion of child protection in the mandates of all UN peace operations; the development of a systematic and concerted monitoring and reporting mechanism to provide objective, regular and accurate reports on violations against children by parties to conflict; the deployment of child protection advisers in peace operations; encouraging regional organizations to strengthen their activities for war-affected children, particularly advocacy, cross-border initiatives, monitoring and peer review; targeting measures against parties responsible for and complicit in the illicit exploitation of natural resources and, in that context, establishing an effective monitoring mechanism for the application of the certification scheme under the Kimberley Process (the regime established in 2000 to stem the illicit flow of rough diamonds used to finance armed conflict and to protect the legitimate diamond industry [YUN 2000, p. 76]). Other recommendations for action by the Council included travel restrictions, a ban on arms supply and military assistance, and restricting the flow of financial resources in cases where insufficient or no progress had been made by parties in adhering to its resolutions 1379 (2001) [YUN 2001, p. 684] and 1460(2003); updating annually the list of parties that recruited or used children in armed conflict, of which a currently updated version was annexed to the report; specific steps to ensure that persons responsible for crimes against children were prosecuted by the International Criminal Court; and deploying greater and more concerted efforts to end ongoing conflicts, which were destroying the lives of millions of children, and addressing the key factors that facilitated those conflicts.

GENERAL ASSEMBLY ACTION

On 23 December [meeting 79], the General Assembly, on the recommendation of the Third Committee [A/58/504], adopted **resolution 58/245** by recorded vote (115-20-28) [agenda item 113].

Office of the Special Representative of the Secretary-General for Children and Armed Conflict

The General Assembly,

Recalling paragraphs 35 to 37 of its resolution 51/77 of 12 December 1996 on the rights of the child, in which the mandate of the Special Representative of the Secretary-General for Children and Armed Conflict was established,

Recalling also its resolution 57/190 of 18 December 2002, in which it requested the Secretary-General to undertake a comprehensive assessment of the scope and effectiveness of the United Nations system response to the issue of children affected by armed conflict, including recommendations for strengthening, mainstreaming, integrating and sustaining those activities,

Taking note of the report of the Special Representative of the Secretary-General for Children and Armed Conflict and his oral statement to the Third Committee of the General Assembly on 20 October 2003,

Recalling the role of the General Assembly in promoting the protection of children affected by armed conflict,

Recognizing the progress achieved since the establishment of the mandate of the Special Representative and the recommendation by which the Secretary-General extended the mandate of the Special Representative for a further period of three years,

Commending the support and the voluntary contributions of donor countries for the work of the Special Representative in the fulfilment of his mandate,

Expressing concern about the financial instability of the Office of the Special Representative and its adverse impact on the implementation of the mandate,

Decides that the activities under the mandate of the Special Representative of the Secretary-General for Children and Armed Conflict shall be supported through regular budgetary funding.

RECORDED VOTE ON RESOLUTION 58/245:

In favour: Algeria, Angola, Antigua and Barbuda, Armenia, Austria, Azerbaijan, Bahrain, Bangladesh, Belarus, Belize, Benin, Bolivia, Botswana, Brunei Darussalam, Burkina Faso, Burundi, Cambodia, Cameroon, Cape Verde, Central African Republic, Chile, China, Colombia, Comoros, Congo, Costa Rica, Côte d'Ivoire, Cuba, Cyprus, Democratic People's Republic of Korea, Djibouti, Dominica, Dominican Republic, Ecuador, Egypt, Eritrea, Ethiopia, France, Gabon, Gambia, Ghana, Greece, Grenada, Guatemala, Guyana, Haiti, Honduras, India, Indonesia, Iran, Ireland, Italy, Jamaica, Jordan, Kenya, Kuwait, Lao People's Democratic Republic, Lebanon, Lesotho, Libyan Arab Jamahiriya, Liechtenstein, Madagascar, Malawi, Malaysia, Maldives, Mali, Malta, Mauritania, Mauritius, Mexico, Monaco, Morocco, Mozambique, Myanmar, Namibia, Nepal, Nicaragua, Niger, Nigeria, Oman, Pakistan, Papua New Guinea, Peru, Philippines, Qatar, Romania, Russian Federation, Rwanda, Saint Lucia, Saudi Arabia, Senegal, Singapore, Slovenia, Somalia, South Africa, Sri Lanka, Sudan, Suriname, Syrian Arab Republic, Thailand, Timor-Leste, Togo, Tonga, Trinidad and Tobago, Tunisia, Turkmenistan, Ukraine, United Arab Emirates, United Republic of Tanzania, Uruguay, Uzbekistan, Viet Nam, Yemen, Zambia, Zimbabwe.

Against: Australia, Belgium, Canada, Denmark, Finland, Georgia, Germany, Iceland, Israel, Japan, Lithuania, Luxembourg, Netherlands, New Zealand, Poland, Sweden, Switzerland, Uganda, United Kingdom, United States.

Abstaining: Albania, Andorra, Argentina, Bosnia and Herzegovina, Brazil, Bulgaria, Croatia, Czech Republic, Estonia, Fiji, Hungary, Latvia, Mongolia, Norway, Panama, Paraguay, Portugal, Republic of Korea, Republic of Moldova, San Marino, Serbia and Montenegro, Slovakia, Solomon Islands, Spain, The former Yugoslav Republic of Macedonia, Turkey, Tuvalu, Venezuela.

Abduction of children in Africa

On 25 April [res. 2003/85], the Commission, deeply alarmed at the spread of the practice of abduction of children during armed conflicts in many African countries, demanded the immediate demobilization and disarmament of child soldiers and the unconditional release and safe return of those abducted. The Commission called on African States to prohibit and criminalize such practices and asked them, in cooperation with UN agencies, to assist the victims and their families and to support sustainable rehabilitation and reintegration programmes for them, taking into account the special needs of abducted girls. The donor community was called on to provide financial assistance to existing national mechanisms in African countries, with a view to complementing national efforts.

Freedom of movement

Mass exoduses

Report of High Commissioner. In response to a 2000 Commission request [YUN 2000, p. 688], the High Commissioner, in a January report [E/CN.4/2003/84], described activities carried out by OHCHR, Member States, UN bodies, specialized agencies and other organizations to address the problem of mass exoduses. The High Commissioner said that, although the international community had become more aware of the global problem of mass exoduses and displacements, there was a need to further strengthen efforts and for worldwide cooperation and assistance to address those situations.

Commission action. On 24 April [res. 2003/52], the Commission requested the High Commissioner to pay particular attention to human rights situations that caused or threatened to cause mass exoduses and to contribute to efforts to address such situations through promotion and protection measures, emergency preparedness and response mechanisms, early warning and information-sharing, technical advice and expertise and cooperation in countries of origin and host countries. He was further asked to report in 2005, taking into account information and comments provided by Governments, intergovernmental organizations, specialized agencies and NGOs, and to annex to the report a thematic compilation of relevant Commission and Subcommission reports and resolutions.

Reports of Secretary-General. Pursuant to General Assembly resolution 56/166 [YUN 2001, p. 651], the Secretary-General, in a July report [A/58/186] on human rights and mass exoduses, described UN efforts to protect and assist those displaced during mass exoduses and to facilitate their return and reintegration. The report contained information on continuing efforts to enhance the UN capacity to avert new flows of refugees and other displaced persons and to tackle the root causes of such flows. The Secretary-General said that human rights violations were a cause of mass exoduses. The United Nations, through technical cooperation, peacekeeping operations and development programmes, played a central role in ensuring that the human rights situations in places of origin were suitable for the return and reintegration of displaced persons. It also had at its disposal mechanisms that could provide crucial early warning information. The challenge for the United Nations was to implement effectively action plans to assist States and avert mass exoduses.

An October bulletin of the Secretary-General [ST/SGB/2003/13], taking into account General Assembly resolution 57/306 (see p. 1237) on the sexual exploitation of refugees by aid workers in West Africa, presented special measures for protection from sexual exploitation and abuse.

GENERAL ASSEMBLY ACTION

On 22 December [meeting 77], the General Assembly, on the recommendation of the Third Committee [A/58/508/Add.2], adopted **resolution 58/169** without vote [agenda item 117 (b)].

Human rights and mass exoduses

The General Assembly,

Deeply disturbed by the scale and magnitude of exoduses and displacements of people in many regions of the world and by the human suffering of refugees and displaced persons, a high proportion of whom are women and children,

Recalling its previous resolutions on this subject, as well as those of the Commission on Human Rights, and the conclusions of the World Conference on Human Rights, which recognized, inter alia, that gross violations of human rights, persecution, political and ethnic conflicts, famine and economic insecurity, poverty and generalized violence are among the root causes leading to mass exoduses and displacements of people,

Mindful of the open debates that have been held within the Security Council on the protection of civilians in armed conflict, the three reports of the Secretary-General on that subject and the related resolutions adopted,

Reaffirming the continuing relevance of the provisions of the 1951 Convention relating to the Status of Refugees and the 1967 Protocol thereto to the situation of people in mass exoduses, and welcoming in this respect the process of Global Consultations on International Protection and the Agenda for Protection and other follow-up processes endorsed by States as a result, which sought, inter alia, to strengthen international responses to mass influx situations,

Welcoming the increased attention being given by the United Nations to the problem of refugee camp security, including through the development of operational guidelines on the separation of armed elements from refugee populations, and the increasing attention to registration and camp layout and design,

Stressing the importance of adherence to international humanitarian, human rights and refugee law in order to avert mass exoduses and to protect refugees and internally displaced persons, and expressing its deep concern at the lack of respect for those laws and principles, especially during armed conflict, including the denial of safe and unimpeded access to the displaced,

Reaffirming the primary responsibility of States to ensure the protection of refugees and internally displaced persons,

Noting with satisfaction the efforts of the United Nations system to develop a comprehensive approach to addressing the root causes and effects of movements of refugees and other displaced persons and strengthening emergency preparedness and response mechanisms,

Recognizing that the human rights machinery of the United Nations, including the mechanisms of the Commission on Human Rights and the human rights treaty bodies, has important capabilities to address human rights violations that cause movements of refugees and displaced persons or prevent durable solutions to their plight,

Taking note of the work in progress of the United Nations system to clarify the role of the United Nations in post-conflict transition situations, including mass exodus situations,

Recognizing the complementarity between the systems for the protection of human rights and for humanitarian action, in particular the mandates of the United Nations High Commissioner for Human Rights and the United Nations High Commissioner for Refugees, as well as the work of the Office for the Coordination of Humanitarian Affairs of the Secretariat, the Representative of the Secretary-General on internally displaced persons and the Special Representative of the Secretary-General for Children and Armed Conflict, and that cooperation between them, in accordance with their respective mandates, as well as coordination between the human rights, humanitarian, development, political and security components of the United Nations system, makes important contributions to the promotion and protection of the human rights of persons forced into mass exodus and displacement,

Acknowledging with appreciation the important and independent work of the International Red Cross and Red Crescent Movement and other humanitarian agencies in protecting and assisting refugees and internally displaced persons, in cooperation with relevant international bodies,

1. *Takes note* of the report of the Secretary-General;

2. *Strongly deplores* ethnic and other forms of intolerance as one of the major causes of forced migratory movements, and urges States to take all necessary steps to ensure respect for human rights, especially the rights of persons belonging to minorities;

3. *Reaffirms* the need for all Governments, intergovernmental bodies and relevant international organizations to intensify their cooperation and assistance in worldwide efforts to address human rights situations that lead to, as well as the serious protection and assistance problems that result from, mass exoduses of refugees and displaced persons;

4. *Urges* the Secretary-General to continue to give high priority to the consolidation and strengthening of emergency preparedness and response mechanisms, including early warning activities in the humanitarian area, so that, inter alia, effective action is taken to identify all human rights abuses that contribute to mass exoduses of persons;

5. *Encourages* States that have not already done so to consider acceding to the 1951 Convention and the 1967 Protocol relating to the Status of Refugees and to other relevant regional instruments concerning refugees, as applicable, and relevant international instruments of human rights and humanitarian law, to take appropriate measures to disseminate and implement those instruments domestically, to encourage compliance with provisions against arbitrary and forcible displacement and greater respect for the rights of those who flee and, as appropriate, to address the situation of the forcibly displaced in their reports to the human rights treaty bodies;

6. *Calls upon* States to ensure the effective protection of refugees by, inter alia, respecting the principle of non-refoulement, emphasizes the responsibility of all States and international organizations to cooperate with those countries, particularly developing countries, which are affected by mass exoduses of refugees and displaced persons, and also calls upon all relevant

international and non-governmental organizations to continue to respond to the assistance and protection needs of refugees and displaced persons, including through the promotion of durable solutions to their plight;

7. *Urges* States to uphold the civilian and humanitarian character of refugee camps and settlements, consistent with international law, inter alia, through effective measures to prevent the infiltration of armed elements, to identify and separate any such armed elements from refugee populations, to settle refugees at safe locations, where possible away from the border, and to afford prompt and unhindered access to them by humanitarian personnel;

8. *Condemns* all incidents of sexual exploitation and abuse and violence against refugees and internally displaced persons, encourages Governments to adopt and implement initiatives aimed at preventing, and at addressing allegations of, sexual exploitation and abuse in emergency situations, and calls upon all relevant United Nations agencies to ensure the effective implementation and monitoring of the Secretary-General's bulletin, the Inter-Agency Standing Committee Plan of Action on Protection from Sexual Exploitation and Abuse in Humanitarian Crises and other relevant codes of conduct;

9. *Encourages* the special rapporteurs, special representatives and working groups of the Commission on Human Rights and the United Nations human rights treaty bodies, acting within their mandates, to seek information, where appropriate, on human rights problems that may result in mass exoduses of populations or impede their voluntary return home, where appropriate, to include such information, together with recommendations thereon, in their reports and to bring such information to the attention of the United Nations High Commissioner for Human Rights for appropriate action in fulfilment of his mandate, in consultation with the United Nations High Commissioner for Refugees;

10. *Requests* all United Nations bodies, acting within their mandates, the specialized agencies and governmental, intergovernmental and non-governmental organizations to cooperate fully with all mechanisms of the Commission on Human Rights and, in particular, to provide them with all relevant information in their possession on the human rights situations creating or affecting refugees and displaced persons, and to exchange such information among themselves, within their mandates, in order to encourage effective international responses;

11. *Requests* the United Nations High Commissioner for Human Rights, in the exercise of his mandate, as set out in General Assembly resolution 48/141 of 20 December 1993, and in cooperation with the United Nations High Commissioner for Refugees, to pay particular attention to situations that cause or threaten to cause mass exoduses or displacements and to contribute to efforts to address such situations effectively and promote sustainable returns through promotion and protection measures, including human rights monitoring of those who have fled or returned as part of mass exoduses, emergency preparedness and response mechanisms, early warning and information-sharing, technical advice, expertise and cooperation in countries of origin as well as host countries;

12. *Welcomes* the efforts of the United Nations High Commissioner for Human Rights to contribute to the creation of a viable environment for the sustainable return of displaced persons in post-conflict societies, working in cooperation with the States concerned, through initiatives such as the rehabilitation of the justice system, the creation of national institutions capable of defending human rights and broad-based programmes of human rights education and the strengthening of local non-governmental organizations through field presences and programmes of advisory services and technical cooperation;

13. *Requests* the Secretary-General to prepare and submit to the General Assembly at its sixtieth session a report on the implementation of the present resolution as it pertains to all aspects of human rights and mass exoduses, with particular emphasis on the efforts of the United Nations system to enhance the protection of those who become displaced during mass exoduses, and to facilitate their return and reintegration, as well as information on efforts to continue to enhance the capacity of the United Nations to avert new flows of refugees and other displaced persons and to tackle the root causes of such flows;

14. *Decides* to continue its consideration of this question at its sixtieth session.

Internally displaced persons

Report of Secretary-General's Representative. In January [E/CN.4/2003/86], the Secretary-General's Representative, Francis M. Deng (Sudan), updated developments regarding the promotion, dissemination and application of the Guiding Principles on Internal Displacement [YUN 1998, p. 675] and efforts to develop an institutional framework for internally displaced persons. He gave an overview of the progress made over the preceding decade and the remaining challenges in responding effectively to the global crisis of internal displacement, as well as the evolution of the international response and activities he had undertaken. Overall, he said, important progress had been made, as reflected particularly in a heightened worldwide awareness of the problem, the development and increasing use of the Guiding Principles, the development of policies at the international, regional and national levels, and various improvements in institutional arrangements and response. However, internal displacement remained a worldwide crisis of epic proportions, affecting some 25 million people, of whom many were without adequate assistance and protection.

Commission action. On 23 April [res. 2003/51], the Commission called on the High Commissioner, in cooperation with Governments, the Representative and other relevant parts of the UN system, to promote the rights of internally displaced persons, enhance their protection and develop projects to address their plight as part of the programme of technical cooperation and advisory services (see p. 678), and to provide information thereon to the Representative for inclusion in his report. The Representative was asked to continue to report on his activities and the Secretary-General to assist him.

Further reports of Representative. In Uganda (10-16 August) [E/CN.4/2004/77/Add.1], where an estimated 1.4 million persons had been displaced mainly by conflict between the Government and the Lord's Resistance Army, the Representative, among other things, consulted with the Government on a proposed national policy on internal displacement. The Representative said Uganda's internal displacement problem, largely neglected outside the country and described as a "forgotten crisis", was one of the world's gravest humanitarian crises, and recommended that the Government adopt its draft policy on the issue and ensure its quick and effective implementation. He further recommended that the Government consider all options for durable solutions and encouraged support by UN, international humanitarian and development organizations, and international donors and other actors.

The Representative summarized the proceedings of an experts' meeting on internal displacement (Khartoum, Sudan, 30 August-1 September) [E/CN.4/2004/77/Add.4], which he had organized in cooperation with the Inter-Governmental Authority on Development (IGAD) and the UN Office for the Coordination of Humanitarian Affairs, at which participants adopted recommendations that formed the basis for the Khartoum Declaration on Internally Displaced Persons in the IGAD Subregion, adopted on 2 September by Ministers of IGAD member States (Djibouti, Eritrea, Ethiopia, Kenya, Somalia, Sudan, Uganda).

The Representative visited the Russian Federation (7-13 September) [E/CN.4/2004/77/Add.2], where hundreds of thousands of persons had been displaced by the conflict in the Chechen Republic and other conflicts elsewhere in the Federation. In the Northern Caucasus (Chechnya and Ingushetia), the Representative engaged the Government, international agencies, NGOs and other relevant actors in a dialogue aimed at ensuring effective responses to internal displacement, and encouraged the various actors to make increased use of the Guiding Principles. The Representative recommended that all actors, particularly the Government, give due consideration to the programme of action adopted at the International Conference on Internal Displacement in the Russian Federation [YUN 2002, p. 761]. He proposed that the Government improve relations between ethnic and national groups in areas of integration, and guarantee that international humanitarian principles regarding the safety of humanitarian workers would be respected and upheld. Further areas for action were presented to the Governments of the Russian Federation, Ingushetia and Chechnya to improve the situation.

In a September report [A/58/393], submitted pursuant to General Assembly resolution 56/164 [YUN 2001, p. 654] and Commission resolution 2003/51 (see p. 793), the Representative further reviewed progress made in addressing the global crisis of internal displacement and outlined the challenges ahead. He noted that significant progress had been made with regard to norm-setting, institutional arrangements and operational responses to the needs of the internally displaced, but that the most progress had been made on the Principles, which were widely accepted. However, there remained a disturbing gap between expressed commitments and actual national and international action. There was a need, said the Representative, for a more thorough appraisal of the system of assistance and protection, and its operations.

Communication. On 14 March [E/CN.4/2003/G/56], Mexico transmitted its comments regarding the Representative's report on his visit to the country [YUN 2002, p. 760].

GENERAL ASSEMBLY ACTION

On 22 December [meeting 77], the General Assembly, on the recommendation of the Third Committee [A/58/508/Add.2], adopted **resolution 58/177** without vote [agenda item 117 (b)].

Protection of and assistance to internally displaced persons

The General Assembly,

Deeply disturbed by the alarmingly high numbers of internally displaced persons throughout the world, for reasons including armed conflict, violations of human rights and natural or human-made disasters, who receive inadequate protection and assistance, and conscious of the serious challenges that this is creating for the international community,

Conscious of the human rights and the humanitarian dimensions of the problem of internally displaced persons and the responsibilities of States and the international community to strengthen further their protection and assistance,

Emphasizing that States have the primary responsibility to provide protection and assistance to internally displaced persons within their jurisdiction as well as to address the root causes of the displacement problem in cooperation with the international community,

Noting the growing awareness of the international community of the issue of internally displaced persons worldwide and the urgency of addressing the root causes of their displacement and finding durable solutions, including voluntary return in safety and with dignity, or local integration,

Recalling the relevant norms of international human rights law, international humanitarian law and international refugee law, and recognizing that the protection of internally displaced persons has been strengthened by identifying, reaffirming and consolidating specific standards for their protection, in particular through the Guiding Principles on Internal Displacement,

Emphasizing the central role of the Emergency Relief Coordinator for the inter-agency coordination of protection of and assistance to internally displaced persons, and welcoming initiatives taken in order to ensure better protection, assistance and development strategies for internally displaced persons, as well as better coordination of activities regarding them,

Commending the Representative of the Secretary-General on internally displaced persons for the activities undertaken so far, for the catalytic role that he plays in raising the level of consciousness about the plight of internally displaced persons and for his efforts to promote a comprehensive strategy that focuses on prevention as well as better protection and assistance and addressing the development needs of internally displaced persons,

Taking note of Commission on Human Rights resolution 2003/51 of 23 April 2003, and recalling the Vienna Declaration and Programme of Action, adopted by the World Conference on Human Rights on 25 June 1993, regarding the need to develop global strategies to address the problem of internal displacement,

Deploring practices of forced displacement and their negative consequences for the enjoyment of human rights and fundamental freedoms by large groups of populations, and noting that the Rome Statute of the International Criminal Court defines the deportation or forcible transfer of population as a crime against humanity and the unlawful deportation or transfer of the civilian population, as well as ordering the displacement of the civilian population, as war crimes,

Noting the increasing dissemination, promotion and application of the Guiding Principles on Internal Displacement when dealing with situations of internal displacement,

Welcoming the cooperation established between the Representative of the Secretary-General and the United Nations and other international and regional organizations, and encouraging further strengthening of this collaboration in order to promote better protection, assistance and development strategies for internally displaced persons,

Acknowledging with appreciation the important and independent contribution of the International Red Cross and Red Crescent Movement and other humanitarian agencies in protecting and assisting internally displaced persons, in cooperation with relevant international bodies,

Recalling its resolution 56/164 of 19 December 2001,

1. *Welcomes* the report of the Representative of the Secretary-General on internally displaced persons;

2. *Expresses its appreciation* to those Governments and intergovernmental and non-governmental organizations that have provided protection and assistance to internally displaced persons and have supported the work of the Representative of the Secretary-General;

3. *Encourages* the Representative of the Secretary-General, through continuous dialogue with Governments and all intergovernmental and non-governmental organizations concerned, to continue his analysis of the causes of internal displacement, the needs and rights of those displaced, measures of prevention and ways to strengthen protection, assistance and solutions for internally displaced persons, taking into account specific situations, and to include information thereon in his reports to the Commission on Human Rights and the General Assembly;

4. *Expresses particular concern* at the grave problems faced by many internally displaced women and children, including violence and abuse, sexual exploitation, forced recruitment and abduction, and welcomes the commitment of the Representative of the Secretary-General to pay more systematic and in-depth attention to their particular assistance, protection and development needs, as well as to other groups with special needs such as older persons and persons with disabilities, taking into account the relevant resolutions of the General Assembly and bearing in mind Security Council resolution 1325(2000) of 31 October 2000;

5. *Notes with appreciation* the increasing role of national human rights institutions in assisting internally displaced persons and in promoting and protecting their human rights;

6. *Notes* the importance of taking the human rights and the specific protection and assistance needs of internally displaced persons into consideration, when appropriate, in peace processes and reintegration and rehabilitation processes;

7. *Expresses its appreciation* of the Guiding Principles on Internal Displacement as an important tool for dealing with situations of internal displacement, welcomes the fact that an increasing number of States, United Nations agencies and regional and non-governmental organizations are applying them as a standard, and encourages all relevant actors to make use of the Guiding Principles when dealing with situations of internal displacement;

8. *Welcomes* the fact that the Representative of the Secretary-General continues to use the Guiding Principles in his dialogue with Governments and intergovernmental and non-governmental organizations and other relevant actors, and requests him to continue his efforts to further the dissemination, promotion and application of the Guiding Principles;

9. *Urges* all Governments to continue to facilitate the activities of the Representative of the Secretary-General, in particular Governments with situations of internal displacement, and to give serious consideration to inviting the Representative to visit their countries so as to enable him to study and analyse more fully the issues involved, and thanks those Governments that have already done so;

10. *Invites* Governments to give serious consideration, in dialogue with the Representative of the Secretary-General, to the recommendations and suggestions addressed to them, in accordance with his mandate, and to inform him of measures taken thereon;

11. *Calls upon* Governments to provide protection and assistance, including reintegration and development assistance, to internally displaced persons, and to

facilitate the efforts of relevant United Nations agencies and humanitarian organizations in these respects, including by further improving access to internally displaced persons;

12. *Emphasizes* the central role of the Emergency Relief Coordinator for the inter-agency coordination of protection of and assistance to internally displaced persons, notes the work of the Internal Displacement Unit within the Office for the Coordination of Humanitarian Affairs of the Secretariat, and encourages further strengthening of the collaboration with the Representative of the Secretary-General in line with the memorandum of understanding of 17 April 2002 between the Representative and the Emergency Relief Coordinator;

13. *Emphasizes also* the need to strengthen further inter-agency arrangements and the capacities of the United Nations agencies and other relevant actors to meet the immense humanitarian challenges of internal displacement, and underlines in this regard the importance of an effective, accountable and predictable collaborative approach;

14. *Encourages* all relevant United Nations agencies and humanitarian assistance, human rights and development organizations to enhance further their collaboration and coordination, through the Inter-Agency Standing Committee and in countries with situations of internal displacement, and to provide all possible assistance and support to the Representative of the Secretary-General;

15. *Notes with appreciation* the increased attention paid to the issue of internally displaced persons in the consolidated inter-agency appeals process, and encourages further efforts in this regard;

16. *Recognizes* the relevance of the global database on internally displaced persons advocated by the Representative of the Secretary-General, and encourages the members of the Inter-Agency Standing Committee and Governments to continue to collaborate and support this effort, including by providing relevant data on situations of internal displacement and financial resources;

17. *Welcomes* the initiatives undertaken by regional organizations, such as the African Union, the Organization of American States, the Organization for Security and Cooperation in Europe, the Intergovernmental Authority on Development, the Council of Europe, the Commonwealth and the Economic Community of West African States, to address the protection, assistance and development needs of internally displaced persons, and encourages them and other regional organizations to strengthen their activities and their cooperation with the Representative of the Secretary-General;

18. *Requests* the Secretary-General to provide his Representative, from within existing resources, with all necessary assistance to carry out his mandate effectively, and encourages the Representative to continue to seek the contributions of States, relevant organizations and institutions in order to create a more stable basis for his work;

19. *Requests* the Representative of the Secretary-General to prepare, for consideration by the General Assembly at its sixtieth session, a report on the implementation of the present resolution;

20. *Decides* to continue its consideration of the question of protection of and assistance to internally displaced persons at its sixtieth session.

Housing and property restitution

Commission action. On 24 April [dec. 2003/109], the Commission endorsed the Subcommission's 2002 decision [YUN 2002, p. 761] to appoint Paulo Sérgio Pinheiro (Brazil) as Special Rapporteur to prepare a comprehensive study on housing and property restitution in the context of the return of internally displaced persons and refugees, and its request to him to submit a preliminary report in 2003, a progress report in 2004 and a final report in 2005.

The Economic and Social Council endorsed the Commission's decision on 23 July (**decision 2003/266**).

Report of Special Rapporteur. In response to a 2002 Subcommission request [YUN 2002, p. 761], the Special Rapporteur on housing and property restitution, Mr. Pinheiro, submitted a June preliminary report [E/CN.4/Sub.2/2003/11] on a study on housing and property restitution in the context of the return of refugees and internally displaced persons. The report presented an overview of selected housing and property restitution programmes, instituted as a result of internal conflict and mass displacement, such as those in Bosnia and Herzegovina, Croatia, Georgia, Guatemala, Kosovo (Serbia and Montenegro) and Rwanda. It illustrated that the programmes had been used in many post-conflict situations, and, when properly implemented, were indispensable to creating a durable peace. However, success was varied, mostly because of the lack of a comprehensive approach, governed by international human rights law. The Special Rapporteur recommended that the Subcommission develop, in consultation with relevant UN agencies and organs, Governments and NGOs, universal principles and guidelines, and a model policy on housing and property restitution for refugees and other displaced persons.

Subcommission action. On 13 August [res. 2003/18], the Subcommission urged States to ensure the free and fair exercise of the right to return to one's home and place of habitual residence by all refugees and internally displaced persons and to develop effective and expeditious legal, administrative and other procedures to ensure the exercise of the right.

Indigenous people

Reports of Special Rapporteur. In response to a 2002 Commission request [YUN 2002, p. 763], the Special Rapporteur on the situation of human rights and fundamental freedoms of indigenous people, Rodolfo Stavenhagen (Mexico), submitted a January report [E/CN.4/2003/90] on the impact of large-scale or major development projects on the human rights and fundamental freedoms of indigenous communities. He said that sometimes the projects were beneficial, but very often they were devastating and related to the loss of traditional territories and land, eviction, migration and eventual resettlement, depletion of resources necessary for physical and cultural survival, destruction and pollution of the traditional environment, social and community disorganization, long-term negative health and nutritional impacts, and, in some cases, harassment and violence. The Special Rapporteur advocated that indigenous peoples participate freely as equal partners and citizens in the decision-making processes that affected their future survival as specific peoples. Their voices should be heard and their demands and grievances met when major decisions were taken at national and international levels regarding development priorities and resource allocation.

In a later report [E/CN.4/2004/80/Add.1], the Special Rapporteur summarized communications he had sent to Governments and replies received during the year. He transmitted 20 urgent appeals and 11 letters alleging violations of indigenous peoples' rights to 12 Governments, some of which were sent jointly with other thematic and country mechanisms. He had received replies pertaining to 22 of a total of 31 cases addressed. The Special Rapporteur noted an increase in the number and substance of communications he had received, as well as severe human rights violations against indigenous peoples worldwide. He was particularly concerned about the status of indigenous women and children.

The Special Rapporteur visited Mexico (1-18 June) [E/CN.4/2004/80/Add.2], where the indigenous population, estimated at 13 million and comprising 62 ethnic groups, accounted for about 12 per cent of the total population and resided mostly in the poorest parts of the country. Current violations of their rights frequently occurred during periods of high tension and dispute. Notable problems related to agrarian conflicts involving the question of land and resources; political disputes regarding the exercise of power and access to public resources; discrimination in the justice system; the conflict in the state of Chiapas; the situation of indigenous women, children and migrants; education, language and culture; and constitutional reform and reconciliation. The Special Rapporteur concluded that, despite Mexico's long history of pro-indigenous policy, accumulated setbacks suffered by the indigenous population placed them at a disadvantage in relation to the rest of the population. He recommended measures for improving indigenous peoples' status, with regard to issues concerning constitutional legislation, the Chiapas peace process, the ILO Indigenous and Tribal Peoples Convention (Convention No. 169), adopted in 1957 [YUN 1957, p. 428], revised in 1989 [YUN 1989, p. 917] and which entered into force in 1991 [YUN 1991, p. 936], agrarian and environmental conflicts, internally displaced persons, the justice system, militarization and armed groups, indigenous migrants, education and culture, as well as the role of OHCHR and relevant UN agencies.

In Chile (18-29 July) [E/CN.4/2004/80/Add.3], which had an indigenous population of some 700,000 persons comprising 4.6 per cent of the total population, the Special Rapporteur, while noting the Government's readiness to cooperate with the international community in addressing questions concerning indigenous populations' rights, said that there were some human rights issues of grave concern. He drew attention to the failure to monitor and deal properly with the needs of indigenous communities in terms of their economic, social and cultural rights, and highlighted a situation of vulnerability and extreme poverty. Recommendations to the Government related to legislation and other legal measures, poverty reduction, land acquisition, sustainable development, the administration of justice, educational and social policy, publicizing indigenous issues in order to combat discrimination and the establishment of a national institution for the promotion and protection of human rights. Additional recommendations were addressed to the international community, civil society, the media and the academic community.

The Special Rapporteur visited Copenhagen, Denmark (6-7 October) [E/CN.4/2004/80/Add.1], where he focused on the right to return of the relocated Inughuit in Greenland, forcibly moved from their ancestral lands in 1953 to make way for the construction of an air base, and on the country's legal system and the administration of justice.

In Norway and Finland (10-14 October), the Special Rapporteur considered the situation of Sami communities, the original indigenous inhabitants of northern Scandinavia, residing in the polar region extending from Norway, Sweden and Finland to the Kola Peninsula in the Russian Federation. In Norway, a major concern related to a proposed land-management bill—the Finnmark Act—under consideration in the Norwegian Parliament, which was not in compliance with ILO Convention No. 169. In Finland, where the Sami population numbered some 6,500 persons, the Special Rapporteur found that, under Finnish law, the Sami did not have any special rights to use public land for securing their livelihoods. They claimed that their culture was being destroyed, demanded the return of their lands and protested the increasing presence of and ownership of land by tourists in the area.

Commission action. On 24 April [res. 2003/56], the Commission requested the Special Rapporteur to request, receive and exchange information on violations of indigenous people's rights from Governments, UN human rights treaty bodies, specialized agencies, Commission and Subcommission special mechanisms, intergovernmental organizations, relevant UN system organizations and civil society, and to respond to the information; to consider the recommendations of the World Conference against Racism, Racial Discrimination, Xenophobia and Related Intolerance [YUN 2001, p. 615], of the Permanent Forum on Indigenous Issues (see p. 803) and of the Working Group on Indigenous Populations (see below); to continue working on the topics included in his first report [YUN 2002, p. 762]; and to report in 2004. The Secretary-General and the High Commissioner were asked to assist him. The Commission took note of the intention of OHCHR to organize, with the participation of governmental, indigenous, non-governmental and independent experts, a seminar on the administration of justice (see below) to assist the Special Rapporteur in examining the main topic of his annual report for 2004.

Expert seminar. The Special Rapporteur transmitted to the Commission the report of the expert seminar on indigenous peoples and the administration of justice (Madrid, Spain, 12-14 November) [E/CN.4/2004/80/Add.4], organized by OHCHR in cooperation with the National University for Distance Education in Madrid, pursuant to Commission resolution 2003/56 (see above). The experts discussed issues relating to discrimination against indigenous peoples in the judicial system and indigenous peoples' own legal systems. They concluded that indigenous peoples' rights were often violated within judicial systems, particularly regarding indigenous women and children, and identified the causes of the problem. The experts adopted recommendations addressed to Governments, UN bodies, specialized agencies and human rights mechanisms, and indigenous peoples.

Communication. On 13 February [E/CN.4/2003/G/59], Guatemala stated that, while the Special Rapporteur's report on his visit to the country [YUN 2002, p. 762] contained many elements reflecting the reality of the situation of the rights of indigenous peoples, it did not constitute a fair assessment of the Government's efforts.

Working Group on Indigenous Populations

Commission action. On 24 April [res. 2003/55], by a recorded vote of 34 to 15, with 4 abstentions, the Commission, noting that the respective mandates of the Working Group on Indigenous Populations (see below), the Permanent Forum on Indigenous Issues (see p. 803) and the Special Rapporteur on the situation of human rights and fundamental freedoms of indigenous people were complementary and did not give rise to duplication, recommended that the Economic and Social Council, in 2003, take into account the contents of its current resolution when reviewing existing UN mechanisms, procedures and programmes regarding indigenous issues. It endorsed the recommendations contained in the Subcommission's 2002 resolutions [YUN 2002, p. 764].

Also on 24 April [res. 2003/58], the Commission recommended that the Council authorize the Group to meet for five working days prior to the Subcommission's 2003 session.

ECONOMIC AND SOCIAL COUNCIL ACTION

On 23 July, the Economic and Social Council, on the recommendation of the Commission on Human Rights [E/2003/23], adopted **decision 2003/254** by recorded vote (52-1-1) [agenda item 14 (g)].

Working Group on Indigenous Populations of the Subcommission on the Promotion and Protection of Human Rights and the International Decade of the World's Indigenous People

At its 46th plenary meeting, on 23 July 2003, the Economic and Social Council took note of Commission on Human Rights resolution 2003/58 of 24 April 2003, and authorized the Working Group on Indigenous Populations to meet for five working days prior to the fifty-fifth session of the Subcommission.

RECORDED VOTE ON DECISION 2003/254:
 In favour: Andorra, Argentina, Azerbaijan, Benin, Bhutan, Brazil, Burundi, Chile, China, Congo, Cuba, Ecuador, Egypt, El Salvador, Ethiopia, Finland, France, Georgia, Germany, Ghana, Greece, Guatemala, Hungary, India, Iran, Ireland, Italy, Jamaica, Japan, Kenya, Libyan Arab Jamahiriya, Malaysia, Mozambique, Nepal, Netherlands, Nicaragua, Nigeria, Pakistan, Peru, Portugal, Qatar, Republic of Korea, Romania, Russian Federation, Saudi Arabia, Senegal, South Africa, Sweden, Uganda, Ukraine, United Kingdom, Zimbabwe.
 Against: United States.
 Abstaining: Australia.

Working Group activities. The Working Group on Indigenous Populations held its twenty-first session (Geneva, 21-25 July) [E/CN.4/Sub.2/2003/22] to review developments pertaining to the promotion and protection of human rights and fundamental freedoms of indigenous populations and to give special attention to the evolution of standards regarding their rights. In annotations to the provisional agenda [E/CN.4/Sub.2/AC.4/2003/1/Add.1], the Secretariat presented background information on indigenous peoples and globalization; cooperation with other UN bodies regarding indigenous issues; follow-up to the World Conference against Racism, Racial Discrimination, Xenophobia and Related Intolerance [YUN 2001, p. 615]; the International Decade of the World's Indigenous People (1995-2004) (see p. 800); and standard-setting activities.

The Group had before it May working papers on the possible development of draft guidelines relating to TNCs whose activities affected indigenous communities [E/CN.4/Sub.2/AC.4/2003/5] and on cooperation between the Special Rapporteur and the Group [E/CN.4/Sub.2/AC.4/2003/7], both submitted by Yozo Yokota (Japan). It also considered a list with commentaries on possible studies to be undertaken by the Group, prepared by Miguel Alfonso Martínez (Cuba) [E/CN.4/Sub.2/AC.4/2003/4], working papers on globalization and the economic, social and cultural rights of indigenous populations, submitted by Mr. Guissé [E/CN.4/Sub.2/AC.4/2003/14], and on ways and means of developing cooperation between the Group and the Permanent Forum on Indigenous Issues, prepared by Mr. Martínez [E/CN.4/Sub.2/AC.4/2003/8], a list of standard-setting activities that could be considered by the Group, submitted by Ms. Motoc [E/CN.4/Sub.2/AC.4/2003/3], and a note by the Secretariat on follow-up to the 2001 World Conference. It further considered a report on a workshop (Washington, D.C., 19-20 February) [E/CN.4/Sub.2/AC.4/2003/10], organized by OHCHR, which reviewed indigenous peoples' participation at the World Summit on Sustainable Development [YUN 2002, p. 821] and discussed a rights-based approach to sustainable development. Regarding the session's principal theme—indigenous peoples and globalization—the Group considered a Secretariat note [E/CN.4/Sub.2/AC.4/2003/2], which highlighted related themes such as migration/urbanization, communication/technology and culture, poverty, development policies, and trade and intellectual property.

In its recommendations, the Group decided to maintain on its agenda for 2004 a sub-item on globalization and indigenous peoples, to allow for a follow-up discussion on the issue, and asked Mr. Guissé to submit in 2004 a supplementary working paper on the topic that would provide an outline for a possible future study; invited OHCHR to organize a second workshop on indigenous peoples, mining companies and human rights, the first having been held in 2001 [YUN 2001, p. 688], with a view to preparing guidelines for companies when planning activities on indigenous peoples' lands; and recommended to the coordinator of the International Decade of the World's Indigenous People that OHCHR organize an international seminar at the end of the Decade in December 2004 to evaluate the Decade and determine the extent to which the Programme of Action had been implemented. In other action, the Group invited Ms. Motoc to prepare a preliminary working paper as a basis for a future standard-setting activity; decided to start at its 2004 session a review of the 1995 draft principles and guidelines on the heritage of indigenous people, developed by Erica-Irene A. Daes (Greece) [YUN 1995, p. 780]; and requested Mr. Yokota to prepare a working paper on possible approaches to the issue. It decided to adopt as the principal theme for its 2004 session indigenous peoples and conflict resolution, asked its Chairperson/Rapporteur to prepare a background paper on the topic and invited Governments, indigenous peoples, the UN system and NGOs to provide relevant information on the theme. The Group decided to invite WTO, WIPO and the World Bank to present at its 2004 session their work relevant to indigenous peoples.

Subcommission action. On 14 August [res. 2003/29], the Subcommission asked the Secretary-General to transmit the Working Group's report on its 2003 session to the High Commissioner, indigenous organizations, Governments, intergovernmental organizations, concerned NGOs, treaty bodies and all thematic rapporteurs, special representatives, independent experts and working groups, and asked that it be made available to the Commission in 2004. It recommended that the Group, upon request, assist the open-ended intersessional working group to elaborate further the draft UN declaration on the rights of indigenous people (see p. 802). The Subcommission decided that the Group, in 2004, should adopt as its principal theme "Indigenous peoples and conflict resolution" and review the revised draft principles and guidelines on the heritage of indigenous people elaborated by Ms. Daes. It decided on the Group's agenda for 2004 and agreed with the Group's decision to establish as principal themes for its 2005 and 2006 sessions "Domestic and international protection of indigenous traditional knowledge" and "Indigenous children and youth", respectively. The Subcommission called for working papers in 2004 from: Mr. Yokota, to serve as a guideline for the review of the draft principles and guidelines; Mr. Guissé, on globalization and indigenous peoples; Ms. Motoc, on the principle of free, prior and informed consent of indigenous people in relation to development affecting their land and natural resources that would serve as a framework for the drafting of a legal commentary on that concept; Ms. Hampson, on possible follow-up by the Group on the human rights situation of indigenous peoples in States and territories threatened with extinction for environmental reasons; and

Mr. Martínez, on indigenous peoples and conflict resolution. The Secretary-General was asked to prepare an annotated agenda for the 2004 session. OHCHR was asked to organize, as a matter of priority and in consultation with the Group's Chairperson/Rapporteur, a second workshop on indigenous peoples, mining and other private sector companies and human rights; to invite Governments, intergovernmental and indigenous organizations and NGOs to provide information and data relevant to the Group's 2004 agenda, particularly on the principal theme; to organize, in consultation with interested Governments, meetings on indigenous issues in different parts of the world to provide greater opportunity for indigenous peoples' participation and to raise public awareness about issues affecting them, particularly in Africa, Asia, Oceania and Latin America; and to encourage studies with respect to the rights to food and adequate nutrition of indigenous peoples, and indigenous peoples and poverty. The Subcommission emphasized that the Economic and Social Council, in reviewing all UN mechanisms relating to indigenous peoples, take into account the fact that the mandates of the Group, the Special Rapporteur and the Permanent Forum were distinct and complementary. It requested the Commission to endorse that view, as well as the participation of the Group's Chairperson/Rapporteur at the Forum's third session, and recommended that the Council approve the participation and that the Commission request the Council to authorize the Group to meet for five working days prior to the Subcommission's 2004 session.

Voluntary Fund for Indigenous Populations

The Board of Trustees of the United Nations Voluntary Fund for Indigenous Populations, at its sixteenth session (Geneva, 31 March–4 April) [E/CN.4/Sub.2/AC.4/2003/12], recommended travel grants totalling $144,000 to enable 80 representatives of indigenous communities and organizations to attend the Working Group on Indigenous Populations (see p. 798), and other travel grants amounting to $41,000 to allow 15 indigenous representatives to attend the working group on the draft UN declaration on the rights of indigenous peoples (see p. 802). The Board's recommendations were approved by the High Commissioner on the Secretary-General's behalf on 9 April and 6 May. Annexed to the report was a list of beneficiaries.

Subcommission action. On 14 August [res. 2003/29], the Subcommission appealed to Governments, organizations, NGOs, indigenous groups and other potential donors in a position to do so to contribute to the Fund.

International Decade of the World's Indigenous People

Commission action. On 24 April [res. 2003/58], the Commission invited the Working Group to continue its review of activities undertaken during the International Decade of the World's Indigenous People (1995-2004), proclaimed by the General Assembly in resolution 48/163 [YUN 1993, p. 865]. The High Commissioner, in his capacity as coordinator of the Decade, was asked to submit in 2004 an updated annual report on activities within the UN system under the Decade's programme of activities (see p. 801), to ensure that OHCHR's indigenous people's unit was adequately staffed and resourced, and to give due regard to developing human rights training for indigenous people. UN financial and development institutions, operational programmes and specialized agencies were asked to give increased priority and resources to improving the conditions of indigenous people; launch special projects to strengthen their community-level initiatives and facilitate the exchange of information and expertise among indigenous people and other relevant experts; and designate focal points or other mechanisms to coordinate with the High Commissioner activities relating to the Decade. The Commission recommended that the situation of indigenous people be taken into account in forthcoming relevant UN conferences, including the World Summit on the Information Society (see p. 857), and requested the Secretary-General to begin implementing the evaluation of the Decade, as called for by the World Conference against Racism, Racial Discrimination, Xenophobia and Related Intolerance [YUN 2001, p. 615]. The Commission requested the Economic and Social Council, within the context of the Council's intended review of all existing UN mechanisms, procedures and programmes concerning indigenous issues, to take into account the views expressed by Governments, NGOs, indigenous people's organizations, the Permanent Forum and all existing mechanisms, the Working Group and the Subcommission.

On 25 April [dec. 2003/117], the Commission, taking note of a 2002 Subcommission resolution [YUN 2002, p. 766], recommended that the Council request the High Commissioner to organize, before the Decade's end, a seminar on treaties, agreements and other constructive arrangements between States and indigenous peoples to explore possible ways to follow up on the recommendations contained in the 1999 report of the Special Rapporteur [YUN 1999, p. 686].

ECONOMIC AND SOCIAL COUNCIL ACTION

On 23 July, the Economic and Social Council, on the recommendation of the Commission on Human Rights [E/2003/23], adopted **decision**

2003/271 by recorded vote (50-1-3) [agenda item 14 (g)].

International Decade of the World's Indigenous People

At its 46th plenary meeting, on 23 July 2003, the Economic and Social Council took note of Commission on Human Rights decision 2003/117 of 25 April 2003, and endorsed the Commission's recommendation that it request the United Nations High Commissioner for Human Rights to organize, before the end of the International Decade of the World's Indigenous People, a seminar on treaties, agreements and other constructive arrangements between States and indigenous peoples to explore possible ways and means to follow up on the recommendations included in the final report of the Special Rapporteur, Mr. Miguel Alfonso Martínez.

RECORDED VOTE ON DECISION 2003/271:

In favour: Andorra, Argentina, Azerbaijan, Benin, Bhutan, Brazil, Burundi, Chile, China, Congo, Cuba, Ecuador, Egypt, El Salvador, Ethiopia, Finland, France, Georgia, Germany, Ghana, Greece, Guatemala, Hungary, India, Iran, Ireland, Italy, Jamaica, Japan, Kenya, Libyan Arab Jamahiriya, Malaysia, Mozambique, Nepal, Netherlands, Nicaragua, Nigeria, Pakistan, Peru, Portugal, Republic of Korea, Romania, Russian Federation, Senegal, South Africa, Sweden, Uganda, Ukraine, United Kingdom, Zimbabwe.
Against: United States.
Abstaining: Australia, Qatar, Saudi Arabia.

Note by Secretary-General. In August [A/58/289], the Secretary-General summarized implementation of the Decade's programme of activities undertaken by OHCHR during the period from August 2002 to July 2003. Of particular note were the second session of the Permanent Forum on Indigenous Issues (see p. 803), the twenty-first (2003) session of the Working Group (see p. 798) and the activities undertaken by the Special Rapporteur (see p. 796). OHCHR continued to promote inter-agency cooperation and the mainstreaming of indigenous rights into technical cooperation programmes. Other ongoing programmes included a joint research project with UN-Habitat on indigenous peoples and their housing rights and the Indigenous Fellowship Programme.

Subcommission action. On 14 August [res. 2003/30], the Subcommission, welcoming the observance in 2003 of the International Day of the World's Indigenous People (24 July), recommended that it be held on the fourth day of the Working Group's 2004 session to ensure as large a participation of indigenous peoples as possible. It recommended that the Decade's coordinator appeal to Governments and other donors to contribute to the Voluntary Fund for the Decade (see below), and that attention be given to improving the extent of indigenous peoples' participation in planning and implementing the Decade's activities. It also recommended that the High Commissioner, in consultation with interested Governments, organize meetings, particularly in Africa, Asia, Oceania and Latin America, prior to the completion of the Decade, to raise public awareness about indigenous issues, and organize an international seminar at the Decade's end to evaluate its impact and to recommend future action in relation to indigenous peoples. The Subcommission further recommended that a second international decade of the world's indigenous people be proclaimed by the General Assembly, which would focus on promoting and protecting their rights.

Report of High Commissioner. A November report of the High Commissioner [E/CN.4/2004/79] reviewed UN activities undertaken to implement the programme for the Decade. OHCHR held the Indigenous Fellowship Programme (28 April–3 October) for five fellows from Burundi, Chile, India, Indonesia and the United States, and cooperated with the University of Deusto (Bilbao, Spain) to provide training for five additional indigenous fellows from Bolivia, Colombia, Guatemala, Paraguay and Venezuela, and with the University of Bourgogne (Dijon, France) to offer similar training to five fellows from Algeria, Canada, Morocco and the Niger. The report described activities regarding inter-agency cooperation on indigenous issues and the work of the Voluntary Fund for the Decade (see below) and the Voluntary Fund for Indigenous Populations (see p. 800).

Voluntary Fund for International Decade

The Advisory Group of the United Nations Voluntary Fund for the International Decade of the World's Indigenous People, at its eighth session (Geneva, 7-11 April) [E/CN.4/Sub.2/AC.4/2003/13], recommended 46 project grants, which were approved for a total of $274,000, and the allocation of $46,600 on a contingency basis for programmes to be implemented by the indigenous projects team, of which $12,000 would be spent on a community-led human rights training programme and $34,600 for the participation of 10 indigenous representatives in a seminar on indigenous peoples and the administration of justice. It proposed to the High Commissioner that the cost of workshops and seminars be met from OHCHR's regular budget and extrabudgetary resources, and that, subject to the availability of funds, a minimum of $50,000 be set aside for organizing at least one workshop or seminar for the remaining year of the Decade. Based on requests received and activities financed in 2003, the Group recommended a minimum allocation of $200,000 for new projects and programmes in 2004.

Draft declaration

Working group activities. The working group established to elaborate a draft declaration on the rights of indigenous peoples, at its eighth session (Geneva, 2-13 December 2002) [E/CN.4/AC.4/2003/92], focused on articles relating to the rights to self-determination; treaties, agreements and other constructive arrangements concluded with States; lands, territories and other resources; cultural and intellectual property; not to be subjected to ethnocide and genocide; their distinct identities and characteristics; and special protection and security in periods of armed conflict. A lack of consensus persisted within the group regarding the term "indigenous peoples". Annexed to the report was a compilation of amendments put forth by States, indigenous representatives and one NGO on the articles examined. An addendum to the report [E/CN.4/2003/92/Add.1] contained the articles, which were discussed and supported by all indigenous organizations, and information on participating Governments and NGOs and on working papers and background documents considered by the group.

On 1 May (**decision 2003/218**), the Economic and Social Council, in accordance with its resolution 1995/32 [YUN 1995, p. 777], authorized three indigenous organizations (Chickaloon Village Traditional Council, Indigenous Peoples and Nations Coalition, United Native Nations) to participate in the group's work.

At its ninth session (Geneva, 15-26 September) [E/CN.4/2004/81], the working group continued to discuss various proposed amendments or new language for 26 of the articles contained in the draft declaration, of which a summary was annexed to the report. An addendum to the report [E/CN.4/2004/81/Add.1] listed the documents considered and the participants who attended. It contained the text of the articles discussed and supported by all indigenous organizations and a proposal submitted by one indigenous organization.

Commission action. On 24 April [res. 2003/57], the Commission recommended that the group meet for 10 working days prior to its 2004 session and asked the group to report in 2004.

On 23 July, the Economic and Social Council authorized the group to meet (**decision 2003/253**).

Note by Secretariat. A June note [E/CN.4/Sub.2/AC.4/2003/6] of the Secretariat stated that, as at 4 June, it had not received the working paper containing commentaries on the most important provisions of the draft declaration, which the Subcommission had entrusted Ms. Hampson to prepare [YUN 2002, p. 765].

Subcommission action. On 14 August [res. 2003/30], the Subcommission recommended the adoption of the draft declaration as early as possible, in accordance with General Assembly resolution 50/157 [YUN 1995, p. 772], and appealed to the group's participants and others concerned to accelerate its preparation.

GENERAL ASSEMBLY ACTION

On 22 December [meeting 77], the General Assembly, on the recommendation of the Third Committee [A/58/505], adopted **resolution 58/158** without vote [agenda item 114].

International Decade of the World's Indigenous People

The General Assembly,

Recalling its resolution 57/192 of 18 December 2002 and previous resolutions on the International Decade of the World's Indigenous People, including resolution 50/157 of 21 December 1995, by which it adopted the programme of activities for the Decade,

Recalling also its resolution 40/131 of 13 December 1985, by which it established the United Nations Voluntary Fund for Indigenous Populations, and its resolution 57/191 of 18 December 2002, as a result of which the Trust Fund in Support of the Permanent Forum on Indigenous Issues was established,

Recalling further that the goal of the Decade is to strengthen international cooperation for the solution of problems faced by indigenous people in such areas as human rights, the environment, development, education and health, and that the theme of the Decade is "Indigenous people: partnership in action",

Welcoming, in this respect, the contributions to the realization of the goals of the Decade made by the Permanent Forum on Indigenous Issues at its first and second sessions, held in New York from 13 to 24 May 2002 and from 12 to 23 May 2003, respectively,

Welcoming also the contributions to the realization of the goals of the Decade made by the World Conference against Racism, Racial Discrimination, Xenophobia and Related Intolerance, held at Durban, South Africa, from 31 August to 8 September 2001, and the World Summit on Sustainable Development, held at Johannesburg, South Africa, from 26 August to 4 September 2002,

Welcoming further the reports of the Special Rapporteur of the Commission on Human Rights on the situation of human rights and fundamental freedoms of indigenous people, submitted to the Commission on Human Rights at its fifty-eighth and fifty-ninth sessions,

Recognizing the importance of consultation and cooperation with indigenous people in planning and implementing the programme of activities for the Decade, the need for adequate financial support from the international community, including support from within the United Nations system, and the need for adequate coordination and communication channels,

Urging all parties to continue to use their best efforts to achieve the goals of the Decade,

1. *Takes note* of the note by the Secretary-General transmitting the report of the United Nations High Commissioner for Human Rights on the implementation of the programme of activities for the International Decade of the World's Indigenous People;

2. *Affirms its conviction* of the value and diversity of the cultures and forms of social organization of indigenous people and its conviction that the development of indigenous people within their countries will contribute to the socio-economic, cultural and environmental advancement of all the countries of the world;

3. *Emphasizes* the importance of strengthening the human and institutional capacity of indigenous people to develop their own solutions to their problems;

4. *Requests* the United Nations High Commissioner for Human Rights, as coordinator for the Decade:

(a) To continue to promote the objectives of the Decade, taking into account, in the fulfilment of his or her functions, the special concerns of indigenous people;

(b) To give due regard to the dissemination, from within existing resources and voluntary contributions, of information on the situation, cultures, languages, rights and aspirations of indigenous people and, in that context, to consider the possibility of organizing projects, special events, exhibitions and other activities addressed to the public, in particular to young people;

(c) To submit, through the Secretary-General, an annual report to the General Assembly on the implementation of the programme of activities for the Decade;

5. *Reaffirms* the adoption of a declaration on the rights of indigenous people as a major objective of the Decade, and underlines the importance of effective participation by indigenous representatives in the open-ended intersessional working group of the Commission on Human Rights charged with elaborating a draft declaration on the rights of indigenous people, established pursuant to Commission resolution 1995/32 of 3 March 1995;

6. *Welcomes* the active consideration by the Permanent Forum on Indigenous Issues of a number of topics pertaining to the Decade, as reflected in its report to the Economic and Social Council on its second session, and encourages the Forum to continue to work towards the realization of the goals of the Decade;

7. *Encourages* Governments to support the Decade by:

(a) Preparing relevant programmes, plans and reports in relation to the Decade, in consultation with indigenous people;

(b) Seeking means, in consultation with indigenous people, of giving indigenous people greater responsibility for their own affairs and an effective voice in decisions on matters that affect them;

(c) Establishing national committees or other mechanisms involving indigenous people to ensure that the objectives and activities of the Decade are planned and implemented on the basis of full partnership with indigenous people;

(d) Contributing to the following funds:

(i) The United Nations Trust Fund for the International Decade of the World's Indigenous People;

(ii) The United Nations Voluntary Fund for Indigenous Populations, in order to assist indigenous representatives in participating in the Permanent Forum on Indigenous Issues, the Working Group on Indigenous Populations of the Subcommission on the Promotion and Protection of Human Rights and the open-ended intersessional working group of the Commission on Human Rights charged with elaborating a draft declaration on the rights of indigenous people;

(iii) The Trust Fund in Support of the Permanent Forum on Indigenous Issues;

(iv) The Fund for the Development of Indigenous Peoples in Latin America and the Caribbean;

(e) Identifying resources for activities designed to implement the goals of the Decade, in cooperation with indigenous people and intergovernmental and non-governmental organizations;

8. *Invites* United Nations financial and development institutions, operational programmes and the specialized agencies and secretariats, as well as other regional and international organizations, in accordance with the existing procedures of their governing bodies:

(a) To give increased priority and resources to improving the conditions of indigenous people, with particular emphasis on the needs of those people in developing countries, inter alia, through the preparation of specific programmes of action for the implementation of the goals of the Decade, within their areas of competence;

(b) To launch special projects, through appropriate channels and in cooperation with indigenous people, to strengthen their community-level initiatives and to facilitate the exchange of information and expertise among indigenous people and other relevant experts;

(c) To designate focal points for the coordination of activities relating to the Decade with the Office of the United Nations High Commissioner for Human Rights; and commends those institutions, programmes, agencies and regional and international organizations that have already done so;

9. *Recommends* that the Secretary-General ensure coordinated follow-up to the recommendations concerning indigenous people of relevant United Nations conferences;

10. *Requests* the United Nations High Commissioner for Human Rights to submit, through the Secretary-General, a report on the implementation of the programme of activities for the Decade to the General Assembly at its fifty-ninth session;

11. *Takes note* of Economic and Social Council decision 2003/306 of 25 July 2003 concerning the initiation of its review of the Decade, pursuant to General Assembly resolution 50/157;

12. *Decides* to include in the provisional agenda of its fifty-ninth session an item entitled "Programme of activities for the International Decade of the World's Indigenous People, 1995-2004".

Permanent Forum on Indigenous Issues

Commission action. On 24 April [dec. 2003/111], the Commission, taking note of a 2002 Subcommission resolution [YUN 2002, p. 769], approved the Subcommission's invitation to the Chairperson/Rapporteur of the Working Group on Indigenous Populations to attend the second session of the Permanent Forum on Indigenous Issues (see p. 803) and recommended that the Economic and Social Council endorse its decision.

Note by Secretariat. By a 22 April note [E/2003/52], the Secretariat transmitted to the Economic and Social Council the provisional agenda for the second session of the Permanent Forum on Indigenous Issues for review and approval.

On 1 May, the Council approved the provisional agenda (**decision 2003/219**).

Permanent Forum session. The 16-member Permanent Forum on Indigenous Issues, established by Economic and Social Council resolution 2000/22 [YUN 2000, p. 731] to address indigenous issues relating to economic and social development, the environment, health, education and culture, and human rights, at its second session (New York, 12-23 May) [E/2003/43], considered the theme, "Indigenous children and youth". It recommended seven draft decisions for adoption by the Council (see below). Matters brought to the Council's attention were indigenous children and youth, economic and social development, the environment, health, human rights, culture, education, the Forum's methods of work with the UN system and the future of its work.

An annex to the Forum's report listed the documents considered.

ECONOMIC AND SOCIAL COUNCIL ACTION

On 25 July, the Council authorized the UN Department of Economic and Social Affairs to convene a three-day workshop on the collection of data concerning indigenous peoples, and decided that the workshop would produce a report containing recommendations for the Forum's consideration in 2004 (**decision 2003/300**); decided to consider indigenous issues as a theme for its high-level segment in 2006 (**decision 2003/301**); taking into account the importance for the Forum to be represented by its Chairperson or designated members at meetings of relevance to its mandate, confirmed such representation as one of the Forum's methods of work (**decision 2003/302**); taking note that the Forum had considered it useful to designate six members for its Bureau at its first and second sessions, confirmed the practice as a method of the Forum's work (**decision 2003/303**); decided that the Forum's third session would be held in New York from 10 to 21 May 2004 (**decision 2003/304**) and approved that session's provisional agenda and documentation (**decision 2003/305**); and decided to transmit to the General Assembly the Forum's recommendation regarding a second international decade of the world's indigenous people, with a view to initiating consideration of the decade, taking into account the forthcoming review by the Council, and further decided to initiate the review (**decision 2003/306**).

Review of existing mechanisms

Pursuant to Economic and Social Council resolution 2000/22 [YUN 2000, p. 731], the Secretary-General, in a June report [E/2003/72], summarized information received from eight Governments, 21 NGOs and indigenous organizations, one member each of the Working Group on Indigenous Populations and of the Permanent Forum on Indigenous Issues, one official of an indigenous community and 20 UN system bodies and agencies, and other relevant intergovernmental organizations, in response to a questionnaire regarding the Council's planned review of all existing UN mechanisms, procedures and programmes concerning indigenous issues. The Secretary-General observed that the review, scheduled for 2003, should contribute to determining how best to promote and support the legitimate interests and concerns of indigenous peoples. The key objectives should be to avoid duplication of work, promote effectiveness and rationalize activities. It was important that UN work in that area be in line with the Organization's broader reform objectives, endorsed by the General Assembly in resolution 57/300 [YUN 2002, p. 1353].

The Secretary-General, in a July report [E/2003/CRP.3], summarized additional information received from UN system bodies and other intergovernmental organizations, and the actual questions posed by the questionnaires.

On 25 July (**decision 2003/307**), the Council decided to postpone consideration of the review and requested the Secretary-General to seek information related to the review from Governments, NGOs, indigenous peoples' organizations and relevant UN system organs and bodies, including the special mechanisms seized with indigenous issues that had not yet submitted their views. It also asked him to provide an analysis of elements contained in paragraph 8 of Council resolution 2000/22, which related to a review of all existing UN mechanisms, programmes and procedures regarding indigenous issues.

Study on treaties, agreements and other constructive arrangements

Report of High Commissioner. In response to a 2002 Commission request [YUN 2002, p. 765], the High Commissioner, in a February report [E/CN.4/2003/91], summarized replies received as at 10 January from two Governments, four NGOs and one member of the Permanent Forum regarding the issues raised in a 1999 study on treaties, agreements and other constructive arrangements between States and indigenous populations [YUN 1999, p. 686].

Working paper. In July [E/2003/92], the Secretariat transmitted a working paper prepared by the Special Rapporteur on treaties, agreements and constructive arrangements between States and indigenous populations, Mr. Martínez, which contained suggestions in connection with a seminar on the topic, as called for in Commission decision 2003/117 (see p. 800). The paper reviewed a number of recommendations for follow-up action, put forth in the Special Rapporteur's 1999 study, and proposed issues for discussion at the seminar, including the possibility of undertaking a new study on the question of treaty-based relations between States and indigenous peoples; confidence-building steps to be taken by both indigenous and non-indigenous interested parties facing situations of potential or actual conflict; a review of ways of implementing other recommendations in the 1999 study; and preliminary consideration of other activities that might contribute to harmonious relations between indigenous and non-indigenous peoples.

Seminar. In response to a 2002 Subcommission request [YUN 2002, p. 766] and to Commission decision 2003/117 (see p. 800), the High Commissioner organized an expert seminar on treaties, agreements and other constructive arrangements between States and indigenous peoples (Geneva, 15-17 December) [E/CN.4/2004/111]. Participants considered that the treaties and agreements had not been respected. They recommended that States educate the public, and presented guidelines for conflict resolution on processes. Other recommendations were addressed to the Commission, working groups, treaty bodies and special procedures, UN bodies and specialized agencies and OHCHR.

Indigenous peoples' permanent sovereignty over natural resources

Commission action. By a recorded vote of 34 to 8, with 10 abstentions, the Commission, on 24 April [dec. 2003/110], taking note of a 2002 Subcommission resolution [YUN 2002, p. 771], endorsed the Subcommission's request to appoint Ms. Daes as Special Rapporteur to undertake a study on indigenous peoples' permanent sovereignty over natural resources, and its request to her to submit a preliminary report in 2003 and a final report in 2004, and to the Secretary-General to assist her.

ECONOMIC AND SOCIAL COUNCIL ACTION

On 23 July, the Economic and Social Council, on the recommendation of the Commission on Human Rights [E/2003/23], adopted **decision 2003/267** by recorded vote (36-12-6) [agenda item 14 (g)].

Indigenous peoples' permanent sovereignty over natural resources

At its 46th plenary meeting, on 23 July 2003, the Economic and Social Council took note of Commission on Human Rights decision 2003/110 of 24 April 2003 and endorsed the Commission's decisions:

(a) To approve the appointment of Ms. Erica-Irene Daes as Special Rapporteur to undertake a study on indigenous peoples' permanent sovereignty over natural resources, based on her working paper, and to request her to submit a preliminary report to the Subcommission on the Promotion and Protection of Human Rights at its fifty-fifth session and her final report at its fifty-sixth session;

(b) To request the Secretary-General to provide the Special Rapporteur with all necessary assistance to enable her to carry out her study.

RECORDED VOTE ON DECISION 2003/267:
In favour: Argentina, Azerbaijan, Benin, Bhutan, Burundi, Chile, China, Congo, Cuba, Ecuador, Egypt, El Salvador, Ethiopia, Georgia, Ghana, Greece, Guatemala, India, Iran, Jamaica, Kenya, Libyan Arab Jamahiriya, Malaysia, Mozambique, Nepal, Nicaragua, Nigeria, Pakistan, Peru, Qatar, Russian Federation, Saudi Arabia, Senegal, South Africa, Uganda, Zimbabwe.
Against: Australia, Finland, France, Germany, Hungary, Netherlands, Portugal, Republic of Korea, Sweden, Ukraine, United Kingdom, United States.
Abstaining: Andorra, Brazil, Ireland, Italy, Japan, Romania.

Report of Special Rapporteur. As requested by the Subcommission in 2002 [YUN 2002, p. 771], the Special Rapporteur on indigenous peoples' permanent sovereignty over natural resources, Ms. Daes, submitted a July preliminary report [E/CN.4/Sub.2/2003/20], which examined whether the term "sovereignty" could appropriately be used in reference to indigenous peoples and their natural resources within independent States. She determined that the term referred to legal governmental control and authority over resources, as an aspect of the exercise of self-determination. No State enjoyed unfettered sovereignty, as States' sovereignty was limited by treaties and customary international law. In legal principle, therefore, there was no objection to using the term in reference to indigenous peoples acting in their governmental capacity, but that capacity might be limited in various ways. It would create conceptual problems if the word "sovereignty" was removed from the long-established principle of permanent sovereignty over natural resources, said the Special Rapporteur. Annexed to the report was a preliminary selected bibliography, a list of relevant cases and a compilation of relevant international law standards.

Subcommission action. On 14 August [dec. 2003/113], the Subcommission requested the Secretary-General to transmit the Special Rapporteur's preliminary report to Governments, indigenous peoples' communities and organizations, specialized agencies, other intergovernmental organizations and NGOs concerned for comments, information and data that would be important for the Special Rapporteur in preparing her final report.

Persons with disabilities

Report of High Commissioner. In accordance with a 2002 Commission request [YUN 2002, p. 772], the High Commissioner, in a January report [E/CN.4/2003/88], reviewed progress made in implementing the recommendations contained in a 2002 study on human rights and disability [YUN 2002, p. 771]. The report summarized information received from 12 Governments on measures they had adopted to implement those recommendations, and highlighted action taken by treaty bodies, the Commission, national human rights institutions and NGOs. The report detailed OHCHR's efforts to implement the study's recommendations and its further activities regarding human rights and disability, including its contribution relating to proposals for a new convention on the human rights and dignity of persons with disabilities. Should the Commission decide to appoint a special rapporteur on the rights of persons with disabilities, as recommended by the 2002 study, it was important to ensure complementarity with the Special Rapporteur on disability of the Commission for Social Development. The High Commissioner said it was vital that Governments, relevant UN bodies and organizations, national disability and human rights institutions, NGOs and independent experts contribute to the work of the Ad Hoc Committee on a Comprehensive and Integral International Convention on Protection and Promotion of the Rights and Dignity of Persons with Disabilities established in General Assembly resolution 56/168 [YUN 2001, p. 1012] (see p. 1107).

Commission action. On 23 April [res. 2003/49], the Commission requested the Secretary-General to make the High Commissioner's January report (see above) available to the Ad Hoc Committee and to include in relevant reports to the General Assembly information on progress made to ensure the full recognition and enjoyment of the human rights of persons with disabilities. It called on OHCHR to report to the Commission in 2004. The Special Rapporteur on disability was invited to address the Commission in 2004 on the human rights dimension gained through monitoring the Standard Rules on the Equalization of Opportunities for Persons with Disabilities, adopted by the General Assembly in resolution 48/96 [YUN 1993, p. 978]. Governments were urged to cover the human rights of persons with disabilities in their reporting obligations under relevant UN human rights instruments, while UN organizations and agencies and intergovernmental institutions for development cooperation were called on to integrate disability measures into their activities and to reflect that in their reports.

Report of Secretary-General. In response to a 2002 Commission request [YUN 2002, p. 772], the Secretary-General submitted a July report with later addendum [A/58/181 & Add.1], which focused on the issue of procedural safeguards for persons with mental disabilities and aimed at clarifying the protection afforded them under international human rights law. The report was based on replies to a questionnaire, to which responses were received from 19 States, three UN bodies and several national human rights institutions. It analysed such issues as legal capacity, involuntary institutionalization and involuntary or forced treatment, and defined "mental disability" or "mental illness" to include persons with intellectual and psychiatric disabilities, individuals with no disability but who were subjected to discrimination on the perception that they had a mental illness and those with a background of past treatment or hospitalization as patients with a mental disability. The report concluded that a major obstacle to the implementation of existing human rights standards for persons with mental disabilities was the lack of specific guidelines. Although the Principles for the Protection of Persons with Mental Illness and for the Improvement of Mental Health Care, adopted by the General Assembly in resolution 46/119 [YUN 1991, p. 620], provided a valuable starting point for clarifying the content of those standards, a more detailed analysis of the implementation of State human rights obligations regarding mental health institutions would be desirable. The Secretary-General proposed, among other measures, a review of the criteria set forth in principle 16 (1) for compulsory institutionalization, detailed monitoring of the implementation of the rights of persons with mental disabilities and the provision by Governments to the human rights treaty bodies of information on measures adopted regarding the norms in their periodic report.

In **resolution 58/246** of 23 December, the General Assembly encouraged Member States and observers to participate actively in the Ad Hoc Committee in order to present to the Assembly the draft text of a convention (see p. 1108).

People with HIV/AIDS

Reports of Secretary-General. In response to a 2002 Commission request [YUN 2002, p. 772], the Secretary-General, in a January report and February addendum [E/CN.4/2003/48 & Add.1], summarized information received from 16 States, four UN bodies, three NGOs and one intergovernmental organization on steps they had taken to promote access to medication in the context of pandemics such as HIV/AIDS. The Secretary-General said that, although some countries had succeeded in slowing the spread of the disease, much more needed to be done to ensure the highest attainable standard of health for people living with and affected by it, including through greater access to medication and a comprehensive approach to prevention, treatment, care and support.

In another January report [E/CN.4/2003/81], submitted in response to a 2001 Commission request [YUN 2001, p. 695], the Secretary-General summarized further comments received from Governments, UN bodies, national human rights institutions and NGOs regarding steps they had taken to promote and implement the Guidelines on HIV/AIDS and Human Rights, recommended by the experts who participated in the Second International Consultation on the topic [YUN 1996, p. 617]. The Secretary-General acknowledged that positive steps had been taken at the national and international levels towards ensuring respect for human rights in the context of HIV/AIDS. Legislation had been adopted in some countries to prohibit discrimination against people living with the disease, and policies and strategies had been developed to promote access to prevention, treatment, care and support for those affected. Moreover, Governments had committed themselves to addressing the root causes of vulnerability to HIV infection and had pledged international cooperation and assistance to ensure respect for the human rights of people affected by the disease.

Commission action. On 22 April [res. 2003/29], the Commission called on States, in furtherance of the Declaration of Commitment on HIV/AIDS adopted in General Assembly resolution S-26/2 [YUN 2001, p. 1126], to address factors affecting the provision of drugs related to the treatment of pandemics such as HIV/AIDS. It asked the Secretary-General to solicit comments from Governments, UN organs, programmes and specialized agencies, international organizations and NGOs on steps they had taken to promote and implement the Commission's current resolution, and to report in 2004.

On 23 April [res. 2003/47], the Commission asked its special representatives, special rapporteurs and working groups to integrate the protection of HIV-related human rights within their respective mandates. The Secretary-General was requested to solicit comments from Governments, UN organs, programmes and specialized agencies, international organizations and NGOs on steps taken to promote and implement the Guidelines on HIV/AIDS and Human Rights and to report in 2005.

In **resolution 58/179** (see p. 1253), the Assembly called on States to refrain from taking measures that would deny or limit equal access for all persons to preventive, curative or palliative pharmaceutical products or medical technologies used to treat HIV/AIDS.

Chapter III

Human rights violations

Alleged violations of human rights and international humanitarian law in a number of countries were examined in 2003 by the General Assembly, the Economic and Social Council, the Commission on Human Rights and its Subcommission on the Promotion and Protection of Human Rights, as well as by special rapporteurs, special representatives of the Secretary-General and independent experts.

General aspects

On 28 March and 2 April, pursuant to Economic and Social Council resolution 2000/3 [YUN 2000, p. 596], the Commission on Human Rights [E/2003/23] considered the situation of human rights in Chad, Djibouti, Liberia and Uzbekistan. It decided to discontinue consideration of the situation in Uzbekistan. Under the confidential procedure established by Council resolutions 1503(XLVIII) (1503 procedure) [YUN 1970, p. 530], to deal confidentially with communications alleging denial or violation of human rights, and 2000/3, the Commission decided to discontinue consideration of the situations in Chad and Liberia and to consider them publicly under the item on human rights advisory services and technical cooperation (see p. 678). On 2 April, the Commission decided that its decisions regarding Chad [dec. 2003/104] and Liberia [dec. 2003/105] should be made public. It recommended the appointment of an independent expert for Liberia (see p. 683).

(For information on the right to restitution, compensation and rehabilitation for victims of grave violations of human rights and fundamental freedoms, see p. 726.)

Africa

Burundi

Commission action. On 17 April [E/2003/23 (res. 2003/16)], the Commission on Human Rights expressed concern at the ongoing violence, the violation of human rights and international humanitarian law and the security situation in parts of Burundi and noted efforts by the authorities to ensure respect for human rights safeguards and international standards. It welcomed the willingness of the Transitional Government to find agreed solutions to the problem of war-affected persons through the establishment of the Standing Consultation Machinery for the Protection of Displaced Persons and its technical monitoring group, and called on Burundi to establish a security environment conducive to the work of aid organizations. It urged the Transitional Government to strengthen its efforts to end impunity and all parties to the conflict to cease using children as soldiers.

The Commission decided to extend the Special Rapporteur's mandate for an additional year and asked her to submit an interim report to the General Assembly in 2003 and to report to the Commission in 2004, giving her work a gender-specific dimension. The Economic and Social Council endorsed the Commission's decision and its requests to the Special Rapporteur on 23 July (**decision 2003/241**).

Reports of Special Rapporteur. In her October interim report [A/58/448], Special Rapporteur Marie-Thérèse A. Kéita-Bocoum (Côte d'Ivoire) reviewed the situation in Burundi from March to August, based on her visit to the country (11-19 May). The political climate during the Special Rapporteur's mission was relatively calm owing to the grace period granted to the new President and his team. Subsequently, and fairly rapidly, the situation deteriorated and an atmosphere of violence once again ensued. Throughout the period under review, the security situation was marked by numerous arbitrary arrests, kidnappings and murders, directed especially against local civilian officials and various high-ranking political leaders. Implementation of the Arusha Agreement on Peace and Reconciliation [YUN 2000, p. 146] had been slowed by the lack of a ceasefire, jeopardizing the many reforms envisaged. However, the Special Rapporteur noted some significant advances, such as the transfer of power to the Transitional Government, the installation of the National Commission for the Rehabilitation of *Sinistrés* (survivors) and the restructuring of the government Commission on Human Rights, which had resumed its visits in the field with assistance from the United Nations Development Programme. However, war and a fragile economy continued to alter the social fabric of the country.

The Special Rapporteur reported that attacks on civil and political rights abounded, while the impunity that surrounded the actions of certain groups, especially members of the regular army and the rebel groups, continued to fuel the widespread feeling of insecurity, curtailing the authorities' determination to fight it. She described violations, attributed to agents of the State, rebel groups and persons unknown, of the rights to life, liberty, security and inviolability of the person, freedom of movement and to choose one's residence, freedom of opinion and expression, women's and children's rights, and the proliferation of rape and the situation of the Batwa minority. With regard to justice and the rule of law, laws on genocide and on the Truth and Reconciliation Committee were adopted. However, people were still being detained in military camps, impunity persisted and widespread incidents of rape by both parties to the conflict remained unpunished. Prisons were severely overcrowded and the hygienic conditions were appalling. The Burundi office of the Office of the United Nations High Commissioner for Human Rights (OHCHR) increased its human rights training sessions and organized a seminar for journalists and police representatives on the media's role in combating torture. The Special Rapporteur observed that the improvement in the human rights situation was closely linked to the creation of a climate of stability in the Great Lakes region (see p. 107).

She reiterated the recommendations she had made in 2002 [YUN 2002, p. 774] and urged all parties to the conflict to discontinue hostilities, implement the agreements they had signed, respect civilians' rights, respect international humanitarian law, refrain from attacking economic and social infrastructures, and not involve children or civilians in armed conflict. She recommended that the Burundian authorities combat impunity and cease arbitrary detention and torture, implement the recommendations of the independent commission on issues relating to prisoners, stop child recruitment into the army and demobilize those already enrolled, demobilize and disarm the militias and other civilian self-defence forces, combat discrimination against the Batwa, protect vulnerable populations, end sexual violence, punish the perpetrators and ensure support to victims, respect all conventions on human rights and international humanitarian law to which Burundi was a party and enhance the efficiency of the government Commission on Human Rights and establish a national human rights commission. The international community was encouraged to increase support for the proper implementation of the transition timetable and for regional mediation and the African Union. The Special Rapporteur appealed to donors to continue supporting humanitarian and development assistance and emphasized the urgency of increasing the resources of OHCHR/Burundi. The General Assembly took note of the report on 22 December (**decision 58/539**).

In a later report [E/CN.4/2004/35], the Special Rapporteur reviewed developments from 1 October to 31 December, based on reports received from OHCHR/Burundi and non-governmental organizations (NGOs), and on data provided by the Burundian authorities and UN bodies. She said that a ceasefire agreement between the Transitional Government and the Conseil national pour la défense de la démocratie–Forces pour la défense de la démocratie marked an important step forward in the military and political situation. It was expected that a decrease in acts of violence, especially towards civilians, would follow. Although it seemed premature, it was wise to envisage the creation of a national commission for human rights. The Special Rapporteur made recommendations regarding acts of violence against civilians, the recruitment of children as soldiers, impunity, the protection of vulnerable populations, women's rights and support by the international community.

Democratic Republic of the Congo

Reports of High Commissioner. By a 24 February note [S/2003/216], the Security Council President transmitted the report of the United Nations High Commissioner for Human Rights on the human rights situation in the Democratic Republic of the Congo (DRC) (see p. 117). The report covered the period 18 July 2002 to 30 January 2003. The High Commissioner highlighted specific atrocities perpetrated in the territories controlled by the Government and rebels and pointed to the continuing need for the Council to exert pressure on the Government and the other belligerents and their foreign supporters to end the human rights violations and the culture of impunity.

On 25 June [S/2003/674], the Secretary-General transmitted to the Council President a report of the High Commissioner on the violent events of 3 April in Drodro (Ituri province), which described the findings of a special investigation team charged with supplementing information provided by the United Nations Organization Mission in the DRC (see p. 121).

(For further details on the situation in the DRC, see p. 113 et seq.)

Commission action. On 17 April [res. 2003/15], the Commission expressed concern at the continuing violation of human rights and international humanitarian law in the DRC, especially in Ituri province and the east of the country, and condemned the massacres and violence there. It also condemned reprisals against civilians, cases of summary or arbitrary execution, disappearance, torture, harassment, arrest, widespread persecution and arbitrary detention, the widespread sexual violence against women and children, the recruitment and use of child soldiers, impunity for those responsible for human rights violations and the illegal exploitation of the natural resources of the DRC. All parties to the conflict were urged to cease military activity, protect human rights and respect international humanitarian law, end the recruitment and use of child soldiers, respect women's rights and protect women and children from sexual and other violence, cooperate with the Ituri Pacification Commission to oversee the settlement of the conflict in the north-east, bring to justice those connected with serious violations of international humanitarian law and human rights, ensure the safety and freedom of movement of UN personnel and unhindered access of humanitarian personnel, and cooperate with the UN system, humanitarian organizations and the World Bank to ensure rapid demobilization and reintegration of armed groups and of child soldiers. The High Commissioner was requested to keep the Commission informed of the consultations between the Human Rights Field Office in the DRC and the Secretary-General regarding ways to assist the transitional Government of the DRC to tackle impunity.

The Commission extended the Special Rapporteur's mandate for a further year and requested her to submit an interim report to the General Assembly in 2003 and a report to the Commission in 2004. The Economic and Social Council endorsed the Commission's decisions on 23 July (**decision 2003/240**).

Reports of Special Rapporteur. In April [E/CN.4/2003/43], in response to the Commission's 2002 request [YUN 2002, p. 774], Special Rapporteur Iulia Motoc (Romania) described the human rights situation in the DRC, following her visit to the country (28 February–10 March). In view of the extent of human rights violations in the DRC, she opted to deal in depth with: the protection of civilians in armed conflicts; the situation of women and children victims of sexual violence; the problem of impunity; the administration of justice; and the use of military courts to try cases of mass violations of human rights. She concluded that the situation of human rights and international humanitarian law in the DRC remained tragic, despite some positive developments. The Special Rapporteur made recommendations to the Government, the Rassemblement congolais pour la démocratie, the Mouvement de libération du Congo and the international community.

In October, the Secretary-General, in response to Commission resolution 2003/15 (above), transmitted to the General Assembly the Special Rapporteur's interim report [A/58/534], covering the period up to 4 October, based on information regularly submitted to her by the Human Rights Field Office in the DRC and on her visit to the country (26 August–6 September). She noted that while considerable progress had been made at the political level in recent months (see p. 129), the situation continued to be characterized by mass human rights violations. All violations reflected the constituent elements, as defined in the Rome Statute of the International Criminal Court (ICC) [YUN 1998, p. 1209], of the crime of genocide, crimes against humanity and war crimes. The Special Rapporteur welcomed the decision of the ICC Prosecutor to make the DRC the first State to be the subject of his investigations. Impunity remained a problem, as did difficult conditions of detention and the numerous irregularities committed in prisons and detention centres. As for the justice system, the Special Rapporteur was aware of abuses committed by those responsible for preliminary investigations in criminal proceedings, including security and intelligence officers. Regarding vulnerable populations, the recruitment of children by various groups continued, violence against women had become common practice and indigenous peoples were subjected to large-scale acts of discrimination by the majority of the population. The Special Rapporteur presented recommendations to the parties to the conflict and to the Government.

In a later report [E/CN.4/2004/34], the Special Rapporteur, following her visit to the DRC (29 November–10 December), stated that she was favourably impressed by the progress made at the political level in 2003, but that the process remained fragile and incomplete. She noted the delay in drafting, considering and adopting important legislation indispensable to a successful transition and the holding of elections. She expressed concern about the fate of institutions responsible for human rights and the lack of progress in combating impunity. Civilians lacked security and were subjected to violence by the military and police, while human rights defenders were arrested. Some 3.4 million internally displaced persons faced security problems and lived in precarious conditions. Over the preceding few months, there had been some positive developments regarding the administration of justice, with the adoption of decrees on the organization of the judiciary and the removal of 315 judges from office. The judicial system in Ituri had become operational. Punishment cells (*cachots*) were still in use in prisons and detention centres, in which conditions were inhuman and torture was practised. Little progress had been made towards implementing legislation regarding children associated with armed groups. The Special Rapporteur said that women continued to be subjected to sexual violence and noted a strong reluctance on the part of judges to try and punish rapists. Minority indigenous peoples continued to be discriminated against on a large scale. The Special Rapporteur welcomed the adoption of a national multisectoral programme to combat HIV/AIDS, together with the formation, inside the armed forces and the national police force, of sectoral HIV/AIDS control committees. Although the DRC was one of the world's richest countries in natural resources, its population suffered from ingrained poverty. Some 17 million people, or two thirds of the population, suffered from malnutrition. According to a survey in the equatorial zone, people were living on less than $0.10 per person per day, 85 per cent of the population did not have access to proper food and 80 per cent had no access to medical care.

The Special Rapporteur called on all parties to the conflict to end military activities, respect the obligations relating to the implementation of the Transitional Constitution, implement the Bujumbura agreements of June 2003 (see p. 129), respect women's rights and protect women and children who were victims of sexual violence, cease recruiting and using children in violation of international law, ensure the security and freedom of movement of UN staff and guarantee unhindered access by humanitarian personnel, verify allegations of massive violations of human rights and of humanitarian law, and cooperate with human rights protection mechanisms. The Government should eliminate impunity, cooperate with ICC and the International Criminal Tribunal for Rwanda, implement the Constitution, continue to reform military justice, close unauthorized detention centres, protect children, end discrimination against the Batwa and against persons with HIV/AIDS, and abolish capital punishment. The international community was called on to assist the transition, help formulate strategies to protect refugees, displaced persons and other vulnerable groups, and consider the illegal exploitation of natural resources with a view to creating a mechanism to benefit deprived population groups.

Joint mission. In a July note [A/58/127], the Secretary-General stated that the joint mission of investigation by the Special Rapporteurs on the situation of human rights in the DRC and on extrajudicial, summary or arbitrary executions and a member of the Working Group on Enforced or Involuntary Disappearances, which the General Assembly had requested in resolution 57/233 [YUN 2002, p. 776], did not take place because of the worsening security situation.

GENERAL ASSEMBLY ACTION

On 22 December [meeting 77], the General Assembly, on the recommendation of the Third (Social, Humanitarian and Cultural) Committee [A/58/508/Add.3], adopted **resolution 58/196** by recorded vote (81-2-91) [agenda item 117 (c)].

Situation of human rights in the Democratic Republic of the Congo

The General Assembly,

Guided by the Charter of the United Nations, the Universal Declaration of Human Rights, the International Covenants on Human Rights and other human rights instruments,

Reaffirming that all States Members of the United Nations have an obligation to promote and protect human rights and fundamental freedoms,

Noting that the Democratic Republic of the Congo is a party to several international and regional human rights instruments and to several instruments pertaining to international humanitarian law,

Recalling all its previous resolutions, as well as those of the Commission on Human Rights, on the situation of human rights in the Democratic Republic of the Congo,

Recalling also Security Council resolution 1493(2003) of 28 July 2003,

Bearing in mind Security Council resolution 1325 (2000) of 31 October 2000 on women and peace and security,

Bearing in mind also Security Council resolution 1460 (2003) of 30 January 2003 on children and armed conflict, and the report of the Secretary-General of 10 November 2003 on children and armed conflict,

Welcoming the Final Act of the inter-Congolese political negotiations signed in Sun City, South Africa, on 2 April 2003,

Taking note of the second special report of the Secretary-General on the United Nations Organization Mission in the Democratic Republic of the Congo of 27 May 2003, the report of the Security Council mission to Central Africa, 7 to 16 June 2003, the report of the United Nations High Commissioner for Human Rights of 13 February 2003 and the report of the High Commissioner on the events of 3 April 2003 in Drodro,

Deeply concerned about the continuation of hostilities in the eastern part of the Democratic Republic of the Congo, particularly in North and South Kivu and Ituri, and the grave violations of human rights and international humanitarian law that accompany them, as described in the above-mentioned reports,

Deploring the impunity that characterizes much of the fighting and the accompanying human rights abuses and humanitarian crises in the eastern part of the Democratic Republic of the Congo,

1. *Welcomes*:

(a) The promulgation by the head of State on 4 April 2003 of the Constitution that is to govern the country throughout the transition, the swearing of allegiance to the new Constitution by President Joseph Kabila on 7 April 2003, the installation on 17 July 2003 of the Government of National Unity and Transition in the Democratic Republic of the Congo, the inauguration of the National Assembly and the Senate on 22 August 2003 and the installation of the five transitional institutions on 28 August 2003;

(b) The signing on 18 March 2003 of a ceasefire agreement by the Governments of the Democratic Republic of the Congo and Uganda and six armed groups, which paved the way for the convening of the Ituri Pacification Commission from 4 to 14 April 2003 and the setting up of an interim administration in Ituri;

(c) The ceasefire agreement signed in Dar es Salaam, United Republic of Tanzania, on 16 May 2003, and the signing on 19 June 2003 of the Bujumbura Commitment by the Government of the Democratic Republic of the Congo, the Congolese Rally for Democracy–Goma and the Congolese Rally for Democracy–Liberation Movement;

(d) The abolition of the Military Order Court;

(e) The interim report of the Special Rapporteur of the Commission on Human Rights on the situation of human rights in the Democratic Republic of the Congo and her visits to the country from 26 February to 10 March and from 26 August to 6 September 2003;

(f) The visit by the United Nations High Commissioner for Human Rights to the Democratic Republic of the Congo from 12 to 15 January 2003 and the action taken by his Office in the country;

(g) The consultations between the Secretary-General and the United Nations High Commissioner for Human Rights on ways of dealing with the problem of impunity in the Democratic Republic of the Congo, and takes note of the proposal of the High Commissioner to establish an international body of inquiry to investigate serious violations of human rights and international humanitarian law;

(h) The extension of the mandate, the continuing presence and the increased deployment of the United Nations Organization Mission in the Democratic Republic of the Congo in accordance with Security Council resolution 1493(2003);

(i) The collaboration between the United Nations Organization Mission in the Democratic Republic of the Congo and the Office of the United Nations High Commissioner for Human Rights on the establishment of national institutions and infrastructures to protect human rights as well as transitional justice mechanisms;

(j) The work of the Special Representative of the Secretary-General for the Democratic Republic of the Congo and Chief of the United Nations Organization Mission in the Democratic Republic of the Congo;

2. *Condemns*:

(a) The continuing violations of human rights and international humanitarian law in the Democratic Republic of the Congo, particularly in Ituri, North and South Kivu and other areas in the eastern part of the country;

(b) The persistence, in the eastern part of the country, of the armed violence and reprisals against the civilian population, especially in North and South Kivu and in Ituri;

(c) All the massacres that have occurred in the province of Ituri, particularly the massacres at Drodro, and most recently, at Katchele on 6 October 2003, while supporting the efforts of the United Nations Organization Mission in the Democratic Republic of the Congo and the Office of the United Nations High Commissioner for Human Rights to investigate them;

(d) The reported perpetration of acts of mutilation and cannibalism in the Mambasa region;

(e) The cases of summary or arbitrary execution, disappearance, torture, harassment, unlawful arrest, widespread persecution and arbitrary detention for long periods;

(f) The widespread recourse to sexual violence against women and children, inter alia, as a means of warfare;

(g) The continuing recruitment and use of child soldiers by armed forces and groups, in particular in the eastern part of the Democratic Republic of the Congo, which are contrary to international law;

(h) The impunity of those responsible for violations of human rights and international humanitarian law, and points out in this connection that the Democratic Republic of the Congo is a party to the Rome Statute of the International Criminal Court;

(i) The illegal exploitation of the natural resources of the Democratic Republic of the Congo, in view of the link between that exploitation and the continuation of the conflict;

3. *Expresses its concern* regarding:

(a) The breaches of freedom of expression, opinion, association and assembly and the attacks on human rights defenders throughout the territory of the Democratic Republic of the Congo, in particular in the eastern part of the country;

(b) The continued suspension of the moratorium on the carrying out of the death penalty, in particular the death sentences passed on 7 January 2003 by the Military Order Court which had tried the persons accused of assassinating the former President of the Republic;

(c) The excessive accumulation and spread of small arms and the distribution, circulation and illicit trafficking of arms in the region and their negative impact on human rights;

(d) The increase in the number of refugees and internally displaced persons, in particular in the eastern part of the country;

(e) The continued insecurity, particularly in the east of the country in the zones still held by armed groups, which seriously hampers the efforts of humanitarian organizations to gain access to people affected by the worrying humanitarian situation;

4. *Urges* all parties to the conflict in the Democratic Republic of the Congo:

(a) To cease immediately all military activities, including support for the armed groups allied to them, in order to facilitate the re-establishment of the sovereignty, unity and territorial integrity of the Democratic Republic of the Congo;

(b) To implement fully and without delay both the Bujumbura Commitment of 19 June 2003 and the Dar es Salaam Agreement of 16 May 2003 and to cooperate with the Ituri Interim Administration in overseeing the settlement of the conflict in the north-eastern part of the Democratic Republic of the Congo;

(c) To continue to respect their obligations as regards the implementation of the Transitional Constitution;

(d) To allow free and secure access to all areas so as to permit and support investigations of the presumed serious violations of human rights and international humanitarian law, with a view to bringing those responsible to justice, and to cooperate fully to that end with national and international human rights protection mechanisms to investigate alleged human rights violations and breaches of international humanitarian law in the Democratic Republic of the Congo;

(e) To put an immediate end to the recruitment and use of child soldiers, which are in contravention of international law and the African Charter on the Rights and Welfare of the Child, with the understanding that, under the Convention on the Rights of the Child and the Optional Protocol thereto on the involvement of children in armed conflict, persons under the age of 18 are entitled to special protection, and to provide information without delay on measures taken to discontinue such practices;

(f) To meet the special needs of women and girls in post-conflict reconstruction as well as to ensure the full participation of women in all aspects of conflict resolution and peace processes, including peacekeeping, conflict management and peace-building, as a matter of priority;

(g) To implement all necessary measures to put an end to the widespread violations of human rights and to impunity, in particular with regard to the sexual violence against women and children;

(h) To protect human rights and to respect international humanitarian law, in particular by ensuring the safety, security and freedom of movement of all civilians, as well as United Nations and associated personnel, and the unhindered access of humanitarian personnel to all of the affected population throughout the territory of the Democratic Republic of the Congo;

(i) To prevent conditions that might lead to flows of refugees and displaced persons in the territory of the Democratic Republic of the Congo and across its borders and to take and apply all necessary measures to establish conditions conducive to the voluntary return of refugees and displaced persons;

5. *Urges* the Government of National Unity and Transition to ensure that the protection of human rights and the establishment of a State based on the rule of law and of an independent judiciary are among its highest priorities, including the establishment of the necessary institutions as reflected in the Global and All-Inclusive Agreement on the Transition in the Democratic Republic of the Congo, signed in Pretoria on 17 December 2002;

6. *Calls upon* the Government of National Unity and Transition to take specific measures:

(a) To achieve the objectives of the transitional period as laid down in the Global and All-Inclusive Agreement, in particular the holding of free and transparent elections at all levels, enabling the establishment of a democratic constitutional regime, and the formation of a restructured and integrated national army;

(b) To strengthen the transitional institutions and to re-establish stability and the rule of law over the entire territory of the Democratic Republic of the Congo, thereby returning peace and progress to its people;

(c) To comply fully with its obligations under international human rights instruments and, accordingly, to continue to cooperate with United Nations mechanisms for the protection of human rights and further strengthen its cooperation with the Office of the United Nations High Commissioner for Human Rights in the Democratic Republic of the Congo;

(d) To carry out a comprehensive reform of the judicial system;

(e) To reinstate the moratorium on capital punishment and adhere to its commitment to progressively abolish the death penalty;

(f) To put an end to impunity and to ensure that those responsible for human rights violations and grave breaches of international humanitarian law are brought to justice in accordance with due process;

(g) To cooperate with the International Criminal Court and to continue to cooperate with the International Tribunal for Rwanda;

7. *Calls upon* the United Nations High Commissioner for Human Rights to keep it informed of the consultations between his/her Office and the Secretary-General concerning the ways in which to assist the transitional Government of the Democratic Republic of the Congo in tackling the problem of impunity;

8. *Calls upon* the international community:

(a) To support the human rights field office in the Democratic Republic of the Congo in order to make possible the effective implementation of its programmes;

(b) To support the organization, at the appropriate time and under the aegis of the United Nations and the African Union, of an international conference on peace, security, democracy and development in the Great Lakes region of Africa, with the participation of all the Governments of the region and all other parties concerned, and to support the introduction of human rights and humanitarian issues as one of the main themes of this conference;

9. *Requests*:

(a) The Special Rapporteurs of the Commission on Human Rights on the situation of human rights in the Democratic Republic of the Congo and on extrajudicial, summary or arbitrary executions and a member of the Working Group on Enforced or Involuntary Disappearances of the Commission to carry out a mission of investigation in the Democratic Republic of the Congo and to report to the Commission at its sixtieth session and to the General Assembly at its fifty-ninth session;

(b) The Secretary-General to give the Special Rapporteurs and the joint mission all necessary assistance to enable them to discharge their mandate fully;

(c) The United Nations High Commissioner for Human Rights to provide the technical skills needed by the joint mission to discharge its mandate;

(d) The Secretary-General to encourage the United Nations Organization Mission in the Democratic Republic of the Congo to continue to raise the awareness of and provide training to all Mission staff, including civilian police and military personnel, with respect to the relevant child protection standards, in particular when dealing with child soldiers, and to cooperate closely with the Special Representative of the Secretary-General for Children and Armed Conflict;

(e) The Secretary-General to encourage the United Nations Organization Mission in the Democratic Republic of the Congo to continue to actively address the issues of gender, the full enjoyment of all human rights by women and the fight to eliminate violence against women and to provide adequate training to all Mission personnel in this regard;

10. *Decides* to continue to examine the situation of human rights in the Democratic Republic of the Congo, and requests the Special Rapporteur to report to the General Assembly at its fifty-ninth session.

RECORDED VOTE ON RESOLUTION 58/196:

In favour: Albania, Andorra, Argentina, Armenia, Australia, Austria, Bahamas, Belgium, Bolivia, Bosnia and Herzegovina, Brazil, Bulgaria, Canada, Chile, Colombia, Costa Rica, Croatia, Cyprus, Czech Republic, Denmark, Dominican Republic, Ecuador, El Salvador, Estonia, Finland, France, Georgia, Germany, Greece, Guatemala, Honduras, Hungary, Iceland, Ireland, Israel, Italy, Japan, Kazakhstan, Kyrgyzstan, Latvia, Liechtenstein, Lithuania, Luxembourg, Malta, Mexico, Micronesia, Monaco, Nauru, Netherlands, New Zealand, Nicaragua, Norway, Palau, Panama, Papua New Guinea, Paraguay, Peru, Poland, Portugal, Republic of Korea, Republic of Moldova, Romania, Russian Federation, Samoa, San Marino, Serbia and Montenegro, Slovakia, Slovenia, Spain, Sweden, Switzerland, Tajikistan, The former Yugoslav Republic of Macedonia, Timor-Leste, Turkey, Ukraine, United Kingdom, United States, Uruguay, Uzbekistan, Venezuela.

Against: Rwanda, Uganda.

Abstaining: Algeria, Angola, Antigua and Barbuda, Azerbaijan, Bahrain, Bangladesh, Barbados, Belarus, Belize, Benin, Bhutan, Botswana, Brunei Darussalam, Burkina Faso, Burundi, Cambodia, Cameroon, Cape Verde, Central African Republic, China, Comoros, Congo, Côte d'Ivoire, Cuba, Democratic People's Republic of Korea, Democratic Republic of the Congo, Djibouti, Dominica, Egypt, Eritrea, Ethiopia, Fiji, Gabon, Ghana, Grenada, Guinea, Guinea-Bissau, Guyana, India, Indonesia, Iran, Jamaica, Jordan, Kenya, Kuwait, Lao People's Democratic Republic, Lebanon, Lesotho, Libyan Arab Jamahiriya, Madagascar, Malawi, Malaysia, Maldives, Mali, Mauritania, Mauritius, Mongolia, Morocco, Mozambique, Myanmar, Namibia, Nepal, Niger, Nigeria, Oman, Pakistan, Philippines, Qatar, Saint Lucia, Saint Vincent and the Grenadines, Saudi Arabia, Senegal, Sierra Leone, Singapore, Somalia, South Africa, Sri Lanka, Sudan, Suriname, Syrian Arab Republic, Thailand, Togo, Trinidad and Tobago, Tunisia, Turkmenistan, Tuvalu, United Arab Emirates, United Republic of Tanzania, Yemen, Zambia, Zimbabwe.

The Third Committee retained the fourth preambular paragraph by a recorded vote of 82 to 4, with 75 abstentions, and paragraphs 3 *(b)* and 6 *(e)* by 73 to 50, with 35 abstentions. An oral amendment to paragraph 6 *(g)* by the United States was rejected by a recorded vote of 93 against to 2 in favour, with 55 abstentions. The text as a whole was adopted by a recorded vote of 74 to 3, with 85 abstentions. The Assembly retained the fourth preambular paragraph by a recorded vote of 89 to 3, with 75 abstentions, and paragraphs 3 *(b)* and 6 *(e)* by 73 to 49, with 44 abstentions.

Liberia

(For information on the human rights situation in Liberia, see p. 683.)

Sierra Leone

(For information on the human rights situation in Sierra Leone, see p. 684.)

Somalia

(For information on the human rights situation in Somalia, see p. 685.)

Sudan

During the fifty-ninth session of the Commission on Human Rights [E/2003/23], the Sudan, on 16 April, requested a recorded vote on a draft resolution on the situation of human rights in the Sudan [E/CN.4/2003/L.35]. By that text, the Commission would have expressed deep concern at the continuing violations of human rights and international law in the country and extended the Special Rapporteur's mandate for a further year. The draft was rejected by 26 votes to 24, with 3 abstentions.

(See p. 764 for details of the visit to the Sudan by the independent expert on extreme poverty.)

Zimbabwe

During the fifty-ninth session of the Commission on Human Rights [E/2003/23], South Africa introduced a motion to take no action on a draft resolution on the situation of human rights in Zimbabwe [E/CN.4/2003/L.37]. By that text, the Commission would have expressed deep concern at continuing human rights violations by the Government of Zimbabwe and requested the Special Rapporteurs on torture, on the independence of the judiciary, on the right to freedom of opinion and expression, on extrajudicial, summary or arbitrary executions, on violence against women and on the right to food, and the Secretary-General's Special Representative on human rights defenders to consider missions, including joint missions, to examine alleged human rights violations in the country. The motion was carried by 28 votes to 24, with 1 abstention.

Americas

Colombia

Commission action. The Commission on Human Rights Chairperson, in a 25 April statement regarding the human rights situation in Colombia [E/2003/23], welcomed the new Government's commitment to the principles of democracy, respect for human rights, good governance and the rule of law. The Commission noted government efforts to increase human rights training, but remained concerned at continued reports of human rights abuses attributed to the armed and security forces. Expressing deep concern at reports that the Office of the Attorney-General was not showing sufficient willingness to investigate serious human rights violations, the Commission urged the Attorney-General to secure and strengthen the independence of the Human Rights and International Humanitarian Law Unit within that Office, to guarantee the protection of its prosecutors and investigators and to secure funding to continue its investigations. The Commission urged the Government to end impunity and to guarantee the right to life, physical integrity and the ability of leaders of trade unions and employers' organizations to function freely. It condemned all acts of terrorism and other criminal acts, impunity, the recruitment of children by illegal armed groups, all violent acts and breaches of international humanitarian law committed by paramilitary groups and other illegal armed groups, kidnapping and the campaign of intimidation against mayors and town councillors, which represented an offence against local liberties and the running of democratic institutions. The High Commissioner was requested to report in 2004.

Report of High Commissioner. The High Commissioner's report on the human rights situation in Colombia in 2003 [E/CN.4/2004/13], based on information collected by OHCHR/Bogotá, stated that the office had registered complaints of violations of the right to life, to physical integrity, to personal freedoms and security, to due process and judicial guarantees, to the independence and impartiality of the judicial system, to respect for privacy and intimacy, to the fundamental freedoms of circulation, residence, opinion and expression, and to political rights. Growing numbers of complaints of violations by the security forces and the Attorney-General's Office were received. Of concern was the increase in numbers of complaints regarding arbitrary or illegal detentions, forced disappearances, extrajudicial executions, violations of the right to due process and the right to intimacy. The number of complaints of torture and mistreatment increased. Economic, social and cultural rights continued to be affected by the large gap in the distribution of wealth, extreme poverty, exclusion and social injustice. Although there was a decrease in killings of union leaders, the situation of human rights defenders and union leaders continued to be critical. The internal armed conflict aggravated the situation of indigenous communities and Afro-Colombians. Measures taken against impunity continued to register few concrete results. The High Commissioner's recommendations, which were addressed to the State authorities, illegal armed groups, civil society and the international community, covered matters relating to prevention and protection, the internal armed conflict, the rule of law and impunity, economic and social policies, the promotion of a culture of human rights, and the advisory services and technical cooperation of OHCHR/Bogotá.

Communication. Responding to the High Commissioner's report [E/CN.4/2004/G/23], Colombia observed that the report did not recognize the gravity of the threat to its institutions and society at the hands of the illegal armed groups using terrorist methods. The Government considered that the report undervalued such 2003 achievements as a reduction in the homicide rate, murders of union leaders, forced displacement and massacres, and an increase in freedom of movement. It enumerated action taken to apply the High Commissioner's previous recommendations [YUN 2002, p. 786].

(For information on the visits to Colombia by the Special Rapporteur on contemporary forms of racism, racial discrimination, xenophobia and related intolerance and by the Special Rapporteur on the right to education, see pp. 705 and 770, respectively.)

Cuba

Communication. On 11 February [E/CN.4/2003/G/37], Cuba transmitted its views on Commission resolution 2002/18 [YUN 2002, p. 787]. It summarized its history of international cooperation in human rights matters and set forth the reasons why it did not accept any part of the resolution.

Commission action. A March note by the Secretariat [E/CN.4/2003/36] stated that, pursuant to Commission resolution 2002/18, the High Commissioner, on 27 January, designated Christine Chanet (France) as his Personal Representative for Cuba.

On 17 April [res. 2003/13], by a recorded vote of 24 to 20, with 9 abstentions, the Commission urged the Government of Cuba to receive the High Commissioner's Personal Representative and to assist her to fulfil her mandate.

Report of Personal Representative. In a report to the Commission [E/CN.4/2004/32 & Corr.1], the High Commissioner's Personal Representative stated that in February and May she invited Cuban authorities to meet with her to plan a constructive dialogue. Although the High Commissioner had backed her request, the Cuban authorities notified the High Commissioner in June that they did not recognize the Representative's mandate. Under those circumstances, the Representative gathered information from the Commission's thematic special rapporteurs who had inquired into the human rights situation in

Cuba and from NGOs wishing to express their views. She also held discussions in Geneva with representatives of the Commission's member States who wished to meet her, and familiarized herself with the concluding observations adopted by the treaty bodies to which Cuba had submitted reports, as well as reports drawn up by the Inter-American Commission on Human Rights.

On the positive side, the Representative said that the Government maintained a sound health system, 100 per cent of the children attended school, school success rates were high, particularly in mathematics, and illiteracy stood at just 0.2 per cent. The proportion of women in the National Assembly, the judiciary and decision-making posts had risen. At the time of Pope John Paul II's visit to Cuba in 1998, an improvement was seen in the exercise of freedom of religion. Cuba had ratified human rights conventions and had submitted reports to the respective treaty bodies. During 2003, Cuba responded to urgent appeals launched on 8 April by the Working Group on Arbitrary Detention and on 19 May jointly by the Special Rapporteur on the right to freedom of opinion and expression, the Special Rapporteur on the independence of judges and lawyers, and the Special Representative of the Secretary-General on human rights defenders.

Subjects of concern related to the arbitrary arrest in March/April of some 80 persons, most of whom supported the Varela project, which involved the collection of signatures for the organization of a referendum on changing the electoral system and the fostering of other legislative reforms. Those arrested were charged with such actions as receiving funds from foreign countries or engaging in subversive activities, communicating with international human rights organizations, possessing radio or video equipment, or participating in trade unions, associations or academic groups deemed to be counter-revolutionary. Independent counsel, diplomats and foreign journalists were barred from attending the trials. Prison terms ranging from 6 to 28 years were imposed. In June, the Personal Representative appealed to Cuba's President to pardon the detainees, but no reply had been received. Particularly alarming information on their prison conditions had been communicated to the Representative. Annexed to the report was a list of the persons arrested in March/April. Also of concern was the execution on 11 April of three individuals who had attempted to hijack a ferry carrying many persons and force it to sail to the United States on 2 April.

The Representative recommended that the Government halt the prosecution of citizens exercising the rights enshrined in the Universal Declaration of Human Rights, adopted by the General Assembly in resolution 217 A (III) [YUN 1948-49, p. 535]; release detainees who had not committed violent acts against individuals and property; review laws that led to criminal prosecutions for the exercise of freedom of expression, demonstration, assembly and association; uphold the moratorium on the application of the death penalty introduced in 2000; reform the rules of criminal procedure; establish an independent body to receive complaints of human rights violations; review regulations relating to the freedom of movement; authorize NGOs to enter Cuba; foster pluralism in respect of associations, trade unions, the press and political parties; and accede to the International Covenant on Civil and Political Rights and the Optional Protocols thereto, and the International Covenant on Economic, Social and Cultural Rights (see pp. 669 and 670, respectively).

Haiti

(For information on the human rights situation in Haiti, see p. 683.)

Asia and the Pacific

Afghanistan

(For information on the human rights situation in Afghanistan, see p. 679.)

Cambodia

(For information on the human rights situation in Cambodia, see p. 679.)

Democratic People's Republic of Korea

On 16 April [res. 2003/10], by a recorded vote of 28 to 10, with 14 abstentions, the Commission expressed deep concern about reports of systematic, widespread and grave human rights violations in the Democratic People's Republic of Korea (DPRK), regretted that the DPRK authorities did not permit the international community to verify the reports in an independent manner and called on the Government to respond urgently. Deeply concerned about reports of a precarious humanitarian situation, the Commission called on the DPRK authorities to ensure that humanitarian organizations had free and unimpeded access to all parts of the country. The High Commissioner was requested to engage in a dialogue with the DPRK authorities, with a view to establishing human rights technical cooperation programmes and to report to the Commission in 2004.

Iran

(For information on the human rights situation in Iran regarding arbitrary detention and freedom of opinion and expression, see pp. 733 and 745, respectively.)

GENERAL ASSEMBLY ACTION

On 22 December [meeting 77], the General Assembly, on the recommendation of the Third Committee [A/58/508/Add.3], adopted **resolution 58/195** by recorded vote (68-54-51) [agenda item 117 (c)].

Situation of human rights in the Islamic Republic of Iran

The General Assembly,

Guided by the Charter of the United Nations, the Universal Declaration of Human Rights, the International Covenants on Human Rights and other international human rights instruments,

Reaffirming that all Member States have an obligation to promote and protect human rights and fundamental freedoms and to fulfil the obligations they have undertaken under the various international instruments in this field,

Mindful that the Islamic Republic of Iran is a party to the International Covenant on Civil and Political Rights, the International Covenant on Economic, Social and Cultural Rights, the International Convention on the Elimination of All Forms of Racial Discrimination and the Convention on the Rights of the Child,

Recalling its previous resolutions on the subject, the most recent of which is resolution 56/171 of 19 December 2001, and recalling also Commission on Human Rights resolution 2001/17 of 20 April 2001,

Noting the commitment made by the Government of the Islamic Republic of Iran to strengthen respect for human rights in the country and to promote the rule of law,

1. *Welcomes*:

(*a*) The open invitation extended by the Government of the Islamic Republic of Iran to all human rights thematic monitoring mechanisms in April 2002;

(*b*) The visit of the Working Group on Arbitrary Detention of the Commission on Human Rights to the Islamic Republic of Iran from 15 to 27 February 2003 and its subsequent report;

(*c*) The visit of the Special Rapporteur of the Commission on Human Rights on the promotion and protection of the right to freedom of opinion and expression to the Islamic Republic of Iran from 4 to 10 November 2003 and the scheduled visit of the Working Group on Enforced or Involuntary Disappearances of the Commission in February 2004;

(*d*) The recommendation by the head of the judiciary of the Islamic Republic of Iran to judges that they choose alternative punishment in cases where the sentence of stoning would otherwise be imposed;

(*e*) The efforts of the elected Government to foster the growth of civil society;

(*f*) The opening of human rights dialogues with a number of countries;

(*g*) The efforts made by Parliament, in particular the Article 90 Commission, and by the Islamic Human Rights Commission to improve the situation of human rights in the Islamic Republic of Iran;

2. *Expresses its serious concern* at:

(*a*) The continuing violations of human rights in the Islamic Republic of Iran;

(*b*) The continuing deterioration of the situation with regard to freedom of opinion and expression, especially the increased persecution for the peaceful expression of political views, including arrest and detention without charge or trial; crackdowns by judiciary and security forces against journalists, parliamentarians, students, clerics and academics; and the harsh reactions to student demonstrations, including imprisonment, mistreatment and use of university disciplinary committees against those who participate;

(*c*) The continuing executions in the absence of respect for internationally recognized safeguards, and in particular deplores public executions;

(*d*) The use of torture and other forms of cruel, inhuman and degrading punishment, in particular the practice of amputation and flogging;

(*e*) The continuing restrictions on free assembly and the forcible dissolution of political parties;

(*f*) The failure to comply fully with international standards in the administration of justice, the absence of due process of law, the use of national security laws to deny the rights of the individual and the lack of respect for internationally recognized legal safeguards, inter alia, with respect to persons belonging to religious minorities;

(*g*) The systemic discrimination against women and girls in law and in practice and the refusal of the Guardian Council to take steps to address this systematic discrimination, noting in this context its refusal, in August 2003, to consider the proposal of the elected Parliament to accede to the Convention on the Elimination of All Forms of Discrimination against Women;

(*h*) The continuing discrimination against persons belonging to minorities, including the Baha'is, Christians, Jews and Sunnis, including cases of arbitrary arrest and detention, the denial of free worship or of publicly carrying out communal affairs and the disregard of property rights;

(*i*) The continuing persecution and arbitrary sentencing to prison of human rights defenders, political opponents, religious dissenters and reformists;

3. *Calls upon* the Government of the Islamic Republic of Iran:

(*a*) To abide by its obligations freely undertaken under the International Covenants on Human Rights and other international human rights instruments, including those relating to freedom of opinion and expression, the use of torture and other forms of cruel, inhuman and degrading treatment or punishment and the promotion and protection of the human rights of women and girls, and to continue its efforts to consolidate respect for human rights and the rule of law;

(*b*) To respond fully to the recommendations of the Working Group on Arbitrary Detention of the Commission on Human Rights;

(c) To continue to cooperate with United Nations mechanisms, in particular with the Special Rapporteur on the promotion and protection of the right to freedom of opinion and expression and the Working Group on Enforced or Involuntary Disappearances, and to respond fully to their recommendations;

(d) To expedite judicial reform, to guarantee the dignity of the individual and to ensure the full application of due process of law and fair and transparent procedures by an independent and impartial judiciary, and in this context to ensure respect for the rights of the defence and the equity of verdicts in all instances, including for members of religious minority groups;

(e) To appoint an impartial prosecutor, noting the re-establishment, since December 2001, within the Islamic Republic of Iran of the Office of the Prosecutor General;

(f) To eliminate all forms of discrimination based on religious grounds or against persons belonging to minorities, including the Baha'is, Christians, Jews and Sunnis, and to address this matter in an open manner, with the full participation of the minorities themselves;

(g) To take all necessary measures to end amputation and public flogging and to pursue vigorously penitentiary reform;

4. *Encourages* the thematic mechanisms of the Commission on Human Rights, including the Special Rapporteur on extrajudicial, summary or arbitrary executions and the Special Rapporteur on the question of torture, to visit the Islamic Republic of Iran, and encourages the Government of the Islamic Republic of Iran to cooperate with these special mechanisms and to respond fully to their subsequent recommendations;

5. *Decides* to continue its examination of the situation of human rights in the Islamic Republic of Iran, paying particular attention to further developments, including the situation of the Baha'is and other minority groups, at its fifty-ninth session, under the item entitled "Human rights questions", in the light of additional elements provided by the Commission on Human Rights.

RECORDED VOTE ON RESOLUTION 58/195:

In favour: Albania, Andorra, Australia, Austria, Bahamas, Barbados, Belgium, Belize, Bolivia, Bosnia and Herzegovina, Brazil, Bulgaria, Canada, Chile, Costa Rica, Croatia, Czech Republic, Denmark, Dominican Republic, Ecuador, El Salvador, Estonia, Fiji, Finland, France, Germany, Greece, Grenada, Hungary, Iceland, Ireland, Israel, Italy, Japan, Latvia, Liechtenstein, Lithuania, Luxembourg, Malta, Marshall Islands, Mexico, Micronesia, Monaco, Nauru, Netherlands, New Zealand, Nicaragua, Norway, Palau, Papua New Guinea, Paraguay, Peru, Poland, Portugal, Romania, Samoa, San Marino, Serbia and Montenegro, Slovakia, Slovenia, Solomon Islands, Spain, Sweden, The former Yugoslav Republic of Macedonia, Timor-Leste, Tuvalu, United Kingdom, United States.

Against: Afghanistan, Algeria, Azerbaijan, Bahrain, Bangladesh, Belarus, Benin, Brunei Darussalam, China, Colombia, Comoros, Cuba, Democratic People's Republic of Korea, Democratic Republic of the Congo, Djibouti, Egypt, Gabon, India, Indonesia, Iran, Jordan, Kazakhstan, Kuwait, Kyrgyzstan, Lebanon, Libyan Arab Jamahiriya, Malaysia, Maldives, Mauritania, Morocco, Myanmar, Niger, Oman, Pakistan, Philippines, Qatar, Russian Federation, Saudi Arabia, Senegal, Sierra Leone, Somalia, South Africa, Sri Lanka, Sudan, Syrian Arab Republic, Tajikistan, Togo, Tunisia, Turkmenistan, Ukraine, Venezuela, Viet Nam, Yemen, Zimbabwe.

Abstaining: Angola, Antigua and Barbuda, Argentina, Bhutan, Botswana, Burkina Faso, Burundi, Cambodia, Cameroon, Cape Verde, Central African Republic, Congo, Côte d'Ivoire, Cyprus, Dominica, Eritrea, Ethiopia, Georgia, Ghana, Guatemala, Guinea, Guinea-Bissau, Guyana, Jamaica, Kenya, Lao People's Democratic Republic, Lesotho, Madagascar, Malawi, Mali, Mauritius, Mongolia, Mozambique, Namibia, Nepal, Nigeria, Panama, Republic of Korea, Rwanda, Saint Lucia, Saint Vincent and the Grenadines, Singapore, Suriname, Switzerland, Thailand, Trinidad and Tobago, Uganda, United Arab Emirates, United Republic of Tanzania, Uruguay, Zambia.

Iraq

Commission action. At its fifty-ninth session [E/2003/23], the Commission, on 27 March, rejected, by a roll-call vote of 25 to 18, with 7 abstentions, a proposal by several Commission members to convene a special sitting on the effect of the war against Iraq, which began on 20 March (see p. 333), on the Iraqi people and their humanitarian situation.

On 25 April [res. 2003/84], by a recorded vote of 31 to 3, with 12 abstentions, the Commission strongly condemned the systematic, widespread and extremely grave violations of human rights and international humanitarian law by the Government of Iraq over many years. It requested all parties to the current conflict to abide by their obligations under international humanitarian law. The Commission called on the international community to address urgently the major humanitarian needs of the Iraqi people and to assist in the development of free and democratic institutions. The Commission decided to extend the Special Rapporteur's mandate for a further year and requested him to report to the General Assembly in 2003 and to the Commission in 2004. The Economic and Social Council endorsed the Commission's decision on 23 July (**decision 2003/262**).

Reports of Special Rapporteur. In an addendum [E/CN.4/2003/40/Add.1] to an earlier report [YUN 2002, p. 794], Special Rapporteur Andreas Mavrommatis (Cyprus) described the human rights situation in Iraq covering the period 1 January to 28 February, based on meetings with the Permanent Representative of Iraq to the United Nations Office at Geneva, members of the Human Rights Department of the Iraqi Ministry for Foreign Affairs, representatives of OHCHR and the International Committee of the Red Cross (ICRC), and NGOs. Discussions focused on the abolition of the death penalty for certain crimes, the abolition of decrees on the amputation of hands or the branding of people, the abolition of the Special Courts and their replacement by a State Security Court attached to the Ministry of Justice, and the number of prisoners and detainees having benefited from the amnesty decree. Also discussed were political rights, democracy, a multiparty system and other efforts to establish respect for fundamental freedoms. The Special Rapporteur suggested that a human rights presence in Iraq could assist in developing ways to entrench a human rights culture. He urged the Government to respect the rights of individuals at all times, including in times of war, and to cooperate on the question of Kuwaiti prisoners of war and persons unaccounted for.

By a September note [A/58/338], the Secretary-General transmitted to the General Assembly the interim report of the Special Rapporteur on Iraq, who stated that he had received a positive response from the United States, on behalf of the Coalition Provisional Authority (CPA), in reply to his request to visit Iraq to examine past gross and systematic human rights violations. The Special Rapporteur had proposed the period from 22 to 27 September for his visit. However, his visit had to be postponed for security reasons. The Assembly took note of the report on 22 December (**decision 58/539**).

In a later report [E/CN.4/2004/36], the Special Rapporteur described his activities in the light of his inability to travel to Iraq. In Geneva, he held meetings with the Permanent Representatives of Iraq, Kuwait, the United Kingdom and the United States, and with CPA experts dealing with such issues as transitional justice, the Iraqi Special Tribunal, mass graves and other human rights violations; in New York, with UN bodies and specialized agencies, international NGOs and the Executive Director of the oil-for-food programme; in Madrid, during the Iraq Reconstruction Donor Conference (23-25 October); and in Amman, Jordan, with a Kurdish delegation (7-10 December). However, despite his efforts, it proved almost impossible to collect and appraise any significant new evidence and much remained to be done. From October onwards, he focused on summary executions, mass graves, the Anfal campaign against the Kurds and the Arabization process, including of property rights. The CPA Office of Human Rights and Transitional Justice made available to him evidence recorded in a list cataloguing past atrocities. A selection of 20 serious cases was provided to the Special Rapporteur, describing almost 15 different methods of torture. He recommended that the Iraqi authorities systematize and accelerate the process of investigation and make available to him selected cases of past violations and establish a quick and effective system of communication with him. All investigations should be carried out in full compliance with Iraq's international obligations, and the transfer of power to the Iraqis should take place as soon as possible as part of the democratization process.

Myanmar

Communication. On 18 March [E/CN.4/2003/G/47], Myanmar submitted information to the Commission regarding the country's difficulties in its transition to a new political system and the Government's achievements in many areas. It cited efforts towards peace and stability and progress in economic development, health care, education, the suppression of narcotic drugs, democratization, the right to development, the rights of the child and the status of women. It refuted allegations of violence against women in Shan State, the use of child soldiers and religious intolerance.

Commission action. On 16 April [res. 2003/12], the Commission welcomed positive developments in Myanmar, including the freedom of movement enjoyed by Daw Aung San Suu Kyi, leader of the National League for Democracy (NLD), the release of political detainees, cooperation with ICRC, the dissemination of human rights standards for public officials and some NGOs and ethnic groups, and the establishment by the Government of a committee on human rights as a precursor to the establishment of a human rights commission. However, it expressed grave concern at the ongoing systematic human rights violations. It called on the Government to restore the independence of the judiciary; eradicate forced labour; ensure safe and unhindered access by UN and international humanitarian organizations; end permanently conflict with all ethnic groups; and establish a human rights commission.

The Commission decided to extend the Special Rapporteur's mandate for a further year and asked him to report to the General Assembly in 2003 and to the Commission in 2004. The Economic and Social Council endorsed the Commission's decision on 23 July (**decision 2003/239**).

Reports of Secretary-General. In response to General Assembly resolution 57/231 [YUN 2002, p. 798], the Secretary-General submitted a March report [E/CN.4/2003/33] on his good offices efforts and those of his Special Envoy, Razali Ismail, in facilitating national reconciliation and democratization in Myanmar. Discussions with the Myanmar authorities focused on UN assistance in moving confidence-building talks to a more substantive dialogue. Although Daw Aung San Suu Kyi's freedom of movement had been restored since May 2002 [YUN 2002, p. 797], she had had no substantive dialogue with the Government. The Secretary-General called on both parties to set aside their differences, unite for a larger cause and start their political dialogue as soon as possible.

In August [A/58/325], the Secretary-General described the events of 30 May in northern Myanmar, when pro-Government protesters attacked an NLD convoy carrying Daw Aung San Suu Kyi, NLD members and other supporters.

Several persons were killed and Daw Aung San Suu Kyi, NLD members and other supporters were subsequently arrested and detained. The Secretary-General called on the authorities to remove, without delay, all the restrictions imposed on their freedom of movement and political activities. Although the events of 30 May had seriously undermined it, the national reconciliation process could be saved with the efforts of all parties.

In a November addendum to his report [A/58/325/Add.1], the Secretary-General noted that the situation prevailing in Myanmar had not changed significantly since the issue of his August report (above). The Government had announced a seven-step road map to a democratic transition on 30 August, which, the Secretary-General said, should involve all Myanmar's political parties, national leaders, ethnic nationalities and strata of society from the beginning. He appealed to the Government to lift the remaining restrictions imposed on Daw Aung San Suu Kyi, other NLD leaders and those detained in connection with the 30 May incident, and to allow NLD to reopen its offices across the country.

The General Assembly took note of the report and addendum on 22 December (**decision 58/539**).

Reports of Special Rapporteur. In response to Commission resolution 2003/12 and Economic and Social Council decision 2003/239 (see p. 819), the Secretary-General, by an August note [A/58/219], transmitted the report of Special Rapporteur Paulo Sérgio Pinheiro (Brazil) on the human rights situation in Myanmar, based on his visit to the country (19-24 March) and information received by him up to 28 July. The Special Rapporteur's visit was curtailed when he discovered a listening device in the room at Insein prison where he was interviewing political prisoners on 22 March. The incident constituted a breach of the standard operating procedures relating to the conduct of fact-finding missions by UN special rapporteurs.

The Special Rapporteur said that the 30 May-related developments (above) had constituted a potentially terminal setback on the political and human rights front. The economic and social situation in Myanmar remained precarious, with massive inflation pervading the country. During the reporting period, the Special Rapporteur continued to pursue his efforts to obtain access to ethnic minority areas to investigate allegations of serious human rights violations. He had received informal suggestions from Myanmar regarding the possibility of an independent assessment mission and, in April, he had submitted to Myanmar the draft modalities of the assessment, which were annexed to his report. Since he had been unsuccessful in his attempts to obtain Myanmar's agreement on the modalities, the Special Rapporteur made public the findings of his research on the human rights situation in ethnic areas of Myanmar conducted in Thailand in October and November 2002 [YUN 2002, p. 797]. The research, which was summarized in his report, documented widespread human rights abuses such as forced labour, arbitrary taxation and extortion, forced relocations, torture, rape and extrajudicial executions.

In a later report [E/CN.4/2004/33], the Special Rapporteur described his visit to Myanmar (3-8 November) and provided information received by him up to 17 December. Despite his repeated calls on the Government to refrain from new arrests, he received reports of some 250 new arrests since 30 May. Grounds for arrest remained highly arbitrary, based on the legislation criminalizing the exercise of basic rights and the freedoms of expression, information, movement, assembly and association, including the use of some provisions of the Penal Code. The Special Rapporteur welcomed slight improvements in the conditions of detention of convicted political prisoners since his March visit. However, concerns remained about disparities in the conditions of different prison blocks in terms of food quality and the lack of basic necessities. He continued to be concerned about ill-treatment of detainees in pre-trial detention, detainees kept in incommunicado detention, reports of religious intolerance, allegations of serious human rights violations in ethnic minority areas, including Shan State, the forcible recruitment of boys as child soldiers and the widespread forced military training of civilians. The Special Rapporteur called for a full and independent inquiry into the events of 30 May, restored freedom of movement for Daw Aung San Suu Kyi and other NLD leaders and members, the lifting of remaining restrictions on the freedoms of expression, movement, information, assembly and association, the repeal of security legislation, the opening and reopening of all political parties' offices and the release of all political prisoners.

GENERAL ASSEMBLY ACTION

On 23 December [meeting 79], the General Assembly, on the recommendation of the Third Committee [A/58/508/Add.3], adopted **resolution 58/247** without vote [agenda item 117 (c)].

Situation of human rights in Myanmar

The General Assembly,

Guided by the Charter of the United Nations, the Universal Declaration of Human Rights, the International Covenants on Human Rights and other human rights instruments,

Reaffirming that all States Members of the United Nations have an obligation to promote and protect human rights and fundamental freedoms and to fulfil the obligations they have undertaken under the various international instruments in the field,

Aware that Myanmar is a party to the Convention on the Rights of the Child, the Convention on the Elimination of All Forms of Discrimination against Women, the Convention on the Prevention and Punishment of the Crime of Genocide and the Geneva Conventions of 12 August 1949 for the protection of victims of war, as well as the Convention concerning Forced or Compulsory Labour, 1930 (Convention No. 29) and the Convention concerning Freedom of Association and Protection of the Right to Organize, 1948 (Convention No. 87), of the International Labour Organization,

Bearing in mind Security Council resolution 1460 (2003) of 30 January 2003 on children and armed conflict and the report of the Secretary-General pursuant thereto,

Recalling its previous resolutions on the subject, the most recent of which is resolution 57/231 of 18 December 2002, those of the Commission on Human Rights, the most recent of which is resolution 2003/12 of 16 April 2003, and resolution I adopted by the International Labour Conference at its eighty-eighth session, on 14 June 2000, concerning the practice of forced or compulsory labour in Myanmar,

Affirming that the will of the people is the basis of the authority of government and that the will of the people of Myanmar was clearly expressed in the elections held in 1990,

Affirming also that the establishment of a genuine democratic government in Myanmar is essential for the realization of all human rights and fundamental freedoms,

Recognizing that good governance, democracy, the rule of law and respect for human rights are essential to achieving sustainable development and economic growth,

Taking note of the increasing awareness of the Government of Myanmar of the need to comprehensively address the production of opium in Myanmar,

Taking note also of the road map for the transition to democracy announced by the Prime Minister of Myanmar on 30 August 2003,

1. *Welcomes*:

(a) The visits to Myanmar by the Special Envoy of the Secretary-General for Myanmar during the past year and the visits by the Special Rapporteur of the Commission on Human Rights on the situation of human rights in Myanmar;

(b) Efforts by the international community, including support from countries in the region, to encourage the Government of Myanmar to resume its efforts towards national reconciliation and dialogue, pursuant to acknowledging the importance of strengthening democracy as a fundamental element of regional security;

(c) The report of the Secretary-General;

(d) The interim report of the Special Rapporteur of the Commission on Human Rights on the situation of human rights in Myanmar;

(e) The agreement, reached on 27 May 2003, on the Joint Government of the Union of Myanmar–International Labour Organization Plan of Action for the Elimination of Forced Labour Practices in Myanmar, including the agreement to an independent facilitator to assist possible victims of forced labour, while noting that the conditions for the implementation of the Plan of Action do not exist at present;

(f) The continued cooperation of the Government of Myanmar with the International Committee of the Red Cross;

2. *Expresses its grave concern* at:

(a) The events of 30 May 2003, the corresponding, subsequent and continuing violations of human rights, which constitute a serious setback for the human rights situation in the country, and the apparent involvement of the Government-affiliated Union Solidarity and Development Association in those events;

(b) The detention and the house arrest of Daw Aung San Suu Kyi and the persistent denial of her human rights and fundamental freedoms, including freedom of movement, as well as the continued detention of other senior leaders of the National League for Democracy;

(c) The closure of offices of the National League for Democracy throughout the country and the increased surveillance and imprisonment of members and supporters of the National League for Democracy and other political organizations, as well as the continuing detentions, including of prisoners whose sentences have expired;

(d) The systematic and consistent harassment and intimidation of members of the National League for Democracy by members of the Union Solidarity and Development Association;

(e) The lack of cooperation shown by the Government of Myanmar towards the Special Rapporteur of the Commission on Human Rights on the situation of human rights in Myanmar, in particular with regard to his proposal to visit ethnic nationality areas to investigate allegations of serious human rights violations;

3. *Expresses once again its grave concern* at:

(a) The ongoing systematic violation of the human rights, including civil, political, economic, social and cultural rights, of the people of Myanmar, in particular:

(i) Extrajudicial killing; continuing use of torture; rape and other forms of sexual violence persistently carried out by members of the armed forces; unsatisfactory conditions of detention; forced relocation; wide disrespect for the rule of law and lack of independence of the judiciary; trafficking in persons; forced labour, including child labour; destruction of livelihoods and confiscation of land by the armed forces; and violations of the right to an adequate standard of living, including food, medical care and education;

(ii) Denial of freedom of expression, including freedom of the media, of association, of assembly and of movement;

(iii) Discrimination and persecution on the basis of religious or ethnic background suffered by persons belonging to ethnic minorities, women and children;

(b) The situation of the large number of internally displaced persons and the flow of refugees to neighbouring countries, and recalls in this context the obligations of Myanmar under international law;

4. *Calls upon* the Government of Myanmar:

(a) To initiate a full and independent inquiry, with international cooperation, into the Depayin incident of 30 May 2003;

(b) To immediately facilitate and cooperate fully with the proposed investigation by the Special Rapporteur of the Commission on Human Rights on the situation of human rights in Myanmar into charges of rape and other abuse of civilians carried out by members of the armed forces in Shan and other states, including unhindered access to the region, and to guarantee the safety of those cooperating with and covered by the investigation;

(c) To immediately secure the safe and unhindered access to all parts of Myanmar of the United Nations and international humanitarian organizations to ensure the provision of humanitarian assistance and to guarantee that it reaches the most vulnerable groups of the population;

(d) To pursue through dialogue and peaceful means an immediate end to conflict with all remaining ethnic groups with which ceasefire agreements have not yet been signed, and to live up to its obligations to improve the development and human rights situation in ceasefire areas;

(e) To take all necessary steps to pursue cooperation with the International Labour Organization, with a view to implementing fully the recommendations of the Commission of Enquiry established to examine the observance by Myanmar of the International Labour Organization Convention concerning Forced or Compulsory Labour, and to create an environment in which the Joint Government of the Union of Myanmar–International Labour Organization Plan of Action for the Elimination of Forced Labour Practices in Myanmar, in particular the facilitator mechanism which it established, may be implemented in a credible manner;

5. *Strongly urges* the Government of Myanmar:

(a) To end the systematic violations of human rights in Myanmar and to ensure full respect for all human rights and fundamental freedoms;

(b) To immediately and unconditionally release Daw Aung San Suu Kyi, other leaders of the National League for Democracy and members of the National League for Democracy detained on or after 30 May 2003 and to allow them to play a full role in bringing about national reconciliation and the transition towards democracy;

(c) To immediately and unconditionally release all other political detainees;

(d) To immediately reverse all the other "temporary" measures imposed following the incident of 30 May 2003, including by reopening all the offices of the National League for Democracy throughout the country;

(e) To immediately lift all restraints on peaceful political activity and to fully guarantee freedom of expression, including freedom of the media, association and assembly;

(f) To put an end to impunity by investigating and bringing to justice any perpetrators of human rights violations, including members of the military and of the Union Solidarity and Development Association, and other government agents in all circumstances;

(g) To enhance cooperation with the Special Envoy of the Secretary-General for Myanmar and the Special Rapporteur of the Commission on Human Rights on the situation of human rights in Myanmar in order to assess first-hand the situation after 30 May 2003, to bring the country towards a transition to civilian rule, to ensure that they are both granted full and free access to Myanmar and that all persons cooperating with them are not subjected to any form of intimidation, harassment or punishment and, while in Myanmar, to provide them with equal access to the leaders and members of all the country's political parties, including the National League for Democracy;

(h) To restore democracy and respect the results of the 1990 elections and to enter immediately into substantive and structured dialogue with Daw Aung San Suu Kyi and other leaders of the National League for Democracy towards democratization and national reconciliation and, at an early stage, to include other political leaders in those talks, including representatives of the ethnic groups;

(i) To elaborate the road map, which is still lacking in essential elements such as concrete timing and an adequate plan for the involvement of all political groups and ethnic nationalities, in a way that ensures that the process is transparent and inclusive;

6. *Once again urges* the Government of Myanmar, as stated in its resolution 57/231 and in Commission on Human Rights resolution 2003/12:

(a) To ensure the independence of the judiciary and due process of law;

(b) To consider as a matter of high priority becoming a party to those remaining international human rights instruments to which it is not already party, and to comply fully with its obligations under international human rights instruments;

(c) To put an immediate end to the recruitment and use of child soldiers, inter alia, by some armed ethnic groups, and ensure their disarmament, demobilization and reintegration, to end systematic enforced displacement and provide protection and assistance to internally displaced persons, to allow the safe and dignified voluntary return of refugees, and to carry out the appropriate action to fight the HIV/AIDS epidemic;

7. *Requests* the Secretary-General:

(a) To continue to provide his good offices and to pursue his discussions on the situation of human rights and the restoration of democracy with the Government and people of Myanmar, including all relevant parties to the national reconciliation process in Myanmar;

(b) To report to the General Assembly at its fifty-ninth session and to the Commission on Human Rights at its sixtieth session on the progress made in the implementation of the present resolution;

(c) To give all necessary assistance to enable his Special Envoy to implement the present resolution and, in the context of the facilitation role, to explore any and all possibilities for discharging fully and effectively his mandate;

(d) To continue to give all necessary assistance to the Special Rapporteur of the Commission on Human Rights on the situation of human rights in Myanmar to enable him to discharge his mandate fully;

8. *Decides* to continue the consideration of this question at its fifty-ninth session.

Timor-Leste

During the fifty-ninth session of the Commission on Human Rights [E/2003/23], the Commission Chairperson, in a statement on Timor-Leste, acknowledged the Government's human rights achievements. He noted the steps taken by Indonesia to bring to justice perpetrators of violations of human rights and humanitarian law in Timor-Leste in 1999 [YUN 1999, p. 707] but expressed disappointment at the way in which the trials of those responsible were carried out. The Commission encouraged Indonesia to improve the current legal processes in a transparent way to ensure that justice would be done. The High Commissioner was asked to develop and implement with the Government of Timor-Leste a human rights technical cooperation programme and to report in 2004.

(For information on the human rights situation in Timor-Leste, see p. 685.)

Turkmenistan

Communication. In a 28 March letter to the High Commissioner [E/CN.4/2003/G/65], Austria, Canada, Germany, Greece, Ireland, Italy, Norway, Sweden, the United Kingdom and the United States referred to their request to the Organization for Security and Cooperation in Europe (OSCE) for the establishment of a fact-finding mission to investigate conflicting reports of the circumstances surrounding an alleged attack of 25 November 2002 on the President of Turkmenistan. The countries stated that the report of the mission proceeded with a single rapporteur and was presented to the OSCE Permanent Council on 13 March 2003. They requested that the mission report be circulated to the Commission.

Commission action. On 16 April [res. 2003/11], by a recorded vote of 23 to 16, with 14 abstentions, the Commission, while expressing appreciation at the decision to abolish the death penalty in Turkeminstan, expressed grave concern at the repression of political opposition activities through arbitrary detention, imprisonment and surveillance of persons; the suppression of independent media and freedom of expression; restrictions on the exercise of freedom of thought, conscience and religion; heavy prison sentences given to objectors to compulsory military service on religious grounds; discrimination against minorities; obstacles to marriages of Turkmen with foreigners; curtailment of the right to liberty of movement and freedom to leave the country; and the elections of 6 April, which did not represent a free and fair process. The Commission urged the Government to ensure full respect for all human rights and fundamental freedoms; end forced displacement and guarantee freedom of movement inside the country; bring to justice those responsible for human rights violations; remove restrictions on NGO activities; develop a constructive dialogue with the High Commissioner and OHCHR; cooperate with the Commission's mechanisms; and submit reports to relevant UN treaty bodies and implement their recommendations. The Special Rapporteurs on the independence of judges and lawyers, on the question of torture, on extrajudicial, summary and arbitrary executions, on the right to freedom of opinion and expression and on freedom of religion or belief, the Working Group on Arbitrary Detention, the Secretary-General's Representative on internally displaced persons and the Secretary-General's Special Representative on the situation of human rights defenders were called on to seek invitations to visit the country. The Secretary-General was requested to bring the Commission's resolution to the attention of all relevant parts of the UN system.

GENERAL ASSEMBLY ACTION

On 22 December [meeting 77], the General Assembly, on the recommendation of the Third Committee [A/58/508/Add.3], adopted **resolution 58/194** by recorded vote (73-40-56) [agenda item 117 (c)].

Situation of human rights in Turkmenistan

The General Assembly,

Reaffirming that all States Members of the United Nations have the obligation to promote and protect human rights and fundamental freedoms and the duty to fulfil the obligations that they have undertaken under the various international instruments in this field,

Expressing its grave concern about the serious and continuing human rights violations occurring in Turkmenistan,

Recalling Commission on Human Rights resolution 2003/11 of 16 April 2003,

Taking note of the recommendations outlined in the report of the Rapporteur of the Moscow Mechanism of the Organization for Security and Cooperation in Europe, issued on 12 March 2003,

Noting with appreciation the recent offer of the Government of Turkmenistan to invite a delegation of experts of the Office of the United Nations High Commissioner for Human Rights to provide technical assistance in the area of human rights as well as the recent visits of the Personal Envoy of the Chairman-in-Office of the Organization for Security and Cooperation in Europe for Participating States in Central Asia and of the High Commissioner on National Minorities of the Organization,

Calls upon the Government of Turkmenistan:

(a) To implement fully the measures set out in Commission on Human Rights resolution 2003/11 and to inform the Commission before its sixtieth session of the steps being taken in this regard;

(b) To implement fully the recommendations outlined in the report of the Rapporteur of the Moscow Mechanism of the Organization for Security and Cooperation in Europe, to work constructively with the various institutions of the Organization and to facilitate further visits of the Personal Envoy of the Chairman-in-Office of the Organization for Participating States in Central Asia and of the High Commissioner on National Minorities of the Organization;

(c) To develop a constructive dialogue with the Office of the United Nations High Commissioner for Human Rights and to cooperate fully with all the mechanisms of the Commission on Human Rights;

(d) To grant immediate access by independent bodies, including the International Committee of the Red Cross, as well as lawyers and relatives, to detained persons.

RECORDED VOTE ON RESOLUTION 58/194:

In favour: Albania, Andorra, Angola, Argentina, Australia, Austria, Bahamas, Belgium, Bolivia, Bosnia and Herzegovina, Bulgaria, Canada, Chile, Colombia, Costa Rica, Côte d'Ivoire, Croatia, Cyprus, Czech Republic, Denmark, Dominican Republic, Ecuador, El Salvador, Estonia, Fiji, Finland, France, Germany, Greece, Guatemala, Honduras, Hungary, Iceland, Ireland, Italy, Japan, Latvia, Liechtenstein, Lithuania, Luxembourg, Malta, Marshall Islands, Mauritius, Mexico, Micronesia, Monaco, Nauru, Netherlands, New Zealand, Nicaragua, Norway, Palau, Panama, Paraguay, Peru, Poland, Portugal, Republic of Korea, Romania, Russian Federation, Samoa, San Marino, Serbia and Montenegro, Slovakia, Slovenia, Spain, Sweden, Switzerland, The former Yugoslav Republic of Macedonia, Timor-Leste, United Kingdom, United States, Uruguay.

Against: Afghanistan, Azerbaijan, Bahrain, Bangladesh, Belarus, Brunei Darussalam, Cambodia, China, Cuba, Democratic People's Republic of Korea, Egypt, Georgia, India, Indonesia, Iran, Jordan, Kuwait, Lebanon, Libyan Arab Jamahiriya, Malaysia, Mauritania, Morocco, Myanmar, Niger, Oman, Pakistan, Qatar, Republic of Moldova, Saudi Arabia, Senegal, Sri Lanka, Syrian Arab Republic, Tajikistan, Tunisia, Turkmenistan, Ukraine, United Arab Emirates, Viet Nam, Yemen, Zimbabwe.

Abstaining: Algeria, Antigua and Barbuda, Barbados, Belize, Benin, Bhutan, Botswana, Brazil, Burkina Faso, Burundi, Cameroon, Cape Verde, Central African Republic, Congo, Democratic Republic of the Congo, Djibouti, Dominica, Eritrea, Ethiopia, Gabon, Ghana, Grenada, Guinea, Guinea-Bissau, Guyana, Jamaica, Kazakhstan, Kenya, Lao People's Democratic Republic, Lesotho, Madagascar, Malawi, Maldives, Mali, Mongolia, Mozambique, Namibia, Nepal, Nigeria, Papua New Guinea, Philippines, Rwanda, Saint Lucia, Saint Vincent and the Grenadines, Sierra Leone, Singapore, Somalia, South Africa, Suriname, Thailand, Togo, Trinidad and Tobago, Uganda, United Republic of Tanzania, Venezuela, Zambia.

Europe

Belarus

On 17 April [res. 2003/14], by a recorded vote of 23 to 14, with 16 abstentions, the Commission expressed deep concern at reports from credible sources implicating senior officials of the Government of Belarus in the forced disappearance and/or summary execution of three political opponents of the incumbent authorities and of a journalist. It also expressed concern about reports of arbitrary arrest and detention, harassment of NGOs, opposition political parties and individuals engaged in opposition activities and independent media, and increased restrictions on religious organizations. It urged Belarus to dismiss or suspend law enforcement officers implicated in forced disappearances and/or summary executions, pending an impartial, credible and full investigation; bring the actions of the police and security forces into conformity with its obligations under relevant international standards; establish an independent judiciary and end impunity; and release journalists and others detained for politically motivated reasons and cease harassment of NGOs and political parties. The Government was urged to cooperate with Commission mechanisms, including by extending invitations to the Special Rapporteurs on the question of torture, on extrajudicial, summary or arbitrary executions, and on the right to freedom of opinion and expression, and the Secretary-General's Representative on the situation of human rights defenders and the Working Groups on Arbitrary Detention and on Enforced or Involuntary Disappearances.

Cyprus

Report of Secretary-General. Pursuant to a 2002 Commission request [YUN 2002, p. 802], the Secretary-General transmitted a March OHCHR report, which provided an overview of human rights issues in Cyprus covering the period up to January 2003 [E/CN.4/2003/31].

The human rights concerns in Cyprus derived predominantly from the division of the island and the political situation. The continuing division had consequences for the enjoyment of the freedoms of movement, property rights, expression, religion and economic, social and cultural rights. Voting rights and the human rights issues pertaining to missing persons were also affected. The Secretary-General concluded that the human rights situation would benefit greatly from a comprehensive settlement of the political impasse.

Commission action. On 17 April [dec. 2003/106], the Commission retained the item on Cyprus on its agenda, on the understanding that previous resolutions would continue to remain operative, including its request to the Secretary-General to report on their implementation.

(See also p. 445.)

Russian Federation

At its fifty-ninth session [E/2003/23], the Commission had before it a draft resolution [E/CN.4/2003/L.13/Rev.1] by which the Commission would have expressed deep concern at reported ongoing violations of international human rights law and international humanitarian law in Chechnya. It would also have strongly condemned all terrorist acts and assassinations of local administration officials, religious leaders and other Chechens, as well as two major terrorist attacks in the Russian Federation in 2002—the hostage-taking at a Moscow theatre and the suicide bomb attack on the main government building in Grozny. The draft was rejected by a recorded vote of 21 to 15, with 17 abstentions.

(See p. 794 for details of the visit to the Russian Federation by the Special Representative of the Secretary-General on internally displaced persons.)

Middle East

Lebanon

Commission action. On 16 April [res. 2003/8], by a recorded vote of 32 to 1, with 20 abstentions, the Commission called on Israel to comply with the Geneva Conventions for the protection of war victims of 12 August 1949 and the Additional Protocols thereto [YUN 1977, p. 706], release imprisoned Lebanese citizens held as hostages for bargaining purposes and submit to the United Nations Interim Force in Lebanon all maps of the landmine fields laid throughout civilian areas. The Secretary-General was asked to bring the Commission's resolution to Israel's attention and to report to the General Assembly in 2003 and to the Commission in 2004.

ECONOMIC AND SOCIAL COUNCIL ACTION

In July, the Economic and Social Council, on the recommendation of the Commission on Human Rights [E/2003/23], adopted **decision 2003/238** by recorded vote (26-2-24) [agenda item 14 (g)].

Human rights situation of the Lebanese detainees in Israel

At its 45th plenary meeting, on 23 July 2003, the Economic and Social Council took note of Commission on Human Rights resolution 2003/8 of 16 April 2003, and endorsed the Commission's decision to request the Secretary-General:

(a) To bring Commission resolution 2003/8 to the attention of the Government of Israel and to call upon it to comply with its provisions;

(b) To report to the General Assembly at its fifty-eighth session and to the Commission at its sixtieth session on the results of his efforts in this regard.

RECORDED VOTE ON DECISION 2003/238:

In favour: Argentina, Benin, Bhutan, Brazil, Burundi, Chile, China, Congo, Cuba, Ecuador, Egypt, India, Iran, Jamaica, Kenya, Libyan Arab Jamahiriya, Malaysia, Nigeria, Pakistan, Qatar, Russian Federation, Saudi Arabia, Senegal, South Africa, Uganda, Zimbabwe.
Against: Georgia, United States.
Abstaining: Andorra, Australia, Ethiopia, Finland, France, Germany, Ghana, Greece, Guatemala, Hungary, Ireland, Italy, Japan, Mozambique, Nepal, Netherlands, Nicaragua, Peru, Portugal, Republic of Korea, Romania, Sweden, Ukraine, United Kingdom.

Reports of Secretary-General. In response to a 2002 Commission request [YUN 2002, p. 805], the Secretary-General stated that he had asked Israel for information on the extent of the implementation of the Commission's 2002 resolution on the human rights situation of Lebanese detainees in Israel, but had received no reply [E/CN.4/2003/32].

In August [A/58/218], the Secretary-General reported that, pursuant to Economic and Social Council decision 2003/238 (above), he had asked Israel for information on the implementation of Commission resolution 2003/8 regarding Lebanese detainees in Israel (above) and had received no reply.

The General Assembly took note of the report on 22 December (**decision 58/539**).

Territories occupied by Israel

During 2003, the question of human rights violations in the territories occupied by Israel as a result of the 1967 hostilities in the Middle East was again considered by the Commission on Human Rights. Political and other aspects were considered by the General Assembly, its Special Committee to Investigate Israeli Practices Affecting the Human Rights of the Palestinian People and Other Arabs of the Occupied Territories (Committee on Israeli Practices) and other bodies (see PART ONE, Chapter VI).

Reports of Secretary-General. In response to a 2002 Commission request [YUN 2002, p. 806], the Secretary-General reported that he had brought the Commission's resolution on the occupied Syrian Golan to the attention of all Governments, UN organs, the specialized agencies, regional intergovernmental organizations and international humanitarian organizations [E/CN.4/2003/28]. It was also communicated to the Committee on Israeli Practices, the Committee on the Exercise of the Inalienable Rights of the Palestinian People (Committee on Palestinian Rights) and the United Nations Relief and Works Agency for Palestine Refugees in the Near East (UNRWA).

In a further report [E/CN.4/2003/27], submitted in response to a 2002 Commission request [YUN 2002, p. 806], the Secretary-General stated that he had brought the Commission's resolution on the violation of human rights in the occupied Arab territories to the attention of the Government of Israel and all other Governments, UN organs, the specialized agencies, regional intergovernmental organizations and international humanitarian organizations, the Committee on Israeli Practices, the Committee on Palestinian Rights and UNRWA. He had received no reply from Israel.

A January note by the Secretary-General [E/CN.4/2003/29] listed all General Assembly reports issued since 26 April 2002 on the situation of the population living in the occupied Arab territories.

Commission action. On 15 April [res. 2003/5], by a recorded vote of 31 to 1 with 21 abstentions, the Commission called on Israel to comply with UN resolutions on the occupied Syrian Golan and demanded that it rescind its decision to impose its laws, jurisdiction and administration on the occupied territory. It also called on Israel to desist from changing the physical character, demographic composition, institutional structure and legal status of the area and to desist from imposing Israeli citizenship and identity cards on the Syrian citizens of the Syrian Golan and from its repressive measures against them. The Secretary-General was requested to bring the Commission's resolution to the attention of all Governments, UN organs, the specialized agencies, regional intergovernmental organizations and international humanitarian organizations, to widely publicize the resolution and to report in 2004.

Also on 15 April [res. 2003/6], by a recorded vote of 33 to 5, with 15 abstentions, the Commission condemned Israel's human rights violations in the Occupied Palestinian Territory, its occupation of the territory, the war launched by the Israeli army against Palestinian towns and camps, extrajudicial executions carried out by the Israeli army against Palestinians, the establishment of Israeli settlements, the expropriation of Palestinian homes in Jerusalem and Hebron, the torture of Palestinians during interrogation, the Israeli army's offensives against hospitals and sick persons, and the use of Palestinian citizens as human shields. Israel was called on to desist from all forms of human rights violations in the Occupied Palestinian Territory, including East Jerusalem. The Secretary-General was requested to bring the Commission's resolution to the attention of Israel and all other Governments, UN organs, the specialized agencies, regional intergovernmental organizations and international humanitarian organizations, to disseminate it widely and to report in 2004 on its implementation by Israel. He was also asked to provide the Commission with all UN reports issued between its sessions dealing with Palestinians' living conditions under Israeli occupation.

On the same date [res. 2003/7], by a recorded vote of 50 to 1, with 2 abstentions, the Commission, expressing grave concern at the continued escalation of the Israeli-Palestinian conflict (see p. 458), Israeli settlement activities in the occupied territories, the restriction of freedom of movement of the Palestinians, and the construction of the so-called security fence, and condemning all acts of violence, including terrorist attacks, urged Israel to comply with the Commission's previous resolutions; reverse its settlement policy; prevent any new installation of settlers; stop the construction of the security fence; implement the High Commissioner's recommendations [YUN 2000, p. 777]; and guarantee the safety and protection of Palestinian civilians. The parties were urged to cooperate in implementing the road map endorsed by the Quartet (European Union, Russian Federation, United Nations, United States) [YUN 2002, p. 436], with the aim of resuming negotiations on a political settlement.

Report of Special Rapporteur. In a September report [E/CN.4/2004/6], Special Rapporteur John Dugard (South Africa) described the human rights situation in the occupied territories, based on his visit to Gaza, Ramallah, Nablus, Bethlehem, Jericho and Jerusalem (22-29 June).

The Special Rapporteur stated that Israel was building a wall between Israel and the West Bank that, when completed, would be some 450 kilometres long and would incorporate substantial parts of Palestine within Israel. Much of the Palestinian land on the Israeli side of the wall consisted of fertile agricultural land and some of the most important water wells in the region. The path of the wall changed regularly in response to demands from settlers and other political interest groups within Israel and there was no transparency surrounding its construction. The wall had serious human rights implications, as it further restricted the freedom of movement of Palestinians, restricted access to health and education facilities, and resulted in the unlawful taking of Palestinian property. Furthermore, it violated the prohibition of the forcible acquisition of territory and the right to self-determination. The construction of the wall within the West Bank and the continued expansion of settlements, which, on the face of it, had more to do with territorial expansion, de facto annexation or conquest, raised serious doubts about the good faith of Israel's justifications in the name of security.

The restrictions on the freedom of movement imposed on the Palestinian people continued to create a humanitarian crisis. Curfews continued, but without the severity of 2002. However, people under curfew in Hebron, Jenin and parts of Gaza were frequently under tighter and more continuous curfew in 2003. Checkpoints, closures and curfews had had a major impact on the Palestinian economy, resulting in unemployment and poverty; a drop in health standards resulting from inability to access hospitals and clinics; and the failure to acquire nutritious food and sufficient clean water. Children had suffered from school closings and curfews, which made it difficult to reach schools. Some 22 per cent of children under five suffered from acute or chronic malnutrition, while the breakdown of family life had a severe impact on children. The loss of life and killing of civilians continued to rise, as did administrative detention and the mistreatment of prisoners. The destruction of property continued unabated and was particularly acute in Gaza. New Israeli settlements were being built and existing settlements continued to grow. Further evidence of the Government's determination to entrench the settlements was provided by the construction of the wall.

Communications. Israel, on 28 March [E/CN.4/2003/G/60], responding to the Special Rapporteur's report (above), said that Mr. Dugard continued to view Israel's security measures as taking place in a vacuum, without any recognition of the terrorism and security threats that necessitated them. Among other matters, Israel commented on his assertions regarding the humanitarian crisis, children in the conflict and the security fence.

The Commission also received a number of communications from Palestine regarding the situation in the Occupied Palestinian Territories, describing Israeli military aggression [E/CN.4/2003/G/27, E/CN.4/2003/G/29, E/CN.4/2003/G/30, E/CN.4/2003/G/33, E/CN.4/2003/G/39, E/CN.4/2003/G/40, E/CN.4/2003/G/76, E/CN.4/2003/G/77, E/CN.4/2004/G/2, E/CN.4/2004/G/4, E/CN.4/2004/G/5, E/CN.4/2004/G/7, E/CN.4/2004/G/11, E/CN.4/2004/G/12]. On 15 September [E/CN.4/2004/G/8], Palestine stated its views on the Israeli Government's decision to expel from the Occupied Palestinian Territories President Yasser Arafat, Chairman of the Executive Committee of the Palestine Liberation Organization and President of the Palestinian National Authority.

(See p. 766 for details of the visit to the Occupied Palestinian Territories by the Special Rapporteur on the right to food.)

PART THREE

Economic and social questions

Chapter I

Development policy and international economic cooperation

In 2003, the world economy began to gain momentum following more than two years of sluggish growth. Although the war in Iraq and the outbreak of severe acute respiratory syndrome (SARS) in several countries caused some setbacks early in the year, the global economy experienced a stronger-than-expected upturn in the second half of the year, raising the overall rate of growth of world output to 2.5 per cent. Despite the improved global prospects, large imbalances remained, making it unlikely that most developing countries would attain the rates of growth necessary for the achievement of the primary Millennium Development Goal (MDG), adopted by the General Assembly in 2000, of halving by 2015 the proportion of the world's people living in extreme poverty.

Eradicating poverty and achieving the other MDGs continued to be a focus of the work of UN bodies in 2003. The Assembly emphasized the vital role of the United Nations in promoting development and partnerships in order to meet the challenges of globalization and to realize the key MDGs of poverty reduction and sustainable development. The Assembly also discussed the ongoing implementation of the first United Nations Decade for the Eradication of Poverty (1997-2006) and the preparations for the International Year of Microcredit, 2005. The high-level segment of the Economic and Social Council adopted a ministerial declaration aimed at promoting an integrated approach to rural development as a means for eradicating poverty and achieving sustainable development. The Council also endorsed the establishment of the World Solidarity Fund to eradicate poverty, which was set up as a trust fund of the United Nations Development Programme. In April, the Committee of Experts on Public Administration addressed ways to enhance the capacity of public administration for achieving the MDGs.

Follow-up to the 2002 World Summit on Sustainable Development, which reviewed progress in implementing Agenda 21, the action plan on sustainable development adopted by the 1992 United Nations Conference on Environment and Development, was also a priority. The Commission on Sustainable Development, which was charged with overseeing Summit follow-up, considered its own future role in that regard, as well as that of major groups. The Assembly reviewed plans by the United Nations Educational, Scientific and Cultural Organization for implementing the United Nations Decade of Education for Sustainable Development (2005-2014).

The implications of science and new technologies, especially information and communication technologies (ICTs), for development remained another focus of UN deliberations during the year. In December, the International Telecommunication Union convened the first phase of the World Summit on the Information Society, which adopted the Declaration of Principles and a Plan of Action to build an inclusive information society. The Assembly considered the role of biotechnology in promoting economic development and proposals for increasing global cybersecurity through the protection of critical information infrastructures. The Council welcomed the orientation of the UN ICT Task Force towards the use of ICTs in the advancement of the MDGs. The Commission on Science and Technology considered technology development and capacity-building for competitiveness in a digital society, with particular emphasis on ICTs.

In addition, a variety of UN organs continued efforts to improve the lives of the millions of people living in particularly vulnerable areas of the world, including the least developed countries (LDCs), small island developing States (SIDS) and landlocked developing countries. In April, the Committee for Development Policy conducted the triennial review of the list of officially designated LDCs, adding one country to the list and recommending two countries for future graduation. In August, the International Ministerial Conference on Transit Transport Cooperation adopted the Almaty Declaration and Programme of Action, a global framework for addressing the special needs of landlocked developing countries and their transit developing neighbours. Preparations were under way for the comprehensive review in 2004 of implementation of the Programme of Action for the Sustainable Development of SIDS, adopted at the global conference on the subject in 1994.

International economic relations

Development and international economic cooperation

A number of UN bodies addressed development and international economic cooperation issues during 2003, including the General Assembly and the Economic and Social Council.

The Assembly, by **decision 58/528** of 17 December, deferred consideration of the launching of global negotiations on international economic cooperation for development and included the item in the provisional agenda of its fifty-ninth (2004) session.

On 23 December, the Assembly took note of the reports of the Second (Economic and Financial) Committee on its discussion of macroeconomic policy questions [A/58/481 & Corr.1] (**decision 58/544**) and on sustainable development and international economic cooperation [A/58/483] (**decision 58/548**).

Economic and Social Council consideration. On 14 April, the Economic and Social Council held its sixth special high-level meeting with the Bretton Woods institutions (the World Bank Group and the International Monetary Fund (IMF)) and the World Trade Organization (WTO) [A/58/77-E/2003/62 & Add.1,2]. It had before it a March note [E/2003/50] by the Secretary-General containing background information on increased coherence, coordination and cooperation of economic policy for the implementation of the Monterrey Consensus, adopted at the 2002 International Conference on Financing for Development [YUN 2002, p. 953] (see p. 987).

Globalization and interdependence

In response to resolution 57/274 [YUN 2002, p. 814], the Secretary-General submitted a 26 September report on the role of the United Nations in promoting development in the context of globalization and interdependence [A/58/394]. The report assessed the impact of globalization on the realization of the MDGs, adopted by the Millennium Summit in 2000 [YUN 2000, p. 51]. It also discussed how to manage globalization so as to maintain and translate the momentum created by the consensus forged at the 2001 WTO Ministerial Meeting [YUN 2001, p. 1432], the 2002 International Conference on Financing for Development [YUN 2002, p. 953] and the 2002 World Summit on Sustainable Development [ibid., p. 821] into action to achieve the MDGs. In discussing globalization, poverty reduction and sustainable development, the report called for UN system organizations to undertake mutual reviews of the impact of their work on the MDGs. International financial institutions and WTO should also be part of such evaluation exercises. The Economic and Social Council and the UN System Chief Executives Board for Coordination (CEB) could contribute to the reviews. Also examined were the linkages between international migration, financial flows, especially workers' remittances, and trade; between corruption, organized crime, trafficking, arms trade and terrorism and measures to reduce their negative impact on growth and development; and between globalization of production patterns and environmental protection and sustainability.

The report concluded that Governments, international organizations, business institutions, and all civil society actors should take new steps to ensure that the measures and policies they adopted in areas such as finance, trade, science and technology, population and migration were supportive of the MDGs and of the developing countries' integration into the world economy. The General Assembly had an important role to play in maintaining the focus on ensuring that the MDGs and other development goals were placed at the centre of economic institutions and policies. It could also give guidance for continuing the international debate on the governance of globalization following the conclusion of the work of the World Commission on the Social Dimensions of Globalization, established by the International Labour Organization (ILO) in 2002 [YUN 2002, p. 814].

GENERAL ASSEMBLY ACTION

On 23 December [meeting 78], the General Assembly, on the recommendation of the Second Committee [A/58/490], adopted **resolution 58/225** without vote [agenda item 100].

Role of the United Nations in promoting development in the context of globalization and interdependence

The General Assembly,

Recalling its resolutions 53/169 of 15 December 1998, 54/231 of 22 December 1999, 55/212 of 20 December 2000, 56/209 of 21 December 2001 and 57/274 of 20 December 2002 on the role of the United Nations in promoting development in the context of globalization and interdependence,

Reaffirming the resolve expressed in the United Nations Millennium Declaration to ensure that globalization becomes a positive force for the people of the entire world,

Recognizing that globalization and interdependence are opening new opportunities and posing new challenges through trade, investment and capital flows and advances in technology, including information technology, for the growth of the world economy, development and the improvement of living standards around the world, within which some countries have made progress in successfully benefiting from the opportunities of globalization, while others have faced difficulties in coping with its challenges,

Noting with concern that, notwithstanding the current improvement, global economic growth has slipped since the adoption of the Millennium Declaration, with a negative impact on development prospects for developing countries,

Recognizing the importance of appropriate policy responses at the national level by all countries to the challenges of globalization, in particular by pursuing sound policies, stressing that such national policies can yield better results with international support and with an enabling international economic environment, noting the need for support from the international community for the efforts of the least developed countries, in particular in improving their institutional and management capacities, and recognizing that all countries should pursue policies conducive to economic growth and to promoting a favourable global economic environment,

Noting with serious concern that a large number of developing countries have not yet been able to benefit fully from the existing multilateral trading system, and underlining the importance of promoting the integration of developing countries into the world economy so as to enable them to take the fullest possible advantage of the trading opportunities arising from globalization and liberalization,

Bearing in mind the commitment made at the Fourth Ministerial Conference of the World Trade Organization, held at Doha from 9 to 14 November 2001, to maintain the process of reform and the liberalization of trade policies, thus ensuring that the system plays its full part in promoting recovery, growth and development, to reaffirm strongly the principles and objectives set out in the Agreement Establishing the World Trade Organization and to pledge to reject the use of protectionism and place development at the heart of the Doha work programme, ensuring that globalization benefits all and that the internationally agreed development goals, including those contained in the Millennium Declaration, are achieved,

Stressing that the process of reform for a strengthened and stable international financial architecture should be based on broad participation in a genuine multilateral approach, involving all members of the international community, to ensure that the diverse needs and interests of all countries are adequately represented,

Underlining the urgent need to ensure the effective participation of all developing countries in the process of globalization, as an instrument for economic growth and poverty eradication,

Recognizing that all human rights are universal, indivisible, interdependent and interrelated,

Noting with concern the increasing linkages between corrupt practices and the transfer of illicitly acquired assets, money-laundering and other related organized crimes across national borders, and calling for better international efforts to effectively address these global trends, including through effective economic and banking regulations in all countries and the return of illicitly acquired assets to the countries of origin, in accordance with the United Nations Convention against Corruption, and in this regard welcoming its adoption by the General Assembly,

1. *Takes note with appreciation* of the report of the Secretary-General;

2. *Reaffirms* that the United Nations has a central role in promoting international cooperation for development and in promoting policy coherence on global development issues, including in the context of globalization and interdependence;

3. *Reiterates* that success in meeting the objectives of development and poverty eradication depends, inter alia, on good governance, both within individual countries and at the international level, sound economic policies, solid democratic institutions that are responsive to the needs of the people and improved infrastructure, which are the basis for sustained growth, poverty eradication and employment creation, and that transparency in financial, monetary and trading systems and commitment to an open, equitable, rule-based, predictable and non-discriminatory multilateral trading and financial system, which are equally essential;

4. *Stresses* the need to address asymmetries in the current global system, including those related to the vulnerability of countries to external shocks, the concentration of technical innovation in industrialized countries and the limited international mobility of labour, as well as such issues as increasing the flow of foreign direct investment and enhancing the participation of developing countries in the world trading and financial systems;

5. *Welcomes* the commitment by all countries to promote national and global economic systems based on the principles of justice, equity, democracy, participation, transparency, accountability and inclusion, as contained in the Monterrey Consensus of the International Conference on Financing for Development;

6. *Strongly urges* the international community to take all necessary and appropriate measures, including support for structural and macroeconomic reform, foreign direct investment, enhanced official development assistance, the search for a durable solution to the external debt problem, market access, capacity-building and the dissemination of knowledge and technology, in order to achieve sustainable development and promote the participation in the global economy of all African countries, as well as the least developed countries, the landlocked developing countries and small island developing States;

7. *Stresses* that, in the increasingly globalizing interdependent world economy, a holistic approach to the interconnected national, international and systematic challenges of financing for development, namely, sustainable, gender-sensitive and people-centred development, is essential in order to open up opportunities for all and to ensure that resources are created and used effectively, and that solid and accountable institutions are established at all levels;

8. *Also stresses* the special importance of creating an enabling international economic environment through strong cooperative efforts by all countries and institutions to promote equitable economic development in a world economy that benefits all people, and in that context invites developed countries, in particular the major industrialized countries, which have significant weight in influencing world economic growth, when

formulating their macroeconomic policies, to take into account whether the effects of those policies in terms of the external economic environment would be favourable to growth and development;

9. *Encourages* all countries to consider, in the context of existing regional or subregional arrangements, reviewing the contribution of their national financial, trade, debt relief and other policies to the realization of agreed development goals and commitments;

10. *Reaffirms* the significant importance of an open, universal, equitable, rule-based, predictable, non-discriminatory and balanced multilateral trading system in pursuit of sustained economic growth, poverty eradication and sustainable development, as set out in the United Nations Millennium Declaration;

11. *Stresses* the need to promote corporate responsibility and accountability, including through the full development and effective implementation of intergovernmental agreements and measures, international initiatives and public-private partnerships and appropriate national regulations, and to support continuous improvement in corporate practices in all countries;

12. *Invites* all countries, as well as the United Nations, the Bretton Woods institutions and the World Trade Organization, within their respective mandates, to continue to strengthen interactions with civil society, including the private sector and non-governmental organizations, as important partners in development;

13. *Expresses its concern* about the setback at the Fifth Ministerial Conference of the World Trade Organization, held in Cancún, Mexico, from 10 to 14 September 2003, and stresses the importance of redoubling efforts in working towards the successful, timely and development-oriented conclusion of the Doha negotiations no later than 1 January 2005, as set out in the Ministerial Declaration of the Fourth Ministerial Conference of the World Trade Organization ("Doha Ministerial Declaration");

14. *Notes* the importance of advancing current efforts to reform the international financial architecture, as envisaged in the Monterrey Consensus, emphasizes that those efforts need to include the effective participation of developing countries and countries with economies in transition, and in this regard encourages the International Monetary Fund and the World Bank to continue examining the issues of the voice and effective participation of those countries, as provided for in the communiqués of the International Monetary and Financial Committee and the Development Committee at their last meetings, held in Dubai, United Arab Emirates, on 21 and 22 September 2003, and looks forward to the consideration of a road map on the issue at their next meeting in April 2004;

15. *Underlines* the importance, for the improved access of developing countries to international financial markets, of considering counter-cyclical macroeconomic policies in the face of volatile capital flows and of strengthening macroeconomic stability;

16. *Also underlines* the fact that, in addressing the linkages between globalization and sustainable development, particular focus must be placed on identifying and implementing policies and practices that advance and strengthen the interdependent and mutually reinforcing pillars of sustainable development, namely, economic development, social development and environmental protection, taking into account the Rio principles, including the principle of common but differentiated responsibilities, as set out in principle 7 of the Rio Declaration on Environment and Development, and bearing in mind that good governance, at both national and international levels, is essential for sustainable development and to facilitate the transfer of environmentally sound technologies on concessional and preferential terms as mutually agreed;

17. *Stresses* the need to build an inclusive information society, which is intrinsically global in nature, and that therefore national efforts need to be supported by effective international and regional cooperation among Governments, the private sector, civil society and other stakeholders, including the international financial institutions, in order, inter alia, to assist in bridging the digital divide, promoting access to information and communication technologies, creating digital opportunities and harnessing the potential of information and communication technologies for development, and invites the World Summit on the Information Society to encourage all stakeholders in this regard;

18. *Reiterates* the need to address the specific concerns and needs of the least developed countries and small island developing States, and in this regard calls upon the least developed countries and their development partners, including multilateral financial institutions, to continue to implement expeditiously the Programme of Action for the Least Developed Countries for the Decade 2001-2010 and to adopt further measures to effectively integrate the least developed countries into the global economy and the multilateral trading system;

19. *Welcomes* the Almaty Programme of Action, adopted at the International Ministerial Conference of Landlocked and Transit Developing Countries and Donor Countries and International Financial and Development Institutions on Transit Transport Cooperation, held in Almaty, Kazakhstan, on 28 and 29 August 2003, which addresses the special needs of landlocked developing countries within a new global framework for transit transport cooperation for landlocked and transit developing countries, and calls upon all stakeholders fully and effectively to implement the Programme of Action;

20. *Emphasizes* the importance of recognizing and addressing the specific concerns of countries with economies in transition so as to help them to benefit from globalization, with a view to their full integration into the world economy;

21. *Invites* all relevant agencies of the United Nations system, through, inter alia, the United Nations System Chief Executives Board for Coordination, within existing resources, to review the impact of its work on the achievement of the internationally agreed development goals, including those contained in the Millennium Declaration, and to focus its report to the Economic and Social Council on progress made in this regard;

22. *Stresses* the need for the United Nations system to continue to address the social dimension of globalization, encourages in that regard the work of the International Labour Organization on the social dimension of globalization, and takes note of the ongoing work of its World Commission on the Social Dimensions of Globalization;

23. *Also stresses* the importance of migration as a phenomenon accompanying increased globalization, including its impact on economies, and underlines further the need for greater coordination and cooperation among countries as well as relevant regional and international organizations;

24. *Requests* the Secretary-General to submit to the General Assembly at its fifty-ninth session a report on globalization and interdependence, in the context of the present resolution, which should focus on ways to forge greater coherence in order to advance the internationally agreed development goals, including those contained in the Millennium Declaration;

25. *Decides* to include in the provisional agenda of its fifty-ninth session the item entitled "Globalization and interdependence".

Development through partnership

Commission for Social Development action. In February, the Commission for Social Development [E/2003/26] (see p. 1099), as part of its consideration of its priority theme, "National and international cooperation for social development", discussed the topic of forging partnerships for social development. It recommended for adoption by the Economic and Social Council a set of agreed conclusions calling for renewed and effective partnerships between developed and developing countries and countries with economies in transition, and among all relevant actors, to achieve the internationally agreed social development objectives and commitments. The Council, by **decision 2003/15** of 21 July, endorsed the Commission's conclusions on partnerships (see p. 1100).

Commission on Sustainable Development action. The Commission on Sustainable Development, in April/May [E/2003/29] (see p. 840), discussed the issue of partnership initiatives on the basis of proposals contained in the Secretary-General's February report on the follow-up to the World Summit on Sustainable Development and the future role of the Commission on Sustainable Development: the implementation track [E/CN.17/2003/2]. It proposed criteria and guidelines for the development of partnerships in the context of the World Summit on Sustainable Development process and its follow-up, which were adopted by the Economic and Social Council in **resolution 2003/61** of 25 July (see p. 842).

Private sector partnerships

In response to General Assembly resolution 56/76 [YUN 2001, p. 744], the Secretary-General submitted an 18 August report on enhanced cooperation between the United Nations and all relevant partners, in particular the private sector [A/58/227]. The report reviewed recent developments, including the World Summit on Sustainable Development [YUN 2002, p. 821] and the International Conference on Financing for Development [ibid., p. 953], to illustrate the variety of partnership arrangements between UN entities and the non-State sector, and attempted to derive lessons and formulate proposals for meeting the challenges ahead. It noted that, in recent years, partnerships between the United Nations and non-State actors—including businesses, foundations and other private sector organizations—had played an increasingly important role and were considered an important tool to complement the Organization's efforts to achieve UN goals and objectives, including the MDGs. At the same time, such partnerships contributed to the Organization's renewal by introducing new methods of work. Partnerships took many forms, ranging from time-bound project partnerships involving a small number of actors to global initiatives involving a multitude of actors. They were an integral part of the work of many UN organizations, especially those with on-the-ground capacities to deliver. UN organizations were still learning how best to utilize the potential benefits of partnerships and were learning from experience gained so far. Among the lessons learned were that successful partnerships had to prove their worth in a practical manner by achieving concrete results and that they needed to make good business sense.

However, to exploit fully the potential contribution that partnerships could make to the Organization's work, a more coherent and systematic approach to developing and supporting them across the UN system was needed. Such an approach could include providing stronger incentives for their development, sharing best practices more systematically, developing a stronger skill base and creating more robust processes for reporting and accountability. The new UN Partnership Office, which would bring under one umbrella the Global Compact Office and the UN Fund for International Partnerships (UNFIP), would be well placed to build on lessons learned thus far, enhance quality assurance and provide a more solid institutional framework in support of new and promising partnership initiatives. It would also identify strategies for ensuring a more systematic and coordinated approach to developing effective cooperation with non-State actors and consider the political issues raised by the Organization's increased use of partnership approaches as a modality for delivering its goals.

GENERAL ASSEMBLY ACTION

On 19 December [meeting 76], the General Assembly adopted **resolution 58/129** [draft: A/58/L.51 & Add.1] without vote [agenda item 46].

Towards global partnerships

The General Assembly,

Recalling its resolutions 55/215 of 21 December 2000 and 56/76 of 11 December 2001,

Reaffirming the vital role of the United Nations, in particular the General Assembly, in the promotion of partnerships in the context of globalization,

Underlining the intergovernmental nature of the United Nations,

Reaffirming its resolve to create an environment, at the national and global levels alike, that is conducive to sustainable development and the elimination of poverty,

Recalling the objectives formulated in the United Nations Millennium Declaration, particularly in regard to developing partnerships through the provision of greater opportunities to the private sector, non-governmental organizations and civil society in general so as to enable them to contribute to the realization of the goals and programmes of the Organization, in particular in the pursuit of development and the eradication of poverty,

Underlining the importance of the contribution of the private sector, non-governmental organizations and civil society in general to the implementation of the outcomes of United Nations conferences in the economic, social and related fields,

Recalling the central role and responsibility of Governments in national and international policy-making,

Stressing that efforts to meet the challenges of globalization could benefit from enhanced cooperation between the United Nations and all relevant partners, in particular the private sector, in order to ensure that globalization becomes a positive force for all,

Underlining the fact that cooperation between the United Nations and all relevant partners, in particular the private sector, shall serve the purposes and principles embodied in the Charter of the United Nations and make concrete contributions to the realization of the goals contained in the Millennium Declaration and in the outcomes of major United Nations conferences and summits and their reviews, in particular in the area of development and the eradication of poverty, and shall be undertaken in a manner that maintains the integrity, impartiality and independence of the Organization,

Emphasizing that all relevant partners, in particular the private sector, can contribute in several ways to addressing the obstacles confronted by developing countries in mobilizing the resources needed to finance their sustainable development, and to the realization of the development goals of the United Nations through, inter alia, financial resources, access to technology, management expertise, and support for programmes, including through the reduced pricing of drugs, where appropriate, for the prevention, care and treatment of HIV/AIDS and other diseases,

Encouraging the private sector to engage as reliable and consistent partners in the development process and to take into account not only the economic and financial, but also the developmental, social, human rights, gender and environmental implications of their undertakings and, in general, towards accepting and implementing the principle of good corporate citizenship, that is, bringing social values and responsibilities to bear on a conduct and policy premised on profit incentives, in conformity with national laws and regulations,

Recalling that the International Conference on Financing for Development welcomed all efforts to encourage good corporate citizenship and noted the initiative undertaken in the United Nations to promote global partnerships,

Noting that the World Summit on Sustainable Development, in order to promote the effective implementation of Agenda 21 at the international level, encouraged partnership initiatives for implementation by all relevant stakeholders to support the outcome of the Summit,

Also noting that the Economic and Social Council, in its resolution 2003/61 of 25 July 2003, reiterated, upon the recommendation of the Commission on Sustainable Development at its eleventh session, that partnerships for sustainable development, as voluntary multi-stakeholder initiatives, contribute to the implementation of Agenda 21 and the Plan of Implementation of the World Summit on Sustainable Development ("Johannesburg Plan of Implementation"),

Further noting that the Economic and Social Council, in its resolution 2003/15 of 21 July 2003, endorsed the conclusion adopted by the Commission for Social Development at its forty-first session that, at the international level, recent initiatives towards building voluntary partnerships for social development should be encouraged,

Taking note of the work of the United Nations on partnerships, such as the Global Compact Initiative launched by the Secretary-General, the Information and Communication Technologies Task Force and the United Nations Fund for International Partnerships, and welcoming the establishment of a multitude of partnerships at the field level, entered into by various United Nations agencies, non-State partners and Member States, such as the United Nations Public-Private Alliance for Rural Development,

Stressing that partnerships should focus on the achievement of concrete results,

1. *Takes note* of the report of the Secretary-General;
2. *Stresses* that the principles and approaches that govern such partnerships should be built on the firm foundation of United Nations purposes and principles, as set out in the Charter of the United Nations, and invites the United Nations system to continue to adhere to a common and systematic approach to partnership which, without imposing undue rigidity in partnership agreements, includes the following principles: common purpose, transparency, bestowing no unfair advantages upon any partner of the United Nations, mutual benefit and mutual respect, accountability, respect for the modalities of the United Nations, striving for balanced representation of relevant partners from developed and developing countries and countries with economies in transition, sectoral and geographic balance, and not compromising the independence and neutrality of the United Nations system in general and the agencies in particular;
3. *Encourages* the relevant United Nations bodies and agencies, and invites the Bretton Woods institutions, as well as the World Trade Organization, to continue to explore possibilities of enhancing the use of partnerships to better implement their goals and programmes, in particular in the pursuit of development

and the eradication of poverty, bearing in mind the different mandates, modes of operation and objectives of the bodies and agencies, as well as the particular roles of the non-State partners involved;

4. *Recalls* that the Johannesburg Plan of Implementation designated the Commission on Sustainable Development to serve as a focal point for discussions on partnerships that promote sustainable development, and in this context reaffirms the criteria and guidelines for partnerships in the context of the World Summit on Sustainable Development process and its follow-up, as set out by the Economic and Social Council in its resolution 2003/61;

5. *Stresses* the importance of the contribution of voluntary partnerships to the achievement of the internationally agreed development goals, including those contained in the United Nations Millennium Declaration, while reiterating that they are a complement to but not intended to substitute for the commitments made by Governments with a view to achieving these goals;

6. *Also stresses* that partnerships should be consistent with national laws, national development strategies and plans, as well as the priorities of countries where their implementation takes place, bearing in mind the relevant guidance provided by Governments;

7. *Calls upon* all bodies within the United Nations system that engage in partnerships to ensure the integrity and independence of the Organization and to include information on partnerships in their regular reporting, as appropriate, on their web sites and through other means;

8. *Stresses* that partnerships should be designed and implemented in a transparent and accountable manner, and in that regard calls upon partners to provide to and exchange relevant information with Governments, other stakeholders and the relevant United Nations agencies and bodies and other international organizations in which they engage, in an appropriate way, including through reports, with particular attention to the importance of sharing among partnerships information on their practical experience;

9. *Requests* the Secretary-General to continue to promote the transparency and accountability of partnerships;

10. *Acknowledges* that serving successful partnerships requires specific skills on the part of the Secretariat staff, and calls upon the Secretary-General to continue to support and further to develop such skills, through appropriate training and the sharing of best practices;

11. *Recalls* the relevant paragraph in its resolution 57/300 of 20 December 2002;

12. *Requests* the Secretary-General to report to the General Assembly at its sixtieth session on the implementation of the present resolution.

Progress, challenges and constraints to achieving major UN development goals

In response to General Assembly resolution 57/246 [YUN 2002, p. 818], the Secretary-General submitted a 28 August report on progress towards and challenges and constraints to the achievement of the major development goals and objectives adopted by the United Nations during the past decade [A/58/327]. The report noted that, since the adoption of the 1990 Declaration on International Economic Cooperation, in particular the Revitalization of Economic Growth and Development of the Developing Countries, in General Assembly resolution S-18/3 [YUN 1990, p. 337], and the International Development Strategy for the Fourth United Nations Development Decade (the 1990s), adopted by the Assembly in resolution 45/199 [ibid., p. 343], the United Nations had held a series of global conferences that had contributed to the forging of a new global consensus on development goals and policies. Also, in 2000, the Assembly had adopted, by resolution 55/2 [YUN 2000, p. 49], the Millennium Declaration, in which the international community resolved to move towards the implementation of the commitments made in the conferences by establishing measurable targets, referred to as the MDGs [ibid., p. 51]. The report also addressed a selection of challenges to and opportunities for development in the first decade of the new millennium. Among the positive forces for development, the report identified opportunities offered by technological progress for attaining food security and the contribution of information and communication technologies. Constraints to global development included the fight against HIV/AIDS, the challenges arising from demographic trends, including ageing and social safety nets, youth unemployment and migrant workers, and the reversal of the peace dividend due to increasing global military spending.

The report concluded that the focus of the international community's development efforts should be on implementation of the MDGs and the goals of the global conferences, which provided a concrete agenda for development in the new millennium. However, the progress achieved in the first quarter of the current decade in almost all fields was less than what was required to achieve all the development goals and targets established in recent years. Thus, extraordinary efforts and measures were required by the international community and Governments in all parts of the world to revitalize development.

On 23 December, by **decision 58/549**, the Assembly took note of the report.

Coercive economic measures

In response to General Assembly resolution 56/179 [YUN 2001, p. 746], the Secretary-General submitted an 11 September report [A/58/301] summarizing replies received from 10 Governments in response to his request for information on the issue of unilateral economic measures as a means of political and economic coercion against developing countries.

GENERAL ASSEMBLY ACTION

On 23 December [meeting 78], the General Assembly, on the recommendation of the Second Committee [A/58/481/Add.1], adopted **resolution 58/198** by recorded vote (125-1-37) [agenda item 91 (a)].

Unilateral economic measures as a means of political and economic coercion against developing countries

The General Assembly,

Recalling the relevant principles set forth in the Charter of the United Nations,

Reaffirming the Declaration on Principles of International Law concerning Friendly Relations and Cooperation among States in accordance with the Charter of the United Nations, which states, inter alia, that no State may use or encourage the use of unilateral economic, political or any other type of measures to coerce another State in order to obtain from it the subordination of the exercise of its sovereign rights,

Bearing in mind the general principles governing the international trading system and trade policies for development contained in relevant resolutions, rules and provisions of the United Nations and the World Trade Organization,

Recalling its resolutions 44/215 of 22 December 1989, 46/210 of 20 December 1991, 48/168 of 21 December 1993, 50/96 of 20 December 1995, 52/181 of 18 December 1997, 54/200 of 22 December 1999 and 56/179 of 21 December 2001,

Gravely concerned that the use of unilateral coercive economic measures adversely affects the economy and development efforts of developing countries in particular and has a general negative impact on international economic cooperation and on worldwide efforts to move towards a non-discriminatory and open multilateral trading system,

1. *Takes note* of the report of the Secretary-General;
2. *Urges* the international community to adopt urgent and effective measures to eliminate the use of unilateral coercive economic measures against developing countries that are not authorized by relevant organs of the United Nations or are inconsistent with the principles of international law as set forth in the Charter of the United Nations and that contravene the basic principles of the multilateral trading system;
3. *Requests* the Secretary-General to continue to monitor the imposition of measures of this nature and to study the impact of such measures on the affected countries, including the impact on trade and development;
4. *Also requests* the Secretary-General to submit to the General Assembly at its sixtieth session a report on the implementation of the present resolution.

RECORDED VOTE ON RESOLUTION 58/198:

In favour: Afghanistan, Algeria, Angola, Antigua and Barbuda, Argentina, Armenia, Azerbaijan, Bahamas, Bahrain, Bangladesh, Barbados, Belarus, Belize, Benin, Bolivia, Botswana, Brazil, Brunei Darussalam, Burkina Faso, Burundi, Cambodia, Cameroon, Cape Verde, Central African Republic, Chile, China, Comoros, Congo, Costa Rica, Cuba, Democratic People's Republic of Korea, Denmark, Djibouti, Dominican Republic, Ecuador, Egypt, Eritrea, Ethiopia, Fiji, Gabon, Ghana, Grenada, Guatemala, Guinea, Guinea-Bissau, Guyana, Haiti, India, Indonesia, Iran, Ireland, Italy, Jamaica, Jordan, Kazakhstan, Kenya, Kuwait, Kyrgyzstan, Lao People's Democratic Republic, Latvia, Lebanon, Lesotho, Libyan Arab Jamahiriya, Madagascar, Malaysia, Maldives, Mali, Mauritania, Mauritius, Mexico, Mongolia, Morocco, Mozambique, Myanmar, Namibia, Nauru, Nepal, Netherlands, Nicaragua, Niger, Nigeria, Oman, Pakistan, Panama, Papua New Guinea, Paraguay, Peru, Philippines, Qatar, Romania, Russian Federation, Rwanda, Saint Lucia, Saint Vincent and the Grenadines, Samoa, Saudi Arabia, Serbia and Montenegro, Seychelles, Singapore, Solomon Islands, Somalia, South Africa, Sri Lanka, Sudan, Suriname, Swaziland, Syrian Arab Republic, Tajikistan, Thailand, Timor-Leste, Togo, Tonga, Trinidad and Tobago, Tunisia, Turkmenistan, Uganda, United Arab Emirates, United Kingdom, United Republic of Tanzania, Uruguay, Venezuela, Viet Nam, Yemen, Zambia, Zimbabwe.

Against: United States.

Abstaining: Albania, Andorra, Australia, Austria, Bulgaria, Canada, Croatia, Cyprus, Czech Republic, Estonia, Finland, France, Germany, Greece, Hungary, Iceland, Israel, Japan, Liechtenstein, Lithuania, Luxembourg, Malta, Marshall Islands, Monaco, Norway, Portugal, Republic of Korea, Republic of Moldova, San Marino, Slovakia, Slovenia, Spain, Sweden, Switzerland, The former Yugoslav Republic of Macedonia, Turkey, Ukraine.

The Assembly, on 4 November, adopted **resolution 58/7** on the necessity of ending the economic, commercial and financial embargo imposed by the United States against Cuba (see p. 286).

Sustainable development

Follow-up to the World Summit on Sustainable Development

In 2003, several UN bodies, including the General Assembly, the Economic and Social Council and the Commission on Sustainable Development, addressed implementation of the outcomes of the 2002 World Summit on Sustainable Development [YUN 2002, p. 821], in particular the Johannesburg Declaration and the Plan of Implementation, which outlined actions and targets for stepping up implementation of Agenda 21—a programme of action for sustainable development worldwide, adopted at the 1992 United Nations Conference on Environment and Development (UNCED) [YUN 1992, p. 672]. The actions and targets related to the five priority areas of water and sanitation, energy, health, agriculture and biodiversity (known as the WEHAB issues) and to new partnerships for sustainable development.

Commission on Sustainable Development consideration. As the main body responsible for coordinating and monitoring implementation of the Summit outcomes, the Commission on Sustainable Development, at its eleventh session (New York, 29 January, 28 April–9 May) [E/2003/29], discussed the Summit follow-up during its high-level segment (28-30 April). A multistakeholder dialogue and five regional implementation forums, held during the high-level segment, contributed to the deliberations. The Commission had before it a 21 February report of the Secretary-General on follow-up to the World

Summit and the future role of the Commission: implementation track [E/CN.17/2003/2], which discussed the outcomes of the Summit and their implications for follow-up at all levels, the future role of the Commission and the role of partnerships in meeting the Summit's objectives. The Secretary-General stated that, in order to achieve the specific goals and time-bound targets contained in the Johannesburg Plan of Implementation, the UN system, Governments and other actors would have to significantly change their policies, programmes and modalities of work. While the primary focus of implementation remained at the national level, UN agencies, funds and programmes would assist Governments by supporting national sustainable development strategies. The United Nations Development Group, led by the United Nations Development Programme (UNDP), would play a major role in promoting integration of the follow-up to the Summit and in ensuring that operational activities were coordinated and focused on practical results. At the regional level, the regional commissions and other regional organizations would need to reorient their activities to pursue the goal of sustainable development more effectively. At the global level, the Plan of Implementation required UN system–wide policy coherence and consistency. It called for major changes in the work of the Commission on Sustainable Development, greater involvement of the Economic and Social Council in sustainable development–related work and stronger linkages with the governing bodies of UN agencies, funds and programmes. The Commission would have to integrate the cross-sectoral dimension of the various sectoral issues and focus on the interrelationship between them, devote more attention to reviewing implementation and suggesting measures to overcome obstacles and undertake implementation reviews and policy discussions and negotiations in alternate years. The Commission's methods of work would therefore vary considerably for the two alternating sessions. Changes in the methods of work could include the redesign of the multi-stakeholder dialogues, creating a forum for partnerships and regional implementation forums. The Commission's post-Johannesburg programme of work needed to be linked more directly with practical implementation and progress towards the agreed goals and targets. The programme for the next decade should have the flexibility to allow the Commission to address emerging challenges, which would require changing and modifying the programme of work over the years. The nature of the outcomes of the Commission was also expected to change, with decisions being more specific, action-oriented and focused, based on comprehensive and up-to-date reports on implementation. The Commission could also provide a forum to nurture and foster partnerships. The Secretary-General submitted, in annexes to his report, specific proposals for meeting the new challenges through innovations in the work of the Commission; a proposed matrix of issues on which the Commission could focus; a proposed typical two-year work cycle of the Commission; proposed new organizational arrangements; a flow chart of the Commission's proposed two-year cycle; a flow chart of the Commission's transition work cycle (2003–early 2005); and lessons learned through major group participation in the Commission and the Summit processes.

The Commission recommended to the Economic and Social Council for adoption a draft resolution on the future programme, organization and methods of work of the Commission (**resolution 2003/61**) (see p. 842).

Implementation activities

Report of Secretary-General. In response to General Assembly resolution 57/253 [YUN 2002, p. 825], the Secretary-General submitted an August report on activities undertaken in implementation of Agenda 21, the Programme for the Implementation of Agenda 21 and the outcomes of the World Summit on Sustainable Development [A/58/210]. He provided an overview of initial actions taken by Governments, the UN system, intergovernmental bodies and major groups in follow-up to the World Summit and reviewed activities and proposals by various stakeholders aimed at meeting Summit goals and targets.

In his proposed 2004-2005 programme budget (see p. 1399), the Secretary-General had aligned the activities of the United Nations with the priorities identified by the General Assembly, one of which was the promotion of sustained economic growth and sustainable development. The five UN regional commissions were integrating the Summit outcomes with their ongoing work and reorienting relevant programme activities towards focused implementation. The Economic Commission for Europe agreed to mainstream the dimensions of sustainable development into all areas of its work (see p. 1016) and the other commissions were taking steps to incorporate the Summit outcomes into their intergovernmental and expert group meetings. The Governing Council of the United Nations Environment Programme (UNEP) [A/58/25] (see p. 1036) had called for full and concrete implementation of the Summit outcomes and agreed that UNEP should have an important role to play in helping countries to develop policies and legislation to deal with environmental impacts associated with globalization.

A major international event was the International Expert Meeting on the 10-Year Framework of Programmes for Sustainable Consumption and Production (Marrakech, Morocco, 16-19 June), organized by the UN Department of Economic and Social Affairs, in cooperation with UNEP, which agreed on the Marrakech Process on sustainable consumption and production.

The report noted that there was great enthusiasm and dynamism in the follow-up to the Summit and consensus on the sharper focus needed on implementation. An important thrust of implementation had been to identify obstacles and constraints and to share lessons learned and best practices at all levels. The widely varied actions and partnership initiatives being implemented at the national, regional and international levels demonstrated the imperative of strengthened cooperation and coordination within and between organizations of the UN system and other international institutions. The Commission on Sustainable Development, as the high-level intergovernmental body on sustainable development within the UN system, provided an important forum for reviewing progress in implementation, for sharing experiences and lessons learned in implementation at the country, regional and global levels and for integrating such experiences and lessons with policy review and guidance. The report concluded with several recommendations for General Assembly action.

CEB consideration. The UN System Chief Executives Board for Coordination (CEB), at its first regular session (Paris, 25-26 April) [CEB/2003/1], reviewed the deliberations of its High-level Committee on Programmes (HLCP) at its fifth session (Rome, 26-27 March) [CEB/2003/4] on the UN system's follow-up to the World Summit on Sustainable Development. CEB asked HLCP to further elaborate its recommendations on the overall approaches to the follow-up to the Summit in the light of the Board's observations and to focus its further work on the substance of Summit follow-up. In that regard, CEB highlighted the need for: coherence and consistency and strong linkages among operational, regional and global levels; country ownership of the follow-up process; coordination support for capacity-building and full use of existing country-level mechanisms; a focus on sustainability and productivity, and on natural resources as the engine for sustainable growth; greater attention to the regional dimensions of the follow-up; and linking implementation to the broader processes of integrated follow-up to UN conferences and summits, particularly the Millennium Summit.

At its second regular session (New York, 31 October-1 November) [CEB/2003/2], CEB endorsed the conclusions of HLCP at its sixth session (Rome, 18-19 September) [CEB/2003/7] on inter-agency collaborative arrangements for the integrated follow-up to Summit outcomes in the areas of freshwater, water and sanitation, energy, oceans and coastal areas, and patterns of consumption and production. Executive heads asked the Committee to take account of the multi-year programme of work of the Commission on Sustainable Development (see p. 847) in framing its future work programme on follow-up to the World Summit. The Board requested HLCP to continue to monitor implementation of inter-agency arrangements for follow-up to the Summit to ensure policy and programme coherence.

GENERAL ASSEMBLY ACTION

On 23 December [meeting 78], the General Assembly, on the recommendation of the Second Committee [A/58/485], adopted **resolution 58/218** without vote [agenda item 95].

Implementation of Agenda 21, the Programme for the Further Implementation of Agenda 21 and the outcomes of the World Summit on Sustainable Development

The General Assembly,

Recalling its resolutions 55/199 of 20 December 2000, 56/226 of 24 December 2001, 57/253 of 20 December 2002 and 57/270 A and B of 20 December 2002 and 23 June 2003, respectively,

Recalling also the Rio Declaration on Environment and Development, Agenda 21, the Programme for the Further Implementation of Agenda 21, the Johannesburg Declaration on Sustainable Development and the Plan of Implementation of the World Summit on Sustainable Development ("Johannesburg Plan of Implementation"),

Reaffirming the commitment to implement the Johannesburg Plan of Implementation, including the time-bound goals and targets, and other internationally agreed development goals, including those contained in the United Nations Millennium Declaration,

Expressing its satisfaction that the Commission on Sustainable Development, at its eleventh session, agreed on its new organization of work and multi-year programme of work, as well as new methods of work aimed at promoting and supporting implementation and the provision for the Commission to work in a series of two-year action-oriented implementation cycles, alternating review and policy years,

Noting the adoption by the Commission, at its eleventh session, of criteria and guidelines on partnership initiatives voluntarily undertaken by some Governments, international organizations and major groups, announced at the World Summit on Sustainable Development and in the follow-up to the Summit, as endorsed by the Economic and Social Council,

Reaffirming the continuing need to ensure a balance between economic development, social development and environmental protection as interdependent and mutually reinforcing pillars of sustainable development,

Reaffirming also that poverty eradication, changing unsustainable patterns of production and consumption and protecting and managing the natural resource base of economic and social development are overarching objectives of, and essential requirements for, sustainable development,

Noting the convening in Marrakech, Morocco, from 16 to 19 June 2003, of an international expert meeting on a ten-year framework of programmes for sustainable consumption and production,

Recognizing that good governance within each country and at the international level is essential for sustainable development,

1. *Takes note* of the report of the Secretary-General on the activities undertaken in implementation of Agenda 21, the Programme for the Further Implementation of Agenda 21 and the outcomes of the World Summit on Sustainable Development;

2. *Reiterates* that sustainable development is a key element of the overarching framework for United Nations activities, in particular for achieving the internationally agreed development goals, including those contained in the United Nations Millennium Declaration and in the Johannesburg Plan of Implementation;

3. *Calls upon* Governments, all relevant international and regional organizations, the Economic and Social Council, the United Nations funds and programmes, the regional commissions and specialized agencies, the international financial institutions, the Global Environment Facility and other intergovernmental organizations, in accordance with their respective mandates, as well as major groups, to take action to ensure the effective implementation of and follow-up to the commitments, programmes and time-bound targets adopted at the Summit, and encourages them to report on concrete progress in that regard;

4. *Calls* for the implementation of the commitments, programmes and time-bound targets adopted at the Summit and, to that end, for the fulfilment of the provisions relating to the means of implementation, as contained in the Johannesburg Plan of Implementation;

5. *Requests* the Secretary-General to strengthen system-wide inter-agency cooperation and coordination for the implementation of Agenda 21, the Programme for the Further Implementation of Agenda 21 and the Johannesburg Plan of Implementation, and in that regard to report on such inter-agency cooperation and coordination activities to the Commission on Sustainable Development and the Economic and Social Council in 2004;

6. *Welcomes* the decision of the Commission at its eleventh session to invite the regional commissions, in collaboration with the secretariat of the Commission, to consider organizing regional implementation meetings in order to contribute to the work of the Commission, and in this regard urges the regional commissions to take into account the relevant thematic clusters contained in the Commission's programme of work and to provide inputs as specified by the Commission at its eleventh session;

7. *Also welcomes* the decision of the Commission at its eleventh session to invite other regional and sub-regional bodies and institutions within and outside the United Nations system to contribute to the preparations for the Commission's review and policy sessions and the intergovernmental preparatory meeting;

8. *Requests* the Secretary-General, in reporting to the Commission at its twelfth session on the state of implementation of Agenda 21, the Programme for the Further Implementation of Agenda 21 and the Johannesburg Plan of Implementation, on the basis of inputs from all levels, as specified by the Commission at its eleventh session, to submit:

(*a*) One report on each of the issues of water, sanitation and human settlement, to be addressed in an integrated manner during the session, which should contain a detailed review of the progress of implementation relating to those issues, taking into account, as appropriate, their interlinkages, while addressing the cross-cutting issues identified by the Commission at its eleventh session;

(*b*) A report on overall progress in the implementation of Agenda 21, the Programme for the Further Implementation of Agenda 21 and the Johannesburg Plan of Implementation, reflecting:

(i) Cross-cutting issues identified by the Commission at its eleventh session;

(ii) Progress made in the three dimensions of sustainable development and their integration;

(iii) Constraints, challenges, opportunities, best practices, information-sharing and lessons learned;

9. *Invites* the Bureau of the Commission at its twelfth session to continue to recommend to the Commission the specific organizational modalities through open-ended and transparent consultations to be conducted in a timely manner, following the established United Nations rules of procedure, bearing in mind that the activities during Commission meetings should provide for balanced involvement of participants from all regions, as well as for gender balance;

10. *Decides* to allocate the resources previously devoted to the former ad hoc intersessional working groups of the Commission to support the participation of representatives of member States of the Commission in one of their respective regional meetings in each implementation cycle;

11. *Invites* donor countries to consider supporting the participation of experts from developing countries in the areas of water, sanitation and human settlement in the next review and policy sessions of the Commission;

12. *Decides* that resources released by the termination of the work of the Committee on Energy and Natural Resources for Development, whose work has been transferred to the Commission, shall be used to support the work of the Commission;

13. *Encourages* Governments and organizations at all levels, as well as major groups, including the scientific community and educators, to undertake results-oriented initiatives and activities to support the work of the Commission and to promote and facilitate the implementation of Agenda 21, the Programme for the Further Implementation of Agenda 21 and the Johannesburg Plan of Implementation, including through voluntary multi-stakeholder partnership initiatives;

14. *Encourages* Governments to participate, at the appropriate level, through representatives of relevant departments and agencies responsible for water, sani-

tation and human settlement, in the next review and policy sessions of the Commission,

15. *Requests* the Secretariat to submit a summary report containing synthesized information on partnerships to the Commission at its twelfth session, in accordance with its programme and organization of work, noting the particular relevance of such reports in review years, with a view to sharing lessons learned and best practices and identifying and addressing problems, gaps and constraints in the implementation of Agenda 21, the Programme for the Further Implementation of Agenda 21 and the Johannesburg Plan of Implementation;

16. *Requests* the Commission, in accordance with General Assembly resolution 47/191 of 22 December 1992 and as specified by the Commission at its eleventh session, to examine progress made in the cross-cutting issues in the relevant thematic clusters, utilizing inputs from all levels;

17. *Requests* the Economic and Social Council to implement the provisions of the Johannesburg Plan of Implementation relevant to its mandate, in particular to promote the implementation of Agenda 21 by strengthening system-wide coordination;

18. *Urges* the Secretariat, in the preparation of the reports of the Secretary-General referred to in paragraph 8 above, to take due account of national reports;

19. *Decides* to include in the provisional agenda of its fifty-ninth session the item entitled "Implementation of Agenda 21, the Programme for the Further Implementation of Agenda 21 and the outcomes of the World Summit on Sustainable Development", and requests the Secretary-General, at that session, to submit a report on the implementation of the present resolution.

Commission on Sustainable Development

The Commission on Sustainable Development held an organizational session on 27 January and the second part of its eleventh session in New York from 28 April to 9 May [E/2003/29]. The session's high-level segment focused on the Commission's future role in the context of follow-up to the 2002 World Summit on Sustainable Development (see p. 838) and included three interactive high-level round tables and five regional implementation forums. A multi-stakeholder dialogue addressed the role of major groups in relation to the future work of the Commission and implementation of the Summit outcomes.

The Commission recommended to the Economic and Social Council for adoption two draft resolutions: one on the Commission's future programme, organization and working methods (see below) and the other on preparations for an international meeting to review implementation of the Programme of Action for the Sustainable Development of Small Island Developing States (SIDS) (see p. 871). It also recommended to the Council for adoption a decision on the report of the eleventh session and the provisional agenda for the twelfth. The Commission adopted a decision [dec. 11/1] recommending Council consideration of the status of non-governmental organizations (NGOs) that were accredited to the World Summit so that the Commission could benefit from their contributions, and another decision [dec. 11/2] asking the Council to consider the term of the Commission's Bureau for future sessions, taking into account the Commission's two-year work cycle.

The Commission had before it the report of the Secretary-General on the follow-up to the World Summit on Sustainable Development and the future role of the Commission (see p. 838); a 7 February letter from Austria [E/CN.17/2003/4], transmitting the executive summary of the third meeting of the Global Forum on Sustainable Energy (Graz, Austria, 27-29 November 2002); proposed revisions to subprogramme 4, Sustainable development, of programme 7, Economic and social affairs, of the medium-term plan for 2002-2005 [E/CN.17/2003/4]; and the draft programme of work for the UN Division for Sustainable Development for the 2004-2005 biennium [E/CN.17/2003/5].

ECONOMIC AND SOCIAL COUNCIL ACTION

On 25 July [meeting 49], the Economic and Social Council, on the recommendation of the Commission on Sustainable Development [E/2003/29], adopted **resolution 2003/61** without vote [agenda item 13 (a)].

Future programme, organization and methods of work of the Commission on Sustainable Development

The Economic and Social Council,

Recalling the Rio Declaration on Environment and Development, Agenda 21 and the Programme for the Further Implementation of Agenda 21,

Recalling also the Johannesburg Declaration on Sustainable Development and the Plan of Implementation of the World Summit on Sustainable Development ("Johannesburg Plan of Implementation"), adopted at the World Summit,

Reaffirming in that regard the commitment to achieving the internationally agreed development goals, including those contained in the United Nations Millennium Declaration and in the outcomes of the major United Nations conferences held and international agreements made since 1992,

Recalling that the Johannesburg Plan of Implementation will build further on the achievements made since the United Nations Conference on Environment and Development and that the Plan expedites the realization of the remaining goals; to that end, committing itself to undertaking concrete actions and measures at all levels and to enhancing international cooperation, taking into account the Rio principles, including, inter alia, the principle of common but differentiated responsibilities as set out in principle 7 of the Rio Declaration, efforts that will also promote the integration of the three components of sustainable development—economic development, social development and environmental protection—as interdependent and mutually reinforcing pillars; and recalling that poverty eradication, changing unsustainable patterns of production and consumption, and protecting and managing the natural resource base of economic and social development are overarching objectives of, and essential requirements for, sustainable development,

Reaffirming that the Commission on Sustainable Development should continue to be the high-level commission responsible for sustainable development within the United Nations system,

Reaffirming also the mandate of the Commission on Sustainable Development as stipulated in Agenda 21, General Assembly resolution 47/191 of 22 December 1992 and the Johannesburg Plan of Implementation,

Taking into account General Assembly resolution 57/253 of 20 December 2002,

Having considered the report of the Commission on Sustainable Development on its eleventh session,

Future organization of work of the Commission

1. *Decides* that the organization of work of the Commission on Sustainable Development should contribute to advancing the implementation of Agenda 21, the Programme for the Further Implementation of Agenda 21 and the Johannesburg Plan of Implementation at all levels;

2. *Also decides* that in order to fulfil its mandate the work of the Commission will be organized in a series of two-year action-oriented implementation cycles, which will include a review session and a policy session. The cycles will function as follows:

(a) The review sessions of the Commission, to be held in April/May for a period of two to three weeks in the first year of the cycle, will undertake an evaluation of progress in implementing Agenda 21, the Programme for the Further Implementation of Agenda 21 and the Johannesburg Plan of Implementation, while focusing on identifying constraints and obstacles in the process of implementation with regard to the selected thematic cluster of issues for the cycle;

(b) The review sessions will include a high-level segment, an exchange of regional experiences, dialogues with experts, including scientific experts, and sharing of best practices and lessons learned, with a view to facilitating implementation, as well as capacity-building activities, such as learning centres and partnership fairs;

(c) The review sessions will undertake the above-mentioned evaluation on the basis of:

(i) The reports of the Secretary-General on the state of implementation, which should reflect overall progress in the implementation of Agenda 21, the Programme for the Further Implementation of Agenda 21 and the Johannesburg Plan of Implementation, based on information provided in particular in countries' reports and in reports by United Nations organizations and bodies as identified in subparagraph (ii) below, and on information from regions and subregions, as appropriate, as well as major groups. In addition, the reports of the Secretary-General on the state of implementation should contain a detailed review of progress in implementation in the selected thematic cluster of issues for the cycle at all levels, and should also reflect new challenges and opportunities related to the implementation of Agenda 21;

(ii) The contributions of United Nations agencies, programmes and funds, the Global Environment Facility and international financial and trade institutions;

(iii) The outcomes of regional and subregional meetings and activities, as appropriate;

(iv) The contributions of major groups, including scientific experts, as well as educators, taking into account paragraphs 139 (g) and 149 (c) and (d) of the Johannesburg Plan of Implementation, on their results-oriented activities concerning the implementation of Agenda 21, the Programme for the Further Implementation of Agenda 21 and the Johannesburg Plan of Implementation;

(d) The review session evaluation should enable an improved understanding of priority concerns in the implementation of the selected thematic cluster of issues and facilitate an effective policy discussion in the course of the policy year with a view to strengthening implementation in those areas;

(e) The outcome of the review session will be a report, including a chairperson's summary, identifying constraints and obstacles and possible approaches and best practices for the implementation of Agenda 21, the Programme for the Further Implementation of Agenda 21 and the Johannesburg Plan of Implementation;

(f) In the policy year, the Commission will convene an intergovernmental preparatory meeting for one week in New York in February/March to discuss policy options and possible actions to address the constraints and obstacles in the process of implementation identified during the review year;

(g) The discussions of the intergovernmental preparatory meeting will be based on the outcome of the review session, reports by the Secretary-General as well as other relevant inputs. Based on those discussions, the Chair will prepare a draft negotiating document for consideration at the policy session;

(h) The policy sessions of the Commission, to be held in April/May of the second year of the cycle, will take policy decisions on practical measures and options to expedite implementation in the selected thematic cluster of issues, taking account of the discussions of the intergovernmental preparatory meeting, the reports of the Secretary-General and other relevant inputs;

(i) The review sessions and the policy sessions should mobilize further action by all implementation actors to overcome obstacles and constraints in the implementation of Agenda 21, the Programme for the Further Implementation of Agenda 21 and the Johannesburg Plan of Implementation, and should address new challenges and opportunities and share lessons learned and best practices;

(j) Specific organizational modalities for Commission meetings will be recommended by the Bureau of the Commission through open-ended and transparent consultations conducted in a timely manner, following the established United Nations rules of procedure. Activities during Commission meetings should provide for balanced involvement of participants from all regions, as well as for gender balance;

3. *Decides*, in order to allow effective consideration of regional and subregional inputs throughout the implementation cycle and to ensure maximum flexibility:

(a) To invite the regional commissions, in collaboration with the secretariat of the Commission on Sustainable Development, to consider organizing regional implementation meetings in order to contribute to the work of the Commission, in accordance with the relevant provisions of the Johannesburg Plan of Implementation and in collaboration with other regional and subregional organizations and bodies, as appropriate, as well as the regional offices of funds, programmes and international finance and trade institutions and other organizations and bodies of the United Nations system. Such meetings should preferably take place before the review session of the Commission, and should:
  (i) Contribute to advancing the implementation of Agenda 21, the Programme for the Further Implementation of Agenda 21 and the Johannesburg Plan of Implementation;
  (ii) Focus on the thematic cluster of issues to be addressed in the ongoing implementation cycle;
  (iii) Provide input to the reports of the Secretary-General and the sessions of the Commission. Those inputs may include identification of obstacles and constraints, new challenges and opportunities related to the implementation of Agenda 21, the Programme for the Further Implementation of Agenda 21 and the Johannesburg Plan of Implementation, and sharing of lessons learned and best practices;
  (iv) Provide for contributions from major groups, taking into account paragraphs 139 (g) and 149 (c) and (d) of the Johannesburg Plan of Implementation;
(b) To invite the General Assembly to consider using the resources previously devoted to the former ad hoc intersessional working groups of the Commission to support the participation of representatives of member States of the Commission in one of their respective regional meetings in each implementation cycle;
(c) To invite the regional commissions to provide other inputs to the review and policy sessions of the Commission and the intergovernmental preparatory meeting;
(d) To invite other regional and subregional bodies and institutions within and outside the United Nations system to contribute to the preparations for the review and policy sessions of the Commission and the intergovernmental preparatory meeting;

4. *Recommends* to the General Assembly that resources released by the termination of the work of the Committee on Energy and Natural Resources for Development, whose work has been transferred to the Commission, could be used to support the work of the Commission;

5. *Invites* Governments, as well as organizations at all levels and major groups, to undertake results-oriented initiatives and activities that support the programme of work of the Commission and promote and facilitate the implementation of Agenda 21, the Programme for the Further Implementation of Agenda 21 and the Johannesburg Plan of Implementation. The results of such initiatives and activities should be an input to the work of the Commission, as appropriate;

6. *Decides* that the results of the work of the Commission could also include the sharing of best practices and lessons learned, capacity-building activities, exchange of experiences concerning the implementation of sustainable development strategies, as appropriate, and partnerships that support the implementation of Agenda 21, the Programme for the Further Implementation of Agenda 21 and the Johannesburg Plan of Implementation;

7. *Also decides* that Commission sessions should include high-level segments, involving ministers or their representatives with responsibilities relevant to the thematic cluster of issues under discussion. The segments should be organized so that ministerial leadership, oversight and guidance in decision-making concerning the outcomes of the sessions would be enhanced. High-level segments should include focused dialogue, with the active participation of agencies, funds, programmes and other organizations of the United Nations system, international finance and trade institutions, and representatives of major groups at the appropriate level, taking into account paragraphs 139 (g) and 149 (c) and (d) of the Johannesburg Plan of Implementation;

8. *Further decides* to organize the periodic consideration of sustainable development themes in regard to the implementation of Agenda 21, the Programme for the Further Implementation of Agenda 21 and the Johannesburg Plan of Implementation, including the means of implementation, and invites the Commission to submit recommendations to the Council with regard to such themes, which may include recommendations to assist the Council with its work in the pursuance of paragraph 144 of the Johannesburg Plan of Implementation, including its role in promoting system-wide coordination;

Multi-year programme of work of the Commission for the period after 2003

9. *Decides* to adopt the multi-year programme of work of the Commission for the period after 2003 as outlined in the annex to the present resolution;

10. *Also decides* that the implementation of that programme of work will be guided by the following considerations:

(a) The review and evaluation of the implementation of actions, commitments and targets will be dealt with in accordance with the relevant provisions of Agenda 21, the Programme for the Further Implementation of Agenda 21, the Johannesburg Plan of Implementation and the decisions of the Commission. The thematic clusters should be addressed in an integrated manner, taking into account the economic, social and environmental dimensions of sustainable development. Recognizing that all the issues identified in Agenda 21 and the Johannesburg Plan of Implementation are important, the implementation process should cover all those issues equally, and the selection of some issues during a given cycle does not therefore diminish the importance of the commitments undertaken with respect to the issues to be considered during future cycles;

(b) Means of implementation, as identified in Agenda 21 and chapter X of the Johannesburg Plan of Implementation, should be addressed in every cycle and for every relevant issue, action and commitment;

(c) Other cross-cutting issues, as referred to in the annex to the present resolution, should also be addressed in every cycle;

(d) African and other regional initiatives, as well as initiatives on small island developing States and least developed countries, will be considered in every cycle with respect to all relevant issues, actions and targets;

(e) The Commission should focus on those issues where it can add value to intergovernmental deliberations on cross-sectoral and sectoral issues, in accordance with the provisions of General Assembly resolution 47/191, in particular its paragraphs 3 (h), 21 and 23 thereof, as well as 139 (f) of the Johannesburg Plan of Implementation;

(f) The Commission should take into account the outcome of the work of the Ad Hoc Working Group of the General Assembly on the integrated and coordinated implementation of and follow-up to the outcomes of major United Nations conferences and summits in the economic and social fields;

(g) The Commission may decide to incorporate new challenges and opportunities related to implementation into its multi-year programme of work;

* * *

11. *Emphasizes* that in order to enable the Commission to perform the relevant requirements provided for in chapter XI of the Johannesburg Plan of Implementation, in particular paragraphs 145, 147 and 148 thereof, an effective system of reporting is essential for reviewing, evaluating and monitoring progress in the implementation of Agenda 21, the Programme for the Further Implementation of Agenda 21 and the Johannesburg Plan of Implementation, sharing of lessons learned and best practices, as well as identifying actions taken, opportunities for and obstacles and constraints to implementation;

12. *Encourages* countries to present, on a voluntary basis, national reports, in particular to the review sessions of the Commission, focusing on concrete progress in implementation, including achievements, constraints, challenges and opportunities;

13. *Encourages*, with the purpose of implementing paragraphs 130 and 131 of the Johannesburg Plan of Implementation and paragraph 3 of Commission decision 9/4 of 27 April 2001, further work on indicators for sustainable development by countries at the national level, including integration of gender aspects, on a voluntary basis, in line with national conditions and priorities, and requests the Secretary-General to consider progress made in that regard, including further work on the above-mentioned indicators, in reporting to the Commission, as appropriate;

14. *Underscores* the fact that reporting to the Commission should be guided by the following considerations:

(a) Reporting should reflect the overall progress made on the three dimensions of sustainable development, focusing on the thematic cluster of issues for the cycle, and should include inputs from all levels, as appropriate, including the national, subregional, regional and global levels, and drawing on those sources listed in subparagraphs (ii) to (iv) of paragraph 2 (c) above;

(b) The existing reporting systems should be used to the fullest extent possible and will be expected to provide the bulk of information required;

(c) Reporting should focus on concrete progress in implementation, taking into account the three dimensions of sustainable development and their integration, and should include information-sharing, lessons learned, progress made and best practices, identifying actions taken, constraints, challenges and opportunities;

(d) The effective use of indicators, as described in paragraph 13 above;

(e) Country reporting should provide information on the status of national strategies for sustainable development;

15. *Requests* the secretariat of the Commission, working in close cooperation with other organizations of the United Nations system:

(a) To take measures to streamline reporting in order to avoid duplication and unnecessary burden on States, including in accordance with the report of the Secretary-General on United Nations reform;

(b) To provide focused information that highlights relevant trends, constraints, challenges and emerging issues;

(c) To provide technical assistance to countries, upon their request, in national reporting through regular and extrabudgetary sources;

16. *Invites* the secretariat of the Commission to improve national reporting guidelines and questionnaires with the intention of making reporting more efficient and less burdensome on countries and more focused on implementation, bearing in mind the provisions of the present resolution, in consultation with Governments, United Nations organizations and secretariats of multilateral environmental agreements, and to report to the Commission for its consideration;

* * *

17. *Invites*, further to paragraph 140 of the Johannesburg Plan of Implementation, relevant United Nations agencies, programmes and funds, the Global Environment Facility, and international and regional financial and trade institutions, within their mandates, to participate actively in the work of the Commission in order to inform it of their activities designed to further the implementation of Agenda 21, the Programme for the Further Implementation of Agenda 21 and the Johannesburg Plan of Implementation. To that end, it is essential to undertake further measures:

(a) To promote stronger linkages between global, regional and country-level implementation measures;

(b) To strengthen coherence and collaboration within and between organizations;

(c) To identify areas where further implementation measures may be required in order to improve progress;

(d) To mobilize and increase the effective use of resources from all sources for implementation;

(e) To enhance collaboration and coordination in all areas, including information exchange and knowledge-sharing on all aspects of the implementation of Agenda 21, the Programme for the Further Implementation of Agenda 21 and the Johannesburg Plan of Implementation;

18. *Requests* the Secretary-General, taking into account the ongoing process of United Nations reform and utilizing the United Nations System Chief Executives Board for Coordination, including through informal collaborative efforts, to further promote system-wide inter-agency cooperation and coordination to enhance the implementation of Agenda 21, the Programme for the Further Implementation of Agenda 21 and the Johannesburg Plan of Implementation, and to

report on its activities to the Economic and Social Council and the Commission;

19. *Also requests* the Secretary-General, pursuant to General Assembly resolution 57/253, to include in his report proposals outlining an integrated and comprehensive response of the United Nations system to sustainable development, taking into account the work of the Ad Hoc Working Group of the General Assembly on the integrated and coordinated implementation of and follow-up to the outcomes of major United Nations conferences and summits in the economic and social fields;

* * *

20. *Decides* that contributions to the Commission from major groups, including the scientific community and educators, taking into account paragraphs 139 (*g*) and 149 (*c*) and (*d*) of the Johannesburg Plan of Implementation, while following the established rules of procedure and practices of the Commission, should be further enhanced, taking into account chapter XI of the Johannesburg Plan of Implementation, through such measures as:

(*a*) Strengthening major group involvement in the activities of the Commission, including through the participation of representatives of major groups at the appropriate level in an interactive dialogue during high-level segments, taking into account paragraphs 139 (*g*) and 149 (*c*) and (*d*) of the Johannesburg Plan of Implementation;

(*b*) Making multi-stakeholder dialogues more action- and implementation-oriented;

(*c*) Enhancing the participation and effective involvement of civil society and other relevant stakeholders in the implementation of Agenda 21, the Programme for the Further Implementation of Agenda 21 and the Johannesburg Plan of Implementation, as well as promoting transparency and broad public participation;

(*d*) Striving for a better balance and better representation of major groups from all regions at the Commission;

(*e*) Active involvement in partnership-related and capacity-building activities at all levels, including the partnerships fairs and learning centres organized as part of the meetings of the Commission;

* * *

21. *Recalls* that the Johannesburg Plan of Implementation designated the Commission to serve as the focal point for discussion on partnerships that promote sustainable development, and reiterates that partnerships, as voluntary multi-stakeholder initiatives, contribute to the implementation of intergovernmental commitments contained in Agenda 21, the Programme for the Further Implementation of Agenda 21 and the Johannesburg Plan of Implementation. They are a complement to, but not intended to substitute for, those commitments;

22. Stresses that partnerships in the context of the World Summit on Sustainable Development process and its follow-up should be developed and implemented in accordance with the following criteria and guidelines, taking note in that regard of the preliminary work undertaken on partnerships during the preparatory process for the Summit, including the Bali guiding principles, and General Assembly resolution 56/76 of 11 December 2001:

(*a*) Partnerships are voluntary initiatives undertaken by Governments and relevant stakeholders, such as major groups and institutional stakeholders;

(*b*) Partnerships should contribute to the implementation of Agenda 21, the Programme for the Further Implementation of Agenda 21 and the Johannesburg Plan of Implementation, and should not divert resources from the commitments contained in those agreements;

(*c*) Partnerships are not intended to substitute commitments made by Governments but to supplement the implementation of Agenda 21, the Programme for the Further Implementation of Agenda 21 and the Johannesburg Plan of Implementation;

(*d*) Partnerships should add concrete value to the implementation process and should be new, that is, they should not merely reflect existing arrangements;

(*e*) Partnerships should bear in mind the economic, social and environmental dimensions of sustainable development in their design and implementation;

(*f*) Partnerships should be based on predictable and sustained resources for their implementation, should include the mobilization of new resources and, where relevant, should result in the transfer of technology to, and capacity-building in, developing countries;

(*g*) It is desirable that partnerships have a sectoral and geographical balance;

(*h*) Partnerships should be designed and implemented in a transparent and accountable manner. In that regard, they should exchange relevant information with Governments and other relevant stakeholders;

(*i*) Partnerships should be publicly announced with the intention of sharing the specific contribution that they make to the implementation of Agenda 21, the Programme for the Further Implementation of Agenda 21 and the Johannesburg Plan of Implementation;

(*j*) Partnerships should be consistent with national laws and national strategies for the implementation of Agenda 21, the Programme for the Further Implementation of Agenda 21 and the Johannesburg Plan of Implementation, as well as the priorities of countries where their implementation takes place;

(*k*) The leading partner of a partnership initiative should inform the national focal point for sustainable development of the involved country or countries about the initiation and progress of the partnership, and all partners should bear in mind the guidance provided by Governments;

(*l*) The involvement of international institutions and United Nations funds, programmes and agencies in partnerships should conform to intergovernmentally agreed mandates and should not lead to the diversion to partnerships of resources otherwise allocated for their mandated programmes;

23. *Decides* that the provision of information and reporting by partnerships registered with the Commission should be transparent, participatory and credible, taking into account the following elements:

(*a*) The registration of partnerships should be voluntary and should be based on written reporting to the Commission, taking into account the provisions specified above. Reporting by partnerships should focus on their contribution to the implementation of the goals, objectives and targets of Agenda 21, the Programme for the Further Implementation of Agenda 21 and the Johannesburg Plan of Implementation;

(b) Partnerships should submit a regular report, preferably at least on a biennial basis;

(c) The Secretariat is requested to make information available on partnerships, including their reports, through a database accessible to all interested parties, including through the Commission web site and other means;

(d) The Secretariat is requested to produce a summary report containing synthesized information on partnerships for consideration by the Commission, in accordance with its programme and organization of work, noting the particular relevance of such reports in review years;

(e) The Commission, during review years, should discuss the contribution of partnerships towards supporting the implementation of Agenda 21, the Programme for the Further Implementation of Agenda 21 and the Johannesburg Plan of Implementation with a view to sharing lessons learned and best practices, identifying and addressing problems, gaps and constraints, and providing further guidance, including on reporting, during policy years, as necessary;

24. *Calls* for activities aimed at strengthening partnerships in the context of the World Summit on Sustainable Development process and its follow-up and facilitating new ones, including through such initiatives as partnerships fairs and learning centres, mindful of the importance of sharing information on existing activities, particularly across the United Nations system.

Annex

Multi-year programme of work of the Commission on Sustainable Development

Cycle	Thematic cluster	Cross-cutting issues
2004/2005	• Water • Sanitation • Human settlements	Poverty eradication; changing unsustainable patterns of consumption and production; protecting and managing the natural resource base of economic and social development; sustainable development in a globalizing world; health and sustainable development; sustainable development of small island developing States; sustainable development for Africa; other regional initiatives; means of implementation; institutional framework for sustainable development; gender equality; education
2006/2007	• Energy for sustainable development • Industrial development • Air pollution/atmosphere • Climate change	Poverty eradication; changing unsustainable patterns of consumption and production; protecting and managing the natural resource base of economic and social development; sustainable development in a globalizing world; health and sustainable development; sustainable development of small island developing States; sustainable development for Africa; other regional initiatives; means of implementation; institutional framework for sustainable development; gender equality; education
2008/2009	• Agriculture • Rural development • Land • Drought • Desertification • Africa	Poverty eradication; changing unsustainable patterns of consumption and production; protecting and managing the natural resource base of economic and social development; sustainable development in a globalizing world; health and sustainable development; sustainable development of small island developing States; sustainable development for Africa; other regional initiatives; means of implementation; institutional framework for sustainable development; gender equality; education
2010/2011[a]	• Transport • Chemicals • Waste management • Mining • Ten-year framework of programmes on sustainable consumption and production patterns	Poverty eradication; changing unsustainable patterns of consumption and production; protecting and managing the natural resource base of economic and social development; sustainable development in a globalizing world; health and sustainable development; sustainable development of small island developing States; sustainable development for Africa; other regional initiatives; means of implementation; institutional framework for sustainable development; gender equality; education
2012/2013[a]	• Forests • Biodiversity • Biotechnology • Tourism • Mountains	Poverty eradication; changing unsustainable patterns of consumption and production; protecting and managing the natural resource base of economic and social development; sustainable development in a globalizing world; health and sustainable development; sustainable development of small island developing States; sustainable development for Africa; other regional initiatives; means of implementation; institutional framework for sustainable development; gender equality; education
2014/2015[a]	• Oceans and seas • Marine resources • Small island developing States • Disaster management and vulnerability	Poverty eradication; changing unsustainable patterns of consumption and production; protecting and managing the natural resource base of economic and social development; sustainable development in a globalizing world; health and sustainable development; sustainable development of small island developing States; sustainable development for Africa; other regional initiatives; means of implementation; institutional framework for sustainable development; gender equality; education
2016/2017	• Overall appraisal of the implementation of Agenda 21, the Programme for the Further Implementation of Agenda 21 and the Johannesburg Plan of Implementation	

[a]This thematic cluster will remain as part of the multi-year programme of work as scheduled, unless otherwise agreed by the Commission (applies to clusters for 2010/2011, 2012/2013 and 2014/2015).

The Council, by **decision 2003/289** of 24 July, took note of the report of the Commission on its eleventh session and approved the provisional agenda for the Commission's twelfth (2004) session.

By **decisions 2003/295** and **2003/296** of 25 July, the Council took note of the Commission's decisions on the status of NGOs and the Bureau, respectively, and deferred further consideration of those matters to its resumed 2003 session. On 19 December, by **decision 2003/316**, the Council deferred consideration of those matters until its 2004 organizational session.

Education for sustainable development

In 2003, in accordance with resolution 57/254 [YUN 2002, p. 826], by which the General Assembly proclaimed the United Nations Decade of Education for Sustainable Development (2005-2014), the United Nations Educational, Scientific and Cultural Organization (UNESCO)—lead agency for promoting the Decade—developed a framework for a draft international implementation scheme for the Decade. The framework, which was presented orally to the Assembly in October [A/C.2/58/SR.15], gave a time line for activities in relation to the Decade up to December 2005 and outlined processes, players, outputs and strategies from which the implementation scheme would be developed.

GENERAL ASSEMBLY ACTION

On 23 December [meeting 78], the General Assembly, on the recommendation of the Second Committee [A/58/486], adopted **resolution 58/219** without vote [agenda item 96].

United Nations Decade of Education for Sustainable Development

The General Assembly,

Recalling chapter 36 of Agenda 21, on promoting education, public awareness and training, adopted at the United Nations Conference on Environment and Development, held in Rio de Janeiro, Brazil, from 3 to 14 June 1992,

Recalling also the relevant provisions of the Plan of Implementation of the World Summit on Sustainable Development ("Johannesburg Plan of Implementation") on education, in particular its provision 124 (*d*) on the United Nations Decade of Education for Sustainable Development,

Recalling further its resolution 57/254 of 20 December 2002,

Reaffirming the internationally agreed development goal of achieving universal primary education, in particular that by 2015 children everywhere, boys and girls alike, will be able to complete a full course of primary schooling,

Taking note of the report of the Director-General of the United Nations Educational, Scientific and Cultural Organization on the United Nations Decade of Education for Sustainable Development,

Welcoming the fact that the Commission on Sustainable Development, at its eleventh session, identified education as one of the cross-cutting issues of its multi-year programme of work,

Emphasizing that education is an indispensable element for achieving sustainable development,

1. *Takes note* of the Framework for a Draft International Implementation Scheme prepared by the United Nations Educational, Scientific and Cultural Organization, requests the United Nations Educational, Scientific and Cultural Organization, as the designated lead agency, to promote the United Nations Decade of Education for Sustainable Development, in coordination with other relevant United Nations agencies and programmes, and further requests it to finalize the international implementation scheme, while clarifying its relationship with the existing educational processes, in particular the Dakar Framework for Action adopted at the World Education Forum and the United Nations Literacy Decade, in consultation with Governments, the United Nations and other relevant international organizations, non-governmental organizations and other stakeholders;

2. *Reaffirms* that education for sustainable development is critical for promoting sustainable development, and in this regard encourages Governments to consider the inclusion of measures to implement the United Nations Decade of Education for Sustainable Development in their respective educational strategies and national development plans by 2005;

3. *Invites* Governments to promote public awareness of and wider participation in the United Nations Decade of Education for Sustainable Development, including through cooperation and initiatives engaging civil society and other relevant stakeholders;

4. *Decides* to include in the provisional agenda of its fifty-ninth session, under the item entitled "Environment and sustainable development", a sub-item entitled "United Nations Decade of Education for Sustainable Development".

Eradication of poverty

UN Decade for Eradication of Poverty

In response to General Assembly resolution 57/266 [YUN 2002, p. 828], the Secretary-General submitted a July report on the implementation of the first United Nations Decade for the Eradication of Poverty (1997-2006) and a draft programme of action for observance of the International Year of Microcredit in 2005 (see p. 853) [A/58/179].

The report stated that progress in reducing poverty had been patchy and uneven, with the poorer developing countries, where economic and social development was needed most, still lagging behind the faster-growing developing countries on many fronts. On current performance, many countries, particularly in sub-Saharan Africa, were not likely to achieve the MDG of halving the proportion of the world's people living on less than one dollar a day by 2015. However, there were some fresh developments and results that pointed towards progress in two key areas—governance at the international and national levels and poverty reduction strategies—considered to be among the preconditions necessary for countries to achieve rapid growth and poverty eradication.

The report also described a modest revival of official development assistance (ODA) levels, following the commitments made at the 2002 International Conference on Financing for Development [YUN 2002, p. 953]. Although the levels were still well below their historical highs and considerably below the minimum levels needed to attain the MDGs, there was optimism that ODA would continue to rise.

GENERAL ASSEMBLY ACTION

On 23 December [meeting 78], the General Assembly, on the recommendation of the Second Committee [A/58/488], adopted **resolution 58/222** without vote [agenda item 98].

Implementation of the first United Nations Decade for the Eradication of Poverty (1997-2006)

The General Assembly,

Recalling its resolutions 47/196 of 22 December 1992, 48/183 of 21 December 1993, 50/107 of 20 December 1995, 56/207 of 21 December 2001 and 57/266 of 20 December 2002,

Recalling also the United Nations Millennium Declaration adopted by heads of State and Government on the occasion of the Millennium Summit, and their commitment to eradicate extreme poverty and to halve, by 2015, the proportion of the world's people whose income is less than one dollar a day and the proportion of people who suffer from hunger,

Underlining the priority and urgency given by the heads of State and Government to the eradication of poverty, as expressed in the Monterrey Consensus of the International Conference on Financing for Development and in the outcomes of the World Summit on Sustainable Development,

Recalling the outcomes of the major United Nations conferences and summits in the economic and social fields,

Bearing in mind the outcomes of the World Summit for Social Development and the twenty-fourth special session of the General Assembly,

Expressing its deep concern that the number of people living in extreme poverty in many countries continues to increase, with women and children constituting the majority and the most affected groups, in particular in the least developed countries and in sub-Saharan Africa,

Recognizing that, while the rate of poverty in some countries has been reduced, some developing countries and disadvantaged groups are being marginalized and others are at risk of being marginalized and effectively excluded from the benefits of globalization, resulting in increased income disparity among and within countries, thereby constraining efforts to eradicate poverty,

1. *Takes note* of the report of the Secretary-General;
2. *Reiterates* that eradicating poverty is the greatest global challenge facing the world today and an indispensable requirement for sustainable development, in particular for developing countries, that each country has the primary responsibility for its own sustainable development and poverty eradication, that the role of national policies and development strategies cannot be overemphasized and that concerted and concrete measures are required at all levels to enable developing countries to eradicate poverty and achieve sustainable development;
3. *Recognizes* that, in order for developing countries to reach the targets set in the context of national development strategies for the achievement of the internationally agreed development goals, including those contained in the United Nations Millennium Declaration, in particular the goal of the eradication of poverty, and for such poverty eradication strategies to be effective, it is imperative that they be integrated into the world economy and share equitably in the benefits of globalization;
4. *Reaffirms* that, within the context of overall action for the eradication of poverty, special attention should be given to the multidimensional nature of poverty and the national and international conditions and policies that are conducive to its eradication, fostering, inter alia, the social and economic integration of people living in poverty and the promotion and protection of all human rights and fundamental freedoms for all, including the right to development;

Global response for the eradication of poverty

5. *Stresses* the importance of the follow-up to the outcome of the International Conference on Financing for Development, and calls for the full and effective implementation of the Monterrey Consensus;
6. *Reaffirms* that good governance at the international level is fundamental for achieving poverty eradication and sustainable development; in order to ensure a dynamic and enabling international economic environment, it is important to promote global economic governance by addressing the international finance, trade, technology and investment patterns that have an impact on the development prospects of developing countries; to that end, the international community should take all necessary and appropriate measures, including ensuring support to structural and macroeconomic reform, a comprehensive solution to the external debt problem and increasing market access for developing countries; efforts to reform the international financial architecture need to be sustained with greater transparency and with the effective participation of developing countries in decision-making processes; and that a universal, rule-based, open, non-discriminatory and equitable multilateral trading system, as well as meaningful trade liberalization, can substantially stimulate development worldwide, benefiting countries at all stages of development;
7. *Also reaffirms* that good governance at the national level is essential for poverty eradication and sustainable development, that sound economic policies, solid democratic institutions responsive to the needs of the people and improved infrastructure are the basis

for sustained economic growth, poverty eradication and employment creation, and that freedom, peace and security, domestic stability, respect for human rights, including the right to development, the rule of law, gender equality, market-oriented policies and an overall commitment to just and democratic societies are also essential and mutually reinforcing;

8. *Recognizes* the major role that trade can play as an engine of growth and development and in eradicating poverty, regrets that the Fifth Ministerial Conference of the World Trade Organization, held in Cancún, Mexico, from 10 to 14 September 2003, failed to produce an agreement, and calls for the resumption of the negotiations and the implementation of the Doha agenda, adopted at the Fourth Ministerial Conference of the World Trade Organization, held at Doha from 9 to 14 November 2001;

9. *Also recognizes* the responsibility of all Governments to adopt policies aimed at preventing and combating corrupt practices at the national and international levels, and welcomes in this regard the adoption of the United Nations Convention against Corruption;

10. *Underlines* that, together with coherent and consistent domestic policies, international cooperation is essential in supplementing and supporting the efforts of developing countries to utilize their domestic resources for development and poverty eradication and in ensuring that they will be able to achieve the development goals as envisioned in the Millennium Declaration;

11. *Reiterates* that a substantial increase in official development assistance and other resources will be required if developing countries, in particular the least developed countries, are to achieve the internationally agreed development goals and objectives, including those contained in the Millennium Declaration, and that, to build support for official development assistance, cooperation is necessary to further improve policies and development strategies to enhance aid effectiveness, both nationally and internationally, requests, in that regard, those countries that made announcements of increased official development assistance at the International Conference on Financing for Development to make those resources available as soon as possible, and notes in this context the recent upward trend in official development assistance;

12. *Urges* developed countries that have not done so to make concrete efforts to reach the targets of 0.7 per cent of their gross national product as official development assistance to developing countries and 0.15 to 0.20 per cent of their gross national product to least developed countries, as reconfirmed at the Third United Nations Conference on the Least Developed Countries, held in Brussels from 14 to 20 May 2001, encourages developing countries to build on progress achieved in ensuring that official development assistance is used effectively to help achieve development goals and targets, acknowledges the efforts of all donors, commends those donors whose official development assistance contributions exceed, reach or are increasing towards the targets, and underlines the importance of undertaking to examine the means and time frames for achieving the targets and goals;

13. *Recognizes* that an enabling domestic environment is vital for mobilizing domestic resources, increasing productivity, reducing capital flight, encouraging the private sector and attracting and making effective use of international investment and assistance, and that efforts to create such an environment should be supported by the international community;

14. *Also recognizes* that creditors and debtors must share the responsibility for preventing and resolving unsustainable debt situations and that debt relief can play a key role in liberating resources that should be directed towards activities consistent with attaining poverty eradication, sustainable economic growth, sustainable development and the achievement of the internationally agreed development goals, including those contained in the Millennium Declaration, and in that regard urges countries to direct those resources freed through debt relief, in particular through debt cancellation and reduction, towards these objectives;

15. *Calls upon* the developed countries, by means of intensified and effective cooperation with developing countries, to promote capacity-building and facilitate access to and transfer of technologies and corresponding knowledge, in particular to developing countries, on favourable terms, including concessional and preferential terms, as mutually agreed, taking into account the need to protect intellectual property rights as well as the special needs of developing countries;

16. *Recognizes* the crucial role that microcredit and microfinance could play in the eradication of poverty, the promotion of gender equality, the empowerment of vulnerable groups and the development of rural communities, encourages Governments to adopt policies that support access to microcredit as well as the development of microfinance institutions and their capacities, and calls upon the international community to support those efforts;

Policies for the eradication of poverty

17. *Reaffirms* that the eradication of poverty should be addressed in an integrated way, as set out in the Plan of Implementation of the World Summit on Sustainable Development ("Johannesburg Plan of Implementation"), taking into account the importance of the need for the empowerment of women and sectoral strategies in such areas as education, development of human resources, health, human settlements, rural, local and community development, productive employment, population, environment and natural resources, water and sanitation, agriculture, food security, energy and migration, and the specific needs of disadvantaged and vulnerable groups, in such a way as to increase opportunities and choices for people living in poverty and to enable them to build and strengthen their assets so as to achieve development, security and stability, and in that regard encourages countries to develop their national poverty reduction policies in accordance with their national priorities, including, where appropriate, through poverty reduction strategy papers;

18. *Underlines*, in this context, the importance of further integration of the internationally agreed development goals, including those contained in the Millennium Declaration, in the national development strategies and plans, including the poverty reduction strategy papers where they exist, and calls upon the international community to continue to support developing countries in the implementation of those development strategies and plans;

19. *Recognizes* the importance of disseminating best practices for the reduction of poverty in its various dimensions, taking into account the need to adapt those best practices to suit the social, economic, cultural and historical conditions of each country;

20. *Reaffirms* that all Governments and the United Nations system should promote an active and visible policy of mainstreaming a gender perspective in all policies and programmes aimed at the eradication of poverty, at both the national and the international levels, and encourages the use of gender analysis as a tool for the integration of a gender dimension into planning the implementation of policies, strategies and programmes for the eradication of poverty;

21. *Also reaffirms* that poverty eradication, changing unsustainable patterns of production and consumption and protecting and managing the natural resource base of economic and social development are overarching objectives of, and essential requirements for, sustainable development;

22. *Emphasizes* the critical role of both formal and non-formal education, in particular basic education and training, especially for girls, in empowering those living in poverty, reaffirms in that context the Dakar Framework for Action adopted at the World Education Forum, and recognizes the importance of the United Nations Educational, Scientific and Cultural Organization strategy for the eradication of poverty, especially extreme poverty, in supporting the Education For All programmes as a tool to achieve the millennium development goal on universal primary education by 2015;

23. *Recognizes* the devastating effect of HIV/AIDS, malaria, tuberculosis and other infectious, contagious diseases on human development, economic growth and poverty reduction efforts in all regions, in particular in sub-Saharan Africa, urges Governments and the international community to give urgent priority to combating those diseases, takes note of the convening of the fifteenth International Conference on HIV/AIDS, to be held in Thailand from 11 to 16 July 2004, and in that regard welcomes the recent decision adopted by members of the World Trade Organization on the implementation of paragraph 6 of the Doha Declaration on the Agreement on Trade-Related Aspects of Intellectual Property Rights and Public Health;

24. *Emphasizes* the link between poverty eradication and improving access to safe drinking water, and stresses in this regard the objective to halve, by 2015, the proportion of people who are unable to reach or to afford safe drinking water and the proportion of people who do not have access to basic sanitation, as reaffirmed in the Johannesburg Plan of Implementation;

25. *Recognizes* that the lack of adequate housing remains a pressing challenge in the fight to eradicate extreme poverty, particularly in the urban areas in developing countries, expresses its concern at the rapid growth in the number of slum dwellers in the urban areas of developing countries, particularly in Africa, stresses that, unless urgent and effective measures and actions are taken at the national and international levels, the number of slum dwellers, who constitute one third of the world's urban population, will continue to increase, and emphasizes the need for increased efforts, with a view to significantly improving the lives of at least 100 million slum-dwellers by 2020;

Specific initiatives in the fight against poverty

26. *Also recognizes* the important potential contribution of the World Solidarity Fund to the achievement of the Millennium Development Goals, in particular the objective to halve, by 2015, the proportion of people living on less than one dollar a day and the proportion of the people who suffer from hunger;

27. *Reiterates its endorsement* of the decision of the World Summit on Sustainable Development to establish the World Solidarity Fund to eradicate poverty and to promote social and human development in the developing countries, while stressing the voluntary nature of the contributions and the need to avoid duplication of existing United Nations funds and encouraging the role of the private sector and individual citizens relative to Governments in funding the endeavours, as set out in the Johannesburg Plan of Implementation;

28. *Encourages* Member States, international organizations, the private sector, relevant institutions, foundations and individuals to contribute to the World Solidarity Fund;

29. *Requests* the Administrator of the United Nations Development Programme, in that regard, to take further measures to operationalize the World Solidarity Fund by establishing, on an urgent basis, the high-level committee whose task it is to define the strategy of the Fund and to mobilize resources to enable it to start its activities in the field of poverty alleviation;

30. *Acknowledges* the significance of greater involvement of developing countries in joint efforts, including those among developing countries, to overcome extreme poverty, and in this context takes note of the initiatives undertaken by the developing countries, including those announced at the fifty-eighth session of the General Assembly;

31. *Welcomes* the initiatives undertaken by regional and subregional organizations for overcoming extreme poverty;

Africa, least developed countries, landlocked developing countries and small island developing States

32. *Stresses* the importance, as recognized in the Millennium Declaration, of meeting the special needs of Africa, where poverty remains a major challenge and where most countries have not benefited fully from the opportunities of globalization, which has further exacerbated the continent's marginalization;

33. *Reaffirms its support* for the New Partnership for Africa's Development, encourages further efforts in the implementation of the commitments contained therein in the political, economic and social fields, and calls upon the developed countries and the United Nations system to continue to support the Partnership, the primary objective of which is to eradicate poverty and promote sustainable development on the basis of African ownership and leadership and enhanced partnerships with the international community, in accordance with the principles, objectives and priorities of the Partnership;

34. *Calls upon* the Governments of the least developed countries and their development partners to

implement fully the commitments contained in the Brussels Declaration and the Programme of Action for the Least Developed Countries for the Decade 2001-2010, adopted at the Third United Nations Conference on the Least Developed Countries;

35. *Stresses* the significant challenge to poverty reduction posed by the geographical disadvantages of landlocked developing countries and the vulnerabilities of small island developing States, and in this context welcomes the adoption of the Almaty Programme of Action, at the International Ministerial Conference of Landlocked and Transit Developing Countries and Donor Countries and International Financial and Development Institutions on Transit Transport Cooperation, held in Almaty, Kazakhstan, on 28 and 29 August 2003, and supports the comprehensive review of the implementation of the Programme of Action for the Sustainable Development of Small Island Developing States, to be held in Mauritius from 30 August to 3 September 2004;

The United Nations and the fight against poverty

36. *Calls* for the full implementation of its resolution 57/270 B of 23 June 2003 on the integrated and coordinated implementation of and follow-up to the outcomes of the major United Nations conferences and summits in the economic and social fields, which provides a comprehensive basis for the follow-up to the outcomes of those conferences and summits and contributes to the achievement of the internationally agreed development goals, including those contained in the Millennium Declaration, in particular the goal of the eradication of poverty and hunger, and notes in this context the decision to review in 2005 the progress achieved in implementing all commitments made in the Millennium Declaration and that there is scope for a major event;

37. *Reaffirms* the role of United Nations funds and programmes, in particular the United Nations Development Programme and its associated funds, in assisting the national efforts of developing countries, inter alia, in the eradication of poverty, and the need for their funding in accordance with the relevant resolutions of the United Nations;

38. *Requests* the Secretary-General to submit to the General Assembly at its fifty-ninth session a report on the implementation of the present resolution;

39. *Decides* to include in the provisional agenda of its fifty-ninth session the item entitled "Implementation of the first United Nations Decade for the Eradication of Poverty (1997-2006)".

World Solidarity Fund

In response to General Assembly resolution 57/265 [YUN 2002, p. 831], the Secretary-General transmitted to the Economic and Social Council and the Assembly, in April, the report of the UNDP Administrator on the establishment of the World Solidarity Fund [A/57/72-E/2003/53]. The Administrator described measures taken to operationalize the Fund, which was established by the 2002 World Summit on Sustainable Development [YUN 2002, p. 821] to eradicate poverty and promote social development in developing countries, and endorsed by the Assembly in resolution 57/265 [ibid., p. 831]. The Fund was set up in February as a UNDP trust fund and steps had been taken to operationalize and publicize it. A high-level committee was to be established to define the Fund's strategy.

The Economic and Social Council, in **resolution 2003/4** of 11 July (see p. 889), requested the UNDP Administrator, among other things, to mobilize the financial resources to enable the Fund to start its activities in poverty alleviation.

In **resolution 58/222** (see p. 849), the Assembly encouraged Member States, international organizations, the private sector and others to contribute to the Fund.

Rural poverty

Committee for Development Policy consideration. The Committee for Development Policy (New York, 7-11 April) [E/2003/33] considered the question of promoting an integrated approach to rural development in developing countries for poverty eradication and sustainable development. The Committee noted that rural development as a strategy to eradicate poverty should reflect the multidimensional nature of poverty, be multi-targeted, extend across disciplines and encompass demographic, economic, social, institutional and political factors. That integrated approach would differ from previous, more sector-specific experiences in rural development. Among the major causes of the persistence of rural poverty in most developing countries were low or stagnant economic growth in rural areas, often below the rate of population growth, inadequate investment in human capital, agricultural technology and infrastructure, and inadequacies in institutional mechanisms that addressed the needs of the rural poor. A fundamental reorientation of integrated rural development should focus on enhancing rural employment and income-generation, and more resources had to be directed towards those areas. The Committee reviewed the poor state of health and education in rural areas, excessive rural-urban migration and rural environmental degradation.

The Committee recommended that both developing countries and the international community should focus on four priority areas: expanding education and health services and providing incentives for rural people to take advantage of the services; increasing agricultural productivity and non-farm activities through the use of technology, diversification and access to inputs and credits; improving access to local, national and global markets; and examining all policies through "rural lenses" with a special focus on women.

Economic and Social Council consideration. In accordance with decision 2002/309 [YUN 2002, p. 814], the Economic and Social Council, at the high-level segment of its substantive session (30 June–2 July) [A/58/3/Rev.1], considered the theme "Promoting an integrated approach to rural development in developing countries for poverty eradication and sustainable development". The segment included four ministerial round-table discussions on: natural resources and rural development in developing countries; an integrated approach to the implementation of the MDGs in the area of rural development; global partnerships for rural development; and rural/urban interface and slums.

The Council had before it an April report by the Secretary-General on the theme of the high-level segment [E/2003/51]. He noted that three quarters of the world's poor lived in rural areas of developing countries and depended mainly on agriculture and related activities for their livelihood. In 2025, when the majority of the world population was expected to be urban, 60 per cent of poverty would still be rural. Accelerated rural development was essential to achieve the internationally agreed development goals, including the MDGs. The international community had an important role to play in supporting national efforts and contributing to an enabling environment for poverty eradication and sustainable development. The Secretary-General stated that an integrated approach to rural development had to encompass economic, social and environmental dimensions and consist of mutually reinforcing policies and programmes to address the range of rural development–related issues, while meeting the specific conditions and requirements of a given country. He outlined the common elements of the integrated approach, which included creating an enabling macroeconomic policy environment conducive to poverty eradication and sustainable development in rural areas; reversing the decline in the flow of domestic resources and ODA; strengthening agricultural and food policies, improving agricultural productivity and fostering non-farm rural economic activities and diversification in production; and enhancing the access of poor rural people, especially women and smallholder farmers, to productive assets, such as land and water, and to financial services.

In a ministerial declaration of 2 July, the Council stated, among other things, that rural development should be pursued through an integrated approach, encompassing economic, social and environmental dimensions, taking into account the gender perspective and consisting of mutually reinforcing policies and programmes. It should be balanced, targeted, situation-specific and locally owned, include local synergies and initiatives and be responsive to the needs of rural populations. The Council expressed its commitment to responding effectively to Africa's special needs for achieving sustainable development and reiterated its support for the priorities of the New Partnership for Africa's Development (NEPAD) (see p. 937). It also recognized the special needs of the least developed countries, the small island developing States and the landlocked developing countries. The Council committed itself to implementing its ministerial declaration and called on civil society, the UN system and other relevant actors and organizations to support the realization of the objectives of integrated rural development. It agreed to review the implementation of the declaration in 2005.

On 24 July, the Council decided that the coordination segment of its 2004 substantive session would consider the theme of a coordinated and integrated UN system approach to promote rural development in developing countries for poverty eradication and sustainable development (**decision 2003/287**).

By **decision 2003/290** of 24 July, adopted on the recommendation of the Commission on Science and Technology for Development [E/2003/31], the Council took note of that Commission's contribution to its consideration of the theme of the high-level segment, which was addressed by the Commission in its 2001 deliberations on national capacity-building in biotechnology [YUN 2001, p. 757], in which the Commission had underlined the need for national capacity-building in biotechnology to support efforts in rural development, including food security, agricultural productivity, health and environmental sustainability.

International Year of Microcredit, 2005

In response to General Assembly resolution 53/197 [YUN 1998, p. 785], by which the year 2005 was declared the International Year of Microcredit, the Secretary-General presented a draft programme of action for the observance of the Year [A/58/179].

The Secretary-General said that the International Year would give impetus to microcredit and microfinance programmes and activities around the world. The objectives of the Year might include building upon promoting the contribution of microcredit and microfinance towards achieving the MDGs and the goals of major conferences and summits; promoting awareness and understanding of microcredit and microfinance, and their roles in poverty eradication; identifying critical measures for Governments to stimulate sustainable, pro-poor financial sectors and build strategies to position microcredit and microfinance as integral parts of a country's financial system; increasing the capacity of microcredit and microfinance service providers to address the needs of poor people more efficiently; and promoting and creating strategic partnerships between Governments, UN system organizations and other microcredit and microfinance stakeholders. The report also outlined activities and initiatives that could be undertaken at the national, regional and international levels.

The Secretary-General concluded that observance of the International Year would provide a significant opportunity to raise awareness of the importance of microcredit and microfinance in the eradication of poverty, share good practices and further enhance programmes that supported sustainable pro-poor financial sectors around the world. Expanding outreach could contribute to achieving the MDGs, particularly the poverty reduction targets, and promoting gender equality and the empowerment of women.

GENERAL ASSEMBLY ACTION

On 23 December [meeting 78], the General Assembly, on the recommendation of the Second Committee [A/58/488], adopted **resolution 58/221** without vote [agenda item 98].

Programme of Action for the International Year of Microcredit, 2005

The General Assembly,

Recalling its resolution 53/197 of 15 December 1998, by which it proclaimed 2005 the International Year of Microcredit and requested that the observance of the Year be a special occasion for giving impetus to microcredit programmes in all countries, particularly the developing countries,

Recalling also its resolution 52/194 of 18 December 1997, in which it emphasized the role of microcredit and microfinance as an important anti-poverty tool that promotes asset creation, employment and economic security and empowers people living in poverty, especially women,

Stressing that people living in poverty in rural and urban areas need access to microcredit and microfinance that enhance their ability to increase income, build assets and mitigate vulnerability in times of hardship,

Bearing in mind the importance of microfinance instruments such as credit, savings and related business services in providing access to capital for people living in poverty,

Recognizing the need to facilitate the access of people living in poverty, especially women, to microcredit and microfinance to enable them to undertake microenterprises so as to generate self-employment and contribute to achieving empowerment,

1. *Takes note* of the report of the Secretary-General containing the draft programme of action for the International Year of Microcredit, 2005;

2. *Emphasizes* that the observance of 2005 as the International Year of Microcredit will provide a significant opportunity to raise awareness of the importance of microcredit and microfinance in the eradication of poverty, to share good practices and to further enhance financial sector developments that support sustainable pro-poor financial services in all countries;

3. *Invites* the Department of Economic and Social Affairs of the Secretariat and the United Nations Capital Development Fund to jointly coordinate the activities of the United Nations system regarding the preparations for and observance of the Year;

4. *Recognizes* the importance of scaling up microcredit and microfinance services and of using the Year as a platform to find ways of enhancing development impact and sustainability through the sharing of best practices and lessons learned;

5. *Invites* Member States to consider establishing national coordinating committees or focal points with responsibility for promoting the activities related to the preparations for and observance of the Year;

6. *Invites* Member States, relevant organizations of the United Nations system, non-governmental organizations, the private sector and civil society to collaborate in the preparations for and observance of the Year and to raise public awareness and knowledge about microcredit and microfinance;

7. *Recognizes* that access to microcredit and microfinance can contribute to achieving the goals and targets of major United Nations conferences and summits, including those contained in the United Nations Millennium Declaration, in particular the targets relating to poverty eradication, gender equality and the empowerment of women;

8. *Encourages* the holding of regional and subregional events on microcredit and microfinance, and, in this regard, welcomes the holding of the Asia-Pacific Region Microcredit Summit Meeting of Councils, in Dhaka, from 16 to 19 February 2004;

9. *Encourages* Member States, relevant organizations of the United Nations system, non-governmental organizations, the private sector and foundations to make voluntary contributions and/or to lend other forms of support to the Year, in accordance with the guidelines for international years;

10. *Requests* the Secretary-General to prepare a report on the preparations for the International Year of Microcredit, 2005, in consultation with Member States, relevant organizations of the United Nations system, non-governmental organizations, the private sector and civil society, and to submit it to the General Assembly at its fifty-ninth session under the item entitled "Implementation of the first United Nations Decade for the Eradication of Poverty (1997-2006)".

Science and technology for development

Commission on Science and Technology for Development

The Commission on Science and Technology for Development held its sixth session in Geneva from 5 to 9 May [E/2003/31]. The session had as its main substantive theme "Technology development and capacity-building for competitiveness in a digital society", with particular attention to information and communication technologies (ICT) as pervasive tools of global impact with wide application and growing potential, and considered a report by the Secretary-General on the subject (see below). The Commission also heard country reports on ICT policies. It had before it notes by the Secretariat on: implementation of and progress made on decisions taken at the Commission's fifth (2001) session [E/CN.16/2003/3]; the Commission's budget [E/CN.16/2003/4]; and the functioning of the Commission, including its role in coordinating science and technology for development [E/CN.16/2003/5]. The Commission recommended a draft resolution and three draft decisions for adoption by the Economic and Social Council. It brought to the Council's attention its decisions noting the Secretary-General's synthesis report on its panels on technology development and capacity-building in a digital society (see below) [E/2003/31 (dec. 6/101)] and the report of the Commission's Open-ended Working Group, the text of which it decided to include in its report [dec. 6/102].

Technology development and capacity-building

The Commission had before it a report by the Secretary-General [E/CN.16/2003/2] that provided an overview of the outcomes of three panels, convened during its 2001-2003 intersessional period, on its main substantive theme of technology development and capacity-building for competitiveness in a digital society. The panels discussed indicators of technology development (Geneva, 22-24 May 2002), foreign direct investment and technology capacity-building for strategic competitiveness (Colombo, Sri Lanka, 15-17 October 2002), and enhancing strategic competitiveness in ICT (Luanda, Angola, 15-17 January 2003). The report summarized the main findings and presented the policy recommendations that emerged from the three panels.

The Commission decided that the substantive theme and focus of its work during the 2003-2004 intersessional period would be "Promoting the application of science and technology to meet the MDGs".

On 9 May, the Commission took note of the report [dec. 6/101].

ECONOMIC AND SOCIAL COUNCIL ACTION

On 24 July [meeting 48], the Economic and Social Council, on the recommendation of the Commission on Science and Technology for Development [E/2003/31], adopted **resolution 2003/56** without vote [agenda item 13 (b)].

Science and technology for development

I. Technology development and capacity-building for competitiveness in a digital society

The Economic and Social Council,

Welcoming the work of the Commission on Science and Technology for Development on its theme "Technology development and capacity-building for competitiveness in a digital society", and noting the findings, which indicate, inter alia, the following:

(a) Information and communication technologies create new opportunities to tackle the problems of poverty, poor communications, economic stagnation and environmental degradation. At the same time, they generate new challenges, especially for those countries in which technological capability, skill capacity and supporting infrastructure are not sufficiently developed,

(b) The diffusion of information and communication technologies throughout the world is extremely uneven. Many of the developing countries face significant barriers in access to and effective applications of information and communication technologies owing to limited telecommunications infrastructure, low computer literacy levels and lack of a regulatory framework,

(c) Information and communication technologies will continue to play an increasingly important role in development. Most developing countries are not in a position to compete with industrialized countries at the frontier of innovation. The most effective way of raising the level of technology in developing countries is therefore through acquisition of technology from the industrialized countries. The experience of successful economies suggests that foreign direct investment has a crucial role to play in the acquisition of technology by developing countries,

(d) Mere transfer and imports of new technology through foreign direct investment and other channels do not ensure technology acquisition. In order to build capacity to acquire and master technology, it is essential that Governments build a sound human resources capital and put in place credible and more focused long-term policies and regulations that encourage the active international transfer, effective diffusion and development of technology,

(e) In order to facilitate and promote information and communication technology use in developing countries, there is a need for an enhanced partnership between Governments, the private sector, academic institutions and non-governmental organizations,

Heeding the call of the ministerial declaration adopted at the high-level segment of the substantive session of the Economic and Social Council in 2000 to work cooperatively to bridge the digital divide and to foster "digital opportunity",

Decides to recommend the following actions for consideration by national Governments, the Commission on Science and Technology for Development and the international community:

1. Governments are encouraged to undertake the following actions:

(a) Utilize the benchmarking tools developed by the Commission to assess their progress in information and communication technology development and to establish mechanisms involving all stakeholders for the ongoing review, evaluation and analysis of information and communication technology strategies, programmes and projects, including strategies to facilitate the attraction of foreign direct investment in information and communication technologies;

(b) Accelerate investment in information and communication technology human capacity-building and promote computer literacy and lifelong learning;

(c) Build up physical and institutional infrastructure to facilitate information and communication technology development and improve efficiency and transparency through e-government;

(d) Develop policy initiatives in order to facilitate the building of information and communication technology infrastructure at the regional level;

(e) Develop strategies to facilitate access to and lower costs of information and communication technology hardware and software by providing tax incentives and encouraging the use and further development of free and open source software;

(f) Apply innovative approaches with a focus on shared infrastructure, public access facilities and the use of intermediaries and other services to interact with individuals who may lack functional literacy;

(g) Establish a regulatory framework that supports infrastructure development and accelerate deployment of appropriate and cost-effective technologies;

(h) Promote sustained measures to ensure the mastery and adaptation of technology by creating and/or strengthening local research and development units, promoting foreign direct investment with high-technology content and fostering collaboration in research and development between foreign investors and domestic research institutions;

(i) Develop strategies for local content development, including the use of icon-based programmes and the integration of traditional mass media, print, television and radio, with electronic media;

2. The international community is invited:

(a) To promote the compilation of more appropriate data on technology indicators, taking into account that that there is a lack of data for many developing countries, which typically have a large informal sector so that more accurate information and communication technology and technology development indices could be developed;

(b) To reaffirm the right of developing countries to use to the full the flexibilities provided in international agreements such as the Agreement on Trade-Related Aspects of Intellectual Property Rights;

3. The Commission on Science and Technology for Development is invited:

(a) To interact closely with the Information and Communication Technologies Task Force to promote greater information exchange and coordination of activities in the field of information and communication technologies in order to contribute to the World Summit on the Information Society and, as feasible, update its publication *Knowledge Societies: Information Technologies for Sustainable Development* in order to raise awareness on recent developments in the field of information and communication technologies;

(b) To play an active role within the United Nations system in the analysis, promotion and recommendation of applications of science and technology to meet the development goals contained in the United Nations Millennium Declaration;

(c) To ensure that the Science and Technology for Development Network further develops and expands into an inter-agency gateway on information on science and technology activities, which also links information technology networks at the regional, subregional and interregional levels to the network;

(d) To liaise with the United Nations Conference on Trade and Development to develop further its benchmarking tool in information and communication technologies, promote its use by other relevant United Nations agencies and consider the possibility of carrying out information and communication technology needs assessment for interested developing countries, in particular least developed countries, to help formulate or update national strategies and action plans for information and communication technologies, coordinating efforts with the United Nations Development Programme and other entities carrying out similar work in order to promote complementarity and efficiency.

II. New substantive theme and other activities

The Economic and Social Council

Welcomes the choice of the theme "Promoting the application of science and technology to meet the development goals contained in the United Nations Millennium Declaration" for the work of the Commission on Science and Technology during the intersessional period 2003-2004. In undertaking work on this theme, the Commission is invited to analyse policies and measures that would lead to:

(a) Improving the policy environment for the application of science and technology to development by identifying potential risks and benefits of new and emerging technologies;

(b) Strengthening basic and applied research in developing countries and international scientific networking;

(c) Strengthening technology support institutions and science advisory mechanisms, building human capacity, identifying new technologies and applications, and encouraging international collaboration to support research in neglected fields;

(d) Promoting affordable universal Internet access and building strategic partnerships in the field of science and technology for development and capacity-building for competitiveness, taking care to ensure complementarity with efforts under way by other organizations, such as the United Nations Development Programme, the International Telecommunication Union and the Information and Communication Technologies Task Force, and to promote efficiency. All entities of the United Nations system working in these areas are invited to collaborate and provide input to the work of the Commission on its main theme;

III. Strengthening coordination of science and technology for development in the United Nations system

The Economic and Social Council,

Noting with appreciation the work carried out by the Gender Advisory Board of the Commission on Science and Technology for Development, including at the regional and national levels,

Requests the Commission to take into account the need to integrate meaningfully and systematically a gender component into all its programmes and to improve its collaboration with its Gender Advisory Board.

In other action, the Council, by **decision 2003/291** of 24 July, decided that the duration of the regular sessions of the Commission should be one week. By **decision 2003/293** of the same date, the Council took note of the report of the Commission on its sixth session and approved the provisional agenda and documentation for the Commission's seventh (2004) session.

Information and communication technologies

In 2003, the United Nations continued to ensure that the benefits of new technologies, especially ICTs, were available to all, in conformity with recommendations contained in the ministerial declaration adopted by the Economic and Social Council at its 2000 high-level segment [YUN 2000, p. 799] and the Millennium Declaration [ibid., p. 49]. In December, the first phase of the World Summit on the Information Society adopted a Declaration of Principles and Plan of Action that outlined specific goals for bridging the digital divide. The second phase of the Summit was scheduled to be held in 2005. During the year, the UN ICT Task Force continued its substantive work as a global forum on integrating information on ICT into development programmes.

World Summit on the Information Society (first phase)

The first phase of the World Summit on the Information Society (Geneva, 10-12 December) [WSIS-03/GENEVA/9(Rev.1)-E] was attended by political leaders from 175 countries, including 44 heads of State or Government, and representatives of intergovernmental and non-governmental organizations and the private sector. It adopted the Declaration of Principles and the Plan of Action for establishing the foundations for an information society for all, reflecting all the different interests at stake. In three round tables, the Summit discussed the themes of creating digital opportunities; diversity in cyberspace; and ICT as a tool for achieving the MDGs. It also considered reports on a number of multi-stakeholder events held in preparation for the Summit. Planned in two phases, the Summit was the first multi-stakeholder global effort to share and shape the use of ICTs for a better world. The second phase was to be held in Tunis, Tunisia, in November 2005.

Declaration of Principles and Plan of Action

The Declaration of Principles adopted on 12 December, "Building the information society: a global challenge in the new Millennium", stated the commitment to build a people-centred, inclusive and development-oriented information society to enable people to achieve their full potential in promoting their sustainable development and improving their quality of life. The challenge was to harness the potential of ICT to promote the MDGs [YUN 2000, p. 51]. The Summit committed itself to realizing that vision, focusing especially on young people and paying attention to the needs of women and of vulnerable groups, particularly the poor in remote rural and marginalized urban areas and the peoples of developing countries and economies in transition. Recognizing that building an inclusive information society required new forms of partnerships and cooperation among Governments and other stakeholders to realize the goal of bridging the digital divide and ensuring harmonious, fair and equitable development for all, the Summit called for national and international digital solidarity.

The Declaration enumerated key principles for an information society for all, covering the role of Governments and all stakeholders in the promotion of ICTs for development: information and communication infrastructure as an essential foundation for an inclusive information society; access to information and knowledge; capacity-building; building confidence and security in the use of ICTs; creating an enabling environment at the national and international levels based on the rule of law within a supportive policy and regulatory framework; and the benefits in all aspects of life of ICT applications. The key principles also covered respect for cultural and linguistic diversity, freedom of the press, the ethical dimensions of the information society and international and regional cooperation. All stakeholders were invited to commit to the "Digital Solidarity Agenda" set forth in the Plan of Action (see below). The Summit participants also committed themselves to evaluate and follow up progress in bridging the digital divide and to assess the effectiveness of investment and international cooperation efforts in building the information society.

The Plan of Action, based on the common vision and guiding principles of the Declaration, had as its objectives to build an inclusive information society; to put the potential of knowledge and ICTs at the service of development; to promote the use of information and knowledge to achieve internationally agreed development goals; and to address new challenges of the information society at all levels. Specific targets for improving connectivity and access in the use of ICTs, to be achieved by 2015, included: connecting villages with ICTs and establishing community access points; connecting universities, colleges, secondary schools and primary schools; connecting scientific and research centres; connecting public libraries, cultural centres, museums, post offices and archives; connecting health centres and hospitals; and connecting local and central government departments and establishing web sites and e-mail addresses. Other targets included adapting all primary and secondary school curricula to meet the challenges of the information society, taking into account national circumstances; ensuring that all of the world's population had access to television and radio services; encouraging the development of content and putting in place technical conditions to facilitate the presence and use of all world languages on the Internet; and ensuring that more than half the world's inhabitants had access to ICTs within their reach.

The Plan of Action set out action lines under each of the key principles in the Declaration. It also established the Digital Solidarity Agenda for putting in place the conditions for mobilizing the necessary human, financial and technological resources for including all men and women in the emerging information society. The priorities of the Agenda would be: making national e-strategies an integral part of national development plans, including poverty reduction strategies; and mainstreaming ICTs into ODA through more effective donor information-sharing and coordination and sharing best practices and lessons learned. A task force was established, under the auspices of the Secretary-General, to review the adequacy of all existing financial mechanisms in meeting the challenges of ICT for development by December 2004, for consideration at the second phase of the Summit, with a view to creating a voluntary Digital Solidarity Fund. Countries were asked to consider establishing national mechanisms to achieve universal access in underserved rural and urban areas to bridge the digital divide. International performance evaluation and benchmarking should be developed to follow up on implementation of the objectives, goals and targets in the Plan of Action.

The Summit also adopted a resolution regarding the arrangements for the second phase of the Summit, to be held in Tunis in 2005. It decided that a preparatory meeting would be held in the first half of 2004 to review those issues of the information society that should form the focus of the Tunis phase.

Summit preparations

In accordance with General Assembly resolutions 56/183 [YUN 2001, p. 764] and 57/238 [YUN 2002, p. 836], the Secretary-General transmitted to the Assembly and the Economic and Social Council, in April, the report of the ITU Secretary-General on preparations for the World Summit on the Information Society [A/58/74-E/2003/58]. The second meeting of the Preparatory Committee (Geneva, 17-28 February) agreed on working documents to serve as a basis for further discussions on the draft declaration and draft action plan and established an intersessional mechanism to advance negotiations on the draft texts, including a meeting to be held in Paris (15-18 July). The third meeting was scheduled to be held from 15 to 26 September.

Five regional preparatory meetings were held prior to the second preparatory meeting for Africa (Bamako, Mali, 25-30 May 2002); Europe (Bucharest, Romania, 7-9 November 2002); Asia and the Pacific (Tokyo, 13-15 January 2003); Latin America and the Caribbean (Baváro, Dominican Republic, 29-31 January); and Western Asia (Beirut, Lebanon, 4-6 February) (see p. 1027). Other initiatives included a meeting of the League of Arab States (Cairo, Egypt, 16-18 June); the Mauritius Ministerial Conference on Access to Information and Communication Technologies for All (Pointe aux Piments, 3-5 April); and a meeting of francophone ministers (Rabat, Morocco, 3-5 September).

The Economic and Social Council, by **decision 2003/309** of 25 July, and the Assembly, by **decision 58/546** of 23 December, took note of the ITU report.

ECONOMIC AND SOCIAL COUNCIL ACTION

On 22 July [meeting 44], the Economic and Social Council adopted **resolution 2003/19** [draft: E/2003/L.30/Rev.1] without vote [agenda item 13 (b)].

World Summit on the Information Society

The Economic and Social Council,

Recalling General Assembly resolutions 56/183 of 21 December 2001 and 57/238 of 20 December 2002, related in particular to the launching of the preparatory process of the World Summit on the Information Society, which will be held in two phases, in Geneva, from 10 to 12 December 2003, and in Tunis, from 16 to 18 November 2005,

Welcoming the progress achieved in the preparatory process of the Summit,

Taking note of the contribution of the Information and Communication Technologies Task Force to the preparatory process of the Summit,

Encouraging all countries to continue to support the preparatory process,

Encouraging civil society, non-governmental organizations and the private sector to contribute further to the preparations for the Summit,

Reaffirming the urgent need to harness the potential of knowledge and technology for promoting the goals of the United Nations Millennium Declaration and to find effective and innovative ways to put this potential at the service of development for all,

Reaffirming also the pivotal role of the United Nations system in promoting development, in particular with regard to access to and transfer of technology, especially information and communication technologies and services, inter alia, through partnerships with all relevant stakeholders,

Reaffirming further the need to harness synergies and to create cooperation among the various information and communication technologies initiatives, at both the regional and global levels, currently being undertaken or planned to promote and foster the potential of information and communication technologies for development by other international organizations and civil society,

1. *Takes note* of the report of the Secretary-General of the International Telecommunication Union on the ongoing preparatory process for the World Summit on the Information Society;

2. *Takes note also* of the results of the first two meetings of the intergovernmental Preparatory Committee, held in Geneva from 1 to 5 July 2002 and from 17 to 28 February 2003;

3. *Welcomes* the holding of the regional preparatory conferences in Bamako, from 25 to 30 May 2002, in Bucharest from 7 to 9 November 2002, in Tokyo from 13 to 15 January 2003, in Baváro, Dominican Republic, from 29 to 31 January 2003, in Beirut from 4 to 6 February 2003, and in Cairo from 16 to 18 June 2003;

4. *Encourages* all relevant United Nations bodies and other intergovernmental organizations, including international and regional institutions, as well as the Information and Communication Technologies Task Force, to intensify their work in the preparatory process of the Summit;

5. *Invites* countries to be represented at the highest political level at the two phases of the Summit;

6. *Encourages* civil society, non-governmental organizations and the private sector to contribute further to and participate actively in the intergovernmental preparatory process of the Summit, and in the Summit itself, according to the modalities of participation established by the Preparatory Committee;

7. *Requests* the International Telecommunication Union, in the context of its role in the preparatory process for the Summit, in close cooperation with the Department of Public Information of the Secretariat and other information offices of the United Nations system, to intensify its public information campaign to raise global awareness of the Summit, within existing resources and through voluntary contributions;

8. *Invites* the international community to continue providing extrabudgetary resources, in particular through voluntary contributions, to the special trust fund established by the International Telecommunication Union to support the preparations for and the holding of the two phases of the Summit and to facilitate the effective participation of representatives of developing countries, in particular the least developed countries, in the third meeting of the intergovernmental Preparatory Committee, to be held in Geneva from 15 to 26 September 2003, as well as in future meetings of the Preparatory Committee and in the two phases of the Summit.

UN role

ICT Task Force. In April, the Secretary-General submitted to the Economic and Social Council the first annual report [E/2003/56 & Corr.1] of the Information and Communication Technologies Task Force, which was established in 2001 [YUN 2001, p. 762] to provide a global forum on integrating ICT into development programmes and a platform for promoting public and private partnerships to help bridge the digital divide and foster digital opportunity.

During the first year of its mandate, the Task Force had become a universally recognized forum for the ICT and development communities to interact in support of the MDGs with the use of ICT and had helped to develop a holistic policy response to the challenge of putting ICT in the service of development, paying special attention to Africa. The Task Force had also begun to address policy issues related to the integration of national e-strategies into overall development and poverty eradication strategies and had strongly advocated mainstreaming ICT into ODA policies and programmes. In the coming years, the Task Force would implement a focused strategy to support the realization of the MDGs. A major challenge was awareness-raising and advocacy for policy and regulatory reform, of which a key part would be to help shape an agenda for the World Summit on the Information Society and build a common platform for action.

ECONOMIC AND SOCIAL COUNCIL ACTION

On 24 July [meeting 48], the Economic and Social Council adopted **resolution 2003/54** [draft: E/2003/L.46] without vote [agenda item 7 (i)].

Information and communication technologies for development

The Economic and Social Council,

Taking note of the first annual report of the Information and Communication Technologies Task Force,

Welcomes the achievements of the Task Force thus far, its orientation towards the use of information and communication technologies in the advancement of the development goals contained in the United Nations Millennium Declaration, its support of the preparations for the World Summit on the Information Society and its work, including through its regional networks and working groups and regional nodes on information and communication technology issues.

Development of a system-wide ICT strategy

CEB consideration. At its sixth session (New York, 20-21 October) [CEB/2003/5], the CEB High-level Committee on Management noted progress made by ICT managers on a number of projects, including the UN system Extranet and the search engine, and encouraged all organizations in the system that had not already done so to join the UN system Extranet so that it could truly become a system-wide tool for communication. The Committee also supported increased interaction between ICT managers and programme managers as part of the development of a system-wide ICT strategy and encouraged the exchange of policies on hardware replacement among organizations in the UN system.

Report of Secretary-General. In response to General Assembly resolution 57/295 [YUN 2002, p. 836], the Secretary-General, as Chairman of CEB, submitted a report [A/58/568] on progress in the development of a comprehensive ICT strategy for the UN system. He reviewed the status of collaboration on ICT in the UN system, including the work of the ICT Task Force and the launch of joint work of the UN system and the Task Force, which concluded that a single e-policy for the UN system was not feasible, but coordination and information-sharing should be enhanced towards the elaboration of a system-wide ICT strategy. Regarding future actions, the report stated that to move towards enhanced coordination in ICT, work was needed in parallel at several levels, including that of ICT managers, senior managers and Member States, to overcome a number of basic roadblocks and impediments. In particular, more coherence was required with regard to budget, procurement and financial procedures, which tended to breed isolationist approaches to funding ICT programmes.

The report called for the elaboration of an action plan outlining the building blocks for a system-wide framework of ICTs, including milestones, benchmarks, resources, responsibilities and accountabilities for results. On the basis of consultation among CEB members and with inputs from the ICT Task Force, a proposal for such a strategy and accompanying action plan would be submitted to the Secretary-General in 2004.

By **decision 58/565** of 23 December, the Assembly decided that the agenda item on ICT for development would remain for consideration at its resumed fifty-eighth (2004) session.

Biotechnology

In response to General Assembly resolution 56/182 [YUN 2001, p. 761], the Secretary-General submitted a May report on the impact of new biotechnologies, with particular attention to sustainable development, including food security, health and economic productivity [A/58/76]. The report presented an overview of sectors and countries where biotechnology was making a significant contribution to economic productivity and human welfare and identified measures that needed to be taken in order to build indigenous capabilities in biotechnology. It put forward proposals on the aspects of the transfer of such technologies, particularly to developing countries and countries with economies in transition, while taking into account the need to protect intellectual property rights and the special needs of developing countries.

The Assembly, by **decision 58/545** of 23 December, took note of the Secretary-General's report and asked that it be circulated at the Global Biotechnology Forum (see below).

UNIDO action. The UNIDO Industrial Development Board, at its twenty-seventh session (Vienna, 26-28 August) [GC.10/4], taking note of preparations for the Global Biotechnology Forum [IDB.27/15], scheduled to be held in Concepción, Chile, from 2 to 5 March 2004, requested the UNIDO Director-General to prepare a draft final statement of the Forum and urged member States to participate in the Forum at the highest appropriate level and encourage the participation of all other stakeholders [GC.10/4 (IDB.27/Dec.8)]. The UNIDO General Conference (Vienna, 1-5 December) [GC.10/INF.4] encouraged the Forum to discuss ways of addressing the issues of accelerating the quest for and acquisition, adaptation and dissemination of innovations, creating capacity for utilizing biotechnology and establishing strategic partnerships [GC.10/INF.4 (GC.10/Res. 7)].

The General Assembly, by **decision 58/545** of 23 December, reiterated its invitation to the UNIDO Director-General to report to the Assembly's fifty-ninth (2004) session on the outcome of the Forum.

GENERAL ASSEMBLY ACTION

On 23 December [meeting 78], the General Assembly, on the recommendation of the Second Committee [A/58/481/Add.2], adopted **resolution 58/200** without vote [agenda item 91 (b)].

Science and technology for development

The General Assembly,

Recognizing the role that international cooperation on science and technology can play in addressing the technological gap and the digital divide between the North and the South,

Recognizing also the importance of North-South as well as South-South cooperation in the field of science and technology,

Recognizing further the vital role of new and emerging technologies in raising the productivity and competitiveness of nations and the need, inter alia, for capacity-building, measures promoting the transfer and diffusion of technologies to developing countries, and the promotion of private sector activities and public awareness of science and technology,

Reaffirming the need to enhance the science and technology activities of the organizations of the

United Nations system and the role of the Commission on Science and Technology for Development in providing policy guidance, in particular on issues of relevance to developing countries,

Recognizing the role of information and communication technologies in promoting development as an important step towards addressing the challenges of bridging the digital divide, and in this regard welcoming the convening of the first phase of the World Summit on the Information Society, held in Geneva from 10 to 12 December 2003, and its second phase, to be held in Tunis from 16 to 18 November 2005,

Welcoming the Commission's selection of the substantive theme "Promoting the application of science and technology to meet the development goals contained in the United Nations Millennium Declaration", for its work during the intersessional period 2003-2004, as welcomed by the Economic and Social Council in its resolution 2003/56 of 24 July 2003,

Noting with appreciation the Commission's work during its intersessional period 2001-2003 on its theme "Technology development and capacity-building for competitiveness in a digital society", in particular the information and communication technologies development indices, which serve as an important contribution to the preparation of the World Summit on the Information Society,

Taking note of the report of the Secretary-General on the impact of new biotechnologies, with particular attention to sustainable development, including food security, health and economic productivity,

Taking note also of Economic and Social Council resolution 2003/56, in which the Council invited the Commission to interact closely with the Information and Communication Technologies Task Force to promote greater information exchange and coordination of activities in the field of information and communication technologies in order to contribute to the World Summit on the Information Society,

1. *Urges* the relevant bodies of the United Nations system engaged in biotechnology to work cooperatively so as to ensure that countries receive sound scientific information and practical advice to enable them to take advantage of these technologies, as appropriate, to promote economic growth and development;

2. *Takes note* of the proposal of the Secretary-General for an integrated framework for biotechnology development within the United Nations system, as contained in his report, and requests him to report further on the status of coordination between the relevant organizations and bodies of the United Nations system with a view to strengthening the coordination of activities in the area of biotechnology, in particular in the promotion of biotechnology within the United Nations system;

3. *Also takes note* of the publication entitled *Information and Communication Technology Development Indices*, and invites the United Nations Conference on Trade and Development in collaboration with the Information and Communication Technologies Task Force and the International Telecommunication Union, to update that publication as part of its contribution to the World Summit on the Information Society, recalling General Assembly resolution 56/183 of 21 December 2001, in which the Assembly encouraged effective contributions from and the active participation of all relevant United Nations bodies;

4. *Calls upon* the Secretary-General to continue to ensure that the Commission and its secretariat within the United Nations Conference on Trade and Development are provided with the necessary resources to enable the Commission to better carry out its mandate;

5. *Requests* the Secretary-General to submit to the General Assembly at its sixtieth session a report on the implementation of the present resolution.

Cybersecurity

GENERAL ASSEMBLY ACTION

On 23 December [meeting 78], the General Assembly, on the recommendation of the Second Committee [A/58/481/Add.2], adopted **resolution 58/199** without vote [agenda item 91 *(b)*].

Creation of a global culture of cybersecurity and the protection of critical information infrastructures

The General Assembly,

Recalling its resolutions 57/239 of 20 December 2002 on the creation of a global culture of cybersecurity, 55/63 of 4 December 2000 and 56/121 of 19 December 2001 on establishing the legal basis for combating the criminal misuse of information technologies, and 53/70 of 4 December 1998, 54/49 of 1 December 1999, 55/28 of 20 November 2000, 56/19 of 29 November 2001 and 57/53 of 22 November 2002 on developments in the field of information and telecommunications in the context of international security,

Recognizing the growing importance of information technologies for the promotion of socio-economic development and the provision of essential goods and services, the conduct of business and the exchange of information for Governments, businesses, other organizations and individual users,

Noting the increasing links among most countries' critical infrastructures—such as those used for, inter alia, the generation, transmission and distribution of energy, air and maritime transport, banking and financial services, e-commerce, water supply, food distribution and public health—and the critical information infrastructures that increasingly interconnect and affect their operations,

Recognizing that each country will determine its own critical information infrastructures,

Recognizing also that this growing technological interdependence relies on a complex network of critical information infrastructure components,

Noting that, as a result of increasing interconnectivity, critical information infrastructures are now exposed to a growing number and a wider variety of threats and vulnerabilities that raise new security concerns,

Noting also that effective critical infrastructure protection includes, inter alia, identifying threats to and reducing the vulnerability of critical information infrastructures, minimizing damage and recovery time in the event of damage or attack, and identifying the cause of damage or the source of attack,

Recognizing that effective protection requires communication and cooperation nationally and internationally among all stakeholders and that national efforts should be supported by effective, substantive international and regional cooperation among stakeholders,

Recognizing also that gaps in access to and the use of information technologies by States can diminish the effectiveness of cooperation in combating the criminal misuse of information technology and in creating a global culture of cybersecurity, and noting the need to facilitate the transfer of information technologies, in particular to developing countries,

Recognizing further the importance of international cooperation for achieving cybersecurity and the protection of critical information infrastructures through the support of national efforts aimed at the enhancement of human capacity, increased learning and employment opportunities, improved public services and better quality of life by taking advantage of advanced, reliable and secure information and communication technologies and networks and by promoting universal access,

Noting the work of relevant international and regional organizations on enhancing the security of critical information infrastructures,

Recognizing that efforts to protect critical information infrastructures should be undertaken with due regard for applicable national laws concerning privacy protection and other relevant legislation,

1. *Takes note* of the elements set out in the annex to the present resolution for protecting critical information infrastructures;

2. *Invites* all relevant international organizations, including relevant United Nations bodies, to consider, as appropriate, inter alia, these elements for protecting critical information infrastructures in any future work on cybersecurity or critical infrastructure protection;

3. *Invites* Member States to consider, inter alia, these elements in developing their strategies for reducing risks to critical information infrastructures, in accordance with national laws and regulations;

4. *Invites* Member States and all relevant international organizations to take, inter alia, these elements and the need for critical information infrastructure protection into account in their preparations for the second phase of the World Summit on the Information Society, to be held in Tunis from 16 to 18 November 2005;

5. *Encourages* Member States and relevant regional and international organizations that have developed strategies to deal with cybersecurity and the protection of critical information infrastructures to share their best practices and measures that could assist other Member States in their efforts to facilitate the achievement of cybersecurity;

6. *Stresses* the necessity for enhanced efforts to close the digital divide, to achieve universal access to information and communication technologies and to protect critical information infrastructures by facilitating the transfer of information technology and capacity-building, in particular to developing countries, especially the least developed countries, so that all States may benefit fully from information and communication technologies for their socio-economic development.

Annex

Elements for protecting critical information infrastructures

1. Have emergency warning networks regarding cyber-vulnerabilities, threats and incidents.

2. Raise awareness to facilitate stakeholders' understanding of the nature and extent of their critical information infrastructures and the role each must play in protecting them.

3. Examine infrastructures and identify interdependencies among them, thereby enhancing the protection of such infrastructures.

4. Promote partnerships among stakeholders, both public and private, to share and analyse critical infrastructure information in order to prevent, investigate and respond to damage to or attacks on such infrastructures.

5. Create and maintain crisis communication networks and test them to ensure that they will remain secure and stable in emergency situations.

6. Ensure that data availability policies take into account the need to protect critical information infrastructures.

7. Facilitate the tracing of attacks on critical information infrastructures and, where appropriate, the disclosure of tracing information to other States.

8. Conduct training and exercises to enhance response capabilities and to test continuity and contingency plans in the event of an information infrastructure attack, and encourage stakeholders to engage in similar activities.

9. Have adequate substantive and procedural laws and trained personnel to enable States to investigate and prosecute attacks on critical information infrastructures and to coordinate such investigations with other States, as appropriate.

10. Engage in international cooperation, when appropriate, to secure critical information infrastructures, including by developing and coordinating emergency warning systems, sharing and analysing information regarding vulnerabilities, threats and incidents and coordinating investigations of attacks on such infrastructures in accordance with domestic laws.

11. Promote national and international research and development and encourage the application of security technologies that meet international standards.

Economic and social trends

The *World Economic and Social Survey 2003* [Sales No. E.03.II.C.1], prepared in mid-2003 by the UN Department of Economic and Social Affairs (DESA), observed that the tentative recovery of the world economy from the global slowdown of 2001, which began in the second half of 2002, quickly faded, largely due to the geopolitical uncertainties associated with the looming confrontation in Iraq (see p. 333). Those uncertainties caused oil prices to rise, equity markets to plummet, and consumer and business confidence to fall to their lowest levels in a decade. Gross world product (GWP) increased by less than 2 per cent in 2002, marking a second consecutive year of below-potential growth. China, India and a number of transition economies were notable exceptions to the sub-par performance that characterized the majority of the world's economies. A global recovery was forecast for the second half of 2003, led by the developed countries, notably the United States, which was expected to provide a stimulus to the rest of the world. However, geopolitical uncertainties continued to pose a downside risk to the global economy in early 2003, as did a new economic shock—severe acute respiratory syndrome (SARS). The most important factors that could pose a threat to short-term global growth were the nature and adjustment of the United States external deficit and the possibility of deflation in a growing number of countries.

Growth in the developed economies as a group, which had been below 1.5 per cent for two years, was expected to be only marginally stronger in 2003. Although the prospects for economic growth in North America were improving, the war in Iraq derailed an already anaemic recovery in the United States and moderated substantially the robust domestic demand that had offset external weaknesses in Canada. While some weaknesses could linger, a gradual rebound was expected in the second half of 2003, to be strengthened further in 2004. Business spending, rather than household consumption, was considered crucial for the strength of the recovery. Following growth of only 1 per cent in 2002, Western Europe was expected to recover somewhat in 2003. The region's extended period of below-trend growth had led to higher region-wide unemployment and increased fiscal deficits, which, together with the appreciation of the euro, would dampen the region's recovery. Japan's economy remained fragile, with gross domestic product (GDP) growth forecast at less than 1 per cent in both 2003 and 2004. Despite an improvement in some economic indicators early in 2003, economic fundamentals continued to be weak, with the ongoing decline in asset prices aggravating severe problems in the banking sector and in the real economy. In Australia and New Zealand, GDP growth was expected to moderate in 2003 and 2004, although it would still exceed 3 per cent.

Growth in the economies in transition had decelerated in 2002 but was expected to strengthen again in 2003 and 2004. Economic growth in the Central and Eastern European countries, which decreased from 2.7 per cent in 2001 to 2.5 per cent in 2002, was expected to strengthen to about 3 per cent in 2003. The Commonwealth of Independent States (CIS) economies continued to be largely sheltered from global economic uncertainties, having recorded strong growth each year since 2000. GDP growth for the region was projected at 4.5 per cent in 2003 (compared with 4.7 per cent in 2002).

In the developing countries overall, economic growth was expected to accelerate slightly to 3.5 per cent in 2003, compared with 3.2 per cent in 2002. However, not all regions were participating in that mild recovery: Latin America would record only modest growth; both East Asia and Western Asia would decelerate; and Africa would grow at only 3 per cent. The only bright spots in the outlook were South Asia, where growth was expected to reach 5.75 per cent in 2003, and China, which would continue its strong performance of recent years.

The *Trade and Development Report, 2003* [Sales No. E.03.II.D.7], published by the United Nations Conference on Trade and Development (UNCTAD), stated that the global economy was experiencing an anxious time. The long-anticipated rebound in the United States continued to be delayed and there were concerns that the imbalances and excesses created during the high-tech boom of the 1990s could result in a long period of erratic and sluggish growth. Adverse consequences for the developing countries, even the most resilient, were unavoidable. Brighter political conditions could help avoid a repetition of the previous year's recession in Latin America, but any recovery there would be fragile. Africa appeared to be relatively insulated from global trends, but the continued weakness of many commodity prices meant that it might not be able to repeat its performance of the preceding two years. Given the current level of development cooperation and the structural weaknesses across the region, there was growing consensus that it would be impossible to meet the MDGs even under the most optimistic growth scenario for the world economy.

A report on the world economic situation and prospects [Sales No. E.04.II.C.2], prepared jointly by DESA and UNCTAD, stated that at the end of 2003 the world economy was gaining momentum; GNP for the year as a whole had risen to 2.5 per cent. Despite some lingering uncertainties and downside risks, the recovery was expected to strengthen and broaden further, raising global economic growth to 3.5 per cent in 2004. The recovery was being driven mainly by the United States but with increasing contributions from a number of other economies, notably China. The acceleration in growth was greater in the developed countries than in the developing countries. While growth was highest in North America, Asia and Oceania achieved the greatest improvement because of Japan's return to productive growth. Overall, the Western European economies performed less well than in 2002, but improved as the year progressed. The CIS countries rebounded solidly from the deceleration in 2002 and growth in other economies in transition also improved. The international economic environment for most developing countries improved during 2003, but the long-term downward trend in the real prices of commodities and the pro-cyclical nature of international capital flows would continue to challenge many of them over the longer term. In Africa, progress in political and economic governance and in achieving macroeconomic stability, along with other positive factors, characterized the economy in 2003. Growth in Latin America and the Caribbean was expected to recover, boosted by the improvement in both external conditions and the domestic economic policy environment. In East Asia, the external sector, private consumption, public spending and business investment were all contributing to a strong recovery. In South Asia, the economic spillover from the war in Iraq was relatively modest and favourable agricultural production, rising rural incomes, increased exports, low interest rates, growing remittances and the improved security situation would continue to support a broad recovery in most countries. The prospects for Western Asia depended on developments in Iraq and on the Israeli-Palestinian conflict. Growth in the oil-exporting countries of the region was expected to accelerate. A key feature of the global recovery was the rising economic weight of the two most populous countries, China and India, which were growing at a rate more than twice the world average. Continued strong growth in those two large low-income countries would benefit the world economy as a whole. However, their size meant that their fast growth would have far-reaching implications for international patterns of trade, production and financing, and for the global supply and demand of energy and commodities.

Human Development Report 2003

The *Human Development Report 2003* [Sales No. 03.III.B.1], prepared by UNDP, assessed progress made towards achieving the MDGs of halving extreme poverty by 2015 and advancing other areas of human development. It also reviewed how the MDGs were transforming development, as Governments, aid agencies and civil society reoriented their work around them. The *Report* found that, although much of the world was on track for some of the Goals, when progress was broken down by region and country and within countries, it was clear that a huge amount of work remained. Many had seen life expectancy plummet due to HIV/AIDS, and some of the worst performers—often torn by conflict—were seeing school enrolments shrink and access to basic health care fall. Nearly everywhere the environment was deteriorating. The *Report* also assessed where the problems in achieving the MDGs were, analysed what needed to be done to reverse the setbacks and made proposals for accelerating progress everywhere towards achieving all the Goals. Building on the commitments made at the 2002 Monterrey Conference on Financing for Development [YUN 2002, p. 953], the *Report* also set out a Millennium Development Compact that provided a broad framework for how national development strategies and international support from donors and others could be better aligned, commensurate with the scale of the challenge of the MDGs.

In addition to providing a critical analysis of a different theme each year, the *Report* assessed the state of human development across the globe, involving country data that focused on human well-being, not just economic trends. In 2003, it ranked 175 countries in its human development index by combining indicators of life expectancy, educational attainment and adjusted per capita income, among other factors. Of the 175 countries listed, 55 were in the high human development category, 87 were in the medium category and 33 were in the low category. The *Report* also included a special set of tables containing indicators relating to the MDGs.

UNDP consideration. In June [E/2003/35 (dec. 2003/21)], the UNDP/United Nations Population Fund Executive Board took note of a report of the UNDP Administrator [DP/2003/17] on strengthening consultations with Member States on the *Human Development Report*, in accordance with General Assembly resolution 57/264 [YUN 2002, p. 841]. The Administrator made proposals for improving the consultation process by increasing the number and enhancing the quality of consultations, and by holding special consultations on specific issues.

By **decision 2003/225** of 11 July, the Economic and Social Council took note of the report.

Development policy and public administration

Committee for Development Policy

The Committee for Development Policy (CDP), at its fifth session (New York, 7-11 April) [E/2003/33], considered the issues of promoting an integrated approach to rural development in developing countries for poverty eradication and sustainable development (see p. 852) and global public goods and financial mechanisms in the pursuit of sustainable development. It also reviewed the list of least developed countries (LDCs), including criteria for their identification (see p. 867).

Concerning global public goods (GPGs) and innovative financial mechanisms in the pursuit of sustainable development, CDP focused on the contribution of the perspective on GPGs to thinking regarding development in developing countries and to accelerated progress towards meeting the MDGs. The Committee considered GPGs as those goods whose benefits had strong qualities of publicness and were global in terms of countries, people and generations. It agreed that GPGs had the potential for generating a better formulation of effective, efficient and equitable paths towards development. However, the concept needed further clarification. Limited until recently to the provision of national or local public goods, the concept had been extended to the international context. CDP suggested: raising public awareness about the nature and role of GPGs; developing new institutional and finance arrangements; identifying the financing gap and developing realistic estimates of financing requirements for the provision of GPGs by category; and considering new potential sources to supplement existing resources to help ensure the provision of GPGs and increasing the role of the private sector.

On 24 July, the Economic and Social Council (**decision 2003/281**) took note of chapters I, II, III and V of the CDP report on its fifth session.

Public administration

As decided by the Economic and Social Council on 28 January (**decision 2003/207**), the Committee of Experts on Public Administration held its second session (New York, 7-11 April) [E/2003/44]. The Committee had before it Secretariat reports on: status of and trends in the development of e-Government [E/C.16/2003/2]; basic data on the public sector [E/C.16/2003/3]; strategies for high-quality staffing in the public sector [E/C.16/2003/4]; and the role of public administration in mainstreaming poverty reduction strategies within the MDGs [E/C.16/2003/5].

The Committee concluded that it was an overarching priority for all countries to revitalize and revalidate public administration. Given the importance of efficient public administration systems for the attainment of social development goals, the Committee recommended that the Economic and Social Council establish linkages between the Committee's work and that of the Commission for Social Development. The Council should bring the issue of governance and public administration to the forefront of the development agenda and consider devoting its next high-level segment to that topic. The Committee further recommended that public administration issues should become an integral part of the process of follow-up to UN conferences and summits, and that the Committee could serve as a valuable source of advice to the intergovernmental machinery in that respect.

The Committee also reviewed and commented and made recommendations on the United Nations Programme in Public Administration and Finance. In particular, it recommended that the Secretariat continue to provide, at the request of Member States, technical advisory support for enhancing the quality of personnel in the public sector; reinforcing governance and public administration systems and institutions; and fostering transparency and accountability, as well as reconstructing public administration in post-conflict countries and in situations of decentralized governance. The Secretariat should further analyse and delineate the role of the State as enabler and user of knowledge and technology to support and encourage innovation throughout public administration and society as a whole. It should also continue its work on basic data on the public sector and expand the number of indicators, in partnership with agencies and institutes currently working on the topic, focusing in particular on government efficiency, transparency and participation.

The Committee commended the *World Public Sector Report* as being an extremely valuable tool for policy makers and practitioners in Member States; recommended that the Secretariat should focus, in its next issue, on human resources development; and advised the Secretariat of the usefulness of having the publication translated into other languages. The Committee stressed the importance of capitalizing on the successes of the United Nations Online Network in Public Administration and Finance (UNPAN) by expanding its reach to the subregional level in order to strengthen the capacity of subregional institutions in public administration.

ECONOMIC AND SOCIAL COUNCIL ACTION

On 25 July [meeting 49], the Economic and Social Council [draft: E/2003/L.45, orally revised] adopted **resolution 2003/60** without vote [agenda item 13 *(g)*].

Public administration and development

The Economic and Social Council,
Recalling its resolution 2002/40 of 19 December 2002,

1. *Takes note* of the report of the Committee of Experts on Public Administration on its second session;

2. *Reiterates* that efficient, accountable, effective and transparent public administration, at both the national and the international levels, has a key role to play in the implementation of the internationally agreed development goals, including those contained in the United Nations Millennium Declaration, and in that context stresses the need to strengthen national public sector administrative and managerial capacity-building, in particular in developing countries and countries with economies in transition;

3. *Reiterates also* that strengthening public administration and the State are at the forefront of the development agenda to achieve the internationally agreed development goals, including those contained in the Millennium Declaration, and that revitalizing public administration is considered to be one of the essential components of economic and social development, and in this context decides to explore the possibility of considering this theme at a future high-level segment;

4. *Decides* that the Committee shall meet annually, instead of biennially, for one week, given the need to adapt to the ever-changing environment and owing to the fact that rapidly emerging issues need to be addressed in a timely manner, with a focus on the need to modernize in all countries public sector human resource systems, strengthen systems of accountability and transparency and explore the potential of e-government to develop innovative public administrative tools;

5. *Decides also* that the Committee, within the framework decided upon in General Assembly resolution 57/270 B of 23 June 2003, should contribute to the integrated and coordinated follow-up to major United Nations conferences and summits in the economic and social fields;

6. *Approves* the following agenda for the next meeting of the Committee, to be held at United Nations Headquarters from 29 March to 2 April 2004:
   1. Revitalizing public administration.
   2. Public sector institutional capacity for African renewal.
   3. Analysis of existing basic data on the public sector.
   4. Review of the United Nations Programme in Public Administration and Finance.

7. *Urges* the Committee to continue to work in accordance with its mandate.

Report of Secretary-General. In response to General Assembly resolution 57/277 [YUN 2002, p. 843], the Secretary-General submitted an 11 July report on the role of public administration in the implementation of the United Nations Millennium Declaration [YUN 2000, p. 49]. International organizations and bodies had been invited to provide information on: initiatives undertaken to improve the capacity of the public sector of Member States to meet the MDGs; and innovative and successful practices that contributed directly to those Goals. The information collected revealed five areas of interventions that were conducive to the attainment of the MDGs: decentralization; transparency and accountability; "engaged governance" or mainstreaming citizens' voices in public policy; the application of ICT; and capacity-building in statistics. The report found that the first four reforms reinforced each other to transform traditional public administration into a public sector that emphasized participation, partnership and openness. Describing capacity-building in statistics as a cross-cutting need, the Secretary-General stated that, to help replicate best practices, the United Nations would regularly document those practices for knowledge transfer, while offering technical and advisory services to Member States for capacity-building.

Global Forum. On 12 September [A/58/383], Morocco transmitted to the Assembly the text of the Marrakech Declaration, adopted by the Fourth Global Forum on Reinventing Government (Marrakech, 11-12 December 2002), devoted to the theme "Citizens, Businesses and Governments: dialogue and partnerships for democracy and development".

Santa Cruz Consensus. On 28 July [A/58/193], Bolivia transmitted to the Secretary-General the texts of the Santa Cruz Consensus and the Ibero-American Charter for the Public Service, adopted at the fifth Ibero-American Conference of Ministers for Public Administration and State Reform (Santa Cruz de la Sierra, Bolivia, 26-27 June 2003).

GENERAL ASSEMBLY ACTION

On 23 December [meeting 78], the General Assembly, on the recommendation of the Second Committee [A/58/495 & Corr.1], adopted **resolution 58/231** without vote [agenda item 12].

Public administration and development

The General Assembly,

Recalling its resolutions 50/225 of 19 April 1996, 53/201 of 15 December 1998, 56/213 of 21 December 2001 and 57/277 of 20 December 2002 on public administration and development, as well as Economic and Social Council resolution 2001/45 of 20 December 2001,

Stressing the need for capacity-building initiatives aimed at institution-building, human resources development, strengthening financial management and harnessing the power of information and technology,

Recalling that 2006 will mark the tenth anniversary of the resumed fiftieth session of the General Assembly, on public administration and development,

Welcoming the adoption of the Ibero-American Charter for the Public Service at the fifth Ibero-American Conference of Ministers for Public Administration and State Reform, held in Santa Cruz de la Sierra, Bolivia, on 26 and 27 June 2003,

Expressing its deep appreciation for the generosity of the Government of Mexico in hosting the fifth Global Forum on Reinventing Government, held in Mexico City from 3 to 7 November 2003,

Welcoming e-Government initiatives as a tool to promote development,

Welcoming also the adoption of the United Nations Convention against Corruption,

1. *Takes note* of the report of the Secretary-General on the role of public administration in the implementation of the United Nations Millennium Declaration;

2. *Reiterates* that efficient, accountable, effective and transparent public administration, at both the national and international levels, has a key role to play in the implementation of the internationally agreed development goals, including those contained in the United Nations Millennium Declaration, and in that context stresses the need to strengthen national public sector administrative and managerial capacity-building, in particular in developing countries and countries with economies in transition;

3. *Takes note with appreciation* of the commemoration of 23 June as United Nations Public Service Day and the granting of the United Nations Public Service Awards, which provide motivation for public servants all over the world to enhance public administration as a tool for development, and in this regard encourages Member States to participate in the award process by nominating candidates;

4. *Also takes note with appreciation* of the Marrakech Declaration, adopted by the Fourth Global Forum on Reinventing Government, held in Marrakech, Morocco, from 11 to 13 December 2002;

5. *Welcomes with appreciation* the offer of the Government of the Republic of Korea to host the Sixth Global Forum on Reinventing Government in Seoul in 2005;

6. *Requests* the Secretary-General to make proposals for commemorating the tenth anniversary of the resumed fiftieth session of the General Assembly, on public administration and development, during the sixty-first session of the General Assembly, in 2006;

7. *Also requests* the Secretary-General to support information exchange and research and to disseminate successful practices and advisory services in public administration that contribute to achieving the internationally agreed development goals, including those contained in the Millennium Declaration;

8. *Encourages* the Secretary-General to continue supporting the e-Government initiatives in the African, Asian, Central American and Caribbean regions as a tool for development;

9. *Requests* the Secretary-General to submit a report to the General Assembly at its fifty-ninth session on the implementation of the present resolution.

Developing countries and transition economies

Least developed countries

The special problems of the officially designated LDCs were considered in several UN forums in 2003, especially through the implementation of the Brussels Declaration and the Programme Action for the LDCs for the Decade 2001-2010, adopted at the Third UN Conference on the LDCs in 2001 [YUN 2001, p. 770] and endorsed by the General Assembly in resolution 55/279 in July of that year [ibid., p. 771]. In April, CDP undertook the triennial review of the official LDC list, recommending one country for addition to and two countries for future graduation from the list (see below).

LDC list

The number of countries officially designated as LDCs increased to 50, when the Economic and Social Council endorsed the CDP recommendation to add Timor-Leste to the list.

The full list of LDCs comprised: Afghanistan, Angola, Bangladesh, Benin, Bhutan, Burkina Faso, Burundi, Cambodia, Cape Verde, Central African Republic, Chad, Comoros, Democratic Republic of the Congo, Djibouti, Equatorial Guinea, Eritrea, Ethiopia, Gambia, Guinea, Guinea-Bissau, Haiti, Kiribati, Lao People's Democratic Republic, Lesotho, Liberia, Madagascar, Malawi, Maldives, Mali, Mauritania, Mozambique, Myanmar, Nepal, Niger, Rwanda, Samoa, Sao Tome and Principe, Senegal, Sierra Leone, Solomon Islands, Somalia, Sudan, Timor-Leste, Togo, Tuvalu, Uganda, United Republic of Tanzania, Vanuatu, Yemen, Zambia.

Triennial review

CDP, which was responsible for adding countries to or graduating them from the LDC list, conducted, in accordance with Economic and Social Council resolution 1998/46 [YUN 1998, p. 1262], a triennial review of the list of LDCs at its fifth session in April [E/2003/33]. As requested by the Council in resolution 2002/36 [YUN 2002, p. 847], the Expert Group Meeting on the Review of the List of Least Developed Countries (New York, 23-24 January) continued to revise the criteria for identification of LDCs, reviewed eligibility for inclusion and graduation, examined the situation of certain economies in transition and discussed the issue of smooth graduation from LDC status.

Based on the Expert Group proposals and its own review, CDP adopted a three-year average of $750 per capita as the threshold for inclusion in the category under the gross national income per capita criterion and increased the margin for graduation from 15 to 20 per cent above the threshold for inclusion, making the graduation threshold a three-year average of $900 per capita. The Committee agreed that the threshold for inclusion with regard to both the human assets index and the economic vulnerability index criteria should be chosen so that three quarters of the most disadvantaged countries would be eligible under each of those criteria. The margin between the thresholds for inclusion and graduation should be decreased from 15 to 10 per cent for those indicators.

Applying those thresholds, the Committee concluded that Timor-Leste qualified for inclusion in the list of LDCs; Cape Verde and Maldives qualified for graduation from the list in 2006; and Samoa was eligible to be considered for graduation in 2006. The Committee emphasized the need for a smooth transition for countries that graduated from the list and called on the international community to give urgent attention to the matter. Since all of the countries that qualified or were eligible for graduation were small island developing States, CDP considered it imperative that the international meeting on small island developing States in 2004 should make progress in formulating policies and actions to address the development challenges faced by that group of countries, particularly those that qualified for graduation from LDC status.

Economic and Social Council action. By **decision 2003/280** of 24 July, the Economic and Social Council included Timor-Leste in the list of LDCs. By **decision 2003/281** of the same date, the Council deferred consideration of the review of the list of LDCs, including the question of graduating Cape Verde and Maldives, to a resumed session. The Secretary-General was asked to provide the Council with technical support in that regard.

GENERAL ASSEMBLY ACTION

On 17 December [meeting 75], the General Assembly adopted **resolution 58/112** [draft: A/58/L.36 & Add.1] without vote [agenda item 12].

Report of the Committee for Development Policy

The General Assembly,

Noting that Timor-Leste became a member of the United Nations on 27 September 2002,

Recalling Economic and Social Council decisions 2003/280 and 2003/281 of 24 July 2003 on the report of the Committee for Development Policy,

Noting that Timor-Leste has given its consent to be included in the list of least developed countries,

Endorses the recommendation of the Economic and Social Council that Timor-Leste be added to the list of the least developed countries.

Programme of Action (2001-2010)

In response to General Assembly resolution 57/276 [YUN 2002, p. 846] and Economic and Social Council resolution 2002/33 [ibid., p. 845], the Secretary-General issued a May report [A/58/86-E/2003/81] on implementation of the Brussels Programme of Action for the LDCs, adopted at the Third United Nations Conference on the LDCs (LDC-III) in 2001 [YUN 2001, p. 770]. The report chronicled the policies adopted by LDCs and progress made and challenges remaining in implementing the Brussels Programme of Action. It also examined the decisions and programmes undertaken by the international development partners, including the UN system, the Bretton Woods institutions, other multilateral organizations, the donor community, civil society and the private sector, in mainstreaming the Brussels Programme of Action.

The report concluded that LDC actions to fulfil the Brussels Programme of Action commitments were yet to materialize, given the limited time since its adoption, the lack of data, the complexity of the issues involved and capacity constraints. While LDC Governments had shown a willingness to reverse the fortunes of their peoples, the right economic and social policies had to be pursued and suitable international conditions should prevail in order for them to make meaningful progress towards achieving the Programme of Action's commitments and targets. In addition, only a few LDCs had established national forums or designated national focal points, both of which were crucial for facilitating follow-up and monitoring the implementation of the Programme of Action.

The report recommended a number of actions to address the challenges that were impeding implementation of the Programme of Action. They covered: the need for international support; a clearly defined operational plan designating the roles of stakeholders, sequenced priorities and coordinated actions at the national, regional/subregional and global levels; and the effective functioning of arrangements for follow-up, coordination, monitoring and review.

ECONOMIC AND SOCIAL COUNCIL ACTION

On 22 July [meeting 44], the Economic and Social Council adopted **resolution 2003/17** [draft: E/2003/L.15/Rev.1] without vote [agenda item 6 (b)].

Programme of Action for the Least Developed Countries for the Decade 2001-2010

The Economic and Social Council,

Recalling the Brussels Declaration and the Programme of Action for the Least Developed Countries for the Decade 2001-2010,

Recalling also its decision 2001/320 of 24 October 2001 on the establishment of a regular sub-item entitled "Review and coordination of the implementation of the Programme of Action for the Least Developed Countries for the Decade 2001-2010",

Recalling further its resolution 2002/33 of 26 July 2002, in which it took note of the oral report of the High Representative for the Least Developed Countries, Landlocked Developing Countries and Small

Island Developing States on the implementation of the Programme of Action for the Least Developed Countries for the Decade 2001-2010,

1. *Takes note* of the progress report of the Secretary-General on the implementation of the Programme of Action for the Least Developed Countries for the Decade 2001-2010;

2. *Expresses its deep concern* over the weak implementation of the Programme of Action, and expresses its expectation of more vigorous implementation by all partners;

3. *Calls upon* the Secretary-General, while stressing the central role of the Economic and Social Council in the coordination of actions in the United Nations system for the implementation of the Programme of Action, to take appropriate measures to strengthen the efficiency and effectiveness of the Office of the High Representative for the Least Developed Countries, Landlocked Developing Countries and Small Island Developing States so that it can fulfil its functions in accordance with General Assembly resolution 56/227 of 24 December 2001;

4. *Urges* all Member States and the organizations and bodies of the United Nations system and invites the international financial institutions and other multilateral organizations to extend to the Office of the High Representative their full support for the fulfilment of its mandate, including through staffing support;

5. *Stresses* the need for the effective implementation of the Programme of Action and its annual assessment at the substantive session of the Council, recognizes in this regard the critical importance of the participation of the least developed countries in the assessment process of the Programme of Action, and requests the Secretary-General to make, in consultation with Member States, recommendations to facilitate the participation of the delegations of the least developed countries at the annual substantive sessions of the Council and to report thereon to the General Assembly at its fifty-eighth session;

6. *Reiterates* that the Programme of Action offers a framework for partnership, based on mutual commitments by least developed countries and their development partners to undertake concrete actions in a number of interlinked areas set out in the Programme of Action;

7. *Calls upon* least developed countries, with the support of their development partners, to continue to fulfil their commitments and to promote the implementation of the actions contained in the Programme of Action by translating them into specific measures within their national development frameworks and poverty eradication strategies, in particular poverty reduction strategy papers, where they exist, with the involvement of civil society, including the private sector, on the basis of a broad-based inclusive dialogue, as well as to continue to promote an enabling environment for the effective mobilization and utilization of resources consistent with paragraph 82 of the Programme of Action;

8. *Calls upon* all development partners of the least developed countries, including multilateral financial institutions, to continue to fulfil their commitments regarding the effective and expeditious implementation of the Programme of Action, and urges the developed countries that have not yet done so to make concrete efforts to implement effectively their commitments on official development assistance to the least developed countries, as contained in paragraph 83 of the Programme of Action;

9. *Invites* the organizations and bodies of the United Nations system, including the Bretton Woods institutions, and all other international organizations, within their respective mandates, to support, as a priority, the implementation of the Programme of Action, including programmes of financial and technical cooperation devoted to least developed countries in support of their national development programmes, including their poverty reduction strategies;

10. *Welcomes* the initiatives of the United Nations and the Group of Eight to bridge the digital divide that has further marginalized the least developed countries, particularly in the area of information technology, calls upon the international community to address the special needs of the least developed countries therein, and in this regard invites the forthcoming World Summit on the Information Society to adopt concrete actions to bridge the digital divide in the least developed countries;

11. *Invites* the forthcoming Ministerial Conference of the World Trade Organization, to be held in Cancún, Mexico, in September 2003, to address the marginalization of the least developed countries in international trade and to adopt further measures to integrate effectively the least developed countries into the multilateral trading system and the global economy;

12. *Invites* the members of the World Trade Organization to facilitate and accelerate accession to the organization for those least developed countries that are candidates by expeditiously implementing the guidelines to facilitate and accelerate the accession of the least developed countries to the World Trade Organization, which were adopted by the General Council of the World Trade Organization on 10 December 2002;

13. *Calls upon* the Secretary-General to submit his annual progress report on the implementation of the Programme of Action in such a way as to make it more analytical and results-oriented by putting greater emphasis on concrete results and indicating the progress achieved in the implementation of the Programme of Action.

The Council, by **decision 2003/287** of 24 July, decided that the high-level segment of its 2004 substantive session would consider the theme "Resources mobilization and enabling environment for poverty eradication in the context of the implementation of the Programme of Action for the Least Developed Countries for the Decade 2001-2010".

Report of Secretary-General. In response to Economic and Social Council resolution 2003/17 (above), the Secretary-General submitted a 24 October report [A/58/532] containing recommendations for facilitating the participation of delegations of LDCs at the Council's annual substantive sessions.

Trade and Development Board. The UNCTAD Trade and Development Board (TDB), at its fiftieth session (Geneva, 6-17 October) [A/58/15], having considered the third progress report of the UNCTAD secretariat on UNCTAD-wide activities in favour of LDCs [TD/B/50/3], an UNCTAD secretariat note on preliminary impact assessment of the main recent initiatives in favour of LDCs in the area of preferential market access [TD/B/50/5 & Corr.1] and a conference room paper describing progress on the implementation of the Integrated Framework for Trade-Related Technical Assistance for LDCs (IF), adopted agreed conclusions [A/58/15 (agreed conclusions 476(L))] in which it urged the secretariat to work with donors to reverse the declining share of LDCs in UNCTAD's technical cooperation resources and intensify its activities in support of LDCs and to report thereon, including on IF-related activities, and to continue to contribute to the Economic and Social Council's reviews of the Brussels Programme of Action. It urged development partners and others in a position to do so to implement market access commitments in favour of LDCs, give priority to enhancing LDCs' supply capacities and address bottlenecks hindering market entry. The secretariat should also undertake further work on how to enhance the benefits to LDCs from preferential market access and other international support measures. In the run-up to UNCTAD XI, to be held in 2004, the secretariat should address the issues of supply capacities and diversification with a view to enabling LDCs to benefit more effectively from preferential market access. TDB encouraged the secretariat to intensify activities for strengthening country ownership of the IF process and called for donor support through the IF Trust Fund. In the area of commodities, the secretariat should strengthen activities in commodity diversification, technical assistance and capacity-building. TDB invited bilateral donors to regularly replenish the UNCTAD Trust Fund for LDCs and asked the secretariat to mobilize adequate extrabudgetary resources for the participation of LDCs in the UNCTAD XI preparatory process and in the conference itself; donors were invited to earmark contributions for that purpose. TDB called for further strengthening of cooperation between UNCTAD and the Office of the High Representative for the Least Developed Countries, Landlocked Developing Countries and Small Island Developing States.

GENERAL ASSEMBLY ACTION

On 23 December [meeting 78], the General Assembly, on the recommendation of the Second Committee [A/58/492], adopted resolution **58/228** without vote [agenda item 102].

Third United Nations Conference on the Least Developed Countries

The General Assembly,

Recalling its resolution 55/279 of 12 July 2001, in which it endorsed the Brussels Declaration and the Programme of Action for the Least Developed Countries for the Decade 2001-2010, and its resolution 57/276 of 20 December 2002 on the Third United Nations Conference on the Least Developed Countries,

Reaffirming its resolution 55/2 of 8 September 2000, by which it adopted the United Nations Millennium Declaration, in particular paragraph 15 thereof, in which the heads of State and Government undertook to address the special needs of the least developed countries,

Recalling Economic and Social Council decision 2001/320 of 24 October 2001, in which the Council decided to establish a regular sub-item entitled "Review and coordination of the implementation of the Programme of Action for the Least Developed Countries for the Decade 2001-2010",

Taking note of Economic and Social Council resolution 2003/17 of 22 July 2003, in which the Council took note of the progress report of the Secretary-General on the implementation of the Programme of Action for the Least Developed Countries,

Taking note also of Economic and Social Council decision 2003/287 of 24 July 2003, in which the Council adopted the theme "Resources mobilization and enabling environment for poverty eradication in the context of the implementation of the Programme of Action for the Least Developed Countries for the Decade 2001-2010" as the theme of its high-level segment of 2004,

Taking note further of the report of the Secretary-General,

1. *Expresses its deep concern* over the weak implementation of the Programme of Action for the Least Developed Countries for the Decade 2001-2010, and expresses its expectation of more vigorous implementation by all partners;

2. *Reiterates* that the Programme of Action offers a framework for partnership, based on mutual commitments by the least developed countries and their development partners to undertake concrete actions in a number of interlinked areas, as set out in the Programme of Action;

3. *Calls upon* the least developed countries to continue, with the support of their development partners, to fulfil their commitments and to promote the implementation of the actions contained in the Programme of Action by translating them into specific measures within their national development frameworks and poverty eradication strategies, in particular poverty reduction strategy papers, where they exist, with the involvement of civil society, including the private sector, on the basis of a broad-based inclusive dialogue, as well as to continue to promote an enabling environment for the effective mobilization and utilization of resources consistent with paragraph 82 of the Programme of Action;

4. *Calls upon* the development partners of the least developed countries, including the multilateral financial institutions, to fulfil their commitments regarding the effective and expeditious implementation of the Programme of Action, and urges the developed countries that have not yet done so to make concrete efforts to effectively implement their commitments on official development assistance to the least developed countries, as contained in paragraph 83 of the Programme of Action;

5. *Urges* the least developed countries and their development partners to make the Programme of Action an effective tool for the implementation of the poverty reduction strategies at the national level for the achievement of the internationally agreed development goals, including those contained in the United Nations Millennium Declaration;

6. *Invites* the United Nations system, including the Bretton Woods institutions, and all other international organizations, within their respective mandates, to support as a priority the implementation of the Programme of Action, including programmes of financial and technical cooperation devoted to the least developed countries in support of their national development programmes, including their poverty reduction strategies;

7. *Stresses* the need for the effective implementation of the Programme of Action and its annual assessment at the substantive session of the Economic and Social Council, and recognizes in this regard the critical importance of the participation of the least developed countries in the assessment process of the Programme of Action;

8. *Requests* the Secretary-General to take appropriate measures to facilitate the participation of government representatives from the least developed countries in the annual assessment by the Economic and Social Council of the Programme of Action within the context of the overall financial provisions established by the General Assembly in its resolution 1798(XVII) of 11 December 1962 and subsequent amendments;

9. *Also requests* the Secretary-General to take appropriate measures, within existing resources and with the full participation of the regional commissions and relevant United Nations bodies, to support the participation of the least developed countries in international meetings, as well as in their preparation and consultation processes;

10. *Emphasizes* the importance of coordinating action within the United Nations system for the implementation of the Programme of Action, and calls upon the Secretary-General to take appropriate measures to ensure the efficiency and effectiveness of the Office of the High Representative for the Least Developed Countries, Landlocked Developing Countries and Small Island Developing States to fulfil its functions in accordance with General Assembly resolution 56/227 of 24 December 2001;

11. *Calls upon* the Secretary-General to submit, through the Economic and Social Council, an annual progress report on the implementation of the Programme of Action in a more analytical and results-oriented way by placing greater emphasis on concrete results and indicating the progress achieved in its implementation.

Island developing countries

Implementation of the Programme of Action

Preparations for international review meeting

Commission on Sustainable Development. Pursuant to resolution 57/262 [YUN 2002, p. 848], by which the General Assembly decided to convene in 2004 an international meeting to undertake a comprehensive review of the implementation of the Barbados Programme of Action for the Sustainable Development of Small Island Developing States (SIDS), adopted at the 1994 Global Conference on the subject [YUN 1994, p. 783], the Commission on Sustainable Development considered, at its eleventh session (27 January and 28 April–9 May) [E/2003/29], its role in the preparatory process for the conduct of that review. There was broad agreement that the Commission should act as the high-level policy forum for the preparatory process. The review should not renegotiate the Programme of Action but should assess the successes and failures of its implementation and focus on developing actions and modalities to further implementation and provide a strong foundation for the sustainable development of SIDS. There was general agreement also that effective regional, subregional and major group input into the preparatory process should be assured through regional preparatory meetings.

The Commission recommended to the Economic and Social Council for adoption a draft resolution on the preparations for the international review meeting.

ECONOMIC AND SOCIAL COUNCIL ACTION

On 24 July [meeting 48], the Economic and Social Council, on the recommendation of the Commission on Sustainable Development [E/2003/29], adopted **resolution 2003/55** without vote [agenda item 13 *(a)*].

Preparations for an international meeting to review the implementation of the Programme of Action for the Sustainable Development of Small Island Developing States

The Economic and Social Council,

Recalling the decision of the General Assembly in its resolution 57/262 of 20 December 2002 to convene an international meeting in 2004 in Mauritius, including a high-level segment, for a full and comprehensive review of the implementation of the Programme of Action for the Sustainable Development of Small Island Developing States,

Recalling also the decision to convene regional and interregional preparatory meetings of small island developing States,

Recalling further the decision to invite the Commission on Sustainable Development, at its eleventh session, to consider its role in the preparatory process for the comprehensive review of the implementation of the Programme of Action,

Noting the preliminary discussion of the issues by the Commission at its eleventh session in its consideration of its role in the preparations for the international meeting,

1. *Decides* that the Commission on Sustainable Development, during its twelfth session, in 2004, shall convene a three-day preparatory meeting for an international meeting for an in-depth assessment and appraisal of the implementation of the Programme of Action for the Sustainable Development of Small Island Developing States, and shall finalize the preparations for the international meeting, including its agenda;

2. *Also decides* that the three-day preparatory meeting shall consider a synthesis report, to be prepared by the Secretary-General on the basis of the recommendations contained in:

(a) National assessment reports of small island developing States, where available;

(b) Expert thematic workshop reports;

(c) Reports of the regional and interregional preparatory meetings referred to in paragraph 6 below on the implementation of the Programme of Action;

3. *Invites* the international donor and development community and international organizations to provide information, on or before 31 January 2004, on their activities in support of the Programme of Action, as well as on recommendations for further action in support of its full implementation, and requests that the information provided be considered by the Secretary-General in the preparation of the synthesis report referred to in paragraph 2 above;

4. *Welcomes* the work in progress in all small island developing States to continue and to enhance their preparations for the international meeting, and calls upon the international community, United Nations agencies and intergovernmental bodies to support the efforts of small island developing States in their preparations of national assessment reports to be completed by July 2003, given that national reports are a critical component for the comprehensive review of the Programme of Action in providing information on respective national circumstances;

5. *Emphasizes* that in the preparation of the reporting referred to in paragraphs 2, 3 and 4 above, the provisions of paragraph 9 of General Assembly resolution 57/262 should be taken into account, and invites the Secretary-General to make full use of the Small Island Developing States Information Network in his efforts to disseminate the various reports;

6. *Welcomes*, in accordance with paragraph 7 of General Assembly resolution 57/262, the regional preparatory meetings for:

(a) Pacific small island developing States, to be held in Apia from 4 to 8 August 2003;

(b) Caribbean small island developing States, to be held in Port of Spain from 18 to 22 August 2003;

(c) Atlantic, Indian Ocean, Mediterranean and South China Seas small island developing States, to be held in Praia from 1 to 5 September 2003;

as well as an interregional preparatory meeting, with ministerial participation, for all small island developing States, to be held in Nassau from 26 to 30 January 2004;

7. *Encourages* Governments and participants at the high-level segment of the twelfth session of the Commission on Sustainable Development to also address, within the thematic cluster of issues for that session, matters related to the sustainable development of small island developing States and the Programme of Action;

8. *Invites* the international community, United Nations agencies and intergovernmental bodies to support regional initiatives and to collaborate closely, in partnership with the regional organizations and institutions, to expedite preparations for the review, noting the work already done by the regional organizations and institutions, bearing in mind the coordinating role assigned to the Department of Economic and Social Affairs of the Secretariat by the General Assembly, and to the Water, Natural Resources and Small Island Developing States Branch of the Department in its capacity as Chair of the inter-agency task force for the international meeting;

9. *Reiterates* the need for the full participation of small island developing States in the preparatory process leading up to, as well as during, the international meeting, and invites Governments and international and regional intergovernmental organizations to contribute to the voluntary fund called for in paragraph 15 of General Assembly resolution 57/262;

10. *Reiterates also* the need for the effective participation of associate members of the regional commissions, and calls for their participation to be facilitated through the voluntary fund referred to in paragraph 9 above;

11. *Invites* interested Governments and donor organizations to support the participation of major groups in the preparatory process and in the international meeting itself;

12. *Requests* the Secretary-General to work within existing resources and especially to utilize fully the savings from the budget that would result from not implementing the two intersessional meetings of the Commission on Sustainable Development as programmed in 2003 and voluntary contributions, as necessary, for the preparatory process referred to above.

Also on 24 July, by **decision 2003/283**, the Council recommended to the Assembly that travel and subsistence allowances for participants from SIDS in the preparatory meetings and the international review meeting should be provided from the funds designated by donors for that purpose in the voluntary fund established by the Assembly in resolution 57/262 [YUN 2002, p. 848].

Report of Secretary-General. In response to General Assembly resolution 57/262 [YUN 2002, p. 848], the Secretary-General submitted an 18 July report on further implementation of the outcome of the Global Conference on the Sustainable Development of SIDS [A/58/170]. He provided an overview of activities planned at the national, regional and international levels in anticipation of the international review meeting, to be hosted by Mauritius in 2004. The report, which included input from the Inter-Agency Task Force established by the Secretary-General for the purpose of preparing the international meeting, also gave information on the schedule of regional preparatory meetings that would coordinate regional platforms based on the national assessment reports of small island developing States, which were expected to play a key role in the preparatory process.

Three regional preparatory meetings were held in 2003: for Pacific SIDS (Apia, Samoa, 4-8 August) [A/58/303]; for Caribbean SIDS (Port of Spain, Trinidad and Tobago, 6-10 October) [A/C.2/58/14]; and SIDS of the Atlantic, Indian Ocean, Mediterranean and South China Seas (Praia, Cape Verde, 1-5 September) [A/C.2/58/12]. Other regional-level preparations included the Expert Meeting on Capacity-Building for Renewable Energy and Energy Efficiency in SIDS (Niue, 7-11 July) [A/58/675] and a workshop on the vulnerability of SIDS (Dominica, 29 September–3 October). Those regional preparatory and expert meetings would culminate in the convening of an interregional preparatory meeting with ministerial-level participation to harmonize the platform for all SIDS, to be held in Nassau, Bahamas, in January 2004. In addition, the SIDS Unit of the Secretariat was compiling best practices and success stories regarding field projects and programmes in SIDS aimed at implementing the Programme of Action at the international, regional and local levels. A publication and web-based databank were envisaged in time for the Mauritius meeting.

The report concluded that preparatory work for the international meeting was progressing steadily, but there was a need for high-level regional and global advocacy in support of the preparations.

The Secretary-General, by a November note [A/58/567 & Corr.1], submitted to the General Assembly the draft provisional rules of procedure of the 2004 International Meeting to Review the Implementation of the Programme of Action for the Sustainable Development of SIDS.

GENERAL ASSEMBLY ACTION

On 23 December [meeting 78], the General Assembly, on the recommendation of the Second Committee [A/58/484/Add.4], adopted **resolution 58/213 A** without vote [agenda item 94 (d)].

Further implementation of the Programme of Action for the Sustainable Development of Small Island Developing States

The General Assembly,

Recalling the Declaration of Barbados and the Programme of Action for the Sustainable Development of Small Island Developing States, adopted by the Global Conference on the Sustainable Development of Small Island Developing States, and recalling also its resolution 49/122 of 19 December 1994 on the Global Conference,

Recalling also its resolutions 51/183 of 16 December 1996, 52/202 of 18 December 1997 and 53/189 of 15 December 1998, the review document adopted by the Assembly at its twenty-second special session, and its resolutions 54/224 of 22 December 1999, 55/199 and 55/202 of 20 December 2000, 56/198 of 21 December 2001 and 57/262 of 20 December 2002,

Recalling further the Johannesburg Declaration on Sustainable Development and the Plan of Implementation of the World Summit on Sustainable Development ("Johannesburg Plan of Implementation"), in particular the emphasis given to small island developing States in chapter VII of the Johannesburg Plan of Implementation, as well as the references to the specific needs of small island developing States contained in the United Nations Millennium Declaration and the Monterrey Consensus of the International Conference on Financing for Development,

Recalling its decision to convene an international meeting in 2004, including a high-level segment, to undertake a full and comprehensive review of the implementation of the Programme of Action, as called for in the Johannesburg Plan of Implementation,

Welcoming the preparatory activities undertaken at the national and regional levels for the international meeting, and expressing its appreciation to the Governments of Samoa, Cape Verde and Trinidad and Tobago for hosting regional preparatory meetings,

Reaffirming the political importance of the forthcoming ten-year review of the progress achieved since the Global Conference, and stressing that the risk from the vulnerabilities of and challenges to small island developing States has increased and requires the strengthening of cooperation and more effective development assistance towards achieving the goals of sustainable development,

1. *Takes note* of the report of the Secretary-General;
2. *Approves* the provisional rules of procedure of the International Meeting to Review the Implementation of the Programme of Action for the Sustainable Development of Small Island Developing States, as contained in the note by the Secretary-General;
3. *Decides* that the International Meeting shall be open to all States Members of the United Nations and States members of the specialized agencies, with the participation of observers, in accordance with the established practice of the General Assembly and its conferences and with the rules of procedure of the International Meeting;
4. *Welcomes* the efforts made at the national, subregional and regional levels to implement the Programme of Action, and takes note of the reports of the regional preparatory meetings for the Pacific, the Atlantic, Indian Ocean, Mediterranean and South China Seas and the Caribbean regions of small island developing States;
5. *Reiterates* the urgent need for the full and effective implementation of the Programme of Action, the Declaration of Barbados and the review document adopted by the General Assembly at its twenty-second special session so as to assist small island developing States in their efforts to achieve sustainable development;

6. *Decides* that the International Meeting will be convened from 30 August to 3 September 2004 and will include a high-level segment to undertake a full and comprehensive review of the implementation of the Programme of Action, as called for in the Johannesburg Plan of Implementation, and welcomes the offer of the Government of Mauritius to host the International Meeting;

7. *Also decides* to hold, if deemed necessary by an open-ended preparatory meeting, and if funded from voluntary resources, two days of informal consultations in Mauritius, on 28 and 29 August 2004, to facilitate the effective preparation of the International Meeting;

8. *Urges* that representation and participation at the International Meeting be at the highest possible level;

9. *Decides* that the International Meeting will seek a renewed political commitment by the international community and will focus on practical actions for the further implementation of the Programme of Action, taking into consideration new and emerging issues, challenges and situations since the adoption of the Programme of Action;

10. *Endorses* Economic and Social Council resolution 2003/55 of 24 July 2003, in which it decided, on the recommendation of the Commission on Sustainable Development at its eleventh session, to convene an interregional preparatory meeting for small island developing States in Nassau from 26 to 30 January 2004, expresses its appreciation to the Government of the Bahamas for hosting the meeting, and encourages participation in the meeting at the ministerial level;

11. *Also endorses* the decision of the Economic and Social Council in its resolution 2003/55, on the recommendation of the Commission on Sustainable Development at its eleventh session, to convene during the twelfth session of the Commission a three-day preparatory meeting for the International Meeting, from 14 to 16 April 2004, for an in-depth assessment and appraisal of the implementation of the Programme of Action and to finalize the preparations for the International Meeting, including its agenda;

12. *Decides* that the preparatory meeting shall be open-ended and shall be held in accordance with the rules of procedure of the functional commissions of the Economic and Social Council and the supplementary arrangements established for the Commission on Sustainable Development by the Council in its decisions 1993/215 of 12 February 1993 and 1995/201 of 8 February 1995, applied to all Member States and other participants, as was the practice in the preparatory committee for the World Summit on Sustainable Development, while maintaining the provisions of the Commission in relation to travel assistance, in accordance with the provisions of Economic and Social Council decision 2003/283 of 24 July 2003;

13. *Encourages* associate members of the regional commissions that are small island developing States to participate in the International Meeting, and decides that their participation shall be in accordance with rule 61 of the provisional rules of procedure of the International Meeting;

14. *Decides* that the participation of major groups, including non-governmental organizations, in the International Meeting shall be in accordance with rule 65 of the provisional rules of procedure of the International Meeting;

15. *Also decides* that non-governmental organizations whose work is relevant to the subject of the International Meeting, that are not currently accredited by the Economic and Social Council, may submit applications to participate as observers in the International Meeting, as well as its preparatory meeting, subject to the approval of the open-ended preparatory meeting;

16. *Takes note* of the appointment of a Secretary-General of the International Meeting;

17. *Requests* the Secretary-General, in consultation with the relevant United Nations agencies and organizations, and taking into account the submissions he may receive from bilateral, regional and multilateral donor agencies as well as from major groups, including non-governmental organizations, to ensure the timely submission to the Commission on Sustainable Development at its twelfth session of a synthesis report on the basis of the national, regional and interregional preparations and reports by small island developing States and other parties;

18. *Requests* that the necessary resources, from within existing resources, be provided to the Department of Public Information of the Secretariat to ensure that the goals and purposes of the International Meeting receive the widest possible dissemination within Member States, major groups, including non-governmental organizations, and national, regional and international media, including through the Small Island Developing States Information Network, with a view to encouraging contributions to and support for the International Meeting and its preparatory process;

19. *Expresses its appreciation* for the contributions made to the voluntary trust fund established for the purpose of assisting small island developing States to participate fully and effectively in the International Meeting and its preparatory process, as approved by the Economic and Social Council in resolution 2003/55 and decision 2003/283, and urges all Member States and organizations to contribute generously to the fund;

20. *Encourages* the full and effective participation of developing countries in the International Meeting, and invites donor countries and agencies to provide additional extrabudgetary resources, in particular through voluntary contributions to the trust fund, to facilitate their participation;

21. *Welcomes* the coordinating efforts undertaken in the United Nations system through the creation of an inter-agency task force to enable the United Nations system to improve coordination and enhance cooperation on matters pertaining to the preparatory process and to the International Meeting itself;

22. *Calls upon* the Department of Economic and Social Affairs of the Secretariat, through the Division for Sustainable Development and its Small Island Developing States Unit, to undertake activities in both the preparatory processes and the International Meeting to enhance coordination and cooperation within the United Nations system as well as with other relevant multilateral organizations to ensure the effective implementation and monitoring of and follow-up to the outcomes of the ten-year review of the Programme of Action;

23. *Calls upon* the Office of the High Representative for the Least Developed Countries, Landlocked Developing Countries and Small Island Developing States to fulfil its mandate and to advocate strongly, in partnership with the relevant parts of the United Nations as well as with major groups, media, academia and foundations, for the mobilization of international support and resources for the successful outcome of the International Meeting and for the follow-up to the outcomes of the ten-year review of the Programme of Action;

24. *Welcomes* the generous contributions by donors to provide for staffing of the Small Island Developing States Unit, and calls upon the Secretary-General to explore practical options for strengthening the Unit, including by redeployment of resources, on a permanent basis during the biennium 2004-2005, pursuant to resolutions 56/198 and 57/262, with a view to facilitating the full and effective implementation of the Declaration of Barbados and the Programme of Action and the outcomes of the International Meeting;

25. *Decides* to include in the provisional agenda of its fifty-ninth session, under the item entitled "Environment and sustainable development", a sub-item entitled "Further implementation of the outcome of the Global Conference on the Sustainable Development of Small Island Developing States: follow-up to the outcomes of the International Meeting to Review the Implementation of the Barbados Programme of Action", and requests the Secretary-General to submit to the General Assembly at its fifty-ninth session the report of the International Meeting.

Landlocked developing countries

In 2003, the International Ministerial Conference of Landlocked and Transit Developing Countries and Donor Countries and International Financial and Development Institutions on Transit Transport Cooperation (Almaty, Kazakhstan, 28-29 August) adopted the Almaty Declaration and Programme of Action, a global framework outlining partnerships, objectives and priorities for addressing the special needs of landlocked developing countries [A/CONF.202/3].

In December, the General Assembly, in **resolution 58/201** (see p. 877), endorsed the Almaty Programme of Action and called for its effective implementation.

Ministerial communiqué. On 2 October [A/C.2/58/3], the Lao People's Democratic Republic transmitted to the Secretary-General the ministerial communiqué adopted at the Fourth Annual Ministerial Meeting of Landlocked Developing Countries (New York, 30 September) and the communiqué issued by the ministers of landlocked developing countries attending the fifth session of the WTO Ministerial Conference (Cancún, Mexico, 13 September) (see p. 1535).

International Ministerial Conference

In accordance with General Assembly resolutions 56/180 [YUN 2001, p. 777] and 57/242 [YUN 2002, p. 850], the International Ministerial Conference of Landlocked and Transit Developing Countries and Donor Countries and International Financial and Development Institutions on Transit Transport Cooperation was held in Almaty, Kazakhstan, on 28 and 29 August [A/CONF.202/3]. The Conference reviewed the current situation of transit transport systems in landlocked developing countries and the implementation of the 1995 Global Framework for Transit Transport Cooperation between Landlocked and Transit Developing Countries and the Donor Community [YUN 1995, p. 876] and formulated policy measures and action-oriented programmes aimed at developing efficient transit transport systems. At the conclusion of the Conference, the ministers adopted the Almaty Declaration and the Almaty Programme of Action: Addressing the Special Needs of Landlocked Developing Countries within a New Global Framework for Transit Transport Cooperation for Landlocked and Transit Developing Countries.

In conjunction with the Conference, three parallel events were organized by UNCTAD (on trade facilitation); by the World Bank (a high-level investment forum); and by the Economic Commission for Europe (regional initiatives on trade and transport facilitation).

Almaty Programme of Action and Declaration

The Almaty Programme of Action stated that landlocked developing countries, as a group, were among the poorest of developing countries. Lack of territorial access to the sea, remoteness and isolation from world markets contributed to their relative poverty, substantially inflating transportation costs and lowering their effective participation in international trade. High transit transport costs constrained export development and caused the price of imports to soar. The transit neighbours of landlocked developing countries were themselves mostly developing countries, often of broadly similar economic structure, beset by similar scarcities of resources, and burdened by the financial, infrastructural and social impacts deriving from transit transport. The transit developing countries were in need of improved technical and administrative arrangements in their transport and customs and administrative systems to which their landlocked neighbours were expected to link.

The objective of the Programme of Action was to address the special needs of landlocked developing countries and establish a new global framework for action for developing efficient transit transport systems in landlocked and transit developing countries, taking into account the interests of both groups. It aimed to: secure access to and from the sea by all means of transport according to applicable rules of international law; reduce costs and improve services so as to increase the competitiveness of their exports; reduce the delivered costs of imports; address problems of delays and uncertainties in trade routes; develop adequate national networks; reduce loss, damage and deterioration en route; open the way for export expansion; and improve safety of road transport and security of people along the corridors.

The Programme of Action outlined five priorities: fundamental transit policy issues; infrastructure development and maintenance, including rail transport, road transport, ports, inland waterways, pipelines, air transport and communications; international trade and trade facilitation; international support measures; and implementation and review. The Conference recommended specific actions under each priority. In terms of international support measures, the Conference recommended that the international community, including financial and development institutions and donor countries, should assist landlocked and transit developing countries to deal effectively with their transit problems and requirements by, among other actions, facilitating an external supporting environment for the timely realization of the objectives of the Programme of Action, providing technical support through partnerships and encouraging increased foreign direct investment. Donor countries and multilateral financial and development institutions should provide landlocked and transit developing countries with financial and technical assistance in the form of grants and/or concessional loans for the needs identified in the Programme of Action. Special attention should be given to institutional capacity-building to promote effective government policy-making and practices addressing transport and transit needs. The Programme of Action identified areas for priority financing, including investments to complete "missing links" in the transit transport chain to extend railways and roads to landlocked developing countries; maintenance of existing physical transit transport infrastructure; development and maintenance of cost-effective routes; development of dry port projects; projects to improve existing or establish adjacent border points; and rehabilitation and reconstruction of transport infrastructure, especially in countries or regions emerging from war and internal conflict and natural disasters.

The Programme of Action stated that implementation required individual and concerted efforts by the landlocked and transit developing countries, their development partners, the UN system, relevant international organizations, including the World Bank and regional development banks, WTO, and the World Customs Organization and regional and other organizations. International and regional organizations should give priority to requests for technical assistance to supplement national and regional efforts to promote efficient use of existing transit facilities. The private sector should be actively involved in implementing the Programme of Action, and South-South cooperation and triangular cooperation with the involvement of donors should be promoted, as should cooperation among subregional and regional organizations. The UN regional commissions should expand their programmes consistent with the Programme of Action and specific subregional meetings should be organized to consider how to implement the Programme of Action effectively.

The UN Secretary-General should report on the implementation of the Programme of Action to the Assembly, which would decide on periodicity. The Assembly was invited to conduct a comprehensive review of the implementation of the Programme of Action at a time to be decided. The Office of the High Representative for the Least Developed Countries, Landlocked Developing Countries and Small Island Developing States should coordinate the preparatory review process, and UNCTAD, the World Bank and the regional commissions were invited to provide substantive assistance for that process. The Office of the High Representative was asked to enhance cooperation and coordination with UN system organizations, particularly those engaged in operational activities on the ground in landlocked and transit developing countries, and to carry out advocacy work to mobilize international awareness and focus attention on the implementation of the Programme of Action.

In the Almaty Declaration, participating Governments recognized that high trade transaction costs were a major reason for the marginalization of landlocked developing countries from the global trading system and committed themselves to minimizing that marginalization and enhancing the beneficial integration of landlocked developing countries into the global economy through the establishment of efficient transit transport systems in both landlocked and transit developing countries, and through genuine partnerships between landlocked and transit developing countries and their development partners at the national, bilateral, subregional, regional and global levels. They reaffirmed the right of access of landlocked countries to and from the sea and freedom of transit through transit countries. They also reaffirmed that transit countries had the right to take all measures necessary to ensure that the rights and facilities provided for landlocked countries in no way infringed upon their legitimate interests. They emphasized the importance of effective implementation of and regular follow-up to the Almaty Programme of Action and committed themselves to that end, and requested the High Representative to ensure that the Conference was effectively followed up. The Conference also adopted a resolution thanking the people and Government of Kazakhstan for hosting the Conference.

Report of Secretary-General. In response to General Assembly resolution 57/242 [YUN 2002, p. 850], the Secretary-General submitted a 23 September report [A/58/388] on the outcome of the International Ministerial Conference and some aspects of the preparatory process that preceded it. He concluded that the Conference successfully galvanized international solidarity and partnerships to address the special needs of landlocked developing countries as called for in the Millennium Declaration [YUN 2002, p. 49]. Implementation of the specific actions in the five priority areas agreed upon in the Almaty Programme of Action would facilitate establishing the efficient transit transport systems in landlocked and transit developing countries that were inevitably required for landlocked developing countries to be effectively integrated into the international trading system.

Preparatory meetings

In accordance with General Assembly resolution 57/242 [YUN 2002, p. 850], the Intergovernmental Preparatory Committee for the International Ministerial Conference held two sessions during 2003. The sixth Meeting of Governmental Experts from Landlocked and Transit Developing Countries and Representative Donor Countries and Financial and Development Institutions (New York, 23-27 June) served as the first preparatory session [A/CONF.202/PC/5]. It included a high-level panel discussion and considered a draft outcome document [A/CONF.202/PC/L.1 & Corr.1]. The session also had before it a May report of the Secretary-General [A/CONF.202/PC/2] on the state of preparations for the Conference, including the outcomes of regional and subregional preparations. Annexed to the report were the Asunción Programme of Action, adopted in Asunción, Paraguay (12-13 March); the Asian Action Plan on Transit Transport Cooperation, adopted at the fifty-ninth session of the Economic and Social Commission for Asia and the Pacific (Bangkok, 24-25 April); and the African Action Plan, adopted in Addis Ababa, Ethiopia (7 May). The report also highlighted other aspects of the preparatory process for the Ministerial Conference, including support from the UN system, consultations with the host Government, mobilization of resources, and advocacy and promotion of the Conference. In addition, the structure and format of the Conference were reviewed. The report concluded that the Conference would need to agree on action-oriented measures that took into account a broad range of factors, such as unfettered access to the sea by all means of transport, inadequate infrastructure, imbalance of trade, inefficient transport organization, poor utilization of assets, reform of transit transport policies and weak managerial, procedural, regulatory and institutional systems, and international support measures.

A Meeting of Senior Officials (Almaty, 25-27 August) served as the second preparatory session [A/CONF.202/PC.2/1], which finalized the draft outcome document, the Almaty Programme of Action, and recommended it to the Conference for adoption.

GENERAL ASSEMBLY ACTION

On 23 December [meeting 78], the General Assembly, on the recommendation of the Second Committee [A/58/481/Add.3], adopted **resolution 58/201** without vote [agenda items 91 (c) & (f)].

Almaty Programme of Action: Addressing the Special Needs of Landlocked Developing Countries within a New Global Framework for Transit Transport Cooperation for Landlocked and Transit Developing Countries

The General Assembly,

Recalling its resolution 56/180 of 21 December 2001, in which it requested the Secretary-General to convene in 2003 the international ministerial meeting now known as the International Ministerial Conference of Landlocked and Transit Developing Countries and Donor Countries and International Financial and Development Institutions on Transit Transport Cooperation, as well as its resolution 57/242 of 20 December 2002,

1. *Takes note* of the report of the Secretary-General on the outcome of the International Ministerial Conference of Landlocked and Transit Developing Countries and Donor Countries and International Financial and Development Institutions on Transit Transport Cooperation;

2. *Expresses its deep appreciation* to the Government of Kazakhstan for hosting the International Ministerial Conference in Almaty on 28 and 29 August 2003;

3. *Endorses* the Almaty Programme of Action: Addressing the Special Needs of Landlocked Developing Countries within a New Global Framework for Transit Transport Cooperation for Landlocked and Transit Developing Countries and the Almaty Declaration, adopted by the International Ministerial Conference;

4. *Calls* for full and effective implementation of the Almaty Programme of Action;

5. *Decides* to include in the provisional agenda of its fifty-ninth session an item entitled "Specific actions related to the particular needs and problems of landlocked developing countries: outcome of the International Ministerial Conference of Landlocked and Transit Developing Countries and Donor Countries and International Financial and Development Institutions on Transit Transport Cooperation";

6. *Requests* the Secretary-General to submit to the General Assembly at its fifty-ninth session a report on the progress made in the implementation of the Almaty Programme of Action.

On 23 December, the Assembly took note of a report by the UNCTAD Secretary-General [A/58/209] on the transit environment in the landlocked States in Central Asia and their transit developing neighbours (**decision 58/547**) (see p. 1010).

Chapter II

Operational activities for development

In 2003, the United Nations system continued to provide development assistance to developing countries and countries with economies in transition through the United Nations Development Programme (UNDP), the central United Nations funding body for technical assistance. UNDP's income in 2003 amounted to $3.2 billion, a 10 per cent increase over 2002. Total expenditure for all programme activities and support costs in 2003 was $2.6 billion as compared with $2.8 billion the previous year. Technical cooperation funded through other sources included $50.7 million provided through the programme executed by the UN Department of Economic and Social Affairs, $73.7 million through the United Nations Fund for International Partnerships and $21.1 million through the United Nations Capital Development Fund. In July, the Economic and Social Council endorsed the establishment of the World Solidarity Fund, as a UNDP trust fund, for the eradication of poverty and the promotion of social and human development in developing countries.

In April, the General Assembly confirmed the appointment of Mark Malloch Brown as Administrator of UNDP for a further four-year term of office beginning on 1 July. The Administrator submitted an end-of-cycle assessment of the multi-year funding framework (MYFF), 2002-2003, which highlighted the progress achieved in meeting the MYFF goals, and the 2004-2007 MYFF, which set out the strategic goals and service lines to be pursued by UNDP. He also presented a review of the implementation of the UNDP Business Plans, 2002-2003.

The Secretary-General reported in May on progress in implementing General Assembly resolution 56/201 on the triennial comprehensive policy review of UN operational activities for development. In July, the Economic and Social Council reviewed progress in implementing the resolution and called for continued reform of the UN development system. In particular, it noted that most UN organizations were realigning their policies, strategies, programmes and activities on the basis of internationally agreed development goals, including the Millennium Development Goals. In the context of his programme for strengthening the United Nations: an agenda for change, the Secretary-General submitted a report reviewing the functioning of UN technical cooperation and how the clarification of roles and responsibilities could help improve its overall impact.

The United Nations Office for Project Services had a project delivery of $490.6 million, an increase of 1 per cent over its original target for the year.

The United Nations Volunteers programme expanded for the seventh consecutive year, with over 5,600 volunteers carrying out more than 5,800 assignments in 150 countries.

In December, the Assembly called for an intensification of efforts to mainstream technical and economic cooperation among developing countries and declared 19 December as the UN Day for South-South Cooperation.

System-wide activities

Review of UN technical cooperation

The Secretary-General, responding to General Assembly resolution 57/300 on strengthening of the United Nations: an agenda for further change [YUN 2002, p. 1353], submitted a report reviewing technical cooperation of the United Nations [A/58/382]. The objective was to provide information on a representative selection of UN technical cooperation issues in order to assist programme countries in their decision-making with regard to technical cooperation and donors in adjusting their funding decisions. It examined how UN system technical cooperation functioned and reviewed how clarification of roles and responsibilities might help to improve overall impact. The issues examined were chosen to illustrate the breadth and differing natures of UN technical cooperation undertakings. Some were traditional sectoral issues, such as natural disasters, trade and energy; others were cross-cutting, such as women and gender, peace-building and information and communication technologies; and some reflected new and emerging issues of a sensitive political and cultural nature, such as the rule of law and peace-building. Yet another, HIV/AIDS, reflected a primary preoccupation for the UN system. For each issue, the report documented the main focus and type of activity carried out by each UN entity; identified current structural challenges within the UN system to the effective and efficient delivery of technical cooperation; and highlighted areas where future work might be required to determine if some form of consolidation, transfer or clarification of responsibilities was required.

The report stated that the complex and at times under-resourced system of UN technical cooperation appeared to be performing reasonably well. Managers were aware of their mandates and of the need to work with others to achieve the range of inputs required. The system had not been designed for optimal efficiency, but had evolved over decades as a result of incremental decision-making by governance bodies and the system's funders. The variety of differing mechanisms in the system for the delivery of technical cooperation continued to attract funding support, and their services continued to be of value to developing countries.

Any major structural rationalization would be complex, involving the fundamental questioning of the continued relevance of some existing mandates and an assessment of donors' willingness to support any such rationalization with a reform of their own funding practices. Rationalization that imperiled resource flows could prove counterproductive. Donor funding practices had a major impact on the structure of the system. Rationalization of the supply-side structure therefore had to be carefully addressed, as there was no guarantee that existing funding arrangements would continue following any functional reorganization in the system. The report emphasized the linkages between the supply side, the demand side and the system of financing. Each had to complement and support the others if an optimal system was to be achieved. Despite the large number of entities involved overall and actions taken by them on any single issue, duplication was limited.

The Secretary-General concluded that follow-up to the main recommendations contained in the report, to be undertaken by the UN Deputy Secretary-General, would ensure that optimum synergies within the system were achieved. The UNDP Administrator would undertake, in collaboration with UN department heads, a review of a few key issues on which the division of labour could be improved and report to the Deputy Secretary-General. Attention would be given to ensuring effective collaboration between the regional commissions and the funds and programmes, in cases where there was shared sectoral priority and where the required expertise existed. Member States would be informed of the follow-up actions as part of the triennial comprehensive review of operational activities in 2004.

The General Assembly, in **resolution 58/270** of 23 December, requested the Secretary-General to undertake a comprehensive review of the regular programme of technical cooperation and to make proposals to the Assembly at its fifty-ninth (2004) session.

Operational activities segment of the Economic and Social Council

The Economic and Social Council, at its 2003 substantive session [A/58/3/Rev.1], considered the question of operational activities of the United Nations for international development cooperation at meetings on 3, 4, 7, 10 and 11 July, based on the programme of work for that segment, which it had noted on 5 March (**decision 2003/211**). The Council held discussions on the follow-up to policy recommendations of the General Assembly and the Council; the reports of the Executive Boards of UNDP/United Nations Population Fund (UNFPA), the United Nations Children's Fund (UNICEF) and the World Food Programme (WFP); and economic and technical cooperation among developing countries (see p. 910), including high-level panel discussions on resources for operational activities for development and on an impartial and independent assessment of the extent to which UN funds, programmes and agencies at the field level learned lessons from their evaluations, and proposals for improving the feedback mechanisms at the field level.

Among the documents before the Council were the Secretary-General's reports on progress in the implementation of Assembly resolution 56/201 on the triennial policy review of operational activities for development [E/2003/61], comprehensive statistical data on operational activities for development for 2001 [E/2003/57], assessment of the lessons learned by UN organizations from evaluation activities at the field level [E/2003/64] and funding of UN system development cooperation activities [E/2003/89] (see sections below).

On 4 July, the Council held a dialogue with the UN country team for Senegal.

Implementation of resolution 56/201

In May [E/2003/61], the Secretary-General reported to the Economic and Social Council on progress in the implementation of General Assembly resolution 56/201 [YUN 2001, p. 784] on the triennial policy review of operational activities for development of the UN system, in the areas of funding, capacity-building, strategic frameworks (common country assessment (CCA) and the United Nations Development Assistance

Framework (UNDAF)), evaluation, field-level coordination, gender mainstreaming, humanitarian assistance, regional and subregional dimensions and South-South cooperation, and technical and economic cooperation among developing countries.

Progress was assessed in the light of the outcomes of a number of high-level conferences and summits (the Millennium Declaration [YUN 2000, p. 49], the Monterrey Consensus of the 2002 International Conference on Financing for Development [YUN 2002, p. 953], the Doha Development Agenda of the fourth World Trade Organization Ministerial Conference [YUN 2001, p. 1432], and the Johannesburg Declaration on Sustainable Development and the Plan of Implementation of the 2002 World Summit on Sustainable Development [YUN 2002, p. 821]), which reflected agreement within the international community on an overarching policy framework to support national efforts to fight poverty through a global partnership between developed and developing countries, and on the basis of the Millennium Development Goals (MDGs) [YUN 2000, p. 51]. The Council was invited to undertake the progress review with the aim of preparing the ground for the next triennial comprehensive policy review of operational activities, which the Assembly would conduct in 2004, and to provide guidance to the Secretary-General. Recommendations were made to the Council on action it might consider for further implementation of resolution 56/201.

The Secretary-General reported that the UN system had improved coherence and coordination at the country level in support of the MDGs and other internationally agreed goals, linking regional and country dimensions and adjusting to complex development situations, including humanitarian emergencies and post-conflict situations. Guidance and training were provided to country teams, encouraging learning and the sharing of experience, and establishing quality assurance and support mechanisms at country, regional and global levels. The system assisted recipient countries in integrating macroeconomic imperatives with social concerns and addressing challenges, such as achieving budget trade-offs between economic and social objectives. While significant progress was made in harmonizing and simplifying processes, improving efficiency and reducing transaction costs for government partners, more could be done to improve the mix of skills, expertise and services that the UN system could mobilize to support countries in implementing development strategies.

For capacity-building—a long-term, country-driven process at the core of development—the report suggested that external support should focus on developing existing national capacities and address institutional, organizational and societal dimensions. CCA, UNDAF and the poverty reduction strategy papers (PRSPs) processes should be used as entry points for the system's support. The report suggested that UN organizations devise country-level strategies for capacity-building and reflect them in CCA and UNDAF, and intensify information-sharing on experience gained, benchmarks and indicators concerning capacity-building as linked to the MDGs.

The focus of CCA and UNDAF on the MDGs was strengthened, thereby improving their quality, enhancing UNDAF's role in supporting coordinated implementation of the outcome of major UN conferences and summits, and providing an integrated response to national priorities. The United Nations Development Group (UNDG) was developing a new support and oversight system for the CCA and UNDAF processes through a comprehensive system of quality support and assurance for country teams. The new support system would provide consolidated inter-agency feedback with a view to creating a learning development system and a greater sense of accountability at all levels. The CCA and UNDAF guidelines had promoted a results-based approach; the UNDAF results matrix harmonized result-based management terminology to establish a link with national priorities and organizations' country programmes as the basis for increased inter-agency coordination, joint or collaborative programming and improved evaluations.

In terms of field-level coordination, in response to the Assembly's request in resolution 56/201 that UN system organizations simplify and harmonize rules and procedures for operational activities, UN funds and programmes had submitted a programme of work to the Council, including proposals to phase out redundant rules and procedures, with benchmarks and time-bound targets to be achieved by 2004. That programme of work was being implemented. New harmonized procedures adopted by UNDP/UNFPA, UNICEF and WFP included simplification and harmonization modalities regarding standard instruments such as: the UNDAF results matrix; the country programme action plan, a standard document highlighting commitments of each UN agency and the Government concerned; the annual output work plan, a standardized document that provided an activity plan for each output; and the UNDAF monitoring and evaluation plan and the UNDAF final evaluations.

Progress in joint programming was still limited, but new guidelines were being completed, which would require new financial mechanisms for reducing transaction costs and increasing the emphasis on capacity-building and effectiveness and efficiency. The full range of new modalities was being phased in, beginning in five countries with country programmes, starting in 2004.

With regard to decentralization, UN funds and programmes that were members of the UNDG Executive Committee concluded that a high degree of delegation and decentralization of authority had been reached in their country and regional offices and that no further action was needed in that area. However, in other UN agencies, different degrees of decentralization and different levels of authorization still prevailed, hindering collaborative programming. Greater attention was still needed to harmonize recruitment, remuneration and training of national project personnel and information technology platforms.

The Secretary-General pursued the "United Nations House" initiative and had supported the development of shared administrative services since his 1997 reform programme [YUN 1997, p. 1390], so as to increase efficiency at the country level. A total of 52 UN Houses had been established, and five new ones were planned to open in 2003.

The resident coordinator system played a central role in field-level coordination, and its responsibilities had become more complex. Practical measures were being implemented to enhance the effectiveness of the system in facilitating joint programming, pooling of resources, and establishing common databases and knowledge networks. Mechanisms to select, train and appraise the performance of resident coordinators had improved, broadening the pool of candidates, while attempting to improve the gender balance. Major challenges to the optimal functioning of the system continued to be the mobilization of technical expertise and resources, and more active participation of all UN organizations, in particular specialized and technical agencies and regional commissions. More extensive use of information and communication technologies might lead to improvement.

UN organizations and the Bretton Woods institutions (the World Bank Group and the International Monetary Fund (IMF)) had been working over the past few years to create new opportunities for country-level cooperation, provide greater avenues for joint actions and increase interaction between their respective instruments. Both of them, in particular the World Bank, were recasting their priorities so as to focus on poverty and the MDGs. Areas for further cooperation included: support to national capacity development for policy design and budget management; support to more systematic monitoring and reporting on policy trends; development of policy and reform scenarios for the macro-economic frameworks underpinning PRSPs; alignment of donor assistance to PRSP priorities; efforts to address statistical deficiencies to monitor progress on the MDGs; and building results-based indicators into the PRSP framework.

Efforts to mainstream gender into programmes and policies were carried out through mechanisms such as thematic groups, CCAs and UNDAFs. The Inter-Agency Network on Women and Gender Equality (see p. 1187), chaired by the United Nations Development Fund for Women (UNIFEM), coordinated an assessment of 15 CCAs and UNDAFs, and a parallel assessment was led by UNICEF on CCA and UNDAF initiatives in West Africa. Both called for measures to clarify roles and responsibilities in respect of gender equality and women's rights at the country level, strengthen the capacity of gender theme groups in the CCA and UNDAF processes, improve availability of gender-disaggregated data, promote capacity-building, and ensure that lessons learned were shared within the system and with Governments and other partners. Concrete initiatives focused on the development of country-specific gender equality indicators and the identification of intermediary targets for achieving the MDGs.

The work of the United Nations in humanitarian assistance was linked to that in operational activities for development, especially for complex emergency situations such as civil strife and armed conflicts. There was increasing awareness among humanitarian agencies of the need to tailor emergency assistance in support of recovery and development and by development assistance providers for early involvement in rehabilitation efforts. There was also a growing recognition of the need for an integrated approach among all donors to ensure field-level coordination in transition periods. The use of ad hoc approaches and appeals processes in post-conflict periods, using a combination of methodological tools available to country teams, suggested that those teams needed more flexible mechanisms to support Governments and institutions in the early stages of post-conflict, while meeting urgent humanitarian needs.

Regional and subregional coordination of operational activities was encouraged through the involvement of the regional bureaux, among other things, in support of country-level preparation of CCAs and UNDAFs. A more systematic participation of the regional commissions in their preparation would be mutually beneficial.

UNDP played a lead role in promoting technical and economic cooperation among developing countries, and all UN system organizations had focal points for technical cooperation among developing countries. Advisory services provided by UN system organizations to developing countries increasingly relied on experts from those countries in such fields as judicial reform, local government, and information and communication technologies.

The Secretary-General, in an April report [E/2003/57] issued to complement his report on progress in implementing resolution 56/201, provided detailed statistical data on resources channelled through the organizations of the UN system for 2001, which the Council noted on 11 July (**decision 2003/225**).

The General Assembly, in **resolution 57/270 B** of 23 June (see p. 1468), recognized the progress achieved towards a more coherent UN performance in the development field, as reflected by the shared responsibility, cooperation and coordination among members of UNDG, and invited the UNDP Administrator, in his capacity as chair of UNDG, to report regularly to the Council on the Group's activities relating to the integrated and coordinated implementation of the outcome of major UN conferences and summits.

ECONOMIC AND SOCIAL COUNCIL ACTION

On 11 July [meeting 30], the Economic and Social Council adopted **resolution 2003/3** [draft: E/2003/L.20] without vote [agenda item 3 (a)].

Progress in the implementation of General Assembly resolution 56/201 on the triennial comprehensive policy review of operational activities for development of the United Nations system

The Economic and Social Council,

Recalling General Assembly resolution 56/201 of 21 December 2001 on the triennial comprehensive policy review of operational activities for development of the United Nations system and Economic and Social Council resolution 2002/29 of 25 July 2002,

Reiterating that the fundamental characteristics of the operational activities of the United Nations system should be, inter alia, their universal, voluntary and grant nature, their neutrality and their multilateralism as well as their ability to respond to development needs in a flexible manner, and that the operational activities of the United Nations system are carried out for the benefit of recipient countries, at the request of those countries and in accordance with their own policies and priorities for development,

Reaffirming and underscoring the collective commitment and political will of Member States to strengthening the role and capacity of the United Nations development system to assist developing countries in the implementation of the goals, targets and commitments set out in the United Nations Millennium Declaration and by the major United Nations conferences and summits,

Stressing that national Governments have the primary responsibility for their countries' development, and recognizing the importance of national ownership of development programmes,

Reiterating the need for all organizations of the United Nations development system, in accordance with their respective mandates, to focus their efforts at the field level in accordance with the priorities identified by recipient countries and with the goals, targets and commitments set in the Millennium Declaration and by the major United Nations conferences and summits,

1. *Takes note* of the reports of the Secretary-General on the progress in the implementation of General Assembly resolution 56/201, on assessment of the lessons learned by United Nations organizations from evaluation activities at the field level and on funding of development cooperation activities of the United Nations system;

2. *Takes note also* of the request contained in General Assembly resolution 57/270 B of 23 June 2003 to invite the Administrator of the United Nations Development Programme, in his capacity as chair of the United Nations Development Group, to present, on a regular basis, to the Economic and Social Council at its coordination segment, the activities carried out by the United Nations Development Group related to the integrated and coordinated implementation of the outcomes of the major United Nations conferences and summits;

3. *Takes note further* of the progress made in the reform of the United Nations development system, and calls for its continuation;

4. *Takes note* of the fact that most organizations of the United Nations system, within their respective mandates, are currently realigning their policies, strategies, programmes and activities on the basis of internationally agreed development goals, including those contained in the United Nations Millennium Declaration, including through mechanisms such as multi-year strategic frameworks, where they exist, the common country assessment and the United Nations Development Assistance Framework, as well as in the context of their contribution to national poverty reduction strategies, including poverty reduction strategy papers, where they exist;

Funding of operational activities for development of the United Nations system

5. *Reiterates* that regular/core resources, inter alia, because of their untied nature, are the bedrock of the operational activities of the United Nations and essential for the maintenance of the multilateral, neutral and universal nature of the United Nations development system;

6. *Notes with regret* that, although significant progress has been achieved with regard to the governance and functioning of the United Nations development system, there has not been, as part of that overall process of change, a significant increase in core resources for operational activities for development;

7. *Recognizes* that strengthening the role and capacity of the United Nations development system to assist countries in achieving their development goals requires continuing improvement in its effectiveness, efficiency, coherence and impact, along with a significant increase in and expansion of its resource base on a continuous, more predictable and assured basis;

8. *Invites* all United Nations funds and programmes, as well as the specialized agencies, to further explore possibilities to strengthen their resource base, including, as appropriate, through multi-year funding frameworks as resource management tools integrating programme objectives, results and resources;

9. *Calls upon* all donor countries and countries in a position to do so to substantially increase their contributions to the core/regular budgets of the United Nations development system, in particular the funds and programmes, and wherever possible, to contribute on a multi-year basis, and also stresses the need for further exploration of other sources of funding that could complement but should not replace traditional sources;

10. *Requests* the Secretary-General to undertake further analytical work on the issue of funding and to report to the General Assembly at its fifty-ninth session in the context of the triennial comprehensive policy review;

Capacity-building

11. *Reaffirms* the need for all organizations of the United Nations development system at the country level to focus on capacity-building as one of their primary objectives, within their respective mandates, and urges these organizations:

(a) To support recipient Governments and other relevant stakeholders in devising country-level strategies for capacity-building in the pursuit of internationally agreed development goals;

(b) To intensify inter-agency information sharing at the system-wide level on good practices and experience gained, results achieved, benchmarks and indicators, monitoring and evaluation criteria concerning capacity-building, and reflect them in the common country assessment and the United Nations Development Assistance Framework;

(c) To invite all organizations to include reporting on capacity-building in their annual reports to their respective governing bodies;

12. *Reiterates* that the United Nations development system should use, to the fullest extent possible and practical, national execution and available national expertise and technologies as the norm in the implementation of the operational activities;

Common country assessment and the United Nations Development Assistance Framework

13. *Requests* the United Nations development system and its country-level structures to continue their efforts to enhance the quality of the common country assessment, in particular its analytical aspects, and to strengthen the operational impact of the United Nations Development Assistance Framework, including by inviting the active engagement of the specialized agencies and other partners, as appropriate, in the formulation and the use of these instruments, under the leadership of national Governments;

14. *Welcomes* efforts by the members of the Executive Committee of the United Nations Development Group to explicitly link their programme support to national development goals and priorities, through the revised Framework and its results matrix, invites other United Nations funds and programmes and the specialized agencies to use the results matrix, and requests that the matrix be submitted to the Executive Boards as an annex to the country programme;

15. *Requests* United Nations funds, programmes and the specialized agencies to continue to ensure the alignment and integration of their operational activities for development with national development efforts and priorities, through the active and full government participation and leadership at all stages of the common country assessment and Framework processes, as well as broader involvement of all relevant stakeholders;

16. *Notes* the increased collaboration between the United Nations system and the Bretton Woods institutions, and invites the United Nations system and the Bretton Woods institutions to explore further ways to enhance cooperation, collaboration and coordination, including through greater harmonization of strategic frameworks, instruments, modalities and partnership arrangements, in full accordance with the priorities of the recipient Governments, and in this regard emphasizes the importance of ensuring, under the leadership of national authorities, greater consistency between the strategic frameworks developed by the United Nations funds, programmes and agencies and the Bretton Woods institutions, and the national poverty reduction strategies, including the poverty reduction strategy papers, where they exist;

17. *Also notes* the efforts of the United Nations Development Group to promote the role of the regional bureaux of the funds and programmes in assisting country teams in the preparation of the common country assessment and the Framework;

18. *Encourages* the regional commissions to provide, when requested, their inputs for the preparation of those frameworks;

Evaluation of operational activities for development

19. *Emphasizes* the importance of monitoring and evaluation of operational activities of the United Nations system in order to enhance their effectiveness and impact, and calls upon the Secretary-General to integrate in future reports a stronger focus on lessons learned, results and outcomes;

20. *Stresses* the need to ensure the full participation of national authorities as well as the involvement of relevant stakeholders in the design, programming, implementation and evaluation processes, as well as in the drafting of the terms of reference, the development of methodologies and indicators and the selection of teams in all evaluation exercises conducted at the field level;

21. *Recommends* that United Nations funds, programmes and the specialized agencies make systematic efforts to enhance the capacity for identifying, documenting and synthesizing lessons learned from evaluation activities in order to retain and absorb their results, ensure their dissemination, in particular at the country level, by placing the evaluation reports in the public domain using the Internet, and use evaluation findings and lessons learned in the design and implementation of programmes and projects, and also recommends that they assist national efforts to create country-level repositories of evaluation findings and lessons learned that are relevant in each national context, supporting the use of information and communication technology, national databases of lessons

learned from evaluation, the development of analysis, documentation, distillation and synthesis of those lessons learned, and promoting the development of publications and the use of other means of communication;

22. *Calls upon* all organizations of the United Nations system to make additional efforts to promote the development of national evaluation capacities, including capacities to make use of lessons learned from past United Nations activities that are relevant in each national context, and encourages them to communicate findings of evaluation activities and disseminate corresponding lessons learned to national entities, also, as appropriate, through more frequent use of local national languages;

23. *Recommends* that all organizations of the United Nations development system consider lessons learned and their dissemination as a specific required component of their activities and designate those responsible for monitoring the effectiveness of the lessons learned process both at Headquarters and at the country level;

24. *Requests* the organizations of the United Nations development system to encourage country teams to make greater use of lessons learned from evaluations in the preparation of the common country assessment, the United Nations Development Assistance Framework, individual country programmes and other relevant country documents and to encourage enhanced country-level absorption of lessons learned, including through the intensification of activities such as joint evaluations, as appropriate under the Framework umbrella, of programmes and joint support to national databases of lessons learned from evaluation;

Simplification and harmonization of rules and procedures on operational activities

25. *Welcomes* progress made by the members of the Executive Committee of the United Nations Development Group in the harmonization and simplification of rules and procedures, and requests the United Nations funds and programmes to enhance and accelerate their simplification and harmonization efforts to ensure full implementation of the programme of work submitted in 2002 before the end of 2004;

26. *Requests* that efforts be undertaken across the United Nations system, including the specialized agencies, to make progress in all the areas of simplification and harmonization of rules and procedures at the field level, taking into account efforts and ongoing initiatives by bilateral donors and multilateral development banks, with the ultimate intent of reducing transaction costs, increasing effectiveness and efficiency in aid delivery and enhancing government ownership of development processes through better coordination and management of external assistance;

27. *Requests* the funds and programmes of the United Nations system, through their Executive Boards, to include in their programmes of work the harmonization and simplification of recovery policies for non-core resources contributions;

28. *Requests* the Secretary-General, in due consultation with the funds and programmes, through the Executive Committee of the United Nations Development Group, to submit to the next substantive session of the Economic and Social Council, in 2004, a report on the assessment of the value added of the joint meetings of the Executive Boards and their impact on the operational activities segment of the Economic and Social Council and to make recommendations as appropriate;

Common premises and shared services

29. *Encourages* the members of the United Nations Development Group to continue their efforts in the area of common premises, shared services and joint offices, with the objective of ensuring higher quality and cost-effectiveness of country-level functioning of the United Nations system;

Resident coordinator system

30. *Reiterates* the need for greater participation by the specialized and technical agencies in the functioning of the resident coordinator system, encouraging all the organizations of the United Nations system to set in place innovative and collaborative ways to enable the resident coordinator system to tap, to an even greater degree, into the wealth of expertise in those areas that are relevant to support national efforts towards internationally agreed development goals;

31. *Also reiterates* the need to increase the number of women resident coordinators;

32. *Encourages* the resident coordinators to continue to work closely with the country representatives of individual agencies, including the World Bank and other relevant partners, in order to ensure effective coordination and collaboration under the leadership of national authorities, including in post-conflict situations;

33. *Requests* the United Nations Development Group and the Executive Committee on Humanitarian Affairs to continue their efforts to provide a coordinated response to the needs of countries in transition from relief to development;

34. *Encourages* the resident coordinator system to facilitate the formulation and use of integrated and flexible approaches in complex emergency and post-conflict situations, ensuring that all relevant partners, including those outside the United Nations system, are involved under the leadership and with the fullest involvement of the Government, wherever possible;

Gender mainstreaming in operational activities

35. *Calls upon* the organizations of the United Nations system to improve their gender mainstreaming efforts in operational activities of the United Nations system in all fields, including in support of poverty eradication, reiterating that the empowerment of women is a development priority, and to strengthen their efforts in support of the development of national capacities to improve the status of women in the context of development and poverty eradication policies;

South-South cooperation/economic and technical cooperation among developing countries

36. *Requests* the organizations of the United Nations system to take appropriate measures to improve the effective incorporation of technical cooperation among developing countries into their programmes and projects and to intensify efforts towards mainstreaming the modality of technical cooperation among developing countries, including through support for the activities of the Special Unit for Technical Cooperation among Developing Countries, and

encourages other relevant international institutions to take similar measures;

Guidelines for the next triennial comprehensive policy review

37. *Requests* the Secretary-General to focus the analysis for the triennial comprehensive policy review in 2004, in the context of the implementation of the internationally agreed development goals, including those contained in the Millennium Declaration, on:

(a) Assessment of the assistance that the United Nations development system provides to developing countries in order to support their efforts to pursue poverty eradication, economic growth and sustainable development;

(b) Integration of operational activities for development of the United Nations system with national efforts and priorities;

(c) Identification of measures for further improvement in coherence and efficiency of the United Nations system at the country level;

(d) Harmonization and simplification processes, further identifying possible areas for an agenda for the period from 2004 to 2007;

(e) Identification of ways to enhance capacity-building in order to assist developing countries to pursue poverty eradication, economic growth and sustainable development;

(f) Adequacy of United Nations development funding, in the light of the challenges that internationally agreed development goals present to the developing countries and the international community, and to make recommendations accordingly, and the identification of ways to ensure adequate funding for operational activities in this context;

(g) Adequacy of human resources and necessary skills available at the country level within the United Nations system to support national efforts and priorities;

(h) Effectiveness of the reforms of the operational activities of the United Nations in improving development results and outcomes and increasing the coherence, efficiency and quality of programming at the country level, ensuring in this regard that particular attention is paid to the contribution of the common country assessment and the United Nations Development Assistance Framework and the associated results matrix in improving operational effectiveness;

(i) Contribution of the Millennium Development Goals as a framework to support the alignment of the operational activities of the United Nations system with national development efforts and priorities;

(j) Results identified, outcomes and lessons learned at the country level from evaluation activities.

Assessment of lessons learned

In response to General Assembly resolution 56/201 [YUN 2001, p. 784], the Secretary-General, in May [E/2003/64], issued an assessment of the lessons learned by UN organizations from field-level evaluation activities.

He stated that the demand for lessons from evaluation had been changing as the content and context of operational activities had changed, shifting the focus of evaluations away from input-oriented accountability towards strategic and policy issues and questions of development success. Evaluation ultimately had to satisfy the requirements of accountability, better programme management and lesson learning. Major contributors to development cooperation activities, in particular bilateral agencies, had devoted considerable attention to evaluation issues and to lesson learning and feedback. However, those considerations focused on management and accountability issues. The evaluation of UN operational activities, however, required special consideration because of the UN role as an advocate and catalyst of developing countries' efforts to pursue agreed goals. The evaluation of the effectiveness of UN system activities should be able to identify both lessons learned and good practices that might assist Member States in pursuing policies or programmes that moved towards those goals and had a direct bearing on the immediate impact of operational activities.

The report identified weaknesses and strengths in identifying lessons learned from evaluations. In general, it found that not enough efforts were invested in documenting and synthesizing lessons learned from evaluations carried out at the project, programme, thematic and country levels. The capacity to identify lessons learned was small, a major cause of the limited institutional memory of the UN system at the field level. There was a lack of sufficient professional evaluation staff at the headquarters and country levels. The process for incorporating lessons learned from evaluations in training courses and other learning mechanisms was lengthy, and evaluation results were not well disseminated across projects, offices and organizational units.

Among strengths of the lesson learning process, the report noted that most organizations had set up evaluation processes, providing coverage of most activities. Evaluation was often decentralized and linked to demand from local managers and country offices for project evaluations, and from headquarters managers and governing bodies for country programme evaluations and thematic studies. Current practice often relied on external evaluators, so as to preserve independence, with increasing emphasis being placed on the use of local evaluators. Evaluations were participatory, allowing for inputs by stakeholders, thereby increasing national ownership of the results. A small number of UN organizations used evaluation lessons learned in preparing CCAs and UNDAFs and in the collective evaluation of UNDAF outcomes.

The methods used to disseminate lessons learned included country-level workshops, publication of evaluation reports in several languages, the development of newsletters, the compilation of annual evaluation reports at the agency level, discussion among agency staff, posting lessons learned on intranets, and use of the Internet to reach a wider community. However, on the whole, the way UN system organizations planned and implemented strategies for communicating and disseminating lessons learned from evaluations at both the country and headquarters level was inadequate.

To improve learning from evaluations, the report listed a number of needs that had been identified in its analysis, including: a strong commitment by senior management to organizational learning and to holding managers accountable for taking lessons learned into account; enhancing the independence of the office managing evaluations and producing lessons, and giving it adequate resources; preparing a management response to each major evaluation, along with follow-up proposals; organizing wide dissemination of evaluation findings and lessons in accessible summary formats; greater use of self-evaluation using appropriate evaluation methods; and allocating adequate resources to extracting lessons from evaluations. The report suggested that UN organizations make efforts to enhance the capacity for identifying, documenting and synthesizing lessons learned from evaluation activities in order to absorb their results and to ensure their dissemination and use in project design and implementation. They should also consider lesson learning and dissemination as a specific component of their annual plans and identify the persons to be responsible for monitoring their effectiveness at headquarters and in the field.

Funding of development cooperation activities

The Secretary-General, in response to General Assembly resolution 56/201 [YUN 2001, p. 784], reported in June on the funding of development cooperation activities of the UN system [E/2003/89]. He analysed the issue in the new context emerging from the 2000 United Nations Millennium Summit [YUN 2000, p. 47] and the 2002 International Conference on Financing for Development [YUN 2002, p. 953], and highlighted the development role of the UN system through its operational structures. The report reviewed the pattern of UN development funding, its trends and current modalities, outlined traditional public funding sources, private initiatives and domestic resources, and described the implications of the relationships with the Bretton Woods institutions and the consequences of the core funding shortfall. It recommended renewed dialogue among Member States with a view to reaching agreement at the 2004 triennial comprehensive policy review on strengthening the resource foundation for the operational work of the system.

The Secretary-General said that, as the Millennium Summit and the International Conference on Financing for Development had created a new development context with a broad consensus on a shared agenda and had given renewed impetus to international development cooperation and a new global partnership, it was time to address the role of UN operational activities for development in helping to achieve those goals. The UN development system needed to be strengthened with increased funding in order to work effectively with national authorities and other bilateral and multilateral actors at the country level, but the issue was how to ensure that UN system operational activities were funded at an adequate level and on a stable footing. The system of annual voluntary contributions for funding UN system operational activities for development had served reasonably well over the past 50 years, and the recent introduction of multi-year funding frameworks (MYFFs) [YUN 1999, p. 806] was intended to reduce the annual volatility of multi-year programming. However, in spite of reforms to increase effectiveness and efficiency, and the increase in overall funding for UN development activities from $5.61 billion in 1992 to $7.73 billion in 2001 (excluding the World Bank Group), core or regular resources of UN funds and programmes had, with the exception of WFP, remained stagnant or declined, although they improved slightly in 2002. The long-term stagnation in resource flows, when adjusted for inflation, resulted in a decline of the resource base in real terms. Moreover, while development dynamics had not kept pace with the changing demands placed on the system, there was a need not only for new money but for new partners and new ways of working with them. Also, increases in humanitarian assistance needs had tended to crowd out the resources required for long-term development, especially in the case of WFP and UNICEF, and reconstruction and post-conflict recovery initiatives arising from post-emergency situations, were increasingly absorbing resources, making them unavailable for regular development programmes.

Within the UN development cooperation system, the funding of the four funds and programmes—UNDP, UNFPA, UNICEF and WFP—was based on annual voluntary contributions, split between core (or regular) and non-core (or supplementary) funds. Over 95 per cent of their core resources came from member countries of the Development Assistance Committee of the Organisation for Economic Co-operation and Development (OECD/DAC), and efforts to broaden that donor base had not borne fruit. While core funding remained the backbone of their development work, non-core funding had increased in recent years, becoming larger than core funding for UNDP and UNICEF. A major concern was the continuing decline in UNDP core funding, from a peak of $1.2 billion for 1992 to a low of $634 million in 2000, while non-core contributions, in the form of third-party cost-sharing arrangements, trust funds and extrabudgetary resources, increased fourfold, from $408 million in 1992 to over $1.6 billion in 2001. UNFPA regular resources were unstable, reaching $337 million in 1997, declining to $244 million in 1999 and returning to $260 million in 2001. Non-core funding had increased over those years. UNICEF funding followed the same pattern, while regular contributions to WFP (which included a considerable portion for humanitarian purposes) rose sharply in 1999, as a result of a change in the criteria for distinguishing between core and non-core resources. Other UN entities, such as the United Nations Human Settlements Programme (UN-Habitat), the United Nations Environment Programme (UNEP), the United Nations Conference on Trade and Development, the Department of Economic and Social Affairs and the regional commissions, were funded largely by extrabudgetary resources. The specialized and technical agencies' activities had been adversely affected by the paucity of programmable funds, and their assessed funding had remained stagnant. Their long-term pattern of technical co-operation funding had also been affected by the reduction of UNDP funding for their activities.

The effectiveness of all the modalities used for funding UN system development cooperation—voluntary contributions, including annual contributions to the core or regular resources and ad hoc non-core or supplementary contributions, the MYFF initiated in UNDP, UNICEF and UNFPA, assessed contributions, such as the Indicative Scale of Contributions used by UNEP, "negotiated replenishment" adopted by the International Development Association and the International Fund for Agricultural Development, and the "programme approach", based on the provision of ad hoc funds linked to a specific thematic issue, such as the Joint United Nations Programme on HIV/AIDS—could not be judged only on technical grounds, since their suitability depended on the political will of potential contributors and none of them per se could protect the UN system from volatility or inadequacy of funding, unless there was a clear political will on the part of a wide donor base to provide sufficient funding.

However, while funding of operational activities was the primary responsibility of Governments, there was room for intensifying collaborative approaches between the UN development system and the private sector, both domestic private firms and foreign companies. Involvement of the business community was increasing. Collaboration with the private sector had traditionally taken the form of participation of international financial institutions, such as the International Finance Corporation of the World Bank Group, but other schemes included management contracts, private financing of programme components, joint ventures, leasing contracts and arrangements for contracting out services. In spite of those opportunities, public financing, principally official development assistance (ODA), would continue to play the main role in funding UN system development activities, with traditional donors (OECD/DAC countries) being its major donors, although it would be desirable to expand the donor base by increasing the share of other countries and new constituencies, including some developing countries. Moreover, there were encouraging signs that the donor community was making significant progress in fulfilling its commitment to deliver ODA equal to 0.7 per cent of its gross national product. New thinking was also needed on the relationship between UN development funding and domestic financial resources, which bore the brunt of development financing in the vast majority of countries, usually in the form of national contributions to co-finance budgets and in-kind contributions. Tighter links would therefore be required between financial disbursements for UN activities funded by donors and domestic contributions provided by government or non-government sources. Collaboration between the United Nations and the Bretton Woods institutions had increased, including through joint funding, and there had been a shift towards grant funding through the World Bank.

The report noted that all the organizations had implemented reforms designed to bolster their performance, intensifying collaboration to harmonize support for recipient countries, with the expectation that donors would respond with substantial additional and predictable resources. However, there had not been any significant change in the funding dynamics of the UN development system. If the internationally agreed development goals were to be achieved, all countries would have to commit themselves in terms of policies, actions and resource allocations, on a sustained basis, and the international community would have to match its declarations of support with real and substantial increases in ODA over a sustained period.

Financing of operational activities in 2002

Expenditures of the UN system on operational activities, excluding loans through the World Bank Group, totalled $7.3 billion in 2002 [A/59/84-E/2004/53], the most recent year for which figures were available, as compared to $7.1 billion in 2001. Of the 2002 amount, $2,138 million was distributed in development grants by UNDP and UNDP-administered funds, $1,772.4 million by specialized agencies and other organizations from extrabudgetary sources, $1,592.2 million by WFP, $1,043.9 million by UNICEF, $479.3 million by specialized agencies and other organizations from regular budgets, and $312.5 million by UNFPA.

The UNDP Administrator, in an August report on UN system technical cooperation expenditures in 2002 [DP/2003/30 & Add.1], said that the $7.3 billion in technical cooperation between the UN system and the developing world in 2002 was an all-time high, representing a 2.4 per cent increase over the previous year. The high delivery rate by the UN system was due to the positive growth rates attained by other specialized agencies, funds and programmes, UNDP and UNICEF, which posted respective increases of 10.6 per cent (at $2.3 billion), 5.5 per cent (at $2.1 billion) and 3.2 per cent (at $1 billion) in 2002. Although WFP and UNFPA experienced a slight contraction in their delivery levels, their respective performances nevertheless allowed UN system technical cooperation to reach an all-time high.

By region, Africa was the largest recipient, with 25.1 per cent, or $1.8 billion of development assistance. The Asia and Pacific region received the second largest amount, $1.7 billion or 23.1 per cent, reflecting an increase of 9 per cent over the 2001 figure. Latin America and the Caribbean received the third largest share (19 per cent, or $1.4 billion), followed by the Arab States (17 per cent, or $1.2 billion), and Europe and the Commonwealth of Independent States (CIS) (6.6 per cent, or $483 million). Other global and interregional activities received 9.2 per cent, or $678 million. The three countries receiving the most development assistance were Afghanistan ($355 million), Brazil ($344 million) and Iraq ($340 million).

The health and humanitarian assistance sectors accounted for 41.2 per cent of the total technical cooperation expenditure, or $3 billion, an increase of 2.3 per cent.

On 12 September [E/2003/35 (dec. 2003/29)], the UNDP/UNFPA Executive Board took note of the Administrator's report on technical cooperation expenditure for 2002.

At the 2003 United Nations Pledging Conference for Development Activities (New York, 4 November) [A/CONF.204/3], Governments made pledges to UN programmes and funds concerned with development. The Conference noted that several Governments were not in a position to announce their contributions but proposed to communicate such contributions when they were able to do so.

The Secretary-General provided a statement of contributions pledged or paid at the 2002 Pledging Conference, as at 30 June 2003, to 21 funds and programmes [A/CONF.200/2]. The total amounted to some $0.8 billion.

Establishment of World Solidarity Fund

In April, the Secretary-General transmitted to the General Assembly and the Economic and Social Council a progress report of the UNDP Administrator on measures taken to operationalize the World Solidarity Fund [A/58/72-E/2003/53], submitted in accordance with Assembly resolution 57/265 [YUN 2002, p. 831]. The Fund was established in February as a UNDP trust fund, whose purpose was to eradicate poverty and promote social and human development in developing countries. It would operate by encouraging the private sector and individual citizens to fund its endeavours, and would support requests received from developing countries for financing poverty alleviation projects, including initiatives from community-based organizations and small private sector entities. Following its establishment, steps were taken to operationalize and publicize the Fund, but at the time of the report, the Fund had not received contributions.

The Administrator proposed the establishment of a high-level committee to define the strategy of the Fund.

ECONOMIC AND SOCIAL COUNCIL ACTION

On 11 July [meeting 31], the Economic and Social Council adopted **resolution 2003/4** [draft: E/2003/L.21] without vote [agenda item 3 (a)].

World Solidarity Fund

The Economic and Social Council,

Recalling General Assembly resolutions 55/210 of 20 December 2000, 56/207 of 21 December 2001 and 57/265 of 20 December 2002,

Recalling also the United Nations Millennium Declaration adopted on 8 September 2000 by heads of State and Government,

Recalling further the Monterrey Consensus, of the International Conference on Financing for Development, and the Johannesburg Declaration on Sustainable Development, as well as the Plan of Implementation of the World Summit on Sustainable Development

("Johannesburg Plan of Implementation"), adopted at the World Summit on Sustainable Development,

1. *Takes note* of the note of the Secretary-General transmitting the report of the Administrator of the United Nations Development Programme on the establishment of the World Solidarity Fund;

2. *Endorses* the decision of the World Summit on Sustainable Development to establish the World Solidarity Fund to eradicate poverty and to promote social and human development in the developing countries, while stressing the voluntary nature of the contributions and the need to avoid duplication of existing United Nations funds and encouraging the role of the private sector and individual citizens relative to Governments in funding the endeavours, as set out in the Johannesburg Plan of Implementation;

3. *Recognizes* the important potential contribution of the Fund to the achievement of the Millennium Development Goals, in particular the objective to halve, by 2015, the proportion of people living on less than one dollar a day and the proportion of the people who suffer from hunger;

4. *Takes note* of the setting up in February 2003 of the World Solidarity Fund as a trust fund of the United Nations Development Programme, subject to the financial rules and regulations as adopted by the Executive Board of the United Nations Development Programme/United Nations Population Fund;

5. *Encourages* Member States, international organizations, the private sector, relevant institutions, foundations and individuals to contribute to the Fund;

6. *Requests*, in this regard, the Administrator of the United Nations Development Programme to take further measures to operationalize the Fund by establishing on an urgent basis the high-level committee whose task it is to define the strategy of the Fund, inter alia, to mobilize the financial resources to enable it to start its activities in the field of poverty alleviation;

7. *Also requests* the Administrator of the United Nations Development Programme to take all necessary measures to publicize the Fund and to raise awareness of its existence among the public and private sectors as well as civil society;

8. *Invites* developing countries, as soon as resources are made available to the Fund, to identify indicative projects to be submitted for financing by the Fund, and requests the United Nations Development Programme to cooperate with national authorities in this regard;

9. *Requests* the Secretary-General to request the Administrator of the United Nations Development Programme to submit a progress report on the operationalization of the Fund to the Economic and Social Council at its substantive session in 2004.

Technical cooperation through UNDP

The UNDP Administrator, in his annual report for 2003 [DP/2004/16], described the results of the internal reform that was initiated in the UNDP Business Plans 2000-2003 [YUN 1999, p. 802]. Those results illustrated the transformation that had taken place in the organization and were reported against each of the five pillars and projected outcomes of the original Business Plans: policy, partnerships, people, performance and resources. In terms of policy, UNDP had become a stronger global advocate for human development. It had worked to operationalize the UN strategy for implementing the MDGs, linking global and country-level campaigning for the MDGs with research, and the institutional and financial reforms needed to achieve them. The United Nations Development Assistance Framework (UNDAF) guidelines had placed the MDGs at the centre of the UN system work at the country level. UNDP also played a leading role in discussions with other development actors on ways to strengthen linkages between the MDGs and the poverty reduction strategy papers (PRSPs), resulting in a joint UNDG/World Bank/IMF statement on the relationship between the two instruments and their respective roles. UNDP's advocacy work related to the *Human Development Report* was complemented by regional and national human development reports. The multi-year funding framework (MYFF) 2004-2007 (see p. 901) grouped UNDP's work around five strategic areas within the MDG framework and reduced by 25 per cent the number of service lines in which UNDP was involved. As a result, UNDP withdrew its programme and technical capacity in non-priority areas and refined a niche in areas such as HIV/AIDS and crisis prevention and recovery. Resident representatives were equipped to respond more swiftly and comprehensively to programme country partner needs, and development policy staffing had been radically restructured. More than two thirds of the international policy experts were located in nine subregional resource facilities. Knowledge management was being consolidated for all practice areas, and UNDP staff were held accountable for their contributions to knowledge networking and organizational learning. UNDP had also become a highly networked organization, creating new development opportunities through strategic partnerships, including with the World Bank, the European Commission and non-State actors, particularly the business sector. Progress in the engagement of UNDP with civil society, a critical element to achieving the MDGs, was evidenced by the positive response of those organizations' partners.

The challenges ahead for UNDP needed to be viewed in the context of the new security environment facing the organization and the constraints it imposed on many aspects of its programmes.

Against that backdrop, analysis of the 2000-2003 MYFF and the formulation of the 2004-2007 MYFF, the reformed UNDP programming process had identified a number of key challenges for the organization over the coming years, including the need to improve conceptual clarity and sharpen strategic focus by aligning results, organizational capacities and resources, and better reflect the MDGs; strengthen the coherence and effectiveness of the UN system at the country level; move results orientation to the next stage by encouraging knowledge sharing and skills development; and consolidate reform into a framework to improve performance, advance the UNDP mission, promote partnerships and expand the external support base for the organization.

The Administrator stated in his report to the Economic and Social Council [E/2004/4-DP/2004/12] that UNDP continued to assist developing countries in strengthening governance and enabling all actors in the national development context to play a mutually supportive role in achieving economic growth by harnessing the knowledge potential of the Internet and attracting international financial flows. UNDP support to the information and communication technologies (ICT) for development programme had expanded from 16 to 52 countries between 2000 and 2002. Some 26 countries had received UNDP support in preparing national ICT strategies and policies. Its support to national economies in attracting international financial flows facilitated by globalization was reflected in its support of the New Partnership for Africa's Development [YUN 2002, p. 907]. Those efforts led to UNDP support of the development of African stock exchanges and of the African Capital Markets Development Forum in April 2003, a joint initiative with the African Stock Exchanges Association and the New York Stock Exchange. In late 2003, UNDP decided to mainstream ICT elements into all of its practice areas.

As part of UNDP's work towards achieving the MDGs, the Millennium Project put a basic infrastructure in place and a first set of outputs was delivered by mid-2003. Twenty-five eminent experts were recruited to serve as task force coordinators. Task forces held their second meetings in 2003. A major contribution was made by the task forces and by the secretariat of the *Human Development Report* towards achieving the MDGs, which included the Millennium Development Compact, a joint effort of the Human Development Report Office and the Millennium Project that outlined how the MDGs could form the core of a goal-oriented development system. The Millennium Development Goals Campaign unit was in place and the building blocks of the Campaign were taking shape. A key focus would be to promote campaigns in developing countries, building on awareness-raising initiatives launched by UNDP country offices and UN country teams. Almost 50 MDG country reports had been produced, and production was planned for 60 more. Five countries had produced their second reports. UNDP took the lead in revising the UNDG guidance note on country monitoring with inputs from several UN organizations.

UNDP/UNFPA Executive Board

In 2003, the UNDP/UNFPA Executive Board held two regular sessions (20-23 January and 8-12 September) and an annual session (6-19 June), all in New York [E/2003/35].

At the first regular session, the Board adopted six decisions, including one that gave an overview of the Board's actions taken at that session [E/2003/35 (dec. 2003/6)]. Other decisions dealt with improvement of the Board's working methods (see p. 892); assistance to Myanmar (see p. 893); the financial situation of the United Nations Office for Project Services (UNOPS) (see p. 908); an independent review of UNOPS (see p. 907); and implementation of the recommendations of the Board of Auditors (see p. 904).

The Executive Board, at its annual session, adopted 15 decisions. In addition to an overview decision that summarized the action taken at that session [dec. 2003/21], the Board adopted decisions regarding UNFPA funding commitments, joint programming, assessment of its MYFF, delegation of personnel authority and its annual report (see PART THREE, Chapter VIII), and others on joint programming with UNDP (see p. 898); assessment of the UNDP MYFF, 2000-2003, and guidance in preparing the new MYFF, 2004-2007 (see p. 901); the United Nations Capital Development Fund (UNCDF) (see p. 914); technical cooperation among developing countries (see p. 911); funding commitments to UNDP (see p. 903); UNOPS (see p. 907); internal audit and oversight for UNDP, UNFPA and UNOPS (see p. 910); joint field visits (see p. 893); and the Global Environment Facility (see p. 1046).

At its second regular session, the Board adopted eight decisions, including an overview decision [dec. 2003/29]. The other decisions concerned the UNDP biennial support budget, 2004-2005 (see p. 903); the biennial support budgets, 2004-2005, for UNCDF (see p. 914) and the United Nations Development Fund for Women (see p. 1194); the UNDP MYFF, 2004-2007 (see p. 901); UNDP evaluation (see p. 899); UNOPS revised budget estimates for 2002-2003 and budget estimates for 2004-2005 (see p. 909); an independent review of UNOPS (see p. 908); and the UNFPA support budget for 2004-2005 (see p. 1091).

The Economic and Social Council, by **decision 2003/225** of 11 July, took note of the reports of the UNDP/UNFPA Executive Board on its 2002 second regular session and its 2003 first regular session.

Working methods

At its first regular session in January, the UNDP/UNFPA Executive Board approved its work plan for 2003 [DP/2003/CRP.1]. It considered a follow-up report on the rationalization of documentation and the streamlining of its working methods [DP/2003/CRP.6], submitted by the secretariat in response to a request by Board members. The report stated that, although there had been a net improvement in the size, content and quality of documents submitted to the Board, a more focused, action-oriented and clearer presentation was still needed, providing a range of options to facilitate policy formulation. The Board should also restrict the number of documents it received for discussion. As to organizational and procedural changes, the report suggested that: informal thematic meetings should take place during Board sessions; UNDP and UNFPA country programmes should be discussed together; interaction between programme and donor countries should be improved through thematic working sub-groups; Board decisions should be communicated more quickly to Member States and its contacts with programme countries improved; and terms of reference should be drawn up for field visits. Other proposals called for a joint informal meeting between the Board and the OECD Development Assistance Committee to exchange views on development policy, shifting from informal to formal discussions with regard to issues such as field visits and joint meetings of the Boards, at which cross-cutting issues of a more strategic nature should be proposed for discussion.

Taking note of the follow-up report, the Board, in January [dec. 2003/1], encouraged a closer relationship between its deliberations and the work in the field, keeping in mind the need to enhance country-driven programming. It decided to include the item on improving its working methods in the agenda of its 2003 annual session and invited Member States, through its Bureau, to submit contributions before 15 May on the rationale for doing so and specific proposals in that regard.

At the Board's annual session in June [E/2003/35], a number of areas for improvement were proposed, including expediting the submission of reports to delegations to allow sufficient time for review; ensuring that meetings of the Board were more focused, while encouraging informal and joint statements; and abolishing the Board's second regular session as it coincided with the opening of the General Assembly. The Board called on its Bureau to follow up on those suggestions and to report accordingly.

Reappointment of UNDP Administrator

The Secretary-General, in an April note [A/57/110], informed the General Assembly that, following consultations with members of the UNDP Executive Board, he was seeking the Assembly's confirmation of the appointment of Mark Malloch Brown as Administrator of UNDP for a further four-year term of office beginning on 1 July 2003. Mr. Malloch Brown was first appointed to that position on 1 July 1999.

By **decision 57/415** of 15 April, the Assembly confirmed the reappointment of Mr. Malloch Brown.

UNDP/UNFPA reports

In January [dec. 2003/6], the UNDP/UNFPA Executive Board took note of the reports of the UNDP Administrator [DP/2003/5] and the UNFPA Executive Director [DP/FPA/2003/2] to the Economic and Social Council and agreed to transmit them to the Council.

In June [dec. 2003/21], the Board took note of the UNDP Administrator's 2002 annual report [YUN 2002, p. 862].

The Council, by **decision 2003/225** of 11 July, took note of the combined annual reports of the UNDP Administrator and the UNFPA Executive Director to the Council [E/2003/13].

In response to General Assembly resolution 57/264 [YUN 2002, p. 841], the Administrator reported in April [DP/2003/17] on strengthening consultations with member States on the *Human Development Report* (see p. 864). Since 1994, UNDP had sought to improve the process of consultation with member States to refine the methodologies used in preparing the *Report*, with a view to improving quality and accuracy without compromising editorial independence. Over the years, those consultations had taken place at three points in the preparation process, and provided an opportunity for an exchange of information between the Human Development Report Office and the Board. The Office made three proposals for improving the consultation process: increasing the number of consultations with the Executive Board to five; improving the quality of consultation by circulating the proposed "messages" of the report earlier than in previous years; and holding special consultations on specific issues.

In June [dec. 2003/21], the Executive Board took note of the report on strengthening consultations with member States on the *Human Development Report* and the comments made thereon.

By **decision 2003/225** of 11 July, the Council also took note of the Administrator's report.

UNDP operational activities

Country programmes

The UNDP/UNFPA Executive Board, at its first regular session in January [dec. 2003/6], approved country programmes for Bahrain, Bolivia, Botswana, Cameroon, Cape Verde, the Comoros, Côte d'Ivoire, Cuba, the Democratic Republic of the Congo, the Dominican Republic, Equatorial Guinea, Guinea-Bissau, India, Jordan, Liberia, the Libyan Arab Jamahiriya, Malaysia, Maldives, Mali, Mauritania, Nigeria, Papua New Guinea, Samoa, Seychelles, Timor-Leste and Venezuela, and multi-country programmes for the Cook Islands, Niue and Tokelau, and the Pacific island countries. It approved the extensions of country cooperation frameworks (CCFs) for the Central African Republic and Thailand [DP/2003/8], and took note of the corrigendum to the second CCF for Panama [DP/CCF/PAN/2/Corr.1].

Also at its January session [dec. 2003/2], the Board, recognizing the critical humanitarian and basic human development needs of the people of Myanmar, took note of the Administrator's note on assistance to that country [DP/2003/3] and of the report submitted by the independent assessment mission to Myanmar, in particular the strategic issues and challenges it raised. The Board encouraged UNDP to enhance the impact of the Human Development Initiative, phase IV, taking into account the report submitted by the independent assessment mission.

At its annual session in June [dec. 2003/21], the Board took note of the first country programme outlines for Benin, Croatia, Ecuador, Kenya, the Niger, Pakistan, the Russian Federation and Thailand. It took note of the first one-year extensions of second CCFs for Angola, Mauritius, Tajikistan, the former Yugoslav Republic of Macedonia, Uruguay and Zimbabwe [DP/2003/16], and approved the two-year extension of the second CCF for Georgia [DP/2003/16] and the one-year extension of the second global cooperation framework. The Board took note [dec. 2003/15] of the reports on the field visits to Mozambique [DP/2003/CRP.10 & Add.1] and Ecuador [DP/2003/CRP.11]. It considered those visits an important contribution to its engagement in the work of the funds and programmes at the country level, and, in particular, to understanding the contribution made by the UN country team to national development strategies. Future joint field visits should focus on themes of common interest to the Executive Boards of UNDP/UNFPA, UNICEF and WFP, such as the UNDAF arrangements, the work of the UN country team on the MDGs and/or other cross-cutting themes. Noting that joint field visits could place a burden on host Governments and the United Nations, the Board requested that that be taken into account in deciding on destinations and the duration of future visits and called for cooperation between the Boards in preparing future joint field visits.

At its second regular session in September [dec. 2003/29], the Board took note of draft country programme documents for the Central African Republic, the Congo, Lithuania, Poland and Sierra Leone. It approved a two-year extension of the CCF for Peru and took note of the one-year extensions of the CCFs for Bosnia and Herzegovina and Chile [DP/2003/37/Rev.1]. The Board took note of the Administrator's note on UNDP assistance to Afghanistan [DP/2003/36] and an oral report on assistance to Myanmar.

UNDP programme results

Poverty reduction

UNDP's efforts to reduce poverty had progressed in recent years from implementing scattered, local poverty reduction projects to supporting national poverty reduction frameworks. The World Bank/IMF PRSP process, which promoted poverty reduction strategies, had given additional impetus to that transformation.

The 1999 results-oriented annual report [YUN 1999, p. 795] revealed that the bulk of UNDP support to poverty reduction was targeted at the community level, with "downstream" expenditures twice as high as "upstream" expenditures. More recently, support in that area had achieved greater focus and strategic coherence. UNDP support to national poverty reduction strategies focused on poverty monitoring and participation, but more needed to be done to strengthen government capacity to develop pro-poor policies and budgets. UNDP provided advice on resource and policy implications and options on human development and poverty reduction. Its support was also effective in facilitating the participation of civil society organizations in the PRSP process, particularly in Southern Africa.

UNDP's expanding role at the country level in furthering the MDG agenda through national goal setting and building capacity for monitoring, reporting and advocacy was reflected in the rapid increase in MDG-linked outcomes. In striving to build national ownership of, and broader participation in, the MDG campaign, UNDP was putting emphasis on partnering with civil society on MDG monitoring, reporting and advocacy. The challenges were to further cement the relationship between PRSPs and the MDGs, and to meet the deadline of producing MDG reports in every country by the end of 2004.

In the area of employment, although country offices had reported numerous small-scale interventions for generating self-employment, UNDP had not moved far enough upstream on employment issues to strengthen the strategic links between employment generation and poverty reduction. In order to increase the access of the poor to productive assets and resources, UNDP, in collaboration with UNCDF, had moved upstream to influence national legal and regulatory frameworks and develop national strategies for sustainable financial services for the poor. In the area of aid, trade and debt relief, through a series of high-profile publications on globalization and participation in initiatives, such as the Integrated Framework (for trade-related technical assistance to least developed countries), UNDP had positioned itself as an advocate for making aid, trade and debt relief work for the poor. Country reports showed, however, that those initiatives had not been translated into national and regional programmes.

UNDP role in the PRSP process

The UNDP Evaluation Office assessed the organization's role in the PRSP process from August 2002 to March 2003. The evaluation examined UNDP's role in the achievement of six key PRSP outcomes: increased country ownership of the preparation process; participation of civil society and the private sector; the multidimensional nature of poverty and pro-poor growth; coherence between PRSPs and other long-term national planning instruments; development partnerships; and poverty monitoring capacity at national and local levels. In a June report [DP/2003/24] on its findings, the evaluation team noted that PRSP represented an area of strategic importance to UNDP and a priority for its key global practice of poverty reduction, in particular through partnerships with the UN system, the World Bank and IMF.

Among its other findings, the report noted that only a few PRSPs had benefited from an analysis of the MDGs. Most countries had simply adopted the MDGs as opposed to adapting them through a national consultative process to make them country-specific. There was no clear link in PRSPs between poverty diagnosis and poverty reduction policies; rather, poverty reduction policies tended to be an "add-on" to a general growth strategy. Lack of clarity of the respective roles of the United Nations and the Bretton Woods institutions had hampered the development of a coherent approach by the UN country team in engaging the PRSP process at the country level. UN organizations did not always understand the relationship between the PRSP process and key UN coordination mechanisms, such as the common country assessment and UNDAF.

In terms of PRSP outcomes, progress was made in fostering government ownership of the PRSP process; however, in most cases progress was limited. Broad-based participation facilitated efforts to transform government ownership of the PRSP process into national ownership, and involved participation by civil society, including the private sector, in the drafting process. Fostering broad-based participation was the weakest outcome for UNDP. The pro-poor content of PRSPs increased when UNDP focused on promoting national discussions on the nature and social costs of poverty and on helping to give a voice to the poor. For long-term planning, PRSPs needed to be integrated into sectoral and thematic programmes. UNDP's partnerships with government and civil society were its strength, yet the full potential of strong partnerships had not been fully realized. Institutional arrangements for poverty monitoring to ensure PRSP implementation were inadequate.

Among the recommendations for strengthening UNDP's capacity to respond to requests from Governments for assistance in the PRSP process, the evaluation report suggested that the UNDP and UN country teams should influence the PRSP framework and support the process in a manner that promoted national ownership of the MDGs. UNDP and the Bretton Woods institutions should act together within the context of a UN team effort led by the resident coordinator, with UNDP taking the lead in UN commitment to the outcomes of the PRSP process. UNDP should make PRSP play a more central role in its country-level operations, and thus a more central role in its policy development and support activities. It should also maximize its potential to provide critical international input to the PRSP process. The success of the PRSP process depended in part on the ability to measure and assess progress in relation to intended outcomes, requiring clear benchmarks and performance criteria for making an evaluation and performance assessment possible. Strengthening evaluation capacity should be an integral part of PRSP assistance provided by external organizations.

The UNDP/UNFPA Executive Board, at its annual session in June [dec. 2003/21], took note of the evaluation of the UNDP role in the PRSP process.

UNDP management, responding to the PRSP evaluation in an August report [DP/2003/35], covered the issues of linking PRSPs to the MDGs, and growth and democratic governance, respectively, to poverty reduction and made recommendations for enhancing UNDP's role in the PRSP process. Overall, management agreed with the central point of the evaluation that the substantial and substantive roles of UNDP in the PRSP process should be enhanced and that the comparative advantage of UNDP lay in its ability to help Governments establish coordinated monitoring systems for poverty and the MDGs, particularly at the local level, and in supporting MDG reports and human development reports as tools for public advocacy and policy advocacy, respectively.

In September, the Executive Board, having considered the UNDP secretariat report containing the management response to the evaluation of UNDP's role in the PRSP process, encouraged UNDP to take into account that response in its PRSP work and requested the Administrator to make recommendations to the Board in 2004 [dec. 2003/25].

Democratic governance

The two most widely practised areas of democratic governance supported by UNDP at the country level were decentralized local governance and public administration reform, with outcomes reported in 90 and 80 countries, respectively. Recently, rapid growth had been observed in decentralization and local governance programme interventions. The major lessons learned in democratic governance involved garnering good practice and moving more rapidly to support integrated decentralization, local governance and public administration reform. Positive results were emerging in the Lao People's Democratic Republic and Mozambique. The area of electoral assistance was a starting point from which UNDP could move to support a broader governance programme. The challenge was to effect a better balance between short-term, event-specific election support projects and longer-term, development-oriented support to electoral systems. While some countries, such as Bangladesh, took a development-related approach, most UNDP projects in that sphere were of less than one year's duration.

In support of parliamentary development, a number of programmes had strengthened rules of procedure, administrative structures, information bases and training of elected members and staff. Several programmes worked to strengthen parliamentary oversight capacity.

Support to justice and human rights was among the fastest growing areas of the governance goal, focusing on strengthening the capacity and functioning of the formal justice sector (courts, prosecutors, justice ministries and police). The next step would be to link support to improved access to justice for the poor.

UNDP supported a number of "e-governance" programmes, with their focus ranging from increased transparency and accountability of national and local governments to the participation of civil society in governance issues. However, despite the demand, UNDP programmes were limited in scope and size by the lack of resources.

Demand had increased for UNDP assistance in multi-stakeholder dialogues on governance priorities and support for national capacities for an independent media and information. Approximately 30 countries had outcomes in that area, ranging from civic dialogue programmes in Latin America to independent media development support in the Gambia and Kazakhstan.

Crisis prevention and recovery

Crisis prevention was a key UNDP priority, with support falling into two categories: downstream support for dealing with the immediate impact of disasters, ranging from the removal of illicit small arms and landmines to the promotion of short-term economic recovery for the worst-affected communities; and upstream support aimed at building capacity for dialogue, facilitating multi-stakeholder consensus on divisive national issues, ranging from constitutional reform to the equitable distribution of natural resources, and addressing the deep-seated inequities and underdevelopment that often constituted the root causes of conflict. In the first category, UNDP provided short-term support for countries emerging from conflict. Joint programmes were launched with the World Bank and the Office of the United Nations High Commissioner for Refugees (UNHCR) to reintegrate refugees and displaced persons into their communities in Afghanistan, Sierra Leone and Sri Lanka. Assistance was provided to the Governments of Angola, Colombia and the Democratic Republic of the Congo. UNDP supported multi-stakeholder dialogue in Fiji, Guatemala, the Niger, Peru, Sao Tome and Principe and Venezuela. Training support in peaceful conflict resolution was provided to national stakeholders in a wide range of countries. In Guyana, UNDP was working with stakeholders to implement constitutional reforms vital to the management of internal tensions and to build dialogue and social cohesion. UNDP provided support for the revival of the civil service in Afghanistan and in other countries emerging from conflict.

Nearly half of UNDP programme countries were afflicted by crisis situations or were in some stage of post-crisis recovery. UNDP was increasingly regarded as a critical partner of the UN humanitarian and political arms, in particular for its role in helping to bridge the gap between humanitarian and reconstruction work in post-crisis countries. In 2003, that aspect was central to the corporate agenda as reflected in the MYFF. The UNDP/UNFPA Executive Board decided to strengthen the Bureau for Crisis Prevention and Recovery with 15 additional core posts, and to increase crisis funding from 5 per cent to 7.2 per cent of the UNDP core budget.

UNDP led the initial recovery effort in Afghanistan, organizing the UN system-wide immediate and transitional assistance programme. Building on that experience, UNDP, on behalf of UNDG, led the Iraq reconstruction process, for which it coordinated a needs assessment and led discussions on the establishment of the United Nations/ World Bank International Reconstruction Fund Facility for Iraq (see p. 353). Another example of collaboration on needs assessment was Liberia, for which the international reconstruction conference pledged $520 million for 2004-2005. Recognizing that collaboration had to go beyond assessment, UNDP, the World Bank and UNHCR addressed critical gaps in repatriation, reintegration, rehabilitation and reconstruction.

In an effort to remove explosive remnants of war and small arms in post-crisis countries, UNDP supported the collection and destruction of 123,730 weapons and 170 tons of ammunition. UNDP advocated for the inclusion of mine action considerations into the development plans and multi-year strategies of countries, donors and aid agencies. In Cambodia, mine action was integrated into the national poverty reduction strategy and adopted by the Government as a specific national MDG. Support in that area was also provided to Afghanistan, Albania, Colombia, Papua New Guinea, the Serbia and Montenegro province of Kosovo, Solomon Islands and Timor-Leste, which were all emerging from violent conflict, and to countries that might have been made vulnerable as a result of conflicts in their neighbourhood.

Environment and energy

UNDP's activities on the environment and natural resources, particularly with regard to water, energy, agriculture and biodiversity, was aimed at supporting poverty reduction and sustainable development. Most funding for environment and energy was derived from non-core sources, such as global trust funds, including the Global Environment Facility (GEF) (see p. 1045) and the Multilateral Fund for Implementation of the Montreal Protocol on Substances that Deplete the Ozone Layer [YUN 1987, p. 686] (see p. 1050). Capacity development to support national and local sustainable development strategies involved development frameworks and policies linked to environmental and human welfare. Country-level efforts included decentralization and governance issues critical to the sustainable use of natural resources, pollution reduction and the generation of livelihoods.

Water governance issues involving access to water resources and related services were increasing in importance. UNDP supported systems of water governance to ensure both ecological integrity and access to adequate safe water resources and services by poor people, as, for example, in Honduras. Other concerns were: strengthening water oversight institutions, legislation and policies, transboundary water issues, and community engagement for improved water management, water supply and sanitation services.

UNDP addressed both poverty and environmental concerns related to access to energy and the consequences of climate change. Significant strides were made in renewable energy, energy efficiency, clean energy technologies and reporting on implementation of the 1992 United Nations Framework Convention on Climate Change [YUN 1992, p. 681] (see p. 1049) in over 70 per cent of country operations. In support of agriculture and drylands management, UNDP worked on local and national planning and management frameworks to address legal, institutional and capacity needs, especially in least developed countries, focusing on the local resource base, agricultural viability and human vulnerability to desertification. In many countries, challenges related to land tenure, access to common lands and the legal status of rural populations. UNDP supported country efforts to maintain biodiversity and related ecosystem services. GEF expanded its mandate to include land degradation and persistent organic pollutants. With respect to ozone layer protection, the Montreal Protocol programme was moving away from individual projects towards multi-year, performance-based national and sectoral programmes requiring policy and institutional support, which were operational in 68 countries and were a significant source of programme resources.

Response to HIV/AIDS

The number of country offices reporting activities undertaken regarding HIV/AIDS had increased rapidly. Results were achieved in developing leadership skills and capacity for advocating, planning, managing and implementing HIV/AIDS responses at the national and local levels. Given the limited availability of resources, the main challenge for UNDP was to increase synergies between activities in order to achieve society-wide impact.

Leadership development programmes were implemented in 19 countries, with requests received from over 40 more. Six countries in the Caribbean participated in a regional leadership development programme. Those programmes supported a broad range of actors and sectors (government, civil society, the private sector and the UN system) working together for optimum results. In Ukraine, the programme generated partnerships among participants from several ministries, civil society and the private sector. In Senegal, 180 participants from Government, civil society and the private sector participated in the programmes and 65 per cent of them subsequently underwent HIV/AIDS testing.

Community capacity enhancement initiatives were implemented in nine countries, mainly in Africa and Asia, to strengthen the response of community-based organizations to HIV/AIDS, including community capacity for action and social change, and to link communities to national processes and responses. In Cambodia, the initiative addressed discrimination and domestic violence within communities and helped to link community action with national strategic planning and implementation at the local level. In Ethiopia, the programme was expanded to an additional 100 districts, and led to shifts in behaviour to control the spread of HIV/AIDS, including the commitment by communities to stop practices such as female genital mutilation.

Development planning activities introduced innovative approaches to strengthen governance, development planning and systems to respond comprehensively to HIV/AIDS across sectors, and at the national, sub-national and community levels. UNDP supported national strategic planning and implementation, addressing the gender dimensions of the epidemic in development plans. The "City Responses to HIV/AIDS" project was established in Brazil, Cambodia, Côte d'Ivoire, India, Lebanon, Malawi, Senegal and Trinidad and Tobago, and was strengthening local responses to the epidemic and helping to align city plans with national strategies.

UNDP worked with artists and the media in a number of countries, including Botswana, Ethiopia, Ghana, India, Lesotho, Malaysia, Nepal, South Africa and Swaziland, to generate a gender-sensitive response that respected the rights of people living with HIV/AIDS. In the Arab States, a regional programme motivated media and entertainment personalities to respond to HIV/AIDS, helping to break the silence surrounding the epidemic. In South Africa, an arts, film and media festival was held in Johannesburg in October.

The Southern Africa Capacity Initiative, a collaborative effort led by UNDP, aimed to address the challenges that Southern African countries faced in the loss of their most productive people. The Initiative worked to accelerate capacity development by synergizing the efforts of nine countries with the highest prevalence rates in the Southern African Development Community to stem the loss of capacity for planning and managing key sectors. Microsoft was a key partner in the Initiative, developing ways to help Governments use ICT to upgrade services, including distance learning and telemedicine.

Programme planning and management

UNDP Business Plans 2000-2003

In January, the Executive Board heard an oral presentation by the Administrator on the implementation of the UNDP Business Plans 2000-2003 [YUN 2000, p. 831], and considered a conference room paper [DP/2003/CRP.8], which articulated UNDP's strategy in five areas (policy, partnerships, people, performance and resources) (see p. 890). To measure the progress in UNDP's transformation, the Business Plans contained a scorecard with indicators that were distributed to all country offices and headquarters units.

The Administrator reported that the agenda for transformation was currently taking hold. UNDP was becoming a more practice-oriented, knowledge-driven organization and its outward-looking, more accountable approach had changed its relationship with both development partners and programme countries. The organization was making its voice heard, advocating and acting on the MDGs. Internally, UNDP had integrated learning and accountability for performance more coherently in its development agenda, while focusing on meeting its own performance targets, and it had progressively transformed itself into a field-oriented, decentralized, networked and service-focused organization. It had sharpened its focus in six priority areas: democratic governance, poverty reduction, crisis prevention and recovery, information and communication technology, energy and environment, and HIV/AIDS, which had become its practice areas. Thematic trust funds had been introduced for each practice area to promote the development of signature products and services. The transformation had created a totally new "business line" for UNDP and, in addition to contributing financial resources to programme country Governments, UNDP was currently providing timely, high-quality, knowledge-based advisory services. In the area of crisis prevention and recovery, UNDP assumed the unprecedented role in Afghanistan of bringing together the entire UN system around a single coherent strategy. From a risk-averse culture, UNDP had evolved into a more opportunity-driven organization, resulting in an array of partnerships with more than 30 foundations on every continent.

While internal restructuring had resulted in a more responsive Strategic Management Team within a leaner and more efficient headquarters structure, UNDP had also realigned its entire staff profile. The alignment of competencies with needs was implemented at all levels. In particular, an assessment centre, administered by an outside firm, was launched to evaluate candidates for resident representative/resident coordinator positions. The organization's culture of performance and accountability was reinforced, with leadership management being more performance driven. On the development effectiveness side, results-oriented annual reports were prepared each year for presentation at the annual sessions of the Executive Board. A more systematic performance rating of managers was introduced and staff performance was continuously evaluated through the Results and Competency Assessment instrument.

UNDP's transformation culminated in the adoption of the new UNDP brand, which was formally unveiled at the 2002 World Summit on Sustainable Development [YUN 2002, p. 821]. It was designed to represent the organization's integral connection to the United Nations and commitment to the goals of the UN Charter. UNDP was thus better placed to lead a concerted effort to help developing countries meet the MDGs.

An assumption of the Business Plans was that the changes would result in increased funding and the expansion of UNDP's resource base for development services. Realistic considerations reduced the initial MYFF targets for regular (core) resources to $900 million in 2003. While that target was not achieved, the negative trend in core resources was reversed.

Based on positive feedback from donor and programme country Governments, UNDP decided that its corporate priorities for 2003 would consist of the four 2002 priorities—the practice areas; the MDGs; performance and staff development; and the new ICT platform—and two additional ones, namely, UN reform, to ensure that UNDP supported the Secretary-General's reform agenda, and resources, to ensure that it had sufficient funds to do its work. In each of the six areas, the emphasis was being placed on integration. In the practice areas, UNDP intended to broaden its global network, elaborate concrete service lines and mobilize funds for the thematic trust funds. It would also introduce a more consistent thematic trust fund allocation process. Its results-based management, talent management and cost-sharing systems would be improved. The crisis prevention and recovery practice would receive special focus in 2003. As for the MDGs, UNDP would focus on capturing results at the country level, including improving the MDG reporting process, involving country teams in spreading awareness, developing capacity for monitoring and analysis, promoting national ownership, cooperating with the World Bank and regional development banks, and aligning policy and programme work to reflect the importance of the new MDG mandate.

As 2003 was the final year of the Business Plans, 2000-2003, and with the preparation of the 2004-2007 MYFF process and the 2004-2005 biennium budget (see p. 903), and the design of the new Enterprise Resource Planning System, UNDP would further align its global and country programmes with its practice areas, business processes, resource mobilization and advocacy efforts to ensure that each complemented the others in a focused and strategic manner. It would also further strengthen in 2003 its external partnerships and widen its geographical coverage with a view to enhancing its development impact.

In January [dec. 2003/6], the Executive Board took note of the oral presentation and the conference room paper on the UNDP Business Plans, 2000-2003.

Programme arrangements

The Executive Board, in a June decision [dec. 2003/7], requested the Administrator to submit in 2004 a written report containing an assessment, based on specific country examples, of UNDP experience in joint programming and other innovative and collaborative approaches aimed at improving programming effectiveness and reducing transaction costs for programme countries.

Monitoring and evaluation

In August [DP/2003/33], the UNDP Administrator, in his annual report on evaluation covering the period from July 2002 to June 2003, examined progress made by UNDP in deepening the culture of performance within the organization. The report, which drew upon evaluative evidence from a global trends analysis of development effectiveness and key country-level and corporate evaluations from UNDP to assess development results, elaborated UNDP efforts to promote more dynamic interaction between country operations and the evaluation function in order to improve the link between evaluations, substantive learning, decision-making and partnerships.

UNDP launched a number of initiatives to revamp its approach to managing for results, including an outreach strategy for promoting knowledge-sharing and lessons-learning throughout the organization and with partners, which was critical for improving development results at the country level. The report emphasized the importance of accessing "real-time" lessons where evaluation recommendations were fed back into decision-making for more effective learning and accountability, especially in view of the challenges in aligning UNDP strategic goals to the MDGs and fostering a broader range of partners for development effectiveness.

In December [E/2004/4-DP/2004/12], the Administrator said that the demand for evaluation and learning had improved substantially. A major focus was "real-time" lessons, which resulted in more effective learning and accountability. Together with outcome evaluations at the programme level and a select number of country evaluations, the development effectiveness report had emerged as a major platform for that perspective. The report assessed country-level development results, as well as global trends and efforts needed to improve effectiveness.

The 2003 development effectiveness report analysed more than 1,000 UNDP project and programme evaluations, country case studies and reports, which indicated that UNDP interventions were becoming more sustainable.

In August [DP/2003/35], UNDP management responded to the evaluation of the role of UNDP in the PRSP process (see p. 895).

The Executive Board, in September [dec. 2003/25], took note of the report on evaluation for 2002. It appreciated the feeding of lessons learned from previous evaluations into the second MYFF (2004-2007) (see p. 901). The Board encouraged UNDP's work in promoting partnerships on evaluation capacity with development with national administrations and welcomed the partnership on evaluation capacity development with other development partners in strengthening national evaluation capacity, such as cooperation through the International Development Evaluation Association and the Inter-Agency Working Group on Evaluation. It stressed the importance of using indicators developed with national Governments' participation.

The Board requested UNDP to enhance the evaluation of strategic and cross-cutting issues, such as the UNDP role in the UNDAF process and gender. Encouraging UNDP to continue linking UNDP policy work to its operational activities, the Board stressed the need to strengthen the lessons-learned process, especially at the country level. It welcomed the focus on deepening the performance culture and encouraged UNDP to continue working on capacity-building in evaluation. UNDP was urged to submit more thorough evaluation reports on UNIFEM, the United Nations Volunteers Programme and UNCDF. The Board encouraged UNDP to take into account the management response to the evaluation of the UNDP role in the PRSP process in its PRSP work, and requested the Administrator to report to the Board with recommendations in 2004.

Assessing MDG reports

The Evaluation Office conducted an assessment of the MDG reports in early 2003 and submitted in August an executive summary [DP/2003/34] of its report in preparation for a presentation of the full report in 2004. The objective was to assist UNDP and UN country teams to improve reporting on the progress made towards the attainment of the MDGs. The reports were emerging also as an important instrument for tracking and monitoring progress at the national level and for putting into place public campaign strategies for attaining the MDGs. Reporting on the MDGs began in 2001, with seven countries producing reports that year. By April 2003, 23 countries had produced MDG reports and another 50 reports were expected by the end of the year.

Overall, there were wide variations in country ownership, authorship and value added of the reports as advocacy tools and, contrary to expectations, those reports had not yet filtered into national debates on the MDGs. There was a need for convergence and stronger links between the monitoring and reporting processes of the MDGs, PRSPs and other comprehensive national development frameworks and reporting instruments, such as national human development reports, the common country assessment and UNDAFs. UNDP country offices in particular needed to focus on coordinating and harmonizing UN system-wide efforts in support of the MDGs and PRSPs and their alignment with national development frameworks.

There was a lack of clarity on the real value added of the MDG reports and there were major data gaps in reporting. Participation in the preparatory process was often constrained by a country's capacity. Statistical capacity varied within a country from one goal to another. UN system capacity also varied from one country to another and in-house UNDP capacities for policy advice, monitoring, reporting, advocacy, communication and coordination were limited. The assessment identified seven challenges (communication, participation, reporting, statistical, campaign, evaluation, global cooperation) that had to be met as UNDP and the United Nations moved to strengthen reporting on the MDGs.

The assessment report made recommendations for the UN system, specifically UNDP, and global development partners to meet those challenges. It called on the UN system to focus on the real value added of the reports and to position them to generate maximum debate and public action for the MDGs. A strategy was needed for establishing and nurturing partnerships with civil society organizations at both the global and country levels. The resident coordinator should develop a long-term strategic plan on MDG reporting that took into account key considerations at the country level, together with an effective advocacy and dissemination plan. UNDP should develop new programmes for the capacity-building of civil society organizations. UNDP and the UN system as a whole should mobilize global partners to mount a global initiative on statistics that would bring together international and national statistical organizations to engage in a comprehensive assessment of data needed for monitoring the MDGs. Global development partners should collectively explore collaborative mechanisms that would ensure regular reporting on the MDGs by countries.

The UNDP Administrator, in August [DP/2003/41], commenting on the report on the assessment of MDG reports, remarked that the findings were encouraging. UNDP appreciated the objective nature of the assessment, had taken note of the gaps and limitations identified, and agreed with most of the proposed actions. Consequently, it had revised the MDG report guidance note. The country teams were working to bring more civil society organizations into the process of preparing the MDG reports. It was working to differentiate the national human development reports from the MDG reports and to tap the potential synergies between the two.

On 12 September [dec. 2003/29], the Executive Board took note of the report on the assessment of the MDG reports and of the Administrator's note on that report.

Funding strategy

Multi-year funding framework

In May [DP/2003/12], the Administrator submitted an end-of-cycle assessment of performance of the multi-year funding framework (MYFF), 2000-2003, UNDP's primary strategic management tool for guiding its work, comprising a strategic results framework (SRF) and an integrated resources framework (IRF). The report examined the transformation of the organization over three years, provided a summary assessment of progress made towards each SRF goal and an in-depth analysis of specific achievements and trends. It also looked at the IRF for 2000-2002, which presented an overview of the use of UNDP resources during that period.

The Administrator, in a conference room paper [DP/2003/CRP.14], highlighted some substantive lessons learned from the MYFF, relating particularly to service lines within the major areas of UNDP activities. He also explored how the organization implemented and internalized results-based management, and analysed programme expenditures for 2000-2002.

The Executive Board, in June [dec. 2003/8], took note of the 2000-2003 MYFF end-of-cycle assessment and the supplementary information, and welcomed the progress achieved during 2000-2003 towards meeting the MYFF goals. It requested that, in the MYFF, 2004-2007, UNDP align and clarify the relationship between the MDGs, the strategic goals and the practice areas with a view to establishing a consistent framework. It should also revisit the practice areas to sharpen the organization's focus, taking into account the potential for added value and comparative advantages within the multilateral development system. Recognizing UNDP's progress in results orientation, human resource and knowledge management, and re-profiling of country offices, it urged the Administrator to continue efforts to make UNDP a more effective development partner and to strengthen the results-based management system, including improving its performance indicators.

Expressing concern that progress in gender mainstreaming, the empowerment of women and in achieving gender equality was uneven, the Board encouraged UNDP to strengthen those efforts with UNIFEM. It also expressed concern that the level of regular resources during 2000-2003 had remained far below target, but welcomed the modest upward trend in those resources. It urged member States in a position to do so to increase their contributions. UNDP was encouraged, within the context of the next MYFF, to take account of current estimates. The Board stressed the need to clarify and develop the relationship between the priorities in the MYFF, the biennial support budget and the programming arrangements. It urged UNDP to simplify the content and format of the next MYFF to ensure that it became the main policy document as well as its strategic resource and management tool.

2004-2007 MYFF

In response to the Board's request (see p. 900), UNDP, in an August report, submitted the second MYFF, 2004-2007 [DP/2003/32]. The document described the strategic goals and service lines to be pursued by the organization, and detailed the organizational strategies that would be followed over that period. It extended and refined the goals and strategies set out in the UNDP Business Plans, 2000-2003 [YUN 2000, p. 831]. The planned use of resources contained in the 2004-2005 biennial budget estimates (see p. 903) reflected the strategies enumerated in the 2004-2007 MYFF. The strategic goals and service lines of that MYFF were influenced primarily by country-level demand for UNDP support as reflected in the approved UNDAF, the Millennium Declaration, the MDGs, the Secretary-General's reform programme and the transformation of UNDP in terms of operational effectiveness. The proposed core goals were: achieving the MDGs and reducing human poverty; fostering democratic governance; managing energy and the environment for sustainable development; supporting crisis prevention and recovery; and responding to HIV/AIDS. Those goals provided the basis for UNDP services over the next four years, expressed under the corporate SRF as a series of specific service lines (specific areas in which UNDP would contribute to development results at the country level). Unlike the first MYFF, the SRF under the MYFF, 2004-2007, was streamlined into a simpler two-tiered arrangement, with a reduced set of 30 service lines within five goals. UNDP applied strict criteria in selecting the service lines, each of which demonstrated to some degree the following characteristics: record of results; contribution to advancing the MDGS; institutional capacity; UNDP's mandate; resource mobilization potential; and the value of UNDP's country network. Annexed to the report was a list of the strategic goals and corresponding service lines.

In terms of organizational strategies for the second MYFF period, 2004-2007, UNDP intended to consolidate and build on the change initiatives introduced during the MYFF, 2000-2003, focusing on three groups of action: building national capacities, promoting national ownership, advocating and fostering an enabling policy environment, promoting gender equity and forging strategic partnerships; building UNDP's organizational capacities, including initiatives to provide broad-based knowledge services and improve internal efficiency and performance; and deepening partnerships within the UN system and the development community at operational and programme levels.

The IRF, together with the SRF for the second MYFF, was based on the income assumptions that voluntary contributions to core resources would increase to $800 million in 2004, $900 million in 2005, $1,000 million in 2006 and $1,100 million in 2007; donor co-financing in the form of cost-sharing and trust fund contributions would reach $3,600 million during 2004-2007; and other (local) resources, such as Government cost-sharing contributions, would reach $4,200 million for that period. Thus, total projected resources would amount to $11,600 million, or about 15 per cent more than the original 2000-2003 estimates, and about 23 per cent more than the revised estimates for 2000-2003. About 86 per cent of the total would be invested in programme activities, and the remaining 14 per cent would support budget activities. Total donor resources (regular and co-financing) were projected to be $7,761 million, or 67 per cent of the total. Approximately 20 per cent of total donor resources were earmarked for support budget activities.

In September [dec. 2003/24], the Executive Board reaffirmed that the objective of the MYFF was to serve as the main policy document and as a strategic resource and management tool. It endorsed the 2004-2007 MYFF and, recognizing that implementation would depend on the attainment of the targeted level of income and the use of nationally owned development strategies, requested UNDP to report thereon. The Board reaffirmed its 2002 decision on the funding target of $1.1 billion [YUN 2002, p. 870]. Welcoming that the MDGs, particularly poverty reduction, were recognized as the overarching basis for all UNDP activities, it underscored the importance of a balanced approach in achieving the internationally agreed development goals. The Board urged UNDP to strengthen support to national development frameworks and priorities through developing partnerships, and to enhance the role of South-South cooperation in poverty eradication and in promoting the sustained growth of developing countries. It also reiterated that the special needs of the least developed countries be taken into account in the implementation of the MYFF, 2004-2007. The Board recognized the need for an improved reporting mechanism for the MYFF, including on gender and other cross-cutting issues, and based on performance indicators. It requested UNDP to submit proposals on the matter in 2004 and encouraged UNDP to strengthen the relationship between the MYFF, the biennial support budget and the programming arrangements.

Thematic trust funds

In August [DP/2003/31], UNDP provided a summary of the operation of the thematic trust funds (TTFs) mechanism, its programme orientation and initial results achieved during the first year of implementation, with observations regarding key lessons learned, the main challenges and the way forward.

TTFs were established in 2001 as a new instrument to help UNDP address the development priorities expressed in the MYFF, which were referred to as the UNDP practice areas, while allowing donors to provide additional (non-core) resources in support of those areas. Of the eight approved TTFs, seven corresponded to the practice areas (democratic governance, crisis prevention and recovery, poverty reduction, ICT for development, HIV/AIDS, energy and environment) and an additional fund covered gender for development. While some TTFs performed better than others, in general the introduction of the funding mechanism had positive results. Two well-funded TTFs supported country offices in generating significant results at the country level (the governance TTF and the crisis prevention and recovery TTF), while two remained unfunded and non-operational (the environment TTF and the gender and development TTF). The remaining four were in the start-up phase and had only limited resources, supporting the process of catalysing country-level alignment with strategic corporate priorities. While the democratic governance TTF had completed two tranches and the crisis prevention and recovery TTF was making allocations as needs arose, most of the other TTFs would complete their first cycle in the third or fourth quarter of 2003.

On 12 September [dec. 2003/29], the Executive Board took note of the report on TTFs.

Financing

The Administrator, in his annual review of the financial situation [DP/2004/34], said UNDP continued to witness a consistent growth in resources, reaching $3.2 billion in 2003, a 10 per cent increase over the 2002 level of $2.9 billlion. Compared to 2002, regular resources also continued an upward trend, increasing by 15 per cent to $770 million, as a result of renewed donor support and a weaker United States dollar, while total expenditure under regular resources increased by 12 per cent to $745 million. The resource balance, exclusive of operational reserves but including after-service health insurance costs, increased by 60 per cent. Contributions received from the top 15 non-programme country donors (Belgium, Canada, Denmark, Finland, France, Germany, Ireland, Italy, Japan, Netherlands, Norway, Sweden, Switzerland, United Kingdom, United States) increased by 15 per cent.

Programme expenditure, including programme support to the resident coordinator system, increased by 11 per cent, from $363 million to $404 million. By appropriation group, 59 per cent of expenditure went to programme support activities, 22 per cent to management and administration and 19 per cent to operational activities. In terms of the percentage share of programme expenditure among regions, Latin America and the Caribbean continued to record the highest share of programme delivery ($21 million or 5 per cent and $1.1 billion or 50 per cent for regular and other expenditures, respectively), followed by Asia and the Pacific ($109 million or 27 per cent and $301 million or 14 per cent, respectively), Africa ($175 million or 43 per cent and $184 million or 9 per cent, respectively), the Arab States $29 million or 7 per cent and $268 million or 13 per cent, respectively), and Europe and the Commonwealth of Independent States (CIS) ($30 million or 7 per cent and $146 million or 7 per cent, respectively).

The percentage share for execution modalities showed that national execution represented 66 per cent of the overall UNDP figure; direct execution, 18 per cent; UNOPS, 10 per cent; the "big five" entitities (UN Department of Economic and Social Affairs, Food and Agriculture Organization of the United Nations, International Labour Organization, United Nations Educational, Scientific and Cultural Organization, United Nations Industrial Development Organization), 2 per cent; other agencies, 3 per cent; and non-governmental organizations (NGOs), 1 per cent.

The growth of direct execution was mainly in crises countries, representing 70 per cent of the total execution.

As at 31 December, the balance of unexpended regular resources stood at $154 million, an increase of 85.5 per cent from the 2002 figure of $83.3 million. UNDP held cash and investments for regular resources totalling $282 million, excluding the operational reserve.

For other resources activities, which comprised local resources (government cost-sharing and cash-counterpart contributions), donor cost-sharing, trust funds, management services agreements, the Junior Professional Officer programme and the reserve for field accommodation, overall income increased from $2.2 billion to $2.3 billion. Overall expenditure increased by 12 per cent ($241 million). Net contributions received totalled $2.3 billion, of which 46 per cent ($1.07 billion) accounted for local resources. Contributions from the OECD/DAC countries increased 13 per cent from $496 million in 2002 to $561 million in 2003.

In September [dec. 2003/29], the Executive Board took note of the Administrator's annual review of the financial situation for 2002 [YUN 2002, p. 871].

Regular funding commitments to UNDP

In June [DP/2003/15], UNDP submitted a report on the status of regular resources funding commitments to the organization and its associated funds and programmes for 2003 and onward. According to the provisional data for 2002, total net income reached $670 million, a 1.5 per cent increase over the previous year. Current projections for gross contributions to regular resources for 2003, using the UN official exchange rate as at 1 May 2003, were $746 million, an 11 per cent increase over the 2002 level. The figure for 2002 resulted from increased contributions in local currency from nine members of OECD/DAC, three of them by over 10 per cent. In United States dollar terms, four of them made contributions in excess of $1 million. Some 33 programme countries made contributions to the regular resource base in 2002, including 7 that increased or resumed their contributions. There were indications that some donors might be in a position to make additional pledges and payments to regular resources during 2003, which was particularly important since the 2003 anticipated income levels were far below the requirements. A total of 14 OECD/DAC countries had provided fixed payment schedules in 2002, compared to 17 in 2001. While the number of donors providing payment schedules had declined over the years, a core group of 12 had systematically done so every year. Donors that had communicated their payment schedules accounted for 77 per cent of the estimated income for 2002. Although adherence to payment schedules was also a concern, 62 per cent of estimated gross income had been received by July 2002, allowing the cash-flow problem to be brought under control and eliminating the need to use the operational reserve. For 2003, five donors had already paid their contributions in full.

In June [dec. 2003/11], the Executive Board welcomed the encouraging, albeit modest, increase in regular resources for the second consecutive year in 2002 and noted the increase in other (non-core) resources. Recognizing that the level of growth in regular contributions continued to be far below target, it urged countries to increase core funding so as to rebuild UNDP's regular resource base. It looked forward to discussing further UNDP funding requirements when adopting the MYFF 2004-2007 (see p. 901).

Budget estimates for 2004-2005

In June, the Administrator submitted budget estimates for the 2004-2005 biennium [DP/2003/28], which formed part of, and underpinned, the MYFF, 2004-2007 (see p. 901). He proposed a budget in net terms of $575.2 million for 2004-2005, an increase of $72.6 million over the net approved budget for 2002-2003 [YUN 2001, p. 809], and which incorporated total net volume increases of $18.6 million, net cost increases of $54 million, and an increase of $6 million to projected income that offset the gross support budget, amounting to $70.3 million, compared to $64.3 million in 2002-2003. The proposals represented a real growth budget in both gross and net terms.

In another document [DP/2003/CRP/20], the Administrator proposed that the Board grant him exceptional authority to access up to 2 per cent of the 2004-2005 support budget as additional funding for security measures amounting to $11.5 million.

In September [DP/2003/29], the Advisory Committee on Administrative and Budgetary Question (ACABQ) submitted its comments on the 2004-2005 budget estimates.

In September [dec. 2003/22], the Executive Board approved gross appropriations in the amount of $645,478,400 for the 2004-2005 biennial support budget, and resolved that the income estimates of $70,310,000 should be used to offset the gross appropriations, resulting in estimated net appropriations of $575,168,400. The Board endorsed the Administrator's proposal to grant him exceptional authority during 2004-2005 to access up to $11.5 million as additional funding for security measures. It also endorsed the establishment of a base structure concept funded by the regular support budget for both headquarters and country offices, with the aim of progressively increasing the proportionate share for augmentation over the base structure between regular and other resources, and requested UNDP to report back on the application of that approach in the context of the proposed 2006-2007 budget. It further endorsed the proposed increase in cost-recovery rates as a provisional arrangement. It requested the Administrator to report in 2004 on the cost-recovery policy, including the methodology used for calculating the rates, and to provide an update on the adequacy of the provisional rates, options for transparent reporting on income from cost recovery, including the possibility of adding that income in the calculation of the next biennial support budget, and a comparison with the practice of the other funds and programmes within UNDG.

The Board approved the Administrator's proposals for the reclassification of posts and requested UNDP to exercise restraint in future proposals for upward reclassifications. It also approved the proposals on government contributions towards local office costs. Recognizing the need to reach an understanding on the distinction between programme and overhead costs, the Board requested the Administrator to consult with ACABQ, the Board and other UNDG members to address those issues prior to submission of the 2006-2007 biennial support budget. He should also consult with the Board should the level of regular resources available for programming fall below $450 million. It authorized him to redeploy resources between appropriation lines to a maximum of 5 per cent of the appropriation line to which the resources were redeployed.

Audit reports

The Executive Board, at its January session, considered the Administrator's report [DP/2003/6] on implementation of the recommendations of the Board of Auditors for the 2000-2001 biennium [YUN 2002, p. 1388], which contained an update of the actions taken by UNDP on the Board's recommendations, including the status of follow-up action and the target date for completion. The Administrator reported that progress had been achieved in most areas and that efforts were being made to address the issues that were still outstanding.

In January [DP/2003/CRP.7], the Administrator provided an update on the implementation of those recommendations, which highlighted UNDP's ongoing efforts to address the concerns raised by the Board since the earlier report.

In January [dec. 2003/5], the Executive Board took note of those reports and one on the implementation of the recommendations of the Board of Auditors for the 2000-2001 biennium relating to UNOPS [DP/2003/7 & Corr.1] (see p. 909), and welcomed the improvements made in implementing the Board of Auditor's recommendations. It encouraged UNDP to continue follow-up action with respect to the audits of nationally executed expenditures and welcomed the imminent completion of the service-level agreements for services provided by UNDP to UNFPA and UNOPS. It also welcomed the ongoing consultations between UNDP, UNFPA and UNOPS to develop a fraud-prevention strategy by the end of 2003. Those three organizations were encouraged to take further steps to simplify, harmonize and standardize their financial reporting.

In May [DP/2003/21], the Administrator submitted the annual report on the internal audit and oversight services provided by the Office of Audit and Performance Review, covering 2002. Of the 42 audits conducted, 8 piloted a new approach, which included: sharing audit criteria with country offices to improve transparency and encourage them to undertake regular self-assessments; completing official draft reports within four weeks of field work; limiting the number of recommendations to 30; revising the standard system for rating offices; conducting balanced assessments of performance rather than focusing only on negative findings; and broadening the scope of the audit to include programme as well as financial and administrative aspects. In 2002, 44 internal audit reports were issued, containing 1,336 recommendations, of which 1,264 (95 per cent) were accepted by UNDP management.

In June [dec. 2003/14], the Executive Board encouraged the Administrator and the Executive Directors of UNFPA and UNOPS to address the issues in those reports and to report to the Board in 2004.

Other technical cooperation

UN activities

Department of Economic and Social Affairs

During 2003, the UN Department of Economic and Social Affairs (DESA) had more than 600 technical cooperation projects under execution in a dozen substantive sectors, with a total project expenditure of $50.7 million. Projects financed by UNDP represented $20.1 million; those by trust funds, $30.2 million; and those by UNFPA, $0.5 million.

On a geographical basis, DESA's technical cooperation programme included expenditures of $26.8 million for interregional and global programmes, $9.6 million in Africa, $6.7 million in Asia and the Pacific, $6 million in the Middle East and $0.5 million in Europe.

Distribution of expenditures by substantive sectors was as follows: associate expert programme, $18.9 million; socio-economic policy, $10.5 million; governance and public administration, $7.1 million; energy, $6.8 million; water, $2 million; Information and Communication Technologies (ICT) Task Force, $1.3 million; infrastructure, $1 million; programme support,

$0.9 million; social development, $0.7 million; knowledge management, $0.6 million; statistics, $0.5 million; and minerals, $0.4 million. Of the total delivery of $50.7 million, the associate expert programme comprised 37 per cent; socio-economic policy, 21 per cent; and governance and public administration, 14 per cent.

On a component basis, DESA's delivery in 2003 included $37 million for project personnel; $7.4 million for subcontracts; $3.4 million for training; $2.2 million for equipment; and $0.7 million for miscellaneous expenses.

The total expenditure for DESA against the UN regular programme of technical cooperation was $8.5 million. Distribution of expenditures by sector was as follows: sustainable development, $3 million; public administration and socio-economic issues, $2.9 million; social development, $1.1 million; statistics, $1 million; gender issues, $0.2 million; population, $0.2 million; and administrative support, $0.1 million. On a component basis, expenditures for the year included $6.8 million for the provision of advisory services, including travel; $1.1 million for training activities; and $0.6 million for consultancy services.

Development Account

The Secretary-General, in response to General Assembly resolution 56/237 [YUN 2001, p. 810], issued, in October [A/58/404], the third progress report on the implementation of projects financed from the Development Account, which was funded through savings derived from efficiencies in the regular programme budget. Activities under the Account were aimed at capacity-building through subregional, regional and interregional economic and technical cooperation among developing countries, and implemented as individual projects to achieve distinct development impact.

Since the Account's establishment by the Assembly in resolution 52/12 B [YUN 1997, p. 1392], 43 projects had been approved for a total of $39.2 million. An additional 23 projects were proposed for approval for the fourth tranche (2004-2005) of the Account, which would bring total funding to $52.3 million. As at 30 June, the seven projects of the first tranche had utilized 80 per cent of allotted resources. Four of those projects had been or were about to be completed and the remaining three were expected to be finished by the end of 2003. The second tranche spent 76.5 per cent of allocated resources. Of the 16 projects, 5 were completed, 4 were close to completion and 7 would be completed in 2004. The third tranche, launched in 2002, had an implementation rate of 36.3 per cent, with 3 projects well advanced, 11 on schedule, 3 with an implementation rate of under 15 per cent and 2 just starting. The number of jointly executed projects had increased from zero in the first tranche to 12 in the fourth. Preliminary thematic evaluations were undertaken under two large clusters of projects: sustainable development and statistics. The reviews covered project execution, the effect networking and capacity-building had on the long-term impact of projects on beneficiaries, and lessons learned.

Development Account projects contributed to capacity-building in developing countries in specific areas related to follow-up to global conferences in the economic and social fields. Learning from experience, including the slow start of the first tranche, and following on guidance received from the intergovernmental process, both the implementation rate and the reporting on results had improved.

ACABQ, in October [A/58/7/Add.5], reviewed the report and stated that more emphasis should be placed on the pace of implementation of projects and on the results achieved, rather than on a description of efforts made and processes followed in implementing projects. It recommended that the Secretary-General incorporate information on the implementation of projects financed from the Development Account in his proposed programme budgets, thus obviating the need for a separate report.

On 23 December, the General Assembly, in section XVIII of **resolution 58/272** (see p. 1419), took note of the Secretary-General's report on the Development Account and concurred with the ACABQ recommendations thereon.

Also, in **resolution 58/270** of the same date (see p. 1399), the Assembly requested the Secretary-General to submit a comprehensive report in 2004 addressing measures to improve the performance of the Development Account, including ways to bring a more focused approach to project formulation, complementarity, implementation and evaluation, and to make proposals for increasing its funding.

UN Fund for International Partnerships

The Secretary-General, in his report on the 2003 activities of the United Nations Fund for International Partnerships (UNFIP) [A/59/170], established in 1998 [YUN 1998, p. 1297] to manage the process of grant allocations through the United Nations Foundation, a public charity founded by Robert E. Turner to channel his gift to the United Nations of stock valued at some $1 billion, provided data on the thirteenth and fourteenth funding cycles, information on progress in each programmatic area and a description of UNFIP activities in advocacy and partnership-building. A total of $73.7 million was programmed for 2003, $16 million in the thirteenth funding cycle and $33 million in the fourteenth. Of the total, $44 million was for nine projects related to children's health; $18.4 million for 18 projects for the environment; $6.2 million for 14 projects for population and women; $2.9 million for five projects for peace, security and human rights; and $2.2 million for four projects outside the four thematic areas. As at 31 December 2003, a total of $563 million had been allocated to fund 292 projects, with activities in 121 countries involving 35 UN organizations.

The General Assembly, in section XXI of **resolution 58/272** of 23 December (see p. 1420), took note of the Secretary-General's report on UNFIP's 2002 activities [YUN 2002, p. 874].

UN Office for Project Services

The United Nations Office for Project Services (UNOPS), established in 1995 [YUN 1995, p. 900] in accordance with General Assembly decision 48/501 [YUN 1994, p. 806] as a separate and self-financing entity of the UN system to act as a service provider to UN organizations, offered a broad range of services, from overall project management to the provision of single inputs.

2003 activities

The year 2003 was the first in a multi-year transition and recovery phase for UNOPS, as the Executive Director reported in his annual report on UNOPS activities for 2003 [DP/2004/23]. UNOPS recorded income exceeding recurring and non-recurring administrative expenditures for the year, thereby adhering to its self-financing principle.

UNOPS project delivery remained on track for the year, reaching $490.6 million. Delivery increased by $6.2 million, or 1 per cent over an original target of $484.4 million. Management service agreements provided for 22 per cent of that total, UNDP for 16 per cent, other UN organizations for 40 per cent, trust funds for 17 per cent, and UNOPS as implementing agent for 5 per cent.

By commodity type, 44 per cent was spent on services and works contracting, 28 per cent on personnel contracting services, 24 per cent on equipment and goods, 3 per cent on training services and 1 per cent on miscellaneous activities.

By geographic region, the Arab States received 24 per cent of the total; Africa, 21 per cent; Asia and the Pacific, 18 per cent; Europe and CIS, 15 per cent; Latin America and the Caribbean, 12 per cent; and global and interregional programmes, 10 per cent.

In 2003, UNOPS generated $66.2 million in total revenues, well above the 2003 approved revised estimates of $44.5 million (see below), mainly as the result of one-time advisory services for contract amendments that UNOPS was requested to provide under the United Nations Office of the Iraq Programme. Of the total, project services (total support costs and fees) provided the largest share of total UNOPS revenue ($34.5 million, or 52 per cent). UNDP remained the primary client of UNOPS, accounting for 41 per cent of support costs and fee revenue ($14.3 million). Revenue generated from the loan supervision and administration portfolio—primarily the International Fund for Agricultural Development loans—increased from $6.4 million in 2002 to $7 million in 2003. Interest income remained low during 2002 and 2003, and a small income was generated by subleasing office space in New York.

Administrative expenditures totalled $47.8 million in 2003, or $2.5 million over 2002 actual expenditures. Staff costs for 2002-2003 ($57.8 million) declined from the 2000-2001 biennium ($66.7 million), reflecting the impact of staff reductions. Contractual services, equipment, communications, travel and general operating expenses equalled $9.2 million. UNOPS paid $5.4 million in reimbursements to UNDP and the United Nations for a range of central and operational support services.

The introduction of a single-instance enterprise resource planning system, known as Atlas, increased the UNOPS cost base. UNOPS spent $3.1 million, or 7 per cent of its expenditure base and twice the budgeted amount, on design, gap analysis, technical interfaces with legacy systems, testing, conversion, data scrubbing and training activities. UNOPS paid $1.7 million as a one-time, lump sum settlement for outstanding reimbursements to the United Nations and UNDP for administrative services and costs.

As at 31 December 2003, UNOPS had a fund balance of $23.2 million, composed of $6 million in operational reserve and $17.2 million in working capital.

Independent review

In January [DP/2003/CRP.4], the UNOPS Executive Director and the Management Coordination Committee (MCC) submitted jointly a detailed budget estimate totalling $225,750 for an independent review pertaining to the business model and related UNOPS issues, as requested by the UNDP/UNFPA Executive Board in 2002 [YUN 2002, p. 878]. Under the terms of reference annexed to the note, the review would formulate a strategy for the long-term growth and sustainability of UNOPS. It would make proposals for aligning its cost and revenue structures and identifying areas of business expansion.

In January [dec. 2003/4], the Board approved a maximum of $255,000 for the budget for the independent review and requested UNDP to prefinance the study and arrange for reimbursement from interested member countries. The Board amended the terms of reference (paragraph 16) of the review relating to the core team. It decided that the review should be undertaken by a consultancy firm selected through tender and requested MCC to initiate the process, bearing in mind the amended terms of reference. The Board also requested that a preliminary report on the review mission's recommendations be presented to the Board in June and that the final report be made available to the Board before its September session.

In response to the Board's request, the UNOPS Executive Director submitted a June progress report summarizing activities undertaken by UNOPS, MCC and the consultancy firm [DP/2003/CRP.15]. In June [dec. 2003/12], the Board took note of the progress report and requested that comments by UNOPS and MCC be submitted before its September session.

In August [DP/2003/40], the UNOPS Executive Director transmitted the final report of the independent review, prepared by management consultants Goss Gilroy Inc. It gave an overview of the recent history and the current state of affairs, including recent evaluations of UNOPS, covered the UNOPS business model and compared it with similar organizations, assessed the market for UNOPS services, discussed organizational issues such as human resources management development, financial systems and practices, procurement and governance, and presented a framework for moving forward. The review included development of a cost model to project various scenarios of UNOPS operations in order to assess the viability of the organization. It made 57 recommendations on all aspects of UNOPS operations, including on enhancement of viability by making changes so that the organization would be less vulnerable to external pressures and changes in the business environment.

The report noted that, upon becoming a separate, independent, self-financing agency in 1995, UNOPS retained most of the project workload and revenues from UNDP. Initially, UNOPS revenue levels permitted a considerable operational reserve fund to be built up. However, between 1998 and 2001, UNDP core funding was reduced, leaving UNOPS with lower net revenue margin projects. Facing a financial crisis in 2002, UNOPS implemented drastic cost-cutting measures in administrative expenditures totalling $9.3 million. Although UNOPS ended the year with a small excess of income over administrative expenditure, the budget reduction exercise, the staff reductions and the atmosphere of uncertainty regarding UNOPS's future caused mutual staff-management mistrust. With the diminished operating reserve and the forecast requirement to reduce it further, UNOPS had lost much of its capacity for enhancing project delivery capabilities, and its capacity to promote the agency and reinvest in systems had almost totally been eliminated. Moreover, the draft 2003 Business Plan specified that forecasting delivery volumes, income and project acquisition might be difficult beyond a one-year planning horizon.

The consultants found that the UNOPS business model resembled, in part, that of a for-profit consultancy firm in the private sector. For several years the business model appeared to work well, but its viability was undermined by the change in the premise that UNOPS would be UNDP's administrative and implementing arm with the advent of national and direct execution, and the failure of UNOPS management to provide the required leadership to adapt to the new environment and context. The business model had changed as a result of the recent financial difficulties, but further change was required to render it viable and sustainable. It was restricted by its revenue dependency, the condition that it function within the UN system and work through UNDP field offices, and its inability to do its own fundraising. The business model was also affected by the relationship of fees and level of effort, the control of costs in relation to fee income and the fragmentation of the organization.

The consultants were of the view that UNOPS was viable and sustainable within the limitation and independence of a revenue dependency business model, which should allow UNOPS a certain degree of independence, including the loosening of restraints and the removal of barriers. They recommended that the UNOPS Executive Director seek confirmation from the Executive Board that the revenue dependency business model, together with all its implications in terms of changes, removal of barriers and lessening of restrictions, should be the approach to establishing UNOPS long-term viability and sustainability. It should be based on a fee-for-service business model concept with a system to track project-related activities. However, UNOPS needed to undertake considerable change in its organization operations and mechanisms for reducing costs, and prepare a rational market development programme. To that end, UNOPS should prepare a change management plan. Once a new business plan was prepared, the Executive Director should seek the necessary bridge financing to cover the cost of restoring UNOPS to financial health and ensuring its viability and sustainability.

The UNOPS Executive Director, in his August comments on the independent review [DP/2003/CRP.19], summarized actions being taken to address the concerns raised in the review and presented an overview of the business and financial prospects for the remainder of 2003 and for 2004.

On 12 September [dec. 2003/27], the Board expressed concern that, despite the anticipated upturn in revenue in late 2003, current business projections for 2004 fell far short of levels needed to sustain the financial viability of UNOPS. It encouraged the Executive Director in his intent to focus on further business acquisition, including through analysing opportunities to build new relationships. It supported his approach with regard to the immediate steps to be taken and welcomed his intention to implement internal changes immediately. He was requested to develop, in consultation with the Board, a full response to the review's recommendations for the Board to consider in 2004. Noting that the question of UNOPS long-term sustainability was linked to broader issues, such as vision, mandate and governance, the Board considered that that discussion needed to take place in parallel with the implementation of internal reforms, and requested the Executive Director to facilitate that broader consultation process as soon as possible. He should report to the Board in 2004 on the strategy for business acquisition and progress in implementing internal changes; present a comprehensive timetable, detailed budget, benchmarks for monitoring the progress and modalities for meeting the costs of the change process; and report on the broader consultation process.

Budget estimates

Revised 2002 budget and 2003 forecast

The Executive Board, at its January session, considered the report [DP/2003/CRP.3] of the UNOPS Executive Director on implementation of the UNOPS revised 2002 budget. Notwithstanding the significant difficulties faced in 2002 to align its income and expenditure, UNOPS was able to stay on track with its project delivery targets. As at 31 October, UNOPS income totalled $34.8 million, of which $28.8 million was from project delivery, $5.4 million from its services-only portfolio and $0.6 million as other income. That amount represented 79 per cent of the approved target of $44.3 million [YUN 2002, p. 879]. Based on estimated project delivery of $503 million, total income for 2002 was projected at $43.1 million. Administrative expenditures for the same period totalled $36.7 million, exceeding earned income by $1.9 million, which was projected to increase to $3.6 million by the end of the year. Staff separation costs directly charged to the operational reserve amounted to $1 million against the projection of $2 million.

The level of the operational reserve stood at $2.5 million as at 31 October and was projected to fall to $2 million. As there continued to be a number of risk factors that could affect the achievement of targets, UNOPS was ready to implement the contingency plan approved by the Executive Board in 2002 [YUN 2002, p. 878].

A paper [DP/2003/CRP.2] on the special reserve for separations, established by the Executive Board in 2002 [YUN 2002, p. 878], provided information on UNOPS and the liabilities affecting UNDP. It was reported that, as a result of the workforce reduction at UNOPS, 16 people were displaced from their positions, at an estimated cost of $2.3 million. Based on the apportionment agreement between UNDP and UNOPS, the total cost to UNDP would be $1.1 million. As at 30 November 2002, eight other staff were in the process of being separated at an estimated cost of $0.5 million to UNDP. The estimated cost for separating the other eight if needed was $0.6 million.

In January [dec. 2003/3], the Board noted the UNOPS report on implementation of the revised 2002 budget and that the preliminary 2002 year-end figures were close to those in the revised budget report. It expressed concern over the continued reduction in the operational reserve and requested the Executive Director to submit a report, through MCC, on updated actual end-of-year figures for 2002 and projected income, expenditure and level of the operational reserve for 2003. The Board also noted the report on the special reserve for separation [dec. 2003/6].

As requested, the Executive Director issued an April report [DP/2003/18] providing UNOPS 2002 year-end figures and revised projections for 2003. Delivery, income and administrative expenditures were all slightly lower than the targets approved by the Board in 2002. When compared with the preliminary year-end projections presented to the Board in January (above), UNOPS achieved better results in all of its business parameters. The level of the operational reserve, carried forward at the end of 2002, stood at $4.2 million, which was $0.9 million higher than projected in June 2002.

UNOPS total 2002 year-end income amounted to $43.7 million, or 99 per cent of the approved income target of $44.3 million, comprising $35.4 million (100 per cent) in project delivery income, $7.5 million (96 per cent) from the service portfolio and $0.8 million (73 per cent) from other income, including rental income of $0.6 million. Expenditures amounted to $43.5 million, compared to the approved figure of $44 million, resulting in $0.2 million in excess of recurrent administrative expenditures, reversing the trend for the past two years. Staff separation costs charged to the operational reserve totalled $1.1 million in 2002, less than was anticipated due to fewer separations. Project delivery reached $485.1 million or 96 per cent of the target of $503.2 million.

For 2003, estimated project delivery was revised to $484.4 million. Income was projected at $44.5 million, comprising $35.3 million in project delivery income, $8.2 million in service portfolio income and $1 million in other income. Estimated expenditure was revised to $45.5 million. Staff separation costs were budgeted at $0.3 million, bringing total estimated staff separation costs to $1.4 million, a savings of $0.6 million. The 2003 year-end balance of the operational reserve was projected to be $3.2 million.

In June [dec. 2003/21], the Executive Board took note of the report on year-end figures for UNOPS in 2002 and projected income, expenditure and level of the operational reserve for 2003.

Revised 2002-2003 budget, 2004-2005 budget and operational reserve

In a July report [DP/2003/38], the Executive Director submitted revised budget estimates for the 2002-2003 biennium, based on actual delivery, income and expenditure for 2002 and on projections for 2003 (see above).

The 2002-2003 target for project delivery was revised to $969.5 million, $294.5 million or 23.3 per cent and $46.7 million or 4.6 per cent below the estimates approved in 2001 and 2002, respectively. Total estimated income was revised to $88.2 million, significantly lower than the original projection of $116.2 million, later revised to $87.9 million in 2002. The 2002-2003 expenditures were revised to $90.7 million, $22.3 million or 19.7 per cent less than the level approved in 2001, but $2.79 million or 3.2 per cent more than the 2002 revised estimate.

The Executive Director also submitted budget estimates for 2004-2005. He reported that a review of the UNOPS portfolio for 2004 and beyond revealed that it did not have the required budgets to support an annual project delivery of some $500 million, which would be comparable to what was achieved in 2002 and likely to be realized in 2003. While UNDP remained the main client of UNOPS, the UNDP portfolio had continued to decline, and increases in the project portfolio from other organizations had not been able to compensate for that decline. In addition, increasingly shorter duration of its business acquisition and reductions in delivery budgets, owing to political and economic upheavals, had made forecasting beyond a one-year horizon difficult, forcing UNOPS to change its planning and forecasting cycle from a two-year to a one-year cycle. The 2004-2005 budget was also expected to be influenced by the outcome of the independent review of UNOPS (see p. 906), as well as by the vision and strategy to be articulated by the new UNOPS Executive Director.

In the light of those considerations, UNOPS deferred the detailed formulation of the 2004-2005 biennium budget and proposed to use instead the same level of project delivery, income and expenditure estimated for the 2002-2003 biennium.

With regard to the operational reserve, the Executive Director proposed that the end 2004-2005 operational reserve be estimated at $4.2 million, equivalent to the end of 2002 level.

In August [DP/2003/39], ACABQ recommended that the Executive Board approve the revised budget estimates for 2002-2003, the proposed staffing level and the projections for 2004-2005.

The Board, in September [dec. 2003/26], approved the revised budget estimates for 2002-2003 in the amount of $90.7 million, the budget estimates for 2004-2005 at $87 million and the staffing level as proposed for 2002-2003.

Audit reports

The UNDP Executive Director submitted to the Executive Board in January [DP/2003/7 & Corr.1] a report on implementation of the recommendations of the Board of Auditors for the 2000-2001 biennium [YUN 2002, p. 1388]. Of the 18 recommendations of the Board of Auditors, 15 concerned financial issues and 3 management issues. At the time of the report, 6 of the 18 recommendations had not been completed, although progress was being made towards their completion. The Board, in January [dec. 2003/5], noted that the opinion of the Board of Auditors on UNOPS financial statements was unqualified and expressed concern that a modified report on UNOPS had been issued.

In May [DP/2003/22], the UNDP Office of Audit and Performance Review (OAPR) and the UNOPS Project Services Audit Section reported on internal audit services for UNOPS operations in 2002. The report presented findings in relation to 19 internal audits in 2002 for which reports were issued, covering operational activities in the field (7 audits) and at headquarters (5 audits), and those under management service agreements (7 audits). Together, the reports contained 135 recommendations, of which 51 were in the area of administration (which included contracts and procurement), 36 in finance, 19 in programme, 16 in personnel, 11 in organization and 2 in the area of policy. Based on an arrangement between UNOPS and OAPR, the UNOPS organizational units concerned provided written comments on all the draft audit reports. UNOPS did not agree with only one of the 135 recommendations; in general, the comments indicated that actions had been taken or were being taken to address the audit issues and recommendations.

The Executive Board, in June [dec. 2003/14], strongly encouraged the Executive Director to address the issues contained in the report on internal audit and oversight and to report in 2004.

UN Volunteers

In 2003, the number of volunteers working for the United Nations Volunteers (UNV) programme—administered by UNDP—increased to 5,635 from 5,234 in 2002. The volunteers, from 165 countries, carried out 5,832 assignments in 150 nations. Seventy-two per cent of them were from developing countries and served either in their home countries or abroad. The number of women volunteers grew in absolute terms by 9 per cent during the 2002-2003 biennium, accounting for 37 per cent of all volunteers; however, in percentage terms, the proportion of women volunteers remained unchanged compared to male volunteers. By region, 41 per cent of assignments were carried out in Africa, 25 per cent in Asia and the Pacific, 15 per cent in Latin America and the Caribbean, 12 per cent in Europe and CIS, and 7 per cent in the Arab States.

UN volunteers supported communities and organizations in programme countries through initiatives that brought direct quality-of-life benefits to target populations. Development cooperation activities remained the hallmark of UNV programme implementation. Support was provided to partners in electoral processes, peace-building and humanitarian relief. In those activities, UNV combined the expertise and knowledge of international and national volunteers to enhance capacity development, reinforce sustainability and promote the spirit of volunteerism and global solidarity.

In his report on the UNV financial situation in 2003 [DP/2004/34], the UNDP Administrator stated that income recorded in 2003 for UNV amounted to $23.5 million, slightly below the 2002 level of $23.7 million, due mainly to a decrease in cost-sharing income from $2.6 million in 2002 to $1.4 million in 2003. Programme expenditure in 2003 also decreased to $21.8 million from $23.1 milllion in 2002. The balance of the operational reserve as at 31 December 2003 was $1.2 million.

Economic and technical cooperation among developing countries

The UNDP Administrator reported in May [DP/2003/14] on the implementation of the second cooperation framework for technical cooperation among developing countries (TCDC) (2001-2003) [YUN 2001, p. 818]. The report assessed the progress made by the Special Unit for TCDC in implementing that framework from 2001 to 2003. The Special Unit continued to promote South-South cooperation in general, including economic and technical cooperation. It developed a strategy for mainstreaming TCDC in the organization, especially in the area of partnerships. It supported strategic interventions to benefit groups of developing countries and to pilot initiatives with the potential for replication in several countries. Particular emphasis was placed on South-South and triangular partnerships, and exchanges of information and expertise. Programme achievements were recorded in the areas of policy dialogue and consensus-building, strengthening multilateral efforts for South-South cooperation, support for South-South sharing of development information, increased economic cooperation among developing countries (ECDC), and cooperation in social policies and social development. Cooperation among Southern countries was also enhanced in science and technology. The Special Unit was the liaison between UNDP and the Group of 77 developing countries, and worked to raise awareness of the importance of ownership by Southern countries in initiating, promoting and building South-South cooperation.

Of the total regular (core) resources of $7,406,000 allocated to the Special Unit for 2001-2003, $2,506,000 was disbursed during 2001-2002, and the remaining resources were fully programmed for implementation in 2003. Other (non-core) resources mobilized for the same period, totalling $9,737,000, were allocated to specific programmes. Of that amount, $8,150,000 was donated by Japan for 17 projects.

In June [dec. 2003/10], the UNDP/UNFPA Executive Board took note of decisions adopted at the thirteenth session of the High-level Committee on the Review of TCDC (see p. 911) and of the Administrator's report on implementation of the second cooperation framework for TCDC. It encouraged further efforts to make South-South cooperation contribute to the development outcomes of UN conferences and summits, including those contained in the UN Millennium Declaration [YUN 2000, p. 49], and to the mainstreaming of TCDC dimensions in implementing UNDP programme activities. The Board recognized the significant role of South-South cooperation in poverty eradication and in promoting the sustained growth and development of all developing countries, particularly the least developed, landlocked and transit developing countries and small island developing States. Welcoming General Assembly resolution 57/263 [YUN 2002, p. 883], which included the Voluntary Trust Fund for the Promotion of South-South Cooperation in the United Nations Pledging Conference for Development Activities, the Board invited developed and developing countries to contribute to the Fund. It noted with appreciation the lessons learned from the second cooperation framework, which would provide useful inputs in formulating the third cooperation framework to be presented in 2004.

High-level Committee on TCDC

The High-level Committee on the Review of Technical Cooperation among Developing Countries, at its thirteenth session (New York, 27-30 May) [A/58/39], considered a comprehensive biennial report of the progress made in the implementation of the 1978 Buenos Aires Plan of Action for Promoting and Implementing TCDC [YUN 1978, p. 467] and the new directions strategy for TCDC [YUN 1995, p. 902], as well as reports of the UNDP Administrator. It held a thematic discussion on enhancing the role of the private sector in promoting South-South cooperation, including triangular cooperation. The Committee commemorated the twenty-fifth anniversary of the adoption of the Buenos Aires Plan of Action.

The Committee adopted two substantive decisions. In the first [A/58/39 (dec. 13/1)], it encouraged developing countries that had not done so to establish a national South-South cooperation policy and coordination mechanism, including a clear delineation of the roles of the national focal point and of the various partners for such cooperation. It also encouraged developing countries, regional and subregional institutions and centres of excellence, with assistance from the Special Unit for TCDC, to draw lessons from experiences in triangular cooperation and design innovative South-South cooperation programmes. Member States and international institutions were encouraged, in designing, formulating and executing TCDC projects, to give priority to local capabilities and resources. The Committee requested the Special Unit to promote the use of ICT, with a view to sharing knowledge and benefits, and called on it to assist developing countries to facilitate and enable their connectivity and use of ICT and the establishment of home pages on the Internet. Commending the Special Unit's efforts in establishing an Internet-based gateway for South-South cooperation, the Web of Information for Development (WIDE), it requested UN development system institutions to make information in their databases on South-South cooperation activities accessible through WIDE. The Special Unit should assist in documenting and disseminating the particular problems of the least developed countries, small island developing States and landlocked developing countries to help address their needs. Developed and developing countries and the UN system should intensify efforts to support South-South initiatives designed to benefit those countries, and countries in post-conflict and crisis situations. The Committee requested UN bodies to take further measures to integrate systematically the use of TCDC/ECDC modalities into their cooperation programmes in line with the new directions strategy. It requested the Administrator to report at its fourteenth (2005) session on progress in implementing South-South cooperation and on implementation of its decision.

In a decision on the overall framework for promoting and applying TCDC [dec. 13/2], the Committee approved the revised Guidelines for the Review of Policies and Procedures concerning TCDC, including its annex on the United Nations Common Results Framework on Technical and Economic Cooperation among Developing Countries. The guidelines had been applied on an experimental basis since 1993 and revised in 1997 [YUN 1997, p. 891]. Welcoming the emphasis on the promotion of South-South cooperation in the Administrator's Business Plans (see p. 897), the Committee called on the Administrator to promote the focal point mechanism relating to TCDC, especially at the regional and country levels through the resident coordinator system. The Committee decided to change the name of the Special Unit for TCDC to the Special Unit for South-South Cooperation and to periodically review its functioning. It called for raising the volume of UNDP resources available for promoting South-South cooperation activities and requested the executive boards of other funds and programmes to review, and to consider increasing, the allocation of resources for such activities. It requested the Administrator to report on the implementation of its decision in 2005.

The Executive Board, in June [dec. 2003/10], took note of the Committee's decisions.

The Economic and Social Council, by **decision 2003/225** of 11 July, took note of the Committee's report on its thirteenth session.

South-South cooperation

The Secretary-General, in response to General Assembly resolution 56/202 [YUN 2001, p. 820], reported in August [A/58/319] on the state of South-South cooperation, covering the 2001-2002 biennium, in particular with regard to monetary, financial, investment and trade arrangements.

At the global level, the Group of 77 developing countries and China and the Non-Aligned Movement continued to serve as the broadest mechanisms for consultation and policy coordination among developing countries. Most South-South and North-South activities occurred within the framework of regional and subregional arrangements, and most of those were oriented towards promoting flows of trade. By the end of 2002, the World Trade Organization had recognized nearly 250 regional and subregional free-trade arrangements intended to promote economic and social development.

In Africa, the largest integration effort in terms of number of countries and long-term scope was the African Union (AU), which envisaged the eventual formation of a common market. A significant initiative at the first summit meeting of the AU was the launching of the New Partnership for Africa's Development [YUN 2002, p. 907], designed to consolidate democracy and sound economic management on the continent. In Asia, the Association of South-East Asian Nations continued as a leader in South-South cooperation, pursuing digital readiness in the region and launching an agricultural Internet hub. In Latin America and the Caribbean, the five-member Andean Community agreed to a new system of intellectual property rights, among other trade issues, while the Andean Community and the Southern Cone Common Market issued a joint communiqué in April 2002 on economic, social and political priorities. The Caribbean Community worked towards a common external tariff and common protective policy, harmonization of fiscal and taxation arrangements, and coordination of economic policies and development planning.

Owing to volatility in the global economy in 2001-2002, South-South cooperation in trade was mixed. Aggregate exports of developing countries accounted for 31.5 per cent of world exports in 2001, with a shift from mainly commodities to manufactures (over 70 per cent). During that period, South-South trade represented 40 per cent of the trade of developing countries. Those figures, however, varied greatly by region, with African countries accounting for 1.9 per cent of world exports in 2001, developing countries in the Americas for 5.5 per cent and Asian developing countries for 23.7 per cent.

Donor countries facilitated South-South cooperation by supporting centres of excellence and knowledge networks. Notable examples of triangular cooperation were Japan's Third Countries Training Programme and the Third Countries Experts Programme and Partnership Programme. Other significant triangular initiatives were the African Capacity-Building Foundation, an initiative of the African Development Bank, UNDP, the World Bank, African Governments and bilateral donors, created in response to the severity of capacity deficits in Africa, European Union support for programmes engaging African countries in trade expansion, environmental protection and the development of human resources, and support by the Netherlands for sectoral programmes in 22 developing countries through multi-donor basket funds.

The report observed that the basic concept of South-South cooperation was having a positive impact on global, regional and national policies and actions relating to trade, investment, monetary and financial arrangements, and on human development in general in the developing world. The emphasis placed on South-South cooperation at UN conferences reaffirmed the relevance of that approach to international development cooperation. As the number of regional and subregional groups grew, efforts needed to be made to expand the scope of South-South and triangular partnerships within the framework of such collaborative arrangements. Rapid globalization underscored the need for a more strategic approach to South-South cooperation, and cooperation in monetary and financial areas should be strengthened. Developing countries needed to avoid counterproductive competition against one another. Growing participation by the private sector, NGOs and civil society organizations in South-South cooperation was a welcome development to be strengthened in future South-South and triangular initiatives.

In September [A/58/345], the Secretary-General, also in response to resolution 57/263, submitted a report on raising public awareness of and support for South-South cooperation, which highlighted the value added and implications of the proposed international decade on South-South cooperation and a UN day for South-South cooperation. It concluded that the proposed UN day and/or an international decade would, on a South-South basis, present new opportunities to mobilize the increasing human and financial resources in the South towards the objective of meeting internationally agreed development goals, including the MDGs. Outlining objectives of the decade and possible activities, the report recommended that the Assembly declare a UN day for South-South cooperation to be held on 12 September and/or an international decade from 2005 to 2015.

The Ministers for Foreign Affairs of the Group of 77 and China, in a Ministerial Declaration issued at their twenty-seventh annual meeting (New York, 25 September) [A/58/413], affirmed the importance of strengthening South-South cooperation in the UN system, particularly the Special Unit for TCDC, and called on UNDP to provide it with the necessary support. It decided that the High-level Conference on South-South Cooperation (see below) would consider the progress in the implementation of the outcomes of the 2000 South Summit [YUN 2000, p. 894], as identified in the Havana Programme of Action.

The High-level Conference on South-South Cooperation (Marrakech, Morocco, 16-19 December) [A/58/683] adopted the Marrakech Declaration on South-South Cooperation and the Marrakech Framework for the Implementation of South-South Cooperation.

GENERAL ASSEMBLY ACTION

On 23 December [meeting 78], the General Assembly, on the recommendation of the Second (Economic and Financial) Committee [A/58/487], adopted **resolution 58/220** without vote [agenda item 97 (b)].

Economic and technical cooperation among developing countries

The General Assembly,

Stressing that South-South cooperation, as an important element of international cooperation for development, offers viable opportunities for developing countries and countries with economies in transition in their individual and collective pursuit of sustained economic growth and sustainable development,

Recognizing that developing countries have the primary responsibility for promoting and implementing South-South cooperation, not as a substitute for but rather as a complement to North-South cooperation, and in this context reiterating the need for the international community to support the efforts of the developing countries to expand South-South cooperation,

Taking note of the Ministerial Declaration adopted by the Ministers for Foreign Affairs of the States members of the Group of 77 at their twenty-seventh annual meeting, held in New York on 25 September 2003, in which the increased importance and relevance of South-South cooperation were re-emphasized,

1. *Takes note* of the report of the High-level Committee on the Review of Technical Cooperation among Developing Countries on its thirteenth session, endorses the decisions adopted by the High-level Committee at that session, and decides to change the name of the Committee to High-level Committee on South-South Cooperation, with no change in its mandate or in the scope of its activities;

2. *Also takes note* of the reports of the Secretary-General on the state of South-South cooperation and on raising public awareness of and support for South-South cooperation;

3. *Reaffirms* the need to strengthen further, within its available resources, the Special Unit for South-South Cooperation of the United Nations Development Programme as a separate entity and a focal point for South-South cooperation within the United Nations system, recognizes that its activities should be perceived as an integral part of the overall development policy of the United Nations system and the United Nations Development Programme, and in this context calls upon United Nations funds and programmes and other entities of the United Nations development system to intensify efforts to mainstream technical and economic co-operation among developing countries by using relevant national, regional and international mechanisms in consultation with Member States;

4. *Notes with interest* that South-South cooperation can have a positive impact on global, regional and national policies and actions in the economic, social and development fields in the developing countries, and urges developing countries and their partners to intensify South-South and triangular cooperation in these areas, as they contribute to the achievement of the internationally agreed development goals, including those contained in the United Nations Millennium Declaration;

5. *Recognizes* that regional integration initiatives between developing countries constitute an important and valuable form of South-South cooperation and that regional integration is a step towards beneficial integration into the world economy;

6. *Also recognizes* the urgent need to help to strengthen the capacities of the developing countries, especially the least developed countries, to participate in and benefit from globalization and liberalization processes, and to this end welcomes the initiatives being undertaken at the subregional, regional, interregional and global levels towards establishing public-private partnership mechanisms aiming to enhance and expand South-South cooperation in trade and investment, and in this context notes the initiatives of the World Trade Forum;

7. *Reiterates* the urgent need to help to strengthen institutions and centres of excellence in the South, especially at the regional and interregional levels, with a view to making more effective use of such entities towards improved South-South knowledge-sharing, networking, capacity-building, information and best practices exchanges, policy analysis and coordinated action among developing countries on major issues of common concern, and in this context encourages such institutions and centres of excellence, as well as regional and subregional economic groupings, to establish closer links and bridges among themselves, including through the Web of Information for Development of the Special Unit for South-South Cooperation;

8. *Notes with interest* the holding of the High-level Conference on South-South Cooperation in Marrakech, Morocco, from 16 to 19 December 2003, and calls upon developing countries, and encourages their development partners and relevant international organizations, to participate actively in the Conference in order to ensure its success and increase the momentum and intensity of South-South cooperation;

9. *Urges* all relevant United Nations organizations and multilateral institutions to intensify their efforts

to effectively mainstream the use of South-South cooperation in the design, formulation and implementation of their regular programmes and to consider increasing allocations of human, technical and financial resources for supporting South-South cooperation initiatives, and in this regard takes note of the initiatives contained in the Havana Programme of Action adopted by the first South Summit and the follow-up to the High-level Conference on South-South Co-operation in Marrakech, as well as the preparations for the second South Summit in 2005;

10. *Recognizes* the need to mobilize additional resources for enhancing South-South cooperation, reiterates in this context its decision in its resolution 57/263 of 20 December 2002 to include the Voluntary Trust Fund for the Promotion of South-South Co-operation in the United Nations Pledging Conference for Development Activities, as long as it exists, and in the same manner decides to include the Pérez-Guerrero Trust Fund for Economic and Technical Co-operation among Developing Countries in the same Pledging Conference, and invites all countries, in particular developed countries, to support South-South and triangular cooperation through, inter alia, these funds, bearing in mind the need for these funds to continue to use such resources in an effective manner;

11. *Decides* to declare 19 December, the date on which the General Assembly endorsed the Buenos Aires Plan of Action for Promoting and Implementing Technical Cooperation among Developing Countries, as the United Nations Day for South-South Cooperation;

12. *Also decides* to include in the provisional agenda of its sixtieth session a sub-item entitled "South-South cooperation for development", and requests the Secretary-General to submit at that session a comprehensive report on the state of South-South cooperation and on the implementation of the present resolution.

UN Capital Development Fund

Contributions to the United Nations Capital Development Fund (UNCDF) regular resources increased by $4.7 million, or 21 per cent, in 2003, bringing the total to $26.9 million, from $22.2 million in 2002 [DP/2004/34]. That increase resulted mainly from the fluctuation of the United States dollar against the euro, and the increased contribution of one donor. Contributions to trust funds and cost-sharing more than doubled, to $10.7 million compared to $3.4 million in 2002. Expenditures decreased from $24.8 million in 2002 to $21.1 million in 2003. Although regular resources programme expenditures declined by $6.2 million, or 28 per cent, other resources expenditures increased from $2.2 million in 2002 to $4.8 million in 2003. Unexpended resources at the end of 2003 totalled $64.5 million, including an operational reserve of $22.6 million that had decreased from $33 million in 2002. That level of unexpended resources, including the operational reserve, represented 26 months' expenditure.

In May [DP/2003/13 & Corr.1], UNCDF presented to the UNDP/UNFPA Executive Board its 2002 results-oriented annual report (ROAR). The report covered the results achieved in 2002 within the UNCDF strategic results framework for 2002-2003.

In 2002, UNCDF operational activities were severely affected by the low level of contributions to its core resources, which were far short of the $30 million target, forcing UNCDF to reduce expenditures significantly. Starting with a planned budget of about $40 million based on previous years' programme commitments, UNCDF had to align target programme expenditures with actual resources available. Despite the reduction in programme expenditures, results attained in 2002 were robust in a few areas, while others suffered. The area of local governance showed performance gains, mainly as a result of local resource mobilization. Progress was made towards operational self-sufficiency of microfinance institutions. UNCDF made considerable progress in establishing technical advisory services on local governance and microfinance on a cost-recovery basis. It strengthened cooperation with development partners, especially UNDP, through formal partnership agreements. The results attracted additional non-core resource commitments.

In 2002, UNCDF had an active project portfolio of 93 projects, 54 of which met the criteria for reporting (projects lasting more than five months or with expenditure over $50,000). More than half of those were local development projects, followed by infrastructure, microfinance and eco-development projects.

In June [dec. 2003/9], the Executive Board took note of the 2002 ROAR, welcomed the articulation of the complementarity and partnership between UNDP and UNCDF as reflected in two memorandums of understanding, one on collaboration in microfinance and the other on local governance. The Board took note of the independent impact assessment of UNCDF to be submitted in 2004 and invited countries to make financial or in-kind contributions towards that initiative. It noted with concern that the regular (core) resources fell far below the demand of programme countries, in particular the least developed countries, in its two areas of concentration—microfinance and local governance/decentralization. Recognizing UNCDF efforts to broaden the donor base, the Board requested UNCDF to inform it of a strategy to achieve the objectives set out in 2002 on achieving goals and obtaining resources [YUN 2002, p. 884].

The Board, in September [dec. 2003/23], took note of the UNDP Administrator's budget estimates for 2004-2005 for UNCDF [DP/2003/28], and approved a gross appropriation for UNCDF for the 2004-2005 biennial support budget in the amount of $14,376,800.

Chapter III

Humanitarian and special economic assistance

In 2003, the United Nations, through the Office for the Coordination of Humanitarian Affairs (OCHA), continued to mobilize and coordinate humanitarian assistance to respond to international emergencies. During the year, consolidated inter-agency appeals were launched for Afghanistan, Angola, the northern Caucasus, the Central African Republic, Côte d'Ivoire, Côte d'Ivoire + 5 (Burkina Faso, Ghana, Guinea, Liberia, Mali), the Democratic People's Republic of Korea, Eritrea, the Great Lakes region and Central Africa (Burundi, Congo, Democratic Republic of the Congo, Uganda), Guinea, Indonesia, Iraq, Liberia, the Occupied Palestinian Territory, Sierra Leone, Somalia, the Southern Africa region (Lesotho, Malawi, Mozambique, Swaziland, Zambia, Zimbabwe), the Sudan and Tajikistan. The appeals sought $5.2 billion to assist some 83 million people. Some $3.9 billion was made available, meeting 75.3 per cent of requirements. Excluding contributions in kind and services not costed, OCHA contributions for natural disaster assistance totalled $57 million.

At the request of Burundi, an ad hoc advisory group to elaborate a long-term programme of support was established, while the group created in 2002 on Guinea-Bissau continued its work.

During the year, the Economic and Social Council considered ways to strengthen the coordination of UN emergency humanitarian assistance, including the financing of humanitarian assistance and the transition from relief to development.

Humanitarian assistance

Coordination

Humanitarian affairs segment of the Economic and Social Council

The humanitarian affairs segment of the Economic and Social Council (11 and 14-15 July) [A/58/3/Rev.1] considered the strengthening of the coordination of UN emergency humanitarian assistance, with particular attention to humanitarian financing and the effectiveness of humanitarian assistance and the transition from relief to development; it convened a panel on the sub-theme of responding to the effects of HIV/AIDS and other widespread diseases on humanitarian relief operations (**decision 2003/210**). Panel discussions were also held on humanitarian financing and the effectiveness of humanitarian assistance and on the transition from relief to development.

The Council considered the Secretary-General's June report [A/58/89-E/2003/85] on strengthening the coordination of UN emergency humanitarian assistance, submitted in response to General Assembly resolutions 46/182 [YUN 1991, p. 421] and 57/153 [YUN 2002, p. 889] and Council resolution 2002/32 [ibid., p. 886]. Following a summary of humanitarian developments over the preceding year, the report addressed the themes of the Council's humanitarian affairs segment (see above) and issues related to the protection of civilians, internally displaced persons, contingency planning, natural disasters and HIV/AIDS in the context of emergencies.

During the preceding year, developments in the humanitarian environment were mixed, with progress seen in ending conflict for some of the world's longer-running emergencies, but others continued to threaten whole regions. The situation in Iraq (see p. 315) underlined the importance of promoting principled humanitarian interaction to address humanitarian needs in the country. Collaborative partnerships among the humanitarian community, Governments and local actors were needed to ensure that durable solutions were found, thus setting the stage for sustainable development. The contribution of regional organizations to humanitarian assistance efforts was becoming increasingly important. A number of issues presented further challenges, including the protection of civilians in armed conflict, safeguarding the security of humanitarian personnel, the resettlement of internally displaced persons, greater integration of a gender perspective into emergency humanitarian assistance, protection from sexual exploitation and abuse, proper preparedness and contingency planning regarding natural disasters and complex humanitarian emergencies, the lack of capacity to reduce the impact of natural hazards and environmental emergencies, and the development of an emergency response to ensure the integration of the HIV/AIDS components into relevant programming areas. In response to the challenge of the involvement of military forces in humanitarian activities, "Guidelines on the Use of Military and Civil Defence Assets to Support United Nations Humanitarian Activities in Complex Emergencies" were developed and released in March. To address civil-military relations in the context of Iraq, the document "General Guidance for Interaction between United Nations Personnel and Military and Civilian Representatives of the Occupying Power in Iraq" was endorsed and released by the Secretary-General, also in March.

The report said that the importance of promoting effective coordination lay at the core of the themes related to transition and humanitarian financing. Coordination in the context of the transition from relief to development required the full engagement of Governments and donors at the earliest stages and a coherent strategy for restoring stability and normalcy. In addition to rebuilding structures or institutions, recovery assistance was needed to aid the consolidation of peace, counter the negative societal transformations that occurred during the crisis and counteract the tensions that led to the conflict. A joint Working Group on Transition Issues had been established by the Secretariat's Executive Committee on Humanitarian Affairs (ECHA) and the United Nations Development Group (UNDG), with the involvement of the International Organization for Migration, the International Red Cross and Red Crescent Movement and non-governmental organizations (NGOs), to improve the UN response to transition through more coherent planning, effective handover of coordination responsibilities and appropriate resource mobilization. The report of the 22-member Working Group was based on case studies of UN experiences in Afghanistan, Angola, the Congo, the Great Lakes region (Burundi, Democratic Republic of the Congo, Rwanda, United Republic of Tanzania), Sierra Leone, Sri Lanka, Tajikistan and Timor-Leste.

The report recommended that UN transition activities be field-driven from conception to implementation and based on a common analysis, a system-wide assessment of needs and a clear identification of the potential UN role. In response to the report, a standing mechanism of the ECHA and UNDG secretariats, as well as a group of senior task teams, was established to provide continuing guidance and practical support to UN country teams engaged in transition planning. A separate report of the Secretary-General on reform measures [A/58/351] (see p. 1384) further discussed the Group's recommendations.

The Secretary-General proposed a series of actions for the Assembly and the Council regarding the protection of civilians, internally displaced persons, gender mainstreaming, sexual violence and exploitation, emergency preparedness and contingency planning, natural disasters, HIV/AIDS in the context of emergencies, transition from relief to development and humanitarian financing.

JIU coordination assessment

JIU evaluation. By a May note [A/58/85-E/2003/80], the Secretary-General transmitted a report of the Joint Inspection Unit (JIU) on its evaluation of the UN system response in East Timor (renamed Timor-Leste), conducted with a view to improving coordination among UN organizations and maximizing the impact and effectiveness of their operations in emergency and post-conflict situations.

On 15 July (**decision 2003/226**), the Economic and Social Council took note of the Secretary-General's note transmitting the JIU report.

Note of Secretary-General. A June note of the Secretary-General [A/58/85/Add.1-E/2003/80/Add.1] transmitted, for the consideration of the General Assembly, his comments, and those of the United Nations System Chief Executives Board for Coordination (CEB), on the JIU report. CEB members noted the actions already taken to address the weaknesses identified in the report.

Communication. On 1 July [A/58/99-E/2003/94], Sweden transmitted the Principles and Good Practice of Humanitarian Donorship and Implementation Plan for Good Humanitarian Donorship, endorsed by the participants of the International Meeting on Good Humanitarian Donorship (Stockholm, 16-17 June).

ECONOMIC AND SOCIAL COUNCIL ACTION

On 15 July [meeting 35], the Economic and Social Council adopted **resolution 2003/5** [draft: E/2003/L.28] without vote [agenda item 5].

Strengthening of the coordination of emergency humanitarian assistance of the United Nations

The Economic and Social Council,

Reaffirming General Assembly resolution 46/182 of 19 December 1991, recalling that humanitarian assistance should be provided in accordance with and with due respect for the guiding principles contained in the annex to that resolution and recognizing other relevant resolutions of the Assembly and resolutions and agreed conclusions of the Economic and Social Council,

Recalling its resolution 2002/32 of 26 July 2002 and General Assembly resolution 57/153 of 16 December 2002,

Recognizing that the affected State has the primary role in the initiation, organization, coordination and implementation of humanitarian assistance within its territory and in the facilitation of the work of humanitarian organizations,

Recognizing also the importance of the principles of neutrality, humanity and impartiality for the provision of humanitarian assistance,

Emphasizing the importance of the discussion of humanitarian policies and activities in the Economic and Social Council,

Welcoming the fact that at the humanitarian affairs segment of 2003 the Economic and Social Council considered the theme "Strengthening of the coordination of the United Nations humanitarian assistance, with particular attention to humanitarian financing and effectiveness of humanitarian assistance and the transition from relief to development" and that the Council held a panel, within the framework of the theme, on "Responding to the effects of HIV/AIDS and other widespread diseases on humanitarian relief operations",

Emphasizing the importance of continued international cooperation in support of the efforts of affected States in dealing with natural disasters and complex emergencies in all their phases,

Reiterating that humanitarian assistance should be provided in a way that is not to the detriment of resources made available for international cooperation for development,

Welcoming positive developments towards the resolution of some long-standing conflicts, while remaining deeply concerned about the outbreak of new conflicts and the protracted nature of other conflicts,

Noting with grave concern the growing intensity and recurrence of natural disasters, and reaffirming the importance of sustainable measures to reduce the vulnerability of societies to natural hazards using an integrated, multi-hazard and participatory approach to address vulnerability, risk assessment and disaster prevention, mitigation, preparedness, response and recovery,

Taking note of the 2003 "Guidelines on the Use of Military and Civil Defence Assets to Support United Nations Humanitarian Activities in Complex Emergencies", as well as of the 1994 "Guidelines on the Use of Military and Civil Defence Assets in Disaster Relief",

Bearing in mind the review of the Yokohama Strategy for a Safer World: Guidelines for Natural Disaster Prevention, Preparedness and Mitigation and the Plan of Action therein,

Expressing grave concern about the tragic loss of lives of humanitarian staff while providing humanitarian assistance and the increased insecurity encountered by humanitarian staff as well as the acts of violence committed against them, in particular deliberate attacks, and mindful of the need to provide the fullest possible protection for their security,

Recalling the inclusion of attacks intentionally directed against personnel involved in a humanitarian assistance or peacekeeping mission in accordance with the Charter of the United Nations as a war crime in the Rome Statute of the International Criminal Court, which was adopted on 17 July 1998 and entered into force on 1 July 2002, and noting the role that the Court could play in appropriate cases in bringing to justice those responsible for serious violations of international humanitarian law,

Bearing in mind that reaching the vulnerable is essential for providing adequate protection and assistance in context of natural disasters and complex emergencies as well as for strengthening local capacity to cope with humanitarian needs in such contexts,

Noting the grave humanitarian and development implications of the HIV/AIDS pandemic and other widespread major infectious diseases prevalent in the humanitarian context, such as malaria, tuberculosis and cholera, on the affected countries,

1. *Takes note with appreciation* of the report of the Secretary-General;

Humanitarian developments and challenges

2. *Calls upon* all parties to armed conflicts to comply with their obligations under international humanitarian law, human rights law and refugee law;

3. *Reaffirms* the obligation of all States and parties to armed conflict to protect civilians in armed conflicts in accordance with international humanitarian law, and invites States to promote a culture of protection, taking into account the particular needs of women, children, older persons and persons with disabilities;

4. *Urges* the international community and the relevant organizations of the United Nations system to strengthen humanitarian and other assistance to civilians under foreign occupation;

5. *Urges* all States to take measures necessary to ensure the safety and security of humanitarian personnel and United Nations and associated personnel;

6. *Strongly condemns* any act, or failure to act, contrary to international law, which obstructs or prevents humanitarian personnel and United Nations personnel from discharging their humanitarian functions;

7. *Calls upon* all Governments and parties in complex humanitarian emergencies, in particular in armed conflicts and in post-conflict situations, in countries in which humanitarian personnel are operating, in conformity with the relevant provisions of international law and national laws, to cooperate fully with the United Nations and other humanitarian agencies and organizations and to ensure the safe and unhindered access of humanitarian personnel, as well as supplies and equipment, in order to allow them to perform efficiently their task of assisting the affected civilian population, including refugees and internally displaced persons;

8. *Strongly urges* States to ensure that those responsible for attacks against humanitarian staff are promptly brought to justice, as provided by national law and obligations under international law, and notes the need for States to end impunity for such acts;

9. *Notes* that an increasing number of States, United Nations organizations and regional and non-governmental organizations are making use of the Guiding Principles on Internal Displacement, encourages the strengthening of legal frameworks for the protection of internally displaced persons, and urges the international community to strengthen its support to affected States in their efforts to provide, through national plans or initiatives, protection and assistance to their internally displaced persons;

10. *Stresses* the continued need and relevance of integrating, through implementation of existing policies, commitments and guidelines on gender mainstreaming, a gender perspective in the planning,

programming and implementation of humanitarian assistance activities;

11. *Welcomes* the establishment by the Inter-Agency Standing Committee of the six core principles in the Plan of Action on Protection from Sexual Exploitation and Abuse in Humanitarian Crises, representing minimum standards of behaviour required of all United Nations civilian staff members, and urges the United Nations to take appropriate follow-up action in response to allegations of sexual violence and exploitation by humanitarian workers;

12. *Encourages* Governments as well as international humanitarian organizations, as appropriate, to take further initiatives to prevent, address and follow up on allegations of sexual exploitation and abuse in humanitarian emergencies, and emphasizes that the highest standards of conduct and accountability are required of all personnel serving in humanitarian and peacekeeping operations;

13. *Stresses* the need to strengthen institutional capacity at all levels as well as disaster risk reduction programmes, particularly in developing countries and countries with economies in transition, in order to minimize vulnerabilities and disaster risks as well as to avoid or to limit adverse impact of natural hazards within the broad context of sustainable development;

14. *Encourages* the United Nations Development Programme, the Office for the Coordination of Humanitarian Affairs of the Secretariat and the secretariat of the International Strategy for Disaster Reduction to continue to strengthen their coordination with the view, inter alia, to advancing the implementation of provisions of vulnerability, risk assessment and disaster management, including prevention, mitigation, preparedness, response and recovery as contained in the Plan of Implementation of the World Summit on Sustainable Development ("Johannesburg Plan of Implementation");

15. *Encourages* humanitarian agencies to ensure, to the extent possible, the participation of those affected by humanitarian situations in the design, implementation and evaluation of humanitarian assistance activities, while respecting the role of authorities of affected countries;

16. *Recalls* paragraph 3 of Article 101 of the Charter of the United Nations, and invites the United Nations organizations to enhance geographical balance in terms of humanitarian personnel employed by them;

17. *Stresses* the need for increased national and regional capacity-building in early warning and monitoring of natural hazards, natural disaster preparedness, mitigation and response, including by strengthening coordination in the areas of information sharing and analysis, logistics support, response coordination and strengthening enhanced relationships with existing regional structures, and encourages the international community to provide necessary technical assistance to States in this regard;

18. *Welcomes* the convening of the Second International Conference on Early Warning: Integration of the Early Warning Process into Public Policy, to be held from 16 to 18 October 2003 in Bonn, Germany, under the auspices of the United Nations;

19. *Encourages* States that have not done so to consider ratifying or acceding to the Tampere Convention on the Provision of Telecommunication Resources for Disaster Mitigation and Relief Operations, adopted at Tampere, Finland, on 18 June 1998;

20. *Recalls* General Assembly resolution 57/150 of 16 December 2002 on strengthening the effectiveness and coordination of international urban search and rescue assistance, and welcomes the work that is being undertaken to further strengthen the effectiveness and coordination of international urban search and rescue assistance;

21. *Affirms* the leading role of civilian organizations in implementing humanitarian assistance, particularly in areas affected by conflicts, and also affirms the need, in situations where military capacity and assets are used to support the implementation of humanitarian assistance, that their use be in conformity with international humanitarian law and humanitarian principles;

22. *Urges* States to implement outcomes and commitments of United Nations conferences on the HIV/AIDS pandemic as well as other major infectious diseases, including malaria and tuberculosis, with particular focus on the time-bound targets related to those diseases in complex emergencies and natural disaster-affected countries and regions;

23. *Recognizes* the important role of humanitarian agencies in addressing HIV/AIDS and other major infectious diseases, such as malaria, tuberculosis and cholera, in emergencies, and urges them to factor considerations pertaining to these major infectious diseases into their planning and coordination efforts, including in the areas of early warning and contingency planning;

24. *Calls upon* humanitarian and development organizations to strengthen their cooperation, between themselves and with Governments of affected States, in order to ensure that the longer-term developmental implications of the HIV/AIDS epidemic and of the other major infectious diseases are adequately addressed in emergency situations;

Transition from relief to development

25. *Takes note* of the work in progress by the United Nations system to clarify the role of the United Nations in post-conflict transition situations;

26. *Reiterates* that emergency assistance must be provided in ways that will support recovery and long-term development;

27. *Also reiterates* the need to address the strategic planning gap between relief and development activities in the context of natural disasters and complex emergencies;

28. *Notes with concern* the disturbing trend of low or late funding for rehabilitation programmes aimed at helping affected communities to attain self-sufficiency;

29. *Recognizes* that, inter alia, early engagement in planning, fuller coverage of the needs of all sectors, more support for recovery and long-term development activities, capacity-building at all relevant levels and enhancement of national ownership are critical to managing the transition from relief to development;

30. *Reiterates* the need for coordinated humanitarian assistance and adequate financial resources to ensure ongoing capacity for prompt, timely and effective response by the United Nations system to natural dis-

asters and other emergencies, both for immediate relief and also for the smooth transition between relief, rehabilitation, reconstruction and long-term sustainable development;

31. *Stresses* the importance of addressing, based on need, the situation of the least developed countries affected by conflict, natural disasters and other humanitarian situations and of improving their institutional capacity and providing adequate support for rehabilitation, reconstruction, long-term sustainable development, poverty reduction and, where appropriate, peace-building efforts of least developed countries emerging from those situations;

32. *Recognizes* that the need for coordination increases and becomes more complex in post-conflict transition, and encourages States and the United Nations system, as appropriate, to enhance their efforts towards the early assumption of the coordination role of the Government as well as integrated coordination, including information management, inclusive planning, donor coordination, strengthening the United Nations resident coordinator system and the full participation of concerned Governments in needs assessment, planning mechanisms and coordination processes;

33. *Stresses* the need to consider the issue of the transition from relief to development in an integrated manner at a substantive session of the Economic and Social Council in the near future, in view of the importance of getting humanitarian and development organizations, including international and regional financial institutions and non-governmental organizations, to discuss the implications of these situations more fully in their programming;

Humanitarian financing and effectiveness of humanitarian assistance

34. *Reaffirms* the responsibility of States, first and foremost, to take care of the victims of humanitarian emergencies within their own borders, while recognizing that the magnitude and duration of many emergencies may be beyond the response capacity of many affected countries;

35. *Recognizes* the role of the Emergency Relief Coordinator, and calls upon relevant United Nations organizations as well as other humanitarian actors to enhance the coordination, effectiveness and efficiency of their humanitarian activities, including by:

(*a*) Enhancing their commitment to system-wide coordination both at Headquarters and in the field;

(*b*) Strengthening efforts to report on results, activities and financial matters, including to donors, in a timely and comprehensive manner, and, where possible, to strive for harmonized reporting, bearing in mind specific requirements of donors;

(*c*) Developing further methods for monitoring and evaluation, including independent evaluations;

(*d*) Maximizing the portion of humanitarian assistance contributions that directly benefits people in need;

(*e*) Addressing mutual safety and security concerns at the field level;

36. *Calls upon* the organizations of the United Nations system to improve and increase consistency in the way in which humanitarian needs are assessed, inter alia, by:

(*a*) Enhancing the quality, accuracy and transparency of needs assessments;

(*b*) Agreeing upon minimum standards in order to properly assess needs;

(*c*) Including States and other humanitarian actors in assessment missions;

(*d*) Addressing all humanitarian needs;

(*e*) Taking into account safety and security of humanitarian personnel;

(*f*) Undertaking joint agency assessments;

37. *Urges* the Emergency Relief Coordinator to further develop the global humanitarian financial tracking system and to refine the comprehensive system for the collection and dissemination of data on humanitarian needs and contributions;

38. *Encourages* the donor community to improve its response to humanitarian emergencies through policies and practices of good donorship, along with mechanisms for their review, and welcomes steps taken in that direction;

39. *Also encourages* the donor community to provide humanitarian assistance in proportion to needs and on the basis of needs assessments, with a view to ensuring a more equitable distribution of humanitarian assistance across humanitarian emergencies, including those of a protracted nature, as well as fuller coverage of the needs of all sectors;

40. *Further encourages* the donor community to establish reliable, predictable and timely funding to meet humanitarian needs and to consider increasing the flexibility of funding and the share of non-earmarked contributions to United Nations agencies in response to humanitarian emergencies, including within the consolidated appeals;

41. *Encourages* donors to consider taking steps to harmonize reporting requirements, based on United Nations standards for financial reporting, as well as to enhance reporting to the financial tracking system;

42. *Requests* the Secretary-General to reflect the progress made in the implementation of and follow-up to the present resolution in his next report to the Council and the General Assembly on the coordination of emergency humanitarian assistance of the United Nations.

Also on 15 July, by **decision 2003/226**, the Council took note of the Secretary-General's report on strengthening the coordination of UN emergency humanitarian assistance (see p. 915).

GENERAL ASSEMBLY ACTION

On 17 December [meeting 75], the General Assembly adopted **resolution 58/114** [draft: A/58/L.39 & Add.1] without vote [agenda item 40 (*a*)].

Strengthening of the coordination of emergency humanitarian assistance of the United Nations

The General Assembly,

Recalling its resolution 46/182 of 19 December 1991 and the guiding principles contained in the annex thereto, other relevant General Assembly and Economic and Social Council resolutions and agreed conclusions of the Council,

Taking note of the report of the Secretary-General,

Taking note also of the report of the Secretary-General on the status of implementation of actions described in the report of the Secretary-General entitled "Strengthening of the United Nations: an agenda for further change",

Reaffirming the principles of neutrality, humanity and impartiality for the provision of humanitarian assistance,

Recognizing that independence, meaning the autonomy of humanitarian objectives from the political, economic, military or other objectives that any actor may hold with regard to areas where humanitarian action is being implemented, is also an important guiding principle for the provision of humanitarian assistance,

Gravely concerned about the acts of violence against humanitarian personnel and United Nations and its associated personnel, in particular deliberate attacks, which are in violation of international humanitarian law or other international law that may be applicable,

Gravely concerned also about the lack of access by humanitarian personnel to victims of humanitarian emergencies, in particular in armed conflict and in post-conflict situations, in many regions of the world,

Reaffirming the responsibility first and foremost of States to take care of the victims of humanitarian emergencies within their own borders, while recognizing that the magnitude and duration of many emergencies may be beyond the response capacity of many affected countries,

Concerned about the need to mobilize adequate levels of financing for emergency humanitarian assistance,

Emphasizing that the Office for the Coordination of Humanitarian Affairs of the Secretariat should benefit from adequate and more predictable funding, while stressing the importance for the Office to continue to make efforts to broaden its donor base,

Recognizing the importance of humanitarian assistance in ensuring the effective transition from conflict to peace and in preventing the recurrence of armed conflict, and that humanitarian assistance must be provided in ways that will be supportive of recovery and long-term development,

Recognizing also the importance of adequate assistance in the transition from relief to development,

1. *Takes note with appreciation* of the outcome of the sixth humanitarian affairs segment of the Economic and Social Council, during its substantive session of 2003;

2. *Welcomes* the appointment of the new Emergency Relief Coordinator, encourages the Office for the Coordination of Humanitarian Affairs of the Secretariat to continue its efforts to strengthen the coordination of humanitarian assistance of the United Nations, including through the consolidated appeals process, and calls upon relevant United Nations organizations as well as other humanitarian and development actors to work with the Office in enhancing the coordination, effectiveness and efficiency of humanitarian assistance;

3. *Stresses* the need to increase in an incremental way, in the normal course of the budget process, the share of the budget of the Office for the Coordination of Humanitarian Affairs borne by the United Nations regular budget;

4. *Emphasizes* the importance of the discussion of humanitarian policies and activities in the General Assembly and the Economic and Social Council;

5. *Calls upon* relevant organizations of the United Nations system, other relevant international organizations, Governments and non-governmental organizations to cooperate with the Secretary-General and the Emergency Relief Coordinator to ensure timely implementation of and follow-up to resolutions of the Economic and Social Council adopted at the humanitarian affairs segment of its substantive session;

6. *Encourages* the Economic and Social Council to consider the issue of the transition from relief to development in an integrated manner, through a possible joint meeting of the humanitarian and operational segments, during its substantive session in the near future, in view of the importance of getting humanitarian and development organizations, including international and regional financial institutions and non-governmental organizations, to discuss and review more fully the implications of the transition from relief to development in their programming, and invites the Council to take into account, inter alia, the work in progress by the United Nations system to clarify its role in post-conflict transition situations as well as other relevant information in its consideration;

7. *Strongly condemns* all forms of violence to which humanitarian personnel and United Nations and its associated personnel are increasingly subjected, as well as any act or failure to act, contrary to international law, which obstructs or prevents humanitarian personnel and United Nations and its associated personnel from discharging their humanitarian functions;

8. *Urges* all States to take necessary measures to ensure the safety and security of humanitarian personnel and United Nations and its associated personnel;

9. *Reaffirms* the leading role of civilian organizations in implementing humanitarian assistance, particularly in areas affected by conflicts, affirms the need, in situations where military capacity and assets are used to support the implementation of humanitarian assistance, for their use to be in conformity with international humanitarian law and humanitarian principles, and in this regard takes note of the 2003 "Guidelines on the Use of Military and Civil Defence Assets to Support United Nations Humanitarian Activities in Complex Emergencies", as well as of the 1994 "Guidelines on the Use of Military and Civil Defence Assets in Disaster Relief";

10. *Calls upon* all Governments and parties in complex humanitarian emergencies, in particular in armed conflicts and in post-conflict situations, in countries in which humanitarian personnel are operating, in conformity with the relevant provisions of international law and national laws, to cooperate fully with the United Nations and other humanitarian agencies and organizations and to ensure the safe and unhindered access of humanitarian personnel as well as supplies and equipment in order to allow them to perform efficiently their task of assisting the affected civilian population, including refugees and internally displaced persons;

11. *Encourages* Member States with internally displaced persons to develop or strengthen, as appropriate, national laws, policies and minimum standards on internal displacement, inter alia, taking into account

the Guiding Principles on Internal Displacement, and to continue to work with humanitarian agencies in endeavours to provide a more predictable response to the needs of internally displaced persons, and in this regard calls for international support, upon request, to capacity-building efforts of Governments;

12. *Reaffirms* the obligation of all States and parties to an armed conflict to protect civilians in armed conflicts in accordance with international humanitarian law, and invites States to promote a culture of protection, taking into account the particular needs of women, children, older persons and persons with disabilities;

13. *Welcomes* the continued efforts to address the issue of sexual exploitation and sexual abuse in the context of humanitarian crises, and notes with interest the bulletin of the Secretary-General on special measures for protection from sexual exploitation and sexual abuse;

14. *Encourages* the donor community to improve its response to humanitarian emergencies through policies and practices of good donorship, together with mechanisms for their review, and welcomes steps taken in this direction;

15. *Calls upon* relevant United Nations organizations to improve and increase consistency in the way in which humanitarian needs are assessed;

16. *Requests* the Secretary-General to report to the General Assembly at its fifty-ninth session, through the Economic and Social Council at its substantive session of 2004, on progress made in strengthening the coordination of emergency humanitarian assistance of the United Nations, including the implementation of and follow-up to Economic and Social Council resolution 2003/5 of 15 July 2003.

UN and other humanitarian personnel

During the year, the Security Council and the General Assembly called for measures to ensure the security and safety of humanitarian personnel and United Nations and associated personnel (see also p. 1452).

SECURITY COUNCIL ACTION

On 26 August [meeting 4814], the Security Council unanimously adopted **resolution 1502(2003)**. The draft [S/2003/581] was prepared in consultations among Council members.

The Security Council,

Reiterating its primary responsibility for the maintenance of international peace and security and, in this context, the need to promote and ensure respect for the principles and rules of international humanitarian law,

Reaffirming its resolutions 1265(1999) of 17 September 1999 and 1296(2000) of 19 April 2000 on protection of civilians in armed conflict, and its resolution 1460 (2003) of 30 January 2003 on children and armed conflict, as well as other relevant resolutions, and recalling the statements by its President on protection of civilians in armed conflict (S/PRST/1999/6, S/PRST/ 2002/6, S/PRST/2002/41) and on protection of United Nations personnel, associated personnel and humanitarian personnel in conflict zones (S/PRST/2000/4),

Welcoming the adoption by the General Assembly of resolution 57/28 of 19 November 2002 entitled "Scope of legal protection under the Convention on the Safety of United Nations and Associated Personnel" and resolution 57/155 of 16 December 2002 entitled "Safety and security of humanitarian personnel and protection of United Nations personnel",

Reaffirming the obligation of all humanitarian personnel and United Nations and associated personnel to observe and respect the laws of the country in which they are operating, in accordance with international law and the Charter of the United Nations, and underlining the importance for humanitarian organizations of upholding the principles of neutrality, impartiality and humanity in their humanitarian activities,

Emphasizing that there are existing prohibitions under international law against attacks knowingly and intentionally directed against personnel involved in a humanitarian assistance or peacekeeping mission undertaken in accordance with the Charter which in situations of armed conflict constitute war crimes, and recalling the need for States to end impunity for such criminal acts,

Aware that the protection of humanitarian personnel and United Nations and associated personnel is a concern in situations of armed conflict and otherwise,

Gravely concerned at the acts of violence in many parts of the world against humanitarian personnel and United Nations and associated personnel, in particular deliberate attacks, which are in violation of international humanitarian law as well as other international law that may be applicable, such as the attack against the headquarters of the United Nations Assistance Mission for Iraq in Baghdad on 19 August 2003,

1. *Expresses its strong condemnation* of all forms of violence, including, inter alia, murder, rape and sexual assault, intimidation, armed robbery, abduction, hostage-taking, kidnapping, harassment and illegal arrest and detention, to which those participating in humanitarian operations are increasingly exposed, as well as attacks on humanitarian convoys and acts of destruction and looting of their property;

2. *Urges* States to ensure that crimes against such personnel do not remain unpunished;

3. *Reaffirms* the obligation of all parties involved in an armed conflict to comply fully with the rules and principles of international law applicable to them related to the protection of humanitarian personnel and United Nations and associated personnel, in particular international humanitarian law, human rights law and refugee law;

4. *Urges* all those concerned, as set forth in international humanitarian law, including the Geneva Conventions of 12 August 1949 and the Regulations annexed to the Hague Convention of 18 October 1907, to allow full unimpeded access by humanitarian personnel to all people in need of assistance and to make available, as far as possible, all necessary facilities for their operations, and to promote the safety, security and freedom of movement of humanitarian personnel and United Nations and associated personnel and their assets;

5. *Expresses its determination* to take appropriate steps in order to ensure the safety and security of hu-

manitarian personnel and United Nations and associated personnel, including, inter alia, by:

(a) Requesting the Secretary-General to seek the inclusion of, and requesting that host countries include, key provisions of the Convention on the Safety of United Nations and Associated Personnel of 9 December 1994, among others, those regarding the prevention of attacks against members of United Nations operations, the establishment of such attacks as crimes punishable by law and the prosecution or extradition of offenders, in future as well as, if necessary, in existing status-of-forces, status-of-mission and host country agreements negotiated between the United Nations and those countries, mindful of the importance of the timely conclusion of such agreements;

(b) Encouraging the Secretary-General, in accordance with his prerogatives under the Charter of the United Nations, to bring to the attention of the Security Council situations in which humanitarian assistance is denied as a consequence of violence directed against humanitarian personnel and United Nations and associated personnel;

(c) Issuing the declaration of exceptional risk for the purposes of article 1 (c) (ii) of the Convention on the Safety of United Nations and Associated Personnel in situations where, in its assessment, circumstances would support such a declaration, and inviting the Secretary-General to advise the Council where, in his assessment, circumstances would support such a declaration;

6. *Requests* the Secretary-General to address in all his country-specific situation reports the issue of the safety and security of humanitarian personnel and United Nations and associated personnel, including specific acts of violence against such personnel, remedial actions taken to prevent similar incidents and actions taken to identify and hold accountable those who commit such acts, and to explore and propose additional ways and means to enhance the safety and security of such personnel.

Report of Secretary-General. In response to General Assembly resolution 57/155 [YUN 2002, p. 1414], the Secretary-General, in a September report [A/58/344], described threats against humanitarian and UN personnel over the preceding year. He noted that, while fatalities had decreased significantly in recent years, there were instances in which the Organization's efforts were being frustrated.

The Assembly, in **resolution 58/122** of 17 December (see p. 1453), called on Governments and parties in complex humanitarian emergencies to ensure the safe and unhindered access of humanitarian personnel.

Resource mobilization

Central Emergency Revolving Fund

In 2003, the Central Emergency Revolving Fund, established in 1992 [YUN 1992, p. 584] as a cash-flow mechanism for the initial phase of humanitarian emergencies, granted 12 advances, amounting to $7.2 million.

Consolidated appeals

The consolidated appeals process continued to coordinate and facilitate the capacity of the UN system to meet its inter-agency resource requirements. In 2003, the United Nations and its humanitarian partners issued consolidated appeals seeking $5.2 billion in assistance to Afghanistan, Angola, the northern Caucasus, the Central African Republic, Côte d'Ivoire, Côte d'Ivoire + 5 (Burkina Faso, Ghana, Guinea, Liberia, Mali), the Democratic People's Republic of Korea, Eritrea, the Great Lakes region and Central Africa (Burundi, Congo, Democratic Republic of the Congo, Uganda), Guinea, Indonesia, Iraq, Liberia, the Occupied Palestinian Territory, Sierra Leone, Somalia, the Southern Africa region (Lesotho, Malawi, Mozambique, Swaziland, Zambia, Zimbabwe), the Sudan and Tajikistan.

The latest available data indicated that 75.3 per cent ($3.9 billion) of requirements had been met.

White Helmets

In response to General Assembly resolution 56/102 [YUN 2001, p. 827], the Secretary-General, in an August report [A/58/320], described the status of implementation of the "White Helmets" initiative, which was established by Argentina in 1993 to promote the concept of pre-identified standby and trained teams of volunteers from various national volunteer corps to support immediate relief, rehabilitation, construction and development activities and was administered by the United Nations Development Programme (UNDP). The report, which covered the period from March 2001 to July 2003, highlighted programme activities and their results, existing mechanisms and partnerships, financing and resources mobilization, and underscored opportunities for widening the operationalization of the concept.

GENERAL ASSEMBLY ACTION

On 17 December [meeting 75], the General Assembly adopted **resolution 58/118** [draft: A/58/L.43 & Add.1] without vote [agenda item 40 (d)].

Participation of volunteers, "White Helmets", in the activities of the United Nations in the field of humanitarian relief, rehabilitation and technical cooperation for development

The General Assembly,

Reaffirming its resolutions 50/19 of 28 November 1995, 52/171 of 16 December 1997, 54/98 of 8 December 1999 and 56/102 of 14 December 2001,

Reaffirming also its resolutions 46/182 of 19 December 1991, 47/168 of 22 December 1992, 48/57 of 14 December 1993, 49/139 A and B of 20 December 1994, 50/57 of 12 December 1995 and 51/194 of 17 December 1996 and Economic and Social Council resolutions 1995/56 of 28 July 1995 and 1996/33 of 25 July 1996,

Emphasizing the need to address the strategic planning gap between relief and development activities in the context of humanitarian emergencies, taking into account the internationally agreed development goals, including those contained in the United Nations Millennium Declaration,

Recognizing that the international community, in addressing the growing magnitude and complexity of man-made and natural disasters and chronic situations characterized by hunger, malnutrition and poverty, must rely not only on the formulation of a well-coordinated global response within the framework of the United Nations but also on the promotion of a smooth transition from relief to rehabilitation, reconstruction and development,

Recalling once again that prevention, preparedness and contingency planning for emergencies on a global level depend, for the most part, on the strengthening of local and national response capacities as well as on the availability of financial resources, both domestic and international,

1. *Takes note* of the report of the Secretary-General, prepared in pursuance of its resolution 56/102 on the participation of volunteers, "White Helmets", in the activities of the United Nations in the field of humanitarian relief, rehabilitation and technical cooperation for development;

2. *Recognizes* the value of domestic and regional actions aimed at making pre-identified, standby and trained national volunteer corps such as the White Helmets available to the United Nations system, through the United Nations Volunteers and other agencies, and in accordance with accepted United Nations procedures and practices, in order to provide specialized human and technical resources for emergency relief and rehabilitation;

3. *Expresses its satisfaction* for the progress of the White Helmets initiative as a singular voluntary international effort to provide the United Nations system with voluntary expertise to respond, in a quick and coordinated manner, to United Nations appeals concerning humanitarian relief, rehabilitation, reconstruction and development, while preserving the non-political, neutral and impartial character of humanitarian action;

4. *Encourages* Member States to identify their respective national focal points for the White Helmets in order to continue to provide the United Nations system with an accessible global network of rapid response facilities in case of humanitarian emergencies;

5. *Recognizes with appreciation* the progress made by the States members of the Common Market of the South and its associated partners in strengthening and broadening the regional role of the White Helmets initiative, and encourages Member States in other regional associations to make similar joint efforts;

6. *Encourages* operational partners of the United Nations system, in particular United Nations Volunteers and the United Nations Development Programme, to draw upon the voluntary expertise of the White Helmets, as appropriate, including in their response to chronic situations characterized by hunger, malnutrition and poverty;

7. *Recognizes* that the White Helmets initiative can play an important role in the promotion, diffusion and fulfilment of the decisions achieved in the United Nations Millennium Declaration, and invites Member States in a position to do so to consider means to ensure the integration of the White Helmets initiative into their programme activities and to make the commensurate financial resources available through the special financing window of the Special Voluntary Fund of the United Nations Volunteers, or in coordination with it;

8. *Invites* the Secretary-General, on the basis of the experience acquired, to consider further the potential use of White Helmets as a resource for preventing and mitigating the effects of post-conflict humanitarian emergencies and, in this context, to maintain adequate support for the White Helmets liaison functions, taking into account the ongoing reforms process;

9. *Requests* the Secretary-General to take into consideration the ten years that will have passed since the adoption of its resolution 49/139 B, the first resolution on the White Helmets initiative, and, in view of the success of coordinated actions carried out since then with, inter alia, the United Nations Children's Fund, the World Food Programme, the Office for the Coordination of Humanitarian Affairs of the Secretariat, the United Nations Development Programme and the United Nations Volunteers, to consider their impact and to analyse possible steps and modalities to enhance the integration of the White Helmets initiative within the work of the United Nations system, suggesting appropriate mechanisms and areas, and to report thereon to the General Assembly at its sixtieth session.

Mine clearance

In response to General Assembly resolution 57/159 [YUN 2002, p. 891], the Secretary-General, in an August report [A/58/260], described progress in implementing the goals and objectives of the UN mine-action strategy for the period 2001-2005 [YUN 2001, p. 828]. A review of the six strategic goals identified progress in each goal as follows: increased information and improved information technology through the production of information related to mine-action problems, interagency assessment missions to mine-affected countries, enhancement of the Web-based information network E-mine, and installations and upgrading of the software, Information Management System for Mine Action (goal 1); improved capacity to respond to emergencies through the endorsement of an operational framework for rapid response, implementation of a rapid-response plan in Iraq, and the provision of emergency mine-action assistance to seven countries (goal 2); sustained efforts to build national mine-action capacity in over 30 countries (goal 3); significant improvements in quality management realized through strengthened management and oversight of the International Mine Action Standards (IMAS) (goal 4); successful resource mobilization leading to increased resources for mine-action programmes and the issue of the *Portfolio of Mine-related Projects: 2003* to coincide with the launch of consolidated appeals (goal 5); and increased advocacy in support of relevant legal instruments through the provision of expert information to Member States considering legislation to regulate explosive remnants of war and assistance in codifying the rights of persons living with disabilities, including landmine survivors (goal 6).

The Secretary-General concluded that the UN mine-action strategy for 2001-2005 had provided valuable direction and guidance for all UN entities involved in its implementation and had fostered coordination and accountability across the mine-action community. He recommended that the Inter-Agency Coordination Group on Mine Action should continuously monitor the 2001-2005 strategy and report annually to the Assembly, and called for the development, in 2005, of a UN mine-action strategy for the period 2005-2009.

An addendum to the report [A/58/260/Add.1] presented the text of the revised strategy.

GENERAL ASSEMBLY ACTION

On 19 December [meeting 76], the General Assembly adopted **resolution 58/127** [draft: A/58/L.50 & Add.1, orally revised] without vote [agenda item 22].

Assistance in mine action

The General Assembly,

Recalling its resolution 57/159 of 16 December 2002 and all its previous resolutions on assistance in mine clearance and mine action, all adopted without a vote,

Recognizing that, in addition to the primary role of States, the United Nations has a significant role to play in the field of assistance in mine action, and considering mine action to be an important and integrated component of United Nations humanitarian and development activities,

Reaffirming its deep concern at the tremendous humanitarian and development problems caused by the presence of mines and other unexploded ordnance that constitute an obstacle to the return of refugees and other displaced persons, to humanitarian aid operations and to reconstruction and economic development, as well as to the restoration of normal social conditions, and that have serious and lasting social and economic consequences for the populations of mine-affected countries,

Bearing in mind the serious threat that mines and other unexploded ordnance pose to the safety, health and lives of local civilian populations, as well as of personnel participating in humanitarian, peacekeeping and rehabilitation programmes and operations,

Encouraged by the reduction in the number of new mine victims, but reiterating its dismay at the existing high number of victims of mines and other unexploded ordnance, especially among civilian populations, including women and children, and recalling in this context its resolution 57/190 of 18 December 2002 and Commission on Human Rights resolutions 2003/49 of 23 April 2003, on the human rights of persons with disabilities, and 2003/86 of 25 April 2003, on the rights of the child,

Deeply alarmed by the number of mines that continue to be laid each year, as well as the presence of a decreasing but still very large number of mines and other unexploded ordnance as a result of armed conflicts, and therefore remaining convinced of the necessity and urgency of a significant increase in mine-clearance efforts by the international community with a view to eliminating the threat of landmines to civilians as soon as possible,

Noting the inclusion in Amended Protocol II to the Convention on Prohibitions or Restrictions on the Use of Certain Conventional Weapons Which May Be Deemed to Be Excessively Injurious or to Have Indiscriminate Effects of a number of provisions of importance for mine-clearance operations, notably the requirement of detectability, and provision of information and technical and material assistance necessary to remove or otherwise render ineffective minefields, mines and booby traps, and noting also that Amended Protocol II to the Convention entered into force on 3 December 1998,

Noting also the conclusions and recommendations adopted at the Fourth and Fifth Annual Conferences of the States Parties to Amended Protocol II to the Convention on Prohibitions or Restrictions on the Use of Certain Conventional Weapons Which May Be Deemed to Be Excessively Injurious or to Have Indiscriminate Effects, held in Geneva on 11 December 2002 and on 26 November 2003, respectively,

Noting further the new additional Protocol to address the post-conflict impact of explosive remnants of war adopted by the Meeting of States Parties to the Convention on Prohibitions or Restrictions on the Use of Certain Conventional Weapons Which May Be Deemed to Be Excessively Injurious or to Have Indiscriminate Effects, held in Geneva on 27 and 28 November 2003, and noting the agreement reached on mandates for further work by the same Meeting,

Noting that additional States have ratified or acceded to the Convention on the Prohibition of the Use, Stockpiling, Production and Transfer of Anti-personnel Mines and on Their Destruction, which entered into force on 1 March 1999, bringing the total number of States that have formally accepted the obligations therein to one hundred and forty-one,

Noting also the conclusions of the Fifth Meeting of the States Parties to the Convention on the Prohibition of the Use, Stockpiling, Production and Transfer of Anti-personnel Mines and on Their Destruction, held in Bangkok from 15 to 19 September 2003, taking note of the reaffirmed commitments that were made by the States parties in the Bangkok Declaration, among other things, to pursue efforts related to the core humanitarian objectives of the Convention, urging all States parties and relevant organizations to participate actively in the work of the intersessional programme established by States parties to the Convention, and taking note also that the First Review Conference, to which the Secretary-General will be invited, will be held in Nairobi, from 29 November to 3 December 2004,

Stressing the need to convince mine-affected States to halt new deployments of anti-personnel mines in order to ensure the effectiveness and efficiency of mine-clearance operations,

Stressing also the pressing need to urge non-State actors to halt immediately and unconditionally new deployments of mines and other associated explosive devices,

Recognizing the importance of assisting mine clearance in mine-affected countries by ensuring that the necessary maps and information and appropriate technical and material assistance are provided to help to remove existing minefields, mines, booby traps and other unexploded ordnance,

Noting that the resources allocated to mine-action activities have increased in recent years, but stressing the need to mobilize additional resources and to secure the best possible utilization of such resources, particularly for victim assistance, in order to meet increasing requirements, and encouraging all States, the United Nations and other international, regional and non-governmental and private organizations to continue their efforts in this regard,

Concerned at the limited availability of safe and cost-effective mine-detection and mine-clearance equipment, as well as the need for effective global coordination in research and development to improve relevant technologies, and conscious of the need to promote further and more rapid progress in this field and to foster international, national and local technical cooperation to that end,

Reaffirming the need to reinforce cooperation and coordination in the area of mine action at all levels and to devote the necessary resources to that end, including resources to support national and regional capacity-building initiatives, where applicable, and the work of the United Nations in this regard,

Noting with appreciation the finalization of an emergency response plan by the United Nations to respond to emergency mine-action requirements,

Welcoming the various established mine-action coordination centres, as well as the creation and existence of international trust funds for mine-action activities,

Noting with satisfaction the inclusion in the mandates of several peacekeeping operations of provisions relating to mine-action work carried out under the direction of the Department of Peacekeeping Operations of the Secretariat, in the context of such operations,

Commending the action taken by donor and recipient Governments, the United Nations system, regional organizations, the International Committee of the Red Cross and non-governmental organizations to coordinate their efforts and seek solutions to the problems related to the presence of mines and other unexploded ordnance, as well as their assistance to victims of mines,

Welcoming the role of the Secretary-General in increasing public awareness of the problem of landmines,

1. *Welcomes* the report of the Secretary-General on assistance in mine action and the recommendations contained therein, and takes note with appreciation of the revised mine-action strategy contained in the addendum to the report;

2. *Calls*, in particular, for the continuation of the efforts of States, with the assistance of the United Nations and relevant organizations involved in mine action, as appropriate, to foster the establishment and development of national mine-action capacities in countries in which mines and other unexploded ordnance constitute a serious threat to the safety, health and lives of the local population or an impediment to social and economic development efforts at the national and local levels, and urges all Member States, in particular those that have the capacity to do so, to assist mine-affected countries in the establishment and development of national capacities in mine action;

3. *Invites* Member States to develop and support national programmes, where appropriate, in cooperation with the relevant bodies of the United Nations system and relevant regional, governmental and non-governmental organizations, to reduce the risks posed by landmines and other unexploded ordnance, including among women and children;

4. *Expresses its appreciation* to Governments, regional organizations and other donors for their financial and in-kind contributions to mine action, including contributions for emergency operations, peacekeeping operations and for national and local capacity-building programmes;

5. *Encourages* efforts to conduct mine action in accordance with accepted national and international standards, including International Mine Action Standards, and also encourages all States involved in mine action, including troop-contributing countries conducting mine action in peacekeeping operations, to follow these standards, as applicable;

6. *Emphasizes* the importance of using an information management system, such as the Information Management System for Mine Action, in full coordination with the United Nations Mine Action Service and with the instrumental support of the Geneva International Centre for Humanitarian Demining;

7. *Appeals* to Governments, regional organizations and other donors to continue and, whenever possible, increase their support to mine action through reliable, predictable and timely contributions, including contributions through the Voluntary Trust Fund for Assistance in Mine Action as well as to national mine-action efforts and humanitarian mine-action programmes of non-governmental organizations, to allow for the timely delivery of mine-action assistance, and stresses that such assistance should be integrated into broader humanitarian, development and other strategies;

8. *Stresses* the importance of international support for emergency assistance to victims of mines and other unexploded ordnance and for the care, rehabilitation and social and economic reintegration of the victims, and also stresses that such assistance should be integrated into broader public health and socio-economic strategies;

9. *Encourages* all relevant multilateral and national programmes and bodies to include, in coordination with the United Nations, activities related to mine action in their humanitarian, rehabilitation, reconstruction and development assistance activities, where appropriate, bearing in mind the need to ensure national and local ownership, sustainability and capacity-building;

10. *Encourages* Member States, the United Nations system, international and regional organizations and

relevant non-governmental organizations to take further action to mainstream a gender perspective and integrate gender and age-appropriate considerations in all aspects of mine-action programming, particularly including programmes to reduce the number of child victims and relieve their plight;

11. *Stresses* the importance of cooperation and coordination in mine action, while emphasizing once again the important role of the United Nations in the effective coordination of mine-action activities, based on the United Nations policy on mine action and effective coordination, and especially the role of the Mine Action Service, stresses also the important role that national authorities and regional organizations can play in this regard, as well as the important role of relevant non-governmental organizations, and underlines the need for the continuous assessment of these roles by the General Assembly;

12. *Emphasizes* the role of the Mine Action Service as the focal point for mine action within the United Nations system and its ongoing collaboration with and coordination of all mine-related activities of the United Nations agencies, funds and programmes, and in this regard expresses its appreciation of the roles played by other bodies of the United Nations system, in accordance with United Nations mine-action policy;

13. *Urges* Member States and regional, governmental and non-governmental organizations and foundations to continue to extend full assistance and cooperation to the Secretary-General and, in particular, to provide him with information and data, as well as other appropriate resources that could be useful in strengthening the coordination role of the United Nations in mine action;

14. *Takes note with appreciation* of the Mine Action Guidelines for Ceasefire and Peace Agreements, requests the Secretary-General to make them widely available to United Nations mediators, moderators, special representatives of the Secretary-General and others, as appropriate, and calls upon all parties to conflict to incorporate provisions on mine action, where relevant, in ceasefire and peace agreements or other relevant arrangements;

15. *Takes note* of the potential that mine action can have as a peace and confidence-building measure in post-conflict situations among concerned parties;

16. *Encourages* the Secretary-General to continue to propose, where appropriate, provisions related to mine action in his recommendations to the Security Council for peacekeeping operations;

17. *Emphasizes* the importance of undertaking further multisectoral assessments and surveys to better define the nature, scope and impact of the landmine and other unexploded ordnance problem in affected countries and to support the establishment of clear priorities and national economic and development plans of action, underlining the need for the participation of populations of mine-affected areas in this regard;

18. *Notes with appreciation* the ongoing development by the United Nations of the International Mine Action Standards, with the assistance of the Geneva International Centre for Humanitarian Demining and other partners in mine action, to support the safe and effective conduct of mine-action activities, and emphasizes the need for an inclusive process to be followed in the development and review of such standards and the importance of developing in mine-affected countries national mine-action standards based on the International Mine Action Standards;

19. *Recognizes* the importance of building national capacities for and ownership of mine-action programmes, encourages the further establishment of national mine-action centres, including those supported by the United Nations Development Programme and the United Nations Children's Fund as well as those established under the auspices of the Mine Action Service in emergency situations, and encourages States to support the activities of those centres and the trust funds established for the coordination of assistance in mine action and the promotion of national ownership;

20. *Requests* the Mine Action Service to continue developing the electronic mine information network as a user-friendly repository of mine-related information and as a means for mine-action programmes to circulate on a regular basis to donors and other partners standard reports on the scope and impact of the mine problem, available mine-action resources and capacities and the progress achieved in the field;

21. *Emphasizes* the importance of recording the location of mines, of retaining all such records and making them available to concerned parties upon cessation of hostilities, and welcomes the strengthening of the relevant provisions in international law;

22. *Calls upon* Member States, especially those that have the capacity to do so, to provide the necessary information and technical, financial and material assistance, as appropriate, and to locate, remove, destroy or otherwise render ineffective minefields, mines, booby traps and other devices, in accordance with international law, as soon as possible;

23. *Urges* Member States and regional, intergovernmental and non-governmental organizations and foundations that have the ability to do so to provide, as appropriate, technological assistance to mine-affected countries and to promote user-oriented scientific research on and development of mine-action techniques and technology, within reasonable time frames, so that mine-action activities may be carried out more safely and cost-effectively, and also urges them to promote collaboration at all levels in this regard;

24. *Invites* States to explore the possibility of strengthening internationally negotiated and non-discriminatory legal instruments that address landmines and other unexploded ordnance, as well as their victims;

25. *Takes note with appreciation* of the ongoing efforts of the Secretary-General to increase public awareness of the impact of the problem of landmines and unexploded ordnance;

26. *Requests* the Secretary-General to submit to the General Assembly at its fifty-ninth session a report on the progress achieved on all relevant issues outlined both in his previous reports to the Assembly on assistance in mine action and in the present resolution, including the progress made by the International Committee of the Red Cross and other international and regional organizations as well as national programmes, and on the operation of the Voluntary Trust Fund for Assistance in Mine Action and other mine-action programmes, as well as a report on the first implementation of the emergency response plan and lessons

learned from this experience and on the implementation of the strategy for the period 2001-2005;

27. *Decides* to include in the provisional agenda of its fifty-ninth session the item entitled "Assistance in mine action".

Humanitarian activities

Africa

Angola

The UN Consolidated Inter-Agency Appeal for Angola, launched for a total of $314 million to assist 3.7 million beneficiaries during 2003, received 55.1 per cent ($173 million) of requirements.

The humanitarian situation in Angola improved significantly during 2003 in all areas accessible to humanitarian partners. However, about 100,000 people with critical needs remained in areas where access was hampered by mine infestation, broken bridges and poor road conditions. According to government figures, more than 3.8 million persons returned to their areas of origin. Some 500,000 remained in camps and temporary settlement areas and centres; about 400,000 persons were living with host families in urban centres; and 350,000 refugees were still in the Democratic Republic of the Congo (DRC).

Humanitarian partners adopted a new programme approach for the 2003 appeal, which focused on unifying programmes around a limited set of time-bound and realistic objectives through programme blocs in food security, public health, protection and education, and access and coordination.

Central African Republic

A Flash Appeal for Humanitarian Assistance to the Central African Republic sought $9.1 million to cover assistance for 2.2 million people from April to June, of which 38.8 per cent ($3.5 million) was received.

Since 15 March, the political and military situation in the Central African Republic had changed with the overthrow of the former regime (see p. 155). However, populations in the former conflict-stricken areas were experiencing a serious humanitarian situation. Lack of access to supplies from the capital deprived the local population of basic commodities and basic health services, whose infrastructure had been consistently looted. Incidence of diseases had increased as had cases of malnutrition among children, and there was serious risk of losing the 2003 crop year due to the lack of seeds that either had been looted or consumed by households. Insecurity across the country constrained humanitarian assistance activities.

Eritrea

The UN Consolidated Inter-Agency Appeal for Eritrea, launched for a total of $160 million to assist 2.3 million beneficiaries during 2003, met 77.3 per cent ($124 million) of requirements.

The humanitarian situation in Eritrea, which deteriorated throughout 2003, was defined by the effect of another year of severe drought, which threatened the country with widespread crop failures and water shortages, in addition to the continuing effects of war, generalized poverty, the imperative of creating a safe environment for the return of thousands of internally displaced persons, expellees, and returning refugees and their reintegration. The 2002 crop production, at only 9 per cent of the national consumption requirement, led 2.3 million people to depend on food aid. In addition, reports of livestock deaths, increased grain prices and deflated livestock prices indicated a significant reduction of purchasing power and increased food insecurity countrywide.

Great Lakes region and Central Africa

The UN Consolidated Inter-Agency Appeal for the Great Lakes Region and Central Africa, launched for a total of $115 million to cover 2003, received 100 per cent of that amount. Neither Rwanda nor the United Republic of Tanzania issued appeals in 2003, but chose instead to rely on alternative funding mechanisms or targeted development assistance.

Key issues were the region's vulnerability to natural disasters and the impact of climatic trends, peace, security and human rights, health and HIV/AIDS, internally displaced persons, refugees and vulnerable groups, and human rights violations targeting women and children.

Burundi

The UN Consolidated Inter-Agency Appeal for Burundi, launched to assist 415,531 beneficiaries in 2003, sought $72 million, of which 44.1 per cent ($32 million) was received.

In 2003, the security situation deteriorated in Burundi, hampering the work of the United Nations and its partners. Acts of abduction, banditry, robbery, looting and assassination of local administrative officials rose markedly. Looting by the rebels and uncontrolled elements of the armed forces stripped communities of their self-sufficiency.

(See also p. 947 for information on the Ad Hoc Advisory Group on Burundi.)

Congo (Republic of the)

The UN Consolidated Inter-Agency Appeal for the Republic of the Congo to cover 2003, amounting to $28 million, met 35 per cent ($10 million) of requirements.

The UN Plan for 2003-2004 described strategies to reduce poverty, enhance the role and status of women in society, support national efforts to stop the spread of HIV/AIDS and assist infected and affected persons, strengthen the rule of law and protect human rights, and improve food security and nutrition. Other areas of concern were children and the family, culture and communications, education and science, employment and income generation, the environment, health, refugees, the reintegration of ex-combatants and water, hygiene and sanitation.

Democratic Republic of the Congo

The UN Consolidated Inter-Agency Appeal for the DRC sought $229 million for assistance to 2.6 million beneficiaries during 2003, of which 47.1 per cent ($108 million) was received.

A fifth year of uninterrupted war in large parts of the DRC further eroded coping mechanisms, and pushed entire populations to near exhaustion, which was reflected in the increase in internally displaced persons from 2.7 million in January to 3.4 million in August. On the positive side, the previous Government and former rebel groups united to form a new transitional Government (see p. 113), which established a new Ministry for Solidarity and Humanitarian Affairs as part of its strategy for consolidating peace and security.

(See also p. 943 under "Special economic assistance".)

Uganda

The UN Consolidated Inter-Agency Appeal for Uganda, launched for a total of $127 million to cover 2003, received 97.6 per cent ($124 million) of that amount to assist 750,000 beneficiaries.

While steady economic progress was made in the south, a serious humanitarian crisis was ongoing in the northern and north-eastern parts of the country, where an estimated 1 million persons had been displaced, with most of them living in heavily congested camps or public buildings under appalling health and sanitary conditions. Limited access to the camps had been possible through government-provided armed escorts. The most vulnerable groups—internally displaced persons, refugees and drought-affected people, mainly in Karamoja—were unable to access adequate agricultural land or find employment because of displacement, lack of income-generating activities and, specific to the drought-affected areas, poor weather and soil conditions.

Somalia

In response to General Assembly resolution 57/154 [YUN 2002, p. 896], the Secretary-General, in a July report [A/58/133], reviewed conditions in Somalia and the humanitarian relief and rehabilitation assistance provided by the United Nations and its partners from 22 May 2002 to 22 May 2003.

Somalia remained one of the poorest countries in the world. About 350,000 internally displaced persons were living in desperate conditions, with no access to international assistance or protection. Chronic food instability exacerbated the plight of the poorer groups, especially in drought-prone areas. Deterioration in the security situation resulted in the United Nations and other international agencies losing access to large areas, and prevented vulnerable Somalis from rebuilding sustainable livelihoods. In collaboration with implementing partners, the United Nations continued to deliver humanitarian aid and development assistance and remained committed to assisting the country. However, the low donor response to the consolidated appeals process prevented UN agencies from fully addressing Somalia's emergency needs. The United Nations, with the assistance of the international community, would continue to support national reconciliation and social and economic development, employing an incremental approach of increased engagement. It would also undertake inter-agency peace-building strategies to strengthen communities and encourage reconciliation between rival factions.

The UN Consolidated Inter-Agency Appeal for Somalia sought $71 million to assist 750,000 beneficiaries in 2003, of which 63.4 per cent ($45 million) was received.

GENERAL ASSEMBLY ACTION

On 17 December [meeting 75], the General Assembly adopted **resolution 58/115** [draft: A/58/L.40 & Add.1] without vote [agenda item 40 (b)].

Assistance for humanitarian relief and the economic and social rehabilitation of Somalia

The General Assembly,

Recalling its resolution 47/160 of 18 December 1992 and subsequent relevant resolutions, in particular resolutions 56/106 of 14 December 2001 and 57/154 of 16 December 2002,

Noting with serious concern that the current four-year drought in Somalia threatens the lives of Somali nomads as well as livestock,

Noting with grave concern the high mortality rates of over 80 per cent of livestock in the worst-affected areas of the Sool and Sanaag plateau of Somalia and the high risk of starvation of Somali nomads,

Noting with serious concern the threat, as a result of this drought, of an imminent collapse of the Somali economy, and in particular of the pastoral economy and social support systems,

Underlining the urgent need for humanitarian assistance, relief and reconstruction,

Noting the linkage between the search for peace and alleviation of the humanitarian crisis in Somalia,

Welcoming the continued focus of the United Nations, in partnership with civil society at the grassroots level, on programmes of assistance, including both humanitarian and development approaches, taking into consideration the conditions on the ground,

Recalling statements by the President of the Security Council of 31 October 2001 and 28 March 2002, by which the Security Council condemned attacks on humanitarian personnel and called upon all parties in Somalia to respect fully the security and safety of personnel of the United Nations, the International Committee of the Red Cross and non-governmental organizations, and to guarantee their complete freedom of movement and access throughout Somalia,

Re-emphasizing the importance of the further implementation of its resolutions 47/160, 56/106 and 57/154 to rehabilitate basic social and economic services throughout the country,

Taking note of the reports of the Secretary-General,

1. *Expresses its appreciation* to the Secretary-General for his continued and tireless efforts to mobilize assistance for the Somali people;

2. *Reiterates its firm support* for the national reconciliation process sponsored by the Intergovernmental Authority on Development, and in particular for the ongoing peace conference in Kenya and the efforts of the Facilitation Committee in this regard, urges all parties throughout Somalia to participate in the process, and invites the Intergovernmental Authority and its member States to continue their efforts to promote national reconciliation in Somalia;

3. *Encourages* the further implementation of its resolution 47/160 to rehabilitate basic social and economic services throughout Somalia;

4. *Welcomes* the strategy of the United Nations focusing on the implementation of community-based interventions aimed at rebuilding local infrastructures and increased self-reliance of the local population, and the ongoing efforts by the United Nations agencies, their Somali counterparts and their partner organizations to establish and maintain close coordination and cooperation mechanisms available for the implementation of the relief, rehabilitation and reconstruction programme;

5. *Notes* the incremental and prioritized approach of the United Nations system to addressing the continuing crisis and needs in Somalia while maintaining long-term commitments to rehabilitation, recovery and development activities;

6. *Commends* the Office for the Coordination of Humanitarian Affairs of the Secretariat for its response, and underlines the urgent need for putting in place practical measures aimed at the alleviation of the consequences of the drought in Somalia;

7. *Urges* all States and intergovernmental and non-governmental organizations concerned to continue to implement further its resolutions 47/160, 56/106 and 57/154 in order to assist the Somali people in embarking on the rehabilitation of basic social and economic services, as well as institution-building aimed at the restoration of structures of civil governance at all levels in all parts of the country in which peace and security prevail;

8. *Calls upon* the Secretary-General to continue to mobilize international humanitarian, rehabilitation and reconstruction assistance for Somalia;

9. *Calls upon* all Somali parties to respect the security and safety of the personnel of the United Nations, the specialized agencies and non-governmental organizations and to guarantee their complete freedom of movement and safe access throughout Somalia;

10. *Urges* the international community to provide as a matter of urgency humanitarian assistance and relief to the Somali people to alleviate in particular the consequences of the prevailing drought;

11. *Calls upon* the international community to provide continuing and increased assistance in response to the United Nations 2004 Consolidated Inter-Agency Appeal for relief, rehabilitation and reconstruction assistance for Somalia;

12. *Commends* the Secretary-General for the establishment of the Trust Fund for Peace-Building in Somalia, welcomes the contributions made thus far to the Fund, and appeals to Member States to contribute to it;

13. *Requests* the Secretary-General, in view of the critical situation in Somalia, to take all necessary and practicable measures for the implementation of the present resolution and to report thereon to the General Assembly at its fifty-ninth session.

Sudan

In response to General Assembly resolution 56/112 [YUN 2001, p. 836], the Secretary-General, in August [A/58/225], described the emergency situation and recovery, rehabilitation and development activities in the Sudan from 15 July 2001 to 22 May 2003.

During the reporting period, positive changes occurred in the operational environment in which humanitarian aid was provided. Nevertheless, the need for such assistance remained high, as armed conflict and ethnic violence continued to destroy infrastructure, isolate populations, erode coping mechanisms and limit access to markets, and also resulted in significant human rights violations. Natural calamities further diverted and drained government resources and caused additional large-scale displacement. In Upper Nile, Kassala, Darfur and the Sobat corridor, the presence of militias constituted a serious impediment to access. Road operations remained hampered by the presence of landmines and conditions were not established to allow internally displaced persons, refugees and ex-combatants to return voluntarily to their homes. From May 2003, some humanitarian workers holding Sudanese visas were not permitted entry to areas in the south. The issuance of travel permits and visas took from three days to three months, and some staff received permits for one month only. Other restrictions were also imposed. Humanitarian access to previously denied or war-affected areas was expected to improve with the conclusion of a peace agreement.

The Secretary-General presented recommendations regarding a coherent transitional assistance programme, which called for sustaining the current multifaceted approach, covering diplomatic, political and economic factors; ensuring adequate funding facilities were responsive to humanitarian and transitional needs prior to the signing of a peace agreement; and the reintegration of internally displaced persons, ex-combatants and refugees into affected communities. He said assistance partners should act urgently to ensure that effective mechanisms were in place for consolidating any peace that was negotiated but not fully implemented.

The UN Consolidated Inter-Agency Appeal for the Sudan, launched for $263 million to cover the needs of 2.8 million beneficiaries in 2003, received 74.2 per cent ($195 million) of requirements.

West Africa

The UN Consolidated Inter-Agency Flash Appeal, launched in 2002 [YUN 2002, p. 898] for $22 million to assist 3.9 million people in Côte d'Ivoire and Burkina Faso, Ghana and Mali from November 2002 to January 2003, received 55.6 per cent ($12 million) of the requirement.

The West Africa subregion had suffered chronic instability, with a coup d'état on 14 September (Guinea-Bissau), state collapse and violent conflict (Côte d'Ivoire and Liberia), disputed governance (Guinea and Togo), weakened economies linked to the crisis in Côte d'Ivoire (Burkina Faso, Ghana, Mali), outburst of political tensions (Mauritania), and increased vulnerability in rural areas due to drought in the Sahel region and civilians seeking asylum in the border areas of Burkina Faso, Ghana, Guinea and Mali.

An appeal for the subregion was planned for 2004.

Côte d'Ivoire + 5

A UN Consolidated Inter-Agency Appeal for Côte d'Ivoire and the five neighbouring countries of Burkina Faso, Ghana, Guinea, Liberia and Mali, to cover the period from April to December 2003, sought $91 million to assist 3 million beneficiaries. Of the total, 54.3 per cent ($49 million) was received.

The humanitarian situation in Côte d'Ivoire steadily deteriorated and was marked by widespread human rights abuses, continuing insecurity and uncertainty about the political/military situation, and the economic downturn and virtual collapse of basic social services. The crisis portended ominous trends for the wider West Africa subregion.

In Liberia, which was already facing a deep political, economic and humanitarian crisis, the situation worsened due to the spillover effects of the Côte d'Ivoire conflict. The ongoing conflict in Côte d'Ivoire and the resultant closure of its borders with Burkina Faso had a severe impact on the latter country's economy, given its structural links with Côte d'Ivoire, including higher transport action costs, loss of income and rising prices. An estimated 3 million Burkinabé lived in Côte d'Ivoire. Despite its own precarious situation, Guinea continued to bear the burden of a constant flow of refugees from its neighbours. Continuing tensions along the Liberian/Guinean border presented a further security obstacle to the population and critical humanitarian assistance operations. The appeal would target about 176,000 people.

The impact of the Côte d'Ivoire crisis on Mali was seen against the background of an economy vulnerable to world commodity price fluctuations and the effects of recurrent Sahelian droughts. Up to 2 million Malian nationals resided in Côte d'Ivoire. An increase in the prices of basic commodities, food and petroleum products, a shortfall in rain and the unexpected return of thousands of Malians, along with a substantial drop in remittances, meant diminishing opportunities in Côte d'Ivoire and a deepening of poverty in Mali. The ramifications of the crisis in Côte d'Ivoire on Ghana mainly resulted in the influx of third-country nationals transiting to their countries of origin, and Ivorian asylum-seekers, challenging the capacity of the Government, the humanitarian community and host communities to identify and respond to their needs adequately.

Guinea

The UN Consolidated Inter-Agency Appeal for Guinea, launched for a total of $48 million to assist 400,000 beneficiaries in 2003, received 61.2 per cent ($29 million) of the requirement.

Guinea provided a safe haven for refugees fleeing conflicts in Côte d'Ivoire, Guinea-Bissau, Liberia and Sierra Leone. Populations in its refugee-hosting and war-affected areas near the border with Liberia and Sierra Leone remained vulnerable and in need of aid, due to the volatile security situation linked to the alleged presence of armed militants. Building the country's capacity to manage complex emergencies and natural disasters remained a key priority.

Liberia

The UN Consolidated Inter-Agency Appeal for Liberia, which sought $47 million to cover 1.3 million beneficiaries in 2003, received 39.6 per cent ($18 million) of that amount from the donor community.

In 2003, the humanitarian situation in Liberia was severely affected by the continuing escalation of conflict. During the first half of the year, humanitarian agencies had poor access to only one third of the country. Assistance to vulnerable populations in accessible areas also became increasingly difficult. Public social services collapsed and schools closed down prematurely. However, there were signs of hope that enabled greater humanitarian access and assistance, including the signing of the Accra Peace Agreement (see p. 192), the inauguration of an interim president and the arrival of Economic Community of West African States troops in early August. As a result, the humanitarian community was able to return to the capital, Monrovia, in mid-August.

Sierra Leone

The UN Consolidated Inter-Agency Appeal for Relief and Recovery for Sierra Leone sought $126 million to assist 1.3 million beneficiaries in 2003. Of the total, 75.6 per cent ($95.1 million) was received from the donor community.

The stable environment in Sierra Leone enabled continued opportunities for reintegration and recovery efforts and accelerated repatriation, while the instability in Liberia generated additional influxes of refugees. Although progress was achieved in meeting humanitarian and recovery needs, delays in the commitment of resources early in the year hampered efforts to implement activities in time for the planting season and before the heavy rains undermined rehabilitation. Priorities for the country during the year included assistance and protection to Liberian refugees; support for the repatriation of Sierra Leonean refugees from neighbouring countries and for reintegration efforts; and enhanced delivery of education, health, agriculture, water and sanitation, and shelter services.

Southern Africa

The UN Consolidated Inter-Agency Appeal in Response to the Humanitarian Crisis in Southern Africa, launched for a total of $464 million to cover 14.4 million beneficiaries from July 2003 to June 2004, received 65.9 per cent ($306 million) of the requirement.

Although conditions had improved in Southern Africa, primarily in the northern region, as a result of a massive humanitarian response and a reasonable 2002-2003 agricultural season, the overall levels of vulnerability remained high and the underlying causes of the crisis (food insecurity, HIV/AIDS, poor social and economic conditions) remained. The combination of a lack of funding for critical assistance activities and prospects for food production once again compromised by drought continued to expose millions to a life-threatening mix of vulnerability. However, longer-term prospects for addressing the crisis seemed healthier, as there were indications that resources to combat HIV/AIDS would become increasingly available.

Lesotho

For Lesotho, the UN Consolidated Inter-Agency Appeal in Response to the Humanitarian Crisis in Southern Africa sought $3.6 million to cover assistance needs from July 2003 to June 2004, of which 25.9 per cent ($949,322) was received.

Pervasive HIV/AIDS continued to adversely impact livelihoods and incomes in Lesotho. Chronic poverty was still growing owing to the lack of employment opportunities to compensate for income losses due to retrenchment of migrant Basotho workers from South African mines and farms in Free State. For the third consecutive year, bad weather conditions led to drastically reduced agricultural production and severe food insecurity.

Malawi

For Malawi, the UN Consolidated Inter-Agency Appeal in Response to the Humanitarian Crisis in Southern Africa sought $11 million to cover assistance from July 2003 to June 2004, of which 20.1 per cent ($2.2 million) was received.

While progress had been tangible in Malawi, the confluence of chronic poverty, HIV/AIDS and the regular disruptions to food security caused by variable rainfall, among other factors, indicated the need for ongoing emergency assistance. A shortage of qualified staff affected the quality of health services. Sanitation and water supply were of increasing concern as large inequities existed in the distribution of water. The macroeconomic environment had deteriorated, with inflation at 9.5 per cent in October.

GENERAL ASSEMBLY ACTION

On 5 December [meeting 69], the General Assembly adopted **resolution 58/26** [draft: A/58/L.35 & Add.1] without vote [agenda item 40 (b)].

Emergency humanitarian assistance to Malawi

The General Assembly,

Recalling its relevant resolutions in particular, resolutions 46/182 of 19 December 1991, 54/219 and 54/233 of 22 December 1999, 55/163 of 14 December

2000 and 56/103 of 14 December 2001, and Economic and Social Council resolution 2002/32 of 26 July 2002,

Convinced that all people have the right to a standard of living adequate for the health and well-being of themselves and their families, including food, medical care, necessary social services and security in the event of lack of livelihood in circumstances beyond their control,

Noting that drought and other types of natural disasters have proved to be recurring phenomena in Malawi,

Reiterating that natural disasters damage the social and economic infrastructure of affected countries, although the long-term consequences of such natural disasters are especially severe for poor developing countries, including Malawi, and hamper sustainable development,

Concerned that Malawi continues to face natural catastrophes such as drought, floods and heavy rains, causing serious crop failure, loss of life and extensive damage to property and infrastructure,

Noting that an increasing number of cases of malnutrition, particularly among children, and deaths due to hunger-related diseases continue to occur in Malawi, with adverse long-term consequences,

Deeply alarmed that the rapid spread of HIV/AIDS has increased the vulnerability of communities, creating greater levels of dependency and severely reducing their ability to cope with humanitarian crises,

Gravely concerned that the capability of the national economy to absorb such shocks has been seriously eroded and that the frequent occurrence of extreme natural disasters has increasingly contributed to the stagnation of social and economic development,

Acknowledging that national efforts are critical to prevent the deepening of the humanitarian crisis,

Noting with appreciation the mobilization and allocation of resources by States, relevant organizations of the United Nations system and intergovernmental and non-governmental organizations to complement the national efforts of Malawi,

Aware that international cooperation remains a critical factor for the success of all national efforts to address the crisis situation,

1. *Welcomes* the positive role of the Government of Malawi in the relief operations, in particular the close coordination between the United Nations system and the Government;

2. *Also welcomes* the launching by the Office for the Coordination of Humanitarian Affairs of the Secretariat of the consolidated appeal for Malawi on 18 July 2002 and the humanitarian appeal for 2004 on 18 November 2003, as well as the continued monitoring of the situation, including through the activities of the Special Envoy of the Secretary-General for Humanitarian Needs in Southern Africa;

3. *Requests* the Office for the Coordination of Humanitarian Affairs to continue to seek ways and means of improving the effectiveness of the United Nations consolidated appeals process;

4. *Calls upon* all States to adopt, where required, and to continue to implement effectively, the legislative and other appropriate measures necessary to mitigate the effects of natural disasters, inter alia, in the areas of disaster prevention, including building regulations and appropriate land use, as well as early warning, disaster preparedness and capacity-building in disaster response, and in that context requests the international community to continue to assist Malawi as the need arises;

5. *Emphasizes* the importance of enhanced international cooperation, including with the United Nations and regional organizations, to assist Malawi in its efforts to build capacity and to predict, prepare for and respond to natural disasters;

6. *Stresses*, in that context, the need to further strengthen international cooperation in the provision of emergency humanitarian assistance in support of the efforts of Malawi to deal with natural disasters in all their phases, from relief and mitigation to development, including through the provision of adequate resources, and encourages the effective use of multilateral mechanisms;

7. *Also stresses* that emergency humanitarian assistance for natural disasters should be provided in accordance with the guiding principles contained in the annex to resolution 46/182, on the basis of human dimensions and needs;

8. *Urges* the international community to continue to support the efforts of Malawi to fight the HIV/AIDS pandemic, poverty and malnutrition in order to increase its capacity to cope during natural disasters;

9. *Requests* the Secretary-General to submit to the General Assembly for consideration at its fifty-ninth session a report on the implementation of the present resolution.

Mozambique

For Mozambique, the UN Consolidated Inter-Agency Appeal in Response to the Humanitarian Crisis in Southern Africa sought $20 million to cover assistance from July 2003 to June 2004, of which 13.7 per cent ($2.8 million) was received.

Monitoring assessments, carried out in November, suggested that, while ongoing interventions had a significant effect in stabilizing the food security status of vulnerable people, the sustainability of progress was contingent on the rainy season in January-March 2004. The southern and central parts of the country remained extremely vulnerable due to the prevalence of HIV/AIDS. A growing concern was the unfolding orphan crisis due to AIDS.

Swaziland

For Swaziland, the UN Consolidated Inter-Agency Appeal in Response to the Humanitarian Crisis in Southern Africa sought $6 million to cover assistance needs from July 2003 to June 2004, of which 39 per cent ($2.3 million) was received.

The humanitarian crisis in Swaziland arose from drought and land degradation, deepening poverty and HIV/AIDS, with mutually reinforcing disastrous effects. Many families that would have weathered the drought through family remittances or employment in local industries no

Zambia

For Zambia, the UN Consolidated Inter-Agency Appeal in Response to the Humanitarian Crisis in Southern Africa sought $15 million to cover assistance needs from July 2003 to June 2004, of which 22 per cent ($3.2 million) was received.

A good harvest and a favourable humanitarian response took Zambia off the critical list of countries requiring emergency food support. However, the recovery was fragile, as by December over 1 million people required emergency food assistance in the southern and western provinces. At the national level, the problems of HIV/AIDS, chronic malnutrition, water and sanitation had reached critical proportions and 73 per cent of the population were living in poverty.

Zimbabwe

For Zimbabwe, the UN Consolidated Inter-Agency Appeal in Response to the Humanitarian Crisis in Southern Africa sought $95 million to cover assistance needs from July 2003 to December 2004, of which 12.8 per cent ($12.3 million) was received.

The general humanitarian situation in Zimbabwe did not improve in 2003. A combination of the constrained policy environment, economic decline, climatic instability and HIV/AIDS continued to plague the population. The cumulative effect of five years of humanitarian crisis had resulted in a dramatic depletion of the country's assets, including human health and productivity, essential services, and economic and vital natural resources.

Asia

Afghanistan

The Transitional Assistance Programme for Afghanistan (TAPA), which covered the period from January 2003 to March 2004, sought $728 million to assist 4.1 million people; as at late May, 31 per cent ($225 million) of the requirements were met.

TAPA sought to address the underlying causes of the crisis in Afghanistan—poverty, debt, environmental degradation, insecurity—as well as urgent recovery and reconstruction priorities. It provided support for mine/unexploded ordnance (UXO) victims, returned land for productive use, clearance for reconstruction projects and education for adults and children on the dangers of mines and UXO. TAPA prioritized integrated national and UN agency action in communities of return, to help assure sustainable livelihoods, essential community services, potable water supply and sanitation, and to address problems of debt and asset depletion. It also aimed to promote environmental protection and recovery, arrest environmental degradation, develop a national counter-narcotics strategy and address food insecurity.

Report of Secretary-General. In response to General Assembly resolution 57/113 B [YUN 2002, p. 900], the Secretary-General, in a December report covering the period from July 2002 to November 2003 [A/58/616], described key political and humanitarian developments in Afghanistan (for political aspects, see p. 304).

The report stated that Afghanistan had made progress towards post-war recovery. Gross domestic product grew by 30 per cent and was expected to grow by a further 20 per cent in 2004. Other achievements included the rehabilitation of the national primary education system and the successful management of one of the largest UN-assisted refugee repatriation efforts in history. However, serious challenges remained, the most important being the creation of a secure environment in the south so that reconstruction activities could take place. Equally crucial were government efforts to extend its authority, enhance its administrative capacity and deliver socio-economic benefits nationwide. UN assistance was channelled through TAPA (see above), which reflected an agreement between the Transitional Administration and the United Nations to ensure that UN humanitarian programming supported the national priorities identified by the Government in the national development budget and strengthened the Government's implementation capacity.

During the review period, some 2.2 million highly vulnerable Afghans, mainly in the north, west and central highlands, received winter assistance. As at June 2003, some 10 million people had received 535,000 metric tons of food commodities; an estimated 6 million Afghans still required food assistance for the remainder of 2003. The majority of food aid projects focused on the restoration of agricultural opportunities, the recovery of agricultural land, seed stocks, irrigation systems, the rehabilitation of pasturelands and the recuperation of livestock, as well as environmental protection. The Ministry of Health, with donor support, focused on providing rural communities with access to primary care by year's end and was establishing an emergency obstetric care centre in each province. A birth registration campaign and national immunization days were launched for children. Progress was made in providing safe drinking water and sanitation facilities to schools, vulnerable villages affected by drought, communities with high numbers of refugee returns and camps for internally displaced persons. The main constraints of the sector were a low funding response, a shortage of sufficient implementing partners and appropriate drilling equipment, and insufficient capacities to plan and manage the sector.

School enrolment increased significantly and 292 schools countrywide were identified for rehabilitation or reconstruction. Efforts to reduce illiteracy among women were under way. Cultural sites and monuments were being restored, and national archives, public libraries and the Kabul theatre were rehabilitated. According to the Office of the United Nations High Commissioner for Refugees (UNHCR), over 2.5 million individuals had received repatriation assistance since March 2002. Afghanistan, Iran and UNHCR signed a joint agreement in June 2003, which provided for the gradual return of some 1 million Afghans from Iran over the next two years. UNHCR suspended its repatriation programme from Pakistan in the wake of the killing of one of its staff members in November. Significant efforts were made to combat the threat of landmines and UXO. Road construction began in July on six sectors of the Kabul-Kandahar highway, totalling 439 kilometres. Reconstruction of the Salang Tunnel, the main road link between the north and the south, began in July.

GENERAL ASSEMBLY ACTION

On 5 December [meeting 70], the General Assembly adopted **resolution 58/27 B** [draft: A/58/L.32 & Add.1] without vote [agenda item 40 (f)].

Emergency international assistance for peace, normalcy and reconstruction of war-stricken Afghanistan

The General Assembly,

Recalling its resolution 57/113 B of 6 December 2002 and all other relevant resolutions,

Recalling also the agreement reached among various Afghan groups in Bonn, Germany, on 5 December 2001 and the International Conference on Reconstruction Assistance to Afghanistan, held in Tokyo on 21 and 22 January 2002,

Expressing its grave concern about the continuing effects of decades of conflict in Afghanistan, which have resulted in massive loss of life, extensive human suffering, serious violations of human rights, destruction of property, serious damage to the economic and social infrastructure, refugee flows and other forcible displacements of large numbers of people,

Mindful that Afghanistan is highly vulnerable to natural disasters and that some parts of its territory continue to be affected by serious drought,

Noting the accession of Afghanistan to the Convention on the Prohibition of the Use, Stockpiling, Production and Transfer of Anti-personnel Mines and on Their Destruction,

Remaining deeply concerned about the problem of millions of anti-personnel landmines and unexploded ordnance, which constitutes a great danger for the civilian population and a major obstacle for the return of refugees and displaced populations and for the resumption of agricultural and other economic activities, the provision of humanitarian assistance and rehabilitation and reconstruction efforts,

Welcoming the positive steps taken so far towards an improved situation of human rights and fundamental freedoms for many Afghans, in particular women and children, and commending in this regard the positive role played by the Afghan Independent Human Rights Commission and Afghan civil society organizations, while noting with grave concern, however, that there remain discriminatory practices that hinder the full enjoyment of their human rights and fundamental freedoms,

Expressing its deep concern about reports of violations of human rights and of international humanitarian law in parts of the country,

Reminding the Transitional Administration and all Afghan groups of their commitment to respect human rights in the country, as contained in the Bonn Agreement,

Reaffirming the importance of the safety and security of the humanitarian personnel and United Nations and associated personnel in Afghanistan, and alarmed by the increase in attacks on humanitarian personnel, including Afghan nationals, in parts of the country,

Noting with concern that the increase in such attacks has limited access to certain areas of Afghanistan and led to inadequate conditions for the delivery of aid for internally displaced persons and vulnerable sectors of the civilian population,

Recognizing that a secure environment is indispensable for the safe and effective delivery and distribution of humanitarian assistance and is a precondition for rehabilitation, reconstruction efforts and long-term development, and welcoming the expansion of the mandate of the International Security Assistance Force to allow it, as resources permit, to support the Afghan Transitional Administration and its successors in the maintenance of security in areas of Afghanistan outside Kabul and its environs, so that the Afghan authorities, as well as the personnel of the United Nations and other international civilian personnel engaged, in particular, in reconstruction and humanitarian efforts, can operate in a secure environment, and to provide security assistance for the performance of other tasks in support of the Bonn Agreement,

Welcoming the ownership of the rehabilitation and reconstruction efforts by the Transitional Administration through the National Development Framework and national budget,

Reiterating the importance of a seamless transition from humanitarian relief to the rehabilitation and reconstruction of Afghanistan, and welcoming the important contribution that the integrated approach of the United Nations Assistance Mission in Afghanistan and of members of the donor community has made in this regard,

Expressing its appreciation to the Special Representative of the Secretary-General for Afghanistan and the United Nations Assistance Mission in Afghanistan for their continued efforts in coordinating, planning and implementing humanitarian and other assistance in cooperation with the Transitional Administration,

Welcoming the return of large numbers of refugees and internally displaced persons, while noting with concern that displacement remains a widespread phenomenon and that the conditions in certain parts of Afghanistan are not yet conducive to safe and sustainable returns to places of origin,

Expressing gratitude to those countries that continue to host Afghan refugee populations, and at the same time once again calling upon all groups to continue to fulfil their obligations for the protection of refugees and internally displaced persons and to allow international access for their protection and care,

Expressing its appreciation to the United Nations system and to all States and international and non-governmental organizations whose international and local staff continue to respond positively to the humanitarian needs of Afghanistan, as well as to the Secretary-General for mobilizing and coordinating the delivery of appropriate humanitarian assistance,

1. *Takes note* of the report of the Secretary-General;
2. *Stresses* that the responsibility for the solution of the humanitarian crisis lies above all with the Afghan people themselves, and urges them to continue their efforts to achieve national reconciliation;
3. *Urges* all Afghan groups to actively support the Transitional Administration in meeting the responsibilities under the Convention on the Prohibition of the Use, Stockpiling, Production and Transfer of Anti-personnel Mines and on Their Destruction, to cooperate fully with the mine action programme coordinated by the United Nations and to execute the destruction of all existing stocks of landmines;
4. *Stresses* the coordinating role of the Special Representative of the Secretary-General for Afghanistan for the United Nations system in ensuring a seamless transition from humanitarian relief to the rehabilitation and reconstruction of Afghanistan, including the cooperation of the United Nations system with other actors in the international community, in particular with the international financial institutions;
5. *Commends* the Special Representative of the Secretary-General, the United Nations Assistance Mission in Afghanistan and the Emergency Relief Coordinator for the work accomplished;
6. *Welcomes* the recent substantial contributions to the Law and Order Trust Fund, and at the same time regrets that the funding provided to the Afghanistan Reconstruction Trust Fund and the Law and Order Trust Fund, which were designed to contribute to the mobilization of international support to Afghanistan, remains inadequate;
7. *Urges* the international community to actively participate in and financially contribute to these rehabilitation and reconstruction efforts, and encourages the international community to channel assistance through the national development budget of the Afghan Transitional Administration and to focus attention on building the capacity of Afghans;
8. *Strongly condemns* the recent deliberate attacks and all other acts of violence and intimidation directed against humanitarian personnel and United Nations and associated personnel, and regrets the loss of life and physical harm suffered among such staff;
9. *Urges* the Transitional Administration and local authorities to ensure the safety, security and free movement of all United Nations and humanitarian personnel, as well as their safe and unimpeded access to all affected populations, and to protect the property of the United Nations and of humanitarian organizations, including non-governmental organizations;
10. *Notes* the ratification by Afghanistan of the Convention on the Elimination of All Forms of Discrimination against Women on 5 March 2003, and at the same time strongly condemns once again continuing discrimination against women and girls, as well as against persons belonging to ethnic and religious groups, including minorities;
11. *Emphasizes* the importance of actively involving all elements of Afghan society, in particular women, in the development and implementation of relief, rehabilitation and reconstruction programmes;
12. *Reminds* all Afghan groups of their commitment to the Bonn Agreement, and calls upon them to respect fully the human rights and fundamental freedoms of all, without discrimination of any kind, including on the basis of gender, ethnicity or religion, in accordance with their obligations under international law, and to protect and promote the equal rights of women and men;
13. *Welcomes* the start of the disarmament, demobilization and reintegration process by the Transitional Administration and the efforts of the international observer group to verify the fairness of the process, and calls upon the international community to assist the Transitional Administration in these efforts;
14. *Also welcomes*, in this regard, the accession of the Transitional Administration on 24 September 2003 to the Optional Protocol to the Convention on the Rights of the Child on the involvement of children in armed conflict, and urges Afghan groups to refrain from the recruitment or use of children contrary to international standards, while stressing the importance of demobilizing and reintegrating child soldiers and other war-affected children;
15. *Emphasizes* the necessity of investigating allegations of violations of human rights and of international humanitarian law, including violations committed against persons belonging to ethnic and religious minorities, as well as against women and girls, of facilitating the provision of efficient and effective remedies to the victims and of bringing the perpetrators to justice in accordance with international law;
16. *Appeals* to the Transitional Administration and the international community to mainstream gender issues into all humanitarian assistance and future rehabilitation and reconstruction programmes and to actively promote the full and equal participation of and benefit to both women and men in respect of those programmes, underlining the importance of a senior gender adviser position in this context;
17. *Calls upon* the Transitional Administration to provide Afghan children with educational and health facilities in all parts of the country, recognizing the special needs of girls, and to ensure their full access to those facilities;

18. *Expresses its appreciation* to those Governments that continue to host Afghan refugees, and reminds them of their obligations under international refugee law with respect to the protection of refugees and the right to seek asylum;

19. *Calls upon* the Transitional Administration, acting with the support of the international community, to create the conditions for the voluntary, safe, dignified and sustainable return of Afghan refugees and internally displaced persons, welcomes in this respect the initiation of the National Area-Based Development Programme and the National Solidarity Programme, and calls upon the international community to provide adequate funding to these programmes which, inter alia, assist in the resettlement of Afghan refugees and internally displaced persons;

20. *Urges* donors to fulfil promptly the funding commitments made in Tokyo at the International Conference on Reconstruction Assistance to Afghanistan and reiterated in Dubai, United Arab Emirates, on 21 September 2003, and invites them to provide additional resources beyond those pledged so far;

21. *Urgently appeals* to all States, the United Nations system and international and non-governmental organizations to continue to provide, in close collaboration with the Transitional Administration and Afghan civil society, all possible and necessary humanitarian, financial, technical and material assistance for the Afghan population, inter alia, a minimal degree of health care and health services in all parts of the country;

22. *Calls upon* the international community to continue and strengthen its coordination of humanitarian assistance to Afghanistan, bearing in mind the role of the Special Representative of the Secretary-General and the United Nations Assistance Mission in Afghanistan;

23. *Also calls upon* the international community to respond generously and without delay to the national development budget, as well as long-term interventions towards rehabilitation and reconstruction;

24. *Requests* the Secretary-General to report to the General Assembly every four months during its fifty-eighth session on the progress of the United Nations and the efforts of his Special Representative to promote peace in Afghanistan, and to report to the Assembly at its fifty-ninth session on progress made in the implementation of the present resolution;

25. *Decides* to include in the provisional agenda of its fifty-ninth session the sub-item entitled "Emergency international assistance for peace, normalcy and reconstruction of war-stricken Afghanistan".

In **resolution 58/27 A** of the same date (see p. 304), the Assembly called on the international community to support the efforts of the Transitional Administration.

Democratic People's Republic of Korea

The UN Consolidated Inter-Agency Appeal for the Democratic People's Republic of Korea (DPRK), launched for a total of $229 million to cover assistance for 6.4 million beneficiaries, received 58.1 per cent ($133 million) of requirements.

The humanitarian situation in the DPRK was impacted by increasing security tension on the peninsula following the re-emergence of the nuclear issue. While most donors continued to separate politics from humanitarian aid, the serious deterioration in the external environment affected the level of assistance to the country. The situation was compounded by the severe acute respiratory syndrome (SARS) epidemic. While no SARS was reported in the DPRK, national authorities took measures beyond the World Health Organization (WHO) technical measures to prevent the introduction of the disease into the country, which were seen as an overriding need to avoid a SARS outbreak.

Indonesia

The UN Consolidated Inter-Agency Appeal for Indonesia, which sought $55 million to assist 3 million beneficiaries in 2003, received 55.3 per cent ($31 million) of the requirements.

Significant progress had been made in restoring relative social and political stability in most of the conflict-affected regions of Indonesia, enabling thousands of internally displaced persons to return to their villages of origin. Humanitarian and development assistance continued to be required to help the Government rehabilitate infrastructure, restore social services facilities and assist the communities affected by the conflict.

Iraq

A Flash Appeal for the Humanitarian Requirements of the Iraq Crisis sought $2,223 million to cover assistance from April to December 2003, of which the donor community committed 90.9 per cent ($2,020 million).

Although the conflict had not resulted in a major humanitarian crisis, the humanitarian situation in Iraq remained serious. The high levels of vulnerability and dependence on government services that existed before the conflict had increased further. The conflict and its aftermath resulted in a widespread breakdown of essential services, severely affecting the population. The lack of security and law and order remained the most serious obstacle to the restoration of basic services and the humanitarian community's ability to conduct assistance activities. It also had a severe impact on the lives of women and children in their ability to access basic services and live normal lives.

Palestine

The UN Consolidated Inter-Agency Appeal for the Occupied Palestinian Territory, which sought $294 million to assist 1.5 million people in

2003, received 60.5 per cent ($178 million) of the requirements.

Israel's closure policy, involving checkpoints and roadblocks, had crippled the Palestinian economy. The situation was further compounded by continued expansion of settlements and bypass roads. The number of Palestinians unable to cope had increased, with 60 per cent living below the poverty line and 40 per cent of the workforce unemployed. Half the population was unable to access their usual health services due to closures and curfews. Children's school performance declined due to a disruption of school life. Assistance focused on recovery and infrastructure, food aid, health, education and psychosocial services.

Tajikistan

The UN Consolidated Inter-Agency Appeal for Tajikistan, which sought $62 million to assist 1 million people in 2003, received 78.5 per cent ($49 million) of the requirements.

Despite positive economic growth indicators for Tajikistan, there was little change in the humanitarian context for the most vulnerable groups. Complex and deep-rooted poverty had left many families with few, if any, coping mechanisms for survival, triggering internal population movements and labour migration to neighbouring countries. Lack of access to food and productive resources, including land, seeds and water, remained the root of food insecurity. The weakened capacity of families to look after their children resulted in increasing numbers of street children and children in conflict with the law. Nearly 20 per cent of the country's schools were destroyed during the civil war, while about 80 per cent of the remaining schools were in need of major repair. With 43 per cent of the population not having access to safe drinking water, unprotected water reservoirs and irrigation canals were the main source of water for many households and public facilities. Outbreaks of water-borne diseases and epidemic levels of malaria and tuberculosis regularly overwhelmed national capacities.

Europe

North Caucasus (Russian Federation)

The UN Consolidated Inter-Agency Appeal for Chechnya and Neighbouring Republics (North Caucasus–Russian Federation), which sought $30 million to assist 1.2 million beneficiaries, received 91.1 per cent ($28 million) of the requirements.

The situation in Chechnya and neighbouring republics continued to be characterized by complexity, instability and unpredictability. Low-intensity hostilities continued in some regions, sometimes resulting in civilian casualties. Chechnya remained one of the world's areas most heavily affected by landmines and UXO. Insecurity remained the biggest hindrance to providing aid to the population and the largest obstacle to recovery and economic development. Pervasive unemployment gave rise to the need for food aid and access to social services, such as potable water, health care and education.

Special economic assistance

On 23 December, the General Assembly decided that the item on special economic assistance to individual countries or regions would remain on the agenda of its resumed fifty-eighth (2004) session (**decision 58/565**).

African economic recovery and development

New Partnership for Africa's Development

The General Assembly, by resolutions 57/2 [YUN 2002, p. 908] and 57/7 [ibid., p. 910], decided to bring the United Nations New Agenda for the Development of Africa in the 1990s [YUN 1991, p. 402] to a close and endorsed the Secretary-General's recommendation [YUN 2002, p. 909] that the New Partnership for Africa's Development (NEPAD), adopted in 2001 by the Assembly of Heads of State and Government of the Organization of African Unity (African Union (AU)) [YUN 2001, p. 900], should be the framework within which the international community should concentrate its efforts for Africa's development.

Reports of Secretary-General. In February, the Commission for Social Development (see p. 1099) considered a report of the Secretary-General on national and international cooperation for social development [E/CN.5/2003/5 & Corr.1], which discussed NEPAD in the context of State to State partnerships.

In response to General Assembly resolution 57/7, the Secretary-General, in August, submitted the first consolidated report [A/58/254] on progress made to implement and support NEPAD. The report was compiled from information provided by the NEPAD secretariat and from information and data generated from responses to questionnaires sent to Member States and UN agencies and organizations. It also drew on ideas and suggestions from meetings with the private sector and civil society groups on NEPAD.

Regarding implementation activities by African countries, the Assembly of Heads of State and Government of the AU (second ordinary session, Maputo, Mozambique, 10-12 July) [A/58/626] adopted a declaration on NEPAD's implementation. The African Peer Review Mechanism—a mutually agreed instrument voluntarily acceded to by AU members as an African self-monitoring, peer-review and peer-learning mechanism—was established and acceded to by 16 members as at July. The Mechanism, which was fundamental to the implementation of the NEPAD priorities of political, economic and corporate governance, had as its primary purpose to foster the adoption of policies, standards and practices that led to political stability and economic growth. Several African countries had taken steps to create a national focal point for NEPAD, and the work programmes of the regional economic communities were reoriented to reflect NEPAD priorities. At the sectoral level, a plan for comprehensive African agricultural development had been completed. NEPAD was also working with the Joint United Nations Programme on HIV/AIDS to prepare a multisectoral AIDS strategy, and had developed a full programme on the environment, which was approved at the second ordinary session of the AU Assembly of Heads of State and Government. Constraints to implementation by African countries were a weak link between the Heads of State and Government Implementation Committee and the regional economic communities; weak institutional capacity to plan and implement the development programmes at the country and regional levels; a lack of sufficient effort in popularizing NEPAD at the country level; and inadequate funding.

Assistance to Africa by the international community through increases in official development assistance (ODA) had been directed to critical sectors, particularly health and education. Closely related to the increase in the volume of ODA was an effort at improving aid effectiveness, including steps by donor countries to untie their aid. It was expected that African countries would benefit from the Rome Declaration on Harmonization, adopted by the heads of multilateral and bilateral development institutions and representatives of the International Monetary Fund (IMF), other multilateral financial institutions and partner countries (Rome, 24-25 February) [A/57/763] to simplify and harmonize programming, reporting and disbursement procedures. Several donor countries made pledges to meet the estimated shortfall of $1 billion in the Trust Fund for the Heavily Indebted Poor Countries (HIPC) Initiative. In addition, some HIPC-eligible African countries had benefited from bilateral debt cancellations announced by several donor countries. In the area of trade, there had been a limited positive international policy response, mainly centring on the granting by some developed countries of duty-free and quota-free access to products of African least developed countries. A number of Africa's partner countries took steps to assist the promotion of foreign direct investment in Africa. The trend towards increased economic and technical cooperation between Africa and other developing regions, especially with countries in Asia and Latin America and the Caribbean, continued. Intergovernmental events offering impetus for cooperation between African and Asian countries were the Asian-African Subregional Organizations Conference (Bandung, Indonesia, 29-30 July), the third Tokyo International Conference on African Development (Tokyo, Japan, 29 September-2 October) and the Second Ministerial Conference of the China-Africa Cooperation Forum (Addis Ababa, Ethiopia, December). Challenges to support to Africa included insufficient levels of ODA for Africa to meet the Millennium Development Goals (MDGs) [YUN 2000, p. 51] and problems within the HIPC Initiative, such as the slow redemption of pledges to the HIPC Trust Fund and a combination of difficulties in preparing poverty reduction strategy papers (PRSPs) and implementing macroeconomic reforms.

Several UN agencies and organizations had aligned their activities with NEPAD priorities. The UN system had also developed an operational framework to support NEPAD at the national, regional and global levels and adopted the cluster approach for pooling its efforts in support of NEPAD. Various UN system entities were engaged in human and institutional development efforts to support NEPAD, and were working with African regional and subregional organizations on policy issues. The Secretary-General established the Office of the Under-Secretary-General and Special Adviser on Africa, effective 1 May, which served as the focal point for NEPAD at Headquarters and supported the promotion of a coordinated, system-wide response to assist Africa's development, particularly implementation of NEPAD, through CEB. The Secretary-General issued a report on the future engagement of the UN system with NEPAD (see p. 939).

The private sector had responded favourably to NEPAD. A NEPAD Business Group, formed to promote cooperation between NEPAD and the private companies that supported it, shared information on trade and investment opportunities in Africa and encouraged private sector involvement in NEPAD and other projects. The African Business Round Table, in collaboration with the United Nations Industrial Development Organization and other sponsors, organized the NEPAD–Economic Community of West African States Business Forum (Abuja, Nigeria, 3-5 March), which underlined the need for more forums modelled on the Abuja meeting, for business associations to disseminate information on NEPAD and for promoting the establishment of business consultative groups to monitor the recommendations of the Forum. The Africa Economic Summit 2003 of the World Economic Forum (Durban, South Africa, June) examined how business could play its part in NEPAD implementation and assist African Governments. Several factors continued to impede private sector development in Africa, including the poor policy environment in most countries; weak institutional mechanisms for policy dialogue and consultation between the corporate sector and the Government in some countries; poor infrastructure facilities; the lack of an enabling governance environment; and limited use of public-private partnerships to address NEPAD priorities. Major constraints for civil society included lack of communication between and among civil society organizations, Government and the private sector and between civil society organizations and the NEPAD secretariat; a lack of resources to implement NEPAD; poor coordination and synergy among civil society organizations in their engagement with NEPAD; and the tendency of African Governments to cooperate mainly with organizations that were created or financed by donors or government departments, while often neglecting others.

The Secretary-General proposed that African countries take measures to integrate NEPAD priorities into their development process; development partners strive to achieve coherence and complementarity in their trade and aid policies; and the private sector and civil society adopt a proactive orientation towards NEPAD.

UN future engagement with NEPAD

Report of Secretary-General. The Secretary-General, responding to a 2002 request of the Committee for Programme and Coordination (CPC), submitted an April report [E/AC.51/2003/6] on the future engagement of the UN system with NEPAD, which described the UN system's role in support of NEPAD as mandated by the General Assembly in resolution 57/7 [YUN 2002, p. 910]. A three-tier operational framework was in place to help implement NEPAD. At the country level, the main framework for engaging with African Governments would be the United Nations Development Assistance Framework and the common country assessments, complemented by PRSPs. At the regional level, the framework for coordination and collaboration among UN entities would be the regional consultative meetings, chaired by the Economic Commission for Africa (ECA), working among the five clusters corresponding to the NEPAD priorities under the convenership of a UN agency: infrastructure development (ECA), governance, peace and security (UNDP), agriculture, trade and market access (Food and Agriculture Organization of the United Nations); environment, population and urbanization (UN Human Settlements Programme (UN-Habitat)); and human resources development, employment and HIV/AIDS (United Nations Children's Fund).

At the global level, CEB was providing oversight and policy guidance, while the new Office of the Special Adviser on Africa would assist the Secretary-General in the coordination of global advocacy and support to NEPAD.

The report concluded that NEPAD's implementation was a work in progress and the UN system had demonstrated a strong commitment to adopting a coherent framework. The active involvement of the NEPAD secretariat and the AU Commission at virtually every stage of the UN system's support to NEPAD augured well for the idea of partnership embodied in NEPAD.

CPC action. CPC, at its forty-third session (New York, 9 June–3 July and 9 July) [A/58/16], recommended that relevant UN system organizations assume the role of convener of the clusters, consistent with their fields of competence and capacity, while avoiding inter-agency rivalry, and strengthening coordination and collaboration so as to ensure their effective involvement in providing added value to NEPAD's implementation. CPC stressed that the coordination function should be carried out at the regional and subregional levels by ECA and coordinated by the Office of the Special Adviser on Africa. It stressed the need for CEB to keep under regular review the issue of inter-agency coordination on NEPAD. The Committee recommended that the Assembly request the Secretary-General to report in 2004 on the further future engagement of the UN system with NEPAD and to submit an annual progress report on the implementation of NEPAD.

Following consideration of the proposed revisions to programme 8, UN support for NEPAD, of the medium-term plan for the period 2002-2005 [A/58/83], CPC recommended that the Assembly approve the revisions with modifications as set out in its report.

ECONOMIC AND SOCIAL COUNCIL ACTION

On 21 July [meeting 42], the Economic and Social Council, on the recommendation of the Commission for Social Development [E/2003/26], adopted **resolution 2003/13** without vote [agenda item 14 (b)].

National and international cooperation for social development: implementation of the social objectives of the New Partnership for Africa's Development

The Economic and Social Council,

Recalling the World Summit for Social Development, held in Copenhagen from 6 to 12 March 1995, and the twenty-fourth special session of the General Assembly entitled "World Summit for Social Development and beyond: achieving social development for all in a globalizing world", held in Geneva from 26 June to 1 July 2000,

Recalling also General Assembly resolution 56/218 of 21 December 2001, by which the Assembly established the Ad Hoc Committee of the Whole of the General Assembly for the Final Review and Appraisal of the Implementation of the United Nations New Agenda for the Development of Africa in the 1990s to conduct, during the fifty-seventh session of the Assembly, the final review and appraisal of the United Nations New Agenda for the Development of Africa in the 1990s and related initiatives on the basis of the report of the Secretary-General on the independent high-level quality evaluation, as well as on the basis of proposals by the Secretary-General on the modalities of the future engagement of the United Nations with the New Partnership for Africa's Development, and Assembly resolution 56/508 of 27 June 2002,

Reaffirming the United Nations Millennium Declaration of 8 September 2000, the United Nations Declaration on the New Partnership for Africa's Development of 16 September 2002 and General Assembly resolution 57/7 of 4 November 2002 on the final review and appraisal of the United Nations New Agenda for the Development of Africa in the 1990s and support for the New Partnership for Africa's Development,

Welcoming the adoption of the chapter VIII, entitled "Sustainable development for Africa", of the Plan of Implementation of the World Summit on Sustainable Development ("Johannesburg Plan of Implementation"),

Cognizant of the link between the priorities of the New Partnership for Africa's Development and the Millennium Declaration, in which the international community committed itself to addressing the special needs of Africa, and of the need to achieve the internationally agreed development goals, including those set out in the Millennium Declaration,

Bearing in mind the reports of the Secretary-General of 20 June 1995 and 12 June 2001, submitted to the Economic and Social Council at its high-level segments devoted to the consideration of the development of Africa,

Bearing in mind also that, while the primary responsibility for the development of Africa remains with African countries, the international community has a stake in that development and in supporting the efforts of those countries in that regard,

Underlining the fact that international cooperation based on a spirit of partnership and solidarity among all countries contributes to creating an enabling environment conducive to the achievement of the goals of social development,

Recognizing the urgent need to continue to assist African countries in their efforts to diversify their economies as well as enhance capacity-building and promote regional cooperation,

Recognizing also the serious challenges facing social development in Africa, in particular illiteracy, poverty and HIV/AIDS,

1. *Emphasizes* that economic development, social development and environmental protection are interdependent and mutually reinforcing components of sustainable development;

2. *Recognizes* that, while social development is primarily the responsibility of Governments, international cooperation and assistance are essential for the full achievement of that goal;

3. *Reiterates* the importance of all human rights and fundamental freedoms, including the right to development;

4. *Reaffirms* the need to strengthen, inter alia, in a spirit of partnership, international, regional and subregional cooperation for social development and implementation of the outcome of the World Summit for Social Development and the twenty-fourth special session of the General Assembly entitled "World Summit for Social Development and beyond: achieving social development for all in a globalizing world";

5. *Also reaffirms* the need for effective partnership and cooperation between Governments and the relevant actors of civil society for the achievement of social development;

6. *Welcomes* the New Partnership for Africa's Development as a programme of the African Union for peace and sustainable development that embodies the vision and commitment of all African Governments and peoples;

7. *Stresses* the need for renewed political will at the national, regional and international levels to invest in people and their well-being so as to achieve the objectives of social development;

8. *Emphasizes* that democracy, respect for all human rights and fundamental freedoms, transparent and accountable governance and administration in all sectors of society, as well as effective participation by civil society, are among the indispensable foundations for the realization of social and people-centred sustainable development;

9. *Also emphasizes* the New Partnership objectives of eradicating poverty in Africa and placing African countries, both individually and collectively, on a path of sustainable growth and development and thus facilitating Africa's participation in the globalization process;

10. *Underlines* the need for effective partnership and cooperation between Governments and the relevant actors of civil society, including non-governmental organizations and the private sector, in the implementation of and follow-up to the Copenhagen Declaration on Social Development and the Programme of Action of the World Summit for Social Development and the twenty-fourth special session of the General Assembly, and the need for ensuring, within the framework of the New Partnership, their involvement in the planning, elaboration, implementation and evaluation of

social policies at the national, regional and international levels;

11. *Welcomes with appreciation* actions already under way at the regional level to organize the activities of the United Nations system around thematic clusters covering the priority areas of the New Partnership, and in this regard urges the strengthening of that process as a means of enhancing the coordinated response of the United Nations system in support of the New Partnership;

12. *Stresses*, in this context, the vital role of the United Nations in assisting Member States to achieve the development objectives and targets of the United Nations Millennium Declaration and to mainstream them in an integrated and coordinated manner in United Nations development activities;

13. *Welcomes* the commitment of African countries to peace, security, democracy, good governance, human rights and sound economic management, as well as their commitment to taking concrete measures to strengthen mechanisms for conflict prevention, management and resolution as embodied in the New Partnership, as an essential basis for sustainable development in Africa, and in this context welcomes the ongoing efforts of African countries to develop further the African peer review mechanism which is an important and innovative feature of the New Partnership;

14. *Recognizes* that illiteracy, poverty, HIV/AIDS and other major communicable diseases add challenges to Africa's development, and urges the international community to continue to increase its assistance to African countries in their efforts to address these challenges;

15. *Urges* the international community and the United Nations system to organize support for African countries in accordance with the principles, objectives and priorities of the New Partnership in the new spirit of partnership;

16. *Invites* the international financial institutions to ensure that their support for Africa is compatible with the principles, objectives and priorities of the New Partnership;

17. *Urges* the United Nations system, in coordinating its activities at the national, regional and global levels, to foster a coherent response, inter alia, through close collaboration with bilateral donors in the implementation of the New Partnership in response to the needs of individual countries within the larger framework of the New Partnership;

18. *Welcomes* the decision of the General Assembly to invite the Economic and Social Council, pursuant to its role in respect of system-wide coordination, to consider how to support the objectives of Assembly resolution 57/7;

19. *Calls upon* the Secretary-General, in his efforts to harmonize the current initiatives on Africa, to enhance coordination between the United Nations and the specialized agencies, programmes and funds of the United Nations system;

20. *Acknowledges* the reflection by the Secretary-General of the social dimensions of the New Partnership in his report on the priority theme for the forty-first session of the Commission for Social Development, "National and international cooperation for social development", and invites him to continue to reflect those dimensions in future reports submitted to the Commission on its priority themes;

21. *Recommends* that the Commission for Social Development continue to give due prominence to the social dimensions of the New Partnership in its future priority themes;

22. *Decides* to bring the present resolution to the attention of the General Assembly at its fifty-eighth session during its consideration of the agenda item entitled "New Partnership for Africa's Development: progress in implementation and international support".

The Council, on 24 July, decided to consider, pursuant to its role in respect of system-wide coordination, how to support the objectives of General Assembly resolution 57/7 at its resumed session in 2003 (**decision 2003/282**).

GENERAL ASSEMBLY ACTION

On 23 December [meeting 78], the General Assembly adopted **resolution 58/233** [draft: A/58/L.17/Rev.1 & Add.1] without vote [agenda item 39 *(a)*].

New Partnership for Africa's Development: progress in implementation and international support

The General Assembly,

Recalling its resolution 57/2 of 16 September 2002 on the United Nations Declaration on the New Partnership for Africa's Development,

Recalling also its resolution 57/7 of 4 November 2002 on the final review and appraisal of the United Nations New Agenda for the Development of Africa in the 1990s and support for the New Partnership for Africa's Development,

Recalling further its resolution 57/297 of 20 December 2002 on the Second Industrial Development Decade for Africa,

Mindful of the Programme of Action for the Least Developed Countries for the Decade 2001-2010, the Declaration of Commitment on HIV/AIDS, the Doha Ministerial Declaration, the Monterrey Consensus of the International Conference on Financing for Development and the Plan of Implementation of the World Summit on Sustainable Development ("Johannesburg Plan of Implementation"),

Noting with appreciation the commitment of the international community in its support of the New Partnership, and welcoming in this regard the outcome of the third Tokyo International Conference on African Development,

Noting with appreciation also that the Group of Eight summit in Evian, France, in June 2003 devoted a significant part of its deliberations to the New Partnership, welcoming in this regard the endorsement of the report on the implementation of the Group of Eight Africa Action Plan, and also welcoming the inaugural meeting, in Paris in November 2003, of the Africa Partnership Forum in support of the New Partnership,

Having considered the report of the Secretary-General entitled "The New Partnership for Africa's Development: first consolidated report on progress in implementation and international support",

1. *Welcomes* the report of the Secretary-General;
2. *Reaffirms its full support* for the implementation of the New Partnership for Africa's Development;

3. *Recognizes* the progress made in the implementation of the New Partnership and regional and international support for the New Partnership;

4. *Also recognizes* that much needs to be done to achieve the objectives of the New Partnership, particularly with regard to economic growth and poverty reduction;

5. *Reaffirms* that the international community, Africa and its development partners should further cooperate with one another to achieve the objectives and priorities of the New Partnership, on the basis of the principles of ownership and partnership;

6. *Calls upon* Member States and the international community, and invites the United Nations system, to enhance their support for the implementation of the New Partnership, in accordance with its principles, objectives and priorities;

I
Action by African countries and organizations

7. *Notes with satisfaction* efforts made by the African countries in fulfilling their commitments, in implementation of the New Partnership for Africa's Development, to deepen democracy, human rights, good governance and sound economic management, and encourages African countries to continue to strengthen their efforts in this regard by developing and strengthening institutions for governance and the development of the region;

8. *Welcomes* the efforts of African countries in the management and resolution of conflicts in the region, in particular their determination to establish a Peace and Security Council within the African Union, African mediation in a number of conflicts and the efforts of the African Union and African regional organizations to develop their capabilities for peace-support operations;

9. *Takes note* of the adoption of the Memorandum of Understanding on the African Peer Review Mechanism, signed in Abuja on 9 March 2003, and welcomes in this regard the progress made with respect to the Mechanism, in particular the accession of a number of States members of the African Union and the appointment of the panel of eminent persons, and encourages other States members of the African Union to accede to the Mechanism as well;

10. *Welcomes* the priorities identified in the New Partnership and the progress made in the development of programmes in the areas of agricultural development, environment and infrastructure development, as well as the ongoing work in the areas of health and education and science and technology;

11. *Also welcomes* the efforts of African countries to fulfil their commitments to promote gender equality, the empowerment of women and the mainstreaming of gender perspectives in the implementation of the New Partnership;

12. *Further welcomes* the adoption by the African Union in Maputo, on 12 July 2003, of the Convention on the Prevention and Combating of Corruption;

13. *Encourages* African countries to take further concrete steps to deepen the process of integrating the priorities of the New Partnership into their national development plans and frameworks, including poverty reduction strategies, where they exist, to mobilize public and political support for the New Partnership, to develop sound programmes in the designated priority areas of the New Partnership and to mobilize resources for those priority areas;

14. *Emphasizes* the role of national focal points in monitoring the implementation of the New Partnership and the need to build and strengthen human and institutional capacities in order to effectively implement it in all its aspects;

15. *Also emphasizes* that regional economic communities are effective vehicles for the development and integration of the African continent, and in this regard calls for the strengthening of their role in the coordination and implementation of programmes and projects of the New Partnership at the subregional level;

16. *Encourages* the further integration of the priorities and objectives of the New Partnership into the programmes of the regional structures and organizations, as well as programmes for the African least developed countries;

17. *Calls upon* African countries to promote the development and strengthening of their domestic private sectors and to facilitate their effective involvement in the growth and development of, and economic integration among, the African economies;

18. *Recognizes* the efforts of African countries to raise awareness of the New Partnership and to involve all African stakeholders, namely, Governments, the private sector and civil society, including women's organizations and community-based organizations, in its implementation;

19. *Welcomes* the decision taken by the Executive Council of the African Union in Maputo to integrate the New Partnership into the African Union structures and processes;

II
Action by the international community

20. *Welcomes* the pledges of increased official development assistance made by many of the development partners, also welcomes the contributions that have been made, and urges that partners take steps to continue to disburse the assistance they have pledged;

21. *Notes with satisfaction* that some developed countries have untied their official development assistance, and encourages countries that have not yet done so to untie their aid, in accordance with the relevant recommendation of the Development Assistance Committee of the Organisation for Economic Co-operation and Development;

22. *Calls upon* the international community, relevant multilateral institutions and developed countries to enhance coherence in their trade, investment and aid policies towards African countries;

23. *Stresses* the need to find a durable solution to the problem of external indebtedness of heavily indebted poor countries in Africa, including through debt cancellation and other arrangements, and the need to encourage innovative mechanisms to comprehensively address the debt problem of low- and middle-income African countries, bearing in mind that external debt relief can release resources that may be utilized in the successful implementation of the New Partnership for Africa's Development, taking into account initiatives that have been taken to reduce outstanding indebtedness and the need to pursue debt relief measures vigorously and expeditiously, including

within the context of the Paris Club, the London Club and other relevant forums;

24. *Welcomes* the actions taken by creditor countries within the framework of the Paris Club and by some creditor countries through the cancellation of bilateral debts, urges all creditor countries to participate in efforts to remedy the external debt and debt-servicing problems of African countries, notes the Evian Approach of the Paris Club of October 2003, and also notes that debt relief does not replace alternative sources of financing;

25. *Encourages* developed countries and other partners to support the promotion of private investment in African countries from their countries, in particular in the key productive sectors of the economy, to provide investment guarantees for such investment and to support policies of African countries aimed at promoting a conducive environment to attract foreign investment;

26. *Underlines* the need to take concrete steps to implement existing frameworks and programmes of South-South cooperation, including through triangular cooperation in support of the New Partnership;

27. *Acknowledges* the activities in African countries of the Bretton Woods institutions and of the African Development Bank, and encourages them to continue their support for the implementation of the priorities and objectives of the New Partnership;

28. *Notes* the growing collaboration among the entities of the United Nations system in support of the New Partnership, and requests the Secretary-General to promote greater coherence in the work of the United Nations system in support of the New Partnership, on the basis of the agreed clusters;

29. *Calls upon* the United Nations funds, programmes and specialized agencies to strengthen further their existing coordination and programming mechanisms, as well as the simplification and harmonization of planning, disbursement and reporting procedures, as a means of enhancing support for African countries in the implementation of the New Partnership;

30. *Notes* that the entities of the United Nations system have been actively using the regional consultation mechanism as a vehicle for fostering collaboration and coordination at the regional level, and encourages them to intensify their efforts in developing and implementing joint programmes in support of the New Partnership at the regional level;

31. *Requests* the United Nations system to continue to provide assistance to the secretariat of the New Partnership and to African countries in developing projects and programmes within the scope of the priorities of the New Partnership;

32. *Welcomes* the cooperation and the support granted by the United Nations to the African regional and subregional organizations in conflict prevention and conflict management, takes note with appreciation of the work carried out by the Economic and Social Council ad hoc advisory groups on African countries emerging from conflict, while looking forward to the evaluation of their work during the substantive session of the Council in 2004, and encourages the pursuit of these activities in support of African efforts for conflict prevention and conflict management and in post-conflict situations;

33. *Also welcomes* the creation of the Office of the Special Adviser on Africa, and requests the Secretary-General to continue to take measures to strengthen the Office to enable it to effectively fulfil its mandate;

34. *Requests* the Secretary-General to submit a comprehensive report on the implementation of the present resolution to the General Assembly at its fifty-ninth session on the basis of inputs from Governments, organizations of the United Nations system and the other stakeholders in the New Partnership for Africa's Development, such as the private sector and civil society.

Democratic Republic of the Congo

In response to General Assembly resolution 57/146 [YUN 2002, p. 915], the Secretary-General, in August [A/58/273], described economic recovery and reconstruction assistance provided by the UN system to the DRC.

A series of encouraging prospects for a peaceful resolution of the country's political crisis followed the signing of the Final Act of the inter-Congolese political negotiations in April (see p. 113). However, in May, after the withdrawal of Ugandan troops, the district of Ituri, particularly the city of Bunia, was the scene of violent clashes between ethnic Hema and Lendu militias, which triggered a major humanitarian crisis (for Security Council action, see p. 123). Those and other clashes weakened the ceasefire, continued to threaten the peace process and exacerbated the already precarious humanitarian situation. Despite significant macroeconomic advances, particularly in controlling inflation, the social situation remained precarious. The great majority of the population continued to live below the poverty line. Faced with the various challenges, UN system agencies provided technical, material and financial assistance to support the transition process, democratic governance and poverty reduction, and for emergency humanitarian assistance.

The Secretary-General encouraged all parties to the conflict in the DRC to pursue efforts to accelerate the establishment of the transitional institutions. He invited donors to stress their support for the efforts of the United Nations Organization Mission in the Democratic Republic of the Congo (MONUC) to ensure the disarmament, demobilization and repatriation of foreign armed groups and to encourage the Government of Rwanda and its allies to cooperate with MONUC for that purpose; the multinational financial institutions and DRC's principal creditors to speed up the country's admission to the HIPC Initiative in order to alleviate its debt service; and development partners to support the implementation of financial mechanisms designed to discharge the public debt, and to cover the funding shortfall of the Emergency Multisectoral Rehabilitation and Reconstruction Programme 2003-2005, approved by the Congolese parties, and support civil service reform and efforts to reunify the country.

GENERAL ASSEMBLY ACTION

On 17 December [meeting 75], the General Assembly adopted **resolution 58/123** [draft: A/58/L.31/Rev.1 & Add.1] by recorded vote (169-1) [agenda item 40 (b)].

Special assistance for the economic recovery and reconstruction of the Democratic Republic of the Congo

The General Assembly,

Recalling its previous resolutions on special assistance for the economic recovery and reconstruction of the Democratic Republic of the Congo,

Recalling also all resolutions of the Security Council and the statements by its President regarding the Democratic Republic of the Congo,

Reaffirming the sovereignty, territorial integrity and political independence of the Democratic Republic of the Congo and all States in the region,

Gravely concerned at the dire humanitarian, economic and social situation in the Democratic Republic of the Congo, and at the effects on the inhabitants of the continued fighting in the eastern part, resulting in the continuing plight of the civilian population, and calling for its protection, taking into account the particular needs of women and girls,

Deeply concerned at the HIV/AIDS pandemic, and at its disproportionate effect on women and girls,

Expressing its deep concern at the dire consequences of the conflict for the humanitarian and human rights situations in the country, and at the continuing lack of sufficient access to vulnerable people,

Gravely concerned by the continued illegal exploitation of the natural resources of the Democratic Republic of the Congo as a source of further conflict, and reaffirming in this regard its commitment to respect the sovereignty of the Democratic Republic of the Congo over its natural resources,

Gravely concerned also at the negative impact of war on the promotion of sustainable development in the Democratic Republic of the Congo and the Great Lakes region,

Deeply concerned about the continued extensive destruction of life and property, as well as the severe damage to infrastructure and the environment suffered by the Democratic Republic of the Congo,

Bearing in mind the fact that the Democratic Republic of the Congo hosts thousands of refugees from neighbouring countries, which places a great burden on its limited resources, and expressing the hope that conditions will be created that facilitate a safe and voluntary return of refugees,

Recalling that the Democratic Republic of the Congo is a least developed country with severe economic and social problems arising from its weak economic infrastructure and aggravated by the ongoing conflict,

Bearing in mind the close interrelationship between ensuring peace and security and the ability of the country to meet the humanitarian needs of its people and to take effective steps towards the rapid revitalization of the economy, and reaffirming the urgent need to assist the Democratic Republic of the Congo in the rehabilitation and reconstruction of its damaged economy and in its efforts to restore basic services and the infrastructure of the country,

1. *Takes note* of the report of the Secretary-General;
2. *Welcomes* the conclusion of the Global and All-Inclusive Agreement on the Transition in the Democratic Republic of the Congo, signed in Pretoria on 17 December 2002 and the subsequent establishment of the Government of National Unity and Transition, and encourages the effective establishment of all transitional institutions;
3. *Also welcomes* the declaration of Principles on Good-Neighbourly Relations and Cooperation between the Democratic Republic of the Congo and Burundi, Rwanda and Uganda, which marked the successful conclusion of the high-level meeting held on 25 September 2003 under the auspices of the Secretary-General;
4. *Further welcomes* the efforts of the Republic of South Africa, the Republic of Angola, and all the Central African countries, as well as the important role of the Secretary-General, in facilitating the adoption of these agreements;
5. *Urges* all parties concerned in the region to cease military activities and to cease any support for armed groups, and rather to use their influence to support the transition and bring all within the dynamic of the transition;
6. *Strongly condemns* the acts of violence, including the latest massacres in Ituri, systematically perpetrated against civilians, including the massacres, as well as other atrocities and violations of international humanitarian law and human rights, in particular sexual violence against women and girls, stresses the need to bring to justice those responsible, including those at the command level, and urges all parties, including the Government of the Democratic Republic of the Congo, to take all necessary steps to prevent further violations of human rights and international humanitarian law, in particular those committed against civilians;
7. *Welcomes* the work of the Interim Emergency Multinational Force in Bunia led by the European Union, and the subsequent efforts of the United Nations Organization Mission in the Democratic Republic of the Congo to help secure the Ituri region;
8. *Recognizes* the importance of an effective withdrawal of all foreign troops from the territory of the Democratic Republic of the Congo;
9. *Urges* all parties concerned in the region to cease any recruitment, training and use of child soldiers, which are contrary to international law, welcomes the initial steps taken by the Government of the Democratic Republic of the Congo to demobilize and reintegrate child soldiers, in particular through education, and urges the Government and all parties to continue their efforts in this context, and to take into account the particular needs of girl ex-combatants;
10. *Invites* donors to strengthen their support for the efforts of the United Nations Organization Mission in the Democratic Republic of the Congo to demobilize and repatriate armed groups currently in the Democratic Republic of the Congo and to encourage the transitional Government and all parties to the conflict to cooperate with the Organization Mission in achieving a

climate of security and trust, the support of neighbouring countries in this process being essential;

11. *Emphasizes* that the consolidation of peace and the resumption of economic activity in the Democratic Republic of the Congo are inextricably linked, and calls for further international economic assistance in this regard;

12. *Encourages* the Government of the Democratic Republic of the Congo to pursue the implementation of economic reforms aimed at stabilizing the macroeconomic framework so that conditions for sustainable growth can be created;

13. *Urges* all parties to fully respect international humanitarian law and to ensure the safe and unhindered access of humanitarian personnel to all affected populations throughout the territory of the Democratic Republic of the Congo and the safety of United Nations and humanitarian personnel;

14. *Calls upon* the international community to increase its support for humanitarian relief activities within the Democratic Republic of the Congo;

15. *Urges* all parties to permit free and unhindered movement of the population, which is essential, inter alia, to the resumption of economic activities;

16. *Expresses its deep concern* especially at the very serious, dire humanitarian situation in Ituri, and calls on all Congolese parties on the ground to cooperate fully, in general, with the institutions of the transition, and, in particular, with the Ituri Pacification Commission;

17. *Also expresses its deep concern* over the dire humanitarian situation throughout the country and the very high number of internally displaced persons in the eastern part and, in particular, in the Ituri region, and urges all parties to avoid further population displacement and to facilitate the safe and voluntary return of refugees and internally displaced persons to their places of origin;

18. *Stresses* the importance of the restoration of river traffic, welcomes in this regard the reopening of the Congo and Oubangui Rivers, and expresses its support for the establishment of a Congo River Basin Commission;

19. *Calls* for the reopening of the Kisangani-Kindu rail and river link to facilitate the delivery of humanitarian assistance, as well as the resupply access for humanitarian personnel;

20. *Encourages* the continued cooperation of the Government of the Democratic Republic of the Congo with the United Nations, the specialized agencies, international financial institutions and other organizations, including non-governmental organizations, in addressing the need for rehabilitation and reconstruction, and welcomes in this regard their renewed dialogue and cooperation;

21. *Renews its urgent appeal* to the executive boards of the United Nations funds and programmes to continue to keep under consideration the special needs of the Democratic Republic of the Congo, and stresses the need to mainstream an appropriate gender perspective within overall reconstruction efforts;

22. *Welcomes* the inclusion of the Democratic Republic of the Congo in the Heavily Indebted Poor Countries Initiative;

23. *Urges* the Government of the Democratic Republic of the Congo to implement national comprehensive strategies to monitor and manage external liabilities, embedded in the domestic preconditions for debt sustainability, including sound macroeconomic and public resource management;

24. *Welcomes* initiatives that have been undertaken to reduce outstanding indebtedness, and invites further national and international measures in that direction, including, as appropriate, debt cancellation and other arrangements;

25. *Invites* the development partners to cover the funding shortfall of the Emergency Multisectoral Rehabilitation and Reconstruction Programme and support civil service reform and efforts to reunify the country;

26. *Invites* Governments to continue providing support to the Democratic Republic of the Congo;

27. *Requests* the Secretary-General:

(a) To ensure through his Special Representative for the Democratic Republic of the Congo, who convenes the International Committee in Support of the Transition, the coordination of all the activities of the United Nations system in the Democratic Republic of the Congo and the facilitation of the coordination with other national and international actors of activities in support of the transition, and welcomes to that effect the adoption of new coordination mechanisms aimed at ensuring a coherent and effective response to the multifaceted humanitarian crisis in the Democratic Republic of the Congo;

(b) To continue to consult with regional leaders, in coordination with the President of the African Union, about ways to bring about a peaceful and durable solution to the conflict;

(c) To continue to consult with regional leaders, in coordination with the President of the African Union, in order to prepare an international conference on peace, security and development in Central Africa and in the Great Lakes region, under the auspices of the United Nations and the African Union, to address the problems of the region in a comprehensive manner;

(d) To keep under review the humanitarian and economic situation in the Democratic Republic of the Congo with a view to promoting participation in and support for a programme of financial and material assistance to the country to enable it to meet urgent needs in terms of economic recovery and reconstruction;

(e) To submit to the General Assembly at its fifty-ninth session a report on the actions taken pursuant to the present resolution.

RECORDED VOTE ON RESOLUTION 58/123:

In favour: Afghanistan, Albania, Algeria, Andorra, Angola, Antigua and Barbuda, Argentina, Armenia, Australia, Austria, Azerbaijan, Bahamas, Bahrain, Bangladesh, Belarus, Belgium, Belize, Bolivia, Bosnia and Herzegovina, Botswana, Brazil, Brunei Darussalam, Bulgaria, Burundi, Cambodia, Canada, Central African Republic, Chile, China, Colombia, Comoros, Congo, Costa Rica, Côte d'Ivoire, Croatia, Cuba, Cyprus, Czech Republic, Democratic People's Republic of Korea, Democratic Republic of the Congo, Denmark, Djibouti, Dominica, Dominican Republic, Ecuador, Egypt, El Salvador, Eritrea, Estonia, Ethiopia, Fiji, Finland, France, Gabon, Gambia, Georgia, Germany, Ghana, Greece, Grenada, Guatemala, Guinea, Guyana, Honduras, Hungary, Iceland, India, Indonesia, Iran, Ireland, Israel, Italy, Jamaica, Japan, Jordan, Kazakhstan, Kenya, Kuwait, Kyrgyzstan, Latvia, Lebanon, Lesotho, Libyan Arab Jamahiriya, Liechtenstein, Lithuania, Luxembourg, Madagascar, Malaysia, Maldives, Mali, Malta, Marshall Islands, Mauritania, Mauritius, Mexico, Micronesia, Monaco, Mongolia, Morocco, Mozambique, Myanmar, Namibia, Nauru, Nepal, Netherlands, New Zealand, Nicaragua, Niger, Nigeria, Norway, Oman, Pakistan, Palau, Panama, Papua New Guinea, Paraguay, Peru, Philippines, Poland, Portugal, Qatar, Republic of Korea, Republic of Moldova, Romania, Russian Federation, Saint Lucia, San Marino, Saudi Arabia, Senegal, Serbia and Montenegro, Sierra Leone, Singapore, Slovakia, Slovenia, Solomon Islands, Somalia, South Africa, Spain, Sri Lanka, Sudan, Suriname, Swaziland, Sweden, Switzerland,

Syrian Arab Republic, Tajikistan, Thailand, The former Yugoslav Republic of Macedonia, Timor-Leste, Togo, Tonga, Trinidad and Tobago, Tunisia, Turkey, Turkmenistan, Tuvalu, Ukraine, United Arab Emirates, United Kingdom, United Republic of Tanzania, United States, Uruguay, Uzbekistan, Vanuatu, Venezuela, Viet Nam, Yemen, Zambia, Zimbabwe.
Against: Rwanda.

Djibouti

In response to General Assembly resolution 56/108 [YUN 2001, p. 853], the Secretary-General submitted an August report [A/58/285] describing the political and socio-economic situation in Djibouti and progress made in providing assistance for reconstruction and development over the past four years to March 2003.

Djibouti's development challenges were related to the country's economic and financial crisis, which resulted from civil strife and changes in the international and subregional context. In addition, recurring emergency situations, including drought, flood and epidemics, combined with large-scale destruction of livestock, water points and health and educational facilities as a result of the internal conflict, led to the large-scale movement of displaced populations and considerably increased Djibouti's need for further emergency and humanitarian assistance. As drought had affected both the rural and urban populations, there was an urgent need to make better use of rainwater and to explore country-wide water resources. Djibouti needed to rebuild much of the rural infrastructure to enable people to return to their homelands. Most schools, roads, hospitals, water facilities and dispensaries had to be reconstructed. Microcredit programmes and highly labour-intensive projects and programmes were needed to encourage people to return to their villages. Also needed was the promotion of income-generating activities. It was estimated that at least $100 million was required to mitigate the socio-economic impact of the civil war. Further assistance was necessary for governance, administrative reform and economic management, and to train national officials to contribute to the rebuilding of a fragile economy.

GENERAL ASSEMBLY ACTION

On 17 December [meeting 75], the General Assembly adopted **resolution 58/116** [draft: A/58/L.41 & Add.1] without vote [agenda item 40 (b)].

Economic assistance for the reconstruction and development of Djibouti

The General Assembly,

Recalling its resolution 56/108 of 14 December 2001 and its previous resolutions on economic assistance to Djibouti,

Recalling also the United Nations Millennium Declaration,

Recalling further the Brussels Declaration and the Programme of Action for the Least Developed Countries for the Decade 2001-2010, adopted by the Third United Nations Conference on the Least Developed Countries on 20 May 2001, as well as the mutual commitments undertaken on that occasion and the importance attached to follow-up and the implementation of the Programme of Action,

Aware that Djibouti is included in the list of least developed countries and that it is ranked 153rd out of the 175 countries studied in the *Human Development Report 2003,*

Noting that the economic and social development efforts of Djibouti are constrained by the extremes of the local climate, in particular cyclical droughts, and that the implementation of reconstruction and development programmes requires the deployment of substantial resources which exceed the limited capacity of the country,

Noting also that the situation in Djibouti has been made worse by the disastrous drought situation prevailing in the Horn of Africa and by the absence of natural resources, which continues to place serious constraints on the fragile economic, budgetary, social and administrative infrastructure of the country,

Expressing its concern at the severe shortage of drinkable water and the dramatic projected figures for the year 2020 as reflected in the report of the Secretary-General,

Noting with satisfaction that the Government of Djibouti is pursuing the implementation of a reform programme and is about to finalize with the international financial institutions a poverty reduction strategy paper,

Noting with gratitude the support provided by various countries, as well as intergovernmental and non-governmental organizations, to meet the humanitarian needs of the country,

1. *Takes note* of the report of the Secretary-General;
2. *Declares its solidarity* with the Government and the people of Djibouti, who continue to face critical developmental and humanitarian challenges owing, in particular, to the scarcity of natural resources, coupled with harsh climatic conditions and the acute issue of water supply impacting on the development aspirations of the country;
3. *Encourages* the Government of Djibouti, despite difficult economic and regional situations, to continue its serious efforts towards the consolidation of democracy;
4. *Notes with satisfaction* the implementation of a reform programme by Djibouti, and in that context appeals to all Governments, international financial institutions, the specialized agencies and non-governmental organizations to respond adequately to the financial and material needs of the country in line with the poverty reduction strategy paper;
5. *Expresses its gratitude* to the intergovernmental organizations and the specialized agencies of the United Nations for their contributions to the national rehabilitation of Djibouti, and invites them to continue their efforts;
6. *Expresses its appreciation* to the Secretary-General for his continued efforts to make the international community aware of the difficulties faced by Djibouti, and welcomes his initiative to appoint a special envoy for humanitarian affairs for the Horn of Africa, with

the objective of mobilizing resources for relief support as well as sustainable development;

7. *Requests* the Secretary-General to continue, in close cooperation with the Government of Djibouti, his efforts to mobilize resources necessary for an effective programme of financial, technical and material assistance to Djibouti;

8. *Also requests* the Secretary-General to report to the General Assembly at its sixtieth session on the humanitarian situation of Djibouti and on the progress made with regard to economic assistance to Djibouti and the implementation of the present resolution.

African countries emerging from conflict

The Economic and Social Council, in resolution 2002/1 [YUN 2002, p. 919], created an ad hoc advisory group, at the request of any African country emerging from conflict, to assess humanitarian and economic needs and develop a programme of long-term support.

In 2003, an Ad Hoc Advisory Group on Burundi was established, while the Group on Guinea-Bissau, mandated by Council decision 2002/304 [YUN 2002, p. 920], continued its activities (see below).

ECONOMIC AND SOCIAL COUNCIL ACTION

On 24 July [meeting 47], the Economic and Social Council adopted **resolution 2003/50** [draft: E/2003/L.22] without vote [agenda item 7 *(h)*].

Ad hoc advisory groups on African countries emerging from conflict

The Economic and Social Council,

Recalling its resolution 2002/1 of 15 July 2002 on the establishment of an ad hoc advisory group on African countries emerging from conflict,

1. *Reiterates* the need to undertake an assessment of lessons learned based on the initial experience of such ad hoc advisory groups, no later than at its substantive session of 2004;

2. *Stresses* the need to assess also progress made in the implementation of recommendations made by the ad hoc advisory groups;

3. *Requests* the Secretary-General to submit a report on this subject to the Council at its substantive session of 2004.

Burundi

In 2003, the Economic and Social Council set up an Ad Hoc Advisory Group on Burundi to study and monitor the country's economic and humanitarian situation with a view to post-conflict reconstruction, following Burundi's request [E/2002/86] to do so.

(For information on the Security Council mission to Burundi in June, see p. 149.)

ECONOMIC AND SOCIAL COUNCIL ACTION

On 21 July [meeting 43], the Economic and Social Council adopted **resolution 2003/16** [draft: E/2003/L.34/Rev.1] without vote [agenda item 7 *(h)*].

Ad Hoc Advisory Group on Burundi

The Economic and Social Council,

Recalling its resolution 2002/1 of 15 July 2002 on the establishment of an ad hoc advisory group on African countries emerging from conflict, in which it decided to consider creating, at the request of any African country emerging from conflict, a limited but flexible and representative ad hoc advisory group at the ambassadorial level, in consultation with all regional groups and the national authorities of the country concerned, drawn from the membership of the Economic and Social Council and its observer States, including representation from the country concerned, and in so doing to take into account the need to include countries that could make a positive contribution to the objectives of such a group,

Recalling also its decision 2002/302 of 4 October 2002, in which it decided to entrust the President of the Economic and Social Council with the holding of consultations regarding the modalities for establishing an ad hoc advisory group on Guinea-Bissau, and its decision 2002/304 of 25 October 2002, in which it established that group,

Taking note of the letter dated 26 September 2002 from the Permanent Representative of Burundi to the United Nations addressed to the President of the Council, in which the authorities of Burundi requested the Council to set up an ad hoc advisory group on Burundi to study and assess the economic and humanitarian situation in that country, with a view to post-conflict reconstruction, in accordance with resolution 2002/1,

Taking note also of the report of the Security Council mission to Central Africa, which visited Burundi from 12 to 14 June 2003, in which the mission expressed its satisfaction as to the peaceful transfer of power in Burundi,

Conscious of the need for providing adequate budgetary and economic support to the transitional Government, given the risk that all gains achieved thus far could collapse if such assistance was not provided immediately,

Urging donor countries to fulfil the commitments that they made at the Paris and Geneva conferences on assistance to Burundi, and welcoming the convening of a donor round table organized by the Government of Burundi, in collaboration with the United Nations Development Programme, scheduled for September 2003,

1. *Decides* to establish the Ad Hoc Advisory Group on Burundi;

2. *Also decides* to entrust the President of the Economic and Social Council with the task of holding consultations and making recommendations, within the framework outlined in resolution 2002/1, on the composition, terms of reference and relevant modalities for the creation of the Advisory Group by the end of August 2003, so as to enable it to participate in the donor round table.

In August, the Council adopted **decision 2003/311** [draft: E/2003/L.48] without vote [agenda item 7 *(h)*].

Ad Hoc Advisory Group on Burundi

At its 50th plenary meeting, on 22 August 2003, the Economic and Social Council, recalling its resolution 2002/1 of 15 July 2002 on the establishment of an ad hoc advisory group on African countries emerging from conflict and resolution 2003/16 of 21 July 2003, by which it established the Ad Hoc Advisory Group on Burundi, decided:

(a) To appoint the Permanent Representatives to the United Nations of Belgium, Burundi, Ethiopia, France, Japan and South Africa to the Ad Hoc Advisory Group on Burundi and to appoint the Permanent Representative of South Africa to the United Nations as Chairperson of the Group;

(b) That the Ad Hoc Advisory Group on Burundi would invite the participation in its work of the Permanent Representative of Guatemala to the United Nations, in his capacity as President of the Economic and Social Council, and the Permanent Representative of Angola to the United Nations, in his capacity as Chairperson of the Ad Hoc Working Group on Conflict Prevention and Resolution in Africa;

(c) That the Ad Hoc Advisory Group would examine the humanitarian and economic needs of Burundi and review relevant programmes of support and prepare recommendations for a long-term programme of support, based on Burundi's development priorities, through the integration of relief, rehabilitation, reconstruction and development into a comprehensive approach to peace and stability, as well as provide advice on how to ensure that the assistance of the international community was adequate, coherent, well-coordinated and effective and promoted synergy;

(d) To request the Ad Hoc Advisory Group on Burundi, taking into consideration the unique character and needs of the situation in Burundi, to submit a report on its recommendations to the Council by mid-January 2004.

On 25 August [S/2003/836], the Council President informed the Security Council of the establishment of the Ad Hoc Advisory Group on Burundi.

Advisory Group activities. Following its first meeting on 11 September, the Group held a series of briefing sessions and meetings in New York with major UN and international interlocutors to discuss various aspects of development assistance to Burundi [E/2004/11]. From 19 to 26 November, the Group undertook a mission to Burundi to meet with government authorities, major socio-economic interlocutors, UN entities active on the ground and other development partners. During its visit, the Group observed a strong UN involvement regarding political support, humanitarian assistance, rural development, health and education.

Guinea-Bissau

Advisory Group activities. A January report of the Ad Hoc Advisory Group on Guinea-Bissau [E/2003/8] described its visit to the country from 9 to 16 November 2002 and the role of the United Nations and of the international community in addressing post-conflict needs.

During its visit, the Group participated in tripartite consultations between the Government, the UN system and the donor community. It drafted a discussion document containing an outline of a possible compact between the Government and the donor community, which was transmitted to the country's President and annexed to the Group's report. On its return from Guinea-Bissau, the Group gave an account of its impressions and continued consultations with key stakeholders, including with high-level UN officials and with the Bretton Woods institutions (the World Bank Group and IMF).

The Group recommended a partnership between the Government and the international community, based on common objectives and on a long-term development strategy. For short-term assistance, the Group recommended to the Economic and Social Council that the partnership be in the form of a compact, which could be based on the discussion document (see above). The proposed compact would have a high-level national steering committee to provide political oversight and monitoring of its performance, and a supporting operational committee composed of government representatives, the UN system and principal donors. It could have, as a central instrument, a temporary trust fund to address urgent short-term needs, to which the donor community could contribute $12 million to $15 million. Trust fund management could be linked to a set of policy benchmarks critical to improving economic and political governance and could include election planning and preparations, a time line for Supreme Court elections, a time line, strategy and process to clarify and promulgate the Constitution, and stability and continuity of the ministerial team. Further short-term recommendations were addressed to the UN system, the Bretton Woods institutions and the donor and international communities. Long-term recommendations to the Government included the promotion of political stability, the development of an economic diversification strategy and improved conditions for private sector activity. Further long-term recommendations were made to the Bretton Woods institutions, the UN system and the donor community.

ECONOMIC AND SOCIAL COUNCIL ACTION (January)

On 31 January, the Economic and Social Council adopted **resolution 2003/1** [draft: E/2003/L.2] without vote [agenda item 2].

Ad Hoc Advisory Group on Guinea-Bissau

The Economic and Social Council,

Recalling its resolution 2002/1 of 15 July 2002, in which it decided to consider creating, at the request of any African country emerging from conflict, an ad hoc advisory group at the ambassadorial level, inter alia, to examine the economic and humanitarian situation of the country concerned, prepare recommendations for a long-term programme of support and provide advice on how to ensure that the assistance of the international community was adequate, coherent, well-coordinated and effective,

Recalling also its decision 2002/304 of 25 October 2002, in which it decided to establish an Ad Hoc Advisory Group on Guinea-Bissau, appointed the members of the Advisory Group and requested the Advisory Group to submit a report on its recommendations to the Economic and Social Council by mid-January 2003,

Recognizing the importance of respecting the sovereignty of Guinea-Bissau and its full participation in the implementation of the mandate of the Advisory Group,

Taking into account the current and specific circumstances prevailing in Guinea-Bissau and the urgent need to address the critical situation that persists in the country,

1. *Takes note with appreciation* of the report of the Ad Hoc Advisory Group on Guinea-Bissau, welcomes the recommendations contained therein and endorses the partnership approach it sets out;

2. *Invites* the Government of Guinea-Bissau and, within their respective mandates, the United Nations system and the Bretton Woods institutions, the donor community and the international community as a whole, to give full consideration to the recommendations formulated by the Advisory Group and to take specific and concrete steps to give effect to the partnership approach, with a view to addressing the short-term needs and implementing a long-term programme of support;

3. *Decides* to extend the mandate of the Advisory Group until the substantive session of the Economic and Social Council to be held in July 2003;

4. *Also decides* that the Advisory Group shall invite the participation in its work of the Permanent Representative of Guatemala to the United Nations, in his capacity as President of the Economic and Social Council for 2003, the Permanent Representative of the Gambia to the United Nations, in his capacity as Chairperson of the Group of Friends of Guinea-Bissau, and the Permanent Representative of Angola to the United Nations, in his capacity as Chairperson of the Ad Hoc Working Group of the Security Council on Conflict Prevention and Resolution in Africa;

5. *Requests* the Secretary-General and the United Nations Development Group, as well as other relevant funds, programmes and specialized agencies of the United Nations system, to continue to assist the Advisory Group in accomplishing its mandate, and invites the Bretton Woods institutions to continue to cooperate to that end;

6. *Recognizes* that the present resolution is specific to the situation prevailing in Guinea-Bissau and that future decisions and resolutions will continue to take into account the specific circumstances of any other African country emerging from conflict that requests the establishment of an ad hoc advisory group.

Further Group activities. By a 1 July letter [E/2003/95], South Africa, in its capacity as Chairman of the Advisory Group, transmitted a supplementary report updating the Group's activities. The Group visited Guinea-Bissau from 26 to 28 June, jointly with the Security Council (see p. 226). The Group met with high-level government representatives, including the country's President, and members of political parties and civil society organizations and NGOs, the private sector and religious leaders. It learned that the political, economic and social situation had deteriorated; donors were willing to assist Guinea-Bissau; and the electoral process was deadlocked. The elections, scheduled for July, were postponed to October. The Group recommended that the Economic and Social Council further appeal to donors to consider funding the elections.

An 18 September statement by the Group [E/2003/105] called on donors to consider extending emergency assistance for Guinea-Bissau to enable it to return to democratic rule following the resignation of its President. It hoped that the emergency assistance would improve the socio-economic conditions in the country.

(For reports of the Secretary-General to the Security Council regarding developments in Guinea-Bissau and the activities of the United Nations Peace-building Support Office in Guinea-Bissau, see p. 223.)

ECONOMIC AND SOCIAL COUNCIL ACTION (July)

On 24 July [meeting 48], the Economic and Social Council adopted **resolution 2003/53** [draft: E/2003/L.23/Rev.1] without vote [agenda item 7 *(h)*].

Ad Hoc Advisory Group on Guinea-Bissau

The Economic and Social Council,

Recalling its resolution 2002/1 of 15 July 2002, in which the Council decided to consider creating, at the request of any African country emerging from conflict, an ad hoc advisory group, and its decision 2002/304 of 25 October 2002, in which the Council decided to establish such a group on Guinea-Bissau,

Recalling also its resolution 2003/1 of 31 January 2003, in which the Council took note with appreciation of the report of the Ad Hoc Advisory Group on Guinea-Bissau, welcomed its recommendations, endorsed the partnership approach it set out and decided to extend the mandate of the Advisory Group until the substantive session of the Council in July 2003,

1. *Takes note with appreciation* of the supplementary report of the Ad Hoc Advisory Group on Guinea-Bissau, and welcomes the interaction and cooperation that has taken place between the Economic and Social Council and the Security Council, within their respective mandates, on the situation in Guinea-Bissau;

2. *Reiterates* the need to foster a comprehensive approach to the problems faced by Guinea-Bissau in its post-conflict phase, in particular to prepare a long-term programme of support, based on its development priorities, through the integration of relief, rehabilitation, reconstruction and development needs;

3. *Reiterates its invitation* to the Government of Guinea-Bissau, and, within their respective mandates, to the organizations of the United Nations system, including the Bretton Woods institutions, the donor community and the international community as a whole to give full consideration to the recommendations formulated by the Advisory Group and to take specific and concrete steps to give effect to the partnership approach that it set out, with a view to addressing the short-term needs and implementing a long-term programme of support;

4. *Welcomes* the progress made with the creation by the United Nations Development Programme of the Emergency Economic Management Fund, following the recommendations made by the Advisory Group in its report and the trust fund set up for the elections, and appeals to donor countries to contribute to these funds;

5. *Decides* to extend the mandate of the Advisory Group until the organizational session of the Economic and Social Council in January 2004, with the current membership, including those invited members, with the purpose of monitoring the implementation of its recommendations, following closely the humanitarian situation and economic and social conditions prevailing in the country and providing an assessment of its work through a report to be submitted to the Council;

6. *Requests* the Secretary-General, the United Nations Development Group, as well as other relevant United Nations funds, programmes and the specialized agencies to continue to assist the Advisory Group in accomplishing its mandate, and invites the Bretton Woods institutions to continue to cooperate to that end.

Other economic assistance

Central America

In response to General Assembly resolution 56/105 [YUN 2001, p. 854], the Secretary-General, in an August report [A/58/286], described the activities of UNDP and other UN system entities, during the period from August 2001 to December 2002, to implement a new sustainable development strategy in Central America. The region received support for consensus-building processes, the strengthening of democratic institutions, social vulnerability and poverty eradication, agricultural development, health and nutrition, public finance and economic growth, and the environment and sustainable development.

Non-reimbursable cooperation in the region had been reduced significantly over the past two years. Donor countries had targeted their work at the national level, focusing on some themes common to the region (see above). In order to cover their investment priorities, Central American countries were forced to increase their levels of debt. In addition, domestic resources for investment had declined considerably as a result of natural disasters and a crisis in the coffee sector.

That had taken place against the background of a competitive international context and as Central American economies went through a process of economic restructuring.

The Secretary-General urged the international community to offer concessional support to reintegrate Central America into the world economy, and for its political and economic integration. The region required continuity in bilateral and multilateral cooperation in the priority areas of strengthening democracy and its institutions, and support to the dialogue and consultation process; and overcoming poverty throughout the region. Other priority areas were food security, health care and the promotion of sustainable development and the environment.

GENERAL ASSEMBLY ACTION

On 17 December [meeting 75], the General Assembly adopted **resolution 58/117** [draft: A/58/L.42 & Add.1] without vote [agenda item 40 *(b)*].

International assistance to and cooperation with the Alliance for the Sustainable Development of Central America

The General Assembly,

Reaffirming all relevant resolutions of the General Assembly that emphasize and acknowledge the importance of international, bilateral and multilateral economic, financial and technical support, cooperation and assistance given by the United Nations system, the international community and non-governmental organizations, which provide a framework for the provision of aid to the Alliance for the Sustainable Development of Central America, in support of national efforts to make the region a zone of peace, freedom, democracy and development,

Noting that the Central American countries have achieved significant progress towards the consolidation of democracy and good governance, the strengthening of civilian Governments and respect for human rights and the rule of law, all as a tool for promoting sustainable development and regional integration, reflecting the desire of the Central American peoples to live and prosper in a climate of peace, solidarity and social justice,

Stressing the importance of the commitments, and their implementation, as undertaken by the regional summits and ministerial meetings, in particular in those areas included in the programme initiatives of the Alliance for the Sustainable Development of Central America in the political, economic, social and ecological fields, which allow a progressive improvement in the quality of life of the people of the region,

Noting that the various natural phenomena which have affected the region are one of the factors that have put at risk the biodiversity of Central America,

Emphasizing that the progress made in complying with the commitments established in the programme of the Alliance for the Sustainable Development of Central America creates the necessary conditions for implementing the policies for reducing the vulnerability of the region to natural disasters,

Noting that the framework of the Puebla-Panama Plan includes the Mesoamerican Initiative for the Prevention and Mitigation of Natural Disasters, as well as others that promote the conservation and sustainable management of natural resources, and encompasses the strategy for the transformation and modernization of Central America in the twenty-first century, presented during the Regional Consultative Group meeting, held in Madrid on 8 and 9 March 2001, and the Strategy for the South-Southeast of Mexico,

Noting also the adoption in 2001 of the Regional Mechanism of Coordination of Mutual Assistance in Case of Disasters, as well as the successful work of the Coordination Centre for the Prevention of Natural Disasters in Central America and, in particular, its mandate to hold the Mitch +5 Regional Forum, and the Regional Programme for Risk Management in Central America of the Coordination Centre and the United Nations Development Programme,

Welcoming the adoption of the Political Dialogue and Cooperation Agreement between the European Union and Central America, which should result in the conclusion of future agreements strengthening the San José Dialogue process and expanding it to, inter alia, economic areas, migration and the campaign against international terrorism,

Recognizing the progress made in the elimination of anti-personnel mines from Central American territory, as well as the need to rehabilitate and reintegrate mine victims in their communities in order to restore normal conditions for the full development of the region,

1. *Takes note with satisfaction* of the report of the Secretary-General;

2. *Notes* the significant reduction in the last two years of the non-reimbursable international assistance and cooperation extended to the Alliance for the Sustainable Development of Central America, as indicated in the report of the Secretary-General;

3. *Supports* the decision of the Central American Governments to promote in a harmonious and balanced way the sustained economic, social, cultural, environmental and political development of its member States and the development of the region as a whole through programmes which help to consolidate democracy and resolve social inequalities and extreme poverty;

4. *Reiterates* the importance of supporting and strengthening the efforts of the Central American countries in the implementation of the Regional Mechanism of Coordination of Mutual Assistance in Case of Disasters and the Regional Plan for Disaster Reduction as well as the implementation of the Strategic Framework for the Reduction of Vulnerability and Disasters in Central America and, in particular, of taking measures for the prevention and mitigation of damage, with special emphasis on the most vulnerable groups and sectors;

5. *Requests* the Secretary-General, the organs, organizations and programmes of the United Nations system and all States, international financial institutions and regional and subregional organizations, as appropriate, to continue providing the support needed to attain the objectives of the programme for the sustainable development of Central America, including those which are being pursued within the framework of the Quinquennium for the Reduction of Vulnerability to and the Impact of Natural Disasters in Central America;

6. *Notes with appreciation* the revision of the subregional cooperation programme in Central America of the United Nations Development Programme, launched in 1996, and of the national programmes of other United Nations agencies and other humanitarian agencies on the basis of the priorities established in the regional development strategy for the transformation and modernization of Central America, contained in the initiatives of the Puebla-Panama Plan;

7. *Encourages* the Governments and disaster-related organizations of Central America to continue implementing the International Strategy for Disaster Reduction in order to reduce the vulnerability to hazards, and urges the international community to contribute to these efforts, including, as appropriate, through cooperation and technical assistance;

8. *Notes with satisfaction* the renewal, in December 2002, of the commitment by the bilateral and the multilateral development organizations to the Meso-American Biological Corridor as one of the pillars for sustainable development comprising the conservation of natural resources, economic competitiveness and efforts to alleviate poverty, which is being developed with assistance from the United Nations Development Programme's own funds, the Global Environment Facility through the World Bank, the United Nations Environment Programme, the Inter-American Development Bank, the German Agency for Technical Cooperation and the United States Agency for International Development;

9. *Recognizes* the efforts and achievements relating to mine clearance in Central America, and calls upon the relevant organs of the United Nations system, the Organization of American States, as well as the international community, to continue providing the material, technical and financial support needed by the Central American Governments to complete mine-clearance, mine-awareness and victim assistance activities in the region, in conformity with the relevant resolutions of the United Nations and the Convention on the Prohibition of the Use, Stockpiling, Production and Transfer of Anti-personnel Mines and on Their Destruction;

10. *Requests* the Secretary-General to report to the General Assembly at its sixtieth session on the implementation of the present resolution as part of a consolidated report under the item entitled "The situation in Central America: progress in fashioning a region of peace, freedom, democracy and development".

Comoros

On 17 December [meeting 75], the General Assembly adopted **resolution 58/120** [draft: A/58/L.45 & Add.1] without vote [agenda item 40 (b)].

Special emergency economic assistance for the recovery and the development of the Comoros

The General Assembly,

Recalling its resolutions 51/30 F of 13 December 1996 and 53/1 F of 16 November 1998 on special emergency economic assistance to the Comoros,

Noting that since 1995, the Comoros has been subjected to several major events, including a secessionist conflict, which created serious political instability and caused economic and social trauma,

Considering that the unfavourable and insular situation of the Comoros, which is among the least developed countries, the decline in the gross domestic product of the country caused by the fall in the prices of its export products, the poverty of its soil, the scarcity of its natural resources and the diminutive size of its domestic market have adverse economic consequences and increase the impoverishment of the population,

Aware of the efforts made by the Government of the Comoros to assist the most affected and deprived sectors of the population and to reallocate to that end, as a matter of great urgency, the major part of the budget required for the functioning of the State,

1. *Welcomes* the signing of the Fomboni Agreement of February 2001, which created prospects for a peaceful resolution of the separatist crisis;

2. *Reaffirms its support* for South Africa, the African Union, the International Organization of la Francophonie and other countries of the region in the mediation efforts to resolve the Comorian crisis;

3. *Welcomes* the recommendations contained in the statement signed by the Friends of the Comoros in Paris on 29 October 2003 and the declaration of the Indian Ocean Commission issued in Moroni on 30 October 2003;

4. *Urges* the Government of the Comoros and the governments of the autonomous islands to pursue the efforts under way, to accelerate the organization of legislative elections and to establish the remaining national institutions as stipulated by the Constitution;

5. *Reaffirms* that the primary responsibility for the well-being of the people and the development of the economy rests firmly with the Government of the Comoros and the governments of the autonomous islands;

6. *Expresses its appreciation* to all States and to all the international organizations concerned, including United Nations bodies and specialized agencies, for the assistance they have provided for the relief of the Comoros;

7. *Stresses* that the financial resources available remain nonetheless insufficient vis-à-vis the most basic needs for ensuring the humanitarian, economic and political recovery of the country;

8. *Requests* Member States, international organizations and other relevant organizations of the United Nations system, in the event of an agreement between the Comoros and the authorities of the autonomous islands, and while awaiting the finalization of the Fomboni Agreement by early 2004, to direct their financial and technical assistance towards assisting the most affected sectors of the population during and after the transition period, achieving reconstruction and sustainable development and enabling the country to re-engage with the international financial institutions;

9. *Requests* the Secretary-General to make efforts to mobilize Member States, relevant United Nations specialized agencies and other organizations in order to provide the Comoros with necessary financial, economic and technical assistance, particularly in debt forgiveness, in order to enable it to fully implement the Fomboni Agreement, particularly to organize legislative elections;

10. *Also requests* the Secretary-General, in collaboration with all relevant United Nations departments and specialized agencies, as well as international organizations already working in the Comoros, to gather relevant information and assess the needs of the country and the possible assistance from the international community;

11. *Further requests* the Secretary-General to report to the General Assembly at its fifty-ninth session on the implementation of the present resolution.

Haiti

In response to Economic and Social Council resolution 2002/22 [YUN 2002, p. 922], the Secretary-General submitted an April report [E/2003/54] on progress achieved in implementing a long-term programme of support for Haiti. A governance support programme, covering the period from 2003 to 2006, was drawn up and approved by the Government in January, which aimed at facilitating cooperation among all partners contributing to improving governance. Its main objective was to support Haiti's institutional normalization, build democratic institutions and strengthen governance. The programme also had a sustainable development component and dimensions relating to advocacy, public debates, the issue of parity and methods of drawing up strategies and policies. The UN system, together with bilateral and multilateral donors and NGOs, finalized an integrated humanitarian programme of assistance to vulnerable populations, which sought to strengthen medium- and long-term development efforts while supporting vulnerable populations to access essential services and vital commodities. The report also detailed progress made regarding Haiti's report on the MDGs [YUN 2000, p. 51], assistance by the Global Fund to Fight AIDS, Tuberculosis and Malaria (see p. 1248), UNDP activities in the area of justice, the compilation of social data, such as living conditions, relief operations and activities to manage risks and calamities resulting from natural disasters, and a national plan of action on education for all.

ECONOMIC AND SOCIAL COUNCIL ACTION

On 23 July [meeting 46], the Economic and Social Council adopted **resolution 2003/46** [draft: E/2003/L.35] without vote [agenda item 7 (e)].

Long-term programme of support for Haiti

The Economic and Social Council,

Recalling its resolutions 1999/11 of 27 July 1999, 2001/25 of 26 July 2001 and 2002/22 of 24 July 2002, and its decision 2000/235 of 27 July 2000,

Taking note of the comprehensive report of the Secretary-General,

Welcoming the efforts of the Organization of American States, including its Special Mission to Strengthen Democracy in Haiti, and of the Caribbean Community to mediate dialogue and promote reconciliation in order to strengthen the political environment in Haiti necessary for the promotion of economic and social development and the alleviation of poverty,

Welcoming also the report of the United Nations independent expert on the situation of human rights in Haiti, noting the statement by the Chairperson of the Commission on Human Rights at its fifty-ninth session, and further encouraging the work of the Inter-American Commission on Human Rights and the Commission on Human Rights in this regard,

Noting the launching of the Integrated Emergency Response Programme: Targeting Vulnerable Groups and Communities in Haiti by the United Nations country team for Haiti on 22 April 2003,

1. *Requests* that the Secretary-General, in coordination with the United Nations resident coordinator in Haiti, report on progress achieved in implementing the long-term programme of support for Haiti and that the report be prepared for the Economic and Social Council on the basis of developments in Haiti;

2. *Decides* to include the item entitled "Long-term programme of support for Haiti" in the provisional agenda of its substantive session of 2004.

(For information regarding the human rights situation in Haiti, see p. 683.)

Timor-Leste

In response to General Assembly resolution 57/105 [YUN 2002, p. 921], the Secretary-General, in August [A/58/280], reported on the status of implementation of assistance for humanitarian relief, rehabilitation and development for Timor-Leste, covering the period from July 2002 to July 2003.

Recognizing that security and stability were a prerequisite for the rehabilitation and development of the country, the United Nations Mission of Support in East Timor (see p. 370) and the UN system intensified efforts to address key institutional challenges of the National Police Force of Timor-Leste, while taking into account the national security and defence framework. Considerable progress was made in developing civil and criminal codes and a review of the justice system identified areas needing technical assistance and support from the international community in order to establish strategies to improve access to justice for Timorese citizens. On the civilian side, the administrative capacity of public servants was being strengthened through on-the-job training. A civil service act, targeting gender equality, was drafted. Progress was also made regarding rural and agricultural development, the delivery of health services and increasing access to primary and junior high school education, together with improving internal efficiency and reducing inequality. During the reporting period, much work was undertaken regarding gender-based violence, including domestic violence and sexual assault. Significant progress had been made in rehabilitating infrastructure, particularly in the power sector, water management and construction-related activities, and the telecommunications sector.

GENERAL ASSEMBLY ACTION

On 17 December [meeting 75], the General Assembly adopted **resolution 58/121** [draft: A/58/L.46 & Add.1] without vote [agenda item 40 *(b)*].

Assistance for humanitarian relief, rehabilitation and development for Timor-Leste

The General Assembly,

Recalling all of its relevant resolutions on the situation in Timor-Leste,

Recalling also all of the relevant Security Council resolutions and decisions on the situation in Timor-Leste, in particular resolutions 1473(2003) of 4 April 2003 and 1480(2003) of 19 May 2003, acknowledging the ongoing crucial role of the United Nations Mission of Support in East Timor and the leadership of the Special Representative of the Secretary-General in assisting the people of Timor-Leste,

Recognizing the essential role played by the international community, including the United Nations, other intergovernmental organizations, Member States and non-governmental organizations, in supporting the nation-building process of Timor-Leste,

Acknowledging the progress made in the transition from relief and rehabilitation to development in Timor-Leste, while noting continuing vulnerabilities, including the need to strengthen the preparedness and response capacity of the Government of Timor-Leste for addressing humanitarian emergencies, and the significant challenges of rehabilitation, reconstruction and development, in particular in the initial years of independence,

Emphasizing the need for continued international assistance to support the development of Timor-Leste in, inter alia, the education, health, agriculture, infrastructure, judicial, public administration and law enforcement sectors,

Welcoming the efforts of the Government of Indonesia and relevant intergovernmental and non-governmental organizations in providing humanitarian assistance to the refugees of Timor-Leste in the Indonesian province of East Nusa Tenggara, in facilitating their return to and reintegration in Timor-Leste or in assisting with their local integration and resettlement, as appropriate, in Indonesia,

1. *Welcomes* the report of the Secretary-General;

2. *Also welcomes* the commitment of the international community to meet the external requirements for rehabilitation, reconstruction and development activities for Timor-Leste;

3. *Urges* the United Nations, other intergovernmental organizations, Member States and non-governmental organizations to continue to support the Government and the people of Timor-Leste in their endeavours towards self-sustainable nation-building and in facing

the remaining vulnerabilities and challenges, such as nationwide capacity-building in all sectors, national reconciliation and the voluntary return of the remaining refugees to Timor-Leste, and sustainable development;

4. *Acknowledges* that a transparent, effective and functioning democratic governmental administration is crucial to fostering a stable and secure social, economic and political environment in Timor-Leste, and in this regard urges the international community to continue to support efforts aimed at institution-building and the training of civil servants, in particular in the areas of public finances and senior management and in the development and maintenance of central and local administrative systems of government;

5. *Also acknowledges* the need to expedite the development of the justice sector of Timor-Leste, and in this regard urges further international support in the areas of law enforcement, the judiciary and the prison system;

6. *Welcomes* the continuing response of the international community to the need for food aid, and calls upon the United Nations, other intergovernmental organizations, Member States and non-governmental organizations to assist Timor-Leste in ensuring sustainable development in the areas of agriculture, livestock and fisheries;

7. *Welcomes with appreciation* the assistance provided by Member States, the Office for the Coordination of Humanitarian Affairs of the Secretariat, the World Food Programme and all other international and non-governmental organizations in response to the appeals by the Government of Timor-Leste during the floods and drought;

8. *Takes note with appreciation* of the progress made in rehabilitating infrastructure, and recommends that outstanding infrastructure needs remain a focus of international assistance in such areas as the reconstruction and rehabilitation of public buildings, educational facilities, roads and public services;

9. *Commends* the continuous international response in providing health services to the general population, including the early deployment of immunization and disease prevention programmes and reproductive health-care and child nutrition programmes, while recognizing the need for further assistance to rebuild hospitals, train health-care professionals and enhance capacity-building to meet the challenges to public health posed by such diseases as tuberculosis, malaria and HIV/AIDS;

10. *Welcomes* the progress made in the rehabilitation of schools, the supply and distribution of educational materials and teacher training, while emphasizing the need for capacity-building, particularly in the area of secondary and higher education, and for continued attention to the rehabilitation needs, including psychosocial support, of children affected by violence;

11. *Also welcomes* the growing participation of the women of Timor-Leste in all aspects of society, and encourages further efforts to address gender issues, including the needs for research, services and appropriate legislation in order to combat domestic violence and other gender-related crimes;

12. *Further welcomes* the continuing efforts made by the Commission for Reception, Truth and Reconciliation to facilitate national reconciliation and the return of refugees to Timor-Leste;

13. *Welcomes* the commitment and contribution made by the Government of Indonesia and by the international community to the Special Fund established for former employees and pensioners of the Government of Indonesia in Timor-Leste and the progress made by the United Nations Development Programme in disbursing funds from the Special Fund, and encourages the international community to consider increasing its contributions;

14. *Also welcomes* the holding, in Dili in September 2003, of the second meeting of the Joint Ministerial Commission for Bilateral Cooperation between Indonesia and Timor-Leste, which emphasized the importance of good relations and of further enhancing and facilitating cooperation in all areas of common interest;

15. *Requests* the Secretary-General to submit a report on the implementation of the present resolution to the General Assembly for consideration at its sixtieth session.

Third States affected by sanctions

In response to General Assembly resolution 56/110 [YUN 2001, p. 857], the Secretary-General submitted a September report [A/58/358 & Corr.1] on economic problems confronting the Eastern European States affected by the developments in the Balkans, particularly their impact on regional trade and economic relations and on navigation along the Danube and the Adriatic Sea. The report summarized information received from 10 Governments, 8 specialized agencies and various relevant international organizations and concerned regional bodies.

Disaster relief

In 2003, 700 natural events resulted in 75,000 deaths and economic losses of more than $65 billion. One third of the deaths resulted from the Bam earthquake in Iran, which killed 26,000 people (see p. 962). Other types of disasters, such as floods, cyclones and droughts, occurred in vulnerable countries and regions.

In Africa, more than two thirds of the population of Eritrea were exposed to the risk of famine during 2003, following the severe drought of 2002. Successive climatic shocks and their cumulative effects had made some 13 million people in Ethiopia dependent on emergency food aid and on non-food assistance. During the year, Guinea was subjected to a substantial deficit in rainfall in the north-west, a flash flood along the Guinea-Bissau border and a series of bush fires in Forest Guinea and in the Sahel region bordering Mali.

The Southern Africa region was prone to a variety of natural disasters, including drought, floods and cyclones. A severe drought in 2002 and 2003 endangered the lives of 14.4 million people in Lesotho, Malawi, Mozambique, Swaziland, Zambia and Zimbabwe. Severe drought and perennial flooding affected Somalia. Drought and floods in parts of the Sudan affected over 800,000 people.

Natural disasters were a major cause of severe economic distress for the Pacific region. In 2003, OCHA responded to 24 natural disasters (13 floods/landslides, seven typhoons/storms, two earthquakes, two extremes of temperature). The year began with Cyclone Zoë in Solomon Islands, and Cyclone Ami, which caused far greater losses across Eastern Fiji. Two additional cyclones struck Solomon Islands and another hit New Caledonia. Heavy rain caused a series of landslides in Papua New Guinea, and American Samoa also suffered a disastrous landslide. Meanwhile, Timor-Leste experienced drought and floods through the wet and the dry seasons, respectively.

In Asia, torrential rains led to the most serious flooding and landslides in Sri Lanka since 1947. Severe and continual rainfall that began in late June led to flooding in several provinces of China, affecting 130 million people and resulting in the evacuation of more than 3 million people from their homes and the death of more than 800 persons. Viet Nam suffered serious floods in October for the fifth year in a row.

In May, earthquakes occurred in Algeria and Turkey.

In Latin America and the Caribbean, OCHA assisted the Dominican Republic to cope with floods in November; Mexico with an earthquake in January; and Peru with floods in January.

Excluding contributions in kind and services not costed, OCHA contributions for natural disaster assistance totalled $104.5 million.

International cooperation

Report of Secretary-General. In response to General Assembly resolution 57/152 [YUN 2002, p. 925], the Secretary-General, in an October report [A/58/434], highlighted key activities undertaken in response to natural disasters and described initiatives to strengthen disaster management at the national and regional levels. The report also provided information on the funding trends for natural disaster response.

The report concluded that it was crucial for the international community to collaborate with vulnerable countries and regions to ensure optimal use of available disaster management tools and initiatives. Member States in disaster-prone regions were encouraged to familiarize themselves with the guidelines of the International Search and Rescue Advisory Group to ensure a coordinated, rapid response of international urban search-and-rescue teams in the event of a sudden disaster. The United Nations Disaster Assessment and Coordination system continued to be a valuable tool through which disaster management expertise was made available by Member States to respond to sudden emergencies. The system was deploying an increasing number of personnel from disaster-prone regions, although its membership needed to be expanded to Africa. A more precise understanding was also needed of the impact of funding levels on natural disaster response, as it was not clear if adequate support was being provided to address capacity-building and post-disaster recovery needs.

GENERAL ASSEMBLY ACTION

On 5 December [meeting 69], the General Assembly adopted **resolution 58/25** [draft: A/58/L.34 & Add.1] without vote [agenda item 40 (a)].

International cooperation on humanitarian assistance in the field of natural disasters, from relief to development

The General Assembly,

Reaffirming its resolution 46/182 of 19 December 1991, the annex to which contains the guiding principles for the strengthening of the coordination of emergency humanitarian assistance of the United Nations system, as well as all its resolutions on international cooperation on humanitarian assistance in the field of natural disasters, from relief to development, and recalling the resolutions of the humanitarian segments of the substantive sessions of the Economic and Social Council,

Recognizing the importance of the principles of neutrality, humanity and impartiality for the provision of humanitarian assistance,

Emphasizing that the affected State has the primary responsibility in the initiation, organization, coordination and implementation of humanitarian assistance within its territory, and in the facilitation of the work of humanitarian organizations in mitigating the consequences of natural disasters,

Emphasizing also the importance of integrating risk reduction into development planning and post-disaster recovery,

Emphasizing further, in this context, the important role of development organizations in supporting national efforts to mitigate the consequences of natural disasters,

Emphasizing the responsibility of all States to undertake disaster preparedness, response and mitigation efforts in order to minimize the impact of natural disasters, while recognizing the importance of international cooperation in support of the efforts of affected countries which may have limited capacities to fulfil this requirement,

Welcoming the International Strategy for Disaster Reduction,

Stressing that national authorities need to enhance the resilience of populations to disasters through, inter alia, implementation of the International Strategy for Disaster Reduction so as to reduce risks to people, their livelihoods, the social and economic infrastructure and environmental resources,

Taking into account the outcome of the Second International Conference on Early Warning, held in Bonn, Germany, from 16 to 18 October 2003, under the auspices of the United Nations,

Noting the critical role played by local resources, as well as by existing in-country capacities, in natural disaster response,

Recognizing the significant role played by national Red Cross and Red Crescent societies in disaster preparedness and risk reduction, disaster response, rehabilitation and development,

Emphasizing the importance of raising awareness among developing countries of the capacities existing at the national, regional and international levels that could be deployed to assist them,

Emphasizing also the importance of international cooperation in support of the efforts of the affected States in dealing with natural disasters in all their phases, including prevention, preparedness, mitigation and recovery and reconstruction, and of strengthening the response capacity of affected countries,

Welcoming the efforts of Member States, with facilitation by the Office for the Coordination of Humanitarian Affairs of the Secretariat, and in cooperation with the International Search and Rescue Advisory Group, to improve efficiency and effectiveness in the provision of international urban search and rescue assistance, and in this context noting its resolution 57/150 of 16 December 2002 entitled "Strengthening the effectiveness and coordination of international urban search and rescue assistance",

Encouraging, in this regard, efforts aiming at the strengthening of the International Search and Rescue Advisory Group and its regional groups, particularly through the participation in its activities of representatives of a larger number of countries,

Mindful of the effects that shortfalls in resources can have on the preparedness for and response to natural disasters, and underscoring, in this regard, the need to gain a more precise understanding of the impact of levels of funding on natural disaster response,

Underlining the need for further improvement in information and analyses available regarding needs, responses and funding related to natural disasters,

1. *Takes note* of the reports of the Secretary-General entitled "International cooperation on humanitarian assistance in the field of natural disasters, from relief to development" and "Strengthening the coordination of emergency humanitarian assistance of the United Nations";

2. *Expresses its deep concern* at the number and scale of natural disasters and their increasing impact, resulting in massive losses of life and property worldwide, in particular in vulnerable societies lacking adequate capacity to mitigate effectively the long-term negative social, economic and environmental consequences of natural disasters;

3. *Calls upon* all States to adopt, where required, and to continue to implement effectively necessary legislative and other appropriate measures to mitigate the effects of natural disasters, inter alia, by disaster prevention, including appropriate land use and building regulations, as well as disaster preparedness and capacity-building in disaster response and mitigation, and requests the international community to continue to assist developing countries in this regard;

4. *Stresses*, in this context, the importance of strengthening international cooperation, particularly through the effective use of multilateral mechanisms, in the provision of humanitarian assistance through all phases of a disaster, from relief and mitigation to development, including the provision of adequate resources;

5. *Also stresses* that humanitarian assistance for natural disasters should be provided in accordance with and with due respect for the guiding principles contained in the annex to resolution 46/182 and should be determined on the basis of the human dimension and needs arising out of the particular natural disasters;

6. *Recognizes* that economic growth and sustainable development contribute to improving the capacity of States to mitigate, respond to and prepare for natural disasters;

7. *Reaffirms* that disaster risk analysis and vulnerability reduction form an integral part of humanitarian assistance, poverty eradication and sustainable development strategies and need to be considered in the development plans of all vulnerable countries and communities, including, where appropriate, in plans relating to the transition from relief to development, and affirms that within such preventive strategies, disaster preparedness and early warning systems must be further strengthened at the country and regional levels, inter alia, through better coordination among relevant United Nations bodies and cooperation with Governments of affected countries and regional and other relevant organizations with the aim of maximizing the effectiveness of natural disaster response and reducing the impact of natural disasters, particularly in developing countries;

8. *Emphasizes* the importance of establishing or updating, as appropriate, national disaster preparedness plans, as agreed upon at the twenty-seventh International Conference of the Red Cross and Red Crescent, held in Geneva in 1999;

9. *Also emphasizes* the importance of enhanced international cooperation, including through the United Nations and regional organizations, to assist developing countries in their efforts to build capacities and to predict, prepare for and respond to natural disasters;

10. *Stresses* the need for partnerships among Governments, organizations of the United Nations system, relevant humanitarian organizations and specialized companies to promote training to strengthen preparedness for and response to natural disasters;

11. *Also stresses* the need to promote the access to and transfer of technology related to early warning systems and to mitigation programmes to developing countries affected by natural disasters;

12. *Encourages* the further use of space-based and ground-based remote-sensing technologies for the prevention, mitigation and management of natural disasters, where appropriate;

13. *Also encourages* in such operations the sharing of geographical data, including remotely sensed images and geographic information system and global posi-

tioning system data, among Governments, space agencies and relevant international humanitarian organizations, as appropriate, and also notes in that context initiatives such as those undertaken by the International Charter on Space and Major Disasters and the Global Disaster Information Network;

14. *Stresses* that particular international cooperation efforts should be undertaken to enhance and broaden further the utilization of national and local capacities and, where appropriate, regional and sub-regional capacities of developing countries for disaster preparedness and response, which may be made available in closer proximity to the site of a disaster, more efficiently and at lower cost;

15. *Recognizes*, in this regard, that the United Nations Disaster Assessment and Coordination system continues to be a valuable tool by which disaster management expertise is made available by Member States to respond to the sudden onset of emergencies;

16. *Welcomes* the role of the Office for the Coordination of Humanitarian Affairs of the Secretariat as the focal point within the overall United Nations system for the promotion and coordination of disaster responses among United Nations humanitarian agencies and other humanitarian partners;

17. *Takes note with interest* of the initiatives taken by the Office for the Coordination of Humanitarian Affairs and the United Nations Development Programme for the establishment of regional positions of disaster response advisers and disaster reduction advisers to assist developing countries in capacity-building for disaster prevention, preparedness, mitigation and response in a coordinated and complementary manner;

18. *Encourages* further cooperation between the United Nations system and regional organizations in order to increase the capacity of these organizations to respond to natural disasters;

19. *Encourages* States that have not acceded to or ratified the Tampere Convention on the Provision of Telecommunication Resources for Disaster Mitigation and Relief Operations, adopted at Tampere, Finland, on 18 June 1998, to consider doing so;

20. *Requests* the Secretary-General, in collaboration with relevant organizations and partners, to finalize establishment of, and then update periodically, the Directory of Advanced Technologies for Disaster Response as a new part of the Central Register of Disaster Management Capacities;

21. *Encourages* donors to consider the importance of ensuring that assistance in the case of higher-profile natural disasters does not come at the expense of those that may have a relatively lower profile, bearing in mind that the allocation of resources should be driven by needs, as well as the importance of making efforts to increase the level of assistance for disaster reduction and preparedness programmes and for disaster response and mitigation activities;

22. *Requests* the Secretary-General to examine ways to further improve the assessment of needs and responses and to enhance the availability of data regarding funding in response to natural disasters and to consider concrete recommendations to improve the international response to natural disasters, as necessary, based on his examination, keeping in mind also the need to address any geographical and sectoral imbalances and shortfalls in such responses, where they exist, as well as the more effective use of national emergency response agencies, and to report thereon to the General Assembly at its fifty-ninth session.

International Strategy for Disaster Reduction

In response to General Assembly resolution 57/256 [YUN 2002, p. 928], the Secretary-General, in an August report [A/58/277], described UN activities to implement the International Strategy for Disaster Reduction (ISDR), which was adopted by the programme forum of the International Decade for Natural Disaster Reduction (1990-2000) in 1999 [YUN 1999, p. 859] and endorsed by the Assembly in resolution 54/219 [ibid, p. 861]. The Inter-Agency Task Force for Disaster Reduction and the ISDR secretariat served as the main mechanisms for the Strategy's implementation by the UN system.

The Johannesburg Plan of Implementation [YUN 2002, p. 822], adopted by the World Summit on Sustainable Development, included commitments relating to disaster and vulnerability reduction and improved early warning. Some of the partnerships launched at the Summit in the area of early warning and disaster preparedness, involving ISDR, led to the convening of the Second International Conference on Early Warning (Bonn, Germany, October), in order to consolidate a global programme to integrate early warning into public policies. The partnership for integrating prevention of, preparedness for and response to environmental emergencies in support of sustainable development, led by OCHA and the United Nations Environment Programme, used existing resources and distributed responsibilities and efforts among partners and key stakeholders. Other partnerships were led by the International Council for Local Environmental Initiatives, the United Nations Educational, Scientific and Cultural Organization (UNESCO), the World Meteorological Organization and the Economic and Social Commission for Asia and the Pacific.

A review of the Inter-Agency Task Force for Disaster Reduction, which had met seven times since 2000, concluded that it represented an essential process for enabling the international community to develop a better understanding of and strategic direction on disaster reduction as a long-term undertaking. However, the review also identified a number of weaknesses and shortcomings. At its seventh meeting, in April, the Task Force discussed the nature and prospective role of its working groups, and the appropriate balance between its own role as an international forum for discussion and the need to produce tangible guidelines and results-oriented products. Its 2004 work programme included support for the development of a framework for guidance and monitoring of disaster risk reduction; urban risk and vulnerability; integration of disaster reduction in sustainable development; linking climate change adaptation and disaster reduction; and special attention to Africa.

The Task Force and the ISDR secretariat initiated the 10-year review of the Yokohama Strategy for a Safer World: Guidelines for Natural Disaster Prevention, Preparedness and Mitigation and its Plan of Action [YUN 1994, p. 851] to examine progress made to implement disaster reduction, identify gaps and prepare recommendations to guide Member States. The Task Force welcomed Japan's offer to host the 2005 Second World Conference on Disaster Reduction in Kobe, which was expected to discuss and adopt a set of principles and substantive activities for 2005-2015. A series of regional and thematic consultations regarding achievements and shortcomings in disaster reduction were held. The first regional consultation was convened in Asia and hosted by the Government of Japan (Hyogo Prefecture, January). The South Pacific island States discussed achievements, shortcomings and requirements for the future (Fiji, May), as did the Euro-Mediterranean Forum on Disaster Reduction (Madrid, Spain, October). Progress was made in engaging additional partner organizations to improve implementation of ISDR, including agreements reached on issues such as urban risk through UN-Habitat; study of the interface between natural and technological disasters with the European Commission Joint Research Centre; the impacts of climate variability and change with the International Research Institute for Climate Prediction; and support for public awareness, education and policy integration for disaster risk reduction with the Central American Centre for Coordination of Natural Disaster Prevention. The ISDR secretariat participated in the steering committee of the International Consortium on Landslides and continued to collaborate with the ProVention Consortium, a project-oriented global coalition and flexible network of Governments, international organizations, academic institutions, the private sector and civil society organizations. The Strategy's regional outreach programmes operated in Africa, Asia, Europe, Latin America and the Caribbean and the Pacific. Other activities that contributed to the implementation of ISDR focused on capacity-building, public awareness, advocacy and guidelines, urban risk, water-related disasters and solutions, and space applications and telecommunications.

The Secretary-General recommended that Member States and international organizations ensure that development plans and poverty reduction strategies included disaster risk assessment as an integral component, and increase their investments to reduce risk and vulnerability. He proposed strengthening the Strategy secretariat by providing it with a more stable and predictable financial base.

GENERAL ASSEMBLY ACTION

On 23 December [meeting 78], the General Assembly, on the recommendation of the Second (Economic and Financial) Committee [A/58/484/Add.5], adopted **resolution 58/214** without vote [agenda item 94 (e)].

International Strategy for Disaster Reduction

The General Assembly,

Recalling its resolutions 44/236 of 22 December 1989, 49/22 A of 2 December 1994, 49/22 B of 20 December 1994, 53/185 of 15 December 1998, 54/219 of 22 December 1999, 56/195 of 21 December 2001 and 57/256 of 20 December 2002 and Economic and Social Council resolutions 1999/63 of 30 July 1999 and 2001/35 of 26 July 2001, and taking into due consideration its resolution 57/270 B of 23 June 2003 on integrated and coordinated implementation of and follow-up to the outcomes of the major United Nations conferences and summits in the economic and social fields,

Recalling also the inclusion of the item "disaster management and vulnerability" in the multi-year programme of work of the Commission on Sustainable Development,

Emphasizing that disaster reduction, including reducing vulnerability to natural disasters, is an important element that contributes to the achievement of sustainable development,

Noting the relevant provisions of the Ministerial Declaration of the Ministerial Conference of the Third World Water Forum, held in Kyoto, Japan, on 22 and 23 March 2003, on water-related disasters,

Reiterating that, although natural disasters damage the social and economic infrastructure of all countries, the long-term consequences of natural disasters are especially severe for developing countries and hamper the achievement of their sustainable development,

Recognizing the urgent need to further develop and make use of the existing scientific and technical knowledge to reduce vulnerability to natural disasters, and emphasizing the need for developing countries to have access to technology so as to tackle natural disasters effectively,

Expressing its deep concern at the number and scale of natural disasters and their increasing impact within recent years, which have resulted in massive loss of life and long-term negative social, economic and environmental consequences for vulnerable societies throughout the world, in particular in developing countries,

Recognizing the need to continue to develop an understanding of, and to address, socio-economic activities that exacerbate the vulnerability of societies to natural disasters and to build and further strengthen community capability to cope with disaster risks,

1. *Takes note* of the report of the Secretary-General on the implementation of the International Strategy for Disaster Reduction;

2. *Invites* Governments and relevant international organizations to consider disaster risk assessment as an integral component of development plans and poverty eradication programmes;

3. *Stresses* that continued cooperation and coordination among Governments, the United Nations system, other international organizations, regional organizations, non-governmental organizations and other partners, as appropriate, are considered essential to address effectively the impact of natural disasters;

4. *Recognizes* the importance of linking disaster risk management to regional frameworks, as appropriate, such as with the New Partnership for Africa's Development, to address issues of poverty eradication and sustainable development;

5. *Also recognizes* the importance of integrating a gender perspective as well as of engaging women in the design and implementation of all phases of disaster management, particularly in the disaster reduction stage;

6. *Further recognizes* the importance of early warning as an essential element of disaster reduction, and recommends the implementation of the outcome of the Second International Conference on Early Warning, held in Bonn, Germany, from 16 to 18 October 2003, which highlighted the importance of strengthened coordination and cooperation to integrate activities and expertise of the various sectors involved in the early warning process and has contributed to the review of the Yokohama Strategy for a Safer World: Guidelines for Natural Disaster Prevention, Preparedness and Mitigation and its Plan of Action;

7. *Decides* to convene a World Conference on Disaster Reduction in 2005, at the senior-official level, designed to foster specialized discussions and produce concrete changes and results, with the following objectives:

(*a*) To conclude the review of the Yokohama Strategy and its Plan of Action, with a view to updating the guiding framework on disaster reduction for the twenty-first century;

(*b*) To identify specific activities aimed at ensuring the implementation of relevant provisions of the Plan of Implementation of the World Summit on Sustainable Development ("Johannesburg Plan of Implementation") on vulnerability, risk assessment and disaster management;

(*c*) To share best practices and lessons learned to further disaster reduction within the context of attaining sustainable development and identify gaps and challenges;

(*d*) To increase awareness of the importance of disaster reduction policies, thereby facilitating and promoting the implementation of those policies;

(*e*) To increase the reliability and availability of appropriate disaster-related information to the public and disaster management agencies in all regions, as set out in the relevant provisions of the Johannesburg Plan of Implementation;

8. *Accepts with deep appreciation* the generous offer of the Government of Japan to host the Conference, and decides that the Conference will be held at Kobe, Hyogo, Japan, from 18 to 22 January 2005;

9. *Decides* to establish an open-ended intergovernmental preparatory committee for the Conference to review the organizational and substantive preparations for the Conference, approve the programme of work of the Conference and propose rules of procedure for adoption by the Conference, and also decides that the preparatory committee will meet at Geneva, following the 2004 semi-annual sessions of the Inter-Agency Task Force for Disaster Reduction, for up to two days each time, and that it will hold a one-day meeting at Kobe within the dates mentioned in paragraph 8 above, as necessary;

10. *Also decides* that the intergovernmental preparatory committee will have a bureau consisting of five representatives of Member States elected on the basis of equitable geographical representation;

11. *Invites* regional groups to nominate their candidates for the bureau of the preparatory committee by the end of January 2004, so that they can be involved in the preparations for the first meeting of the preparatory committee, and to notify the secretariat of the Conference of those nominations;

12. *Requests* the inter-agency secretariat for the International Strategy for Disaster Reduction to serve as the secretariat of the Conference and to coordinate preparatory activities, the costs of which will be funded extrabudgetarily through the Trust Fund for the International Strategy for Disaster Reduction and in close cooperation with the host country and the preparatory committee for the Conference, with the full support of the relevant departments of the Secretariat;

13. *Understands* that the activities set out in paragraph 12 above will not hinder the other existing work and priorities of the inter-agency secretariat for the Strategy;

14. *Invites* Member States, all United Nations bodies and specialized agencies and other relevant intergovernmental agencies and organizations, in particular the members of the Inter-Agency Task Force for Disaster Reduction, to participate actively in the Conference, as well as its preparatory process;

15. *Welcomes* contributions from all regions that could provide substantive inputs to the preparatory process and the Conference itself;

16. *Encourages* effective contributions from major groups, as identified in Agenda 21, invites them to seek accreditation to the Conference and its preparatory process, and decides that their accreditation and participation will be in accordance with the rules of procedure of the Commission on Sustainable Development, the rules of procedure of the World Summit on Sustainable Development and the established practice of the Commission on the participation and engagement of major groups;

17. *Decides* that the actual additional costs of the preparatory process and the Conference itself should be funded through extrabudgetary resources, without negatively affecting programmed activities, and through specific voluntary contributions to the Trust Fund for the Strategy;

18. *Requests* the Secretariat to provide conference services for the preparatory process and the Confer-

ence itself, the costs thereof to be borne by the host country, on the understanding that the Secretariat will ensure that its existing human resources are utilized to the maximum extent possible, without further charge to the host country;

19. *Encourages* the international community to provide the necessary financial resources to the Trust Fund for the Strategy and to provide the necessary scientific, technical, human and other resources to ensure adequate support for the activities of the inter-agency secretariat for the Strategy and the Inter-Agency Task Force for Disaster Reduction and its working groups, as well as to facilitate the preparations for the Conference;

20. *Expresses its appreciation* to those countries that have provided financial support for the activities of the Strategy by making voluntary contributions to its Trust Fund;

21. *Requests* the Secretary-General to allocate adequate financial and administrative resources, within existing resources, for the effective functioning of the inter-agency secretariat for the Strategy;

22. *Also requests* the Secretary-General to submit to the General Assembly at its fifty-ninth session a report on the implementation of the present resolution, in particular on the state of preparations for the World Conference on Disaster Reduction, under the item entitled "Environment and sustainable development".

On 23 December [meeting 78], the Assembly, also on the recommendation of the Second Committee [A/58/484/Add.5], adopted **resolution 58/215** without vote [agenda item 94 (*e*)].

Natural disasters and vulnerability

The General Assembly,

Recalling its decision 57/547 of 20 December 2002,

Taking into account the Johannesburg Declaration on Sustainable Development and the Plan of Implementation of the World Summit on Sustainable Development ("Johannesburg Plan of Implementation"),

Recognizing the need to continue to develop an understanding of, and to address, socio-economic activities that exacerbate the vulnerability of societies to natural disasters and to build and further strengthen community capacity to cope with disaster risks,

Noting that the global environment continues to suffer degradation, adding to economic and social vulnerabilities, in particular in developing countries,

Taking into account the various ways and forms in which all countries, in particular the more vulnerable developing countries, are affected by severe natural hazards, such as earthquakes, volcanic eruptions and extreme weather events such as heatwaves, severe droughts, floods and storms, and El Niño/La Niña events, which have global reach,

Expressing its deep concern at the frequency and intensity of extreme weather events and associated natural disasters,

Expressing its deep concern also at the enormous negative impact of severe natural hazards, including extreme weather events and associated natural disasters, which continues to hinder social and economic progress, in particular in developing countries,

Reiterating that, although natural disasters damage the social and economic infrastructure of all countries, the long-term consequences of natural disasters are especially severe in developing countries and hamper their achievement of sustainable development,

Stressing that national authorities need to undertake disaster preparedness and mitigation efforts, in particular through the implementation of the International Strategy for Disaster Reduction, so as to enhance the resilience of populations to disasters and reduce the risks to them, their livelihoods, the social and economic infrastructure and environmental resources,

Recalling that the International Strategy for Disaster Reduction provides a framework for collaboration on the development of methodologies to systematically characterize, measure, assess and respond to natural disasters, including weather-related disasters, hazards and vulnerabilities,

Taking into account the fact that extreme weather events and associated natural disasters and their reduction must be dealt with in a coherent manner,

Noting the need for international cooperation to increase the capacity of countries to respond to the negative impacts of all natural hazards, including extreme weather events and associated natural disasters, particularly in developing countries,

Emphasizing the importance of raising awareness among developing countries of the capacities existing at the national, regional and international levels that could be deployed to assist them,

Taking note of the outcome of the Second International Conference on Early Warning, held in Bonn, Germany, from 16 to 18 October 2003,

1. *Takes note* of the report of the Secretary-General on the implementation of the International Strategy for Disaster Reduction, in particular the section on the negative impacts of extreme weather events and associated natural disasters on vulnerable countries, in particular developing countries, as requested by the Assembly in its decision 57/547;

2. *Urges* the international community to continue to address ways and means, including through cooperation and technical assistance, to reduce the adverse effects of natural disasters, including those caused by extreme weather events, in particular in vulnerable developing countries, through the implementation of the International Strategy for Disaster Reduction, and encourages the Inter-Agency Task Force for Disaster Reduction to continue its work in this regard;

3. *Encourages* Governments to establish effective national platforms or focal points for disaster reduction, and to strengthen them where they already exist;

4. *Also encourages* Governments, in cooperation with the United Nations system and other stakeholders, to strengthen capacity-building in the most vulnerable regions, to enable them to address the socio-economic factors that increase vulnerability, and encourages the international community to provide effective assistance to developing countries in this regard;

5. *Encourages* the Inter-Agency Task Force for Disaster Reduction to enhance the coordination on the promotion of disaster reduction as well as to make available to the relevant United Nations entities information on options for natural disaster reduction, including severe natural hazards and extreme weather-related disasters and vulnerabilities;

6. *Encourages* the Conference of the Parties to the United Nations Framework Convention on Climate Change and the parties to the Kyoto Protocol to the United Nations Framework Convention on Climate Change to continue to address the adverse effects of climate change, especially in those developing countries that are particularly vulnerable, in accordance with the provisions of the Convention, and also encourages the Intergovernmental Panel on Climate Change to continue to assess the adverse effects of climate change on the socio-economic and natural disaster reduction systems of developing countries;

7. *Requests* the Secretary-General to report to the General Assembly at its fifty-ninth session on the implementation of the present resolution in a separate section of his report on the implementation of the International Strategy for Disaster Reduction, and decides to consider the issue of natural disasters and vulnerability at that session, under the sub-item "International Strategy for Disaster Reduction" of the item entitled "Environment and sustainable development".

Also on 23 December, the Assembly decided that the sub-item on ISDR would remain for consideration at its resumed fifty-eighth (2004) session (**decision 58/565**).

El Niño

On 5 February [A/57/727], Ecuador transmitted to the Secretary-General the Constitution of the International Research Center on El Niño, which was signed at a meeting of the sponsors of and participants in the Center (Guayaquil, 9-10 January).

Disaster assistance

Ethiopia

In response to General Assembly resolution 57/149 [YUN 2002, p. 931], the Secretary-General, in an August report [A/58/224], reviewed the political, economic and humanitarian situation in Ethiopia and the assistance provided by the United Nations and its partners.

The report said that Ethiopia was subject to drastic weather patterns, with cyclical periods of drought and heavy rain. The rains, combined with an already weakened population, were creating an environment conducive to the spread of infectious diseases, including water-borne diseases and malaria. Certain areas and large population segments were immediately affected by more severe poverty as soon as harvests were endangered by inadequate rainfall patterns. Despite high levels of emergency assistance, the number of people defined as chronically food-insecure was growing yearly, as a result of inadequate development assistance over the preceding decade. A new approach was required to separate chronic and acute food insecurity, and immediate and substantial action was needed to prevent further deterioration. Special emphasis should be placed on improving nutritional capacity to meet emerging needs, emergency water activities and vaccination campaigns. The outlook for 2004 was difficult to anticipate before the "belg" (cropping season) assessment in November/December, but it was expected that relief needs would continue to grow. A robust rehabilitation strategy for pastoral and agricultural areas and a greater focus on resettlement and policy issues affecting development were critical in alleviating the impact of future droughts.

The joint Government-UN appeal "Emergency Assistance Requirements and Implementation Options for 2003, a March update, referred to as the "Addendum", and the appeal update of August identified 11.3 million people in need of 1.4 million tons of food and an additional 3 million at risk. Against the total relief food requirements of 1.8 million tons, 94 per cent was covered by the end of October. Against $108 million required for non-food, about 70 per cent was covered. Revised non-food needs to the end of the year of some $40.4 million were largely unfunded by the end of October, with the exception of support for malaria control.

GENERAL ASSEMBLY ACTION

On 5 December [meeting 69], the General Assembly adopted **resolution 58/24** [draft: A/58/L.22 & Add.1] without vote [agenda item 40 (*b*)].

Emergency humanitarian assistance to Ethiopia
The General Assembly,
Recalling its resolution 57/149 of 16 December 2002 on emergency humanitarian assistance to Ethiopia,
Noting with concern the recurrent drought that affects Ethiopia, and its consequences,
Recalling the initiatives of the Secretary-General to improve food security, including the appointment of the Special Envoy for the Humanitarian Crisis in the Horn of Africa,
Gravely concerned at the magnitude of the recurrent drought, which affects millions owing to the serious crop failures in drought-prone parts of the country that have weak infrastructures and low development capacities,
Bearing in mind the joint 2004 appeal of the United Nations and the Government of Ethiopia for emergency assistance for Ethiopia, to respond to the food and non-food requirements of households in need so as to prevent the worsening of the current humanitarian crisis,
Noting with serious concern the significant and persistent humanitarian needs in such areas as health, water and acute malnutrition that still exist in parts of the country,
Noting also with serious concern the dire humanitarian situation and its long-term socio-economic and environmental impacts,

Emphasizing the need to address the crisis, bearing in mind the importance of the transition from relief to development, and acknowledging the underlying structural causes of recurrent drought in Ethiopia,

Recognizing that the main responsibility for improving the humanitarian situation and creating conditions for long-term development lies with the Government of Ethiopia, while bearing in mind the important role played by the international community,

Emphasizing the importance of establishing a strong early warning system in order to predict better and respond as early as possible to disasters and to minimize their consequences,

1. *Takes note* of the report of the Secretary-General;
2. *Welcomes* the coordinated and collaborative efforts of the Government of Ethiopia, agencies, funds and programmes of the United Nations system, the donor community, non-governmental organizations and other entities to avert, through their timely and generous response, a major humanitarian crisis in Ethiopia in 2003;
3. *Calls upon* the international community to respond in a timely manner to the joint 2004 appeal of the United Nations and the Government of Ethiopia for emergency assistance for Ethiopia, covering food and non-food needs, as well as to the urgent needs of programme interventions for 2004, aimed at addressing the underlying causes of food insecurity, and issues of recovery, asset protection and the sustainable development of the affected areas;
4. *Welcomes* the programme prepared by the Coalition for Food Security in Ethiopia, and encourages the international community to support the Coalition in realizing its main objective, namely, breaking the cycle of food aid dependency within the next three to five years, thereby enabling fifteen million vulnerable people to engage in sustainable productive activities;
5. *Also welcomes* the efforts of the Government of Ethiopia, the international community and civil society, including non-governmental organizations, to strengthen mechanisms already in place to respond to such emergency situations, and appreciates their endeavours to increase the availability of food through domestic production and to ensure the access of households in need to food, health and water facilities;
6. *Further welcomes* the initiative taken by the Secretary-General in appointing a Special Envoy for the Humanitarian Crisis in the Horn of Africa, with the objective of mobilizing resources for relief support as well as the sustainable development of the affected areas;
7. *Invites* the Office for the Coordination of Humanitarian Affairs of the Secretariat to continue considering ways to enhance the mobilization of emergency relief assistance to cover the remaining humanitarian needs in Ethiopia;
8. *Calls upon* all development partners to integrate relief efforts with recovery, asset protection and long-term development and to address the underlying structural causes of recurrent drought in Ethiopia in a way that is, inter alia, in line with the poverty reduction strategy paper, including strategies that are aimed at preventing such crises in the future and that improve the resilience of the population;
9. *Encourages* the Government of Ethiopia to further strengthen its efforts to address the underlying structural causes of recurrent threats of drought as part of its overall economic development programme;
10. *Requests* the Secretary-General to report to the General Assembly at its fifty-ninth session on the implementation of the present resolution.

Iran

On 26 December, an earthquake measuring 6.5 on the Richter scale struck the city of Bam and its surrounding villages in Kerman province in south-eastern Iran, killing some 26,0000 people and rendering 75,000 people homeless. It also severely damaged or destroyed about 85 per cent of the houses, commercial units, health facilities and administrative buildings in Bam and surrounding villages, including the 2,500 year-old historic citadel of Bam. The Iranian Red Crescent Society launched a massive rescue and relief operation, which was supported by the international community. Within hours of the disaster, the United Nations dispatched its Disaster Assessment and Coordination Team, which, with UN agencies, mobilized relief items and technical support. The UN resident coordinator initiated the preparation of a Flash Appeal in December, with the support of the UN country team and OCHA.

Chernobyl aftermath

In response to General Assembly resolution 56/109 [YUN 2001, p. 870], the Secretary-General, in an August report [A/58/332], described international efforts to study, mitigate and minimize the consequences of the 1986 Chernobyl nuclear accident [YUN 1986, p. 584].

The report of the multidisciplinary international inter-agency mission [YUN 2001, p. 869], which studied the consequences of Chernobyl 15 years after the accident, was launched under the title "The Human Consequences of the Chernobyl Nuclear Accident: A Strategy for Recovery". The report made several recommendations for recovery and sustainable development. In order to promote the new strategy for recovery with government agencies and international donors, and to help initiate the implementation of its recommendations, the United Nations Coordinator of International Cooperation on Chernobyl visited the region. At the field level, concrete actions were taken by the UN country teams in the three most affected countries—Belarus, the Russian Federation and Ukraine. The disbursement of seed money from the United Nations Chernobyl Trust Fund was authorized for three pilot projects, prepared by the country teams in the affected countries, which aimed to support socio-economic rehabilitation and to improve people's health. Another recommendation of the report was implemented with the launch, in June, of the International Chernobyl Research and Information Network, to support ongoing international, national and civil society efforts for the sustainable development of the affected regions by compiling, consolidating and coordinating scientific research, commissioning further research, and ensuring its effective dissemination to all stakeholders.

The United Nations saw the need to energize work with donors to secure more systematic support and focused on a number of modalities for approaching them. UN programmes aimed at addressing the consequences of the disaster had been chronically underfunded for many years, and because of the constraints felt by some donors, Chernobyl fell into a budgetary gap. Substantial resources were needed to sustain the international community's recent initiatives. Annexed to the report were accounts by the Governments of the three most affected States regarding their efforts to overcome the consequences of the catastrophe.

GENERAL ASSEMBLY ACTION

On 17 December [meeting 75], the General Assembly adopted **resolution 58/119** [draft: A/58/L.44 & Add.1] without vote [agenda item 40 (c)].

Strengthening of international cooperation and coordination of efforts to study, mitigate and minimize the consequences of the Chernobyl disaster

The General Assembly,

Reaffirming its resolutions 45/190 of 21 December 1990, 46/150 of 18 December 1991, 47/165 of 18 December 1992, 48/206 of 21 December 1993, 50/134 of 20 December 1995, 52/172 of 16 December 1997, 54/97 of 8 December 1999 and 56/109 of 14 December 2001, as well as its resolution 55/171 of 14 December 2000 on closure of the Chernobyl nuclear power plant, and taking note of the decisions adopted by the organs, organizations and programmes of the United Nations system in the implementation of those resolutions,

Recalling Economic and Social Council resolutions 1990/50 of 13 July 1990, 1991/51 of 26 July 1991 and 1992/38 of 30 July 1992 and Council decision 1993/232 of 22 July 1993,

Conscious of the long-term nature of the consequences of the disaster at the Chernobyl nuclear power plant, which was a major technological catastrophe in terms of its scope and complexity and created humanitarian, environmental, social, economic and health consequences and problems of common concern, requiring for their solution wide and active international cooperation and coordination of efforts in this field at the international and national levels,

Expressing profound concern at the ongoing effects of the consequences of the accident on the lives and health of people, in particular children, in the affected areas of Belarus, the Russian Federation and Ukraine, as well as in other affected countries,

Acknowledging the importance of the national efforts being undertaken by the Governments of Belarus, the Russian Federation and Ukraine to mitigate and minimize the consequences of the Chernobyl disaster,

Noting with appreciation the contribution made by States and by organizations of the United Nations system to the development of cooperation to mitigate and minimize the consequences of the Chernobyl disaster, the activities of regional and other organizations and those of non-governmental organizations, as well as bilateral activities,

Recognizing the importance of continuing international support to the national efforts of the Governments and civil societies of Belarus, the Russian Federation and Ukraine, as the most affected countries, to mitigate and minimize the persisting negative effects of the Chernobyl disaster on the sustainable development of the affected areas as a result of the radiological, health, socio-economic, psychological and environmental consequences of the disaster,

Welcoming the increased role played by the United Nations Development Programme, the United Nations resident coordinators and the United Nations country teams in Belarus, the Russian Federation and Ukraine in helping to address both the developmental and the humanitarian consequences of the catastrophe,

Taking note of the United Nations report entitled "The Human Consequences of the Chernobyl Nuclear Accident: A Strategy for Recovery", prepared on the basis of an international needs assessment undertaken in mid-2001 in the affected areas of Belarus, the Russian Federation and Ukraine,

Emphasizing the importance of the new developmental approach to tackling the problems caused by the Chernobyl accident, aimed at normalizing the situation of the individuals and communities concerned in the medium and long term,

Stressing the continued need for a response to the exceptional Chernobyl-related needs, in particular in the areas of health, ecology and research, as the transition is made from the emergency to the recovery phase of mitigation of the consequences of the Chernobyl disaster, as mentioned in the United Nations report entitled "The Human Consequences of the Chernobyl Nuclear Accident: A Strategy for Recovery",

Welcoming the launch of the International Chernobyl Research and Information Network, with the aim of supporting the ongoing international, national and civil society efforts towards the sustainable development of the affected territories by compiling, consolidating and coordinating relevant scientific research, commissioning further research where required, and making available and ensuring the effective dissemination of its findings, which should allow informed decision-making on the phases of long-term recovery and management with a view to improving the complex and diverse humanitarian, ecological, economic, social and medical situations in those territories,

Welcoming also the establishment of the Chernobyl Forum by the International Atomic Energy Agency, with the participation of the Food and Agriculture Organization of the United Nations, the Office for the Coordination of Humanitarian Affairs of the Secretariat, the United Nations Development Programme, the United Nations Environment Programme, the United

Nations Scientific Committee on the Effects of Atomic Radiation, the World Health Organization, the World Bank and representatives of the three most affected States,

Welcoming further the coordination of the activities of the International Chernobyl Research and Information Network and the Chernobyl Forum, and efforts to ensure the substantial integration of the Forum's assessment of environmental and health consequences into the Network process,

Taking note of the report of the Secretary-General concerning the implementation of resolution 56/109,

1. *Reaffirms* that the United Nations plays an important catalytic and coordinating role in the strengthening of international cooperation to study, mitigate and minimize the consequences of the Chernobyl disaster, and commends the contribution made by all other relevant multilateral mechanisms to this end;

2. *Welcomes* the further practical measures that have been taken by the Secretary-General and the United Nations Coordinator of International Cooperation on Chernobyl to strengthen coordination of the international efforts in that area, especially the launch of the International Chernobyl Research and Information Network;

3. *Also welcomes* the efforts undertaken by the agencies of the United Nations system and other international organizations members of the Inter-Agency Task Force on Chernobyl to implement a new developmental approach to studying, mitigating and minimizing the consequences of the Chernobyl disaster, in particular through the development of specific projects, and requests the Inter-Agency Task Force to continue its activities to that end, including through coordinating efforts in the field of resource mobilization;

4. *Acknowledges* the difficulties faced by the most affected countries in minimizing the consequences of the Chernobyl disaster, and invites States, in particular donor States and all relevant agencies, funds and programmes of the United Nations system, in particular the Bretton Woods institutions, as well as non-governmental organizations, to continue to provide support to the ongoing efforts of Belarus, the Russian Federation and Ukraine to mitigate the consequences of the Chernobyl disaster, including through the allocation of adequate funds to support medical, social, economic and ecological programmes related to the disaster;

5. *Takes note with satisfaction* of the recent development of the Cooperation for Rehabilitation Programme, aimed at promoting better living conditions in and the sustainable development of the affected territories;

6. *Emphasizes* the important role of the authorities of the affected countries in mitigating the humanitarian and other consequences of the Chernobyl catastrophe, and welcomes the continued efforts of the affected countries in this regard, including the measures taken with a view to facilitating the work of humanitarian organizations, including non-governmental organizations, to mitigate the humanitarian and other consequences of the Chernobyl catastrophe;

7. *Stresses* the need for coordinated international cooperation in studying the consequences of the Chernobyl catastrophe, in particular through effective work of the International Chernobyl Research and Information Network, the Chernobyl Forum, the International Chernobyl Centre for nuclear safety, radioactive waste and radioecology, and other research centres from the most affected countries, and invites Member States and all interested parties to take part in their activities;

8. *Welcomes* the decision of the Council of Heads of State of the Commonwealth of Independent States to proclaim 26 April the International Day Commemorating Victims of Radiation Accidents and Catastrophes in the States members of the Commonwealth;

9. *Invites* Member States to observe this Day and to conduct appropriate activities to commemorate victims of radiation accidents and catastrophes and to enhance public awareness of their consequences for human health and the environment throughout the world;

10. *Requests* the Secretary-General to continue his efforts in the implementation of the relevant General Assembly resolutions and, through existing coordination mechanisms, in particular the United Nations Coordinator of International Cooperation on Chernobyl, to continue to maintain close cooperation with the agencies of the United Nations system, as well as with regional and other relevant organizations, while implementing specific Chernobyl-related programmes and projects;

11. *Also requests* the Secretary-General to consider possible ways to strengthen further the coordination, analytical, advocacy and technical capacities of the United Nations in the field, as well as at Headquarters, as described in the report of the Secretary-General, with due regard to the existing administrative and budgetary capacity of the Organization;

12. *Further requests* the Secretary-General to submit to the General Assembly at its sixtieth session, under a separate sub-item, a report containing a comprehensive assessment of the implementation of all aspects of the present resolution and proposals for innovative measures for optimizing the effectiveness of the response of the international community, including the United Nations, to the Chernobyl disaster, as well as to consider how better to focus international cooperation to achieve a long-term developmental approach for the affected areas, bearing in mind the exceptional Chernobyl-related needs.

Chapter IV

International trade, finance and transport

Growth in the volume of world merchandise trade in 2003 accelerated to an estimated 4.7 per cent, from 3 per cent in 2002. The improved performance was attributed mainly to increased import demand in developing countries, particularly in Asia, and in the transition economies. Most of the growth occurred during the second half of the year. Among the developed countries, exports of the United States rebounded in the third quarter and those of Japan recovered in the second half of the year. However, Western Europe experienced low growth in both import and export volumes, while the export performance of Central and Eastern Europe was mixed. On the other hand, the external trade of developing countries grew by 9 per cent, well over the world average. International commodity prices improved slightly in 2003, largely reflecting the weakening of the value of the United States dollar. The General Assembly convened an open-ended panel in October to consider the report of the Meeting of Eminent Persons on Commodity Issues, which made recommendations for improving the conditions in commodity markets and for alleviating the poverty of many commodity producers.

The net transfer of financial resources from developing countries in 2003 was similar in magnitude to that in 2002, when it reached a peak of $192 billion. There was also a net outward transfer from economies in transition. In Latin America, the increase in exports and deceleration in the decline in imports were not enough to reverse the large net outward transfers experienced in 2002. Likewise, the large net transfers from East Asia resulting from its strong export growth continued in 2003.

In September, the multilateral trading system suffered a major setback as the Fifth World Trade Organization (WTO) Ministerial Conference failed to advance the negotiations on key aspects of the Doha work programme adopted at the Fourth (2001) Ministerial Conference. In December, the General Assembly called on WTO members to engage in negotiations with a renewed sense of urgency and to redouble efforts to achieve a successful outcome.

In April, the high-level meeting between the Economic and Social Council and the Bretton Woods institutions (the World Bank Group and the International Monetary Fund) discussed coordination and cooperation in the implementation of the Monterrey Consensus adopted at the 2002 International Conference on Financing for Development and identified significant gaps in some key areas. In October, the Assembly held its first high-level Dialogue on Financing for Development, which called for a more precise mechanism for monitoring implementation of the Monterrey Consensus commitments and of related targets in the Millennium Development Goals, adopted by the Assembly in 2000.

The Trade and Development Board, the governing body of the United Nations Conference on Trade and Development (UNCTAD), adopted agreed conclusions on Africa's trade performance. It also recommended that the secretariat implement its new strategy for technical cooperation and initiated preparations for the convening in 2004 of UNCTAD XI in Brazil.

The International Trade Centre, operated jointly by UNCTAD and WTO, increased its delivery of technical cooperation programmes for developing countries and economies in transition by some 20 per cent.

International trade

The *Trade and Development Report, 2003* [Sales No. E.03.II.D.7] stated that world trade registered a modest recovery in 2002 following the marked deceleration of 2001. Import volumes rose by 1.6 per cent and export volumes by 2 per cent, having fallen by -0.1 and -0.9 per cent, respectively, in 2001. However, the trade volume growth rate exceeded world output by only a narrow margin. The recovery was due to the rise in United States imports, which increased by nearly 4 per cent in 2002, after a 3 per cent decline the previous year, and the recovery of Japan's imports, which rose by 1.6 per cent, and exports, which attained their 2000 levels. In Asia, China's export growth rate tripled in 2002, matched by the growth in imports following its accession to membership of the World Trade Organization (WTO). On the other hand, trade volume in the European Union (EU) was low due to slow growth in the region, and Latin America experienced one of the worst years since the debt crisis, with an 8 per cent drop in imports; in Argentina, imports fell to half their 2001 level. Exports from that region held up slightly, due to strong demand from the United States combined with currency declines against the dollar. In Africa, the volume of both imports and exports grew by 2.6 per cent despite weak demand from Western Europe. The terms of trade for the region as a whole deteriorated for the second consecutive year, with import growth exceeding export growth in value by a wide margin. Although sub-Saharan Africa's terms of trade recovered moderately in 2002, reflecting a price increase in exports of non-fuel commodities, that upturn was insufficient to make up for 2001 losses. In the transition economies, both imports and exports decelerated but still exceeded world averages by a wide margin. Many of the candidates for EU membership were integrating more closely into a single market, but weakening growth in the EU caused their exports to slow in late 2002. Export earnings increased for most Commonwealth of Independent States (CIS) countries, notably the Russian Federation, due to rising prices and volume of oil exports.

The *World Economic and Social Survey 2003* [Sales No. E.03.II.C.1] stated that the volume of world merchandise trade grew by 1.8 per cent in 2002, the second weakest performance in two decades. However, in dollar terms, world trade expanded by 4 per cent, reflecting modest increases in the prices of commodities and manufactured goods and a weaker dollar. International trade performance was uneven in 2002, with strong recovery in the first half of the year because of improved economic conditions in many countries and a revival in manufacturing. However, by the last quarter, the recovery of global trade decelerated, with new shocks to consumer and investor confidence, slower demand and loss of momentum in industrial production. That weakness intensified in early 2003 as conflict in Iraq loomed.

A joint report on the world economic situation and prospects [Sales No. E.04.II.C.2], issued by the Department of Economic and Social Affairs (DESA) and the United Nations Conference on Trade and Development (UNCTAD), stated that the volume of merchandise trade grew from 3 per cent in 2002 to an estimated 4.7 per cent in 2003, due to increased import demand in developing countries, particularly in Asia, and the transition economies. Most of the growth occurred in the second half of the year. In dollar terms, world trade grew by almost 13 per cent, reflecting not only increased volume but also a continuing weakening of the dollar. Among the developed economies, the merchandise exports of the United States rebounded in the third quarter of 2003, with exports of capital goods leading the recovery. United States real imports grew by almost 4 per cent. Japan's exports also recovered in the second half of the year, reaching an estimated 6 per cent, while imports were expected to continue their growth of around 5 per cent. In Western Europe, the growth of import and export volumes was low as the euro continued to appreciate in value, increasing competitive pressure on many EU exporters. However, growth in world demand partially offset the negative impact of the stronger euro on exports. Robust domestic demand and currency appreciation weakened exports and increased imports of both Australia and New Zealand, while increased international competition, trade disputes and the appreciation of its currency reduced Canada's share in the United States market. In the CIS countries, strong regional economic growth and higher oil prices drove rapid trade growth. However, export performance in Central and Eastern Europe was mixed, with exports stalling in some cases because of earlier currency appreciation, and increasing in other cases as competitiveness improved. Imports remained strong due to higher disposable income in most countries and strong investment in others.

In developing economies, external trade grew by 9 per cent in 2003, well above the world average, though imports grew more slowly than exports because of external financial constraints and weak domestic conditions in several economies. Africa recorded a modest trade growth in 2003 as high oil-import bills impacted negatively on the volume of imports of many countries. China continued to play a dominant role in the trade performance of East Asia, as its exports and imports grew by some 30 per cent in nominal terms. Export growth was robust in South Asia in 2003, particularly because Pakistan's preferential textile export quotas to the EU and the United States were expanded. Western Asia's trade performance was boosted by the rise in oil prices. Latin America and the Caribbean achieved a more balanced trade performance, with exports growing by only 1.4 per cent, due to Mexico's poor performance, lower oil exports by Venezuela and weak exports from Argentina. Brazil's exports benefited from both higher prices and greater external demand, resulting from a diversification of its trading partners, particularly China.

Africa's trade performance

At its fiftieth session (Geneva, 6-17 October), the UNCTAD Trade and Development Board

(TDB) had before it a July report by the UNCTAD secretariat on economic development in Africa: issues in Africa's trade performance [TD/B/50/6 & Corr.1]. The report examined the structure of trade and Africa's performance, price volatility and terms of trade losses, the beneficiaries, past policy responses and policy issues. It noted that Africa's share in world trade had been falling consistently since 1980. The continent remained heavily dependent on the export of a few primary commodities, most of which had suffered a decline in prices leading to large terms-of-trade losses. Its share in world exports fell from 6 per cent in 1980 to 2 per cent in 2002, and its share of world imports fell from 4.6 to 2.1 per cent during the same period. Unlike other developing regions, Africa had by and large not been able to diversify into manufactures or market-dynamic products and had even lost market shares for its traditional exports. Although the value of Africa's manufactures was increasing by 6.3 per cent annually, that rate was low compared with 14 and 12 per cent for Asia and Latin America, respectively. Market-oriented policies had not been able to reverse the situation. In addition to providing better market access and reductions in subsidies for products competing with African exports, external resources were required to compensate for losses and to fill the resource gap in order to ensure adequate investment in the development of human and physical infrastructure, institution-building and diversification.

In agreed conclusions adopted on 17 October [A/58/15 (agreed conclusions 477(L))], TDB noted with concern that Africa's share in international trade had fallen considerably in the past 20 years; its share in commodity exports, where it traditionally had had comparative advantage, had also decreased. It encouraged African countries to continue to promote peace and stability and strengthen their economic and legal framework, which were essential factors for strengthening economic and social development and enhancing their participation in international trade.

TDB agreed that the ability of African producers to retain and increase market share and move up the value chain should be enhanced through such measures as providing extension services and farm inputs, transportation, market information, quality control and assistance to farmers. TDB encouraged the design and delivery of technical assistance to realize those objectives. It called for support for efforts to develop and upgrade African countries' productive capacity, increase their export earnings and adjust to fluctuating commodity prices. TDB called for support and exchanges of experiences in the better promotion of commodities of export interest to Africa, including non-traditional exports. It requested UNCTAD, in collaboration with regional economic communities, to further study interregional trade in Africa, with a view to identifying the potential for its future expansion. The international community should complement the efforts of African countries in the context of the New Partnership for Africa's Development (NEPAD) [YUN 2002, p. 907], to improve the application of the Highly Indebted Poor Countries (HIPC) Initiative and to supply additional public and private resources to bridge the investment gap. It agreed that UNCTAD should continue to support African countries to meet NEPAD's aims and objectives and to provide analysis and policy advice on African development.

The multilateral trading system

Report of Secretary-General. In response to General Assembly resolution 57/235 [YUN 2002, p. 934], the Secretary-General submitted an October report [A/58/414], prepared in collaboration with UNCTAD, on international trade and development, which discussed recent trends in international trade, developments in the multilateral trading system, particularly the results of the Fifth Ministerial Conference of the World Trade Organization (WTO) (Cancún, Mexico, 10-14 September), regional arrangements and other trade measures, UNCTAD's role and development benchmarks.

The report said the Fifth WTO Ministerial Conference had been expected to ensure that political impetus was given to advancing negotiations on key aspects of the Doha (Qatar) work programme, adopted by WTO's Fourth Ministerial Conference in 2001 [YUN 2001, p. 1432], build greater confidence for the future of the trading system and provide fresh impetus to the world economy and global trade. Despite intensive negotiations since the Doha Conference, progress in advancing the work programme encountered a number of limitations, including the failure to reach agreement on issues of priority concern to developing countries. Those countries found it difficult to compromise in stalled negotiations on agricultural and non-agricultural products and on Singapore issues (trade and competition policy, transparency in government procurement and trade facilitation). On the eve of the Conference, agreement was reached on some issues, including trade-related aspects of intellectual property rights (TRIPS) and public health. Other steps forward included the conclusion of the accession process of Cambodia and Nepal and the adoption of modalities for special treatment of least developed countries (LDCs) in services negotiations. Consensus was not achieved on other key

Doha work programme issues, such as agriculture, non-agricultural market access, special and differential treatment, implementation-related issues and Singapore issues. A revised draft Cancún ministerial text (also known as the Derbez text) was submitted on 13 September, on the basis of which negotiations continued. The Conference Chairman, in a statement issued at the end of the Conference, indicated that the WTO General Council would convene no later than 15 December 2003 to work towards concluding the negotiations. There was concern, however, that the stalemate in the negotiations could lead to a more vigorous pursuit of bilateral and regional trade agreements, the number of which (over 200) had grown rapidly during the 1990s. The cause of trade liberalization could be affected and protectionist sentiment could gain ground.

The report concluded that all countries had shared interests in the success of the Doha work programme and the realization of its core development agenda, which, if effectively pursued and implemented, could put in place important elements for achieving the Millennium Development Goal (MDG) [YUN 2001, p. 51] of "an open, equitable, rule-based, predictable and non-discriminatory multilateral trading . . . system".

UNCTAD consideration. At its fiftieth session (Geneva, 6-17 October) [A/58/15], TDB reviewed an UNCTAD secretariat paper on developments and issues in the post-Doha work programme of practical concern to developing countries: outcome of the Fifth WTO Ministerial Conference [TD/B/50/8]. Summarizing the Board's discussion, the President highlighted the importance, in the post-Cancún phase, of concentrating on the Doha mandate, addressing the legitimate concerns of developing countries on new and complicated issues on which no consensus existed for new WTO disciplines, and addressing coherence and consistency between trade, financial, monetary and technological policies in support of development. Future negotiations should take into account the considerable adjustment and social costs for developing countries of the negotiations and implementation of their results. The special needs of LDCs should be adequately addressed, including binding duty-free and quota-free access for LDC products, along with improvements in preferential schemes and rules, the removal of non-tariff barriers and avoidance of safeguards and contingency measures on their products.

UNCTAD could provide a forum for consensus-building in negotiating areas for further treatment in WTO, and so contribute to putting the Doha work programme back on track. Equally important was the support provided by UNCTAD to countries in the accession process. The international community was called on to provide greater resources to UNCTAD so that it could play fully its trade and development role.

GENERAL ASSEMBLY ACTION

On 23 December [meeting 78], the General Assembly, on the recommendation of the Second (Economic and Financial) Committee [A/58/481/Add.1], adopted **resolution 58/197** without vote [agenda item 91 (a)].

International trade and development

The General Assembly,

Recalling its resolutions 55/182 of 20 December 2000, 56/178 of 21 December 2001 and 57/235 of 20 December 2002 on international trade and development,

Recalling also the Plan of Action adopted at the tenth session of the United Nations Conference on Trade and Development, held in Bangkok from 12 to 19 February 2000,

Reaffirming the role of the United Nations Conference on Trade and Development as focal point within the United Nations for the integrated treatment of trade and development and the interrelated issues in the areas of finance, technology, investment and sustainable development,

Recalling the provisions of the United Nations Millennium Declaration pertaining to trade and related development issues, as well as the outcomes of the International Conference on Financing for Development, held in Monterrey, Mexico, from 18 to 22 March 2002, and the World Summit on Sustainable Development, held in Johannesburg, South Africa, from 26 August to 4 September 2002,

Recalling also its resolutions 57/250 of 20 December 2002 and 57/270 B of 23 June 2003, in which it invited the United Nations Conference on Trade and Development, as well as the Trade and Development Board, to contribute, within its mandate, to the implementation and to the review of the progress made in the implementation of the outcomes of the major United Nations conferences and summits and invited the President of the Trade and Development Board to present the outcomes of such reviews to the Economic and Social Council,

Taking note of the report of the Meeting of Eminent Persons on Commodity Issues, held in Geneva on 22 and 23 September 2003, and expressing appreciation for the work of the eminent persons,

Recalling that, to benefit fully from trade, which in many cases is the single most important external source of development financing, the establishment and the enhancement of appropriate institutions and policies in developing countries, as well as in countries with economies in transition, are needed and that, in this context, enhanced market access, balanced rules and well-targeted, sustainably financed technical assistance and capacity-building programmes for developing countries also play important roles,

Noting the significant contribution of the multilateral trading system to economic growth, development and employment and the importance of maintaining the process of reform and liberalization of trade policies, as well as the importance of rejecting the use of protectionism, so that the system plays its full part in promoting recovery, growth and development, in particular of developing countries, bearing in mind paragraph 10 of resolution 55/182,

Recognizing with concern that the benefits from global economic prosperity and trade liberalization have not fully accrued to all developing countries,

Recognizing that a number of developing countries have undertaken significant trade and investment liberalization unilaterally, regionally and/or multilaterally, both within and outside the context of structural adjustment programmes,

Reaffirming the urgency, subject to national legislation, of recognizing the rights of local and indigenous communities that are holders of traditional knowledge, innovations and practices and, with the approval and involvement of the holders of such knowledge, innovations and practices, of developing and implementing benefit-sharing mechanisms on mutually-agreed terms for the use of such knowledge, innovations and practices,

Recognizing that countries must take appropriate and necessary security measures, but also underlining the importance of taking these measures in the manner that is least disruptive of normal trade and related practices,

Taking note of the in-depth review undertaken by the Trade and Development Board at its fiftieth session with respect to developments and issues in the post-Doha work programme of particular concern to developing countries, including the outcome of the Fifth Ministerial Conference of the World Trade Organization, held in Cancún, Mexico, from 10 to 14 September 2003, and its contribution to an understanding of the actions required to help developing countries secure beneficial and meaningful integration into the multilateral trading system and the global economy and to achieve a balanced, development-oriented and successful conclusion of the Doha negotiations,

Taking note also of the report of the Trade and Development Board and the report of the Secretary-General,

Noting the proposals made to implement the work programme of the World Trade Organization, including those to liberalize international agricultural and non-agricultural trade,

Underlining the development potential of a balanced outcome of the negotiations under the Doha work programme, which reflects the interests of all World Trade Organization members, particularly the developing countries,

1. *Reaffirms* the great importance of promoting the objectives set out in the United Nations Millennium Declaration of ensuring an open, equitable, rule-based, predictable and non-discriminatory multilateral trading system in pursuit of economic growth and development, fairness and a level playing field as well as human development and poverty eradication goals, and reiterates its commitment to achieving those objectives;

2. *Reiterates* the commitment made at the Fourth Ministerial Conference of the World Trade Organization, held in Doha from 9 to 14 November 2001, to place development at the heart of the Doha work programme and to continue to make positive efforts to ensure that developing countries, especially the least developed among them, secure a share in the growth of world trade commensurate with the needs of their economic development;

3. *Expresses its concern* about the insufficient progress in the Doha negotiations, especially in areas of interest to developing countries, as manifested, inter alia, by missed deadlines in relation to special and differential treatment, implementation-related issues and concerns and modalities for agricultural negotiations;

4. *Also expresses its concern* about the setback at the Fifth Ministerial Conference of the World Trade Organization, and stresses the importance of redoubling efforts in working towards a successful, timely and development-oriented conclusion of the Doha negotiations no later than 1 January 2005 as set out in the Ministerial Declaration of the Fourth Ministerial Conference of the World Trade Organization ("Doha Ministerial Declaration");

5. *Further expresses its concern* about the adverse consequences that the setback of the Fifth Ministerial Conference may have for the multilateral trading system, including a possible surge in protectionist measures;

6. *Expresses its concern* about the adoption of a number of unilateral actions that are not consistent with the rules of the World Trade Organization, harm the exports of all countries, in particular those of developing countries, and have a considerable bearing on the ongoing World Trade Organization negotiations and on the achievement and further enhancement of the development dimension of the trade negotiations;

7. *Considers* that the political will and commitment of World Trade Organization members to address the unresolved questions under the Doha work programme promptly and fully and to focus on the key development issues are essential for bringing the negotiations back on track;

8. *Underscores* the need for concerted political will and efforts to address the challenges of globalization, including by improving market access and market entry for the export products of particular interest to developing countries so that they can benefit more from the globalization process;

9. *Recognizes* that it is important for developing countries and countries with economies in transition to consider reducing trade barriers among themselves;

10. *Stresses* the importance of an open, transparent, inclusive and democratic process and of procedures for the effective functioning of the multilateral trading system that allow for internal transparency and the effective participation of members, including in the decision-making process, and that enable them to have their vital interests duly reflected in the outcome of trade negotiations;

11. *Also stresses* the need to place the interests and concerns of developing countries at the heart of the Doha work programme and to revive faith in it, and, in this regard, calls upon members of the World Trade Organization to engage in negotiations with a renewed sense of urgency and purpose and to redouble their efforts to achieve a successful outcome of the Doha work programme, including on the following issues of particular interest to the developing countries:

(*a*) The expeditious and appropriate resolution of outstanding implementation issues, consistent with paragraph 12 of the Doha Ministerial Declaration;

(b) The completion of the review of all provisions relating to special and differential treatment with a view to strengthening them and making them more precise, effective and operational, recognizing the importance of paragraph 12.1 (i) of the decision on implementation-related issues and concerns of 14 November 2001, adopted by the Fourth Ministerial Conference of the World Trade Organization;

(c) Substantial improvements in market access, the reduction of, with a view to phasing out, all forms of export subsidies, substantial reductions in trade-distorting domestic support in agriculture and the expeditious adoption of appropriate modalities for reduction commitments in agriculture negotiations, with operationally effective special and differential treatment and non-trade concerns being taken into account, in accordance with paragraphs 13 and 14 of the Doha Ministerial Declaration;

(d) Abusive application of anti-dumping, sanitary and phytosanitary standards and other trade-distorting measures;

(e) The positive consideration of trade-related issues pertaining to the commodity sector in the multilateral trading system;

(f) An effective solution to address the problems reflected in the sectoral initiative in favour of cotton proposed by a group of African countries within the context of negotiations on agriculture under the Doha work programme;

(g) Negotiations on trade in services conducted with a view to promoting the economic growth of all trading partners and the development of developing countries and the least developed countries, without a priori exclusion of any service sector or mode of supply and with special attention given to sectors and modes of supply of export interest to developing countries, recognizing the work already undertaken in the negotiations and the large number of proposals submitted by members on a wide range of sectors and on several horizontal issues, as well as on the movement of natural persons;

(h) Appropriate modalities for reduction or elimination commitments in negotiations on market access for non-agricultural products, as provided for in paragraph 16 of the Doha Ministerial Declaration, in particular on products of export interest to developing countries, and taking into account the special needs and interests of developing and least developed country participants, including through less than full reciprocity in reduction commitments;

(i) The review of the Agreement on Trade-related Aspects of Intellectual Property Rights, taking fully into account its development dimension;

(j) In accordance with paragraph 16 of the Doha Ministerial Declaration, on market access for non-agricultural products, reduction or elimination of high tariffs, tariff peaks and tariff escalation, as well as non-tariff barriers, on those products, in particular on products of export interest to developing countries;

(k) The clarification and improvement of disciplines in the areas of anti-dumping, subsidies and countervailing measures, taking into account the needs of developing countries, including the least developed among them, while preserving the basic concepts, principles and effectiveness of those agreements and their instruments and objectives in non-agricultural market access;

(l) The examination, in the context of paragraphs 36 and 37 of the Doha Ministerial Declaration, of the relationship between trade, debt and finance and between trade and transfer of technology, and possible recommendations thereon, taking into account their development dimension;

(m) Making the World Trade Organization operations more transparent, including through more effective and prompt dissemination of information;

12. *Recognizes* the crucial role that the expeditious implementation of World Trade Organization agreements and improved World Trade Organization rules, reflective of the development dimension of the Doha Ministerial Declaration, can play with regard to the development opportunities of developing countries and their capacity to integrate into the global economy;

13. *Takes note* of the provisions of the Doha Ministerial Declaration with respect to the relationship between trade and investment, the interaction between trade and competition policy, transparency in government procurement and trade facilitation;

14. *Reaffirms* that agriculture remains a fundamental and key sector for the overwhelming majority of developing countries, and stresses the importance of a successful conclusion of the Doha work programme in this regard;

15. *Also reaffirms* the commitment to the full and faithful implementation of the Agreement on Textiles and Clothing, and calls for further progress in its implementation, which is a necessary and inherent condition of full implementation of the agreements arising from the Uruguay Round of Multilateral Trade Negotiations;

16. *Further reaffirms* that preferences granted to developing countries, pursuant to the "enabling clause", should be generalized, non-reciprocal and non-discriminatory;

17. *Reaffirms* the need for the implementation of paragraph 4 of the Marrakesh Ministerial Decision on Measures Concerning the Possible Negative Effects of the Reform Programme on Least Developed and Net Food-importing Developing Countries;

18. *Welcomes* the decision adopted by the General Council of the World Trade Organization on the implementation of paragraph 6 of the Doha Declaration on the Agreement on Trade-related Aspects of Intellectual Property Rights and Public Health to address the problems faced by countries with insufficient or no manufacturing capacity in the pharmaceutical sector in accessing medicines at affordable prices when combating serious public health problems afflicting many developing and least developed countries, especially those resulting from HIV/AIDS, tuberculosis, malaria and other epidemics, and invites all members to work towards an expeditious and permanent solution to the issue by, inter alia, amending the Agreement on Trade-related Aspects of Intellectual Property Rights within the agreed time frame, to ensure that the solution will be simple to use, sustainable, predictable and legally secure;

19. *Emphasizes* that bilateral and regional trade arrangements should contribute to the multilateral trading system, and in this context stresses the importance of clarifying and improving disciplines and proce-

dures under the existing provisions of the World Trade Organization applying to regional trade agreements in accordance with paragraph 29 of the Doha Ministerial Declaration, taking into account the implications of those agreements for development, and urges the United Nations Conference on Trade and Development, in accordance with its mandate, to provide technical inputs in this respect;

20. *Reaffirms* the commitments made at the Fourth Ministerial Conference of the World Trade Organization, and at the Third United Nations Conference on the Least Developed Countries, held in Brussels from 14 to 20 May 2001, in this regard calls upon developed countries that have not already done so to work towards the objective of duty-free, quota-free market access for all least developed country exports, and notes that the consideration of proposals for developing countries to contribute to improved market access for the least developed countries would also be helpful;

21. *Welcomes* the approval of the accession of Cambodia and Nepal to the World Trade Organization, stresses the importance of facilitating the accession of all developing countries, in particular the least developed countries, as well as countries with economies in transition, that apply for membership in the World Trade Organization, bearing in mind paragraph 21 of resolution 55/182 and subsequent developments, and calls for the effective and faithful application of the World Trade Organization guidelines on accession of the least developed countries;

22. *Invites* members of the international community to consider the interests of non-members of the World Trade Organization in the context of trade liberalization;

23. *Reaffirms* the commitment to actively pursue the work programme of the World Trade Organization with respect to addressing the trade-related issues and concerns affecting the fuller integration of countries with small, vulnerable economies into the multilateral trading system in a manner commensurate with their special circumstances and in support of their efforts towards sustainable development, in accordance with paragraph 35 of the Doha Ministerial Declaration;

24. *Acknowledges* the seriousness of the concerns expressed in the Almaty Programme of Action adopted at the International Ministerial Conference of Landlocked and Transit Developing Countries and Donor Countries and International Financial and Development Institutions on Transit Transport Cooperation, held in Almaty, Kazakhstan, on 28 and 29 August 2003, and stresses the need for the special problems and needs of landlocked developing countries, including those contained in paragraph 33 of the Programme of Action, as well as other relevant issues contained in the section on international trade and trade facilitation of the Programme of Action, to be effectively addressed by the relevant international organizations and donors in a multi-stakeholder approach;

25. *Notes* the health- and environment-related measures that have an impact on exports, stresses that the adoption or enforcement of any measures necessary to protect human, animal or plant life or health should not be applied in a manner that would constitute arbitrary or unjustified discrimination or a disguised restriction on international trade, and recognizes the importance of capacity-building support to enable developing countries to put in place measures that are appropriate and necessary for meeting standards consistent with those of the World Trade Organization;

26. *Encourages* the United Nations Conference on Trade and Development, the World Trade Organization, the World Bank, the United Nations Industrial Development Organization, the United Nations Development Programme and other relevant international organizations to continue to cooperate on trade-related capacity-building in developing countries, including, as appropriate, under the Integrated Framework for Trade-related Technical Assistance to Least Developed Countries and the Joint Integrated Technical Assistance Programme;

27. *Requests* the United Nations Conference on Trade and Development to continue its work, within its mandate, on trade-related issues and policies, from the development perspective, including its contribution to the Plan of Implementation of the World Summit on Sustainable Development ("Johannesburg Plan of Implementation"), and notes its work on development benchmarks of the international trading system and trade negotiations;

28. *Reiterates* the importance of supporting United Nations Conference on Trade and Development programmes of technical cooperation and capacity-building that assist developing countries, especially the least developed countries, countries with economies in transition and countries with small and vulnerable economies, in particular those programmes that support their participation in the Doha work programme, in accordance with the technical cooperation strategy of the United Nations Conference on Trade and Development;

29. *Emphasizes* the importance of and invites Member States to support the activities of the United Nations Conference on Trade and Development, and invites donors and other countries in a position to do so to continue to provide the United Nations Conference on Trade and Development with the resources necessary to effectively implement its technical cooperation activities by giving priority to longer-term sustainable activities, particularly through multi-year funding mechanisms and inter-divisional operations based on the thematic priorities set by the United Nations Conference on Trade and Development in its work programme;

30. *Takes note* of the substantive item of the provisional agenda of the eleventh session of the United Nations Conference on Trade and Development, to be held in São Paulo, Brazil, from 13 to 18 June 2004, entitled "Enhancing coherence between national development strategies and global economic processes towards economic growth and development, particularly of developing countries", and in this context stresses the importance of the role and mandate of the United Nations Conference on Trade and Development;

31. *Requests* the Secretary-General of the United Nations, in collaboration with the secretariat of the United Nations Conference on Trade and Development, to report to the General Assembly at its fifty-ninth session on the implementation of the present resolution and on developments in the multilateral trading system under the sub-item entitled "International trade and development".

Trade policy

Trade in goods and services, and commodities

The Commission on Trade in Goods and Services, and Commodities, at its seventh session (Geneva, 3-6 February) [TD/B/EX(31)/4], had before it the following documentation: a note by the UNCTAD secretariat on export diversification, market access and competitiveness [TD/B/COM.1/54]; the 2002 report of the Expert Meeting on the Diversification of Production and Exports in Commodity-dependent Developing Countries, Including Single-commodity Exporters, for Industrialization and Development, Taking into Account the Special Needs of LDCs [TD/B/COM.1/50] [YUN 2002, p. 939]; a note by the UNCTAD secretariat on trade in services and development implications [TD/B/COM.1/55]; the report of the Expert Meeting on Audiovisual Services: Improving Participation of Developing Countries [TD/B/COM.1/56] [YUN 2002, p. 939]; a note by the UNCTAD secretariat on trade, environment and development [TD/B/COM.1/52]; the report of the Expert Meeting on Environmental Requirements and International Trade [TD/B/COM.1/53] [YUN 2002, p. 939]; and a progress report on the implementation of agreed conclusions and recommendations, including the post-Doha follow-up [TD/B/COM.1/57].

In agreed recommendations of 6 February, the Commission called on UNCTAD to intensify its work and activities, particularly in the follow-up to the post-Doha work programme, taking into account the special needs of LDCs; to monitor the progress on the Doha work programme regularly from the point of view of development issues; and to provide substantive support to various WTO bodies.

The Commission recommended that UNCTAD continue its policy-oriented analysis and capacity-building activities and undertake work on: the impacts of multilateral negotiations and preferential arrangements, particularly with respect to the competitiveness of commodities produced and traded by developing countries; the distribution of value added along the supply chain for commodities of export interest to developing countries, and the opportunities for diversification of the commodity sector in developing countries; policy options for dealing with commodity market imbalances and their negative impact on development and disadvantaged groups; assistance to developing countries in formulating policies for diversifying their exports and increasing their competitiveness; assessing the service sectors in developing countries and improving statistics and data on services production and trade, identifying export opportunities in services sectors of interest to developing countries; identifying modalities to operationalize article IV in the context of the negotiations under the General Agreement on Trade in Services (GATS); analysing ways to facilitate exports of labour-intensive services through GATS mode 4 (temporary movement of natural persons), and assisting developing countries to strengthen their negotiating capacities, particularly in the GATS requests and offers process; exploring the possibility of creating a consultative group on environmental requirements and international trade; promoting the UNCTAD/Food and Agriculture Organization of the United Nations (FAO)/IFOAM (International Federation of Organic Agriculture Movements) Task Force on Harmonization and Equivalence in Organic Agriculture; facilitating access to scientific and technical advice on environmental, sanitary and phytosanitary measures and the impact of new technologies, particularly in the context of the UNCTAD Science and Technology Diplomacy Initiative; strengthening the Capacity-Building Task Force of the United Nations Environment Programme (UNEP)/UNCTAD, particularly in the post-Doha context; strengthening work under the BIOTRADE programme, in particular in the follow-up to partnerships launched at the World Summit on Sustainable Development [YUN 2002, p. 821], to promote trade, export diversification and investment in support of the sustainable use of biodiversity; continuing work on standard-setting and harmonization of environmental and health regulations, considering the development dimension; and analysing the trade investment implications of multilateral environmental agreements.

The Commission encouraged Governments to support UNCTAD's work on commodities and its application in developing countries through the provision of extrabudgetary resources for expanded research, country-level activities and technical cooperation.

At its thirty-first executive session on 10 March [A/58/15], TDB took note of the Commission's report and endorsed its recommendations.

Subsidiary bodies. In 2003, a number of expert meetings took place, all in Geneva, on issues to be considered by the Commission in 2004.

The Expert Meeting on Definitions and Dimensions of Environmental Goods and Services in Trade and Development (9-11 July) [TD/B/COM.1/59] had before it an UNCTAD background note on the subject [TD/B/COM.1/EM.21/2], which discussed definitions; trade; the WTO Doha work programme; and potential benefits for developing countries.

The Meeting recommended action to be taken at the national level, including development of a list of environmental goods that reflected a country's sustainable development and trade interests; the implementation of measures that translated environmental, human health and resource management needs into demand for environmental goods and services; and policy coordination aimed at the development of the various related sectors and trade liberalization. It requested the international community to, among other things, develop a consensus on environmental services classification and greater policy coherence between provisions on environmental goods and services in the trading system. UNCTAD should continue to assist developing countries in organizing national policy dialogues, and undertake studies to clarify issues related to the liberalization of trade in environmental services. It should also assist those countries to promote exports of environmentally preferable products through appropriate capacity-building activities.

The Expert Meeting on the Market Access Issues in Mode 4 (Movement of Natural Persons to Supply Services) and Effective Implementation of Article IV on Increasing the Participation of Developing Countries (29-31 July) [TD/B/COM.1/64] had before it an UNCTAD secretariat note [TD/B/COM.1/EM.22/2] on the subject.

The Expert Meeting invited UNCTAD to continue working in trade-related areas of the movement of natural persons. In particular, it should continue the dialogue on conceptual, policy, legal, institutional and administrative frameworks facilitating movement of natural persons to supply services; explore mechanisms for granting GATS visas and for expediting administrative services; help improve mode 4 statistics and strengthen the capacities of Governments in managing the trade agenda surrounding mode 4 issues; analyse national and regional experiences; and undertake studies and organize ad hoc expert meetings to discuss specific issues.

The Expert Meeting on Market Entry Conditions Affecting Competitiveness and Exports of Goods and Services of Developing Countries: Large Distribution Networks, Taking into Account the Special Needs of LDCs (3-5 November) [TD/B/COM.1/66] had before it an UNCTAD secretariat note on the subject [TD/B/COM.1/EM.23/2]. The Expert Meeting concluded that negotiations on distribution services were related to those on the other service sectors, and with agriculture and industry. It highlighted a number of issues to be explored in informing developing countries' negotiations on distribution services, including the effect of the evolution of those services on small and medium-sized enterprises in developing countries; ways to enable developing countries to gain access to new distribution technologies; and how to help developing countries overcome the risks related to liberalization of distribution services through a safeguard mechanism. Participants agreed that UNCTAD would continue to investigate those questions and to provide developing countries with analytical inputs and technical assistance to enhance their ability to assess the challenges and opportunities in distribution services and participate effectively in WTO-related negotiations.

Interdependence and global economic issues

TDB, at its fiftieth session (Geneva, 6-17 October) [A/58/15], considered interdependence and global economic issues from a trade and development perspective: capital accumulation, economic growth and structural change. Participants agreed that short-term prospects for global growth, though more positive than suggested in the *Trade and Development Report, 2003* [Sales No. E.03.II.D.7], continued to be troubled by uncertainties and imbalances, with negative consequences for developing countries. They underlined the need for firm action by developed countries to stimulate growth and ensure a smooth and orderly rebalancing of the world economy. While a more favourable global environment was required to accelerate development, developing countries should engage in market-oriented reforms and the formulation of proactive monetary, financial and industrial policies. They should open to the world economy gradually and reduce their dependence on primary commodities. There was agreement about the need to resume multilateral trade negotiations as soon as possible, as further progress in reforming the international trading system was desirable for the entire international community. Developing countries in particular stressed the urgency of strengthening the development dimension in the multilateral trading system if globalization was to generate benefits for all countries. To put the Doha round of trade negotiations back on track, the particular needs and interests of developing countries, particularly in agriculture, should be taken into account. Developed countries were called upon to liberalize their trade regimes further, while developing countries were encouraged to open their markets increasingly to each other's exports. Systematic efforts were also needed to achieve greater coherence between the international trading and financial systems. There was also a need for an integrated approach to global economic governance and for concrete and sufficiently funded programmes to protect developing countries against the impact of exter-

Trade promotion and facilitation

In 2003, UN bodies continued to assist developing countries and transition economies in promoting their exports and facilitating their integration into the multilateral trading system. The International Trade Centre was the main originator of technical cooperation projects in that area.

International Trade Centre

During 2003, the International Trade Centre (ITC), under the joint sponsorship of UNCTAD and WTO, increased its delivery of technical cooperation programmes by 19 per cent to $20.1 million from $16.9 million in 2002 [ITC/AG (XXXVII)/197].

ITC focused on positioning, performance and partnership. It consolidated its niche position in trade-related technical assistance by fostering and contributing specialized and business-oriented inputs to inter-agency consortiums, building field-level interventions around competitiveness enhancement tools and advocating the international competitiveness of the small and medium-sized enterprises sector in global initiatives. ITC's Competitive Tool Kit was packaged into customized bundles relevant to specific needs, and was actively promoted through Competitiveness Tools Fairs. ITC's Latin American and Caribbean programme expanded, while its Africa programme achieved modest growth. However, overall, the cooperation programme with LDCs declined, as did the programme covering Central and Eastern Europe and CIS countries.

Africa continued to be the region of focus, with the Joint ITC/UNCTAD/WTO Integrated Technical Assistance Programme in Selected Least-Developed and Other African Countries (JITAP) entering its second phase. JITAP's focus continued to be on capacity-building within the public sector for WTO compliance and negotiations, and enhancing the private sector's ability to respond competitively to the emerging multilateral trading system. However, ITC's component was adjusted to highlight local design and implementation, with ITC providing support tools and related guidance. In collaboration with the Trade Facilitation Office Canada (TFOC), ITC launched the pilot phase of the multi-year Programme for Building African Capacity for Trade, in Ghana, Senegal, South Africa and the United Republic of Tanzania, which sought to have an impact on trade performance through the joint application of customized tools from ITC, TFOC and other sources. A subregional economic integration project for Central African States also became operational, with UNDP funding. ITC implemented national-level projects in the Gambia, Mauritania, Uganda and the United Republic of Tanzania, and carried out project design work in Burundi, Ethiopia, Guinea, Lesotho, Madagascar and Senegal.

In the Arab region, technical cooperation in Algeria and Mauritania focused on trade information and institution-strengthening and on banking and financial sector reform in Algeria. It also supported the competitiveness of specific export-oriented companies in Morocco. Other countries benefiting from its support included Djibouti, the United Arab Emirates and Yemen.

In Asia, ITC collaborated with UNCTAD in implementing a multilateral trading system–related project in Bangladesh and undertook programme development activities for large-scale, integrated projects in Pakistan, Sri Lanka and Viet Nam. National projects were designed in Cambodia and the Lao People's Democratic Republic. The first phase of a regional trade promotion programme covering Kazakhstan, Kyrgyzstan, Tajikistan and Uzbekistan was completed and follow-up national assistance projects approved. Export-led poverty reduction pilot projects became operational in Cambodia and in China's Shaanxi Province.

In Eastern Europe, comprehensive technical cooperation projects were designed in Bulgaria, the Republic of Moldova and Romania, and programme activities undertaken in Serbia and Montenegro and the Russian Federation. A regional executive forum was organized in Sofia, Bulgaria, with the participation of strategy teams from Albania, Belarus, Bosnia and Herzegovina, Bulgaria, Moldova, Romania, Serbia and Montenegro and Ukraine, in conjunction with Bulgarian institutions, to review strategic approaches to competitiveness enhancement and export development, identify technical cooperation needs and broaden ITC partnerships.

In Latin America and the Caribbean, where its presence had been limited, ITC's priority objective in 2003 was to increase its involvement in the region. In its only large-scale national project, in Bolivia, emphasis was placed on upgrading the export support programmes of public and private sector trade support institutions and on developing the management competencies of participating enterprises. In Haiti, it completed a project covering the legal aspects of trade, institutional support to the Ministry of Trade and Industry and the assessment of export potential. Elsewhere in the region, assistance was provided to Cuba and El Salvador to prepare for changes in global trade in textiles and clothing, and to strategy teams in Jamaica and Saint Lucia piloting ITC's strategy process tool, the National Export Strategy Template. Technical cooperation in trade support network building was provided to Brazil, Panama and Venezuela, and in the development of information technology exports to Cuba. The TradeMap and ProductMap programmes were launched in Cuba and Guatemala, together with market analysis and associated capacity-building activities, while the E-Trade Bridge Programme supported Ecuador and El Salvador, which, with Bolivia and Brazil, launched initiatives under ITC's Export-led Poverty Reduction Programme.

JAG action. The ITC Joint Advisory Group (JAG) held its thirty-sixth session in Geneva from 28 April to 2 May [ITC/AG(XXXVI)/195]. It had before it reports on ITC activities in 2002 [YUN 2002, p. 940] and technical cooperation projects in 2002 [ITC/AG(XXXVI)/193/Add.1,2] and the report of the ITC Global Trust Fund's Consultative Committee [ITC/AG(XXXVI)/194].

The Group endorsed ITC's planned strategy to maintain focus on areas where it had been successful and welcomed its readiness to venture into new areas. It also endorsed the ITC plan to increase support to the building of public-private sector partnerships and to strengthening business advocacy. It was suggested that ITC establish a special division devoted entirely to the development and management of technical cooperation for the economies in transition, in recognition of the growing importance of those activities in the ITC work programme. In terms of ITC's response to UN issues of common concern—poverty reduction, gender, the environment and technical cooperation among developing countries—the Group noted that ITC's Export-led Poverty Reduction Programme was well under way, and suggested that increased attention be paid to the other areas of concern. Noting the value of ITC's work in sectoral and national export strategy, representatives encouraged ITC to continue its work with a view to becoming the lead reference centre in strategy design and management. The Group recommended that ITC should take a medium-term approach to technical assistance, irrespective of the programme, and emphasized the importance of ITC ensuring that resources were available to maintain field-level support once initial interventions had been completed. It generally endorsed the ITC strategy for growth, based on the three principles outlined by the Executive Director: remaining focused on what it did best; continuing to innovate technical assistance approaches and programmes; and working towards greater field-level impact. The Group urged ITC to continue to measure its performance in terms of quality of contribution and impact, rather than in terms of number of activities.

The Group endorsed a proposal for an independent, external evaluation of ITC.

Pledges of trust fund contributions to ITC were announced by Canada, Denmark, Finland, France, India, Ireland, Italy, the Netherlands, Norway, Sweden, Switzerland, the United Kingdom and the United States.

TDB, at its thirty-first executive session on 10 March, adopted a decision [A/58/15 (dec. 475(EX-31))] in which it took the view that JAG documentation should be issued in all six official languages. It recommended that the General Assembly consider the proposal.

In **resolution 57/312** of 18 June (see below), the Assembly requested the Secretary-General to provide for documentation services in Arabic and Chinese for JAG in the proposed programme budget for the 2004-2005 biennium.

ITC administrative arrangements

In accordance with arrangements approved by the General Assembly in resolution 53/411 B [YUN 1998, p. 888], the Secretary-General, in March, submitted an outline of the proposed programme budget for ITC for the 2004-2005 biennium [A/57/761], which contained the ITC budget for the first year of activities for the biennium and a projection of requirements for the second year. Requirements, expressed in Swiss francs (SwF) at 2004-2005 rates, were estimated at SwF 33,126,300 for 2004 and SwF 33,523,500 for 2005. Since SwF 347,500 from various sources would be available to ITC annually, the annual contribution of each organization (the United Nations and WTO) was estimated at SwF 16,389,400 for 2004 and SwF 16,588,000 for 2005.

Having considered the Secretary-General's report, the Advisory Committee on Administrative and Budgetary Questions (ACABQ), in May [A/57/7/Add.26], recommended that the Assembly take note of the resources proposed in the ITC budget outline.

GENERAL ASSEMBLY ACTION

On 18 June [meeting 90], the General Assembly, on the recommendation of the Fifth (Administrative and Budgetary) Committee [A/57/649/Add.2], adopted **resolution 57/312** without vote [agenda item 112].

Outline of the proposed programme budget for the biennium 2004-2005 for the International Trade Centre UNCTAD/WTO

The General Assembly

1. *Takes note* of the report of the Secretary-General on the outline of the proposed programme budget for

the biennium 2004-2005 for the International Trade Centre UNCTAD/WTO, and concurs with the observations and recommendations of the Advisory Committee on Administrative and Budgetary Questions thereon;

2. *Requests* the Secretary-General to provide for documentation services in Arabic and Chinese for the Joint Advisory Group of the International Trade Centre UNCTAD/WTO in the proposed programme budget of the Centre for the biennium 2004-2005;

3. *Recalls* its decision 57/572 of 20 December 2002, and requests the Secretary-General to initiate consultations with the International Trade Centre UNCTAD/WTO and the World Trade Organization for a joint review of the administrative arrangements for the Centre and to submit a report thereon to the General Assembly at its fifty-eighth session;

4. *Reaffirms* paragraph 30 of its resolution 56/253 of 24 December 2001.

ACABQ, having considered the proposed programme budget for 2004-2005 for ITC [A/58/6 (sect. 13)/Add.1], recommended, in its October report [A/58/7/Add.7], that the resources for ITC be reduced by SwF 26,000 to an amount of SwF 64,268,400 for the biennium.

The Assembly, in **resolution 58/272**, section XII of 23 December (see p. 1419), approved an amount of $23,472,200 for the 2004-2005 biennium.

Enterprise, business facilitation and development

The Commission on Enterprise, Business Facilitation and Development, at its seventh session (Geneva, 24-27 February) [TD/B/EX(31)/5], had before it an UNCTAD secretariat report on improving the competitiveness of small and medium-sized enterprises (SMEs) through enhancing productive capacity [TD/B/COM.3/51 & Corr.1 & Add.1], a background paper on developments and main issues in e-commerce and information and communication technologies (ICT) [TD/B/COM.3/49], an UNCTAD secretariat note on efficient transport and trade facilitation to improve participation by developing countries in international trade [TD/B/COM.3/53] and a progress report on the implementation of the Commission's agreed conclusions and recommendations at its sixth session [YUN 2002, p. 942], including post-Doha follow-up [TD/B/COM.3/54]. It also had before it a number of reports of expert meetings held in 2002 [YUN 2002, p. 943].

In agreed recommendations, the Commission requested UNCTAD, in order to improve coherence between macroeconomic and microeconomic policies, to disseminate as widely as possible its findings on the main components of proactive competitiveness policies, as contained in the issues paper on improving the competitiveness of SMEs through enhancing productive capacity [TD/B/COM.3/51/Add.1]. It should assess the competitiveness policies of developing countries that had widely improved their performance; assess the linkage between investment, trade and technology transfer; and explore measures that promoted access to technology by developing countries and built domestic capacities. UNCTAD should further investigate the coherence between competitiveness policies for microstimulation and multilateral commitments and requirements, taking into account national development strategies and objectives.

The Commission also requested UNCTAD to enhance efforts to help developing countries and transition economies to promote dynamic and competitive enterprises through the EMPRETEC programme, including through implementation of the recommendations arising from its evaluation. The programme should also be strengthened and expanded.

UNCTAD should monitor developments relating to efficient transport and trade facilitation, including multimodal transport and logistic services, and analyse their implications for developing countries, and continue to provide guidance and assistance to developing countries in the use of ICT for international transport services and trade facilitation. It should study, analyse and disseminate information on the impact of new security initiatives on the international trade and transport of developing countries, contribute to the work of intergovernmental organizations in developing uniform international legal instruments affecting international transport, and disseminate information on their implications for developing countries.

UNCTAD should continue to analyse developments in trade facilitation and assist developing countries in establishing their related needs and priorities and provide them with negotiating assistance in transport services in the context of GATS, and in identifying international best practices regarding policies promoting and facilitating the adoption of ICT and e-business practices, in coordination with other international organizations.

UNCTAD should continue to promote the elaboration of national and regional e-commerce strategies for development, including by organizing regional events. It should carry out research and analysis regarding e-commerce on issues relevant to the development dimension, including major trends in technology; industries and sectors of development and commercial relevance to developing countries; Internet regulation; and the implications of various legislative approaches to e-commerce, with a view to enhancing the capacity of developing countries to formulate adequate strategies to promote the adoption of ICT, e-business and e-commerce practices by their enterprises and to participate in relevant international discussions. UNCTAD should analyse issues related to the measurement and benchmarking of e-commerce and of the use of ICT by enterprises, and help developing countries to develop indicators and data on e-commerce. As the UN focal point for trade and development, it should continue to make a substantive contribution to the outcome of and follow-up to the World Summit on Sustainable Development [YUN 2002, p. 821].

At its thirty-first executive session in March [A/58/15], TDB took note of the Commission's report and endorsed its recommendations.

Subsidiary bodies. In 2003, a number of expert meetings took place, all in Geneva, on issues to be considered by the Commission in 2004.

The Expert Meeting on Measuring Electronic Commerce as an Instrument for the Development of the Digital Economy (8-10 September) [TD/B/COM.3/61] had before it an UNCTAD secretariat background paper on the subject [TD/B/COM.3/EM.19/2]. The meeting suggested that UNCTAD continue providing forums for experts to further develop conceptual and methodological work on information economy statistics and share best practices. A proposal was made on a set of core indicators for ICT measurement that could be collected by all countries; they would focus on e-readiness and usage indicators for businesses and households. Experts considered that working towards a basic set of core indicators would be the starting point for the creation of an international database on ICT and e-business statistics and would be a desirable objective for future work. They also considered that UNCTAD should assist developing countries to develop their national e-measurement strategies and share models of some specific national/regional surveys on ICT and e-commerce.

The Expert Meeting on the Development of Multimodal Transport and Logistic Services (24-26 September) [TD/B/COM.3/59 & Corr.1] had before it an UNCTAD secretariat paper on the subject [TD/B/COM.3/EM.20/2]. The experts agreed that access to logistics and multimodal transport services was crucial to competitiveness in a globalized economy and many developing countries, especially small island, landlocked and least developed ones, had limited access to those services. To prevent the persistent exclusion of those countries from global production processes, a concerted effort by national Governments and international organizations was needed. UNCTAD, in cooperation with other organizations and developing countries' regional and subregional organizations, was called on to put in place mechanisms to support developing countries' endeavours to participate in and fully benefit from opportunities offered by modern multimodal transport and logistic services. That was considered a crucial element of a coherent strategy for integrating developing countries into the world economy and enhancing a trade-based development process.

Commodities

A joint UNCTAD/DESA report on the world economic situation and prospects [Sales No. E.04.II.C.2] stated that commodity prices improved slightly in 2003, with non-fuel commodity prices increasing by 5.8 per cent in nominal dollar terms over the first 10 months of the year. Over the first three quarters of the year, the UNCTAD combined index for minerals and metals rose by 7.4 per cent and for agricultural raw materials by 11.4 per cent. In contrast, the food index fell by 10 per cent. The recovery largely reflected the weakening of the dollar. However, the economic upturn in major developed economies in the second half of the year and continued high growth of Chinese demand also influenced raw material prices.

Meeting of eminent persons on commodity issues. Pursuant to General Assembly resolution 57/236 [YUN 2002, p. 945], the UNCTAD Secretary-General established a group of eminent persons to examine and report on commodity issues. The report of the group's meeting (Geneva, 22-23 September) [TD/B/50/11] contained recommendations for improving the conditions in commodity markets and for alleviating the poverty of many commodity producers.

TDB, at its fiftieth session (6-17 October) [A/58/15], took note of the group's report and transmitted it to the Assembly for consideration.

The report, which the Secretary-General transmitted to the Assembly by a 2 October note [A/58/401], stated that there was a wide range of actions for improving the conditions on the commodity markets and alleviating the poverty of many commodity producers, including through better crop management systems. The group made short-, medium- and long-term recommendations, drawing particular attention to those for enhanced, equitable and predictable market access for commodities of key importance to developing countries; addressing the problems of oversupply for many commodities; making compensatory financing schemes user-friendly and operational; strengthening capacity and institutions; and pursuing the possibilities for creating a new international diversification fund.

Open-ended panel on commodities

GENERAL ASSEMBLY ACTION

On 16 October [meeting 34], the General Assembly adopted **resolution 58/2** [draft: A/58/L.1] without vote [agenda item 12].

Open-ended panel of the General Assembly on commodities

The General Assembly,

Recalling its resolution 57/236 of 20 December 2002,

1. *Decides* to convene an open-ended panel of the General Assembly on commodities, to be chaired by the President of the General Assembly, with a maximum of six panellists from among the independent eminent persons and lead discussants, on 27 October 2003, from 3 to 5 p.m.;

2. *Also decides* that the President of the General Assembly will present a summary of the discussions of the open-ended panel at the beginning of the debate in the Second Committee on the item dealing with commodities.

Summary of discussions. As requested in resolution 58/2, the Assembly President, in a 2 December note [A/58/615], presented a summary of the discussions of the Assembly's open-ended panel on commodities, which took place on 27 October. The panellists emphasized the long-standing dependence of numerous developing countries on a few commodities for a major part of their income and export earnings. For them, the performance of commodities markets had a major impact on their macroeconomic stability, capacity to meet foreign debt obligations, balance-of-payments performance, success in poverty reduction and overall sustainable development efforts.

Panellists and participants identified a number of macroeconomic patterns of central importance requiring renewed attention by the international community and raised a number of pertinent "new" matters, together with comments/issues raised during the discussions. They emphasized that developing countries alone could not solve the problems in commodities markets arising from defects in the global market. A viable and long-term solution required action by individual countries, as well as joint action by consumers and producers of commodities from developing and developed countries.

Suggestions for future action included calls for the resumption of the Doha negotiations, giving special attention to negotiations on cotton and other commodities; the International Monetary Fund (IMF) should consider the connection between structural adjustment programmes and commodities and the importance of well-functioning compensatory finance systems; UNCTAD, at its eleventh (2004) session, should consider the need to enhance capacity-building initiatives, establish new multi-stakeholder partnerships on commodities and examine the inter-relationship between national development and the global market in detail; commodity-dependency matters should be considered in the implementation of the MDGs; and the United Nations Global Compact [YUN 2000, p. 989] and individual commodity firms and their trade associations should incorporate a commodity focus into ongoing corporate social responsibility efforts.

GENERAL ASSEMBLY ACTION

On 23 December [meeting 78], the General Assembly, on the recommendation of the Second Committee [A/58/481/Add.6], adopted **resolution 58/204** without vote [agenda item 91 *(g)*].

Commodities

The General Assembly,

Recalling its resolution 57/236 of 20 December 2002, and stressing the urgent need to ensure its full implementation,

Recalling also the United Nations Millennium Declaration adopted by heads of State and Government on 8 September 2000,

Taking note of the Programme of Action for the Least Developed Countries for the Decade 2001-2010 and the *Least Developed Countries Report, 2002,*

Taking note also of the Ministerial Declaration of the Fourth Ministerial Conference of the World Trade Organization, held at Doha from 9 to 14 November 2001,

Taking note further of the Monterrey Consensus of the International Conference on Financing for Development,

Taking note of the targets set out in the Rome Declaration on World Food Security and the Plan of Action of the World Food Summit and the outcome document of the World Food Summit: five years later, which reaffirms the pledge to end hunger,

Taking note also of the Plan of Implementation of the World Summit on Sustainable Development ("Johannesburg Plan of Implementation"),

Taking note further of the report of the Trade and Development Board on its fiftieth session and the report of the Secretary-General of the United Nations Conference on Trade and Development on world commodity trends and prospects, containing recommendations for specific actions relating to the particular needs and problems of commodity-dependent developing countries,

Mindful of the opportunity that the eleventh session of the United Nations Conference on Trade and Development, to be held in São Paulo, Brazil, from 13 to 18 June 2004, will offer for the further consideration of proposals to address commodity issues within the framework of the links among trade, investment and finance,

Mindful also that, in 2004, the International Monetary Fund will review its role in assisting low-income countries over the medium term,

Taking note of the summary by the President of the General Assembly of the open-ended panel of the Assembly on commodities,

1. *Takes note* of the report of the Meeting of Eminent Persons on Commodity Issues, held at Geneva on 22 and 23 September 2003, and expresses appreciation for the work of the eminent persons;

2. *Emphasizes* the need for efforts by the developing countries that are heavily dependent on primary commodities to continue to promote a domestic policy and an institutional environment that encourage diversification and liberalization of the trade and export sectors and enhance competitiveness;

3. *Encourages* donor Governments and organizations to increase their financial and technical support for activities aimed at addressing commodity issues, in particular the needs and problems of commodity-dependent developing countries;

4. *Stresses* the importance of a speedy resumption and successful conclusion of the work programme adopted at the Fourth Ministerial Conference of the World Trade Organization, taking into account the needs of the commodity-dependent developing countries;

5. *Invites* the United Nations Conference on Trade and Development and other relevant bodies and organs of the United Nations system to continue to mainstream and accord high priority to programmes on commodity-related issues within their respective mandates;

6. *Welcomes* regular consideration of commodity issues by the Trade and Development Board of the United Nations Conference on Trade and Development;

7. *Invites* non-governmental organizations, civil society and the private sector to initiate programmes of assistance and other innovative initiatives in support of commodity-dependent developing countries;

8. *Notes* the relevance to appropriate governing bodies in the United Nations system and to international commodity bodies of the report of the Meeting of Eminent Persons on Commodity Issues, as well as the summary of discussions in the Trade and Development Board and the Second Committee of the General Assembly, which highlight the importance of finding lasting solutions to the problems faced by commodity-dependent developing countries in their pursuit of the internationally agreed development goals, including those contained in the United Nations Millennium Declaration;

9. *Urges* Governments and invites international financial institutions to continue to assess the effectiveness, including the operationalization and user-friendliness, of the systems for compensatory financing of export-earnings shortfalls, and in this regard stresses the importance of empowering developing-country commodity producers to insure themselves against risk, including natural disasters;

10. *Invites* donor countries and development partners to support the efforts of commodity-dependent developing countries to add value to their products, and reiterates the importance of making progress on the Doha work programme to ensure the sustainability of those efforts;

11. *Requests* the Secretary-General to undertake further open and transparent discussions with all relevant stakeholders on enhancing the impact of the set of existing instruments to support commodity-dependent developing countries in their efforts to diversify their exports, overcome supply-side constraints, strengthen institutions and build knowledge and technical capacity;

12. *Calls upon* the United Nations Conference on Trade and Development and invites other relevant bodies and organs of the United Nations system, as well as other relevant international organizations, to strengthen coherently and within their respective mandates their capacity-building and technical co-operation activities in the fields of policy design and implementation, institution-building, management and utilization of commodity revenues, management of price risk and improvement of supply capacities, including the ability to satisfy quality and other requirements for market entry, and to enhance activities aimed at South-South cooperation in the field of commodities, share experiences and identify best practices for dealing with oversupply situations;

13. *Invites* the United Nations Conference on Trade and Development and all relevant international organizations to continue to analyse trends in commodities and their impact on the development of commodity-dependent developing countries, including on debt sustainability;

14. *Invites* the United Nations Conference on Trade and Development, the Common Fund for Commodities and all other relevant organizations to provide useful, timely, accurate, comprehensive and user-friendly information and analysis on commodities and to enable the use of this information by commodity-dependent developing countries;

15. *Requests* the Department of Public Information of the Secretariat to undertake, within existing budgetary resources, initiatives and activities to raise awareness of the commodities issue and keep it a high priority of Governments, the international community, media, academia and all other relevant stakeholders;

16. *Requests* the Secretary-General to submit to the General Assembly at its fifty-ninth session a report on the implementation of the present resolution, taking into account the provisions of Assembly resolution 57/236.

Individual commodities

Olive oil and table olives. The International Olive Council (23-25 June) extended the International Agreement on Olive Oil and Table Olives, 1986, as amended and extended, 1993 [YUN 1993, p. 760], until 31 December 2004, with effect from 1 July 2003. It also extended until 31 December 2003 the time limit for the deposit of the instrument of accession by Iran. In 2003, the Libyan Arab Jamahiriya acceded to the Agreement, bringing the number of parties to 15.

Coffee. As at 31 December, the International Coffee Agreement 2001 [YUN 2000, p. 905] had 35 signatories and 55 parties. During the year, Benin, Ethiopia, Guatemala, Guinea, Malawi, Portugal, Togo and Zambia became parties. On 21 May, the International Coffee Council extended to 31 May 2004 the time limit for the deposit of instruments of ratification, acceptance, approval or accession and of instruments of ratification, acceptance or approval by States applying the Agreement provisionally.

Cocoa. As at 31 December, the International Cocoa Agreement, 2001 [YUN 2001, p. 880] had 11 signatories and 12 parties. During the year, the Dominican Republic and Papua New Guinea signed the Agreement, while Cameroon, Ecuador, Gabon, Ghana, Nigeria, Slovakia and Switzerland became parties. At meetings in March, June and September, the International Cocoa Council extended until 30 September 2010 the period for signing the Agreement, and the time limit for the deposit of instruments of ratification, acceptance or approval. It also agreed that the Agreement would enter into force provisionally on 1 October 2003.

Common Fund for Commodities

The 1980 Agreement establishing the Common Fund for Commodities [YUN 1980, p. 621], a mechanism intended to stabilize the commodities market by helping to finance buffer stocks of specific commodities, as well as commodity development activities such as research and marketing, had entered into force in 1989 and the Fund became operational later that year.

As at 31 December 2003, the number of parties to the Agreement stood at 110.

Finance

Financial policy

The *World Economic and Social Survey 2003* [Sales No. E.03.II.C.1] stated that the immediate reaction to the economic slowdown in 2001 was substantial reductions in policy interest rates in developed countries. Inflation was not seen as a major threat in the majority of developed countries and low interest rates were maintained in most countries throughout the year and into early 2003. Some central banks, notably the Federal Reserve of the United States, brought interest rates to unusually low levels. The inflation-targeting rule followed by the European Central Bank until early 2003 delayed its cuts in policy interest rates until March. At the same time, it changed its inflation objective of 2 per cent from a ceiling to a target, allowing greater flexibility in its monetary policy. In several countries in Eastern Europe, interest rates were reduced in 2002, primarily to dampen any appreciation of the exchange rate so as to maintain competitiveness.

Most countries had less scope for expansionary fiscal policies because of the size of their fiscal deficits. The major exception was the United States, where increased central government expenditures and reduced taxation in 2002 produced a sizeable fiscal stimulus and a growing fiscal deficit. In Western Europe, fiscal policy was slightly expansionary in 2002, although some countries were under pressure to meet the 3 per cent deficit ceiling of the Stability and Growth Pact. Japan was in a difficult financial position and any further sizeable fiscal stimulus would risk damaging economic confidence. Many developing countries and some economies in transition improved their fiscal positions in the 1990s, but deficits remained a problem. China and most economies in East Asia were able to use monetary and fiscal instruments in the appropriate counter-cyclical manner during the period of slow growth. In contrast, most economies in Africa and Latin America had to give priority to addressing their macroeconomic imbalances, which usually required using their macroeconomic policy instruments in a restrictive, currently pro-cyclical manner, rather than as a means of offsetting sluggish conditions.

A joint DESA/UNCTAD report on the world economic situation and prospects [Sales No. E.04.II.C.2], based on information available as at 30 November, stated that, with economic recovery continuing, macroeconomic policy in many economies, particularly the largest, was accommodating or stimulatory, but was expected to shift to neutral. A three-year phase of global monetary easing was about to end, to be replaced by a phase of tightening. Since late 2000, the central banks in a majority of economies had been reducing interest rates to alleviate the adverse effects of the cyclical downturn, to stabilize financial markets amidst plummeting equity markets and exogenous shocks, and to stimulate demand. Interest rates were further reduced in 2003, particularly during the period of heightened uncertainties associated with the possibility of war in Iraq and the outbreak of the SARS virus. The central banks in a few developed economies had already started tightening monetary policy and, as the recovery strengthened further, central banks in other major developed countries were expected to raise interest rates, probably in the second half of 2004.

Fiscal policy actions were much less homogeneous across countries. Some economies, such as the United States and a number of Asian countries, adopted sizeable stimuli, but the policy stance in many other economies was only modestly stimulatory or neutral, while a third group of economies adhered to restrictive fiscal policies. It was suggested that policy makers might consider whether rule-based policies, such as the inflation-targeting mechanism adopted by a growing number of economies in recent years, were too rigid to respond effectively to shocks, particularly in an economic downturn.

Among developing countries, the key questions were whether the conditionalities associated with the programmes of the international financial institutions were pro-cyclical, leading to unnecessary losses in output and employment, and how to enhance macroeconomic management for those developing countries facing global economic integration.

Financial flows

The joint DESA/UNCTAD report on the world economic situation and prospects [Sales No. E.04.II.C.2] stated that the net transfer of financial resources from developing countries in 2003 was similar in magnitude to that in 2002, when it reached a peak of $192 billion. There was also a net outward financial transfer from economies in transition in 2003. Among the financial components of the net transfer were an increase in capital flows to some countries and an increase in foreign exchange reserves by others, particularly those with large trade surpluses. At the regional level, Latin America experienced an increase in exports and a deceleration in the decline in imports, but that was not enough to reverse the large net outward transfer. Likewise, the large net transfer from East Asia resulting from its strong export growth continued in 2003.

In terms of inflows, developing countries received an estimated $95 billion in net capital flows in 2003, a modest increase from 2002, in the form of foreign direct investment (FDI), official loans and grants. However, FDI in developing countries did not rebound from the decline of 2002. FDI flows to Latin America continued to decrease, while those to Africa rose. A small increase in FDI to Eastern and Southern Asia was largely due to record flows to China. FDI in transition economies remained strong. Official financial flows reflected a mix of reduced anticrisis multilateral lending, especially by IMF, and increased aid flows. Major disbursements in 2003 were made to Argentina, Brazil and Turkey.

International financial system

Report of Secretary-General. In response to General Assembly resolution 57/241 [YUN 2002, p. 949], the Secretary-General submitted a 16 September report on the international financial system and development [A/58/369]. He highlighted recent developments in the international financial system that had special relevance to development, provided estimates of the mainly negative net transfer of financial resources of groups of developing countries in 2002 and updated developments in international financial reform. The issues highlighted in the report were among those discussed in the Secretary-General's report prepared for the High-level Dialogue on Financing for Development [A/58/216] (see p. 988). Specific conclusions and recommendations on relevant issues were addressed in that report.

IMF/World Bank Development Committee. The Joint IMF/World Bank Development Committee, in a communiqué issued following its meeting on 22 September (Dubai, United Arab Emirates), renewed its commitment to achieving the MDGs and to continuing its work on implementing the strategies, partnerships and actions agreed at the Fifth WTO Ministerial Meeting (see p. 1535), the International Conference on Financing for Development [YUN 2002, p. 953] and the World Summit on Sustainable Development [ibid., p. 821]. It agreed on the urgent need to intensify efforts if the MDGs were to be met, with enhanced concerted actions by developing and developed countries and international institutions.

GENERAL ASSEMBLY ACTION

On 23 December [meeting 78], the General Assembly, on the recommendation of the Second Committee [A/58/481/Add.4], adopted **resolution 58/202** without vote [agenda item 91 (d)].

International financial system and development
The General Assembly,

Recalling its resolutions 55/186 of 20 December 2000 and 56/181 of 21 December 2001, both entitled "Towards a strengthened and stable international financial architecture responsive to the priorities of growth and development, especially in developing countries, and to the promotion of economic and social equity", as well as its resolution 57/241 of 20 December 2002,

Recalling also the United Nations Millennium Declaration adopted by the heads of State and Government on 8 September 2000, its resolution 56/210 B of 9 July 2002, in which it endorsed the Monterrey Consensus of the International Conference on Financing for Development, and the Plan of Implementation of the World Summit on Sustainable Development ("Johannesburg Plan of Implementation"), adopted on 4 September 2002,

Emphasizing that the international financial system should support sustainable development, sustained economic growth and poverty reduction while allowing for the coherent mobilization of all sources of financing for development, including the mobilization of domestic resources, international investment flows, official development assistance, external debt relief and an open, equitable, rule-based, predictable and non-discriminatory global trading system,

Reiterating that success in meeting the objectives of development and poverty eradication depends on good governance within each country and at the international level, and stressing that sound economic policies, solid democratic institutions responsive to the needs of the people and improved infrastructure are the basis for sustained economic growth, poverty eradication and employment creation,

Reiterating also the need to strengthen the leadership role of the United Nations in promoting development,

Welcoming the growing interaction between the United Nations and the international financial and trade institutions, consistent with the relevant provisions of the Charter of the United Nations and in accordance with related agreements,

Encouraging further progress on the issue of participation of developing countries in international economic decision-making and norm-setting processes, including those of the Bretton Woods institutions and other economic and financial institutions and ad hoc groupings, while welcoming the steps that have been taken with a view to strengthening the capacity of developing countries to participate effectively in the international financial institutions,

Recognizing the urgent need to enhance the coherence, governance and consistency of the international monetary, financial and trading systems, and the importance of ensuring their openness, fairness and inclusiveness in order to complement national development efforts to ensure sustained economic growth and the achievement of the internationally agreed development goals, including those contained in the Millennium Declaration,

1. *Takes note* of the report of the Secretary-General;

2. *Recognizes* the increasing initial signs that economic activity is gradually strengthening in many economies, while noting with concern the unevenness of the recovery of the global economy, which challenges efforts of developing countries to eradicate poverty and ensure sustained economic growth, and stresses the importance of cooperative efforts by all countries and institutions to cope with risks of financial instability and ensure a strong and steady recovery;

3. *Invites* developed countries, in particular major industrialized economies, to take into account the effect of their macroeconomic policies on international growth and development;

4. *Recognizes* the concern about the fact that in 2002 developing countries as a whole made net outward transfers of financial resources for the sixth consecutive year, and underscores the need for measures, as appropriate, at the national and international levels to address this issue, while taking note of the efforts that have been made thus far to this end and of the fact that for some developing countries those transfers, at the present time, indicate positive developments in the trade balance, which are required, inter alia, for debt repayment and which allow for the purchase of foreign assets;

5. *Underlines* the importance of adopting effective measures, including new financial mechanisms, as appropriate, to support the efforts of developing countries to achieve sustained economic growth, sustainable development, poverty reduction and the strengthening of their democratic systems, while reaffirming that each country has primary responsibility for its own economic and social development and that national policies have the leading role in the development process;

6. *Stresses* the importance of strong domestic institutions to promote business activities and financial stability for the achievement of growth and development, inter alia, through sound macroeconomic policies and policies aimed at strengthening the regulatory systems of the corporate, financial and banking sectors, and also stresses that international cooperation initiatives in those areas should encourage flows of capital to developing countries;

7. *Underlines* the importance of promoting international financial stability and sustainable growth, and welcomes the efforts undertaken to this end by the International Monetary Fund and the Financial Stability Forum, as well as the International Monetary and Financial Committee's consideration of ways to sharpen tools designed to promote international financial stability and enhance crisis prevention, including through an even-handed implementation of surveillance and a sharpening of surveillance on capital markets and systemically and regionally important countries, with a view, inter alia, to early identification of problems and risks and the fostering of appropriate policy responses; the provision of adequate precautionary support to deal with external crises; and further improvements in the transparency of macroeconomic data and statistical information on international capital flows;

8. *Reiterates* in this regard that measures to mitigate the impact of excessive volatility of short-term capital flows and to improve transparency of and information about financial flows are important and must be considered;

9. *Notes* the impact of financial crises and risks of contagion on developing countries and countries with economies in transition, regardless of their size, and underlines the need to ensure that the international financial institutions, including the International Monetary Fund, have a suitable array of financial facilities and resources to respond in a timely and appropriate way, in accordance with their policies, to such crises;

10. *Notes also* the importance of advancing current efforts to reform the international financial architecture, as envisaged in the Monterrey Consensus, emphasizes that those efforts need to include the effective participation of developing countries and countries with economies in transition, and in this regard encourages the International Monetary Fund and the World Bank to continue examining the issues of the voice and effective participation of those countries, as provided for in the communiqués of the International Monetary and Financial Committee and the Development Committee at their last meetings, held in Dubai, United Arab Emirates, on 21 and 22 September 2003, and looks forward to the consideration of a road map on the issue at their next meeting, in April 2004;

11. *Welcomes* the ongoing work of the International Monetary Fund on quotas, and notes the conclusion of the Fund's Twelfth General Review of Quotas, the report on which indicated the adequacy of the current level of Fund resources and the intention of the Executive Board, during the period of the Thirteenth General Review, to monitor closely and assess the adequacy of Fund resources, to consider measures to achieve a

distribution of quotas that reflects developments in the world economy and to consider measures to strengthen the governance of the Fund;

12. *Emphasizes* that it is essential to ensure the effective and equitable participation of developing countries in the formulation of financial standards and codes, and underscores the need to ensure their implementation, on a voluntary and progressive basis, as a contribution to reducing vulnerability to financial crisis and contagion;

13. *Invites* the multilateral and regional development banks and development funds to continue to play a vital role in serving the development needs of developing countries and countries with economies in transition, including through coordinated action, as appropriate, and stresses that strengthened regional development banks and subregional financial institutions add flexible financial support to national and regional development efforts, enhancing their ownership and overall efficiency, and are an essential source of knowledge and expertise for their developing country members;

14. *Calls upon* multilateral financial institutions, in providing policy advice and financial support to member countries, to work on the basis of nationally owned reform and development strategies, to pay due regard to the special needs and implementing capacities of developing countries and countries with economies in transition and to minimize the negative impacts of the adjustment programmes on the vulnerable segments of society, while taking into account the importance of gender-sensitive employment and poverty eradication policies and strategies;

15. *Reiterates* the importance of the orderly resolution of sovereign debt crises, notes the increasing voluntary use of collective action clauses in international sovereign bonds, and takes note of the efforts led by sovereign debtors and private creditors to develop a voluntary code of conduct for the resolution of sovereign debt crises;

16. *Encourages* the efforts, including those of the Bretton Woods institutions, to improve the assessment of debt sustainability in low- and middle-income countries through, inter alia, the development of better tools to deal with exogenous shocks and the need to take country-specific factors into account;

17. *Also encourages* the consideration of proposals to generate innovative public and private mechanisms for financing development, without unduly burdening developing countries, and the study, in the appropriate forums, of the results of the analysis requested from the Secretary-General on possible innovative sources of finance, taking note of the proposal to use special drawing rights allocations for development purposes, bearing in mind that any assessment of special drawing rights allocations must respect the Articles of Agreement of the International Monetary Fund and the established rules of procedure of the Fund, which requires taking into account the global need for liquidity at the international level;

18. *Requests* the Secretary-General to report to the General Assembly at its fifty-ninth session on the implementation of the present resolution;

19. *Decides* to include in the provisional agenda of its fifty-ninth session, under the item entitled "Macro-economic policy questions", the sub-item entitled "International financial system and development".

Debt problems of developing countries

Report of Secretary-General. In response to General Assembly resolution 57/240 [YUN 2002, p. 951], the Secretary-General submitted a September report [A/58/290] on the external debt crisis and development. It described recent trends in international debt indicators and capital flows; reserve accumulation and net transfer of resources; private capital flows to developing countries in a longer-term perspective; official debt, in particular issues related to the implementation of the Heavily Indebted Poor Countries (HIPC) Initiative and the Paris Club (a group of creditor countries) agreements; and sovereign debt restructuring. The report complemented the Secretary-General's report for the High-level Dialogue on Financing for Development (see p. 988), which recommended steps towards a more lasting solution to developing countries and transition economies' debt problems.

The Secretary-General stated that the total stock of external debt of developing countries and economies in transition increased by about $52 billion, or 2.2 per cent, in 2002, while both private debt and short-term debt declined. Debt-service payments fell by almost 10 per cent in 2002 because of lower international interest rates. The ratios of total debt and debt service to exports of goods and services continued to decline. Among developing regions, Latin America had the highest debt/export ratio with external debt equivalent to 173.6 per cent of exports. The unprecedented increase (some $163 billion) in the international reserves of developing countries and economies in transition led to a strong improvement in the ratio of short-term debt to international reserves in all regions, with the exception of Latin America. Despite some further improvement in 2002, that indicator continued to be the highest for sub-Saharan Africa, excluding South Africa, where short-term debt at the end of 2002 was equivalent to 76 per cent of international reserves.

Although the HIPC Initiative was recognized for addressing development constraints and poverty alleviation in many of the poorest countries, there had been doubts in recent years that the Initiative in its current form and scope could meet those objectives. HIPC ministers had suggested that the Initiative should be surrounded with a wider framework of measures to overcome shocks and stressed the need for cheap, automatic and rapidly available contingency financing by the international financial institutions, based on annual reassessments of debt sustainability.

Recent Paris Club activity continued to focus on HIPC Initiative implementation. In late 2002/early 2003, 10 countries (8 of them HIPCs) concluded new agreements on debt rescheduling or restructuring. The G-8 (major industrialized countries) Finance Ministers, at their meeting in Deauville, France, in May, made proposals for reforming the Paris Club, including measures to remove the artificial ceiling on debt rescheduling or cancellation, for debt reduction in exceptional cases for countries not qualifying for debt relief under the HIPC Initiative, and comparable treatment by both private and Paris Club creditors.

The Secretary-General concluded that although bilateral official creditors continued to provide relief to low-income countries, it was not sufficient to achieve long-term debt sustainability and significant poverty reduction. Given the continuing difficulties facing HIPCs and other heavily indebted countries in complying with debt relief conditionality, he suggested that donors and international financial institutions provide additional support in the design and implementation of their Poverty Reduction Strategy Papers, giving greater attention to poverty and social impact analysis and technical assistance to conduct such analyses on their own. The number of low- and middle-income developing countries and economies in transition with large debt burdens that were not eligible for debt relief under the HIPC Initiative raised the need for a greater safety margin to protect against unanticipated adverse developments, which, with effective contingency financing mechanisms, including grant financing, could help eliminate the need for repeated rescheduling. A framework was also needed to deal comprehensively with international sovereign debt of insolvent developing countries.

Other actions. The WTO Working Group on Trade, Debt and Finance, established by the Fourth WTO Ministerial Conference [YUN 2001, p. 1432] to examine the relationship between trade, debt and finance and to recommend steps for enhancing the capacity of the multilateral trading system to contribute to a durable solution to the problem of external indebtedness of developing and least developed countries, met on 28 March and 5 June. Its report, which described progress in examining its mandate, was submitted to the WTO General Council on 11 July [WT/WORKING GROUP/GTDF/2].

The Joint IMF/World Bank Development Committee (Dubai, 22 September) urged all official and commercial creditors that had not yet done so to participate in the HIPC Initiative. It looked forward to a report being prepared by the Bank and the Fund on a forward-looking framework for debt sustainability in low-income countries, for review at its next meeting. It also encouraged further work on ways to help reduce the vulnerability of those countries to exogenous shocks.

The joint DESA/UNCTAD report on the world economic situation and prospects 2004 [Sales No. E.04.II.C.2] reported that, in October, the Paris Club agreed to change the approach to its treatment of the external debt of debt-crisis countries not covered by the HIPC Initiative. The new policy, called the Evian Approach, which put into effect the May agreement of the G-8 Finance Ministers (see above), outlined more flexible procedures and established a set of exceptional circumstances when it might agree to reduce the debt of countries previously eligible only for postponement of debt-servicing payments.

GENERAL ASSEMBLY ACTION

On 23 December [meeting 78], the General Assembly, on the recommendation of the Second Committee [A/58/481/Add.5], adopted **resolution 58/203** without vote [agenda item 91(e)].

External debt crisis and development

The General Assembly,

Recalling its resolutions 51/164 of 16 December 1996, 52/185 of 18 December 1997, 53/175 of 15 December 1998, 54/202 of 22 December 1999, 55/184 of 20 December 2000, 56/184 of 21 December 2001 and 57/240 of 20 December 2002 on enhancing international cooperation towards a durable solution to the external debt problems of developing countries,

Recalling also the United Nations Millennium Declaration adopted by heads of State and Government on 8 September 2000,

Reaffirming the Monterrey Consensus of the International Conference on Financing for Development, which recognizes sustainable debt financing as an important element for mobilizing resources for public and private investment,

Recalling its resolution 57/270 B of 23 June 2003 on the integrated and coordinated implementation of and follow-up to the outcomes of the major United Nations conferences and summits in the economic and social fields,

Concerned that the current global economic recovery is uneven but determined to ensure that it leads to sustained world economic growth, to sustainable development and to a durable solution of the external debt problems of developing countries,

Noting in this regard that the total debt stock of the developing countries rose from 1,421.6 billion dollars in 1990 to 2,384.2 billion dollars in 2002,

Noting with great concern that the continuing debt and debt-servicing problems of the heavily indebted poor developing countries constitute one of the many elements that adversely affect their sustainable development efforts, and bearing in mind their impact on the achievement of the internationally agreed development goals, including those contained in the Millennium Declaration,

Noting with concern the fact that some highly indebted, low- and middle-income developing countries continue to face serious difficulties in meeting their external debt-servicing obligations, which constitutes an element that seriously constrains their efforts to ensure sustained economic growth and sustainable development,

Noting that, in 2002, developing countries as a whole made net outward transfers of financial resources for the sixth consecutive year, and underscoring the need for measures, as appropriate, at the national and international levels to address this issue to enhance the prospects for debt sustainability, while noting also the fact that for some developing countries those transfers, at the present time, indicate positive developments in the trade balance, and were required, inter alia, for debt repayment,

Convinced that enhanced market access for goods and services of export interest to developing countries contributes significantly to debt sustainability in developing countries,

Welcoming the positive impact of the enhanced Heavily Indebted Poor Countries Initiative, while recognizing that significant challenges remain, and inviting all developed bilateral creditors to forgive on a unilateral basis up to 100 per cent of all remaining claims after HIPC debt relief,

Welcoming also the actions taken by creditor countries within the framework of the Paris Club and by some creditor countries through the cancellation of bilateral debts, urging all creditor countries to participate in efforts to remedy the external debt and debt-servicing problems of developing countries, and noting the Evian Approach of the Paris Club of October 2003 and that debt relief does not replace alternative sources of financing,

Emphasizing the important role that private sector creditors play in debt relief and debt sustainability,

Welcoming the call in the communiqué issued by the joint International Monetary Fund/World Bank Development Committee on 22 September 2003 in Dubai, United Arab Emirates, urging all official and commercial creditors to participate in the Heavily Indebted Poor Countries Initiative,

Recognizing the current debate on sovereign debt restructuring, especially the efforts led by sovereign debtors and private creditors to develop a voluntary code of conduct, and stressing that modalities for sovereign debt restructuring should be voluntary, market-friendly and flexible, with due consideration of the specific circumstances of individual countries, and should result from the participation of all relevant stakeholders,

Noting the increasing voluntary use of collective action clauses in sovereign bond contracts by both developing and developed countries,

1. *Takes note* of the report of the Secretary-General;

2. *Reaffirms* the determination, as expressed in the United Nations Millennium Declaration, to deal comprehensively and effectively with the debt problems of low- and middle-income developing countries, through various national and international measures designed to make their debt sustainable in the long term;

3. *Emphasizes* that the international financial system, along with enhanced official and private external financing and foreign direct investment, are key elements for a durable solution to the external debt problems of developing countries;

4. *Stresses* that sustainable debt financing is an important element for mobilizing resources for public and private investment, and that national comprehensive strategies to monitor and manage the external liabilities embedded in the domestic preconditions for debt sustainability, including sound macroeconomic policies and public resource management, are a key element in reducing national vulnerabilities;

5. *Welcomes* the World Trade Organization Working Group on Trade, Debt and Finance and its mandate to examine the relationship between trade, debt and finance so as to enhance the capacity of the multilateral trading system to contribute to a durable solution to the problem of external indebtedness of the developing and least developed countries, and to strengthen the coherence of international trade and financial policies, with a view to safeguarding the multilateral trading system from the effects of financial and monetary instability, and takes note of its report of 11 July 2003 to the General Council of the World Trade Organization;

6. *Recognizes* that creditors and debtors must share the responsibility for preventing and resolving unsustainable debt situations and that debt relief can play a key role in liberating resources that should be directed towards activities consistent with attaining poverty eradication, sustainable economic growth and sustainable development and with the achievement of the internationally agreed development goals, including those contained in the Millennium Declaration, and in this regard urges countries to direct those resources freed through debt relief, in particular through debt cancellation and reduction, towards these objectives;

7. *Stresses* that debt sustainability depends upon a confluence of many factors at the international and national levels, underscores that no single indicator should be used to make definitive judgements about debt sustainability, and emphasizes that country circumstances should be taken into account;

8. *Recalls* the call upon industrialized countries, as expressed in the Millennium Declaration, to implement the enhanced programme of debt relief for the heavily indebted poor countries without further delay and to agree to cancel all official bilateral debts of those countries in return for their making demonstrable commitments to poverty reduction, and in this regard welcomes the decision of those countries that have already taken action to do so, emphasizing that debt relief complementary to the framework should be treated as additional;

9. *Calls upon* those heavily indebted poor countries that have not already done so, to take, as soon as possible, the policy measures necessary to become eligible for the enhanced Heavily Indebted Poor Countries Initiative and to reach the decision point, inter alia, through the formulation of poverty reduction strategies, where they exist;

10. *Stresses* the need to pursue, where appropriate, debt relief measures vigorously and expeditiously, by all creditors, including within the Paris and London Clubs and other relevant forums, and welcomes other

bilateral initiatives that have been undertaken to reduce outstanding indebtedness, so as to contribute to debt sustainability and facilitate sustainable development;

11. *Calls upon* the international community, including the United Nations system, and invites the Bretton Woods institutions as well as the private sector to take appropriate measures and actions for the implementation of the commitments, agreements and decisions of the major United Nations conferences and summits, in particular those relating to the question of the external debt problem of developing countries, and in this regard stresses the need:

(*a*) To implement speedily, effectively and fully the enhanced Heavily Indebted Poor Countries Initiative, which should be fully financed through additional resources, while stressing the need for fair, equitable and transparent burden-sharing among the international public creditor community and other donor countries, and take into consideration, as appropriate, measures to address any fundamental changes in the economic circumstances of those developing countries that have an unsustainable debt burden, including those caused by natural catastrophes, severe terms-of-trade shocks or conflict, taking into account initiatives that have been undertaken to reduce outstanding indebtedness;

(*b*) To continue to bring about a sustained commitment on the part of the heavily indebted poor countries to improvements in domestic policies and economic management, to support capacity-building for the management of financial assets and liabilities, to ensure full participation and delivery of relief by all affected creditors, to ensure adequate and sufficiently concessional financing by international financing institutions and the donor community, and to further explore options to address the difficult issues of HIPC-to-HIPC debt relief and creditor litigation;

(*c*) To continue to bring together international debtors and creditors in relevant international forums to restructure unsustainable debt in a timely and efficient manner, taking into account the need to involve the private sector in the resolution of crises;

(*d*) To acknowledge the problems of the debt sustainability of some low-income countries that are not heavily indebted, in particular those facing exceptional circumstances, and in this regard to note the tailored treatment for non-HIPC developing debtor countries adopted by the Paris Club to ensure that debt restructuring provides non-HIPC debtor countries with a debt treatment that reflects their financial needs and the objective of ensuring long-lasting debt sustainability;

(*e*) To reduce the unsustainable debt burden of developing countries through such actions as debt relief and, as appropriate, debt cancellation and other innovative mechanisms geared to comprehensively addressing the debt problems of developing countries, in particular the poorest and most heavily indebted ones;

(*f*) To encourage exploring innovative mechanisms to comprehensively address the debt problems of developing countries, including middle-income countries, and countries with economies in transition; such mechanisms may include debt-for-sustainable-development swaps, or multi-creditor debt swap arrangements, as appropriate;

(*g*) To establish effective debt-tracking mechanisms in developing countries and strengthen technical assistance for external debt management and debt tracking, including through enhanced cooperation and coordination between organizations providing assistance in this regard;

(*h*) To take steps to ensure that resources provided for debt relief do not detract from official development assistance resources intended to be available for developing countries and that the debt-relief arrangements seek to avoid imposing any unfair burden on other developing countries;

(*i*) To welcome consideration by all relevant stakeholders of an international debt-work-out mechanism, in the appropriate forums, the adoption of which should not preclude emergency financing in times of crisis, to promote fair burden-sharing and minimize moral hazard, which will engage debtors and creditors to come together to restructure unsustainable debts in a timely and efficient manner;

(*j*) To establish a set of clear principles for the management and resolution of financial crises that provide for fair burden-sharing between the public and private sectors and among debtors, creditors and investors, while recognizing that a flexible mix of instruments is needed to respond appropriately to the varying economic circumstances and capacities of different countries;

12. *Stresses* the importance of continued flexibility with regard to the eligibility criteria for the enhanced Heavily Indebted Poor Countries Initiative, in particular for countries in post-conflict situations, and the need to keep the computational procedures and assumptions underlying debt sustainability analysis under review;

13. *Emphasizes* the need to help bring about initial recovery in heavily indebted poor post-conflict countries, in coordination with the international financial institutions, to help clear, as appropriate, the arrears of those countries vis-à-vis international financial institutions;

14. *Reaffirms* that reviews of debt sustainability should also bear in mind the impact of debt relief on progress towards the achievement of the development goals set out in the Millennium Declaration and the fact that debt sustainability analysis at the completion point needs to take into account any change in the global growth prospects or in the terms of trade, especially for commodity export developing countries;

15. *Notes* that it is important for the International Monetary Fund and the World Bank to continue their efforts to strengthen the transparency and integrity of debt sustainability analysis and to consider any fundamental changes in countries' debt sustainability caused by natural catastrophes, severe terms-of-trade shocks or conflict when making policy recommendations, including for debt relief, as appropriate;

16. *Stresses* the need to strengthen the institutional capacity of developing countries in debt management, calls upon the international community to support the efforts made towards this end, and in this regard stresses the importance of such initiatives as the Debt Management and Financial Analysis System, the International Monetary Fund and World Bank guidelines for public debt management, and the debt-management capacity-building programme;

17. *Invites* the United Nations Conference on Trade and Development, the International Monetary Fund

and the World Bank, in cooperation with the regional banks, regional commissions and multilateral institutions, to study the possibility of creating a consultative group on external debt management aimed at developing best practices and strengthening the institutional capacity of developing countries in debt management, taking into account work that has already been done;

18. *Requests* the Secretary-General to submit to the General Assembly at its fifty-ninth session a report on the implementation of the present resolution and to include in that report a comprehensive and substantive analysis of the external debt and debt-servicing problems of developing countries, inter alia, those resulting from global financial instability;

19. *Decides* to include in the provisional agenda of its fifty-ninth session, under the item entitled "Macroeconomic policy questions", the sub-item entitled "External debt crisis and development".

Financing for development

Follow-up to the International Conference on Financing for Development

High-level meeting of Economic and Social Council, Bretton Woods institutions and WTO. In accordance with General Assembly resolution 50/227 [YUN 1996, p. 1249] and Economic and Social Council decision 2003/206 of 28 January, the sixth special high-level meeting of the Economic and Social Council, the Bretton Woods institutions (the World Bank Group and IMF) and WTO took place in New York on 14 April. The theme "Increased coherence, coordination and cooperation for the implementation of the Monterrey Consensus of the International Conference on Financing for Development at all levels one year after the Conference" was adopted by the Council in **decision 2003/209** of 30 January. It had before it a note by the Secretary-General on the subject [E/2003/50].

The Council President, in his summary of the high-level meeting [A/58/77-E/2003/62 & Add.1,2], said that the discussions showed that, despite some progress in the implementation of the Monterrey Consensus [YUN 2002, p. 953], there were still significant gaps in implementation in some key areas. The Assembly's High-level Dialogue on Financing for Development (see p. 988) would be an important opportunity for taking stock more fully of progress made and for considering further steps.

In preparation for that Dialogue, the Council suggested that the Assembly address the following key issues: improved measurement of national and international efforts and outcomes in the implementation of the Monterrey Consensus, including aid flows and their impact; additional steps to be taken by the Assembly to increase the chances of completing on time the multilateral trade negotiations under the Doha Development Agenda; national and international measures to reduce the risks of external debt problems; further exploration of international approaches to orderly debt workouts; strengthened participation of developing countries in decision-making processes on international economic policy; and increased coherence in a number of policy areas.

ECONOMIC AND SOCIAL COUNCIL ACTION

On 24 July [meeting 47], the Economic and Social Council adopted **resolution 2003/47** [draft: E/2003/L.39] without vote [agenda item 6 (a)].

International Conference on Financing for Development

The Economic and Social Council,

Recalling General Assembly resolution 56/210 B of 9 July 2002, in which the Assembly endorsed the Monterrey Consensus of the International Conference on Financing for Development, adopted on 22 March 2002,

Recalling also its resolution 2002/34 of 26 July 2002,

Recalling further General Assembly resolution 57/270 A of 20 December 2002 on the integrated and coordinated implementation of and follow-up to the outcomes of the major United Nations conferences and summits in the economic and social fields,

Recognizing the crucial importance of proper follow-up to and implementation of the Monterrey Consensus and other agreements and commitments reached at the International Conference on Financing for Development,

Stressing the importance of staying fully engaged, nationally, regionally and internationally, in order both to ensure proper follow-up to the implementation of agreements and commitments reached at the International Conference on Financing for Development and to continue to build bridges between development, finance and trade organizations and initiatives, within the framework of the holistic agenda of the Conference,

Recognizing the link between financing for development and attaining internationally agreed development goals and objectives, including those contained in the United Nations Millennium Declaration, in measuring development progress and helping to guide development priorities, as well as achieving sustained economic growth and sustainable development, bearing in mind the Plan of Implementation of the World Summit on Sustainable Development ("Johannesburg Plan of Implementation"),

1. *Takes note with appreciation* of the summary by the President of the Economic and Social Council of the special high-level meeting of the Council with the Bretton Woods institutions and the World Trade Organization, held in New York on 14 April 2003, which constitutes an important input provided by the Council to the high-level dialogue on financing for development, which is to be held by the General Assembly in October 2003;

2. *Takes note* of the report of the Secretary-General on the follow-up efforts to the International Conference on Financing for Development;

3. *Takes note also* of the establishment of the Financing for Development Office in the Department of Economic and Social Affairs of the Secretariat, in accordance with General Assembly resolution 57/273 of 20 December 2002;

4. *Reaffirms its commitment* to contribute to the implementation of the Monterrey Consensus of the International Conference on Financing for Development, both in the context of its general mandate to follow up and support the implementation of commitments adopted at all major United Nations conferences, including the Millennium Summit, and as an important process in its own right, and in that regard attaches priority to four broad tasks related to follow-up activities:

(*a*) To promote coherence and an integrated approach within the United Nations;

(*b*) To intensify interactions with the World Bank, the International Monetary Fund and the World Trade Organization, as well as other institutional stakeholders;

(*c*) To continue involving other relevant stakeholders, including civil society organizations and the private sector; and

(*d*) To prepare inputs for consideration by the General Assembly;

5. *Expresses its satisfaction* with the interactive dialogue of the special high-level meeting of the Council with the Bretton Woods institutions and the World Trade Organization, which constituted an important and successful step in the follow-up process provided for in paragraph 69 of the Monterrey Consensus;

6. *Decides* to build on the experience accumulated during the high-level meeting of the Council in 2003 in convening and organizing the next high-level spring meeting to address issues of coherence, coordination and cooperation in the context of the implementation of the Monterrey Consensus, examining further specific steps that could be taken by each of the stakeholders to move the Monterrey process forward;

7. *Decides also* to include representatives of the Trade and Development Board of the United Nations Conference on Trade and Development in the high-level meeting of the Council with the Bretton Woods institutions and the World Trade Organization;

8. *Decides further* that the Department of Economic and Social Affairs, in collaboration with the secretariats of the Bretton Woods institutions, the World Trade Organization, the United Nations Conference on Trade and Development and other institutional stakeholders, will prepare the necessary documentation for the next high-level meeting of the Economic and Social Council, and decides to invite all institutional stakeholders to provide the Secretary-General with interim reports during the first quarter of 2004 on the work undertaken and planned in their respective areas of competence regarding implementation of the different components of the Monterrey Consensus, with the understanding that those reports will be essential inputs to the preparation of the meeting;

9. *Welcomes* the continued participation of non-governmental organizations and the business sector in the Monterrey process, expresses its readiness to continue its work in the innovative and participatory spirit that characterized the International Conference on Financing for Development, strengthening the role of the Council in its interaction with non-governmental organizations and the business sector at its annual spring meetings with the Bretton Woods institutions and the World Trade Organization, and stresses that the specific modalities and formats to give concrete expression to that commitment should continue to be decided by the Council, in accordance with its rules of procedure and the accreditation procedures and modalities of participation utilized at the Conference and in its preparatory process.

High-level Dialogue on Financing for Development

The General Assembly's first High-level Dialogue on Financing for Development was held on 29 and 30 October in New York, under the theme "The Monterrey Consensus: status of implementation and tasks ahead". Organized in response to Assembly resolution 57/250 [YUN 2002, p. 961], the High-level Dialogue was attended by more than 190 Governments, 35 intergovernmental organizations and 50 civil society stakeholders from the business sector, academia and NGOs.

The Dialogue consisted of a series of plenary and informal meetings and eight ministerial interactive round tables, which were organized around the various themes to be discussed: regional dimensions of the implementation of the results of the International Conference on Financing for Development (round tables 1 and 2); coherence and consistency of the international monetary, financial and trading systems in support of development (round tables 3 and 4); the link between the progress in the implementation of the agreements and commitments reached at the International Conference and the achievement of internationally agreed development goals, including those contained in the United Nations Millennium Declaration [YUN 2000, p. 49] (round tables 5 and 6); and the link between the progress in the implementation of the agreements and commitments reached at the International Conference and the promotion of sustainable development, sustained economic growth and the eradication of poverty, with a view to achieving an equitable global economic system (round tables 7 and 8).

The Assembly President, in his summary of the proceedings [A/58/555 & Corr.1], said that participants welcomed progress where it had occurred, but insisted that much more was required. Participants noted that there had been slippage in some areas, manifested by disappointing developments in international trade and financial transfers, and called for a more precise mechanism for monitoring implementation of both the Monterrey commitments and the targets embodied in the MDGs. The main themes addressed during the Dialogue were: mobilizing domestic resources; private capital flows; international trade; official development assistance and other resources; external debt; systemic and institutional issues; and staying engaged in the Monterrey Consensus follow-up process.

The Assembly President also submitted summaries of the informal hearings of civil society [A/58/555/Add.1] and the business sector [A/58/555/Add.2], both held on 28 October.

Documentation. The High-level Dialogue had before it a note by the Secretary-General on organizational and procedural matters concerning the High-level Dialogue [A/58/436], documents transmitted by Italy on its contribution to the HIPC Initiative [A/58/437] and on the European Union's Barcelona Commitments for following up the Monterrey Consensus [A/58/ 529], and Denmark's first progress report on the MDG of developing a global partnership for development [A/58/542]. It also had before it the Secretary-General's report [A/58/216] on implementation of and follow-up to the commitments and agreements made at the International Conference on Financing for Development, prepared in collaboration with major institutional stakeholders. He highlighted the most important areas of progress, or lack thereof, in implementing the commitments, suggested guidelines for policies and processes and identified issues for further study in order to operationalize and build on the Monterrey Consensus.

Organizational matters. By **decision 57/593** of 15 September, the General Assembly decided to accredit to the High-level Dialogue several intergovernmental organizations. By **decisions 57/594** of 15 September and **58/509** of 27 October, it decided to accredit a number of business entities/organizations and NGOs to the Dialogue and to the earlier hearings of the business sector and civil society.

GENERAL ASSEMBLY ACTION

On 23 December [meeting 78], the General Assembly, on the recommendation of the Second Committee [A/58/494, as orally revised], adopted **resolution 58/230** without vote [agenda item 104].

Follow-up to and implementation of the outcome of the International Conference on Financing for Development

The General Assembly,

Recalling the International Conference on Financing for Development, held in Monterrey, Mexico, from 18 to 22 March 2002, and its resolutions 56/210 B of 9 July 2002, 57/250 of 20 December 2002, 57/270 B of 23 June 2003 and 57/272 and 57/273 of 20 December 2002, as well as Economic and Social Council resolutions 2002/34 of 26 July 2002 and 2003/47 of 24 July 2003,

Taking note of the report of the Secretary-General on the implementation of and follow-up to commitments and agreements made at the International Conference on Financing for Development, prepared in collaboration with the major institutional stakeholders,

Having considered the summary presented by the President of the General Assembly of the High-level Dialogue on Financing for Development, held in New York on 29 and 30 October 2003,

Having also considered the summary presented by the President of the Economic and Social Council of the special high-level meeting of the Council with the Bretton Woods institutions and the World Trade Organization, held in New York on 14 April 2003,

Determined to continue to implement and build further on the commitments made and agreements reached at the International Conference on Financing for Development and to strengthen the coordinated and coherent engagement of all relevant stakeholders in the financing for development process,

1. *Welcomes* the holding of the first High-level Dialogue on Financing for Development;

2. *Reiterates* the call to fully implement and to build further on the commitments made and agreements reached at the International Conference on Financing for Development;

3. *Notes* the progress made in the implementation of these commitments and agreements and that much remains to be done in this context;

4. *Emphasizes* the link between financing for development and the achievement of the internationally agreed development goals, including those contained in the United Nations Millennium Declaration;

5. *Stresses,* in order to complement national development efforts, the importance of full implementation of the commitment to enhance further the coherence and consistency of international monetary, financial and trading systems, and in this context requests the Secretary-General to keep actions under review;

6. *Recognizes* initiatives taken to enhance the voice, participation and representation of developing countries and countries with economies in transition in the work and decision-making processes of the intergovernmental bodies of institutional stakeholders, and invites them to continue and strengthen actions aimed at reaching decisions in this regard;

7. *Invites* the World Trade Organization to strengthen its institutional relationship with the United Nations, in particular through its active involvement in the meetings of the General Assembly and the Economic and Social Council devoted to financing for development, and through its participation in the preparation of the annual report on the implementation of and follow-up to the commitments made and agreements reached at the International Conference on Financing for Development;

8. *Welcomes* the decisions by the major institutional stakeholders of the International Conference on Financing for Development to include in the agendas of their intergovernmental bodies relevant items on the implementation of the Monterrey Consensus of the International Conference on Financing for Development, and invites all major institutional stakeholders to consider doing so, in accordance with paragraph 70 of the Monterrey Consensus, and to make a contribution to the assessment of progress made to the High-level Dialogue on Financing for Development of the General Assembly and to the spring meeting of the Economic and Social Council;

9. *Requests* the United Nations Conference on Trade and Development, in cooperation with other relevant stakeholders, to continue to address in a comprehensive way commodities issues and their impact on financing for development;

10. *Requests* the Economic and Social Council, in its examination of the report of the Ad Hoc Group of Experts on International Cooperation in Tax Matters at its next substantive session to give consideration to the institutional framework for international cooperation in tax matters;

11. *Recalls* paragraph 69 of the Monterrey Consensus and building on the experience of the high-level spring meeting of the Economic and Social Council and the High-level Dialogue of the General Assembly in 2003, in the context of the integrated approach to the follow-up to and implementation of the commitments made and agreements reached at the International Conference on Financing for Development, requests:

(a) The President of the General Assembly, in coordination with the President of the Economic and Social Council, to strengthen the preparations, with all major institutional and other stakeholders, of matters relevant to the organization of the High-level Dialogue, in consultation with all Member States;

(b) The President of the Economic and Social Council, with support from the Vice-Presidents, to enhance the Council's interactions through regular exchanges with the Bretton Woods institutions, the World Trade Organization and the United Nations Conference on Trade and Development on organizational matters related to the follow-up to the International Conference on Financing for Development, within the context of the preparations for the high-level meeting with these institutions, bearing in mind General Assembly resolution 57/270 B and Economic and Social Council resolution 2003/47, and to report thereon to the Council;

(c) The President of the Economic and Social Council, in consultation with all major institutional stakeholders, to focus the annual special high-level meeting on specific issues, within the holistic integrated approach of the Monterrey Consensus, and to report thereon to the Council;

12. *Invites* the regional commissions, with the support of regional development banks, as appropriate, and in cooperation with United Nations funds and programmes, to use the opportunity of their regular intergovernmental sessions to hold special meetings within existing resources, as necessary, to address the regional and interregional aspects of the follow-up to the International Conference on Financing for Development and thus help to bridge any gaps between the national, regional and international dimensions of the implementation of the Monterrey Consensus and serve as inputs to the High-level Dialogue as well as to the spring meeting of the Economic and Social Council;

13. *Welcomes* the establishment of the Financing for Development Office in the Department of Economic and Social Affairs of the Secretariat, and in this regard reiterates the need to fully implement resolution 57/273 to enable the Office to provide effective support to the intergovernmental process entrusted with the follow-up to the International Conference on Financing for Development, and to facilitate the participation of all stakeholders in accordance with the rules of procedure of the United Nations, in particular the accreditation procedures and modalities of participation utilized at the Conference and in its preparatory process, as well as to continue within its mandate:

(a) To organize workshops and multi-stakeholder consultations, including experts from the official and private sectors, as well as academia and civil society, to examine issues related to the mobilization of resources for financing development and poverty eradication;

(b) To convene activities involving various stakeholders, including the private sector and civil society, as appropriate, to promote best practices and exchange information on the implementation of the commitments made and agreements reached at the International Conference for Financing for Development;

14. *Decides* to consider at its fifty-ninth session possible innovative sources of financing for development, and requests the Secretary-General to submit the result of the analysis on this issue as called for in paragraph 44 of the Monterrey Consensus;

15. *Invites* countries to report by 2005, inter alia, through existing reporting mechanisms, on their efforts to implement the Monterrey Consensus, bearing in mind the need to achieve the internationally agreed development goals, including those contained in the Millennium Declaration;

16. *Decides* to hold the 2005 High-level Dialogue on Financing for Development at the ministerial level; the time and modalities of the High-level Dialogue will be set by the General Assembly at its fifty-ninth session, taking into account other major events in the same year and the need for adequate provisions for an enhanced dialogue;

17. *Also decides* to include in the provisional agenda of its fifty-ninth session an item entitled "Follow-up to and implementation of the outcome of the International Conference on Financing for Development", and requests the Secretary-General to submit an annual analytical assessment of the state of the implementation of the Monterrey Consensus, including the implementation of the present resolution, to be prepared in full collaboration with the major institutional stakeholders.

Investment, technology and related financial issues

The UNCTAD Commission on Investment, Technology and Related Financial Issues held its seventh session in Geneva from 20 to 24 January [TD/B/EX(31)/3].

At its thirty-first executive session in March [A/58/15], TDB took note of the Commission's report and endorsed its recommendations.

Investment and development. For its consideration of policy issues related to investment and development, the Commission had before it an UNCTAD secretariat note on the subject [TD/B/COM.2/44]; the report of the Expert Meeting on the Development Dimension of FDI: policies to enhance the role of FDI in support of the competitiveness of the enterprise sector and the economic performance of host economies, taking into account the trade/investment interface, in the national and international context [YUN 2002, p. 966]; and an UNCTAD secretariat note on the development dimension of FDI: policies to enhance the role of FDI in the international context—policy issues to consider [TD/B/COM.2/EM.12/2].

The Commission recommended that the secretariat continue its post-Doha technical assistance and capacity-building work, facilitate an ongoing exchange of information and experiences among investment negotiators, and continue its in-depth analysis of policies and measures to help developing countries attract and benefit more from FDI. The secretariat should also complement its analytical work with technical and capacity-building assistance, including helping countries to modernize relevant laws, and continue to assist in the development of inter-enterprise relations.

Investment arrangements. For its consideration of issues related to investment arrangements, the Commission had before it an UNCTAD secretariat note on the subject [TD/B/COM.2/45]; the report of the Expert Meeting on Experiences with Bilateral and Regional Approaches to Multilateral Cooperation in the Area of Long-term Cross-border Investment, particularly FDI [YUN 2002, p. 966]; and a related UNCTAD secretariat note [TD/B/COM.2/EM.11/2].

The Commission welcomed the interface between policy makers and investment promotion practitioners in the format of a joint session with the World Association of Investment Promotion Agencies, which it invited to contribute to the UNCTAD XI preparatory process (see p. 998).

Investment policy reviews. For its consideration of investment policy reviews: exchange of national experiences, the Commission had before it the summary of the deliberations of the Investment Policy Review of Botswana and Ghana [TD/B/COM.2/49].

The Commission encouraged the secretariat to devote sufficient time to investment policy reviews covering member States during the session, to enable their presentation and exchange of national experiences. It encouraged the UN regional commissions to participate in the Commission's work, thereby enhancing its role as a forum for exchange among member States and intergovernmental agencies on issues related to investment.

Subsidiary bodies. In 2003, two expert meetings took place, both in Geneva. The Expert Meeting on Effectiveness of FDI Policy Measures (25-27 June) [TD/B/COM.2/51] had before it an UNCTAD secretariat note on the subject [TD/B/COM.2/EM.13/2]. The Expert Meeting focused on selected general policy measures (labour, business immigration and taxation) and proactive measures in selected industries important for developing countries (garments/textiles, agribusiness, tourism and information and communication technology). It also considered the investment policy review of Nepal.

In considering the general regulatory environment, the experts emphasized the need for effective policy measures in the areas of labour, business immigration and taxation, and in competition policy, exchange control, intellectual property protection, and sectoral and environmental regulation. In all areas, the effectiveness of measures depended on policy transparency, good governance, social consensus and economic and political stability. Home country measures, such as tax incentives and trade preferences, using ODA for capacity-building, infrastructure development, enterprise support and training and technological upgrading, could contribute to encouraging FDI inflows and to enhancing the benefits of FDI, particularly in LDCs and other structurally weak economies. Together with host country proactive measures, they could be a powerful stimulus to attracting FDI in developing countries.

The Expert Meeting on FDI and Development (29-31 October) [TB/B/COM.2/57] had before it an UNCTAD secretariat note on the subject [TD/B/COM.2/EM.14/2]. The Expert Meeting discussed the role of FDI in the development of services industries and related policy challenges, including FDI and competitiveness, the growth of export-oriented FDI in services, and the role and impact of FDI in the context of privatization of services. Experts noted that although services often represented the largest sector of the economy, the importance of FDI in services had not been adequately reflected in research and policy analysis. They suggested that policy formulation should go beyond the standard economic analysis and agreed that both analysis and policy formulation needed to reflect the wide diversity among different kinds of services.

Competition law and policy

The Intergovernmental Group of Experts on Competition Law and Policy, at its fifth session (Geneva, 2-4 July) [TD/B/COM.2/52], considered consultations on competition law and policy, including the model law and studies related to the provisions of the 1980 Set of Multilaterally Agreed Equitable Principles and Rules for the Control of Restrictive Business Practices (known as the Set) [YUN 1980, p. 626]; and the UNCTAD work programme, including technical assistance, and advisory and training programmes on competition law and policy. It had before it UNCTAD secretariat reports on: experiences gained so far on international cooperation in competition policy issues and the mechanisms used [TD/B/COM.2/CLP/21/Rev.2]; roles of possible dispute mediation mechanisms and alternative arrangements, including voluntary peer reviews, in competition law and policy [TD/B/COM.2/CLP/37]; a review of capacity-building and technical assistance in competition law and policy [TD/B/COM.2/CLP/36]; the proposed handbook on competition legislation [TD/B/COM.2/CLP/33]; the updated Directory of Competition Authorities [TD/B/COM.2/CLP/34]; and the revised Model Law on Competition [TD/B/RBP/CONF.5/7/Rev.2].

In agreed conclusions, the Group of Experts recommended to UNCTAD XI, to be held in 2004, the continuation and strengthening of the work programme on competition law and policy within UNCTAD's secretariat and the Group. It invited the secretariat to continue its efforts related to the implementation of the Doha Declaration [YUN 2001, p. 1432] in technical assistance and capacity-building. The secretariat was asked to revise/update the documents before the Group, for submission to its 2004 session. It was also asked to prepare for that session, which would act as the preparatory meeting for the Fifth UN Conference to Review All Aspects of the Set in 2005, a number of studies on the implications of closer multilateral cooperation in competition policy for the development objectives of developing and least developed countries.

The Group recommended that for better implementation of the Set, it would consider in 2004 the strengths and weaknesses of peer review related to competition policy, cooperation and dispute mediation mechanisms in regional integration agreements related to competition law and policy, evidence gathering and cooperation issues in hard-core cartel investigations, and advocacy in promoting awareness of competition policy and law in developing countries.

The secretariat should expand its capacity-building and technical cooperation activities in all regions and prepare for consideration at its next session an updated review of capacity-building and technical assistance, a further revised and updated version of the Model Law on Competition, and an information note on recent important cases, with special reference to cases involving more than one country.

The Commission, at its seventh session [TD/B/EX(31)/3], took note of the report of the fourth (2002) session of the Intergovernmental Group of Experts [YUN 2002, p. 967] and endorsed its agreed conclusions.

International standards of accounting and reporting

The Intergovernmental Working Group of Experts on International Standards of Accounting and Reporting, at its twentieth session (Geneva, 29 September–1 October) [TD/B/COM.2/58], had before it UNCTAD secretariat reports on: major issues on implementation of corporate disclosure requirements [TD/B/COM.2/ISAR/19 & Add.1-5 & Add.2/Corr.1]; disclosures of the impact of corporations on society: current trends and issues [TD/B/COM.2/ISAR/20]; and a revised model accounting curriculum [TD/B/COM.2/ISAR/21].

In its agreed conclusions, the Working Group requested the UNCTAD secretariat to publish and disseminate a paper on transparency and disclosure requirements for corporate governance. The secretariat should continue to assist countries in developing and implementing their own guidelines and benchmarking systems, and form partnerships with private and public intergovernmental organizations promoting corporate governance. The Working Group, noting the work being done by various groups, including the Global Reporting Initiative, to develop different indicators, agreed to begin examining existing indicators so that corporate social responsibility reports would be comparable and not impose unreasonable burdens on enterprises in developing countries. In terms of the draft guidance relating to accounting by small and medium-sized enterprises, the Working Group agreed that small groups be established to monitor changes made to existing and new standards issued by the International Accounting Standards Board and the results obtained through field testing. It requested the secretariat to continue its efforts on national and international requirements for the qualification of professional accountants and to finalize and widely disseminate the Model Curriculum. It recommended that the work on environmental accounting and eco-efficiency indicators be brought to the notice of the International Federation of Accountants and that UNCTAD conduct additional field testing of the guideline on eco-efficiency indicators in developing countries and across industry sectors.

The Commission, at its seventh session [TD/B/EX(31)/3], endorsed the report of the nineteenth (2002) session of the Intergovernmental Working Group of Experts on International Standards of Accounting and Reporting [YUN 2002, p. 967].

Taxation

On 5 March (**decision 2003/214**), the Economic and Social Council endorsed the decision of the Ad Hoc Group of Experts on International Cooperation in Tax Matters to change the dates and venue of its eleventh meeting from 7 to 11 April in New York to 10 to 14 November in Geneva. On 31 October (**decision 2003/313**), the Council endorsed the Ad Hoc Group's decision to change the date of that meeting to 15 to 19 December.

The eleventh meeting of the Ad Hoc Group of Experts on International Cooperation in Tax Matters (Geneva, 15-19 December) [E/2004/51] discussed mutual assistance in the collection of tax debts and a protocol for mutual assistance procedures; treaty shopping and treaty abuses; interaction of tax, trade and investment; financial taxation and equity market development; transfer pricing; cross-border interest income and capital flight; e-commerce and developing countries; revision of the United Nations Model Double Taxation Convention and the *Manual for the Negotiation of Bilateral Tax Treaties;* and the institutional framework for strengthening international cooperation in tax matters.

Transport

Maritime transport

The *Review of Maritime Transport 2003* [Sales No. E.03.II.D.10] stated that world seaborne trade rebounded slightly in 2002, reaching 5.88 billion tons after a 2001 contraction. The annual growth rate was 0.8 per cent compared to a negative 1 per cent in 2001.

The world merchant fleet expanded to 844.2 million deadweight tons (dwt) at the end of 2002, an increase of 2.3 per cent. New building deliveries were up by an impressive 8.4 per cent to 49 million dwt, and tonnage broken up and lost increased by 9.7 per cent to 30.5 million dwt, leaving a net gain of 18.5 million dwt. The fleets of oil tankers and dry bulk carriers together made up 71.6 per cent of the total world fleet. The fleet of oil tankers increased by 6.6 per cent, while that of dry bulk carriers increased by 1.9 per cent. There was a 7.4 per cent increase to 82.8 million dwt in the container fleet and a 2.1 per cent increase to 19.5 million dwt in the liquefied gas carriers fleet. Registration of ships by developed market-economy countries and major open-registry countries accounted for 25.7 and 47.2 per cent, respectively, of the world fleet. Open registries saw their tonnage contract by almost 1 per cent and two thirds of that beneficial fleet was owned by market economies and developing countries. Developing countries' share of the world fleet was 20.3 per cent, or 171.3 million dwt, of which 126.9 million dwt was registered in Asia.

Transport of dangerous goods

In response to Economic and Social Council resolutions 2001/34 [YUN 2001, p. 893] and 2001/44 [ibid.], the Secretary-General submitted a May report [E/2003/46] on the work during 2001-2002 of the Committee of Experts on the Transport of Dangerous Goods and on the Globally Harmonized System of Classification and Labelling of Chemicals.

The report stated that the Committee had adopted amendments to the twelfth revised edition of the *Recommendations on the Transport of Dangerous Goods: Model Regulations* and to the *Recommendations on the Transport of Dangerous Goods: Manual of Tests and Criteria*. Both revisions had been published by the secretariat.

Following the events of 11 September 2001 [YUN 2001, p. 60], the Committee had developed and adopted new security provisions for inclusion in the *Model Regulations* that were intended to minimize theft and misuse of dangerous goods, especially "high-consequence" dangerous goods. The Committee also adopted the final version of the *Globally Harmonized System of Classification and Labelling of Chemicals*, which would become operational by 2008, in accordance with the Johannesburg Plan of Implementation, adopted by the 2002 World Summit on Sustainable Development [YUN 2002, p. 821].

The Committee adopted a programme of work for the 2003-2004 biennium and recommended a draft resolution on its work for adoption by the Council (see below).

The Committee's two subsidiary bodies held two sessions each, in Geneva: the Subcommittee of Experts on the Transport of Dangerous Goods held its twenty-third (30 June-4 July) [ST/SG/AC.10/C.3/46 & Add.1] and twenty-fourth (3-10 December) [ST/SG/AC.10/C.3/48 & Add.1] sessions; and the Subcommittee of Experts on the Globally Harmonized System of Classification and Labelling of Chemicals held its fifth (7-9 July) [ST/SG/AC.10/C.4/10] and sixth (10-12 December) [ST/SG/AC.10/C.4/12] sessions.

By **decision 2003/309** of 25 July, the Economic and Social Council took note of the Secretary-General's report on the work of the Committee of Experts.

ECONOMIC AND SOCIAL COUNCIL ACTION

On 25 July [meeting 49], the Economic and Social Council adopted **resolution 2003/64** [draft: E/2003/46] without vote [agenda item 13 (*l*)].

Work of the Committee of Experts on the Transport of Dangerous Goods and on the Globally Harmonized System of Classification and Labelling of Chemicals

The Economic and Social Council,

Recalling its resolutions 1999/65 of 26 October 1999, 2001/34 of 26 July 2001 and 2001/44 of 20 December 2001,

Having considered the report of the Secretary-General on the work of the Committee of Experts on the Transport of Dangerous Goods and on the Globally Harmonized System of Classification and Labelling of Chemicals during the biennium 2001-2002,

A. Work of the Committee regarding the transport of dangerous goods

Recognizing the importance of the work of the Committee for the harmonization of codes and regulations relating to the transport of dangerous goods,

Bearing in mind the need to maintain safety standards at all times and to facilitate trade, as well as the importance of this to the various organizations responsible for modal regulations, while meeting the growing concern for the protection of life, property and the environment through the safe transport of dangerous goods, including their security in transport,

Noting the increasing volume of dangerous goods being introduced into worldwide commerce and the rapid expansion of technology and innovation,

1. *Expresses its appreciation* for the work of the Committee with respect to matters relating to the transport of dangerous goods, including their security in transport;

2. *Requests* the Secretary-General:

(a) To circulate the new and amended recommendations on the transport of dangerous goods to the Governments of Member States, the specialized agencies, the International Atomic Energy Agency and other international organizations concerned;

(b) To publish the thirteenth revised edition of the *Recommendations on the Transport of Dangerous Goods: Model Regulations* and the fourth revised edition of the *Recommendations on the Transport of Dangerous Goods: Manual of Tests and Criteria* in all the official languages of the United Nations, in the most cost-effective manner, not later than the end of 2003;

(c) To make these publications available on the web site of the Economic Commission for Europe, which also provides secretariat services to the Committee, and to make them available also on CD-ROM;

3. *Invites* all Governments, the specialized agencies, the International Atomic Energy Agency and the other international organizations concerned to transmit to the secretariat of the Committee their views on the work of the Committee, together with any comments that they may wish to make on the amended recommendations;

4. *Invites* all interested Governments, the regional commissions, the specialized agencies and the international organizations concerned, when developing or updating appropriate codes and regulations, to consider taking into account the recommendations of the Committee;

5. *Requests* the Secretary-General to submit a report on the status of the effective implementation of the Model Regulations on the Transport of Dangerous Goods by Member States and international organizations on a worldwide level;

B. Work of the Committee regarding the Globally Harmonized System of Classification and Labelling of Chemicals

Bearing in mind that, pursuant to paragraph 19.27 of Agenda 21, the Inter-Organization Programme for the Sound Management of Chemicals has cooperated for a decade with the International Labour Organization, the Organisation for Economic Co-operation and Development and the Subcommittee of Experts on the Transport of Dangerous Goods to develop a globally harmonized hazard classification and compatible labelling system for chemicals,

Bearing in mind also that the Subcommittee of Experts on the Globally Harmonized System of Classification and Labelling of Chemicals was created pursuant to resolution 1999/65 to make the Globally Harmonized System available worldwide, to keep it up to date and to promote and monitor its implementation,

Noting with satisfaction that the Committee could reach consensus on the Globally Harmonized System after consideration of a draft consolidated by the Inter-Organization Programme for the Sound Management of Chemicals on the basis of input from the Subcommittee of Experts on the Transport of Dangerous Goods, the International Labour Organization and the Organisation for Economic Co-operation and Development,

Aware that, in paragraph 23 (c) of the Plan of Implementation of the World Summit on Sustainable Development ("Johannesburg Plan of Implementation"), the World Summit encouraged countries to implement the Globally Harmonized System as soon as possible with a view to having the System fully operational by 2008,

Also aware that the General Assembly, in its resolution 57/253 of 20 December 2002, endorsed the Johannesburg Plan of Implementation and requested the Economic and Social Council to implement the provisions of the Plan relevant to its mandate and, in particular, to promote the implementation of Agenda 21 by strengthening system-wide coordination,

Aware of and recognizing the significance of the United Nations Institute for Training and Research/International Labour Organization/Organisation for Economic Co-operation and Development Global Partnership for Capacity-building to Implement the Globally Harmonized System for building capacities at all levels to achieve the 2008 target,

1. *Expresses its deep appreciation* to the Committee and other organizations concerned for their fruitful cooperation;

2. *Requests* the Secretary-General:

(a) To publish the Globally Harmonized System of Classification and Labelling of Chemicals in all the official languages of the United Nations, in the most cost-effective manner, and to circulate it to the Governments of Member States, the specialized agencies and the other international organizations concerned as soon as possible and no later than 2004;

(b) To consider disseminating the Globally Harmonized System as a CD-ROM;

(c) To make the Globally Harmonized System available on the web site of the secretariat of the Economic

Commission for Europe, which also provides secretariat services to the Committee;

3. *Invites* all Governments to take the necessary steps, through appropriate national procedures and/or legislation, to implement the Globally Harmonized System, as soon as possible and no later than 2008;

4. *Reiterates* the call for support to developing countries in strengthening their capacity of the sound management of chemicals by providing technical and financial assistance;

5. *Invites* the regional commissions, United Nations programmes, the specialized agencies and other organizations concerned to promote the implementation of the Globally Harmonized System and, where relevant, to amend their respective legal international instruments addressing transport safety, work safety, consumer protection or the protection of the environment so as to give effect to the Globally Harmonized System through such instruments;

6. *Invites* Governments, the regional commissions, United Nations programmes, the specialized agencies and the other organizations concerned to provide feedback to the Subcommittee of Experts on the Globally Harmonized System of Classification and Labelling of Chemicals;

7. *Requests* the Secretary-General to submit a report on the status of implementation of the Globally Harmonized System;

8. *Encourages* Governments, the regional commissions, United Nations programmes, the specialized agencies and other relevant international organizations and non-governmental organizations, in particular industry, to support implementation of the Globally Harmonized System and capacity-building activities in developing countries and countries in transition by providing financial contributions and/or technical assistance;

C. Programme of work of the Committee

Taking note of the programme of work of the Committee for the biennium 2003-2004 as contained in paragraphs 29 to 31 of the report of the Secretary-General,

Noting the relatively poor representation of experts from developing countries and countries with economies in transition in the work of the Committee and the need to ensure their wider participation in its work,

1. *Decides* to approve the programme of work of the Committee;

2. *Stresses* the importance of the participation of experts from developing countries as well as countries with economies in transition in the work of the Committee, calls, in this regard, for voluntary contributions to facilitate their participation, including through support for travel and daily subsistence allowance, and invites Member States and international organizations in a position to do so to contribute;

3. *Notes* the recommendations of the Committee regarding staff resources and invites the General Assembly to consider this issue in the context of its review of the proposed programme budget for the biennium 2004-2005;

4. *Requests* the Secretary-General to submit a report to the Economic and Social Council in 2005 on the implementation of the present resolution.

UNCTAD institutional and organizational questions

In 2003, the Trade and Development Board (TDB)—the executive body of UNCTAD—held its twentieth (27 January) special session, its thirty-first (10 March) and thirty-second (28 July) executive sessions, and its fiftieth (6-17 October) session [A/58/15], and the first part of its thirty-third (23 September) executive session [A/59/15]. All sessions took place in Geneva.

In January, at its twentieth special session, the Board adopted a decision [dec. 474(S-XX)] on the financing of the participation of experts from developing countries and countries with economies in transition in UNCTAD expert meetings (see p. 997). In March, it adopted a decision on the preparations for UNCTAD XI, to be held in 2004 [dec. 475(EX-31)], and took note of the reports of its subsidiary bodies (see above).

In March, TDB adopted a decision on the languages for official documentation of the ITC Joint Advisory Group [dec. 475(EX-31)]. It also considered preparations for UNCTAD XI and reports of its subsidiary bodies.

In July, TDB considered activities undertaken by UNCTAD in favour of Africa and in support of the New Partnership for Africa's Development (NEPAD) (see p. 937), preparations for UNCTAD XI and reports on the activities of its subsidiary bodies.

In September, it continued consideration of the financing of the participation of experts from developing countries and countries with economies in transition.

In October, TDB adopted agreed conclusions on the review of progress in the implementation of the Programme of Action for LDCs for the Decade 2001-2010 [agreed conclusions 476(L)] (see p. 870); and on economic developments in Africa: issues of Africa's trade performance [agreed conclusions 477(L)] (see p. 966). It adopted a decision on review of technical cooperation activities of UNCTAD [dec. 478(L)] (see below). It also considered UNCTAD's assistance to the Palestinian people (see p. 504), the preparatory process for UNCTAD XI, the law on international trade (see p. 1374) and the report of the Meeting of Eminent Persons on Commodity Issues (see p. 977).

Technical cooperation

In a July report [TD/B/50/2 & Add.1,2], the UNCTAD Secretary-General provided an overview of technical cooperation activities in 2002, which continued to emphasize capacity-building. Major programmes in order of expenditure were the Automated System for Customs Data (ASYCUDA), investment policies and capacity-building, the Debt Management and Financial Analysis System (DMFAS), trade negotiations and commercial diplomacy, trade logistics, technology and enterprise, and trade and environment. Expenditures totalled $21.8 million, a 5.9 per cent decrease in delivery compared to 2001, due to a drop in expenditures on UNDP-supported projects and projects financed by trust funds. Of the total, $3.4 million was financed by UNDP, $15.3 million from trust fund contributions and $3.1 million from the programme budget.

By region, approximately $3.02 million went to Africa, $3.9 million to Asia and the Pacific, $2.01 million to Latin America and the Caribbean, $1.01 million to Europe and $11.87 million to interregional projects. LDCs' share of technical cooperation expenditures decreased to 29 per cent compared to 43 per cent in 2001.

By programme, services infrastructure for development and trade efficiency accounted for 36.7 per cent of total expenditures; international trade in goods and services, and commodities, 20.1 per cent; investment, technology and enterprise development, 19.5 per cent; and globalization and development strategies, 12.9 per cent. The balance (8.8 per cent) was represented by cross-divisional advisory services (4.8 per cent), the Office of the Special Coordinator for Least Developed, Landlocked and Island Developing Countries (1.7 per cent), and executive direction and management (4.3 per cent).

Technical cooperation strategy

In May [TD/B/WP/161], the UNCTAD secretariat reported on consultations with member States, in response to requests of the Working Party on the Medium-term Plan and the Programme Budget at its thirty-ninth session [YUN 2002, p. 970] and TDB, in decision 472(XLIX) [ibid., p. 969], on integrating into UNCTAD's technical cooperation strategy elements of the thematic evaluation on capacity-building [ibid., p. 970]. The consultations resulted in an understanding that the issues emanating from the evaluation should be dealt with in the context of a new strategy for technical cooperation. It was agreed that the 1997 technical cooperation strategy [YUN 1997, p. 959] should be updated and reinforced by incorporating elements from the recommendations of the thematic evaluation of capacity-building. It was proposed that a draft of a new strategy of UNCTAD technical cooperation be prepared and submitted to the September session of the Working Party for consideration.

The Working Party, at its forty-first session (15-19 September) [TD/B/50/12], had before it the draft technical cooperation strategy of UNCTAD [TD/B/50/7], which set out UNCTAD's operational activities to address the problems of trade and development in an era of globalization and liberalization, emphasizing the development of human, institutional, productive and export capacities of developing countries and economies in transition, particularly LDCs, with a view to supporting poverty reduction policies and the achievement of the MDGs [YUN 2000, p. 51]. It also had before it an UNCTAD secretariat note on capacity development [TD/B/50/9], submitted in response to TDB decision 472(XLIX), which discussed definitions of capacity-building/development: elements relevant for UNCTAD's conceptual framework for capacity development; the goals and instruments of UNCTAD's capacity development; and the specific capacity development needs of LDCs.

The Working Party adopted a draft decision for consideration by TDB.

On 10 October [A/58/15 (dec. 478(L))], TDB recommended that the secretariat implement the strategy for UNCTAD's technical cooperation activities, the text of which was attached to its decision, taking into account the ideas contained in the secretariat note on capacity development (see above). It invited the secretariat to further strengthen coordination among its different entities with a view to integrated approaches and through dissemination of the strategy among its staff, particularly project managers. TDB also invited the secretariat to report on the strategy and its implementation to UNCTAD XI in 2004 and promote it among donors and beneficiary countries.

Evaluation

In August, an independent team submitted an evaluation of UNCTAD's trade, environment and development programme [TD/B/WP/165], which aimed to build capacity to handle WTO negotiation issues, and trade and environment issues of importance to developing countries. While the programme's activities, such as workshops and seminars, were considered to be good, the link with the immediate work of participant countries and follow-up were weak, outreach was not as good as intended and both beneficiaries and donors had difficulty in obtaining information about the programme and had experienced varying standards of service. It was recommended that the programme create a vision and a strategy for its work, develop a communication strategy, work out measurable performance indicators, undertake internal staff training, improve follow-up, pay attention to the value chain, improve outreach and plan how to withdraw after completion of activities.

At its forty-first session [TD/B/50/12], the Working Party on the Medium-term Plan and the Programme Budget endorsed the recommendations contained in the evaluation report and encouraged the secretariat to make further improvements. It should submit a progress report to the Working Party's forty-third session in 2004.

TDB, in October [A/58/15], endorsed the conclusions of the Working Party.

Participation in expert meetings

TDB, at its twentieth special session (Geneva, 27 January) [A/58/15], continued its 2002 consideration [YUN 2002, p. 971] of the financing of the participation of experts from developing countries and countries with economies in transition in UNCTAD expert meetings. In a decision [A/58/15 (dec. 474(S-XX))], the Board, noting that funding would cover the participation of 10 experts at each of eight expert meetings per annum, selected according to geographical distribution, beneficiary needs and expertise, agreed, on an experimental basis, to finance the participation of experts in UNCTAD expert meetings from extrabudgetary contributions and from a reserve fund in the event such contributions were insufficient. It decided that funds currently available to finance participation in expert meetings should constitute the reserve fund; the process of obtaining extrabudgetary contributions should begin immediately; funding for each expert meeting should be secured not later than three months prior to the meeting; if sufficient funding was not available, use should be made of the reserve fund; and it would discuss the working of the scheme, including its replenishment, in September, and regularly thereafter, based on an evaluation by the UNCTAD Secretary-General, in the light of criteria established by TDB at its nineteenth (2002) special session [YUN 2002, p. 971].

At the first part of its thirty-third executive session (23 September) [A/59/15], the UNCTAD secretariat, in a 17 September note [TD/B/EX(33)/2], stated that by the end of September the participation of 58 experts in six expert meetings would have been financed. Since only one pledge of an extrabudgetary contribution ($10,000) had been received so far, all six expert meetings had been financed from the reserve fund. The balance in the fund, which totalled $219,000 at the beginning of 2003, stood at $45,822 (including the pledge). The reserve fund was likely to be depleted by the end of the year, the first year of the scheme, and financing to fund the participation of experts in 2004 was uncertain. The experimental scheme based on extrabudgetary contributions, agreed to by TDB in January, did not seem to meet the requirement of providing a long-term solution for predictable and regular financing of participation in expert meetings. TDB would therefore have to consider other means of replenishing the reserve fund and ensuring extrabudgetary contributions for 2004 if it wished to continue the experimental scheme.

The UNCTAD Deputy Secretary-General informed the Board that the secretariat's note had omitted to mention a pledge of 100,000 euros made in 2002, before the introduction of the scheme for financing the participation of LDC experts, and which would finance those experts for 2004 and beyond. However, there were no funds to finance the 70 per cent of experts who did not come from LDCs. He suggested the use of regular budget resources as one option to fund the scheme, since previous options proposed, such as using unspent project balances, would not produce enough resources to sustain it.

TDB decided to suspend its session and requested the President to hold informal consultations with interested delegations on the matter.

Medium-term plan and programme budget

The UNCTAD Working Party on the Medium-term Plan and the Programme Budget held two sessions in 2003, both in Geneva.

At the first part of its fortieth session (13-17 January) [TD/B/EX(31)/2], the Working Party reviewed proposals for the draft programme budget on trade and development for the 2004-2005 biennium [UNCTAD/EDM/Misc.241/Rev.1]. In agreed conclusions, it concurred with the revised text and considered that the work programme should take into account the outcome of the Fifth WTO Ministerial Conference (see p. 1535), the results of UNCTAD XI (2004) and other relevant UN meetings. It encouraged the UNCTAD secretariat to further develop its cooperation with other related UN organizations, WTO and the Bretton Woods institutions. It stressed that, as a crosscutting issue, the question of LDCs should be further integrated in all UNCTAD subprogrammes. The Working Party requested the secretariat to consider compiling internally, on a specific web site, the main country and regional data on UNCTAD technical assistance programmes to complement the UNCTAD database on bilateral technical assistance, including through a link with the Organisation for Economic Co-operation and Development/WTO database on trade-related capacity-building, and report to the Working Party at its forty-first session. It supported the efforts of African countries in the framework of the implementation of the objectives of NEPAD [YUN 2002, p. 907]. It invited member States to contribute to a better definition of indicators, particularly qualitative indicators, and encouraged further interaction between the secretariat and member States.

In March [A/58/15], TDB took note of the Working Party's report on the first part of its fortieth session and endorsed the agreed conclusions.

At the second part of its fortieth session (21-22 May) [TD/B/EX(32)/3], the Working Party reviewed the draft programme budget on trade and development for the 2004-2005 biennium [A/56/6 (Sect. 12)] and concurred with the programmatic content. In agreed conclusions, the Working Party emphasized the importance of UNCTAD's role in implementing the outcomes of major international conferences and of its assistance to member States in implementing the WTO post-Doha work programme and NEPAD. It also emphasized the importance of the *Least Developed Countries Report* and requested TDB to consider publishing that report annually.

In July [A/58/15], TBD took note of the Working Party's report on the second part of its fortieth session and endorsed the agreed conclusions.

At its forty-first session [TD/B/50/12], the Working Party approved a draft decision for adoption by TDB on technical cooperation (see p. 995); a decision on the in-depth evaluation of the technical assistance programme on trade, environment and development (see p. 996); and agreed conclusions on the progress report on the implementation of the second phase of UNCTAD's web site (see below).

UNCTAD web site

At its forty-first session [TD/B/50/12], the Working Party on the Medium-term Plan and the Programme Budget welcomed the new functionalities of UNCTAD's web site. It requested the secretariat to develop the Newsroom facility for sessional documents and to make documents available to missions in a secure manner. It should also develop a web information diffusion policy, particularly with regard to embargoed and restricted documents, to ensure immediate and full access to all documents by member States. The secretariat should enhance the search facility of its web site and consider organizing a briefing session for delegates on the best use of the web site.

Preparations for UNCTAD XI

At its thirty-first executive session (10 March) [A/58/15], TDB asked its President to conduct consultations, with a view to reaching agreement on the substantive agenda item for UNCTAD XI, to be held in 2004, specific themes to be taken up within the framework of the agenda item, and the arrangements for the preparatory process. It requested the UNCTAD Secretary-General, for the purpose of those consultations, to present proposals in that regard. TDB set the end of April as the deadline for reaching agreement.

At the Board's thirty-second executive session (28 July) [A/58/15], the UNCTAD Deputy Secretary-General reported that both substantive and logistic preparations for UNCTAD XI were proceeding apace. Efforts were currently concentrated on the secretariat's submission, the first part of which would provide a historical perspective and assess global developments since UNCTAD X [YUN 2000, p. 890], while the second part, intended to serve as a basis for negotiations, would outline the issues involved, provide policy options and suggest how UNCTAD could contribute in its future work.

At its fiftieth session (6-17 October) [A/58/15], TDB approved the draft provisional agenda for UNCTAD XI. The substantive agenda item was established as: enhancing coherence between national development strategies and global economic processes towards economic growth and development, particularly of developing countries. The Board also established an open-ended Preparatory Committee for UNCTAD XI, under the chairmanship of the Board's President.

The Preparatory Committee, at its first session (Geneva, 15-16 November) [TD(XXI)/PC/2], considered a submission by the UNCTAD Secretary-General entitled "Preparations for UNCTAD XI" [TD/(XI)/PC/1], in which he gave a historical perspective of trade and development and presented the pre-conference text, which discussed the sub-themes: development strategies in a globalizing world economy; building productive capacity and international competitiveness; assuring development gains from the international trading system and trade negotiations; and partnerships for development. Annexed to the document were proposed arrangements for collaboration between UNCTAD and civil society organizations prior to and during the conference. The Preparatory Committee decided to discuss the sub-themes in a committee of the whole from 17 to 21 November and 4 to 5 December.

UNCTAD Secretary-General

By **decision 57/417** of 6 June, the General Assembly, on the proposal of the Secretary-General [A/57/109], confirmed the extension of the appointment of Rubens Ricupero as Secretary-General of UNCTAD for a period of one year, from 15 September 2003 to 14 September 2004.

Chapter V

Regional economic and social activities

The five regional commissions continued in 2003 to provide technical cooperation, including advisory services, to their member States, promote programmes and projects and provide training to enhance national capacity-building in various sectors. Four of them held regular sessions during the year—the Economic Commission for Africa (ECA), the Economic Commission for Europe (ECE), the Economic and Social Commission for Asia and the Pacific (ESCAP) and the Economic and Social Commission for Western Asia (ESCWA). The Economic Commission for Latin America and the Caribbean (ECLAC) did not meet in 2003 but was scheduled to meet in 2004. The executive secretaries of the commissions continued to hold periodic meetings to exchange views and coordinate activities and positions on major development issues and preparations for and follow-up to UN conferences.

During the year, ECA placed particular emphasis on development issues related to social policy and poverty, and issues related to trade, in the context of the priorities set by the Millennium Development Goals (MDGs) and the New Partnership for Africa's Development. In July, the Economic and Social Council welcomed the cooperation between ECA and ECE on the project for the link through the Strait of Gibraltar and in deep-sea drilling work. ESCAP, in the review of its programmes, focused on the impact of HIV/AIDS on development, poverty reduction, the effects of globalization and implementation of the MDGs. It also considered issues related to landlocked developing countries and called for cooperation in transit transport in the ESCAP region, in accordance with the Almaty Programme of Action on the special transport needs of landlocked developing countries in Central Asia and their neighbours. In July, the Economic and Social Council admitted Timor-Leste as a full member of ESCAP.

The Council decided to establish within ESCWA a committee on women to identify, among other things, women-related priorities of its programme of work and medium-term plan, and to prepare and implement field projects for their advancement and empowerment. It called on the ESCWA secretariat to consider establishing a UN Arabic language centre to raise the technical and linguistic level of Arabic terminology used in UN documents. Other ESCWA activities concerned transport and trade, sustainable development and economic analysis and statistics. Among its activities, ECE focused on trade cooperation and industrial standards, particularly for transition economies. ECLAC continued activities in numerous areas, especially sustainable development and poverty reduction.

Regional cooperation

In 2003, the United Nations continued to strengthen cooperation among its regional commissions, between them and other UN entities, and with regional and international organizations.

On 28 January (**decision 2003/205**), the Economic and Social Council decided that the theme for the regional cooperation item of its 2003 substantive session would be "Development dimensions of trade negotiations: a regional perspective".

Meetings of executive secretaries. The executive secretaries of the five regional commissions met on 12 February (New York), 17 July (Geneva), 29 October (New York) and 9 December (Geneva) [E/2003/15, E/2004/15].

At their February meeting and meetings held in the latter half of 2002 [YUN 2002, p. 973], the executive secretaries exchanged views on, among other topics, the commissions' preparations for the World Summit on the Information Society (see p. 857); the Secretary-General's second set of major reforms contained in his report "Strengthening the United Nations: An Agenda for Further Change" [ibid., p. 1352]; global development issues as they related to their respective regions; and areas of cooperation among the commissions and the relationship between them and their UN system partners. They also exchanged views on the commissions' main strategic tasks in assisting their member States to implement the Millennium Declaration commitments [YUN 2000, p. 49] and those arising from other UN conferences, and on how to reflect those tasks in setting priorities for preparing their 2004-2005 programme budgets.

The executive secretaries agreed that the commissions provided an important regional forum for exchanging policies and best practices among member States and other stakeholders, bringing global concerns to their regions and regional concerns to global forums, and assisting member countries in peer reviews and the exchange of information, including on lessons learned. They also agreed to continue to highlight the role of the commissions in forging common regional positions as well as special concerns that were unique to the regions.

The executive secretaries concurred that, although the dual role of the regional commissions as regional outposts of the United Nations and as its regional expression had been reaffirmed by the Economic and Social Council in resolution 1998/46 [YUN 1998, p. 1262], the Secretary-General's proposals for further reform, including results-based budgeting [YUN 2002, p. 1368], should bring greater convergence of the commissions' activities with the priorities of the Millennium Declaration and the outcomes of major world conferences. For that purpose, through the 2004-2005 budget preparation process, the commissions had further strengthened their priority setting and strategic planning. They had also streamlined their organizational structures and the functioning of their subsidiary governmental forums and reinforced their outreach activities, including through improved dissemination of information about their activities.

Regarding the Secretary-General's proposals for reforming technical cooperation and his intention to clarify roles so as to achieve greater coherence and complementarity in providing those services (see p. 879), the executive secretaries affirmed that the commissions should play the overall leadership role in facilitating cooperation and coordination of technical cooperation activities provided by UN entities to regional and subregional processes, and that the regional coordination meetings mandated by the Council should be utilized for that purpose.

The executive secretaries found the regional coordination meetings useful for information exchange, and agreed to make them more strategic in their approach to coordination and more effective for coordination of follow-up to world conferences and other global intergovernmental commitments, in particular for regional monitoring of the Millennium Development Goals (MDGs) [YUN 2000, p. 51]. The meetings should encourage collaboration among UN entities and linkages of their activities to ensure a more coherent UN system response to agreed priorities for their respective regions. They noted that the ECA mandate for coordinating and monitoring UN activities in support of the New Partnership for Africa's Development (NEPAD) (see p. 937), and its endorsement by the United Nations System Chief Executives Board for Coordination, had ensured a stronger direction for the regional coordination meetings while maintaining their simple structure and lack of bureaucratic layers.

The executive secretaries reviewed the Secretary-General's proposals for strengthening the role of the Executive Committee on Economic and Social Affairs for strategic planning and policy coherence, and noted that the Committee's work had led to improved interaction between the regional commissions and other relevant UN entities working at the global level. They agreed to involve the United Nations Development Programme (UNDP) more actively in the Executive Committee's work and in the regional coordination meetings to ensure improved coordination of regional programmes and activities, and in the preparation of the *Human Development Report*.

The executive secretaries noted the importance of the timely and successful conclusion of the Doha Development Agenda [YUN 2001, p. 1432], and reviewed the regional commissions' role in extending technical assistance to developing countries in preparing for the multilateral trade negotiations. They exchanged views on cooperation between the commissions and subregional organizations and integration groupings in their respective regions. They were of the view that the two projects submitted by the commissions for funding under the UN Development Account (see p. 905)—capacity-building in trade and environment, and interregional partnership for promoting trade as an engine of growth through knowledge management and information and communication technology—should strengthen interregional cooperation and cooperation among the commissions.

Review and reform of the regional commissions

In a May report [E/2003/15], the Secretary-General updated action taken by the regional commissions to implement the guidance given by the Economic and Social Council in resolution 1998/46 [YUN 1998, p. 1262] on restructuring and revitalizing the United Nations. In particular, the report described the commissions' dual role as UN outposts and as the regional expression of the Organization, discussed the theme for the Council's substantive session on regional cooperation (development dimensions of trade negotiations) and cooperation among the regional commissions in given areas, and reported on the meetings of the executive secretaries (see above).

In addenda to the report, the Secretary-General submitted resolutions and decisions adopted at recent meetings of the regional commissions calling for action by the Council [E/2003/15/Add.1] and a summary of resolution 59/1 (see p. 1013), adopted at ESCAP's fifty-ninth session [E/2003/15/Add.2], on regional follow-up to the Declaration of Commitment on HIV/AIDS, adopted at the twenty-sixth special session of the General Assembly by resolution S-26/2 [YUN 2001, p. 1126]

By **decision 2003/274** of 24 July, the Council took note of the Secretary-General's reports on regional cooperation (above) and the summaries of the economic and social situation in Africa, 2002 [E/2003/17]; the economic and social survey of Asia and the Pacific, 2003 [E/2003/18]; the economic survey of Europe, 2002 [E/2003/16]; the economic survey of Latin America and the Caribbean, 2002 [E/2003/19]; and the survey of economic and social developments in the ESCWA region, 2002-2003 [E/2003/20].

The Council adopted resolutions on the admission of Timor-Leste as a full member of ESCAP (**resolution 2003/7**); the establishment within ESCWA of a committee on women (**resolution 2003/9**) and of a UN Arabic language centre (**resolution 2003/8**); and the project for a Europe-Africa link through the Strait of Gibraltar (**resolution 2003/52**). It adopted a decision on the date and venue of ESCAP's sixtieth (2004) session (**decision 2003/228**).

(Summaries of the surveys and the texts of the resolutions are found in the relevant sections of this chapter.)

The General Assembly, in **resolution 58/272** of 23 December (see p. 1447), took note of the Secretary-General's report on the proportion of General Service staff to Professional staff in the regional commissions [A/58/403] and the related report of the Advisory Committee on Administrative and Budgetary Questions [A/58/7/Add.5] (see p. 1447).

Review of regional commission subprogrammes

In April [E/AC.51/2003/4], the Secretary-General transmitted to the Committee for Programme and Coordination (CPC) the report of the Office of Internal Oversight Services on the triennial review of the implementation of the recommendations made by CPC on the in-depth evaluation of global development trends, issues and policies, global approaches to social and microeconomic issues and policies, and the corresponding subprogrammes in the regional commissions. The review, submitted in accordance with General Assembly resolution 54/244 [YUN 1999, p. 1274], concluded that the Department of Economic and Social Affairs (DESA) and the regional commissions had improved the quality and presentation of those reports to ensure that their findings and proposals could more easily reach government officials and the specialized public. The programmes concerned had applied good practices that were increasing the dissemination of analyses, such as the timely release of publications, more targeted distribution and special briefings to government officials and the press. Greater efforts were needed to ensure that economic analyses served as a source for understanding long-term trends, thereby contributing to the achievement of the MDGs. The exchange of information between DESA and the regional commissions would benefit from a more focused and institutionalized approach; for example, standard procedures should be followed during the planning stage of global and regional economic surveys.

At its forty-third session (New York, 9 June–3 July and 9 July) [A/58/16], CPC stressed the need for regional commissions to redouble their efforts in establishing strong linkages with regional and national institutions that were end-users of the outputs of the commissions' work on regional socio-economic analysis, in order to ensure that the findings of such studies could be taken into account at the country and regional levels.

Africa

The Economic Commission for Africa (ECA) held its thirty-sixth session/Conference of African Ministers of Finance, Planning and Economic Development (Addis Ababa, Ethiopia, 29 May–1 June) [E/ECA/CM.36/4] under the theme "Towards greater coherence and mutual accountability for development effectiveness". It considered the modalities and terms of reference for an external review of ECA's work since 1996, the proposed programme of work and priorities for 2004-2005 and the Commission's annual report for the 12-month period beginning 1 June 2002.

The Conference of African Ministers adopted a ministerial statement in which Ministers recognized the emerging consensus in the international community on the importance to development effectiveness of mutual accountability, harmonization and policy coherence. They considered their deliberations as a critical African effort to operationalize mutual accountability, promote policy coherence, contribute to making the International Monetary Fund (IMF) work better for Africa, and overcome the macroeconomic challenges of HIV/AIDS and thereby contribute to meeting the MDGs.

The Conference was preceded by the twenty-second meeting of the Committee of Experts of the Conference of African Ministers of Finance, Planning and Economic Development (Addis Ababa, 29-30 May), which discussed the items on the Commission's agenda.

The third Tokyo International Conference on African Development (TICAD III) (Tokyo, 29 September–1 October) reviewed the achievements of the 10-year TICAD process and discussed its future direction. The Conference adopted the TICAD Tenth Anniversary Declaration, affirming the ideal of partnership based on mutual trust and respect between Africa and the international community. The Chairman issued a summary of the proceedings.

The Second Ministerial Conference of the China-Africa Cooperation Forum (Addis Ababa, December) adopted the Addis Ababa Action Plan (2004-2006), which would serve as a guideline for cooperation between Africa and China.

Economic trends

In 2003, Africa's gross domestic product (GDP) grew by 3.6 per cent, compared to 3.2 per cent in 2002, making it the second fastest growing region in the developing world, behind Eastern and Southern Asia, according to the "Economic report on Africa 2004: unlocking Africa's potential in the global economy" [E/2004/17]. That performance was due largely to higher oil prices and production, rising commodity prices, increased foreign direct investment and good macroeconomic fundamentals, backed by good weather conditions. North Africa showed the strongest performance with a 4.7 per cent growth in GDP, followed by Central Africa at 3.7 per cent and West Africa at 3.6 per cent. East and Southern Africa both registered a paltry growth of 2.5 per cent. At the country level, there was a greater disparity in growth, with seven countries experiencing negative rates.

Fiscal deficits were largely kept under control, despite the challenge faced by many African countries in balancing spending on poverty reduction and preserving macroeconomic stability. Inflation rose slightly to 10.6 per cent, compared to 9.3 per cent in 2002, reflecting higher food and oil-import prices and currency depreciation in several countries. The regional current account deficit fell from 1.6 per cent of GDP in 2002 to 0.7 per cent in 2003, driven by robust oil and commodity prices and high worker remittances.

There was a slight deterioration in aggregate economic performance for sub-Saharan Africa, down from 3.5 per cent in 2002 to 2.9 per cent in 2003 and, in terms of per capita growth rates, North Africa and sub-Saharan Africa, with the highest rates of demographic expansion in the world, registered rates of 2.7 per cent and 1.7 per cent, respectively, which were clearly inadequate to achieve the MDGs for poverty reduction.

Activities in 2003

ECA activities in 2003 were undertaken through the following subprogrammes: facilitating economic and social policy analysis; fostering sustainable development; strengthening development management; harnessing information for development; promoting trade and regional integration; promoting the advancement of women; and supporting subregional activities for development [E/ECA/CM.36/4, E/ECA/CM.37/4].

Development policy and regional economic development

African recovery and development

ECA continued in 2003 to strengthen the capacity of member States to design and implement appropriate economic and social policies and strategies to achieve sustained economic growth for poverty reduction, in line with the priorities of the Millennium Declaration [YUN 2000, p. 49] and the New Partnership for Africa's Development (NEPAD) [YUN 2001, p. 899]. Particular emphasis was placed on economic policy analysis, development issues related to social policy and poverty analysis, trade and finance, and statistical development.

In the area of economic policy analysis, ECA published the 2003 edition of the *Economic Report on Africa* under the theme "Accelerating the pace of development". ECA's work in social policy and poverty analysis focused on support for member States in achieving the goals of NEPAD and the Millennium Declaration, including the preparation of analytical studies and other research activities, to help them understand the structural causes of poverty in order to design and implement effective pro-poor policies and strategies. Several other studies examined the policy and methodological issues involved in poverty measurement in Africa. The secretariat organized an ad hoc expert group meeting (Kampala, Uganda, June) to analyse the impact of pro-poor growth strategies on such sectors as education, labour, health, tourism and agriculture. It also convened the third meeting of the African Learning Group on the Poverty Reduction Strategy Paper (PRSP) (Addis Ababa, 3-5 December), which examined the PRSP process, the extent to which African countries were using the framework to focus on poverty reduction, and how it was influencing Africa's major development partners and shaping the new aid relationship. Two workshops were held on capital markets development in October (Johannesburg, South Africa, and Cairo, Egypt), and an ad hoc expert group meeting (Addis Ababa) was held on fiscal policy and growth in Africa to examine the challenges of decentralization, fiscal federalism and taxation and their implications for growth and poverty reduction.

As a follow-up to ECA's discussion on mutual accountability and policy coherence, the secretariat convened a special session of the ECA Big Table (Washington, D.C., October) to review how policies and practices of the Bretton Woods institutions (the World Bank Group and IMF) could contribute to Africa's realization of the MDGs.

New Partnership for Africa's Development

ECA continued to chair the regional consultative meetings of UN agencies working in Africa, which constituted the framework for coordination of UN system support for NEPAD [E/AC.51/2003/6]—a programme for the continent's development, initiated by African leaders in 2001 [YUN 2001, p. 899]. Under the infrastructure development cluster, one of the five clusters around which the UN system organized support for NEPAD [YUN 2002, p. 977], ECA and the World Bank, in collaboration with other partners, developed a long-term plan for the Sub-Saharan Africa Transport Programme, which was to be adopted by the Programme's General Meeting (Kigali, Rwanda, May). ECA and the African Development Bank carried out a study on the Trans African Highways, which was reviewed by stakeholders (Addis Ababa, 30-31 January). With regard to air transport, ECA and the World Bank helped the Economic Community of West African States (ECOWAS) and the Economic and Monetary Community of Central Africa (CEMAC) to organize a ministerial meeting for West and Central Africa (25-28 February) to consider economic regulatory and safety oversight programmes. To that end, a plan was adopted, and ECA and the World Bank agreed to evaluate the Bank-supported capacity-building programmes for air transport at ECOWAS and CEMAC. Under the human resources development, employment and HIV/AIDS cluster, ECA supported the new commission on HIV/AIDS in Africa and the regional programme for HIV/AIDS.

In **resolution 58/233** of 23 December (see p. 941), the General Assembly, noting the growing collaboration among UN system entities in support of NEPAD, requested the Secretary-General to promote greater coherence in the work of the UN system in support of NEPAD, on the basis of the agreed clusters.

(For more on NEPAD, see p. 937.)

Information technology

ECA activities under the subprogramme on harnessing information for development focused on promoting the growth of an information society in Africa through harnessing information and communication technologies (ICTs). The Commission assisted African countries in preparing for the World Summit on the Information Society (see p. 857), including through follow-up activities to the African Regional Preparatory Conference [YUN 2002, p. 978], such as the African media practitioners' forum (Addis Ababa, May) and the African Engineers' Day (Tunis, Tunisia, October). ECA continued to provide support to its member States in preparing for the second phase of the World Summit, scheduled to be held in Tunis in 2005. It participated in the launch of several initiatives and projects at the Summit, including the Global e-Policy Resource Network, thereby setting up the African regional node to coordinate demand from African institutions seeking guidance on e-strategies. ECA successfully completed the task of ensuring that information fed into the *Spatial Data Infrastructures Africa: An Implementation Guide,* launched in 2003 to provide guidelines on such national and regional infrastructures, was compatible and complementary. It worked closely with UNDP in the formulation of national information and communications infrastructure policies and plans for Cameroon, Malawi, Mozambique, Rwanda and Swaziland. Collaboration was also strengthened with other UN agencies within the context of the activities of the African Stakeholders Network of the UN ICT Task Force, which ECA coordinated. ECA and the World Intellectual Property Organization organized a subregional workshop (Addis Ababa, November) to address issues related to strategies for the acquisition, management and dissemination of intellectual property information.

The third meeting of the Committee on Development Information (CODI III) (Addis Ababa, 10-16 May), held under the theme "Information and governance", underscored the importance of information and good governance in Africa and made recommendations on strategies for harnessing information to enhance good governance practices. As part of CODI III activities, the Global Knowledge Partnership Africa Day was held on 13 May, focusing on, among other things, ICT and governance experiences in African countries, strategies for promoting e-governance, progress on ICT policies, and information and knowledge developments.

Transport and communications

Europe-Africa permanent link

In response to Economic and Social Council resolution 1999/37 [YUN 1999, p. 918], the Secretary-General submitted a May report [E/2003/45] by the executive secretaries of ECA and ECE on the work done in connection with the project to establish a Europe-Africa permanent link through the Strait of Gibraltar. The report described the work carried out by two research companies in the areas of topographic mapping and related activities, geological mapping, oceanography, geotechnical tests and traffic monitoring. The information gathered so far seemed to indicate that the temporarily suspended studies and activities, particularly offshore deep drilling activities, should be restarted. That, together with the possible construction of a submarine exploration tunnel, should clear up remaining doubts as to the technical feasibility of a bored rail tunnel.

ECONOMIC AND SOCIAL COUNCIL ACTION

On 24 July [meeting 47], the Economic and Social Council adopted **resolution 2003/52** [draft: E/2003/L.16] without vote [agenda item 10].

Europe-Africa permanent link through the Strait of Gibraltar

The Economic and Social Council,

Recalling its resolutions 1982/57 of 30 July 1982, 1983/62 of 29 July 1983, 1984/75 of 27 July 1984, 1985/70 of 26 July 1985, 1987/69 of 8 July 1987, 1989/119 of 28 July 1989, 1991/74 of 26 July 1991, 1993/60 of 30 July 1993, 1995/48 of 27 July 1995, 1997/48 of 22 July 1997, 1999/37 of 28 July 1999 and 2001/29 of 26 July 2001,

Referring to resolution 912(1989) adopted on 1 February 1989 by the Parliamentary Assembly of the Council of Europe regarding measures to encourage the construction of a major traffic artery in southwestern Europe and to study thoroughly the possibility of a permanent link through the Strait of Gibraltar,

Referring also to the Barcelona Declaration adopted at the Euro-Mediterranean Conference, held at Barcelona, Spain, in November 1995, and to the work programme annexed thereto, aimed at connecting the Mediterranean transport networks to the trans-European transport networks so as to ensure their interoperability,

Referring further to the Lisbon Declaration adopted at the Conference on Transport in the Mediterranean, held at Lisbon in January 1997, and to the conclusions of the Pan-European Transport Conference, held at Helsinki in June 1997, on corridors in the Mediterranean incorporating the permanent link,

Taking note of the conclusions of the second and third meetings of the Western Mediterranean Transport Group, held at Rabat in September 1995 and at Madrid in January 1997, and of the conclusions of the meeting held at Brussels in 2000 by the Euro-Mediterranean Forum on Transport, which constitutes a framework for coordination among the countries of the Mediterranean basin, for the development of integrated transport networks,

Taking note also of the conclusions of the study on transport infrastructure in the six countries of the western Mediterranean, carried out by the Western Mediterranean Transport Group in 1998, which is currently being updated with funding by the European Commission, for the establishment of an integrated network in the Mediterranean basin,

Taking note further of the follow-up report prepared jointly by the Economic Commission for Africa and the Economic Commission for Europe in accordance with resolution 2001/29, which refers to further project studies, with the aim, in particular, of supplementing the related geological and geotechnical research,

1. *Welcomes* the cooperation on the project for the link through the Strait of Gibraltar between the Economic Commission for Africa, the Economic Commission for Europe, the Governments of Morocco and Spain and specialized international organizations;

2. *Also welcomes* the efforts made to date in deep-sea drilling work, which have provided a decisive impetus to geological and geotechnical knowledge of undersea formations, and invites the two sponsoring countries and the organizations concerned to intensify their cooperation in order to finalize the project studies;

3. *Commends* the Economic Commission for Africa and the Economic Commission for Europe on the work done in preparing the project follow-up report requested by the Council in its resolution 2001/29;

4. *Renews* its invitation to the competent organizations of the United Nations system and to specialized governmental and non-governmental organizations to participate in the studies and operations on the permanent link through the Strait of Gibraltar;

5. *Requests* the Executive Secretaries of the Economic Commission for Africa and the Economic Commission for Europe to continue to take an active part in the follow-up to the project and to report to the Council at its substantive session of 2005;

6. *Requests* the Secretary-General to provide formal support and, to the extent that priorities permit, the resources necessary, within the regular budget, to the Economic Commission for Africa and the Economic Commission for Europe, to enable them to carry out the activities mentioned above.

Industrial development

The sixteenth meeting of the Conference of African Ministers of Industry (Vienna, 28 November), convened in cooperation with the African Union (AU) and the NEPAD secretariat, requested the Director-General of the United Nations Industrial Development Organization to support African industrialization under the framework of NEPAD, in line with General Assembly resolution 57/297 [YUN 2002, p. 979] on the Second Industrial Development Decade for Africa (1993-2002). The Conference adopted the African Productive Capacity Initiative (APCI), with the objective of providing further impetus to structural change in Africa, encouraging economic growth and sustainable development, promoting intra-trade and regional production processes, removing constraints and reducing transaction costs. It established the African Productive Capacity Facility to finance implementation of APCI.

Food security and sustainable development

ECA activities under the subprogramme on food security and sustainable development were aimed at enhancing the awareness and understanding of policy makers of the environmental foundations of sustainable development, with particular focus on strengthening their capacities for better integrating the nexus of food security, population growth, environmental sustainability and sustainable natural resources management into national development plans and poverty reduction strategies. ECA also helped to create awareness of the potential contribution of science and technology, including biotechnology, to achieving food security and sustainable development. The secretariat assisted member States in defining their environmental challenges and priorities and identifying strategies for addressing them.

ECA organized the third meeting of the Committee on Sustainable Development (Addis Ababa, 7-10 October), under the theme "Making technology work for the poor". The Committee adopted recommendations on harmonizing its work with that of the Commission on Sustainable Development (see p. 838) and making the Committee serve as a regional review forum for the Commission. Six ad hoc expert group meetings were organized to address land tenure policies and their implications for food security and sustainable development, indicators for measuring food security in Africa, assessment of power pooling arrangements, the green revolution in Africa, the regional 10-year review of the International Conference on Population and Development [YUN 1994, p. 955], and minerals cluster development. ECA also undertook research and prepared studies on a variety of related subjects. As a follow-up to the ad hoc expert group meeting that helped develop the road map to a green revolution in Africa, the secretariat organized an advocacy ministerial round table on the topic at the high-level segment of the Economic and Social Council (Geneva, July) (see p. 853). It also implemented a field project in Kampala, Uganda, in December, bringing together key African researchers to identify indicators and contribute to designing a strategy for agricultural modernization.

The secretariat supported implementation of the NEPAD mining chapter, providing, in collaboration with the United Nations Educational, Scientific and Cultural Organization, technical assistance for revamping African science and technology, including commissioning working papers for an experts' preparatory meeting (Nairobi, Kenya, October). It participated in the ministerial meeting in Johannesburg, which adopted an action plan and established a Ministerial Council for Managing Science and Technology in Africa.

Development management

The issue of governance in Africa was centred on the "capable State"—one in which the public service, legislature, judiciary and statutory bodies could provide an enabling environment for all sectors of society to play their respective roles in improving governance and consolidating the foundations for sustainable development. Activities under the subprogramme of strengthening development management focused on promoting good governance and enhancing broad-based stakeholder participation in the development process. In that regard, ECA continued its project on "Measuring and monitoring progress towards good governance in Africa", in order to prepare for the first edition of the African Governance Report, to be launched in 2004. Activities under that project included extensive fieldwork and country-level research, in collaboration with several national institutions, to develop 83 core indicators assessing three broad areas of governance: political representation, institutional effectiveness and economic management, and corporate governance. In preparation for the Fourth African Development Forum, to be held in 2004, ECA organized three subregional workshops in 2003—for Eastern and Southern Africa (Lusaka, Zambia, November); Central and West Africa (Accra, Ghana, December); and North Africa, including the Horn of Africa (Cairo, Egypt, December). A meeting of the Forum's Steering Committee was held in July in Addis Ababa to agree on the issues paper and the overall approach to the Forum's work.

The second meeting of the Committee on Human Development and Civil Society (Addis Ababa, 26-27 May), organized in collaboration with the Joint United Nations Programme on HIV/AIDS, deliberated on the theme of participation and partnership in Africa's development. Some of the Committee's recommendations served as the basis for the regional input to the high-level panel discussion on HIV/AIDS, organized as part of the General Assembly's fifty-eighth (2003) session (see p. 1243). The meeting developed a framework for promoting the creation of modalities for the dissemination of "best practices", institutional reforms and capacity-building initiatives needed to meet the MDGs by 2015. A list of indicators for monitoring the effectiveness of that framework was also developed.

Promoting trade and regional integration

ECA's Trade and Regional Integration Division continued to promote the integration and participation of African countries in the global economy and to strengthen the regional integration process, focusing on policy issues and infrastructure development. To realize that objective, the Division undertook activities in the areas of trade promotion and multilateral trade negotiations; facilitating the process of regional economic integration; and transportation infrastructure development. It initiated or participated in analytical studies in support of trade promotion and multilateral trade negotiations, including the Economic Report, 2004, on the theme "Unlocking Africa's trade potential in the global economy".

At the request of member States, ECA undertook several initiatives and activities to strengthen their capacities for effective participation in the new multilateral trade arrangements; for example, it collaborated with the AU Commission and other organizations to organize the second high-level brainstorming meeting of African trade negotiators (Grand Baie, Mauritius, June), which formed the basis for the African common position for the fifth World Trade Organization (WTO) ministerial meeting (Cancún, Mexico, September) (see p. 1535). As a follow-up to the WTO meeting, the secretariat, in collaboration with the AU Commission and Ghana, organized an expert group meeting (Accra, 28-29 November) to evaluate the implications of the Cancún meeting for African countries, assist countries to develop strategies for further negotiations, and identify research needs for those negotiations. Other trade-related activities included the convening of an expert group meeting (Addis Ababa, October) on the impact of trade liberalization on the fiscal revenue base of African countries. To support the NEPAD goal of mobilizing resources for poverty reduction and development, progress was made in establishing the African Trade Policy Centre, with the objective of strengthening Africa's trading capacity through research, training and capacity-building.

The third session of the Committee on Regional Cooperation and Integration (Addis Ababa, 30-31 October) brought together representatives of member States, the AU, the World Bank and other regional and international organizations dealing with air transport issues to consider matters pertaining to ECA's activities in support of the African economic integration process. The meeting reviewed reports on the status of regional integration in Africa, the implementation of the 1988 Yamoussoukro Declaration on air transport [YUN 1988, p. 273] and air transport liberalization in Africa. In the area of transport infrastructure development, a study was undertaken on multimodal transport development in Africa, which was reviewed by an ad hoc expert group meeting (Addis Ababa, October). The meeting recommended the establishment of a regional dispute settlement mechanism to arbitrate disputes between and among member States and that a study be conducted on the impact of liberalization in America and Europe.

Integration of women in development

In 2003, ECA continued to develop instruments for measuring progress in attaining the priorities identified in the Dakar [YUN 1994, p. 696] and Beijing [YUN 1995, p. 1170] Platforms for Action on the advancement of women. It developed an Africa-specific guidebook on mainstreaming gender into national planning instruments, including national accounts and national budgetary instruments. The guidebook contained a set of methodologies and tools as an easy reference for mainstreaming gender and provided guidelines in such areas as the collection of gender-disaggregated data through time-use studies, and evaluation of policy impacts on poverty reduction and welfare. The guidebook, reviewed by an ad hoc expert group meeting in December, was intended to inform decision makers about the importance of women's contribution to the national product and enhance their capacity for mainstreaming that contribution into national budgetary processes. The African Gender and Development Index, launched in 2002 [YUN 2002, p. 980], moved into a second phase with trials in Benin, Burkina Faso, Cameroon, Ethiopia, Ghana, South Africa, Uganda and the United Republic of Tanzania. The process of compiling country gender profiles for all 53 African countries was completed. The secretariat finalized a programme for the Africa Decade Review of the implementation of the Dakar and Beijing Platforms for Action, which was endorsed in September by the Bureau of the Committee on Women and Development.

ECA continued to support the economic empowerment of women through assistance for subregional enterprise development facilities. In May, it launched the facility for the East Africa subregion, based in Kampala.

Subregional Offices

The Subregional Offices (formerly called Subregional Development Centres), located in Central, East, North, Southern and West Africa, continued to promote policy dialogue and support development initiatives through collaborative arrangements with member States or through regional economic communities and intergovernmental bodies. They also provided technical assistance and promoted regional integration initiatives among the constituencies they served.

Construction of office facilities at ECA

In July [A/58/154], the Secretary-General, in response to resolution 56/270 [YUN 2002, p. 1459], reported on progress in the construction of additional office facilities at ECA headquarters in Addis Ababa (see p. 1500), including a revised project schedule of design consultancy and construction activities and a proposed site plan.

Asia and the Pacific

The Economic and Social Commission for Asia and the Pacific (ESCAP) held its fifty-ninth session in Bangkok, Thailand, in two phases: the first on 24 and 25 April [E/2003/39]; and the second from 1 to 4 September [E/2003/39/Add.1], under the theme "Integrating economic and social concerns, especially HIV/AIDS, in meeting the needs of the region". The Commission also held a two-part ministerial round table: one part on HIV/AIDS and the other on the first regional report on the MDGs [YUN 2000, p. 51].

The Commission reviewed programme planning and evaluation, resource mobilization, including technical cooperation, transit transport issues in landlocked and transit developing countries, policy and management questions, emerging regional issues and developments, least developed, landlocked and island developing countries, and reports of regional intergovernmental bodies.

The Commission agreed that the theme of its sixtieth session would be "Meeting the challenges in an era of globalization by strengthening regional development cooperation".

Economic trends

According to the summary of the economic and social survey of Asia and the Pacific, 2004 [E/2004/18], the developing economies of the region continued to show strong growth in 2003, achieving a real GDP growth rate of 6 per cent. ESCAP developing countries' GDP grew faster than the global economy and other groups of developing countries as a result of forces within the region, such as intraregional trade and strong domestic demand. China's performance in just three years (2001-2003) was central in sustaining the momentum of growth in the region as a whole. Regional developed countries achieved a GDP growth rate of 2.7 per cent, due to a strong revival of growth in Japan, for the first time in 10 years, and continued dynamism in Australia and New Zealand.

In the North and Central Asia subregion, GDP growth accelerated by an impressive 2.3 percentage points to reach 7.7 per cent. The already high rates of growth in economies such as Armenia, Azerbaijan, Georgia, Tajikistan and Turkmenistan increased further, while the economy of the Russian Federation exceeded expectations and reached 7.3 per cent. The latter's performance was driven by the strong energy and other natural resource sectors, aided by the continued diversification of the economy. The collective GDP rate in South and South-West Asia showed marked improvement, reaching 6.6 per cent. That growth was almost exclusively accounted for by India, although Bangladesh, Pakistan and Sri Lanka also experienced better growth rates to varying degrees. The growth in India (7.5 per cent) and Pakistan (5.1 per cent) was facilitated by more favourable weather, which aided a stronger output in agriculture. The GDP growth rate of the South-East Asian countries reached 4.5 per cent, a slight improvement over the previous year's performance, but nowhere near the momentum of growth in the 1980s and 1990s. East and North-East Asia was the only subregion not to experience a more rapid GDP growth rate in 2003 (6 per cent), as the rapid growth of the Chinese economy failed to offset the slowdown in the Republic of Korea and weaker growth in the Taiwan Province of China. The Pacific island countries emerged from two years of recession to achieve a GDP growth rate of 2.8 per cent, stimulated by higher agricultural commodity prices. However, inflationary pressures intensified, especially in the larger economies of Papua New Guinea and Fiji, due to higher energy prices.

The developed economies of the region saw a strong revival of growth, with Japan showing signs of durable growth (2.7 per cent compared to negative growth in 2002) for the first time in 10 years and Australia (2.8 per cent) and New Zealand (2.7 per cent) continuing to show dynamism.

Policy issues

Even with relatively buoyant economic growth, some problematic policy issues faced the region, such as the unwinding of global imbalances and the weakening of the dollar, from which individual economies needed to shield themselves, and the appreciation of regional exchange rates, which required flexibility of response buttressed by stronger regional cooperation. Another policy issue was the possible emergence of asset bubbles in stock markets and in real estate and whether pre-emptive action was the appropriate response. Other regional issues included the outbreak of avian influenza, requiring strong cooperation in containing the spread of the disease, and the need for Governments to place short-term issues within their longer-term commitments, such as those in the MDGs.

The need for fiscal consolidation was becoming paramount. Governments had to adopt strict debt-to-GDP ratios and annual budgetary deficits as the European Union (EU) had done in its Stability and Growth Pact, aimed at introducing an element of predictability in their public finances, and providing a more secure and informed basis for investment decisions. The consolidation of public debt should be approached within a long-term programme of fiscal reform. All national tax systems in the region needed to be more equitable and efficient. One problematic element in national tax systems was the discretionary powers given to tax officials, which tended to erode accountability, open up opportunities for corrupt practices and lower efficiency. Corporate and financial sector reform had made significant progress in the region as a whole, but needed to be accelerated.

The key to steady development in the medium term was maintaining and enhancing competitiveness, and investment in human resources development was a critically important element in that regard. Many regional countries were not doing enough in that area and risked falling behind in competitiveness.

Financial market infrastructure was poorly developed to assist small and medium-sized enterprises, a major source of employment, in growing to an efficient size. Many of them found it difficult to access financing in order to expand. Governments should reinforce training, technology transfer, information dissemination and the formation of networks to improve the performance of small and medium-sized enterprises.

Governance remained a policy challenge throughout the region, despite some progress in private and public sector governance. The lack of, or differential access to, administrative or legal redress reduced productivity. Governments should correct shortcomings, such as counterproductive State bureaucracy and delays in the legal process. Corporate malfeasance and corruption by public officials also needed to be tackled vigorously.

At its 2003 session, ESCAP considered reports on the current economic situation in the region and related policy issues [E/ESCAP/1266/Rev.1 & Corr.1] and the economic and social survey of Asia and the Pacific in 2003 (see p. 1007). The Commission noted that, in 2003, the region had to face further difficulties, such as the war in Iraq (see p. 315), the outbreak of severe acute respiratory syndrome (SARS) and new terrorist attacks. Although those developments had adversely affected the economic outlook for the region, economic performance remained satisfactory. However, Governments would have to improve public and private sector governance and transparency. In the medium to long term, poverty was the major policy challenge facing the region's developing countries. To attain the MDGs and improve the people's well-being, national economic and social policies had to be integrated. The Commission suggested that the secretariat evaluate the interaction between economic and social policies and examine the mechanisms by which social expenditures acted as productive factors in the development process.

The Commission urged that special attention be given to the integration of least developed countries into the multilateral trading system on fair terms, including duty-free and quota-free access for their products and a guaranteed increase in the market share of unskilled and semi-skilled providers of goods and services in world trade. It agreed that the problem of HIV/AIDS (see p. 1013) was no longer simply a health problem, but a serious threat to development, security and stability, and had to be dealt with in a holistic manner.

Activities in 2003

Poverty reduction

For its discussion of poverty reduction, the Commission had before it a document on related developments, issues and strategies [E/ESCAP/1268/Rev.1] and the report of the Committee on Statistics on its thirteenth (November 2002) session [E/ESCAP/1269].

The Commission supported the secretariat's plan to assist members in reducing poverty in a strategy comprising research on economic development prospects and policies that influenced poverty reduction, disseminating good practices in poverty reduction, and adopting and replicating those practices in trade and entrepreneurial development, environment, information, communication and space technology, and social development. It recommended that the secretariat explore financial frameworks to ensure equal access of the poor to credit facilities and promote domestic financial institutions working for the poor. The Commission agreed that poverty should be tackled through the enhancement of agricultural productivity, health care, educational standards, affordable access to information, communication and space technology, advancement of the status of women and weaker sections of society and the promotion of wider political participation. Noting the linkages between poverty and environmental degradation, the Commission requested the secretariat to propose poverty reduction programmes and activities to assist countries in promoting sustainable development practices and in implementing the Monterrey Consensus, adopted at the 2002 International Conference on Financing for Development [YUN 2002, p. 953], and the Johannesburg Declaration and Plan of Implementation, adopted at the World Summit on Sustainable Development [ibid., p. 821]. The Commission stressed the importance of human security within the framework of poverty reduction and development, based on the empowerment of individuals, and underlined the importance of indicators in illuminating policy matters with regard to poverty.

The Committee on Poverty Reduction, at its first session (Bangkok, 8-10 October) [E/ESCAP/1306], discussed financial and other key resource mobilization issues in implementing the MDGs, and issues related to poverty statistics and measurement, the transfer of good and innovative practices, and information and communication technology for poverty reduction. The Committee recommended that stakeholders coordinate their efforts to achieve the MDGs, with UN assistance. It noted the need to strengthen national statistical infrastructure and improve the quality of statistics, and encouraged the secretariat to provide more coherence in the identification and replication of poverty reduction interventions and to place emphasis on the capacity-building of the agencies involved in poverty reduction programmes.

The Commission also endorsed the report of the Steering Group of the Committee on Regional Economic Cooperation on its fourteenth meeting (2-4 December 2002) [E/ESCAP/1276], and urged that the recommendations contained therein be implemented. It requested the secretariat to continue its assistance in capacity-building in trade and investment, paying particular attention to sustained investment liberalization, strengthening the legal framework, institutional capacity-building, development of infrastructure for trade and investment, human resources development and private sector development, with special attention to the development of small and medium-sized enterprises and microenterprises.

Statistics

The Commission endorsed the report of the Committee on Statistics on its thirteenth (2002) session [E/ESCAP/1269] and supported its recommendations, including initiatives on statistical capacity-building. It recommended the sharing of good practices on poverty statistics and urged the secretariat to contribute to the preparation of a handbook on concepts, methods and practices in poverty statistics being developed by the United Nations Statistics Division.

Noting the inadequacy of economic statistics in many countries, resulting in a lack of basic data on such subjects as capital stocks, the Commission requested the secretariat to provide assistance in that regard. It also noted the Committee's efforts to improve the measurement of economic activity, including of the informal sector and the informal economy. The Commission considered it important that countries be informed of new data collection techniques and methods to capture and estimate the full production of the informal economy. It further noted the progress made on preparations for the 2004 round of the International Comparison Programme, but expressed concern about the adequacy of the funding. It requested the secretariat to provide assistance and capacity-building in statistics related to the measurement of the information society and knowledge-based economy, which had become a priority in the region.

The Commission also considered the report of the Governing Board of the Statistical Institute for Asia and the Pacific [E/ESCAP/1270], which gave an overview of training activities implemented in 2002/03 and highlighted issues for the Commission's attention, including the Institute's 2003/04 programme of work.

Managing globalization

The Commission considered a secretariat note [E/ESCAP/1297] on progress in the implementation of Commission resolutions relating to the theme of managing globalization. Those resolutions dealt with transport infrastructure development, space applications for sustainable development, environment and sustainable development, information and communication technologies for development, the 2002 World Summit on Sustainable Development [YUN 2002, p. 821] and establishment of the Asian and Pacific Centre for Agricultural Engineering and Machinery [ibid., p. 990].

The Commission noted that, although the region had benefited from globalization, the impact had been uneven. It underscored the need for concerted efforts among countries at different development levels and for creating a conducive environment for regional cooperation that would encourage the forces of globalization to promote economic and social development in the region.

The first session of the Committee on Managing Globalization (Bangkok, 19-21 November) [E/ESCAP/1307] reviewed selected cross-cutting issues (trade and transport facilitation, sustainable consumption and production, regional cooperation for bridging the digital divide) and sectoral developments, and provided guidance on the future work of its subcommittees on international trade and investment, transport infrastructure and facilitation and tourism, environment and sustainable development, and information, communications and space technology. It recommended an integrated approach to addressing trade and transport facilitation issues and requested the secretariat to assist countries in applying the Trade Facilitation Framework and the time and cost-distance model. It recognized the secretariat's lead role in the shift towards sustainable consumption and production. The Committee commended the secretariat's work in the area of trade and investment, with a focus on the Doha Development Agenda [YUN 2001, p. 1432]. It requested the secretariat to give priority to a study on current regional trade arrangements and bilateral trade initiatives, and to issues relating to the importance of foreign direct investment in the development process.

The Committee endorsed the ESCAP strategy on infrastructure development and transport facilitation and supported a revised plan for the Asian land transport infrastructure project (see p. 1011). It recommended that a ministerial conference on transport be organized in 2006 and an intergovernmental meeting on sustainable tourism development in 2005. It urged member countries to sign or accede to the Intergovernmental Agreement on the Asian Highway Network, adopted by the Intergovernmental Meeting to Develop an Intergovernmental Agreement on the Asian Highway Network (Bangkok, 17-18 November) [E/ESCAP/TTD/AHN/Rep].

The Committee endorsed the use of the regional road map towards an information society in Asia and the Pacific for the formulation of an action plan. It urged the convening of an intergovernmental meeting to analyse the outcome of the World Summit on Sustainable Development and requested the secretariat to continue its efforts in the areas of the environment, energy and water and water-related disaster mitigation and preparedness.

Least developed, landlocked and island developing countries

Special Body on Least Developed and Landlocked Developing Countries

The Commission considered the report of the Special Body on Least Developed and Landlocked Developing Countries on its sixth session (Bangkok, 1-2 September) [E/ESCAP/1303 & Corr.1], which reviewed the outcome of the International Ministerial Conference of Landlocked and Transit Developing Countries and Donor Countries and International Financial and Development Institutions on Transit Transport Cooperation (Almaty, Kazakhstan, 28-29 August) [E/ESCAP/1309]. The Conference adopted the Almaty Programme of Action: Addressing the Special Needs of Landlocked Developing Countries within a New Global Framework for Transit Transport Cooperation for Landlocked and Transit Developing Countries (see p. 875), which set out measures for establishing efficient transit transport systems in five areas—transit policy issues, infrastructure development and maintenance, international trade and trade facilitation, international support measures and implementation and review. The Commission urged all stakeholders to implement the Programme of Action.

Landlocked States in Central Asia

In August [A/58/209], the Secretary-General transmitted to the General Assembly the report of the Secretary-General of the United Nations Conference on Trade and Development (UNCTAD) on the transit environment in landlocked States in Central Asia and their transit developing neighbours, in response to General Assembly resolution 55/181 [YUN 2000, p. 933]. The report discussed the transit environment in Central Asia and current measures to improve that environment and reduce non-physical barriers to transit transport through national laws and increased regional and international cooperation. The report also discussed complementary new actions to improve the transit environment, such as harmonization and simplification of transit procedures and documentation, increased use of information technology to speed up border-crossing procedures, efforts to reduce trade and transit transport barriers, measures to strengthen regional cooperation and policies to promote the private sector.

By **decision 58/547** of 23 December, the Assembly took note of the UNCTAD report.

Least developed countries

The Commission, on 4 September [E/2003/39/Add.1 (res. 59/4)], adopted a resolution on the implementation of the Programme of Action for the Least Developed Countries (LDCs) for the Decade 2001-2010 [YUN 2001, p. 770], in which it requested the Executive Secretary, in line with the Programme of Action, to review, analyse and disseminate annually information on economic and social developments in LDCs, assist them in formulating sectoral development strategies, paying due regard to the diverse development circumstances and constraints facing them, and conduct, in 2005, a regional midterm review of the implementation of the Programme of Action.

The Commission agreed that the eighth session of the Special Body on Pacific Island Developing Countries, scheduled for Shanghai, China, in 2004, would consider as its theme "Experiences and challenges in urban management issues in Pacific island countries".

Economic and technical cooperation

In 2003, ESCAP received $13.6 million for technical cooperation activities [E/ESCAP/1321], a slight decrease from the $14 million for 2002. Of that amount, $5.3 million was received from the UN system and $7.6 million from individual States, including developing countries, and $0.7 million from intergovernmental organizations and nongovernmental organizations (NGOs). Contributions from four developed countries (Australia, Finland, Japan, United States) provided just under 50 per cent of the total bilateral assistance, with Japan contributing the most. Among the developing country members and associate members, China, India and the Republic of Korea were the largest contributors. In addition to cash contributions, donor countries provided some 126 work-months of experts on a non-reimbursable loan basis. Twenty-four new projects were launched during the year.

As part of its revitalization process, ESCAP launched a new technical cooperation strategy, focusing on three priority thematic areas—poverty reduction, managing globalization and emerging social issues—in order to assist countries to attain internationally agreed development goals.

Transport, communications, tourism and infrastructure development

The Commission had before it the report of the Committee on Transport, Communications, Tourism and Infrastructure Development on its fourth session (Bangkok, 13-15 November 2002) [E/ESCAP/1274] and a report on progress in the implementation of resolutions relating to the theme of managing globalization [E/ESCAP/1297], including implementation of the New Delhi Action Plan on Infrastructure Development in Asia and the Pacific [YUN 1995, p. 1012]. The Commission endorsed the Committee's recommendations and reiterated its commitment to and support for the Seoul Declaration on Infrastructure Development in Asia and the Pacific, including phase II of the Regional Action Programme (2002-2006) of the New Delhi Action Plan [YUN 2001, p. 910]. Recognizing the importance of private sector investment in the development of transport infrastructure, the Commission requested the secretariat to study approaches to promote such investment and prepare models of funding in the framework of private sector partnerships. It also endorsed the plan of action for phase VI (2004-2005) of the Asian land transport infrastructure development project, and requested the secretariat to update the route alignment of the Trans-Asian Railway prior to the establishment of a Trans-Asian Railway Working Group. Noting the two ESCAP projects relating to the development of an integrated shipping and port system in the North-East Asian subregion and an integrated international transport and logistics system for North-East Asia, the Commission requested the secretariat to undertake a study on best practices in the subregion and disseminate the results.

In the area of tourism, the Commission reaffirmed its commitment to implementing the Plan of Action for Sustainable Tourism Development in the Asian and Pacific Region [YUN 1999, p. 929]. It noted the capacity-building seminars related to sustainable tourism development held in 2003 for specific countries and those planned for 2004 and the seminar on poverty alleviation (Kathmandu, Nepal, August), which discussed measures to alleviate poverty through tourism. It asked the secretariat to further strengthen activities to enhance the contribution of tourism to poverty alleviation.

Science and technology

The Commission considered the February report [E/ESCAP/1278] of the Asian and Pacific Centre for Transfer of Technology (APCTT) on its activities, including the report of the APCTT Governing Board (seventeenth session, Hanoi,

Viet Nam, 31 October and 1 November 2002). The Commission, noting the APCTT review, advised that, to improve its effectiveness, the Centre should conduct a more thorough needs assessment of its members, with emphasis on technology commercialization, high-technology transfer, technology parks and business incubator development, tech-entrepreneurship development, the building of information technology–powered regional and cross-regional technology transfer networks, transfer of environmentally sound technologies, e-commerce and private sector involvement in the Centre's activities. APCTT should promote the sharing of experiences and best practices with regard to the transfer and adoption of relevant technologies in rural areas, set up working groups on its key areas and establish comprehensive programme planning to ensure allocation of reasonable financial resources. The Commission requested APCTT to finalize a strategy for establishing an endowment fund.

Environment and sustainable development

The Commission, having considered the report of the Committee on Environment and Natural Resources Development on its fourth session (Bangkok, 19-21 November 2002) [E/ESCAP/1275] and a report on regional follow-up [E/ESCAP/1302] to the Johannesburg Plan of Implementation of the World Summit on Sustainable Development [YUN 2002, p. 822], endorsed the latter, including its conclusions and recommendations. The Commission recommended that ESCAP play a substantive role in implementing the Johannesburg Plan. Noting that several regional initiatives in the Phnom Penh Regional Platform on Sustainable Development for Asia and the Pacific [YUN 2001, p. 911] were echoed in the outcome of the World Summit, the Commission decided to implement programmes in conformity with the decisions of the Johannesburg Plan and of the Commission on Sustainable Development at its eleventh session (see p. 838). It urged the secretariat to mobilize additional resources for implementing the outcome of the World Summit, supported the regional meeting (October) to review implementation of the Plan in relation to the first cluster areas of water, sanitation and human settlements, and asked it to report to the Commission on Sustainable Development in 2004.

The Commission supported the secretariat's capacity-building programmes in strategic planning and management for integrated water resources management to meet the MDG targets in a holistic approach. The secretariat should promote, among other things, public awareness of water conservation, water-use efficiency and groundwater contamination and increase cooperation to commemorate the International Year of Freshwater 2003 (see p. 1033). The secretariat was also called on to assist ESCAP members in assessing water resources and monitoring the freshwater situation.

The Commission noted the Asia-Pacific Expert Meeting on Promoting Sustainable Production and Consumption Patterns (Yogyakarta, Indonesia, 21-23 May), which identified priorities for regional and subregional frameworks and initiatives, and the international expert group meeting, organized by the Department of Economic and Social Affairs (Marrakech, Morocco, June), which adopted a 10-year framework of programmes for sustainable production and consumption patterns.

Agriculture and development

The Commission had before it a July report [E/ESCAP/1277/Rev.1] on the Asian and Pacific Centre for Agricultural Engineering and Machinery (APCAEM), which detailed the activities related to the establishment of the Centre and the recommendations of its Governing Board (Beijing, 26-27 November 2002). The Commission requested the Centre to develop a medium- to long-term road map by prioritizing its work programme, and recommended that activities in agro-electronics, rural energy and other poverty alleviation activities be accorded priority, with a view to making APCAEM a centre of excellence. It recommended that the Centre disseminate information on technologies for promoting the involvement of rural women in agro-processing activities, strengthen activities in farm machinery and agro-engineering that were beneficial to the poor and engage in new technologies, especially in biotechnology. The Centre was urged to mobilize additional resources, with a view to becoming self-supporting.

A later report [E/ESCAP/1320] indicated that the Host Country Headquarters Agreement and its Supplementary Agreement on Administrative and Financial Arrangements were signed between China and ESCAP in November, making the Centre operational. The second session of the APCAEM Governing Board (Beijing, 26-27 November) adopted a number of conclusions and recommendations, and the 2004-2005 APCAEM work programme and financial resources plan and its 2004-2008 medium- and long-term strategy.

The Commission also considered the report of the Regional Coordination Centre for Research and Development of Coarse Grains, Pulses, Roots and Tuber Crops in the Humid Tropics of Asia and the Pacific [E/ESCAP/1272], including the report of its Governing Board on its twenty-first session (Bogor, Indonesia, 14-15 January). The Executive Secretary summarized the report of the Governing Board on its extraordinary session (20-21 August), at which the findings and recommendations of an external evaluation of the Centre were reviewed. The Board agreed that the work of the Centre should be aligned with the ESCAP programme of work, medium-term plan and thematic priorities, particularly poverty reduction issues. The Commission accepted the findings and recommendations of the Board at its extraordinary session, emphasized the importance of the Centre's activities for the development of sustainable agriculture, and suggested that another review be conducted in 2006.

Social development

The Commission endorsed the report of the Fifth Asian and Pacific Population Conference (Bangkok, 11-17 December 2002) [E/ESCAP/1271 & Corr.1], including the Plan of Action on Population and Poverty. It stressed that demographic and population factors should be fully integrated into national, sectoral and local planning. The Commission recommended that efforts to provide access to basic needs and services be strengthened and integrated into the planning process at all levels, and that a pro-poor macroeconomic model be accompanied by a people-centred development approach, based on good governance at the local and international levels.

The Commission, in a September resolution [E/2003/39/Add.1 (res. 59/1)] on regional action to follow up the Declaration of Commitment on HIV/AIDS contained in General Assembly resolution S-26/2 [YUN 2001, p. 1126], called on members and associate members to implement the Declaration, respond to the HIV/AIDS pandemic with high-level political commitment, maintain high levels of investment to prevent the epidemic's spread, promote policies that prevented the spread of HIV/AIDS, including interventions among drug users, address the gender-specific dimensions of the epidemic, support action to reduce infection among young people aged 15 to 24, and strengthen support for children living with HIV/AIDS. The Executive Secretary was requested to strengthen UN regional coordination to promote accelerated action in addressing issues of stigma and discrimination relevant to HIV/AIDS prevention and treatment, cooperate with subregional groupings to strengthen the subregional capability to deal with HIV/AIDS, mainstream HIV/AIDS prevention, treatment, care and support in the ESCAP programme of work, and initiate measures to build national capacity to meet the HIV/AIDS challenge.

The Commission stressed the importance of gender mainstreaming in education and of eliminating barriers to women's and girls' access to education, in order to promote gender equality. It called for increasing women's access to paid employment and for strengthening their social protection and security coverage.

In a September resolution on strengthening social safety in Asia and the Pacific [res. 59/2], the Commission called on members and associate members to increase resources for education, vocational and management training, occupational safety and health by strengthening technical cooperation with the private sector; improve methods for collecting and analysing basic employment data; assess mechanisms to measure unremunerated work; devise arrangements to meet the needs of the poor and vulnerable groups; and strengthen partnerships with the public and private sectors and other stakeholders concerned with social welfare and social safety. The Executive Secretary was requested to design an action-oriented programme of work and assist members and associate members in developing social safety policies, including employment data collection and analysis. He was urged to promote experience-sharing and best-practice learning on social integration within the ESCAP region, paying attention to disadvantaged, marginalized and unskilled groups in formulating the 2004 programme of work.

The Committee on Emerging Social Issues, at its first session (Bangkok, 4-6 September) [E/ESCAP/1310], reviewed issues concerning socially vulnerable groups, health and development, programme planning and the evaluation of two flagship projects in the area of emerging social issues. It also reviewed the regional situation concerning HIV/AIDS and SARS and the proposed 2006-2009 medium-term plan. It requested the secretariat to support capacity-building on emerging social issues through technical assistance, training, expert group meetings and the sharing of good practices and experiences.

The Commission endorsed the Shanghai Regional Implementation Strategy [E/ESCAP/1280] for the Madrid International Plan of Action on Ageing 2002 [YUN 2002, p. 1194] and the 1998 Macao Plan of Action on Ageing for Asia and the Pacific [YUN 1998, p. 942]. The Strategy recommended major areas for action—older persons and development; advancing health and well-being into old age; ensuring enabling and supportive environments; and implementation and follow-up.

The Commission noted the February report [E/ESCAP/1281] of the High-level Intergovernmental Meeting to Conclude the Asian and Pacific Decade of Disabled Persons, 1993-2002 [YUN

2002, p. 991], and supported the rights-based approach to the social integration of persons with disabilities, as specified in the Biwako Millennium Framework for Action towards an Inclusive, Barrier-free and Rights-based Society for Persons with Disabilities in Asia and the Pacific, adopted at the meeting. The Framework, which incorporated the MDGs and their targets, would act as a guide for the next Decade (2003-2012).

The Commission, in a September resolution [res. 59/3], took note of the Biwako Millennium Framework for Action and requested members and associate members to support its implementation nationally and internationally. It invited donors and the private sector to contribute to the technical assistance trust fund for the next Decade to ensure implementation of the Framework, and invited relevant UN organizations, the World Bank and the Asian Development Bank, in cooperation with ESCAP, to strengthen support for developing national capabilities to implement the Framework. It requested the Executive Secretary to collaborate with UN agencies and civil society to develop regional activities for implementing the Framework; to support Governments in fulfilling the Framework's targets; and to provide them with technical support in formulating a regional approach for an international convention on the rights and dignity of persons with disabilities (see p. 1107) by organizing regional meetings and training workshops.

Natural disasters

The Commission, having considered the report of the Mekong River Commission on its 2002 activities [E/ESCAP/1292], noted achievements in consolidating core, support and sector programmes, by adopting a comprehensive programme approach to support basin-wide strategies of member countries. Further efforts were made in the flood management and mitigation programme and other aspects of water management in the Mekong River basin, such as fisheries, watershed management, hydrology, navigation and capacity-building programmes.

The Commission also considered the report of the Typhoon Committee [E/ESCAP/1293], noting achievements in 2002 in the meteorological component, including observations, forecasts and warnings of typhoons, in the hydrological component, including flood forecasts and warning, and on natural disaster reduction. It noted the improvement in meteorological satellite facilities and observations and the increase in subregional activities in meteorology, hydrology, training and research and disaster prevention and preparedness. The Committee decided to adopt the strategic approach in implementing the 2002 Regional Cooperation Programme Implementation Plan [YUN 2002, p. 992] to ensure effective achievement of the Committee's priority objectives.

Also before the Commission was the report of the Panel on Tropical Cyclones [E/ESCAP/1294]. The Commission noted the improvement in monitoring facilities and data exchange among member countries to enhance the effectiveness of flood forecasting in international river basins, and the comprehensive review aimed at strengthening cooperation among the members on cyclone-related disaster reduction, carried out with ESCAP secretariat assistance, in cooperation with the World Meteorological Organization and the Panel's Technical Support Unit. The Commission urged donor countries and institutions to support the Panel's work.

Programme and organizational questions

The Commission endorsed the realignment of ESCAP's 2002-2003 programme of work [E/ESCAP/1285 & Corr.1 & Add.1] based on the new programme structure, as reflected in the revised 2002-2005 medium-term plan, and the implementation status of the 2002-2003 programme of work. Noting that a detailed report on the implementation of the programme of work would be submitted in 2004, it requested the secretariat to report on the new methodologies for monitoring and evaluating the programme of work that were being developed by UN Headquarters. The Commission endorsed the proposed changes for 2003 [E/ESCAP/1296 & Corr.1,2] as a result of the realignment of the 2002-2003 work programme, and the draft 2004-2005 programme of work [E/ESCAP/1284 & Corr.1,2].

The Commission also had before it the tentative calendar of meetings and training programmes for the period April 2003 to March 2004 [E/ESCAP/1287].

ESCAP reform

The Commission considered a report [E/ESCAP/1283] by the Executive Secretary on the implementation of Commission resolution 58/1 [YUN 2002, p. 993] on the restructuring of its conference structure. Among his recommendations for improving Commission sessions, the Executive Secretary called for focusing a session's theme more on current and emerging economic and social issues, making the agenda more issue-related, and periodically holding sessions outside Bangkok on the initiative of individual host countries. The secretariat proposed changes to the organization of the ministerial segment, including occasional presentations by eminent persons on particular issues, informal meetings among ministers, and side events involving NGOs, the business sector, civil society organizations and the media. Another proposal was for the Commission to adopt declarations on issues of particular interest to the region.

The Commission noted the progress made with the restructuring process and requested the secretariat, in consultation with members and associate members, to further prioritize that focus, discontinue obsolete activities and promote the sharing of best practices among regional countries. While noting the secretariat's efforts to improve the Commission's format, the Commission raised a number of concerns for examination by the Advisory Committee of Permanent Representatives and Other Representatives Designated by Members of the Commission (ACPR), especially the financial implications of holding sessions outside Bangkok, the risk of diluting the focus on important issues owing to the large number of proposed activities, the delegations' capacity to attend the sessions organized around the thematic clusters, and time constraints of ministers with regard to the organization of events. The Commission emphasized the importance of a midterm review of the new ESCAP conference structure to monitor its effectiveness and to make any necessary adjustments.

The Commission endorsed the report [E/ESCAP/1286] on the evaluation of ESCAP publications conducted in 2002, including the plan of action to improve their planning, production, processing and dissemination. It noted the 47 per cent reduction in the number of publications, and requested the secretariat to reduce that number further. The Commission supported the secretariat's proposals for enhancing the quality and impact of ESCAP publications. It felt that cooperation between the secretariat and national focal points would contribute to improving the quality of the publications. The secretariat was requested to explore additional means of disseminating its publications to maximize their impact and readership.

The Commission, noting the report on the activities of ACPR and its open-ended informal working group [E/ESCAP/1288 & Add.1,2], requested that ACPR's guiding and monitoring role be strengthened. ACPR should discuss significant programme activities during the implementation stage to ensure their implementation, and focus on issues related to Commission resolutions and decisions, including resolution 58/1 [YUN 2002, p. 993].

Evaluations

The Commission considered reports on the outcome of the evaluation of its regional institutions [E/ESCAP/1299] and of the ESCAP Pacific Operations Centre (EPOC) [E/ESCAP/1300]. The EPOC evaluation reviewed the relevance, performance and sustainability of its activities, while that of the other three institutions (the Statistical Institute for Asia and the Pacific, the Regional Coordination Centre for Research and Development of Coarse Grains, Pulses, Roots and Tuber Crops in the Humid Tropics of Asia and the Pacific and the Asian and Pacific Centre for Transfer of Technology) reviewed their operational, institutional and programming needs to ascertain how they could best serve members and associate members. The Commission expressed satisfaction with the findings of the evaluation reports, the implementation of which should increase efficiency and effectiveness. It noted that the forthcoming review of the Pacific Islands Forum secretariat would take into account the institutional implications of the relocaton of EPOC from Port Vila, Vanuatu, to Suva, Fiji, expected to be completed in 2004.

Admission of Timor-Leste

The Commission welcomed the application of Timor-Leste for admission to membership in ESCAP [E/ESCAP/1265] and recommended to the Economic and Social Council a draft resolution for adoption (see below).

ECONOMIC AND SOCIAL COUNCIL ACTION

On 18 July [meeting 41], the Economic and Social Council, on the recommendation of ESCAP [E/2003/15/Add.1], adopted **resolution 2003/7** without vote [agenda item 10].

Admission of the Democratic Republic of Timor-Leste as a full member of the Economic and Social Commission for Asia and the Pacific: amendment of the terms of reference of the Commission

The Economic and Social Council,

Noting that the Democratic Republic of Timor-Leste became a Member of the United Nations on 27 September 2002,

Noting also that, in accordance with paragraph 3 of the terms of reference of the Economic and Social Commission for Asia and the Pacific, the Democratic Republic of Timor-Leste shall thereupon be admitted as a member of the Commission,

Decides to amend paragraphs 2 and 3 of the terms of reference of the Commission accordingly.

Venue of ESCAP sixtieth session

By **decision 2003/228** of 18 July, the Economic and Social Council approved the ESCAP decision to hold its sixtieth session in Shanghai in April 2004 and expressed its gratitude to the Government of China for its offer to host the meeting.

Europe

The Economic Commission for Europe (ECE), at its fifty-eighth session (Geneva, 4-6 March) [E/2003/37], considered economic developments in the region and sustainable development, particularly national sustainable development strategies (main problems, lessons and implications for ECE work), and regional perspectives on sustainable development, notably ECE follow-up to the World Summit on Sustainable Development [YUN 2002, p. 821]. The Commission agreed in general with ECE's role in follow-up to the World Summit on the understanding that the format and modalities would be decided following the debate by the Commission on Sustainable Development (see p. 838) and at an ad hoc informal meeting of the Commission (see below).

The Commission also considered a paper on ECE reform [E/ECE/1399], which was a follow-up to the paper on strengthening the organization presented in 2002 [YUN 2002, p. 1003]. The paper provided information on the state of the UN reform process and that of ECE, focusing on adjustments to the intergovernmental structure, strengthening of the secretariat and technical cooperation. The Commission affirmed that the Group of Experts on the Programme of Work would continue deliberations on ECE reform, including the points made by delegations at the Commission's session, and make recommendations. The Commission expressed general agreement with the concept of the paper on major policy directions of ECE's work [E/ECE/1400], and supported the ECE approach of mainstreaming the three dimensions of sustainable development into all ECE areas of work as a way to further integrate sustainable development concerns into its activities, in response to the World Summit's Plan of Implementation [YUN 2002, p. 822].

Having considered a report by the Executive Secretary on ECE achievements and constraints during 2002 and perspectives for 2003 [E/ECE/1401], the Commission expressed satisfaction with the work of the Principal Subsidiary Bodies (PSBs) but underlined that some future streamlining and restructuring of those bodies and related groups should be considered to ensure their relevance and effectiveness. Decision-making by the Commission would be assisted by evaluations of the effectiveness and impact of ECE's work, and gender issues needed to be further incorporated into the work of all subprogrammes. The Commission underlined the role of the PSB Bureaux in overall programme coordination with other organizations involved in the same areas to avoid duplication and strengthen complementarity.

The Commission also considered reports on preparations for and follow-up to world and regional conferences, including preparations for the World Summit on the Information Society in December 2003 (see p. 857) [E/ECE/1402], on technical cooperation activities [E/ECE/1403] and on cooperation and coordination with other organizations [E/ECE/1404 & Add.1], and the report of the Group of Experts on the Programme of Work [E/ECE/1405].

The Commission held two ad hoc informal meetings, on 26 June [E/ECE/1407] and 2 September [E/ECE/1408]. In June, the Commission endorsed the recommendations on reform of the Group of Experts in regard to monitoring and evaluation of technical cooperation, and adopted guidelines for the operations of specialist teams of ECE working parties, on the understanding that PSBs would set the procedure for establishing the teams. In September, the Commission decided to hold the first regional implementation meeting on the World Summit on Sustainable Development in January 2004 in order to contribute to the work of the Commission on Sustainable Development.

Economic trends

According to ECE's summary of the economic survey of Europe, 2003 [E/2004/16], a global economic recovery took hold in the second half of 2003, led by the United States, and was supported by expansionary economic policies. By contrast, the euro area remained the principal weak spot in the global economy due to sluggish activity in the three largest economies (France, Germany and Italy), while economic activity in Eastern Europe as a whole strengthened, particularly in the Commonwealth of Independent States (CIS). In the United States, GDP growth accelerated to 3.1 per cent, while in the euro area GDP rose by only 0.5 per cent. In the EU, real GDP grew by 0.8 per cent, because of the resilience of the United Kingdom economy.

In Eastern Europe, GDP growth accelerated to 3.8 per cent, led by strong domestic demand, improved financial intermediation and a booming credit market: a consequence of successful banking reforms. However, economic performance among regional States varied considerably, with GDP growth in Poland, the largest Eastern European economy, rising by 3.7 per cent, while Hungary and Slovenia experienced a slowdown. Latvia and Lithuania were the fastest-growing East European economies, with GDP increasing by 7 and 8.9 per cent, respectively. Growth also remained relatively strong (above 4 per cent) in Albania, Bulgaria, Croatia, Estonia, Romania and Slovakia. In parts of South-East Europe, economic activity remained weak, particularly in Serbia and Montenegro, where it was almost stagnant, reflecting the difficulty in opening up the economy and starting major reforms, and in Bosnia and Herzegovina, where it slowed down for the fourth consecutive year.

In the CIS region, economic activity surged with aggregate GDP growing by 7.6 per cent, making it one of the fastest-growing regions in the world. The strong performance of the three largest CIS economies—the Russian Federation, Ukraine and Kazakhstan, where GDP grew by 7.3 per cent, 8.5 per cent and 9.1 per cent, respectively—contributed to the robust performance. The upturn in the Russian Federation was underpinned by an expansionary monetary policy and signs of a deeper restructuring of the Russian enterprise sector, partly in response to growing competitive pressure. Kazakhstan's economic growth was mostly due to the rapid expansion of fuel-related exports, while in Ukraine it resulted from a sharp export-driven upturn in the manufacturing sector. Although the other CIS economies were unusually buoyant, a sign of the general strength of growth was the fact that in Uzbekistan, the slowest-growing economy in the CIS region, GDP still increased by some 5 per cent.

Activities in 2003

Trade, industry and enterprise development

The Committee for Trade, Industry and Enterprise Development, at its seventh session (Geneva, 13 and 16 May) [ECE/TRADE/306], approved: the expansion of its Multiplier Point Network to include the entire region and to better serve large transition economies, such as Ukraine and the Russian Federation; the change of the name of the Working Party on Standardization of Perishable Produce and Quality Development to the Working Party on Agricultural Quality Standards; a new ad hoc team of experts on market surveillance to assist in developing controls for the conformance of products in the marketplace to standards and regulations; a proposal for revising the work programme format and related procedures; its 2003-2005 work programme; and new procedures for approval of its reports and the organization of its sessions. It endorsed a pilot project for implementing the International Model for Regulatory Harmonization in earth-moving equipment and the decision to issue a joint publication with the Inland Transport Committee on "Trade and Transport Facilitation Instruments and Recommendations". The Committee agreed to hold a forum, in conjunction with its 2004 session, on the challenges the region would face in trade, industry and enterprise following the enlargement of the EU, and especially those challenges facing the "new neighbours".

The Regional Forum on Social Aspects and Financing of Industrial Restructuring (Moscow, Russian Federation, 26-27 November) [TRADE/WP.8/AC.1/SEM.22/2003/3], co-sponsored by ECE and the International Labour Organization, discussed ways to resolve the social issues arising during the restructuring of uncompetitive industries, measures required by the European Commission from enterprises to mitigate the adverse consequences of restructuring on employment and workers' incomes, support to start-up companies and industries, and the scope of industrial and territorial clustering as a means of economic revitalization of underdeveloped and depressed regions.

The Working Party on Agricultural Quality Standards continued to update and create internationally harmonized quality standards, and to work on internationally harmonized trade descriptions for fruit and vegetables, to be used in electronic commerce, and internal quality and maturity requirements.

Timber

The Timber Committee, at its sixty-first session (Geneva, 7-10 October) [ECE/TIM/2003/2], held a policy forum on wood and energy, in cooperation with the Committee on Sustainable Energy. The forum reviewed energy policies, especially those concerning renewable energies and interactions between energy policies and those for forests and timber, and sector market developments. The Committee also reviewed markets for forest products, including the consequences of illegal logging, and approved a statement. It discussed the policy conclusions and recommendations of the European Forest Sector Outlook Study and the ECE/Food and Agriculture Organization of the United Nations (FAO) contribution to global and regional forest dialogues. The Committee adopted its work programme and launched a process of strategic review of the integrated ECE/FAO 2003/04 programme.

The ECE secretariat presented information on the state of Europe's forests to the Fourth Ministerial Conference on the Protection of Forests in Europe (Vienna, 28-30 April). The data were based on a set of indicators of sustainable forest management.

Transport

The Inland Transport Committee, at its sixty-fifth session (Geneva, 18-20 February) [ECE/TRANS/152 & Corr.1], reviewed, among other things, its draft strategic objectives, the transport situation in ECE member countries and emerging development trends, transport and security, assistance to countries with economies in transition, and the status of application of ECE transport agreements and conventions. The Committee also considered transport trends and economics, road transport, road traffic safety, safety in tunnels, harmonization of vehicle regulations, rail transport, inland water transport, combined transport, border crossing facilitation, transport of dangerous goods and perishable foodstuffs, and transport statistics.

The Committee adopted a resolution on the Fourth Road Safety Week in the ECE region and requested the secretariat to publicize the campaign and to seek partnerships to give it maximum impact. It also adopted a resolution on the implementation of the European Agreement on Main Inland Waterways of International Importance, and endorsed resolutions of the Working Party on Inland Water Transport on the inventory of bottlenecks and missing links in the European waterway network, and on technical requirements for preventing pollution from vessels.

The Committee also endorsed proposals for requiring digital tachographs (an on-board device in commercial vehicles designed to measure the driver's working hours and rest periods) on new vehicles assigned to international road transport under the European Agreement concerning the Work of Crews of Vehicles Engaged in International Road Transport (AETR). They would become mandatory for AETR contracting parties four years after the entry into force of the proposed amendments.

Energy

The Committee on Sustainable Energy, at its thirteenth session (Geneva, 19-21 November) [ECE/ENERGY/53], having considered renewable energy sources and sustainable energy development in the ECE region, expressed appreciation to the secretariat for a discussion paper and draft terms of reference on renewable energy sources, decided that technical assistance should be developed for ECE economies in transition, and requested the Steering Committee of the Energy Efficiency 21 Project to consider a draft work programme for technical assistance on renewable sources of energy to those countries. The Committee concluded that energy security was a key element of sustainable energy policy, deserving the attention of the Energy Security Forum launched by the Committee during its 2003 session. It noted the statement signed by all Forum participants, which was annexed to the Committee's report, and requested the secretariat to convene the first meeting of the Forum's Executive Board.

Noting that the Guidelines on Reforming Energy Prices and Subsidies had been endorsed by the Fifth Ministerial Conference on the Environment for Europe (see below), the Committee recommended that the ECE transition economies implement them in accordance with the declaration adopted by the Conference, and requested the task force on the Guidelines to assess their implementation in 2005 and 2006. The Committee noted the successful implementation of the Energy Efficiency 21 Project, in accordance with the 2000-2003 project plan, and requested the Bureau and the secretariat to complete a project plan for a second phase (2003-2006), including a financing mechanism, and to explore extra-budgetary support with interested Governments and institutions.

The Committee considered the documentation of the Working Party on Gas, and of the Ad Hoc Group of Experts on the Supply and Use of Gas, and the Gas Centre, and renewed the mandate of the Group of Experts for two years. It also renewed the mandate of the Ad Hoc Group of Experts on Coal in Sustainable Development and that of the Ad Hoc Group of Experts on Electric Power and approved its terms of reference. The Committee endorsed the Regional Strategy for the Efficient Use of Energy and Water Resources in Central Asia.

Environment

The Fifth Ministerial Conference "Environment for Europe" (Kiev, Ukraine, 21-23 May) adopted three new protocols to ECE conventions: the Protocol on Strategic Environmental Assessment to the 1991 Convention on Environmental Impact Assessment in a Transboundary Context (Espoo Convention); the Protocol on Pollutant Release and Transfer Registers to the 1998 Convention on Access to Information, Public Participation in Decision-making and Access to Justice in Environmental Matters (Aarhus Convention) [YUN 1998, p. 952]; and the Protocol on Civil Liability and Compensation for Damage Caused by the Transboundary Effects of Industrial Accidents on Transboundary Waters to the 1992 Convention on the Protection and Use of Transboundary Watercourses and International Lakes and to the 1992 Convention on the Transboundary Effects of Industrial Accidents [YUN 1992, p. 501]. The Conference also adopted Guidelines for Strengthening

Compliance with and Implementation of Multilateral Environmental Agreements in the ECE region and a regional Convention on the Carpathians (Mountains), and launched the Environment Strategy for Countries of Eastern Europe, the Caucasus and Central Asia and preparations for the environment, water and security partnership in Central Asia. Other decisions related to energy and water for sustainable development, biodiversity and education.

The Committee on Environmental Policy held a special session (Geneva, 18-19 February) [ECE/CEP/91] and its tenth session (20-22 October) [ECE/CEP/116 & Add.1]. The special session discussed future ECE strategic directions in environmental policy around the themes of pan-European harmonization and governance, programmes and strategies, and cross-sectoral cooperation and integration. The Committee reviewed the environmental performance of Georgia and discussed policy issues emerging from the review. At a joint session with the Working Group of Senior Officials, the Committee approved the Group's recommendations for a second round of environmental performance reviews.

At its tenth session, the Committee hosted a round-table discussion on the theme "The environment in a changing region", which assessed the implications of EU enlargement for the environment and highlighted future challenges. It adopted the strategic goals contained in the document on future ECE strategic directions for the environment, and reviewed the environmental performance of Azerbaijan and adopted related recommendations. It also considered the outcome of the Kiev Ministerial Conference (see p. 1018) and how it should best reflect the relevant commitments of the Kiev Ministerial Declaration in its work programme. It adopted a work programme for environmental monitoring and updated the terms of reference of the Working Group on Environmental Monitoring and Assessment, and agreed to work on education for sustainable development, implementation of the Environment Strategy for Eastern Europe, the Caucasus and Central Asia, and the development of a communication strategy.

The first meeting of the Steering Committee for Transport, Health and Environment Pan-European Programme (PEP), organized jointly with the Regional Office of the World Health Organization, was held in April. The PEP Steering Committee endorsed its 2003-2005 programme of work.

Human settlements

The Committee on Human Settlements, at its sixty-fourth session (Geneva, 15-17 September) [ECE/HBP/129], held in-depth discussions on reforms and social equity in human settlements and decided to integrate the results of those discussions into its contribution to the Regional Implementation Forum on Sustainable Development, to be held in January 2004, as a follow-up to the World Summit on Sustainable Development [YUN 2002, p. 821]. It acknowledged that policy reforms on social stability and equity should become a critical element of the national, regional and local strategies for sustainable human settlements. It stressed the importance of linking the priorities of the Habitat Agenda [YUN 1996, p. 994], the World Summit on Sustainable Development Plan of Implementation and the Millennium Declaration [YUN 2000, p. 49] with its programme of work. The Committee adopted its 2003-2005 programme of work, and confirmed the priority of the country profile programme for the housing sector and land administration activities. It agreed to start preparation of a regional profile of the housing sector in South-East European countries, based on the decisions of the High-level Conference on Housing Reforms in South-East Europe (Paris, April). It commended the Guidelines on Condominium Ownership of Housing. It agreed on the outline for and composition of the task force for guidelines on social housing development and to prepare guidelines on spatial planning systems. The Committee also agreed to cooperate with the Conference of European Statisticians on the preparation of a new set of ECE recommendations for housing censuses.

Statistics

The Conference of European Statisticians (fifty-first session, Geneva, 10-12 June) [ECE/CES/64] considered the implications of the meetings of its parent bodies—the March session of ECE (see p. 1016) and the March session of the UN Statistical Commission (see p. 1289). The Conference asked the Bureau to continue to review how the Conference could further incorporate cross-sectoral concerns into the work of all its subprogrammes, such as sustainable development, gender, security, and information and communication technology. It agreed that the ECE Statistical Division should be closely involved in operational activities addressing economies in transition through the Regional Adviser Programme. The Conference agreed to review the Integrated Presentation of International Statistics by examining two topics in great depth and the remaining programme elements on the basis of recommendations by the Bureau. The two topics chosen for the current session were "families and households", and "crime and criminal justice statistics".

Operational activities

Operational activities in 2002, as described in a note by the Executive Secretary [E/ECE/1403], were carried out in the areas of capacity-building, assistance with attracting partners/investors for local projects at countries' request, project elaboration/implementation, resource mobilization, building up institutions and policy formulation. Most of ECE's operational activities, with a total value of $1,527,501, were funded from the regular budget, of which 48 per cent went to activities related to trade, followed by transport (21 per cent), environment (12 per cent), energy (11 per cent) and statistics (8 per cent). It also received $693,232 from the UN Development Account. Total extrabudgetary expenditure under the 11 ECE general trust funds totalled $2,642,066, and $2,132,825 under the 22 local technical cooperation trust funds.

The Commission welcomed the formation of a new Technical Cooperation Unit in the secretariat and supported the setting up of a joint committee in the secretariat to improve the overall coordination of technical cooperation activities.

Latin America and the Caribbean

The Economic Commission for Latin America and the Caribbean (ECLAC) did not meet in 2003. The Commission's thirtieth session was to be held in 2004.

Economic trends

In 2003, the economies of Latin America and the Caribbean grew by 1.7 per cent, contrasting favourably with the 0.6 per cent reduction in GDP recorded for 2002, according to the summary of the economic survey of Latin America and the Caribbean, 2003 [E/2004/19]. However, the recovery was not strong enough to offset the economic stagnation of recent years, and per capita GDP was still 1.2 per cent lower than in 1997. The region's stronger performance was linked to the situation in the international economy, which brightened with the recovery in the United States and Japan and the continuing rapid expansion of the Asian economies, led by China. The combined effect of those factors was a 15.4 per cent increase in the price of export commodities, which, however, was reduced to 7.2 per cent when oil was excluded. The upswing in export prices, although partially offset by a 1.5 per cent rise in import prices, was sufficient to halt the 3.3 per cent deterioration in the terms of trade between 1998 and 2002. The buoyancy of exports was widespread, as growth rates for the year were 5.9 per cent for Central America and the Caribbean, 7.8 per cent for the Andean Community and Chile, 18.9 per cent for the Southern Cone Common Market (MERCOSUR) and 8.3 per cent for the regional average. Increased volumes and higher prices turned 2003 into a record year in terms of the region's trade surplus ($41.8 billion), which contributed to a $5.6 billion surplus on the balance-of-payments current account, the first time in 50 years.

Capital flows to the region were also positive, reaching $4.4 billion net, as compared with an outflow of $14.4 billion the previous year. Financial flows were negative, but direct investment more than offset that outflow. Foreign direct investment, which amounted to $30.1 billion, was 23 per cent lower than the 2002 figure. Despite the significant level of financing, the net transfer of resources continued to be negative ($33.3 billion), equivalent to 7.9 per cent of exports. Most countries consolidated their use of flexible exchange-rate regimes and were phasing out restrictions on foreign exchange operations, except Venezuela. In addition, various countries maintained a high degree of dollarization in their economies or had simply adopted the dollar as legal tender. The region returned to single digit levels of inflation as a result of the implementation of various fiscal and monetary instruments. In 2003, prices increased by 8.5 per cent, four percentage points less than the previous year.

The positive economic outlook led to a slight increase in the employment rate. However, at 10.7 per cent, unemployment remained high and was expected to rise during the year. Poverty and indigence in the region increased, with 227 million people (44 per cent of the population) living below the poverty line.

Activities in 2003

Development policy and regional economic cooperation

The ECLAC Economic Development Division continued to report on the macroeconomic performance of the region as a whole and individual countries in its publications *Economic Survey of Latin America and the Caribbean* and *Preliminary Overview of the Economies of Latin America and the Caribbean*. It provided technical assistance to Bolivia, Colombia, the Dominican Republic, Ecuador, Mexico and Paraguay, particularly on issues of fiscal reform, and organized the fourteenth regional seminar on fiscal policy (Santiago, Chile, 27-29 January). It secured funding for two new projects: e-fiscal concepts and issues in Latin America and Euro-Latin American research of macroeconomic coordination experts. As to the macroeconomic dimension of regional integration, ECLAC consolidated its coordination position through a network of macroeconomists from national and regional institutions. Its macroeconomic dialogue network, implemented with EU financial support, provided a forum for discussion and an exchange of experiences among government officials on macroeconomic issues linked to integration. The Division, at the request of Governments, focused on the analysis of short-term issues related to external and internal macroeconomic imbalances, mainly through technical assistance missions and relevant policy research. It continued to address emerging key structural issues in the region, mainly through its publications on issues of interest to Governments, particularly economic growth, employment, the development challenges faced by landlocked countries and the coordination of macroeconomic policies. It organized an international seminar on "Latin American growth: Why so slow?" (Santiago, Chile, December).

The Latin American and Caribbean Institute for Economic and Social Planning (ILPES) continued to enhance the capacity of member States to apply the basic principles of efficient public administration planning and State regulation by organizing 25 expert meetings, seminars and workshops, reaching some 1,750 participants. It updated its capacity to respond to member countries' growing demand for new information, studies and technical support regarding such public planning issues as decentralization and administration of public decisions, local development, regulation of public services and noncompetitive sectors. ILPES provided technical assistance to governmental bodies in regional countries and was confirmed as the ECLAC training hub for standardizing all procedural matters regarding the design, implementation and evaluation of training activities carried out by ECLAC substantive divisions.

Noteworthy events during 2002-2003 were the eleventh Conference of Ministers and Heads of Planning of Latin America and the Caribbean and the twelfth meeting of the ILPES Regional Council for Planning (Madrid, Spain, 6 November 2002). ECLAC also convened the Regional Preparatory Ministerial Conference of Latin America and the Caribbean for the World Summit on the Information Society (Bávaro, Dominican Republic, 29-31 January 2003).

International trade and integration

The activities of ECLAC's Division of International Trade and Integration were aimed at strengthening the decision-making capacity of institutions in member countries to generate progress in subregional, regional and hemispheric integration, including the provision of technical assistance to member States in building their capacity for negotiating the Free Trade Area of the Americas initiative and during the Fifth Ministerial Conference of the World Trade Organization (WTO) (see p. 1535). To help countries in the region better understand the domestic implications of the international commitments undertaken in bilateral, regional and multilateral trade negotiations, ECLAC prepared numerous documents containing policy recommendations to strengthen the international competitiveness of Latin American and Caribbean countries in areas relating to trade promotion, product diversification and export markets. The Division paid close attention to improving the analysis of the impact of trade on selected groups, placing emphasis on the need to incorporate developing countries' small and medium-sized enterprises into the area of e-commerce.

Social development and equity

In 2003, the efforts of the ECLAC Social Development Division were focused on strengthening countries' capacity to design and implement policies targeting the most underprivileged social sectors, so as to increase the quality of human and social capital, foster social equity and reduce poverty, with a focus on overcoming gender inequity. The Division published its 2001-2002 and 2002-2003 editions of the *Social Panorama of Latin America*, which included an evaluation of progress and difficulties in regional efforts to achieve the MDGs [YUN 2000, p. 51] in the areas of poverty reduction, education and health. It conducted substantial research within the context of the regional project "Policy strategies for sustainable development in Latin America and the Caribbean: promotion of a socially sustainable policy (Equity II)", and continued its collaboration with the Integrated Project Formulation, Evaluation and Monitoring System, providing regional Governments with a methodological tool for use as a guide in designing, implementing and following up social policy. The Division also started developing an Internet directory of social institutions in Latin America and the Caribbean (DISALC), which was currently being used for social policy coordination and the sharing of experiences by more than 700 institutions and officials.

With regard to drug abuse prevention policies, ECLAC continued to develop a comprehensive vision by incorporating socio-economic and cultural aspects into its analyses, including the way in which the drug problem impacted on the more vulnerable sectors of society. The Division also supported Chile in implementing a comprehensive system of specialized information for its National Drug Control Council.

Environment and human settlements

The ECLAC Sustainable Development and Human Settlements Division focused its work on international environmental agreements, environmental management, sustainable development trends, and urban management and property. Countries in the region gave priority to implementing the 2002 Latin American and Caribbean Initiative for Sustainable Development [YUN 2002, p. 1012]. The Division was particularly active in launching an innovative approach to the interrelationship between trade and environment by integrating issues such as intellectual property rights, investment, services and environment, leading to the publication of the study "Latin America and the Caribbean: from a strategy on trade and environment towards a strategy on trade for sustainable development". The Division offered several training courses and seminars as part of the training programme on sustainable development and environmental management. It provided technical assistance to Argentina, Colombia, the Dominican Republic and Puerto Rico in the systematization and application of sustainable development indicators, resulting in a reduction of gaps in the availability of empirical information. It also provided technical assistance to Argentina, Bolivia, the Dominican Republic, Ecuador and Mexico in urban management practices and policies, and conducted a number of courses and workshops on urban management. With respect to urban poverty, the Division organized in January a meeting of experts in the framework of a project entitled "Urban poverty: an action-oriented strategy for urban governments and institutions in Latin America and the Caribbean".

Population and development

The ECLAC Population Division continued to incorporate sociodemographic elements into gender and social programming by supporting countries of the region in strengthening their capacity to produce updated and reliable sociodemographic information. Among other methods, it developed new or improved methodologies for population estimates and projections on such topics as social vulnerability, fertility, housing deficits, residential segregation and internal migration. It organized (Santiago, 19-21 November) the Regional Intergovernmental Conference on Ageing: Towards a regional strategy for the implementation in Latin America and the Caribbean of the Madrid International Plan of Action on Ageing [YUN 2002, p. 1194], and published a document entitled "Older persons in Latin America and the Caribbean: situation and policies".

The Division's activities in technical cooperation and regional training in population and development were conducted to foster the exchange of experiences and lessons learned in relation to implementation of the Programme of Action of the International Conference on Population and Development (ICPD) [YUN 1994, p. 956]. Together with the United Nations Population Fund, it provided support to the Caribbean subregional meeting to assess implementation of the ICPD Programme of Action 10 years after its adoption (Port of Spain, Trinidad and Tobago, 11-12 November), and hosted an open-ended meeting of the Presiding Officers of the ECLAC Ad Hoc Committee on Population and Development (Santiago, December). To help countries devise and update appropriate indicators for national and regional follow-up to ICPD, the Division developed and updated the regional system of indicators and, with the support of the Women and Development Unit, developed indicators for monitoring the Beijing Platform for Action [YUN 1995, p. 1170]. Two subregional training workshops (one for South America and the other for Central America, Mexico and the Caribbean) were conducted to discuss the most appropriate indicators and to train technicians from national statistical offices in the design, development and implementation of national indicator systems.

Integration of women in development

The work of ECLAC's Women and Development Unit centred on the follow-up to the Regional Programme of Action for the Women of Latin America and the Caribbean, 1995-2001 [YUN 1994, p. 739] and the Beijing Platform for Action [YUN 1995, p. 1170], and organization of the thirty-fifth (Havana, Cuba, 28-29 April) meeting of the Presiding Officers of the Regional Conference on Women in Latin America and the Caribbean. By agreements adopted at that meeting and at the thirty-fourth meeting (Santiago, 5-6 September 2002), the countries welcomed the methodology and modality of technical assistance being implemented in the region by the Women and Development Unit. At the 2003 meeting, the Presiding Officers commended ECLAC for developing a system of gender indicators to facilitate regional comparability and requested technical assistance from the Commission for the definition of national systems of gender indicators for use in carrying out comparative analyses within countries.

As follow-up to the recommendations of the eighth session of the Regional Conference on Women in Latin America and the Caribbean [YUN 2000, p. 950], particularly those concerning impediments to an evaluation of the objectives of the Beijing Platform for Action, ECLAC developed a strategy for collaboration with UN system agencies. As a result, seven countries (Argentina, Brazil, Chile, Ecuador, Mexico, Nicaragua, Panama) had developed gender indicator subsystems, some of which incorporated systems for follow-up to international commitments (Mexico, Panama). The other regional countries had basic information disaggregated by sex, and all used the regional system of gender indicators. Eleven countries had prepared civil society reports using the ECLAC indicators, and nine had national reports on progress towards meeting the MDGs.

An international meeting (September) of producers and users of the ECLAC indicators of violence and poverty from a gender perspective was held as part of the work of the Statistical Conference of the Americas, in collaboration with national women's offices.

Economic statistics and technical cooperation

The ECLAC Statistics and Economic Projections Division strengthened the regional framework of statistical information with respect to databanks of statistics on current economic trends, household surveys, foreign trade and national accounts. To improve the dissemination of statistics, it created a web page providing online access to the Division's databases, which offered, in 2003, three new online products: the *Statistical Yearbook*, a database on international trade and an information system on social statistics and indicators. The Division created a database on microdata from household surveys for the use of specialized research and policy-making institutions. New dimensions related to environment and gender indicators were added to its databanks. Those improvements were recognized in the conclusions of the second meeting of the Statistical Conference of the Americas (Santiago, 18-20 June).

The Division carried out a large number of technical cooperation missions and there was a strong demand for meetings, seminars and training workshops in relation to national accounts, international classifications and household surveys. Activities were aimed at improving countries' technical capacity to produce statistics and forecasts as inputs for economic and social programmes, with emphasis on harmonizing methodologies and concepts at the regional level, in order to enhance the comparability of national statistics and adherence to international standards. The Division continued to prepare manuals and transfer methodological and technological advances, especially with respect to the full implementation of the new System of National Accounts in the region.

Natural resources and infrastructure

The ECLAC Natural Resources and Infrastructure Division provided technical expertise to member countries in designing policies for the sustainable development of natural resources and infrastructure. It played a leading role in promoting a regional dialogue on renewable sources of energy at the Regional Conference for Latin America and the Caribbean on Renewable Energies (Brasília, Brazil, October), which, in its Brasília Platform, requested ECLAC to prepare the regional document to be submitted to the 2004 International Conference on Renewable Energies. ECLAC presented the region's vision on water and governance and indigenous rights at the Third World Water Forum (Japan, March). Among its efforts to increase the capacity of countries to manage natural resources, energy, infrastructure and transport at the decentralized regional and local levels, ECLAC and ILPES trained 57 professionals from 12 countries at the fourth (Santiago, 2-6 September 2002) and fifth (8-12 September 2003) courses on public utilities regulation. The Division strengthened the negotiating capacity of regional countries in international and regional mechanisms dealing with sustainable development of natural resources and infrastructure.

ECLAC hosted the fifth ministerial meeting of the Executive Steering Committee of the Initiative for Regional Infrastructure Integration in South America (Santiago, 4-5 December) and convened a meeting of regional energy institutions, with a view to coordinating their activities (Santiago, 2 December). It organized the regional preparatory meeting (Asunción, Paraguay, 12-13 March) for the International Ministerial Conference of Landlocked and Transit Developing Countries and Donor Countries and International Financial and Development Institutions on Transit Transport Cooperation (see p. 875). As part of those preparations, it conducted a study on the economic costs of being landlocked, which was taken into account in the Almaty Programme of Action adopted at the Conference.

Subregional activities

Caribbean

The ECLAC subregional headquarters for the Caribbean—the secretariat of the Caribbean Development and Cooperation Committee (CDCC) in Port of Spain, Trinidad and Tobago—worked towards improving policies, programmes and projects to facilitate Caribbean societies' adjustment to rapid change on the international scene, particularly globalization; boost the subregional integration process; alleviate poverty and reduce gender inequalities; strengthen member States' capacity to develop and apply indicators to measure the catalytic effect of science and technology on economic and social development; and strengthen national capacities to implement the Programme of Action for the Sustainable Development of Small Island Developing States [YUN 1994, p. 783]. It convened the eleventh meeting of the CDCC Monitoring Committee and a joint meeting with the Inter-Agency Collaborative Group (Puerto Rico, 10-11 April); the Caribbean subregional meeting to assess the implementation of the ICPD Programme of Action [YUN 1994, p. 956] (Trinidad and Tobago, 11-12 November); and the Caribbean preparatory meeting (Trinidad and Tobago, 6-10 October) at the technical level for the 2004 international meeting to undertake a comprehensive review of the implementation of the Programme of Action for the Sustainable Development of Small Island Developing States.

Technical assistance and training workshops were held in such areas as trade and social statistics, information technology, disaster assessment, human and social development, environmental sustainability, water resources and trade. Activities undertaken through extrabudgetary projects included the completion of an assessment of the social impact of the closure of the sugar industry in Saint Kitts and Nevis, a marine-based tourism project focusing on the yachting sector in the eastern Caribbean, the development and establishment of databases for trade and social statistics and the development of a draft national human development agenda for Belize.

Mexico and Central America

In 2003, the ECLAC subregional headquarters in Mexico provided analyses and training and expanded its technical assistance to build capacity in the countries of the subregion to adjust to rapid changes in the international scene, maximizing the benefits and mitigating the adverse effects of globalization; improve policies and mechanisms for reducing poverty and gender inequality; and harmonize energy policies and boost the efficiency of energy management. Activities included work on economic, industrial and agricultural development, trade negotiations, the environment and natural disasters, subregional integration and cooperation processes. That support helped to increase the capacity to negotiate trade agreements for 34 member States in the case of the Free Trade Area of the Americas and for five States in the case of the United States–Central American Free Trade Agreement, including the preparation of national strategies to strengthen trade-related capacities in another four member States.

The subregional headquarters continued to act as the ECLAC focal point for natural disaster issues and to evaluate disasters on request. On poverty reduction and gender inequality, work performed by ECLAC contributed to a new law on responsible fatherhood in one case and an implementation policy in another; improvements in three poverty reduction strategies/national action plans for children; incorporation of the subject into two public training programmes; preparation of a training manual; and a proposal for related indicators. The subregional headquarters began to process and analyse microdata from household surveys in the Central American countries, and provided comparative analyses on unmet needs, poverty levels, social vulnerability, public social expenditures and the relationship between gender and poverty. It provided technical assistance and analyses to public institutions, NGOs and regional forums on the relationship between gender and poverty/economic development to support policy-making. In the field of energy, support was provided for the harmonization of energy policies and for increasing the efficiency of energy management. Emphasis was placed on sustainable energy development, particularly environmental externality guidelines and options for biofuels.

The General Assembly, on 17 December, adopted **resolution 58/117** on international assistance to and cooperation with the Alliance for the Sustainable Development of Central America (see p. 950).

Western Asia

The Economic and Social Commission for Western Asia (ESCWA) held its twenty-second session in Beirut, Lebanon, from 14 to 17 April [E/2003/41/Rev.1]. The Commission adopted two resolutions for action by the Economic and Social Council, on the establishment within ESCWA of a

UN Arabic language centre and of a committee on women.

Economic and social trends

Economic trends

For the ESCWA region, 2003 was a good year in terms of overall economic growth, notwithstanding the negative consequences of the war in Iraq (see p. 333), according to the survey of economic and social developments in the region [E/2004/20]. The survey estimated that GDP, excluding Iraq and the West Bank and Gaza Strip, grew by 5 per cent compared to the meagre 1.25 per cent growth of the previous year. With a regional population growth rate of 2.4 per cent, overall GDP per capita increased by 2.5 per cent, as compared with the contraction of 1.2 per cent in 2002. However, economic performance was very distinct for the two subgroups: the Gulf Cooperation Council (GCC) States (Bahrain, Kuwait, Oman, Qatar, Saudi Arabia, United Arab Emirates) and the more diversified economies (Egypt, Iraq, Jordan, Lebanon, Palestine, Syrian Arab Republic, Yemen). The GCC States enjoyed an upturn in GDP real growth, which increased from 0.4 per cent in 2002 to 5.8 per cent in 2003, resulting in a per capita GDP growth of 2.8 per cent, up from a negative 2.5 per cent in 2002. All GCC economies improved as a result of increased oil production and revenues, but the non-oil sectors also performed well, boosted by restored confidence and better economic prospects after the war in Iraq. Strong public expenditure, high domestic liquidity and low interest rates, which enhanced domestic consumption and investment, also contributed. Qatar achieved the highest GDP growth rate (5.44 per cent), while Oman recorded a negative 0.80 per cent. In the more diversified economies, political instability remained the most influential factor determining growth. The combined GDP growth of that subgroup remained almost constant at 3.14 per cent in 2003 and 3.15 per cent in 2002, with overall GDP per capita growth stagnating at a low 0.8 per cent. The most negatively affected countries were Jordan and Syria. In the conflict zones in the ESCWA region, the Occupied Palestinian Territories showed signs of a marginal recovery from a very low base, while in Iraq, the war, occupation and the subsequent difficult political and security situation restrained an upturn in economic activity, despite the lifting of UN sanctions and the termination of the oil-for-food programme (see p. 338).

Inflation rates remained relatively moderate, despite the depreciation of the United States dollar against the euro (to which the national currencies of the GCC countries were pegged), and the increase in the price of imports from the euro zone. Consumer price inflation increased modestly in most countries, ranging from 0.6 per cent in Oman to 4.4 per cent in the Occupied Palestinian Territories, except Yemen and Iraq, where inflation soared to a double-digit rate and an estimated 33 per cent, respectively.

Oil

In 2003, the basket price of crude oil of the Organization of Petroleum Exporting Countries was $28.10 a barrel, the highest nominal average since 1984. The 6.3 per cent increase in oil output over 2002 allowed most ESCWA oil-producing countries to reap the benefits of high prices, with total oil export revenues for the region estimated at $161 billion in 2003, up by 22 per cent from the previous year. Iraq and the Syrian Arab Republic were the only exceptions, as their oil exports plunged due to the war and ensuing political and security conditions.

Trade

The total gross value of merchandise exports of ESCWA member countries was estimated at $228 billion, while that of merchandise imports was estimated at $143 billion. The GCC countries accounted for 88 per cent of those exports and 72 per cent of all imports. Gross total exports from the ESCWA region increased by 17.2 per cent in 2003, and by 21.2 per cent from the GCC countries, owing to their increased energy exports, while in the more diversified economies, gross total exports decreased by 4.7 per cent. Gross total imports increased by 9.3 per cent. The value of total imports of the GCC countries went up by 15.4 per cent, due to the expansion of domestic demand, while total imports of the more diversified economies dropped by 3.8 per cent, owing to a substantial decrease in the imports of Egypt and Iraq.

Social trends

Social conditions declined in Iraq and the Occupied Palestinian Territories. In Iraq, with more than 40 per cent of the labour force unemployed, the extent to which poverty rose was significant, while in the Occupied Palestinian Territories, where 28 per cent of the labour force was unemployed, conditions were also bleak; however, the real catastrophe was the human toll of the conflict. In terms of unemployment data, real wages in the ESCWA region had declined, while the labour supply continued to outgrow demand. In the absence of adequate official social safety nets to protect the unemployed and the marginalized, informal social nets and sector activities proliferated, particularly the cultural principle of *al-takaful* (mutual support), which mitigated the effects of abject poverty and hunger. There were, however, certain bright spots in terms of a marked increase in life expectancy and the educational attainment of women.

Activities in 2003

Economic development and cooperation

The third session of the Technical Committee on the Liberalization of Foreign Trade and Economic Globalization in the Countries of the ESCWA Region (Muscat, Oman, 24-25 February) [E/ESCWA/GRID/2003/IG.1/7] reviewed action taken in trade liberalization and economic globalization and considered proposals regarding its 2004-2005 programme of work and priorities.

The Committee proposed, among other recommendations, that ESCWA include in its 2004-2005 programme of work training on WTO-related issues for media officials as well as judges, their assistants and lawyers, in order to prepare the judicial sector to work with WTO-related issues. ESCWA should also monitor and keep member countries updated on the progress of current WTO negotiations and should publish studies and reports on the Internet. Other recommendations called for documents to be translated into Arabic and Committee sessions to be held annually instead of biennially.

In the area of technology, the Commission, on 17 April [E/2003/41/Rev.1 (res. 245(XXII))], adopted the recommendations of the Forum on Technology, Employment and Poverty Alleviation in the Arab Countries [YUN 2002, p. 1018] and of the first meeting of the ESCWA Consultative Committee on Scientific and Technological Development and Technological Innovation [ibid.], particularly with respect to a new vision for the future of science, technology and technological innovation and related national policies; the establishment of a new institutional framework in ESCWA member countries; the strengthening and coordination of research and development; and the development of national education and vocational training systems.

The Commission requested the secretariat to prepare a study on countries' positions on vital technology in agriculture, food and medicines production; formulate priorities for the region in those fields; and propose initiatives to assist countries in confronting international trends in the sector. The secretariat should follow up those recommendations through a regional initiative to achieve specific goals within an appropriate time frame. The Executive Secretary was asked to report to the Commission in 2005.

Transportation

The Committee on Transport, at its fourth session (Beirut, 14-16 January) [E/ESCWA/TRANS/2003/IG.1/6], urged member States to complete measures for the ratification of the Agreement on International Roads in the Arab Mashreq [YUN 2001, p. 928], with a view to ensuring that it entered into force as soon as possible. It also urged Saudi Arabia's Ministry of Communications to complete the specifications for the sign for international roads and to inform ESCWA thereof by the end of March.

The Committee recommended that the proposals by the United Nations Office of Legal Affairs on the Agreement on International Railways in the Arab Mashreq [YUN 2002, p. 1019], which were included in the amended text of the Agreement, should be approved. The Agreement, having been finalized, was opened for signature during ESCWA's April 2003 session (see p. 1024) and thereafter at UN Headquarters until 31 December 2004 [E/ESCWA/22/5].

The Committee also recommended that the national committees for the facilitation of trade and transport be renamed national committees "for the facilitation of transport and trade". The Commission should follow up with member countries on the steps adopted to establish national committees and report in 2004 to the Committee on Transport. The amended draft memorandum of understanding (MOU) concerning cooperation in the field of maritime transport in the Arab Mashreq should be adopted and a working group of maritime transport experts should be established to study member countries' comments and proposals. The group should meet on 2 April and its outcome submitted to ESCWA's April 2003 session. Member countries should be urged to add, through ESCWA, ports and harbours to the network of maritime routes contained in the draft MOU. The Committee further recommended that the tables of the international roads in the Arab Mashreq should be amended in the schedule distributed to member countries, to be completed no later than 15 April. It recommended a 2004-2005 draft programme of work and priorities for approval and that the Commission include air transport and transport safety in future work programmes.

The Commission, on 17 April [E/2003/41/Rev.1 (res. 243(XXII))], adopted the Agreement on International Railways in the Arab Mashreq and urged member countries to make the necessary arrangements for its signature and ratification so that it might enter into force as soon as possible.

Statistics

The Commission, on 17 April [res. 247(XXII)], noting the regional countries' need to develop national statistical bodies and update mechanisms and methods for preparing and analysing their economic and social data and indicators, requested the secretariat to assist those countries in adopting and applying the international standards for amassing, analysing and disseminating statistics so that they could formulate economic and social policies and monitor progress towards national development objectives. The secretariat was requested to provide technical support to enable them to become parties to the Special Data Dissemination Standard applied by IMF. The Commission urged member countries to participate in the project for the development of national gender statistics.

On the same date [res. 248(XXII)], the Commission urged member countries that had not done so to join the International Comparison Programme, cooperate with those responsible for it and provide it with financial support. It recommended that the secretariat include activities related to the Programme in its work.

Natural resources, energy and environment

On 17 April [res. 244(XXII)], the Commission urged member countries to complete the procedures for officially approving MOUs relating to bilateral shared water resource cooperation projects and to support the technical task forces carrying out such projects. It adopted the recommendation of the Committee on Water Resources at its fifth session [YUN 2002, p. 1019] for the establishment of an Arab network for integrated management of water resources and the activation of its role, in coordination with the ESCWA secretariat. The Commission urged specialist water training and research centres and institutes in Arab countries to become members of that network, and member countries, international organizations and donors to provide the funding necessary to activate the network. The Executive Secretary was asked to promote projects and activities relating to shared water resources and the Arab network for the integrated management of water resources and to follow up their implementation, with a view to supporting national and regional capacity-building in the integrated management of water resources.

Information

The Commission, on 17 April [res. 246(XXII)], noted the work of the Western Asia Preparatory Conference (Beirut, 4-6 February) for the forthcoming World Summit on the Information Society (see p. 857), and affirmed ESCWA's intention to play a role, in consultation with regional and international organizations working in Arab countries, with a view to formulating a single regional plan of action for the Arab region, given that those countries were culturally and historically related. The Commission called on the secretariat to propose a regional plan of action for building the information society that respected the particularities and linguistic and cultural priorities of the region, and to coordinate in that regard with the League of Arab States. It also requested the secretariat to amend the 2002-2003 work programme to take into consideration the preparatory work, to review the 2004-2005 work programme in order to ensure that it contained activities relating to the regional plan, and to continue participating in the preparations for the World Summit.

Quality of life

The Commission, on 17 April [res. 241(XXII)], noting with concern the impact of the lack of stability in the Arab region on the economic, social and environmental situation and on the development process in general, requested the secretariat to study the impact of war on economic and social development and the environment in Iraq, ensuring that its related activities were coordinated with those of other UN bodies and relevant regional organizations, and to provide the necessary assistance. The secretariat was asked to identify activities that ESCWA should undertake as part of the post-war reconstruction and rehabilitation process and to incorporate them into its programme of work and specializations. It was also asked to establish a mechanism for monitoring the effects of crises, with a view to identifying and analysing their impact on economic and social development in the region, and to assist countries in dealing with them. The Commission requested the Executive Secretary to report in 2005.

In another resolution of the same date [res. 252(XXII)], the Commission requested the secretariat to exert efforts to increase Arab participation in reconstruction and rehabilitation in Palestine and to link such participation to relevant international programmes. It affirmed the role of the Palestinian Authority (PA) and Palestinian civil society institutions in formulating the reconstruction and rehabilitation plan, and the need for the secretariat to assist the PA by delegating experts to evaluate economic and social losses and assisting in finding a relevant mechanism, through international organizations, for compensating such losses. The Commission requested the Executive Secretary to follow up implementation of the resolution and submit a progress report in 2005.

Programme and organizational questions

On 17 April [res. 242(XXII)], the Commission approved the amendments to the revised 2002-2003 programme of work and requested the secretariat to follow up its implementation and assume responsibility for activities that addressed any changes in the ESCWA region. It asked the Executive Secretary to inform member countries of any further modifications to the 2002-2003 work programme and to include that information in the progress report to be submitted to member countries in the years between Commission sessions.

By other resolutions of the same date, the Commission: approved the proposed 2004-2005 programme budget [res. 251(XXII)]; affirmed the importance of extrabudgetary resources in enabling the secretariat to expand its activities and deal with unforeseen developments in the ESCWA region, and urged member countries to increase their donations to other UN regional commissions [res. 253(XXII)]; called on the secretariat to strengthen consultancy services and technical cooperation activities, and requested it to better coordinate its research and analysis activities with its technical cooperation activities and consultancy services; urged member countries and donors to increase financial support for the Commission's consultancy services and technical cooperation activities [res. 249(XXII)]; and adopted the recommendations contained in the reports of its subsidiary bodies and requested member countries to cooperate with ESCWA in measures to promote their implementation [res. 250(XXII)].

Establishment of UN Arabic language centre

On 17 April [res. 239(XXII)], the Commission decided to submit to the Economic and Social Council for adoption a resolution on the establishment within ESCWA of a UN Arabic language centre.

ECONOMIC AND SOCIAL COUNCIL ACTION

On 18 July [meeting 41], the Economic and Social Council, on the recommendation of ESCWA [E/2003/15/Add.1], adopted **resolution 2003/8** without vote [agenda item 10].

Consideration of the establishment within the Economic and Social Commission for Western Asia of a United Nations Arabic language centre

The Economic and Social Council,

Referring to General Assembly resolution 54/248 of 23 December 1999 concerning the pattern of conferences,

Referring also to the requests and suggestions put forward to the Secretariat of the United Nations by the delegations of Arab States Members of the United Nations concerning Arabic language services and, in particular, to the proposal of the delegation of Egypt that is set forth in annex II to the report of the Committee on Conferences and the letter dated 31 July 2001 from the Permanent Representative of Qatar to the United Nations addressed to the Secretary-General, written in his capacity as Chairman of the Arab Group for the month of July 2001, concerning multilingualism,

Recognizing the importance of the coordinating role that could be played by the Economic and Social Commission for Western Asia, given that it is located in the Arab region, with respect to strengthening Arabic language services in the United Nations system in close cooperation with United Nations Headquarters Arabic translation and editorial services and benefiting from the high level of expertise in the region,

1. *Calls upon* the secretariat of the Economic and Social Commission for Western Asia to consider the establishment of a United Nations Arabic language centre, based at the Commission, of which the objective, in cooperation with the Secretariat of the United Nations, and taking into consideration the requisite technical, financial and administrative needs, shall be to raise the technical and linguistic level of the Arabic terminology used in United Nations documents, in order to facilitate the use of the Arabic language in such documents;

2. *Also calls upon* the secretariat of the Commission, in cooperation with the Secretariat of the United Nations, to undertake the establishment of a committee responsible for determining the competencies of the aforementioned centre;

3. *Requests* the Executive Secretary of the Economic and Social Commission for Western Asia to follow up implementation of the present resolution and to submit a report on the progress achieved in that regard to the Commission at its twenty-third session.

Establishment of a committee on women

On 17 April [res. 240(XXII)], the Commission decided to submit to the Economic and Social Council for adoption a resolution on the establishment within ESCWA of a committee on women.

ECONOMIC AND SOCIAL COUNCIL ACTION

On 18 July [meeting 41], the Economic and Social Council, on the recommendation of ESCWA [E/2003/15/Add.1], adopted **resolution 2003/9** without vote [agenda item 10].

Establishment within the Economic and Social Commission for Western Asia of a committee on women

The Economic and Social Council,

Aware of the importance of action relating to the empowerment of women and the improvement of their status, and of making available equal opportunities for their empowerment and increased participation at all levels of the development process,

Aware also of the importance of coordination with regard to the empowerment of women and of respect for the particularities, customs and culture of each Arab country in order to harmonize Arab positions at global conferences and in the follow-up to global conferences organized by the United Nations, with a view to incorporating the regional dimension in international documents,

Affirming the importance of the involvement of the interested parties in member countries of the Economic and Social Commission for Western Asia in the planning, development and follow-up to implementation of secretariat programmes relating to the empowerment of women and of mainstreaming the gender perspective in activities and policies,

Guided by the action taken by the other United Nations regional commissions that have established special committees on women,

Taking into consideration the recommendation made by the Committee on Social Development of the Commission at its fourth session, held in Beirut from 3 to 5 July 2002, concerning the establishment within the Commission of a committee on women,

1. *Decides* to establish within the Economic and Social Commission for Western Asia a committee on women comprising representatives of member countries who are specialists in women's issues, to be responsible for the following:

(a) Identifying the women-related priorities of the programmes of work and medium-term plans of the Commission;

(b) Monitoring developments with respect to the status of women and evaluating indicators and statistics with a view to formulating an integrated policy for the advancement and empowerment of women;

(c) Monitoring the progress made in women-related activities of the Commission secretariat;

(d) Following up global and regional conferences and the participation of member countries therein and coordinating the endeavours of member countries and regional organizations with regard to implementation of the resolutions and recommendations adopted at such conferences;

(e) Coordinating action at the regional level towards the adoption of unified positions on the issue at international gatherings and in follow-up to the performance by member countries of the undertakings to which they made a commitment in human rights instruments concerning women;

(f) Preparing and implementing field projects for the advancement and empowerment of women in member countries of the Commission and finding the necessary funding for such projects;

(g) According the requisite importance to women in the regions in which wars and conflicts are prevalent, and in particular to Palestinian women, who are suffering in the conditions in which the Palestinian people is living under continuing Israeli occupation;

2. *Decides also* that the Committee on Women shall hold its sessions biennially, with effect from 2004, and that an inaugural session should be held before the end of 2003;

3. *Requests* the Executive Secretary of the Commission to establish a women's centre within the secretariat of the Commission with responsibility for acting as the secretariat of the Committee on Women;

4. *Also requests* the Executive Secretary to follow up implementation of the present resolution and to submit a report on the matter to the Commission at its twenty-third session.

Chapter VI

Energy, natural resources and cartography

The conservation, development and use of natural resources and energy were considered by several UN bodies in 2003, including the Commission on Sustainable Development, which recommended the theme of water for the Commission's first two-year work cycle (2004-2005) and energy for its second (2006-2007).

During 2003, action was taken to promote new and renewable sources of energy, including the effective implementation of, and mobilization of resources for, the World Solar Programme 1996-2005. In December, the General Assembly encouraged national and regional initiatives on renewable sources of energy to promote access to energy for the poorest and to improve energy efficiency and conservation.

Amid significant challenges and achievements, the International Atomic Energy Agency (IAEA) in 2003 marked the fiftieth anniversary of its dedication to the achievement and promotion of "Atoms for Peace"—the prevention of nuclear weapons proliferation, which had led to the establishment of the Agency. Speaking before the Assembly in November, the IAEA Director General stated that nuclear power continued to contribute to the world's electricity supply, and was the only source of large-scale electricity provision with comparatively minimal environmental impact.

The United Nations observed the International Year of Freshwater, 2003, with activities supported system-wide and at the national and international levels. On the World Day for Water (22 October), the Secretary-General launched the first edition of the *World Water Development Report*. In December, the Assembly proclaimed the International Decade for Action "Water for Life" (2005-2015), to commence on World Water Day in 2005.

The Sixteenth United Nations Regional Cartographic Conference for Asia and the Pacific adopted resolutions on the Asia-Pacific spatial data infrastructure; regional geodesy; policies for sharing fundamental data and developing regional fundamental data sets; cadastre and spatial data infrastructure; and capacity-building.

The recommendations of the Eighth (2002) United Nations Conference on the Standardization of Geographical Names were endorsed by the Council in July.

Energy and natural resources

The Commission on Sustainable Development (CSD), which assumed the work of the Committee on Energy and Natural Resources for Development following its termination by Economic and Social Council decision 2002/303 [YUN 2002, p. 1022], held its eleventh session (New York, 27 January and 28 April–9 May) [E/2003/29] (see p. 838).

CSD's high-level segment (28-30 April; 5 and 9 May) discussed a February report of the Secretary-General [E/CN.17/2003/2] on follow-up to the World Summit on Sustainable Development, held in 2002 [YUN 2002, p. 821], and the Commission's future role in sustainable development. The report proposed a matrix of issues on which the Commission might focus, among them, natural resources, water and sanitation, and energy. The Chairperson's summary of the high-level segment [E/2003/29] stated that the segment's participants had agreed on the concept of a two-year work cycle, and recommended the overarching theme of water for the first two-year cycle (2004-2005) and energy for the second (2006-2007). He noted that those focus areas underpinned poverty eradication, sustainable production and consumption of natural resources, which, if dealt with successfully, would send a positive message to Governments and the world's poor that the World Summit was delivering real results.

On 9 May [E/2003/29], the Commission adopted a draft resolution on the future programme, organization and methods of work of the Commission, in which it decided to include the themes of water and energy in its multi-year programme of work for the years 2004-2005 and 2006-2007, respectively. On 25 July (**resolution 2003/61**), the Council adopted the draft (see p. 842).

Energy

World Solar Programme (1996-2005)

In response to General Assembly resolution 56/200 [YUN 2001, p. 934], the Secretary-General submitted a July report [A/58/164] on action taken to promote new and renewable sources of energy, including the effective implementation of, and mobilization of resources for, the World Solar Programme 1996-2005. The report described efforts to promote new and renewable sources of energy carried out at the international level by the United Nations and its member organizations, the World Bank, the Global Environment Facility (see p. 1045), other international organizations, non-governmental organizations (NGOs) and partnerships. The United Nations Educational, Scientific and Cultural Organization (UNESCO), as initiator of the World Solar Programme 1996-2005, continued to pursue its twofold strategy of stimulating advocacy and investment mobilization, and promoting education, training and information efforts; and encouraging regional cooperation. It also played an advocacy role in promoting renewable energy technologies for sustainable development, and continued to implement the Global Renewable Energy Education and Training programme, with particular emphasis on Africa. Other activities included regional forums for renewable energy sources; an international symposium on wind energy (Nouakchott, Mauritania, January); and the launching of an international network for sustainable energy. UNESCO continued to assist the task force established to restructure the World Solar Commission, which had finalized statutes that specified the adoption of a new name, the "World Commission on Renewable Energy", and the re-establishment of that Commission as an autonomous organization. Notable developments included the establishment of the Johannesburg Renewable Energy Coalition (see below), which involved 82 member States, and the decision by Germany to host the International Conference for Renewable Energy in June 2004. The Secretary-General concluded that, while challenges and obstacles to the promotion of new and renewable sources of energy remained, there was justification for guarded optimism. The twin concerns of poverty elimination and climate change had produced an unprecedented level of interest in new and renewable sources of energy.

Communication. On 16 October [A/C.2/58/10], Italy, on behalf of the European Union (EU), transmitted a joint declaration entitled "The way forward on renewable energy", launched at the World Summit on Sustainable Development [YUN 2002, p. 821] by the EU and like-minded countries, known as the Johannesburg Renewable Energy Coalition.

GENERAL ASSEMBLY ACTION

On 23 December [meeting 78], the General Assembly, on the recommendation of the Second (Economic and Financial) Committee [A/58/484/Add.1 & Corr.1], adopted **resolution 58/210** without vote [agenda item 94 (a)].

Promotion of new and renewable sources of energy, including the implementation of the World Solar Programme 1996-2005

The General Assembly,

Recalling its resolutions 53/7 of 16 October 1998, 54/215 of 22 December 1999, 55/205 of 20 December 2000 and 56/200 of 21 December 2001 on the World Solar Programme 1996-2005,

Recalling also the recommendations and conclusions contained in the Plan of Implementation of the World Summit on Sustainable Development ("Johannesburg Plan of Implementation") concerning energy for sustainable development,

Welcoming initiatives that aim to improve access to reliable, affordable, economically viable, socially acceptable and environmentally sound energy services for sustainable development in order to contribute to the achievement of the internationally agreed development goals, including those set out in the United Nations Millennium Declaration,

Emphasizing that the World Solar Programme 1996-2005 is aimed at encompassing all forms of new and renewable energy, including solar, thermal, photovoltaic, biomass, wind, hydro, tidal, ocean and geothermal forms,

1. *Takes note* of the report of the Secretary-General;
2. *Reaffirms* that the Johannesburg Plan of Implementation is the intergovernmental framework for energy for sustainable development agreed to at the World Summit on Sustainable Development, and calls for its full implementation;
3. *Notes* the role that the World Solar Commission continues to play in the mobilization of international support and assistance for the implementation of many of the national high-priority projects on renewable sources of energy included in the World Solar Programme 1996-2005, many of which are being executed with national funding;
4. *Notes also* that although significant financial support has been provided by some developed countries that are Members of the United Nations and by some intergovernmental organizations, both within and outside the United Nations system, in the implementation of the World Solar Programme 1996-2005, more action still needs to be taken in this regard;
5. *Recognizes* that rural energy services, including their financing, should be designed to maximize local ownership, as appropriate;
6. *Encourages* the United Nations system to continue to raise awareness of the importance of energy for sustainable development, including the need for the promotion of new and renewable sources of energy and the implementation of the World Solar Programme 1996-2005, particularly in the context of sustainable development and poverty eradication;
7. *Emphasizes* the need to intensify research and development in support of energy for sustainable development, which will require increased commitment on the part of all stakeholders, including Governments and the private sector, to deploy financial and human resources for accelerating research efforts;

8. *Stresses* that the wider use of available renewable sources of energy requires technology transfer and diffusion on a global scale, including through North-South and South-South cooperation;

9. *Calls upon* Governments, as well as relevant regional and international organizations and other relevant stakeholders, to combine, as appropriate, the increased use of renewable energy resources, more efficient use of energy, greater reliance on advanced energy technologies, including advanced and cleaner fossil fuel technologies, and the sustainable use of traditional energy resources, which could meet the growing need for energy services in the longer term to achieve sustainable development;

10. *Encourages* national and regional initiatives on renewable energies to promote access to energy, including renewable energy, for the poorest and to improve energy efficiency and conservation by resorting to a mix of available technologies, taking into full account the provisions of the Johannesburg Plan of Implementation concerning energy for sustainable development;

11. *Welcomes* the initiative by the Government of Germany to host the International Conference for Renewable Energies, in Bonn, from 1 to 4 June 2004;

12. *Invites* the Director-General of the United Nations Educational, Scientific and Cultural Organization to continue to make effective the implementation of the Global Renewable Energy Education and Training Programme 1996-2005 in the various regions;

13. *Requests* the Secretary-General to submit to the General Assembly at its sixtieth session a report on the implementation of the present resolution;

14. *Decides* to include in the provisional agenda of its sixtieth session, under the item entitled "Environment and sustainable development", the sub-item entitled "Promotion of new and renewable sources of energy, including the implementation of the World Solar Programme 1996-2005".

Nuclear energy

By an August note [A/58/312], the Secretary-General transmitted to the General Assembly the 2002 report of the International Atomic Energy Agency (IAEA). Presenting and updating the report in the Assembly on 3 November [A/58/PV.52], the IAEA Director General said that nuclear power continued to contribute to the world's electricity supply, and was the only source that could provide electricity on a large scale with comparatively minimal environmental impact. In 2002, nuclear power supplied 16 per cent of the world's electricity, down from 16.2 per cent in 2001. Asia remained the largest centre of expansion, accounting for 20 of the 33 power reactors under construction.

The safety and security of nuclear activities worldwide remained a key factor and continued to improve at nuclear power plants during 2002. The development, adoption and implementation of legally binding norms had proved to be a powerful mechanism for enhancing safety. Conventions continued to be implemented on early notification of a nuclear accident and assistance in the case of a nuclear accident or radiological emergency; nuclear safety; and the safety of spent-fuel management and on the safety of radioactive waste management (see p. 553). Work progressed to amend and broaden the scope of the 1979 Convention on the Physical Protection of Nuclear Material [YUN 1979, p. 1239], and in the Agency's continued revision and updating of international nuclear safety standards. In services to member States, IAEA undertook more than 60 safety missions, conducted nearly 40 advisory and evaluation missions and convened more than 50 training courses. Despite increased attention to the security of radioactive sources since the 11 September 2001 terrorist attacks in the United States [YUN 2001, p. 60], deficiencies remained and a market continued to exist for such sources for malevolent purposes.

The Director General reported that the situation in the Democratic People's Republic of Korea (DPRK) continued to pose a serious and immediate challenge to the nuclear non-proliferation regime. Since December 2002, no verification activities were performed in the DPRK and the Agency could not provide any level of assurance about the non-diversion of nuclear material. As a result of Security Council resolution 1441(2002) [YUN 2002, p. 292], the Agency had resumed verification activities in Iraq (November 2002–March 2003), and reported that it had found no evidence of the revival of nuclear activities. However, in the light of the Agency's four-year absence, the renewed inspection period was not sufficient for it to complete its overall review and assessment. In May, the Security Council adopted resolution 1483(2003) (see p. 338), in which it expressed the intention to revisit the mandates of IAEA and the United Nations Monitoring, Verification and Inspection Commission. No progress had resulted from consultations with the States of the Middle East region on the application of full-scope safeguards to all nuclear activities (see p. 550) and on the development of model agreements relevant to the establishment of a nuclear-weapon-free zone in that region (see p. 556). Regarding the implementation of the Treaty on the Non-Proliferation of Nuclear Weapons (NPT) safeguards agreements in Iran, the IAEA Board of Governors adopted a resolution urging Iran to show proactive and accelerated cooperation and to demonstrate full transparency by providing the Agency with a declaration of all its nuclear activities. IAEA was in the process of verifying a declaration received from Iran, and a status report on safeguards implementation would be given at a later date (see p. 550). The Agency continued its technical cooperation programme, providing about $80 million annually. Within the programme, nuclear applications were gaining increasing importance as tools for economic and social development, including such areas as human health, water resources management and mutation breeding of major food crops.

IAEA marked the fiftieth anniversary of its dedication to the achievement and promotion of "Atoms for Peace"—the prevention of nuclear weapons proliferation, which had led to the establishment of the Agency.

GENERAL ASSEMBLY ACTION

On 4 November [meeting 55], the General Assembly adopted **resolution 58/8** [draft: A/58/L.10 & Add.1] by recorded vote (129-1) [agenda item 14].

Report of the International Atomic Energy Agency

The General Assembly,

Having received the report of the International Atomic Energy Agency for 2002,

Taking note of the statement of the Director General of the International Atomic Energy Agency, in which he provided additional information on the main developments in the activities of the Agency during 2003,

Recognizing the importance of the work of the Agency,

Recognizing also the cooperation between the United Nations and the Agency and the Agreement governing the relationship between the United Nations and the Agency as approved by the General Conference of the Agency on 23 October 1957 and by the General Assembly in the annex to its resolution 1145(XII) of 14 November 1957,

1. *Takes note with appreciation* of the report of the International Atomic Energy Agency;

2. *Takes note* of resolutions GC(47)/RES/7 A on measures to strengthen international cooperation in nuclear, radiation and transport safety and waste management, GC(47)/RES/7 B on the code of conduct on the safety and security of radioactive sources, GC(47)/RES/7 C on transport safety, GC(47)/RES/8 on nuclear and radiological security—progress on measures to protect against nuclear and radiological terrorism, GC(47)/RES/9 on strengthening of the Agency's technical cooperation activities, GC(47)/RES/10 A on strengthening the Agency's activities related to nuclear science, technology and applications, GC(47)/RES/10 B on nuclear knowledge, GC(47)/RES/10 C on Agency activities in the development of innovative nuclear technology, GC(47)/RES/10 D on the use of isotope hydrology for water resources management, GC(47)/RES/10 E on a plan for producing potable water economically using small and medium-sized nuclear reactors, GC(47)/RES/11 on strengthening the effectiveness and improving the efficiency of the safeguards system and application of the Model Additional Protocol, GC(47)/RES/12 on implementation of the Agreement between the Agency and the Democratic People's Republic of Korea for the application of safeguards in connection with the Treaty on the Non-Proliferation of Nuclear Weapons, GC(47)/RES/13 on the application of Agency safeguards in the Middle East, GC(47)/RES/14 A on staffing of the Agency's secretariat and GC(47)/RES/14 B on women in the secretariat, and decisions GC(47)/DEC/12 on implementation of United Nations Security Council resolutions relating to Iraq, GC(47)/DEC/13 on Israeli nuclear capabilities and threat and GC(47)/DEC/14 on the amendment to article VI of the statute, adopted on 19 September 2003 by the General Conference of the Agency at its forty-seventh regular session;

3. *Affirms its support* for the indispensable role of the Agency in encouraging and assisting the development and practical application of atomic energy for peaceful uses, in technology transfer to developing countries and in nuclear safety, verification and security;

4. *Appeals* to Member States to continue to support the activities of the Agency;

5. *Requests* the Secretary-General to transmit to the Director General of the Agency the records of the fifty-eighth session of the General Assembly relating to the activities of the Agency.

RECORDED VOTE ON RESOLUTION 58/8:

In favour: Albania, Algeria, Andorra, Angola, Argentina, Armenia, Australia, Austria, Bahamas, Bahrain, Belarus, Belgium, Belize, Benin, Bolivia, Bosnia and Herzegovina, Brazil, Brunei Darussalam, Bulgaria, Cambodia, Cameroon, Canada, Cape Verde, Central African Republic, Chile, China, Colombia, Costa Rica, Croatia, Cyprus, Czech Republic, Democratic Republic of the Congo, Denmark, Dominican Republic, Egypt, El Salvador, Eritrea, Estonia, Ethiopia, Fiji, Finland, France, Georgia, Germany, Ghana, Greece, Guatemala, Guyana, Honduras, Hungary, Iceland, India, Indonesia, Iran, Ireland, Israel, Italy, Jamaica, Japan, Kazakhstan, Kuwait, Lao People's Democratic Republic, Latvia, Lebanon, Libyan Arab Jamahiriya, Liechtenstein, Lithuania, Luxembourg, Malaysia, Maldives, Mali, Malta, Mexico, Monaco, Mongolia, Morocco, Mozambique, Myanmar, Nepal, Netherlands, New Zealand, Nicaragua, Nigeria, Norway, Oman, Pakistan, Panama, Papua New Guinea, Paraguay, Peru, Philippines, Poland, Portugal, Qatar, Republic of Korea, Russian Federation, San Marino, Senegal, Serbia and Montenegro, Seychelles, Sierra Leone, Singapore, Slovakia, Slovenia, Spain, Sri Lanka, Sudan, Suriname, Sweden, Switzerland, Syrian Arab Republic, Tajikistan, Thailand, The former Yugoslav Republic of Macedonia, Togo, Tonga, Tunisia, Turkey, Ukraine, United Arab Emirates, United Kingdom, United Republic of Tanzania, United States, Uruguay, Venezuela, Viet Nam, Yemen, Zambia, Zimbabwe.

Against: Democratic People's Republic of Korea.

Natural resources

Water resources

International Year of Freshwater (2003)

A report of the Secretary-General [A/59/167] described activities taken during the International Year of Freshwater, 2003, proclaimed by the General Assembly in resolution 55/196 [YUN 2001, p. 963]; the year was launched on 12 December 2002 in parallel events at UN Headquarters and at UNESCO (Paris). The report covered institutional arrangements and inter-agency coordination, international and national activities, public outreach and educational projects, and UN partnerships with NGOs, the private sector and other members of civil society.

Activities supported by UN agencies and launched during the Year were as follows: UNESCO and the World Water Council established a new Water Cooperation Facility; the

United Nations Children's Fund (UNICEF) and the Water Supply and Sanitation Collaborative Council launched the Water, Sanitation and Hygiene for All in Schools campaign in a number of countries; the United Nations Development Programme (UNDP) launched its Community Water Initiative and its Gender and Water Resource Guide (with the Gender and Water Alliance); and the United Nations Human Settlements Programme (UN-Habitat) signed a memorandum of understanding with the Asian Development Bank to create the Water for Asian Cities programme. Also, the Secretary-General launched the first edition of the *World Water Development Report* on World Day for Water (22 March); and CSD selected water, sanitation and human settlements as the main themes for its first two-year cycle (2004-2005) (see p. 847). In further international activities, the Third World Water Forum (Kyoto, Osaka and Shiga, Japan, 16-23 March), which adopted a Ministerial Declaration "Message from the Lake Biwa and Yodo River Basin" [A/57/785], led to specific commitments by international organizations, Governments and major stakeholders; the International Freshwater Forum (Dushanbe, Tajikistan, 29 August-1 September) adopted the Dushanbe Water Appeal [A/58/362], which called for an International Decade for Action: "Water for Life" (2005-2015) (see below for General Assembly action); the International Conference on Water for the Poorest: Responding to the Millennium Development Goals (Stavanger, Norway, 4-5 November), held under the aegis of the International Water Academy in cooperation with NGOs, focused on how to implement the Millennium Development Goals for water [YUN 2000, p. 52]; the Pan-African Implementation and Partnership Conference on Water (Addis Ababa, Ethiopia, 8-13 December), held under the aegis of the African Ministerial Council on Water, the New Partnership for Africa's Development and the United Nations Economic Commission for Africa [E/AC.5/2004/6], discussed water sector development in Africa; and the international symposium "Basis of Civilization: Water Sciences" (Rome, Italy, 3-6 December) contributed to the advancement of the issue of water. At the national level, Governments created and implemented water policies and agreements.

The Secretary-General noted that it would be useful to have guidelines for national focal points on how to approach the private sector for funding and partnerships, as well as a person to work with the private sector and negotiate and secure partnerships to provide microcredit, scholarships and grants to groups working at the local and national levels; that might be explored for the Water for Life Decade (below). He also proposed setting up UN agency and national focal points, providing materials appropriate for youth groups and updating relevant web sites.

International Decade for Action, "Water for Life", 2005-2015

On 23 December [meeting 78], the General Assembly, on the recommendation of the Second Committee [A/58/485], adopted **resolution 58/217** without vote [agenda item 95].

International Decade for Action, "Water for Life", 2005-2015

The General Assembly,

Recalling its resolution 55/196 of 20 December 2000, by which it proclaimed the year 2003 the International Year of Freshwater,

Emphasizing that water is critical for sustainable development, including environmental integrity and the eradication of poverty and hunger, and is indispensable for human health and well-being,

Recalling the provisions of Agenda 21, the Programme for the Further Implementation of Agenda 21 adopted at its nineteenth special session, the Plan of Implementation of the World Summit on Sustainable Development ("Johannesburg Plan of Implementation") and the decisions of the Economic and Social Council and of the Commission on Sustainable Development at its sixth session relating to freshwater,

Reaffirming the internationally agreed development goals on water and sanitation, including those contained in the United Nations Millennium Declaration, and determined to achieve the goal to halve, by the year 2015, the proportion of people who are unable to reach or to afford safe drinking water, and a similar goal set out in the Johannesburg Plan of Implementation to halve the proportion of people without access to basic sanitation,

Taking note of the contents of the *United Nations World Water Development Report: Water for People, Water for Life*, a joint project of twenty-three specialized agencies and other United Nations entities, and other water-related collaborative mechanisms and initiatives,

Taking note also of the Ministerial Declaration entitled "Message from the Lake Biwa and Yodo River Basin", adopted on 23 March 2003, at the Ministerial Conference on the occasion of the Third World Water Forum, held in Kyoto, Japan, and the Dushanbe Water Appeal, proclaimed on 1 September 2003 at the International Freshwater Forum, held in Dushanbe from 29 August to 1 September 2003,

1. *Proclaims* the period from 2005 to 2015 the International Decade for Action, "Water for Life", to commence on World Water Day, 22 March 2005;

2. *Decides* that the goals of the Decade should be a greater focus on water-related issues at all levels and on the implementation of water-related programmes and projects, while striving to ensure the participation and involvement of women in water-related development efforts, and the furtherance of cooperation at all levels, in order to help to achieve internationally agreed water-related goals contained in Agenda 21, the Programme for the Further Implementation of Agenda

21, the United Nations Millennium Declaration and the Johannesburg Plan of Implementation, and, as appropriate, those identified during the twelfth and thirteenth sessions of the Commission on Sustainable Development;

3. *Welcomes* the decision of the Commission on Sustainable Development at its eleventh session, as reflected in its multi-year programme of work, to consider water, sanitation and human settlements as the thematic cluster in the first cycle, 2004-2005, and invites the Commission to work within existing resources to identify possible activities and programmes in connection with the Decade within the framework of its consideration of the thematic cluster of issues on water, sanitation and human settlements at its twelfth and thirteenth sessions, as provided for by its multi-year programme of work;

4. *Invites* the Secretary-General to take the appropriate steps to organize the activities of the Decade, taking into account the results of the International Year of Freshwater and the work of the Commission on Sustainable Development at its twelfth and thirteenth sessions;

5. *Calls upon* the relevant United Nations bodies, specialized agencies, regional commissions and other organizations of the United Nations system to deliver a coordinated response, utilizing existing resources and voluntary funds, to make "Water for Life" a decade for action.

JIU report

A 2 May note [A/57/497/Add.1] of the Secretary-General transmitted his comments and those of the UN System Chief Executives Board for Coordination (CEB) on the JIU report on the extension of water-related technical cooperation projects to end-beneficiaries: bridging the gap between the normative and the operational in the United Nations system (case studies in two African countries (Madagascar, Zambia)) [YUN 2002, p. 1027]. Among other things, the report questioned the need to enforce some JIU recommendations such as the setting up of joint and comprehensive guidelines for the implementation of water-related projects. The need to establish a database and a web site was not convincing, in view of duplication with already established web sites and the issue of the cost factor. On operational issues, CEB stated that irrespective of inter-agency coordination for intervention, the most effective form of coordination was at the country level.

On 11 July (**decision 2003/225**), the Economic and Social Council took note of the Secretary-General's notes transmitting the JIU report and his comments and those of CEB thereon.

Cartography

UN Regional Cartographic Conference for Asia and the Pacific

In accordance with Economic and Social Council decisions 2000/229 [YUN 2000, p. 964] and 2002/229 [YUN 2002, p. 1028], the Secretary-General submitted a report on the Sixteenth United Nations Regional Cartographic Conference for Asia and the Pacific (Okinawa, Japan, 14-18 July) [E/2004/57 & Corr.1]. The work of the Conference was organized around three technical committees on development needs and institutional capacity-building, fundamental data and spatial data infrastructures and their development in Asia and the Pacific.

The Conference adopted resolutions regarding the Asia-Pacific spatial data infrastructure; regional geodesy; policies for sharing fundamental data and developing regional fundamental data sets; cadastre and spatial data infrastructure; and capacity-building. A further resolution called for the Seventeenth United Nations Regional Cartographic Conference for Asia and the Pacific to be convened for five working days in 2006, with a primary focus on the continued and strengthened contribution of cartography and geographic information in support of the implementation of Agenda 21 [YUN 1992, p. 672].

The Conference recommended that the Council endorse its recommendation regarding the Seventeenth Regional Conference, to be held in 2006 (see above), and requested the Secretary-General to implement its other recommendations.

Standardization of geographical names

In a report [E/2003/4] to the Economic and Social Council, the Secretary-General presented information on the Eighth (2002) United Nations Conference on the Standardization of Geographical Names, and on the Conference's recommendations [YUN 2002, p. 1029].

On 24 July, the Council took note of the report (**decision 2003/309**) and endorsed the Conference's recommendations (**decision 2003/294**).

Chapter VII

Environment and human settlements

In 2003, the United Nations and the international community continued efforts to protect the environment through legally binding instruments and the activities of the United Nations Environment Programme (UNEP).

The UNEP Governing Council/fourth Global Ministerial Environment Forum adopted a programme for international action to deal with mercury contamination. Further decisions concerned early warning assessment and monitoring, water, climate and atmosphere, chemicals, forest-related issues, support for Africa and small island developing States, and long-term strategies for sport and the environment and for the engagement of young people in environmental issues.

UNEP continued efforts to implement the environment-related elements of the Johannesburg Plan of Implementation of the 2002 World Summit on Sustainable Development, including regional implementation.

The Conference of the Parties to the 1992 United Nations Framework Convention on Climate Change adopted new emissions-reporting guidelines based on good-practice guidance on land use, land-use change and forestry. The 2000 Cartagena Protocol on Biosafety to the 1992 Convention on Biodiversity entered into force on 11 September. Heads of State and Government participating in a special session of the Conference of the Parties to the 1994 United Nations Convention to Combat Desertification in those Countries Experiencing Serious Drought and/or Desertification, particularly in Africa, adopted the Havana Declaration, which invited all affected parties to integrate the Convention into national strategies for sustainable development. In December, the General Assembly declared 2006 the International Year of Deserts and Desertification.

The Governing Council of the United Nations Human Settlements Programme (UN-Habitat) held its first session, which was designated as its nineteenth session to signify continuity between the former Commission on Human Settlements and the Governing Council. The Council took action in support of the implementation of the 1996 Habitat Agenda; the 2000 UN Millennium Declaration; the 2001 Declaration on Cities and Other Human Settlements in the New Millennium; and the human settlements–related elements of the Johannesburg Plan of Implementation. UN-Habitat established a Water and Sanitation Trust Fund to facilitate the achievement of the Millennium Development Goal to reduce by half by 2015 the proportion of people without sustainable access to safe water and sanitation. The Governing Council endorsed the establishment of the Special Human Settlements Programme for the Palestinian People and a Technical Cooperation Fund of $5 million for an initial period of two years.

Environment

UN Environment Programme

Governing Council/Ministerial Forum

The fourth Global Ministerial Environment Forum (GMEF), also serving as the twenty-second session of the Governing Council (GC) of the United Nations Environment Programme (UNEP), was held at UNEP headquarters in Nairobi, Kenya, from 3 to 7 February [A/58/25]. On 7 February [dec. 22/24], the Governing Council decided to hold its eighth special session in Seoul, Republic of Korea, from 29 to 31 March 2004 and its twenty-third session in Nairobi from 21 to 25 February 2005; it also approved the provisional agenda for those sessions.

Ministerial consultations (5-6 February) [UNEP/GC.22/11] discussed the implementation of the outcome of the 2002 World Summit on Sustainable Development (Johannesburg Plan of Implementation) [YUN 2002, p. 821], with a focus on the New Partnership for Africa's Development (NEPAD) (see p. 937), the implications of regional implementation of the Summit's outcomes for UNEP's work and the promotion of sustainable consumption and production patterns. UNEP's Executive Director presented papers on UNEP's regional efforts (see p. 1043); Africa and NEPAD (see p. 1040); the living natural resource base to fight poverty: UNEP's contribution to the biodiversity commitments of the World Summit (see p. 1042); and promoting sustainable consumption and production patterns [YUN 2002, p. 1065].

The Committee of the Whole (3-7 February) [UNEP/GC.22/11] considered the state of the environment; coordination and cooperation issues (see p. 1044); the role of civil society (see p. 1046); international environmental governance (see p. 1038); follow-up to General Assembly resolutions (see p. 1047); UNEP's contribution to future sessions of the Commission on Sustainable Development; UNEP's 2004-2005 programme of work; the Environment Fund (see p. 1047); and administrative and other budgetary matters (see p. 1047).

On 10 July, the Economic and Social Council took note of the Governing Council's report on its twenty-second session (**decision 2003/309**).

Subsidiary body

In 2003, the Committee of Permanent Representatives, which was open to representatives of all UN Member States and members of specialized agencies, met in Nairobi on 17 March [UNEP/CPR/83/2], 17 June [UNEP/CPR/84/2], 17 September [UNEP/CPR/85/2] and 9 December [UNEP/CPR/86/2]; an extraordinary meeting was held on 22 January [UNEP/CPR/82/3]. The Committee discussed, among other matters, the implementation of the programme of work and the relevant decisions of the Governing Council's twenty-first [YUN 2001, p. 943] and twenty-second (2003) sessions and seventh special session [YUN 2002, p. 1030]; UNEP relations with the United Nations Office at Nairobi (UNON); and the status of the Environment Fund.

GENERAL ASSEMBLY ACTION

On 23 December [meeting 78], the General Assembly, on the recommendation of the Second (Economic and Financial) Committee [A/58/484/Add.8], adopted **resolution 58/209** without vote [agenda item 94].

Report of the Governing Council of the United Nations Environment Programme on its twenty-second session

The General Assembly,

Recalling its resolution 2997(XXVII) of 15 December 1972, by which it established the Governing Council of the United Nations Environment Programme,

Recalling also its resolutions 53/242 of 28 July 1999, 56/193 of 21 December 2001 and 57/251 of 20 December 2002 on the report of the Governing Council,

Taking note of the report of the Governing Council on its seventh special session,

Reaffirming the role of the United Nations Environment Programme as the principal body within the United Nations system in the field of environment, which should take into account, within its mandate, the sustainable development needs of developing countries as well as countries with economies in transition,

Taking into account the Plan of Implementation of the World Summit on Sustainable Development ("Johannesburg Plan of Implementation"),

Recalling the need to enhance the provisions of the Johannesburg Plan of Implementation concerning support for capacity-building in developing countries and countries with economies in transition,

1. *Takes note* of the report of the Governing Council of the United Nations Environment Programme on its twenty-second session and the decisions contained therein;

2. *Emphasizes* the need for the United Nations Environment Programme, within its mandate, to further contribute to sustainable development programmes, the implementation of Agenda 21 and the Johannesburg Plan of Implementation at all levels, bearing in mind the mandate of the Commission on Sustainable Development;

3. *Reiterates* the need to ensure that capacity-building and technical assistance to developing countries remain important components of the work of the United Nations Environment Programme, and in this regard emphasizes the need for full and effective implementation of relevant decisions of the Governing Council/Global Ministerial Environment Forum;

4. *Calls upon* the United Nations Environment Programme to contribute, within its mandate, to the preparations for the twelfth session of the Commission on Sustainable Development, while avoiding duplication and overlap in the work of the two bodies;

5. *Also calls upon* the United Nations Environment Programme to contribute, within its mandate and as a member of the Inter-Agency Task Force, to the preparations for the international meeting to review the implementation of the Programme of Action for the Sustainable Development of Small Island Developing States, to be held in Mauritius from 30 August to 3 September 2004, including its preparatory process;

6. *Encourages* Member States, the Governing Council and the relevant bodies of the United Nations system to submit their comments, in a timely manner, on the important but complex issue of establishing universal membership of the Governing Council/Global Ministerial Environment Forum, including its legal, political, institutional, financial and system-wide implications, in order to contribute to the report of the Secretary-General to be submitted to the General Assembly for consideration before its sixtieth session, in accordance with resolution 57/251;

7. *Encourages* Member States to participate in the ongoing intergovernmental consultation process on the strengthening of the scientific base of the United Nations Environment Programme;

8. *Notes,* in regard to strengthening the overall financial situation of the United Nations Environment Programme, the various available options and the efforts being undertaken to enhance predictability in financing its programme of work and broadening its base of contributions;

9. *Invites* the Governing Council/Global Ministerial Environment Forum to review its methods, agenda and programme of work, in view of the mandate of the United Nations Environment Programme, with the aim of enhancing manageability and the effective participation of States Members of the United Nations in its sessions, and taking into account recent work

thereon by the Committee of Permanent Representatives of the United Nations Environment Programme;

10. *Emphasizes* the need to further enhance coordination and cooperation among the relevant United Nations organizations in the promotion of the environmental dimension of sustainable development, and in this respect welcomes the participation of the United Nations Environment Programme in the United Nations Development Group;

11. *Requests* that the reports on the work of the Environmental Management Group be made available to the General Assembly at its next session through the Governing Council of the United Nations Environment Programme;

12. *Reiterates* the need for stable, adequate and predictable financial resources for the United Nations Environment Programme, and in accordance with resolution 2997(XXVII) underlines the need to consider adequate reflection of all administrative and management costs of the Programme in the context of the United Nations regular budget;

13. *Requests* the Secretary-General to keep the resource needs of the United Nations Environment Programme and the United Nations Office at Nairobi under review so as to permit the delivery, in an effective manner, of necessary services to the Programme and to the other United Nations organs and organizations in Nairobi.

International environmental governance

In a decision on follow-up to General Assembly resolution 57/251 [YUN 2002, p. 1031], the Governing Council, on 7 February [A/58/25 (dec. 22/17 I)], requested the Executive Director to invite Governments to submit written comments by 31 October regarding the establishment of universal membership of GC/GMEF [YUN 2002, p. 1033] and to submit a report incorporating the comments to the eighth (2004) special session of GC/GMEF. He was asked, in collaboration with the United Nations Development Programme (UNDP), the Global Environment Facility (GEF) (see p. 1045) and other organizations, in compliance with a 2002 Governing Council decision [ibid.], to develop an intergovernmental strategic plan for technology support and capacity-building and to submit a draft strategic plan and a report in 2004.

A June issue paper on the universal membership of GC/GMEF [UNEP/GCSS.VIII/INF/11] was circulated to all Governments together with a letter from the Executive Director seeking their views on the matter.

Environmental Management Group

The Environmental Management Group (EMG), an inter-agency advisory group set up in 1999 to coordinate UN system activities in addressing the major challenges in the UNEP work programme [YUN 1999, p. 974], was reinvigorated and made fully operational in 2003 with the establishment of its permanent secretariat in Geneva; it met several times to develop its programme of work for the short and medium term. Taking into account developments in international cooperation, particularly the outcomes of the 2002 World Summit on Sustainable Development [YUN 2002, p. 821], recent GC/GMEF sessions, the eleventh session of the Commission on Sustainable Development (see p. 842), and the first session of the Governing Council of UN-Habitat (see p. 1078), EMG, in July, considered how it could best contribute to implementing the sustainable development agenda in the areas of environment and human settlements. In line with a call in the World Summit's Johannesburg Plan of Implementation for coordination among international and intergovernmental bodies and processes working on water-related issues, EMG members, in September, provided their views on environmental aspects of water, sanitation and human settlements. The outcomes of that discussion were to be incorporated in a background paper for ministerial-level consultations at the eighth (2004) special session of the Governing Council on that topic.

UNEP activities

UNEP's proposed 2004-2005 programme of work included activities in the five areas of concentration as defined by the Governing Council in a 1998 decision [YUN 1998, p. 982]: environmental assessment and early warning; enhanced coordination of environmental conventions and development of environmental policy instruments; freshwater; technology transfer and industry; and support to Africa. UNEP strengthened coherence and integration in its 2004-2005 work programme by linking programme priorities with environmental monitoring, assessment and early warning; the water and sanitation, energy, health, agriculture and biodiversity (WEHAB) initiative, proposed by the Secretary-General in 2002 [YUN 2002, p. 1036]; and the promotion of policy integration.

Monitoring and assessment

A January note by the Executive Director [UNEP/GC.22/INF/15] discussed a 2002 proposal to strengthen UNEP's scientific base through the establishment of an intergovernmental panel on global environmental change [YUN 2002, p. 1034]. It stated that the design of the proposed intergovernmental panel as a multidisciplinary advisory organ of GC/GMEF with open-ended membership should be considered in the light of several closely interrelated needs, among them the need to implement fully the 2002 GC/GMEF decision on international environmental governance [ibid., p. 1033]. The panel's mandate would be to provide scientific and technical advice to GC/GMEF regarding implementation of the responsibilities assigned to it by the General Assembly. It would play a key role in keeping under review the world environment situation and in mobilizing the scientific community towards that end. It would act upon requests from GC/GMEF and advise on global and regional issues. The panel would also analyse gaps in the assessment process and consider initiating assessments to cover the gaps.

Governing Council action. On 7 February [A/58/25 (dec. 22/1 I A)], the Governing Council invited Governments, intergovernmental organizations, non-governmental organizations (NGOs) and scientific institutions to submit to the Executive Director their views on the likely gaps and types of assessment needs with respect to the environment; how UNEP and other organizations were meeting those needs; and existing options for meeting any needs within UNEP's mandate. They were invited to address scientific credibility, saliency, legitimacy and relevance in the assessment process; interaction between science and policy development; the role of existing institutions; strengthening existing institutions and mechanisms and establishing an intergovernmental panel on global environmental change; links and sectoral integrations; duplication, cooperation, complementarity and added value to the work of other assessment processes, international agencies and multilateral environmental agreements (MEAs); cost-effectiveness and efficiency; and developing country participation and capacity-building. The Executive Director was asked to make submissions publicly available and to prepare a synthesis report in 2004. He was also asked to facilitate an intergovernmental consultation taking into account available funding, transparency, regional balance and developing country participation.

On the same date [dec. 22/1 I B], the Council requested the Executive Director to keep the world environmental situation under review, and provide early warning on emerging environmental issues of international significance by producing annual global environment outlook statements; preparing the comprehensive Global Environment Outlook report series every five years, with the next report for 2007; supporting sub-global integrated environmental assessment processes; supporting thematic assessments on emerging or cross-cutting issues; cooperating with Governments and organizations to develop up-to-date and integrated databases and indicators that provided for early warning, monitoring and assessment; and promoting networking with relevant institutions to enhance the exchange and dissemination of environmental data and information. Governments were urged to provide additional funding to strengthen targeted capacity-building by UNEP in integrated environmental assessment and related data, information and knowledge management, and the identification of emerging issues.

Post-conflict assessments

The Governing Council, on 7 February [dec. 22/1 IV], requested the Executive Director to strengthen UNEP's ability to assess environmental impacts in post-conflict situations and called on Governments to support countries or regions in need of assessments. It invited Governments and other concerned parties to provide UNEP with assistance for conducting post-conflict environmental assessments. The Executive Director was asked to enable UNEP to conduct post-conflict environmental assessments at the request of States and to report to the relevant UN bodies for follow-up; inform Governments of current post-conflict environmental assessment activities; and report to the Governing Council in 2005.

A December report by the Executive Director [UNEP/GCSS.VIII/2] summarized the state of the environment relating to UNEP's activities in environmental assessment and early warning, thematic assessments, assessing the environmental contribution to development, and the state of the environment in various regions. It emphasized activities related to water, sanitation and human settlements, and addressed areas of special geographic focus, taking into account the region where the Council's eighth (2004) special session was to be held (Jeju, Republic of Korea).

UNEP's post-conflict environmental activities included the clean-up of environmental hot spots in Kosovo; an environmental assessment of Afghanistan; a study of the state of the environment in the Occupied Palestinian Territories (see p. 1073); a study on the environmental impacts of the use of depleted uranium in Bosnia and Herzegovina; and the development of an environmental database and analysis service for the United Nations Compensation Commission (see p. 369) to assess claims for environmental damages from the 1990 hostilities in the Gulf region [YUN 1990, p. 189]. In response to requests from several African countries, UNEP was preparing an assessment to be carried out in Africa during 2003-2004. UNEP published a desk study outlining the environmental vulnerabilities in Iraq resulting from years of conflict, the low priority attached to environment by the previous regime and the unintended effects of sanctions imposed in the 1990s (see p. 361); a final report on the environmental assessment in Iraq was envisaged for 2004.

Support to Africa

A January discussion paper of the Executive Director [UNEP/GC.22/8/Add.1/Rev.1] provided information on: UNEP's support to Africa, including assistance for implementing the NEPAD environment initiative [YUN 2002, p. 1035], which targeted desertification, wetland conservation, invasive alien species, coastal management, global warming, transboundary conservation areas, environmental governance and financing; its work in Africa in the light of the 2002 Johannesburg Plan of Implementation [YUN 2002, p. 821]; its regional programmes in Africa; and its partnerships for implementation.

UNEP supported the African Ministerial Conference on the Environment (AMCEN) establishing the African Environmental Information Network (AEIN) (see below), and assisted the steering committee in finalizing an action plan for NEPAD's environment initiative. It would organize thematic workshops on the finalization of the action plan until its adoption by the second special session of AMCEN (Maputo, Mozambique, 9-10 June) [UNEP/AMCEN/SS/II/16], prior to the endorsement by the second ordinary session of the African Union (AU) Assembly (Maputo, 10-12 July) [Assembly/AU/dec.6-31(II)]. UNEP would also assist in strengthening the African Ministerial Conference on Water (AMCOW), established as part of the NEPAD initiative, regional institutions and civil society organizations, and AMCEN's operational mechanisms.

In the area of assessment, UNEP launched AEIN, which was aimed at strengthening the capacities of the UNEP Collaborating Centres and some key national institutions, as well as establishing a collaborative institutional framework to support the overall production process for the Africa Environment Outlook report and subregional State of the Environment reports, which in turn would provide input into the Global Environment Outlook report.

Regarding shared freshwater resources, UNEP would support the development and implementation of AMCOW's programme of work, the strengthening of river and lake basin authorities, and the promotion of energy self-sufficiency. Other industry and trade-related activities would receive special attention.

In 2003, 35 UNEP/GEF projects devoted exclusively to Africa were approved, with total funding of $60.9 million, including $28.9 million in GEF resources. UNEP supported African countries in the development of the Action Plan for implementation of the NEPAD environment initiative (see above) through a GEF-funded medium-sized project.

Governing Council action. On 7 February [dec. 22/9], the Governing Council requested the Executive Director to: establish working relationships with AU specialized technical committees to facilitate the integration of environmental issues in the work of the institutional dispensation of the AU and NEPAD; work closely with UN and African partners in implementing the 2002 United Nations Declaration on NEPAD, adopted by General Assembly resolution 57/2 [YUN 2002, p. 908]; and continue to assist in developing NEPAD's environment initiative and to support African countries in implementing it. He was asked to support the production of the Africa Environment Outlook report and the establishment of AEIN, as called for by AMCEN in 2002 [YUN 2002, p. 1035]; the annual celebrations of African Environment Day on 3 March; and AMCOW. The Governing Council also requested the Executive Director, in collaboration with EMG, to support the work of any Economic and Social Council ad hoc advisory group, established in accordance with Council resolution 2002/1 [YUN 2002, p. 919], on the advisory group's request; to develop and promote in Africa understanding of the linkages between poverty, health, trade and the environment; and to mobilize resources to assist African countries, in collaboration with Governments, in the preparations for the conferences of the parties to MEAs. The Governing Council called on African Governments to take primary action and responsibility for the sustainable development of their countries. Governments and the donor community were called on to enhance their support for the implementation of NEPAD and AMCEN priority programmes through, among other things, contributions to the General Trust Fund for AMCEN. The Executive Director was called on to strengthen UNEP collaboration with UN organizations working in Africa and with the United Nations Human Settlements Programme. The Governing Council took note of the progress made by the Executive Director in the revitalization of the 1981 Abidjan Convention for Cooperation in the Protection and Development of the Marine and Coastal Environment of the West and Central African Region [YUN 1981, p. 833] and the 1985 Nairobi Convention for the Protection, Management and Development of the Marine and Coastal Environment of the East African Region [YUN 1985, p. 816] by the successful launch of the African Process on the development and management of the coastal and marine environment, and requested him to strengthen the two conventions. The Executive Director was asked to report to the Committee of Permanent Representatives and the next session of GC/GMEF.

On 7 February [dec. 22/10], the Governing Council called on all Governments, international organizations, donor organizations and major groups to work towards poverty eradication, as committed to in the Johannesburg Plan of Implementation, and towards operationalizing the World Solidarity Fund, which was endorsed by the General Assembly in resolution 57/265 [YUN 2002, p. 831]. The Executive Director was requested to develop a strategy to implement those actions within UNEP's mandate and, in collaboration with UNDP and other organizations, particularly NEPAD and AMCEN, to explore opportunities for greater cooperation with the AU on the NEPAD initiative and to provide input on the linkages between poverty and the environment. The Executive Director and AMCEN were asked to continue UNEP's work in promoting greater understanding of those linkages and to assist Governments to integrate environmental decision-making into social and economic policy towards poverty eradication, using the note by the Executive Director on the conceptual framework on poverty and ecosystems [UNEP/GC.22/INF/30/Rev.1] (see p. 1044) as a guide. The Executive Director was also asked, in collaboration with UNDP and other organizations, to operationalize the conceptual framework on poverty and ecosystems, using the Executive Director's note as a guide; to test the approach through country studies with a focus on Africa, working through NEPAD, towards the development of country-specific poverty-environment strategies; and to report to the next GC/GMEF session.

Water policy and strategy

A January discussion paper by the Executive Director [UNEP/GC.22/10/Add.3/Rev.1] on the implementation of the water-related outcomes of the World Summit on Sustainable Development [YUN 2002, p. 821] outlined current challenges regarding access to safe drinking water and sanitation, the links between the freshwater, coastal and marine environments, the management of coasts, seas and oceans, the special issues facing small island developing States and the response of international forums. It laid out the targets and goals of the water-related outcomes of the World Summit and UNEP's response, and presented questions related to water to be discussed during the ministerial segment of the twenty-second (2003) GC/GMEF session. The report recommended that steps be taken to: enhance implementation of UNEP's water policy and strategy; consolidate UNEP's progress in water assessment by building on achievements; support implementation of the Montreal Declaration on the Protection of the Marine Environment [YUN 2001, p. 965], taking into account the related outcomes of the World Summit; and strengthen UNEP's role in freshwater management.

On 7 February [dec. 22/2 I], the Governing Council decided that UNEP should play an active role in the follow-up to the water-related outcomes of the World Summit, particularly the Johannesburg Plan of Implementation [YUN 2002, p. 821]. It requested the Executive Director to implement UNEP's water policy and strategy and urged him to assist regional bodies and Governments to develop and implement strategies, plans and programmes with regard to integrated river basin, watershed and groundwater management. He was asked to strengthen the freshwater component of the policy and strategy with respect to: the transfer of environmentally sound technologies for water management; integrated river basin, watershed and groundwater management; regional and global assessments of water resources; international and regional cooperation on the environmental aspects of water (freshwater, coastal and marine environment); integrated freshwater–coastal area management; groundwater vulnerability assessment and sustainable groundwater resource management; and ongoing collaboration between UNEP and UN-Habitat in the area of water, including projects on water for cities and industrial waste-water management (see p. 1082). He was further requested to strengthen: the implementation of the Global International Waters Assessment project (see p. 1065); in consultation with Governments, support for the regional implementation of the UNEP water policy and strategy; cooperation with other UN agencies and international and regional organizations; and support for the efforts of MEAs and national Governments when undertaking UNEP activities on the environmental aspects of water. The Executive Director was asked to play an active role in the observance of World Day for Water, 2003 (22 March); the International Year of Freshwater, 2003 (see p. 1033); and the Third World Water Forum and ministerial conference (Kyoto, Osaka and Shiga, Japan, 16-23 March 2003). He was also asked to participate in the follow-up to the 2002 WEHAB initiative [YUN 2002, p. 1036] and the activities of the Millennium Task Force on Water and Sanitation.

The Governing Council decided to review the UNEP water policy and strategy at the twenty-third (2005) GC/GMEF session; for that purpose, the Executive Director should prepare an updated version of the water policy and strategy.

The atmosphere

To help reduce greenhouse gas emissions, UNEP promoted sustainable energy through such initiatives as the Sustainable Energy Finance Initiative, a joint venture of UNEP and the Basel Agency for Sustainable Energy launched in October and aimed at encouraging investment in renewable energy and energy efficiency, and the Mediterranean Renewable Energy Programme, a new UNEP initiative supported by Italy, which sought to increase financing for clean energy in the Mediterranean, with an initial focus on Egypt, Morocco and Tunisia.

In response to the 2002 UNEP-sponsored report on the vast haze cloud that appeared seasonally over much of Asia as a result of biomass burning and industrial emissions [YUN 2002, p. 1035], UNEP brought together a team of international scientists to study the impacts of aerosol pollution. The Atmospheric Brown Cloud Project was establishing a network of ground-based monitoring stations to assess the phenomenon; initial results suggested that the amount of sunlight reaching the Earth's surface could be reduced by as much as 15 per cent, affecting monsoon patterns and triggering unseasonal drought and floods across Asia.

Environment and sustainable development

A January policy statement of the Executive Director [UNEP/GC.22/9] regarding the development of policies on the environment and sustainable development presented information on UNEP's proposed 2004-2005 programme of work. The report stated that the proposed work programme represented UNEP's contribution towards international consensus for action on sustainable development, and that UNEP was committed to enhancing the understanding that sustainable development and environmental security were essential pillars of peace.

By **decision 58/550** of 23 December, the General Assembly took note of the report of the Second Committee on environment and sustainable development [A/58/484].

Governing Council action. On 7 February, the Governing Council adopted decisions on UNEP's activities related to the Arctic, least developed countries (LDCs) and small island developing States (SIDS).

The Council, noting the inclusion of concerns relevant to the Arctic in the Johannesburg Plan of Implementation [YUN 2002, p. 821], especially those dealing with ocean issues, sustainable use of natural resources, the eradication of poverty among indigenous communities, the impact of climate change, persistent organic pollutants and heavy metals, requested the Executive Director to provide assessments and early warning on emerging issues related to the Arctic environment, in particular its impact on the global environment [dec. 22/11].

Regarding LDCs [dec. 22/12], the Council invited the Executive Director to take steps to ensure that implementation of the Brussels Programme of Action for the Least Developed Countries for the Decade 2001-2010, adopted in 2001 [YUN 2001, p. 770], was fully included in UNEP's programme activities and in its intergovernmental processes within its mandate and resources.

In a decision on SIDS [dec. 22/13], the Governing Council decided to strengthen the institutional capacity of SIDS to achieve the sustainable development goals outlined in the 1994 Barbados Programme of Action for the Sustainable Development of Small Island Developing States [YUN 1994, p. 783] by providing technical and financial support, and to provide support for partnership initiatives within the context of implementation of the Johannesburg Plan of Implementation [YUN 2002, p. 821]. The Executive Director was asked to identify appropriate modalities for implementing those objectives and to report in 2004 and to increase funding for UNEP activities related to SIDS during the 2004-2005 biennium, particularly those concerning the preparations for and the implementation of the outcomes of the international review meeting on SIDS, to be held in Mauritius in 2004 (see p. 871). He was also asked to identify appropriate modalities for the effective implementation of the decision's recommendations and to report in 2004.

Follow-up to World Summit on Sustainable Development (2002)

In response to a 2002 Governing Council decision [YUN 2002, p. 1036], the Council had before it a report of the Executive Director [UNEP/GC.22/5] on UNEP's actions to implement the Johannesburg Plan of Implementation, adopted at the 2002 World Summit on Sustainable Development [YUN 2002, p. 821]. UNEP held consultations with UN bodies and agencies and other organizations to provide a coherent contribution from the UN system; environmental policy dialogues were held with civil society organizations. A number of Type II voluntary initiatives—those jointly implemented by Governments, the private sector, civil society and international organizations—involving UNEP constituted the concrete outcome of the coordination and dialogue process. In response to the Secretary-General's WEHAB initiative [YUN 2002, p. 1036], UNEP was tasked to take the lead on biodiversity issues and actively contributed to all other WEHAB areas. UNEP's 2002-2003 programme of work addressed a broad range of activities identified in the Plan of Implementation; following the Summit, further adjustments were made to the work programme to match the Plan's requirements. The proposed 2004-2005 programme of work fully integrated the relevant elements of the Plan with UNEP's main activities and thematic focus (see p. 1038). The Executive Director's report also covered the emerging issue of the interlinkages between the environment and cultural diversity and proposed Governing Council action on that subject as well as on other issues.

On 7 February [dec. 22/16], the Governing Council requested the Executive Director, subject to the availability of voluntary funds, to examine the issue of environment and cultural diversity by, among other measures, conducting a survey, in cooperation with the United Nations Educational, Scientific and Cultural Organization (UNESCO) and relevant stakeholders, on the state of current work and relevant developments, with particular attention to human well-being, and to report in 2005.

In a discussion paper [UNEP/GC.22/8 & Corr.1] on regional implementation of the outcomes of the World Summit, the Executive Director said that UNEP was working towards an increased policy dialogue and cooperation at the regional level. The role of regional and subregional ministerial forums and the work of the regional offices with those forums were providing a crucial link between UNEP's policy and programme development and the actual concerns in the regions. To enhance that connection, the involvement of civil society organizations in UNEP's work at the regional level would be strengthened.

The proposed UNEP 2004-2005 programme of work included activities that stemmed from work with regional ministerial forums and aimed to strengthen UNEP's participation in the development and implementation of regional initiatives. It included involvement in NEPAD's environment initiative (see p. 1040); the Latin American and Caribbean Initiative on Sustainable Development; the Arab Initiative for Sustainable Development; the Environment for Europe Conference (Kiev, Ukraine, 21-23 May) (see p. 1018), which addressed strengthening environmental governance structures in the region; and participation in and support for relevant ministerial forums in Asia and the Pacific, including those of the Association of South-East Asian Nations (ASEAN), the South Asia Cooperative Environment Programme, the South Asian Association for Regional Cooperation and the South Pacific Regional Environment Programme.

The Governing Council had before it a note by the Executive Director [UNEP/GC.22/INF/34] containing extracts from the Johannesburg Declaration on Sustainable Development and the Plan of Implementation that were relevant to regionalization.

On 7 February [dec. 22/21], the Governing Council endorsed the priorities for attention and action in the regions, as contained in the regional annexes to the Executive Director's discussion paper, and requested him to promote and support the work, activities and initiatives of regional and subregional environmental forums, with a view to maximizing their involvement in preparing and implementing GC/GMEF decisions. The Executive Director was asked to ensure the adequate capacity of the regional offices for the UNEP work programme and to respond adequately to the World Summit's call to strengthen and support regional and subregional initiatives and actions, and the interregional aspects of the 1994 Barbados Programme of Action for the Sustainable Development of Small Island Developing States [YUN 1994, p. 783]. He was asked to include in the programme of work, beginning with the 2006-2007 biennium, regional annexes identifying the percentage of the Environment Fund budget from each of the divisions that would be implemented at the regional level, to be presented for a decision at the twenty-third (2005) GC/GMEF session, with preliminary data to be presented to the eighth GC/GMEF special session (2004). The Council requested the Executive Director to establish and strengthen partnerships at the regional and subregional levels with other UN bodies, development banks and other institutions, including civil society groups; it also called on member States to support UNEP's work in the regions.

Also on 7 February [dec. 22/14], the Governing Council welcomed the outcome of the first Environmental Ministerial Meeting of the Economic Cooperation Organization (ECO) (Tehran, Iran, 15 December 2002) and requested the Executive Director to support the subregional environmental initiatives of the ECO region (Western and Central Asia). He was also asked to promote the work of the regional offices and increase their financial capacities for fulfilling the goals of capacity-building and technology transfer to ECO member countries; establish and reinforce linkages and partnerships among other UN bodies, development banks and the Bretton Woods institutions (the World Bank Group and the International Monetary Fund (IMF)) to enable the regional offices and ECO member countries to deliver the regional UNEP programme of work; and report to the next GC/GMEF meeting. Governments were called on to contribute to UNEP's work concerning regional offices in the ECO region.

A discussion paper presented by the Executive Director described UNEP's activities to contribute to the UN system-wide efforts to eradicate the environmental causes of poverty [UNEP/GC.22/8/Add.3]. It stated that the living resource base provided many of the renewable goods and services that underpinned sustainable development, and the abundance or scarcity of those goods and services was an important factor in poverty eradication. As the living natural resource base was degraded, and options for change were diminished, communities and society became more vulnerable. The paper outlined poverty-related commitments, targets and time frames agreed to at the 2002 World Summit; discussed UNEP's response to those outcomes; presented questions and issues related to poverty and the environment for discussion at the current GC/GMEF session; and recommended action by the Governing Council.

In keeping with a 2001 Governing Council decision [YUN 2001, p. 946], the Executive Director, in a January note [UNEP/GC.22/INF/30/Rev.1], outlined linkages between poverty and the environment and provided a synopsis of "Poverty and Ecosystems: A Conceptual Framework". UNEP envisioned operationalizing the Framework and testing the approach in several country studies, focusing on Africa. The plan called for the initiation of a national dialogue on the poverty-environment links with five countries in Africa. National workshops would be convened, followed by a detailed country assessment exercise, and task forces would carry out assessments and document opportunities to be strengthened and barriers to be overcome. A final report would address specific poverty-environment linkages and discuss possible trade-off issues. The work was scheduled to take three years.

Policy and advisory services

Economics, trade and sustainable development

A January discussion paper on economics, trade and sustainable development [UNEP/GC.22/10/Add.2/Rev.1] outlined the current international debate on the environmental impacts of trade and trade liberalization; the use of economic instruments to achieve environmental objectives in other areas; the role of subsidies in the agriculture, fisheries and energy sectors in contributing to overconsumption and environmentally damaging production and consumption patterns; the relationship between MEAs and the World Trade Organization (WTO); the relationship between the 1994 WTO Agreement on Trade-Related Aspects of Intellectual Property Rights (TRIPS Agreement) [YUN 1994, p. 1475], the environment and the 1992 Convention on Biological Diversity [YUN 1992, p. 683] (see p. 1051); the role of environmental goods and services, including environmentally sustainable technologies, in trade and in achieving environmental objectives and supporting sustainable development; and capacity-building and the provision of technical assistance. The report described UNEP activities relating to economics, trade, investment and finance, as called for by the Governing Council most recently in 2001 [YUN 2001, p. 948]. The paper suggested issues for discussion at the Council's 2003 session.

Institution-building

On 7 February [dec. 22/17 B], the Governing Council requested the Executive Director to intensify the provision of policy and advisory services in the areas of capacity- and institution-building, in response to requests and in cooperation with other organizations, for assistance in applying principle 10 of the 1992 Rio Declaration on Environment and Development [YUN 1992, p. 670], which related to public awareness and access to information held by public authorities, public participation in decision-making and access to justice in environmental matters. He was also asked to assess the possibility of promoting, at the national and international levels, the application of principle 10 to determine, among other things, if there was value in initiating an intergovernmental process to prepare global guidelines on the application, and to report in 2005 on progress made in preparing the guidelines. The Governing Council invited Governments and intergovernmental and civil society organizations to participate in the process and to provide financial or other contributions.

Coordination and cooperation

Business and industry

On 7 February [dec. 22/7], the Governing Council, having considered the Executive Director's 2002 report on UNEP's policy responses to tackle emerging environmental problems, in particular those engaging business and industry [YUN 2002, p. 1038], requested member States to submit to the Executive Director elements for guidelines for cooperation between UNEP and business and industry, in order for UNEP to begin developing

Environmental emergencies

On 7 February [dec. 22/8], the Governing Council invited Governments and relevant UN agencies and bodies, other international organizations and NGOs to cooperate with UNEP in providing assistance to countries, particularly developing countries and countries with economies in transition, to prevent, prepare for and respond to environmental emergencies. It recommended that Governments develop and improve prevention, preparedness and response arrangements to deal with environmental emergencies, and urged them to develop joint contingency arrangements on a regional, subregional or bilateral basis. Governments and international organizations were urged to contribute to the General Trust Fund for Environmental Emergencies, and States were invited to become parties to relevant legal instruments and to implement and enforce them. The Executive Director was requested to: establish a process, with government participation, for regular review of the 2001 Strategic Framework on Emergency Prevention, Preparedness, Assessment, Mitigation and Response [YUN 2001, p. 950] and to facilitate the implementation of its Agenda for Action; develop and pursue, in cooperation with other agencies, programmes on capacity-building with respect to improving the ability of developing countries and countries with economies in transition to prevent, prepare for and respond to environmental emergencies; provide support to refugee-hosting countries in making assessments and rehabilitating environments, including ecosystems and habitats, that had been damaged while receiving and resettling refugees; and report to GC/GMEF in 2005. The Governing Council urged the Executive Director to support the regional offices in developing and implementing capacity-building programmes for dealing with environmental emergencies. It decided that work on capacity-building should focus on those regions most in need of assistance, consistent with the Johannesburg Plan of Implementation [YUN 2002, p. 821].

In 2003, the Joint UNEP/Office for the Coordination of Humanitarian Affairs (OCHA) Environment Unit coordinated responses to the environmental aspects of emergencies resulting from a phenol spill into a river system in Serbia and Montenegro and in its province of Kosovo, a tropical storm in Seychelles, an inland oil spill in Morocco and an oil spill in the port of Karachi, Pakistan. The fifth meeting of the Advisory Group on Environmental Emergencies (AGEE) (Geneva, 14 May) reviewed the work of the Joint Unit and provided guidance on areas for development and future activities. A joint meeting of AGEE and the UNEP Awareness and Preparedness for Emergencies at Local Level (APELL) programme (15 May) was dedicated to the implementation of the Partnership on an Integrated Approach to Prevention, Preparedness for and Response to Environmental Emergencies, launched in 2002 [YUN 2002, p. 1039] during the World Summit. On 16 May, the APELL Senior-level Expert Advisory Group discussed implementation of its programme and improvement of coordination with partners.

Global Environment Facility

The Global Environment Facility (GEF), a joint programme of UNDP, UNEP and the World Bank established in 1991 [YUN 1991, p. 505] to help solve global environmental problems, was the designated financial mechanism for the 1992 Convention on Biological Diversity [YUN 1992, p. 683] (see p. 1051), the 1992 United Nations Framework Convention on Climate Change [ibid., p. 681] (see p. 1049), and the 1994 United Nations Convention to Combat Desertification in those Countries Experiencing Serious Drought and/or Desertification, particularly in Africa [YUN 1994, p. 944], and served as the interim financial mechanism for the 2001 Stockholm Convention on Persistent Organic Pollutants (POPs) in those Countries Experiencing Serious Drought and/or Desertification, particularly in Africa [YUN 2001, p. 971] (see p. 1072), pending the Convention's entry into force.

At year's end, the cumulative UNEP/GEF work programme was financed to $710 million, including $381 million in GEF resources, involving activities in more than 150 countries. Through GEF enabling activities related to biodiversity, climate change, POPs and capacity-building needs assessment for global environmental management, UNEP assisted 138 countries to meet their obligations to the global environmental conventions and build capacity to implement them.

Ninety-seven new UNEP/GEF initiatives were approved in 2003, with funding of $183 million, including $90 million in GEF grant financing.

UNDP action. The UNDP/United Nations Population Fund (UNFPA) Executive Board, following a briefing on GEF held during its first regular session (New York, 20-23 January), decided, on 23 January [E/2003/35 (dec. 2003/6)], that delegations needed more time to review with their capitals the Beijing Declaration adopted by the Second (2002) GEF Assembly [YUN 2002, p. 1039], and proposed that the item be taken up at its annual session (New York, 6-9 June).

At that session, the Board considered a March note by the UNDP Administrator [DP/2003/23], which set forth amendments to the Instrument for the Establishment of the Restructured Global Environment Facility, approved by the 2002 GEF Assembly, consequent upon its decision, as contained in the Beijing Declaration, to add two new GEF focal areas (land degradation and POPs). The note also outlined the implications for UNDP of those two new focal areas.

On 19 June [dec. 2003/20], the Executive Board adopted the amendments and requested the UNDP Administrator to transmit the decision to the Chief GEF Executive Officer/Chairperson.

Governing Council action. On 7 February [dec. 22/19], the UNEP Governing Council adopted the amendments to the Instrument for the Establishment of the Restructured Global Environment Facility. The Executive Director was requested to transmit the decision to the GEF Chief Executive Officer/Chairperson.

Memorandums of understanding

In 2003, UNEP signed memorandums of understanding with the South Asia Cooperative Environment Programme (February), under which UNEP would assist in capacity-building activities and in the implementation of MEAs through regional cooperation and promote public awareness; with the Foundation for Environmental Education (March), to provide a framework for long-term cooperation on education, training and public awareness for sustainable development globally; with the Philippine Institute of Industrial Engineers (August), to foster cleaner/sustainable production practices as a main strategy for industry; and with the World Conservation Union (September), to provide a framework for the work of the World Database on Protected Areas Consortium.

Participation of civil society

The UNEP Tunza children and youth strategy [YUN 2002, p. 1040], a six-year plan to create a global movement in which children and youth would participate in activities and be given a voice in policy-making to help improve the global environment, was endorsed by the Governing Council (see below) and launched during the year. The *Tunza* quarterly magazine was also launched. UNEP published *Tunza: Acting for a Better World*, a book containing information on environmental issues, tips on how to carry out community-based environmental projects and advice from young people. The first Tunza International Youth Conference (Dubna, Russian Federation, 25-27 August) resulted in a series of regional action plans, 10 commitments on sustainable development and the compilation of a how-to-do online database and action kit. Delegates discussed the long-term strategy and elected members of the Tunza Youth Advisory Council to advise UNEP on better ways of engaging young people in UNEP's work. A further Tunza event was Eco-Innovate (Sydney, Australia, 14-18 July), a regional conference for young entrepreneurs in the Asia-Pacific region.

In a January report [UNEP/GC.22/3/Add.3/Rev.1], the Executive Director presented UNEP's long-term strategy for sport and the environment, aimed at integrating environmental ethics and values at all levels of sport, including recreational sport. The core objectives of the strategy, which complemented the Tunza strategy, under an overall concept called "Michezo" (meaning "sports" and "play" in Kishwahili, a subregional language in Eastern Africa), were to promote the integration of environmental considerations of sports; to use the popularity of sports to promote environmental awareness and respect for the environment among the public, especially young people; and to promote the development of environmentally friendly sports facilities and the manufacturing of environmentally friendly sporting goods.

Governing Council action. On 7 February, the Governing Council decided that the Committee of Permanent Representatives (see p. 1037) should continue, as mandated [YUN 2002, p. 1039], to enhance the engagement of civil society in UNEP's work in considering the amendment of rule 69 of the Council's rules of procedure and any consequential amendments of the Rules, taking into account the evolving relationship between civil society and the UN system and the ongoing UN reform process [dec. 22/18 I].

The Council endorsed the Tunza strategy and decided to implement it [dec. 22/18 II]. The Executive Director was invited to seek additional private sector funding to ensure implementation as well as extrabudgetary resources to implement the strategy, with support to developing countries for local training programmes, and to present a midterm progress report on the implementation of the strategy to GC/GMEF in 2006 and a final report in 2009. Governments were invited to develop programmes to sensitize and educate youth in sustainable development, particularly in environmental matters.

Noting the links between the Tunza and Michezo programmes and the fact that the Executive Director had consolidated them, the Governing Council endorsed the activities contained in UNEP's sport and environment programme strategy [dec. 22/18 III]. It requested the Executive Director to explore ways to expand UNEP's efforts in sport and the environment and to increase resources from the Environment Fund (see below) to the programme and to seek extrabudgetary resources. Governments were asked to inform UNEP of any sport and environment activities being undertaken in their countries so that UNEP could share the information through its sport and environment web site.

General Assembly issues

The Executive Director provided information on issues arising from resolutions adopted by the General Assembly in 2002 that called for action by, or were of relevance to, UNEP [UNEP/GC.22/INF/7].

Global Environment Outlook Year Book

In response to Governing Council decision 22/1 I B (see p. 1039), UNEP published the Global Environment Outlook (GEO) *GEO Year Book 2003*. An overall objective of the *Year Book* was to present an analytical overview of issues which had most influenced the environment and might continue to be major factors.

UNEP secretariat

OIOS audit and inspection services

In September, the Secretary-General transmitted to the General Assembly the ninth annual Office of Internal Oversight Services (OIOS) report [A/58/364], covering activities from 1 July 2002 to 30 June 2003, including an audit of UNEP's publication function. The audit showed that UNEP did not have a viable approach to managing its publications and did not know whether the $10 million reported as expenditures on publications for 2000-2001 was an accurate figure or whether that level of effort met its needs and those of its clients. To address those issues, UNEP was analysing and revising its publication planning, monitoring and budgeting mechanisms to assess the relevance, usefulness, value and affordability of UNEP publications.

Regarding the audit of the UNEP World Conservation Monitoring Centre, OIOS was concerned that the Centre had not been established in compliance with UN regulations and rules, as UNEP staff had not adequately consulted relevant UN and UNEP regulations and rules and responsible offices, including the UN Office of Legal Affairs. Action was under way to implement the audit recommendations.

Administrative and budgetary matters

Environment Fund

Following consideration of the Executive Director's report on the proposed 2004-2005 biennial programme and support budget [UNEP/GC.22/6] and the related report of the Advisory Committee on Administrative and Budgetary Questions (ACABQ) [UNEP/GC.22/6/Add.1], the Governing Council, on 7 February [dec. 22/20], approved appropriations for the Environment Fund in the amounts of: $110 million for the programme of work; $15 million for the biennial budget; and $5 million for the Fund programme reserve. It noted that an increase in funding from the UN regular budget for the United Nations Office at Nairobi (UNON) and/or UNEP in 2004-2005 would decrease the requirement under the Environment Fund biennial support budget, and the released resources would be reallocated for programme activities and/or the Environment Fund financial reserve. The Council requested the Executive Director to ensure that all Fund programme activities were provided with resources from the Fund. It reconfirmed the Executive Director's authority to reallocate resources between programmes up to 20 per cent of the appropriation to which the resources were reallocated, and urged him to increase the financial reserve to $20 million as and when carry-over resources became available. While welcoming the recent increase in the number of contributors, the Council expressed concern over the fluctuation in the overall contributions to the Fund and in the number of countries that had contributed during 1999-2002. It requested the Executive Director to broaden the donor base, and the Committee of Permanent Representatives to consult with him on ways to provide the Council and the Committee with information on the distribution of work programme activities at the regional level. The Council noted the launching of a pilot phase for a voluntary indicative scale of contributions aimed at enhancing predictability in financing and at broadening the base of contributions. It requested the Executive Director to include in a report on UNEP's overall financial situation, as called for by GC/GMEF [YUN 2002, p. 1033], an analysis of the 2003 pilot phase.

The Executive Director was requested to provide financial details of work programmes to Governments and to make available to Governments, twice yearly, information on implementation of the work programme. He was also asked to ensure that earmarked contributions to UNEP, apart from those for which UNEP acted as treasurer, funded activities that were in line with the work programme. The Council authorized him to enter into commitments not exceeding $20 million for 2006-2007 Fund programme activities. It requested him to prepare a programme of work consisting of Fund programme activities amounting to $120 million and to adapt that amount, if necessary and in consultation with the Committee of Permanent Representatives; to submit a finalized draft budget and work programme for 2006-2007 for approval by GC/GMEF in 2005; and to include in the work programme, beginning with the 2006-2007 biennium, regional annexes identifying the percentage of the Environment Fund budget from each division that would be implemented at the regional level, and to present that information for a decision in 2005, and preliminary data in 2004.

Trust funds

A note by the Executive Director [UNEP/GC.22/INF/8] contained programmatic descriptions and expenditures of UNEP trust funds for the 2000-2001, 2002-2003 and 2004-2005 bienniums.

On 7 February [dec. 22/23 I], the Governing Council approved the establishment of 11 trust funds and the extension of 32 others.

For the 98 active UNEP trust funds (as at 15 November 2002), revised projections of income and expenditures for 2002 and 2003 totalled $557.99 million and $499.68 million, respectively.

Financial reserve loan

On 7 February [dec. 22/23 II], the Governing Council noted a report of the Executive Director [UNEP/GC.22/7 & Corr.1,2], which, in accordance with a 2001 Council decision [YUN 2001, p. 953], provided information on the loan from the Environment Fund financial reserve and the progress achieved in the first phase of the construction of additional office accommodation at UNON [YUN 2002, p. 1041]. It requested the Executive Director to report to the Committee of Permanent Representatives on further progress of loan drawdowns and the status of the construction project, and to report to GC/GMEF in 2005.

Board of Auditors report

At its twenty-second session, GC/GMEF had before it the report of the Board of Auditors, which included the financial report and audited financial statements of the UNEP Fund for the 2000-2001 biennium [A/57/5/Add.6 & Corr.1]. UNEP's financial statements covered the major funds, including the Environment Fund, general trust funds, the Multilateral Fund for the Implementation of the Montreal Protocol on Substances that Deplete the Ozone Layer (see p. 1050), technical cooperation trust funds and other trust funds. The Environment Fund reported a total income of $95.1 million against expenditures of $106.33 million, showing a net shortfall of $11.23 million (12 per cent), as compared with a net excess of income over expenditures of $14.59 million in 1998-1999. The Multilateral Fund reported a shortfall of income relative to expenditures of $32.24 million, compared with an excess of income over expenditures of $102.95 million in 1998-1999.

The Board made recommendations to improve investment procedures, update the recording of bank reconciling items, ensure agreement of databases and assess the efficiency and effectiveness of administrative arrangements with the Economic Commission for Latin America and the Caribbean.

Financial rules

On 7 February [dec. 22/22], the Governing Council, having considered the Executive Director's report containing proposals for a revision of the Financial Rules of the UNEP Fund, the General Procedures governing the Operations of the Fund, the general guidelines for the execution of projects and the institutional and financial arrangements for international environment cooperation [UNEP/GC.22/7 & Corr.1,2], approved the proposed revisions.

Indicative scale of contributions

A January note by the Executive Director [UNEP/GC.22/INF/20/Rev.1] contained information on the proposed indicative scale of contributions for a pilot phase. The pilot phase using the indicative scale would give UNEP experience in further financing its programme and broadening the base of donors, as well as in preparing a detailed report for 2004. The note discussed UNEP's financial situation in 2000-2001 and 2002-2003 and provided a comparative analysis of systems for assessing contributions used by UN organizations and the environmental conventions under UNEP and the first comments by countries on the pilot phase.

International conventions and mechanisms

Implementation of environment conventions

The Governing Council, on 7 February [dec. 22/17 II C], authorized the Executive Director to transmit a chapter of his report on the status of international environment conventions and protocols [UNEP/GC.22/3/Add.2] and his note on changes to the status of ratification of and/or accession to those treaties [UNEP/GC.22/INF/12], together with comments by delegations, to the General Assembly at its fifty-eighth (2003) session. The chapter mentioned listed relevant instruments that entered into force during the period from 1 January 2001 to 20 October 2002 and new conventions and protocols concluded during that period.

Climate change convention

As at 31 December, the number of parties to the United Nations Framework Convention on Climate Change (UNFCCC), which opened for signature in 1992 [YUN 1992, p. 681] and entered into force in 1994 [YUN 1994, p. 938], stood at 187 States and the European Community (EC).

At year's end, 119 States and the EC were parties to the Kyoto Protocol to the Convention [YUN 1997, p. 1048]. During the year, six States ratified the Protocol and 13 acceded to it.

Conference of Parties

The ninth session of the Conference of the Parties to UNFCCC (Milan, Italy, 1-12 December) [FCCC/CP/2003/6 & Add.1,2] adopted new emission reporting guidelines based on the good-practice guidance for land use, land-use change and forestry provided by the Intergovernmental Panel on Climate Change (see p. 1056); the emission reports were due in 2005. The Conference also adopted modalities and procedures for afforestation and reforestation project activities under the Kyoto Protocol's clean development mechanism (CDM) (see below). Other decisions related to: GEF's report to the Conference; an extension of the mandate of the Least Developed Countries Expert Group; guidelines for the preparation of national adaptation programmes of action; capacity-building; various aspects of the impacts of, and vulnerability and adaptation to, climate change, and of mitigation; global climate observing systems; and issues relating to the technical review of greenhouse gas inventories from UNFCCC parties included in annex I (industrialized countries). In decisions on national communications from UNFCCC parties, the Conference welcomed information from parties included in annex I on policies and measures to mitigate climate change and requested the secretariat to propose the information contained in all initial national communications submitted before 1 April 2005 for consideration at its eleventh (2005) session. Regarding the Kyoto Protocol, the Conference adopted decisions on technical guidance on methodologies for adjustments under the Protocol's article 5, issues relating to the implementation of article 8 and forest management activities in Croatia under article 3. Further decisions dealt with the Convention's financial mechanism, the operation of its Special Climate Change and Least Developed Countries Funds [YUN 2001, p. 954], and other administrative and budgetary questions.

In September, the Executive Board of CDM issued its second annual report [FCCC/CP/2003/2 & Add.1], covering the period from November 2002 to July 2003. At its ninth session, the Conference of the Parties adopted a decision providing guidance to the Board.

The Subsidiary Body for Scientific and Technological Advice (SBSTA) [FCCC/SBSTA/2003/10 & Add.1-3] and the Subsidiary Body for Implementation (SBI) [FCCC/SBI/2003/8] held their eighteenth sessions (Bonn, Germany, 4-13 June). The nineteenth sessions of SBSTA (1-9 December) [FCCC/SBSTA/2003/15] and SBI (1-10 December) [FCCC/SBI/2003/19] were held in Milan.

Note by Secretary-General. Pursuant to General Assembly resolution 57/257 [YUN 2002, p. 1043], the Secretary-General, in August [A/58/308], transmitted the report of the UNFCCC Executive Secretary on the work of the eighth (2002) session of the Conference of the Parties [YUN 2002, p. 1042].

GENERAL ASSEMBLY ACTION

On 23 December [meeting 79], the General Assembly, on the recommendation of the Second Committee [A/58/484/Add.6], adopted **resolution 58/243** without vote [agenda item 94 (f)].

Protection of global climate for present and future generations of mankind

The General Assembly,

Recalling its resolution 54/222 of 22 December 1999, its decision 55/443 of 20 December 2000 and its resolutions 56/199 of 21 December 2001 and 57/257 of 20 December 2002 and other resolutions relating to the protection of the global climate for present and future generations of mankind,

Recalling also the provisions of the United Nations Framework Convention on Climate Change, including the acknowledgement that the global nature of climate change calls for the widest possible cooperation by all countries and their participation in an effective and appropriate international response, in accordance with their common but differentiated responsibilities and respective capabilities and their social and economic conditions,

Recalling further the Johannesburg Declaration on Sustainable Development, the Plan of Implementation of the World Summit on Sustainable Development ("Johannesburg Plan of Implementation") and the Delhi Ministerial Declaration on Climate Change and Sustainable Development, adopted by the Conference of the Parties to the United Nations Framework Convention on Climate Change at its eighth session, held in New Delhi from 23 October to 1 November 2002,

Noting that one hundred and eighty-eight States and one regional economic integration organization have ratified the Convention,

Remaining deeply concerned that all countries, in particular developing countries, including the least developed countries and small island developing States, face increased risks from the negative impacts of climate change,

Noting the work of the Intergovernmental Panel on Climate Change and the need to build and enhance scientific and technological capabilities, inter alia, through continuing support to the Panel for the exchange of scientific data and information, especially in developing countries,

Noting also that, to date, the Kyoto Protocol to the United Nations Framework Convention on Climate Change has attracted one hundred and nineteen ratifications, including from parties mentioned in annex I to the Convention, who account for 44.2 per cent of emissions,

Recalling the United Nations Millennium Declaration, in which heads of State and Government resolved to make every effort to ensure the entry into force of the Kyoto Protocol, preferably by the tenth anniversary of the United Nations Conference on Environment and Development in 2002, and to embark on the required reduction in emissions of greenhouse gases,

Taking note of the report of the Executive Secretary of the United Nations Framework Convention on Climate Change on the work of the Conference of the Parties to the Convention,

1. *Calls upon* States to work cooperatively towards achieving the ultimate objective of the United Nations Framework Convention on Climate Change;

2. *Notes* that States that have ratified the Kyoto Protocol to the United Nations Framework Convention on Climate Change strongly urge States that have not already done so to ratify it in a timely manner;

3. *Notes with interest* the preparations undertaken for the implementation of the flexible mechanisms established by the Kyoto Protocol;

4. *Notes* the ongoing work of the liaison group of the secretariats and officers of the relevant subsidiary bodies of the United Nations Framework Convention on Climate Change, the United Nations Convention to Combat Desertification in Those Countries Experiencing Serious Drought and/or Desertification, Particularly in Africa, and the Convention on Biological Diversity, and encourages cooperation to promote complementarities among the three secretariats while respecting their independent legal status;

5. *Requests* the Secretary-General to make provisions for the sessions of the Conference of the Parties to the United Nations Framework Convention on Climate Change and its subsidiary bodies in his proposal for the programme budget for the biennium 2004-2005;

6. *Invites* the Executive Secretary of the United Nations Framework Convention on Climate Change to report to the General Assembly at its fifty-ninth session on the work of the Conference of the Parties;

7. *Invites* the conferences of the parties to the multilateral environmental conventions, when setting the dates of their meetings, to take into consideration the schedule of meetings of the General Assembly and the Commission on Sustainable Development so as to ensure the adequate representation of developing countries at those meetings;

8. *Decides* to include in the provisional agenda of its fifty-ninth session the sub-item entitled "Protection of global climate for present and future generations of mankind".

Vienna Convention and Montreal Protocol

As at 31 December, 186 States and the EC were parties to the 1985 Vienna Convention for the Protection of the Ozone Layer [YUN 1985, p. 804], which entered into force in 1998 [YUN 1998, p. 810]. In 2003, the Cook Islands and Niue acceded to the Convention and to the Montreal Protocol on Substances that Deplete the Ozone Layer.

Parties to the Montreal Protocol, which was adopted in 1987 [YUN 1987, p. 686], numbered 185 States and the EC; to the 1990 Amendment to the Protocol, 169 and the EC; to the 1992 Amendment, 157 and the EC; to the 1997 Amendment, 111 and the EC; and to the 1999 Amendment, 62 and the EC.

The Fifteenth Meeting of the Parties to the Montreal Protocol (Nairobi, Kenya, 10-14 November) [UNEP/OzL.Pro.15/9] adopted decisions on: the production of ozone-depleting substances (ODS) for basic domestic needs; obligations of parties to the 1999 Amendment to the Protocol [YUN 1999, p. 986] with respect to hydrochlorofluorocarbons; promotion of the closure of essential-use nominations for metered-dose inhalers; the use of controlled substances as process agents; the status of destruction technologies for ODS and the "Code of Good Housekeeping", a set of measures on reducing ODS releases, which was annexed to the Meeting's report; the handling and destruction of foams containing ODS; a plan of action to modify regulations mandating the use of halons on new airframes; the use of methyl bromide for treating high-moisture dates; the report of the Executive Committee of the Multilateral Fund for the Implementation of the Montreal Protocol [UNEP/OzL.Pro.15/8]; South Africa's application for GEF technical and financial assistance; GEF assistance to countries with economies in transition; terms of reference for a study of the Protocol's financial mechanism (the Multilateral Fund) and for the Scientific Assessment Panel, the Environmental Effects Panel and the Technology and Economic Assessment Panel; and compliance issues.

Convention on air pollution

As at 31 December, the number of parties to the 1979 Convention on Long-range Transboundary Air Pollution [YUN 1979, p. 710], which entered into force in 1983 [YUN 1983, p. 645], remained at 48 States and the EC. Eight protocols to the Convention dealt with the programme for monitoring and evaluation of the pollutants in Europe (1984), the reduction of sulphur emissions or their transboundary fluxes by at least 30 per cent (1985), the control of emissions of nitrogen oxides or their transboundary fluxes (1988), the control of volatile organic compounds or their transboundary fluxes (1991), further reduction of sulphur emissions (1984), heavy metals (1998), persistent organic pollutants (POPs) (1998) and the abatement of acidification, eutrophication and ground-level ozone (1999).

The twenty-first session of the Executive Body for the Convention (Geneva, 15-18 December) [ECE/EB.AIR/79 & Add.1,2] established a task force on POPs to address the technical needs of the reviews required by the 1998 Protocol on POPs, which entered into force in October. It adopted decisions on compliance and the facilitation of participation in the Convention of countries with economies in transition, and its 2004 work plan.

Convention on Biological Diversity

As at 31 December, 187 States and the EC were parties to the 1992 Convention on Biological Diversity [YUN 1992, p. 638], which entered into force in 1993 [YUN 1993, p. 210]. During 2003, Thailand ratified the Convention.

At year's end, 78 States and the EC were parties to the Cartagena Protocol on Biosafety, which was adopted in 2000 [YUN 2000, p. 973]. During the year, 27 States ratified the Protocol, 12 States acceded to it and France approved it. The Protocol entered into force on 11 September, 90 days after the deposit of the fiftieth instrument of ratification. The first meeting of the Conference of the Parties serving as the Meeting of the Parties to the Cartagena Protocol on Biosafety was scheduled to take place in February 2004.

The eighth (10-14 March) [UNEP/CBD/COP/7/3] and ninth (10-14 November) [UNEP/CBD/COP/7/4] meetings of the Subsidiary Body on Scientific, Technical and Technological Advice, both held in Montreal, adopted recommendations for consideration by the seventh (2004) meeting of the Conference of the Parties to the Convention. Recommendations on mountain biodiversity were among those adopted by the meetings.

The second meeting of the Working Group on Access and Benefit-Sharing (Montreal, 1-5 December) [UNEP/CBD/COP/7/6] adopted recommendations for consideration by the seventh (2004) Conference of the Parties on terms of reference for negotiations regarding an international regime on access and benefit-sharing and measures to support compliance. The Open-ended Intersessional Meeting on the Multi-year Programme of Work of the Conference of the Parties up to 2010 (Montreal, 17-20 March) [UNEP/CBD/COP/7/5] adopted recommendations on the outcome of the 2002 World Summit on Sustainable Development [YUN 2002, p. 821] as it related to the Convention process; the Convention's contribution to the Millennium Development Goals (MDGs) [YUN 2000, p. 51]; the Commission on Sustainable Development process (see p. 838); and other issues. The meeting "2010—The Global Biodiversity Challenge" (London, 21-23 May) [UNEP/CBD/COP/7/INF/22], organized by the Convention secretariat in partnership with the UNEP World Conservation Monitoring Centre and UNDP, considered approaches for measuring biodiversity loss; reviewed the 2010 target for a significant reduction in the rate of biodiversity loss, adopted in 2002 [YUN 2002, p. 1045]; and identified initiatives in addressing the loss.

Note by Secretary-General. In accordance with General Assembly resolution 57/260 [YUN 2002, p. 1046], the Secretary-General transmitted, in July [A/58/191], a report of the Executive Secretary of the Convention on principal activities undertaken within the framework of the Convention and ongoing work and cooperation with the Assembly and other UN institutions.

Report of Secretary-General. In response to Economic and Social Council resolution 2002/18 [YUN 2002, p. 1062], the Secretary-General submitted a March report [E/CN.15/2003/8 & Corr.1 & Add.1] to supplement the 2002 progress report [YUN 2002, p. 1045] on implementation of Council resolution 2001/12 [YUN 2001, p. 968] regarding illicit trafficking in protected species of wild flora and fauna (see p. 1069) and illicit access to genetic resources. With regard to the latter, the report discussed the legal framework dealing with illicit access to genetic material and the possible involvement of organized criminal groups. The Secretary-General concluded that, while organized crime did not yet seem to be involved in that area, such involvement might not be reported; greater detection and reporting efforts were desirable to provide the basis for the establishment of a repository of information and the creation of a database. Biotechnology and pharmaceutical companies carried some responsibility for ensuring that organized crime was not able to infiltrate and influence their industries; a key component would be the creation of a compliance system to ensure that the companies had no links to organized crime or with other individuals or groups engaged in biopiracy.

GENERAL ASSEMBLY ACTION

On 23 December [meeting 78], the General Assembly, on the recommendation of the Second Committee [A/58/484/Add.3], adopted **resolution 58/212** without vote [agenda item 94 (c)].

Convention on Biological Diversity

The General Assembly,

Recalling its resolutions 55/201 of 20 December 2000, 56/197 of 21 December 2001 and 57/253 and 57/260 of 20 December 2002,

Reiterating that the Convention on Biological Diversity is the key international instrument for the conservation and sustainable use of biological resources and the fair and equitable sharing of benefits arising from the use of genetic resources,

Recalling the World Summit on Sustainable Development commitments to pursue a more efficient and coherent implementation of the three objectives of the Convention and the achievement by 2010 of a significant reduction in the current rate of loss of biological diversity, which will require action at all levels, including the implementation of national biodiversity strategies and action plans and the provision of new and additional financial and technical resources to developing countries,

Reaffirming the urgency to recognize, subject to national legislation, the rights of local and indigenous communities that are holders of traditional knowledge, innovations and practices, and, with the approval and involvement of the holders of such knowledge, innovations and practices, to develop and implement benefit-sharing mechanisms, on mutually agreed terms, for the use of such knowledge, innovations and practices,

Expressing its deep appreciation for the generous offer of the Government of Malaysia to host the seventh meeting of the Conference of the Parties to the Convention on Biological Diversity and the first meeting of the Conference of the Parties to the Convention serving as the meeting of the Parties to the Cartagena Protocol on Biosafety, to be held at Kuala Lumpur, respectively, from 9 to 20 February and from 23 to 27 February 2004,

1. *Takes note* of the report of the Executive Secretary of the Convention on Biological Diversity, submitted by the Secretary-General to the General Assembly at its fifty-eighth session;

2. *Notes* the outcome of the open-ended intersessional meeting on the multi-year programme of work of the Conference of the Parties to the Convention on Biological Diversity up to 2010, held at Montreal, Canada, from 17 to 20 March 2003;

3. *Notes also* the outcomes of the eighth and ninth meetings of the Subsidiary Body on Scientific, Technical and Technological Advice of the Conference of the Parties to the Convention on Biological Diversity, held at Montreal, Canada, from 10 to 14 March and from 10 to 14 November 2003;

4. *Reiterates* the World Summit on Sustainable Development commitment to negotiate within the framework of the Convention on Biological Diversity, bearing in mind the Bonn Guidelines on Access to Genetic Resources and Fair and Equitable Sharing of the Benefits Arising out of their Utilization, an international regime to promote and safeguard the fair and equitable sharing of benefits arising out of the utilization of genetic resources;

5. *Reiterates also* the World Summit on Sustainable Development commitment to promote the wide implementation of and continued work on the Bonn Guidelines, as an input to assist the parties when developing and drafting legislative, administrative or policy measures on access and benefit-sharing as well as contract and other arrangements under mutually-agreed terms for access and benefit-sharing;

6. *Invites* the countries that have not yet done so to ratify the Convention on Biological Diversity;

7. *Welcomes* the entry into force of the Cartagena Protocol on Biosafety to the Convention on Biological Diversity, on 11 September 2003, and the convening of the first meeting of the Conference of the Parties serving as the meeting of the Parties to the Cartagena Protocol on Biosafety, and invites the parties to the Convention that have not yet ratified or acceded to the Protocol to consider doing so;

8. *Emphasizes* that the effective implementation of the Cartagena Protocol on Biosafety will require full support from parties and relevant international organizations, and further urges parties to facilitate capacity-building in biosafety in developing countries as well as countries with economies in transition, including to develop and strengthen national capacities for making the required information available to and interacting with the Biosafety Clearing House;

9. *Invites* countries to consider ratifying or acceding to the International Treaty on Plant Genetic Resources for Food and Agriculture;

10. *Encourages* developed countries parties to the Convention to contribute to the relevant trust funds of the Convention, in particular so as to enhance the full participation of the developing countries parties in all its activities;

11. *Urges* parties to the Convention on Biological Diversity to facilitate the transfer of technology for the effective implementation of the Convention in accordance with its provisions;

12. *Underlines* the need for increased financial and technical resources for the implementation of the Convention on Biological Diversity and the Cartagena Protocol on Biosafety by developing countries as well as countries with economies in transition, and in this regard welcomes the successful and substantial third replenishment of the Global Environment Facility;

13. *Takes note* of the ongoing work of the liaison group of the secretariats and offices of the relevant subsidiary bodies of the United Nations Framework Convention on Climate Change, the United Nations Convention to Combat Desertification in Those Countries Experiencing Serious Drought and/or Desertification, Particularly in Africa, and the Convention on Biological Diversity, and further encourages continuing cooperation in order to promote complementarities among the secretariats, while respecting their independent legal status;

14. *Stresses* the importance of harmonizing the reporting requirements of the biodiversity-related conventions while respecting their independent legal status;

15. *Invites* the Executive Secretary of the Convention on Biological Diversity to continue reporting to the General Assembly on the ongoing work regarding the Convention, including its Cartagena Protocol;

16. *Decides* to include in the provisional agenda of its fifty-ninth session the sub-item entitled "Convention on Biological Diversity".

Convention to combat desertification

In 2003, Bhutan, the Democratic People's Republic of Korea, Lithuania, the Russian Federation and Timor-Leste acceded to the 1994 United Nations Convention to Combat Desertification in those Countries Experiencing Serious Drought and/or Desertification, particularly in Africa [YUN 1994, p. 944], which entered into force in 1996 [YUN 1996, p. 958], bringing the total number of parties to 191.

The Conference of the Parties, at its sixth session (Havana, Cuba, 25 August–5 September) [ICCD/COP(6)/11 & Corr.1 & Add.1], decided to accept GEF as a financial mechanism of the Convention. It resolved to strengthen implementation of the Convention in line with the outcome of the 2002 World Summit on Sustainable Development [YUN 2002, p. 821] through action to: mobilize adequate and predictable financial resources; formulate national action programmes (NAPs) as priority tools; encourage the secretariats of UNFCCC (see p. 1049), the 1992 Convention on Biological Diversity [ibid., p. 683] (see p. 1051) and the Convention to Combat Desertification to enhance synergies; integrate measures to prevent and combat desertification and mitigate the effects of drought; provide affordable access to information to improve monitoring and early warning; and improve the sustainability of grassland resources. Other decisions related to the secretariat's activities and implementation by affected country parties; the Global Mechanism, which mobilized resources to combat land degradation and poverty; implementation of the 2000 Declaration on commitments to enhance the Convention's implementation [YUN 2000, p. 976]; strengthening of relationships with other conventions, international organizations, institutions and agencies; traditional knowledge; benchmarks and indicators; early warning systems; the Land Degradation Assessment in Drylands and the Millennium Ecosystem Assessment (see p. 1055); and administrative issues. The seventh session was scheduled for October 2005 in Bonn. The Conference adopted the Havana Declaration on the Implementation of the United Nations Convention to Combat Desertification, which, among other things, invited all affected parties to the Convention to integrate the Convention in national strategies for sustainable development and include programmes to combat desertification in policies on land, water, rural development, forests, energy, education and culture.

The second session of the Committee for the Review of the Implementation of the Convention (Havana, 26-29 August) had before it a summary of the reports submitted by States parties up until 2002 [ICCD/CRIC(2)/3]; a note on developments regarding the operational programme on sustainable land management, approved by the GEF Council in May [ICCD/CRIC(2)/6]; a note describing progress by affected country parties to implement the Convention [ICCD/CRIC(2)/2]; and further notes on the Global Mechanism [ICCD/CRIC/(2)/4 & 5]. The Conference of the Parties adopted the programme of work for the Committee's third session, to be held in Bonn in 2004.

The Committee on Science and Technology (Havana, 26-29 August), a Conference subsidiary body, considered a preliminary report of the 19-member group of experts (Bonn, 2-7 June) [ICCD/COP(6)/CST/3], which reviewed desertification activities from November 2002 to May 2003, and reports on traditional knowledge [ICCD/COP(6)/CST/4], benchmarks and indicators [ICCD/COP(6)/CST/5], early warning systems [ICCD/COP(6)/CST/6] and other issues. The Committee submitted recommendations to the Conference.

Report of Secretary-General. As requested in General Assembly resolution 57/259 [YUN 2002, p. 1048], the Secretary-General, in July [A/58/158], reported on the implementation of the Convention, including the work of the Committee for the Review of the Implementation of the Convention in 2002 [YUN 2002, p. 1047] and measures called for in the Johannesburg Plan of Implementation [YUN 2002, p. 821] to strengthen the prevention and/or reduction of land degradation, rehabilitation of partly degraded land and reclamation of desertified land in semi-arid and dry sub-humid areas.

GENERAL ASSEMBLY ACTION

On 23 December [meeting 79], the General Assembly, on the recommendation of the Second Committee [A/58/484/Add.2], adopted **resolution 58/242** without vote [agenda item 94 (*b*)].

Implementation of the United Nations Convention to Combat Desertification in Those Countries Experiencing Serious Drought and/or Desertification, Particularly in Africa

The General Assembly,

Recalling its resolutions 56/196 of 21 December 2001 and 57/259 of 20 December 2002 and other resolutions relating to the United Nations Convention to Combat Desertification in Those Countries Experiencing Serious Drought and/or Desertification, Particularly in Africa,

Recognizing the strong commitment of the international community, demonstrated at the World Summit on Sustainable Development and the Second Assembly of the Global Environment Facility, to make the Facility available as a financial mechanism of the Convention, pursuant to article 21 of the Convention,

Recognizing also the role of the Conference of the Parties to the Convention, as the highest decision-making body, in providing guidance on matters regarding the implementation of the Convention and in encouraging financial mechanisms to seek to maximize the availability of resources for affected developing countries, while respecting the respective mandates of the mechanisms,

Reaffirming that the Convention is an important tool for poverty eradication, particularly in Africa, and recognizing the importance of the implementation of the Convention for meeting the internationally agreed development goals, including those contained in the United Nations Millennium Declaration,

Reaffirming also the universal membership of the Convention, and acknowledging that desertification and drought are problems of a global dimension, in that they affect all regions of the world,

Expressing its deep appreciation and gratitude to the Government of Cuba for hosting the sixth session of the Conference of the Parties to the Convention in Havana from 25 August to 5 September 2003,

1. *Takes note* of the report of the Secretary-General;

2. *Welcomes* the decision of the Conference of the Parties to the United Nations Convention to Combat Desertification in Those Countries Experiencing Serious Drought and/or Desertification, Particularly in Africa, at its sixth session, to accept the Global Environment Facility as a financial mechanism of the Convention, pursuant to article 21 of the Convention;

3. *Also welcomes* the decision of the Council of the Global Environment Facility at its meeting, held in Washington, D.C., from 14 to 16 May 2003, to establish a new operational programme on sustainable land management, and, in that regard, urges the Executive Secretary, in collaboration with the Managing Director of the Global Mechanism, to consult with the Chief Executive Officer and Chairman of the Global Environment Facility, with a view to preparing and agreeing upon a memorandum of understanding, as mandated by the Conference of the Parties, for the consideration of and adoption by the Conference of Parties and the Council of the Global Environment Facility;

4. *Further welcomes* the outcome of the Second Assembly of the Global Environment Facility, held in Beijing from 16 to 18 October 2002, in particular the decision to designate land degradation as a new focal area of the Facility, which will, inter alia, support the implementation of the Convention;

5. *Notes with appreciation* the increased number of affected developing country parties that have adopted their national, subregional and regional action programmes, and urges affected developing countries that have not yet done so to accelerate the process of elaboration and adoption of their action programmes, with a view to finalizing them as soon as possible;

6. *Invites* affected developing countries to place the implementation of their action programmes to combat desertification high among their priorities in their dialogue with their development partners;

7. *Calls upon* affected parties, with the collaboration of relevant multilateral organizations, including the Global Environment Facility implementation agencies, to integrate desertification into their strategies for sustainable development;

8. *Urges* the international community to take effective measures for the implementation of the Convention through bilateral and multilateral cooperation programmes;

9. *Urges* the United Nations funds and programmes, the Bretton Woods institutions, the donor countries and other development agencies to integrate actions in support of the Convention in their strategies to support the achievement of internationally agreed development goals, including those contained in the United Nations Millennium Declaration;

10. *Welcomes* the strengthened cooperation between the secretariat of the Convention and the Global Mechanism through the elaboration and implementation of a joint work plan aimed at maximizing the impact of resources and actions, avoiding duplication and overlap and tapping into the expertise, added value and network of each organization in a collaborative manner as action programmes are implemented;

11. *Invites* all parties to pay promptly and in full the contributions required for the core budget of the Convention for the biennium 2002-2003, and urges all parties that have not yet paid their contributions for the year 1999 and/or the biennium 2000-2001 to do so as soon as possible in order to ensure continuity in the cash flow required to finance the ongoing work of the Conference of the Parties, the secretariat and the Global Mechanism;

12. *Calls upon* Governments, and invites multilateral financial institutions, regional development banks, regional economic integration organizations and all other interested organizations, as well as non-governmental organizations and the private sector, to contribute generously to the General Fund, the Supplementary Fund and the Special Fund, in accordance with the relevant paragraphs of the financial rules of the Conference of the Parties, and welcomes the financial support already provided by some countries;

13. *Takes note* of Conference of the Parties decision 23/COP.6 of 5 September 2003 on the programme and budget for the biennium 2004-2005, as an ongoing process of the Conference of the Parties to undertake a comprehensive review of the activities of the secretariat, as defined in article 23, paragraph 2, of the Convention;

14. *Requests* the Secretary-General to make provision for the sessions of the Conference of the Parties and its subsidiary bodies, including the seventh ordinary session of the Conference and the meetings of its subsidiary bodies, in his proposal for the programme budget for the biennium 2004-2005;

15. *Also requests* the Secretary-General to report to the General Assembly at its fifty-ninth session on the implementation of the present resolution;

16. *Decides* to include in the provisional agenda of its fifty-ninth session the sub-item entitled "Implementation of the United Nations Convention to Combat Desertification in Those Countries Experiencing Serious Drought and/or Desertification, Particularly in Africa".

International Year of Deserts and Desertification

On 7 February [dec. 22/15], the Governing Council, concerned by the exacerbation of desertification, particularly in Africa, and its far-reaching implications for the implementation of the MDG on poverty alleviation [YUN 2000, p. 51], invited the General Assembly to consider declaring an international year of deserts and desertification as soon as possible and designating UNEP as focal point of the international year, in conjunction with the Convention to Combat Desertification (see p. 1053) and UNDP. It requested the Secretary-General to designate a special representative for the international year, in the event it was declared; invited concerned countries to establish national committees and to celebrate the year with appropriate activities; and called on relevant international organizations and developed countries to support activities organized by affected countries, in particular African countries and LDCs.

GENERAL ASSEMBLY ACTION

On 23 December [meeting 78], the General Assembly, on the recommendation of the Second Committee [A/58/484/Add.2], adopted **resolution 58/211** without vote [agenda item 94 (b)].

International Year of Deserts and Desertification, 2006

The General Assembly,

Recalling chapter 12 of Agenda 21 adopted by the United Nations Conference on Environment and Development,

Recalling also the United Nations Convention to Combat Desertification in Those Countries Experiencing Serious Drought and/or Desertification, Particularly in Africa,

Recalling further the Plan of Implementation of the World Summit on Sustainable Development ("Johannesburg Plan of Implementation") and the Johannesburg Declaration on Sustainable Development,

Having considered decision 22/15 of 7 February 2003 of the Governing Council of the United Nations Environment Programme on an international year of deserts and desertification,

Deeply concerned by the exacerbation of desertification, particularly in Africa, and its far-reaching implications for the implementation of the Millennium Development Goals, in particular on poverty eradication,

Recalling the environment initiative of the New Partnership for Africa's Development,

Conscious of the need to raise public awareness and to protect the biological diversity of deserts as well as indigenous and local communities and the traditional knowledge of those affected by this phenomenon,

1. *Decides* to declare 2006 the International Year of Deserts and Desertification;
2. *Designates* the Executive Secretary of the United Nations Convention to Combat Desertification in Those Countries Experiencing Serious Drought and/or Desertification, Particularly in Africa, as focal point of the Year, in conjunction with the United Nations Environment Programme, the United Nations Development Programme, the International Fund for Agricultural Development and other relevant bodies of the United Nations;
3. *Invites* all countries to establish national committees or focal points and to celebrate the Year by arranging appropriate activities;
4. *Calls upon* all relevant international organizations and Member States to support the activities related to desertification, including land degradation, to be organized by affected countries, in particular African countries and the least developed countries;
5. *Encourages* countries to contribute, as they are able, to the Convention and to undertake special initiatives in observance of the Year with the goal of enhancing the implementation of the Convention;
6. *Requests* the Secretary-General to report to the General Assembly at its sixtieth session on the status of preparations for the Year.

Environmental activities

Follow-up to the Millennium Summit

In September [A/58/323], the Secretary-General reported on the implementation of the Millennium Declaration, adopted by the General Assembly in resolution 55/2 [YUN 2000, p. 49], including progress towards the MDG of ensuring environmental sustainability. He stated that the 1987 Montreal Protocol on Substances that Deplete the Ozone Layer [YUN 1987, p. 686] to the 1985 Vienna Convention for the Protection of the Ozone Layer [YUN 1985, p. 804] (see p. 1050) had demonstrated the effectiveness of concerted multilateral action, resulting in a large decrease in global consumption of chlorofluorocarbons, primarily in developed countries, and a decrease in developing countries by about half since 1995. Progress in other areas had been less encouraging and included a decline in the proportion of land covered by forests in developing regions. The Johannesburg Plan of Implementation [YUN 2002, p. 821] committed signatories to responsible and equitable management of the Earth's resources and highlighted the critical role of the private sector and public-private partnerships in addressing key environmental challenges ranging from biodiversity protection to renewable energy.

Millennium Ecosystem Assessment

A December report of the Executive Director [UNEP/GCSS.VIII/2] provided information on the Millennium Ecosystem Assessment, a four-year international assessment launched in 2001 [YUN 2001, p. 961] to evaluate the state of major ecosystems and their links with human well-being.

UNEP coordinated the Assessment's secretariat and was one of the implementing agencies, together with the World Fish Center and the World Resources Institute. The Assessment's first report, *Ecosystems and Human Well-being—A Framework for Assessment*, was released in 2003. The report offered decision makers a mechanism to identify options to achieve core human development and sustainability goals and understand the trade-offs in decisions regarding development and environment. A Caribbean Sea assessment was implemented with technical and financial assistance from UNEP, and other joint ventures were under negotiation. Approved sub-global assessments were under way in Canada, India, Norway, Papua New Guinea, the Philippines, Southern Africa, Sweden and western China, and at tropical benchmark sites around the world.

The Assessment's Sub-Global, Condition, Scenarios and Responses Working Groups all met in 2003, and a combined working group meeting was held (Prague, Czech Republic, 13-17 October). The 2003 meeting of the Millennium Assessment Board (Gland, Switzerland, 11-12 February) reviewed and approved the Assessment's first report.

The atmosphere

Intergovernmental Panel on Climate Change

The Intergovernmental Panel on Climate Change (IPCC), at its twentieth session (Paris, 19-21 February), adopted a framework and criteria for establishing priorities for special reports, methodological reports and technical papers for the fourth assessment period (2004-2007). It decided to hold two meetings to develop submissions to the Panel's twenty-first session (see below), to conduct stakeholder consultations with business and NGO communities, to conduct a climate sensitivity workshop in 2004, and that water would be a cross-cutting theme in the fourth assessment. The Panel decided to hold a scientific meeting to survey the current understanding of the processes affecting carbon stocks and human influences thereon. It decided to produce a report entitled "Safeguarding the ozone layer and the global climate system: issues related to hydrofluorocarbons and perfluorocarbons", and that its Working Group III should prepare a report on carbon dioxide capture and storage. Other decisions related to procedural and budgetary matters.

At its twenty-first session (Vienna, 3 and 6-7 November), IPCC further discussed criteria for reports and adopted decisions on its 2004-2007 work programme and budget.

Governing Council action. On 7 February [dec. 22/3 I], the Governing Council decided that UNEP should strengthen its role in supporting regional and national actions and programmes, in cooperation with the secretariat of the United Nations Framework Convention on Climate Change (UNFCCC) and other relevant bodies, to ensure that UNEP activities were complementary to and not duplicative of work carried out by other agencies. It asked the Executive Director to assist, upon request by developing countries, in undertaking activities related to adaptation and the transfer of technology, to meet the specific needs arising from the adverse effects of climate change without duplicating UNFCCC activities. He was asked to strengthen cooperation between UNEP and scientific organizations to advance policy and know-how for reducing vulnerability to climate change in various sectors, in particular water resources, biodiversity, agriculture, coastal zone management and health, in the context of sustainable development, and to seek contributions from Governments for those activities. It invited States that had not signed, ratified or acceded to UNFCCC [YUN 1992, p. 681] and the 1997 Kyoto Protocol to the Convention [YUN 1997, p. 1048] (see p. 1049) to do so and invited the Executive Director to raise public awareness of IPCC's findings.

Regarding IPCC, the Governing Council requested the Executive Director, in cooperation with the Secretary-General of the World Meteorological Organization (WMO), to continue arrangements to carry on IPCC's work, ensuring a wide and effective participation of developing country experts in the process [dec. 22/3 II]. He was asked to disseminate IPCC's findings widely, complementing the efforts undertaken in the context of UNFCCC on implementing its article 6 on education, training and public awareness. Governments were urged to provide financial, technical and scientific support to the IPCC process. IPCC was requested to report on progress to GC/GMEF in 2005.

World Climate Change Conference

The World Climate Change Conference (Moscow, 29 September–3 October), an initiative of the Russian Federation, discussed climate change, including natural and anthropogenic factors driving the climate; approaches to reducing anthropogenic emissions; and impacts and adaptation measures. During the Conference, detailed scientific reports were presented on the science of climate change; ecological, social and economic impacts of climate change; mitigation of

Terrestrial ecosystems

In 2003, drylands supported 1 billion rural poor across 110 countries. UNEP increased its support for the implementation of the United Nations Convention to Combat Desertification in those Countries Experiencing Serious Drought and/or Desertification, particularly in Africa (see p. 1053), through the development of an ecosystem approach to dryland environmental management. In partnership with the Consultative Group for International Agricultural Research (CGIAR), UNEP developed a renewed collaborative thrust on sustainable dryland management and the environment and worked on a new CGIAR Challenge Programme on Desertification, Drought, Poverty and Agriculture and on improved science-policy linkages. Norway agreed to support the three-year UNEP project on an ecosystem approach to restoring West African drylands and improving rural livelihoods through agroforestry-based land management interventions.

Deforestation and forest degradation

United Nations Forum on Forests

The Governing Council, on 7 February [dec. 22/5], took action on enhancing UNEP's role in forest-related issues. It requested the Executive Director, in collaboration with the Coordinator and secretariat of the United Nations Forum on Forests (UNFF), to cooperate with other organizations, in response to a 2002 UNFF decision on rehabilitation and conservation strategies for countries with low forest cover [YUN 2002, p. 1051] and other decisions, and to support the Tehran Process, established in 1999 to bring together low-forest-cover countries and provide a forum for addressing the specific needs of developing countries with low forest cover, in order to strengthen the capacity of those countries.

UNFF, at its third session (Geneva, 26 May–6 June) [E/2003/42], adopted five resolutions and three decisions, which were brought to the Economic and Social Council's attention. The Forum adopted resolutions on the economic aspects of forests [res. 3/1], forest health and productivity [res. 3/2], maintaining forest cover to meet present and future needs [res. 3/3], enhancing cooperation and policy and programme coordination with the support of the Collaborative Partnership on Forests [YUN 2001, p. 964] and other organizations [res. 3/4], and strengthening the UNFF secretariat [res. 3/5]. The Forum accorded observer status to three intergovernmental organizations [dec. 3/1]; requested its secretariat to develop, at its fourth (2004) session, a suggested format for countries to use in reporting on implementation of the Intergovernmental Panel on Forests [YUN 1995, p. 1080] and the Intergovernmental Forum on Forests [YUN 1997, p. 1057] (IPF/IFF) proposals for action [dec. 3/2]; and took note of documents before the Forum [dec. 3/3] (see below).

The Forum recommended a draft resolution for adoption by the Council on the Trust Fund for UNFF and a draft decision on the establishment of ad hoc expert groups on approaches and mechanisms for monitoring, assessment and reporting, on finance and transfer of environmentally sound technologies (ESTs), and on the parameters of a mandate for developing a legal framework on all types of forests. (See pp. 1058 and 1062 for Economic and Social Council action.) Other draft decisions dealt with the date, venue and agenda for UNFF's fourth (2004) session and the report on the Forum's third session.

The Forum had before it reports of the Secretary-General on progress in implementing the IPF/IFF proposals on forest health and productivity [E/CN.18/2003/5]; economic aspects of forests [E/CN.18/2003/7]; and maintaining forest cover to meet current and future needs [E/CN.18/2003/8]. The Secretary-General also provided information on the Forum's second multi-stakeholder dialogue [E/CN.18/2003/2 & Add.1-6], which took place during UNFF's third session, and on enhanced cooperation and policy and programme coordination in and outside the forest sector in the management of forests and other natural resources [E/CN.18/2003/6]. Secretariat notes contained the draft negotiating text on the titles, composition, terms of reference, scheduling and reporting of the ad hoc expert groups [E/CN.18/2003/3], and guidelines for the preparation of voluntary national reports to UNFF at its third session [E/CN.18/2003/4]. A further Secretariat note [E/CN.18/2003/12] listed three intergovernmental organizations requesting UNFF accreditation, and recommended that they be granted observer status. Also before the Forum was the Collaborative Partnership on Forests Framework 2003 [E/CN.18/2003/INF/1] outlining the Partnership's work plan and progress report; the report of the UNFF Intersessional Experts Meeting (Wellington, New Zealand, 25-27 March) on the role of planted forests in sustainable forest management [E/CN.18/2003/10]; a report on the Regional Initiative for the Transfer of Environmentally Sound Technologies for the Sustainable Management of Mangrove Ecosystems in Latin America and the Wider Caribbean: a regional approach initiated by the Government of Nicaragua [E/CN.18/2003/11]; and a report on lessons learned in monitoring, assessment and reporting on the implementation of IPF/IFF proposals for action, reflecting the results of a UNFF country-led initiative (Viterbo, Italy, 17-20 March) [E/CN.18/2003/9 & Corr.1].

ECONOMIC AND SOCIAL COUNCIL ACTION

On 25 July [meeting 49], the Economic and Social Council, on the recommendation of the United Nations Forum on Forests [E/2003/42, orally amended], adopted **decision 2003/299** [agenda item 13 (i)].

Intersessional work by ad hoc expert groups

At its 49th plenary meeting, on 25 July 2003, the Economic and Social Council, bearing in mind paragraph 4 (k) of its resolution 2000/35 of 18 October 2000, and recalling the multi-year programme of work of the United Nations Forum on Forests, adopted by the Forum in its resolution 1/1, in particular its paragraphs 23 and 24:

(a) Decided to establish three ad hoc expert groups to support the work of the Forum, as set out in the annex to the present decision;

(b) Decided that the meetings of the ad hoc expert groups on approaches and mechanisms for monitoring, assessment and reporting, and on finance and transfer of environmentally sound technologies should be convened in Geneva from 8 to 19 December 2003. The Council also decided that the date of the meeting in New York of the ad hoc expert group on "consideration, with a view to recommending the parameters of a mandate for developing a legal framework on all types of forests" should be decided at the resumed session of the Council of 2003;

(c) Invited each of the five United Nations regional groups to nominate to the Secretariat six country experts for the ad hoc expert group on approaches and mechanisms for monitoring, assessment and reporting, and six country experts for the ad hoc expert group on finance and transfer of environmentally sound technologies, by 15 September 2003;

(d) Invited States members of the United Nations Forum on Forests to nominate to the Secretariat a country expert for the ad hoc expert group on consideration, with a view to recommending the parameters of a mandate for developing a legal framework on all types of forests, by 31 March 2004;

(e) Decided that, to ensure efficiency, transparency and balanced reflection of the range of views, the following preparations should be performed for the meeting of the ad hoc expert group meeting on consideration, with a view to recommending the parameters of a mandate for developing a legal framework on all types of forests:

(i) Presentation of factual and technical information, including updated information on existing regional and international binding and non-binding instruments and processes relevant to forests and that of other relevant organizations and agreements, including multilateral environmental agreements and regional conventions and processes;

(ii) Compilation of the progress made and catalysts and obstacles encountered by States members and member organizations of the Collaborative Partnership on Forests in implementing the proposals for action of the Intergovernmental Panel on Forests/Intergovernmental Forum on Forests and the decisions and resolutions of sessions of the United Nations Forum on Forests;

(iii) Presentation and detailed description of a range of options, including their legal, financial and institutional modalities;

The States members of the United Nations Forum on Forests were invited to submit their views on (i), (ii) and (iii) above. The member organizations of the Collaborative Partnership on Forests were invited to provide information on (i) and (ii) above. These views and information should be provided to the Forum secretariat by 31 January 2004.

Accordingly, the United Nations Forum on Forests secretariat should compile the views submitted by the States members and the information provided by the member organizations of the Collaborative Partnership on Forests in preparation for the ad hoc expert group meeting.

For its fourth session, the Bureau of the United Nations Forum on Forests should keep States members apprised of the progress made in the preparation of documentation for the ad hoc expert group. The Bureau would undertake consultations with the member States by convening a one-day informal meeting in New York immediately after a meeting of the Bureau prior to the fourth session of the Forum.

The United Nations Forum on Forests would receive an information note at its fourth session on progress in the preparation of documentation for the ad hoc expert group meeting. This note was subject to neither discussion nor negotiation in the Forum.

The official documentation for the consideration of the ad hoc expert group should be made available to countries sixty days in advance of the meeting of the ad hoc expert group.

Annex

A. Ad hoc expert group on approaches and mechanisms for monitoring, assessment and reporting

Scope and work programme

1. The ad hoc expert group shall provide scientific and technical advice to the United Nations Forum on Forests on approaches and mechanisms for the work of the Forum on monitoring, assessment and reporting. Its work should be undertaken within the context of Economic and Social Council resolution 2000/35 and relevant resolutions adopted by the Forum at its sessions, and should also consider, inter alia, related proposals for action of the Intergovernmental Panel on Forests (IPF)/Intergovernmental Forum on Forests (IFF) and the outcomes of Forum sessions, including its reports.

Tasks

2. For monitoring, assessment and reporting on progress in implementing IPF/IFF proposals for action and progress towards sustainable forest management, the ad hoc expert group shall:

(a) Assess existing reporting requirements under relevant international conventions, processes, instruments and organizations in order to identify strengths, weaknesses and duplication in reporting processes, taking into account the relevant work undertaken by member organizations of the Collaborative Partnership on Forests;

(b) Assess existing monitoring and assessment procedures in international conventions, processes, instruments and organizations related to forests in order to identify strengths, weaknesses and duplications, taking into account the relevant work undertaken by member organizations of the Collaborative Partnership on Forests;

(c) Propose ways for the Forum to monitor and assess progress, based on:
  (i) Voluntary reporting by countries on implementing the IPF/IFF proposals for action;
  (ii) Voluntary reporting by member organizations of the Collaborative Partnership on Forests and other relevant organizations and international and regional processes on implementing the IPF/IFF proposals for action;
  (iii) Ongoing work on criteria and indicators for sustainable forest management being undertaken at the national, regional and international levels;
  (iv) Existing data and information, as well as reporting systems and structures;

(d) Propose an outline for voluntary reporting to the Forum;

(e) Recommend options for drawing upon the reports provided to Forum sessions to identify trends and lessons learned;

(f) Develop recommendations on how to build capacity in countries, including the increase of resources for that goal, for monitoring, assessment and reporting, taking into account the special needs of developing countries.

3. In carrying out these tasks, the ad hoc expert group should take into account the results of intersessional activities related to monitoring, assessment and reporting led by countries, organizations and international and regional processes. Its reports should be made available as a contribution to the discussions at country- and organization-led initiatives of the Forum that are related to the present terms of reference. As relevant, the ad hoc expert group should also take into account the results of the work undertaken by member organizations of the Collaborative Partnership on Forests on forest-related concepts, terminology and definitions.

Composition and participation

4. The ad hoc expert group shall be composed of thirty experts in accordance with Economic and Social Council decision 2003/299, to which the present annex is attached, six from each of the five United Nations regional groups.

5. The experts shall have well-recognized scientific and technical expertise in monitoring, assessment and reporting, and knowledge of the intergovernmental forest policy deliberations of IPF, IFF and the Forum.

6. Representatives of the States members of the United Nations Forum on Forests shall be allowed to participate in the first two days of the meeting of the ad hoc expert group and remain as observers for the last three days of the meeting.

7. The Collaborative Partnership on Forests shall be invited to make scientific and technical contributions to the work of the ad hoc expert group to support the work of the ad hoc expert group in a resource capacity.

8. Intergovernmental organizations and representatives of major groups with relevant expertise may participate in the meeting, in accordance with the rules of procedure of the functional commissions of the Economic and Social Council, as well as practices established by the Commission on Sustainable Development, IPF and IFF. They may be invited to make scientific and technical contributions.

Travel assistance

9. Travel support and a daily subsistence allowance at established United Nations rates will be provided to each of the experts, if the budget allows, with priority to developing countries, particularly least developed countries, as well as countries with economies in transition.

Officers

10. The chairman of the ad hoc expert group shall be elected from among the experts at its meeting.

Duration of work

11. The ad hoc expert group shall initiate its work after the third session of the Forum and complete its work at least three months in advance of the fourth session of the Forum.

Meeting

12. The ad hoc expert group shall hold one meeting for up to five days before the end of 2003. It shall also use electronic means of communication to the greatest extent possible. The ad hoc expert group meeting shall be organized at a United Nations venue where meeting facilities are available, preferably in New York, taking into account cost-effectiveness. To the extent possible, the ad hoc expert group shall hold its meeting back to back with the meeting of the ad hoc expert group on finance and transfer of environmentally sound technologies.

Proposals and recommendations for consideration by the Forum

13. The proposals and recommendations of the ad hoc expert group should be provided by consensus. In the absence of consensus, the report of the ad hoc expert group shall fully reflect the diversity of views expressed.

Reports

14. The ad hoc expert group shall prepare its report, taking into consideration the views of all participants and contributions received, and shall submit its report to the Forum at its fourth session for consideration. The report shall specify the major outcomes of the ad hoc expert group's work, including proposals and recommendations for further consideration by the Forum.

Secretariat

15. The Forum secretariat shall serve as the secretariat for the ad hoc expert group, supported by the Collaborative Partnership on Forests.

B. Ad hoc expert group on finance and transfer of environmentally sound technologies

Scope and work programme

16. The ad hoc expert group shall provide scientific and technical advice to the Forum for its work on

finance and transfer of environmentally sound technologies. The work of the ad hoc expert group should be undertaken within the context of Economic and Social Council resolution 2000/35 and relevant resolutions adopted by the Forum at its sessions, and should also consider, inter alia, related IPF/IFF proposals for action and outcomes of Forum sessions, including its reports.

Tasks

17. The ad hoc expert group shall undertake the following specific tasks on finance:

Finance

(a) Consider previous initiatives on finance, including recommendations from the Croydon, Oslo and Pretoria workshops, as well as the relevant IPF/IFF proposals for action, background papers and strategy documents of member organizations of the Collaborative Partnership on Forests;

(b) Assess the role and status of official development assistance directed towards sustainable forest management and consider ways for enhancing its availability and effectiveness; in this regard, identify possible means to enhance the efforts of developed countries to fulfil their commitments on official development assistance;

(c) Review the effectiveness of existing international financing for sustainable forest management, including methods and mechanisms; analyse opportunities, country-level gaps, limitations and donor and recipient priorities, as well as the contribution of the Collaborative Partnership on Forests towards financing sustainable forest management; propose measures to improve the effectiveness of that financing for enhancing the enabling environment at both the national and international levels and to attract increased financing from all sources;

(d) Explore the potential of new and innovative approaches to attract increased financing for sustainable forest management; discuss and make suggestions for expanded use of those approaches to address the need for financial resources for financing sustainable forest management, including through national forest programmes or equivalent processes;

(e) Assess country experiences in the mobilization of financial resources to support sustainable forest management; in this regard, identify gaps in, and the potential and limitations of, current financing sources and financial mechanisms in implementing sustainable forest management; propose approaches to enhance and more effectively use and mobilize national and international financial resources;

(f) Assess and consider the role of the private sector in financing sustainable forest management; in this regard, recommend measures to improve the enabling environment for private investment in sustainable forest management, at both the national and international levels; and encourage increased private resource flows to the forest sector, in particular in developing countries and countries with economies in transition.

18. The ad hoc expert group shall undertake the following specific tasks on the transfer of environmentally sound technologies:

Transfer of environmentally sound technologies

(a) Review and assess existing initiatives on the transfer of environmentally sound technologies and knowledge diffusion for the promotion of sustainable forest management among countries and sectors and stakeholders, including through North-South, North-North and South-South cooperation and programmes of member organizations of the Collaborative Partnership on Forests. This should include an analysis of incentives that promote, and obstacles that inhibit, the transfer of forest-related environmentally sound technologies between and/or within countries, in particular to developing countries and countries with economies in transition, in both the private and public sectors;

(b) Recommend approaches to improve transfer of forest-related environmentally sound technologies. The recommendation may include the role of various policy instruments, such as concessional and preferential terms, public/private partnerships and research cooperation, as well as capacity-building in the use and application of current and emerging environmentally sound technologies, including remote sensing.

Composition and participation

19. The ad hoc expert group shall consist of thirty experts, six from each of the five regional groups.

20. The experts shall have well-recognized scientific and technical expertise in finance and transfer of environmentally sound technologies and knowledge of the intergovernmental forest policy deliberations of IPF, IFF and the Forum.

21. Representatives of the States members of the United Nations Forum on Forests shall be allowed to participate in the first two days of the meetings of the ad hoc expert group and remain as observers for the last three days of the meeting.

22. The Collaborative Partnership on Forests shall be invited to make scientific and technical contributions to the work of the ad hoc expert group to support the work of the ad hoc expert group in a resource capacity.

23. Intergovernmental organizations and representatives of major groups with relevant expertise may participate in the meeting, in accordance with the rules of procedure of the functional commissions of the Economic and Social Council, as well as practices established by the Commission on Sustainable Development, IPF and IFF. They may be invited to make scientific and technical contributions.

Travel assistance

24. Travel support and a daily subsistence allowance at established United Nations rates shall be provided to each of the experts, if the budget allows, with priority to developing countries, particularly least developed countries, as well as countries with economies in transition.

Officers

25. The chairman of the ad hoc expert group shall be elected from among the experts at its meeting.

Duration of work

26. The ad hoc expert group shall initiate its work after the third session of the Forum and complete its work at least three months in advance of the fourth session of the Forum.

Meeting

27. The ad hoc expert group shall hold one meeting for up to five days before the end of 2003. It shall

also use electronic means of communication to the greatest extent possible. The ad hoc expert group meeting shall be organized at a United Nations venue where meeting facilities are available, preferably in New York, taking into account cost-effectiveness. To the extent possible, the ad hoc expert group will hold its meeting back to back with the meeting of the ad hoc expert group on approaches and mechanisms for monitoring, assessment and reporting.

Proposals and recommendations for consideration by the Forum

28. The proposals and recommendations of the ad hoc expert group should be provided by consensus. In the absence of consensus, the reports of the ad hoc expert group shall fully reflect the diversity of views expressed.

Reports

29. The ad hoc expert group shall prepare its report, taking into consideration the views of all participants and contributions received, and shall submit its report to the Forum at its fourth session for consideration. The report shall specify major outcomes of the ad hoc expert group's work, including proposals and recommendations for further consideration by the Forum.

Secretariat

30. The Forum secretariat shall serve as the secretariat for the ad hoc expert group, supported by the Collaborative Partnership on Forests.

C. Ad hoc expert group on consideration, with a view to recommending the parameters of a mandate for developing a legal framework on all types of forests

Scope and work programme

31. The ad hoc expert group shall provide scientific and technical advice to the Forum for its work on consideration, with a view to recommending the parameters of a mandate for developing a legal framework on all types of forests. The work of the ad hoc expert group should be undertaken within the context of Economic and Social Council resolution 2000/35 and resolutions adopted by the Forum at its sessions, in particular those referring to the creation and scope of the ad hoc expert groups.

Tasks

32. The reports of the ad hoc expert groups on approaches and mechanisms for monitoring, assessment and reporting and on finance and transfer of environmentally sound technologies shall serve as inputs to the work of this ad hoc expert group.

33. The ad hoc expert group shall undertake the following specific tasks on consideration, with a view to recommending the parameters of a mandate for developing a legal framework on all types of forests:

(a) Assess existing regional and international binding and non-binding instruments and processes relevant to forests; the assessment should include, inter alia, analysis of complementarities, gaps and duplications, and should take into account Forum resolution 2/3 on specific criteria for the review of the effectiveness of the international arrangement on forests;

(b) Consider reports prepared by countries, as referred to in decision 2003/299 to which the present annex is attached, the member organizations of the Collaborative Partnership on Forests and the Forum secretariat, as well as outcomes of Forum sessions;

(c) Consider other outcomes of the international arrangement on forests, inter alia, the efforts of countries to implement the IPF/IFF proposals for action, other expert groups, country- and organization-led initiatives of the Forum and previous relevant initiatives, and forest-related work undertaken by the member organizations of the Collaborative Partnership on Forests;

(d) Review the relevant experiences of existing forest-related and other relevant organizations and agreements, including multilateral environmental agreements and regional conventions and processes, focusing on complementarities, gaps and duplications;

(e) Provide for the consideration of the Forum at its fifth session, a balanced range of options with respect to "consideration, with a view to recommending the parameters of a mandate for developing a legal framework on all types of forests".

Composition and participation

34. The ad hoc expert group shall be composed of experts of the States members of the Forum.

35. The experts shall have well-recognized scientific and technical expertise on the forest regime and the Rio conventions and knowledge of the intergovernmental forest policy deliberations of IPF, IFF and the Forum.

36. The Collaborative Partnership on Forests shall be invited to make scientific and technical contributions to the work of the ad hoc expert group to support the work of the ad hoc expert group in a resource capacity.

37. Intergovernmental organizations and representatives of major groups with relevant expertise may participate in the meeting, in accordance with the rules of procedure of the functional commissions of the Economic and Social Council, as well as practices established by the Commission on Sustainable Development, IPF and IFF. They may be invited to make scientific and technical contributions.

Travel assistance

38. Travel support and a daily subsistence allowance at the established United Nations rates shall be provided to one country expert from each developing country, as well as to one country expert from countries with economies in transition, to the maximum extent from the budget, supplemented by voluntary extrabudgetary contributions.

Officers

39. Two co-chairpersons of the ad hoc expert group shall be elected from among experts at its meeting, one from a developing country and one from a developed country.

Duration of work

40. The ad hoc expert group shall initiate its work immediately after the fourth session of the Forum and complete its work at least three months in advance of the fifth session of the Forum.

Meeting

41. The ad hoc expert group shall hold one meeting for up to five days. It shall also use electronic means of communication to the greatest extent possible. The ad hoc expert group meeting shall be organ-

ized at a United Nations venue where meeting facilities are available, preferably in New York, taking into account cost-effectiveness.

Proposals and recommendations for consideration by the Forum

42. The proposals and recommendations of the ad hoc expert group should be provided by consensus. In the absence of consensus, the reports of the ad hoc expert group shall fully reflect the diversity of views expressed.

Reports

43. The ad hoc expert group shall adopt a report at its meeting, for submission to the Forum at its fifth session. The report shall specify major outcomes of the ad hoc expert group's work, including proposals and recommendations for further consideration by the Forum.

Secretariat

44. The Forum secretariat shall serve as the secretariat for the ad hoc expert group, supported by the Collaborative Partnership on Forests.

(For information on expert group meetings in 2003, see below.)

On 25 July, [meeting 49], the Council, on the recommendation of the United Nations Forum on Forests [E/2003/42, orally amended], adopted **resolution 2003/63** without vote [agenda item 13 (i)].

Trust Fund for the United Nations Forum on Forests

The Economic and Social Council,

Recalling its resolution 2000/35 of 18 October 2000, in particular paragraph 4, by which it established the United Nations Forum on Forests as a subsidiary body of the Council composed of all States Members of the United Nations and States members of the specialized agencies with full and equal participation,

Recalling also paragraph 6 of the same resolution, in which it invited voluntary extrabudgetary contributions in support of the participation of representatives of developing countries that are not members of the Commission on Sustainable Development in sessions of the Forum and its subsidiary bodies,

Recalling further paragraph 16 of the same resolution, in which it called upon interested donor Governments, financial institutions and other organizations to make voluntary financial contributions to a trust fund in order to facilitate the continuing work of the Forum and its secretariat,

Taking note of the oral report on the status of the secretariat presented by the secretariat to the Forum at its third session, and the views expressed by many countries on the need for enhanced participation of Member States that are developing countries, least developed countries or countries with economies in transition in the sessions of the Forum,

Noting that the Trust Fund is an important resource for carrying out activities to support the work of the Forum and to ensure the increased participation of representatives of developing countries, least developed countries and countries with economies in transition, as well as experts from those countries, in the sessions of the Forum, and other meetings aimed at supporting the work of the Forum, and ad hoc expert groups,

Acknowledging with appreciation the voluntary extrabudgetary contributions made by a number of donor Governments to the Trust Fund to support the Forum and its secretariat, and recognizing the need for additional resources,

1. *Invites* donor Governments, institutions and other organizations to provide contributions to the Trust Fund;

2. *Recommends* that the General Assembly decide that support to participants from developing countries, with priority to the least developed countries, as well as from countries with economies in transition may be provided from the Trust Fund for travel and daily subsistence from funds designated for that purpose.

On the same date, the Council decided that UNFF's fourth session would be held in Geneva from 3 to 14 May 2004 (**decision 2003/297**) and took note of the Forum's report on its third session and approved the provisional agenda for the fourth session (**decision 2003/298**).

Note by Secretariat. An October Secretariat note [A/C.2/58/6] stated that, by its resolution 2003/63 (see above), the Economic and Social Council recommended that the General Assembly decide that support to participants from developing countries, with priority to LDCs, and from countries with economies in transition could be provided from the Trust Fund for travel and daily subsistence from funds designated for that purpose. The Assembly so decided on 23 December (**decision 58/554**).

Expert group meetings. The Ad Hoc Expert Group on Approaches and Mechanisms for Monitoring, Assessment and Reporting (Geneva, 8-12 December) [E/CN.18/2004/2] transmitted to the fourth (2004) UNFF session conclusions and recommendations covering its tasks as envisaged in Economic and Social Council decision 2003/299 (see p. 1058), including on existing monitoring, assessment and reporting procedures under relevant international conventions, processes, instruments and organizations; ways for UNFF to monitor and assess progress towards sustainable forest management and implementation of the IPF/IFF proposals for action [YUN 1997, p. 1057]; an outline for voluntary reporting to UNFF; the use of reports provided to UNFF to identify trends and lessons learned; and building national capacity for monitoring, assessment and reporting. The Group considered an October Secretariat note [E/CN.18/AC.1/2003/2], which provided background information to assist it in carrying out its tasks.

The meeting of the Ad Hoc Expert Group on the Finance and Transfer of Environmentally Sound Technologies (Geneva, 15-19 December) [E/CN.18/2004/5] considered previous initiatives on finance and transfer of ESTs for sustainable forest management, with particular attention given to lessons learned from existing initiatives and constraints affecting the effectiveness and efficiency of financing and transfer of ESTs. It made recommendations for improving the transfer of such technologies for UNFF's consideration at its 2004 session; the recommendations were divided into those directed at Member States, members of the Collaborative Partnership on Forests and the Forum itself. Recommendations on improving forest management financing were directed at the national and international levels, both within and outside the forest sector. The Expert Group considered October Secretariat notes on challenges in the current financial environment for financing sustainable forest management [E/CN.18/AC.2/2003/2] and an overview of the transfer of ESTs for such management [E/CN.18/AC.2/2003/3].

On 19 December, the Economic and Social Council decided that the UNFF ad hoc expert group on consideration, with a view to recommending the parameters of a mandate for developing a legal framework on all types of forests, would meet in New York from 6 to 10 September 2004 (**decision 2003/315**).

International Year of Mountains (2002)

Note by Executive Director. A January note by the Executive Director [UNEP/GC.22/INF/37] summarized UNEP's contribution to the International Year of Mountains, 2002 [YUN 2002, p. 1052], including awareness-raising and an outreach campaign to promote the Year; efforts to build coalitions and organize events; environmental assessments and preparation of the first report on the global status of mountain ecosystems (Mountain Watch); and technical assistance for negotiating legal instruments for transboundary cooperation. Under the International Partnership for Sustainable Development in Mountain Regions, launched in 2002 [YUN 2002, p. 1053], UNEP was requested to lead efforts on networking and regional agreements; transboundary cooperation in the Carpathian, Central Asia, Caucasus, Altai, African and Latin American mountain ranges; and public-private partnerships. UNEP began work on addressing the environmental aspects of sustainable development of mountain regions under the auspices of an interim secretariat for the International Partnership, with support from Italy and Switzerland.

Note by Secretary-General. In accordance with General Assembly resolution 57/245 [YUN 2002, p. 1053], the Secretary-General transmitted, in July [A/58/134], a report on activities related to the International Year of Mountains, prepared by the Director-General of the Food and Agriculture Organization of the United Nations (FAO), the Year's lead agency. It described achievements made at the national, regional and international levels in 2002, emphasizing activities that would lead to long-term, concrete action for sustainable mountain development. The Year stimulated the establishment of 78 national committees or similar mechanisms to develop plans and policies to achieve such development. Reports from countries suggested that many of those committees would become permanent bodies. Long-term action was needed to implement chapter 13 of Agenda 21 [YUN 1992, p. 672] on sustainable mountain development and the Johannesburg Plan of Implementation [YUN 2002, p. 821], requiring national involvement in and support for follow-up to the Year. The report recommended, for the Assembly's consideration, action by Governments to build on results achieved so far.

Communication. In October, Italy transmitted the conclusions of the First Global Meeting of Members of the International Partnership for Sustainable Development in Mountain Regions (Merano, Italy, 5-6 October) [A/C.2/58/8].

GENERAL ASSEMBLY ACTION

On 23 December [meeting 78], the General Assembly, on the recommendation of the Second Committee [A/58/484/Add.7], adopted **resolution 58/216** without vote [agenda item 94 (g)].

Sustainable development in mountain regions

The General Assembly,

Recalling its resolution 53/24 of 10 November 1998, by which it proclaimed 2002 the International Year of Mountains,

Recalling also its resolutions 55/189 of 20 December 2000 and 57/245 of 20 December 2002,

Recognizing chapter 13 of Agenda 21 and all relevant paragraphs of the Plan of Implementation of the World Summit on Sustainable Development ("Johannesburg Plan of Implementation"), in particular paragraph 42 thereof, as the overall policy frameworks for sustainable development in mountain regions,

Noting the International Partnership for Sustainable Development in Mountain Regions ("Mountain Partnership"), launched during the World Summit on Sustainable Development with the committed support of thirty-eight countries, fifteen intergovernmental organizations and thirty-eight organizations from major groups, as an important approach to addressing the various interrelated dimensions of sustainable development in mountain regions,

Taking note of the Bishkek Mountain Platform, the outcome document of the Bishkek Global Mountain Summit, held in Bishkek from 28 October to 1 November 2002, which was the concluding event of the International Year of Mountains,

1. *Takes note* of the report transmitted by the Secretary-General on the International Year of Mountains, 2002;

2. *Welcomes* the significant results achieved during the Year, which substantially increased awareness of and strengthened interest in sustainable development and poverty eradication in mountain regions, as well as acting as a catalyst for long-term effective action to implement chapter 13 of Agenda 21 and paragraph 42 of the Johannesburg Plan of Implementation;

3. *Notes with appreciation* that a growing network of Governments, organizations, major groups and individuals around the world know that mountains are globally important as the source of most of the Earth's freshwater, as repositories of rich biological diversity, as popular destinations for recreation and tourism and as areas of important cultural diversity, knowledge and heritage;

4. *Also notes with appreciation* the effective role played by Governments, as well as major groups, academic institutions and international organizations and agencies, in the activities related to the Year, including the establishment of seventy-eight national committees or similar mechanisms;

5. *Appreciates* the work undertaken by the Food and Agriculture Organization of the United Nations as the lead agency for the Year, as well as the valuable contributions made by the United Nations Environment Programme, the United Nations University, the United Nations Educational, Scientific and Cultural Organization, the United Nations Development Programme and the United Nations Children's Fund;

6. *Underlines* the fact that there remain key challenges to implementing sustainable development and eradicating poverty in mountain regions as well as challenges in the areas of national involvement, international cooperation, support for partnerships and mobilization of financial resources, and against this background:

(*a*) Encourages the United Nations system to enhance efforts to strengthen inter-agency collaboration to achieve more effective implementation of chapter 13 of Agenda 21 and paragraph 42 of the Johannesburg Plan of Implementation;

(*b*) Also encourages the continued establishment and development of mountain-related national committees, focal points and other multi-stakeholder mechanisms at the national level for sustainable development in mountain regions;

(*c*) Supports national efforts, within the framework of national development plans, to develop goals and strategic plans for the sustainable development of mountains, as well as enabling policies and laws, programmes and projects;

(*d*) Encourages transboundary approaches, where the States concerned agree, to the sustainable development of mountain ranges and information-sharing in this regard;

(*e*) Also encourages Member States to collect and produce information and to establish databases devoted to mountains so as to capitalize on knowledge to support interdisciplinary research, programmes and projects and to improve decision-making and planning;

(*f*) Supports the development and implementation of global, regional and national communication programmes to build on the awareness and momentum for change established by the Year;

(*g*) Stresses the importance of capacity-building and educational programmes to enhance awareness of good practices in sustainable development in mountain regions and the nature of relationships between highland and lowland areas;

(*h*) Calls for the improvement of mountain women's access to resources and the strengthening of their role in their communities and cultures, and in this context takes note of the recommendations of the Thimpu Declaration adopted at the Celebrating Mountain Women conference, held at Thimpu from 1 to 4 October 2002;

7. *Notes* the entry into force of the nine Protocols to the Convention on the Protection of the Alps as a contribution to regional cooperation for sustainable development in that mountain region;

8. *Notes also* the adoption and signing of the Framework Convention on the Protection and Sustainable Development of the Carpathians by the countries of the region;

9. *Notes further* that a consultative process has been conducted with all Mountain Partnership stakeholders, in particular donor countries, with a view to determining the best options for further assisting all stakeholders in the implementation of the Partnership;

10. *Takes note* of the conclusions of the first global meeting of the members of the Mountain Partnership, held in Merano, Italy, on 5 and 6 October 2003, at the invitation of the Government of Italy;

11. *Notes* that the next global meeting of the members of the Mountain Partnership will be organized during the second half of 2004, and welcomes in this context the offer of the Government of Peru to host the meeting;

12. *Notes also*, in this context, that the Mountain Partnership is a cooperation mechanism that is dynamic, transparent, flexible and participatory in nature and that it is open to all Governments, including local and regional authorities, as well as to intergovernmental, non-governmental and other organizations whose objectives and activities are consistent with the vision and mission of the Partnership;

13. *Notes further* that Mountain Partnership members committed themselves to implement the Partnership in accordance with Economic and Social Council resolution 2003/61 of 25 July 2003, and calls upon them to comply with the criteria and guidelines agreed in the decision taken by the Commission on Sustainable Development at its eleventh session;

14. *Invites* the international community and other relevant partners to consider joining the Mountain Partnership;

15. *Encourages* all relevant entities of the United Nations system, within their respective mandates, to continue their constructive collaboration in the context of the follow-up to the Year, taking into account the inter-agency group on mountains and the need for the further involvement of the United Nations system, in particular the Food and Agriculture Organization of the United Nations, the United Nations Environment Programme, the United Nations University, the United Nations Development Programme, the United Nations Educational, Scientific and Cultural Organization and the United Nations Children's Fund, international financial institutions and other relevant in-

ternational organizations, taking into account the recommendations formulated in the Bishkek Mountain Platform;

16. *Encourages* Governments, the United Nations system, the international financial institutions, the Global Environment Facility and other relevant United Nations funding mechanisms, such as the Global Mechanism of the United Nations Convention to Combat Desertification in Those Countries Experiencing Drought and/or Desertification, Particularly in Africa, as well as all relevant stakeholders from civil society organizations and the private sector, to provide support, including through voluntary financial contributions, to local, national and international programmes and projects for sustainable development in mountain regions;

17. *Requests* the Secretary-General to report to the General Assembly at its sixtieth session on the status of sustainable development in mountain regions, including an overall analysis of the challenges that lie ahead and appropriate policy recommendations, under a sub-item entitled "Sustainable development in mountain regions" of the item entitled "Environment and sustainable development".

Marine ecosystems

Oceans and seas

In preparation for World Water Day (22 March), UNEP launched *Vital Water Graphics*, a publication providing a visual guide to the problems of deteriorating freshwater and marine resources. In October, UNEP published the *World Atlas of Seagrasses*, which described the status of seagrass, a fragile coastal ecosystem, and indicated that it had declined by 15 per cent worldwide in the previous decade.

Among issues suggested by the fourth meeting of the United Nations Open-ended Informal Consultative Process on Oceans and the Law of the Sea (New York, 2-6 June) [A/58/95] (see p. 1355), for consideration by the General Assembly, was the protection of vulnerable marine ecosystems.

On 3 November, Azerbaijan, Iran, Kazakhstan, the Russian Federation and Turkmenistan signed the Framework Convention for the Protection of the Marine Environment of the Caspian Sea, which would coordinate regional efforts to address the environmental crisis resulting from habitat destruction, pollution and the overexploitation of fish and other marine life.

Global waters assessment

The Global International Waters Assessment (GIWA), inaugurated in 2000 [YUN 2000, p. 982] to assess international waters and causes of environmental problems in 66 water regions, focusing on the aquatic environment in transboundary waters, released results for the Amazon Basin, the Caspian Sea and the Indian Ocean islands at the thirteenth Stockholm water symposium (11-14 August).

Governing Council action. On 7 February [dec. 22/1 II], the Governing Council, having considered the 2002 report of the Executive Director on the global assessment of the marine environment [YUN 2002, p. 1054], requested him to make arrangements for UNEP's participation in preparations for establishing a regular global reporting process and assessment of the state of the marine environment, as called for in General Assembly resolution 57/141 [YUN 2002, p. 1322]. It called on the Executive Director to identify existing UNEP resources that could be applied to the process, and urged regional seas programmes (see p. 1067) to participate and contribute as appropriate. The Executive Director was asked to report to the Secretary-General in 2003 and to GC/GMEF in 2004 on UNEP's contribution to the process, and was authorized to seek extrabudgetary resources, including through the establishment of a trust fund, to support the participation of developing countries. Governments were urged to contribute to the trust fund, once established, and were called on to focus on coastal areas, in collaboration with regional institutions.

Report of Secretary-General. In response to General Assembly resolution 57/141 [YUN 2002, p. 1322], the Secretary-General, in October [A/58/423], reported on proposals to establish a regular process for the assessment of the state of the marine environment, drawing on, among other things, UNEP's work pursuant to a 2001 Governing Council decision on the subject [YUN 2001, p. 964], and taking into account a review by the Joint Group of Experts on the Scientific Aspects of Marine Environmental Protection (GESAMP). The report also described existing global and regional assessment programmes and how they differed from the envisaged global marine assessment (GMA) process, and summarized replies to the request contained in resolution 57/141 for proposals on the process. It concluded that GMA would be a global, comprehensive assessment of the marine environment, including socio-economic aspects, and would take into consideration all activities affecting the oceans and the interrelationship of all the elements of the ocean environment, including biodiversity (the ecosystem approach). It was to be regular, with general assessments to be completed possibly every five years. It should operate under the authority of the Assembly, with substantive discussions by all interested parties on the process and its results taking place either at the Informal Consultative Process or at associated meetings. Capacity-building would be an essential element of GMA and would require special arrangements. Due to its step-by-step structure, its clear separation of science and policy and its provision for consultations among all interested parties at the outset, the organizational model for the global assessment process proposed by GESAMP, which was annexed to the report, appeared to be the most compelling.

For Assembly action regarding the establishment of GMA, see **resolution 58/240** (p. 1355).

Report of Executive Director. A December report of the Executive Director [UNEP/GCSS.VIII/6] outlined progress made in response to Governing Council decision 22/1 II on GMA (see p. 1065). In March, the UNEP secretariat held internal consultations to identify existing programmatic and budgetary resources that could contribute to the GMA process. In support of the Governing Council's decision, UNEP, on 9 April, established a trust fund and requested contributions from Governments. UNEP organized an informal consultative meeting (The Hague, Netherlands, 26-27 May), which concluded that UNEP's competency lay in its expertise and experience in environmental assessment; its extensive global and regional networks of institutions and scientists; its interaction and collaboration with relevant global and regional programmes; and a strong capability-building component targeting developing countries. It recommended convening an inter-agency consultation meeting between UN agencies, and a meeting to explore the scope and methodology of GMA, including links between UNEP's science-based activities and other endeavours, such as the 1992 Convention on Biological Diversity [YUN 1992, p. 683] (see p. 1051), the Global Programme of Action for the Protection of the Marine Environment from Land-based Activities (see below) and regional seas programmes (see p. 1067). UNEP conveyed the findings of that meeting to the fourth meeting of the United Nations Open-ended Informal Consultative Process on Oceans and the Law of the Sea (see p. 1355), which agreed on the date and venue of the recommended inter-agency meeting, to be organized by the UN Division for Ocean Affairs and the Law of the Sea (see p. 1362).

The inter-agency consultative meeting on the establishment of GMA (Paris, 8-9 September) discussed general modalities of GMA in terms of a coordinating mechanism, secretariat, involvement of existing assessments, funds, new resources and capacity-building. UNEP presented "A Survey of Global and Regional Marine Environmental Assessments and Related Scientific Activities", together with a proposal on the modular partnership approach as a possible modality for GMA, whereby each UN agency would take responsibility in the assessment according to its mandate.

UNEP organized a planning meeting (Nairobi, 19-21 November) to develop a multi-purpose module for assessing the coastal and marine environment that would address the needs of relevant policy instruments, including the Convention on Biological Diversity (see p. 1051), GPA (see below) and the regional seas programmes (see p. 1067). The meeting discussed how current UNEP assessments could contribute to the module and identified areas of cooperation with key partners.

Global Programme of Action

On 7 February [dec. 22/2 II], the Governing Council requested the Executive Director to address, in the implementation of the Global Programme of Action (GPA) for the Protection of the Marine Environment from Land-based Activities [YUN 1995, p. 1081], the 2001 Montreal Declaration on the implementation of GPA [YUN 2001, p. 965], the Monterrey Consensus, adopted at the 2002 International Conference on Financing for Development [YUN 2002, p. 953], and the Johannesburg Plan of Implementation [ibid., p. 821] as they related to GPA objectives. He was asked to continue to contribute to the work of the Informal Coordinating Group on Oceans, Coasts and Islands formed for the 2002 World Summit on Sustainable Development, with a view to providing input to the Commission on Sustainable Development when considering the Summit's results and creating synergies among the Type II partnerships relating to coastal and marine issues; to promote the concept of integrated coastal area and river basin management, and to facilitate scientific, management and institutional links between freshwater and coastal/marine management, taking into consideration existing national and regional experience; to develop a strategy paper on the environmental dimensions of water supply and sanitation in the context of integrated water resource and waste-water management, and cooperate with relevant UN bodies in developing indicators to assess the impact of improved sanitation on the environment; and to further develop the principles of guidance on municipal waste-water management [YUN 2002, p. 1055] for submission to the Governing Council in 2005. The Executive Director was further requested to assess the feasibility of organizing regional consultations on the development of waste-water emission targets at the national and subnational levels, including reference to ecological benefits. The Council urged Governments to adopt, and the Executive Director to integrate into UNEP's work, a holistic environmental approach to sanitation and the implementation of the World Summit sanitation target [YUN 2002, p. 822], incorporating the provision of household sanitation services and all other components of the water management process. He was asked to submit to the Governing Council in 2005 a report on action taken by the UNEP secretariat to implement the decision, including on preparations for the second Intergovernmental Review Meeting of the Global Programme of Action in 2006.

In **resolution 58/240** of 23 December (see p. 1355), the General Assembly called on States to advance the implementation of GPA and the 2001 Montreal Declaration.

Coral reefs

On 7 February [dec. 22/2 IV], the Governing Council extended the scope of its 2001 decision [YUN 2001, p. 965] on the International Coral Reef Initiative (ICRI) [YUN 1995, p. 1084] to cover the period 2003-2004. It requested the Executive Director to continue to support ICRI to enhance its development and impact, and to support the International Coral Reef Action Network (ICRAN), set up in 2001 to address the state of the declining coral reefs by facilitating implementation of the priorities identified by ICRI [YUN 2001, p. 966]. The Council noted that, at the World Summit on Sustainable Development [YUN 2002, p. 821], ICRI had been expanded to include three additional tropical seas containing coral communities. The Executive Director was asked to promote the participation of industries in the Network; to continue giving effect to the 2001 Governing Council decision as it related to collaborative efforts between UNEP's coral-related activities and multilateral environmental conventions, and collaborative approaches with UN agencies; and to submit a progress report on the conservation and sustainable use of coral reefs to the Governing Council in 2005.

Regional Seas Programme

On 7 February, the Governing Council adopted a series of decisions regarding the Regional Seas Programme. A decision on regional seas strategies for sustainable development [dec. 22/2 III A] requested the Executive Director to support regional seas conventions and action plans to incorporate a series of strategic elements, as specified in the decision, in their programmes of work and to bring those elements to the attention of the conventions' member States. He was asked to develop activities aimed at securing long-term sustainability, taking into account the outcome of the 2002 World Summit on Sustainable Development [YUN 2002, p. 821]. The Governing Council also asked him to facilitate the establishment of mechanisms and instruments to protect inland waters, mainly through UNEP regional offices, and to support the establishment of new regional seas conventions and action plans. The Governing Council called on littoral States of shared inland waters to establish collectively legal instruments to protect the environment of those areas as soon as possible, and called on the Executive Director and countries of regional seas programmes to mobilize resources for implementing the programmes' plans of action. Governments were invited to: take a more proactive role in implementing the programme of work of their respective regional seas conventions and action plans and strengthen and develop "ownership" over them; broaden governmental participation through the involvement of all relevant national ministries; and broaden monitoring, assessment and training activities.

Regarding the Action Plan for the Protection, Management and Development of the Marine Coastal Environment of the North-West Pacific Region (NOWPAP), established in 2001 [YUN 2001, p. 966], the Governing Council [dec. 22/2 III B] requested the Executive Director to facilitate the finalization of the host country agreements for the co-hosted regional coordinating unit with Japan and the Republic of Korea and to facilitate the recruitment process for the unit's staff; to continue to serve as NOWPAP's interim secretariat until the unit was established and operational, and support the unit's activities; and to facilitate the development and implementation of a Global Environment Facility (GEF) project on land-based activities in the NOWPAP region.

The Governing Council [dec. 22/2 III C] invited countries that had not become party to the Convention for Cooperation in the Protection and Sustainable Development of the Marine and Coastal Environment of the North-East Pacific, initially signed by six States in 2002 [YUN 2002, p. 1055], to do so and to take steps to implement the Convention; recommended that the Governments of the region convene a second intergovernmental meeting of the Convention's Plan of Action and requested the Executive Director to assist in that task (see p. 1068); and called on Governments of the region to establish a regional coordinating unit (RCU) for the Action Plan following offers made by countries.

In a decision on the 1981 Abidjan Convention for Cooperation in the Protection and Development of the Marine and Coastal Environment of the West and Central African Region [YUN 1981, p. 840] and the 1985 Nairobi Convention for the Protection, Management and Development of the Marine and Coastal Environment of the Eastern African Region [YUN 1985, p. 816] [dec. 22/2 III D], the Governing Council requested the Executive Director to provide technical and financial support to ensure coordination of the programmes of work for the two conventions through UNEP's Regional Seas Programme and to focus on activities that made the conventions effective instruments for sustainable development. He was also asked to provide support and delegate additional responsibilities to RCUs to ensure their coordination of regional consensus-building, intergovernmental dialogue and resource mobilization, and to undertake coordination activities for implementing the outcomes of the New Partnership for Africa's Development (NEPAD) (see p. 937). Countries within the Nairobi and Abidjan Convention areas that had not ratified or acceded to the conventions were invited to do so and to implement them; the Executive Director was asked to provide technical and legal assistance to facilitate ratifications. Parties to the conventions were invited to make contributions to their trust funds.

With regard to the South-East Pacific Action Plan, created in 1981 [YUN 1981, p. 833], the Governing Council [dec. 22/2 III E] asked the Executive Director to strengthen horizontal cooperation and twinning arrangements established by the Permanent Commission for the South Pacific and the South Pacific Regional Environment Programme, and to support the organization of an interregional conference between those two regions, in addition to a conference between the regional seas programmes of the Pacific basin in 2004.

Recalling its 2001 decision in which it called for the establishment of a joint International Maritime Organization (IMO)/UNEP forum on emergency response to marine pollution [YUN 2001, p. 967], the Governing Council [dec. 22/2 V] invited IMO to review international regulations regarding single-hull tankers, especially those transporting heavy fuel oil, and to consider their more timely phasing out, with a view to reducing serious risk to the environment. IMO was invited to consider establishing a supplementary compensation fund for oil pollution victims, and for remediation of environmental damage through a protocol that could be considered for adoption during a diplomatic conference to be convened by IMO in London during May (see p. 1529). Coastal and flag States that had not done so were invited to ratify the 1990 International Convention on Oil Pollution Preparedness, Response and Cooperation [YUN 1990, p. 1108] and the 2000 Protocol on Preparedness, Response and Cooperation on Pollution Incidents by Hazardous and Noxious Substances [YUN 2000, p. 1438], and to implement the commitments of those instruments. UNEP and IMO were invited to strengthen their cooperation for implementation at the regional level of the global rules and regulations on preventing and combating pollution from ships. The Executive Director was requested to support, in the framework of the Regional Seas Programme, regional implementation of the Governing Council decision, in cooperation with IMO.

The second Intergovernmental Meeting of the Plan of Action for the Protection and Sustainable Development of the Marine and Coastal Environment of the North-East Pacific was held in Managua, Nicaragua, on 6 and 7 March. The first Intergovernmental Meeting was held in 2002 (Guatemala City, 19-22 February 2002).

In keeping with the Governing Council's 2003 decision on regional seas strategies for sustainable development (see p. 1067), the Fifth Global Meeting of Regional Seas Conventions and Action Plans (Nairobi, 26-28 November) agreed on the Strategic Guidelines for the Regional Seas Programme for 2004-2007.

Conservation of wildlife

As at 31 December, the 1994 Lusaka Agreement on Cooperative Enforcement Operations Directed at Illegal Trade in Wild Fauna and Flora [YUN 1994, p. 951], which entered into force in 1996 [YUN 1996, p. 970], had been ratified or acceded to by six States (Congo, Kenya, Lesotho, Uganda, United Republic of Tanzania, Zambia). The Agreement aimed to reduce, and ultimately eliminate, illegal trafficking in African wildlife.

The sixth meeting of the Governing Council of the Parties to the Lusaka Agreement (Nairobi, 21-22 July) adopted decisions on the development and harmonization of wildlife laws and regulations, institutional capacity-building, co-operation with partners, an evaluation of the Agreement, and administrative and budgetary matters.

Governing Council action. In a 7 February decision on the UNEP World Conservation Monitoring Centre (WCMC) [dec. 22/1 III], the Governing Council requested the Executive Director to support the Centre's development, establish a network of collaborating centres in developing countries to cooperate with WCMC and assist them in undertaking their work programmes. In collaboration with UNESCO and FAO, he was asked to seek a renewed mandate from the Economic and Social Council/General Assembly for the United Nations List of National Parks and Protected Places, compiled by WCMC, reflecting UNEP's role and its agreement with the World Conservation Union on new partnership arrangements for the World Database on Protected

Areas. The Governing Council endorsed the strengthening of the Database, including linking it with other databases on biodiversity and ecology; the establishment of a global consortium; and the strengthening of the relationship between UNEP and the World Conservation Union on global protected area issues.

Report of Secretary-General. In response to Economic and Social Council resolution 2002/18 [YUN 2002, p. 1062], the Secretary-General submitted a March report [E/CN.15/2003/8 & Corr.1 & Add.1] on illicit trafficking in protected species of wild flora and fauna and illicit access to genetic resources (see p. 1051). The report, which was aimed at completing the 2002 progress report [YUN 2002, p. 1045] on the implementation of Council resolution 2001/12 [YUN 2001, p. 968], summarized replies received from 21 Member States in response to a 2002 request by the Secretary-General for comments on the progress report and for information on relevant national legislation, practical experience, statistics and measures taken. It discussed the involvement of organized criminal groups in such trafficking.

ECONOMIC AND SOCIAL COUNCIL ACTION

On 22 July [meeting 44], the Economic and Social Council, on the recommendation of the Commission on Crime Prevention and Criminal Justice [E/2003/30], adopted **resolution 2003/27** without vote [agenda item 14 (c)].

Illicit trafficking in protected species of wild flora and fauna

The Economic and Social Council,

Aware that the conservation of wild flora and fauna is essential for the maintenance of biological diversity, preservation of the environment and sustainable development,

Recalling the Convention on International Trade in Endangered Species of Wild Fauna and Flora and the Convention on Biological Diversity and action taken to implement those conventions,

Aware of the existence of organized criminal groups operating transnationally that specialize in trafficking in protected species of wild flora and fauna, and concerned at the adverse environmental, economic and social repercussions of their activities,

Convinced that international cooperation and mutual legal assistance are both essential to prevent, combat and eradicate trafficking in protected species of wild flora and fauna,

Recalling its resolution 2001/12 of 24 July 2001, in which it urged States to adopt the legislative or other measures necessary for establishing trafficking in protected species of wild flora and fauna as a criminal offence in their domestic legislation,

Recalling also its resolution 2002/18 of 24 July 2002, in which it urged all Member States to cooperate with the Secretary-General and other competent entities of the United Nations system so that the report of the Secretary-General on progress made in the implementation of resolution 2001/12 might be finalized,

Taking note of the replies received from Member States concerning their national legislation and practical experience in the area of trafficking in protected species of wild flora and fauna, contained in the report of the Secretary-General,

1. *Welcomes with satisfaction* the report of the Secretary-General on trafficking in protected species of wild flora and fauna and illicit access to genetic resources;

2. *Urges* all Member States to cooperate, as appropriate, with the Secretary-General and competent entities of the United Nations system, in particular the Centre for International Crime Prevention of the United Nations Office on Drugs and Crime, the secretariat of the Convention on International Trade in Endangered Species of Wild Fauna and Flora and the secretariat of the Convention on Biological Diversity, with a view to preventing, combating and eradicating trafficking in protected species of wild flora and fauna;

3. *Urges* Member States to adopt preventive measures, where necessary, as well as to review their criminal legislation with a view to ensuring that offences relating to trafficking in protected species of wild flora and fauna are punishable by appropriate penalties that take into account the serious nature of those offences;

4. *Encourages* Member States to undertake awareness-raising activities to improve understanding of the serious impact of trafficking in protected species of wild flora and fauna;

5. *Calls upon* Member States to promote international cooperation as well as the conclusion of mutual legal assistance agreements, as appropriate, with a view to preventing, combating and eradicating trafficking in protected species of wild flora and fauna;

6. *Requests* the Secretary-General to report to the Commission on Crime Prevention and Criminal Justice at its fourteenth session on the implementation of the present resolution.

Protection against harmful products and waste

Chemical safety

As at 31 December, 72 States and the EC had signed and 53 States and the EC were parties to the 1998 Rotterdam Convention on the Prior Informed Consent (PIC) Procedure for Certain Hazardous Chemicals and Pesticides in International Trade [YUN 1998, p. 997]. During the year, 10 States ratified the Convention and seven acceded to it. The Convention was to enter into force on 24 February 2004, 90 days following the deposit of the fiftieth instrument of ratification.

Pending the entry into force of the Convention, the PIC procedure, which promoted a shared responsibility between exporting and importing countries in protecting human health and the environment from the harmful effects of certain hazardous chemicals that were traded internationally, was applied voluntarily by Governments.

The 29-member Interim Chemical Review Committee, a subsidiary body of the Intergovernmental Negotiating Committee (INC) for an International Legally Binding Instrument for the Application of the PIC Procedure, established in 1999 [YUN 1999, p. 997] to make recommendations on specific chemicals or hazardous pesticide formulations for inclusion in the PIC procedure, held its fourth session (Rome, 3-7 March) [UNEP/FAO/PIC/ICRC.4/18], at which it made recommendations on chemicals that were subsequently banned by INC.

The tenth session of INC (Geneva, 17-21 November) [UNEP/FAO/PIC/INC.10/24] resumed consideration of issues associated with the implementation of the interim PIC procedure and preparations for the first Conference of the Parties, scheduled for September 2004. Drafts of rules of procedure, financial rules, rules on arbitration and conciliation, and compliance mechanisms and procedures were prepared for that meeting, as was a draft decision on cooperation between the interim secretariat and the World Trade Organization (WTO). Following recommendations made by the Interim Chemical Review Committee in 2002 [YUN 2002, p. 1063] and 2003 (see below), INC made four forms of asbestos (actinolite, anthophyllite, amosite, tremolite) subject to the interim PIC procedure, along with the chemical pesticide dinitro-ortho-cresol (DNOC)—an insecticide, weedkiller and fungicide—and its salts, such as ammonium, potassium and sodium salts. It also made severely hazardous pesticide formulations of a dustable powder containing a combination of benomyl at or above 7 per cent, carbofuran at or above 10 per cent, and thiram at or above 15 per cent subject to the interim procedure. Other INC action dealt with inconsistencies within the Convention and between the Convention and decision guidance documents, and a strategic approach to technical assistance to parties to the Convention. INC decided to hold its eleventh session, as a conference of plenipotentiaries, immediately before the first meeting of the Conference of the Parties, to decide whether to include in the voluntary PIC procedure chrysotile (a form of asbestos), tetraethyl lead and tetramethyl lead (gasoline additives), and the chemical pesticide parathion.

Notes by Executive Director. A note by the Executive Director [UNEP/GC.22/INF/22] outlined progress in implementing a 2002 Governing Council decision on a strategic approach to international chemicals management [YUN 2002, p. 1063]. An initial steering committee, comprising the participating organizations of the Inter-Organization Programme for the Sound Management of Chemicals (IOMC) (FAO, the International Labour Organization, the Organisation for Economic Co-operation and Development, UNEP, the United Nations Industrial Development Organization, the United Nations Institute for Training and Research, the World Health Organization (WHO)), together with the Intergovernmental Forum on Chemical Safety (IFCS), UNDP and the World Bank, was formed to deal with the practical aspects of developing a strategic approach. The committee proposed that the strategic approach development process should culminate in a high-level, multisectoral conference in late 2005.

A discussion paper by the Executive Director [UNEP/GC.22/10/Add.1] provided an overview of UNEP activities in the area of chemicals, including its provision of secretariats for the Rotterdam Convention (see above) and the 2001 Stockholm Convention on Persistent Organic Pollutants [YUN 2001, p. 971] (see p. 1072); its chemical safety capacity-building programme; assessment projects; policy development efforts, including the development of the strategic approach to international chemicals management (see below); and coordination with other international organizations in chemical safety.

In response to Governing Council decisions of 2001 [YUN 2001, p. 969] and 2002 [YUN 2002, p. 1063], the Executive Director, in a January note [UNEP/GC.22/INF/38], described UNEP's contribution to the implementation of IFCS's Bahia Declaration and Priorities for Action beyond 2000 [YUN 2001, p. 969].

A February note by the Executive Director [UNEP/GC.22/INF/39] provided an overview of the Partnership for Clean Fuels and Vehicles, launched during the 2002 World Summit on Sustainable Development [YUN 2002, p. 821] as a Type II project—projects jointly implemented by Governments, the private sector, civil society and international organizations—aimed at supporting the introduction of clean fuels and vehicles in developing countries for improved air quality. The Partnership held its first meeting in New York in November 2002.

A February addendum to a 2002 note by the Executive Director on progress in phasing out lead in gasoline [YUN 2002, p. 1063] updated information on the use of leaded gasoline in Africa [UNEP/GC.22/INF/23/Add.1].

Governing Council action. In February, the Governing Council adopted a series of decisions relating to chemical safety.

The Council invited States and regional economic integration organizations to ratify, accept, approve or accede to the Rotterdam Convention on the PIC procedure, make contributions to the trust fund which supported the interim arrangements and operation of the Conference of the Parties, and ensure the participation of developing countries and countries with economies in transition in INC's work. The Executive Director was requested, in consultation with the FAO Director-General, to promote cooperation between the Convention's interim secretariat and the secretariats of other relevant conventions [dec. 22/4 I].

Regarding chemicals management [dec. 22/4 IV], the Council: decided to proceed with the development of a strategic approach as it envisioned in 2002 [YUN 2002, p. 1063]; underlined that the scope of the approach should be defined and take into account economic, social and environmental aspects of chemicals management, with a view to contributing to sustainable development; and decided that the approach should be regularly reviewed to assess progress on chemical safety, in the light of the targets set at the 2002 World Summit. It requested the Executive Director to compile draft elements of a strategic approach for consideration by the first preparatory meeting (see below), and invited contributions from Governments, relevant international organizations and others. It endorsed the concept of an open-ended consultative process involving representatives of all stakeholder groups, at preparatory meetings and an international conference. It asked the Executive Director to propose that the international conference be held in conjunction with the ninth GC/GMEF special session in 2006, with a view to the latter serving as a high-level segment of the conference that would consider adopting the completed strategic approach document on UNEP's behalf and inviting the other relevant organizations to endorse it. The Council invited major agencies responsible for international development cooperation, and other relevant organizations and stakeholders, to collaborate in the further development of the strategic approach, and called on Governments and other stakeholders to contribute the required extra-budgetary resources. The Executive Director was requested to: report in 2004 on progress to develop the strategic approach; report in 2005 on progress and the outcomes of the preparatory meetings; and provide additional resources to cover core infrastructure costs.

In a decision on lead [dec. 22/4 III], the Governing Council called on Governments to act urgently to eliminate the use of lead in gasoline and on the commitment of the 2002 World Summit [YUN 2002, p. 821] to phase out lead-based paint and other sources of human exposure, to prevent exposure, in particular children's exposure, and to strengthen monitoring and treatment of lead poisoning. The Executive Director, in cooperation with other IOMC members, was asked to assist Governments in their efforts to phase out sources of human exposure and to strengthen monitoring, surveillance and treatment. He was also asked to provide additional resources to cover its core infrastructure costs, estimated at $500,000 for the 2004-2005 biennium.

IFCS session. The fourth session of IFCS (Bangkok, Thailand, 1-7 November) [IFCS/FORUM IV/16w] focused on topics relating to children and chemical safety; occupational safety and health; hazard data generation and availability; acutely toxic pesticides; and capacity-building. It adopted decisions on the globally harmonized system for the classification and labelling of chemicals and illegal international traffic in toxic and dangerous products.

Preparatory Committee meeting. Participants in the first session of the Preparatory Committee for the Development of a Strategic Approach to International Chemicals Management (SAICM) (Bangkok, Thailand, 9-13 November) [SAICM/PREPCOM.1/7] discussed potential issues to be addressed during the development of the strategy, examined ways to structure discussions and considered possible outcomes of the process.

Mercury assessment

In response to a 2001 Governing Council decision [YUN 2001, p. 969], the Executive Director submitted a note containing the global mercury assessment report [UNEP/GC.22/INF/3], which was produced within the IOMC framework and issued by UNEP. The key findings of the assessment had been presented in a 2002 report to the Governing Council [YUN 2002, p. 1064].

On 7 February [dec. 22/4 V], the Governing Council accepted the key findings of the mercury assessment and found that there was sufficient evidence of significant global adverse impacts from mercury and its compounds to warrant further international action to reduce the risks to human health and the environment. It decided that national, regional and global actions should be initiated as soon as possible, and urged all countries to take action to identify exposed populations and ecosystems and to reduce anthropogenic mercury releases. The Governing Council requested the Executive Director to facilitate and conduct technical assistance and capacity-building activities to support countries' efforts regarding mercury pollution, with the objectives outlined in the decision, in the light of the options for immediate action mentioned in the global mercury assessment. He was asked to cooperate with other international organizations that addressed mercury-related issues. The Governing Council invited the Executive Director to seek partnerships with NGOs and the private sector to support the implementation of actions on mercury. He was also asked to report on progress in 2005 and to compile a synthesis of views and options, including on the possibility of developing a legally binding instrument, a non-legally binding instrument or other measures. The Council decided to consider, in 2005, any further action that might be taken with regard to other heavy metals, for example, lead and cadmium.

Persistent organic pollutants

As at 31 December, 42 States were parties to the 2001 Stockholm Convention on Persistent Organic Pollutants (POPs) [YUN 2001, p. 971]. During the year, 15 States ratified the Convention and three acceded to it. The Convention would enter into force 90 days after the deposit of the fiftieth instrument of ratification, acceptance, approval or accession.

The seventh session of the Intergovernmental Negotiating Committee for an International Legally Binding Instrument for Implementing International Action on Certain POPs (Geneva, 14-18 July) [UNEP/POPS/INC.7/28] reviewed ongoing international activities relating to the Committee's work and considered secretariat activities, preparation for the Conference of the Parties to the Convention and administrative matters. It adopted decisions on reporting DDT use; a register for specific exemptions; exempted use of POPs; identification and quantification of releases of the toxic chemicals dioxin and furan; technical guidelines on the environmentally sound management of POP wastes; national implementation plans; technical assistance; a draft memorandum of understanding with GEF; reporting; and effectiveness evaluation.

The Expert Group on Best Available Techniques/ Best Environmental Practices, established by the Committee in 2002 [YUN 2002, p. 1064], held its first (Triangle Research Park, North Carolina, United States, 10-14 March) [UNEP/POPS/INC.7/6] and second (Villarrica, Chile, 8-12 December) [UNEP/POPS/EGB.2/3] sessions.

Governing Council action. On 7 February [dec. 22/4 II], the Governing Council invited States and regional economic integration organizations to ratify, accept, approve or accede to the Stockholm Convention, with a view to its entry into force by 2004, and authorized the continued participation of UNEP's secretariat in an interim secretariat of the Convention, as requested by the 2001 Conference of Plenipotentiaries [YUN 2001, p. 971]. The Executive Director was requested to promote cooperation between the interim secretariat and the secretariats of other conventions and to take actions regarding reduction of POPs as requested by the Governing Council in 1997 [YUN 1997, p. 1065].

He was urged to assist in implementing relevant resolutions of the Conference of Plenipotentiaries and the 2002 decisions of the Intergovernmental Negotiating Committee [YUN 2002, p. 1064]. The Executive Director was invited to facilitate voluntary implementation of the Convention prior to its entry into force. The Council appealed to Governments, intergovernmental organizations, NGOs and the private sector to provide financial resources for implementing interim arrangements prior to the first session of the Convention's Conference of the Parties.

Hazardous wastes

As at 31 December, the number of parties to the 1989 Basel Convention on the Control of Transboundary Movements of Hazardous Wastes and their Disposal [YUN 1989, p. 420], which entered into force in 1992 [YUN 1992, p. 685], rose to 158, with the accession of Equatorial Guinea, Ghana, Jamaica, Kazakhstan and the Marshall Islands. The 1995 amendment to the Convention [YUN 1995, p. 1333], not yet in force, had been ratified, accepted or approved by 43 parties. The 1999 Basel Protocol on Liability and Compensation for Damage Resulting from Transboundary Movements of Hazardous Wastes and their Disposal [YUN 1999, p. 998] had 13 signatories and one party (Ethiopia) at year's end.

The first session of the Open-ended Working Group of the Convention (Geneva, 28 April-2 May) [UNEP/CHW/OEWG/1/16] selected project proposals under the strategic plan for the implementation of the Convention to 2010, adopted by the Conference of the Parties to the Convention in 2002 [YUN 2002, p. 1065], and approved project funding of up to $880,000 for 2003-2004. Other decisions related to annexes II and IX to the Convention; management of end-of-life mobile phones; partnership with NGOs, industry and the business sector; hazardous characteristics listed in annex III to the Convention; identification of hazardous wastes; disposal of polyvinyl chloride (PVC); guidelines on management of waste POPs and on wastes from metals and plastics; and recycling/reclamation of metals.

The second session of the Working Group (Geneva, 20-24 October) [UNEP/CHW/OEWG/2/12] selected further project proposals and adopted an interim work plan for partnership with NGOs and the industry and business sectors. Other decisions concerned implementing the Basel Protocol on Liability and Compensation [YUN 1999, p. 998]; legal aspects of dismantling ships; national definitions of hazardous wastes; annexes II, VII and IX to the Convention; and guidelines on the management of wastes with POPs.

Cleaner production and sustainable consumption patterns

On 7 February [dec. 22/6], the Governing Council requested the Executive Director to strengthen UNEP's sustainable consumption and production activities, and existing eco-efficiency and cleaner production activities. He was further asked to support initiatives and activities to enhance corporate responsibility and accountability, and develop and facilitate consumer awareness campaigns; develop training, awareness-raising and capacity-building programmes in support of Governments, business and others, particularly in developing countries and countries with economies in transition, on sustainable production and consumption; take into account gender issues and differing circumstances in regions and countries; and take an active role in developing a 10-year framework of programmes to support regional and national initiatives on sustainable consumption and production, as set out in the Johannesburg Plan of Implementation [YUN 2002, p. 821]. The Executive Director was asked to report regularly to GC/GMEF and to the Commission on Sustainable Development.

International Expert Meeting. A December report of the Executive Director [UNEP/GCSS.VIII/6] provided information on activities to accelerate the shift to sustainable consumption and production patterns, including the outcome of the International Expert Meeting on the 10-Year Framework of Programmes for Sustainable Consumption and Production (Marrakech, Morocco, 16-19 June) (see p. 840).

Other matters

Environmental law

On 7 February [dec. 22/17 A], the Governing Council, taking note of the Executive Director's report on the 2002 Global Judges' Symposium on the Role of Law and Sustainable Development [YUN 2002, p. 1065], called on him to support, within the framework of the Programme for the Development and Periodic Review of Environmental Law for the First Decade of the Twenty-first Century (Montevideo Programme III), adopted by the Governing Council in 2001 [YUN 2001, p. 972], the improvement of the capacity of those involved in promoting, implementing, developing and enforcing environmental law at the national and local levels to carry out their functions with the necessary skills, information and material.

(For information on the human rights aspects of the illicit movement and dumping of toxic and dangerous products and wastes, see p. 771.)

The Executive Director was asked to report on progress in 2005.

In a further decision [dec. 22/17 D], the Executive Director was asked to report to the Council in 2005 on the implementation of Montevideo Programme III.

Occupied Palestinian and other Arab territories

In accordance with a 2002 Governing Council decision [YUN 2002, p. 1066], the Executive Director submitted a January note containing the Desk Study on the Environment in the Occupied Palestinian Territories [UNEP/GC.22/INF/31]. The Study, conducted by a team of environmental experts that visited the region in October 2002, contained recommendations on increasing transboundary and international cooperation concerning the environment in the region; developing a work plan from the Palestinian Authority's (PA) National Environment Action Plan and strengthening its Environmental Quality Authority, which was responsible for environmental administration in the Occupied Palestinian Territories; improving land-use planning; encouraging NGO cooperation between Palestinians and Israelis; increasing the private sector's involvement in environmental issues; and strengthening freshwater and wastewater management. The Study put forth short-, medium- and long-term recommendations to deal with solid wastes and hazardous wastes, and measures aimed at conservation and the protection of biodiversity.

Governing Council action. The Governing Council, on 7 February [dec. 22/1 V], requested the Executive Director to implement the Desk Study's recommendations. It asked him to make UNEP available to act as a facilitator and impartial moderator to assist in solving urgent environmental problems. It further requested him to facilitate the identification of technical and financial solutions to implement the recommendations; promote capacity-building programmes; encourage technology transfer; and promote the PA's participation in meetings and processes of multilateral environmental agreements. The Council called on Governments and international organizations to support the rehabilitation of the environment and reconstruction of damaged environmental infrastructure. The Executive Director was asked to report in 2005.

Follow-up to the International Year of Ecotourism (2002)

In accordance with Economic and Social Council resolution 1998/40 [YUN 1998, p. 999], the Secretary-General transmitted, in June, a report [A/58/96] prepared by the Secretary-General of the World Tourism Organization (WTO/OMT) on results of the International Year of Ecotourism, 2002 [YUN 2002, p. 1066], proclaimed by the General Assembly in resolution 53/200 [YUN 1998, p. 1000]. The report outlined activities undertaken by WTO/OMT, UNEP and other international organizations, and by Governments, in preparation for and during the Year. It also provided information on follow-up activities and recommendations for further action by UNEP and WTO/OMT, including guidelines for ecotourism and sustainable tourism policies, training in the public use of parks and nature interpretation, and fostering public-private partnerships.

Human settlements

Follow-up to the 1996 UN Conference on Human Settlements (Habitat II) and the 2001 General Assembly special session

Report of Executive Director. In January [HSP/GC/19/4], the Executive Director of the United Nations Human Settlements Programme (UN-Habitat) reported on follow-up to the General Assembly's twenty-fifth (2001) special session [YUN 2001, p. 973] to review implementation of the Habitat Agenda [YUN 1996, p. 994], adopted by the 1996 United Nations Conference on Human Settlements (Habitat II) [ibid., p. 992]. The report summarized highlights from the special session, the implementation process of the Declaration on Cities and Other Human Settlements in the New Millennium, adopted by the special session in resolution S-25/2 [YUN 2001, p. 974], and the transformation of the UN Centre for Human Settlements into UN-Habitat, and of the Commission on Human Settlements into UN-Habitat's Governing Council (see p. 1078). It also described the reorganization and upgrading of UN-Habitat and its enhanced focus on both process and substance.

Report of Secretary-General. In July [A/58/178], the Secretary-General, in response to General Assembly resolution 57/275 [YUN 2002, p. 1070], reported on follow-up to the special session. As requested by the 2002 International Conference on Financing for Development [ibid., p. 953] and Assembly resolution 56/206 [YUN 2001, p. 987], Governments worked with UN-Habitat to explore ways to mobilize domestic financial resources for sustainable urbanization, especially in developing countries and countries with economies in transition. Following a review of the UN Habitat and Human Settlements Foundation (see p. 1084), UN-Habitat proposed a global shelter facility or similar mechanism to fight urban poverty. Governments reiterated the need for increased financial support for UN-Habitat, resulting in a predicted 28 per cent rise in general-purpose contributions, from $6 million in 2002 to $7.7 million by July 2003. UN-Habitat collaborated with international financial institutions to encourage implementation of the Habitat Agenda and the MDG target of significantly improving the lives of at least 100 million slum-dwellers by 2020 [YUN 2000, p. 52]. The Cities Alliance partnership between the World Bank and UN-Habitat continued to provide a forum for policy coordination and support for pro-poor city development strategies and slum-upgrading programmes. UN-Habitat established a Water and Sanitation Trust Fund within the Habitat and Human Settlements Foundation to facilitate the achievement of the MDG and the related targets of reducing by half the proportion of people without sustainable access to safe water and sanitation (see below).

The Fourth Global Forum of Parliamentarians on Habitat (Berlin, 12-14 May) adopted the Berlin Declaration, which called on Governments to increase financial support for the realization of the MDG on slums and ensure predictable financial resources for UN-Habitat to strengthen its work on poverty alleviation. Follow-up activities to the UN-Habitat campaigns on secure tenure and urban governance, launched in 2000 [YUN 2000, p. 995], were supported by the Cities Alliance, with a view to preparing participatory pro-poor strategies. Seven city development strategy exercises were completed and a synthesis was prepared through the Urban Management Programme, an effort by UN-Habitat, UNDP and other support agencies.

In the light of water- and infrastructure-related activities of NEPAD (see p. 937), UN-Habitat was formulating a second phase of the Managing Water for African Cities Programme, the first activity to be funded from the Water and Sanitation Trust Fund (see above), to promote increased investment in the seven cities already involved (Abidjan, Côte d'Ivoire; Accra, Ghana; Addis Ababa, Ethiopia; Dakar, Senegal; Johannesburg, South Africa; Lusaka, Zambia; and Nairobi) and to promote improved sanitation and pro-poor governance structures.

Following the decision of the eleventh (2003) session of the Commission on Sustainable Development to focus on water, sanitation and human settlements at its 2004 and 2005 sessions (see p. 842), UN-Habitat was designated the task manager for drafting a scoping paper on human settlements. It entered a partnership with the

United Nations Statistics Division for monitoring the implementation of the MDG target on slums; created 11 partnerships in the Coalition for Sustainable Urbanization aimed at implementing the 2002 Johannesburg Declaration and Plan of Implementation [YUN 2002, p. 821]; entered into the Partnership for Local Capacity Development, designed to promote cohesion and collective efficiency in making international support available for the development of local capacities for sustainable urbanization; and monitored relevant partnerships.

The Secretary-General encouraged Governments to increase their contributions in order to ensure the viability of the UN Habitat and Human Settlements Foundation in its enhanced role [YUN 2002, p. 1068] (see p. 1084); to review UN-Habitat's Partnership Agreement to determine how it might fit into countries' development assistance programmes; to facilitate partnerships at the national and local levels, in implementing the Habitat Agenda and the relevant MDGs; to facilitate the participation of representatives of the poor and vulnerable in the second (2004) World Urban Forum; and to establish national urban observatories and urge local urban observatories to collect, analyse and report information on urban conditions and trends in order to formulate urban development policies. They were called on to incorporate the question of human settlements in their national development policy plans, their United Nations Development Assistance Frameworks (UNDAFs), poverty reduction strategy papers and other relevant development plans.

Coordinated implementation of Habitat Agenda

In May [E/2003/76], the Secretary-General reported on the implementation of Economic and Social Council resolution 2002/38 [YUN 2002, p. 1069] regarding the coordinated implementation of the Habitat Agenda. The report discussed the recent increase in contributions to the United Nations Habitat and Human Settlements Foundation (see p. 1084) and collaboration with international financial institutions and regional development banks. It outlined UN-Habitat's cooperation with local authorities, relations with NGOs, partnership with civil society organizations, and relations with the private sector and with youth organizations and women's groups. It described the establishment of the Habitat Agenda Task Manager System, which was supported by the Assembly in the 2001 Declaration on Cities and Other Human Settlements [YUN 2001, p. 974], and collaboration between UN-Habitat and other UN system entities.

The Secretary-General encouraged Governments to increase their contributions for implementation of the Habitat Agenda, the 2001 Declaration and the MDGs, and facilitate partnerships at the national and local levels with civil society organizations, local authorities and the business sector. They were called on to support UN-Habitat's youth programme, especially in Africa, in the areas of youth employment and crime prevention. Members of UN country teams working on the common country assessment (CCA) and UNDAF, together with national partners, were urged to call on UN-Habitat to include the issues of shelter, sustainable human settlements and urban poverty in preparing the CCA and UNDAF.

ECONOMIC AND SOCIAL COUNCIL ACTION

On 25 July [meeting 49], the Economic and Social Council adopted **resolution 2003/62** [draft: E/2003/L.12] without vote [agenda item 13 (d)].

Coordinated implementation of the Habitat Agenda

The Economic and Social Council,

Recalling its resolution 2002/38 of 26 July 2002 and General Assembly resolutions 3327(XXIX) of 16 December 1974, 32/162 of 19 December 1977, 56/206 of 26 December 2001 and 57/275 of 20 December 2002,

Recalling also the Istanbul Declaration on Human Settlements, the Habitat Agenda and the Declaration on Cities and Other Human Settlements in the New Millennium, which focused on adequate shelter for all and sustainable human settlements,

Recalling further the goal contained in the United Nations Millennium Declaration of achieving a significant improvement in the lives of at least 100 million slum-dwellers by 2020, and the relevant decisions contained in the Plan of Implementation of the World Summit on Social Development ("Johannesburg Plan of Implementation"), to halve, by 2015, the proportion of people who are unable to reach or to afford safe drinking water, as outlined in the Millennium Declaration, and the proportion of people who do not have access to basic sanitation,

Recalling that Governments have the primary responsibility for the sound and effective implementation of the Habitat Agenda and the Declaration on Cities and Other Human Settlements in the New Millennium, and stressing that the international community should fully implement its commitments to support Governments of developing countries and countries with economies in transition in their efforts, through the provision of requisite resources, capacity-building, transfer of technology and the creation of an international enabling environment,

Welcoming the progress made in the revitalization of the United Nations Human Settlements Programme (UN-Habitat) and the United Nations Habitat and Human Settlements Foundation,

Commending those countries which have contributed to the Foundation, as indicated in the report of the Secretary-General,

Expressing concern at the relatively low level of non-earmarked contributions, leading to the continuing and growing imbalance between earmarked and non-earmarked contributions to the Foundation,

Recognizing the need for increased and predictable financial contributions to the Foundation in the new millennium to ensure timely, effective and concrete results in the implementation of the Habitat Agenda, the Declaration on Cities and Other Human Settlements in the New Millennium and the relevant internationally agreed development goals, including those contained in the Millennium Declaration and the Johannesburg Plan of Implementation, particularly in developing countries,

Taking note of efforts by UN-Habitat to implement the Habitat Agenda and the Declaration on Cities and Other Human Settlements in the New Millennium,

Taking note also of the report of the Secretary-General,

1. *Underlines* the commitments made by Governments to implement the Habitat Agenda, the Declaration on Cities and Other Human Settlements in the New Millennium, and the development goal contained in the United Nations Millennium Declaration of achieving a significant improvement in the lives of at least 100 million slum-dwellers by 2020;

2. *Invites* Governments in a position to do so to increase their financial contributions to the United Nations Habitat and Human Settlements Foundation, and invites international financial institutions, as appropriate, to assist developing countries in the implementation of the Habitat Agenda, the Declaration on Cities and Other Human Settlements in the New Millennium and the goal contained in the Millennium Declaration of achieving a significant improvement in the lives of at least 100 million slum-dwellers by 2020, while giving due consideration to marginalized groups;

3. *Welcomes* decision 19/18 of 9 May 2003 of the Governing Council of UN-Habitat endorsing the establishment of the Special Human Settlements Programme for the Palestinian people and the Technical Cooperation Trust Fund of 5 million United States dollars for an initial period of two years, and urges the international donor community and all financial institutions to support UN-Habitat in the immediate mobilization of financial resources for the establishment and operation of the Programme and the Fund;

4. *Invites* Governments to facilitate furthering of partnerships at the national and local levels, as appropriate, with civil society organizations, local authorities, women's groups, the business sector and other Habitat Agenda partners in implementing the Habitat Agenda and the relevant targets of the Millennium Declaration;

5. *Encourages* Governments to support and enable the participation of youth in the implementation of the Habitat Agenda through social, cultural and economic activities at the city level and in other national and local activities;

6. *Encourages* UN-Habitat to continue to implement the Habitat Agenda and the Declaration on Cities and Other Human Settlements in the New Millennium, including by promoting partnerships with local authorities, non-governmental organizations and private sector and other Habitat Agenda partners;

7. *Requests* the Executive Director of UN-Habitat to strengthen the implementation of the Habitat Agenda Task Manager System to allow better monitoring and mutual enforcement of actions taken in the implementation of the Habitat Agenda;

8. *Calls* for increased cooperation between UN-Habitat and other members of the United Nations Development Group through existing coordination mechanisms such as the common country assessment and the United Nations Development Assistance Framework processes;

9. *Encourages* Governments to include issues pertaining to shelter and sustainable human settlements and urban poverty in their national development strategies, including poverty reduction strategy papers, where they exist;

10. *Requests* the Secretary-General to submit a report to the Council at its substantive session of 2004 on the implementation of the present resolution.

GENERAL ASSEMBLY ACTION

On 23 December [meeting 78], the General Assembly, on the recommendation of the Second Committee [A/58/491], adopted **resolution 58/226** without vote [agenda item 101].

Implementation of the outcome of the United Nations Conference on Human Settlements (Habitat II) and the strengthening of the United Nations Human Settlements Programme (UN-Habitat)

The General Assembly,

Recalling its resolutions 3327(XXIX) of 16 December 1974, 32/162 of 19 December 1977, 34/115 of 14 December 1979, 56/205 and 56/206 of 21 December 2001 and 57/275 of 20 December 2002,

Taking note of Economic and Social Council resolutions 2002/38 of 26 July 2002 and 2003/62 of 25 July 2003,

Recalling the Habitat Agenda and the Declaration on Cities and Other Human Settlements in the New Millennium,

Recalling also the goal contained in the United Nations Millennium Declaration of achieving a significant improvement in the lives of at least 100 million slum-dwellers by 2020, as proposed in the Cities Without Slums Initiative, and recalling further the goal contained in the Plan of Implementation of the World Summit on Sustainable Development ("Johannesburg Plan of Implementation") to halve, by the year 2015, the proportion of people who are unable to reach or afford safe drinking water and the proportion of people who do not have access to basic sanitation,

Taking into account the Johannesburg Declaration on Sustainable Development and the Johannesburg Plan of Implementation, as well as the Monterrey Consensus of the International Conference on Financing for Development,

Recognizing that the overall thrust of the new strategic vision of the United Nations Human Settlements Programme (UN-Habitat) and its emphasis on the two global campaigns on secure tenure and urban governance are strategic points of entry for the effective implementation of the Habitat Agenda, especially for guiding international cooperation in respect of adequate shelter for all and sustainable human settlements development,

Conscious of the need to achieve greater coherence and effectiveness in the implementation of the Habitat

Agenda, the Declaration on Cities and Other Human Settlements in the New Millennium and the relevant internationally agreed development goals, including those contained in the Millennium Declaration,

Recognizing the need for increased and predictable financial contributions to the United Nations Habitat and Human Settlements Foundation in the new millennium to ensure timely, effective and concrete results in the implementation of the Habitat Agenda, the Declaration on Cities and Other Human Settlements in the New Millennium and the relevant internationally agreed development goals, including those contained in the Millennium Declaration and the Johannesburg Declaration and Plan of Implementation, particularly in developing countries,

Welcoming the establishment by the Executive Director of UN-Habitat of a Water and Sanitation Trust Fund as a financing mechanism to support the creation of enabling environments for pro-poor investment in water and sanitation in developing-country cities,

Commending those countries that have contributed to the United Nations Habitat and Human Settlements Foundation, as indicated in the report of the Secretary-General to the Economic and Social Council,

Reiterating the call to the Executive Director of UN-Habitat to increase her efforts to strengthen the Foundation in order to achieve its primary operative objective, as set out in resolution 3327(XXIX), of supporting the implementation of the Habitat Agenda, including supporting shelter, related infrastructure-development programmes and housing-finance institutions and mechanisms, particularly in developing countries,

Recalling the decision of the Commission on Sustainable Development at its eleventh session to address the themes of water, sanitation and human settlements in its next review and policy sessions,

Noting the efforts by UN-Habitat to forge partnerships with Habitat Agenda partners, other United Nations funds and programmes and international financial institutions, such as the World Bank,

Recognizing that shelter and human settlements planning and administration are important sectors in humanitarian efforts,

Expressing its appreciation to the Government of Spain and the city of Barcelona for their willingness to host the second session of the World Urban Forum in 2004 and to the Government of Canada and the city of Vancouver for their willingness to host the third session of the World Urban Forum in 2006,

1. *Takes note* of the report of the Governing Council of the United Nations Human Settlements Programme (UN-Habitat) on the work of its nineteenth session and the report of the Secretary-General on the special session of the General Assembly for an overall review and appraisal of the implementation of the outcome of the United Nations Conference on Human Settlements (Habitat II) and the strengthening of UN-Habitat;

2. *Recognizes* that Governments have the primary responsibility for the sound and effective implementation of the Habitat Agenda and the Declaration on Cities and Other Human Settlements in the New Millennium, and stresses that the international community should fully implement its commitments to support the Governments of developing countries and countries with economies in transition in their efforts, through the provision of the requisite resources, capacity-building, the transfer of technology and the creation of an international enabling environment;

3. *Encourages* Governments to include issues pertaining to shelter and sustainable human settlements and urban poverty in their national development strategies, including poverty reduction strategy papers, where they exist;

4. *Urges* Governments to promote pro-poor investments in services and infrastructure, in particular water and sanitation, in order to improve living environments, in particular in slums and informal settlements;

5. *Encourages* Governments to establish local, national and regional urban observatories and to provide financial and substantive support to UN-Habitat for the further development of methodologies for data collection, analysis and dissemination;

6. *Also encourages* Governments to support and enable the participation of youth in the implementation of the Habitat Agenda through social, cultural and economic activities at the city level and other national- and local-level activities;

7. *Encourages* Governments and UN-Habitat to continue to promote partnerships with local authorities, non-governmental organizations, the private sector and other Habitat Agenda partners, including women's groups and academic and professional groups, in order to empower them, within the legal framework and conditions of each country, to play a more effective role in the provision of adequate shelter for all and sustainable human settlements development in an urbanizing world;

8. *Encourages* UN-Habitat to continue to work closely with other relevant agencies within the United Nations system, in particular members and observers of the United Nations Development Group and the members of the Inter-Agency Standing Committee;

9. *Requests* UN-Habitat to strengthen further its efforts to make the Cities Alliance initiative an effective means for the implementation of the twin goals of the Habitat Agenda, namely, adequate shelter for all and sustainable human settlements development in an urbanizing world;

10. *Takes note with appreciation* of the efforts by the Cities Alliance partnership between the World Bank and UN-Habitat, and other donor countries, to continue to provide an important forum for policy coordination and development, as well as to provide support for the preparation of pro-poor city development strategies and slum-upgrading programmes within the legal framework and conditions of each country;

11. *Invites* the Secretary-General to incorporate the assessment of the progress towards the target of achieving a significant improvement in the lives of at least 100 million slum-dwellers by 2020 in his report on the review in 2005 of the implementation of the United Nations Millennium Declaration;

12. *Welcomes* the fund-raising efforts of the Executive Director of UN-Habitat, which realized an increase in the general-purpose contributions of the United Nations Habitat and Human Settlements Foundation for the year 2003;

13. *Calls* for continued financial support to UN-Habitat through increased voluntary contributions to

the Foundation, and invites Governments to provide multi-year funding to support programme implementation;

14. *Requests* UN-Habitat to collaborate with the Division for Sustainable Development of the Department of Economic and Social Affairs of the Secretariat in the preparations for the twelfth session of the Commission on Sustainable Development to promote a fruitful discussion on the thematic cluster of issues on water, sanitation and human settlements;

15. *Requests* the Executive Director of UN-Habitat to inform the Governing Council of the United Nations Human Settlements Programme of the results of the discussions on the topics of water, sanitation and human settlements at the twelfth session of the Commission on Sustainable Development;

16. *Notes* that the upcoming sessions of the World Urban Forum, a non-legislative technical forum, which will be held in Barcelona in 2004 and in Vancouver in 2006, will offer an opportunity to experts to exchange experiences, best practices and lessons learned in the field of human settlements;

17. *Invites* donor countries to support the participation of representatives of the developing countries in the second and future sessions of the World Urban Forum;

18. *Requests* the Secretary-General to keep the resource needs of UN-Habitat and the United Nations Office at Nairobi under review so as to permit the delivery, in an effective manner, of necessary services to UN-Habitat and the other United Nations organs and organizations in Nairobi;

19. *Requests* UN-Habitat, as the focal point for human settlements development and for coordination of human settlements activities within the United Nations system, to work towards coordination of human settlements issues as inputs to the overall coordination of humanitarian efforts, including through its participation in the consideration by the Economic and Social Council, in the near future, of the issue of the transition from relief to development;

20. *Requests* the Secretary-General to submit a report to the General Assembly at its fifty-ninth session on the implementation of the present resolution;

21. *Decides* to include in the provisional agenda of its fifty-ninth session an item entitled "Special session of the General Assembly for an overall review and appraisal of the implementation of the outcome of the United Nations Conference on Human Settlements (Habitat II) and the strengthening of the United Nations Human Settlements Programme (UN-Habitat)".

UN Human Settlements Programme

Governing Council

The Governing Council of the United Nations Human Settlements Programme (UN-Habitat), which was transformed from the former Commission on Human Settlements in 2001 by the General Assembly in resolution 56/206 [YUN 2001, p. 987], held its first session in 2003. To signify the continuity and relationship between the former Commission and the Governing Council, the session was designated as the nineteenth session (Nairobi, 5-9 May) [A/58/8]. The Council adopted 18 resolutions, one of which recommended the adoption of its draft rules of procedure by the General Assembly [res. 19/1] (see p. 1079). In a resolution on countries with economies in transition [res. 19/15], the Council asked the Executive Director to assist in mobilizing additional funding from sources indicated in the 2001 Declaration on Cities and Other Human Settlements, adopted by the twenty-fifth special session of the General Assembly in resolution S-25/2 [YUN 2001, p. 974], and from other sources; invited her to incorporate countries with economies in transition in UN-Habitat's global programmes and campaigns; and requested her to report in 2005. A further resolution [res. 19/17] requested UN-Habitat to continue to give special attention to LDCs in its programme activities; the Council asked the Executive Director to mainstream the implementation of the 2001 Programme of Action for the Least Developed Countries for the Decade 2001-2010, adopted by General Assembly resolution 55/279 [YUN 2001, p. 771], in UN-Habitat activities and intergovernmental processes, and called on her to cooperate with the Office of the High Representative for the Least Developed Countries, Landlocked Developing Countries and Small Island Developing States to ensure implementation of the 2001 Brussels Declaration on LDCs [ibid., p. 770] and the Programme of Action for the Decade.

The Executive Director was asked to advance UN-Habitat's work programme in the engagement of youth in urban governance and in addressing the problem of youth at risk; ensure UN-Habitat's participation in the Secretary-General's initiative on youth employment [YUN 2002, p. 1192]; develop a Global Partnership Initiative on Urban Youth Development in Africa; establish an interim youth consultative mechanism and initiate a draft strategy on enhancing youth engagement in UN-Habitat's work; and report in 2005 [res. 19/13].

Having considered a report of the Executive Director on decentralization [HSP/GC/19/14], the Council decided that the special themes of its twentieth (2005) session would be involvement of civil society in improving local governance, and post-conflict and natural and human-made disaster assessment and reconstruction [res. 19/9]. Taking note of the secretariat report on the rural dimension of sustainable urban development [HS/GC/19/6], the Council requested the Executive Director to raise awareness regarding positive urban-rural development linkages and sustainable urbanization, disseminate good practices and policies, and report in 2005 [res. 19/10]. The Council endorsed a proposal made in the Executive Director's report on dialogues on effective decentralization and strengthening of local authorities [HSP/GC/19/7] to establish a multidisciplinary ad hoc advisory panel on decentralization. She was asked to intensify dialogue on decentralization and strengthening local authorities among Governments, local authorities and other Habitat Agenda partners, and report in 2005 [res. 19/12]. In another resolution [res. 19/8], the Council decided on arrangements for the accreditation of local authorities and other Habitat Agenda partners. Regarding the second (2004) session of the World Urban Forum [res. 19/14], the Council requested the Executive Director to take into account the work of the Council's current session in preparing the Forum's provisional agenda and documentation, and report in 2005.

Regarding UN-Habitat's global campaigns on secure tenure and urban governance, launched in 2000 [YUN 2000, p. 995], the Executive Director was asked to expand the campaigns; further mainstream the campaigns' principles through UN-Habitat regional offices, regional anchor institutions, urban observatories, national and local institutions, and other networks; enhance synergy with UN organizations; and report in 2005 [res. 19/3].

On 9 May [res. 19/2], the Council approved the 2004-2005 draft work programme [HSP/GC/19/8 & Add.1 & Add.1/Corr.1] and budget of $44.4 million for 2004-2005 [HSP/GC/19/9/Add.3], as presented by the Executive Director, following the submission of an earlier budget proposal [HSP/GC/19/9], a review by the Advisory Committee on Administrative and Budgetary Questions (ACABQ) [HSP/GC/19/9/Add.1] and supplementary information [HSP/GC/19/9/Add.2]. It authorized the Executive Director to make commitments up to $50.5 million and approved an increase in the 2004-2005 general-purpose statutory reserve from $1 million to $2.4 million. The Executive Director was asked to submit in 2005 the 2006-2007 budget and work programme and to report regularly on the work programme.

Resolutions on implementing the MDG on slum-dwellers [res. 19/5], cooperation between UN-Habitat and UNEP [res. 19/4], water and sanitation in cities [res. 19/6], regional and technical cooperation [res. 19/7], strengthening the United Nations Habitat and Human Settlements Foundation [res. 19/11], women's role and rights in human settlements development and slum upgrading [res. 19/16], and human settlements in the Occupied Palestinian Territory [res. 19/8] are covered below.

The Commission considered a theme paper on urban development and shelter strategies in favour of the urban poor [HSP/GC/19/5]; and reports on cooperation with UN system agencies and organizations, intergovernmental organizations and NGOs [HSP/GC/19/12] and on matters arising from the resolutions adopted by UN bodies [HSP/GC/19/13]. It also considered a note by the Executive Director [HSP/GC/19/10] on the proposed UN-Habitat 2006-2009 medium-term plan.

On 10 July, the Economic and Social Council took note of the Governing Council's report [A/58/8] (**decision 2003/309**).

Rules of procedure

Annexed to the Governing Council's report was the report of the Working Group on the Rules of Procedure of the Governing Council, established by the Council on 5 May to consider the draft rules of procedure set forth by the Executive Director [HSP/GC/19/3/Add.2]. The draft rules were prepared by the Committee of Permanent Representatives to UN-Habitat and adopted by the Working Group. Also annexed to the Working Group's report was the statement by the Chairman of the Group giving a legal interpretation of the phrase "recognized by the United Nations" in draft rule 64. On 9 May [res. 19/1], the Governing Council recommended to the General Assembly the adoption of the Council's draft rules of procedure, which were attached to the resolution. The draft rules dealt with the duration and place of Council sessions; provisional agendas; representation and credentials; Bureau officers and their functions; subsidiary organs; duties of the Executive Director and the secretariat; official and working languages; public meetings; the conduct of Council business; the decision-making process; participation of non-members; and changes to the rules of procedure.

GENERAL ASSEMBLY ACTION

On 23 December [meeting 78], the General Assembly, on the recommendation of the Second Committee [A/58/491], adopted **resolution 58/227** without vote [agenda item 101].

Rules of procedure of the Governing Council of the United Nations Human Settlements Programme (UN-Habitat)

The General Assembly,

Recalling its resolution 32/162 of 19 December 1977, in which it established the Commission on Human Settlements and the United Nations Centre for Human Settlements (Habitat),

Recalling also its resolution 56/206 of 21 December 2001, in which it decided to transform the United Nations Centre for Human Settlements (Habitat) into the secretariat of the United Nations Human Settlements Programme (UN-Habitat), and the Commission on Human Settlements into the Governing Council of UN-Habitat, a subsidiary organ of the General Assembly,

Having considered the recommendation of the Governing Council, in its resolution 19/1 of 9 May 2003, that the General Assembly adopt its draft rules of procedure as contained in the annex to that resolution, and the oral statement by the Chairman of the Working Group on Rules of Procedure of the Governing Council,

Adopts the draft rules of procedure of the Governing Council of the United Nations Human Settlements Programme (UN-Habitat) as contained in the annex to Governing Council resolution 19/1.

UN-Habitat activities

UN-Habitat's operational activities in 2003 helped Governments create policies and strategies aimed at strengthening a self-reliant management capacity at the national and local levels, and focused on promoting shelter for all, improving urban governance, reducing urban poverty, improving the environment, and managing disaster mitigation and post-conflict rehabilitation.

Under the Safer Cities Programme, UN-Habitat organized the International Safer Cities Conference "Sustainable Safety: Municipalities at the Crossroads" (Durban, South Africa, 25-28 November) and the Africities Summit (Yaoundé, Cameroon, 2-6 December). A safer cities training manual for local authorities was developed. UN-Habitat had some 154 technical projects in 61 countries, most of them in LDCs, including projects in the post-war societies of Afghanistan, the Democratic Republic of the Congo, Iraq, Kosovo, Rwanda and Somalia.

UN-Habitat's Global Campaign for Urban Governance, which supported sustainable human settlements development in urban areas through improved governance [YUN 2000, p. 995], and its Global Campaign for Secure Tenure, an advocacy instrument [ibid.], were helping to transform institutional structures, initiate policy and legislative changes, and enhance organizational capacities in 27 countries. In 2003, governance and secure tenure campaigns were launched at the national level in Brazil; an expert group meeting was organized in Egypt as part of the regional campaigns on those issues in the Arab States; preparations for campaign launches were initiated in Cuba, Ghana, Indonesia, Mexico, Nepal, Peru and Uganda, and preparations were advanced in Burkina Faso, Morocco and Senegal; and follow-up activities were held in Afghanistan, Bangladesh, Cambodia, India, Jamaica, the Philippines and South Africa.

The fourth phase (2001-2005) of the Urban Management Programme (UMP), a joint technical assistance project of UN-Habitat and UNDP, focused on achieving maximum impact at the city level through consolidating and enhancing the city consultation process. UMP also provided a platform for its partners—19 anchor institutions and over 40 local and national institutions—to work on emerging urban management themes. The Sustainable Cities Programme focused on environmental planning and management capacities in the Gambia, Nigeria, Sri Lanka and other countries, and management tools were locally adapted and translated in Cuba, Morocco, the Russian Federation and Sri Lanka.

UN-Habitat continued in-country activities to achieve the MDG on slums [YUN 2000, p. 52]. Activities related to the Three Cities Project (Durban, South Africa; Mumbai, India; and Manila, Philippines) and to the cities without slums subregional programme for Eastern and Southern Africa [YUN 2002, p. 1072], which were initiated in Lesotho, Mozambique, South Africa, Uganda and the United Republic of Tanzania. UN-Habitat published *Guidelines for National Implementation of the Global Campaign for Secure Tenure* and a revised concept paper on the campaign. The Housing Rights Programme, a joint initiative of UN-Habitat and the Office of the UN High Commissioner for Human Rights, developed indicators to monitor realization of the human right to adequate housing. To monitor achievement of the MDG on slums, UN-Habitat implemented its first survey for monitoring urban inequities in Addis Ababa; five other such surveys were implemented as a part of demographic and health surveys of Bangladesh, Bolivia, Egypt, Ghana, the Philippines and Turkey. Ten urban observatories and local indicators facilities were set up in Africa, the Far East and Latin America. UN-Habitat's flagship report, *The Challenge of Slums: Global Report on Human Settlements 2003*, provided a baseline for the global monitoring of progress towards the realization of the MDG on slums by assessing globally the number of slum-dwellers and the physical extent and characteristics of slums; determining the forces underlying the emergence and development of slums; assessing their social, spatial and economic characteristics; assessing policy responses to slums, including those of the private sector, international organizations and civil society; and exploring future policy directions.

UN-Habitat expanded its training and capacity-building programmes in Africa and the Arab States, providing technical and methodological support through training of trainers and ongoing technical cooperation projects. It also produced training publications, implemented subregional and national training of trainers workshops, and conducted six major training workshops.

In 2003, UN-Habitat organized an expert group meeting on gender and women's issues in human settlements, which recommended priority areas for action at the local, national, regional and international levels, and led to the adoption by the Governing Council of a resolution on women's roles and rights in human settlements development and slum upgrading (see p. 1083). Other outcomes included adoption of a women's development code, in collaboration with governmental and women's organizations, and initiation of the Akshara Visakha literacy programme in India, in which 11,000 women from 208 slums were enrolled. UN-Habitat published its *Gender Evaluation Report, June 2003*.

Throughout 2003, UN-Habitat continued to implement the settlements rehabilitation programme in Iraq, addressing the needs of over 800,000 internally displaced persons and other vulnerable groups. The handover of the programme to the Coalition Provisional Authority on 21 November included 2,854 completed projects valued at $234 million, 185 ongoing projects valued at $94.5 million, assets amounting to $39.8 million and international purchase orders of $61.7 million. UN-Habitat formed a High-level Advisory Panel for the Reconstruction of Iraq to engage with Iraqi professionals and Ministers of Planning and Development Cooperation and to place a new UN-Habitat programme under Iraqi ownership. It also produced two publications: *UN-Habitat in Iraq, April 2003* and *Rebuilding Iraq—Iraq Reconstruction Plan for Shelter and Urban Development, October 2003*.

A new governance and development planning programme was formulated in Kosovo, and the disaster management programme continued its activities there in collaboration with the United Nations Interim Administration Mission in Kosovo (UNMIK).

In 2003, 63 projects and programmes were under way in 30 countries in the Africa and Arab States region, including a regional urban profile study, to be completed in 2004. In collaboration with UNDP, UN-Habitat programme manager offices were set up in Burundi, Cameroon, the Democratic Republic of the Congo, Egypt, Ethiopia, Nigeria, South Africa and the United Republic of Tanzania. UN-Habitat was producing profiles of the cities of Bamako (Mali), Douala (Cameroon), Durban (South Africa), Lagos (Nigeria), Lusaka (Zambia), Nairobi (Kenya) and Rabat (Morocco) as a basis for development plans and investment project identification. In Asia and the Pacific, 40 projects were under way in 2003. Projects in the Latin America and the Caribbean region included the Central American programme on vulnerability reduction and the programme on urban security. Reports were issued covering gender, participatory monitoring of programmes, upgrading policies in Central America, urban water and sanitation, and a review of best practices in the region.

Strategic vision

An April secretariat note [HSP/GC/19/INF/10] updated information on UN-Habitat's strategic vision, which was adopted by the Governing Council in 1999 [YUN 1999, p. 1003]. The strategic vision comprised: knowledge management and reporting, expanding the global understanding of urban development, shelter and poverty, and tracking progress in implementing the Habitat Agenda; advocacy of norms for sustainable urbanization and urban poverty reduction, through two global campaigns (see p. 1080) and a number of global programmes; technical cooperation in linking norms and campaign/programme goals to urban poverty reduction activities; innovative financing for urbanization and specific shelter needs of the urban poor; and strategic partnerships to leverage resources and coordinate international programme activities. The note also discussed the urbanization of poverty and the need to strengthen local authorities to address that challenge; the UN response to urbanization; and the programmatic framework for the strategic vision.

Cooperation with UNEP

On 9 May [res. 19/4], the Governing Council, having considered a joint progress report of the Executive Directors of UN-Habitat and of UNEP on cooperation between the two programmes [HSP/GC/19/11], requested the UN-Habitat Executive Director to continue to implement General Assembly resolution 53/242 [YUN 1999, p. 975] and to expand cooperation between UN-Habitat and UNEP. She was asked to intensify joint work in the sustainable cities, managing water for African cities, and disaster management programmes and similar joint programmes, and establish a mechanism for coordinated oversight; make effective the Habitat Agenda task manager system (see p. 1075) to promote efficiency among Habitat Agenda partners in relation to the biennial session of the World Urban Forum, taking into account UN system-wide coordination mechanisms; and report in 2005.

MDG implementation

With a view to achieving the MDG of significantly improving the lives of 100 million slum-dwellers by 2020 [YUN 2000, p. 52], the Governing Council [res. 19/5] requested the Executive Director to present a strategy paper to the Committee of Permanent Representatives for its approval; explore options to increase financial resources to support the Goal, taking into account the Monterrey Consensus of the International Conference on Financing for Development [YUN 2002, p. 953]; further develop and strengthen UN-Habitat's collaboration with the Cities Alliance, all relevant stakeholders and other UN agencies, including the Bretton Woods institutions; assist Governments in developing policy guidelines and action plans, in particular through implementing the Global Campaigns for Secure Tenure and for Urban Governance; establish an advisory group to monitor, identify and promote alternatives to unlawful evictions; strengthen the Global Urban Observatory; and report in 2005. Governments and local authorities were invited to allocate the necessary resources to meet the human settlements Goals of the 2000 United Nations Millennium Declaration [YUN 2000, p. 49], and to develop and implement national and local action plans for upgrading slums. Member States and Habitat Agenda partners were invited to support UN-Habitat in developing methodologies for data collection and dissemination and to evaluate concepts and sources of city and intra-city statistics.

Water and sanitation

An April secretariat note [HSP/GC/19/INF/6] discussed the report *Water and Sanitation in the World's Cities: Local Action for Global Goals*, a UN-Habitat contribution to the International Year of Freshwater, 2003 (see p. 1033). The report called for local and national action to achieve the MDG to reduce by half the proportion of people without sustainable access to safe drinking water by 2015 [YUN 2000, p. 52] and the MDG on slums [ibid.]. It focused on knowledge and information gaps in vital areas that affected decision-making, analysed the causes of deficiencies in services and suggested priority actions.

On 9 May [res. 19/6], the Governing Council requested the Executive Director to strengthen and promote UN-Habitat's work in urban drinking water and sanitation. She was asked to develop a programme for water and sanitation in human settlements in countries with economies in transition; to consult with Governments in other regions on the possibility of establishing or strengthening water and sanitation programmes in cities; and to publish *Water and Sanitation in the World's Cities* as a recurrent publication every three years.

Regional and technical cooperation

The Governing Council, on 9 May [res. 19/7], urged the Executive Director to strengthen efforts to make the Cities Alliance initiative an effective means for implementing the goals of the Habitat Agenda—adequate shelter for all and sustainable human settlements in an urbanizing world—as requested by the General Assembly in resolution 57/275 [YUN 2002, p. 1070], and invited host countries to support the placement of locally recruited UN-Habitat programme managers in selected UNDP offices. Noting the emerging cooperation between UN-Habitat and regional development banks to promote sustainable urbanization in developing countries, it called on the Executive Director to pursue such initiatives in other regions. The Executive Director was asked, in the context of the update of the UN-Habitat regionalization strategy [HSP/GC/19/INF/9], to strengthen UN-Habitat's regional presence, including by strengthening the existing regional offices, and to study the establishment of new offices. The Council recommended that UN-Habitat operational activities be associated with the Global Campaigns for Secure Tenure and for Urban Governance, and focus on the MDGs and the Plan of Implementation of the 2002 World Summit on Sustainable Development [YUN 2002, p. 821] related to water, sanitation, waste management, integrated transportation systems and slum upgrading, and on capacity-building in support of sustainable urbanization policies at the country and city levels. It also recommended that UN-Habitat devote specific attention to human settlements needs in the reconstruction of countries and territories affected by armed conflicts or by other disasters, in close coordination with multilateral and bilateral agencies, and that it ensure links and continuity between the humanitarian and developmental requirements of the human settlements sector.

Occupied Palestinian Territory

Pursuant to a 2001 Commission on Human Settlements resolution [YUN 2001, p. 984], the Executive Director submitted a March report on the housing situation in the Occupied Palestinian Territory and establishment of a human settlements fund for Palestinians living in that Territory [HSP/GC/19/2/Add.3]. It found that the key housing challenge was the lack of control over the limited land available to Palestinians. Among the negative impacts on land were the expansion of Israeli settlements and the building of bypass roads; closures for military and other purposes; confiscation of Palestinian land; limitations on granting building permits; house demolition by Israel; deterioration of access to basic services, especially water; and environmental degradation.

The report recommended that UN-Habitat provide long-term technical assistance for shelter delivery; support land titling and registration of apartments; assist in preparing regional and local master plans and granting building permits; support the Palestinian Authority (PA) in formulating a social housing strategy for vulnerable groups; review laws and regulations governing financial institutions to expand financing for housing; and assess institutional capacities. It contained a proposal for a special human settlements programme for the Territory, to be financed by a technical cooperation trust fund that would be used for reconstruction once peace was attained. The report recommended that UN-Habitat formulate the programme, with an initial funding of $5 million, in cooperation with the PA and others, focusing on building capacity for good governance at the central and municipal levels; promoting tenure security including legal rights; and mobilizing resources to support shelter for poor people. UN-Habitat should establish the technical cooperation fund and launch a campaign to raise financial contributions.

On 9 May [res. 19/18], the Governing Council endorsed the establishment of the Special Human Settlements Programme for the Palestinian People and the Technical Cooperation Fund of $5 million for an initial period of two years. It urged the international community and financial institutions to support the mobilization of financial resources for the Programme and Fund. The Executive Director was requested to report in 2005.

Role of women

On 9 May [res. 19/16], the Governing Council requested the Executive Director to promote the integration of gender perspectives in all activities, especially in the Global Campaigns for Secure Tenure and for Urban Governance, and in slum-upgrading projects. She was asked to develop mechanisms to monitor the impact of human settlements policies and programmes on women in cities, especially those in low-income areas, or to strengthen such mechanisms where they already existed. Governments were invited to increase assistance to UN-Habitat for mainstreaming gender issues and the work of the Gender Coordinating Unit, in particular for gender-specific slum-upgrading projects. They were requested to promote and protect women's equal access to adequate housing, property and land, including rights to inheritance, and access to credit. Governments were urged to address forced relocation and forced evictions, to promote participation of women in human settlements planning and development to ensure gender-sensitive implementation of slum-upgrading programmes, and to promote credit schemes for shelter and income-generating activities that were affordable to poor women, particularly those affected by HIV/AIDS. The Executive Director was asked to report on the implementation of the resolution in her progress reports to the Governing Council beginning in 2005.

OIOS audit

In September, the Secretary-General transmitted to the General Assembly the ninth annual Office of Internal Oversight Services (OIOS) report [A/58/364], which covered UN-Habitat activities from 1 July 2002 to 30 June 2003. During that period, OIOS issued 17 critical recommendations, of which two were implemented, and satisfactory progress was under way to implement the remaining 15.

A follow-up audit of the settlement rehabilitation programme in northern Iraq found that UN-Habitat had not implemented audit recommendations made by OIOS and the Board of Auditors in 2002 [YUN 2002, p. 1074], even though the OIOS recommendations had been accepted by UN-Habitat's senior management. UN-Habitat's failure to mitigate the high risks relating to the inclusion of a currency fluctuation clause in construction contracts, as recommended by OIOS, resulted in losses to the United Nations of more than $2 million and could result in significant additional losses if the exchange rate for the Iraqi dinar remained the same or appreciated further against the United States dollar. The bidding process for construction contracts had serious internal control weaknesses. There was no assurance that management had exercised due diligence and that the Organization was receiving best value for its money; nor was there an established project management reporting and approval structure, a lack which prevented senior management from monitoring project activities and taking timely corrective action. UN-Habitat accepted most of the recommendations and took measures to implement them.

An audit of the UN-Habitat publication function showed that useful work had been done to achieve an integrated, coordinated operation, but a publication initiative launched in 2001 had not fully achieved its goals. UN-Habitat agreed to re-examine its organizational structure, policies and planning mechanisms to ensure that publication activities were cost-effective.

UN Habitat and Human Settlements Foundation

Report by Executive Director. In response to General Assembly resolution 56/206 [YUN 2001, p. 987], the Executive Director reported in March on progress made in strengthening the United Nations Habitat and Human Settlements Foundation [HSP/GC/19/2/Add.4]. The report summarized the results of two studies—one finalized in March 2002, the other begun in September 2002—on options to strengthen the Foundation and its contribution to the implementation of the Habitat Agenda [YUN 1996, p. 992] and the MDGs [YUN 2000, p. 51], particularly the MDG on slums. It provided information on two suggested financial instruments. One was a domestic currency loan guarantee facility (Global Shelter Facility) with a proposed initial capitalization of $200 million, to play a catalytic role in mobilizing public and private sector domestic resources to meet the housing and infrastructure needs of the urban poor; the other was a complementary fund (Shelter Assistance Fund), with a funding target of $100 million over five years, to finance technical assistance and provide seed capital, capacity-building grants and challenge funds to help put in place the preconditions for slum upgrading and other interventions.

The report recommended that UN-Habitat's Governing Council endorse the establishment of a loan guarantee facility. It proposed that the Executive Director act to strengthen the Foundation to provide financial support for: UN-Habitat's core staff and programmes; seed capital, challenge funds and grants to encourage the mobilization of domestic resources for shelter and infrastructure; technical support services in developing countries; and local currency guarantees. It recommended that the Council endorse the suggested financing targets for the proposed Global Shelter Facility and the Shelter Assistance Fund. It also recommended that the Council establish an Executive Board for the Foundation to oversee its operations, particularly financial instruments and facilities, and approval of loans and grants. The appointment of Board members and the rules of procedure would be subject to the approval of the Governing Council, or, during the intersessional period, of the Committee of Permanent Representatives.

Governing Council action. On 9 May [res. 19/11], the Governing Council urged the international community to extend financial support so that the Foundation could mobilize domestic resources, from both the private and public sectors, for shelter and infrastructure in developing countries, focusing on slum-dwellers and low-income people. It requested the Executive Director to strengthen the Foundation so as to provide finance for UN-Habitat core staff and programmes; mobilization of seed capital, domestic and other financial resources for shelter and infrastructure with priority to the needs of low-income households; and technical support services to developing countries and countries with economies in transition for mobilizing and utilizing domestic resources to improve human settlements and to assist countries in preparing and implementing projects. It also requested the Executive Director to work with the World Bank Group and other development banks, the private sector and other partners to field test approaches through pilot projects and to develop longer-term programmes to mobilize resources for increased affordable credit for pro-poor human settlements development in developing countries and countries with economies in transition. She was asked to report in 2005. The Governing Council deferred decisions on setting funding targets for Foundation activities, as set out above, to the 2005 Governing Council session, pending review.

Chapter VIII

Population

In 2003, the world's population reached 6.3 billion. The population activities of the United Nations continued to be guided by the Programme of Action adopted at the 1994 International Conference on Population and Development (ICPD) and the key actions for its further implementation adopted at the twenty-first special session of the General Assembly in 1999. In December, the Assembly decided to devote one day during its fifty-ninth (2004) session to the commemoration of ICPD's tenth anniversary. It also decided to devote a high-level dialogue to international migration and development in 2006.

The United Nations Population Fund (UNFPA), the largest internationally funded source of population assistance, was the lead UN organization for advancing the ICPD Programme of Action. It continued its work in reproductive health, HIV/AIDS, adolescent and youth needs, humanitarian assistance and partnership brokering. In 2003, UNFPA's donor base grew to 151, comprising 149 donor Governments, the Mars Trust and the grass-roots campaign, the "34 Million Friends". The Fund's income from all sources increased to $397.9 million from $373.2 million in 2002 and programme expenditure decreased to $380 million from $410.1 million in 2002.

The Commission on Population and Development, at its thirty-sixth session, considered the central theme of population, education and development, and adopted a resolution on the subject. Other matters discussed by the Commission included financial resources to implement the ICPD Programme of Action, world population monitoring and the activities of the UN Population Division.

New publications of the Population Division included the *World Fertility Report 2003* and *World Population Prospects: The 2002 Revision*.

Follow-up to 1994 Conference on Population and Development

On 17 December, the General Assembly decided to devote one day during its fifty-ninth (2004) session to commemorate the tenth anniversary of the 1994 International Conference on Population and Development (ICPD) (**decision 58/529**).

Implementation of the Programme of Action

Commission on Population and Development action. In follow-up to the recommendations of ICPD [YUN 1994, p. 955], the Commission on Population and Development, at its thirty-sixth session (New York, 31 March–4 April) [E/2003/25], considered the central theme of population, education and development. That subject was one of the key actions for the further implementation of the ICPD Programme of Action, contained in resolution S-21/2 [YUN 1999, p. 1006], which was adopted in 1999 at the twenty-first special session of the General Assembly (ICPD+5) [ibid., p. 1005]. The Commission also discussed the flow of financial resources for assisting in the implementation of the Programme of Action.

Population, education and development

As decided at its 2000 session [YUN 2000, p. 1007], the central theme for the Commission's 2003 session was "Population, education and development". For the Commission's discussion of the theme, the Secretary-General submitted a concise report on world population monitoring, 2003 [E/CN.9/2003/2], which summarized recent information on selected aspects of population, education and development, examining the topics of: trends in population, education and development; education and entry into reproductive life; interrelationships between education and fertility; education, health and mortality; and education and international migration.

The report found that education played a key role in national development, besides being a prime component of individual well-being. Through education, individuals were enabled to have choices and empowered to make decisions in such areas as work, place of residence, family size, health and lifestyles, and personal development. The Secretary-General's conclusions were summarized under the broad headings of interrelationships among population, education and development; expected changes in the school-age population and the achievement of internationally recognized goals; the impact of education on patterns of marriage, onset of sexual activity, fertility and contraceptive use; relationships among education, health and mortality; and the role of education in international migration.

The Commission also considered the Secretary-General's report on the monitoring of population programmes focusing on population, education and development [E/CN.9/2003/3]. The report highlighted progress towards implementing the ICPD Programme of Action as it related to education, population and reproductive health. It emphasized education as a human right and as a key factor in sustainable development, noting that reductions in fertility, morbidity and mortality rates and the empowerment of women were largely assisted by progress in education. Particular attention was paid to the education of young people, especially girls. Major challenges outlined in the report included illiteracy, eliminating gender disparities and reducing gaps in financing, in information and in the capacity to deliver quality education for all.

The Secretary-General concluded that education was the common denominator for managing such world challenges as globalization of production and trade, conflicts and increased ethnic rivalries, the widening digital divide and persistent problems of famine, pandemics and unequal resource distribution. Currently, about 1 billion young people between the ages of 15 and 24 needed to learn how to keep themselves healthy, provide for their families and find new jobs or remain employed. Using the vehicles of public statements and policy guidelines, the UN family and its partners should advocate the formulation of national education policies and programmes that maximized female enrolment and continuation at school, promoted the value of girl children to their families and society, and mobilized community participation in support of education for all.

The Commission, by a 4 April resolution [E/2003/25 (res. 2003/1)], which it brought to the attention of the Economic and Social Council, requested the UN Population Division to continue its research and the United Nations Population Fund (UNFPA) to continue its programming on the linkages between population, education and development, including the relationships between population factors and the attainment of the goals of the 1990 World Conference on Education for All [YUN 1990, p. 763]. The Population Division was also asked to contribute its research findings to the implementation of the outcomes relevant to population, education and development of the UN conferences and summits. The Commission encouraged the Population Division to disseminate the results of its research, as a contribution to the greater understanding and awareness of the interrelationships among population, education and development. UNFPA was encouraged to continue its support for population, education and development programmes so as to accelerate the implementation of the ICPD Programme of Action.

Financial resources

In accordance with General Assembly resolutions 49/128 [YUN 1994, p. 963] and 50/124 [YUN 1995, p. 1094], the Secretary-General submitted to the Commission a report on the flow of financial resources for assisting in the implementation of the ICPD Programme of Action [E/CN.9/2003/4]. The report examined trends in bilateral, multilateral and foundation/non-governmental assistance to population activities in developing countries for 2000 and provisional figures for 2001, and provided estimates of domestic expenditures reported by developing countries for 2001. International population assistance and domestic expenditures declined in 2001, according to preliminary figures. External assistance for population was estimated at $2.3 billion in 2001, compared with $2.6 billion in 2000. Domestic governmental and non-governmental expenditures in developing countries were estimated at $7.1 billion in 2001, compared with $8.6 billion in 2000. Together, external assistance and domestic expenditures for population activities yielded a global estimate of $9.4 billion in 2001, compared with a target figure of $17 billion for 2000, as estimated in the Programme of Action.

International migration and development

In response to General Assembly resolution 56/203 [YUN 2001, p. 993], the Secretary-General submitted a July report on international migration and development [A/58/98]. The report summarized activities relating to international migration undertaken by organizations within and outside the UN system, taking account of lessons learned and best practices on migration management and policies. Also discussed were the actual and potential UN system mechanisms to address related issues, including the possibility of convening a conference on international migration and development.

The report described activities of UN departments, programmes, funds, specialized agencies and other bodies in respect of international migration. It also gave an overview of activities undertaken by several intergovernmental organizations on migration issues, particularly in providing assistance to migrants.

The Secretary-General noted that the lessons learned and best practices regarding international migration management, as well as policy guidance emanating from them, had helped to address some of the consequences of international migration for development and to clarify aspects of the migration and development nexus that provided insights into ways of maximizing the development benefits of international migration.

In accordance with Assembly resolution 56/203, the Secretary-General again solicited the views of Member States on the possibility of convening a UN conference on international migration and development. Governments had been asked for their views on the issue in 1995 [YUN 1995, p. 1096], 1997 [YUN 1997, p. 1072] and 1999 [YUN 1999, p. 1020]. Of the 46 Member States and one non-member State that had responded, 25 were in favour of convening a conference and 22 expressed reservations.

A majority of the Governments in favour of a conference considered that it should be of a technical and analytical nature. It was envisaged that the proposed conference would debate major issues and deepen theoretical and empirical knowledge of the trends, causes and consequences of international migration on development. A few countries suggested that the conference could provide a forum for dialogue among concerned Governments, strengthen cooperation between countries of origin and of destination, and establish a system of collaboration to maximize the benefits of international migration. It was frequently suggested that the conference outcome could be the adoption of recommendations or principles, especially relative to migration policies in origin and destination countries or with respect to the establishment of an institutional framework to foster cooperation. Several Governments mentioned that the conference could be held in 2004 or 2005 and last from 2 to 10 days.

Most of the 22 Governments not in favour of a conference did, however, underscore the importance of international migration and development. Many considered that existing mechanisms, such as the Commission on Population and Development or a General Assembly special session, could provide appropriate forums for discussion of the issue. Some countries felt that the Organization's financial constraints should be considered and one country stressed that a regional approach was more appropriate.

The Secretary-General stated that while the possibility of convening a UN conference on international migration and development remained uncertain, the international community's expectation that the United Nations should address that global challenge in a comprehensive manner had grown. Areas in which the Organization was expected to play a key role included data collection, research, coordination of activities among concerned organizations, provision of advisory services and technical assistance, advocacy, and promotion of the ratification of international instruments related to international migration.

GENERAL ASSEMBLY ACTION

On 23 December [meeting 78], the General Assembly, on the recommendation of the Second (Economic and Financial) Committee [A/58/483/Add.3], adopted **resolution 58/208** without vote [agenda item 93 *(c)*].

International migration and development
The General Assembly,

Recalling the Programme of Action of the International Conference on Population and Development adopted at Cairo, in particular chapter X on international migration, and the key actions for the further implementation of the Programme of Action, set out in the annex to General Assembly resolution S-21/2 of 2 July 1999, in particular section II.C on international migration, as well as the relevant provisions contained in the Copenhagen Declaration on Social Development, the Programme of Action of the World Summit for Social Development, the Platform for Action adopted by the Fourth World Conference on Women and the outcome documents of the twenty-fourth and twenty-fifth special sessions of the General Assembly,

Recalling also its resolutions 49/127 of 19 December 1994, 50/123 of 20 December 1995, 52/189 of 18 December 1997, 54/212 of 22 December 1999 and 56/203 of 21 December 2001 on international migration and development, as well as Economic and Social Council decision 1995/313 of 27 July 1995,

Recalling further its resolution 57/270 B of 23 June 2003 on the integrated and coordinated implementation of and follow-up to the outcomes of the major United Nations conferences and summits in the economic and social fields,

Reaffirming the obligations of all States to promote and protect all human rights and fundamental freedoms, reaffirming also the Universal Declaration of Human Rights, and recalling the International Convention on the Elimination of All Forms of Racial Discrimination, the Convention on the Elimination of All Forms of Discrimination against Women and the Convention on the Rights of the Child,

Recalling the International Convention on the Protection of the Rights of All Migrant Workers and Members of Their Families, which entered into force in July 2003,

Recalling also that heads of State and Government at the United Nations Millennium Summit resolved to take measures, inter alia, to ensure respect for and protection of the human rights of migrants, migrant workers and their families, to eliminate the increasing acts of racism and xenophobia in many societies and to promote greater harmony and tolerance in all societies,

Reaffirming that the General Assembly and the Economic and Social Council should carry out their respective responsibilities as entrusted to them in the Charter of the United Nations, and that Member States should strive to achieve the goals set at the relevant United Nations conferences in the formulation of policies and the provision of guidance to and coordination of United Nations activities in the field of population and development, including activities on international migration,

Reaffirming also the need for the relevant United Nations organizations and other international organizations to enhance their financial and technical support to developing countries, as well as countries with economies in transition, to foster migration that contributes to development,

Taking note of the views of Member States on the question of convening a United Nations conference on international migration, its scope, form and agenda, and noting the low number of respondents to the survey of the Secretariat, and in this context inviting the Secretary-General to continue considering the issue,

Noting the work undertaken under the International Migration Policy Programme by the United Nations Institute for Training and Research, the International Organization for Migration and the United Nations Population Fund, in partnership with the International Labour Office, the Office of the United Nations High Commissioner for Refugees, the Office of the United Nations High Commissioner for Human Rights and other relevant international and regional institutions, with a view to strengthening the capacity of Governments to manage migration flows at the national and regional levels and thus foster greater cooperation among States towards orderly migration,

Aware that, among other important factors, both domestic and international, the widening economic and social gap between and among many countries and the marginalization of some countries in the global economy, due in part to the uneven impact of the benefits of globalization and liberalization, have contributed to large flows of people between and among countries and to the intensification of the complex phenomenon of international migration,

Aware also that, in spite of the existence of an already established body of principles, there is a need to enhance international cooperation on migration issues and make further efforts, including through appropriate mechanisms, to ensure that the human rights and dignity of all migrants and their families, in particular of women migrant workers, are respected and protected,

Taking note of the rights of all migrants and their obligation to respect national legislation, including legislation on migration,

Noting that an overall commitment to multiculturalism helps to provide a context for the effective integration of migrants, preventing and combating discrimination and promoting solidarity and tolerance in receiving societies,

Recognizing the need for further studies and analyses of the effects of the movements of highly skilled migrant workers and those with advanced education on economic and social development in developing countries, and emphasizing the need for further studies and analysis of the effects of those movements on development in the context of globalization,

Noting the importance of remittances by migrant workers, which for many countries are one of the major sources of foreign exchange and can make an important contribution to developmental potential, and stressing the need to consider the various dimensions of this issue in a sustainable development perspective,

1. *Takes note* of the report of the Secretary-General;
2. *Urges* Member States and the United Nations system to continue strengthening international cooperation and arrangements at all levels in the area of international migration and development in order to address all aspects of migration and to maximize the benefits of international migration to all those concerned;
3. *Calls upon* all relevant bodies, agencies, funds and programmes of the United Nations system and other relevant intergovernmental, regional and subregional organizations, within their continuing mandated activities, to continue to address the issue of international migration and development, with a view to integrating migration issues, including a gender perspective and cultural diversity, in a more coherent way within the broader context of the implementation of agreed economic and social development goals and respect for all human rights;
4. *Requests* the Secretary-General, in cooperation with relevant bodies, agencies, funds and programmes of the United Nations system and other relevant international, regional and subregional organizations, to continue convening meetings, as necessary, in order to coordinate their activities regarding international migration, and to collect information to assist States in identifying critical issues and discussing future steps;
5. *Takes note* of the initiatives undertaken by Member States to continue to identify the many dimensions of international migration and development in order to better understand international migration processes and their linkages with globalization and development, to address the issues related to international migration, to analyse the gaps and shortcomings in the current approaches, to maximize the benefits of international migration and to strengthen international, regional and subregional cooperation;
6. *Encourages* Governments of countries of origin, countries of transit and countries of destination to increase cooperation on issues related to migration, and notes with appreciation the numerous meetings and conferences convened relating to migration and development, in particular in the context of regional cooperation;
7. *Invites* Governments, with the assistance of the international community, where appropriate, to seek to make the option of remaining in one's country viable for all people, in particular through efforts to achieve sustainable development, leading to a better economic balance between developed and developing countries;
8. *Requests* the Secretary-General, as an exception, to submit a report to the General Assembly at its fifty-ninth instead of its sixtieth session on the implementation of the present resolution, which, inter alia, provides an update of the results of relevant activities within the United Nations system and of United

Nations cooperation with the International Organization for Migration and other relevant intergovernmental organizations concerning international migration and development, including best practices on managed migration and polices to increase understanding and strengthen cooperation in the area of international migration and development among States and other stakeholders, reviews major initiatives of Member States and suggests action-oriented options for the consideration of the General Assembly;

9. *Decides* that in 2006 the General Assembly will devote a high-level dialogue to international migration and development, in accordance with the rules and procedures of the Assembly;

10. *Requests* the Secretary-General to report to the General Assembly at its sixtieth session on the organizational details of the high-level dialogue, bearing in mind that:

(*a*) The purpose of the high-level dialogue is to discuss the multidimensional aspects of international migration and development in order to identify appropriate ways and means to maximize its development benefits and minimize its negative impacts;

(*b*) The high-level dialogue should have a strong focus on policy issues, including the challenge of achieving the internationally agreed development goals;

(*c*) Round tables and informal exchanges are useful for dialogue;

(*d*) The outcome of the high-level dialogue will be a Chairperson's summary, which will be widely distributed to Member States, observers, United Nations agencies and other appropriate organizations;

11. *Decides* to include in the provisional agenda of its fifty-ninth session the sub-item entitled "International migration and development".

UN Population Fund

2003 activities

In her report covering 2003 [DP/FPA/2004/9 (Part I)] to the United Nations Development Programme (UNDP)/UNFPA Executive Board, the UNFPA Executive Director described the Fund's activities in programme priority areas and noted that assisting countries to achieve the ICPD goals [YUN 1994, p. 955], the ICPD+5 key actions [YUN 1999, p. 1005] and the Millennium Development Goals (MDGs) [YUN 2000, p. 51] was central to the Fund's mission. She said that UNFPA was also committed to strengthening results-based management and organizational effectiveness, as it focused strategically on consolidating and building on its 18-month transition exercise that ended in December 2002 [YUN 2002, p. 1078].

The number of UNFPA donors grew to 151 in 2003, comprising 149 donor Governments, the Mars Trust and the grass-roots campaign called "34 Million Friends". In 2003, the Fund's regular income increased by 12.7 per cent to $293.1 million, following its efforts to attract larger contributions from major donor countries of the Organisation for Economic Co-operation and Development (OECD). Contributions to related resources (trust funds, cost-sharing and other programme arrangements) amounted to $103.6 million.

The implementation of country and subregional programmes continued as the Fund's core work during 2003. By programme area, the largest share of resources, 61.5 per cent, went to reproductive health activities; 19.8 per cent went to population and development strategies; 12.1 per cent to advocacy activities; and 6.7 per cent to multisectoral activities. The highest priority for allocation of assistance, 65.5 per cent, was for Group A countries (those most in need), which included all the least developed countries (see p. 867). By region, sub-Saharan Africa accounted for 36 per cent of programme assistance; Asia and the Pacific for 30.2 per cent; the Arab States and Europe for 13 per cent; and Latin America and the Caribbean for 7.6 per cent. Interregional and global activities accounted for 13.1 per cent of programme assistance.

UNFPA's investment in reproductive health was intended to enhance women's access to quality services and female-controlled methods and to promote male involvement. Activities encompassed reducing maternal mortality and morbidity, family planning and reproductive health commodity security.

HIV/AIDS prevention was another key component of the Fund's work in 2003. The Fund focused on three core areas, namely, the prevention of HIV infection among young people, the prevention of HIV infection in pregnant women and comprehensive condom programming. It maintained its role as the convening agency in the two important areas of focusing on young people and condom programming and worked to strengthen UN partnership and collaboration. The Fund provided a strong presence in country-level theme groups on HIV/AIDS.

The needs of adolescents and youth in developing countries remained an urgent priority for UNFPA in 2003, particularly in the fight against poverty and HIV/AIDS. The Fund's flagship publication, *State of World Population 2003* [Sales No. E.03.III.H.1], stressed that HIV/AIDS had become a disease of the young, with half of all new HIV infections, and at least a third of more than 333 million new cases of curable sexually transmitted infections (STIs) each year, occurring in people aged 15 to 24. However, only a small percentage knew that they were infected and the majority were ignorant about how HIV was transmitted.

UNFPA continued to support efforts to expand information and education on reproductive health issues to young people.

UNFPA provided humanitarian assistance to more than 20 countries and territories. As part of the UN emergency response system, it supplied reproductive health kits valued at some $2.15 million to 59 emergency destinations. It provided support to conduct and facilitate rapid reproductive health assessments, train field staff and national counterparts, prepare project documents and consolidated appeals processes, advocacy, supply reproductive health kits and commodities, mobilize resources and conduct emergency and post-conflict programme evaluation. The Fund also contributed to the first-ever interagency global evaluation of reproductive health services. It led an evaluation of worldwide delivery of the Minimum Initial Services Package of reproductive health services to refugees, and an analysis of financial resource trends for emergency reproductive health programming.

Throughout 2003, UNFPA was involved in partnerships with a variety of development partners, working with civil society coalitions at the country level and collaborating with the New Partnership for Africa's Development (see p. 937), among others. It also continued to promote South-South cooperation as an integral strategy for implementing the ICPD Programme of Action goals, to focus on the incorporation of population dimensions into development policies and plans to address the overall goal of poverty reduction, and to support work on population dynamics and demographic trends.

Gender issues were mainstreamed throughout UNFPA's programmes in both reproductive health and population and development areas. The Fund continued to address structural and cultural barriers in the context of a rights-based approach to development. At the inter-agency level, it worked to advance the Secretary-General's human rights plan of action "Strengthening human rights–related United Nations action at country level: National protection systems and country teams", while at the policy level it supported the development and enforcement of laws prohibiting all forms of gender-based violence.

On 19 June [E/2003/35 (dec. 2003/16)], the UNDP/UNFPA Executive Board welcomed the report of the Executive Director for 2002 [YUN 2002, p. 1077] and invited her to consider merging the various parts of the annual report into a single, concise, performance- and results-oriented annual report, taking into account the priorities, goals and outputs contained in the multi-year funding framework.

By **decision 2003/225** of 11 July, the Economic and Social Council took note of the annual reports of the UNDP Administrator and the UNFPA Executive Director to the Council [E/2003/13] and the Executive Board's reports on its 2002 second regular session [DP/2003/1] and its first regular session in 2003 [DP/2003/9].

Country and intercountry programmes

UNFPA's provisional project expenditures for country and intercountry (regional and interregional) programmes in 2003 totalled $176.4 million, compared to $203.6 million in 2002, according to the Executive Director's statistical overview report [DP/FPA/2004/9 (Part I, Add.1)]. The 2003 figure included $140.5 million for country programmes and $35.9 million for intercountry programmes. In accordance with the procedure for allocating resources according to categorization of countries into groups, laid down in a 1996 UNDP/UNFPA decision [YUN 1996, p. 989] and updated in 2000 [YUN 2000, p. 1005], total expenditures in 2003 to Group A countries (those most in need) amounted to $92.1 million, compared to $116.5 million in 2002.

Africa. Provisional expenditures for UNFPA programmes in sub-Saharan Africa totalled $63.5 million in 2003, compared to $73.3 million in 2002. Most of those resources (60.4 per cent) went to reproductive health and family planning, followed by population and development strategies (25.8 per cent), multisectoral activities (8 per cent) and advocacy (5.8 per cent).

On 23 January [E/2003/35 (dec. 2003/6)], the UNDP/UNFPA Executive Board approved country programmes for Botswana, Burundi, Cameroon, the Comoros, Côte d'Ivoire, Equatorial Guinea, Guinea-Bissau, Mali, Mauritania and Nigeria. On 19 June [dec. 2003/21], the Board took note of the country programme outlines for Benin, Kenya and the Niger.

Arab States and Europe. Provisional expenditures for UNFPA programmes in the Arab States and Europe totalled $23 million in 2003, compared to $23.8 million in 2002. Most of the resources (71.4 per cent) went to reproductive health and family planning, followed by population and development strategies (17.7 per cent), advocacy (5.9 per cent) and multisectoral activities (5 per cent).

On 23 January [dec. 2003/6], the UNDP/UNFPA Executive Board approved country programmes for Djibouti and Jordan.

Asia and the Pacific. Provisional expenditures for UNFPA programmes in Asia and the Pacific totalled $53.3 million in 2003, compared to $63.8 million in 2002. Most of the resources

(71.8 per cent) went to reproductive health and family planning, followed by population and development strategies (13.3 per cent), advocacy (10.6 per cent) and multisectoral activities (4.3 per cent).

On 23 January [dec. 2003/6], the UNDP/UNFPA Executive Board approved country programmes for Bangladesh, China, India, Maldives, Papua New Guinea, Timor-Leste and the South Pacific region. On 19 June [dec. 2003/21], the Board took note of the country programme outlines for Afghanistan, the Democratic People's Republic of Korea and Pakistan; and took note of the report on the implementation of UNFPA's special programme of assistance to Myanmar [DP/FPA/2003/9].

Latin America and the Caribbean. Provisional expenditures for UNFPA programmes in Latin America and the Caribbean totalled $13.5 million in 2003, compared to $21.8 million in 2002. Most of the resources (54.8 per cent) went to reproductive health and family planning, followed by population and development strategies (28.6 per cent), advocacy (8.7 per cent) and multisectoral activities (8 per cent).

On 23 January [dec. 2003/6], the UNDP/UNFPA Executive Board approved country programmes for Bolivia, Colombia, El Salvador and Venezuela. On 19 June [dec. 2003/21], it took note of the country programme outline for Cuba.

Interregional programmes. Provisional expenditures for UNFPA's interregional and global programmes totalled $23.2 million in 2003, compared to $20.9 million in 2002. Of that total, 41.3 per cent went to advocacy, 34.5 per cent to reproductive health and family planning, 15 per cent to population and development strategies, and 9.3 per cent to multisectoral activities.

Financial and administrative questions

UNFPA's income from all sources totalled $397.9 million in 2003, compared to $373.2 million in 2002 [DP/FPA/2004/15], comprising $292.3 million in regular resources and $105.6 million from other resources. Expenditures totalled $380 million in 2003, down from $410.1 million in 2002, comprising $270.8 million from regular resources and $109.2 million from other resources, resulting in a net excess of $21.5 million in regular resources and a net deficit of $3.6 million in other resources.

Contributions to regular resources increased in 2003 by 15.4 per cent ($38.4 million) to $288.5 million, continuing the trend of the preceding five years. Income to other resources decreased by 5.4 per cent ($5.9 million) to $103.6 million, which also continued a recent trend. Total expenditure decreased by 7.3 per cent ($30.1 million) to $380 million. Programme expenditure decreased to $303.6 million in 2003, down from $343.3 million in 2002.

2004-2005 support budget

In a July report [DP/FPA/2003/11], the Executive Director submitted to the UNDP/UNFPA Executive Board the estimates for the 2004-2005 biennial support budget, totalling $169.6 million (gross) and $155 million (net). The estimates were based on a resource framework of $750.6 million for total income.

The proposal provided for greater support to country offices by consolidating the cost of establishing a new typology for the Fund's country offices and incorporating the resources needed to strengthen country offices in such areas as audit services, human resources management and the integrated Enterprise Resource Planning (ERP) system. It provided for growth because the higher income estimate of $584.1 million from regular resources was $39.1 million, or 7.2 per cent, higher than in the revised proposal for the 2002-2003 biennium [YUN 2002, p. 1081], despite the loss of a major donor's contribution. It also provided cost containment for several operating costs that had been limited to their 2002-2003 levels or adjusted downward.

Commenting on the estimates for the 2004-2005 biennial support budget in August [DP/FPA/2003/12], the Advisory Committee on Administrative and Budgetary Questions (ACABQ) stated that the time had come to introduce results-based budgeting techniques in preparing budget estimates; requested that future UNFPA budget documents contain a separate annex indicating actions taken to implement previous ACABQ recommendations, as approved by the Executive Board; and expressed appreciation for the Fund's efforts to increase resources.

On 10 September [E/2003/35 (dec. 2003/28)], the Executive Board approved gross appropriations of $169.6 million for the 2004-2005 biennial support budget and resolved that income estimates of $14.6 million should be used to offset the gross appropriations, resulting in estimated net appropriations of $155 million. It authorized the Executive Director to redeploy resources between appropriation lines up to 5 per cent of the appropriation to which the resources were redeployed; and additional extrabudgetary expenditures up to $3.8 million for the implementation of the ERP project.

Multi-year funding commitments

In May [DP/FPA/2003/6], the Executive Director submitted to the UNDP/UNFPA Executive Board updated estimates of regular and other resources for 2003 and future years. As at 28 February, 60 countries had submitted written pledges to UNFPA for 2003, of which only 15 were multi-year pledges.

In 2002, UNFPA exceeded its pledging target of 125 countries, reaching an all-time high of 136 donor countries by the end of the year: 36 from Africa, 33 from Asia and the Pacific, 32 from Europe, 20 from Latin America and the Caribbean, 13 from the Arab States, 1 from North America, and a private contribution from the Mars Trust in the amount of $1.1 million. Total contributions received from donor Governments and from the interest from the Mars Trust for UNFPA's regular resources in 2002 amounted to $260 million. As at 28 February, $281 million had been pledged for 2003, including a projected interest receivable amount of $4 million; $63 million for 2004; $63 million for 2005; and $8,000 for 2006. Of UNFPA's 15 major donors (those contributing $1 million or more), which together provided an estimated 95 per cent of the total contributions to regular resources, only five countries were in a position to make multi-year pledges.

UNFPA called on Executive Board members and the Fund's donors to consider increasing their contributions for 2003 and future years and to ensure the early and timely payment of pledges. The Fund hoped that the increases in official development assistance (ODA) announced at the 2002 International Conference on Financing for Development [YUN 2002, p. 953] would lead to increased contributions to UNFPA.

On 19 June [E/2003/35 (dec. 2003/19)], the UNDP/ UNFPA Executive Board encouraged UNFPA to broaden its donor base; welcomed the contributions and commitments made by programme countries; encouraged all countries to commit to multi-year pledges and make early contribution payments; and urged them, in the spirit of the Monterrey Consensus [YUN 2002, p. 953], to increase regular (core) funding to UNFPA in order to secure a stable regular resource base.

Assessment of the 2000-2003 multi-year funding framework

In response to UNDP/UNFPA Executive Board decision 2000/9 [YUN 2000, p. 1005], UNFPA submitted a cumulative report on its first multi-year funding framework (MYFF) for 2000-2003 [DP/ FPA/2003/4 (Part II)], which outlined the Fund's key contributions in assisting countries to implement the ICPD Programme of Action [YUN 1994, p. 955] and ICPD+5 key actions [YUN 1999, p. 1005] and in achieving the MDGs [YUN 2000, p. 51]; outlined the context in which UNFPA worked during the 2000-2003 MYFF period; described progress in achieving MYFF goals and outputs; discussed lessons learned in the implementation process; indicated steps taken towards results-based management; presented an integrated resources framework; and highlighted strategic considerations for the next MYFF cycle.

Although there was a lack of data for reporting on the MYFF goal indicators over such a short period of time, there had been a marked improvement in the availability and quality of data at the output level, and a notable increase in the recording and reporting of data at the country level. Continued efforts were necessary to build capacity in data collection and in monitoring and reporting programme results. Results-based management had led to the formulation of a common strategic direction and results-oriented approaches to processes and systems that were being implemented throughout UNFPA. Under the resources framework, the report updated income estimates; reported on resource mobilization; and indicated how programme funds were distributed, in accordance with Executive Board decision 2000/19 [YUN 2000, p. 1005].

The strategic considerations for the implementation of the next MYFF cycle (2004-2007) would place greater emphasis on shared goals and outcomes; accelerate progress towards ICPD goals and the MDGs; link programme support to national policy development and poverty reduction; reinvigorate work in population and development; promote gender equality and women's empowerment; give special attention to the needs of adolescents and youth in the face of the HIV/ AIDS epidemic; increase access to reproductive health information and services, and reduce maternal morbidity and mortality; and implement results- and competency-based mechanisms in human resources management.

On 19 June [E/2003/35 (dec. 2003/17)], the Executive Board approved the strategic considerations for the 2004-2007 MYFF cycle; urged UNFPA to simplify and refine the content and format of the 2004-2007 MYFF; and requested the Executive Director to develop her proposal to report on the MYFF every second year, and to continue to hold open-ended informal consultations on the development of the 2004-2007 MYFF.

Audit reports

The Executive Director submitted to the UNDP/UNFPA Executive Board a status report [DP/FPA/2003/1] describing action taken in response to recommendations on UNFPA by the Board of Auditors for the 2000-2001 biennium [YUN 2002, p. 1082]. On 23 January [E/2003/35 (dec. 2003/5)], the Executive Board took note of the report.

In an April report [DP/FPA/2003/3], the Executive Director described UNFPA's internal audit and oversight activities in 2002, stating that management audits had been carried out in 28 country offices, one Country Technical Services Team office, one division and one functional area at headquarters. Contracted audits were undertaken in 13 country offices. In addition, 542 audit reports covering 2001 activities for projects executed by Governments and non-governmental organizations (NGOs) were reviewed. Of 41 reports issued in 2002 (including 9 on 2001 audits), the level of internal controls and the compliance with financial and administrative requirements were found to be satisfactory in 14 offices. Twenty-two offices were rated partially satisfactory and five offices/divisions were deficient.

The UNFPA Office of Oversight and Evaluation analysed 20 midterm reviews of UNFPA-assisted country programmes undertaken during 2001-2002; conducted a policy application review of one country programme in the Latin American region; and continued to follow up on the implementation of recommendations of similar reviews conducted in previous years.

On 19 June [E/2003/35 (dec. 2003/14)], the Executive Board encouraged the Executive Director to take the necessary steps to address the issues contained in the report on internal audit and oversight and to report to the Board in 2004.

Technical Advisory Programme

In response to Executive Board decision 2002/3 [YUN 2002, p. 1083], the Executive Director submitted a report on the Technical Advisory Programme (TAP) monitoring and evaluation system for 2003-2005 [DP/FPA/2003/7].

TAP, an inter-agency arrangement through which UNFPA technical assistance was provided to countries in support of population and development activities, was established in 1992 and had evolved in terms of both its substantive areas of focus and its method of servicing country programme needs. TAP was a three-tiered arrangement: the first tier was composed of national and regional expertise; the second was a group of technical specialists assigned to multidisciplinary regional Country Technical Services Teams (CSTs); and the third was made up of Technical Advisory Services (TAS) specialists posted at the headquarters or regional offices of relevant UN agencies and regional commissions.

The monitoring and evaluation process had three components: CSTs would collect information on technical support activities; CSTs, along with relevant UN organizations, would analyse the collected information to identify strengths and weaknesses and make recommendations for corrective action—the analysis would also include midterm review findings that would assess the quality and usefulness of the TAP outputs; and an external and internal evaluation would be undertaken in the third year of the TAP implementation to assess its contribution to the MYFF goals and outcomes.

On 19 June [E/2003/35 (dec. 2003/21)], the Executive Board took note of the report.

Delegation of formal authority on personnel matters

The Executive Director submitted a March report [DP/FPA/2003/5] on the delegation of formal authority to the Executive Director in matters concerning UNFPA personnel. Formal authority had resided with UNDP's Administrator since 1969 and remained there even after UNFPA was placed under the General Assembly's authority in 1972 by Assembly resolution 3019(XXVII) [YUN 1972, p. 378]. The Executive Director stated that the delegation of authority to UNFPA, endorsed by UNDP, would improve the Fund's management, efficiency and accountability of personnel services. Although the change in delegation of authority would incur no direct financial implications or added costs, UNFPA would continue to make use of, and pay for, certain personnel services provided by UNDP. The cost of the personnel services assumed by the Fund would be offset by a corresponding reduction in the amount paid to UNDP.

In a May report [DP/FPA/2003/10], ACABQ endorsed UNFPA's recommendation on delegating formal authority in its personnel matters to the Executive Director.

On 17 June [E/2003/35 (dec. 2003/13)], the UNDP/UNFPA Executive Board recommended to the General Assembly, through the Economic and Social Council, that formal authority in matters of UNFPA personnel be delegated by the Secretary-General to the Executive Director. By **decision 2003/224** of 11 July, the Council took note of the Executive Board decision and made that recommendation to the Assembly. A 22 September Secretariat note [A/C.5/58/2 & Corr.1] drew the Fifth (Administrative and Budgetary) Committee's attention to the Council's decision.

By **decision 58/555** of 23 December, the Assembly decided that formal authority in matters of UNFPA personnel should be delegated by the Secretary-General to the Fund's Executive Director.

UN Population Award

The 2003 United Nations Population Award was presented to Werner Fornos (United States),

President of the Population Institute, in the individual category, and to the Family Planning Association of Kenya in the institutional category. Mr. Fornos was selected for his outstanding contributions in the population field, primarily in advocacy. The Family Planning Association of Kenya was selected for its advocacy efforts to promote gender equality and to eradicate female genital mutilation.

The Award was established by General Assembly resolution 36/201 [YUN 1981, p. 792], to be presented annually to individuals or institutions for outstanding contributions to increasing awareness of population problems and to their solutions. In July, the Secretary-General transmitted to the Assembly the report of the UNFPA Executive Director on the Population Award [A/58/151]. By **decision 58/552** of 23 December, the Assembly took note of the report.

Other population activities

Commission on Population and Development

The Commission on Population and Development, at its thirty-sixth session (New York, 31 March–4 April) [E/2003/25], considered as its central theme "Population, education and development", which was discussed in the context of the follow-up to the 1994 International Conference on Population and Development (ICPD) (see p. 1085). Documents before the Commission that focused on the theme were reports of the Secretary-General on world population monitoring, 2003 [E/CN.9/2003/2] (see p. 1085); the monitoring of population programmes [E/CN.9/2003/3] (see p. 1086); the flow of financial resources for assisting in the implementation of the ICPD Programme of Action [E/CN.9/2003/4] (see p. 1086); and world demographic trends [E/CN.9/2003/5]. The Commission also had before it the Secretary-General's report [E/CN.9/2003/6] on programme implementation and progress of work in the field of population in 2002 [YUN 2002, p. 1084].

The Commission adopted and brought to the Economic and Social Council's attention a resolution on population, education and development [E/2003/25 (res. 2003/1)] (see p. 1086). It also decided that the special theme for its thirty-eighth (2005) session would be "Population, development and HIV/AIDS, with particular emphasis on poverty" [dec. 2003/1] and took note of the documents it had considered [dec. 2003/2].

By **decision 2003/229** of 21 July, the Economic and Social Council took note of the Commission's report on its thirty-sixth session and approved the provisional agenda for its thirty-seventh (2004) session.

In preparation for the thirty-seventh session, the Commission's Bureau held an intersessional meeting (Vilnius, Lithuania, 13-14 November) [E/CN.9/2004/2].

2003 UN activities

In a report on programme implementation and progress of work of the UN Population Division in 2003 [E/CN.9/2004/5], the Secretary-General described the Division's activities dealing with the analysis of fertility, mortality and migration; world population estimates and projections; population policies and population ageing; population and development; monitoring, coordination and dissemination of population information; and technical cooperation in population. The report also highlighted the Division's major accomplishments during the year.

The Population Division's work in fertility and family planning analysis included the issuance of the *World Fertility Report 2003*, which presented data on fertility, nuptiality, contraceptive use and national policies with respect to fertility and family planning for 194 countries and various areas of the world. Work also progressed on setting up a fertility database, which would complement the *Report*.

On mortality and health, the Population Division organized a workshop on HIV/AIDS and adult mortality in developing countries (New York, 8-13 September) for specialists from African countries most affected by the epidemic. It discussed ways to improve communication, especially through the media; the social and economic effects of the epidemic; and opportunities and constraints in the use of demographic information as an advocacy tool.

On international migration, the Population Division organized the Second Coordination Meeting on International Migration (New York, 15-16 October), which discussed, among other issues, workers' remittances; undocumented migration, with special attention to human trafficking; and international migration and security. The Division prepared and submitted to the General Assembly the Secretary-General's report on international migration and development (see p. 1086).

With regard to population projections, the Population Division completed *World Population Prospects: The 2002 Revision,* which presented estimates and projections to the year 2050 and a new set of long-range projections, extending the projection horizon by country of the *2002 Revision* to the year 2300. The Division held a technical working group meeting on long-range population projections (New York, 30 June) and an Expert Group Meeting on World Population in 2300 (New York, 9 December). The "2003 Revision of World Urbanization Prospects" was completed as a working paper and would be issued in 2004.

In the area of population policies, the Population Division completed "National Population Policies 2003"; a study on fertility, contraception and population policies; and a study on HIV/AIDS policies, "National responses to HIV/AIDS: a review of progress". The United Nations Ninth Inquiry among Governments on Population and Development was finalized and sent to all permanent missions to the United Nations.

Other issuances included a report on living arrangements of older persons around the world, which was being finalized for formal publication, and a preliminary version of *The Impact of AIDS*. Work continued on the fourth version of the Population, Resources, Environment and Development database.

During 2003, the Population Division prepared the second quinquennial review and appraisal of the progress made in achieving the ICPD Programme of Action goals and objectives, to be considered by the Commission on Population and Development in 2004. It also continued to maintain and develop the Population Information Network (POPIN), a major channel for information dissemination.

The Population Division continued to implement a programme of technical assistance for capacity-building among population research centres in developing countries in the effective use of new information and communication technologies, particularly the Internet; and to maintain three web sites associated with the networks of population research and training institutions.

The Population Division's technical cooperation programme launched an automatic e-mail announcement service for new publications and produced and distributed MORTPAK for Windows, the Division's software package for demographic estimation. It convened an international panel of eminent specialists (Bangkok, Thailand, January) that developed a blueprint for a multistage research training programme on population ageing in developing countries and organized a briefing on its work for about 100 specially invited students from over 60 countries at the Population Association of America annual meeting (Minneapolis, United States, May).

Chapter IX

Social policy, crime prevention and human resources development

In 2003, the United Nations continued to promote social, cultural and human resources development, and to strengthen its crime prevention and criminal justice programme.

The Commission for Social Development, in May, considered as its priority theme national and international cooperation for social development and adopted agreed conclusions on the theme, which were endorsed by the Economic and Social Council. The General Assembly considered follow-up to the 1995 World Summit for Social Development and to the Assembly's twenty-fourth (2000) special session, which adopted further initiatives, and preparations for the observance of the tenth anniversary of the International Year of the Family in 2004.

In December, the Assembly endorsed a June decision of the Ad Hoc Committee on a Comprehensive and Integral International Convention on the Protection and Promotion of the Rights and Dignity of Persons with Disabilities to establish a working group to prepare a draft text for the convention, which would be the basis for negotiation by Member States. The Assembly proclaimed 2005 the International Year for Sport and Physical Education, as a means to promote education, health, development and peace. As preparations gathered momentum for the twenty-eighth (2004) Olympic Games, the Assembly urged Governments to observe the Olympic Truce while the Games were under way.

In the area of crime prevention, the Assembly, in October, adopted the United Nations Convention against Corruption, which was opened for signature (December, Merida, Mexico). The United Nations Convention against Transnational Organized Crime entered into force in September, as did its Protocol to Prevent, Suppress and Punish Trafficking in Persons, Especially Women and Children in December. Preparations continued for the Eleventh United Nations Congress on Crime Prevention and Criminal Justice, to be held in 2005.

The Commission on Crime Prevention and Criminal Justice considered trafficking in persons, transnational organized crime, preparations for the Eleventh United Nations Congress on Crime Prevention and Criminal Justice, the work of the Centre for International Crime Prevention of the United Nations Office on Drugs and Crime, international cooperation and technical assistance in preventing and combating terrorism, urban crime, kidnapping, crimes against cultural heritage, UN standards and norms in crime prevention, the Commission's functioning and illicit trafficking in protected species of wild flora and fauna.

The Secretary-General, in September, described the need to increase investment in human resources development and to promote strategies for information technologies. Also calling for increased investment, the Assembly recognized the importance of developing human resources as a means to promote sustained economic growth and eradicate poverty.

Social policy and cultural issues

Social development

**Follow-up to 1995 World Summit
and to General Assembly special session**

The Secretary-General, in response to General Assembly resolution 57/163 [YUN 2002, p. 1087], submitted a July report [A/58/172] on the implementation of the Copenhagen Declaration on Social Development and the Programme of Action, adopted at the 1995 World Summit for Social Development [YUN 1995, p. 1113], and of the further initiatives for social development adopted by the Assembly's twenty-fourth (2000) special session [YUN 2000, p. 1012]. The report focused on the coherence of policies to promote social development, and participation and partnership as objectives and means of social development, and brought to the Assembly's attention the agreed conclusions on national and international cooperation for social development [E/2003/26], adopted by the Commission for Social Development (see p. 1099). The report stated that the Commission approached the coherence of policies to promote social development from four angles: policies in relation to the goals and objectives of social development; the integration of social and economic policies; the coherence between national and international cooperation for development policies; and the specific case of employment. Regarding participation and partnership, which had emerged as objectives and instruments of social development, three main elements were found in the Commission's agreed conclusions: the participation of developing countries in international affairs; partnership among all actors of the development process: the private sector and civil society; and the New Partnership for Africa's Development (NEPAD) (see p. 937) as an example of partnerships. The report made a series of recommendations to the Assembly, which were incorporated into resolution 58/130 (below).

GENERAL ASSEMBLY ACTION

On 22 December [meeting 77], the General Assembly, on the recommendation of the Third (Social, Humanitarian and Cultural) Committee [A/58/496], adopted **resolution 58/130** without vote [agenda item 105].

Implementation of the outcome of the World Summit for Social Development and of the twenty-fourth special session of the General Assembly

The General Assembly,

Recalling the World Summit for Social Development, held at Copenhagen from 6 to 12 March 1995, and the twenty-fourth special session of the General Assembly, entitled "World Summit for Social Development and beyond: achieving social development for all in a globalizing world", held at Geneva from 26 June to 1 July 2000,

Reaffirming that the Copenhagen Declaration on Social Development and the Programme of Action and the further initiatives for social development adopted by the General Assembly at its twenty-fourth special session constitute the basic framework for the promotion of social development for all at the national and international levels,

Recalling the United Nations Millennium Declaration and the development goals contained therein, as well as the commitments made at major United Nations conferences, special sessions and summits,

Recalling also the commitment to promote national and global economic systems based on the principles of justice, equity, democracy, participation, transparency, accountability and inclusion,

Recalling further its resolution 57/270 B of 23 June 2003 on the integrated and coordinated implementation of and follow-up to the outcomes of the major United Nations conferences and summits in the economic and social fields,

Considering that, despite the efforts made and the progress achieved in some areas of economic and social development, vast sectors of our societies, in particular in the developing and the least developed countries, are still facing serious challenges, including serious financial crises, insecurity, poverty, exclusion and inequality in income growth and distribution, education and health,

Noting that the Commission for Social Development, at its forty-third session in 2005, will consider as its priority theme "Review of the further implementation of the World Summit for Social Development and the outcome of the twenty-fourth special session of the General Assembly",

1. *Takes note with appreciation* of the report of the Secretary-General;

2. *Reaffirms* the need to take effective measures to implement the commitments made by heads of State and Government at the World Summit for Social Development, contained in the Copenhagen Declaration on Social Development and the Programme of Action, which established a new consensus to place people at the centre of development policies and pledged to eradicate poverty, promote full and productive employment and foster social integration so as to achieve stable, safe and just societies for all;

3. *Also reaffirms* the decisions on further action and initiatives to accelerate social development for all, adopted by the General Assembly at its twenty-fourth special session and contained in the further initiatives for social development;

4. *Further reaffirms* that the aim of social integration is to create a "society for all", in which every individual, each with rights and responsibilities, has an active role to play, and that such an inclusive society must be based on respect for all human rights and fundamental freedoms, cultural and religious diversity, social justice and the special needs of vulnerable and disadvantaged groups, democratic participation and the rule of law;

5. *Recognizes* the need to promote respect for human rights and fundamental freedoms in order to address the most pressing social needs of people living in poverty, including through the design and development of appropriate mechanisms to strengthen and consolidate democratic institutions and governance;

6. *Reaffirms* the commitment to gender equality and to strengthening policies and programmes that improve, ensure and broaden the full participation of women in all spheres of political, economic, social and cultural life, as equal partners, and to improving their access to all resources needed for the full exercise of all their human rights and fundamental freedoms by removing persistent barriers;

7. *Stresses* that, in addition to social policies, progress in the realization of long-term goals, such as equity, social cohesion and an adequate accumulation of human capital, requires supportive and coherent short-term and long-term economic policies at the national and international levels;

8. *Emphasizes* the importance of integrating economic and social policies in promoting human resources development and enhancing the process of development, invites the Economic and Social Council, at the highest possible level, to assess the effectiveness of such integration and make recommendations in this regard to the General Assembly, requests the Commission for Social Development to continue giving particular attention to this issue in its forthcoming sessions, and invites the different entities of the United Nations system, within their respective mandates, to take into account the integration of economic and social policies in their respective domains;

9. *Stresses* the necessity of ensuring the effective involvement of developing countries in the international economic decision-making process through, inter alia, greater participation in international economic forums, thereby ensuring the transparency and accountability of international financial institutions with respect to according a central position for social development in their policies and programmes;

10. *Reaffirms* that, given the growing and multifaceted interdependence of all regions and countries, coherent and strengthened international cooperation as well as a favourable external economic environment are indispensable complements to the efforts of developing countries, including least developed countries and countries with economies in transition, to promote their social development and eradicate poverty;

11. *Recognizes* that achieving the internationally agreed development goals, including those contained in the United Nations Millennium Declaration, demands a new partnership between developed and developing countries, and in this context stresses the importance of achieving sound policies, good governance at all levels and the rule of law, as well as mobilizing domestic resources, attracting international flows, promoting international trade as an engine for development, increasing international and financial and technical cooperation for development, sustainable debt financing and external debt relief and enhancing the coherence and consistency of the international monetary, financial and trading systems;

12. *Also recognizes* that a substantial increase in official development assistance and other resources will be required if developing countries are to achieve the internationally agreed development goals and objectives, including those contained in the Millennium Declaration, and further recognizes that, in order to build support for official development assistance, heads of State and Government have pledged further to improve policies and development strategies, both nationally and internationally, to enhance aid effectiveness;

13. *Urges* developed countries that have not done so to make concrete efforts towards achieving the target of providing 0.7 per cent of their gross national product as official development assistance to developing countries and from 0.15 to 0.20 per cent of their gross national product as official development assistance to least developed countries, as reconfirmed at the Third United Nations Conference on the Least Developed Countries, held at Brussels from 14 to 20 May 2001, encourages developing countries to build on progress achieved in ensuring that official development assistance is used effectively to help to achieve development goals and targets, acknowledges the efforts of all donors, commends those donors whose official development assistance contributions exceed, reach or are increasing towards the targets, and underlines the importance of undertaking an examination of the means and time frames for achieving the targets and goals;

14. *Reaffirms* that recipient and donor countries, as well as international institutions, should strive to make official development assistance more effective;

15. *Underlines* the importance of adopting effective measures, including new financial mechanisms, as appropriate, to support the efforts of developing countries to achieve sustained economic growth, sustainable development, poverty reduction and the strengthening of their democratic systems, while reaffirming that each country has primary responsibility for its own economic and social development and that national policies have the leading role in the development process;

16. *Reaffirms* that social development requires the active involvement of all actors in the development process, including civil society organizations, corporations and small businesses, and that partnerships among all relevant actors are increasingly becoming part of national and international cooperation for social development, reaffirms also that, within countries, partnerships among the Government, civil society and the private sector can contribute effectively to the achievement of social development goals, and underlines the fact that, at the international level, the recent initiatives towards building voluntary partnerships for social development should be encouraged and discussed further at, inter alia, the intergovernmental level;

17. *Underlines* the responsibility of the private sector, at both the national and the international levels, including small and large companies and transnational corporations, regarding not only the economic and financial, but also the development, social, gender and environmental implications of their activities, their obligations towards their workers and their contributions to achieving sustainable development, including social development, and emphasizes the need to take concrete actions within the United Nations system and through the participation of all relevant stakeholders on corporate responsibility and accountability;

18. *Reaffirms* that education, employment creation and improvement in working conditions, which are some of the indispensable elements of poverty eradication, social integration, gender equality and overall development, should be at the centre of development strategies and international cooperation in support of national policies, and recognizes the need to promote employment that meets labour standards as defined in relevant instruments of the International Labour Organization and other international instruments;

19. *Encourages*, in this context, current initiatives of the United Nations system on the elaboration of comprehensive employment strategies and measures to foster youth employment, bearing in mind relevant international instruments pertaining to youth;

20. *Reaffirms* the call of the Economic and Social Council for enhanced coordination within the United Nations system and the ongoing efforts to harmonize the current initiatives on Africa, and requests the Commission for Social Development to continue to give due prominence in its work to the social dimension of the New Partnership for Africa's Development;

21. *Welcomes* the contribution of the Commission for Social Development in the follow-up to and review of the further implementation of the commitments made at the World Summit for Social Development and the further initiatives agreed upon at the twenty-fourth special session of the General Assembly, reaffirms that the Commission will continue to have the primary responsibility in this regard, and encourages Governments, the relevant specialized agencies, funds and programmes of the United Nations system and civil society to enhance their support to its work;

22. *Recalls*, in this regard, its request to each functional commission of the Economic and Social Council to examine its methods of work in order to better pursue the implementation of the outcomes of the major United Nations conferences and summits, recognizing that there is no need for a uniform approach since each functional commission has its own specificity, while also noting that modern methods of work can better guarantee the review of progress made in implementation at all levels, on the basis of a report with recommendations to be submitted by the Secretary-General to each functional commission and relevant subsidiary body of the Council on its methods of work, in accordance with the provisions defined by the respective outcomes and relevant decisions taken by each body, bearing in mind the progress recently achieved in this regard by certain commissions, in particular by the Commission on Sustainable Development; the functional commissions and other relevant bodies of the Council should report to it no later than 2005 on the outcome of this examination;

23. *Notes* its decision to review in 2005 the progress achieved in implementing all the commitments made in the Millennium Declaration, and notes also that there is scope for a major event in this context, and in this regard calls upon the Commission for Social Development to transmit to the General Assembly, through the Economic and Social Council, the substantive outcome of its review of the further implementation of the World Summit for Social Development and the outcome of the twenty-fourth special session of the General Assembly for its consideration in 2005;

24. *Invites* the Secretary-General, the Economic and Social Council, the Commission for Social Development, the regional commissions, the relevant specialized agencies, funds and programmes of the United Nations system and other intergovernmental forums, within their respective mandates, to continue to integrate into their work programmes and give priority attention to the commitments and undertakings contained in the Copenhagen Declaration and the Programme of Action and in the further initiatives for social development, to continue to be actively involved in their follow-up and to monitor the achievement of those commitments and undertakings;

25. *Decides* to include in the provisional agenda of its fifty-ninth session the item entitled "Implementation of the outcome of the World Summit for Social Development and of the twenty-fourth special session of the General Assembly", and requests the Secretary-General to submit a report on this question to the Assembly at that session.

Commission for Social Development

The Commission for Social Development, at its forty-first session (New York, 10-21 February) [E/2003/26], adopted agreed conclusions on its priority theme, "National and international cooperation for social development" (see p. 1100). The Commission made recommendations for action by the Economic and Social Council on: the drafting of an international convention to promote and protect the rights and dignity of persons with disabilities (see p. 1107); national and international cooperation for social development, in particular the implementation of the social objectives of NEPAD (see p. 937); policies and programmes involving youth (see p. 1216); and modalities for reviewing the 2002 Madrid International Plan of Action on Ageing (see p. 1219). A text on preparations for the observance of the tenth anniversary of the International Year of the Family in 2004 was recommended to the Council for adoption by the General Assembly (see p. 1103).

The Commission reviewed the proposed work programme of the Division for Social Policy and Development of the Department of Economic and Social Affairs (DESA) for the 2004-2005 biennium [E/CN.5/2003/8], and took note of the report of the Board of the United Nations Research Institute for Social Development (UNRISD) on UNRISD's work during 2001-2002 [YUN 2002, p. 1089]. The Commission nominated, for confirmation by the Council, four candidates for membership to the Board for a four-year term beginning 1 July 2003 [E/CN.5/2003/3 & Add.1].

In an effort to link the Commission's normative work with its work in the field, a presentation was made on technical cooperation activities. A dialogue with non-governmental organizations (NGOs) was also held.

On 21 July, the Council took note of the Commission's report on its forty-first session and approved the provisional agenda and documentation for its forty-second (2004) session (**decision 2003/230**).

Cooperation for social development

The Secretary-General, in response to Economic and Social Council decision 2002/237 [YUN 2002, p. 1089], submitted to the Commission for Social Development a report on national and international cooperation for social development [E/CN.5/2003/5 & Corr.1], the priority theme for the Commission's 2003 session. The priority theme had five sub-themes: the sharing of experiences and practices in social development; forging partnerships for social development; the social responsibility of the private sector; the impact of employment strategies on social development; and the policies and role of international financial institutions and their effect on national social development strategies. The report analysed the sub-themes, covering such issues as capacity-building for social development, priority-setting and financing, information and evaluation, lessons learned from recent experiences with social development partnerships and approaches to the social responsibility of the private sector. It also reviewed the impact of employment strategies on social development and provided a critical appraisal of the activities and impact of international financial institutions on national social development strategies.

To study the priority theme, the Secretariat organized expert group meetings on the sharing of experiences and practices in social development (Havana, Cuba, 12-14 June 2002), and on forging partnerships for social development and the social responsibility of the private sector (Copenhagen, Denmark, 26-29 June 2002). The report said that, while economic and social development was generally considered to be a national concern, international support was important for developing countries to achieve development objectives within reasonable time frames, including the Millennium Development Goals (MDGs) [YUN 2000, p. 51]. The report proposed policy recommendations for the Commission's consideration.

ECONOMIC AND SOCIAL COUNCIL ACTION

On 21 July [meeting 42], the Economic and Social Council, on the recommendation of the Commission for Social Development [E/2003/26], adopted **resolution 2003/15** without vote [agenda item 14 (*b*)].

Agreed conclusions on national and international cooperation for social development

The Economic and Social Council

Endorses the following agreed conclusions adopted by the Commission for Social Development at its forty-first session with respect to its priority theme:

1. The Commission stresses that national and international cooperation for social development should aim at solidarity, equality within and among countries, social justice, good governance at all levels, tolerance and full respect for all human rights and fundamental freedoms.

2. The Commission recognizes that globalization and interdependence are opening new opportunities through trade, investment and capital flows and advances in technology, including information technology, for the growth of the world economy and the development and improvement of living standards around the world. At the same time, there remain serious challenges, including serious financial crises, insecurity, poverty, exclusion and inequality within and among societies. Considerable obstacles to further integration and full participation in the global economy remain for developing countries, in particular the least developed countries, as well as for some countries with economies in transition. Unless the benefits of social and economic development are extended to all countries, a growing number of people in all countries and even entire regions will remain marginalized from the global economy. The Commission reiterates the need for immediate action in order to overcome those obstacles affecting peoples and countries and to realize the full potential of opportunities presented for the benefit of all. The Commission stresses that the social impact and dimension of globalization deserves further attention.

3. Globalization offers opportunities and challenges. The developing countries and countries with economies in transition face special difficulties in responding to those challenges and opportunities. Globalization should be fully inclusive and equitable, and there is a strong need for policies and measures at the national and international levels, formulated and implemented with the full and effective participation of developing countries and countries with economies in transition to help them to respond effectively to those challenges and opportunities.

4. In an increasingly globalizing world, renewed and effective partnerships between developed countries and developing countries as well as countries with economies in transition are required to achieve the internationally agreed social development objectives and commitments, including those adopted at the World Summit for Social Development and the further initiatives adopted at the twenty-fourth special session of the General Assembly, and the internationally agreed development goals, including those contained in the United Nations Millennium Declaration.

5. The Commission welcomes the prominence given to the New Partnership for Africa's Development in the report of the Secretary-General on national and international cooperation for social development as an example of a partnership among Governments. It also recognizes that the objectives and action plans enunciated in the New Partnership are consistent with the internationally agreed development goals, including those contained in the Millennium Declaration, as well as those spelled out in the Copenhagen Declaration on Social Development, particularly its commitment 7 on accelerating the economic, social and human resource development of Africa and the least developed countries, and the outcome document of the twenty-fourth special session of the General Assembly.

6. The Commission invites the General Assembly and the Economic and Social Council to continue to include consideration of the integration of economic and social policies as one of the thematic areas to be addressed in future debates.

7. National capacity is one of the key factors in implementing social development policies and fulfilling national responsibilities. Each country has primary responsibility for its own economic and social development and the role of national policies and development strategies cannot be overemphasized. Enhanced international cooperation is essential to implement the Copenhagen Declaration on Social Development and the Programme of Action of the World Summit for Social Development as well as the further initiatives for social development and to address the challenges of globalization. In this regard, international cooperation has a vital role in assisting developing countries as well as some countries with economies in transition in the strengthening of their human, institutional and technological capacity. Without the building of such capacity, it will be difficult to ensure that social policy concerns are integrated within the policy planning and budgeting processes. The Commission therefore urges the international community to continue to assist developing countries in their capacity-building in order to promote social development.

8. Given the importance of education as a primary and critical component in any development strategy, in particular for the elimination of illiteracy, the Commission emphasizes the relevance of cooperation in educational matters at the national and international levels.

9. Achieving the internationally agreed development goals, including those contained in the Millennium Declaration, demands a new partnership between developed and developing countries. In this context, the Commission stresses the importance of the commitment recently made by heads of State and Government to achieving sound policies, good governance at all levels and the rule of law, as well as to mobilizing domestic resources, attracting international flows, promoting international trade as an engine for development, increasing international financial and technical cooperation for development, sustainable debt financing and external debt relief, and enhancing the coherence and consistency of the international monetary, financial and trading systems.

10. The Commission recognizes that a substantial increase in official development assistance and other resources will be required if developing countries are to achieve the internationally agreed development goals and objectives, including those contained in the Millennium Declaration. To build support for official development assistance, heads of State and Government have pledged to further improve policies and development strategies, both nationally and internationally, to enhance aid effectiveness.

11. In that context, the Commission urges developed countries that have not done so to make concrete efforts towards achieving the target of providing 0.7 per cent of their gross national product as official development assistance to developing countries and from 0.15 to 0.20 per cent of their gross national product as official development assistance to least developed countries, as reconfirmed at the Third United Nations Conference on the Least Developed Countries, and encourages developing countries to build on progress achieved in ensuring that official development assistance is used effectively to help achieve development goals and targets. The Commission acknowledges the efforts of all donors, commends those donors whose official development assistance contributions exceed, reach or are increasing towards the targets, and underlines the importance of undertaking an examination of the means and time frames for achieving the targets and goals.

12. Recipient and donor countries, as well as international institutions, should strive to make official development assistance more effective.

13. The Commission underlines the responsibility of the private sector at the national and international levels, including small and large companies and transnational corporations, regarding not only the economic and financial but also the development, social, gender and environmental implications of their activities, their responsibilities towards their workers and their contributions to achieving sustainable development including social development. In this context, the Commission emphasizes the need to take concrete actions within the United Nations system and through the participation of all relevant stakeholders on corporate responsibility and accountability.

14. Partnerships among all relevant actors are increasingly becoming part of national and international cooperation for social development. Within countries, partnerships among the Government, civil society and the private sector can contribute effectively to the achievement of social development goals. At the international level, the recent initiatives towards building voluntary partnerships for social development should be encouraged and discussed further at, inter alia, the intergovernmental level.

15. Cross-sectoral and integrated policies that take into account the needs and interests of all members of society, as well as their contributions to national development, and that mainstream a gender perspective should be promoted.

16. The Commission calls upon all relevant development partners to give adequate attention to productive and sustainable employment, as appropriate, in their development policies. Employment strategies can have a substantial impact on poverty eradication, social development and gender equality and should be developed in harmony with economic growth strategies and structural reforms. The Commission sees the involvement of social partners in cooperating with Governments in the formulation and implementation of employment strategies as an important element in ensuring their success. The Commission stresses the need to design appropriate labour and employment policies that will support both growth with employment and employment that supports social development goals.

17. Fulfilment of sustainable development objectives should aim at ensuring, inter alia, quality employment and defending workers' rights and interests and, to this effect, the Commission notes the need to promote respect for the relevant conventions of the United Nations and the International Labour Organization.

18. The Commission encourages the strengthening of cooperation among countries, inter alia, to address the issues of labour-market information and skills standards certification as well as transnational issues on labour migration, with a view to protecting the rights and dignity of migrant workers.

19. The Commission stresses the necessity of ensuring the effective involvement of developing countries in the international economic decision-making process through, inter alia, greater participation in international economic forums, thereby ensuring the transparency and accountability of international financial institutions with respect to according a central position to social development in their policies and programmes.

20. The Commission notes the increasing operational coordination and cooperation achieved between the United Nations funds and programmes and the international financial institutions, while taking into account their respective competencies and mandates. In this context, the Commission invites the international financial institutions to strengthen further their efforts to ensure that an improved social outcome is incorporated into their programmes of assistance, taking into account the fact that poverty reduction strategies should be nationally owned. Where poverty reduction strategy papers exist, a broad platform is necessary to place them within a wider context where all social objectives would be adequately taken into account.

In **resolution 2003/13** of 21 July (see p. 940), the Council underlined the need for partnership and cooperation between Governments and civil society in implementing the outcomes of the World Summit for Social Development [YUN 1995, p. 1114] and the twenty-fourth special session of the

General Assembly [YUN 2000, p. 1012], and the need to ensure, within the NEPAD framework, their involvement in the planning, elaboration, implementation and evaluation of social policies at the national, regional and international levels.

UN Research Institute for Social Development

During 2003, the United Nations Research Institute for Social Development (UNRISD) continued to conduct research on the social dimensions of development problems. It sought to promote a holistic and multidisciplinary approach to social development by focusing on decision-making processes, often-conflicting social forces and the effects of growing or contracting economies.

Among issues addressed in its 2003 publications and research papers were communicating in the information society; gender, health and human rights; the expansion of information technology in Senegal; marginalized rural youth in Brazil, Egypt and Nepal; agrarian change in the first half of 2003; global media governance; and citizenship rights and obligations of people of African descent.

UNRISD participated in the second meeting of the Preparatory Committee for the World Summit on the Information Society and participated in the Summit's first phase (see p. 857). It organized a conference entitled "Corporate Social Responsibility and Development: Towards a New Agenda?" (Geneva, 17-18 November), and collaborated in organizing the conference "Promoting Corporate Social and Environmental Responsibility in the Philippines" (7 March). UNRISD launched a new research project on UN world summits and civil society engagement to assess the impact of various UN summits on civil society activism at global, national and local levels. UNRISD also expanded its access to public media.

Cooperatives in social development

In response to General Assembly resolution 56/114 [YUN 2001, p. 1007], the Secretary-General, in July [A/58/159], submitted the replies he had received from Governments and international organizations on progress achieved in the resolution's implementation, particularly in promoting a supportive environment for the development of cooperatives and their contribution to poverty eradication, the generation of full and productive employment, and the enhancement of social integration.

The Secretary-General concluded that efforts were being made to create a supportive environment for cooperative development in many countries, particularly in revamping cooperative regulations and legislation. Initiatives had been taken to enhance capacity, efficiency and management to better serve members and communities. Suggestions were made for promoting the development of cooperatives, including strengthening national training and information centres; focusing on integrating and strengthening national and international cooperative networks; research on the cooperative model by the Committee for the Promotion and Advancement of Cooperatives; and UN assistance for human resources development, technical advice and training.

GENERAL ASSEMBLY ACTION

On 22 December [meeting 77], the General Assembly, on the recommendation of the Third Committee [A/58/497], adopted **resolution 58/131** without vote [agenda item 106].

Cooperatives in social development

The General Assembly,

Recalling its resolutions 47/90 of 16 December 1992, 49/155 of 23 December 1994, 51/58 of 12 December 1996, 54/123 of 17 December 1999 and 56/114 of 19 December 2001, concerning cooperatives in social development,

Recognizing that cooperatives, in their various forms, promote the fullest possible participation in the economic and social development of all people, including women, youth, older persons and persons with disabilities, and are becoming a major factor of economic and social development,

Recognizing also the important contribution and potential of all forms of cooperatives to the follow-up to the World Summit for Social Development, held at Copenhagen from 6 to 12 March 1995, the Fourth World Conference on Women, held at Beijing from 4 to 15 September 1995, the second United Nations Conference on Human Settlements (Habitat II), held at Istanbul, Turkey, from 3 to 14 June 1996, and their five-year reviews, the World Food Summit, held at Rome from 13 to 17 November 1996, the Second World Assembly on Ageing, held at Madrid from 8 to 12 April 2002, the International Conference on Financing for Development, held at Monterrey, Mexico, from 18 to 22 March 2002, and the World Summit on Sustainable Development, held at Johannesburg, South Africa, from 26 August to 4 September 2002,

1. *Takes note* of the report of the Secretary-General;
2. *Draws the attention* of Member States to the proposals contained in the report of the Secretary-General for further action to promote a supportive environment for the development of cooperatives;
3. *Also draws the attention* of Member States to the revised guidelines aimed at creating a supportive environment for the development of cooperatives, to be considered by them in developing or revising their national policies on cooperatives;
4. *Encourages* Governments to keep under review, as appropriate, the legal and administrative provisions governing the activities of cooperatives, with a view to ensuring a supportive environment for them and to protecting and advancing the potential of cooperatives to help them to achieve their goals;
5. *Urges* Governments, relevant international organizations and specialized agencies, in collaboration

with national and international cooperative organizations, to give due consideration to the role and contribution of cooperatives in the implementation of and follow-up to the outcomes of the World Summit for Social Development, the Fourth World Conference on Women, the second United Nations Conference on Human Settlements (Habitat II) and their five-year reviews, the World Food Summit, the Second World Assembly on Ageing, the International Conference on Financing for Development and the World Summit on Sustainable Development by, inter alia:

(a) Utilizing and developing fully the potential and contribution of cooperatives for the attainment of social development goals, in particular the eradication of poverty, the generation of full and productive employment and the enhancement of social integration;

(b) Encouraging and facilitating the establishment and development of cooperatives, including taking measures aimed at enabling people living in poverty or belonging to vulnerable groups to engage on a voluntary basis in the creation and development of cooperatives;

(c) Taking appropriate measures aimed at creating a supportive and enabling environment for the development of cooperatives by, inter alia, developing an effective partnership between Governments and the cooperative movement, promoting and implementing better legislation, training, research, sharing of good practices and human resources development;

6. *Invites* Governments, in collaboration with the cooperative movement, to develop programmes to promote and strengthen the education of members, the elected leadership and professional cooperative management, where appropriate, and to create or improve statistical databases on the development of cooperatives and on their contribution to national economies;

7. *Invites* Governments, relevant international organizations, specialized agencies and local, national and international cooperative organizations to continue to observe the International Day of Cooperatives annually, on the first Saturday of July, as proclaimed by the General Assembly in its resolution 47/90;

8. *Requests* the Secretary-General, in cooperation with the relevant United Nations and other international organizations and national, regional and international cooperative organizations, to render support to Member States, as appropriate, in their efforts to create a supportive environment for the development of cooperatives, to continue to provide assistance for human resources development, technical advice and training, and to promote an exchange of experience and best practices, through, inter alia, conferences, workshops and seminars at the national and regional levels;

9. *Also requests* the Secretary-General to submit to the General Assembly at its sixtieth session a report on the implementation of the present resolution, focusing on the role of cooperatives in the eradication of poverty.

Follow-up to
International Year of the Family (1994)

By a March note [A/58/67-E/2003/49], the Secretary-General, in response to General Assembly resolution 57/164 [YUN 2002, p. 1090], submitted a report on preparations for the tenth (2004) anniversary of the International Year of the Family [E/CN.5/2003/6], proclaimed by the Assembly in resolution 44/82 [YUN 1989, p. 612] and observed in 1994 [YUN 1994, p. 1144].

At the national level, organizational arrangements had been made, partnerships formed and promotional activities undertaken. The UN regional commissions were playing a lead role and, at the international level, NGOs were acting as partners in the preparation and observance of the anniversary. At the United Nations, DESA promoted awareness of the economic, social and demographic processes affecting families and their members. The report recommended that Governments promote and facilitate the observance of the anniversary, with the participation of all segments of society; raise awareness of family issues; formulate national strategies for enhancing the well-being of families; enlist all segments of society in the development and implementation of national plans; and strengthen partnerships with NGOs working on family issues, particularly with regard to advocacy and policy formulation. Concerned UN agencies and bodies were called on to emphasize the family perspective in development cooperation and encourage regional and subregional cooperation in matters relating to families, monitor progress in the regions, identify needs, collect and analyse information, sponsor research and development, and provide advisory services and training for personnel.

The Economic and Social Council, on 24 July, took note of the Secretary-General's note (**decision 2003/310**), as did the Assembly on 22 December (**decision 58/530**).

ECONOMIC AND SOCIAL COUNCIL ACTION

On 21 July [meeting 42], the Economic and Social Council, on the recommendation of the Commission for Social Development [E/2003/26], adopted **resolution 2003/10** without vote [agenda item 14 (b)].

**Preparations for and observance of the
tenth anniversary of the
International Year of the Family in 2004**

The Economic and Social Council
Recommends to the General Assembly the adoption of the following draft resolution:
[For text, see General Assembly resolution 58/15 below.]

GENERAL ASSEMBLY ACTION

On 3 December [meeting 68], the General Assembly, on the recommendation of the Third Committee [A/58/497], adopted **resolution 58/15** without vote [agenda item 106].

**Preparations for and observance of the
tenth anniversary of the
International Year of the Family in 2004**

The General Assembly,
Recalling its resolutions 44/82 of 8 December 1989, 45/133 of 14 December 1990, 46/92 of 16 December

1991, 47/237 of 20 September 1993, 50/142 of 21 December 1995, 52/81 of 12 December 1997, 54/124 of 17 December 1999, 56/113 of 19 December 2001 and 57/164 of 18 December 2002 concerning the proclamation of, preparations for and observance of the International Year of the Family in 1994 and its tenth anniversary in 2004,

Recognizing that the tenth anniversary of the International Year of the Family constitutes an important opportunity to strengthen and enhance the effectiveness of efforts at all levels to carry out specific programmes within the framework of the objectives of the Year,

Recognizing also that 2004 is to be viewed as a target year by which time concrete achievements will have been produced with respect to identifying and elaborating issues of direct concern to families and mechanisms will have been set up to plan and coordinate activities by the appropriate governmental and non-governmental bodies and agencies,

Emphasizing that equality between women and men and respect for all human rights and fundamental freedoms of all family members are essential to family well-being and to society at large, noting the importance of reconciliation of work and family life, and recognizing the principle that both parents have common responsibilities for the upbringing and development of the child,

Noting with satisfaction the close collaboration of the Department of Economic and Social Affairs of the Secretariat with intergovernmental and non-governmental organizations active in the family field, as well as its research efforts and preparations for the tenth anniversary of the International Year of the Family,

Appreciating the active role of the regional commissions in the preparatory process of the tenth anniversary of the International Year of the Family, particularly in facilitating regional cooperation in that regard,

Recalling that one plenary meeting at its fifty-ninth session, in 2004, will be devoted to the observance of the tenth anniversary of the International Year of the Family, building upon the events to be held on 15 May 2004 on the occasion of the International Day of Families,

1. *Welcomes* the decision of Benin to host a regional preparatory conference in Benin in May 2004 in collaboration with the United Nations, within existing resources;

2. *Also welcomes* the decision of the State of Qatar to host an international conference to celebrate the tenth anniversary of the International Year of the Family in November 2004;

3. *Welcomes* the launching by the Secretary-General of the celebration of the tenth anniversary of the International Year of the Family on 4 December 2003;

4. *Further welcomes* decisions by members of the international community (Governments, non-governmental organizations, civil society) to host events in observance of the tenth anniversary of the International Year of the Family;

5. *Encourages* Governments to make every possible effort to realize the objectives of the tenth anniversary of the International Year of the Family and to integrate a family perspective in the planning process;

6. *Recalls its invitation* to all States to set the end of 2003 as a target date for finalizing a programme for the observance of the tenth anniversary of the International Year of the Family;

7. *Also recalls its invitation* to Governments that had not already done so to set up national coordinating committees or similar mechanisms, as appropriate, for the tenth anniversary of the International Year of the Family, and invites them, as well as the Governments of countries with existing bodies responsible for preparations and observance, to intensify preparatory measures already under way;

8. *Recommends* that all relevant actors, inter alia, Governments, civil society, including relevant non-governmental organizations, and research and academic institutions, contribute to developing strategies and programmes aimed at strengthening the livelihood of families;

9. *Encourages* United Nations agencies and bodies, including the regional commissions, as well as intergovernmental and non-governmental organizations and research and academic institutions, to work closely with the Department of Economic and Social Affairs of the Secretariat in a coordinated manner on family-related issues, inter alia, by sharing experience and findings, in recognition of their valuable role in family policy development at all levels;

10. *Calls upon* United Nations agencies and bodies, including the regional commissions, within existing resources, and invites intergovernmental organizations and research and academic institutions to support regional events of the year 2004 to contribute to the success of those events;

11. *Requests* the Secretary-General:

(*a*) To strengthen the programme of work of the Department of Economic and Social Affairs on family pursuant to the objectives of the tenth anniversary of the International Year of the Family in the context of national family-related provisions of the outcomes of the United Nations conferences and summits, and in the context of the internationally agreed development goals, including those contained in the United Nations Millennium Declaration, to enhance the unique role of the family in society, in particular through:

(i) The development and strengthening of a family-focused perspective in relevant policies and programmes of United Nations bodies as well as in the follow-up to the outcomes of the relevant United Nations conferences and summits in the economic and social fields;

(ii) The provision of policy guidance on emerging issues and trends affecting the family, through the preparation of studies and research papers aimed in particular at enhancing the role of the family in society;

(iii) The provision of technical assistance to countries, upon request, to enhance, where appropriate, their national capacities in the area of family-related work;

(*b*) To address family issues, where relevant, in his report on the integrated and coordinated implementation of and follow-up to the outcomes of the major United Nations conferences and summits in the economic and social fields;

12. *Also requests* the Secretary-General to submit an interim report to the Commission for Social Development at its forty-second session and a substantive report to the General Assembly at its fifty-ninth session

Persons with disabilities

World Programme of Action concerning Disabled Persons

The Secretary-General, in response to General Assembly resolution 56/115 [YUN 2001, p. 1010], submitted the fourth five-year review and appraisal of the 1982 World Programme of Action concerning Disabled Persons [A/58/61-E/2003/5], adopted by Assembly resolution 37/52 [YUN 1982, p. 981]. The report assessed trends in policies and programmes since the previous review [YUN 1997, p. 1117], noting the widespread support for the goals and objectives of the Programme of Action and for the guidance provided by the Standard Rules on the Equalization of Opportunities for Persons with Disabilities, adopted by Assembly resolution 48/96 [YUN 1993, p. 977], on disability-sensitive policy design, planning, evaluation and drafting of national legislation. However, Governments had yet to pronounce on the proposed supplement to the Standard Rules, contained in a 2002 report of the Special Rapporteur on disability [YUN 2002, p. 1091]. Views of Governments on the proposed supplement would be considered by the Commission for Social Development in 2004. Recommendations for further action included identifying options to bring a disability perspective into international development instruments, such as the MDGs, which did not address specifically the situation of persons with disabilities; and defining disability within the proposed convention (see p. 1107). Three priorities were identified for action: the dimension of environmental accessibility; ways in which persons with disabilities could benefit from measures for implementing the MDGs by 2015 on the basis of equality with non-disabled populations; and the development of international agreements on employment indicators, such as labour force participation and unemployment rates for persons with disabilities. Proposals for action to the Assembly involved identifying policy options and target areas that could be used by UN funds and programmes to incorporate a disability perspective in their activities; identifying priorities for action related to statistics and indicators; and expressing its views on options and priorities to strengthen joint planning and evaluation of the outcomes of the UN system in promoting the advancement of persons with disabilities in the context of development.

Annexed to the report was an overview of recent policy and programme activities taken by Governments.

The Economic and Social Council, by **decision 2003/310** of 24 July, took note of the Secretary-General's report.

GENERAL ASSEMBLY ACTION

On 22 December [meeting 77], the General Assembly, on the recommendation of the Third Committee [A/58/497], adopted **resolution 58/132** without vote [agenda item 106].

Implementation of the World Programme of Action concerning Disabled Persons: towards a society for all in the twenty-first century

The General Assembly,

Recalling the purposes and principles of the Charter of the United Nations, and reaffirming the obligations contained in relevant human rights instruments, including the Convention on the Elimination of All Forms of Discrimination against Women and the Convention on the Rights of the Child,

Recalling also its relevant resolutions, in particular resolution 37/52 of 3 December 1982, by which it adopted the World Programme of Action concerning Disabled Persons, resolution 48/96 of 20 December 1993, by which it adopted the Standard Rules on the Equalization of Opportunities for Persons with Disabilities, and resolution 56/115 of 19 December 2001, as well as the relevant resolutions of the Economic and Social Council and its functional commissions,

Recalling further the United Nations Millennium Declaration, adopted on 8 September 2000 by heads of State and Government at the Millennium Summit of the United Nations, stressing the need to promote and protect the full enjoyment of all human rights and fundamental freedoms by persons with disabilities, and recognizing the importance of incorporating the disability perspective in the implementation of the outcomes of the major United Nations conferences and summits, with a view to achieving the internationally agreed development goals, including those contained in the Millennium Declaration,

Noting with appreciation the initiatives and actions of Governments to implement relevant sections of the Standard Rules and of relevant resolutions that give special attention to the questions of accessible environments and information and communication technologies, health, education and social services, employment and sustainable livelihoods, including the relevant activities of intergovernmental and non-governmental organizations,

Reaffirming the outcomes of the major United Nations conferences and summits and their respective follow-up reviews,

Noting that the Madrid International Plan of Action on Ageing, 2002, adopted by the Second World Assembly on Ageing, considers "older persons and disabilities" as a specific issue for policy concern,

Noting also the preparatory work of the Ad Hoc Committee on a Comprehensive and Integral International Convention on the Protection and Promotion of the Rights and Dignity of Persons with Disabilities in establishing a working group with the aim of preparing and presenting a draft text that would be the basis for the negotiation of the draft convention,

Recognizing the strong commitment of Governments to the equalization of opportunities and to the rights of persons with disabilities and the promotion and protection of the full enjoyment of all human rights by persons with disabilities, including in the context of development,

Acknowledging the important role of non-governmental organizations in the promotion and protection of the full enjoyment of all human rights by persons with disabilities, and noting in this regard their work in promoting the elaboration of an international convention on the rights of disabled persons,

Noting with appreciation the important contributions of regional intergovernmental organizations and the regional commissions of the United Nations in promoting awareness and building capacities for the full participation and equality of persons with disabilities, as well as the outcome of international conferences relating to persons with disabilities,

Mindful of the need to adopt and implement effective policies and strategies to promote the rights and the full and effective participation of persons with disabilities at all levels,

Recognizing the importance of accessibility both of the physical environment and of information and communication in enabling persons with disabilities to enjoy fully their human rights,

Reiterating that technology, in particular information and communication technologies, provides new possibilities for improving accessibility and employment for persons with disabilities and for facilitating their full and effective participation and equality, and welcoming the initiatives of the United Nations and contributions from regional groups in promoting information and communication technologies as a means of achieving the universal goal of a society for all,

Recognizing the importance of timely and reliable data on disability-sensitive topics, programme planning and evaluation and the need for the further development of practical statistical methodology for the collection and compilation of data on populations with disabilities,

Recognizing also the challenge of better incorporating the disability perspective in development and technical cooperation activities,

Recognizing further the need to improve the quality of life of persons with disabilities worldwide through the enhancement of awareness of and sensitivity to disability issues and respect for the full enjoyment of all human rights by persons with disabilities,

Recognizing that, in the elaboration of national and international development strategies, consideration needs to be given to the impact of poverty, especially in rural areas, on the conditions of persons with disabilities,

Expressing grave concern that situations of armed conflict continue to have especially devastating consequences for the human rights of persons with disabilities,

1. *Takes note with appreciation* of the report of the Secretary-General on the implementation of the World Programme of Action concerning Disabled Persons, including the recommendations of the Secretary-General relating to policy options to promote the full enjoyment of all human rights by persons with disabilities in the context of development;

2. *Welcomes* the work of the Special Rapporteur on disability of the Commission for Social Development to promote the full enjoyment of all human rights by, and the equalization of opportunities for, persons with disabilities;

3. *Calls upon* Governments to take all necessary measures to advance beyond the adoption of national plans for people with disabilities through, inter alia, the creation or reinforcement of arrangements for the promotion and awareness of disability issues and the allocation of sufficient resources for the full implementation of existing plans and initiatives, and emphasizes in this regard the importance of supporting national efforts through international cooperation;

4. *Encourages* Governments, intergovernmental and non-governmental organizations and the private sector, as appropriate, to continue to take concrete measures to mainstream the disability perspective into the development process and promote the implementation of relevant United Nations resolutions and agreed international standards concerning persons with disabilities, in particular the Standard Rules on the Equalization of Opportunities for Persons with Disabilities, and for the further equalization of opportunities for persons with disabilities;

5. *Encourages* Governments to continue their support to non-governmental organizations and other groups, including organizations of persons with disabilities, that contribute to the fulfilment of the implementation of the World Programme of Action;

6. *Also encourages* Governments to involve persons with disabilities in the formulation of strategies and plans, in particular those pertaining to them;

7. *Urges* relevant organizations and bodies of the United Nations system, including relevant human rights treaty bodies and the regional commissions, as well as intergovernmental and non-governmental organizations and institutions, to incorporate the disability perspective in their activities, as appropriate, and to continue to work closely with the Division for Social Policy and Development of the Secretariat for the promotion of the full enjoyment of all human rights and fundamental freedoms by persons with disabilities, including activities at the field level, by sharing experiences, findings and recommendations on persons with disabilities;

8. *Stresses* the importance of improving data and statistics on persons with disabilities, in compliance with national legislation on the protection of personal data, so that they can be compared internationally and domestically for purposes of policy design, planning and evaluation from the disability perspective, urges Governments, in this regard, to cooperate with the Statistics Division of the Secretariat in the continuing development of global statistics and indicators on disability, and encourages them to avail themselves of the technical assistance of the Division to build national capacities for national data-collection systems;

9. *Urges* Governments, intergovernmental organizations and non-governmental organizations to provide special protection to persons with mental or physical disabilities, who may experience multiple or aggravating forms of discrimination, with special emphasis on integrating them into society and protecting

and promoting their full enjoyment of all human rights;

10. *Urges* Governments to address the situation of persons with disabilities with respect to all actions taken to implement existing human rights treaties to which they are parties;

11. *Invites* States to continue to participate actively in the negotiations within the Ad Hoc Committee on a Comprehensive and Integral International Convention on the Protection and Promotion of the Rights and Dignity of Persons with Disabilities;

12. *Encourages* Governments, intergovernmental organizations, concerned non-governmental organizations and the private sector to continue to support the United Nations Voluntary Fund on Disability, with a view to strengthening its capacity to support catalytic and innovative activities to implement fully the World Programme of Action and the Standard Rules, including the work of the Special Rapporteur, and to support activities to build national capacities, with emphasis on priorities for action identified in the present resolution;

13. *Requests* the Secretary-General to continue to support the initiatives of relevant organizations and bodies of the United Nations system, as well as those of regional, intergovernmental and non-governmental organizations and institutions, for the promotion of the full enjoyment of all human rights by, and non-discrimination in respect of, persons with disabilities and the further implementation of the World Programme of Action, as well as their efforts to integrate persons with disabilities in technical cooperation activities, both as beneficiaries and as decision makers;

14. *Expresses its appreciation* to the Secretary-General for his efforts in improving the accessibility of the United Nations for persons with disabilities, and urges him to continue to implement plans to provide a barrier-free environment;

15. *Welcomes* the review by the Secretary-General in his current report on the fourth quinquennial review and appraisal of the World Programme of Action, and requests the Secretary-General to submit to the General Assembly at its sixtieth session a report on the implementation of the present resolution.

International convention on the rights of persons with disabilities

In accordance with General Assembly resolution 57/229 [YUN 2002, p. 1095], the Ad Hoc Committee on a Comprehensive and Integral International Convention on Protection and Promotion of the Rights and Dignity of Persons with Disabilities, established by Assembly resolution 56/168 [YUN 2001, p. 1012], held its second session (New York, 16-27 June). It established a working group to prepare a draft text for a convention, which would be the basis for negotiation by Member States. The working group would be composed of 27 governmental representatives and 12 NGO representatives. The Committee recommended holding its third session in 2004 and invited the Assembly to examine further the provision of reasonable accommodation for persons with disabilities in order to facilitate accessibility to UN premises, technology and documents.

ECONOMIC AND SOCIAL COUNCIL ACTION

On 21 July [meeting 42], the Economic and Social Council, on the recommendation of the Commission for Social Development [E/2003/26], adopted **resolution 2003/12** without vote [agenda item 14 (b)].

Comprehensive and integral international convention to promote and protect the rights and dignity of persons with disabilities

The Economic and Social Council,

Recalling relevant provisions of the major United Nations conferences and summits, and their respective follow-up reviews, for the promotion of the rights and well-being of persons with disabilities on an equal and participatory basis,

Encouraged by the increased interest of the international community in the promotion and protection of the rights and dignity of persons with disabilities under a comprehensive and integral approach,

Recalling General Assembly resolution 56/168 of 19 December 2001, by which the Assembly established an Ad Hoc Committee to consider proposals for a comprehensive and integral international convention to promote and protect the rights and dignity of persons with disabilities, based on the holistic approach in the work carried out in the fields of social development, human rights and non-discrimination, and taking into account the recommendations of the Commission on Human Rights and the Commission for Social Development,

Recalling also General Assembly resolution 57/229 of 18 December 2002, in which the Assembly took note with appreciation of the report of the Ad Hoc Committee on a Comprehensive and Integral International Convention on the Protection and Promotion of the Rights and Dignity of Persons with Disabilities on its first session, and reaffirmed the need to promote and protect the equal and effective enjoyment of all human rights and fundamental freedoms by persons with disabilities, aware of the contribution that a convention could make in that regard and thus convinced of the need to continue to consider proposals,

Recalling further its resolution 2002/7 of 24 July 2002 on a comprehensive and integral international convention to promote and protect the rights and dignity of persons with disabilities,

Stressing the primary responsibility of Governments in the promotion and protection of all human rights and fundamental freedoms and their full enjoyment by persons with disabilities,

Welcoming the work of national, regional and international meetings of Governments, experts and non-governmental organizations that contribute to the work of the Ad Hoc Committee, including the regional initiatives taken previous to the second session of the Ad Hoc Committee in Africa, Latin America, Asia and Europe,

Taking note of the report of the Secretary-General on the fourth quinquennial review and appraisal of the World Programme of Action concerning Disabled Persons,

Stressing the need for additional efforts to ensure accessibility with reasonable accommodation regarding facilities and documentation at the United Nations for all persons with disabilities, in accordance with General Assembly decision 56/474 of 23 July 2002,

Deeply concerned about the disadvantaged and vulnerable situation faced by 600 million persons with disabilities around the world,

1. *Acknowledges* the contributions of the Special Rapporteur on disability of the Commission for Social Development to the process established by the General Assembly in resolution 56/168 on a comprehensive and integral international convention to promote and protect the rights and dignity of persons with disabilities, and encourages the Special Rapporteur to continue to contribute to this process in accordance with Assembly resolution 57/229;

2. *Also acknowledges* the contributions of the Office of the United Nations High Commissioner for Human Rights and the Department of Economic and Social Affairs of the Secretariat to the process established by the General Assembly in resolution 56/168, and encourages them to continue to contribute to this process;

3. *Requests* the Commission for Social Development to continue to contribute to the process established by the General Assembly in resolution 56/168 by, inter alia, providing its views regarding the social development of persons with disabilities, bearing in mind the experience in the implementation of the Standard Rules on the Equalization of Opportunities for Persons with Disabilities and the World Programme of Action concerning Disabled Persons;

4. *Invites* bodies, organs and entities of the United Nations system, including the funds and programmes, particularly those working in the fields of social and economic development and human rights, within their respective mandates, as well as non-governmental organizations, national disability and human rights institutions and independent experts with an interest in the matter, to make available to the Ad Hoc Committee on a Comprehensive and Integral International Convention on Protection and Promotion of the Rights and Dignity of Persons with Disabilities suggestions and possible elements to be considered in proposals for a convention;

5. *Encourages* the relevant bodies of the United Nations to continue to promote and support the active participation of civil society, including interested non-governmental organizations, in the process established by the General Assembly in resolution 56/168, in accordance with Assembly resolutions 56/510 of 23 July 2002 and 57/229, and requests the Secretary-General to disseminate widely to the community of non-governmental organizations all available information on accreditation procedures as well as information on supportive measures and modalities for their participation in the work of the Ad Hoc Committee;

6. *Invites* Governments, civil society and the private sector to contribute to the voluntary fund established by the General Assembly to support the participation of non-governmental organizations and experts from developing countries, in particular from the least developed countries, in the work of the Ad Hoc Committee;

7. *Underlines* the importance of strengthening the United Nations Programme on Disability in order to provide support to the Ad Hoc Committee, as requested by the General Assembly in resolution 57/229.

GENERAL ASSEMBLY ACTION

On 23 December [meeting 79], the General Assembly, on the recommendation of the Third Committee [A/58/508/Add. 2], adopted **resolution 58/246** without vote [agenda item 117(*b*)].

Ad Hoc Committee on a Comprehensive and Integral International Convention on the Protection and Promotion of the Rights and Dignity of Persons with Disabilities

The General Assembly,

Recalling its resolution 56/168 of 19 December 2001, by which it decided to establish an Ad Hoc Committee open to the participation of all Member States and observers to the United Nations, to consider proposals for a comprehensive and integral international convention to promote and protect the rights and dignity of persons with disabilities, based on a holistic approach in the work done in the fields of social development, human rights and non-discrimination and taking into account the recommendations of the Commission on Human Rights and the Commission for Social Development,

Recalling also its resolution 57/229 of 18 December 2002, as well as relevant resolutions of the Commission for Social Development and the Commission on Human Rights,

Reaffirming the universality, indivisibility and interdependence of all human rights and fundamental freedoms and the need for persons with disabilities to be guaranteed their full enjoyment without discrimination,

Convinced of the contribution that a convention can make in this regard,

Encouraging Member States and observers to participate actively in the Ad Hoc Committee in order to present to the General Assembly, as a matter of priority, a draft text of a convention,

Stressing the importance of the active participation of intergovernmental and non-governmental organizations and national human rights institutions in the work of the Ad Hoc Committee, and their valuable contribution to the promotion of the full enjoyment of all human rights and fundamental freedoms by persons with disabilities,

Recognizing the important contributions made thus far to the Ad Hoc Committee by all stakeholders,

1. *Welcomes* the report of the Ad Hoc Committee on a Comprehensive and Integral International Convention on the Protection and Promotion of the Rights and Dignity of Persons with Disabilities;

2. *Requests* the Secretary-General to transmit the report of the Ad Hoc Committee to the Commission for Social Development at its forty-second session and to the Commission on Human Rights at its sixtieth session, and further requests both Commissions to continue to contribute to the work of the Ad Hoc Committee;

3. *Endorses* the decision of the Ad Hoc Committee to establish a Working Group with the aim of preparing and presenting a draft text, which would be the basis for negotiations on the draft convention in the Ad Hoc Committee, taking into account all contributions;

4. *Notes* that the Working Group will present the outcome of its work on a draft text to the Ad Hoc Committee at the third session of the Committee;

5. *Decides* that the Ad Hoc Committee shall start the negotiations on a draft convention at its third session;

6. *Decides also* that the Ad Hoc Committee shall hold, within existing resources, two sessions in 2004 of ten working days each, prior to the fifty-ninth session of the General Assembly;

7. *Underlines* the importance of strengthening the cooperation and coordination between the Office of the United Nations High Commissioner for Human Rights and the Department of Economic and Social Affairs of the Secretariat in order to support jointly the work of the Ad Hoc Committee;

8. *Urges* that further efforts be made to ensure the active participation of non-governmental organizations in the Ad Hoc Committee, in accordance with General Assembly resolution 56/510 of 23 July 2002 and based on the decision of the Ad Hoc Committee on the modalities for the participation of non-governmental organizations in its work;

9. *Stresses* the need for additional efforts to ensure accessibility at the United Nations, with reasonable accommodation regarding facilities and documentation, for all persons with disabilities, in accordance with General Assembly decision 56/474 of 23 July 2002;

10. *Requests* the Secretary-General to continue to provide the Ad Hoc Committee with the facilities necessary for the performance of its work;

11. *Encourages* Member States to continue to include in their delegations to the meetings of the Ad Hoc Committee persons with disabilities and/or other experts in the field;

12. *Urges* Member States, observers, civil society and the private sector to contribute to the voluntary fund established pursuant to its resolution 57/229 to support the participation of non-governmental organizations and experts from developing countries, in particular least developed countries, in the work of the Ad Hoc Committee;

13. *Requests* the Secretary-General to transmit a comprehensive report of the Ad Hoc Committee to the General Assembly at its fifty-ninth session and to report on the implementation of paragraphs 7, 8 and 9 of the present resolution.

Cultural development

Follow-up to United Nations Year for Cultural Heritage

Following the observance of the United Nations Year for Cultural Heritage in 2002 [YUN 2002, p. 1096], the United Nations Educational, Scientific and Cultural Organization (UNESCO) General Conference, on 17 October 2003, adopted the Convention for the Safeguarding of the Intangible Cultural Heritage and the Declaration concerning the Intentional Destruction of Cultural Heritage. The Convention, the fifth of its kind adopted by UNESCO for the protection of cultural heritage, was designed to make the States parties take measures to ensure the safeguarding of the international cultural heritage and to strengthen solidarity and cooperation at regional and international levels. The Declaration outlined possible protection measures by States to combat the intentional destruction of cultural heritage, in both peacetime and in the event of armed conflict, including during an occupation.

GENERAL ASSEMBLY ACTION

On 17 December [meeting 75], the General Assembly adopted **resolution 58/124** [draft: A/58/L.11/Rev.2 & Add.1] without vote [agenda item 42].

United Nations Year for Cultural Heritage, 2002

The General Assembly,

Recalling the international conventions dealing with the protection of cultural and natural heritage, including the Convention for the Protection of Cultural Property in the Event of Armed Conflict adopted at The Hague in 1954 and the two Protocols thereto, the 1970 Convention on the Means of Prohibiting and Preventing the Illicit Import, Export and Transfer of Ownership of Cultural Property, and the 1972 Convention for the Protection of the World Cultural and Natural Heritage, as well as the 1989 Recommendation on the Safeguarding of Traditional Culture and Folklore and the 2001 Universal Declaration on Cultural Diversity of the United Nations Educational, Scientific and Cultural Organization,

Welcoming the ratification of the Convention for the Protection of the World Cultural and Natural Heritage by one hundred and seventy-six States parties, and noting the inscription of seven hundred and fifty-four sites on the World Heritage List,

Noting the adoption of the Convention on the Protection of the Underwater Cultural Heritage by the General Conference of the United Nations Educational, Scientific and Cultural Organization on 2 November 2001,

Mindful of the importance of protecting the world cultural tangible and intangible heritage as a common ground for the promotion of mutual understanding and enrichment among cultures and civilizations,

Noting the work already undertaken to protect the world cultural and natural heritage by the United Nations Educational, Scientific and Cultural Organization, including international campaigns,

Recalling its resolutions 56/8 of 21 November 2001, in which it proclaimed 2002 the United Nations Year for Cultural Heritage, and 57/158 of 16 December 2002, in which it declared the Year concluded,

1. *Notes* the activities of the United Nations Educational, Scientific and Cultural Organization undertaken during the United Nations Year for Cultural Heritage;

2. *Takes note with appreciation* of the adoption of the Convention for the Safeguarding of the Intangible Cultural Heritage by the General Conference of the United Nations Educational, Scientific and Cultural Organization at its thirty-second session, on 17 October 2003;

3. *Welcomes* the adoption of the Declaration concerning the Intentional Destruction of Cultural Heritage by the General Conference of the United Nations

Educational, Scientific and Cultural Organization on 17 October 2003;

4. *Invites* the United Nations Educational, Scientific and Cultural Organization, in collaboration with Member States, observers, relevant United Nations bodies, within their respective mandates, other international organizations and relevant non-governmental organizations, to continue to intensify the implementation of programmes, activities and projects aimed at the promotion and protection of the world cultural heritage;

5. *Invites* Member States and observers to continue to promote education and raise public awareness so as to foster respect for national and world cultural heritage.

Culture of peace

The General Assembly, by **decision 58/565** of 23 December, decided that the agenda item on the culture of peace would remain for consideration during its resumed fifty-eighth (2004) session.

Religious and cultural understanding

On 19 December [meeting 76], the General Assembly adopted **resolution 58/128** [draft: A/58/L.52 & Add.1] without vote [agenda item 44].

Promotion of religious and cultural understanding, harmony and cooperation

The General Assembly,

Reaffirming the purposes and principles enshrined in the Charter of the United Nations and the Universal Declaration of Human Rights,

Underlining the importance of promoting understanding, tolerance and friendship among human beings in all their diversity of religion, belief, culture and language, and recalling that all States have pledged themselves under the Charter to promote and encourage universal respect for and observance of human rights and fundamental freedoms for all, without distinction as to race, sex, language or religion,

Affirming that inter-religious dialogue is an integral part of the efforts to translate shared values, as reflected in the United Nations Millennium Declaration, into actions, in particular the efforts to promote a culture of peace and dialogue among civilizations,

Recalling its resolution 57/6 of 4 November 2002, in which it invited Member States to expand their activities promoting a culture of peace and non-violence at the national, regional and international levels,

Recalling also its other relevant resolutions,

Recalling with satisfaction the proclamation of the Global Agenda for Dialogue among Civilizations, bearing in mind the valuable contribution that dialogue among civilizations can make to an improved awareness and understanding of the common values shared by all humankind,

Recalling the Universal Declaration on Cultural Diversity of the United Nations Educational, Scientific and Cultural Organization and the principles contained therein,

Emphasizing the need, at all levels of society and among nations, for strengthening freedom, justice, democracy, tolerance, solidarity, cooperation, pluralism, respect for diversity of culture and religion or belief, dialogue and understanding, which are important elements for peace,

Reaffirming that freedom of expression, media pluralism, multilingualism, equal access to art and to scientific and technological knowledge, including in digital form, and the possibility for all cultures to have access to the means of expression and dissemination are the guarantees of cultural diversity, and that in ensuring the free flow of ideas by word and image, care should be exercised that all cultures can express themselves and make themselves known,

Recognizing all efforts made by the United Nations system to promote understanding, tolerance and friendship among human beings in all their diversity of culture, religion, belief and language,

Alarmed that serious instances of intolerance and discrimination on the grounds of religion or belief, including acts of violence, intimidation and coercion motivated by religious intolerance, are on the increase in many parts of the world and threaten the enjoyment of human rights and fundamental freedoms,

Considering that tolerance for cultural, ethnic, and religious and linguistic diversities, as well as dialogue among and within civilizations, is essential for peace, understanding and friendship among individuals and people of different cultures and nations of the world, while manifestations of cultural prejudice, intolerance and xenophobia towards different cultures and religions generate hatred and violence among peoples and nations throughout the world,

Emphasizing that combating hatred, prejudice, intolerance and stereotyping on the basis of religion or culture represents a significant global challenge that requires further action,

1. *Acknowledges* that respect for the diversity of religions and cultures, tolerance, dialogue and cooperation in a climate of mutual trust and understanding can contribute to the combating of ideologies and practices based on discrimination, intolerance and hatred and help to reinforce world peace, social justice and friendship among peoples;

2. *Reaffirms* the solemn commitment of all States to fulfil their obligations to promote universal respect for, and observance and protection of, all human rights and fundamental freedoms for all in accordance with the Charter of the United Nations, other instruments relating to human rights, and international law; the universal nature of these rights and freedoms is beyond question;

3. *Also reaffirms* the importance for all peoples and nations to hold, develop and preserve their cultural heritage and traditions in a national and international atmosphere of peace, tolerance and mutual respect;

4. *Recognizes* that respect for religious and cultural diversity in an increasingly globalizing world contributes to international cooperation, promotes enhanced dialogue among religions, cultures and civilizations, and helps to create an environment conducive to the exchange of human experience;

5. *Also recognizes* that all cultures and civilizations share a common set of universal values;

6. *Further recognizes* that, while the significance of national and regional particularities and various historical, cultural and religious backgrounds must be borne in mind, it is the duty of States, regardless of

their political, economic and cultural systems, to promote and protect all human rights and fundamental freedoms;

7. *Reaffirms* that the promotion and protection of the rights of persons belonging to national or ethnic, religious and linguistic minorities contribute to political and social stability and peace and enrich the cultural diversity and heritage of society as a whole in the States in which such persons live, and urges States to ensure that their political and legal systems reflect the multicultural diversity within their societies and, where necessary, to improve democratic and political institutions, organizations and practices so that they are more fully participatory and avoid the marginalization and exclusion of, and discrimination against, specific sectors of society;

8. *Encourages* Governments to promote, including through education, understanding, tolerance and friendship among human beings in all their diversity of religion, belief, culture and language, which will address the cultural, social, economic, political and religious sources of intolerance, and to apply a gender perspective while doing so, in order to promote understanding, tolerance, peace and friendly relations among nations and all racial and religious groups, recognizing that education at all levels is one of the principal means to build a culture of peace;

9. *Calls upon* all States to exert their utmost efforts to ensure that religious sites are fully respected and protected in compliance with their international obligations and in accordance with their national legislation, and to adopt adequate measures aimed at preventing acts or threats of damage to and destruction of these sites;

10. *Urges* States, in compliance with their international obligations, to take all necessary action to combat incitement to or acts of violence, intimidation and coercion motivated by hatred and intolerance based on culture, religion or belief, which may cause discord and disharmony within and among societies;

11. *Also urges* States to take effective measures to prevent and eliminate discrimination on the grounds of religion or belief in the recognition, exercise and enjoyment of human rights and fundamental freedoms in all fields of civil, economic, political, social and cultural life and to make all efforts to enact or rescind legislation, where necessary, to prohibit any such discrimination, and to take all appropriate measures to combat intolerance on the grounds of religion or beliefs;

12. *Further urges* States to ensure that, in the course of their official duties, members of law enforcement bodies and the military, civil servants, educators and other public officials respect different religions and beliefs and do not discriminate against persons professing other religions or beliefs, and that any necessary and appropriate education or training is provided;

13. *Welcomes* the efforts of States, relevant entities of the United Nations system and other intergovernmental organizations, civil society, including religion-based and other non-governmental organizations, and the media in developing a culture of peace, and encourages them to continue such efforts, including the promotion of inter-religious and intercultural interaction within and among societies through, inter alia, congresses, conferences, seminars, workshops, research work and related processes;

14. *Requests* the Secretary-General to ensure the widest dissemination of the relevant United Nations material related to the present resolution in as many different languages as possible through the United Nations system, including the United Nations information centres, within available resources;

15. *Also requests* the Secretary-General to present to the General Assembly at its fifty-ninth session a report on the implementation of the present resolution.

Sport for development and peace

In October, the Secretary-General published the report of the United Nations Inter-Agency Task Force on Sport for Development and Peace, entitled *Sport for Development and Peace: Towards Achieving the Millennium Development Goals* [ODG/2004/12]. The report provided a synthesis of the relationship between the world of sport and the UN system. It found that sports-based initiatives were practical and cost-effective tools to achieve objectives in development and peace. Sport could cut across barriers that divided societies, making it a means to support conflict prevention and peace-building efforts, both symbolically and practically. Sport programmes could promote social integration and foster tolerance, help to reduce tension and generate dialogue. Sport could be an effective tool for advocacy and communication.

International Year of Sport and Physical Education (2005)

On 3 November [meeting 52], the General Assembly adopted **resolution 58/5** [draft: A/58/L.2 & Add.1] without vote [agenda item 23 *(b)*].

Sport as a means to promote education, health, development and peace

The General Assembly,

Recalling its decision to include in its agenda an item entitled "Sport for peace and development" and a sub-item thereof entitled "International Year of Sport and Physical Education",

Considering the role of sport and physical education as a means to promote education, health, development and peace,

Acknowledging the major role of the United Nations, its funds and programmes and the United Nations Educational, Scientific and Cultural Organization and other specialized agencies, in promoting human development through sport and physical education, through its country programmes,

Taking note of the communiqué issued by the round table of ministers responsible for sports and physical education, held in Paris on 9 and 10 January 2003, in which they expressed their commitment to ensuring that the role of physical education and sport is fully recognized and developed,

Recalling the Convention on the Rights of the Child and the outcome document of the special session of the General Assembly on children, entitled "A world fit for children", stressing that education shall be directed to the development of children's personality, talents and mental and physical abilities to their fullest potential,

Recalling also the International Charter of Physical Education and Sport of the United Nations Educational, Scientific and Cultural Organization and the Dakar Framework for Action adopted at the World Education Forum in April 2000, as well as other relevant documents emphasizing the role of sport and physical education,

Taking note of the report of the United Nations Inter-agency Task Force on Sport for Development and Peace,

Noting that sport and physical education in many countries face increasing marginalization within education systems even though they are a major tool not only for health and physical development but also for acquiring values necessary for social cohesion and intercultural dialogue,

Acknowledging with concern the dangers faced by sportsmen and sportswomen, in particular young athletes, including, inter alia, child labour, violence, doping, early specialization, over-training and exploitative forms of commercialization, as well as less visible threats and deprivations, such as the premature severance of family bonds and the loss of sporting, social and cultural ties,

Recognizing the need for greater coordination of efforts at the international level to facilitate a more effective fight against doping, and noting in this regard the Anti-Doping Convention established by the Council of Europe, the Copenhagen Declaration on Anti-doping in Sport, adopted during the World Conference on Doping in Sport, held from 3 to 5 March 2003, and any other relevant international instrument,

1. *Invites* Governments, the United Nations, its funds and programmes, the specialized agencies, where appropriate, and sport-related institutions:

(a) To promote the role of sport and physical education for all when furthering their development programmes and policies, to advance health awareness, the spirit of achievement and cultural bridging and to entrench collective values;

(b) To include sport and physical education as a tool to contribute towards achieving the internationally agreed development goals, including those contained in the United Nations Millennium Declaration and the broader aims of development and peace;

(c) To work collectively so that sport and physical education can present opportunities for solidarity and cooperation in order to promote a culture of peace and social and gender equality and to advocate dialogue and harmony;

(d) To recognize the contribution of sport and physical education towards economic and social development and to encourage the building and restoration of sports infrastructures;

(e) To further promote sport and physical education, on the basis of locally assessed needs, as a tool for health, education, social and cultural development;

(f) To strengthen cooperation and partnership between all actors, including family, school, clubs/ leagues, local communities, youth sports associations and decision makers as well as the public and private sectors, in order to ensure complementarities and to make sport and physical education available to everyone;

(g) To ensure that young talents can develop their athletic potential without any threat to their safety and physical and moral integrity;

2. *Encourages* Governments, international sports bodies and sport-related organizations to elaborate and implement partnership initiatives and development projects compatible with the education provided at all levels of schooling to help achieve the Millennium Development Goals;

3. *Invites* Governments and international sports bodies to assist developing countries, in particular the least developed countries and small island developing States, in their capacity-building efforts in sport and physical education;

4. *Encourages* the United Nations to develop strategic partnerships with the range of stakeholders involved in sport, including sports organizations, sports associations and the private sector, to assist in the implementation of sport for development programmes;

5. *Encourages* Governments and the United Nations system to seek new and innovative ways to use sport for communication and social mobilization, particularly at the national, regional and local levels, engaging civil society through active participation and ensuring that target audiences are reached;

6. *Stresses* the need for all parties to cooperate closely with international sports bodies to elaborate a "code of good practice";

7. *Invites* Governments to accelerate the elaboration of an international anti-doping convention in all sports activities, and requests the United Nations Educational, Scientific and Cultural Organization, in cooperation with other relevant international and regional organizations, to coordinate the elaboration of such a convention;

8. *Decides* to proclaim 2005 the International Year for Sport and Physical Education, as a means to promote education, health, development and peace, and invites Governments to organize events to underline their commitment and to seek the assistance of sports personalities in this regard;

9. *Requests* the Secretary-General to report to the General Assembly at its fifty-ninth session on the implementation of the present resolution and on the preparation of events at the national and international levels to celebrate the year 2005, under the sub-item entitled "International Year of Sport and Physical Education".

Olympic Truce and ideal

On 3 November [meeting 52], the General Assembly adopted **resolution 58/6** [draft: A/58/L.9 & Add.1] without vote [agenda item 23 (a)].

Building a peaceful and better world through sport and the Olympic ideal

The General Assembly,

Recalling its resolution 56/75 of 11 December 2001, in which it decided to include in the provisional agenda of its fifty-eighth session the item entitled "Building a peaceful and better world through sport and the Olympic ideal" and its decision to consider this item every two years in advance of each Summer and Winter Olympic Games,

Recalling also its resolution 48/11 of 25 October 1993, which, inter alia, revived the ancient Greek tradition of *ekecheiria* or "Olympic Truce" calling for a truce during the Games that would encourage a peaceful environment and ensuring the safe passage and participation of athletes and others at the Games and, thereby, mobilizing the youth of the world to the cause of peace,

Taking into account the inclusion in the United Nations Millennium Declaration of an appeal for the observance of the Olympic Truce now and in the future and support for the International Olympic Committee in its efforts to promote peace and human understanding through sport and the Olympic ideal,

Noting that the Games of the XXVIII Olympiad will take place from 13 to 29 August 2004 in Athens, in Greece, where the Olympic Games were born in ancient times and revived in 1896, and where the tradition of the Olympic Truce was first established,

Welcoming the initiative of the Secretary-General to establish the United Nations Inter-agency Task Force on Sport for Development and Peace,

Recognizing the important role of sport in the implementation of the internationally agreed development goals, including those contained in the Millennium Declaration,

Recognizing also the valuable contribution that the appeal launched by the International Olympic Committee for an Olympic Truce, with which the National Olympic Committees of the Member States are associated, could make towards advancing the purposes and principles of the Charter of the United Nations,

Noting with satisfaction the flying of the United Nations flag at all competition sites of the Olympic Games, and the joint endeavours of the International Olympic Committee and the United Nations system in fields such as poverty alleviation, human and economic development, humanitarian assistance, education, health promotion, gender equality, environmental protection and HIV/AIDS prevention,

Welcoming the establishment by the International Olympic Committee of an International Olympic Truce Foundation and an International Olympic Truce Centre to promote further the ideals of peace and understanding through sport, on whose Board the President in office of the General Assembly sits and the Secretary-General and the Director-General of the United Nations Educational, Scientific and Cultural Organization are represented,

Welcoming also the individual support of world personalities for the promotion of the Olympic Truce,

1. *Urges* Member States to observe, within the framework of the Charter of the United Nations, the Olympic Truce, individually and collectively, during the Games of the XXVIII Olympiad, to be held in Athens;

2. *Welcomes* the decision of the International Olympic Committee to mobilize all international sports organizations and the National Olympic Committees of the Member States to undertake concrete actions at the local, national, regional and world levels to promote and strengthen a culture of peace based on the spirit of the Olympic Truce;

3. *Calls upon* all Member States to cooperate with the International Olympic Committee in its efforts to use the Olympic Truce as an instrument to promote peace, dialogue and reconciliation in areas of conflict during and beyond the Olympic Games period;

4. *Welcomes* the increased implementation of projects for development through sport, and encourages Member States and all concerned agencies and programmes of the United Nations system to strengthen their work in this field, in cooperation with the International Olympic Committee;

5. *Requests* the Secretary-General to promote the observance of the Olympic Truce among Member States and support for human development initiatives through sport, and to cooperate with the International Olympic Committee in the realization of these objectives;

6. *Decides* to include in the provisional agenda of its sixtieth session the sub-item entitled "Building a peaceful and better world through sport and the Olympic ideal" and to consider this sub-item before the XX Olympic Winter Games.

On 23 December, the Assembly decided that the agenda item entitled "Building a peaceful and better world through sport and the Olympic ideal" would remain for consideration at its resumed fifty-eighth (2004) session (**decision 58/565**).

Cultural property

Return of cultural property

The Secretary-General, in August [A/58/314], transmitted to the General Assembly the UNESCO Director-General's report on action taken by the organization to implement the 2001 recommendations adopted by the Intergovernmental Committee for Promoting the Return of Cultural Property to its Countries of Origin or its Restitution in Case of Illicit Appropriation [YUN 2001, p. 1017]. Submitted in response to General Assembly resolution 56/97 [ibid.], the report contained seven recommendations adopted by the Committee at its twelfth session (Paris, 25-28 March).

The Committee recommended that the Director-General assist in facilitating a meeting between the United Kingdom and Greece to discuss the latter's proposal that the United Kingdom, in view of the planned Olympic Games in Athens in 2004, grant a long-term loan of the Parthenon marbles. He should continue his good offices towards resolving the issue of Turkey's request that Germany return the Boguskoy Sphinx and report to the Committee at its next session. The Committee invited UNESCO to submit examples of returns and restitutions upon which a database might be developed, to examine the dissemination of information on returns and restitution, and to promote the implementation of an identification standard system and the International Code of Ethics for Dealers in Cultural Property, adopted by UNESCO. Member States were called on to implement the relevant UNESCO conventions and take security measures to protect cultural property. The Director-General should establish a database on cultural heritage legislation, including import and export certificates, and prepare an explanatory note on the procedure for assessing projects submitted pursuant to the Operational Guidelines of the Fund of the Intergovernmental Committee. He should also communicate to all UNESCO member States the report of the meetings of experts on the settlement of disputes concerning cultural objects displaced as a result of the Second World War and the non-binding Principles on the settlement of such disputes elaborated at those meetings so that they could submit their observations.

GENERAL ASSEMBLY ACTION

On 3 December [meeting 68], the General Assembly adopted **resolution 58/17** [draft A/58/L.20 & Add.1] without vote [agenda item 43].

Return or restitution of cultural property to the countries of origin

The General Assembly,

Reaffirming the relevant provisions of the Charter of the United Nations,

Recalling its resolutions 3026 A(XXVII) of 18 December 1972, 3148(XXVIII) of 14 December 1973, 3187 (XXVIII) of 18 December 1973, 3391(XXX) of 19 November 1975, 31/40 of 30 November 1976, 32/18 of 11 November 1977, 33/50 of 14 December 1978, 34/64 of 29 November 1979, 35/127 and 35/128 of 11 December 1980, 36/64 of 27 November 1981, 38/34 of 25 November 1983, 40/19 of 21 November 1985, 42/7 of 22 October 1987, 44/18 of 6 November 1989, 46/10 of 22 October 1991, 48/15 of 2 November 1993, 50/56 of 11 December 1995, 52/24 of 25 November 1997, 54/190 of 17 December 1999 and 56/97 of 14 December 2001,

Recalling also its resolution 56/8 of 21 November 2001, in which it proclaimed 2002 the United Nations Year for Cultural Heritage,

Recalling further the Convention for the Protection of Cultural Property in the Event of Armed Conflict, adopted at The Hague on 14 May 1954, and the two Protocols thereto, adopted in 1954 and 1999,

Recalling the Convention on the Means of Prohibiting and Preventing the Illicit Import, Export and Transfer of Ownership of Cultural Property, adopted on 14 November 1970 by the General Conference of the United Nations Educational, Scientific and Cultural Organization,

Recalling also the Convention concerning the Protection of the World Cultural and Natural Heritage, adopted on 16 November 1972 by the General Conference of the United Nations Educational, Scientific and Cultural Organization,

Recalling further the Convention on Stolen or Illegally Exported Cultural Objects, adopted in Rome on 24 June 1995 by the International Institute for the Unification of Private Law,

Taking note of the adoption of the Convention on the Protection of the Underwater Cultural Heritage by the General Conference of the United Nations Educational, Scientific and Cultural Organization on 2 November 2001,

Recalling the Medellin Declaration for Cultural Diversity and Tolerance and the Plan of Action on Cultural Cooperation, adopted at the first Meeting of the Ministers of Culture of the Movement of Non-Aligned Countries, held in Medellin, Colombia, on 4 and 5 September 1997,

Noting the adoption of the Universal Declaration on Cultural Diversity and the Action Plan for its implementation, adopted by the General Conference of the United Nations Educational, Scientific and Cultural Organization on 2 November 2001,

Welcoming the report of the Secretary-General submitted in cooperation with the Director-General of the United Nations Educational, Scientific and Cultural Organization,

Aware of the importance attached by some countries of origin to the return of cultural property that is of fundamental spiritual and cultural value to them, so that they may constitute collections representative of their cultural heritage,

Expressing concern about the illicit traffic in cultural property and its damage to the cultural heritage of nations,

Expressing concern also about the loss, destruction, removal, theft, pillage, illicit movement or misappropriation of and any acts of vandalism or damage directed against cultural property, in particular in areas of armed conflict, including territories that are occupied, whether such conflicts are international or internal,

Recalling Security Council resolution 1483(2003), adopted on 22 May 2003, in particular paragraph 7 relating to the restitution of the cultural property of Iraq,

1. *Commends* the United Nations Educational, Scientific and Cultural Organization and the Intergovernmental Committee for Promoting the Return of Cultural Property to its Countries of Origin or its Restitution in Case of Illicit Appropriation on the work they have accomplished, in particular through the promotion of bilateral negotiations, for the return or restitution of cultural property, the preparation of inventories of movable cultural property and the implementation of the Object-ID standard related thereto, as well as for the reduction of illicit traffic in cultural property and the dissemination of information to the public;

2. *Calls upon* all relevant bodies, agencies, funds and programmes of the United Nations system and other relevant intergovernmental organizations to work in coordination with the United Nations Educational, Scientific and Cultural Organization, within their mandates and in cooperation with Member States, in order to continue to address the issue of return or restitution of cultural property to the countries of origin and to provide appropriate support accordingly;

3. *Welcomes* the adoption of the Declaration concerning the Intentional Destruction of Cultural Heritage, adopted by the General Conference of the

United Nations Educational, Scientific and Cultural Organization on 17 October 2003;

4. *Reaffirms* the importance of the principles and provisions of the Convention for the Protection of Cultural Property in the Event of Armed Conflict, and invites Member States that have not already done so to become parties to the Convention and to promote its implementation;

5. *Also reaffirms* the importance of the Second Protocol to the Convention, adopted at The Hague on 26 March 1999, and invites all States Parties to the Convention to consider becoming parties to the Second Protocol;

6. *Welcomes* the most recent efforts made by the United Nations Educational, Scientific and Cultural Organization for the protection of the cultural heritage of countries in conflict, including the safe return to those countries of cultural property and other items of archaeological, historical, cultural, rare scientific and religious importance that have been illegally removed, and calls upon the international community to contribute to these efforts;

7. *Invites* Member States to consider adopting and implementing the Convention on the Means of Prohibiting and Preventing the Illicit Import, Export and Transfer of Ownership of Cultural Property;

8. *Urges* Member States to introduce effective national and international measures to prevent and combat illicit trafficking in cultural property, including special training for police, customs and border services;

9. *Reaffirms* the importance of the provisions of the Convention on Stolen or Illegally Exported Cultural Objects of the International Institute for the Unification of Private Law, and invites Member States that have not already done so to consider becoming parties to it;

10. *Invites* Member States, in cooperation with the United Nations Educational, Scientific and Cultural Organization, to continue to draw up systematic inventories of their cultural property, as well as to work towards the creation of a database of the cultural legislation of Member States, in particular in an electronic form;

11. *Reaffirms* the efforts of the United Nations Educational, Scientific and Cultural Organization to promote the use of identification systems, in particular the application of the Object-ID standard, and to encourage the linking of identification systems and existing databases, including the one developed by the International Criminal Police Organization-Interpol, to allow for the electronic transmission of information in order to reduce illicit trafficking in cultural property, and encourages the United Nations Educational, Scientific and Cultural Organization to make further efforts in this regard in cooperation with Member States, where appropriate;

12. *Recognizes* the public awareness and increased mobilization and action in favour of heritage values that was achieved in 2002, the United Nations Year for Cultural Heritage, and calls upon the international community and the United Nations to continue to cooperate with the United Nations Educational, Scientific and Cultural Organization on the basis of that work;

13. *Welcomes* the adoption of the International Code of Ethics for Dealers in Cultural Property by the General Conference of the United Nations Educational, Scientific and Cultural Organization on 16 November 1999, and invites those who deal with trade in cultural property and their associations, where they exist, to encourage the implementation of the Code;

14. *Recognizes* the importance of the creation, by the General Conference of the United Nations Educational, Scientific and Cultural Organization, of the International Fund for the Return of Cultural Property to its Countries of Origin or its Restitution in Case of Illicit Appropriation, launched in November 2000, and encourages the United Nations Educational, Scientific and Cultural Organization to promote the Fund and render it operational;

15. *Requests* the Secretary-General to cooperate with the United Nations Educational, Scientific and Cultural Organization in its efforts to bring about the attainment of the objectives of the present resolution;

16. *Also requests* the Secretary-General, in cooperation with the Director-General of the United Nations Educational, Scientific and Cultural Organization, to submit to the General Assembly at its sixtieth session a report on the implementation of the present resolution;

17. *Decides* to include in the provisional agenda of its sixtieth session the item entitled "Return or restitution of cultural property to the countries of origin".

Prevention of crimes against cultural heritage

On 22 July [meeting 44], the Economic and Social Council, on the recommendation of the Commission on Crime Prevention and Criminal Justice [E/2003/30], adopted **resolution 2003/29** without vote [agenda item 14 *(c)*].

Prevention of crimes that infringe on the cultural heritage of peoples in the form of movable property

The Economic and Social Council,

Aware of the serious harm done to States and to the objects themselves by the theft and illicit export of objects regarded as part of States' cultural heritage, in particular as a result of the plundering of archaeological sites and of other sites of historical and cultural value,

Recognizing the importance for States of protecting and preserving their cultural heritage in accordance with the Convention on the Means of Prohibiting and Preventing the Illicit Import, Export and Transfer of Ownership of Cultural Property, adopted by the United Nations Educational, Scientific and Cultural Organization on 14 November 1970, the preamble to which refers, inter alia, to the duty of every State to protect the cultural property existing within its territory against the dangers of theft, clandestine excavation and illicit export, and also the commitment by States and relevant international organizations to combat such practices with all the means at their disposal, in particular with regard to international cooperation on the return of such property,

Wishing to promote mutual cooperation in preventing illegal acts against the historical and cultural legacy of peoples,

Aware of the urgent need to establish standards for the restitution and return of movable property forming part of the cultural heritage of peoples after it has been stolen or illicitly exported, and for its protection and preservation,

Recognizing that one of the main objectives of the United Nations in the field of crime prevention and criminal justice is the promotion and strengthening of international cooperation in the fight against transnational organized crime,

Recalling General Assembly resolution 45/121 of 14 December 1990 on the Eighth United Nations Congress on the Prevention of Crime and the Treatment of Offenders, held in Havana from 27 August to 7 September 1990,

Recalling also the model treaty for the prevention of crimes that infringe on the cultural heritage of peoples in the form of movable property, adopted by the Eighth Congress,

Welcoming the organization by the Andean Community of Nations and the Government of France of a regional workshop on theft and illicit trafficking of cultural property, held in Lima from 14 to 16 May 2003,

1. *Encourages* Member States to consider, where appropriate and in accordance with national law, when concluding relevant agreements with other States, the model treaty for the prevention of crimes that infringe on the cultural heritage of peoples in the form of movable property, adopted by the Eighth United Nations Congress on the Prevention of Crime and the Treatment of Offenders;

2. *Calls upon* all Member States to continue to strengthen international cooperation and mutual assistance in the prevention and prosecution of crimes against movable property that forms part of the cultural heritage of peoples;

3. *Requests* the Secretary-General to report to the Commission on Crime Prevention and Criminal Justice at its thirteenth session on the implementation of the present resolution.

Crime prevention and criminal justice

Commission on Crime Prevention and Criminal Justice

The Commission on Crime Prevention and Criminal Justice, at its twelfth session (Vienna, 13-22 May) [E/2003/30], recommended to the Economic and Social Council four draft resolutions for adoption by the General Assembly and eight draft resolutions and two draft decisions for adoption by the Council. The draft resolutions related to trafficking in persons, transnational organized crime, preparations for the Eleventh United Nations Congress on Crime Prevention and Criminal Justice, the work of the Centre for International Crime Prevention of the United Nations Office on Drugs and Crime (UNODC), international cooperation and technical assistance in preventing and combating terrorism, urban crime, kidnapping, crimes against the cultural heritage of peoples, UN standards and norms in crime prevention, and the functioning of the Commission (see specific headings below). A draft text on illicit trafficking in protected species of wild flora and fauna, adopted by the Council in **resolution 2003/27** of 22 July, urged Member States to cooperate with the relevant UN system entities to prevent, combat, and eradicate the trafficking (see p. 1069). A thematic discussion was held on trafficking in human beings, especially women and children. The Commission also considered strategic management and programme questions and the provisional agenda for its 2004 session.

ECONOMIC AND SOCIAL COUNCIL ACTION

On 22 July [meeting 44], the Economic and Social Council, on the recommendation of the Commission on Crime Prevention and Criminal Justice [E/2003/30], adopted **resolution 2003/31** without vote [agenda item 14 (c)].

Functioning of the Commission on Crime Prevention and Criminal Justice

The Economic and Social Council,

Mindful of the statement of principles and programme of action of the United Nations Crime Prevention and Criminal Justice Programme, annexed to General Assembly resolution 46/152 of 18 December 1991,

Recalling resolutions 1/1 of 29 April 1992, 4/3 of 9 June 1995, 5/3 of 31 May 1996 and 6/1 of 9 May 1997 of the Commission on Crime Prevention and Criminal Justice, on strategic management and programme questions,

Recalling in particular Commission resolution 5/3, in which the Commission requested member States to submit to the Bureau draft proposals, together with the information required in accordance with the annex to Commission resolution 4/3, one month prior to the commencement of the session of the Commission, in order to ensure the smooth and effective functioning of the Commission,

Recognizing the need for the Bureau of the Commission to have adequate time to prepare for sessions of the Commission,

Recalling its resolution 1999/30 of 28 July 1999, in particular paragraph 3 of section I thereof regarding the method of election of the Bureau of the Commission on Narcotic Drugs,

1. *Encourages* States members of the Commission on Crime Prevention and Criminal Justice to submit their draft proposals to it in accordance with Commission resolution 5/3 and to include in such proposals the information required in accordance with the annex to Commission resolution 4/3, including information on the proposed activity, the timetable and the identification of the United Nations or other body that could carry out the activity, one month prior to the commencement of the session of the Commission;

2. *Endorses* the request of the Commission to its Bureau to report on its intersessional work annually, including on its experience with regard to the adherence of member States to the procedural requirements for the submission of draft proposals;

3. *Decides* that the Commission shall examine during the intersessional period, with a view to taking a decision at its thirteenth session, the duration of the session of the Commission on the basis of the experience gained from its twelve sessions held so far and taking into account the requirements of the United Nations Crime Prevention and Criminal Justice Programme, the requirements of the work of the Commission, the judicious use of the resources allocated to the Commission and the experience to be gained from its intersessional meetings;

4. *Requests* the Centre for International Crime Prevention of the United Nations Office on Drugs and Crime to submit to the Commission at its thirteenth session a report on the status of implementation of the mandates assigned to it by or through the recommendation of the Commission, including information on the requirements of that implementation;

5. *Decides* that, with effect from 2004, the Commission shall, at the end of its session, elect its Bureau for the subsequent session and encourage it to play an active role in the preparation of the regular as well as the informal intersessional meetings of the Commission, so as to enable the Commission to provide continuous and effective policy guidance to the United Nations Crime Prevention and Criminal Justice Programme, and also decides that the Chairman shall, whenever appropriate, invite the chairmen of the five regional groups, the chairman of the Group of 77 and China and the Presidency of the European Union to participate in the meetings of the Bureau.

Also on 22 July, the Council took note of the Commission's report on its twelfth session and approved the provisional agenda and documentation for its thirteenth (2004) session (**decision 2003/233**).

Preparations for Eleventh Crime Congress

The Commission on Crime Prevention and Criminal Justice considered a March report with later addenda [E/CN.15.2003/11 & Corr.1 & Add.1,2] by the Secretary-General on preparations for the Eleventh United Nations Congress on Crime Prevention and Criminal Justice, scheduled for 2005 in Thailand. The report presented the views of States, specialized agencies and UN programmes, intergovernmental organizations and NGOs on agenda items and workshop topics planned for the Congress and on documentation and public information activities.

In accordance with Assembly resolution 57/171 [YUN 2002, p. 1109], the Secretary-General, in May [A/58/87-E/2003/82], described preparations for the Congress, including a summary of the views in his report (above), and highlighted the organizational arrangements. The Commission's recommendations regarding substantive issues, such as the provisional agenda of the Congress and guidance on workshops during the Congress, were incorporated into General Assembly resolution 58/138 (below).

On 24 July, the Economic and Social Council took note of the Secretary-General's May report on preparations for the Congress (**decision 2003/310**), as did the General Assembly on 22 December (**decision 58/531**). The Council, in **resolution 2003/26** of 22 July (see p. 1154), recommended that the issue of urban crime be given due attention in the Congress programme.

ECONOMIC AND SOCIAL COUNCIL ACTION

On 22 July [meeting 44], the Economic and Social Council, on the recommendation of the Commission on Crime Prevention and Criminal Justice [E/2003/30], adopted **resolution 2003/23** without vote [agenda item 14 (c)].

Preparations for the Eleventh United Nations Congress on Crime Prevention and Criminal Justice

The Economic and Social Council
Recommends to the General Assembly the adoption of the following draft resolution:
[For text, see General Assembly resolution 58/138 below.]

GENERAL ASSEMBLY ACTION

On 22 December [meeting 77], the General Assembly, on the recommendation of the Third Committee [A/58/499], adopted **resolution 58/138** without vote [agenda item 108].

Preparations for the Eleventh United Nations Congress on Crime Prevention and Criminal Justice

The General Assembly,
Recalling its resolution 56/119 of 19 December 2001 on the role, function, periodicity and duration of the United Nations congresses on the prevention of crime and the treatment of offenders, and its resolution 57/171 of 18 December 2002 on preparations for the Eleventh United Nations Congress on Crime Prevention and Criminal Justice,

Considering that, pursuant to its resolutions 415(V) of 1 December 1950 and 46/152 of 18 December 1991, the Eleventh Congress is to be held in 2005,

Bearing in mind the guidelines for and the new format of the United Nations congresses, as stipulated in paragraph 2 of resolution 56/119, as well as paragraphs 29 and 30 of the statement of principles and programme of action of the United Nations Crime Prevention and Criminal Justice Programme, annexed to resolution 46/152,

Recognizing the significant contributions of the United Nations congresses in promoting the exchange of experience in research, law and policy development and the identification of emerging trends and issues in crime prevention and criminal justice among States, intergovernmental organizations and individual experts representing various professions and disciplines,

Recalling that, in its resolution 57/171, it requested the Commission on Crime Prevention and Criminal

Justice, at its twelfth session, to finalize the programme for the Eleventh Congress and to make its final recommendations, through the Economic and Social Council, to the General Assembly,

Recalling also that, in its resolution 57/171, it decided that the main theme of the Eleventh Congress should be "Synergies and responses: strategic alliances in crime prevention and criminal justice",

Recalling further its resolution 57/170 of 18 December 2002 on the follow-up to the plans of action for the implementation of the Vienna Declaration on Crime and Justice: Meeting the Challenges of the Twenty-first Century,

Stressing the importance of undertaking all the preparatory activities for the Eleventh Congress in a timely and concerted manner,

Having considered the report of the Secretary-General,

1. *Notes* the progress made thus far in the preparations for the Eleventh United Nations Congress on Crime Prevention and Criminal Justice;

2. *Decides* to hold the Eleventh Congress from 18 to 25 April 2005, with pre-congress consultations to be held on 18 April 2005;

3. *Also decides* that the high-level segment of the Eleventh Congress shall be held during the last three days of the Congress in order to allow heads of State or Government or government ministers to focus on the main substantive agenda items of the Congress;

4. *Approves* the following provisional agenda for the Eleventh Congress, finalized by the Commission on Crime Prevention and Criminal Justice at its twelfth session:
   1. Opening of the Congress.
   2. Organizational matters.
   3. Effective measures to combat transnational organized crime.
   4. International cooperation against terrorism and links between terrorism and other criminal activities in the context of the work of the United Nations Office on Drugs and Crime.
   5. Corruption: threats and trends in the twenty-first century.
   6. Economic and financial crimes: challenges to sustainable development.
   7. Making standards work: fifty years of standard-setting in crime prevention and criminal justice.
   8. Adoption of the report of the Congress;

5. *Decides* that the following issues shall be considered by workshops within the framework of the Eleventh Congress:

   (a) Enhancing international law enforcement cooperation, including extradition measures;

   (b) Enhancing criminal justice reform, including restorative justice;

   (c) Strategies and best practices for crime prevention, in particular in relation to urban crime and youth at risk;

   (d) Measures to combat terrorism, with reference to the relevant international conventions and protocols;

   (e) Measures to combat economic crime, including money-laundering;

   (f) Measures to combat computer-related crime;

6. *Reiterates its request* to the Secretary-General to prepare, in cooperation with the institutes of the United Nations Crime Prevention and Criminal Justice Programme network, a discussion guide for the regional preparatory meetings and the workshops of the Eleventh Congress;

7. *Urges* the regional preparatory meetings to examine the substantive items on the agenda and the workshop topics of the Eleventh Congress and to make action-oriented recommendations to serve as a basis for the draft recommendations and conclusions for consideration by the Congress and the Commission at its fourteenth session;

8. *Emphasizes* the importance of the workshops, and invites Member States, intergovernmental and non-governmental organizations and other relevant entities to provide financial, organizational and technical support to the Centre for International Crime Prevention of the United Nations Office on Drugs and Crime and to the institutes of the United Nations Crime Prevention and Criminal Justice Programme network for the preparations for the workshops, including the preparation and circulation of relevant background material;

9. *Requests* the Secretary-General to include in the discussion guide requested in paragraph 6 above consideration of technical cooperation ideas, projects and documents related to enhancing bilateral and multilateral efforts in technical assistance activities in crime prevention and criminal justice;

10. *Invites* donor countries to cooperate with developing countries to ensure their full participation in the workshops;

11. *Approves* the plan for documentation for the Eleventh Congress, as proposed by the Secretary-General in his report on preparations for the Congress, taking into account the recommendations of the Commission related thereto;

12. *Invites* Governments and relevant intergovernmental and non-governmental organizations to inform the Eleventh Congress about their activities with a view to the implementation of the plans of action for the implementation of the Vienna Declaration on Crime and Justice: Meeting the Challenges of the Twenty-first Century, as guidance for the formulation of legislation, policies and programmes in the field of crime prevention and criminal justice at the national and international levels;

13. *Reiterates its request* to the Secretary-General to make available the necessary resources for the participation of the least developed countries in the regional preparatory meetings for the Eleventh Congress and at the Congress itself, in accordance with past practice;

14. *Encourages* Governments to undertake preparations for the Eleventh Congress at an early stage by all appropriate means, including, where appropriate, the establishment of national preparatory committees, with a view to contributing to a focused and productive discussion on the topics and to participating actively in the organization of and follow-up to the workshops;

15. *Requests* the Secretary-General to provide resources, as required, in accordance with established United Nations budgetary practice and within the overall appropriations of the programme budget for the biennium 2004-2005, in order to ensure a wide and effective programme of public information relating to the preparations for the Eleventh Congress, to the Congress itself and to the follow-up to and implementation of its recommendations;

16. *Reiterates its invitation* to Member States to be represented at the Eleventh Congress at the highest possible level, for example, by heads of State or Government or government ministers and attorneys general, to make statements on the theme and topics of the Congress and to participate in thematic interactive round tables;

17. *Requests* the Secretary-General to facilitate the organization of ancillary meetings of non-governmental and professional organizations participating in the Eleventh Congress, in accordance with past practice, as well as meetings of professional and geographical interest groups, and to take appropriate measures to encourage the participation of the academic and research community in the Congress;

18. *Again encourages* the relevant specialized agencies, United Nations programmes and intergovernmental and non-governmental organizations, as well as other professional organizations, to cooperate with the Centre for International Crime Prevention in the preparations for the Eleventh Congress;

19. *Requests* the Secretary-General to appoint a Secretary-General and an Executive Secretary of the Eleventh Congress, in accordance with past practice, to perform their functions under the rules of procedure for United Nations congresses on crime prevention and criminal justice;

20. *Requests* the Commission to accord sufficient time at its thirteenth session to reviewing the progress made in the preparations for the Eleventh Congress, to finalize in good time all the necessary organizational and substantive arrangements and to make its recommendations through the Economic and Social Council to the General Assembly;

21. *Requests* the Secretary-General to ensure the proper follow-up to the present resolution and to report thereon to the General Assembly through the Commission on Crime Prevention and Criminal Justice at its thirteenth session.

Crime prevention programme

In response to General Assembly resolution 57/173 [YUN 2002, p. 1112], the Secretary-General, in an August report on strengthening the United Nations Crime Prevention and Criminal Justice Programme, in particular its technical cooperation capacity [A/58/222], reviewed progress in the negotiation of the United Nations Convention against Corruption (see p. 1126) and in promoting the ratification of the United Nations Convention against Transnational Organized Crime, which, together with one of its supplementary Protocols, entered into force in 2003 (see p. 1125). The report also covered the global programmes for countering terrorism, organized crime, trafficking in human beings and corruption, and supporting reconstruction of criminal justice systems, justice reform and crime prevention. Other areas discussed were research, the implementation of standards and norms, the dissemination of information, coordination of activities and the mobilization of resources (see also under relevant headings below).

Overall, the Programme's technical assistance activities had increased, particularly in criminal justice reform, reconstruction and crime prevention and terrorism prevention. Technical cooperation was provided by the Centre for International Crime Prevention for four global projects: assistance to signatories of the United Nations Convention against Transnational Organized Crime (see p. 1125); establishing a database on flows of trafficking in persons; enhancing judicial integrity; and strengthening the legal regime against terrorism.

Contributions and pledges to the United Nations Crime Prevention and Criminal Justice Fund from January 2002 to June 2003 totalled $9,546,300, of which 95 per cent was earmarked for specific projects. As at 1 January 2003, the authority to manage the Fund, as well as the sub-account for the United Nations Interregional Crime and Justice Research Institute, was delegated to the Executive Director of UNODC.

ECONOMIC AND SOCIAL COUNCIL ACTION

On 22 July [meeting 44], the Economic and Social Council, on the recommendation of the Commission on Crime Prevention and Criminal Justice [E/2003/30], adopted **resolution 2003/25** without vote [agenda item 14 (c)].

International cooperation, technical assistance and advisory services in crime prevention and criminal justice

The Economic and Social Council,

Recalling the Vienna Declaration on Crime and Justice: Meeting the Challenges of the Twenty-first Century, adopted by the Tenth United Nations Congress on the Prevention of Crime and the Treatment of Offenders and endorsed by the General Assembly in its resolution 55/59 of 4 December 2000,

Recalling also General Assembly resolution 57/173 of 18 December 2002 on strengthening the United Nations Crime Prevention and Criminal Justice Programme, in particular its technical cooperation capacity,

Recalling further its resolution 1998/24 of 28 July 1998 on technical cooperation and advisory services in crime prevention and criminal justice, and its resolution 2002/19 of 24 July 2002 on strengthening international cooperation and technical assistance within the framework of the activities of the Centre for International Crime Prevention of the United Nations Office on Drugs and Crime in preventing and combating terrorism,

Emphasizing the importance of enhancing international cooperation and coordination among Member States in the field of crime prevention and criminal justice for the achievement of the objectives of the United Nations, including sustainable development, improved quality of life, democracy and human rights,

Noting the increasing number of requests for technical assistance received by the Centre from least developed countries, developing countries, countries with economies in transition and countries emerging from conflict,

Expressing its appreciation for funding provided by Member States in 2002, which has permitted the Centre to enhance its capacity to conduct an increasing number of technical assistance activities,

1. *Takes note with appreciation* of the report of the Executive Director of the United Nations Office on Drugs and Crime on the work of the Centre for International Crime Prevention, in particular its technical cooperation activities, and the reports of the Secretary-General on ratification of the United Nations Convention against Transnational Organized Crime and the Protocols thereto and on strengthening international cooperation and technical assistance in preventing and combating terrorism;

2. *Commends* the Centre for assisting Member States in the improvement of their criminal justice systems by responding to an increasing number of requests for technical assistance in the implementation of projects;

3. *Recognizes* the expansion of technical assistance activities of the Centre, and encourages international, regional and national funding agencies, as well as international financial institutions, to support the technical cooperation activities and interregional advisory services of the Centre;

4. *Urges* relevant entities of the United Nations system, including the United Nations Development Programme, the World Bank and the International Monetary Fund, as well as other international and regional organizations, to increase their interaction with the Centre in order to ensure that, as appropriate, activities in the fields of crime prevention and criminal justice, including activities to combat terrorism and corruption, are considered in their country and regional programmes and development frameworks, to ensure the full utilization of the expertise of the Centre in activities related to crime prevention and criminal justice and to promotion of the rule of law and to avoid duplication of effort;

5. *Expresses its appreciation* to Member States for supporting the technical assistance activities of the Centre by providing financial or in-kind contributions to the United Nations Crime Prevention and Criminal Justice Programme;

6. *Expresses the need* to have adequate resources available in order to make progress in the further operationalization of the activities of the Centre and in order to implement the projects carried out under its global programmes against trafficking in human beings, terrorism, corruption and organized crime;

7. *Urges* Member States to make or increase, as appropriate, voluntary contributions to the United Nations Crime Prevention and Criminal Justice Fund, as well as to make or increase, as appropriate, contributions in direct support of activities and projects of the Centre, including through contributions to institutes of the United Nations Crime Prevention and Criminal Justice Programme network, in order to strengthen further the capacity of the Centre to provide technical assistance;

8. *Encourages* Member States, in particular, developing countries and countries with economies in transition, that are beneficiaries of technical assistance provided by the Centre and are in a position to do so to contribute to the activities of the Centre through such means as the provision of necessary infrastructure or human resources or by allotting national funds to projects implemented in partnership with the Centre;

9. *Encourages* developing countries and countries with economies in transition to include in their requests for assistance from the United Nations Development Programme, in particular within its country programme framework, projects and/or elements on crime prevention and criminal justice;

10. *Requests* the Secretary-General to enhance further the resources available within the existing overall budgetary framework of the United Nations for the operational activities and, in particular, the interregional advisory services of the Centre under section 23, Regular programme of technical cooperation, of the programme budget of the United Nations;

11. *Also requests* the Secretary-General to make all possible efforts, including appeals to donors in the private sector, mobilization of resources and fundraising, to increase extrabudgetary resources, including general-purpose funds, bearing in mind the need to safeguard the independence and international character of the Centre.

GENERAL ASSEMBLY ACTION

On 22 December [meeting 77], the General Assembly, on the recommendation of the Third Committee [A/58/499], adopted **resolution 58/140** without vote [agenda item 108].

Strengthening the United Nations Crime Prevention and Criminal Justice Programme, in particular its technical cooperation capacity

The General Assembly,

Recalling its resolution 46/152 of 18 December 1991 on the creation of an effective United Nations crime prevention and criminal justice programme, in which it approved the statement of principles and programme of action annexed to that resolution,

Recalling also its resolution 57/173 of 18 December 2002 on strengthening the United Nations Crime Prevention and Criminal Justice Programme, in particular its technical cooperation capacity,

Bearing in mind its resolution 58/135 of 22 December 2003 on international cooperation in the fight against transnational organized crime: assistance to States in capacity-building with a view to facilitating the implementation of the United Nations Convention against Transnational Organized Crime and the Protocols thereto,

Bearing in mind also its resolution 58/136 of 22 December 2003 on strengthening international cooperation and technical assistance in promoting the implementation of the universal conventions and protocols related to terrorism within the framework of the activities of the Centre for International Crime Prevention of the United Nations Office on Drugs and Crime,

Recalling Economic and Social Council resolution 2003/24 of 22 July 2003 on the work of the Centre for International Crime Prevention, including the management of the United Nations Crime Prevention and Criminal Justice Fund,

Recalling also Economic and Social Council resolution 2003/28 of 22 July 2003 on international cooperation in the prevention, combating and elimination of kidnapping and in providing assistance to victims,

Emphasizing the role of the United Nations in the field of crime prevention and criminal justice, specifically the reduction of criminality, more efficient and effective law enforcement and administration of justice, respect for human rights and the rule of law, and promotion of the highest standards of fairness, humanity and professional conduct,

Recognizing that action against global criminal activity is a common and shared responsibility,

Convinced of the desirability of closer coordination and cooperation among States in combating crime, including organized crime, corruption, the smuggling of migrants and trafficking in persons, especially women and children, drug-related crimes, money-laundering, the illicit manufacturing of and trafficking in firearms, their parts and components and ammunition and the criminal misuse of information technologies, as well as criminal activities carried out for the purpose of furthering terrorism in all its forms and manifestations, bearing in mind the role that could be played by both the United Nations and regional organizations in this respect,

Recognizing existing efforts at the regional level that complement the work of the United Nations Crime Prevention and Criminal Justice Programme in combating the smuggling of migrants and trafficking in persons, especially women and children, and noting in this context the ongoing work of the Bali and Puebla Processes,

Recognizing also existing efforts that complement the work of the United Nations Crime Prevention and Criminal Justice Programme in combating corruption, and noting the outcome of the third Global Forum on Fighting Corruption and Safeguarding Integrity, held at Seoul from 28 to 31 May 2003,

Acknowledging the role of United Nations standards and norms in crime prevention and criminal justice and their development, as reflected in Economic and Social Council resolution 2003/30 of 22 July 2003,

Recognizing the urgent need to increase technical cooperation activities to assist countries, in particular developing countries and countries with economies in transition, with their efforts in translating United Nations conventions and other legal instruments and policy guidelines into practice,

Recalling its resolution 55/25 of 15 November 2000, by which it adopted the United Nations Convention against Transnational Organized Crime, the Protocol to Prevent, Suppress and Punish Trafficking in Persons, Especially Women and Children, supplementing the United Nations Convention against Transnational Organized Crime, and the Protocol against the Smuggling of Migrants by Land, Sea and Air, supplementing the United Nations Convention against Transnational Organized Crime, and its resolution 55/255 of 31 May 2001, by which it adopted the Protocol against the Illicit Manufacturing of and Trafficking in Firearms, Their Parts and Components and Ammunition, supplementing the United Nations Convention against Transnational Organized Crime,

Welcoming the adoption of its resolution 58/4 of 31 October 2003 on the United Nations Convention against Corruption,

Recognizing the need to maintain a balance in the technical cooperation capacity of the United Nations Office on Drugs and Crime between all priorities identified by the General Assembly and the Economic and Social Council,

Recalling its relevant resolutions, in which it requested the Secretary-General, as a matter of urgency, to provide the United Nations Crime Prevention and Criminal Justice Programme with sufficient resources for the full implementation of its mandate, in conformity with the high priority attached to the Programme,

Bearing in mind the Vienna Declaration on Crime and Justice: Meeting the Challenges of the Twenty-first Century,

Recalling the plans of action for the implementation of the Vienna Declaration on Crime and Justice: Meeting the Challenges of the Twenty-first Century,

Recalling also Economic and Social Council resolution 2003/25 of 22 July 2003 on international cooperation, technical assistance and advisory services in crime prevention and criminal justice,

Aware of the continued increase in requests for technical assistance forwarded to the United Nations Office on Drugs and Crime by least developed countries, developing countries, countries with economies in transition and countries emerging from conflict,

Appreciating the funding provided by certain Member States in 2002 and 2003 that has permitted the United Nations Office on Drugs and Crime to enhance its capacity to execute an increased number of projects in the field of crime prevention and criminal justice,

1. *Takes note with appreciation* of the report of the Secretary-General on the progress made in the implementation of General Assembly resolution 57/173;

2. *Affirms* the importance of the work of the United Nations Office on Drugs and Crime in the fulfilment of its mandate in crime prevention and criminal justice, including to prevent and combat terrorism, in particular in strengthening international cooperation and providing technical assistance, upon request, which complements the work of the Security Council Committee established pursuant to resolution 1373 (2001) concerning counter-terrorism;

3. *Reaffirms* the importance of the United Nations Crime Prevention and Criminal Justice Programme in promoting effective action to strengthen international cooperation in crime prevention and criminal justice, in responding to the needs of the international community in the face of both national and transnational criminality and in assisting Member States in achieving the goals of preventing crime within and among States and improving the response to crime;

4. *Reiterates its appreciation* of the decision of the Commission on Crime Prevention and Criminal Justice to mainstream a gender perspective into its activities and its request that a gender perspective be integrated into all activities of the United Nations Office on Drugs and Crime;

5. *Reaffirms* the role of the United Nations Office on Drugs and Crime in providing to Member States, upon request, technical cooperation, advisory services and other forms of assistance in the field of crime prevention and criminal justice, including in the areas of prevention and control of transnational organized

crime, corruption and terrorism as well as in the area of reconstruction of national criminal justice systems;

6. *Recognizes* the progress made in the implementation of the global programmes addressing the trafficking in human beings, corruption, organized crime and terrorism, formulated on the basis of close consultations with Member States and review by the Commission on Crime Prevention and Criminal Justice, and calls upon the Secretary-General to enhance further the visibility of those programmes and to strengthen the United Nations Office on Drugs and Crime by providing it with the resources necessary for the full implementation of its mandate in crime prevention and criminal justice;

7. *Supports* the high priority given to technical cooperation and advisory services in the field of crime prevention and criminal justice, including in the areas of prevention and control of transnational organized crime, corruption and terrorism, and stresses the need to enhance the operational activities of the United Nations Office on Drugs and Crime to assist, in particular, developing countries, countries with economies in transition and countries emerging from conflict;

8. *Urges* States and relevant international organizations to develop national, regional and international strategies and other necessary measures which complement the work of the United Nations Crime Prevention and Criminal Justice Programme in addressing effectively the significant problems posed by the smuggling of migrants and trafficking in persons and related activities;

9. *Invites* all States to support the operational activities of the United Nations Crime Prevention and Criminal Justice Programme, through voluntary contributions to the United Nations Crime Prevention and Criminal Justice Fund, or through voluntary contributions in direct support of such activities, including for the provision of technical assistance for the implementation of the commitments entered into at the Tenth United Nations Congress on the Prevention of Crime and the Treatment of Offenders, including the measures outlined in the plans of action for the implementation of the Vienna Declaration on Crime and Justice: Meeting the Challenges of the Twenty-first Century;

10. *Encourages* relevant programmes, funds and organizations of the United Nations system, in particular the United Nations Development Programme, international financial institutions, in particular the World Bank, and regional and national funding agencies, to support the technical operational activities of the United Nations Office on Drugs and Crime in the field of crime prevention and criminal justice;

11. *Urges* States and funding agencies to review, as appropriate, their funding policies for development assistance and to include a crime prevention and criminal justice component in such assistance;

12. *Welcomes* the efforts undertaken by the Commission on Crime Prevention and Criminal Justice to exercise more vigorously its mandated function of resource mobilization, and calls upon the Commission to strengthen further its activities in this direction, in accordance also with Economic and Social Council resolution 2003/31 of 22 July 2003 on the functioning of the Commission;

13. *Notes with appreciation* the decision to organize a senior-level discussion during the thirteenth session of the Commission on Crime Prevention and Criminal Justice on progress made with regard to the criminal justice aspects of terrorism and international conventions and protocols related to terrorism;

14. *Expresses its appreciation* to non-governmental organizations and other relevant sectors of civil society for their support to the United Nations Crime Prevention and Criminal Justice Programme;

15. *Invites* relevant entities of the United Nations system, including the United Nations Development Programme and the World Bank, and other international funding agencies to increase their interaction with the United Nations Office on Drugs and Crime in order to benefit from synergies and avoid duplication of effort, and to ensure that, as appropriate, activities on crime prevention and criminal justice, including activities related to the prevention of corruption, are considered in their sustainable development agenda and that the expertise of the Office in activities related to crime prevention and criminal justice, including activities related to the prevention of corruption and the promotion of the rule of law, is fully utilized;

16. *Requests* the Secretary-General to take all necessary measures to provide adequate support to the Commission on Crime Prevention and Criminal Justice, as the principal policy-making body in this field, in performing its activities, including cooperation and coordination with the institutes of the United Nations Crime Prevention and Criminal Justice Programme network and other relevant bodies;

17. *Welcomes* the entry into force of the United Nations Convention against Transnational Organized Crime (Palermo Convention) and the forthcoming entry into force of the Protocol to Prevent, Suppress and Punish Trafficking in Persons, Especially Women and Children, supplementing the United Nations Convention against Transnational Organized Crime, and the results of the treaty event "Focus 2003: treaties against transnational organized crime and terrorism", organized by the Secretary-General in New York from 23 to 26 September 2003;

18. *Emphasizes* the importance of the expeditious entry into force of the remaining Protocols to the Convention;

19. *Urges* all States and regional economic organizations that have not yet done so to ratify or accede to the Convention as soon as possible, so as to participate in the conference of the States parties at its inaugural session, to be held at Vienna from 28 June to 9 July 2004;

20. *Welcomes* the voluntary contributions already made, and encourages States to make adequate and regular voluntary contributions for the implementation of the Convention and the Protocols thereto, through the United Nations funding mechanism specifically designed for that purpose in the Convention or in direct support of implementation activities and initiatives;

21. *Also welcomes* the successful outcome of the negotiations on the United Nations Convention against Corruption and the participation of States and competent regional economic integration organizations in the High-level Political Conference for the Purpose of Signing the Convention, held at Mérida, Mexico, from 9 to 11 December 2003, and urges them to take all nec-

essary measures to ratify the Convention as soon as possible;

22. *Requests* the Secretary-General to take all necessary measures and provide adequate support to the United Nations Office on Drugs and Crime so as to enable it to promote the speedy entry into force of the United Nations Convention against Corruption;

23. *Encourages* States to make adequate and regular voluntary contributions for the entry into force of the United Nations Convention against Corruption, through the United Nations funding mechanism specifically designed for that purpose in the Convention or in direct support of implementation activities and initiatives;

24. *Requests* the Secretary-General to submit a report on the implementation of the present resolution to the General Assembly at its fifty-ninth session.

Work of the Centre for International Crime Prevention

The Executive Director of the Centre for International Crime Prevention of the United Nations Office on Drugs and Crime reported in March [E/CN.15/2003/2] on the Centre's activities in 2002. One of the Centre's core activities was the promotion of the ratification process of the United Nations Convention against Transnational Organized Crime and its Protocols (see p. 1125) and the provision of assistance to States seeking to ratify them. A Global Programme against Terrorism was launched in 2002 to respond to requests for counter-terrorism assistance by the Security Council's Counter-Terrorism Committee (see p. 63) or directly from requesting States. Thirteen Member States responded to the Secretary-General's request for information on steps taken to implement the plans of action for the implementation of the Vienna Declaration on Crime and Justice: Meeting the Challenges of the Twenty-first Century, annexed to General Assembly resolution 56/261 [YUN 2002, p. 1099]; a number of them indicated that they were being guided by the plans of action. The Centre published statistical information on crime and criminal justice for the period 1998-2000 received from over 80 Member States and expanded its dissemination of information by electronic means. Work focused on initiating the Centre's global trends study, which examined the links between institutional arrangements and organized crime and public sector corruption. The report presented statistical data on the Centre's technical cooperation activities and described coordination with the United Nations Crime Prevention and Criminal Justice Programme network.

A March report of the Secretary-General [E/CN.15/2003/4] summarized the activities of the institutions comprising the United Nations Crime Prevention and Criminal Justice Programme network—the United Nations Interregional Crime and Justice Research Institute (UNICRI), 11 regional and affiliated institutes and the International Scientific and Professional Advisory Council—based on their contributions submitted pursuant to General Assembly resolution 58/170 [YUN 2002, p. 1108]. UNICRI activities focused on juvenile justice; criminal justice reform; trafficking in persons; terrorism; and the production of crime surveys. The regional and affiliated institutes emphasized similar activities, in addition to those relating to prison conditions, extradition and legal assistance, trafficking in illicit firearms and ammunition, restorative justice, violence, property crime and drugs, transnational organized crime, extradition and terrorism, and high-technology and computer-related crime.

ECONOMIC AND SOCIAL COUNCIL ACTION

On 22 July [meeting 44], the Economic and Social Council, on the recommendation of the Commission on Crime Prevention and Criminal Justice [E/2003/30], adopted **resolution 2003/24** without vote [agenda item 14 (*c*)].

Work of the Centre for International Crime Prevention, including the management of the United Nations Crime Prevention and Criminal Justice Fund

The Economic and Social Council,

Recalling General Assembly resolution 46/152 of 18 December 1991, in which the Assembly approved the statement of principles and programme of action of the United Nations Crime Prevention and Criminal Justice Programme,

Recalling also General Assembly resolutions 56/123 of 19 December 2001 and 57/173 of 18 December 2002 on strengthening the United Nations Crime Prevention and Criminal Justice Programme, in particular its technical cooperation capacity,

Welcoming the increase in voluntary contributions made by donors to the United Nations Crime Prevention and Criminal Justice Fund, which enables the Centre for International Crime Prevention of the United Nations Office on Drugs and Crime to execute a larger number of technical assistance projects,

Welcoming also other contributions made by donors in direct support of activities and projects of the Centre, including through contributions made to institutes of the United Nations Crime Prevention and Criminal Justice Programme network,

Recognizing the importance of transparency and close communication between the Centre and Member States in order to raise the confidence of Member States in the work of the Centre,

1. *Takes note with appreciation* of the report of the Executive Director of the United Nations Office on Drugs and Crime on the work of the Centre for International Crime Prevention;

2. *Invites* Member States to make appropriate voluntary contributions to the United Nations Crime Prevention and Criminal Justice Fund in order to strengthen the capacity of the Centre to provide technical assistance to requesting States;

3. *Encourages* Member States to continue to make contributions in direct support of activities and projects of the Centre, including through contributions to institutes of the United Nations Crime Prevention and Criminal Justice Programme network;

4. *Welcomes* the efforts being made by the United Nations Office on Drugs and Crime to ensure transparency in its work, as well as to maintain a continuous dialogue with Member States, including through appropriate informative documentation, with a view to enhancing its accountability to Member States, and to improve the synergy between the activities of the Centre and those of the United Nations International Drug Control Programme;

5. *Encourages* the Centre to provide Member States with more information on a regular basis on funding requirements for projects in order to increase voluntary contributions;

6. *Encourages* the United Nations Office on Drugs and Crime, subject to the availability of extrabudgetary financial resources, to extend the Programme and Financial Information Management System to the activities funded by the United Nations Crime Prevention and Criminal Justice Fund, so that Member States are provided with up-to-date online financial information on those activities;

7. *Stresses* the importance of monitoring and evaluation of projects financed by the Fund, and welcomes in that respect the recent decision to establish an independent evaluation function in the United Nations Office on Drugs and Crime;

8. *Welcomes* the recent delegation of authority from the Secretary-General to the Director-General of the United Nations Office at Vienna for the management of the Fund, which should increase the efficiency of the Centre in managing its financial resources and enhance its reporting to the Commission on Crime Prevention and Criminal Justice on the financial status of the Fund;

9. *Encourages* the Executive Director of the United Nations Office on Drugs and Crime to use the experience of the Fund-Raising Unit of the United Nations International Drug Control Programme in areas such as broadening the donor base, cost-sharing, private sector funding and other innovative means to increase the resources of the Centre;

10. *Requests* the Executive Director of the United Nations Office on Drugs and Crime to include in his annual report to the Commission information on the financial status of the Fund and the results of the evaluation of projects financed by the Fund;

11. *Also requests* the Executive Director of the United Nations Office on Drugs and Crime to provide Member States with relevant information on the Fund when required.

UN African crime prevention institute

In an August report [A/58/223], submitted in response to General Assembly resolution 57/172 [YUN 2002, p. 1114], the Secretary-General highlighted the activities of the African Institute for the Prevention of Crime and the Treatment of Offenders (UNAFRI), including the medium-term strategy and action plan for 2002-2007, approved by the UNAFRI Governing Board (Addis Ababa, Ethiopia, 17-18 March), fund-raising efforts and strategies for sustaining the Institute.

UNAFRI, as part of the main focus of its activities, held a series of national workshops with a view to sharing valuable experience and disseminating information regarding the prevalence of transnational criminality and the need for concerted action at the regional and subregional levels. It informed countries about relevant UN conventions as an effective means of combating crime. Other activities related to a draft convention on mutual legal assistance and extradition to control transnational organized crime, combating trafficking in firearms and ammunition in Africa, a UN survey on kidnapping, means to combat terrorism, workshops on crime prevention strategies and preventing trafficking in women and children.

The Institute's total resources for 2002-2003 amounted to $952,691, which came from member States, assessed contributions, a UN grant, and rent and interest income.

Proposals to strengthen the Institute included increasing cooperation and partnership with UNODC; calling on potential donors and relevant international funding agencies for contributions for the effective implementation of the UNAFRI work programme; and urging members to meet their financial obligations to the Institute.

GENERAL ASSEMBLY ACTION

On 22 December [meeting 77], the General Assembly, on the recommendation of the Third Committee [A/58/499], adopted **resolution 58/139** without vote [agenda item 108].

United Nations African Institute for the Prevention of Crime and the Treatment of Offenders

The General Assembly,

Recalling its resolution 57/172 of 18 December 2002 and all other relevant resolutions,

Taking note of the report of the Secretary-General,

Bearing in mind the urgent need to establish effective crime prevention strategies for Africa, as well as the importance of law enforcement agencies and the judiciary at the regional and subregional levels,

Noting that the financial situation of the United Nations African Institute for the Prevention of Crime and the Treatment of Offenders has greatly affected its capacity to deliver its services to African Member States in an effective and comprehensive manner,

1. *Commends* the United Nations African Institute for the Prevention of Crime and the Treatment of Offenders for its efforts to promote and coordinate regional technical cooperation activities related to crime prevention and criminal justice systems in Africa;

2. *Commends* the Secretary-General for his efforts to mobilize the financial resources necessary to provide the Institute with the core professional staff required

to enable it to function effectively in the fulfilment of its mandated obligations;

3. *Reiterates* the need to strengthen further the capacity of the Institute to support national mechanisms for crime prevention and criminal justice in African countries;

4. *Urges* the States members of the Institute to make every possible effort to meet their obligations to the Institute;

5. *Calls upon* all Member States and non-governmental organizations to adopt concrete practical measures to support the Institute in the development of the requisite capacity and to implement its programmes and activities aimed at strengthening crime prevention and criminal justice systems in Africa;

6. *Requests* the Secretary-General to intensify efforts to mobilize all relevant entities of the United Nations system to provide the necessary financial and technical support to the Institute to enable it to fulfil its mandate;

7. *Also requests* the Secretary-General to continue his efforts to mobilize the financial resources necessary to maintain the Institute with the core professional staff required to enable it to function effectively in the fulfilment of its mandated obligations;

8. *Calls upon* the United Nations Crime Prevention and Criminal Justice Programme and the United Nations International Drug Control Programme to work closely with the Institute;

9. *Requests* the Secretary-General to enhance the promotion of regional cooperation, coordination and collaboration in the fight against crime, especially in its transnational dimension, which cannot be dealt with adequately by national action alone;

10. *Also requests* the Secretary-General to make concrete proposals, including the provision of additional core professional staff, to strengthen the programmes and activities of the Institute and to report to the General Assembly at its fifty-ninth session on the implementation of the present resolution.

Transnational crime

In 2003, the United Nations continued its efforts to counter transnational organized crime by promoting the signature and ratification of the United Nations Convention against Transnational Organized Crime and its supplementary protocols. In September, the Convention entered into force, as did its Protocol to Prevent, Suppress and Punish Trafficking in Persons, Especially Women and Children in December.

The Economic and Social Council, in **resolution 2003/36** (see p. 1267), called on States to counter transnational criminal acts regarding money-laundering within the context of international and national drug control plans.

International convention

In 2003, the United Nations Convention against Transnational Organized Crime and one of its supplementary Protocols—the Protocol to Prevent, Suppress and Punish Trafficking in Persons, Especially Women and Children—entered into force (on 29 September and 25 December, respectively), while the Protocol against the Smuggling of Migrants by Land, Sea and Air and the Protocol against the Illicit Manufacturing of and Trafficking in Firearms, Their Parts and Components and Ammunition had yet to fulfil the criteria to do so. The Convention and Protocols thereto on trafficking and migrants were adopted by the General Assembly in resolution 55/25 [YUN 2000, p. 1048] and the Protocol on firearms in resolution 55/255 [YUN 2001, p. 1036]. The first meeting of the Conference of the Parties to the Convention and its Protocols was scheduled for 2004.

As at 31 December, there were 59 parties and 147 signatories to the Convention, 45 parties and 117 signatories to the Protocol on trafficking, 40 parties and 112 signatories to the Protocol on migrants, and 12 parties and 52 signatories to the Protocol on firearms.

In a March report [E/CN.15/2003/5], updated by a July report [A/58/165] prepared by the UNODC Centre for International Crime Prevention, the Secretary-General described efforts to promote the signature and ratification of the Convention and Protocols thereto. On 22 December, the Assembly took note of the July report (**decision 58/531**).

Communication. Egypt, on 14 October [A/C.3/58/4], transmitted the Cairo Declaration issued by the Regional Ministerial Conference of French-speaking Countries of Africa for the promotion of ratification of the UN Convention against Transnational Organization Crime and the Protocols thereto (Cairo, 2-4 September) and the report of the Conference. The ministers recommended that the French-speaking countries of Africa that were not party to the Convention and its Protocols accede to them as soon as possible.

ECONOMIC AND SOCIAL COUNCIL ACTION

On 22 July [meeting 44], the Economic and Social Council, on the recommendation of the Commission on Crime Prevention and Criminal Justice [E/2003/30], adopted **resolution 2003/21** without vote [agenda item 14 *(c)*].

International cooperation in the fight against transnational organized crime: assistance to States in capacity-building with a view to facilitating the implementation of the United Nations Convention against Transnational Organized Crime and the Protocols thereto

The Economic and Social Council
Recommends to the General Assembly the adoption of the following draft resolution:
[For text, see General Assembly resolution 58/135 below.]

GENERAL ASSEMBLY ACTION

On 22 December [meeting 77], the General Assembly, on the recommendation of the Third Committee [A/58/499], adopted **resolution 58/135** without vote [agenda item 108].

International cooperation in the fight against transnational organized crime: assistance to States in capacity-building with a view to facilitating the implementation of the United Nations Convention against Transnational Organized Crime and the Protocols thereto

The General Assembly,

Recalling its resolution 55/25 of 15 November 2000, by which it adopted the United Nations Convention against Transnational Organized Crime, the Protocol to Prevent, Suppress and Punish Trafficking in Persons, Especially Women and Children, supplementing the United Nations Convention against Transnational Organized Crime, and the Protocol against the Smuggling of Migrants by Land, Sea and Air, supplementing the United Nations Convention against Transnational Organized Crime,

Recalling also its resolution 55/255 of 31 May 2001, by which it adopted the Protocol against the Illicit Manufacturing of and Trafficking in Firearms, Their Parts and Components and Ammunition, supplementing the United Nations Convention against Transnational Organized Crime,

Recalling further its resolution 56/120 of 19 December 2001 on action against transnational organized crime: assistance to States in capacity-building with a view to facilitating the implementation of the Convention and the Protocols thereto,

Reaffirming its deep concern at the impact of transnational organized crime on the political, social and economic stability and development of societies,

Reaffirming that the adoption of the Convention and the Protocols thereto is a significant development in international criminal law and that they constitute important instruments for effective international cooperation against transnational organized crime,

1. *Takes note with appreciation* of the report of the Secretary-General on the ratification of the United Nations Convention against Transnational Organized Crime and the Protocols thereto;

2. *Welcomes* the entry into force of the United Nations Convention against Transnational Organized Crime, and notes the number of signatures and ratifications of the three Protocols to the Convention, which is likely to lead to the expected entry into force at an early date of the Protocol to Prevent, Suppress and Punish Trafficking in Persons, Especially Women and Children, supplementing the United Nations Convention against Transnational Organized Crime, and the Protocol against the Smuggling of Migrants by Land, Sea and Air, supplementing the United Nations Convention against Transnational Organized Crime;

3. *Commends* the Centre for International Crime Prevention of the United Nations Office on Drugs and Crime for its work in promoting the ratification of the Convention and the Protocols thereto, including, in particular, the preparation of legislative guides designed to facilitate the ratification and subsequent implementation of those instruments, and invites the Centre to finalize the legislative guides and to disseminate them as widely as possible;

4. *Welcomes* the organization by the Secretary-General, in cooperation with the Centre and the Office of Legal Affairs of the Secretariat, of the treaty event "Focus 2003: treaties against transnational organized crime and terrorism", held at United Nations Headquarters from 23 to 26 September 2003, in accordance with General Assembly resolution 57/173 of 18 December 2002, welcomes the participation of Member States in that event, and urges Member States that have not yet done so to deposit their instruments of ratification or approval of or accession to the Convention and the Protocols thereto, in order to ensure the widest possible participation in those instruments and thus to maximize their effectiveness;

5. *Also welcomes* the financial support provided by several donors to promote the entry into force and implementation of the Convention and the Protocols thereto, and encourages Member States to make sufficient voluntary contributions to the United Nations Crime Prevention and Criminal Justice Fund, as well as contributions in direct support of activities and projects of the Centre, including through contributions to the institutes of the United Nations Crime Prevention and Criminal Justice Programme network, for the provision of technical assistance to developing countries and countries with economies in transition for the implementation of those international legal instruments;

6. *Requests* the Centre, in its capacity as secretariat of the Conference of the Parties to the Convention, to undertake all activities necessary to ensure the efficient preparation of the inaugural session of the Conference of the Parties, in 2004;

7. *Also requests* the Centre, within existing regular or extrabudgetary resources, in preparing to provide services to the Conference of the Parties, as mandated, to develop a guide containing elements that would be useful to States parties in meeting their reporting requirements to the Conference of the Parties and to undertake a study on the functioning of extradition and mutual legal assistance through existing mechanisms, including bilateral, regional and multilateral agreements or arrangements;

8. *Requests* the Secretary-General to continue to provide the Centre with the resources necessary to enable it to promote, in an effective manner, the implementation of the Convention and the Protocols thereto and to discharge its functions as the secretariat of the Conference of the Parties in accordance with its mandate;

9. *Also requests* the Secretary-General to report on the implementation of the present resolution in his report on the work of the Centre to be submitted to the General Assembly at its fifty-ninth session.

Corruption

Convention against Corruption

In 2003, negotiations were concluded on the United Nations Convention against Corruption by the Ad Hoc Committee for the Negotiation of a Convention against Corruption. The Ad Hoc Committee, which held its first three sessions in

2002 [YUN 2002, p. 1119] and its fourth (13-24 January) [A/AC.261/13], fifth (10-21 March) [A/AC.261/16], sixth (21 July–8 August) [A/AC.261/22] and seventh (29 September–1 October) [A/AC.261/25] sessions in 2003, all in Vienna, issued an October report [A/58/422 & Add.1] summarizing its work, pursuant to General Assembly resolutions 56/260 [YUN 2002, p. 1118] and 57/169 [ibid., p. 1119]. Annexed to the report was a draft resolution for adoption by the Assembly, which incorporated the draft text of the Convention.

In March [E/CN.15/2003/6], the Secretary-General described the outcomes of the Ad Hoc Committee's first four sessions and urged the Commission on Crime Prevention and Criminal Justice to provide its views on the Committee's progress achieved thus far and to explore ways to support the Committee's work.

GENERAL ASSEMBLY ACTION

On 31 October [meeting 51], the General Assembly, on the recommendation of Ad Hoc Committee for the Negotiation of a Convention against Corruption [A/58/422], adopted **resolution 58/4** without vote [agenda item 108].

United Nations Convention against Corruption

The General Assembly,

Recalling its resolution 55/61 of 4 December 2000, in which it established an ad hoc committee for the negotiation of an effective international legal instrument against corruption and requested the Secretary-General to convene an intergovernmental open-ended expert group to examine and prepare draft terms of reference for the negotiation of such an instrument, and its resolution 55/188 of 20 December 2000, in which it invited the intergovernmental open-ended expert group to be convened pursuant to resolution 55/61 to examine the question of illegally transferred funds and the return of such funds to the countries of origin,

Recalling also its resolutions 56/186 of 21 December 2001 and 57/244 of 20 December 2002 on preventing and combating corrupt practices and transfer of funds of illicit origin and returning such funds to the countries of origin,

Recalling further its resolution 56/260 of 31 January 2002, in which it requested the Ad Hoc Committee for the Negotiation of a Convention against Corruption to complete its work by the end of 2003,

Recalling its resolution 57/169 of 18 December 2002, in which it accepted with appreciation the offer made by the Government of Mexico to host a high-level political conference for the purpose of signing the convention and requested the Secretary-General to schedule the conference for a period of three days before the end of 2003,

Recalling also Economic and Social Council resolution 2001/13 of 24 July 2001, entitled "Strengthening international cooperation in preventing and combating the transfer of funds of illicit origin, derived from acts of corruption, including the laundering of funds, and in returning such funds",

Expressing its appreciation to the Government of Argentina for hosting the informal preparatory meeting of the Ad Hoc Committee for the Negotiation of a Convention against Corruption in Buenos Aires from 4 to 7 December 2001,

Recalling the Monterrey Consensus, adopted by the International Conference on Financing for Development, held in Monterrey, Mexico, from 18 to 22 March 2002, in which it was underlined that fighting corruption at all levels was a priority,

Recalling also the Johannesburg Declaration on Sustainable Development, adopted by the World Summit on Sustainable Development, held in Johannesburg, South Africa, from 26 August to 4 September 2002, in particular paragraph 19 thereof, in which corruption was declared a threat to the sustainable development of people,

Concerned about the seriousness of problems and threats posed by corruption to the stability and security of societies, undermining the institutions and values of democracy, ethical values and justice and jeopardizing sustainable development and the rule of law,

1. *Takes note* of the report of the Ad Hoc Committee for the Negotiation of a Convention against Corruption, which carried out its work at the headquarters of the United Nations Office on Drugs and Crime in Vienna, in which the Ad Hoc Committee submitted the final text of the draft United Nations Convention against Corruption to the General Assembly for its consideration and action, and commends the Ad Hoc Committee for its work;

2. *Adopts* the United Nations Convention against Corruption annexed to the present resolution, and opens it for signature at the High-level Political Signing Conference to be held in Merida, Mexico, from 9 to 11 December 2003, in accordance with resolution 57/169;

3. *Urges* all States and competent regional economic integration organizations to sign and ratify the United Nations Convention against Corruption as soon as possible in order to ensure its rapid entry into force;

4. *Decides* that, until the Conference of the States Parties to the Convention established pursuant to the United Nations Convention against Corruption decides otherwise, the account referred to in article 62 of the Convention will be operated within the United Nations Crime Prevention and Criminal Justice Fund, and encourages Member States to begin making adequate voluntary contributions to the above-mentioned account for the provision to developing countries and countries with economies in transition of the technical assistance that they might require to prepare for ratification and implementation of the Convention;

5. *Also decides* that the Ad Hoc Committee for the Negotiation of a Convention against Corruption will complete its tasks arising from the negotiation of the United Nations Convention against Corruption by holding a meeting well before the convening of the first session of the Conference of the States Parties to the Convention in order to prepare the draft text of the rules of procedure of the Conference of the States Parties and of other rules described in article 63 of the Convention, which will be submitted to the Conference

of the States Parties at its first session for consideration;

6. *Requests* the Conference of the States Parties to the Convention to address the criminalization of bribery of officials of public international organizations, including the United Nations, and related issues, taking into account questions of privileges and immunities, as well as of jurisdiction and the role of international organizations, by, inter alia, making recommendations regarding appropriate action in that regard;

7. *Decides* that, in order to raise awareness of corruption and of the role of the Convention in combating and preventing it, 9 December should be designated International Anti-Corruption Day;

8. *Requests* the Secretary-General to designate the United Nations Office on Drugs and Crime to serve as the secretariat for and under the direction of the Conference of the States Parties to the Convention;

9. *Also requests* the Secretary-General to provide the United Nations Office on Drugs and Crime with the resources necessary to enable it to promote in an effective manner the rapid entry into force of the United Nations Convention against Corruption and to discharge the functions of secretariat of the Conference of the States Parties to the Convention, and to support the Ad Hoc Committee in its work pursuant to paragraph 5 above;

10. *Further requests* the Secretary-General to prepare a comprehensive report on the High-level Political Signing Conference to be held in Merida, Mexico, in accordance with resolution 57/169, for submission to the General Assembly at its fifty-ninth session.

Annex

United Nations Convention against Corruption

Preamble

The States Parties to this Convention,

Concerned about the seriousness of problems and threats posed by corruption to the stability and security of societies, undermining the institutions and values of democracy, ethical values and justice and jeopardizing sustainable development and the rule of law,

Concerned also about the links between corruption and other forms of crime, in particular organized crime and economic crime, including money-laundering,

Concerned further about cases of corruption that involve vast quantities of assets, which may constitute a substantial proportion of the resources of States, and that threaten the political stability and sustainable development of those States,

Convinced that corruption is no longer a local matter but a transnational phenomenon that affects all societies and economies, making international cooperation to prevent and control it essential,

Convinced also that a comprehensive and multidisciplinary approach is required to prevent and combat corruption effectively,

Convinced further that the availability of technical assistance can play an important role in enhancing the ability of States, including by strengthening capacity and by institution-building, to prevent and combat corruption effectively,

Convinced that the illicit acquisition of personal wealth can be particularly damaging to democratic institutions, national economies and the rule of law,

Determined to prevent, detect and deter in a more effective manner international transfers of illicitly acquired assets and to strengthen international cooperation in asset recovery,

Acknowledging the fundamental principles of due process of law in criminal proceedings and in civil or administrative proceedings to adjudicate property rights,

Bearing in mind that the prevention and eradication of corruption is a responsibility of all States and that they must cooperate with one another, with the support and involvement of individuals and groups outside the public sector, such as civil society, non-governmental organizations and community-based organizations, if their efforts in this area are to be effective,

Bearing also in mind the principles of proper management of public affairs and public property, fairness, responsibility and equality before the law and the need to safeguard integrity and to foster a culture of rejection of corruption,

Commending the work of the Commission on Crime Prevention and Criminal Justice and the United Nations Office on Drugs and Crime in preventing and combating corruption,

Recalling the work carried out by other international and regional organizations in this field, including the activities of the African Union, the Council of Europe, the Customs Cooperation Council (also known as the World Customs Organization), the European Union, the League of Arab States, the Organisation for Economic Cooperation and Development and the Organization of American States,

Taking note with appreciation of multilateral instruments to prevent and combat corruption, including, inter alia, the Inter-American Convention against Corruption, adopted by the Organization of American States on 29 March 1996, the Convention on the Fight against Corruption involving Officials of the European Communities or Officials of Member States of the European Union, adopted by the Council of the European Union on 26 May 1997, the Convention on Combating Bribery of Foreign Public Officials in International Business Transactions, adopted by the Organisation for Economic Cooperation and Development on 21 November 1997, the Criminal Law Convention on Corruption, adopted by the Committee of Ministers of the Council of Europe on 27 January 1999, the Civil Law Convention on Corruption, adopted by the Committee of Ministers of the Council of Europe on 4 November 1999, and the African Union Convention on Preventing and Combating Corruption, adopted by the Heads of State and Government of the African Union on 12 July 2003,

Welcoming the entry into force on 29 September 2003 of the United Nations Convention against Transnational Organized Crime,

Have agreed as follows:

Chapter I
General provisions

Article 1
Statement of purpose

The purposes of this Convention are:

(*a*) To promote and strengthen measures to prevent and combat corruption more efficiently and effectively;

(b) To promote, facilitate and support international cooperation and technical assistance in the prevention of and fight against corruption, including in asset recovery;

(c) To promote integrity, accountability and proper management of public affairs and public property.

Article 2
Use of terms

For the purposes of this Convention:

(a) "Public official" shall mean: (i) any person holding a legislative, executive, administrative or judicial office of a State Party, whether appointed or elected, whether permanent or temporary, whether paid or unpaid, irrespective of that person's seniority; (ii) any other person who performs a public function, including for a public agency or public enterprise, or provides a public service, as defined in the domestic law of the State Party and as applied in the pertinent area of law of that State Party; (iii) any other person defined as a "public official" in the domestic law of a State Party. However, for the purpose of some specific measures contained in chapter II of this Convention, "public official" may mean any person who performs a public function or provides a public service as defined in the domestic law of the State Party and as applied in the pertinent area of law of that State Party;

(b) "Foreign public official" shall mean any person holding a legislative, executive, administrative or judicial office of a foreign country, whether appointed or elected; and any person exercising a public function for a foreign country, including for a public agency or public enterprise;

(c) "Official of a public international organization" shall mean an international civil servant or any person who is authorized by such an organization to act on behalf of that organization;

(d) "Property" shall mean assets of every kind, whether corporeal or incorporeal, movable or immovable, tangible or intangible, and legal documents or instruments evidencing title to or interest in such assets;

(e) "Proceeds of crime" shall mean any property derived from or obtained, directly or indirectly, through the commission of an offence;

(f) "Freezing" or "seizure" shall mean temporarily prohibiting the transfer, conversion, disposition or movement of property or temporarily assuming custody or control of property on the basis of an order issued by a court or other competent authority;

(g) "Confiscation", which includes forfeiture where applicable, shall mean the permanent deprivation of property by order of a court or other competent authority;

(h) "Predicate offence" shall mean any offence as a result of which proceeds have been generated that may become the subject of an offence as defined in article 23 of this Convention;

(i) "Controlled delivery" shall mean the technique of allowing illicit or suspect consignments to pass out of, through or into the territory of one or more States, with the knowledge and under the supervision of their competent authorities, with a view to the investigation of an offence and the identification of persons involved in the commission of the offence.

Article 3
Scope of application

1. This Convention shall apply, in accordance with its terms, to the prevention, investigation and prosecution of corruption and to the freezing, seizure, confiscation and return of the proceeds of offences established in accordance with this Convention.

2. For the purposes of implementing this Convention, it shall not be necessary, except as otherwise stated herein, for the offences set forth in it to result in damage or harm to state property.

Article 4
Protection of sovereignty

1. States Parties shall carry out their obligations under this Convention in a manner consistent with the principles of sovereign equality and territorial integrity of States and that of non-intervention in the domestic affairs of other States.

2. Nothing in this Convention shall entitle a State Party to undertake in the territory of another State the exercise of jurisdiction and performance of functions that are reserved exclusively for the authorities of that other State by its domestic law.

Chapter II
Preventive measures

Article 5
Preventive anti-corruption policies and practices

1. Each State Party shall, in accordance with the fundamental principles of its legal system, develop and implement or maintain effective, coordinated anti-corruption policies that promote the participation of society and reflect the principles of the rule of law, proper management of public affairs and public property, integrity, transparency and accountability.

2. Each State Party shall endeavour to establish and promote effective practices aimed at the prevention of corruption.

3. Each State Party shall endeavour to periodically evaluate relevant legal instruments and administrative measures with a view to determining their adequacy to prevent and fight corruption.

4. States Parties shall, as appropriate and in accordance with the fundamental principles of their legal system, collaborate with each other and with relevant international and regional organizations in promoting and developing the measures referred to in this article. That collaboration may include participation in international programmes and projects aimed at the prevention of corruption.

Article 6
Preventive anti-corruption body or bodies

1. Each State Party shall, in accordance with the fundamental principles of its legal system, ensure the existence of a body or bodies, as appropriate, that prevent corruption by such means as:

(a) Implementing the policies referred to in article 5 of this Convention and, where appropriate, overseeing and coordinating the implementation of those policies;

(b) Increasing and disseminating knowledge about the prevention of corruption.

2. Each State Party shall grant the body or bodies referred to in paragraph 1 of this article the necessary independence, in accordance with the fundamental

principles of its legal system, to enable the body or bodies to carry out its or their functions effectively and free from any undue influence. The necessary material resources and specialized staff, as well as the training that such staff may require to carry out their functions, should be provided.

3. Each State Party shall inform the Secretary-General of the United Nations of the name and address of the authority or authorities that may assist other States Parties in developing and implementing specific measures for the prevention of corruption.

Article 7
Public sector

1. Each State Party shall, where appropriate and in accordance with the fundamental principles of its legal system, endeavour to adopt, maintain and strengthen systems for the recruitment, hiring, retention, promotion and retirement of civil servants and, where appropriate, other non-elected public officials:

(a) That are based on principles of efficiency, transparency and objective criteria such as merit, equity and aptitude;

(b) That include adequate procedures for the selection and training of individuals for public positions considered especially vulnerable to corruption and the rotation, where appropriate, of such individuals to other positions;

(c) That promote adequate remuneration and equitable pay scales, taking into account the level of economic development of the State Party;

(d) That promote education and training programmes to enable them to meet the requirements for the correct, honourable and proper performance of public functions and that provide them with specialized and appropriate training to enhance their awareness of the risks of corruption inherent in the performance of their functions. Such programmes may make reference to codes or standards of conduct in applicable areas.

2. Each State Party shall also consider adopting appropriate legislative and administrative measures, consistent with the objectives of this Convention and in accordance with the fundamental principles of its domestic law, to prescribe criteria concerning candidature for and election to public office.

3. Each State Party shall also consider taking appropriate legislative and administrative measures, consistent with the objectives of this Convention and in accordance with the fundamental principles of its domestic law, to enhance transparency in the funding of candidatures for elected public office and, where applicable, the funding of political parties.

4. Each State Party shall, in accordance with the fundamental principles of its domestic law, endeavour to adopt, maintain and strengthen systems that promote transparency and prevent conflicts of interest.

Article 8
Codes of conduct for public officials

1. In order to fight corruption, each State Party shall promote, inter alia, integrity, honesty and responsibility among its public officials, in accordance with the fundamental principles of its legal system.

2. In particular, each State Party shall endeavour to apply, within its own institutional and legal systems, codes or standards of conduct for the correct, honourable and proper performance of public functions.

3. For the purposes of implementing the provisions of this article, each State Party shall, where appropriate and in accordance with the fundamental principles of its legal system, take note of the relevant initiatives of regional, interregional and multilateral organizations, such as the International Code of Conduct for Public Officials contained in the annex to General Assembly resolution 51/59 of 12 December 1996.

4. Each State Party shall also consider, in accordance with the fundamental principles of its domestic law, establishing measures and systems to facilitate the reporting by public officials of acts of corruption to appropriate authorities, when such acts come to their notice in the performance of their functions.

5. Each State Party shall endeavour, where appropriate and in accordance with the fundamental principles of its domestic law, to establish measures and systems requiring public officials to make declarations to appropriate authorities regarding, inter alia, their outside activities, employment, investments, assets and substantial gifts or benefits from which a conflict of interest may result with respect to their functions as public officials.

6. Each State Party shall consider taking, in accordance with the fundamental principles of its domestic law, disciplinary or other measures against public officials who violate the codes or standards established in accordance with this article.

Article 9
Public procurement and management of public finances

1. Each State Party shall, in accordance with the fundamental principles of its legal system, take the necessary steps to establish appropriate systems of procurement, based on transparency, competition and objective criteria in decision-making, that are effective, inter alia, in preventing corruption. Such systems, which may take into account appropriate threshold values in their application, shall address, inter alia:

(a) The public distribution of information relating to procurement procedures and contracts, including information on invitations to tender and relevant or pertinent information on the award of contracts, allowing potential tenderers sufficient time to prepare and submit their tenders;

(b) The establishment, in advance, of conditions for participation, including selection and award criteria and tendering rules, and their publication;

(c) The use of objective and predetermined criteria for public procurement decisions, in order to facilitate the subsequent verification of the correct application of the rules or procedures;

(d) An effective system of domestic review, including an effective system of appeal, to ensure legal recourse and remedies in the event that the rules or procedures established pursuant to this paragraph are not followed;

(e) Where appropriate, measures to regulate matters regarding personnel responsible for procurement, such as declaration of interest in particular public procurements, screening procedures and training requirements.

2. Each State Party shall, in accordance with the fundamental principles of its legal system, take appro-

priate measures to promote transparency and accountability in the management of public finances. Such measures shall encompass, inter alia:

(a) Procedures for the adoption of the national budget;

(b) Timely reporting on revenue and expenditure;

(c) A system of accounting and auditing standards and related oversight;

(d) Effective and efficient systems of risk management and internal control; and

(e) Where appropriate, corrective action in the case of failure to comply with the requirements established in this paragraph.

3. Each State Party shall take such civil and administrative measures as may be necessary, in accordance with the fundamental principles of its domestic law, to preserve the integrity of accounting books, records, financial statements or other documents related to public expenditure and revenue and to prevent the falsification of such documents.

Article 10
Public reporting

Taking into account the need to combat corruption, each State Party shall, in accordance with the fundamental principles of its domestic law, take such measures as may be necessary to enhance transparency in its public administration, including with regard to its organization, functioning and decision-making processes, where appropriate. Such measures may include, inter alia:

(a) Adopting procedures or regulations allowing members of the general public to obtain, where appropriate, information on the organization, functioning and decision-making processes of its public administration and, with due regard for the protection of privacy and personal data, on decisions and legal acts that concern members of the public;

(b) Simplifying administrative procedures, where appropriate, in order to facilitate public access to the competent decision-making authorities; and

(c) Publishing information, which may include periodic reports on the risks of corruption in its public administration.

Article 11
Measures relating to the judiciary and prosecution services

1. Bearing in mind the independence of the judiciary and its crucial role in combating corruption, each State Party shall, in accordance with the fundamental principles of its legal system and without prejudice to judicial independence, take measures to strengthen integrity and to prevent opportunities for corruption among members of the judiciary. Such measures may include rules with respect to the conduct of members of the judiciary.

2. Measures to the same effect as those taken pursuant to paragraph 1 of this article may be introduced and applied within the prosecution service in those States Parties where it does not form part of the judiciary but enjoys independence similar to that of the judicial service.

Article 12
Private sector

1. Each State Party shall take measures, in accordance with the fundamental principles of its domestic law, to prevent corruption involving the private sector, enhance accounting and auditing standards in the private sector and, where appropriate, provide effective, proportionate and dissuasive civil, administrative or criminal penalties for failure to comply with such measures.

2. Measures to achieve these ends may include, inter alia:

(a) Promoting cooperation between law enforcement agencies and relevant private entities;

(b) Promoting the development of standards and procedures designed to safeguard the integrity of relevant private entities, including codes of conduct for the correct, honourable and proper performance of the activities of business and all relevant professions and the prevention of conflicts of interest, and for the promotion of the use of good commercial practices among businesses and in the contractual relations of businesses with the State;

(c) Promoting transparency among private entities, including, where appropriate, measures regarding the identity of legal and natural persons involved in the establishment and management of corporate entities;

(d) Preventing the misuse of procedures regulating private entities, including procedures regarding subsidies and licences granted by public authorities for commercial activities;

(e) Preventing conflicts of interest by imposing restrictions, as appropriate and for a reasonable period of time, on the professional activities of former public officials or on the employment of public officials by the private sector after their resignation or retirement, where such activities or employment relate directly to the functions held or supervised by those public officials during their tenure;

(f) Ensuring that private enterprises, taking into account their structure and size, have sufficient internal auditing controls to assist in preventing and detecting acts of corruption and that the accounts and required financial statements of such private enterprises are subject to appropriate auditing and certification procedures.

3. In order to prevent corruption, each State Party shall take such measures as may be necessary, in accordance with its domestic laws and regulations regarding the maintenance of books and records, financial statement disclosures and accounting and auditing standards, to prohibit the following acts carried out for the purpose of committing any of the offences established in accordance with this Convention:

(a) The establishment of off-the-books accounts;

(b) The making of off-the-books or inadequately identified transactions;

(c) The recording of non-existent expenditure;

(d) The entry of liabilities with incorrect identification of their objects;

(e) The use of false documents; and

(f) The intentional destruction of bookkeeping documents earlier than foreseen by the law.

4. Each State Party shall disallow the tax deductibility of expenses that constitute bribes, the latter being one of the constituent elements of the offences established in accordance with articles 15 and 16 of this Convention and, where appropriate, other expenses incurred in furtherance of corrupt conduct.

Article 13
Participation of society

1. Each State Party shall take appropriate measures, within its means and in accordance with fundamental principles of its domestic law, to promote the active participation of individuals and groups outside the public sector, such as civil society, non-governmental organizations and community-based organizations, in the prevention of and the fight against corruption and to raise public awareness regarding the existence, causes and gravity of and the threat posed by corruption. This participation should be strengthened by such measures as:

(a) Enhancing the transparency of and promoting the contribution of the public to decision-making processes;

(b) Ensuring that the public has effective access to information;

(c) Undertaking public information activities that contribute to non-tolerance of corruption, as well as public education programmes, including school and university curricula;

(d) Respecting, promoting and protecting the freedom to seek, receive, publish and disseminate information concerning corruption. That freedom may be subject to certain restrictions, but these shall only be such as are provided for by law and are necessary:

   (i) For respect of the rights or reputations of others;
   (ii) For the protection of national security or *ordre public* or of public health or morals.

2. Each State Party shall take appropriate measures to ensure that the relevant anti-corruption bodies referred to in this Convention are known to the public and shall provide access to such bodies, where appropriate, for the reporting, including anonymously, of any incidents that may be considered to constitute an offence established in accordance with this Convention.

Article 14
Measures to prevent money-laundering

1. Each State Party shall:

(a) Institute a comprehensive domestic regulatory and supervisory regime for banks and non-bank financial institutions, including natural or legal persons that provide formal or informal services for the transmission of money or value and, where appropriate, other bodies particularly susceptible to money-laundering, within its competence, in order to deter and detect all forms of money-laundering, which regime shall emphasize requirements for customer and, where appropriate, beneficial owner identification, record-keeping and the reporting of suspicious transactions;

(b) Without prejudice to article 46 of this Convention, ensure that administrative, regulatory, law enforcement and other authorities dedicated to combating money-laundering (including, where appropriate under domestic law, judicial authorities) have the ability to cooperate and exchange information at the national and international levels within the conditions prescribed by its domestic law and, to that end, shall consider the establishment of a financial intelligence unit to serve as a national centre for the collection, analysis and dissemination of information regarding potential money-laundering.

2. States Parties shall consider implementing feasible measures to detect and monitor the movement of cash and appropriate negotiable instruments across their borders, subject to safeguards to ensure proper use of information and without impeding in any way the movement of legitimate capital. Such measures may include a requirement that individuals and businesses report the cross-border transfer of substantial quantities of cash and appropriate negotiable instruments.

3. States Parties shall consider implementing appropriate and feasible measures to require financial institutions, including money remitters:

(a) To include on forms for the electronic transfer of funds and related messages accurate and meaningful information on the originator;

(b) To maintain such information throughout the payment chain; and

(c) To apply enhanced scrutiny to transfers of funds that do not contain complete information on the originator.

4. In establishing a domestic regulatory and supervisory regime under the terms of this article, and without prejudice to any other article of this Convention, States Parties are called upon to use as a guideline the relevant initiatives of regional, interregional and multilateral organizations against money-laundering.

5. States Parties shall endeavour to develop and promote global, regional, subregional and bilateral cooperation among judicial, law enforcement and financial regulatory authorities in order to combat money-laundering.

Chapter III
Criminalization and law enforcement

Article 15
Bribery of national public officials

Each State Party shall adopt such legislative and other measures as may be necessary to establish as criminal offences, when committed intentionally:

(a) The promise, offering or giving, to a public official, directly or indirectly, of an undue advantage, for the official himself or herself or another person or entity, in order that the official act or refrain from acting in the exercise of his or her official duties;

(b) The solicitation or acceptance by a public official, directly or indirectly, of an undue advantage, for the official himself or herself or another person or entity, in order that the official act or refrain from acting in the exercise of his or her official duties.

Article 16
Bribery of foreign public officials and
officials of public international organizations

1. Each State Party shall adopt such legislative and other measures as may be necessary to establish as a criminal offence, when committed intentionally, the promise, offering or giving to a foreign public official or an official of a public international organization, directly or indirectly, of an undue advantage, for the official himself or herself or another person or entity, in order that the official act or refrain from acting in the exercise of his or her official duties, in order to obtain or retain business or other undue advantage in relation to the conduct of international business.

2. Each State Party shall consider adopting such legislative and other measures as may be necessary to establish as a criminal offence, when committed intentionally, the solicitation or acceptance by a foreign public official or an official of a public international organization, directly or indirectly, of an undue advantage, for the official himself or herself or another person or entity, in order that the official act or refrain from acting in the exercise of his or her official duties.

Article 17
Embezzlement, misappropriation or other diversion of property by a public official

Each State Party shall adopt such legislative and other measures as may be necessary to establish as criminal offences, when committed intentionally, the embezzlement, mis-appropriation or other diversion by a public official for his or her benefit or for the benefit of another person or entity, of any property, public or private funds or securities or any other thing of value entrusted to the public official by virtue of his or her position.

Article 18
Trading in influence

Each State Party shall consider adopting such legislative and other measures as may be necessary to establish as criminal offences, when committed intentionally:

(a) The promise, offering or giving to a public official or any other person, directly or indirectly, of an undue advantage in order that the public official or the person abuse his or her real or supposed influence with a view to obtaining from an administration or public authority of the State Party an undue advantage for the original instigator of the act or for any other person;

(b) The solicitation or acceptance by a public official or any other person, directly or indirectly, of an undue advantage for himself or herself or for another person in order that the public official or the person abuse his or her real or supposed influence with a view to obtaining from an administration or public authority of the State Party an undue advantage.

Article 19
Abuse of functions

Each State Party shall consider adopting such legislative and other measures as may be necessary to establish as a criminal offence, when committed intentionally, the abuse of functions or position, that is, the performance of or failure to perform an act, in violation of laws, by a public official in the discharge of his or her functions, for the purpose of obtaining an undue advantage for himself or herself or for another person or entity.

Article 20
Illicit enrichment

Subject to its constitution and the fundamental principles of its legal system, each State Party shall consider adopting such legislative and other measures as may be necessary to establish as a criminal offence, when committed intentionally, illicit enrichment, that is, a significant increase in the assets of a public official that he or she cannot reasonably explain in relation to his or her lawful income.

Article 21
Bribery in the private sector

Each State Party shall consider adopting such legislative and other measures as may be necessary to establish as criminal offences, when committed intentionally in the course of economic, financial or commercial activities:

(a) The promise, offering or giving, directly or indirectly, of an undue advantage to any person who directs or works, in any capacity, for a private sector entity, for the person himself or herself or for another person, in order that he or she, in breach of his or her duties, act or refrain from acting;

(b) The solicitation or acceptance, directly or indirectly, of an undue advantage by any person who directs or works, in any capacity, for a private sector entity, for the person himself or herself or for another person, in order that he or she, in breach of his or her duties, act or refrain from acting.

Article 22
Embezzlement of property in the private sector

Each State Party shall consider adopting such legislative and other measures as may be necessary to establish as a criminal offence, when committed intentionally in the course of economic, financial or commercial activities, embezzlement by a person who directs or works, in any capacity, in a private sector entity of any property, private funds or securities or any other thing of value entrusted to him or her by virtue of his or her position.

Article 23
Laundering of proceeds of crime

1. Each State Party shall adopt, in accordance with fundamental principles of its domestic law, such legislative and other measures as may be necessary to establish as criminal offences, when committed intentionally:

(a) (i) The conversion or transfer of property, knowing that such property is the proceeds of crime, for the purpose of concealing or disguising the illicit origin of the property or of helping any person who is involved in the commission of the predicate offence to evade the legal consequences of his or her action;

(ii) The concealment or disguise of the true nature, source, location, disposition, movement or ownership of or rights with respect to property, knowing that such property is the proceeds of crime;

(b) Subject to the basic concepts of its legal system:

(i) The acquisition, possession or use of property, knowing, at the time of receipt, that such property is the proceeds of crime;

(ii) Participation in, association with or conspiracy to commit, attempts to commit and aiding, abetting, facilitating and counselling the commission of any of the offences established in accordance with this article.

2. For purposes of implementing or applying paragraph 1 of this article:

(a) Each State Party shall seek to apply paragraph 1 of this article to the widest range of predicate offences;

(b) Each State Party shall include as predicate offences at a minimum a comprehensive range of criminal offences established in accordance with this Convention;

(c) For the purposes of subparagraph (b) above, predicate offences shall include offences committed both within and outside the jurisdiction of the State Party in question. However, offences committed outside the jurisdiction of a State Party shall constitute predicate offences only when the relevant conduct is a criminal offence under the domestic law of the State where it is committed and would be a criminal offence under the domestic law of the State Party implementing or applying this article had it been committed there;

(d) Each State Party shall furnish copies of its laws that give effect to this article and of any subsequent changes to such laws or a description thereof to the Secretary-General of the United Nations;

(e) If required by fundamental principles of the domestic law of a State Party, it may be provided that the offences set forth in paragraph 1 of this article do not apply to the persons who committed the predicate offence.

Article 24
Concealment

Without prejudice to the provisions of article 23 of this Convention, each State Party shall consider adopting such legislative and other measures as may be necessary to establish as a criminal offence, when committed intentionally after the commission of any of the offences established in accordance with this Convention without having participated in such offences, the concealment or continued retention of property when the person involved knows that such property is the result of any of the offences established in accordance with this Convention.

Article 25
Obstruction of justice

Each State Party shall adopt such legislative and other measures as may be necessary to establish as criminal offences, when committed intentionally:

(a) The use of physical force, threats or intimidation or the promise, offering or giving of an undue advantage to induce false testimony or to interfere in the giving of testimony or the production of evidence in a proceeding in relation to the commission of offences established in accordance with this Convention;

(b) The use of physical force, threats or intimidation to interfere with the exercise of official duties by a justice or law enforcement official in relation to the commission of offences established in accordance with this Convention. Nothing in this subparagraph shall prejudice the right of States Parties to have legislation that protects other categories of public official.

Article 26
Liability of legal persons

1. Each State Party shall adopt such measures as may be necessary, consistent with its legal principles, to establish the liability of legal persons for participation in the offences established in accordance with this Convention.

2. Subject to the legal principles of the State Party, the liability of legal persons may be criminal, civil or administrative.

3. Such liability shall be without prejudice to the criminal liability of the natural persons who have committed the offences.

4. Each State Party shall, in particular, ensure that legal persons held liable in accordance with this article are subject to effective, proportionate and dissuasive criminal or non-criminal sanctions, including monetary sanctions.

Article 27
Participation and attempt

1. Each State Party shall adopt such legislative and other measures as may be necessary to establish as a criminal offence, in accordance with its domestic law, participation in any capacity such as an accomplice, assistant or instigator in an offence established in accordance with this Convention.

2. Each State Party may adopt such legislative and other measures as may be necessary to establish as a criminal offence, in accordance with its domestic law, any attempt to commit an offence established in accordance with this Convention.

3. Each State Party may adopt such legislative and other measures as may be necessary to establish as a criminal offence, in accordance with its domestic law, the preparation for an offence established in accordance with this Convention.

Article 28
Knowledge, intent and purpose as elements of an offence

Knowledge, intent or purpose required as an element of an offence established in accordance with this Convention may be inferred from objective factual circumstances.

Article 29
Statute of limitations

Each State Party shall, where appropriate, establish under its domestic law a long statute of limitations period in which to commence proceedings for any offence established in accordance with this Convention and establish a longer statute of limitations period or provide for the suspension of the statute of limitations where the alleged offender has evaded the administration of justice.

Article 30
Prosecution, adjudication and sanctions

1. Each State Party shall make the commission of an offence established in accordance with this Convention liable to sanctions that take into account the gravity of that offence.

2. Each State Party shall take such measures as may be necessary to establish or maintain, in accordance with its legal system and constitutional principles, an appropriate balance between any immunities or jurisdictional privileges accorded to its public officials for the performance of their functions and the possibility, when necessary, of effectively investigating, prosecuting and adjudicating offences established in accordance with this Convention.

3. Each State Party shall endeavour to ensure that any discretionary legal powers under its domestic law relating to the prosecution of persons for offences established in accordance with this Convention are exercised to maximize the effectiveness of law enforcement measures in respect of those offences and with due re-

gard to the need to deter the commission of such offences.

4. In the case of offences established in accordance with this Convention, each State Party shall take appropriate measures, in accordance with its domestic law and with due regard to the rights of the defence, to seek to ensure that conditions imposed in connection with decisions on release pending trial or appeal take into consideration the need to ensure the presence of the defendant at subsequent criminal proceedings.

5. Each State Party shall take into account the gravity of the offences concerned when considering the eventuality of early release or parole of persons convicted of such offences.

6. Each State Party, to the extent consistent with the fundamental principles of its legal system, shall consider establishing procedures through which a public official accused of an offence established in accordance with this Convention may, where appropriate, be removed, suspended or reassigned by the appropriate authority, bearing in mind respect for the principle of the presumption of innocence.

7. Where warranted by the gravity of the offence, each State Party, to the extent consistent with the fundamental principles of its legal system, shall consider establishing procedures for the disqualification, by court order or any other appropriate means, for a period of time determined by its domestic law, of persons convicted of offences established in accordance with this Convention from:

(a) Holding public office; and

(b) Holding office in an enterprise owned in whole or in part by the State.

8. Paragraph 1 of this article shall be without prejudice to the exercise of disciplinary powers by the competent authorities against civil servants.

9. Nothing contained in this Convention shall affect the principle that the description of the offences established in accordance with this Convention and of the applicable legal defences or other legal principles controlling the lawfulness of conduct is reserved to the domestic law of a State Party and that such offences shall be prosecuted and punished in accordance with that law.

10. States Parties shall endeavour to promote the reintegration into society of persons convicted of offences established in accordance with this Convention.

Article 31
Freezing, seizure and confiscation

1. Each State Party shall take, to the greatest extent possible within its domestic legal system, such measures as may be necessary to enable confiscation of:

(a) Proceeds of crime derived from offences established in accordance with this Convention or property the value of which corresponds to that of such proceeds;

(b) Property, equipment or other instrumentalities used in or destined for use in offences established in accordance with this Convention.

2. Each State Party shall take such measures as may be necessary to enable the identification, tracing, freezing or seizure of any item referred to in paragraph 1 of this article for the purpose of eventual confiscation.

3. Each State Party shall adopt, in accordance with its domestic law, such legislative and other measures as may be necessary to regulate the administration by the competent authorities of frozen, seized or confiscated property covered in paragraphs 1 and 2 of this article.

4. If such proceeds of crime have been transformed or converted, in part or in full, into other property, such property shall be liable to the measures referred to in this article instead of the proceeds.

5. If such proceeds of crime have been intermingled with property acquired from legitimate sources, such property shall, without prejudice to any powers relating to freezing or seizure, be liable to confiscation up to the assessed value of the intermingled proceeds.

6. Income or other benefits derived from such proceeds of crime, from property into which such proceeds of crime have been transformed or converted or from property with which such proceeds of crime have been intermingled shall also be liable to the measures referred to in this article, in the same manner and to the same extent as proceeds of crime.

7. For the purpose of this article and article 55 of this Convention, each State Party shall empower its courts or other competent authorities to order that bank, financial or commercial records be made available or seized. A State Party shall not decline to act under the provisions of this paragraph on the ground of bank secrecy.

8. States Parties may consider the possibility of requiring that an offender demonstrate the lawful origin of such alleged proceeds of crime or other property liable to confiscation, to the extent that such a requirement is consistent with the fundamental principles of their domestic law and with the nature of judicial and other proceedings.

9. The provisions of this article shall not be so construed as to prejudice the rights of bona fide third parties.

10. Nothing contained in this article shall affect the principle that the measures to which it refers shall be defined and implemented in accordance with and subject to the provisions of the domestic law of a State Party.

Article 32
Protection of witnesses, experts and victims

1. Each State Party shall take appropriate measures in accordance with its domestic legal system and within its means to provide effective protection from potential retaliation or intimidation for witnesses and experts who give testimony concerning offences established in accordance with this Convention and, as appropriate, for their relatives and other persons close to them.

2. The measures envisaged in paragraph 1 of this article may include, inter alia, without prejudice to the rights of the defendant, including the right to due process:

(a) Establishing procedures for the physical protection of such persons, such as, to the extent necessary and feasible, relocating them and permitting, where appropriate, non-disclosure or limitations on the disclosure of information concerning the identity and whereabouts of such persons;

(b) Providing evidentiary rules to permit witnesses and experts to give testimony in a manner that ensures the safety of such persons, such as permitting testimony to be given through the use of communications technology such as video or other adequate means.

3. States Parties shall consider entering into agreements or arrangements with other States for the relocation of persons referred to in paragraph 1 of this article.

4. The provisions of this article shall also apply to victims insofar as they are witnesses.

5. Each State Party shall, subject to its domestic law, enable the views and concerns of victims to be presented and considered at appropriate stages of criminal proceedings against offenders in a manner not prejudicial to the rights of the defence.

Article 33
Protection of reporting persons

Each State Party shall consider incorporating into its domestic legal system appropriate measures to provide protection against any unjustified treatment for any person who reports in good faith and on reasonable grounds to the competent authorities any facts concerning offences established in accordance with this Convention.

Article 34
Consequences of acts of corruption

With due regard to the rights of third parties acquired in good faith, each State Party shall take measures, in accordance with the fundamental principles of its domestic law, to address consequences of corruption. In this context, States Parties may consider corruption a relevant factor in legal proceedings to annul or rescind a contract, withdraw a concession or other similar instrument or take any other remedial action.

Article 35
Compensation for damage

Each State Party shall take such measures as may be necessary, in accordance with principles of its domestic law, to ensure that entities or persons who have suffered damage as a result of an act of corruption have the right to initiate legal proceedings against those responsible for that damage in order to obtain compensation.

Article 36
Specialized authorities

Each State Party shall, in accordance with the fundamental principles of its legal system, ensure the existence of a body or bodies or persons specialized in combating corruption through law enforcement. Such body or bodies or persons shall be granted the necessary independence, in accordance with the fundamental principles of the legal system of the State Party, to be able to carry out their functions effectively and without any undue influence. Such persons or staff of such body or bodies should have the appropriate training and resources to carry out their tasks.

Article 37
Cooperation with law enforcement authorities

1. Each State Party shall take appropriate measures to encourage persons who participate or who have participated in the commission of an offence established in accordance with this Convention to supply information useful to competent authorities for investigative and evidentiary purposes and to provide factual, specific help to competent authorities that may contribute to depriving offenders of the proceeds of crime and to recovering such proceeds.

2. Each State Party shall consider providing for the possibility, in appropriate cases, of mitigating punishment of an accused person who provides substantial cooperation in the investigation or prosecution of an offence established in accordance with this Convention.

3. Each State Party shall consider providing for the possibility, in accordance with fundamental principles of its domestic law, of granting immunity from prosecution to a person who provides substantial cooperation in the investigation or prosecution of an offence established in accordance with this Convention.

4. Protection of such persons shall be, mutatis mutandis, as provided for in article 32 of this Convention.

5. Where a person referred to in paragraph 1 of this article located in one State Party can provide substantial cooperation to the competent authorities of another State Party, the States Parties concerned may consider entering into agreements or arrangements, in accordance with their domestic law, concerning the potential provision by the other State Party of the treatment set forth in paragraphs 2 and 3 of this article.

Article 38
Cooperation between national authorities

Each State Party shall take such measures as may be necessary to encourage, in accordance with its domestic law, cooperation between, on the one hand, its public authorities, as well as its public officials, and, on the other hand, its authorities responsible for investigating and prosecuting criminal offences. Such cooperation may include:

(a) Informing the latter authorities, on their own initiative, where there are reasonable grounds to believe that any of the offences established in accordance with articles 15, 21 and 23 of this Convention has been committed; or

(b) Providing, upon request, to the latter authorities all necessary information.

Article 39
Cooperation between national authorities and the private sector

1. Each State Party shall take such measures as may be necessary to encourage, in accordance with its domestic law, cooperation between national investigating and prosecuting authorities and entities of the private sector, in particular financial institutions, relating to matters involving the commission of offences established in accordance with this Convention.

2. Each State Party shall consider encouraging its nationals and other persons with a habitual residence in its territory to report to the national investigating and prosecuting authorities the commission of an offence established in accordance with this Convention.

Article 40
Bank secrecy

Each State Party shall ensure that, in the case of domestic criminal investigations of offences established in accordance with this Convention, there are appropriate mechanisms available within its domestic legal system to overcome obstacles that may arise out of the application of bank secrecy laws.

Article 41
Criminal record

Each State Party may adopt such legislative or other measures as may be necessary to take into consideration, under such terms as and for the purpose that it deems appropriate, any previous conviction in another State of an alleged offender for the purpose of using such information in criminal proceedings relating to an offence established in accordance with this Convention.

Article 42
Jurisdiction

1. Each State Party shall adopt such measures as may be necessary to establish its jurisdiction over the offences established in accordance with this Convention when:

(a) The offence is committed in the territory of that State Party; or

(b) The offence is committed on board a vessel that is flying the flag of that State Party or an aircraft that is registered under the laws of that State Party at the time that the offence is committed.

2. Subject to article 4 of this Convention, a State Party may also establish its jurisdiction over any such offence when:

(a) The offence is committed against a national of that State Party; or

(b) The offence is committed by a national of that State Party or a stateless person who has his or her habitual residence in its territory; or

(c) The offence is one of those established in accordance with article 23, paragraph 1 (b) (ii), of this Convention and is committed outside its territory with a view to the commission of an offence established in accordance with article 23, paragraph 1 (a) (i) or (ii) or (b) (i), of this Convention within its territory; or

(d) The offence is committed against the State Party.

3. For the purposes of article 44 of this Convention, each State Party shall take such measures as may be necessary to establish its jurisdiction over the offences established in accordance with this Convention when the alleged offender is present in its territory and it does not extradite such person solely on the ground that he or she is one of its nationals.

4. Each State Party may also take such measures as may be necessary to establish its jurisdiction over the offences established in accordance with this Convention when the alleged offender is present in its territory and it does not extradite him or her.

5. If a State Party exercising its jurisdiction under paragraph 1 or 2 of this article has been notified, or has otherwise learned, that any other States Parties are conducting an investigation, prosecution or judicial proceeding in respect of the same conduct, the competent authorities of those States Parties shall, as appropriate, consult one another with a view to coordinating their actions.

6. Without prejudice to norms of general international law, this Convention shall not exclude the exercise of any criminal jurisdiction established by a State Party in accordance with its domestic law.

Chapter IV
International cooperation

Article 43
International cooperation

1. States Parties shall cooperate in criminal matters in accordance with articles 44 to 50 of this Convention. Where appropriate and consistent with their domestic legal system, States Parties shall consider assisting each other in investigations of and proceedings in civil and administrative matters relating to corruption.

2. In matters of international cooperation, whenever dual criminality is considered a requirement, it shall be deemed fulfilled irrespective of whether the laws of the requested State Party place the offence within the same category of offence or denominate the offence by the same terminology as the requesting State Party, if the conduct underlying the offence for which assistance is sought is a criminal offence under the laws of both States Parties.

Article 44
Extradition

1. This article shall apply to the offences established in accordance with this Convention where the person who is the subject of the request for extradition is present in the territory of the requested State Party, provided that the offence for which extradition is sought is punishable under the domestic law of both the requesting State Party and the requested State Party.

2. Notwithstanding the provisions of paragraph 1 of this article, a State Party whose law so permits may grant the extradition of a person for any of the offences covered by this Convention that are not punishable under its own domestic law.

3. If the request for extradition includes several separate offences, at least one of which is extraditable under this article and some of which are not extraditable by reason of their period of imprisonment but are related to offences established in accordance with this Convention, the requested State Party may apply this article also in respect of those offences.

4. Each of the offences to which this article applies shall be deemed to be included as an extraditable offence in any extradition treaty existing between States Parties. States Parties undertake to include such offences as extraditable offences in every extradition treaty to be concluded between them. A State Party whose law so permits, in case it uses this Convention as the basis for extradition, shall not consider any of the offences established in accordance with this Convention to be a political offence.

5. If a State Party that makes extradition conditional on the existence of a treaty receives a request for extradition from another State Party with which it has no extradition treaty, it may consider this Convention the legal basis for extradition in respect of any offence to which this article applies.

6. A State Party that makes extradition conditional on the existence of a treaty shall:

(a) At the time of deposit of its instrument of ratification, acceptance or approval of or accession to this Convention, inform the Secretary-General of the United Nations whether it will take this Convention as the legal basis for cooperation on extradition with other States Parties to this Convention; and

(b) If it does not take this Convention as the legal basis for cooperation on extradition, seek, where appropriate, to conclude treaties on extradition with other States Parties to this Convention in order to implement this article.

7. States Parties that do not make extradition conditional on the existence of a treaty shall recognize offences to which this article applies as extraditable offences between themselves.

8. Extradition shall be subject to the conditions provided for by the domestic law of the requested State Party or by applicable extradition treaties, including, inter alia, conditions in relation to the minimum penalty requirement for extradition and the grounds upon which the requested State Party may refuse extradition.

9. States Parties shall, subject to their domestic law, endeavour to expedite extradition procedures and to simplify evidentiary requirements relating thereto in respect of any offence to which this article applies.

10. Subject to the provisions of its domestic law and its extradition treaties, the requested State Party may, upon being satisfied that the circumstances so warrant and are urgent and at the request of the requesting State Party, take a person whose extradition is sought and who is present in its territory into custody or take other appropriate measures to ensure his or her presence at extradition proceedings.

11. A State Party in whose territory an alleged offender is found, if it does not extradite such person in respect of an offence to which this article applies solely on the ground that he or she is one of its nationals, shall, at the request of the State Party seeking extradition, be obliged to submit the case without undue delay to its competent authorities for the purpose of prosecution. Those authorities shall take their decision and conduct their proceedings in the same manner as in the case of any other offence of a grave nature under the domestic law of that State Party. The States Parties concerned shall cooperate with each other, in particular on procedural and evidentiary aspects, to ensure the efficiency of such prosecution.

12. Whenever a State Party is permitted under its domestic law to extradite or otherwise surrender one of its nationals only upon the condition that the person will be returned to that State Party to serve the sentence imposed as a result of the trial or proceedings for which the extradition or surrender of the person was sought and that State Party and the State Party seeking the extradition of the person agree with this option and other terms that they may deem appropriate, such conditional extradition or surrender shall be sufficient to discharge the obligation set forth in paragraph 11 of this article.

13. If extradition, sought for purposes of enforcing a sentence, is refused because the person sought is a national of the requested State Party, the requested State Party shall, if its domestic law so permits and in conformity with the requirements of such law, upon application of the requesting State Party, consider the enforcement of the sentence imposed under the domestic law of the requesting State Party or the remainder thereof.

14. Any person regarding whom proceedings are being carried out in connection with any of the offences to which this article applies shall be guaranteed fair treatment at all stages of the proceedings, including enjoyment of all the rights and guarantees provided by the domestic law of the State Party in the territory of which that person is present.

15. Nothing in this Convention shall be interpreted as imposing an obligation to extradite if the requested State Party has substantial grounds for believing that the request has been made for the purpose of prosecuting or punishing a person on account of that person's sex, race, religion, nationality, ethnic origin or political opinions or that compliance with the request would cause prejudice to that person's position for any one of these reasons.

16. States Parties may not refuse a request for extradition on the sole ground that the offence is also considered to involve fiscal matters.

17. Before refusing extradition, the requested State Party shall, where appropriate, consult with the requesting State Party to provide it with ample opportunity to present its opinions and to provide information relevant to its allegation.

18. States Parties shall seek to conclude bilateral and multilateral agreements or arrangements to carry out or to enhance the effectiveness of extradition.

Article 45
Transfer of sentenced persons

States Parties may consider entering into bilateral or multilateral agreements or arrangements on the transfer to their territory of persons sentenced to imprisonment or other forms of deprivation of liberty for offences established in accordance with this Convention in order that they may complete their sentences there.

Article 46
Mutual legal assistance

1. States Parties shall afford one another the widest measure of mutual legal assistance in investigations, prosecutions and judicial proceedings in relation to the offences covered by this Convention.

2. Mutual legal assistance shall be afforded to the fullest extent possible under relevant laws, treaties, agreements and arrangements of the requested State Party with respect to investigations, prosecutions and judicial proceedings in relation to the offences for which a legal person may be held liable in accordance with article 26 of this Convention in the requesting State Party.

3. Mutual legal assistance to be afforded in accordance with this article may be requested for any of the following purposes:

(a) Taking evidence or statements from persons;

(b) Effecting service of judicial documents;

(c) Executing searches and seizures, and freezing;

(d) Examining objects and sites;

(e) Providing information, evidentiary items and expert evaluations;

(f) Providing originals or certified copies of relevant documents and records, including government, bank, financial, corporate or business records;

(g) Identifying or tracing proceeds of crime, property, instrumentalities or other things for evidentiary purposes;

(h) Facilitating the voluntary appearance of persons in the requesting State Party;

(i) Any other type of assistance that is not contrary to the domestic law of the requested State Party;

(j) Identifying, freezing and tracing proceeds of crime in accordance with the provisions of chapter V of this Convention;

(k) The recovery of assets, in accordance with the provisions of chapter V of this Convention.

4. Without prejudice to domestic law, the competent authorities of a State Party may, without prior request, transmit information relating to criminal matters to a competent authority in another State Party where they believe that such information could assist the authority in undertaking or successfully concluding inquiries and criminal proceedings or could result in a request formulated by the latter State Party pursuant to this Convention.

5. The transmission of information pursuant to paragraph 4 of this article shall be without prejudice to inquiries and criminal proceedings in the State of the competent authorities providing the information. The competent authorities receiving the information shall comply with a request that said information remain confidential, even temporarily, or with restrictions on its use. However, this shall not prevent the receiving State Party from disclosing in its proceedings information that is exculpatory to an accused person. In such a case, the receiving State Party shall notify the transmitting State Party prior to the disclosure and, if so requested, consult with the transmitting State Party. If, in an exceptional case, advance notice is not possible, the receiving State Party shall inform the transmitting State Party of the disclosure without delay.

6. The provisions of this article shall not affect the obligations under any other treaty, bilateral or multilateral, that governs or will govern, in whole or in part, mutual legal assistance.

7. Paragraphs 9 to 29 of this article shall apply to requests made pursuant to this article if the States Parties in question are not bound by a treaty of mutual legal assistance. If those States Parties are bound by such a treaty, the corresponding provisions of that treaty shall apply unless the States Parties agree to apply paragraphs 9 to 29 of this article in lieu thereof. States Parties are strongly encouraged to apply those paragraphs if they facilitate cooperation.

8. States Parties shall not decline to render mutual legal assistance pursuant to this article on the ground of bank secrecy.

9. (a) A requested State Party, in responding to a request for assistance pursuant to this article in the absence of dual criminality, shall take into account the purposes of this Convention, as set forth in article 1;

(b) States Parties may decline to render assistance pursuant to this article on the ground of absence of dual criminality. However, a requested State Party shall, where consistent with the basic concepts of its legal system, render assistance that does not involve coercive action. Such assistance may be refused when requests involve matters of a *de minimis* nature or matters for which the cooperation or assistance sought is available under other provisions of this Convention;

(c) Each State Party may consider adopting such measures as may be necessary to enable it to provide a wider scope of assistance pursuant to this article in the absence of dual criminality.

10. A person who is being detained or is serving a sentence in the territory of one State Party whose presence in another State Party is requested for purposes of identification, testimony or otherwise providing assistance in obtaining evidence for investigations, prosecutions or judicial proceedings in relation to offences covered by this Convention may be transferred if the following conditions are met:

(a) The person freely gives his or her informed consent;

(b) The competent authorities of both States Parties agree, subject to such conditions as those States Parties may deem appropriate.

11. For the purposes of paragraph 10 of this article:

(a) The State Party to which the person is transferred shall have the authority and obligation to keep the person transferred in custody, unless otherwise requested or authorized by the State Party from which the person was transferred;

(b) The State Party to which the person is transferred shall without delay implement its obligation to return the person to the custody of the State Party from which the person was transferred as agreed beforehand, or as otherwise agreed, by the competent authorities of both States Parties;

(c) The State Party to which the person is transferred shall not require the State Party from which the person was transferred to initiate extradition proceedings for the return of the person;

(d) The person transferred shall receive credit for service of the sentence being served in the State from which he or she was transferred for time spent in the custody of the State Party to which he or she was transferred.

12. Unless the State Party from which a person is to be transferred in accordance with paragraphs 10 and 11 of this article so agrees, that person, whatever his or her nationality, shall not be prosecuted, detained, punished or subjected to any other restriction of his or her personal liberty in the territory of the State to which that person is transferred in respect of acts, omissions or convictions prior to his or her departure from the territory of the State from which he or she was transferred.

13. Each State Party shall designate a central authority that shall have the responsibility and power to receive requests for mutual legal assistance and either to execute them or to transmit them to the competent authorities for execution. Where a State Party has a special region or territory with a separate system of mutual legal assistance, it may designate a distinct central authority that shall have the same function for that region or territory. Central authorities shall ensure the speedy and proper execution or transmission of the requests received. Where the central authority transmits the request to a competent authority for execution, it shall encourage the speedy and proper execution of the request by the competent authority. The Secretary-General of the United Nations shall be notified of the central authority designated for this purpose at the time each State Party deposits its instrument of ratification, acceptance or approval of or accession to this Convention. Requests for mutual legal assistance and any communication related thereto shall be transmitted to the central authorities designated by the States Parties. This requirement shall be without prejudice to the right of a State Party to require that such requests and communications be addressed to it through diplomatic channels and, in ur-

gent circumstances, where the States Parties agree, through the International Criminal Police Organization, if possible.

14. Requests shall be made in writing or, where possible, by any means capable of producing a written record, in a language acceptable to the requested State Party, under conditions allowing that State Party to establish authenticity. The Secretary-General of the United Nations shall be notified of the language or languages acceptable to each State Party at the time it deposits its instrument of ratification, acceptance or approval of or accession to this Convention. In urgent circumstances and where agreed by the States Parties, requests may be made orally but shall be confirmed in writing forthwith.

15. A request for mutual legal assistance shall contain:

(a) The identity of the authority making the request;

(b) The subject matter and nature of the investigation, prosecution or judicial proceeding to which the request relates and the name and functions of the authority conducting the investigation, prosecution or judicial proceeding;

(c) A summary of the relevant facts, except in relation to requests for the purpose of service of judicial documents;

(d) A description of the assistance sought and details of any particular procedure that the requesting State Party wishes to be followed;

(e) Where possible, the identity, location and nationality of any person concerned; and

(f) The purpose for which the evidence, information or action is sought.

16. The requested State Party may request additional information when it appears necessary for the execution of the request in accordance with its domestic law or when it can facilitate such execution.

17. A request shall be executed in accordance with the domestic law of the requested State Party and, to the extent not contrary to the domestic law of the requested State Party and where possible, in accordance with the procedures specified in the request.

18. Wherever possible and consistent with fundamental principles of domestic law, when an individual is in the territory of a State Party and has to be heard as a witness or expert by the judicial authorities of another State Party, the first State Party may, at the request of the other, permit the hearing to take place by video conference if it is not possible or desirable for the individual in question to appear in person in the territory of the requesting State Party. States Parties may agree that the hearing shall be conducted by a judicial authority of the requesting State Party and attended by a judicial authority of the requested State Party.

19. The requesting State Party shall not transmit or use information or evidence furnished by the requested State Party for investigations, prosecutions or judicial proceedings other than those stated in the request without the prior consent of the requested State Party. Nothing in this paragraph shall prevent the requesting State Party from disclosing in its proceedings information or evidence that is exculpatory to an accused person. In the latter case, the requesting State Party shall notify the requested State Party prior to the disclosure and, if so requested, consult with the requested State Party. If, in an exceptional case, advance notice is not possible, the requesting State Party shall inform the requested State Party of the disclosure without delay.

20. The requesting State Party may require that the requested State Party keep confidential the fact and substance of the request, except to the extent necessary to execute the request. If the requested State Party cannot comply with the requirement of confidentiality, it shall promptly inform the requesting State Party.

21. Mutual legal assistance may be refused:

(a) If the request is not made in conformity with the provisions of this article;

(b) If the requested State Party considers that execution of the request is likely to prejudice its sovereignty, security, *ordre public* or other essential interests;

(c) If the authorities of the requested State Party would be prohibited by its domestic law from carrying out the action requested with regard to any similar offence, had it been subject to investigation, prosecution or judicial proceedings under their own jurisdiction;

(d) If it would be contrary to the legal system of the requested State Party relating to mutual legal assistance for the request to be granted.

22. States Parties may not refuse a request for mutual legal assistance on the sole ground that the offence is also considered to involve fiscal matters.

23. Reasons shall be given for any refusal of mutual legal assistance.

24. The requested State Party shall execute the request for mutual legal assistance as soon as possible and shall take as full account as possible of any deadlines suggested by the requesting State Party and for which reasons are given, preferably in the request. The requesting State Party may make reasonable requests for information on the status and progress of measures taken by the requested State Party to satisfy its request. The requested State Party shall respond to reasonable requests by the requesting State Party on the status, and progress in its handling, of the request. The requesting State Party shall promptly inform the requested State Party when the assistance sought is no longer required.

25. Mutual legal assistance may be postponed by the requested State Party on the ground that it interferes with an ongoing investigation, prosecution or judicial proceeding.

26. Before refusing a request pursuant to paragraph 21 of this article or postponing its execution pursuant to paragraph 25 of this article, the requested State Party shall consult with the requesting State Party to consider whether assistance may be granted subject to such terms and conditions as it deems necessary. If the requesting State Party accepts assistance subject to those conditions, it shall comply with the conditions.

27. Without prejudice to the application of paragraph 12 of this article, a witness, expert or other person who, at the request of the requesting State Party, consents to give evidence in a proceeding or to assist in an investigation, prosecution or judicial proceeding in the territory of the requesting State Party shall not be prosecuted, detained, punished or subjected to any other restriction of his or her personal liberty in that territory in respect of acts, omissions or convictions prior to his or her departure from the territory of the

requested State Party. Such safe conduct shall cease when the witness, expert or other person having had, for a period of fifteen consecutive days or for any period agreed upon by the States Parties from the date on which he or she has been officially informed that his or her presence is no longer required by the judicial authorities, an opportunity of leaving, has nevertheless remained voluntarily in the territory of the requesting State Party or, having left it, has returned of his or her own free will.

28. The ordinary costs of executing a request shall be borne by the requested State Party, unless otherwise agreed by the States Parties concerned. If expenses of a substantial or extraordinary nature are or will be required to fulfil the request, the States Parties shall consult to determine the terms and conditions under which the request will be executed, as well as the manner in which the costs shall be borne.

29. The requested State Party:

(a) Shall provide to the requesting State Party copies of government records, documents or information in its possession that under its domestic law are available to the general public;

(b) May, at its discretion, provide to the requesting State Party in whole, in part or subject to such conditions as it deems appropriate, copies of any government records, documents or information in its possession that under its domestic law are not available to the general public.

30. States Parties shall consider, as may be necessary, the possibility of concluding bilateral or multilateral agreements or arrangements that would serve the purposes of, give practical effect to or enhance the provisions of this article.

Article 47
Transfer of criminal proceedings

States Parties shall consider the possibility of transferring to one another proceedings for the prosecution of an offence established in accordance with this Convention in cases where such transfer is considered to be in the interests of the proper administration of justice, in particular in cases where several jurisdictions are involved, with a view to concentrating the prosecution.

Article 48
Law enforcement cooperation

1. States Parties shall cooperate closely with one another, consistent with their respective domestic legal and administrative systems, to enhance the effectiveness of law enforcement action to combat the offences covered by this Convention. States Parties shall, in particular, take effective measures:

(a) To enhance and, where necessary, to establish channels of communication between their competent authorities, agencies and services in order to facilitate the secure and rapid exchange of information concerning all aspects of the offences covered by this Convention, including, if the States Parties concerned deem it appropriate, links with other criminal activities;

(b) To cooperate with other States Parties in conducting inquiries with respect to offences covered by this Convention concerning:

(i) The identity, whereabouts and activities of persons suspected of involvement in such offences or the location of other persons concerned;

(ii) The movement of proceeds of crime or property derived from the commission of such offences;

(iii) The movement of property, equipment or other instrumentalities used or intended for use in the commission of such offences;

(c) To provide, where appropriate, necessary items or quantities of substances for analytical or investigative purposes;

(d) To exchange, where appropriate, information with other States Parties concerning specific means and methods used to commit offences covered by this Convention, including the use of false identities, forged, altered or false documents and other means of concealing activities;

(e) To facilitate effective coordination between their competent authorities, agencies and services and to promote the exchange of personnel and other experts, including, subject to bilateral agreements or arrangements between the States Parties concerned, the posting of liaison officers;

(f) To exchange information and coordinate administrative and other measures taken as appropriate for the purpose of early identification of the offences covered by this Convention.

2. With a view to giving effect to this Convention, States Parties shall consider entering into bilateral or multilateral agreements or arrangements on direct cooperation between their law enforcement agencies and, where such agreements or arrangements already exist, amending them. In the absence of such agreements or arrangements between the States Parties concerned, the States Parties may consider this Convention to be the basis for mutual law enforcement cooperation in respect of the offences covered by this Convention. Whenever appropriate, States Parties shall make full use of agreements or arrangements, including international or regional organizations, to enhance the cooperation between their law enforcement agencies.

3. States Parties shall endeavour to cooperate within their means to respond to offences covered by this Convention committed through the use of modern technology.

Article 49
Joint investigations

States Parties shall consider concluding bilateral or multilateral agreements or arrangements whereby, in relation to matters that are the subject of investigations, prosecutions or judicial proceedings in one or more States, the competent authorities concerned may establish joint investigative bodies. In the absence of such agreements or arrangements, joint investigations may be undertaken by agreement on a case-by-case basis. The States Parties involved shall ensure that the sovereignty of the State Party in whose territory such investigation is to take place is fully respected.

Article 50
Special investigative techniques

1. In order to combat corruption effectively, each State Party shall, to the extent permitted by the basic principles of its domestic legal system and in accordance with the conditions prescribed by its domestic law, take such measures as may be necessary, within its means, to allow for the appropriate use by its compe-

tent authorities of controlled delivery and, where it deems appropriate, other special investigative techniques, such as electronic or other forms of surveillance and undercover operations, within its territory, and to allow for the admissibility in court of evidence derived therefrom.

2. For the purpose of investigating the offences covered by this Convention, States Parties are encouraged to conclude, when necessary, appropriate bilateral or multilateral agreements or arrangements for using such special investigative techniques in the context of cooperation at the international level. Such agreements or arrangements shall be concluded and implemented in full compliance with the principle of sovereign equality of States and shall be carried out strictly in accordance with the terms of those agreements or arrangements.

3. In the absence of an agreement or arrangement as set forth in paragraph 2 of this article, decisions to use such special investigative techniques at the international level shall be made on a case-by-case basis and may, when necessary, take into consideration financial arrangements and understandings with respect to the exercise of jurisdiction by the States Parties concerned.

4. Decisions to use controlled delivery at the international level may, with the consent of the States Parties concerned, include methods such as intercepting and allowing the goods or funds to continue intact or be removed or replaced in whole or in part.

Chapter V
Asset recovery

Article 51
General provision

The return of assets pursuant to this chapter is a fundamental principle of this Convention, and States Parties shall afford one another the widest measure of cooperation and assistance in this regard.

Article 52
Prevention and detection of transfers of proceeds of crime

1. Without prejudice to article 14 of this Convention, each State Party shall take such measures as may be necessary, in accordance with its domestic law, to require financial institutions within its jurisdiction to verify the identity of customers, to take reasonable steps to determine the identity of beneficial owners of funds deposited into high-value accounts and to conduct enhanced scrutiny of accounts sought or maintained by or on behalf of individuals who are, or have been, entrusted with prominent public functions and their family members and close associates. Such enhanced scrutiny shall be reasonably designed to detect suspicious transactions for the purpose of reporting to competent authorities and should not be so construed as to discourage or prohibit financial institutions from doing business with any legitimate customer.

2. In order to facilitate implementation of the measures provided for in paragraph 1 of this article, each State Party, in accordance with its domestic law and inspired by relevant initiatives of regional, interregional and multilateral organizations against money-laundering, shall:

(*a*) Issue advisories regarding the types of natural or legal person to whose accounts financial institutions within its jurisdiction will be expected to apply enhanced scrutiny, the types of accounts and transactions to which to pay particular attention and appropriate account-opening, maintenance and record-keeping measures to take concerning such accounts; and

(*b*) Where appropriate, notify financial institutions within its jurisdiction, at the request of another State Party or on its own initiative, of the identity of particular natural or legal persons to whose accounts such institutions will be expected to apply enhanced scrutiny, in addition to those whom the financial institutions may otherwise identify.

3. In the context of paragraph 2 (*a*) of this article, each State Party shall implement measures to ensure that its financial institutions maintain adequate records, over an appropriate period of time, of accounts and transactions involving the persons mentioned in paragraph 1 of this article, which should, as a minimum, contain information relating to the identity of the customer as well as, as far as possible, of the beneficial owner.

4. With the aim of preventing and detecting transfers of proceeds of offences established in accordance with this Convention, each State Party shall implement appropriate and effective measures to prevent, with the help of its regulatory and oversight bodies, the establishment of banks that have no physical presence and that are not affiliated with a regulated financial group. Moreover, States Parties may consider requiring their financial institutions to refuse to enter into or continue a correspondent banking relationship with such institutions and to guard against establishing relations with foreign financial institutions that permit their accounts to be used by banks that have no physical presence and that are not affiliated with a regulated financial group.

5. Each State Party shall consider establishing, in accordance with its domestic law, effective financial disclosure systems for appropriate public officials and shall provide for appropriate sanctions for non-compliance. Each State Party shall also consider taking such measures as may be necessary to permit its competent authorities to share that information with the competent authorities in other States Parties when necessary to investigate, claim and recover proceeds of offences established in accordance with this Convention.

6. Each State Party shall consider taking such measures as may be necessary, in accordance with its domestic law, to require appropriate public officials having an interest in or signature or other authority over a financial account in a foreign country to report that relationship to appropriate authorities and to maintain appropriate records related to such accounts. Such measures shall also provide for appropriate sanctions for non-compliance.

Article 53
Measures for direct recovery of property

Each State Party shall, in accordance with its domestic law:

(*a*) Take such measures as may be necessary to permit another State Party to initiate civil action in its courts to establish title to or ownership of property acquired through the commission of an offence established in accordance with this Convention;

(*b*) Take such measures as may be necessary to permit its courts to order those who have committed offences established in accordance with this Convention to pay compensation or damages to another State Party that has been harmed by such offences; and

(c) Take such measures as may be necessary to permit its courts or competent authorities, when having to decide on confiscation, to recognize another State Party's claim as a legitimate owner of property acquired through the commission of an offence established in accordance with this Convention.

Article 54
Mechanisms for recovery of property through international cooperation in confiscation

1. Each State Party, in order to provide mutual legal assistance pursuant to article 55 of this Convention with respect to property acquired through or involved in the commission of an offence established in accordance with this Convention, shall, in accordance with its domestic law:

(a) Take such measures as may be necessary to permit its competent authorities to give effect to an order of confiscation issued by a court of another State Party;

(b) Take such measures as may be necessary to permit its competent authorities, where they have jurisdiction, to order the confiscation of such property of foreign origin by adjudication of an offence of money-laundering or such other offence as may be within its jurisdiction or by other procedures authorized under its domestic law; and

(c) Consider taking such measures as may be necessary to allow confiscation of such property without a criminal conviction in cases in which the offender cannot be prosecuted by reason of death, flight or absence or in other appropriate cases.

2. Each State Party, in order to provide mutual legal assistance upon a request made pursuant to paragraph 2 of article 55 of this Convention, shall, in accordance with its domestic law:

(a) Take such measures as may be necessary to permit its competent authorities to freeze or seize property upon a freezing or seizure order issued by a court or competent authority of a requesting State Party that provides a reasonable basis for the requested State Party to believe that there are sufficient grounds for taking such actions and that the property would eventually be subject to an order of confiscation for purposes of paragraph 1 (a) of this article;

(b) Take such measures as may be necessary to permit its competent authorities to freeze or seize property upon a request that provides a reasonable basis for the requested State Party to believe that there are sufficient grounds for taking such actions and that the property would eventually be subject to an order of confiscation for purposes of paragraph 1 (a) of this article; and

(c) Consider taking additional measures to permit its competent authorities to preserve property for confiscation, such as on the basis of a foreign arrest or criminal charge related to the acquisition of such property.

Article 55
International cooperation for purposes of confiscation

1. A State Party that has received a request from another State Party having jurisdiction over an offence established in accordance with this Convention for confiscation of proceeds of crime, property, equipment or other instrumentalities referred to in article 31, paragraph 1, of this Convention situated in its territory shall, to the greatest extent possible within its domestic legal system:

(a) Submit the request to its competent authorities for the purpose of obtaining an order of confiscation and, if such an order is granted, give effect to it; or

(b) Submit to its competent authorities, with a view to giving effect to it to the extent requested, an order of confiscation issued by a court in the territory of the requesting State Party in accordance with articles 31, paragraph 1, and 54, paragraph 1 (a), of this Convention insofar as it relates to proceeds of crime, property, equipment or other instrumentalities referred to in article 31, paragraph 1, situated in the territory of the requested State Party.

2. Following a request made by another State Party having jurisdiction over an offence established in accordance with this Convention, the requested State Party shall take measures to identify, trace and freeze or seize proceeds of crime, property, equipment or other instrumentalities referred to in article 31, paragraph 1, of this Convention for the purpose of eventual confiscation to be ordered either by the requesting State Party or, pursuant to a request under paragraph 1 of this article, by the requested State Party.

3. The provisions of article 46 of this Convention are applicable, mutatis mutandis, to this article. In addition to the information specified in article 46, paragraph 15, requests made pursuant to this article shall contain:

(a) In the case of a request pertaining to paragraph 1 (a) of this article, a description of the property to be confiscated, including, to the extent possible, the location and, where relevant, the estimated value of the property and a statement of the facts relied upon by the requesting State Party sufficient to enable the requested State Party to seek the order under its domestic law;

(b) In the case of a request pertaining to paragraph 1 (b) of this article, a legally admissible copy of an order of confiscation upon which the request is based issued by the requesting State Party, a statement of the facts and information as to the extent to which execution of the order is requested, a statement specifying the measures taken by the requesting State Party to provide adequate notification to bona fide third parties and to ensure due process and a statement that the confiscation order is final;

(c) In the case of a request pertaining to paragraph 2 of this article, a statement of the facts relied upon by the requesting State Party and a description of the actions requested and, where available, a legally admissible copy of an order on which the request is based.

4. The decisions or actions provided for in paragraphs 1 and 2 of this article shall be taken by the requested State Party in accordance with and subject to the provisions of its domestic law and its procedural rules or any bilateral or multilateral agreement or arrangement to which it may be bound in relation to the requesting State Party.

5. Each State Party shall furnish copies of its laws and regulations that give effect to this article and of any subsequent changes to such laws and regulations

or a description thereof to the Secretary-General of the United Nations.

6. If a State Party elects to make the taking of the measures referred to in paragraphs 1 and 2 of this article conditional on the existence of a relevant treaty, that State Party shall consider this Convention the necessary and sufficient treaty basis.

7. Cooperation under this article may also be refused or provisional measures lifted if the requested State Party does not receive sufficient and timely evidence or if the property is of a *de minimis* value.

8. Before lifting any provisional measure taken pursuant to this article, the requested State Party shall, wherever possible, give the requesting State Party an opportunity to present its reasons in favour of continuing the measure.

9. The provisions of this article shall not be construed as prejudicing the rights of bona fide third parties.

Article 56
Special cooperation

Without prejudice to its domestic law, each State Party shall endeavour to take measures to permit it to forward, without prejudice to its own investigations, prosecutions or judicial proceedings, information on proceeds of offences established in accordance with this Convention to another State Party without prior request, when it considers that the disclosure of such information might assist the receiving State Party in initiating or carrying out investigations, prosecutions or judicial proceedings or might lead to a request by that State Party under this chapter of the Convention.

Article 57
Return and disposal of assets

1. Property confiscated by a State Party pursuant to article 31 or 55 of this Convention shall be disposed of, including by return to its prior legitimate owners, pursuant to paragraph 3 of this article, by that State Party in accordance with the provisions of this Convention and its domestic law.

2. Each State Party shall adopt such legislative and other measures, in accordance with the fundamental principles of its domestic law, as may be necessary to enable its competent authorities to return confiscated property, when acting on the request made by another State Party, in accordance with this Convention, taking into account the rights of bona fide third parties.

3. In accordance with articles 46 and 55 of this Convention and paragraphs 1 and 2 of this article, the requested State Party shall:

(*a*) In the case of embezzlement of public funds or of laundering of embezzled public funds as referred to in articles 17 and 23 of this Convention, when confiscation was executed in accordance with article 55 and on the basis of a final judgement in the requesting State Party, a requirement that can be waived by the requested State Party, return the confiscated property to the requesting State Party;

(*b*) In the case of proceeds of any other offence covered by this Convention, when the confiscation was executed in accordance with article 55 of this Convention and on the basis of a final judgement in the requesting State Party, a requirement that can be waived by the requested State Party, return the confiscated property to the requesting State Party, when the requesting State Party reasonably establishes its prior ownership of such confiscated property to the requested State Party or when the requested State Party recognizes damage to the requesting State Party as a basis for returning the confiscated property;

(*c*) In all other cases, give priority consideration to returning confiscated property to the requesting State Party, returning such property to its prior legitimate owners or compensating the victims of the crime.

4. Where appropriate, unless States Parties decide otherwise, the requested State Party may deduct reasonable expenses incurred in investigations, prosecutions or judicial proceedings leading to the return or disposition of confiscated property pursuant to this article.

5. Where appropriate, States Parties may also give special consideration to concluding agreements or mutually acceptable arrangements, on a case-by-case basis, for the final disposal of confiscated property.

Article 58
Financial intelligence unit

States Parties shall cooperate with one another for the purpose of preventing and combating the transfer of proceeds of offences established in accordance with this Convention and of promoting ways and means of recovering such proceeds and, to that end, shall consider establishing a financial intelligence unit to be responsible for receiving, analysing and disseminating to the competent authorities reports of suspicious financial transactions.

Article 59
Bilateral and multilateral agreements and arrangements

States Parties shall consider concluding bilateral or multilateral agreements or arrangements to enhance the effectiveness of international cooperation undertaken pursuant to this chapter of the Convention.

Chapter VI
Technical assistance and information exchange

Article 60
Training and technical assistance

1. Each State Party shall, to the extent necessary, initiate, develop or improve specific training programmes for its personnel responsible for preventing and combating corruption. Such training programmes could deal, inter alia, with the following areas:

(*a*) Effective measures to prevent, detect, investigate, punish and control corruption, including the use of evidence-gathering and investigative methods;

(*b*) Building capacity in the development and planning of strategic anti-corruption policy;

(*c*) Training competent authorities in the preparation of requests for mutual legal assistance that meet the requirements of this Convention;

(*d*) Evaluation and strengthening of institutions, public service management and the management of public finances, including public procurement, and the private sector;

(*e*) Preventing and combating the transfer of proceeds of offences established in accordance with this Convention and recovering such proceeds;

(*f*) Detecting and freezing of the transfer of proceeds of offences established in accordance with this Convention;

(*g*) Surveillance of the movement of proceeds of offences established in accordance with this Convention and of the methods used to transfer, conceal or disguise such proceeds;

(h) Appropriate and efficient legal and administrative mechanisms and methods for facilitating the return of proceeds of offences established in accordance with this Convention;

(i) Methods used in protecting victims and witnesses who cooperate with judicial authorities; and

(j) Training in national and international regulations and in languages.

2. States Parties shall, according to their capacity, consider affording one another the widest measure of technical assistance, especially for the benefit of developing countries, in their respective plans and programmes to combat corruption, including material support and training in the areas referred to in paragraph 1 of this article, and training and assistance and the mutual exchange of relevant experience and specialized knowledge, which will facilitate international cooperation between States Parties in the areas of extradition and mutual legal assistance.

3. States Parties shall strengthen, to the extent necessary, efforts to maximize operational and training activities in international and regional organizations and in the framework of relevant bilateral and multilateral agreements or arrangements.

4. States Parties shall consider assisting one another, upon request, in conducting evaluations, studies and research relating to the types, causes, effects and costs of corruption in their respective countries, with a view to developing, with the participation of competent authorities and society, strategies and action plans to combat corruption.

5. In order to facilitate the recovery of proceeds of offences established in accordance with this Convention, States Parties may cooperate in providing each other with the names of experts who could assist in achieving that objective.

6. States Parties shall consider using subregional, regional and international conferences and seminars to promote cooperation and technical assistance and to stimulate discussion on problems of mutual concern, including the special problems and needs of developing countries and countries with economies in transition.

7. States Parties shall consider establishing voluntary mechanisms with a view to contributing financially to the efforts of developing countries and countries with economies in transition to apply this Convention through technical assistance programmes and projects.

8. Each State Party shall consider making voluntary contributions to the United Nations Office on Drugs and Crime for the purpose of fostering, through the Office, programmes and projects in developing countries with a view to implementing this Convention.

Article 61
Collection, exchange and analysis of information on corruption

1. Each State Party shall consider analysing, in consultation with experts, trends in corruption in its territory, as well as the circumstances in which corruption offences are committed.

2. States Parties shall consider developing and sharing with each other and through international and regional organizations statistics, analytical expertise concerning corruption and information with a view to developing, insofar as possible, common definitions, standards and methodologies, as well as information on best practices to prevent and combat corruption.

3. Each State Party shall consider monitoring its policies and actual measures to combat corruption and making assessments of their effectiveness and efficiency.

Article 62
Other measures: implementation of the Convention through economic development and technical assistance

1. States Parties shall take measures conducive to the optimal implementation of this Convention to the extent possible, through international cooperation, taking into account the negative effects of corruption on society in general, in particular on sustainable development.

2. States Parties shall make concrete efforts to the extent possible and in coordination with each other, as well as with international and regional organizations:

(a) To enhance their cooperation at various levels with developing countries, with a view to strengthening the capacity of the latter to prevent and combat corruption;

(b) To enhance financial and material assistance to support the efforts of developing countries to prevent and fight corruption effectively and to help them implement this Convention successfully;

(c) To provide technical assistance to developing countries and countries with economies in transition to assist them in meeting their needs for the implementation of this Convention. To that end, States Parties shall endeavour to make adequate and regular voluntary contributions to an account specifically designated for that purpose in a United Nations funding mechanism. States Parties may also give special consideration, in accordance with their domestic law and the provisions of this Convention, to contributing to that account a percentage of the money or of the corresponding value of proceeds of crime or property confiscated in accordance with the provisions of this Convention;

(d) To encourage and persuade other States and financial institutions as appropriate to join them in efforts in accordance with this article, in particular by providing more training programmes and modern equipment to developing countries in order to assist them in achieving the objectives of this Convention.

3. To the extent possible, these measures shall be without prejudice to existing foreign assistance commitments or to other financial cooperation arrangements at the bilateral, regional or international level.

4. States Parties may conclude bilateral or multilateral agreements or arrangements on material and logistical assistance, taking into consideration the financial arrangements necessary for the means of international cooperation provided for by this Convention to be effective and for the prevention, detection and control of corruption.

Chapter VII
Mechanisms for implementation

Article 63
Conference of the States Parties to the Convention

1. A Conference of the States Parties to the Convention is hereby established to improve the capacity of

and cooperation between States Parties to achieve the objectives set forth in this Convention and to promote and review its implementation.

2. The Secretary-General of the United Nations shall convene the Conference of the States Parties not later than one year following the entry into force of this Convention. Thereafter, regular meetings of the Conference of the States Parties shall be held in accordance with the rules of procedure adopted by the Conference.

3. The Conference of the States Parties shall adopt rules of procedure and rules governing the functioning of the activities set forth in this article, including rules concerning the admission and participation of observers, and the payment of expenses incurred in carrying out those activities.

4. The Conference of the States Parties shall agree upon activities, procedures and methods of work to achieve the objectives set forth in paragraph 1 of this article, including:

(a) Facilitating activities by States Parties under articles 60 and 62 and chapters II to V of this Convention, including by encouraging the mobilization of voluntary contributions;

(b) Facilitating the exchange of information among States Parties on patterns and trends in corruption and on successful practices for preventing and combating it and for the return of proceeds of crime, through, inter alia, the publication of relevant information as mentioned in this article;

(c) Cooperating with relevant international and regional organizations and mechanisms and non-governmental organizations;

(d) Making appropriate use of relevant information produced by other international and regional mechanisms for combating and preventing corruption in order to avoid unnecessary duplication of work;

(e) Reviewing periodically the implementation of this Convention by its States Parties;

(f) Making recommendations to improve this Convention and its implementation;

(g) Taking note of the technical assistance requirements of States Parties with regard to the implementation of this Convention and recommending any action it may deem necessary in that respect.

5. For the purpose of paragraph 4 of this article, the Conference of the States Parties shall acquire the necessary knowledge of the measures taken by States Parties in implementing this Convention and the difficulties encountered by them in doing so through information provided by them and through such supplemental review mechanisms as may be established by the Conference of the States Parties.

6. Each State Party shall provide the Conference of the States Parties with information on its programmes, plans and practices, as well as on legislative and administrative measures to implement this Convention, as required by the Conference of the States Parties. The Conference of the States Parties shall examine the most effective way of receiving and acting upon information, including, inter alia, information received from States Parties and from competent international organizations. Inputs received from relevant non-governmental organizations duly accredited in accordance with procedures to be decided upon by the Conference of the States Parties may also be considered.

7. Pursuant to paragraphs 4 to 6 of this article, the Conference of the States Parties shall establish, if it deems it necessary, any appropriate mechanism or body to assist in the effective implementation of the Convention.

Article 64
Secretariat

1. The Secretary-General of the United Nations shall provide the necessary secretariat services to the Conference of the States Parties to the Convention.

2. The secretariat shall:

(a) Assist the Conference of the States Parties in carrying out the activities set forth in article 63 of this Convention and make arrangements and provide the necessary services for the sessions of the Conference of the States Parties;

(b) Upon request, assist States Parties in providing information to the Conference of the States Parties as envisaged in article 63, paragraphs 5 and 6, of this Convention; and

(c) Ensure the necessary coordination with the secretariats of relevant international and regional organizations.

Chapter VIII
Final provisions

Article 65
Implementation of the Convention

1. Each State Party shall take the necessary measures, including legislative and administrative measures, in accordance with fundamental principles of its domestic law, to ensure the implementation of its obligations under this Convention.

2. Each State Party may adopt more strict or severe measures than those provided for by this Convention for preventing and combating corruption.

Article 66
Settlement of disputes

1. States Parties shall endeavour to settle disputes concerning the interpretation or application of this Convention through negotiation.

2. Any dispute between two or more States Parties concerning the interpretation or application of this Convention that cannot be settled through negotiation within a reasonable time shall, at the request of one of those States Parties, be submitted to arbitration. If, six months after the date of the request for arbitration, those States Parties are unable to agree on the organization of the arbitration, any one of those States Parties may refer the dispute to the International Court of Justice by request in accordance with the Statute of the Court.

3. Each State Party may, at the time of signature, ratification, acceptance or approval of or accession to this Convention, declare that it does not consider itself bound by paragraph 2 of this article. The other States Parties shall not be bound by paragraph 2 of this article with respect to any State Party that has made such a reservation.

4. Any State Party that has made a reservation in accordance with paragraph 3 of this article may at any time withdraw that reservation by notification to the Secretary-General of the United Nations.

Article 67
Signature, ratification, acceptance, approval and accession
1. This Convention shall be open to all States for signature from 9 to 11 December 2003 in Merida, Mexico, and thereafter at United Nations Headquarters in New York until 9 December 2005.
2. This Convention shall also be open for signature by regional economic integration organizations provided that at least one member State of such organization has signed this Convention in accordance with paragraph 1 of this article.
3. This Convention is subject to ratification, acceptance or approval. Instruments of ratification, acceptance or approval shall be deposited with the Secretary-General of the United Nations. A regional economic integration organization may deposit its instrument of ratification, acceptance or approval if at least one of its member States has done likewise. In that instrument of ratification, acceptance or approval, such organization shall declare the extent of its competence with respect to the matters governed by this Convention. Such organization shall also inform the depositary of any relevant modification in the extent of its competence.
4. This Convention is open for accession by any State or any regional economic integration organization of which at least one member State is a Party to this Convention. Instruments of accession shall be deposited with the Secretary-General of the United Nations. At the time of its accession, a regional economic integration organization shall declare the extent of its competence with respect to matters governed by this Convention. Such organization shall also inform the depositary of any relevant modification in the extent of its competence.

Article 68
Entry into force
1. This Convention shall enter into force on the ninetieth day after the date of deposit of the thirtieth instrument of ratification, acceptance, approval or accession. For the purpose of this paragraph, any instrument deposited by a regional economic integration organization shall not be counted as additional to those deposited by member States of such organization.
2. For each State or regional economic integration organization ratifying, accepting, approving or acceding to this Convention after the deposit of the thirtieth instrument of such action, this Convention shall enter into force on the thirtieth day after the date of deposit by such State or organization of the relevant instrument or on the date this Convention enters into force pursuant to paragraph 1 of this article, whichever is later.

Article 69
Amendment
1. After the expiry of five years from the entry into force of this Convention, a State Party may propose an amendment and transmit it to the Secretary-General of the United Nations, who shall thereupon communicate the proposed amendment to the States Parties and to the Conference of the States Parties to the Convention for the purpose of considering and deciding on the proposal. The Conference of the States Parties shall make every effort to achieve consensus on each amendment. If all efforts at consensus have been exhausted and no agreement has been reached, the amendment shall, as a last resort, require for its adoption a two-thirds majority vote of the States Parties present and voting at the meeting of the Conference of the States Parties.
2. Regional economic integration organizations, in matters within their competence, shall exercise their right to vote under this article with a number of votes equal to the number of their member States that are Parties to this Convention. Such organizations shall not exercise their right to vote if their member States exercise theirs and vice versa.
3. An amendment adopted in accordance with paragraph 1 of this article is subject to ratification, acceptance or approval by States Parties.
4. An amendment adopted in accordance with paragraph 1 of this article shall enter into force in respect of a State Party ninety days after the date of the deposit with the Secretary-General of the United Nations of an instrument of ratification, acceptance or approval of such amendment.
5. When an amendment enters into force, it shall be binding on those States Parties which have expressed their consent to be bound by it. Other States Parties shall still be bound by the provisions of this Convention and any earlier amendments that they have ratified, accepted or approved.

Article 70
Denunciation
1. A State Party may denounce this Convention by written notification to the Secretary-General of the United Nations. Such denunciation shall become effective one year after the date of receipt of the notification by the Secretary-General.
2. A regional economic integration organization shall cease to be a Party to this Convention when all of its member States have denounced it.

Article 71
Depositary and languages
1. The Secretary-General of the United Nations is designated depositary of this Convention.
2. The original of this Convention, of which the Arabic, Chinese, English, French, Russian and Spanish texts are equally authentic, shall be deposited with the Secretary-General of the United Nations.

IN WITNESS WHEREOF, the undersigned plenipotentiaries, being duly authorized thereto by their respective Governments, have signed this Convention.

High-level Political Conference. The Convention was opened for signature at the High-level Political Conference for the Purpose of Signing the United Nations Convention against Corruption (Merida, Mexico, 9-11 December) [A/CONF.205/2], in accordance with General Assembly resolutions 57/169 [YUN 2002, p. 1119] and 58/4 (above), and would remain open for signature thereafter at UN Headquarters until 9 December 2005. The Convention would enter into force 90 days following the deposit of the thirtieth instrument of ratification, acceptance, approval or accession. In addition to signing the Convention, participants discussed follow-up activities for its implementation and future work in four round tables on: the role of the private and public sectors in preventive measures against corruption; the role of civil society and the media in building a culture against corruption; legislative measures to implement the Convention; and measures to fight corruption in national and international financial systems.

As at 31 December, the Convention had been signed by 98 countries and ratified by Kenya.

Corrupt practices and illegal transfer of funds

In response to General Assembly resolution 57/244 [YUN 2002, p. 1120], the Secretary-General transmitted a July report [A/58/125] prepared by the UN Centre for International Crime Prevention on preventing and combating corrupt practices and the transfer of funds of illicit origin and returning such assets to the countries of origin. The report also reflected the content of a global study [A/AC.261/12] on the transfer of funds of illicit origin, especially funds derived from acts of corruption, which was submitted to the Ad Hoc Committee for the Negotiation of a Convention against Corruption (see p. 1126). The report contained a series of recommendations for removing the impediments to the recovery of funds of illicit origin, and for the return of such funds, including through national capacity-building, UN technical assistance and the negotiation of a future convention.

On 22 December, the Assembly took note of the Secretary-General's report (**decision 58/531**).

GENERAL ASSEMBLY ACTION

On 23 December [meeting 78], the General Assembly, on the recommendation of the Second (Economic and Financial) Committee [A/58/482], adopted **resolution 58/205** without vote [agenda item 92].

Preventing and combating corrupt practices and transfer of assets of illicit origin and returning such assets to the countries of origin

The General Assembly,

Recalling its resolution 54/205 of 22 December 1999 and its resolutions 56/186 of 21 December 2001 and 57/244 of 20 December 2002, both on preventing and combating corrupt practices and transfer of funds of illicit origin and returning such funds to the countries of origin,

Recalling also the Monterrey Consensus of the International Conference on Financing for Development, which underlined that fighting corruption at all levels is a priority, and the Plan of Implementation of the World Summit on Sustainable Development ("Johannesburg Plan of Implementation"),

Deeply concerned about the seriousness of problems posed by continuing corrupt practices and transfer of assets of illicit origin and return of such funds and assets to the countries of origin, which may endanger the stability and security of societies, undermine the values of democracy and civil ethics and jeopardize sustainable and political development, in particular when an inadequate national and international response leads to impunity,

Taking note of the global study on the transfer of funds of illicit origin, especially funds derived from acts of corruption, submitted to the Ad Hoc Committee for the Negotiation of a Convention against Corruption, which noted the substantial amounts of money involved, the economic hardships for countries that are victims of such corruption and the enormous obstacles to recovery faced by those countries,

Noting that Member States have different institutional arrangements and capacities to ensure the implementation of legislation on preventing corrupt practices and transfer of assets of illicit origin and returning such assets to the countries of origin,

Considering that the prevention of corrupt practices and transfer of assets of illicit origin and the return of such assets to the countries of origin have not been adequately regulated by all national legislations and international legal instruments,

Emphasizing the responsibilities of all Governments to enact laws aimed at preventing and combating corrupt practices and transfer of assets of illicit origin and return of such assets to the countries of origin,

1. *Takes note* of the report of the Secretary-General on preventing and combating corrupt practices and transfer of funds of illicit origin and returning such assets to the countries of origin;

2. *Welcomes* the entry into force of the United Nations Convention against Transnational Organized Crime;

3. *Notes with appreciation* the report of the Ad Hoc Committee for the Negotiation of a Convention against Corruption on the work of its first to seventh sessions;

4. *Welcomes* the adoption of the United Nations Convention against Corruption;

5. *Also welcomes* the participation of Member States at a high level, including at the ministerial level, in the High-level Political Conference for the Purpose of Signing the United Nations Convention against Corruption, held at Merida, Mexico, from 9 to 11 December 2003;

6. *Invites* all Member States and competent regional economic integration organizations to sign, ratify and fully implement the United Nations Convention against Corruption as soon as possible in order to ensure its rapid entry into force;

7. *Encourages* all Member States that have not yet done so to enact laws to prevent and combat corrupt practices and the transfer of illicitly acquired assets and for the return of such assets to the countries of origin, in accordance with the United Nations Convention against Corruption;

8. *Also encourages* all Member States that have not yet done so to require financial institutions to properly implement comprehensive due diligence and vigilance programmes that could facilitate transparency and prevent the placement of illicitly acquired funds;

9. *Encourages* subregional and regional cooperation, where appropriate, in the efforts to prevent and combat corrupt practices and the transfer of assets of

illicit origin and for the return of such assets to the countries of origin;

10. *Calls* for further international cooperation, inter alia, through the United Nations system, in support of national, subregional and regional efforts to prevent and address the transfer of assets of illicit origin, as well as to return such assets to the countries of origin;

11. *Requests* the international community to provide, inter alia, technical assistance to support national efforts to strengthen human and institutional capacity aimed at preventing corrupt practices and the transfer of assets of illicit origin, returning such assets to the countries of origin and formulating strategies for mainstreaming and promoting transparency and integrity in both the public and private sector;

12. *Requests* the Secretary-General to submit to the General Assembly at its fifty-ninth session a report on the implementation of the present resolution;

13. *Decides* to include in the provisional agenda of its fifty-ninth session a sub-item entitled "Preventing and combating corrupt practices and transfer of funds and assets of illicit origin and returning such funds and assets to the countries of origin".

Strategies for crime prevention

Combating terrorism

In response to Economic and Social Council resolution 2002/19 [YUN 2002, p. 1121], the Secretary-General, in March [E/CN.15/2003/9], summarized information received from 19 Member States on measures they had taken to strengthen international cooperation and technical assistance in preventing and combating terrorism, particularly on such matters as adherence to international instruments, implementation of relevant Security Council resolutions, regional instruments, bilateral agreements, national and international action to combat terrorism, national legal frameworks against terrorism, terrorism and organized crime, and support for the work UNODC against terrorism.

The report also described UN activities, particularly those of UNODC as part of its Global Programme against Terrorism. To support the establishment of a global legal framework against terrorism, a preparatory assistance project on strengthening the legal regime against terrorism was being implemented. As part of the project, a UN legislative guide to the 12 international anti-terrorism conventions and protocols and to the legislative actions required for their ratification was reviewed by a group of international experts (Siracusa, Italy, 3-5 December 2002). A web page containing the UN legislative guide and examples of national counter-terrorism legislation was also created.

The Secretary-General concluded that UN activities should be part of a tripartite strategy supporting global efforts to: dissuade disaffected groups from embracing terrorism; deny groups or individuals the means to carry out acts of terrorism; and sustain broad-based international cooperation in the struggle against terrorism.

The Ad Hoc Committee established by General Assembly resolution 51/210 [YUN 1996, p. 1208] continued work on a draft comprehensive convention on international terrorism (see p. 1338).

ECONOMIC AND SOCIAL COUNCIL ACTION

On 22 July [meeting 44], the Economic and Social Council, on the recommendation of the Commission on Crime Prevention and Criminal Justice [E/2003/30], adopted **resolution 2003/22** without vote [agenda item 14 *(c)*].

Strengthening international cooperation and technical assistance in promoting the implementation of the universal conventions and protocols related to terrorism within the framework of the activities of the Centre for International Crime Prevention

The Economic and Social Council

Recommends to the General Assembly the adoption of the following draft resolution:

[For text, see General Assembly resolution 58/136 below.]

GENERAL ASSEMBLY ACTION

On 22 December [meeting 77], the General Assembly, on the recommendation of the Third Committee [A/58/499], adopted **resolution 58/136** without vote [agenda item 108].

Strengthening international cooperation and technical assistance in promoting the implementation of the universal conventions and protocols related to terrorism within the framework of the activities of the Centre for International Crime Prevention

The General Assembly,

Recalling its relevant resolutions related to the prevention and suppression of terrorism, as well as Security Council resolutions 1373(2001) of 28 September 2001, 1377 (2001) of 12 November 2001 and 1456(2003) of 20 January 2003,

Recalling also its resolution 56/1 of 12 September 2001, in which it strongly condemned the heinous acts of terrorism of 11 September 2001, and its resolution 57/27 of 19 November 2002, in which it also condemned those in Bali and Moscow and urgently called for international cooperation to prevent and eradicate acts of terrorism, as well as Security Council resolution 1465(2003) of 13 February 2003, in which the Council condemned the bombing attack in Bogotá on 7 February 2003,

Recalling further its resolution 57/173 of 18 December 2002, in which it affirmed the importance of the role of the Centre for International Crime Prevention of the United Nations Office on Drugs and Crime in the fulfilment of its mandate, including to prevent and combat terrorism, and in particular in strengthening international cooperation and providing technical assistance, upon request, which complements the work of the Security Council Committee established pursuant to resolution 1373(2001) concerning counter-terrorism,

Recalling its resolution 57/292 of 20 December 2002, in section IV of which it approved the strengthening of the Terrorism Prevention Branch of the Secretariat, given that terrorism was one of the priorities of the medium-term plan for the period 2002-2005,

Mindful of its resolution 56/261 of 31 January 2002 on the plans of action for the implementation of the Vienna Declaration on Crime and Justice: Meeting the Challenges of the Twenty-first Century, which includes a plan of action against terrorism,

Supporting the ongoing efforts of the Executive Director of the United Nations Office on Drugs and Crime to enhance an integrated approach to combating terrorism, drug trafficking, transnational organized crime and other related forms of criminal activity,

Stressing the need for close coordination and cooperation between States, international, regional and subregional organizations and the Counter-Terrorism Committee, as well as the Centre, in preventing and combating terrorism and criminal activities carried out for the purpose of furthering terrorism in all its forms and manifestations,

Convinced of the need, as asserted by the General Assembly and the Security Council in various resolutions, in particular Council resolution 1373(2001), to prevent and suppress acts of terrorism, and noting with deep concern the links between terrorism and transnational organized crime, drug trafficking, money-laundering and trafficking in arms, as well as illegal transfers of nuclear, chemical and biological materials,

Expressing its appreciation to the Government of Austria and the Centre for the organization of the symposium on the theme "Combating international terrorism: the contribution of the United Nations", held in Vienna on 3 and 4 June 2002, and taking note of the report of the Executive Director,

Recalling that Member States must ensure that any measures taken to combat terrorism comply with all their obligations under international law and that such measures are adopted in accordance with international law, in particular international human rights, refugee and humanitarian law, as appropriate,

Noting with appreciation that the Ad Hoc Committee established by General Assembly resolution 51/210 of 17 December 1996 is continuing the preparation of a draft comprehensive convention on international terrorism and of a draft international convention for the suppression of acts of nuclear terrorism,

1. *Encourages* the activities of the Centre for International Crime Prevention of the United Nations Office on Drugs and Crime within its mandates in the area of preventing terrorism by providing Member States, upon request, with technical assistance, specifically to implement the universal conventions and protocols related to terrorism, thereby strengthening international cooperation in preventing and combating terrorism, working in close coordination with the Security Council Committee established pursuant to resolution 1373(2001) concerning counter-terrorism and the Office of Legal Affairs of the Secretariat, as well as with international, regional and subregional organizations;

2. *Welcomes* the establishment of the Global Programme against Terrorism, launched by the Centre, which provides the appropriate framework for activities supporting Member States in their fight against terrorism, in particular through the implementation of the universal conventions and protocols related to terrorism;

3. *Calls upon* Member States that have not yet done so to become parties to and implement the universal conventions and protocols related to terrorism and, where appropriate, to request assistance to that end from the Centre;

4. *Notes* the preparation of a United Nations legislative guide to the universal conventions and protocols related to terrorism, which was reviewed by an expert group hosted by the International Institute of Higher Studies in Criminal Sciences in Siracusa, Italy, from 3 to 5 December 2002, and invites States that have not yet ratified or acceded to the universal conventions and protocols related to terrorism to make use of the legislative guide in their efforts to incorporate the provisions of those instruments into their national legislation;

5. *Urges* Member States to continue working together, as well as on a regional and bilateral basis and in close cooperation with the United Nations, to prevent and combat acts of terrorism by strengthening international cooperation and technical assistance within the framework of Security Council resolutions 1373 (2001), 1377(2001) and 1456(2003) and other relevant international instruments and in accordance with the Charter of the United Nations and international law;

6. *Requests* the Centre, subject to the availability of regular or extrabudgetary resources, to prepare guidelines on technical assistance according to which the Centre, acting in areas within its competence and in coordination with the Counter-Terrorism Committee, will provide assistance related to promoting the ratification of, accession to and implementation of the universal conventions and protocols related to terrorism and to identify concrete elements of such assistance with a view to facilitating cooperation among Member States in combating terrorism, and to submit those guidelines to Member States for their consideration;

7. *Also requests* the Centre, subject to the availability of extrabudgetary funds, to intensify its efforts to provide technical assistance, upon request, in preventing and combating terrorism through the implementation of the universal conventions and protocols related to terrorism, with particular emphasis on the need to coordinate its work with the Counter-Terrorism Committee and international, regional and subregional organizations;

8. *Expresses its appreciation* to donor countries that have supported, through voluntary contributions to the United Nations Crime Prevention and Criminal Justice Fund or through direct contributions to the United Nations Crime Prevention and Criminal Justice Programme network, the launching of the Global Programme against Terrorism, and invites all States to make adequate voluntary contributions to the Fund in order to strengthen the capacity of the Centre to provide technical assistance to requesting Member States, in particular for promoting the ratification of, accession to and implementation of the universal conventions and protocols related to terrorism;

9. *Recommends* that the Commission on Crime Prevention and Criminal Justice, in coordination with other United Nations entities, in particular the Counter-Terrorism Committee, keep under regular review the progress made by Member States in becoming parties to and implementing the universal conventions and protocols related to terrorism and the needs of Member States requesting technical assistance;

10. *Requests* the Secretary-General to organize a senior-level discussion during the thirteenth session of the Commission on Crime Prevention and Criminal Justice on progress made with regard to the criminal justice aspects of terrorism and international cooperation and to the universal conventions and protocols related to terrorism, and invites the Counter-Terrorism Committee and relevant international organizations to participate in that discussion;

11. *Invites* Member States to provide the Secretary-General with information on the nature of links between terrorism and other forms of crime in order to increase synergies in the delivery of technical assistance by the Centre, and requests the Secretary-General to include an analysis of that information in his report on the implementation of the present resolution;

12. *Requests* the Secretary-General to report to the General Assembly at its fifty-ninth session on the implementation of the present resolution.

Trafficking in persons

In a March note on trafficking in human beings, especially women and children [E/CN.15/2003/3], the Secretary-General outlined topics that the Commission might wish to consider under the sub-themes: trends in trafficking human beings; investigating and prosecuting cases of trafficking in human beings at the national and international levels; and awareness-raising and social intervention, including victim support and the role of civil society. A research workshop on trafficking in human beings, especially women and children: lessons learned and policy implications was held during the Commission's session on 16 May.

ECONOMIC AND SOCIAL COUNCIL ACTION

On 22 July, the Economic and Social Council, on the recommendation of the Commission on Crime Prevention and Criminal Justice [E/2003/30], adopted **resolution 2003/20** without vote [agenda item 14 (c)].

Strengthening international cooperation in preventing and combating trafficking in persons and protecting victims of such trafficking

The Economic and Social Council

Recommends to the General Assembly the adoption of the following draft resolution:

[For text, see General Assembly resolution 58/137, below.]

GENERAL ASSEMBLY ACTION

On 22 December [meeting 77], the General Assembly, on the recommendation of the Third Committee [A/58/499], adopted **resolution 58/137** without vote [agenda item 108].

Strengthening international cooperation in preventing and combating trafficking in persons and protecting victims of such trafficking

The General Assembly,

Recalling the Declaration of Basic Principles of Justice for Victims of Crime and Abuse of Power,

Taking note of guideline 8, Special measures for the protection and support of child victims of trafficking, contained in the report of the United Nations High Commissioner for Human Rights,

Recalling the Convention on the Rights of the Child, and noting the entry into force of the Optional Protocol to the Convention on the Rights of the Child on the sale of children, child prostitution and child pornography,

Recalling also the International Labour Organization Convention concerning the Prohibition and Immediate Action for the Elimination of the Worst Forms of Child Labour, 1999 (Convention No. 182), which prohibits forced or obligatory labour of all people under the age of 18,

Recalling further paragraphs 25 and 27 of the Vienna Declaration on Crime and Justice: Meeting the Challenges of the Twenty-first Century,

Recalling its resolution 55/25 of 15 November 2000, by which it adopted the United Nations Convention against Transnational Organized Crime, and in particular the Protocol to Prevent, Suppress and Punish Trafficking in Persons, Especially Women and Children, supplementing the United Nations Convention against Transnational Organized Crime,

Condemning trafficking in persons as an abhorrent form of modern-day slavery and as an act that is contrary to universal human rights,

Decrying the treatment of human beings as commodities bartered, bought or sold by traffickers, in particular exploiters,

Deeply concerned at the worldwide occurrence of trafficking in persons for the purpose of exploitation of all kinds by transnational organized criminal groups, many of which are also involved in other forms of illegal activity, including trafficking in firearms, money-laundering, drug trafficking and corruption,

Profoundly alarmed by the fact that trafficking in persons is a growing and profitable trade in most parts of the world, aggravated by, inter alia, poverty, armed conflict, inadequate social and economic conditions and demand in the illicit labour and sex markets,

Expressing dismay at the ability of criminal networks to avoid punishment while preying on the vulnerabilities of their victims,

Noting the distinctions and interlinkages between the two criminal behaviours of trafficking in persons, as set forth in the Protocol to Prevent, Suppress and Punish Trafficking in Persons, Especially Women and Children, supplementing the United Nations Convention against Transnational Organized Crime, and of smuggling of migrants, as set forth in the Protocol against the Smuggling of Migrants by Land, Sea and Air, supplementing the United Nations Convention against Transnational Organized Crime,

Convinced of the urgent need for broad and concerted international cooperation among all Member

States, employing a multidisciplinary, balanced and global approach, including adequate technical assistance, in order to prevent and combat trafficking in persons,

Convinced also that civil society, including non-governmental organizations, can play a role in reducing existing and future opportunities for victimization in the field of trafficking and in assisting Governments in promoting the protection of victims through comprehensive and non-stigmatizing social and appropriate economic assistance to victims, including in the areas of health, education, housing and employment,

Welcoming efforts of Member States, in particular countries of origin, transit and destination, to create awareness in civil society concerning the seriousness of the crime of trafficking and of its various forms, as well as the role of the public in preventing victimization and assisting victims of trafficking,

Noting the thematic discussion on trafficking in human beings, especially women and children, held by the Commission on Crime Prevention and Criminal Justice at its twelfth session,

1. *Urges* Member States to employ a comprehensive approach to combating trafficking in persons, incorporating law enforcement efforts and, where appropriate, the confiscation and seizure of the proceeds of trafficking, the protection of victims and preventive measures, including measures against activities that derive profit from the exploitation of victims of trafficking;

2. *Calls upon* Member States to collaborate with a view to preventing trafficking in persons, especially for the purpose of sexual exploitation, through:

(a) Improved technical cooperation to strengthen local and national institutions aimed at preventing trafficking in persons, especially women and children, in countries of origin;

(b) Information campaigns on the techniques and methods of traffickers, programmes of education aimed at prospective targets, as well as vocational training in social skills and assistance in the reintegration of victims of trafficking into society;

(c) A focus on post-conflict regions where patterns of human trafficking are emerging as a new phenomenon and the incorporation of anti-trafficking measures into early intervention;

3. *Recognizes* that broad international cooperation between Member States and relevant intergovernmental and non-governmental organizations is essential to counter effectively the threat of trafficking in persons;

4. *Urges* Member States to take measures to ratify or accede to the United Nations Convention against Transnational Organized Crime, the Protocol to Prevent, Suppress and Punish Trafficking in Persons, Especially Women and Children, supplementing the United Nations Convention against Transnational Organized Crime and the Optional Protocol to the Convention on the Rights of the Child on the sale of children, child prostitution and child pornography and to implement those instruments by, inter alia:

(a) Criminalizing trafficking in persons;

(b) Promoting cooperation among law enforcement authorities in combating trafficking in persons;

(c) Establishing the offence of trafficking in persons as a predicate offence for money-laundering offences;

5. *Invites* Member States to adopt measures, in accordance with their domestic law and capacity, inter alia:

(a) To fight sexual exploitation with a view to abolishing it, by prosecuting and punishing those who engage in that activity;

(b) To raise awareness, especially through training, among criminal justice officials and others, as appropriate, of the needs of victims of trafficking and of the crucial role of victims in detecting and prosecuting this crime by, inter alia:

(i) Investigating all cases reported by victims, preventing further victimization and, in general, treating victims with respect;

(ii) Treating victims and witnesses with sensitivity throughout criminal judicial proceedings, in accordance with articles 24 and 25 of the United Nations Convention against Transnational Organized Crime and article 6, paragraph 2, of the Protocol to Prevent, Suppress and Punish Trafficking in Persons, Especially Women and Children;

6. *Also invites* Member States to adopt measures, in accordance with their domestic law and capacity, inter alia:

(a) To provide assistance and protection to victims of trafficking in persons, including measures to permit victims of trafficking to remain in their territory temporarily or permanently, as appropriate;

(b) To promote the legislative and other measures necessary to establish a wide range of assistance, including legal, psychological, medical and social assistance and, if appropriate, compensation or restitution, to the actual victims of trafficking, subject to the determination of the existence of victimization;

(c) To provide humane treatment for all victims of trafficking, taking into account their age, gender and particular needs, in accordance with article 6, paragraphs 3 and 4, of the Protocol to Prevent, Suppress and Punish Trafficking in Persons, Especially Women and Children;

(d) To assist in the reintegration of victims of trafficking into society;

7. *Further invites* Member States, as appropriate, to develop guidelines for the protection of victims of trafficking before, during and after criminal proceedings;

8. *Urges* Member States to ensure that measures taken against trafficking in persons, especially women and children, are consistent with internationally recognized principles of non-discrimination and that they respect the human rights and fundamental freedoms of victims;

9. *Invites* Member States to set up mechanisms for coordination and collaboration between governmental and non-governmental organizations with a view to responding to the immediate needs of victims of trafficking;

10. *Also invites* Member States to allocate appropriate resources for victim services, public awareness campaigns and law enforcement activities directed at eliminating trafficking and exploitation and to foster international cooperation, including adequate technical assistance and capacity-building programmes, to improve the ability of Member States to take effective measures against trafficking in persons;

11. *Encourages* Member States to examine the role of the exploitation of the prostitution of others in encouraging trafficking in persons;

12. *Also encourages* Member States to adopt legislative or other measures to reduce the demand that fosters all forms of trafficking in persons, including by cooperating with non-governmental organizations and civil society and by raising public awareness of how sexual and other forms of exploitation degrade their victims and the related risks of trafficking in persons, especially women and children;

13. *Further encourages* Member States to take measures, including raising public awareness, to discourage, especially among men, the demand that fosters sexual exploitation, in accordance with article 9, paragraph 5, of the Protocol to Prevent, Suppress and Punish Trafficking in Persons, Especially Women and Children;

14. *Encourages* Member States to target the link, where appropriate, between trafficking in persons for purposes of sexual and other forms of exploitation and other types of crime;

15. *Encourages* the Centre for International Crime Prevention of the United Nations Office on Drugs and Crime to continue its close cooperation and coordination with relevant international and regional organizations in this area;

16. *Encourages* Member States to make voluntary contributions to further strengthen and support the Centre and its Global Programme against Trafficking in Human Beings, in particular in the area of technical assistance activities;

17. *Requests* the Secretary-General to report to the Commission on Crime Prevention and Criminal Justice at its fourteenth session on the implementation of the present resolution.

Kidnapping

In response to Economic and Social Council resolution 2002/16 [YUN 2002, p. 1117], the Secretary-General submitted a March report [E/CN.15/2003/7 & Add.1] on international cooperation to prevent, combat and eliminate kidnapping and to provide assistance to victims. The report summarized replies received from 64 Member States and three UN entities to a survey on the practice and extent of kidnapping, and the legislative, law enforcement, victim support and international cooperative initiatives taken in response to the problem. All responding countries considered kidnapping to be a serious crime and treated it accordingly. They noted that the various types of kidnapping suggested that the role of organized criminal and terrorist groups differed from jurisdiction to jurisdiction. The report pointed to a relatively dramatic increase in some States in kidnappings carried out within and between criminal groups and the development of new varieties of kidnapping. Although steps had been taken in a number of jurisdictions to counter kidnapping, it was too early to judge their success; lessons were emerging on countering the crime and there was scope for increased exchange of information on best practices and technical cooperation.

ECONOMIC AND SOCIAL COUNCIL ACTION

On 22 July [meeting 44], the Economic and Social Council, on the recommendation of the Commission on Crime Prevention and Criminal Justice [E/2003/30], adopted **resolution 2003/28** without vote [agenda item 14 (c)].

International cooperation in the prevention, combating and elimination of kidnapping and in providing assistance to victims

The Economic and Social Council,

Concerned at the practice of kidnapping in various countries of the world and at the harmful effects of that crime on victims and their families, and resolved to support measures to assist and protect them and to promote their recovery,

Reiterating that the kidnapping of persons under any circumstances and for any purpose constitutes a serious crime and a violation of individual freedom and undermines human rights,

Noting the transnational nature of organized crime and the tendency of organized criminal groups and terrorist groups to expand their illegal operations,

Concerned at the growing tendency of organized criminal groups and terrorist groups to resort to kidnapping, especially for the purpose of extortion, as a method of accumulating capital with a view to consolidating their criminal operations and undertaking other illegal activities, such as trafficking in firearms, drugs and persons, money-laundering and crimes related to terrorism,

Convinced that the links between various illegal activities, including terrorism, and organized crime pose an additional threat to security and the quality of life, hindering economic and social development,

Convinced also that the United Nations Convention against Transnational Organized Crime provides the legal framework necessary for international cooperation in the fight against kidnapping,

Recalling its resolution 2002/16 of 24 July 2002, in which it requested the Secretary-General, in coordination with competent entities of the United Nations system, to submit a progress report to the Commission on Crime Prevention and Criminal Justice at its twelfth session on the factual and legal situation of kidnapping throughout the world, including the situation of victims,

1. *Vigorously condemns and rejects once again* the practice of kidnapping, in any circumstances and for any purpose, including kidnapping by organized criminal groups and terrorist groups;

2. *Stresses* that organized criminal groups and terrorist groups as well as all perpetrators are responsible for any harm or death that results from a kidnapping committed by them and should be punished accordingly;

3. *Takes note with appreciation* of the progress report of the Secretary-General, submitted pursuant to resolution 2002/16;

4. *Urges* Member States that have taken new measures in the context of the present resolution to co-

operate with the Secretary-General and competent entities of the United Nations system, in particular the Centre for International Crime Prevention of the United Nations Office on Drugs and Crime, inter alia, by submitting comments on the progress report of the Secretary-General and by providing information on national legislation and on practical measures and experience at the domestic level in that connection;

5. *Invites* Member States that have not yet done so to provide the Secretary-General with information on the practice of kidnapping and on relevant domestic measures that have been adopted, including any related to support and assistance to the victims and their families;

6. *Invites* Member States that have not yet done so to adopt the legislative or other measures necessary to establish kidnapping as a serious crime in their domestic legislation, in accordance with the definition of "serious crime" contained in the United Nations Convention against Transnational Organized Crime;

7. *Encourages* Member States to continue to foster international cooperation, especially extradition, mutual legal assistance, collaboration between law enforcement authorities and information exchange, with a view to preventing, combating and eradicating kidnapping;

8. *Calls upon* Member States that have not yet done so, in furtherance of the fight against kidnapping, to strengthen their measures against money-laundering and to engage in international cooperation and mutual assistance, inter alia, in the tracing, detection, freezing and confiscation of proceeds of kidnapping in order to combat organized criminal groups and terrorist groups;

9. *Requests* the Secretary-General, drawing on extrabudgetary funds or voluntary contributions, to provide technical assistance to States, upon request, to enable them to strengthen their capacity to combat kidnapping, including establishing, as appropriate, special law enforcement and prosecution units and mechanisms for cooperation with civil society and international cooperation;

10. *Also requests* the Secretary-General to complete his report on the implementation of resolution 2002/16, including in it information on the practice of kidnapping and on relevant domestic measures that have been taken, including those related to support and assistance to the victims and their families, and to submit it to the Commission on Crime Prevention and Criminal Justice at its thirteenth session.

Urban crime

On 22 July [meeting 44], the Economic and Social Council, on the recommendation of the Commission on Crime Prevention and Criminal Justice [E/2003/30], adopted **resolution 2003/26** without vote [agenda item 14 (c)].

Prevention of urban crime

The Economic and Social Council,

Recalling General Assembly resolutions 55/59 of 4 December 2000, in which the Assembly endorsed the Vienna Declaration on Crime and Justice: Meeting the Challenges of the Twenty-first Century, adopted by the Tenth United Nations Congress on the Prevention of Crime and the Treatment of Offenders, held in Vienna from 10 to 17 April 2000, resolution 56/261 of 31 January 2002, in which the Assembly took note with appreciation of the plans of action for the implementation of the Vienna Declaration, annexed to the resolution, including the plan of action on crime prevention, and resolution 57/170 of 18 December 2002, in which the Assembly again invited Governments to use the plans of action as a guide in their efforts to formulate legislation, policies and programmes in the field of crime prevention and criminal justice,

Recalling also its resolution 1995/9 of 24 July 1995, by which it adopted guidelines for cooperation and technical assistance in the field of urban crime prevention,

Recalling further its resolution 2002/13 of 24 July 2002 on action to promote effective crime prevention, in which it accepted the Guidelines for the Prevention of Crime, annexed to the resolution,

Concerned at the continuing rise in urban crime of an increasingly serious nature in many parts of the world,

Mindful of the clear linkages between urban crime and drug trafficking, organized crime and the illegal possession and use of firearms,

Recognizing that, in many countries, criminal activities have become a major threat to public safety in large urban areas,

Expressing particular concern for children at risk in large urban areas,

Recognizing that urban criminality in specific situations hampers economic growth and weakens state institutions, thereby undermining efforts to promote sustainable development and reduce poverty,

Recognizing also the need for a balanced, integrated approach to fighting urban crime, including activities addressing such root causes as poverty, social marginalization and exclusion and lack of opportunities for young people,

Recognizing further that crime prevention strategies and actions should be based on a broad, gender-sensitive, multidisciplinary foundation of knowledge about proven and promising practices,

Reiterating the need for more regional and international collaboration in the fight against urban crime,

1. *Encourages* Member States to draw upon the Guidelines for the Prevention of Crime, annexed to its resolution 2002/13, when developing, implementing and evaluating urban crime prevention programmes and projects, and to share their experience gained in that regard, including in their inputs to the report of the Secretary-General requested in that resolution;

2. *Also encourages* Member States to establish effective policies and to pursue the implementation of such policies, where appropriate, to protect children at risk in urban areas;

3. *Requests* the Centre for International Crime Prevention of the United Nations Office on Drugs and Crime, in consultation with Member States, the institutes of the United Nations Crime Prevention and Criminal Justice Programme network, the United Nations Human Settlements Programme (UN-Habitat) and other relevant entities of the United Nations system to continue to assist Member States, upon request, to prepare proposals for the provision of technical assistance in the area of crime prevention, in accordance with the

Guidelines, including through capacity-building and training;

4. *Also requests* the Centre, subject to the availability of extrabudgetary resources and with the assistance of Governments, the institutes of the United Nations Crime Prevention and Criminal Justice Programme network and relevant United Nations entities, to compile an overview of proven and promising practices in the area of urban crime prevention, including in criminal justice, to develop a practical manual on the use and application of the Guidelines and to convene for that purpose an expert group meeting, with participants to be selected on the basis of equitable geographical representation;

5. *Again calls upon* all relevant United Nations organizations and bodies and international financial institutions to give appropriate consideration to the inclusion of urban crime prevention and law enforcement projects in their assistance programmes;

6. *Recommends* that, in the programme of the Eleventh United Nations Congress on Crime Prevention and Criminal Justice, due attention be given to the issue of urban crime;

7. *Welcomes* the inclusion of urban crime and youth at risk as one of the issues for the workshops to be held at the Eleventh Congress, which will permit an in-depth discussion of the subject at the regional preparatory meetings for the Congress.

UN standards and norms

In response to Economic and Social Council resolution 2002/15 [YUN 2002, p. 1124], the Secretary-General convened the Meeting of Experts on the Application of United Nations Standards and Norms in Crime Prevention and Criminal Justice (Stadtschlaining, Austria, 10-12 February) [E/CN.15/2003/10/Add.1]. The Meeting evaluated the progress made in the application of the standards and norms, reviewed the current system of reporting on their application and presented proposals on the future application of the standards and norms. The Meeting adopted a series of recommendations addressed to the Commission on Crime Prevention and Criminal Justice, Member States and other entities and UNODC.

The Secretary-General submitted to the Commission a March report and later addendum [E/CN.15/2003/10 & Add.2] on UN standards and norms in crime prevention and criminal justice, in response to Council resolutions 2002/12 [YUN 2002, p. 1129], 2002/13 [ibid., p. 1125], 2002/14 [ibid., p. 1116] and 2002/15 [ibid., p. 1124]. The report summarized replies received from Member States, UN entities, other intergovernmental organizations, NGOs and institutes comprising the UN Crime Prevention and Criminal Justice Programme network on their initiatives and accomplishments in the use and application of the standards and norms. The Secretary-General concluded that the information provided indicated that the use and application of the standards and norms resulted in changes and reforms being introduced in legal systems in many parts of the world with a view to upgrading and strengthening the capacity of criminal justice systems.

ECONOMIC AND SOCIAL COUNCIL ACTION

On 22 July [meeting 44], the Economic and Social Council, on the recommendation of the Commission on Crime Prevention and Criminal Justice [E/2003/30], adopted **resolution 2003/30** without vote [agenda item 14 (c)].

United Nations standards and norms in crime prevention and criminal justice

The Economic and Social Council,

Recalling its resolution 2002/15 of 24 July 2002, in which it reaffirmed the importance of United Nations standards and norms in crime prevention and criminal justice, including within the framework of peacekeeping and post-conflict reconstruction, and requested the Secretary-General to convene a meeting of a group of experts, subject to the availability of extrabudgetary funds, to make concrete proposals on the application of United Nations standards and norms to be considered by the Commission on Crime Prevention and Criminal Justice at its twelfth session,

Recalling also its resolution 2002/17 of 24 July 2002 on international cooperation, technical assistance and advisory services in crime prevention and criminal justice, in which it invited potential donors to make significant and regular contributions, and requested the Secretary-General to enhance further the resources available for operational activities and interregional advisory services,

Recalling further its resolution 1993/34 of 27 July 1993, in particular section III, paragraph 7 (c), thereof, in which it requested the Secretary-General to commence without delay a process of information-gathering to be undertaken by means of surveys, such as reporting systems, and contributions from other sources,

Welcoming the ongoing collaboration between the United Nations Office on Drugs and Crime and the Office of the United Nations High Commissioner for Human Rights in the areas of juvenile justice, human rights education, professional education for judges and lawyers, technical cooperation, counter-terrorism and human rights, trafficking in persons, the rights of victims, the independence of the judiciary and post-conflict reconstruction,

Desirous of reforming and streamlining the current process of information-gathering with respect to the application of United Nations standards and norms in crime prevention and criminal justice in order to make the process more efficient and cost-effective for all those concerned,

Aware of the resources that past surveys have required from Member States, and acknowledging the workload of the Centre for International Crime Prevention of the United Nations Office on Drugs and Crime and Member States in relation to the present priorities set by the Commission on Crime Prevention and Criminal Justice,

1. *Takes note with appreciation* of the report of the Secretary-General;

2. *Expresses its appreciation* for the work undertaken by the Meeting of Experts on the Application of United Nations Standards and Norms in Crime Prevention and Criminal Justice, held in Stadtschlaining, Austria, from 10 to 12 February 2003, takes note of the recommendations of the Meeting of Experts contained in the annex to the present resolution, and expresses its appreciation to the Governments of Austria, Canada and Germany for their financial support in the organization of the Meeting;

3. *Decides* to group United Nations standards and norms in crime prevention and criminal justice in the following categories for the purpose of targeted collection of information, in order to better identify the specific needs of Member States and to provide an analytical framework with a view to improving technical cooperation:

(a) Standards and norms related primarily to persons in custody, non-custodial sanctions and juvenile and restorative justice;

(b) Standards and norms related primarily to legal, institutional and practical arrangements for international cooperation;

(c) Standards and norms related primarily to crime prevention and victim issues;

(d) Standards and norms related primarily to good governance, the independence of the judiciary and the integrity of criminal justice personnel;

4. *Calls upon* Member States, intergovernmental and non-governmental organizations, the institutes of the United Nations Crime Prevention and Criminal Justice Programme network and United Nations entities, in responding to targeted inquiries on the application of United Nations standards and norms in crime prevention and criminal justice, to focus on identifying difficulties that have been encountered in their application, ways in which technical assistance to requesting States can overcome those difficulties and desirable practices in the prevention and control of crime;

5. *Requests* the Centre for International Crime Prevention of the United Nations Office on Drugs and Crime, in collaboration with the institutes of the United Nations Crime Prevention and Criminal Justice Programme network:

(a) To provide support to Member States requesting assistance with specific issues in the use and application of United Nations standards and norms in crime prevention and criminal justice, including by developing resource materials and organizing training courses and workshops;

(b) To collaborate with other United Nations entities, intergovernmental and non-governmental organizations and national institutions to promote the widest possible dissemination of United Nations standards and norms in crime prevention and criminal justice and to identify experts in that field who may be available to assist requesting Member States;

(c) To provide advisory services in relation to United Nations standards and norms in crime prevention and criminal justice;

6. *Requests* the Secretary-General to convene, subject to the availability of extrabudgetary funds, an intergovernmental expert group meeting on the basis of adequate and equitable geographical representation to prepare proposals to be considered by the Commission on Crime Prevention and Criminal Justice at its thirteenth session in relation to:

(a) The design of information-gathering instruments that are short, simple, complete and understandable in relation to select groups of standards and norms referred to in paragraph 3 above and that are aimed at identifying and addressing specific problems in Member States requesting assistance and at providing an analytical framework with a view to improving technical cooperation;

(b) New ways and means for maximizing the effectiveness of technical assistance to Member States in specific areas of crime prevention and criminal justice, including in the context of the reconstruction of criminal justice institutions in peacekeeping and post-conflict situations, in particular as regards capacity-building and the promotion of the rule of law;

7. *Also requests* the Secretary-General to report to the Commission at its fifteenth session on progress made in the first targeted collection of information on the group of standards and norms referred to in paragraph 3 (a) and (b) above, including how that collection of information relates to requests by Member States for technical assistance.

Annex

Recommendations of the Meeting of Experts on the Application of United Nations Standards and Norms in Crime Prevention and Criminal Justice

Recommendations to the Commission on Crime Prevention and Criminal Justice

1. The application and formulation of United Nations standards and norms in crime prevention and criminal justice should continue to be accorded high priority by the Commission on Crime Prevention and Criminal Justice. The standing agenda item on those standards and norms should be maintained and appropriate time and resources should be devoted to it.

2. Possible future United Nations standards and norms in crime prevention and criminal justice should focus on emerging practices in crime prevention or criminal justice, in order to facilitate the development of detailed practical guidelines for use by interested States in carrying out specific tasks.

3. The Commission should establish a mechanism, such as a group of experts and/or a special rapporteur, to supplement existing procedures for undertaking periodic reviews of the application of selected United Nations standards and norms in crime prevention and criminal justice in order to ensure their promotion, as well as to make appropriate recommendations to the Commission.

4. The focus in subsequent review cycles should be on identifying difficulties that have been encountered in the application of United Nations standards and norms, in crime prevention and criminal justice, ways in which technical assistance can be used to overcome those difficulties and desirable practices in crime prevention and control.

5. The resulting data and other information should be shared in order to enhance the level and impact of technical cooperation in the world, the overall objective being to promote criminal justice reform in

line with applicable United Nations standards and norms in crime prevention and criminal justice.

6. The entire review process should be guided by the need to relate it to the main programme priorities of the United Nations, as noted in the United Nations Millennium Declaration and the Vienna Declaration on Crime and Justice: Meeting the Challenges of the Twenty-first Century, including strengthening the rule of law, good governance, sustainable development and the alleviation of poverty.

7. In line with the programme priorities of the United Nations, the Commission, at each of its sessions, should seek to focus on the application of a cluster of United Nations standards and norms in crime prevention and criminal justice. The Commission may wish to consider the possibility of reviewing a presentation of a particular cluster of standards and norms and their application in specific countries. Such a presentation could be prepared in cooperation with the institutes of the United Nations Crime Prevention and Criminal Justice Programme network.

8. In redesigning the information-gathering mechanisms and within the limits of current programme budget resources, the Commission should examine and propose focusing the future review process on selected clusters of instruments with the most widespread potential and relevance for application in criminal justice reforms in the world, in the following order of priority, bearing in mind gender as a cross-cutting issue, and grouped into clusters as follows:

(*a*) Juvenile justice and prison reform, including alternatives to imprisonment and restorative justice;

(*b*) The conduct of law enforcement and criminal justice practitioners, including the integrity of the judiciary;

(*c*) Public security and crime prevention;

(*d*) The treatment of victims and witnesses;

(*e*) Legal, institutional and practical arrangements for international cooperation (model treaties).

9. The Commission should request donor States and relevant intergovernmental and non-governmental institutions to support criminal justice reforms, in accordance with United Nations standards and norms in crime prevention and criminal justice, in countries requesting assistance. The Commission could rely on a roster of national and regional experts who could, upon request, provide technical assistance and advice on the use and application of selected standards and norms.

10. The Commission should encourage donor countries to make financial contributions to the United Nations Crime Prevention and Criminal Justice Fund. Contributions should be directed towards technical cooperation projects for implementing and promoting United Nations standards and norms in crime prevention and criminal justice, as well as organizing meetings of experts to identify priority areas for the development of future standards and norms.

Recommendations to Member States and other entities

11. Each of the Member States should be encouraged to identify at least one contact person who could serve as a knowledgeable source for the analysis of the State's response concerning the application of United Nations standards and norms in crime prevention and criminal justice.

12. Member States should establish mechanisms and provide resources at the national level for promoting and monitoring the application of United Nations standards and norms in crime prevention and criminal justice.

13. Focused efforts should be made to obtain the commitment of policy makers and criminal justice managers to the implementation of United Nations standards and norms in crime prevention and criminal justice.

14. Member States should publish and disseminate, in their local languages, the United Nations standards and norms in crime prevention and criminal justice.

15. United Nations standards and norms in crime prevention and criminal justice should be easily accessible and explained in understandable language.

16. Member States, financial institutions and development agencies should support projects for the implementation of United Nations standards and norms in crime prevention and criminal justice.

17. Member States, intergovernmental and non-governmental organizations and interregional, regional and national training and educational institutions should vigorously promote programmes and projects that advance the United Nations standards and norms in crime prevention and criminal justice.

18. National institutions and non-governmental organizations should integrate United Nations standards and norms fully into their relevant training programmes.

Recommendations to the United Nations Office on Drugs and Crime

19. The United Nations Office on Drugs and Crime should emphasize in its organizational structure and operations the essential role of United Nations standards and norms in crime prevention and criminal justice.

20. The United Nations Office on Drugs and Crime should assist Member States, upon request, in the application of United Nations standards and norms in crime prevention and criminal justice and in the development of projects.

21. The United Nations Office on Drugs and Crime should seek to ensure that the relevant entities within the Secretariat and in the field are fully aware of the importance of United Nations standards and norms in crime prevention and criminal justice for building and maintaining the rule of law.

22. Well-focused efforts should be undertaken to encourage officials in peacekeeping and peace-building operations and their counterparts to apply United Nations standards and norms in crime prevention and criminal justice.

23. The United Nations Office on Drugs and Crime should identify opportunities for sharing data and other information on United Nations standards and norms in crime prevention and criminal justice with Governments and with intergovernmental and non-governmental organizations.

24. The information provided by Member States on the application of United Nations standards and norms in crime prevention and criminal justice should be distributed by the United Nations Office on Drugs and Crime via the World Wide Web.

25. The United Nations Office on Drugs and Crime should encourage financial institutions, development agencies and non-governmental organizations to expand their technical assistance programmes for improving access to justice and the rule of law.

26. The information-gathering mechanisms used by the United Nations Office on Drugs and Crime should be reviewed in order to bring them in line with the overall programme priorities of the United Nations. The goal should be to redesign the mechanisms in a more comprehensive, consistent and operational manner, so that the collected data and other information are more relevant to those priorities. The goal should also be to enhance cooperation among respondents, both in the collection of data and in the execution of technical cooperation projects.

27. New information-gathering mechanisms should be focused on identifying difficulties encountered in application and desirable practices. The mechanisms should be based on the present United Nations priorities unless the Eleventh United Nations Congress on Crime Prevention and Criminal Justice, to be held in 2005, identifies new priorities.

28. Bearing in mind the priorities, the new information-gathering mechanisms should be conceptualized and existing mechanisms reviewed along the following parameters:

(a) Standards and norms related primarily to persons in custody, non-custodial sanctions and juvenile and restorative justice;

(b) Standards and norms related primarily to good governance, the independence of the judiciary and the integrity of criminal justice personnel;

(c) Standards and norms related primarily to crime prevention and victim issues;

(d) Standards and norms related primarily to legal, institutional and practical arrangements for international cooperation.

29. Reviews of United Nations standards and norms related primarily to capital punishment should be conducted pursuant to Economic and Social Council resolution 1995/57 of 28 July 1995, in which the Council recommended that the quinquennial reports of the Secretary-General should continue to cover the implementation of the safeguards guaranteeing protection of the rights of those facing the death penalty.

30. In gathering information on the above-mentioned priorities, the United Nations Office on Drugs and Crime should also focus its efforts on practical measures that make it possible to determine their operational usefulness in restoring or maintaining law and order, with particular reference to developing countries, countries with economies in transition and post-conflict situations.

31. The United Nations Office on Drugs and Crime should continue to explore the possibility of additional approaches and techniques in information-gathering in order to develop even more concise, simplified and cross-sectoral methods.

32. The survey instruments should be designed to be short, easy to complete and comprehensible.

33. The Secretary-General is requested to involve the regional institutes of the United Nations Crime Prevention and Criminal Justice Programme network in the review and design of the information-gathering instruments and the analysis of information collected.

34. Procedures should be developed according to which the Secretary-General, in reporting on the application of United Nations standards and norms in crime prevention and criminal justice, would be able to utilize not only other relevant information available within the United Nations, but also the expertise of specialized agencies, relevant intergovernmental and non-governmental organizations and academic institutions.

Recommendations on training

35. The United Nations Office on Drugs and Crime should continue to develop and produce manuals, modules and tools to be used in providing training on United Nations standards and norms in crime prevention and criminal justice, to carry out a limited number of such training courses and workshops and to coordinate such training with other United Nations entities.

36. A training unit should be created within the United Nations Office on Drugs and Crime and resources should be allocated for training and coordination functions.

37. To the maximum extent possible, the institutes of the United Nations Crime Prevention and Criminal Justice Programme network should be utilized in the planning and conduct of such training activities.

38. In cooperation with the Department of Peacekeeping Operations and the Department of Political Affairs of the Secretariat, the United Nations Office on Drugs and Crime should develop basic training materials for peacekeeping and peace-building operations.

Recommendations on technical cooperation

39. The United Nations Office on Drugs and Crime should establish rosters of national and regional experts who would be able to provide, upon request, technical assistance and advice on the application of particular types of United Nations standards and norms in crime prevention and criminal justice. Such rosters should be developed in accordance with the different clusters of such standards and norms.

40. The advisory services of the United Nations Office on Drugs and Crime in relation to United Nations standards and norms in crime prevention and criminal justice should be enhanced. Projects should be evaluated in the light of the information gathered. The lessons learned should be incorporated into future planning so that the capacity to execute technical assistance projects can be improved.

41. At the request of Member States, practical projects should be developed, in particular for victims' support services and witness protection, prison reform and alternatives to imprisonment, juvenile justice and restorative justice.

Human resources development

In response to General Assembly resolution 56/189 [YUN 2001, p. 1047], which recognized the importance of developing human resources as a means of promoting economic growth, eradicating poverty, participating more effectively in the world economic system and benefiting from globalization, the Secretary-General, in a September report [A/58/348], described measures to implement the resolution. The report focused on the issues addressed in resolution 56/189, particularly the need to adopt a comprehensive approach to human resources development, increase investment in human resources development and promote strategies for information and communication technologies, collaboration with the private sector and NGOs, and the harmonization of UN system efforts and partnerships. The report called for human resources development strategies to include developing capacities for all generations and for groups of special concern, such as persons with disabilities, older persons, youth and indigenous peoples, taking into consideration gender equality. It recommended increasing investments to provide access to health care and education to all persons living in poverty, including groups with special needs. The HIV/AIDS pandemic required combining short-term humanitarian responses with long-term development measures to rebuild the human capacity lost to AIDS. The development of core work skills (such as communication and problem-solving) should form an important part of basic education and literacy programmes. Policies for expanding the use of technologies should encourage the use of local resources, including traditional information systems. Efforts should be made to increase the flow of development financing and its greater allocation to human resources development.

GENERAL ASSEMBLY ACTION

On 23 December [meeting 78], the General Assembly, on the recommendation of the Second Committee [A/58/483/Add.2], adopted **resolution 58/207** without vote [agenda item 93 (b)].

Human resources development

The General Assembly,

Recalling its resolutions 52/196 of 18 December 1997, 54/211 of 22 December 1999 and 56/189 of 21 December 2001, as well as the relevant sections of the Agenda for Development,

Reaffirming internationally agreed development goals, including those contained in the United Nations Millennium Declaration,

Recalling the outcomes of the major United Nations conferences and summits in the economic, social and related fields,

Recalling also the ministerial declaration of the high-level segment of the substantive session of 2002 of the Economic and Social Council, on the contribution of human resources development, including in the areas of health and education, to the process of development,

Stressing that health and education are at the core of human resources development and the need to ensure that, by 2015, children everywhere, boys and girls alike, will be able to complete a full course of primary schooling and will have equal access to all levels of education, as expressed at the World Education Forum, held at Dakar from 26 to 28 April 2000, and in the Millennium Declaration,

Recognizing that human beings are at the centre of concerns for sustainable development and that human resources development is a fundamental aspect of poverty eradication and is vital to the process of sustainable development, contributing to sustained economic growth, social development and environmental protection,

Recognizing also that there is a need to integrate human resources development into comprehensive strategies that mainstream a gender perspective,

Stressing that Governments have the primary responsibility for defining and implementing appropriate policies for human resources development and the need for greater support from the international community for the national efforts of developing countries,

Stressing also the need for enabling national and international environments that will enhance human resources development in developing countries so that they can face the challenges of and benefit from globalization,

Recognizing the need for adequate financial resources to increase investment in human resources development,

Expressing its concern at the increasing development gap between developed and developing countries, including the gap in knowledge and in access to information and communication technologies, and the disparity of income within and among nations and its adverse impact on human resources development in developing countries,

Expressing deep concern at the devastating impact of the HIV/AIDS pandemic, malaria, tuberculosis and other major infectious diseases on human resources development in developing countries, especially in sub-Saharan Africa,

Noting the impact of the movement of highly skilled people and those with an advanced education on human resources development and sustainable development in developing countries, and recognizing the need for further studies and analyses of its effects in the context of globalization,

Emphasizing the continuing need for coordination and integration among the organs and organizations of the United Nations system in assisting developing countries, in particular the least developed among them, in fostering the development of their human resources, especially that of the most vulnerable groups, and for the United Nations to continue to give priority to human resources development in developing countries,

1. *Takes note* of the report of the Secretary-General;
2. *Recognizes* the importance of developing human resources as a means, inter alia, of promoting sustained economic growth and sustainable development and eradicating poverty, as well as of participating more effectively in the world economic system and benefiting from globalization;
3. *Urges* increased investments by all countries, the United Nations system, international organizations,

the private sector, non-governmental organizations and civil society in all aspects of human development, such as health, nutrition, education, training and further capacity-building, with a view to achieving sustainable development and the well-being of all;

4. *Also urges* the adoption of comprehensive approaches to human resources development in designing and implementing development strategies at the national, subregional, regional and international levels and the sharing of best practices, while recognizing the role that local knowledge systems could play;

5. *Further urges* the adoption of cross-sectoral approaches to human resources development, which combine, among other factors, economic growth, poverty eradication, provision of basic social services, sustainable livelihoods, empowerment of women, involvement of young people, the needs of vulnerable groups of society, the needs of local indigenous communities, political freedom, popular participation and respect for human rights, justice and equity, all of which are essential for enhancing human capacity in order to meet the challenge of development;

6. *Encourages* all countries to ensure local and community-level engagement in the formulation and implementation of national and local policies to promote human resources development, and in this regard also encourages them to continue developing individual capacity as well as empowering communities;

7. *Emphasizes* the need to ensure the full participation of women in the formulation and implementation of national and local policies to promote human resources development;

8. *States* the importance of ensuring adequate resources for education as a fundamental aspect of eradicating poverty and promoting development with a view to achieving sustainable economic growth and human development;

9. *Encourages* Governments to manage resources assigned to education in a responsible, accurate and transparent way and to ensure accountability;

10. *Recognizes* the lack of adequate resources in many developing countries to expand access to and improve the quality of education, and, in particular, to provide free universal primary education;

11. *Encourages* the international community to provide greater technical assistance, financial support and allocation to human resources development in developing countries in support of their national efforts;

12. *Encourages* the United Nations system to focus in its cooperation activities on building human and institutional capacity, giving specific attention to women, girls and vulnerable groups;

13. *Calls upon* the United Nations system to harmonize further its collective human resources development efforts, in accordance with national policies and priorities;

14. *Encourages* the United Nations system to continue engaging in partnerships with the private sector and other relevant stakeholders, where appropriate, in accordance with United Nations resolutions and national priorities, so as to contribute further to the building of human resources development capacity in developing countries;

15. *Recognizes* the role of information and communication technologies in promoting human resources development, and in this regard welcomes the World Summit on the Information Society, the first phase of which was held in Geneva from 10 to 12 December 2003 and the second phase of which will be held in Tunis from 16 to 18 November 2005, as an important step towards addressing the challenges of bridging the digital divide as well as identifying a truly information and knowledge-based approach towards the achievement of the internationally agreed development goals, including those contained in the United Nations Millennium Declaration, in developing countries;

16. *Also recognizes* the need to direct concerted efforts at enhancing the technical skills and know-how of people living in rural and agricultural areas, with a view to improving their means of livelihood and material well-being, and in this regard encourages the allocation of more resources for this purpose so as to facilitate access to appropriate technology and know-how from within countries as well as from other countries, in particular the developed countries, and through South-South cooperation, including triangular arrangements;

17. *Invites* international organizations, including international financial institutions, within their respective mandates, to give greater priority to supporting the objectives of human resources development and to integrating them into their policies, projects and operations;

18. *Requests* the Secretary-General to submit to the General Assembly at its sixtieth session a report on the implementation of the present resolution and to include a separate section therein on the effect of the movement of highly skilled people and those with an advanced education on human resources development in developing countries;

19. *Decides* to include in the provisional agenda of its sixtieth session, under the item entitled "Sustainable development and international economic cooperation", the sub-item entitled "Human resources development".

UN research and training institutes

UN Institute for Training and Research

A report [A/59/14] of the Executive Director of the United Nations Institute for Training and Research (UNITAR) described the Institute's activities during the period from 1 July 2002 to 31 December 2003. He reviewed UNITAR's programmes in international affairs management, which had increased to 150 different programmes and workshops or seminars organized annually, benefiting over 7,600 participants yearly; the activities of outposted offices in New York and at the regional office for Asia and the Pacific in Hiroshima, Japan, which was established in July; and activities related to training and capacity-building in sustainable development.

In response to General Assembly resolution 57/268 [YUN 2002, p. 1132], the Secretary-General, in July [A/58/183], provided an overview of UNITAR programmes. He said that, while the financial situation of the programmes funded through special-purpose grants was satisfactory, the UNITAR General Fund, made up of non-earmarked voluntary contributions, remained weak and vulnerable. The Secretariat and UNITAR had considered ways to solve the long-standing issue of rental and maintenance costs of the premises used in Geneva and New York and the payment of the accumulated debt of UNITAR to the United Nations.

An October report [A/58/544] of the Secretary-General on the financial viability of UNITAR, submitted in response to General Assembly resolution 57/292 [YUN 2002, p. 1375], covered the status of all voluntary contributions and the payment of the accumulated debt of the Institute, as well as provisions offered to other comparable organizations. Based on his consultations with the Institute, the Secretary-General put forward proposals on how to address the issue of past and future maintenance and rental costs. In order to compensate UNITAR for its expenditures under the General Fund relating to the provision of training in multilateral diplomacy and international affairs management to the diplomatic personnel of the missions to the United Nations free of charge, the Secretary-General proposed providing UNITAR with an annual subvention in an amount not exceeding its annual rental and maintenance costs ($165,630 in 2002), to be paid from the UN regular budget. That would require an additional provision of $331,300 over the resources proposed under section 29, Management and central support services, of the 2004-2005 biennial programmme budget. He also proposed that UNITAR's debt of $321,184 to the United Nations should be paid within a five-year period.

In November [A/58/7/Add.10], the Advisory Committee on Administrative and Budgetary Questions (ACABQ) presented its comments on the Secretary-General's report. It believed that the five-year period was too long to repay UNITAR's debt and recommended that the UNITAR Executive Director repay the amount as soon as possible. The possibility of releasing part of the accrued interest on special-purpose grants so that it could be applied towards loan repayment should be explored.

GENERAL ASSEMBLY ACTION

On 23 December [meeting 78], the General Assembly, on the recommendation of the Second Committee [A/58/489, as orally revised], adopted **resolution 58/223** without vote [agenda item 99 (a)].

United Nations Institute for Training and Research

The General Assembly,

Recalling its resolutions 51/188 of 16 December 1996, 52/206 of 18 December 1997, 53/195 of 15 December 1998, 54/229 of 22 December 1999, 55/208 of 20 December 2000, 56/208 of 21 December 2001 and 57/268 of 20 December 2002,

Welcoming the recent progress made by the United Nations Institute for Training and Research in its various programmes and activities, including the improved cooperation that has been established with other organizations of the United Nations system and with regional and national institutions,

Expressing its appreciation to the Governments and private institutions that have made or pledged financial and other contributions to the Institute,

Noting with concern that contributions to the General Fund have not increased, while the participation of the developed countries in training programmes in New York and Geneva is increasing,

Noting that the bulk of the resources contributed to the Institute is directed to the Special Purpose Grants Fund rather than to the General Fund, and stressing the need to address that unbalanced situation,

Noting also that the Institute receives no subsidy from the United Nations regular budget and that it provides training programmes to all Member States free of charge,

Reiterating that training activities should be accorded a more visible and larger role in support of the management of international affairs and in the execution of the economic and social development programmes of the United Nations system,

1. *Takes note* of the report of the Secretary-General;

2. *Reaffirms* the importance of a coordinated United Nations system-wide approach to research and training, based on an effective coherent strategy and an effective division of work among the relevant institutions and bodies;

3. *Also reaffirms* the relevance of the United Nations Institute for Training and Research in view of the growing importance of training within the United Nations and the training requirements of States and the relevance of the training-related research activities undertaken by the Institute within its mandate;

4. *Welcomes* the progress made in building partnerships between the Institute and other organizations and bodies of the United Nations system with respect to their training programmes, and in this context underlines the need to develop further and to expand the scope of those partnerships, in particular at the country level;

5. *Also welcomes* the establishment of the Institute's Hiroshima Office for Asia and the Pacific in Hiroshima, Japan;

6. *Requests* the Board of Trustees of the Institute to continue to ensure fair and equitable geographical distribution and transparency in the preparation of the programmes and in the employment of experts, and in this regard stresses that the courses of the Institute should focus primarily on development issues and the management of international affairs;

7. *Renews its appeal* to all Governments, in particular those of developed countries, and to private institutions that have not yet contributed financially or otherwise to the Institute, to give it their generous financial and other support, and urges the States that have interrupted their voluntary contributions to consider resuming them in view of the successful restructuring and revitalization of the Institute;

8. *Encourages* the Board of Trustees of the Institute to continue its efforts to resolve the critical financial situation of the Institute, in particular with a view to broadening its donor base and to increasing the contributions to the General Fund;

9. *Also encourages* the Board of Trustees to consider diversifying further the venues of the events organized by the Institute and to include the cities hosting regional commissions, in order to promote greater participation and reduce costs;

10. *Stresses* the need to take action to resolve expeditiously the issues related to the Institute's rent, debt, rental rates and maintenance costs, taking into account its financial situation, and welcomes the consideration of those issues by the Fifth Committee;

11. *Requests* the Secretary-General to submit to the General Assembly at its fifty-ninth session a report on the implementation of the present resolution, including details on the status of contributions to and the financial situation of the Institute.

Also on 23 December, the Assembly, in **resolution 58/272** (see p. 1417), decided to cancel UNITAR's debt in respect of rent and maintenance charges in the amount of $321,184 and requested the Secretary-General to invite the UNITAR Board of Trustees to rationalize the financial structure of the Institute, including through the possible application of a consistent programme support rate to the Special Purpose Grants Fund in order to bring it in line with the standard rate applied by the United Nations. It decided to revert to the matter at its fifty-ninth (2004) session.

University for Peace

In response to General Assembly resolution 56/2 [YUN 2001, p. 1050], the Secretary-General, in October [A/58/430], described progress in revitalizing the Costa Rica–based University for Peace. As part of its five-year expansion and revitalization plan, a newly designed academic programme was being implemented, including five new master's degree programmes on peace and security issues and a number of short courses for mid-career professionals. The course materials would be disseminated to partner universities worldwide. The Secretary-General noted that the University's five-year development strategy would be concluded by December 2005. The first phase of development of the academic programme would be financed from tuition and scholarship fees, the regional activities would be self-sustaining and the distance education programme would be revenue generating. Full implementation of the programme depended on broad government support and on financial resources for the University's institutional functioning and the implementation and dissemination of its academic programme.

GENERAL ASSEMBLY ACTION

On 10 November [meeting 59], the General Assembly adopted **resolution 58/12** [draft: A/58/L.26 & Add.1] without vote [agenda item 25].

University for Peace

The General Assembly,

Recalling its resolution 56/2 of 22 October 2001, in which it recalled that, in its resolution 34/111 of 14 December 1979, it had approved the idea of establishing the University for Peace as a specialized international centre for higher education, research and the dissemination of knowledge relative to peace and its universal promotion within the United Nations system, and in which it also recalled its resolution 35/55 of 5 December 1980, in which it approved the establishment of the University for Peace, as well as all preceding resolutions on this item,

Noting that in 1991 the Secretary-General, with the assistance of the United Nations Development Programme, established a Trust Fund for Peace consisting of voluntary contributions in order to provide the University with the means necessary to extend its sphere of activity to the whole world, taking full advantage of its potential capacity for education, research and support of the United Nations and to carry out its mandate of promoting peace in the world,

Noting with appreciation the vigorous actions taken by the Secretary-General, in consultation with the Director-General of the United Nations Educational, Scientific and Cultural Organization and with the encouragement and support of the Government of Costa Rica, to revitalize the University,

Recognizing the important and varied activities carried out by the University during the period from 2001 to 2003, with the valuable assistance and contributions of Governments, foundations and non-governmental organizations, in particular the progress made in the development and implementation of the academic programme and the expansion of its scope worldwide as part of a five-year programme of expansion and revitalization,

Noting with satisfaction the activities directed towards expanding the University's educational and research programmes to Africa, Asia and the Pacific, Central Asia and Latin America and the Caribbean,

Also noting with satisfaction the progress made in the development of teaching programmes at the master's level, short courses, programmes to disseminate course materials and distance education and the establishment of a digital library on peace-related issues,

Noting that the University has placed special emphasis on the areas of conflict prevention, peacekeeping, peace-building and the peaceful settlement of disputes, and that it has launched programmes in the areas of democratic consensus-building and the techniques of peaceful settlement of conflicts,

Noting also that the University has launched a broad programme for building a culture of peace in Central America and the Caribbean in the context of the efforts being made by the United Nations and the United Nations Educational, Scientific and Cultural Organization for the development and promotion of a culture of peace,

Noting with appreciation the intensifying collaboration between the University and organizations and agencies of the United Nations, particularly the United Nations University, the United Nations Educational, Scientific and Cultural Organization, the Department of Political Affairs and the Department for Disarmament Affairs of the Secretariat, the United Nations Development Programme, the United Nations Institute for Training and Research and others,

Considering the importance of promoting education that fosters peaceful coexistence among people, including respect for the life, dignity and integrity of human beings, irrespective of their nationality, race, sex, religion or culture, as well as friendship and solidarity among peoples,

1. *Takes note with appreciation* of the report of the Secretary-General outlining the progress made in revitalizing the University for Peace, especially in regard to implementation of the five-year programme of expansion and revitalization;

2. *Requests* the Secretary-General, in view of the important work of the University for Peace and its potential role in developing new concepts and approaches to security through research and dialogue in order to respond effectively to emerging threats to peace, to consider further ways to strengthen cooperation between the United Nations and the University for Peace;

3. *Also requests* the Secretary-General to consider using the services of the University as part of his conflict-resolution and peace-building efforts and in the promotion of the Declaration and Programme of Action on a Culture of Peace;

4. *Invites* Member States, intergovernmental bodies, non-governmental organizations and interested individuals to contribute to the Trust Fund for Peace or to the budget of the University;

5. *Invites* Member States to accede to the International Agreement for the Establishment of the University for Peace, thereby demonstrating their support for an educational institution devoted to the promotion of a universal culture of peace;

6. *Decides* to include in the provisional agenda of its sixtieth session the item entitled "University for Peace".

On 23 December, the Assembly decided that the agenda item on the University for Peace would remain for consideration during its resumed fifty-eighth (2004) session (**decision 58/565**).

United Nations University

The Council of the United Nations University (UNU) (Tokyo, Japan 1-5 December) [A/59/31] considered the 2004-2005 academic programme and budget; a review of the financial situation of UNU, including the management of the UNU Endowment Fund; the UNU personnel policy; a policy paper on new UNU associated institutions; a policy on the role of UNU support groups and associations; a UNU-wide strategy for follow-up of the 2002 World Summit on Sustainable Development [YUN 2002, p. 821]; and a report on UNU's strategy for future activities in and on Africa.

During 2003, the UNU peace and governance programme focused its research and policy analysis activities in four thematic areas: conflict and security; human rights and ethics; policy and institutional frameworks; and international order and international justice. The focus of the UNU environment and sustainable development programme was on the interactions between human activities and the natural environment, and the implications for sustainable human management of natural resources. Networking and capacity-building, particularly in developing countries, were given high priority. In 2003, the programme regrouped its activities under four broad themes: sustainable urbanization; managing fragile ecosystems; solutions to water crises; and environmental governance and information.

Chapter X

Women

During 2003, United Nations efforts to advance the status of women and ensure their rights continued to be guided by the Beijing Declaration and Platform for Action, adopted by the Fourth (1995) World Conference on Women. The outcome of the General Assembly's twenty-third (2000) special session, to appraise and assess implementation of the Beijing Declaration and Platform for Action (Beijing+5), prompted further action and initiatives for the advancement of women.

The Commission on the Status of Women, at its forty-seventh session in March, recommended to the Economic and Social Council for adoption agreed conclusions on women's participation in and access to the media and information and communication technologies and their impact on and use as an instrument for the advancement and empowerment of women, which the Council endorsed in July. The Council also took action on assistance to Palestinian women; women and girls in Afghanistan; mainstreaming a gender perspective into all policies and programmes in the UN system; and the revitalization and strengthening of the International Research and Training Institute for the Advancement of Women (INSTRAW). The Commission also adopted and brought to the attention of the Council a resolution on women, the girl child and HIV/AIDS; and a decision on communications concerning the status of women.

The Assembly adopted resolutions on women and political participation; violence against women migrant workers; improvement of the situation of women in rural areas; elimination of domestic violence against women; the girl child; an in-depth study on all forms of violence against women; women in development; improvement of the status of women in the United Nations; and the Convention on the Elimination of All Forms of Discrimination against Women. The United Nations Development Fund for Women continued to focus on women's economic security and political empowerment, and to advocate gender mainstreaming and equality.

INSTRAW continued its research and training, and networking and information dissemination, in particular through the gender awareness information and networking system. Economic and Social Council amendments to the Institute's statute included the replacement of its Board of Trustees with an Executive Board and the empowerment of the Secretary-General to appoint its Director, taking into account the list of candidates proposed by the Board. In December, the Secretary-General appointed Carmen Moreno as the Institute's new Director.

Follow-up to the Fourth World Conference on Women and Beijing+5

During 2003, the Commission on the Status of Women, the Economic and Social Council and the General Assembly considered follow-up to the 1995 Fourth World Conference on Women, particularly the implementation of the Beijing Declaration and Platform for Action [YUN 1995, p. 1170], and the political declaration and further actions and initiatives to implement the Beijing Declaration and Platform for Action, adopted at the twenty-third (2000) special session of the Assembly (Beijing+5) by resolution S/23-2 [YUN 2000, p. 1084]. The political declaration had reaffirmed the commitment of Governments to the goals and objectives of the Fourth World Conference and to the implementation of the 12 critical areas of concern set forth in the Platform for Action: women and poverty; education and training of women; women and health; violence against women; women and armed conflict; women and the economy; women in power and decision-making; institutional mechanisms for the advancement of women; human rights and women; women and the media; women and the environment; and the girl child (see pp. 1167-1190 for action taken regarding the critical areas of concern). In the context of the follow-up, the issue of mainstreaming a gender perspective into UN policies and programmes was also addressed (see p. 1188).

Report of Secretary-General. In response to General Assembly resolution 57/182 [YUN 2002, p. 1137], the Secretary-General, in a July report [A/58/166], described the steps taken by the Assembly and its Main Committees, the Economic and Social Council and the United Nations Office of the Special Adviser on Gender Issues and Advancement of Women to promote the mainstreaming of gender perspectives into UN policies and programmes. The report highlighted action taken relating to the follow-up to the United Nations Millennium Declaration [YUN 2000, p. 49], the World Summit on Sustainable Development [YUN 2002, p. 821] and the World Summit on the Information Society (see p. 857).

The Secretary-General recommended that the Assembly call for continued efforts to include gender equality in reports; take further steps to provide greater attention to the follow-up and implementation of the resolutions and decisions addressing gender equality and the empowerment of women; ensure that gender perspectives were an integral part of all aspects of the implementation of the Millennium Declaration; and call for further attention to gender perspectives in the follow-up to and reporting on the Johannesburg Declaration and Plan of Implementation adopted by the World Summit on Sustainable Development. It might also wish to encourage further systematic attention to gender perspectives in the preparatory process for and outcome of the World Summit on the Information Society.

GENERAL ASSEMBLY ACTION

On 22 December [meeting 77], the General Assembly, on the recommendation of the Third (Social, Humanitarian and Cultural) Committee [A/58/502], adopted **resolution 58/148** without vote [agenda item 111].

Follow-up to the Fourth World Conference on Women and full implementation of the Beijing Declaration and Platform for Action and the outcome of the twenty-third special session of the General Assembly

The General Assembly,

Recalling its previous resolutions on the question, including resolution 57/182 of 18 December 2002,

Recalling also the outcome of the twenty-third special session of the General Assembly, entitled "Women 2000: gender equality, development and peace for the twenty-first century", and the proposed actions and initiatives to overcome obstacles and challenges thereto,

Deeply convinced that the Beijing Declaration and Platform for Action and the outcome of the twenty-third special session are important contributions to the advancement of women worldwide in the achievement of gender equality and must be translated into effective action by all States, the United Nations system and other organizations concerned, as well as by non-governmental organizations,

Stressing the importance of strong, sustained political will and commitment at the national, regional and international levels for achieving full and accelerated implementation of the Beijing Declaration and Platform for Action and the outcome of the twenty-third special session,

Recognizing that the responsibility for the implementation of the Beijing Declaration and Platform for Action and the outcome of the twenty-third special session rests primarily at the national level and that strengthened efforts are necessary in this respect, and reiterating that enhanced international cooperation is essential for the effective implementation of the Beijing Declaration and Platform for Action and the outcome of the twenty-third special session,

Welcoming the increased attention to the situation of women and girls and the integration of a gender perspective in the work of the United Nations, in particular in the outcomes of major conferences, special sessions and summit conferences and their follow-up processes, and reaffirming its commitment to building on progress achieved in this respect,

Emphasizing the importance of Economic and Social Council decision 2003/287 of 24 July 2003, in which the Council decided to undertake, during the coordination segment of its substantive session of 2004, a review and appraisal of the system-wide implementation of agreed conclusions 1997/2 on mainstreaming a gender perspective into all policies and programmes in the United Nations system, adopted by the Council on 18 July 1997, and taking note of Council resolution 2003/49 of 24 July 2003,

Reaffirming the primary and essential role of the General Assembly and the Economic and Social Council in promoting the advancement of women and gender equality, while noting the open debate on women and peace and security held in the Security Council on 28 and 29 October 2002 and on 29 October 2003,

Bearing in mind its relevant resolutions and Security Council resolution 1325(2000) of 31 October 2000,

1. *Reaffirms* the goals, objectives and commitments contained in the Beijing Declaration and Platform for Action and also in the political declaration and further actions and initiatives to implement the Beijing Declaration and Platform for Action adopted by the General Assembly at its twenty-third special session;

2. *Takes note with appreciation* of the report of the Secretary-General on the follow-up to and progress made in the implementation of the Beijing Declaration and Platform for Action and the outcome of the twenty-third special session;

3. *Calls upon* Governments, the relevant entities of the United Nations system, within their respective mandates, and all relevant actors of civil society, including non-governmental organizations, to continue to take effective action to achieve the full and effective implementation of the Beijing Declaration and Platform for Action and the outcome of the twenty-third special session;

4. *Reaffirms* its decision that the General Assembly, the Economic and Social Council and the Commission on the Status of Women, in accordance with their respective mandates and with General Assembly resolutions 48/162 of 20 December 1993 and 57/270 B of 23 June 2003 and other relevant resolutions, constitute a three-tiered intergovernmental mechanism that plays the primary role in overall policy-making and follow-up and in coordinating the implementation and monitoring of the Beijing Platform for Action and the outcome of the twenty-third special session;

5. *Also reaffirms* that the follow-up to the Fourth World Conference on Women and the twenty-third special session will be undertaken within the framework of an integrated and coordinated follow-up to

major international conferences and summits in the economic, social and related fields;

6. *Strongly encourages* Governments to continue to support the role and contribution of civil society, in particular non-governmental organizations and women's organizations, in the implementation of the Beijing Declaration and Platform for Action and the outcome of the twenty-third special session;

7. *Calls upon* Governments and all other relevant actors to continue to integrate a gender perspective into the implementation of and follow-up to recent United Nations conferences, summits and special sessions and in future reports on this subject;

8. *Invites* States parties to the Convention on the Elimination of All Forms of Discrimination against Women to include information on measures taken to implement the outcome of the twenty-third special session, as well as the Beijing Platform for Action, in their reports to the Committee on the Elimination of Discrimination against Women under article 18 of the Convention;

9. *Urges* Member States to consider signing, ratifying or acceding to the United Nations Convention against Transnational Organized Crime and the Protocols thereto, in particular the Protocol to Prevent, Suppress and Punish Trafficking in Persons, Especially Women and Children, supplementing the United Nations Convention against Transnational Organized Crime, and welcomes the imminent entry into force of that Protocol on 25 December 2003;

10. *Invites* Member States to submit, before 30 April 2004, responses to the questionnaire of the Secretariat on the implementation of the Beijing Platform for Action and the outcome of the twenty-third special session, in preparation for the review and appraisal mandated in the multi-year programme of work of the Commission on the Status of Women;

11. *Invites* the Economic and Social Council to continue its efforts to ensure that gender mainstreaming is an integral part of all activities in its work and that of its subsidiary bodies, building upon agreed conclusions 1997/2 adopted by the Council on 18 July 1997, and in this regard welcomes the inclusion of the question of gender mainstreaming in its agenda, the consideration of annual progress made in gender mainstreaming and the attention given to the gender perspective in the outcomes of the substantive session of 2003 of the Council;

12. *Encourages* the Economic and Social Council to request the regional commissions, within their respective mandates and resources, to intensify efforts to build up a database, to be updated regularly, in which all programmes and projects carried out in their respective regions by organizations or bodies of the United Nations system are listed, and to facilitate the dissemination of information on such programmes and projects, as well as the evaluation of their impact on the empowerment of women through the implementation of the Beijing Platform for Action;

13. *Welcomes* the contribution of the Commission on the Status of Women to the follow-up and review of the future implementation of the commitments made in the Beijing Declaration and Platform for Action and the outcome of the twenty-third special session, reaffirms that the Commission will continue to play a central role in this regard, and encourages Governments, the relevant specialized agencies, funds and programmes of the United Nations system and civil society to continue to support its work;

14. *Recognizes* the importance attached to the regional and subregional monitoring of the global and regional platforms for action and of the implementation of the outcome of the twenty-third special session by regional commissions and other regional or subregional structures, within their mandates, in consultation with Governments, and calls for the promotion of further cooperation in that respect among Governments and, where appropriate, national machineries of the same region;

15. *Also recognizes* that sustained political will and commitment at the national, regional and international levels are essential elements for the full and accelerated implementation of the Beijing Platform for Action and the outcome of the twenty-third special session;

16. *Emphasizes* that the promotion of gender equality and of women's empowerment and participation, together with the mainstreaming of a gender perspective, are among the essential elements for advancing the implementation of the United Nations Millennium Declaration, with a view, in particular, to achieving the internationally agreed development goals, including those contained in the Millennium Declaration and the outcomes of United Nations summits, conferences and special sessions;

17. *Recognizes* that adequate mobilization of resources at the national and international levels, as well as new and additional resources for the developing countries, including the least developed countries and countries with economies in transition, from all available funding mechanisms, including multilateral, bilateral and private sources, will also be required;

18. *Emphasizes* that the creation of an enabling environment at the national and international levels, including by ensuring the participation of women on an equal basis with men at all levels of decision-making, is necessary to ensure the full participation of women in economic activities, and calls upon States to remove obstacles to the full implementation of the Beijing Declaration and Platform for Action and the outcome of the twenty-third special session;

19. *Reaffirms* that, in order to ensure the effective implementation of the strategic objectives of the Beijing Platform for Action and the outcome of the twenty-third special session, the United Nations system should promote an active and visible policy of mainstreaming a gender perspective, including through the work of the Division for the Advancement of Women and the Office of the Special Adviser on Gender Issues and Advancement of Women and the maintenance of gender units and focal points;

20. *Also reaffirms* that United Nations bodies that focus on gender issues, such as the United Nations Population Fund, the United Nations Development Fund for Women, the International Research and Training Institute for the Advancement of Women and the United Nations Children's Fund, have a critical role to play in the implementation of the objectives of the Beijing Declaration and Platform for Action and the outcome of the twenty-third special session, and recognizes that gender specialists throughout the United Nations system also have an important role to play in this regard;

21. *Recognizes* the important role of women in the prevention and resolution of conflicts and in peacebuilding, the importance of their equal participation and full involvement in all efforts for the maintenance and promotion of peace and security and the need to increase their role in decision-making with regard to conflict prevention and resolution, and urges the United Nations system and Governments to make further efforts in this regard and to take steps to ensure and support the full participation of women at all levels of decision-making and implementation in development activities and peace processes, including conflict prevention and resolution, post-conflict reconstruction, peacemaking, peacekeeping and peacebuilding, as well as through the integration of a gender perspective into those United Nations processes;

22. *Expresses its appreciation* for the efforts made by all relevant organizations of the United Nations system in promoting the role of women in conflict prevention and resolution;

23. *Welcomes* the convening of the World Summit on the Information Society in Geneva in 2003 and in Tunis in 2005, and encourages Governments and all other stakeholders to integrate a gender perspective into the preparatory processes and outcome documents, taking into account the agreed conclusions on women's participation in and access to the media, and information and communication technologies and their impact on and use as an instrument for the advancement and empowerment of women, adopted by the Commission on the Status of Women at its forty-seventh session, and the report of the Secretary-General;

24. *Also welcomes* the entry into force of the Optional Protocol to the Convention on the Elimination of All Forms of Discrimination against Women, and urges States parties to the Convention that have not yet done so to consider signing, ratifying or acceding to the Optional Protocol;

25. *Requests* all bodies that deal with programme and budgetary matters, including the Committee for Programme and Coordination, to ensure that all programmes, medium-term plans and programme budgets visibly mainstream a gender perspective;

26. *Requests* the Secretary-General to continue to disseminate the Beijing Declaration and Platform for Action and the outcome of the twenty-third special session as widely as possible in all the official languages of the United Nations;

27. *Also requests* the Secretary-General to integrate a gender perspective in his reporting to the General Assembly, in order to support gender-sensitive policy formulation;

28. *Further requests* the Secretary-General to report annually to the General Assembly, the Economic and Social Council and the Commission on the Status of Women on the follow-up to and progress made in the implementation of the Beijing Declaration and Platform for Action and the outcome of the twenty-third special session, with an assessment of progress made in mainstreaming a gender perspective within the United Nations system, including by providing information on key achievements, lessons learned and best practices, and to recommend further measures and strategies for future action within the United Nations system;

29. *Requests* the Secretary-General to include in his annual and quinquennial reports on the follow-up to the United Nations Millennium Declaration an assessment of the progress made in promoting the goal of gender equality, in particular in relation to the development goals set forth in the Millennium Declaration, and recommendations to improve the measurement and coverage of indicators so that progress towards gender equality can be evaluated over time;

30. *Also requests* the Secretary-General to ensure that all United Nations personnel and officials at Headquarters and in the field, especially in field operations, receive training on mainstreaming a gender perspective in their work, including gender impact analysis, and to ensure appropriate follow-up to such training;

31. *Further requests* the Secretary-General to provide, by the end of 2004, a compilation of updated and substantiated statistics from Member States and other relevant sources on the situation of women and girls, including older women, in countries around the world, including by issuing a new volume of *The World's Women: Trends and Statistics*;

32. *Recognizes* the need to further include a gender perspective in the work of its Main Committees;

33. *Recalls*, in this regard, its request to each functional commission of the Economic and Social Council to examine its methods of work in order to better pursue the implementation of the outcomes of major United Nations conferences and summits, recognizing that there is no need for a uniform approach since each functional commission has its own specificity, while noting that modern methods of work can better guarantee the review of progress made in implementation at all levels, on the basis of a report containing recommendations to be submitted by the Secretary-General to each functional commission and relevant subsidiary body of the Economic and Social Council on its methods of work, in accordance with the provisions defined by the respective outcomes and relevant decisions taken by each body, bearing in mind the progress recently achieved in this regard by certain commissions, in particular the Commission on Sustainable Development, and recalling that the functional commissions and other relevant bodies of the Economic and Social Council should report to it no later than 2005 on the outcome of this examination;

34. *Decides* to include in the provisional agenda of its fifty-ninth session the item entitled "Implementation of the outcome of the Fourth World Conference on Women and of the twenty-third special session of the General Assembly, entitled 'Women 2000: gender equality, development and peace for the twenty-first century'".

Critical areas of concern

Women in power and decision-making

On 22 December [meeting 77], the General Assembly, on the recommendation of the Third Committee [A/58/501], adopted **resolution 58/142** without vote [agenda item 110].

Women and political participation

The General Assembly,

Reaffirming the obligations of all States to promote and protect human rights and fundamental freedoms as stated in the Charter of the United Nations, and guided by the purposes and principles of human rights instruments,

Reaffirming also the Universal Declaration of Human Rights, which states that everyone has the right to take part in the government of his or her country and the right of equal access to public service,

Recalling the International Covenant on Civil and Political Rights, which states, inter alia, that every citizen shall have the right and opportunity to take part in the conduct of public affairs, directly or through freely chosen representatives, to vote and to be elected at genuine periodic elections and to have access, on general terms of equality, to public service in his or her country,

Recalling also the Convention on the Elimination of All Forms of Discrimination against Women, which states, inter alia, that States parties shall take all appropriate measures to eliminate discrimination against women in the political and public life of the country,

Recalling further the Convention on the Political Rights of Women, which states that women shall be, on equal terms with men and without any discrimination, entitled to vote in all elections, eligible for election to all publicly elected bodies established by national law and entitled to hold public office and to exercise all public functions established by national law,

Recalling the Beijing Declaration and Platform for Action, the outcome of the twenty-third special session of the General Assembly, entitled "Women 2000: gender equality, development and peace for the twenty-first century", the United Nations Millennium Declaration and agreed conclusions 1997/2 on women in power and decision-making, adopted by the Commission on the Status of Women on 21 March 1997,

Affirming that the empowerment and autonomy of women and the improvement of their political, social and economic status are essential to the achievement of representative, transparent and accountable government, democratic institutions and sustainable development in all areas of life,

Affirming also that the active participation of women, on equal terms with men, at all levels of decision-making is essential to the achievement of equality, sustainable development, peace and democracy,

Concerned that, despite general acceptance of the need for gender balance in decision-making bodies at all levels, women are still largely underrepresented at most levels of government, especially in ministerial and other executive bodies, and in legislative bodies,

Recognizing that women have demonstrated considerable leadership in community and informal organizations, as well as in public office,

Recognizing also that women's full and equal participation in the political process and decision-making will provide a balance that more accurately reflects the composition of society, is needed to strengthen democracy and promote its proper functioning, plays a pivotal role in furthering women's equal status, including improving women's socio-economic status, and contributes to redefining political priorities and providing new perspectives on political issues,

Recognizing further that women's participation in decision-making and in political, civil, economic, social and cultural life is negatively affected by poverty, which disproportionately affects women, particularly in developing countries,

Reaffirming the important role of women in the prevention and resolution of conflicts and in peace-building, and stressing the importance of their full and equal participation in all efforts to maintain and promote peace and security and the need to increase their role in decision-making with regard to conflict prevention and resolution and the rebuilding of post-conflict society, in accordance with Security Council resolution 1325(2000) of 31 October 2000 and the relevant resolutions of the General Assembly,

Recognizing the importance of education and training from an early age in government, public policy, economics, civics, information technology and science to ensure that women develop the knowledge, skills, confidence and ethical values needed to participate fully in society and the political process,

1. *Urges* States:

(*a*) To promote and protect the right of women to associate freely, express their views publicly, openly debate political policy and petition and participate in their Government at all levels, including in the formulation and implementation of government policy, on equal terms with men;

(*b*) To eliminate laws, regulations and practices that, in a discriminatory manner, prevent or restrict women's participation in the political process and to implement positive measures that would accelerate the achievement of equality between men and women;

(*c*) To ensure equal access to education, property rights and inheritance rights and to promote equal access to information technology and business and economic opportunities, including in international trade, in order to provide women with the tools that enable them to take part fully and equally in decision-making processes at all levels;

(*d*) To counter, as appropriate, negative societal attitudes about women's capacity to participate equally in the political process that contribute to the low proportion of women among political decision makers at the local, national and international levels;

(*e*) To promote the goal of gender balance in all public positions and to take all appropriate measures to encourage political parties to ensure that women have a fair and equal opportunity to compete for all elective and non-elective public positions;

(*f*) To review the differential impact of their electoral systems on the political representation of women in elected bodies and to adjust or reform those systems where appropriate;

(*g*) To institute educational programmes, as appropriate, in the school curriculum that sensitize young people about the equal rights of women, teach civic responsibilities, promote confidence-building and counter negative societal attitudes that discourage women's political participation;

(*h*) To monitor progress in the representation of women through the regular collection, analysis and dissemination of data on the political participation of women and men at all levels and the progress of political parties in providing equal and fair opportunities for women to participate;

(*i*) To identify and propose more women candidates for senior and decision-making positions in the United Nations system and for appointment or election to intergovernmental expert and treaty bodies, and to encourage more women to apply for those positions;

(j) To promote gender balance for their delegations to United Nations and other international meetings and conferences;

(k) To encourage greater involvement of indigenous and other marginalized women in decision-making at all levels and to address and counter the barriers faced by marginalized women in accessing and participating in politics and decision-making;

(l) To ensure that measures to reconcile family and professional life apply equally to women and men, bearing in mind that the sharing of family responsibilities between women and men creates an enabling environment for women's political participation;

2. *Invites* Governments, as well as the private sector, non-governmental organizations and other actors of civil society:

(a) To develop mechanisms and training programmes that encourage women to participate in the electoral process and improve women's capacity to cast informed votes in free and fair elections;

(b) To encourage political parties to remove all barriers that directly or indirectly discriminate against the participation of women, in order to ensure that women have the right to participate fully at all levels of decision-making in all internal policy-making structures and nominating processes and in the leadership of political parties on equal terms with men;

(c) To encourage political parties to actively seek qualified women candidates, to provide training in conducting campaigns, public speaking, fund-raising and parliamentary procedure and to include qualified women and men on their party lists for elective office, where such lists exist;

(d) To strive to ensure that information about candidates, political party platforms, voting procedures, including voter registration, and electoral law is available to women on an equal basis with men;

(e) To support initiatives, including public-private partnerships and exchange programmes, to expand women's political skills, which include imparting or enhancing skills on how to vote, advocate, manage and govern, run for public office and serve as elected and appointed officials;

(f) To promote the participation of young people, especially women, in civil society organizations to enable them to acquire experience, skills and capacities that are transferable to the field of political participation;

(g) To encourage the establishment of and the support of existing non-governmental organizations that provide training in leadership, decision-making, public-speaking skills, use of information and communication technologies, confidence-building and political campaigning;

(h) To intensify efforts to increase the number of women in public bodies, including through research into barriers to women's access to high-level public appointments;

(i) To promote recruitment and career-development programmes that provide women equal access to managerial, entrepreneurial, technical and leadership training, in order to better enable them to assume legislative, judicial and executive positions in government;

(j) To continue to study links between poverty eradication, the empowerment of women, in particular with regard to women's political participation, and to compile and widely disseminate good practices and lessons learned;

(k) To promote equal opportunities for women to gain appointment to advisory and decision-making bodies and promotion to senior positions by, inter alia, reviewing the criteria for recruitment, appointment and promotion, to ensure that such criteria are relevant to and do not discriminate against women;

(l) To develop programmes to educate and train women and girls in using the media and information and communication technologies in order to obtain and impart information, be informed voters, network, communicate with potential voters and raise campaign funds;

(m) To encourage the media to recognize the importance of women's participation in the political process, provide fair and balanced coverage of male and female candidates, cover participation in women's political organizations and ensure coverage of issues that have a particular impact on women;

3. *Urges* States and the United Nations system to increase the participation of women at all levels of decision-making in conflict resolution and peace processes;

4. *Invites* non-governmental organizations and other actors of civil society:

(a) To advocate at all levels to enable women to influence political, economic and social decisions, processes and systems, including by building and strengthening networks among women;

(b) To establish, consistent with data-protection legislation, databases on women and their qualifications for use in appointing women to senior decision-making and advisory positions, for dissemination to Governments, regional and international organizations and private enterprise, political parties and other relevant bodies;

(c) To increase coordination and cooperation in supporting women and to continue to present women's concerns and experiences to Governments;

5. *Requests* the Secretary-General, in his report to the Commission on the Status of Women at its fiftieth session, to include information on the participation of women in politics at all levels, bearing in mind that in 2006 the Commission will consider the item entitled "Equal participation of women and men in decision-making processes at all levels", and encourages Governments to cooperate with the Secretary-General by providing precise data on the political participation of women at all levels.

Violence against women

In accordance with the multi-year (2002-2006) programme of work adopted by Economic and Social Council resolution 2001/4 [YUN 2001, p. 1084], the Commission on the Status of Women had before it a report of the Secretary-General [E/CN.6/2003/7 & Corr.1] on women's human rights and elimination of all forms of violence against women and girls, as defined in the Beijing Platform for Action, [YUN 1995, p. 1170] and the outcome documents of the twenty-third special session of the General Assembly, as annexed to Assembly resolutions S/23-2 [YUN 2000, p. 1084] and S/23-3 [ibid., p. 1085]. Owing to the broad nature of violence, the report focused on the one form of violence that had reached worldwide proportions—trafficking in women and girls.

The report reviewed activities undertaken by the UN system regarding trafficking in women and girls, which, the Secretary-General said, had expanded since the Assembly's 2000 special session. It described regional efforts against trafficking and summarized the discussion and recommendations of an expert group meeting on the issue in November 2002.

Commission action. In March, the Commission on the Status of Women held a panel discussion on women's human rights and elimination of all forms of violence against women and girls, as defined in the Beijing Platform for Action and the outcome document of the Assembly's twenty-third special session, which focused on domestic violence and trafficking in women and girls.

On 25 March [E/2003/27 (dec. 47/103)], the Commission took note of the Secretary-General's report (above).

GENERAL ASSEMBLY ACTION

On 22 December [meeting 77], the General Assembly, on the recommendation of the Third Committee [A/58/501], adopted **resolution 58/147** without vote [agenda item 110].

Elimination of domestic violence against women

The General Assembly,

Reaffirming the obligation of all States to promote and protect all human rights and fundamental freedoms, as stated in the Universal Declaration of Human Rights as well as in other relevant international instruments, and reaffirming also that discrimination on the basis of sex is contrary to the Charter of the United Nations, the Convention on the Elimination of All Forms of Discrimination against Women and other international human rights instruments and that its elimination is an integral part of efforts towards the elimination of violence against women,

Recalling the Vienna Declaration and Programme of Action adopted by the World Conference on Human Rights, the Declaration on the Elimination of Violence against Women, the Beijing Declaration and Platform for Action adopted by the Fourth World Conference on Women and the Programme of Action of the International Conference on Population and Development, as well as the follow-up action by the Commission on the Status of Women on violence against women and the outcome documents of the twenty-third special session of the General Assembly, entitled "Women 2000: gender equality, development and peace for the twenty-first century",

Recalling also all its previous resolutions on the elimination of violence against women,

Taking note of Commission on Human Rights resolution 2003/45 of 23 April 2003 on the elimination of violence against women, as well as all its previous relevant resolutions on this issue,

Bearing in mind that domestic violence against women and girls is a human rights issue,

Recognizing that domestic violence against women is, inter alia, a societal problem and a manifestation of unequal power relations between women and men,

Recognizing also that both men and women have and should take responsibility for promoting gender equality,

Recognizing further the serious immediate and long-term implications for health, including sexual and reproductive health, that domestic violence against women can present for individuals and families,

Recognizing the implications of domestic violence for the social and economic development of communities and States,

Underlining the importance of the empowerment of women and their economic independence as critical tools to prevent and eliminate domestic violence against women,

1. *Recognizes:*

(a) That domestic violence is violence that occurs within the private sphere, generally between individuals who are related through blood or intimacy;

(b) That domestic violence is one of the most common and least visible forms of violence against women and that its consequences affect many areas of the lives of victims;

(c) That domestic violence can take many different forms, including physical, psychological and sexual violence;

(d) That domestic violence is of public concern and requires States to take serious action to protect victims and prevent domestic violence;

(e) That domestic violence can include economic deprivation and isolation and that such conduct may cause imminent harm to the safety, health or well-being of women;

2. *Welcomes:*

(a) The activities and initiatives of States aimed at the elimination of domestic violence against women, including legal, educational, economic, social and other measures;

(b) The work of the Special Rapporteur of the Commission on Human Rights on violence against women, its causes and consequences, and takes note of the report entitled "Developments in the area of violence against women (1994-2002)";

(c) The efforts undertaken by United Nations bodies, funds and programmes, including the United Nations Children's Fund and the United Nations Population Fund, to address the issue of domestic violence and encourages them to coordinate their efforts, and, in particular, expresses its appreciation for the initiatives of the United Nations Development Fund for Women to combat violence against women at the international, regional and national levels, as well as the *World Report on Violence and Health* launched by the World Health Organization in 2002, particularly its consideration of gender-based violence;

(d) The work carried out by civil society, including non-governmental organizations, such as women's organizations, and community-based organizations and individuals, aimed at the elimination of domestic violence against women, inter alia, by raising awareness of its harmful effects, and in the provision of support services to women victims of violence;

3. *Strongly condemns* all forms of domestic violence against women and girls, and in this regard, calls for the elimination of all forms of gender-based violence in the family, including where condoned by the State;

4. *Expresses its concern:*

(a) That women continue to be victims of domestic violence and at the continuing occurrence in all regions of the world of domestic violence, which takes many different forms, and at failure to prosecute and punish the perpetrators;

(b) That domestic violence, including sexual violence in marriage, is still treated as a private matter in some countries;

5. *Stresses* that States have an obligation to exercise due diligence to prevent, investigate and punish the perpetrators of domestic violence against women and to provide protection to the victims, and also stresses that not to do so violates and impairs or nullifies the enjoyment of their human rights and fundamental freedoms;

6. *Reaffirms* the commitment of States to establish legislation and/or strengthen appropriate mechanisms to handle criminal matters relating to all forms of domestic violence, including marital rape and sexual abuse of women and girls, and to ensure that such cases are brought to justice swiftly;

7. *Calls upon* States:

(a) To adopt, strengthen and implement legislation that prohibits domestic violence, prescribes punitive measures and establishes adequate legal protection against domestic violence and periodically to review, evaluate and revise these laws and regulations so as to ensure their effectiveness in eliminating domestic violence;

(b) To make domestic sexual violence a criminal offence and to ensure proper investigation and prosecution of perpetrators;

(c) To adopt and/or strengthen policies and legislation in order to strengthen preventive measures, protect the human rights of victims, ensure proper investigation and prosecution of perpetrators and provide legal and social assistance to victims of domestic violence, and to adopt policies with regard to the rehabilitation of perpetrators;

(d) To intensify measures aimed at preventing domestic violence against women;

(e) To ensure greater protection for women, inter alia, by means of, where appropriate, orders restraining violent spouses from entering the family home, or by banning violent spouses from contacting the victim;

(f) To provide or facilitate the provision of adequate training, inter alia, gender-awareness training, to all professionals who deal with domestic violence, in particular with victims of domestic violence, police officers, judicial and legal personnel, health personnel, educators, youth workers and social workers;

(g) To provide or facilitate the provision of assistance to victims of domestic violence in lodging police reports and receiving treatment and support, which may include the setting up of one-stop centres, as well as the establishment of safe shelters and centres for victims of domestic violence;

(h) To protect women in the process of seeking redress from further victimization because of gender-insensitive laws or practices;

(i) To establish and/or strengthen police response protocols and procedures to ensure that all appropriate actions are taken to protect victims of domestic violence and to prevent further acts of domestic violence;

(j) To take measures to ensure the protection of women subjected to violence, access to just and effective remedies, inter alia, through compensation and indemnification and healing of victims, and the rehabilitation of perpetrators;

(k) To intensify efforts to raise collective and individual awareness about violence against women, including through human rights education, to highlight the role of men and boys in the prevention and elimination of domestic violence against women, and to encourage and support initiatives to promote attitudinal and behavioural change on the part of, and the rehabilitation of, perpetrators of violence against women;

(l) To encourage the efforts of the media to engage in awareness-raising campaigns;

(m) To take all measures to empower women and strengthen their economic independence, including through equal remuneration for equal work, and increased job opportunities for women, as well as equal access to and control over economic resources, including land, credit, microcredit and traditional saving schemes such as women's banks and cooperatives, and by ensuring property rights and the right to inheritance, with a view to reducing women's vulnerability to all forms of violence, including domestic violence;

(n) Not to invoke any custom, tradition or religious consideration to avoid their obligations to eliminate violence against women;

(o) To consider, as a matter of priority, becoming parties to the Convention on the Elimination of All Forms of Discrimination against Women;

(p) That are parties to the Convention to include in their reports to the Committee on the Elimination of Discrimination against Women information on legal and policy measures adopted and implemented in their efforts to prevent and eliminate domestic violence against women and to cross-reference that information, where appropriate, in reports to other human rights treaty bodies;

(q) To cooperate closely with relevant specialized agencies and United Nations funds and programmes, as well as with regional intergovernmental organizations, as appropriate, and relevant community and non-governmental organizations, including women's organizations, in an effort to eliminate violence against women;

(r) To collect, update and improve the collection of data on violence against women, including through sex-disaggregated information systems, which should be made public and disseminated widely;

8. *Emphasizes* the need for technical and financial assistance to developing countries in their efforts to eliminate domestic violence against women from United Nations funds and programmes, international and regional financial institutions and bilateral and multilateral donors, and civil society, as well as the need for assistance from the international community to non-governmental organizations and community-based groups active in this field;

9. *Encourages* States to contribute or increase their contribution to the Trust Fund in Support of Actions

to Eliminate Violence against Women managed by the United Nations Development Fund for Women;

10. *Invites:*

(a) Relevant specialized agencies, United Nations bodies, regional intergovernmental organizations and non-governmental organizations to exchange information on the subject of the present resolution, and encourages the exchange of such information between non-governmental organizations active in this field and the relevant human rights treaty bodies;

(b) The relevant human rights treaty bodies to continue to address this issue, where appropriate;

11. *Decides* to continue its consideration of this question at its sixtieth session under the item entitled "Advancement of women".

Also on 22 December [meeting 77], the Assembly, on the recommendation of the Third Committee [A/58/508/Add.2], adopted **resolution 58/185** without vote [agenda item 117(*b*)].

In-depth study on all forms of violence against women

The General Assembly,

Affirming that the term "violence against women" means any act of gender-based violence that results in, or is likely to result in, physical, sexual or psychological harm or suffering to women, including threats of such acts, coercion or arbitrary deprivation of liberty, whether occurring in public or in private life,

Requests the Secretary-General:

(a) To conduct an in-depth study, from existing available resources and, if necessary, supplemented by voluntary contributions, on all forms and manifestations of violence against women, as identified in the Beijing Declaration and Platform for Action adopted at the Fourth World Conference on Women and the outcome of the twenty-third special session of the General Assembly entitled "Women 2000: gender equality, development and peace for the twenty-first century", and relevant documents, disaggregated by type of violence, and based on research undertaken and data collected at the national, regional and international levels, in particular in the following fields:

  (i) A statistical overview on all forms of violence against women, in order to better evaluate the scale of such violence, while identifying gaps in data collection and formulating proposals for assessing the extent of the problem;

  (ii) The causes of violence against women, including its root causes and other contributing factors;

  (iii) The medium and long-term consequences of violence against women;

  (iv) The health, social and economic costs of violence against women;

  (v) The identification of best practice examples in areas including legislation, policies, programmes and effective remedies, and the efficiency of such mechanisms to the end of combating and eliminating violence against women;

(b) To cooperate closely with all relevant United Nations bodies, as well as with the Special Rapporteur of the Commission on Human Rights on violence against women, its causes and consequences, when preparing the study;

(c) To solicit information, including on strategies, policies, programmes and best practices, from Member States as well as relevant non-governmental organizations in the preparation of the study;

(d) To make the study available to all Member States and observers, as well as other United Nations stakeholders, and, on the basis of the study, to submit a report, with the study as an annex, to the General Assembly at its sixtieth session, under the item entitled "Advancement of women", including action-oriented recommendations, for consideration by States, encompassing, inter alia, effective remedies and prevention and rehabilitation measures;

(e) To submit a progress report on the study to the General Assembly at its fifty-ninth session under the item entitled "Advancement of women".

(See also pp. 777 and 780.)

Women migrant workers

In response to General Assembly resolution 56/131 [YUN 2001, p. 1058], the Secretary-General, in a July report [A/58/161], summarized information received from Member States, UN system entities and intergovernmental bodies on measures they had taken to address the issue of violence against women migrant workers. The Secretary-General stated that, although a number of countries had taken measures to address the violence, information on their impact remained limited. The lack of comprehensive and timely data on the number of women migrants and the violence and discrimination they suffered remained an obstacle to understanding the scale of the phenomenon and made it more difficult to design policies to combat such violence and discrimination. Information was also needed on the gender-specific impact of labour and immigration legislation, especially in respect of the enjoyment by women migrant workers of the full range of human rights. The Secretary-General called for improving access to legal protection for women seeking to migrate in search of work, in order to reduce their vulnerability to exploitation, ill-treatment and trafficking; exploring the link between migration and trafficking and addressing the two issues, with a particular focus on the need to protect women from all forms of violence, irrespective of their immigrant status; encouraging Governments and other actors to provide information on migration and trafficking in their legislative and other measures; and encouraging other actors to place enhanced emphasis on migration and trafficking. Governments were urged to ratify international instruments dealing with migration issues, particularly the International Convention on the Protection of the Rights of All Migrant Workers and Members of Their Families (see p. 676), and the United Nations Convention against Transnational Organized Crime and its supplementary Protocols on trafficking in persons and on migrant smuggling (see p. 1125).

GENERAL ASSEMBLY ACTION

On 22 December [meeting 77], the General Assembly, on the recommendation of the Third Committee [A/58/501], adopted **resolution 58/143** without vote [agenda item 110].

Violence against women migrant workers

The General Assembly,

Recalling all of its previous resolutions on violence against women migrant workers and those adopted by the Commission on the Status of Women, the Commission on Human Rights and the Commission on Crime Prevention and Criminal Justice, and the Declaration on the Elimination of Violence against Women,

Reaffirming the provisions concerning women migrant workers contained in the outcome documents of the World Conference on Human Rights, the International Conference on Population and Development, the Fourth World Conference on Women and the World Summit for Social Development and their five-year reviews,

Noting the various activities initiated by entities in the United Nations system, such as the Hemispheric Conference on International Migration: Human Rights and the Trafficking in Persons in the Americas, organized by the Economic Commission for Latin America and the Caribbean and the International Organization for Migration, held at Santiago from 20 to 22 November 2002, as well as other activities that continue to assess and alleviate the plight of women migrant workers,

Emphasizing the need for objective, comprehensive, broad-based information, possibly including a database for research and analysis, and a wide exchange of experience and lessons learned by individual Member States and civil society in the formulation of policies and concrete strategies to address the problem of violence against women migrant workers,

Encouraging the continuing participation of civil society in developing and implementing appropriate measures to support innovative partnerships among public agencies, non-governmental organizations and other members of civil society for combating violence against women migrant workers,

Noting the large numbers of women from developing countries and some countries with economies in transition who continue to venture forth to more affluent countries in search of a living for themselves and their families as a consequence of poverty, unemployment and other socio-economic conditions, and acknowledging the duty of the countries of origin to try to create conditions that provide employment and economic security for their citizens,

Expressing deep concern at the continuing reports of grave abuses and acts of violence committed against women migrant workers,

Realizing that the movement of a significant number of women migrant workers may be facilitated and made possible by means of fraudulent or irregular documentation and sham marriages with the object of migration, that this may be facilitated through, among other things, the Internet, and that these women migrant workers are more vulnerable to abuse and exploitation,

Acknowledging the economic benefits that accrue to both the country of origin and the country of destination from the employment of women migrant workers,

Recognizing the importance of joint and collaborative approaches and strategies at the bilateral, regional, interregional and international levels in protecting and promoting the rights and welfare of women migrant workers,

Recognizing also the importance of exploring the link between migration and trafficking,

Encouraged by some measures adopted by some countries of destination to alleviate the plight of women migrant workers residing in their areas of jurisdiction,

Underlining the important role of relevant United Nations treaty bodies in monitoring the implementation of human rights conventions and the relevant special procedures, within their respective mandates, in addressing the problem of violence against women migrant workers and in protecting and promoting their rights and welfare,

1. *Takes note* of the report of the Secretary-General;

2. *Also takes note* of the reports of the Special Rapporteur of the Commission on Human Rights on the human rights of migrants and of the Special Rapporteur of the Commission on Human Rights on violence against women, its causes and consequences, with regard to violence against women migrant workers, and encourages the Special Rapporteurs to continue to address the issue of violence against women migrant workers and their human rights, in particular the problems of gender-based violence and of discrimination, as well as trafficking in women;

3. *Acknowledges with appreciation* the entry into force of the International Convention on the Protection of the Rights of All Migrant Workers and Members of their Families on 1 July 2003;

4. *Requests* all Governments to continue to cooperate fully with both Special Rapporteurs in the performance of their tasks and mandated duties and to furnish all information requested, including by reacting promptly to the urgent appeals of the Special Rapporteurs;

5. *Encourages* Governments, in particular those of the countries of origin and destination, to make available to the Special Rapporteur on the human rights of migrants information on violence against women migrant workers, with a view to requesting the Special Rapporteur to recommend concrete measures and actions to address the problem;

6. *Also encourages* Governments to give serious consideration to inviting the Special Rapporteur to visit their countries so as to enable her to fulfil the mandate effectively;

7. *Urges* concerned Governments, in particular those of the countries of origin and destination, to strengthen further their national efforts to protect and promote the rights and welfare of women migrant workers, including through sustained bilateral, regional, interregional and international cooperation, by developing strategies and joint action and taking into account the innovative approaches and experiences of individual Member States, and to establish and main-

tain continuing dialogues to facilitate the exchange of information;

8. *Also urges* concerned Governments, in particular those of the countries of origin and destination, to support and allocate appropriate resources for programmes aimed at strengthening preventive action, in particular information for target groups, education and campaigns to increase public awareness of this issue at the national and grass-roots levels, in cooperation with non-governmental organizations;

9. *Notes with appreciation* the adoption by Member States, including countries of origin, transit and destination, of measures to inform women migrant workers of their rights and the benefits to which they are entitled, and encourages other Member States to adopt appropriate measures in this regard;

10. *Calls upon* concerned Governments, in particular those of the countries of origin and destination, if they have not done so, to put in place penal and criminal sanctions to punish perpetrators of violence against women migrant workers and, to the extent possible, to provide and to encourage non-governmental organizations to provide victims of violence with the full range of immediate assistance and protection, such as counselling, legal and consular assistance, temporary shelter and other measures that will allow them to be present during the judicial process, as well as to establish reintegration and rehabilitation schemes for returning women migrant workers to their countries of origin;

11. *Encourages* concerned Governments, in particular those of the countries of origin and destination, to support and, if they have not done so, to formulate and implement training programmes for their law enforcers, prosecutors and service providers with a view to instilling among those public sector workers the necessary skills and attitude to ensure the delivery of proper and professional interventions for women migrant workers who are subjected to abuse and violence;

12. *Also encourages* concerned Governments, in particular those of the countries of origin and destination, to adopt measures or strengthen existing ones to regulate the recruitment and deployment of women migrant workers, and to consider the adoption of appropriate legal measures against intermediaries who deliberately encourage the clandestine movement of workers and who exploit women migrant workers;

13. *Invites* Governments to identify the causes of undocumented migration and its economic, social and demographic impact, as well as its implications for the formulation and application of social, economic and migration policies, including those relating to women migrant workers;

14. *Encourages* concerned Governments, in particular those of the countries of origin, transit and destination, to avail themselves of the expertise of the United Nations, including the Statistics Division of the Secretariat and other relevant bodies, such as the International Research and Training Institute for the Advancement of Women, to develop appropriate national data-collection methodologies that will generate comparable data on violence against women migrant workers as bases for research and analysis of the subject;

15. *Encourages* Member States to consider signing and ratifying or acceding to relevant International Labour Organization conventions and to consider signing and ratifying or acceding to the International Convention on the Protection of the Rights of All Migrant Workers and Members of Their Families, as well as the Slavery Convention of 1926;

16. *Welcomes* the imminent entry into force of the Protocol to Prevent, Suppress and Punish Trafficking in Persons, Especially Women and Children, supplementing the United Nations Convention against Transnational Organized Crime, and the adoption by the General Assembly of the Protocol against the Smuggling of Migrants by Land, Sea and Air, supplementing the United Nations Convention against Transnational Organized Crime, and encourages Governments to consider signing and ratifying or acceding to the Protocols;

17. *Encourages* the Committee on the Elimination of Discrimination against Women to consider developing a general recommendation on the situation of women migrant workers;

18. *Requests* the Secretary-General to report to the General Assembly at its sixtieth session on the problem of violence against women migrant workers and on the implementation of the present resolution, taking into account updated information from the organizations of the United Nations system, in particular the International Labour Organization, the United Nations Development Programme, the United Nations Development Fund for Women and the International Research and Training Institute for the Advancement of Women, as well as the International Organization for Migration and other relevant sources, including non-governmental organizations.

(See also pp. 706 and 778.)

Women's health

Women, the girl child and HIV/AIDS

In a March resolution on women, the girl child and HIV/AIDS [E/2003/27 (res. 47/1)], the Commission on the Status of Women emphasized that the advancement of women was the key to reversing the pandemic. It called for enhanced efforts by all relevant actors to include a gender perspective in developing HIV/AIDS programmes and policies and in training personnel involved in implementing the programmes. The Secretary-General was asked, in his reports on HIV/AIDS (see p. 1241), to take a gender perspective into account.

Traditional practices affecting the health of women and girls

In response to General Assembly resolution 56/128 [YUN 2001, p. 1063], the Secretary-General, in a July report on traditional or customary practices affecting the health of women and girls [A/58/169], summarized information received from 28 Member States regarding measures they had taken to counter the problem. Similar information was provided by UN system entities and non-governmental organizations (NGOs).

The Secretary-General concluded that initiatives at the national, regional and international levels reflected the increased recognition of the need for the prevention and elimination of harmful traditional practices. Consultative and participatory initiatives involving men and women in affected societies, including community and traditional leaders, as well as judicial, legal, healthcare, educational and media personnel, had been effective tools in combating harmful traditional practices. Member States, NGOs and UN entities should continue and strengthen measures to eliminate the harmful practices, and strengthen their cooperation with assistance from donor Governments and international organizations. The Secretary-General advocated expanding information and data collection on the trends and prevalence of the practices and conducting progress assessment and impact-monitoring studies on implemented initiatives so that appropriate and effective strategies could be documented and shared, and lessons learned adapted and replicated in other relevant settings.

Women and human rights

Women in Afghanistan

In response to Economic and Social Council resolution 2002/4 [YUN 2002, p. 1149], the Secretary-General, in a January report on the situation of women and girls in Afghanistan [E/CN.6/2003/4], reviewed developments in 2002, focusing on steps taken by the Afghan Transitional Administration (TA) to raise the status of women and UN system activities to assist the TA. Afghanistan's emergence from 24 years of conflict (see p. 289) had led to positive changes in women's lives. Women were re-emerging as a political and economic force, participated in decision-making on the peace process and reconstruction of the country, appointed to serve in Government and returning to the workforce and gaining access to education. However, many women continued to face gross violations of their rights and were victims of insecurity. In addition, Taliban-like restrictions by local leaders continued to be applied to women in some parts of the country. The Secretary-General made recommendations to the TA and the UN system, donor countries and civil society, in order to further strengthen the status of women and girls in Afghanistan and their full participation in the reconstruction and development of their country.

ECONOMIC AND SOCIAL COUNCIL ACTION

On 22 July [meeting 44], the Economic and Social Council, on the recommendation of the Commission on the Status of Women [E/2003/27], adopted **resolution 2003/43** without vote [agenda item 14 (a)].

Situation of women and girls in Afghanistan

The Economic and Social Council,

Guided by the Charter of the United Nations, the Universal Declaration of Human Rights, the International Covenants on Human Rights, the Convention against Torture and Other Cruel, Inhuman or Degrading Treatment or Punishment, the Convention on the Elimination of All Forms of Discrimination against Women, the Declaration on the Elimination of Violence against Women, the Convention on the Rights of the Child and the Optional Protocols thereto on the involvement of children in armed conflict and on the sale of children, child prostitution and child pornography, the Beijing Declaration and Platform for Action, the further actions and initiatives to implement the Beijing Declaration and Platform for Action, adopted by the General Assembly at its twenty-third special session, accepted humanitarian rules as set out in the Geneva Conventions of 12 August 1949, and other instruments of human rights and international law,

Recalling that Afghanistan is a party to the Convention on the Prevention and Punishment of the Crime of Genocide, the International Covenant on Civil and Political Rights, the International Covenant on Economic, Social and Cultural Rights, the Convention against Torture and Other Cruel, Inhuman or Degrading Treatment or Punishment, the Convention on the Elimination of All Forms of Discrimination against Women, the Convention on the Rights of the Child, the Geneva Conventions of 12 August 1949, and the Rome Statute of the International Criminal Court,

Reaffirming that all States have an obligation to promote and protect human rights and fundamental freedoms,

Recalling the importance of the implementation of Security Council resolution 1325(2000) of 31 October 2000, on women and peace and security, and Council resolution 1460(2003) of 30 January 2003, on children and armed conflict,

Recalling also the Agreement on Provisional Arrangements in Afghanistan pending the Re-establishment of Permanent Government Institutions, signed in Bonn, Germany, on 5 December 2001,

Recalling further the funding commitments made at the International Conference on Reconstruction Assistance to Afghanistan, held in Tokyo on 21 and 22 January 2002,

Welcoming the establishment of the Afghan Independent Human Rights Commission in June 2002,

Welcoming also the holding of the Emergency Loya Jirga in June 2002, establishing the Afghan Transitional Authority, and the participation of more than two hundred women in the meeting,

Welcoming further the continuing commitment of the Afghan Transitional Administration to the full enjoyment of human rights and fundamental freedoms by women and girls, to the active participation of Afghan women in political, economic and social life, to the education of girls as well as boys and to the opportunity for women to work outside the home,

Welcoming the return to school of more than 3 million children, including 1 million girls, since March

2002, and the international support that has made it possible,

Welcoming also the inclusion of women in the Transitional Administration, the Judicial Reform Commission, the Independent Human Rights Commission and the Constitutional Drafting Commission, and stressing the importance of the full and effective participation of women in all decision-making processes regarding the future of Afghanistan,

Welcoming further the fact that the National Development Framework of the Transitional Administration reflects the needs of, and the importance of the role to be taken by, women and girls in the process of peace-building, reconstruction and development,

Welcoming the efforts of Afghanistan's neighbouring countries, which have hosted millions of Afghan refugees, especially women and children, and have provided humanitarian assistance in many areas, such as education, health and other basic services,

Recognizing that Afghan women are primary stakeholders and agents of change, who must have the opportunity to identify their own needs, interests and priorities in all sectors of society as full partners in the rebuilding of their society,

Emphasizing that a safe environment, free from violence, discrimination and abuse, for all Afghans, is essential for a viable and sustainable recovery and reconstruction process,

1. *Welcomes:*

(a) The ongoing commitments made by the Transitional Authority to recognize, protect and promote all human rights and fundamental freedoms, and to respect and promote respect for international humanitarian law;

(b) The ratification by the Transitional Authority of the Convention on the Elimination of All Forms of Discrimination against Women on 5 March 2003;

2. *Also welcomes* the report of the Secretary-General to the Commission on the Status of Women;

3. *Urges* the Transitional Authority:

(a) To ensure that any legislative, administrative and other measures support the full enjoyment of women and girls of human rights and fundamental freedoms;

(b) To enable the full, equal and effective participation of women and girls in civil, cultural, economic, political and social life throughout the country at all levels;

(c) To protect the right to freedom of movement, expression and association for women and girls;

(d) To provide the necessary support and resources to enable the Ministry of Women's Affairs to function effectively, so that the Ministry can fulfil its task in promoting gender equality and the empowerment of women and develop the capacity to act as a catalyst for gender mainstreaming throughout the Transitional Administration;

(e) To ensure that the Judicial Reform Commission, the Constitutional Drafting Commission and the Independent Human Rights Commission have adequate resources to fulfil their mandates and ensure that gender perspectives are consistent with international standards;

(f) To affirm full support for the full, equal and effective participation of women in the constitutional process and in the Constitutional Loya Jirga, and to ensure that the principle of equality between men and women and the full enjoyment of human rights and fundamental freedoms by women and girls are guaranteed by the new Constitution;

(g) To continue its efforts to re-establish the rule of law, in accordance with international standards, including by ensuring that law enforcement agencies respect and uphold human rights and fundamental freedoms, with particular emphasis on access to justice for women;

(h) To continue its efforts to reflect a gender perspective in the training and activities of its police, prosecutors and judiciary, and to promote the recruitment of Afghan women in all ranks;

(i) To review and improve the practices of law enforcement personnel when dealing with women victims of violence, particularly those accused of offences based on tradition or imprisoned for social reasons to protect them from violence by family members;

(j) To ensure that gender-sensitive approaches are applied in the development and application of procedures during data collection for the census and the registration of voters to deliver universal suffrage and the full participation of women in the national elections in 2004;

(k) To ensure the equal right of women and girls to education, the effective functioning of schools throughout the country and the admission of women and girls to all levels of education;

(l) To respect the equal right of women to work and promote their reintegration into employment in all sectors and at all levels of Afghan society;

(m) To protect the equal right of women and girls to security of person, and to bring to justice those responsible for violence against women and girls;

(n) To Initiate rapid demobilization and disarmament and facilitate the reintegration of those, in particular women and girls, who have participated in or have otherwise been affected by war into society and work;

(o) To raise awareness of the need to prevent and eliminate violence, including domestic violence, against women, with the aim of changing the attitudes and behaviour that allow such crimes to take place, and strengthen efforts to prevent and eliminate violence against women by using legislative measures;

(p) To ensure the effective and equal access of women and girls to the facilities necessary to protect the right to the enjoyment of the highest attainable standard of physical and mental health in accordance with the obligations of Afghanistan under the International Covenant on Economic, Social and Cultural Rights;

(q) To ensure the equal right of women to own land and other property, inter alia, through the right to inheritance, and undertake administrative reforms and other necessary measures to give women the same right as men to credit, capital, appropriate technologies and access to and control over natural resources as well as access to markets and information;

4. *Encourages* the continuing efforts of the United Nations and its agencies, donors and civil society, guided by Security Council resolution 1325(2000) on women and peace and security:

(a) To provide financial and technical assistance, including support to the Ministry of Women's Affairs and the Independent Human Rights Commission, to ensure the full enjoyment of human rights and fundamental freedoms by women and girls so as to strengthen the capacity of Afghan women to participate fully and effectively in conflict resolution and peacebuilding efforts and in civil, political, economic, cultural and social life;

(b) To support fully the Transitional Authority regarding the participation of women in society, inter alia, by providing support to ministries to develop their capacity to mainstream gender issues into their programmes;

(c) To provide technical and other relevant assistance so that the judicial system has the capacity to adhere to international standards of human rights;

(d) To support measures to ensure the full enjoyment of human rights and fundamental freedoms by women and girls, and to hold accountable those who were responsible for gross violations of human rights in the past and ensure that full investigations are conducted and perpetrators brought to justice in accordance with international standards in order to combat impunity;

5. *Invites* the United Nations system, international and non-governmental organizations, and donors:

(a) To ensure a human rights–based approach and coherent policy and resources for gender mainstreaming in all programmes and operations, based on the principles of non-discrimination and equality between women and men, and ensure that women benefit equally with men from such programmes in all sectors;

(b) To ensure the full and effective participation of Afghan women in all stages of humanitarian assistance, recovery, reconstruction and development, including planning, programme development, implementation, monitoring and evaluation;

(c) To support the elements of civil society active in the field of human rights and encourage the involvement of women therein;

(d) To ensure that all their international and national personnel, prior to beginning their service, receive training in gender equality as well as appropriate training in the history, culture and traditions of Afghanistan and are fully familiar with and guided by international standards of human rights;

(e) To integrate efforts to improve the health status of women within all reconstruction efforts, especially through access to skilled prenatal care, increasing access to skilled birth attendance, education programmes on basic health issues, community information activities and emergency obstetric care;

(f) To continue to support measures for the employment of women and the integration of a gender perspective into all social, development and reconstruction programmes, taking into account the special needs of widows and returning refugee and displaced women and girls as well as those living in rural areas;

6. *Urges* the Secretary-General to ensure that the post of Senior Gender Adviser in the United Nations Assistance Mission in Afghanistan is filled immediately and with due regard to the need for continuity in this task;

7. *Requests* the Secretary-General to continue to review the situation of women and girls in Afghanistan and to submit to the Commission on the Status of Women at its forty-eighth session a report on progress made in the implementation of the present resolution.

(See also p. 779.)

Palestinian women

In response to Economic and Social Council resolution 2002/25 [YUN 2002, p. 453], a report of the Secretary-General [E/CN.6/2003/3] reviewed the situation of and assistance to Palestinian women during the period from September 2001 to September 2002 (see p. 493).

On 22 July, the Economic and Social Council, in **resolution 2003/42**, took action on the situation of and assistance to Palestinian women (see p. 494).

Older women in society

In response to General Assembly resolutions 57/167 [YUN 2002, p. 1197] and 57/177 [ibid., p. 1153], the Secretary-General submitted a July report [A/58/160] on the follow-up to the 2002 Second World Assembly on Ageing [YUN 2002, p. 1193]. The report introduced the road map for the implementation of the Madrid International Plan of Action on Ageing, which was adopted at the 2002 World Assembly [ibid., p. 1194]; highlighted the Plan's main gender dimensions; reviewed progress in defining the modalities for the review and appraisal of the Plan; and outlined major developments during the first year of the implementation process. (See also p. 1219.)

Women and development

In response to General Assembly resolution 56/188 [YUN 2001, p. 1069], the Secretary-General submitted a July report [A/58/135], which described the attention paid at UN conferences and summits to the concerns of women and gender equality goals in the context of the implementation of the Millennium Declaration [YUN 2000, p. 49] and the promotion of economic growth, poverty eradication and sustainable development.

The Secretary-General concluded that recent UN conferences and summits had made progress in integrating women's concerns and gender perspectives into the preparatory processes and final outcomes. However, progress achieved had to be translated into practical action at the national level and a strong focus on implementing policies, norms and recommendations was required. The Secretary-General proposed a series of recommendations to the Assembly regarding increased attention to gender perspectives and more effective monitoring of progress.

GENERAL ASSEMBLY ACTION

On 23 December [meeting 78], the General Assembly, on the recommendation of the Second (Economic and Financial) Committee [A/58/483/Add.1 & Corr.1], adopted **resolution 58/206** without vote [agenda item 93 (a)].

Women in development

The General Assembly,

Recalling its resolutions 52/195 of 18 December 1997, 54/210 of 22 December 1999 and 56/188 of 21 December 2001 and all its other resolutions on the integration of women in development, and the relevant resolutions and agreed conclusions, including those on women in the economy, adopted by the Commission on the Status of Women,

Recalling also the outcome of the twenty-third special session of the General Assembly, entitled "Women 2000: gender equality, development and peace for the twenty-first century",

Reaffirming the United Nations Millennium Declaration, which affirms that the equal rights and opportunities of women and men must be assured, and calls for, inter alia, the promotion of gender equality and the empowerment of women as being effective and essential in the combat of poverty, hunger and disease and in stimulating development that is truly sustainable,

Reaffirming also that gender equality is of fundamental importance for achieving sustained economic growth and sustainable development, in accordance with the relevant General Assembly resolutions and recent United Nations conferences, and that investing in the development of women and girls has a multiplier effect, in particular on productivity, efficiency and sustained economic growth,

Recognizing the significant contribution that women make to the economy and the major force that they represent for change and development in all sectors of the economy, especially in key areas such as agriculture, industry and services,

Reaffirming that women are key contributors to the economy and to combating poverty through both remunerated and unremunerated work at home, in the community and in the workplace and that the empowerment of women is a critical factor in the eradication of poverty,

Recognizing that population and development issues, education and training, health, nutrition, the environment, water supply, sanitation, housing, communications, science and technology, and employment opportunities are important elements for effective poverty eradication and the advancement and empowerment of women,

Recognizing also, in this context, the importance of respect for all human rights, including the right to development, and of a national and international environment that promotes, inter alia, justice, gender equality, equity, civil and political participation and political freedom for the advancement and empowerment of women,

Recognizing further that equal access to education and training, in particular in business, trade, administration, information and communication technologies and other new technologies, is essential for gender equality, the empowerment of women and poverty eradication,

Recognizing that the difficult socio-economic conditions that exist in many developing countries, in particular the least developed countries, have resulted in the acceleration of the feminization of poverty and that the empowerment of women is a critical factor in the eradication of poverty,

Recognizing also that poverty eradication and the achievement and preservation of peace are mutually reinforcing, and recognizing further that peace is inextricably linked to equality between women and men and to development,

Aware that, while globalization and liberalization processes have created employment opportunities for women in many countries, they have also made women, especially in developing countries and in particular in the least developed countries, more vulnerable to problems caused by increased economic volatility,

Recognizing that some effects of market liberalization may deepen the socio-economic marginalization of women in the agricultural sector, including through the loss of employment among small-scale farmers, who are more likely to be women than men, and emphasizing that women who are small-scale farmers need special support and empowerment in order to be able to meet the challenges and take advantage of the opportunities of agricultural market liberalization,

Recognizing also that enhanced trade opportunities for developing countries, including through trade liberalization, will improve the economic condition of those societies, including women, which is of particular importance in rural communities,

Aware that, while women represent an important and growing proportion of business owners, their contribution to economic and social development is constrained by, inter alia, the lack of equal access of women and men to, and control over, credit, technology, support services, land and information,

Concerned that the continuing discrimination against women, the denial or lack of equal rights and access to education, training and credit facilities and the lack of control over land, capital, technology and other areas of production impede their full and equal contribution to, and equal opportunity to benefit from, development,

Emphasizing the promotion of programmes aimed at financial intermediation, with a view to ensuring the access of rural women to credit and to agricultural inputs and implements and, in particular, to easing collateral requirements for access to finance by women,

Expressing its concern about the underrepresentation of women in economic decision-making, and stressing the importance of mainstreaming a gender perspective in the formulation, implementation and evaluation of all policies,

Noting the importance of the organizations and bodies of the United Nations system, in particular its funds and programmes, including the United Nations Development Fund for Women, in facilitating the advancement of women in development, and recognizing the work done by the International Research and Training Institute for the Advancement of Women,

1. *Takes note* of the report of the Secretary-General entitled "The empowerment of women and integra-

tion of gender perspectives in the promotion of economic growth, poverty eradication and sustainable development";

2. *Reaffirms* the goals and commitments contained in the Beijing Declaration and Platform for Action and also in the political declaration and further actions and initiatives to implement the Beijing Declaration and Platform for Action adopted by the General Assembly at its twenty-third special session;

3. *Calls upon* Governments, the relevant entities of the United Nations system, within their respective mandates, and all relevant actors of civil society, including non-governmental organizations, to continue to take effective action to achieve full and effective implementation of the Beijing Declaration and Platform for Action and the outcome of the twenty-third special session of the General Assembly;

4. *Stresses* the importance of creating a favourable and conducive national and international environment in all fields of life for the effective integration of women in development;

5. *Urges* all Governments to develop and promote strategies to mainstream a gender perspective in the design and implementation of economic and development policies and in the monitoring and evaluation of related programmes of action;

6. *Recognizes* the need to mainstream a gender perspective in budget policies at all levels, and calls upon Governments to increase women's full and equal participation in economic decision-making through, inter alia, their engagement in the budgetary process;

7. *Also recognizes* the mutually reinforcing links between gender equality and poverty eradication, as well as the need to elaborate and implement, where appropriate, in consultation with civil society, comprehensive gender-sensitive poverty eradication strategies that address social, structural and macroeconomic issues;

8. *Further recognizes* the need to strengthen the capacity of Governments to incorporate a gender perspective in policies and decision-making, and encourages all Governments, international organizations, including the United Nations system, and other relevant stakeholders to assist and support developing countries in integrating a gender perspective in all aspects of policy-making, including through the provision of technical assistance and financial resources;

9. *Stresses* the importance of developing national strategies for the promotion of sustainable and productive entrepreneurial activities that will generate income among disadvantaged women and women living in poverty;

10. *Urges* all Governments to ensure women's equal rights with men and their full and equal access to education, training, employment, technology and economic and financial resources, including credit, in particular for rural women and women in the informal sector, and to facilitate, where appropriate, the transition of women from the informal to the formal sector;

11. *Encourages* Governments, the private sector, non-governmental organizations and other actors of civil society to promote and protect the rights of women workers, to take action to remove structural and legal barriers as well as stereotypical attitudes to gender equality at work and to initiate positive steps to promote equal pay for equal work or work of equal value;

12. *Urges* all Governments to take all appropriate measures to eliminate discrimination against women with regard to their access to bank loans, mortgages and other forms of financial credit, giving special attention to poor, uneducated women, and to support women's access to legal assistance;

13. *Calls upon* Governments and entrepreneurial associations to facilitate the access of women, including young women and women entrepreneurs, to education and training in business, administration, and information and communication technologies;

14. *Recognizes* the role of microfinance, including microcredit, in the eradication of poverty, the empowerment of women and the generation of employment, notes in this regard the importance of sound national financial systems, and encourages the strengthening of existing and emerging microcredit institutions and their capacities, including through the support of international financial institutions;

15. *Stresses* the need for assistance to enable women in developing countries, particularly grass-roots women's groups, to have full access to and use of new technologies, including information technologies, for their empowerment;

16. *Urges* States to design and revise laws that ensure that women are accorded full and equal rights to own land and other property, including through inheritance, and to undertake administrative reforms and other necessary measures to give women the same right as men to credit, capital and appropriate technologies and access to markets and information;

17. *Calls upon* Governments to encourage the financial sector to mainstream a gender perspective in its policies and programmes, in particular by:

(*a*) Exploring viable options with respect to reaching people living in poverty, in particular women, including through international public and/or private funds;

(*b*) Designing savings schemes that are attractive to the poor, and to poor women in particular;

(*c*) Undertaking research to learn more about the characteristics, financial needs and performance of businesses owned by women;

(*d*) Working towards equal treatment for women clients through comprehensive gender-awareness training for staff at all levels and better representation of women in decision-making positions;

18. *Requests* Governments to ensure the full and equal participation of women in decision-making and in policy formulation and implementation at all levels so that their priorities, skills and potentials can be adequately reflected in national policy;

19. *Calls upon* Governments to promote, inter alia, through legislation, family-friendly and gender-sensitive work environments, the facilitation of breast-feeding for working mothers and the provision of the necessary care for working women's children and other dependants and to consider promoting policies and programmes, as appropriate, to enable men and women to reconcile their work, social and family responsibilities;

20. *Expresses its concern* that the HIV/AIDS pandemic reinforces gender inequalities, that women and girls bear a disproportionate share of the burden imposed by the HIV/AIDS crisis, that they are more easily infected, that they play a key role in care and that they

have become more vulnerable to poverty as a result of the HIV/AIDS crisis;

21. *Calls upon* the international community to make efforts to mitigate the effects of excess volatility and economic disruption, which have a disproportionately negative impact on women, and to enhance trade opportunities for developing countries in order to improve the economic situation of women;

22. *Urges* the international community, the United Nations system and relevant organizations to give priority to assisting the efforts of developing countries to ensure the full and effective participation of women in deciding and implementing development strategies and integrating gender concerns into national programmes, including by providing adequate resources to operational activities for development in support of the efforts of Governments to ensure full and equal access of women to health care, capital, education, training and technology, as well as full and equal participation in all decision-making;

23. *Recognizes* that a substantial increase in official development assistance and other resources will be required if developing countries are to achieve the internationally agreed development goals and objectives, including those contained in the United Nations Millennium Declaration, and that in order to build support for official development assistance, cooperation will be needed in further improving policies and development strategies, both nationally and internationally, to enhance aid effectiveness;

24. *Urges* developed countries that have not yet done so to make concrete efforts towards the target of 0.7 per cent of gross national product as official development assistance to developing countries and 0.15 to 0.20 per cent of the gross national product of developed countries to least developed countries, as reconfirmed at the Third United Nations Conference on the Least Developed Countries, held in Brussels from 14 to 20 May 2001, encourages developing countries to build on progress achieved in ensuring that official development assistance is used effectively to help to achieve development goals and targets, acknowledges the efforts of all donors, commends those donors whose official development assistance contributions exceed, reach or are increasing towards the targets, and stresses the importance of undertaking to examine the means and time frames for achieving the targets and goals;

25. *Encourages* the international community, the United Nations system, the private sector and civil society to continue to provide the necessary financial resources to assist national Governments in their efforts to meet the development targets and benchmarks agreed upon at the World Summit for Social Development, the Fourth World Conference on Women, the International Conference on Population and Development, the Millennium Summit, the International Conference on Financing for Development, the World Summit on Sustainable Development, the Second World Assembly on Ageing, the twenty-third and twenty-fourth special sessions of the General Assembly and other relevant United Nations conferences and summits;

26. *Encourages* the United Nations system and international and regional organizations, as appropriate, to assist Governments, at their request, in building institutional capacity and developing national action plans or further implementing existing action plans for the implementation of the Beijing Platform for Action;

27. *Urges* Governments to create and maintain a non-discriminatory and gender-sensitive legal environment by reviewing legislation, with a view to striving to remove discriminatory provisions as soon as possible, preferably by 2005, and eliminating legislative gaps that leave women and girls without protection of their rights and without effective recourse against gender-based discrimination, and encourages assistance to countries in achieving this aim;

28. *Urges* multilateral donors, and invites international financial institutions, within their respective mandates, and regional development banks to review and implement policies to support national efforts to ensure that a higher proportion of resources reach women, in particular in rural and remote areas;

29. *Welcomes* the convening of the first phase of the World Summit on the Information Society, held in Geneva from 10 to 12 December 2003, and its second phase, to be held in Tunis from 16 to 18 November 2005, and encourages Governments and all other stakeholders to integrate a gender perspective in the preparatory processes and outcome documents, taking into account the agreed conclusions on women's participation in and access to the media and information and communication technologies and their impact on and use as an instrument for the advancement and empowerment of women, adopted by the Commission on the Status of Women at its forty-seventh session and endorsed by the Economic and Social Council in its resolution 2003/44 of 22 July 2003, and the report of the Secretary-General;

30. *Encourages* Governments, international organizations, including the United Nations system, the private sector and civil society to fully incorporate a gender perspective into the implementation of and follow-up to the World Summit on Sustainable Development and the International Conference on Financing for Development and to implement the specific recommendations on microfinance and microcredit for women and gender budget policies;

31. *Stresses* the importance of collecting all relevant information needed on the role of women in development and statistics disaggregated by sex by all countries, encourages the relevant entities of the United Nations to support national efforts, especially those of developing countries, and in this regard invites developed countries, relevant entities of the United Nations and other international organizations to provide support and assistance to developing countries, upon their request, with respect to establishing, developing and strengthening their databases and information systems, and encourages all Governments and international organizations, including the United Nations system, to collect information needed on the role of women in development and the disaggregation by sex of all statistics;

32. *Urges* all Governments and international organizations, including the United Nations system, to incorporate a gender perspective in their planning and evaluation, including in common country assessments, the United Nations Development Assistance Frame-

work and poverty reduction strategy papers, where they exist;

33. *Encourages* the involvement, as appropriate, of relevant stakeholders, including the private sector and civil society, in mainstreaming a gender perspective in planning and evaluation;

34. *Calls upon* the United Nations system to integrate gender mainstreaming into all its programmes and policies, including in the integrated follow-up to United Nations conferences, in accordance with agreed conclusions 1997/2 on gender mainstreaming adopted by the Economic and Social Council at its substantive session of 1997, and welcomes the decision of the Council to devote one of the two themes of the coordination segment of its substantive session of 2004 to the review and appraisal of the system-wide implementation of those agreed conclusions;

35. *Reiterates its request* to the Secretary-General to update the *World Survey on the Role of Women in Development* for the consideration of the General Assembly at its fifty-ninth session, noting that the survey should focus, as in the past, on selective emerging development issues that have an impact on the role of women in the economy at the national, regional and international levels;

36. *Requests* the Secretary-General to submit to the General Assembly at its sixtieth session a report on the progress made in the implementation of the present resolution, including the impact of globalization on the empowerment of women and their integration in development;

37. *Decides* to include in the provisional agenda of its sixtieth session the sub-item entitled "Women in development".

Women in rural areas

In response to General Assembly resolution 56/129 [YUN 2001, p. 1071], the Secretary-General submitted a July report and September addendum [A/58/167 & Add.1], which reviewed the attention given to the situation of rural women by the Committee on the Elimination of Discrimination against Women, intergovernmental bodies and processes, the UN system and international financial organizations. Also included was a summary of the responses received from Member States on the desirability of convening a high-level policy consultation on the challenges faced by rural women.

The Secretary-General stated that Governments and international organizations, including those of the UN system, should ensure that: the integrated process of follow-up to the major summits and conferences in economic and social areas focused on the situation of rural women; the process of follow-up to the Economic and Social Council high-level segment of the substantive session considered rural women as the key stakeholders in sustainable rural development (see below); the priorities of rural women were addressed in all policies and programmes, and rural women consulted and involved in policy and programme formulation; the World Summit on the Information Society (see p. 857) addressed the priorities and needs of rural women and ensured their participation in developing and implementing global information and communication technology strategies; and rural women's perspectives were taken into account, and they participated in all areas, including in emergencies, humanitarian activities, peace-building and post-conflict reconstruction.

Economic and Social Council action. On 2 July [A/58/3], the Economic and Social Council, at the high-level segment of its substantive session, adopted a ministerial declaration, which, among other things, expressed commitment to the empowerment of rural women at all levels and in all aspects of rural development.

GENERAL ASSEMBLY ACTION

On 22 December [meeting 77], the General Assembly, on the recommendation of the Third Committee [A/58/501], adopted **resolution 58/146** without vote [agenda item 110].

Improvement of the situation of women in rural areas

The General Assembly,

Recalling its resolution 56/129 of 19 December 2001,

Recalling also the importance attached to the problems of rural women in the Nairobi Forward-looking Strategies for the Advancement of Women, the Beijing Declaration and Platform for Action adopted by the Fourth World Conference on Women, the outcome documents of the twenty-third special session of the General Assembly, entitled "Women 2000: gender equality, development and peace for the twenty-first century", and the Convention on the Elimination of All Forms of Discrimination against Women,

Recalling further the United Nations Millennium Declaration, in which Member States resolved, inter alia, to promote gender equality and the empowerment of women as effective ways to combat poverty, hunger and disease and to stimulate development that is truly sustainable,

Welcoming the Monterrey Consensus of the International Conference on Financing for Development, as well as the Johannesburg Declaration on Sustainable Development and the Plan of Implementation of the World Summit on Sustainable Development ("Johannesburg Plan of Implementation"), which called upon Governments to mainstream the gender perspective into development at all levels and in all sectors,

Welcoming also the agreed conclusions on women's participation in and access to the media, and information and communication technologies and their impact on and use as an instrument for the advancement and empowerment of women, adopted by the Commission on the Status of Women at its forty-seventh session,

Welcoming further the ministerial declaration of the high-level segment of the substantive session of 2003 of the Economic and Social Council, adopted on 2 July 2003, which stressed the need for rural development to become an integral part of national and international development policies and of the activities and programmes of the United Nations system, and called for an enhanced role for rural women at all levels of rural development, including decision-making,

Recognizing the critical role and contribution of rural women in enhancing agricultural and rural development, improving food security and eradicating rural poverty,

Noting that some effects of globalization may deepen the socio-economic marginalization of rural women,

Noting also that the globalization process has had some benefits by providing opportunities for wage employment for rural women in new sectors,

Mindful of the fact that the available data and existing tools of measurement and analysis are insufficient for a full understanding of the gender implications of the processes of globalization and rural change, and their impact on rural women,

Recognizing the urgent need to take appropriate measures aimed at further improving the situation of women in rural areas,

1. *Takes note* of the report of the Secretary-General;

2. *Requests* the Secretary-General and all relevant United Nations bodies to take into account, while developing future policies, plans and activities, the views expressed by Member States in their replies concerning the desirability of convening a high-level policy consultation at the governmental level, with a view to setting priorities and developing critical strategies that would meet the manifold challenges faced by rural women;

3. *Invites* Member States, in collaboration with the organizations of the United Nations and civil society, as appropriate, to continue their efforts to implement the outcome of and to ensure an integrated and coordinated follow-up to United Nations conferences and summits, including their five-year reviews, and to attach greater importance to the improvement of the situation of rural women in their national, regional and global development strategies by, inter alia:

(a) Creating an enabling environment for improving the situation of rural women, including integrating a gender perspective in macroeconomic policies and developing appropriate social support systems;

(b) Pursuing the political and socio-economic empowerment of rural women by supporting their full and equal participation in decision-making at all levels, including in rural institutions through, inter alia, the provision of training and capacity-building programmes, including legal literacy;

(c) Integrating a gender perspective into the design, implementation, monitoring and evaluation of development policies and programmes, including budget policies, paying increased attention to the needs of rural women so as to ensure that they benefit from policies and programmes adopted in all spheres and that the disproportionate number of rural women living in poverty is reduced;

(d) Ensuring that the perspectives of rural women are taken into account and that they participate in the design, implementation, monitoring and evaluation of policies and activities related to emergencies, natural disasters, humanitarian assistance, peace-building and post-conflict reconstruction;

(e) Investing in and strengthening efforts to meet the basic needs of rural women through capacity-building and human resources development measures and the provision of a safe and reliable water supply and sanitation, nutritional programmes, education and literacy programmes, and health and social support measures, including in the area of sexual and reproductive health and HIV/AIDS treatment, care and support;

(f) Designing and implementing policies that promote and protect the enjoyment by women of all human rights and fundamental freedoms and creating an environment that does not tolerate violations of the rights of women and girls, including domestic violence;

(g) Developing specific assistance programmes and advisory services to promote economic skills of rural women in banking, modern trading and financial procedures and providing microcredit and other financial and business services to a greater number of women in rural areas for their economic empowerment;

(h) Taking steps towards ensuring that women's unpaid work and contributions to on-farm and off-farm production, including income generated in the informal sector, are visible, and assessing the feasibility of developing and improving mechanisms, such as time-use studies, to measure in quantitative terms unpaid work, recognizing the potential for it to be reflected in the formulation and implementation of policies and programmes at the national and regional levels;

(i) Designing and revising laws to ensure that, where private ownership of land and property exists, rural women are accorded full and equal rights to own land and other property, including through the right to inheritance, and undertaking administrative reforms and other necessary measures to give women the same right as men to credit, capital, appropriate technologies and access to markets and information;

(j) Promoting programmes to enable rural women and men to reconcile their work and family responsibilities and to encourage men to share equally with women household and childcare responsibilities;

4. *Invites* the Commission on the Status of Women to continue to pay due attention to the situation of rural women in the consideration of the priority themes identified in its multi-year programme of work for the period 2002-2006;

5. *Invites* the relevant organizations of the United Nations system dealing with issues of development to address and support the empowerment of rural women and their specific needs in their programmes and strategies, including in the context of globalization;

6. *Stresses* the need to identify the best practices for ensuring that rural women have access to and full participation in the area of information and communication technologies, inter alia, through specific studies, and invites the World Summit on the Information Society, in Geneva and Tunis, to take into consideration, while addressing gender issues, the priorities and needs of rural women and girls as active users of information and ensure their participation in developing and implementing global information and communication technology strategies;

7. *Invites* Member States, the United Nations and the relevant organizations of its system to ensure that the needs of rural women are mainstreamed into the integrated process of follow-up to the major summits and conferences in the economic and social fields, in

particular the World Summit on Sustainable Development and the International Conference on Financing for Development, and the 2005 review of the progress achieved in implementing all the commitments made in the United Nations Millennium Declaration, the Beijing Platform for Action and the outcome documents of the twenty-third special session of the General Assembly, entitled "Women 2000: gender equality, development and peace for the twenty-first century";

8. *Invites* Member States to take into consideration the concluding comments and recommendations of the Committee on the Elimination of Discrimination against Women concerning their reports to the Committee when formulating policies and designing programmes focused on the improvement of the situation of rural women, including those to be developed and implemented in cooperation with relevant international organizations;

9. *Requests* the Secretary-General to report to the General Assembly at its sixtieth session on the implementation of the present resolution, addressing different aspects of the empowerment of rural women, including the impact of macroeconomic policy frameworks on their situation.

Women and the media

In accordance with the multi-year (2002-2006) programme of work of the Commission on the Status of Women, adopted by the Economic and Social Council in resolution 2001/4 [YUN 2001, p. 1084], the Secretary-General submitted a report [E/CN.6/2003/6] summarizing UN system efforts in the area of women and the media and information and communication technologies (ICT). The report, which was based on the analysis and conclusions of two expert meetings (Seoul, Republic of Korea, 11-14 November 2002; Beirut, Lebanon, 12-15 November 2002) and contributions by UN entities and civil society, focused on the opportunities and challenges to women's empowerment through ICT and the media.

The Secretary-General's recommendations to the Commission included the creation of a gender-sensitive enabling environment and integration of gender perspectives in the development and implementation of national policies and strategies in ICT and media and communication policies; the promotion of women's participation and employment in the information society; the mobilization of resources to promote gender equality in the media and in ICT; inclusiveness and participation in the promotion of gender equality in the information society; and the inclusion of a gender perspective in every facet of the World Summit on the Information Society (see p. 857).

On 14 March, the Commission adopted agreed conclusions on women's participation in and access to the media and ICT and their impact on and use as an instrument for women's advancement and empowerment and requested that the Economic and Social Council endorse them (see below). On 25 March [E/2003/27 (dec. 47/103)], it took note of the Secretary-General's report.

ECONOMIC AND SOCIAL COUNCIL ACTION

On 22 July [meeting 44], the Economic and Social Council, on the recommendation of the Commission on the Status of Women [E/2003/27], adopted **resolution 2003/44** without vote [agenda item 14 (a)].

Agreed conclusions of the Commission on the Status of Women on women's participation in and access to the media, and information and communication technologies and their impact on and use as an instrument for the advancement and empowerment of women

The Economic and Social Council,

Endorses the following agreed conclusions adopted by the Commission on the Status of Women at its forty-seventh session with respect to women's participation in and access to the media, and information and communication technologies and their impact on and use as an instrument for the advancement and empowerment of women:

1. The Commission on the Status of Women recalls and reiterates the strategic objectives and actions of the Beijing Declaration and Platform for Action and the outcome document adopted at the twenty-third special session of the General Assembly entitled "Women 2000: gender equality, development and peace in the twenty-first century", on the potential of the media and of information and communication technologies to contribute to the advancement and empowerment of women. It also recalls the United Nations Millennium Declaration and the development goals contained therein to promote gender equality and the empowerment of women as effective ways to combat poverty, hunger and disease, to stimulate development that is truly sustainable and to ensure that the benefits of new technologies, especially information and communication technologies, are available to all.

2. The Commission notes that, globally, there are substantial differences in participation in, access to and use of media and information and communication technologies, their content and production. Such differences have important implications for policy development at the national, regional and international levels. A focus on the gender dimensions of information and communication technologies is essential in order to prevent and combat any adverse impact of the digital revolution on gender equality and the perpetuation of existing inequalities and discrimination, including the sexual exploitation of women both through the traditional media and through new technologies. The media and information and communication technologies also offer tools for enhancing women's full access to the benefits of information and new technologies and can become central tools for the empowerment of women and the promotion of gender equality. Efforts are therefore necessary to increase women's access to and participation in the media and information and communication technologies, including in their decision-making processes and new opportunities created through information and communication technologies.

3. The Commission welcomes the convening of the World Summit on the Information Society, which is to be held in Geneva in December 2003 and in Tunis in 2005, and urges all participants to take the following recommendations into account and to integrate gender perspectives in every facet of the Summit. It further encourages the participation of women in the Summit, including significant numbers of gender equality experts and women experts in the field of information and communication technologies as members of national delegations, organizations of civil society and the business community.

4. The Commission urges Governments and, as appropriate, the relevant funds and programmes, organizations and specialized agencies of the United Nations system, the international financial institutions, civil society, including the private sector and non-governmental organizations, and other stakeholders to take the following actions:

(a) Prioritize the integration of gender perspectives and ensure early and full participation of women in the development and implementation of national policies, legislation, programmes, projects, strategies and regulatory and technical instruments in the field of information and communication technologies and media and communications, and create monitoring and accountability mechanisms to ensure implementation of gender-sensitive policies and regulations as well as to analyse the gender impact of such policies in consultation and collaboration with women information technology specialists, women's organizations and gender equality advocates;

(b) Encourage regulatory bodies, where they exist, to promote full participation of women in ownership, control and management in the information and communication technology and media sectors;

(c) Include gender perspectives and measurable gender-specific targets in all programmes and projects on information and communication technologies for development, as well as specific activities, as appropriate, for women and girls as active users of information;

(d) Remove infrastructural barriers related to information and communication technologies that disproportionately affect women and girls, and promote the establishment of affordable and accessible infrastructure related to information and communication technologies for all women and girls, bearing in mind the specific needs and interests of women and girls living in countries in the process of peace-building and reconstruction;

(e) Invite, as appropriate, through partnerships, or through the use of self-regulatory gender-sensitive guidelines for media coverage and representation, public and community media to work in support of gender equality, bearing in mind the importance of providing financial resources and other support;

(f) Support research into all aspects of the impact of the media and information and communication technologies on women and girls, in particular into their information needs and interests, review existing media and information and communication technologies policies and find ways to adapt information and communication technologies to the needs of poor and, in particular, illiterate women in order to overcome barriers and support the empowerment of women;

(g) Make education, formal and non-formal, a priority, in particular for the development of information and communication technologies, and take measures to promote girls' education so as to enable girls and women to gain access to those technologies;

(h) Include, at appropriate levels of government, education in information and communication technologies for girls and women in curricula at all educational levels, from early childhood to tertiary level, as well as in continuing education, in order to promote and ensure the full participation of women in the information society;

(i) Take concrete steps to increase the number of female students at all educational levels in subjects related to the media and information and communication technologies, including science, mathematics and technology, including through such methods as distance- and e-learning;

(j) Establish or, where they already exist, expand skills training, vocational and employment training and capacity-building programmes for women and girls and women's non-governmental organizations on the use, design and production of information and communication technologies, including preparing them to take on leadership roles and promoting their participation in the political process, and integrate a gender perspective in training programmes in those technologies for teachers and in training programmes for media professionals;

(k) Enable equal access for women to information and communication technology–based economic activities, such as small business and home-based employment, to information systems and improved technologies and to new employment opportunities in this area, and consider developing tele-centres, information centres, community access points and business incubators;

(l) Strengthen partnerships among all stakeholders to build the capacity of women to participate fully in and enjoy the benefits of the information society, including e-governance, where it exists and as it is developed, and participatory approaches;

(m) Ensure equal opportunities for women and monitor gender representation in different categories and levels of work, education and training in the media and information and communication technology areas, with a view to increasing the participation of women in decision-making at all levels of information and communication technology and the media;

(n) Provide management, negotiation and leadership training for women, as well as mentoring systems and other support strategies and programmes to enhance women's capabilities and potential for advancement in the media and information and communication technology sectors;

(o) Take effective measures, to the extent consistent with freedom of expression, to combat the growing sexualization and use of pornography in media content, in terms of the rapid development of information and communication technologies, encourage the media to refrain from presenting women as inferior beings and exploiting them as sexual objects and commodities, combat information and communication technology– and media-based violence against women, including the criminal misuse of information and communication technology for sexual harassment, sexual exploitation and trafficking in women and girls, and support the development and use of such technologies as a resource for the empowerment of women and girls, including those affected by violence, abuse and other forms of sexual exploitation;

(*p*) Respect the value of different and local languages and promote and encourage local knowledge systems and locally produced content in media and communications, support the development of a wide range of information and communication technology-based programmes in local languages, as appropriate, with content relevant to different groups of women, and build the capacity of girls and women to develop information and communication technology content;

(*q*) Encourage South-South cooperation to facilitate transfer and exchange of low-cost technologies and appropriate information and communication technology content between developing countries for the benefit of women and girls;

(*r*) Strengthen and encourage the use of existing information and communication technologies, such as radio, television, telecommunications and print, in parallel, in order to enhance the use of new technologies for gender equality and the economic, political and social empowerment of women as leaders, participants and consumers, and recognize that women and girls are potentially large-scale consumers, users and producers of information and communication technologies and media;

(*s*) Collect, share, positively recognize and widely publicize good practices to counter gender stereotyping, negative portrayals and exploitation of women in all forms of the media and information and communication technologies as part of their efforts to eliminate discrimination and violence against women;

(*t*) Increase efforts to compile, and disaggregate by sex and age, statistics on the use of information and communication technologies, in order to develop gender-specific indicators on information and communication technology use and needs and to collect gender-specific data on employment and education patterns in the media and in information and communication technology professions;

(*u*) Provide adequate and appropriate resources for innovative, affordable, accessible and sustainable programmes, projects and products on the media and information and communication technologies that support gender equality and gender mainstreaming, are relevant to the concerns of women and girls and provide support to women's online communities and networks that promote gender equality;

(*v*) Prioritize the allocation of resources to support programmes, projects and strategies that aim at increasing women's participation in and equal access to the information society, including vocational, scientific and technical training, literacy training and capacity-building programmes;

(*w*) Enhance, for the benefit of women and girls, international cooperation in support of national efforts to create an enabling environment to reduce the digital and information divide between developed and developing countries and promote, develop and enhance access to information and communication technologies, including the Internet infrastructure, by facilitating access to and transfer of knowledge and technology on concessional, preferential and favourable terms for the developing countries, as mutually agreed, taking into account the need to protect intellectual property rights and the special needs of developing countries;

(*x*) Strengthen the capacity of national machineries for the advancement of women, including through the allocation of adequate and appropriate resources and the provision of technical expertise, to take a lead advocacy role with respect to media and information and communication technologies and gender equality, support their involvement in national, regional and international processes related to media and information and communication technology issues and enhance coordination among ministries responsible for information and communication technologies, national machineries for the advancement of women, the private sector and national non-governmental organizations working in the field of gender advocacy.

The girl child

On 22 December [meeting 77], the General Assembly, on the recommendation of the Third Committee [A/58/504], adopted **resolution 58/156** without vote [agenda item 113].

The girl child

The General Assembly,

Recalling its resolution 57/189 of 18 December 2002 and all relevant resolutions, including the agreed conclusions of the Commission on the Status of Women, in particular those relevant to the girl child,

Reaffirming the equal rights of women and men as enshrined, inter alia, in the Preamble to the Charter of the United Nations, the Convention on the Elimination of All Forms of Discrimination against Women and the Convention on the Rights of the Child,

Welcoming the entry into force of the Optional Protocols to the Convention on the Rights of the Child on the involvement of children in armed conflict and on the sale of children, child prostitution and child pornography,

Welcoming also the imminent entry into force, on 25 December 2003, of the Protocol to Prevent, Suppress and Punish Trafficking in Persons, Especially Women and Children, supplementing the United Nations Convention against Transnational Organized Crime,

Recalling the United Nations Millennium Declaration adopted on 8 September 2000,

Reaffirming the outcome document entitled "A world fit for children" adopted by the General Assembly at its special session on children, on 10 May 2002,

Reaffirming also the Declaration of Commitment on HIV/AIDS adopted by the General Assembly at its twenty-sixth special session, on 27 June 2001,

Recalling all other relevant United Nations conferences, the Beijing Declaration and Platform for Action adopted at the Fourth World Conference on Women, the outcome of the twenty-third special session of the General Assembly, entitled "Women 2000: gender equality, development and peace for the twenty-first century", and the outcome documents of the recent five-year reviews of the implementation of the Programme of Action of the International Conference on Population and Development and the Programme of Action of the World Summit for Social Development,

Reaffirming the Dakar Framework for Action adopted at the World Education Forum,

Recalling the Declaration and Agenda for Action adopted at the World Congress against Commercial Sexual Exploitation of Children, held at Stockholm from 27 to 31 August 1996, and welcoming the Yokohama Global Commitment 2001, adopted at the Second World Congress against Commercial Sexual Exploitation of Children, held at Yokohama, Japan, from 17 to 20 December 2001,

Recognizing the efforts of the international community to strengthen the standards for combating sexual abuse and exploitation, and in this regard taking note of the Secretary-General's bulletin on special measures for protection from sexual exploitation and sexual abuse and other policies and codes of conduct developed by the United Nations system to prevent and address such incidents,

Recalling the International Conference on War-Affected Children, held at Winnipeg, Canada, from 10 to 17 September 2000, and affirming the ongoing importance of the Winnipeg Agenda for War-Affected Children for all children affected by armed conflict,

Recognizing the need to achieve gender equality to ensure a just and equitable world for girls,

Deeply concerned about discrimination against the girl child and the violation of the rights of the girl child, which often result in less access for girls to education, nutrition and physical and mental health care and in girls enjoying fewer of the rights, opportunities and benefits of childhood and adolescence than boys and often being subjected to various forms of cultural, social, sexual and economic exploitation and to violence and harmful practices, such as female infanticide, incest, early marriage, prenatal sex selection and female genital mutilation,

Deeply concerned also that, in situations of poverty, war and armed conflict, girl children are among those most affected and that their potential for full development is thus limited,

Concerned that the girl child has furthermore become the victim of sexually transmitted diseases and increasingly of the human immunodeficiency virus, which have a serious impact on the quality of her life and leave her open to further discrimination,

Concerned also by the increasing number of child-headed households particularly orphan girls, including those orphaned by the HIV/AIDS pandemic,

Convinced that racism, racial discrimination, xenophobia and related intolerance reveal themselves in a differentiated manner for women and girls and can be among the factors leading to a deterioration in their living conditions, poverty, violence, multiple forms of discrimination and limitation or denial of their human rights,

1. *Stresses* the need for full and urgent implementation of the rights of the girl child as guaranteed to her under all human rights instruments, including the Convention on the Rights of the Child and the Convention on the Elimination of All Forms of Discrimination against Women, as well as the need for universal ratification of those instruments;

2. *Urges* States to consider signing, ratifying or acceding to the Optional Protocol to the Convention on the Elimination of All Forms of Discrimination against Women and the Optional Protocols to the Convention on the Rights of the Child;

3. *Urges* all States to take all necessary measures and to institute legal reforms to ensure the full and equal enjoyment by the girl child of all human rights and fundamental freedoms and to take effective action against violations of those rights and freedoms;

4. *Urges* all Governments and the United Nations system to strengthen efforts bilaterally and with international organizations and private sector donors in order to achieve the goals of the World Education Forum, in particular that of eliminating gender disparities in primary and secondary education by 2005, and to implement the United Nations Girls' Education Initiative as a means of reaching this goal, and reaffirms the commitment contained in the United Nations Millennium Declaration in this regard;

5. *Calls upon* all States to take measures to address the obstacles that continue to affect the achievement of the goals set forth in the Beijing Platform for Action, as contained in paragraph 33 of the further actions and initiatives to implement the Beijing Declaration and Platform for Action, where appropriate, including the strengthening of national mechanisms to implement policies and programmes for the girl child and, in some cases, to enhance coordination among responsible institutions for the realization of the human rights of girls, as indicated in the further actions and initiatives;

6. *Urges* States to enact and strictly enforce laws to ensure that marriage is entered into only with the free and full consent of the intending spouses, to enact and strictly enforce laws concerning the minimum legal age of consent and the minimum age for marriage and to raise the minimum age for marriage where necessary;

7. *Also urges* States to fulfil their obligations under the Convention on the Rights of the Child and the Convention on the Elimination of All Forms of Discrimination against Women, as well as the commitment to implement the Beijing Platform for Action and the outcomes of the twenty-third special session of the General Assembly, entitled "Women 2000: gender equality, development and peace for the twenty-first century" and the special session on children;

8. *Urges* all States to promote gender equality and equal access to basic social services, such as education, nutrition, health care, including sexual and reproductive health care, vaccinations, and protection from diseases representing the major causes of mortality, and to mainstream a gender perspective in all development policies and programmes;

9. *Also urges* all States to enact and enforce legislation to protect girls from all forms of violence and exploitation, including female infanticide and prenatal sex selection, female genital mutilation, rape, domestic violence, incest, sexual abuse, sexual exploitation, child prostitution and child pornography, trafficking and forced labour, and to develop age-appropriate safe and confidential programmes and medical, social and psychological support services to assist girls who are subjected to violence;

10. *Urges* States to formulate comprehensive, multidisciplinary and coordinated national plans, programmes or strategies to eliminate all forms of violence against women and girls, which should be widely disseminated and should provide targets and timetables for implementation, as well as effective domestic enforcement procedures through the establishment of monitoring mechanisms involving all parties con-

cerned, including consultations with women's organizations, giving attention to the recommendations relating to the girl child of the Special Rapporteur of the Commission on Human Rights on violence against women, its causes and consequences;

11. *Calls upon* all States and international and non-governmental organizations, individually and collectively, to implement further the Beijing Platform for Action, in particular the strategic objectives relating to the girl child, and the further actions and initiatives to implement the Beijing Declaration and Platform for Action;

12. *Urges* States to ensure that the right of children to express themselves and participate in all matters affecting them, in accordance with their age and maturity, is fully and equally enjoyed by girls;

13. *Recognizes* that a considerable number of children, including orphans, children living on the street, internally displaced and refugee children, children affected by trafficking and sexual and economic exploitation and children who are incarcerated, live without parental support, and in this regard urges States to take special measures to support such children and the institutions, facilities and services that care for them, and to build and strengthen children's abilities to protect themselves;

14. *Urges* States to take appropriate measures to address the needs of orphan girls by implementing national policies and strategies to build and strengthen governmental, family and community capacities to provide a supportive environment for orphans and girls and boys infected with and affected by HIV/AIDS, including by providing appropriate counselling and psychosocial support, and ensuring their enrolment in school and access to shelter, good nutrition and health and social services on an equal basis with other children; and to protect orphans and vulnerable children from all forms of abuse, violence, exploitation, discrimination, trafficking and loss of inheritance;

15. *Also urges* States to take special measures for the protection of girls affected by armed conflicts and in particular to protect them from sexually transmitted diseases, such as HIV/AIDS, gender-based violence, including rape and sexual abuse, and sexual exploitation, torture, abduction and forced labour, paying special attention to refugee and displaced girls, and to take into account the special needs of girls affected by armed conflict in the delivery of humanitarian assistance and disarmament, demobilization, rehabilitation assistance and reintegration processes;

16. *Deplores* all the cases of sexual exploitation and abuse of women and children, especially girls, in humanitarian crises, including those cases involving humanitarian workers and peacekeepers;

17. *Urges* all States and the international community to respect, protect and promote the rights of the child, taking into account the particular vulnerabilities of the girl child in pre-conflict, conflict and post-conflict situations, and calls for special initiatives designed to address all of the rights and needs of girls affected by armed conflicts;

18. *Calls upon* Governments, civil society, including the media, and non-governmental organizations to promote human rights education and the full respect for and enjoyment of the human rights of the girl child, inter alia, through the translation, production and dissemination of age-appropriate information material on those rights to all sectors of society, in particular to children;

19. *Calls upon* States and international and non-governmental organizations to mobilize all necessary resources, support and efforts to realize the goals, strategic objectives and actions set out in the Beijing Platform for Action and the further actions and initiatives to implement the Beijing Declaration and Platform for Action;

20. *Requests* the Secretary-General, as Chairman of the United Nations System Chief Executives Board for Coordination, to ensure that all organizations and bodies of the United Nations system, individually and collectively, in particular the United Nations Children's Fund, the United Nations Educational, Scientific and Cultural Organization, the World Food Programme, the United Nations Population Fund, the United Nations Development Fund for Women, the World Health Organization, the United Nations Development Programme, the Office of the United Nations High Commissioner for Refugees and the International Labour Organization, take into account the rights and the particular needs of the girl child in the country programme of cooperation in accordance with the national priorities, including through the United Nations Development Assistance Framework;

21. *Requests* all human rights treaty bodies, special procedures and other human rights mechanisms of the Commission on Human Rights and its Subcommission on the Promotion and Protection of Human Rights to adopt regularly and systematically a gender perspective in the implementation of their mandates and to include in their reports information on the qualitative analysis of violations of the human rights of women and girls, and encourages the strengthening of cooperation and coordination in that regard;

22. *Stresses* the importance of a substantive assessment of the implementation of the Beijing Platform for Action with a life-cycle perspective so as to identify gaps and obstacles in the implementation process and to develop further actions for the achievement of the goals of the Platform for Action;

23. *Requests* Member States to ensure that, in preventing and addressing HIV/AIDS, particular attention is paid to the girl child infected with and affected by HIV/AIDS;

24. *Decides* to review the progress made in the protection and promotion of the rights and well-being of the girl child, and requests the Secretary-General to provide information relating to the girl child in his report on the follow-up to and implementation of the outcomes of the United Nations conferences and summits to be considered during the sixtieth session of the General Assembly.

(See also p. 780.)

Institutional mechanisms for the advancement of women

Inter-Agency Network. The United Nations Inter-Agency Network on Women and Gender Equality, at its second session (New York, 24-27 February) [IANWGE/2003/12/Rev.1], endorsed decisions and recommendations made by task forces and working groups regarding women, peace and security; gender mainstreaming in programme budgets; gender and financing for development; gender and ICT; gender mainstreaming in the common country assessment and United Nations Development Assistance Framework process; database activities including WomenWatch, an Internet portal to UN gender resources; working methods and the link between the United Nations System Chief Executives Board for Coordination and the Network; and the regional commissions' projects on gender indicators. The Network established three new task forces on the gender perspectives of the MDGs, gender and trade, and gender and water. It also held a workshop on incorporating gender perspectives into the preparation of and follow-up to global conferences.

Report of Secretary-General. In response to General Assembly resolution 56/132 [YUN 2001, p. 1055], the Secretary-General, in a report [E/CN.6/2003/2] to the Commission on the Status of Women, summarized progress made in mainstreaming gender perspectives within the UN system, based on input received from UN system entities since his 2002 report on the issue [YUN 2002, p. 1154]. He concluded that there had been a marked increase in the number of gender units/focal points, networks, task forces and similar institutional mechanisms established to provide catalytic support and to strengthen capacity for gender mainstreaming in sectoral areas. Other measures included the training of staff and establishment of monitoring mechanisms. Inter-agency activities at global and regional levels remained a vehicle for coordination, information-sharing and joint activities. Further efforts should focus on identifying the remaining gaps in policy frameworks and strategies, and assessing the impact of the strategies, which should provide critical input towards the review of the progress made in implementing Economic and Social Council agreed conclusions 1997/2 on gender mainstreaming [YUN 1997, p. 1186]. The Secretary-General recommended that the Commission request that the following be included in the next report: assessments of the impact of policies and strategies, of the most pertinent gaps in sex-disaggregated data and gender-specific information, by sector, of remaining gaps in the policy and strategy framework for gender equality and mainstreaming in sectoral areas in UN entities, and of the effectiveness of existing institutional mechanisms. He also proposed an overview of monitoring mechanisms for gender mainstreaming in place in the UN system.

Commission on the Status of Women. On 13 March [E/2003/27 (res. 47/2)], the Commission requested the Secretary-General to include in his next report the assessments and overview of monitoring mechanisms proposed in his report (above). It asked the Economic and Social Council to consider devoting its 2004 coordination segment to a review and appraisal of the system-wide implementation of agreed conclusions 1997/2.

Further report of Secretary-General. In response to General Assembly resolution 57/182 [YUN 2002, p. 1137] and Economic and Social Council resolution 2002/23 [ibid., p. 1154], the Secretary-General, in a May report [E/2003/69], described progress made by the Council in mainstreaming a gender perspective in its work during 2002, and that of its functional commissions in 2003. Also reviewed was the work of the Inter-Agency Network on Women and Gender Equality (see p. 1187). The Secretary-General concluded that the Council and all subsidiary bodies that had completed their sessions reflected, to some degree, the concerns of women or gender perspectives in their work. However, interaction between the Commission on the Status of Women and other functional commissions, and use of the Commission's work by the Council and its subsidiary machinery had been uneven. Recommendations to the Council proposed devoting its 2004 coordination segment to a review and appraisal of the system-wide implementation of agreed conclusions 1997/2; encouraging its subsidiary machinery to strengthen practical guidance provided in resolutions, decisions and agreed conclusions; encouraging relevant commissions to address gender aspects within their mandates; urging the commissions to use more systematically the work of the Commission on related topics under their consideration; and calling for efforts to include attention to gender equality in reports submitted to the Council and its subsidiary machinery.

ECONOMIC AND SOCIAL COUNCIL ACTION

On 24 July [meeting 47], the Economic and Social Council adopted **resolution 2003/49** [draft: E/2003/L.24/Rev.1] without vote [agenda item 7 (f)].

Mainstreaming a gender perspective into all policies and programmes in the United Nations system

The Economic and Social Council,

Recalling its resolution 2002/23 of 24 July 2002, and the decision taken in its resolution 2001/41 of 26 July 2001 to establish the regular sub-item entitled "Mainstreaming a gender perspective into all policies and programmes of the United Nations system" in order to, inter alia, monitor and evaluate achievements made and obstacles encountered by the United Nations system, and to consider further measures to strengthen the implementation and monitoring of gender mainstreaming within the United Nations system,

Recalling Also its agreed conclusions 1997/2 of 18 July 1997 on mainstreaming a gender perspective into all policies and programmes in the United Nations system, and its subsequent decision to devote a coordination segment before 2005 to a review and appraisal of the system-wide implementation of those agreed conclusions,

Affirming that gender mainstreaming is a globally accepted strategy for promoting gender equality,

Reaffirming that gender mainstreaming constitutes a critical strategy in the implementation of the Beijing Platform for Action and the outcome of the twenty-third special session of the General Assembly,

Underlining the catalytic role played by the Commission on the Status of Women in promoting gender mainstreaming,

1. *Welcomes* the report of the Secretary-General on follow-up to and progress in the implementation of the Beijing Declaration and Platform for Action and the outcome of the twenty-third special session of the General Assembly, especially on measures taken by the Economic and Social Council and its subsidiary bodies to mainstream a gender perspective into their work;

2. *Decides* to undertake, during the coordination segment of its substantive session in 2004, a review and appraisal of the system-wide implementation of its agreed conclusions 1997/2 on mainstreaming a gender perspective into all policies and programmes in the United Nations system;

3. *Calls upon* Member States and all other actors of the United Nations system to continue to mainstream a gender perspective into all activities at all levels;

4. *Decides* to intensify its efforts to ensure that gender mainstreaming is an integral part of all activities in its work, and therefore to give appropriate attention to gender perspectives and the particular obstacles that women face in all its segments and agenda items, both during discussions and in outcomes;

5. *Expresses its appreciation* to its subsidiary bodies for the progress made in giving attention to situations that are specific to women and to the mainstreaming of gender perspectives into their work, for example by:

(a) Reiterating that gender equality is a goal in itself as well as a means in the more effective pursuit of their specific mandates;

(b) Highlighting gender equality as a cross-cutting issue;

6. *Calls upon* its subsidiary bodies to intensify further their efforts to mainstream gender perspectives in their work, and encourages them to strengthen the practical guidance provided in resolutions, decisions, agreed conclusions and other outcomes so as to accelerate the consistent use of gender mainstreaming in all policies and programmes at all levels;

7. *Also calls upon* its subsidiary bodies to continue their efforts to address gender perspectives in relation to the thematic issues of their multi-year programmes of work or in relation to their annual themes;

8. *Calls upon* the bureaux of its subsidiary bodies to consider how best to facilitate the inclusion of a gender perspective in their work;

9. *Emphasizes* the importance of its subsidiary bodies increasing their collaboration with the Commission on the Status of Women, including by making more systematic use of the output of the Commission, and encourages the Commission to continue its efforts to identify gender issues in the work of the Council and its other subsidiary bodies and assist them in pursuing these issues;

10. *Invites* its Bureau to include in the agenda of meetings with the bureaux of its subsidiary bodies an item on progress made and obstacles encountered in gender mainstreaming;

11. *Encourages* the President of the Economic and Social Council to include, in the agenda of meetings with the chairpersons of its subsidiary bodies, an item on enhanced coordination on gender mainstreaming between the Council and its subsidiary bodies;

12. *Encourages* the collection, analysis and dissemination of sex-disaggregated data and other gender-specific studies and information and all gender-analysis budgets by the United Nations system and its subsidiary bodies;

13. *Encourages also* the Special Adviser to the Secretary-General on Gender Issues and Advancement of Women and the Division for the Advancement of Women of the Secretariat to maintain their efforts to raise awareness of gender issues across the United Nations system;

14. *Notes with appreciation* the expanded efforts of the Inter-Agency Network on Women and Gender Equality to support gender mainstreaming in a growing number of sectors, especially its efforts to ensure that gender perspectives are addressed systematically by the United Nations System Chief Executives Board for Coordination, and in this regard encourages the Board in its efforts to mainstream gender perspectives throughout the United Nations system;

15. *Encourages* United Nations bodies to promote inter-agency arrangements through the Inter-Agency Network on Women and Gender Equality for increased coordination and partnership on gender issues across the United Nations system;

16. *Welcomes* the efforts by the regional commissions to promote gender mainstreaming and improve the situation of women, and encourages the regional commissions to intensify those efforts;

17. *Underlines* the importance of reports to intergovernmental bodies consistently giving attention to gender equality through systematic and rigorous analysis of the issues involved, and presenting issues and approaches in a gender-sensitive manner so as to give concrete and practical recommendations and serve as an analytical basis for those bodies to undertake gender-responsive policy formulation in accordance with its agreed conclusions 1997/2;

18. *Requests* the Secretary-General to submit a report on implementation of and follow-up to the Beijing Declaration and Platform for Action and the outcome of the twenty-third special session of the General Assembly, including on progress in gender mainstreaming, to the next substantive session of the Council;

19. *Also requests* the Secretary-General to include in his report recommendations for the review and appraisal of the system-wide implementation of its agreed conclusions 1997/2 on mainstreaming a gender perspective into all policies and programmes in the United Nations system.

Status of women in the United Nations

In response to General Assembly resolution 57/180 [YUN 2002, p. 1411], the Secretary-General, in a January report [E/CN.6/2003/8], updated information on women's representation in the UN

Secretariat since the submission of his last report [YUN 2002, p. 1410] and focused on the implementation of gender equality goals in the staffing process. He recommended discontinuing the present report and replacing it with a report to the General Assembly at the session immediately preceding that of the Commission on the Status of Women, accompanied by an oral update to the Commission if needed. On 25 March, the Commission took note of the Secretary-General's report [E/2003/27 (dec. 47/103)].

Also in response to resolution 57/180, the Secretary-General submitted a September report [A/58/374] on improving the status of women in the UN system (see p. 1448).

In **resolution 58/144** of 22 December, the Assembly requested the Secretary-General to provide a verbal update to the Commission and to report to the Assembly in 2004 (see p. 1449).

CPC action. In June [A/58/16], the Committee for Programme and Coordination (CPC), having considered a report of the Office of Internal Oversight Services [E/AC.51/2003/5 & Corr.1] on the triennial review of the implementation of CPC recommendations on the evaluation of the advancement of women programme in 2000 [YUN 2000, p. 1123], recommended that the review's conclusions be approved and submitted to the Commission on the Status of Women. On 22 December, the General Assembly endorsed CPC's recommendations (**decision 58/532**).

UN machinery

Convention on the elimination of discrimination against women

As at 31 December 2003, 175 States were parties to the 1979 Convention on the Elimination of All Forms of Discrimination against Women, adopted by the General Assembly in resolution 34/180 [YUN 1979, p. 895]. During the year, Afghanistan, San Marino and Sao Tome and Principe ratified the Convention and the Syrian Arab Republic and Timor-Leste acceded to it. At year's end, 42 States parties had also accepted the amendment to article 20, paragraph 1, of the Convention in respect of the meeting time of the Committee on the Elimination of Discrimination against Women, which was adopted by the States parties in 1995 [YUN 1995, p. 1178]. The amendment would enter into force when accepted by a two-thirds majority of States parties.

The Optional Protocol to the Convention, adopted by the Assembly in resolution 54/4 [YUN 1999, p. 1100] and which entered into force in 2000 [YUN 2000, p. 1123], had 59 States parties by year's end.

The Secretary-General submitted his annual report to the Assembly on the status of the Convention as at 31 July [A/58/341].

CEDAW

In 2003, the Committee on the Elimination of Discrimination against Women (CEDAW), established in 1982 [YUN 1982, p. 1149] to monitor compliance with the 1979 Convention, held two regular sessions in New York [A/58/38].

At its twenty-eighth session (13-31 January), CEDAW reviewed the initial or periodic reports of Albania, Canada, the Congo, El Salvador, Kenya, Luxembourg, Norway and Switzerland on measures they had taken to implement the Convention. CEDAW considered a Secretariat report on ways and means of expediting its work [CEDAW/C/2003/I/4] and a note by the Secretary-General on the reports of specialized agencies [CEDAW/C/2003/I/3] and the reports of specialized agencies on the implementation of the Convention in areas falling within the scope of their activity [CEDAW/C/2003/I/3/Add.1,3,4]. CEDAW appointed five members to the Working Group on Communications under the Optional Protocol (see below) for a two-year period starting in January [A/58/38 (dec. 28/I)]; decided to convene a meeting during its twenty-ninth session in July with States whose reports under the Convention had been due for over five years [dec. 28/II]; decided, subject to the availability of resources, to nominate two of its members, in addition to its Chairperson, to participate in the May workshop, held by the Office of the United Nations High Commissioner for Human Rights (OHCHR), on reform proposals for treaty bodies [dec. 28/III] (see p. 668); and, subject to the availability of resources, decided to nominate four members, including the Chairperson, to participate in OHCHR's second (June) inter-committee meeting of treaty bodies [dec. 28/IV] (see p. 668). The Committee decided to change the name of the Working Group on the Optional Protocol to the Working Group on Communications under the Optional Protocol. The Group met (25-27 June) to review its methods of work and to consider cooperation between the UN Division for the Advancement of Women and OHCHR. It decided to register its first communication.

At its twenty-ninth session (30 June-18 July), CEDAW reviewed the initial or periodic reports of Brazil, Costa Rica, Ecuador, France, Japan, Morocco, New Zealand and Slovenia, and considered the Secretariat report submitted to its twenty-eighth session (above). The Committee decided that those States parties whose initial reports under article 18 were more than five years overdue as at 18 July would be reminded of their reporting obligations [A/58/38 (dec. 29/I)].

GENERAL ASSEMBLY ACTION

On 22 December [meeting 77], the General Assembly, on the recommendation of the Third Committee [A/58/501], adopted **resolution 58/145** without vote [agenda item 110].

Convention on the Elimination of All Forms of Discrimination against Women

The General Assembly,

Recalling its resolution 57/178 of 18 December 2002 and its previous resolutions on the elimination of discrimination against women,

Bearing in mind that one of the purposes of the United Nations, as stated in Articles 1 and 55 of the Charter, is to promote universal respect for human rights and fundamental freedoms for all without distinction of any kind, including distinction as to sex,

Reiterating the need to intensify efforts to eliminate all forms of discrimination against women throughout the world,

Affirming that women and men should participate equally in social, economic and political development, should contribute equally to such development and should share equally in improved conditions of life,

Recalling the Vienna Declaration and Programme of Action adopted by the World Conference on Human Rights on 25 June 1993, in which the Conference reaffirmed that the human rights of women and the girl child were an inalienable, integral and indivisible part of universal human rights,

Acknowledging the need for a comprehensive and integrated approach to the promotion and protection of the human rights of women, which includes the integration of the human rights of women into the mainstream of United Nations activities system-wide,

Reaffirming the commitments made in the political declaration and the outcome document of the twenty-third special session of the General Assembly, entitled "Women 2000: gender equality, development and peace for the twenty-first century", in particular paragraphs 68 *(c)* and *(d)* concerning the Convention on the Elimination of All Forms of Discrimination against Women and the Optional Protocol thereto,

Recalling that, in the United Nations Millennium Declaration, heads of State and Government resolved to implement the Convention,

Recognizing that the equal enjoyment by women of all human rights and fundamental freedoms will promote the realization of the rights of the child, bearing in mind the special needs of girls, and acknowledging the mutual reinforcement of the implementation of the Convention on the Elimination of All Forms of Discrimination against Women and the Convention on the Rights of the Child and the Optional Protocols thereto,

Welcoming the progress made in the implementation of the Convention on the Elimination of All Forms of Discrimination against Women, but expressing concern about the remaining challenges,

Welcoming also the growing number of States parties to the Convention, which now stands at one hundred and seventy-five,

Recalling the entry into force on 22 December 2000 of the Optional Protocol to the Convention on the Elimination of All Forms of Discrimination against Women,

Bearing in mind the recommendation of the Committee on the Elimination of Discrimination against Women that national reports should contain information on the implementation of the Beijing Platform for Action, in accordance with paragraph 323 of the Platform,

Having considered the report of the Committee on its twenty-eighth and twenty-ninth sessions,

Expressing concern at the great number of reports that are overdue and that continue to be overdue, in particular initial reports, which constitutes an obstacle to the full implementation of the Convention,

1. *Welcomes* the report of the Secretary-General on the status of the Convention on the Elimination of All Forms of Discrimination against Women;

2. *Expresses disappointment* that universal ratification of the Convention was not achieved by 2000, and urges all States that have not yet ratified or acceded to the Convention to do so;

3. *Urges* States parties to comply fully with their obligations under the Convention and the Optional Protocol thereto and to take into consideration the concluding comments as well as the general recommendations of the Committee on the Elimination of Discrimination against Women;

4. *Encourages* all relevant entities of the United Nations system, within their mandates, as well as Governments, intergovernmental and non-governmental organizations and, in particular, women's organizations, as appropriate, to strengthen assistance to States parties, upon their request, in implementing the Convention;

5. *Welcomes* the rapidly growing number of States parties to the Optional Protocol, which now stands at fifty-nine, and urges other States parties to the Convention to consider signing and ratifying or acceding to the Optional Protocol;

6. *Notes* the closed meeting held by the Committee on 16 July 2003 with States parties whose reports were more than five years overdue;

7. *Takes note with appreciation* of the fact that the Committee has commenced its work under the Optional Protocol;

8. *Notes* that some States parties have modified their reservations, expresses satisfaction that some reservations have been withdrawn, and urges States parties to limit the extent of any reservations that they lodge to the Convention, to formulate any such reservations as precisely and as narrowly as possible, to ensure that no reservations are incompatible with the object and purpose of the Convention, to review their reservations regularly with a view to withdrawing them and to withdraw reservations that are contrary to the object and purpose of the Convention;

9. *Welcomes* the adoption by the Committee of revised reporting guidelines, and urges States parties to adhere to the revised guidelines, in particular with regard to the content and length of reports;

10. *Recalls* the great number of overdue reports, in particular initial reports, and urges States parties to the Convention to make every possible effort to submit their

reports on the implementation of the Convention in a timely manner in accordance with article 18 thereof;

11. *Encourages* the Secretariat to extend further technical assistance to States parties, upon their request, to strengthen their capacity in the preparation of reports, in particular initial reports, and invites Governments to contribute to those efforts;

12. *Invites* States parties to make use of the technical assistance provided by the Secretariat to facilitate the preparation of reports, in particular initial reports;

13. *Commends* the Committee on its contributions to the effective implementation of the Convention;

14. *Strongly urges* States parties to the Convention to take appropriate measures so that acceptance of the amendment to article 20, paragraph 1, of the Convention by a two-thirds majority of States parties can be reached as soon as possible so that the amendment may enter into force;

15. *Expresses its appreciation* for the efforts made so far by the Committee to improve the efficiency of its working methods, and encourages the Committee to continue its activities in this regard;

16. *Encourages* the continued participation of members of the Committee in inter-committee meetings and meetings of persons chairing the human rights treaty bodies, including those on methods of work relating to the State reporting system;

17. *Encourages* the Committee, within its mandate, to continue to contribute to the efforts to strengthen cooperation and coordination between the treaty bodies;

18. *Requests* the Secretary-General, in accordance with General Assembly resolution 54/4 of 6 October 1999, to provide the resources, including staff and facilities, necessary for the effective functioning of the Committee within its full mandate, taking into account in particular the entry into force of the Optional Protocol;

19. *Urges* Governments, organizations and bodies of the United Nations system and intergovernmental and non-governmental organizations to disseminate the Convention and the Optional Protocol thereto;

20. *Encourages* States parties to disseminate the concluding comments adopted in relation to the consideration of their reports as well as the general recommendations of the Committee;

21. *Encourages* all relevant entities of the United Nations system to continue to build women's knowledge and understanding of and capacity to utilize human rights instruments, in particular the Convention and the Optional Protocol thereto;

22. *Urges* the specialized agencies, at the invitation of the Committee, to submit reports on the implementation of the Convention in areas falling within the scope of their activities;

23. *Welcomes* the contribution of non-governmental organizations to the work of the Committee;

24. *Requests* the Secretary-General to submit to the General Assembly at its sixtieth session a report on the status of the Convention on the Elimination of All Forms of Discrimination against Women and the implementation of the present resolution.

Commission on the Status of Women

The Commission on the Status of Women, at its forty-seventh session (New York, 3-14 and 25 March) [E/2003/27], recommended three draft resolutions to the Economic and Social Council for adoption on the situation of and assistance to Palestinian women (see p. 494); the situation of women and girls in Afghanistan (see p. 1175); and its agreed conclusions on the participation in and access of women to the media and information and communication technologies and their impact on and use as an instrument for the advancement and empowerment of women (see p. 1183). The Commission also adopted and brought to the Council's attention resolutions on women, the girl child and HIV/AIDS (see p. 1174); and mainstreaming a gender perspective into all policies and programmes in the UN system (see p. 1188). A draft decision for adoption by the Council related to the Commission's report on its forty-seventh (2003) session and the provisional agenda for the forty-eighth (2004) session (see below). The Commission further adopted three decisions, which were brought to the Council's attention, regarding the United Nations International Research and Training Institute for the Advancement of Women [dec. 47/101] (see p. 1194) and the Working Group on Communications on the Status of Women [dec. 47/102] (see p. 1193); and it took note of the documents before it [dec. 47/103], among them, the Secretary-General's report summarizing steps taken by the Commission to follow up on policy guidance provided by the Council to its functional commissions in 2002 [E/CN.6/2003/10]; and on the joint work plan of the Division for the Advancement of Women and OHCHR for 2003 [E/CN.4/ 2003/73-E/CN.6/2003/5] (see p. 779).

By **decision 2003/237** of 22 July, the Economic and Social Council took note of the Commission's report on its forty-seventh session and approved the provisional agenda for its forty-eighth session.

Communications on the status of women

Working Group. At three meetings in March, including one closed meeting [E/2003/27], the Commission considered the report of the Working Group on Communications on the Status of Women, established in 1993 [YUN 1993, p. 1050] to consider ways of making the communications procedure more transparent and efficient. The Working Group considered seven confidential communications received directly by the Division for the Advancement of Women and 15 confidential communications received by OHCHR. The Group noted that Governments had replied to three of the seven communications received by the Division and to 14 of the 15 transmitted by OHCHR. Due to the limited number (22) of communications received, the Group was unable to assess the existence of a consistent pattern of reliably proven injustice and discriminatory practices against women, as defined by its mandate in Economic and Social Council resolution 1983/27 [YUN 1983, p. 923]. However, it ascertained that communications were most frequently submitted on sexual violence against women, including rape, perpetrated by State agents, such as members of the police force, security forces, prison guards and members of the army; violations of the rights of female human rights defenders, in particular the violation of the freedom of expression and assembly; violations of the rights of women belonging to ethnic or religious minorities, including killings, inhuman and degrading treatment and discrimination; and violations of women's human rights in the context of internal conflicts, including killings, torture and enforced or involuntary disappearances. The Group was concerned about a communication received indicating the existence of legal practices that prescribed cruel, inhuman or degrading punishment of women.

In a March decision [E/2003/27 (dec. 47/102)], the Commission decided that at its forty-eighth (2004) session, it would continue to consider the Working Group's future work, and requested the Secretary-General to submit a report for that purpose.

UN Development Fund for Women (UNIFEM)

During 2003 [A/59/135], the United Nations Development Fund for Women (UNIFEM) continued to focus on strengthening women's economic security and rights; enhancing women's leadership in governance and peace-building; and promoting women's human rights by highlighting the gender dimensions of the HIV/AIDS pandemic and eliminating violence against women. UNIFEM's activities were defined in its 2000-2003 strategy and business plan, endorsed by the Executive Board of the United Nations Development Programme/United Nations Population Fund (UNDP/UNFPA) in 2000 [YUN 2000, p. 1127].

UNIFEM's work in support of women's economic security and rights focused on promoting an enabling environment for women's equal ownership and access to economic resources and assets; incorporating a gender perspective in macroeconomic frameworks and building the capacity of countries to manage globalization and economic transition from the perspective of poor women; and strengthening women's economic capacity and rights. Results in those areas were greatly enhanced through gender-responsive budget initiatives and promoting the use of gender-sensitive data and statistics. UNIFEM's work regarding women's leadership in governance and peace-building achieved significant results in strengthening gender-focused information collection and on conflict prevention and early warning mechanisms; enhancing humanitarian assistance and protection for women in conflict situations; making women and gender perspectives central to peace processes; supporting gender justice in post-conflict peace-building; and strengthening women's political participation. In its programme to promote women's human rights by highlighting the gender dimensions of the HIV/AIDS pandemic and eliminating violence against women, UNIFEM expanded capacity for effective implementation at the national level of the Convention on the Elimination of All Forms of Discrimination against Women (see p. 1190); strengthened policies and programmes to end violence against women and girls; and increased awareness and action in response to the gender and human rights dimensions of the HIV/AIDS pandemic.

UNIFEM's initiatives to enhance the capacity of the UN system to support women's empowerment and gender mainstreaming in policies and programmes resulted in increased attention to gender equality in coordination mechanisms and stronger collaboration with strategic UN partner organizations. Strengthening the Fund's effectiveness by incorporating the principles of a learning organization and building strategic partnerships resulted in the refinement of knowledge "products" to capture and make accessible learning in key thematic areas.

In 2003, UNIFEM's resources totalled $34 million, of which $21.7 million was in core resources and $12.3 million in non-core resources. A total of 38 Member States contributed to the core resources. Contributions from bilateral donors accounted for 88 per cent of the resource base, as in 2002.

By a January note [E/CN.6/2003/11-E/CN.4/2003/121], the Secretary-General transmitted to the Commission on Human Rights and the Commission on the Status of Women UNIFEM's report on the 2002 activities of its Trust Fund in Support of Actions to Eliminate Violence against Women [YUN 2002, p. 1165], prepared pursuant to General Assembly resolution 50/166 [YUN 1995, p. 1188]. On 25 March [E/2003/27 (dec. 47/103)], the Commission on the Status of Women took note of UNIFEM's report. A later report of UNIFEM [E/CN.6/2004/8-E/CN.4/ 2004/117 & Corr.1] stated that the Fund approved over $600,000 in grants for eight new projects in 2003, in an enhanced attempt to address diverse forms of violence against women. Since its establishment in 1996, the Trust Fund had awarded $8.4 million in grants to 155 projects in more than 70 countries.

The UNDP/UNFPA Executive Board, on 10 September [E/2003/35 (dec. 2003/23)], took note of the UNDP Administrator's report [DP/2003/28] on budget estimates for the 2004-2005 biennium, and approved $14.9 million for UNIFEM.

In July [A/58/168], the Secretary-General transmitted to the General Assembly a report on UNIFEM's 2002 activities [YUN 2002, p. 1164]. The Assembly noted the report, on the recommendation of the Third Committee [A/58/501], by **decision 58/533** of 22 December, and, on the recommendation of the Second Committee [A/58/487], by **decision 58/551** of 23 December.

International Research and Training Institute (INSTRAW)

A May report of the Board of Trustees of the International Research and Training Institute for the Advancement of Women (INSTRAW) [E/2003/59] stated that the Board's twenty-second session, which was postponed in 2002 [YUN 2002, p. 1165] pending the recommendations of the Working Group on the Future Operation of INSTRAW (see below), still had not taken place. However, the Board electronically approved a brief on INSTRAW developments and challenges during 2002 and current status, prepared by INSTRAW, which was annexed to the report.

INSTRAW's financial situation remained precarious in 2003 (see p. 1200).

Working Group report. The Working Group on the Future Operation of INSTRAW, established by General Assembly resolution 56/125 [YUN 2001, p. 1089], submitted a preliminary report [A/AC.266/1] in February on activities undertaken pursuant to Assembly resolution 57/175 [YUN 2002, p. 1167] relating to its recommendations [ibid., p. 1166]. The Working Group held a 10 February meeting with UN Secretariat representatives to request the Secretary-General to appoint an INSTRAW Director to provide leadership and initiate fund-raising activities. The Secretariat expressed the view that such an appointment was not currently possible because the funds available for INSTRAW would be sufficient only to cover the salaries of the current staff, contracts and operational expenses until 31 May, after which additional fund-raising would be necessary through voluntary contributions. Following a 12 February meeting on the status of INSTRAW's voluntary contributions, the Secretary-General received a pledge of $100,000 from Spain, with the promise of a further similar amount once a Director had been appointed, and $5,520 from Venezuela. INSTRAW's host country, the Dominican Republic, reiterated its support to the Institute. The Under-Secretary-General of the UN Department of Economic and Social Affairs (DESA) said that the pledges made, together with the existing funds, should be enough to permit the prompt appointment of a Director. He intended to meet with the UN Controller to coordinate the appointment. On 20 February, the Working Group decided to consult with the Secretary-General regarding the appointment of a Director. It also decided to raise with the Secretariat the possibility of postponing the election, scheduled for the Economic and Social Council's resumed 2003 organizational session, of the five members of INSTRAW's Board of Trustees whose mandates would end on 30 June. The Working Group discussed the procedural steps that should be taken to fulfil its mandate and highlighted the need for the Council to amend the Institute's statute.

In March, [E/2003/27 (dec. 47/101)], the Commission on the Status of Women took note of the report and recommended that the Economic and Social Council consider the Group's reports to the Assembly in 2003.

Note by Secretary-General. In an April note [E/2003/L.3/Add.6], the Secretary-General stated that, on 18 March, he informed all Member States that the Council would be called on to appoint five members to serve on INSTRAW's Board of Trustees. He drew the Council's attention to Assembly resolution 57/175, which endorsed and requested the Secretary-General to implement the Working Group's recommendation that the Board of Trustees be abolished and replaced with an advisory board composed of Member States. In the light of that information, the Secretary-General recommended that the Council extend the mandate of the existing members of the Board and postpone the election of Board members until the Council had taken action on the Working Group's recommendation.

Communication. On 20 June [E/2003/93], Spain, as Chairman of the Working Group on the future of INSTRAW, transmitted to the President of the Economic and Social Council a note presenting the Working Group's recommendations regarding the amendment of INSTRAW's statute [YUN 2002, p. 1166]. The Group proposed that the Council adopt a resolution in order to achieve those changes, which would allow the Institute to achieve its mandate properly.

Note by Secretary-General. In response to General Assembly resolution 57/175, the Secretary-General submitted a July note [E/2003/101], which contained the Secretariat's comments on the recommendations of the Working Group as transmitted by its Chairman (see above). The Secretariat noted that some of the proposed amendments did not adequately reflect the full scope of the effect that the Assembly's endorsement of the Working Group's recommendations in resolution 57/175 had on INSTRAW's statute. In particular, the new recommendations did not address the abolition of INSTRAW's autonomous status nor the establishment of institutional linkage to DESA under the direct authority of the Under-Secretary-General of that Department. In addition, the proposed amendments did not address the requirement that the Institute work closely and in close coordination with the other UN bodies involved in gender equality and the advancement of women. Also, the amendment proposed to article III, which referred to an Executive Board, should instead refer to an Advisory Board; article III, which referred to members of the Executive Board, should in fact refer to Member States instead of individual representatives since the Board should be composed of Member States; article IV, which provided that the Director should be appointed by the Secretary-General from a pool of three candidates proposed by the Executive Board, in fact interfered with the Secretary-General's prerogative as the Organization's Chief Administrative Officer; and the same reasoning applied to the amendments proposed in article IV, dealing with the authority vested in the Secretary-General to retain, confirm or replace the Institute's Director. With regard to the appointment of a Director, an understanding could be reached whereby the Secretary-General would present the Board with a list of candidates, from which the Board would select up to three, one of whom should be appointed by the Secretary-General. A revised statute of the Institute was annexed to the note.

ECONOMIC AND SOCIAL COUNCIL ACTION

On 24 July [meeting 48], the Economic and Social Council adopted **resolution 2003/57** [draft: E/2003/L.44] without vote [agenda item 14 (a)].

Revitalization and strengthening of the International Research and Training Institute for the Advancement of Women

The Economic and Social Council,

Recalling all of its resolutions aimed at the revitalization and strengthening of the International Research and Training Institute for the Advancement of Women, in particular its resolutions 1999/54 of 29 July 1999, 2000/24 of 28 July 2000 and 2001/40 of 26 July 2001,

Recalling also General Assembly resolution 56/125 of 19 December 2001, by which the Assembly decided to establish the Working Group on the Future Operation of the International Research and Training Institute for the Advancement of Women,

Taking note of the report of the Working Group, which contains a series of recommendations aimed at the revitalization and strengthening of the Institute,

Recalling General Assembly resolution 57/175 of 18 December 2002, in which the Assembly endorsed the recommendations of the Working Group and requested the Secretary-General to implement the measures recommended by the Group in that regard,

Taking note of the preliminary report of the Working Group submitted to the Commission on the Status of Women at its forty-seventh session, which highlights the need for the Economic and Social Council to amend the statute of the Institute,

Recalling Commission on the Status of Women decision 47/101, of 13 March 2003, in which the Commission recommended that the Economic and Social Council should consider the report of the Working Group to the General Assembly under the appropriate agenda item at its substantive session of 2003,

Recalling also General Assembly decision 57/580 of 20 December 2002 and Assembly resolution 57/311 of 18 June 2003 on the financial situation of the Institute,

1. *Takes note* of the report of the Board of Trustees of the International Research and Training Institute for the Advancement of Women;

2. *Takes note with appreciation* of the note by the Chairman of the Working Group on the Future Operation of the International Research and Training Institute for the Advancement of Women;

3. *Takes note* of the note by the Secretary-General on the Board of Trustees of the International Research and Training Institute for the Advancement of Women;

4. *Decides* to amend article III of the statute of the International Research and Training Institute for the Advancement of Women, in order to replace the Board of Trustees with an Executive Board, by replacing paragraphs 1, 2, 3 (c) and 4 with the following:

"1. The Institute and its work shall be governed by an Executive Board composed of ten Member States (hereinafter referred to as 'the Board');

"2. The Board shall be composed as follows:

"(a) Two governmental representatives from each of the five regional groups of the United Nations. The Economic and Social Council shall elect the members of the Board and they shall serve in their national capacities for a term of three years. They shall be eligible for reappointment by the Economic and Social Council for one further term. If a casual vacancy occurs in the membership of the Board, the Economic and Social Council shall appoint a new member to serve for the unexpired portion of the term of office of the former member concerned;

"(b) The Director of the Institute, the Under-Secretary-General for Economic and Social Affairs, a representative of the host country and a representative of each of the regional commissions of the Economic and Social Council shall serve as ex officio members of the Board.

"3. . . .

"(c) Make recommendations for the operations of the Institute;

. . .

"4. The Board shall meet at least once a year, at United Nations Headquarters in New York, in accordance with article VII of the present Statute. It shall elect its own officers, including its President, in accordance with the adopted rules of procedure. It shall take its decisions for in the manner provided in its rules of procedure."

"(e) Review the list of candidates for Director of the Institute proposed by the Secretary-General in accordance with the Charter of the United Nations, and identify several candidates from the list for the final appointment to be made by the Secretary-General";

5. *Decides also* to amend article IV of the statute of the Institute, with regard to the Director and the staff, by replacing paragraphs 1, 2 (introductory part and subparagraph (e)) and 5 of with the following:

"1. The Secretary-General of the United Nations shall appoint the Director, taking into account the list of candidates proposed by the Board.

"2. The Director shall have overall responsibility for the organization, direction and administration of the Institute in accordance with general directives by the Board and within the terms of the authority delegated to the Director by the Secretary-General. The Director shall, including through the delegation of responsibilities, where appropriate, inter alia:

...

"(e) Appoint and direct the staff of the Institute, including a Deputy Director, on behalf of the Secretary-General;

...

"5. The terms and conditions of service of the Director, the Deputy Director and the staff shall be those provided in the Staff Regulations and Rules of the United Nations, subject to such arrangements for special rules or terms of appointment as may be approved by the Secretary-General after consultations with the Board. The salaries, allowances and other expenses of the Director and the staff shall be borne by the Trust Fund for the International Research and Training Institute for the Advancement of Women";

6. *Requests* the General Assembly at its fifty-eighth session to consider the final report of the Working Group;

7. *Requests* the Director of the Institute, in consultation with the Board, to report on the implementation of the present resolution to the Economic and Social Council at its substantive session of 2004;

8. *Requests* the Secretary-General to report to the General Assembly at its fifty-ninth session on the implementation of the present resolution.

Annex

Statute of the United Nations International Research and Training Institute for the Advancement of Women

Article I
Status and purposes

The United Nations International Research and Training Institute for the Advancement of Women was established by the Economic and Social Council (Council resolution 1998(LX) of 12 May 1976) in conformity with an earlier decision of the General Assembly (resolution 3520(XXX) of 15 December 1975), which was based on a recommendation made by the World Conference of the International Women's Year, held at Mexico City from 19 June to 2 July 1975. The Institute is an autonomous institution within the framework of the United Nations established in accordance with the Charter of the United Nations to serve as a vehicle on the international level for the purpose of undertaking research and establishing training programmes to contribute to the integration and mobilization of women in development, to raise awareness of women's issues worldwide and better to assist women to meet new challenges and directions. The Institute, as part of the United Nations, enjoys the status, privileges and immunities provided in Articles 104 and 105 of the Charter and other relevant international agreements and United Nations resolutions relating to the status, privileges and immunities of the Organization.

Article II
Objectives and functions

1. The objectives of the Institute are to stimulate and assist, through research, training and the collection and dissemination of information, the advancement of women and their integration in the development process both as participants and as beneficiaries. The Institute is to assist the efforts of intergovernmental, governmental and non-governmental organizations in this regard. Accordingly, the principal functions of the Institute shall be:

(a) To conduct research and studies which would enhance the effective integration and mobilization of women in development; the research and studies programmes of the Institute, including, in particular, action-oriented ones, shall give particular attention to the problems facing women in developing countries and to the integration of women in the formulation, design and implementation of development activities at all levels;

(b) To establish training programmes, including a fellowship programme and advisory services, through which the Institute shall endeavour to raise awareness on issues concerning women and development and shall strive to achieve equal participation of women in all aspects of economic and social development and to increase the opportunities for women to acquire new skills in order to meet the challenges of rapid change in today's society;

(c) To establish and maintain a system of information, documentation and communication so as to enable the Institute to respond to the need for disseminating information worldwide on women's issues.

2. In view of its catalytic role, the Institute shall make every effort to develop and utilize networking, as appropriate, in carrying out its functions. This should be done at the international, regional and national levels.

3. In the pursuit of its objectives, the Institute shall carry out its activities in close collaboration and coordination with institutes and other bodies within and outside the United Nations system.

Article III
Executive Board

1. The Institute and its work shall be governed by an Executive Board composed of ten Member States (hereinafter referred to as "the Board").

2. The Board shall be composed as follows:

(a) Two governmental representatives from each of the five regional groups of the United Nations. The Economic and Social Council shall elect the members of the Board and they shall serve in their national capacities for a term of three years. They shall be eligible for reappointment by the Economic and Social Council for one further term. If a casual vacancy occurs in the membership of the Board, the Economic and Social Council shall appoint a new member to serve for the unexpired portion of the term of office of the former member concerned;

(b) The Director of the Institute, the Under-Secretary-General for Economic and Social Affairs, a representative of the host country and a representative of each of the regional commissions of the Economic and Social Council shall serve as ex officio members of the Board.

3. The Board shall:

(a) Formulate principles, policies and guidelines for the activities of the Institute;

(b) Consider and approve the work programmes and the budget proposals of the Institute on the basis of recommendations submitted to it by the Director of the Institute;

(c) Make recommendations for the operations of the Institute;

(d) Report periodically to the Economic and Social Council and, where appropriate, to the General Assembly;

(e) Review the list of candidates for Director of the Institute proposed by the Secretary-General in accordance with the Charter of the United Nations, and identify several candidates from the list for the final appointment to be made by the Secretary-General.

4. The Board shall meet at least once a year, at United Nations Headquarters in New York, in accordance with article VII of the present statute. It shall elect its own officers, including its President, in accordance with the adopted rules of procedure. It shall take its decisions in the manner provided for in its rules of procedure.

5. The Board shall consider methods for enhancing the financial resources of the Institute with a view to ensuring the effectiveness of its future operations, their continuity and the Institute's autonomous character within the framework of the United Nations.

6. Members of the Board, in furtherance of the principles and policies of the Institute, may be invited to help in achieving the goals of the Institute by attending meetings on behalf of the Institute, raising funds for the Institute's operations and helping to establish national support teams, if possible, in their respective countries for the attainment of the objectives of the Institute.

7. Organizations of the United Nations system and other institutions may be represented, as appropriate, at meetings of the Board in respect of activities of interest to them under the conditions outlined in the rules of procedure of the Board.

Article IV
The Director and the staff

1. The Secretary-General of the United Nations shall appoint the Director, taking into account the list of candidates proposed by the Board.

2. The Director shall have overall responsibility for the organization, direction and administration of the Institute in accordance with general directives by the Board and within the terms of the authority delegated to the Director by the Secretary-General. The Director shall, including through the delegation of responsibilities, where appropriate, inter alia:

(a) Submit the work programmes and the budget estimates of the Institute to the Board for its consideration and adoption;

(b) Oversee the execution of the work programmes and make the expenditures envisaged in the budget of the Institute as adopted by the Board;

(c) Submit to the Board annual and ad hoc reports on the activities of the Institute and the execution of its work programmes;

(d) Submit to the Economic and Social Council or to the General Assembly, as appropriate, reports approved by the Board;

(e) Appoint and direct the staff of the Institute, including a Deputy Director, on behalf of the Secretary-General;

(f) Coordinate the work of the Institute with that of other organs and bodies of the United Nations, the specialized agencies and international, regional and national institutions in similar fields;

(g) Negotiate arrangements with Governments and intergovernmental organizations as well as non-governmental organizations, academic and philanthropic institutions with a view to offering and receiving services related to the activities of the Institute;

(h) Actively seek appropriate funding for the implementation of the work programme of the Institute;

(i) Accept, subject to the provisions of article VI, paragraph 2, of the present Statute, voluntary contributions to the Institute;

(j) Make the necessary arrangements for securing established and continuous contact with and support from United Nations Headquarters;

(k) Undertake other assignments or activities as may be determined by the Board or requested by the Secretary-General, provided that any such requests are consistent with the programme budget approved by the Board.

3. The staff of the Institute shall be appointed by the Director on behalf of the Secretary-General and in accordance with modalities established by the Secretary-General, within the staffing table approved by the Board. Such appointment shall be limited to service with the Institute. The staff shall be responsible to the Director in the exercise of their functions.

4. The staff of the Institute shall be recruited on as wide a geographical basis as possible, full consideration being given to the particular requirements of and qualifications for each post needed by the Institute.

5. The terms and conditions of service of the Director, the Deputy Director and the staff shall be those provided in the Staff Regulations and Rules of the United Nations, subject to such arrangements for special rules or terms of appointment as may be approved by the Secretary-General after consultations with the Board. The salaries, allowances and other expenses of the Director and the staff shall be borne by the Trust Fund for the International Research and Training Institute for the Advancement of Women.

6. The Director and the staff of the Institute shall not seek or receive instructions from any Government or from any authority external to the United Nations. They shall refrain from any action which might reflect on their position as international officials responsible only to the Organization.

7. The Director and the staff of the Institute are officials of the United Nations and are therefore covered by Article 105 of the Charter of the United Nations and by other international agreements and United Nations resolutions defining the status of officials of the Organization.

Article V
Fellows, consultants, correspondents and focal points

1. The Board may designate as honorary fellows individuals who could contribute substantively to the Institute's objectives.

2. The Director may designate a limited number of especially qualified persons to serve as senior fellows of the Institute, for a period not longer than one year, in accordance with criteria established by the Board and procedures formulated by the Secretary-General. Such persons, who may be invited to participate as lecturers or research scholars, shall be selected on the basis of outstanding contributions they have made in fields germane to the work of the Institute.

3. The Director may also designate junior fellows as part of the Institute's ongoing fellowship programmes. All fellowships will be granted within the financial provisions of the Institute's programme budget.

4. The Director may also arrange for the services of consultants for the purpose of contributing to the analysis and planning of the activities of the Institute or for special assignments in connection with the Institute's programmes. Such consultants shall be engaged in accordance with policies established by the Secretary-General.

5. Correspondents and focal points in countries or regions may be used by the Institute to assist in maintaining contact with national or regional institutions and in carrying out or advising on studies and research.

6. Honorary, senior or junior fellows, consultants and correspondents shall not be considered to be members of the staff of the Institute.

Article VI
Finance

1. The activities of the Institute shall be funded by voluntary contributions from States, intergovernmental and non-governmental organizations, foundations, including the United Nations Foundation, private sources and other sources in accordance with article VII of the present Statute.

2. Contributions to the Institute may be accepted provided that they are consistent with the purposes and policies of the Institute. Voluntary contributions that are unrestricted or that are designated for the implementation of an activity approved by the Board may be accepted by the Director after obtaining the concurrence of the Controller of the United Nations. Other voluntary contributions may be accepted only with the approval of the Board, which shall take into account the comments of the Secretary-General. Contributions which may directly or indirectly involve an immediate or ultimate financial liability for the United Nations may be accepted only with the approval of the General Assembly.

3. The funds of the Institute derived from voluntary contributions shall be kept in the Trust Fund for the International Research and Training Institute for the Advancement of Women established by the Secretary-General in accordance with the Financial Regulations and Rules of the United Nations.

4. The funds in the Trust Fund of the Institute shall be held and administered solely for the purposes of the Institute. The Controller of the United Nations shall perform all necessary financial and accounting functions for the Institute, including the custody of its funds, and shall prepare and certify the annual accounts of the Institute.

5. The Financial Regulations and Rules of the United Nations and the financial policies and procedures established by the Secretary-General shall apply to the financial operations of the Institute. Funds of the Institute shall be subject to audit by the United Nations Board of Auditors.

6. The Institute may, in accordance with the Financial Regulations and Rules of the United Nations, enter into contracts with organizations, institutions or firms for the purpose of carrying out its operations. The Institute may acquire or dispose of real and movable property in accordance with the same Regulations and Rules.

Article VII
Administrative and other support

The Secretary-General of the United Nations shall provide the Institute with appropriate administrative and other support, including financial and personnel services, in accordance with the Financial Regulations and Rules of the United Nations and on conditions determined after consultations between the Secretary-General and the Director of the Institute, it being understood that no extra costs to the regular budget of the United Nations are incurred.

Article VIII
Cooperation with other organizations and institutions

1. The Institute shall develop arrangements for active and close cooperation with the specialized and related agencies of the United Nations as well as with other organs, programmes and institutions within the United Nations system.

2. The Institute shall endeavour to develop arrangements for cooperation with other organizations or institutions involved in training and research activities which are relevant to the work of the Institute and which may be of assistance to the Institute in the performance of its functions.

Article IX
Location

The headquarters of the Institute shall be located in the Dominican Republic at Santo Domingo. The Institute may, with the approval of the Board and after consultations with the Secretary-General of the United Nations, establish other offices elsewhere.

Article X
Amendments

1. Amendments to the present Statute may be made by the Economic and Social Council.

2. The Board may review the provisions of the present Statute and propose to the Economic and Social Council such amendments as it may consider necessary.

3. The Secretary-General may submit to the Board or, if necessary, to the Economic and Social Council,

after consultation with the President of the Board, proposals for the revision of the present Statute.

Future operation of INSTRAW

Report of Secretary-General. In response to General Assembly resolution 57/175 [YUN 2002, p. 1167], the Secretary-General submitted an October report [A/58/417], which reviewed progress in the implementation of reform measures proposed by the Working Group on the Future Operation of INSTRAW in 2002 [YUN 2002, p. 1166], including the revision of INSTRAW's statute (see p. 1195), the implementation of its work programme, the creation of the post of Deputy Director with specific fund-raising responsibilities and the establishment of a liaison function for INSTRAW in DESA, the appointment of a Director (see below), increased coordination between INSTRAW and other relevant UN bodies and the management of INSTRAW. An external audit was conducted (26-30 May) on follow-up to audit recommendations, including recommendations made by the Office of Internal Oversight Services [YUN 2002, p. 1165] and progress in the implementation of the work programme for 2002 [ibid., p. 1166], the results of which would be reported to Member States once a management letter had been received.

The Secretary-General said that, as requested by Assembly resolution 57/311 (see p. 1200), the Secretariat had transferred $250,000 to the Trust Fund for INSTRAW in June, which represented the second tranche of the regular budget subsidy of $500,000 that was set aside in the contingency fund for the 2002-2003 biennium, in accordance with Assembly decision 57/580 [YUN 2002, p. 1167]. Largely due to the subsidy and savings from vacancies in INSTRAW, the Institute would be able to continue to operate at a minimal level until the end of May 2004. INSTRAW's precarious financial situation precluded long-term planning and programming, and its capacity to contribute to the advancement of women and gender equality continued to deteriorate. He concluded that, despite the efforts of the Working Group and the Secretariat, no progress had been made in the implementation of INSTRAW's institutional reform.

Working Group report. In response to General Assembly resolution 57/175, the Working Group on the Future Operation of INSTRAW, in an October report [A/58/540], updated the status of implementation of its recommendations. The Economic and Social Council had decided to amend the INSTRAW statute in order to transform the Board of Directors into an Executive Board (see p. 1195), the $500,000 subsidy was allocated (see above) and the creation of a post of Deputy Director had been enabled by the changes to the statute.

By **decision 58/533** of 22 December, the Assembly took note of the Secretary-General's and the Working Group's reports on the future operation of INSTRAW.

Appointment. In December, the Secretary-General announced the appointment of Carmen Moreno as Director of the Institute.

GENERAL ASSEMBLY ACTION

On 23 December [meeting 79], the General Assembly, on the recommendation of the Third Committee [A/58/501], adopted **resolution 58/244** by recorded vote (126-5-30) [agenda item 110].

Future operation of the International Research and Training Institute for the Advancement of Women

The General Assembly,

Recalling its previous resolutions on the subject, in particular resolutions 55/219 of 23 December 2000, 56/125 of 19 December 2001 and 57/175 of 18 December 2002,

Recalling also that, in its resolution 56/125, it decided to establish a working group mandated to make recommendations to the General Assembly on the future operation of the International Research and Training Institute for the Advancement of Women,

Reaffirming its resolution 57/311 of 18 June 2003 on the financial situation of the Institute,

Welcoming Economic and Social Council resolution 2003/57 of 24 July 2003, in which the Council decided to amend articles III and IV of the statute of the Institute,

Welcoming also the efforts and the consistency in the work of the Working Group on the Future Operation of the International Research and Training Institute for the Advancement of Women in promoting a comprehensive approach to the revitalization and strengthening of the Institute, which has led to the adoption of important institutional and political changes that are contributing to the strengthening of the Institute,

1. *Welcomes* the report of the Working Group on the Future Operation of the International Research and Training Institute for the Advancement of Women, in which the Working Group, inter alia, reaffirmed the mandate of the Institute in the field of gender equality and the advancement of women and stressed the need for it to be reformed and revitalized, as recommended in its previous report and endorsed by the General Assembly in its resolution 57/175;

2. *Decides* to continue monitoring the implementation of the measures recommended by the Working Group in its report, in close consultation with the Secretary-General;

3. *Stresses* the critical importance of voluntary financial contributions by Member States to the United Nations Trust Fund for the International Research and Training Institute for the Advancement of Women to enable it to carry out its mandate;

4. *Urges* Member States to make voluntary contributions to the Trust Fund, particularly during this critical transitional period;

5. *Decides* to continue to provide its full support to the current efforts to revitalize the Institute and, in this regard, to provide funds complementary to the existing ones, if needed, to ensure that the Institute will have adequate resources to function for a period of one year and to submit its report to the General Assembly as requested in resolution 57/311, in the light of the delay in appointing a Director to implement a feasible work programme and fund-raising activities;

6. *Also decides* to request the Working Group to continue monitoring the implementation of the recommendations and measures contained in its report until the new executive board convenes its first session;

7. *Requests* the Secretary-General to report to the General Assembly at its fifty-ninth session on the implementation of the present resolution.

RECORDED VOTE ON RESOLUTION 58/244:

In favour: Algeria, Andorra, Angola, Antigua and Barbuda, Argentina, Armenia, Azerbaijan, Bahrain, Bangladesh, Belarus, Belize, Benin, Bolivia, Bosnia and Herzegovina, Botswana, Brazil, Brunei Darussalam, Burkina Faso, Burundi, Cambodia, Cameroon, Cape Verde, Central African Republic, Chile, China, Colombia, Comoros, Congo, Costa Rica, Côte d'Ivoire, Cuba, Cyprus, Djibouti, Dominica, Dominican Republic, Ecuador, Egypt, Eritrea, Ethiopia, Fiji, Gabon, Gambia, Ghana, Greece, Grenada, Guatemala, Guyana, Haiti, India, Indonesia, Iran, Italy, Jamaica, Jordan, Kenya, Kuwait, Kyrgyzstan, Lao People's Democratic Republic, Lebanon, Lesotho, Libyan Arab Jamahiriya, Madagascar, Malawi, Malaysia, Maldives, Mali, Malta, Marshall Islands, Mauritania, Mauritius, Mexico, Monaco, Mongolia, Morocco, Mozambique, Myanmar, Namibia, Nepal, Nicaragua, Niger, Nigeria, Oman, Pakistan, Panama, Papua New Guinea, Paraguay, Peru, Philippines, Portugal, Qatar, Republic of Moldova, Romania, Russian Federation, Rwanda, Saint Lucia, Saudi Arabia, Senegal, Serbia and Montenegro, Singapore, Slovakia, Slovenia, Solomon Islands, Somalia, Spain, Sri Lanka, Sudan, Suriname, Syrian Arab Republic, Thailand, The former Yugoslav Republic of Macedonia, Timor-Leste, Togo, Tonga, Trinidad and Tobago, Tunisia, Turkey, Turkmenistan, Tuvalu, United Arab Emirates, United Republic of Tanzania, Uruguay, Venezuela, Viet Nam, Yemen, Zambia, Zimbabwe.

Against: Australia, Canada, Japan, New Zealand, United States.

Abstaining: Albania, Austria, Belgium, Bulgaria, Croatia, Czech Republic, Denmark, Estonia, Finland, France, Georgia, Germany, Hungary, Iceland, Ireland, Israel, Latvia, Liechtenstein, Lithuania, Luxembourg, Netherlands, Norway, Poland, Republic of Korea, San Marino, Sweden, Switzerland, Ukraine, United Kingdom, Uzbekistan.

Financial situation

During 2003, INSTRAW's financial situation remained precarious. In an April report [A/57/797] on INSTRAW's financial situation, submitted in response to General Assembly decision 57/580 [YUN 2002, p. 1167], the Secretary-General stated that, in accordance with the decision, $250,000 was transferred to the Institute's Trust Fund in January, resulting in a balance of $687,780, which was sufficient to finance the Institute's operations and related operating expenses until 31 May. However, contributions pledged during the Pledging Conference for Development Activities (New York, November 2002) had not been received. The Trust Fund's income during the first four months of 2003 amounted to $138,919, including $127,925 in government contributions and $10,994 in miscellaneous income. On that basis, and taking into account that the Institute's Director was expected to be appointed as from 1 May, it was estimated that the Trust Fund's balance as at 31 May would amount to approximately $481,900, which was considered sufficient for maintaining its operations until the end of November. An additional amount of $100,000 would, however, be required to sustain the Institute's operations until 31 December. The Secretary-General concluded that it was not possible to be definitive as to any contributions that might be made subsequent to the issuance of the current report. He recommended that the General Assembly take note of the current report and request a further report on the Institute's financial situation at its fifty-eighth (2003) session.

In May [A/57/7/Add.27], the Advisory Committee on Administrative and Budgetary Questions endorsed the Secretary-General's recommendation.

GENERAL ASSEMBLY ACTION

On 18 June [meeting 90], the General Assembly, on the recommendation of the Fifth (Administrative and Budgetary) Committee [A/57/649/Add.2], adopted **resolution 57/311** without vote [agenda item 112].

Financial situation of the International Research and Training Institute for the Advancement of Women

The General Assembly,

Recalling its decision 57/580 of 20 December 2002,

Having considered the report of the Secretary-General on the financial situation of the International Research and Training Institute for the Advancement of Women and the related report of the Advisory Committee on Administrative and Budgetary Questions,

Having also considered the report of the Office of Internal Oversight Services on the audit of the Institute,

1. *Takes note* of the report of the Secretary-General and of the observations and recommendations of the Advisory Committee on Administrative and Budgetary Questions;

2. *Takes note also* of the report of the Office of Internal Oversight Services;

3. *Regrets* that the nomination of a Director of the Institute, a post classified at the D-2 level, has not yet taken place, impairing the capacity of the Institute to function properly;

4. *Urges* the Secretary-General to appoint immediately a Director at the D-2 level, to be based at the headquarters of the Institute in the Dominican Republic, and thereafter to inform the Working Group on the Future Operation of the International Research and Training Institute for the Advancement of Women of the designation of the nominee;

5. *Approves* the release of the amount of 250,000 United States dollars that was set aside in the contingency fund for the biennium 2002-2003, in conformity with the provisions of General Assembly decision 57/580, as an additional provision for the continuation of the core activities of the Institute in 2003, and decides to appropriate the amount of 250,000 dollars for this purpose;

6. *Recalls* its resolutions 41/213 of 19 December 1986 and 42/211 of 21 December 1987, and in this connection stresses that the contingency fund is not in-

tended to be used as a recurring source of programme funding;

7. *Requests* the Institute to report to the General Assembly, one year after the appointment of a Director, on its programme of work and on the implementation of the recommendations contained in the report of the Office of Internal Oversight Services;

8. *Requests* the Secretary-General to report further to the General Assembly at its fifty-eighth session on the financial situation of the Institute.

As requested by Assembly resolution 57/311 (above), the Secretary-General submitted an October report [A/58/426] on INSTRAW's financial situation. During the reporting period (17 April–30 September), additional income to the Trust Fund amounted to $10,421, which included $2,999 in government contributions and $7,452 in miscellaneous income. As at 30 September, unpaid pledges to the Institute amounted to $76,074. The level of expenditures for the period from 1 January to 30 September was lower than expected. That, coupled with the additional grant of $250,000 from the UN regular budget, resulted in the Trust Fund's projected unencumbered balance as at 31 December 2003 being $450,000, an amount that would allow the Institute's operations to continue until the end of May 2004.

Chapter XI
Children, youth and ageing persons

In 2003, the United Nations Children's Fund (UNICEF) continued its efforts to ensure that every child received the best start in life; was fully immunized and protected from disease and disability; completed a quality primary education; and was protected from harm, abuse and violence in times of war and peace and in emergencies. All young people were to be given reliable information on HIV/AIDS prevention.

Progress towards the implementation of "A world fit for children", the final document of the General Assembly's twenty-seventh (2002) special session on children, continued in the four major goal areas of the document's Plan of Action—promoting healthy lives, providing quality education, protecting children against abuse, exploitation and violence, and combating HIV/AIDS.

UNICEF continued work on its five organizational priorities for 2002-2005: girls education; fighting HIV/AIDS; integrated early childhood development; immunization "plus"; and improved protection from violence, exploitation, abuse and discrimination.

The World Youth Report 2003, a comprehensive analysis of the global situation of youth, reviewed the 10 priority areas of the 1995 World Programme of Action for Youth to the Year 2000 and Beyond, and identified five new concerns that had emerged since the Programme's adoption. The second meeting of the High-level Panel of the Youth Employment Network considered a draft action programme, which recommended the next five steps to be taken by the Network.

In 2003, the United Nations continued its efforts to implement the Madrid International Plan of Action on Ageing, adopted in 2002 by the Second World Assembly on Ageing. The Secretariat proposed a "bottom-up" approach to the review and appraisal of the Plan of Action, and a road map for its implementation was introduced by the Secretary-General in July.

Children

Follow-up to the 2002 General Assembly special session on children

In response to General Assembly resolution 57/190 [YUN 2002, p. 749], the Secretary-General, in August [A/58/333], described follow-up to the Assembly's twenty-seventh (2002) special session on children [YUN 2002, p. 1168], including progress in realizing the commitments of the session's final document, "A world fit for children", consisting of a Declaration and Plan of Action, adopted in resolution S-27/2 [ibid., p. 1169]. The report covered global and regional actions taken by non-governmental organizations (NGOs) and civil society organizations, and the UN system's response. It also highlighted action taken in the four major goal areas of the Plan of Action—promoting healthy lives, providing quality education, protecting children against abuse, exploitation and violence, and combating HIV/AIDS.

Although Governments, foundations, NGOs, civil society organizations, the private sector and UN agencies had worked together to ensure that the Declaration and Plan of Action were enthusiastically and diligently pursued, follow-up actions had not received high priority in all countries or regions, and more systematic efforts and exchanges of experience were called for to fulfil the pledges made at the special session. Nearly 140 countries had taken concrete actions to translate their commitments into national action plans and/or to integrate them into specific plans and policies. Information received by UNICEF, as at the end of July, indicated that 29 countries had completed or drafted new national plans of action for children; 64 countries were in the process of or would start to develop such plans. In addition, 10 countries had updated their existing national plans and 46 had integrated the agenda of "A world fit for children" into existing national plans and policies, poverty reduction strategies and sectoral policies. The report provided regional information on progress in sub-Saharan Africa; Asia; Central and Eastern Europe, the Commonwealth of Independent States (CIS) and the Baltic States; Latin America and the Caribbean; the Middle East and North Africa; and industrialized countries.

Follow-up by the UN system focused on programmatic support and inter-agency collaboration, advocacy, communication strategies, resource mobilization, building partnerships and alliances, and the quantitative and qualitative review of progress made by Member States. Efforts were under way to ensure that the goals, targets and strategies of "A world fit for children" were adequately reflected in the common country assessment (CCA) and the United Nations Development Assistance Framework (UNDAF) processes. The UN system was also working with the World Bank and bilateral agencies to include the agenda of "A world fit for children" and the Millennium Development Goals (MDGs) of the Millennium Declaration, adopted by the General Assembly in resolution 55/2 [YUN 2000, p. 49], in poverty reduction strategies and sector-wide approaches.

The Secretary-General concluded that the progress made represented a good start, but tremendous challenges remained. He urged countries that were developing or would develop national action plans to complete them by year's end. Countries that had chosen to use other mechanisms should ensure that those plans and frameworks reflected the key goals and targets of "A world fit for children" to enable periodic monitoring and future review of progress. It was imperative that a broad consensus be built, and that civil society organizations, NGOs, families, children and young people be engaged in the development and monitoring of national and subnational plans of action for children. All countries should follow up the Monterrey Consensus, adopted at the 2002 International Conference on Financing for Development [YUN 2002, p. 953], to increase financing for development. They should also consider establishing or strengthening national institutions to promote and protect children's rights; establish or strengthen national and subnational monitoring systems to assess progress towards key, child-related goals and increase national capacities to collect, analyse and disaggregate data by sex, age and other factors; and conduct periodic reviews of progress at national and subnational levels to address obstacles and accelerate progress. Countries might wish to develop closer linkages between the mechanisms established for monitoring and reporting on the 1989 Convention on the Rights of the Child, adopted by General Assembly resolution 44/25 [YUN 1989, p. 560] (see p. 780). The Secretary-General proposed providing to the Assembly an in-depth progress report on implementation of the Declaration and Plan of Action every five years—in 2006, 2011 and 2016—based on national, regional and global reviews. All countries were encouraged to conduct in-depth reviews of progress in or before 2005 for the first review process, which would lead to the 2006 report.

A final report on the use of funds for UNICEF support to the special session [E/ICEF/2003/AB/L.12] indicated that UNICEF received 40 contributions from 22 Member States, six national committees and one foundation, totalling $7,417,439; total expenditures as at 30 June amounted to $7,415,324, leaving a balance of $2,115.

On 22 December, the General Assembly, in **resolution 58/157** (see p. 781), requested the Secretary-General to prepare an updated report on progress achieved in realizing the commitments set out in "A world fit for children" and to report to the Assembly at its fifty-ninth (2004) session.

On 23 December, the Assembly decided that the item on follow-up to the outcome of the special session on children would remain for consideration during its resumed fifty-eighth (2004) session (**decision 58/565**).

United Nations Children's Fund

UNICEF was committed to the realization of the MDGs [YUN 2000, p. 51], and the goals set out by the Assembly's twenty-seventh (2002) special session on children [YUN 2002, p. 1168] in its outcome document, "A world fit for children" [ibid., p. 1169]. Its mission was to defend children's rights, help meet their basic needs, ensure their survival and increase their opportunities to flourish; rally political will to invest in children's well-being; respond to emergencies and strengthen the ability of children and their families to handle crises, including armed conflict, natural disasters and HIV/AIDS; assist countries in transition to protect young people's rights and provide vital services to children and their families; advance equal rights for boys and girls and encourage their full participation in the development of their communities; and work towards the human development goals adopted by the world community and the peace, justice and social progress enshrined in the Charter of the United Nations.

UNICEF's flagship publication, *The State of the World's Children 2003*, sought to draw public attention to the importance of young people's active participation in family, school, community and national life; encourage States, civil society organizations and the private sector to promote children's involvement in decisions that affected their lives; present examples of how the lives of children, families and communities had been changed when children had the opportunity to contribute on matters that affected them; and spark action that included children and young people in meeting the goals of "A world fit for children" and the MDGs.

In 2003, UNICEF cooperated with 158 countries, areas and territories: 46 in sub-Saharan Africa; 35 in Latin America and the Caribbean; 35 in Asia; 20 in the Middle East and North Africa; and 22 in Central and Eastern Europe, CIS and the Baltic States.

Total expenditures, including write-offs, amounted to $1,480 million (compared with $1,273 million in 2002), of which 93 per cent ($1,382 million) was for country programmes of cooperation; 6 per cent ($87 million) for management and administration of the organization; and about 1 per cent ($11 million) for write-offs and other charges. Programme expenditures by priorities were: $442 million for early childhood development; $258 million for immunization "plus"; $233 million for girls' education; $123 million for the improved protection of children; and $110 million for HIV/AIDS. UNICEF operations in 2003 were described in the *UNICEF Annual Report* covering the period 1 January to 31 December 2003, the annual report of its Executive Director [E/ICEF/2004/4] and a report of the Executive Director [E/ICEF/2004/9] on results achieved for children during the year in support of UNICEF's 2002-2005 medium-term strategic plan, which was approved by the Executive Board in 2001 [YUN 2001, p. 1094].

The UNICEF Executive Board held its first regular session of 2003 (13-17 January), the annual session (2-6 and 9 June), the second regular session (15-19 September) and an extraordinary budgetary session (1-2 December), all in New York [E/2003/34/Rev.1]. The Board adopted 18 decisions during those sessions.

By **decision 2003/225** of 11 July, the Economic and Social Council took note of the Board's report on its first regular session; the Board's decisions at its annual session [E/2003/L.8]; and the annual report of the Executive Director covering the year 2002 [E/2003/48], which was transmitted in accordance with a January decision of the Board [E/2003/34/Rev.1 (dec. 2003/1)].

On 19 September [dec. 2003/14], the Executive Board, having considered a July report on its working methods [E/ICEF/2003/12], requested the Bureau to enter into dialogue with representatives of other UN funds, programmes and organizations to explore approaches to improving working methods and to report back to the Board in 2004. On the same date, the Board adopted the programme of work and dates for its 2004 sessions [dec. 2003/15].

Programme policies

In January, the Executive Board considered a progress report on UNICEF engagement in sector-wide approaches to development (SWAps) [E/ICEF/2003/6]. The report discussed SWAps in the context of existing and emerging development financing initiatives; UNICEF's contribution to SWAps; benefits and constraints of UNICEF participation; and UNICEF's efforts to develop staff capacities to participate meaningfully in policy dialogue on SWAps and in their implementation. UNICEF was participating in evolving SWAps and sectoral development programmes in 20 countries, mostly in the health and education sectors.

Medium-term financial plan (2003-2006)

While the medium-term financial plan was contained in each medium-term strategic plan (MTSP) (the 2002-2005 MTSP was approved by the Executive Board in 2001 [YUN 2001, p. 1094]), it was updated annually. The Board considered a July report [E/ICEF/2003/AB/L.7], which presented the financial plan for 2003-2006 and projected total planned programme expenditures with an upward trend to reflect increased income. The Executive Director recommended that the Board approve the medium-term financial plan as a framework of projections for 2003-2006, including preparation of up to $151 million in programme expenditures from regular resources to be submitted to the Board in 2004. The amount was subject to the availability of resources and to the condition that estimates of income and expenditure continued to be valid. The Executive Director also recommended that the Board authorize the establishment of a funded reserve to count towards the contingent liability of after-service health insurance, with $30 million allocated to the reserve in 2003 and $10 million per year for the period 2004-2006.

On 17 September [dec. 2003/11], the Board approved the 2003-2006 medium-term plan and the establishment of a funded reserve for after-service health insurance, as recommended by the Executive Director.

Evaluation system

A November report of the Executive Director [E/2004/3-E/ICEF/2004/4] stated that a senior-level Evaluation Committee was created in 2003 to advise her on evaluation matters and to provide oversight of the evaluation function. Its mandate was to review evaluation reports produced by UNICEF that had relevance at the global governance level and to endorse the recommendations made in the reports. The Committee examined the work of UNICEF's Evaluation Office and cleared the release of reports to the public domain; it also adopted rules and procedures that clarified the accountabilities for the evaluation function at all levels of UNICEF and its own modus operandi. Training workshops were held as part of ongoing evaluations, so as to disseminate results-based approaches to programming and evaluation. Integrated monitoring and evaluation planning within the country programme management plan were promoted through workshops and inclusion in the United Nations Development Group (UNDG) harmonized and simplified country programme cycle. In compliance with a multi-year evaluation plan in support of the MTSP, evaluation work was conducted in areas related to HIV/AIDS and education as prevention against child labour. An assessment of the *ChildInfo* web site, which provided access to UNICEF's key statistical database, was completed. The Evaluation Office assessed programmes of cooperation for Mauritius, the Pacific island countries and Peru, in an effort to develop and test a broad-based methodology for country programme evaluation. To strengthen evaluation capacity-building within UNICEF, a meta-evaluation of the quality of evaluations performed by country offices, together with national authorities, identified areas requiring improvement.

Emergency assistance

In 2003, UNICEF updated its Core Commitments for Children in Emergencies (CCCs). Efforts focused on the comparative advantage of UNICEF in the light of enhanced coordination by humanitarian actors. The purpose of the revised CCCs was to enhance the timeliness, effectiveness and predictability of the UNICEF humanitarian response, and to reinforce the link between the UNICEF response to crises and its mandate to promote and help ensure the rights of children and women.

About one third of the countries in which UNICEF operated in 2003 were responding to crises and emergencies, and 25-30 per cent of UNICEF funding was dedicated emergency funding. UNICEF continued to participate actively in the United Nations inter-agency consolidated appeals process (see p. 922).

In 2003, humanitarian support extended by donors included secondment of emergency response personnel, in-kind donations and other forms of assistance to enable improved response to children's needs in crisis situations. Emergency funding reached $401.4 million. Of that amount, UNICEF received $345.2 million (86 per cent) from government and intergovernmental donors and $52.1 million (13 per cent) from national committees. During the year, UNICEF humanitarian programmes received support from 38 Governments, 29 national committees and 5 other donors.

UNICEF programmes by region

In 2003, UNICEF regional programme expenditures totalled $1,208 million, of which $493 million (41 per cent) went to programmes in sub-Saharan Africa; $388 million (32 per cent) to programmes in Asia; $160 million (13 per cent) to programmes in the Middle East and North Africa; $69 million (6 per cent) to programmes in the Americas and the Caribbean; and $53 million (4 per cent) to programmes in Central and Eastern Europe, CIS and the Baltic States. Another $45 million (4 per cent) went to interregional programmes. Programme support costs amounted to an additional $155 million.

Programme expenditures continued to be concentrated in countries with low income and high or very high under-five mortality rates. The 63 low-income countries—those with a per capita gross national income of $745 and less—had a total child population of 1 billion or about 55 per cent of all children worldwide; they received 65 per cent of the total programme expenditure, 6 per cent less than in 2002 [YUN 2002, p. 1185].

Field visits

In Mozambique (10-19 March), Executive Board members noted that UNICEF activities had achieved a good balance between efforts to promote survival and health care for children and interventions aimed at promoting long-term human development. In supporting community-based action aimed at engaging people in the development process, the country team had achieved impressive outcomes while ensuring that the methodology used supported long-term project sustainability. UNICEF had taken innovative approaches in implementing its priorities, including in combating HIV/AIDS through active support for peer education, and in its vision of extending services to the aged who cared for HIV/AIDS orphans and other orphaned children; there was a need to encourage and support community-based monitoring of the impact of those approaches, with a view to ensuring that they were maintained and strengthened. UNICEF's involvement of community volunteers working in the supplementary feeding programme in the detection of severe malnutrition increased the community's ability to monitor the nutritional status of children for referral to health centres. A joint segment of the field visit by members of the Executive Boards of the United Nations Development Programme (UNDP)/United Nations Population Fund (UNFPA), UNICEF and the World Food Programme (WFP) took place during the same period; it was recommended that such joint visits be continued.

Executive Board members who visited Tajikistan and Uzbekistan (10-19 March) concluded that both countries had successfully established political stability and were seriously committed to and involved in implementing the 1989 Convention on the Rights of the Child (see p. 780). The country programmes in both countries were well-focused and characterized by a decentralized approach; they forged strong partnerships with institutions, the community, NGOs and children, while remaining action-oriented, cost-effective and catalytic. UNICEF's role as catalyst was especially evident in the pursuit of child-related issues within the framework of the Convention. The programme reviews, particularly the midterm reviews in Tajikistan and Uzbekistan, had resulted in a better-focused set of key priorities and targets. The current thrust of building the capacity of local NGOs and community participation should be reinforced. In the light of funding constraints, which could seriously hamper programme delivery and progress, it would be desirable for UNICEF to reinforce its fund-raising strategies for the region through the Central Asian Republics and Kazakhstan Forum, as well as horizontal cooperation.

At the initiative of the Executive Board President, Bureau members visited Bolivia (7-10 April), marking the first-ever field visit explicitly for Bureau members. The team found that the empowerment of communities, particularly of women, was evident in most programmes visited, including in the management of the microcredit scheme and of water and sanitation systems. Literacy programmes had proved very effective in empowering community members and as an entry point for other initiatives. The sustainability of most projects appeared to be linked to low cost, the use of simple technologies and the commitment of local authorities and community members. In addition to direct interventions in basic services, the country programme was also successful in advocacy, policy dialogue and capacity-building. UNICEF was able to influence national policies in bilingual education and in basic health insurance schemes for women and for children under the age of five. The Bureau members were convinced of the importance of field visits in future and recommended that the practice continue annually.

UNICEF programmes by sector

In 2003, UNICEF programme expenditures were linked to the five organizational priorities established in 2001 under the 2002-2005 MTSP [YUN 2001, p. 1093], with the largest share of the $1,208 million total expenditure made in the area of early childhood development (ECD) ($440 million or 36 per cent). Significant shares also went to immunization "plus" ($260 million or 22 per cent); girls' education ($233 million or 19 per cent); child protection ($123 million or 10 per cent); and HIV/AIDS ($111 million or 9 per cent). Expenditures in other areas amounted to $41 million or 3 per cent of the total. Programme support costs amounted to an additional $155 million.

The Executive Director allocated $24.9 million in 2003 to country programmes from the global set-aside of 7 per cent of regular resources. The funds were allocated in support of strategic initiatives, in line with the Executive Board decision establishing the set-aside [YUN 1997, p. 1220]. The largest portion of the set-aside—41 per cent—was used to combat HIV/AIDS and its effects, while 16 per cent supported girls' education initiatives and 12 per cent went to child protection. The remaining funds were allocated to support arsenic mitigation, ECD, polio eradication, and health initiatives in Haiti. Forty-three per cent of the set-aside funds were allocated to countries in Asia and 30 per cent to sub-Saharan Africa.

Early childhood development

In 2003, UNICEF supported various components of the early childhood approach that addressed improving the situation of children living in poverty, their families and communities. Some 57 countries had national coordinating mechanisms for early childhood development, compared to 41 in 2002. The number of programme countries with official policies on early childhood increased from 17 in 2002 to 30 in 2003. Together with other UN agencies, UNICEF worked in Azerbaijan, Burkina Faso, Mongolia, the Republic of Moldova and Serbia and Montenegro to promote an emphasis on young children in new or revised poverty reduction strategy papers (PRSPs). In Uganda, health and education SWAps were used to help ensure a policy focus on young children.

UNICEF and the World Bank teamed up to support the use in several countries of the "marginal budgeting to bottlenecks" tool, which helped to identify implementation constraints in the health-care system and the marginal costs of overcoming them. The tool had been used in preparing medium-term expenditure frameworks in Mali and Mauritania, where it helped to increase allocations to child and maternal survival, and for policy dialogue in Madagascar and the state of Madhya Pradesh in India.

Regarding basic delivery service in key areas of maternal and child health, water and sanitation, prevention of iodine deficiency disorders, malaria prevention, the control of diarrhoeal diseases, and pre-school and early learning programmes, some countries in West Africa used "zones of convergence" to deliver a coordinated package of services and commodities to young children. The convergence approach to basic service provision was also used in places with large populations of displaced people or refugees, such as Guinea and

Liberia. In Angola, "child-friendly" spaces were used to provide a range of assistance to war-affected children and adolescents, including nutrition rehabilitation, birth registration, family tracing and psychosocial recovery. The Integrated Management of Childhood Illness (IMCI) strategy, a major effort for the convergent delivery of services for child survival, growth and development, focused on malnutrition, acute respiratory infections, diarrhoeal diseases and malaria—conditions that combined to cause nearly 4 million child deaths every year. In 77 countries, UNICEF supported a "community focus" on IMCI, including strengthening the local health system, the case management skills of health workers, and family health practices in the management of diarrhoea, pneumonia and malaria. The Accelerated Child Survival and Development (ACSD) programme, a complementary initiative piloted by UNICEF and the Canadian International Development Agency (CIDA), supported cost-effective interventions in 11 countries in West and Central Africa, including immunization and case management of the main childhood killer diseases, vitamin A supplementation and antenatal care. It was estimated that some 130 million people in 86 developing countries were covered by IMCI and ACSD in 2003.

A range of sectoral interventions continued to be supported by UNICEF, such as the improvement of emergency obstetric care in 3,400 health facilities in 80 countries during 2003. The use of insecticide-treated nets (ITNs) to combat malaria expanded in 38 countries. At least 12 African countries were expected to reach 60 per cent usage rates among young children and women in 2005. Procurement of nets and insecticide, a priority of the UNICEF supply operation (see p. 1214), had more than doubled, from 2.3 million nets in 2001 to nearly 4.8 million—worth $13.5 million—in 2003, as part of UNICEF's contribution to the Roll Back Malaria partnership (see p. 1251). Insecticide worth some $3.7 million was also supplied. UNICEF supported the training of health workers in diarrhoea management and strengthening of systems for the distribution of essential commodities such as oral rehydration salts (ORS); it supplied 43.2 million sachets of ORS in 33 countries in 2003, a 38 per cent increase compared to 2002.

In 2003, UNICEF supported programmes for clean water, sanitation and hygiene in 91 countries, assisting in policy reform, capacity-building and improved service delivery for poor and marginalized populations, with a major focus on rural water supply and sanitation in countries with low coverage rates. In Iraq, UNICEF supported the repair of damaged infrastructure and supplied 825,000 people with water on a daily basis. It also led the UN coordinating unit for Iraq, based in Amman, Jordan. Emergency support was provided in response to an earthquake in Iran and to a major typhoid outbreak in Tajikistan.

During the year, participatory approaches were applied to nutrition, HIV/AIDS and malaria control, and were implemented successfully in drought- and AIDS-affected countries in Southern Africa, especially Mozambique and Zambia. Responding to the potential danger of arsenic poisoning in several countries in Asia, affecting an estimated 50 million people, Governments, with the support of UNICEF and other agencies, initiated arsenic mitigation programmes to raise awareness about the danger, identify contaminated wells and establish alternative water systems. UNICEF was involved in testing household filter technologies in Bangladesh, India and Viet Nam, and it continued to focus on finding alternative arsenic-free water sources.

During 2003, UNICEF supported birth registration campaigns in 40 least developed countries (LDCs) and 25 countries facing emergency situations, indicating that registration had become an important part of crisis response. The number of countries that had developed key parental care practices, based on UNICEF/World Health Organization (WHO) recommendations, for promoting among families and communities the need to secure a child's best start in life, increased to 83, compared with 67 in 2002; the total included some 60 per cent of LDCs and nearly two thirds of countries with current humanitarian appeals. About 60 countries also undertook baseline surveys during 2002-2003 to improve the understanding of existing family-care practices. Ten countries suffering the burden of HIV/AIDS revitalized efforts to support infant feeding and the Baby-Friendly Hospital Initiative, and the introduction of the UNICEF/WHO Global Strategy for Infant and Young Child Feeding, endorsed by UNICEF's Executive Board in 2002 [YUN 2002, p. 1184], refocused efforts on support to women and families. The number of countries making efforts to strengthen the role of fathers in child care increased from 10 in 2002 to 28 in 2003. UNICEF continued its support for child-care centres in about two thirds of programme countries, and for home-based care in about half. In 38 countries, UNICEF also supported early learning initiatives that incorporated specific measures to prepare girls for school.

Immunization "plus"

At current levels of immunization coverage, it was estimated that the lives of 2.5 million children were saved each year worldwide, but there were about 2.2 million preventable deaths. In 2003, UNICEF procured some 2.5 billion doses of vaccines to support immunization programmes and campaigns, including nearly 1.9 billion doses of oral polio vaccine. UNICEF continued to work for global polio eradication in partnership with Governments and international organizations, including the United States Centers for Disease Control (CDC), Rotary International and WHO. Following a rise in the number of confirmed cases of wild polio virus to 1,918 in 2002 from 483 in 2001, renewed progress was seen in 2003 towards the eradication goal, with some 733 cases confirmed. By the end of the year, polio transmission had become more localized and confined to a few states or provinces of Afghanistan, Egypt, India, the Niger, Nigeria and Pakistan. UNICEF assisted in the vaccination of 4 million children against polio before the conflict in Iraq (see p. 333), and its provision of 25 million doses of vaccine and cold-chain equipment helped to re-establish the routine immunization system soon after.

The MTSP target of reducing measles mortality by one half was likely to be reached and even surpassed. By 2002, the death toll from measles had been reduced to 611,000—an estimated 30 per cent decrease from 869,000 in 1990. Ninety-six per cent of those deaths occurred in 45 priority countries, mainly in Africa and Asia, where UNICEF and its partners were focusing their efforts. Of the 45 countries, 10 completed "catch-up" vaccination campaigns in 2003 and another eight mounted campaigns as part of multi-year efforts to reach all children. UNICEF supplied about 160 million doses of measles vaccines compared to 145 million in 2002. UNICEF, the United States CDC and WHO supported the planning and management of the campaigns and the exclusive use of auto-disable (AD) syringes. However, funding shortfalls and logistical constraints, injection safety and waste management still needed to be addressed to achieve and sustain national measles reduction targets. The Measles Initiative, whose members included the American Red Cross, the United States CDC, CIDA, the International Federation of Red Cross and Red Crescent Societies, the United Nations Foundation, UNICEF and WHO, continued to support efforts towards the measles mortality reduction targets.

Maternal and neonatal tetanus (MNT) remained a public health problem in 52 countries. With widespread funding shortages, tetanus campaigns in 2003 aimed to cover 5.5 million women in high-risk areas that had poor infrastructure—a substantial decrease from 2002. Despite that setback, UNICEF supported Governments in formulating and implementing MNT activities in 37 of the priority countries, compared with 26 in 2002. In Afghanistan, a three-year elimination plan was developed and almost 760,000 women received three doses of tetanus toxoid vaccine.

Some 60 countries—half of those reporting—used AD syringes for all routine immunization activities during 2003, up from 45 in 2002. UNICEF supplied $31 million worth of AD syringes, an increase from $18 million the year before, contributing to limiting the spread of infections such as hepatitis B and HIV, and to strengthening awareness of immunization safety. UNICEF collaborated with the United States CDC, WHO and other partners in support of countries in the context of the Safe Injection Global Network.

UNICEF supplied nearly 511 million high-dose vitamin A supplement capsules to 82 countries through a donation in kind from the Micronutrient Initiative, a not-for-profit organization specializing in addressing micronutrient malnutrition. The UNICEF Vaccine Independence Initiative continued to contribute to national self-sufficiency procurement, including in the Pacific and Central Asian subregions. In 69 of the 130 programme countries for which information was available, routine vaccine spending was fully met by Governments. However, some 25 countries, predominantly in Africa, remained completely dependent on external support for their vaccine needs in 2003.

In Latin America and the Caribbean, UNICEF co-sponsored the first vaccination week, which brought immunization to indigenous populations and border areas, and continued to promote expanded coverage of routine services to the poorest families through its participation in health SWAps and PRSPs. The joint UNICEF/WHO Reach Every District immunization initiative was introduced in nine countries in 2003.

More than 16 million doses of measles vaccine had been delivered in Afghanistan since 2001, preventing an estimated 30,000 deaths. In Angola, a post-conflict country, over 7 million children of up to 14 years of age received measles vaccine and nearly 3 million received vitamin A supplements during two months in 2003. In Peru, the Ministry of Health and UNICEF initiated a hepatitis B immunization campaign, in response to an outbreak that threatened the survival of two ethnic groups in the Amazon region.

Girls' education

The number of countries with girls' net enrolment ratios below 85 per cent was estimated at 65 in 2003, about the same as in 2002. UNICEF had become a more responsive and strategic partner for meeting the MDG on education [YUN 2000, p. 52] and the goal to provide quality education for all by 2015, with particular emphasis on girls' schooling, to which Governments committed themselves at the 2000 World Education Forum [ibid., p. 1081]. In 2003, the United Nations Girls' Education Initiative [ibid.] was evaluated and revitalized, and was focusing on joint action by UN partners at the country level. Efforts were intensified and some advances were made by countries with low or stagnating levels of school enrolment and persistent gender disparities, including Afghanistan, Benin, Burkina Faso, Chad, Mali, Pakistan and Yemen. UNICEF played a leading role in the formulation of national education plans and their review against the indicative framework of the Fast-Track Initiative, a partnership of developing countries and donors created to help low-income countries achieve the MDG on education. It also increased its emphasis on advocacy for sustained investments in basic education, including through SWAps and PRSPs.

Enrolment gains reported in UNICEF-assisted zones were higher than the national averages in 53 countries in 2003, compared to 38 in 2002, but it was not clear that such gains were occurring at a rate that would make possible the achievement of the MDG goal on education with regard to gender disparity, particularly in south Asia and sub-Saharan Africa. In all, UNICEF spent some $31 million on educational supplies in 2003, a significant increase over earlier years. UNICEF-assisted community approaches to schooling were taken up by Governments and other partners and expanded in Egypt, Malawi, Sierra Leone and elsewhere.

The number of countries reporting that their national Education For All (EFA) plans included explicit measures for reducing the number of out-of-school girls increased from 66 in 2002 to 71 in 2003, and included 40 of the 65 countries that had an estimated net enrolment rate of less than 85 per cent, and 20 of the 25 priority countries for acceleration. The number of countries where a gender review of the education sector had been undertaken within the previous three years increased to 56 in 2003 from 37 in 2002, although only 28 of the countries with low girls' net enrolment had undertaken such a study.

Although UNICEF continued to support more specific interventions to promote quality learning, especially in curriculum development and teacher training, it needed to develop clearer strategies for such support, in order to avoid piecemeal approaches. Policies were needed to address the educational needs of orphans and adolescent girls, especially in countries with high HIV/AIDS prevalence.

UNICEF support for school environments with a clean water supply and sanitation expanded to 73 countries in 2003 from 50 in 2002, and was reported to be effective in promoting the enrolment and retention of girls. Practical hygiene education formed part of the interventions, either as a part of life-skills education or through the Participatory Hygiene and Sanitation Transformation approach.

Protection from violence, abuse, exploitation and discrimination

In 2003, 80 UNICEF offices reported Government-issued public statements on trafficking in children, compared with 64 in 2002, and 84 public statements on sexual exploitation, up from 14 in 2002. UNICEF stepped up efforts to emphasize, with national and UN partners, the close linkages between child protection and the MDGs and the relevant provisions of the Millennium Declaration, adopted by the General Assembly in resolution 55/2 [YUN 2000, p. 49].

UNICEF documented 1,037 cases of gross violations of child rights in Sierra Leone. It supported databases on abducted children in Uganda and child soldiers in Sri Lanka. In Liberia, it assisted in the establishment of a child protection group of more than 40 NGOs, and a task force that had reunited over 100 children with their families. The number of UNICEF offices undertaking general advocacy on behalf of children in armed conflict increased from 21 in 2002 to 29 in 2003; on the demobilization of child soldiers, from 15 to 18; and on internally displaced children, from 12 to 15. At the global level, UNICEF worked with partners to produce the Inter-Agency Guiding Principles on Unaccompanied and Separated Children. It also continued close collaboration with the Office of the Special Representative of the Secretary-General for Children and Armed Conflict (see p. 789), including the finalization and piloting of a training package for peacekeeping personnel.

A major consultation (New York, November), convened by UNICEF with NGO and UN partners, identified potential indicators for children in formal care, juvenile justice, female genital mutilation and child marriage. One hundred and nine UNICEF offices reported that a child protection analysis was either in place or under development, up from 91 in 2002. In 2003, only 23 UNICEF offices indicated that national standards adequately protected children deprived of their liberty or in formal care. UNICEF worked with Armenia to shift funding from institutional care to support for vulnerable families, and supported the development of foster care systems. In Bosnia and Herzegovina, it worked with partners to ensure the inclusion of provisions in the PRSP aimed at reducing institutionalization. The promotion of inclusive education was the major emphasis of UNICEF work to support children with disabilities during the MTSP period.

By the end of 2003, the International Labour Organization (ILO) Worst Forms of Child Labour Convention (No. 182) [YUN 1999, p. 1388] had been ratified by 147 countries. UNICEF worked with ILO in over 60 countries to combat the worst forms of child labour. Joint activities in 2003 included a programme combining education for working children with financial credit for their families in Paraguay, a child labour survey in Jamaica and a time-bound plan of action in Indonesia. UNICEF developed Guidelines for Protection of the Rights of Children Victims of Trafficking in South-Eastern Europe, which were adopted by the Stability Pact, a security mechanism for South-Eastern Europe adopted in 1999 [YUN 1999, p. 398]. Limited progress was made regarding child labour issues in national statistical systems in 2003.

Regarding child soldiers, UNICEF worked with partners, including the United Nations Department of Peacekeeping Operations, the World Bank and NGOs, in Côte d'Ivoire and the Democratic Republic of the Congo (DRC), where 814 and 846 children were demobilized, respectively. Parties to the conflict in Sri Lanka agreed, with UNICEF facilitation, on a plan that established a formal release and reintegration system for child soldiers.

In 2003, 78 UNICEF offices reported that a review of legal standards to protect children from violence had been undertaken either by the Government or others within the last three years, up by 17 from 2002, while three quarters of country offices continued to promote awareness-raising on violence against children. Over 4,000 humanitarian relief workers were trained in Africa on a code of conduct applicable to international and national staff for the protection of women and children from sexual violence in humanitarian crises. In the DRC, Guinea and Sierra Leone, UNICEF developed programmes to respond to gender-based violence, which included components on HIV transmission.

UNICEF expanded its activities relating to landmines to 31 countries, from 18 at the start of the MTSP period, with particular emphasis on Asia and Eastern and Southern Africa. It produced its first mine-action strategy and strengthened its capacity to support mine-action in the field, with financial assistance from the United Kingdom Department for International Development and the Swedish Development Agency.

(See also pp. 780-91.)

HIV/AIDS

Since the inception of the 2002-2005 MTSP [YUN 2002, p. 1184], UNICEF had made major advances in establishing HIV/AIDS as an organizational priority. Key challenges continued to include the interaction of HIV/AIDS with poverty and humanitarian crises, the effects of stigma, silence and discrimination, and the weakness of local capacities for prevention, treatment and care. In 2003, all UNICEF country offices were cooperating to combat HIV/AIDS. The UNICEF supply operation (see p. 1214) was assisting Governments in over 40 countries to purchase antiretroviral drugs and diagnostic equipment as access to therapies expanded with the support of the WHO-led initiative to reach 3 million people by 2005 (the "3 by 5" initiative) (see p. 1248). A national situational analysis on HIV/AIDS, children and young people was undertaken in 78 countries and was planned for a further 21.

Preventing HIV/AIDS among young people was the core of the UNICEF global response to the epidemic and was a priority in all regions. UNICEF continued to work with Governments to develop or update national plans in that regard. In 2003, national plans were in place for some 88 countries, compared with 80 in 2002, but many of the plans were not supported with adequate resources. UNICEF supported life-skills-based education for HIV prevention in most countries with high prevalence rates, and many programmes were operating on a large scale through schools. National strategies in HIV prevention education had been adopted by 71 countries in 2003, compared with 64 in 2002. In Andhra Pradesh, India, approximately 1.3 million young people were reached through 11,500 schools. Curriculum reform and teacher training were taking place with UNICEF support in East Asia, sub-Saharan Africa and the Eastern Caribbean.

During 2003, UNICEF continued to be a lead supporter of prevention of parent-to-child transmission (PPTCT) programmes worldwide. A major development was the reduction in price of antiretroviral drugs and their increased availability for treatment through new global initiatives, with impetus from WHO and the United States. The priority for UNICEF and its partners was to move forward with PPTCT Plus, incorporating care and support for mothers, their children and families. The PPTCT Plus initiative, led by Columbia University (New York) and operated with UNICEF assistance in eight countries during 2003, was designed to increase synergy among PPTCT programmes by reducing stigma and offering mothers an additional incentive to participate. In 2003, UNICEF and its partners provided direct support to PPTCT programmes in 70 countries, up from 58 in 2002; five countries had nationwide programmes and 26 were in the process of scaling up.

Regarding the protection of children orphaned or made vulnerable by HIV/AIDS, the first forum of global partners on orphans and vulnerable children, convened by UNICEF (Geneva, October), agreed on a framework for responding to the crisis. UNICEF also issued *Africa's Orphaned Generations*, a report which stressed both the protection and material needs of orphans and raised the visibility of children within the global response to HIV/AIDS. National strategies for the protection of orphans and vulnerable children were in place in 36 countries in 2003, compared to 31 in 2002, and were under development in a further 32 countries. UNICEF was supporting relevant programmes in 38 countries in sub-Saharan Africa.

(For further information on HIV/AIDS prevention and control, see p. 1243.)

Operational and administrative matters

UNICEF finances

UNICEF income totalled $1,680 million, an increase of $226 million (16 per cent) over 2002, which resulted from substantial increases in emergency contributions and some growth in regular resource contributions and exchange rate gains. The total was higher than the financial plan forecast by 20 per cent. UNICEF derived its income primarily from Governments, which contributed $1,127 million (67 per cent of total income), and from private sector or non-government sources, which provided $516 million (31 per cent). The balance of $37 million (2 per cent) was derived from other miscellaneous sources.

During its second regular session in September, the Executive Board took note of the UNICEF interim financial report and statements for the year ended 31 December 2002 [E/ICEF/2003/AB/L.9].

Budget appropriations

In June [dec. 2003/6], the Board approved recommendations for the aggregate indicative budgets for 12 country programmes and a programme for Palestinian children and women, amounting to the following amounts for regular and other resources, respectively, by region: Africa, $108,188,000 and $201,744,000; the Americas and the Caribbean, $3,912,000 and $10,000,000; Asia, $67,124,000 and $79,000,000; and the Middle East and North Africa, $3,200,000 and $9,230,000. On 17 September [dec. 2003/12], the Board approved recommendations for funding of $13,023,000 from other resources only for country programmes in two countries and a Gulf Area subregional programme; $2,208,730 in additional resources to fund the approved country programmes of eight countries; and $789,594 from regular resources to cover overexpenditures from four programmes. A report of the Executive Board summarized the regular resources and other resources programmed for 2003 [E/ICEF/2003/P/L.25].

Also in June [dec. 2003/7], the Board approved an increase of $100 million in the other resources ceiling for intercountry programmes, from $203 million to $303 million, for the 2002-2003 biennium, as recommended by the Executive Director [E/ICEF/2003/P/L.14].

During its extraordinary budgetary session (New York, 1-2 December), the Executive Board considered an October report of the Advisory Committee on Administrative and Budgetary Questions (ACABQ) [E/ICEF/2003/AB/L.15] on UNICEF's supplementary support budget for 2002-2003 [E/ICEF/2003/AB/L.13] and biennial support budget for 2004-2005 [E/ICEF/2003/AB/L.14]. Acting on the comments of ACABQ, the Executive Board, in December [dec. 2003/16], approved supplementary budget appropriations of $8 million to cover salary increases and additional requirements for security, and approved gross appropriations in the amount of $684,906,000 for UNICEF programme support in the field and at headquarters, and for management and administration [dec. 2003/17]. It resolved that income estimates of $156,400,000 would be used to offset the gross appropriations, resulting in estimated net appropriations of $528,506,000. The Board authorized the Executive Director to redeploy resources between appropriation lines up to a maximum of 5 per cent of the appropriation to which the resources were redeployed. The Board also approved an additional allocation of $14 million for security-related provisions. It requested the Executive Director to continue to develop results-based budgeting for the 2006-2007 biennium, in close collaboration with other funds and programmes; to consult the Board if the level of resources available for programming fell significantly below the level projected in the 2004-2005 budget; and to explore options for timing the approval of the biennial support budget in the context of one of the existing regular board sessions and to report during the 2004 annual session.

As a result of the harmonization of the budgets of UNICEF, UNDP and UNFPA, proposals relating to intercountry programmes were presented separately from the support budget. Based on those proposals [E/ICEF/2003/P/L.29], the Executive Board, on 2 December [dec. 2003/18], approved a regular resources programme budget of $25.19 million (other than the Emergency Programme Fund) for 2004-2005. The Emergency Programme Fund budget was approved at $25 million. The Board also approved an other resources-funded programme budget of $302.2 million for the 2004-2005 biennium, subject to the availability of specific-purpose contributions. Further, a total recommendation of $302.2 million for other resources funding was approved for the biennium.

In July [E/ICEF/2003/P/L.21], the Executive Director reported on the implementation of the modified system for allocation of regular resources for programmes, which was endorsed by the Board in 1997 [YUN 1997, p. 1220]. Since the system's introduction in 1999, the secretariat had implemented all of its features. The report described results of the implementation; links between the modified system and the 2002-2005 MTSP and with integrated budgeting; and measures for improving system implementation performance. On 19 September [dec. 2003/13], the Executive Board decided to continue to apply the modified system. It requested the Executive Director to intensify efforts to reach the target of 60 per cent of regular resources to be allocated to LDCs and maintain at least 50 per cent for sub-Saharan Africa, and to report to the Board no later than the second regular session of 2004. She was also asked to continue to review the modified system.

Audits

On 14 January [dec. 2002/3], the Executive Board took note of the UNICEF financial report and audited financial statements for the biennium ended 31 December 2001 and the report of the Board of Auditors [A/57/5/Add.2 & Corr.1]. In October [E/ICEF/2003/AB/L.10], UNICEF reported on steps taken or to be taken in response to the recommendations of the Board of Auditors on the UNICEF accounts for the 2000-2001 biennium.

In its sixth annual report [E/ICEF/2003/AB/L.11 & Corr.1], the Office of Internal Audit stated that it completed 36 audits in 2002, including two audits at headquarters locations and three global summary reports. It found that overall, UNICEF controls were generally satisfactory, no location was found to be unsatisfactory in all audited areas, and most country offices and headquarters auditees took timely and adequate actions to address both the audit observations issued in 2002 and those that remained open from previous years.

Operational reserve

In response to a 2001 Executive Board decision [YUN 2001, p. 1098], the Executive Director, in March, reviewed the issue of establishing an operational reserve [E/ICEF/2003/AB/L.4]. The report stated that since the issue was last discussed by the Board in 2001, UNICEF had exceeded the requirement, under its current policy, to maintain year-end cash balances of regular resources income equal to about 10 per cent of the following year's regular resources income, as it had done since the measure was established in 1987 [YUN 1987, p. 862]. In addition, UNICEF had met the informal liquidity ratio reported in its financial statements. While an operational reserve could provide a short-term response mechanism to address an unforeseen shortfall in receipts and income, and afford an opportunity to earn marginally increased interest income through longer-term investments, it also created a balance sheet asset at the expense of funding programmes, and might engender increased costs if it became necessary to break long-term investment commitments to utilize the funds. A 12 May letter from the ACABQ Chairman to the Executive Director [E/ICEF/2003/AB/L.6 & Corr.1] contained ACABQ's comments on the report.

On 4 June [dec. 2003/8], the Executive Board recommended that UNICEF continue to manage its liquidity in accordance with the requirement approved by the Board, and that it not establish a funded operational reserve.

Recovery policy

In January, the Executive Board considered a review of the current recovery policy for support costs for programmes funded from other resources [E/ICEF/2003/AB/L.1], which the Executive Board approved in 1998 [YUN 1998, p. 1100] as an interim policy and was a core part of the financial procedures related to supplementary-funded projects. The review recommended action to the Board regarding revisions to the policy. The Board also had before it ACABQ's comments on the review [E/ICEF/2003/AB/L.2]. An April report [E/ICEF/2003/AB/L.5] discussed consultations by UNICEF with regional groups, national committees and, in some cases, bilateral consultations on the policy, which identified key areas of consensus on the underlying principles of the recovery policy and key areas of concern, including harmonization; thematic and private sector fundraising; simplification of the proposal; interest income on other resources cash balances; and UN reform and new funding modality. A 12 May letter from the ACABQ Chairman to the Executive Director [E/ICEF/2003/AB/L.6 & Corr.1] presented ACABQ's comments on the April report.

On 5 June [dec. 2003/9], the Executive Board requested all donors to strive to increase contributions to regular resources, and requested the Executive Director to hold consultations to encourage donors to increase the proportion of contributions to regular resources. It endorsed the objectives that other resources support the MTSP priorities and that regular resources should not subsidize the support costs for other resources programmes, and it encouraged UNICEF to apply procedures that reduced transaction costs for other resources programmes (see below). It also endorsed the aim of eliminating, in the medium term, the subsidy of support costs for other resources programmes by regular resources. The Board called on donors contributing to other resources to consider directing those contributions to the five thematic areas of the MTSP (see p. 1206) and called on all donors to simplify their administrative and reporting requirements to significantly reduce the administrative costs of their contributions to other resources. The Board decided to apply, as an interim measure, the methodology, as described in the review report (see p. 1212). It authorized the Executive Director to apply the following rates to new agreements to be signed after Executive Board approval of the revised policy on an interim basis: 5 per cent for all resources raised from the private sector in the programme countries; for other private sector resources, 5 per cent for thematic contributions and 7 per cent for non-thematic contributions; for other contributions to thematic areas, 8 per cent; and an additional reduction of 1 per cent for 90 per cent of up-front payments. For non-thematic contributions, the Board authorized 12 per cent and additional reductions of 1 per cent for 90 per cent of up-front payments, 1 per cent for contributions over $500,000, 2 per cent for contributions over $2 million, 3 per cent for contributions over $10 million, and, as a transitional arrangement through 2004, 4 per cent for contributions over $40 million. The Board requested the Executive Director to bring the issue of the recovery policy to the attention of the UNDG working group on harmonization and simplification, with a view to harmonizing the methodology used by UNDG members in devising their recovery policies. It also requested the Executive Director to report to the Board on the experiences of the recovery policy, especially on actual cost recovery achieved and recovery rates applied to projects during this period, on its effects on the regular resources and on the harmonization efforts undertaken, and to submit proposals for further steps towards the elimination of any remaining subsidy of support costs of other resources programmes by regular resources at the second regular session of the Executive Board in 2005, for a review of the interim policy.

Also on 5 June [dec. 2003/10], the Executive Board requested the Executive Director to submit, in 2004, an assessment report, based on country-specific examples, of the UNICEF experience of joint programming and other innovative and collaborative approaches aimed at improving programming and reducing transaction costs for programme countries and their associated costs and benefits.

Resource mobilization

UNICEF continued to collaborate with Governments to mobilize both regular and other resources, holding 17 consultations or high-level visits with donor Governments. A further 59 discussions and presentations were held on thematic, technical or programmatic issues. The discussions increasingly focused on UNICEF's strategic contributions to the MDGs [YUN 2000, p. 51]; the need to obtain regular resources contributions to strengthen UNICEF's core capacity to support national priorities over the medium term; and flexible, thematic contributions that did not entail high transaction costs.

At a January pledging event, 62 Governments pledged a total of $392 million to regular resources, and, by year's end, 90 Governments had contributed $403 million, an increase of 10 per cent compared to 2002; some 28 Governments increased their contributions. The United States remained the largest donor with a contribution of $119.2 million, followed by Norway ($46.2 million), Sweden ($36.3 million), the Netherlands ($32.7 million), the United Kingdom ($27.8 million) and Denmark ($26.9 million).

In the area of thematic funding for MTSP priorities, a total of $29.4 million was mobilized from four Governments ($24.4 million from Andorra, Finland, Norway and Sweden) and eight national committees ($5 million from the committees in Belgium, France, Italy, Japan, Spain, Sweden, the United Kingdom, and the United States).

Private Sector Division

Net income from UNICEF Private Sector Division (PSD) activities for the year ending 31 December 2003 totalled $289.4 million for regular resources, $8 million (2.9 per cent) higher than the $281.4 million achieved in 2002 [E/ICEF/2004/AB/L.9]. That amount included $47.1 million from UNICEF card and gift sales, $249.5 million from private sector fund-raising activities, a positive exchange rate adjustment of $6.3 million and investment fund expenditures of $13.5 million. In addition, $172.2 million ($141.9 million in 2002) was raised from private sector fund-raising activities that were earmarked for other resources. The net consolidated income, including both regular and other resources, amounted to $461.6 million, an increase of $38.3 million compared to the 2002 net consolidated income of $423.3 million. Excluding a one-time legacy in 2002 of $56.2 million, the net increase in 2003 was $94.5 million (25.8 per cent).

On 15 January [dec. 2003/4], the Executive Board approved budgeted expenditures of $80.9 million for the PSD work plan for 2003 [E/ICEF/2003/AB/L.3]. The Executive Director was authorized to redeploy resources between various budget lines up to a maximum of 10 per cent of the amounts approved, and to spend an additional amount between Executive Board sessions, when necessary, up to the amount caused by currency fluctuations, to implement the 2003 approved work plan. The Board renewed investment funds with $14.2 million established for 2003; authorized the Executive Director to incur expenditures in 2003 related to the cost of goods delivered (production/purchase of raw materials, cards and other products) for 2004, up to $30.5 million; and approved the PSD medium-term plan for 2004-2007.

JIU report

In January, the Executive Board had before it a secretariat note [E/ICEF/2003/5] on the reports of the Joint Inspection Unit concerning issues of relevance to UNICEF, prepared between September 2001 and September 2002. On 13 January [dec. 2003/2] the Board took note of the document.

Joint Committee on Education

The Executive Board considered a report of the eighth meeting of the United Nations Educational, Scientific and Cultural Organization (UNESCO)/UNICEF Joint Committee on Education (Paris, 25 November 2002) [E/ICEF/2003/8], which addressed collaboration in the two core areas of EFA and girls' education at the international, regional and national levels, focusing on results, impacts and major challenges ahead. The Joint Committee, having decided that it had fulfilled its original mandate, agreed to recommend to the UNESCO and UNICEF Executive Boards that it be discontinued and asked the secretariats of both agencies to propose ways of strengthening coordination.

On 15 January [dec. 2003/5], the UNICEF Executive Board agreed with the Joint Committee's recommendation and requested the UNICEF secretariat to work with the UNESCO secretariat on strengthening coordination.

Supply operations

The Executive Board had before it a review of the UNICEF supply function in the context of the MTSP, which provided an overview of the UNICEF Supply Division and discussed the supply component of the five organizational priorities of the MTSP [E/ICEF/2003/7]. It also reviewed the Division's procurement services for governmental and non-governmental partners and its work with the oil-for-food programme in Iraq (see p. 362), and discussed steps taken to improve the efficiency of UNICEF's global supply operation and the Division's alliances and partnerships. The report addressed future challenges, including the issue of vaccine security; the increased demand for antiretroviral medicines for the treatment of people with HIV/AIDS and for insecticide-impregnated bednets to help prevent malaria in young children and pregnant women; the procurement of key commodities in a more complex business environment; and the procurement of supporting supplies.

Youth

Implementation of the World Programme of Action for Youth

UN policies and programmes on youth in 2003 continued to focus on efforts to implement the 1995 World Programme of Action for Youth to the Year 2002 and Beyond, adopted by the General Assembly in resolution 50/81 [YUN 1995, p. 1211]. The Programme of Action addressed the problems faced by youth worldwide and outlined ways to enhance youth participation in national and international policy- and decision-making.

An expert group meeting on jobs for youth: national strategies for employment promotion (Geneva, 15-16 January) was organized by the UN Division for Social Policy and Development in collaboration with ILO.

World Youth Report 2003

In response to General Assembly resolution 56/117 [YUN 2001, p. 1100], the Secretary-General, by a May note [A/58/79], transmitted the World Youth Report 2003 [E/CN.5/2003/4], a comprehensive report on the global situation of youth, which he had presented to the forty-first session of the Commission for Social Development (New York, 27 February 2002 and 10-21 February 2003) [E/2003/26] (see p. 1099). The report stated that from 1995 to 2000, the world's youth population was estimated to have grown by an average of 0.7 per cent, from 1.025 billion to 1.061 billion, with 85 per cent living in developing countries. Based on the findings of an expert group meeting on global priorities for youth (Helsinki, Finland, October 2002), the report contained a review of the 10 priority areas of the World Programme of Action for Youth to the Year 2000 and Beyond, namely education, employment, hunger and poverty, health issues, environment, drug abuse, juvenile delinquency, leisure, girls and young women, and youth participation. It also reviewed five new concerns that had emerged since the adoption of the Programme of Action, including the impact of globalization on young people; the use of and access to information and communication technologies; the dramatic increase in HIV infections among young people and the epidemic's impact on their lives; the active involvement of young people in armed conflict; and the increased importance of addressing intergenerational issues in an ageing society. The report presented recommendations on those priorities and concerns.

The report evaluated the 2001 World Youth Forum of the United Nations System [YUN 2001, p. 1100] and recommended that future sessions of the Forum be based on an intergovernmental mandate emanating from the Assembly. It also suggested that, in order to promote meaningful youth participation, Governments should take a more positive stance when addressing young people's ideas and questions.

Youth employment

Pursuant to General Assembly resolution 57/165 [YUN 2002, p. 1192], the Secretary-General, in August [A/58/229], reported on the promotion of youth employment and progress achieved by the Youth Employment Network, formed by the Secretary-General in collaboration with ILO in 2001 [YUN 2001, p. 1100]. ILO estimated that about 74 million young women and men were unemployed worldwide, accounting for 41 per cent of the 180 million unemployed globally; many more were working long hours for low pay. An estimated 59 million young people between the ages of 15 and 17 were engaged in hazardous work. In response to a questionnaire on the current status of national action plans for youth employment, 19 of the 37 responding Member States reported that they had not prepared a national action plan; of those, 11 reported that they were planning to do so. Several Member States reported that they did not have a specific action plan for youth employment because the issue was already being addressed as part of an overall action plan for employment or that there were already programmes in place addressing the issue.

The report stated that the Network's High-level Panel on Youth Employment had set up Working Groups on employability, equal opportunities, entrepreneurship and employment creation, corresponding to the four priority areas for national action plans identified in 2001 [ibid.]. The results of the Working Groups were integrated into a consolidated document that provided further guidance in the four areas and were the subject of discussion at the Panel's second High-level Meeting (Geneva, 30 June–1 July) (see below). The Network's activities were being coordinated with the work of UNDG, the United Nations Millennium Development Project—an advisory body launched by the Secretary-General and the UNDP Administrator to recommend strategies for achieving the MDGs [YUN 2000, p. 51]—and with the overall strategy for implementation of the Millennium Declaration, adopted by the General Assembly in resolution 55/2 [ibid., p. 49].

The fifth session of the High-level Committee on Programmes of the United Nations System Chief Executives Board for Coordination (Rome, 26-27 March) [CEB/2003/4] confirmed its strong support for the Network. It called on its members to contribute actively to Governments' efforts to develop national reviews and action plans and to provide inputs to the Secretary-General's report to the Assembly's fifty-eighth (2003) session.

The second meeting of the Network's High-level Panel (Geneva, 30 June–1 July) discussed a draft action programme recommending the next five steps to be taken by the Network, including a call for the Network to endorse the Panel's recommendations on the four priorities for national action plans, based on road maps produced by the Panel's four Working Groups; initiatives to stimulate and encourage Governments to design and implement national action plans, as called for in Assembly resolution 57/165 [YUN 2002, p. 1192]; a proposal for social dialogue on youth employment; an invitation to youth organizations worldwide to advise on the design of youth employment programmes, contribute to the implementation of those programmes, help Governments monitor progress towards their youth employment commitments, and work with the Panel in an advisory capacity; and a call for the World Bank and ILO to develop jointly an initiative for mobilizing funding for national youth employment programmes and for the work of the Network's secretariat. Following the meeting, the secretariat undertook joint consultations on strengthening the coherence of its youth employment activities in three areas, including a political process: linking policy to action; mapping the challenge of youth employment; and promoting initiatives and programmes with proven impact through network development.

In March, ILO's Governing Body called on the Youth Employment Network and its core partner institutions (ILO, the World Bank and the UN Secretariat) to support Member States in carrying out national reviews and action plans on youth employment. A guidance note for the preparation of reviews and action plans, which was annexed to the report, was sent to all Member States. The Network, under ILO's leadership, was called on to carry out from 2004 to early 2005, in cooperation with the Secretariat, the World Bank and other relevant agencies, a global analysis and evaluation of the reviews and plans and of progress made by the Network. ILO intended to prepare the global analysis and evaluation in the framework of its World Employment Report 2005. The analysis would also contribute to the five-year review of the MDGs in 2005.

The report concluded that, to prepare for the next phase of the Network's activities, which focused on country-level action, it was urgent that Member States submit their national reviews and action plans and that steps be taken to mobilize the necessary resources for implementation.

ECONOMIC AND SOCIAL COUNCIL ACTION

On 21 July [meeting 42], the Economic and Social Council, on the recommendation of the Commission for Social Development [E/2003/26], adopted **resolution 2003/11** without vote [agenda item 14 (b)].

Policies and programmes involving youth

The Economic and Social Council,

Recalling the United Nations Millennium Declaration, and recognizing that the Declaration includes important goals and targets pertaining to youth,

Recalling and reaffirming the commitments made at the major United Nations conferences and summits held since 1990 and their follow-up processes,

Guided by the Charter of the United Nations as well as other relevant international instruments,

Reaffirming the obligation of States to promote and protect human rights and fundamental freedoms and their full enjoyment by young people,

Recalling General Assembly resolution 50/81 of 14 December 1995, by which the Assembly adopted the World Programme of Action for Youth to the Year 2000 and Beyond,

1. *Takes note* of the report of the Secretary-General on the implementation of the World Programme of Action for Youth to the Year 2000 and Beyond;

2. *Reaffirms* that the ten priority areas identified in the Programme of Action, namely, education, employment, hunger and poverty, health issues, environment, drug abuse, juvenile delinquency, leisure, girls and young women, and youth participation, remain areas of crucial importance;

3. *Recognizes* the importance of the five issues of concern to young people identified in the report of the Secretary-General, namely, the mixed impact of globalization on young women and men; the use of and access to information and communication technologies; the dramatic increase of HIV infections among young people and the impact of the epidemic on their lives; the active involvement of young people in armed conflict, both as victims and as perpetrators; and the increased importance of addressing intergenerational issues in an ageing society;

4. *Also recognizes* the importance of the full and effective participation of youth and youth organizations at the local, national, regional and international levels in promoting and implementing the Programme of Action and in evaluating the progress achieved and the obstacles encountered in its implementation, and the need to support the activities of youth mechanisms that have been set up by youth and youth organizations, bearing in mind that girls, boys, young women and young men have the same rights but different needs and strengths and are active agents for decision-making processes, positive change and development in society;

5. *Calls upon* all States, all United Nations bodies, the specialized agencies, the regional commissions and the intergovernmental and non-governmental organizations concerned, in particular youth organizations, to make every possible effort towards the implementation of the Programme of Action, aiming at cross-sectoral youth policies by integrating a youth perspective into all planning and decision-making processes relevant to youth;

6. *Recommends* that the United Nations system, on the basis of the positive experience of youth participation in the work of the United Nations, inter alia, at the World Summit on Sustainable Development and the special session of the General Assembly on children, continue to provide opportunities for dialogue between Governments and representatives of youth organizations in consultative status with the Economic and Social Council through forums, open-ended dialogues, meetings and debates;

7. *Also recommends* that the convening of a future world youth forum be based on an intergovernmental decision emanating from the General Assembly;

8. *Invites* the General Assembly to consider devoting, at its sixtieth session, in 2005, two plenary meetings to reviewing the situation of youth and achievements produced in the implementation of the Programme of Action ten years after its adoption;

9. *Also invites* the General Assembly to request the Secretary-General to provide the Assembly, at its sixtieth session, through the Commission for Social Development at its forty-third session, with a comprehensive report on the priority areas of youth identified in the Programme of Action, calling upon the experience of the Member States, organizations, programmes and specialized agencies of the United Nations system, as well as the regional commissions, and youth organizations, in their multidisciplinary work for and with youth;

10. *Further invites* the General Assembly to request the Secretary-General, in preparing the report requested in paragraph 9 above, to take into account the five concerns identified in paragraph 3 above.

GENERAL ASSEMBLY ACTION

On 22 December [meeting 77], the General Assembly, on the recommendation of the Third (Social, Humanitarian and Cultural) Committee

[A/58/497 (Part II)], adopted **resolution 58/133** without vote [agenda item 106].

Policies and programmes involving youth

The General Assembly,

Guided by the Charter of the United Nations as well as other relevant international instruments, including the Convention on the Rights of the Child and the two Optional Protocols thereto,

Reaffirming the obligation of States to promote and protect human rights and fundamental freedoms and their full enjoyment by young people,

Recalling the United Nations Millennium Declaration, and recognizing that the Millennium Declaration includes important goals and targets pertaining to youth,

Recalling and reaffirming the commitments made at the major United Nations conferences and summits held since 1990 and their follow-up processes, in particular those commitments that are related to youth, including youth employment,

Recognizing that the participation of young people is an asset and a prerequisite for sustainable economic growth and social development, and expressing deep concern about the magnitude of youth unemployment and underemployment throughout the world and its profound implications for the future of our societies, particularly those in developing countries,

Acknowledging that poverty, among other factors, represents a serious challenge to the full and effective participation and contribution of young people to society,

Recalling its resolution 50/81 of 14 December 1995, by which it adopted the World Programme of Action for Youth to the Year 2000 and Beyond, annexed thereto,

Recalling also its resolution 54/120 of 17 December 1999, in which it took note with appreciation of the Lisbon Declaration on Youth Policies and Programmes adopted at the World Conference of Ministers Responsible for Youth in 1998, and its resolutions 56/117 of 19 December 2001 and 57/165 of 18 December 2002,

1. *Takes note* of the reports of the Secretary-General on the World Youth Report 2003 and on promoting youth employment;

2. *Reaffirms* that the ten priority areas identified in the World Programme of Action for Youth to the Year 2000 and Beyond, namely, education, employment, hunger and poverty, health issues, environment, drug abuse, juvenile delinquency, leisure, girls and young women, and youth participation, remain areas of crucial importance;

3. *Takes note* of the five issues of concern to young people identified in the World Youth Report 2003, namely, the mixed impact of globalization on young women and men, the use of and access to information and communication technologies, the dramatic increase of human immunodeficiency virus infections among young people and the impact of the epidemic on their lives, the active involvement of young people in armed conflict, both as victims and as perpetrators, and the increased importance of addressing intergenerational issues in an ageing society;

4. *Recognizes* the importance of the full and effective participation of young people and youth organizations at the local, national, regional and international levels in promoting and implementing the World Programme of Action and in evaluating the progress achieved and the obstacles encountered in its implementation, as well as the need to support the activities of mechanisms that have been set up by young people and youth organizations, bearing in mind that girls, boys, young women and young men have the same rights but different needs and strengths and are active agents in decision-making processes and for positive change and development in society;

5. *Also recognizes* the great importance of empowering young people by building their capacity to achieve greater independence, overcoming constraints to their participation and providing them with opportunities to make decisions that affect their lives and well-being;

6. *Calls upon* all Member States, United Nations bodies, specialized agencies, regional commissions and intergovernmental and non-governmental organizations concerned, in particular youth organizations, to make every possible effort to implement the World Programme of Action, aiming at cross-sectoral youth policies, by integrating a youth perspective into all planning and decision-making processes relevant to youth;

7. *Takes note with appreciation* of the work done by the regional commissions to implement the World Programme of Action, to follow up the World Conference of Ministers Responsible for Youth in their respective regions, in coordination with regional meetings of ministers responsible for youth and regional non-governmental youth organizations, and to provide advisory services to support national youth policies and programmes in each region, and encourages them to continue to do so;

8. *Recommends* that the United Nations system, on the basis of the positive experience of youth participation in the work of the United Nations, inter alia, at the World Summit on Sustainable Development and the special session of the General Assembly on children, continue to provide opportunities for dialogue between Governments and representatives of youth organizations in consultative status with the Economic and Social Council through forums, open-ended dialogues, meetings and debates;

9. *Decides* that the organization of a future world youth forum should be based on a decision of the General Assembly;

10. *Notes* the decision of eight countries to volunteer as lead countries in the preparation of national reviews and action plans on youth employment;

11. *Encourages* Member States to prepare national reviews and action plans on youth employment, either integrated into their national action plans on employment or issued as separate documents, to make full use of existing data and statistics and to involve young people and youth organizations in this process, taking into account, inter alia, the commitments made by Member States in this regard, in particular those included in the World Programme of Action, and, where such reviews and action plans exist, to submit them to the Secretariat by September 2004;

12. *Invites*, within the context of the Youth Employment Network, the International Labour Organization, in collaboration with the Secretariat and the World Bank and other relevant specialized agencies, to assist and support, upon request, the efforts of Governments in the elaboration of national reviews and action plans and to undertake a global analysis and evaluation of progress made in this regard;

13. *Recommends* devoting two plenary meetings at its sixtieth session, in 2005, to review the situation of youth and achievements attained in the implementation of the World Programme of Action ten years after its adoption;

14. *Requests* the Secretary-General, with regard to paragraph 4 above, to consider organizing a consultative meeting with youth organizations and youth representatives, taking into account equitable geographical distribution, on the evaluation of the progress made and obstacles encountered in the implementation of the World Programme of Action in preparation for the two plenary meetings of the General Assembly to be held in 2005, and to include the outcome of the meeting in his report to the Assembly at its sixtieth session;

15. *Invites* all Governments and intergovernmental and non-governmental organizations to contribute to the United Nations Youth Fund, and requests the Secretary-General to take appropriate actions to encourage contributions;

16. *Notes with appreciation* the provision by some Member States of expertise and financial resources to support the activities of the Youth Employment Network, and invites all Member States and intergovernmental and non-governmental organizations to contribute to the Network in support of action taken at the country level within the framework of the Network;

17. *Reiterates* the call made in the World Programme of Action to Member States to consider including youth representatives in their delegations to the General Assembly and other relevant United Nations meetings, thus broadening the channels of communication and enhancing the discussion of youth-related issues, and requests the Secretary-General to convey this invitation again to Member States;

18. *Requests* the Secretary-General to provide the General Assembly at its sixtieth session, through the Commission for Social Development at its forty-third session, with a comprehensive report including an evaluation of the implementation since 1995 of the priority areas identified in the World Programme of Action, including actions taken by Member States, United Nations bodies, specialized agencies, regional commissions and youth organizations in their multidisciplinary work for and with youth;

19. *Also requests* the Secretary-General, in preparing the report requested in paragraph 18 above, to bear in mind the five issues identified in paragraph 3 above and discuss them in an annex to the report;

20. *Further requests* the Secretary-General to include in his report to the General Assembly at its sixtieth session a global analysis and evaluation of national action plans on youth employment.

Ageing persons

Follow-up to the Second World Assembly on Ageing (2002)

Note by Secretariat. The Commission for Social Development, at its forty-first session (New York, 27 February 2002 and 10-21 February 2003) [E/2003/26] (see p. 1099), considered a Secretariat note [E/CN.5/2003/7] on the Commission's role in integrating the different dimensions of population ageing in its work and the modalities for the review and appraisal of the Madrid International Plan of Action on Ageing [YUN 2002, p. 1194], which was adopted in 2002 by the Second World Assembly on Ageing [ibid., p. 1193]. The note underscored ageing as a cross-cutting theme and the need to integrate it into the broader agendas of the Economic and Social Council, General Assembly and other relevant functional commissions. As for the Commission, its role in the follow-up became more important in the light of the Regional Implementation Strategy for the Madrid International Plan of Action on Ageing, 2002, adopted by the Economic Commission for Europe Ministerial Conference on Ageing (Berlin, 11-13 September 2002) [ECE/AC.23/2002/2/Rev.6], whose follow-up process was made contingent on what was decided by the Commission.

The note presented a proposal for a "bottom-up "approach to the review and appraisal of the Madrid International Plan of Action on Ageing that would involve open-ended dialogues, meetings and forums with various stakeholders at local levels both in and outside of government, and in partnership and coordination with national actors. Regional entities, notably the regional commissions and their intergovernmental bodies, should play an active role in implementation assessment by networking with their member countries, national committees and other stakeholders in the exchange of information and the gathering and compiling of data and research findings. It was envisaged that the Commission would provide the forum in which stakeholders would present and elaborate on their findings. The Commission was invited to consider the review and appraisal approach and to reach an understanding on the format and substantive outcome. The note recommended that the Commission consider a review and appraisal of the Madrid Plan of Action every four or five years. In identifying the themes or issues for the review, it recommended that the Commission adhere to the Plan's recommendations and its priority directions, namely, ageing and development, advancing health and well-being into old age, and ensuring enabling and supportive environments [YUN 2002, p. 1193]. It also recommended that the Commission adopt the "bottom-up" review and appraisal approach.

The UN Department of Economic and Social Affairs (DESA) would facilitate the review process, including the preparation of materials for a review strategy, advocacy, and information dissemination and exchange. Under the Commission's guidance, DESA could also develop guidelines for the review of the Madrid Plan of Action.

ECONOMIC AND SOCIAL COUNCIL ACTION

On 21 July [meeting 42], the Economic and Social Council, on the recommendation of the Commission for Social Development [E/2003/26], adopted **resolution 2003/14** without vote [agenda item 14 (b)].

Modalities for the review and appraisal of the Madrid International Plan of Action on Ageing, 2002

The Economic and Social Council,

Recalling that the goals and targets in the economic, social and related fields contained in the United Nations Millennium Declaration and the outcomes of the major United Nations conferences and summits, supplemented by the outcomes of their reviews, constitute a comprehensive basis for actions at the national, regional and international levels,

Recalling also General Assembly resolution 57/167 of 18 December 2002 and all previous Assembly resolutions on ageing and the International Year of Older Persons,

Recalling further the resolutions adopted by the Commission for Social Development on ageing and on the preparations for the Second World Assembly on Ageing,

Bearing in mind that, in its resolution 57/167, the General Assembly invited the Commission to consider the modalities for reviews and appraisals of the follow-up to the Second World Assembly on Ageing,

Bearing in mind also that the Commission is responsible for follow-up to and appraisal of the implementation of the Madrid International Plan of Action on Ageing, 2002, and that it should consider integrating into its work the different dimensions of population ageing as contained in the Madrid Plan of Action,

Bearing in mind further the work of the open-ended Ad Hoc Working Group of the General Assembly on the integrated and coordinated implementation of and follow-up to the outcomes of the major United Nations conferences and summits in the economic and social fields, established pursuant to Assembly resolution 57/270 A of 20 December 2002,

1. *Invites* all actors at all levels, as appropriate, to participate in the implementation of and follow-up to the Madrid International Plan of Action on Ageing, 2002;

2. *Invites* the organizations of the United Nations system to consider mainstreaming ageing issues into their work plans;

3. *Invites* Members States and other stakeholders to mainstream ageing into the design and implementation of their policies and programmes;

4. *Invites* Governments as well as the United Nations system and civil society to participate in a "bottom-up" approach to the review and appraisal of the Madrid Plan of Action, through, inter alia, sharing of ideas, data collection and best practices;

5. *Requests* the Secretary-General to include in his report to the General Assembly at its fifty-eighth session information on the implementation of the present resolution.

Report of Secretary-General. In response to General Assembly resolution 57/167 [YUN 2002, p. 1197] on follow-up to the Second World Assembly on Ageing (2002) [ibid., p. 1193] and resolution 57/177 on the situation of older women in society [ibid., p. 1153], the Secretary-General, in July [A/58/160], reported on the implementation of the Madrid International Plan of Action on Ageing [YUN 2002, p. 1194]. During the first year following the World Assembly, progress was seen in several areas, including intergovernmental processes, inter-agency activities, regional actions, research and information dissemination.

The report introduced the road map for the implementation of the Plan of Action, which was intended to assist countries in developing implementation strategies at the national level by helping to set priorities, select approaches and stimulate international cooperation. It took into consideration the Plan's recommendations for implementation and follow-up, and incorporated the Plan's priorities for international cooperation on ageing. National capacity-building and mainstreaming of ageing into the national development agenda were two universal and essential facets of the implementation process, particularly in developing countries and those with economies in transition. The DESA Programme on Ageing, as the UN focal point on ageing, would facilitate the evolving road map project through networking within and outside the UN system. National action would include the convening of workshops. At the international level, ageing would need to be linked to the global agendas on poverty, children and youth, the advancement of women, rural development and HIV/AIDS. The report identified the lack of age-disaggregated data in many countries as a serious limitation to policy formulation and development, and recommended that the Assembly consider requesting the Statistical Commission to develop modalities for disaggregating statistics on the basis of age and sex. While dialogue on ageing had increased significantly among stakeholders, the inclusion of ageing in development processes was constrained by the lack of data and formulation of indicators. The report recommended that the Assembly ensure the incorporation of ageing into actions to achieve the MDG on the eradication of poverty, adopted by the General Assembly in resolution 55/2 [YUN 2000, p. 49], and that it consider requesting UN organizations and specialized agencies to take up the issue of mainstreaming ageing in their work programmes and to report on progress to the Commission for Social Development.

The situation of older women and the gender aspects of ageing should receive explicit attention from Governments and other stakeholders. The report proposed that the Assembly recommend the establishment or strengthening of institutional linkages at the national level between national machineries for the advancement of women and governmental bodies responsible for developing, coordinating and/or implementing age-related policies and programmes. Opportunities for systematic attention to the gender aspects of ageing and the situation of older women should continue to be enhanced within the UN system, and the mainstreaming of ageing should be undertaken from a gender perspective. Opportunities should be explored for further coordination and collaboration between the Commission for Social Development and the Commission on the Status of Women (see p. 1192), with regard to older women and in the framework of their multi-year programmes of work.

Regarding the proposed "bottom-up" narrative approach to the review and appraisal of the implementation of the Madrid Plan of Action (see p. 1218), the Secretary-General stated that additional efforts were required to clarify the content of modalities and periodicity of the review and appraisal process, and recommended that the Assembly request the Commission for Social Development to take up that task in 2004. He also recommended that the Assembly suggest that the Commission apply an ageing perspective in its consideration of priority themes related to the follow-up to the 1995 World Summit for Social Development [YUN 1995, p. 1113].

GENERAL ASSEMBLY ACTION

On 22 December [meeting 77], the General Assembly, on the recommendation of the Third Committee [A/58/498], adopted **resolution 58/134** without vote [agenda item 107].

Follow-up to the Second World Assembly on Ageing

The General Assembly,

Recalling its resolution 57/167 of 18 December 2002, in which it endorsed the Political Declaration and the Madrid International Plan of Action on Ageing, 2002, and welcomed the preparation by the Programme on Ageing of the Division for Social Policy and Development of the Department of Economic and Social Affairs of the Secretariat of a road map for the process of implementing the Madrid Plan of Action, as well as its resolution 57/177 of 18 December 2002, in which it stressed, inter alia, the importance of mainstreaming a gender perspective,

Recalling also Economic and Social Council resolution 2003/14 of 21 July 2003, in which the Council invited Governments, the United Nations system and civil society to participate in a "bottom-up" approach to the review and appraisal of the Madrid Plan of Action,

Recalling further its resolution 57/270 B of 23 June 2003, in which it agreed to the framework for an integrated and coordinated implementation of and follow-up to the outcomes of the major United Nations conferences and summits in the economic and social fields and reaffirmed the importance of regularly reviewing the progress made in the implementation of the commitments undertaken at individual major United Nations conferences and summits in the economic, social and related fields,

Recognizing that the follow-up to and the implementation of the outcome of the Second World Assembly on Ageing is an integral part of the integrated and coordinated implementation of and follow-up to the outcomes of the major United Nations conferences and summits,

Recognizing also that a tremendous global demographic change is to be expected during the next fifty years, in both developing and developed countries, as well as in countries with economies in transition, and that since this change will be the most rapid in developing countries, where the older population is expected to quadruple over the same period of time, it is imperative that ageing be integrated into development policies for the attainment of internationally agreed development goals, including those contained in the United Nations Millennium Declaration,

Aware that the lack of data disaggregated by age and sex is an impediment to the consideration of ageing issues and the situation of older persons at both the international and the national policy levels,

1. *Takes note* of the report of the Secretary-General;
2. *Also takes note* of the road map for the implementation of the Madrid International Plan of Action on Ageing, 2002, contained in the report of the Secretary-General;
3. *Invites* Member States and the organizations and bodies of the United Nations system to incorporate ageing, as appropriate, into actions to achieve the internationally agreed development goals, including those contained in the United Nations Millennium Declaration, in particular the goal on the eradication of poverty;
4. *Stresses* the need for action at the national and international levels to implement the Madrid Plan of Action, including the need to set national and international priorities and to select appropriate approaches to ensure that countries achieve a society for all ages;
5. *Encourages* the establishment of institutional linkages at the national level between national machineries for the advancement of women and those governmental entities responsible for the development, implementation and coordination of ageing-related policies and programmes;
6. *Stresses* that the role of civil society, including non-governmental organizations, is important in supporting Governments in their implementation and assessment of and follow-up to the Madrid Plan of Action;
7. *Requests* the Economic and Social Council to consider ageing when elaborating its list of cross-sectoral thematic issues common to the outcomes of major United Nations conferences and summits for the establishment of the multi-year programme of work for the coordination segment of its substantive session;
8. *Requests* the Commission for Social Development to integrate an ageing perspective in its consideration

of priority themes related to the follow-up to the World Summit for Social Development;

9. *Requests* the Commission for Social Development and the Commission on the Status of Women to further coordinate and collaborate through their respective bureaux on the issue of older women within the framework of their respective multi-year programmes of work;

10. *Recalls*, in this regard, its request to each functional commission of the Economic and Social Council to examine its methods of work in order to better pursue the implementation of the outcomes of the major United Nations conferences and summits, recognizing that there is no need for a uniform approach since each functional commission has its own specificity, while noting that modern methods of work can better guarantee the review of progress made in implementation at all levels, on the basis of a report containing recommendations to be submitted by the Secretary-General to each functional commission and relevant subsidiary body of the Economic and Social Council on its methods of work, in accordance with the provisions defined by the respective outcomes and relevant decisions taken by each body, bearing in mind the progress recently achieved in this regard by certain commissions, in particular the Commission on Sustainable Development, and recalling that the functional commissions and other relevant bodies of the Council should report to it no later than 2005 on the outcome of this examination;

11. *Requests* the Commission for Social Development to take up the issue of the periodicity and the format of the review of the implementation of the Madrid Plan of Action at its forty-second session, taking into account the provisions of resolution 57/270 B;

12. *Stresses* the importance of the collection of data and population statistics disaggregated by age and sex on all aspects of policy formulation by all countries, and encourages the relevant entities of the United Nations to support national efforts in capacity-building, especially those of developing countries and countries with economies in transition, takes note in this context of the establishment by the United Nations of an Internet-accessible database on ageing, and invites States to submit, whenever possible, information for inclusion in the database;

13. *Requests* the Statistical Commission to assist Member States in developing modalities for disaggregating data by age and sex;

14. *Requests* the organizations and bodies of the United Nations system and the specialized agencies to integrate ageing, including from a gender perspective, into their programmes of work and to report on their progress to the Commission for Social Development;

15. *Invites* the international financial institutions and the regional development banks to take older persons into account in their policies and projects as part of the effort to assist developing countries and countries with economies in transition in the implementation of the Madrid Plan of Action;

16. *Recommends* that the institutional linkages between United Nations gender focal points and focal points on ageing be strengthened in order to enhance the integration of the gender aspects of ageing within the system;

17. *Welcomes* the progress made in the work of some of the regional commissions in implementing the objectives and recommendations of the Madrid Plan of Action, and encourages other regional commissions to make progress in this regard;

18. *Requests* the Secretary-General to forward his report to the Commission for Social Development at its forty-second session and to make available any other relevant information related to this issue that may assist the Commission in its deliberations;

19. *Also requests* the Secretary-General to report to the General Assembly at its fifty-ninth session on the implementation of the present resolution.

Chapter XII

Refugees and displaced persons

In 2003, the total number of persons of concern to the Office of the United Nations High Commissioner for Refugees (UNHCR) dropped to approximately 17 million, from 20.8 million in 2002, due largely to the return home of millions of refugees following the end of prolonged crises, mainly in Africa and Afghanistan. Almost 5 million people who had fled their homes found a solution through resettlement or local integration.

UNHCR achieved success in addressing the refugee situation in some regions, while problems in other areas undermined progress. Positive developments included the repatriation of over half a million Afghan refugees in the largest return movement of the year. Despite persisting insecurity in parts of Afghanistan, UNHCR maintained the momentum of returns and made considerable progress in ensuring that returnees were included in national development programmes. In other large-scale repatriations, thousands were assisted to return to their places of origin in Angola, Bosnia and Herzegovina, Burundi, Côte d'Ivoire, Eritrea, Iraq, Liberia, Rwanda, Sierra Leone and Somalia. On the negative side, persons of concern in some 38 protracted refugee crises worldwide still awaited durable solutions. Notable situations of concern in that regard included millions of Afghans and half a million Angolans remaining in neighbouring countries, and 700,000 Burundian refugees and internally displaced persons (IDPs) whose hope of return faded as the country's peace process faltered. Others included some 165,000 refugees from Western Sahara living in camps in south-western Algeria for over 25 years and an increasing number of IDPs, estimated at 2 million, uprooted by the conflict in Colombia, of whom 290,000 were displaced during the year. In other fresh outflows, over 300,000 refugees fled several African countries, creating large-scale emergencies in some cases.

During the year, UNHCR finalized the report on the "UNHCR 2004" process, designed to strengthen the Office and better position it to carry out its mandate. In December, the General Assembly removed the time limitation on the continuation of UNHCR and decided to continue the Office until the refugee problem was solved. It also enlarged the UNHCR Executive Committee membership from 64 to 66 States. In October, the Assembly extended the term of office of Ruud Lubbers as UN High Commissioner for Refugees for a period of two years beginning on 1 January 2004.

Office of the United Nations High Commissioner for Refugees

Programme policy

Executive Committee action. At its fifty-fourth session (Geneva, 29 September–3 October) [A/58/12/Add.1], the Executive Committee of the UNHCR Programme, in a conclusion on proposals [A/AC.96/980] arising from the "UNHCR 2004" process [YUN 2001, p. 1107], recognized UNHCR's leading role in international protection of refugees and supported the continuation of the Office until the refugee problem was solved, thereby removing the time limitation contained in General Assembly resolution 57/186 [YUN 2002, p. 1203] (see also p. 1225). Highlighting the importance of joint efforts by UN departments and UNHCR in seeking solutions for refugees, the Committee encouraged UNHCR to play a more active role in that regard and recommended that the High Commissioner review, every 10 years, the global situation of refugees and UNHCR's role, and report thereon to the Assembly as from its sixty-eighth (2013) session. The Committee also adopted conclusions on international protection, including the Agenda for Protection adopted in 2002 [ibid., p. 1205] and statelessness; the return of persons found not to be in need of international protection; protection safeguards in interception measures; and protection from sexual abuse and exploitation. Decisions were adopted on administrative, programme and financial, and institutional matters.

In his opening statement to the Committee, the High Commissioner, describing the negative impact on UNHCR operations of the 19 August terrorist attack on the UN headquarters in Baghdad, Iraq (see p. 346), stated that the challenge facing the Office was finding a balance between continued assistance to the Iraqi people and ensuring staff security. The High Commissioner highlighted positive developments in Afghanistan and in several African countries, including Angola, the Democratic Republic of the Congo (DRC), Liberia and Sierra Leone. However, he noted that although over half a million Afghan refugees returned home during the year, millions of others remained in neighbouring countries, particularly in Iran and Pakistan, and finding durable solutions for them remained a top priority. In Africa, UNHCR continued to seek durable solutions for the refugees in the United Republic of Tanzania; difficulties in Burundi's peace process left over 300,000 refugees and some 400,000 internally displaced persons (IDPs) with limited prospects of returning home; and intense fighting in the Darfur region of the Sudan compelled up to 65,000 refugees to flee to Chad. The priority in Asia remained the resolution of the stalemate on finding solutions for 100,000 Bhutanese people in camps in Nepal. In China, the plight of North Koreans who left their country illegally remained a serious concern. In the Americas, UNHCR continued to coordinate the UN response in Colombia, where the total number of IDPs stood at well over 2 million. In Europe, attention focused on the difficulties facing the displaced population of Chechnya, Russian Federation, while the ongoing asylum debate in the European Union (EU), despite prompting new thinking on ways of enhancing refugee protection, also tended to encourage increasingly restrictive legal asylum measures. The High Commissioner, announcing the finalization of the report on the "UNHCR 2004" process to strengthen the Office [YUN 2001, p. 1107] and better position it to carry out its mandate (see p. 1225), noted that a panel discussion was planned on the implementation of the conclusions contained in the report.

The High Commissioner reported significant progress in the ongoing review of human resources management. Steps had also been taken to enhance transparency and accountability in the management of UNHCR operations, and revised guidelines on preventing and responding to sexual and gender-based violence, intended for the staff of UNHCR and its humanitarian and development partners, had been launched. With regard to finances, UNHCR was required to cut its budget twice during the year, reducing the level of allocations by $54 million, freezing $37 million of the operational reserve, and making additional cuts to compensate for $42 million in increased costs resulting from exchange rate fluctuations and UN salary increases. To avoid further cuts, $56 million in new contributions was needed towards the 2003 annual budget. The High Commissioner also highlighted ongoing efforts to strengthen UNHCR's partnerships.

By **decision 2003/310** of 24 July, the Economic and Social Council took note of the High Commissioner's report covering the period from 1 January 2002 to 30 April 2003 [A/58/12].

Extension of High Commissioner

By **decision 58/402** of 6 October, the General Assembly, on the 30 September proposal of the Secretary-General [A/58/396], extended for a period of two years the term of Office of the High Commissioner, Ruud Lubbers, beginning on 1 January 2004.

Coordination of emergency humanitarian assistance

In 2003 [A/59/12], UNHCR, in a continuing effort to strengthen its partnerships within the UN system, joined the United Nations Development Group, an inter-agency forum established to help improve the effectiveness of UN development initiatives at the country level. Within that framework, UNHCR co-chaired, with the United Nations Development Programme (UNDP), a working group to develop guidelines for UN resident coordinators and country teams in achieving durable solutions for target groups. UNHCR continued to participate in the work of the Executive Committee for Humanitarian Affairs (ECHA) and the Inter-Agency Standing Committee (IASC). It also remained active in the Inter-Agency Advisory Group on AIDS and the IASC Task Force on HIV/AIDS in Emergency Settings (see p. 1245). During the year, UNHCR continued to work closely with the IDP Unit of the UN Office for the Coordination of Humanitarian Affairs (OCHA) on measures to strengthen collaboration for protecting IDPs, and further strengthened collaboration with the World Food Programme (WFP), the International Labour Organization (ILO) and the United Nations Human Settlements Programme (UN-Habitat) on refugee issues. With over 600 United Nations Volunteers (UNVs) participating in some 60 UNHCR operations worldwide during the year, a memorandum of understanding (MOU) was being finalized to further strengthen cooperation with the UNV Office. In the area of refugee health, UNHCR cooperated with the World Health Organization (WHO) in addressing refugee health and nutrition, and in preparing technical guidelines, including the New Emergency Health Kit and the Tuberculosis (TB) Control Manual. The Office also continued collaboration with the International Organization for Migration (IOM) and participated in furthering the objectives of the New Partnership for Africa's Development (NEPAD) (see p. 937) to ensure a stake for returnees and IDPs in their countries of origin, and to help avert renewed displacement. During the year, UNHCR channelled $223 million (one quarter of its annual budget) through over 500 non-governmental organizations (NGOs), covering sectors such as shelter/ other infrastructure; transport/logistics; health and nutrition; education; legal assistance/protection; and agency operational support. UNHCR initiated consultations to involve strategic NGO partners more closely in assessing planning processes so as to avoid duplicating efforts and better target humanitarian assistance and protection. The Office launched a protection learning programme for its partners: a pilot project designed to promote a team-based approach, mainstream gender and age issues, and demonstrate the importance of accountability.

Evaluation activities

UNHCR, in an August report [A/AC.96/976], described developments in its evaluation function, explained its evaluation policy, examined the challenge of ensuring that related findings and recommendations were effectively utilized, and described the evaluation activities of its Evaluation and Policy Analysis Unit (EPAU). In January, the new evaluation policy, contained in a policy statement adopted in 2002 [YUN 2002, p. 1201], took effect. To ensure the effective use of evaluation findings and recommendations, UNHCR introduced a management response requirement, obliging the manager responsible for an evaluated policy or programme to explain how the findings and recommendations of the evaluation would be used. EPAU was also considering several other mechanisms for further strengthening the evaluation function.

Completed evaluation projects were related to health and community services; reproductive health services to refugees; monitoring the protection, rights and well-being of refugees; protracted refugee situations, particularly in Africa; refugees in urban areas; management learning programmes; country programmes; facilitation and internal consultancy; and strategic reviews of UNHCR operations. Other activities during the year included reviews of UNHCR operations in Afghanistan, Guinea, Tajikistan, Timor-Leste and Western Europe, and of UNHCR office staffing parameters, emergency procurement arrangements, indicators for implementing the High Commissioner's commitments regarding refugee women and freedom of movement issues in refugee situations.

Inspections

In 2003 [A/59/12], regular inspections of UNHCR operations by its Inspector General's Office (IGO) were conducted in Gabon, Greece, Pakistan and Turkey. In order to assess strategy and policy from a subregional perspective and to ascertain where UNHCR might strengthen partnerships with other members of the UN system, international organizations and NGOs, IGO undertook its first operational reviews of Somalia, Sri Lanka, the Sudan and Turkey. It also carried out a comprehensive review and revision of its inspection strategy. IGO expanded its work to include ad hoc inspections focusing on specific management issues requiring a separate assessment. In 2003, IGO received 158 complaints alleging misuse of assets, medical insurance fraud, sexual harassment of staff, sexual exploitation of refugees and other improper conduct. In 40 per cent of those cases, it recommended administrative or disciplinary action; in another 40 per cent, it concluded that the allegations were unfounded or insufficiently established.

The UN Office of Internal Oversight Services (OIOS) audited UNHCR's staffing of emergency operations; decentralized personnel administration; housing maintenance element (HOME) entitlement; the Media Relations and Public Information Service; central emergency and regional stockpiles; air operations; various aspects of the Management System Renewal Project; and operations in 29 countries. It also reviewed two NGOs to assess their systems and procedures and to advise on how to comply with UNHCR requirements. OIOS audits covered operations and activities amounting to $218 million or 22 per cent of UNHCR's total expenditure of $983 million in 2003. It issued 34 audit reports to senior management and over 66 audit observations to managers in the field.

GENERAL ASSEMBLY ACTION

On 22 December [meeting 77], the General Assembly, on the recommendation of the Third (Social, Humanitarian and Cultural) Committee [A/58/503], adopted **resolution 58/151** without vote [agenda item 112].

Office of the United Nations High Commissioner for Refugees

The General Assembly,

Having considered the report of the United Nations High Commissioner for Refugees on the activities of his Office and the report of the Executive Committee of the Programme of the United Nations High Commissioner for Refugees on the work of its fifty-fourth session and the conclusions and decisions contained therein,

Recalling its previous annual resolutions on the work of the Office of the United Nations High Commissioner for Refugees since its establishment by the General Assembly,

Expressing its appreciation for the leadership shown by the High Commissioner, commending the staff and implementing partners of the Office of the High Commissioner for the competent, courageous and dedicated manner in which they discharge their responsibilities, and underscoring its strong condemnation of all forms of violence to which humanitarian personnel and United Nations and associated personnel are increasingly exposed,

1. *Endorses* the report of the Executive Committee of the Programme of the United Nations High Commissioner for Refugees on the work of its fifty-fourth session;

2. *Welcomes* the important work undertaken by the Office of the United Nations High Commissioner for Refugees and its Executive Committee in the course of the year, and notes in this context the conclusions adopted on international protection, on the return of persons found not to be in need of international protection, on protection safeguards in interception measures, and on protection from sexual abuse and exploitation, which are aimed at strengthening the international protection regime, consistent with the Agenda for Protection resulting from the Global Consultations on International Protection, and at assisting Governments in meeting their protection responsibilities in today's changing international environment;

3. *Reaffirms* the 1951 Convention relating to the Status of Refugees and its 1967 Protocol as the foundation of the international refugee protection regime, and recognizes the importance of their full and effective application by States parties and the values they embody, notes with satisfaction that one hundred and forty-five States are now parties to one instrument or to both, encourages States not parties to consider acceding to those instruments, underlines in particular the importance of full respect for the principle of non-refoulement, and recognizes that a number of States not parties to the international refugee instruments have shown a generous approach to hosting refugees;

4. *Notes* that fifty-five States are now parties to the 1954 Convention relating to the Status of Stateless Persons and that twenty-seven States are parties to the 1961 Convention on the Reduction of Statelessness, and encourages the High Commissioner to continue his activities on behalf of stateless persons;

5. *Re-emphasizes* that the protection of refugees is primarily the responsibility of States, whose full and effective cooperation, action and political resolve are required to enable the Office of the High Commissioner to fulfil its mandated functions;

6. *Emphasizes* that international protection is a dynamic and action-oriented function that is at the core of the mandate of the Office of the High Commissioner and which includes, in cooperation with States and other partners, the promotion and facilitation of, inter alia, the admission, reception and treatment of refugees and the ensuring of durable, protection-oriented solutions, bearing in mind the particular needs of vulnerable groups, and notes in this context that the delivery of international protection is a staff-intensive service that requires adequate staff with the appropriate expertise, especially at the field level;

7. *Welcomes* the High Commissioner's "Convention Plus" initiative, and encourages the High Commissioner and those States that have offered to facilitate Convention Plus agreements to strengthen the international protection regime through the development of comprehensive approaches to resolving refugee situations, including improving international burden- and responsibility-sharing and realizing durable solutions;

8. *Recalls* the important role of effective partnerships and coordination in meeting the needs of refugees and other displaced persons and in finding durable solutions to their situations, and welcomes the efforts under way, in cooperation with other United Nations agencies and development actors, to promote a framework for durable solutions, particularly in protracted refugee situations, including the "4Rs" approach (repatriation, reintegration, rehabilitation and reconstruction) to sustainable return;

9. *Urges* all States and relevant non-governmental and other organizations, in conjunction with the Office of the High Commissioner, in a spirit of international solidarity and burden- and responsibility-sharing, to cooperate and to mobilize resources with a view to enhancing the capacity of, and reducing the heavy burden borne by, countries that have received large numbers of refugees and asylum-seekers, and calls upon the Office to continue to play its catalytic role in mobilizing assistance from the international community to address the root causes as well as the economic, environmental and social impact of large-scale refugee populations in developing countries, particularly least developed countries, and countries with economies in transition;

10. *Strongly reaffirms* the fundamental importance and the purely humanitarian and non-political character of the function of the Office of the High Commissioner of providing international protection to refugees and seeking permanent solutions to refugee problems, and recalls that these solutions include voluntary repatriation and, where appropriate and feasible, local integration and resettlement in a third country, while reaffirming that voluntary repatriation, supported by necessary rehabilitation and development assistance to facilitate sustainable reintegration, remains the preferred solution;

11. *Emphasizes* the obligation of all States to accept the return of their nationals, calls upon States to facilitate the return of their nationals who have been determined not to be in need of international protection, and affirms the need for the return of persons to be undertaken in a safe and humane manner and with full respect for their human rights and dignity, irrespective of the status of the persons concerned;

12. *Encourages* the Office of the High Commissioner to continue to improve its management systems and to ensure effective and transparent use of its resources, recognizes that adequate and timely resources are essential for the Office to continue to fulfil the mandate conferred upon it through its statute and by subsequent General Assembly resolutions concerning refugees and other persons of concern, and urges Governments and other donors to respond promptly to annual and supplementary appeals issued by the Office for requirements under its programmes;

13. *Requests* the High Commissioner to report on his activities to the General Assembly at its fifty-ninth session.

Strengthening UNHCR

In response to General Assembly resolution 57/186 [YUN 2002, p. 1203], the Secretary-General, in October, transmitted the report of the High Commissioner on strengthening the capacity of

UNHCR to carry out its mandate [A/58/410]. The report was the outcome of the "UNHCR 2004" process, launched in 2001 [YUN 2001, p. 1107], to determine how UNHCR could be better positioned to meet new challenges that had affected its capacity to carry out its mandate. It was prepared in consultation with the UNHCR Executive Committee, the Secretary-General and partner agencies and NGOs. The High Commissioner noted that, although the primary role of the Office had not changed, new categories of persons of concern had been added to its responsibilities, raising the need to ensure that it was sufficiently equipped to do its work and to respond to related challenges. The actions proposed, some of which depended on Assembly decisions, covered the time-limited nature of the Office; implementation of the Agenda for Protection [YUN 2002, p. 1205]; accessions to the Conventions on stateless persons and statelessness; IDPs; protection and assistance for returnees; the targeting of development assistance to facilitate durable solutions; addressing the asylum and migration nexus; convening periodic ministerial meetings, normally every five years, of States parties to the 1951 Convention relating to the Status of Refugees [YUN 1951, p. 520] and its 1967 Protocol [YUN 1967, p. 477]; streamlining UNHCR reporting, strengthening the linkages between UNHCR and peace and security, development and humanitarian pillars, and with human rights bodies; partnerships with NGOs; and diversifying and broadening UNHCR funding.

GENERAL ASSEMBLY ACTION

On 22 December [meeting 77], the General Assembly, on the recommendation of the Third Committee [A/58/503], adopted **resolution 58/153** without vote [agenda item 112].

Implementing actions proposed by the United Nations High Commissioner for Refugees to strengthen the capacity of his Office to carry out its mandate

The General Assembly,

Recalling its resolution 428(V) of 14 December 1950, the annex to which contains the statute of the Office of the United Nations High Commissioner for Refugees, and its resolution 57/186 of 18 December 2002 on the continuation of the Office of the High Commissioner,

Appreciating the concerted efforts of the High Commissioner in undertaking consultations with the Secretary-General, the members of the Executive Committee of the Programme of the United Nations High Commissioner for Refugees and observers of its Standing Committee, through the process known as "UNHCR 2004", on how the Office of the High Commissioner could be better equipped to carry out its mandate in the changing context of the global situation, and noting that this is in support and in the context of the goals, objectives and commitments contained in the United Nations Millennium Declaration, as well as the efforts of the Secretary-General to strengthen the United Nations system,

1. *Welcomes* the report of the United Nations High Commissioner for Refugees on strengthening the capacity of the Office of the United Nations High Commissioner for Refugees to carry out its mandate, as called for in resolution 57/186;

2. *Reaffirms* that international protection and the search for durable solutions for refugees and, as applicable, other persons of concern to the Office of the High Commissioner, which were examined, inter alia, in the Global Consultations on International Protection process and are reflected in the Agenda for Protection, are the core of the mandate of the Office;

3. *Welcomes* the efforts of the Office of the High Commissioner to strengthen its linkages with the other parts of the United Nations system in order to enhance refugee protection and to identify and implement durable solutions for refugees and other persons of concern to the Office, and appreciates its efforts to strengthen partnerships with operational and implementing partners;

4. *Welcomes* the admission of the Office to the United Nations Development Group, and invites the Development Group to include, through the resident coordinator system and in full consultation with the Government concerned, consideration of the needs of refugees and, as applicable, other persons of concern to the Office of the High Commissioner in the common country assessment process and the subsequent formulation and implementation of their development programmes;

5. *Notes* the importance of the support of the Office of the High Commissioner, within its mandate, to the efforts of the Emergency Relief Coordinator to promote predictable and timely United Nations strategies that, inter alia, integrate durable solutions for refugees with those for internally displaced persons;

6. *Highlights* the importance of joint efforts of the Department of Political Affairs and the Department of Peacekeeping Operations of the Secretariat, together with those of the Office of the High Commissioner, which contribute to durable solutions for refugees in conflict and post-conflict situations, encourages the Office to play a more active role, including by sharing information with relevant United Nations forums, and stresses that all of these activities should be undertaken in a manner consistent with the mandate of the Office;

7. *Recalls* paragraph 20 of the statute of the Office of the High Commissioner, and calls for its application;

8. *Reaffirms* the continued voluntary nature of the funding of the Office of the High Commissioner in accordance with its statute, while recognizing the importance of contributions made by countries hosting refugees, especially developing countries, notes the need for more equitable international responsibility and burden-sharing and expresses concern over the recurring shortfall in the funding of the Office, requests that States, within their capacities, contribute to the full funding of the budget level approved by the Executive Committee, and encourages the Office to continue its efforts to expand its donor base and to diver-

sify funding sources, including through the private sector;

9. *Decides* to remove the temporal limitation on the continuation of the Office of the High Commissioner contained in its resolution 57/186 and to continue the Office until the refugee problem is solved;

10. *Decides also* that the High Commissioner shall make an annual oral report to the Economic and Social Council to keep it informed of the coordination aspects of the work of the Office and shall continue the existing practice, as established in paragraph 11 of its statute, of presenting an annual written report to the General Assembly, on the understanding that every ten years, beginning at the sixty-eighth session, the report will include a strategic review of the global situation of refugees and the role of the Office, prepared in consultation with the Secretary-General and the Executive Committee.

Enlargement of Executive Committee

On 24 July, the Economic and Social Council, by **decision 2003/285**, noted Egypt's request [E/2003/3] for membership in the UNHCR Executive Committee and recommended that the General Assembly decide on the question of enlarging the Committee's membership from 64 to 65 States at its fifty-eighth (2003) session. By **decision 2003/286** of the same date, the Council noted Zambia's request [E/2003/77] for membership and recommended that the Assembly decide on the question of enlarging the membership from 65 to 66 States at its fifty-eighth session.

GENERAL ASSEMBLY ACTION

On 22 December [meeting 77], the General Assembly, on the recommendation of the Third Committee [A/58/503], adopted **resolution 58/152** without vote [agenda item 112].

Enlargement of the Executive Committee of the Programme of the United Nations High Commissioner for Refugees

The General Assembly,

Taking note of Economic and Social Council decisions 2003/285 and 2003/286 of 24 July 2003 concerning the enlargement of the Executive Committee of the Programme of the United Nations High Commissioner for Refugees,

Taking note also of the requests regarding the enlargement of the Executive Committee contained in the letter dated 23 September 2002 from the Permanent Representative of Egypt to the United Nations addressed to the Secretary-General and the note verbale dated 25 April 2003 from the Permanent Mission of Zambia to the United Nations Office at Geneva addressed to the Secretary-General,

1. *Decides* to increase the number of members of the Executive Committee of the Programme of the United Nations High Commissioner for Refugees from sixty-four to sixty-six States;

2. *Requests* the Economic and Social Council to elect the additional members at its resumed organizational session for 2004.

Financial and administrative questions

UNHCR's initial annual programme budget target for 2003 was set at $836.3 million [A/59/12] by the Executive Committee in 2002 [YUN 2002, p. 1204]. Supplementary programmes established during the year totalled $330.6 million. Contributions to the annual programme budget totalled $652.2 million plus $8.1 million for the Junior Professional Officers (JPO) programme. The UN regular budget provided $28.2 million and contributions towards supplementary programmes totalled $268.2 million, $18.6 million of which was transferred to the annual programme budget to cover supplementary programme activities. Expenditures during the year totalled some $983 million, $714.8 million of which was from the annual programme budget. UNHCR expenditure by region was as follows: Africa, $376 million; Central Asia, South-West Asia, North Africa and the Middle East, $225 million; Asia and the Pacific, $54.4 million; Europe, $120.5 million; and the Americas, $24.3 million.

In October, the Executive Committee approved the revised 2003 annual programme budget amounting to $809.1 million, which, together with the UN regular budget contribution of $20.4 million, provisions for JPOs of $7 million and needs under supplementary programmes of $313.3 million, brought total requirements for the year to $1,150 million.

For the 2004 annual programme budget, the Committee approved $923 million, including an operational reserve of $61 million (representing 7.5 per cent of programmed activities) and $50 million, introduced on a trial basis for one year, for funding activities not included in the annual programme budget. The Committee decided to review in 2004 the issue of additional contributions for such activities and took note of the UN regular budget contribution of $25 million, and of the sum of $7 million for JPOs, which brought total requirements for 2004 to $955 million.

Accounts (2002)

The audited financial statements of voluntary funds administered by UNHCR for the year ending 31 December 2002 [A/58/5/Add.5] showed total expenditures of some $908.4 million and total income of $858.2 million, with a reserve balance of $120 million.

The Board of Auditors found that: unallocated available reserves at the end of 2002 ($50 million) were insufficient to cover the staff termination liabilities of some $263 million; the value of non-expendable property as at 31 December 2002 was understated by some $70 million; invalid expenditure, valued at $5.9 million, showed the need to set up a proper accounting policy; the 2002 operational expenditure not supported by implementing partners' financial reports totalled $14.2 million as at 11 June 2003; as at 31 January 2003, UNHCR had not received audit certificates for 52.5 per cent of expenditure on 2001 operational projects; the share of non-programme expenditure (28 per cent) had to be reviewed in view of the shortfall of $50 million in 2002; between 1998 and 2002, staff employed constantly exceeded the number of posts; some 75 per cent of staff held de facto permanent appointments as at 1 July 2002, versus 16 per cent in 1998; at the end of 2002, 113 Professionals were "staff-in-between-assignment", being paid but without assignment; the creation of the housing maintenance element (HOME) for staff exceeded the delegation of authority granted to the High Commissioner and was not in line with standard UN provisions; and the accounting systems did not enable UNHCR to report what was paid in respect of each entitlement and each staff member. The Board made a series of recommendations to improve management, noting that UNHCR had mostly actively responded to earlier recommendations, although some had not been implemented.

UNHCR, in August [A/AC.96/978/Add.1], reported on measures taken or proposed to respond to the recommendations of the Board of Auditors.

In a September report [A/58/384], the Advisory Committee on Administrative and Budgetary Questions (ACABQ) observed that the Board had modified its opinion, drawing attention to its finding on the adequacy of assurance obtained by UNHCR that funds were properly used for the purpose intended and on the understatement of some $70 million in the disclosure of non-expendable property. ACABQ noted that the statement of income and expenditure and changes in reserve and fund balances of the voluntary funds administered by the Office did not include $21 million received from the UN regular budget. As to human resources management, ACABQ shared the Board's concern about the gap between staff members with appointments and posts. ACABQ expressed concern about UNHCR's management of staff-in-between-assignments, citing the Board's finding that, as at December 2002, some 113 Professional staff and 16 General Service staff, although their assignments had expired, remained on special leave with full pay, which had cost the Office several million dollars between 1998 and 2002. ACABQ requested that the High Commissioner take urgent action to comply with the Board's recommendations in that regard and to report on the management of affected staff in the next budget report. It welcomed the High Commissioner's intention to introduce reforms, transparency and stronger control of the staffing table. ACABQ agreed with the Board's view that the creation of the HOME allowance exceeded the authority delegated to the High Commissioner.

The Executive Committee, in a decision on administrative, financial and programme matters [A/58/12/Add.1], requested that it be informed regularly on measures taken to address the recommendations and observations made by the Board of Auditors and ACABQ.

Standing Committee

The UNHCR Standing Committee held three meetings in 2003 (4-6 March [A/AC.96/974]; 24-26 June [A/AC.96/984]; and 25 September [A/AC.96/985]). It reviewed UNHCR's programmes and activities in various regions and considered updates on overall programme and funding issues; protection/programme policy issues, including the safety and security of staff and refugees, and the economic and social impact of massive refugee populations on developing host countries and other countries; international protection; statelessness; coordination issues within the UN system; and issues relating to management, finance, oversight and human resources, and governance.

In October [A/58/12/Add.1], the Executive Committee adopted the following items for the Standing Committee's 2004 programme of work: international protection; programme/protection policy; programme and funding; governance; coordination; and management, financial, oversight and human resources. The Standing Committee was authorized to add or delete items, as appropriate, to its intersessional work programme.

Staff safety

At its March meeting [A/AC.96/974], the Standing Committee discussed staff and refugee safety and security. The Director of UNHCR's Emergency Security Service drew attention to increasing threats to the physical safety of UNHCR staff and past and current initiatives to address those threats. The establishment of a qualified cadre of professional security officers had been accompanied by measures to develop a wider culture of security awareness to help all staff become more effective in managing their own security and that of their colleagues. That resulted in the establishment of the UNHCR security policy, which was complementary to the system-wide accountability scheme of the United Nations Security Coordinator (UNSECOORD). Further measures included training sessions and tools development, notably the CD-ROM interactive self-learning course, which had been adopted by other UN system agencies as a mandatory basic security training. Additional initiatives would extend training support further across the system, and possibly to NGO and governmental partners. Work was ongoing, in collaboration with the UN Department of Peacekeeping Operations and Governments, to find ways to improve UNHCR's response to refugee security.

Refugee protection and assistance

Protection issues

In his annual report covering 2003 [A/59/12], the High Commissioner described significant challenges facing States and UNHCR in securing and upholding international protection of refugees, which included safeguarding humanitarian principles in a frequently precarious security environment, ensuring access to international protection, planning and supporting major repatriation movements, and promoting the resolution of protracted situations. He stated that the goals and related objectives of the Agenda for Protection, adopted in 2002 [YUN 2002, p. 1205] as a multi-year programme of action for improving the protection of refugees and asylum-seekers, had been mainstreamed into UNHCR strategies, policies, practices and reporting processes, from country operations plans to protection learning programmes. Measures taken by UNHCR to meet the goals of the Agenda for Protection included: strengthening implementation of the 1951 Convention relating to the Status of Refugees [YUN 1951, p. 520] and its 1967 Protocol [YUN 1967, p. 477]; protecting refugees within broader migration movements; sharing burdens and responsibilities more equitably and building capacities to receive and protect refugees; addressing security-related concerns more effectively; redoubling the search for durable solutions; and meeting the protection needs of refugee women and children.

In a July note on international protection [A/AC.96/975], the High Commissioner focused on the mechanics of protection, highlighting how States, UNHCR and other actors were using various tools to ensure that those needing international protection benefited from it. He discussed operational, legal and policy, and promotional protection tools, covering the period from September 2002 to July 2003, highlighted developments in different countries where they indicated broader trends, and outlined UNHCR's actions in response to protection challenges within the framework of follow-up action to the Agenda for Protection.

The High Commissioner stated that the effects of globalization and contemporary security concerns had brought to the fore problems resulting from mixed migratory flows. UNHCR had suggested ways to develop a comprehensive framework for improving national asylum systems in destination States, establish cooperative regional processing systems among those States and improve access to durable solutions in regions of origin. Nonetheless, the protection of refugees faced significant challenges, especially in situations of conflict, such as in West and Central Africa, where insecurity remained an endemic problem. UNHCR was also concerned at the proliferation of international organizations describing their work as protection, which could lead to a confusion of roles and dilution of expertise, ultimately detrimental to protection. Elsewhere, asylum processes had increasingly been tightened to the detriment of refugees and there was a strong tendency towards harmonization, at the level of the lowest common denominator, in the development of regional asylum systems.

The Executive Committee, in October [A/58/12/Add.1], stressed the value of strengthening protection capacities in host countries, encouraged follow-up activities towards the implementation of the Agenda for Protection and urged cooperation between States and UNHCR on methods to resolve cases of statelessness. The Committee highlighted the need to provide protection safeguards to intercepted persons within the framework of international human rights and refugee law, and recommended measures to guide such interception and ways to protect refugees and asylum-seekers from sexual abuse and exploitation.

International instruments

In 2003, Timor-Leste acceded to the 1951 Convention relating to the Status of Refugees [YUN 1951, p. 520], bringing the total number of parties to the Convention to 142. With the accession of Saint Vincent and the Grenadines and Timor-Leste, the total number of States party to the Convention's 1967 Protocol [YUN 1967, p. 477] rose to 141. Albania's accession to the 1954 Convention relating to the Status of Stateless Persons [YUN 1954, p. 416] and the 1961 Convention on the Reduction of Statelessness [YUN 1961, p. 533] increased the number of States party to those instruments to 55 and 27, respectively.

Convention Plus

In 2003, the High Commissioner for Refugees launched the "Convention Plus" initiative to help strengthen the commitment of States and UNHCR partners to resolving refugee situations, notably through multilateral special agreements, and develop comprehensive action plans for resolving specific refugee situations, particularly protracted ones. Dialogue and negotiations on multilateral special agreements began within groups of States and other stakeholders, convened around each of the three central strands of the initiative: the strategic use of resettlement; ways to address irregular secondary movements of refugees and asylum-seekers; and the strategic targeting of development assistance to achieve solutions to refugee problems. A comprehensive plan of action to address the Somali refugee crisis was being considered.

Assistance measures

The global population of concern to UNHCR dropped to 17 million in 2003 from 20.8 million in 2002, due largely to the return of millions of refugees following the end of prolonged crises in Africa and Afghanistan. An estimated 5 million persons who had fled their homes found a solution through voluntary repatriation, resettlement or local integration. Those assisted included asylum-seekers, refugees, returning refugees in the early stages of their reintegration, IDPs and other persons of concern, mainly victims of conflict. During the year, some 1.1 million refugees repatriated voluntarily to their countries of origin, with the largest number (644,500) repatriating to Afghanistan from Iran and Pakistan. Many others returned to Angola, Bosnia and Herzegovina, Burundi, Eritrea, Iraq, Liberia, Rwanda, Sierra Leone and Somalia. The number of those resettled during the year rose to 26,000 from 20,000 in 2002, owing to a relative rise in acceptance levels for resettlement. Also, efforts to encourage local integration and to implement self-reliance strategies for refugees made limited but tangible progress in many countries. Nonetheless, millions in some 38 protracted refugee situations still awaited durable solutions, with new outflows reported in several African countries and in Colombia. UNHCR continued to accord high priority to developing effective responses for such situations.

In 2003, UNHCR received a total of some $929 million in voluntary contributions towards its annual programme budget.

Refugees and the environment

In 2003, UNHCR, in a bid to limit environmental damage and degradation caused by the presence of refugees, continued efforts to mainstream sound environmental management into all phases of refugee operations, with the active participation of refugees and host communities. It emphasized cost-effective, community-based projects and strengthened collaboration with partners in addressing post-repatriation environmental rehabilitation. It also planned to produce guidelines on the assessment, monitoring and evaluation of environmental activities, for field testing and finalization in 2004.

Refugees and HIV/AIDS

Under UNHCR's 2002-2004 strategic plan on HIV/AIDS, launched in 2002 [YUN 2002, p. 1207], which included plans to standardize and align programmes within country operations, the Office was making efforts to develop a subregional approach to combating the disease, one example of which was the World Bank–funded Great Lakes Initiative programme, which aimed to achieve more effective coordination and cooperation between donors, host populations and Governments. Within the IASC Task Force on HIV/AIDS in Emergency Settings, UNHCR, together with WFP and the United Nations Children's Fund (UNICEF), was reviewing nutrition and food aid policies to ensure that sufficient food was provided to those suffering from the disease.

Refugee women

In May, UNHCR issued its response to the 2002 [YUN 2002, p. 1202] evaluations on refugee women, refugee children and the community service function, which drew particular attention to the need for increased ownership of existing policies and the involvement of all staff. The implementation of a three-year action plan drawn up in that regard was being overseen by a Steering Committee. During the year, a pilot project developed in Latin America and Turkey, on the basis of earlier UNHCR experiences, was launched in 10 countries. The project aimed to facilitate the integration of a gender and age perspective into UNHCR operations. UNHCR revised its Guidelines for Prevention and Response to Sexual and Gender-based Violence in refugee and refugee-like settings and disseminated it to field offices and partners. Numerous training workshops on prevention were organized.

Refugee children

In 2003, UNHCR maintained a strong emphasis on education as a protection tool for refugee children, focusing on ensuring access to primary education. To overcome low enrolment rates, particularly among girl refugees at the primary school level, projects were launched in Ethiopia, Kenya and Somalia, in partnership with private corporations. Tertiary-level scholarships and secondary-level trust fund education support continued. A UNHCR report on education indicators in 118 refugee camps in 23 asylum countries identified areas where future planning for refugee children's education could be improved.

Report of Secretary-General. In response to General Assembly resolution 56/136 [YUN 2001, p. 1115], the Secretary-General submitted an August report on assistance to unaccompanied refugee minors [A/58/299]. The report provided information on UNHCR action to protect and assist minors and on activities by other UN entities, including UNICEF, the Office of the United Nations High Commissioner for Human Rights, OCHA and the Office of the Special Representative of the Secretary-General for Children and Armed Conflict, among others. The report discussed a rights-based approach to securing the interests of affected minors and global priority issues relating to refugee children, including family tracing and reunification, military recruitment, sexual exploitation, abuse and violence, and education. It also highlighted other concerns and challenges such as the special protection needs of refugee girls and of internally displaced children.

The Secretary-General observed that progress had been made over the past two years in addressing the protection and assistance needs of unaccompanied or separated refugee children. Cooperation among UN system bodies and with other partners, notably the International Committee of the Red Cross, NGOs and Governments, had been strengthened. Positive results were evident in terms of training and capacity-building, commitments to common goals on critical child protection and assistance issues, the entry into force of new human rights instruments, and legislative changes raising child protection standards. The inter-agency agreement on common Guiding Principles on Unaccompanied and Separated Children was a noteworthy example of progress. Nonetheless, serious challenges remained, including security concerns, insufficient human and material resources, inadequate law enforcement systems for the effective pursuit of child rights violations, and, in some cases, insufficient political will by States to comply with international standards relating to children. The Secretary-General urged States that had not done so to ratify the two optional protocols to the Convention on the Rights of the Child, adopted by the General Assembly in resolution 54/263 [YUN 2000, p. 615], and to ensure the implementation and monitoring of compliance with international instruments and accountability for violations. States and other stakeholders in civil society were encouraged to ensure that adequate resources were provided to enable refugee children to enjoy rights to which they were entitled, such as the right to education, and to avoid being recruited into armed forces or groups, or falling victim to sexual exploitation and abuse. More attention was needed by all actors involved with unaccompanied or separated children towards achieving more effective identification, registration, tracing and family reunification systems.

GENERAL ASSEMBLY ACTION

On 22 December [meeting 77], the General Assembly, on the recommendation of the Third Committee [A/58/503], adopted **resolution 58/150** without vote [agenda item 112].

Assistance to unaccompanied refugee minors

The General Assembly,

Recalling its resolutions 49/172 of 23 December 1994, 50/150 of 21 December 1995, 51/73 of 12 December 1996, 52/105 of 12 December 1997, 53/122 of 9 December 1998, 54/145 of 17 December 1999 and 56/136 of 19 December 2001,

Aware of the fact that the majority of refugees are children and women,

Bearing in mind that unaccompanied refugee minors are among the most vulnerable refugees and the most at risk of neglect, violence, forced military recruitment, sexual assault, abuse and vulnerability to infectious disease, such as human immunodeficiency virus/acquired immunodeficiency syndrome, malaria and tuberculosis, and therefore require special assistance and care,

Mindful of the fact that the ultimate solution to the plight of unaccompanied minors is their return to and reunification with their families,

Bearing in mind that the most important steps in working with unaccompanied minors are rapid identification, immediate registration and documentation and tracing of family,

Recalling the outcome document entitled "A world fit for children", adopted on 10 May 2002 by the General Assembly at its twenty-seventh special session,

Noting with appreciation the efforts of the Office of the United Nations High Commissioner for Refugees and the United Nations Children's Fund in the identification and tracing of unaccompanied minors, and welcoming their efforts in reunifying families of refugees,

Welcoming the efforts exerted by the United Nations High Commissioner for Refugees to reunite refugees with their families,

Noting the efforts of the High Commissioner to ensure the protection of and assistance to refugees, including children and unaccompanied minors, and that further enhanced efforts need to be exerted to this effect,

Recalling the provisions of the Convention on the Rights of the Child, and the 1951 Convention and the 1967 Protocol thereto relating to the Status of Refugees,

1. *Takes note* of the report of the Secretary-General;
2. *Expresses its deep concern* at the continuing plight of unaccompanied refugee minors, and emphasizes once again the urgent need for their early identification and for timely, detailed and accurate information on their number and whereabouts;

3. *Stresses* the importance of providing adequate resources for programmes of identification, registration, documentation and tracing of unaccompanied minors and their reunification with their families;

4. *Calls upon* the Office of the United Nations High Commissioner for Refugees, in cooperation with other relevant United Nations bodies, to incorporate into its programmes policies that aim at preventing the separation of refugee families, conscious of the importance of family unity;

5. *Calls upon* all Governments, the Secretary-General, the Office of the High Commissioner, all United Nations organizations, as well as other international organizations and non-governmental organizations concerned to exert the maximum effort to assist and protect refugee minors and to expedite the return and reunification with their families of unaccompanied refugee minors;

6. *Urges* the Office of the High Commissioner, all United Nations organizations, as well as other international organizations and non-governmental organizations concerned to take appropriate steps to mobilize resources commensurate with the needs of unaccompanied refugee minors and for their reunification with their families;

7. *Calls upon* all States and other parties to armed conflict to comply with their obligations under international humanitarian law, human rights law and refugee law and, in this regard, calls upon States parties to respect fully the provisions of the Geneva Conventions of 12 August 1949 and related instruments, and to respect the provisions of the Convention on the Rights of the Child, which accord children affected by armed conflict special protection and treatment;

8. *Condemns* all acts of exploitation of unaccompanied refugee minors, including their use as soldiers or human shields in armed conflict and their forced recruitment into military forces, and any other acts that endanger their safety and personal security;

9. *Acknowledges* that education is among the most effective initial means of ensuring protection for unaccompanied minors, especially girls, by shielding them from exploitative activities such as child labour, military recruitment or sexual exploitation and abuse;

10. *Calls upon* the Secretary-General, the United Nations High Commissioner for Refugees, the Office for the Coordination of Humanitarian Affairs of the Secretariat, the United Nations Children's Fund, other United Nations organizations and other international organizations to mobilize adequate assistance to unaccompanied refugee minors in the areas of relief, education, recreational activities, health and psychological rehabilitation;

11. *Encourages* the Special Representative of the Secretary-General for Children and Armed Conflict in his efforts to raise awareness worldwide and mobilize official and public opinion for the protection of children affected by armed conflict, including refugee minors;

12. *Requests* the Secretary-General to report to the General Assembly at its sixtieth session on the implementation of the present resolution and to give special attention in his report to the girl-child refugee.

Regional activities

Africa

Report of Secretary-General. In response to General Assembly resolution 57/183 [YUN 2002, p. 1209], the Secretary-General submitted a September report on assistance to refugees, returnees and displaced persons in Africa [A/58/353], updating information contained in his 2002 report [YUN 2002, p. 1208]. He stated that, in early 2003, Africa was hosting 3.3 million refugees, 32 per cent of the global refugee population. Almost 350,000 African refugees were repatriated during the reporting period, mainly Angolan, Burundian, Sierra Leonean and Somalian nationals. The main African refugee groups continued to originate from Angola, Burundi, the DRC, Eritrea, Somalia and the Sudan, with major new refugee outflows reported from Burundi, the Central African Republic, Côte d'Ivoire, the DRC and Liberia in 2002.

In East Africa and the Horn of Africa, which was hosting some 940,000 refugees, persistent political, humanitarian and socio-economic challenges, including acute food shortages in Eritrea and Ethiopia, continued to take their toll on refugee operations. However, progress on a few of the major political and humanitarian problems in the subregion opened the way for voluntary repatriation operations, notably for Eritrean and Somali refugees. Hopes of resolving the crisis in the Sudan prompted preparation of contingency plans for the return and reintegration of half a million Sudanese refugees from six neighbouring States. However, rebel attacks on refugee settlements in Uganda, persistent insecurity in western Ethiopia and violence in parts of Kenya undermined UNHCR operations, displacing thousands of Sudanese refugees in those countries.

The Central Africa and the Great Lakes subregion was host to an estimated 1.3 million refugees. In the Central African Republic, UNHCR continued to protect and assist thousands of refugees from neighbouring States, despite the general insecurity and political and economic turmoil prevailing in that country. UNHCR began to promote the voluntary return of Rwandan refugees. By the end of 2002, 23,800 Rwandan refugees had returned from the United Republic of Tanzania and 14,000 from the DRC. In 2003, 4,000 Rwandan refugees were assisted to return from the DRC and Tanzania. In Burundi, the peaceful handover of power to a new regime opened further possibilities for addressing the situation of an estimated 574,000 Burundian refugees in exile. In Tanzania, some of the largest refugee caseloads in Africa posed major challenges to the international community in terms of providing protection and assistance, including the provision of adequate food. In the DRC, a peace agreement with Rwanda renewed impetus for the voluntary repatriation of Rwandan refugees residing there, some 6,000 of whom returned home during the year. However, persistent instability in eastern DRC, among other factors, obstructed the anticipated repatriation from neighbouring countries of over 350,000 refugees, and affected the humanitarian community's response to the protection and assistance needs of over half a million IDPs in the country. In Angola, the Government took measures to further consolidate and enhance the refugee protection mandate, and the peace process between the Government and the National Union for the Total Independence of Angola (UNITA) enabled the repatriation of thousands of Angolan refugees from the DRC.

In West Africa, where 1 million persons of concern resided, the end of the civil war in Sierra Leone and renewed hostilities in some host countries paved the way for many Sierra Leonean refugees to return home. Since the beginning of the return programme in 2000, up to 213,000 refugees had repatriated voluntarily, 115,000 of whom were assisted by UNHCR. In total, some 300,000 Sierra Leoneans had benefited from assistance in returnee areas through community-based projects. In contrast, the ongoing war in Liberia resulted in hundreds of thousands of IDPs and forced some 275,000 Liberians to flee to neighbouring countries, mostly to Guinea. In Côte d'Ivoire, where a 2002 coup d'état sparked a civil war and significant population movements, UNHCR continued to ensure the safety of some 45,000 refugees and to meet basic protection and assistance needs. In Guinea, the Office continued to assist the refugee population in camps and to promote voluntary repatriation.

In Southern Africa, which was hosting 685,000 persons of concern to UNHCR, the consolidation of peace in Angola allowed some 130,000 Angolan refugees to return home spontaneously, and assistance measures helped reintegrate them in their home villages. In Zambia, which hosted over 250,000 refugees, the largest refugee population in the subregion, the Government, with support from UNHCR, the United Nations Office for Project Services and the international community, continued to implement local integration projects. Peace prospects in the DRC and Rwanda had also raised hopes for the return of refugees from both countries who had fled to other Southern African States. Nonetheless, critical food shortages continued to affect the subregion, with some 6 million people in need of support.

Describing cooperation with regional bodies and initiatives, the Secretary-General stated that an important development was the signing, in May, of a memorandum of understanding between the African Commission on Human and Peoples' Rights and UNHCR, designed to strengthen cooperation and to promote and protect the human rights of refugees and other persons of concern.

UNHCR report. According to UNHCR's *Global Report 2003*, persons of concern in Africa during the year totalled 4.5 million, comprising some 3.3 million refugees, 180,639 asylum-seekers, 669,655 IDPs and 329,528 returnee refugees.

In Central Africa and the Great Lakes, UNHCR's major preoccupation was the influx into Chad of tens of thousands of people from the Darfur region of the Sudan. The emergency posed a major challenge, owing mainly to the length and inaccessibility of the borderland to which the refugees fled. Other challenges affecting humanitarian operations related to continuing insecurity in Burundi, the Central African Republic and the DRC, and to environmental degradation in Tanzania. Despite those problems, UNHCR was able to either repatriate or settle thousands of Burundian, Rwandan and Somali refugees. Positive developments in East Africa and the Horn of Africa included the repatriation and reintegration of some 9,444 Eritreans, 10,227 Somalis and 281 Ugandans. Following the outbreak of fighting in the Sudan's Darfur region, however, and the killing of three humanitarian workers in north-west Somalia (Somaliland), hopes of further progress were dashed. In West Africa, UNHCR assisted over 33,000 Sierra Leonean refugees to return home and facilitated the local integration of urban refugees in the country. Major concerns in West Africa included sporadic and complex population flows, resulting mainly from the conflicts in Côte d'Ivoire and Liberia. Significant developments in Southern Africa included the repatriation of 76,674 Angolan refugees and the resettlement in the country of another 435 from neighbouring States. Combating HIV/AIDS was a priority and emphasis was placed on ensuring that related refugee care was included in host countries' health programmes. Challenges in the subregion included restrictive refugee legislation, irregular refugee movements and a backlog of asylum applications, and the limited capacity of some countries, most notably Angola, to receive and reintegrate returnees.

UNHCR assisted 1.3 million persons in Central Africa and the Great Lakes region, which received $101.3 million in agency expenditures. In West Africa, $110.8 million was spent on 1.5 million persons of concern, while some $107 million was spent on programmes assisting 1 million persons in need in East Africa and the Horn of Africa. In Southern Africa, $57.5 million was spent on over half a million persons of concern.

GENERAL ASSEMBLY ACTION

On 22 December [meeting 77], the General Assembly, on the recommendation of the Third Committee [A/58/503], adopted **resolution 58/149** without vote [agenda item 112].

Assistance to refugees, returnees and displaced persons in Africa

The General Assembly,

Recalling its resolution 57/183 of 18 December 2002,

Recalling also the provisions of its resolution 2312 (XXII) of 14 December 1967, by which it adopted the Declaration on Territorial Asylum,

Recalling further the Organization of African Unity Convention governing the specific aspects of refugee problems in Africa of 1969 and the African Charter on Human and Peoples' Rights,

Recalling the Khartoum Declaration and the Recommendations on Refugees, Returnees and Internally Displaced Persons in Africa adopted by the Organization of African Unity at the ministerial meeting held at Khartoum on 13 and 14 December 1998,

Welcoming decision EX/CL/Dec.46(III) on the situation of refugees, returnees and displaced persons in Africa adopted by the Executive Council of the African Union at its third ordinary session, held at Maputo from 4 to 8 July 2003,

Welcoming also decision AHG/Dec.165(XXXVII) on the fiftieth anniversary of the adoption of the 1951 Convention relating to the Status of Refugees, adopted by the Assembly of Heads of State and Government of the Organization of African Unity at its thirty-seventh ordinary session, held at Lusaka from 9 to 11 July 2001,

Recalling its resolution 57/2 of 16 September 2002 on the United Nations Declaration on the New Partnership for Africa's Development, and affirming that international support for the implementation of the New Partnership for Africa's Development is essential, notably as it relates to refugees, returnees and displaced persons,

Reaffirming that the 1951 Convention relating to the Status of Refugees, together with the 1967 Protocol thereto, as complemented by the Organization of African Unity Convention of 1969, remains the foundation of the international refugee protection regime in Africa,

Recognizing that the fundamental principles and rights embodied in those conventions have provided a resilient protection regime within which millions of refugees have been able to find safety from armed conflicts and persecution,

Welcoming in that regard the Declaration adopted at the Ministerial Meeting of States Parties to the 1951 Convention and/or its 1967 Protocol relating to the Status of Refugees, held at Geneva on 12 and 13 December 2001, as an expression of their collective commitment to full and effective implementation of the Convention and the Protocol,

Recalling the Comprehensive Implementation Plan adopted by the Special Meeting of Governmental and Non-Governmental Technical Experts convened by the Organization of African Unity and the Office of the United Nations High Commissioner for Refugees at Conakry from 27 to 29 March 2000 on the occasion of the thirtieth anniversary of the adoption of the Organization of African Unity Convention governing the specific aspects of refugee problems in Africa of 1969, and noting its endorsement by the Council of Ministers of the Organization of African Unity at its seventy-second ordinary session, held at Lomé from 6 to 8 July 2000,

Commending the convening of the first African Union Ministerial Conference on Human Rights in Africa at Kigali on 8 May 2003, and recalling the attention paid to issues relevant to refugees and displaced persons in the Kigali Declaration adopted by the Conference,

Recognizing the contributions made by African States to the development of regional standards for the protection of refugees and returnees, and noting with appreciation that countries of asylum are hosting refugees in a humanitarian spirit and in a spirit of African solidarity and brotherhood,

Recognizing also the need for States to address resolutely the root causes of forced displacement and to create conditions that facilitate durable solutions for refugees and displaced persons, and stressing in that regard the need for States to foster peace, stability and prosperity throughout the African continent to forestall large refugee flows,

Convinced of the need to strengthen the capacity of States to provide assistance to and protection for refugees, returnees and displaced persons and of the need for the international community, within the context of burden-sharing, to increase its material, financial and technical assistance to the countries affected by refugees, returnees and displaced persons, to simultaneously address the inadequacies of existing assistance arrangements and to support initiatives in this regard,

Acknowledging with appreciation that some assistance is already rendered by the international community to refugees, returnees and displaced persons and host countries in Africa,

Noting the "Convention Plus" initiative of the United Nations High Commissioner for Refugees, which is aimed at strengthening the international protection regime through the development of comprehensive approaches to resolving refugee situations, including improving international burden- and responsibility-sharing and realizing durable solutions,

Deeply concerned about the continuing critical humanitarian situation in African countries, in particular in the Horn of Africa and Southern Africa, aggravated, among other things, by persistent natural disasters, including drought, floods and desertification, which can precipitate the displacement of people,

Noting with great concern that, despite all the efforts made so far by the United Nations, the African Union and others, the situation of refugees and displaced persons in Africa remains precarious,

Stressing that the provision of relief and assistance to African refugees by the international community should be on an equitable and non-discriminatory basis,

Considering that, among refugees, returnees and internally displaced persons, women and children are the majority of the population affected by conflict and bear the brunt of atrocities and other consequences of conflict,

1. *Takes note* of the reports of the Secretary-General and the United Nations High Commissioner for Refugees;

2. *Notes with concern* that the deteriorating socio-economic situation, compounded by political instability, internal strife, human rights violations and natural disasters, has led to increased numbers of refugees and displaced persons in some countries of Africa, and remains particularly concerned about the impact of large-scale refugee populations on the security, socio-economic situation and environment of countries of asylum;

3. *Encourages* African States to ensure the full implementation of and follow-up to the Comprehensive Implementation Plan adopted by the Special Meeting of Governmental and Non-Governmental Technical Experts convened by the Organization of African Unity and the Office of the United Nations High Commissioner for Refugees at Conakry from 27 to 29 March 2000 on the occasion of the thirtieth anniversary of the adoption of the Organization of African Unity Convention governing the specific aspects of refugee problems in Africa of 1969;

4. *Calls upon* States and other parties to armed conflict to observe scrupulously the letter and the spirit of international humanitarian law, bearing in mind that armed conflict is one of the principal causes of forced displacement in Africa;

5. *Expresses its appreciation* for the leadership shown by the United Nations High Commissioner for Refugees since assuming office in January 2001, and commends the Office of the High Commissioner for its ongoing efforts, with the support of the international community, to assist African countries of asylum and to respond to the protection and assistance needs of refugees, returnees and displaced persons in Africa;

6. *Reaffirms* that international protection and the search for durable solutions for refugees and, as appropriate, other persons of concern to the Office of the High Commissioner, which were examined, inter alia, in the Global Consultations on International Protection process and are reflected in the Agenda for Protection, are at the core of the mandate of the Office;

7. *Welcomes* the efforts of the Office of the High Commissioner to strengthen its linkages with the other parts of the United Nations system in order to enhance refugee protection and to identify and implement durable solutions for refugees and other persons of concern to the Office, and appreciates the efforts of the Office to strengthen partnerships with operational and implementing partners;

8. *Takes note* of the Ministerial Meeting of States Parties to the 1951 Convention and/or its 1967 Protocol relating to the Status of Refugees as an expression of their collective commitment to full and effective implementation of the Convention and the Protocol;

9. *Reaffirms* that the 1951 Convention and the 1967 Protocol relating to the Status of Refugees, as complemented by the Organization of African Unity Convention of 1969, remain the foundation of the international refugee protection regime in Africa, encourages African States that have not yet done so to accede to those instruments, and calls upon States parties to the Conventions to reaffirm their commitment to their ideals and to respect and observe their provisions;

10. *Notes* the need for States to address the root causes of forced displacement in Africa, and calls upon African States, the international community and relevant United Nations organizations to take concrete action to meet the needs of refugees, returnees and displaced persons for protection and assistance and to contribute generously to national projects and programmes aimed at alleviating their plight;

11. *Also notes* the link, inter alia, between human rights violations, poverty, natural disasters and environmental degradation and population displacement, and calls for redoubled and concerted efforts by States, in collaboration with the African Union, to promote and protect human rights for all and to address those problems;

12. *Encourages* the Office of the United Nations High Commissioner for Refugees to continue to cooperate with the Office of the United Nations High Commissioner for Human Rights and the African Commission on Human and Peoples' Rights, within their respective mandates, in the promotion and protection of the human rights and fundamental freedoms of refugees, returnees and displaced persons in Africa, and welcomes in this regard the signing of the memorandum of understanding between the African Commission on Human and Peoples' Rights and the Office of the United Nations High Commissioner for Refugees on 26 May 2003;

13. *Notes with appreciation* the ongoing mediation and conflict resolution efforts carried out by African States, the African Union and subregional organizations, as well as the establishment of regional mechanisms for conflict prevention and resolution, and urges all relevant parties to address the humanitarian consequences of conflicts;

14. *Expresses its appreciation and strong support* for those African Governments and local populations that, in spite of the general deterioration of socio-economic and environmental conditions and overstretched national resources, continue to accept the additional burden imposed upon them by increasing numbers of refugees and displaced persons, in compliance with the relevant principles of asylum;

15. *Welcomes* the decision of African heads of State and Government to address the situation of refugees, returnees and displaced persons in Africa within the context of the New Partnership for Africa's Development;

16. *Expresses its concern* about instances in which the fundamental principles of asylum are jeopardized by unlawful expulsion or refoulement or by threats to the life, physical security, integrity, dignity and well-being of refugees;

17. *Reaffirms* that host States have the primary responsibility to ensure the civilian and humanitarian character of asylum, and calls upon States, in cooperation with international organizations, within their mandates, to take all necessary measures to ensure respect for the principles of refugee protection and, in particular, to ensure that the civilian and humanitarian nature of refugee camps is not compromised by the presence or the activities of armed elements or

used for purposes that are incompatible with their civilian character;

18. *Deplores* the deaths, injuries and other forms of violence sustained by staff members of the Office of the High Commissioner, urges States, parties to conflict and all other relevant actors to take all necessary measures to protect activities related to humanitarian assistance, prevent attacks on and kidnapping of national and international humanitarian workers and ensure their safety and security, calls upon States to investigate fully any crime committed against humanitarian personnel and to bring to justice persons responsible for such crimes, and calls upon organizations and aid workers to abide by the national laws and regulations of the countries in which they operate;

19. *Condemns* any exploitation of refugees, especially their sexual abuse and exploitation, calls for those responsible for such deplorable acts to be brought to justice, welcomes in this regard the conclusion on protection from sexual abuse and exploitation adopted by the Executive Committee of the Programme of the United Nations High Commissioner for Refugees at its fifty-fourth session, and notes with deep concern that inadequate protection and/or inappropriate assistance, particularly concerning the quantity and quality of food and other material assistance, increases the vulnerability of refugees and asylum-seekers to sexual abuse and exploitation;

20. *Welcomes* the decision of the Office of the High Commissioner to put in place a code of conduct for humanitarian personnel aimed at preventing the exploitation of refugees, especially in the area of sexual exploitation;

21. *Calls upon* the Office of the High Commissioner, the African Union, subregional organizations and all African States, in conjunction with agencies of the United Nations system, intergovernmental and non-governmental organizations and the international community, to strengthen and revitalize existing partnerships and forge new ones in support of the international refugee protection system;

22. *Calls upon* the Office of the High Commissioner, the international community and other concerned entities to intensify their support to African Governments through appropriate capacity-building activities, including training of relevant officers, disseminating information about refugee instruments and principles, providing financial, technical and advisory services to accelerate the enactment or amendment and implementation of legislation relating to refugees, strengthening emergency response and enhancing capacities for the coordination of humanitarian activities;

23. *Reaffirms* the right of return and the principle of voluntary repatriation, appeals to countries of origin and countries of asylum to create conditions that are conducive to voluntary repatriation, and recognizes that, while voluntary repatriation remains the pre-eminent solution, local integration and third-country resettlement, where appropriate and feasible, are also viable options for dealing with the situation of African refugees who, owing to prevailing circumstances in their respective countries of origin, are unable to return home;

24. *Notes with satisfaction* the voluntary return of millions of refugees to their homelands following the successful repatriation and reintegration operations carried out by the Office of the High Commissioner with the cooperation and collaboration of countries hosting refugees and countries of origin, and welcomes the efforts under way, in cooperation with other United Nations agencies and development actors, to promote a framework for durable solutions, particularly in protracted refugee situations, including the "4Rs" approach (repatriation, reintegration, rehabilitation and reconstruction) to sustainable return;

25. *Appeals* to the international community to respond positively, in the spirit of solidarity and burden-sharing, to the third-country resettlement requests of African refugees, and notes with appreciation that some African countries have offered resettlement places for refugees;

26. *Calls upon* the international donor community to provide financial and material assistance that allows for the implementation of community-based development programmes that benefit both refugees and host communities, as appropriate, in agreement with host countries and consistent with humanitarian objectives;

27. *Welcomes* the programmes carried out by the Office of the High Commissioner with host Governments, the United Nations, non-governmental organizations and the international community to address the environmental and socio-economic impact of refugee populations;

28. *Calls upon* the international donor community to provide material and financial assistance for the implementation of programmes intended for the rehabilitation of the environment and infrastructure affected by refugees in countries of asylum;

29. *Expresses its concern* about the long stay of refugees in certain African countries, and calls upon the Office of the High Commissioner to keep its programmes under review, in conformity with its mandate in the host countries, taking into account the increasing needs of refugees;

30. *Notes* the conclusion adopted by the Executive Committee of the Programme of the United Nations High Commissioner for Refugees at its fifty-fourth session on the importance of early and effective registration systems and censuses as a tool of protection and as a means to enable the quantification and assessment of needs for the provision and distribution of humanitarian assistance and to implement appropriate durable solutions;

31. *Emphasizes* the need for the Office of the High Commissioner to collate statistics, on a regular basis, on the number of refugees living outside refugee camps in certain African countries with a view to evaluating and addressing the needs of those refugees;

32. *Urges* the international community, in a spirit of international solidarity and burden-sharing, to continue to fund generously the refugee programmes of the Office of the High Commissioner and, taking into account the substantially increased needs of programmes in Africa, to ensure that Africa receives a fair and equitable share of the resources designated for refugees;

33. *Requests* all Governments and intergovernmental and non-governmental organizations to pay particular attention to meeting the special needs of refugee women and children and displaced persons, including those with special protection needs;

34. *Calls upon* States and the Office of the High Commissioner to make renewed efforts to ensure that

the rights, needs and dignity of elderly refugees are fully respected and addressed through appropriate programme activities;

35. *Expresses grave concern* about the plight of internally displaced persons in Africa, calls upon States to take concrete action to pre-empt internal displacement and to meet the protection and assistance needs of internally displaced persons, recalls in that regard the Guiding Principles on Internal Displacement, and urges the international community, led by relevant United Nations organizations, to contribute generously to national projects and programmes aimed at alleviating the plight of internally displaced persons;

36. *Invites* the Representative of the Secretary-General on internally displaced persons to continue his ongoing dialogue with Member States and the intergovernmental and non-governmental organizations concerned, in accordance with his mandate, and to include information thereon in his reports to the Commission on Human Rights and the General Assembly;

37. *Requests* the Secretary-General to submit a comprehensive report on assistance to refugees, returnees and displaced persons in Africa to the General Assembly at its fifty-ninth session, taking fully into account the efforts expended by countries of asylum, under the item entitled "Report of the United Nations High Commissioner for Refugees, questions relating to refugees, returnees and displaced persons and humanitarian questions", and to present an oral report to the Economic and Social Council at its substantive session of 2004.

Sexual exploitation of refugees in West Africa

The General Assembly, in April, considered the 2002 [YUN 2002, p. 1202] OIOS report [A/57/465] on its investigation of allegations of sexual exploitation of female refugees by UN and NGO staff and peacekeepers in West Africa (Guinea, Liberia, Sierra Leone).

GENERAL ASSEMBLY ACTION

On 15 April [meeting 83], the General Assembly, on the recommendation of the Fifth (Administrative and Budgetary) Committee [A/57/604/Add.1], adopted **resolution 57/306** without vote [agenda item 122].

Investigation into sexual exploitation of refugees by aid workers in West Africa

The General Assembly,

Recalling its resolutions 48/218 B of 29 July 1994 and 54/244 of 23 December 1999,

Recalling also paragraph 14 of Security Council resolution 1400(2002) of 28 March 2002 and paragraph 10 of Council resolution 1460(2003) of 30 January 2003,

Having considered the report of the Office of Internal Oversight Services on the investigation into sexual exploitation of refugees by aid workers in West Africa,

Recognizing the important roles and responsibilities that humanitarian and peacekeeping personnel have in protecting and assisting vulnerable populations, especially refugees and internally displaced persons, and expressing appreciation for the valuable efforts of the vast majority of such personnel in this regard,

Expressing its grave concern at incidents of sexual exploitation and abuse against vulnerable populations, in particular refugees and internally displaced persons in West Africa and elsewhere,

Emphasizing that the highest standards of conduct and accountability are required of all personnel serving in humanitarian and peacekeeping operations,

1. *Takes note* of the report of the Office of Internal Oversight Services on the investigation into sexual exploitation by aid workers in West Africa;

2. *Expresses its serious concern* that the conditions in refugee camps and communities may make refugees, especially women and children, vulnerable to sexual and other forms of exploitation;

3. *Condemns* any exploitation of refugees and internally displaced persons, especially sexual exploitation, and calls for those responsible for such deplorable acts to be brought to justice;

4. *Emphasizes* the need to create an environment free of sexual exploitation and abuse in humanitarian crises by, inter alia, integrating the prevention of and response to sexual exploitation and abuse into the protection and assistance functions of all humanitarian and peacekeeping personnel;

5. *Notes with appreciation* the Plan of Action developed by the Inter-Agency Standing Committee Task Force on Protection from Sexual Exploitation and Abuse in Humanitarian Crises, and encourages all relevant agencies to pursue its effective and appropriate implementation;

6. *Requests* the Secretary-General to ensure that the remedial and preventive measures taken by the Office of the United Nations High Commissioner for Refugees and its implementing partners, the Inter-Agency Standing Committee and the Department of Peacekeeping Operations of the United Nations Secretariat, in response to recommendations of the Office of Internal Oversight Services are extended, as appropriate, to all peacekeeping missions, refugee camps, refugee-related operations and other humanitarian operations;

7. *Also requests* the Secretary-General to ensure that, in response to recommendations of the Office of Internal Oversight Services, clear and consistent procedures for impartially reporting and investigating instances of sexual exploitation and related offences are in place in all United Nations peacekeeping missions and humanitarian operations;

8. *Encourages* all United Nations organizations, funds and programmes, and specialized agencies and non-governmental organizations, to incorporate into codes of conduct specific responsibilities of humanitarian aid workers to prevent and respond appropriately to sexual exploitation and abuse and to adopt appropriate disciplinary procedures for dealing with such violations when they occur;

9. *Recognizes* the shared responsibility, within their respective competencies, of United Nations organizations and agencies and troop-contributing countries to ensure that all personnel are held accountable for sexual exploitation and related offences committed while serving in humanitarian and peacekeeping operations;

10. *Requests* the Secretary-General, in response to recommendations of the Office of Internal Oversight Services, to maintain data on investigations into sexual exploitation and related offences, irrespective of age

and gender, by humanitarian and peacekeeping personnel, and all relevant actions taken thereon;

11. *Recalls* its decision that reports of the Office of Internal Oversight Services should be considered under the relevant items of the agenda of the General Assembly;

12. *Requests* the Secretary-General, in his implementation of the measures pursuant to the report of the Office of Internal Oversight Services, to proceed expeditiously also with the implementation of the present resolution, inter alia, by issuing as soon as possible his bulletin on sexual exploitation and abuse, and to report thereon to the General Assembly at its fifty-eighth session, including information on any new cases of sexual exploitation revealed and the measures taken to deal with such cases.

Note by Secretary-General. In response to Assembly resolution 57/306 (see p. 1237), the Secretary-General, on 10 November [A/58/559], summarized actions he had taken to address the problem of sexual exploitation and abuse. He had issued an October bulletin on the issue, emphasized the significance of the problem to the Senior Management Group of the common system and indicated plans to implement the bulletin in the field. The UN Office of Human Resources Management would collect information on investigations into cases of sexual exploitation and abuse for preparation of the report requested by the Assembly. The Secretariat had received no reports of investigations into such allegations in 2003.

On 23 December (**decision 58/558**), the General Assembly noted the information.

The Americas

Developments in North America and the Caribbean during the year included Canada's plans to reorganize its national refugee system, assigning responsibility for some issues relating to citizenship and immigration, including detention and removals, to a newly created Department of Public Safety and Emergency Preparedness. The United States maintained primary focus on threats posed by international terrorism and the Iraq war, with the resulting restrictive asylum environment. The newly created Department of Homeland Security incorporated the former Immigration and Naturalization Service, which was in turn split into three agencies with practical implications for the implementation of national immigration, refugee and asylum policies. UNHCR monitored those policy developments in both countries, especially the adverse effects of the ongoing emphasis on security on the United States resettlement programme. In 2003, arrivals totalled 28,422, well below the approved ceiling of 70,000. Continuing unrest in Haiti and the potential for a mass exodus prompted UNHCR to step up contingency plans with States likely to be affected. In Central America and Mexico, restrictive migratory and security concerns in some countries posed difficulties for persons seeking access. A major challenge for UNHCR remained the identification of asylum-seekers among mixed flows of migrants and ensuring alternatives to detention. Also, UNHCR's reduced presence in the subregion affected its capacity to protect refugees and other persons of concern at entry points; economic and social factors hampered local integration, particularly in Costa Rica; and Belize lacked a functioning asylum procedure. In South America, there were fewer newly displaced persons in 2003 than in previous years. However, the conflict in Colombia continued to cause major population displacement and an outward flow to neighbouring States. The presence of illegal armed groups along the borders with Colombia had a negative impact on the asylum policies of those countries. UNHCR's response focused on ensuring that asylum-seekers were protected and assisted, consolidating the legal and institutional asylum framework, and coordinating protection and assistance networks. It opened a representative office in Panama, helped to enhance institutional capacity-building in Peru and established quick-impact projects to benefit some 26,000 persons of concern in 27 communities in Venezuela. The integration of groups of resettled refugees remained difficult in some Latin American countries, notably in Brazil and Chile, because of limited opportunities open to them for self-reliance.

Total UNHCR expenditure in the Americas in 2003 was $24.3 million, for a population of concern numbering approximately 3 million.

Asia and the Pacific and the Arab States

In 2003, UNHCR spent a total of $54.4 million on activities in Asia and the Pacific, for a total population of concern of 1.4 million. For operations in Central Asia, South-West Asia, North Africa and the Middle East, a total of $225 million was spent for a population of concern of 4 million.

South Asia

During the year, the refugee situation in South Asia was affected by a deteriorating situation in Nepal, following resumed hostilities between government forces and Maoist rebels, and by a continuing stalemate in the Bhutan-Nepal bilateral process, which had kept over 100,000 people in Nepalese camps for several years. In another protracted situation, 19,700 Myanmar Muslims had been living in temporary asylum in Bangladesh for more than a decade. Relative progress was made in that situation as UNHCR facilitated the voluntary return to Myanmar of some 3,231 refugees and proposed self-reliance projects for several thousand of the others remaining in Bangladesh. In Sri Lanka, the 2002 ceasefire agreement [YUN 2002, p. 1213] paved the way for the return of 345,734 IDPs to their home areas and 5,964 refugees from India. UNHCR strengthened its operational capacity in the country and expanded its field presence to monitor more closely the human rights situation in return areas.

East Asia and the Pacific

In East Asia and the Pacific, renewed fighting in Indonesia's Aceh province resulted in a sharp increase in asylum-seekers into neighbouring Malaysia, another 8,000 persons from Myanmar requested UNHCR protection and assistance, and the plight of North Koreans in China remained a cause of concern to UNHCR. UNHCR was constrained by lack of access to asylum-seekers and populations of concern throughout the subregion, especially in Cambodia, Viet Nam and areas along China's border with North Korea. Efforts by the Office to find durable solutions for former East Timorese refugees in Indonesia were constrained by ongoing UN security restrictions in West Timor. In Viet Nam, UNHCR intervened with authorities on the naturalization and local integration of 2,400 Cambodians residing in Vietnamese camps since 1979. In Papau New Guinea, it supported the registration of 2,500 refugees, an essential step to obtaining residency certificates. In West Timor, the construction of 870 houses enabled the closure of several camps for East Timorese refugees and helped reduce tension along the border with Timor-Leste. At year's end, only 385 files of East Timorese separated children remained open.

Central Asia, South-West Asia, North Africa and the Middle East

In Central Asia, UNHCR became a partner in implementing an EU border management programme that would ensure that the rights and needs of refugees and asylum-seekers were respected. Although progress was made in developing and strengthening refugee protection and in establishing related national structures, particularly in Kyrgyzstan and Tajikistan, challenges remained in a number of other countries in the region. During the year, UNHCR assisted 362 Afghans to return from Central Asian States and 76 Chechen asylum-seekers in Kyrgyzstan and 143 Tajik refugees to return to their homes. It resettled some 208 refugees in third countries. In South-West Asia, UNHCR continued to facilitate the voluntary repatriation of Afghan refugees and IDPs, some 485,400 of whom were assisted, particularly from Iran and Pakistan. The low rate of return in 2003, compared to the 2002 figure of 1.8 million, was attributed to instability and economic underdevelopment in potential high return areas and the slow imposition of the rule of law in Afghanistan. In Iran, UNHCR's agreement with the authorities to introduce a screening mechanism ensured that repatriated Afghans had access to UNHCR for continuing protection. UNHCR signed a tripartite agreement with Pakistan and Afghanistan, which committed the two Governments to a policy of voluntary return. However, security problems in parts of both countries, as well as the conflict in Iraq, continued to affect UNHCR operations. In November, the return operation was suspended temporarily following the murder of a UNHCR staff member in Afghanistan.

In North Africa, UNHCR's main concern was the situation of some 165,000 refugees from Western Sahara living in camps in south-western Algeria for more than 25 years. A breakthrough in the political stalemate between the parties to the Western Saharan conflict allowed the implementation of confidence-building measures, including opportunities for separated families to meet.

In the Middle East, UNHCR assisted some 9,000 Iraqis who had sought asylum in Iran, Lebanon, Saudi Arabia and the Syrian Arab Republic to return to their homes, despite continuing insecurity in the country. At UNHCR's request, Iraq's neighbours introduced a temporary protection regime, banning the forced return of Iraqis, and strengthened protection and assistance to refugee women and children in the region. UNHCR worked to raise public awareness of its activities and concerns through the establishment of a web site in Arabic and the work of its Goodwill Ambassador, Adel Imam. Following the 19 August attack on the UN complex in Baghdad (see p. 346) and the withdrawal of international staff members, the responsibility for maintaining UNHCR's programme there devolved to locally recruited staff and UNHCR's implementing partners.

Europe

In 2003, UNHCR's expenditure for activities in Europe totalled $120.5 million for a population of concern of over 5 million. Over half of that amount ($66 million) was for 1 million persons of concern in South-Eastern Europe.

Western, Central and Eastern Europe

In Western Europe, although asylum claims fell dramatically to 288,100, from 425,528 in 2002, and despite ongoing negotiations to harmonize asylum systems at the EU level, 12 States amended their national asylum legislation, incorporating restrictive concepts into the system. Some 79 per cent of all new claims in 2003 were received by Austria, France, Germany, Sweden and the United Kingdom. A number of States showed increased interest in resettlement as a durable solution, with the United Kingdom introducing a first annual quota of 500 resettlement cases. Voluntary repatriation gained momentum and some Governments indicated support for initiatives under Convention Plus (see p. 1229). Public information activities remained a key element of UNHCR's Europe strategy, designed to increase awareness and understanding of asylum and related issues. UNHCR expressed concern with regard to proposals within the context of EU negotiations on harmonizing asylum systems, particularly those relating to the draft qualification directive and the draft asylum procedures directive. It proposed, as an alternative approach, improving access to protections and solutions in regions of origin. Other concerns included access to and conditions in reception facilities for asylum-seekers and the mandatory detention of asylum-seekers.

In Central Europe and the Baltic States, where asylum applications rose to 43,320, the year marked a critical transition period for the five newly admitted EU members (Cyprus, Czech Republic, Malta, Poland, Slovenia) as they undertook the challenge of revising or adopting asylum legislation to meet international and EU standards. To meet those new imperatives, UNHCR began taking stock of its programme and management structure in the subregion. Other challenges included the introduction of restrictive bilateral visa regimes; the need to upgrade asylum systems and to enhance refugee status determination capacity; the lack of opportunities for the sustainable integration of recognized refugees, which continued to encourage secondary movements; inadequate safety conditions in reception and detention centres; disappearance of separated children from reception facilities; gender-based violence; discrepancies in asylum procedures among States; and weak implementation of asylum systems. However, progress was made in strengthening asylum structures and procedure. The number of successful appeals against first instance rejections and cases of detention increased and the quality of NGO interventions also improved. UNHCR placed special emphasis on preventing and responding to sexual and gender-based violence at all stages of the asylum process, improving the protection of refugee women, and on their participation in decisions affecting them.

In Eastern Europe, UNHCR increased focus on building asylum systems in fragile environments where there were ongoing conflicts. In the Russian Federation, progress was made in building the capacity of authorities responsible for persons of concern. In Georgia, the profiling of Chechen refugees considerably reduced tensions in the Pankisi Valley and facilitated the definition of a range of durable solutions. In the light of the impending EU enlargement, which highlighted the need to strengthen asylum systems in the western Commonwealth of Independent States (CIS) countries (Belarus, Moldova, Ukraine), UNHCR strengthened its regional representation in Ukraine to enable it to coordinate its activities. In Armenia and Azerbaijan, UNHCR, in partnership with the European Commission, initiated activities to strengthen reception facilities and the capacity of Governments to address asylum issues.

Follow-up to 1996 conference of CIS countries and neighbouring States

In response to General Assembly resolution 56/134 [YUN 2001, p. 1122], the Secretary-General submitted an August report [A/58/281] on follow-up to the 1996 Regional Conference to Address the Problems of Refugees, Displaced Persons, Other Forms of Involuntary Displacement and Returnees in the Countries of the Commonwealth of Independent States and Relevant Neighbouring States [YUN 1996, p. 1117]. The report provided information on progress in the implementation of the Conference's Programme of Action [ibid., p. 1118] and reviewed progress made and future plans.

GENERAL ASSEMBLY ACTION

On 22 December [meeting 77], the General Assembly, on the recommendation of the Third Committee [A/58/503], adopted **resolution 58/154** without vote [agenda item 112].

Follow-up to the Regional Conference to Address the Problems of Refugees, Displaced Persons, Other Forms of Involuntary Displacement and Returnees in the Countries of the Commonwealth of Independent States and Relevant Neighbouring States

The General Assembly,

Recalling its resolutions 48/113 of 20 December 1993, 49/173 of 23 December 1994, 50/151 of 21 December 1995, 51/70 of 12 December 1996, 52/102 of 12 December 1997, 53/123 of 9 December 1998 and, in particular, resolutions 54/144 of 17 December 1999 and 56/134 of 19 December 2001,

Taking note of the report of the Secretary-General,

Having considered the report of the United Nations High Commissioner for Refugees,

Reaffirming the importance and continuing validity of the Programme of Action, adopted in 1996 by the Regional Conference to Address the Problems of Refugees, Displaced Persons, Other Forms of Involuntary Displacement and Returnees in the Countries of the Commonwealth of Independent States and Relevant

Neighbouring States, as a basic guiding tool for future activities,

Recognizing the ongoing acuteness of the migration and displacement problems in the countries of the Commonwealth of Independent States and the necessity to follow up the Conference,

Recalling the decision of the Steering Group of the Conference at its fifth meeting to continue activities in the process entitled "Follow-up to the 1996 Geneva Conference on the Problems of Refugees, Displaced Persons, Migration and Asylum Issues" for a period of five years,

Recalling also the Work Plan for the Thematic Issues, prepared jointly by the Office of the United Nations High Commissioner for Refugees, the International Organization for Migration, the Organization for Security and Cooperation in Europe and the Council of Europe, in accordance with the recommendations adopted by the Steering Group at its fifth meeting,

Welcoming the convening, in Moscow from 20 to 23 November 2001, of the second meeting of experts within the framework of the Work Plan for the Thematic Issues, on the topic of asylum system development and treatment of asylum-seekers, as well as international efforts aimed at improving migration regulation and border management, with due regard for refugee protection matters, and encouraging all lead agencies to continue to implement the Work Plan,

Welcoming also the subregional initiatives within the framework of transboundary cooperation and the convening, in Kolmården, Sweden, in September 2002, of the senior-level review meeting,

Reaffirming the view of the Conference that the primary responsibility for tackling population displacement problems lies with the affected countries themselves and that these issues are to be regarded as national priorities, while at the same time recognizing the need for enhancing international support for the national efforts of the countries of the Commonwealth of Independent States aimed at the effective implementation of such responsibilities within the framework of the Programme of Action adopted by the Conference,

Noting with satisfaction the efforts of the Office of the United Nations High Commissioner for Refugees, the International Organization for Migration and the Organization for Security and Cooperation in Europe in developing strategies and practical tools for more effective capacity-building in countries of origin and enhancing programmes to address the needs of various categories of concern to the countries of the Commonwealth of Independent States,

Taking note of the positive results emanating from the implementation of the Programme of Action,

Convinced of the necessity of further strengthening practical measures and of continuing to maintain the regional approach for the achievement of effective implementation of the Programme of Action,

Noting with concern the decision to postpone the high-level review meeting concerning the implementation of the decisions of the Conference,

Recalling that the protection and promotion of human rights and the strengthening of democratic institutions are essential to prevent mass population displacement,

Mindful that adherence to the principles and the recommendations contained in the Programme of Action should be facilitated and that they can be ensured only through cooperation and coordinated activities undertaken in this respect by all interested States, intergovernmental and non-governmental organizations and other actors,

1. *Takes note* of the report of the United Nations High Commissioner for Refugees;

2. *Calls upon* the Governments of the countries of the Commonwealth of Independent States, in cooperation with the Office of the United Nations High Commissioner for Refugees, the International Organization for Migration and the Organization for Security and Cooperation in Europe, to strengthen their efforts and mutual cooperation relating to the follow-up to the Regional Conference to Address the Problems of Refugees, Displaced Persons, Other Forms of Involuntary Displacement and Returnees in the Countries of the Commonwealth of Independent States and Relevant Neighbouring States, and welcomes the positive results achieved by them in the implementation of the Programme of Action adopted by the Conference;

3. *Invites* all States that have not yet done so to accede to and implement fully the 1951 Convention and the 1967 Protocol relating to the Status of Refugees;

4. *Calls upon* States and interested international organizations, in a spirit of solidarity and burden-sharing, to provide appropriate forms and levels of support for activities undertaken in follow-up to the Programme of Action;

5. *Invites* international financial and other institutions to contribute to the financing of projects and programmes within the framework of such follow-up activities;

6. *Invites* the countries of the Commonwealth of Independent States to intensify bilateral, subregional and regional cooperation in maintaining the balance of commitments and interests in such activities;

7. *Calls upon* the Governments of the countries of the Commonwealth of Independent States to continue to strengthen their commitment to the principles underpinning the Programme of Action, in particular principles of human rights and refugee protection, and to lend high-level political support to ensure the implementation of activities undertaken in follow-up to the Programme of Action;

8. *Invites* the Office of the United Nations High Commissioner for Refugees and the International Organization for Migration to enhance their mutual relationship with other key international actors, such as the Council of Europe, the European Commission and human rights, development and financial institutions, in order better to address the wide-ranging and complex issues in activities undertaken in follow-up to the Programme of Action;

9. *Welcomes* the progress made in building civil society, in particular through the development of the non-governmental sector and the development of cooperation between non-governmental organizations and the Governments of a number of countries of the Commonwealth of Independent States, and notes in this regard the relationship between adherence to the principles of the Programme of Action and success in promoting civil society, especially in the field of human rights;

10. *Encourages* the involvement of intergovernmental and non-governmental organizations in the follow-

up to the Conference, and invites them to demonstrate stronger support for the process of multinational constructive dialogue among a wide range of countries concerned;

11. *Emphasizes* the necessity of undertaking follow-up activities to the Programme of Action in relation to ensuring respect for human rights as an important factor in the management of migration flows, the consolidation of democracy, the rule of law and stability;

12. *Recognizes* the importance of taking measures, on the basis of strict adherence to all of the principles of international law, including humanitarian, human rights and refugee law, to prevent situations that lead to new flows of refugees, displaced persons and other forms of involuntary displacement;

13. *Requests* the Secretary-General to report to the General Assembly at its sixtieth session on the progress achieved in the implementation of activities undertaken in follow-up to the Programme of Action;

14. *Decides* to continue its consideration of the question at its sixtieth session.

South-Eastern Europe

In South-Eastern Europe, the political environment in the Balkans deteriorated and progress slowed down for refugees in Serbia and Montenegro and IDPs in Bosnia and Herzegovina. Also, the economic situation offered a bleak prospect for the welfare of the most vulnerable refugees and displaced persons and stifled hopes of sustainable return. There was also slow progress on property repossession and tenancy rights, which impacted negatively on the repatriation of Croatian refugees. Thus, contrary to earlier expectations that most of the affected refugees and IDPs would be repatriated by year's end, the need for UNHCR's protection and assistance would continue in 2004. Positive developments in the subregion included the fact that the property (restitution) law implementation plan in Bosnia and Herzegovina facilitated the resolution of 92.5 per cent of all property claims and the majority of the subregional States adopted new asylum legislation consistent with international standards. A total of 9,280 refugees repatriated to Croatia, and in Serbia and Montenegro some 44,000 refugees were granted citizenship and deregistered. In Bosnia and Herzegovina, 54,300 returns were recorded, while the Kosovo province of Serbia and Montenegro witnessed 3,629 minority returns, a 31 per cent increase over the previous year. Another 2,014 refugees repatriated from Kosovo to the former Yugoslav Republic of Macedonia.

Chapter XIII

Health, food and nutrition

In 2003, the United Nations continued to promote human health, coordinate food aid and food security, and support research in nutrition.

At the end of 2003, about 37.8 million people were living with HIV/AIDS. During the year, an estimated 4.8 million people became infected with the virus and 2.9 million died as a result. In September, the General Assembly held four high-level plenary meetings devoted to follow-up to the outcome of its twenty-sixth (2001) special session and the implementation of the Declaration of Commitment on HIV/AIDS, adopted during the special session. The Joint United Nations Programme on HIV/AIDS (UNAIDS) continued to coordinate UN activities for AIDS prevention and control, including the implementation of the Declaration. In December, UNAIDS and the World Health Organization (WHO) launched the "3 by 5" initiative, a global project to provide antiretroviral therapy to 3 million people in developing countries by the end of 2005. Efforts also continued towards meeting the UN Millennium Development Goal of halting and beginning to reverse the spread of HIV/AIDS by 2015.

In support of the Decade to Roll Back Malaria in Developing Countries, Particularly in Africa, 2001-2010, the General Assembly called on the international community to support the development of the capacity to manufacture insecticide-treated nets (ITNs) in Africa and to encourage and facilitate the transfer of technology needed to make ITNs more effective and long-lasting. Measures were taken to strengthen the Roll Back Malaria initiative, launched by WHO in 1998 with the goal of halving the world's malaria burden by 2010. The Assembly also took action to address the global road safety crisis. The text of the WHO Framework Convention on Tobacco Control was finalized in February and adopted by the World Health Assembly in May.

The World Food Programme (WFP)—a joint undertaking of the United Nations and the Food and Agriculture Organization of the United Nations (FAO)—assisted a record 104.2 million people, providing 6 million tons of food aid. Through WFP's relief operation in Iraq, 2.1 million tons of food reached the entire Iraqi population of around 27 million. FAO continued to implement the Plan of Action adopted at the 1996 World Food Summit and the Declaration of the 2002 World Food Summit: five years later, which called on the international community to fulfil the pledge made at the Summit to halve the number of hungry to about 400 million by 2015.

Health

AIDS prevention and control

Follow-up to the twenty-sixth special session

The Declaration of Commitment on HIV/AIDS, adopted at the twenty-sixth special session of the General Assembly by resolution S-26/2 [YUN 2001, p. 1126], called for an expanded global response to the epidemic and established time-bound targets relating to the prevention, care, support and treatment, impact alleviation, and children orphaned and made vulnerable by HIV/AIDS. As pledged by the session's participants, one full day of high-level plenary meetings during the Assembly's annual session was devoted to the follow-up to the outcome of the special session and implementation of the Declaration (see p. 1244). The first of the Declaration's time-bound commitments were due to be met in 2003.

GENERAL ASSEMBLY ACTION (May)

On 22 May [meeting 86], the General Assembly adopted **resolution 57/308** [draft: A/57/L.78] without vote [agenda item 42].

High-level plenary meetings devoted to the follow-up to the outcome of the twenty-sixth special session: implementation of the Declaration of Commitment on HIV/AIDS

The General Assembly,

Recalling its resolution 57/299 of 20 December 2002, entitled "Follow-up to the outcome of the twenty-sixth special session: implementation of the Declaration of Commitment on HIV/AIDS", in which it decided to convene a day of high-level plenary meetings devoted to the follow-up to the outcome of its twenty-sixth special session and the implementation of the Declaration of Commitment on HIV/AIDS, and to hold, in parallel with the afternoon plenary meeting, an informal interactive panel discussion with the theme "Implementation of the Declaration of Commitment on HIV/AIDS: from policy to practice—progress achieved, lessons learned and best practices",

Recalling also that, in accordance with its resolution 57/299, the statements in the debate in the plenary meetings should not exceed five minutes each,

Recalling further that in its resolution 57/299, it invited the President of the General Assembly to finalize any outstanding organizational matters in consultation with the Member States,

1. *Decides* to amend paragraph 2 of its resolution 57/299 to read "*Decides* to convene a day of high-level plenary meetings of the General Assembly devoted to the follow-up to the outcome of its twenty-sixth special session and the implementation of the Declaration of Commitment on HIV/AIDS, to be held on 22 September 2003";

2. *Also decides* that the list of speakers for the debate in plenary will be organized on a first-come, first-served basis, the order of precedence being as follows:
    (a) Heads of State and Government;
    (b) Vice-Presidents/Crown Princes or Princesses;
    (c) Deputy Prime Ministers;
    (d) The highest ranking official of the Holy See, in its capacity as observer State, and of Palestine, in its capacity as observer;
    (e) Ministers;
    (f) Vice-Ministers;
    (g) Heads of delegations;
and, should the level of participation change, the replacement speaker will be accommodated in the last position available in the appropriate category;

3. *Further decides* that, in accordance with paragraph 5 of its resolution 57/299, an invitation to the informal interactive panel discussion, to be held in parallel with the afternoon plenary meeting, will be extended to those on the list of civil society representatives submitted on 25 April 2003 by the President of the General Assembly to Member States and to which no objection has been received.

In accordance with the above resolution, the Assembly, on 22 September, held four high-level plenary meetings [A/58/PV.3-6] devoted to the follow-up to the outcome of the twenty-sixth special session and the implementation of the Declaration of Commitment on HIV/AIDS.

Report of Secretary-General. Pursuant to the Declaration of Commitment and in accordance with General Assembly resolution 57/299 [YUN 2002, p. 1218], the Secretary-General submitted a July report [A/58/184] on progress made to implement the Declaration. The report, which was based primarily on responses provided by 100 Member States on 18 global and national indicators developed by UNAIDS, said that there had been significant progress in the global response to HIV/AIDS since the Secretary-General's first (2002) progress report [YUN 2002, p. 1217]. The number of Member States meeting the policy targets for 2003 set forth in the Declaration had increased significantly, but many countries risked falling behind in certain aspects of the implementation if immediate action was not taken. Political intervention at the highest level was required in many countries to ensure that obstacles to coordination, implementation and reinforcement of HIV/AIDS strategies were rapidly addressed. Organizations representing people living with the disease, faith-based groups, workers' organizations and the business sector had extended the reach of essential HIV/AIDS programmes and services, but such engagement remained inadequate. Only 62 per cent of responding States had laws and policies in place to protect against discrimination towards people living with or affected by HIV/AIDS, and only 38 per cent had policies prohibiting discrimination against vulnerable populations. Investment in HIV/AIDS programmes in low- and middle-income developing countries had grown significantly and was estimated at $4.7 billion during 2003, including both national and international spending. The Global Fund to Fight AIDS, Tuberculosis and Malaria, established in 2002 [YUN 2002, p. 1217], had received almost $4.6 billion in financial pledges and approved proposals worth $1.5 billion in 93 countries. However, current financing trends still suggested that global funding for HIV/AIDS programmes would fall far short of the estimated $10.5 billion required annually by 2005.

While virtually all heavily affected countries had adopted multisectoral HIV/AIDS strategies, most were experiencing difficulty in converting those strategies into broad-based programmes. The problem hindered obtaining basic information on HIV/AIDS, access to voluntary counselling and testing services, antenatal care for pregnant women regarding the prevention of mother-to-child transmission of the virus and access to antiretroviral treatment. More than one in four countries identified a need for greater attention to programmes for vulnerable populations. A shortage of financial, human and technical resources and limited monitoring and evaluation capacity were among the primary impediments to programmatic reinforcement. Agricultural production was declining in many heavily affected countries in sub-Saharan Africa as a result, in part, of the loss of workers to HIV/AIDS, and education systems were being undermined by the loss of teachers to HIV-related illness and death. Women and girls represented half of all cases of HIV infection globally and as high as 58 per cent of cases in Africa. Thirty-nine per cent of countries with generalized epidemics—defined as adult prevalence consistently greater than 1 per cent in both urban and rural areas—had no formal strategy to address the needs of orphans and other vulnerable children, but many States indicated that such policies were in development.

The report described efforts to increase leadership on HIV/AIDS at the national, regional and global levels and to ensure the engagement of civil society partners; protect and promote human rights as an effective response to HIV/AIDS; prevent infection and reduce vulnerability to the disease; increase access to care, support and treatment; alleviate the social and economic impacts of the epidemic; strengthen research and development; address HIV/AIDS in conflict- and disaster-affected regions; mobilize resources; and monitor and evaluate follow-up to the Declaration of Commitment on HIV/AIDS.

The report recommended that countries assess their national policies in relation to the Declaration's provisions for 2003 and accelerate the development and implementation of policies needed to come into compliance with them. Areas needing emphasis were national leadership; the engagement of civil society, especially people living with HIV/AIDS; human rights, stigmatization and discrimination; prevention through the provision of information, services and support to young people; reducing the vulnerability of women and girls and other groups; comprehensive prevention, treatment and support programmes; the needs of children orphaned and made vulnerable by the epidemic; capacity-building and sustainability; urgent sustained and coordinated action to respond to crisis conditions in Southern Africa; and monitoring, evaluation and follow-up. Financing the global response needed to achieve the Declaration's future commitments required a threefold increase over current levels of annual funding for HIV/AIDS programmes by 2005 and a fivefold increase by 2007.

On 22 December, the General Assembly took note of the Secretary-General's report (**decision 58/534**); on 23 December, it decided that the agenda item on the follow-up to the outcome of the twenty-sixth special session: implementation of the Declaration of Commitment on HIV/AIDS would remain for consideration at its resumed fifty-eighth (2004) session (**decision 58/565**).

IASC Task Force. In June, the Inter-Agency Standing Committee (IASC) Task Force on HIV/AIDS in Emergency Settings, formally established by the IASC working group in 2002 as a reference group [YUN 2002, p. 1220], completed a draft revision of guidelines for HIV/AIDS interventions in emergency settings, originally produced in 1996 by the Office of the United Nations High Commissioner for Refugees, UNAIDS and WHO. The purpose of the guidelines was to enable Governments and cooperating agencies, including UN agencies and non-governmental organizations, to give the minimum required multisectoral response to HIV/AIDS during the early phase of emergency situations. A final version of the guidelines would be published in 2004. The Task Force also continued its activities in the areas of advocacy and training.

GENERAL ASSEMBLY ACTION (December)

On 23 December [meeting 78], the General Assembly adopted **resolution 58/236** [draft: A/58/L.54] without vote [agenda item 47].

Follow-up to the outcome of the twenty-sixth special session: implementation of the Declaration of Commitment on HIV/AIDS

The General Assembly,

Recalling the goals and targets set forth in the Declaration of Commitment on HIV/AIDS adopted by the General Assembly at its twenty-sixth special session, in 2001, and the HIV/AIDS-related goals contained in the United Nations Millennium Declaration of 2000,

Reaffirming the commitment made by all States at the twenty-sixth special session of the General Assembly,

Noting with profound concern that 42 million people worldwide are living with HIV/AIDS, that the HIV/AIDS pandemic claimed 3.1 million lives in 2002 and to date has orphaned 14 million children,

Noting with grave concern that the majority of new HIV infections occur among young people and that women and girls are disproportionately affected by the pandemic,

Noting that the unequal legal and social status of women heightens their vulnerability to HIV,

Expressing serious concern about the continued global spread of HIV/AIDS, which exacerbates poverty and poses a major threat to economic and social development and to food security in heavily affected regions, while recognizing that poverty, underdevelopment and illiteracy are among the principal contributing factors to the spread of the disease,

Noting that the epidemic affects every region and, while sub-Saharan Africa remains worst affected, serious epidemics are present or emerging in the Caribbean, Eastern Europe and Asia and the Pacific,

Acknowledging that prevention, care, support and treatment for those infected and affected by HIV/AIDS are mutually reinforcing elements of an effective response and must be integrated in a comprehensive approach to combat the epidemic,

Also acknowledging the importance of maintaining an emphasis on prevention measures in countries with low prevalence rates,

Recognizing that, while the primary responsibility for responding to HIV/AIDS rests with Governments, the efforts and engagement of all sectors of society are essential to generating an effective response,

Reaffirming that the full realization of human rights and fundamental freedoms for all is an essential element in a global response to the HIV/AIDS pandemic, and reaffirming also the importance of the elimination of all forms of discrimination against people living with or at risk of HIV/AIDS, including those most vulnerable,

Recognizing that populations destabilized by armed conflict, humanitarian emergencies and natural disasters, including refugees, internally displaced persons and, in particular, women and children, are at increased risk of exposure to HIV infection,

Encouraged that civil society, especially organizations representing people living with HIV/AIDS, women, young persons, orphans, faith-based organizations and the private sector, is increasingly involved in national responses to HIV/AIDS, while noting the need for further engagement of these stakeholders at all levels,

Acknowledging the efforts of international humanitarian organizations, including the International Federation of Red Cross and Red Crescent Societies, in combating the epidemic in the most affected areas of the world,

Noting that strengthened political commitment, including at the highest level, as witnessed, inter alia, at the high-level General Assembly meeting on HIV/AIDS, held on 22 September 2003, demonstrates the resolve of Governments and the international community to intensify implementation and cooperation in order to meet the goals and targets contained in the Declaration of Commitment,

Noting with appreciation the support for national responses provided by the United Nations system, especially the secretariat of the Joint United Nations Programme on HIV/AIDS and Co-sponsors, inter alia, for effective country-led mechanisms, including the mobilization of financial resources, the facilitation and provision of technical assistance and support to the Global Fund to Fight AIDS, Tuberculosis and Malaria and applicant countries, at every level of the grant-making process,

Also noting with appreciation the new strategic direction taken by the Joint Programme after the five-year evaluation of the Programme by its Programme Coordinating Board, encompassing, in particular, a greater focus on national-level processes, continued global leadership and advocacy, and a focus on the gender implications of HIV/AIDS,

Encouraged that the United Nations system has made progress towards integrating the consideration of HIV/AIDS in its activities, including addressing HIV/AIDS in the United Nations workplace, the appointment of HIV/AIDS focal points in peacekeeping operations and the work on guidelines for HIV/AIDS in emergency settings,

Recognizing the emergence of the World Bank Multi-Country HIV/AIDS Programme and the Global Fund to Fight AIDS, Tuberculosis and Malaria and the contributions of private foundations as important sources of new and additional funding,

Noting with concern that, although many Member States have met the 2003 targets contained in the Declaration of Commitment, considerable gaps remain,

Also noting with concern that, at the current rate of implementation and fulfilment of commitments, many countries are unlikely to meet the targets for 2005,

Recognizing that many developing countries may not have the financial or human resources capacity to mount an effective response to the HIV/AIDS epidemic, and in this context underlining the importance of international cooperation,

Noting that, despite improvement, current global resources available for HIV/AIDS are less than half of the 10 billion United States dollars considered necessary for an effective response in 2005 alone and that substantial new funding will be required in order to meet the global resource targets,

Also noting that intensified implementation will require partnership and enhanced cooperation at all levels, as well as enhanced support for human and institutional capacity development and considerably increased financial resources,

Further noting that implementation has to be intensified through partnerships at the national, regional and international levels in order to offer infected and affected people and communities in developing countries and countries with economies in transition medicines and related technology which are affordable, easy to use and readily available,

Encouraged that an increasing number of companies in the private sector are offering prevention, care and treatment services to employees and their families, while noting the need for continued efforts in this regard,

Recalling Commission on Human Rights resolution 2003/47 of 23 April 2003,

1. *Welcomes* the report of the Secretary-General on progress towards implementation of the Declaration of Commitment on HIV/AIDS;

2. *Reaffirms its commitment* to the goals and targets contained in the Declaration of Commitment on HIV/AIDS and the United Nations Millennium Declaration and to their implementation;

3. *Stresses with deep concern* that the HIV/AIDS emergency, with its devastating scale and impact, requires urgent actions in all fields and at all levels;

4. *Urges* relevant United Nations organizations, as well as other relevant international organizations, to further support national efforts for implementation of the Declaration of Commitment and address the issue of the cost, availability and affordability of drugs and related technology;

5. *Urges* Member States to intensify national efforts and international cooperation in the implementation of the Declaration of Commitment in order to meet the goals and targets contained therein based on national plans, where they exist, and, in particular, where gaps have been identified in the report of the Secretary-General by, inter alia:

(*a*) Providing stronger and more visible leadership in response to the epidemic;

(*b*) Creating an environment that encourages the engagement of and partnerships with all stakeholders, including civil society, people living with HIV/AIDS, marginalized and vulnerable groups, cultural and faith-based organizations, non-governmental organizations, traditional health practitioners, the private sector, international institutions and the media;

(*c*) Strengthening policies and programmes for combating HIV/AIDS, including those relating to the protection and promotion of all human rights and fundamental freedoms for all, including eliminating stigmas and discrimination against people living with and/or affected by HIV/AIDS, ensuring gender equality, assisting orphans and children and expanding access to treatment, care and support;

(*d*) Building and scaling up a comprehensive response to achieve broad multisectoral coverage for prevention, care, treatment and support and recognizing the need to seriously address impact mitigation issues, in particular in the worst affected countries, and specifically within this context:

(i) Intensifying prevention measures, especially those directed at vulnerable groups, in particular women and young persons, bearing in mind that prevention is the mainstay of the national, regional and international response;
(ii) Expanding access to treatment, in a progressive and sustainable manner, including the prevention and treatment of opportunistic diseases and the effective use of antiretroviral medication;
(iii) Improving the provision of care and support to those infected and affected by HIV/AIDS, including orphans;
(iv) Mitigating the social and economic impact of the epidemic;
(v) Promoting access to low-cost and effective drugs and related pharmaceutical products;
(vi) Strengthening health-care systems and integrating HIV/AIDS programmes into current health services;
(vii) Strengthening HIV/AIDS surveillance and systems for evaluating programme effectiveness;

(e) Strengthening pharmaceutical policies and practices, including those applicable to generic drugs and intellectual property regimes, in order to further promote innovation and the development of domestic industries consistent with international law;

(f) Intensifying training and research initiatives or programmes to strengthen the capacities of Governments to manage the epidemic;

(g) Sharing experiences and exchanging information on key areas of intervention, such as prevention, the provision of care and support for HIV/AIDS-infected persons and the treatment of HIV/AIDS-related conditions;

(h) Addressing the human resource crisis affecting the effective implementation of comprehensive national HIV/AIDS programmes, including supporting the development of monitoring and evaluation capacities and working at the national and international levels to generate flexible solutions;

(i) Mobilizing financial resources and providing the support necessary to ensure that they are targeted effectively and absorbed quickly and deliver equitable and sustainable coverage of services, particularly to those most in need;

6. *Welcomes with appreciation* the Declaration on the Agreement on Trade-Related Aspects of Intellectual Property Rights and Public Health, adopted on 14 November 2001 at the Fourth Ministerial Conference of the World Trade Organization, held in Doha, and the decision dated 30 August 2003 of the General Council of the World Trade Organization on the implementation of paragraph 6 of the Declaration;

7. *Welcomes* the commitment by the World Health Organization and the Joint United Nations Programme on HIV/AIDS to work with the international community to support developing countries in achieving the target of providing antiretroviral medicines to 3 million people infected with HIV/AIDS by the end of 2005, the "3 by 5" target, recalling Commission on Human Rights resolution 2003/29 of 22 April 2003 entitled "Access to medication in the context of pandemics such as HIV/AIDS, tuberculosis and malaria";

8. *Urges* the mobilization of additional resources from national, bilateral, multilateral and private sources, including but not limited to additional support to the Global Fund to Fight AIDS, Tuberculosis and Malaria, in order to address the growing need;

9. *Also urges* the provision of additional financial resources to the United Nations system, especially the Joint Programme's secretariat and Co-sponsors, in order that they may intensify their support for national responses to HIV/AIDS;

10. *Emphasizes* that, with the increasing number of HIV/AIDS initiatives at the global, regional and national levels, there is a need for close coordination at all levels, including under government leadership at the national level to ensure a harmonized approach and to increase the effectiveness of the response;

11. *Encourages* the private sector to become fully engaged in the fight against HIV/AIDS, including by adopting relevant workplace non-discrimination policies;

12. *Encourages* the private sector and the pharmaceutical industry to contribute to the fight against AIDS by, inter alia, continuing to provide key AIDS pharmaceuticals that meet the standards of the World Health Organization, at the lowest possible prices;

13. *Recognizes* the importance of young men and women having access to information, education, including peer education and youth-specific HIV education, and services necessary to develop the life skills required to reduce their vulnerability to HIV infection, in full partnership with young persons, parents, families, educators and health-care providers;

14. *Reiterates* the need to respond urgently to the dire situation in sub-Saharan Africa and in particular the crisis conditions in the southern African region, in order to minimize the loss of institutional capacity in key national sectors and mitigate the threat of accelerating the cycle of poverty, food insecurity, instability and heightened vulnerability to HIV/AIDS;

15. *Stresses* the need for intensified action in all regions, especially the Caribbean, Eastern Europe and Asia and the Pacific;

16. *Decides* to hold a high-level meeting in 2005 to review the progress achieved in realizing the commitments set out in the Declaration of Commitment, and decides also that the scheduling, format, participation, including civil society participation, and other organizational details will be further considered during the fifty-eighth session of the General Assembly;

17. *Requests* the Secretary-General, in this regard, to submit a comprehensive and analytical report on progress achieved in realizing the commitments set out in the Declaration of Commitment, in particular those set out for 2005, with a view to identifying problems and constraints and making recommendations on action needed to make further progress;

18. *Decides* to include in the provisional agenda of its fifty-ninth session the item entitled "Follow-up to the outcome of the twenty-sixth special session: implementation of the Declaration of Commitment on HIV/AIDS".

Joint UN Programme on HIV/AIDS

UNAIDS, which became fully operational in 1996 [YUN 1996, p. 1121] and served as the main advocate for global action on HIV/AIDS, had nine co-sponsors: the International Labour Organization (ILO), the United Nations Development Programme (UNDP), the United Nations Children's Fund (UNICEF), the United Nations Educational, Scientific and Cultural Organization (UNESCO), the United Nations International Drug Control Programme, the United Nations Population Fund (UNFPA), WHO, the World Food Programme (WFP) and the World Bank. UNAIDS was mandated to lead, strengthen and support an expanded response to the epidemic, mainly through facilitation and coordination, best-practice development and advocacy. The key goals of the response were to prevent the spread of HIV; to provide support for those infected and affected by the disease; to reduce the vulnerability of individuals and communities to HIV/AIDS; and to alleviate the socioeconomic and human impact of the virus.

According to UNAIDS, at the end of 2003 an estimated 37.8 million people were living with HIV/AIDS, of whom 35.7 million were adults and 2.1 million were children under the age of 15. Globally, nearly 50 per cent of those living with the virus were women. During the year, an estimated 4.8 million people became infected with the virus and 2.9 million died as a result. The epidemic continued to expand in sub-Saharan Africa, where an estimated 3 million new infections occurred in 2003 and 25 million were living with the virus; an estimated 2.2 million Africans died of the disease. In Asia, an estimated 1.1 million people became infected, and 7.4 million people were living with HIV; in India, about 5.1 million people were living with the disease at year's end. In the Middle East and North Africa, some 480,000 people were living with HIV. In Eastern Europe and Central Asia, 1.3 million people were living with HIV and an estimated 360,000 became infected. In Latin America, around 1.6 million people were living with HIV and around 430,000 were living with the disease in the Caribbean region.

The fourteenth meeting of the UNAIDS Programme Coordinating Board (PCB) (Geneva, 26-27 June) [UNAIDS/PCB(14)/03.8] considered, among other things, the 2002-2003 report of its Executive Director [UNAIDS/PCB(14)/03.2]; financial and budgetary updates for the period 1 January 2002 to 31 March 2003; a report from the working group on UNAIDS governance; and the UN system strategic plan on HIV/AIDS (2001-2005). PCB endorsed the strategies and approaches contained in the 2004-2005 unified budget and work plan [UNAIDS/PCB(14)/03.3], particularly its strategic thrust to enable countries to enhance their national response to the epidemic. The Board approved a core budget of $250.5 million and an additional inter-agency core budget of $20 million, subject to availability of funding beyond the $250.5 million core budget. It also approved, with amendments, a memorandum of understanding [UNAIDS/PCB(14)/03.7] between UNAIDS and the Global Fund to Fight AIDS, Tuberculosis and Malaria, established in 2002 [YUN 2002, p. 1217] as an enabling framework for further collaboration.

On World AIDS Day, 1 December, WHO and UNAIDS launched the "3 by 5" initiative, a global project to provide antiretroviral therapy to 3 million people in developing countries by the end of 2005 (see p. 1514). The initiative came in response to a 22 September declaration by UNAIDS, WHO and the Global Fund that the lack of access to the therapy was a global health emergency.

On 5 March (**decision 2003/210**), the Economic and Social Council decided that the theme for the humanitarian affairs segment of its 2003 substantive session (Geneva, 30 June-25 July) would be "Strengthening of the coordination of United Nations humanitarian assistance, with particular attention to humanitarian financing and effectiveness of humanitarian assistance and the transition from relief to development"; within the context of that theme it decided to convene a panel on the sub-theme "Responding to the effects of HIV/AIDS and other widespread diseases on humanitarian relief operations". On 14 July, the Council held the panel discussion with the participation of the Director of the UNAIDS Country and Regional Support Department, among others.

Report of UNAIDS Executive Director. In response to Economic and Social Council resolution 2001/23 [YUN 2001, p. 1137], the Secretary-General, by a May note [E/2003/66], transmitted a report of the UNAIDS Executive Director, which updated the status of the epidemic; summarized steps taken by UNAIDS to promote the implementation of the 2001 Declaration of Commitment on HIV/AIDS; and summarized key developments in advancing a more effective and coordinated UN system response to the epidemic. It also provided an overview of the future direction of UNAIDS in response to decisions made by PCB at its thirteenth meeting in 2002 [YUN 2002, p. 1219], following an external evaluation of the Programme [ibid., p. 1220].

The report recommended that the Council consider endorsing the decisions of the thirteenth PCB meeting and the five cross-cutting functions applicable at all levels of UNAIDS set out in the Board's decisions. It should encourage UNAIDS and the broader UN system to pursue full achievement of the Millennium Development Goals (MDGs) of the 2000 Millennium Declaration, adopted by the General Assembly in resolution 55/2 [YUN 2000, p. 49], and the goals and targets of the Declaration of Commitment on

HIV/AIDS. It should also encourage the further development of UNAIDS as a positive, ongoing example of UN system reform; support to periodic and comprehensive multi-stakeholder reviews of national AIDS programmes; the formulation of joint UN programmes to support national responses to HIV/AIDS; and more systematic reporting on the activities of UN theme groups on HIV/AIDS, through the annual reports submitted by the UN resident coordinators to the Secretary-General. The Council should urge UN funds, programmes and specialized agencies, through the resident coordinators, to include the UNAIDS country coordinators as regular members in the UN country teams; all Governments, especially donors, to provide full funding for the 2004-2005 biennium; and PCB and the governing boards of co-sponsoring agencies to develop closer links and more effective coordination.

ECONOMIC AND SOCIAL COUNCIL ACTION

On 22 July [meeting 44], the Economic and Social Council adopted **resolution 2003/18** [draft: E/2003/L.25/Rev.1] without vote [agenda item 7 (g)].

Joint United Nations Programme on HIV/AIDS (UNAIDS)

The Economic and Social Council,

Recalling its resolution 1994/24 of 26 July 1994, by which it created the Joint United Nations Programme on HIV/AIDS (UNAIDS), and its resolution 2001/23 of 26 July 2001,

Having considered the report of the Executive Director of the Joint United Nations Programme on HIV/AIDS (UNAIDS),

Recalling the goals and targets set forth in the Declaration of Commitment on HIV/AIDS adopted by the General Assembly at its twenty-sixth special session, held from 25 to 27 June 2001, and the HIV/AIDS-related goals contained in the United Nations Millennium Declaration of 8 September 2000,

Encouraged by the resolve of Governments to intensify implementation of the Declaration of Commitment on HIV/AIDS in order to meet the goals and targets contained therein,

Reaffirming the importance of the follow-up process prescribed by the Declaration, which included the setting of specific time-bound targets, which fall due in 2003, 2005 and 2010,

Noting with profound concern that 42 million people worldwide are living with HIV/AIDS and that the HIV/AIDS pandemic claimed 3.1 million lives in 2002,

Expressing serious concern about the continued global spread of HIV/AIDS, which exacerbates poverty and poses a major threat to economic and social development and to food security in heavily affected regions,

Welcoming the establishment of the Global Fund to Fight AIDS, Tuberculosis and Malaria, and the memorandum of understanding concluded between the Programme and the Global Fund,

Acknowledging other national, bilateral and multilateral resources available to fight the HIV/AIDS epidemic and the need to mobilize additional resources,

1. *Urges* the Joint United Nations Programme on HIV/AIDS (UNAIDS) and the organizations and bodies of the United Nations system to intensify their support to Governments, with a view to achieving the goals contained in the United Nations Millennium Declaration, as well as the goals and targets contained in the Declaration of Commitment on HIV/AIDS;

2. *Encourages* Governments to participate in the high-level plenary meetings and informal interactive panel discussion of the General Assembly, which are to be held on 22 September 2003, and which will be devoted to the follow-up to the outcome of the twenty-sixth special session of the Assembly and the implementation of the Declaration of Commitment on HIV/AIDS;

3. *Welcomes* the decisions of the Programme Coordinating Board of UNAIDS, taken in response to the five-year evaluation of the Programme, which set out five cross-cutting functions to apply at all levels of the Programme, namely: *(a)* leadership and advocacy for effective action on the epidemic; *(b)* strategic information required to guide the efforts of the partners; *(c)* tracking, monitoring and evaluation of the epidemic and actions responding to it; *(d)* civil society engagement and partnership development; and *(e)* financial, technical and political resources mobilization;

4. *Also welcomes* the decision of the Programme Coordinating Board calling for significantly increased efforts and resources in the unified budget and work plan devoted to scaling up the response to HIV/AIDS at the country level;

5. *Commends* the Programme as a positive example of collaborative action of the United Nations system, and encourages the further refinement of the work of the Programme;

6. *Invites* the Chairperson of the Programme Coordinating Board to continue consultations with the members of the Board and with Observer States in order to improve further the working methods of the Programme, its subcommittees and ad hoc working groups, with a view to further enhancing participation in the work of the Programme;

7. *Calls upon* the Chairperson of the United Nations Development Group to ensure, through the resident coordinators, the inclusion of the country coordinators of the Programme as members of United Nations country teams, in order to strengthen United Nations coordination in the fight against HIV/AIDS at the country level, and to mobilize intensified assistance to Governments in mounting and sustaining effective responses to HIV/AIDS;

8. *Invites* the governing bodies of the co-sponsoring organizations of the Programme, as well as the Programme Coordinating Board, to develop closer links and more effective coordination in order to ensure that clear and effective guidance is provided to the secretariat of the Programme and to co-sponsoring organizations, including through the annual consideration by the governing body of each sponsoring organization of its engagement in the Programme;

9. *Urges* Governments, bilateral and multilateral donors, civil society, the private sector and other partners to increase their funding for HIV/AIDS-related activities, including funding of the unified budget and work plan of the Programme, in order to ensure a level of financial and other resources that are fully com-

mensurate with the multisectoral challenges of the epidemic;

10. *Encourages* the Programme to continue to foster efficient and effective cooperation with financing mechanisms, such as the World Bank Multi-Country HIV/AIDS Programme and the Global Fund to Fight AIDS, Tuberculosis and Malaria, bearing in mind the complementarity of the role of those mechanisms, based on their respective comparative advantages;

11. *Requests* the Secretary-General to transmit to the Economic and Social Council, at its substantive session of 2005, a report prepared by the Executive Director of the Programme, in collaboration with other relevant organizations and bodies of the United Nations system, which should include information on progress made in developing the coordinated response of the United Nations system to the HIV/AIDS pandemic, as well as the decisions, recommendations and conclusions of the Programme Coordinating Board taken subsequent to the substantive session of the Council in 2003.

HIV/AIDS and food insecurity

The High-level Committee on Programmes (HLCP) of the United Nations System Chief Executives Board for Coordination (CEB), at its fifth session (Rome, Italy, 26-27 March) [CEB/2003/4], discussed the issue of linkages between HIV/AIDS and food security and governance, based on a note introduced by the UNAIDS secretariat, which had convened an ad hoc group to prepare the Committee's consideration of the issue. The Committee noted that the projected 10 to 30 per cent reduction of the labour force by 2020 in countries with a high prevalence of HIV/AIDS showed the indomitable nature of the threat to public institutional capacity and its far-reaching impact on the ability of the affected States to provide effective governance. In turn, lack of food security and deepening poverty were exacerbating the more rapid spread of the pandemic, while erosion of public institutional capacity, especially in rural areas, was debilitating the capacity of many countries to deal with the pandemic and to strengthen food production capacity. The Committee emphasized that HIV/AIDS not only detracted from progress towards sustainable development and the achievement of the MDGs, but had emerged as a major security threat at the national, regional and global levels. The Committee requested the UNAIDS secretariat to continue to convene the open-ended group with WFP as co-convenor. While not ignoring other regions, the group should focus on Southern and Eastern Africa as the areas where the triple crisis of HIV/AIDS, food security and governance was most manifest, provide an overview of relevant UN system initiatives, and prepare a policy paper and present it to the Committee and CEB (see p. 1260). The group was asked to develop a matrix of initiatives under way on AIDS, food security and governance to encourage transparency and information-sharing. The CEB secretariat was requested to consult with the Office of the Secretary-General on possible approaches to advocacy and outreach. At its first 2003 intersessional meeting (Geneva, 2 July) [CEB/2003/6], HLCP endorsed the content and time frame of the paper on HIV/AIDS, and food security and governance.

At its sixth session (Rome, 18-19 September) [CEB/2003/7], HLCP considered HIV/AIDS, and food security and governance on the basis of a paper prepared collaboratively by 11 agencies with UNAIDS and WFP as task leaders. A revised paper was issued during the meeting and endorsed by the Committee on an ad referendum basis. The Committee agreed that a revised version should be circulated by 24 September so that its members might consult their executive heads and a final text prepared for submission to CEB. The final paper, entitled "Organizing the United Nations response to the triple threat of food insecurity, weakened capacity for governance and AIDS, particularly in Southern and Eastern Africa", was annexed to the meeting report. The paper presented a coherent UN system-wide policy and programming approach on HIV/AIDS with specific recommendations to be endorsed by CEB. It summarized the interlinkages between HIV/AIDS, and food security and governance, and identified the paradigm shift required in the UN system to meet the new challenges. Appended to the paper was a declaration adopted by UN regional directors at their meeting in Maputo, Mozambique, on 9 July to accelerate country and regional action on HIV/AIDS in Southern and Eastern Africa. The Committee called for urgent, collective and intensified commitment and action by the UN system to assist affected countries in responding to HIV/AIDS and to demonstrate in the process that the system could make a visible difference and impact on the ground.

At its second regular session of 2003 (New York, 31 October-1 November) [CEB/2003/2], CEB endorsed the general analysis and programming approach and the series of programmatic and institutional actions set out in the paper on the triple threat of HIV/AIDS, and food insecurity and weak governance, and concurred with the thrust of the recommendations contained therein. It called on its members to: provide the necessary support to carry out the action points of the paper; strive to increase financial investments in country-level actions directed at HIV/AIDS in Southern and Eastern Africa; draw on the paper as a tool for advocacy and communication with regard to the interlinked crises of food security, weakened capacity for governance and AIDS in that region; adopt the paper as a guide for action by their country representatives and by UN country teams in areas threatened by AIDS; and request the United Nations Development Group (UNDG), in coordination with IASC and in consultation with the Regional Inter-Agency Coordination and Support Office, as appropriate, to take the lead on follow-up and to report on progress in implementing the actions set out in the paper. HLCP, at its second intersessional meeting of 2003 (New York, 3 November) [CEB/2003/8], invited UNDG to report on progress to the Committee's February 2004 session.

Tobacco

The sixth and final session of the Intergovernmental Negotiating Body on the WHO Framework Convention on Tobacco Control (Geneva, 17-28 February) finalized the draft text of the Framework Convention and transmitted it to the fifty-sixth session of the WHO World Health Assembly (Geneva, 19-28 May) (see p. 1514). The Convention, which governed tobacco taxation, smoking prevention and treatment, illicit trade, advertising, sponsorship and promotion, and product regulation, was adopted by the World Health Assembly on 21 May. It was opened for signature from 16 to 22 June at WHO headquarters in Geneva and would remain open for signature at UN Headquarters in New York from 30 June 2003 to 29 June 2004. The Convention would enter into force 90 days after the fortieth instrument of ratification, approval, acceptance, formal confirmation or accession was deposited with the UN depositary.

As at 31 December, 85 States had signed the Convention. During the year, Fiji, Malta, Seychelles and Sri Lanka ratified the Convention, and Norway approved it.

Ad Hoc Inter-Agency Task Force

The Ad Hoc Inter-Agency Task Force on Tobacco Control, established in 1999 [YUN 1999, p. 1151], at its fifth session (Washington, D.C., 21-22 October), discussed the new orientation of the Task Force and the activities it should focus on following the adoption of the Framework Convention. Task Force members highlighted areas of concern in which tobacco use had had a significant adverse impact, including on health, economic growth and poverty, as well as its fiscal impact and the impact of globalization on tobacco use at the country level.

Roll Back Malaria initiative

In a July report [A/58/136 & Corr.1], the Secretary-General provided an update, prepared by WHO, of the implementation of General Assembly resolution 57/294 [YUN 2002, p. 1223] on the Decade to Roll Back Malaria in Developing Countries, Particularly in Africa (2001-2010), which was proclaimed by the Assembly in resolution 55/284 [YUN 2001, p. 1139]. The report reviewed the state of resource mobilization and financing of malaria control; presented steps to finance malaria control in Africa; and provided examples of successful ways in which malaria-endemic countries were tackling the disease through sector-wide approaches for health and the prioritization of malaria control in debt relief. It also discussed government action to reduce or waive taxes and tariffs on mosquito nets; technology transfer for the production of long-lasting insecticidal nets and increased access to antimalarial medicines; and WHO's enhanced technical support to countries for effective disease management in resource development planning.

The report drew significantly on *The Africa Malaria Report—2003*, published by UNICEF and WHO and launched on Africa Malaria Day, which described the malaria burden and trends, policies and implementation of key interventions, constraints and obstacles to implementation, and financing south of the Sahara. Data were mainly from the period 1998 to 2002 and, as such, provided a baseline against which to evaluate progress by 2005. The report also described efforts to strengthen the Roll Back Malaria (RBM) Partnership, which was founded by WHO in 1998 [YUN 1998, p. 1384] with the goal of halving the world's malaria burden by 2010. Following an internal review and an external evaluation in 2002, steps were taken to restructure the Partnership secretariat. In May, a Monitoring and Evaluation Reference Group (MERG) was established as an advisory body of RBM partners to establish robust systems to reliably monitor the malaria situation and evaluate the effectiveness of RBM interventions. At its first meeting (Arlington, Virginia, United States, 8-9 May), MERG, which was chaired by WHO and co-chaired by UNICEF, established task forces on five priority issues: malaria mortality trends; the development of a malaria prevalence indicator of the MDGs; malaria-related anaemia; strengthening national monitoring and evaluation capacity for RBM activities; and developing population-based surveys.

The 2005 evaluation of the midterm (2005) targets of the Decade to Roll Back Malaria in Developing Countries, Particularly in Africa, as set by the 2000 Abuja Declaration and Plan of Action on Roll Back Malaria in Africa [YUN 2001, p. 1139], and laid out in resolution 55/284 [ibid.], was discussed by MERG at its second meeting (Kampala, Uganda, 17-18 November).

The report concluded that although progress was made in malaria control, it was still too slow. It proposed a series of recommendations to the General Assembly, which were incorporated into resolution 58/237 (see below).

Maputo Declaration. On 11 December [A/58/626], Mozambique transmitted the decisions and declarations adopted by the Assembly of the African Union (AU) at its second ordinary session (Maputo, Mozambique, 10-12 July), including the Maputo Declaration on Malaria, HIV/AIDS, Tuberculosis and Other Related Infectious Diseases. In the Declaration, the heads of State and Government of the AU reaffirmed the commitments enshrined in the 2000 Abuja Declaration and Plan of Action and the 2001 Abuja Declaration and Framework Plan of Action on HIV/AIDS, Tuberculosis and Other Related Infectious Diseases, adopted by the heads of State and Government of the Organization of African Unity during an extraordinary summit meeting on the subject. They also reiterated their commitment to intensify and consolidate efforts for the implementation of those Declarations.

GENERAL ASSEMBLY ACTION

On 23 December [meeting 78], the General Assembly adopted **resolution 58/237** [draft: A/58/L.53 & Add.1] without vote [agenda item 51].

2001-2010: Decade to Roll Back Malaria in Developing Countries, Particularly in Africa

The General Assembly,

Recalling its resolutions 49/135 of 19 December 1994, 50/128 of 20 December 1995, 55/284 of 7 September 2001 and 57/294 of 20 December 2002 concerning the struggle against malaria in developing countries, particularly in Africa,

Bearing in mind the relevant resolutions of the Economic and Social Council relating to the struggle against malaria and diarrhoeal diseases, in particular resolution 1998/36 of 30 July 1998,

Taking note of the declarations and decisions on health issues adopted by the Organization of African Unity, in particular the declaration and plan of action on the "Roll Back Malaria" initiative adopted at the Extraordinary Summit of Heads of State and Government of the Organization of African Unity, held in Abuja on 24 and 25 April 2000, as well as decision AHG/Dec.155(XXXVI) concerning the implementation of that declaration and plan of action, adopted by the Assembly of Heads of State and Government of the Organization of African Unity at its thirty-sixth ordinary session, held in Lomé from 10 to 12 July 2000,

Also taking note of the Maputo Declaration on Malaria, HIV/AIDS, Tuberculosis and Other Related Infectious Diseases, adopted by the Assembly of the African Union at its second ordinary session, held in Maputo from 10 to 12 July 2003,

Recognizing the linkages in efforts being made to reach the targets set in the Abuja Summit as necessary and important for the attainment of the "Roll Back Malaria" goal and the targets of the United Nations Millennium Declaration by 2010 and 2015, respectively,

Also recognizing the urgent need for scaling up national malaria control programmes if African countries are to meet the intermediate target set by the Abuja Summit for the five-year period of 2000-2005,

Further recognizing that malaria-related ill health and deaths throughout the world can be eliminated with political commitment and commensurate resources if the public is educated and sensitized about malaria and appropriate health services are made available, particularly in countries where the disease is endemic,

Emphasizing the importance of implementing the Millennium Declaration, and welcoming in this connection the commitment of Member States to respond to the specific needs of Africa,

Commending the efforts of the World Health Organization and the United Nations Children's Fund and other partners to fight malaria over the years, including the launching of the Roll Back Malaria Partnership in 1998,

1. *Takes note* of the report of the Secretary-General, and calls for support for the recommendations contained therein;

2. *Calls upon* the international community to continue to support the "Roll Back Malaria" partner organizations, including the World Health Organization and the United Nations Children's Fund, as vital complementary sources of support for the efforts of malaria-endemic countries to combat the disease;

3. *Appeals* to the international community to ensure that the Global Fund to Fight AIDS, Tuberculosis and Malaria receives increased funding to support sound national plans to control malaria in endemic countries to be implemented in a sustained and equitable way that contributes to health system development;

4. *Urges* malaria-endemic countries to increase domestic resource allocation to malaria control;

5. *Encourages* all African countries that have not yet done so to implement the recommendations of the Abuja Summit to reduce or waive taxes and tariffs for nets and other products needed for malaria control, both to reduce the price of nets to consumers and to stimulate free trade in insecticide-treated nets;

6. *Calls upon* the international community to support ways of stimulating the development of manufacturing capacity of insecticide-treated nets in Africa and, in this connection, to encourage and facilitate the transfer of technology needed to make insecticide-treated nets more effective and long-lasting;

7. *Recognizes* the importance of the development of effective vaccines and new medicines to prevent and treat malaria, and the need for further research, including through effective global partnerships such as the various malaria vaccine initiatives and the Medicines for Malaria Venture, in securing their development;

8. *Reiterates* the need for expanded public-private partnerships for malaria control and prevention, and in this context urges petroleum companies operating in Africa to consider providing polymer for the manufacture of mosquito nets at reduced prices as a contribution to rolling back malaria in Africa;

9. *Urges* the pharmaceutical industry to take note of the increasing need for effective combination treatment for malaria, particularly in Africa, and to form additional alliances and partnerships to help to ensure that all people at risk have access to prompt, affordable and quality treatment;

10. *Requests* the Secretary-General, in close collaboration with the World Health Organization, developing countries and regional organizations, including the African Union, to conduct in 2005 an evaluation of the measures taken and progress made towards the achievement of the mid-term targets, the means of implementation provided by the international community in this regard and the overall goals of the Decade, and to report thereon to the General Assembly at its sixtieth session;

11. *Also requests* the Secretary-General to report to the General Assembly at its fifty-ninth session on the implementation of the present resolution, under the agenda item entitled "2001-2010: Decade to Roll Back Malaria in Developing Countries, Particularly in Africa".

Access to medication

In 2003, the Secretary-General reported to the Commission on Human Rights on measures States had taken to promote access to medication in the context of pandemics such as HIV/AIDS (see p. 806). In furtherance of the Declaration of Commitment on HIV/AIDS, adopted in General Assembly resolution S-26/2 [YUN 2001, p. 1126], the Commission called on States to address factors affecting the provision of drugs related to pandemics (see p. 807). In related action, the Commission's Special Rapporteur on the right to the highest attainable standard of physical and mental health presented an overview of good practices for the right (see p. 772).

On 30 August, the World Trade Organization General Council adopted a decision on the implementation of the 2001 Doha Declaration on the Agreement on Trade-Related Aspects of Intellectual Property Rights and Public Health [YUN 2001, p. 1432], which would make it easier for poorer countries to import cheaper generic drugs made under compulsory licensing if they were unable to manufacture the medicines themselves.

GENERAL ASSEMBLY ACTION

On 22 December [meeting 77], the General Assembly, on the recommendation of the Third (Social, Humanitarian and Cultural) Committee [A/58/508/Add.2], adopted **resolution 58/179** by recorded vote (181-1) [agenda item 117 (b)].

Access to medication in the context of pandemics such as HIV/AIDS, tuberculosis and malaria

The General Assembly,

Reaffirming the Universal Declaration of Human Rights and the International Covenant on Economic, Social and Cultural Rights,

Reaffirming also that the right of everyone to the enjoyment of the highest attainable standard of physical and mental health is a human right,

Recalling Commission on Human Rights resolutions 2001/33 of 23 April 2001, 2002/32 of 22 April 2002 and 2003/29 of 22 April 2003,

Acknowledging that prevention and comprehensive care and support, including treatment and access to medication for those infected and affected by pandemics such as HIV/AIDS, tuberculosis and malaria, are inseparable elements of an effective response and must be integrated into a comprehensive approach to respond to such pandemics,

Stressing the importance of fully implementing the Declaration of Commitment on HIV/AIDS, "Global Crisis—Global Action", and taking note of the report of the Secretary-General,

Welcoming the continuing political commitment demonstrated at the high-level plenary meetings of the General Assembly devoted to the follow-up to the outcome of its twenty-sixth special session and the implementation of the Declaration of Commitment on HIV/AIDS, "Global Crisis—Global Action", held on 22 September 2003,

Expressing its support for the work of the Global Fund to Fight AIDS, Tuberculosis and Malaria and that of other international bodies combating such pandemics,

Bearing in mind World Health Assembly resolutions WHA55.12 and WHA55.14, both of 18 May 2002, and WHA56.30 of 28 May 2003,

Bearing in mind also the International Labour Organization Code of Practice on HIV/AIDS and the World of Work, adopted by the Governing Body of the International Labour Organization in June 2001,

Taking note of general comment No. 14 (2000) on the right to the highest attainable standard of physical and mental health (article 12 of the International Covenant on Economic, Social and Cultural Rights), adopted by the Committee on Economic, Social and Cultural Rights at its twenty-second session,

Taking note also of general comment No. 3 (2003) on HIV/AIDS and the rights of the child, adopted by the Committee on the Rights of the Child at its thirty-second session,

Alarmed that the HIV/AIDS pandemic claimed 3.1 million lives in 2002, that about 42 million people were living with HIV by the end of 2002 and that 25 million children under the age of 15, including 20 million in Africa, are projected to lose one or both parents by 2010 owing to HIV/AIDS,

Fully aware that the failure to deliver antiretroviral treatment for HIV/AIDS to the millions of people who need it is a global health emergency,

Recalling its resolution 57/294 of 20 December 2002, entitled "2001-2010: Decade to Roll Back Malaria in Developing Countries, Particularly in Africa",

Alarmed that, according to the global Roll Back Malaria Partnership, malaria annually causes more than 1 million deaths, around 90 per cent of which are in Africa, that it is the leading cause of death in young children and that it causes at least 300 million cases of acute illness each year,

Also alarmed that, according to the World Health Organization global tuberculosis control report of 2003, tuberculosis kills about 2 million people each year, that 7 to 8 million people around the world become sick with tuberculosis each year and that it is projected that 36 million people will die of tuberculosis between 2002 and 2020 if control is not further strengthened,

Acknowledging the significance of HIV/AIDS in the increase in tuberculosis and other opportunistic diseases,

Welcoming the initiatives of the Secretary-General and relevant United Nations agencies, States and civil society, including the private sector, to make drugs related to HIV/AIDS, tuberculosis and malaria more accessible and affordable to infected persons, especially in developing countries, and noting that much more could be done in this regard,

Recalling the Declaration on the Agreement on Trade-Related Aspects of Intellectual Property Rights (TRIPS Agreement) and Public Health adopted at the Fourth World Trade Organization Ministerial Conference in Doha in November 2001, and welcoming the World Trade Organization General Council decision of 30 August 2003 on the implementation of paragraph 6 of the Declaration,

Recognizing that the spread of HIV/AIDS can have a uniquely devastating impact on all sectors and levels of society, and stressing that the HIV/AIDS pandemic, if unchecked, may pose a risk to stability and security, as stated in Security Council resolution 1308(2000) of 17 July 2000,

Emphasizing, in view of the increasing challenges presented by pandemics such as HIV/AIDS, tuberculosis and malaria, the need for intensified efforts to ensure universal respect for and observance of human rights and fundamental freedoms for all, including by reducing vulnerability to pandemics such as HIV/AIDS, tuberculosis and malaria and by preventing related discrimination and stigma,

1. *Recognizes* that access to medication in the context of pandemics such as HIV/AIDS, tuberculosis and malaria is one fundamental element for achieving progressively the full realization of the right of everyone to the enjoyment of the highest attainable standard of physical and mental health;

2. *Welcomes* the commitment of the World Health Organization and the Joint United Nations Programme on HIV/AIDS to work with the international community to support developing countries in achieving the global target of providing antiretroviral medicines to 3 million people infected with HIV/AIDS by the end of 2005, the "3 by 5" target;

3. *Takes note with interest* of the interim report of the Special Rapporteur of the Commission on Human Rights on the right of everyone to the enjoyment of the highest attainable standard of physical and mental health;

4. *Calls upon* States to develop and implement national strategies, in accordance with applicable international law, including international agreements acceded to, to progressively realize access for all to prevention-related goods, services and information as well as access to comprehensive treatment, care and support for all individuals infected and affected by pandemics such as HIV/AIDS, tuberculosis and malaria;

5. *Also calls upon* States to establish or strengthen national health and social infrastructures and healthcare systems, with the assistance of the international community as necessary, for the effective delivery of prevention, treatment, care and support to respond to pandemics such as HIV/AIDS, tuberculosis and malaria;

6. *Further calls upon* States to pursue policies, in accordance with applicable international law, including international agreements acceded to, which would promote:

(a) The availability in sufficient quantities of pharmaceutical products and medical technologies used to treat pandemics such as HIV/AIDS, tuberculosis and malaria or the most common opportunistic infections that accompany them;

(b) The accessibility and affordability for all, without discrimination, including the most vulnerable or socially disadvantaged groups of the population, of pharmaceutical products or medical technologies used to treat pandemics such as HIV/AIDS, tuberculosis and malaria or the most common opportunistic infections that accompany them;

(c) The assurance that pharmaceutical products or medical technologies used to treat pandemics such as HIV/AIDS, tuberculosis and malaria or the most common opportunistic infections that accompany them, irrespective of their sources and countries of origin, are scientifically and medically appropriate and of good quality;

7. *Calls upon* States, at the national level, on a non-discriminatory basis, in accordance with applicable international law, including international agreements acceded to:

(a) To refrain from taking measures that would deny or limit equal access for all persons to preventive, curative or palliative pharmaceutical products or medical technologies used to treat pandemics such as HIV/AIDS, tuberculosis and malaria or the most common opportunistic infections that accompany them;

(b) To adopt and implement legislation or other measures, in accordance with applicable international law, including international agreements acceded to, to safeguard access to such preventive, curative or palliative pharmaceutical products or medical technologies from any limitations by third parties;

(c) To adopt all appropriate positive measures, to the maximum of the resources allocated for this purpose, to promote effective access to such preventive, curative or palliative pharmaceutical products or medical technologies;

8. *Also calls upon* States, in furtherance of the Declaration of Commitment on HIV/AIDS, to address factors affecting the provision of drugs related to the treatment of pandemics such as HIV/AIDS and the most common opportunistic infections that accompany them, as well as to develop integrated strategies to strengthen healthcare systems, including voluntary counselling and testing, laboratory capacities and the training of healthcare providers and technicians, in order to provide treatment and monitor the use of medications, diagnostics and related technologies;

9. *Further calls upon* States to take all appropriate measures, nationally and through cooperation, to promote the research and development of new and more effective preventive, curative or palliative pharmaceutical products and diagnostic tools, in accordance with applicable international law, including international agreements acceded to;

10. *Calls upon* States, at the international level, to take steps, individually and/or through international

cooperation, in accordance with applicable international law, including international agreements acceded to, such as:

(a) Facilitating, wherever possible, access in other countries to essential preventive, curative or palliative pharmaceutical products or medical technologies used to treat pandemics such as HIV/AIDS, tuberculosis and malaria or the most common opportunistic infections that accompany them, as well as extending the necessary cooperation, wherever possible, especially in times of emergency;

(b) Ensuring that their actions, as members of international organizations, take due account of the right of everyone to the enjoyment of the highest attainable standard of physical and mental health and that the application of international agreements is supportive of public health policies that promote broad access to safe, effective and affordable preventive, curative or palliative pharmaceutical products or medical technologies;

11. *Welcomes* the financial contributions made to date to the Global Fund to Fight AIDS, Tuberculosis and Malaria, urges that further contributions be made to sustain the Fund, and calls upon all States to encourage the private sector to contribute to the Fund as a matter of urgency;

12. *Calls upon* the Joint United Nations Programme on HIV/AIDS to mobilize further resources to combat the HIV/AIDS pandemic and upon all Governments to take measures to ensure that the necessary resources are made available to the Programme, in line with the Declaration of Commitment on HIV/AIDS;

13. *Calls upon* States to ensure that those at risk of contracting malaria, in particular pregnant women and children under 5 years of age, benefit from the most suitable combination of personal and community protective measures, such as insecticide-treated bed nets and other interventions that are accessible and affordable, in order to prevent infection and suffering;

14. *Also calls upon* States to provide the necessary support for the World Health Organization Roll Back Malaria and Stop Tuberculosis Partnerships in their ongoing measures to combat malaria and tuberculosis;

15. *Calls upon* the international community, in particular the developed countries, to continue to assist developing countries in the fight against pandemics such as HIV/AIDS, tuberculosis and malaria, through financial and technical support as well as through the training of personnel;

16. *Invites* the Committee on Economic, Social and Cultural Rights to give attention to the issue of access to medication in the context of pandemics such as HIV/AIDS, tuberculosis and malaria, and invites States to include appropriate information thereon in the reports they submit to the Committee.

RECORDED VOTE ON RESOLUTION 58/179:

In favour: Afghanistan, Albania, Algeria, Andorra, Angola, Antigua and Barbuda, Argentina, Armenia, Australia, Austria, Azerbaijan, Bahamas, Bahrain, Bangladesh, Barbados, Belarus, Belgium, Belize, Benin, Bhutan, Bolivia, Bosnia and Herzegovina, Botswana, Brazil, Brunei Darussalam, Bulgaria, Burkina Faso, Burundi, Cambodia, Cameroon, Canada, Cape Verde, Central African Republic, Chile, China, Colombia, Comoros, Congo, Costa Rica, Côte d'Ivoire, Croatia, Cuba, Cyprus, Czech Republic, Democratic People's Republic of Korea, Democratic Republic of the Congo, Denmark, Djibouti, Dominica, Dominican Republic, Ecuador, Egypt, El Salvador, Eritrea, Estonia, Ethiopia, Fiji, Finland, France, Gabon, Gambia, Georgia, Germany, Ghana, Greece, Grenada, Guatemala, Guinea, Guinea-Bissau, Guyana, Haiti, Honduras, Hungary, Iceland, India, Indonesia, Iran, Ireland, Israel, Italy, Jamaica, Japan, Jordan, Kazakhstan, Kenya, Kuwait, Kyrgyzstan, Lao People's Democratic Republic, Latvia, Lebanon, Lesotho, Libyan Arab Jamahiriya, Liechtenstein, Lithuania, Luxembourg, Madagascar, Malawi, Malaysia, Maldives, Mali, Malta, Marshall Islands, Mauritania, Mauritius, Mexico, Micronesia, Monaco, Mongolia, Morocco, Mozambique, Myanmar, Namibia, Nauru, Nepal, Netherlands, New Zealand, Nicaragua, Niger, Nigeria, Norway, Oman, Pakistan, Palau, Panama, Papua New Guinea, Paraguay, Peru, Philippines, Poland, Portugal, Qatar, Republic of Korea, Republic of Moldova, Romania, Russian Federation, Rwanda, Saint Lucia, Saint Vincent and the Grenadines, Samoa, San Marino, Saudi Arabia, Senegal, Serbia and Montenegro, Seychelles, Sierra Leone, Singapore, Slovakia, Slovenia, Solomon Islands, Somalia, South Africa, Spain, Sri Lanka, Sudan, Suriname, Sweden, Switzerland, Syrian Arab Republic, Tajikistan, Thailand, The former Yugoslav Republic of Macedonia, Timor-Leste, Togo, Tonga, Trinidad and Tobago, Tunisia, Turkey, Turkmenistan, Tuvalu, Uganda, Ukraine, United Arab Emirates, United Kingdom, United Republic of Tanzania, Uruguay, Uzbekistan, Venezuela, Viet Nam, Yemen, Zambia, Zimbabwe.

Against: United States.

Follow-up to Millennium Summit

In response to General Assembly resolution 56/95 [YUN 2001, p. 1279], the Secretary-General submitted, in September, the second annual report [A/58/323] on progress achieved by the UN system and Member States to implement the United Nations Millennium Declaration, adopted in Assembly resolution 55/2 [YUN 2000, p. 49]. The Secretary-General noted the lack of progress made to reverse the rate of the spread of HIV/AIDS, malaria and tuberculosis. HIV/AIDS had already had a devastating social and economic impact in sub-Saharan Africa and, to a lesser extent, in the Caribbean. Infection rates in most countries of South-Central and South-Eastern Asia were already at least comparable to those in most developed countries, where the pandemic started much earlier, and there were signs that the disease was breaking out of high-risk pockets into the general population. The incidence of malaria might also be on the rise, as increasing resistance to the available drugs, and of mosquitoes to available pesticides, made both treatment and prevention more difficult. The best estimates available indicated that the incidence of tuberculosis was increasing. However, the Secretary-General said, rapid improvements were possible by learning and building on success stories such as in Thailand, where a strong prevention campaign since 1990 had contained the HIV/AIDS pandemic; in Uganda, where infection rates were down for eight consecutive years in the 1990s; and in Senegal and Cambodia, where the spread of HIV was also contained. Countries had the opportunity to make sizeable inroads into the incidence of tuberculosis by adopting a relatively inexpensive but sustained treatment programme. Efforts to combat HIV/AIDS, as well as tuberculosis and malaria, were being supported by a major global mobilization that combined new commitments to advocacy and political action in many of the most affected countries and a new drive to raise international resources commensurate with the scale of the challenge.

The Secretary-General, as patron of the Global Fund to Fight HIV/AIDS, Tuberculosis and Malaria, was encouraged by the increase in support for that body and for broader efforts by UN agencies, the World Bank and others. Private foundations were also increasingly supporting research, treatment and prevention. Some pharmaceutical firms were offering steeply discounted drug supplies, and an increasing number of countries were able to provide inexpensive generic drugs to their populations. Nevertheless, with commitments for the Global Fund still significantly short of the $3 billion required in 2004 and the $4.5 billion needed in 2005, it was imperative that donors make a renewed effort to increase their support. With immediate action, there was still reasonable hope to meet the MDG of halting and beginning to reverse the spread of HIV/AIDS and the incidence of malaria and other major diseases by 2015.

GENERAL ASSEMBLY ACTION

On 27 October [meeting 43], the General Assembly adopted **resolution 58/3** [draft: A/58/L.5 & Add.1] without vote [agenda item 60].

Enhancing capacity-building in global public health

The General Assembly,

Recalling the United Nations Millennium Declaration, adopted by heads of State and Government at the Millennium Summit of the United Nations, and the development goals contained therein, in particular the health-related development goals, and its resolutions 55/162 of 14 December 2000, 56/95 of 14 December 2001 and 57/144 of 16 December 2002,

Bearing in mind World Health Assembly resolutions 48.13 of 12 May 1995, 54.14 of 21 May 2001 and 56.28 and 56.29 of 28 May 2003,

Recognizing that Member States have to strengthen their efforts to halt and begin to reverse, by 2015, the spread of HIV/AIDS and the incidence of malaria and other major diseases,

Reaffirming its Declaration of Commitment on HIV/AIDS,

Recognizing that the globalization of trade and increased international travel have increased the risk of a rapid worldwide spread of infectious diseases, posing new challenges to public health,

Noting with concern the deleterious impact on humankind of HIV/AIDS, tuberculosis, malaria and other major infectious diseases and epidemics, and the heavy disease burden borne by poor people, especially in developing countries,

Welcoming the current success of the affected countries in combating the severe acute respiratory syndrome, the first severe infectious disease to emerge in the twenty-first century, the political commitment and strong leadership shown in the affected countries and the role of the World Health Organization in controlling the epidemic, while mindful of the fact that the fight against the severe acute respiratory syndrome and other epidemics is far from over,

Convinced that strengthening public health is critical to the development of all Member States, and that economic and social development are enhanced through measures that strengthen capacity-building in public health, including systems of prevention of and immunization against infectious diseases,

Emphasizing that Member States have primary responsibility for strengthening their capacity-building in public health to detect and respond rapidly to outbreaks of major infectious diseases, through the establishment and improvement of effective public health mechanisms, while recognizing that the magnitude of the necessary response may be beyond the capabilities of many developing countries,

Convinced that the control of outbreaks of diseases, particularly new diseases whose origins remain unknown, requires international and regional cooperation,

Recognizing the need for greater international and regional cooperation to meet new and existing challenges to public health, in particular in promoting effective measures such as vaccines, as well as to assist developing countries in securing vaccines against preventable infectious diseases,

Recognizing also the expertise of the World Health Organization and its role in, inter alia, coordinating actions with Member States in the areas of information exchange, personnel training, technical support, resource utilization, the improvement of global public health preparedness and response mechanisms and stimulating and advancing work on the prevention, control and eradication of epidemic, endemic and other diseases, as well as the work of the World Health Organization office dedicated to communicable diseases surveillance and response,

Underscoring the continued importance of the International Health Regulations as an instrument for ensuring the maximum possible protection against the international spread of diseases with minimum interference in international traffic, and urging Member States to give high priority to the work on the revision of the Regulations,

Welcoming the efforts of the World Health Organization, in cooperation with Member States, the United Nations system, the Bretton Woods institutions, the private sector and civil society, in enhancing capacity-building in global public health and in promoting public health at the country level,

Welcoming also the Doha Declaration on the Agreement on Trade-Related Aspects of Intellectual Property Rights and Public Health, adopted on 14 November 2001, and noting the decision of the World Trade Organization General Council of 30 August 2003 on the implementation of paragraph 6 of the Declaration,

Recognizing the need to strengthen national health and social infrastructures to reinforce measures to eliminate discrimination in access to public health, information and education for all people, and especially for the most underserved and vulnerable groups,

1. *Urges* Member States to further integrate public health into their national economic and social development strategies, including through the establishment and improvement of effective public health mechanisms, in particular networks of disease surveillance, response, control, prevention, treatment and information exchange and the recruitment and training of national public health personnel;

2. *Calls upon* Member States and the international community to raise awareness of good public health practices, including through education and the mass media;

3. *Emphasizes* the importance of active international cooperation in the control of infectious diseases, based on the principles of mutual respect and equality, with a view to strengthening capacity-building in public health, especially in developing countries, including through the exchange of information and the sharing of experience, as well as research and training programmes focusing on surveillance, prevention, control, response, and care and treatment in respect of infectious diseases, and vaccines against them;

4. *Calls* for the improvement of the global public health preparedness and response systems, including systems of prevention and monitoring of infectious diseases, to better cope with major diseases, including in cases of global outbreaks of new diseases;

5. *Encourages* Member States to participate actively in the verification and validation of surveillance data and information concerning public health emergencies of international concern and, in close collaboration with the World Health Organization, to exchange information and experience in a timely and open manner on epidemics and the prevention and control of emerging and re-emerging infectious diseases that pose a risk to global public health;

6. *Invites* the regional commissions of the Economic and Social Council, as appropriate, to cooperate closely with Member States, the private sector and civil society, when requested, in their capacity-building in public health, as well as in regional cooperation to diminish and eliminate the deleterious impact of major infectious diseases;

7. *Encourages* Member States, as well as United Nations agencies, bodies, funds and programmes, in accordance with their respective mandates, to continue to address public health concerns in their development activities and programmes, and to actively support capacity-building in global public health and health care institutions;

8. *Requests* the Secretary-General to include observations on the issue of enhancing capacity-building in global public health in his report on the follow-up to the outcome of the Millennium Summit of the United Nations to be submitted to the General Assembly at its fifty-ninth session.

Road safety

In a letter of 28 January [A/57/235], Oman requested the inclusion of an additional item in the agenda in the fifty-seventh session of the General Assembly on the global road safety crisis; an explanatory memorandum included facts about road traffic injuries.

WHO designated "Safe roads" as the theme of World Health Day 2004, to be observed on 7 April of that year.

GENERAL ASSEMBLY ACTION (May)

On 22 May [meeting 86], the General Assembly adopted **resolution 57/309** [draft: A/57/L.77 & Add.1] without vote [agenda item 169].

Global road safety crisis

The General Assembly,

Noting the rapid increase in road traffic deaths, injuries and disabilities globally,

Recognizing the disproportionate fatality rate in developing countries,

Taking note of the negative impact of road traffic injuries on national and global economies,

Affirming the need for a worldwide effort to raise awareness of the importance of road safety as a public policy issue, especially through education and the dissemination of information,

Convinced that responsibility for road safety rests at the local, municipal and national levels,

Affirming that the road safety crisis has multiple dimensions requiring collaborative efforts at all levels, including through appropriate public health education programmes,

1. *Welcomes* the efforts of the World Health Organization to designate "Safe roads" as the theme of World Health Day 2004, to be observed on 7 April of that year, and to undertake the development of a world report on road traffic injury prevention, to be issued in April 2004;

2. *Encourages* Governments and civil society to raise awareness of the widespread problem of preventable road traffic deaths and injuries, targeting especially the young in educational establishments;

3. *Urges* all Governments to promulgate and to continue to enforce existing traffic laws;

4. *Requests* the Secretary-General to submit a report to the General Assembly on the global road safety crisis, through the appropriate United Nations body, taking into consideration the views expressed by Member States and the relevant organs and agencies within the United Nations system, for consideration by the Assembly at its fifty-eighth session.

Report of Secretary-General. In response to resolution 57/309 (above), the Secretary-General submitted an August report [A/58/228] on the global road safety crisis, prepared by WHO and revised to include comments from Secretariat departments and other UN system entities. It emphasized that road traffic injuries posed a global public health crisis requiring action at the national and international levels. The report discussed the magnitude of the problem; who was affected; the social and economic consequences of road traffic injuries; the lack of information to assess road safety; risk factors and determinants that predisposed certain groups to vulnerability to road traffic injuries; and successful intervention strategies.

An estimated 1.26 million people worldwide died as a result of road traffic injuries in 2000; such injuries accounted for 2.2 per cent of global mortality and were responsible for 25 per cent of all deaths due to injury. Road traffic crashes ranked as the ninth leading cause of mortality and morbidity, accounting for 2.8 per cent of all global deaths and disability. WHO projections suggested that by 2020 road traffic injuries could rank third among causes of death and disability, ahead of malaria, tuberculosis and HIV/AIDS. More than a third—435,000—of annual road crash deaths in 2000 occurred in South-East Asia, but Africa had the highest road traffic death rate, at 28 deaths per 100,000 people. Road traffic injuries affected disproportionately the poor in developing countries, where the majority of road crash victims were vulnerable road users (pedestrians, cyclists, children, passengers). In developed countries, children of lower socio-economic status were more likely to die in collisions involving pedestrians than their more affluent counterparts. Poorer socio-economic groups also had less access to medical services, leading to disparities in chances of recovery or survival. More than 50 per cent of global mortality due to road traffic injury occurred among young adults, aged 15 to 44. The road traffic injury mortality rate for males was almost three times as high as it was for females.

The report identified a number of risk factors and determinants that affected the probability of a road traffic injury, which could be modified by intervention, including speeding; alcohol use; the use of helmets for motorbike riders; safety devices, such as seat belts and child restraints; access to trauma care; road design and roadway environment; implementation of road safety standards; enforcement of traffic safety regulations; improving vehicle safety; and the lack of vehicle inspection programmes.

The report made a series of recommendations to the General Assembly to address the global road safety crisis, particularly regarding the identification of a coordinating body within the UN system; the assessment by Member States of their road traffic safety problem and situation; increased funding for the inclusion of the problem of road traffic injuries in priority programmes in UN organizations, especially for low- and middle-income countries; and the development and implementation of a national strategy for Member States on road traffic injury prevention and appropriate action plans, and multisectoral collaboration between various ministries and sectors. It also proposed that the Assembly call on the UN regional commissions to expand their work programmes to include activities on: promoting regional best practices regarding matters related to road safety; assisting Member States in drawing up road safety standards appropriate to their setting; supporting human and technical capacity-building programmes pertaining to road safety; developing and implementing sustainable transport policies that incorporated road safety; adopting multisectoral approaches to road safety with clear targets and appropriate management structures; and developing short- and medium-term strategies to address road safety priorities.

GENERAL ASSEMBLY ACTION (November)

On 5 November [meeting 56], the General Assembly adopted **resolution 58/9** [draft: A/58/L.3/Rev.1 & Add.1] without vote [agenda item 160].

Global road safety crisis

The General Assembly,

Recalling its resolution 57/309 of 22 May 2003,

Welcoming the report of the Secretary-General on the global road safety crisis,

Expressing great concern at the rapid increase, particularly in developing countries, in traffic fatalities and injuries worldwide, which accounted for an estimated 1.26 million deaths in 2000 and which disproportionately affect people in low- and middle-income countries, and also expressing concern at the economic costs of road traffic injuries, which amount to 518 billion United States dollars per annum worldwide, with developing countries bearing 100 billion dollars of the cost,

Convinced that road traffic injuries are a major public health problem requiring concerted multisectoral efforts for effective and sustainable prevention,

Affirming the need for a worldwide effort to raise awareness about the health impact and social and economic costs of injuries caused by road traffic accidents,

Recognizing that effective action requires strong political commitment, in particular at the national but also at the international level,

Recognizing also that road traffic injuries are a preventable and treatable problem,

Emphasizing the need for the private sector and relevant non-governmental organizations to participate actively in promoting road traffic safety,

Convinced that road safety requires partnerships, bridging many sectors of society, to promote and facilitate efforts to prevent road traffic injuries,

Convinced also that responsibility for road safety rests at the local, municipal and national levels, and recognizing that many developing countries have limited capacities to address these issues,

Recognizing the importance of further strengthening the efforts of developing countries to build capacities in the field of road safety, and of providing financial and technical support for those efforts,

Welcoming the efforts of the relevant United Nations agencies and many other organizations in promoting road traffic safety,

Commending the World Health Organization for its important work, and welcoming the selection of the theme "Road safety" for the observance of World Health Day on 7 April 2004, when the World Health Organization will release its *World Report on Road Traffic Injury Prevention*,

1. *Decides* to hold a plenary meeting of the General Assembly on 14 April 2004 in connection with World Health Day and the launching of the *World Report on Road Traffic Injury Prevention* to increase awareness at a high level of the magnitude of the road traffic injury problem, and invites Governments to participate, as appropriate;

2. *Invites* the President of the General Assembly, the Secretary-General, the Director-General of the World Health Organization, the President of the World Bank, the Executive Director of the United Nations Children's Fund and the Administrator of the United Nations Development Programme to address the Assembly;

3. *Invites* the Economic and Social Council, working with other relevant organizations and bodies of the United Nations system, and through its regional commissions, to facilitate the exchange of information on best road traffic safety practices and the development of recommendations for road traffic injury control;

4. *Requests* the Department of Public Information of the Secretariat to organize a meeting of experts, the private sector, relevant non-governmental organizations, members of civil society and other interested parties, including the media, on the morning of 15 April 2004, in conjunction with the plenary meeting, to raise awareness and exchange information on best road practices;

5. *Underlines* the need for international cooperation to deal with issues of road safety;

6. *Requests* the Secretary-General, through an appropriate United Nations body, to submit a report to the General Assembly at its sixtieth session on the progress made in improving global road safety and the issues referred to in the present resolution, also taking into consideration the views expressed during the meetings on 14 and 15 April 2004;

7. *Decides* to include in the provisional agenda of its sixtieth session the item entitled "Global road safety crisis".

On 23 December, the General Assembly decided that the agenda item on the global road safety crisis would remain for consideration at the resumed fifty-eighth (2004) session (**decision 58/565**).

Food and agriculture

Food aid

World Food Programme

In July, the Economic and Social Council had before it two reports pertaining to the work of the World Food Programme (WFP): the annual report of the Executive Director of WFP for 2002 [E/2003/14] and a report of the WFP Executive Board containing the decisions and recommendations of its 2002 sessions [E/2003/36]. The Council, by **decision 2003/225** of 11 July, took note of the reports.

The WFP Executive Board decided on organizational and programme matters and approved a number of projects at its 2003 sessions [E/2004/36], all held in Rome: first regular session (5-7 February), annual session (28-30 May), second regular session (2-3 June) and third regular session (20-24 October). In October, the Board approved the WFP 2004-2005 biennial management plan and the WFP strategic plan (2004-2007), which outlined five core strategic priorities and identified nine management priority areas.

WFP activities

According to the WFP annual performance report for 2003 [WFP/EB.A/2004/4-A & Corr.1], WFP reached a record 104.2 million people in 81 countries in 2003, a 44.7 per cent increase from the 72 million assisted in 2002. Of those assisted, 61.2 million benefited from emergency operations, 26.8 million benefited from protracted relief and recovery operations and 16.2 million benefited from development programmes. The beneficiaries included 55.5 million children, including 15.2 million assisted through school feeding programmes; 53.5 million women and girls, representing 51.3 per cent of all beneficiaries; and 2.6 million refugees and 5.7 million internally displaced persons.

WFP delivered 6 million tons of food, including more than 2 million tons in Iraq alone; the volume of food shipped increased by 57 per cent compared to 2002.

Global food aid deliveries amounted to 10.2 million tons in 2003, an increase of about 5.2 per cent from the 9.7 million tons delivered in 2002. Bilateral deliveries accounted for 22.4 per cent of the total, a 9.7 per cent decrease from the previous year's 32.1 per cent. Nearly 67 per cent of the food aid delivered for the year was provided as relief aid to people affected by man-made or natural emergency situations. WFP's relief operation in Iraq was by far the largest: 2.1 million tons of food from donor contributions and from the oil-for-food programme reached the entire Iraqi population of approximately 27 million people. (For more information on the situation in Iraq in 2003, see p. 315.)

The portion of food aid channelled multilaterally increased from 39 per cent in 2002 to 49 per cent in 2003. WFP initiated 56 new operational activities and four new country programmes worldwide.

At the regional level, sub-Saharan Africa received the largest share of WFP assistance, with 48.8 per cent of operational expenditures spent in 40 countries; the Middle East and North Africa received 37.1 per cent for nine countries; Asia, 12.3 per cent for 19 countries; Eastern Europe and the Commonwealth of Independent States, 2.3 per cent for nine countries; and Latin America and the Caribbean, 1.7 per cent for 11 countries.

Administrative and financial matters

The first joint session of the Executive Boards of UNDP/UNFPA and UNICEF, with the participation of WFP (New York, 6 and 9 June) [E/2003/35], discussed the simplification and harmonization process undertaken by the United Nations Development Group (UNDG) Executive Committee; the transition from relief to development; building on the Monterrey Consensus, reached at the 2002 International Conference on Financing for Development [YUN 2002, p. 953]; the five-year evaluation of UNAIDS, which was concluded in 2002 [ibid., p. 1220]; and the implementation in Nepal of the MDGs, adopted in General Assembly resolution 55/2 [YUN 2000, p. 49].

Resources and financing

WFP operational expenditures for 2003 amounted to an all-time high of $3.3 billion for development and relief activities in the least developed countries and low-income food-deficit countries [WFP/EB.A/2004/4-A & Corr.1]. Contributions totalled a record $2.6 billion [E/2004/14], a 43 per cent increase over 2002. More than half of WFP's resources continued to be provided by the United States, which contributed $1.4 billion. Of the total contributed, $1.4 billion went to emergency operations, $240 million to development activities and $824 million to protracted relief and recovery operations.

Food security

Follow-up to 1996 World Food Summit

By a June note [E/2003/87], the Director-General of the Food and Agriculture Organization of the United Nations (FAO) transmitted to the Economic and Social Council a report prepared by FAO's Committee on World Food Security on progress made to implement the Plan of Action adopted at the 1996 World Food Summit [YUN 1996, p. 1129]. The report highlighted linkages with the coordinated and integrated follow-up to major UN conferences and summits. It consisted of extracts from a number of Committee reports, including the Declaration of the 2002 World Food Summit: five years later [YUN 2002, p. 1225], which, among other things, called on the international community to fulfil the pledge made at the 1996 Summit to reduce the number of hungry by half, to about 400 million, by 2015. The report also contained extracts from Committee decisions regarding a 2000 review of the first cluster of Plan of Action commitments, relating to people-centred objectives, and a 2002 review of the second cluster, consisting of commitments related to development-centred activities. Based on its findings and conclusions, the Committee made recommendations to implement the Plan of Action by Governments, the international community, international institutions, and FAO and its secretariat. National reports showed that countries had policies and programmes in place to implement the Plan, but the specific impact of each policy in improving food security and reducing the number of undernourished was seldom articulated in quantitative terms, making an analysis of progress difficult. A limited number of countries had succeeded in reducing the number of undernourished; in a large number of countries, the number of undernourished was growing.

On 16 July (**decision 2003/227**), the Council took note of the report.

CEB consideration. The CEB High-level Committee on Programmes (HLCP) considered the issue of linkages between HIV/AIDS and food security and governance (see p. 1250) at its fifth session (Rome, 26-27 March) [CEB/2003/4], at its first intersessional meeting of 2003 (Geneva, 2 July) [CEB/2003/6] and at its sixth session (Rome, 18-19 September) [CEB/2003/7]. Over the course of the meetings, HLCP prepared an analytical policy paper on the UN response to the threats of food insecurity, weakened capacity for governance and AIDS. CEB, at its second regular session of 2003 (New York, 31 October–1 November) [CEB/2003/2], endorsed the general analysis and programming approach and the series of programmatic and institutional actions set out in the paper, and concurred with the thrust of its recommendations. HLCP, at its second intersessional meeting of 2003 (New York, 3 November) [CEB/2003/8], invited UNDG to report on progress in implementing the actions contained in the paper to the Committee's February 2004 session.

International Year of Rice (2004)

FAO continued to coordinate preparations for the International Year of Rice in 2004, declared by the General Assembly in resolution 57/162 [YUN 2002, p. 1226] as a major international effort to increase rice production. A meeting of the Steering Committee of the International Rice Commission on the International Year of Rice (Rome, 17 January) discussed a proposed road map for the Year and the terms of reference and membership of the FAO Organizing Committee. On 30 October, FAO's secretariat for the Year produced a concept paper, with inputs from members of the Organizing Committee and participants of the international planning and coordination meeting for the Year (Rome, 6-7

March), which discussed the background and history of the Year, aspects of rice-based systems, challenges and opportunities for the Year and a conceptual framework for implementation.

The Year was officially launched at UN Headquarters in New York on 31 October.

Nutrition

Standing Committee on Nutrition

The thirtieth session of the UN System Standing Committee on Nutrition (SCN) (Chennai, India, 3-7 March) reviewed reports of working groups on nutrition throughout the life cycle; nutrition in emergencies; nutrition and HIV/AIDS; micronutrients; nutrition, ethics and human rights; capacity development in food and nutrition; the nutrition of school-age children; breastfeeding and complementary feeding; and household food security. During the session, a task force formed to draft an SCN position statement on nutrition and the MDGs reported to the Committee. The position statement would set out the role that nutrition improvement played in achieving the MDGs and would cover nutrition interventions and enabling environmental factors. On 4 March, the M. S. Swaminathan Research Foundation hosted a symposium on mainstreaming nutrition to improve development outcomes.

Based on a request from the twenty-ninth (2002) SCN session [YUN 2002, p. 1226], an international technical working group was formed to explore current information on the impact of iron deficiency in children less than 2 years of age and to recommend strategies to eliminate it in children of that age group by 2008.

UNU activities

The United Nations University Food and Nutrition Programme for Human and Social Development (UNU-FNP) assisted developing regions to enhance individual, organizational and institutional capacity, carried out coordinated global research activities and served as the academic arm for the UN system in areas of food and nutrition that were best addressed in a non-regulatory, non-normative environment.

In 2003, UNU-FNP activities included the Latin America Initiative, which focused on leadership training and leveraging of funds in the region to strengthen local and regional capacity for action in health/nutrition promotion, micronutrient fortification, and prevention of nutrition-related chronic diseases and other forms of malnutrition. Regarding its African Initiative, UNU-FNP completed the initial two-year implementation phase of the 10-year action plans for strengthening capacity in the area of food and nutrition, and an assessment of lessons learned and action plan updates were under way. Capacity had been strengthened in the areas of HIV and nutrition and the enhancement of advocacy skills. At the thirtieth SCN session (see above), the Task Force for Capacity Strengthening in Nutrition in Asia presented its 10-year plan. A five-year grant of $1 million per year from the Ellison Medical Foundation would support a fellowship programme coordinated with UNU's capacity development efforts. The programme, to be administered by the International Nutrition Foundation, had obligated funds for the first two years and would be limited to about 16 developing country institutions recognized as leaders in their respective regions; the fellowships would be used to help develop or maintain a critical mass of well-trained personnel. The data collection phase of the Multi-Country Growth Reference Study was completed, with studies in six countries involving some 8,000 children; construction of the world's first truly international growth standards had begun.

Under the University's capacity development training programme, cooperation between UNU and FAO in the area of nutrition data management continued with a three-week course on production and the use of food composition data in nutrition (Wageningen, Netherlands, October), with the participation of seven UNU fellows. Five fellows began a year-long training programme in food science and technology organized by UNU at the National Food Research Institute in Tsukuba, Japan; five others completed their training and received grants to return to their home countries for follow-up research projects. UNU also awarded a fellowship to one student from the Sudan for a 10-month course at the Central Food Technological Research Institute in Mysore, India. In the degree-oriented programme, one UNU fellow was admitted to the two-year Master's Programme in Applied Human Nutrition offered by the University of Nairobi. UNU continued its quarterly publication of the *Food and Nutrition Bulletin* and the *Journal of Food Composition and Analysis*.

Chapter XIV

International Drug Control

During 2003, the United Nations, through the Commission on Narcotic Drugs, the International Narcotics Control Board (INCB) and the United Nations Office on Drugs and Crime (UNODC), reaffirmed its commitment to strengthen international cooperation and increase efforts to counter the world drug problem. Drug control activities throughout the UN system focused mainly on implementation of the 1999 Action Plan for the Implementation of the Declaration on the Guiding Principles of Drug Demand Reduction, which served as a guide for Member States in adopting strategies and programmes for reducing illicit drug demand in order to achieve significant results by 2008.

UNODC assisted States in complying with international drug control treaties and supported the international community in achieving the objectives of the measures adopted by the General Assembly at its 1998 special session on the world drug problem. Through its technical cooperation programmes, UNODC promoted drug control activities at the national, regional and international levels and initiatives to suppress drug trafficking, prevent drug abuse and strengthen treatment and rehabilitation services. It supported national efforts to reduce or eliminate illicit cultivation of opium poppy, coca bush and cannabis through alternative development projects and to estimate the extent of illicit crop cultivation in key illicit production areas.

The Commission on Narcotic Drugs—the main UN policy-making body dealing with drug control—recommended a number of draft resolutions to the Economic and Social Council and adopted resolutions on such issues as the reduction of demand for illicit drugs and prevention of drug abuse, illicit drug trafficking and supply, implementation of the international drug control treaties, administrative and budgetary matters and strengthening UN machinery for international drug control. In July, the Council urged Governments to continue contributing to the maintenance of a balance between the licit supply of and demand for opiate raw materials for medical and scientific purposes.

INCB reviewed the impact of illicit drugs on economic development and continued to oversee the implementation of the three major international drug control conventions, to analyse the drug situation worldwide and to draw Governments' attention to weaknesses in national control and treaty compliance, making suggestions and recommendations for improvements at the national and international levels.

Follow-up to the twentieth special session

In response to General Assembly resolution 57/174 [YUN 2002, p. 1229], the Secretary-General, in an August report [A/58/253], presented a quinquennial evaluation of the implementation of the outcome of the Assembly's twentieth special session on countering the world drug problem [YUN 1998, p. 1135], including the Action Plan for the Implementation of the Declaration on the Guiding Principles of Drug Demand Reduction, adopted by the Assembly in resolution 54/132 [YUN 1999, p. 1157]. The report reviewed the 2003 ministerial segment of the Commission on Narcotic Drugs (see p. 1263); the adoption of national drug control strategies and plans; the Action Plan for implementing the Declaration on the Guiding Principles; the Action Plan against Illicit Manufacture, Trafficking and Abuse of Amphetamine-type Stimulants and Their Precursors, adopted by Assembly resolution S-20/4 A [YUN 1998, p. 1139]; countering money-laundering linked to drug trafficking; the Action Plan on International Cooperation on the Eradication of Illicit Drug Crops and on Alternative Development, adopted by Assembly resolution S-20/4 E [ibid., p. 1148]; judicial cooperation; and the control of precursors. The Secretary-General concluded that positive developments in countering the drug problem were mixed with some alarming signals. He noted that, while heroin and cocaine abuse had stabilized or declined in some countries, trends in synthetic drugs were worrying, with illicit manufacture spreading beyond the traditional centres in North America, Europe and East Asia. Cannabis abuse was also on the rise. On the supply side, illicit coca cultivation was declining, but the total output volume of illicitly cultivated opium poppy remained stable.

The number of producing countries had been reduced significantly, reflecting the positive impact of alternative development programmes, as in Pakistan and Thailand. The Secretary-General asserted that drug control policy, demand reduction, alternative development and international cooperation had yielded positive results in countering the drug problem.

In February, the UNODC Executive Director submitted his second biennial report on the implementation of the outcome of the Assembly's special session [E/CN.7/2003/2 & Add.1-6]. The report, prepared pursuant to Commission resolutions 42/11 [YUN 1999, p. 1191] and 44/2 [YUN 2001, p. 1143], was based on an analysis of information received from States. It reviewed national, regional and global efforts to counter the world drug problem, identified the major difficulties faced by Governments and provided guidance as to the areas requiring action.

In July [A/58/124], the Commission on Narcotic Drugs, in response to Assembly resolutions 55/65 [YUN 2000, p. 1175] and 56/124 [YUN 2001, p. 1144], reported on progress achieved in meeting the goals and targets set out in the Political Declaration, adopted at the Assembly's special session in resolution S-20/2 [YUN 1998, p. 1136], based on an evaluation conducted by the Commission during a ministerial segment at its forty-sixth session (Vienna, 16-17 April). The Commission adopted a Joint Ministerial Statement, in which it recognized that Member States' efforts in implementing the action plans and measures adopted by the Assembly were uneven, and made recommendations for the period 2003-2007. The report also contained the outcomes of round-table discussions held during the segment on challenges, new trends and patterns of the world drug problem; countering illicit drug supply; strengthening international cooperation, based on the principle of shared responsibility; and demand reduction and preventive policies. A Secretariat note [E/CN.7/2003/3] provided information on the substantive organization of the Commission's ministerial segment.

Conference on drug routes. At the initiative of France, the Foreign Ministers of 55 countries seriously affected by the traffic of opium and heroin produced in Afghanistan and originating from Central and South-West Asia attended the Conference on Drug Routes from Central Asia to Europe (Paris, 21-22 May) [S/2003/641]. The Conference adopted the Paris Statement, which addressed many facets of the issue.

GENERAL ASSEMBLY ACTION

On 22 December [meeting 77], the General Assembly, on the recommendation of the Third (Social, Humanitarian and Cultural) Committee [A/58/500], adopted **resolution 58/141** without vote [agenda item 109].

International cooperation against the world drug problem

The General Assembly,

Recalling the United Nations Millennium Declaration, its resolution 57/174 of 18 December 2002 and its other previous resolutions,

Reaffirming its commitment to the outcome of the twentieth special session of the General Assembly, devoted to countering the world drug problem together, held in New York from 8 to 10 June 1998, and welcoming the continuing determination of Governments to overcome the world drug problem by a full and balanced application of national, regional and international strategies to reduce the demand for, production of and trafficking in illicit drugs,

Reaffirming the importance of the commitments of Member States in meeting the objectives targeted for 2003 and 2008, as set out in the Political Declaration adopted by the General Assembly at the twentieth special session, and welcoming the guidelines and elements recommended by the Commission on Narcotic Drugs to the Executive Director of the United Nations International Drug Control Programme for the preparation of subsequent reports on the follow-up to the twentieth special session,

Emphasizing the importance of the Action Plan for the Implementation of the Declaration on the Guiding Principles of Drug Demand Reduction, which introduces a new global approach balanced between illicit supply and demand reduction, under the principle of shared responsibility, and of the Action Plan on International Cooperation on the Eradication of Illicit Drug Crops and on Alternative Development, which recognizes the importance of supply reduction as an integral part of a balanced drug control strategy,

Recognizing the efforts of all countries, in particular those that produce narcotic drugs for scientific and medical purposes, and of the International Narcotics Control Board in preventing the diversion of such substances to illicit markets and in maintaining production at a level consistent with licit demand, in line with the Single Convention on Narcotic Drugs of 1961 and the Convention on Psychotropic Substances of 1971,

Aware that progress has been uneven in meeting the goals set in the Political Declaration, as also reflected in the biennial reports of the Executive Director of the United Nations Office on Drugs and Crime, and recognizing that the drug problem is still a global challenge that constitutes a serious threat to public health and safety and the well-being of humankind, in particular children and young people, and that it undermines socio-economic and political stability and sustainable development, including efforts to reduce poverty, and causes violence and crime, including in urban areas,

Deeply concerned by the serious challenges and threats posed by the continuing links between illicit drug trafficking and terrorism and other national and transnational criminal activities, such as trafficking in human beings, especially women and children, money-laundering, corruption and trafficking in arms and chemical precursors, and reaffirming that strong and effective international cooperation is needed to counter these threats,

Gravely concerned about policies and activities in favour of the legalization of illicit narcotic drugs and psychotropic substances that are not in accordance with the international drug control treaties and that might jeopardize the international drug control regime,

Acknowledging that international cooperation in countering drug abuse and illicit production and trafficking has shown that positive results can be achieved through sustained and collective efforts, and expressing its appreciation for the initiatives in this regard,

Welcoming the holding of the ministerial segment of the forty-sixth session of the Commission on Narcotic Drugs in Vienna on 16 and 17 April 2003,

I

Respect for the principles enshrined in the Charter of the United Nations and international law in countering the world drug problem

1. *Reaffirms* that countering the world drug problem is a common and shared responsibility that must be addressed in a multilateral setting, requires an integrated and balanced approach, and must be carried out in full conformity with the purposes and principles of the Charter of the United Nations and international law, and in particular with full respect for the sovereignty and territorial integrity of States, the principle of non-intervention in the internal affairs of States and all human rights and fundamental freedoms, and on the basis of the principles of equal rights and mutual respect;

2. *Urges* all States to ratify or accede to and implement all the provisions of the Single Convention on Narcotic Drugs of 1961 as amended by the 1972 Protocol, the Convention on Psychotropic Substances of 1971 and the United Nations Convention against Illicit Traffic in Narcotic Drugs and Psychotropic Substances of 1988;

II

International cooperation to counter the world drug problem and follow-up to the twentieth special session

1. *Reaffirms* the Joint Ministerial Statement and further measures to implement the action plans emanating from the twentieth special session of the General Assembly, adopted during the ministerial segment of the forty-sixth session of the Commission on Narcotic Drugs, which emphasizes that the world drug problem must be addressed in multilateral, regional, bilateral and national settings and that, in order to succeed, action to counter it has to involve all Member States, that action must be supported by strong international and development cooperation and must be further included in national development priorities, and that it requires a balance between supply reduction and demand reduction, as well as a comprehensive strategy that combines alternative development, including, as appropriate, preventive alternative development, eradication, interdiction, law enforcement, prevention, treatment and rehabilitation as well as education;

2. *Calls upon* all relevant actors to continue their close cooperation with Governments in promoting and implementing the outcome of the twentieth special session and of the ministerial segment of the forty-sixth session of the Commission on Narcotic Drugs;

National drug control strategies

3. *Stresses* that, in order to be able to further develop sound, evidence-based drug control policies, data collection and analysis and evaluation of the results of ongoing policies are essential tools;

Demand reduction

4. *Urges* all Member States to implement the Action Plan for the Implementation of the Declaration on the Guiding Principles of Drug Demand Reduction and to strengthen their national efforts to counter the abuse of illicit drugs in their population, in particular among children and young people, noting with concern the increasing levels of drug abuse among them;

5. *Urges* States, in order to achieve a significant and measurable reduction of drug abuse by 2008:

(a) To further implement comprehensive demand reduction policies and programmes, including research, covering all drugs under international control, in order to raise public awareness of the drug problem, paying special attention to prevention and education and providing, especially to young people and others at risk, information on developing life skills, making healthy choices and engaging in drug-free activities;

(b) To further develop and implement comprehensive demand reduction policies, including risk reduction activities, that are in line with sound medical practice and the international drug control treaties and that reduce the adverse health and social consequences of drug abuse, and to provide a wide range of comprehensive services for the treatment, rehabilitation and social reintegration of drug abusers, with appropriate resources being devoted to such services, since social exclusion constitutes an important risk factor for drug abuse;

(c) To enhance early intervention programmes that dissuade children and young people from the use of illicit drugs, including polydrug use and the recreational use of substances such as cannabis and synthetic drugs, especially amphetamine-type stimulants, and to encourage the active participation of the younger generation in campaigns against drug abuse;

(d) To provide a comprehensive range of services for preventing the transmission of HIV/AIDS and other infectious diseases associated with drug abuse, including education, counselling and drug abuse treatment, and in particular to assist developing countries in their efforts to deal with these issues;

Illicit synthetic drugs

6. *Urges* States to renew their efforts, at the national, regional and international levels, to implement the comprehensive measures covered in the Action Plan against Illicit Manufacture, Trafficking and Abuse of Amphetamine-type Stimulants and Their Precursors, to make special efforts to counter the abuse and recreational use of amphetamine-type stimulants, especially by young people, and to disseminate information on the adverse health, social and economic consequences of such abuse;

Control of precursors

7. *Encourages* States:

(a) To establish or strengthen mechanisms for making the most effective use of existing systems and for ensuring strict control of chemical precursors used to manufacture illicit drugs;

(b) To support international operations aimed at preventing the diversion of chemical precursors used in the illicit manufacture of cocaine, heroin and amphetamine-type stimulants by exchanging information with other States and conducting timely joint law enforcement operations, including the use of controlled deliveries;

(c) To further international cooperation in the implementation of article 12, on control of precursors, of the United Nations Convention against Illicit Traffic in Narcotic Drugs and Psychotropic Substances of 1988, in close cooperation with the International Narcotics Control Board, and the measures agreed upon at the twentieth special session;

Judicial cooperation

8. *Calls upon* all States to strengthen international cooperation among judicial and law enforcement authorities at all levels in order to prevent and combat illicit drug trafficking and to share and promote best operational practices in order to interdict illicit drug trafficking, including by establishing and strengthening regional mechanisms, providing technical assistance and establishing effective methods for cooperation, in particular in the areas of air, maritime and port control;

Countering money-laundering

9. *Urges* States to strengthen action, in particular international cooperation and technical assistance aimed at preventing and combating the laundering of proceeds derived from drug trafficking and related criminal activities, with the support of the United Nations system, international institutions such as the World Bank and regional development banks, to develop and strengthen comprehensive international regimes to combat money-laundering, and to improve information-sharing among financial institutions and agencies in charge of preventing and detecting the laundering of those proceeds;

10. *Calls upon* States to consider including provisions in their national drug control plans for the establishment of national networks to enhance their respective capabilities to prevent, monitor, control and suppress serious offences connected with money-laundering and the financing of terrorist acts, and in general to counter all acts of transnational organized crime, and to supplement existing regional and international networks dealing with money-laundering;

International cooperation in illicit crop eradication and alternative development

11. *Calls upon* States, where appropriate:

(a) To enhance support, including, where appropriate, through the provision of new and additional financial resources, for alternative development and elimination programmes undertaken by countries affected by the illicit cultivation of cannabis, especially in Africa, of opium poppy and of coca bush, in particular national programmes that seek to reduce social marginalization and promote sustainable economic development;

(b) To enhance joint strategies, through international and regional cooperation, to strengthen, including by training and education, alternative development, eradication and interdiction capacity, with the aim of eliminating illicit crop cultivation;

(c) To encourage international cooperation, including, as appropriate, preventive alternative development, to prevent illicit crop cultivation from emerging in or being relocated to other areas;

(d) To provide, in accordance with the principle of shared responsibility, greater access to their markets for products of alternative development programmes, which are necessary for the creation of employment and the eradication of poverty;

(e) To establish or reinforce, where appropriate, national mechanisms to monitor and verify illicit crops;

(f) To continue to contribute to the maintenance of a balance between the licit supply of and demand for opiate raw materials used for medical and scientific purposes and to cooperate in preventing the proliferation of sources of production of opiate raw materials;

12. *Welcomes* the adoption by the Transitional Government of Afghanistan of a national drug strategy, and notes the need for continued coordination with the international efforts;

13. *Recommends* that adequate help be provided to Afghanistan within the framework of the comprehensive international strategy, carried out, inter alia, under the auspices of the United Nations and through other multilateral forums, in support of the commitment of the Transitional Government of Afghanistan, including the strengthening of "security belts" in the region, and reaffirms that the response to this unique situation will not detract from the commitments and resources devoted to the fight against drugs in other parts of the world;

III

Action by the United Nations system

1. *Emphasizes* that the multidimensional nature of the world drug problem calls for the promotion of integration and coordination of drug control activities throughout the United Nations system, including in the follow-up to major United Nations conferences, as well as other relevant multilateral institutions and organizations;

2. *Reaffirms its resolve* to continue to strengthen the United Nations machinery for international drug control, in particular the Commission on Narcotic Drugs, the United Nations International Drug Control Programme and the International Narcotics Control Board, in order to enable them to fulfil their mandates, bearing in mind the recommendations contained in Economic and Social Council resolution 1999/30 of 28 July 1999 and the measures taken and recommendations adopted by the Commission on Narcotic Drugs at its forty-fourth, forty-fifth and forty-sixth sessions, aimed at the enhancement of its functioning, in particular in its resolutions 44/16 of 29 March 2001, 45/17 of 15 March 2002 and 46/8 of 15 April 2003;

3. *Encourages* the Commission on Narcotic Drugs, as the global coordinating body in international drug control and as the governing body of the United Nations International Drug Control Programme, and the International Narcotics Control Board to continue their useful work on the control of precursors and other chemicals used in the illicit manufacture of narcotic drugs and psychotropic substances;

4. *Notes* that the International Narcotics Control Board needs sufficient resources to carry out all its mandates, and therefore urges Member States to commit themselves in a common effort to assigning adequate and sufficient budgetary resources to the Board, in accordance with Economic and Social Council resolution 1996/20 of 23 July 1996, and emphasizes the need to maintain its capacity, inter alia, through the provision of appropriate means by the Secretary-General and adequate technical support by the United Nations International Drug Control Programme, and calls for enhanced cooperation and understanding between Member States and the Board in order to enable it to implement all its mandates under the international drug control conventions;

5. *Welcomes* the efforts of the United Nations International Drug Control Programme to implement its mandate, and requests the Programme to continue:

(a) To strengthen dialogue with Member States and also to ensure continued improvement in management, so as to contribute to enhanced and sustainable programme delivery and further encourage the Executive Director to maximize the effectiveness of the Programme, inter alia, through the full implementation of Commission on Narcotic Drugs resolutions 44/16 and 45/17, in particular the recommendations contained therein;

(b) To strengthen cooperation with Member States and with United Nations programmes, funds and relevant agencies, as well as relevant regional organizations and agencies and non-governmental organizations, and to provide, on request, assistance in implementing the outcome of the twentieth special session;

(c) To increase its assistance, within the available voluntary resources, to countries that are deploying efforts to reduce illicit crop cultivation by, in particular, adopting alternative development programmes, and to explore new and innovative funding mechanisms;

(d) To allocate, while keeping the balance between supply and demand reduction programmes, adequate resources to allow it to fulfil its role in the implementation of the Action Plan for the Implementation of the Declaration on the Guiding Principles of Drug Demand Reduction, and support countries, upon their request, to further develop and implement drug demand reduction policies;

(e) To strengthen dialogue and cooperation with multilateral development banks and with international financial institutions so that they may undertake lending and programming activities related to drug control in interested and affected countries to implement the outcome of the twentieth special session, and to keep the Commission on Narcotic Drugs informed of further progress made in this area;

(f) To take into account the outcome of the twentieth special session, to include in its report on the illicit traffic in drugs an updated, objective and comprehensive assessment of worldwide trends in illicit traffic and transit in narcotic drugs and psychotropic substances, including methods and routes used, and to recommend ways and means of improving the capacity of States along those routes to address all aspects of the drug problem;

(g) To publish the *World Drug Report*, with comprehensive and balanced information about the world drug problem, and to seek additional extrabudgetary resources for its publication in all the official languages;

(h) To provide technical assistance, from available voluntary contributions for that purpose, to those States identified by relevant international bodies as the most affected by the transit of drugs, in particular developing countries in need of such assistance and support;

(i) To develop action-oriented strategies to assist Member States to implement the Action Plan for the Implementation of the Declaration, and to report to the Commission on Narcotic Drugs at its forty-seventh session on the follow-up to the Action Plan;

(j) To provide assistance, subject to the availability of resources, at the request of States and respecting fully their sovereignty and territorial integrity, and with the support of the United Nations Office for Outer Space Affairs and the European Space Agency, among others, in detecting on time the emergence or relocation of illicit crop cultivation;

6. *Welcomes* the holding in Paris, on 21 and 22 May 2003, of the Conference on Drug Routes from Central Asia to Europe, and encourages the United Nations Office on Drugs and Crime and other relevant international institutions to continue in their follow-up action on the recommendations of the Conference (the Paris Pact);

7. *Requests* the United Nations Office on Drugs and Crime, subject to the availability of resources and the Commission on Narcotic Drugs guidelines for the use of general-purpose funds, together with international financial institutions and the organizations involved in preventing and suppressing money-laundering and drug trafficking, to facilitate the provision of training and advice through technical cooperation in States, when requested, taking into account, inter alia, the recommendations on money-laundering and the financing of terrorism formulated by the Financial Action Task Force on Money Laundering and its regional groups;

8. *Urges* all Governments to provide the fullest possible financial and political support to the United Nations International Drug Control Programme by widening its donor base and increasing voluntary contributions, in particular general-purpose contributions, to enable it to continue, expand and strengthen its operational and technical cooperation activities, and recommends that a sufficient share of the regular budget of the United Nations be allocated to the Programme to enable it to fulfil its mandates and to work towards securing assured and predictable funding;

9. *Encourages* the meetings of Heads of National Drug Law Enforcement Agencies and of the Subcommission on Illicit Drug Traffic and Related Matters in the Near and Middle East of the Commission on Narcotic Drugs to continue to contribute to the strengthening of regional and international cooperation, taking into account the outcome of the twentieth special session and the ministerial segment of the forty-sixth session of the Commission on Narcotic Drugs;

10. *Calls upon* the relevant United Nations agencies and entities, other international organizations and international financial institutions, including regional development banks, to mainstream drug control issues into their programmes;

11. *Takes note* of the report of the Commission on Narcotic Drugs and the report of the Secretary-General, and, taking into account the promotion of in-

tegrated reporting, requests the Secretary-General to submit to the General Assembly at its fifty-ninth session a report on the implementation of the present resolution.

Money-laundering

On 22 July [meeting 44], the Economic and Social Council, on the recommendation of the Commission on Narcotic Drugs [E/2003/28/Rev.1], adopted **resolution 2003/36** without vote [agenda item 14 (d)].

Establishment of national networks to counter money-laundering in the framework of national and international drug control plans

The Economic and Social Council,

Bearing in mind the United Nations Convention against Illicit Traffic in Narcotic Drugs and Psychotropic Substances of 1988, the International Convention for the Suppression of the Financing of Terrorism, the United Nations Convention against Transnational Organized Crime and the Inter-American Convention against Terrorism,

Taking into account the Financial Action Task Force on Money Laundering and its regional groups,

Taking into account also the Political Declaration adopted by the General Assembly at its twentieth special session, devoted to countering the world drug problem together, which called for Member States to make special efforts against the laundering of money linked to drug trafficking and recommended that States adopt by the year 2003 national money-laundering legislation and programmes in accordance with the 1988 Convention, as well as the measures for countering money-laundering adopted at the twentieth special session,

Considering that multilateral action against the modern global phenomenon of transnational organized crime and the illicit activities connected with it, in particular drug trafficking, money-laundering, corruption and the financing of terrorism, represents a commitment by States that calls for shared responsibility and coordinated activities with a view to achieving a coherent global approach in accordance with multilateral instruments,

Recognizing that the laundering of proceeds derived from drug trafficking and other serious offences has increased throughout the world to become a global threat to the stability and security of the financial and commercial system, and even to government structures, and that concerted efforts by the international community are required in order to deal with the problems posed by organized crime and the proceeds derived from it,

Emphasizing the need for States to harmonize their legislation in order to ensure adequate coordination of their policies for preventing, monitoring, controlling and suppressing money-laundering and the financing of terrorism,

Recognizing that effective action to counter the problem of money-laundering will be possible only through international cooperation and the utilization of networked information systems that facilitate collaboration and the exchange of information between the relevant authorities of the States concerned,

Recognizing also the strategic necessity for States to have the appropriate infrastructure for analysis and financial investigation in order to combat money-laundering and the financing of transnational organized crime in a coordinated manner, using national, regional and international strategies,

Reiterating the importance of establishing and implementing national plans or strategies to combat the laundering of the proceeds of crime,

1. *Recommends* that States, in conformity with their legislation and in accordance with their capabilities, set up national networks to supplement existing regional and international networks dealing with money-laundering;

2. *Calls upon* States to consider including provisions in their national drug control plans for the establishment of national networks to enhance their respective capabilities to prevent, monitor, control and suppress serious offences connected with money-laundering and the financing of terrorist acts and, in general, to counter all transnational organized criminal acts;

3. *Requests* the United Nations Office on Drugs and Crime, subject to the availability of resources and the Commission on Narcotic Drugs guidelines for the use of general-purpose funds, together with international financial institutions and the organizations involved in preventing and suppressing money-laundering and drug trafficking, to facilitate the provision of training and advice through technical cooperation in States, when requested, taking into account, inter alia, the recommendations on money-laundering and the financing of terrorism formulated by the Financial Action Task Force on Money Laundering and its regional groups.

Conventions

In 2003, international efforts to control narcotic drugs were governed by three global conventions: the 1961 Single Convention on Narcotic Drugs [YUN 1961, p. 382], which, with some exceptions of detail, replaced earlier narcotics treaties and was amended in 1972 by a Protocol [YUN 1972, p. 397] intended to strengthen the role of the International Narcotics Control Board (INCB); the 1971 Convention on Psychotropic Substances [YUN 1971, p. 380]; and the 1988 United Nations Convention against Illicit Traffic in Narcotic Drugs and Psychotropic Substances [YUN 1988, p. 690].

As at 31 December 2003, 175 States were parties to the 1961 Convention, as amended by the 1972 Protocol. During the year, Algeria and Myanmar acceded to the Convention.

The number of parties to the 1971 Convention stood at 174 as at 31 December 2003, with the accession of Albania and Saint Lucia.

At year's end, 167 States and the European Community were parties to the 1988 Convention, with Mongolia acceding in 2003.

Commission action. At its forty-sixth session in April [E/2003/28/Rev.1], the Commission on Narcotic Drugs reviewed implementation of international drug control treaties. It had before it the INCB report covering 2002 [YUN 2002, p. 1235]; the 2002 INCB technical report on the implementation of article 12 of the 1988 Convention, entitled "Precursors and chemicals frequently used in the illicit manufacture of narcotic drugs and psychotropic substances" [ibid., p. 1236]; and a Secretariat note on changes in the scope of control of substances [E/CN.7/2003/12 & Add.1], which contained recommendations for Commission action and a proposal from the World Health Organization (WHO) to place amineptine in schedule II of the 1971 Convention.

Pursuant to its mandate under the 1961 Convention, as amended by the 1972 Protocol, the Commission called on Governments of producing countries to adhere to the Convention's provisions and prevent illicit production or diversion of opiate raw materials. Regarding implementation of article 12 of the 1988 Convention, the Commission noted the Board's overview of the global situation regarding control of precursor chemicals and its efforts to improve information exchange between Governments in order to prevent their diversion. Recognizing that the control of precursor chemicals was one of the most effective tools in addressing the illicit manufacture of amphetamine-type stimulants (ATS), the Commission urged Governments to support Project Prism [YUN 2002, p. 1235], an INCB initiative to address diversions of ATS precursors and materials and equipment used in their illicit manufacture. The Commission commended the Board for its efforts as the focal point for the exchange of information under Operation Purple and Operation Topaz, the international programmes focusing on potassium permanganate and acetic anhydride, respectively. Governments were urged to submit annual information to the Board.

On 8 April [E/2003/28/Rev.1 (dec. 46/1)], the Commission decided to include amineptine in schedule II of the 1971 Convention.

On 15 April [res. 46/4], the Commission called on Member States to implement the international treaties fully and to avoid adopting policies and measures facilitating access to drugs for non-medical or non-scientific purposes. It urged States to engage non-governmental organizations (NGOs) and other civil society organizations in their efforts to address the world drug problem. The Executive Director was requested to report in 2004.

INCB action. In its report covering 2003 [Sales No. E.04.XI.1], INCB called on States that had not done so to become parties to the 1961 Convention on Narcotic Drugs and to accede to or ratify the 1972 Protocol amending it. It reiterated its request to States to implement the 1971 Convention on Psychotropic Substances and become parties thereto. Noting that almost all of the world's major drug and chemical manufacturing, exporting and importing countries were parties to the 1988 Convention against Illicit Traffic in Narcotic Drugs and Psychotropic Substances, the Board called on States that had not done so to implement the Convention and become parties to it.

ECONOMIC AND SOCIAL COUNCIL ACTION

On 22 July [meeting 44], the Economic and Social Council, on the recommendation of the Commission on Narcotic Drugs [E/2003/28/Rev.1], adopted **resolution 2003/40** without vote [agenda item 14 (d)].

Demand for and supply of opiates for medical and scientific purposes

The Economic and Social Council,

Recalling its resolution 2002/20 of 24 July 2002 and previous relevant resolutions,

Emphasizing that the need to balance the global licit supply of opiates against the legitimate demand for opiates for medical and scientific purposes is central to the international strategy and policy of drug control,

Noting the fundamental need for international cooperation with the traditional supplier countries in drug control to ensure universal application of the provisions of the Single Convention on Narcotic Drugs of 1961 and that Convention as amended by the 1972 Protocol,

Reiterating that a balance between consumption and production of opiate raw materials was achieved in the past as a result of efforts made by the two traditional supplier countries, India and Turkey, together with other producer countries,

Expressing deep concern at the increase in the global production of opiate raw materials and the significant accumulation of stocks over the past few years as a consequence of the operation of market forces, which has the potential to upset the delicate balance between the licit supply of and demand for opiates for medical and scientific purposes,

Noting the importance of opiates in pain relief therapy as advocated by the World Health Organization,

Noting also that countries differ significantly in their level of consumption of narcotic drugs and that, in most developing countries, the use of narcotic drugs for medical purposes has remained at an extremely low level,

1. *Urges* all Governments to continue to contribute to the maintenance of a balance between the licit supply of and demand for opiate raw materials for medical and scientific purposes, the achievement of which would be facilitated by maintaining, insofar as their constitutional and legal systems permit, support to the traditional and legal supplier countries, and to cooperate in preventing the proliferation of sources of production of opiate raw materials;

2. *Urges* Governments of all producer countries to adhere strictly to the provisions of the Single Convention on Narcotic Drugs of 1961 and that Convention as amended by the 1972 Protocol, to take effective measures to prevent illicit production or diversion of opiate raw materials to illicit channels, especially when in-

creasing licit production, and welcomes the study carried out by the International Narcotics Control Board on the relative merits of different methods of producing opiate raw materials;

3. *Urges* Governments of consumer countries to assess their licit needs for opiate raw materials realistically and to communicate those needs to the International Narcotics Control Board in order to ensure easy supply, and requests the Governments of producer countries to ensure that their future production of opiate raw materials is adjusted to conform to the actual requirements for opiate raw materials worldwide, bearing in mind the current level of global stocks of opiate raw materials, and to cooperate in preventing the proliferation of sources of production of opiate raw materials;

4. *Commends* the International Narcotics Control Board for its efforts in monitoring the implementation of the relevant Economic and Social Council resolutions and, in particular:

(a) In urging the Governments concerned to adjust global production of opiate raw materials to a level corresponding to actual licit needs and to avoid unforeseen imbalances between the licit supply of and demand for opiates caused by the exportation of products manufactured from seized and confiscated drugs;

(b) In inviting the Governments concerned to ensure that opiates imported into their countries for medical and scientific use do not originate in countries that transform seized and confiscated drugs into licit opiates;

(c) In arranging informal meetings, during the sessions of the Commission on Narcotic Drugs, with the main States that import and produce opiate raw materials;

5. *Requests* the International Narcotics Control Board to continue its efforts in monitoring the implementation of the relevant Economic and Social Council resolutions in full compliance with the Single Convention on Narcotic Drugs of 1961 and with that Convention as amended by the 1972 Protocol;

6. *Requests* the Secretary-General to transmit the text of the present resolution to all Governments for consideration and implementation and to report to the Commission on Narcotic Drugs at its forty-seventh session on progress made in the implementation of the present resolution.

On the same day [meeting 44], the Council, on the recommendation of the Commission [E/2003/28/Rev.1], adopted **resolution 2003/41** without vote [agenda item 14 (d)].

Efforts to counter the trend towards the legalization of drugs for non-medical use

The Economic and Social Council,

Taking into account the policies adopted by organizations of the United Nations system concerning the Single Convention on Narcotic Drugs of 1961, that Convention as amended by the 1972 Protocol, the Convention on Psychotropic Substances of 1971, the United Nations Convention against Illicit Traffic in Narcotic Drugs and Psychotropic Substances of 1988 and the Convention on the Rights of the Child, in particular article 33 thereof,

Recalling the Political Declaration adopted by the General Assembly at its twentieth special session, devoted to countering the world drug problem together, the Declaration on the Guiding Principles of Drug Demand Reduction and the Action Plan for the Implementation of the Declaration on the Guiding Principles of Drug Demand Reduction,

Recalling also that narcotic drugs and psychotropic substances are controlled under the 1961 Convention, that Convention as amended by the 1972 Protocol and the 1971 Convention, which call for the States parties to those conventions to adopt all possible measures to limit the production, manufacture, export, import and distribution of, trade in and use and possession of those drugs for medical and scientific purposes if those States consider that to be the most appropriate means of protecting health and public welfare,

Conscious that increased availability of narcotic drugs and psychotropic substances, without the appropriate controls, could facilitate the diversion of those drugs,

Taking into account the reports of the International Narcotics Control Board for 2001 and 2002,

Bearing in mind that countering the world drug problem is a shared responsibility calling for coordinated action in conformity with the relevant multilateral instruments in force at the international level,

Concerned about the increasing levels of illicit drug consumption, in particular among children, young people and groups at risk of abusing narcotic drugs and psychotropic substances,

Concerned also about the trend towards the development of lenient policies relating to cannabis and other drugs that are not in accordance with international drug control treaties and about the fact that such trends may have a negative impact on efforts being made to eradicate cannabis cultivation and to combat drug trafficking,

1. *Invites* the International Narcotics Control Board to continue to monitor and report on the application of the international drug control treaties by Member States with regard to cannabis and other drugs;

2. *Requests* the United Nations International Drug Control Programme, in collaboration with the World Health Organization, to report on new trends with regard to cannabis.

Also on the same date [meeting 44], the Council, on the recommendation of the Commission [E/2003/28/Rev.1], adopted **resolution 2003/39** without vote [agenda item 14 (d)].

Strengthening systems of control over chemical precursors and preventing their diversion and trafficking

The Economic and Social Council,

Convinced that the transnational nature of the world drug problem and related offences requires the effective application of the principles of shared responsibility and a holistic and balanced approach,

Noting that the availability of chemical precursors makes it possible to extract, refine and synthesize illicit drugs of natural or synthetic origin,

Noting also General Assembly resolution S-20/4 B of 10 June 1998 on the control of precursors, adopted by the Assembly at its twentieth special session, devoted to countering the world drug problem together,

Stressing the importance of Commission on Narcotic Drugs resolution 45/12 of 12 March 2002 on the diversion of precursors and prompt reporting to competent authorities of the countries of origin and the countries of transit and the International Narcotics Control Board,

Concerned at the fact that the diversion of chemical precursors is related to, inter alia, the manufacture of illicit drugs,

Observing that transnational criminal organizations have taken advantage of the benefits of globalization and the use of new technology to broaden the scope of their activity in this area and that, therefore, combating those organizations and the methods they use constitutes one of the greatest challenges facing the international community today,

Noting with concern the widespread use of substances substituted for controlled substances in Tables I and II of the United Nations Convention against Illicit Traffic in Narcotic Drugs and Psychotropic Substances of 1988, for the purposes of extracting and refining drugs of natural or synthetic origin,

Noting the important problems posed by the diversion, smuggling and illicit trading of chemical precursors needed for the production of drugs of natural or synthetic origin,

Aware that the availability of chemical precursors continues, despite the success of "Operation Topaz" and "Operation Purple" and the efforts of all countries to prevent the access of drug traffickers to chemical precursors needed in the manufacture of illicit drugs of natural and synthetic origin,

Committed to preventing, through all legal means available, access to chemical precursors by those engaged in or attempting to engage in the processing of illicit drugs,

Concerned at the fact that illicit drugs of natural and synthetic origin have spread worldwide, and recognizing that that represents a threat to all States,

1. *Urges* all States, including producing, exporting, transit and importing States, in accordance with the principle of shared responsibility, to exchange information, through the competent authorities established in accordance with the United Nations Convention against Illicit Traffic in Narcotic Drugs and Psychotropic Substances of 1988 or through law enforcement authorities, regarding suspicious transactions or shipments of substances suspected of being diverted for use in illicit drug production;

2. *Recommends* that all States ensure that they have in place fully effective systems for chemical precursor control and procedures for training personnel of control agencies and operational, regulatory and administrative staff;

3. *Calls upon* all States to inform, through the International Narcotics Control Board, the competent authorities of States about matters concerning the introduction of substances substituted for controlled substances and the use of new techniques in the synthesis, refining and extraction of illicit drugs, with a view to strengthening controls;

4. *Encourages* all States, including producing, exporting, transit and importing States, to make full use of existing channels of communication for the timely exchange of information, where possible, on enterprises that have been given penalties for improper management of chemicals, in accordance with their national legislation, as well as on routes and means of trafficking and diversion, on methods of camouflaging and on means of falsifying and manipulating customs documents, and any other information necessary to exercise more effective control;

5. *Reiterates* the vital importance of the process of prior notification of export of chemicals used in the manufacture of organic and synthetic drugs, established pursuant to article 12 of the 1988 Convention, as a mechanism for preventing the diversion of chemicals into illicit channels, and stresses the need for timely feedback following such prior notification;

6. *Reiterates also* the need to adopt measures for the application of the "know-your-customer" principle by enterprises involved in production and distribution;

7. *Encourages* States and relevant international organizations to provide technical assistance that can be used to exercise more effective precursor control.

International Narcotics Control Board

The 13-member International Narcotics Control Board held its seventy-sixth (3-7 February), seventy-seventh (26 May–6 June) and seventy-eighth (29 October–14 November) sessions, all in Vienna.

In performing the tasks assigned to it under the international conventions, the Board maintained a permanent dialogue with Governments, and used the information received from them to identify the enforcement of treaty provisions requiring them to limit to medical and scientific purposes the licit manufacture of, trade in and distribution and use of narcotic drugs and psychotropic substances. The Board, which was requested by the international drug control treaties to report annually on the drug control situation worldwide, noted weaknesses in national control and treaty compliance and made recommendations for improvements at both the national and international levels.

The Board's 2003 report [Sales No. E.04.XI.1] reviewed the impact of drugs, crime and violence at the microlevel in society, addressing the relationship among drug abuse, crime and violence with respect to individuals, families, neighbourhoods and communities, and taking into account both criminality and victimization.

INCB concluded that drug trafficking and related crime and violence linked local communities with transnational criminal networks, and a targeted intervention was essential to deal with traffickers operating at the microlevel. The law enforcement response should include community-based policing, pre-emptive intervention and greater cooperation among criminal justice agencies, social welfare agencies and specialized NGOs. More timely and targeted efforts should be made at the local, national and international levels through partnerships with a diverse range of organizations, and programmes introducing community-based microlevel interventions should be established. The Board stressed the importance of introducing a comprehensive demand reduction programme.

The Board expressed concern at the failure of many States, including some that manufactured, imported, exported or used narcotic drugs, to comply with their treaty obligation to submit timely annual statistical reports. It encouraged States and territories for which it had established estimates of narcotic drug requirements for 2004 to review and revise them.

As to the diversion of narcotic drugs and psychotropic substances, INCB noted that the diversion of pharmaceutical products containing narcotic drugs from domestic licit distribution channels, occurring in many countries, was underreported. Noting that the diversion and abuse of opioids prescribed for substitution treatment was also reported in many countries, the Board reiterated its request to prevent their diversion. The Board called on Governments to prohibit the import and export of narcotic drugs and psychotropic substances through the mail in order to prevent the selling of illegal supplies by Internet pharmacies.

In the light of continued attempts by traffickers to divert precursors, it was imperative for Governments to verify the intended end use of orders of precursor chemicals and the volumes required, particularly ATS precursors, ephedrine and pseudoephedrine. Operational activities commenced in January under Project Prism (see p. 1268) to address the diversion of ATS precursors and equipment and materials used in their illicit manufacture, and the use of the Internet for their sale. The second meeting of the Project Prism working groups (Bangkok, Thailand, June) reviewed those activities. The Board noted the continued success of Operation Purple, involving the international tracking programme for potassium permanganate used in the illicit manufacture of cocaine, and of Operation Topaz, involving the international tracking of acetic anhydride used in heroin manufacture. With illicit opium production in Afghanistan increasing, it was essential for countries in the region to implement the working mechanisms and operating procedures established for Operation Topaz to prevent acetic anhydride from being diverted and smuggled into and through the region to Afghanistan. The Board convened a round-table consultation (Vienna, March) to address the diversion of acetic anhydride uncovered in Europe.

As to ensuring the availability of drugs for medical purposes, INCB noted that global production and stocks of opiate raw materials rich in both morphine and thebaine reached a record high in 2002, well in excess of global demand. The Board requested producing countries not to exceed their 2004 estimates for the cultivation and production of opiate raw materials, and urged them, in accordance with international drug control objectives and policies, to adjust their future production to meet actual worldwide requirements. However, in view of the continued low availability of opiates in many countries for the treatment of pain, the Board had no objection to increasing the production of opiate raw materials in response to increased global demand. It called on Governments to contribute to the maintenance of a balance between the supply of opiate raw materials and the demand for opiates.

The Board, aware of continued use by some military forces of drugs scheduled under the 1961 and the 1971 conventions, mainly of the amphetamine-type group, and the ongoing research into their further possible uses, appealed to Governments to ensure that military and law enforcement sectors followed the principles of sound medical practice in their use of internationally controlled substances and that the international conventions were respected.

By **decision 2003/236** of 22 July, the Economic and Social Council took note of the INCB report for 2002 [E/INCB/2002/1 (Sales No. E.03.XI.1)].

The Council, by **decision 2003/220** of 1 May, decided to include the issue of honorariums payable to INCB members in the agenda of its substantive 2003 session.

World drug situation

In its 2003 report [Sales No. E.04.XI.1], INCB presented a regional analysis of world drug abuse trends and control efforts, so that Governments would be kept aware of situations that might endanger the objectives of international drug control treaties.

Africa

Throughout Africa, cannabis was the most widely grown, trafficked and abused drug, accounting for one quarter of global seizures. The bulk was seized by South Africa, but large cannabis seizures were also reported in Egypt, Ghana, Kenya, Malawi, Morocco, Nigeria and the United Republic of Tanzania. Morocco remained one of the world's leading cannabis producers and the source of 60 to 70 per cent of the cannabis resin seized in Europe. In Egypt, cannabis continued to be illicitly cultivated in the northern part of the Sinai. In the Sudan, a shift from the cultivation of food crops to cannabis resulted in food shortages. In Western and Central Africa, where cultivation was traditionally limited to the local market, cannabis became a significant economic crop following the fall in prices of cash crops in international markets. It was produced on a large scale, in particular in Ghana, Nigeria and Senegal, and continued to be cultivated in Eastern Africa. Southern Africa remained the major source of cannabis in Africa.

Illicit opium poppy cultivation in the Sinai peninsula in Egypt was declining. While heroin abuse in Africa was relatively low, trends showed an increase, particularly from the spillover effects of drug trafficking. Heroin from South-East and South-West Asia continued to be smuggled through Eastern and Western Africa to illicit markets in Europe and, to some extent, the United States. Some heroin was also smuggled into South Africa, where its abuse was rising, particularly among youth.

Cocaine originating in South America and shipped mainly from Brazil continued to transit Western and Southern Africa to Europe. Cocaine abuse in Africa was limited to the spillover effects of trafficking.

The abuse of psychotropic substances was of concern in Southern, Eastern and Western Africa. In Western Africa, especially in the Sahelian countries, the abuse of amphetamine, ephedrine and pemoline was widespread. Most psychotropic substances continued to be diverted mainly from licit distribution channels. A major problem was the abuse of prescription pharmaceutical products that were being sold over the counter or in the streets, particularly in several Western and Central African countries. The diversion of drugs intended for the licit market into illicit channels became an issue in South Africa. Methcathinone ("cat") appeared on illicit markets in South Africa, and, despite law enforcement efforts aimed at interrupting the supply of methaqualone (Mandrax), its abuse continued unabated in Eastern and Southern Africa, above all in South Africa, where it remained the second most commonly abused illicit drug. Methaqualone continued to enter that country from India and China and from clandestine laboratories in Southern Africa. The abuse of methylenedioxymethamphetamine (MDMA (Ecstasy)) occurred in Southern Africa, particularly in South Africa.

Illicit drug trafficking remained a major problem in the region. Information gathered from war-torn countries in Western and Central Africa indicated that the arms and ammunition used by rebel groups and criminal organizations to destabilize those subregions might have been partly procured with the proceeds of illicit drug trafficking.

As to regional cooperation, collaboration targeting the drug problem continued within intergovernmental organizations such as the African Union (AU), the Economic Community of West African States (ECOWAS), the Southern African Development Community (SADC) and the East African Community (EAC). Arab ministers of information and of the interior held a meeting (Tunis, Tunisia, January) to discuss money-laundering, terrorism and organized crime. Ministers of the interior of the Western Mediterranean States coalition met (Tripoli, Libyan Arab Jamahiriya, July) to discuss cooperation in fighting terrorism, drug trafficking and organized crime, among other issues. A regional workshop (Accra, Ghana, May) brought together the coordinators of inter-ministerial drug committees, national project coordinators and NGO representatives of ECOWAS members. The third annual meeting of the East Africa Drug Information System took place in Nairobi, Kenya, in October. At the national level, Ethiopia introduced draft legislation against money-laundering, while Nigeria enacted legislation against money-laundering in 2002.

The Board welcomed action by Morocco to conduct a comprehensive survey in 2003 to determine the extent, locations and patterns of cannabis cultivation in the northern part of the country. In South Africa, the demand reduction campaign "Ke Moja" was launched nationwide in June, and legislation to combat money-laundering was implemented.

An INCB mission to Mali in March found that various drugs, mainly diverted from licit distribution channels and humanitarian aid, were sold in street markets. In April, an INCB mission visited Algeria, where diversions of psychotropic substances occurred after they had been licitly imported. The Board called on the Government to strengthen its control of the distribution of pharmaceutical products and to undertake an assessment of drug abuse.

Americas

Central America and the Caribbean

Drug trafficking in Central America and the Caribbean involved mostly cannabis and cocaine, although heroin seizures increased. Trafficking contributed to the increase in drug abuse in Central America and the Mexican corridor and the Caribbean, which remained the transit route for smuggling cocaine and heroin from Colombia into North America.

Cannabis cultivation continued in all countries in Central America, mainly for local abuse or smuggling into neighbouring countries, and it remained the most widely abused substance, with El Salvador and Honduras reporting the highest prevalence. The largest seizures in the Caribbean continued to be made in Jamaica, an important source of the cannabis trafficked outside the subregion. In the Eastern Caribbean, it was grown mainly in Saint Vincent and the Grenadines, Saint Lucia and Dominica, primarily for local abuse. The smuggling of cannabis from the Caribbean into Europe and North America continued to decline; cannabis produced in the subregion was increasingly abused locally or trafficked within the subregion.

Cocaine production remained insignificant, with only Panama reporting minor coca bush cultivation and cocaine laboratories. However, the transit traffic in cocaine continued to affect all countries, especially Puerto Rico, the main entry point for cocaine smuggled through the Caribbean into the United States. Countries through which the substance was trafficked had a higher level of abuse. Cocaine abuse increased and the age of initiation into illicit drug consumption decreased. Cocaine, or crack cocaine, was the second most widely abused drug in the Caribbean among students in secondary school. In Curaçao, crack abuse became a major problem.

Guatemala was the only Central American country to report minimal cultivation of opium poppy. Heroin abuse was marginal, except in Puerto Rico. Heroin seizures, which were reported in all countries in Central America and most countries in the Caribbean, reached unprecedented levels. Most of the heroin originated in Colombia. Trinidad and Tobago continued to be affected by trafficking in cocaine and heroin, mainly from Venezuela.

Central America was a transit area for shipments of precursor chemicals used in the manufacture of narcotic drugs and destined mainly for Colombia. There were shortcomings with respect to their control. Some Central American countries reported sporadic seizures of Ecstasy, mostly originating in Europe, abuse of which was emerging in the region.

The Inter-American Drug Abuse Control Commission (CICAD) of the Organization of American States was the main forum of regional cooperation. Coordination in areas such as judicial cooperation, law enforcement operations and border control was usually in the form of bilateral agreements between countries. The United States remained the single most important bilateral partner in drug control matters for most countries and territories, providing assistance in the interdiction of drug trafficking. The Board welcomed the increased attention given to demand reduction in the region, and the cooperation of Caribbean countries with the Netherlands and the United Kingdom to address the smuggling of drugs into Europe by individual couriers.

At the national level, Central American countries continued to seek ways to strengthen their capabilities to combat trafficking. The Board noted the strengthening of legislation against money-laundering and of the drug control infrastructure in Costa Rica. It urged the Bahamas to adopt a national drug control plan and implement regulations on precursor chemicals. Progress was achieved in combating money-laundering activities in the Caribbean. However, some of the islands in the Eastern Caribbean were still vulnerable.

An INCB mission to Panama in February noted its vulnerability to trafficking due to its geographical location, economic structure and intense commercial traffic. While Panama had adequate drug control legislation, it had limited resources to implement it. The Board encouraged the Government to ensure coordination and communication between government entities and the inter-institutional commission for chemical control. INCB reviewed action taken by El Salvador to implement its recommendations following a 2000 Board mission to that country [YUN 2000, p. 1184]. It noted the adoption of a national drug control plan, covering supply reduction, demand reduction and the control of licit activities related to narcotic drugs, psychotropic substances and precursors.

North America

Cannabis, the most abused drug in Canada, Mexico and the United States, was produced in large quantities in all three countries. Almost 40 per cent of cannabis herb seizures reported worldwide were made in Mexico.

The demand for cocaine fell in some areas of the United States. While there appeared to be an overall decline in drug abuse among teenagers with regard to some drugs, cocaine and crack abuse remained at the same level. In Mexico, the abuse of cocaine and crack increased, in particular among youth, and they were increasingly used as initiation drugs.

Heroin abuse was rising in Mexico, with increased availability, lower prices and higher purity levels. Though the majority of heroin smuggled into the United States and Canada was of Colombian origin, a significant share was also manufactured in Mexico, where, despite efforts by the Government to reduce it, illicit opium poppy cultivation continued. In the United States, a field with 40,000 opium poppies was discovered in June in a remote area in California, raising concern that trafficking organizations were attempting to establish large-scale cultivation sites within the country.

The abuse of Ecstasy among teenagers in the United States declined in 2002 for the first time in several years, though it remained at high levels. The abuse of amphetamine and methamphetamine remained high. In Mexico, ATS abuse increased significantly among young persons. Abuse of prescription drugs in the United States continued, exacerbated by the unlawful selling of narcotic drugs and psychotropic substances by online pharmacies within and outside the country.

The North American countries cooperated closely in their drug control efforts, resulting in the arrest by Mexico and the United States of a number of powerful drug traffickers. Mexico extradited to the United States numerous suspected drug traffickers, including major figures in drug trafficking organizations. In April, Canada and the United States completed a joint operation targeting trafficking in pseudoephedrine, a precursor used in methamphetamine manufacture.

As to national legislation, new regulations came into force in Canada, completing the inclusion under appropriate national control of all internationally controlled psychotropic substances. Canada's Drug Strategy was adopted, increasing the funding of drug control activities. Noting with concern that, in June, Canada had approved the establishment of a drug injection room in Vancouver, the Board reiterated its view that such sites were contrary to the fundamental provisions of the international treaties.

In October, INCB visited Canada and noted the strong coordination among various ministries and agencies in drug control and initiatives to deal with the problem of indoor cannabis production.

South America

In South America, the political threat of the drug problem led many Governments to devote more of their limited resources to reducing illicit drug supply, including by the eradication of illicit crops, the interdiction of drug trafficking and the introduction of measures against money-laundering. There were continued reports of arms being exchanged for illicit drugs. What was originally known as Plan Colombia, sponsored by the United States and aimed at reducing the illicit supply from Colombia and other South American countries, evolved into a broader effort named the Andean Counter-drug Initiative. Colombia remained the main recipient of assistance.

Cannabis, the most widely abused illicit drug in South America, was cultivated in almost every country, mainly for local or regional markets. One half of its seizures were accounted for by Brazil and one third by Colombia, both of which ranked among the top 10 countries in the world in terms of cannabis herb seizures.

In Colombia, coca bush cultivation fell by 58 per cent compared with 2000, the peak year. Most of the reduction was attributed to aerial fumigation. However, illicit cultivation increased sharply in the Nariño area bordering Ecuador. In Peru, the total area under cultivation remained stable, while in Bolivia, there was a slight increase in 2002.

The potential total manufacture of cocaine remained at approximately 800 tons in 2002, the bulk of which took place in Colombia, mainly in areas under the control of armed groups. Some 80 tons of potassium permanganate were seized in Colombia in 2002, the largest quantity ever in one year. Apart from the coca-producing countries, the transit countries of Brazil, Ecuador and Venezuela reported the largest seizures of cocaine. The United States remained the main market for South American cocaine. Other trafficking routes were uncovered, such as a route leading from Peru to Australia via Argentina.

Colombia estimated that in 2002, some 4,200 hectares were under opium poppy cultivation in the central and southern parts of the country. Peru also reported a small increase in opium poppy cultivation. In South America, there was an increasing trend in heroin manufacture and trafficking, mainly from Colombia into the United States, using individual carriers.

Regional cooperation often took the form of bilateral or multilateral agreements between States with common interests and shared geographical traits. Cooperation between Brazil and Colombia was enhanced, and joint police force operations were extended to Peru, Suriname and Venezuela. The United States remained the principal contributor of resources, mostly through bilateral agreements. Cooperation agreements also existed between South American and European countries. Various regional operations were initiated in South America to address the diversion of and trafficking in chemicals.

At the national level, new legislation on chemical precursors increased the number of chemicals monitored in Brazil. In Peru, new legislation for strengthening the control of precursor chemicals was adopted and a financial intelligence unit was created. In Uruguay, the legal framework for the control of precursor chemicals was strengthened. However, control provisions against money-laundering needed to be expanded.

In February, a Board mission to Colombia, recognizing the importance of providing alternative development for the local population in coca-growing areas, noted that increased resources were needed and invited the international community to support Colombia in alternative development and demand reduction. In July, an INCB mission visited Ecuador which, as a result of measures taken in neighbouring Andean countries, had become more vulnerable to drug trafficking activities. The Board welcomed the establishment in 2002 of the Drug Observatory and appreciated the initiatives taken to combat corruption, drug trafficking and money-laundering. It noted the need for increased international assistance to Ecuador to tackle illicit cultivation and trafficking in the Andean subregion. Also in July, a Board mission to Peru noted efforts towards the elimination of coca bush cultivation. It expressed appreciation for Peru's decision to update the registry of farmers for the licit production of coca leaf, and to estimate actual needs for coca leaf to evaluate the required cultivation area. The Board acknowledged the improvements made by the Government, in follow-up to its 2000 recommendations [YUN 2000, p. 1186], particularly in streamlining the functions of agencies involved in drug control, but noted that some recommendations had not been addressed.

Asia

East and South-East Asia

In all the countries of East and South-East Asia, cannabis abuse was widespread. However, it was limited in China, Japan and the Republic of Korea and declined in Malaysia and Thailand, where abusers shifted to other drugs, mainly methamphetamine and various stimulants. The Philippines reported a significant reduction in cultivation, as a result of an eradication campaign, but it continued to be cultivated in and smuggled out of Cambodia, Indonesia, the Lao People's Democratic Republic, Myanmar and Thailand. Indonesia and Thailand were also sources of cannabis resin.

In East and South-East Asia, the total area under illicit opium poppy cultivation declined further. As a result of government efforts, illicit opium production fell in Myanmar and Laos, the two major producers. In Myanmar, the world's second largest producer of illicit opium and heroin after Afghanistan, the area under opium poppy cultivation had decreased by almost two thirds since 1996, and by 55 per cent since 1998 in Laos, the third largest producer. In Thailand and Viet Nam, production levels remained insignificant. Opium was abused in countries where cultivation took place, but the number of abusers decreased, as many addicts turned to heroin, the drug of choice. In East and South-East Asia, there was little cocaine trafficking and abuse.

Methamphetamine continued to be manufactured, mainly in China, Myanmar and, to a lesser extent, in the Philippines. Over two thirds of the global seizures took place in the region, mainly in China, Myanmar and Thailand, although they had declined since 2001. Precursors for methamphetamine continued to be smuggled into Myanmar and the Philippines out of China and India. Methamphetamine was the most widely abused drug in Japan, the Republic of Korea and Thailand. Its abuse increased in most parts of the region coupled with a rise in the abuse of other ATS, particularly Ecstasy. Seizures of Ecstasy were reported mainly in China and Japan. The illicit trade in precursor chemicals continued to be a major concern.

The Board commended the cooperation of the Association of Southeast Asian Nations (ASEAN) with China. In September, the six signatories to the 1993 memorandum of understanding on drug control between the countries in the Mekong area (Cambodia, China, Laos, Myanmar, Thailand, Viet Nam) reconfirmed their agreement to strengthen subregional cooperation across borders. China, Laos, Myanmar and Thailand agreed to establish a network among their ports along the Mekong to reinforce their national campaigns against drug traffickers, and Malaysia launched a joint police initiative with Australia, Brunei Darussalam, Singapore and Thailand. In May, the border liaison offices of Laos and Thailand pledged to strengthen cross-border law enforcement. China and Thailand provided assistance for alternative development in Laos and Myanmar.

In March, an INCB mission visited Laos. It noted that the Government had enhanced its national drug legislation and that the opium elimination programme had led to a significant decline in illicit cultivation. However, as a result of enhanced law enforcement measures in some neighbouring countries, Laos was increasingly targeted by drug traffickers. Also in March, a Board mission visited Viet Nam to review the drug control situation and progress made following its 1997 mission there [YUN 1997, p. 1274]. The Government made progress in drug control, particularly in strengthening the national drug control legislation and institutions, the implementation of the national drug master plan and the eradication of illicit opium poppy cultivation. The Board encouraged the Government to take measures to exercise control over its financial institutions and enact a law against money-laundering. In April, an INCB mission visited Cambodia, where the abuse of drugs, particularly methamphetamine and heroin, had increased. The Board urged the Government to develop a national drug control master plan.

South Asia

South Asian countries continued to be used by drug traffickers as transit countries because of their proximity to the world's most prolific opiate production areas in South-East and South-West Asia. Drug trafficking was believed to be one of the major sources of funds for terrorist groups in the region. In most countries, licitly manufactured narcotic drugs were diverted to the illicit markets, and the region faced increasing abuse of pharmaceutical products containing controlled narcotic drugs and psychotropic substances.

Cannabis was illicitly cultivated in all countries except Maldives and was smuggled out of India and Nepal. Scattered but increasing illicit cultivation was reported in Bangladesh, which had also become a transit point for cannabis resin, originating in India and Pakistan, on its way to Europe. The north-west of India emerged as a significant source of cannabis resin. In Nepal, the abuse of locally grown and wild cannabis remained widespread. Cannabis grew wild in the high hills of the central, mid-western and far western parts of the country, where eradication was expensive due to the difficult terrain. In the southern part, its cultivation increased, the crops mostly destined for the illicit market in India. Cannabis was illicitly cultivated in Sri Lanka for the local illicit markets.

In India, a traditional producer of opium for medical and scientific purposes, opium poppy was grown under a stringent licensing policy controlled by the Central Bureau of Narcotics, but diversion of opium to illicit channels still occurred. The bulk of the illicit opium poppy cultivation was confined to the remote north-eastern states. The production of opium for local abuse and for sale to cross-border heroin manufacturers in Myanmar increased. Illicit laboratories throughout India manufactured the low-quality brown heroin base known as "brown sugar". Most of the heroin from Afghanistan, which was smuggled through the border between India and Pakistan, was destined for Europe. In Bangladesh, a large number of abusers of phensedyl (codeine-based cough syrup) changed to heroin because of its increased availability and the high price of phensedyl. Most of the heroin abused in Bangladesh originated in India. In Nepal, illicit opium poppy cultivation was increasing, and the smuggling and abuse of heroin from South-West and South-East Asia were on the rise. In Sri Lanka, a transit point for shipments of heroin from Asia to Europe, the percentage of injecting drug abusers remained low and opium abuse became insignificant.

India manufactured a wide range of precursor chemicals. Despite strict controls and training for law enforcement officials, diversion from licit channels occurred. The most commonly abused precursors were benzodiazepines (alprazolam, diazepam, nitrazepam). Bangladesh and Nepal reported the abuse of diverted diazepam and nitrazepam, mainly of Indian origin. Benzodiazepines were also abused in Sri Lanka, where they were diverted from the retail trade. In India, control over the licit distribution of buprenorphine was strengthened, but its diversion still occurred. In Sri Lanka, the import and distribution of psychotropic substances continued to take place without adequate control.

As to regional cooperation, Bangladesh signed a bilateral agreement with Myanmar for combating illicit trafficking in narcotic drugs, psychotropic substances and precursors. India concluded two bilateral agreements and held meetings with Myanmar, Pakistan and Sri Lanka. It hosted a number of exchange programmes. Nationally, the Board urged Nepal to adopt legislation on precursor control.

An INCB mission to India in May concluded that the licit production and processing of opiates were well regulated and the Government continued to tighten controls to make diversion of licitly produced opium more difficult. As the main exporter of licitly produced opium in the world, India cooperated with the Board in ensuring a lasting balance between the supply of and demand for opium worldwide. Although control over precursors was well implemented, controls over the licit manufacture of, trade in and distribution of narcotic drugs and psychotropic substances were inadequate. INCB urged the Government to enforce laws at the retail level to prevent illicit sales of psychotropic substances and to streamline the administrative structure for drug control at the national level.

West and Central Asia

The drug problem remained a major challenge for West Asia, undermining the social and economic stability of some countries and jeopardizing peace and security in the region. Corruption linked to drug trafficking was also a serious problem. In several countries, initiatives to assess the extent of drug abuse and establish demand reduction activities revealed worrying levels of abuse, including an increase in abuse by injection. The main drugs of abuse were cannabis and opiates. In addition, Ecstasy became increasingly available. In Afghanistan, despite the armed intervention and political change (see p. 289) and the fight against terrorism, cultivation and trafficking in opiates expanded, resulting in increased political instability. In 2003, seizures of opiates increased, particularly in Central Asia. Precursor chemicals continued to flow into the region along the same routes used for smuggling opiates but in the opposite direction.

Cannabis was the most widely grown and abused drug in West Asia. Illicit cannabis cultivation took place in several countries, and the plant grew wild in Afghanistan, Kazakhstan and Pakistan. Some cultivation was destroyed in Tajikistan, where a few cases of opium poppy cultivation were also discovered. Cannabis continued to be smuggled in large quantities, mainly in the form of cannabis resin, out of South-West Asia and into Europe. In Lebanon, despite regular eradication campaigns, illicit cultivation of both cannabis and opium poppy re-emerged in the Bekaa valley and was linked to the area's economically deprived status.

In Afghanistan, opium poppy cultivation, which had re-emerged on a large scale in 2002, spread further in 2003, as farmers grew it increasingly in remote and inaccessible areas. Production of opium increased, despite significant eradication efforts in some traditional cultivation areas. The Board noted with concern the resurgence of opium poppy cultivation in Pakistan, mostly in non-traditional poppy-growing areas.

Large-scale heroin manufacture in West Asia persisted, primarily in Afghanistan, although hardly any laboratories were detected. Opiate smuggling from Afghanistan continued into other countries in West Asia, destined for Europe and other regions, as well as for abuse in the region. Seizures of opiates, mainly heroin and morphine, increased in Iran, Pakistan, Tajikistan, Turkey and several countries of the Commonwealth of Independent States (CIS).

Drug abuse assessments revealed alarming trends. In Pakistan, drug abuse increased in urban and rural areas, with cannabis-type drugs (cannabis resin and "charas"), heroin, psychotropic substances and alcohol being the most commonly abused substances. In Afghanistan, cannabis resin was the most commonly abused substance, followed by pharmaceutical drugs, opium, heroin and alcohol. A major concern was the rate of drug injection. In Turkey, drug abuse, though relatively low, was increasing. The Board expressed concern about the high level of drug abuse in West Asia and the increasing trend with regard to injecting drug abuse.

Trafficking in and abuse of illicitly manufactured stimulants (often reported as Captagon) continued in the Eastern Mediterranean area and on the Arabian peninsula. Rising trends in West Asia were noted in the abuse of Ecstasy. In Turkey, seizures of Ecstasy originating from Western Europe increased considerably. Israel made several large seizures of Ecstasy in 2002, and its availability also increased in Iran. In several countries, the abuse of benzodiazepines was widespread, particularly among women.

At the regional level, Afghanistan participated in meetings and other activities, such as the fourth meeting of drug liaison officers, hosted by Iran in March. At the Conference on Drug Routes from Central Asia to Europe (see also p. 1263), ways for strengthening cooperation in stemming the illicit production of and trade in heroin and opium from Afghanistan to Central Asia were discussed. Kazakhstan, Kyrgyzstan, Tajikistan and Uzbekistan—members of the Central Asian Cooperation Organization (CACO)—discussed the development of multilateral regional cooperation within the framework of CACO (Almaty, Kazakhstan, July) [A/58/131-S/2003/703]. In West Asia, regional and subregional cooperation, especially regarding drug law enforcement, was well developed. Steps were taken to integrate Afghanistan in regional law enforcement activities, and cooperation activities continued to be carried out between Iran and Pakistan.

At the national level, a new drug control law was adopted in Afghanistan, and a national drug control strategy was endorsed by the President in May. The Board noted with concern that Afghanistan's commitment to drug control, as expressed by the Transitional Administration, was not followed throughout the country, due to lack of nationwide control and insufficient support by provincial authorities. It welcomed the drug law enforcement initiatives in Central Asia. The Board noted that information about drug abuse in most countries was fragmented and demand reduction activities received less priority than those in supply reduction.

In June, an INCB mission to Turkey noted that the country had made efforts to improve its position as a competitive supplier of opiate raw materials on the world market, while ensuring the implementation of control measures and achieving a balance between supply and demand. The Board welcomed the activities undertaken by the Turkish International Academy against Drugs and Organized Crime, which focused on drug law enforcement training and promoted national and regional cooperation.

In September, the Board visited Iran, where drug abuse and illicit trafficking created significant problems, as the country was a main conduit for illicit drugs originating in Afghanistan. INCB appreciated the Government's increased demand reduction efforts and welcomed its co-operation with the other countries in the region. It encouraged the Government to strengthen support to Afghanistan and to enact and implement legislation on money-laundering and the control of precursors.

Europe

Cannabis remained the most commonly abused drug in Europe and was increasingly cultivated and trafficked in the region. In Switzerland, between 300 and 500 hectares were cultivated for production, and in the United Kingdom it was estimated that about 50 per cent of all abusers grew their cannabis. Albania was a large supplier of cannabis, which was smuggled into Europe and West Asia. Its abuse was on the increase in Central and Eastern Europe. Cannabis seizures showed a stable or upward trend in many countries.

The cocaine market in Europe was second only to that in North America. The abuse of all forms of cocaine increased in Western Europe; however, crack cocaine abuse was confined to metropolitan areas in some countries. The volume of cocaine from South America smuggled into Europe continued to increase, with Spain, the Netherlands and the United Kingdom being the three main ports of entry. Spain ranked third in the world (after the United States and Colombia) for the volume of cocaine seized.

Heroin abuse spread in Central and Eastern Europe, replacing the abuse of locally produced opiates in most countries. HIV infection among injecting drug abusers spread alarmingly in the Baltic States, the Russian Federation and Ukraine. Heroin on the illicit market was mainly of Afghan origin. In Western Europe, heroin seizures remained stable or declined. In South-Eastern Europe, trafficking continued via the Balkan route. Drug abuse in the countries along that route showed an upward trend. In Western Europe, drug abuse prevention and treatment efforts contributed to the stable or declining levels of heroin abuse. In Eastern Europe, however, it continued to increase.

Europe remained a major producer of synthetic drugs, particularly those of the MDMA variety, which were trafficked worldwide. While Ecstasy and related drugs were mostly manufactured in and distributed from Belgium and the Netherlands, amphetamine was increasingly manufactured all over Europe, especially in Poland, the Baltic States and Romania. Home-cooked methamphetamine (pervitin) was still being manufactured in the Czech Republic, and its trafficking was no longer confined to the local illicit markets, but had spread to Austria, Germany and Slovakia. The percentage of ATS abusers was highest in Ireland, the United Kingdom and the Netherlands.

The Board noted the efforts by Greece, holding the Presidency of the European Council during the first half of 2003, to forge a common European Union (EU) drug control policy. It also noted that the EU Council of Ministers of Justice and Home Affairs had adopted an implementation plan of action against the illicit supply of synthetic drugs in November 2002, and urged EU members to ensure its implementation.

The Board acknowledged national legislation, policy and action, including in the Netherlands, where cannabis became available as a prescription drug; a new drug action plan, which entered into force in Norway; a national action plan on drugs and addiction adopted by Germany; Spain's decision to use funds generated by the forfeiture of assets seized in drug trafficking cases for supporting drug control activities carried out by UNODC; and efforts in countries on the Balkan route, in particular Serbia and Montenegro, to thwart the diversion of precursor chemicals for international trade for the illicit manufacture of drugs.

Following an INCB mission to Poland (February), where ATS manufacture and abuse took place at significant levels, the Board urged the Government to take steps for more effective repression of ATS manufacture and trafficking. An INCB mission visited the Czech Republic (March), where the Board noted the commitment of the Government to deal with drug abuse and trafficking. In July, the Board sent a mission to Germany to visit drug injection rooms and to discuss its concerns. It noted that there was little evidence that drug injection rooms ensured treatment or contributed to a reduction in drug-related deaths, reiterated that those rooms were not in compliance with the international drug control treaties and urged the Government to take steps to ensure compliance. The Board, reviewing progress by Ireland in implementing its 2000 recommendations [YUN 2000, p. 1189], noted that a number of controlled substances under the 1961 and the 1971 Conventions had not been placed under adequate control and urged the Government to adopt legislative provisions required by the two conventions. In January, the Board, during a technical visit to Slovakia, noted that legislation for opium poppy cultivation and poppy straw was in line with its position and appreciated the efforts of the law enforcement authorities to counteract diversion and trafficking in psychotropic substances.

Oceania

Although cannabis abuse declined in Oceania, it remained at a high level and cannabis was the drug of choice in Australia and New Zealand. More sophisticated hydroponic growing techniques contributed to increased yields, especially in Australia. Significant cultivation was found also in Fiji and Papua New Guinea.

Australia and New Zealand were among the main destinations for shipments of heroin and ATS from South-East Asia. However, successful law enforcement operations in Australia led to a sharp reduction in heroin supply to illicit markets. At the same time, the abuse of cocaine and synthetic drugs increased despite record seizures at borders. In all countries in Oceania, except Australia and New Zealand, heroin and cocaine trafficking and abuse were sporadic and at a low level.

In Australia, border detections of synthetic drugs, ATS and Ecstasy increased, as did the number of uncovered clandestine laboratories for ATS manufacture. In both Australia and New Zealand, local illicit manufacture and distribution of ATS increased. In some parts of New Zealand, cannabis abuse was surpassed by ATS abuse, and Ecstasy abuse continued to spread. In Australia, gamma-hydroxybutyric acid, ketamine and various antidepressants became popular party drugs.

At the regional level, the Pacific Islands Forum maintained an essential role in coordinating drug control efforts in Oceania. In March, Australia and Indonesia signed a memorandum of understanding on the exchange of information to enforce customs laws. The Australian Federal Police and the New Zealand Police played a key role in terms of regional technical assistance, and the police and customs of Australia and Papua New Guinea continued to participate in joint border patrols.

At the national level, New Zealand tightened its control over domestic licit distribution of ephedrine and pseudoephedrine through close cooperation between police and pharmacists. The Board noted that both Australia and New Zealand had strengthened their legislation to detect and prevent clandestine ATS manufacture and to intercept consignments of such stimulants and their precursors. The Board noted progress achieved in the fight against money-laundering in several Pacific island States.

In January, the Board sent missions to Fiji and Papua New Guinea. It invited the Government of Fiji to establish a comprehensive national master plan for drug control. It noted that further efforts were required to ensure adequate availability of drugs for medical purposes and to provide scientific support for drug law enforcement. Papua New Guinea needed to revise its drug control legislation. INCB invited the Government to conduct an assessment of the drug abuse situation with a view to introducing proper treatment and rehabilitation programmes.

UN action to combat drug abuse

UN Office on Drugs and Crime

The United Nations Office on Drugs and Crime (UNODC), formerly the Office of Drug Control and Crime Prevention [YUN 2002, p. 1247], implemented the Organization's drug programme and crime programme (see p. 1116) in an integrated manner, addressing the interrelated issues of drug control, crime prevention and international terrorism in the context of sustainable development and human security. The drug programme continued to be implemented in accordance with General Assembly resolution 45/179 [YUN 1990, p. 874]. The Office served as the central drug control entity responsible for coordinating all UN drug control activities, and as the repository of technical expertise in international drug control for the UN Secretariat. It acted on behalf of the Secretary-General in fulfilling his responsibilities under international treaties and resolutions relating to drug control; and provided services to the Assembly, the Economic and Social Council, and committees and conferences dealing with drug control matters.

The UNODC Executive Director described the Office's 2003 activities in a report to the Commission on Narcotic Drugs and the Commission on Crime Prevention and Criminal Justice [E/CN.7/2004/9-E/CN.15/2004/2]. UNODC assisted States in complying with international conventions to counter the world drug problem and supported INCB in monitoring their implementation. It identified and promoted best policing practices, facilitating cross-border law enforcement cooperation, and worked closely with the relevant law enforcement agencies, such as Interpol, the Customs Cooperation Council (also known as the World Customs Organization), the European Police Office (Europol) and the Southeast European Cooperative Initiative. Technical law enforcement assistance was provided to countries in Southern and East Africa, Central Asia, South-East Asia and Central and Eastern Europe.

In the alternative development area, UNODC supported Governments in reducing the cultivation of illicit drug crops, particularly opium poppy and coca bush. UNODC programmes focused on poverty reduction, the empowerment of women, the creation of new sources of livelihood and the protection of the environment. The programmes targeted peasant families in isolated areas, where illicit drug production and trafficking thrived. The Office promoted best practices in alternative development in Afghanistan, Bolivia, Colombia, the Lao People's Democratic Republic, Myanmar, Peru and Viet Nam.

As to drug demand reduction, UNODC assisted Member States in establishing national drug abuse information systems, promoting best practices in drug abuse prevention and the treatment and rehabilitation of addicts, and implementing projects for reducing drug dependence. UNODC developed the tool kit on drug abuse epidemiology to support the development of an integrated drug information system and supported drug abuse education in schools, and projects targeting youth at risk. The UNODC/World Health Organization (WHO) Global Initiative on Primary Prevention of Substance Abuse was finalized, reaching thousands of people in Belarus, the Philippines, the Russian Federation, South Africa, Thailand, the United Republic of Tanzania, Viet Nam and Zambia. A local expert network on demand reduction was launched in Western Africa.

UNODC launched regional treatment and rehabilitation projects aimed at diversifying services to injecting drug users, including HIV/AIDS treatment and prevention in Belarus, the Republic of Moldova, the Russian Federation, Ukraine and the Central Asian States. To strengthen its capacity to respond to HIV/AIDS drug abuse–related issues, the Office established a new unit for HIV/AIDS work to implement preventive projects among abusers. HIV/AIDS advisers were placed in the UNODC regional offices in Bangkok, Moscow and Tashkent. The Office maintained the UN Reference Group on HIV/AIDS Prevention and Care among Injecting Drug Users in Developing and Transitional Countries, whose members completed a mapping of the global, regional and national epidemiology of injecting drug use and HIV infection.

In Afghanistan, UNODC assisted the Counter-Narcotics Directorate of the National Security Council in building capacities in drug law enforcement and in the criminal justice sector. The Office engaged the agencies involved in post-conflict reconstruction to ensure that the elimination of illicit drug crops remained a priority, and it helped to develop the national drug control strategy aimed at the elimination of illicit cultivation of opium poppy within 10 years. Central Asia and the countries bordering the region were affected by the export of Afghan opium. UNODC followed up on the recommendations of the Conference on Drug Routes from Central Asia to Europe (see pp. 1263 and 1277) with an initiative aimed at achieving effective cross-border cooperation in countries along the drug trafficking routes.

In Africa, the Office supported the AU in integrating drug- and crime-related issues into the New Partnership for Africa's Development (see p. 937). It continued to work with Governments to strengthen judicial integrity and promoted the development of multisectoral programmes to combat drug trafficking and abuse, corruption, organized crime and terrorism. It helped to improve the seaport and airport law enforcement capabilities in Eastern and Southern Africa, and provided specialized training for judges, prosecutors and investigators to improve treaty implementation. In various African countries, an initiative launched jointly by UNODC and the Joint United Nations Programme on HIV/AIDS (UNAIDS) (see p. 1247) resulted in several preventive actions. In Eastern Africa, projects were revised to include training professionals to provide services to prevent HIV/AIDS transmission. Small grants were given to NGOs to support activities targeting drug abuse and HIV/AIDS.

The operational priorities that were agreed by Member States in January 2003, reflected in the consolidated budget for the 2004-2005 biennium (see p. 1281), set the resource requirements at $180.4 million. The UNODC budget (mostly funded through voluntary contributions by a small number of Member States) increased by 12.7 per cent. General-purpose income increased to $18.5 million in 2003 (23 per cent above the 2002 level). The increase, coupled with cost-saving measures introduced in mid-2002, prevented a potential default during the year.

Training

On 22 July [meeting 44], the Economic and Social Council, on the recommendation of the Commission on Narcotic Drugs [E/2003/28/Rev.1], adopted **resolution 2003/32** without vote [agenda item 14 (d)].

Training in precursor control, countering money-laundering and drug abuse prevention

The Economic and Social Council,

Conscious that offences connected with drug trafficking depend on the availability of chemical precursors, without which the illicit manufacture of cocaine, heroin and amphetamine-type stimulants would not have become a problem,

Concerned at the escalation of the problem of illicit supply, diversion and substitution of precursors and at the use of sophisticated technologies,

Concerned also at the increase in the laundering of money derived from drug trafficking, which is detrimental to national economies and fosters corruption,

Noting that the supply of and demand for illicit drugs are harmful to public health and that children and young persons are among the consumers of such drugs,

Recognizing that education and training are basic prerequisites for the efficient performance of the various tasks that institutions and their officials must carry out in order to deal with the world drug problem and drug-related offences,

Urges relevant international organizations, in consultation with the United Nations Office on Drugs and Crime, to provide financing and other support for the training of experts in various subjects related to the fight against the world drug problem, with particular emphasis on preventive measures and areas such as precursor control, drug-testing laboratories and laboratory quality assurance, countering money-laundering and drug abuse prevention, bearing in mind that such training may often be best delivered on a regional basis.

Administrative and budgetary matters

2002-2003 programme budget

The Commission on Narcotic Drugs considered the proposed revised budget for 2002-2003 [E/CN.7/2003/15] for the Fund of the United Nations International Drug Control Programme (UNDCP), as presented by the Executive Director in January [E/CN.7/2003/15]. The revised 2002-2003 support budget amounted to $34.2 million, reflecting a nominal decrease of $1.1 million, or 3.3 per cent, compared with the initial support budget amount of $35.4 million. It included a proposed volume decrease of $1.5 million or 4.2 per cent, and cost changes of $341,300, or 1 per cent, compared with the initial budget [YUN 2001, p. 1166]. The Commission also considered an overview of UNDCP's financial situation, which showed that total income for the 2002-2003 biennium was revised upwards by $0.9 million to $137.2 million. However, general-purpose income had to be revised downwards by $5 million, while special-purpose or earmarked income was revised upwards by $5.9 million. The change in the mix of income would result in a decline in the general-purpose fund balance by $5.3 million by the end of 2003, well below the $8 million minimum balance required to maintain sufficient cash flow in 2004. To address the cash-flow and structural problem in financing, the Secretariat proposed a number of options, including finding alternative sources of financing.

The Advisory Committee on Administrative and Budgetary Questions (ACABQ), in a February report [E/CN.7/2003/16], recommended approval of the proposed revised support budget for the 2002-2003 biennium

By a 15 April resolution [E/2003/28/Rev.1 (res. 46/10)], the Commission approved an appropriation in the amount of $34.2 million for the Fund's revised 2002-2003 support budget. It authorized the Executive Director to redeploy resources between appropriation lines up to 5 per cent of the appropriation to which the resources were redeployed, and endorsed the revised resource allocation for programme activities in the amount of $130.2 million. Also on 15 April [res. 46/9], the Commission, noting that the Executive Director's initiatives to increase general-purpose contributions and contributions to the support budget, encouraged him to continue further cost savings and/or reduce the burden on the support budget; to broaden, in cooperation with Member States, the donor base; and to increase voluntary contributions to the Fund. He should also explore innovative means for increasing the resources for drug control programmes.

The Executive Director, in a September performance review of the 2002-2003 budget [E/CN.7/2003/20 & Add.1], noted that the final 2002-2003 budget for the UNDCP Fund amounted to $144.2 million, comprising a programme budget of $106.3 million, a final support budget of $35.4 million and agency support costs of $2.5 million. The final support budget of $35.4 million increased by $3 million (9.2 per cent), as compared with the revised support budget for 2002-2003.

By a 27 November resolution [E/2003/28/Rev.1 (res. 46/11)], the Commission approved an appropriation in the amount of $38 million for the final support budget for the 2002-2003 biennium funded under the UNDCP Fund, of which $27.6 million was allocated for programme support and $10.3 million for management and administration. It endorsed the final resource allocation for programme activities of $106.3 million for 2002-2003.

Proposed 2004-2005 budget

The budget outline for UNDCP for 2004-2005, as proposed by the Executive Director in January [E/CN.7/2003/15], amounted to $170.9 million, compared with the 2002-2003 revised budget of $166.4 million, reflecting an increase of $4.5 million, or 2.7 per cent. Of that amount, $132.2 million would be allocated for programme activities, $28.3 million for programme support, and $10.4 million for management and administration. ACABQ, in February [E/CN.7/2003/15], recommended approval of the proposed outline for the 2004-2005 biennium.

On 15 April [E/2003/28/Rev.1 (res. 46/10)], the Commission endorsed the programme and budget strategy for 2004-2005 and took note of the outline for 2004-2005 totalling $171 million, which it considered a basis for the submission of the proposed initial budget for 2004-2005 by the UNODC Executive Director.

At its reconvened forty-sixth session in November, the Commission considered a September report on the 2004-2005 UNODC consolidated budget [E/CN.7/2003/20 & Add.1]. For 2004-2005, the total budget for the UNDCP Fund amounted to $187.4 million, comprising a programme budget of $146.9 million, a support budget of $35.9 million and agency support costs of $4.6 million. Total projected resources amounted to $196 million. The proposed 2004-2005 UNODC budget was predicated on a projected total income from voluntary sources of $155.8 million, of which $141.8 million covered the drug programme, a decrease of about 1 per cent compared with the income for 2002-2003. Total income resources projected for 2004-2005 for the Office would amount to $183.7 million, of which $160.3 million was for the drug programme. General-purpose funds of $35.2 million were expected to remain at about the same level; of the total, $33 million was for the drug programme.

A November ACABQ report [E/CN.7/2003/21] stated that the consolidated budget document was a step in the UNODC reform process. It recommended that the budget should indicate the extent to which expected results would contribute to the attainment of the stated objectives, within defined time frames. It urged the Office to maintain better coordination with the Budget Division of the UN Secretariat and close collaboration with other UN entities that had introduced results-based management systems, encouraged the Executive Director's efforts, including increasing cooperation with the private sector, and stressed the need for complete transparency.

A November note by the Secretariat [E/CN.7/2003/22], submitted in response to Commission resolution 46/9 (see p. 1281), stated that the proposed 2004-2005 budget relating to section 17 of the UN regular budget was under consideration by the General Assembly, and that further consultations would be held in early 2005 when the regular budget for the 2006-2007 biennium would be prepared.

By a 27 November resolution [E/2003/28/Rev.1 (res. 46/11)], the Commission approved an appropriation of $40.5 million for the 2004-2005 initial support budget and an appropriation of $15.1 million for the initial core programme budget. It authorized the Executive Director to redeploy resources between appropriation lines in the support and core budgets of up to 5 per cent of the appropriation to which the resources were redeployed, and endorsed the initial resource allocation for technical cooperation activities in the amount of $131.8 million for 2004-2005. The Commission also endorsed the 2004-2005 programme and budget strategy and noted that implementation of the budget and additional priority programmes was subject to the availability of funding.

National Drug Control System

The Commission, in a 15 April resolution [E/2003/28/Rev.1 (res. 46/5)] on improving the exchange of electronic information among Member States and communication with international organizations, commended the broadening of the mandate and scope of the National Drug Control System to cover the collection, exchange and processing of data relevant to national and international drug control, and the provision of support to States in using it. The Commission requested that data be provided to Member States by electronic means and asked that the possibility of obtaining secure funds to deploy the System in more countries be explored and that the System be enhanced. Member States were encouraged to expand the System's use.

Commission on Narcotic Drugs

The Commission on Narcotic Drugs held its forty-sixth session in Vienna from 8 to 17 March, during which it adopted 10 resolutions and one decision and recommended to the Economic and Social Council for adoption 10 draft resolutions and two draft decisions. It held a reconvened forty-sixth session on 26 and 27 November, also in Vienna, at which it adopted a resolution on the 2002-2003 final budget and the initial budget for 2004-2005 for the UNDCP Fund (see p. 1281 and above), and brought it to the Council's attention.

Following the closure of the forty-sixth session on 27 November, the Commission opened its forty-seventh session to elect the new chairman and other bureau members.

By **decision 2003/235** of 22 July, the Council took note of the Commission's report on its forty-sixth session [E/2003/28/Rev.1] and approved the provisional agenda and documentation for the forty-seventh (2004) session, on the understanding that intersessional meetings would be held inVienna, at no additional cost, to finalize the items to be included in the provisional agenda and the documentation requirements for the forty-seventh session.

Demand reduction

In 2003, the Commission on Narcotic Drugs had before it a February report by the Executive Director on optimizing systems for collecting information and identifying the best practices to counter the demand for illicit drugs [E/CN.7/2003/8]. The report, submitted in response to

Commission resolution 45/13 [YUN 2002, p. 1248], reviewed the implementation of demand reduction activities and contained a proposed programme of work for 2003-2008 intended to achieve measurable results in demand reduction by 2008 by improving information systems for reporting on activities for reducing demand; facilitating the sharing of information on best practices; and supporting Member States seeking expertise in developing their own strategies and activities. An addendum to the report [E/CN.7/2003/8/Add.1] summarized some main principles of best practices to counter the demand for illicit drugs as reflected in the Declaration on the Guiding Principles of Drug Demand Reduction, adopted in General Assembly resolution S-20/3 [YUN 1998, p. 1137].

In a 15 April resolution [E/2003/28/Rev.1 (res. 46/1)], the Commission urged States to allocate sufficient resources to demand reduction; to ensure that reduction programmes were based on effective, evidence-based standards of research; and to develop a framework for assessing and reporting on the achievements of their national strategies, in line with the Declaration. The Commission encouraged States to share best practices and requested UNDCP to ensure that the programmes promoted had effectiveness in reducing the illicit use of drugs and in facilitating recovery from dependence or addiction. It called on States to develop knowledge of drug abuse and dependence; to use evidence-based interventions to develop prevention programmes; to develop and implement intervention programmes targeting non-dependent drug users; and to improve treatment and rehabilitation programmes for drug-dependent users as well as in community-based services.

ECONOMIC AND SOCIAL COUNCIL ACTION

On 22 July [meeting 44], the Economic and Social Council, on the recommendation of the Commission on Narcotic Drugs [E/2003/28/Rev.1], adopted **resolution 2003/33** without vote [agenda item 14 (d)].

Reduction of illicit drug demand

The Economic and Social Council,

Recalling the Declaration on the Guiding Principles of Drug Demand Reduction and the measures to enhance international cooperation to counter the world drug problem, adopted by the General Assembly at its twentieth special session,

Recognizing that the rapid evolution of the socio-economic situation, combined with cultural, personal and social factors and compounded by the availability of illicit drugs, has exacerbated the global problem of consumption of psychoactive substances,

Conscious that the problem of consumption has a greater impact on populations at risk, in particular children and young people, who, for various family and cultural reasons, have become more vulnerable and susceptible to illicit drug consumption and hazardous behaviour regarding illicit drugs,

Aware that programmes for the reduction of illicit drug demand must form part of a global strategy and that, if they are integrated and coordinated so as to offer a wide variety of appropriate measures in the community and in the education, health, labour and social welfare sectors, they will enable the targeted persons, families and communities to diminish the adverse effects of improper drug use,

Considering that the world drug problem must be dealt with on the basis of shared responsibility, which requires an integrated and balanced approach, offering people comprehensive care that will foster their development as individuals and within the community,

1. *Supports* the implementation of programmes for the reduction of illicit drug demand with global impact and scope that target the people at risk of consuming illicit drugs and the problems associated with illicit drug consumption, to be implemented in an integrated and coordinated manner in the community and in the education, health, labour and social welfare sectors;

2. *Invites* Member States to share their experience with models for intervention in the various sectors with a view to restructuring their programmes for the reduction of illicit drug demand so that the programmes will have greater impact.

Drug abuse

The Commission considered a January Secretariat report [E/CN.7/2003/4], which reviewed global patterns and trends in illicit drug consumption covering 2001 and analysed abuse patterns by drug type. It also discussed developments in the capacity to monitor illicit drug abuse. The analysis was based on the responses submitted by the 103 countries (54 per cent) that had completed and returned the annual reports questionnaire for the year 2001 by 20 November 2002, in compliance with their obligations under the international treaties.

The Commission, by a 15 April resolution [E/2003/28/Rev.1 (res. 46/7)] on measures to promote the exchange of information on new patterns of drug use and on psychoactive substances consumed, urged States to implement its resolution 45/6 [YUN 2002, p. 1248]. It invited UNODC and WHO to convene a meeting of experts to establish guidelines applicable to recording cases of drug abuse and dependence, to improve the assessment of the potential of abuse and dependence of psychoactive substances, and to establish a worldwide databank. The UNODC Executive Director was requested to report in 2004.

HIV/AIDS and other blood-borne viruses

A January report by the Executive Director [E/CN.7/2003/5], submitted in response to Commission decision 45/1 [YUN 2002, p. 1249], provided an overview of the status of the HIV/AIDS epidemic, in particular its linkage with drug use, and highlighted activities as reported by Member States through the annual reports questionnaire for the reporting period 2001, and the biennial questionnaire for the reporting cycle 2000-2002. At the end of 2002, an estimated 42 million people were living with HIV/AIDS; over 95 per cent of them were in developing countries. More than 130 countries reported the injecting of illicit drugs, and more than 110 reported HIV infections among injectors. Between 5 and 10 per cent of HIV/AIDS cases were attributable to injecting drug use, which was a major driving force of the epidemic in East Asia and the Pacific, Eastern Europe and Central Asia, where it continued to expand the fastest. In East and South-East Asia, the epidemic spread rapidly through injections, and in many Latin American and Caribbean countries, its spread through the sharing of injecting equipment was a growing concern. In North America, injecting drug use was a prominent route of HIV infection in the United States, whereas the HIV prevalence in Canada remained very low. Although the Middle East and North Africa region was one of the least affected by the epidemic, injecting drug use was a major mode of transmission. Both hepatitis B and hepatitis C were also highly prevalent among injecting drug users.

On 15 April [E/2003/28/Rev.1 (res. 46/2)], the Commission encouraged Member States to strengthen efforts to achieve the targets set in the Declaration of Commitment on HIV/AIDS, contained in General Assembly resolution S-26/2 [YUN 2001, p. 1126], in the area of HIV prevention, and to ensure that prevention, education, treatment and rehabilitation measures were accessible to all individuals, including HIV-infected drug abusers. Reiterating its concern at the negative consequences of injecting drug abuse, the Commission called on States to implement measures to reduce it; to take into account issues involving drug-related HIV infection in their national policies; and to establish monitoring and evaluation systems to assess progress. It called on the international community to invest in programmes to prevent the spread of HIV related to drug abuse. The Executive Director was requested to report in 2004.

Guidelines for travellers

The Commission, in a 15 April resolution on provisions regarding travellers under medical treatment with drugs containing narcotic drugs and psychotropic substances under international control [E/2003/28/Rev.1 (res. 46/6)], encouraged the States parties to the drug conventions (see p. 1267) to notify INCB of restrictions applicable to those travellers and requested INCB to publish that information in a unified form, in order to ensure wide dissemination and facilitate the task of government agencies. States were urged to implement recommendations on national regulations relating to travellers under medical treatment, taking into account national legal requirements and practical considerations. The UNODC Executive Director was requested to report in 2004.

Illicit cultivation and trafficking

The Commission considered a report by the Executive Director on international assistance to the States most affected by the transit of drugs [E/CN.7/2003/11], prepared in response to Economic and Social Council resolution 2002/21 [YUN 2002, p. 1250]. The report reviewed activities to support transit States through programmes in Asia and the Pacific, Latin America and the Caribbean, Eastern Europe, Central Asia and Africa. Assistance was provided to upgrade technical skills and strengthen competencies, such as data collection in support of informed responses to illicit trafficking; the provision of equipment to front-line operations; projects to build cross-border and regional cooperation; and self-sustaining instruction to provide agency training in best operating practices.

A January report by the Executive Director on strengthening international cooperation in the control of opium poppy cultivation [E/CN.7/2003/10], submitted pursuant to Commission resolution 45/10 [YUN 2002, p. 1246], stated that advisory and technical support was provided to the Transitional Administration of Afghanistan and to the United Nations Assistance Mission in Afghanistan (UNAMA) through policy support, legislation and advocacy; elimination of illicit crops; suppression of illicit drug trafficking; and drug abuse prevention and reduction. The potential positive role of microcredit and other financing schemes was studied to dissuade farmers from cultivating opium poppy.

Another January report of the Executive Director [E/CN.7/2003/9], submitted in response to Commission resolution 44/6 [YUN 2001, p. 1170], reviewed action to develop technical assistance and training on cooperation against illicit drug trafficking by sea. It analysed progress made in developing a guide for national authorities responsible for receiving and responding to requests made pursuant to article 17 of the 1988 Convention (see p. 1267). The guide contained an overview of maritime cooperation under the provisions of the Convention, provided guidelines on the establishment of a legal framework at the national level and reviewed the tasks of national authorities. To support States in their cooperation against illicit trafficking by sea, the directory of competent national authorities under the 1988 Convention was published on a quarterly basis.

On 15 April [E/2003/28/Rev.1 (res. 46/3)], the Commission, noting progress made by UNDCP in developing a practical guide for national authorities, invited States to evaluate its usefulness as an instrument for enhancing international cooperation against drug trafficking by sea. States were encouraged to establish channels for the exchange of information and to provide to UNDCP information to enable the preparation, distribution and maintenance of a directory of a national contact or contacts. The Commission also urged States with expertise in maritime interdiction to provide, in cooperation with UNDCP, assistance, training and equipment to interested States.

ECONOMIC AND SOCIAL COUNCIL ACTION

On 22 July [meeting 44], the Economic and Social Council, on the recommendation of the Commission on Narcotic Drugs [E/2003/28/Rev.1], adopted **resolution 2003/34** without vote [agenda item 14 (d)].

International assistance to the States affected by the transit of illicit drugs

The Economic and Social Council,

Recalling its resolution 2002/21 of 24 July 2002 and the Political Declaration adopted by the General Assembly at its twentieth special session, devoted to countering the world drug problem together, the Action Plan for the Implementation of the Declaration on the Guiding Principles of Drug Demand Reduction and the measures to enhance international cooperation to counter the world drug problem,

Reaffirming its resolution 2001/16 of 24 July 2001 on international assistance to the States most affected by the transit of drugs,

Taking note of the second biennial report of the Executive Director of the United Nations Office on Drugs and Crime on the implementation of the outcome of the twentieth special session of the General Assembly, his report on international assistance to the States most affected by the transit of drugs and other relevant reports submitted to the Commission on Narcotic Drugs at its forty-sixth session,

Bearing in mind the principle of shared responsibility and the need for all States to promote and implement the actions necessary to counter the world drug problem and crimes related to that problem,

Acknowledging efforts by national authorities and the international community, including the United Nations International Drug Control Programme, to reduce the demand for and to combat international trafficking in illicit drugs,

Noting the fact that the transit States continue to face grave and multifaceted challenges, owing to both the problems related to illicit drug trafficking and supply and the rising levels of drug abuse resulting from the transiting of illicit drugs through their territories,

Bearing in mind the need to strengthen law enforcement capacities at all levels and the importance of inter-agency coordination to the achievement of effective drug control strategies addressing all aspects of the world drug problem,

Recognizing the need to provide, for that purpose, international assistance to the States affected by the transit of illicit drugs,

1. *Encourages* the States affected by the transit of illicit drugs to continue to implement and strengthen law enforcement initiatives at all levels and cross-border cooperation between transit States, as well as countries of destination, with a view to promoting coordinated drug control activities and unified responses to drug trafficking;

2. *Also encourages* the States affected by the transit of illicit drugs to continue to implement and strengthen comprehensive policies for the reduction of illicit drug demand;

3. *Calls upon* the States affected by the transit of illicit drugs to ensure well-coordinated and focused policies to suppress drug trafficking through greater coordination between key agencies responsible for drug law enforcement;

4. *Calls upon* the United Nations International Drug Control Programme, subject to the availability of voluntary funds and in accordance with the guidelines for the use of general-purpose funds, adopted by the Commission on Narcotic Drugs, and Member States to facilitate such initiatives by providing assistance and technical support to the drug control authorities of the States affected by the transit of illicit drugs, in particular developing countries, including countries with economies in transition, that are in need of such assistance and support;

5. *Requests* the United Nations International Drug Control Programme and Member States, in providing such assistance to the States affected by the transit of illicit drugs, to integrate, subject to availability of voluntary funds and in accordance with guidelines for the use of general-purpose funds adopted by the Commission, projects for the reduction of illicit drug demand and the strengthening of treatment and rehabilitation services for drug abusers;

6. *Urges* the international financial institutions and other potential donors to provide financial assistance to the States affected by the transit of illicit drugs, including for empowering and building the capacity of locally available human resources, so that those States may intensify their efforts to combat drug trafficking and deal with its consequences, in particular increased drug addiction;

7. *Requests* the Executive Director of the United Nations Office on Drugs and Crime to report to the Commission on Narcotic Drugs at its forty-seventh session on the implementation of the present resolution.

On the same day [meeting 44], the Council, also on the recommendation of the Commission [E/2003/28/Rev.1], adopted **resolution 2003/35** without vote [agenda item 14 (d)].

Strengthening the prevention and suppression of illicit drug trafficking

The Economic and Social Council,

Recognizing that, in order to be effective, the elimination of illicit drug crops must be based on a regional strategy that involves international cooperation, including the strengthening of capacity to prevent trafficking in illicit drugs from producer countries, taking into account the need to make alternative development products competitive,

Recalling that Governments have adopted various measures to promote multilateral, regional, subregional and bilateral cooperation between judicial, law enforcement and tax authorities so as to deal in a comprehensive manner with criminal groups involved in drug trafficking,

1. *Reaffirms* the importance of broad policies to eliminate illicit drug crops and of the implementation of legislation, in particular legislation to facilitate the interdiction of illicit drug shipments, in support of illicit drug crop eradication and elimination, alternative development and strong law enforcement efforts at reducing the supply of illicit drugs;

2. *Calls upon* States to adopt effective measures to strengthen international cooperation projects aimed at the prohibition and control of drug trafficking and to deal with the activities of criminal groups involved in such trafficking and the diversification of their methods and transport routes;

3. *Urges* States to include among those measures the exchange of mutual legal and investigatory assistance to combat criminal groups involved in drug trafficking, and to promote the further development of effective models for cooperation, in particular in the areas of air, sea and port control, and the enhanced monitoring of controlled precursors and chemical components.

Secretariat report. A report by the Secretariat [E/CN.7/2004/4] described global trends and patterns in illicit drug production during 2002-2003 and trafficking up to 2002. Information on illicit cultivation and production was drawn from the illicit crop-monitoring surveys presented by UNODC. Information on seizures in 2002 was drawn from the annual reports questionnaire submitted by Governments to UNODC, and, in 2003, it was drawn from government reports on significant seizures. Other sources included country reports received by UNODC or submitted to the Commission and reports from UNODC field offices.

Alternative development

A February report [E/CN.7/2003/17] by the Executive Director, prepared in response to Commission resolution 45/14 [YUN 2002, p. 1250], described development-oriented drug control mechanisms and discussed possibilities for innovative funding mechanisms. UNODC undertook pilot projects and advocated and built alternative development interventions and projects. At the country level, the United Nations Development Assistance Framework (UNDAF) and the resident coordinator system helped to integrate the drug component in the UN agenda and promoted inter-agency cooperation. In most countries with alternative development schemes, including in Bolivia, Colombia, the Lao People's Democratic Republic, Lebanon, Peru and Viet Nam, the drug aspect was addressed through UNDAF. In the area of alternative product marketing, partnerships with the private sector, foundations and corporate entities facilitated the sharing of commitments and resources for alternative development. Regarding possibilities for innovative funding mechanisms, the report stated that, although UNODC had not established a special funding mechanism for alternative development, it had made approaches to secure more attention, support and resources. The report concluded that efforts to support alternative development would be positively affected by a stable and predictable core funding base; the long-term commitment of resources to alternative development projects; and the inclusion of alternative development in sustainable development policies and operations by the major development and financial institutions.

ECONOMIC AND SOCIAL COUNCIL ACTION

On 22 July [meeting 44], the Economic and Social Council, on the recommendation of the Commission on Narcotic Drugs [E/2003/28/Rev.1], adopted **resolution 2003/37** without vote [agenda item 14 *(d)*].

Strengthening alternative development through trade and socio-environmental preservation

The Economic and Social Council,

Recalling the Action Plan on International Cooperation on the Eradication of Illicit Drug Crops and on Alternative Development, adopted by the General Assembly at its twentieth special session, which states that alternative development is an important component for generating and promoting lawful, viable and sustainable economic options to illicit drug crop cultivation, that States with illicit drug crops will need continued funding to support national efforts to eliminate drug crops and that the success of alternative development programmes depends, inter alia, on the long-term political and financial commitment of the Governments of the affected countries and the international community,

Reaffirming Commission on Narcotic Drugs resolution 45/14 of 15 March 2002, in which the Commission invited Member States to make more comprehensive and determined efforts in the area of financial and technical cooperation aimed at promoting alternative development, including, where appropriate, preventive alternative development, and urged the United Nations International Drug Control Programme to enlarge its base of donors and to use available voluntary resources to increase the financial and technical assistance that it provides to alternative development programmes, including, where appropriate, preventive alternative development,

Aware of the importance of programmes promoting alternative development, including, where appropriate, preventive alternative development,

Urging Member States to consider that the presence of illicit drug crops and illicit cultivation and production leads to the degradation of the environment,

Noting with concern that the existence of illicit crops and illicit cultivation and production seriously damages the environment and causes severe socio-economic problems, in particular for highly vulnerable populations, and that effective crop control strategies require an integrated and balanced approach, in particular alternative development, including, where appropriate, preventive alternative development,

1. *Urges* the United Nations International Drug Control Programme and all Member States to continue to cooperate effectively on programmes to promote alternative development, including, where appropriate, preventive alternative development, in accordance with the provisions of Commission on Narcotic Drugs resolution 45/14;

2. *Calls upon* the international community and Member States to promote an economic environment that is favourable to products from alternative development and that facilitates the access of such products to international markets as an effective and efficient means of eliminating the illicit economy;

3. *Reiterates* the necessity of encouraging access to international markets for products, including produce, from alternative development areas;

4. *Urges* Member States, in accordance with the principle of shared responsibility and as a sign of their commitment to the fight against illicit drugs, to extend cooperation in the area of alternative development to include technical assistance, support for the protection of the environment, sustainable development of forest resources, creation of social and productive infrastructure and promotion of private investment and agro-industry, as well as facilitation of the access of alternative development products to markets;

5. *Calls upon* Member States to share their experience in programmes to eliminate or reduce illicit crop cultivation, thereby taking into account common socio-economic and environmental factors, and to encourage the participation of local inhabitants in such programmes;

6. *Encourages* Member States, multilateral financial institutions, regional development banks and non-governmental organizations to focus attention on measures designed to protect society, in particular highly vulnerable populations, and the environment from the harmful effects of illicit drugs;

7. *Resolves* to promote the implementation of programmes of the United Nations Office on Drugs and Crime, subject to the availability of voluntary funds, which might be from general-purpose funds, in accordance with the guidelines adopted by the Commission on Narcotic Drugs, or from earmarked funds, and programmes of other relevant organizations for alternative development, including, where appropriate, preventive alternative development, through an integrated approach to the development of vulnerable areas that includes strategies for the preservation of the environment, security, monitoring, education, health, sanitation and community development.

Regional cooperation

In a report to the Commission [E/CN.7/2004/5], the Secretariat reviewed action taken by the Commission's subsidiary bodies in 2003. Following a review of trafficking trends and regional and subregional cooperation, each subsidiary body addressed drug law enforcement issues of priority concern to its region and made recommendations. The thirty-eighth session of the Subcommission on Illicit Drug Traffic and Related Matters in the Near and Middle East (Amman, Jordan, 23-27 June) [UNODC/SUBCOM/2003/5], considered regional trends in opiate trafficking; identifying traffickers through effective document control; and illicit manufacture and distribution of stimulants. The thirteenth meeting of Heads of National Drug Law Enforcement Agencies (HONLEA), Africa (Port Louis, Mauritius, 8-12 September) [UNODC/HONLAF/2003/5] considered regional trends in opiate and cannabis trafficking; illicit manufacture and distribution of stimulants; identifying sound practice in training for Africa's law enforcement officials; and mobilizing community support for law enforcement anti-drug strategies. The thirteenth meeting of HONLEA, Latin America and the Caribbean (Salvador, Brazil, 20-24 October) [UNODC/HONLAC/2003/5] examined the value of effective controlled delivery operations; strengthening information exchange and operational cooperation at the interagency, cross-border and regional levels; and new global threats: challenges to law enforcement from globalization. The twenty-seventh meeting of HONLEA, Asia and the Pacific (Bangkok, Thailand, 8-12 December) [UNODC/HONLAP/2003/5] reviewed effective mechanisms to support operational cross-border cooperation; the appropriateness of national drug law enforcement strategies to the current world situation; identifying traffickers through effective document control; and the region's response to the increasing availability of ATS.

ECONOMIC AND SOCIAL COUNCIL ACTION

On 22 July [meeting 44], the Economic and Social Council, on the recommendation of the Commission on Narcotic Drugs [E/2003/28/Rev.1], adopted **resolution 2003/38** without vote [agenda item 14 (d)].

Funding of travel for participants in meetings of heads of national drug law enforcement agencies

The Economic and Social Council,

Recalling General Assembly resolutions 53/115 of 9 December 1998, 54/132 of 17 December 1999, 55/65 of 4 December 2000 and 56/124 of 19 December 2001, in which the Assembly stressed the importance of the meetings of Heads of National Drug Law Enforcement Agencies, in all regions of the world, and the Subcommission on Illicit Drug Traffic and Related Matters in the Near and Middle East of the Commission on Narcotic Drugs, and encouraged them to continue to contribute to the strengthening of regional and international cooperation, taking into account the outcome of the twentieth special session of the General Assembly,

Recalling also its resolution 1985/11 of 28 May 1985, in which it requested the Secretary-General to convene regular meetings of the operational heads of the national drug control and law enforcement agencies of States in the African region to study questions related to illicit drug traffic in the region and to establish more effective mechanisms for cooperation and mutual assistance in the suppression of illicit drug traffic within, from and into the region,

Recalling further its resolution 1987/34 of 26 May 1987, in which it invited the Governments of the Latin American and the Caribbean countries and other interested Governments to participate in the regional meeting of the heads of national drug law enforcement agencies with a view to establishing the Meeting of Heads of National Drug Law Enforcement Agencies, Latin America and the Caribbean, and requested the Secretary-General to adopt the necessary measures and to provide the financial resources required for holding the regional meeting,

Recalling its resolution 1988/15 of 25 May 1988, in which it requested the Secretary-General to take the necessary measures to convene annually the Meetings of Heads of National Drug Law Enforcement Agencies, Asia and the Pacific, Africa, and Latin America and the Caribbean, and to provide the financial resources required from available resources and, if necessary, to seek additional extrabudgetary resources,

Recalling also its resolution 1992/28 of 30 July 1992 on improvement of the functioning of the subsidiary bodies of the Commission on Narcotic Drugs, in which it requested the Commission to examine further, on a regular basis, the functioning of the subsidiary bodies of the Commission,

Recalling further Commission on Narcotic Drugs resolution 45/2 of 15 March 2002, in which the Commission reiterated its request to the Secretary-General to provide the regional meetings of Heads of National Drug Law Enforcement Agencies with the financial resources to assist those States which could not otherwise be represented, by defraying the travel expenses for one participant from each of those States,

1. *Confirms* that the meetings of Heads of National Drug Law Enforcement Agencies, as subsidiary bodies of the Commission on Narcotic Drugs, have the same status as the Subcommission on Illicit Drug Traffic and Related Matters in the Near and Middle East;

2. *Recognizes* that the annual meetings of Heads of National Drug Law Enforcement Agencies relate to the programme of work of the United Nations International Drug Control Programme, which is funded from the regular budget of the United Nations;

3. *Requests* the Secretary-General to provide, from within available resources of the regular budget of the United Nations, the meetings of Heads of National Drug Law Enforcement Agencies with the financial resources to assist those States which could not otherwise be represented, by defraying the travel expenses for one participant from each of those States, as is done for the Subcommission on Illicit Drug Traffic and Related Matters in the Near and Middle East.

Strengthening UN mechanisms

The Commission on Narcotic Drugs had before it a report by the UNDCP Executive Director on strengthening the drug control programme and the role of the Commission [E/CN.7/2003/14]. The report, prepared in response to Commission resolution 45/17 [YUN 2002, p. 1252], reviewed progress made to implement its resolution 44/16 [YUN 2001, p. 1172] regarding strengthening dialogue between Member States and the programme; improving the effectiveness of the Commission's work; the programme's operations and management; and funding.

On 15 April [E/2003/28/Rev.1 (res. 46/8)], the Commission urged the continued reform of the drug control programme, based on resolutions 44/16 and 45/17 and the recommendations contained in the reports of the Office of Internal Oversight Services [YUN 2001, p. 1167], the Board of Auditors and the Joint Inspection Unit [YUN 2002, p. 1358], and called on the Executive Director to complete their implementation and develop existing reforms. Reaffirming its governing role in the programme's budget process, the Commission requested UNDCP to continue to present briefings and reports to States, such as the progress report on management reform entitled "Commitment to good governance". The Commission called on the Executive Director to consider as priorities the development and application of expertise in evaluation and monitoring. He was requested to report in 2004.

Chapter XV

Statistics

The United Nations continued its statistical work programme in 2003, mainly through the Statistical Commission and the United Nations Statistics Division. In March, the Commission endorsed the Division's proposed actions in support of the 2010 round of population and housing censuses; approved the draft terms of reference for the newly established Advisory Committee on Indicators; and endorsed the draft work programme of the Statistics Division for the 2004-2005 biennium.

The Commission reviewed the work of groups of countries and international organizations in various areas of economic, social, demographic and environment statistics and made specific recommendations and suggestions.

Work of Statistical Commission

The Statistical Commission held its thirty-fourth session in New York from 4 to 7 March [E/2003/24]. Actions included: endorsement of the proposed activities to be undertaken by the United Nations Statistics Division in support of the 2010 round of population and housing censuses and of the scope of the updating process of the 1993 System of National Accounts (SNA), with a view to maintaining the current system's fundamentals and its consistency with related manuals. The Commission also endorsed the managing and coordinating role of the Intersecretariat Working Group on National Accounts (ISWGNA) in the updating process, with the assistance of an Advisory Group on National Accounts (AGNA), and further endorsed the targeted publication date of 2008.

Having reviewed the statistical work of groups of countries and international organizations, the Commission requested the creation of a "Friends of the Chair" group to examine coordination in the production and dissemination of health statistics and to recommend improvements. It endorsed the Division's proposal to hold, in collaboration with the Siena Group for Social Statistics, an expert group meeting on setting the scope of social statistics and to prepare a compendium on best practices in poverty statistics. The Commission welcomed the report of the Office for National Statistics (United Kingdom), which summarized topical issues concerning the new economy; noted the progress made in agricultural statistics, in particular the modernization of FAOSTAT (the corporate statistical database of the Food and Agriculture Organization of the United Nations (FAO)); and agreed with the proposal to create an international advisory panel on agricultural statistics. The Commission also welcomed the Australian Bureau of Statistics report on service statistics activities and suggested that the Organisation for Economic Co-operation and Development (OECD) take the lead in project management and coordination of work in that field. It commended the World Bank's efforts that had resulted in significant developments in the International Comparison Programme (ICP), endorsed the composition of ICP's new Executive Board and welcomed the progress made by the Programme's new Global Office in coordinating work on purchasing power parities. It also supported the Statistics Division's work outline for environment statistics and agreed that an inter-agency working group should be set up on that subject. It further noted the proposal by OECD, the Statistical Office of the European Communities (Eurostat) and the Economic Commission for Europe (ECE) to establish a steering committee on sustainable development statistics. The Commission supported the need for a "concepts paper" to provide a basis for the revisions of the International Standard Industrial Classification of All Economic Activities (ISIC) and the Central Product Classification (CPC), and reiterated its expectation of a positive outcome of the convergence between the General Industrial Classification of Economic Activities within the European Communities (NACE) and the North American Industry Classification System (NAICS). The Commission authorized its Chairman to finalize the report on indicators, which was requested by the Economic and Social Council in 2002 [YUN 2002, p. 1254]; asked that the report emphasize the need for international support to statistical capacity-building in developing countries; stressed the need to pay attention to indicators for monitoring implementation of the UN Millennium Development Goal (MDG) [YUN 2000, p. 51] on developing a global partnership for development; and approved the draft terms of reference for the Advisory Committee on Indicators. The Commission emphasized the importance of statistical capacity-building, stressing that statistical capacity-building efforts needed to be an integral part of development programmes, and endorsed the Statistics Division's technical cooperation programme. It agreed that Commission and Division actions were consistent with Economic and Social Council policy decisions. The Commission welcomed the establishment of the Committee for the Coordination of Statistical Activities and requested that it work on a common approach to data quality assessment. It also requested that the Statistics Division and the Committee continue to work on the issue of reviewing and resolving data-collection duplication. The Commission endorsed the Division's proposed draft work programme for the 2004-2005 biennium and approved the revised 2003 work programme. The Commission noted or gave direction to the work of a number of statistical groups (see below).

On 24 July (**decision 2003/284**), the Economic and Social Council deferred consideration of the item on statistics to its resumed 2003 session. On 19 December (**decision 2003/317**), the Council deferred consideration of the Statistical Commission's report on its thirty-fourth session to its organizational session in 2004.

Economic statistics

National accounts

In response to a 2002 Statistical Commission request [YUN 2002, p. 1254], the Secretary-General submitted the report of the Task Force on National Accounts [E/CN.3/2003/9]. The report assessed the implementation of the 1993 SNA [YUN 1993, p. 1112] and reviewed coordination of related work programmes. It discussed the treatment of a number of issues in applying SNA: accrual accounting of interest; repurchase agreements; interest under conditions of high inflation; pension funds; employee stock option plans; non-performing loans; insurance/reinsurance; financial services; software; and taxes on capital gains. It also reviewed the current procedure for updating the 1993 SNA.

The report also contained the recommendations of ISWGNA for the future updating of the SNA and other ISWGNA actions to strengthen the updating procedure.

With regard to the assessment of the implementation of the 1993 SNA, it was reported that the conceptual compliance questionnaire was sent to all countries by the end of September 2002. The assessment report would be submitted to the Commission in 2004.

The Commission had recommended in 2002 [YUN 2002, p. 1254] that the Statistics Division collect data on national accounts quarterly, in addition to annual data. ISWGNA recommended that the Division not replicate International Monetary Fund (IMF) and OECD work in that area.

In March [E/2003/24], the Commission endorsed the scope of the updating process, with a view to maintaining the fundamentals of the current 1993 SNA and its consistency with related publications like the *Balance of Payments Manual*, the *Government Finance Statistics Manual* and the *Monetary and Financial Statistics Manual*. It supported the three criteria for identifying issues for SNA updating and recommended the inclusion of two additional criteria: user needs and feasibility. The Commission also endorsed the managing and coordinating role of ISWGNA in the updating process, requested the preparation of a project document describing the 1993 SNA updating and delineating AGNA's role, and advised ISWGNA to circulate the document to member countries for input. It further endorsed the list of issues to be updated, recommending that it be an open-ended list, and the targeted publication date of 2008 for the updated 1993 SNA. It considered the deadline of 2005 for the conclusions to be submitted to the Commission too optimistic and suggested that it be moved to mid-2006. The Commission noted the concerns of some member countries about the decision-making process regarding past ISWGNA submissions of solutions and recognized the desirability of arriving at solutions in a spirit of compromise, ensuring a thorough analysis of issues by set deadlines. It further noted the concerns of developing countries and international bodies about the challenges faced in implementing the current 1993 SNA and the need to maintain international comparability. The Commission emphasized the need to widen the participation of Member States in the updating process and urged timely translation of the officially approved document in all the official languages of the United Nations.

Services statistics

The Commission considered a report by the Australian Bureau of Statistics on the statistics of services [E/CN.3/2003/12], which gave particular attention to the classification of services and products, price indexes for services, international trade in services and short-term indicators in services. Conceptual and measurement issues in emerging areas of information and communication technology, knowledge-based economy, innovation, globalization and non-profit institutions were also covered. The report concluded that the main issues were: whether the international statistical community needed to increase the priority of and resources devoted to services statistics; whether current coordination mechanisms could be made more efficient; and how the provision of practical measurement guidance to developing countries might be coordinated. The Commission also had before it the Secretary-General's note transmitting the report of the Task Force on Statistics of International Trade in Services [E/CN.3/2003/15], which noted the publication of its *Manual on Statistics of International Trade in Services*.

The Commission noted the activities related to services statistics of the city and expert groups, and emphasized that participation of developing countries in those groups needed to be facilitated. It noted the need for a "project management" approach and coordination of work in services statistics, and suggested that OECD take the lead in that regard; agreed that the coordination function should not be carried out by existing city groups, whose work should remain focused on methodological issues; and noted that the coordination function would include a continuous overview of activities, ensuring and facilitating communication between the different groups involved, and identifying overlaps, links and gaps in data-collection, in methodological issues and in setting work priorities. The Commission encouraged the preparation of a single annual report on the work of the various expert and city groups, which should be submitted to the Commission. It suggested that the future work on implementation of the *Manual on Statistics of International Trade in Services* should focus on increasing data quality rather than on introducing more detailed statistics.

International Comparison Programme

The Commission had before it the Secretary-General's note transmitting a World Bank report on ICP [E/CN.3/2003/13] [YUN 2002, p. 1255]. The Commission acknowledged the important role of the Friends of the Chair as an interim governing body and noted that, with ICP's new management structure, the group would be disbanded. It commended the World Bank's work, which had resulted in significant developments, endorsed the ICP Executive Board's composition and welcomed the progress achieved by the ICP Global Office in centrally coordinating purchasing power parities. The Commission stressed that country ownership of the Programme should be strongly emphasized and that continuous communication with national statistical offices was essential. It recognized the interrelationship between scope, coverage and funding issues; noted that alternative proposals had been elaborated in case of budget constraints, resulting in the necessity of reconsidering limiting the Programme to the comparison of consumption for a smaller number of countries; and encouraged additional funding and in-kind Programme support at the regional and global levels and bilateral support to countries seeking technical assistance. The Commission concluded that the Programme timetable provided an adequate basis for implementing ICP in a timely fashion, and noted that its presentation in a room document had contributed to its transparency. It welcomed the preparation of the draft ICP handbook and supported the initiative for wider information dissemination on the Programme through the ICP newsletter and web site. The Commission supported the ICP implementation, emphasizing its capacity-building potential in consumer price and national accounts statistics, as well as price and household consumption surveys, and stressed the need to develop the Programme so as to ensure its sustainability beyond the current phase.

A December World Bank report [E/CN.3/2004/14] discussed ICP's organizational and financial status at the regional and global levels, noting that, although significant progress had been made in resource mobilization, response to fund-raising had not met expectations and the Programme faced a shortfall of $6.8 million.

Finance statistics

The Commission had before it the report of the Task Force on Finance Statistics [E/CN.3/2003/16] on activities undertaken to improve the methodological soundness, transparency, timeliness and availability of data on external debt and international reserves.

The Commission welcomed the cooperation among international organizations within the Task Force, congratulated the Task Force on completing *External Debt Statistics: Guide for Compilers and Users*, and welcomed IMF's training seminars for managers and external debt data compilers on collection, quality improvement and cross-country data comparability. It endorsed the Task Force as a forum to address external debt statistics issues and encouraged research on vulnerability assessment. The Commission supported Task Force and IMF efforts to develop a centralized external debt statistics database to complement the joint Bank for International Settlements/IMF/OECD/World Bank statistics (BIOWS) database; develop further BIOWS with regard to short-term debt data; identify information repositories so as to assess external debt data gaps; and analyse and reconcile statistics compiled by debtors and creditors. It acknowledged the Task Force's effort to assist IMF in developing a data quality assessment framework.

Other economic statistics

Measuring the new economy

The Secretary-General transmitted to the Commission a report by the United Kingdom Office for National Statistics on the International Association for Official Statistics conference on "official statistics and the new economy" (London, 27-29 August 2002) [E/CN.3/2003/10].

The Commission recognized that the "new economy" involved advanced levels of knowledge and information and communication technologies; it had led to rapid changes on a global scale, affecting many statistical domains, especially services statistics, and entailing highly complex conceptual issues, including measurement, one of which could involve changes in comparative advantage and how wealth was created. The Commission endorsed the recommendation that international bodies set clear research priorities and agreed that close cooperation between international bodies and national statistical offices and the sharing of good practice were required to move the agenda forward.

Agriculture statistics

The Secretary-General transmitted to the Commission the FAO report on recent developments in agricultural statistics and future plans [E/CN.3/2003/11 & Corr.1]. The Commission noted the progress made in agricultural statistics, particularly the modernization of FAOSTAT, the promotion of the decennial Programme of the World Census of Agriculture and the renewed activities in agricultural producer price statistics. It welcomed FAO's monitoring of two indicators among the MDGs: prevalence of undernourishment and percentage of forest cover. The Commission expressed support for the future methodological development plans that would broaden the scope of agricultural statistics, move towards demand-side statistics and develop a framework of new concepts and methods for rural statistics. It affirmed that more resources would be needed for FAO to fulfil its leadership role and extend its programme in agricultural statistics and agreed with the proposal to create an international advisory panel on agricultural statistics.

International trade statistics

The Secretary-General transmitted to the Commission the report of the Task Force on International Trade Statistics [E/CN.3/2003/14], which discussed the impact of e-commerce on international trade statistics; international trade statistics according to CPC; and alternative trade data sources. The Task Force identified the need for a manual on international trade indices and IMF had agreed to explore the possibility of leading that effort. The Commission took note of the work and plans of the Task Force; endorsed its plans to develop a manual on import and export price indices; and welcomed IMF's intention to develop that manual.

Price indexes and statistics

The Commission had before it the report of the Ottawa Group on Price Indexes [E/CN.3/2003/17]. It took note of the Group's report and its plan to hold a meeting in 2003 to provide a forum for sharing experience on crucial problems of measuring price change.

ISWGPS

Having considered the report of the Intersecretariat Working Group on Price Statistics (ISWGPS) [E/CN.3/2003/18], the Commission noted that the Manual on Consumer Price Indexes was almost completed and that its improved structure reflected stronger emphasis on practical issues of compilation of consumer price indexes. It also noted that the work on the Producer Price Index Manual was well advanced, with an expected late 2003 publication date. The Commission recommended that ISWGPS explore the possible future direction of its work after its initial mandate on the elaboration of the manuals was accomplished.

Environment statistics

The Commission had before it the Secretary-General's report on environment statistics [E/CN.3/2003/19], which summarized the results of two international collections of environmental data carried out by the Statistics Division in 1999 and 2001. It also outlined a work programme for the improvement of the regular collection, compilation and dissemination of international environment statistics.

The Commission underlined the complexity of environment statistics, acknowledged existing methodological and institutional difficulties, and emphasized the high priority to be given at the international level to the new and developing area of environment statistics. It supported the work programme outlined in the report; emphasized the need for a continuous review of data collection; and stressed the need to intensify work in the development of standards, concepts and methods. The Commission also underlined the need to link development of environment statistics with statistics on sustainable development; recognized the importance of national collaboration between data producers and policy makers; and stressed the role of training and national capacity-building in developing environment statistics. It agreed that the Statistics Division should set up an inter-agency working group on environment statistics; and took note of the OECD/Eurostat/ECE joint proposal to establish a steering group on statistics of sustainable development.

Demographic and social statistics

Population and housing censuses

The Commission considered the Secretary-General's report on population and housing censuses [E/CN.3/2003/2], which summarized activities undertaken during 2002, approved for 2003, proposed for the 2004-2005 biennium and requested by the Commission for inclusion in the Statistics Division's work programme in subsequent bienniums.

During 2002, the Division conducted training programmes to strengthen national capabilities in census operations, analysis, dissemination and the promotion of census results; drafted the handbook on the collection of fertility and mortality data and submitted it for publication; and issued a technical report on the collection of economic characteristics in population censuses. It also published the proceedings of the 2001 global review of the 2000 round of population and housing censuses, on the theme "Mid-decade assessment and future prospects"; and began to draft a handbook on household demographic and social surveys.

The approved activities for 2003 included an expert group meeting to review the handbook on household demographic and social surveys, and workshops and meetings to consider concerns expressed by the Commission. Activities for the 2004-2005 biennium included two specific Commission requests from its thirty-third (2002) session: a follow-up symposium in 2004 on the experience of the 2000 round of censuses and a report on the collection, compilation and dissemination of international migration statistics [E/CN.3/2003/2].

The Commission endorsed the activities proposed in the report, emphasizing that they would need to be completed by 2006 in order to respond to country requirements and contribute to the 2010 planning of population and housing censuses. It recommended the inclusion of other activities: the development of guidelines and sharing of experience in the use of the Internet in census data collection and dissemination, and development of new technologies for data capturing to improve efficiency and cost-effectiveness; the preparation of technical documents on successes and failures in the 2000 round of national censuses, post-enumeration surveys based on national experience from the 2000 round and the use of geographical information systems and digital mapping in data collection and dissemination; and further work on the use of new technology to capture data on human settlements, including slums. The Commission suggested themes for the 2004 symposium: mobilization of broad public acceptance and support for census activities; approaches to the collection and dissemination of data on race and ethnicity; and cost-effectiveness of post-enumeration surveys. It requested the development of a handbook to complement the *Recommendations on Statistics of International Migration, Revision 1* [Sales No. E. 98.XVII.14], and the organization of workshops to review and assess national experience in implementating the recommendations; that population and housing censuses be an integral part of national statistical systems; and that work be undertaken to identify instruments that could be used to ensure accurate and reliable measurement of population change during intercensal periods.

Health statistics

The Secretary-General transmitted to the Commission a report by the World Health Organization (WHO) on its recent work in health statistics [E/CN.3/2003/3]. WHO worked with countries to strengthen their capacity to collect and analyse their own data, and to measure and report indicators; it was in the process of establishing additional advisory committees using external experts.

The Commission also had before it reports on health statistics submitted by the Australian Bureau of Statistics [E/CN.3/2003/4], the Central Statistics Office of Botswana [E/CN.3/2003/5 & Corr.1] and Eurostat [E/CN.3/2003/6].

The Commission expressed concern about the lack of consultation, coordination and collaboration between WHO and national statistical offices and regional and international organizations. It emphasized that primary data collection was the responsibility of countries, while international organizations were responsible for assistance in statistical standards development and technical support to countries. The Commission reiterated the need for transparency and openness in methods used to compile and generate health statistics, and for coordination in the use of existing national sources. It expressed support for WHO's work on international classifications, and requested that guidelines be prepared on national health accounts and on the implementation of the automated coding system for recording cause of death.

It also requested WHO, in collaboration with the Statistics Division and other relevant UN bodies, to explore alternative methods of estimating the prevalence of HIV/AIDS. The Commission further requested the creation of a Friends of the Chair group to examine coordination among international organizations and between international organizations and national statistical offices in the production and dissemination of health statistics and to recommend improvements.

Social statistics

The Commission considered the Secretary-General's report on social statistics [E/CN.3/2003/7], which described activities to be carried out by the Statistics Division in response to the expressed need for a more systematic development of social statistics, improved measurement of disability and the preparation of a poverty compendium on best practices. The Commission also had before it the report of the Office for National Statistics of the United Kingdom on the theme "Official statistics and the new economy" (see p. 1292).

The Commission welcomed the Secretary-General's report and endorsed the activities proposed therein, including the holding of an expert group meeting in May, in collaboration with the Siena Group for Social Statistics, on setting the scope of social statistics. That meeting, it underscored, needed to deliver clear outcomes and develop a time frame for achieving set goals; review current coordinating activities, with particular attention to setting good practices and standards; take into account the progress made in the area of development indicators; and consider the implications for social statistics contained in the report of the Office for National Statistics of the United Kingdom on official statistics and the new economy. The Commission supported the collection of disability statistics through the *Demographic Yearbook* system; emphasized the need to ensure the collection of internationally comparable disability statistics; encouraged the Statistics Division to work with the Washington Group on Disability Measurement (see below) to identify items for which statistical disability information was comparable; and advised the judicious and complementary use of sources of disability statistics, namely, censuses, surveys and administrative records. The Commission endorsed the proposal to prepare a compendium on best practices in poverty statistics, which should address the needs of developing countries and have an applied focus; it stressed the importance of the compendium's timely and progressive release. The Commission urged proactive consultation with other institutions that had expertise in poverty data collection and measurement and recommended the compilation of gender-relevant statistics.

The Expert Group Meeting on Setting the Scope of Social Statistics took place in New York from 6 to 9 May [ESA/STAT/AC.88/04]. The Expert Group Meeting to Review the United Nations *Demographic Yearbook* System took place in New York from 10 to 14 November [ESA/STAT/AC.91/L4].

Disability measurement

The Commission had before it the report of the Washington Group on Disability Measurement [E/CN.3/2003/8], which discussed the dissemination of the results of the first meeting of the Washington Group and outlined plans for future meetings. The Commission noted that disability was a complex and difficult area of statistical measurement. It advised caution in the policy use of information generated from general measures of disability since the purpose and use of such data might require a range of disability measures.

Other statistical activities

International economic and social classifications

The Commission considered the Secretary-General's report on international economic and social classifications [E/CN.3/2003/20], which outlined how the Commission's 2002 recommendations [YUN 2002, p. 1257] had been addressed. The Commission also had before it background documents on the 2007 revision of ISIC and CPC: a draft concepts paper, and on the report of the Working Group on the Convergence of NACE and NAICS.

The Commission supported the need for the concepts paper to provide a conceptual basis for the ISIC and CPC revisions, and noted that country consultations would facilitate further discussion and refinement. It stressed the need for a link between activity and product classifications, and for continuity through links to previous versions of the classifications; it cautioned against substantial changes. The Commission reiterated its expectation of a positive outcome of the convergence process between NACE and NAICS, welcomed the steps taken and emphasized the need to continue consultations in Europe. It noted the need for funding in some regions to ensure inclusion of the countries concerned in the revision process; recommended that national consultations on classifications involve a variety of users; and noted the need for increased integration of classifications activities, products and occupations. The Commission requested that the International Standard Classification of Occupations (ISCO) revision timetable be reviewed, noting that moving deadlines forward was necessary to meet the needs of the next census rounds, and suggested the creation of a technical subgroup to assist in the ISCO revision.

Follow-up to UN conferences and summits

In response to a 2002 Statistical Commission request [YUN 2002, p. 1258], the Secretary-General submitted a report on the harmonization of indicators and progress towards realizing the MDGs [E/CN.3/2003/21], in the context of the United Nations Millennium Declaration [YUN 2000, p. 49] follow-up process [YUN 2001, p. 1278]. The Statistics Division's work had primarily focused on following up the Economic and Social Council's mandate in resolution 2000/27 [YUN 2000, p. 1377] to harmonize and rationalize conference indicators and prepare the statistical base material for the annual report on progress towards the MDGs (see p. 1384). The Commission also had before it the Secretary-General's note transmitting the report of the United Nations Development Programme on the status of MDG country reporting [E/CN.3/2003/22].

The Commission authorized its Chairman to finalize the report on indicators that was requested in Council decision 2002/311 [YUN 2002, p. 1254], requesting that the report emphasize the need for international support for statistical capacity-building in developing countries to meet the needs for development indicators on a sustainable basis. It stressed the need to pay particular attention to indicators for monitoring implementation of the MDG to develop a global partnership for development and recommended that developed countries prepare progress reports on assistance to developing countries for the achievement of the goals contained in the Millennium Declaration, with at least one such report being prepared by each developed country by 2004, in time for the Secretary-General's 2005 comprehensive review. The Commission approved the draft terms of reference for the Standing Advisory Committee on Development Indicators, requested that they be sent to Commission members within two weeks, and decided that the Advisory Committee should submit recommendations for Commission approval. It agreed that further harmonization and prioritization in the field of development indicators were needed, particularly with regard to MDG indicators and the indicator architecture recommended by the Friends of the Chair and endorsed by the Commission in 2002 [ibid., p. 1258]. The Commission emphasized that internationally recommended indicators should be adapted in each country and that national statistical services played a leading role in developing national country reports. It noted the progress in preparing the next ICP round and the value of those data in preparing internationally comparable estimates for the indicator for the MDG of eradicating extreme poverty and hunger. The Commission called on the international statistical services to provide developing countries with more extensive guidance, documentation and training materials on international standards and best practices in data collection and analysis relating to development indicators and monitoring of progress towards the MDGs, and their role in policy planning and implementation.

Report of Secretary-General. In response to Economic and Social Council decision 2002/311 [YUN 2002, p. 1254], the Statistical Commission submitted a May report [E/2003/83], in which it presented an overview of its work on development indicators, as reported at the Commission's thirty-third (2002) session [YUN 2002, p. 1258] and as described in the Secretary-General's 2002 report on basic indicators for the integrated and coordinated follow-up to major UN conferences and summits at all levels [ibid., p. 1436]. The report included proposals for future activities.

By **decision 2003/227** of 15 July, the Council took note of the report.

(See also p. 1467.)

Statistical capacity-building

The Commission considered the Secretary-General's report [E/CN.3/2003/23], which described the Statistics Division's technical cooperation activities that sought to build the statistical capacity of countries and regions. The Commission also had before it the annual report of the Steering Committee of the Partnership in Statistics for Development in the Twenty-first Century (PARIS 21) [E/CN.3/2003/24], which provided an update on the work of PARIS 21, the programme of regional workshops and the activities and outputs of the task teams, including the completion of the report on indicators of statistical capacity-building. It also discussed future plans, including the 2003 evaluation of PARIS 21 achievements.

The Commission emphasized the importance of statistical capacity-building, stressing that efforts in that regard needed to be an integral part of development programmes. It also emphasized the importance of effective collaboration of all technical cooperation providers. The Commission endorsed the Statistics Division's technical cooperation programme, took note of the indicator framework for statistical capacity and encouraged PARIS 21 to conduct further testing in member States, and welcomed the offer of PARIS 21 to submit a report on the dissemination of statistics at the Commission's next (2004) session.

Coordination and integration of statistical programmes

The Commission considered the report of the inter-agency meeting on coordination of statistical activities (New York, 17-19 September 2002) [E/CN.3/2003/25], which discussed the need to develop a new coordination system, given that the Administrative Committee on Coordination Subcommittee on Statistical Activities had been disbanded in 2001 [YUN 2002, p. 1259]. The meeting established a Committee for the Coordination of Statistical Activities. Also before the Commission was the Secretary-General's report on the coordination of statistical data collection from countries [E/CN.3/2003/26], which described the Statistics Division's efforts to eliminate duplication in data collection.

The Commission welcomed the establishment of the Committee for the Coordination of Statistical Activities and requested that it work on a common approach to data quality assessment. It endorsed the Statistics Division's and the Committee's approach to reviewing and resolving examples of data collection duplication, and requested them to continue work on that issue. The Commission also encouraged Member States to bring instances of data collection duplication at the international level to the Division's attention.

Follow-up to Economic and Social Council policy decisions

The Commission had before it a note of the Secretary-General on action taken in response to 2002 policy decisions of the Economic and Social Council that were relevant to the Commission's work [E/CN.3/2003/28]. The Commission agreed that the actions outlined in the note were consistent with the Council's requests.

Programme and institutional questions

The Commission endorsed the Statistics Division's draft programme of work for the 2004-2005 biennium [E/CN.3/2003/29] and approved the revised list of expert group meetings and workshops to be held in 2003 [E/CN.3/2003/30].

The Commission approved its multi-year (2002-2005) programme of work for the period 2003-2006, as amended [E/CN.3/2003/31]; took note of the activities of the Commission for Social Development [E/CN.3/2003/32] and the Commission on Sustainable Development [E/CN.3/2003/33] that were relevant to its work; and recommended that its thirty-fifth session be held in New York from 2 to 5 March 2004. It also approved the provisional agenda and documentation for that session.

PART FOUR

Legal questions

Chapter I

International Court of Justice

In 2003, the International Court of Justice (ICJ) delivered three Judgments, made 12 Orders and had 26 contentious cases and one request for an advisory opinion pending before it.

In a 31 October address to the General Assembly, the ICJ President explained that many cases had been rendered more complex as a result of preliminary objections by respondents to jurisdiction or admissibility, counterclaims and applications for permission to intervene, and requests for the indication of provisional measures, which were dealt with as a matter of urgency. He stated that in performing its dispute resolution function, the Court, which embodied the principle of equality of all before the law, acted as guardian of international law and ensured the maintenance of a coherent international legal order. The President assured the Assembly that the Court would pursue its efforts to respond to the hopes placed in it.

Judicial work of the Court

During 2003, the Court delivered a Judgment on the merits in the case concerning *Oil Platforms (Iran v. United States)* and two Judgments on the admissibility of the request for revision, in the cases concerning *Application for Revision of the Judgment of 11 July 1996 in the Case concerning Application of the Convention on the Prevention and Punishment of the Crime of Genocide (Bosnia and Herzegovina v. Yugoslavia), Preliminary Objections (Yugoslavia v. Bosnia and Herzegovina)* and *Application for Revision of the Judgment of 11 September 1992 in the Case concerning the Land, Island and Maritime Frontier Dispute (El Salvador/Honduras: Nicaragua intervening) (El Salvador v. Honduras)*.

During the year, the Court was seized of four new cases: *Avena and Other Mexican Nationals (Mexico v. United States)*; *Certain Criminal Proceedings in France (Republic of the Congo v. France)*; *Sovereignty over Pedra Branca/Pulau Batu Puteh, Middle Rocks and South Ledge (Malaysia/Singapore)*; and the General Assembly's request for an advisory opinion on *Legal Consequences of the Construction of a Wall in the Occupied Palestinian Territory*. On 4 August, Liberia filed an Application in respect of a dispute with Sierra Leone concerning the indictment and international arrest warrant of 7 March, issued against Charles Ghankay Taylor, President of Liberia, by a decision of the Special Court for Sierra Leone at Freetown. In the Application, Liberia also requested the Court to indicate provisional measures. Regarding the Court's jurisdiction, Liberia referred to its own declaration of 1952 accepting the Court's jurisdiction as compulsory [YUN 1952, p. 150], and stated that "[w]ith a view to Article 38 (5) of the Rules of the Court, [it] expects the Republic of Sierra Leone to accede for the purpose of this Application to the jurisdiction of the Court pursuant to Article 36 (2) of the Statute of the Court ...". In accordance with Article 38, paragraph 5, of the Rules of the Court, a copy of the Application, together with the request for provisional measures, was transmitted to Sierra Leone. However, as at 31 December, Sierra Leone had not given its consent to the Court's jurisdiction in the case and, accordingly, the Court took no action in the matter.

The Court or its President made Orders on the conduct of the proceedings in the cases concerning *Armed Activities on the Territory of the Congo (Democratic Republic of the Congo v. Uganda)*; *Territorial and Maritime Dispute (Nicaragua v. Colombia)*; *Frontier Dispute (Benin/Niger)*; *Avena and Other Mexican Nationals (Mexico v. United States)*; *Certain Criminal Proceedings in France (Republic of the Congo v. France)*; *Sovereignty over Pedra Branca/Pulau Batu Puteh, Middle Rocks and South Ledge (Malaysia/Singapore)*; and *Legal Consequences of the Construction of a Wall in the Occupied Palestinian Territory* (request for advisory opinion). It held hearings in the cases concerning *Oil Platforms (Iran v. United States)*; *Frontier Dispute (Benin/Niger)*; *Application for Revision of the Judgment of 11 September 1992 in the Case concerning the Land, Island and Maritime Frontier Dispute (El Salvador/Honduras: Nicaragua intervening) (El Salvador v. Honduras)*; *Avena and Other Mexican Nationals (Mexico v. United States)* (provisional measures and merits); and *Certain Criminal Proceedings in France (Republic of the Congo v. France)* (provisional measures).

In the case of *Questions of Interpretation and Application of the 1971 Montreal Convention arising from the Aerial Incident at Lockerbie (Libyan Arab Jamahiriya v. United Kingdom)* and *(Libyan Arab Jamahiriya v. United States)*, the Court, following notifications by the Parties, discontinued proceedings and removed the case from its List.

During the year, there were no new developments in the cases concerning *Legality of Use of Force (Serbia and Montenegro v. Belgium), (Serbia and Montenegro v. Canada), (Serbia and Montenegro v. France), (Serbia and Montenegro v. Germany), (Serbia and Montenegro v. Italy), (Serbia and Montenegro v. Netherlands), (Serbia and Montenegro v. Portugal)* and *(Serbia and Montenegro v. United Kingdom)* [YUN 1999, p. 1207], and *Certain Property (Liechtenstein v. Germany)* [YUN 2001, p. 1194].

ICJ activities in 2003 were covered in two reports to the General Assembly, for the periods 1 August 2002 to 31 July 2003 [A/58/4 & Corr.1] and 1 August 2003 to 31 July 2004 [A/59/4]. On 31 October, the Assembly took note of the 2002/03 report (**decision 58/510**).

Questions of interpretation and application of the 1971 Montreal Convention arising from the aerial incident at Lockerbie (Libyan Arab Jamahiriya v. United Kingdom) and (Libyan Arab Jamahiriya v. United States)

The Libyan Arab Jamahiriya instituted in 1992 [YUN 1992, p. 982] separate proceedings against the United Kingdom and the United States in respect of a dispute over the interpretation and application of the 1971 Montreal Convention for the Suppression of Unlawful Acts against the Safety of Civil Aviation [YUN 1971, p. 739], which arose from its alleged involvement in the crash of Pan Am flight 103 over Lockerbie, Scotland, on 21 December 1988. In the Applications, Libya referred to the charging and indictment of two of its nationals by the Lord Advocate of Scotland and by a United States Grand Jury for having caused a bomb to be placed aboard Pan Am flight 103, which exploded, caused the aircraft to crash and killed all 270 persons aboard.

The United Kingdom and the United States, on 16 and on 20 June 1995, respectively [YUN 1995, p. 1306], filed preliminary objections to the jurisdiction of the Court to entertain Libya's Applications. Public sittings to hear the oral arguments of the Parties on the preliminary objections were held in October 1997 [YUN 1997, p. 1313]. In February 1998 [YUN 1998, p. 1184], the Court delivered the two Judgments on the preliminary objections, by which it rejected the objection to jurisdiction raised by the United Kingdom and the United States; found that it had jurisdiction, on the basis of article 14, paragraph 1, of the Convention, to hear the disputes between Libya and the United Kingdom and Libya and the United States concerning the interpretation or application of the provisions of the Convention; rejected the objection to admissibility derived by the United Kingdom and the United States from Security Council resolutions 748(1992) [YUN 1992, p. 55] and 883 (1993) [YUN 1993, p. 101]; found that the Applications filed by Libya on 3 March 1992 were admissible; and declared that the objection raised by both countries according to which the same Council resolutions had rendered the claims of Libya without object did not, in the circumstances of the case, have an excessively preliminary character.

The time limit of 30 December 1998 fixed by the Court [YUN 1998, p. 1185] for the filing of the Counter-Memorials of the United Kingdom and the United States was extended to 31 March 1999 following a proposal of the United Kingdom and the United States, which referred to diplomatic initiatives [ibid., p. 163], and after the views of Libya had been ascertained. The Counter-Memorials were filed within the time limit.

The Court, by Orders of 29 June 1999 [YUN 1999, p. 1203], authorized the submission of a Reply by Libya and a Rejoinder by the United Kingdom and the United States, which fixed 29 June 2000 as the time limit for the filing of the Reply. The Court fixed no date for the filing of the Rejoinders; the representatives of the Respondent States had expressed the desire that no such date be fixed at that stage of the proceedings, "in view of the new circumstances consequent upon the transfer of the two accused to the Netherlands for trial by a Scottish court". Libya's Reply was filed within the prescribed time limit.

By Orders of 6 September 2000 [YUN 2000, p. 1211], the President of the Court, taking account of the Parties' views, fixed 3 August 2001 as the time limit for filing the Rejoinder of the United Kingdom and the United States. The Rejoinders were filled within the prescribed time limit [YUN 2001, p. 1183].

By two letters of 9 September 2003, the Governments of Libya and the United Kingdom and of Libya and the United States notified the Court that they had "agreed to discontinue with prejudice the proceedings". Following the notifications, the President of the Court, on 10 September 2003, made an Order in each of the cases, placing on record the discontinuance of the proceedings with prejudice, by agreement of the Parties, and directing the removal of the case from the Court's List.

Oil platforms (Iran v. United States)

Iran instituted proceedings against the United States in 1992 [YUN 1992, p. 983] regarding a dispute in which Iran alleged that the destruction by United States warships, on 19 October 1987 and 18 April 1988, of three offshore oil production complexes owned and operated by the National Iranian Oil Company constituted a breach of international law and the 1955 Iran/United States

Treaty of Amity, Economic Relations and Consular Rights. Iran requested the Court to rule on the matter.

Orders of the Court in 1992 [YUN 1992, p. 983] and 1993 [YUN 1993, p. 1138] fixed time limits for the filing of the Memorial by Iran and for a Counter-Memorial by the United States. Iran filed its Memorial, while the United States filed certain preliminary objections to the jurisdiction of the Court. In 1994 [YUN 1994, p. 1280], Iran presented a written statement of its observations and submissions on the United States objections, in accordance with an Order of the Court.

The Court delivered its Judgment in 1996 [YUN 1996, p. 1178], by which it rejected the preliminary objection of the United States and found that it had jurisdiction to entertain the claims made by Iran.

By an Order of 16 December 1996 [YUN 1996, p. 1178], the President of the Court fixed 23 June 1997 as the time limit for the filing of the Counter-Memorial of the United States. Within that time limit, the United States filed the Counter-Memorial and a counterclaim [YUN 1997, p. 1313].

In November and December 1997, respectively, Iran and the United States submitted written observations on the question of the admissibility of the United States counterclaim.

In 1998 [YUN 1998, p. 1185], the Court found that the counterclaim presented by the United States in its Counter-Memorial was admissible. It further directed Iran to submit a Reply and the United States to submit a Rejoinder, fixing the time limits for those pleadings at 10 September 1998 and 23 November 1999, respectively. Also in 1998, the Vice-President of the Court, as Acting President, twice extended the time limits for Iran's Reply and the United States Rejoinder, which finally were set at 10 March 1999 for Iran's Reply and 23 November 2000 for the United States Rejoinder. Iran's Reply was filed within the time limit. However, in September 2000 [YUN 2000, p. 1211], the President of the Court extended, at the request of the United States and taking into account the agreement between the Parties, the time limit for filing the United States Rejoinder to 23 March 2001. The Rejoinder was filed within the extended time limit.

By an Order of 28 August 2001 [YUN 2001, p. 1183], the Vice-President of the Court, taking account of the agreement of the Parties, authorized Iran's submission of an additional pleading relating solely to the United States counterclaim and fixed 24 September 2001 as the time limit for the filing of that pleading. Iran filed the additional pleading within the prescribed time limit.

At the conclusion of public hearings on the merits of the case, held from 17 February to 7 March 2003, the Parties presented their final submissions. Iran requested the Court to adjudge and declare that: the United States breached its obligations to Iran under the 1955 Treaty, and bore responsibility for the attacks; the United States was accordingly under obligation to make full reparation to Iran in a form and amount to be determined by the Court, the right being reserved to Iran to introduce and present to the Court a precise evaluation of the reparation owed, and any other remedy the Court might deem appropriate; and the United States counterclaim be dismissed. The United States asked the Court to adjudge and declare that it did not breach its obligations to Iran under the 1955 Treaty, and Iran's claims were accordingly dismissed. With respect to its counterclaim, it asked the Court to adjudge and declare, rejecting all submissions to the contrary, that Iran, in attacking vessels in the Gulf with mines and missiles and otherwise engaging in military actions that were dangerous and detrimental to commerce and navigation between the territories of the United States and Iran, had breached its obligations to the United States under the 1955 Treaty, and was accordingly under an obligation to make full reparation to the United States in a form and amount to be determined by the Court.

In its Judgment of 6 November 2003, the Court, by 14 votes to 2, found that the actions of the United States against the Iranian oil platforms could not be justified as measures necessary to protect the essential security interests of the United States under the 1955 Treaty, as interpreted in the light of international law on the use of force; the Court could not, however, uphold Iran's submission that those actions constituted a breach of the United States obligations under the Treaty regarding freedom of commerce between the Parties' territories, and, accordingly, Iran's claim for reparations also could not be upheld. By 15 votes to 1, the Court found that the United States claim concerning the breach of Iran's obligations under the 1955 Treaty, regarding freedom of commerce and navigation between the Parties' territories, could not be upheld and, accordingly, that the United States counterclaim for reparation also could not be upheld.

Appended to the Judgment were: declarations by Vice-President Ranjeva and Judge Koroma; separate opinions by Judges Buergenthal, Higgins, Parra-Aranguren, Kooijmans, Owada and Simma; dissenting opinions by Judges Al-Khasawneh and Elaraby; and a separate opinion by Judge ad hoc Rigaux.

Application of the Convention on the Prevention and Punishment of the Crime of Genocide (Bosnia and Herzegovina v. Serbia and Montenegro)

Bosnia and Herzegovina instituted proceedings in 1993 [YUN 1993, p. 1138] against Serbia and Montenegro, then known as the Federal Republic of Yugoslavia, for alleged violations of the 1948 Convention on the Prevention and Punishment of the Crime of Genocide, adopted by the General Assembly in resolution 260 A (III) [YUN 1948-49, p. 959]. The Court delivered its Judgment in 1996 [YUN 1996, p. 1179], rejecting the preliminary objections raised by Serbia and Montenegro in 1995 [YUN 1995, p. 1307]. In 1997, Serbia and Montenegro filed a Counter-Memorial that included counterclaims against Bosnia and Herzegovina [YUN 1997, p. 1315]. Bosnia and Herzegovina filed a Reply in 1998 [YUN 1998, p. 1186], and Serbia and Montenegro filed a Rejoinder in 1999 [YUN 1999, p. 1204].

By an Order of 10 September 2001, the President of the Court placed on record the withdrawal by Serbia and Montenegro of the counterclaims submitted in its Counter-Memorial [YUN 2001, p. 1184].

Serbia and Montenegro had submitted to the Court, on 4 May 2001, a document entitled "Initiative to the Court to reconsider ex officio Jurisdiction over Yugoslavia". Submissions presented in the document were, firstly, that the Court had no jurisdiction *ratione personae* over Serbia and Montenegro and, secondly, that the Court should suspend proceedings regarding the merits of the case until a decision on the jurisdictional issue had been rendered. In a 12 June 2003 letter, the ICJ Registrar informed the Parties that the Court had decided it could not effect a suspension of the proceedings in the circumstances of the case.

Application for Revision of the Judgment of 11 July 1996 concerning Application of the Convention on the Prevention and Punishment of the Crime of Genocide (Bosnia and Herzegovina v. Yugoslavia), Preliminary Objections (Yugoslavia v. Bosnia and Herzegovina)

On 24 April 2001 [YUN 2001, p. 1184], the Federal Republic of Yugoslavia (FRY), currently known as Serbia and Montenegro, filed an Application for revision of the Judgment delivered by the Court on 11 July 1996 in the case concerning *Application of the Convention on the Prevention and Punishment of the Crime of Genocide (Bosnia and Herzegovina v. Yugoslavia), Preliminary Objections* [YUN 1996, p. 1179] (see above).

Public hearings were held on the question of the admissibility of the Application for revision in 2002 [YUN 2002, p. 1264].

On 3 February 2003, the Court delivered its Judgment. By 10 votes to 3, it found that the Application submitted by FRY for revision of the Judgment of 11 July 1996 was inadmissible. Judge Koroma appended a separate opinion to the Judgment; Judge Vereshchetin a dissenting opinion; and Judge Rezek a declaration. Judges ad hoc Mahiou and Dimitrijevic appended a separate opinion and a dissenting opinion, respectively.

Ahmadou Sadio Diallo (Guinea v. Democratic Republic of the Congo)

In 1998 [YUN 1998, p. 1190], Guinea instituted proceedings against the Democratic Republic of the Congo (DRC) by an "Application with a view to diplomatic protection", in which it requested the Court to condemn the DRC for the grave breaches of international law perpetrated upon the person of a Guinean national, Ahmadou Sadio Diallo.

According to Guinea, Mr. Diallo, a businessman who had been a resident of the DRC for 32 years, was "unlawfully imprisoned by the authorities of that State" for two and a half months, "divested from his important investments, companies, bank accounts, movable and immovable properties, then expelled". The expulsion took place on 2 February 1996, as a result of his attempts to recover sums owed to him by the DRC (especially by Gécamines, a State enterprise and mining monopoly) and by oil companies operating in that country (Zaïre Shell, Zaïre Mobil and Zaïre Fina), by virtue of contracts concluded with businesses owned by him, namely Africom-Zaïre and Africacontainers-Zaïre.

In 1999 [YUN 1999, p. 1206], the Court fixed 11 September 2000 as the time limit for the filing of a Memorial by Guinea and 11 September 2001 for the filing of a Counter-Memorial by the DRC. By an Order of 8 September 2000 [YUN 2000, p. 1213], the President of the Court, at Guinea's request and after the views of the other Party had been ascertained, extended to 23 March 2001 and 4 October 2002 the respective time limits for the Memorial and Counter-Memorial. The Memorial was filed within the extended time limit.

On 3 October 2002 [YUN 2002, p. 1266], within the time limit as extended for the deposit of its Counter-Memorial, the DRC filed certain preliminary objections to the Court's jurisdiction and the admissibility of Guinea's Application; the proceedings on the merits were accordingly suspended, in accordance with Article 79 of the Rules of the Court. By an Order of 7 November 2002 [ibid.], the Court fixed 7 July 2003 as the time limit within which Guinea might present a written statement of its observations and submissions on the preliminary objections raised by the DRC.

The written statement was filed within the time limit.

Armed activities on the territory of the Congo (Democratic Republic of the Congo v. Uganda)

The DRC instituted proceedings against Burundi, Uganda and Rwanda on 23 June 1999 [YUN 1999, p. 1209] for acts of armed aggression perpetrated in flagrant violation of the Charter of the United Nations and the Charter of the Organization of African Unity (OAU). In 2001 [YUN 2001, p. 1191], the DRC notified the Court that it wished to discontinue the proceedings against Burundi and Rwanda. The President of the Court, in Orders of 30 January 2001, placed the discontinuance by the DRC on record and ordered the removal of the case from the List. In its Applications, the DRC contended that "such armed aggression... involved inter alia violation of the sovereignty and territorial integrity of the [DRC], violations of international humanitarian law and massive human rights violations". The DRC sought the cessation of the aggression against it; reparation for acts of intentional destruction and looting; and restitution of national property and resources appropriated for the benefit of the respective respondent States.

In the case against Uganda, the Court, taking into account an agreement of the Parties in 1999 [YUN 1999, p. 1210], fixed 21 July 2000 as the time limit for the filing of a Memorial by the DRC and 21 April 2001 for the filing of a Counter-Memorial by Uganda. The Memorial of the DRC was filed within the prescribed time limit.

On 19 June 2000 [YUN 2000, p. 1218], the DRC requested the Court to indicate provisional measures requiring, among other things, the withdrawal of Uganda's army from Kisangani and the cessation of military and other activities by Uganda within the territory of the DRC. Public sittings to hear the oral observations of the Parties on the request for the indication of provisional measures were held on 26 and 28 June 2000. On 1 July 2000 [ibid.], the Court rendered its Order on the DRC's request for provisional measures, which stated that both Parties must, forthwith, prevent and refrain from any action, particularly armed action, which might prejudice the rights of the other Party in respect of whatever judgment the Court might render, or which might aggravate or extend the dispute before the Court or make it more difficult to resolve; both Parties must, forthwith, take measures to comply with all their obligations under international law; and both Parties must, forthwith, take measures to ensure full respect within the zone of conflict for fundamental human rights and for the applicable provisions of humanitarian law. Judges Oda and Koroma appended declarations to the Order.

Uganda filed its Counter-Memorial, which contained counterclaims, within the time limit set by the Court's Order of 21 October 1999 [YUN 1999, p. 1210].

By an Order of 29 November 2001 [YUN 2001, p. 1192], the Court found that two of the counterclaims submitted by Uganda against the DRC were "admissible as such and [formed] part of the current proceedings", but that the third was not. In view of those conclusions, the Court considered it necessary for the DRC to file a Reply and Uganda a Rejoinder, addressing the claims of both Parties, and fixed 29 May 2002 as the time limit for the filing of the Reply and 29 November 2002 for the Rejoinder. Further, in order to ensure strict equality between the Parties, the Court reserved the right of the DRC to present its views in writing a second time on the Uganda counterclaims, in an additional pleading to be the subject of a subsequent Order. The Reply was filed within the time limit [YUN 2002, p. 1268]. By an Order of 7 November 2002 [ibid.], the Court extended the time limit for the filing by Uganda of its Rejoinder to 6 December 2002. The Rejoinder was filed within the extended time limit.

By an Order of 29 January 2003, the Court authorized the DRC's submission of an additional pleading relating solely to the counterclaims submitted by Uganda, and fixed 28 February 2003 as the time limit for its filing. The written pleading was filed within the fixed time limit. The Court then fixed 10 November 2003 as the date for the opening of the hearings.

In a 5 November 2003 letter, the DRC raised the question of whether the hearings might be adjourned to a later date, in April 2004, to enable the diplomatic negotiations engaged by the Parties to be conducted in an atmosphere of calm. A 6 November 2003 letter by Uganda indicated that it supported the proposal and adopted the DRC's request.

By a 6 November 2003 letter, the ICJ Registrar informed the Parties that the Court, acting under Article 54, paragraph 1, of the Rules of the Court, and taking account of the representations made to it by the Parties, had decided that the opening of the oral proceedings would be postponed and that it was impossible to fix a date in April 2004 for the adjourned hearings. As the Court's judicial calendar until well into 2004 had been adopted some time before, a new date for the opening of oral proceedings would have to be fixed subsequently.

Application of the genocide convention (Croatia v. Serbia and Montenegro)

Croatia instituted proceedings against Serbia and Montenegro, then known as FRY, on 2 July 1999 [YUN 1999, p. 1210] for alleged violations of the 1948 Convention on the Prevention and Punishment of the Crime of Genocide, adopted by the General Assembly in resolution 260 A (III) [YUN 1948-49, p. 959], said to have been committed between 1991 and 1995. In its Application, Croatia contended that by "directly controlling the activity of its armed forces, intelligence agents, and various paramilitary detachments, on the territory of . . . Croatia, in the Knin region, eastern and western Slovenia, and Dalmatia, [Serbia and Montenegro] is liable [for] the 'ethnic cleansing' of Croatian citizens from these areas . . . and is required to provide reparation for the resulting damage". It further alleged that, "by directing, encouraging, and urging Croatian citizens of Serb ethnicity in the Knin region to evacuate the area in 1995, as . . . Croatia reasserted its legitimate governmental authority . . . [Serbia and Montenegro] engaged in conduct amounting to a second round of 'ethnic cleansing'". Croatia invoked the jurisdiction of the Court based on Article 36, paragraph 1, of the Statute and on article IX of the Convention. Croatia reserved the right to introduce to the Court at a future date a precise evaluation of the damages.

By an Order of 14 September 1999, the Court took account of an agreement of the Parties expressed on 13 September and fixed 14 March 2000 as the time limit for the filing of the Memorial of Croatia and 14 September 2000 for the filing of the Counter-Memorial of Serbia and Montenegro.

In 2000 [YUN 2000, p. 1219], at Croatia's request, the President of the Court twice extended the time limits, which finally were set at 14 March 2001 for the Memorial of Croatia and at 16 September 2002 for the Counter-Memorial of Serbia and Montenegro. The Memorial of Croatia was filed within the time limit thus extended. On 11 September 2002 [YUN 2002, p. 1268], within the extended time limit for filing its Counter-Memorial, Serbia and Montenegro filed certain preliminary objections to jurisdiction and admissibility. The proceedings on the merits were suspended, in accordance with Article 79 of the Rules of the Court.

On 25 April 2003, within the time limit fixed by an Order of the Court of 14 November 2002 [YUN 2002, p. 1268], Croatia filed a written statement of its observations and submissions on the preliminary objections raised by Serbia and Montenegro.

Maritime delimitation (Nicaragua v. Honduras)

In 1999 [YUN 1999, p. 1210], Nicaragua instituted proceedings against Honduras in respect of a dispute concerning the delimitation of the maritime zones appertaining to each of those States in the Caribbean Sea. In its Application, Nicaragua stated that it had maintained for decades the position that its maritime Caribbean border with Honduras had not been determined, while the position of Honduras allegedly was that a delimitation line was fixed by the King of Spain in an Arbitral Award of 23 December 1906, which was found valid and binding by ICJ on 18 November 1960 [YUN 1960, p. 536]. According to Nicaragua, the position adopted by Honduras had brought repeated confrontations and mutual capture of vessels of both nations in and around the general border area, and diplomatic negotiations had failed. Nicaragua founded the jurisdiction of the Court on declarations under Article 36, paragraph 2, of the Court's Statute, by which both States accepted the compulsory jurisdiction of the Court, and also article XXXI of the American Treaty on Pacific Settlement (officially known as the "Pact of Bogotá"), signed on 30 April 1948, to which both Nicaragua and Honduras were parties.

Nicaragua requested the Court to determine the course of the single maritime boundary between areas of territorial sea, continental shelf and exclusive economic zone appertaining to Nicaragua and Honduras.

By an Order of 21 March 2000 [YUN 2000, p. 1219], the Court, taking into account the agreement of the Parties, fixed 21 March 2001 as the time limit for the filing of a Memorial by Nicaragua and 21 March 2002 for the filing of the Counter-Memorial by Honduras. The Memorial [YUN 2001, p. 1193] and Counter-Memorial [YUN 2002, p. 1269] were filed within the prescribed time limits. Copies of the pleadings and annexed documents were made available to Colombia [YUN 2001, p. 1193] and Jamaica [YUN 2002, p. 1269], at their request.

By an Order of 13 June 2002 [YUN 2002, p. 1269], the Court authorized the submission of a Reply by Nicaragua and a Rejoinder by Honduras and fixed 13 January 2003 and 13 August 2003, respectively, as the time limits for the filing of those pleadings. The Reply of Nicaragua and the Rejoinder of Honduras were filed within the fixed time limits.

Territorial and maritime dispute (Nicaragua v. Colombia)

In 2001 [YUN 2001, p. 1195], Nicaragua instituted proceedings against Colombia in respect of a dispute concerning "a group of related legal issues subsisting" between the two States "concerning title to territory and maritime delimitation". In its Application, Nicaragua requested the Court to adjudge and declare, first, that Nicaragua had sovereignty over the islands of Providencia, San Andres and Santa Catalina and all the appurtenant islands and keys, and also over the Roncador, Serrana, Serranilla and Quitasueño keys (insofar as they were capable of appropriation); and, second, in the light of the determinations concerning the title requested above, the Court was asked further to determine the course of the single maritime boundary between the areas of continental shelf and exclusive economic zone appertaining to Nicaragua and Colombia, in accordance with equitable principles and relevant circumstances recognized by general international law as applicable to such a delimitation of a single maritime boundary. Nicaragua reserved the right to claim compensation for elements of unjust enrichment consequent upon Colombian possession of the islands of San Andres and Providencia, as well as the keys and maritime spaces up to the 82 meridian, in the absence of lawful title. It also reserved the right to claim compensation for interference with fishing vessels of Nicaraguan nationality or vessels licensed by Nicaragua.

By an Order of 26 February 2002 [YUN 2002, p. 1271], the Court fixed 28 April 2003 and 28 June 2004, respectively, as the time limits for the filing of a Memorial by Nicaragua and of a Counter-Memorial by Colombia. The Memorial of Nicaragua was filed within the time limit.

On 21 July 2003, Colombia filed preliminary objections to the jurisdiction of the Court; under Article 79 of the Rules of the Court, proceedings on the merits were suspended accordingly. By an Order of 24 September 2003, the Court fixed 26 January 2004 as the time limit for the filing by Nicaragua of a written statement of its observations and submissions on Colombia's preliminary objections.

Frontier dispute (Benin/Niger)

In 2002 [YUN 2002, p. 1271], Benin and the Niger jointly notified the Court of a Special Agreement, which was signed between them on 15 June 2001 and entered into force on 11 April 2002. Under article 1 of the Agreement, the Parties agreed to submit their boundary dispute to a chamber to be formed by the Court, pursuant to Article 26, paragraph 2, of the Court's Statute, and that each of them would choose a judge ad hoc. Article 2 of the Agreement stated that the Court was requested to determine the course of the boundary between Benin and the Niger in the River Niger sector; specify which State owned each of the islands in the River Niger, in particular Lété Island; and determine the course of the boundary between the two States in the River Mekrou sector. Article 10 contained a "special undertaking" as follows: "Pending the judgment of the Chamber, the Parties undertake to preserve peace, security and quiet among the peoples of the two States". By an Order of 27 November 2002 [ibid.], the Court decided to accede to the Parties' request and form a special chamber of five judges; the Court formed a Chamber of three members of the Court together with two judges ad hoc chosen by the Parties. The Court fixed 27 August 2003 as the time limit for the filing of a Memorial by each Party. The Memorials were filed within the time limit.

By an Order of 11 September 2003, the President of the Chamber fixed 28 May 2004 as the time limit for the filing of a Counter-Memorial by each of the Parties. On 20 November 2003, the Chamber held its first public sitting to enable the two judges ad hoc to make the solemn declaration required by the Statute and the Rules of the Court.

Armed activities on the territory of the Congo (New Application: 2002)
(Democratic Republic of the Congo v. Rwanda)

On 28 May 2002 [YUN 2002, p. 1271], the DRC filed an Application instituting proceedings against Rwanda in respect of a dispute concerning "massive, serious and flagrant violations of human rights and of international humanitarian law" resulting "from acts of armed aggression perpetrated by Rwanda on the territory of the Democratic Republic of the Congo in flagrant breach of the sovereignty and territorial integrity of the [latter], as guaranteed by the United Nations and OAU Charters". The DRC requested the Court to adjudge and declare that, by violating human rights, Rwanda had violated and was violating the UN Charter as well as articles 3 and 4 of the OAU Charter; that it further had violated a number of instruments protecting human rights; that, by shooting down a Boeing 727 owned by Congo Airlines on 9 October 1998 in Kindu, thereby causing the death of 40 civilians, Rwanda had also violated certain conventions regarding international civil aviation; and that, by engaging in killing, slaughter, rape, throat-slitting and crucifying, Rwanda was guilty of genocide against more than 3.5 million Congolese, including the victims of massacres in the city of Kisangani, and had violated the sacred right to life provided for in certain instruments protecting human rights, as well as the 1948 Convention on the Prevention and Punishment of the Crime of Genocide [YUN 1948-49, p. 959]. It further asked the Court to adjudge and declare that all Rwandan armed forces should be withdrawn from Congolese territory and that the DRC was entitled to compensation. In its Application, the DRC, in order to found the jurisdiction of the Court, relied on a number of compromissory clauses in treaties.

Also on 28 May 2002 [YUN 2002, p. 1272], the DRC submitted a request for the indication of provisional measures. Following public hearings on the request, the Court delivered its Order, by which, having found that it had no prima facie jurisdiction, it rejected the request of the DRC. In the Order, the Court also rejected the submissions by Rwanda seeking the removal of the case from the Court's List.

By an Order of 18 September 2002 [ibid.], the Court decided, in accordance with Article 79, paragraphs 2 and 3, of the revised Rules of the Court, that the written pleadings would first be addressed to the questions of the jurisdiction of the Court and the admissibility of the Application, and fixed 20 January 2003 as the time limit for the Memorial of Rwanda and 20 May 2003 for the DRC's Counter-Memorial. The pleadings were filed within the time limits.

Revision of the Judgment of 11 September 1992 in the Case concerning the Land, Island and Maritime Frontier Dispute (El Salvador/Honduras: Nicaragua intervening) (El Salvador v. Honduras)

In September 2002 [YUN 2002, p. 1272], El Salvador filed an Application for revision of a Judgment delivered in 1992 by the Chamber of the Court in the case concerning *Land, Island and Maritime Frontier Dispute (El Salvador/Honduras: Nicaragua intervening)* [YUN 1992, p. 983]. El Salvador indicated that the "sole purpose of the application is to seek revision of the course of the boundary decided by the Court for the sixth disputed sector of the land boundary between El Salvador and Honduras". El Salvador based its Application for revision on Article 61, paragraph 1, of the ICJ Statute. El Salvador requested the Court to proceed to form the chamber that would hear the Application, bearing in mind the terms agreed upon by El Salvador and Honduras in a Special Agreement of 24 May 1986 [YUN 1986, p. 984]; to declare the Application of El Salvador admissible; and, following the admission of the Application, to proceed to the revision of the 1992 Judgment.

By an Order of 27 November 2002 [YUN 2002, p. 1273], the Court, after its President had been informed of the view of the Parties on the composition of the chamber and had reported to it, decided to accede to the request of both Parties that it should form a special chamber of five judges, and formed a Chamber of three members of the Court together with the two judges ad hoc chosen by the Parties. The Court further fixed 1 April 2003 as the time limit for the filing of written observations by Honduras on the admissibility of the Application for revision. The observations were deposited within the prescribed time limit.

Hearings on the admissibility of the request for revision were held from 8 to 12 September 2003. At the conclusion of the hearings, the Parties presented submissions to the Court. El Salvador requested the Chamber, rejecting all contrary claims and submissions, to declare that its Application was admissible based on new facts of such a nature as to leave the case open to revision, pursuant to Article 61 of the ICJ Statute, and, once the request was admitted, to proceed to a revision of the 1992 Judgment, so that a new judgment fixed the boundary line in the sixth disputed sector of the land boundary between El Salvador and Honduras as specified by El Salvador in its submission. Honduras, in its submission, requested the Chamber to declare the inadmissibility of El Salvador's Application for revision.

On 18 December 2003, the Chamber delivered its Judgment, which, by 4 votes to 1, found that the Application submitted by El Salvador for revision of the 1992 Judgment was inadmissible.

Judge ad hoc Paolillo appended a dissenting opinion to the Judgment.

(See also p. 286.)

Avena and other Mexican nationals (Mexico v. United States)

On 9 January 2003, Mexico instituted proceedings before the Court against the United States in a dispute concerning alleged violations of articles 5 and 36 of the 1963 Vienna Convention on Consular Relations [YUN 1963, p. 510] with respect to 54 Mexican nationals who had been sentenced to death in the States of Arizona, Arkansas, California, Florida, Illinois, Nevada, Ohio, Oklahoma, Oregon and Texas.

In its Application, Mexico maintained that the 54 cases (later adjusted by Mexico to 52) illustrated the systemic nature of the United States violation of its obligation under article 36 of the Vienna Convention to inform nationals of Mexico of their right to consular assistance and to provide relief adequate to redress such a violation. Mexico claimed that in at least 49 of the cases, it had found no evidence that the competent United States authorities attempted to comply with article 36 before Mexico's nationals were tried, convicted and sentenced to death. It further noted that in four cases, some attempt was apparently made to comply with article 36, but that the authorities still failed to provide the required notification "without delay"; and in one case, the detained national was informed of his rights to consular notification and access in connection with immigration proceedings, but not in connection with pending capital charges. The Application briefly described each case, catalogued by state. Mexico invoked as a basis for the Court's jurisdiction article I of the Vienna Convention's Optional Protocol concerning the Compulsory Settlement of Disputes [YUN 1963, p. 512], which provided that "disputes arising out of the interpretation or application of the Convention shall lie within the compulsory jurisdiction of the International Court of Justice".

Also on 9 January, Mexico, "in view of the extreme gravity and immediacy of the threat that authorities in the United States will execute a Mexican citizen in violation of obligations the United States owes to [it]", filed an urgent request for the indication of provisional measures, asking that, pending final judgment in the case, the Court indicate that the United States should take all measures necessary to ensure that no Mexican national was executed and that no execution dates were set for any Mexican national, report to the Court the actions it had taken in that respect, and ensure no action was taken that might prejudice the rights of Mexico or its nationals with respect to any decision the Court might render on the merits of the case. At hearings held on 21 January, Mexico confirmed its request for the indication of provisional measures, while the United States asked the Court to reject the request and not to indicate any such measures.

On 5 February, the Court unanimously adopted an Order indicating provisional measures. In the Order, it decided that the United States should take "all measures necessary" to ensure that César Roberto Fierro Reyna, Roberto Moreno Ramos and Osvaldo Torres Aguilera, of Mexican nationality, were not executed pending a final judgment of the Court; the United States should inform the Court of all measures taken to implement the Order; and the Court would remain seized of the matters which formed the subject of the Order until it had rendered its final judgment.

A further separate Order of 5 February, taking into account the views of the Parties, fixed 6 June as the time limit for the filing of a Memorial by Mexico and 6 October as the time limit for the filing of a Counter-Memorial by the United States. By an Order of 22 May, the President of the Court, at the joint request of the Parties, extended the time limits to 20 June for the Memorial of Mexico and to 3 November for the Counter-Memorial of the United States. The Memorial and Counter-Memorial were filed within the extended time limits.

At the conclusion of public hearings held from 15 to 19 December, the Parties presented final submissions to the Court. In its submission, Mexico requested the Court to adjudge and declare: that the United States, in arresting, detaining, trying, convicting and sentencing the 52 Mexican nationals on death row, had violated its international legal obligations to Mexico, in its own right and in the exercise of its right to diplomatic protection of its nationals, by failing to inform, without delay, the nationals after their arrest of their right to consular notification and access under article 36 (1) *(b)* of the 1963 Vienna Convention, and by depriving Mexico of its right to provide consular protection and the nationals' rights to receive such protection as Mexico would provide under article 36 (1) *(a)* and *(c)* of the Convention (the obligation in article 36 (1) of the Vienna Convention required notification of consular rights and a reasonable opportunity for consular access before the competent authorities of the receiving State took any action potentially detrimental to the foreign nationals' rights); and that the United States had violated its obligations under article 36 (2) of the Vienna Convention by failing to provide meaningful and effective review and reconsideration of convictions and sentences impaired by a violation of article 36 (1), by substituting for the review and the reconsideration clemency proceedings and by applying the "procedural default" doctrine and other municipal law doctrines that failed to attach legal significance to an article 36 (1) violation on its own terms. Pursuant to the injuries suffered by Mexico in its own right and in the exercise of diplomatic protection of its nationals, Mexico also asked the Court to adjudge and declare that: Mexico was entitled to full reparation for the injuries in the form of *restitutio in integrum*; such restitution consisted of the obligation to restore the status quo ante by annulling or otherwise depriving of full force or effect the convictions and sentences of all 52 Mexican nationals; the restitution also included the obligation to take all measures necessary to ensure that a prior violation of article 36 would not affect the subsequent proceedings; to the extent that any of the 52 convictions or sentences were not annulled, the United States would provide, by means of its own choosing, meaningful and effective review and reconsideration of the convictions and sentences of the 52 nationals, and the obligation could not be satisfied by means of clemency proceedings or if any municipal law, rule or doctrine inconsistent with Mexico's request regarding the United States obligations under article 36 (1) and (2) of the Vienna Convention was applied (see p. 1307); and the United States should cease violations of article 36 with regard to Mexico and its 52 nationals and should provide appropriate guarantees and assurances that it would take measures to achieve increased compliance with article 36 (1) and to ensure compliance with article 36 (2).

The United States, on the basis of the facts and arguments it had made in its Counter-Memorial and in the proceedings, requested that the Court, taking into account that the United States had conformed its conduct to the Court's 2001 Judgment in the case concerning *LaGrand (Germany v. United States)* [YUN 2001, p. 1188], with respect not only to German nationals but also, consistent with the declaration of the President of the Court in that case [ibid., p. 1189], to all detained foreign nationals, adjudge and declare that Mexico's claims were dismissed.

Certain criminal proceedings in France (Republic of the Congo v. France)

On 9 December 2002 [YUN 2002, p. 1263], the Republic of the Congo filed an Application by which it sought to institute proceedings against France seeking the annulment of the investigation and prosecution measures taken by the French judicial authorities further to a complaint for crimes against humanity and torture filed by various associations against the President of the Congo, Denis Sassou Nguesso, the Congolese Minister of the Interior, Pierre Oba, and other individuals including General Norbert Dabira, Inspector General of the Congolese Armed Forces. The Application further stated that, in connection with the proceedings, an investigating judge of the Meaux (France) tribunal de grande instance had issued a warrant for the President of the Congo to be examined as witness.

The Congo contended that by "attributing to itself universal jurisdiction in criminal matters and by arrogating to itself the power to prosecute and try the Minister of the Interior of a foreign State for crimes allegedly committed by him in connection with the exercise of his powers for the maintenance of public order in his country", France violated "the principle that a State may not, in breach of the principle of sovereign equality among all Members of the United Nations . . . exercise its authority on the territory of another State". The Congo further submitted that, in issuing a warrant instructing police officers to examine the President of the Congo as witness in the case, France violated "the criminal immunity of a foreign head of State, an international customary rule recognized by the jurisprudence of the Court".

In its Application, the Congo indicated that it sought to found the jurisdiction of the Court, pursuant to Article 38, paragraph 5, of the Rules of the Court, "on the consent of the French Republic, which will certainly be given". In accordance with that provision, the Application by the Congo was transmitted to France and no further action was taken in the proceedings at that stage.

By an 8 April letter, France stated that it "consent[ed] to the jurisdiction of the Court to entertain the Application pursuant to Article 38, paragraph 5". That consent made it possible to enter the case in the Court's List and to open the proceedings. In its letter, France added that its consent to the Court's jurisdiction applied strictly within the limits "of the claims formulated by the Republic of the Congo" and that "Article 2 of the Treaty of Co-operation signed on 1 January 1974 by the French Republic and the People's Republic of the Congo, to which the latter refers in its Application, does not constitute a basis of jurisdiction for the Court in the present case".

The Application of the Congo was accompanied by a request for the indication of a provisional measure "seek[ing] an order for the immediate suspension of the proceedings being conducted by the investigating judge of the Meaux tribunal de grande instance".

Taking into account the consent given by France and in accordance with Article 74, paragraph 3, of the Rules of the Court, the President of the Court fixed 28 April as the date for the opening of the public hearings on the request for the indication of a provisional measure submitted by the Congo. The hearings were held on 28 and 29 April.

On 17 June, the President of the Court read the Order, by which the Court found, by 14 votes to 1, that the circumstances, as they presented themselves to the Court, were not such as to require the exercise of its power under Article 41 of the Statute to indicate provisional measures. Judges Koroma and Vereshchetin appended a joint separate opinion to the Order, and Judge ad hoc de Cara a dissenting opinion.

By an Order of 11 July, the President of the Court fixed 11 December as the time limit for the Memorial of the Congo and 11 May 2004 as the time limit for the Counter-Memorial of France. The Memorial was filed within the time limit.

Sovereignty over Pedra Branca/Pulau Batu Puteh, Middle Rocks and South Ledge (Malaysia/Singapore)

On 24 July, Malaysia and Singapore jointly notified the Court of a Special Agreement that was signed between them on 6 February at Putrajaya, Malaysia, and entered into force on 9 May.

In article 2 of the Special Agreement, the Parties requested the Court to determine whether sovereignty over Pedra Branca/Pulau Batu Puteh, Middle Rocks and South Ledge belonged to Malaysia or Singapore. In article 6, the Parties agreed to accept the judgment of the Court as final and binding upon them. The Parties further set out their views on the procedure to be followed.

By an Order of 1 September, the President of the Court, taking into account the provisions of article 4 of the Special Agreement, fixed 25 March 2004 and 25 January 2005 as the respective time limits for the filing, by each of the Parties, of a Memorial and of a Counter-Memorial.

Legal consequences of the construction of a wall in the Occupied Palestinian Territory

In response to General Assembly **resolution ES-10/14** of 8 December 2003 (see p. 480), which requested the Court to urgently render an advisory opinion on the legal consequences arising from the construction of the wall being built by Israel in the Occupied Palestinian Territory, ICJ, by an Order of 19 December, decided that the United Nations and its Member States were likely, in accordance with Article 66, paragraph 2, of the ICJ Statute, to be able to furnish information on all aspects raised by the question submitted to the Court for an advisory opinion, and fixed 30 January 2004 as the time limit within which written statements might be submitted, in accordance with Article 66, paragraph 4, of the Statute. By the same Order, the Court further decided that, in the light of resolution ES-10/14 and the report of the Secretary-General transmitted with the request (see p. 478), and taking into account the fact that the Assembly had granted Palestine a special status of observer and that the latter was co-sponsor of the draft resolution requesting the advisory opinion, Palestine might also submit a written statement on the question within the time limit. Also by the Order, the Court decided, in accordance with Article 105, paragraph 4, of the Rules of the Court, to hold public hearings, during which oral statements and comments might be presented to it by the United Nations and its Member States, regardless of whether or not they had submitted written statements, and fixed 23 February 2004 as the date for the opening of the hearings. In the Order, the Court also decided that, for the reasons set out above, Palestine might take part in the hearings. Lastly, it invited the United Nations, its Member States and Palestine to inform the Registry, by 13 February 2004 at the latest, if they intended to take part in the hearings. By letters of 19 December 2003, the Registrar informed them of the Court's decisions and transmitted to them a copy of the Order.

Other questions

1999 advisory opinion

On 22 May [E/2003/78], the Secretary-General, further to his letters of 15 December 1999 [YUN 1999, p. 1212] and 26 April 2002 [YUN 2002, p. 1273], informed the President and the members of the Economic and Social Council that he remained concerned that the United Nations had not been reimbursed for the legal expenses of Dato' Param Cumaraswamy, a Special Rapporteur of the Commission on Human Rights, in accordance with ICJ's advisory opinion of 29 April 1999 [YUN 1999, p. 1211]. The legal expenses were incurred as a result of suits filed in Malaysia against Mr. Cumaraswamy in 1996 and 1997, which were dismissed by the Kuala Lumpur High Court. It was the considered view of the United Nations that the costs imposed by the Malaysian courts, within the meaning of the advisory opinion, included all legal expenses imposed on Mr. Cumaraswamy by virtue of the court orders and proceedings in the Malaysian courts, and Malaysia was ultimately responsible for those expenses. The United Nations maintained that, in order to fulfil its obligations to hold Mr. Cumaraswamy financially harmless, Malaysia should reimburse the United Nations the amount of $118,145.91 for the legal expenses it had paid on his behalf.

Trust Fund to Assist States in the Settlement of Disputes

In August [A/58/295], the Secretary-General reported on the activities and status of the Trust Fund to Assist States in the Settlement of Disputes through ICJ since the submission of his 2002 report [YUN 2002, p. 1274]. The Fund, established in 1989 [YUN 1989, p. 818], provided financial assistance to States for expenses incurred in connection with a dispute submitted to ICJ by way of a special agreement or the execution of a judgment resulting from such an agreement.

The Fund received no applications during the period under review (1 January 2002–30 June 2003). Two States contributed to the Fund, which, as at 31 July, had a total balance of $1,863,162, excluding awards already paid.

Chapter II

International tribunals

In 2003, the International Tribunal for the Prosecution of Persons Responsible for Serious Violations of International Humanitarian Law Committed in the Territory of the Former Yugoslavia since 1991 (ICTY) moved forward with its strategy to complete investigations in 2004 and first instance trials in 2008. In May, the Security Council amended the ICTY statute to permit ad litem judges, during the period of their appointments to a trial, also to adjudicate in pre-trial proceedings in other cases. The Council reappointed Carla Del Ponte as the Tribunal's Prosecutor for a four-year term with effect from 15 September 2003.

During the year, the International Criminal Tribunal for the Prosecution of Persons Responsible for Genocide and Other Serious Violations of International Humanitarian Law Committed in the Territory of Rwanda and Rwandan Citizens Responsible for Genocide and Other Such Violations Committed in the Territory of Neighbouring States between 1 January and 31 December 1994 (ICTR) rendered five judgements, the greatest number delivered in a single year. The Council amended the ICTR statute in order to increase the number of ad litem judges who might be used at any given time from four to nine and to empower them to adjudicate in pre-trial proceedings in cases other than those they had been appointed to try. The Council further amended the ICTR statute to establish a new position of ICTR Prosecutor, and subsequently appointed Hassan Bubacar Jallow as Prosecutor for a four-year term with effect from 15 September 2003. Until then, the ICTY Prosecutor had also acted as the ICTR Prosecutor.

International Tribunal for the Former Yugoslavia

In 2003, the International Tribunal for the Former Yugoslavia (ICTY) moved forward with its completion strategy [YUN 2002, p. 1275], adopting internal reforms to ensure compliance with Security Council resolution 1503(2003), adopted in August (see p. 1330). It also continued to prepare the States in the Balkan region for the prosecution of war crimes cases. It reached agreement with the Office of the High Representative for Bosnia and Herzegovina (see p. 399) regarding the establishment of a special chamber for war crimes prosecutions in the State Court of Bosnia and Herzegovina. That special chamber, endorsed on 12 June by the Steering Board of the Peace Implementation Council, was expected to enable ICTY to begin transferring some cases of mid- and lower-level accused by the end of 2004 or early 2005.

The Council, by resolution 1481(2003) (see p. 1315), amended the ICTY statute to permit ad litem judges to do pre-trial work in addition to participating in the trials to which they were assigned.

The judges amended the ICTY Rules of Procedure and Evidence to clarify the standards for the referral of cases to competent national courts; to permit the replacement of a judge in certain cases of judicial disability, even without the consent of the accused, when the interests of justice so warranted; and to give the Trial Chambers greater power to limit the amount of evidence presented by the prosecution.

During the year, the ICTY judicial database, providing the judges, the Chambers, the Registry and the Office of the Prosecutor with electronic access to court records of most of the cases, became operational.

The activities of ICTY, established by Security Council resolution 827(1993) [YUN 1993, p. 440], were covered in two reports to the Council and the General Assembly, for the periods 1 August 2002 to 31 July 2003 [A/58/297-S/2003/829 & Corr.1] and 1 August 2003 to 31 July 2004 [A/59/215-S/2004/627]. On 9 October, the Assembly took note of the 2002/03 report (**decision 58/505**).

The Chambers

The judicial activities of the Tribunal's three Trial Chambers, which ran six trials simultaneously throughout the year, and of its Appeals Chamber included first instance and appeals proceedings—against judgements, interlocutory decisions and State requests for review—proceedings regarding the Tribunal's primacy and contempt cases. ICTY had a total of 25 judges—16 permanent judges, including 2 ICTR judges serving in the Appeals Chamber, and 9 ad litem judges.

New arrests, surrenders and indictments

Milan Milutinovic, charged jointly with Slobodan Milosevic, Nikola Sainovic, Dragoljub Ojdanic and Vlajko Stojlkovic in 1999 [YUN 1999, p. 1214] but still at large in 2002 [YUN 2002, p. 1278], surrendered to the Tribunal on 20 January, making his initial appearance before the Trial Chamber on 27 January. His motion challenging the jurisdiction of ICTY was dismissed on 6 May and his 13 May appeal of that decision was suspended as he no longer had legal representation. On 10 June, he confidentially filed an application for leave to appeal the Trial Chamber's decision rejecting his 23 January application for provisional release, which the Appeals Chamber refused on the ground that he had not shown good cause.

Four members of the Kosovo Liberation Army who had served at the Lapusnik Prison Camp in Glogovac (Kosovo province of Serbia and Montenegro) were arrested for crimes against Kosovo Serbs. Haradin Bala and Isak Musliu were arrested in Kosovo on 17 February by the international security force (KFOR) and transferred to the Tribunal the following day. At their initial appearance on 20 February, Mr. Bala pleaded not guilty to four counts and Mr. Musliu to three counts of crimes against humanity (imprisonment, cruel treatment, torture, murder), alternatively charged as violations of the laws or customs of war. Fatmir Limaj, arrested on 18 February by police in Slovenia and transferred to ICTY on 4 March, pleaded not guilty to those same charges at his initial appearance on 5 March. On 31 October, the Chamber denied a request filed by all three for provisional release. Agim Murtezi, also an indictee in the case, was arrested by KFOR in February and transferred to the Tribunal; he was released upon determination that he was not the person thought to be responsible for the crimes alleged in the indictment.

Vojislav Seselj, who surrendered to the Tribunal on 24 February, was charged with crimes against humanity and violations of the laws or customs of war in a 14-count indictment. The indictment alleged that as president of the Serbian Radical Party he participated in a plan for the forcible removal of a majority of the Croat, Muslim and other non-Serb populations from about one third of the territory of Croatia, large parts of Bosnia and Herzegovina and parts of Vojvodina in Serbia in order to make those areas part of a new Serb-dominated State. On 25 March, he pleaded not guilty to all counts.

Ivica Rajic, arrested by the Croatian authorities in April, was surrendered to the Tribunal on 24 June. Originally indicted [YUN 1996, p. 1186] for crimes committed in 1993 against the civilian Muslim population in Stupni Do [YUN 1993, p. 461] and Vares [ibid., p. 462] in central Bosnia and Herzegovina, the accused pleaded not guilty to two counts of war crimes (wilful killing, destruction of property) and one count of violations of the laws and customs of war (attack on civilians), at his initial appearance on 27 June.

Naser Oric was arrested in Tuzla, Bosnia and Herzegovina, on 10 April by the multinational Stabilization Force and transferred to the Tribunal the following day. At his initial appearance on 15 April, he pleaded not guilty to two counts of violations of the laws or customs of war under article 7(1) of the ICTY statute (wanton destruction of cities, towns or villages not justified by military necessity, plunder of public or private property) and four counts of violations of the laws or customs of war under article 7(3) (murder, cruel treatment, wanton destruction of cities, towns or villages not justified by military necessity, plunder of public or private property). On 25 July, the Trial Chamber denied his request for provisional release, and, on 17 October, the Appeals Chamber affirmed that decision.

Franko Simatovic and Jovica Stanisic, who surrendered from Belgrade (Serbia) on 30 May and 11 June, respectively, pleaded not guilty, in June, to charges of four counts of crimes against humanity (persecutions, murder, deportation, inhumane acts (forcible transfer)) and one count of violating the laws or customs of war (murder).

Miroslav Radic, who surrendered to the Tribunal from Belgrade on 17 May, and Veselin Sljivancanin, arrested by the authorities of Serbia and Montenegro and transferred to ICTY on 1 July, made their initial appearance on 21 May and 10 July, respectively. Both had been at large since their indictment in 1997 [YUN 1997, p. 1322] jointly with two other accused in connection with the alleged execution in Ovcara (near Vukovar, Croatia) of some 200 Croatian and other non-Serb persons removed from Vukovar Hospital in 1991.

In the case against Dusen Fustar, Pedrag Banovic, Dusko Knezevic, Momcilo Gruban and Zeljko Meakic, who were charged in the Omarska [YUN 1995, p. 1314] and Keraterm [YUN 1998, p. 1193] indictments, which were joined into a single case in 2002 [YUN 2002, p. 1279], Mr. Meakic surrendered to the Tribunal from Belgrade on 4 July and made his initial appearance on 7 July. On 18 March, the Trial Chamber dismissed Mr. Knezevic's motion for provisional release and Mr. Gruban's application in May to vary the terms of his provisional release. On 26 June, the Trial Chamber, having accepted a guilty plea by Mr. Banovic to one count of persecution, pursuant to a plea agreement, withdrew the other four counts in the indictment against him. In October, he was sentenced to eight years in prison.

Mitar Rasevic, indicted on 11 June 1997 regarding events that took place in Bosnia and Herzegovina at the Kazneno Popravni Dom detention centre at Foca from April 1992 until October 1994 against Muslim and other non-Serb civilians [YUN 1996, p. 1186], surrendered on 10 August in Serbia. He was charged with seven counts of crimes against humanity (persecutions, torture, inhumane acts, murder, imprisonment, enslavement) and five counts of violations of the laws or customs of war (torture, cruel treatment, murder, slavery). At his 16 September initial appearance, the accused declined to enter a plea; therefore the judge entered pleas of not guilty to all charges on his behalf. The prosecution requested the Trial Chamber to hold its decision in abeyance on the challenge to the indictment, filed by the defence on 20 November, pending the filing of an amended indictment. The defence did not oppose the prosecution's motion, filed on 2 December, for leave to amend the indictment.

Vladimir Kovacevic was arrested in Serbia on 25 September and transferred to the Tribunal on 23 October. His case was entwined with that of Miodrag Jokic, Pavle Strugar and Milan Zec (see p. 1314).

Milan Babic's testimony at the trial of Slobodan Milosevic (see p. 1313) led to an indictment filed against him in November for one count of persecution as a crime against humanity and four counts of murder, cruel treatment, wanton destruction of cities and destruction of religious institutions, as violations of the laws and customs of war. The accused, who had held various political positions in the Serb-dominated part of Croatia known as Krajina, surrendered voluntarily to the Tribunal and agreed to cooperate with the prosecution.

In 2003, public indictments were made against Vlastimir Dordevic, Vladimir Lazarevic, Sreten Lukic and Nebojsa Pavkovic, all of whom remained at large.

Ongoing cases and trials

On 27 January, independent medical experts confirmed that Janko Bobetko was unfit to travel and stand trial, as purported by Croatia in 2002 [YUN 2002, p. 1277]. As Croatia had failed to serve the indictment on the accused or his counsel, the judge issued an order on 19 March directing it to do so. Croatia, on 4 April, informed the Tribunal that it had served the indictment. On 29 April, the accused died; on 24 June, the case was declared closed causa mortis.

Dragoljub Ojdanic and Nikola Sainovic, charged in 1999 (see p. 1311), whose requests for provisional release in 2002 had been denied [YUN 2002, p. 1278], filed, on 7 and 10 February, respectively, their second motions for provisional release, which were again denied. Also in February, the Trial Chamber held that the Registrar should carry out a new assessment of Mr. Sainovic's ability to remunerate counsel. (Mr. Sainovic in 2002 had challenged the Registrar's decision requiring him to bear the cost of 1,700 hours of pre-trial investigative work.) In April, Mr. Ojdanic applied to the Trial Chamber for review of the Registrar's decision not to provide additional funds for his pre-trial proceedings. The Chamber upheld that decision and, on 16 July, certified the matter for interlocutory appeal.

Mitar Vasiljevic, who had pleaded not guilty to charges against him in 2000 [YUN 2000, p. 1221], whose trial began in 2001 [YUN 2001, p. 1201] and who was sentenced in 2002 and filed a notice of appeal at that time [YUN 2002, p. 1280], filed a new notice of appeal on 12 February. In November, the Appeals Chamber heard oral arguments on the appeal.

Biljana Plavsic, who surrendered voluntarily in 2001 [YUN 2001, p. 1198] and changed her plea in 2002 to guilty in respect of one charge (persecution) [YUN 2002, p. 1279], was sentenced on 27 February to 11 years in prison. In June, she was transferred to Sweden to serve her sentence.

On 31 March, a judgement against Vinko Martinovic and Mladen Naletilic, who had pleaded not guilty in 1999 [YUN 1999, p. 1216] and 2000 [YUN 2000, p. 1223], sentenced them to 18 years and 20 years in prison, respectively. Both accused filed notices of appeal on 29 April, as did the prosecution on 2 May, and all parties filed appeal briefs between July and October. The accused also filed motions for the admission of additional evidence.

In the Celebici case (Hazim Delic, Esad Landzo, Zdravko Mucic), the Appeals Chamber, on 8 April, rejected appeals filed in 2002 [YUN 2002, p. 1280] and confirmed the sentences imposed by the Trial Chamber in 2001 [YUN 2001, p. 1201]. On 9 July, Messrs. Delic and Landzo were transferred to serve their sentences in Finland. On the same date, Mr. Mucic's request for early release was granted, effective 18 July, as he had served two thirds of his sentence at The Hague, having been in pre-trial and trial custody since 18 March 1996 [YUN 1996, p. 1186].

The trial of Vidoje Blagojevic, Dragan Obrenovic, Dragan Jokic and Momir Nikolic, charged jointly in 2001 [YUN 2001, p. 1199] with crimes allegedly committed following the fall of Srebrenica in 1995 [YUN 1995, p. 529], began in May. In a plea agreement, Mr. Nikolic, on provisional release since 2002 [YUN 2002, p. 1276], agreed to testify against the co-accused, and both the defence and prosecution requested that sentencing be delayed until after he had testified to allow the Trial

Chamber to assess the extent of his cooperation with the prosecution. The proceedings against Mr. Nikolic were separated from those against the other three accused. Following his testimony, a sentencing hearing was held in October. As part of Mr. Nikolic's plea agreement, the prosecution recommended a 15-to-20-year sentence, while the defence submitted that the sentence should not exceed 10 years. On 2 December, the Trial Chamber sentenced Mr. Nikolic to 27 years in prison, which he appealed. Similarly, Mr. Obrenovic entered into a plea agreement to testify against his co-accused; the proceedings against him were separated from those against the remaining two accused. Following his testimony, he was sentenced on 10 December to 17 years in prison. The trial of the remaining co-accused began on 14 May and would continue into 2004.

Goran Jelisic, whose motion for review of his 1999 sentence [YUN 1999, p. 1216; YUN 2001, p. 1201] was dismissed in 2002 [YUN 2002, p. 1280], was transferred in May to Italy to serve his sentence.

The trial of Momcilo Krajisnik [YUN 2000, p. 1221; YUN 2002, p. 1279], scheduled to begin in May, was postponed to 2004. The Registrar was compelled to withdraw the defence counsel because he had been disbarred in his home country. By decisions of 30 July and 16 September, he appointed a new defence team.

In the trial of Slobodan Milosevic [YUN 1999, p. 1214; YUN 2001, p. 1201; YUN 2002, p. 1277], the Trial Chamber, on 20 May, issued an oral ruling rejecting the prosecution's argument that the case should be allowed to proceed for as long as it took to hear the testimony of all the witnesses it wished to call, stating that the trial would become excessively long and oppressive to all concerned. On 30 September, the Trial Chamber ruled that, in view of medical advice concerning the health of the accused, the Chamber would sit three days weekly. In addition to interlocutory appeals, the case had generated a number of ancillary proceedings, including prosecution applications for binding orders directed to Serbia and Montenegro for the production of documentation relevant to the proceedings.

In the case of Pasko Ljubicic, who had pleaded not guilty in 2001 [YUN 2001, p. 1200] and whose indictment was amended in 2002 [YUN 2002, p. 1279], pre-trial briefs were filed by the prosecution and the defence, in June and July, respectively. The case would not be ready for trial until a large number of documents sought by the defence were produced by the Governments of Bosnia and Herzegovina and Croatia. The Trial Chamber had issued a binding order to the Government of Bosnia and Herzegovina in February, but the defence had not received all the documents sought.

In the case against General Rahim Ademi, who surrendered voluntarily and pleaded not guilty in 2001 [YUN 2001, p. 1199], pre-trial briefs were filed in June and July. However, the Prosecutor announced in July the intention to co-indict other perpetrators charged with crimes against civilian Serbs in the Medak pocket region of Croatia [YUN 1993, p. 490]. The Chamber was thus asked to defer General Ademi's trial until the new indictments were brought.

Darko Mrda, arrested and charged in 2002 [YUN 2002, p. 1276], entered into a plea agreement with the prosecutor on 24 July, according to which he pleaded guilty to murder and inhumane acts but not to extermination. The Chamber verified that there was a sufficient factual basis for the crimes and for the accused's participation therein, and accordingly entered a finding of guilt. Sentencing briefs were filed by the parties on 13 October and a sentencing hearing was held on 22 October.

In the trial of Milomir Stakic, who had pleaded not guilty in 2001 [YUN 2001, p. 1199] and whose defence case began in 2002 [YUN 2002, p. 1278], the Trial Chamber, on 31 July, handed down its judgement: it found the accused guilty and sentenced him to life imprisonment, with a minimum term of 20 years. In September, the prosecution and the accused filed notices of appeal.

Radislav Krstic, who was sentenced in 2001 [YUN 2001, p. 1201] and whose appeal briefs were filed in 2002 [YUN 2002, p. 1278], filed two applications for the admission of additional evidence in January and August 2003. The Appeals Chamber issued its decision on the first additional evidence motion on 5 August and on the second additional evidence motion on 15 September, with reasons to follow. On 19 November, the Chamber dismissed the prosecution's motion of 11 November to adduce additional evidence. On 20 November, the Chamber granted a supplementary motion to adduce additional evidence filed by Mr. Krstic on 4 November. The Chamber conducted evidentiary hearings and heard oral arguments on the appeal on 21, 26 and 27 November.

The trial of Radoslav Brdanin, which began in 2002 [YUN 2002, p. 1277] on charges of genocide and crimes against humanity to which he had pleaded not guilty in 1999 [YUN 1999, p. 1215] and again in 2000 [YUN 2000, p. 1222], continued in 2003. Following the close of the prosecution case, the defence submitted, on 22 August, a partly confidential motion for judgement of acquittal, to which the prosecution responded. The Trial Chamber delivered its oral decision on 9 October, followed by a written decision on 28 November. The decision granted the defence motion insofar as the accused was acquitted of genocide in the context of the third category of joint criminal enterprise, and certain factual allegations were struck out with respect to four of the municipalities cited in the indictment; it dismissed the remaining issues raised in the defence motion, with one of the judges dissenting in part, favouring the acquittal of the accused on the counts of genocide and complicity in genocide. The prosecution subsequently filed the sixth amended indictment to comply with the Trial Chamber's ruling. It appealed the decision of the Trial Chamber, which the Appeals Chamber upheld, and reinstated the charge of genocide with respect to the third category of joint criminal enterprise, finding that the Trial Chamber had erroneously conflated the mens rea requirements for genocide with the mental requirement of the mode of liability. Co-accused Momir Talic died on 28 May.

In the case against Miodrag Jokic, Vladimir Kovacevic, Pavle Strugar and Milan Zec [YUN 2001, p. 1200], Mr. Jokic, who was provisionally released on 20 February, entered into a plea agreement on 25 August, according to which he pleaded guilty to six counts in an amended indictment in exchange for his full cooperation with the prosecution and a joint recommendation for a maximum sentence of 10 years in prison. On 17 September, the case against Mr. Jokic was severed from the case against Messrs. Strugar and Kovacevic. Mr. Jokic's sentencing hearing was held on 26 November. Mr. Kovacevic, arrested in Belgrade in September and transferred to the Tribunal on 23 October, was found in a state of mental disorder upon his arrival, which prevented him from entering a plea. At two initial appearances in November, he was found not fit to enter a plea. Also in November, his case was severed from the case against Mr. Strugar. A medical examination of Mr. Kovacevic by two experts concluded that he was unable to understand fully the context of the charges against him, but that he might recover if adequately treated at a mental health institution in a Bosnian/Croatian/Serbian-speaking environment; a similar finding was made by a defence psychiatrist and by the consulting psychiatrist of the Tribunal's Detention Unit. As for Mr. Strugar, a third amended indictment alleged six counts of violations of the laws or customs of war, three of which related to crimes against persons (murder, cruel treatment, attacks on civilians) and three related to crimes against property (devastation not justified by military necessity, attacks on civilian objects, destruction of institutions dedicated to religion and the arts and sciences). Prior to his trial, the defence raised the question of the fitness of the accused to stand trial. The Trial Chamber, having examined a report it had ordered on his medical condition and his medical records, found no justification for ordering any further examination. His trial began on 16 December. The indictment against Milan Zec was withdrawn in 2002.

In the case of Milorad Krnojelac, who was sentenced in 2002 [YUN 2002, p. 1278], the Appeals Chamber dismissed all grounds of his appeal in September. It introduced new convictions and revised the sentence, raising it from seven and a half years of imprisonment to 15 years.

A third amended indictment, dated 26 September, charged Enver Hadzihasanovic and Amir Kubura, who had pleaded not guilty in 2001 [YUN 2001, p. 1199], with violations of the laws or customs of war (two counts of murder, two counts of cruel treatment, one count of wanton destruction of cities, towns or villages not justified by military necessity, one count of destruction or wilful damage of institutions dedicated to religion, one count of plunder of public and private property). Regarding the interlocutory appeal, jointly filed in 2002, of the Trial Chamber's decision that the doctrine of command responsibility was applicable in their case [YUN 2002, p. 1279], the Appeals Chamber affirmed it in part and reversed it in part on 16 July. It held that command responsibility in non-international conflicts was established but that the principle of a commander's being criminally liable for acts by his subordinates committed before he assumed command had not been sufficiently clearly established as a rule of customary international law at the time of the alleged offences to form a basis for criminal liability under the Tribunal's statute. The two accused, on provisional release since December 2001, surrendered to the custody of the Tribunal on 27 November 2003. Their trial started on 2 December. On 29 December, the Prosecutor filed an appeal regarding the Trial Chamber's decision on the refreshment of a witness's memory and on a 19 December motion for certification to appeal. Proceedings against the third co-accused, Mehmed Alagic, were terminated following his death in March.

Dragan Nikolic, who had pleaded not guilty in 2000 [YUN 2000, p. 1221] and again in 2002 to new charges contained in a second amended indictment [YUN 2002, p. 1278], entered a further plea of not guilty to a third amended indictment in 2003. In a September plea agreement, the accused pleaded guilty to counts one to four of the indictment related to persecution, murder, rape and torture. In December, the Trial Chamber entered a single conviction for persecutions as subsuming all crimes and sentenced the accused to 23 years in prison.

Preliminary motions by Milan Martic against the form of his indictment, to which he had pleaded not guilty in 2002 [YUN 2002, p. 1276], triggered several amendments to the indictment, which was finally approved by the Trial Chamber on 30 May. He pleaded not guilty to a second amended indictment of 5 September of 10 counts of crimes against humanity (persecution, extermination, murder, imprisonment, torture, inhumane acts, deportation) and to nine charges of violations of the laws or customs of war (murder, torture, cruel treatment, wanton destruction of villages and religions institutions, plunder of private property, attack on civilians).

Miroslav Deronjic, arrested in 2002 [YUN 2002, p. 1276], entered a guilty plea on 30 September to a second amended indictment, which incorporated the six counts previously charged against him [ibid., p. 1277].

On 7 October, Ranko Cesic, arrested in 2002 [YUN 2002, p. 1276], filed a plea agreement in which he pleaded guilty to the 12 counts charged against him [ibid.]. The prosecutor made further submissions at a sentencing hearing held on 27 November.

The Trial Chamber delivered its judgement in the trial of Blagoje Simic, Miroslav Tadic and Simo Zaric, jointly charged in 2002 under a fifth amended indictment [YUN 2002, p. 1278]. The judgement, delivered on 17 October, found Mr. Simic guilty of a crime against humanity for persecutions based on the unlawful arrest and detention of Bosnian Muslim and Croat civilians, cruel and inhumane treatment and deportation and forcible transfer, for which he was sentenced to 17 years in prison. He filed a notice of appeal on 17 November. Mr. Tadic, found guilty of a crime against humanity for persecutions based on deportation and forcible transfer, was sentenced to eight years in prison. Mr. Zaric, pronounced guilty of a crime against humanity for persecutions based on cruel and inhumane treatment, was sentenced to six years in prison.

Regarding notices of appeals filed by Tihomir Blaskic [YUN 2000, p. 1223; YUN 2002, p. 1280], following his 1999 trial [YUN 1999, p. 1216], the Appeals Chamber, on 31 October, admitted 108 items as additional evidence, as well as rebuttal material proffered by the prosecution. Appeals against his conviction were pending.

Stanislav Galic, who had pleaded not guilty in 1999 [YUN 1999, p. 1215] and whose trial began in 2001 [YUN 2001, p. 1201] and continued in 2002 [YUN 2002, p. 1279] and 2003, was sentenced, on 5 December, to 20 years in prison. One of the three judges filed a separate and partially dissenting opinion, challenging the majority's finding of certain facts and of some of the legal findings, and recommending a sentence of 10 years in prison. On 18 December, the prosecution filed a notice of appeal from the judgement.

An amicus curiae was appointed in a confidential contempt of court case pending before the Trial Chamber, which was seized of two other contempt cases.

Ad litem judges

The Secretary-General, on 7 May [S/2003/530], transmitted to the Security Council President a 1 May letter from the ICTY President requesting the Council to amend the ICTY statute so that ad litem judges, during the period of their appointment to a trial, could also adjudicate in pre-trial proceedings in other cases.

SECURITY COUNCIL ACTION

On 19 May [meeting 4759], the Security Council unanimously adopted **resolution 1481(2003)**. The draft [S/2003/546] was prepared in prior consultations among Council members.

The Security Council,

Reaffirming its resolutions 827(1993) of 25 May 1993, 1166(1998) of 13 May 1998, 1329(2000) of 30 November 2000, 1411(2002) of 17 May 2002 and 1431(2002) of 14 August 2002,

Having considered the letter dated 18 March 2002 from the Secretary-General addressed to the President of the Security Council and the letter annexed thereto dated 12 March 2002 from the President of the International Tribunal for the Former Yugoslavia addressed to the Secretary-General,

Having considered also the letter dated 7 May 2003 from the Secretary-General to the President of the Security Council and the letter annexed thereto dated 1 May 2003 from the President of the International Tribunal for the Former Yugoslavia addressed to the President of the Security Council,

Convinced of the advisability of enhancing the powers of ad litem judges in the International Tribunal for the Former Yugoslavia so that, during the period of their appointment to a trial, they might also adjudicate in pre-trial proceedings in other cases, should the need arise and should they be in a position to do so,

Acting under Chapter VII of the Charter of the United Nations,

1. *Decides* to amend article 13 quater of the statute of the International Tribunal for the Former Yugoslavia and to replace that article with the provisions set out in the annex to the present resolution;

2. *Decides* to remain seized of the matter.

Annex

Amendment to the statute of the International Tribunal for the Former Yugoslavia

Replace article 13 quater by the following:

Article 13 quater
Status of ad litem judges

1. During the period in which they are appointed to serve in the International Tribunal, ad litem judges shall:

(a) Benefit from the same terms and conditions of service mutatis mutandis as the permanent judges of the International Tribunal;

(b) Enjoy, subject to paragraph 2 below, the same powers as the permanent judges of the International Tribunal;

(c) Enjoy the privileges and immunities, exemptions and facilities of a judge of the International Tribunal;

(d) Enjoy the power to adjudicate in pre-trial proceedings in cases other than those that they have been appointed to try.

2. During the period in which they are appointed to serve in the International Tribunal, ad litem judges shall not:

(a) Be eligible for election as, or to vote in the election of, the President of the Tribunal or the Presiding Judge of a Trial Chamber pursuant to article 14 of the statute;

(b) Have power:
 (i) To adopt rules of procedure and evidence pursuant to article 15 of the statute. They shall, however, be consulted before the adoption of those rules;
 (ii) To review an indictment pursuant to article 19 of the statute;
 (iii) To consult with the President in relation to the assignment of judges pursuant to article 14 of the statute or in relation to a pardon or commutation of sentence pursuant to article 28 of the statute.

Office of the Prosecutor

The Prosecutor's policy continued to be directed at the highest-level political and military leaders responsible for the gravest crimes, leaving middle- and lower-ranking criminals to be tried by national courts. The Office of the Prosecutor implemented the completion strategy it had defined in 2002 [YUN 2002, p. 1275] and which the Security Council approved in resolution 1503(2003) (see p. 1330). Particular efforts were made to obtain the cooperation of countries on which ICTY relied to carry out its mandate and to assist in the reform of the judicial systems of the countries of the former Yugoslavia—key elements of the ICTY completion strategy. The Prosecutor continued to review regularly all ongoing and pending investigations in order to ensure that all resources adequately targeted the highest-level suspects. The Office also continued its pre-trial, trial and appeals activities and developed measures to enhance its operations, such as streamlining its procedure and consolidating its use of electronic systems.

The cooperation of Croatia had improved considerably. Following the change of Government in December, it acted immediately in regard to two new indictments and facilitated the surrender of all accused, while undertaking measures to locate and arrest Ante Gotovina, who had been indicted in 2001 [YUN 2001, p. 1199]. Cooperation by Serbia and Montenegro improved but continued to be complex, partial and variable and affected by political uncertainties and developments, such as the assassination of Serbia's Prime Minister (see p. 415). Cooperation at the federal level was minimal and, in spite of some positive developments under new leadership in February/March, the overall assessment was that the State's cooperation was hostage to political developments. The cooperation of Bosnia and Herzegovina remained satisfactory, while that of Republika Srpska remained insufficient, notably in regard to the fugitives and access to wartime documentation. Since the Prosecutor's decision to apply the Tribunal's primacy regarding the investigation of allegations of war crimes committed between the security forces of the former Yugoslav Republic of Macedonia (FYROM) and organized Albanian rebel groups in 2001 [YUN 2001, p. 1204], two investigations had been opened involving perpetrators on both sides of the conflict. Following a deferral hearing, held before an ICTY Trial Chamber on 25 September to resolve the issue of primacy, national authorities continued to cooperate with the Office of the Prosecutor after a change of Government. FYROM authorities were cooperating with the Office with respect to the ongoing investigations.

Communication. In a July letter [S/2003/766] to the Security Council President, the Secretary-General, in accordance with the ICTY statute providing for the appointment of the Prosecutor by the Council on nomination by the Secretary-General, put forth the name of Carla Del Ponte as his nominee for reappointment to that position at the end of her current term as Prosecutor on 14 September.

SECURITY COUNCIL ACTION

On 4 September [meeting 4819], the Security Council unanimously adopted **resolution 1504 (2003)**. The draft [S/2003/846] was prepared in consultations among Council members.

The Security Council,

Recalling its resolution 1503(2003) of 28 August 2003,

Noting that by that resolution the Council created a new position of Prosecutor for the International Tribunal for Rwanda,

Noting also that by its resolution 1503(2003) the Council welcomed the intention of the Secretary-General to submit to the Council the name of Ms. Carla Del Ponte as nominee for Prosecutor for the International Tribunal for the Former Yugoslavia,

Having regard to Article 16, paragraph 4, of the statute of the International Tribunal for the Former Yugoslavia,

Having considered the nomination by the Secretary-General of Ms. Carla Del Ponte as Prosecutor of the International Tribunal for the Former Yugoslavia,

Appoints Ms. Carla Del Ponte as Prosecutor of the International Tribunal for the Former Yugoslavia with effect from 15 September 2003 for a four-year term.

The Registry

The Registry continued to exercise its responsibilities in the administration and servicing of the Tribunal, and provided support to the Chambers and the Office of the Prosecutor. The Registry also managed the Victims and Witnesses Section, the Detention Unit, the legal aid system and information technology instruments, facilitated court management functions and provided general administrative services.

On 4 April, in Arusha, United Republic of Tanzania, the Registrars of ICTY and ICTR signed a joint statement of implementation of the inter-Tribunal (ICTY-ICTR) project, sponsored by the European Commission. In September, the Commission approved the extension of the project's grant to include cooperation initiatives between ICTY-ICTR and the Special Court for Sierra Leone (see p. 213).

In May, the Registrar visited the ICTY field office in Kosovo and conducted inter-agency meetings with the United Nations Interim Administration Mission in Kosovo and other international organizations, judges and prosecutors on a range of operational and administrative matters.

The Registry Advisory Section participated in working groups regarding the establishment of the Special War Crimes Chamber at the State Court of Bosnia and Herzegovina, in cooperation with the Office of the High Representative.

In keeping with recommendations in Security Council resolution 1503(2003) (see p. 1330), the Tribunal, as part of its completion strategy, continued to develop and improve its outreach programme, paying special attention to improving the capacity of national jurisdictions to prosecute war crimes cases. The outreach programme enhanced its activities to strengthen national jurisdictions in their handling of war crimes cases, assisting in the creation of a responsible body of lawyers, prosecutors and other legal professionals through a broad range of training programmes. The programme organized a conference (Sarajevo, December), which brought together victims' associations and legal professionals to discuss the impact of ICTY judgements on specific communities.

Report of Secretary-General. In response to General Assembly resolution 57/288 [YUN 2002, p. 1283], the Secretary-General, in an August report [A/58/288], described progress made by ICTY to reform its legal aid system, particularly with regard to rationalizing the costs of defence counsel and establishing indigence. A new system regarding defence counsel promised greater efficiency and eliminated time- and resource-consuming litigation of invoices before the Chambers or the ICTY President. As to the establishment of indigence, the Registry developed a financial formula that took into account the accused's income and assets, expenses for dependants and the costs and necessary duration of legal aid and other measures, such as means in relation to the projected cost of legal representation. The ability of the accused to contribute to defence costs was reassessed regularly. The report reviewed other issues related to the legal aid system, including financial investigations to address the issue of fee splitting, in which counsel and the accused arranged to share lawyer fees; the Association of Defence Counsel, established in 2002 [YUN 2002, p. 1275]; a Disciplinary Panel to address ethical violations; external factors affecting legal aid costs; and future reforms.

ACABQ report. In an October report [A/58/449], the Advisory Committee on Administrative and Budgetary Questions (ACABQ) said that, from the available documentation, it was not in a position to ascertain the effect of the measures taken to reform the legal aid system on the estimated resource requirements of $29.5 million for defence counsel for the 2004-2005 biennium, even though, according to supplementary information provided to it, the estimates took into account the application of a revised system of paying for trials adopted as from July 2002. It requested detailed information in the context of the next budget estimates for ICTY on the effectiveness of the measures outlined in the Secretary-General's August report.

Financing

2002-2003 biennium

Report of Secretary-General. A November report of the Secretary-General [A/58/593], submitted in response to General Assembly resolution 57/288 [YUN 2002, p. 1283], contained the second performance report of ICTY for the 2002-2003 biennium. The report reflected a net additional requirement of $18.8 million over the revised appropriation for that biennium. The increased requirements included changes with respect to exchange rates ($20.4 million) attributable mainly to the weakening of the United States dollar against the euro and inflation ($3.8 million). The Assembly was requested to revise the appropriation for 2002-2003 to $288.3 million gross ($255 million net) to the ICTY Special Account.

ACABQ report. ACABQ, in November [A/58/605], recommended the revision of the 2002-2003 appropriation to the ICTY Special Account as requested by the Secretary-General.

GENERAL ASSEMBLY ACTION

On 23 December [meeting 79], the General Assembly, on the recommendation of the Fifth (Administrative and Budgetary) Committee [A/58/580], adopted **resolution 58/254** without vote [agenda item 132].

Second performance report for the biennium 2002-2003 on the International Tribunal for the Prosecution of Persons Responsible for Serious Violations of International Humanitarian Law Committed in the Territory of the Former Yugoslavia since 1991

The General Assembly,

Having considered the second performance report of the Secretary-General for the biennium 2002-2003 on the International Tribunal for the Prosecution of Persons Responsible for Serious Violations of International Humanitarian Law Committed in the Territory of the Former Yugoslavia since 1991 and the related report of the Advisory Committee on Administrative and Budgetary Questions,

Recalling its resolution 47/235 of 14 September 1993 on the financing of the International Tribunal for the Former Yugoslavia and its subsequent resolutions thereon, the latest of which were resolutions 56/247 A of 24 December 2001, 56/247 B of 27 March 2002 and 57/288 of 20 December 2002,

1. *Takes note* of the second performance report of the Secretary-General for the biennium 2002-2003 on the International Tribunal for the Prosecution of Persons Responsible for Serious Violations of International Humanitarian Law Committed in the Territory of the Former Yugoslavia since 1991 and the related report of the Advisory Committee on Administrative and Budgetary Questions;

2. *Endorses* the conclusions and recommendations contained in the report of the Advisory Committee on Administrative and Budgetary Questions;

3. *Notes with concern* the late issuance of the second performance report of the Secretary-General for the biennium 2002-2003, bearing in mind the nature of the report and the period covered therein;

4. *Resolves* that, for the biennium 2002-2003, the amount of 262,653,700 United States dollars gross (235,955,000 dollars net) approved in its resolution 57/288 of 20 December 2002 for the budget of the International Tribunal for the Former Yugoslavia shall be adjusted by the amount of 25,668,500 dollars gross (18,803,200 dollars net) for a total amount of 288,322,200 dollars gross (254,603,800 dollars net).

2004-2005 biennium

Reports of Secretary-General. In response to General Assembly resolution 57/288 [YUN 2002, p. 1283], the Secretary-General submitted an August report [A/58/226], containing the ICTY resource requirements for the 2004-2005 biennium. The requirements before recosting amounted to $262 million gross ($235 million net) and reflected a decrease in real terms of $992,500 net, compared to the revised 2002-2003 appropriation (see p. 1317). The changes reflected a proposed reorganization and initial downsizing of the staffing table as a first step to implement the completion strategy [YUN 2002, p. 1275]. In nominal terms, the estimate for 2004-2005 amounted to $330 million gross ($299 million net) and reflected an increase of $64 million net, mostly due to the decline of the United States dollar against the euro.

A September report of the Secretary-General [A/58/368] estimated a reduction in ICTY requirements for 2004-2005 of $2.3 million gross ($1.9 million net) in the light of Security Council resolution 1503(2003) (see p. 1330), which established the new position of ICTR Prosecutor and thus reduced the number of posts from the ICTY budget. Therefore, the overall requirements for 2004-2005 in nominal terms were reduced from $330 million gross ($299 million net) to $327.3 million gross ($297 million net).

ACABQ report. In an October report [A/58/449], ACABQ commented on the potential for economies under a number of objects of expenditure, and recommended that the estimated ICTY requirements for 2004-2005 be reduced by $20 million gross.

GENERAL ASSEMBLY ACTION

On 23 December [meeting 79], the General Assembly, on the recommendation of the Fifth Committee [A/58/580], adopted **resolution 58/255** without vote [agenda item 132].

Financing of the International Tribunal for the Prosecution of Persons Responsible for Serious Violations of International Humanitarian Law Committed in the Territory of the Former Yugoslavia since 1991

The General Assembly,

Having considered the reports of the Secretary-General on the financing for the biennium 2004-2005 of the International Tribunal for the Prosecution of Persons Responsible for Serious Violations of International Humanitarian Law Committed in the Territory of the Former Yugoslavia since 1991 and the related report of the Advisory Committee on Administrative and Budgetary Questions,

Recalling its resolution 47/235 of 14 September 1993 on the financing of the International Tribunal for the Former Yugoslavia and its subsequent resolutions thereon, the latest of which were resolutions 56/247 B of 27 March 2002 and 57/288 of 20 December 2002,

Recalling also Security Council resolution 1503(2003) of 28 August 2003 concerning the creation of a new position of Prosecutor of the International Tribunal for Rwanda,

Welcoming the developments and improvements in the management and the activities of the International Tribunal for the Former Yugoslavia thus far achieved during the biennium 2002-2003,

1. *Takes note* of the reports of the Secretary-General on the financing for the biennium 2004-2005 of the International Tribunal for the Prosecution of Persons Responsible for Serious Violations of International Humanitarian Law Committed in the Territory of the Former Yugoslavia since 1991 and the related report of the Advisory Committee on Administrative and Budgetary Questions;

2. *Endorses* the conclusions and recommendations contained in the report of the Advisory Committee, subject to the provisions of the present resolution;

3. *Notes with concern* the levels of unpaid assessed contributions, and urges Member States to pay their assessed contributions on time, in full and without conditions;

4. *Concurs* with the view of the Advisory Committee that continued close collaboration between the International Tribunal for the Former Yugoslavia and the International Tribunal for Rwanda is essential, and urges the Secretary-General to take all necessary measures to ensure this;

5. *Decides* not to endorse the recommendation contained in paragraph 38 of the report of the Advisory Committee;

6. *Encourages* Member States to consider paying their assessments in euros, consistent with regulation 3.9 and rule 103.3 of the Financial Regulations and Rules of the United Nations;

7. *Requests* the Secretary-General to ensure that the report requested by the General Assembly in paragraph 2 of its resolution 55/225 A of 23 December 2000, including the views of the Board of Auditors thereon, is submitted to the Assembly at the main part of its fifty-ninth session;

8. *Welcomes* the efforts of the Secretary-General to present the proposed programme budget for the biennium 2004-2005 in a results-based budgeting format, and encourages the Secretary-General to make further progress in this regard;

9. *Invites* the Security Council to continue to monitor closely the progress made by the Tribunal towards completing its mandate, in accordance with the completion strategy;

10. *Requests* the Secretary-General to develop further the link between the Tribunal's completion strategy and objectives and the resources requested in future budget proposals;

11. *Also requests* the Secretary-General to continue, where appropriate, to prioritize and deploy resources in support of the completion strategy and to report thereon in the context of his first and second performance reports for the biennium 2004-2005;

12. *Further requests* the Secretary-General to undertake efficiency measures to streamline the work of the Tribunal and to provide an assessment of the financial impact of those measures in the context of future budget proposals;

13. *Encourages* the Tribunal to continue to implement and closely monitor reforms to its legal aid system, and requests the Secretary-General to report thereon, in particular on consequent savings in defence costs, in his first performance report for the biennium 2004-2005;

14. *Recalls* paragraph 25 of its resolution 58/253 of 23 December 2003, and requests the Secretary-General to include, where appropriate, the International Tribunal for the Former Yugoslavia in the scope of his consideration and recommendations referred to in paragraphs 38 and 39 of his comprehensive report on the progress made by the International Tribunal for Rwanda in reforming its legal aid system;

15. *Decides* that vacancy rates of 10.2 per cent for Professional staff and 7.3 per cent for General Service staff shall be used as a basis for the calculation of the budget for the biennium 2004-2005;

16. *Decides also* not to approve the proposed increase in resources for consultants and experts;

17. *Decides further* to approve the proposed post and non-post resources for the Investigations Division for 2004 and to defer consideration of the resource requirements for the Division for 2005 until its fifty-ninth session;

18. *Requests* the Secretary-General to resubmit, in the context of his first performance report for the biennium 2004-2005, a proposal for the resource requirements for the Investigations Division for 2005, and to ensure that the proposal is adequate for the effective implementation of the completion strategy;

19. *Endorses* the conclusions and recommendations of the Advisory Committee contained in paragraph 28 of its report;

20. *Concurs* with the Advisory Committee that the volume of work and the pace of completion should be monitored continuously in order to determine whether some of the posts identified for abolition or redeployment could be abolished or released for transfer to other areas of the Tribunal before the second half of 2005;

21. *Decides* to reduce the appropriation for contractual services to the level proposed in the second performance report of the Secretary-General on the programme budget for the biennium 2002-2003 as the proposed final appropriation, before recosting, given the savings achieved in respect of defence counsel during the biennium;

22. *Decides also* to reduce the proposed resources for travel of Registry staff by 200,000 United States dollars;

23. *Decides further* to appropriate to the Special Account for the International Tribunal for the Prosecution of Persons Responsible for Serious Violations of International Humanitarian Law Committed in the Territory of the Former Yugoslavia since 1991 the total amount of 298,226,300 dollars for the biennium 2004-2005, as detailed in the annex to the present resolution;

24. *Decides* that the financing of the appropriation for the biennium 2004-2005 under the Special Account shall take into account the estimated income of 184,000 dollars for the biennium 2004-2005, which shall be set off against the aggregate amount of the appropriation;

25. *Decides also* that the total assessment for 2004 under the Special Account, amounting to 174,689,650 dollars, shall consist of:

(*a*) 149,021,150 dollars, being half of the estimated appropriation approved for the biennium 2004-2005;

(*b*) 25,668,500 dollars, being the increase in the final appropriation for the biennium 2002-2003 approved by the General Assembly in its resolution 58/254 of 23 December 2003;

26. *Decides further* to apportion the amount of 87,344,825 dollars, being half of the total assessment for 2004, among Member States in accordance with the

scale of assessments applicable to the regular budget of the United Nations for 2004, as set out in its resolution 58/1 B of 23 December 2003;

27. *Decides* to apportion the amount of 87,344,825 dollars, being half of the total assessment for 2004, among Member States in accordance with the rates of assessment applicable to peacekeeping operations for 2004;

28. *Decides also* that, in accordance with the provisions of its resolution 973(X) of 15 December 1955, there shall be set off against the apportionment among Member States, as provided for in paragraphs 26 and 27 above, the amount of 20,051,150 dollars, consisting of:

(a) 13,185,850 dollars, being half of the estimated staff assessment income approved for the Tribunal for the biennium 2004-2005;

(b) 6,865,300 dollars, being the increase in staff assessment income for the biennium 2002-2003 approved by the General Assembly in its resolution 58/254.

Annex

Financing for the biennium 2004-2005 of the International Tribunal for the Prosecution of Persons Responsible for Serious Violations of International Humanitarian Law Committed in the Territory of the Former Yugoslavia since 1991

	Gross	Net
	(United States dollars)	
1. Estimated appropriation for the biennium 2004-2005	327,323,000	296,955,800
2. Recommendations of the Advisory Committee on Administrative and Budgetary Questions	(20,000,000)	(19,948,800)
3. Recommendations of the Fifth Committee	(9,096,700)	(5,152,400)
4. Revised estimated appropriation for the biennium 2004-2005	298,226,300	271,854,600
Less:		
5. Estimated income for the biennium 2004-2005	(184,000)	(184,000)
6. Total assessment for 2004, comprising:	**174,689,650**	**154,638,500**
(a) Requirements representing half of the estimated appropriation for the biennium 2004-2005	149,021,150	135,835,300
(b) Requirements arising from the final appropriation for the biennium 2002-2003	25,668,500	18,803,200
Including:		
7. Contributions assessed on Member States in accordance with the scale of assessments applicable to the regular budget of the United Nations for 2004	87,344,825	77,319,250
8. Contributions assessed on Member States in accordance with the rates of assessment applicable to peacekeeping operations of the United Nations for 2004	87,344,825	77,319,250

Also on 23 December, the Assembly decided that the item on the financing of ICTY would remain for consideration during its resumed fifty-eighth (2004) session (**decision 58/565**).

International Tribunal for Rwanda

In 2003, ICTR, in Arusha, United Republic of Tanzania, rendered five judgements, the greatest number delivered in a single year. ICTR continued to explore innovative measures to expedite trials, which included amendments to its statute by the Security Council (see p. 1324) in order to increase the number of ad litem judges that might be used at any given time from four to nine and to expand their competence by empowering them to adjudicate over pre-trial matters. The Council further amended the statute to allow for an ICTR Prosecutor (see p. 1325). In September, Hassan Bubacar Jallow joined ICTR as its Prosecutor.

In the light of Council resolution 1503(2003) (see p. 1330), the ICTR President submitted a revised completion strategy [S/2003/946] based on information available as at 29 September.

In 2003, ICTR was awarded the Friedrich-Ebert-Stiftung Human Rights Award for its contribution to human rights.

The 2003 activities of ICTR, established by Council resolution 955(1994) [YUN 1994, p. 299], were covered in two reports to the Council and the General Assembly, for the periods 1 July 2002 to 30 June 2003 [A/58/140-S/2003/707] and 1 July 2003 to 30 June 2004 [A/59/183-S/2004/601]. On 9 October, the Assembly took note of the 2002/03 report (**decision 58/504**).

The Chambers

New cases

On 16 February, Ildephonse Hategekimana, former commander of the Ngoma camp, was arrested in Brazzaville, Congo, and transferred to ICTR three days later. He appeared before the Tribunal on 28 February for arraignment and pleaded not guilty to charges of genocide and crimes against humanity.

On 13 August, Juvenal Rugumbarara, former Bourgmestre of Bicumbi commune, was arrested in Uganda and transferred to Arusha. At his initial appearance, on 15 August, he pleaded not guilty to charges of genocide, crimes against humanity and serious violations of the Geneva Conventions of 12 August 1949 and of Additional Protocol II [YUN 1977, p. 706].

Ongoing trials

In February, the Chamber sentenced Elizaphan Ntakirutimana and his son, Gerard Ntakirutimana, to 10 and 25 years in prison, respectively. Both accused, whose trial began in

2001 [YUN 2001, p. 1208] and was ongoing in 2002 [YUN 2002, p. 1285], lodged appeals against the judgement.

In May, the Chamber rendered a judgement in the case of Eliezer Niyitegeka, who had pleaded not guilty in 1999 [YUN 1999, p. 1223] and whose trial was ongoing in 2002 [YUN 2002, p. 1285]. The accused, who was sentenced to life in prison, filed a notice of appeal on 20 June.

Also in May, Laurent Semanza, whose trial began in 2000 [YUN 2000, p. 1226] and was ongoing in 2001 [YUN 2001, p. 1208] and 2002 [YUN 2002, p. 1286], was sentenced to 25 years in prison. Both the accused and the prosecutor appealed the judgement.

The trial of Sylvestre Gacumbitsi, who was arrested and pleaded not guilty in 2001 [YUN 2001, p. 1207], began on 28 July.

The joint trial of André Ntagerura, Emmanuel Bagambiki and Samuel Imanishimwe, referred to as the "Cyangugu" case [YUN 1999, p. 1222], which began in 2000 [YUN 2000, p. 1226] and was ongoing in 2001 [YUN 2001, p. 1208] and 2002 [YUN 2002, p. 1286], closed on 15 August.

The trial of Emmanuel Ndindabahizi, who was arrested and pleaded not guilty in 2001 [YUN 2001, p. 1207], began on 1 September.

On 6 November, the trial began against Casimir Bizimungu, Justin Mugenzi, Jerome Bicamumpaka and Prosper Mugiraneza, referred to as the Government II case [YUN 1999, pp. 1222 & 1223].

On 27 November, the trial began against Edouard Karemera, Andre Rwamakuba, Matthieu Ngirumpatse and Joseph Nzirorera, referred to as the Government I case [YUN 1999, pp. 1222 & 1223].

In December, the Chamber sentenced Juvénal Kajelijeli, whose trial began in 2001 [YUN 2001, p. 1208] and was ongoing in 2002 [YUN 2002, p. 1286], to three concurrent sentences: a life sentence each for genocide and for a crime against humanity (extermination) and 15 years in prison for direct and public incitement to commit genocide. He was acquitted of a crime against humanity (rape). The accused appealed the judgement.

In the "Media" case [YUN 1999, p. 1222], which was ongoing in 2002 [YUN 2002, p. 1285], Ferdinand Nahimana and Hassan Ngeze, in December, were sentenced to life in prison, while Jean-Bosco Barayagwiza was sentenced to 35 years in prison. They filed appeals against the judgement.

The following trials remained ongoing in 2003: the joint trial begun in 2002 [YUN 2002, p. 1285] of four senior Rwandan military officers (Théoneste Bagosora, Anatole Nsengiyumva, Aloys Ntabakuze, Gratien Kabiligi), consolidated as the "Military" case in 1999 [YUN 1999, p. 1222] and regarding which an interlocutory appeal was disposed of in 2001 [YUN 2001, p. 1209]; the joint trial in the "Butare" case (Pauline Nyiramasuhuko, Arsène Shalom Ntahobali, Sylvain Nsabimana, Alphonse Nteziryayo, Joseph Kanyabashi, Elie Ndayambaje), which began in 2001 [YUN 2001, p. 1208] and continued in 2002 [YUN 2002, p. 1286]; and the trial of Jean de Dieu Kamuhanda, which also began in 2001 [YUN 2001, p. 1208] and continued in 2002 [YUN 2002, p. 1285].

Regarding an appeal by Georges Anderson Nderubumwe Rutaganda against his life sentence [YUN 1999, p. 1221], the Appeals Chamber, on 26 May, quashed the conviction on count 7 of the indictment (crime against humanity (murder)), overturned his acquittal on counts 4 and 6 of the indictment (murder as a violation of the 1949 Geneva Conventions) and rejected the remainder of his grounds for appeal. The Appeals Chamber confirmed the life sentence imposed by the Trial Chamber.

An accused, Samuel Musabyimana, who was arrested in 2001 [YUN 2001, p. 1207], passed away on 24 January.

Election of judges

In 2003, the General Assembly elected 11 ICTR judges for terms of office to expire on 24 May 2007. In addition, 18 ad litem judges were elected.

In order to achieve the target for the Tribunal to complete all trial activities at first instance by the end of 2008, as set by the Security Council in resolution 1503(2003) (see p. 1330), the Council amended the ICTR statute to permit an ad litem judge who was appointed to serve for a trial to adjudicate in pre-trial proceedings. The statute was also amended to authorize the use of up to nine ad litem judges at any one trial, rather than a maximum of four.

Permanent judges

In January, the General Assembly adopted **decision 57/414 A** without vote [agenda item 18].

Election of judges of the International Criminal Tribunal for the Prosecution of Persons Responsible for Genocide and Other Serious Violations of International Humanitarian Law Committed in the Territory of Rwanda and Rwandan Citizens Responsible for Genocide and Other Such Violations Committed in the Territory of Neighbouring States between 1 January and 31 December 1994

At its 80th plenary meeting, on 31 January 2003, the General Assembly, in accordance with article 12 of the statute of the International Criminal Tribunal for the Prosecution of Persons Responsible for Genocide and Other Serious Violations of International Humanitarian Law Committed in the Territory of Rwanda and Rwandan Citizens Responsible for Genocide and Other Such Violations Committed in the Territory of

Neighbouring States between 1 January and 31 December 1994, elected the following eleven judges to serve in the Trial Chambers of the Tribunal for a term of office of four years, that is until 24 May 2007:

Mr. Mansoor AHMED (Pakistan)
Mr. Sergei Alekseevich EGOROV (Russian Federation)
Mr. Asoka de Zoysa GUNAWARDANA (Sri Lanka)
Mr. Mehmet GÜNEY (Turkey)
Mr. Erik MØSE (Norway)
Ms. Arlette RAMAROSON (Madagascar)
Mr. Jai Ram REDDY (Fiji)
Mr. William Hussein SEKULE (United Republic of Tanzania)
Ms. Andrésia VAZ (Senegal)
Ms. Inés Mónica WEINBERG DE DOCA (Argentina)
Mr. Lloyd George WILLIAMS (Saint Kitts and Nevis)

Communications. In identical letters of 16 April [A/57/790-S/2003/431] to the Presidents of the Security Council and the General Assembly, the Secretary-General transmitted a March letter of the ICTR President, Judge Navanethem Pillay, requesting extensions of the term of office of four permanent judges who were not elected to a new term, in order to allow them to dispose of a number of ongoing cases expected to continue beyond the end of their term on 24 May. The requests raised institutional and budgetary questions regarding the status of a judge beyond his/her elected term of office and related financial arrangements. Approval by the Council, as the parent organ of the Tribunal, and of the Assembly, as the organ that elected its judges, would be desirable to preclude any question on the legality of the extensions. The Registry estimated the associated costs at $1,893,800.

The Council President, in a 30 April letter [S/2003/550] to the Secretary-General, presented the views of Council members on the requested extensions to the effect that each request raised a different set of legal and practical issues. Council members had asked him to seek the advice of the President of the International Criminal Court (ICC) regarding the extension of Judge Pillay, who, on 4 February, had been elected an ICC judge for a term that had started on 11 March. Furthermore, Council members asked Judge Pillay for clarification of the issues raised and for quarterly reports on the progress of the cases in question, once the Council took action on the requests.

Mexico, on 19 May [S/2003/554], transmitted a 30 April letter from the Council President to the ICC President seeking advice on Judge Pillay's availability and the ICC Vice-President's 2 May reply, stating that it was not envisaged that she would be assigned substantive case work before year's end.

An 8 May letter [S/2003/551] from the Secretary-General to the Council President transmitted the views of Judge Pillay on the requests contained in her March letter (above), particularly regarding the extension of Judge Winston Churchill Matanzima Maqutu's term to December 2005 in order to complete the "Butare" case (see p. 1321). Regarding her election to ICC judge, Judge Pillay confirmed that she would be fully available as an ICTR judge and would not engage in substantive work as an ICC judge during the period required to complete the "Media" case (see p. 1321), which was expected to be completed no later than year's end.

SECURITY COUNCIL ACTION

On 19 May [meeting 4760], the Security Council unanimously adopted **resolution 1482(2003)**. The draft [S/2003/549] was prepared in consultations among Council members.

The Security Council,

Taking note of the letter dated 16 April 2003 from the Secretary-General addressed to the President of the Security Council attaching the letter dated 26 March 2003 from the President of the International Tribunal for Rwanda addressed to him,

Taking note also of the letter dated 30 April 2003 from the President of the Security Council addressed to the President of the International Criminal Court and the reply from the Vice-President of the International Criminal Court dated 2 May 2003, and of the letter dated 30 April 2003 from the President of the Security Council addressed to the Secretary-General and the reply from the Secretary-General dated 8 May 2003, to which is attached the letter addressed to him from the President of the International Tribunal for Rwanda dated 6 May 2003,

1. *Decides*, in response to the request by the Secretary-General, that:

(a) Judge Dolenc, once replaced as a member of the International Tribunal for Rwanda, finish the *Cyangugu* case which he has begun before expiry of his term of office;

(b) Judge Maqutu, once replaced as a member of the Tribunal, finish the *Kajelijeli* and *Kamuhanda* cases which he has begun before expiry of his term of office;

(c) Notwithstanding article 11, paragraph 1, of the statute of the Tribunal and on an exceptional basis, Judge Ostrovsky, once replaced as a member of the Tribunal, finish the *Cyangugu* case which he has begun before expiry of his term of office;

(d) Judge Pillay, once replaced as a member of the Tribunal, finish the *Media* case which she has begun before expiry of her term of office;

2. *Takes note*, in this regard, of the intention of the Tribunal to finish the *Cyangugu* case before the end of February 2004 and the *Kajelijeli*, *Kamuhanda* and *Media* cases before the end of December 2003;

3. *Requests* the President of the Tribunal to provide it, by 1 August 2003, 15 November 2003 and 15 January 2004, respectively, with reports on the progress of the cases referred to in paragraph 1 above.

Also on 19 May [A/57/814], the Secretary-General transmitted the Council's resolution to the General Assembly.

International tribunals

GENERAL ASSEMBLY ACTION

On 22 May, the General Assembly adopted **decision 57/414 B** without vote [agenda item 18].

Election of judges of the International Criminal Tribunal for the Prosecution of Persons Responsible for Genocide and Other Serious Violations of International Humanitarian Law Committed in the Territory of Rwanda and Rwandan Citizens Responsible for Genocide and Other Such Violations Committed in the Territory of Neighbouring States between 1 January and 31 December 1994

At its 86th plenary meeting, on 22 May 2003, the General Assembly decided to endorse those recommendations of the Secretary-General that were endorsed by the Security Council in its resolution 1482(2003) of 19 May 2003, that Judge Dolenc, once replaced as a member of the Tribunal, would finish the *Cyangugu* case which he had begun before expiry of his term of office; Judge Maqutu, once replaced as a member of the Tribunal, would finish the *Kajelijeli* and *Kamuhanda* cases which he had begun before expiry of his term of office; notwithstanding article 11, paragraph 1, of the statute of the Tribunal and on an exceptional basis, Judge Ostrovsky, once replaced as a member of the Tribunal, would finish the *Cyangugu* case which he had begun before expiry of his term of office; Judge Pillay, once replaced as a member of the Tribunal, would finish the *Media* case which she had begun before expiry of her term of office. The Assembly also took note of the intention of the Tribunal to finish the *Cyangugu* case before the end of February 2004 and the *Kajelijeli*, *Kamuhanda* and *Media* cases before the end of December 2003.

Ad litem judges

Communications. On 6 March [S/2003/290], the Secretary-General forwarded to the Security Council a list of the 26 nominations, together with their curricula vitae, that he had received for election to 18 ICTR posts for ad litem judges. Member States and non-member States maintaining permanent missions at Headquarters were invited, by a 3 January letter, to nominate candidates within the stipulated 60-day submission period. A list of a minimum of 36 candidates was required to be established by the Council for transmittal to the General Assembly. On 28 March [S/2003/382], the Council President informed the Secretary-General that the Council had extended the deadline for submitting nominations until 15 April 2003.

The Secretary-General, on 21 April [S/2003/467], forwarded to the Council a list of 35 nominations and their curricula vitae, noting that the list remained short of the minimum number of 36.

SECURITY COUNCIL ACTION

On 29 April [meeting 4745], the Security Council unanimously adopted **resolution 1477(2003)**. The draft [S/2003/505] was prepared in consultations among Council members.

The Security Council,

Recalling its resolutions 955(1994) of 8 November 1994, 1165(1998) of 30 April 1998, 1329(2000) of 30 November 2000, 1411(2002) of 17 May 2002 and 1431 (2002) of 14 August 2002,

Having considered the nominations for ad litem judges of the International Tribunal for Rwanda received by the Secretary-General,

Forwards the following nominations to the General Assembly in accordance with article 12 ter, paragraph 1 (d), of the statute of the International Tribunal:

Ms. Achta Saker Abdoul (Chad)
Mr. Aydin Sefa Akay (Turkey)
Ms. Florence Rita Arrey (Cameroon)
Mr. Abdoulaye Barry (Burkina Faso)
Mr. Miguel Antonio Bernal (Panama)
Ms. Solomy Balungi Bossa (Uganda)
Mr. Robert Fremr (Czech Republic)
Mr. Silvio Guerra Morales (Panama)
Ms. Taghreed Hikmat (Jordan)
Ms. Karin Hökborg (Sweden)
Mr. Vagn Joensen (Denmark)
Mr. Gberdao Gustave Kam (Burkina Faso)
Mr. Joseph-Médard Kaba Kashala Katuala (Democratic Republic of the Congo)
Ms. Engera A. Kileo (United Republic of Tanzania)
Ms. Nathalia P. Kimaro (United Republic of Tanzania)
Ms. Agnieszka Klonowiecka-Milart (Poland)
Ms. Flavia Lattanzi (Italy)
Mr. Kenneth Machin (United Kingdom of Great Britain and Northern Ireland)
Mr. Joseph Edward Chiondo Masanche (United Republic of Tanzania)
Mr. Patrick Matibini (Republic of Zambia)
Mr. Edouard Ngarta Mbaïouroum (Chad)
Mr. Antoine Kesia-Mbe Mindua (Democratic Republic of the Congo)
Mr. Tan Sri Dato' Hj. Mohd. Azmi Dato' Hj. Kamaruddin (Malaysia)
Mr. Lee Gacuiga Muthoga (Kenya)
Mr. Laurent Ngaoundi (Chad)
Ms. Beradingar Ngonyame (Chad)
Mr. Daniel David Ntanda Nsereko (Uganda)
Mr. Seon Ki Park (Republic of Korea)
Ms. Tatiana Raducanu (Republic of Moldova)
Mr. Mparany Mamy Richard Rajohnson (Madagascar)
Mr. Edward Mukandara K. Rutakangwa (United Republic of Tanzania)
Mr. Emile Francis Short (Ghana)
Mr. Albertus Henricus Joannes Swart (Netherlands)
Mr. Xenofon Ulianovschi (Republic of Moldova)
Ms. Aura Emérita Guerra de Villalaz (Panama)

Also on 29 April [A/57/800], the Council President transmitted the Council's resolution to the General Assembly.

Communications by Secretary-General. By a 30 April memorandum [A/57/801], the Secretary-General submitted the list of candidates selected by the Security Council to the General Assembly. He transmitted their curricula vitae through a separate note, also in April [A/57/802]. By further memorandums issued between 16 May and 26 June [A/57/801/Add.1-5], the Secretary-General indicated withdrawals of candidatures and presented consequent revised lists of candidates.

GENERAL ASSEMBLY ACTION

In June, the General Assembly adopted **decision 57/414 C** without vote [agenda item 18].

Election of judges of the International Criminal Tribunal for the Prosecution of Persons Responsible for Genocide and Other Serious Violations of International Humanitarian Law Committed in the Territory of Rwanda and Rwandan Citizens Responsible for Genocide and Other Such Violations Committed in the Territory of Neighbouring States between 1 January and 31 December 1994

At its 92nd plenary meeting, on 25 June 2003, the General Assembly, in accordance with articles 12 and 12 ter of the statute of the Tribunal, elected the following eighteen ad litem judges for a four-year term of office beginning on 25 June 2003:

Mr. Aydin Sefa AKAY (Turkey)
Ms. Florence Rita ARREY (Cameroon)
Ms. Solomy Balungi BOSSA (Uganda)
Mr. Robert FREMR (Czech Republic)
Ms. Taghreed HIKMAT (Jordan)
Ms. Karin HÖKBORG (Sweden)
Mr. Vagn JOENSEN (Denmark)
Mr. Gberdao Gustave KAM (Burkina Faso)
Mr. Tan Sri Dato' Hj. Mohd. Azmi Dato' Hj. KAMARUDDIN (Malaysia)
Ms. Flavia LATTANZI (Italy)
Mr. Kenneth MACHIN (United Kingdom of Great Britain and Northern Ireland)
Mr. Joseph Edward Chiondo MASANCHE (United Republic of Tanzania)
Mr. Lee Gacuiga MUTHOGA (Kenya)
Mr. Seon Ki PARK (Republic of Korea)
Mr. Mparany Mamy Richard RAJOHNSON (Madagascar)
Mr. Emile Francis SHORT (Ghana)
Mr. Albertus Henricus Joannes SWART (Netherlands)
Ms. Aura Emérita GUERRA DE VILLALAZ (Panama)

Amendment of statute

The Secretary-General transmitted to the Security Council President an 8 September letter [S/2003/879] from the ICTR President requesting that the Council amend the ICTR statute so that, during the period in which an ad litem judge was appointed to serve for a trial, he/she could also adjudicate in pre-trial proceedings in other cases. The amendment would facilitate the conduct of judicial business and enable the Tribunal to make better use of the time and abilities of the ad litem judges.

In a 29 September letter [S/2003/946], the President stated that if ICTR's judicial capacity remained unchanged, it would take until 2011 to complete the trials of all persons currently being, or who might in the future be, prosecuted before it. For ICTR to achieve completion by the end of 2008, the target set by the Council in resolution 1503 (2003) (see p. 1330), he requested that the Council amend the ICTR statute so that it would be authorized to make use of up to nine ad litem judges at any one time, rather than the current maximum of four. The related increase in the ICTR budget was estimated at $12.4 million for the 2004-2005 biennium for an additional five ad litem judges and support staff. ICTR's updated completion strategy was enclosed with the letter.

SECURITY COUNCIL ACTION

On 27 October [meeting 4849], the Security Council unanimously adopted **resolution 1512(2003)**. The draft [S/2003/1033] was prepared in consultations among Council members.

The Security Council,

Reaffirming its resolutions 955(1994) of 8 November 1994, 1165(1998) of 30 April 1998, 1329(2000) of 30 November 2000, 1411(2002) of 17 May 2002, 1431(2002) of 14 August 2002 and 1503(2003) of 28 August 2003,

Having considered the letter dated 12 September 2003 from the Secretary-General addressed to the President of the Security Council and the letter annexed thereto dated 8 September 2003 from the President of the International Tribunal for Rwanda addressed to the Secretary-General,

Having considered also the letter from the Secretary-General dated 3 October 2003 addressed to the President of the Security Council and the letter annexed thereto dated 29 September 2003 from the President of the International Tribunal for Rwanda addressed to the Secretary-General,

Convinced of the advisability of enhancing the powers of ad litem judges in the International Tribunal for Rwanda so that, during the period of their appointment to a trial, they might also adjudicate in pre-trial proceedings in other cases, should the need arise and should they be in a position to do so,

Convinced also of the advisability of increasing the number of ad litem judges that may be appointed at any one time to serve in the Trial Chambers of the International Tribunal for Rwanda, so that the Tribunal might be better placed to complete all trial activities at first instance by the end of 2008, as envisaged in its Completion Strategy,

Acting under Chapter VII of the Charter of the United Nations,

1. *Decides* to amend articles 11 and 12 quater of the Statute of the International Tribunal for Rwanda and to replace those articles with the provisions set out in the annex to the present resolution;

2. *Decides* to remain actively seized of the matter.

Annex

Article 11
Composition of the Chambers

1. The Chambers shall be composed of sixteen permanent independent judges, no two of whom may be nationals of the same State, and a maximum at any one

time of nine ad litem independent judges appointed in accordance with article 12 ter, paragraph 2, of the present statute, no two of whom may be nationals of the same State.

2. Three permanent judges and a maximum at any one time of six ad litem judges shall be members of each Trial Chamber. Each Trial Chamber to which ad litem judges are assigned may be divided into sections of three judges each, composed of both permanent and ad litem judges. A section of a Trial Chamber shall have the same powers and responsibilities as a Trial Chamber under the present statute and shall render judgement in accordance with the same rules.

3. Seven of the permanent judges shall be members of the Appeals Chamber. The Appeals Chamber shall, for each appeal, be composed of five of its members.

4. A person who for the purposes of membership of the Chambers of the International Tribunal for Rwanda could be regarded as a national of more than one State shall be deemed to be a national of the State in which that person ordinarily exercises civil and political rights.

Article 12 quater
Status of ad litem judges

1. During the period in which they are appointed to serve in the International Tribunal for Rwanda, ad litem judges shall:

(a) Benefit from the same terms and conditions of service mutatis mutandis as the permanent judges of the International Tribunal for Rwanda;

(b) Enjoy, subject to paragraph 2 below, the same powers as the permanent judges of the International Tribunal for Rwanda;

(c) Enjoy the privileges and immunities, exemptions and facilities of a judge of the International Tribunal for Rwanda;

(d) Enjoy the power to adjudicate in pre-trial proceedings in cases other than those that they have been appointed to try.

2. During the period in which they are appointed to serve in the International Tribunal for Rwanda, ad litem judges shall not:

(a) Be eligible for election as, or to vote in the election of, the President of the International Tribunal for Rwanda or the Presiding Judge of a Trial Chamber pursuant to article 13 of the present statute;

(b) Have power:
 (i) To adopt rules of procedure and evidence pursuant to article 14 of the present statute. They shall, however, be consulted before the adoption of those rules;
 (ii) To review an indictment pursuant to article 18 of the present statute;
 (iii) To consult with the President of the International Tribunal for Rwanda in relation to the assignment of judges pursuant to article 13 of the present statute or in relation to a pardon or commutation of sentence pursuant to article 27 of the present statute.

Office of the Prosecutor

The Office of the Prosecutor had instituted internal reforms to increase the trial capacity of ICTR to the level of prosecuting up to six different cases every day. The Office focused on individuals who allegedly were in positions of leadership and bore the gravest responsibility for the crimes committed in 1994. Accused and suspects alleged to have been mid- to low-level participants in those crimes were to be transferred to national jurisdictions, including Rwanda, for trial. An updated version of the completion strategy for ICTR's work was submitted to the Security Council on 29 September [S/2003/946] (see p. 1320).

By **resolution 1503(2003)** (see p. 1330), the Security Council established the position of Prosecutor of ICTR and appointed Hassan Bubacar Jallow as Prosecutor for a four-year term with effect from 15 September 2003.

SECURITY COUNCIL ACTION

On 4 September [meeting 4819], the Security Council unanimously adopted **resolution 1505 (2003)**. The draft [S/2003/847] was prepared in consultations among Council members.

The Security Council,

Recalling its resolution 1503(2003) of 28 August 2003,

Noting that by that resolution the Council created a new position of Prosecutor of the International Tribunal for Rwanda,

Having regard to article 15, paragraph 4, of the statute of the International Tribunal for Rwanda, as adopted by the Council in its resolution 1503(2003),

Having considered the nomination by the Secretary-General of Mr. Hassan Bubacar Jallow as Prosecutor of the International Tribunal for Rwanda,

Appoints Mr. Hassan Bubacar Jallow as Prosecutor of the International Tribunal for Rwanda with effect from 15 September 2003 for a four-year term.

The Registry

In the light of the completion strategy (see p. 1320), management reforms and organizational restructuring were undertaken in the Office of the Registrar. Significant changes included the re-amalgamation of the witnesses and victims support mechanisms of the Registry into a single section and the remerging of the management of the United Nations Detention Facility with that of the Defence Counsel to form the Defence Counsel and Detention Management Section.

In March, the Registrar signed an agreement with France on the enforcement of sentences.

The recruitment, in June, of a Gender Adviser within the Gender Advisory Unit of the Office provided the impetus for more strategic action in gender-sensitive areas. The Unit contributed to the establishment of policy guidelines aimed at encouraging a more conducive environment for the participation of victims and witnesses in the judicial proceedings. Physical and psychological support measures were provided to victims, especially those who had been subjected to rape and sexual assault, summoned to testify before the Tribunal.

Report of Secretary-General. In response to General Assembly resolution 57/289 [YUN 2002, p. 1291], the Secretary-General, in September [A/58/366], described progress made in the reform of the ICTR legal aid system, particularly with regard to rationalizing the costs of defence counsel and establishing indigence. The Defence Counsel and Detention Management Section instituted measures to monitor and control the upward trend of defence costs. The report of a consultant, which was annexed to the main report, stated that the systems at both ICTY and ICTR were flawed and open to abuse and made recommendations regarding defence team costs and indigency.

ACABQ report. A November report of ACABQ [A/58/554] commended the course of action proposed in the Secretary-General's report. However, it did not share the concern raised in the report as to the discriminatory effect of restricting the lists of lead counsel, co-counsel, legal assistants and investigators to persons residing in Africa, or that all co-counsel, legal assistants and investigators should be from Africa. The Committee was of the view that the effect of implementing the recommendations on the cost of defence counsel was not yet clear, but that it was bound to be considerable. Information on progress made in that regard should be provided.

Financing

2002-2003 biennium

Report of Secretary-General. A November report of the Secretary-General [A/58/597], submitted in response to General Assembly resolution 57/289 [YUN 2002, p. 1291], contained the second performance report of ICTR for the 2002-2003 biennium. The report indicated an additional requirement of $4.5 million gross ($4.4 million net) over the revised appropriation for that biennium. The increased requirements pertained to changes with respect to the combined effect of exchange rates and inflation ($7.5 million gross ($7.5 million net)), partially offset by decreases in post incumbency and other changes ($3 million gross ($3.1 million net)). The Assembly was requested to revise the appropriation for the 2002-2003 biennium to $208.5 million gross ($187.3 million net) to the ICTR Special Account.

ACABQ report. A November report of ACABQ [A/58/605] recommended that the General Assembly approve the revision of the 2002-2003 appropriation to the ICTR Special Account as requested by the Secretary-General's report (above).

GENERAL ASSEMBLY ACTION

On 23 December [meeting 79], the General Assembly, on the recommendation of the Fifth Committee [A/58/579], adopted **resolution 58/252** without vote [agenda item 131].

Second performance report for the biennium 2002-2003 on the International Criminal Tribunal for the Prosecution of Persons Responsible for Genocide and Other Serious Violations of International Humanitarian Law Committed in the Territory of Rwanda and Rwandan Citizens Responsible for Genocide and Other Such Violations Committed in the Territory of Neighbouring States between 1 January and 31 December 1994

The General Assembly,

Having considered the second performance report of the Secretary-General for the biennium 2002-2003 on the International Criminal Tribunal for the Prosecution of Persons Responsible for Genocide and Other Serious Violations of International Humanitarian Law Committed in the Territory of Rwanda and Rwandan Citizens Responsible for Genocide and Other Such Violations Committed in the Territory of Neighbouring States between 1 January and 31 December 1994 and the related report of the Advisory Committee on Administrative and Budgetary Questions,

Recalling its resolution 49/251 of 20 July 1995 on the financing of the International Tribunal for Rwanda and its subsequent resolutions thereon, the latest of which were resolutions 56/248 A of 24 December 2001, 56/248 B of 27 March 2002 and 57/289 of 20 December 2002,

1. *Takes note* of the second performance report of the Secretary-General for the biennium 2002-2003 on the International Criminal Tribunal for the Prosecution of Persons Responsible for Genocide and Other Serious Violations of International Humanitarian Law Committed in the Territory of Rwanda and Rwandan Citizens Responsible for Genocide and Other Such Violations Committed in the Territory of Neighbouring States between 1 January and 31 December 1994 and the related report of the Advisory Committee on Administrative and Budgetary Questions;

2. *Endorses* the conclusions and recommendations contained in the report of the Advisory Committee on Administrative and Budgetary Questions;

3. *Notes with concern* the late issuance of the second performance report of the Secretary-General for the biennium 2002-2003, bearing in mind the nature of the report and the period covered therein;

4. *Resolves* that, for the biennium 2002-2003, the amount of 203,962,600 United States dollars gross (182,870,700 dollars net) approved in its resolution 57/289 of 20 December 2002 for the budget of the International Tribunal for Rwanda, shall be adjusted by the amount of 4,517,100 dollars gross (4,392,200 dollars net) for a total amount of 208,479,700 dollars gross (187,262,900 dollars net).

2004-2005 biennium

Reports of Secretary-General. An August report of the Secretary-General [A/58/269] contained the ICTR resource requirements for the 2004-2005 biennium. Those requirements, before recosting, amounted to $209 million gross ($187.3 million net), including growth of $4.8 million gross ($4.4 million net), or 2.4 per cent, compared with the revised 2002-2003 appropriation (see p. 1326). The real resource changes included provisions for the delayed impact of 109 new posts and the ad litem judges approved for 2002-2003 (see p. 1323). In nominal terms, the estimate for 2004-2005 amounted to $235 million gross ($213 million net) and reflected an increase of $26 million net mostly due to the impact of changes in inflation, offset by a decrease in exchange rates.

A September report of the Secretary-General [A/58/368] estimated additional ICTR requirements for 2004-2005 of $4 million gross ($3.4 million net) in the light of Security Council resolution 1503 (2003) (see p. 1330), which established the new position of ICTR Prosecutor. Thus, the overall requirements for 2004-2005 in nominal terms increased from $235 million gross ($213 million net) to $239.2 million gross ($216.3 million net).

A September note by the Secretary-General [A/58/367] stated that, as at 12 September, the Council, pursuant to General Assembly resolution 57/289 [YUN 2002, p. 1291], had taken no action on the long-term financial obligations of the United Nations regarding the enforcement of sentences. He proposed, therefore, that the Assembly continue the temporary arrangements set out in resolution 57/289, for which resources in the amount of $250,000 were included in the proposed 2004-2005 budget.

In a November report [A/58/550], the Secretary-General set out the resource requirements for 2004-2005 in the light of Council resolution 1512 (2003) (see p. 1324), which established five additional ICTR posts for ad litem judges. The estimated additional requirements would amount to $12.2 million gross ($11.2 million net), with an additional 45 temporary posts, thus increasing the overall requirements from $239.2 million gross ($216.3 million net) to $251.4 million gross ($227.5 million net).

ACABQ report. In a November report [A/58/554], ACABQ recommended approval of the estimated ICTR requirements for the 2004-2005 biennium of $251.4 million gross ($227.5 million net).

GENERAL ASSEMBLY ACTION

On 23 December [meeting 79], the General Assembly, on the recommendation of the Fifth Committee [A/58/579], adopted **resolution 58/253** without vote [agenda item 131].

Financing of the International Criminal Tribunal for the Prosecution of Persons Responsible for Genocide and Other Serious Violations of International Humanitarian Law Committed in the Territory of Rwanda and Rwandan Citizens Responsible for Genocide and Other Such Violations Committed in the Territory of Neighbouring States between 1 January and 31 December 1994

The General Assembly,

Having considered the documents submitted by the Secretary-General on the financing for the biennium 2004-2005 of the International Criminal Tribunal for the Prosecution of Persons Responsible for Genocide and Other Serious Violations of International Humanitarian Law Committed in the Territory of Rwanda and Rwandan Citizens Responsible for Genocide and Other Such Violations Committed in the Territory of Neighbouring States between 1 January and 31 December 1994 and the related report of the Advisory Committee on Administrative and Budgetary Questions,

Recalling its resolution 49/251 of 20 July 1995, on the financing of the International Tribunal for Rwanda, and its subsequent resolutions thereon, the latest of which were resolutions 56/248 A of 24 December 2001, 56/248 B of 27 March 2002 and 57/289 of 20 December 2002,

Recalling also Security Council resolution 1503(2003) of 28 August 2003 concerning the creation of a new position of Prosecutor of the International Tribunal for Rwanda,

Recalling further Security Council resolution 1512 (2003) of 27 October 2003 concerning the authorization for the use of up to nine additional ad litem judges in the International Tribunal for Rwanda,

Welcoming the developments and improvements in the management and the activities of the Tribunal thus far achieved during the biennium 2002-2003,

1. *Takes note* of the documents submitted by the Secretary-General on the financing for the biennium 2004-2005 of the International Criminal Tribunal for the Prosecution of Persons Responsible for Genocide and Other Serious Violations of International Humanitarian Law Committed in the Territory of Rwanda and Rwandan Citizens Responsible for Genocide and Other Such Violations Committed in the Territory of Neighbouring States between 1 January and 31 December 1994 and the related report of the Advisory Committee on Administrative and Budgetary Questions;

2. *Endorses* the conclusions and recommendations contained in the report of the Advisory Committee on Administrative and Budgetary Questions, subject to the provisions of the present resolution;

3. *Notes with concern* the levels of unpaid assessed contributions, and urges Member States to pay their assessed contributions on time, in full and without conditions;

4. *Welcomes* the efforts of the Secretary-General to present the proposed budget for the biennium 2004-2005 in a results-based format, and encourages him to make further progress in this regard;

5. *Requests* the Secretary-General to ensure that the report requested in paragraph 2 of General Assembly resolution 55/226 of 23 December 2000, as well as the views of the Board of Auditors thereon, is submitted to the Assembly during the main part of its fifty-ninth session;

6. *Welcomes* the appointment of a Prosecutor and the authorization for the use of up to nine ad litem judges, as approved by the Security Council in its resolutions 1503(2003) and 1512(2003), and stresses the importance of ensuring that the Tribunal receives adequate financial and human resources to support its strengthened judicial capacity and to enable it to meet the targets set out in its completion strategy;

7. *Welcomes also* the efforts made by the Tribunal to enhance coordination between the Chambers, the Office of the Prosecutor and the relevant sections of the Registry, through the establishment of the various management committees;

8. *Requests* the Tribunal to continue to enhance its engagement with the defence counsel establishment in the facilitation of trial work;

9. *Welcomes* the development of the completion strategy, and invites the Tribunal to revise the strategy, where appropriate, to take into account the provisions of Security Council resolutions 1503(2003) and 1512 (2003) and the resultant increased judicial capacity of the Tribunal;

10. *Requests* the Secretary-General to develop further the link between the Tribunal's completion strategy and objectives and the resources requested in future budget proposals;

11. *Concurs* with the view of the Advisory Committee on Administrative and Budgetary Questions that continued close collaboration between the International Tribunal for the Former Yugoslavia and the International Tribunal for Rwanda is essential, and urges the Secretary-General to take all necessary measures to ensure such collaboration;

12. *Notes with concern* that the vacancy rate at the International Tribunal for Rwanda remains high, while acknowledging that the level has been reduced during the biennium 2002-2003, and requests the Secretary-General to take the necessary measures, as a matter of priority, to reduce the vacancy rate during the biennium 2004-2005, including, if appropriate, through delegating authority to the Registrar for recruitment in the Professional category and considering extending the contracts of core staff for longer periods, consistent with the staff regulations and rules, and bearing in mind the targets set in the completion strategy;

13. *Requests* the Secretary-General to continue, where appropriate, to prioritize and deploy resources in support of the completion strategy and to report thereon in his first and second performance reports;

14. *Also requests* the Secretary-General to undertake efficiency measures to streamline the work of the Tribunal and to provide an assessment of the financial impact of those measures in future budget proposals;

15. *Invites* the Security Council to continue to monitor closely the progress made by the Tribunal towards completing its mandate, in accordance with the completion strategy;

16. *Also invites* the Security Council to request the Secretary-General to make initial preparations, including establishing the rules of procedure, for the transfer of cases to national jurisdictions;

17. *Requests* the Secretary-General to report to the General Assembly at its fifty-ninth session on proposals for the resources necessary to aid in the transfer of cases to national jurisdictions;

18. *Decides* to maintain the current level of funding for consultants and experts;

19. *Also decides* to approve the proposed post and non-post resources for the Investigations Division for 2004 and to defer consideration of the resource requirements for the Investigations Division for 2005 until the fifty-ninth session of the General Assembly;

20. *Requests* the Secretary-General to resubmit, in his first performance report for the biennium 2004-2005, proposals for the resource requirements for the Investigations Division for 2005 and to ensure that the proposals are adequate for the effective implementation of the completion strategy;

21. *Also requests* the Secretary-General to review the outreach programme of the Tribunal and to report to the General Assembly during the main part of its fifty-ninth session on optimal media for the dissemination of information on the work of the Tribunal and on the resources allocated to this function, and on how future outreach initiatives and coordination with other parts of the United Nations system support the completion strategy and contribute to the reconciliation process in Rwanda;

22. *Further requests* the Secretary-General to report on oversight functions in the Tribunal in his first performance report for the biennium 2004-2005, with specific reference to oversight of resources allocated for the upgrading of prison facilities to international standards;

23. *Requests* the Secretary-General to pursue the possibility of assistance to the Tribunal from the United Nations Office at Nairobi and other offices of the United Nations system to increase remote translation capabilities and to report on cost comparisons in his first performance report;

24. *Welcomes* the comprehensive report of the Secretary-General on the progress made by the Tribunal in reforming its legal aid system;

25. *Requests* the Secretary-General to continue to reform the legal aid system, taking into account the recommendations contained in the comprehensive report or other reforms deemed more appropriate by the Tribunal, as a top priority, and to report on the implementation and consequent savings in defence costs in his performance report for the biennium 2004-2005;

26. *Decides* that a vacancy rate of 18.2 per cent for Professional staff and 9.7 per cent for General Service staff shall be used as a basis for the calculation of the budget for the biennium 2004-2005;

27. *Recalls* paragraph 3 of its resolution 57/289, in which it urged the Secretary-General to request the Office of Internal Oversight Services to conduct a management review of the Office of the former Prosecutor, and requests the Secretary-General to submit the report on the matter to the General Assembly no later than at its resumed fifty-eighth session;

28. *Decides* to appropriate to the Special Account for the International Criminal Tribunal for the Prosecution of Persons Responsible for Genocide and Other Serious Violations of International Humanitarian Law Committed in the Territory of Rwanda and Rwandan Citizens Responsible for Genocide and Other Such Violations Committed in the Territory of Neighbouring States between 1 January and 31 December 1994 the total amount of 235,324,200 United States dollars

for the biennium 2004-2005, as detailed in the annex to the present resolution;

29. *Decides also* that the total assessment for 2004 under the Special Account, amounting to 122,179,200 dollars, shall consist of:

(a) 117,662,100 dollars, being half of the estimated appropriation approved for the biennium 2004-2005;

(b) 4,517,100 dollars, being the increase in the final appropriation for the biennium 2002-2003 approved by the General Assembly in its resolution 58/252 of 23 December 2003;

30. *Decides further* to apportion the amount of 61,089,600 dollars, being half of the total assessment for 2004, among Member States in accordance with the rates of assessment applicable to the regular budget of the United Nations for 2004, as set out in its resolution 58/1 B of 23 December 2003;

31. *Decides* to apportion the amount of 61,089,600 dollars, being half of the total assessment for 2004, among Member States in accordance with the rates of assessment applicable to peacekeeping operations for 2004;

32. *Decides also* that, in accordance with the provisions of its resolution 973(X) of 15 December 1955, there shall be set off against the apportionment among Member States, as provided for in paragraphs 30 and 31 above, the amount of 11,149,250 dollars, consisting of:

(a) 11,024,350 dollars, being half of the estimated staff assessment income approved for the Tribunal for the biennium 2004-2005;

(b) 124,900 dollars, being the increase in staff assessment income for the biennium 2002-2003 approved by the General Assembly in its resolution 58/252 of 23 December 2003.

Annex

Financing for the biennium 2004-2005 of the International Criminal Tribunal for the Prosecution of Persons Responsible for Genocide and Other Serious Violations of International Humanitarian Law Committed in the Territory of Rwanda and Rwandan Citizens Responsible for Genocide and Other Such Violations Committed in the Territory of Neighbouring States between 1 January and 31 December 1994

	Gross	Net
	(United States dollars)	
1. Estimated appropriation for the biennium 2004-2005	251,388,400	227,469,200
2. Recommendations of the Advisory Committee on Administrative and Budgetary Questions	-	-
3. Recommendations of the Fifth Committee	(16,064,200)	(14,193,700)
4. Revised estimated appropriation for the biennium 2004-2005	235,324,200	213,275,500
5. Estimated income for the biennium 2004-2005	-	-
6. Total assessment for 2004, comprising:	**122,179,200**	**111,029,950**
(a) Requirements representing half of the estimated appropriation for the biennium 2004-2005	117,662,100	106,637,750
(b) Requirements arising from the final appropriation for the biennium 2002-2003	4,517,100	4,392,200

	Gross	Net
	(United States dollars)	
Including:		
Contributions assessed on Member States in accordance with the rates of assessment applicable to the regular budget of the United Nations for 2004	61,089,600	55,514,975
Contributions assessed on Member States in accordance with the rates of assessment applicable to peacekeeping operations of the United Nations for 2004	61,089,600	55,514,975

Also on 23 December, the Assembly decided that the item on financing of ICTR would remain for consideration during its resumed fifty-eighth (2004) session (**decision 58/565**).

Prison facilities

Following the Security Council's adoption of resolution 1512(2003) (see p. 1324), the Council President, on 27 October [meeting 4849], made statement **S/PRST/2003/18** on behalf of the Council:

The Security Council notes the invitation of the General Assembly contained in paragraph 7 of its resolution 57/289 of 20 December 2002 that it address uncertainties regarding the power of the International Tribunal for Rwanda under its statute to finance the upgrading of prison accommodation in which persons convicted by the Tribunal are to serve their sentences.

The Council confirms that it is within the lawful powers of the International Tribunal for Rwanda under its statute to fund the renovation and refurbishment of prison facilities in States that have concluded agreements with the United Nations for the carrying out of prison sentences of the Tribunal. Such funds shall be used to bring up to international minimum standards the prison accommodation to be occupied or used pursuant to those agreements.

The Council will remain seized of this matter.

Functioning of the tribunals

Office of the Prosecutor

On 28 July [S/2003/766], the Secretary-General informed the Security Council President that, in view of his consultations with Council members, he had concluded that it was time to split the role of the Prosecutor, heretofore shared by both ICTY and ICTR. He felt that, as the two Tribunals moved towards implementing their completion strategies, it seemed essential, in the interests of efficiency and effectiveness, for each to have its own Prosecutor. To that end, he proposed amendments to the ICTR statute, as set out in the annex to his letter, to permit the appointment of a separate Prosecutor for ICTR.

SECURITY COUNCIL ACTION

On 28 August [meeting 4817], the Security Council unanimously adopted **resolution 1503(2003)**. The draft [S/2003/835] was prepared in consultations among Council members.

The Security Council,

Recalling its resolutions 827(1993) of 25 May 1993, 955(1994) of 8 November 1994, 978(1995) of 27 February 1995, 1165(1998) of 30 April 1998, 1166(1998) of 13 May 1998, 1329(2000) of 30 November 2000, 1411 (2002) of 17 May 2002, 1431(2002) of 14 August 2002, and 1481(2003) of 19 May 2003,

Noting the letter dated 28 July 2003 from the Secretary-General to the President of the Security Council,

Commending the important work of the International Tribunal for the Former Yugoslavia and the International Tribunal for Rwanda in contributing to lasting peace and security in the former Yugoslavia and Rwanda, and the progress made since their inception,

Noting that an essential prerequisite for achieving the objectives of the completion strategies of the International Tribunal for the Former Yugoslavia and the International Tribunal for Rwanda is full cooperation by all States, especially in apprehending all remaining at-large persons indicted by the Tribunals,

Welcoming steps taken by States in the Balkans and the Great Lakes region of Africa to improve cooperation and apprehend at-large persons indicted by the Tribunals, but noting with concern that certain States are still not offering full cooperation,

Urging Member States to consider imposing measures against individuals and groups or organizations assisting indictees at large to continue to evade justice, including measures designed to restrict the travel and freeze the assets of such individuals, groups, or organizations,

Recalling and reaffirming in the strongest terms the statement of 23 July 2002 made by the President of the Security Council, endorsing the strategy of the International Tribunal for the Former Yugoslavia for completing investigations by the end of 2004, all trial activities at first instance by the end of 2008, and all of its work in 2010 (the International Tribunal for the Former Yugoslavia Completion Strategy), by concentrating on the prosecution and trial of the most senior leaders suspected of being most responsible for crimes within the jurisdiction of the Tribunal and transferring cases involving those who may not bear this level of responsibility to competent national jurisdictions, as appropriate, as well as the strengthening of the capacity of such jurisdictions,

Urging the International Tribunal for Rwanda to formalize a detailed strategy, modelled on the International Tribunal for the Former Yugoslavia Completion Strategy, to transfer cases involving intermediate- and lower-rank accused to competent national jurisdictions, as appropriate, including Rwanda, in order to allow the International Tribunal for Rwanda to achieve its objective of completing investigations by the end of 2004, all trial activities at first instance by the end of 2008, and all of its work in 2010 (International Tribunal for Rwanda Completion Strategy),

Noting that the above-mentioned completion strategies in no way alter the obligation of Rwanda and the countries of the former Yugoslavia to investigate those accused whose cases would not be tried by International Tribunal for Rwanda or the International Tribunal for the Former Yugoslavia and take appropriate action with respect to indictment and prosecution, while bearing in mind the primacy of the Tribunals over national courts,

Noting also that the strengthening of national judicial systems is crucially important to the rule of law in general and to the implementation of the completion strategies of the International Tribunal for the Former Yugoslavia and International Tribunal for Rwanda in particular,

Noting further that an essential prerequisite for achieving the objectives of the International Tribunal for the Former Yugoslavia Completion Strategy is the expeditious establishment under the auspices of the High Representative and early functioning of a special chamber within the State Court of Bosnia and Herzegovina (the "War Crimes Chamber") and the subsequent referral by the International Tribunal for the Former Yugoslavia of cases of lower- or intermediate-rank accused to the Chamber,

Convinced that the International Tribunal for the Former Yugoslavia and the International Tribunal for Rwanda can most efficiently and expeditiously meet their respective responsibilities if each has its own Prosecutor,

Acting under Chapter VII of the Charter of the United Nations,

1. *Calls upon* the international community to assist national jurisdictions, as part of the completion strategies, in improving their capacity to prosecute cases transferred from the International Tribunal for the Former Yugoslavia and the International Tribunal for Rwanda, and encourages the Presidents, Prosecutors, and Registrars of the Tribunals to develop and improve their outreach programmes;

2. *Calls upon* all States, especially Serbia and Montenegro, Croatia, and Bosnia and Herzegovina, and on the Republika Srpska within Bosnia and Herzegovina, to intensify cooperation with and render all necessary assistance to the International Tribunal for the Former Yugoslavia, particularly to bring Radovan Karadzic and Ratko Mladic, as well as Ante Gotovina and all other indictees to the Tribunal, and calls upon these and all other at-large indictees of the Tribunal to surrender to it;

3. *Calls upon* all States, especially Rwanda, Kenya, the Democratic Republic of the Congo, and the Republic of the Congo, to intensify cooperation with and render all necessary assistance to the International Tribunal for Rwanda, including on investigations of the Rwandan Patriotic Army and efforts to bring Felicien Kabuga and all other such indictees to the Tribunal, and calls upon these and all other at-large indictees of the Tribunal to surrender to it;

4. *Calls upon* all States to cooperate with the International Criminal Police Organization (ICPO-Interpol) in apprehending and transferring persons indicted by the International Tribunal for the Former Yugoslavia and the International Tribunal for Rwanda;

5. *Calls upon* the donor community to support the work of the High Representative for Bosnia and Herzegovina in creating a special chamber, within the State Court of Bosnia and Herzegovina, to adjudicate allegations of serious violations of international humanitarian law;

6. *Requests* the Presidents of the International Tribunal for the Former Yugoslavia and the International Tribunal for Rwanda and their Prosecutors, in their annual reports to the Council, to explain their plans to implement the completion strategies of the International Tribunal for the Former Yugoslavia and the International Tribunal for Rwanda;

7. *Calls upon* the International Tribunal for the Former Yugoslavia and the International Tribunal for Rwanda to take all possible measures to complete investigations by the end of 2004, to complete all trial activities at first instance by the end of 2008, and to complete all of their work in 2010 (the completion strategies);

8. *Decides* to amend article 15 of the statute of the International Tribunal for Rwanda and to replace that article with the provision set out in the annex to the present resolution, and requests the Secretary-General to nominate a person to be the Prosecutor of the International Tribunal for Rwanda;

9. *Welcomes* the intention expressed by the Secretary-General in his letter dated 28 July 2003 to submit to the Security Council the name of Ms. Carla Del Ponte as nominee for Prosecutor of the International Tribunal for the Former Yugoslavia;

10. *Decides* to remain actively seized of the matter.

Annex

Article 15
The Prosecutor

1. The Prosecutor shall be responsible for the investigation and prosecution of persons responsible for serious violations of international humanitarian law committed in the territory of Rwanda and Rwandan citizens responsible for such violations committed in the territory of neighbouring States between 1 January and 31 December 1994.

2. The Prosecutor shall act independently as a separate organ of the International Tribunal for Rwanda. He or she shall not seek or receive instructions from any government or from any other source.

3. The Office of the Prosecutor shall be composed of a Prosecutor and such other qualified staff as may be required.

4. The Prosecutor shall be appointed by the Security Council on nomination by the Secretary-General. He or she shall be of high moral character and possess the highest level of competence and experience in the conduct of investigations and prosecutions of criminal cases. The Prosecutor shall serve for a four-year term and be eligible for reappointment. The terms and conditions of service of the Prosecutor shall be those of an Under-Secretary-General of the United Nations.

5. The staff of the Office of the Prosecutor shall be appointed by the Secretary-General on the recommendation of the Prosecutor.

OIOS report

Pursuant to General Assembly resolution 57/289 [YUN 2002, p. 1291], the Secretary-General transmitted a review by the Office of Internal Oversight Services (OIOS) [A/58/677] of the Office of the Prosecutor of ICTR and of ICTY. The review, conducted in June and July, concluded that the then sole Prosecutor for both Tribunals had taken initiatives to improve the performance of the two Offices through the use of information technology and changing working methods, such as the way translations were carried out. However, best practices were not always shared between the Offices, resulting in missed opportunities for building synergies. In addition, arrangements for planning and monitoring needed internal strengthening, in coordination with the other organs of the Tribunals. There was insufficient information to confirm the Tribunals' contention to the Security Council that investigation and prosecution mandates would be completed by 2004 and 2008, respectively. The Offices lacked a strategy document that formed part of a coordinated Tribunal-wide approach and that identified the factors that impacted on the Tribunals' ability to achieve the completion dates. While certain elements were present in the ICTR and ICTY proposed 2004-2005 budgets, which included a revised management structure, reduction and redeployment of staff of the Office of the Prosecutor of both Tribunals, nowhere were those clearly indicated as requirements to achieve the completion dates. The review found delays in recruiting the ICTR Deputy Prosecutor and the Chief of Prosecutions to be due to inappropriate recruitment procedures on the part of the Offices and the Registries. The Secretary-General took note of the OIOS findings and concurred with the recommendations. The ICTR and ICTY Prosecutors had accepted the recommendations and were in the process of implementing them.

Chapter III

Legal aspects of international political relations

During 2003, the International Criminal Court (ICC), established by the 1998 Rome Statute of the International Criminal Court, became an operational judicial institution. Following the election of its 18 judges and Prosecutor at the resumed first session of the Assembly of States Parties to the Rome Statute, ICC held its inaugural meeting in The Hague, Netherlands, on 11 March. Its administrative set-up was completed with the appointment of its Presidency and constitution of its chambers by ICC and appointment of its most senior officials and subsidiary bodies at the second session of the Assembly of States Parties. In December, the General Assembly called on States not yet parties to the Rome Statute to consider ratifying or acceding to it and on all States to consider becoming parties to the Agreement on the Privileges and Immunities of the International Court.

The International Law Commission continued its examination of topics suitable for the progressive development and codification of international law, provisionally adopting additional draft guidelines and draft articles on reservations to treaties and on diplomatic protection. It also adopted the first three draft articles on the responsibility of international organizations.

The Ad Hoc Committee on the convention for suppression of nuclear terrorism and the Sixth (Legal) Committee of the General Assembly continued work on the elaboration of a draft comprehensive convention on international terrorism and a draft international convention for the suppression of acts of nuclear terrorism.

The Ad Hoc Committee on the Scope of Legal Protection under the 1994 Convention on the Safety of United Nations and Associated Personnel continued to consider measures to enhance the existing protective legal regime for UN and associated personnel.

Establishment of the International Criminal Court

The 1998 Rome Statute of the International Criminal Court [YUN 1998, p. 1209], which established ICC as a permanent institution with the power to exercise jurisdiction over persons for the most serious crimes of international concern—genocide, crimes against humanity, war crimes and the crime of aggression—entered into force on 1 July 2002 [YUN 2002, p. 1298]. As at 31 December 2003, the Statute had 139 signatories and 92 States parties.

During 2003, the Assembly of States Parties to the Rome Statute, the management oversight and legislative body of ICC, fully constituted ICC by electing its 18 judges and Prosecutor, appointing its other senior officials and completing its administrative set-up, thus making ICC operational.

Peacekeeping and ICC

The Security Council, by **resolution 1487 (2003)** of 12 June (see p. 77), renewed its request contained in resolution 1422(2002) [YUN 2002, p. 70] that ICC delay for a 12-month period, from 1 July 2003, investigation or prosecution of any case involving current or former officials from a State not party to the Rome Statute. The Council further expressed its intention to renew that request each 1 July for as long as might be necessary.

Assembly of States Parties

The Assembly of States Parties to the Rome Statute of the International Criminal Court met in New York for the first (3-7 February) and second (21-23 April) resumptions of its first (2002) annual session [YUN 2002, p. 1300] and for its second annual session (8-12 September). The reports summarizing the proceedings of the resumptions [ICC-ASP/1/3/Add.1] and of the second session [ICC-ASP/2/10] were adopted by the Assembly on 23 April and 12 September, respectively.

In February, the Assembly elected the required 18 judges of the Court, all beginning their terms of three, six and nine years (six judges for each term) on 11 March. At their inaugural meeting on that date, in The Hague, Netherlands, the judges took their oath of office.

In April, the Assembly unanimously elected the Prosecutor, Luis Moreno Ocampo (Argentina), who took office on 16 June. It recommended that the judges proceed to elect the Registrar on the basis of a list submitted by the

Assembly Presidency, elected 10 of the 12 members of the Committee on Budget and Finance and authorized the Committee to begin functioning as partially constituted. The Bureau, acting under the delegated authority of the Assembly, appointed the National Audit Office of the United Kingdom as External Auditor for ICC for a four-year period.

At the September session, the Assembly elected the Deputy Prosecutor, Serge Brammertz (Belgium), for a six-year term starting on 3 November. It completed the election, begun in April, of the 12-member Committee on Budget and Finance, 6 to serve for two years and 6 for three, and elected the Board of Directors of the trust fund for the victims of crimes within ICC's jurisdiction and their families (Victims Trust Fund). It took note of the oral report of the Special Working Group on the Crime of Aggression, which met for the first time during the September session.

In other action, the Assembly established its permanent secretariat; approved the 2004 programme budget of ICC, which included 53,071,846 euros for the major programmes; approved the ICC staff regulations; sought to strengthen ICC and the Assembly; established a trust fund for the participation of least developed countries (LDCs) in the Assembly's work; and acknowledged the facilitating role of the non-governmental organization (NGO) Coalition for the International Criminal Court and of the United Nations in the establishment of ICC. It also considered the conditions of service and compensation of the ICC judges; the ratification status of the Agreement on the Privileges and Immunities of the International Criminal Court [YUN 2002, p. 1301]; and the establishment of an international criminal bar.

The Assembly decided to hold its third session in The Hague from 6 to 10 September 2004. It also decided that the Committee on Budget and Finance would meet in The Hague from 29 to 31 March and from 2 to 6 August 2004.

ICC report. In August, ICC submitted a report [ICC-ASP-2/5 & Corr.1] for consideration by the Assembly of States Parties at its September session, describing: coordination within the Court; the election in March of its three-member Presidency—composed of the President (Judge Philippe Kirsch) and the First and Second Vice-Presidents—together with its judicial, administrative and external-relations functions; the Pre-Trial, Trial and Appeals Divisions (Chambers) into which the judges constituted themselves; the functions of the Office of the Prosecutor; and the election of the Registrar in June and the core mission of the Registry. Also described were the Court's relations with the States parties and with the host State with regard to interim and permanent premises and a headquarters agreement.

Report of Secretary-General. In a September report [A/58/372], submitted pursuant to General Assembly resolution 57/23 [YUN 2002, p. 1301], the Secretary-General described the sessions of the Assembly of States Parties and the substantive and technical services of the UN Secretariat in its capacity as provisional secretariat for the Assembly of States Parties. He stated that he had taken steps within the Secretariat to expand the mandate of the fund established by General Assembly resolution 51/207 of 17 December 1996 [YUN 1996, p. 1205] for voluntary contributions towards meeting the costs of LDC participation in the work of the Assembly of States Parties. A total of 64 LDC delegates to the two-part resumption of the first session and to the second session received assistance from the fund in the form of air tickets. Since a similar fund had been established under the ICC Registrar's authority, the Assembly of States Parties requested the Secretary-General to close the special fund established by resolution 51/207.

GENERAL ASSEMBLY ACTION

On 9 December [meeting 72], the General Assembly, on the recommendation of the Sixth Committee [A/58/516], adopted **resolution 58/79** without vote [agenda item 154].

International Criminal Court

The General Assembly,

Recalling its resolutions 47/33 of 25 November 1992, 48/31 of 9 December 1993, 49/53 of 9 December 1994, 50/46 of 11 December 1995, 51/207 of 17 December 1996, 52/160 of 15 December 1997, 53/105 of 8 December 1998, 54/105 of 9 December 1999, 55/155 of 12 December 2000, 56/85 of 12 December 2001 and 57/23 of 19 November 2002,

Noting that the Rome Statute of the International Criminal Court was adopted on 17 July 1998 and entered into force on 1 July 2002,

Noting also that with the election of the judges and the Prosecutor and the appointment of the Registrar, the International Criminal Court is fully constituted,

Reiterating the historic significance of the adoption of the Rome Statute of the International Criminal Court,

1. *Calls upon* all States that are not yet parties to the Rome Statute of the International Criminal Court to consider ratifying it or acceding to it without delay, and encourages efforts aimed at promoting awareness of the results of the United Nations Diplomatic Conference of Plenipotentiaries on the Establishment of an International Criminal Court, held in Rome from 15 June to 17 July 1998, the provisions of the Statute and the process leading to the establishment of the International Criminal Court;

2. *Calls upon* all States to consider becoming parties to the Agreement on the Privileges and Immunities of the International Criminal Court without delay;

3. *Welcomes* the holding of the first and second resumptions of the first session and the second session of the Assembly of States Parties, in New York from 3 to 7 February and 21 to 23 April 2003 and from 8 to 12 September 2003, respectively, and also welcomes the election of judges and the Prosecutor and the adoption of a number of instruments;

4. *Takes note* of the establishment of the Special Working Group on the Crime of Aggression by the Assembly of States Parties to the Rome Statute of the International Criminal Court, open to all States on an equal footing, and of the possibility that at some future time the meeting of that working group may be held at United Nations Headquarters;

5. *Expresses its appreciation* to the Secretary-General for providing effective and efficient assistance in the establishment of the International Criminal Court;

6. *Welcomes* the establishment of the Permanent Secretariat of the Assembly of States Parties to the Rome Statute of the International Criminal Court;

7. *Recognizes* the need for an orderly and smooth transition of work from the Secretariat of the United Nations to the secretariat of the Assembly of States Parties to the Rome Statute of the International Criminal Court;

8. *Invites* the Secretary-General to take steps to conclude a relationship agreement between the United Nations and the International Criminal Court and to submit the negotiated draft agreement to the General Assembly for approval;

9. *Decides* to include in the provisional agenda of its fifty-ninth session the item entitled "International Criminal Court".

International Law Commission

The International Law Commission (ILC) held its fifty-fifth session in Geneva in two parts (5 May–6 June; 7 July–8 August) [A/58/10]. During the second part, the International Law Seminar held its thirty-ninth session, which was attended by 24 participants, mostly from developing countries. They observed ILC meetings, attended specially arranged lectures and participated in working groups on specific topics.

ILC, assisted by working groups and a Drafting Committee, advanced its work on reservations to treaties by adopting further guidelines on the formulation and communication of reservations and interpretive declarations. It considered several draft articles on diplomatic protection, reviewed the progress on the topic of unilateral acts of States and agreed on a conceptual outline for the topic of international liability in case of loss from transboundary harm arising from hazardous activities. It considered the first reports on two of three new topics in its work programme, namely, the responsibility of international organizations and shared natural resources. It decided, in the case of the third new topic, fragmentation of international law: difficulties arising from the diversification and expansion of international law, to begin by studying the *lex specialis* rule and the question of self-contained regimes. (For details on those topics, see pp. 1336 and 1337.)

In furtherance of cooperation with other bodies concerned with international law, ILC continued its traditional information exchanges with the International Court of Justice, the Inter-American Juridical Committee, the Asian-African Legal Consultative Organization, the European Committee on Legal Cooperation and the Committee of Legal Advisers on Public International Law. ILC members also held informal meetings with other bodies and associations on matters of mutual interest.

Among its other decisions, ILC reconstituted the working group on its long-term programme of work and reiterated that the page limitations for reports of subsidiary bodies, as endorsed by General Assembly resolution 57/21 [YUN 2002, p. 1302], could not be applied to its documentation because of the characteristics of its work. It further reiterated that Assembly resolution 56/272 [ibid., p. 1402], which reduced the payment of honorariums to the nominal amount of $1, contradicted the Secretary-General's 1998 recommendations on the subject [YUN 1998, p. 1304], was taken without consultation with ILC and was not consistent with the principle of fairness on the basis of which the United Nations conducted its affairs. It stressed that the decision especially affected special rapporteurs, as it compromised support for their research. ILC decided to hold its fifty-sixth session in Geneva in two parts: from 3 May to 4 June and from 5 July to 6 August 2004.

GENERAL ASSEMBLY ACTION

On 9 December [meeting 72], the General Assembly, on the recommendation of the Sixth Committee [A/58/514], adopted **resolution 58/77** without vote [agenda item 152].

Report of the International Law Commission on the work of its fifty-fifth session

The General Assembly,

Having considered the report of the International Law Commission on the work of its fifty-fifth session,

Emphasizing the importance of furthering the codification and progressive development of international law as a means of implementing the purposes and principles set forth in the Charter of the United Nations and in the Declaration on Principles of International Law concerning Friendly Relations and Cooperation among States in accordance with the Charter of the United Nations,

Recognizing the desirability of referring legal and drafting questions to the Sixth Committee, including topics that might be submitted to the International

Law Commission for closer examination, and of enabling the Sixth Committee and the Commission to enhance further their contribution to the progressive development of international law and its codification,

Recalling the need to keep under review those topics of international law which, given their new or renewed interest for the international community, may be suitable for the progressive development and codification of international law and therefore may be included in the future programme of work of the International Law Commission,

Welcoming the holding of the International Law Seminar, and noting with appreciation the voluntary contributions made to the United Nations Trust Fund for the International Law Seminar,

Stressing the usefulness of focusing and structuring the debate on the report of the International Law Commission in the Sixth Committee in such a manner that conditions are provided for concentrated attention to each of the main topics dealt with in the report and for discussions on specific topics,

Wishing to enhance further, as proposed at the fifty-eighth session of the General Assembly by the Austrian-Swedish initiative to revitalize the debate on the report of the International Law Commission, the interaction between the Sixth Committee as a body of governmental representatives and the Commission as a body of independent legal experts, with a view to improving the dialogue between the two bodies,

1. *Takes note with appreciation* of the report of the International Law Commission on the work of its fifty-fifth session, and recommends that the Commission continue its work on the topics in its current programme, taking into account the comments and observations of Governments, whether submitted in writing or expressed orally in debates in the General Assembly;

2. *Draws the attention* of Governments to the importance for the International Law Commission of having their views on the various aspects involved in the topics on the agenda of the Commission, in particular on all the specific issues identified in chapter III of its report;

3. *Reiterates its invitation* to Governments, within the context of paragraph 2 above, to provide information to the International Law Commission regarding State practice on the topic "Unilateral acts of States";

4. *Invites* Governments, within the context of paragraph 2 above, to provide information to the International Law Commission regarding national legislation, bilateral and other agreements and arrangements with regard to the use and management of transboundary groundwaters, in particular those governing quality and quantity of such waters, relevant to the topic currently entitled "Shared natural resources";

5. *Requests* the Secretary-General to invite States and international organizations to submit information concerning their practice relevant to the topic "Responsibility of international organizations", including cases in which States members of an international organization may be regarded as responsible for acts of the organization;

6. *Invites* the International Law Commission to continue taking measures to enhance its efficiency and productivity;

7. *Encourages* the International Law Commission to continue taking cost-saving measures at its future sessions;

8. *Takes note* of paragraph 448 of the report of the International Law Commission, and decides that the next session of the Commission shall be held at the United Nations Office at Geneva from 3 May to 4 June and from 5 July to 6 August 2004;

9. *Welcomes* the enhanced dialogue between the International Law Commission and the Sixth Committee at the fifty-eighth session of the General Assembly, stresses the desirability of further enhancing the dialogue between the two bodies, and in this context encourages, inter alia, the continued practice of informal consultations in the form of discussions between the members of the Sixth Committee and the members of the Commission attending the fifty-ninth session of the Assembly;

10. *Encourages* delegations, during the debate on the report of the International Law Commission to adhere as far as possible to the structured work programme agreed to by the Sixth Committee and to consider presenting concise and focused statements;

11. *Encourages* Member States to consider being represented at the level of legal adviser during the first week in which the report of the International Law Commission is discussed in the Sixth Committee to enable high-level discussions on issues of international law, and decides that the week shall henceforth be known as "International Law Week";

12. *Requests* the International Law Commission to continue to pay special attention to indicating in its annual report, for each topic, any specific issues on which expressions of views by Governments, either in the Sixth Committee or in written form, would be of particular interest in providing effective guidance for the Commission in its further work;

13. *Takes note* of paragraphs 449 to 455 of the report of the International Law Commission with regard to cooperation with other bodies, and encourages the Commission to continue the implementation of article 16, paragraph *(e)*, and article 26, paragraphs 1 and 2, of its statute in order to further strengthen cooperation between the Commission and other bodies concerned with international law, having in mind the usefulness of such cooperation;

14. *Notes* that consulting with national organizations and individual experts concerned with international law may assist Governments in considering whether to make comments and observations on drafts submitted by the International Law Commission and in formulating their comments and observations;

15. *Reaffirms* its previous decisions concerning the indispensable role of the Codification Division of the Office of Legal Affairs of the Secretariat in providing assistance to the International Law Commission;

16. *Approves* the conclusions reached by the International Law Commission in paragraphs 440 to 443 of its report regarding documentation of the Commission, and reaffirms its previous decisions concerning the summary records of the International Law Commission;

17. *Expresses the hope* that the International Law Seminar will continue to be held in connection with the sessions of the International Law Commission and that an increasing number of participants, in particular

from developing countries, will be given the opportunity to attend the Seminar, and appeals to States to continue to make urgently needed voluntary contributions to the United Nations Trust Fund for the International Law Seminar;

18. *Requests* the Secretary-General to provide the International Law Seminar with adequate services, including interpretation, as required, and encourages him to continue considering ways to improve the structure and content of the Seminar;

19. *Also requests* the Secretary-General to forward to the International Law Commission, for its attention, the records of the debate on the report of the Commission at the fifty-eighth session of the General Assembly, together with such written statements as delegations may circulate in conjunction with their oral statements, and to prepare and distribute a topical summary of the debate, following established practice;

20. *Requests* the Secretariat to circulate to States, as soon as possible after the conclusion of the session of the International Law Commission, chapter II of its report containing a summary of the work of that session, chapter III containing the specific issues on which the views of Governments would be of particular interest to the Commission and the draft articles adopted on either first or second reading by the Commission;

21. *Recommends* that the debate on the report of the International Law Commission at the fifty-ninth session of the General Assembly commence on 1 November 2004.

International liability

Under the topic of international liability for injurious consequences arising out of acts not prohibited by international law, ILC considered the first report by Special Rapporteur Pemmaraju Sreenivasa Rao (India) on the legal regime for the allocation of loss in case of transboundary harm arising out of hazardous activities [A/CN.4/531]. The report reviewed previous ILC work on the topic, analysed the liability regimes of various instruments and offered a series of conclusions that could be a basis for drafting more precise formulations. ILC established an open-ended working group to assist the Special Rapporteur in considering the future orientation of the topic in the light of the ILC debate on his report.

Unilateral acts of States

ILC considered the sixth report on unilateral acts of States [A/CN.4/534] by Special Rapporteur Victor Rodríguez Cedeño (Venezuela), dealing in a preliminary and general manner with the unilateral act of recognition, with emphasis on recognition of States. It analysed the act of recognition in its various forms (conduct and acts, silence and acquiescence, tacit recognition through implicit or explicit acts and conventional recognition), especially with regard to the criteria for the formulation of such an act and its discretionary nature. It examined the conditions required for the validity of the act (formulation (intent), lawfulness of the object and conformity with imperative norms of international law); its legal effects and the basis for its binding nature; and the application of the act of recognition in order to draw conclusions as to whether an author State could modify, suspend or revoke the act unilaterally. The report yielded an outline definition that could be aligned with the draft definition of unilateral acts in general.

Following the debate on the report, the open-ended working group on the subject submitted its recommendations on the scope of the topic, with commentaries, and on the methodological approach, which ILC adopted on 31 July.

Responsibility of international organizations

ILC considered the first report on the topic of responsibility of international organizations [A/CN.4/532] by Special Rapporteur Giorgio Gaja (Italy). The report proposed articles 1 to 3, on the scope of those articles, the use of terms and general principles, which ILC referred to the Drafting Committee. On the Committee's recommendation, ILC, in July, adopted the three articles and, in August, the commentaries thereto.

Fragmentation of international law

In 2003, ILC appointed Martti Koskenniemi (Finland) as Chairman of the open-ended study group, established in 2002 [YUN 2002, p. 1304], on the topic of fragmentation of international law: difficulties arising from the diversification and expansion of international law. The group set a tentative schedule of work for the remainder (2004-2006) of the current quinquennium (2002-2006). It distributed work among its members on the preparation of the outlines of four studies endorsed by ILC in 2002 [ibid., p. 1305] on: the interpretation of treaties in the light of "any relevant rules of international law applicable in the relations between the parties" (article 31 (3) (c) of the 1969 Vienna Convention on the Law of Treaties [YUN 1969, p. 734]), in the context of general developments in international law and concerns of the international community; the application of successive treaties relating to the same subject matter (article 30 of the Vienna Convention); agreements to modify multilateral treaties between certain of the parties only (article 41 of the same Convention); and hierarchy in international law: *jus cogens*, obligations *erga omnes*, Article 103 of the Charter of the United Nations, as conflict rules.

The group agreed that the outlines should focus on the nature of the topic in relation to fragmentation; the acceptance and rationale of the relevant rule; the operation of that rule; and conclusions, including possible draft guidelines. It held a preliminary discussion on the Chairman's outline on the questions of the function and scope of the *lex specialis* rule and "self-contained regimes".

Shared natural resources

In July 2003, ILC considered the first report on shared natural resources [A/CN.4/533 & Add.1] by Special Rapporteur Chusei Yamada (Japan). The report described the background to the topic and proposed limiting its scope to confined transboundary groundwaters, oil and gas, beginning with the first item. The addendum provided an overview of groundwater resources and dealt with basic terminology and related issues. ILC was informally briefed by groundwater experts from the Food and Agriculture Organization of the United Nations and the International Association of Hydrogeologists.

International State relations and international law

Jurisdictional immunities of States and their property

In accordance with General Assembly resolution 57/16 [YUN 2002, p. 1305], the Ad Hoc Committee on Jurisdictional Immunities of States and Their Property, established by resolution 55/150 [YUN 2000, p. 1246], reconvened (New York, 24-28 February 2003) to make a final attempt to consolidate areas of agreement and resolve outstanding issues, with a view to elaborating a generally acceptable instrument based on the draft articles on jurisdictional immunities of States and their property, adopted by ILC in 1991 [YUN 1991, p. 829], and on the results of the discussions of the Ad Hoc Committee and the open-ended working group of the Sixth Committee established by resolution 53/98 [YUN 1998, p. 1215], and to recommend a form for the instrument.

The Working Group of the Whole established two informal consultative groups—the first to consider the outstanding issue of the criteria for determining the commercial character of a contract or transaction, and the second to consider those related to the concept of a State enterprise or other entity in relation to commercial transactions, contracts of employment, the question of non-applicability of the draft articles to criminal proceedings, and the articles' relationship with other agreements. The pending issues concerning ownership, possession and use of property; intellectual and industrial property; the effect of an arbitration agreement; and State immunity from prejudgement measures of constraint were considered by the Working Group of the Whole, as was the form of the future instrument. All outstanding issues were resolved by the Working Group.

On 28 February, the Ad Hoc Committee adopted its report [A/58/22], to which were annexed the text of the draft articles on jurisdictional immunities of States and their property and the understandings with respect to certain of the articles' provisions. The Committee recommended that the Assembly take a decision on the form of the draft articles, noting that, if and when it decided to adopt the articles as a convention, they would need a preamble and final clauses, including a general saving provision concerning the relationship between the articles and other international agreements relating to the same subject.

GENERAL ASSEMBLY ACTION

On 9 December [meeting 72], the General Assembly, on the recommendation of the Sixth Committee [A/58/512], adopted **resolution 58/74** without vote [agenda item 150].

Convention on jurisdictional immunities of
States and their property

The General Assembly,

Recalling its resolutions 46/55 of 9 December 1991, 49/61 of 9 December 1994, 52/151 of 15 December 1997, 53/98 of 8 December 1998, 54/101 of 9 December 1999, 55/150 of 12 December 2000, 56/78 of 12 December 2001 and 57/16 of 19 November 2002,

Having considered the report of the Ad Hoc Committee on Jurisdictional Immunities of States and Their Property, established pursuant to resolution 55/150,

Noting the adoption of the draft articles and the understandings by the Ad Hoc Committee,

Noting also the broad support for the conclusion of a convention on jurisdictional immunities of States and their property,

Stressing the importance of uniformity and clarity in the law applicable to jurisdictional immunities of States and their property,

1. *Takes note with appreciation* of the report of the Ad Hoc Committee on Jurisdictional Immunities of States and Their Property;

2. *Decides* that the Ad Hoc Committee shall be reconvened from 1 to 5 March 2004, with the mandate to formulate a preamble and final clauses, with a view to completing a convention on jurisdictional immunities of States and their property, which will contain the results already adopted by the Ad Hoc Committee;

3. *Requests* the Ad Hoc Committee to report to the General Assembly at its fifty-ninth session on the outcome of its work;

4. *Decides* to include in the provisional agenda of its fifty-ninth session the item entitled "Convention on jurisdictional immunities of States and their property".

International terrorism

Conventions on international terrorism and for suppression of acts of nuclear terrorism

Ad Hoc Committee

In accordance with General Assembly resolution 57/27 [YUN 2002, p. 1307], the Ad Hoc Committee on the convention for suppression of nuclear terrorism, established by Assembly resolution 51/210 [YUN 1996, p. 1208], held its seventh session (New York, 31 March–2 April) to continue, within the framework of a working group of the Sixth Committee, to elaborate a draft comprehensive convention on international terrorism, with appropriate time allocated to the continued consideration of outstanding issues relating to the elaboration of a draft international convention for the suppression of acts of nuclear terrorism. It kept on its agenda the question of convening a high-level conference under UN auspices to formulate a joint organized response of the international community to terrorism in all its forms and manifestations.

The Ad Hoc Committee held a general exchange of views and proceeded with informal bilateral consultations in two stages: the first on the outstanding issues pertaining to articles 2, 2 bis and 18 and to the preamble of the draft comprehensive convention; and the second on issues pertaining to the draft international convention for the suppression of acts of nuclear terrorism, the principal one of which related to article 4, on the scope of application of the convention. The results were orally presented by the coordinators for those two consultations.

The Committee Chairman said he had received no specific proposal on the question of convening a high-level conference but that some delegations had had informal contacts on the matter, which he urged them to continue.

On 2 April, the Ad Hoc Committee adopted its report [A/58/37], to which were annexed the Chairman's informal summary of the general discussion and the reports of the coordinators. The Ad Hoc Committee recommended that the Sixth Committee, at the Assembly's fifty-eighth (2003) session, establish a working group to continue the elaboration of the two draft conventions and to keep on its agenda the question of convening a high-level conference.

Sixth Committee working group

As recommended by the Ad Hoc Committee (see above), the Sixth Committee established an open-ended working group on measures to eliminate international terrorism, which held three meetings (New York, 6, 8 and 10 October). Before it were the reports of the Ad Hoc Committee on its sixth [YUN 2002, p. 1306] and seventh [A/58/37] sessions; the 2002 report of the Sixth Committee working group [YUN 2002, p. 1306], annexing the lists of written amendments and proposals on the draft comprehensive convention on international terrorism; and the 1998 report of the Sixth Committee working group [YUN 1998, p. 1216], annexing a revised text of the draft international convention for the suppression of acts of nuclear terrorism, with written amendments and proposals.

The working group began with a general exchange of views and then held informal consultations on the outstanding issues of the two draft conventions. On 8 October, the consultation coordinators orally reported on the results of those consultations. The working group was informed by its Chairman that consultations by several delegations on the question of convening a high-level conference were continuing at the political level in their capitals. On 10 October, the group adopted its report [A/C.6/58/L.10], which it referred to the Sixth Committee with a recommendation that work on finalizing the texts of the two draft conventions should continue, building on what had already been accomplished.

Measures to eliminate terrorism

In accordance with General Assembly resolution 50/53 [YUN 1995, p. 1330], the Secretary-General, in July, issued his annual report with later addendum [A/58/116 & Add.1] containing information on measures taken at the national and international levels by 28 States and 13 international organizations and UN agencies and bodies to implement the 1994 Declaration on Measures to Eliminate International Terrorism, approved by Assembly resolution 49/60 [YUN 1994, p. 1294], and Security Council resolution 1269(1999) [YUN 1999, p. 1240]. It listed 21 international instruments pertaining to terrorism, indicating the status of State participation in each, and provided information on workshops and training courses on combating terrorist crimes by four UN bodies and one regional intergovernmental organization. The report noted that the Secretariat was in the process of compiling material to be included in a second volume of the *United Nations Legislative Series* entitled "National Law and Regulations on the Prevention and Suppression of International Terrorism, Part II".

GENERAL ASSEMBLY ACTION

On 9 December [meeting 72], the General Assembly, on the recommendation of the Sixth Committee [A/58/518], adopted **resolution 58/81** without vote [agenda item 156].

Measures to eliminate international terrorism

The General Assembly,

Guided by the purposes and principles of the Charter of the United Nations,

Recalling the Declaration on the Occasion of the Fiftieth Anniversary of the United Nations,

Recalling also the United Nations Millennium Declaration,

Recalling further all General Assembly and Security Council resolutions on measures to eliminate international terrorism,

Convinced of the importance of the consideration of measures to eliminate international terrorism by the General Assembly as the universal organ having competence to do so,

Deeply disturbed by the persistence of terrorist acts, which have been carried out worldwide,

Reaffirming its strong condemnation of the heinous acts of terrorism that have caused enormous loss of human life, destruction and damage, including those which prompted the adoption of General Assembly resolution 56/1 of 12 September 2001, as well as Security Council resolutions 1368(2001) of 12 September 2001, 1373(2001) of 28 September 2001 and 1377(2001) of 12 November 2001, and those that have occurred since the adoption of General Assembly resolution 57/27 of 19 November 2002,

Recalling its strong condemnation of the atrocious and deliberate attack against the headquarters of the United Nations Assistance Mission for Iraq in Baghdad on 19 August 2003 in General Assembly resolution 57/338 of 15 September 2003 and Security Council resolution 1502(2003) of 26 August 2003,

Stressing the need to strengthen further international cooperation among States and among international organizations and agencies, regional organizations and arrangements and the United Nations in order to prevent, combat and eliminate terrorism in all its forms and manifestations, wherever and by whomsoever committed, in accordance with the principles of the Charter, international law and the relevant international conventions,

Noting the role of the Security Council Committee established pursuant to resolution 1373(2001) concerning counter-terrorism in monitoring the implementation of that resolution, including the taking of the necessary financial, legal and technical measures by States and the ratification or acceptance of the relevant international conventions and protocols,

Mindful of the need to enhance the role of the United Nations and the relevant specialized agencies in combating international terrorism, and of the proposals of the Secretary-General to enhance the role of the Organization in this respect,

Mindful also of the essential need to strengthen international, regional and subregional cooperation aimed at enhancing the national capacity of States to prevent and suppress effectively international terrorism in all its forms and manifestations,

Recalling the Declaration on Measures to Eliminate International Terrorism, contained in the annex to General Assembly resolution 49/60 of 9 December 1994, wherein the Assembly encouraged States to review urgently the scope of the existing international legal provisions on the prevention, repression and elimination of terrorism in all its forms and manifestations, with the aim of ensuring that there was a comprehensive legal framework covering all aspects of the matter,

Taking note of the final document of the Thirteenth Conference of Heads of State or Government of Non-Aligned Countries, adopted in Kuala Lumpur on 25 February 2003, which reiterated the collective position of the Movement of Non-Aligned Countries on terrorism and reaffirmed the previous initiative of the Twelfth Conference of Heads of State or Government of Non-Aligned Countries, held at Durban, South Africa, from 29 August to 3 September 1998, calling for an international summit conference under the auspices of the United Nations to formulate a joint organized response of the international community to terrorism in all its forms and manifestations, as well as other relevant initiatives,

Bearing in mind the recent developments and initiatives at the international, regional and subregional levels to prevent and suppress international terrorism,

Recalling its decision in resolutions 54/110 of 9 December 1999, 55/158 of 12 December 2000, 56/88 of 12 December 2001 and 57/27 that the Ad Hoc Committee established by General Assembly resolution 51/210 of 17 December 1996 should address, and keep on its agenda, the question of convening a high-level conference under the auspices of the United Nations to formulate a joint organized response of the international community to terrorism in all its forms and manifestations,

Aware of General Assembly resolution 57/219 of 18 December 2002,

Noting regional efforts to prevent, combat and eliminate terrorism in all its forms and manifestations, wherever and by whomsoever committed, including through the elaboration of and adherence to regional conventions,

Having examined the report of the Secretary-General, the report of the Ad Hoc Committee established by General Assembly resolution 51/210 of 17 December 1996 and the report of the Working Group of the Sixth Committee established pursuant to resolution 57/27,

1. *Strongly condemns* all acts, methods and practices of terrorism as criminal and unjustifiable, wherever and by whomsoever committed;

2. *Reiterates* that criminal acts intended or calculated to provoke a state of terror in the general public, a group of persons or particular persons for political purposes are in any circumstances unjustifiable, whatever the considerations of a political, philosophical, ideological, racial, ethnic, religious or other nature that may be invoked to justify them;

3. *Reiterates its call* upon all States to adopt further measures in accordance with the Charter of the United Nations and the relevant provisions of international law, including international standards of human rights, to prevent terrorism and to strengthen international cooperation in combating terrorism and, to that end, to consider in particular the implementation of

the measures set out in paragraphs 3 (a) to (f) of resolution 51/210;

4. *Also reiterates its call* upon all States, with the aim of enhancing the efficient implementation of relevant legal instruments, to intensify, as and where appropriate, the exchange of information on facts related to terrorism and, in so doing, to avoid the dissemination of inaccurate or unverified information;

5. *Reiterates its call* upon States to refrain from financing, encouraging, providing training for or otherwise supporting terrorist activities;

6. *Reaffirms* that international cooperation as well as actions by States to combat terrorism should be conducted in conformity with the principles of the Charter, international law and relevant international conventions;

7. *Urges* all States that have not yet done so to consider, as a matter of priority, and in accordance with Security Council resolution 1373(2001), becoming parties to the relevant conventions and protocols as referred to in paragraph 6 of General Assembly resolution 51/210, as well as the International Convention for the Suppression of Terrorist Bombings and the International Convention for the Suppression of the Financing of Terrorism, and calls upon all States to enact, as appropriate, the domestic legislation necessary to implement the provisions of those conventions and protocols, to ensure that the jurisdiction of their courts enables them to bring to trial the perpetrators of terrorist acts, and to cooperate with and provide support and assistance to other States and relevant international and regional organizations to that end;

8. *Urges* States to cooperate with the Secretary-General and with one another, as well as with interested intergovernmental organizations, with a view to ensuring, where appropriate within existing mandates, that technical and other expert advice is provided to those States requiring and requesting assistance in becoming parties to the conventions and protocols referred to in paragraph 7 above;

9. *Notes with appreciation and satisfaction* that, consistent with the call contained in paragraph 7 of resolution 57/27, a number of States became parties to the relevant conventions and protocols referred to therein, thereby realizing the objective of wider acceptance and implementation of those conventions;

10. *Reaffirms* the Declaration on Measures to Eliminate International Terrorism, contained in the annex to resolution 49/60, and the Declaration to Supplement the 1994 Declaration on Measures to Eliminate International Terrorism, contained in the annex to resolution 51/210, and calls upon all States to implement them;

11. *Urges* all States and the Secretary-General, in their efforts to prevent international terrorism, to make the best use of the existing institutions of the United Nations;

12. *Welcomes* the efforts of the Terrorism Prevention Branch of the United Nations Office on Drugs and Crime in Vienna, after reviewing existing possibilities within the United Nations system, to enhance, through its mandate, the capabilities of the United Nations in the prevention of terrorism, and recognizes, in the context of Security Council resolution 1373(2001), its role in assisting States in becoming parties to, and implementing, the relevant international conventions and protocols relating to terrorism;

13. *Invites* regional intergovernmental organizations to submit to the Secretary-General information on the measures they have adopted at the regional level to eliminate international terrorism;

14. *Welcomes* the important progress attained in the elaboration of the draft comprehensive convention on international terrorism during the meetings of the Ad Hoc Committee established by General Assembly resolution 51/210 of 17 December 1996 and the Working Group of the Sixth Committee established pursuant to General Assembly resolution 57/27;

15. *Decides* that the Ad Hoc Committee shall continue to elaborate a draft comprehensive convention on international terrorism, shall continue its efforts to resolve the outstanding issues relating to the elaboration of a draft international convention for the suppression of acts of nuclear terrorism as a means of further developing a comprehensive legal framework of conventions dealing with international terrorism, and shall keep on its agenda the question of convening a high-level conference under the auspices of the United Nations to formulate a joint organized response of the international community to terrorism in all its forms and manifestations;

16. *Decides also* that the Ad Hoc Committee shall meet from 28 June to 2 July 2004 to continue the elaboration of a draft comprehensive convention on international terrorism, with appropriate time allocated to the continued consideration of outstanding issues relating to the elaboration of a draft international convention for the suppression of acts of nuclear terrorism, that it shall keep on its agenda the question of convening a high-level conference under the auspices of the United Nations to formulate a joint organized response of the international community to terrorism in all its forms and manifestations, and that the work shall continue, if necessary, during the fifty-ninth session of the General Assembly, within the framework of a working group of the Sixth Committee;

17. *Requests* the Secretary-General to continue to provide the Ad Hoc Committee with the necessary facilities for the performance of its work;

18. *Requests* the Ad Hoc Committee to report to the General Assembly at its fifty-eighth session in the event of the completion of the draft comprehensive convention on international terrorism or the draft international convention for the suppression of acts of nuclear terrorism;

19. *Also requests* the Ad Hoc Committee to report to the General Assembly at its fifty-ninth session on progress made in the implementation of its mandate;

20. *Decides* to include in the provisional agenda of its fifty-ninth session the item entitled "Measures to eliminate international terrorism".

Safety and security of United Nations and associated personnel

Ad Hoc Committee consideration. The Ad Hoc Committee on the Scope of Legal Protection under the 1994 Convention on the Safety of United Nations and Associated Personnel [YUN 1994, p. 1289], established by General Assembly resolution 56/89 [YUN 2001, p. 1227], held its second session (New York, 24-28 March) to continue considering measures to enhance the existing protective legal regime for UN and associated personnel, including addressing the application of the Convention to all UN operations, taking into account the Secretary-General's 2000 report [YUN 2000, p. 1347] and the Ad Hoc Committee's discussions at its 2002 session [YUN 2002, p. 1311].

Accordingly, a working group of the whole of the Committee deliberated on the questions of removing from the Convention the requirement of a declaration of an exceptional risk (the "trigger" mechanism) and of the inclusion of UN operations other than those foreseen under article 1 *(c)* (i) within the scope of the Convention. It considered the first two of three proposals that were introduced: one by New Zealand, containing a draft optional additional protocol aimed at extending the application of the Convention to all UN operations by removing the "trigger" mechanism contained in article 1 *(c)* (ii) [A/AC.264/2003/DP.1]; the second, by Pakistan, representing a short-term measure aimed at improving the existing regime [A/AC.264/2003/DP.2]; and the third, by Greece on behalf of the European Union (EU), providing a replacement text for article 1 *(c)* of the Convention regarding the definition of UN operations [A/AC.264/2003/DP.3].

As an alternative to an optional protocol, it was suggested that a stand-alone instrument be drafted to include some of the Convention's provisions while updating certain others in the light of the relevant treaties, such as the 1997 International Convention for the Suppression of Terrorist Bombings [YUN 1997, p. 1348] and the 1999 International Convention for the Suppression of the Financing of Terrorism [YUN 1999, p. 1233].

On 28 March, the Ad Hoc Committee adopted its report [A/58/52], which annexed the proposals and recommended that the Assembly renew its mandate for 2004 and request the Secretary-General to provide for its next session a report elaborating on his report on the implementation of the short-term measures agreed in Assembly resolution 57/28 [YUN 2002, p. 1311], as well as on any measures undertaken on his own initiative to achieve the goals of the Convention, taking into account the Committee's discussions and including an assessment of the overall effectiveness of such measures.

Report of Secretary-General. In response to General Assembly resolution 57/28 and the Ad Hoc Committee's recommendation (above), the Secretary-General prepared a report [A/58/187] focusing on: the incorporation of the key provisions of the Convention into status-of-forces and status-of-mission agreements; a procedure to initiate a declaration of an exceptional risk pursuant to article 1 *(c)* (ii); and standardization of relevant provisions in agreements between the United Nations and humanitarian NGOs.

The Secretary-General observed that, in the light of the short period that had elapsed since the adoption of resolution 57/28 and of the 2003 report of the Ad Hoc Committee, it would be premature to assess the effectiveness of measures taken to strengthen the Convention's protective regime. Its key provisions had been introduced in a small number of status-of-forces and status-of-mission agreements, most of them currently under negotiation. In the absence of any request for information on matters relevant to the application of the Convention, the role of the Secretary-General as "certifying authority" for the purposes of attesting to a declaration of an exceptional risk had not been tested. A standard provision in agreements between the United Nations and NGOs was in no way likely to affect the application of the Convention or strengthen its protective regime if the host country was not otherwise bound by the Convention, although a list of NGOs operating in the UN area of operation and contractually linked to the Organization might be submitted to the host country, at its request.

The Secretary-General said that the difficulty of initiating a declaration of exceptional risk remained the single most important limitation to the protective regime of the Convention and observed that the strength of the Convention's protective regime lay in the readiness of Member States to ensure its implementation. Annexed to his report was a list of the 198 civilian personnel who had lost their lives as a result of malicious acts while performing services for the Organization since January 1992, indicating the States in whose territories those acts were committed. Also listed were 21 cases in which the Secretariat had been advised by the Member States concerned that they had taken legal action to bring the perpetrators to justice.

Sixth Committee working group. On 29 September, the Sixth Committee established a working group to continue the work of the Ad Hoc Committee. The report on the group's work [A/C.6/58/L.16] contained details of its discussions on a proposal by New Zealand and the EU amendment thereto (see above) and a proposal by Jordan that sought to fill the gaps found in the Convention and addressed the concerns that had hindered universal adherence to it. The report also described the discussions on options for the form of the document to be elaborated, whether it should be an additional protocol, optional protocol, amendment to the 1994 Convention or a stand-alone protocol. A proposal by Costa Rica on the subject was introduced for discussion at a later stage.

GENERAL ASSEMBLY ACTION

On 9 December [meeting 72], the General Assembly, on the recommendation of the Sixth Committee [A/58/519], adopted **resolution 58/82** without vote [agenda item 157].

Scope of legal protection under the Convention on the Safety of United Nations and Associated Personnel

The General Assembly,

Recalling its resolution 57/28 of 19 November 2002 on the scope of legal protection under the Convention on the Safety of United Nations and Associated Personnel, as well as the adoption by the Security Council of resolution 1502(2003) on 26 August 2003,

Recalling also its resolution 57/338 of 15 September 2003, in which it strongly condemned the atrocious and deliberate attack against the headquarters of the United Nations Assistance Mission for Iraq in Baghdad on 19 August 2003,

Recalling further its resolution 49/59 of 9 December 1994, by which it adopted the Convention on the Safety of United Nations and Associated Personnel,

Recalling the letter dated 24 October 2000 addressed to the President of the Security Council on behalf of the global staff of the United Nations system, drawing attention to the safety and security problems faced by United Nations and associated personnel,

Recalling also the report of the Secretary-General on the scope of legal protection under the Convention on the Safety of United Nations and Associated Personnel and the recommendations contained therein, and also recalling the further report of the Secretary-General on this issue,

Reaffirming the need to promote and ensure respect for the principles and rules of international law, including international humanitarian law, as well as relevant provisions of human rights and refugee law,

Reaffirming also the obligation of all humanitarian personnel and United Nations and associated personnel to respect the national laws of the country in which they are operating, in accordance with international law and the Charter of the United Nations,

Deeply concerned by the increasing dangers and security risks faced by United Nations and associated personnel at the field level, and mindful of the need to provide the fullest possible protection for their security,

Expressing its concern that locally recruited personnel are particularly vulnerable to attacks directed at the United Nations,

Deeply concerned that perpetrators of attacks against United Nations and associated personnel seemingly operate with impunity,

Welcoming the recent increase in the number of States that have become parties to the Convention, which entered into force on 15 January 1999, and noting that the Convention has been ratified or acceded to by sixty-nine States as at the date of the present resolution,

Mindful of the need to promote the universality of the Convention,

Having considered the report of the Ad Hoc Committee on the Scope of Legal Protection under the Convention on the Safety of United Nations and Associated Personnel, established pursuant to resolution 56/89 of 12 December 2001, and the report of the Working Group of the Sixth Committee,

1. *Expresses its appreciation* for the work done by the Ad Hoc Committee on the Scope of Legal Protection under the Convention on the Safety of United Nations and Associated Personnel;

2. *Urges* States to take all necessary measures, in accordance with their international obligations, to prevent crimes against United Nations and associated personnel from occurring;

3. *Also urges* States to ensure that crimes against United Nations and associated personnel do not go unpunished and that the perpetrators of such crimes are brought to justice;

4. *Affirms* the obligation of all States to comply fully with their obligations under the relevant rules and principles of international law in relation to the safety and security of United Nations and associated personnel;

5. *Calls upon* all States to consider becoming parties to and to respect fully their obligations under the relevant international instruments, in particular the Convention on the Safety of United Nations and Associated Personnel;

6. *Recommends* that the Secretary-General continue to seek the inclusion of, and that host countries include, key provisions of the Convention, including those regarding the prevention of attacks against members of the operation, the establishment of such attacks as crimes punishable by law and the prosecution or extradition of offenders, in future as well as, if necessary, in existing status-of-forces, status-of-mission and host country agreements negotiated between the United Nations and those countries, mindful of the importance of the timely conclusion of such agreements;

7. *Recommends also* that, consistent with his existing authority, the Secretary-General advise the Security Council or the General Assembly, as appropriate, where in his assessment circumstances would support a declaration of exceptional risk for the purposes of article 1 (c) (ii) of the Convention;

8. *Confirms* that, consistent with his existing authority, the Secretary-General, who has knowledge of the facts and easy access to the information, may provide information, upon the request of a State, on matters of fact relevant to the application of the Convention, such as the fact and content of any declaration of exceptional risk by the Security Council or the General Assembly or any agreement concluded between the United Nations and a humanitarian non-governmental organization or agency;

9. *Notes* that the Secretary-General has prepared a standardized provision for incorporation into the agreements concluded between the United Nations and humanitarian non-governmental organizations or agencies for the purposes of clarifying the application of the Convention to persons deployed by those organizations or agencies, and requests the Secretary-General to make available to Member States the names of organizations or agencies that have concluded such agreements;

10. *Urges* the Secretary-General and relevant bodies to continue to take such other practical measures as

are within their authority and existing institutional mandates to strengthen protection for United Nations and associated personnel, including locally recruited personnel, who are particularly vulnerable and account for the majority of casualties among United Nations or associated personnel;

11. *Decides* that the Ad Hoc Committee established under resolution 56/89 shall reconvene for one week from 12 to 16 April 2004, with a mandate to expand the scope of legal protection under the Convention on the Safety of United Nations and Associated Personnel, including, inter alia, by means of a legal instrument, and that the work shall continue during the fifty-ninth session of the General Assembly within the framework of a working group of the Sixth Committee;

12. *Requests* the Ad Hoc Committee to submit a report on its work to the General Assembly at the fifty-ninth session;

13. *Requests* the Secretary-General to report to the General Assembly at its fifty-ninth session on the measures taken to implement the present resolution;

14. *Decides* to include in the provisional agenda of its fifty-ninth session the item entitled "Scope of legal protection under the Convention on the Safety of United Nations and Associated Personnel".

Diplomatic relations

Protection of diplomatic and consular missions and representatives

As at 31 December 2003, the States parties to the following conventions relating to the protection of diplomats and diplomatic and consular relations were: 180 States parties to the 1961 Vienna Convention on Diplomatic Relations [YUN 1961, p. 512], 50 parties to the Optional Protocol concerning the acquisition of nationality [ibid., p. 516] and 62 parties to the Optional Protocol concerning the compulsory settlement of disputes [ibid.].

The 1963 Vienna Convention on Consular Relations [YUN 1963, p. 510] had 165 parties, the Optional Protocol concerning the acquisition of nationality [ibid., p. 512] had 39 and the Optional Protocol concerning the compulsory settlement of disputes [ibid.] had 46.

Parties to the 1973 Convention on the Prevention and Punishment of Crimes against Internationally Protected Persons, including Diplomatic Agents [YUN 1973, p. 775], numbered 144.

ILC consideration. ILC, at its fifty-fifth session [A/58/10], had before it the fourth report of Special Rapporteur John R. Dugard (South Africa) on diplomatic protection, specifically with regard to corporations and shareholders [A/CN.4/530 & Add.1]. ILC considered the first part of the report covering draft articles 17 to 20 in May and the second part covering draft articles 21 and 22 in July. It established an open-ended working group on article 17, paragraph 2, which concerned, in respect of an injury to a corporation, the determination of its State nationality. ILC subsequently referred to the Drafting Committee article 17 as proposed by the working group, together with articles 18 to 22.

In June, ILC considered the Drafting Committee's report on draft articles 8 [10], 9 [11] and 10 [14], with the commentaries thereon. It provisionally adopted those articles and reproduced in its report the draft articles on diplomatic protection that it had so far adopted.

Treaties and agreements

Reservations to treaties

In July 2003, ILC [A/58/10] considered the eighth report of Special Rapporteur Alain Pellet (France) relating to withdrawal and modification of reservations to treaties and interpretative declarations, as well as to the formulation of objections to them [A/CN.4/535 & Add.1]. ILC referred to the Drafting Committee draft guidelines 2.3.5 (enlargement of the scope of a reservation), 2.4.9 (modification of interpretative declarations), 2.4.10 (modification of a conditional interpretative declaration), 2.5.12 (withdrawal of an interpretative declaration) and 2.5.13 (withdrawal of a conditional interpretative declaration).

Earlier, in May, ILC considered and provisionally adopted the following draft guidelines referred to the Drafting Committee in 2002 [YUN 2002, p. 1314]: 2.5.1 (withdrawal of reservations), 2.5.2 (form of withdrawal), 2.5.3 (periodic review of the usefulness of reservations), 2.5.4 [2.5.5] (formulation of the withdrawal of a reservation at the international level), 2.5.5 [2.5.5 bis, 2.5.5 ter] (absence of consequences at the international level of the violations of internal rules regarding the withdrawal of reservations), 2.5.6 (communication of a withdrawal of a reservation), 2.5.7 [2.5.7, 2.5.8] (effect of withdrawal of a reservation), 2.5.8 [2.5.9] (effective date of withdrawal of a reservation) (together with model clauses A, B and C), 2.5.9 [2.5.10] (cases on which a reserving State or international organization may unilaterally set the effective date of withdrawal of a reservation), 2.5.10 [2.5.11] (partial withdrawal of a reservation) and 2.5.11 [2.5.12] (effect of a partial withdrawal of a reservation). In August, ILC adopted the commentaries to those draft guidelines and reproduced in its report the text of the draft guidelines on reservations to treaties it had so far provisionally adopted, together with the commentaries pertaining thereto.

Treaties involving international organizations

The 1986 Vienna Convention on the Law of Treaties between States and International Organizations or between International Organizations [YUN 1986, p. 1006], which had not entered into force, had 37 States parties as at 31 December 2003.

UN registration and publication of treaties

During 2003, 1,214 international agreements were received and 955 were registered; 1,251 subsequent actions were registered or filed and recorded by the Secretariat. In addition, 1,008 formalities concerning agreements for which the Secretary-General performed depositary functions were registered. Twelve issues of the *Monthly Statement of Treaties and International Agreements* were published.

Also in 2003, the texts of international agreements registered or filed and recorded were published in the UN *Treaty Series* in 47 volumes in the original languages, with translations into English and French where necessary. The drop in the number of volumes published was due mainly to the lack of translations. Volume 38 of the *Cumulative Index to the Treaty Series* was published in English and French. The new edition of the *Final Clauses of Multilateral Treaties Handbook* [Sales No. E.04.V.3] was also published.

Multilateral treaties

The UN *Treaty Series* (in 2,228 printed volumes as at the end of 2003) and the regularly updated status of multilateral treaties deposited with the Secretary-General were available on the Internet at the UN Treaty Collection web site (http://untreaty.un.org).

New multilateral treaties concluded under UN auspices

The following treaties, concluded under UN auspices, were deposited with the Secretary-General during 2003:

Agreement on International Railways in the Arab Mashreq, adopted in Beirut, Lebanon, on 14 April 2003

Regulation No. 114. Uniform provisions concerning the approval of: I. An airbag module for a replacement airbag system; II. A replacement steering wheel equipped with an airbag module of an approved type; III. A replacement airbag system other than that installed in a steering wheel, adopted in Geneva on 1 February 2003

Protocol on Civil Liability and Compensation for Damage Caused by the Transboundary Effects of Industrial Accidents on Transboundary Waters to the 1992 Convention on the Protection and Use of Transboundary Watercourses and International Lakes and to the 1992 Convention on the Transboundary Effects of Industrial Accidents, adopted in Kiev, Ukraine, on 21 May 2003

Protocol on Pollutant Release and Transfer Registers (to the *Convention on Access to Information, Public Participation in Decision-Making and Access to Justice in Environmental Matters*, adopted in Aarhus, Denmark, on 25 June 1998), adopted in Kiev on 21 May 2003

Protocol on Strategic Environmental Assessment to the Convention on Environmental Impact Assessment in a Transboundary Context, adopted in Kiev on 21 May 2003

Framework Convention on Tobacco Control, adopted in Geneva on 21 May 2003

Regulation No. 115. Uniform provisions concerning the approval of: I. Specific LPG (Liquefied Petroleum Gases) retrofit systems to be installed in motor vehicles for the use of LPG in their propulsion systems; II. Specific CNG (Compressed Natural Gas) retrofit systems to be installed in motor vehicles for the use of CNG in their propulsion systems, adopted in Geneva on 30 October 2003

United Nations Convention against Corruption, adopted by General Assembly resolution 58/44 of 31 October 2003

Intergovernmental Agreement on the Asian Highway Network, adopted in Bangkok, Thailand, on 18 November 2003

Additional Protocol to the Convention on Prohibitions or Restrictions on the Use of Certain Conventional Weapons Which May Be Deemed to Be Excessively Injurious or to Have Indiscriminate Effects (Protocol V, entitled Protocol on explosive remnants of war), adopted in Geneva on 28 November 2003

Multilateral treaties deposited with the Secretary-General

At the end of 2003, the Secretary-General performed depositary functions for 509 multilateral treaties. During the year, 371 signatures were affixed to treaties for which he performed depositary functions and 1,282 instruments of ratification, accession, acceptance and approval were deposited.

The following multilateral treaties, among others, in respect of which the Secretary-General acted as depositary came into force in 2003:

International Convention on the Protection of the Rights of All Migrant Workers and Members of Their Families, adopted by General Assembly resolution 45/158 of 18 December 1990

Regulation No. 114. Uniform provisions concerning the approval of: I. An airbag module for a replacement airbag system; II. A replacement steering wheel equipped with an airbag module of an approved type; III. A replacement airbag system other than that installed in a steering wheel, adopted in Geneva on 1 February 2003

Regulation No. 115. Uniform provisions concerning the approval of: I. Specific LPG (Liquefied Petroleum Gases) retrofit systems to be installed in motor vehicles for the use of LPG in their propulsion systems; II. Specific CNG (Compressed Natural Gas) retrofit systems to be installed in motor vehicles for the use of CNG in their propulsion systems, adopted in Geneva on 30 October 2003

Agreement on International Roads in the Arab Mashreq, adopted in Beirut, Lebanon, on 10 May 2001

United Nations Convention against Transnational Organized Crime, adopted by General Assembly resolution 55/25 of 15 November 2000

Protocol to Prevent, Suppress and Punish Trafficking in Persons, Especially Women and Children, supplementing the United Nations Convention against Transnational Organized Crime, adopted by General Assembly resolution 55/25 of 15 November 2000

International Cocoa Agreement, 2001, adopted in Geneva on 2 March 2001

Protocol on the Privileges and Immunities of the International Seabed Authority, adopted in Kingston, Jamaica, on 27 March 1998

Protocol to the 1979 Convention on Long-Range Transboundary Air Pollution on Heavy Metals, adopted in Aarhus, Denmark, on 24 June 1998

Protocol to the 1979 Convention on Long-Range Transboundary Air Pollution on Persistent Organic Pollutants, adopted in Aarhus on 24 June 1998

Cartagena Protocol on Biosafety to the Convention on Biological Diversity, adopted in Montreal, Canada, on 29 January 2000

Information for 2003 regarding all multilateral treaties deposited with the Secretary-General was contained in *Multilateral Treaties Deposited with the Secretary-General: Status as at 31 December 2003*, Vols. I & II [ST/LEG/SER.E/22], Sales No. E.04.V.2.

Chapter IV

Law of the Sea

The United Nations continued in 2003 to promote universal acceptance of the 1982 United Nations Convention on the Law of the Sea and its two implementing Agreements, on the conservation and management of straddling fish stocks and highly migratory fish stocks and on the privileges and immunities of the International Tribunal for the Law of the Sea.

The three institutions created by the Convention—the International Seabed Authority, the International Tribunal for the Law of the Sea and the Commission on the Limits of the Continental Shelf—held sessions during the year.

On 31 May 2003, the 1998 Protocol on the Privileges and Immunities of the International Seabed Authority entered into force.

UN Convention on the Law of the Sea

Signatures and ratifications

In 2003, Albania, Canada, Kiribati and Lithuania ratified or acceded to the United Nations Convention on the Law of the Sea (UNCLOS), bringing the number of parties to 145. The Convention, which was adopted by the Third United Nations Conference on the Law of the Sea in 1982 [YUN 1982, p. 178], entered into force on 16 November 1994 [YUN 1994, p. 1301].

Meeting of States Parties

The thirteenth Meeting of States Parties to the Convention (New York, 9-13 June) [SPLOS/103 & Corr.1] discussed the 2002 activities of the International Tribunal for the Law of the Sea [YUN 2002, p. 1321] and took action on a number of Tribunal-related financial and administrative issues, including: approving the 2004 budget in the amount of $8.04 million and a new budget line providing for the Tribunal's liability coverage in the event of service-related death, injury or illness; reducing the ceiling rate of the assessment scale for States parties for the Tribunal budget from the current 25 per cent to 24 per cent for the 2004 budget and to 22 per cent for the 2005-2006 budget; deciding to deduct on a pro rata basis from the contributions of States parties to the 2004 budget the $2.3 million that had accrued in the staff assessment account at the end of 2002; and adopting the Tribunal's Financial Regulations, to become effective on 1 January 2004. Also discussed were the 2002 activities of the International Seabed Authority and of the Commission on the Limits of the Continental Shelf [ibid.], and the possible inclusion in the agenda of future Meetings of issues arising from the implementation of UNCLOS.

On 2 September, a Special Meeting of States Parties elected Judge Anthony Amos Lucky (Trinidad and Tobago) to fill the vacancy in the Tribunal created by the death on 29 March of Judge Lennox Fitzroy Ballah (Trinidad and Tobago). Judge Lucky would serve on the Tribunal until 30 September 2011.

Agreement relating to the Implementation of Part XI of the Convention

During 2003, the number of parties to the 1994 Agreement relating to the Implementation of Part XI of the Convention (governing exploitation of seabed resources beyond national jurisdiction), adopted by General Assembly resolution 48/263 [YUN 1994, p. 1301], reached 117. The Agreement, which entered into force on 28 July 1996 [YUN 1996, p. 1215], was to be interpreted and applied together with the Convention as a single instrument, and, in the event of any inconsistency between the Agreement and Part XI of the Convention, the provisions of the Agreement would prevail. Any ratification of or accession to the Convention after 28 July 1994 represented consent to be bound by the Agreement also. Parties to the Convention prior to the Agreement's adoption had to deposit a separate instrument of ratification of or accession to the Agreement.

Agreement relating to conservation and management of straddling fish stocks and highly migratory fish stocks

As at 31 December 2003, the number of parties to the 1995 Agreement for the Implementation of the Provisions of the United Nations Convention on the Law of the Sea of 10 December 1982 relating to the Conservation and Management of Straddling Fish Stocks and Highly Migratory Fish Stocks [YUN 1995, p. 1334] reached 51. Referred to as the Fish Stocks Agreement, it entered into force on 11 December 2001 [YUN 2001, p. 1232].

Report of Secretary-General. In response to General Assembly resolutions 56/13 [YUN 2001, p. 1232] and 57/143 [YUN 2002, p. 1318], the Secretary-General submitted an August report [A/58/215] on the status and implementation of the Fish Stocks Agreement and its impact on related or proposed instruments throughout the UN system, with special reference to the implementation of Part VII of the Agreement dealing with the requirements of developing States. The report discussed the role of all States in the implementation of the Agreement and of States acting through subregional and regional fisheries management organizations (RFMOs) and arrangements; peaceful dispute settlement; Part VII of the Agreement; and the impact of the Agreement's entry into force on related or proposed international instruments.

The report concluded that the Agreement had had an important impact on the conservation and management of international fisheries, representing a benchmark for many States and recognized by the Plan of Implementation of the 2002 World Summit on Sustainable Development [YUN 2002, p. 821]; its full effect would only be achieved, however, by the wider acceptance and implementation of its provisions by all States. The current depleted state of stocks covered by the Agreement and the costs associated with implementing the Agreement were likely to mean that the short-term focus would be on distribution of actual fishing opportunities and full recovery of management costs, rather than on development of new fisheries. The report recommended specific action by coastal, flag and port States; global coverage of stocks by RFMOs and strengthening of RFMOs; priority areas of assistance to developing States parties to the Agreement under a new Part VII trust fund; and co-operation and coordination at the State and UN inter-agency levels and among RFMOs.

GENERAL ASSEMBLY ACTION

On 24 November [meeting 64], the General Assembly adopted **resolution 58/14** [draft: A/58/L.18 & Add.1] without vote [agenda item 52 *(b)*].

Sustainable fisheries, including through the 1995 Agreement for the Implementation of the Provisions of the United Nations Convention on the Law of the Sea of 10 December 1982 relating to the Conservation and Management of Straddling Fish Stocks and Highly Migratory Fish Stocks, and related instruments

The General Assembly,

Reaffirming its resolutions 46/215 of 20 December 1991, 49/116 and 49/118 of 19 December 1994, 50/25 of 5 December 1995 and 57/142 of 12 December 2002, as well as other resolutions on large-scale pelagic drift-net fishing, unauthorized fishing in zones of national jurisdiction and on the high seas, fisheries by-catch and discards, and other developments, and its resolutions 56/13 of 28 November 2001 and 57/143 of 12 December 2002 on the Agreement for the Implementation of the Provisions of the United Nations Convention on the Law of the Sea of 10 December 1982 relating to the Conservation and Management of Straddling Fish Stocks and Highly Migratory Fish Stocks ("the Agreement"),

Recalling the relevant provisions of the United Nations Convention on the Law of the Sea ("the Convention"), and bearing in mind the relationship between the Convention and the Agreement,

Recognizing that, in accordance with the Convention, the Agreement sets forth provisions concerning the conservation and management of straddling fish stocks and highly migratory fish stocks, including provisions on subregional and regional cooperation in enforcement, binding dispute settlement and the rights and obligations of States in authorizing the use of vessels flying their flags for fishing on the high seas,

Noting that the Code of Conduct for Responsible Fisheries of the Food and Agriculture Organization of the United Nations ("the Code") and its associated international plans of action set out principles and global standards of behaviour for responsible practices to conserve, manage and develop fisheries, including guidelines for fishing on the high seas and in areas under the national jurisdiction of other States, and on fishing gear selectivity and practices, with the aim of reducing by-catch and discards,

Noting with satisfaction the Strategy for Improving Information on Status and Trends of Capture Fisheries recently adopted by the Food and Agriculture Organization of the United Nations, and recognizing that the long-term improvement of the knowledge and understanding of fishery status and trends is a fundamental basis for fisheries policy and management for implementing the Code,

Recognizing the need to implement, as a matter of priority, the Plan of Implementation of the World Summit on Sustainable Development ("Johannesburg Plan of Implementation"), in relation to achieving sustainable fisheries,

Deploring the fact that fish stocks, including straddling fish stocks and highly migratory fish stocks, in many parts of the world are overfished or subject to sparsely regulated and heavy fishing efforts, mainly as a result of, inter alia, unauthorized fishing, inadequate regulatory measures and excess fishing capacity,

Concerned that illegal, unreported and unregulated fishing threatens seriously to deplete populations of certain fish species and to significantly damage marine ecosystems, to the detriment of sustainable fisheries as well as the food security and the economies of many States, particularly developing States,

Recognizing that inadequate flag State control over fishing vessels, including those fishing for straddling fish stocks and highly migratory fish stocks, and insufficient monitoring, control and surveillance measures exacerbate the problem of overfishing,

Recognizing also that the interrelationship between ocean activities, such as shipping and fishing, and environmental issues needs further consideration,

Calling attention to the circumstances affecting fisheries in many developing States, in particular African States and small island developing States, and recognizing the urgent need for capacity-building to assist such States in meeting their obligations under international instruments and realizing the benefits from fisheries resources,

Noting the obligation of all States, pursuant to the provisions of the Convention, to cooperate in the conservation and management of straddling fish stocks and highly migratory fish stocks, and recognizing the importance of coordination and cooperation at the global, regional, subregional as well as national levels in the areas, inter alia, of data collection, information-sharing, capacity-building and training for the conservation, management and sustainable development of marine living resources,

Recognizing the duty provided in the Convention, the Agreement to Promote Compliance with International Conservation and Management Measures by Fishing Vessels on the High Seas ("the Compliance Agreement"), the Agreement and the Code for flag States to exercise effective control over fishing vessels flying their flag and vessels flying their flag which provide support to such vessels, and to ensure that the activities of such vessels do not undermine the effectiveness of conservation and management measures taken in accordance with international law and adopted at the national, subregional, regional or global levels,

Recognizing also the urgent need for action at all levels to ensure the long-term sustainable use and management of fisheries resources,

Recognizing further the economic and cultural importance of sharks in many countries, the biological importance of sharks in the marine ecosystem, the vulnerability of some shark species to over-exploitation and the need for measures to promote the long-term sustainability of shark populations and fisheries,

Reaffirming its support for the initiative of the Food and Agriculture Organization of the United Nations and relevant regional and subregional fisheries management organizations and arrangements on the conservation and management of sharks, while noting with concern that only a small number of countries have implemented the International Plan of Action for the Conservation and Management of Sharks, adopted by the Food and Agriculture Organization in 1999,

Noting with satisfaction the outcomes of the second round of informal consultations of States parties to the Agreement, held in New York from 23 to 25 July 2003,

Taking note with appreciation of the report of the Secretary-General, and emphasizing the useful role that the report plays in bringing together information relating to the sustainable development of the world's marine living resources provided by States, relevant international organizations, regional and subregional fisheries organizations and non-governmental organizations,

Noting with satisfaction that the incidence of reported large-scale pelagic drift-net fishing activities in most regions of the world's oceans and seas has continued to be low,

Expressing concern that the practice of large-scale pelagic drift-net fishing remains a threat to marine living resources,

Emphasizing that efforts should be made to ensure that the implementation of resolution 46/215 in some parts of the world does not result in the transfer to other parts of the world of drift nets that contravene the resolution,

Expressing concern at the reports of continued loss of seabirds, particularly albatrosses, as a result of incidental mortality from longline fishing operations, and the loss of other marine species, including sharks and finfish species, as a result of incidental mortality, and noting with satisfaction the imminent entry into force of the Agreement for the Conservation of Albatrosses and Petrels under the Convention on the Conservation of Migratory Species of Wild Animals,

Welcoming the fact that a growing number of States, and entities referred to in the Convention and in article 1, paragraph 2 *(b)*, of the Agreement, as well as regional and subregional fisheries management organizations and arrangements, have enacted legislation, established regulations, adopted conventions or taken other measures as steps towards implementation of the provisions of the Agreement,

Recognizing the significant contribution of sustainable fisheries to food security, income and wealth for present and future generations,

I
Achieving sustainable fisheries

1. *Reaffirms* the importance it attaches to the long-term conservation, management and sustainable use of the marine living resources of the world's oceans and seas and the obligations of States to cooperate to this end, in accordance with international law, as reflected in the relevant provisions of the Convention, in particular the provisions on cooperation set out in Part V and Part VII, section 2, of the Convention regarding straddling stocks, highly migratory species, marine mammals, anadromous stocks and marine living resources of the high seas, and where applicable, the Agreement;

2. *Calls upon* all States that have not done so, in order to achieve the goal of universal participation, to become parties to the Convention, which sets out the legal framework within which all activities in the oceans and seas must be carried out, taking into account the relationship between the Convention and the Agreement;

3. *Reaffirms* the importance of the Johannesburg Plan of Implementation in relation to fisheries, in particular the commitment made therein to restore depleted fish stocks on an urgent basis and, where possible, not later than 2015;

4. *Urges* all States to apply the precautionary approach widely to the conservation, management and exploitation of fish stocks, including straddling fish stocks and highly migratory fish stocks, and calls upon States parties to the Agreement to implement fully the provisions of article 6 of the Agreement as a matter of priority;

II
Implementation of the 1995 Agreement for the Implementation of the Provisions of the United Nations Convention on the Law of the Sea of 10 December 1982 relating to the Conservation and Management of Straddling Fish Stocks and Highly Migratory Fish Stocks

5. *Calls upon* all States, and entities referred to in the Convention and in article 1, paragraph 2 *(b)*, of the

Agreement, that have not done so to ratify or accede to the Agreement and to consider applying it provisionally;

6. *Emphasizes* the importance of the effective implementation of the provisions of the Agreement, including those provisions relating to bilateral, regional and subregional cooperation in enforcement, and urges continued efforts in this regard;

7. *Welcomes* the entry into force of the Convention on the Conservation and Management of Fishery Resources in the South-East Atlantic Ocean on 13 April 2003, and invites signatory States and other States with real interest whose vessels fish in the Convention area for fishery resources covered by that Convention to ratify or to accede to the Convention;

8. *Calls upon* all States to ensure that their vessels comply with the conservation and management measures that have been adopted by subregional and regional fisheries management organizations and arrangements in accordance with relevant provisions of the Convention and of the Agreement;

9. *Invites* States and international financial institutions and organizations of the United Nations system to provide assistance according to Part VII of the Agreement, including, if appropriate, the development of special financial mechanisms or instruments to assist developing States, in particular the least developed among them and small island developing States, to enable them to develop their national capacity to exploit fishery resources, including developing their domestically flagged fishing fleet, value-added processing and the expansion of their economic base in the fishing industry, consistent with the duty to ensure the proper conservation and management of those fisheries resources;

10. *Decides* to establish an Assistance Fund under Part VII of the Agreement to assist developing States parties in the implementation of the Agreement, to be administered by the Food and Agriculture Organization of the United Nations, which should act as the implementing office for the Fund, in collaboration with the United Nations, in accordance with the terms of reference as agreed at the second round of informal consultations of the States parties to the Agreement and appropriate arrangements made between them;

11. *Emphasizes* the importance of outreach to potential donor organizations to contribute to the programme of assistance, including the Assistance Fund newly established under Part VII of the Agreement;

12. *Recalls* paragraph 6 of its resolution 56/13, and requests the Secretary-General to convene a third round of informal consultations of States parties to the Agreement, for the purposes and objectives of considering the national, regional, subregional and global implementation of the Agreement, in particular by conducting an evaluation of the implementation of the Agreement by regional fisheries management organizations as well as considering initial preparatory steps for the review conference to be convened by the Secretary-General pursuant to article 36 of the Agreement, and making any appropriate recommendation to the General Assembly;

13. *Requests* the Secretary-General to invite States, and entities referred to in the Convention and in article 1, paragraph 2 (b), of the Agreement, not party to the Agreement, as well as the United Nations Development Programme, the Food and Agriculture Organization of the United Nations and other specialized agencies, the Commission on Sustainable Development, the World Bank, the Global Environment Facility and other relevant international financial institutions, regional fishery bodies and arrangements and relevant non-governmental organizations to attend the third round of informal consultations of States parties to the Agreement as observers;

III
Related fisheries instruments

14. *Welcomes* the entry into force of the Compliance Agreement, and calls upon all States and other entities referred to in article 10, paragraph 1, of the Compliance Agreement that have not yet deposited instruments of acceptance to do so as a matter of priority;

15. *Urges* parties to the Compliance Agreement to exchange information in the implementation of that Agreement;

16. *Urges* States and subregional and regional fisheries management organizations and arrangements to promote the application of the Code within their areas of competence;

17. *Invites* States to support implementation of the Strategy for Improving Information on Status and Trends of Capture Fisheries at the national and regional levels, giving particular emphasis to capacity-building in developing countries;

18. *Urges* States to develop and implement national and, as appropriate, regional plans of action to put into effect the international plans of action of the Food and Agriculture Organization of the United Nations, namely the International Plan of Action for the Management of Fishing Capacity, the International Plan of Action for Reducing Incidental Catch of Seabirds in Longline Fisheries, the International Plan of Action for the Conservation and Management of Sharks and the International Plan of Action to Prevent, Deter and Eliminate Illegal, Unreported and Unregulated Fishing;

IV
Illegal, unreported and unregulated fishing

19. *Calls upon* States not to permit vessels flying their flag to engage in fishing on the high seas or in areas under the national jurisdiction of other States, unless duly authorized by the authorities of the States concerned and in accordance with the conditions set out in the authorization, without having effective control over their activities, and to take specific measures, including deterring the reflagging of vessels by their nationals, in accordance with the relevant provisions of the Convention, the Agreement and the Compliance Agreement, to control fishing operations by vessels flying their flag;

20. *Affirms* the need to strengthen, where necessary, the international legal framework for intergovernmental cooperation, in particular at the regional and subregional levels, in the management of fish stocks and in combating illegal, unreported and unregulated fishing, in a manner consistent with international law, and for States and entities referred to in the Convention and in article 1, paragraph 2 (b), of the Agreement to collaborate in efforts to address these types of fishing activities;

21. *Encourages* States to consider becoming members of the International Monitoring, Control, and Surveillance Network for Fisheries-Related Activities,

a voluntary network of monitoring, control and surveillance professionals designed to facilitate exchange of information and to support countries in discharging their obligations pursuant to international agreements, in particular the Compliance Agreement;

22. *Invites* the International Maritime Organization and other relevant competent international organizations to study, examine and clarify the role of the "genuine link" in relation to the duty of flag States to exercise effective control over ships flying their flag, including fishing vessels;

23. *Calls upon* flag and port States to take all measures consistent with international law necessary to prevent the operation of sub-standard vessels and illegal, unreported and unregulated fishing activities;

24. *Encourages* States in their work with regional and subregional fisheries management organizations and arrangements to develop and implement vessel monitoring systems and, where appropriate and consistent with international law, trade monitoring schemes;

25. *Urges* States to develop and implement national and, where appropriate, regional plans of action, to put into effect by 2004 the International Plan of Action to Prevent, Deter and Eliminate Illegal, Unreported and Unregulated Fishing and to establish effective monitoring, reporting and enforcement and control of fishing vessels, including by flag States, to further the International Plan of Action;

26. *Urges* relevant regional and subregional fisheries management organizations and arrangements to implement effective measures against illegal, unreported and unregulated fishing, inter alia, by compiling a record of vessels authorized to fish in their area of competence, in accordance with the Code;

27. *Urges* States to eliminate subsidies that contribute to illegal, unreported and unregulated fishing and to overcapacity, while completing the efforts undertaken at the World Trade Organization to clarify and improve its disciplines on fisheries subsidies, taking into account the importance of this sector to developing countries;

28. *Commends* the Food and Agriculture Organization of the United Nations for its activities in combating illegal, unreported and unregulated fishing, including its initiative to organize the intergovernmental technical consultation on illegal, unreported and unregulated fishing and fleet overcapacity, to be held in June 2004, and the intergovernmental technical consultation on the role of the port State in combating illegal, unreported and unregulated fishing, to be held in September 2004;

29. *Recognizes* the need for enhanced port State controls to combat illegal, unreported and unregulated fishing, urges States to cooperate, in particular at the regional level, and through regional and subregional fisheries management organizations and arrangements, as well as through participation, where appropriate, in the efforts of the Food and Agriculture Organization of the United Nations in cooperation with the International Maritime Organization to address substantive issues relating to the role of the port State, noting that such efforts include the elaboration of principles and guidelines for the establishment of regional memorandums of understanding on port State measures to prevent, deter and eliminate illegal, unreported and unregulated fishing;

V
Fishing overcapacity

30. *Calls upon* States and relevant regional fisheries management organizations, as a matter of priority, to take effective measures to improve the management of fishing capacity and to put into effect by 2005 the International Plan of Action for the Management of Fishing Capacity, taking into account the need, through these actions, to avoid the transfer of fishing capacity to other fisheries or areas including, but not limited to, those areas where fisheries are overexploited or in a depleted condition;

31. *Urges* those States and other entities referred to in article X, paragraph 1, of the Compliance Agreement that have become parties to it to establish a record of fishing vessels authorized to fish on the high seas and, pursuant to articles IV and VI thereof, to make such a record available to the Food and Agriculture Organization of the United Nations as a matter of priority, and urges the Food and Agriculture Organization to quickly establish the record of fishing vessels as called for in the Compliance Agreement;

32. *Calls upon* all States to assist this work of the Food and Agriculture Organization of the United Nations, to take measures to halt the increase of large-scale fishing vessels in accordance with the International Plan of Action for the Management of Fishing Capacity and to participate in the intergovernmental technical consultation on illegal, unreported and unregulated fishing and fleet overcapacity to be organized by the Food and Agriculture Organization in 2004;

VI
Large-scale pelagic drift-net fishing

33. *Reaffirms* the importance it attaches to continued compliance with its resolution 46/215 and other subsequent resolutions on large-scale pelagic drift-net fishing, and urges States and entities referred to in the Convention and in article 1, paragraph 2 (*b*), of the Agreement to enforce fully the measures recommended in those resolutions;

VII
Fisheries by-catch and discards

34. *Urges* States, relevant international organizations and regional and subregional fisheries management organizations and arrangements that have not done so to take action to reduce or eliminate by-catch, catch by lost or abandoned gear, fish discards and post-harvest losses, including juvenile fish, consistent with international law and relevant international instruments, including the Code, and in particular to consider measures including, as appropriate, technical measures related to fish size, mesh size or gear, discards, closed seasons and areas and zones reserved for selected fisheries, particularly artisanal fisheries, the establishment of mechanisms for communicating information on areas of high concentration of juvenile fish, taking into account the importance of ensuring confidentiality of such information, and support for studies and research that will reduce or eliminate by-catch of juvenile fish;

35. *Encourages* States and entities referred to in the Convention and in article 1, paragraph 2 (*b*), of the Agreement to give due consideration to participation, as appropriate, in regional and subregional organizations with mandates to conserve non-target species

taken incidentally in fishing operations, and notes in particular the Inter-American Convention for the Protection and Conservation of Sea Turtles and Their Habitats, regional sea turtle conservation instruments in the West African, the wider Caribbean, and the Indian Ocean/South-East Asia regions, the work of the Southeast Asian Fisheries Development Centre on turtle conservation and management, the Agreement on the Conservation of Small Cetaceans of the Baltic and North Seas and the Agreement on the Conservation of Albatrosses and Petrels under the Convention on the Conservation of Migratory Species of Wild Animals in this regard;

36. *Notes with satisfaction* the activities of the Food and Agriculture Organization of the United Nations, in cooperation with relevant United Nations agencies, in particular the United Nations Environment Programme and the Global Environment Facility, aimed at promoting the reduction of by-catch and discards in fisheries activities;

VIII
Subregional and regional cooperation

37. *Urges* coastal States and States fishing on the high seas, in accordance with the Convention and the Agreement, to pursue cooperation in relation to straddling fish stocks and highly migratory fish stocks, either directly or through appropriate subregional or regional fisheries management organizations or arrangements, to ensure the effective conservation and management of such stocks;

38. *Encourages* States fishing for straddling fish stocks and highly migratory fish stocks on the high seas, and relevant coastal States, where a subregional or regional fisheries management organization or arrangement has the competence to establish conservation and management measures for such stocks, to give effect to their duty to cooperate by becoming members of such an organization or participants in such an arrangement, or by agreeing to apply the conservation and management measures established by such an organization or arrangement;

39. *Invites*, in this regard, subregional and regional fisheries management organizations and arrangements to ensure that all States having a real interest in the fisheries concerned may become members of such organizations or participants in such arrangements, in accordance with the Convention and the Agreement;

40. *Encourages* relevant coastal States and States fishing on the high seas for a straddling fish stock or a highly migratory fish stock, where there is no subregional or regional fisheries management organization or arrangement to establish conservation and management measures for such stock, to cooperate to establish such an organization or enter into another appropriate arrangement to ensure the conservation and management of such stocks, and to participate in the work of the organization or arrangement;

41. *Welcomes* the initiation of negotiations and ongoing preparatory work to establish regional and subregional fisheries management organizations or arrangements in several fisheries, and urges participants in those negotiations to apply provisions of the Convention and the Agreement to their work;

42. *Encourages* States to develop ocean policies and mechanisms on integrated management, including at the subregional and regional levels, and also including assistance to developing States in accomplishing these objectives, as well as by promoting improved cooperation between regional fisheries management organizations and other regional entities, such as the United Nations Environment Programme regional seas programmes and conventions;

IX
Responsible fisheries in the marine ecosystem

43. *Encourages* States to apply by 2010 the ecosystem approach, notes the Reykjavik Declaration on Responsible Fisheries in the Marine Ecosystem and decisions V/6 and VI/12 of the Conference of the Parties to the Convention on Biological Diversity, encourages States to consider the guidelines of the Food and Agriculture Organization of the United Nations for the implementation of ecosystem considerations in fisheries management, and notes the importance to this approach of relevant provisions of the Agreement and the Code;

44. *Calls upon* the Food and Agriculture Organization of the United Nations, the United Nations Environment Programme, in particular its Regional Seas programme, the International Maritime Organization, regional and subregional fisheries management organizations and arrangements and other appropriate intergovernmental organizations to take up, as a matter of priority, the issue of marine debris as it relates to fisheries and, where appropriate, to promote better coordination and help States to implement fully relevant international agreements, including annex V to the International Convention for the Prevention of Pollution from Ships, 1973, as modified by the Protocol of 1978 relating thereto;

45. *Urges* all States to implement the Global Programme of Action for the Protection of the Marine Environment from Land-based Activities and to accelerate activity to safeguard the marine environment against pollution and physical degradation;

46. *Requests* the Secretary-General, in close cooperation with the Food and Agriculture Organization of the United Nations, and in consultation with States, regional and subregional fisheries management organizations and arrangements and other relevant organizations, in his next report concerning fisheries to include a section outlining current risks to the marine biodiversity of vulnerable marine ecosystems including, but not limited to, seamounts, coral reefs, including cold water reefs and certain other sensitive underwater features, related to fishing activities, as well as detailing any conservation and management measures in place at the global, regional, subregional or national levels addressing these issues;

47. *Calls upon* States, the Food and Agriculture Organization of the United Nations and subregional or regional fisheries management organizations and arrangements to implement fully the International Plan of Action for the Conservation and Management of Sharks as a matter of priority, inter alia, by conducting assessments of shark stocks and developing and implementing national plans of action, recognizing the need of some States, in particular developing States, for assistance in this regard;

48. *Urges* States, including those working through subregional or regional fisheries management organizations and arrangements in implementing the Inter-

national Plan of Action for the Conservation and Management of Sharks, to collect scientific data regarding shark catches and to consider adopting conservation and management measures, particularly where shark catches from directed and non-directed fisheries have a significant impact on vulnerable or threatened shark stocks, in order to ensure the conservation and management of sharks and their long-term sustainable use, including by banning directed shark fisheries conducted solely for the purpose of harvesting shark fins and by taking measures for other fisheries to minimize waste and discards from shark catches, and to encourage the full use of dead sharks;

49. *Urges* all States to cooperate with the Food and Agriculture Organization of the United Nations in order to assist developing States in implementing the International Plan of Action for the Conservation and Management of Sharks, including through voluntary contributions to work of the organization, such as its FishCODE programme;

50. *Invites* the Food and Agriculture Organization of the United Nations, in consultation with relevant subregional or regional fisheries management organizations or arrangements, to prepare a study relating to the impact on shark populations of shark catches from directed and non-directed fisheries and their impact on ecologically related species, taking into account the nutritional and socio-economic considerations as reflected in the International Plan of Action for the Conservation and Management of Sharks, particularly as they relate to small-scale, subsistence and artisanal fisheries and communities, as well as updating Technical Paper 389 of the Food and Agriculture Organization, entitled "Shark utilization, marketing and trade", in order to facilitate improved shark conservation, management and utilization, and to report to the Secretary-General for inclusion in a fisheries-related report as soon as practicable;

X
Capacity-building

51. *Reiterates* the crucial importance of cooperation by States directly or, as appropriate, through the relevant regional and subregional organizations, and by other international organizations, including through financial and/or technical assistance, in accordance with the Agreement, the Compliance Agreement, the Code and the International Plan of Action to Prevent, Deter and Eliminate Illegal, Unreported and Unregulated Fishing, to increase the capacity of developing States to achieve the goals and implement the actions called for in the present resolution;

52. *Invites* States and relevant intergovernmental organizations to develop projects, programmes and partnerships with relevant stakeholders and mobilize resources for the effective implementation of the outcome of the African Process for the Protection and Development of the Marine and Coastal Environment, and to consider the inclusion of fisheries components in this work;

53. *Also invites* States and relevant intergovernmental organizations to further implement sustainable fisheries management and improve financial returns from fisheries by supporting and strengthening relevant regional fisheries management organizations, as appropriate, such as the Caribbean Regional Fisheries Mechanism and such agreements as the Convention on the Conservation and Management of Highly Migratory Fish Stocks in the Western and Central Pacific;

XI
Cooperation within the United Nations system

54. *Requests* the relevant parts of the United Nations system, international financial institutions and donor agencies to support increased enforcement and compliance capabilities for regional fisheries management organizations and their member States;

55. *Invites* the Food and Agriculture Organization of the United Nations to continue its cooperative arrangements with United Nations agencies on the implementation of the international plans of action and to report to the Secretary-General, for inclusion in his annual report on oceans and the law of the sea, on priorities for cooperation and coordination in this work;

XII
Fifty-ninth session of the General Assembly

56. *Requests* the Secretary-General to bring the present resolution to the attention of all members of the international community, relevant intergovernmental organizations, the organizations and bodies of the United Nations system, regional and subregional fisheries management organizations and relevant non-governmental organizations, and to invite them to provide the Secretary-General with information relevant to the implementation of the present resolution;

57. *Also requests* the Secretary-General to submit to the General Assembly at its fifty-ninth session a report on "Sustainable fisheries, including through the 1995 Agreement for the Implementation of the Provisions of the United Nations Convention on the Law of the Sea of 10 December 1982 relating to the Conservation and Management of Straddling Fish Stocks and Highly Migratory Fish Stocks, and related instruments", taking into account information provided by States, relevant specialized agencies, in particular the Food and Agriculture Organization of the United Nations, and other appropriate organs, organizations and programmes of the United Nations system, regional and subregional organizations and arrangements for the conservation and management of straddling fish stocks and highly migratory fish stocks, as well as other relevant intergovernmental bodies and non-governmental organizations, and consisting, inter alia, of elements provided in relevant paragraphs in the present resolution;

58. *Decides* to include in the provisional agenda of its fifty-ninth session, under the item entitled "Oceans and the law of the sea", a sub-item entitled "Sustainable fisheries, including through the 1995 Agreement for the Implementation of the Provisions of the United Nations Convention on the Law of the Sea of 10 December 1982 relating to the Conservation and Management of Straddling Fish Stocks and Highly Migratory Fish Stocks, and related instruments".

Institutions created by the Convention

International Seabed Authority

Through the International Seabed Authority, established by UNCLOS and the 1994 Implementation Agreement [YUN 1994, p. 1301], States organized and conducted exploration of the resources of the seabed and ocean floor and subsoil beyond the limits of national jurisdiction. In 2003, the Authority, which had 145 members as at 31 December, held its ninth annual session (Kingston, Jamaica, 28 July-8 August) [ISBA/10/A/3]. Its subsidiary bodies, namely, the Assembly, the Council, the Legal and Technical Commission and the Finance Committee, also met during the session.

The Assembly considered the report of the Authority's Secretary-General covering July 2002 to June 2003 [ISBA/9/A/3], who indicated that, in view of the increasing technical emphasis in the Authority's work, he had begun developing a comprehensive three-year work plan to incorporate a review of existing staff positions and job descriptions and detailed budgetary implications of planned training programmes, with a view to strengthening the secretariat's technical expertise in marine scientific research. He would keep the pattern of meetings under review to ensure that it met the requirements of the various organs and bodies involved and represented the most efficient mechanism for carrying out the necessary technical work.

The Legal and Technical Commission, reporting to the Council on its work during the current session [ISBA/9/C/4], acknowledged that, from its evaluation of the first set of annual (2002) reports by the seven contractors engaged in the exploration for polymetallic nodules, the contractors had taken note of the format and structure recommended by the Commission [YUN 2002, p. 1321]. It stated that, of the second set of annual reports due by the end of March, five had been received as at 10 June. The Council noted the Commission's progress in formulating draft rules, regulations and procedures for the prospecting and exploration of polymetallic sulphides and cobalt-rich ferromanganese crusts in the Area (the seabed area beyond the limits of national jurisdiction), including regulations for the protection and preservation of the marine environment during those operations. The Council further noted the need for a flexible approach, given the lack of scientific knowledge relating to deep sea ecosystems, and for any proposed regulations to be consistent with the existing regulatory regime for polymetallic nodules [YUN 2000, p. 1257].

On 31 May, the 1998 Protocol on the Privileges and Immunities of the International Seabed Authority [YUN 1998, p. 1226] entered into force, following the accession to it of the tenth member of the Authority, Nigeria.

In a ceremony at the Authority's headquarters on 17 December, the Supplementary Agreement between the Authority and the Government of Jamaica regarding the headquarters of the Authority and the use of the Jamaica Conference Centre complex was signed. Negotiations towards the Agreement, begun in 2000 [YUN 2000, p. 1257], concluded in November. The Agreement, to be applied provisionally upon signature, would enter into force upon its approval by the Assembly of the Authority and the Government of Jamaica.

International Tribunal for the Law of the Sea

The International Tribunal for the Law of the Sea held its fifteenth (10-21 March) and sixteenth (8-19 September) sessions at its seat in Hamburg, Germany [SPLOS/109].

The Tribunal met from 20 September to 8 October to deal with the *Case concerning Land Reclamation by Singapore in and around the Straits of Johor (Malaysia v. Singapore)*. The judicial deliberations in the case were held in conjunction with the Tribunal's September session. On 5 September, Malaysia submitted a request for the prescription of provisional measures under article 290, paragraph 5, pending the constitution of an arbitral tribunal to be established under annex VII to the Convention. A copy of a 4 July document instituting arbitral proceedings against Singapore accompanied the request, which was entered in the list of cases as Case No. 12. Pursuant to article 17, paragraph 3, of the statute, Malaysia nominated Kamal Hossain and Singapore nominated Bernard H. Oxman as judges ad hoc, who were admitted to participate in the case. By a 10 September Order, the Tribunal fixed 25 September for the opening of the hearing. On 20 September, Singapore filed its response. On 24 September, prior to the opening of the hearing, the Tribunal held initial deliberations. At five public sittings on 25, 26 and 27 September, the Tribunal heard oral arguments from the parties and their final submissions at the end of the hearing. On 8 October, the Tribunal delivered its Order.

In the *Case concerning the Conservation and Sustainable Exploitation of Swordfish Stocks in the South-Eastern Pacific Ocean (Chile/European Community)*, the Tribunal considered the requests of Chile and the European Community dated 31 October and 11 November, respectively, to continue suspension of the time limit for a further two years. By an order of 16 December, the Tribunal extended the time limit for making preliminary objections until 1 January 2006.

The thirteenth Meeting of States Parties to the Convention approved the Tribunal's proposed 2004 budget in the amount of $8,039,000.

Commission on the Limits of the Continental Shelf

In 2003, the Commission on the Limits of the Continental Shelf, established in 1997 [YUN 1997, p. 1362], held its twelfth session (New York, 28 April–2 May) [CLCS/36]. Its thirteenth session, scheduled for 25 to 29 August, was not held as no submission from a coastal State had been received by 25 May.

At the twelfth session, the Commission considered a number of items to facilitate the process of dealing with coastal States' submissions regarding the establishment of the outer limits of the continental shelf beyond 200 nautical miles, including a review of its procedural and organizational documents with a view to aligning their provisions. It decided that the operational provisions contained in its modus operandi would be combined with the internal procedure of the subcommissions set up to examine submissions into one document, and to make only editorial amendments to its Rules of Procedure and reissue it as a separate document. To address concerns of confidentiality in connection with the need of States for information and data contained in coastal States' submissions and relevant Commission recommendations, the Commission decided that its recommendations should include an executive summary containing a general description of the extended continental shelf and a set of coordinates to identify the line describing the outer limits recommended by the Commission and illustrative charts, if appropriate. The Secretary-General would then be in a position to publicize the summary at his discretion, without causing prejudice to confidentiality requirements. Also considered was the status of the training manual to assist States in preparing submissions in respect of the outer limits of the continental shelf, for which a master plan had already been prepared by the two coordinators who were members of the Commission.

Other developments related to the Convention

In response to General Assembly resolution 57/141 [YUN 2002, p. 1322], the Secretary-General submitted a March report with later addendum on oceans and the law of the sea [A/58/65 & Add.1], in which he described the status of UNCLOS and its two implementing Agreements and discussed issues related to maritime space; safety of navigation; crimes at sea; marine resources, the marine environment and sustainable development; marine science and technology; settlement of disputes; and international cooperation and coordination.

According to the report, issues dominating discussions in several forums in the area of navigation were the accelerated phase-out of single-hull oil tankers, the transport of dangerous goods by sea, coastal States' jurisdiction, capacity-building for the production of nautical charts, flag State implementation and enforcement, ports of refuge, the provision of a place of safety for persons rescued at sea, and the freedom of movement of seafarers balanced against security concerns. Urgent action to ensure the effective conservation and sustainable use of marine and coastal biodiversity was underscored. So was the role of the International Maritime Organization in establishing international rules and standards for the prevention, reduction and control of marine environment pollution from vessels (see p. 1529) and in providing a forum for the consideration of new measures, such as the designation of a large area off the coasts of several Western European countries as a particularly sensitive sea area.

The Secretary-General considered it necessary for all States to ratify or accede to UNCLOS and its implementing Agreements and to the many other agreements giving substance and detail to the basic UNCLOS principles; to implement those agreements in their national laws and administrative structures; and actively to apply and enforce those laws and regulations. It was essential to reinforce the control of flag States over their vessels and to ensure that States did not register any vessels unless they had a truly effective means of enforcing on them all the relevant international rules and standards. To enhance and facilitate inter-agency cooperation, a flexible and transparent mechanism needed to be established to review ongoing ocean-related work in each agency, fund and programme, and to prepare coordinated responses to emerging challenges or urgent issues; it should work within UN established structures, such as the United Nations System Chief Executives Board for Coordination and its High-level Committee on Programmes. Mindful that the annual report on oceans and the law of the sea could play a role in facilitating international coordination and cooperation, the Secretary-General proposed submitting two separate reports to the Assembly: one, to be prepared in time for the meeting of the United Nations Open-ended Informal Consultative Process on Oceans and the Law of the Sea (see p. 1355), would report on the areas of focus recommended by the Assembly and on international coordination and cooperation; the other, to be prepared for the Assembly's consideration under the agenda item on oceans and the law of the sea, would provide the traditional

Marine environment: reporting and assessment

In response to General Assembly resolution 57/141 [YUN 2002, p. 1322], the Secretary-General submitted an October report [A/58/423] providing an overview of the main developments concerning the proposed establishment of a regular process for the reporting and assessment of the state of the marine environment, including socioeconomic aspects, that would build on ongoing assessments. The report focused on steps towards such a process and reflected some of the discussions on global marine assessment (GMA) at an inter-agency consultative meeting of the Intergovernmental Oceanographic Commission of the United Nations Educational, Scientific and Cultural Organization (Paris, 8-9 September).

The report concluded that: the GMA process should operate under the authority of the General Assembly; capacity-building would be among its essential elements; funding required to support a secretariat and a global scientific panel could be considerable and would also have to cover preparatory work to establish the process; the organizational model proposed by the Joint Group of Experts on the Scientific Aspects of Marine Environmental Protection (GESAMP) appeared the most compelling; and the status of GESAMP as an existing inter-agency mechanism and its long-standing experience (since its founding in 1967) in marine assessment qualified it for a leading role in the global scientific panel. Although enough preparatory work had already been done, the practical modalities involved were complex and required further expert consideration.

United Nations Open-ended Informal Consultative Process

Pursuant to General Assembly resolution 57/141 [YUN 2002, p. 1322], the fourth meeting of the United Nations Open-ended Informal Consultative Process on Oceans and the Law of the Sea (New York, 2-6 June) [A/58/95] focused its discussions on the protection of vulnerable marine ecosystems and on the safety of navigation. In that regard, and also with respect to Assembly resolutions 57/142 [ibid., p. 1058] and 57/143 [ibid., p. 1318], the Consultative Process presented proposals for the Assembly's consideration.

Established by Assembly resolution 54/33 [YUN 1999, p. 994] to facilitate the Assembly's annual review of developments in ocean affairs, the Consultative Process, in 2003, began the new three-year period for which it had been extended by Assembly resolution 57/141. It noted that the period since its third (2002) meeting had seen a heightened awareness of oceans issues, with the observation of the twentieth anniversary of the opening for signature of UNCLOS [YUN 2002, p. 1316] and the convening of the 2002 World Summit on Sustainable Development [ibid., p. 821].

GENERAL ASSEMBLY ACTION

On 23 December [meeting 79], the General Assembly adopted **resolution 58/240** [draft: A/58/L.19 & Add.1] by recorded vote (156-1-2) [agenda item 52 (a)].

Oceans and the law of the sea

The General Assembly,

Recalling its resolutions 49/28 of 6 December 1994, 52/26 of 26 November 1997, 54/33 of 24 November 1999, 57/141 of 12 December 2002 and other relevant resolutions adopted subsequent to the entry into force of the United Nations Convention on the Law of the Sea ("the Convention") on 16 November 1994,

Emphasizing the universal and unified character of the Convention and its fundamental importance for the maintenance and strengthening of international peace and security, as well as for the sustainable development of the oceans and seas,

Reaffirming that the Convention sets out the legal framework within which all activities in the oceans and seas must be carried out and is of strategic importance as the basis for national, regional and global action and cooperation in the marine sector, and that its integrity needs to be maintained, as recognized also by the United Nations Conference on Environment and Development in chapter 17 of Agenda 21,

Conscious that the problems of ocean space are closely interrelated and need to be considered as a whole through an integrated, interdisciplinary and intersectoral approach,

Convinced of the need, building on arrangements established in accordance with the Convention, to improve coordination at the national level and cooperation and coordination at both intergovernmental and inter-agency levels, in order to address all aspects of oceans and seas in an integrated manner,

Recognizing the important role that the competent international organizations have in relation to ocean affairs, in implementing the Convention and in promoting the sustainable development of the oceans and seas,

Recalling the essential role of international cooperation and coordination in promoting the integrated management and sustainable development of the oceans and seas, and recalling also that the role of international cooperation and coordination on a bilateral basis and, where applicable, within a subregional, regional, interregional or global framework is to support and supplement the national efforts of all States, including coastal States, in promoting the implementation and observance of the Convention and the integrated management and sustainable development of coastal and marine areas,

Underlining once again the essential need for capacity-building to ensure that all States, especially developing countries, in particular least developed countries and small island developing States, as well as coastal African States, are able both to implement the Convention and to benefit from the sustainable development of the oceans and seas,

Underlining the essential need for capacity-building to ensure that all States, especially developing countries, in particular least developed countries and small island developing States, are able to participate fully in global and regional forums and processes dealing with oceans and law of the sea issues,

Emphasizing the need to strengthen the ability of competent international organizations to contribute, at the global, regional, subregional and bilateral levels, including through cooperation programmes with Governments, to the development of national and local capacity in marine science and the sustainable management of oceans and their resources,

Recalling the recommendations of the World Summit on Sustainable Development, including to establish by 2004 a regular process under the United Nations for global reporting and assessment of the state of the marine environment, including socio-economic aspects, both current and foreseeable, building on existing regional assessments, and the decision of the General Assembly in its resolution 57/141 to establish such a process by 2004,

Reiterating its deep concern at the situation of many of the world's fisheries, caused principally by overcapacity, overfishing and illegal, unregulated and unreported fishing, as well as, in many areas, pollution,

Reiterating its concern at the adverse impacts on the marine environment, in particular on vulnerable marine ecosystems, including coral, of human activities, such as overutilization of living marine resources, the use of destructive fishing practices, physical impacts by ships, the introduction of alien invasive species and marine pollution from all sources, including from land-based sources and vessels, in particular through the illegal release of oil and other harmful substances and from dumping, including the dumping of hazardous waste such as radioactive materials, nuclear waste and dangerous chemicals,

Recognizing that hydrographic surveys and nautical charting are critical to the safety of navigation and life at sea, environmental protection, including vulnerable marine ecosystems and the economics of the global shipping industry, and recognizing in this regard that the move towards electronic charting not only provides significantly increased benefits for safe navigation and management of ship movement, but also provides data and information that can be used for sustainable fisheries activities and other sectoral uses of the marine environment, the delimitation of maritime boundaries and environmental protection,

Welcoming the convening by the International Atomic Energy Agency of the International Conference on the Safety of Transport of Radioactive Material, as well as the outcomes of the Conference, which provided an opportunity for States to address issues relating to the transport of radioactive materials, including by sea,

Taking note of the report of the Secretary-General, and emphasizing in this regard the critical role of the annual comprehensive report of the Secretary-General, which integrates information on developments relating to the implementation of the Convention and the work of the Organization, its specialized agencies and other institutions in the field of ocean affairs and the law of the sea at the global and regional levels, and as a result constitutes the basis for the annual consideration and review of developments relating to ocean affairs and the law of the sea by the General Assembly as the global institution having the competence to undertake such a review,

Taking note also of the report on the work of the United Nations Open-ended Informal Consultative Process on Oceans and the Law of the Sea ("the Consultative Process"), established by the General Assembly in its resolution 54/33 in order to facilitate the annual review by the Assembly of developments in ocean affairs, at its fourth meeting,

Noting the responsibilities of the Secretary-General under the Convention and related resolutions of the General Assembly, in particular resolutions 49/28, 52/26 and 54/33, and in this context the expected increase in responsibilities of the Division for Ocean Affairs and the Law of the Sea of the Office of Legal Affairs of the Secretariat in view of the anticipated receipt of submissions from States to the Commission on the Limits of the Continental Shelf ("the Commission"), in addition to the expected growing involvement of the Division with new developments such as the regular process for global reporting and assessment of the state of the marine environment, including socio-economic aspects, and with requests for technical assistance from States, and the role of the Division in inter-agency coordination and cooperation,

I
Implementation of the Convention and related agreements and instruments

1. *Calls upon* all States that have not done so, in order to achieve the goal of universal participation, to become parties to the Convention and the Agreement relating to the Implementation of Part XI of the United Nations Convention on the Law of the Sea of 10 December 1982 ("the Agreement");

2. *Reaffirms* the unified character of the Convention;

3. *Calls upon* States that have not done so to become parties to the Agreement for the Implementation of the Provisions of the United Nations Convention on the Law of the Sea of 10 December 1982 relating to the Conservation and Management of Straddling Fish Stocks and Highly Migratory Fish Stocks;

4. *Once again calls upon* States to harmonize, as a matter of priority, their national legislation with the provisions of the Convention, to ensure the consistent application of those provisions and to ensure also that any declarations or statements that they have made or make when signing, ratifying or acceding to the Convention are in conformity therewith and, otherwise, to withdraw any of their declarations or statements that are not in conformity;

5. *Encourages* States parties to the Convention to deposit with the Secretary-General charts and lists of geographical coordinates, as provided for in the Convention;

6. *Emphasizes* the essential need to improve the implementation of international agreements referred to in article 311 of the Convention and, where appropriate, to foster the conditions for the application of in-

struments of a voluntary nature, and recalls the important role of international organizations in achieving these goals;

II
Meeting of States Parties

7. *Takes note* of the report of the thirteenth Meeting of States Parties to the Convention;

8. *Requests* the Secretary-General to convene the fourteenth Meeting of States Parties to the Convention in New York from 14 to 18 June 2004 and to provide the services required;

III
Settlement of disputes

9. *Notes with satisfaction* the continued contribution of the International Tribunal for the Law of the Sea ("the Tribunal") to the peaceful settlement of disputes in accordance with Part XV of the Convention, underlines the important role and authority of the Tribunal concerning the interpretation or application of the Convention and the Agreement, once again encourages States parties to the Convention that have not yet done so to consider making a written declaration choosing from the means set out in article 287 for the settlement of disputes concerning the interpretation or application of the Convention and the Agreement, and invites States parties to note the provisions of annexes V, VI, VII and VIII to the Convention concerning, respectively, conciliation, the Tribunal, arbitration and special arbitration;

10. *Equally pays tribute* to the important and long-standing role of the International Court of Justice with regard to the peaceful settlement of disputes concerning the law of the sea;

11. *Recalls* the obligation under article 296 of the Convention requiring all parties to a dispute before a court or a tribunal referred to in article 287 of the Convention to comply promptly with any decisions rendered by such court or tribunal;

12. *Encourages* States parties to the Convention that have not yet done so to nominate conciliators and arbitrators in accordance with annexes V and VII to the Convention, and requests the Secretary-General to continue to update and circulate lists of these conciliators and arbitrators on a regular basis;

IV
The Area

13. *Notes* the progress of the discussion of issues relating to the regulations for prospecting and exploration for polymetallic sulphides and cobalt-rich crusts in the Area;

14. *Reiterates* the importance of the ongoing elaboration by the International Seabed Authority ("the Authority"), pursuant to article 145 of the Convention, of rules, regulations and procedures to ensure the effective protection of the marine environment, the protection and conservation of the natural resources of the Area and the prevention of damage to its flora and fauna from harmful effects that may arise from activities in the Area;

V
Effective functioning of the Authority and the Tribunal

15. *Appeals* to all States parties to the Convention to pay their assessed contributions to the Authority and to the Tribunal in full and on time, and appeals also to all former provisional members of the Authority to pay any outstanding contributions;

16. *Calls upon* States that have not done so to consider ratifying or acceding to the Agreement on the Privileges and Immunities of the Tribunal and to the Protocol on the Privileges and Immunities of the Authority;

VI
The continental shelf and the work of the Commission

17. *Encourages* States parties that are in a position to do so to make every effort to make submissions regarding the establishment of the outer limits of the continental shelf beyond 200 nautical miles to the Commission within the time period established by the Convention, taking into account the decision of the eleventh Meeting of States Parties to the Convention;

18. *Approves* the convening by the Secretary-General of the thirteenth session of the Commission in New York from 26 to 30 April 2004, followed by two weeks of meetings of a subcommission in the event that a submission is made to the Commission, and of the fourteenth session of the Commission from 30 August to 3 September 2004, also followed by two weeks of meetings of a subcommission in the event that a submission is made;

19. *Encourages* States and relevant international organizations and institutions to consider developing and making available training courses to assist developing States in the preparation of such submissions, based on the outline for a five-day training course prepared by the Commission in order to facilitate the preparation of submissions in accordance with its Scientific and Technical Guidelines;

VII
Capacity-building

20. *Calls upon* bilateral and multilateral donor agencies and international financial institutions to keep their programmes systematically under review to ensure the availability in all States, particularly in developing States, of the economic, legal, navigational, scientific and technical skills necessary for the full implementation of the Convention and the objectives of the present resolution as well as the sustainable development of the oceans and seas nationally, regionally and globally, and in so doing to bear in mind the rights of landlocked developing States;

21. *Calls upon* States and international financial institutions, including through bilateral, regional and global cooperation programmes and technical partnerships, to continue to strengthen capacity-building activities, in particular in developing countries, in the field of marine scientific research by, inter alia, training the necessary skilled personnel, providing the necessary equipment, facilities and vessels, and transferring environmentally sound technologies;

22. *Encourages* States to assist developing States, and especially least developed States and small island developing States, as well as coastal African States, on a bilateral and, where appropriate, regional level, in the preparation of submissions to the Commission, including the assessment of the nature of the continental shelf of a coastal State made in the form of a desktop study, and the mapping of the outer limits of its continental shelf;

VIII
Safety of navigation and flag State implementation

23. *Encourages* States to ratify or accede to international agreements addressing the safety of navigation and to adopt the necessary measures consistent with the Convention, aimed at implementing and enforcing the rules contained in those agreements;

24. *Urges* States and regional economic integration organizations to work within the framework of the International Maritime Organization and in accordance with the Convention and international rules and regulations regarding measures related to the phase-out of single-hull tankers, and welcomes the organization's giving priority to the consideration of any proposals related thereto;

25. *Welcomes* the work of the International Maritime Organization in developing guidelines on places of refuge for ships in need of assistance, and encourages States to draw up plans and to establish procedures to implement those guidelines for ships in waters under their jurisdiction;

26. *Also welcomes* the adoption by the General Conference of the International Atomic Energy Agency at its forty-seventh session of resolution GC(47)/RES/7, concerning measures to strengthen international cooperation in nuclear, radiation and transport safety and waste management, including those aspects relating to maritime transport safety, in which it requested the Agency to develop an action plan, in consultation with its member States and for approval by the Board of the Agency, if possible in March 2004, based on the results of the International Conference on the Safety of Transport of Radioactive Material and within the competence of the Agency;

27. *Urges* flag States without an effective maritime administration and appropriate legal frameworks to establish or enhance the necessary infrastructure, legislative and enforcement capabilities to ensure effective compliance with, and implementation and enforcement of, their responsibilities under international law and, until such action is undertaken, to consider declining the granting of the right to fly their flag to new vessels, suspending their registry or not opening a registry;

28. *Invites* the International Maritime Organization and other relevant competent international organizations to study, examine and clarify the role of the "genuine link" in relation to the duty of flag States to exercise effective control over ships flying their flag, including fishing vessels;

29. *Requests* the Secretary-General, in cooperation and consultation with relevant agencies, organizations and programmes of the United Nations system, to prepare and disseminate to States a comprehensive elaboration of the duties and obligations of flag States, including the potential consequences for non-compliance prescribed in the relevant international instruments;

30. *Encourages* the acceleration of the work of the International Maritime Organization in developing a voluntary model audit scheme, and urges the organization to strengthen its draft implementation code;

31. *Welcomes* the work of the Food and Agriculture Organization of the United Nations in promoting compliance by States and their fishing vessels with conservation and management measures, and requests the International Maritime Organization and the Food and Agriculture Organization to enhance their cooperation and coordination in their efforts with regard to flag State duties relating thereto, including through the Inter-Agency Consultative Group on Flag State Implementation during the period of the Group's existence;

32. *Also welcomes* the work of the International Labour Organization to consolidate and modernize international maritime labour standards, and calls upon Member States to take an active interest in the development of these new standards for seafarers and fishers;

33. *Recognizes* the important role of port State controls in promoting the effective enforcement by flag States of, and compliance by shipowners and charterers with, flag States' and internationally agreed safety, labour and pollution standards, as well as maritime security regulations and conservation and management measures, and further encourages Member States to improve the exchange of appropriate information between port States control authorities;

34. *Invites* the International Maritime Organization to strengthen its functions with regard to port State control in relation to safety and pollution standards as well as maritime security regulations and, in collaboration with the International Labour Organization, labour standards so as to promote the implementation of globally agreed minimum standards by all States, and invites the Food and Agriculture Organization of the United Nations to continue its work in promoting port State measures in relation to fishing vessels in order to combat illegal, unreported and unregulated fishing;

35. *Calls upon* flag and port States to take all measures consistent with international law necessary to prevent the operation of sub-standard vessels and illegal, unreported and unregulated fishing activities;

36. *Urges* all States, in cooperation with the International Maritime Organization, to combat piracy and armed robbery at sea by adopting measures, including those relating to assistance with capacity-building through training of seafarers, port staff and enforcement personnel in the prevention, reporting and investigation of incidents, bringing the alleged perpetrators to justice, in accordance with international law, and by adopting national legislation, as well as providing enforcement vessels and equipment and guarding against fraudulent ship registration;

37. *Calls upon* all States and relevant international bodies to cooperate in the prevention and combating of piracy and armed robbery at sea, and urges States to give urgent attention to promoting, concluding and implementing cooperation agreements, in particular at the regional level and in high-risk areas;

38. *Urges* States to become parties to the Convention for the Suppression of Unlawful Acts against the Safety of Maritime Navigation and its Protocol, invites States to participate in the review of those instruments by the Legal Committee of the International Maritime Organization to strengthen the means of combating such unlawful acts, including terrorist acts, and further urges States to take appropriate measures to ensure the effective implementation of those instruments, in particular through the adoption of legislation, where appropriate, aimed at ensuring that there is a proper framework for responses to incidents of armed robbery and terrorist acts at sea;

39. *Calls upon* States to work together cooperatively and with the International Maritime Organization to

strengthen measures to prevent the embarkation of ships involved in the smuggling of migrants;

40. *Once again urges* States that have not yet done so to become parties to the Protocol against the Smuggling of Migrants by Land, Sea and Air, supplementing the United Nations Convention against Transnational Organized Crime, and to take appropriate measures to ensure its effective implementation;

41. *Welcomes* the work of the International Maritime Organization in developing amendments to the International Convention for the Safety of Life at Sea and to the International Convention on Maritime Search and Rescue on the delivery of persons rescued at sea to a place of safety;

IX
Capacity-building for the production of nautical charts

42. *Welcomes* the work of the International Hydrographic Organization and its fourteen regional hydrographic commissions and encourages increased membership of the organization, noting the capacity of the organization to provide technical assistance, facilitate training and identify potential funding sources for the development or improvement of hydrographic services, and calls upon States and agencies to support the trust fund of the organization and examine the possibility of partnerships with the private sector;

43. *Invites* the International Hydrographic Organization and the International Maritime Organization to continue their coordinated efforts, to jointly adopt measures with a view to encouraging greater international cooperation and coordination for the transition to electronic nautical charts and to increase the coverage of hydrographic information on a global basis, especially in the areas of international navigation and ports and where there are vulnerable or protected marine areas;

44. *Encourages* intensified efforts to build capacity for developing countries, in particular for the least developed countries and small island developing States, as well as coastal African States, to improve hydrographic services and the production of nautical charts, including the mobilization of resources and building of capacity with support from international financial institutions and the donor community, recognizing that economies of scale can apply in some instances at the regional level through shared facilities, technical capabilities and information for the provision of hydrographic services and the preparation of and access to nautical charts;

45. *Welcomes* the adoption of criteria and guidelines on the transfer of marine technology by the Intergovernmental Oceanographic Commission;

X
Marine environment, marine resources and the protection of vulnerable marine ecosystems

46. *Emphasizes once again* the importance of the implementation of Part XII of the Convention in order to protect and preserve the marine environment and its living marine resources against pollution and physical degradation, and calls upon all States to cooperate and take measures, directly or through competent international organizations, for the protection and preservation of the marine environment;

47. *Calls upon* States to continue to prioritize action on marine pollution from land-based sources as part of their national sustainable development strategies and programmes, in an integrated and inclusive manner, as a means of implementing the Global Programme of Action for the Protection of the Marine Environment from Land-based Activities;

48. *Welcomes* the continued work of States, the United Nations Environment Programme and regional organizations in the implementation of the Global Programme of Action for the Protection of the Marine Environment from Land-based Activities, and encourages increased emphasis on the link between freshwater, the coastal zone and marine resources in the implementation of the Millennium Development Goals, taking into account the time-bound targets in the Plan of Implementation of the World Summit on Sustainable Development ("Johannesburg Plan of Implementation"), in particular the target on sanitation, and the Monterrey Consensus of the International Conference on Financing for Development;

49. *Calls upon* States to advance the implementation of the Global Programme of Action for the Protection of the Marine Environment from Land-based Activities and the Montreal Declaration on the Protection of the Marine Environment from Land-based Activities, to enhance maritime safety and the protection of the marine environment from pollution and other physical impacts, and to improve the scientific understanding and assessment of marine and coastal ecosystems as a fundamental basis for sound decision-making through the actions identified in the Johannesburg Plan of Implementation;

50. *Welcomes* the work of the Convention on Biological Diversity, the Food and Agriculture Organization of the United Nations and other relevant global and regional organizations in the development of strategies and programmes for the implementation of an integrated ecosystem-based approach to management, and urges those organizations to cooperate in the development of practical guidance in this regard;

51. *Reiterates its call* for urgent consideration of ways to integrate and improve, on a scientific basis, the management of risks to the marine biodiversity of seamounts, cold water coral reefs and certain other underwater features;

52. *Invites* the relevant global and regional bodies, in accordance with their mandates, to investigate urgently how to better address, on a scientific basis, including the application of precaution, the threats and risks to vulnerable and threatened marine ecosystems and biodiversity in areas beyond national jurisdiction; how existing treaties and other relevant instruments can be used in this process consistent with international law, in particular with the Convention, and with the principles of an integrated ecosystem-based approach to management, including the identification of those marine ecosystem types that warrant priority attention; and to explore a range of potential approaches and tools for their protection and management; and requests the Secretary-General to cooperate and liaise with those bodies and to submit an addendum to his annual report to the General Assembly at its fifty-ninth session, describing the threats and risks to such marine ecosystems and biodiversity in areas beyond national jurisdiction as well as details on any conservation and management measures in place at the global, regional, subregional or national levels addressing these issues;

53. *Notes* the scientific and technical work under the Convention on Biological Diversity relating to marine and coastal biodiversity;

54. *Reaffirms* the efforts of States to develop and facilitate the use of diverse approaches and tools for conserving and managing vulnerable marine ecosystems, including the establishment of marine protected areas, consistent with international law and based on the best scientific information available, and the development of representative networks of such marine protected areas by 2012;

55. *Encourages* States, in accordance with the Convention and other relevant instruments, either bilaterally or regionally, to jointly develop and promote contingency plans for responding to pollution incidents, as well as other incidents that are likely to have significant adverse effects on marine biodiversity;

56. *Urges* States and relevant global and regional bodies to enhance their cooperation in the protection and preservation of coral reefs, mangroves and seagrass beds, including through the exchange of information;

57. *Reiterates its support* for the International Coral Reef Initiative and welcomes the outcomes of the Second International Tropical Marine Ecosystems Management Symposium, held in Manila in 2003, supports the work under the Jakarta Mandate on the Conservation and Sustainable Use of Marine and Coastal Biological Diversity, and notes that the International Coral Reef Initiative and other relevant bodies are considering incorporating cold water coral ecosystems into their programmes of activities;

58. *Encourages* States to cooperate, directly or through competent international bodies, in exchanging information in the event of accidents involving foreign vessels on coral reefs, and in promoting the development of economic assessment techniques for both restoration and non-use values of coral reef systems;

59. *Emphasizes* the need to mainstream coral reef management approaches into national development strategies, as well as into the activities of relevant United Nations agencies and programmes, international financial institutions and the donor community;

60. *Welcomes* the convening by the International Maritime Organization of a diplomatic conference to adopt an international convention for the control and management of ships' ballast waters and sediments;

61. *Notes with interest* the ongoing discussions in the Marine Environment Protection Committee of the International Maritime Organization on the designation of the Western European Atlantic coast and the English Channel as a particularly sensitive sea area, and encourages the organization to consider the eventual adoption of the proposed associated protective measure as long as it is consistent with the Convention;

XI
Regional cooperation

62. *Emphasizes once again* the importance of regional organizations and arrangements for cooperation and coordination in integrated oceans management, and, where there are separate regional structures for different aspects of oceans management, such as environmental protection, fisheries management, navigation, scientific research and maritime delimitation, calls for those different structures, where appropriate, to work together for optimal cooperation and coordination;

63. *Notes* that there have been a number of initiatives at the regional level, in various regions, to further the implementation of the Convention, and in this context notes the results of the Second Plenary Meeting of the Conference on Maritime Delimitation in the Caribbean, held in Mexico City on 13 and 14 October 2003, as well as of the functioning of its Caribbean-focused Assistance Fund, which is intended to facilitate, mainly through technical assistance, the voluntary undertaking of maritime delimitation negotiations between Caribbean States, takes note once again of the Fund for Peace: Peaceful Settlement of Territorial Disputes established by the General Assembly of the Organization of American States in 2000 as a primary mechanism, given its broader regional scope, for the prevention and resolution of pending territorial, land border and maritime boundary disputes, and calls upon States and others in a position to do so to contribute to these Funds;

XII
Regular process for global reporting and assessment of the state of the marine environment, including socio-economic aspects

64. *Welcomes* the report of the Secretary-General containing proposals on modalities for the establishment of a regular process under the United Nations for global reporting and assessment of the state of the marine environment, including socio-economic aspects, and requests the Secretary-General, in close collaboration with Member States, relevant organizations and agencies and programmes of the United Nations system, other competent intergovernmental organizations and relevant non-governmental organizations, to take the following steps to establish the regular process by 2004:

(*a*) Convene a group of experts of no more than twenty-four participants, comprising representatives of States, including all regional groups, and representatives from intergovernmental organizations and non-governmental organizations, including scientists and policy makers, to produce, including by possibly hiring a consultant, a draft document with details on the scope, general framework and outline of the regular process, peer review, secretariat, capacity-building and funding, and to consider, review and refine the draft document;

(*b*) Transmit the draft document to States and relevant intergovernmental organizations, non-governmental organizations, scientific associations, funding mechanisms and other parties for written comments and for indication of specific issues to be addressed in the first assessment;

(*c*) Request the group of experts to revise the draft document in the light of comments made;

(*d*) Convene an international workshop with representatives from all interested parties, in conjunction with the fifth meeting of the Consultative Process, to further consider and review the draft document;

(*e*) Convene an intergovernmental meeting to finalize and adopt the document and to formally establish the regular process;

65. *Accepts* the offer of the Government of Iceland to host this intergovernmental meeting in Reykjavik in 2004, in accordance with paragraph 17 of resolution 47/202 A of 22 December 1992;

66. *Requests* the Secretary-General to report to the General Assembly at its fifty-ninth session on the development of the regular process;

XIII
Open-ended informal consultative process on oceans and the law of the sea

67. *Requests* the Secretary-General to convene the fifth meeting of the Consultative Process in New York from 7 to 11 June 2004, and to provide it with the necessary facilities for the performance of its work and to arrange for support to be provided by the Division for Ocean Affairs and the Law of the Sea, in cooperation with other relevant parts of the Secretariat, including the Division for Sustainable Development of the Department of Economic and Social Affairs, as appropriate;

68. *Recommends* that, in its deliberations on the report of the Secretary-General on oceans and the law of the sea at its meeting, the Consultative Process should organize its discussions around the following areas:

New sustainable uses of the oceans, including the conservation and management of the biological diversity of the seabed in areas beyond national jurisdiction;

as well as issues discussed at previous meetings;

XIV
Inter-agency coordination and cooperation

69. *Reiterates its request* to the Secretary-General to establish an effective, transparent and regular inter-agency coordinating mechanism for issues relating to oceans and seas within the United Nations system, taking into account paragraph 49 of Part A of the report of the Consultative Process at its third meeting;

70. *Requests* the Secretary-General to bring the present resolution to the attention of heads of intergovernmental organizations, the specialized agencies and funds and programmes of the United Nations engaged in activities relating to ocean affairs and the law of the sea, drawing their attention to paragraphs of particular relevance to them, and underlines the importance of their constructive and timely input for the report of the Secretary-General on oceans and the law of the sea and of their participation in relevant meetings and processes;

71. *Invites* the competent international organizations, as well as funding institutions, to take specific account of the present resolution in their programmes and activities and to contribute to the preparation of the comprehensive report of the Secretary-General on oceans and the law of the sea;

XV
Activities of the Division for Ocean Affairs and the Law of the Sea

72. *Expresses its appreciation* to the Secretary-General for the annual comprehensive report on oceans and the law of the sea, prepared by the Division for Ocean Affairs and the Law of the Sea, as well as for the other activities of the Division, in accordance with the provisions of the Convention and the mandate set forth in resolutions 49/28, 52/26, 54/33 and 56/12 of 28 November 2001;

73. *Requests* the Secretary-General to continue to carry out the responsibilities entrusted to him in the Convention and related resolutions of the General Assembly, including resolutions 49/28 and 52/26, and to ensure that appropriate resources are made available to the Division for Ocean Affairs and the Law of the Sea for the performance of such responsibilities under the approved budget for the Organization;

74. *Invites* Member States and others in a position to do so to support the training activities under the TRAIN-SEA-COAST Programme of the Division for Ocean Affairs and the Law of the Sea;

XVI
Trust funds and fellowships

75. *Recognizes* the importance of assisting developing countries, in particular the least developed countries and small island developing States, in implementing the Convention, and urges States, intergovernmental organizations and agencies, national institutions, non-governmental organizations and international financial institutions, as well as natural and juridical persons, to make voluntary financial or other contributions to the trust funds, as referred to in resolution 57/141, established for this purpose;

76. *Also recognizes* the importance of the Trust Fund for preparation of submissions to the Commission in assisting developing States, in particular the least developed countries and small island developing States, in preparing their submissions where their continental shelves extend beyond 200 nautical miles and, in order to facilitate the management of the Trust Fund, amends, as set out in the annex to the present resolution, sections 1, 4 and 6 of the terms of reference, guidelines and rules of the Trust Fund, as contained in annex II to resolution 55/7 of 30 October 2000, in accordance with paragraph 31 of the annex;

77. *Urges* Member States and others in a position to do so to contribute to the further development of the Hamilton Shirley Amerasinghe Memorial Fellowship Programme on the Law of the Sea established by the General Assembly in its resolution 35/116 of 10 December 1980;

XVII
Fifty-ninth session of the General Assembly

78. *Requests* the Secretary-General to report to the General Assembly at its fifty-ninth session on the implementation of the present resolution, including other developments and issues relating to ocean affairs and the law of the sea, in connection with his annual comprehensive report on oceans and the law of the sea, and to provide the report in accordance with the modalities set out in resolutions 49/28, 52/26 and 54/33, and also requests the Secretary-General to make the report available, in its current comprehensive format, at least six weeks in advance of the meeting of the Consultative Process;

79. *Decides* to include in the provisional agenda of its fifty-ninth session the item entitled "Oceans and the law of the sea".

Annex

Amendments to the terms of reference, guidelines and rules of the Trust Fund for the purpose of facilitating the preparation of submissions to the Commission on the Limits of the Continental Shelf for developing States, in particular the least developed countries and small island developing States, and compliance with article 76 of the United Nations Convention on the Law of the Sea

1. Reasons for establishing the Trust Fund

In paragraph 2, amend the last sentence to read:

"The earliest deadline for submission for States is 13 May 2009."

4. Application for financial assistance
In paragraph 17, amend sub-item (a) (iv) to read:
"(iv) The curriculum vitae of the trainees, including their date of birth;"

6. Granting of assistance
Amend paragraph 23 to read:
"23. The Secretary-General will provide financial assistance from the Fund for requests approved on the basis of the evaluation and recommendation of the Division on the advice of the Panel of Experts. Payments will be processed by the Organization in accordance with standard practices."

RECORDED VOTE ON RESOLUTION 58/240:

In favour: Albania, Algeria, Andorra, Angola, Antigua and Barbuda, Argentina, Armenia, Australia, Austria, Azerbaijan, Bahrain, Bangladesh, Belarus, Belgium, Belize, Benin, Bolivia, Bosnia and Herzegovina, Botswana, Brazil, Brunei Darussalam, Bulgaria, Burkina Faso, Burundi, Cambodia, Canada, Cape Verde, Central African Republic, Chile, China, Comoros, Congo, Costa Rica, Côte d'Ivoire, Croatia, Cuba, Cyprus, Czech Republic, Denmark, Djibouti, Dominica, Dominican Republic, Ecuador, Egypt, Eritrea, Estonia, Fiji, Finland, France, Gabon, Gambia, Georgia, Germany, Ghana, Greece, Grenada, Guatemala, Haiti, Honduras, Hungary, Iceland, India, Indonesia, Ireland, Israel, Italy, Jamaica, Japan, Jordan, Kazakhstan, Kenya, Kuwait, Kyrgyzstan, Lao People's Democratic Republic, Latvia, Lebanon, Lesotho, Libyan Arab Jamahiriya, Liechtenstein, Lithuania, Luxembourg, Malawi, Malaysia, Maldives, Mali, Malta, Marshall Islands, Mauritania, Mauritius, Mexico, Micronesia, Monaco, Mongolia, Morocco, Mozambique, Myanmar, Namibia, Nauru, Nepal, Netherlands, New Zealand, Nicaragua, Niger, Nigeria, Norway, Oman, Pakistan, Panama, Papua New Guinea, Paraguay, Peru, Philippines, Poland, Portugal, Qatar, Republic of Korea, Republic of Moldova, Romania, Russian Federation, Saint Lucia, San Marino, Saudi Arabia, Senegal, Serbia and Montenegro, Singapore, Slovakia, Slovenia, Solomon Islands, Somalia, South Africa, Spain, Sri Lanka, Sudan, Suriname, Sweden, Switzerland, Tajikistan, Thailand, The former Yugoslav Republic of Macedonia, Timor-Leste, Togo, Tonga, Trinidad and Tobago, Tunisia, Tuvalu, Uganda, Ukraine, United Arab Emirates, United Kingdom, United Republic of Tanzania, United States, Uruguay, Viet Nam, Yemen, Zambia, Zimbabwe.
Against: Turkey.
Abstaining: Colombia, Venezuela.

Division for Ocean Affairs and the Law of the Sea

During 2003, the Division for Ocean Affairs and the Law of the Sea of the Office of Legal Affairs continued to fulfil its role as the substantive unit of the UN Secretariat responsible for reviewing and monitoring all developments related to the law of the sea and ocean affairs, as well as for the implementation of UNCLOS and related General Assembly resolutions.

Under its TRAIN-SEA-COAST programme [YUN 1998, p. 1232], designed to build in-country capacity to improve skills in integrated coastal and ocean management, the Division conducted three training courses on responsible fisheries in the Pacific islands (June), and on ships' ballast water management (Brazil, 12-16 June).

In December, the eighteenth Hamilton Shirley Amerasinghe Fellowship on the Law of the Sea, established in 1981 [YUN 1981, pp. 130 & 139], was awarded to Fernanda Millicay of Argentina.

Evaluation of programme on law of the sea and ocean affairs

By an April note [E/AC.51/2003/3], the Secretary-General transmitted to the Committee for Programme and Coordination (CPC) the report of the Office of Internal Oversight Services (OIOS) on its in-depth evaluation of the work of the programme on the law of the sea and ocean affairs, implemented since 1992 by the Division for Ocean Affairs and the Law of the Sea (see above), with a focus on the period 1998-2002. OIOS recommended that consultations among secretariats of the treaty system of institutions be held periodically and that the new inter-agency coordinating mechanism on oceans and coastal areas called for by General Assembly resolution 57/141 [YUN 2002, p. 1322] be task-oriented and involve all relevant UN agencies and programmes. It recommended that the Division promote universal acceptance of UNCLOS and its two related Agreements, participate actively in regional seas meetings and action plans, further analyse and synthesize information on new developments in ocean affairs, assess the needs of the readership of its publications to increase their usefulness, and maintain its capacity to fulfil its different responsibilities, taking account of existing specialized expertise throughout the UN system. The Secretary-General took note of the findings of OIOS and concurred with its recommendations. CPC [A/58/16], in approving the recommendations, stated that the annual report on oceans and the law of the sea should neither include assessments of the overall impact of the efforts of the competent organizations nor suggest future activities; rather it should focus on issues pertinent to oceans and seas in a systematic and integrated way.

Chapter V

Other legal questions

The Special Committee on the Charter of the United Nations and on the Strengthening of the Role of the Organization continued in 2003 to consider, among other items, proposals relating to the maintenance of international peace and security in order to strengthen the Organization and the implementation of Charter provisions on assistance to third States affected by the application of sanctions under Chapter VII.

The Committee on Relations with the Host Country continued to address complaints by permanent missions to the United Nations. Matters discussed included delays in issuing visas, transportation problems, security and safety, and travel regulations.

The Ad Hoc Committee on an International Convention against the Reproductive Cloning of Human Beings continued its consideration of the elaboration of a mandate for negotiating an international convention, within the framework of a working group of the Sixth (Legal) Committee.

The United Nations Commission on International Trade Law adopted the Model Legislative Provisions on Privately Financed Infrastructure Projects. In December, the General Assembly took note of the Model and requested the Secretary-General to consolidate that text and the *Legislative Guide on Privately Financed Infrastructure Projects* into a single publication.

In other action, the Assembly approved the guidelines and recommendations proposed by the Secretary-General for the United Nations Programme of Assistance in the Teaching, Study, Dissemination and Wider Appreciation of International Law, and appointed 25 Members to the Programme's Advisory Committee for a four-year period beginning 1 January 2004.

International organizations and international law

Strengthening the role of the United Nations

Special Committee on United Nations Charter

In accordance with General Assembly resolution 57/24 [YUN 2002, p. 1331], the Special Committee on the Charter of the United Nations and on the Strengthening of the Role of the Organization, at its fifty-eighth session (New York, 7-16 April) [A/58/33], continued to consider proposals relating to: the maintenance of international peace and security, according priority to the implementation of the provisions of the Charter of the United Nations on assistance to third States affected by the application of sanctions; the peaceful settlement of disputes between States; the future of the Trusteeship Council; the improvement of the Committee's working methods; and the status of the publications *Repertory of Practice of United Nations Organs* and *Repertoire of the Practice of the Security Council*.

In an exchange of views on the first item, the point was made that the question of sanctions as an effective policy tool to modify the behaviour of a State, entity or group of individuals posing a threat to international peace and security should be addressed in a holistic manner to include their impact on target States. In that connection, support was expressed for the revised working paper submitted by the Russian Federation entitled "Declaration on the basic conditions and standard criteria for the introduction of sanctions and other coercive measures and their implementation". The Committee's working group of the whole completed its first reading of the preamble and operative part of the draft declaration, subject to the amendments proposed, and agreed that the sponsor should prepare a revised version for a second reading.

Support was also expressed for the revised working paper on the strengthening of certain principles concerning the impact and application of sanctions, submitted by the Libyan Arab Jamahiriya [YUN 2002, p. 1329], which said that it complemented the Russian Federation's paper.

Discussions continued on the proposal submitted by the Russian Federation (1998) entitled "Fundamentals of the legal basis for United Nations peacekeeping operations in the context of Chapter VI of the Charter of the United Nations". Its key elements included: a clear definition of the mandate of peacekeeping operations, including humanitarian assistance; establishing the limits to peacekeepers' right to self-defence while strengthening their protection; analysing the mechanism of apportioning responsibility between the United Nations and troop-contributing States for damage caused during peacekeeping operations; and specifying basic peacekeeping principles, including non-interference in the internal affairs of States parties to the conflict, neutrality and impartiality.

The working papers submitted by Cuba (1997 and 1998) entitled "Strengthening the role of the Organization and enhancing its effectiveness" contained proposals aimed at analysing the functions and powers of the General Assembly and Security Council for the maintenance of international peace and security. On the basis of those proposals, Cuba hoped a consensus could be reached on measures to strengthen the relevant provisions of the Charter.

As to the revised proposal submitted by the Libyan Arab Jamahiriya (1998) on strengthening the role of the United Nations in the maintenance of international peace and security, the sponsor noted that it was complementary to Cuba's proposals. It reiterated its concerns over the existing imbalance of powers exercised by the principal UN organs, as underscored by the situation in Iraq (see p. 315), and therefore the importance of the Special Committee's consideration of its revised proposal.

Discussions continued on the revised working paper jointly submitted by Belarus and the Russian Federation (2001) proposing that an advisory opinion be sought from the International Court of Justice (ICJ) on the legal consequences of a State's resort to the use of force without prior Council authorization, except in the exercise of the right to self-defence.

On the peaceful settlement of disputes, the primacy of the principle of free choice of means was emphasized. The Committee noted that recourse to dispute-settlement mechanisms required the disputing parties' consent. In singling out the importance of the judicial settlement of disputes, it stressed the role of ICJ, reaffirmed its authority and emphasized the need to ensure adequacy of its resources.

On the future of the Trusteeship Council, it was reiterated that to abolish it or change its status would be premature, since its existence entailed no financial implications for the United Nations and the purpose for which it had been established remained relevant.

With regard to measures to improve the Special Committee's working methods, a further revised working paper on the subject, submitted by Japan and the Republic of Korea and subsequently co-sponsored by Thailand, was reviewed by the working group, which provisionally adopted several of the proposed paragraphs, as amended. The remaining provisions would be taken up at the 2004 session.

As to the *Repertory of Practice of United Nations Organs* and *Repertoire of the Practice of the Security Council*, the Legal Counsel reported to the working group on the status of both publications, including the Secretary-General's proposal to discontinue work on the *Repertory*, the instructions not to provide for it in the proposed 2004-2005 programme budget and an option that an academic institution might consider taking over the publication. The Special Committee recommended that the Assembly, at its fifty-eighth session, should encourage the Secretary-General in his efforts to eliminate the backlog in both publications, including by exploring options involving cooperation with academic institutions without prejudice to the continuation of timely publication; commend him for his initiative to make *Repertory* studies available on the Internet; and request him to exert every effort to make electronically available all versions of the *Repertory* as early as possible.

Report of Secretary-General. In response to General Assembly resolution 57/24 [YUN 2002, p. 1331], the Secretary-General submitted a September report [A/58/347] outlining the steps taken by the Secretariat to reduce the backlog in the publication of the supplements to the *Repertory of Practice of United Nations Organs* and *Repertoire of the Practice of the Security Council*, including consideration of alternative courses of action relating to the *Repertory*. For the *Repertoire*, it proposed a two-track approach to address current developments in the procedure and practice of the Council, and to expedite elimination of the backlog. The Assembly was invited, in the context of the approval of the 2004-2005 budget, to take action in the light of the information presented.

ACABQ report. Having considered the Secretary-General's September report and additional information provided by his representatives, the Advisory Committee on Administrative and Budgetary Questions (ACABQ), in October [A/58/537], recalled that any Assembly decision entailing financial requirements was subject to the provision of a statement of programme budget implications and its consideration by the Fifth (Administrative and Budgetary) Committee, which would make the appropriate recommendation.

GENERAL ASSEMBLY ACTION

On 23 December [meeting 79], the General Assembly, on the recommendation of the Sixth (Legal) Committee [A/58/517], adopted **resolution 58/248** without vote [agenda item 155].

Report of the Special Committee on the Charter of the United Nations and on the Strengthening of the Role of the Organization

The General Assembly,

Recalling its resolution 3499(XXX) of 15 December 1975, by which it established the Special Committee on the Charter of the United Nations and on the Strengthening of the Role of the Organization, and its relevant resolutions adopted at subsequent sessions,

Recalling also its resolution 47/233 of 17 August 1993 on the revitalization of the work of the General Assembly,

Recalling further its resolution 47/62 of 11 December 1992 on the question of equitable representation on and increase in the membership of the Security Council,

Taking note of the report of the Open-ended Working Group on the Question of Equitable Representation on and Increase in the Membership of the Security Council and Other Matters Related to the Security Council,

Recalling the elements relevant to the work of the Special Committee contained in its resolution 47/120 B of 20 September 1993,

Recalling also its resolution 51/241 of 31 July 1997 on the strengthening of the United Nations system and its resolution 51/242 of 15 September 1997, entitled "Supplement to an Agenda for Peace", by which it adopted the texts on coordination and the question of sanctions imposed by the United Nations, which are annexed to that resolution,

Recalling further that the International Court of Justice is the principal judicial organ of the United Nations, and reaffirming its authority and independence,

Considering the desirability of finding practical ways and means to strengthen the Court, taking into consideration, in particular, the needs resulting from its increased workload,

Taking note of the progress achieved on the revised working paper on the working methods of the Special Committee, as amended,

Taking note also of the report of the Secretary-General on the *Repertory of Practice of United Nations Organs* and the *Repertoire of the Practice of the Security Council*,

Recalling its resolution 57/24 of 19 November 2002,

Having considered the report of the Special Committee on the work of its session held in 2003,

Noting with appreciation the work done by the Special Committee to encourage States to focus on the need to prevent and to settle peacefully their disputes which are likely to endanger the maintenance of international peace and security,

1. *Takes note* of the report of the Special Committee on the Charter of the United Nations and on the Strengthening of the Role of the Organization;

2. *Decides* that the Special Committee shall hold its next session from 29 March to 8 April 2004;

3. *Requests* the Special Committee, at its session in 2004, in accordance with paragraph 5 of General Assembly resolution 50/52 of 11 December 1995:

(a) To continue its consideration of all proposals concerning the question of the maintenance of international peace and security in all its aspects in order to strengthen the role of the United Nations and, in this context, to consider other proposals relating to the maintenance of international peace and security already submitted or which may be submitted to the Special Committee at its session in 2004;

(b) To continue to consider, on a priority basis, the question of the implementation of the provisions of the Charter of the United Nations related to assistance to third States affected by the application of sanctions under Chapter VII of the Charter by commencing a substantive debate on all of the related reports of the Secretary-General and the proposals submitted on the question;

(c) To keep on its agenda the question of the peaceful settlement of disputes between States;

(d) To continue to consider proposals concerning the Trusteeship Council in the light of the report of the Secretary-General submitted in accordance with General Assembly resolution 50/55 of 11 December 1995, the report of the Secretary-General entitled "Renewing the United Nations: a programme for reform" and the views expressed by States on this subject at previous sessions of the Assembly;

(e) To continue to consider, on a priority basis, ways and means of improving its working methods and enhancing its efficiency with a view to identifying widely acceptable measures for future implementation;

4. *Invites* the Special Committee at its session in 2004 to continue to identify new subjects for consideration in its future work with a view to contributing to the revitalization of the work of the United Nations;

5. *Notes* the readiness of the Special Committee, in the context of its consideration of the subject of assistance to working groups on the revitalization of the work of the United Nations and coordination between the Special Committee and other working groups dealing with the reform of the Organization, to provide, within its mandate, such assistance as may be sought at the request of other subsidiary bodies of the General Assembly in relation to any issues before them;

6. *Requests* the Special Committee to submit a report on its work to the General Assembly at its fifty-ninth session;

7. *Takes note* of paragraphs 42 and 43 of the report of the Secretary-General, commends the Secretary-General for his continued efforts to reduce the backlog in the publication of the *Repertory of Practice of United Nations Organs*, and endorses the efforts of the Secretary-General to eliminate the backlog in the publication of the *Repertoire of the Practice of the Security Council;*

8. *Encourages* the Secretary-General in his continuous efforts to eliminate the backlog in the publication of the *Repertory of Practice of United Nations Organs* and of the *Repertoire of the Practice of the Security Council*, including by exploring options involving cooperation with academic institutions as a means to achieve this aim without prejudice to the continuation of their timely publication;

9. *Commends* the Secretary-General for his initiative to make *Repertory* studies available on the Internet;

10. *Requests* the Secretary-General to make every effort, within the level of the currently approved budget, towards making available electronically all versions of the *Repertory of Practice of United Nations Organs* as early as possible;

11. *Also requests* the Secretary-General to submit a report on both the *Repertory of Practice of United Nations Organs* and the *Repertoire of the Practice of the Security*

Council to the General Assembly at its fifty-ninth session;

12. *Decides* to include in the provisional agenda of its fifty-ninth session the item entitled "Report of the Special Committee on the Charter of the United Nations and on the Strengthening of the Role of the Organization".

Charter provisions relating to sanctions

Special Committee consideration. During the Special Committee's consideration of the implementation of the Charter provisions related to assistance to third States affected by sanctions [A/58/33], it was suggested that, given the length of time that the Committee had been considering the question, it should recommend the establishment of a working group of the Sixth Committee as a framework for a focused discussion of the issue. The Security Council was called upon to be fair and equitable in its application of sanctions. Prior to their imposition, the Council should make an objective evaluation and assessment, without overestimation, of their short-, medium- and long-term impact on third States, as well as on the target States, giving special consideration to their humanitarian impact. Sanctions should be clearly defined, targeted, imposed for a specific time frame, subject to periodic review and lifted as soon as the reason for their imposition had ceased to exist. Practical measures to alleviate the hardships encountered by third States included granting commercial exemptions, concessions or preferential treatment to such States or their suppliers; granting priority to their contractors for investment in the target State; and allowing their participation in the provision of supplies for peacekeeping operations or in the post-conflict rehabilitation, reconstruction and development. Maintaining direct consultations between the Council and the affected States was also mentioned. Delegations welcomed the Council's recent practice of imposing targeted sanctions of limited duration, and its adoption of the de-listing procedure (enabling individuals listed as targets to submit information to the sanctions committee concerned showing that the listing should not apply or no longer applied) and of technical resolutions on humanitarian exemptions. Targeted sanctions (arms embargoes, travel restrictions, freezing of personal assets and exclusion from participation in international forums) were viewed as appropriate interventions to address concerns regarding the humanitarian impact of sanctions. The initiatives undertaken outside the UN framework to establish targeted sanctions as regular tools for application by the Council were commended, such as the Interlaken (Switzerland) process on targeted financial sanctions [YUN 2001, p. 1246] and the Bonn-Berlin (Germany) process on arms embargoes and travel-related restrictions [ibid.].

The Committee recommended that the Assembly continue to consider the 1998 expert group's deliberations and main findings on developing a methodology for assessing the consequences incurred by third States as a result of preventive or enforcement measures [YUN 1998, p. 1235], taking into account the Committee's current debate; views presented in the Secretary-General's 1999 [YUN 1999, p. 1252] and 2000 [YUN 2000, p. 1270] reports; his most recent views on the main findings of the ad hoc expert group [YUN 2002, p. 1333]; and information he was to submit on the follow-up to a 1999 Security Council note [YUN 1999, p. 1252] and on assistance to third States affected by sanctions under Chapter VII and the implementation of Assembly resolution 57/25 [YUN 2002, p. 1333].

Security Council consideration. The Security Council met on 25 February 2003 [meeting 4713] to discuss general issues relating to sanctions and to consider the report of the Stockholm Process on the Implementation of Targeted Sanctions presented by Sweden. Begun in November 2001 [YUN 2001, p. 1246], the Stockholm Process lasted for more than a year. Its goal was to suggest ways to strengthen the capacity to implement targeted sanctions, both within the UN system and among Member States, and to minimize unintentional negative consequences. One priority was to identify measures to enhance planning, monitoring, reporting and coordination among sanctions committees and monitoring bodies.

By an 18 December note [S/2003/1185], the Council President announced that the Council had agreed to extend until 31 December 2004 the mandate of its informal working group established to examine specific issues from which to develop recommendations on how to improve the effectiveness of UN sanctions [YUN 2000, p. 1270].

Report of Secretary-General. In response to General Assembly resolution 57/25 [YUN 2002, p. 1333], the Secretary-General submitted a September report [A/58/346] highlighting measures for further improving the procedures and working methods of the Security Council and its sanctions committees related to assistance to third States affected by the application of sanctions. It reviewed the role of the Assembly, the Economic and Social Council and the Committee for Programme and Coordination in the area of such assistance. It also reviewed the Secretariat's capacity and modality for implementing relevant intergovernmental mandates and for addressing the main findings and recommendations of the

Other legal questions 1367

1998 ad hoc expert group meeting [YUN 1998, p. 1235].

By **decision 2003/309** of 24 July 2003, the Economic and Social Council took note of the Secretary-General's 2002 report [YUN 2002, p. 1333] on the subject.

GENERAL ASSEMBLY ACTION

On 9 December [meeting 72], the General Assembly, on the recommendation of the Sixth Committee [A/58/517], adopted **resolution 58/80** without vote [agenda item 155].

Implementation of the provisions of the Charter of the United Nations related to assistance to third States affected by the application of sanctions

The General Assembly,

Concerned about the special economic problems confronting certain States arising from the carrying out of preventive or enforcement measures taken by the Security Council against other States, and taking into account the obligation of Members of the United Nations under Article 49 of the Charter of the United Nations to join in affording mutual assistance in carrying out the measures decided upon by the Security Council,

Recalling the right of third States confronted with special economic problems of that nature to consult the Security Council with regard to a solution of those problems, in accordance with Article 50 of the Charter,

Recognizing the desirability of the consideration of further appropriate procedures for consultations to deal in a more effective manner with the problems referred to in Article 50 of the Charter,

Recalling:

(a) The report of the Secretary-General entitled "An Agenda for Peace", in particular paragraph 41 thereof,

(b) Its resolution 47/120 A of 18 December 1992, entitled "An Agenda for Peace: preventive diplomacy and related matters", its resolution 47/120 B of 20 September 1993, entitled "An Agenda for Peace", in particular section IV thereof, entitled "Special economic problems arising from the implementation of preventive or enforcement measures", and its resolution 51/242 of 15 September 1997, entitled "Supplement to an Agenda for Peace", in particular annex II thereto, entitled "Question of sanctions imposed by the United Nations",

(c) The position paper of the Secretary-General entitled "Supplement to an Agenda for Peace",

(d) The statement by the President of the Security Council of 22 February 1995,

(e) The report of the Secretary-General prepared pursuant to the statement by the President of the Security Council regarding the question of special economic problems of States as a result of sanctions imposed under Chapter VII of the Charter,

(f) The annual overview reports of the Administrative Committee on Coordination for the period from 1992 to 2000 and the annual overview reports of the United Nations System Chief Executives Board for Coordination for 2001 and 2002, in particular the sections on assistance to countries invoking Article 50 of the Charter,

(g) The reports of the Secretary-General on economic assistance to States affected by the implementation of the Security Council resolutions imposing sanctions against the Federal Republic of Yugoslavia and General Assembly resolutions 48/210 of 21 December 1993, 49/21 A of 2 December 1994, 50/58 E of 12 December 1995, 51/30 A of 5 December 1996, 52/169 H of 16 December 1997, 54/96 G of 15 December 1999, 55/170 of 14 December 2000 and 56/110 of 14 December 2001,

(h) The reports of the Special Committee on the Charter of the United Nations and on the Strengthening of the Role of the Organization on the work of its sessions held in the years 1994 to 2003,

(i) The reports of the Secretary-General on the implementation of the provisions of the Charter related to assistance to third States affected by the application of sanctions under Chapter VII of the Charter,

(j) The report of the Secretary-General to the Millennium Assembly of the United Nations, in particular section IV.E thereof, entitled "Targeting sanctions",

(k) The United Nations Millennium Declaration, in particular paragraph 9 thereof,

(l) The report of the Secretary-General entitled "Road map towards implementation of the United Nations Millennium Declaration", in particular paragraphs 56 to 61 thereof,

(m) The report of the Committee for Programme and Coordination on the work of its forty-third session, in particular the recommendation that the Chief Executives Board play a role in better coordinating the analysis of the problems of the countries invoking Article 50 of the Charter, and the development of new methodologies to identify the damage to affected States and new mechanisms to determine the appropriate compensation for them,

Taking note of the report of the Secretary-General on the work of the Organization, in particular paragraphs 68 and 69 thereof,

Recalling that the question of assistance to third States affected by the application of sanctions has been addressed recently in several forums, including the General Assembly, the Security Council, the Economic and Social Council and their subsidiary organs,

Recalling also the measures taken by the Security Council, in accordance with the statement by the President of the Security Council of 16 December 1994, that, as part of the effort of the Council to improve the flow of information and the exchange of ideas between members of the Council and other States Members of the United Nations, there should be increased recourse to open meetings, in particular at an early stage in its consideration of a subject,

Recalling further the measures taken by the Security Council in accordance with the note by the President of the Security Council of 29 January 1999 aimed at improving the work of the sanctions committees, including increasing the effectiveness and transparency of those committees,

Stressing that, in the formulation of sanctions regimes, due account should be taken of the potential effects of sanctions on third States,

Stressing also, in this context, the powers of the Security Council under Chapter VII of the Charter and the primary responsibility of the Council under Article 24 of the Charter for the maintenance of international peace and security in order to ensure prompt and effective action by the United Nations,

Recalling that, under Article 31 of the Charter, any Member of the United Nations that is not a member of the Security Council may participate, without vote, in the discussion of any question brought before the Council whenever the latter considers that the interests of that Member are specially affected,

Recognizing that the imposition of sanctions under Chapter VII of the Charter has been causing special economic problems in third States and that it is necessary to intensify efforts to address those problems effectively,

Taking into consideration the views of third States which could be affected by the imposition of sanctions,

Recognizing that assistance to third States affected by the application of sanctions would further contribute to an effective and comprehensive approach by the international community to sanctions imposed by the Security Council,

Recognizing also that the international community at large and, in particular, international institutions involved in providing economic and financial assistance should continue to take into account and address in a more effective manner the special economic problems of affected third States arising from the carrying out of preventive or enforcement measures taken by the Security Council under Chapter VII of the Charter, in view of their magnitude and of the adverse impact on the economies of those States,

Recalling the provisions of its resolutions 50/51 of 11 December 1995, 51/208 of 17 December 1996, 52/162 of 15 December 1997, 53/107 of 8 December 1998, 54/107 of 9 December 1999, 55/157 of 12 December 2000, 56/87 of 12 December 2001 and 57/25 of 19 November 2002,

1. *Renews its invitation* to the Security Council to consider the establishment of further mechanisms or procedures, as appropriate, for consultations as early as possible under Article 50 of the Charter of the United Nations with third States which are or may be confronted with special economic problems arising from the carrying out of preventive or enforcement measures imposed by the Council under Chapter VII of the Charter, with regard to a solution of those problems, including appropriate ways and means for increasing the effectiveness of its methods and procedures applied in the consideration of requests by the affected States for assistance;

2. *Welcomes* the measures taken by the Security Council since the adoption of General Assembly resolution 50/51, most recently the note by the President of the Security Council of 15 January 2002, whereby the members of the Security Council agreed to extend the mandate of the informal working group of the Council established in 2000 to develop general recommendations on how to improve the effectiveness of United Nations sanctions, looks forward to the adoption of the proposed outcome document of the working group, in particular those provisions thereof regarding the issues of the unintended impact of sanctions and assistance to States in implementing sanctions, and strongly recommends that the Council continue its efforts to enhance further the effectiveness and transparency of the sanctions committees, to streamline their working procedures and to facilitate access to them by representatives of States that find themselves confronted with special economic problems arising from the carrying out of sanctions;

3. *Invites* the Security Council, its sanctions committees and the Secretariat to continue to ensure, as appropriate, that:

(*a*) Both pre-assessment reports and ongoing assessment reports include as part of their analysis the likely and actual unintended impact of the sanctions on third States and recommend ways in which the negative impact of sanctions can be mitigated;

(*b*) Sanctions committees provide opportunities for third States affected by sanctions to brief them on the unintended impact of sanctions they are experiencing and on assistance needed by them to mitigate the negative impact of sanctions;

(*c*) The Secretariat continues to provide, upon request, advice and information to third States to help them to pursue means to mitigate the unintended impact of sanctions, for example, on invoking Article 50 of the Charter for consultation with the Security Council;

(*d*) Where economic sanctions have had severe effects on third States, the Security Council is able to request the Secretary-General to consider appointing a special representative or dispatching, as necessary, fact-finding missions on the ground to undertake necessary assessments and to identify, as appropriate, possible ways of assistance;

(*e*) The Security Council is able, in the context of situations referred to in subparagraph (*d*) above, to consider establishing working groups to consider such situations;

4. *Requests* the Secretary-General to pursue the implementation of General Assembly resolutions 50/51, 51/208, 52/162, 53/107, 54/107, 55/157, 56/87 and 57/25 and to ensure that the competent units within the Secretariat develop the adequate capacity and appropriate modalities, technical procedures and guidelines to continue, on a regular basis, to collate and coordinate information about international assistance available to third States affected by the implementation of sanctions, to continue developing a possible methodology for assessing the adverse consequences actually incurred by third States and to explore innovative and practical measures of assistance to the affected third States;

5. *Welcomes* the report of the Secretary-General containing a summary of the deliberations and main findings of the ad hoc expert group meeting on developing a methodology for assessing the consequences incurred by third States as a result of preventive or enforcement measures and on exploring innovative and practical measures of international assistance to the affected third States, and renews its invitation to States and relevant international organizations within and outside the United Nations system which have not yet done so to provide their views regarding the report of the ad hoc expert group meeting;

6. *Takes note* of the most recent report of the Secretary-General on this question and, in particular, of his views on the deliberations and main findings, including the recommendations of the ad hoc expert group on the implementation of the provisions of the Charter related to assistance to third States affected by the application of sanctions, as well as the views of

States, the organizations of the United Nations system, international financial institutions and other international organizations, as contained in the previous reports of the Secretary-General;

7. *Reaffirms* the important role of the General Assembly, the Economic and Social Council and the Committee for Programme and Coordination in mobilizing and monitoring, as appropriate, the economic assistance efforts of the international community and the United Nations system on behalf of States confronted with special economic problems arising from the carrying out of preventive or enforcement measures imposed by the Security Council and, as appropriate, in identifying solutions to the special economic problems of those States;

8. *Takes note* of the decision of the Economic and Social Council, in its resolution 2000/32 of 28 July 2000, to continue its consideration of the question of assistance to third States affected by the application of sanctions, invites the Council, at its organizational session for 2004, to make appropriate arrangements for this purpose within its programme of work for 2004, further invites the Council to continue its consideration of the question of assistance to third States affected by the application of sanctions, and decides to transmit the most recent report of the Secretary-General on the implementation of the provisions of the Charter related to assistance to third States affected by the application of sanctions, together with the relevant background materials, to the Council at its substantive session of 2004;

9. *Invites* the organizations of the United Nations system, international financial institutions, other international organizations, regional organizations and Member States to address more specifically and directly, where appropriate, the special economic problems of third States affected by sanctions imposed under Chapter VII of the Charter and, for this purpose, to consider improving procedures for consultations to maintain a constructive dialogue with such States, including through regular and frequent meetings, as well as, where appropriate, special meetings between the affected third States and the donor community, with the participation of United Nations agencies and other international organizations;

10. *Requests* the Special Committee on the Charter of the United Nations and on the Strengthening of the Role of the Organization, at its session in 2004, to continue to consider on a priority basis the question of the implementation of the provisions of the Charter related to assistance to third States affected by the application of sanctions under Chapter VII of the Charter by commencing a substantive debate on all of the related reports of the Secretary-General, in particular the 1998 report containing a summary of the deliberations and main findings of the ad hoc expert group meeting convened pursuant to paragraph 4 of General Assembly resolution 52/162, together with the most recent report of the Secretary-General on this question, taking into consideration the forthcoming report of the informal working group of the Security Council on general issues relating to sanctions, the proposals submitted on the question, the debate on the question in the Sixth Committee during the fifty-eighth session of the Assembly and the text on the question of sanctions imposed by the United Nations contained in annex II to Assembly resolution 51/242, as well as the implementation of the provisions of Assembly resolutions 50/51, 51/208, 52/162, 53/107, 54/107, 55/157, 56/87, 57/25 and the present resolution;

11. *Decides* to consider within the Sixth Committee or a working group of the Committee, at the fifty-ninth session of the General Assembly, further progress in the elaboration of effective measures aimed at the implementation of the provisions of the Charter related to assistance to third States affected by the application of sanctions under Chapter VII of the Charter;

12. *Requests* the Secretary-General to submit a report on the implementation of the present resolution to the General Assembly at its fifty-ninth session, under the agenda item entitled "Report of the Special Committee on the Charter of the United Nations and on the Strengthening of the Role of the Organization".

UN Programme for the teaching and study of international law

In response to General Assembly resolution 56/77 [YUN 2001, p. 1250], the Secretary-General submitted an October report [A/58/446] on the United Nations Programme of Assistance in the Teaching, Study, Dissemination and Wider Appreciation of International Law during 2002 and 2003. The report described UN efforts to implement the Programme, among them the holding of the thirty-ninth session of the International Law Seminar (Geneva, 7-25 July) (see p. 1334). Under the fellowship programme in international law, the Secretary-General awarded, at the request of Governments of developing countries, 18 fellowships in 2002 and 19 in 2003, and a series of lectures, seminars and complementary study visits were organized by the UN Office of Legal Affairs (OLA) and the United Nations Institute for Training and Research (UNITAR).

The OLA Codification Division assisted in the electronic dissemination of information regarding UN work on codification and the progressive development of international law, and created web sites on other legal information. The United Nations Commission on International Trade Law (UNCITRAL) organized seminars and symposiums for the study of international law in many developing countries. The Treaty Section of OLA, jointly with UNITAR, organized two training sessions at UN Headquarters on treaty law and practice and a meeting of a panel of international experts on multilateral treaties against transnational organized crime and terrorism (New York, 8 July), in preparation for the 2003 treaty event on that theme (see p. 1125). Other programmes included the Hamilton Shirley Amerasinghe Fellowship on the Law of the Sea (see p. 1362), awarded annually by OLA, and the Fellowship Programme on the International Civil Service, a training programme organized by UNITAR in cooperation with other organizations.

The report also described the legal publications issued during the year, proposed guidelines and recommendations regarding the execution of the Programme of Assistance in the 2004-2005 biennium, and outlined the administrative and financial implications of UN participation in the Programme for the 2002-2003 and 2004-2005 bienniums.

The Advisory Committee on the Programme held its thirty-seventh and thirty-eighth sessions on 21 November 2002 and on 16 October 2003, respectively, at which it considered the Secretary-General's report in interim and draft forms.

GENERAL ASSEMBLY ACTION

On 9 December [meeting 72], the General Assembly, on the recommendation of the Sixth Committee [A/58/511], adopted **resolution 58/73** without vote [agenda item 149].

United Nations Programme of Assistance in the Teaching, Study, Dissemination and Wider Appreciation of International Law

The General Assembly,

Taking note with appreciation of the report of the Secretary-General on the implementation of the United Nations Programme of Assistance in the Teaching, Study, Dissemination and Wider Appreciation of International Law and the guidelines and recommendations on future implementation of the Programme which were adopted by the Advisory Committee on the Programme and are contained in section III of the report,

Considering that international law should occupy an appropriate place in the teaching of legal disciplines at all universities,

Noting with appreciation the efforts made by States at the bilateral level to provide assistance in the teaching and study of international law,

Convinced, nevertheless, that States and international organizations and institutions should be encouraged to give further support to the Programme and increase their activities to promote the teaching, study, dissemination and wider appreciation of international law, in particular those activities which are of special benefit to persons from developing countries,

Reaffirming its resolutions 2464(XXIII) of 20 December 1968, 2550(XXIV) of 12 December 1969, 2838 (XXVI) of 18 December 1971, 3106(XXVIII) of 12 December 1973, 3502(XXX) of 15 December 1975, 32/146 of 16 December 1977, 36/108 of 10 December 1981 and 38/129 of 19 December 1983, in which it stated or recalled that in the conduct of the Programme it was desirable to use as far as possible the resources and facilities made available by Member States, international organizations and others, as well as its resolutions 34/144 of 17 December 1979, 40/66 of 11 December 1985, 42/148 of 7 December 1987, 44/28 of 4 December 1989, 46/50 of 9 December 1991, 48/29 of 9 December 1993, 50/43 of 11 December 1995, 52/152 of 15 December 1997, 54/102 of 9 December 1999 and 56/77 of 12 December 2001, in which, in addition, it expressed or reaffirmed the hope that, in appointing lecturers for the seminars to be held within the framework of the fellowship programme in international law, account would be taken of the need to secure the representation of major legal systems and balance among various geographical regions,

1. *Approves* the guidelines and recommendations contained in section III of the report of the Secretary-General and adopted by the Advisory Committee on the United Nations Programme of Assistance in the Teaching, Study, Dissemination and Wider Appreciation of International Law, in particular those designed to achieve the best possible results in the administration of the Programme within a policy of maximum financial restraint;

2. *Authorizes* the Secretary-General to carry out in 2004 and 2005 the activities specified in his report, including the provision of:

(*a*) A number of international law fellowships in both 2004 and 2005, to be determined in the light of the overall resources for the Programme and to be awarded at the request of Governments of developing countries;

(*b*) A minimum of one scholarship in both 2004 and 2005 under the Hamilton Shirley Amerasinghe Memorial Fellowship on the Law of the Sea, subject to the availability of new voluntary contributions made specifically to the fellowship fund;

(*c*) Subject to the overall resources for the Programme, assistance in the form of a travel grant for one participant from each developing country, who would be invited to possible regional courses to be organized in 2004 and 2005;

and to finance the above activities from provisions in the regular budget, when appropriate, as well as from voluntary financial contributions earmarked for each of the activities concerned, which would be received as a result of the requests set out in paragraphs 11 to 13 below;

3. *Expresses its appreciation* to the Secretary-General for his constructive efforts to promote training and assistance in international law within the framework of the Programme in 2002 and 2003, in particular for the organization of the thirty-eighth and thirty-ninth sessions of the International Law Seminar, held at Geneva in 2002 and 2003, respectively, and for the activities of the Office of Legal Affairs of the Secretariat related to the fellowship programme in international law and to the Hamilton Shirley Amerasinghe Memorial Fellowship on the Law of the Sea, carried out, respectively, through its Codification Division and its Division for Ocean Affairs and the Law of the Sea;

4. *Requests* the Secretary-General to consider the possibility of admitting, for participation in the various components of the Programme, candidates from countries willing to bear the entire cost of such participation;

5. *Also requests* the Secretary-General to consider the relative advantages of using available resources and voluntary contributions for regional, subregional or national courses, as against courses organized within the United Nations system;

6. *Further requests* the Secretary-General to continue to provide the necessary resources to the programme budget for the Programme for the next and the future bienniums with a view to maintaining the effectiveness of the Programme;

7. *Welcomes* the efforts undertaken by the Office of Legal Affairs to bring up to date the United Nations *Treaty Series* and the *United Nations Juridical Yearbook*, as well as efforts made to place on the Internet the *Treaty Series* and other legal information;

8. *Expresses its appreciation* to the United Nations Institute for Training and Research for its participation in the Programme through the activities described in the report of the Secretary-General;

9. *Also expresses its appreciation* to The Hague Academy of International Law for the valuable contribution it continues to make to the Programme, which has enabled candidates under the fellowship programmes in international law to attend and participate in the Programme in conjunction with the Academy courses;

10. *Notes with appreciation* the contributions of The Hague Academy to the teaching, study, dissemination and wider appreciation of international law, and calls upon Member States and interested organizations to give favourable consideration to the appeal of the Academy for a continuation of support and a possible increase in their financial contributions, to enable the Academy to carry out its activities, particularly those relating to the summer courses, regional courses and programmes of the Centre for Studies and Research in International Law and International Relations;

11. *Requests* the Secretary-General to continue to publicize the Programme and periodically to invite Member States, universities, philanthropic foundations and other interested national and international institutions and organizations, as well as individuals, to make voluntary contributions towards the financing of the Programme or otherwise to assist in its implementation and possible expansion;

12. *Reiterates its request* to Member States and to interested organizations and individuals to make voluntary contributions, inter alia, for the International Law Seminar, the fellowship programme in international law, the Hamilton Shirley Amerasinghe Memorial Fellowship on the Law of the Sea and the United Nations Audiovisual Library in International Law, and expresses its appreciation to those Member States, institutions and individuals that have made voluntary contributions for this purpose;

13. *Urges*, in particular, all Governments to make voluntary contributions for the organization of regional refresher courses in international law by the United Nations Institute for Training and Research, especially with a view to covering the amount needed for the financing of the daily subsistence allowance for up to twenty-five participants in each regional course, thus alleviating the burden on prospective host countries and making it possible for the Institute to continue to organize the regional courses;

14. *Requests* the Secretary-General to report to the General Assembly at its sixtieth session on the implementation of the Programme during 2004 and 2005 and, following consultations with the Advisory Committee on the Programme, to submit recommendations regarding the execution of the Programme in subsequent years;

15. *Decides* to appoint twenty-five Member States, six from Africa, five from Asia, three from Eastern Europe, five from Latin America and the Caribbean and six from Western Europe and other States, as members of the Advisory Committee on the United Nations Programme of Assistance in the Teaching, Study, Dissemination and Wider Appreciation of International Law, for a period of four years beginning on 1 January 2004;

16. *Decides* to include in the provisional agenda of its sixtieth session the item entitled "United Nations Programme of Assistance in the Teaching, Study, Dissemination and Wider Appreciation of International Law".

Host country relations

In five meetings held in New York between 13 February and 16 October, the Committee on Relations with the Host Country considered the following aspects of relations between the UN diplomatic community and the United States, the host country: entry visas to the host country; transportation issues regarding the use of motor vehicles, parking and related matters; the security of missions and the safety of their personnel; and host country travel regulations. The recommendations and conclusions on those items, approved by the Committee at its 16 October meeting, were incorporated in its report [A/58/26].

Entry visas

On 13 February, the Committee heard complaints from Iraq regarding delays in issuing entry or re-entry visas to Iraqi diplomats and experts, which impeded its Mission's work and, in particular, interfered with Iraq's participation in UN meetings. Iraq also reported that its diplomats had been harassed and followed within and outside the UN Headquarters premises.

In response, the United States referred to the new security requirements of its Government, which inevitably resulted in long visa delays. In the circumstances, it advised allowing at least 20 days for the processing of visa applications. It also denied Iraq's allegation that its diplomats were being followed or harassed by the United States authorities.

On 21 May, the Committee heard another complaint of a visa delay from Zimbabwe, which stated that, although established policy required 15 business days for the processing of visa applications, its mission application, submitted five months prior to the date of the official business for which the visa was needed, had yet to be issued. The United States, recalling that the application period had increased to 20 business days after the events of 11 September 2001 [YUN 2001, p. 60], said it would look into the particular case.

The Committee anticipated that the host country would continue to ensure the timely issuance of entry visas to representatives of Member States, including to attend official UN meetings.

Transportation

Throughout its meetings, the Committee heard complaints from 11 permanent missions to the United Nations—notably from Costa Rica, Cuba and the Russian Federation—regarding difficulties experienced in the implementation of the Parking Programme for Diplomatic Vehicles, in force since November 2002 [YUN 2002, p. 1338]. They complained of recurrent or daily use of their designated parking spaces by unauthorized vehicles and claimed that the remedial steps had not been successful, the appeals procedure was not functioning properly and fines were being imposed without explanation as required by the Programme.

The host country regretted the problems raised and confirmed its commitment and that of the city to resolve them, noting that an official had been designated in the United States Mission to deal solely with the Parking Programme. It reminded the permanent missions to refer their parking problems to the New York City Commission for the United Nations, Consular Corps and Protocol and/or to the United States Mission. It reiterated that the appeals procedure did not subject missions to the administrative or judicial jurisdiction of the host city or country. Addressing the Committee, the New York City Commissioner undertook to work expeditiously to resolve all problems brought to its attention. She confirmed that the Parking Programme was fully operational but that human error could not be discounted. She also offered additional information briefings for the benefit of the permanent missions and their personnel.

In May and October, the host country reported on progress made in the Parking Programme's implementation: parking violations had declined and summonses had decreased by 87 per cent. It commended the missions' compliance with paying or protesting violation notices and requested the timely notification of cases of illegal parking in their designated parking spaces. In September, the host country said that the United States Mission had exerted good-faith efforts by holding briefings, sending out notes verbales, setting up a special e-mail address and web site, and designating a focal point for parking issues. It praised as useful reminders the monthly reports issued by the Department of Finance of the City of New York listing all unpaid notices issued to mission vehicles and their staff. It invited the missions to avail themselves of the forms of recourse provided for in the Programme rather than wait for the non-renewal of their diplomatic plates.

While the host country did not object to a review of the Programme's implementation, it made clear that such a review would not entail any revision of the Programme.

The Committee decided to conduct a detailed review of the implementation of the Parking Programme, as recommended by the Legal Counsel in 2002 [YUN 2002, p. 1338], with a view to ensuring that it was fair, non-discriminatory, effective and consistent with international law. It asked the host country to continue to bring to the attention of New York City officials, the problems experienced by the permanent missions or their staff with regard to the Programme, in order to improve their functioning and to promote compliance with international norms regarding diplomatic privileges and immunities.

Security and safety of permanent missions

On 21 May, Cuba drew to the Committee's attention its notes verbales of 11 March and 12 May to the United States Mission concerning the reduction of the security perimeter around the Cuban Mission. Fearing the resultant easy pedestrian access to the Mission and an increased likelihood of threats to it, Cuba called on the host country immediately to restore the previous security perimeter. The host country indicated that the security zone around the Cuban Mission had been established years ago in a period of numerous attacks and that the Mission was the only one with such a security zone. The host country concluded that the Police Department's objective assessment might have indicated that the situation no longer necessitated the special security measure in question. Cuba reiterated that it had provided the Security Council with a chronological account of terrorist attacks emanating from United States soil against Cuba, including on its Permanent Mission to the United Nations. It did not consider attacks or threats against its Mission to be a thing of the past and called on the host country to fulfil its obligations in respect of the security of missions.

On 3 September, China stated that, in the light of the terrorist incidents around the world, the security of permanent missions needed to be strengthened and reinforced. It called for more stationary and mobile police. Expressing concern about the number of unauthorized vehicles in the vicinity of its Mission and fear of what could happen, China called for the establishment of a regular police presence and a no-parking zone.

The Committee appreciated the efforts made by the host country in the security of the missions accredited to the United Nations and the safety of their personnel and anticipated that it would

Host country travel regulations

On 9 October, the Committee heard complaints from Cuba and the Libyan Arab Jamahiriya regarding the host country's policy of restricting the movement and travel of personnel of their permanent missions to the United Nations and of Secretariat officials of certain nationalities. The complaints concerned denial of requests to travel outside the 25-mile radius, beyond which the movement of certain mission personnel was restricted; denial or delays in the issuance of visas; restrictions on travel of non-dependant family members; and the degrading treatment of diplomats at New York airports, which Libya characterized as beyond what was acceptable in the name of security. In connection with its complaints, Libya invoked the Convention on the Privileges and Immunities of the United Nations [YUN 1946-47, p. 100, GA res. 22 A (I)], the Agreement between the United Nations and the United States of America regarding the Headquarters of the United Nations [YUN 1947-48, p. 1376, GA res. 169(II)] and the Vienna Convention on Diplomatic Relations [YUN 1961, p. 512].

The host country confirmed that there were no restrictions on official UN travel, only on personal or recreational travel, and that United States policy on official visas for dependants was very specific. The host country was sensitive to cultural differences regarding secondary or over-age dependants and did everything possible to accommodate requests to keep families together. It confirmed that arrangements had been made to ensure the privacy and courtesy of security measures directed at diplomats other than heads of State and cabinet-rank ministers. It referred to a circular issued by the United States Mission on those arrangements and to the seriousness with which the host country dealt with infractions thereof.

The Committee, in continuing to urge the host country to remove the remaining travel restrictions as soon as possible, noted the positions of the affected Member States, of the Secretary-General and of the host country.

GENERAL ASSEMBLY ACTION

On 9 December [meeting 72], the General Assembly, on the recommendation of the Sixth Committee [A/58/515], adopted **resolution 58/78** without vote [agenda item 153].

Report of the Committee on Relations with the Host Country

The General Assembly,

Having considered the report of the Committee on Relations with the Host Country,

Recalling Article 105 of the Charter of the United Nations, the Convention on the Privileges and Immunities of the United Nations, the Agreement between the United Nations and the United States of America regarding the Headquarters of the United Nations and the responsibilities of the host country,

Recalling also that, in accordance with paragraph 7 of General Assembly resolution 2819(XXVI) of 15 December 1971, the Committee should consider, and advise the host country on, issues arising in connection with the implementation of the Agreement between the United Nations and the United States of America regarding the Headquarters of the United Nations,

Recalling further its resolution 43/172 of 9 December 1988, in which it stressed the importance of a positive perception of the work of the United Nations, and urged that efforts be continued to build up public awareness by explaining, through all available means, the importance of the role played by the United Nations and the missions accredited to it in the strengthening of international peace and security,

Recognizing that effective measures should continue to be taken by the competent authorities of the host country, in particular to prevent any acts violating the security of missions and the safety of their personnel,

1. *Endorses* the recommendations and conclusions of the Committee on Relations with the Host Country contained in paragraph 52 of its report;

2. *Considers* that the maintenance of appropriate conditions for the normal work of the delegations and the missions accredited to the United Nations and the observance of their privileges and immunities, which is an issue of great importance, are in the interest of the United Nations and all Member States, and requests the host country to continue to solve, through negotiations, problems that might arise and to take all measures necessary to prevent any interference with the functioning of missions;

3. *Welcomes* the decision of the Committee to conduct a detailed review of the implementation of the Parking Programme for Diplomatic Vehicles, as recommended by the Legal Counsel in his opinion on 24 September 2002, with a view to addressing the problems experienced by some permanent missions during the first year of the Programme, and ensuring its proper implementation in a manner that is fair, non-discriminatory, effective and consistent with international law;

4. *Expresses its appreciation* for the efforts made by the host country, and hopes that the issues raised at the meetings of the Committee will continue to be resolved in a spirit of cooperation and in accordance with international law;

5. *Notes* that during the reporting period the travel controls previously imposed by the host country on staff of certain missions and staff members of the Secretariat of certain nationalities remained in effect, and requests the host country to consider removing such travel controls, and in this regard notes the positions of affected States, of the Secretary-General and of the host country;

6. *Notes also* that the Committee anticipates that the host country will continue to ensure the issuance, in a timely manner, of entry visas to representatives of Member States, pursuant to article IV, section 11, of the

Agreement between the United Nations and the United States of America regarding the Headquarters of the United Nations, inter alia, for the purpose of their attending official United Nations meetings;

7. *Requests* the Secretary-General to remain actively engaged in all aspects of the relations of the United Nations with the host country;

8. *Requests* the Committee to continue its work in conformity with General Assembly resolution 2819 (XXVI);

9. *Decides* to include in the provisional agenda of its fifty-ninth session the item entitled "Report of the Committee on Relations with the Host Country".

International law

International bioethics law

Convention against cloning of human beings

Pursuant to General Assembly decision 57/512 [YUN 2002, p. 1340], an open-ended working group of the Sixth Committee met in New York from 29 September to 3 October 2003 to continue the consideration, begun in 2002 [ibid., p. 1339], of the elaboration of a mandate for the negotiation of an international convention against the reproductive cloning of human beings. Among the documents before the group were the previous year's working group report [A/C.6/57/L.4] and Sixth Committee report [A/57/569]; the revised Secretariat information document containing, among other things, a list of selected international instruments concerning the reproductive cloning of human beings [A/AC.263/2002/INF/1/Rev.1]; a paper submitted by the Holy See [A/C.6/58/WG.1/CRP.1]; and a 2 April letter from Costa Rica [A/58/73] transmitting a draft international convention on the prohibition of all forms of human cloning, with an explanatory commentary. The working group's report [A/C.6/58/L.9] was referred to the Sixth Committee.

A November report of the Sixth Committee [A/58/520] contained two draft resolutions, one introduced by Costa Rica and the other by Belgium, by which the Assembly would decide that the Ad Hoc Committee established by Assembly resolution 56/93 [YUN 2001, p. 1255] should be reconvened in 2004 to prepare, as a matter of urgency, a draft international convention against the reproductive cloning of human beings.

On 9 December, having considered the report of the Sixth Committee (above), the Assembly decided to include in the provisional agenda of its fifty-ninth (2004) session the item entitled "International convention against the reproductive cloning of human beings" (**decision 58/523**).

International economic law

In 2003, legal aspects of international economic law continued to be considered by the United Nations Commission on International Trade Law (UNCITRAL) and the by Sixth Committee of the General Assembly.

International trade law

At its thirty-sixth session (New York, 30 June–11 July), UNCITRAL finalized and adopted the UNCITRAL Model Legislative Provisions on Privately Financed Infrastructure Projects and approved in principle the draft UNCITRAL legislative guide on insolvency law. It continued work on arbitration, transport law, electronic commerce and security interests. It monitored the implementation of the 1958 New York Convention on the Recognition and Enforcement of Foreign Arbitral Awards (the New York Convention) [YUN 1958, p. 390], the work on the collection and dissemination of case law on UNCITRAL texts (CLOUT), and training and technical assistance activities. It also considered possible future work in public procurement and commercial fraud.

The report on the session [A/58/17] described actions taken on those topics (for details, see below).

GENERAL ASSEMBLY ACTION

On 9 December [meeting 72], the General Assembly, on the recommendation of the Sixth Committee [A/58/513], adopted **resolution 58/75** without vote [agenda item 151].

Report of the United Nations Commission on International Trade Law on the work of its thirty-sixth session

The General Assembly,

Recalling its resolution 2205(XXI) of 17 December 1966, by which it established the United Nations Commission on International Trade Law with a mandate to further the progressive harmonization and unification of the law of international trade and in that respect to bear in mind the interests of all peoples, in particular those of developing countries, in the extensive development of international trade,

Reaffirming its belief that the progressive modernization and harmonization of international trade law, in reducing or removing legal obstacles to the flow of international trade, especially those affecting the developing countries, would contribute significantly to universal economic cooperation among all States on a basis of equality, equity and common interest and to the elimination of discrimination in international trade and, thereby, to the well-being of all peoples,

Having considered the report of the Commission on its thirty-sixth session,

Concerned that activities undertaken by other bodies in the field of international trade law without adequate coordination with the Commission might lead to undesirable duplication of efforts and would not be in keeping with the aim of promoting efficiency, consistency and coherence in the unification and harmonization of international trade law,

Reaffirming the mandate of the Commission, as the core legal body within the United Nations system in the field of international trade law, to coordinate legal activities in this field, in particular to avoid duplication of efforts, including among organizations formulating rules of international trade, and to promote efficiency, consistency and coherence in the modernization and harmonization of international trade law, and to continue, through its secretariat, to maintain close cooperation with other international organs and organizations, including regional organizations, active in the field of international trade law, as stated in General Assembly resolution 50/47 of 11 December 1995,

Taking note of the proposals made by the Secretary-General in the proposed programme budget for the biennium 2004-2005 with a view to strengthening the secretariat of the Commission within the bounds of the resources available in the Organization so as to enable it to deal with the increased workload arising, inter alia, from the coordination of work with other organizations and growing demands for legislative technical assistance,

1. *Takes note with appreciation* of the report of the United Nations Commission on International Trade Law on its thirty-sixth session;

2. *Takes note with satisfaction* of the completion and adoption by the Commission of the Model Legislative Provisions on Privately Financed Infrastructure Projects;

3. *Commends* the Commission for its approval in principle of the draft legislative guide on insolvency law, elaborated in close cooperation with other international organizations, including the World Bank, the International Monetary Fund, the Asian Development Bank, the International Bar Association and the International Federation of Insolvency Professionals, and requests that the draft legislative guide be made available for comment to Member States, relevant intergovernmental and non-governmental organizations, as well as private sector and regional organizations and individual experts;

4. *Also commends* the Commission for the progress made in the work on the draft legislative guide on secured transactions, on model legislative provisions on interim measures in international commercial arbitration and on issues of electronic contracting and transport law;

5. *Requests* the Commission and its secretariat, relying on its role as the core legal body within the United Nations system in the field of international trade law, to take the lead in assuring cooperation and coordination with the World Bank, the International Monetary Fund, regional economic commissions and other international organizations in the work on international legal texts and propose appropriate and widely accepted international standards with due respect to the distinct objectives of the Commission and the international financial institutions;

6. *Reaffirms* the importance, in particular for developing countries, of the work of the Commission concerned with training and legislative technical assistance in the field of international trade law, and in this connection:

(a) Expresses its appreciation to the Commission for organizing seminars and briefing missions in Bangladesh, Botswana, Burkina Faso, Cuba, Kazakhstan, Mongolia, New Zealand, Peru, the Republic of Korea, the Russian Federation, Serbia and Montenegro, Thailand and Viet Nam;

(b) Expresses its appreciation to the Governments whose contributions enabled the seminars and briefing missions to take place, and appeals to Governments, the relevant bodies of the United Nations system, organizations, institutions and individuals to make voluntary contributions to the United Nations Commission on International Trade Law Trust Fund for Symposia and, where appropriate, to the financing of special projects, and otherwise to assist the secretariat of the Commission in carrying out training and legislative technical assistance activities, in particular in developing countries;

(c) Reiterates its appeal to the United Nations Development Programme and other bodies responsible for development assistance, such as the World Bank and regional development banks, as well as to Governments in their bilateral aid programmes, to support the training and legislative technical assistance programme of the Commission and to cooperate and coordinate their activities with those of the Commission;

7. *Appeals* to Governments, the relevant bodies of the United Nations system, organizations, institutions and individuals to make voluntary contributions to the trust fund established to provide travel assistance to developing countries that are members of the Commission, at their request and in consultation with the Secretary-General;

8. *Decides*, in order to ensure full participation by all Member States in the sessions of the Commission and its working groups, to continue, in the competent Main Committee during the fifty-eighth session of the General Assembly, its consideration of granting travel assistance to the least developed countries that are members of the Commission, at their request and in consultation with the Secretary-General;

9. *Stresses* the importance of bringing into effect the conventions emanating from the work of the Commission for the global unification and harmonization of international trade law, and, to this end, urges States that have not yet done so to consider signing, ratifying or acceding to those conventions;

10. *Requests* the Secretary-General, in view of the continuing demands on personnel resources of the secretariat of the Commission resulting, inter alia, from the need for coordination among a growing number of international organizations in the field of international trade law and the growing demand for legislative technical assistance, to keep under review the level of resources available to the Commission in order to ensure its ability to carry out its mandate.

Also on 9 December, the Assembly, by **decision 58/522**, took note of the consideration of the item entitled "Progressive development of the principles and norms of international law relating to the new international economic order", and noted that the question could be considered in the future.

International commercial arbitration

At its 2003 session [A/58/17], UNCITRAL took note of the reports of the Working Group on Arbitration and Conciliation on its thirty-seventh (Vienna, 7-11 October 2002) [A/CN.9/523 & Add.1,2] and thirty-eighth (New York, 12-16 May 2003) [A/CN.9/524] sessions, commending the Group for the progress accomplished on the issue of interim measures of protection.

At its thirty-seventh session, the Working Group continued deliberations on the power of a court or arbitral tribunal to order interim measures of protection on the basis of a draft text proposed by the United States for a revision of article 17 of the UNCITRAL Model Law on International Commercial Arbitration. Court-ordered interim measures of protection were also discussed, as were draft texts on the recognition and enforcement of interim measures issued by an arbitral tribunal for possible inclusion as a new provision in the Model Law. At its thirty-eighth session, the Working Group continued consideration of, among other things, the question of recognition and enforcement.

With respect to future work, UNCITRAL was informed that an expert group meeting held at the initiative of the Organisation for Economic Co-operation and Development had found that arbitration was an appropriate method for resolving intra-corporate disputes, in particular where the disputes involved parties from different States. The question of arbitrability, considered central to that work, was a topic that UNCITRAL felt could be reassessed when considering its future programme of work. Revision of the UNCITRAL Arbitration Rules (1976) and of the UNCITRAL Notes on Organizing Arbitral Proceedings (1996) could also be considered for inclusion in future work.

Implementation of the 1958 New York Convention

Under the ongoing project, approved by UNCITRAL in 1995 [YUN 1995, p. 1364], aimed at monitoring the legislative implementation of the 1958 New York Convention [YUN 1958, p. 390], UNCITRAL, at its 2003 session [A/58/17], noted that replies from 66 States parties to the Convention (out of the current 133) had been received to the questionnaire relating to the legal regime in those States governing the recognition and enforcement of foreign arbitral awards. UNCITRAL requested the secretariat to intensify efforts to obtain the information necessary for preparing its report and, for that purpose, to recirculate the questionnaire to States parties that had yet to reply and to request those that had replied to submit information on any new developments. The secretariat was further requested to obtain information from other sources, including from intergovernmental and non-governmental organizations.

Model Legislative Provisions on Privately Financed Infrastructure Projects

In 2003, UNCITRAL had before it the draft model law on privately financed infrastructure projects, which had been completed in 2002 [YUN 2002, p. 1344]; an explanatory note by the Secretariat on the draft model provisions [A/CN.9/522]; the text of the draft model provisions as approved by the Working Group on Privately Financed Infrastructure Projects [A/CN.9/522/Add.1]; a concordance table presenting side by side the draft model provisions and the legislative recommendations to which they related [A/CN.9/522/Add.2]; and a compilation of the comments received from Governments and international organizations on the draft model provisions [A/CN.9/533 & Add.1-7].

On 7 July, having concluded its review of the draft model provisions as revised by a drafting group, UNCITRAL adopted the Model Legislative Provisions on Privately Financed Infrastructure Projects as reproduced in annex I to its report [A/58/17]; requested the Secretary-General to transmit the text, along with the *UNICTRAL Legislative Guide on Privately Financed Infrastructure Projects*, to Governments, relevant international intergovernmental and non-governmental organizations, private sector entities and academic institutions; and requested the Secretariat, subject to the availability of resources, to consolidate in due course the Model Legislative Provisions and the *UNCITRAL Legislative Guide* into a single publication and to retain the legislative recommendations contained in the *Legislative Guide* as a basis of the development of the Model Legislative Provisions.

GENERAL ASSEMBLY ACTION

On 9 December [meeting 72], the General Assembly, on the recommendation of the Sixth Committee [A/58/513], adopted **resolution 58/76** without vote [agenda item 151].

Model Legislative Provisions on Privately Financed Infrastructure Projects of the United Nations Commission on International Trade Law

The General Assembly,

Bearing in mind the role of public-private partnerships to improve the provision and sound management of infrastructure and public services in the interest of sustainable economic and social development,

Recognizing the need to provide an enabling environment that both encourages private investment in infrastructure and takes into account the public interest concerns of the country,

Emphasizing the importance of efficient and transparent procedures for the award of privately financed infrastructure projects,

Stressing the desirability of facilitating project implementation by rules that enhance transparency, fairness and long-term sustainability and remove undesirable restrictions on private sector participation in infrastructure development and operation,

Recalling the valuable guidance that the United Nations Commission on International Trade Law has provided to Member States towards the establishment of a favourable legislative framework for private participation in infrastructure development through the *UNCITRAL Legislative Guide on Privately Financed Infrastructure Projects*,

Believing that the Model Legislative Provisions on Privately Financed Infrastructure Projects of the United Nations Commission on International Trade Law will be of further assistance to States, in particular developing countries, in promoting good governance and establishing an appropriate legislative framework for such projects,

1. *Expresses its appreciation* to the United Nations Commission on International Trade Law for the completion and adoption of the Model Legislative Provisions on Privately Financed Infrastructure Projects, the text of which is contained in annex I to the report of the United Nations Commission on International Trade Law on its thirty-sixth session;

2. *Requests* the Secretary-General to publish the Model Legislative Provisions and to make all efforts to ensure that the Model Legislative Provisions along with the *UNCITRAL Legislative Guide on Privately Financed Infrastructure Projects* become generally known and available;

3. *Also requests* the Secretary-General, subject to availability of resources, to consolidate in due course the text of the Model Legislative Provisions and the *Legislative Guide* into one single publication and, in doing so, to retain the legislative recommendations contained in the *Legislative Guide* as a basis of the development of the Model Legislative Provisions;

4. *Recommends* that all States give due consideration to the Model Legislative Provisions and the *Legislative Guide* when revising or adopting legislation related to private participation in the development and operation of public infrastructure.

Transport law

UNCITRAL, at its thirty-sixth session, had before it the reports of the Working Group on Transport Law on its tenth [YUN 2002, p. 1345] and eleventh (New York, 24 March–4 April 2003) [A/CN.9/526] sessions, describing its continuing discussions on the provisions of a draft instrument on transport law covering door-to-door transport operations. It was noted that a number of controversial issues remained open for discussion regarding the scope and individual provisions of the draft instrument. The view was expressed that increased flexibility in the design of the proposed instrument should continue to be explored by the Group to allow States to opt for all or part of the door-to-door regime. To expedite the Group's work within an acceptable time frame, UNCITRAL authorized the Group, on an exceptional basis, to hold its twelfth and thirteenth sessions on the basis of two-week sessions and, if possible, hold intersessional consultations, including through electronic mail.

The Working Group's report on its twelfth session (Vienna, 6-17 October) [A/CN.9/544] began its review of the draft instrument on the carriage of goods [wholly or partly] [by sea] contained in a secretariat note and discussed various proposals on 10 of its aspects. Based on its deliberations and conclusions, the Group requested the secretariat to prepare a revised draft of a number of provisions.

Electronic commerce

UNCITRAL, at its thirty-sixth session, took note of the reports of the Working Group on Electronic Commerce on its fortieth [YUN 2002, p. 1344] and forty-first (New York, 5-9 May 2003) [A/CN.9/528] sessions, during which it continued deliberations on a preliminary draft international convention on electronic commerce dealing with selected issues related to electronic contracting.

At its forty-first session, the Group resumed deliberations by holding a general discussion on the purpose and nature of the draft convention. The question before the Group was whether and to what extent the solutions for electronic contracting being considered in the context of the preliminary draft convention could also apply to transactions involving licensing of intellectual property rights and similar arrangements. The secretariat was to seek the views of relevant international organizations on the question, in particular the World Intellectual Property Organization.

The report of the Working Group on its forty-second session (Vienna, 17-21 November) [A/CN.9/546] covered its general exchange of views on the purpose and scope of the preliminary draft convention, which had been extensively revised and restructured to reflect the Group's deliberations at its previous session. The Group was reminded of the concerns expressed at its thirty-ninth (2002) session [YUN 2002, p. 1344] concerning the risk of establishing a duality of regimes for contract formation: a uniform regime for electronic contracts under the new instrument and a different, not harmonized, regime for contract formation by any other means, except for the few types of contract already covered by uniform law, such as sales contracts falling under the 1980 United Nations Sales Convention on Contracts for the International Sale of Goods [YUN 1980, p. 1131].

Case law on UNCITRAL texts

UNCITRAL noted the ongoing work under the established system for the collection and dissemination of case law on UNCITRAL texts (CLOUT), consisting of the preparation of case abstracts and of research aids and analytic tools, such as thesauri and indices, and the compilation of full texts of decisions. A total of 41 issues of CLOUT had been published, dealing with 476 cases.

New enhancements to the CLOUT system included the addition of a table of cases in each print edition, hyperlinks to the full text of a decision in the original language and to its translation into a UN official language, and keywords for cases interpreting the 1985 UNCITRAL Model Law on International Commercial Arbitration [YUN 1985, p. 1192]. UNCITRAL was also informed of the preparation of a new thesaurus on the Model Law.

The Commission expressed appreciation to the national correspondents for their work in selecting decisions and preparing case abstracts. The wide distribution of CLOUT in both print and electronic formats promoted the uniform interpretation and application of UNCITRAL texts by facilitating access to decisions and awards from other jurisdictions.

Insolvency law

UNCITRAL, at its thirty-sixth session, took note of the reports of the Working Group on Insolvency Law at its twenty-seventh [YUN 2002, p. 1346] and twenty-eighth (New York, 24-28 February) [A/CN.9/530] sessions. It expressed satisfaction with the Group's progress in developing the draft legislative guide on insolvency law, commending the level of consensus achieved and the comprehensive and balanced nature of the draft text.

At its twenty-eighth session, the Group, after completing its review of the core substance of the draft legislative guide, recommended that UNCITRAL approve the scope of the work as responsive to the Group's mandate; give preliminary approval to the key objectives, general features and structure of the insolvency regimes set forth in part one of the draft legislative guide; direct the secretariat to make the draft available for comment to all Member States, relevant intergovernmental and non-governmental international organizations, the private sector and regional organizations; and direct the Group to complete its work on the legislative guide for presentation in 2004 for UNCITRAL's approval and adoption.

Following its consideration of the draft legislative guide on insolvency law, UNCITRAL adopted a resolution approving, in principle, the policy considerations reflected in the draft legislative guide and the key objectives. It asked the secretariat to disseminate the draft legislative guide as requested by the Working Group; recommended that the secretariat coordinate and cooperate with the World Bank to identify points of difference between its *Principles and Guidelines for Effective Insolvency and Creditor Rights Systems*, currently under revision, and the draft legislative guide and identify a process for achieving alignment of those texts; and also recommended the continued collaboration between the Working Group on Insolvency Law and the Working Group on Security Interests (see below).

The Working Group on Insolvency Law, at its twenty-ninth session (Vienna, 1-5 September) [A/CN.9/542], reviewed the draft legislative guide and considered and revised the glossary of terms, which it could not complete for lack of time.

Security interests

UNCITRAL, at its thirty-sixth session, took note of the reports of the Working Group on Security Interests on its second (Vienna, 17-20 December 2002) [A/CN.9/531] and third (New York, 3-7 March 2003) [A/CN.9/532] sessions, at which the Working Group continued its work on the development of an efficient legal regime for security rights in goods involved in a commercial activity, in the form of a legislative guide. Also before it was the report of the first joint session (Vienna, 16-17 December 2002) of that Working Group and the Working Group on Insolvency Law [A/CN.9/535].

At the joint session, the two working groups deliberated on how to coordinate their work on the treatment of security interests in the case of insolvency proceedings, and requested the secretariat to prepare a revised version of chapter IX, Insolvency, of the draft legislative guide on secured transactions.

UNCITRAL commended the progress made at the sessions and noted plans for future joint expert meetings, the presentation of the modern registration systems of security rights in movable property and the secretariat's plan to prepare a paper dealing with technical issues arising in the context of such registries.

The Working Group on Security Interests, at its fourth session (Vienna, 8-12 September) [A/CN.9/543], continued to develop a legal regime for security rights in goods involved in a commercial activity. The secretariat was requested to prepare, on the basis of the Working Group's deliberations and decisions, a revision of the chapters of the draft guide that were discussed.

Training and technical assistance

UNCITRAL had before it a note by the secretariat [A/CN.9/536] describing training and technical assistance activities it had undertaken since 2002 and the direction of future activities. Reported, among other things, were nine seminars and briefing missions organized to promote understanding of international commercial law conventions, model laws and other legal texts, and participation in 45 seminars, conferences and courses examining UNCITRAL texts for possible adoption or use. UNCITRAL also co-sponsored the tenth Willem C. Vis International Commercial Arbitration Moot (Vienna, 11-17 April), to disseminate information about uniform law texts and teaching international trade law.

UNCITRAL reiterated its appeal to all States, international organizations and other interested entities to consider making contributions to its trust funds to enable it to meet increasing demands on its training and technical assistance programme. It requested the secretariat to consider making an assessment of the effectiveness of the programme, as had been suggested by the Office of Internal Oversight Services in 2002 [YUN 2002, p. 1360]. UNCITRAL also noted the initial steps taken by the Secretary-General to increase substantially the human and financial resources to the secretariat, for its implementation of the programme and the timely publication and dissemination of UNCITRAL's work.

Future work

In 2003, UNCITRAL held discussions on its future work programme on the basis of two secretariat notes: one set out activities of international and regional organizations in the area of government procurement [A/CN.9/539 & Add.1] since the adoption of the UNCITRAL Model Law on Procurement of Goods, Construction and Services [YUN 1994, p. 1328]; the other studied the impact and significance of commercial fraud, its meaning and nature, general issues of commercial law affected by it and possible courses of UNCITRAL action [A/CN.9/540].

In the light of certain issues that had arisen from the practical application of the Model Law that might justify adjustment of its text, UNCITRAL requested the secretariat to prepare detailed studies on those issues and proposals on how to address them for consideration by a working group in 2004. The secretariat's recommendation to organize an international colloquium on the various aspects of commercial fraud from the point of view of private law was strongly supported.

PART FIVE

Institutional, administrative and budgetary questions

Chapter I

Strengthening and restructuring of the United Nations system

During 2003, the continued implementation of the Secretary-General's programme of reform of the Organization began to yield results in terms of improved servicing of the General Assembly, a sharpened focus in public information activities and results-based budgeting. In highlighting progress towards realizing the key goal of strengthening the Organization, as set out in the Millennium Declaration, the Secretary-General reported that the United Nations had become more efficient, transparent and creative. It was at the forefront of the battle against poverty and HIV/AIDS; its capacity to deploy its peacekeeping and peace-building operations had improved; and the disparate elements of the UN system worked with better coherence.

To further advance the reforms, the Secretary-General proposed reorganizing the Departments for General Assembly and Conference Management, and of Public Information, establishing a strategic planning capacity in the Department of Economic and Social Affairs, and strengthening the management of the Office of the United Nations High Commissioner for Human Rights.

The Assembly, in order to revitalize its own work, adopted measures to enhance its authority and role and improve its working methods. It requested the Secretary-General to seek the views of Member States on improving the effectiveness of the First (Disarmament and International Security) Committee. It urged the Open-ended Working Group on the Question of Equitable Representation on and Increase in the Membership of the Security Council and Other Matters related to the Security Council to achieve progress on all aspects of the question, and encouraged the Office of Internal Oversight Services to continue to strengthen accountability throughout the Organization.

Programme of reform

General aspects

In his annual report on the work of the Organization (see p. 3), the Secretary-General noted that the ongoing UN programme of reform, initiated in 1997 [YUN 1997, p. 1389], had taken effect in several areas. Efforts to improve the servicing of the General Assembly and to sharpen the focus of public information activities had begun to yield results. The role of the Special Adviser on Africa had been strengthened to ensure a coherent and integrated approach to UN efforts in support of the region. Delegation of administrative authority to Secretariat departments and offices and the associated accountability of programme managers had been enhanced by results-based budgeting and management. The Departments of Management and of Peacekeeping Operations were working jointly to increase support to peacekeeping missions through new field procurement arrangements. Human resources management had improved further since the introduction of, among other measures, new staff selection and revised performance appraisal systems, targeted training, managed reassignments and flexible working arrangements. Despite new security arrangements, the 19 August attack on the United Nations Office in Baghdad (see p. 346) forced the Organization to re-examine those arrangements and consider fundamental changes.

To implement the refurbishment of the UN Headquarters complex authorized under the capital master plan, a financial package from the host country and public and private contributions were being explored. The UN financial situation had shown a positive trend in the last two years, with the indicators (cash on hand, debt to Member States, unpaid UN assessments) continuing to improve. The Office of Internal Oversight Services (OIOS) remained active in maintaining the Organization's integrity and ethics system. Major efforts were made towards ensuring that the 2004-2005 programme budget reflected the goal of the Secretary-General's agenda for further change, namely, the alignment of UN activities with the priorities agreed upon at the Millennium Summit [YUN 2000, p. 47] and global conferences. He proposed the reorganization of the Department for General Assembly and Conference Management and the Department of Public Information. He stated his intention to establish a strategic planning capacity in the Department of Economic and Social Affairs (DESA) and to strengthen the management of the Office of the United Nations High Commissioner for Human Rights (OHCHR).

Work was under way to bolster country-level actions relating to human rights, clarify roles and responsibilities in technical cooperation, streamline reporting and publications, and review the relationship between the Organization and civil society. UN funds and programmes had their impact at the country level by joint programming and pooling of resources; those measures were to be extended to more than 80 country programmes by 2006.

On 23 December, the General Assembly decided that the item on United Nations reform: measures and proposals would remain for consideration during its resumed fifty-eighth (2004) session (**decision 58/565**).

Agenda for change

Strengthening of the UN system

The Secretary-General, in response to General Assembly resolution 57/300 [YUN 2002, p. 1353], reported in September [A/58/351] on progress in implementing the reform measures proposed by him in 2002 [YUN 2002, p. 1352] and considered in resolution 57/300. Those measures included the alignment of UN activities with agreed priorities; strengthening human rights; enhancing public information; streamlining publications and reports; managing conferences and meetings; strengthening the effectiveness of the UN presence in developing countries; clarifying roles and responsibilities for technical cooperation; strengthening the management capacity of DESA; establishment of the Office of the Under-Secretary-General and Special Adviser on Africa; promoting partnerships; allocating resources to priorities; human resources management; and managing change. The report noted that the rationale of the Secretary-General's agenda for further change was to ensure that the Organization devoted attention to the priorities established in the Millennium Declaration [YUN 2000, p. 49] and in the outcomes of recent global conferences. The nature and pace of implementation currently under way also depended on progress made in a number of intergovernmental forums, the most significant being the Assembly, which would discuss at its fifty-eighth (2003) session systemic improvements to the planning and budgeting system. Other issues requiring further deliberation included funding for operational activities for development and the reform of treaty bodies. The report stressed that a stronger United Nations depended on commensurate changes in its intergovernmental organs, notably the Assembly, the Economic and Social Council and the Security Council. Revitalizing their agendas and improving their working methods would be an essential step towards improving UN efficiency and effectiveness. The implementation of the reforms also required the continued collective commitment of UN staff, managers and Member States.

Also in response to resolution 57/300, the Secretary-General submitted additional reports on a review of technical cooperation in the United Nations [A/58/382] (see p. 879), on the intergovernmental review of the medium-term plan and the programme budget [A/57/786], and on improvements to the current planning and budgeting process [A/58/395 & Corr.1, A/58/600], which the Assembly considered in **resolution 58/269** of 23 December (see p. 1395).

By **decision 58/565** of 23 December, the Assembly decided that the item on strengthening of the United Nations system would remain for consideration during its resumed fifty-eighth (2004) session.

Implementation of the Millennium Declaration

Note by Secretary-General. The Secretary-General, by a 4 February note [A/57/372/Add.1], transmitted his comments and those of the United Nations System Chief Executives Board for Coordination (CEB) on the 2002 Joint Inspection Unit (JIU) report [YUN 2002, p. 1356] entitled "The results approach in the United Nations: implementing the United Nations Millennium Declaration". The comments related to the two parts of the report: part one, on the results-based budgeting and planning procedures practised in the United Nations; and part two, proposing the creation of new instruments and processes to enable the UN system to adopt effective results-based approaches and to provide Member States with effective monitoring of progress towards the objectives of the Millenium Declaration [YUN 2000, p. 49]. The report was seen as a timely reminder of the need to keep the results approach under review. Finding the report too wide-ranging to permit a judicious overall assessment that could lead to concrete follow-up action, particularly with regard to the linkages it attempted to establish between its two parts, CEB proposed that the two parts be taken up seriatim at the intergovernmental level.

GENERAL ASSEMBLY ACTION

On 15 April [meeting 83], the General Assembly, on the recommendation of the Fifth (Administrative and Budgetary) Committee [A/57/649/Add.1], adopted **resolution 57/303** without vote [agenda item 112].

Report of the Joint Inspection Unit entitled "The results approach in the United Nations: implementing the United Nations Millennium Declaration"

The General Assembly,

Reaffirming its resolution 55/231 of 23 December 2000 and the Regulations and Rules Governing Programme Planning, the Programme Aspects of the Budget, the Monitoring of Implementation and the Methods of Evaluation,

Recalling its resolutions 56/253 of 24 December 2001 and 57/284 A and B of 20 December 2002 and its decision 57/575 of 20 December 2002,

Having considered the report of the Joint Inspection Unit entitled "The results approach in the United Nations: implementing the United Nations Millennium Declaration" and the comments of the Secretary-General and those of the United Nations System Chief Executives Board for Coordination thereon,

1. *Takes note with appreciation* of the report of the Joint Inspection Unit and the comments of the Secretary-General and those of the United Nations System Chief Executives Board for Coordination thereon;

2. *Requests* the Committee for Programme and Coordination to consider the report of the Joint Inspection Unit and the comments of the Secretary-General and those of the Chief Executives Board at its forty-third session and to report thereon to the General Assembly at its fifty-eighth session.

CPC action. In keeping with the foregoing Assembly resolution, the Committee for Programme and Coordination (CPC), at its forty-third session (New York, 9 June–3 July and 9 July 2003) [A/58/16], considered the 2002 JIU report, together with the related comments of the Secretary-General and CEB (see p. 1384). CPC noted that, while the report highlighted important conceptual elements and addressed a multiplicity of issues, it was complex and not readily accessible, and its recommendations were too sweeping, ambitious and impractical.

CPC recommended that the Assembly take note of JIU's recommendations on the subject; urge JIU to improve the presentation and format of its reports, making them focused, concise and reader-friendly; and review those efforts during its fifty-eighth (2003) session.

Report of Secretary-General. In his September annual report [A/58/323], the Secretary-General evaluated the progress achieved by the UN system and Member States in implementing the United Nations Millennium Declaration [YUN 2000, p. 49] in the areas of peace and security (see p. 48), development, and human rights, democracy and good governance (see p. 736), and the obstacles encountered, and re-examined some of the underlying assumptions of the Declaration. He pointed out that the United Nations was at the forefront of the fight against poverty and HIV/AIDS, and its peacekeeping and peace-building operations had improved and, by and large, had responded well to unexpected challenges in Afghanistan, Kosovo (Serbia and Montenegro), Sierra Leone and Timor-Leste. Overall, the United Nations, with its disparate elements, worked with greater coherence and had built fruitful partnerships with a wide range of non-State actors. As it evolved with the times, it had become more efficient, more transparent and more creative.

The Secretary-General said he had appointed a high-level panel to review the whole range of relations between the United Nations and global civil society, the essential counterpart of which had to be a review of the UN principal organs—the General Assembly, the Security Council, the Economic and Social Council and the Trusteeship Council—in terms of their effectiveness, coherence, and the balance of roles and responsibilities among them. All needed to be reinvigorated or reformed. He said the Member States might wish to set 2005, the year scheduled for the five-year review of the implementation of the Millennium Declaration commitments, as a deadline for reaching agreement on the reforms needed to enable those organs to meet the new challenges outlined in his report.

By **decision 58/565** of 23 December, the General Assembly decided that the item on the follow-up to the outcome of the Millennium Summit would remain for consideration during its resumed fifty-eighth (2004) session.

Preparation for 2005 review

CEB action. CEB, at its first 2003 regular session (Paris, 25-26 April) [CEB/2003/1], addressed the follow-up to the Millennium Summit [YUN 2000, p. 47], focusing on "Strategies for sustainable development", one of the themes to be given special attention in the Secretary-General's 2003 report on implementation of the United Nations Millennium Declaration [ibid., p. 49] (see p. 840).

CEB also considered the report of its High-level Committee on Programmes (HLCP) on its fifth session (Rome, 26-27 March) [CEB/2003/4] regarding its work on preparations for the 2005 comprehensive review of follow-up to the Millennium Declaration, specifically on how the UN system should position itself in relation to that review. CEB emphasized the importance of HLCP in shaping the structure and content of the review. Accordingly, HLCP, at its sixth session (Rome, 18-19 September) [CEB/2003/7], agreed that its contribution to the review should focus on the three major themes: peace and security; human rights and governance; and development and protection of the environment. Its report should take the form of a strategic document demonstrating

Managerial reform and oversight

Procurement

OIOS report. Pursuant to General Assembly resolutions 48/218 B [YUN 1994, p. 1362] and 54/244 [YUN 1999, p. 1274], the Secretary-General, by an October note [A/58/294], transmitted to the Assembly an OIOS report on its audit of the functioning of the Headquarters Committee on Contracts (HCC) during the period from January 2000 to August 2002. HCC's primary function was to advise the Office of Central Support Services (OCSS) as to whether proposed procurement in excess of $200,000 and contracts involving income in excess of $40,000 complied with the Financial Regulations and Rules of the United Nations, procedures, administrative issuances and instructions.

The audit found that 1,498 procurement cases valued at about $3 billion were submitted for HCC review; cases valued under $1 million totalled around 68 per cent in number but only about 11 per cent in value; 90 cases valued at about $81 million (about 10 per cent of all cases reviewed) were reviewed on an ex post facto/partial ex post facto basis (after complete or partial procurement had transpired). Most of the cases did not meet the Procurement Manual's definition of exigency. Records also revealed that HCC spent only two working days for the review of certain cases with significant monetary value. In addition, the Procurement Manual did not clearly describe the provisions and criteria governing the tenure of HCC members, the voting process or the pre-clearance procedure, as established by HCC in 2000.

OIOS made 10 recommendations, among which it called for transferring HCC from the administrative authority of OCSS to that of the Office of the Under-Secretary-General for Management; an increase of the current procurement threshold for review to $500,000 or $1 million; a monitoring of "walk-in", "special meeting" and "telephonic" presentations; limiting non-regular presentations to exceptions and the rejection of all submissions giving less than the required number of review days; referring ex post facto cases to the Controller; an extension of the current minimum review time for cases; assessment by HCC as to whether its review time was sufficient prior to accepting complex cases and those with high monetary value; and a revision of the Procurement Manual to clarify the tenure of HCC members, the criteria and process for their selection, voting and pre-clearance procedures.

The Under-Secretary-General for Management generally concurred with the recommendations but disagreed with some of the findings, as well as with the need to transfer HCC from its current placement.

By **decision 58/564 A** of 23 December, the Assembly deferred until its resumed fifty-eighth (2004) session consideration of the agenda item on the report of OIOS on the audit of HCC.

Oversight activities

Internal oversight

At its resumed fifty-seventh session, the General Assembly, by **decision 57/556 B** of 15 April, took note of the 2002 OIOS report [YUN 2002, p. 615] on the management review of OHCHR.

At its fifty-eighth session, the Assembly had before it the reports of OIOS on its own activities for the period from 1 July 2001 to 30 June 2002 [YUN 2002, p. 1359] and on the 2002 investigation into sexual exploitation of female refugees by aid workers and peacekeepers in West Africa [ibid., p. 1202].

OIOS activities. In September, the Secretary-General transmitted the ninth annual report of OIOS covering its activities from 1 July 2002 to 30 June 2003 [A/58/364].

During that period, OIOS issued nine reports for transmittal by the Secretary-General to the General Assembly. Those issued in 2003, in addition to its report on its own activities (above), were on: procurement of goods and services through letters of assist [A/57/718]; implementation of all provisions of Assembly resolution 55/258 [YUN 2001, p. 1337] on human resources management [A/57/726]; review of the structure and operations of UN information centres (UNICs) [A/57/747]; audit of the Investment Management Service of the United Nations Joint Staff Pension Fund [A/58/81]; review of duplication, complexity and bureaucracy in UN administrative processes and procedures [A/58/211]; audit of the functioning of HCC [A/58/294]; the UN capital master plan for the period January to July 2003 [A/58/342]; investigation into the fraudulent diversion of $4.3 million by a senior staff member of the reconstruction pillar of the United Nations Interim Administration Mission in Kosovo [A/58/592]; and the administration of peacekeeping trust funds [A/58/613].

The OIOS reports for transmittal to CPC included a proposal for two evaluation themes: post-conflict peace-building and integrated water management, for a pilot thematic evaluation [E/AC.51/2003/2]; an in-depth evaluation of the programme on the law of the sea and ocean affairs [E/AC.51/2003/3]; and two triennial reviews of the implementation of the recommendations made by CPC in 2000 on the in-depth evaluations of global development trends, issues and policies, global approaches to social and microeconomic issues and policies and the corresponding subprogrammes in the regional commissions [E/AC.51/2003/4], and of the advancement of women programme [E/AC.51/2003/5 & Corr.1].

During the reporting period, OIOS issued 2,737 recommendations, of which 789 were classified as critical. The overall implementation rate for all recommendations was 50.6 per cent; that for critical recommendations was 32.6 per cent. As at June 2003, the implementation of 72 (including 10 critical) recommendations issued during 2000/01 and 185 (including 31 critical) recommendations issued during 2001/02 had not started owing to their complexity or to the lengthy negotiations on modalities required for implementation. Of the 789 critical recommendations, 50 per cent aimed to improve operational efficiency and effectiveness; 35 per cent to improve administration and management; 11 per cent to improve accuracy of management information; and 4 per cent to improve security and disclosure of mismanagement, misconduct or fraud.

Savings and recoveries from OIOS audits and investigations totalled $15.4 million, compared to the $27.6 million reported in the previous period [YUN 2002, pp. 1359 & 1360].

The report outlined the oversight results and assessments for various UN departments and offices, which were the outcome of audit, evaluation, inspection, investigation and management consulting activities undertaken during the reporting period. It described the risk-management framework that had guided the planning of oversight assignments.

OIOS received 630 new cases for investigation, a 17 per cent increase from the previous reporting period [YUN 2002, p. 1359]. In addition to some 50 cases under investigation, 200 backlog cases were awaiting sufficient resources for resolution.

To enable it to meet the goals and objectives of the internal oversight programme and to contribute to the Organization's priorities for 2003, OIOS developed a strategy centred on five main themes: utilizing a risk-management framework to guide oversight activities; establishing an organizational integrity programme to combat fraud and corruption; promoting results-based management through enhanced monitoring and evaluation; providing change management consulting services; and rationalizing and prioritizing its investigation services. To underpin the strategy, OIOS strengthened its resource and information technology management.

GENERAL ASSEMBLY ACTION

On 15 April [meeting 83], the General Assembly, on the recommendation of the Fifth Committee [A/57/604/Add.1], adopted **resolution 57/287 C** without vote [agenda item 122].

Report of the Secretary-General on the activities of the Office of Internal Oversight Services

The General Assembly,

Recalling its resolutions 48/218 B of 29 July 1994 and 54/244 of 23 December 1999,

Recalling also its resolution 56/246 of 24 December 2001,

Having considered the annual report of the Office of Internal Oversight Services of the Secretariat for the period from 1 July 2001 to 30 June 2002,

1. *Notes with appreciation* the work of the Office of Internal Oversight Services;

2. *Takes note* of the annual report of the Office of Internal Oversight Services;

3. *Welcomes* the continuing efforts of the Office of Internal Oversight Services to coordinate its programme with other oversight bodies, including the Board of Auditors and the Joint Inspection Unit;

4. *Stresses* the need for adequate supervision and record-keeping of peacekeeping equipment, proper inventory and internal control systems, sufficient control over mission accounts and compliance with procurement guidelines, and requests the Secretary-General to ensure that the applicable recommendations of the Office of Internal Oversight Services are implemented fully by the relevant departments and peacekeeping missions;

5. *Encourages* the Office of Internal Oversight Services to continue to help to ensure better use of the resources of the Organization and to strengthen accountability throughout the Organization;

6. *Notes with concern* the findings of the Office of Internal Oversight Services on problem areas in the functioning and administration of the Investment Management Service of the United Nations Joint Staff Pension Fund, and requests the Secretary-General to ensure full and expeditious implementation of the relevant recommendations of the Office that are of critical importance.

On 23 December, the Assembly, by **decision 58/564 A**, deferred to its resumed fifty-eighth (2004) session consideration of the OIOS report on its activities for the period 1 July 2002 to 30 June 2003.

External oversight

Joint Inspection Unit

In its thirty-fifth report to the General Assembly [A/59/34], JIU gave an overview of its activities in 2003, during which it issued seven reports, on:

review of management and administration in the United Nations Industrial Development Organization [JIU/REP/2003/1]; review of the UN budgetary process [JIU/REP/2003/2]; from the optical disk system to the official document system: status of implementation and evaluation [JIU/REP/2003/3]; multilingualism and access to information: case study on the World Health Organization [JIU/REP/2003/4]; achieving the universal primary education goal of the Millennium Declaration: new challenges for development cooperation [JIU/REP/2003/5]; management review of OHCHR [JIU/REP/2003/6]; and evaluation of the UN Volunteers programme [JIU/REP/2003/7].

During 2003, JIU began a comprehensive review to identify impediments to its effective functioning and to design possible solutions. The review stemmed from its conclusion that it needed to improve its functioning and the quality and impact of its activities and from a CPC recommendation that it undertake an in-depth review of its statute and working methods and present to the Assembly proposals for addressing its weaknesses. Accordingly, the Secretary-General, by a September note [A/58/343], transmitted to the Assembly the report of JIU on its preliminary review, identifying the weaknesses and issues to be addressed, among them the selection of inspectors, their term of office and the ratio of inspectors to research staff; meaningful follow-up of JIU's accepted recommendations, which were advisory rather than mandatory; improvement of its annual programme of work, based on suggestions received from participating organizations; and the limited powers granted by the statute to its Chairman. Annexed to the report was the outline of a strategic framework for identifying programmatic, managerial and administrative areas in the UN system that presented an element of risk.

By a November addendum to his note [A/58/343/Add.1], the Secretary-General transmitted JIU's in-depth analysis of the issues previously identified as the most problematic with corresponding proposals for Assembly action.

The Secretary-General transmitted to the Assembly, on 28 February, the JIU work programme for 2003 [A/58/64] and, on 19 August, the preliminary list of reports for possible inclusion in the work programme for 2004 and beyond [A/58/291].

On 6 August [A/58/220], the Secretary-General transmitted to the Assembly information on the status of implementation of the recommendations contained in the JIU reports on strengthening the UN system capacity for conflict prevention; sharing responsibilities in peacekeeping: the United Nations and regional organizations; and travel in the United Nations: issues of efficiency and cost savings.

By **decision 58/564 A** of 23 December, the Assembly deferred until its resumed fifty-eighth (2004) session consideration of the item on the report of JIU; the programme of work of JIU for 2003; the preliminary list of potential reports for its work programme for 2004 and beyond; the implementation of recommendations contained in JIU reports; and the JIU reports on the preliminary and in-depth reviews of its statute and working methods.

The Assembly, in **resolution 58/272** (section VI) of the same date (see p. 1418), approved the gross budget for JIU for 2004 in the amount of $4,900,800, and decided to take action on the gross budget for JIU for 2005 in the context of the first performance report on the programme budget for the biennium 2004-2005.

Intergovernmental machinery

Revitalization of the work of the General Assembly

By an 8 September note [A/57/861], the General Assembly President indicated that, in the continuing process of revitalizing the Assembly, open-ended informal consultations in the plenary had been held from November 2002 to June 2003 on the subject. The outcome of those consultations, which contained suggested reform measures, including those proposed in 2002 [YUN 2002, p. 1363], was summarized in the annex to the note.

The President announced that the amendment to rule 1 of the rules of procedure of the Assembly regularizing the opening of its annual session and of the general debate, including its duration, would take effect as from the fifty-eighth (2003) session, as decided by the Assembly in resolution 57/301 (see p. 1464). Also, in accordance with the earlier amendments contained in resolution 56/509 [YUN 2002, p. 1429], the Assembly, on 6 June, elected the incoming Assembly President, 21 Vice-Presidents and the Chairpersons of the Main Committees (see p. 1556) to allow ample time for the smooth transition to those officials and thereby contribute to improving the Assembly's work.

The Assembly also recommended for further discussion in informal consultations the report of a seminar (New York, 16-17 May) [A/57/836] entitled "From promise to practice: revitalizing the General Assembly for the new millennium", organized by the Netherlands, in collaboration with the New York–based International Peace Academy. Participants discussed issues relating to the role of and priority issues for the Assembly, the streamlining of its agenda, its decision-making processes, organization of work and suggestions for improving its efficiency and effectiveness.

By **decision 57/595** of 15 September, the Assembly included in the draft agenda of its fifty-eighth (2003) session the item entitled "Revitalization of the work of the General Assembly".

GENERAL ASSEMBLY ACTION

On 19 December [meeting 76], the General Assembly adopted **resolution 58/126** [draft: A/58/L.49/Rev.1, orally revised], without vote [agenda item 55].

Revitalization of the work of the General Assembly

The General Assembly,

Recalling its previous resolutions relating to the revitalization of its work,

Aware of the need to enhance its authority and role and to improve its working methods,

Decides to adopt the text contained in the annex to the present resolution.

Annex

A. Enhancing the authority and role of the General Assembly

In order to enhance the authority and role of the General Assembly, it is decided that:

1. Member States reaffirm the relevant provisions of the Charter of the United Nations and the United Nations Millennium Declaration on the central position of the General Assembly.

2. The Security Council is invited to submit periodically, in accordance with Article 24 of the Charter, special subject-oriented reports to the General Assembly for its consideration on issues of current international concern.

3. The Security Council is invited to continue with initiatives to improve the quality of its annual report to the General Assembly, mandated by Article 24, paragraph 3, of the Charter, in order to provide the Assembly with a substantive, analytical and material account of its work, in accordance with resolution 51/193.

4. In carrying out the assessment of the debate on the annual report of the Security Council called for in resolution 51/241, annex, paragraph 12, the President shall inform the General Assembly of his decision regarding the need for further consideration of the Security Council report, including in respect of the convening of informal consultations, on the need for, and content of, any action by the Assembly based on the debate, as well as on any matters to be brought to the attention of the Security Council.

5. The President of the General Assembly should continue to be briefed regularly by the President of the Security Council on the work of the Council. The President of the Assembly may wish to inform Member States about the substantive issues raised during these meetings.

6. The Presidents of the General Assembly, the Security Council and the Economic and Social Council should meet together periodically with a view to ensuring increased cooperation, coordination and complementarity of the work programmes of the three organs in accordance with their respective responsibilities under the Charter. In this connection, the President of the Security Council may wish to discuss the plans of the Security Council for thematic debates with the President of the General Assembly and the President of the Economic and Social Council. The President of the Assembly will inform Member States about the outcome of these meetings.

7. In June of each year, the President-elect of the General Assembly, after taking into account the views provided by Member States and following consultations with the incumbent President and the Secretary-General, will suggest an issue, or issues, of global concern upon which Member States will be invited to comment during the general debate at the forthcoming session of the Assembly. The views provided by Member States should also be summarized and circulated to Member States. Such suggestions regarding the issue(s) for comment will be without prejudice to the sovereign right of Member States to solely and entirely determine the content of their general debate statements.

8. The work and decisions of the General Assembly should be better publicized. Accordingly, the support provided by the Department of Public Information of the Secretariat for these purposes should be intensified and strengthened. The Secretary-General is requested to present a plan to this end, within existing resources, to the next session of the Committee on Information, so that recommendations can be made to the Assembly.

9. Member States and the Secretariat should consider initiatives that might be taken for better monitoring of the follow-up of resolutions of the General Assembly, such as the provision of timely inputs for reports of the Secretary-General and giving effect to proposals that would advance the follow-up of major United Nations conferences and summits.

10. The resources available to the Office of the President of the General Assembly in personnel and other support shall be augmented from within existing resources, bearing in mind the provisions of paragraph 22 of the annex to resolution 55/285. Five additional posts shall be made available to supplement current support, of which three shall be filled on an annual basis, following consultations with the incoming President, beginning at the fifty-ninth session of the Assembly.

11. Transitional office accommodation and other support shall be provided to the President-elect of the General Assembly. The Secretary-General is requested to make the necessary arrangements for the provision of such support, within existing resources, beginning with the President-elect of the fifty-ninth session of the Assembly.

B. Improving the working methods of the General Assembly

The working methods of the General Assembly need to be further rationalized in order to improve its efficiency and effectiveness and to make its outcomes more productive. Towards this end:

1. The General Committee shall meet throughout the session and further improve its working methods to increase its efficiency and effectiveness. It will play

the leading role in advising the General Assembly on the efficient organization, coordination and management of its work. In this connection, the Assembly will also consider proposals to reform the General Committee.

2. The work of the Main Committees of the General Assembly might benefit if it is scheduled over two substantive periods during the session. The rescheduling of the work of the Main Committees should not lead to additional costs, additional or longer meetings, or staggered work schedules of the Main Committees. With a view to enabling the Assembly to consider changes in this regard, with effect from the sixtieth session of the Assembly, the Secretary-General is requested to present, by 1 February 2004, various options for consideration by the General Committee, taking into account the requirements of the relevant intergovernmental bodies and the different locations of their meetings and the budget cycle. The General Committee shall hold open-ended discussions on the options presented by the Secretary-General before making recommendations to the Assembly for its decision by 1 July 2004.

3. The General Assembly will consider convening more interactive debates. At the beginning of each session, the General Committee, following recommendations from the President of the General Assembly, shall recommend to the Assembly a programme of, and format for, interactive debates during that session on items on its agenda.

4. With a view to better conceptualization of the content of the agenda of the General Assembly, the Secretary-General is requested to submit to the Assembly, for its consideration by 1 March 2004, an illustrative agenda of the Assembly, based on all the agenda items of the fifty-eighth session, organized around the priorities of the Organization for the period 2002-2005. The General Committee shall hold open-ended discussions on the illustrative agenda before making recommendations on the matter to the Assembly for its decision by 1 July 2004.

5. It would be advantageous for the General Assembly to have a shorter agenda to ensure the fullest discussion of all issues, so that its decisions may have greater impact. Accordingly, the President of the General Assembly at its fifty-eighth session, in consultation with the Secretary-General, and following consultations with concerned Member States, is requested to make proposals for the further biennialization, triennialization, clustering and elimination of items of the customary agenda of the Assembly for the consideration of the General Committee by 1 April 2004. The General Committee shall hold open-ended discussions on the proposals before making recommendations on the matter to the Assembly for its decision by 1 July 2004.

6. General Assembly resolutions should be more concise, focused and action-oriented. Where practical, more actions taken by the Assembly should be in the form of decisions. Preambular paragraphs in resolutions of the Assembly should normally be kept to the minimum.

7. The heavy volume of documentation that is submitted to the General Assembly for its consideration should be reduced. In this regard, the Secretary-General is requested to continue his efforts to make proposals to Member States for the consolidation of reports on related subjects in accordance with the provisions of paragraph 20 of resolution 57/300. The proposals on a shorter agenda should be accompanied by related proposals for a reduction in the volume of documentation.

8. The Main Committees of the General Assembly are bound by the rules of procedure of the General Assembly, although they have different practices and working methods. With a view to identifying best practices and working methods, and recognizing the ongoing efforts of the Main Committees to streamline their work, the Secretary-General, drawing on the experience of previous Chairmen of the Main Committees, is requested to submit a historical and analytical note on the practices and working methods of the Main Committees for the consideration of the General Committee by 1 April 2004. The General Committee shall hold open-ended discussions on the note before making recommendations on the matter to the Assembly for its decision by 1 July 2004.

9. In accordance with paragraph 2 *(a)* and *(c)* of resolution 56/509, the General Assembly elects the President of the Assembly, the Vice-Presidents of the Assembly, and the Chairmen of the Main Committees at least three months before the opening of the session in which they will serve. In order to foster better advance planning and preparation of the work of the Main Committees, the full Bureaux of the Main Committees shall similarly be elected three months in advance of the next session.

On 23 December, the Assembly decided that the item entitled "Revitalization of the work of the General Assembly" would remain for consideration during its resumed fifty-eighth (2004) session (**decision 58/565**).

Improving the methods of work of the First Committee

On 8 December [meeting 71], the General Assembly, on the recommendation of the First Committee [A/58/462], adopted **resolution 58/41** without vote [agenda item 73].

Improving the effectiveness of the methods of work of the First Committee

The General Assembly,

Expressing grave concern over both existing threats to international peace and security and new threats that have become manifest in the post–September 11, 2001 period,

Reaffirming the role of the First Committee of the General Assembly in dealing with questions of disarmament and related international security issues, consistent with the functions and powers of the Assembly in the maintenance of international peace and security, including the principles governing disarmament and the regulation of armaments, as stipulated in Article 11, paragraph 1, of the Charter of the United Nations,

Considering that the improvement of the methods of work of the First Committee would complement and facilitate the broader effort to revitalize the General Assembly,

Noting in this regard the relevant reports of the Secretary-General and related General Assembly resolutions on this subject, as well as the ongoing process in the open-ended informal consultations in the plenary on the revitalization of the Assembly chaired by its President, and seeking to contribute to this effort,

1. *Requests* the Secretary-General, within existing resources, to seek the views of Member States on the issue of improving the effectiveness of the methods of work of the First Committee, to prepare a report compiling and organizing the views of Member States on appropriate options, and to submit the report to the General Assembly for consideration at its fifty-ninth session;

2. *Decides* to include in the provisional agenda of its fifty-ninth session an item entitled "Improving the effectiveness of the methods of work of the First Committee".

Review of Security Council membership and related matters

The Open-ended Working Group on the Question of Equitable Representation on and Increase in the Membership of the Security Council and Other Matters related to the Security Council, established by General Assembly resolution 48/26 [YUN 1993, p. 212], submitted a report on its work during five substantive sessions held between 29 January and 20 June [A/57/47 & Corr.1]. Discussions continued on the issues under cluster I: decision-making, including the veto, the Council's expansion and periodic review of an enlarged Council; and on those under cluster II: the Council's working methods and transparency of its work. The Working Group had before it conference papers prepared by its Bureau.

At its first session (29 January), the Working Group adopted its programme of work. At its second session (10, 12-13 February), it began consideration of clusters I and II issues, which continued into the third (18, 20-21 March) and fourth (5-8 May) sessions, on the basis of two related conference room papers annexed to the Group's previous report [YUN 2002, p. 1364]. At the third session, proposals on decision-making procedures in an enlarged Council were submitted by Italy and Japan, while the Council President (Guinea) and two other Council members (Mexico and United Kingdom), at the Group's invitation, discussed steps taken by the Council to ensure greater openness and transparency in its procedures and working methods. At its fourth session, the Assembly President briefed the Group on the results of a questionnaire that he had formulated in his personal capacity on the Group's work and working methods and distributed informally to the Group prior to the session. At its fifth session (2-20 June), the Group considered and adopted its report to the Assembly.

By **decision 57/591** of 3 July, the Assembly took note of the Working Group's report; welcomed the progress achieved on issues dealing with the Security Council's working methods; and urged the Group to continue efforts during the Assembly's fifty-eighth session to achieve progress in all aspects of the question of equitable representation on and increase in the Council's membership and other related matters, taking account of progress achieved during the forty-eighth (1993) through the fifty-seventh Assembly sessions, and the views to be expressed on the question during the fifty-eighth session, and to report to the Assembly before the end of that session.

On 23 December, the Assembly decided that the item on the question of equitable representation on and increase in the membership of the Security Council and related matters would remain for consideration during its resumed fifty-eighth (2004) session (**decision 58/565**).

Revitalization of the United Nations in the economic, social and related fields

Report of Secretary-General. The Secretary-General, in a May report to the Economic and Social Council [E/2003/74], highlighted progress in implementing the key provisions of the Council's agreed conclusions 2002/1 [YUN 2002, p. 1365] on strengthening the Council further, building on its recent achievements, to help it fulfil the role ascribed to it in the Charter of the United Nations, as contained in the UN Millennium Declaration [YUN 2000, p. 49], and of the related provisions of General Assembly resolution 45/264 [YUN 1991, p. 749], which had called for annual reporting on the restructuring and revitalization of the United Nations in the economic, social and related fields. The report also addressed the implementation of the provisions on that subject, as contained in Assembly resolutions 50/227 [YUN 1996, p. 1249] and 52/12 B [YUN 1997, p. 1392] and in Council resolutions 1998/46 [YUN 1998, p. 1262] and 1999/51 [YUN 1999, p. 1281].

The report observed that, while the Council's working methods had significantly improved in their efficiency and in the increased involvement of its subsidiary bodies and other stakeholders in its work, modalities needed to be developed further for the integrated and effective consideration in the UN intergovernmental structure of the follow-up to the common agenda emerging from major conferences. The report recommended that the Council adopt omnibus resolutions, especially on subjects relating to the follow-up to a major UN conference or summit; continuously seek to maximize its support to, and complement, the

Assembly's work, to avoid overlap; consider ways to further enhance its annual spring meetings with the Bretton Woods institutions (the World Bank Group and the International Monetary Fund) and the World Trade Organization as a global forum for advancing the commitments made at the 2002 International Conference on Financing for Development [YUN 2002, p. 953]; invite non-governmental organizations to contribute to the work of its various segments; examine its Bureau's suggestions regarding the modalities of its work and provide guidance on how to put them into practice in preparing for its 2004 session; and invite its Bureau to monitor the timeliness of documentation.

Other recommendations called on the Council to: further build its operational activities segment as a global forum for providing overall policy guidance to the UN system's operational activities for development and to encourage the full cooperation of the funds and programmes; use its coordination, operational, humanitarian and general segments to mainstream implementation of conference goals in the system's work programmes and recommend new policies and measures to that end; recommend that, at the organizational session, its Bureau make further proposals for consolidating reports to be submitted at the general segment; and further encourage its subsidiary bodies to schedule their meetings at least eight weeks before the Council session so that their outcomes were fully reflected in the Council's work.

The Council, by **decision 2003/308** of 25 July, deferred consideration of the item on the implementation of General Assembly resolutions 50/227 and 52/12 B until its resumed substantive session.

On 23 December, the Assembly decided that the item on the restructuring and revitalization of the United Nations in the economic, social and related fields would remain for consideration at its resumed fifty-eighth (2004) session (**decision 58/565**).

Work of the functional commissions

The Secretary-General, responding to the agreed conclusions 2002/1 [YUN 2002, p. 1365], submitted a consolidated report in June, with a later addendum [E/2003/90 & Add.1], on the work of the functional commissions of the Economic and Social Council in 2003, aimed at assisting the Council in providing policy guidance to them and in coordinating their work. The report analysed selected major policy issues addressed by the commissions and highlighted their contributions to the various segments of the 2003 substantive Council session. It further examined the commissions' follow-up action to policy guidance provided by the Council in 2002, reviewed key issues relating to the coordination or procedural aspects of their work and made recommendations for the Council's consideration and action.

The Council, by **decision 2003/314** of 19 December, deferred consideration of the item entitled "Implementation of General Assembly resolutions 50/227 and 52/12 B: Consolidated report on the work of the functional commissions of the Economic and Social Council in 2003" until its 2004 organizational session.

Chapter II

United Nations financing and programming

The overall financial situation of the United Nations continued to be generally positive in 2003, although there was some cause for concern. By year's end, unpaid assessments were significantly lower than in 2002 and the number of Member States paying their regular budget contribution in full and on time increased appreciably. However, aggregate cash fell and the cash balances of the tribunals were negative. Unpaid assessments reached $1,603 million, compared with $1,684 million in 2002, and debt to Member States for troops and contingent-owned equipment was $449 million as against $703 million at the end of 2002.

The General Assembly adopted revised budget appropriations for the 2002-2003 biennium of $2,967,727,800, an increase of $76,659,100 over the initial appropriation of $2,891,068,700. It approved appropriations totalling $3,160,860,300 for the 2004-2005 biennium.

The Assembly examined the Secretary-General's proposals for reforming the procedure for reviewing the programme budget and the medium-term plan, and for simplifying and improving the planning and budgetary processes. It agreed that the Committee for Programme and Coordination would no longer review the budget outline and asked the Secretary-General to prepare, for consideration in 2004, a strategic framework to replace the current four-year medium-term plan.

The Committee on Contributions continued to review the methodology for preparing the scale of assessments of Member States' contributions to the UN budget.

The Assembly adopted revisions to the 2002-2005 medium-term plan.

Financial situation

Although the overall financial picture of the United Nations continued to be positive in 2003, some disturbing elements began to reappear. In October [A/58/531], the Secretary-General stated that aggregate assessments increased to $3.9 billion as at 30 September, compared to $3.4 billion in 2002, and were likely to exceed $4 billion if additional peacekeeping assessments were approved before the end of the year. Cash availability under the regular budget and related reserve accounts had become critical by October, necessitating borrowing from peacekeeping accounts. On the positive side, the United States, having paid $31 million earlier in 2003, expected to make regular budget payments of between $233 million and $341 million by the end of December.

As at 30 September, unpaid assessments for the regular budget, peacekeeping, the two international tribunals and the capital master plan totalled $2.4 billion, the same as in 2002. That figure included $1,559 million for peacekeeping (compared to $1,776 million in 2002), $693 million for the regular budget, $117 million for the tribunals (the highest ever) and $11 million for the capital master plan. Member States paying their regular budget assessment in full for 2003 and prior years numbered 113 at the end of September, slightly more than the 105 at the end of September 2002.

In his end-of-year review of the financial situation [A/58/531/Add.1], the Secretary-General said that the performance of the three indicators of the Organization's financial health reflected a mixed financial picture: aggregate cash was lower, at $1,352 million, with the tribunals showing a deficit of $73 million; total unpaid assessments had been reduced to $1,603 million; and debt to Member States for troops and contingent-owned equipment was significantly lower at $439 million. The number of Member States paying their regular budget assessments in full and on time increased to 131 in 2003 as against 117 in 2002.

On 15 September, the General Assembly included in the draft agenda of its fifty-eighth (2003) session the item entitled "Improving the financial situation of the United Nations" (**decision 57/598**).

UN budget

Reforming the process

Intergovernmental review

The Secretary-General, in response to General Assembly resolution 57/300 [YUN 2002, p. 1353], submitted an April report [A/57/786] on strengthening of the United Nations: an agenda for further change, which sought to clarify his 2002 proposal [YUN 2002, p. 1368] for a single-stage intergovernmental review of the programme budget and medium-term plan, within the context of his overall proposals for simplifying and improving the current planning and budgetary processes (see below). That review, currently performed by both the Fifth (Administrative and Budgetary) Committee and the Committee for Programme and Coordination (CPC), would be conducted by the Fifth Committee, which would continue to take into account the recommendations of the Advisory Committee on Administrative and Budgetary Questions (ACABQ). Specialized intergovernmental bodies would continue to review those portions of the plan and programme of work relevant to their areas of expertise. CPC would continue to hold annual sessions, but its programme of work would concentrate on monitoring and evaluation.

The report recommended that the Assembly approve the Secretary-General's proposals for a single-stage intergovernmental review of the medium-term plan, the budget outline and the programme budget, to become effective in 2004, and for the review of the functions of CPC in order to enhance its effectiveness in monitoring and evaluation.

By **decision 57/587** of 18 June, the Assembly deferred consideration of the Secretary-General's report until its fifty-eighth (2003) session, under the agenda item entitled "Strengthening of the United Nations system".

Improving the planning and budgetary processes

The Secretary-General, in a September report on strengthening of the United Nations: an agenda for further change—improvements to the current process of planning and budgeting [A/58/395 & Corr.1], submitted in response to General Assembly resolution 57/300 [YUN 2002, p. 1353], discussed in greater detail his 2002 proposals [ibid., p. 1368] for improving those processes, including a shorter, more strategic medium-term plan linked to the budget outline. Shortcomings of the current system of programme planning, budgeting, monitoring and evaluation included a lack of precision in defining expected accomplishments, duplication between the text of the medium-term plan and the programme budget, and the considerable time spent on their review rather than on their implementation and evaluation. As exemplified by the improved format and content of the current 2002-2005 plan based on results-based budgeting, the medium-term plan should not be a listing of activities but a policy instrument that distinguished mandates requiring particular activities or delivery of specific outputs from general mandates providing the overall orientation of programmes and subprogrammes. CPC's review of the plan had consisted mainly of making editorial changes rather than in providing overall direction and guidance. Identifying common priorities often proved difficult, given the varying programme objectives of Member States, resulting in the designation of priorities for a wide range of issues covering almost every programme, with no demonstrated linkage between such designations and resource allocation. A two-year plan period, instead of the current four-year one, would ensure up-to-date mandates and limit expected accomplishments to those achievable within the reduced period. The proposal to synchronize the plan and budget outline to allow their concurrent consideration by the Assembly would ensure that decisions on resource levels were based on a clear linkage between programmatic needs and resource provisions.

As to monitoring and evaluation, the Secretary-General proposed a revamped biennial programme performance report for 2002-2003, providing more information on the attainment of expected results, rather than just a quantitative listing of outputs delivered, with more emphasis on evaluation by programme managers. CPC would continue to review the medium-term plan (to be renamed the "biennial programme plan"), while ACABQ and the Fifth Committee would review the budget outline and programme budgets, thus eliminating duplicative reviews.

The Secretary-General recommended that the Assembly approve a two-year medium-term plan, to be renamed "part one, biennial programme plan" and combined with "part two, budget outline" to constitute a "strategic framework" for the Organization; expansion of the detail contained in the budget outline, including additional information on programmatic and resource changes; further improvement to the format and content of the proposed programme budget to facilitate decision-making at the policy level; revision of CPC's role to encompass the review of "part one, biennial programme plan", but to exclude review of "part two, budget outline"; a modified biennial programme performance report focusing on the achievement of expected results; an improved format and timing of evaluation reports; identification of resources for monitoring and evaluation activities in all budget sections; and strengthening of CPC's monitoring and evaluation functions in order to determine the continuing relevance, efficiency, effectiveness and impact of the Organization's work.

JIU report. In a September note [A/58/375], the Secretary-General transmitted a report of the

Joint Inspection Unit (JIU) on the review of the UN budgetary process, which appraised the efficiency and effectiveness of the current UN budgetary process and presented alternatives to the General Assembly for an improved planning, programming, budgeting, monitoring and evaluation process, taking into account experiences and practices in a number of UN system organizations.

ACABQ consideration. ACABQ, in its sixth report on the 2004-2005 programme budget [A/58/7/Add.5], stated that the proposals to replace the current medium-term plan by a biennial programme plan and to revise CPC's role required a policy decision by the General Assembly. It therefore asked the Secretary-General to submit mock-ups of the medium-term plan and a new budget outline for the Assembly's consideration. Depending on the Assembly's action, he would then report to it, through ACABQ, any consequential amendments to the Financial Regulations and Rules of the United Nations and to the Regulations and Rules Governing Programme Planning, the Programme Aspects of the Budget, the Monitoring of Implementation and the Methods of Evaluation for further consideration. He was also to clarify, in that report, the proposed measures to improve the process of programme performance, monitoring and evaluation, including a modified biennial programme performance report and improved format and timing of evaluation reports.

Fifth Committee consideration. On 10 November, during its consideration of the Secretary-General's report on strengthening of the United Nations, including improving the current process of planning, programming and budgeting (see p. 1394), the Fifth Committee generally supported the Secretary-General's proposals and ACABQ's related recommendations. The Assistant Secretary-General for Programme Planning, Budget and Accounts said that the Secretariat would provide the requested mock-ups and flow charts and any other relevant information.

Note of Secretary-General. The Secretary-General, by an 18 November note [A/58/600], submitted the requested mock-ups based on current documents to illustrate the proposed formats of a biennial programme plan and budget outline to be incorporated as parts one and two of his proposed strategic framework. Programme 5, Legal affairs, of the medium-term plan was chosen to illustrate the type of changes that would be made to the plan's format.

GENERAL ASSEMBLY ACTION

On 23 December [meeting 79], the General Assembly, on the recommendation of the Fifth Committee [A/58/587], adopted **resolution 58/269** without vote [agenda item 59].

Strengthening of the United Nations: an agenda for further change

The General Assembly,

Reaffirming its determination to strengthen further the role, capacity, effectiveness and efficiency of the United Nations and thus improve its performance in order to realize the full potential of the Organization, in accordance with the purposes and principles of the Charter of the United Nations, and to respond more effectively to the needs of Member States and existing and new global challenges facing the United Nations in the twenty-first century,

Recalling Articles 17, 18, 97 and 100 of the Charter of the United Nations,

Recalling also its resolutions 41/213 of 19 December 1986, 42/211 of 21 December 1987 and 55/234 of 23 December 2000,

Recalling further the relevant provisions of its resolution 57/300 of 20 December 2002,

Recalling the terms of reference of the Committee for Programme and Coordination, as outlined in the annex to Economic and Social Council resolution 2008(LX) of 14 May 1976,

Emphasizing that resources provided to the Secretary-General should be commensurate with all mandated programmes and activities,

Reaffirming the role of the General Assembly and its relevant intergovernmental and expert bodies, within their respective mandates, in planning, programming, budgeting, monitoring and evaluation,

Having considered the reports of the Secretary-General entitled "Intergovernmental review of the medium-term plan and the programme budget" and "Improvements to the current process of planning and budgeting", the note by the Secretary-General entitled "Improvements to the current process of planning and budgeting" and the reports of the Advisory Committee on Administrative and Budgetary Questions thereon,

Taking into account the views expressed by the Member States during the consideration of this item at its fifty-seventh and fifty-eighth sessions,

1. *Welcomes* the commitment of the Secretary-General to strengthening the United Nations, including its planning, programming and budgetary process;

2. *Stresses* that setting the priorities of the United Nations is the prerogative of the Member States, as reflected in legislative mandates;

3. *Stresses also* the need for the Member States to participate fully in the budget preparation process, from its early stages and throughout the process;

4. *Emphasizes* the importance of providing the information necessary to enable Member States to make well-informed decisions;

5. *Requests* the Secretary-General to prepare, on a trial basis, for submission to the General Assembly at its fifty-ninth session, a strategic framework to replace the current four-year medium-term plan, which would comprise in one document:

(*a*) Part one: a plan outline, reflecting the longer-term objectives of the Organization;

(*b*) Part two: a biennial programme plan, to cover two years;

6. *Decides* that:

(a) The budget outline shall continue to provide the same level of detail as at present, in accordance with regulation 3.2 of the Regulations and Rules Governing Programme Planning, the Programme Aspects of the Budget, the Monitoring of Implementation and the Methods of Evaluation;

(b) The budget outline shall be submitted and considered for approval after consideration and adoption of the strategic framework;

(c) After their approval, the budget outline and strategic framework shall together form the basis for preparing the proposed programme budget;

7. *Affirms* that the strategic framework, as outlined above, shall constitute the principal policy directive of the United Nations and shall serve as the basis for programme planning, budgeting, monitoring and evaluation;

8. *Decides* to review, with a view to taking a final decision at its sixty-second session, the format, content and duration of the strategic framework, including the necessity of maintaining part one, and requests the Secretary-General to submit a report, through the Committee for Programme and Coordination, reviewing the experiences gained with the changes made in the planning and budgeting process;

9. *Decides also* that the programme narratives of the programme budget fascicles shall be identical to the biennial programme plan;

10. *Decides further* to keep the current format of the proposed programme budget and to maintain the level of information contained therein;

11. *Decides* that the Committee for Programme and Coordination shall no longer consider the budget outline;

12. *Requests* the Secretary-General to include in the introduction of the budget fascicles information on the new and/or revised mandates approved by the General Assembly subsequent to the adoption of the biennial programme plan;

13. *Requests* the Committee for Programme and Coordination, in performing its programmatic role in the planning and budgeting process, to review the programmatic aspects of the new and/or revised mandates referred to above, as well as any differences that arise between the biennial programme plan and the programmatic aspects of the proposed programme budget;

14. *Also requests* the Committee for Programme and Coordination, in the context of its report on its forty-fifth session, to provide comments on the various aspects of the review process referred to above;

15. *Emphasizes* the importance of the intergovernmental nature of the Committee for Programme and Coordination in discharging its functions;

16. *Invites* the Committee for Programme and Coordination to submit at its forty-fourth session proposals on enhancing its role in monitoring and evaluation;

17. *Recalls* paragraph 34 of General Assembly resolution 57/300, in which the Assembly invited the Committee for Programme and Coordination to continue to improve its working methods;

18. *Invites* the Committee for Programme and Coordination to submit, at its forty-fourth session, recommendations on improving its effectiveness;

19. *Emphasizes* the need to strengthen the monitoring and evaluation system, and in this regard urges the Secretary-General to improve the format and timing of programme performance and evaluation reports;

20. *Requests* the Secretary-General to ensure that resources are clearly identified in all the sections of the proposed programme budget for the performance of the monitoring and evaluation functions;

21. *Also requests* the Secretary-General to entrust the Office of Internal Oversight Services, in collaboration with the Joint Inspection Unit, with submitting to the General Assembly for consideration at its sixtieth session proposals on the strengthening and monitoring of programme performance and evaluation.

On 23 December, the Assembly decided that the agenda item on strengthening of the UN system would remain for consideration during its resumed fifty-eighth (2004) session (**decision 58/565**).

Budget for 2002-2003

Final appropriation

In 2003, the General Assembly adopted final budget appropriations for the 2002-2003 biennium, increasing the amount of $2,891,068,700 approved in resolutions 57/293 A [YUN 2002, p. 1373] and 57/311 (see p. 1200) by $76,659,100 to $2,967,727,800, and income estimates by $13,660,500 to $428,090,100.

Report of Secretary-General. In his second performance report on the 2002-2003 programme budget [A/58/558], the Secretary-General provided estimates of the anticipated final levels of expenditure and income for the biennium, based on actual expenditures for the first 20 months, projections for the last four months, and changes in inflation and exchange rates and cost-of-living adjustments.

The anticipated final level of expenditures and of income represented a net increase of $49.6 million, reflecting projected additional requirements of $86.5 million due to changes in exchange rates ($59.1 million), changes in inflation ($7.7 million), commitments entered into under the provisions of General Assembly resolution 56/256 [YUN 2001, p. 1322] ($19.7 million); and reduced requirements of $36.9 million due to variations in post costs and adjustments to other objects of expenditure, based on actual anticipated requirements ($23.7 million), and an increase in income ($13.2 million).

The projected expenditure for the biennium was estimated at $2,953.9 million gross, an increase of $62.8 million compared with the revised appropriation of $2,891.1 million approved in 2002. The projected income was estimated at $427.6 million, an increase of $13.2 million, compared with the revised income estimates of $414.4 million.

ACABQ, in November [A/58/604], stated that the current practice of reporting on programme and financial performance separately and on separate cycles should be reformed to make it consistent with and supportive of results-based budgeting. It recommended that a single report be issued covering both programme and financial performance for the same period, and made available during the formulation and consideration of the proposed programme budget. The first such report should be submitted to the Assembly in 2004.

GENERAL ASSEMBLY ACTION

On 23 December [meeting 79], the General Assembly, on the recommendation of the Fifth Committee [A/58/572/Add.1], adopted **resolution 58/267 A** and **B** without vote [agenda item 120].

Programme budget for the biennium 2002-2003

A

Final budget appropriations for the biennium 2002-2003

The General Assembly

1. *Takes note* of the second performance report of the Secretary-General on the programme budget for the biennium 2002-2003 and the related report of the Advisory Committee on Administrative and Budgetary Questions;

2. *Resolves* that, for the biennium 2002-2003:

(a) The amount of 2,891,068,700 United States dollars appropriated by it in its resolutions 57/293 A of 20 December 2002 and 57/311 of 18 June 2003 shall be increased by 76,659,100 dollars, as follows:

Section		Amount approved by the General Assembly in its resolutions 57/293 A and 57/311	Increase/ (decrease)	Final appropriation
		(United States dollars)		
	Part I. Overall policy-making, direction and coordination			
1.	Overall policy-making, direction and coordination	50,628,800	1,207,300	51,836,100
2.	General Assembly affairs and conference services	470,592,900	18,320,700	488,913,600
	Total, part I	521,221,700	19,528,000	540,749,700
	Part II. Political affairs			
3.	Political affairs	251,550,300	12,023,700	263,574,000
4.	Disarmament	15,821,100	330,800	16,151,900
5.	Peacekeeping operations	78,200,100	(1,668,400)	76,531,700
6.	Peaceful uses of outer space	4,315,300	(182,500)	4,132,800
	Total, part II	62,070,400	1,640,600	63,711,000
	Part III. International justice and law			
7.	International Court of Justice	26,315,900	1,964,900	28,280,800
8	Legal affairs	35,754,500	(324,300)	35,430,200
	Total, part III	62,070,400	1,640,600	63,711,000
	Part IV. International cooperation for development			
9.	Economic and social affairs	123,902,200	2,987,200	126,889,400
9A.	Office of the High Representative for the Least Developed Countries	3,099,500	(865,900)	2,233,600
10.	Africa: New Agenda for Development	6,052,300	46,300	6,098,600
11A.	Trade and development	91,295,800	1,778,200	93,074,000
11B.	International Trade Centre UNCTAD/WTO	19,373,900	997,900	20,371,800
12.	Environment	8,355,100	500,300	8,855,400
13.	Human settlements	12,794,200	847,800	13,642,000
14.	Crime prevention and criminal justice	6,339,800	1,074,900	7,414,700
15.	International drug control	16,293,700	1,551,800	17,845,500
	Total, part IV	287,506,500	8,918,500	296,425,000
	Part V. Regional cooperation for development			
16.	Economic and social development in Africa	83,865,900	(5,009,200)	78,856,700
17.	Economic and social development in Asia and the Pacific	58,821,300	(253,100)	58,568,200
18.	Economic development in Europe	43,798,800	3,551,200	47,350,000
19.	Economic and social development in Latin America and the Caribbean	73,210,500	189,300	73,399,800
20.	Economic and social development in Western Asia	49,842,800	(467,500)	49,375,300
21.	Regular programme of technical cooperation	42,871,500	1,034,100	43,905,600
	Total, part V	352,410,800	(955,200)	351,455,600
	Part VI. Human rights and humanitarian affairs			
22.	Human rights	47,576,300	534,500	48,110,800

Section		Amount approved by the General Assembly in its resolutions 57/293 A and 57/311	Increase/ (decrease)	Final appropriation
		(United States dollars)		
23.	Protection of and assistance to refugees	45,956,000	3,315,500	49,271,500
24.	Palestine refugees	28,278,700	1,250,800	29,529,500
25.	Humanitarian assistance	20,577,400	168,300	20,745,700
	Total, part VI	142,388,400	5,269,100	147,657,500
	Part VII. *Public information*			
26.	Public information	147,107,600	278,200	147,385,800
	Total, part VII	147,107,600	278,200	147,385,800
	Part VIII. *Common support services*			
27.	Management and central support services	451,342,100	6,748,000	458,090,100
	Total, part VIII	451,342,100	6,748,000	458,090,100
	Part IX. *Internal oversight*			
28.	Internal oversight	20,946,600	82,300	21,028,900
	Total, part IX	20,946,600	82,300	21,028,900
	Part X. *Jointly financed administrative activities and special expenses*			
29.	Jointly financed administrative activities	8,759,600	(647,900)	8,111,700
30.	Special expenses	77,085,600	4,820,800	81,906,400
	Total, part X	85,845,200	4,172,900	90,018,100
	Part XI. *Capital expenditures*			
31.	Construction, alteration, improvement and major maintenance	88,341,100	529,900	88,871,000
	Total, part XI	88,341,100	529,900	88,871,000
	Part XII. *Staff assessment*			
32.	Staff assessment	368,936,500	19,943,200	388,879,700
	Total, part XII	368,936,500	19,943,200	388,879,700
	Part XIII. *Development Account*			
33.	Development Account	13,065,000	—	13,065,000
	Total, part XIII	13,065,000	—	13,065,000
	Grand total	**2,891,068,700**	**76,659,100**	**2,967,727,800**

(b) The Secretary-General shall be authorized to transfer credits between sections of the budget, with the concurrence of the Advisory Committee;

(c) In addition to the appropriations approved under subparagraph (a) above, an amount of 125,000 dollars is appropriated for each year of the biennium 2002-2003 from the accumulated income of the Library Endowment Fund for the purchase of books, periodicals, maps and library equipment and for such other expenses of the Library at the Palais des Nations as are in accordance with the objects and provisions of the endowment.

B
Final income estimates for the biennium 2002-2003

The General Assembly

Resolves that, for the biennium 2002-2003:

(a) The estimates of income of 414,429,600 United States dollars approved by it in its resolution 57/293 B of 20 December 2002 shall be increased by 13,660,500 dollars, as follows:

Income section	Amount approved by the General Assembly in its resolution 57/293 B	Increase/ (decrease)	Final estimate
	(United States dollars)		
1. Income from staff assessment	373,048,100	20,053,100	393,101,200
Total, income section 1	**373,048,100**	**20,053,100**	**393,101,200**

Income section	Amount approved by the General Assembly in its resolution 57/293 B	Increase/ (decrease)	Final estimate
	(United States dollars)		
2. General income	41,953,200	(8,211,000)	33,742,200
3. Services to the public	(571,700)	1,818,400	1,246,700
Total, income sections 2 and 3	**41,381,500**	**(6,392,600)**	**34,988,900**
Grand total	**414,429,600**	**13,660,500**	**428,090,100**

(b) The income from staff assessment shall be credited to the Tax Equalization Fund in accordance with the provisions of General Assembly resolution 973(X) of 15 December 1955;

(c) Direct expenses of the United Nations Postal Administration, services to visitors, catering and related services, garage operations, television services and the sale of publications, not provided for under the budget appropriations, shall be charged against the income derived from those activities.

Also on 23 December, the Assembly, by **decision 58/565,** decided that the agenda item on the programme budget for the biennium 2002-2003 would remain for consideration during its resumed fifty-eighth (2004) session.

Budget for 2004-2005

In introducing the proposed programme budget for the 2004-2005 biennium [A/58/6] before the Fifth Committee on 28 October, the Secretary-General said that the proposed budget of $2.9 billion before recosting represented minimal real growth of 0.5 per cent ($15 million) over the 2002-2003 programme budget, and was in accordance with the outline figure endorsed by the General Assembly in resolution 57/280 [YUN 2002, p. 1382]. It also represented a projected net increase of 117 posts. The proposed budget activities were aligned with the priorities set out in his report on strengthening of the United Nations: an agenda for further change [YUN 2002, p. 1352]. Additional resources were allocated for development and the special needs of Africa, and modest increases for drug control, crime prevention and human rights. A significant reallocation of resources ($100 million) was being proposed between subprogrammes, as were the redeployment of 810 posts and the discontinuation of more than 900 outputs that had become obsolete or marginally useful. The proposed budget also incorporated the results of the reviews of the Organization's public information and human rights activities, reflected efforts to modernize conference- servicing and to strengthen the UN Department of Economic and Social Affairs, set out the requirements to implement the information and communication technology strategy, and proposed more funds for training. It also represented the next stage in the implementation of results-based budgeting.

The Secretary-General was concerned that some of the recommendations already made by ACABQ regarding the proposed programme budget might subject the Organization to undue constraints, especially in its reform efforts. Recalling his proposals [YUN 2002, p. 1368] for improving the budget and planning process, the medium-term plan, the role of CPC and the system of monitoring and evaluation, he hoped that the Assembly would take decisions on those issues before the end of 2003 so that the changes could be introduced in the next budget cycle.

CPC considered the proposed programme budget at its 2003 session (New York, 9 June–3 July and 9 July) [A/58/16] and recommended that the Assembly approve the narratives of the majority of the budget sections subject to certain modifications. It took note of the preliminary estimates for the International Trade Centre (ITC) and of the submission directly to the Assembly of its detailed 2004-2005 proposed programme budget, which should reflect resolution 57/312 on the ITC budget outline (see p. 975). CPC recommended that a revised fascicle of section 14, Environment, be issued to reflect the decisions adopted by the Governing Council of the United Nations Environment Programme at its twenty-second session (see p. 1036) and submitted to the Assembly's fifty-eighth (2003) session for consideration; and that, at that session, the Assembly review section 24, Human rights, including the programme content, in the light of all relevant Assembly mandates. CPC took note of the programme narrative of section 28, Public information, and recommended that the Assembly further consider it, taking into account the modifications it had suggested.

As requested, the Secretary-General submitted the reformulated narratives of section 13, International Trade Centre UNCTAD/WTO (United Nations Conference on Trade and Development/World Trade Organization) [A/58/6 (Sect. 13)/Add.1], and section 14, Environment [A/58/6 (Sect. 14)/Rev.1].

GENERAL ASSEMBLY ACTION

On 23 December [meeting 79], the General Assembly, on the recommendation of the Fifth Committee [A/58/573], adopted **resolution 58/270** without vote [agenda item 121].

Questions relating to the proposed programme budget for the biennium 2004-2005

The General Assembly,

Reaffirming its resolutions 41/213 of 19 December 1986, 42/211 of 21 December 1987, 45/248 B, section VI, of 21 December 1990 and 56/253 of 24 December 2001,

Recalling its resolutions 57/280 and 57/282 of 20 December 2002,

Recalling also its resolutions 57/292 of 20 December 2002 and 57/311 of 18 June 2003,

Reaffirming the respective mandates of the Advisory Committee on Administrative and Budgetary Questions and the Committee for Programme and Coordination in the context of the proposed programme budget for the biennium 2004-2005,

Having considered the proposed programme budget for the biennium 2004-2005 and the relevant reports of the Advisory Committee on Administrative and Budgetary Questions and the Committee for Programme and Coordination thereon,

1. *Reaffirms* that the Fifth Committee is the appropriate Main Committee of the General Assembly entrusted with responsibilities for administrative and budgetary matters;
2. *Also reaffirms* rule 153 of its rules of procedure;
3. *Further reaffirms* the Regulations and Rules Governing Programme Planning, the Programme Aspects of the Budget, the Monitoring of Implementation and the Methods of Evaluation and the Financial Regulations and Rules of the United Nations;
4. *Welcomes* the timely submission of the proposed programme budget for the biennium 2004-2005;
5. *Endorses* the conclusions and recommendations of the Committee for Programme and Coordination on the programme narratives of the proposed programme budget for the biennium 2004-2005 con-

tained in the report of the Committee on the work of its forty-third session, subject to the provisions of the present resolution, as reflected in annex I;

6. *Approves* the programme narratives of section 14, Environment, and section 24, Human rights, as also reflected in annex I;

7. *Endorses* the conclusions and recommendations of the Advisory Committee on Administrative and Budgetary Questions concerning posts and non-post resources contained in its report on the proposed programme budget for the biennium 2004-2005, subject to the provisions of the present resolution;

8. *Decides* that a vacancy rate of 5.5 per cent for Professional staff and 3.8 per cent for General Service staff shall be used as a basis for the calculation of the budget for the biennium 2004-2005;

9. *Also decides* to maintain the current practice of recosting for the forthcoming biennium, except with respect to section 23, Regular programme of technical cooperation, of the proposed programme budget, to which recosting should not be applied;

10. *Further decides* to revert to the question of recosting at its fifty-ninth session in the context of the first performance report on the programme budget for the biennium 2004-2005, and in this regard requests the Secretary-General to include in that report information on the variation between the projected recosting needs arising from inflation and currency movements as at October 2003 and at the time of the preparation of the report;

11. *Requests* the Board of Auditors, in consultation with the Secretary-General, to examine the recosting methodology and to report thereon to the General Assembly at its fifty-ninth session, including proposing the most appropriate mechanism for managing the currency aspects of the recosting methodology;

12. *Notes* the observations of the Advisory Committee on Administrative and Budgetary Questions related to the concept of managing the staffing table as a whole, contained in paragraphs 73 to 78 and 143 of its report;

13. *Reaffirms* paragraph 35 of its resolution 57/300 of 20 December 2002;

14. *Requests* the Secretary-General, during the course of the programme budget for the biennium 2004-2005, to commence, on an experimental basis, with the redeployment of posts as necessary to meet the evolving needs of the Organization in attaining its mandated programmes and activities, in accordance with the following principles:

(*a*) The experiment shall be limited to the redeployment of up to 50 posts Organization-wide;

(*b*) The experiment shall not imply any change in the human resources management policies of the Organization;

(*c*) The proposed programme budget shall remain the principal instrument in which the Secretary-General sets out the resources and staffing requirements of the Organization;

(*d*) The authority to redeploy posts shall in no way prevent the Secretary-General from requesting additional posts during the course of the experiment;

(*e*) The experiment shall not exacerbate high vacancy rates in any budget sections;

(*f*) The experiment shall not apply to language services;

(*g*) Redeployment between sections shall be carried out only after all possibilities of using resources available within budget sections that will benefit from the transfer have been exhaustively explored;

(*h*) The experiment shall not be implemented as a result of General Assembly resolutions calling for the implementation of decisions "within existing resources";

(*i*) Reporting to the General Assembly shall be carried out in the context of the annual budget performance reports;

(*j*) The Secretary-General is requested to provide information periodically to the Advisory Committee on Administrative and Budgetary Questions on actions taken;

15. *Also requests* the Secretary-General to ensure that the experiment shall in no way limit opportunities for external recruitment for posts at any level;

16. *Further requests* the Secretary-General to report to the General Assembly at its resumed fifty-ninth session on the implications of the experiment for human resources management policies;

17. *Requests* the Secretary-General to submit, through the Advisory Committee on Administrative and Budgetary Questions, a comprehensive report for consideration by the General Assembly at its sixtieth session on the progress of and lessons learned from the experiment, including the following aspects:

(*a*) Implications for the relevant financial regulations and rules of the Organization;

(*b*) Additional implications, if any, for human resources management policies;

(*c*) Constraints encountered by the Secretary-General in exercising the flexibility granted to him in General Assembly resolutions 48/228 C of 29 July 1994 and 50/214 of 23 December 1995, as well as in regulation 5.6 of the Financial Regulations and Rules of the United Nations;

(*d*) Measures to ensure that such a policy will not have any negative impact on sections with high vacancy rates;

(*e*) An elaboration of the elements requested in paragraph 35 of its resolution 57/300;

(*f*) Recommendations concerning the possible application of this approach to managing the staffing table in future;

18. *Decides* that the staffing table for each year of the biennium 2004-2005 shall be as set out in annex II to the present resolution;

19. *Also decides*, notwithstanding the proposal of the Secretary-General and the recommendations of the Advisory Committee on Administrative and Budgetary Questions, to approve new posts to be funded from the regular budget for the biennium 2004-2005, as set out in annex III to the present resolution;

20. *Recalls* paragraphs 8 and 9 of its resolution 57/300, and in this regard notes the proposal of the Secretary-General in his report on the administration and management of the Office of the United Nations High Commissioner for Human Rights regarding the establishment of two posts, one P-5 and one P-4, under subprogramme 2, as well as two posts, one D-1 and one P-4, under subprogramme 3 of section 24, Human rights, of the proposed programme budget for the biennium 2004-2005 related to the implementation of actions 3 and 4 of his report entitled "Strengthening of the United Nations: an agenda for further change";

21. *Decides* to establish the above-mentioned posts, as set out in annex III to the present resolution;

22. *Also decides* to consider this issue further in the context of the decisions of the relevant intergovernmental bodies on the issues referred to in paragraphs 8 and 9 of resolution 57/300;

23. *Further decides* to reclassify four P-4 posts to the P-5 level, one in section 15, Human settlements, one in section 17, International drug control, and two in section 22, Economic and social development in Western Asia, one D-1 post to the D-2 level in section 30, Internal oversight, and one D-2 post to the Assistant Secretary-General level in section 27, Humanitarian assistance;

24. *Decides* to approve the post conversions requested by the Secretary-General and recommended by the Advisory Committee on Administrative and Budgetary Questions, as set out in annex IV to the present resolution, with the exception of two posts, one P-4 and one P-3, that had been proposed for conversion to section 5, Peacekeeping operations, from the Voluntary Trust Fund for Assistance in Mine Action;

25. *Requests* the Secretary-General to suspend recruitment action for new vacancies in General Service posts for the biennium 2004-2005, with the exception of safety and security personnel and editorial assistants (text processors) in language functions, and to report on the progress made and on the impact of those measures in the context of his performance reports;

26. *Decides* to abolish six General Service posts, three in the Department of Economic and Social Affairs of the Secretariat and three in the Economic Commission for Europe;

27. *Also decides* to reduce further, by 3.2 million United States dollars, the proposed provision for restoration of common services;

28. *Further decides* to reduce the provision for general temporary assistance by 2.5 million dollars;

29. *Decides* that the reduction described in paragraph 28 above should not be applied to section 2, General Assembly affairs and conference services;

30. *Also decides* to reduce by 2 million dollars the provision for overtime and night differential, as set out in paragraph 84 of the first report of the Advisory Committee on Administrative and Budgetary Questions on the proposed programme budget for the biennium 2004-2005, further decides that the relevant reductions should not be applied to security operations, and invites the Secretary-General to elaborate on resource needs for overtime and night differential in the context of his first budget performance report;

31. *Requests* the Secretary-General to discontinue the practice of paying higher subsistence rates to middle- and senior-level United Nations staff members;

32. *Decides* to reduce the total appropriation for publications by 400,000 dollars;

33. *Also decides* to maintain provisions for the United Nations Truce Supervision Organization at the level recommended by the Secretary-General;

34. *Further decides* to appropriate an amount of 38,200 dollars, under section 9, Economic and social affairs, requested for the preparation of Executive Committee papers on common strategic policy issues and/or support for the Committee's work on publications in advancing the Millennium Development Goals;

35. *Decides* to appropriate an amount of 78,500 dollars, under section 9, Economic and social affairs, requested under subprogramme 2 for consultants and experts;

36. *Also decides* to defer the appropriation of the budgetary provisions for the Joint Inspection Unit for 2005;

37. *Further decides* to appropriate an amount of 1,858,600 dollars for consultants and experts for the United Nations Conference on Trade and Development;

38. *Decides* to appropriate an amount of 56,731,900 dollars for the Office of the United Nations High Commissioner for Refugees for the biennium 2004-2005;

39. *Also decides* to reduce the allocation for United Nations information centres by 2 million dollars;

40. *Further decides* to defer consideration of 590,000 dollars for a network back-up system at the United Nations Office at Geneva until such time as all viable alternatives have been explored and reported to the General Assembly;

41. *Decides* to restore an amount of 105,200 dollars under section 28, Public information, for supplies and materials under outreach services;

42. *Recalls* its decision 57/579 of 20 December 2002, and requests the Secretary-General to continue to strengthen the United Nations web site through further redeployment to the required language posts and to report on the status of its implementation to the General Assembly at its fifty-ninth session;

43. *Decides* to consider the proposal of the Secretary-General regarding the transfer of the technical secretariats of the Fifth and Sixth Committees at its fifty-ninth session, with a view to taking a decision in the context of the proposed programme budget for the biennium 2006-2007;

44. *Recalls* its resolution 57/24 of 19 November 2002 and regulation 5.6 and the criteria set forth in rule 105.6 (*a*) of the Regulations and Rules Governing Programme Planning, the Programme Aspects of the Budget, the Monitoring of Implementation and the Methods of Evaluation, and requests the Secretary-General to report, in the context of his first performance report, on the possibilities for absorptions or the mobilization of extrabudgetary resources for the *Repertory of Practice of United Nations Organs;*

45. *Requests* the Secretary-General to submit a report to the General Assembly at its fifty-ninth session on improving the implementation of regulation 5.6 and rule 105.6 of the Regulations and Rules Governing Programme Planning;

46. *Also requests* the Secretary-General to continue to implement the information and communication technology strategy and to provide to the General Assembly at its fifty-ninth session a progress report on the impact of investments in information and communication technology;

47. *Further requests* the Secretary-General to review the structure and functions of all liaison or representation offices in New York of organizations headquartered elsewhere funded from the regular budget and to report to the General Assembly at its resumed fifty-eighth session on possibilities for improving their effectiveness;

48. *Requests* the Secretary-General to undertake a fundamental and comprehensive review of the regular programme of technical cooperation and to make ap-

propriate proposals to the General Assembly at its fifty-ninth session;

49. *Also requests* the Secretary-General to submit to the General Assembly at its fifty-ninth session a proposal for the progressive implementation of article 20 of the statute of the Office of the United Nations High Commissioner for Refugees with a view to its full implementation;

50. *Further requests* the Secretary-General to conduct, through the Office of Internal Oversight Services, a review of the operation and management of United Nations libraries, with a view to assessing staffing requirements for those libraries in the light of technological advances in the delivery of information services, and to report thereon to the General Assembly at its fifty-ninth session;

51. *Requests* the Secretary-General to report to the General Assembly at its fifty-ninth session on proposals for developing a more robust capability within the Office of Human Resources Management of the Secretariat to enable it to reduce the level of underrepresentation of Member States and the number of unrepresented Member States;

52. *Also requests* the Secretary-General to entrust the Office of Internal Oversight Services with the task of conducting a study on the availability in local labour markets of the skills for which international recruitment for posts in the General Service category now takes place and to report to the General Assembly at its fifty-ninth session on the findings and their implications;

53. *Reaffirms* the provisions of paragraph 5 of General Assembly resolution 57/307 of 15 April 2003, requests the Secretary-General to ensure the independence of the United Nations Administrative Tribunal and the separation of its secretariat from the Office of Legal Affairs of the Secretariat, and also requests the Secretary-General to submit to it at its fifty-ninth session the report on the financial independence of the Tribunal requested in the above-mentioned resolution;

54. *Requests* the Secretary-General to report on further progress made to increase the capacity of the Economic Commission for Africa to communicate and transmit data electronically in the context of the proposed programme budget for the biennium 2006-2007;

55. *Reaffirms* paragraphs 15 and 17 of its resolution 57/300, in particular where the General Assembly requests the Secretary-General, with assistance from the Office of Internal Oversight Services, to proceed as quickly as possible to conduct a systematic evaluation of the impact, efficiency and cost-effectiveness of all activities of the Department of Public Information, and to report on progress made to the General Assembly at its fifty-ninth session through the Committee on Information and the Fifth Committee;

56. *Also reaffirms* that the Official Document System of the United Nations, as an archival and retrieval system of official documents, should cover the entire Organization, including the United Nations Office at Nairobi and all regional commissions, and in this regard requests the Secretary-General to pursue vigorous implementation and to report to the General Assembly at its fifty-ninth session on the progress made;

57. *Emphasizes* the priority it attaches to the necessity of improving and modernizing the conference facilities at the United Nations Office at Nairobi, and in this regard requests the Secretary-General to keep under review the issue of the construction of additional facilities at the Office and to report thereon to the General Assembly in the context of the proposed programme budget for the biennium 2006-2007, in the light of experience gained from operating the modernized conference facilities;

58. *Requests* the Secretary-General to submit a comprehensive report to the Assembly at its fifty-ninth session addressing possible measures to improve the performance of the Development Account, including ways and means aimed at bringing a more focused approach to project formulation, complementarity, implementation and evaluation, as well as to make proposals on increasing its funding in accordance with General Assembly resolutions 52/12 B of 19 December 1997 and 54/15 of 29 October 1999.

Annex I

Changes to the programme narratives of the proposed programme budget for the biennium 2004-2005 as reflected in the conclusions and recommendations of the Committee for Programme and Coordination at its forty-third session and additional modifications

Section 1
Overall policy-making, direction and coordination

Table 1.21

Under indicator of achievement (*e*) (i), after "of the Secretary-General's reform", insert "as mandated by General Assembly resolutions", bearing in mind the provisions of Article 97 of the Charter of the United Nations.

Table 1.34

Add an indicator of achievement (*a*), reading: "*(a)* The number of conflicts referred to the Ombudsman for which the Ombudsman facilitated a resolution"; and insert "*(b)*" before the existing indicator.

Section 2
General Assembly affairs and conference services

Tables 2.15, 2.17, 2.19, 2.22, 2.24, 2.26, 2.33, 2.35, 2.41 and 2.43

In table 2.15, add the entry "*(d)* Increased productivity" under both *Expected accomplishments* and *Indicators of achievement*.

In tables 2.17, 2.19 and 2.26, add the entry "*(b)* Increased productivity" under both *Expected accomplishments* and *Indicators of achievement*.

In table 2.22, add the entry "*(e)* Increased productivity" under both *Expected accomplishments* and *Indicators of achievement*.

In tables 2.24, 2.33, 2.35, 2.41 and 2.43, add the entry "*(c)* Increased productivity" under both *Expected accomplishments* and *Indicators of achievement*.

Table 2.9

Add an expected accomplishment (*c*), reading: "*(c)* Improvement of conference service performance in New York and all other duty stations".

Add an indicator of achievement (*c*), reading:

"*(c)* (i) Optimization of use of technology in key processes;

"(ii) Updated proposals for workload standards, efficiency and related performance indicators;

"(iii) Issuance of updated bulletins of the Secretary-General that set out the relationship between Headquarters and conference-servicing units in other duty stations".

Table 2.13

Delete footnote a and the indicator thereto.

Add an indicator of achievement (iii), reading: "(iii) Presentation of documentation on time, with full respect for the six-week rule".

Tables 2.17, 2.19, 2.24, 2.26, 2.33, 2.35, 2.41 and 2.43

Under *Indicators of achievement, Performance measures,* replace "2004-2005: to be determined through a survey" with "2004-2005: 90 per cent (to be determined through a survey)".

Tables 2.15, 2.22, 2.31 and 2.39

Add an expected accomplishment *(c)*, reading: "*(c)* Improvement in the timeliness of the production and distribution of parliamentary documentation in the six official languages of the Organization"; and, in table 2.22, reletter existing expected accomplishment *(c)* as *(d)*.

Add an indicator of achievement *(c)* reading: "*(c)* The amount and percentage of parliamentary documentation produced and distributed in the six official languages of the Organization within established deadlines"; and, in table 2.22, reletter existing indicator of achievement *(c)* as *(d)*

Paragraph 2.33 (a) (ii) d.

Add the following activity element: "iii. Meetings of regional and other major groupings on the basis of existing practice, bearing in mind further consideration of this issue by the General Assembly during its fifty-eighth session, in accordance with its resolution 57/283 B".

Table 2.15

In indicator of achievement *(a)*, after "relevant rules", add ", especially the six-week rule for submission of documents".

Table 2.17

Add an indicator of achievement *(b)*, reading: "*(b)* Presentation of documentation on time, observing the six-week rule"; and insert "*(a)*" before the preceding indicator.

Paragraph 2.43

In the third sentence, after "Official Document System (ODS)", add ", without negatively affecting the quality of services provided and the quantity of documents required by Member States".

Paragraph 2.45 (b)

Add the following output:

"(vi) Meetings of regional and other major groupings on the basis of existing practice, bearing in mind further consideration of this issue by the General Assembly during its fifty-eighth session, in accordance with its resolution 57/283 B".

Paragraph 2.46

In the third sentence, after "amounting to $459,200", add ", without negatively affecting the quality of services provided and the quantity of documents required by Member States".

Tables 2.22, 2.31 and 2.39

In indicator of achievement *(a)*, after "in accordance with relevant rules", add ", in particular regarding the six-week rule for issuance and distribution of parliamentary documentation simultaneously in the six official languages".

Tables 2.24, 2.33, 2.35, 2.41 and 2.43

Add an expected accomplishment *(b)*, reading: "*(b)* Presentation of documentation on time, observing the six-week rule"; and insert "*(a)*" before the preceding expected accomplishment.

Add an indicator of achievement *(b)*, reading: "*(b)* The degree of satisfaction expressed by Member States with the presentation of the documentation on time"; and insert "*(a)*" before the preceding indicator of achievement.

Section 3
Political affairs

Paragraph 3.7

After "for further change (A/57/387)", add "approved in paragraph 26 of General Assembly resolution 57/300".

Paragraph 3.16

In the fourth sentence, delete "the Security Council Committee established by resolution 661(1990) concerning the situation between Iraq and Kuwait", and replace the figure 11 at the beginning of the sentence with the figure 10.

Table 3.13

At the end of indicator of achievement (i), add "through peaceful means".

In indicator of achievement (ii), after "in which", add "conflicts or situations of conflict exist, and in which", and delete ", including in cooperation with partners,".

Table 3.19

Objective 1

After "Non-Self-Governing Territories" at the end of expected accomplishment *(a)*, add "in accordance with the relevant resolutions of the United Nations".

Add an indicator of achievement *(a)* (ii) reading: "(ii) The effectiveness of servicing provided to the Special Committee, its seminars and the General Assembly; the effectiveness of research and analytical studies and reports on conditions in the Territories; and the effectiveness of publicity campaigns"; and renumber indicator of achievement *(a)* as *(a)* (i).

Objective 2

After "Non-Self-Governing Territories" at the end of the objective, add "in accordance with the relevant resolutions of the United Nations".

Paragraph 3.44 (d)

Replace the text of subparagraph *(d)* of paragraph 3.44 with the following: "the administering Powers will cooperate with the Special Committee in the implementation of the relevant resolutions and decisions of the United Nations".

Paragraph 3.47

In the last sentence, after "international legitimacy", insert "and legality".

At the end of the paragraph, add "in accordance with relevant Security Council resolutions".

Table 3.21

In indicator of achievement (i), delete ", as evidenced by the voting on the relevant resolutions".

Table 3.25

In indicators of achievement *(b)* (i) and (ii), delete "and incontrovertible".

Section 4
Disarmament

Paragraph 4.39

Replace the seventh to ninth lines, after "mandated by the General Assembly:", with "compilation of information on measures taken by Member States and international organizations to prevent terrorists from acquiring weapons of mass destruction; making accessible to Member States information on national legislation on transfer of arms, military equipment and dual use of goods and technology;".

Section 5
Peacekeeping operations

Paragraph 5.5

Before the last sentence, insert the following sentence: "The Department will also continue to improve representation of underrepresented and unrepresented Member States in future recruitment".

In the fifth sentence, delete "also".

Table 5.9

In expected accomplishment *(c)* and indicator of achievement *(c)*, after "gender issues", insert "and their geographical balance".

Table 5.12

In indicator of achievement (i), performance measures (target 2004-2005), replace "10 weeks" with "8 weeks".

In indicator of achievement (ii), performance measures (target 2004-2005), replace "80 per cent of benchmarks" with "100 per cent of benchmarks within expected time frame".

Table 5.14

In indicator of achievement *(b)* (ii), performance measures (target 2004-2005), replace "6 months" with "4 months".

Table 5.16

Reword indicator of achievement *(a)* (ii) to read: "An increase in the number of Member States with which the Secretariat has concluded standby arrangements".

Under indicator of achievement *(b)*, reword the performance measures to read:

"2000-2001: __ per cent of all personnel deployment needs met by utilizing the United Nations standby arrangements system and rapid deployment levels or the on-call list

"Estimate 2002-2003: __ per cent of all personnel deployment needs met by utilizing the United Nations standby arrangements system and rapid deployment levels or the on-call list

"Target 2004-2005: __ per cent of all personnel deployment needs met by utilizing the United Nations standby arrangements system and rapid deployment levels or the on-call list".

Paragraph 5.29

Delete paragraph 5.29 and renumber the subsequent paragraphs accordingly.

Former paragraph 5.39

Replace former paragraph 5.39 with the following: "The subprogramme is expected to achieve its objectives and expected accomplishments on the assumption that the Mine Action Service receives an adequate level of resources to respond to General Assembly and Security Council mandates."

Section 8
Legal affairs

Paragraph 8.3, last line

Before "registers and publishes treaties", insert as an objective "assists Member States regarding implementation of the international legal order for seas and oceans as well as the law of treaties;".

Paragraph 8.12

Rephrase the third task of the Division to read: "The Division will provide services for the effective application of the international judicial order of the sea and the ocean, thus helping in the understanding, acceptance and consequent application of the United Nations Convention on the Law of the Sea (1982) and the related agreements."

Paragraph 8.31 (b) (ix)

At the end of subparagraph (ix) of paragraph 8.31 *(b)*, add "meeting the requests of Governments on questions relating to international public law through the relevant subsidiary organs in accordance with the existing practice".

Table 8.14

Under indicator of achievement (a) (iv), performance measures (2000-2001, estimate 2002-2003 and target 2004-2005), replace "1 week" with "1 week, observing the 6-week rule for documentation".

Paragraph 8.39 (a) (v)

Replace the title "Ad Hoc Committee on the Elaboration of Legal Instruments for the Prevention of Terrorist Acts" with "Ad Hoc Committee established in accordance with General Assembly resolution 51/210 of 17 December 1996".

Paragraph 8.39 (b) (i)

Under recurrent publications, include "and *Yearbook of the International Law Commission,* 2002, volumes I and II (General Assembly resolution 987(X), judgements, advisory opinions, consultations and orders of the International Court of Justice)".

Table 8.18

Under indicator of achievement *(a)*, add a subparagraph (ix) reading: "(ix) Higher number of international transactions and higher volume of international debt trade carried out under the regime of UNCITRAL".

Section 9
Economic and social affairs

Paragraph 9.3

In the first sentence, insert "and social" after "sustained economic".

Table 9.12

At the end of indicator of achievement *(a)* (iii), add "with the assistance of the Secretariat".

In the second line of expected accomplishment *(b)*, after "that assist", replace "developing countries and countries with economies in transition" with "all countries".

At the end of indicator of achievement *(d)* (iii), add "taking into account the provisions of Article 101 of the Charter of the United Nations".

At the end of indicator of achievement *(f)*, add "with the assistance of the Secretariat".

Table 9.16
Expected accomplishment *(a)* should read: "*(a)* Effective implementation of the outcomes of the World Summit on Sustainable Development at all levels, including through partnership initiatives according to the modalities agreed upon in the Commission on Sustainable Development that support implementation of the commitments agreed at the World Summit".

In expected accomplishment *(b)*, delete "in all activities of sustainable development".

Replace indicator of achievement *(b)* (i) with the following: "(i) Progress in the achievement of United Nations objectives and goals on sustainable development, in particular those related to water, sanitation and human settlements, and the 10-year framework of programmes on sustainable consumption and production".

Replace expected accomplishment *(e)* with the following: "*(e)* Enabling the Commission to effectively review and facilitate partnerships that support the implementation of Agenda 21, the Programme for the Further Implementation of Agenda 21 and the Johannesburg Plan of Implementation".

Replace indicator of achievement *(e)* with the following: "*(e)* Provision of information and summary reports on partnerships in a transparent, participatory and credible manner, according to the procedures which were agreed upon in the Commission on Sustainable Development at its eleventh session".

In expected accomplishment *(f)*, after "in particular", insert "North-South and".

Table 9.22
Add an expected accomplishment *(f)*, reading: "*(f)* Improved access by Governments and international bodies to analytical tools, options and adequate methodologies regarding the linkages between political and economic issues and policies, such as economic sanctions, imposition of coercive economic measures, the relationship between disarmament and development and relevant aspects of post-conflict rehabilitation and reconstruction".

Add an indicator of achievement *(f)* and corresponding performance measures, reading:
"*(f)* Feedback from Member States on their access to analytical tools, options and adequate methodologies regarding the linkages between political and economic issues and policies
"*Performance measures:*
"2000-2001: to be determined
"Estimate 2002-2003: to be determined
"Target 2004-2005: to be determined".

Table 9.30
In expected accomplishment *(a)*, delete "multi-stakeholder".

Replace the text of expected accomplishment *(e)* with the following: "*(e)* Enhanced capacity of Governments, in particular that of developing countries and countries with economies in transition, to participate actively in the financing for development process".

Add an expected accomplishment *(f)*, reading: "*(f)* Fuller engagement of Governments to ensure proper follow-up to the implementation of agreements and commitments reached at the Conference and to continue to build bridges between development, finance and trade organizations and initiatives within the framework of the holistic agenda of the Conference".

Add an indicator of achievement *(f)* and corresponding performance measures, reading:
"*(f)* Feedback from Member States on the contribution of the subprogramme to the fuller engagement of Governments in the follow-up to the implementation of the outcome of the Conference
"*Performance measures:*
"2000-2001: not available
"Estimate 2002-2003: to be determined
"Target 2004-2005: to be determined".

Section 10
Least developed countries, landlocked developing countries and small island developing States

Paragraph 10.1
At the end of the paragraph, add the following sentence: "In addition, the programme is responsible for the provision of effective follow-up support to the further implementation of the Programme of Action for the Sustainable Development of Small Island Developing States, taking fully into account the relevant outcomes of the Plan of Implementation of the World Summit on Sustainable Development and General Assembly resolution 57/262 relating to the convening of an international meeting in Mauritius in 2004 to undertake a full and comprehensive review of the implementation of the Programme of Action for the Sustainable Development of Small Island Developing States."

Paragraph 10.4
In the first sentence, after "Transport Cooperation and the", insert "further implementation of the".

In the third sentence, after "Department of Economic and Social Affairs", insert ", the regional commissions and the South Centre" and delete "and the regional commissions".

Table 10.5
In the objective, replace "progress towards the achievement of" with "realize".

At the end of the expected accomplishment, add "and the relevant General Assembly resolutions".

Paragraph 10.14 (d)
Replace "political situation of", with "political situation in".

Section 11
United Nations support for the New Partnership for Africa's Development

Paragraph 11.16
Replace the text of external factor *(b)* with the following: "(b) the agencies of the United Nations system

collaborate and coordinate their activities in a coherent and effective manner".

Delete "and" before external factor "*(d)*" and, at the end of the external factor, add "and *(e)* all stakeholders implement their financial pledges and other commitments to support the New Partnership for Africa's Development".

Table 11.10

In expected accomplishment *(a)*, insert "academic institutions," before "the media".

Section 12
Trade and development

Replace, in every paragraph where the reference is made, "Millennium Development Goals" with "goals of the United Nations Millennium Declaration, as identified in section III of General Assembly resolution 55/2".

Paragraph 12.7

In the first sentence, replace "sectoral" with "national".

Paragraph 12.29 (a) (i)

Before subparagraph (i) of paragraph 12.29 *(a)*, reading "United Nations Conference on Trade and Development", insert a subparagraph (i), reading "(i) General Assembly: substantive servicing of and inputs to the high-level dialogue on strengthening international economic cooperation for development through partnership, in accordance with the relevant provisions of Assembly resolution 57/250"; and renumber the subsequent subparagraphs accordingly.

Table 12.10

In indicator of achievement *(e)*, after "technical cooperation projects", add "that improve the areas of trade, competition, enterprise development and investment".

Table 12.11

In indicator of achievement *(b)*, replace "Increased number of cross-sectoral activities" with "Significant increase in the number of cross-sectoral activities".

Table 12.15

In indicator of achievement *(a)* (ii), replace "this area" with "the trade-related capacity-building area".

Paragraph 12.54 (a) (i)

At the end of subparagraph (i) of paragraph 12.54, after "multilateral trading system (2);", add "contributions to the report on the implementation of the International Conference on Financing for Development concerning trade".

Annex

Retain the output contained in document A/56/6, paragraph 11A.31 *(d)* (i), reading: "Advisory services to developing countries to enhance their capacity to attract foreign portfolio investment funds, and to optimize their developmental impact", and the output contained in A/56/6, paragraph 11A.43 *(a)* (i) *b*, reading: "Inputs to the report of the Secretary-General on the implementation of the Barbados Programme of Action for the Sustainable Development of Small Island Developing States".

Section 14
Environment

Paragraph 14.4

At the end of the second sentence, add "as well as at the seventh special session of the Governing Council of UNEP, held in Cartagena, and the World Summit on Sustainable Development".

Table 14.18

Indicator of achievement *(d)* should read: "*(d)* Increased cooperation with UNCTAD, WTO and the multilateral environmental agreement secretariats to promote the mutual support of trade and environmental policies".

Indicator of achievement *(e)* (i) should read: "(i) Increased number of companies adhering to the relevant provisions of the World Summit on Sustainable Development with regard to corporate responsibility and the Global Compact".

Paragraph 14.47 (b) (ii)

Replace "reports of surveys and studies on appropriate policies, practices and indicators to improve products and services from a life-cycle perspective" with "reports of surveys and studies on appropriate practices to improve products and services from a life-cycle perspective".

Replace "technical documents (including guidelines, case studies and training packages) on policies and practices related to life-cycle management of production processes, products and services" with "technical documents (including guidelines, case studies and training packages) on practices related to life-cycle management of production processes, products and services".

Paragraph 14.47 (c) (i)

After "provision of targeted technical advice to financial institutions to influence investment decisions favouring energy efficiency and renewable energy", add "and advanced fossil fuel technology".

Table 14.26

Under "Action taken to implement the recommendation", replace the paragraph reading:

"It is expected that, after use of the indicative scale of contributions during a pilot phase in 2003, UNEP will analyse the accumulated experience and develop a new scale for the biennium 2004-2005, inviting all Member States to make adequate and predictable contributions"

with the paragraph reading:

"The Governing Council/Global Ministerial Environment Forum of UNEP in 2004 will review the effectiveness of the system and take a decision, as appropriate".

Section 15
Human settlements

Table 15.10

Replace expected accomplishment *(i)* with the following: "*(i)* Increased awareness of and sensitivity to the plight of the urban poor, and enhanced cooperation and partnership in slum upgrading initiatives in line with the Millennium Development Goal 'cities without slums'".

Insert in indicator of achievement *(i)* after "countries" "and other Habitat Agenda partners".

Delete in expected accomplishment *(j)* "renewable energy and".

Replace indicator of achievement *(j)* with the following: "*(j)* Number of countries working with UN-Habitat to promote access to diverse and efficient energy services as well as public and non-motorized transport".

Section 16
Crime prevention and criminal justice
Table 16.7
In indicator of achievement *(e)*, replace "Number" with "Percentage" and adjust the performance measures accordingly.

Section 17
International drug control
Table 17.7
In indicator of achievement (ii), after "Full", add "and efficient".

Table 17.10
In indicator of achievement *(c)*, replace "Timely receipt by" with "Availability of information for".

Table 17.12
Under indicator of achievement *(c)* (i), performance measures (target 2004-2005), replace "an average rating of 'fully satisfactory'" with "a 75 per cent rating 'fully satisfactory'".

Delete indicator of achievement *(c)* (ii), and delete "(i)" in indicator of achievement *(c)* (i).

Under indicators of achievement *(f)* and *(h)*, performance measures (target 2004-2005), replace "average survey rating of 'fully satisfactory'" with "a 75 per cent rating 'fully satisfactory'".

Table 17.13
Expected accomplishment *(b)* should read: "*(b)* Enhanced treaty adherence, at the request of Governments".

Indicator of achievement *(b)* should read: "*(b)* Number of Member States that received support from the Secretariat to become parties to one of the three drug control treaties".

In indicator of achievement *(c)*, insert ",with the assistance of the Secretariat," after "Governments".

Table 17.15
In indicators of achievement *(a)*, *(b)*, *(c)* and *(d)*, insert ", with the assistance of the Secretariat," after "Member States".

Table 17.17
Objective 1
Replace the text of indicator of achievement *(a)* with the following: "*(a)* Enhanced assistance by UNDCP to Member States to establish or strengthen national strategies to reduce and eliminate illicit cultivation, including comprehensive measures such as programmes in alternative development, law enforcement and eradication".

In indicators of achievement *(b)*, *(c)* and *(d)*, insert ", with the assistance of the Secretariat," after "countries".

In indicator of achievement *(e)* (i), insert ", with the assistance of the Secretariat," after "Member States".

Objective 2
In indicator of achievement *(a)*, insert ", with the assistance of the Secretariat," after "transit States".

Section 18
Economic and social development in Africa
Paragraph 18A.25
In the second sentence, after "This goal", insert ", while taking into account the new organization and programme of work of the Commission on Sustainable Development with regard to the regional implementation forum,".

Table 18A.10
Expected accomplishment *(a)* should read: "*(a)* Improved capacity of member States to design, implement and monitor development policies and strategies that address the needs of the poor, taking into account the goals of the Millennium Declaration and the priorities of NEPAD".

Table 18A.12
Expected accomplishment *(a)* should read: "*(a)* Increased awareness of policy makers of the interrelationship between and the need for integration of the three dimensions of sustainable development".

In indicator of achievement *(a)*, replace "the number of citations of" with "the number of times reference was made to". In the performance measures, replace "citations" with "references".

Expected accomplishment *(c)* should read: "*(c)* Effective incorporation of the interrelated issues of food security, population, environment and human settlements into sustainable development policies".

Table 18A.18
In indicator of achievement *(a)*, replace "trained by ECA" with "with the assistance of ECA".

Section 19
Economic and social development in Asia and the Pacific
Subprogramme 7
Replace the title with "Social development, including persistent and emerging issues".

Paragraph 19.7
Replace "least developed and landlocked countries as well as other developing countries" with "the developing countries and countries with economies in transition, particularly the least developed countries, landlocked developing countries and small island developing States".

Paragraph 19.40 (c) (ii)
At the beginning and at the end of the paragraph, replace "in the least developed countries and the countries with economies in transition" with "especially in the developing countries and countries with economies in transition, in particular the least developed countries, landlocked developing countries and small island developing States".

Paragraph 19.48 (c) (ii), (iii) and (iv)
After "energy efficiency", add ", advanced fossil fuel technology".

Table 19.22
In expected accomplishment *(a)*, replace "social issues" with "social development issues".

Delete indicator of achievement *(a)* (i) and delete "(ii)" in indicator of achievement *(a)* (ii).

Section 21
Economic and social development in Latin America and the Caribbean

Table 21.10

Add, as indicators of achievement *(c)* and *(d)*, indicators of achievement *(d)* and *(e)* of paragraph 17.9 of the medium-term plan for the period 2002-2005, as revised.

Table 21.12

Add, as indicators of achievement (iii), (iv) and (v), the indicators of achievement of paragraph 17.13 of the medium-term plan for the period 2002-2005, as revised.

Table 21.14

In expected accomplishment *(c)*, after "Enhanced regional", insert "technical".

Add, as indicators of achievement *(c)* (ii) and *(c)* (iii), indicators of achievement *(a)* and *(b)* of paragraph 17.18 of the medium-term plan for the period 2002-2005, as revised; and renumber the existing indicator of achievement as *(c)* (i).

Table 21.16

In indicator of achievement *(c)*, after "guidelines" insert ", with the assistance of ECLAC,".

Paragraph 21.60

Replace paragraph 21.60 with the following: "The subprogramme is expected to achieve its objectives and expected accomplishments on the assumption that: *(a)* gender mainstreaming in the region continues to receive full support from the countries of the region; and *(b)* member States continue to support the activities of the subprogramme."

Table 21.20

Add indicators of achievement *(a)* and *(c)* of paragraph 17.33 of the medium-term plan for the period 2002-2005, as revised, as indicators of achievement *(a)* (iv) and *(a)* (v). Add to the end of each "with the assistance or collaboration of ECLAC".

Table 21.22

Add indicator of achievement *(b)* of paragraph 17.37 of the medium-term plan for the period 2002-2005, as revised, as indicator of achievement *(b)* (ii); and renumber the existing indicator of achievement as *(b)* (i).

Table 21.24

Add expected accomplishment *(a)* of paragraph 17.41 and indicator of achievement *(a)* of paragraph 17.42 of the medium-term plan for the period 2002-2005, as revised, as expected accomplishment *(e)* and indicator of achievement *(e)*.

Table 21.28

At the end of indicator of achievement *(a)* (ii), after "coding systems", add "with the assistance and/or collaboration of ECLAC".

Add indicators of achievement *(d)* and *(e)* of paragraph 17.50 of the medium-term plan for the period 2002-2005, as revised, as indicators of achievement *(a)* (iii) and *(a)* (iv).

Table 21.30

Add, as expected accomplishments and indicators of achievement *(c)*, *(d)* and *(e)*, expected accomplishments *(a)*, *(c)* and *(d)* of paragraph 17.54 and indicators of achievement *(a)*, *(b)* and *(c)* of paragraph 17.55 of the medium-term plan for the period 2002-2005, as revised.

Table 21.32

Add indicator of achievement *(b)* of paragraph 17.59 of the medium-term plan for the period 2002-2005, as revised, as indicator of achievement *(c)* (ii); and renumber indicator of achievement *(c)* (ii) as *(c)* (iii).

Section 23
Regular programme of technical cooperation

Paragraph 23.35

(a) (i) In the first of the advisory services, replace "especially in least developed, landlocked and island developing countries and countries with economies in transition" with "especially in the developing countries and countries with economies in transition, in particular least developed, landlocked and island developing countries";

(e) (i) In the tenth line, after "developing", insert "energy efficiency, advanced fossil fuel technology and";

(e) (ii) Replace "renewable energy" with "implementation of paragraph 20 of the Johannesburg Plan of Implementation, on energy";

(f) (i) In the first of the advisory services, replace "particularly of least developed, landlocked and island developing countries and countries with economies in transition" with "especially of the developing countries and countries with economies in transition, in particular least developed, landlocked and island developing countries";

(g) (iii) Replace the text with the following: "(iii) Field project on addressing social development, including emerging social issues".

Section 24
Human rights

Paragraph 24.3

Delete the final sentence.

Paragraph 24.4

Delete the final sentence.

Paragraph 24.5

Delete the final sentence.

Paragraph 24.6

The final sentence should read: "During the biennium, OHCHR will work towards the goal of increased effectiveness and improved management, taking into account relevant resolutions and decisions, as well as the recommendations already made in that regard."

Paragraph 24.8 (a) (ii)

Subparagraph (ii) of paragraph 24.8 *(a)* should read: "(ii) Under subprogramme 1, one new P-4 post to direct research and analysis in the implementation of the right to development, including strategies to achieve the Millennium Development Goals".

Paragraph 24.15 (e)

Delete subparagraph *(e)* of paragraph 24.15 and reletter the subsequent subparagraphs accordingly.

Paragraph 24.29

At the end of the paragraph, add the sentence: "Specific proposals in this regard will be submitted to the General Assembly in line with the decision contained in paragraph 4 of its resolution 54/244".

Table 24.11

Add an expected accomplishment *(e)* reading: "*(e)* Strengthened efforts that contribute to the elimination of racism, racial discrimination, xenophobia and related intolerance" and an indicator of achievement *(e)* reading: "*(e)* An increased number of activities carried out to fulfil the mandates".

Paragraph 24.39 (c)

Subparagraph *(c)* of paragraph 24.39 should read: "the establishment of 1 new P-4 post to strengthen capacity in the area of the implementation of the right to development, including strategies to achieve the Millennium Development Goals, by directing research and analysis".

Paragraph 24.58

The second sentence should read: "OHCHR establishes presences in the field as a response to decisions of relevant intergovernmental bodies of the United Nations, including the Commission on Human Rights, in accordance with their respective mandates."

In the fifth sentence, replace "creating a culture of human rights" with "creating human rights education and training".

Section 25
Protection of and assistance to refugees

Paragraph 25.4

In the last sentence, replace "programme of work will" with "work under the subprogramme on international protection will also".

Table 25.5

Replace expected accomplishment *(d)* with the following: "*(d)* Progress towards a durable solution through the formulation, facilitation and active implementation of voluntary repatriation operations in conditions of safety and dignity, followed up by the monitoring of the situations in countries to which the refugees return".

At the end of indicator of achievement *(d)*, add "in the framework of voluntary repatriation operations".

Replace expected accomplishment *(e)* with the following: "*(e)* The promotion of local integration as a possible durable solution, where feasible, in accordance with the High Commissioner's strategy of development through local integration".

Under indicator of achievement *(f)* (ii), add the following:

"*Performance measures:*
"2000-2001: not available
"Estimate 2002-2003: to be determined
"Target 2004-2005: to be determined"

To indicator of achievement *(f)*, add a subparagraph (iii), reading:

"(iii) The extent to which tools to improve monitoring and oversight of resettlement have been adopted
"*Performance measures:*
"2000-2001: not available
"Estimate 2002-2003: to be determined
"Target 2004-2005: to be determined".

Add a full stop at the end of expected accomplishment *(c)* and add the text of expected accomplishment *(g)* to expected accomplishment *(c)*.

Merge indicator of achievement *(g)* with indicator of achievement *(c)*, producing two subparagraphs, as follows:

"*(c)* (i) Decrease in the number of incidents related to sexual and gender-based violence reported to health clinics in refugee camps"
"(ii) The number of UNHCR country operations plans reflecting the five priority categories and key sectors"

To indicator of achievement *(c)*, add a subparagraph (iii) and performance measures, reading:

"(iii) Development of measurable indicators corresponding to the High Commissioner's five commitments
"*Performance measures:*
"2000-2001: not available
"Estimate 2002-2003: to be determined
"Target 2004-2005: to be determined".

Table 25.6

Replace the text of indicator of achievement *(b)* (i) with the following: "(i) The number of initiatives incorporating quality of life of refugees and the surrounding local communities into national development plans".

In indicator of achievement *(b)* (ii), delete "against core standards".

In indicator of achievement *(b)* (iii), replace "microfinance" with "self-reliance".

In expected accomplishment *(d)*, replace "protect" with "assist" and at the end of the expected accomplishment, add "through the provision of sufficient voluntary contributions by the international community, in a spirit of burden-sharing and international solidarity".

In indicator of achievement *(d)* (ii), delete "as well as in the development through local integration strategy".

Under indicator of achievement *(d)*, add a subparagraph (iii), reading: "(iii) Increase in the level of voluntary contributions provided by the international community". To this indicator of achievement, add "Performance measures: to be determined".

Section 28
Public information

Paragraph 28.3

Replace the first two sentences with the following sentence: "The overarching mandate of the Department of Public Information is contained in General Assembly resolution 13(I) of 13 February 1946, and its primary mission is to provide, through its outreach activities, accurate, impartial, comprehensive and timely information to the public on the tasks and responsibilities of the United Nations in order to strengthen international support for the activities of the Organization with the greatest transparency, respecting existing mandates and in line with regulation 5.6 of the Regulations and Rules Governing Programme Planning, the Programme Aspects of the Budget, the Monitoring of Implementation and the Methods of Evaluation, to focus its message and better concentrate its efforts and, as a function of performance management, to match its programmes to the needs of its target audiences, on the basis of improved feedback and evaluation mechanisms, as set out in General Assembly resolution 57/130 B".

In the last sentence, after "has been formulated,", insert "as welcomed by the Committee on Information".

Paragraph 28.4

The second sentence should read: "Its core message, with the medium-term plan priorities as the main guide, and taking into consideration General Assembly resolution 55/2 (the Millennium Declaration), will focus on the eradication of poverty, conflict prevention, sustainable development, human rights, the HIV/AIDS epidemic, the battle against international terrorism and the needs of the African continent (see resolution 57/130 B), as well as on international cooperation, the transfer of technology and transparency in international trade".

Paragraph 28.11

After "in Western Europe" at the end of the third sentence, add "in accordance with resolutions 57/130 B and 57/300, in particular paragraphs 44 and 15 respectively".

Table 28.7

At the end of the objective, add "and assessing that impact through annual programme reviews".

At the beginning of the last paragraph under *Indicators of achievement*, insert "*(d)*"; and at the end of the paragraph, add "in the implementation of the results of the Department's annual programme impact reviews".

Paragraph 28.29

In the first sentence, delete "and established by the Secretary-General".

In the second sentence, replace ", using the Millennium Declaration as its guide" with "of the medium-term plan and of the Millennium Declaration (General Assembly resolution 55/2)".

Paragraph 28.30

The second sentence should read: "Under the guidance of the Information Centres Service at Headquarters, the United Nations information centres and information components and regional hubs, as applicable, will play a significant role in disseminating information about the work of the Organization to the peoples of the world, including the areas outlined in the United Nations Millennium Declaration, with the information centres as the 'field voice' of the Department of Public Information, and will work through local intermediaries to promote public awareness of and mobilize support for the work of the United Nations at the local level, bearing in mind that information in the local languages has the strongest impact on the local populations."

Paragraph 28.31

After "regional information hubs in strategic locations" in the first sentence, insert "in accordance with resolutions 57/130 B and 57/300, in particular paragraphs 44 and 15 respectively".

Paragraph 28.33

Delete the last sentence.

Table 28.10

In the objective, after "on priority issues" add "of the medium-term plan and the Millennium Declaration (General Assembly resolution 55/2)".

In expected accomplishment *(a)*, replace "on priority issues" with "in accordance with priorities established by the General Assembly".

Paragraph 28.50

At the end of the first sentence, replace "the Member States" with "intergovernmental organs in collaboration with the Member States".

Table 28.18

Insert "*(a)*" before the expected accomplishment and the indicator of achievement. Add the following to indicator of achievement *(a)*: "; the number of hits on the United Nations web site, sorted by official language, and the number of radio programmes broadcast, by language".

Add an expected accomplishment *(b)*, reading: "*(b)* Timeliness in the submission of photographic and video material".

Add an indicator of achievement *(b)*, reading: "*(b)* Period of time within which photographic and video material is available to news organizations and media after an event takes place".

Table 28.22

At the end of indicator of achievement *(a)*, add "; number of joint and/or coordinated projects by the Dag Hammarskjöld Library and other United Nations libraries; and number of hits on the Dag Hammarskjöld Library web sites, sorted by official language".

Paragraph 28.66

After "on priority issues", replace the rest of the text with the following: "using the priorities of the medium-term plan as the main guide and taking into consideration General Assembly resolution 55/2 (the Millennium Declaration)."

Table 28.24

In the objective, replace "using the Millennium Declaration as a guide" with "using the priorities of the medium-term plan and taking into consideration General Assembly resolution 55/2 (the Millennium Declaration)".

Add the following to the indicator of achievement: "; the number of readers of the *UN Chronicle*, sorted by official language; and the number of times articles appearing in the *UN Chronicle* are cited in newspapers and journals".

Section 29A
Office of the Under-Secretary-General for Management

Table 29A.5

In indicator of achievement *(c)*, insert "efficient" before "support services".

Table 29A.8

In objective 1, replace "Secretary-General's vision for reform" with "reforms in the United Nations".

Under objective 1, add an indicator of achievement (ii) reading: "(ii) Level of satisfaction expressed by the intergovernmental organs" and a corresponding performance measure reading: "Periodic surveys among

Member States"; and renumber the existing indicator of achievement as "(i)".

Table 29A.10

At the end of the expected accomplishment, add "related to disciplinary affairs, claims and appeals of the staff".

Section 29B
Office of Programme Planning, Budget and Accounts

Table 29B.5

In the objective, after "procedures", insert "contained in the Financial Regulations and Rules and the Regulations and Rules Governing Programme Planning, the Programme Aspects of the Budget, the Monitoring of Implementation and the Methods of Evaluation".

Table 29B.8

Objective 1

Add an expected accomplishment *(b)* reading: "*(b)* Better implementation of and compliance by departments and offices of the Secretariat with the Financial Regulations and Rules of the United Nations and the Regulations and Rules Governing Programme Planning, the Programme Aspects of the Budget, the Monitoring of Implementation and the Methods of Evaluation"; and add "*(a)*" before the existing expected accomplishment.

Add an indicator of achievement *(b)* reading: "*(b)* Fewer findings by the oversight bodies of non-compliance with the Financial Regulations and Rules of the United Nations and the Regulations and Rules Governing Programme Planning, the Programme Aspects of the Budget, the Monitoring of Implementation and the Methods of Evaluation and other approved budgetary procedures and guidelines for the regular budget, peacekeeping budgets, extrabudgetary resources and budgets of the Tribunals". Indicators of achievement *(a)* and *(b)* become indicators of achievement *(a)* (i) and (ii).

Objective 2

In indicator of achievement *(a)*, after "travel claims", add "payroll, insurance, invoices and claims processing"; and add an indicator of achievement *(c)* reading: "*(c)* The availability of financial reports by the required dates".

Table 29B.10

Under objective 1, change indicator of achievement *(b)* to *(b)* (i), and add an indicator of achievement *(b)* (ii) reading: "(ii) Availability of budgetary documents by the required dates".

Under objective 1, add an expected accomplishment *(c)* reading: "*(c)* Improved compliance with regulation 5.6 of the Regulations and Rules Governing Programme Planning, the Programme Aspects of the Budget, the Monitoring of Implementation and the Methods of Evaluation"; and add an indicator of achievement *(c)*, reading: "*(c)* Number of sections of the proposed programme budget for the biennium 2006-2007 that reflect a number of outputs deleted because they are obsolete, irrelevant or of marginal usefulness".

Paragraph 29B.31

In subparagraph *(a)* (ii) after "measures to encourage payment of assessed contributions and related issues", add "if mandated".

Section 29C
Office of Human Resources Management

Table 29C.9

At the end of the expected accomplishment, add ", taking into account Article 101 of the Charter".

At the end of indicator of achievement (ii), add ", taking into account Article 101 of the Charter".

Under indicator of achievement (iii), performance measures, before "Number of unrepresented Member States", add a performance measure, reading: "Level of under-representation of Member States: to be determined".

Paragraph 29C.22

In subparagraph *(a)* (ii), after "gender balance," add ", geographical representation,".

At the end of subparagraph *(b)* (i) *e*, add "and taking into account planning for the replacement of retiring staff".

Section 29D
Office of Central Support Services

Table 29D.5

At the end of expected accomplishment *(a)*, add ", improving the application of the Financial Regulations and Rules of the United Nations and the Regulations and Rules Governing Programme Planning, the Programme Aspects of the Budget, the Monitoring of Implementation and the Methods of Evaluation".

In indicator of achievement *(a)* (iii), replace "Full" with "Effective and efficient".

Table 29D.12

The objective should read: "To ensure efficient, effective and diversified procurement opportunities and high-quality procurement services for the Organization."

Add an expected accomplishment *(c)* reading: "*(c)* Improvement in efforts to diversify United Nations suppliers", and a corresponding indicator of achievement *(c)* reading: "*(c)* Number of new suppliers registered".

Section 29E
Administration, Geneva

Section 29F
Administration, Vienna

Section 29G
Administration, Nairobi

Table 29E.12

At the end of expected accomplishment *(f)*, add "and improvement in efforts to diversify United Nations suppliers".

Paragraph 29F.20

At the end of subparagraphs *(a)* and *(b)*, add "observing the principle of geographical representation, taking into account Article 101 of the Charter".

Table 29G.12
At the end of expected accomplishment (f), add "and improvement in efforts to diversify United Nations suppliers".

Tables 29E.6 (Objective), 29E.8 (Objective 1), 29F.7 (Objective), 29F.9 (Objective 1), 29G.6 (Objective), 29G.8 (Objective 1)
At the end of the objectives, add ", with the goal of achieving greater efficiency and effectiveness of operations".

Add an indicator of achievement (ii) reading: "(ii) Savings achieved from efficiency measures" and renumber the existing indicator of achievement as (i).

Section 30
Internal oversight

Table 30.8
In indicator of achievement (a), after "non-compliance" add "by programme managers".

In expected accomplishment (b), after "the Organization" add "and increased efficiency".

In indicator of achievement (b), replace "audit recommendations calling for formal" with "audits on".

Indicator of achievement (c) should become (c) (i); add an indicator (c) (ii), reading: "(ii) The level of recovery of erroneous or unauthorized expenditures"; and add under the corresponding performance measures "To be determined".

In indicator of achievement (d), delete "and assignments".

Table 30.10
At the end of expected accomplishment (a), add "in accordance with the mandates".

Table 30.12
Add an indicator of achievement (iii) reading:
"(iii) Number of cases resolved
 "Performance measures:
 "To be determined".

Annex, column headed "Reason for discontinuation"
In the entry for paragraph 28.22 (a) (ii) b., after "Organization" insert "included in the medium-term plan and to enhance support for self-evaluation by other departments and offices".

Section 31
Jointly financed administrative activities

Table 31.9
Under indicator of achievement (a), add the following:

"Performance measures:
"2000-2001: to be determined
"Estimate 2002-2003: to be determined
"Target 2004-2005: to be determined".

Table 31.24
Under objective 1, add an expected accomplishment (b) reading: "(b) Ensuring adequate coordination among United Nations agencies to provide for the safety and security of staff"; and reletter the existing expected accomplishment as (a).

Add an indicator of achievement (b), reading:
"(b) (i) Reduction in the number of preventable security incidents in the field
 "(ii) Increase in attendance at joint security training sessions run by the United Nations Security Coordinator in the field
 "(iii) Compliance by all resident coordinators/ humanitarian coordinators with their responsibilities as 'designated officials' for security";
and reletter the existing indicator of achievement as (a).

Annex II
Staffing table for 2004 and 2005

Category	2004	2005
Professional and above		
Deputy Secretary-General	1	1
Under-Secretary-General	27	27
Assistant Secretary-General	21	21
D-2	84	84
D-1	253	253
P-5	706	706
P-4/3	2,341	2,342
P-2/1	477	477
Subtotal	3,910	3,911
General Service		
Principal level	274	274
Other level	2,673	2,673
Subtotal	2,947	2,947
Other		
Security Service	218	218
Local level	1,677	1,677
Field Service	185	185
Trades and Crafts	181	181
Subtotal	2,261	2,261
Total	9,118	9,119

Annex III
New posts approved in the context of the review of the initial proposal of the Secretary-General

Section 1. Overall policy-making, direction and coordination
Office of the Ombudsman — 1 D-1
Office of the Director-General, United Nations Office at Nairobi — 1 P-5

Section 3. Political affairs
Office of the United Nations Special Coordinator for the Middle East Peace Process — 1 P-3, 1 Security Service

Section 4. Disarmament
Weapons of mass destruction — 1 P-5
Regional disarmament — 1 D-1

Section 8. Legal affairs

Progressive harmonization and unification of the law of international trade — 1 D-2, 1 P-5, 1 P-2

Section 9. Economic and social affairs

Executive direction and management — 1 Assistant Secretary-General, 1 P-5
Economic and Social Council support and coordination — 1 P-5
Population — 1 P-5, 1 P-3
Financing for development — 1 P-5, 1 P-4, 1 P-3
Secretariat of the Permanent Forum on Indigenous Issues — 1 P-3, 1 P-2

Section 10. Least developed countries, landlocked developing countries and small island developing States
1 D-1

Section 12. Trade and development

Investment, enterprise development and technology — 1 P-4
Programme support — 1 D-2

Section 14. Environment

Executive direction and management — 1 P-5

Section 15. Human settlements

Shelter and sustainable human settlements development — 1 P-4
Monitoring the Habitat agenda — 1 P-5

Section 16. Crime prevention and criminal justice
1 P-4

Section 19. Economic and social development in Asia and the Pacific

Poverty and development — 1 P-2
Statistics — 1 P-2
Environment and sustainable development — 1 P-2
Social development, including emerging social issues — 1 P-2

Section 21. Economic and social development in Latin America and the Caribbean

Environment and human settlements — 1 P-2
Subregional activities in Mexico and Central America — 1 P-4

Section 24. Human rights

Right to development, research and analysis — 1 P-4
Supporting human rights bodies and organs — 1 P-5, 1 P-4
Advisory services, fact-finding and field activities — 1 D-1, 1 P-5, 1 P-4

Section 26. Palestine refugees
1 D-1, 1 P-5, 1 P-4, 2 P-3

Section 27. Humanitarian assistance

Complex emergencies — 1 P-4, 1 P-3
Disaster relief — 1 P-3

Section 29. Management and central support services

Management services, Nairobi — 1 General Service (Local level)
Programme planning, budget and accounts, Nairobi — 1 P-4, 5 General Service (Local level)
Human resources management, Nairobi — 2 P-4, 1 P-3, 1 P-2, 5 General Service

Total 62

Annex IV

Conversions of temporary resources to established posts

Section 2. General Assembly affairs and conference services

Interpretation, meeting and publishing services, New York — 2 P-5, 3 P-4, 5 P-3

Section 3. Political affairs

Security Council affairs — 1 P-5, 1 P-3, 1 P-2/1, 5 General Service (Other level)

Section 7. International Court of Justice

The Registry — 5 P-2/1

Section 10. Least developed countries, landlocked developing countries and small island developing States
1 Under-Secretary-General, 1 D-2, 2 P-5, 3 P-4, 1 P-3, 5 General Service (Other level)

Section 11. United Nations support for the New Partnership for Africa's Development

Mobilization of international support — 1 Under-Secretary-General, 1 D-1, 1 P-4, 2 P-3, 2 General Service (Other level)

Section 24. Human rights

Advisory services, fact-finding and field activities — 1 P-5, 1 P-4, 3 P-3

Section 29C. Human Resources Management

Office of Operational Services — 1 P-3, 1 P-2, 2 General Service (Other level)

Total 52

Appropriations

In his proposed programme budget for the 2004-2005 biennium [A/58/6], the Secretary-General recommended expenditures of $3,031.6 million and income of $26.6 million and staff assessment income of $380.7 million (an increase of $7.6 million), resulting in a net budget estimate of $2,650.9 million and representing a 7 per cent real growth over the 2002-2003 budget.

Extrabudgetary resources for the 2004-2005 biennium were estimated at $4,220.1 million, comprising $700 million for support activities, $1,237.9 million for substantive activities and $2,282.2 million for operational activities.

ACABQ, in its first report on the 2004-2005 programme budget [A/58/7], noting that the overall real growth in resources for the proposed budget before recosting would amount to just 0.5 per cent, was of the opinion that, should the General Assembly approve the budget at a level lower than that proposed by the Secretary-General, such reductions as might be decided by the Assembly should be based on an analysis of specific items; it accordingly proposed specific reductions in a number of areas. Regarding requests for new posts, ACABQ, taking account of the ratio of General Service to Professional posts and of the impact of the investment made in information and communication technology, recommended against additional support staff but in favour of an additional Professional post. It trusted that redeployments would be effected Secretariat-wide, with no post being "owned" by any particular unit.

The budgetary reductions resulting from ACABQ's recommendations on posts and reclassifications totalled $12.5 million gross at 2004-2005 rates, and $437,800 in respect of consultants and experts. It recommended full restoration of the cuts in respect of information and communication technology; reductions totalling $7.5 million relating to common services facility infrastructure; cuts of $3.3 million relating to furniture and equipment, including the computer replacement cycle; and $1.9 milllion for general operating expenses. Owing to the sharp decline of the United States dollar since the 2004-2005 budget was first costed and the likelihood of its further fluctuation, the appropriated and assessed amounts resulting from a recosting exercise might considerably be at variance with actual requirements. ACABQ thus recommended that the Assembly schedule its consideration of additional requirements arising from currency movements and inflation when a more complete picture had emerged, such as during its consideration of the first performance report.

In October [A/58/528], the Secretary-General recommended revised estimates reflecting the latest data on actual inflation experience, the outcome of salary surveys, the movement of post adjustment indices in 2003, salary expenditure experience and the effect of the evolution of operational rates of exchange in 2003 on the proposed 2004-2005 programme budget. The recosted level of expenditure amounted to $3,167.6 million; revised estimates of income amounted to $419.4 million.

ACABQ, in its twelfth report on the 2004-2005 programme budget [A/58/7/Add.11], found no technical basis for objecting to the Secretary-General's revised estimates and transmitted them to the Fifth Committee.

GENERAL ASSEMBLY ACTION

On 23 December [meeting 79], the General Assembly, on the recommendation of the Fifth Committee [A/58/573], adopted **resolution 58/271 A-C** without vote [agenda item 121].

Programme budget for the biennium 2004-2005

A

Budget appropriations for the biennium 2004-2005
The General Assembly
Resolves that, for the biennium 2004-2005:
1. Appropriations totalling 3,160,860,300 United States dollars are hereby approved for the following purposes:

United Nations financing and programming

Section			Amount (Thousands of United States dollars)
	Part I. Overall policy-making, direction and coordination		
1.	Overall policy-making, direction and coordination		58,504.4
2.	General Assembly affairs and conference services		535,380.5
		Subtotal	593,884.9
	Part II. Political affairs		
3.	Political affairs		239,595.4
4.	Disarmament		18,048.2
5.	Peacekeeping operations		86,124.2
6.	Peaceful uses of outer space		5,484.4
		Subtotal	349,252.2
	Part III. International justice and law		
7.	International Court of Justice		31,537.9
8.	Legal affairs		38,707.5
		Subtotal	70,245.4
	Part IV. International cooperation for development		
9.	Economic and social affairs		137,739.4
10.	Least developed countries, landlocked developing countries and small island developing States		4,231.9
11.	United Nations support for the New Partnership for Africa's Development		9,344.0
12.	Trade and development		106,241.8
13.	International Trade Centre UNCTAD/WTO		23,472.2
14.	Environment		10,530.1
15.	Human settlements		15,536.2
16.	Crime prevention and criminal justice		9,392.8
17.	International drug control		20,006.9
		Subtotal	336,495.3
	Part V. Regional cooperation for development		
18.	Economic and social development in Africa		95,617.0
19.	Economic and social development in Asia and the Pacific		66,644.0
20.	Economic development in Europe		50,196.8
21.	Economic and social development in Latin America and the Caribbean		80,804.0
22.	Economic and social development in Western Asia		52,480.4
23.	Regular programme of technical cooperation		42,871.5
		Subtotal	388,613.7
	Part VI. Human rights and humanitarian affairs		
24.	Human rights		56,794.5
25.	Protection of and assistance to refugees		56,731.9
26.	Palestine refugees		33,851.8
27.	Humanitarian assistance		23,292.3
		Subtotal	170,670.5
	Part VII. Public information		
28.	Public information		155,869.9
		Subtotal	155,869.9
	Part VIII. Common support services		
29.	Management and central support services		516,168.9
		Subtotal	516,168.9
	Part IX. Internal oversight		
30.	Internal oversight		23,227.2
		Subtotal	23,227.2
	Part X. Jointly financed administrative activities and special expenses		
31.	Jointly financed administrative activities		22,990.2
32.	Special expenses		79,455.1
		Subtotal	102,445.3
	Part XI. Capital expenditures		
33.	Construction, alteration, improvement and major maintenance		58,651.3
		Subtotal	58,651.3
	Part XII. Staff assessment		
34.	Staff assessment		382,270.7
		Subtotal	382,270.7
	Part XIII. Development Account		
35.	Development Account		13,065.0
		Subtotal	13,065.0
		Total	**3,160,860.3**

2. The Secretary-General shall be authorized to transfer credits between sections of the budget with the concurrence of the Advisory Committee on Administrative and Budgetary Questions;

3. The total net provision made under the various sections of the budget for contractual printing shall be administered as a unit under the direction of the United Nations Publications Board;

4. In addition to the appropriations approved under paragraph 1 above, an amount of 125,000 dollars is appropriated for each year of the biennium 2004-2005 from the accumulated income of the Library Endowment Fund for the purchase of books, periodicals, maps and library equipment and for such other expenses of the library at the Palais des Nations in Geneva as are in accordance with the objects and provisions of the endowment.

B
Income estimates for the biennium 2004-2005
The General Assembly
Resolves that, for the biennium 2004-2005:

1. Estimates of income other than assessments on Member States totalling 415,291,800 United States dollars are approved as follows:

Income section	Amount (Thousands of United States dollars)
1. Income from staff assessment	386,491.7
2. General income	24,043.2
3. Services to the public	4,756.9
Total	415,291.8

2. The income from staff assessment shall be credited to the Tax Equalization Fund in accordance with the provisions of General Assembly resolution 973(X) of 15 December 1955;

3. Direct expenses of the United Nations Postal Administration, services to visitors, the sale of statistical products, catering operations and related services, garage operations, television services and the sale of publications not provided for under the budget appropriations shall be charged against the income derived from those activities.

C
Financing of appropriations for the year 2004
The General Assembly
Resolves that, for the year 2004:

1. Budget appropriations consisting of 1,580,430,150 United States dollars, being half of the appropriation of 3,160,860,300 dollars approved for the biennium 2004-2005 by the General Assembly in paragraph 1 of resolution A above, plus 76,909,100 dollars, being the increase in revised appropriations for the biennium 2002-2003 approved by the Assembly in its resolutions 57/311 of 18 June 2003 and 58/267 A of 23 December 2003, shall be financed in accordance with regulations 3.1 and 3.2 of the Financial Regulations of the United Nations, as follows:

(a) 8,007,450 dollars, consisting of 14,400,050 dollars, being the net of half of the estimated income other than staff assessment approved for the biennium 2004-2005 under resolution B above, less 6,392,600 dollars, being the decrease in income other than staff assessment for the biennium 2002-2003;

(b) 1,649,331,800 dollars, being the assessment on Member States in accordance with its resolution 58/1 B of 23 December 2003;

2. There shall be set off against the assessment on Member States, in accordance with the provisions of General Assembly resolution 973(X) of 15 December 1955, their respective share in the Tax Equalization Fund in the total amount of 213,298,950 dollars, consisting of:

(a) 193,245,850 dollars, being half of the estimated staff assessment income approved for the biennium 2004-2005 in resolution B above;

(b) 20,053,100 dollars, being the increase in income from staff assessment for the biennium 2002-2003 approved by the Assembly in its resolution 58/267 B of 23 December 2003.

On 23 December, the Assembly decided that the item on the proposed programme budget for the 2004-2005 biennium would remain for consideration during its resumed fifty-eighth (2004) session (**decision 58/565**).

Other questions relating to the programme budget

The Fifth Committee considered a number of special subjects relating to the 2004-2005 programme budget, among them special political missions; estimates in respect of matters of which the Security Council was seized; revised estimates resulting from resolutions and decisions adopted by the Economic and Social Council at its 2003 substantive session; the contingency fund; the effect of changes in rates of exchange or inflation and additional expenditures deriving therefrom, the Working Capital Fund; and unforeseen and extraordinary expenses (see sections below).

Other subjects concerned the administrative expenses of the United Nations Joint Staff Pension Fund (see p. 1457); the UN information and communication technology strategy (see p. 630); the comprehensive review of the post structure of the UN Secretariat (see p. 1446); the request for a subvention to the United Nations Institute for Disarmament Research (UNIDIR) (see p. 586); improving and modernizing the conference facilities at the United Nations Office at Nairobi (see p. 1490); the International Trade Centre UNCTAD/WTO (see. p. 974); cost implications of providing more predictable and adequate conference services to meetings of regional and other major groupings of Member States (see p. 1491); conference and support services for the Counter-Terrorism Committee (see p. 66); the Development Account (see p. 905); the proportion of General Service staff to Professional staff in the regional commissions (see p. 1447); the United Nations Fund for International Partnerships (see p. 905); the capital master plan (see p. 1500); the administration and management of the Office of the United Nations High Commissioner for Human Rights (see p. 657); administrative and financial implications of the decisions and recommendations of the report of the International Civil Service Commission (ICSC) for 2003 (see p. 1431); improvements in the current process of planning and budgeting (see p. 1394); interorganizational security measures (see p. 1501); and the gross budgets for JIU (see p. 1467), ICSC (see p. 1432) and the Office of the United Nations Security Coordinator (see p. 1456).

GENERAL ASSEMBLY ACTION

On 23 December [meeting 79], the General Assembly, on the recommendation of the Fifth Committee [A/58/573], adopted **resolution 58/272** without vote [agenda item 121].

Special subjects relating to the proposed programme budget for the biennium 2004-2005

The General Assembly,

I

Information and communication technology strategy

Recalling its resolution 57/304 of 15 April 2003,

Having considered the report of the Secretary-General entitled "Information and communication technology strategy: implementation of General Assembly resolution 57/304 of 15 April 2003",

Having also considered the report of the Joint Inspection Unit entitled "Managing information in the United Nations system organizations: management information systems", the comments of the Secretary-General and those of the United Nations System Chief Executives Board for Coordination thereon and the related report of the Advisory Committee on Administrative and Budgetary Questions,

1. *Takes note* of the report of the Secretary-General, and welcomes the steps being taken to address all requests contained in its resolution 57/304;

2. *Reiterates* the need to indicate the return on investment for planned and proposed major projects in terms that are as quantitative as possible;

3. *Takes note* of the report of the Joint Inspection Unit, the comments of the Secretary-General and those of the United Nations System Chief Executives Board for Coordination thereon and the related report of the Advisory Committee on Administrative and Budgetary Questions;

II

Comprehensive review of the post structure of the United Nations Secretariat

Recalling its resolution 56/253 of 24 December 2001 and its decision 57/574 of 20 December 2002,

Takes note of the report of the Secretary-General on the comprehensive review of the post structure of the United Nations Secretariat and the related report of the Advisory Committee on Administrative and Budgetary Questions;

III

Request for a subvention to the United Nations Institute for Disarmament Research

Having considered the note by the Secretary-General on the request for a subvention to the United Nations Institute for Disarmament Research resulting from the recommendations of the Board of Trustees of the Institute on the work programme of the Institute for 2004 and the related report of the Advisory Committee on Administrative and Budgetary Questions,

1. *Approves* the request for a subvention by the General Assembly of 227,600 United States dollars for the United Nations Institute for Disarmament Research for 2004 from the approved regular budget of the United Nations, on the understanding that no additional appropriation would be required under section 4, Disarmament, of the programme budget for the biennium 2004-2005;

2. *Requests* the Secretary-General to report to the General Assembly at the main part of its fifty-ninth session on the continuing need for a subvention to the Institute, taking into account previous reports and any relevant decisions on the question of subventions;

IV

Improving and modernizing the conference facilities at the United Nations Office at Nairobi in order to accommodate adequately major meetings and conferences

Recalling its resolutions 55/222 of 23 December 2000, 56/242 of 24 December 2001 and 57/283 B of 15 April 2003,

Having considered the report of the Secretary-General on improving and modernizing the conference facilities at the United Nations Office at Nairobi in order to accommodate adequately major meetings and conferences and the related report of the Advisory Committee on Administrative and Budgetary Questions,

1. *Authorizes* the modernization of the existing conference facilities at the United Nations Office at Nairobi;

2. *Decides* to appropriate related resources under section 33, Construction, alteration, improvement and major maintenance, of the proposed programme budget for the biennium 2004-2005, to finance the modernization of the existing conference facilities at the United Nations Office at Nairobi in the amount of 1,032,000 United States dollars as a charge against the contingency fund;

3. *Also decides* to approve the utilization of an amount of 1,020,000 dollars for the modernization of the existing conference facilities at the United Nations Office at Nairobi, to be financed within the available balance of the construction-in-progress account;

4. *Requests* the Secretary-General to report to the General Assembly on the experience gained from operating the modernized conference facilities of the United Nations Office at Nairobi during the biennium 2006-2007;

V

Special political missions: estimates in respect of matters of which the Security Council is seized

Having considered the report of the Secretary-General on the estimates in respect of special political missions, good offices and other political initiatives authorized by the General Assembly and/or the Security Council and the related report of the Advisory Committee on Administrative and Budgetary Questions,

1. *Takes note* of the report of the Secretary-General on estimates in respect of special political missions, good offices and other political initiatives authorized by the General Assembly and/or the Security Council;

2. *Endorses* the observations and recommendations of the Advisory Committee on Administrative and Budgetary Questions contained in its report, subject to the provisions of the present resolution;

3. *Decides* not to endorse the observation of the Advisory Committee contained in paragraph 26 of its report;

4. *Requests* the Secretary-General to further explore synergies and complementarities between various missions and other relevant entities of the United Nations in order to ensure efficiency and optimum use of resources and to report thereon in the context of future budget proposals on special political missions;

5. *Also requests* the Secretary-General to expand the treatment of larger missions with a view to providing a level of information similar to that contained in the proposed budgets of peacekeeping operations, taking into account relevant resolutions of the General Assembly;

6. *Approves* a charge of 133,119,500 United States dollars for the 17 special political missions presented in table 1, section II, of the report of the Secretary-General, emanating from decisions taken or to be taken by the Security Council, against the provision of 169,431,700 dollars for special political missions under section 3, Political affairs, of the proposed programme budget for the biennium 2004-2005;

7. *Also approves* a further charge of 2,172,400 dollars for the United Nations Mission in Côte d'Ivoire for the period from 1 January to 4 February 2004, consequent to the adoption of resolution 58/275 of 23 December 2003, against the provision of 169,431,700 dollars for special political missions under section 3, Political affairs, of the proposed programme budget for the biennium 2004-2005;

8. *Further approves* a charge of 7,185,000 dollars for the three special political missions presented in table 1, section I, of the report of the Secretary-General, emanating from decisions taken or to be taken by the General Assembly, against the provision of 169,431,700 dollars for special political missions under section 3, Political affairs, of the proposed programme budget for the biennium 2004-2005;

VI
Joint Inspection Unit

1. *Approves* the gross budget for the Joint Inspection Unit for 2004 in the amount of 4,900,800 United States dollars;

2. *Decides* to take action on the gross budget for the Joint Inspection Unit for 2005 in the context of the first performance report on the programme budget for the biennium 2004-2005;

VII
International Civil Service Commission

Approves a gross budget for the International Civil Service Commission for the biennium 2004-2005 in the amount of 14,724,100 United States dollars;

VIII
Office of the United Nations Security Coordinator

Approves the gross budget for the Office of the United Nations Security Coordinator for the biennium 2004-2005 in the amount of 86,375,800 United States dollars;

IX
Revised estimates resulting from resolutions and decisions of the Economic and Social Council at its substantive session of 2003

1. *Takes note* of the report of the Secretary-General on the revised estimates resulting from resolutions and decisions adopted by the Economic and Social Council at its substantive and resumed substantive sessions of 2003 and the related report of the Advisory Committee on Administrative and Budgetary Questions;

2. *Notes* that additional financial requirements for the meeting of the Committee of Experts on Public Administration in the amount of 58,300 United States dollars are no longer required;

3. *Invites* the Economic and Social Council to review its decision 2003/264 of 23 July 2003 regarding the arrangement of the Social Forum, invites the Council, in this regard, to hold the Social Forum immediately before the sessions of the Subcommission on the Promotion and Protection of Human Rights, and decides that the related resources of 12,800 dollars will be a charge against the contingency fund;

4. *Also invites* the Economic and Social Council to review its decision 2003/269 of 23 July 2003 with a view to examining the possibility that additional meetings of the Commission on Human Rights may not be required in connection with its sixtieth session, requests the Secretary-General to provide such conference services as might be required consequent to Council decision 2003/269, as reviewed, and to report to the General Assembly at its fifty-ninth session on the related expenditures in the context of his first performance report on the programme budget for the biennium 2004-2005, and decides that an amount of 193,800 dollars shall be set aside in the contingency fund in the event that additional requirements arise from providing such services;

X
Administrative expenses of the United Nations Joint Staff Pension Fund

Having considered the report of the Standing Committee of the United Nations Joint Staff Pension Board on the administrative expenses of the United Nations Joint Staff Pension Fund, the report of the Secretary-General on the administrative and financial implications arising from the report of the Standing Committee of the United Nations Joint Staff Pension Board and the related reports of the Advisory Committee on Administrative and Budgetary Questions,

1. *Concurs* with the recommendations contained in the reports of the Advisory Committee on Administrative and Budgetary Questions on the administrative expenses of the United Nations Joint Staff Pension Fund and on the administrative and financial implications arising from the report of the Standing Committee of the United Nations Joint Staff Pension Board;

2. *Approves* expenses, chargeable directly to the Fund, totalling 80,770,800 United States dollars net for the biennium 2004-2005 and no change in the initial appropriation of 74,384,900 dollars net for the biennium 2002-2003 for the administration of the Fund;

3. *Also approves* an additional amount of 1,504,500 dollars above the level of resources set out in section 1, Overall policy-making, direction and coordination, of the proposed programme budget for the biennium

2004-2005 as the United Nations share of the cost of the administrative expenses of the central secretariat of the Fund;

4. *Authorizes* the United Nations Joint Staff Pension Board to supplement the voluntary contributions to the Emergency Fund for the biennium 2004-2005 by an amount not exceeding 200,000 dollars;

XI
Special political missions

Notes that an unallocated balance of 26,954,800 United States dollars remains against the provision of 169,431,700 dollars for special political missions;

XII
Proposed programme budget for the International Trade Centre UNCTAD/WTO

Having considered the programme budget proposals for the International Trade Centre UNCTAD/WTO for the biennium 2004-2005 and the related report of the Advisory Committee on Administrative and Budgetary Questions,

Decides to approve resources in the amount of 23,472,200 United States dollars proposed for the biennium 2004-2005 under section 13, International Trade Centre UNCTAD/WTO, of the proposed programme budget for the biennium 2004-2005;

XIII
Effect of changes in rates of exchange and inflation

Having considered the report of the Secretary-General on the revised estimates resulting from the effect of changes in rates of exchange and inflation and the related report of the Advisory Committee on Administrative and Budgetary Questions,

Takes note of the revised estimates arising from recosting due to the effects of changes in the rates of exchange and inflation;

XIV
Financial viability of the United Nations Institute for Training and Research

Having considered the report of the Secretary-General on the United Nations Institute for Training and Research and the related report of the Advisory Committee on Administrative and Budgetary Questions,

1. *Decides* to cancel the debt of the United Nations Institute for Training and Research in respect of rent and maintenance charges in the amount of 321,184 United States dollars;

2. *Requests* the Secretary-General to invite the Board of Trustees of the United Nations Institute for Training and Research to rationalize the financial structure of the Institute, including through the possible application of a consistent programme support rate to the Special Purpose Grants Fund in order to bring it in line with the standard rate applied by the United Nations, and decides to revert to the question at its fifty-ninth session;

XV
Cost implications of providing more predictable and adequate conference services to the meetings of regional and other major groupings of Member States

Recalling its resolutions 56/242 of 24 December 2001 and 57/283 B of 15 April 2003,

Having considered the report of the Secretary-General on the cost implications of providing more predictable and adequate conference services to the meetings of regional and other major groupings of Member States and the related report of the Advisory Committee on Administrative and Budgetary Questions,

Takes note of the report of the Secretary-General on the cost implications of providing more predictable and adequate conference services to the meetings of regional and other major groupings of Member States and the related report of the Advisory Committee on Administrative and Budgetary Questions, and notes in this regard that there would be no effect on the budget estimates of the United Nations;

XVI
Contingency fund

Notes that a balance of 11,314,500 United States dollars remains in the contingency fund;

XVII
Conference and support services extended to the Counter-Terrorism Committee in the implementation of Security Council resolution 1373(2001)

Recalling its resolutions 56/288 of 27 June 2002 and 57/292 of 20 December 2002,

Having considered the report of the Secretary-General on conference and support services extended to the Counter-Terrorism Committee in the implementation of Security Council resolution 1373(2001) and the related report of the Advisory Committee on Administrative and Budgetary Questions,

1. *Reiterates* paragraph 2 of its resolution 56/288, in which it requested the Secretary-General to ensure the provision of conference and support services to the Counter-Terrorism Committee without adversely affecting other conference services;

2. *Decides* to appropriate an amount of 8,193,000 United States dollars to support the meeting requirements of the Counter-Terrorism Committee for the biennium 2004-2005 in the programme budget as follows: 7,958,900 dollars under section 2, General Assembly affairs and conference services, and 234,100 dollars under section 29D, Office of Central Support Services;

XVIII
Development Account

Takes note of the report of the Secretary-General entitled "Implementation of projects financed from the Development Account: third progress report", and concurs with the recommendations of the Advisory Committee on Administrative and Budgetary Questions thereon;

XIX
Additional expenditures deriving from inflation and currency fluctuations

1. *Reaffirms* its resolution 41/213 of 19 December 1986;

2. *Notes* that the effects on the budget of inflation and currency fluctuations can be both positive and negative;

3. *Takes note* of the report of the Secretary-General on additional expenditures deriving from inflation and currency fluctuations and the related report of the

Advisory Committee on Administrative and Budgetary Questions;

4. *Requests* the Secretary-General to explore the possibility of establishing a reserve fund to utilize currency gains and to report thereon, through the Advisory Committee, to the General Assembly at its sixtieth session;

XX
Proportion of General Service staff to Professional staff in the regional commissions

Takes note of the report of the Secretary-General on the proportion of General Service staff to Professional staff in the regional commissions and the related report of the Advisory Committee on Administrative and Budgetary Questions;

XXI
United Nations Fund for International Partnerships

Takes note of the report of the Secretary-General on the United Nations Fund for International Partnerships;

XXII
Capital master plan

Takes note of the first annual progress report of the Secretary-General on the implementation of the capital master plan, the note by the Secretary-General transmitting the report of the Office of Internal Oversight Services on the capital master plan for the period from January to July 2003, the note by the Secretary-General transmitting the progress report of the Board of Auditors on the capital master plan and the related report of the Advisory Committee on Administrative and Budgetary Questions;

XXIII
Administration and management of the Office of the United Nations High Commissioner for Human Rights

Takes note of the report of the Secretary-General on the administration and management of the Office of the United Nations High Commissioner for Human Rights and the related report of the Advisory Committee on Administrative and Budgetary Questions;

XXIV
Administrative and financial implications of the decisions and recommendations contained in the report of the International Civil Service Commission for 2003

Recalling its resolution 58/251 of 23 December 2003, entitled "United Nations common system", in particular section I.D concerning hazard pay,

Takes note of the statement of the Secretary-General on the administrative and financial implications of the decisions and recommendations contained in the report of the International Civil Service Commission for 2003 and the related report of the Advisory Committee on Administrative and Budgetary Questions.

Contingency fund

The contingency fund, established by General Assembly resolution 41/213 [YUN 1986, p. 1024], accommodated additional expenditures relating to each biennium that derived from legislative mandates not provided for in the proposed programme budget or from revised estimates. Guidelines for its use were annexed to Assembly resolution 42/211 [YUN 1987, p. 1098].

The Fifth Committee considered the Secretary-General's December report [A/C.5/58/34] containing a consolidated statement of all programme budget implications and revised estimates falling under the guidelines for use of the fund. The consolidated amount of $23,020,100 exceeded by $1,420,100 the approved level of the fund of $21,600,000. The Secretary-General proposed adjustments of $7,869,300 to bring the overall level of charges to $15,150,800, well within the balance in the fund.

ACABQ, in its thirtieth report on the 2004-2005 programme budget [A/58/7/Add.29], said that, should the Assembly accept the assumptions and suggestions contained in the Secretary-General's report, the balance available in the contingency fund would amount to $6,449,200.

Revised estimates in respect of matters of which the Security Council was seized

As a result of action taken by the General Assembly and/or the Security Council in 2003, the Secretary-General submitted on 1 December estimated resource requirements of $140,304,500 for 20 political missions [A/C.5/58/20]. That amount would be charged against the $163,178,100 (before recosting) proposed for special political missions under section 3, Political affairs, of the 2004-2005 proposed programme budget.

In a 15 December note [A/C.5/58/33], the Secretary-General indicated that, after charging the recosted amount of $142,476,900 against the recosted provision of $169,431,700 under section 3 of the programme budget, the remaining unallocated balance for special political missions amounted to $26,954,800.

ACABQ [A/58/7/Add.28] recommended that the Assembly take note of the Secretary-General's 15 December note.

Revised estimates resulting from Economic and Social Council action

By an October report [A/C.5/58/10], the Secretary-General submitted estimates of requirements totalling $2,040,400 additional to the resources initially proposed in the 2004-2005 programme budget, of which $1,197,700 could be absorbed, leaving a net requirement of $842,700 resulting from Economic and Social Council resolution 2003/60 (see p. 865), and decisions 2003/242 (see p. 670), 2003/261 (see p. 754), 2003/264 (see p. 760), 2003/269 (see p. 656), 2003/280 (see p. 868) and 2003/291 (see p. 857). The net requirement, which would be charged against the contingency fund, related to section 1, Overall policy-making, direction and coordination ($91,900); section 2, General Assembly affairs and conference services ($557,300); section 9, Economic and social affairs ($58,300); section 24, Human rights ($135,200); and section 29D, Office of Central Support Services ($72,600), offset by an equivalent reduction under section 9.

Additional requirements of up to $326,200 for the Social Forum (see p. 760), approved as an annual meeting by Council decision 2003/264, could be avoided by scheduling the Forum during the session of the Subcommission on the Promotion and Protection of Human Rights. Assembly approval of that proposal would reduce the appropriation requirement from $842,700 to $616,500.

ACABQ, in its related report [A/58/7/Add.8], recommended that the Fifth Committee take note of the estimate of $842,700, on the understanding that such appropriations as might be necessary would be requested by the Secretary-General in the context of a consolidated statement of programme budget implications and revised estimates to be submitted to the Assembly. Should the Assembly decide to proceed with the proposed scheduling of the Social Forum (see above), appropriation requirements for 2004-2005 would amount to $616,500.

Inflation and currency fluctuation

In response to General Assembly decision 57/576 [YUN 2002, p. 1381], the Secretary-General submitted an October report [A/58/400] on additional expenditures derived from inflation and currency fluctuations. Annexed to the report was tabular information on the practices followed by UN system organizations to deal with currency fluctuations and inflation. Those practices, namely, split assessments, forward purchasing and reserve accounts, which had been previously considered by the Assembly [YUN 1997, p. 1416; YUN 2002, p. 1381], entailed unavoidable costs, including the inability to realize savings in times of a strengthening of the United States dollar, or, in the case of a reserve, presenting Member States with the financial burden of advanced assessments that might prove unnecessary. The Assembly might therefore wish to continue the current system of periodically adjusting the estimate of requirements on the basis of the Secretary-General's latest forecast of inflation and exchange rates.

ACABQ, in a related report [A/58/7/Add.5], recommended that the Assembly note the Secretary-General's report.

Subvention to UNIDIR

The Secretary-General, in September [A/C.5/58/3], transmitted for the General Assembly's approval a request for a subvention of $227,600 from the UN regular budget to the United Nations Institute for Disarmament Research (UNIDIR), following a review by the UNIDIR Board of Trustees of the Director's report on UNIDIR's activities from August 2002 to July 2003.

Working capital fund

In December, the General Assembly established the Working Capital Fund for the 2004-2005 biennium at $100 million, the same level as for the 2002-2003 biennium [YUN 2001, p. 1321]. As in the past, the Fund was to be used to finance appropriations pending the receipt of assessed contributions, to pay for unforeseen and extraordinary expenses, as well as for miscellaneous self-liquidating purchases and advance insurance premiums, and to enable the Tax Equalization Fund to meet current commitments pending the accumulation of credits.

GENERAL ASSEMBLY ACTION

On 23 December [meeting 79], the General Assembly, on the recommendation of the Fifth Committee [A/58/573], adopted **resolution 58/274** without vote [agenda item 121].

Working Capital Fund for the biennium 2004-2005
The General Assembly
Resolves that:
1. The Working Capital Fund shall be established for the biennium 2004-2005 in the amount of 100 million United States dollars;
2. Member States shall make advances to the Working Capital Fund in accordance with the scale of assessments adopted by the General Assembly for contributions of Member States to the budget for the year 2004;
3. There shall be set off against this allocation of advances:
(a) Credits to Member States resulting from transfers made in 1959 and 1960 from the surplus account to the Working Capital Fund in an adjusted amount of 1,025,092 dollars;
(b) Cash advances paid by Member States to the Working Capital Fund for the biennium 2004-2005 in accordance with General Assembly resolution 56/257 of 24 December 2001;
4. Should the credits and advances paid by any Member State to the Working Capital Fund for the biennium 2002-2003 exceed the amount of that Member State's advance under the provisions of paragraph 2 above, the excess shall be set off against the amount of the contributions payable by the Member State in respect of the biennium 2004-2005;
5. The Secretary-General is authorized to advance from the Working Capital Fund:
(a) Such sums as may be necessary to finance budgetary appropriations pending the receipt of contribu-

tions; sums so advanced shall be reimbursed as soon as receipts from contributions are available for that purpose;

(b) Such sums as may be necessary to finance commitments that may be duly authorized under the provisions of the resolutions adopted by the General Assembly, in particular resolution 58/273 of 23 December 2003 relating to unforeseen and extraordinary expenses; the Secretary-General shall make provision in the budget estimates for reimbursing the Working Capital Fund;

(c) Such sums as may be necessary to continue the revolving fund to finance miscellaneous self-liquidating purchases and activities, which, together with net sums outstanding for the same purpose, do not exceed 200,000 dollars; advances in excess of 200,000 dollars may be made with the prior concurrence of the Advisory Committee on Administrative and Budgetary Questions;

(d) With the prior concurrence of the Advisory Committee, such sums as may be required to finance payments of advance insurance premiums where the period of insurance extends beyond the end of the biennium in which payment is made; the Secretary-General shall make provision in the budget estimates of each biennium, during the life of the related policies, to cover the charges applicable to each biennium;

(e) Such sums as may be necessary to enable the Tax Equalization Fund to meet current commitments pending the accumulation of credits; such advances shall be repaid as soon as credits are available in the Tax Equalization Fund;

6. Should the provision in paragraph 1 above prove inadequate to meet the purposes normally related to the Working Capital Fund, the Secretary-General is authorized to utilize, in the biennium 2004-2005, cash from special funds and accounts in his custody, under the conditions approved by the General Assembly in its resolution 1341(XIII) of 13 December 1958, or the proceeds of loans authorized by the Assembly.

Unforeseen and extraordinary expenses

Under specific circumstances, the Secretary-General was authorized by the General Assembly to enter into commitments for activities of an urgent nature, without reverting to it for approval under the terms of resolution 56/256 [YUN 2001, p. 1322].

GENERAL ASSEMBLY ACTION

On 23 December [meeting 79], the General Assembly, on the recommendation of the Fifth Committee [A/58/573], adopted **resolution 58/273** without vote [agenda item 121].

Unforeseen and extraordinary expenses for the biennium 2004-2005

The General Assembly

1. *Authorizes* the Secretary-General, with the prior concurrence of the Advisory Committee on Administrative and Budgetary Questions and subject to the Financial Regulations and Rules of the United Nations and the provisions of paragraph 3 below, to enter into commitments in the biennium 2004-2005 to meet unforeseen and extraordinary expenses arising either during or subsequent to the biennium, provided that the concurrence of the Advisory Committee shall not be necessary for:

(a) Such commitments not exceeding a total of 8 million United States dollars in any one year of the biennium 2004-2005 as the Secretary-General certifies relate to the maintenance of peace and security;

(b) Such commitments as the President of the International Court of Justice certifies relate to expenses occasioned by:

(i) The designation of ad hoc judges (Statute of the International Court of Justice, Article 31), not exceeding a total of 330,000 dollars;

(ii) The calling of witnesses and the appointment of experts (Statute, Article 50) and the appointment of assessors (Statute, Article 30), not exceeding a total of 50,000 dollars;

(iii) The maintenance in office for the completion of cases of judges who have not been re-elected (Statute, Article 13, paragraph 3), not exceeding a total of 40,000 dollars;

(iv) The payment of pensions and travel and removal expenses of retiring judges and travel and removal expenses and installation grant of members of the Court (Statute, Article 32, paragraph 7), not exceeding a total of 410,000 dollars;

(v) The work of the Court or its Chambers away from The Hague (Statute, Article 22), not exceeding a total of 25,000 dollars;

(c) Such commitments not exceeding a total of 500,000 dollars in the biennium 2004-2005 as the Secretary-General certifies are required for inter-organizational security measures pursuant to section IV of General Assembly resolution 36/235 of 18 December 1981;

2. *Resolves* that the Secretary-General shall report to the Advisory Committee and to the General Assembly at its fifty-ninth and sixtieth sessions all commitments made under the provisions of the present resolution, together with the circumstances relating thereto, and shall submit supplementary estimates to the Assembly in respect of such commitments;

3. *Decides* that, for the biennium 2004-2005, if a decision of the Security Council results in the need for the Secretary-General to enter into commitments relating to the maintenance of peace and security in an amount exceeding 10 million dollars in respect of the decision, that matter shall be brought to the General Assembly, or, if the Assembly is suspended or not in session, a resumed or special session of the Assembly shall be convened by the Secretary-General to consider the matter.

Contributions

According to the Secretary-General's report on improving the financial situation of the United Nations [A/58/531/Add.1], unpaid assessed contributions from Member States to the UN budget at the end of 2003 totalled $1,603 million (compared to $1,684 million in 2002); outstanding peacekeeping arrears totalled $1,066 million (compared to $1,335 million in 2002); and total unpaid assessments for the international tribunals more than doubled, to $88 million (compared to $43 million in 2002).

The number of Member States paying their regular budget assessment in full increased from 117 in 2002 to 131 at 31 December 2003.

Assessments

The Committee on Contributions, at its sixty-third session (New York, 2-27 June) [A/58/11], considered a number of issues related to the payment of assessments, including the scale of assessments for the period 2004-2006, multi-year payment plans, the application of Article 19 of the Charter, assessment of non-member States and measures to encourage the payment of arrears. The General Assembly took action on the Committee's recommendations in April, October and December.

Application of Article 19

Committee on Contributions. The Committee on Contributions [A/58/11] reviewed requests for exemption under Article 19, whereby a Member State would lose its vote in the General Assembly if the amount of its arrears should equal or exceed the amount of contributions due from it for the preceding two full years.

Having reviewed requests from nine Member States, the Committee took no action on the request of the Democratic Republic of the Congo (DRC), as it was not submitted within the required two-week period prior to the Committee's session. It determined that the failure of Burundi, the Central African Republic, the Comoros, Georgia, Guinea-Bissau, the Republic of Moldova, Sao Tome and Principe, Somalia and Tajikistan to pay the full minimum amount of their arrears necessary to avoid the application of Article 19 was due to conditions beyond their control and recommended that they be allowed to vote until 30 June 2004. The Committee welcomed the Central African Republic's intention to submit a schedule for the payment of its arrears, but noted that, apart from $513,567 paid in 1998, it had made no other payments since 1994. In noting the substantial reduction in the Central African Republic's rate of assessment from 1998, it urged that country to make some payments to reduce, or at least avoid an increase in, its arrears. It urged the Comoros to do likewise and agreed to review any future request from the Comoros in the light of its payment record. The Committee noted with concern Georgia's failure to meet the terms of its 2002 multi-year payment plan and that the plan did not provide for any payment in 2003 and went well beyond the recommended six-year period for eliminating arrears. On the other hand, the Committee noted that: the Republic of Moldova had substantially adhered to its payment plan in 2001-2002 and had paid more than half the amount scheduled for 2003, despite the serious and continuing difficulties it faced; Sao Tome and Principe had submitted a multi-year payment plan in 2002 and had made the related payment for that year; and Tajikistan, despite its serious problems, had more than met the payments scheduled for 2000-2003 under its 2000 payment plan.

The Committee encouraged all Member States requesting Article 19 exemption to consider presenting a payment plan, taking into account the Committee's 2002 recommendations [YUN 2002, p. 1386], as endorsed by the Assembly in resolution 57/4 B [ibid., p. 1385]. It urged those States to submit as much information as possible in support of their exemption requests and the Secretariat to do likewise on the situation of such States. To facilitate early action on the requests for exemption before it, the Committee authorized its Chairman to convey to the Assembly, without delay, the related section of its report in respect of the requests from the above nine Member States [A/C.5/57/39].

At the conclusion of the Committee's session, nine Member States (Burundi, Central African Republic, DRC, Djibouti, Iraq, Kyrgyzstan, Liberia, Niger, Vanuatu) were in arrears under the terms of Article 19 and had no vote in the Assembly. Seven others (Comoros, Georgia, Guinea-Bissau, Republic of Moldova, Sao Tome and Principe, Somalia, Tajikistan) had been permitted to vote until 30 June 2003, pursuant to Assembly resolution 57/4 A [YUN 2002, p. 1384].

The Committee noted that four Member States (Cyprus, Morocco, Pakistan, Trinidad and Tobago), availing themselves of the opportunity afforded by Assembly resolution 55/5 B [YUN 2000, p. 1311], had paid the equivalent of $1,778,949.63 in currencies other than the United States dollar.

Reports of Secretary-General. During the year, the Secretary-General reported to the General Assembly on payments made by certain Member States to reduce their level of arrears below that specified in Article 19, so that they could vote in the Assembly. As at 15 September [A/58/360], 14 Member States were below the gross amount assessed for the preceding two full years (2001-2002). That number was reduced to 13 by 18 September [A/58/360/Add.1], 12 by 7 October [A/58/360/Add.2], remaining at 12 by 16 October [A/58/440], and 11 by 18 December [A/58/440/Add.1].

Communication. On 1 October [A/C.5/58/4], the General Assembly President transmitted to the Chairman of the Fifth Committee a 26 September request from the Niger for exemption under Article 19 to permit it to retain its vote in the Assembly until June 2004, because of its continuing economic and social difficulties. It planned to submit a schedule for payment of its contributions and arrears at a later date.

GENERAL ASSEMBLY ACTION

On 16 October [meeting 34], the General Assembly, on the recommendation of the Fifth Committee [A/58/432], adopted **resolution 58/1 A** without vote [agenda item 124].

Scale of assessments for the apportionment of the expenses of the United Nations

The General Assembly,

Having considered the letter dated 3 July 2003 from the President of the General Assembly to the Chairman of the Fifth Committee transmitting a letter dated 27 June 2003 from the Chairman of the Committee on Contributions regarding the recommendations of that Committee on requests for exemption under Article 19 of the Charter of the United Nations,

Having also considered the letter dated 1 October 2003 from the President of the General Assembly to the Chairman of the Fifth Committee transmitting a letter dated 26 September 2003 from the Permanent Representative of the Niger to the United Nations,

Reaffirming the obligation of Member States under Article 17 of the Charter to bear the expenses of the Organization as apportioned by the General Assembly,

1. *Reaffirms* its role in accordance with the provisions of Article 19 of the Charter of the United Nations and the advisory role of the Committee on Contributions in accordance with rule 160 of the rules of procedure of the General Assembly;

2. *Also reaffirms* its resolution 54/237 C of 23 December 1999;

3. *Agrees* that the failure of Burundi, the Central African Republic, the Comoros, Georgia, Guinea-Bissau, the Republic of Moldova, Sao Tome and Principe, Somalia and Tajikistan to pay the full minimum amount necessary to avoid the application of Article 19 of the Charter was due to conditions beyond their control, while noting the observations in paragraphs 82 and 90 of the annex to the letter from the Chairman of the Committee on Contributions;

4. *Takes note* of the information provided by the Niger, and welcomes its intention to submit a schedule for the payment of its contributions and arrears;

5. *Concludes* that the failure of the Niger to pay the full minimum amount necessary to avoid the application of Article 19 of the Charter was due to conditions beyond its control, and invites the Niger to submit appropriate information to the Committee on Contributions if similar circumstances prevail in the future;

6. *Decides* that Burundi, the Central African Republic, the Comoros, Georgia, Guinea-Bissau, the Niger, the Republic of Moldova, Sao Tome and Principe, Somalia and Tajikistan should be permitted to vote in the General Assembly until 30 June 2004.

Other matters relating to payment of assessed contributions

The General Assembly also considered the recommendations of the Committee on Contributions relating to the scale of assessment for the period 2004-2006, multi-year payment plans, appeals by Member States for a change of assessment, the assessment of non-member States and the treatment of the outstanding assessed contributions of the former Yugoslavia (see sections below).

GENERAL ASSEMBLY ACTION

On 23 December [meeting 79], the General Assembly, on the recommendation of the Fifth Committee [A/58/432/Add.1], adopted **resolution 58/1 B** without vote [agenda item 124].

Scale of assessments for the apportionment of the expenses of the United Nations

The General Assembly,

Recalling its resolutions 43/223 B of 21 December 1988, 46/221 B of 20 December 1991, 55/5 B, C and D of 23 December 2000, 57/4 B of 20 December 2002 and 57/4 C of 15 April 2003,

Having considered the report of the Committee on Contributions on the work of its sixty-third session,

Having also considered the report of the Secretary-General on multi-year payment plans and his note on the outstanding assessed contributions of the former Yugoslavia, as well as the letter dated 27 December 2001 from the Secretary-General addressed to the President of the General Assembly,

Reaffirming the obligation of all Member States to bear the expenses of the United Nations, as apportioned by the General Assembly, in conformity with Article 17, paragraph 2, of the Charter of the United Nations,

Reaffirming also the fundamental principle that the expenses of the Organization shall be apportioned among Member States broadly according to capacity to pay,

1. *Reaffirms* its earlier decision in its resolution 55/5 B that the elements of the scale of assessments outlined in paragraph 1 of that resolution will be fixed until 2006;

2. *Resolves* that the scale of assessments for the contributions of Member States to the regular budget of the United Nations for the years 2004, 2005 and 2006 shall be as follows:

Member State	Percentage
Afghanistan	0.002
Albania	0.005
Algeria	0.076
Andorra	0.005
Angola	0.001
Antigua and Barbuda	0.003
Argentina	0.956
Armenia	0.002
Australia	1.592
Austria	0.859
Azerbaijan	0.005

United Nations financing and programming

Member State	Percentage	Member State	Percentage
Bahamas	0.013	Iceland	0.034
Bahrain	0.030	India	0.421
Bangladesh	0.010	Indonesia	0.142
Barbados	0.010	Iran	0.157
Belarus	0.018	Iraq	0.016
Belgium	1.069	Ireland	0.350
Belize	0.001	Israel	0.467
Benin	0.002	Italy	4.885
Bhutan	0.001	Jamaica	0.008
Bolivia	0.009	Japan	19.468
Bosnia and Herzegovina	0.003	Jordan	0.011
Botswana	0.012	Kazakhstan	0.025
Brazil	1.523	Kenya	0.009
Brunei Darussalam	0.034	Kiribati	0.001
Bulgaria	0.017	Kuwait	0.162
Burkina Faso	0.002	Kyrgyzstan	0.001
Burundi	0.001	Lao People's Democratic Republic	0.001
Cambodia	0.002	Latvia	0.015
Cameroon	0.008	Lebanon	0.024
Canada	2.813	Lesotho	0.001
Cape Verde	0.001	Liberia	0.001
Central African Republic	0.001	Libyan Arab Jamahiriya	0.132
Chad	0.001	Liechtenstein	0.005
Chile	0.223	Lithuania	0.024
China	2.053	Luxembourg	0.077
Colombia	0.155	Madagascar	0.003
Comoros	0.001	Malawi	0.001
Congo	0.001	Malaysia	0.203
Costa Rica	0.030	Maldives	0.001
Côte d'Ivoire	0.010	Mali	0.002
Croatia	0.037	Malta	0.014
Cuba	0.043	Marshall Islands	0.001
Cyprus	0.039	Mauritania	0.001
Czech Republic	0.183	Mauritius	0.011
Democratic People's Republic of Korea	0.010	Mexico	1.883
Democratic Republic of the Congo	0.003	Micronesia	0.001
Denmark	0.718	Monaco	0.003
Djibouti	0.001	Mongolia	0.001
Dominica	0.001	Morocco	0.047
Dominican Republic	0.035	Mozambique	0.001
Ecuador	0.019	Myanmar	0.010
Egypt	0.120	Namibia	0.006
El Salvador	0.022	Nauru	0.001
Equatorial Guinea	0.002	Nepal	0.004
Eritrea	0.001	Netherlands	1.690
Estonia	0.012	New Zealand	0.221
Ethiopia	0.004	Nicaragua	0.001
Fiji	0.004	Niger	0.001
Finland	0.533	Nigeria	0.042
France	6.030	Norway	0.679
Gabon	0.009	Oman	0.070
Gambia	0.001	Pakistan	0.055
Georgia	0.003	Palau	0.001
Germany	8.662	Panama	0.019
Ghana	0.004	Papua New Guinea	0.003
Greece	0.530	Paraguay	0.012
Grenada	0.001	Peru	0.092
Guatemala	0.030	Philippines	0.095
Guinea	0.003	Poland	0.461
Guinea-Bissau	0.001	Portugal	0.470
Guyana	0.001	Qatar	0.064
Haiti	0.003	Republic of Korea	1.796
Honduras	0.005	Republic of Moldova	0.001
Hungary	0.126	Romania	0.060

Member State	Percentage
Russian Federation	1.100
Rwanda	0.001
Saint Kitts and Nevis	0.001
Saint Lucia	0.002
Saint Vincent and the Grenadines	0.001
Samoa	0.001
San Marino	0.003
Sao Tome and Principe	0.001
Saudi Arabia	0.713
Senegal	0.005
Serbia and Montenegro	0.019
Seychelles	0.002
Sierra Leone	0.001
Singapore	0.388
Slovakia	0.051
Slovenia	0.082
Solomon Islands	0.001
Somalia	0.001
South Africa	0.292
Spain	2.520
Sri Lanka	0.017
Sudan	0.008
Suriname	0.001
Swaziland	0.002
Sweden	0.998
Switzerland	1.197
Syrian Arab Republic	0.038
Tajikistan	0.001
Thailand	0.209
The former Yugoslav Republic of Macedonia	0.006
Timor-Leste	0.001
Togo	0.001
Tonga	0.001
Trinidad and Tobago	0.022
Tunisia	0.032
Turkey	0.372
Turkmenistan	0.005
Tuvalu	0.001
Uganda	0.006
Ukraine	0.039
United Arab Emirates	0.235
United Kingdom	6.127
United Republic of Tanzania	0.006
United States of America	22.000
Uruguay	0.048
Uzbekistan	0.014
Vanuatu	0.001
Venezuela	0.171
Viet Nam	0.021
Yemen	0.006
Zambia	0.002
Zimbabwe	0.007
Total	**100.000**

3. *Also resolves* that:

(*a*) Notwithstanding the terms of financial regulation 3.9, the Secretary-General shall be empowered to accept, at his discretion and after consultation with the Chairman of the Committee on Contributions, a portion of the contributions of Member States for the calendar years 2004, 2005 and 2006 in currencies other than the United States dollar;

(*b*) In accordance with financial regulation 3.8, the Holy See, which is not a Member of the United Nations but which participates in certain of its activities, shall be called upon to contribute towards the expenses of the Organization for 2004, 2005 and 2006 on the basis of a notional assessment rate of 0.001 per cent, which represents the basis for the calculation of the flat annual fees to be charged to the Holy See in accordance with General Assembly resolution 44/197 B of 21 December 1989;

4. *Notes* that the application of the current methodology, as set out above, leads to substantial increases in the rate of assessment of some Member States, including developing countries;

5. *Emphasizes* the need for future scales of assessments to reflect the principle that the expenses of the Organization shall be apportioned broadly according to capacity to pay;

6. *Requests* the Committee on Contributions, in accordance with its mandate and the rules of procedure of the General Assembly, to continue to review the methodology of future scales of assessments based on the principle that the expenses of the Organization shall be apportioned broadly according to capacity to pay;

7. *Recalls* paragraph 7 of its resolution 54/237 D of 7 April 2000, and requests the Committee on Contributions to continue its consideration of possible systematic criteria for deciding when market exchange rates should be replaced with price-adjusted rates of exchange or other appropriate conversion rates for the purposes of preparing the scale of assessments, taking into account the relevant provisions of resolution 46/221 B, and to report thereon to the General Assembly at its fifty-ninth session;

8. *Requests* the Committee on Contributions to continue to make a thorough analysis of the revised method of calculating price-adjusted rates of exchange and to report thereon to the General Assembly at its fifty-ninth session;

9. *Recalls* paragraph 1 of its resolution 48/223 C of 23 December 1993, and reaffirms that the Committee on Contributions as a technical body is required to prepare the scale of assessments strictly on the basis of reliable, verifiable and comparable data;

10. *Takes note* of the report of the Secretary-General on multi-year payment plans;

11. *Urges* all Member States to pay their assessed contributions in full, on time and without imposing conditions;

12. *Reaffirms* paragraph 1 of resolution 57/4 B;

13. *Notes* the decision of the Committee on Contributions, contained in paragraph 130 of its report, to consider further at its sixty-fourth session the question of measures to encourage the payment of arrears, and requests the Committee to report thereon to the General Assembly at its fifty-ninth session;

14. *Endorses* the preliminary observations of the Committee on Contributions concerning criteria for ad hoc adjustments of the rates of assessment, contained in paragraphs 45 and 47 of its report;

15. *Notes* the decision of the Committee on Contributions to consider the question further at its sixty-fourth session, and requests the Committee to report thereon to the General Assembly at its fifty-ninth session;

16. *Reaffirms* paragraph 4 of its resolution 57/4 B, and urges the Committee on Contributions to expedite its work on the criteria regarding ad hoc adjustments of the rates of assessment;

17. *Endorses* the recommendations of the Committee on Contributions contained in paragraph 122 of its report;

18. *Decides* to defer until its fifty-ninth session consideration of the question of the outstanding assessed contributions of the former Yugoslavia.

On 23 December, the Assembly decided that the item on the scale of assessments for the apportionment of the expenses of the United Nations would remain for consideration during its resumed fifty-eighth (2004) session (**decision 58/565**).

Scale of assessments for 2004-2006

The General Assembly decided to conduct its review of the scale of assessments for the period 2004-2006 on the basis of the elements of the methodology for the scale of assessments for the period 2001-2003, as set out in its resolution 55/5 B [YUN 2000, p. 1311].

Requests for change of assessments

The Committee on Contributions [A/58/11] considered requests from Argentina, Iran, Paraguay, Poland and Uruguay for reductions in their rate of assessment. Argentina, referring to its continuing severe economic problems and to its overvalued market exchange rate (MER) that did not accurately reflect its capacity to pay, requested that price-adjusted rates of exchange (PAREs) be used in converting its gross national income (GNI) to United States dollars. Iran requested that market or weighted average exchange rates be used instead of the official rate in preparing the scale of assessment. Paraguay requested that the additional information it had provided on its economic and social situation, in particular its high population growth and unemployment, be taken into account in the scale to be adopted for 2004-2006. Poland also provided supplementary information, including on the economic and social impact of restructuring and of a growing debt problem, which were not adequately reflected in the GNI data. Uruguay requested that PAREs be used to convert GNI for some or all of the years of the base period of the scale.

The Committee decided to replace MERs with PAREs for Argentina for 2000-2001 and for the DRC for 1999-2001. It decided to apply weighted average exchange rates for Iran for 1996-2001, to reflect a more realistic balance between official and market rates, and PAREs for Iraq for the same period; to retain PAREs for Lebanon for the overlapping part of the base period, 1996-1998, but to use MERs for 1999-2001; to apply PAREs for Myanmar for 1996-2001; to retain PAREs for Nigeria for the overlapping part of the base period, 1996-1998, but to use MERs for 1999-2001; and to apply PAREs to the Syrian Arab Republic for the full period 1996-2001, to Uruguay for 1999-2001 and to Venezuela for 1996-2001.

In terms of the criteria for ad hoc adjustments of the rates of assessment, the Committee agreed that the circumstances surrounding those requests for assessment changes should be truly exceptional and extraordinary, and based on the fullest possible information so as to give the Committee and the Assembly a sound basis on which to base their conclusions. It would consider the matter further in 2004, including on the basis of investigations by the Secretariat of the background to rule 160 of the Assembly's rules of procedure concerning the criteria for fixing assessment scales, and would report thereon to the Assembly.

Measures to encourage the payment of arrears

On 15 April [meeting 83], the General Assembly, having considered the Secretary-General's 2002 report on measures to encourage Member States in arrears to reduce and eventually pay their arrears [YUN 2002, p. 1386], adopted, on the recommendation of the Fifth Committee [A/57/492/Add.2], **resolution 57/4 C** without vote [agenda item 117].

Scale of assessments for the apportionment of the expenses of the United Nations

The General Assembly,

Recalling all of its relevant resolutions,

1. *Takes note* of the report of the Secretary-General on measures to encourage Member States in arrears to reduce and eventually pay their arrears;

2. *Requests* the Committee on Contributions to make recommendations on measures with a positive impact to encourage Member States to pay their arrears, and to report thereon to the General Assembly at its fifty-eighth session.

Report of Secretary-General. In response to General Assembly resolution 57/4 B [YUN 2002, p. 1385], the Secretary-General submitted a February report on multi-year payment plans [A/58/63], which provided information on payment plans/schedules submitted earlier by Georgia, the Republic of Moldova, Sao Tome and Principe and Tajikistan and on the status of implementation of those plans as at 31 December 2002. According to the information, Tajikistan had significantly exceeded the payments for 2000, 2001 and 2002 foreseen in its most recent schedule of payments. Sao Tome and Principe had also exceeded the planned figure for the first year of its payment schedule. Payments by the Republic of Moldova were slightly under the total planned amount, as were those by Georgia during the first year of its most recent schedule. The Secretary-General reported that no other Member States had submitted payment plans or schedules for the elimination of their arrears.

Committee on Contributions. The Committee on Contributions [A/58/11] reaffirmed the conclusions and recommendations adopted at its 2002 session [YUN 2002, p. 1386] concerning multi-year payment plans. It noted the substantial effort made by some Member States to reduce their arrears to the Organization and urged them to make every effort to meet the commitments made in their payment plans. It decided to consider further the question of measures to encourage the payment of arrears in 2004 in the light of guidance from the General Assembly and of updated information from the Secretariat on the related experience of other UN system organizations and to report to the Assembly before the end of its fifty-eighth session.

Outstanding assessed contributions

In July [A/58/189], the Secretary-General updated the information on the outstanding assessed contributions of the former Yugoslavia, consequent upon the admission in 2000 of the Federal Republic of Yugoslavia, renamed Serbia and Montenegro (see p. 412), to membership of the United Nations. The updated information indicated a total outstanding assessed amount of $16,165,515 adjusted for credits in 2001-2003.

Accounts and auditing

The General Assembly, at its resumed fifty-seventh (2003) session, considered the report of the Board of Auditors on UN peacekeeping operations for the period 1 July 2001 to 30 June 2002 [A/57/5 (Vol. II) & Corr.5], together with the Secretary-General's report on the implementation of the Board's recommendations [A/57/416/Add.2] and related ACABQ comments and recommendations [A/57/772].

On 18 June, the Assembly, in **resolution 57/278 B**, endorsed the Board's report (see p. 91).

Board of Auditors report. The Assembly, at its fifty-eighth session, had before it the report of the Board of Auditors and audited financial statements of the voluntary funds administered by the Office of the United Nations High Commissioner for Refugees for the 12-month period ended 31 December 2002 [A/58/5/Add.5]. Also before it were the Secretary-General's July note [A/58/114], submitted pursuant to resolution 52/212 B [YUN 1998, p. 1288], transmitting the report of the Board on the implementation of its recommendations relating to the 2000-2001 biennium; his second report on the implementation of the Board's recommendations on the UN accounts for the biennium ended 31 December 2001 [A/58/97]; and his second report on the implementation of the Board's recommendations on the accounts of the UN funds and programmes for the same period [A/58/97/Add.1].

ACABQ's comments and recommendations on those reports were contained in its September report to the Assembly [A/58/384] (see p. 1227).

GENERAL ASSEMBLY ACTION

On 23 December [meeting 79], the General Assembly, on the recommendation of the Fifth Committee [A/58/570], adopted **resolution 58/249 A** without vote [agenda item 118].

Financial reports and audited financial statements, and reports of the Board of Auditors

The General Assembly,

Having considered the audited financial statements and the report of the Board of Auditors on the voluntary funds administered by the United Nations High Commissioner for Refugees for the year ended 31 December 2002, the report of the Board of Auditors on the implementation of its recommendations relating to the biennium 2000-2001, the second report of the Secretary-General on the implementation of the recommendations of the Board of Auditors on the accounts of the United Nations and on the accounts of the United Nations funds and programmes for the biennium ended 31 December 2001, and the related report of the Advisory Committee on Administrative and Budgetary Questions,

Recognizing the difficult conditions under which the Office of the United Nations High Commissioner for Refugees does its work,

1. *Accepts* the financial report and audited financial statements and the report and audit opinion of the Board of Auditors regarding the voluntary funds administered by the United Nations High Commissioner for Refugees for the period from 1 January to 31 December 2002;

2. *Endorses* the recommendations of the Board of Auditors contained in its report;

3. *Also endorses* the observations and recommendation contained in paragraphs 2 to 18 of the report of the Advisory Committee on Administrative and Budgetary Questions;

4. *Notes with concern* the shortcomings identified by the Board of Auditors in the management of financial and human resources by the Office of the United Nations High Commissioner for Refugees, urges the High Commissioner to continue to implement the Board's recommendations, and requests him to report regularly to the relevant governing bodies on progress made in that regard;

5. *Notes* the efforts of the United Nations High Commissioner for Refugees in implementing the recommendations of the Board of Auditors;

6. *Notes with concern* the further depletion of the reserves of the Office of the United Nations High Commissioner for Refugees, and requests the High Commissioner to examine the causes of continued operating

deficits with a view to ensuring that the Office usually operates within its income for each financial year;

7. *Requests* the Secretary-General to report to the General Assembly on the full extent of unfunded staff termination and post-service liabilities in the United Nations and its funds and programmes and to propose measures that would ensure progress towards fully funding such liabilities;

8. *Takes note* of the second report of the Secretary-General on the implementation of the recommendations of the Board of Auditors on the accounts of the United Nations and on the accounts of the United Nations funds and programmes for the biennium ended 31 December 2001 and the report of the Board of Auditors on the implementation of its recommendations;

9. *Notes with appreciation* the recommendation to consolidate the reports of the Secretary-General on the accounts of the United Nations and its funds and programmes in a single report;

10. *Requests* the Secretary-General to continue to include in the consolidated report the status of implementation of the recommendations of the Board of Auditors and to clarify the recommendations that were partially implemented and those that were not implemented;

11. *Requests* the audited organizations to take all steps necessary to implement fully and expeditiously the outstanding audit recommendations.

Also on 23 December, the Assembly, decided that the item on the financial reports and audited financial statements, and reports of the Board of Auditors would remain for consideration at its resumed fifty-eighth (2004) session (**decision 58/565**).

Financial rules and regulations

In May, the Secretary-General promulgated a revised edition of the Financial Regulations and Rules of the United Nations [ST/SGB/2003/7], containing the revisions adopted by the General Assembly in decision 57/573 [YUN 2002, p. 1390], which were to take effect as from 1 June 2003.

Administrative and budgetary coordination

CEB report. By a February note [A/57/442/Add.1], the Secretary-General transmitted to the General Assembly his comments and those of CEB on the JIU report on support costs related to extrabudgetary activities in UN system organizations [YUN 2002, p. 1391]. CEB agreed that a single, system-wide support-cost rate, based on a system-wide cost average that made no distinction among cost structures, the types of extrabudgetary activity being supported and the nature of that support, would hardly have any current value. However, it supported some harmonization of the policies governing the establishment of support-cost rates. CEB noted that the long-established practice of applying a flat rate (13 per cent of project costs) was no longer responsive to the needs of the organizations concerned, and took the view that a policy framework more relevant to real needs should be considered. A new framework (as outlined by JIU) would take into account the increasing diversity of the services currently being provided by various organizations and the requirement for greater flexibility.

By **decision 57/556 B** of 15 April, the Assembly deferred until the second part of its resumed fifty-seventh (2003) session the Secretary-General's notes transmitting the JIU report on support costs related to extrabudgetary activities in organizations of the UN system and his comments and those of CEB thereon, and the related ACABQ report [A/57/434].

By **decision 57/588** of 18 June, the Assembly further deferred consideration of the Secretary-General's notes and the ACABQ report until its fifty-eighth (2003) session.

On 23 December, the Assembly requested JIU to further clarify its recommendations 1, 4, 6, 8 and 9, and decided to continue consideration of the matter at the first part of its resumed fifty-eighth (2004) session (**decision 58/560**). On the same date, the Assembly decided that the item on the review of the efficiency of the administrative and financial functioning of the United Nations would remain for consideration during its resumed fifty-eighth session (**decision 58/565**).

Programme planning

Medium-term plan

CPC, at its June/July session [A/58/16], recommended that the General Assembly, at its fifty-eighth (2003) session, approve the Secretary-General's proposed revisions to the 2002-2005 medium-term plan, with recommended modifications by CPC, in respect of programme 7, Economic and social affairs [A/58/84], and programme 8, United Nations support for the New Partnership for Africa's Development (NEPAD) [A/58/83]. The achievement indicators under programme 8 should reflect action, results and value received; the Bretton Woods institutions (the World Bank Group and the International Monetary Fund) and donors should continue to be sensitized to the need to address the issue of African countries' debts, to ensure that it did not hinder the effective implementation of NEPAD. CPC also recommended further Assembly consideration of the proposed revisions to programme 23, Public information [A/58/90].

The recommendations in respect of programmes 7 and 23 were endorsed, respectively, by the Second (Economic and Financial) Committee in a 22 October letter, which also proposed additional modifications [A/C.5/58/11], and by the Fourth (Special Political and Decolonization) Committee in a 4 November letter [A/C.5/58/14], both addressed to the Assembly President, who transmitted them to the Fifth Committee. On 24 November [A/C.5/58/19], the Assembly advised the Fifth Committee that on that date [meeting 64] it had endorsed CPC's recommendations relating to programme 8.

GENERAL ASSEMBLY ACTION

On 23 December [meeting 79], the General Assembly, on the recommendation of the Fifth Committee [A/58/574], adopted **resolution 58/268** without vote [agenda item 122].

Programme planning

The General Assembly,

Recalling its resolutions 37/234 of 21 December 1982, 38/227 A of 20 December 1983, 41/213 of 19 December 1986, 55/234 of 23 December 2000, 56/253 of 24 December 2001, 57/282 of 20 December 2002 and 58/270 of 23 December 2003,

Having considered the report of the Committee for Programme and Coordination on the work of its forty-third session,

Appreciating the letters from the President of the General Assembly transmitting the recommendations of the Assembly, the Second Committee, the Third Committee and the Special Political and Decolonization Committee (Fourth Committee), on the recommendations of the Committee for Programme and Coordination on proposed revisions to programmes 7, 8 and 23 of the medium-term plan for the period 2002-2005, and on evaluation,

1. *Takes note* of the report of the Committee for Programme and Coordination on the work of its forty-third session;

2. *Endorses* the conclusions and recommendations of the Committee for Programme and Coordination on the proposed revisions to the medium-term plan for the period 2002-2005 as contained in the report of the Committee on the work of its forty-third session and as endorsed by the Second Committee regarding programme 7, Economic and social affairs, by the General Assembly regarding programme 8, United Nations support for the New Partnership for Africa's Development, and by the Special Political and Decolonization Committee (Fourth Committee) regarding programme 23, Public information;

3. *Reaffirms* the relevant paragraphs of its resolution 55/231 of 23 December 2000, and requests the Secretary-General to submit to the General Assembly at its fifty-ninth session, through the Committee for Programme and Coordination, a report on priority-setting;

4. *Endorses* the conclusions and recommendations of the Committee for Programme and Coordination on the review of the efficiency of the administrative and financial functioning of the United Nations, as contained in chapter II of the report of the Committee on the work of its forty-third session; on evaluation, as contained in section C of chapter III and as endorsed by the Third Committee and the General Assembly; on the annual overview report of the United Nations System Chief Executives Board for Coordination for 2002 and on the New Partnership for Africa's Development, as contained in chapter IV; and on the Joint Inspection Unit, as contained in chapter V;

5. *Decides* to consider the report of the Secretary-General on the practice of involving United Nations programme managers in investigative processes, requested in section IV, paragraph 3, of its resolution 57/282, at the first part of its resumed fifty-eighth session under the item entitled "Review of the efficiency of the administrative and financial functioning of the United Nations".

On 23 December, the Assembly decided that the item on programme planning would remain for consideration during its resumed fifty-eighth (2004) session (**decision 58/565**).

Programme performance

Evaluation

CPC, at its June/July session [A/58/16], having considered the report of the Office of Internal Oversight Services (OIOS) on proposed evaluation themes, transmitted by the Secretary-General in April [E/AC.51/2003/2], deferred to its 2004 session the selection of a topic for thematic evaluation for submission to its 2005 session and for review at its 2006 session. It requested OIOS to further develop topics by elaborating the precise and comprehensive context, objective, scope, methodology and intended utilization of the findings of proposals for a pilot evaluation project.

CPC recommended approval of the OIOS recommendations on the in-depth evaluations of the programme on the law of the sea and ocean affairs [E/AC.51/2003/3] (see p. 1362); global development trends, issues and policies, global approaches to social and microeconomic issues and policies, and the corresponding subprogrammes in the regional commissions [E/AC.51/2003/4] (see p. 1001); and the evaluation of the advancement of women programme [E/AC.51/2003/5 & Corr.1] (see p. 1190) for submission to the Commission on the Status of Women for review and action.

By letters dated 10 November [A/C.5/58/15] and 24 November [A/C.5/58/21], the General Assembly President transmitted to the Fifth Committee the endorsements of the Third (Social, Humanitarian and Cultural) Committee and the Assembly, respectively, of CPC's recommendations on the evaluations of the advancement of women programme and of the law of the sea and ocean affairs.

Chapter III

United Nations staff

The United Nations suffered a severe blow on 19 August 2003 when its headquarters in Iraq was subjected to a savage terrorist attack that resulted in the death of 22 people, 15 of them UN staff members, and the wounding of 150. The General Assembly strongly condemned the attack and called for the perpetrators to be brought to justice.

During 2003, the Assembly, through the International Civil Service Commission (ICSC), continued to review the conditions of service of staff of the UN common system. The Assembly adopted ICSC recommendations relating to the base/floor salary scale and methodologies for surveys of best prevailing conditions of employment at Headquarters and non-Headquarters duty stations and requested the Commission to consider and decide on the level of hazard pay for local staff.

The Secretary-General reported on: the conditions of service and compensation for the ICSC Chairman and Vice-Chairman, for the Chairman of the Advisory Committee on Administrative and Budgetary Questions, and for members of the International Court of Justice, and judges of the International Tribunal for the Former Yugoslavia and the International Criminal Tribunal for Rwanda; post structure; staff composition and the proportion of General Service to Professional staff in the regional commissions; use of gratis personnel; the status of women in the Secretariat; multilingualism in the Secretariat; staff rules and regulations; staff safety and security; and requirements for membership in the United Nations Joint Staff Pension Fund (UNJSPF).

The Office of Internal Oversight Services issued an evaluation of the implementation of Assembly provisions on human resources management and of the audit of investment management, procurement and contract administration of UNJSPF, while the Joint Inspection Unit reported on the implementation of multilingualism in the United Nations system.

In continuing efforts to enhance the safety and security of UN staff and associated humanitarian personnel, the Assembly urged States to take stronger action to ensure that any threat or act of violence against staff on their territory was investigated and the perpetrators brought to justice, and requested the Secretary-General to consider ways to strengthen the protection of UN and associated personnel.

Conditions of service

International Civil Service Commission

The International Civil Service Commission (ICSC), a 15-member body established in 1974 by General Assembly resolution 3357(XXIX) [YUN 1974, p. 875], continued in 2003 to regulate and coordinate the conditions of service and the salaries and allowances of the UN common system. The United Nations and 12 related organizations had accepted the ICSC statute: the International Labour Organization (ILO); the Food and Agriculture Organization of the United Nations (FAO); the United Nations Educational, Scientific and Cultural Organization (UNESCO); the International Civil Aviation Organization (ICAO); the World Health Organization (WHO); the Universal Postal Union (UPU); the International Telecommunication Union (ITU); the World Meteorological Organization (WMO); the International Maritime Organization (IMO); the World Intellectual Property Organization (WIPO); the International Atomic Energy Agency (IAEA); and the United Nations Industrial Development Organization (UNIDO). One other organization, the International Fund for Agricultural Development, had not formally accepted the statute but participated fully in ICSC work.

ICSC held its fifty-sixth (Rome, Italy, 31 March–18 April) and fifty-seventh (New York, 14-25 July) sessions, at which it considered, in addition to organizational matters, the conditions of service applicable to both Professional and General Service categories of staff, and those relating specifically to the Professional and higher categories and to the General Service and other locally recruited categories.

The deliberations, recommendations and decisions of ICSC on those matters were detailed in its twenty-ninth annual report to the Assembly [A/58/30] (see sections below).

In an 18 September statement on the administrative and financial implications of ICSC decisions and recommendations for the 2004-2005 programme budget [A/58/378], the Secretary-General estimated the resulting requirements at $1,774,000, to be accommodated within the common staff costs provision in the proposed programme budget currently before the Assembly (see p. 1339).

On 26 September [A/58/7/Add.2], the Advisory Committee on Administrative and Budgetary Questions (ACABQ) recommended approval of the Secretary-General's recommendation on accommodating the estimated additional requirements.

GENERAL ASSEMBLY ACTION

The General Assembly, in section XXIV of **resolution 58/272** of 23 December (see p. 1420), took note of the Secretary-General's statement and the related ACABQ report. In section VII of the same resolution (see p. 1418), the Assembly approved the amount of $14,724,100 for ICSC for the 2004-2005 biennium.

Also on 23 December [meeting 79], the Assembly, on the recommendation of the Fifth (Administrative and Budgetary) Committee [A/58/576], adopted **resolution 58/251** without vote [agenda item 126].

United Nations common system

The General Assembly,

Having considered the report of the International Civil Service Commission for 2003 and the statement submitted by the Secretary-General on the administrative and financial implications of the decisions and recommendations contained in the report of the Commission,

Reaffirming its commitment to a single, unified United Nations common system as the cornerstone for the regulation and coordination of the conditions of service of the United Nations common system,

Convinced that the common system constitutes the best instrument through which to secure staff with the highest standards of efficiency, competence and integrity for the international civil service, as stipulated in the Charter of the United Nations,

Reaffirming the statute of the Commission and its central role in the regulation and coordination of the conditions of service of the United Nations common system,

Takes note with appreciation of the work of the International Civil Service Commission, and takes note of its report for 2003;

I
Conditions of service applicable to both categories of staff

A. Review of the pay and benefits system

Recalling its resolutions 51/216 of 18 December 1996, 52/216 of 22 December 1997, 53/209 of 18 December 1998, 55/223 of 23 December 2000 and 57/285 of 20 December 2002,

1. *Takes note with appreciation* of the continuing progress being made by the Commission in the review of the pay and benefits system in the context of the approved framework for human resources management;

2. *Takes note* of the decisions of the Commission contained in paragraphs 35, 86 and 88 of its report;

B. Contractual arrangements

Recalling section I.A, paragraph 4, of its resolution 57/285,

1. *Notes with appreciation* the collaborative process between the Commission and the organizations to develop a general framework for contractual arrangements within which organizations of the common system could operate;

2. *Takes note* of the decisions of the Commission contained in paragraphs 104 and 105 of its report;

C. Mobility

Recalling section V of its resolution 55/258 of 14 June 2001 and section I.B of its resolution 57/285,

1. *Takes note* of the decision of the Commission contained in paragraph 125 of its report;

2. *Takes note also* of the decision of the Commission contained in paragraph 126 of its report to review the current mobility and hardship scheme in the context of the pay and benefits review;

D. Hazard pay

Recalling section I.D of its resolution 57/285,

Recalls that hazard pay is a payment of a symbolic nature, and requests the Commission to reconsider and decide on a smaller increase in the level of hazard pay for local staff, taking into account the views expressed by Member States, and to report on the implementation of this request to the General Assembly at its fifty-ninth session;

E. Mission subsistence allowance/special operations approach

Takes note of the decision of the Commission contained in paragraph 154 of its report;

II
Conditions of service of staff in the Professional and higher categories

A. Base/floor salary scale

Recalling section I.H of its resolution 44/198 of 21 December 1989, by which it established a floor net salary for staff in the Professional and higher categories with reference to the corresponding base net salary levels of officials in comparable positions serving at the base city of the comparator civil service,

Approves the recommendation of the Commission contained in paragraph 188 of its report;

B. Linkage between the mobility and hardship allowance and the base/floor salary scale

Recalling its resolutions 44/198, 46/191 A of 20 December 1991, 51/216, 55/223 and 57/285,

Looks forward to receiving, at its fifty-ninth session, the reports of the Commission on its review of the mobility and hardship scheme and on the linkage between the mobility and hardship allowance and the base/floor salary scale;

III
Conditions of service of the General Service and other locally recruited categories: methodologies for surveys of best prevailing conditions of employment at Headquarters and non-Headquarters duty stations

Recalling section III, paragraph 1, of its resolution 47/216 of 23 December 1992,

Endorses the decisions of the Commission and the refinements and modifications of the methodologies contained in paragraphs 230, 265 to 269, 279, 288, 302, 311, 312, 326, 354 and 355 of its report.

Annex

Comparison of average net remuneration of United Nations officials in the Professional and higher categories in New York and United States officials in Washington, D.C., by equivalent grades (margin for calendar year 2003)

Grade	Net remuneration (United States dollars) United Nations[a]	Net remuneration (United States dollars) United States	United Nations/ United States ratio (United States, Washington, D.C. = 100)	United Nations/ United States ratio adjusted for cost-of-living differential	Weights for calculation of overall ratio[b]
P-1	58,761	42,420	138.5	120.3	0.2
P-2	73,087	55,169	132.5	115.1	5.3
P-3	89,112	67,748	131.5	114.2	20.9
P-4	106,863	84,642	126.3	109.7	32.1
P-5	125,124	99,430	125.8	109.3	27.5
D-1	144,874	114,817	126.2	109.6	10.4
D-2	151,732	118,923	127.6	110.9	3.7
Weighted average ratio before adjustment for New York/Washington, D.C., cost-of-living differential					127.6
New York/Washington, D.C., cost-of-living ratio					115.1
Weighted average ratio, adjusted for cost-of-living difference					110.9

[a] For the calculation of the average United Nations salaries, personnel statistics of the United Nations System Chief Executives Board for Coordination as at 31 December 2000 were used.

[b] These weights correspond to the United Nations common system staff in grades P-1 to D-2 serving at Headquarters and established offices as at 31 December 2000.

Functioning of ICSC

The Commission had before it information submitted by its secretariat on the implementation or follow-up by common system organizations of its 2000-2002 decisions and/or recommendations. Noting that increased response by organizations in that regard had enabled it to draw more meaningful conclusions concerning the implementation rate of its recommendations and decisions, the Commission requested its Chairman to urge organizations that had not participated in the 2003 implementation exercise to do so in future and requested its secretariat to present in 2004 a statistical report on gender balance at all levels in common system organizations, including with regard to ungraded officials.

Remuneration issues

Pursuant to the standing mandate in General Assembly resolutions 47/216 [YUN 1992, p. 1055] and 55/223 [YUN 2000, p. 1331], ICSC continued to review the relationship between the net remuneration of UN staff in the Professional and higher categories (grades P-1 to D-2) in New York, and that of the current comparator, the United States federal civil service employees in comparable positions in Washington, D.C. (referred to as the margin). In its 2003 report to the Assembly [A/58/30], ICSC noted that a net remuneration margin of 111.9 was forecast for 2003, based on existing grade equivalencies between United Nations and United States officials in comparable positions, as shown in annex II to its report. The comparator had not fully implemented the pay adjustments required to establish pay comparability with its non-federal sector, and the actual year-to-year (2002-2003) gross increase for Washington, D.C., taking into account the employment cost index and the locality pay adjustment, was 4.27 per cent, effective 1 January 2003.

In view of the increase in the comparator's civil service salaries as at 1 January 2003, the Commission found that, based on the 1995 methodology for adjusting the base/floor salary scale [YUN 1995, p. 1405], an 8.4 per cent adjustment of the UN common system's salary scale, effective 1 March 2004 on a no-loss/no-gain basis, would be required to keep it in line with that of the comparator. However, that adjustment would increase the number of duty stations, where the post adjustment classification would be equal or close to zero, resulting in real salary increases for staff at those duty stations and thereby affect the purchasing power parity between duty stations. The Commission recommended that the Assembly revert to the 1989 base/floor salary procedure [YUN 1989, p. 885], using the nationwide General Schedule (excluding locality pay) of the United States federal civil service as a reference point, which would, for the time being, maintain the current level of the UN base/floor scale adopted by the Assembly in resolution 57/285 (annex) [YUN 2002, p. 1397]. The Commission decided to study further in 2004 the issue of duty stations having no or low post adjustment.

The Commission also considered the linkage between the mobility and hardship scheme and the base/floor salary scale (see p. 1438).

Emoluments of top-echelon officials

Secretary-General and UNDP Administrator

ACABQ report (March). In a March report [A/57/7/Add.25], ACABQ recommended that the 6.3 per cent salary increase approved by the General Assembly in resolution 57/285 [YUN 2002, p. 1397] for staff at the D-2 level and above in the Professional and higher categories also be applied to the Secretary-General and the Administrator of the United Nations Development Programme (UNDP), raising their net annual remuneration from $259,097 to $275,420 and from $208,935 to $222,098, respectively.

The financial implications of the recommendations regarding the Secretary-General's salary in the 2002-2003 programme budget were estimated at $18,000 gross ($16,400 net). There would also be a consequential increase in the maximum retirement allowance for the three former Secretaries-General, estimated at $24,000 for 2003.

ACABQ also proposed that the Staff Regulations be amended to avoid recurring inconsistencies between the amount specified in the text as the UNDP Administrator's gross salary and the amount resulting from the application of the revised methodology for determining the salary and emoluments of staff of the UN common system.

GENERAL ASSEMBLY ACTION (June)

On 18 June [meeting 90], the General Assembly, on the recommendation of the Fifth Committee [A/57/649/Add.2], adopted **resolution 57/310** without vote [agenda item 112].

Salary and retirement allowance of the Secretary-General and salary and pensionable remuneration of the Administrator of the United Nations Development Programme

The General Assembly,

Having considered the report of the Advisory Committee on Administrative and Budgetary Questions,

1. *Concurs* with the recommendation of the Advisory Committee on Administrative and Budgetary Questions concerning the salary and retirement allowance of the Secretary-General contained in paragraph 9 of its report;

2. *Also concurs* with the recommendation of the Advisory Committee concerning the salary and pensionable remuneration of the Administrator of the United Nations Development Programme contained in paragraph 9 of its report;

3. *Approves* the amendment to paragraph 1 of annex I to the Staff Regulations of the United Nations with effect from 1 January 2003, as set forth in the annex to the present resolution;

4. *Requests* the Advisory Committee to submit proposals to the General Assembly at its fifty-eighth session with a view to formalizing conditions and procedures related to the salary and retirement allowance of the Secretary-General and the salary and pensionable remuneration of the Administrator of the United Nations Development Programme.

Annex

Amendment to paragraph 1 of annex I to the Staff Regulations of the United Nations

In paragraph 1, the last sentence, "With effect from 1 January 1998, the Administrator of the United Nations Development Programme shall receive a gross salary of 175,344 United States dollars per annum", should be deleted.

ACABQ report (October). In response to the Assembly's request in resolution 57/310 (above) that it submit proposals for formalizing conditions and procedures relating to the Secretary-General's salary and retirement allowance and the UNDP Administrator's salary and pensionable remuneration, ACABQ, in October [A/58/7/Add.3], stated that it did not see a need for changing the current practice whereby the Assembly, on ACABQ's recommendation, approved the adjustments whenever there was a change in the salary scales for the staff in the Professional and higher categories.

GENERAL ASSEMBLY ACTION (December)

On 23 December [meeting 79], the General Assembly, on the recommendation of the Fifth Committee [A/57/572], adopted **resolution 58/265** without vote [agenda item 120].

Salary and retirement allowance of the Secretary-General and salary and pensionable remuneration of the Administrator of the United Nations Development Programme

The General Assembly,

Recalling paragraph 4 of its resolution 57/310 of 18 June 2003,

Having considered the report of the Advisory Committee on Administrative and Budgetary Questions,

Concurs with paragraph 3 of the report of the Advisory Committee on Administrative and Budgetary Questions, and decides, at this time, not to change the current practice regarding the salary and retirement allowance of the Secretary-General and salary and pensionable remuneration of the Administrator of the United Nations Development Programme.

Methodologies for salary surveys

In 2003, ICSC reviewed the Headquarters and non-Headquarters methodologies for surveys of best prevailing conditions of employment for staff in the General Service and other locally recruited categories, based on the recommendations of the working groups it had established for that purpose.

The Commission, having reviewed the 1997 methodologies for salary surveys [YUN 1997, p. 1453], approved, with effect from 1 January 2004, the revised methodology for conducting surveys of the best prevailing conditions of employment at Headquarters duty stations and introduced a standard confidentiality pledge letter to be annexed to the methodology in order to encourage employer participation. It also approved, with effect from 1 January 2004, the revised methodology for conducting surveys at non-Headquarters duty stations, subject to the modifications approved by the staff representatives regarding further clarification of the survey process, the responsibilities of the survey participants and the reflection of some factual changes that had taken place since the last methodology review.

Post adjustment

ICSC continued to keep under review the operation of the post adjustment system, designed to measure cost-of-living movements, and considered, in that regard, the report of its Advisory Committee on Post Adjustment Questions on the work of its twenty-fifth session. It dealt with a range of technical questions concerning the next round of place-to-place surveys, scheduled to take place in 2005. It also considered recommendations addressing a variety of related issues, including the list of items and specifications to be used in the next round of surveys; the use of duty station–specific housing-type weights; alternative sources of price data; seasonal adjustment of prices; duty station–specific weights for the education component of the post adjustment index; the transparency of data processing; cost-of-living manuals; rules and procedures for reviewing the post adjustment classification and rental subsidy thresholds; the new computerized system for processing cost-of-living survey data; and other matters concerning external housing data, including the London congestion charge. The Commission endorsed the recommendations of its Advisory Committee, agreeing that it should hold its next meeting in 2004, prior to the next round of Headquarters duty stations place-to-place surveys.

Other remuneration issues

Conditions of service and compensation for non-Secretariat officials

Members of ICSC and Chairman of ACABQ

In March [A/C.5/57/35], the Secretary-General proposed that the 6.3 per cent salary increase approved by the General Assembly in resolution 57/285 [YUN 2002, p. 1397] for staff at the D-2 level and above in the Professional and higher categories also be applied to the net compensation of the Chairman and Vice-Chairman of ICSC and the Chairman of ACABQ in order to maintain the salary relativity of 97 per cent of the compensation of senior officials. That would raise the net salary of the three officials from $157,266 to $167,174.

The Secretary-General estimated that the financial implications of his proposals would require an additional $20,800 for the 2002-2003 biennium, representing the full cost of provision in respect of the ACABQ Chairman and the net cost to the United Nations of the provisions for the ICSC Chairman and Vice-Chairman, which were jointly financed with other UN system organizations. In accordance with Assembly resolution 55/238 [YUN 2000, p. 1300], the next comprehensive review of the compensation and other conditions of service of the three officials would be undertaken in 2005.

On 18 June, the General Assembly deferred until its fifty-eighth (2003) session consideration of the Secretary-General's report (**decision 57/588**).

GENERAL ASSEMBLY ACTION

On 23 December [meeting 79], the General Assembly, on the recommendation of the Fifth Committee [A/58/572], adopted **resolution 58/266** without vote [agenda item 120].

Conditions of service and compensation for officials, other than Secretariat officials, serving the General Assembly: full-time members of the International Civil Service Commission and the Chairman of the Advisory Committee on Administrative and Budgetary Questions

The General Assembly,

Recalling its resolutions 35/221 of 17 December 1980 and 55/238 of 23 December 2000,

Having considered the report of the Secretary-General,

1. *Approves* the suggestions outlined in paragraphs 4 to 6 of the report of the Secretary-General, due to the increase in the salary scale for staff in certain grades of the Professional and higher categories in accordance with its resolution 57/285 of 20 December 2002, with effect from 1 September 2003;

2. *Decides* that the additional financial requirements stemming from the proposals shall be reflected in its resolution on the second performance report for the biennium 2002-2003;

3. *Also decides* to maintain the procedure for adjusting the compensation of the Chairman and Vice-Chairman of the International Civil Service Commission and the Chairman of the Advisory Committee on Administrative and Budgetary Questions on the basis of the movement of the consumer price index;

4. *Requests* the Secretary-General to bring the issue of conditions of service and compensation of the three officials to the attention of the General Assembly when the annual compensation for the Chairman of the International Civil Service Commission and the Chairman of the Advisory Committee on Administrative and Budgetary Questions falls below the level of the compensation of Assistant Secretaries-General, but no sooner than at its sixty-third session;

5. *Decides* that the procedure outlined above shall replace the requirement for future five-year comprehensive reviews outlined in paragraph 8 of the report of the Secretary-General;

6. *Reaffirms* the principle that the conditions of service and compensation of the three officials shall be separate and distinct from those of officials of the United Nations Secretariat.

Judges of ICJ and the international tribunals

Report of Secretary-General. The Secretary-General submitted to the General Assembly a 12 March report [A/C.5/57/36] on the conditions of service of members of the International Court of Justice (ICJ) and judges of the International Tribunal for the Former Yugoslavia (ICTY) and the International Criminal Tribunal for Rwanda (ICTR). He drew attention to the fact that the pension scheme regulations applicable to judges of ICJ and the two tribunals did not preclude payment of a retirement pension to judges who, having previously served in one of those organs, were subsequently appointed to another one. The Secretary-General recalled the Assembly's ruling contained in resolutions 55/249 [YUN 2001, p. 1335] and 57/289 [YUN 2002, p. 1291], which defined specific conditions under which the payment of such pensions to ad litem judges of the tribunals should cease. He recommended that the Assembly decide that former judges of ICJ, ICTY or ICTR should also cease to receive payment of their retirement pension when serving as judges of another of those organs and, accordingly, amend the pension scheme regulations to reflect the Assembly's decisions in resolutions 55/249 and 57/289. The proposed amended texts of the pension regulations were annexed to the report.

On 18 June, the Assembly deferred until its fifty-eighth (2003) session consideration of the Secretary-General's report (**decision 57/588**).

GENERAL ASSEMBLY ACTION

On 23 December [meeting 79], the General Assembly, on the recommendation of the Fifth Committee [A/58/572], adopted **resolution 58/264** without vote [agenda item 120].

Conditions of service and compensation for officials other than Secretariat officials: members of the International Court of Justice, judges of the International Tribunal for the Former Yugoslavia and judges of the International Criminal Tribunal for Rwanda

The General Assembly,

Recalling section VIII of its resolution 53/214 of 18 December 1998 and its resolution 56/285 of 27 June 2002 on the conditions of service and compensation for officials other than Secretariat officials: members of the International Court of Justice, judges of the International Tribunal for the Prosecution of Persons Responsible for Serious Violations of International Humanitarian Law Committed in the Territory of the Former Yugoslavia since 1991 and judges of the International Criminal Tribunal for the Prosecution of Persons Responsible for Genocide and Other Serious Violations of International Humanitarian Law Committed in the Territory of Rwanda and Rwandan Citizens Responsible for Genocide and Other Such Violations Committed in the Territory of Neighbouring States between 1 January and 31 December 1994, its resolution 55/249 of 12 April 2001 on the conditions of service and compensation for the ad litem judges of the International Tribunal for the Former Yugoslavia and its resolution 57/289 of 20 December 2002 on the financing of the International Criminal Tribunal for Rwanda,

Having considered the report of the Secretary-General,

1. *Decides* to amend article 1 of the Pension Scheme Regulations for the members of the International Court of Justice and to replace that article with the provisions set out in annex I to the present resolution;

2. *Also decides* to amend article 1 of the Pension Scheme Regulations for the judges of the International Tribunal for the Former Yugoslavia and to replace that article with the provisions set out in annex II to the present resolution;

3. *Further decides* to amend article 1 of the Pension Scheme Regulations for the judges of the International Criminal Tribunal for Rwanda and to replace that article with the provisions set out in annex III to the present resolution.

Annex I

Pension Scheme Regulations for the members of the International Court of Justice (based on the provisions of General Assembly resolution 38/239 of 20 December 1983 and section VIII of Assembly resolution 53/214 of 18 December 1998 and applicable as from 1 January 1999)

Replace the text of article 1 with the following:

Article 1
Retirement pension

1. A member of the International Court of Justice who has ceased to hold office and who has reached the age of sixty shall be entitled during the remainder of his or her life, subject to paragraphs 6 and 7 below, to a retirement pension, payable monthly provided that he or she has:

(a) Completed at least three years of service;

(b) Not been required to relinquish his or her appointment under Article 18 of the Statute of the Court for reasons other than the state of his or her health.

2. For a member who has served a full term of nine years, the annual pension entitlement shall be:

(a) For the year 1999, 60,000 United States dollars;

(b) For the year 2000, 70,000 dollars;

(c) With effect from 1 January 2001, one half of the annual salary.

3. A member serving in office as from 31 December 1998, who has been or is re-elected, shall be entitled to an increase in the amount of the pension by one three-hundredth of the amount payable under paragraph 2 for each month of service in excess of nine years, provided that maximum retirement pension shall not exceed two thirds of his or her annual salary.

(a) For the year 1999, a maximum of 81,600 dollars;

(b) For the year 2000, a maximum of 95,200 dollars;

(c) For the year 2001, two thirds of the annual salary, 106,667 dollars.

4. A member who has served for less than a full term of nine years shall be entitled to a retirement pension in the amount of that proportion of one half of the annual salary which the number of months of his or her actual service bears to one hundred and eight.

5. A member who ceases to hold office before the age of sixty and who would be entitled to a retirement pension when he or she reached that age may elect to receive a pension from any date after the date on which he or she ceases to hold office. Should he or she so elect, an actuarial reduction factor of one half of one per cent per month would be applied on the retirement pension which would have been paid to him or her at the age of sixty.

6. No retirement pension shall be payable to a former member who has been re-elected to office until he or she again ceases to hold office. At that time, the amount of his or her pension shall be calculated in accordance with paragraphs 2 to 4 above on the basis of his or her total period of service and shall be subject to a reduction equal in actuarial value to the amount of any retirement pension paid to him or her before he or she reached the age of sixty.

7. No retirement pension shall be payable to a former member who has been elected or appointed a permanent judge of the International Tribunal for the Former Yugoslavia or the International Criminal Tribunal for Rwanda or who has been appointed to serve in the International Tribunal for the Former Yugoslavia or the International Criminal Tribunal for Rwanda as an ad litem judge until he or she ceases to hold that office or appointment.

Annex II

Pension Scheme Regulations for the judges of the International Tribunal for the Former Yugoslavia (based on the provisions of section VIII of General Assembly resolution 53/214 of 18 December 1998 and applicable as from 1 January 1999)

Replace the text of article 1 with the following:

Article 1
Retirement pension

1. A judge of the International Tribunal for the Former Yugoslavia who has ceased to hold office and who has reached the age of sixty shall be entitled during the remainder of his or her life, subject to paragraphs 4 and 5 below, to a retirement pension, payable monthly provided that he or she has:

(a) Completed at least three years of service;

(b) Not been required to relinquish his or her appointment under Article 18 of the Statute of the International Court of Justice for reasons other than the state of his or her health.

2. The amount of the retirement pension shall be determined as follows:

(a) If the judge has served a full term of four years and ceases to hold office after 1 January 2001, the amount of the annual pension shall be two ninths of the annual salary;

(b) If the judge has served a full term of four years and ceases to hold office after 1 January 1999 but before 1 January 2000, the amount of the annual pension shall be 26,500 United States dollars;

(c) If the judge has served a full term of four years and ceases to hold office after 1 January 2000 but before 1 January 2001, the amount of the annual pension shall be 31,000 dollars;

(d) Judges who have served a term of four years and who retire in 1999 or 2000 shall receive an increase in their pension as follows. As noted above, judges retiring in 1999 shall receive an annual pension of 26,500 dollars. Their annual pension shall be increased to 31,000 dollars in 2000 and to 35,500 dollars in 2001. Judges retiring in 2000 shall receive an annual pension of 31,000 dollars. The pension shall be increased to 35,500 dollars in 2001;

(e) With effect from 1 January 1999, all pensions in course of payment as at 31 December 1998, including pensions of judges who retire on or before that date, shall be increased by 10.3 per cent, i.e., the change resulting from the increase in the annual salary;

(f) If a judge served for less than a full term of four years, the amount of the pension shall be that proportion of the annual pension which the number of months of his or her actual service bears to forty-eight;

(g) If the judge came into office prior to 1 January 1999 and has been or is subsequently re-elected for another term, he or she shall continue to receive one one-hundred-and-thirty-third of the International Tribunal's pension benefit for each further month subsequent to his or her initial term, up to a maximum pension equivalent to eight twenty-sevenths of the annual salary. Judges elected to terms of office commencing after 31 December 1998 shall not be entitled to an increase in their pension benefit in case of re-election.

3. A judge who ceased to hold office before the age of sixty and who would be entitled to a retirement pension when he or she reached that age may elect to receive a pension from any date after the date on which he or she ceases to hold office. Should he or she so elect, the amount of such pension shall be that amount which has the same value as the retirement pension which would have been paid to him or her at the age of sixty.

4. No retirement pension shall be payable to a former judge who has been re-elected to office until he or she again ceases to hold office. At that time, the amount of his or her pension shall be calculated in accordance with paragraph 2 above on the basis of his or her total period of service and shall be subject to a reduction equal in actuarial value to the amount of any retirement pension paid to him or her before he or she reached the age of sixty.

5. No retirement pension shall be payable to a former judge who has been elected a member of the International Court of Justice or who has been elected or appointed a permanent judge of the International Criminal Tribunal for Rwanda or who has been appointed to serve on the International Tribunal for the Former Yugoslavia or the International Criminal Tribunal for Rwanda as an ad litem judge until he or she ceases to hold that office or appointment.

Annex III

Pension Scheme Regulations for the judges of the International Criminal Tribunal for Rwanda (based on the provisions of section VIII of General Assembly resolution 53/214 of 18 December 1998 and applicable as from 1 January 1999)

Replace the text of article 1 with the following:

Article 1
Retirement pension

1. A judge of the International Criminal Tribunal for Rwanda who has ceased to hold office and who has reached the age of sixty shall be entitled during the remainder of his or her life, subject to paragraphs 4 and 5 below, to a retirement pension, payable monthly provided that he or she has:

(a) Completed at least three years of service;

(b) Not been required to relinquish his or her appointment under Article 18 of the Statute of the International Court of Justice for reasons other than the state of his or her health.

2. The amount of the retirement pension shall be determined as follows:

(a) If the judge has served a full term of four years and ceases to hold office after 1 January 2001, the amount of the annual pension shall be two ninths of the annual salary;

(b) If the judge has served a full term of four years and ceases to hold office after 1 January 1999 but before 1 January 2000, the amount of the annual pension shall be 26,500 United States dollars;

(c) If the judge has served a full term of four years and ceases to hold office after 1 January 2000 but before 1 January 2001, the amount of the annual pension shall be 31,000 dollars;

(d) Judges who have served a term of four years and who retire in 1999 or 2000 shall receive an increase in their pension as follows. As noted above, judges retiring in 1999 shall receive an annual pension of 26,500 dollars. Their annual pension shall be increased to 31,000 dollars in 2000 and to 35,500 dollars in 2001. Judges retiring in 2000 shall receive an annual pension of 31,000 dollars. The pension shall be increased to 35,500 dollars in 2001;

(e) With effect from 1 January 1999, all pensions in course of payment as at 31 December 1998, including pensions of judges who retire on or before that date, shall be increased by 10.3 per cent, i.e., the change resulting from the increase in the annual salary;

(f) If a judge served for less than a full term of four years, the amount of the pension shall be that proportion of the annual pension which the number of months of his or her actual service bears to forty-eight;

(g) If the judge came into office prior to 1 January 1999 and has been or is subsequently re-elected for another term, he or she shall continue to receive one one-hundred-and-thirty-third of the International Tribunal's pension benefit for each further month subsequent to his or her initial term, up to a maximum pension equivalent to eight twenty-sevenths of the annual salary. Judges elected to terms of office commencing after 31 December 1998 shall not be entitled to an increase in their pension benefit in case of re-election.

3. A judge who ceased to hold office before the age of sixty and who would be entitled to a retirement pension when he or she reached that age may elect to receive a pension from any date after the date on which he or she ceases to hold office. Should he or she so elect, the amount of such pension shall be that amount which has the same value as the retirement pension which would have been paid to him or her at the age of sixty.

4. No retirement pension shall be payable to a former judge who has been re-elected to office until he or she again ceases to hold office. At that time, the amount of his or her pension shall be calculated in accordance with paragraph 2 above on the basis of his or her total period of service and shall be subject to a reduction equal in actuarial value to the amount of any retirement pension paid to him or her before he or she reached the age of sixty.

5. No retirement pension shall be payable to a former judge who has been elected a member of the International Court of Justice or who has been elected or appointed a permanent judge of the International Tribunal for the Former Yugoslavia or who has been appointed to serve in the International Tribunal for the Former Yugoslavia or the International Criminal Tribunal for Rwanda as an ad litem judge until he or she ceases to hold that office or appointment.

Mobility and hardship allowance

As requested by the General Assembly in resolution 57/285 [YUN 2002, p. 1397], ICSC reviewed the linkage between the mobility and hardship allowance and the base/floor salary scale. The Commission recognized that the mobility and hardship allowance, approved in 1989 [YUN 1989, p. 885], was designed to compensate for service at difficult duty stations and to encourage operational mobility. However, concern was expressed about its linkage to the base/floor salary scale, which resulted in an automatic adjustment of the allowance whenever the base/floor scale was revised, leading to increasing costs. The Commission requested its secretariat to provide more detailed information to allow it to study the question at its fifty-ninth (2004) session.

Hazard pay

In response to General Assembly resolution 57/285 [YUN 2002, p. 1397], ICSC reviewed its 2002 decision regarding hazard pay [ibid., p. 1402], particularly the question of increasing the level granted to locally recruited staff. The Commission decided to uphold its decision that the level of hazard pay granted to locally recruited staff should be increased to 30 per cent of the midpoint of the local salary scale, effective 1 January 2004. The financial impact of the increase was estimated at approximately $2,700,000 yearly system-wide.

In response to a request from the Federation of International Civil Servants' Associations (FICSA) concerning hazard pay for staff of the United Nations Relief and Works Agency for Palestine Refugees in the Near East (UNRWA), the Commission recalled its 2002 conclusion [YUN 2002, p. 1402] that UNRWA's Commissioner-General had full authority to deal with the issue by applying the relevant procedures in place for that category of staff.

Mission subsistence allowance

In 2003, ICSC reviewed the criteria and practice for the payment of mission subsistence allowance (MSA) in the UN system, based on updated information provided by its secretariat on the practices of other common system organizations using the special operations approach and the extended monthly evacuation allowance, and the views of those organizations on the feasibility of harmonizing their practices vis-à-vis staff assigned to non-family locations. The information showed that different arrangements existed at different UN organizations regarding remuneration packages and conditions of service of staff assigned to special and non-family missions. The Commission stressed the need for further harmonization of practices with respect to the allowances of staff serving in non-family duty stations, in order to avoid competition and to promote staff mobility. It requested organizations to continue developing arrangements applicable to all and to report on the issue in 2004. Its secretariat, in cooperation with common system organizations, was asked to report on the feasibility of linking the MSA rates to the established rates for daily subsistence allowance.

Other staff matters

Personnel policies

Human resources management

The General Assembly, at its resumed fifty-seventh session in 2003, had before it reports of the Secretary-General, consideration of which had been deferred from previous sessions, on: the employment of retirees in 1998-1999 [YUN 2000, p. 1352]; amendments to the 100, 200 and 300 series of Staff Rules, submitted in 2001 [YUN 2001, p. 1347]; staff composition in 2001 [ibid., p. 1342]; the implications of changing the mandatory age of separation for staff members appointed prior to 1 January 1990 from 60 to 62 years [ibid., p. 1354]; the placement of staff serving in the Executive Office of the Secretary-General [YUN 2002, p. 1407]; the hiring and use of consultants and individual contractors in 2000 [YUN 2001, p. 1343]; the report of ICSC on its fifty-fourth and fifty-fifth (2002) sessions [YUN 2002, p. 1396]; amendments to the 100, 200 and 300 series of Staff Rules, submitted in 2002 [ibid., p. 1413]; establishment of a capacity in the UN Office of Human Resources Management (OHRM) for monitoring all relevant Secretariat activities regardless of the source of funding [ibid., p. 1403]; results of the implementation of the provisions contained in resolution 55/258 [YUN 2001, p. 1337] on human resources management reform [YUN 2002, p. 1403]; the hiring and use of consultants and individual contractors in 2001 [ibid., p. 1409]; the employment of retirees in 2000-2001 [ibid., p. 1418]; staff composition in 2002 [ibid., p. 1407]; and lists of staff of the UN Secretariat in 2001 [A/C.5/56/L.7] and 2002 [A/C.5/57/L.3]. It also had before it a note by the Secretary-General transmitting an Office of Internal Oversight Services (OIOS) report on implementation of the provisions of resolution 55/258 on human resources management [A/57/726] (see below); a Secretariat note on streamlining staff rules and regulations [YUN 2001, p. 1347]; and related ACABQ reports [A/56/7, A/56/846, A/57/469].

OIOS report. Pursuant to General Assembly resolutions 48/218 B [YUN 1994, p. 1362], 54/244 [YUN 1999, p. 1274] and 56/253 [YUN 2001, p. 1297], the Secretary-General transmitted a February OIOS report [A/57/726] on the implementation of Assembly resolution 55/258 [YUN 2001, p. 1337] on human resources management reform. The report focused on a number of critical strategic human resources management reform drivers, including human resources planning, the new staff selection system, mobility, competencies, continuous learning and career development, the performance appraisal system (e-PAS), monitoring, enhanced conditions of service, and the streamlining of rules and procedures.

OIOS observed that, although it was too early to assess the full impact of the human resources reform, OHRM had made significant progress in implementing a number of reform initiatives. It recognized that, although OHRM could take the lead in introducing new initiatives, their successful implementation at the organizational level depended on mutual cooperation between different partners and bodies in the Organization in support of a culture of change. To be perceived as a strategic asset, OHRM should strengthen its ability to measure the impact of its activities on the Organization's performance and, if necessary, refocus initiatives to achieve stronger alignment with the Organization's operational goals.

To further advance the human resources management reform process, OIOS proposed a number of specific actions, grouped under four main themes: strategic orientation, focusing on the functions and activities needed by OHRM's clients to promote productive behaviour in the Organization; result-oriented evaluation systems, involving concise assessments concentrating on the results of new initiatives and demonstrating OHRM's impact on the Organization's performance; enhanced systemic linkages between components of the human resources management reform and parts of the larger organizational reform strategy; and maximized efficiency of administrative human resources processes.

The report also included an overview of the new approach by OIOS to supporting OHRM in fully realizing the reform goals; assessing and refining its primary objectives, current roles, responsibilities and core functions; and aligning them with its ongoing reform efforts. Following consultations, a revised OHRM mission statement was formulated and guiding principles for further implementation of envisaged change were developed.

GENERAL ASSEMBLY ACTION

On 15 April [meeting 83], the General Assembly, on the recommendation of the Fifth Committee [A/57/771], adopted **resolution 57/305** without vote [agenda item 118].

Human resources management

The General Assembly,

Reaffirming its resolutions 49/222 A and B of 23 December 1994 and 20 July 1995, 51/226 of 3 April 1997, 52/219 of 22 December 1997, 52/252 of 8 September 1998, 53/221 of 7 April 1999 and 55/258 of 14 June 2001 and its decision 56/462 of 24 December 2001, as well as its other relevant resolutions and decisions, subject to the provisions of the present resolution,

Having considered the relevant reports on human resources management questions submitted to the General Assembly for its consideration and the related reports of the Advisory Committee on Administrative and Budgetary Questions,

I
Principles and role of the Office of Human Resources Management of the Secretariat

1. *Reaffirms* the principles set out in section I of resolutions 53/221 and 55/258 concerning human resources management and the role of the Office of Human Resources Management of the Secretariat;

2. *Requests* the Secretary-General to ensure that United Nations staff members adhere fully to the United Nations code of conduct as approved by resolution 52/252, in conformity with staff regulation 1.2 of the Staff Regulations of the United Nations and the principle set out in section I, paragraph 6, of resolution 53/221 concerning the integrity and independence of the international civil service;

II
Human resources management reform

1. *Appreciates* the efforts of the Secretary-General aimed at reforming human resources management in the Organization, and in this regard reaffirms the importance of the central role of the Office of Human Resources Management in achieving this objective;

2. *Welcomes* the efforts of the Secretary-General to improve conditions of service within the framework of the common system, and affirms that his endeavours to improve performance, productivity and results across the Organization are a necessary complement to improved conditions of service;

3. *Endorses* the opinions of the Advisory Committee on Administrative and Budgetary Questions contained in paragraph 17 of its report;

4. *Requests* the Secretary-General to report to the General Assembly at its fifty-ninth session in a comprehensive manner on the achievements of the human resources management reform, when sufficient information will be available on the experiences of the Secretariat with the implementation of the reform initiatives as implemented within the prerogative of the Secretary-General or as approved by the Assembly;

5. *Also requests* the Secretary-General to conduct a study, through the Office of Internal Oversight Services of the Secretariat, on the impact of human resources management reform, in particular on the improvement of recruitment, placement, promotion and training, including an assessment of the role of the central review bodies and mobility, within the Secretariat, taking into account, inter alia, the relevant reports of the Joint Inspection Unit, and to report thereon to the General Assembly at its fifty-ninth session;

6. *Further requests* the Secretary-General to ensure that all future reports on the implementation of the human resources management reform focus on the results of such measures;

Recruitment and placement

7. *Reaffirms* the provisions contained in section IV of resolution 55/258, on recruitment, placement and

promotion, and requests the Secretary-General to ensure the full implementation thereof;

8. *Requests* the Secretary-General to ensure that the highest standards of efficiency, competence and integrity serve as the paramount consideration in the employment of staff, with due regard to the principle of equitable geographical distribution, in accordance with Article 101, paragraph 3, of the Charter of the United Nations;

9. *Reiterates* the value of a transparent process of recruitment, placement and promotion in the Organization;

10. *Requests* the Secretary-General to ensure the accountability of programme managers in the staff selection process, in close collaboration with the Office of Human Resources Management, and to report thereon to the General Assembly at its fifty-ninth session;

11. *Also requests* the Secretary-General to develop measures, as necessary, in cooperation with the Office of Internal Oversight Services and the Joint Inspection Unit, to prevent discrimination on the basis of nationality, race, gender, religion or language in the United Nations, in accordance with the principles of the Charter and the provisions of the Staff Regulations and Rules of the United Nations, and to report to the General Assembly at its fifty-ninth session;

12. *Reiterates its concern* about the continuing high vacancy rates at some United Nations duty stations and regional commissions, especially those located in developing countries;

13. *Recalls* the findings, conclusions and recommendations of the Office of Internal Oversight Services following the inspection of the administrative and management practices of the United Nations Office at Nairobi, and in this regard requests the Secretary-General to address the causes of the continuous high vacancy rates at all the heavily affected United Nations offices and regional commissions in developing countries, particularly those located in Africa, and to report thereon to the General Assembly at its fifty-ninth session;

14. *Requests* the Secretary-General to report to the General Assembly at its fifty-ninth session on the differences between the policies and procedures for staff recruitment, selection and appointment of the Secretariat and those of jointly funded organizations, such as the United Nations Joint Staff Pension Fund, the International Civil Service Commission and the Joint Inspection Unit, specifically addressing the mechanisms in those jointly funded organizations to ensure equal access to the opportunity to compete for positions, merit-based staffing and fairness and transparency in the selection process;

15. *Welcomes* the introduction of Galaxy, and requests the Secretary-General to ensure that it will enhance transparency, efficiency and effectiveness in the recruitment process of the United Nations system, subject to the framework of current mandates of human resources management in the Organization;

16. *Notes* that nationals of one hundred and eighty-six Member States have submitted employment applications utilizing Galaxy;

17. *Requests* the Secretary-General to further improve Galaxy, including measures to deal with the increased number of applications, and to invite all the organizations of the United Nations system to use Galaxy for recruitment, and to report on its performance to the General Assembly at its fifty-ninth session;

18. *Also requests* the Secretary-General to inform Member States monthly, through the United Nations web site, and upon request in hard copy, of appointments made;

19. *Further requests* the Secretary-General to ensure that relevant experience, knowledge and institutional memory acquired in the United Nations system are given due consideration in evaluating applications for promotion, consistent with the need to select staff on the basis of merit, demonstrated competencies and performance;

20. *Requests* the Secretary-General, while filling vacant posts in the language services of the Secretariat, to ensure the highest quality of translation and interpretation in all six official languages;

21. *Recalls* resolution 55/258, in particular section IV, paragraph 3, and draws attention to the difficulties relating to access to information technology by some developing countries, including the least developed countries;

22. *Requests* the Secretary-General, in view of the difficulties referred to above, to continue to maintain a system of circulation of hard copies of all vacancy announcements, in accordance with resolution 55/258, for distribution to all delegations, except those that indicate otherwise, as well as to continue the practice of receiving and processing applications in hard copy;

23. *Also requests* the Secretary-General to provide information about Galaxy in all six official languages on the official United Nations web site;

24. *Reaffirms* the need to respect the equality of each of the two working languages of the Secretariat, reaffirms also the use of additional working languages in specific duty stations as mandated, and in this regard requests the Secretary-General to ensure that vacancy announcements specify the need for either of the working languages of the Secretariat, unless the functions of the post require a specific working language;

25. *Affirms* the need for vacant posts to be filled expeditiously, subject to operational requirements, and requests the Secretary-General to make efforts to complete the recruitment process without delay;

26. *Welcomes* the progress made in reducing the number of Member States that are unrepresented in the Secretariat;

27. *Expresses concern*, however, at the number of Member States that continue to be unrepresented and underrepresented in the Secretariat and the increase in the number of overrepresented Member States;

28. *Reaffirms* section IV, paragraph 8, of resolution 55/258, including the requirement for indicative means to measure progress in improving equitable geographical representation;

29. *Requests* the Secretary-General to provide information on these issues, including on section IV, paragraph 8, of resolution 55/258, in a separate, self-contained report for consideration by the General Assembly at its fifty-ninth session;

30. *Also requests* the Secretary-General to include an analysis of the level of underrepresentation in future reports on the composition of the Secretariat;

31. *Recognizes* that Galaxy should have a positive impact on improving equitable geographical distribution

among Member States in the process of recruiting United Nations staff;

32. *Reiterates its request* to the Secretary-General, contained in section X, paragraph 3, of resolution 55/258, to further increase his efforts to improve the composition of the Secretariat by ensuring a wide and equitable geographical distribution of staff in all departments;

33. *Requests* the Secretary-General to hold the heads of relevant departments accountable for the human resources action plans and to ensure that they in turn take due account of equitable geographical representation when considering candidates on the lists endorsed by the central review bodies, as well as on the rosters, and to report to the General Assembly annually on progress made by departments in the implementation of their respective human resources action plans;

34. *Reaffirms* the established policies by which temporary staff are used to replace staff on extended sick leave or maternity leave or to cover essential work which, as a result of vacancies, cannot be performed by regular staff;

35. *Requests* the Secretary-General to report on the function, relevant operational factors and incidence of temporary staff appointed at the Professional level or above for less than one year under the 100 series of the Staff Rules of the United Nations, and the implications for substantive appointments to the Secretariat;

36. *Invites* the Secretary-General to consider including the question of equitable geographical representation in the secretariats of the United Nations system in the agenda of the United Nations System Chief Executives Board for Coordination and to report thereon to the General Assembly at its fifty-ninth session;

37. *Reaffirms* that, in accordance with resolutions 41/206 A of 11 December 1986, 53/221 and 55/258, no post should be considered the exclusive preserve of any Member State or group of States, including at the highest levels, and requests the Secretary-General to ensure that, as a general rule, no national of a Member State succeeds a national of that State in a senior post and that there is no monopoly on senior posts by nationals of any State or group of States, and to report thereon to the General Assembly at its fifty-ninth session;

38. *Reiterates its request* to the Secretary-General to take all necessary measures to ensure, at the senior and policy-making levels of the Secretariat, equitable representation of Member States, especially those with inadequate representation at those levels, including unrepresented and underrepresented States, in particular developing countries, in accordance with the relevant resolutions of the General Assembly, and to continue to include relevant information thereon in all future reports on the composition of the Secretariat;

39. *Reiterates its request*, contained in section XIV, paragraph 2, of resolution 55/258, which recalled resolution 53/221, including the reaffirmation of the goal of 50/50 gender distribution by 2000 in all categories of posts within the United Nations system, especially at the D-1 level and above, with full respect for the principle of equitable geographical distribution, in conformity with Article 101 of the Charter, and taking into account the continuing lack of representation or underrepresentation of women from certain countries, in particular from developing countries and countries with economies in transition;

40. *Reiterates* section III.C, paragraph 8, of resolution 51/226, in which it strongly encouraged Member States to support the efforts of the United Nations and the specialized agencies to increase the percentage of women in Professional posts, especially at the D-1 level and above, by identifying and regularly presenting more women candidates and by encouraging women to apply for posts in the Secretariat and the specialized agencies;

41. *Requests* the Secretary-General, in the light of ongoing concern about the underrepresentation of women in the United Nations, especially at senior levels, to undertake a comprehensive review of progress made towards the goal of 50/50 gender distribution, including, inter alia, the factors affecting progress, and to submit proposals to improve gender representation, particularly in offices in which women are underrepresented, to the General Assembly at its fifty-ninth session;

42. *Reiterates* that the national competitive examination programme is a useful tool for selecting the best-qualified candidates from inadequately represented Member States, and requests the Secretary-General to continue to hold the examinations for posts subject to geographical distribution at the P-2 level and, if necessary, at the P-3 level for those Member States;

43. *Also reiterates* the policy that appointments at the P-3 level shall normally be made through competitive examination;

44. *Notes* that the time needed to complete a national competitive examination cycle from the deadline for the applications until the successful candidate is placed on the roster is one year or more, and requests the Secretary-General to significantly reduce the time needed, and to report thereon to the General Assembly at its fifty-ninth session;

45. *Recalls* paragraph 39 of resolution 57/300 of 20 December 2002, and requests the Secretary-General to ensure that movement from the General Service to the Professional category is consistent with legislative mandates;

46. *Notes with concern* the low proportion of staff below the age of 35, and requests the Secretary-General to examine the factors that inhibit the selection of young people and to report accordingly to the General Assembly at its fifty-ninth session;

Mobility

47. *Welcomes* the efforts of the Secretary-General to develop a more versatile, multi-skilled, mobile and experienced international civil service;

48. *Recalls* section V of resolution 55/258;

49. *Stresses* in this regard that when implementing mobility policies, the Secretary-General should ensure that:

(a) Mobility does not negatively affect the continuity and the quality of services and the institutional memory and capacity of the Organization;

(b) It does not lead to the transfer or abolition of posts as a result of vacancies;

(c) It has a positive impact in filling existing high vacancy rates in some United Nations duty stations and regional commissions;

(d) There is a clear differentiation between mobility within duty stations and mobility across duty stations and that the latter should be a more important factor in career development;

(e) Mobility is encouraged in all categories of Professional and higher level posts;

50. *Acknowledges* that mobility needs to be supported through greater efforts to improve conditions of life and work throughout different duty stations;

51. *Encourages* the Secretary-General to expedite, as appropriate, the agreements between the Secretariat and the United Nations funds and programmes and the specialized agencies for all staff levels in relation to mobility;

52. *Requests* the Secretary-General to take the necessary steps to ensure that mobility will not be used as an instrument of coercion against staff;

53. *Also requests* the Secretary-General to closely monitor mobility and to submit proposals to the General Assembly, for consideration at its fifty-ninth session, in order to solve any problems resulting from increased staff mobility;

Performance management and career development

54. *Acknowledges with appreciation* the achievements to date in establishing and promulgating organizational values and core and managerial competencies, expanded learning and development programmes and a revised performance management system as steps towards developing staff careers;

55. *Notes with appreciation* the efforts of the Secretary-General to create a fair, equitable, transparent and measurable system of performance management for all staff, and encourages the Secretary-General to continue to develop a results-based culture that rewards excellent performance;

56. *Requests* the Secretary-General to implement all necessary measures to further enhance a comprehensive and systematic career development system, including in the areas of the performance appraisal system, training and competitive examinations, in order to provide for the recognition of competence and outstanding performance and to facilitate the continuous professional growth of staff at all levels, and to report to the General Assembly at its fifty-ninth session on the progress made in the implementation of those measures;

57. *Also requests* the Secretary-General to make specific proposals for making full use of the potential contribution of the United Nations System Staff College in the development of a common organizational culture and strengthening managerial skills and competencies;

Contractual arrangements

58. *Reaffirms* section III, paragraph 2, of resolution 55/258, and reiterates its request to the Secretary-General to submit definitive and concrete proposals on new contractual arrangements, specifying the differences between existing and proposed types of appointments, for consideration by the General Assembly as soon as possible, and requests the Secretary-General, in the meantime, to continue current contractual arrangements in accordance with existing mandates;

III
Delegation of authority and accountability

1. *Requests* the Secretary-General, when implementing measures in regard to the delegation of authority to programme managers, strictly to comply with the principles and policies established in section IV of resolution 53/221 and section VII of resolution 55/258;

2. *Also requests* the Secretary-General to report on a biennial basis on the progress made in the implementation of the provisions contained in section IV of resolution 53/221 and section VII of resolution 55/258;

3. *Further requests* the Secretary-General to report on the application of staff rule 104.14 *(b)* in the context of the comprehensive report on the implementation of human resources management reform;

4. *Requests* the Secretary-General to expeditiously finalize and issue new administrative instructions on the implementation of section VII, paragraph 8, of resolution 55/258;

IV
Monitoring capacity in the Office of Human Resources Management

1. *Endorses* the approach outlined by the Secretary-General to developing a more robust monitoring capacity in the Office of Human Resources Management;

2. *Takes note* of the intention of the Advisory Committee to revert to this matter in the context of its review of the proposed programme budget for the biennium 2004-2005;

3. *Emphasizes* the importance of the monitoring of policies, guidelines and practices by the Office of Human Resources Management, and requests the Secretary-General to ensure that the proper screening process for recruitment, identifying the best-qualified candidates, is conducted by the Office, in accordance with section IV, paragraph 7, of resolution 55/258, to continue to develop a comprehensive monitoring system and to report thereon to the General Assembly at its fifty-ninth session;

V
Consultants and individual contractors

1. *Takes note* of the report of the Secretary-General;

2. *Reaffirms* that consultants shall not perform functions of staff members of the Organization or have any representative or supervisory responsibility;

3. *Reiterates* that the Secretary-General should refrain from using consultants to carry out functions assigned to established posts and that consultants should be hired only in strict accordance with existing rules and relevant General Assembly resolutions and where expertise is not available within the Organization;

4. *Also reiterates* that in areas where consultants are frequently hired for a period of more than one year, the Secretary-General should submit proposals, where necessary, for the establishment of posts and should report thereon to the General Assembly at its fifty-ninth session;

5. *Reaffirms* the guidelines, principles and comments contained in section VIII, paragraph 11, of resolution 53/221;

6. *Takes note* of the recommendation contained in paragraph 5 of the report of the Advisory Committee;

7. *Endorses* the recommendation made by the Committee for Programme and Coordination at its forty-second session that the Secretary-General should make greater efforts to ensure geographical balance among qualified consultants and individual contractors;

8. *Requests* the Secretary-General to report biennially, starting at its fifty-ninth session, on the use of consultants and individual contractors within the Secretariat and the regional commissions and the factors

contributing to that, with statistics for each year of the two-year period, including information on their duties;

VI
Employment of retired former staff

1. *Endorses* the conclusions and recommendations on the employment of retired former staff contained in paragraphs 10, 11, 13 and 14 of the report of the Advisory Committee on Administrative and Budgetary Questions;

2. *Requests* the Secretary-General to have recourse to the employment of retired former staff only if the operational requirements of the Organization cannot be met by existing staff;

3. *Also requests* the Secretary-General to ensure that the employment of retired former staff has no adverse effects on the career planning and mobility of other United Nations staff members;

4. *Stresses* that the hiring of retired former staff should be on an exceptional basis, and in this regard encourages the Secretary-General to fill vacant posts at senior and decision-making levels through the established staff selection process;

5. *Requests* the Secretary-General to report to the General Assembly at its fifty-ninth session on the employment of retired former staff, including the criteria for selection of staff in the Professional categories, the number of staff hired for periods exceeding two years and the number of retired former staff serving in posts that affect the decision-making process, in particular in the areas of recruitment and promotion within the Secretariat and in the field, as well as instances in which representative responsibilities before intergovernmental bodies are assigned to retired staff;

6. *Also requests* the Secretary-General to include in the report referred to in paragraph 5 of the present section information on economy and efficiency gains envisaged in the context of language posts;

7. *Discourages* the Secretary-General from using retired former staff to present reports to any intergovernmental body;

VII
Mandatory age of separation

1. *Takes note* of the report of the Advisory Committee, and decides that, in order to prioritize the rejuvenation of the Secretariat, no further changes are required to the rule of the mandatory age of separation established at 60 years;

2. *Reaffirms* that retention in service beyond the mandatory age of separation shall be pursuant to the exceptions provided for in staff regulation 9.5, and requests the Secretary-General to report on the exceptions made and their circumstances on a biennial basis;

VIII
Placement of staff members serving in the Executive Office of the Secretary-General

Approves, in view of the special circumstances, the proposal contained in the report of the Secretary-General, while emphasizing that the process must be transparent and in accordance with the Staff Regulations and Rules, and requests the Secretary-General to report on the implementation of this procedure to the General Assembly as appropriate;

IX
Composition of the Secretariat

1. *Notes* the study conducted by the Secretariat as requested in section X, paragraph 4, of resolution 55/258, and decides to revert to this subject at its fifty-ninth session;

2. *Requests* the Secretary-General, as approved by resolution 42/220 A of 21 December 1987, to fully reach the level of posts subject to geographical distribution, which currently stands at 2,700, and to conduct a study which includes a comprehensive assessment of the system of geographical distribution and an assessment of the issues relating to possible changes in the number of posts subject to the system of geographical distribution, bearing in mind Article 101 of the Charter and the efficiency and effectiveness of the Organization;

3. *Reiterates its request* to the Secretary-General, contained in section IV, paragraph 8, of resolution 55/258, to develop a programme and set specific targets as soon as possible for achieving equitable geographical representation for all unrepresented and underrepresented Member States, bearing in mind the need to increase the number of staff recruited from Member States below the mid-point of their desirable ranges;

4. *Notes with concern* the possibility of an increase in the number of unrepresented and underrepresented Member States within the Secretariat, according to the statistics provided by the Secretariat on the number of retirees for the period from 2003 to 2007;

5. *Requests* the Secretary-General to make efforts to avoid the increase of the number of underrepresented Member States, by paying due attention to equitable geographical distribution in the recruitment and selection process, bearing in mind the large number of retirees projected;

6. *Reaffirms its request* to the Secretary-General not to decrease the proportion of entry-level posts at the P-1 to P-3 levels for budgetary purposes;

7. *Requests* the Secretary-General to include, for informational purposes, in the future report on the composition of the Secretariat statistics on the composition of the General Service and related staff, national staff and project personnel, including, inter alia, nationality, gender and level;

X
Staff-management consultations

Reiterates its request, contained in section XI, paragraph 4, of resolution 53/221, that the Secretary-General take into account the views of staff representatives, in accordance with article VIII of the Staff Regulations and Rules and resolution 35/213 of 17 December 1980;

XI
Amendments to Staff Rules

Takes note of the reports of the Secretary-General.

On 23 December, the Assembly deferred until its resumed fifty-eighth (2004) session consideration of the agenda item on human resources management (**decision 58/564 A**).

Pay and benefits system

ICSC, in its ongoing review of the UN pay and benefits system, endorsed the new conceptual model for reforming the job evaluation system, developed in 2002 [YUN 2002, p. 1404]. Validation exercises to assess its viability provided feedback, particularly on the use of language in the application of the Master Standard and grade level descriptors—the two evaluation tools around which the new model was designed. The model was then revised, in terms of language, design and utility, and a new release of the automated system developed. The new job evaluation system, comprising the Master Standard, grade level descriptors and post illustrators in automated format, was sent to all common system organizations in June and a draft handbook with guidelines was developed. Workshops and management briefings were scheduled to take place between September 2003 and March 2004 to support the implementation of the new system.

The Commission delegated to its Chairman the authority to promulgate the system by 1 January 2004. It asked its secretariat to report annually on the implementation of the new standards in organizations, including information on the number of jobs that, on application of the new standard, were found to be undergraded or overgraded and the levels affected, and the impact of change on, and the difficulties encountered by, the organizations involved. Its secretariat should conduct a comprehensive assessment of the system after 18 to 24 months and submit to the Commission for review and approval any substantive design changes that might be required. The secretariat should also conduct, in consultation with common system organizations and staff representatives, further research on reforming the job evaluation system for the General Service and related categories, and report to the Commission.

Regarding broadbanding/performance pay, under which grades would be grouped into broad salary bands that excluded steps between the minimum and maximum pay within particular bands, ICSC selected three models to be tested in a pilot study. It requested its Chairman to recruit a full-time project manager, subject to the availability of resources, and decided that a task force should be established, led by its secretariat, to further develop reform concepts. A comprehensive project plan should also be developed to guide the preparation for and conduct of the pilot study. The Commission requested its secretariat, in consultation with administration and staff representatives, to present proposals on the conduct of the pilot study.

Contractual arrangements

In accordance with General Assembly resolution 57/285 [YUN 2002, p. 1397], ICSC considered the issue of contractual arrangements, one of the core elements identified in the integrated framework for human resources management [YUN 2000, p. 1337]. It had before it an analysis of the experience of ILO, ITU, the Office of the United Nations High Commissioner for Refugees (UNHCR) and WHO, and proposals for developing a general framework within which organizations could operate, including three types of contractual arrangements that would be common to organizations of the common system.

ICSC agreed that there were too many types of contracts across organizations and that the number should be reduced. However, while considerable information was available on the current situation in common system organizations, more work was needed before a recommendation could be made to the Assembly. To facilitate that, and taking into account the need for flexibility in common system organizations, the Commission requested its secretariat to prepare, for consideration at its fifty-ninth (2004) session, a model contract for each of the three categories proposed, namely, continuing appointments, fixed-term appointments and temporary appointments, with subgroups in each category that would distinguish their key characteristics. The secretariat would also provide for each subgroup details on the conditions of employment; requirements for mobility and for a probationary period; procedures for progression to other contract types; the compensation package; social security and health insurance provisions; and procedures for extension and/or termination.

Mobility

In accordance with General Assembly resolution 55/258 [YUN 2001, p. 1337], ICSC continued its review of staff mobility. Based on information from common system organizations, the Commission examined various rationales for mobility, constraints and a framework for enhancing mobility in the common system. That framework identified areas where supportive programmes could be established to enhance internal or interorganizational mobility, including mobility from Headquarters to the field and vice versa, interagency mobility and mobility between common system organizations and other public or private organizations. Such supportive programmes would facilitate efficient mobility policies and could be developed in the areas of: career management; information technology support; development of a young professionals scheme; transparency of terms of contract; effective recruitment processes; development of induction and orientation programmes; promotion of external mobility; building a culture of mobility;

the role of the United Nations System Staff College (see p. 1456); review of promotions while on inter-agency assignments; amendment of inter-agency agreements; work/family agenda; knowledge management; and financial aspects.

Recognizing that mobility was a key element in the system's reform efforts, ICSC emphasized its importance as a means of developing a more versatile, multi-skilled and experienced international civil service capable of fulfilling complex mandates. It decided to approach staff mobility in a comprehensive manner, in harmony with contractual arrangements, conditions of employment, work/life agendas and spouse employment.

CEB action. The High-level Committee on Management (HLCM) of the United Nations System Chief Executives Board for Coordination (CEB), at its fifth session (New York, 12-13 June) [CEB/2003/3], considered a note by the CEB secretariat on a number of initiatives for enhancing mobility among agencies and perceived impediments to inter-agency mobility. HLCM invited the CEB secretariat to circulate a draft "vision" statement reflecting the UN system's ongoing commitment to inter-agency mobility and the need to develop solutions to its inherent impediments. It asked the secretariat to convene a working group to further examine mobility issues, to pursue its work on the participating agencies' mobility systems and its contacts with international organizations outside the UN system, and with the private sector, in order to boost spouse employment, and to list current provisions for the issuance of work permits for spouses or domestic partners. HLCM also agreed to: invite the human resources network to contribute to the working group's work on the harmonization of entitlements; encourage organizations to join the United Nations Development Group (UNDG) initiative on spouse employment; underline the importance of maintaining the current mobility and hardship scheme as a vital support to mobility in general; discourage duplication of effort in reviewing human resources–related problems and ask the human resources network to report thereon at its next session; request UN resident representatives to facilitate spouse or domestic partner employment; and forge a common approach for recognizing domestic partners.

Post structure

In response to General Assembly decision 57/574 [YUN 2002, p. 1405], the Secretary-General submitted an October report [A/58/398] in which he provided additional information regarding his 2002 comparative review of the UN Secretariat's post structure with that of other UN system organizations [YUN 2002, p. 1405]. He concluded that the comparative review did not reflect any top-heaviness of the UN Secretariat structure compared to those of common system organizations, which supported and further reinforced the findings contained in his 2002 report. He acknowledged, however, that the comparative review was subject to a number of critical constraints, including the fact that the validity of the exercise depended on the establishment of accurate grade equivalencies, which was a complex and sometimes controversial process. Moreover, organizations were different in size, structure and span of control, due to their functions or management philosophy or culture. Also, some organizations, particularly those outside the common system, and some Governments, considered data on grade structure to be sensitive and were reluctant to share such information.

ACABQ report. In October [A/58/7/Add.5], ACABQ, citing the constraints identified in the report, expressed concern that the Secretary-General was not in a position to obtain all the data needed for the purposes of the review.

The Assembly, in section II of **resolution 58/272** (see p. 1417), took note of the Secretary-General's report and the related ACABQ report.

Staff composition

In a December annual report on the UN Secretariat's staff composition [A/58/666], the Secretary-General updated information on the demographic characteristics of the Secretariat's staff and on the system of desirable ranges for geographical distribution. As at 30 June 2003, Secretariat staff numbered 15,082, 551 less than at 30 June 2002. Of the total, 5,525 were in the Professional and higher categories, 8,726 were in the General Service and related categories, and 831 were project personnel; 7,543 were paid from the regular budget and 7,539 from extrabudgetary sources. Staff in posts subject to geographical distribution numbered 2,491, of whom 1,040 (41.8 per cent) were female. Seventeen Member States were unrepresented in all staff categories, while 10 were underrepresented, compared to 16 and 11, respectively, in 2002. Appointments to posts subject to geographical distribution between 1 July 2002 and 30 June 2003 totalled 168. Of those, 34 (20.2 per cent) were nationals of underrepresented Member States, 105 (62.5 per cent) of within-range Member States, 26 (15.5 per cent) of overrepresented Member States, 2 (3.4 per cent) from a newly admitted Member State, and 1 was a stateless person. Changes in representation status resulted from appointments or separation from service, adjustments to desirable ranges, owing to an increase or decrease in the number of posts subject to geographical distribution, and to changes in the number of Member States, scale of assessments, population of Member States and status of individual staff members.

The report also gave information on the demographic profile of Secretariat staff, Secretariat staff movement between 1 July 2002 and 30 June 2003 and forecasts of anticipated retirements between 2003 and 2007.

As requested in Assembly **resolution 57/305** (see p. 1440), the report provided initial information on progress made by UN departments in implementing their human resources action plans, a management scheme established in 1999 throughout the Secretariat, under the central authority of OHRM and in accordance with Assembly resolution 53/221 [YUN 1999, p. 1324]. A pilot programme, launched in 1999-2001, enabled OHRM to develop and define the scope, criteria and tools to be used in those plans, and provided the Secretariat with valuable experience that was used to improve the methodology and tools for the second planning cycle, launched in 2001. In that cycle, covering a two-year period, additional indicators were introduced and progress reviews with departments were increased to two per year. Also, a variety of tools was created to assist departments in monitoring their progress throughout the planning cycle and in preparing for end-of-year assessment meetings between the head of OHRM and heads of departments. The biannual reviews allowed OHRM to provide more timely guidance and assistance to departments/offices in reaching their targets. In addition, new electronic tools were being developed to enable departments and offices to access human resources data online and improve departments' self-monitoring capacity. In 2003, OHRM completed the second planning cycle and began the third, with 26 departments and offices participating. The data and information gathered from the pilot programme and from the second cycle were being compiled and cross-evaluated in order to produce an analytical report at the Secretariat level, and would constitute the baseline for analysis and comparison in subsequent cycles. Comprehensive information on human resources action planning would be submitted to the Assembly at its fifty-ninth (2004) session.

Proportion of General Service to Professional staff in regional commissions

In response to General Assembly resolution 56/253 [YUN 2001, p. 1297], the Secretary-General, in an October report [A/58/403], reviewed the proportion of General Service staff compared to Professional staff in the Economic Commission for Africa (ECA), the Economic and Social Commission for Asia and the Pacific (ESCAP), the Economic Commission for Europe (ECE), the Economic Commission for Latin American and the Caribbean (ECLAC) and the Economic and Social Commission for Western Asia (ESCWA). Information was also gathered from the United Nations Conference on Trade and Development (UNCTAD) and the UN Department of Economic and Social Affairs (DESA) on the number of staff assigned to each function within the General Service and related categories for the 1998-1999, 2000-2001 and 2002-2003 bienniums. Each office or department also estimated resources applied towards technology and innovation to automate support activities during those periods, and which could impact the number of General Service staff assigned to support functions.

The review confirmed an overall higher ratio of General Service staff to Professional staff within four of the regional commissions than in UNCTAD and DESA, the exception being ECE. The situation had resulted from the broader coverage of services under the programme support component in the regional commissions, which, in addition to traditional support functions, included the management of technical cooperation programmes, conference and library services, security and safety and other services. Although investment in information technology could lead to improvements in the efficiency of support services, most regional commissions continued to rely heavily on their own staff for support services owing to limited outsourcing opportunities. Moreover, it was difficult to define an optimal post structure for any regional commission because each of them needed to be viewed as a separate entity to ensure that the requisite resources were available for implementation of mandated activities.

ACABQ report. In October [A/58/7/Add.5], ACABQ recommended that the information contained in the Secretary-General's report be considered in the context of the Assembly's review of the proposed resource requirements for the regional commissions for the 2004-2005 biennium.

The Assembly, in **resolution 58/272**, section XX (see p. 1420), took note of the Secretary-General's report and the related ACABQ report.

Recruitment, promotion and placement

On 15 April, the General Assembly, in **resolution 57/305**, section II (see p. 1440), reiterated the value of a transparent process of recruitment, placement and promotion in the Organization and requested the Secretary-General to ensure the accountability of programme managers in the staff selection process and to report thereon in 2004. On the same date, the Assembly, by **decision 57/556 B**, deferred until the second part of its resumed fifty-seventh (2003) session consideration of the OIOS report on the investigation of possible discrimination due to nationality, race, sex, religion and language in recruitment, promotion and placement and the comments of the Joint Inspection Unit (JIU) thereon [YUN 2002, p. 1406].

By **decision 58/564 A** of 23 December, the Assembly deferred consideration of the agenda item "Human resources management" and related documents to its resumed fifty-eighth (2004) session.

Gratis personnel

Report of Secretary-General. The Secretary-General, in February, submitted to the General Assembly his annual report [A/57/721] on the use of gratis personnel between 1 January and 31 December 2002. Type I gratis personnel serving under an established regime included interns, associate experts and technical cooperation experts obtained on non-refundable loans, while type II gratis personnel comprised personnel provided by a Government or other entity pursuant to Assembly resolution 51/243 [YUN 1997, p. 1469]. The Secretary-General reported that during 2002 the number of type I gratis personnel increased by 60.9 per cent, from 187 to 301. The increase was due mainly to a 108 per cent rise in the number of interns, from 68 to 142. Associate experts rose from 105 to 124 and technical cooperation experts from 14 to 35 during the year. The number of type II gratis personnel decreased from 3 to 1 by the end of 2002. The remaining individual was a hydrology expert, whose services were provided to ESCWA by Germany. He was expected to separate by 31 December 2003.

ACABQ report. In February [A/57/735], ACABQ, having considered the Secretary-General's report (above), noted that, in view of the steps taken, pursuant to General Assembly resolution 51/243, to phase out the number of gratis personnel, the Secretary-General should provide, on a biennial basis, information on their status within the context of his report on the composition of the Secretariat. Information on type I gratis personnel should be expanded to include nationality, duration and functions performed.

By **decision 57/556 B** of 15 April, the Assembly deferred until the second part of its resumed fifty-seventh (2003) session consideration of the Secretary-General's report on gratis personnel and the related ACABQ report.

GENERAL ASSEMBLY ACTION

On 18 June [meeting 90], the General Assembly, on the recommendation of the Fifth Committee [A/57/603/Add.1], adopted **resolution 57/281 B** without vote [agenda items 111 & 118].

Gratis personnel provided by Governments and other entities

The General Assembly,

Reaffirming its resolutions 51/243 of 15 September 1997, 52/234 of 26 June 1998, 53/11 of 26 October 1998, 53/218 of 7 April 1999 and 57/281 of 20 December 2002 and its decision 55/462 of 12 April 2001,

Having considered the annual report of the Secretary-General on gratis personnel provided by Governments and other entities, covering the period from 1 January to 31 December 2002, and the related report of the Advisory Committee on Administrative and Budgetary Questions,

1. *Takes note* of the annual report of the Secretary-General;
2. *Requests* the Secretary-General to provide in subsequent reports, on a biennial basis, information on the use of gratis personnel, indicating, inter alia, their nationality and duration of service, department where employed and functions performed.

Status of women

In a January report [E/CN.6/2003/8] to the Commission on the Status of Women, the Secretary-General provided a statistical update, as at 30 November 2002, of the gender distribution of staff, particularly at the Professional and higher levels, in the UN Secretariat and in organizations of the UN common system (see p. 1189).

In response to General Assembly resolution 57/180 [YUN 2002, p. 1411], the Secretary-General submitted a September report [A/58/374] on the status of women in the UN system. He noted that, as at 30 June 2003, the number of women in the Professional and higher categories with appointments subject to geographical distribution rose, from 1,022 (41 per cent) in 2002 to 1,041 (41.8 per cent). The 0.8 per cent rise was less than the approximately 1 percentage point annual average increase recorded yearly for the group since 1989. At senior policy-making levels (D-1 and above), the overall proportion of women decreased slightly from 33.7 per cent to 33.3 per cent. There were notable increases at the Under-Secretary-General (from 16.7 per cent to 20.8 per cent) and D-2 (from 29.4 per cent to 31.2 per cent) levels, no improvement at the Assistant Secretary-General level, which remained at 23.5 per cent, and a decrease at the D-1 level (from 37.8 to 36.3 per cent). At the P-1 to P-5 levels, where women comprised 43.1 per cent, gender balance was achieved only at the P-2 level (55.3 per cent). The proportion of women holding appointments of one year or more increased slightly from 35 per cent to

35.6 per cent (1,971 out of a total of 5,530 staff members).

The report concluded that, notwithstanding increases in the number of women in some categories of staff, the overall representation of women did not improve significantly during the reporting period. Additional steps to achieve the goal of 50/50 gender balance would include recruitment and retention efforts; establishing the goal of selecting women to 50 per cent or more of vacancies; increasing appointments at the senior and policy-making levels; and extending the ongoing training and sensitization of managers on gender balance issues.

GENERAL ASSEMBLY ACTION

On 22 December [meeting 77], the General Assembly, on the recommendation of the Third (Social, Humanitarian and Cultural) Committee [A/58/501], adopted **resolution 58/144** without vote [agenda item 110].

Improvement of the status of women in the United Nations system

The General Assembly,

Recalling Articles 1 and 101 of the Charter of the United Nations, as well as Article 8, which provides that the United Nations shall place no restrictions on the eligibility of men and women to participate in any capacity and under conditions of equality in its principal and subsidiary organs,

Recalling also the goal, contained in the Platform for Action adopted by the Fourth World Conference on Women, of achieving overall gender equality, particularly at the Professional level and above, by 2000 and the further actions and initiatives set out in the outcome document adopted by the General Assembly at its twenty-third special session, entitled "Women 2000: gender equality, development and peace for the twenty-first century",

Recalling further its resolution 57/180 of 18 December 2002, as well as its resolution 57/305 of 15 April 2003, in particular section II, paragraphs 39 to 41 thereof,

Taking note of Commission on Human Rights resolution 2003/44 of 23 April 2003 on integrating the human rights of women throughout the United Nations system, in particular paragraph 15 thereof, in which the Commission recognized that gender mainstreaming would strongly benefit from the enhanced and full participation of women, including at the higher levels of decision-making within the United Nations system,

Taking into account the continuing lack of representation or underrepresentation of women from certain countries, in particular from developing countries, including least developed countries and small island developing States, from countries with economies in transition and from unrepresented or largely underrepresented Member States,

Noting with appreciation the efforts of the Office of Programme Planning, Budget and Accounts, the Office of Human Resources Management, the Department of Public Information, the Office of the Under-Secretary-General for Management and the Executive Office of the Secretary-General and the United Nations Institute for Training and Research in achieving or maintaining the goal of gender balance, as well as those departments and offices that have met or exceeded the goal of 50 per cent in the selection of women candidates for vacant posts in the past year,

Expressing particular concern that, for the second consecutive year, there was a slowing of progress towards achieving the target of 50/50 gender balance and that between 1998 and 2003 there has been almost no progress in the rate of representation of women in appointments of one year or more at the Professional and higher levels,

Expressing concern that there is still only one female special representative of the Secretary-General,

Welcoming the work of the Department of Peacekeeping Operations of the Secretariat in issuing guidance for field missions on the procedures to be followed for handling disciplinary issues and allegations of serious misconduct involving mission personnel, and encouraged by the agreement in the Staff-Management Coordination Committee that the procedure for dealing with all forms of sexual harassment will be reviewed and incorporated in a new administrative instruction covering all forms of harassment,

Welcoming also the new flexible working arrangements authorized in all departments and offices of the Secretariat,

Noting with concern that the statistics on the representation of women in some organizations of the United Nations system are not fully up to date,

1. *Takes note with appreciation* of the report of the Secretary-General and the actions described therein;

2. *Regrets* that the goal of 50/50 gender distribution was not met by the end of 2000, and urges the Secretary-General to redouble his efforts to realize significant progress towards this goal in the very near future;

3. *Reaffirms* the urgent goal of achieving 50/50 gender distribution in all categories of posts within the United Nations system, especially at senior and policy-making levels, with full respect for the principle of equitable geographical distribution, in conformity with Article 101, paragraph 3, of the Charter of the United Nations, and also taking into account the continuing lack of representation or underrepresentation of women from certain countries, in particular from developing countries, from countries with economies in transition and from unrepresented or largely underrepresented Member States;

4. *Expresses concern* that in three departments and offices of the Secretariat women still account for less than 30 per cent of professional staff and that in three organizations of the United Nations system women still account for less than 20 per cent of professional staff, and encourages the Secretary-General and the executive heads of the organizations of the United Nations system to intensify their efforts to meet the goal of gender balance within the United Nations system;

5. *Welcomes*:

(a) The ongoing personal commitment of the Secretary-General to meeting the goal of gender equality and his assurance that gender balance will be given the highest priority in his continuing efforts to bring about a new management culture in the Organization;

(b) The pledge of the executive heads of the organizations of the United Nations system to intensify their efforts to meet the gender equality goals set out in the Beijing Declaration and Platform for Action;

(c) The inclusion of the objective of improving gender balance in action plans on human resources management for individual departments and offices, and encourages further cooperation, including the sharing of best-practice initiatives, between heads of departments and offices, the Special Adviser on Gender Issues and Advancement of Women and the Office of Human Resources Management of the Secretariat in the implementation of those plans, which include specific targets and strategies for improving the representation of women in individual departments and offices;

(d) The decision, within the context of the new staff selection system, to hold heads of departments and offices accountable for meeting the gender targets in departmental human resource action plans through their performance compacts;

(e) The continuing designation of focal points for women in the United Nations system, and requests the Secretary-General to ensure that the focal points are designated at a sufficiently high level and enjoy full access to senior management, both at Headquarters and in the field;

(f) The continuing provision of specific training programmes on gender mainstreaming and gender issues in the workplace, tailored to meet the special needs of individual departments, commends those heads of departments and offices who have launched gender training for their managers and staff, and strongly encourages those who have not yet organized such training to do so as soon as possible;

(g) The formulation of a project by the Office of the Under-Secretary-General for Management to strengthen the efforts of the Secretary-General to achieve gender balance by adopting a more coordinated and integrated approach to this issue, with the purpose of setting and achieving verifiable goals to ensure that gender balance targets are attained by 2006;

(h) The preparation of a research-based analysis by the Office of the Special Adviser on Gender Issues and Advancement of Women, to be presented to the General Assembly at its fifty-ninth session, of the probable causes of the slow advancement in the improvement of the status of women in the United Nations system, with a view to elaborating new strategies for achieving gender parity;

(i) The commitment of the Office of Human Resources Management and the Office of the Special Adviser on Gender Issues and Advancement of Women to explore ways to better integrate the departmental focal points in the new staffing system, so that the focal points can continue to play an important role for the periodic and systematic monitoring of the recruitment, retention and career advancement of women, and looks forward to information on this matter in the next report;

6. *Requests* the Secretary-General, in order to achieve and maintain the goal of 50/50 gender distribution with full respect for the principle of equitable geographical distribution, in conformity with Article 101, paragraph 3, of the Charter:

(a) To continue to develop innovative recruitment strategies to identify and attract suitably qualified women candidates, particularly from and in developing countries and countries with economies in transition and other Member States that are unrepresented or underrepresented in the Secretariat, and in occupations in which women are underrepresented;

(b) To encourage the United Nations system and its agencies and departments to make more effective use of existing information technology resources and systems and other established methods to disseminate information about employment opportunities for women and to better coordinate rosters of potential women candidates;

(c) To continue to monitor closely the progress made by departments and offices in meeting the goal of gender balance, to ensure that the appointment and promotion of suitably qualified women represents at least 50 per cent of all appointments and promotions until the goal of 50/50 gender distribution is met;

(d) To strongly encourage heads of departments and offices to continue selecting female candidates when their qualifications are the same as, or better than, those of male candidates, and to effectively encourage, monitor and assess the performance of managers in meeting targets for improving women's representation;

(e) To encourage consultation by heads of departments and offices with departmental focal points on women during the selection process and to ensure that the focal points are designated at a sufficiently high level and enjoy full and effective access to senior management;

(f) To extend ongoing training and sensitization of managers on gender balance issues;

(g) To enable the Office of the Special Adviser on Gender Issues and Advancement of Women to effectively contribute to, monitor and facilitate the setting and implementation of gender targets in human resource action plans, including by ensuring access to the information required to carry out that work;

(h) To intensify his efforts to create, within existing resources, a gender-sensitive work environment supportive of the needs of his staff, both women and men, including by actively pursuing appropriate work/life policies, such as flexible working time, flexible workplace arrangements, career development, mentoring programmes and childcare and elder-care needs, as well as through the provision of more comprehensive information to prospective candidates and new recruits on employment opportunities for spouses, the provision of support for the activities of women's networks and organizations within the United Nations system and the expansion of gender-sensitivity training in all departments, offices and duty stations, including more information and training of staff and managers on the benefits of the work/life policies on productivity and effectiveness;

(i) To continue to work to strengthen further the policy against harassment, including sexual harassment, by, inter alia, ensuring the full implementation of the guidelines for its application at Headquarters and in the field;

7. *Strongly encourages* the Secretary-General, in the context of his commitment to set concrete targets for the appointment of women as his special representatives and special envoys in order to reach the target of 50/50 gender balance by 2015, to intensify his efforts to appoint more women as special representatives and envoys to pursue good offices on his behalf, especially in matters related to peacekeeping, peace-building, preventive diplomacy and economic and social development, as well as in operational activities, including appointment as resident coordinators, and to appoint more women to other high-level positions;

8. *Encourages* the Secretary-General and the executive heads of the organizations of the United Nations system to continue to develop common approaches for retaining women, promoting inter-agency mobility and improving career development opportunities;

9. *Encourages* the United Nations and Member States to continue to implement the outcome of the twenty-third special session of the General Assembly, entitled "Women 2000: gender equality, development and peace for the twenty-first century", pertaining to the improvement of the status of women in the United Nations system;

10. *Strongly encourages* Member States:

(a) To support the efforts of the United Nations and the specialized agencies, funds and programmes to achieve the goal of 50/50 gender distribution, especially at senior and policy-making levels, by identifying and regularly submitting more women candidates for appointment to positions in the United Nations system, by identifying and proposing national recruitment sources, including through the establishment of networks with professional organizations, that will assist the organizations of the United Nations system in identifying suitable women candidates, in particular from developing countries and countries with economies in transition, by creating awareness among their nationals, particularly women, of available vacancies throughout the United Nations system, and by encouraging more women to apply for positions within the Secretariat, the specialized agencies, funds and programmes and the regional commissions, including in areas in which women are underrepresented, such as peacekeeping, peace-building and other non-traditional areas;

(b) To identify women candidates for assignment to peacekeeping missions and to improve the representation of women in military and civilian police contingents;

(c) To identify and submit regularly more women candidates for appointment or election to intergovernmental, expert and treaty bodies;

(d) To identify and nominate more women candidates for appointment or election as judges or other senior officials in international courts and tribunals;

(e) To cooperate closely with the United Nations to facilitate spouse employment at all the major duty stations of the Secretariat and the organizations of the United Nations system;

11. *Requests* the Secretary-General to provide a verbal update to the Commission on the Status of Women at its forty-eighth session and to report to the General Assembly at its fifty-ninth session on the implementation of the present resolution, including by providing up-to-date statistics on the number and percentage of women in all organizational units and at all levels throughout the United Nations system, as well as gender-segregated attrition rates for all organizational units and at all levels, as well as on the implementation of departmental human resource action plans, in particular for the achievement of the gender targets;

12. *Requests* the United Nations and the specialized agencies, funds and programmes of the United Nations system, in order to facilitate the preparation of the above-mentioned report, to submit personnel data on all appointments, promotions and mobility as well as to collect and submit data in a timely fashion to measure accurately progress in achieving gender parity for staff.

Multilingualism

JIU report. By a June note [A/58/93], the Secretary-General transmitted to the General Assembly a report of the Joint Inspection Unit (JIU) on the implementation of multilingualism in the UN system. JIU noted that, although most organizations considered multilingualism as a corollary to their universal character and their governing bodies had insisted on the strict application of rules establishing language parity, many meetings attended by Member States continued to be held without interpretation or documents available in all prescribed languages. Such a situation might contribute to the marginalization of some linguistic groups, particularly from developing countries, by not allowing them to contribute on an equal basis to the outcomes of those meetings.

JIU made a number of recommendations for improving the situation, including the holding of a review by common system organizations and legislative bodies to clarify the status of the different languages used in their organization so as to provide further guidance. Executive heads should submit in their budget proposals predefined objectives for improved multilingualism and expected results from phased priorities. They should also indicate the languages in which planned publications would be issued and languages in which information materials would be posted on different web sites.

Report of Secretary-General. In response to General Assembly resolution 56/262 [YUN 2002, p. 1413], the Secretary-General submitted a September report on activities to implement the Assembly's resolution on multilingualism [A/58/363]. He provided information on issues relating to the Secretariat's working languages, the use of languages in meetings and public information, and provided statistical updates on, and a detailed survey of, the language capacities of UN web sites. The Secretary-General observed that the greatest obstacle to multilingualism in outputs was the shortage of resources; while consistent funding was available for translating parliamentary documents into the six official languages, the same was not true for publications. Meanwhile, the maintenance of web sites in various languages was being largely accomplished within existing resources. Departments were therefore preparing their sites in the official languages selectively, in terms of both the materials and the languages covered. The Secretary-General outlined steps to facilitate the further development of competence in the six official languages among Secretariat staff, including training programmes. Secretariat departments were encouraged to identify clearly in their budget submissions the resources required to ensure production of outputs (other than official documents) in the six official languages and in relevant non-official languages, as applicable.

Staff rules and regulations

In accordance with staff regulation 12.3 stipulating that the full text of provisional staff rules and amendments should be reported annually to the General Assembly, the Secretary-General, in August [A/58/283], outlined amendments to the 100 and 200 series of Staff Rules, together with the rationale for the changes. Amendments to the 100 series related to education grant travel, re-employment, permanent appointments, home leave and appeals, while amendments under the 200 series related to education grant and types of appointment and re-employment.

The Secretary-General recommended that the Assembly take note of the amendments in the annex to the report, which he proposed to implement as from 1 January 2004.

Safety and security

Attack on UN offices in Baghdad. On 19 August, the UN headquarters in Baghdad, Iraq, was subjected to a terrorist attack that resulted in the death of 22 persons, including the Secretary-General's Special Representative for Iraq, Sergio Vieira de Mello, and the wounding of more than 150 (see also p. 346). On 20 August, the Security Council President made statement **S/PRST/2003/13** on behalf of the Council, in which members condemned the attack (see p. 347).

GENERAL ASSEMBLY ACTION

On 15 September [meeting 94], the General Assembly adopted **resolution 57/338** [draft: A/57/L.83/Rev.1] without vote [agenda item 10].

Condemnation of the attack on United Nations personnel and premises in Baghdad

The General Assembly,

Guided by the purposes and principles of the Charter of the United Nations,

Recognizing the selfless commitment of the United Nations staff members who serve the ideals of the United Nations around the world,

1. *Strongly condemns* the atrocious and deliberate attack on the United Nations Office in Baghdad on 19 August 2003, which killed fifteen United Nations staff members, the largest number ever in one incident, and seven others, and wounded more than one hundred persons;

2. *Pays special tribute* to Sergio Vieira de Mello, the United Nations High Commissioner for Human Rights and Special Representative of the Secretary-General for Iraq, and his colleagues who perished in this senseless tragedy;

3. *Expresses its condolences* to all the families and loved ones of those who lost their lives;

4. *Urgently calls* for international cooperation to find and bring to justice the perpetrators, organizers and sponsors of this vicious act;

5. *Calls* for intensified international cooperation to prevent and eradicate such acts of terrorism and to hold accountable all those who participate in such acts;

6. *Reaffirms* the determination of the United Nations to assist the Iraqi people to build peace and justice in their country and to determine their own political future by themselves, and welcomes in this regard the determination of the Organization to continue its operation in Iraq to fulfil its mandate in the service of the Iraqi people and not to be intimidated by such attacks.

Report of Secretary-General. In response to General Assembly resolution 57/155 [YUN 2002, p. 1414], the Secretary-General, in a September report [A/58/344], updated information on threats against the safety and security of UN personnel between 1 July 2002 and 30 June 2003. He stated that UN personnel continued to face significant security threats in all regions. Apart from deaths resulting from illness or vehicle and aircraft accidents, 196 UN civilian staff members had been killed since 1992, excluding uniformed peacekeepers and losses resulting from the 19 August attack in Baghdad (see above). During the reporting period, five staff members were killed and seven incidents of hostage-taking and kidnapping occurred, involving 14 UN personnel in the Democratic Republic of the Congo (DRC), Georgia, Nigeria, Pakistan and Somalia. More than 258 incidents of assault were reported, including 69 in Afghanistan, 30 in Israel and the Occupied Palestinian Territory, and 53 in the Kosovo province of Serbia and Montenegro. Also reported were at least 168 incidents of staff harassment, some 270 violent attacks against related compounds and convoys, and 550 incidents of theft of office equipment, official vehicles and staff property. The number of staff arrested, detained or missing, and regarding whom the Organization had been unable to exercise fully its right to protection, declined slightly from the previous reporting period, from 39 to 34 cases. The report described efforts to further improve the current security management system towards strengthening staff security and safety at Headquarters and in the field, including measures relating to accountability, minimum operating security standards, security training programmes, stress management and security collaboration between the United Nations and NGOs. The Secretary-General observed that, while many factors beyond the Organization's control would continue to influence the level of threats and risk faced by UN personnel, the fact that fatality had decreased markedly over the past years gave cause for optimism that ongoing efforts to strengthen the security management system were on the right track. He stated that all aspects of the system had been evaluated and that the findings, currently being reviewed, would be reported in due course.

Security Council action. The Security Council, on 26 August, adopted **resolution 1502(2003)** condemning violence against UN and other humanitarian personnel (see p. 921).

CEB action. CEB, in its annual overview report for 2003 [E/2004/67], noted that a main concern of the system during the period under review was to ensure that urgent measures were taken to strengthen system-wide security policies and infrastructure in the aftermath of the tragic events in Baghdad (see p. 1452). The findings and recommendations of independent panels commissioned by the Secretary-General, as well as internal reviews, had all confirmed the need for such measures. CEB endorsed and/or agreed to reinforce a number of system-wide initiatives covering issues relating to risk and threat assessments, UN premises, accommodation and movement control, and other related issues, including security at headquarters locations, accountability, security for women, air travel safety and consideration of the institution of United Nations Guard Contingents to provide staff security in high-risk areas. During 2003, CEB continued to monitor the development of emergency preparedness plans by common system organizations and knowledge-sharing among them. A comprehensive review of progress in that regard was planned for 2004.

GENERAL ASSEMBLY ACTION

On 17 December [meeting 75], the General Assembly adopted **resolution 58/122** [draft: A/58/L.47 & Add.1] without vote [agenda item 40].

Safety and security of humanitarian personnel and protection of United Nations personnel

The General Assembly,

Reaffirming its resolution 46/182 of 19 December 1991 on strengthening of the coordination of humanitarian emergency assistance of the United Nations,

Recalling its resolutions 53/87 of 7 December 1998, 54/192 of 17 December 1999, 55/175 of 19 December 2000, 56/217 of 21 December 2001 and 57/155 of 16 December 2002 on safety and security of humanitarian personnel and protection of United Nations personnel, as well as resolutions 52/167 of 16 December 1997 on safety and security of humanitarian personnel and 52/126 of 12 December 1997 on protection of United Nations personnel, and Economic and Social Council resolution 2003/5 of 15 July 2003,

Welcoming the adoption by the Security Council of resolution 1502(2003) of 26 August 2003 on the safety and security of humanitarian personnel and United Nations and its associated personnel,

Taking note of the reports of the Secretary-General on the protection of civilians in armed conflict and of Security Council resolutions 1265(1999) of 17 September 1999 and 1296(2000) of 19 April 2000 and the recommendations made therein, as well as the statements by the President of the Council of 30 November 1999, on the role of the Council in the prevention of armed conflicts, 13 January 2000, on humanitarian assistance to refugees in Africa, 9 February 2000, on protection of United Nations personnel, its associated personnel and humanitarian personnel in conflict zones, 9 March 2000, on humanitarian aspects of issues before the Council, and 15 March 2002, on the aide-memoire for the consideration of issues pertaining to the protection of civilians in armed conflict, and noting in that context the range of views expressed during all open debates of the Council on these issues,

Reaffirming the need to promote and ensure respect for the principles and rules of international humanitarian law,

Concerned by the increasingly difficult context in which humanitarian assistance takes place in some areas, in particular the continuous erosion, in many cases, of respect for the principles and rules of international humanitarian law,

Deeply concerned by the dangers and security risks faced by humanitarian personnel and United Nations and its associated personnel at the field level, and mindful of the need to improve the current security management system in order to improve their safety and security,

Gravely concerned at the acts of violence in many parts of the world against humanitarian personnel and United Nations and its associated personnel, in particular deliberate attacks, which are in violation of international humanitarian law as well as other international law that may be applicable,

Expressing profound regret at the deaths of all international and national humanitarian personnel and United Nations and its associated personnel who were involved in the provision of humanitarian assistance, and strongly deploring the rising toll of casualties among such personnel in complex humanitarian emergencies, in particular in armed conflicts and in post-conflict situations,

Commending the courage and commitment of those who take part, often at great personal risk, in humanitarian operations, especially of locally recruited staff,

Strongly condemning acts of murder and other forms of violence, rape and sexual assault, intimidation, armed robbery, abduction, hostage-taking, kidnapping, harassment and illegal arrest and detention to which those participating in humanitarian operations are increasingly exposed, as well as attacks on humanitarian convoys and acts of destruction and looting of their property,

Emphasizing that there are existing prohibitions under international law against attacks knowingly and intentionally directed against personnel involved in a humanitarian assistance or peacekeeping mission undertaken in accordance with the Charter of the United Nations, which in situations of armed conflicts constitute war crimes,

Recalling the inclusion of attacks intentionally directed against personnel involved in a humanitarian assistance or peacekeeping mission in accordance with the Charter as a war crime in the Rome Statute of the International Criminal Court, which entered into force on 1 July 2002, and noting the role that the Court could play in appropriate cases in bringing to justice those responsible for serious violations of international humanitarian law,

Expressing concern that the occurrence of attacks and threats against humanitarian personnel and United Nations and its associated personnel is a factor that increasingly restricts the ability of the Organization to provide assistance and protection to civilians in fulfilment of its mandate under the Charter,

Recalling that primary responsibility under international law for the security and protection of humanitarian personnel and United Nations and its associated personnel lies with the Government hosting a United Nations operation conducted under the Charter or its agreements with relevant organizations,

Urging all other parties involved in armed conflicts, in compliance with international humanitarian law, in particular their obligations under the Geneva Conventions of 12 August 1949 and the obligations applicable to them under the Additional Protocols thereto, of 8 June 1977, to ensure the security and protection of all humanitarian personnel and United Nations and its associated personnel,

Bearing in mind that reaching the vulnerable is essential for providing adequate protection and assistance in the context of natural disasters and complex emergencies as well as for strengthening local capacity to cope with humanitarian needs in such contexts,

Welcoming the fact that the Convention on the Safety of United Nations and Associated Personnel, which entered into force on 15 January 1999, has been ratified or acceded to by sixty-nine States as at the present date, and mindful of the need to promote universality of the Convention,

Reaffirming the need to ensure adequate levels of safety and security for United Nations personnel and humanitarian personnel and a culture of accountability at all levels,

Reaffirming also that ensuring the safety and security of United Nations personnel constitutes an underlying duty of the Organization, which must be based on a necessary cost-sharing arrangement with the relevant agencies, funds and programmes within the United Nations system,

Guided by the relevant provisions on protection contained in the Convention on the Privileges and Immunities of the United Nations of 13 February 1946, the Convention on the Privileges and Immunities of the Specialized Agencies of 21 November 1947, the Convention on the Safety of United Nations and Associated Personnel, the Geneva Convention relative to the Protection of Civilian Persons in Time of War of 12 August 1949 and the Additional Protocols to the Geneva Conventions, and Amended Protocol II of 3 May 1996 to the Convention on Prohibitions or Restrictions on the Use of Certain Conventional Weapons Which May Be Deemed to Be Excessively Injurious or to Have Indiscriminate Effects of 10 October 1980,

1. *Welcomes* the report of the Secretary-General, while noting that it does not cover developments after 30 June 2003;

2. *Urges* all States to take the necessary measures to ensure the full and effective implementation of the relevant principles and rules of international law, including international humanitarian law, as well as the relevant provisions of human rights and refugee law related to the safety and security of humanitarian personnel and United Nations personnel;

3. *Also urges* all States to take the necessary measures to ensure the safety and security of humanitarian personnel and United Nations and its associated personnel and to respect and ensure respect for the inviolability of United Nations premises, which are essential to the continuation and successful implementation of United Nations operations;

4. *Calls upon* all other parties involved in armed conflicts, in compliance with international humanitarian law, in particular their obligations under the 1949 Geneva Conventions and the obligations applicable to them under the Additional Protocols thereto, to ensure the safety and protection of humanitarian personnel and United Nations and its associated personnel, to refrain from abducting or detaining them in violation of their immunity under relevant conventions referred to in the present resolution and applicable international humanitarian law, and speedily to release, without harm, any abductee or detainee;

5. *Calls upon* all Governments and parties in complex humanitarian emergencies, in particular in armed conflicts and in post-conflict situations, in countries in which humanitarian personnel are operating, in conformity with the relevant provisions of international law and national laws, to cooperate fully with the United Nations and other humanitarian agencies and organizations and to ensure the safe and unhindered access of humanitarian personnel in order to allow them to perform efficiently their task of assisting the affected civilian population, including refugees and internally displaced persons;

6. *Strongly condemns* any act or failure to act, contrary to international law, which obstructs or prevents humanitarian personnel and United Nations personnel from discharging their humanitarian functions, or which entails being subjected to threats, the use of force or physical attack, frequently resulting in injury or death, and affirms the need to hold accountable those who commit such acts and, for that purpose, the need to enact national legislation, as appropriate;

7. *Expresses deep concern* that, over the past decade, threats against the safety and security of humanitarian personnel and United Nations and its associated personnel have escalated at an unprecedented rate and that perpetrators of acts of violence seemingly operate with impunity;

8. *Strongly urges* all States to take stronger actions to ensure that any threat or act of violence committed against humanitarian personnel and United Nations and its associated personnel on their territory is investigated fully and to ensure that the perpetrators of such acts are brought to justice in accordance with international law and national law, and notes the need for States to end impunity for such acts;

9. *Calls upon* all States to consider becoming parties to and to respect fully their obligations under the relevant international instruments, in particular the Convention on the Safety of United Nations and Associated Personnel;

10. *Also calls upon* all States to consider becoming parties to the Rome Statute of the International Criminal Court;

11. *Further calls upon* all States to consider becoming parties to and to respect fully their obligations under the Convention on the Privileges and Immunities of the United Nations and the Convention on the Privileges and Immunities of the Specialized Agencies, which have been ratified so far by one hundred and forty-eight States and one hundred and eight States, respectively;

12. *Calls upon* all States to provide adequate and prompt information in the event of the arrest or detention of humanitarian personnel or United Nations and its associated personnel, to afford them the necessary medical assistance and to allow independent medical teams to visit and examine the health of those detained, and urges them to take the necessary measures to ensure the speedy release of United Nations and other personnel carrying out activities in fulfilment of the mandate of a United Nations operation who have been arrested or detained in violation of their immunity, in accordance with the relevant conventions referred to in the present resolution and applicable international humanitarian law;

13. *Reaffirms* the obligation of all humanitarian personnel and United Nations and its associated personnel to observe and respect the national laws of the country in which they are operating, in accordance with international law and the Charter of the United Nations;

14. *Requests* the Secretary-General to take the necessary measures to ensure full respect for the human rights, privileges and immunities of United Nations and other personnel carrying out activities in fulfilment of the mandate of a United Nations operation, and to continue to consider ways and means to strengthen the protection of United Nations and other personnel carrying out activities in fulfilment of the mandate of a United Nations operation, notably by seeking the inclusion, in negotiations of headquarters and other mission agreements concerning United Nations and its associated personnel, of the applicable conditions contained in the Convention on the Privileges and Immunities of the United Nations, the Convention on the Privileges and Immunities of the Specialized Agencies and the Convention on the Safety of United Nations and Associated Personnel;

15. *Recommends* that the Secretary-General continue to seek the inclusion of, and that host countries include, key provisions of the Convention on the Safety of United Nations and Associated Personnel, among others, those regarding the prevention of attacks against members of the operation, the establishment of such attacks as crimes punishable by law and the prosecution or extradition of offenders, in future as well as, if necessary, in existing status-of-forces, status-of-mission and host country agreements negotiated between the United Nations and those countries, mindful of the importance of the timely conclusion of such agreements;

16. *Takes note with appreciation* of the work being done by the Ad Hoc Committee established in accordance with resolution 56/89 of 12 December 2001, which will be reconvened in accordance with resolution 58/82 of 9 December 2003, with a mandate to expand the scope of legal protection under the Convention on the Safety of United Nations and Associated Personnel, including by means of a legal instrument;

17. *Welcomes* the ongoing initiatives undertaken by the Secretary-General following the publication of the report of the Independent Panel on the Safety and Security of United Nations Personnel in Iraq headed by Martti Ahtisaari, and requests the Secretary-General to continue his efforts in this regard as a matter of the highest priority, and to inform the General Assembly accordingly;

18. *Requests* the Secretary-General to take the necessary measures to ensure that United Nations and other personnel carrying out activities in fulfilment of the mandate of a United Nations operation are properly informed about the conditions under which they are called upon to operate, including relevant customs and traditions in the host country, and the standards that they are required to meet, including those contained in relevant domestic and international law, and that adequate training in security, human rights and international humanitarian law is provided so as to enhance their security and effectiveness in accomplishing their functions, and reaffirms the necessity for all other humanitarian organizations to provide their personnel with similar support;

19. *Also requests* the Secretary-General to take the necessary measures to ensure that United Nations and other personnel carrying out activities in fulfilment of the mandate of a United Nations humanitarian assistance operation are properly informed about and operate in conformity with the minimum operating security standards and relevant codes of conduct;

20. *Further requests* the Secretary-General to take the necessary measures, falling within his responsibilities, to promote and enhance the security consciousness within the organizational culture of the Secretariat and the United Nations agencies, funds and programmes, including by disseminating and enhancing the security procedures and regulations, to create awareness and consciousness by the United Nations personnel of those procedures and regulations and the need to follow them, and to ensure that security matters are an integral part of the planning for existing and newly mandated United Nations operations and that such precautions extend to all United Nations and its associated personnel;

21. *Welcomes* the ongoing efforts of the Secretary-General to further enhance the security management system of the United Nations, and in this regard invites the United Nations and other humanitarian organizations to strengthen the analysis of threats to their safety and security in order to minimize security risks and to facilitate informed decisions on the maintenance of an

effective presence in the field, inter alia, to fulfil their humanitarian mandate;

22. *Emphasizes* the need to give further consideration to the safety and security of locally recruited humanitarian personnel, who account for the majority of casualties;

23. *Also emphasizes* the importance of paying special attention to the safety and security of United Nations and its associated personnel engaged in United Nations peacekeeping and peace-building operations;

24. *Stresses* the need to ensure that all United Nations staff members receive adequate security training, including physical and psychological training, prior to their deployment to the field, the need to attach a high priority to the improvement of stress and trauma counselling services available to United Nations staff members, including through the implementation of a comprehensive security and stress and trauma management training, support and assistance programme for United Nations staff throughout the system, before, during and after missions, and the need to make available to the Secretary-General the means for that purpose;

25. *Recognizes* the need for a strengthened and unified security management system for the United Nations, both at the headquarters and the field levels, and requests the United Nations system, as well as Member States, to take all appropriate measures to that end;

26. *Requests* the Office of the United Nations Security Coordinator to continue to play a central role in promoting increased cooperation and collaboration among agencies, funds and programmes in the planning and implementation of measures aimed at improving staff security training and awareness and in strengthening the Inter-Agency Security Management Network, and calls upon all relevant United Nations agencies, funds and programmes to support these efforts;

27. *Recognizes* the need for enhanced coordination and cooperation, both at the headquarters and the field levels, between the United Nations security management system and non-governmental organizations on matters relating to the safety and security of humanitarian personnel and United Nations and its associated personnel, with a view to addressing mutual security concerns in the field;

28. *Underlines* the need to allocate adequate and predictable resources to the safety and security of United Nations personnel, including through the Consolidated Appeals Process, and encourages all States to contribute to the Trust Fund for Security of Staff Members of the United Nations System;

29. *Recalls* the essential role of telecommunication resources in facilitating the safety of humanitarian personnel and United Nations and its associated personnel, calls upon States to consider acceding to or ratifying the Tampere Convention on the Provision of Telecommunication Resources for Disaster Mitigation and Relief Operations of 18 June 1998, and encourages them to facilitate and expedite, consistent with their national laws and regulations, the use of communications equipment in such operations, and emphasizes the importance of States facilitating communications, inter alia, through limiting and, whenever possible, lifting the restrictions placed on the use of communications equipment by United Nations and its associated personnel;

30. *Requests* the Secretary-General to submit to the General Assembly at its fifty-ninth session a comprehensive and updated report on the safety and security situation of humanitarian personnel and protection of United Nations personnel and on the implementation of the present resolution, including the progress made by the Secretary-General in pursuing accountability and assessing responsibility for all individual security incidents that involve United Nations and its associated personnel at all levels throughout the United Nations system, as well as an account of the measures taken by Governments and the United Nations to prevent and respond to such incidents.

In other action, the Assembly, in section VIII of **resolution 58/272** (see p. 1418), approved the gross budget for the Office of the United Nations Security Coordinator for the 2004-2005 biennium in the amount of $86,375,800.

Staff College

In accordance with General Assembly resolution 55/278 [YUN 2001, p. 1355], the Secretary-General, by an August note [A/58/305 & Corr.1], transmitted the first report of the Director of the United Nations System Staff College, covering the period from 1 January 2002, when its new statute, approved by Assembly resolution 55/278, came into force, to 30 June 2003. The report outlined the Staff College's objectives, set out its outputs, activities and projects, described its governance and structure, and outlined its future directions. In May 2003, a new Director was appointed.

In the 18 months covered by the report, the College organized and/or participated in 97 learning events in which 2,456 persons took part. The College also supported UN agencies and organizations with advice and a range of services in adult learning and training.

The report concluded that the College had made considerable progress as a distinct entity within the UN family, and had been supported in its work by Italy, the host country, with which it was to sign a formal host-country agreement. Additional support was provided by key common system organizations, programmes and entities, and by Member States.

GENERAL ASSEMBLY ACTION

On 23 December [meeting 78], the General Assembly, on the recommendation of the Second (Economic and Financial) Committee [A/58/489], adopted **resolution 58/224** without vote [agenda item 99(b)].

United Nations System Staff College in Turin, Italy

The General Assembly,

Recalling its resolutions 54/228 of 22 December 1999, 55/207 of 20 December 2000 and 55/258 of 14 June 2001,

Recalling also its resolution 55/278 of 7 August 2001, by which it approved the statute of the United Nations System Staff College,

Reaffirming the role of the Staff College as an institution for system-wide knowledge management, training and continuous learning for the staff of the United Nations system, in particular in the areas of economic and social development, peace and security and internal management,

1. *Takes note with appreciation* of the note by the Secretary-General and the accompanying report;
2. *Welcomes* the progress made by the United Nations System Staff College since the entry into force of its statute on 1 January 2002 in pursuing the objectives set forth therein;
3. *Calls upon* all organizations of the United Nations system to make full and effective use of the facilities of the Staff College;
4. *Invites* the Staff College, in developing and implementing its work programme, to focus, inter alia, on activities that can serve to maximize system-wide coherence and effectiveness in supporting the coordinated and integrated follow-up to the outcomes of conferences, including, in particular, the United Nations Millennium Declaration, and improving the delivery of services to Member States;
5. *Encourages* the Staff College to provide strategic leadership in order to increase operational effectiveness, promote inter-agency collaboration and strengthen management culture by its own example, including the development of new systems of performance management, flexible and collaborative work structures and cost-effective means of delivering services to clients and beneficiaries;
6. *Calls upon* relevant institutions of the United Nations, including the United Nations University, the United Nations Institute for Training and Research and the Staff College, to collaborate closely to those ends;
7. *Welcomes* the financial and other support extended by Member States to the work of the Staff College, and invites the international community to strengthen its support for the College through voluntary contributions, in accordance with article VII of the statute, to enable the College to consolidate its distinctive contribution to fostering a cohesive management culture across the United Nations system that is responsive to the requirements of Member States;
8. *Invites* the United Nations System Chief Executives Board for Coordination, in accordance with article X of the statute, to make a recommendation that the report of the Secretary-General submitted pursuant to article IV, paragraph 5, of the statute be submitted to the Economic and Social Council rather than to the General Assembly.

Joint Staff Pension Fund

As at 31 December 2003, the United Nations Joint Staff Pension Fund (UNJSPF) had 85,245 active participants compared to 82,715 at the end of 2002; the number of periodic payments in award increased from 51,028 to 52,496 over the year. The breakdown of the periodic benefits in award was 16,713 retirement benefits; 11,730 early retirement benefits; 6,575 deferred retirement benefits; 8,294 widows' and widowers' benefits; 8,221 children's benefits; 921 disability benefits; and 42 secondary dependants' benefits. In the course of the year, 12,978 full withdrawals and other settlements were paid.

The Fund was administered by the 33-member United Nations Joint Staff Pension Board (UNJSPB), which did not meet in 2003 because of the biennialization of the work of the Fifth Committee. Instead, the Board's Standing Committee met on its behalf (New York, 7-11 July) [A/58/214 & Corr.1] and discussed, among other subjects, matters relating to the Fund's administration and operation, revised budget estimates for the 2002-2003 biennium, budget estimates for the 2004-2005 biennium and the authorization for contributions to the Emergency Fund for 2004-2005.

ACABQ, commenting in November [A/58/7/Add.9] on the Standing Committee's report, recommended approval of revised estimates for administrative expenses of $80,278,200 for the 2002-2003 biennium and $94,685,200 for the 2004-2005 biennium. It also agreed with the Standing Committee's proposal to supplement voluntary contributions to the Emergency Fund by an amount not exceeding $200,000 for 2004-2005.

Those recommendations were approved by the General Assembly in **resolution 58/272**, section X, of 22 December (see p. 1418).

Pension Fund investments

The market value of UNJSPF assets as at 31 December 2003 was $26,084 million, an increase of $5,095 million from the previous year. The total investment return for 2003 was 24.8 per cent, which, after adjusting for inflation, represented a "real" rate of return of 22.5 per cent. Investment income for the 2002-2003 biennium from interest and dividends amounted to $1,539.4 million. New funds that became available for investment (contributions plus investment income, less benefit payment and administrative expenses) totalled $1,294.3 million for the biennium. The Fund's investment income during the 2002-2003 biennium amounted to $2.1 billion, comprising $1.6 billion in interest and dividends and $457 million in net profit on sales of investments. Investment management costs amounted to $41.7 million.

The Fund remained one of the most diversified pension funds in the world, with 51.9 per cent of its assets exposed to currencies other than the United States dollar, which was the Fund's unit of account.

OIOS audit

Pursuant to General Assembly resolutions 48/218 B [YUN 1994, p. 1362] and 54/244 [YUN 1999, p. 1274], the Secretary-General, in May [A/58/81], transmitted to the Assembly an OIOS audit of the Investment Management Service of UNJSPF, carried out between September 2001 and March 2002.

In its audit of the Service's investment management activities, OIOS identified weaknesses in the internal control system, inadequate procedures for documenting the investment process and a need to improve the efficiency and transparency of investment operations. Its audit of the Service's procurement and contract administration revealed a number of problems, including the absence of documented procedures, non-compliance with UN procurement policies, inadequate monitoring of vendor performance and insufficient tracking and monitoring of the procurement process and contract administration. OIOS made a series of recommendations to rectify those shortcomings.

The Secretary-General took note of the OIOS findings and concurred with the recommendations made in the report.

GENERAL ASSEMBLY ACTION

On 23 December [meeting 79], the General Assembly, on the recommendation of the Fifth Committee [A/58/571], adopted **resolution 58/279** without vote [agenda item 119].

Report of the Office of Internal Oversight Services on the audit of the Investment Management Service of the United Nations Joint Staff Pension Fund

The General Assembly,

Recalling its resolutions 48/218 B of 29 July 1994 and 54/244 of 23 December 1999,

Having considered the report of the Office of Internal Oversight Services on the audit of the Investment Management Service of the United Nations Joint Staff Pension Fund,

1. *Takes note* of the report of the Office of Internal Oversight Services on the audit of the Investment Management Service of the United Nations Joint Staff Pension Fund;

2. *Notes with concern* the findings of the Office of Internal Oversight Services on problem areas in the functioning, administration and accountability mechanisms of the Investment Management Service;

3. *Requests* the Secretary-General to ensure that all the recommendations of the Office of Internal Oversight Services contained in its report are fully and expeditiously implemented and to submit a report thereon to the General Assembly at its resumed fifty-eighth session.

Admission of the International Criminal Court

At the request of the Netherlands [A/58/234], the General Assembly, on 13 October [A/58/PV.28], on the recommendation of the General Committee [A/58/250/Add.1], included in the agenda of its fifty-eighth (2003) session an additional item entitled "Admission of the International Criminal Court to membership in the United Nations Joint Staff Pension Fund", and allocated it to the Fifth Committee for consideration.

Note by Secretary-General. On 29 October [A/C.5/58/13], the Secretary-General transmitted to the Fifth Committee a note by the UNJSPF Chief Executive Officer concerning the Court's application for membership. The note pointed out that the application met the requirements for admission to the Fund and that the UNJSPB Standing Committee, on behalf of the Pension Board, had recommended to the Assembly that the Court be admitted, effective 1 January 2004, subject to confirmation by the Fund's Secretary/Chief Executive Officer that it had aligned its conditions of service with those prevailing in the common system.

ACABQ report. On 31 October [A/58/545], ACABQ recommended that the Assembly approve the recommendation of the UNJSPB Standing Committee regarding the Court's application for membership in the Fund.

GENERAL ASSEMBLY ACTION

On 23 December [meeting 79], the General Assembly, on the recommendation of the Fifth Committee [A/58/590], adopted **resolution 58/262** without vote [agenda item 166].

Admission of the International Criminal Court to membership in the United Nations Joint Staff Pension Fund

The General Assembly,

Having considered the note by the Secretary-General on the admission of the International Criminal Court to membership in the United Nations Joint Staff Pension Fund and the related report of the Advisory Committee on Administrative and Budgetary Questions,

Decides to admit the International Criminal Court to membership in the United Nations Joint Staff Pension Fund, in accordance with article 3, paragraphs *(b)* and *(c)*, of the Regulations of the Fund, with effect from 1 January 2004.

Travel-related matters

By **decision 57/556 B** of 15 April, the General Assembly deferred until the second part of its resumed fifty-seventh (2003) session consideration of the Secretary-General's 2002 annual report on standards of accommodation for air travel [YUN 2002, p. 1422]. The Assembly, by **decision 57/589** of 18 June, took note of that report and the oral report of the Chairman of ACABQ thereon [A/C.5/57/SR.39], and requested the Secretary-General to

Administration of justice

The General Assembly, at its resumed fifty-seventh (2003) session, considered the Secretary-General's 2002 report on the administration of justice in the Secretariat [YUN 2002, p. 1423], the JIU report on the reform of the administration of justice in the UN system: options for higher recourse instances [ibid., p. 1424], the comments of the Secretary-General and those of CEB thereon [ibid.], the related ACABQ report [ibid., p. 1423] and the letter of the President of the United Nations Administrative Tribunal to the Chairman of the Fifth Committee [ibid., p. 1425].

GENERAL ASSEMBLY ACTION

On 15 April [meeting 83], the General Assembly, on the recommendation of the Fifth Committee [A/57/768], adopted **resolution 57/307** without vote [agenda item 123].

Administration of justice in the Secretariat

The General Assembly,

Recalling section XI of its resolution 55/258 of 14 June 2001,

Recognizing that a transparent, impartial and effective system of administration of justice is a necessary condition for ensuring fair and just treatment of United Nations staff, and important for the success of human resources reform in the Organization,

Having considered the report of the Secretary-General on the administration of justice in the Secretariat,

Having also considered the report of the Joint Inspection Unit entitled "Reform of the administration of justice in the United Nations system: options for higher recourse instances" and the comments of the Secretary-General and those of the United Nations System Chief Executives Board for Coordination thereon,

Having further considered the report of the Advisory Committee on Administrative and Budgetary Questions and the letter from the President of the United Nations Administrative Tribunal to the Chairman of the Fifth Committee,

Affirming the importance of continuing efforts to ensure that the administration of justice within the United Nations is of the highest standard,

Also affirming the importance of the United Nations as an exemplary employer,

1. *Stresses* the urgent need to ensure effective and expeditious administration of justice in the Organization, and requests the Secretary-General to ensure that the highest standards of efficiency, competence and integrity, as well as the principles of fairness and due process, serve as the paramount considerations in the system of administration of justice within the United Nations;

2. *Notes with concern* that the related reports were not introduced at its fifty-sixth session, as requested in its resolution 55/258, in addition to being issued late for consideration at its current session;

3. *Regrets* that the present system of administration of justice in the Secretariat continues to be slow, cumbersome and costly;

4. *Also regrets* the serious delays in the appeals process, and requests the Secretary-General to ensure full cooperation and accountability in the internal system of justice of the department or programme manager whose decision has been challenged by the appellant, at all stages of the process;

5. *Requests* the Secretary-General to take steps to ensure the independence of the United Nations Administrative Tribunal and the separation of its secretariat from the Office of Legal Affairs, to study the possibility of its financial independence and to report thereon to the General Assembly at its fifty-eighth session;

6. *Takes note* of the report of the Secretary-General on the administration of justice in the Secretariat, the report of the Joint Inspection Unit entitled "Reform of the administration of justice in the United Nations system: options for higher recourse instances" and the comments of the Secretary-General and those of the United Nations System Chief Executives Board for Coordination thereon and the report of the Advisory Committee on Administrative and Budgetary Questions;

7. *Endorses* the recommendation of the Advisory Committee contained in paragraph 8 of its report;

8. *Welcomes* the initiative taken by the Secretary-General in requesting the Office of Internal Oversight Services to conduct a management review of the appeals process, and in this regard concurs with the observations and recommendations contained in paragraphs 6 and 7 of the report of the Advisory Committee;

9. *Requests* the Secretary-General, taking due account also of the findings of the Office of Internal Oversight Services, to submit a report containing alternatives on strengthening the administration of justice by means of ensuring transparency and fairness in the provision of justice to staff of the Organization, for consideration by the General Assembly at its fifty-eighth session;

10. *Also requests* the Secretary-General to entrust the Office of Internal Oversight Services with the inclusion in its report of measures to shorten the period required for the disposal of cases, including imposing deadlines at all stages of the process;

11. *Further requests* the Secretary-General to ensure that the Office of Internal Oversight Services includes in its report not only the procedures and functions related to the Joint Appeals Board but also those related to the Panel of Counsel, the Administrative Law Unit and the secretariats of the Joint Appeals Board and the Joint Disciplinary Committee, as well as their impact on and contribution to the administration of justice;

12. *Welcomes* the establishment of the post of Ombudsman to strengthen informal mechanisms for conflict resolution;

13. *Also welcomes* the organization of basic legal training courses for new members of the Joint Appeals Board and the Joint Disciplinary Committee, and encourages the Secretary-General to continue his efforts in this regard without additional budgetary implications;

14. *Agrees* that the United Nations Administrative Tribunal should be strengthened through an amendment to its statute requiring that the candidates for the Tribunal possess judicial experience in the field of administrative law or its equivalent within the candidate's national jurisdiction, as recommended in paragraph 13 of the report of the Advisory Committee, and decides to take a decision on this matter at its fifty-eighth session;

15. *Notes* that the staff of the United Nations Secretariat and the specialized agencies are subject to two different systems of administration of justice, and in this regard requests the Joint Inspection Unit to continue to study the possibility of harmonizing the statutes of the United Nations Administrative Tribunal and the International Labour Organization Administrative Tribunal, bearing in mind the information contained in paragraphs 39 to 42 of the report of the Secretary-General, for consideration by the General Assembly at its fifty-ninth session;

16. *Requests* the Secretary-General to undertake a more in-depth analysis of the implications of ensuring that the executive heads of organizations collaborate with the staff associations in the development of comprehensive legal insurance schemes to cover legal advice and representation for staff, with a view to ensuring equality of all staff in adversary procedures and the widest possible access of staff to the administration of justice;

17. *Also requests* the Secretary-General to strengthen the Panel of Counsel, as appropriate, taking into account the management review report to be submitted by the Office of Internal Oversight Services;

18. *Affirms* that the functions of staff members appointed to serve on joint bodies in the administration of justice are official in nature and are valuable to the Organization;

19. *Encourages* the Secretary-General to ensure that staff members appointed to serve on joint bodies of the internal justice system are given sufficient time off from their substantive responsibilities to discharge their responsibilities, including adjustment of work in their substantive offices;

20. *Requests* the Secretary-General, in consultation with the Ombudsman and staff representatives, to submit detailed proposals on the role and work of the Panel on Discrimination and Other Grievances for consideration by the General Assembly at its fifty-eighth session;

21. *Also requests* the Secretary-General to include statistics on the disposition of cases and information on the work of the Panel of Counsel in his annual report on the administration of justice in the Secretariat;

22. *Further requests* the Secretary-General to distribute a hard copy of the annual report of the Panel of Counsel to Member States, upon request;

23. *Requests* the United Nations Administrative Tribunal to submit a comprehensive report on its activities to the General Assembly;

24. *Reiterates its request* to the Secretary-General to establish a clear linkage between the administration of justice and responsibility and accountability in the United Nations Secretariat when decisions of the Administrative Tribunal result in losses to the Organization due to management irregularities;

25. *Also reiterates its request* to the Secretary-General to develop, as a matter of priority, an effective system of personal responsibility and accountability to recover financial losses to the Organization caused by management irregularities, wrongful actions or gross negligence of officials of the United Nations Secretariat that result in judgements of the Administrative Tribunal, and to report thereon to the General Assembly at its fifty-eighth session;

26. *Requests* the Secretary-General to expeditiously finalize and issue an administrative instruction on the implementation of section XI, paragraph 9, of General Assembly resolution 55/258;

27. *Also requests* the Secretary-General to continue to ensure that all decisions affecting the status of the staff should be communicated to the staff members concerned;

28. *Decides* to amend staff rule 110.4 *(a)* to read: "No disciplinary proceedings may be instituted against a staff member unless he or she has been notified, in writing, of the allegations against him or her and of the right to seek the assistance of counsel in his or her defence at his or her own expense, and has been given a reasonable opportunity to respond to those allegations", and to make similar amendments to staff rules 210.1 *(b)* and 310.1 *(d)*;

29. *Also decides* to amend staff rule 111.2 *(i)* to read: "A staff member may arrange to have his or her appeal presented to the panel on his or her behalf by counsel, at his or her own expense";

30. *Decides* to include in the provisional agenda of its fifty-eighth session the item entitled "Administration of justice at the United Nations".

Joint Appeals Board

In response to section XI of General Assembly resolution 55/258 [YUN 2001, p. 1340], the Secretary-General submitted an August report [A/58/300] in which he provided information on the work of the Joint Appeals Board (JAB) in 2002. He stated that 159 appeals and suspension-of-action cases were filed with JAB in New York, Geneva, Vienna and Nairobi in 2002, compared to 115 cases the previous year. JAB disposed of 119 cases compared to 105 in 2001. Regarding disciplinary cases, which were accorded priority, 11 such cases were considered in 2002, compared to 10 the previous year. The Secretary-General accepted fully or partially 85 per cent of unanimous JAB decisions favourable to appellants in 2002 and rejected 15 per cent, compared to 81 per cent acceptances and 19 per cent rejections in 2001.

UN Administrative Tribunal

In its annual note to the General Assembly [A/INF/58/7], the United Nations Administrative Tribunal reported in December, through the Secretary-General, that it delivered 63 judgements in 2003, relating to cases brought by staff against the Secretary-General or the executive heads of other UN bodies to resolve disputes involving terms of appointment and other issues. The Tribunal met in plenary in New York on 20 October and held two panel sessions (Geneva, 23 June–25 July; New York, 20 October–21 November).

The Assembly, in **resolution 58/270** of 23 December (see p. 1399), requested the Secretary-General to ensure the independence of the Tribunal and the separation of its secretariat from the Office of Legal Affairs and to submit in 2004 a report on the financial independence of the Tribunal.

GENERAL ASSEMBLY ACTION

On 9 December [meeting 72], the General Assembly, on the recommendation of the Fifth Committee [A/58/521], adopted **resolution 58/87** without vote [agenda item 128].

Administration of justice at the United Nations
The General Assembly,
Acknowledging with gratitude the important contribution which the United Nations Administrative Tribunal (the Tribunal) has made to the functioning of the United Nations system, and commending the members of the Tribunal on their valuable work,

Desiring to assist the Tribunal in carrying out its future work as effectively as possible,

Having considered the report of the Advisory Committee on Administrative and Budgetary Questions,

Decides to amend the Statute of the United Nations Administrative Tribunal with effect from 1 January 2004, as follows:

Article 3, paragraph 1, shall be amended to read as follows:

"The Tribunal shall be composed of seven members, no two of whom may be nationals of the same State. Members shall possess judicial or other relevant legal experience in the field of administrative law or its equivalent within the member's national jurisdiction. Only three members shall sit in any particular case."

On 23 December, the Assembly, by **decision 58/564 A**, deferred until its resumed fifty-eighth (2004) session consideration of the agenda item on administration of justice at the United Nations.

Chapter IV

Institutional and administrative matters

In 2003, the United Nations continued to address administrative and institutional matters in order to ensure the efficient functioning of the Organization. The General Assembly resumed its fifty-seventh session and its tenth emergency special session; it opened its fifty-eighth session on 16 September. It granted observer status to the International Institute for Democracy and Electoral Assistance, the Eurasian Economic Community, the GUUAM (a regional agreement among Georgia, Ukraine, Uzbekistan, Azerbaijan and the Republic of Moldova) and the East African Community. The World Tourism Organization became a UN specialized agency.

The Security Council held 208 formal meetings to deal with regional conflicts, peacekeeping operations and a number of other issues related to the maintenance of international peace and security. The expansion of its membership was again considered by the Assembly.

In addition to its organizational and substantive sessions, the Economic and Social Council held a special high-level meeting with the Bretton Woods institutions (the World Bank Group and the International Monetary Fund) and the World Trade Organization.

The Committee on Conferences examined requests for changes to the 2003 calendar of conferences and meetings and sought ways of optimizing the use of conference-servicing resources. It urged the Department for General Assembly and Conference Management to maintain high quality services during its ongoing reform process.

The Joint Inspection Unit made recommendations for the improvement of certain operations of the UN system organizations: the management of information systems; revenue-producing activities; outsourcing practices; and common services for the Vienna-based organizations. The Assembly took note of the review of the duplication in UN administrative processes and procedures conducted by the Office of Internal Oversight Services. It adopted a resolution aimed at strengthening political impetus in the implementation of and follow-up to the outcomes of major UN conferences and summits in the economic, social and related fields.

Progress was reported on the early stages of implementation of the capital master plan for refurbishing the UN complex and on measures to strengthen the security and safety of UN premises.

On 23 December, the Assembly decided that the item entitled "Admission of new Members to the United Nations" would remain for consideration during its resumed fifty-eighth (2004) session (**decision 58/565**).

Institutional machinery

General Assembly

The General Assembly met throughout 2003; it resumed and concluded its fifty-seventh session and held the major part of its fifty-eighth session. The fifty-seventh session was resumed in plenary meetings on 29 January, 13 March, 15 April, 13, 22 and 29 May, 6, 18, 23 and 25 June, 3 July and 15 September. The fifty-eighth session opened on 16 September and continued until its suspension on 23 December.

The Assembly resumed the tenth emergency special session on 19 September, 20-21 October and 8 December to discuss "Illegal Israeli actions in Occupied East Jerusalem and the rest of the Occupied Palestinian Territory" (see p. 472).

Organization of Assembly sessions

2003 sessions

By **decision 58/501** of 16 September, the General Assembly authorized the Committee on Relations with the Host Country, the Committee on the Exercise of the Inalienable Rights of the Palestinian People, the Working Group on the Financing of the United Nations Relief and Works Agency for Palestine Refugees in the Near East and the Executive Board of the United Nations Children's Fund (UNICEF) to meet during the main part of its fifty-eighth session; and, on 20 October, authorized the Working Group on the Future Operation of the International Research and Training Institute for the Advancement of Women (INSTRAW) to do likewise.

By **decision 58/502** of 19 September, the Assembly adopted a number of provisions concerning the organization of the fifty-eighth session, as recommended by the General Committee [A/58/250]. On 17 and 19 December, the Assembly postponed the date of recess of the session to 22 and to 23 December, respectively.

Credentials

The Credentials Committee, at its first meeting on 11 December [A/58/625], had before it a memorandum by the Secretary-General indicating that, as at 9 December, 130 Member States had submitted the formal credentials of their representatives. During the meeting, the Legal Counsel made a statement updating the information contained in the memorandum. Information concerning the representatives of 61 other Member States had been communicated also.

The Committee adopted a resolution accepting the credentials received and recommended a draft resolution to the Assembly for adoption. On 17 December, the Assembly, by **resolution 58/125**, approved the Committee's report.

On 23 December, the Assembly decided that the agenda item on the report of the Credentials Committee would remain for consideration during the resumed fifty-eighth (2004) session (**decision 58/565**).

Agenda

During the resumed fifty-seventh (2003) session, the General Assembly took the following actions relating to its agenda, as listed in **decision 57/503 B**: to consider in plenary the sub-item on the appointment of members of the Advisory Committee on Administrative and Budgetary Questions (ACABQ) [A/57/101/Add.1/Rev.1]; an additional item for inclusion in the agenda, on the General Committee's recommendation [A/57/250/Add.4], entitled "Global road safety crisis"; the item on integrated and coordinated implementation of and follow-up to the outcomes of the major UN conferences and summits in the economic and social fields, in order to consider the report of the Assembly's Ad Hoc Working Group on that subject [A/57/48] (see p. 1467); and the sub-items on the appointment of a member of the United Nations Staff Pension Committee [A/57/111/Add.2], on the convening of the Assembly's fourth special session devoted to disarmament [A/57/848] and on the high-level dialogue on strengthening international economic cooperation for development through partnership [A/57/L.80, A/57/L.82]. It agreed to proceed immediately to the consideration of those sub-items.

On 15 April (**decision 57/556 B**), the Assembly deferred until the second part of its resumed fifty-seventh session consideration of the items on the review of the efficiency of the administrative and financial functioning of the United Nations, human resources management, the 2002-2003 programme budget and the Secretary-General's report on the activities of the Office of Internal Oversight Services (OIOS).

On 18 June, the Assembly deferred until its fifty-eighth session consideration of the Secretary-General's report entitled "Strengthening the United Nations: an agenda for further change—intergovernmental review of the medium-term plan and the programme budget" under the item "Strengthening of the UN system" (**decision 57/587**); and of the items on the 2002-2003 programme budget, human resources management, and administrative and budgetary aspects of the financing of UN peacekeeping operations (**decision 57/588**).

On 15 September, the Assembly included in the draft agenda of its fifty-eighth session the item on revitalization of the work of the General Assembly (**decision 57/595**); and deferred consideration of, and included in the draft agenda of its fifty-eighth session, the items on: the question of Cyprus (**decision 57/596**), armed aggression against the Democratic Republic of the Congo (**decision 57/597**), improving the UN financial situation (**decision 57/598**) and the financing of the United Nations Mission in East Timor (**decision 57/599**).

The Assembly took a number of actions in respect of its fifty-eighth session agenda, as listed in **decision 58/503 A**: on 19 September, on the recommendation of the General Committee [A/58/250], it adopted the agenda [A/58/251 & Corr.1] and allocation of agenda items [A/58/252 & Corr.1], deferred consideration of, and included in the provisional agenda of its fifty-ninth (2004) session, the item "Question of the Malagasy islands of Glorieuses, Juan de Nova, Europa and Bassas da India"; on 13 October, also on the recommendation of the General Committee [A/58/250/Add.1], it included additional items in the agenda, on financing of the United Nations Mission in Liberia and on the admission of the International Criminal Court to membership in the United Nations Joint Staff Pension Fund, and decided to consider in plenary the item "Crime prevention and criminal justice" for the sole purpose of taking action on the draft United Nations Convention against Corruption; and, on 10 November, on the General Committee's recommendation [A/58/250/Add.2], it deferred consideration of, and included in the provisional agenda of its fifty-ninth session, the item "Question of the Comorian Island of Mayotte".

The Assembly also deferred consideration of, and included in the provisional agenda of its fifty-ninth session, the following items: "Question of the Falkland Islands (Malvinas)" (**decision 58/511**); "Declaration of the Assembly of Heads of State and Government of the Organization of African Unity on the aerial and naval military attack against the Socialist People's Libyan Arab Jamahiriya by the present United States Administration in April 1986" (**decision 58/512**); "Consequences of the Iraqi occupation of and aggression against Kuwait" (**decision 58/514**); "Armed Israeli aggression against the Iraqi nuclear installations and its grave consequences for the established international system concerning the peaceful uses of nuclear energy, the non-proliferation of nuclear weapons and international peace and security" (**decision 58/527**); and "Launching of global negotiations on international economic cooperation for development" (**decision 58/528**).

On 8 December, the Assembly included the following items in the provisional agenda of its fifty-ninth session: "Verification in all its aspects, including the role of the United Nations in the field of verification" (**decision 58/515**); "Review of the implementation of the Declaration on the Strengthening of International Security" (**decision 58/516**); "United Nations conference to identify ways of eliminating nuclear dangers in the context of nuclear disarmament" (**decision 58/517**); "Establishment of a nuclear-weapon-free zone in Central Asia" (**decision 58/518**); "Consolidation of peace through practical disarmament measures" (**decision 58/519**); "Relationship between disarmament and development" (**decision 58/520**); and "Convening of the fourth special session of the General Assembly devoted to disarmament" (**decision 58/521**).

On 9 December, the Assembly included in the provisional agenda of its fifty-ninth session the item "International convention against the reproductive cloning of human beings" (**decision 58/523**).

On 23 December, the Assembly deferred until its resumed fifty-eighth (2004) session consideration of the items on human resources management, administration of justice at the United Nations, the Joint Inspection Unit (JIU), the Secretary-General's report on OIOS activities, and administrative and budgetary aspects of the financing of UN peacekeeping operations (**decision 58/564 A**). On the same date, the Assembly decided to retain 45 items for consideration during that session (**decision 58/565**).

Second, Third and Fifth Committees

The General Assembly, on 22 December, approved the organization of work of the Third (Social, Humanitarian and Cultural) Committee and its 2004-2005 programme of work (**decision 58/542**). On 23 December, it approved the provisional programme of work of the Second (Economic and Financial) Committee and invited that Committee's Bureau to continue efforts, in consultation with Member States, to ensure a more practical and coherent organization of the Committee's work, in accordance with Assembly resolution 57/270 B of 23 June (see p. 1468), and to make suggestions for a decision at the fifty-ninth (2004) session (**decision 58/553**). Also on 23 December, it approved the 2004-2005 programme of work of the Fifth (Administrative and Budgetary) Committee (**decision 58/563**).

Resolutions and decisions of the General Assembly

By **decision 58/513** of 3 December, the General Assembly deferred consideration of the agenda item "Implementation of the resolutions of the United Nations" and included it in the provisional agenda of its fifty-ninth (2004) session.

Amendment to rules of procedure

On 13 March [meeting 81], the General Assembly adopted **resolution 57/301** [draft: A/57/L.75] without vote [agenda item 53].

Amendment to rule 1 of the rules of procedure of the General Assembly and opening date and duration of the general debate

The General Assembly,

Recalling its resolutions 51/241 of 31 July 1997, 52/232 of 4 June 1998, 53/224 of 7 April 1999, 53/239 of 8 June 1999 and 55/14 of 3 November 2000 concerning, inter alia, the opening date of the regular session of the General Assembly,

Recalling in particular paragraph 1 of its resolution 55/14, in which it decided to amend rule 1 of the rules of procedure of the General Assembly to read: "The General Assembly shall meet every year in regular session commencing on the Tuesday following the second Monday in September",

Also recalling in particular paragraph 19 of the annex to its resolution 51/241, in which it decided that there should continue to be only one general debate each year, beginning in the third week of September, and paragraph 20 (*a*) of the annex, in which it decided that the general debate should be organized over a period of two weeks so as to maximize possibilities for interministerial contacts,

Recalling that ad hoc arrangements had to be made regarding the dates and duration of the general debate at its fifty-fourth, fifty-fifth and fifty-sixth sessions,

Recalling also its decision 56/468 of 1 May 2002, by which it decided to hold an eight-day general debate at its fifty-seventh session, from Thursday, 12 September, to Sunday, 15 September, and from Tuesday, 17 September, to Friday, 20 September 2002,

Noting that the advancement of the opening date of the regular session as decided in its resolution 55/14

has resulted in insufficient time to ensure preparedness for the session,

Concerned about the impact that the fluctuation of the opening date and the interruption in the course of the general debate have had on its work and on Member States,

Strongly convinced that resetting the opening date of the regular session of the General Assembly and predetermining the dates for the opening and duration of the general debate at future sessions will facilitate the organization of its work, including the work of its Main Committees, and will benefit Member States in their planning,

1. *Decides* to amend rule 1 of the rules of procedure of the General Assembly to read: "The General Assembly shall meet every year in regular session commencing on the Tuesday of the third week in September, counting from the first week that contains at least one working day";

2. *Also decides* that the general debate in the General Assembly shall open on the Tuesday following the opening of the regular session of the General Assembly and shall be held without interruption over a period of nine working days;

3. *Further decides* that the provisions of paragraphs 1 and 2 above shall be implemented as from the fifty-eighth regular session; the fifty-eighth regular session shall therefore open on Tuesday, 16 September 2003, and the general debate shall open on Tuesday, 23 September 2003, and end on Friday, 3 October 2003; the fifty-seventh regular session shall therefore close on Monday, 15 September 2003;

4. *Decides* to annex paragraph 2 above to the rules of procedure of the General Assembly.

Security Council

The Security Council held 208 formal meetings in 2003, adopted 67 resolutions and issued 30 presidential statements. It considered 49 agenda items (see APPENDIX IV). In a September note [A/58/354], the Secretary-General, in accordance with Article 12, paragraph 2, of the Charter of the United Nations and with the consent of the Council, notified the General Assembly of 57 matters relative to the maintenance of international peace and security that the Council had discussed since his previous annual notification [YUN 2002, p. 1430]. The Secretary-General also listed 74 matters that the Council had not discussed since then. The Assembly, on 13 October, took note of the Secretary-General's note (**decision 58/507**).

On 17 October, the Assembly took note of the Council's report for the period 1 August 2002 to 31 July 2003 [A/58/2] (**decision 58/508**). It decided on 23 December that the item on the Council's report would remain for consideration during its resumed fifty-eighth (2004) session (**decision 58/565**).

Membership

The General Assembly continued to examine the question of expanding the Security Council's membership. It considered the report of the Open-ended Working Group on the Question of Equitable Representation on and Increase in the Membership of the Security Council and Other Matters related to the Security Council [A/57/47 & Corr.1]. (For details and related Assembly decisions, see p. 1391.)

Economic and Social Council

The Economic and Social Council held its organizational session for 2003 on 15, 28, 30 and 31 January; a resumed organizational session on 5 and 25 March, 29 April, 1 and 27 May and 24 June; and a special high-level meeting with the Bretton Woods institutions (the World Bank Group and the International Monetary Fund) and the World Trade Organization (WTO) on 14 April, all in New York. It held its substantive session in Geneva from 30 June to 25 July and resumed substantive session in New York on 22 August, 31 October and 19 December.

On 15 January, the Council elected its Bureau (a President and four Vice-Presidents) for 2003 (see APPENDIX III) and adopted the agenda of its organizational session [E/2003/2 & Add.1].

On 28 January, the Council approved the provisional agenda of its 2003 substantive session (**decision 2003/202**) and decided on the working arrangements for that session (**decision 2003/204**). On 30 June, it adopted the agenda [E/2003/100] and approved the proposed programme of work of that session [E/2003/L.5], and, on 1 July, approved the requests for hearings from non-governmental organizations (NGOs) [E/2003/88] (**decision 2003/223**).

Sessions and segments

During 2003, the Economic and Social Council adopted 64 resolutions and 122 decisions. By **decision 2003/204** of 28 January, the Council decided that the high-level segment of its substantive session would be held from 30 June to 2 July; the operational activities segment from 3 to 7 July; the coordination segment from 8 to 10 July; the humanitarian affairs segment from 11 to 15 July; and the general segment from 16 to 23 July. By **decision 2003/206** of the same date, the Council decided that its high-level meeting with representatives of the Bretton Woods institutions and WTO would be held in New York on 14 April.

On 25 July, the Council, by **decision 2003/301**, decided to consider indigenous issues as a theme for its high-level segment in 2006.

The work of the Council in 2003 was covered in its report to the Assembly [A/58/3/Rev.1]. The Assembly took note of various chapters of the report on 22 (**decision 58/543**) and 23 (**decision 58/556**) December. Also on 23 December, it took note of the full report (**decision 58/552**) and decided that the item on the Council's report would remain for consideration at its resumed fifty-eighth (2004) session (**decision 58/565**).

2003 and 2004 sessions

On 28 January, the Council decided that the theme for the regional cooperation item at its 2003 substantive session would be "Development dimensions of trade negotiations: a regional perspective" (**decision 2003/205**). On 5 March, it decided that the theme for the humanitarian affairs segment would be "Strengthening of the coordination of United Nations humanitarian assistance, with particular attention to humanitarian financing and effectiveness of humanitarian assistance and the transition from relief to development", and that it would convene a panel, within the framework of that theme, on the sub-theme "Responding to the effects of HIV/AIDS and other widespread diseases on humanitarian relief operations" (**decision 2003/210**) (see p. 1248); it also took note of the programme of work for the operational activities segment (**decision 2003/211**).

On 24 July, the Council decided that the theme of the high-level segment for its 2004 substantive session would be "Resources mobilization and enabling environment for poverty eradication in the context of the implementation of the Programme of Action for the Least Developed Countries for the Decade 2001-2010"; and that the themes for the coordination segment would be "Review and appraisal of the system-wide implementation of the Council's agreed conclusions 1997/2 on mainstreaming the gender perspective into all policies and programmes in the United Nations system" and "Coordinated and integrated United Nations system approach to promote rural development in developing countries, with due consideration to least developed countries, for poverty eradication and sustainable development" (**decision 2003/287**).

Work programme

On 28 January, the Economic and Social Council, having considered its proposed basic programme of work for 2003 and 2004 [E/2003/1/Rev.1], took note of the list of questions for inclusion in its programme of work for 2004 and the list of documents for each agenda item (**decision 2003/203**).

Coordination, monitoring and cooperation

Institutional mechanisms

CEB activities

According to its annual overview report for 2003 [E/2004/67], the United Nations System Chief Executives Board for Coordination (CEB) continued to focus on ensuring coherent and coordinated UN-system implementation of the Millennium Declaration, adopted by the General Assembly in resolution 55/2 [YUN 2000, p. 49]. The themes around which the CEB agenda was framed included strategies in the context of the follow-up to the 2002 World Conference on Sustainable Development [YUN 2002, p. 821] and the 2002 International Conference on Financing for Development [ibid., p. 953]; curbing transnational crime; bridging the digital divide through projects, including the UN system Extranet (see p. 859); HIV/AIDS and its linkages with food security and governance (see p. 1250); system-wide support for Africa's development and the New Partnership for Africa's Development (NEPAD) (see p. 939); and conflict prevention (see p. 55).

CEB also considered assistance to countries invoking Article 50 of the Charter of the United Nations on assistance to third States affected by the application of sanctions and, through its High-level Committee on Management (HLCM), endorsed and/or agreed to a number of system-wide initiatives to strengthen the security system of the United Nations (see p. 1453).

CEB held two regular sessions in 2003: the first in Paris (25-26 April) [CEB/2003/1] and the second in New York (31 October–1 November) [CEB/2003/2]. Its principal subsidiary bodies met as follows: HLCM, fifth (12-13 June) [CEB/2003/3] and sixth (20-21 October) [CEB/2003/5] sessions, both in New York; HLCP (High-level Committee on Programmes), fifth (26-27 March) [CEB/2003/4] and sixth (18-19 September) [CEB/2003/7] sessions, both in Rome, Italy, with two intersessional meetings (Geneva, 2 July [CEB/2003/6] and New York, 3 November [CEB/2003/8]).

Report for 2002

The Committee for Programme and Coordination (CPC) [A/58/16] considered CEB's annual overview report for 2002 [E/2003/55]. It requested that future reports be results-oriented and incorporate expected accomplishments, indicators of achievement and progress made and called on CEB to strengthen further coordination among

UN agencies at the country level in harmonizing and streamlining their practices and procedures. CPC recommended that CEB play a role in better coordinating analysis of the problems of countries invoking Article 50 of the Charter and develop new methodologies to identify the damage to affected States and mechanisms to determine appropriate compensation. It stressed that CEB keep under review the issue of inter-agency coordination on NEPAD and include in its annual report information on coordination and cooperation in the fields of human resources and finance.

The Economic and Social Council, by **decision 2003/288** of 24 July, took note of CEB's 2002 report.

Programme coordination

The Committee for Programme and Coordination held an organizational meeting on 5 May and its forty-third session from 9 June to 3 July and on 9 July, all in New York [A/58/16].

CPC reviewed the efficiency of the administrative and financial functioning of the United Nations, the proposed 2004-2005 programme budget and the proposed revisions to the 2002-2005 medium-term plan. It considered a number of OIOS reports on proposed evaluation themes, an in-depth programme evaluation, and two triennial reviews of the implementation of CPC recommendations on specific in-depth evaluations (see p. 1387). In addition to its review of CEB's 2002 annual report (see above), CPC also considered the Secretary-General's report on the UN system's future engagement with NEPAD (see p. 939) and the 2002 JIU report on the results approach in the United Nations for implementing the United Nations Millennium Declaration [YUN 2002, p. 1356], together with the related comments of the Secretary-General and CEB (see p. 1384).

The Economic and Social Council, by **decision 2003/288** of 24 July, took note of CPC's report.

Joint Inspection Unit

JIU, in its thirty-fourth report to the General Assembly, covering the period 1 January to 31 December 2002 [A/58/34], examined relations and cooperation with participating organizations and other oversight bodies and follow-up on its reports and recommendations. JIU continued to review the administration and management of its participating organizations (see p. 1387).

As requested by the Assembly in resolution 56/245 [YUN 2001, p. 1286], JIU continued to cooperate and coordinate with other external and internal oversight bodies of the UN system, reaching agreements on the handling of follow-up of its reports with the secretariats of six additional organizations.

Pursuant to Assembly resolution 56/279 [YUN 2002, p. 1457], JIU reported on progress in the development and consolidation of common services at Geneva and other duty stations. The Management Ownership Committee, comprising the heads of all Geneva-based agencies and chaired by the Director-General of the UN Office at Geneva, provided strategic direction and high-level support for all common service initiatives. The Task Force on Common Services had been instrumental in the realization of developments in the areas of travel, the provision of electrical archives and records management (see p. 1494).

By **decision 58/564 A** of 23 December, the Assembly deferred consideration of JIU's report until its resumed fifty-eighth (2004) session. In **resolution 58/272**, section VI (see p. 1418), it approved a gross budget for JIU of $4,900,800 for 2004.

Other coordination matters

Follow-up to international conferences

In a 15 May report [E/2003/67], the Secretary-General analysed how the Economic and Social Council could promote an integrated approach to the follow-up and implementation of the outcomes of recent major UN conferences and summits. It contained suggestions on how the Council could use its segments to sustain progress towards internationally agreed goals and address policy, coordination and operational aspects of common conference themes, and on how it could perform its follow-up functions in respect of recent conferences and summits. It put forward proposals for enhancing the Council's dialogue with and oversight of the boards of UN funds and programmes, improving further the contribution of the functional commissions to the implementation of conference outcomes, and developing the regional commissions' role in reviewing progress towards achieving internationally agreed goals. It also recommended ways to build a closer relationship with the specialized agencies and inter-agency bodies and to foster partnerships and alliances with all stakeholders.

The Secretary-General's report was to be read in conjunction with the report of the open-ended Ad Hoc Working Group of the General Assembly on the integrated and coordinated implementation of and follow-up to the outcomes of the major UN conferences and summits in the economic and social fields, established by General Assembly resolution 57/270 [YUN 2002, p. 1435]. The Group's report [A/57/48] covered its deliberations during its formal meetings on 27 January, 3-4, 7 and 24 February, 27 March, 22 April, 12-13 May and 4-6, 13 and 17 June, and at a series of informal meetings held between January and June.

On 17 June, the Ad Hoc Working Group adopted its report and recommended a draft resolution for adoption by the Assembly (see below).

By **decision 2003/227** of 16 July, the Economic and Social Council took note of the report of the Secretary-General and that of the Ad Hoc Working Group.

(For the Secretary-General's 23 May progress report [E/2003/74] on the implementation of the key provisions of the Economic and Social Council's agreed conclusions 2002/1 [YUN 2002, p. 1365], see p. 1391.)

GENERAL ASSEMBLY ACTION

On 23 June [meeting 91], the General Assembly, on the basis of the report of the Ad Hoc Working Group [A/57/48], adopted **resolution 57/270 B** without vote [agenda item 92].

Integrated and coordinated implementation of and follow-up to the outcomes of the major United Nations conferences and summits in the economic and social fields

The General Assembly,

Recalling its resolutions 50/227 of 24 May 1996 and 57/270 A of 20 December 2002,

Recalling also the outcomes of the major United Nations conferences and summits in the economic, social and related fields,

Considering that, after more than a decade of such events, progress in implementation has been insufficient and therefore the time has come to vigorously pursue effective implementation,

Recalling the United Nations Millennium Declaration,

Recognizing that the internationally agreed development goals, including those contained in the Millennium Declaration, offer a framework for planning, reviewing and assessing the activities of the United Nations for development,

Reaffirming that sustainable development is a key element of the overarching framework for United Nations activities, in particular for achieving the internationally agreed development goals, including those contained in the Millennium Declaration,

Reaffirming also that the internationally agreed development goals, including those contained in the Millennium Declaration and the outcomes of the major United Nations conferences and summits, provide a comprehensive basis for action at the national, regional and international levels with the key objectives of poverty eradication, sustained economic growth and sustainable development,

Recognizing that peace, security, stability and respect for human rights and fundamental freedoms, including the right to development, as well as respect for cultural diversity, are essential for achieving sustainable development and ensuring that sustainable development benefits all,

Emphasizing the importance of integrated and coordinated implementation of and follow-up to the outcomes of the major United Nations conferences and summits, bearing in mind the need to respect the thematic unity of each of the conferences and the interlinkages between them,

Bearing in mind the ongoing process of reform of the United Nations,

Recognizing the need to strengthen political impetus in the implementation of and follow-up to the outcomes of the major United Nations conferences and summits,

I
Integrated and coordinated implementation of the outcomes of the major United Nations conferences and summits at the national, regional and international levels

The role of Member States

1. *Emphasizes* that each country has a primary responsibility for its own economic and social development and that the role of national policies and development strategies cannot be overemphasized; that, at the same time, domestic economies are now interwoven with the global economic system and, inter alia, the effective use of trade and investment opportunities can help countries to fight poverty; and that national development efforts need to be supported by an enabling international economic environment, and encourages and supports development frameworks initiated at the regional level, such as the New Partnership for Africa's Development and similar efforts in other regions;

2. *Reaffirms,* in this context, that the achievement of the internationally agreed development goals, including those contained in the United Nations Millennium Declaration, requires an enhanced partnership between donor and recipient countries, based on the recognition of national leadership and ownership of development plans, as well as sound policies and good governance at the national and international levels;

3. *Stresses,* in this context, that all countries should promote policies consistent and coherent with the commitments of the major United Nations conferences and summits, including those systemic in nature, in order, inter alia, to achieve the internationally agreed development goals, including those contained in the Millennium Declaration;

Means of implementation

4. *Stresses* the importance of means of implementation as identified in the outcomes of the major United Nations conferences and summits, and reaffirms that the implementation of those outcomes requires the urgent fulfilment by all countries of their commitments relating to means of implementation as contained in the relevant paragraphs of the conference outcome documents, including the Plan of Implementation of the World Summit on Sustainable Development ("Johannesburg Plan of Implementation") and the Monterrey Consensus of the International Conference on Financing for Development;

Institutional frameworks

5. *Stresses* the importance of institutional frameworks as identified in the outcomes of the major United Nations conferences and summits;

The role of the United Nations system, including the Bretton Woods institutions, and the World Trade Organization and other relevant institutional stakeholders

6. *Emphasizes* that the United Nations system has an important responsibility to assist Governments to stay fully engaged in the follow-up to and implementation of agreements and commitments reached at the major United Nations conferences and summits, and invites its intergovernmental bodies to further promote the implementation of the outcomes of the major United Nations conferences and summits;

7. *Calls upon* the governing bodies of the United Nations funds and programmes to ensure that policy guidance from the General Assembly and the Economic and Social Council on the implementation of the outcomes of the major United Nations conferences and summits is integrated into their programme of work and translated into their operational activities;

8. *Stresses* that the relevant organs, organizations and bodies of the United Nations system should incorporate in their programme of work, in accordance with their respective mandates, the outcomes of the major United Nations conferences and summits and take them into account in the operational work and country frameworks of the organs of the United Nations system, in accordance with national development objectives and priorities;

9. *Recommends* greater cooperation at the national, regional and international levels among the United Nations organizations and other relevant intergovernmental organizations, based on a clear understanding of and respect for their respective mandates and governance structures;

10. *Calls* for enhanced coordination among heads of international agencies to ensure the integrated and coordinated implementation of the outcomes of the major United Nations conferences and summits;

11. *Underlines*, in this context, that the inter-agency guidelines for operational activities for development of the United Nations system and the work of the United Nations System Chief Executives Board for Coordination and the United Nations Development Group should reflect the agreements and commitments reached at the major United Nations conferences and summits;

12. *Invites* the Secretary-General, utilizing the United Nations System Chief Executives Board for Coordination, to further promote system-wide inter-agency coordination and cooperation to implement the agreements and commitments reached at conferences, and requests him to continue to report on the activities of the Board in this regard;

13. *Recognizes* the progress achieved towards a more coherent United Nations performance in the development field, as reflected by a new culture of shared responsibility, cooperation and coordination among the members of the United Nations Development Group, and, in this regard, invites the Administrator of the United Nations Development Programme, in his capacity as Chair of the United Nations Development Group, to report, on a regular basis, to the Economic and Social Council at its coordination segment, on the activities carried out by the Group relating to the integrated and coordinated implementation of the outcomes of the major United Nations conferences and summits;

14. *Emphasizes* that the agencies should continue to improve their operational guidelines, results-based management and multi-year work programmes and deepen further inter-agency cooperation in the implementation of conference outcomes;

15. *Also emphasizes* the importance of ensuring, under the leadership of national Governments, greater consistency between the strategic frameworks developed by the United Nations funds and programmes and the specialized agencies, including the Bretton Woods institutions, and national poverty reduction strategies, including poverty reduction strategy papers, where they exist;

16. *Calls upon* the regional commissions, within their respective mandates, to further strengthen and enhance the effectiveness of their activities and improve their coordination with the entire United Nations system with regard to the implementation and review of the outcomes of the major United Nations conferences and summits, in order to ensure the achievement of the internationally agreed development goals, including those contained in the Millennium Declaration;

17. *Reiterates* the need for a substantial increase in resources for operational activities for development, on a predictable, continuous and assured basis, to enable the United Nations funds and programmes and the specialized agencies to contribute effectively to the implementation of the outcomes of the major United Nations conferences and summits;

18. *Also reiterates* the need for continuous overall improvement in the effectiveness, efficiency, management and impact of the United Nations system in delivering its development assistance;

19. *Affirms* that the Bretton Woods institutions and the World Trade Organization have an important role to play in the implementation of the outcomes of the major United Nations conferences and summits, and, in this regard, welcomes their efforts to deepen further their interaction with the United Nations and their engagement with the financing-for-development process in particular, and encourages them to continue their efforts to ensure the effective implementation of the commitments reached in the Monterrey Consensus, with the aim of achieving the internationally agreed development goals, including those contained in the Millennium Declaration;

20. *Calls* for greater coherence, coordination and cooperation between the United Nations, the Bretton Woods institutions and the World Trade Organization, and other relevant institutional stakeholders, such as regional development banks and other organizations, at the international, regional and national levels, within their respective competencies, mandates and comparative advantages, and for working with recipient Governments in full accordance with national priorities, with a view to achieving increased complementarity and better division of labour in their activities;

The role of other relevant stakeholders, including civil society and the private sector

21. *Underlines* the importance of the contribution of civil society, including non-governmental organizations and the private sector, to the implementation of conference outcomes;

22. *Stresses* the importance of promoting corporate environmental and social responsibility and accountability; this would include actions at all levels:

(*a*) To encourage industry to improve social and environmental performance through voluntary initiatives, including environmental management systems, codes of conduct, certification and public reporting on environmental and social issues, taking into account such initiatives as the International Organization for Standardization standards and Global Reporting Initiative guidelines on sustainability reporting, bearing in mind principle 11 of the Rio Declaration on Environment and Development;

(*b*) To encourage dialogue between enterprises and the communities in which they operate and other stakeholders;

(*c*) To encourage financial institutions to incorporate sustainable development considerations in their decision-making processes;

(*d*) To develop workplace-based partnerships and programmes, including training and education programmes;

Review of progress made in the implementation of the outcomes of the major United Nations conferences and summits

23. *Stresses* the utmost importance of regular review, in accordance with the provisions defined by the respective outcomes and follow-up processes, of the progress made in the implementation of the commitments undertaken at individual major United Nations conferences and summits in the economic, social and related fields;

24. *Also stresses* that review is important for assessing the progress made in the implementation of commitments at all levels;

25. *Further stresses* that all review and follow-up processes of the major United Nations conferences and summits in the economic, social and related fields must focus on the progress made in the implementation of commitments;

26. *Emphasizes* that the review of the major United Nations conferences and summits should, inter alia, identify constraints and obstacles faced in relation to implementation;

27. *Stresses* the need to make maximum use of existing United Nations mechanisms for the purpose of reviewing the implementation of commitments made within the United Nations system in key areas of development and, in this regard:

(*a*) Recalls the role of the United Nations Conference on Trade and Development as the focal point within the United Nations for the integrated treatment of trade and development and interrelated issues in the areas of finance, technology, investment and sustainable development, and invites the Trade and Development Board to contribute, within its mandate, to the implementation and to the review of progress made in the implementation of the outcomes of the major United Nations conferences and summits, under its relevant agenda items;

(*b*) Invites the Economic and Social Council to invite the President of the Trade and Development Board to present the outcomes of such reviews to the Council;

(*c*) Also invites the Economic and Social Council to include representatives of the Trade and Development Board in the high-level meeting of the Council with the Bretton Woods institutions and the World Trade Organization;

(*d*) Reiterates the importance of making fuller use of and strengthening the General Assembly and the Economic and Social Council, as well as the relevant intergovernmental bodies and the governing bodies of other institutional stakeholders, for the purpose of conference follow-up and coordination, and, in this regard, decides to assess during its fifty-eighth session the functioning of the follow-up mechanisms set up in Monterrey in accordance with chapter III of the Monterrey Consensus;

28. *Invites* Member States, as well as organizations of the United Nations system, including the Bretton Woods institutions, and the World Trade Organization and non-governmental actors, to contribute to the review and follow-up processes of the major United Nations conferences and summits in the economic, social and related fields, consistent with their mandates, through the assessment of progress made in the implementation of their respective commitments, in accordance with the provisions of the outcomes of the respective United Nations conferences and summits;

29. *Reaffirms* the importance of indicators in the review of the progress made in the implementation of all the commitments of the major United Nations conferences and summits;

30. *Emphasizes* that the indicators used by the Secretariat in the context of the integrated and coordinated implementation of and follow-up to the outcomes of the major United Nations conferences and summits should be developed with the full participation of all countries and approved by the relevant intergovernmental bodies;

31. *Reiterates* that the Statistical Commission is the intergovernmental focal point for the elaboration and the review of the indicators used by the United Nations system in the context of the integrated and coordinated implementation of and follow-up to the outcomes of major United Nations conferences and summits at all levels, and, in this regard, encourages continued efforts by the Statistical Commission to further improve the list of indicators on implementation of the outcomes of the major United Nations conferences and summits in the economic, social and related fields, including by means of methodological and technical refinement of the existing indicators;

32. *Stresses* the need to apply and further develop indicators on means of implementation to evaluate progress towards conference goals in creating an enabling environment for development;

33. *Calls upon* the United Nations funds and programmes, the functional and regional commissions and the specialized agencies to keep under review the full range of indicators used in their reports and information networks, with full participation and ownership of Member States, with a view to avoiding duplication, as well as ensuring the transparency, consistency and reliability of those indicators;

34. *Stresses* the importance of building statistical capacity in all countries, including through statistical training, and of effective international support in this context for developing countries, and urges countries, the United Nations funds and programmes, the Secretariat, bilateral funding agencies, the Bretton Woods

institutions and regional funding agencies to mobilize the required resources and coordinate their efforts to support national statistical capacity-building in developing countries, in particular in the least developed countries;

35. *Emphasizes*, in this regard, the importance of the simplification and harmonization of requests of the United Nations system for reports by Member States, encourages further the collaboration between the various international organizations in the field of statistics, and calls upon the concerned United Nations bodies and agencies to adopt, in consultation with Member States, simplified and harmonized methods, and, in this regard, to support developing countries, where needed and requested, in the preparation of reports based on national data and statistics;

36. *Stresses* the need for continued intergovernmental assessment, within existing mechanisms, of the performance of the United Nations system in fulfilling its mandates with regard to the implementation of the outcomes of the major United Nations conferences and summits in the economic, social and related fields, bearing in mind, inter alia, the work of the United Nations Evaluation Group, the results oriented annual report methodologies and practices in other development agencies;

II
Integrated and coordinated follow-up to the outcomes of the major United Nations conferences and summits

The role of the General Assembly

37. *Reiterates* the need to strengthen its role as the highest intergovernmental mechanism for the formulation and appraisal of policy on matters relating to coordinated and integrated follow-up to the major United Nations conferences and summits in the economic and social fields;

38. *Recommends* greater consultation between the presidents and the bureaux of the General Assembly and the Economic and Social Council to improve coordination between the Assembly and the Council, with the objective, inter alia, of contributing to a better consideration of the integrated and coordinated implementation of and follow-up to the outcomes of the major United Nations conferences and summits;

39. *Decides* to include in the annual agenda of the General Assembly an item entitled "Integrated and coordinated implementation of and follow-up to the outcomes of the major United Nations conferences and summits in the economic, social and related fields"; also decides to consider, under this item, the assessment of the implementation of the outcomes of the conferences and summits and its impact on the achievement of the goals and targets of the conferences and summits and to provide the necessary guidance for the further implementation of and follow-up to these outcomes; notes in this regard the emerging practice of holding high-level plenary meetings in the context of the general debate of the General Assembly; and further decides to consider, under this item, the chapters of the annual report of the Economic and Social Council relevant to the integrated and coordinated implementation of and follow-up to the outcomes of the major United Nations conferences and summits, including through the participation in its discussions of the President of the Council, and invites the Secretary-General to submit a report on the integrated and coordinated implementation of and follow-up to the outcomes of the major United Nations conferences and summits in the economic, social and related fields;

The role of the Economic and Social Council

Functional commissions

Regional commissions

Governing bodies of funds and programmes

40. *Reiterates* that the Economic and Social Council should continue to strengthen its role as the central mechanism for system-wide coordination and thus promote the integrated and coordinated implementation of and follow-up to the outcomes of the major United Nations conferences in the economic, social and related fields, in accordance with the Charter of the United Nations and General Assembly resolution 50/227;

41. *Decides* that the Economic and Social Council should review by means of a cross-sectoral approach the progress made in the implementation of the outcomes of the major United Nations conferences and summits and their follow-up processes, and assess its impact on the achievement of the goals and targets of the conferences and summits; this review and assessment should be carried out on an annual basis, focusing on a particular common cross-sectoral thematic issue, at the coordination segment of the substantive session of the Economic and Social Council, on the basis, inter alia, of a report to be submitted by the Secretary-General;

42. *Requests*, in this regard, the Economic and Social Council to establish, no later than 2004, a multi-year work programme for the coordination segment of its substantive session, based on a focused and balanced list of cross-sectoral thematic issues common to the outcomes of major United Nations conferences and summits, including the objectives, goals and targets of the Millennium Declaration while respecting decisions to be taken by the Council regarding themes for 2004, bearing in mind decisions already taken by the Council regarding themes; this multi-year programme will enable the United Nations system and relevant stakeholders to better prepare their contributions to those discussions, in accordance with the rules of procedure of the Economic and Social Council;

43. *Underlines* that the theme of the high-level segment of the substantive session of the Economic and Social Council could be related to the theme of the coordination segment, respecting decisions already made by the Council, thus enabling the Council to address both the policy and system-wide coordination aspects of the theme;

44. *Invites* the Economic and Social Council to consider modalities for implementing the necessary arrangements regarding cross-sectoral thematic issues;

45. *Invites* the functional commissions and relevant follow-up mechanisms, as appropriate, to contribute, from their specific perspectives, to the assessment by the Economic and Social Council of the cross-sectoral thematic issue selected for the coordination segment of its substantive session, including through the possible participation of their chairpersons, suitably mandated, in the discussions on the cross-sectoral thematic issue in the Council;

46. *Requests* each functional commission to examine its methods of work in order to better pursue the implementation of the outcomes of the major United Nations conferences and summits, recognizing that there is no need for a uniform approach since each functional commission has its own specificity, while also noting that modern methods of work can better guarantee the review of progress made in implementation at all levels, on the basis of a report with recommendations to be submitted by the Secretary-General to each functional commission and relevant subsidiary bodies of the Economic and Social Council on their methods of work, in accordance with the provisions defined by the respective outcomes and relevant decisions taken by each body, bearing in mind the progress recently achieved in this regard by certain commissions, especially the Commission on Sustainable Development; the functional commissions and other relevant bodies of the Economic and Social Council should report to the Council no later than 2005 on the outcome of this examination;

47. *Underscores* that the functional commissions, when mandated, should continue to have the primary responsibility for the review and assessment of progress made in implementing United Nations conference documents, while taking on a new focus in their methods of work;

48. *Invites* the functional commissions to consider, in their deliberations, the experience gained and lessons learned by the United Nations funds and programmes in the implementation of the outcomes of the major United Nations conferences and summits;

49. *Urges* the Economic and Social Council to make better use of the existing consolidated report of the Secretary-General on the work of the commissions and to dedicate more time to its review;

50. *Requests* the Statistical Commission to refine and finalize indicators to assess the implementation of commitments and the achievement of the development goals at the national, regional and international levels;

51. *Recognizes* the role of the Commission on Science and Technology for Development, in the area of science and technology for development, as a forum for improving the understanding of science and technology issues and for the formulation of recommendations and guidelines on science and technology matters within both the United Nations system and the framework of integrated and coordinated implementation of the outcomes of the major United Nations conferences and summits;

52. *Invites* the United Nations regional commissions in collaboration with other regional and subregional organizations and processes, as appropriate, to contribute, within their mandates, to the review of progress made in the implementation of and follow-up to the outcomes of the major United Nations conferences and summits and to provide input to the discussions of the Economic and Social Council on the cross-sectoral thematic issues to be addressed in the coordination segment of its substantive session, in accordance with the rules of procedure of the Council;

53. *Invites* the organizations of the United Nations system, including the Bretton Woods institutions, and the World Trade Organization to contribute within their respective mandates, to the consideration by the Economic and Social Council of the cross-sectoral thematic issues;

54. *Invites* the United Nations System Chief Executives Board for Coordination to contribute to the consideration by the Economic and Social Council of the cross-sectoral thematic issues;

55. *Emphasizes* that the contribution of non-governmental organizations and the private sector to the work of the Economic and Social Council should be further encouraged and improved, in accordance with the rules of procedure of the Council;

The role of the United Nations system, including the specialized agencies

56. *Calls* for making the maximum use of the existing coordination mechanisms of the United Nations system in order to contribute to the integrated and coordinated implementation of and follow-up to the outcomes and commitments of the major United Nations conferences and summits in the economic, social and related fields as a focus on the international agenda;

III
Consideration of the work of the General Assembly and its Second and Third Committees relevant to the implementation of and follow-up to the outcomes of the major United Nations conferences and summits, including the modalities of reports submitted to the General Assembly

57. *Stresses* the need to enhance the role of the General Assembly in conference follow-up and in reviewing progress made on implementation, by ensuring that the working methods of its plenary meetings and of its committees allow maximum focus, visibility and political energy in its work;

58. *Decides* to continue to explore ways and means for improving the work of the Second and Third Committees, including through more active participation of the United Nations system and all relevant intergovernmental stakeholders;

59. *Notes* that the consideration by the Second Committee and the Third Committee, as well as by the General Assembly in plenary meeting, of relevant agenda items should be coherent with the process of integrated and coordinated implementation of and follow-up to the major United Nations conferences and summits in the economic and social fields;

60. *Reiterates* the need to promote greater coherence and complementarity between the work of the General Assembly and its Second and Third Committees; for this purpose the General Committee of the General Assembly should ensure better coordination of the agendas of the Second and Third Committees; the bureaus of the two Committees should review their respective programmes of work in order to exchange information on the issues discussed in each, identify potential areas of overlap or duplication and examine means of considering, in a more coordinated manner, issues related to the follow-up to the major United Nations conferences and summits and make recommendations thereon to their respective Committees;

61. *Recommends* that consideration be given to the use of joint informal debate that can inform the work of each Committee; better use could be made of the General Assembly plenary debate for issues that are considered by both Committees;

62. *Also recommends*, in this context, that at the fifty-eighth session of the General Assembly the Second Committee consider the indicative programme of work set out in the annex to the present resolution and take a decision thereon by December 2003;

63. *Invites* the Bureau of the Second Committee to ensure a practical and coherent organization of the work of the Committee, allowing better focus, visibility and participation;

64. *Encourages* the United Nations system to continue to improve its reports and to make them more analytical and action-oriented by highlighting critical areas requiring action by the General Assembly and, as appropriate, by making specific recommendations; all documents should be issued in hard copy within the specific time frames and page limits and in all official United Nations languages simultaneously; efforts should continue to be made to have all the documentation, in all official languages, available in electronic form;

65. *Underlines* that reports under the agenda items of the Second and Third Committees should continue to follow established reporting procedures, taking into account processes launched by General Assembly resolution 57/300 of 20 December 2002;

66. *Recognizes* the need to avoid requesting duplicative reports from the Secretary-General;

67. *Recommends* that debates in the plenary meetings and in the Second and Third Committees be more interactive, encourages the participation of relevant stakeholders in accordance with the rules of procedure of the General Assembly, and, in this regard, invites the bureaux to consider making use of round tables, briefings and panels to inform the intergovernmental deliberations;

68. *Reiterates* that, in order to strengthen the link between the debates and resolutions in the Second Committee, draft resolutions should continue to be tabled shortly after the relevant debate on agenda items and should take account of the debate;

69. *Recommends* that, in order to ensure that they have greater political impact, resolutions should be short, in particular as regards the preambular parts, and should focus more on action-oriented operative paragraphs;

70. *Underlines* that consideration should be given to the biennialization or triennialization of agenda items;

IV

How best to address the review of the implementation of the outcomes of the major United Nations conferences and summits, including format and periodicity

71. *Stresses* that reviews and appraisals of the major United Nations conferences and summits should assess the progress made in the implementation of commitments and provide the occasion to reaffirm the goals and objectives agreed upon at those conferences and summits, share best practices and lessons learned, and identify obstacles and constraints encountered, actions and initiatives to overcome them and important measures for the further implementation of their programmes of action, as well as new challenges and emerging issues;

72. *Recognizes* that United Nations conferences and summits play a crucial role in raising awareness, mobilizing political will and public opinion, engaging civil society and the private sector and for taking stock of the implementation of the outcomes of the major United Nations conferences and summits by all relevant stakeholders at all levels;

73. *Emphasizes* that the periodicity and the format of the review of the implementation of the outcomes of the major United Nations conferences and summits should be decided on a case-by-case basis by the General Assembly, bearing in mind the relevant specific provisions, taking into account the needs, concerns and specific nature of the issue and the economic and political circumstances and developments, and also bearing in mind the need to continue efforts to use the existing structures, as well as the calendar of major United Nations events;

74. *Also emphasizes* that the review processes should be focused on implementation;

75. *Stresses* that there is scope for a major event in 2005, possibly a comprehensive review, which could be politically attractive and powerful, bearing in mind that the General Assembly has decided to review in 2005 the progress achieved in implementing all the commitments made in the Millennium Declaration, on the basis of a comprehensive report of the Secretary-General.

Annex

Indicative programme of work (Second Committee)

1. Macroeconomic policy questions:
 (a) International trade and development;
 (b) Science and technology for development;
 (c) International financial system and development;
 (d) External debt crisis and development;
 (e) Commodities.

2. Implementation of and follow-up to the Monterrey Consensus of the International Conference on Financing for Development:
 (a) Follow-up to the International Conference on Financing for Development;
 (b) High-level dialogue for the implementation of the outcome of the International Conference on Financing for Development (fifty-eighth session);
 (c) High-level dialogue on strengthening international economic cooperation for development through partnership.

3. Globalization and interdependence.

4. Eradication of poverty, capacity-building and other development issues:
 (a) Implementation of the first United Nations Decade for the Eradication of Poverty (1997-2006);
 (b) Women in development;
 (c) Human resources development (fifty-eighth session);
 (d) International migration and development (fifty-eighth session);
 (e) Culture and development (fifty-ninth session);
 (f) Preventing and combating corrupt practices and transfer of funds of illicit origin and returning such assets to the countries of origin;
 (g) Training and research
  (i) United Nations Institute for Training and Research;
  (ii) United Nations System Staff College in Turin, Italy (fifty-eighth session);
  (iii) United Nations University (fifty-ninth session);

(h) Implementation of the Declaration on International Economic Cooperation, in particular the Revitalization of Economic Growth and Development of the Developing Countries, and implementation of the International Development Strategy for the Fourth United Nations Development Decade;
(i) Industrial development cooperation (fifty-ninth session).
5. Sustainable development:
(a) Implementation of Agenda 21, the Programme for the Further Implementation of Agenda 21 and the outcomes of the World Summit on Sustainable Development;
(b) Further implementation of the Programme of Action for the Sustainable Development of Small Island Developing States;
(c) International Strategy for Disaster Reduction;
(d) Protection of global climate for present and future generations of mankind;
(e) Sustainable mountain development;
(f) United Nations Decade of Education for Sustainable Development;
(g) Promotion of new and renewable sources of energy, including the implementation of the World Solar Programme 1996-2005 (fifty-eighth session);
(h) Implementation of the United Nations Convention to Combat Desertification in those Countries Experiencing Serious Drought and/or Desertification, particularly in Africa;
(i) Convention on Biological Diversity.
6. Implementation of the outcome of the Second United Nations Conference on Human Settlements (Habitat II) and of the twenty-fifth special session of the General Assembly.
7. Operational activities for development:
(a) Operational activities for development of the United Nations system;
(b) Triennial policy review of operational activities for development of the United Nations system (fifty-ninth session);
(c) Economic and technical cooperation among developing countries (fifty-eighth session).
8. Groups of countries in special situations:
(a) Third United Nations Conference on the Least Developed Countries;
(b) Specific actions relating to the particular needs and problems of landlocked developing countries (fifty-eighth session);
(c) Outcome of the International Ministerial Conference of Landlocked and Transit Developing Countries and Donor Countries and International Financial and Development Institutions on Transit Transport Cooperation;
(d) Integration of the economies in transition into the world economy (fifty-ninth session).
9. Permanent sovereignty of the Palestinian people in the Occupied Palestinian Territory, including East Jerusalem, and of the Arab population in the occupied Syrian Golan over their natural resources.
10. Report of the Economic and Social Council.

On 23 December, the Assembly decided that the agenda item on the integrated and coordinated implementation of and follow-up to the outcomes of the major UN conferences and summits in the economic, social and related fields would remain for consideration during its resumed fifty-eighth (2004) session (**decision 58/565**).

ECONOMIC AND SOCIAL COUNCIL ACTION

On 16 July [meeting 36], the Economic and Social Council adopted **resolution 2003/6** [draft: E/2003/L.27] without vote [agenda item 4].

The role of the Economic and Social Council in the integrated and coordinated implementation of the outcomes of and follow-up to major United Nations conferences and summits

The Economic and Social Council,
1. *Welcomes* General Assembly resolution 57/270 B of 23 June 2003, entitled "Integrated and coordinated implementation of and follow-up to the outcomes of the major United Nations conferences and summits in the economic and social fields";
2. *Decides* to take the necessary steps for the effective implementation of the provisions of resolution 57/270 B that are relevant to the work of the Economic and Social Council and its subsidiary machinery and to keep this implementation under review;
3. *Welcomes* the request by the General Assembly for the establishment of a multi-year work programme for the coordination segment of the Economic and Social Council, based on a focused and balanced list of cross-sectoral thematic issues common to the outcomes of the major United Nations conferences and summits, including the objectives, goals and targets of the Millennium Declaration;
4. *Expresses*, in this regard, its determination to finalize the list of cross-sectoral thematic issues and the multi-year work programme for its coordination segment, with the aim of reaching a decision before the substantive session of 2004, and in this regard, invites the Bureau to initiate informal consultations by January 2004;
5. *Takes note* of the report of the Secretary-General, and, in this regard, requests the Secretary-General to update the report and its recommendations in the light of resolution 57/270 B and to submit it for consideration by the Council at its next substantive session.

By **decision 2003/227** of 15 July, the Council took note of a Statistical Commission report on basic indicators for the integrated and coordinated follow-up to major UN conferences and summits (see p. 1295).

The UN and other organizations

Requests for conversion to UN specialized agency

World Tourism Organization

In accordance with Economic and Social Council resolution 2002/24 [YUN 2002, p. 1437], the

Council President appointed 26 States as members of the Committee on Negotiations with Intergovernmental Agencies to negotiate a relationship agreement between the United Nations and the World Tourism Organization (WTO/OMT). Five other States participated as observers.

By **decision 2003/215 A** of 25 March, the Council took note of the Council President's 28 February letter [E/2003/12] informing the Secretary-General of the first 13 Committee appointees and one observer, and also noting the subsequent appointment of another six members and four observers.

The Committee (New York, 26 March; 7, 10 and 15-17 April) considered the text of a draft relationship agreement [E/C.1/2003/1], which it amended, approved and transmitted to WTO/OMT. On 14 May [E/C.1/2003/2], the Secretary-General transmitted a communication from WTO/OMT indicating its approval. The text of the agreement was submitted to the Council in the annex to its report [E/2003/60].

Communication. On 3 December [A/C.2/58/13], the WTO/OMT Secretary-General transmitted to the Second Committee Chairman a resolution adopted by its General Assembly proposing that the United Nations establish in the near future an "International Year of Tourism".

ECONOMIC AND SOCIAL COUNCIL ACTION

On 10 July [meeting 29], the Economic and Social Council adopted **resolution 2003/2** [draft: E/2003/L.19] without vote [agenda item 16].

Agreement between the United Nations and the World Tourism Organization

The Economic and Social Council,

Recalling General Assembly resolutions 2529(XXIV) of 5 December 1969, 32/156 and 32/157 of 19 December 1977 and 36/41 of 19 November 1981, as well as its decision 254(LXIII) of 3 August 1977 and its resolution 2002/24 of 24 July 2002,

Having considered the text of the draft agreement negotiated by its Committee on Negotiations with Intergovernmental Agencies and the World Tourism Organization Committee on the Negotiations for the Conversion of the Organization into a Specialized Agency, in accordance with Article 57 and Article 63, paragraph 1, of the Charter of the United Nations,

Aware that the text of the draft agreement was noted with satisfaction by the Executive Council of the World Tourism Organization on 4 June 2003,

Recommends to the General Assembly that it approve at its fifty-eighth session the agreement contained in the annex to the present resolution.

[For text, see General Assembly resolution 58/232 below.]

GENERAL ASSEMBLY ACTION

On 23 December [meeting 78], the General Assembly, on the recommendation of the Second Committee [A/58/495 & Corr.1], adopted **resolution 58/232** without vote [agenda item 12].

Agreement between the United Nations and the World Tourism Organization

The General Assembly,

Recalling its resolutions 2529(XXIV) of 5 December 1969, 32/156 and 32/157 of 19 December 1977 and 36/41 of 19 November 1981,

Having considered Economic and Social Council resolution 2003/2 of 10 July 2003, the annex to which contains the text of the draft agreement negotiated by the Committee on Negotiations with Intergovernmental Agencies of the Economic and Social Council and the World Tourism Organization Committee on the Negotiations for the Conversion of the Organization into a Specialized Agency, intended to transform the World Tourism Organization, an intergovernmental organization, into a specialized agency, in accordance with Articles 57 and 63 of the Charter of the United Nations,

Approves the agreement between the United Nations and the World Tourism Organization as set forth in the annex to the present resolution.

Annex

Agreement between the United Nations and the World Tourism Organization

Recalling resolutions 2529(XXIV) of 5 December 1969 and 32/156 of 19 December 1977 of the General Assembly of the United Nations,

In consideration of the Charter of the United Nations and the Statutes of the World Tourism Organization,

In further consideration of the provisions of Article 57 of the Charter of the United Nations and of article 3, paragraph 3, and article 31 of the Statutes of the World Tourism Organization,

The United Nations and the World Tourism Organization agree as follows:

Article 1
Recognition

1. The United Nations recognizes the World Tourism Organization as a specialized agency of the United Nations responsible for taking such action as may be appropriate under its Statutes for the accomplishment of the objectives set forth therein.

2. The United Nations recognizes the decisive and central role of the World Tourism Organization, as an intergovernmental organization, in world tourism, as enshrined in its Statutes.

3. Convinced that tourism can contribute significantly to the pursuit of the shared objectives of achieving sustainable development and poverty eradication, the United Nations notes that, in accordance with its Statutes, the World Tourism Organization shall pay particular attention to the interests of the developing countries in the field of tourism.

Article 2
Coordination and cooperation

1. In its relations with the United Nations, its organs and the agencies of the United Nations system, the World Tourism Organization recognizes the coordinating role, as well as the comprehensive responsibilities in promoting economic and social development, of the General Assembly and the Economic and Social Council under the Charter of the United Nations.

2. In exercise of its central coordinating role in the field of tourism undertaken in accordance with its Statutes and with a view to contributing to economic and social development, in particular opportunities for poverty eradication and employment creation in the least developed countries, the World Tourism Organization recognizes the need for effective coordination and cooperation with the United Nations, its organs and the agencies of the United Nations system.

3. The World Tourism Organization, accordingly, agrees to cooperate with the United Nations in whatever measure may be necessary to effect the required coordination of policies and activities.

4. The World Tourism Organization agrees further to participate in, and to cooperate with, any body or bodies that have been established or may be established by the United Nations for the purpose of facilitating such cooperation and coordination, in particular through membership in the United Nations System Chief Executives Board for Coordination, and to furnish such information as may be required for the carrying out of this purpose.

5. The World Tourism Organization shall inform the Economic and Social Council of matters of inter-agency concern within its competence and of any formal agreement on such matters to be concluded between the World Tourism Organization and another agency within the United Nations system.

Article 3
Reciprocal representation

1. Representatives of the United Nations shall be invited to attend the meetings of the General Assembly and the Executive Council of the World Tourism Organization and their subsidiary organs, and to participate, without the right to vote, in the deliberations of these bodies. Written statements presented by the United Nations shall be distributed by the secretariat of the World Tourism Organization to the members of the above-mentioned bodies, in accordance with the relevant rules of procedure.

2. Representatives of the World Tourism Organization shall be invited to attend meetings and to participate, without the right to vote and in accordance with the relevant rules of procedure, in the deliberations of the Economic and Social Council, its commissions and its committees, of the Main Committees and other organs of the General Assembly and of the conferences and meetings of the United Nations, with respect to items on their agenda relating to matters within the scope of the activities of the World Tourism Organization and other matters of mutual interest. Written statements presented by the World Tourism Organization shall be distributed by the Secretariat of the United Nations to the members of the above-mentioned bodies, in accordance with the relevant rules of procedure.

3. Representatives of the World Tourism Organization shall be invited, for purposes of consultation, to attend meetings of the General Assembly when matters defined in paragraph 2 of the present article are under consideration.

Article 4
Proposals of agenda items

1. After such preliminary consultations as may be necessary, the World Tourism Organization shall arrange for the inclusion in the agenda of its General Assembly, the Executive Council or their subsidiary bodies, as appropriate, items proposed by the United Nations.

2. After such preliminary consultations as may be necessary, the United Nations shall arrange for the inclusion in the agenda of the Economic and Social Council or, as appropriate and in accordance with the relevant rules of procedure, of other organs or bodies of the United Nations of items proposed by the World Tourism Organization.

Article 5
Recommendations of the United Nations

1. Having regard to the obligations of the United Nations to promote the objectives set forth in Article 55 of the Charter of the United Nations and the functions and powers of the Economic and Social Council, under Article 62 of the Charter, to make or initiate studies and reports with respect to international economic, social, cultural, educational, health and related matters and to make recommendations concerning these matters to the specialized agencies concerned, and having regard also to the responsibility of the United Nations, under Articles 58 and 63 of the Charter, to make recommendations for the coordination of the policies and activities of such specialized agencies, the World Tourism Organization agrees to arrange for the submission, as soon as possible, to the appropriate organ of the World Tourism Organization of all formal recommendations which the United Nations may make to it.

2. The World Tourism Organization agrees to enter into consultations with the United Nations upon request with respect to such recommendations, and in due course to report to the United Nations on the action taken by the World Tourism Organization or by its members to give effect to such recommendations, or on the other results of their consideration.

Article 6
Assistance to the United Nations

In accordance with the Charter of the United Nations and the Statutes of the World Tourism Organization, the World Tourism Organization shall cooperate with the United Nations by furnishing to it to the fullest extent possible such special information or studies, and by rendering such assistance to it as the United Nations may request.

Article 7
Regular reports

The World Tourism Organization shall submit to the United Nations regular reports on its activities.

Article 8
Exchange of information and documents

Subject to such arrangements as may be necessary for the safeguarding of confidential material, full and prompt exchange of appropriate information and documents shall be made between the United Nations and the World Tourism Organization.

Article 9
Public information

Having regard to the aim of the World Tourism Organization, as defined in article 3, paragraph 1, of its Statutes, and with a view to coordinating the activities of the World Tourism Organization in this field with the operations of the information services of the United Nations, supplementary arrangements regarding these matters shall be concluded between the United Nations and the World Tourism Organization.

Article 10
Relations with the International Court of Justice

1. The World Tourism Organization agrees to furnish any information which may be requested by the International Court of Justice in pursuance of Article 34 of the Statute of the Court.

2. The General Assembly of the United Nations authorizes the World Tourism Organization to request advisory opinions of the International Court of Justice on legal questions arising within the scope of its competence other than questions concerning the mutual relationships between the United Nations and the World Tourism Organization or other specialized agencies.

3. Such requests may be addressed to the International Court of Justice by the General Assembly or by the Executive Council of the World Tourism Organization acting in pursuance of an authorization by the General Assembly of the World Tourism Organization.

4. When requesting the International Court of Justice to give an advisory opinion, the World Tourism Organization shall inform the Economic and Social Council of the request.

Article 11
Non-Self-Governing and other Territories

The World Tourism Organization agrees to cooperate within the fields of its competence with the United Nations in giving effect to the principles and obligations set forth in Chapters XI, XII and XIII of the Charter of the United Nations and other internationally recognized principles and obligations regarding colonial countries and peoples, and taking into account the relevant resolutions of the General Assembly of the United Nations, with regard to matters affecting the well-being and development of the peoples of the Non-Self-Governing and other Territories.

Article 12
Technical assistance

The United Nations and the World Tourism Organization undertake to work together in the provision of technical assistance in the field of tourism and tourism development. In particular, they undertake to avoid undesirable duplication of activities and services and agree to take such measures as may be required to achieve effective coordination within the framework of existing coordinating machinery in the field of technical assistance, taking into account the respective roles and responsibilities of the United Nations and the World Tourism Organization under their constituent instruments, as well as those of other organizations participating in technical assistance activities. To this end, the World Tourism Organization recognizes the overall responsibilities of the resident coordinators for operational activities for development, as formulated in the relevant General Assembly resolutions. As one of the smaller specialized agencies without field representation, the World Tourism Organization may use resident coordinators to ensure its representation and promote its role.

Article 13
Statistical services

1. The United Nations and the World Tourism Organization agree to strive for the maximum cooperation, the elimination of all undesirable duplication between them and the most efficient use of personnel in their respective collection, analysis, publication and dissemination of statistical information. They agree to combine their efforts to secure the greatest possible usefulness and utilization of statistical information, to guarantee close coordination in their respective statistical initiatives and to minimize the burden placed upon Governments and other organizations from which such information may be collected.

2. The World Tourism Organization recognizes that the United Nations is the central agency for the collection, analysis, publication, standardization and improvement of tourism statistics serving the general purposes of international organizations.

3. The United Nations recognizes the World Tourism Organization as the appropriate organization to collect, to analyse, to publish, to standardize and to improve the statistics of tourism and to promote the integration of these statistics within the sphere of the United Nations system.

Article 14
Administrative cooperation

1. The United Nations and the World Tourism Organization recognize the desirability of cooperation in administrative matters of mutual interest.

2. Accordingly, the United Nations and the World Tourism Organization undertake to consult together, and with other agencies concerned within the United Nations system, from time to time concerning these matters, particularly the most efficient and harmonized use of facilities, staff and services and appropriate methods of avoiding the establishment and operation of competitive or overlapping facilities and services with a view to securing as much uniformity in these matters as possible.

3. The consultations referred to in the present article shall be utilized to establish the most equitable manner in which any special services or assistance furnished, on request, by the World Tourism Organization to the United Nations or by the United Nations to the World Tourism Organization shall be financed subject to supplementary arrangements to be concluded for that purpose.

4. The consultations referred to in the present article shall also explore the possibility of continuing or establishing common facilities or services in specific areas, including the possibility of one organization providing such facilities or services to one or several other organizations, and establish the most equitable manner in which such facilities or services shall be financed subject to supplementary arrangements to be concluded for that purpose.

Article 15
Regional and branch offices

Any regional or branch offices which the World Tourism Organization may establish shall closely cooperate with the regional or branch offices which the United Nations has established or may establish, in particular the offices of the regional commissions and of the resident coordinators.

Article 16
Personnel arrangements

1. The United Nations and the World Tourism Organization agree to develop, in the interests of uniform standards of international employment and to the extent feasible, common personnel standards, methods and arrangements designed to avoid unjustified differences in terms and conditions of employment, to avoid competition in recruitment of personnel and to facilitate any mutually desirable and beneficial interchange of personnel. For this purpose the World Tourism Organization agrees to accept the Statute of the International Civil Service Commission and participate in the United Nations Joint Staff Pension Fund in accordance with the Regulations of the Fund and accept the jurisdiction of the United Nations Administrative Tribunal in matters involving applications alleging non-observance of those Regulations.

2. The United Nations and the World Tourism Organization agree to cooperate to the fullest extent possible in achieving these ends, and in particular they agree:

(a) To consult together from time to time concerning matters of mutual interest relating to the terms and conditions of employment of the officers and staff, with a view to securing as much uniformity in these matters as may be feasible;

(b) To cooperate in the interchange of personnel when desirable, on a temporary or a permanent basis, making due provision for the retention of seniority and pension rights;

(c) To cooperate with the agencies of the United Nations system in the establishment and operation of suitable machinery for the settlement of disputes arising in connection with the employment of personnel and related matters.

3. The terms and conditions under which any facilities or services of the United Nations or the World Tourism Organization in connection with the matters referred to in the present article are to be extended to the other shall, where necessary, be the subject of supplementary arrangements concluded for this purpose pursuant to article 20 of the present Agreement.

Article 17
Budgetary and financial matters

1. The World Tourism Organization recognizes the desirability of establishing close budgetary and financial relationships with the United Nations in order that the administrative operations of the United Nations and the agencies within the United Nations system shall be carried out in the most efficient and economic manner possible, and that the maximum measure of coordination and uniformity with respect to these operations shall be secured.

2. The World Tourism Organization agrees to accept the Statute of the Joint Inspection Unit.

3. The World Tourism Organization agrees to conform, as far as may be practicable and appropriate, to standard practices and forms recommended by the United Nations.

4. Financial and budgetary arrangements that may be entered into between the United Nations and the World Tourism Organization shall be approved in accordance with their respective constitutive instruments.

5. In the preparation of the budget of the World Tourism Organization, the Secretary-General of the World Tourism Organization shall consult with the Secretary-General of the United Nations with a view to achieving, insofar as practicable, uniformity in presentation of the budgets of the United Nations and of the agencies within the United Nations system for the purposes of providing a basis for comparison of the several budgets without precluding the use by each organization of different currencies to formulate its budget.

6. The World Tourism Organization agrees to transmit its proposed budgets to the United Nations not later than when the said budgets are transmitted to its members so as to enable the General Assembly of the United Nations to examine them and make recommendations, in accordance with Article 17, paragraph 3, of the Charter of the United Nations.

7. Representatives of the World Tourism Organization shall be entitled to participate, without vote, in the deliberations of the General Assembly or any committee thereof established by it, at all times when the budget of the World Tourism Organization or general administrative or financial questions concerning the World Tourism Organization are under consideration.

Article 18
United Nations laissez-passer

Officials of the World Tourism Organization shall be entitled, in accordance with such special arrangements as may be concluded between the Secretary-General of the United Nations and the Secretary-General of the World Tourism Organization, to use laissez-passer of the United Nations.

Article 19
Implementation of the Agreement

The Secretary-General of the United Nations and the Secretary-General of the World Tourism Organization may enter into such supplementary arrangements for the implementation of the present Agreement as may be found desirable.

Article 20
Amendment and revision

The present Agreement may be amended or revised by agreement between the United Nations and the World Tourism Organization, and any such amendment or revision shall come into force on its approval by the General Assembly of the United Nations and the General Assembly of the World Tourism Organization.

Article 21
Entry into force

The present Agreement enters into force on its approval by the General Assembly of the United Nations and the General Assembly of the World Tourism Organization.

International Civil Defence Organization

The Economic and Social Council, by **decision 2003/222** of 24 June, further deferred consideration of the request made in 2002 [YUN 2002, p. 1437] by the International Civil Defence Organization (ICDO), an intergovernmental organization with observer status with the Council, for

Observer status

International Institute for Democracy and Electoral Assistance

The General Assembly, pursuant to decision 57/513 [YUN 2002, p. 1444], resumed consideration of the 2000 request for observer status in the Assembly for the International Institute for Democracy and Electoral Assistance [YUN 2000, p. 1383].

GENERAL ASSEMBLY ACTION

On 9 December [meeting 72], the General Assembly, on the recommendation of the Sixth (Legal) Committee [A/58/522], adopted **resolution 58/83** without vote [agenda item 159].

Observer status for the International Institute for Democracy and Electoral Assistance in the General Assembly

The General Assembly,

Wishing to promote cooperation between the United Nations and the International Institute for Democracy and Electoral Assistance,

1. *Decides* to invite the International Institute for Democracy and Electoral Assistance to participate in the sessions and the work of the General Assembly in the capacity of observer;

2. *Requests* the Secretary-General to take the necessary action to implement the present resolution.

Eurasian Economic Community

On 11 June [A/58/143], Belarus, Kazakhstan, Kyrgyzstan, the Russian Federation and Tajikistan, the five States members of the Eurasian Economic Community (EURASEC), requested the inclusion in the agenda of the General Assembly's fifty-eighth session of an item on observer status for EURASEC in the Assembly. In an explanatory memorandum, EURASEC, which also included Armenia, Moldova and Ukraine as observers, said that its tasks were to set up a customs union and establish a single economic zone. Granting it observer status would strengthen cooperation between EURASEC and the United Nations and expand their mutual capabilities for ensuring peace, security and cooperation on both regional and global scales.

GENERAL ASSEMBLY ACTION

On 9 December [meeting 72], the General Assembly, on the recommendation of the Sixth Committee [A/58/523], adopted **resolution 58/84** without vote [agenda item 162].

Observer status for the Eurasian Economic Community in the General Assembly

The General Assembly,

Wishing to promote cooperation between the United Nations and the Eurasian Economic Community,

1. *Decides* to invite the Eurasian Economic Community to participate in the sessions and the work of the General Assembly in the capacity of observer;

2. *Requests* the Secretary-General to take the necessary action to implement the present resolution.

GUUAM

On 4 September [A/58/231], Georgia, on behalf of the GUUAM States—Georgia, Ukraine, Uzbekistan, Azerbaijan and Moldova—requested the inclusion in the agenda of the General Assembly's fifty-eighth session of an item on observer status in the Assembly for the GUUAM. An explanatory memorandum annexed to the request provided information on the GUUAM's founding, its organizational structure and objectives, namely, to promote social and economic development; strengthen and expand trade and economic links; develop and use transport and communications networks effectively; strengthen regional security; develop relations in the field of science and culture and in the humanitarian sphere; and combat international terrorism, organized crime and drug trafficking. Granting the GUUAM observer status would allow it to contribute to a broader spectrum of activities of concern to the United Nations.

GENERAL ASSEMBLY ACTION

On 9 December [meeting 72], the General Assembly, on the recommendation of the Sixth Committee [A/58/524], adopted **resolution 58/85** without vote [agenda item 163].

Observer status for the GUUAM in the General Assembly

The General Assembly,

Wishing to promote cooperation between the United Nations and the GUUAM,

1. *Decides* to invite the GUUAM to participate in the sessions and the work of the General Assembly in the capacity of observer;

2. *Requests* the Secretary-General to take the necessary action to implement the present resolution.

East African Community

On 4 September [A/58/232], Kenya, Uganda and the United Republic of Tanzania, the partner States of the East African Community (EAC), a regional economic organization, requested the inclusion in the agenda of the General Assembly's fifty-eighth session of an item on observer status for EAC in the Assembly.

An explanatory memorandum annexed to the request described the establishment of EAC under a 1999 treaty stating that its main objectives were consistent with those of the United Nations as contained in the Charter. EAC believed it desirable to consolidate links with the United Nations and that granting it observer status would be mutually beneficial.

GENERAL ASSEMBLY ACTION

On 9 December [meeting 72], the General Assembly, on the recommendation of the Sixth Committee [A/58/525], adopted **resolution 58/86** without vote [agenda item 164].

Observer status for the East African Community in the General Assembly

The General Assembly,

Wishing to promote cooperation between the United Nations and the East African Community,

1. *Decides* to invite the East African Community to participate in the sessions and the work of the General Assembly in the capacity of observer;

2. *Requests* the Secretary-General to take the necessary action to implement the present resolution.

Participation of organizations in UN work

Intergovernmental organizations

The Economic and Social Council included in the agenda of its 2003 substantive session the applications for observer status with the Council of: the Islamic Development Bank [E/2003/6] and the Islamic Educational, Scientific and Cultural Organization (ISESCO) [E/2003/7] on 28 January (**decision 2003/208**); and the Common Fund for Commodities [E/2003/10] on 5 March (**decision 2003/213**).

The Council granted observer status to the Intergovernmental Institution for the Use of Micro-alga Spirulina against Malnutrition on 5 March (**decision 2003/212**); approved the applications from the Common Fund for Commodities, the Islamic Development Bank and ISESCO (see above) to participate in the Council's work in accordance with rule 79 of its rules of procedure on 24 June (**decision 2003/221**); and granted observer status to the Helsinki Commission, an intergovernmental organization that had applied for observer status in September [E/2003/ 104], on 31 October (**decision 2003/312**).

Non-governmental organizations

Committee on NGOs

The Committee on Non-Governmental Organizations, at its resumed 2002 session (New York, 8-24 January 2003) [E/2003/11], considered 147 applications from NGOs for consultative status with the Economic and Social Council, including those deferred from its 1998-2002 sessions, and eight requests for reclassification. It recommended 89 NGOs for consultative status, three for reclassification and three to maintain their current status. It further recommended that three organizations not be granted consultative status, deferred consideration of 52 applications and closed consideration of three. The Committee took note of 11 quadrennial reports submitted by NGOs in general and special consultative status with the Council, deferred consideration of six such reports pending responses to questions posed by the Committee and of two others pending its review of special reports from the NGOs concerned, and recommended three draft decisions for action by the Council.

The Committee reviewed its working methods relating to the implementation of Council resolution 1996/31 [YUN 1996, p. 1360], including the process of NGO accreditation, and of decision 1995/304 [YUN 1995, p. 1445]. It considered the implementation of Council decision 1996/302 [YUN 1996, p. 1368] on NGO applications for consultative status placed on the Roster for the purpose of the work of the Commission on Sustainable Development, five special NGO reports responding to complaints by Iran, and complaints by Member States against five NGOs. The Committee recommended the participation of three NGOs of indigenous people not in consultative status with the Council in the open-ended intersessional working group of the Commission on Human Rights, established pursuant to Council resolution 1995/32 [YUN 1995, p. 777].

On 1 May, the Council noted the Committee's report on its resumed 2002 session, decided that its 2003 session would be held from 5 to 23 May and approved that session's provisional agenda and documentation (**decision 2003/217**). On the same date, it granted special consultative status to 72 NGOs, placed 17 on the Roster and reclassified three from the Roster to special consultative status; it decided not to grant consultative status to three NGOs and not to reclassify three others from special to general consultative status; it took note of 11 quadrennial reports and noted the Committee's decision to close consideration of three NGO applications and its closure of States' complaints against four NGOs (**decision 2003/216**).

The Committee held its 2003 regular session (5-23 May) [E/2003/32 (Parts I & II & Part II/Corr.1)] and its resumed 2003 session (15-19 December) [E/2003/ 32 (Part III)], both in New York. In May, the Committee recommended 57 NGOs for consultative status and deferred consideration of 48 applications (two organizations having withdrawn their applications). It recommended that two of three NGOs requesting reclassification to consultative status be so reclassified, deferring consideration of the third to its resumed 2003 session. It took note of 65 quadrennial reports, deferred consideration of six others already deferred from previous sessions and of four new ones, and closed consideration of two complaints by States.

The Committee adopted a resolution, which it brought to the Council's attention, and recommended five draft decisions for action by the Council. By the resolution, the Committee recommended that the Council decide to introduce for the Committee on NGOs an electronic meeting system ("Paperless Committee") on a one-year trial basis.

On 24 July, the Council, on the Committee's recommendation, granted special consultative status to 57 NGOs, placed 14 others on the Roster, and reclassified two from the Roster to special consultative status, and noted that the Committee had taken note of 65 quadrennial reports and had closed the case of two complaints submitted by States against NGOs (**decision 2003/275**). It suspended for one year the special consultative status of one organization (**decision 2003/276**). It took note of the Committee's resolution on the electronic meeting system, decided that the Committee should try the system for one year and, if successful, implement it permanently; it also requested the Secretary-General to provide adequate staff and facilities in that regard (**decision 2003/277**). It authorized the Committee to hold a resumed session from 15 to 19 December to complete the work of its 2003 session (**decision 2003/278**) and took note of the Committee's report on its 2003 regular session (**decision 2003/279**).

At its resumed 2003 session, the Committee considered 129 NGO applications for consultative status with the Council, including 47 deferred from previous sessions, and six requests for reclassification. It recommended 69 NGOs for consultative status, three for reclassification and one to maintain its current status. It deferred to its 2004 regular session further consideration of 59 applications for consultative status (one application having been withdrawn) and two reclassification applications. It reviewed 65 quadrennial reports and recommended two draft decisions for action by the Council in 2004.

Requests for hearing

On 22 May, the Committee on NGOs approved 20 NGO requests to be heard during the Council's high-level segment, seven during the coordination segment and two during the general segment.

Withdrawal of status

On 16 May, the Committee took note of the request for withdrawal of status submitted by the Inter-Parliamentary Union (IPU) and agreed to remove it from its list. IPU had been granted observer status by the General Assembly in 2002 by resolution 57/32 [YUN 2002, p. 1445].

Conferences and meetings

Committee on Conferences (2002)

The General Assembly, at its resumed fifty-seventh (2003) session, continued consideration of the 2002 reports of the Committee on Conferences and ACABQ [YUN 2002, p. 1450] on the Secretary-General's report on improving the performance of the Department of General Assembly Affairs and Conference Services (DGAACS) [ibid., p. 1459], which changed its name to the Department for General Assembly and Conference Management (DGACM) in 2003.

GENERAL ASSEMBLY ACTION

On 15 April [meeting 83], the General Assembly, on the recommendation of the Fifth Committee [A/57/651/Add.1], adopted **resolution 57/283 B** without vote [agenda item 116].

Pattern of conferences

The General Assembly,

Recalling its relevant resolutions, including resolutions 40/243 of 18 December 1985, 41/213 of 19 December 1986, 43/222 A to E of 21 December 1988, 52/214 of 22 December 1997, 54/248 of 23 December 1999, 55/222 of 23 December 2000, 56/242 of 24 December 2001, 56/254 D of 27 March 2002, 56/262 of 15 February 2002, 56/287 of 27 June 2002 and 57/283 A of 20 December 2002,

Reaffirming its resolution 42/207 C of 11 December 1987, in which it requested the Secretary-General to ensure the equal treatment of the official languages of the United Nations,

Having considered the report of the Committee on Conferences and the reports of the Secretary-General,

Having also considered the report of the Advisory Committee on Administrative and Budgetary Questions,

1. *Endorses* the recommendations of the Advisory Committee on Administrative and Budgetary Questions contained in its report, subject to the provisions of the present resolution;

2. *Takes note* of the report of the Committee on Conferences;

I
Calendar of conferences and meetings

1. *Notes with satisfaction* that the Secretariat took into account the arrangements referred to in General Assembly resolutions 53/208 A of 18 December 1998, 54/248, 55/222 and 56/242 concerning Orthodox

Good Friday and the official holidays of Id al-Fitr and Id al-Adha, and requests all intergovernmental bodies to observe those decisions when planning their meetings;

2. *Reaffirms* its decision that the headquarters rule shall be adhered to by all bodies, and decides that waivers to the headquarters rule shall be granted solely on the basis of the calendar of conferences and meetings of the United Nations as recommended by the Committee on Conferences for adoption by the General Assembly;

3. *Also reaffirms* the relevant provisions established by the General Assembly in resolution 50/11 of 2 November 1995 on multilingualism;

4. *Requests* the Secretary-General, when planning the calendar of conferences and meetings, to avoid simultaneous peak periods at the various duty stations and to avoid scheduling meetings of related intergovernmental bodies too closely together;

5. *Also requests* the Secretary-General to ensure that any modification to the calendar of conferences and meetings is implemented strictly in accordance with the mandate of the Committee on Conferences and other relevant General Assembly resolutions;

6. *Reaffirms* that the Advisory Committee, when deciding upon its meeting schedule, including meetings away from Headquarters, should take into account the programme of work of the Fifth Committee;

II

A. Utilization of conference-servicing resources and facilities

1. *Notes with deep concern* that the overall utilization factor at the four duty stations in 2001 dropped six points below the benchmark of 80 per cent, with a 14 per cent drop in New York, which accounted for the overall decrease;

2. *Urges* the secretariats and bureaux of bodies that underutilize their conference resources to work more closely with the Department for General Assembly and Conference Management and to consider changes to their programme of work, including adjustments based on previous patterns for recurring agenda items, with a view to reducing underutilization;

3. *Notes with appreciation* that, as a result of the establishment of a permanent interpretation service at the United Nations Office at Nairobi, the number of meetings at which interpretation services have been provided increased by 23.5 per cent in 2001 and the number of events held increased by 10 per cent;

4. *Notes with concern* that the severe constraint of adequate conference facilities at the United Nations Office at Nairobi poses a serious challenge for any further increase in utilization;

5. *Reiterates its request* to the Secretary-General, contained in section II, paragraph 24, of its resolution 56/242, to consider improving and modernizing the conference facilities at the United Nations Office at Nairobi in order to accommodate adequately major meetings and conferences and to report thereon to the General Assembly at the main part of its fifty-eighth session through the Advisory Committee and the Committee on Conferences;

6. *Welcomes* the efforts made during the previous year to improve the utilization of conference services at the United Nations Office at Nairobi;

7. *Expresses regret* that the written report on utilization of conference facilities and services at the United Nations Office at Nairobi for the current period was not submitted for consideration by the Committee on Conferences;

8. *Requests* the Secretary-General to submit the written report referred to in paragraph 7 of the present section to the General Assembly for consideration at its fifty-seventh session, through the Committee on Conferences;

9. *Reaffirms* that all meetings of Nairobi-based bodies shall take place in Nairobi, except as otherwise authorized by the General Assembly or the Committee on Conferences acting on its behalf;

10. *Strongly discourages* any invitation for hosting meetings which would violate the headquarters rule, in particular for United Nations centres with a low utilization level;

11. *Reiterates its encouragement* to the Secretary-General to continue to intensify efforts being made by the United Nations Office at Nairobi to attract more meetings to its facilities;

12. *Notes*, in the report of the Secretary-General, that the percentage of requests met for meetings with interpretation in New York by regional and other major groupings of Member States continued to increase, from 92 per cent during the period 2000-2001 to 97 per cent during the period from July 2001 to April 2002, and that overall, for the four duty stations, 98 per cent of the requests were met, and encourages the Secretariat to maintain that trend;

13. *Requests* the Secretary-General, in this regard, to report to the General Assembly at its fifty-eighth session, through the Committee on Conferences, on the methodology that accurately reflects the situation of the provision of conference services to regional and other major groupings of Member States, taking into account the concerns raised in its resolutions 56/254 D and 56/287;

14. *Reaffirms* its decision in its resolution 56/242 to include all necessary resources in the budget for the biennium 2004-2005 to provide interpretation services for meetings of regional and other major groupings of Member States upon request by those groups, on an ad hoc basis, in accordance with established practice, and requests the Secretary-General to submit to the General Assembly at its fifty-eighth session, through the Committee on Conferences, a report on the implementation of this decision;

15. *Requests* the Secretary-General to provide information on meetings of regional and other major groupings of Member States not serviced by conference services in the context of the proposed programme budget for the biennium 2004-2005;

16. *Also requests* the Secretary-General to submit a separate detailed report to the General Assembly at its fifty-seventh session on the cost implications of providing more predictable and adequate conference services to the meetings of regional and other major groupings of Member States, for its consideration in the context of the proposed programme budget for the biennium 2004-2005;

17. *Further requests* the Secretary-General, when preparing budget proposals for conference services, to ensure that the level of resources proposed for temporary assistance is commensurate with the full demand

for services, estimated on the basis of current experience;

18. *Requests* the Secretary-General to continue to report in writing on the utilization rates of interpretation services and conference facilities at all duty stations;

19. *Also requests* the Secretary-General to develop methods and indicators for assessing the performance of conference services from a full-system standpoint, in particular their cost-effectiveness, efficiency and productivity in carrying out their mandates, taking into account the best practices and experiences of other bodies and organizations that provide analogous services, including, specifically, their experience in developing unit cost measures of full work processes, and to report thereon to the General Assembly at its fifty-eighth session, through the Committee on Conferences;

20. *Encourages* the Committee on Conferences to keep under continued review the procedures for the participation of observers in the work of the Committee;

21. *Requests* the Secretary-General to continue to explore all possible options to increase further the utilization of the conference centre at the Economic Commission for Africa and to report thereon to the General Assembly at its fifty-eighth session through the Committee on Conferences;

B. Improving the performance of the Department of General Assembly Affairs and Conference Services

1. *Reaffirms* that the Fifth Committee is the appropriate Main Committee of the General Assembly entrusted with responsibilities for administrative and budgetary matters;

2. *Welcomes* the intention of the Secretary-General to develop, as soon as possible, with the advice and support of the Office of Internal Oversight Services of the Secretariat, an implementation plan for the envisaged improvements, taking into account the provisions of the present resolution, and requests the Secretary-General to include progress indicators in the plan;

3. *Notes* the proposal to integrate the functions of the technical servicing secretariats of the Fifth and Sixth Committees of the General Assembly into the Department, and requests the Secretary-General to submit this proposal in the context of the proposed programme budget for the biennium 2004-2005 for further consideration;

4. *Recognizes* the need to develop or update existing workload standards so as to reflect functions performed by language staff not currently included, taking into account the best practices and experience of other bodies and organizations engaged in analogous work and drawing on expert advice, while taking into consideration the impact of technological innovations;

5. *Invites* the Secretary-General, in the light of the complex intellectual nature of the language services, to develop further the performance indicators in order to evaluate the quality of the functions performed by them to the satisfaction of the Member States;

6. *Reaffirms* the concepts of delegation of authority and enforcement of accountability, which should be applied in accordance with the relevant resolutions of the General Assembly;

7. *Stresses* that the Department is responsible for the implementation of policy, the formulation of standards and guidelines, overseeing and coordinating United Nations conference services and the overall management of resources under the relevant budget section, while the United Nations Offices at Geneva, Vienna and Nairobi remain responsible and accountable for day-to-day operational activities;

8. *Also stresses* that the responsibilities and functions of the Department and major duty stations in the budgetary and human resources areas should be clearly defined in accordance with the relevant mandates, taking into account specificities of the various duty stations and their functioning in the field of conference services, when enhancing global management;

9. *Requests* the Secretary-General, when implementing paragraph 8 of the present section, to ensure a comprehensive dialogue and coordination between the Department and the United Nations Offices at Geneva, Vienna and Nairobi, with advice from the Office of Internal Oversight Services, as required, in accordance with its mandate, in preparing revisions to the relevant secretariat's documents;

10. *Notes* the intention to strengthen and integrate editorial support functions, and stresses the importance of maintaining an official records editing function while strengthening the pre-editing functions in the Department so as to improve the timeliness of submission of documentation, as mandated by the General Assembly;

11. *Requests* the Secretary-General, as a follow-up to his report, to report on how the reform initiative will involve the other major duty stations, taking into account their specificities and operational responsibilities, in the context of the present resolution;

12. *Also requests* the Secretary-General to ensure that the structural and name changes of the Department will be consistent with the existing mandates, inter alia, the medium-term plan, as well as ensuring the implementation of these mandates, and not lead to any involuntary personnel departures, and that they should improve and not negatively affect the quality and timeliness of technical support services being provided to intergovernmental bodies and not negatively affect the quantity of production and distribution of documents in hard copies, as requested by Member States, simultaneously in the six official languages, and to report thereon to the General Assembly at its fifty-eighth session;

13. *Concurs* with the observation of the Advisory Committee contained in paragraph 6 of its report, that a pragmatic approach should be followed in order not to introduce unnecessary restrictions on the ability of an intergovernmental body or conference to reach a successful conclusion;

III
Documentation- and publication-related matters

1. *Notes with deep concern* the low rate of compliance with the six-week rule for the issuance of documentation, and encourages the Secretary-General, in view of the impact of late submissions on the timely issuance of documents, to deal with this alarming situation;

2. *Reiterates its request* to the Secretary-General to ensure that documentation is available in accordance with the six-week rule for the distribution of documents simultaneously in the six official languages of the General Assembly;

3. *Reiterates its deep regret* concerning the failure of author departments to abide by section III, paragraph 5, of its resolution 55/222, and in this regard requests the Secretary-General to take corrective measures to ensure the full implementation of this provision;

4. *Requests* the Secretary-General to take all necessary measures to ensure the compliance of the Secretariat, organizations, bodies and organs with the request contained in paragraph 3 of the present section, and to submit a report on violations to the General Assembly at its fifty-eighth session;

5. *Notes* that the failure to abide by section III, paragraph 5, of its resolution 55/222 also connotes failure to abide by the six-week rule for the availability of documents, as well as resolution 50/11 on multilingualism, in which the General Assembly recalled the need to ensure the simultaneous distribution of documents in the six official languages of the United Nations;

6. *Notes with appreciation* that some progress has been made by the Secretary-General to comply with some of the provisions of section III, paragraph 5, of its resolution 56/242, and requests the Secretary-General to continue to direct all departments to include, where appropriate, the following elements in reports originating in the Secretariat:

(a) A summary of the report;

(b) Consolidated conclusions, recommendations and other proposed actions;

(c) Relevant background information;

7. *Reiterates* that all documents submitted to legislative organs by the Secretariat and expert bodies for consideration and action should have conclusions and recommendations in bold print;

8. *Reiterates its request* to the Office of Internal Oversight Services to submit its reports in accordance with paragraph 12 of resolution 53/208 B of 18 December 1998;

9. *Regrets* that, if a report is issued late, some departments of the Secretariat still do not indicate the reasons for the delay when the report is introduced;

10. *Reiterates* its decision that, if a report is submitted late to conference services, the reasons therefor should be included in a footnote to the document;

11. *Notes with concern* the current situation of late submission and issuance of documents, as well as its negative impact on the functioning of intergovernmental and expert bodies;

12. *Notes* that the Department will assign timing of submission of manuscripts that takes into account the programme of work of the session at which the report is to be considered and the time needed to produce the document simultaneously in the six official languages at a high level of quality;

13. *Also notes* the intention of the Secretary-General to improve the current situation of late submission and issuance of documents with this approach, in order to comply more effectively with the existing rules on the issuance of documentation, and stresses in this regard that such an approach should be aimed at improving the functioning of the Secretariat and, at the same time, facilitating the work of Member States, and requests the Secretary-General to report thereon to the General Assembly at its fifty-eighth session;

14. *Reiterates* the need to develop a responsibility and accountability system within the Secretariat in order to ensure timely submission of documents for processing;

15. *Requests* the Secretary-General to submit a comprehensive report to the General Assembly at its fifty-eighth session on the implementation of paragraph 14 of the present section, taking into consideration section III, paragraph 10, of resolution 56/242;

16. *Reiterates its request* to the Secretary-General to bring to the attention of the organs concerned, when they are taking action on draft resolutions and decisions, rules 78 and 120 of the rules of procedure of the General Assembly;

17. *Notes with concern* the delay in the issuance of verbatim and summary records, and in this regard requests the Secretary-General to take appropriate measures to ameliorate the situation;

18. *Reiterates its request* to the Secretary-General to study the possibility of further measures in this regard, including enhanced cooperation between the preparation of summary records by the Department and the production of press releases by the Department of Public Information of the Secretariat, bearing in mind the different nature of summary records and press releases;

19. *Also reiterates its request* to the Secretary-General to ensure the communication of resolutions adopted by the General Assembly to the Member States within fifteen days of the close of each session in order to overcome regrettable delays;

20. *Notes* the intention of the Economic and Social Commission for Western Asia to increase the percentage of documents available in Arabic to 100 per cent during the biennium 2004-2005, and in this regard reaffirms all its relevant resolutions in which it requested the Secretary-General fully to ensure the issuance of all documents and publications of the Commission in Arabic;

21. *Requests* the Secretary-General to ensure the full implementation of paragraph 20 of the present section and to report thereon to the General Assembly at its fifty-eighth session;

22. *Stresses* the need to maintain the distribution of hard copy documents to Member States simultaneously in all official languages;

23. *Also stresses* that printing on demand should not negatively affect the quality of services provided and the quantity of documents required by Member States;

24. *Notes* the proposal to improve electronic access to United Nations collections, publications and parliamentary documents, and requests the Secretary-General to keep the internal capacity for the provision of hard copies at the request of Member States, subject to the relevant provisions of resolution 56/242;

25. *Welcomes* the elimination of pouch or courier shipments of documents to duty stations in the light of the capability of duty stations to download and print their own copies from the Official Document System or other United Nations databases;

26. *Requests* the Secretary-General to seek confirmation from Member States on the number of hard copy document sets required by each Member State;

27. *Notes* the intention of the Secretary-General to engage in consultations with universities, depository libraries and other institutions regarding the continued provision of United Nations documentation to them;

28. *Requests* the Secretary-General to provide a report on the outcome of the consultations referred to in paragraph 27 of the present section to the General Assembly at its fifty-eighth session;

29. *Reaffirms* section B of resolution 52/214, and re-emphasizes that any reduction in the length of documents should not adversely affect either the quality of the presentation or the substantive content of the documents and that the reduction should be implemented in a flexible manner with respect to the consolidated reports;

30. *Reiterates* paragraph 20 of resolution 54/249 of 23 December 1999, and requests the Secretary-General to address this issue in the context of the proposed programme budget for the biennium 2004-2005;

IV
Translation- and interpretation-related matters

1. *Notes with concern* that the Arabic and English Units in the Interpretation Section at the United Nations Office at Nairobi are not yet fully staffed, and in this regard reiterates its request to the Secretary-General contained in section IV, paragraph 9, of resolution 56/242 to fill expeditiously the remaining vacancies, and requests the Secretary-General to report thereon to the General Assembly at its fifty-seventh session;

2. *Emphasizes* the importance of multilingualism and the equality of the six official languages of the United Nations;

3. *Requests* the Secretary-General, in the context of the proposed programme budget for the biennium 2004-2005, to make proposals so as to fill the de facto gap between the Spanish Translation Service and the other official language services with similar workloads, without any adverse effect on the other official language services;

4. *Takes note with concern* of the high vacancy rate in the Spanish Translation Service;

5. *Requests* the Secretary-General to take all necessary measures to fill expeditiously the vacant posts in all six official language services of the United Nations and to report thereon to the General Assembly at its fifty-eighth session;

6. *Also requests* the Secretary-General to submit a report to the General Assembly at its fifty-eighth session on the implementation of section IV, paragraph 6, of resolution 56/242;

7. *Notes with deep concern* that some official documents are not translated into all the official languages of the Organization, and reiterates its request contained in paragraph 8 of resolution 56/242;

8. *Requests* the Secretary-General to ensure that efforts continue to be made to improve the quality control of language services at all duty stations;

9. *Reiterates its request* to the Secretary-General to ensure that translation, in principle, reflects the specificity of each language;

10. *Also reiterates its request* to the Secretary-General, in order to improve further the quality of translation of documents issued in the six official languages, to ensure continuous dialogue between translation staff and interpretation staff, among United Nations headquarters in New York, Geneva, Vienna and Nairobi, and between translation divisions and Member States with regard to the standardization of the terminology used;

11. *Further reiterates its request* to the Secretary-General to hold informational meetings in order to brief Member States periodically on the terminology used;

12. *Requests* the Secretary-General to conduct consultations, with the Member States concerned, on the improvement of the translation services;

13. *Recalls* section IV, paragraph 1, of its resolution 56/242, in which it requested the Secretary-General not to conduct further pilot projects on remote interpretation until technological developments so warranted, and in this regard requests the Secretary-General to take into consideration the experiences of international institutions and organizations in this area, as expressed in paragraph 102 of the report of the Secretary-General;

V
Information technology

Emphasizes that the primary goal of the introduction of new technology should be to enhance the quality of conference services and to ensure their timely provision;

* * *

Requests the Secretary-General to report to the General Assembly at its fifty-eighth session on the implementation of the present resolution.

Committee on Conferences (2003)

The Committee on Conferences held an organizational meeting on 22 April and its substantive session on 8, 10 and 12 September [A/58/32]. The Committee examined requests for changes to the approved calendar of conferences and meetings for 2003 [A/AC.172/2003/2] and the draft revised calendar for the 2004-2005 biennium [A/AC.172/2003/CRP.1 & Add.1]. On 10 September, the Committee, having considered the biennialization of the item entitled "Pattern of conferences" on the Assembly's agenda, concluded that its current procedures should be retained. The Committee also considered the utilization of conference-servicing resources and facilities, requests for exceptions to General Assembly resolution 40/243 [YUN 1985, p. 1256] concerning meetings of subsidiary bodies, documentation- and publication-related matters (submission, availability and distribution of documents), translation and interpretation, the proposed 2004-2005 programme budget and information technology. (The Committee's deliberations and recommendations on those matters are detailed in the sections below.)

The Committee approved requests from a number of bodies for changes to the approved calendar for 2003. It adopted the draft 2004-2005 calendar of conferences and meetings of subsidiary organs of the Economic and Social Council and recommended that the Assembly approve it, on the understanding that the budgetary implications of certain items, such as the decisions and recommendations of the Council adopted at its 2003 substantive session and included in the calendar, would be reviewed by the responsible legislative bodies, and authorize adjustments to the calendar that might become necessary as a result of actions and decisions taken by the Assembly at its fifty-eighth session.

On 24 July, the Council approved the 2004-2005 calendar of conferences and meetings in the economic, social and related fields (**decision 2003/272**).

GENERAL ASSEMBLY ACTION

On 23 December [meeting 79], the General Assembly, on the recommendation of the Fifth Committee [A/58/575], adopted **resolution 58/250** without vote [agenda item 125].

Pattern of conferences

The General Assembly,

Recalling its relevant resolutions, including resolutions 40/243 of 18 December 1985, 41/213 of 19 December 1986, 43/222 A to E of 21 December 1988, 51/211 A to E of 18 December 1996, 52/214 of 22 December 1997, 53/208 A to E of 18 December 1998, 54/248 of 23 December 1999, 55/222 of 23 December 2000, 56/242 of 24 December 2001, 56/254 D of 27 March 2002, 56/262 of 15 February 2002, 56/287 of 27 June 2002, 57/283 A of 20 December 2002 and 57/283 B of 15 April 2003,

Reaffirming its resolution 42/207 C of 11 December 1987, in which it requested the Secretary-General to ensure the equal treatment of the official languages of the United Nations,

Also reaffirming the provisions relevant to conference services of its resolutions on multilingualism,

Having considered the report of the Committee on Conferences and the relevant reports of the Secretary-General,

Having also considered the first report of the Advisory Committee on Administrative and Budgetary Questions on the proposed programme budget for the biennium 2004-2005, in particular paragraph I.84 thereof, and the second report of the Advisory Committee,

I
Calendar of conferences and meetings

1. *Notes with appreciation* the work of the Committee on Conferences;

2. *Approves* the draft biennial calendar of conferences and meetings of the United Nations for 2004-2005, as submitted by the Committee on Conferences, taking into account the observations of the Committee, and subject to the provisions of the present resolution;

3. *Authorizes* the Committee on Conferences to make any adjustments to the calendar of conferences and meetings for 2004-2005 that may become necessary as a result of actions and decisions taken by the General Assembly at its fifty-eighth session;

4. *Notes with satisfaction* that the Secretariat has taken into account the arrangements referred to in General Assembly resolutions 53/208 A, 54/248, 55/222, 56/242 and 57/283 B concerning Orthodox Good Friday and the official holidays of Id al-Fitr and Id al-Adha, and requests all intergovernmental bodies to continue to observe those decisions when planning their meetings;

II

A. Utilization of conference-servicing resources and facilities

1. *Notes* the improvements in the utilization of the conference centre at the Economic Commission for Africa in response to section II.A, paragraph 21, of its resolution 57/283 B, and requests the Secretary-General to continue to explore all possible options to increase further the utilization of the conference centre;

2. *Requests* the Committee on Conferences to consult with those bodies that have consistently utilized less than the applicable benchmark figure of their allocated resources of the past three sessions, with a view to making appropriate recommendations in order to achieve the optimum utilization of conference-servicing resources, and urges the secretariats and bureaux of bodies that underutilize their conference-servicing resources to work more closely with the Department for General Assembly and Conference Management of the Secretariat and to consider changes to their programme of work, as appropriate, including adjustments based on previous patterns for recurring agenda items, with a view to making improvements in their underutilization factors;

3. *Welcomes* the efforts that are being made to improve utilization of conference facilities at the United Nations Office at Nairobi, as set out in the report of the Secretary-General;

4. *Recalls* its several resolutions, including resolution 57/283 B, section II.A, paragraph 9, and reaffirms that all meetings of Nairobi-based United Nations bodies shall take place in Nairobi, except as otherwise authorized by the General Assembly or the Committee on Conferences acting on its behalf;

5. *Reiterates its encouragement* to the Secretary-General to continue to intensify the efforts being made by the United Nations Office at Nairobi to attract more meetings to its facilities;

6. *Strongly discourages* any invitation to host meetings which would violate the headquarters rule, in particular for the United Nations Office at Nairobi and other United Nations centres with a low utilization level;

7. *Emphasizes* that all duty stations shall be given adequate resources for the effective and efficient discharge of their respective mandates;

8. *Reiterates its concern* over the delay in the process of filling the remaining vacancies in the interpretation and translation services at the United Nations Office at Nairobi and calls for the expeditious filling of the vacancies, and requests the Secretary-General to report thereon, through the Committee on Conferences, to the General Assembly at its fifty-ninth session;

9. *Regrets* the difficulties, including the delay, in fully staffing the Arabic Unit in the Interpretation Section at the United Nations Office at Nairobi and requests the Secretary-General to take adequate measures to ensure the filling of those posts without further delay, and to report thereon, through the Committee on Conferences, to the General Assembly at its fifty-ninth session;

10. *Notes* the importance of meetings of regional and other major groupings of Member States for the smooth functioning of the sessions of intergovernmental bodies, and requests the Secretary-General to ensure that, as far as possible, all requests for conference services for meetings of regional and other major groupings of Member States are met;

11. *Notes with concern* that the rate of provision of interpretation services to the regional and other major groupings has declined;

12. *Notes with appreciation* that 100 per cent of requests by regional and other major groupings for conference facilities were met, according to the current methodology for recording statistics;

13. *Emphasizes* the importance of providing services of the highest quality to Member States in all duty stations and, in this regard, requests the Secretary-General to take appropriate measures in order to address current disparities in the quality of conference services between duty stations;

14. *Requests* the Secretary-General to continue to include in future reports the utilization rates of interpretation services and conference facilities at all duty stations;

15. *Notes* that the Secretary-General has submitted his report pursuant to section II.A, paragraph 14, of its resolution 57/283 B, in which it reaffirmed its decision to include all necessary resources in the budget for the biennium 2004-2005 to provide interpretation services for meetings of regional and other major groupings of Member States upon request by those groups, on an ad hoc basis, in accordance with established practice;

B. Reform of the Department for General Assembly and Conference Management

1. *Reaffirms* that the Fifth Committee is the appropriate Main Committee of the General Assembly entrusted with responsibilities for administrative and budgetary matters;

2. *Welcomes* the initial steps taken by the Secretary-General in the implementation of the reform measures put forward in his report in accordance with section II.B of its resolution 57/283 B, and encourages the continued implementation of the measures described in paragraph 52 of his report on the reform of the Department for General Assembly and Conference Management of the Secretariat, subject to the provisions of the present resolution;

3. *Reiterates its request* contained in section II.B, paragraph 12, of its resolution 57/283 B;

4. *Stresses* that the reform of the Department should be aimed at improving the quality of documents and their timely production and delivery and the quality of conference services provided to Member States, with a view to meeting their needs as efficiently and effectively as possible and in accordance with the relevant resolutions of the General Assembly;

5. *Also stresses* that the reform of the Department should be aimed equally at increasing the productivity of the Department in delivering all services in accordance with relevant resolutions;

6. *Notes* that the reform will include a comprehensive study of the integrated global management, in accordance with section II.B, paragraph 8, of resolution 57/283 B, in consultation with the Office of Internal Oversight Services and with the full participation of all duty stations in a collaborative and consultative process, with a view to reaching conclusions that are both practical and comprehensive, and requests the Secretary-General to keep the General Assembly informed of the matter through the Committee on Conferences;

7. *Requests* the Secretary-General to develop further an effective measure to strengthen the responsibility and accountability system within the Secretariat, in order to ensure the timely submission of documents for processing, and to submit a comprehensive report thereon to the General Assembly at its fifty-ninth session, through the Committee on Conferences;

8. *Notes* the intention of the Secretary-General to establish a Secretariat task force, with broad participation, to conduct a comprehensive study of workload standards and performance measurement and to report thereon to the General Assembly at its fifty-ninth session, through the Committee on Conferences;

9. *Requests* the Secretary-General to conduct a thorough cost-benefit study of summary records and to review the list of bodies entitled to them, in full consultation with all relevant intergovernmental bodies, with a view to assessing the need for such records, and to explore the possibility of delivering them in a more efficient and effective manner, and to report thereon, through the Committee on Conferences, to the General Assembly at its fifty-ninth session;

10. *Also requests* the Secretary-General to ensure that the ongoing and planned work on workload standards and performance measurement specifically develops quantitative methods and indicators to assess productivity, efficiency and cost-effectiveness and to do so also for the quality of services, and to report thereon, through the Committee on Conferences, to the General Assembly at its fifty-ninth session;

11. *Further requests* the Secretary-General to ensure that the ongoing and planned work on workload standards and performance measurement specifically develops qualitative methods and indicators to assess productivity, efficiency and cost-effectiveness and to do so also for the quality of services, and to report thereon, through the Committee on Conferences, to the General Assembly at its fifty-ninth session;

12. *Recognizes* that the satisfaction of Member States is a key performance indicator in conference management and services, and requests the Secretary-General to continue to include a user-oriented approach towards performance management on a wider scope, to make proposals to the General Assembly on the incorporation of such an approach into the performance-management methods of the Department and to incorporate the results of such an approach, as well as the results of his own internal evaluation of the Department, into future proposals for the improvement of the operation of the Department;

III

Documentation- and publication-related matters

1. *Emphasizes* the importance of the equality of the six official languages of the United Nations;

2. *Reaffirms* section B of its resolution 52/214, and emphasizes that any reduction in the length of reports should affect neither the quality of presentation nor the content of the reports;

3. *Notes* that reports not originating from the Secretariat comprise the bulk of the documents issued, and requests the Secretary-General to examine ways and means to achieve compliance with the relevant guideline on page limits and to report on the matter to the General Assembly through the Committee on Conferences;

4. *Also notes* the relative improvement in the timely issuance of documents for the fifty-eighth session;

5. *Notes with concern* that the six-week rule for issuance of documents is not fully complied with owing to, inter alia, the late submission of documents by author departments in violation of relevant rules, and requests the Secretary-General to take corrective measures so as to ensure strict compliance with the six-week rule for the timely issuance of documentation in view of the impact of their late issuance on the functioning of intergovernmental and expert bodies;

6. *Requests* the Secretary-General to ensure that the rules concerning simultaneous distribution of documents in all official languages are followed with respect to the posting of parliamentary documentation on the Official Document System and on the United Nations web site, in keeping with section III, paragraph 5, of General Assembly resolution 55/222;

7. *Notes with concern* paragraph 61 of the report of the Secretary-General, reaffirms that there should be no exceptions to the rule that documents must be distributed in all official languages, and emphasizes the principle that all official documents must be distributed simultaneously in all official languages before they are made available on United Nations web sites;

8. *Reiterates its request* to the Secretary-General to ensure that documents are available in accordance with the six-week rule for their distribution simultaneously in the six official languages;

9. *Also reiterates its request* to the Secretary-General to ensure that translation, in principle, reflects the specificity of each language to the extent possible and that concordance in resolutions is achieved;

10. *Recalls* section III, paragraphs 25, 26 and 27, of resolution 57/283 B, expresses its concern that the report requested in paragraph 28 of the resolution was not submitted, urges the Secretary-General to provide Member States promptly with the outcome of the consultations referred to in this context, and decides to revert to this issue at its fifty-ninth session;

11. *Reiterates its request* to the Secretary-General to direct all departments to include the following elements in reports originating in the Secretariat:

(*a*) A summary of the report;

(*b*) Consolidated conclusions, recommendations and other proposed actions;

(*c*) Relevant background information;

12. *Encourages* intergovernmental and expert bodies to include the above-mentioned elements, where appropriate, in their reports to the General Assembly;

13. *Requests* that all documents submitted to legislative organs by the Secretariat, intergovernmental and expert bodies for consideration and action have conclusions and recommendations in bold print;

14. *Notes with concern* the delay in the issuance of verbatim and summary records and, in this regard, requests the Secretary-General to take appropriate measures to ameliorate the situation, with a view to issuing them in a timely fashion;

15. *Also notes with concern* the non-compliance with rule 59 of the rules of procedures of the General Assembly, and requests the Secretary-General to ensure the communication of resolutions adopted by the General Assembly to Member States within fifteen days after the closure of the session;

16. *Further notes with concern* the decrease in the percentage of documents available in Arabic issued by the Economic and Social Commission for Western Asia, and requests the Secretary-General to take immediate measures to ensure the 100 per cent issuance in Arabic of all the Commission's documents and publications in the biennium 2004-2005;

17. *Reaffirms* section B of its resolution 52/214, and re-emphasizes that any reduction in the length of documents should not adversely affect either the quality of the presentation or the substance of the documents and that the reduction should be implemented in a flexible manner with respect to the consolidated reports;

IV
Translation- and interpretation-related matters

1. *Notes with concern* the high rate of self-revision in some of the official languages, as well as the translation problems in some languages;

2. *Requests* the Secretary-General, in updating the workload standards, to address the question of the appropriate level of self-revision that is consistent with quality in all official languages;

3. *Reiterates its request* to the Secretary-General contained in section IV, paragraph 1, of its resolution 55/222;

V
Information technology

1. *Emphasizes* that the primary goal of the introduction of new technology should be to enhance the quality, production, cost-effectiveness and efficiency of conference services, in accordance with legislative mandates;

2. *Notes* the relative progress achieved thus far across duty stations in integrating information technology into management and documentation- processing systems;

3. *Also notes* the particular situation of the United Nations Office at Nairobi, urges the Secretary-General to take steps to ensure that modern conference management and documentation practices, systems and technology are shared across all duty stations in an institutionalized manner and requests the Secretary-General to report thereon, through the Committee on Conferences, to the General Assembly at its fifty-ninth session;

VI

1. *Requests* the Secretary-General to submit a consolidated report on all actions mandated in the present resolution to the Committee on Conferences at its next session;

2. *Recalls* the need to consider biennialization and triennialization of the agenda items of the Fifth Committee, in accordance with the guidelines on the rationalization of the agenda of the General Assembly outlined in paragraph 5 (*c*) of annex I to its resolution 48/264 of 29 July 1994 and in its resolution 58/126 of 19 December 2003 on the revitalization of the work of the General Assembly;

3. *Requests* the Secretary-General, in the context of paragraph 2 above, to submit to the General Assembly at its fifty-ninth session, through the Committee on Conferences, proposals on the possibility of biennializing this item.

Also on 23 December, the Assembly decided that the item "Pattern of conferences" would remain for consideration during its resumed fifty-eighth (2004) session (**decision 58/565**).

Intergovernmental meetings

At the request of host Governments, the main documents of intergovernmental conferences held in 2003 were transmitted to the Secretary-General for circulation to the General Assembly or the Security Council, or to both, as follows:

The Troika of the Non-Aligned Movement (Cuba, Malaysia, South Africa) (Putrajaya, Malaysia, 19 March) [A/58/68-S/2003/357]; heads of State of members of the Shanghai Cooperation Organization (Moscow, 29 May) [A/58/94-S/2003/642]; International Meeting on Good Humanitarian Donorship (Stockholm, Sweden, 16-17 June) [A/58/99-S/2003/94]; heads of State of the members of the Central Asian Cooperation Organization (Almaty, Kazakhstan, 5 July) [A/58/131-S/2003/703]; thirty-fourth meeting of the Chairmen/Coordinators of the Chapters of the Group of 77 (Geneva, 26-27 June) [A/58/204]; fifth Ibero-American Conference of Ministers for Public Administration and State Reform (Santa Cruz de la Sierra, Bolivia, 26-27 June) [A/58/193]; thirty-fourth Pacific Island Forum (Auckland, New Zealand, 14-16 August) [A/58/304]; twenty-seventh Annual Meeting of the Ministers for Foreign Affairs of the Group of 77 and China (New York, 25 September) [A/58/413]; Ministers for Foreign Affairs of the Non-Aligned Movement (New York, 26 September) [A/58/420]; Ministers for Foreign Affairs of the New Agenda Coalition countries (Brazil, Egypt, Ireland, Mexico, New Zealand, South Africa, Sweden) (New York, 23 September) [A/58/406]; Annual Coordination Meeting of Ministers for Foreign Affairs of the Member States of the Organization of the Islamic Conference (New York, 30 September) [A/58/415-S/2003/952]; Council of Heads of State of the Commonwealth of Independent States (Yalta, Ukraine, 19 September) [A/58/445]; Thirteenth Ibero-American Summit of Heads of State and Government (Santa Cruz de la Sierra, 14-15 November) [A/58/607]; World Economic Development Declaration Conference (Zhuhai, China, 6-7 November) [A/58/614].

Reform of the Department for General Assembly and Conference Management

In response to General Assembly resolution 57/283 B (see p. 1481), the Secretary-General submitted a 5 August report [A/58/213] on the reform of DGACM (formerly the UN Department of General Assembly Affairs and Conference Services). He summarized the measures taken by DGACM during its first year of reform and outlined the future course of action. The Secretary-General noted that, since the second half of 2002, DGACM had instituted proactive managerial policies and working methods in order to implement the reform measures contained in his 2002 report [YUN 2002, p. 1449]. The measures and mechanisms introduced were aimed at achieving full-system benefits by instilling a new managerial culture focused on the Department's overall performance and synergy within and across work units, and closer interdepartmental and intergovernmental coordination; integrated global management of conference-related resources; optimized use of technology; alleviation of the documentation situation; and high-quality performance during the course of reform.

The report concluded that the first year of the reform had laid a solid foundation for fundamentally changing DGACM's existing philosophy and mentality and overhauling its modus operandi. The effort had resulted in considerable reductions in temporary assistance and overtime expenditures, enabling DGACM in New York to stay within its 2002 budget allotment and placing it in a good position to discharge its functions within its 2002-2003 budgetary appropriations.

Recommended follow-up steps included: work towards full electronic processing of documents in all official languages; the replacement of outdated traditional printing equipment and identifying the most appropriate mix of printing and distribution technology; extending the concordance of selected draft resolutions to all Assembly resolutions; upgrading and expanding e-Meets (electronic meetings management) to include information from other duty stations; increasing the integration of the electronic management systems for the meetings and documents chains to synchronize documentation requirements with meeting schedules; undertaking a major study of the integrated global management of conference-related resources in cooperation with OIOS; and a comprehensive study by DGACM of workload standards and performance measurement.

The Committee on Conferences [A/58/32], having considered the Secretary-General's report, sought DGACM's assurance that documents would be equally accessible in all official languages under the electronic documents flow system. The Department was urged to maintain high-quality services during the reform process and assist Member States in the transition to the electronic submission and retrieval of documents. Recommendations on those issues were formulated by the Committee in a proposed draft resolution that was subsequently incorporated in Assembly **resolution 58/250** (see p. 1486).

Use of conference services

The Committee on Conferences [A/58/32] considered a September report of the Secretary-General [A/58/194 & Corr.1,2] providing analytical information on the improved utilization of conference-servicing resources and facilities; documentation- and publication-related matters; translation- and interpretation-related matters; and information technology.

The Committee noted that the 2002 utilization factor for the four duty stations of 75 per cent was one percentage point higher than in 2001, but six percentage points lower than in 2000. The slight improvement was due solely to a decrease in time lost owing to late starts and early endings at three duty stations. There was little change in the number of cancellations. The Committee also noted that the 75 per cent utilization factor was five percentage points lower than the benchmark figure established by the General Assembly and remained an unacceptable loss of resources. The Committee Chairman again conducted consultations with the chairpersons and/or secretaries of those bodies that had underutilized for three consecutive years, urging them to consider changes in their work programme and to introduce more discipline into the way they operated. The Chairman was asked to continue such consultations with a view to making recommendations for achieving optimum utilization of conference-servicing resources.

Use of regional conference facilities

Nairobi

Reports of Secretary-General. In response to General Assembly resolution 57/283 B (see p. 1481), the Secretary-General submitted a May report [A/57/809] providing statistical information on the utilization of conference facilities and services at the United Nations Office at Nairobi (UNON) for the period 2000-2003. The data related to the planning and coordination of meetings, interpretation assignments, translation and editorial services, text processing and printing and distribution.

In response to Assembly resolutions 55/222 [YUN 2000, p. 1387], 56/242 [YUN 2001, p. 1378] and 57/283 B, the Secretary-General, in October [A/58/530], presented the results of a Secretariat review, which indicated a pressing need to modernize the UNON conference facilities. The proposed modernization, at an estimated cost of $3,479,000, would increase seating capacity, install modern simultaneous interpretation equipment and upgrade the sound, air-conditioning and data-distribution systems. The possibility of constructing three additional conference rooms at a cost of $4,228,800 was also considered but the Secretariat felt that such construction should be reviewed at a later stage in the light of experience gained from operating the modernized facilities during the 2006-2007 biennium.

Annexed to the report was information on existing and projected conference facilities capacity, conference services workload and a sketch of possible expansion of conference facilities at UNON.

The Committee on Conferences [A/58/32] noted that further reporting on improving and modernizing the UNON conference facilities would be done through ACABQ, in accordance with established procedures.

ACABQ report. In October [A/58/7/Add.6], ACABQ recommended that the Assembly authorize the modernization of the existing conference facilities at UNON and the funding of the estimated cost of $3,479,000, as described and outlined in the Secretary-General's report.

By **resolution 58/272**, section IV, of 23 December (see p. 1417), the Assembly authorized the proposed modernization and decided to appropriate resources to finance it in the proposed 2004-2005 programme budget.

Vacancies at UNON. In accordance with General Assembly resolution 57/283 B, the Secretary-General reported on 9 April [A/57/783] on efforts to fill vacancies in the Arabic and English Units of UNON's Interpretation Section. He said that unexpected delays in the recruitment process for those vacancies had occurred and that measures had been taken to ensure that by year's end the Section would be completely staffed with Nairobi-based staff.

Economic Commission for Africa

In response to General Assembly resolution 57/283 B (see p. 1481), the Secretary-General, in July [A/58/194 & Corr.1,2], discussed options to increase further the utilization of the conference centre at the Economic Commission for Africa (ECA) (Addis Ababa, Ethiopia). The report noted that, while the high occupancy rate achieved in 2002 as a result of the reorganized management of the centre was maintained in the first half of 2003, there were possibilities for further improvement. To that end, measures being planned included integrating all operating phases of the centre into one system, with standardized procedures to ensure competitive service standards; attracting large-scale events outside the traditional and consultative formats; and adopting international best practices with regard to package rates, and promoting the centre by targeting key publics and forums using advanced channels of communications and the services of a marketing officer.

The Committee on Conferences [A/58/32] expressed appreciation that in 2002 ECA had reorganized its conference centre by establishing a Conference Coordination Unit to enable it to better respond to clients' needs and an Integrated Conference Management System to further enhance the provision of services. It noted that occupancy at the centre in 2002 had increased by more than 80 per cent over the previous year, an increase that was being maintained in 2003. It further noted ECA plans to further increase utilization of the centre.

Interpretation for regional and other groupings

In response to General Assembly resolution 57/283 B (see p. 1481), the Secretary-General, in July [A/58/194 & Corr. 1,2], reported on the provision of interpretation services to the meetings of regional and other major groupings of Member States for the period from 1 May 2002 to 30 April 2003. During that period, New York met 90 per cent of requests for interpretation services (compared to 97 per cent during the 2001/02 period), Geneva 98 per cent and Nairobi 100 per cent. No requests for interpretation were made in Vienna.

The Committee on Conferences [A/58/32] expressed regret that the percentage of meetings held in the four duty stations by regional and other major groupings that were provided with interpretation services in the reporting period had decreased to 92 per cent from 98 per cent over the same period in 2001/02.

Cost implications of providing conference services

In response to General Assembly resolution 57/283 B (see p. 1481), the Secretary-General submitted an October report [A/58/397] on the cost implications of providing more predictable and adequate conference services to the meetings of regional and other major groupings of Member States. The report noted that such meetings were currently serviced on an ad hoc basis from within the existing capacity of DGACM and that no resources had been allocated in the UN programme budget for those services. An analysis of the existing mandate, the capacity of the departments and offices involved in the servicing of conferences and meetings of UN organs and the level of resources currently available for that purpose had led to the conclusion that a change in the mandate for servicing such meetings, dedicated conference-servicing time and the allocation of the related financial resources would be the only means of providing more predictable and adequate conference services to those groupings. Should the Assembly decide to change that mandate and to establish, effective in the 2004-2005 biennium, more predictable and adequate conference-servicing arrangements for the meetings of those groups, an adequate resource provision would need to be made, in addition to the resources initially requested in the proposed 2004-2005 programme budget. Based on average annual demand for such services over the past five years, that provision was estimated at $7,966,000, subject to the procedure for the use and operation of the contingency fund established by Assembly resolution 42/211 [YUN 1987, p. 1098].

The demand for services for such meetings would be kept under review and, should actual demands in 2004-2005 exceed the assumptions in the current report, the financial requirements would be reported to the Assembly in the context of the second budget performance report for that biennium.

ACABQ report. On 23 October [A/58/7/Add.5], ACABQ noted that whether or not to change the existing mandate for the provision of conference services to regional and other major groupings of Member States was a policy decision to be made by the General Assembly. However, should the Assembly decide to approve such a change, ACABQ recommended that an estimate of $4,740,600 be approved, subject to the procedures set out in Assembly resolutions 41/213 [YUN 1986, p. 1024] and 42/211 [YUN 1987, p. 1098] for the use and operation of the contingency fund. It asked the Secretary-General to report on the utilization of the amount appropriated in the context of the first performance report on the 2004-2005 programme budget.

The Assembly, in **resolution 58/272**, section XV, of 23 December (see p. 1419), took note of the reports of the Secretary-General and ACABQ.

Documentation

In response to General Assembly resolution 57/283 B (see p. 1481), the Secretary-General, in July [A/58/194 & Corr.1,2], described measures to ensure compliance with the Assembly's request in resolution 55/222 [YUN 2000, p. 1387] that all documents be distributed simultaneously in the six UN official languages before being made available on UN web sites. The gradual opening of the Official Document System (ODS) to the public represented the single most effective corrective measure to ensure simultaneous availability of parliamentary documentation in the official languages on the UN web site.

In a 5 August report [A/58/213], the Secretary-General said that, to address the late issuance of documents caused by their late and often uncoordinated submission for processing, DGACM had begun implementing on a trial basis in 2003 a slotting system whereby documents were assigned a week-long "slot" based on the scheduled dates on which they were to be considered by intergovernmental bodies, for issuance four weeks at the latest prior to those dates. An initial assessment indicated the author departments' growing awareness of the importance of staying within their assigned slot.

Other matters discussed concerned the enforcement of restrictions and guidelines on the length of reports originating in and outside the Secretariat, including waiver requests for specific documents; the amelioration of the late issuance of summary records; and the concordance of Assembly draft resolutions.

The Committee on Conferences [A/58/32] expressed the view that the simultaneous and timely availability of official documents in all six languages required substantial resources; the consolidation of reports, as called for in the context of DGACM's reform, would contribute in that regard.

ESCWA documents

In response to General Assembly resolution 57/283 B (see p. 1481), which reaffirmed that all documents and publications of the Economic and Social Commission for Western Asia (ESCWA) be issued in Arabic, the Secretary-General reported in July [A/58/194 & Corr.1,2] that ESCWA had kept the matter under review. Based on data available as at July, projections for documents and publications to be issued in Arabic in 2004-2005 were 100 per cent and 92 per cent, respectively (compared to an estimated 82 per cent and 55.5 per cent in 2002-2003 and actual 95 per cent and 62.5 per cent in 2000-2001).

Translation and interpretation matters

Recruitment in language services

In response to General Assembly resolution 57/283 B (see p. 1481), the Secretary-General reported in July [A/58/194 & Corr.1,2] on efforts to fill vacant posts in the UN translation services. Total vacancies for Spanish had dropped from 28 to 16 for all duty stations, with eight vacancy reductions at Headquarters alone, and the six vacancies in the Chinese Translation Service at Headquarters had been filled. The overall vacancy situation at all duty stations, however, needed to be improved further. The depletion of the current roster was a major reason why vacancies in the Arabic, English, French and Spanish services had not been filled. Rosters established after the completion of competitive examinations in those languages during the year would alleviate the high vacancy rate in the translation services.

The Secretary-General noted that the rate of self-revision improved in the first half of 2003 and that efforts would continue to bring the rate closer to the target of 45 per cent set by the Assembly.

The Committee on Conferences [A/58/32], while expressing satisfaction at the vacancy reduction, requested complete vacancy data in all language services. It expressed concern about the number of anticipated retirements and about the working conditions in New York not being as attractive as those in Europe. Concerned also about occasional lapses in the quality of interpretation, it stressed the usefulness of dialogue on terminology between interpreters and delegates, possibly through the format of language-specific informational meetings for delegations organized by DGACM (see below).

Informational meetings

In response to the General Assembly's request in resolution 57/283 B (see p. 1481) that informational meetings be organized to brief Member States on the terminology used and that consultations be held with them on the improvement of translation services, DGACM organized, for each of the six UN official languages, language-specific meetings where delegations posed questions relating to terminology used by the UN language services and on the provision of language services in general.

UN information systems

Information and communication technology

In April, the General Assembly continued consideration of the Secretary-General's 2002 report [A/57/620] on the revised information and communication technology (ICT) strategy [YUN 2002, p. 1454].

GENERAL ASSEMBLY ACTION

On 15 April [meeting 83], the General Assembly, on the recommendation of the Fifth Committee [A/57/649/Add.1], adopted **resolution 57/304** without vote [agenda item 112].

Information and communication technology strategy

The General Assembly,

Recalling its resolutions 56/239 and 56/253 of 24 December 2001,

1. *Takes note* of the report of the Secretary-General on an information and communication technology strategy, and welcomes the significant step it repre-

sents in developing a strategic framework to guide the further development of information and communication technology in the United Nations, as called for in its resolution 56/239;

2. *Stresses* the importance of information and communication technology as a strategic tool for strengthening the functioning of the United Nations, and recognizes its potential for application throughout the Organization to improve effectiveness and work practices, to facilitate multilingualism, including public information activities, and to enhance programme delivery, as mandated;

3. *Notes with interest* key elements of the approach set out by the Secretary-General, notably the three broad areas of sharing and dissemination of information, administration and management, and the servicing of United Nations organs and governing bodies as a framework for classifying initiatives; priority given to robust infrastructure, system security, reliable field connectivity, and internal human resources capacity-building; a governance structure; and the requirement to ensure that investments in information and communication technology generate tangible returns commensurate with their cost;

4. *Requests* the Secretary-General to provide further information and to make proposals, to be considered in the context of the proposed programme budget for the biennium 2004-2005, on the further strengthening of governance and central leadership arrangements, including a mechanism to assess the results achieved and apply the lessons learned and the suggestion made by the Advisory Committee on Administrative and Budgetary Questions that the head of the Information Technology Services Division of the Office of Central Support Services of the Secretariat be enabled to act as a chief information and communication technology officer of the United Nations, and requests the Secretary-General also to make proposals on how best to reflect this function in the organizational structure of the Organization;

5. *Also requests* the Secretary-General to ensure that the information and communication technology requirements for the various duty stations and the regional commissions, in particular those located in developing countries, are fully integrated into the strategy, and that appropriate provision is made to allow for the implementation of information and communication technology in those offices;

6. *Further requests* the Secretary-General to provide, in the context of the proposed programme budget for the biennium 2004-2005, the following additional information:

(*a*) An update on the status of projects identified in the strategy;

(*b*) The return on investment anticipated for planned and proposed major projects, in terms which are as quantitative as possible;

(*c*) Specific plans to strengthen the information and communication technology infrastructure and the functionality this would provide, measures to strengthen system security and the means to ensure system reliability and maintenance, indicating, where possible, how they compare with practices in similar organizations;

(*d*) The specific objectives for the planned or proposed further development of connectivity with the various duty stations, field missions, regional commissions, the International Court of Justice, the International Tribunal for the Prosecution of Persons Responsible for Serious Violations of International Humanitarian Law Committed in the Territory of the Former Yugoslavia since 1991 and the International Criminal Tribunal for the Prosecution of Persons Responsible for Genocide and Other Serious Violations of International Humanitarian Law Committed in the Territory of Rwanda and Rwandan Citizens Responsible for Genocide and Other Such Violations Committed in the Territory of Neighbouring States between 1 January and 31 December 1994;

7. *Requests* the Secretary-General to address, in the context of the proposed programme budget for the biennium 2004-2005, the optimum placement in the Organization of technical functions currently housed in the Information Technology Services Division that are not information and communication technology functions;

8. *Notes* that the provisions of the present resolution include guidelines that should assist the Advisory Committee in its consideration of the information and communication technology strategy, and decides to revert to this question and the report of the Secretary-General in the light of the observations and recommendations of the Advisory Committee thereon, in the context of the proposed programme budget for the biennium 2004-2005.

Report of Secretary-General. In response to the Assembly's request in the above resolution, the Secretary-General, in September [A/58/377], provided further information on the proposals contained in his 2002 report [YUN 2002, p. 1454] on the revised ICT strategy, first outlined in 2001 [YUN 2001, p. 1387]. He updated the status of projects identified in that strategy: of 34 related projects and initiatives, 11 had experienced implementation delays, owing largely to resource constraints and, in some cases, to modifications in initial requirements. He described actions taken with regard to: strengthening governance and central leadership arrangements and ensuring that the ICT requirements of duty stations were integrated into the strategy and provided for adequately; the development of the standard project methodology for projecting returns on investment in major projects; plans to strengthen the ICT infrastructure, including system security, reliability and maintainability; the further development of connectivity with duty stations, field missions, regional commissions, the International Court of Justice and the international tribunals; and the optimum placement in the Organization of support activities that were not ICT functions.

The Secretary-General stated that reduced funding for contractual services and general operating expenses had forced the Secretariat to cancel or cut service coverage for several infrastructure components needed to provide, among other things, Internet services and support for central services. The power outage in the United States on 14 and 15 August 2003 and its impact on UN activities had illustrated the risks in operating an ICT infrastructure with inadequate safeguards and support services. Reliance on a single Internet provider due to the lack of funding for a back-up provider had prevented the immediate reinstatement of Internet services as electrical power was restored and connectivity with the field was interrupted, as were the operations of the Integrated Management Information System, electronic mail, the UN web site and ODS.

JIU report. The Secretary-General transmitted to the General Assembly in May [A/58/82] a JIU report giving an overview of the computerized management information (MI) systems in the human resources, financial and administrative areas in use in the organizations in the UN system.

JIU called on legislative organs of the system's organizations to request their respective executive heads to prepare a comprehensive strategy for MI systems, giving due regard to the UN results-based approach; to designate a chief information officer (CIO) or unit to ensure proper management of the information technology (IT) infrastructure and to seek compatibility in MI systems-related policies and practices with other UN organizations; and to streamline existing work processes, procedures and practices within the UN system, and establish a plan for integrating the various management systems with a view to developing an integrated system-wide MI system. It was recommended that the Secretary-General take steps to enhance transparency and comparability of the financial implications of MI system projects through a standardized cost classification for such projects and enhance cooperation and coordination in designing and implementing MI systems throughout the UN system.

CEB action. CEB [A/58/82/Add.1], while agreeing with the actions recommended by JIU to foster greater cost-effectiveness and inter-organization sharing and learning in the exploitation of modern ICTs to improve management, pointed out that the terms of reference of each proposed CIO should be decided upon by each organization on the basis of its requirements. Standardization of cost classifications would be difficult to implement, as it would need to take account of a range of complex factors, namely, the scope of the MI system projects to be included, business processes and methods of analysis.

ACABQ report. ACABQ [A/58/389] pointed to the continuing need for a technical analysis of the various IT systems to enable decision makers to obtain an understanding of relative costs and benefits and requested clarification of CEB's response to the proposed appointment of a CIO.

General Assembly action. The Assembly, in **resolution 58/272**, section I, of 23 December (see p. 1417), took note of the reports of the Secretary-General and JIU and the related comments of CEB and ACABQ.

International cooperation in informatics

In response to Economic and Social Council resolution 2002/35 [YUN 2002, p. 1455], the Secretary-General submitted a May report [E/2003/75] on international cooperation in the field of informatics, which summarized the activities of the Ad Hoc Open-ended Working Group on Informatics and of the UN Secretariat.

The Working Group continued to coordinate high-level information exchange via conferences and working meetings among Member States, the Secretariat and private and public sector organizations. In addition, it served as a bridge between Member States and the Secretariat on ICT issues. In 2003, the Working Group organized the Global E-commerce Summit: Secure E-commerce and E-government Operations in a Troubled World (New York, 14-15 May), during which expert panels covered the latest developments in software, hardware platforms, network applications, hackers, viruses, worms and terrorist disruptions that had a significant impact on e-commerce and e-government applications and initiatives; and the latest advances in e-commerce and e-government applications and initiatives. Other meetings heard presentations on distance learning, known as e-education or e-learning. A service to allow delegates to download information from the UN web site through palm-sized personal computers or personal digital assistants was proposed by Andorra. With its support, a pilot project was to take place during the year.

The report also described the activities of various Secretariat offices and departments.

ECONOMIC AND SOCIAL COUNCIL ACTION

On 24 July [meeting 47], the Economic and Social Council adopted **resolution 2003/48** [draft: E/2003/L.11/Rev.1] without vote [agenda item 7 (d)].

The need to harmonize and improve United Nations informatics systems for optimal utilization and accessibility by all States

The Economic and Social Council,

Welcoming the report of the Secretary-General on international cooperation in the field of informatics and the initiatives of the Ad Hoc Open-ended Working Group on Informatics,

Recognizing the interest of Member States in taking full advantage of information and communication technologies for the acceleration of economic and social development,

Recalling its previous resolutions on the need to harmonize and improve United Nations information systems for optimal utilization and access by all States, with due regard to all official languages,

1. *Reiterates* the high priority that it attaches to easy, economical, uncomplicated and unhindered access for States Members and observers of the United Nations, as well as non-governmental organizations accredited to the United Nations, to the computerized databases and information systems and services of the United Nations, provided that the unhindered access of non-governmental organizations to such databases, systems and services shall not prejudice the access of Member States nor impose an additional financial burden for their use;

2. *Requests* the President of the Economic and Social Council to convene the Ad Hoc Open-ended Working Group on Informatics for one more year to enable it to carry out, from within existing resources, its work of facilitating the successful implementation of the initiatives being taken by the Secretary-General with regard to the use of information technology and of continuing the implementation of measures required to achieve its objectives, and, in this regard, requests the Working Group to continue its efforts in order to act as a bridge between the evolving needs of Member States and the actions of the Secretariat;

3. *Supports* the efforts of the Working Group to keep intact the network of national focal points established in connection with the year 2000 problem as a vehicle for the diffusion of best practices and lessons learned, in particular for the exchange of information on locally and regionally appropriate solutions, and, in this regard, appeals once again to countries and other sources to provide the extrabudgetary resources necessary to maintain the mailing list of the national focal points;

4. *Requests* the Secretary-General to extend full cooperation to the Working Group and to give priority to implementing its recommendations;

5. *Also requests* the Secretary-General to report to the Council at its substantive session of 2004 on the action taken to follow up the present resolution, including the findings of the Working Group and an assessment of its work and mandate.

Other matters

Common services

Common services at Vienna

JIU report. On 7 August [A/58/258], the Secretary-General transmitted to the General Assembly a JIU report on common and joint services of UN system organizations based at the Vienna International Centre (VIC), which included the United Nations Office at Vienna (UNOV), the United Nations Office on Drugs and Crime, the International Atomic Energy Agency (IAEA), the United Nations Industrial Development Organization (UNIDO) and the Preparatory Commission for the Comprehensive Nuclear-Test-Ban Treaty Organization (CTBTO).

JIU called on the legislative organs of the Vienna-based organizations (VBOs) jointly to draw up proposals for the establishment of a single common services administrative unit under UNOV, to be implemented no later than in the 2006-2007 budget cycle; to decide whether or not the Catering Services and the Commissary should receive subsidies for utilities and/or buildings services, with UNIDO to make available the internal audit of the current catering contract; to request their executive heads jointly to review the costs of running parallel language training services at VIC, renew efforts to expand common services in procurement, ICT, human resources management, and financial and public information services, and monitor the costs of maintaining separate library services for the 2002-2003 and 2004-2005 bienniums; and to request the UNOV, UNIDO, IAEA and CTBTO executive heads to establish a joint management advisory committee for the Joint Medical Service and the Security and Safety Service and jointly to review the cost-sharing formulas, including the costs of administrative support for each common service.

Other recommendations called for proposals for a common printing service for all VBOs; IAEA to consult with UNOV, UNIDO and CTBTO regarding drawing up proposals for a fully unified conference service facility at VIC, to be managed by the United Nations and implemented no later than in the 2006-2007 budget cycle; the renegotiation of the 1977 Memorandum of Understanding (MOU) regarding common services to reflect current realities; and UNIDO and IAEA to report comprehensively every two years on their activities as common and joint services providers and users, in order to improve the effectiveness of Member States' oversight role regarding those services.

CEB action. On 25 August [A/58/258/Add.1], CEB reported that the Consultative Committee on Common Services, which had considered the JIU report, did not believe it desirable to establish a single common services administrative unit under UNOV management, although all common services arrangements would continue to be reviewed with a view to improving administrative efficiency and had concluded that establishing a formal management advisory committee would merely add a bureaucratic layer without advantages. The Secretary-General was of the opinion that the current conference service arrangements should strike an optimal balance between centrally provided common services and IAEA's customized supplementary arrangements. A possible gain through common service arrangements in ICT was acknowledged so that the issue would be carefully studied. On the issue of library services, currently under review pursuant to General Assembly resolution 57/300 [YUN 2002, p. 1353], a physical library facility at any one location might no longer be needed due to rapid changes in the library field. IAEA and UNIDO did not support the need to review cost-sharing formulas, but would take into consideration the biennial reports required of them. Other recommendations were generally acceptable.

ACABQ report. In September [A/58/389], ACABQ stated that it would revert to the JIU report in the context of its future consideration of the issue, which was of continuing concern to it.

GENERAL ASSEMBLY ACTION

On 23 December [meeting 79], the General Assembly, on the recommendation of the Fifth Committee [A/58/571], adopted **resolution 58/278** without vote [agenda item 119].

Report of the Joint Inspection Unit on common and joint services of United Nations system organizations at Vienna

The General Assembly,

Having considered the report of the Joint Inspection Unit on common and joint services of United Nations system organizations at Vienna, the comments of the Secretary-General and the United Nations System Chief Executives Board for Coordination thereon and the related comments of the Advisory Committee on Administrative and Budgetary Questions,

1. *Welcomes* the comprehensive and timely preparation of the report of the Joint Inspection Unit;
2. *Decides* to revert at its fifty-ninth session to the consideration of the report of the Joint Inspection Unit and the comments of the Secretary-General and the United Nations System Chief Executives Board for Coordination thereon upon the issuance of the related report of the Advisory Committee on Administrative and Budgetary Questions.

Common services at Geneva

In response to General Assembly resolution 56/279 [YUN 2002, p. 1457], the Secretary-General submitted an October report [A/58/439] on the implementation of JIU's 2001 recommendations concerning the UN system common services in Geneva [YUN 2001, p. 1391]. He described the most salient joint initiatives carried out towards the development of an action plan for common services in Geneva, including the provision of electricity and travel, mail and banking services. He observed that flexibility was key to enhancing cooperation and that participating organizations tended to favour a pragmatic approach geared towards the completion of specific projects within the existing common services framework, rather than the establishment of additional structures in order to define and implement the action plan. The three-tier mechanism outlined in the Secretary-General's 2001 report [ibid., p. 1392], comprising the Management Ownership Committee, the Task Force on Common Services and the various ad hoc working groups, was under review to enhance its efficiency further.

UN commercial activities

Revenue-producing activities

JIU report. In January [A/57/707], the Secretary-General transmitted to the General Assembly a JIU report on UN system revenue-producing activities. The activities covered were those implemented by common-system organizations as an integral part of their work programmes that also afforded opportunities to generate income, ranging from dispensable product lines (such as the sale of souvenir items) to constitutional fee-for-service activities at the World Intellectual Property Organization and ancillary services (catering, rental, garage and news-stand operations). Others, notably the United Nations Postal Administration (UNPA) and the Visitors' Services (mainly the guided tours), were established purposely to publicize the Charter goals and project the Organization's public image. Considerable attention was given to the sale of publications, currently the most important common revenue-producing activity, and to other activity lines holding promise for effectively promoting the Organization's value system and public visibility, among them audio-visual productions and related products, and electronic databases.

JIU recommended that the Secretary-General consider merging the revenue-producing activities into a single division, relocating such retail operations as bookstores and gift shops to enhance public access and visibility, extending the geographical spread of some activities, and exploring outsourcing possibilities for eligible operations. He should seek from the Assembly the authority to review existing agreements between the United Nations and host countries regarding UNPA to establish the continuing validity of the cost- and revenue-sharing formula for UNPA operations.

Other recommendations urged all UN system organizations to strengthen existing directives covering revenue-producing activities; increase revenue from publications; identify public information products with marketable value that could be developed for advocacy and income-generation; emulate best UN practices in the on-line marketing of databases, and develop and market software programmes that promoted the mandates of organizations; strengthen their comparative advantages in the international procurement of goods and services for third parties; formulate a common science and technology policy on patents; establish substantive training and public-lecture programmes for non-State actors on a fee-paying basis; and reinforce the marketing function through market research studies, price discounts, subscription fees and cooperative distribution strategies.

CEB action. In an April note [A/57/707/Add.1], the Secretary-General transmitted CEB's comments and his own on the JIU report. Although CEB generally found the JIU recommendations to be relevant, in some cases greater specificity and agreement on the means of implementation were essential before they could be considered. CEB observed that the focus tended to be more on the production and sale of publications and related products than on the development of new income-generating activities that were supportive of organizations' mandates. It also expressed reservations with respect to issues raised in the report concerning the sale of publications.

GENERAL ASSEMBLY ACTION

On 23 December [meeting 79], the General Assembly, on the recommendation of the Fifth Committee [A/58/572], adopted **resolution 58/263** without vote [agenda item 120].

Report of the Joint Inspection Unit on the revenue-producing activities of the United Nations system

The General Assembly,

Having considered the report of the Joint Inspection Unit on United Nations system revenue-producing activities and the comments of the Secretary-General and the United Nations System Chief Executives Board for Coordination thereon,

1. *Agrees* with the concepts expressed in paragraph *(a)* of recommendation 1 of the Joint Inspection Unit concerning consolidation of the management of revenue-producing activities on the basis of sound business practices, bearing in mind the related legislative mandates, and awaits with interest the specific proposals of the Secretary-General;

2. *Takes note* of paragraph *(b)* of recommendation 1 of the Unit and the related comments of the Secretary-General;

3. *Endorses* recommendation 2 of the Unit;

4. *Notes* paragraph *(a)* of recommendation 3 of the Unit, and requests the Secretary-General to report to the General Assembly at the second part of its resumed fifty-eighth session on the possibility of operating guided tours, bookstores and gift shops at the United Nations Office at Nairobi and the cost implications thereof;

5. *Requests* the Secretary-General to explore the possibility of selling products of the gift centre and the book shop via the Internet, in addition to existing arrangements;

6. *Endorses* paragraphs *(b)* and *(c)* of recommendation 3 of the Unit, and agrees with the comments of the Secretary-General in connection with paragraph *(a)* of that recommendation;

7. *Recognizes* that in its recommendation 4 the Unit outlines some general factors that should be considered in connection with the outsourcing of revenue-generating activities in the framework of approved outsourcing policies;

8. *Agrees* with the comments of the Secretary-General in connection with recommendation 5, and looks forward to further proposals of the Secretary-General concerning the United Nations Postal Administration consequent to its resolution 57/292 of 20 December 2002;

9. *Agrees also* that the competent legislative organs, when considering strengthening the policy frameworks for revenue-generating activities in their organizations, should consider drawing on the objectives set out by the Unit in its recommendation 6, bearing in mind the specificities of each organization and the comments of the United Nations System Chief Executives Board for Coordination with respect to the generation of income from intellectual property;

10. *Agrees further* with the comments of the Chief Executives Board for Coordination on recommendation 7 of the Unit;

11. *Endorses* recommendation 8, which should not affect existing practices concerning the free distribution of public information materials;

12. *Also endorses* recommendation 9, and agrees with the Chief Executives Board for Coordination that the application of this approach needs to be tailored to the specific objectives and circumstances of the organizations concerned;

13. *Takes note* of recommendations 11 to 13 of the Unit and the related comments of the Chief Executives Board for Coordination.

UN Postal Administration

In response to General Assembly resolution 57/292, section VI [YUN 2002, p. 1378], the Secretary-General submitted a November report [A/58/558/Add.1 & Corr.1] on efforts to reverse the downward trend in the business of UNPA. He stated that, within the context of the second performance report on the 2002-2003 programme budget, a comprehensive review of UNPA's operations had been undertaken, with the involvement of an outside consultant specializing in philatelic market operations. A number of recommendations stemming from the review had been or were in the process of being implemented.

The report concluded that UNPA continued to play an important role in promoting the United Nations through the issuance of stamps and other philatelic products. Initiatives taken to reverse the downward trend in its revenues had shown encouraging results, with a projected modest surplus of $189,000 in the current biennium. The report recommended that the Organization gradually build a financial reserve to meet contingent liabilities arising from the sale of stamps. The current arrangements, whereby a net surplus from revenue-producing activities under Income section 3, Services to the public, of the programme budget was used to offset the expenditure part of the regular budget, should be modified to credit the surplus to a reserve fund to be established as from the 2004-2005 biennium. If that proposal was accepted, any net revenue realized would, as an exception to financial rule 103.7, be retained at the close of the biennium in a revenue account.

ACABQ report. Commenting on the Secretary-General's report on 18 November [A/58/604], ACABQ, referring to the issue of contingent liability, noted that, according to the Secretariat, while in the past only a small percentage of UN stamps sold were actually used for postage by customers, the percentage of postage charges paid to the United States Postal Service of the gross stamp sale revenue had increased from 6 per cent in 1980 to 18 per cent in 2002. More importantly, the United Nations was currently incurring expenditures for products sold in past periods, for which the accounts had been closed. Also, accurate estimates of the contingent liability were not available. ACABQ encouraged efforts to achieve success in the negotiations that were under way between UNPA and the postal authorities of Austria, Switzerland and the United States to obtain more favourable agreements that might positively impact on the contingent liabilities of UNPA. Meanwhile, it recommended the continuation of current accounting arrangements for the sale of UN stamps.

Outsourcing practices

JIU report. In June [A/58/92], the Secretary-General transmitted to the General Assembly a JIU report on its management audit review of outsourcing in the United Nations and its funds and programmes, to establish the extent to which outsourcing practices in 1999 and 2000 were consistent with the policy directives set out in General Assembly resolution 55/232 [YUN 2000, p. 1401]. JIU focused its inquiry on the contractual and managerial phases of outsourcing procedures. It observed that, since its 1997 report on the subject [YUN 1997, p. 1511], outsourced operations had not evolved significantly in value and scope and had remained a relatively small proportion of the financial resources of the United Nations and its funds and programmes.

JIU recommended that the managerial processes of the outsourced service or activity should be owned and controlled by the contractor, outsourcing should be geared mostly to providing services to support the contracting organization's substantive programme requirements, and, as a rule, an outsourcing arrangement implied a business relationship lasting one year or more; the term "outsourcing" should be restricted to contractual relations with commercial vendors, as distinct from "national execution" of technical cooperation, humanitarian and other projects; existing outsourcing policy guidelines should be reinforced by incorporating the policy directives in resolution 55/232 in policy documents, services to be outsourced should be made explicit in the programme budget narrative and the associated resources should be approved; the Inter-Agency Procurement Working Group (IAPWG) should standardize and generalize the application of due diligence procedures; IAPWG should seek agreement on standard contract provisions emphasizing cost-effectiveness and efficiency; arrangements involving the regular presence of supplier personnel on UN premises should include safety and security assessment in the pre-contract phase and periodically thereafter; the Secretary-General should review with national authorities all cases involving the levying of taxes on the organizations for their outsourced services; IAPWG should consider disseminating the evolving experience of the UN Procurement Division in the use of its new formats for monitoring, evaluating and certifying supplier performance under outsourced contracts; and adequate resources should be budgeted for the training of programme managers at all duty stations in contract oversight.

Note by Secretary-General. The Secretary-General, in June [A/58/92/Add.1], commented that the JIU report would have been more useful had it examined the factors that actually influenced the implementation of the basic policy and guidelines in outsourcing experience during 1999-2000 and, more importantly, had derived useful lessons learned. It appeared that events over time had overtaken the usefulness of some of JIU's findings.

ACABQ report. In September [A/58/389], ACABQ concurred with the Secretary-General's comments on the JIU report.

GENERAL ASSEMBLY ACTION

On 23 December [meeting 79], the General Assembly, on the recommendation of the Fifth Committee [A/58/571], adopted two resolutions, both without vote [agenda item 119]: the first was **resolution 58/276;** the second, **resolution 58/277.**

Outsourcing practices

The General Assembly,

Recalling its resolutions 54/256 of 7 April 2000 and 55/232 of 23 December 2000,

Having considered the report of the Secretary-General on outsourcing practices and the related report of the Advisory Committee on Administrative and Budgetary Questions,

1. *Takes note* of the report of the Secretary-General;
2. *Endorses* the recommendations contained in paragraphs 10 and 11 of the report of the Advisory Committee on Administrative and Budgetary Questions;
3. *Requests* the Secretary-General to report to the General Assembly at its fifty-ninth session on the implementation of the provisions of its resolution 55/232 and on activities outsourced during the years 2002 and 2003, including information on the location and type of outsourced activities and more detailed reasoning therefor.

Report of the Joint Inspection Unit on the management audit review of outsourcing in the United Nations and the United Nations funds and programmes

The General Assembly,

Reaffirming its previous resolutions on the Joint Inspection Unit, in particular resolutions 50/233 of 7 June 1996, 54/16 of 29 October 1999, 55/230 of 23 December 2000, 56/245 of 24 December 2001 and 57/284 A and B of 20 December 2002,

Also reaffirming its resolutions 54/256 of 7 April 2000 and 55/232 of 23 December 2000 on outsourcing practices,

Having considered the report of the Joint Inspection Unit on the management audit review of outsourcing in the United Nations and the United Nations funds and programmes, the comments of the Secretary-General thereon and paragraphs 5 to 7 and 9 of the report of the Advisory Committee on Administrative and Budgetary Questions,

1. *Takes note* of recommendation 1 of the Joint Inspection Unit;
2. *Also takes note* of recommendation 2 of the Unit and the related comments of the Secretary-General;
3. *Endorses* recommendation 3 *(a)* of the Unit;
4. *Takes note* of recommendations 4 and 5 of the Unit, as well as the related comments of the Secretary-General and the Advisory Committee on Administrative and Budgetary Questions;
5. *Requests* the Secretary-General to ensure that contractors whose staff are present on the United Nations premises on a regular basis are held accountable for conducting individual background checks at their own expense;
6. *Endorses* recommendations 7 to 9 of the Unit;
7. *Requests* the Secretary-General to share the experience of the Procurement Division of the Office of Central Support Services of the Secretariat in the use of its new formats for monitoring, evaluating and certifying supplier performance under outsourced contracts with the members of the Inter-Agency Procurement Working Group and to report thereon to the General Assembly in the context of his next report on outsourcing practices.

Review of administrative processes and procedures

Pursuant to General Assembly resolutions 48/218 B [YUN 1994, p. 1362], 54/244 [YUN 1999, p. 1274] and 56/253 [YUN 2001, p. 1297], the Secretary-General, on 4 August [A/58/211], transmitted an OIOS report on the review of duplication, complexity and bureaucracy in the UN administrative processes and procedures. The review focused on processes in travel, procurement and the administration of staff entitlements. It found that the Secretariat's administrative environment was not fully leveraging the advantages of technology, nor was it applying modern management processes adopted by other organizations.

OIOS recommended: establishment by the Department of Management of a project team to commission a detailed needs analysis for the automation of the travel process, identification of an Organization-wide application for procurement, and further automation of the processes for rental subsidy, education grant and dependency allowances; streamlining of the travel process, exempting the claims procedure for travel that did not deviate from the authorized itinerary; implementation of an information security and data privacy policy and of employee self-certification, with a mechanism for random check of supporting documentation for rental subsidy and dependency allowances; redefining the role of the executive office and the administrative officers in departments and offices; and the implementation of a central project registry for computerized systems.

The Department of Management agreed with most of the recommendations.

GENERAL ASSEMBLY ACTION

On 23 December [meeting 79], the General Assembly, on the recommendation of the Fifth Committee [A/58/571], adopted **resolution 58/280** without vote [agenda item 119].

Review of duplication, complexity and bureaucracy in United Nations administrative processes and procedures

The General Assembly,

Recalling its resolutions 48/218 B of 29 July 1994, 54/244 of 23 December 1999 and 56/253 of 24 December 2001,

Having considered the report of the Office of Internal Oversight Services on the review of duplication, complexity and bureaucracy in United Nations administrative processes and procedures,

Takes note of the report of the Office of Internal Oversight Services.

UN premises and property

Addis Ababa office facilities

Report of Secretary-General. In response to General Assembly resolution 56/270 [YUN 2002, p. 1459], the Secretary-General reported in July [A/58/154] that the preparations for the construction of additional office facilities at ECA, Addis Ababa, were progressing. The project schedule was revised due to difficulties encountered early in the year that caused a 10-month delay.

ACABQ report. In its first report to the General Assembly on the proposed 2004-2005 programme budget [A/58/7 & Corr.1], ACABQ recommended that the Assembly take note of the Secretary-General's report.

By **decision 58/561** of 23 December, the Assembly took note of the Secretary-General's report and the related ACABQ report.

Transfer of buildings to UNLB

On 14 November [A/58/596], the Secretary-General transmitted to the General Assembly a proposal to accept a pledge by Italy to transfer five additional buildings with a total floor space of 1,760 square metres to the United Nations Logistics Base (UNLB) at Brindisi. Under an MOU between the Government of Italy and the United Nations, the United Nations would renovate the five buildings for some $140,000, and thereafter bear an estimated $15,000 yearly for maintenance. As acceptance of the buildings would involve an additional financial liability in respect of maintenance costs, the Assembly's approval was sought, in line with financial regulation 3.11.

ACABQ report. On 20 November [A/58/609], ACABQ recommended that the Assembly approve acceptance of the five additional buildings pledged by Italy.

The Assembly, by **decision 58/557** of 23 December, expressed appreciation for Italy's offer, took note of the related Secretary-General's note and ACABQ report, approved the transfer of the buildings to UNLB and decided to keep under review during its resumed fifty-eighth (2004) session the question of the financing of the Base.

Capital master plan

Report of Board of Auditors. In response to section II of General Assembly resolution 57/292 [YUN 2002, p. 1375], the Secretary-General, in August [A/58/321], transmitted the report of the Board of Auditors on the capital master plan (CMP), which outlined the broad audit objectives and confirmed the scope of the audit. Noting that the activities and actual expenditures related to CMP were currently limited, the Board stated that the first audit of the financial statements would cover the biennium ending 31 December 2003. Accordingly, the Board's first report on CMP would be transmitted to the Assembly for consideration at its fifty-ninth (2004) session.

OIOS report. Pursuant to General Assembly resolutions 48/218 B [YUN 1994, p. 1362], 54/244 [YUN 1999, p. 1274] and 57/292, the Secretary-General, in September [A/58/342], transmitted a report by OIOS on its monitoring of the CMP project during the period from 1 January to 31 July 2003 to ascertain whether adequate internal controls were in place for the project's design development phase. According to the implementation plan, a key activity to be completed in 2003 and 2004 was the search for competent architectural and engineering firms to design the various CMP components. The Procurement Division of the Office of Central Support Services posted an expression-of-interest notice on its web page, which it followed with requests for proposals to 85 firms, 69 of which expressed interest in the project; from those, 21 were shortlisted. OIOS observed that the design development process had advanced satisfactorily and, thus far, had been transparent and fair. It had developed an oversight strategy and a preliminary audit plan covering the project's design development phase in anticipation of contract negotiations with the firms selected to provide an architectural and engineering design that would meet the requirements set by the Secretariat and the expectations of Member States. Based on projected CMP activities, OIOS would request additional resources for 2004 and beyond, to enable it to provide the necessary oversight as the project progressed.

Report of Secretary-General. Pursuant to General Assembly resolution 57/292 [YUN 2002, p. 1375], the Secretary-General submitted in November his first annual progress report on the implementation of CMP [A/58/599]. He stated that ongoing discussions with the host country were expected to result in a proposal for funding CMP in early 2004, with possible funding availability in 2005. As Member States were still considering the modalities for a financial package, the Secretary-General felt it premature to establish an advisory board or to approach other public and private sources for contributions. Availability of the so-called swing space, that is, the proposed new building to be known as UNDC-5, was projected for the second half of 2007. The architect for that building, Maki and Associates (Japan), was selected in December. In preparation for the detailed design development work, the CMP Office had awarded contracts to 21 vendors for a total of $12.3 million.

Of the $8 million appropriated by General Assembly resolution 55/238 [YUN 2000, p. 1299] for preparing the comprehensive design plan and cost analysis of CMP, $7,996,300 had been expended, leaving a balance of $3,700, reported as savings in the second performance report for the 2000-2001 biennium [YUN 2001, p. 1294]. Resolution 57/292 appropriated a further $25.5 million for the 2002-2003 biennium, of which $16,870,300 had been committed for CMP implementation. It had also authorized the Secretary-General to enter into commitments of up to $26 million for 2004-2005 for the remaining work related to the design, project management and management of pre-construction services.

The Secretary-General believed that tangible progress had been made in all areas of implementation of the CMP project. The final construction schedule would determine the actual completion date of implementation.

ACABQ report. In November [A/58/7/Add.15], ACABQ stated that, as CMP was a time-limited and specialized Secretariat project, to be implemented on a phased basis, additional staffing for it should be requested according to actual workload requirements in each phase. ACABQ trusted that, before such staffing requirements were proposed, full account would be taken of available expertise within the Secretariat.

The Assembly, by **resolution 58/272**, section XXII, of 23 December (see p. 1417), took note of the report of Secretary-General, his notes transmitting the OIOS and Board of Auditors reports, and the related ACABQ report (see above).

Security

Strengthening security of UN premises

Report of Secretary-General. In response to General Assembly resolution 56/286 [YUN 2002, p. 1461], the Secretary-General, in his second performance report on the programme budget for the biennium 2002-2003, submitted in November [A/58/558/Add.1 & Corr.1], summarized work undertaken and/or planned by the Secretariat to strengthen the security and safety of UN premises, the status of the related appropriations and expenditures as at 31 October, and/or projections for the rest of 2003. Construction, training and other projects at Headquarters, Geneva, Nairobi, Vienna and the offices of the UN regional commissions were described.

The report concluded that the approved programme for strengthening the security and safety of UN premises in Vienna, Nairobi, Bangkok, Santiago and Beirut had nearly been completed. At Headquarters, Geneva and Addis Ababa, programme implementation was at an early stage.

ACABQ report. On 18 November [A/58/604], ACABQ noted that the Secretary-General would report in 2004 on additional measures needed to improve the security and safety of UN premises and personnel. After its review of that report, ACABQ would present its comments and recommendations.

PART SIX

Intergovernmental organizations related to the United Nations

Chapter I

International Atomic Energy Agency (IAEA)

In 2003, the International Atomic Energy Agency (IAEA) continued to act as a catalyst for the development and transfer of peaceful nuclear technologies; to build and maintain a global nuclear safety regime; and to assist in efforts to prevent the proliferation of nuclear weapons. The year marked the fiftieth anniversary of the "Atoms for Peace" speech delivered to the General Assembly by United States President Dwight D. Eisenhower, which offered a vision that would enable humanity to make full use of the benefits of nuclear energy and which eventually led to the establishment of IAEA.

The forty-seventh session of the IAEA General Conference (Vienna, 15-19 September) adopted resolutions and decisions on strengthening IAEA's activities in nuclear science, technology and applications; strengthening international cooperation in nuclear, radiation, transport and waste safety; improving the effectiveness and efficiency of the safeguards system; strengthening IAEA technical cooperation activities; applying safeguards in the Middle East; implementing the safeguards agreement between IAEA and the Democratic People's Republic of Korea (DPRK); Security Council resolutions relating to Iraq; Israel's nuclear capabilities; and measures against nuclear and radiological terrorism.

In 2003, IAEA had 137 member States.

Activities

Nuclear safety and security

IAEA continued to provide nuclear safety services and assistance worldwide. During 2003, two publications on safety standards were published, and a strategy to enhance safety standards and their global application was submitted to the Board of Governors and the General Conference. The events of 11 September 2001 [YUN 2001, p. 60] gave rise to a review of IAEA programmes on nuclear and radiological terrorism, which resulted in the adoption of a plan of activities to protect against such acts. The International Nuclear Security Advisory Service was developed to identify measures for additional or improved security for nuclear-related activities. Member States received assistance in evaluating their national physical protection systems through the International Physical Protection Advisory Service missions. Moreover, IAEA delivered an extensive programme of physical protection, which included training courses, workshops and seminars, in addition to border evaluation missions for customs and other personnel.

Radiation safety

IAEA's radiation safety programme continued to focus on the development of a unified set of safety standards and their application; implementation of the Agency's radiation protection rules; and the provision of advice and services to member States. In September, the Board of Governors approved an action plan for improving programmes to protect workers from radiation, based on the findings and recommendations of IAEA's 2002 international conference on occupational radiation protection [YUN 2002, p. 1465]. The IAEA international conference on the security of radioactive sources (Vienna, March) updated the 1999 Action Plan for the Safety of Radiation Sources and the Security of Radioactive Material. IAEA convened a conference on the safety of transport of radioactive material (Vienna, 7-11 July), which addressed radiation protection, compliance and quality assurance, emergency preparedness and response, packaging and transport of radioactive material, and regulatory issues.

Nuclear power

IAEA continued to assist member States in planning and implementing programmes for the utilization of nuclear power, supported them in achieving improved safety and provided them with information and training. Four publications were completed on various aspects of improving nuclear power plant performance and management. IAEA convened an international conference on innovative technologies for nuclear fuel cycles and nuclear power (Vienna, 23-26 June).

Nuclear fuel cycle

In 2003, IAEA and the Nuclear Energy Agency of the Organisation for Economic Co-operation and Development (OECD/NEA) published *Uranium 2003: Resources, Production and Demand*, the foremost reference on uranium supplies. In

June, the Agency hosted an international conference on the storage of spent fuel from power reactors to identify the most important directions for national efforts and international cooperation. Potential initiatives emphasized at the conference included assistance to member States in coordinating research on the long-term behaviour of spent fuel, and the continuing exchange of information on related technology and public acceptance matters.

Radioactive waste management

IAEA's Board of Governors approved the Action Plan on the Safety of Radioactive Waste Management which took into account the findings of a 2002 Agency conference on issues and trends in radioactive waste management [YUN 2002, p. 1466]. In addition, a position paper by international experts was published. During the first Review Meeting of the Contracting Parties to the Joint Convention on the Safety of Spent Fuel Management and on the Safety of Radioactive Waste Management (Vienna, 3-14 November) (see p. 553), participants agreed that it was important for all States to have a long-term strategy for managing spent fuel and radioactive waste. IAEA organized an international conference on the protection of the environment from the effects of ionizing radiation (Stockholm, Sweden, 6-10 October), which recommended the preparation of an international action plan to protect the environment from the effects of radiation exposure.

Marine environment and water resources

In 2003, IAEA's eleventh international symposium on isotope hydrology and integrated water resources management (Vienna, 19-23 May) reviewed isotope techniques and their application to water resources management. IAEA made a substantive contribution to the third World Water Forum (Kyoto, Japan, 16-23 March) and launched the first world water development report. The Agency provided assistance to member States through its analytical quality control service programme for the analysis of radionuclides in the marine environment, and its Marine Environment Laboratory participated in the first global expedition for marine isotope studies in the southern hemisphere oceans.

Food and agriculture

In 2003, the Agency made substantial progress in developing improved crop varieties through mutation induction, particularly in relation to rice. The twenty-sixth session of the Codex Alimentarius Commission (Rome, Italy, 30 June–7 July) adopted a revised "Codex General Standard for Irradiated Foods", and a revised "Codex Recommended International Code of Practice for Radiation Processing of Food". In April, IAEA and the Food and Agriculture Organization of the United Nations agreed on cooperative arrangements in food and agriculture in the event of a nuclear or radiological emergency.

Human health

IAEA continued to address needs related to the prevention, diagnosis and treatment of health problems in developing member States through the development and application of nuclear techniques. It provided radiotherapy equipment and staff training through national and regional technical cooperation projects. An international conference, organized by IAEA (Vienna, June), identified potential opportunities for developing countries to apply a broad range of isotopic and nuclear analytical techniques in health and environmental studies.

Technical cooperation

IAEA's secretariat delivered $76.1 million worth of training, expert services, equipment and other assistance to member States under its technical cooperation programme in 2003, which was $1.3 million higher than in 2002. As a follow-up to the 2002 evaluations of the technical cooperation programme [YUN 2002, p. 1467], in-depth reviews were carried out of internal processes and programming tools to ensure greater performance and better linkage with international development priorities.

Safeguard responsibilities

In 2003, IAEA continued efforts to implement a strengthened safeguard system, though a number of States had yet to bring into force their comprehensive safeguards agreements. The Agency withdrew its inspectors from Iraq on 17 March due to the impending military conflict (see p. 333). IAEA inspectors returned to Iraq in June to verify nuclear material stored at a nuclear material storage facility near the Tuwaitha complex, south of Baghdad. The inspectors found that some dispersal of natural uranium compounds had occurred due to looting (see p. 322). As the DPRK remained in non-compliance with its safeguards agreement, IAEA was unable to verify the non-diversion of nuclear material. IAEA carried out a range of verification activities in the context of Iran's safeguards agreement. In June, IAEA reported that Iran had failed to meet its obligations under its safeguards agreement with respect to the reporting of nuclear material, the subsequent processing and use of that material and the declaration of facilities where the material was stored and processed. It also noted that corrective actions had been taken by Iran. On 18 December, Iran signed a protocol additional to its safeguards agreement and decided to voluntarily suspend all enrichment and reprocessing activities as a confidence-building measure. On 19 December, the Libyan Arab Jamahiriya announced its decision to eliminate all materials, equipment and programmes which led to the production of internationally proscribed weapons. On 27 December, the Agency began an in-depth verification of Libya's undeclared nuclear activities. Libya also announced that, as at 29 December, it would pursue a policy of full transparency and active cooperation with IAEA.

Nuclear information

During 2003, the Agency discussed and explained, in a variety of forums, the importance of verification in preventing the proliferation of nuclear weapons, and, at the same time, the peaceful application of nuclear techniques for the benefit of humanity. The Agency also launched information campaigns on radiation treatment for cancer and the search for sustainable water resources. In September, IAEA, together with OECD/NEA, the World Association of Nuclear Operators and the World Nuclear Association, supported the founding of the World Nuclear University. The International Nuclear Information System, the Agency's largest database, was incorporated as an integral part of its new nuclear knowledge initiative.

Secretariat

At the end of 2003, IAEA secretariat staff totalled 2,255, including 1,048 in the Professional and higher categories and 1,207 in the General Service category.

Budget

The 2003 regular budget amounted to $249 million. Actual budget expenditure amounted to $254.9 million. A total of $39.5 million in extrabudgetary funds was provided by member States, the United Nations, international organizations and other sources.

NOTE: For further information, see *Annual Report 2003*, published by IAEA.

HEADQUARTERS AND OTHER OFFICE

HEADQUARTERS
International Atomic Energy Agency
P.O. Box 100
Wagramerstrasse 5
A-1400 Vienna, Austria
 Telephone: (43) (1) 2600-0
 Fax: (43) (1) 2600-7
 Internet: www.iaea.org
 E-mail: Official.Mail@iaea.org

NEW YORK LIAISON OFFICE
IAEA Office at the United Nations
1 United Nations Plaza, Room 1155
New York, NY 10017, United States
 Telephone: (1) (212) 963-6012/6011
 Fax: (1) (917) 367-4046

Chapter II

International Labour Organization (ILO)

In 2003, the International Labour Organization (ILO) continued to promote social justice and economic stability and improve labour conditions. ILO's strategic objectives were to promote and realize fundamental principles and rights at work; create greater opportunities for women and men to secure decent employment and income; enhance the coverage and effectiveness of social protection; and strengthen tripartism and social dialogue.

In 2003, ILO membership increased to 177.

Meetings

The ninety-first session of the International Labour Conference (ILC) (Geneva, 3-19 June) adopted a new Convention on Seafarers' Identity Documents, replacing ILO Convention No. 108, adopted in 1958 [YUN 1958, p. 436]. The new Convention established a more rigorous seafarers' identity regime, in order to develop effective security from terrorism, ensure that the world's 1.2 million seafarers would be given the freedom of movement necessary for their well-being and facilitate international commerce.

The Director-General submitted to the Conference a global report on equity at work, as follow-up to the 1998 ILO Declaration on Fundamental Principles and Rights at Work [YUN 1998, p. 1375]. The highlight of the Conference was a discussion on the global fight against poverty. The Director-General also submitted a report on the situation of workers in the Occupied Palestinian Territory.

Sectoral and other meetings convened in Geneva during 2003 included: Joint Meeting on Public Emergency Services: Social Dialogue in a Changing Environment (27-31 January); Fourth Meeting of the World Commission on the Social Dimension of Globalization (16-18 February); Tripartite Meeting on the Future of Employment in the Tobacco Sector (24-28 February); Tripartite Meeting on the Employment Effects of Mergers and Acquisitions in Commerce (7-11 April); Tripartite Meeting on Challenges and Opportunities Facing Public Utilities (19-23 May); Meeting of Experts to Develop a Code of Practice on Violence and Stress in Services: A Threat to Productivity and Decent Work (8-15 October); Tripartite Meeting on Best Practices in Work-Flexibility Schemes and their Impact on Quality of Working Life in the Chemical Industries (27-31 October); Seventeenth International Conference of Labour Statisticians (24 November–3 December); Tenth African Regional Meeting (2-5 December); and Tripartite Meeting of Experts on Security, Health and Safety in Ports (8-17 December).

International standards

During 2003, ILO activities with regard to Conventions and Recommendations included standard-setting and the supervision and promotion of the application of standards. Supervisory bodies reviewed existing procedures and standard-setting policy, withdrawing outdated Recommendations.

In June, ILC adopted the Convention on Seafarers' Identity Documents (see above).

Employment and development

ILO continued to help constituents combat unemployment and poverty through the creation of employment opportunities and improvement of existing jobs. It provided advice and guidance on employment and labour market policies and on their labour market information and statistical systems. Activities to promote employment included support to constituents to develop entrepreneurship through the creation of cooperatives and small and micro-enterprises.

Regarding human resources development, ILO emphasized the need for the adaptation of training policy and delivery to the rapidly changing skill requirements and special needs of vulnerable groups. It also responded to the needs of countries affected by conflict.

Field activities

In 2003, expenditure on technical cooperation programmes totalled approximately $138 million compared to $117.4 million in 2002. The leading fields of activity were the standards and fundamental principles and rights at work sector with 37.7 per cent ($52.1 million), followed by the employment sector with 31.4 per cent ($43.4 million), the social dialogue sector with 14.3 per cent ($19.8 million) and the social protection sector with 10.6 per cent ($14.7 million).

In terms of regional distribution, Africa accounted for 23.4 per cent of total expenditure ($32.2 million), Asia and the Pacific for 22.4 per cent ($30.9 million), Latin America and the Caribbean 17.4 per cent ($24 million), Europe 6.4 per cent ($8.8 million) and the Arab States 2.1 per cent ($2.8 million). Interregional and global activities accounted for the greatest share at 28.4 per cent ($39.1 million).

Educational activities

The Turin Centre and the International Institute for Labour Studies, both autonomous institutions within ILO, reported to the ILO Governing Body. The Centre continued to carry out training and related activities in a wide range of technical areas as an integral part of ILO technical cooperation activities. The Institute continued to carry out research, encouraged networking related to emerging labour policy issues, and acted as a catalyst for future ILO programme development. The Institute analysed the relationships between social exclusion, labour institutions and poverty, and explored the changing global organization of production and its social implications at the local level.

Secretariat

As at 31 December 2003, ILO employed a total of 2,418 full-time staff, of whom, 1,019 were in the Professional and higher categories and 1,399 were in the General Service category.

Budget

ILO, in 2001, had adopted a budget of $473 million for the 2002-2003 biennium. At its 2003 session, ILC adopted a budget of $529.6 million for 2004-2005.

NOTE: For further information on ILO, see *Report of the Director-General—ILO programme implementation, 2002-2003.*

HEADQUARTERS AND OTHER OFFICES

HEADQUARTERS
International Labour Organization
4, route des Morillons
CH-1211 Geneva 22, Switzerland
 Telephone: (41) (22) 799-6111
 Fax: (41) (22) 798-8685
 Internet: www.ilo.org
 E-mail: ilo@ilo.org

LIAISON OFFICE
International Labour Organization
Liaison Office with the United Nations
220 East 42nd Street, Suite 3101
New York, NY 10017, United States
 Telephone: (1) (212) 697-0150
 Fax: (1) (212) 697-5218
 E-mail: newyork@ilo.org

ILO maintained regional offices in Abidjan, Côte d'Ivoire; Bangkok, Thailand; Beirut, Lebanon; Geneva, Switzerland; and Lima, Peru.

Chapter III

Food and Agriculture Organization of the United Nations (FAO)

The Food and Agriculture Organization of the United Nations (FAO) continued to work towards achieving sustainable global food security by raising nutrition levels and living standards, improving agricultural productivity and advancing the condition of rural populations.

At its one hundred and twenty-fourth session (Rome, Italy, 23-28 June), the FAO Council reconfirmed the crucial importance of the Code of Conduct for Responsible Fisheries and its related International Plans of Action in promoting long-term sustainable development in fisheries and aquaculture. The FAO Council, in November, endorsed the recommendations of the Joint Meeting of the Programme Committee and the Finance Committee, aimed at strengthening the independent role of the Evaluations Service.

As part of the follow-up to the World Food Summits, held in 1996 [YUN 1996, p. 1129] and 2002 [YUN 2002, p. 1225], FAO helped its members in meeting the goal of halving the number of hungry by 2015 and in the preparation of food security and agricultural development programmes. With the collaboration of financial institutions, FAO also helped to formulate projects that would hasten a reversal of declining resources to agriculture.

In 2003, FAO membership increased to 187 countries and the European Community.

World food situation

World cereal production for 2003 was estimated at 1,874 million tonnes (including rice in milled equivalent), 6 million tonnes lower than the previous year's level, the result of a deliberate national policy to downsize cereal inventories by increasing exports. World livestock production was estimated at 249.1 million tonnes of meat and 599.1 million tonnes of dairy products. World fish output stood at 130 million tonnes, of which about 30 per cent was from aquaculture, a subsector under continuous expansion.

FAO's Global Information and Early Warning System, in cooperation with the World Food Programme, continued to alert the international community to impending emergency situations and fielded crop and food supply to affected countries.

The FAO Trust Fund for Food Security and Food Safety continued through its regional programmes to initiate projects aimed at sustainable increased food availability and to finance projects to combat animal and plant diseases that threatened food security.

Activities

FAO's Emergency Operation and Rehabilitation Division continued to provide emergency assistance in the agricultural, livestock and fisheries sectors to developing countries affected by exceptional natural or man-made calamities. In 2003, FAO's emergency assistance programme received over $73 million to fund 160 projects in more than 50 countries, and $114 million for the execution of the agricultural component of the oil-for-food programme in Iraq.

Through its field programmes, FAO provided technical assistance in food and agriculture, fisheries, forestry and rural development, totalling $405.1 million. FAO's Investment Centre assisted developing and transition countries to identify and assess investment opportunities, and formulated 157 investment projects worth over $5 billion. The Special Programme for Food Security assisted developing countries, particularly low-income food-deficit countries, to improve national and household food security on an economically and environmentally sustainable basis. By the end of 2003, 89 countries were participating in the programme.

In 2003, FAO continued to participate in activities related to plant biological diversity, crop management and diversification, seed production and improvement, crop protection, agricultural engineering, the prevention of food losses, and food and agricultural industries. It also contributed to the development of animal production and health programmes. The Global Rinderpest Eradication Programme continued its work to eliminate the fatal livestock virus by 2010. The 1998 Rotterdam Convention on the Prior Informed Consent Procedure for Certain Hazardous Chemicals and Pesticides in International Trade [YUN 1998, p. 997], which served to protect people and the environment from hazardous chemicals, including pesticides, was ratified in 2003 and would enter into force in 2004.

The FAO Forestry Department continued its work in forest resource management, policy and planning, and forest products. The first International Mountain Day was celebrated on 11 December 2003, as an outgrowth of the International Year of Mountains in 2002.

The FAO Fisheries Department promoted sustainable development of responsible fisheries and contributed to food security through activities in fishery resources, policy, industries and information. The Agreement to Promote Compliance with International Conservation and Management Measures by Fishing Vessels on the High Seas, an integral part of FAO's Code of Conduct for Responsible Fisheries, came into force in 2003.

In 2003, the Codex Alimentarius Commission, responsible for implementing the joint FAO/World Health Organization Food Standards Programme, adopted new assessment guidelines for risks associated with foods derived from biotechnology.

Secretariat

As at 31 December 2003, FAO staff numbered 3,897, of whom 1,610 were in the Professional or higher categories and 2,287 were in the General Service category.

Budget

The regular programme budget for the 2002-2003 biennium was $651.8 million.

HEADQUARTERS AND OTHER OFFICES

HEADQUARTERS
Food and Agriculture Organization of the United Nations
Viale delle Terme di Caracalla
00100 Rome, Italy
  Telephone: (39) (06) 57051
  Fax: (39) (06) 5705 3152
  Internet: www.fao.org
  E-mail: FAO-HQ@fao.org

NEW YORK LIAISON OFFICE
Food and Agriculture Organization Liaison
Office with the United Nations
1 United Nations Plaza, Room 1125
New York, NY 10017, United States
  Telephone: (1) (212) 963-6036
  Fax: (1) (212) 963-5425
  E-mail: FAO-LONY@fao.org

FAO also maintained liaison offices in Brussels, Geneva, Washington, D.C., and Yokohama, Japan; regional offices in Accra, Ghana; Bangkok, Thailand; Cairo, Egypt; and Santiago, Chile; and subregional offices in Apia, Samoa; Bridgetown, Barbados; Budapest, Hungary; Harare, Zimbabwe; and Tunis, Tunisia.

Chapter IV

United Nations Educational, Scientific and Cultural Organization (UNESCO)

The United Nations Educational, Scientific and Cultural Organization (UNESCO) continued in 2003 to promote cooperation in education, science, culture and communication among its member States.

The biennial General Conference, at its thirty-second session (Paris, 29 September–17 October), adopted the organization's 2004-2005 programme budget. The 58-member Executive Board held its one hundred and sixty-sixth (4-16 April), one hundred and sixty-seventh (15 September–15 October) and one hundred and sixty-eighth (20 October) sessions, all in Paris.

In 2003, UNESCO membership increased to 190, plus six associate members.

Activities

Education

UNESCO continued to coordinate Education for All (EFA) partners and maintained their collective momentum through two mechanisms—the Working Group and the High-level Group meetings on EFA. The fourth Working Group meeting (Paris, 22-23 July) sought better ways to ensure the integration of international initiatives into national planning processes and development frameworks. The third meeting of the High-level Group (New Delhi, India, 10-12 November) resulted in an Action Agenda, which focused on immediate supportive and strategic actions towards gender parity by 2005 and gender equality by 2015.

The Director-General convened a Round Table of Ministers of Physical Education and Sport (9-10 January), which recommended that an international convention against doping in sport be prepared, under the coordination of UNESCO and in close cooperation with the UN system, the Council of Europe, the International Olympic Committee, the World Anti-Doping Agency (WADA) and the International Intergovernmental Consultative Group on Anti-Doping in Sport. The convention would provide to WADA and its World Anti-Doping Code a comprehensive set of rules and regulations to bind the sporting movement.

As follow-up to the 1998 World Conference on Higher Education (WCHE) [YUN 1998, p. 1380], UNESCO organized the Meeting of Higher Education Partners (WCHE+5), in June, to review the progress achieved in implementing the Framework for Priority Action for Change and Development, to measure its impact on the development of higher education worldwide and to define the orientations for future action.

Efforts to promote a better understanding among stakeholders and the international community on the importance of secondary education reform and expansion of the EFA process, and more specifically its impact on primary education's expansion, were pursued in 2003 through regional seminars involving high-level officials from ministries of education and other experts. In order to promote and support the New Flagship Programme on the Rights of Persons with Disabilities, UNESCO and the International Working Group on Disability and Development produced the publication *Towards Inclusive Practices in Secondary Education*, which provided a selection of best practices worldwide in that area.

Natural sciences

Through its active involvement in the International Global Observing Strategy, the Committee on Earth Observation Satellites and Earth Observation Ministerial Summit Process, as well as the Group on Earth Observation, created in July, UNESCO contributed to the development of the 10-year (2005-2015) Implementation Plan for an improved, integrated, operational and sustained Earth Observation System of Systems. The System of Systems would strengthen Earth observation monitoring activities for sustainable development planning and for improving the in situ and space-borne sensor measurements of the environment.

UNESCO's Intergovernmental Oceanic Commission (IOC) approved the *Guidelines for the Transfer of Marine Technology* and the new IOC Data Exchange Policy, recognizing the essential nature of the timely, free and unrestricted international exchange of oceanographic data.

In 2003, the First World Water Development Report was published by the World Water Assessment Programme whose secretariat was hosted by UNESCO. UNESCO played a lead role in the International Year of Freshwater 2003 (see p. 1033), and its International Hydrological Programme completed the first global map of groundwater. The UNESCO-IHE (Institute for Hydrological Education) Institute for Water Education in Delft, Netherlands, was established.

Social and human sciences

UNESCO prepared the International Declaration on Human Genetic Data, which was finalized by a meeting of government experts in June and by a working group set up at the thirty-second General Conference. It was adopted unanimously and by acclamation by the General Conference on 16 October.

The Sector for Social and Human Sciences continued to make efforts to respond to the contemporary challenges to democracy and democratic development. UNESCO's Executive Board, at its one hundred and sixty-seventh session, adopted the *Integrated Strategy on Democracy within the Framework of the International Centre for Human Sciences, Byblos*. The Strategy aimed at fostering comparative empirical research on democracy and its relationship to culture; promoting international dialogues and prospective analysis on the future of democracy; and supporting democracy in post-conflict societies.

Culture

At its thirty-second session, the General Conference adopted new standard-setting instruments: the UNESCO Declaration concerning Intentional Destruction of Cultural Heritage, the preparation of which was initiated following the 2001 destruction of the Bamian Buddhas in Afghanistan [YUN 2001, p. 1019]; and the Convention for the Safeguarding of the Intangible Cultural Heritage. The General Conference also approved the elaboration of the International Instrument on Cultural Diversity.

Communication

UNESCO continued its efforts to defend and promote freedom of expression and press freedom, notably through the observance of World Press Freedom Day (3 May) in more than 80 countries. UNESCO also successfully promoted the explicit inclusion of the principle of freedom of expression in the World Summit on the Information Society Declaration of Principles and Plan of Action (see p. 857).

Major reforms were put in place to reinforce and increase the efficiency of the International Programme for the Development of Communication, the only multilateral forum in the UN system that mobilized the international community to support media development in developing countries.

Secretariat

As at 31 December 2003, UNESCO employed 2,156 full-time staff, of whom 1,029 were in the Professional or higher categories and 1,127 were in the General Service category.

Budget

In October 2003, the UNESCO General Conference approved a budget of $610 million for the 2004-2005 biennium.

HEADQUARTERS AND OTHER OFFICES

HEADQUARTERS
UNESCO House
7, Place de Fontenoy
75352 Paris 07-SP, France
 Telephone: (33) (1) 45-68-10-00
 Fax: (33) (1) 45-67-16-90
 Internet: www.unesco.org

UNESCO also maintained a liaison office in Geneva.

NEW YORK LIAISON OFFICE
United Nations Educational, Scientific and Cultural Organization
2 United Nations Plaza, Room 900
New York, NY 10017, United States
 Telephone: (1) (212) 963-5995
 Fax: (1) (212) 963-8014
 E-mail: newyork@unesco.org

Chapter V

World Health Organization (WHO)

In 2003, the World Health Organization (WHO) continued to implement its corporate strategy by addressing the burden of ill-health among poor populations; tracking and assessing health risks and helping societies take action to reduce them; improving the performance of health systems; and encouraging national health policies.

The World Health Assembly, WHO's governing body, at its fifty-sixth session (Geneva, 19-28 May), adopted the Framework Convention on Tobacco Control, the first global health treaty aimed at reducing global tobacco consumption and cutting the number of tobacco-related deaths (see p. 1251). The Assembly also adopted resolutions on tropical diseases, including the pan-African tsetse and trypanosomiasis eradication campaign; control of neurocysticercosis; WHO's contribution to the achievement of the Millennium Development Goals [YUN 2000, p. 51] and to the follow-up to the General Assembly's 2001 special session on HIV/AIDS [YUN 2001, p. 1125]; the World Summit on Sustainable Development [YUN 2002, p. 821]; the strategy for child and adolescent health and development; innovations in public health; strengthening health systems in developing countries; revision of the International Health Regulations; and the joint Food and Agriculture Organization of the United Nations/WHO evaluation of the work of the Codex Alimentarius Commission. WHO observed the twenty-fifth anniversary of the Alma-Ata International Conference on Primary Health Care [YUN 1978, p. 1107].

The one hundred and eleventh session of the WHO Executive Board (Geneva, 20-28 January) endorsed a global health-sector strategy for HIV/AIDS; and adopted resolutions on the reduction of global measles mortality and on the prevention and control of influenza pandemics and annual epidemics. It also implemented the recommendations of the *World Report on Violence and Health*, released by WHO in 2002. At its one hundred and twelfth session (Geneva, 29-30 May), the Board discussed the report of the WHO Advisory Committee on Health Research; human organ and tissue transplantation; a proposal for a ".health" Internet domain; and various staffing matters.

In 2003, WHO membership remained at 192, with two associate members.

2003 activities

In 2003, WHO continued to work with national health authorities worldwide to achieve progress in health care policies, establish better health systems and provide improved health care. A $40 million trust fund was established to help the world's least developed countries set food safety standards through the Codex Alimentarius Commission. A meeting of health experts, international researchers and development and donor agencies from 40 developing countries on the theme "Global Consultation on Increasing Investment in Health Outcomes for the Poor" (Geneva, 28-30 October) resulted in a declaration pledging to establish and strengthen appropriate national and subregional mechanisms for the development of national health investment plans. The plans focused on capacity-building, leadership skills and incentives for retention and utilization of skilled human resources.

WHO investigated reports of several cases of atypical pneumonia in Hong Kong and Viet Nam, the first signs of what was later diagnosed as severe acute respiratory syndrome (SARS). On 12 March, WHO alerted the world to the new disease of undetermined cause. Global cooperation and the collaboration of scientists and public health officials, coordinated by WHO, resulted in the identification of a new coronavirus as the cause of the disease. Following a four-month globally coordinated effort, WHO reported on 5 July that it had broken the chain of human-to-human transmission of SARS worldwide. As at 7 August, 8,422 cases of infection and 916 deaths were attributed to SARS. Due to the risk of a recurrence during the winter season, WHO continued SARS vigilance throughout the year.

On World AIDS Day (1 December), WHO and the Joint United Nations Programme on HIV/AIDS announced an ambitious strategy to provide antiretroviral therapy to 3 million people living with HIV/AIDS by the end of 2005. The "3 by 5" strategy included urgent and sustained country support, and standard procedures for delivery.

Secretariat

As at 31 December 2003, WHO employed a staff of 3,842, including 1,490 in the Professional and higher categories and 2,139 in the General Service category. The remaining 213 were employed under other contracts.

Budget

WHO, in 2001, had adopted a budget of $855.7 million, including miscellaneous income, for the 2002-2003 biennium. Extrabudgetary resources were expected to be about $1.4 million. In 2003, the World Health Assembly appropriated $960.1 million under the regular budget for the biennium 2004-2005.

NOTE: For further details of WHO activities, see the *World Health Report 2003*, published by the organization.

HEADQUARTERS AND OTHER OFFICES

HEADQUARTERS
World Health Organization
20, Avenue Appia
CH-1211 Geneva 27, Switzerland
Telephone: (41) (22) 791-21-11
Fax: (41) (22) 791-31-11
Internet: www.who.int
E-mail: info@who.int

WHO OFFICE AT THE UNITED NATIONS
2 United Nations Plaza, Room 970
New York, NY 10017, United States
Telephone: (1) (212) 963-4388
Fax: (1) (212) 963-8565

WHO also maintained regional offices in Brazzaville, Congo; Cairo, Egypt; Copenhagen, Denmark; Manila, Philippines; New Delhi, India; and Washington, D.C.

Chapter VI

World Bank (IBRD and IDA)

The World Bank consisted of the International Bank for Reconstruction and Development (IBRD) and the International Development Association (IDA). Collectively, the following five institutions were known as the World Bank Group: IBRD, IDA, the International Finance Corporation (IFC), the Multilateral Investment Guarantee Agency (MIGA) and the International Centre for Settlement of Investment Disputes (ICSID).

In fiscal 2003 (1 July 2002–30 June 2003), the World Bank continued to promote sustainable economic development by providing loans, guarantees and related technical assistance for projects and programmes in developing nations. Within the context of the Bank's central objective of poverty reduction, key focal points of its assistance were human development, infrastructure, finance and private sector development, agriculture and the environment, and public sector management.

In April, the Bank and three partner organizations launched the Investment Partnership for Polio, an innovative financing programme that supported the eradication of poliomyelitis worldwide by 2005. In December, the Bank sponsored the first Urban Research Symposium, which focused on urban poverty in developing and transition countries.

At the end of fiscal 2003, IBRD membership had increased to 184.

Lending operations

IBRD continued to promote sustainable development through loans, guarantees and non-lending, including analytical and advisory services. As at 30 June 2003, its cumulative lending totalled $383 billion.

IBRD's loan commitment for fiscal 2003 totalled $11.2 billion for 99 new operations in 37 countries, compared to $11.5 billion in 2002 for 96 new operations. The share of adjustment lending totalled $419 billion in fiscal 2003, down from $738 billion in 2002.

In fiscal 2003, IBRD lending commitments were highest in Latin America ($5.7 billion), followed by Europe and Central Asia ($2 billion) and East Asia and the Pacific ($1.8 billion). Law, justice and public administration was the leading sector for IBRD lending, receiving $2.6 billion, or 23 per cent of the total, followed by lending to health and other social services, representing $2.1 billion, or 18 per cent of the total. In fiscal 2003, Argentina, Brazil, China, Colombia and Mexico had combined commitment volume equalling 49 per cent of total lending.

International Development Association

Established in 1960 as the Bank's concessional lending arm, IDA provided interest-free loans and other services to low-income countries to reduce poverty and improve the quality of life. In fiscal 2003, IDA commitments totalled $7.3 billion in grants, compared to $8.1 billion in 2002. Although below the previous year's record high, IDA lending commitments in fiscal 2003 represented the third highest on record and were above the average annual total for the previous five years. Lending to Africa constituted 51 per cent of total IDA commitments, with $3.7 billion financing 60 new operations. South Asia followed with $2.1 billion for 29 operations. Bangladesh, the Democratic Republic of the Congo, Ethiopia, India and Uganda represented the largest single recipients of IDA financing.

In fiscal 2003, about 17 per cent of total IDA operational financing came in the form of grants in the following categories: operations benefiting the poorest countries ($241 million); poorest and debt-vulnerable countries ($406 million); post-conflict countries ($306 million); HIV/AIDS projects and components ($214 million); and natural disaster reconstruction projects ($65 million). Health, social services, law and justice and public administration were the leading sectors for IDA support, each receiving 19 per cent of the total ($1.4 billion).

Fiscal 2003 marked the first year of IDA-13, which funded commitments for fiscal years 2003 through 2005. IDA-13 provided a total of 18 billion special drawing rights (about $24 billion) of concessional resources to IDA-eligible borrowers over the three-year period.

At the end of fiscal 2003, IDA membership increased to 164 countries.

International Centre for Settlement of Investment Disputes

ICSID, established in 1966, continued to encourage foreign investments by providing international facilities for coordination and arbitration of investment disputes. It also conducted research and publishing activities in the areas of arbitration law and foreign investment law. In 2003, 26 new cases were registered with the Centre.

In 2003, ICSID membership totalled 139.

Multilateral Investment Guarantee Agency

MIGA, established in 1988, continued to encourage foreign direct investment in developing countries by providing guarantees to foreign investors against losses caused by non-commercial risks. MIGA also provided technical assistance and advisory services to help developing countries strengthen the capacity of investment promotion intermediaries and disseminate information on investment opportunities.

In fiscal 2003, MIGA had 162 members and issued $1.4 billion in guarantee coverage, for a cumulative total of $12.4 billion.

World Bank Institute

In 2003, the World Bank Institute continued to organize global training activities in an effort to empower people through knowledge- and capacity-building. The Institute adopted a country-focused business model, customizing its capacity-building programmes to countries' priority needs, applying best-practice pedagogy, maintaining a sustained presence at the country level, and collaborating with key figures who could implement policy decisions. To increase its reach, the Institute helped clients gain access to information resources through e-learning, webcasting facilities, web sites and the Global Development Learning Network, which reached more than 36,000 participants in fiscal 2003 via video conferencing–based distance learning.

Co-financing

In fiscal 2003, co-financing amounted to $3 billion, a decrease of $1.7 billion from 2002. Major co-financing partners included the Inter-American Development Bank, the Global Environment Facility and the European Investment Bank. By region, the majority of co-financing went to Latin America and the Caribbean ($0.87 billion), followed by Africa ($0.85 billion) and Asia and the Pacific ($0.64 billion).

Financial activities

During fiscal 2003, IBRD raised $19 billion in medium- and long-term debt, compared to $22 billion in fiscal 2002. The decrease in funding was primarily attributed to lower borrowing requirements. IBRD followed a strategy of selective bond issuance, composed of cost-effective private placements, public issues placed with large institutional investors, and public issues targeted to retail investors. During fiscal 2003, IBRD repurchased or called $6 billion of its outstanding borrowings (net of unamortized discounts, premiums and issuance costs).

Capitalization

As at 30 June 2003, the total subscribed capital of IBRD was $190.8 billion, of which $189.5 billion had been subscribed. Of the subscribed capital, $11.4 billion had been paid in and $178.1 billion was callable.

Income and reserves

IBRD's net income rose to $5.34 billion in fiscal 2003, from $2.78 billion in fiscal 2002. As at 30 June 2003, the Bank's liquid asset portfolio was $27 billion, up from $25 billion in fiscal 2002.

Secretariat

At the end of fiscal 2003, IBRD's regular, fixed-term and long-term consultants and long-term temporary staff in Washington, D.C., and local offices numbered 8,800.

NOTE: For further details regarding the Bank's activities, see *The World Bank Annual Report 2003*.

HEADQUARTERS AND OTHER OFFICES

HEADQUARTERS
The World Bank
1818 H Street, NW
Washington, DC 20433, United States
Telephone: (1) (202) 473-1000
Fax: (1) (202) 477-6391
Internet: www.worldbank.org
E-mail: feedback@worldbank.org

LIAISON OFFICE
The World Bank Mission to the United Nations
1 Dag Hammarskjöld Plaza
885 Second Avenue, 26th floor
New York, NY 10017, United States
Telephone: (1) (212) 355-5112
Fax: (1) (212) 355-4523

The World Bank also maintained offices in Brussels, Belgium; Frankfurt, Germany; Geneva; London; Paris; Sydney, Australia; and Tokyo, Japan.

Chapter VII

International Finance Corporation (IFC)

The International Finance Corporation (IFC), part of the World Bank Group, continued in fiscal 2003 (1 July 2002–30 June 2003) to promote sustainable growth in developing countries by financing private sector investments, helping to mobilize capital in the international financial markets and providing technical assistance and advice to Governments and businesses. To address the environmental and social consequences of development, IFC made sustainability a top priority in its investment and advisory activities.

During fiscal 2003, IFC's membership remained at 175.

Financial and advisory services

In fiscal 2003, more than 67 per cent of IFC's new investments were in the priority sectors of finance, infrastructure, information technology, health and education. The share of those investments in frontier countries, either high-risk or low-income, was 28 per cent. IFC intensified its efforts in the areas of trade facilities, microfinance, housing finance, risk mitigation, local currency financing and securitization. Its structured finance operations included the use of bond issues to mobilize funding for clients beyond IFC's own exposure. In addition, IFC's activities responded creatively to the evolving needs of the private sector in developing countries and staked out new ways of doing business.

The Private Sector Advisory Services, jointly managed by IFC and the World Bank, continued to advise Governments on policy, regulatory issues related to the investment climate and the private provision of public services. It included the rapid response online knowledge service that offered clients databases of research, case studies, toolkits, benchmarking indicators and online discussion boards on private sector development.

The Foreign Investment Advisory Service (FIAS) continued to assist Governments to develop policies and institutions to attract more foreign investment. FIAS completed 49 advisory projects in fiscal 2003, with the largest programmes in Africa (12 projects), followed by Europe and Central Asia (11), and Asia and the Pacific (11).

Throughout fiscal 2003, the donor community provided cumulative contributions of $178 million to support the technical assistance trust funds (TATF) programme, which included a budgetary allocation from IFC's own resources of $11 million. Since inception of the programme in 1988, donors had approved more than 1,250 technical assistance projects. The TATF programme financed feasibility studies, sector studies, advisory activities on privatization and policies to strengthen the business environment in developing countries, and assessed the environmental and social impacts of investment projects.

Regional projects

In fiscal 2003, the new projects for which IFC committed about $5 billion were grouped under six regions.

In sub-Saharan Africa, despite a difficult political environment, IFC completed projects with significant development impact in particularly challenging countries and sectors and supported leading investments in conflict-affected countries. IFC's commitments in the region amounted to $167 million.

In East Asia and the Pacific, IFC strategic priorities included assistance to improve the investment climate, develop local financial markets, and expand private provision of physical and social infrastructure. IFC also aided domestic enterprises, promoted corporate and financial sector restructuring and reached out to small businesses. IFC's commitments in the region totalled $583 million.

In South Asia, IFC provided loans and technical assistance to help companies restructure their operations, access longer-term funding, forge effective partnerships, adopt innovative technologies and reach new markets. IFC commitments totalled $386 million in new investments in the region.

In Europe and Central Asia, IFC priorities emphasized the financial sector, small businesses and privatization, and focused on investments that had a broad development impact with a commitment to responsible environment and social performance. IFC also provided technical support to small and medium-sized enterprises (SMEs). It committed financing in the region for a total of $1.4 billion.

In Latin America and the Caribbean, political or economic issues hampered the performance of the private sector in Bolivia, Colombia, the Dominican Republic and Jamaica, while Venezuela suffered a serious economic downturn stemming from internal political issues. Given the retreat of external financing, demand for lending was strong. Demand also increased for IFC support for refinance, corporate finance and trade financing. In fiscal 2003, IFC committed financing amounting to $2.1 billion in the region.

In the Middle East and North Africa, increased turmoil marked the year. The war in Iraq, the continued unrest in the West Bank and Gaza, and concerns about spillover effects reduced the economic prospects in much of the region. IFC's focus in the region reflected corporate objectives: frontier markets, high-impact sectors, SMEs and sustainability. IFC commitments in the region amounted to $279 million.

Financial performance

In fiscal 2003, IFC's operating income was $528 million, compared with $161 million in fiscal 2002. IFC's committed portfolio at the end of fiscal 2003 was $16.8 billion, up from $15.1 billion in fiscal 2002. The portfolio consisted of loans, equity investments, risk management products, and guarantees in 1,378 companies in 117 countries.

Capital retained earnings

As at 30 June 2003, IFC's net worth reached $6.8 billion, compared with $6.3 billion at the end of fiscal 2002.

Secretariat

As at 31 December 2003, IFC employed 2,206 staff, of whom 1,487 were in the Professional or higher categories and 719 were in the General Service category.

NOTE: For further details of IFC activities, see *International Finance Corporation 2003 Annual Report*, published by the Corporation.

HEADQUARTERS AND OTHER OFFICE

HEADQUARTERS
International Finance Corporation
2121 Pennsylvania Avenue, NW
Washington, DC 20433, United States
  Telephone: (1) (202) 473-3800
  Fax: (1) (202) 974-4384
  Internet: http://www.ifc.org
  E-mail: webmaster@ifc.org

NEW YORK OFFICE
International Finance Corporation
c/o The World Bank, Office of the Special Representative to the UN
1 Dag Hammarskjöld Plaza
885 Second Avenue, 26th floor
New York, NY 10017, United States
  Telephone: (1) (212) 355-5112
  Fax: (1) (212) 355-4523

Chapter VIII

International Monetary Fund (IMF)

During 2003, the International Monetary Fund (IMF) continued to work with its members to foster sustainable growth and financial stability through its surveillance activities and policy advice; lending in support of stabilization and reform programmes; and technical assistance in formulating sound policies and building robust institutions. IMF supported low-income developing countries through low-interest loans, under the poverty reduction and growth facility, and through debt relief, under the enhanced Heavily Indebted Poor Countries (HIPCs) Initiative. It also continued to counter money-laundering.

In fiscal 2003 (1 May 2002–30 April 2003), IMF membership increased to 184.

IMF facilities and polices

In fiscal 2003, IMF continued to update its lending policies and policy conditionality—the conditions it attached to its financial assistance to guarantee that it was repaid and that external viability, financial stability and sustainable economic growth were restored in the borrowing member country—to ensure that they met member country needs. IMF concluded a two-year review of the conditions attached to IMF-supported programmes and approved new guidelines for designing and implementing the conditionality to enhance country ownership and programme effectiveness.

The Independent Evaluation Office, established in 2001, studied the prolonged use of IMF resources; the Fund's role in three current capital account crises (Brazil, Indonesia, Republic of Korea); and IMF-supported programmes.

In order to enhance surveillance and crisis prevention, IMF's Executive Board proposed improvements to assessment exercises under the Fund's standards and codes initiative and the joint IMF–World Bank Financial Sector Assessment Program, and also adopted a new framework for debt sustainability assessments. After the completion in 2003 of the 12-month IMF–World Bank pilot programme for assessing anti-money-laundering/combating the financing of terrorism policies and practices, the Board decided that such work should be included in all financial sector assessment programme reports and offshore assessments.

Financial assistance

New IMF lending commitments in fiscal 2003 totalled 29.4 billion special drawing rights (SDR) compared with SDR 39.4 billion in fiscal 2002. Commitments were largely dominated by the lending arrangement for Brazil (SDR 22.8 billion), which was approved in September 2002 and was the largest in IMF history. Colombia and Argentina also received new large commitments.

IMF approved 10 new standby arrangements totalling SDR 27.1 billion and an existing commitment to Uruguay was augmented by SDR 1.5 billion. In addition, two new extended fund facility arrangements were approved: SDR 0.7 billion for Serbia and Montenegro and SDR 0.1 billion for Sri Lanka. Drawings under the poverty reduction and growth facility (PRGF) amounted to SDR 1.2 billion compared with SDR 1 billion in fiscal 2002. IMF also committed SDR 1.6 billion in HIPC grants to 27 countries, of which SDR 1 billion was disbursed.

As at April 2003, 15 standby arrangements, 3 extended arrangements and 36 PRGF arrangements were in effect with members, while outstanding IMF credit amounted to SDR 72.9 billion, compared with SDR 58.7 billion a year earlier.

Liquidity

As at 30 April, IMF's usable resources totalled SDR 98 billion, a decrease from SDR 104 billion in fiscal 2002. Net uncommitted usable resources totalled SDR 60.6 billion at the end of fiscal 2003, compared with 64.7 billion in fiscal 2002.

The Fund's liquid liability totalled SDR 68 billion, compared with SDR 55.3 billion in 2002, while the ratio of the Fund's net uncommitted usable resources to its liquid liabilities decreased to 89.1 per cent at the end of April 2003, from 117 per cent a year earlier.

SDR activity

In fiscal 2003, total transfer of SDRs increased to SDR 15.6 billion from SDR 14 billion in fiscal 2002.

Transfers of SDRs among participants and prescribed holders rose to SDR 6 billion in 2003 from SDR 5.1 billion. Transfer from participants to the general resources account (GRA) increased significantly to SDR 4.6 billion, due to increased payments for members' quotas. Drawings from IMF in SDRs continued to decrease to SDR 2.2 billion from SDR 2.4 billion in fiscal 2002, representing the largest category of transfers from the GRA, followed by remuneration payments of SDR 1.2 billion to members with creditor positions.

IMF holdings of SDRs in the GRA declined to SDR 1 billion from SDR 1.5 billion in fiscal 2002, while SDRs held by prescribed holders amounted to SDR 0.6 billion. SDR holdings by participants increased to SDR 19.9 billion from SDR 19.6 billion in fiscal 2002. SDR holdings of industrial and net creditor countries relative to their net cumulative allocations decreased from a year earlier. SDR holdings of non-industrial members amounted to 72 per cent of their net cumulative allocations compared with 56.9 per cent a year earlier.

Policy on arrears

Financial obligations to IMF decreased from SDR 2.36 billion in 2002 to SDR 2 billion as at 30 April 2003. Almost all arrears were protracted (outstanding for more than six months), about evenly divided between overdue principal and overdue charges and interest. The Sudan and Liberia accounted for more than 79 per cent of the overdue financial obligations, while Somalia and Zimbabwe accounted for most of the remainder. The application of remedial measures against Iraq and Somalia had been delayed or suspended because of civil conflicts, the absence of a functioning Government and/or international sanctions. As at 30 April 2003, Liberia, Somalia, the Sudan and Zimbabwe were ineligible to use IMF's general resources. In addition, Liberia's voting and related rights had been suspended; Zimbabwe had been removed from the PRGF list; and for both Liberia and Zimbabwe declarations of non-cooperation had been imposed.

Technical assistance and training

During fiscal 2003, the Executive Board endorsed measures to introduce an institution-wide methodology for monitoring and evaluating technical assistance activities, and for implementing a formal three-year rolling programme of evaluations. It also created a comprehensive financial accounting system to capture the full cost of technical assistance delivery, both in the field and at IMF headquarters.

The IMF Institute continued to strengthen its training curriculum, delivering 119 courses and seminars to over 3,800 participants. A number of courses were cancelled because of the security situation in Côte d'Ivoire, the war in Iraq and the outbreak of severe acute respiratory syndrome in Asia.

Secretariat

As at 31 December 2003, IMF employed 2,693 staff members, of whom 1,954 were Professional staff and 739 assistant staff.

Budget

The Fund's administrative budget for fiscal 2003 was approved at $794.3 million ($746.4 million, net of estimated reimbursements). In April, the Board approved $837.5 million ($785.5 million, net of reimbursements) for fiscal 2004.

NOTE: For further details of IMF activities, see *International Monetary Fund Annual Report 2003*, published by the Fund.

HEADQUARTERS AND OTHER OFFICES

HEADQUARTERS
International Monetary Fund
700 19th Street, NW
Washington, DC 20431, United States
Telephone: (1) (202) 623-7000
Fax: (1) (202) 623-4661
Internet: www.imf.org
E-mail: publicaffairs@imf.org

IMF also maintained offices in Geneva, Paris and Tokyo.

IMF OFFICE, UNITED NATIONS, NEW YORK
International Monetary Fund
885 Second Avenue, 26th floor
New York, NY 10017, United States
Telephone: (1) (212) 893-1700
Fax: (1) (212) 893-1715

Chapter IX

International Civil Aviation Organization (ICAO)

The International Civil Aviation Organization (ICAO) continued in 2003 to promote the safety and efficiency of civil air transport by prescribing standards and recommending practices and procedures for facilitating international civil aviation operations. Its objectives were set forth in annexes to the Convention on International Civil Aviation, adopted in Chicago, United States, in 1944 (the Chicago Convention).

In 2003, domestic and international scheduled traffic of the world's airlines increased to some 404 billion tonne-kilometres. Overall, passenger traffic increased by just over 1 per cent to some 1.66 billion, and freight carriage increased by almost 10 per cent to about 35 million tonnes. The passenger load factor on scheduled services in 2003 remained at approximately 71 per cent. Air freight increased by almost 5 per cent to 125.2 billion tonne-kilometres, and airmail traffic increased by 1 per cent to 4.6 billion tonne-kilometres. Overall passenger/freight/mail tonne-kilometres increased by almost 2 per cent, while there was little change in international tonne-kilometres.

The Council of ICAO held three regular sessions in 2003. The thirty-fourth ICAO Assembly elected a new Council and, among other things, adopted a resolution to finance aviation security activities of member States.

ICAO observed International Civil Aviation Day (7 December) under the theme "For 60 Years . . . Setting the Standards for International Civil Aviation", to mark the creation of ICAO on that day in 1944.

In 2003, ICAO membership remained at 188 countries.

Activities

Air navigation

ICAO continued to update and implement international specifications and regional plans, with particular emphasis on safety, communications, navigation and surveillance/air traffic management (CNS/ATM) systems. The specifications consisted of International Standards and Recommended Practices contained in 18 technical annexes to the 1944 Chicago Convention, and Procedures for Air Navigation Services (PANS).

In 2003, seven air navigation meetings were convened, all in Montreal. The meetings dealt with, among other things, aeronautical telecommunications, airworthiness of aircraft, the safe transport of dangerous goods by air, flight crew licensing and training, standards, and recommended practices relating to aeronautical navigation issues and operational issues.

The Council adopted amendments to 10 technical annexes to the Chicago Convention and approved amendments to three PANS documents.

Other projects that were given special attention in 2003 included accident prevention, investigation and incident data reporting; aviation environmental matters; aerodromes, including licensing/certification; the aeronautical electromagnetic spectrum, with particular regard to ICAO's position for the International Telecommunication Union's World Radiocommunication Conference (2003); aeronautical information services; aeronautical meteorology; airworthiness; aviation medicine; bird strikes to aircraft; controlled flight into terrain; flight safety and human factors; operations; personnel licensing and training; safety aspects of aviation security; safety oversight; and the TRAINAIR Programme, which established and maintained training standards.

Air transport

ICAO's air transport programmes were directed towards economic analysis, policy, forecasting and planning; collection and publication of air transport statistics; airport and route facility management; economic and organizational aspects of CNS/ATM systems coordination; economic aspects of environmental protection; the promotion of greater facilitation in international air transport; and aviation security.

The Fifth Worldwide Air Transport Conference (Montreal, 24-28 March) focused on developing a global framework for ongoing liberalization and adopted a Declaration of Global Principles for Liberalization of International Air Transport.

Significant progress was made in the implementation of the ICAO Aviation Security Plan of Action. The Aviation Security Audit Unit continued the implementation of the Universal Security Audit Programme. Twenty member States were audited by ICAO aviation security audit teams. New and emerging threats to civil aviation, such as man-portable air defence systems (MANPADS), were the subject of the Aviation Security Panel deliberations. In order to assist States in the development of countermeasures against MANPADS, additional guidance material was developed.

ICAO continued to provide secretariat services to three regional civil aviation bodies—the African Civil Aviation Commission, the European Civil Aviation Conference and the Latin American Civil Aviation Commission.

Legal matters

On 9 June, the Council of ICAO approved the draft participation agreement relating to the global aviation war risk insurance scheme. On 4 November, the Convention for the Unification of Certain Rules for International Carriage by Air, signed at Montreal on 28 May 1999, entered into force, having been ratified by 30 States. By the end of the year, the Convention had 34 parties.

Technical cooperation

In 2003, the ICAO technical cooperation programme undertook 123 projects in 59 developing countries. The programme, financed by the United Nations Development Programme (UNDP), trust funds, management service agreements and the Civil Aviation Purchasing Services, had total expenditures of $105.4 million. Some 86.7 per cent of that amount was provided by Governments to fund their own projects on the basis of cost-sharing with UNDP.

A total of 507 fellowships were awarded in 2003, of which 474 were taken up.

ICAO employed 420 experts from 38 countries, of whom 77 were on assignment under UNDP and 358 on trust fund projects. Equipment purchases in 2003 totalled $82.8 million, compared to $39.16 million in 2002. ICAO had resident missions in 68 countries.

Secretariat

As at 31 December 2003, ICAO employed 794 staff members, including 345 in the Professional and higher categories and 449 in the General Service and related categories.

Budget

Appropriations for the ICAO budget in 2003 were $58,415,389.

NOTE: For further details on activities of ICAO in 2003, see *Annual Report of the Council, 2003.*

HEADQUARTERS AND REGIONAL OFFICES

International Aviation Organization
999 University Street
Montreal, Quebec, Canada H3C 5H7
Telephone: (1) (514) 954-8219
Fax: (1) (514) 954-6077
Internet: www.icao.int
E-mail: icaohq@icao.int

ICAO maintained regional offices in Bangkok, Thailand; Cairo, Egypt; Dakar, Senegal; Lima, Peru; Mexico, D.F.; Nairobi, Kenya; and Paris.

Chapter X

Universal Postal Union (UPU)

In 2003, the Universal Postal Union (UPU) continued to promote and develop a fast and reliable universal postal service through international collaboration among its member countries.

UPU's 190 members remained the largest physical distribution network in the world, with more than 5 million postal employees in some 650,000 post offices.

Activities of the UPU organs

Universal Postal Congress

The Universal Postal Congress, UPU's supreme legislative authority, met every five years. It last met in 1999 [YUN 1999, p. 1408] and was scheduled to meet in 2004, in Bucharest, Romania.

Council of Administration

The Council of Administration, which ensured the continuity of the Union's work between Congresses and studied regulatory, administrative, legislative and legal issues, held its annual session in Berne, Switzerland (9-27 October). It adopted a resolution on extraterritorial offices of exchange and approved the objectives of the future World Postal Strategy that would be adopted at the 2004 Bucharest Congress.

Postal Operations Council

During 2003, the Postal Operations Council (POC) dealt with the operational, economic and commercial aspects of international postal services. At its annual session (Berne, 31 March-11 April), POC endorsed the principles of the future terminal dues system and finalized the quality link for industrialized countries, which would be presented to the 2004 Bucharest Congress for final approval.

Actions to combat money-laundering and terrorist-financing activities topped the agenda of the Postal Security Action Group in April. Conferences were also held on postal financial services and international parcels development.

International Bureau

In 2003, UPU continued to provide support, liaison, information and consultation to postal administrations of member countries. It studied developments in the postal environment, monitored the quality of postal service on a global scale, and published information and statistics on international postal services.

UPU's Postal Technology Centre, which was responsible for managing the postal application of electronic data interchange, introduced new technology applications and information solutions to improve the quality, reliability and speed of national and international postal services through, among other methods, tracking-and-tracing of mail items.

As at 31 December 2003, the Bureau's permanent staff numbered 151, of whom 58 were in the Professional or higher categories and 93 were in the General Service category.

Budget

Under UPU's self-financing system, contributions were payable in advance by member States based on the following year's budget. The Council of Administration approved a budget of 71.4 million Swiss francs for the 2003-2004 budget.

NOTE: For further details on UPU's activities in 2003, see *Universal Postal Union Biennial Report 2003-2004*, published by UPU.

HEADQUARTERS

Universal Postal Union
Weltpoststrasse 4
Case postale 13
3000 Berne 15, Switzerland
  Telephone: (41) (31) 350 31 11
  Fax: (41) (31) 350 31 10
  Internet: www.upu.int
  E-mail: info@upu.int

Chapter XI

International Telecommunication Union (ITU)

The International Telecommunication Union (ITU) continued in 2003 to promote the worldwide development and efficient operation of telecommunication systems and to provide technical assistance.

At its annual session (Geneva, 5-16 May), the ITU Council discussed preparations for the World Summit on the Information Society, the first phase of which took place in Geneva (10-12 December) (see p. 857), while the second phase was scheduled for 2005. Other issues addressed were the 2004-2005 biennial budget, international telecommunication regulations and satellite network filings. The Council also considered mechanisms to link strategic, operational and financial planning, in addition to general provisions regarding conferences and assemblies.

During the year, the Union staged numerous events, including ITU TELECOM WORLD 2003 (Geneva, 12-18 October), which focused on restoring confidence and building growth in the industry.

ITU membership remained at 189 in 2003.

Radiocommunication Sector

ITU's Radiocommunication Sector (ITU-R) continued to develop operational procedures and technical characteristics for terrestrial and space-based wireless services and systems. ITU-R study groups prepared over 150 new and revised recommendations for many services, including spectrum management, fixed-satellite and broadcasting. ITU-R convened the 2003 World Radiocommunication Conference (Geneva, 9 June-4 July), which concluded with a blueprint for the global radiocommunication sector that reflected its current and future needs. The Radiocommunication Bureau substantially improved satellite notification and filing by reducing the waiting time for the processing of notices.

Telecommunication Standardization Sector

The Telecommunication Standardization Sector (ITU-T) continued to ensure the efficient and on-time production of high-quality standards covering all areas of telecommunications. It streamlined its work in data networks, open systems communications and telecommunication software, and organized workshops and seminars worldwide.

ITU-T adopted 257 recommendations and supplements, including standards for security architecture for systems providing end-to-end communications, which were expected to quadruple fibre optic transmission capacity and lower costs, and a standard that encouraged innovation in interactive television.

Telecommunication Development Sector

The Telecommunication Development Sector (ITU-D) continued to promote investment and foster expansion of telecommunication infrastructure in developing countries.

The Telecommunication Development Bureau (BDT), the administrative arm of ITU-D, continued to assist countries to reform and restructure their telecommunication sectors through new technologies, developing the human resources necessary to ensure sustainability in management and operations, and promoting financing and partnerships as a strategy to attract investment in the sectors. BDT's Sector Reform Unit carried out an annual survey on telecommunication regulation. The fifth annual *Trends in Telecommunication Reform* report focused on universal access to information and communication technologies.

The fourth annual Global Symposium for Regulators (GSR) (Geneva, 8-9 December) established a set of universal access regulatory best practice principles.

The fourth Forum on Telecommunication Regulation in Africa (Accra, Ghana, November) developed universal access recommendations addressed to Governments, telecommunication regulators and other stakeholders that were presented to GSR.

Secretariat

As at 31 December 2003, ITU had 765 staff members, comprising 5 elected officials, 312 in the Professional and higher categories and 448 in the General Service category.

Budget

The 2002-2003 budget for ITU amounted to 341,947,736 Swiss francs (SwF). The ITU Council set the 2004-2005 budget at SwF 328,872,000.

NOTE: For further details regarding ITU activities, see the *ITU* 2003 Annual Report, published by the Union.

HEADQUARTERS

International Telecommunication Union
Place des Nations
CH-1211, Geneva 20, Switzerland
Telephone: (41) (22) 730-6039
Fax: (41) (22) 733-7256
Internet: http://www.itu.int
E-mail: pressinfo@itu.int

Chapter XII

World Meteorological Organization (WMO)

In 2003, the World Meteorological Organization (WMO) continued to facilitate worldwide cooperation in the generation and exchange of meteorological and hydrological information and the application of meteorology to aviation, shipping, water problems, agriculture and other activities. It also promoted operational hydrology and encouraged research and training in meteorology.

During the year, anniversaries of two initiatives that ultimately led to the establishment of WMO were observed: the one hundred and fiftieth anniversary of the Brussels Maritime Conference (1853), which initiated formal global cooperation in meteorology; and the one hundred and thirtieth anniversary of the first (1873) Congress of the International Meteorological Organization.

The Fourteenth World Meteorological Congress (Geneva, 5-24 May), WMO's governing body, reviewed programme implementation and activities, and adopted the Sixth Long-term Plan (2004-2011) and three new programmes on natural disaster reduction and mitigation, space and the least developed countries. The Congress also established the Consultative Meetings on High-level Policy on Satellite Matters.

The WMO Executive Council, at its fifty-fifth session (Geneva, 26-28 May), re-established the Working Group on Long-term Planning, the Advisory Group on the International Exchange of Data, the Panel of Experts on Education and Training and the Advisory Group of Experts on Technical Cooperation.

WMO's membership increased to 181 States and six Territories in 2003.

World Weather Watch Programme

In 2003, the World Weather Watch Programme marked its fortieth anniversary. Its scientific and technical programme provided meteorological data and products to member States, offering worldwide weather information, analysis and forecasts through its Global Observing System, Global Telecommunications System, Global Data-processing System and data management and system support activities, collectively known as the basic system. It also included the Tropical Cyclone Programme, the Instruments and Methods of Observation Programme and WMO satellite and environmental emergency response activities.

The ITU World Radiocommunication Conference (Geneva, June/July) safeguarded and consolidated several frequency band allocations for meteorological operations. The Commission for Instruments and Methods of Observation (CIMO), at its first session (Los Angeles, United States, 13-15 February), finalized the structure of CIMO Open Programme Area Groups and terms of reference of each expert team. A joint meeting of the CIMO Expert Team on Surface-based Instrument Intercomparisons and Calibration Methods and the International Organizing Committee on Surface-based Instrument Intercomparisons (Trappes, France, 24-28 November) marked the first step in organizing a series of intercomparisons. Substantive work was completed on the Guide to Meteorological Instruments and Methods of Observation (seventh edition); five instrument and observing methods reports were published in CD-ROM format and on the CIMO/Instruments and Methods of Observation Programme web site.

The Second International Conference on Women in Meteorology and Hydrology (Geneva, 24-27 March), organized by WMO, reviewed progress made in women's participation in those areas and developed strategies to increase their involvement.

World Climate Programme

In 2003, the World Climate Application and Service Programme, including Climate Information and Prediction Services, focused on food and agriculture, water resources, health and urban climate, and continued to support regional climate outlook forums, particularly in Africa, where it established a regional climate network for journalists.

In January, the International Research Center on El Niño was established in Guayaquil, Ecuador, to focus on the El Niño/Southern Oscillation and its impacts, and climate applications.

Publications issued in 2003 included the seventh *Global Climate System Review* covering the period from June 1996 to December 2001 and the *Statement on the Status of the Global Climate*.

Atmospheric Research and Environment Programme

During 2003, significant progress was made in the implementation of component programmes of the Atmospheric Research and Environment Programme. The new World Weather Research Programme "THORPEX: a Global Atmospheric Research Programme", which aimed to improve the accuracy of high-impact 1- to 14-day weather forecasts, progressed in its organization and development.

The World Climate Research Programme (WCRP) in 2003 successfully concluded the WCRP Arctic Climate System Study (ACSYS). The aim of the new WCRP core project, Climate and Cryosphere, a sequel to ACSYS, was to enhance systematically monitoring, understanding and modelling of complex processes through which the cryosphere interfaced with the global climate system.

Applications of meteorology

The Applications of Meteorology Programme continued to support member States in a wide range of socio-economic activities, including the protection of life and property and safeguarding the environment. The Agricultural Meteorology Programme held joint activities with the Climate Information and Prediction Services (CLIPS) Programme through the organization of the Regional Technical Meeting on CLIPS and Agrometeorological Applications for the Andean Countries (Guayaquil, 8-12 December). The aeronautical meteorology activities were devoted to putting in place guidance and regulatory material and conducting training events in preparation for the final (2005) phase of the World Area Forecast System.

At its first meeting in February, a task team on resources, established to assist in identifying and securing resources to implement the capacity-building programme of the Joint WMO/Intergovernmental Oceanographic Commission Technical Commission for Oceanography and Marine Meteorology, decided on the development of a database of key funding agencies to link capacity-building projects to potential funding sources and to advise on the project evaluation and selection process.

Hydrology and water resources

The Hydrology and Water Resources Programme continued to provide assistance to national hydrological services, particularly in their water resources assessment activities, through conferences, seminars, training courses and field projects. A meeting on improved meteorological and hydrological forecasting for flood situations (Geneva, 1-2 April) highlighted the need for an action programme to focus on the ability of national meteorological services and hydrological services to cooperate in an effective manner to provide improved flood forecasting services.

Technical cooperation

In 2003, WMO technical assistance, valued at $23.58 million, was financed by the WMO Voluntary Cooperation Programme ($7.7 million), the United Nations Development Programme ($2.19 million), trust funds ($12.76 million) and the WMO regular budget ($0.93 million).

Secretariat

As at 31 December 2003, WMO staff totalled 258, including 116 in the Professional and higher categories and 142 in the General Service category.

Budget

A regular budget of 127,169,800 Swiss francs (SwF) for the 2004-2005 biennium was approved by the WMO Executive Council in 2003. The Fourteenth World Meteorological Congress, also in 2003, approved a maximum expenditure of SwF 253,800,000 for the fourteenth financial period (2004-2007).

NOTE: For further details regarding WMO activities, see *World Meteorological Organization Annual Report 2003*, published by WMO.

HEADQUARTERS AND OTHER OFFICE

World Meteorological Organization
7 bis, avenue de la Paix
(Case postale No. 2300)
CH-1211 Geneva 2, Switzerland
 Telephone: (41) (22) 730-8111
 Fax: (41) (22) 730-8181
 Internet: http://www.wmo.ch
 E-mail: wmo@wmo.int

World Meteorological Organization Liaison Office at the United Nations
2 United Nations Plaza, Room 980
New York, NY 10017, United States
 Telephone: (1) (212) 963-9444
 Fax: (1) (212) 963-6997
 E-mail: DonNanjira@un.org

Chapter XIII

International Maritime Organization (IMO)

In 2003, the International Maritime Organization (IMO) continued to improve the safety and security of international shipping and protect the marine environment from pollution by ships.

IMO's twenty-third Assembly (London, 24 November–5 December) adopted 30 resolutions, including new guidelines on places of refuge for ships in distress and on ship recycling. The Assembly also approved IMO's strategic plan (2004-2010), adopted a resolution on the voluntary IMO member State audit scheme and elected a new 40-member Council for 2004-2005. During 2003, member States worked towards the implementation of the 2002 maritime security measures [YUN 2002, p. 1489].

In 2003, IMO membership increased to 163 with three associate members.

Activities in 2003

Prevention of pollution

In December, IMO's Marine Environment Protection Committee adopted a revised, accelerated phase-out scheme for single hull oil tankers, along with other measures, including a new regulation banning the carriage of heavy grade oil in single-hull tankers. Those amendments to the International Convention for the Prevention of Pollution from Ships, 1973, as modified by the Protocol of 1978 (MARPOL 73/78), were expected to enter into force in April 2005.

IMO designated Paracas National Reserve, Peru, as a particularly sensitive sea area (PSSA). MARPOL 73/78 defined certain areas as PSSAs in which, for technical reasons relating to their sea traffic, the adoption of special mandatory methods for the prevention of sea pollution was required. Other PSSAs included the Great Barrier Reef, Australia; the Sabana-Camagüey Archipelago, Cuba; Malpelo Island, Colombia; the area around the Florida Keys, United States; and the Wadden Sea, Northern Europe.

In May, a diplomatic conference held in London, adopted a Protocol to the International Convention on the Establishment of an International Fund for Compensation for Oil Pollution Damage, 1971, establishing an International Oil Pollution Compensation Supplementary Fund, designed to increase levels of compensation to victims of oil pollution from oil tanker accidents. Total compensation payable for any one incident was limited to 750 million special drawing rights, just over $1.15 billion.

Ship security and safety at sea

During 2003, model courses and guidelines on maritime security were approved and an International Ship and Port Facility Security Code Database was established. IMO's Integrated Technical Cooperation Programme assisted developing countries to contribute to the global effort to protect shipping from terrorist attacks.

The Maritime Safety Committee (MSC) and subsidiary bodies continued to work on technical safety issues. In June, MSC adopted a revised annex to the 1988 Protocol to the International Convention on Load Lines, 1966, which was expected to have a beneficial impact on the safety of bulk carriers in particular.

Secretariat

As at 31 December, IMO employed 276 staff members, of whom 123 were in the Professional and higher categories and 153 were in the General Service category.

Budget

The IMO Assembly, in 2003, approved budget appropriations of 46,194,900 pounds sterling for the 2004-2005 biennium.

NOTE: For further information, see the organization's quarterly magazine, *IMO News*.

HEADQUARTERS

International Maritime Organization
4 Albert Embankment
London SE1 7SR, United Kingdom
Telephone: (44) (207) 735-7611
Fax: (44) (207) 587-3210
Internet: www.imo.org
E-mail: info@imo.org

Chapter XIV

World Intellectual Property Organization (WIPO)

The World Intellectual Property Organization (WIPO) continued to help ensure that the rights of creators and owners of intellectual property were protected worldwide, thus ensuring that inventors and authors were recognized and rewarded for their ingenuity.

The governing bodies of WIPO and the Unions administered by the organization held their thirty-eighth series of meetings (Geneva, 26-27 May).

During 2003, WIPO membership remained at 179. The number of States adhering to the treaties administered by WIPO increased: as at 31 December 2003, 164 States were parties to the Paris Convention for the Protection of Industrial Property, 151 to the Berne Convention for the Protection of Literary and Artistic Works, and 122 to the Patent Cooperation Treaty (PCT). A significant development was the entry into force, on 23 December, of the Geneva Act of the Hague Agreement Concerning the International Registration of Industrial Designs.

World Intellectual Property Day was observed on 26 April, under the theme "Make Intellectual Property Your Business".

Activities in 2003

Development cooperation

During 2003, WIPO continued to assist developing countries in optimizing their intellectual property systems for economic, social and cultural benefit. Some 17,000 representatives from 98 developing countries participated in 228 seminars held under WIPO Cooperation for Development auspices. Staff members undertook some 300 missions to developing countries to implement the organization's work programme, which addressed such areas as intellectual property policy options, intellectual property asset management, training, legislative advice, computerization, administrative advice and public awareness promotion. A cooperation agreement relating to geographical indications was signed by WIPO, the African Intellectual Property Organization and France. In other activities, a second WIPO/League of Arab States regional coordination meeting for heads of industrial property and copyright offices was organized in Muscat, Oman; and the ministerial-level meeting on intellectual property for Caribbean countries (Antigua, November) signed a multilateral agreement to promote the use of intellectual property and the development of intellectual property assets and cultural industries in the region. WIPO organized a forum on the theme "Intellectual Property: A Powerful Tool for Economic Growth" in cooperation with the University of Khartoum and the Sudanese Businessmen and Employers Federation. The first WIPO Worldwide Academy (WWA) session for least developed countries' Ambassadors (Geneva) discussed the role and contribution of the intellectual property system for economic growth and development.

WWA's Distance Learning Programme delivered the "General Course on Intellectual Property" in seven languages; some 8,300 students from 180 countries participated. Three specialized courses, copyright and related rights, traditional knowledge and biotechnology, were pilot-tested for launch in 2004.

Intellectual property law

In 2003, WIPO provided legislative advice on draft intellectual property laws and consultations on the modernization of national intellectual property legislation. It also participated in the drafting of the intellectual property section of the Model Civil Code for the Commonwealth of Independent States and advised officials from six countries concerning the accession to, or implementation of, WIPO-administered treaties.

The Standing Committee on the Law of Patents held one session on the harmonization of substantive aspects of patent law, as set out in the draft Substantive Patent Law Treaty and related Regulations and Practice Guidelines.

The Standing Committee on the Law of Trademarks, Industrial Design and Geographical Indications continued work on the revision of the Trademark Law Treaty, and focused on provisions regarding the electronic filing of trademark applications and other communications.

The Standing Committee on Copyright and Related Rights made progress in identifying beneficiaries and discussing the scope of rights to be granted to broadcasting organizations.

Arbitration and Mediation Centre

In 2003, the Arbitration and Mediation Centre, the leading provider of services for domain name and other intellectual property disputes, received 1,100 new cases. It organized workshops to train intellectual property specialists in the mechanics of dispute resolution procedures, and issued a new publication describing the features of those procedures in comparison with court litigation of intellectual property disputes.

International registration activities

PCT. The number of international patent applications filed in 2003 exceeded 100,000 for the third consecutive year.

Madrid system. In the trademark system under the Madrid Agreement concerning the International Registration of Trademarks and its 1989 Protocol, the number of new international registrations totalled 21,847 in 2003, bringing the total number of international registrations to 412,000 as at 31 December 2003.

Hague system. The Hague Agreement concerning industrial designs registered 13,152 industrial designs in 2003.

Lisbon system. During the year, the International Bureau recorded six new registrations for appellations of origin under the Lisbon system.

Secretariat

As at 31 December 2003, WIPO employed some 980 staff members representing 94 countries.

Budget

The approved programme and budget for 2004-2005 amounted to 638.8 million Swiss francs. Contributions by member States represented 6 per cent of the overall budget. WIPO remained largely a self-funding agency, financing its activities from revenues acquired through the provision of services to the private sector.

NOTE: For further information, see *WIPO Annual Report 2003*, published by WIPO.

HEADQUARTERS AND OTHER OFFICE

HEADQUARTERS
World Intellectual Property Organization
34, Chemin des Colombettes (P.O. Box 18)
CH-1211 Geneva 20, Switzerland
 Telephone: (41) (22) 338-9111
 Fax: (41) (22) 733-5428
 Internet: www.wipo.int
 E-mail: wipo-mail@wipo.int

WIPO OFFICE AT THE UNITED NATIONS
2 United Nations Plaza, Suite 2525
New York, NY 10017, United States
 Telephone: (1) (212) 963-6813
 Fax: (1) (212) 963-4801
 Email: wipo@un.org

Chapter XV

International Fund for Agricultural Development (IFAD)

The International Fund for Agricultural Development (IFAD) continued in 2003 to promote the economic advancement of the rural poor by providing low-interest loans and grants.

The twenty-sixth session of the Governing Council (Rome, Italy, 19-20 February) approved a document entitled "Enabling the rural poor to overcome their poverty: report of the Consultation on the Sixth Replenishment of IFAD's Resources 2004-2006". The document set out guidelines on major policy issues, including a performance-based allocation system, field presence, results and impact measurement, a more independent evaluation function and external evaluation of IFAD.

In 2003, IFAD membership increased to 163 States, of which 23 were in List A (developed countries), 12 in List B (oil-exporting developing countries) and 128 in List C (other developing countries), of which 49 were in Sub-List C1 (Africa), 48 were in Sub-List C2 (Europe, Asia and the Pacific) and 31 in Sub-List C3 (Latin America and the Caribbean).

Resources

The Governing Council adopted the sixth replenishment of IFAD's resources at a target level of $560 million for the 2004-2006 period, which represented the largest negotiated target in the organization's history. The 2003 programme of work was approved for $450 million.

Activities

In 2003, loans approved and finalized through IFAD amounted to $403.6 million; grants worth $20 million were also approved. The total cost of the 25 new projects and programmes was estimated at $712.6 million, of which $124.9 million would be provided by other external financiers, and $184.1 million by financiers in the recipient countries—primarily Governments.

Regular Programme lending was distributed as follows: Asia and the Pacific, $93.5 million for four projects (23.2 per cent); Western and Central Africa, $84.9 million for seven projects (21 per cent); Eastern and Southern Africa, $74.5 million for five projects (18.5 per cent); Latin America and the Caribbean, $74 million for four projects (18.3 per cent); and the Near East and North Africa, $76.8 million for five projects (19 per cent).

During 2003, 30 projects were completed; 195 projects remained effective at the end of the year.

Secretariat

As at 12 November 2003, the IFAD secretariat employed 295 staff members, comprising 118 in the Professional and higher categories and 177 in the General Service category.

Income and expenditure

At the end of 2003, IFAD's income on loans was $47 million and on cash and investments was $114.5 million. Operating expenses for the year totalled $124 million.

NOTE: For further details on IFAD activities in 2003, see *Annual Report 2003*, published by the Fund.

HEADQUARTERS AND OTHER OFFICES

HEADQUARTERS
International Fund for Agricultural Development
Via del Serafico, 107
00142 Rome, Italy
 Telephone: (39) (06) 54591
 Fax: (39) (06) 5043463
 Internet: www.ifad.org
 E-mail: ifad@ifad.org

IFAD LIAISON OFFICE
2 United Nations Plaza, Room 1128-29
New York, NY 10017, United States
 Telephone: (1) (212) 963-0546
 Fax: (1) (212) 963-2787

IFAD also maintained offices in Eschbom, Germany, and in Washington, DC.

Chapter XVI

United Nations Industrial Development Organization (UNIDO)

The United Nations Industrial Development Organization (UNIDO) continued in 2003 to promote the sustainable industrial development of developing countries and economies in transition.

The Industrial Development Board, at its twenty-seventh session (Vienna, 26-28 August), considered UNIDO's programme and budget for the 2004-2005 biennium. Member States welcomed the establishment of an informal consultative group on voluntary contributions and discussed UNIDO's corporate strategy.

The tenth session of the UNIDO General Conference (Vienna, 1-5 December) adopted the medium-term programme framework for 2004-2007 and invited the Director-General to develop a strategic long-term (10 to 15 years) vision statement for adoption at its General Conference in 2005. It also adopted resolutions on, among other things, South-South cooperation, UNIDO's activities in countries emerging from crises and poverty reduction in developing countries, particularly in Latin America and the Caribbean, in the context of sustainable development.

UNIDO membership rose to 171 in 2003.

Global forum activities

Through its global forum activities, UNIDO continued to promote industrial development and cooperation between countries, partnerships, knowledge-sharing, technology and investment. It also assisted developing countries and economies in transition in the implementation of multilateral environmental agreements.

Global forum activities included the compilation and dissemination worldwide of the 2003 edition of UNIDO's industrial statistics databases through various media, including CD-ROM, hard copy publication and the Internet; ongoing implementation of a research programme on combating marginalization and poverty through industrial development; and a workshop on policy tools (Monterrey, Mexico, 6-7 November) for the promotion of industrial clusters in Latin America. The Nordic Partnership's scope of cooperation was extended and members signed an annex to the memorandum of understanding [YUN 2002, p. 1494] that outlined the objectives and modalities.

Technical cooperation

UNIDO continued to provide technical cooperation through its integrated programmes and country service frameworks, most of which dealt with capacity-building; many were geared towards increasing productivity and competitiveness with a particular emphasis on small and medium-sized enterprises and on environmental protection. During 2003, UNIDO's technical cooperation programmes and projects totalled some $94.6 million, compared to $81.8 million in 2002.

Secretariat

As at 31 December 2003, UNIDO employed 645 staff members: 255 were in the Professional or higher categories, 385 were in the General Service category and 5 were national officers.

Budget

The ninth (2001) session of the UNIDO General Conference approved the organization's 2002-2003 regular budget in the amount of 133,689,800 euros. The tenth (2003) session approved the 2004-2005 regular budget in the amount of 142,000,000 euros.

NOTE: For further information about UNIDO, see *Annual Report of UNIDO 2003*, published by UNIDO.

HEADQUARTERS AND OTHER OFFICES

HEADQUARTERS
United Nations Industrial Development Organization
Vienna International Centre
P.O. Box 300
A-1400 Vienna, Austria
 Telephone: (43) (1) 26026-0
 Fax: (43) (1) 269-26-69
 Internet: http://www.unido.org
 E-mail: unido@unido.org

LIAISON OFFICES

UNIDO Office at Geneva
Palais des Nations
Le Bocage, Pavillion 1
8, rue de Pregny
CH-1211 Geneva 10, Switzerland
Telephone: (41) (22) 917-3364
Fax: (41) (22) 917-0059
E-mail: office.geneva@unido.org

UNIDO Office in New York
1 United Nations Plaza, Room DC1-1110
New York, NY 10017, United States
Telephone: (1) (212) 963-6890
Fax: (1) (212) 963-7904
E-mail: office.newyork@unido.org

Chapter XVII

World Trade Organization (WTO)

During 2003, the World Trade Organization (WTO), the legal and institutional foundation of the multilateral trading system, continued to oversee the rules of international trade, settle trade disputes and organize trade negotiations.

WTO's Fifth Ministerial Conference (Cancun, Mexico, 10-14 September), WTO's highest authority, failed to make any significant progress towards the implementation of the Doha Development Agenda, adopted by the Fourth (2001) Ministerial Conference [YUN 2001, p. 1432]. The Conference suggested that work continue to resolve outstanding issues. A General Council meeting was held in December, though no major breakthroughs were reported.

As at 31 December 2003, WTO membership (members and observers) totalled 146.

General activities

The three working groups set up by the First (1996) Ministerial Conference [YUN 1996, p. 1441] met during 2003. Pursuant to directions and guidelines provided by the Doha Development Agenda, the Working Group on the Relationship between Trade and Investment focused on the clarification of core issues related to a possible multilateral framework on investment; investors' and home governments' obligations; and on the question of whether or not it was desirable to launch negotiations on investment in WTO. The Working Group on the Interaction between Trade and Competition Policy focused on the clarification of core principles of transparency, non-discrimination, procedural fairness and provisions on hard-core cartels; modalities for voluntary cooperation; and support for progressive reinforcement of competition institutions in developing countries through capacity-building. The Working Group on Transparency in Government Procurement discussed, among other issues, the definition and scope of government procurement; publication of information on national legislation and procedures; information on procurement opportunities, tendering and qualification procedures; transparency of decisions on qualification and contract awards; domestic review procedures; information to other Governments; WTO dispute settlement procedures; and technical cooperation.

WTO continued to settle trade disputes between members covered by the Understanding on Rules and Procedures Governing the Settlement of Disputes; provided technical assistance and capacity-building to developing countries; and cooperated with the International Monetary Fund and the World Bank in promoting greater coherence in international economic policymaking.

During the year, the Trade Policy Review Body carried out reviews of Bulgaria, Burundi, Canada, Chile, El Salvador, Guyana, Haiti, Honduras, Indonesia, Maldives, Morocco, New Zealand, the Niger, Senegal, the Southern African Customs Union (Bostwana, Lesotho, Namibia, South Africa, Swaziland), Thailand and Turkey.

Trade in goods

During 2003, the Council for Trade in Goods continued to monitor the implementation of multilateral trade agreements and examined and approved requests for waivers and waiver extensions from members in connection with the transposition of their schedules into the Harmonized System. It carried out a transitional review under the Protocol of accession of China, and discussed a review of the operation of the trade-related investment measures agreeement and the work programme on electronic commerce as set out in the Doha Ministerial Declaration.

The Committee on Agriculture continued to review the implementation of WTO commitments resulting from the Uruguay Round agricultural reform programme, or from accession to WTO.

The Committee on Sanitary and Phytosanitary Measures continued to monitor the implementation of the Agreement on the Application of Sanitary and Phytosanitary Measures, which set out the rights and obligations of members to ensure food safety, protect humans from plant- or animal-spread diseases, or protect plants and animals from pests and diseases.

The Committee on Safeguards continued to review national safeguard legislation and/or regulations.

Trade in services

In 2003, the Council for Trade in Services held five formal meetings, which addressed proposals for a technical review of the General Agreement on Trade in Services (GATS) provisions; reviewed air transport under the Annex on Air Transport; conducted a transitional review under the Protocol of accession of China; and discussed Albania's request for a waiver from specific commitments under GATS.

Intellectual property

The TRIPS Agreement provided for minimum international standards of protection in copyright, trademarks, geographic indications, industrial designs, patents, layout designs of integrated circuits and undisclosed information. In 2003, the Council for TRIPS continued to review national implementing legislation of developing countries and economies in transition.

Regional trade agreements

As at December 2003, WTO received notifications of 18 additional regional trade agreements, bringing the total number of notified agreements in force to 193.

Trade and development

The Committee on Trade and Development continued to consider special and differential treatment of developing countries to facilitate their participation in world trade, technical cooperation and training, and market access for least developed countries. It also considered implementation issues and identified and debated the developmental aspects of negotiations.

Plurilateral agreements

The Committee on Government Procurement continued negotiations on expanding the coverage of the Agreement on Government Procurement, its simplification and improvement, including adaptation to advances in information technology and the elimination of discriminatory measures and practices that distorted open procurement.

The Agreement on Trade in Civil Aircraft eliminated customs duties and other charges on imports of civil aircraft products and repairs, bound them at zero level and required the adoption or adaptation of end-use customs administration. Although part of the 1994 WTO Agreement, it remained outside the organization's framework. The Committee on Trade in Civil Aircraft continued to eliminate customs duties and other charges on imports of civil aircraft products and repairs.

International Trade Centre

The International Trade Centre, operated jointly by WTO and the United Nations Conference on Trade and Development (see p. 974), continued to play a crucial role in trade-related technical cooperation and trade-related capacity-building. In 2003, it focused its technical assistance for developing and transition economies on helping businesses understand WTO rules, strengthening enterprises, competitiveness and developing new trade promotion strategies.

Budget

The WTO budget for 2003 totalled 155 million Swiss francs.

Secretariat

As at 31 December 2003, WTO staff numbered 601.

NOTE: For further information on WTO activities, see the organization's *Annual Report 2003*.

HEADQUARTERS

World Trade Organization
Centre William Rappard
154, rue de Lausanne
CH-1211 Geneva, 21, Switzerland
Telephone: (41) (22) 739-5111
Fax: (41) (22) 731-4206
Internet: www.wto.org
E-mail: enquiries@wto.org

Appendices

Appendix I
Roster of the United Nations
There were 191 Member States as at 31 December 2003.

MEMBER	DATE OF ADMISSION	MEMBER	DATE OF ADMISSION	MEMBER	DATE OF ADMISSION
Afghanistan	19 Nov. 1946	Egypt[2]	24 Oct. 1945	Malta	1 Dec. 1964
Albania	14 Dec. 1955	El Salvador	24 Oct. 1945	Marshall Islands	17 Sep. 1991
Algeria	8 Oct. 1962	Equatorial Guinea	12 Nov. 1968	Mauritania	27 Oct. 1961
Andorra	28 July 1993	Eritrea	28 May 1993	Mauritius	24 Apr. 1968
Angola	1 Dec. 1976	Estonia	17 Sep. 1991	Mexico	7 Nov. 1945
Antigua and Barbuda	11 Nov. 1981	Ethiopia	13 Nov. 1945	Micronesia (Federated States of)	17 Sep. 1991
Argentina	24 Oct. 1945	Fiji	13 Oct. 1970	Monaco	28 May 1993
Armenia	2 Mar. 1992	Finland	14 Dec. 1955	Mongolia	27 Oct. 1961
Australia	1 Nov. 1945	France	24 Oct. 1945	Morocco	12 Nov. 1956
Austria	14 Dec. 1955	Gabon	20 Sep. 1960	Mozambique	16 Sep. 1975
Azerbaijan	2 Mar. 1992	Gambia	21 Sep. 1965	Myanmar	19 Apr. 1948
Bahamas	18 Sep. 1973	Georgia	31 July 1992	Namibia	23 Apr. 1990
Bahrain	21 Sep. 1971	Germany[3]	18 Sep. 1973	Nauru	14 Sep. 1999
Bangladesh	17 Sep. 1974	Ghana	8 Mar. 1957	Nepal	14 Dec. 1955
Barbados	9 Dec. 1966	Greece	25 Oct. 1945	Netherlands	10 Dec. 1945
Belarus	24 Oct. 1945	Grenada	17 Sep. 1974	New Zealand	24 Oct. 1945
Belgium	27 Dec. 1945	Guatemala	21 Nov. 1945	Nicaragua	24 Oct. 1945
Belize	25 Sep. 1981	Guinea	12 Dec. 1958	Niger	20 Sep. 1960
Benin	20 Sep. 1960	Guinea-Bissau	17 Sep. 1974	Nigeria	7 Oct. 1960
Bhutan	21 Sep. 1971	Guyana	20 Sep. 1966	Norway	27 Nov. 1945
Bolivia	14 Nov. 1945	Haiti	24 Oct. 1945	Oman	7 Oct. 1971
Bosnia and Herzegovina	22 May 1992	Honduras	17 Dec. 1945	Pakistan	30 Sep. 1947
Botswana	17 Oct. 1966	Hungary	14 Dec. 1955	Palau	15 Dec. 1994
Brazil	24 Oct. 1945	Iceland	19 Nov. 1946	Panama	13 Nov. 1945
Brunei Darussalam	21 Sep. 1984	India	30 Oct. 1945	Papua New Guinea	10 Oct. 1975
Bulgaria	14 Dec. 1955	Indonesia[4]	28 Sep. 1950	Paraguay	24 Oct. 1945
Burkina Faso	20 Sep. 1960	Iran (Islamic Republic of)	24 Oct. 1945	Peru	31 Oct. 1945
Burundi	18 Sep. 1962	Iraq	21 Dec. 1945	Philippines	24 Oct. 1945
Cambodia	14 Dec. 1955	Ireland	14 Dec. 1955	Poland	24 Oct. 1945
Cameroon	20 Sep. 1960	Israel	11 May 1949	Portugal	14 Dec. 1955
Canada	9 Nov. 1945	Italy	14 Dec. 1955	Qatar	21 Sep. 1971
Cape Verde	16 Sep. 1975	Jamaica	18 Sep. 1962	Republic of Korea	17 Sep. 1991
Central African Republic	20 Sep. 1960	Japan	18 Dec. 1956	Republic of Moldova	2 Mar. 1992
Chad	20 Sep. 1960	Jordan	14 Dec. 1955	Romania	14 Dec. 1955
Chile	24 Oct. 1945	Kazakhstan	2 Mar. 1992	Russian Federation[6]	24 Oct. 1945
China	24 Oct. 1945	Kenya	16 Dec. 1963	Rwanda	18 Sep. 1962
Colombia	5 Nov. 1945	Kiribati	14 Sep. 1999	Saint Kitts and Nevis	23 Sep. 1983
Comoros	12 Nov. 1975	Kuwait	14 May 1963	Saint Lucia	18 Sep. 1979
Congo	20 Sep. 1960	Kyrgyzstan	2 Mar. 1992	Saint Vincent and the Grenadines	16 Sep. 1980
Costa Rica	2 Nov. 1945	Lao People's Democratic Republic	14 Dec. 1955	Samoa	15 Dec. 1976
Côte d'Ivoire	20 Sep. 1960	Latvia	17 Sep. 1991	San Marino	2 Mar. 1992
Croatia	22 May 1992	Lebanon	24 Oct. 1945	Sao Tome and Principe	16 Sep. 1975
Cuba	24 Oct. 1945	Lesotho	17 Oct. 1966	Saudi Arabia	24 Oct. 1945
Cyprus	20 Sep. 1960	Liberia	2 Nov. 1945	Senegal	28 Sep. 1960
Czech Republic[1]	19 Jan. 1993	Libyan Arab Jamahiriya	14 Dec. 1955	Serbia and Montenegro[7]	1 Nov. 2000
Democratic People's Republic of Korea	17 Sep. 1991	Liechtenstein	18 Sep. 1990	Seychelles	21 Sep. 1976
Democratic Republic of the Congo	20 Sep. 1960	Lithuania	17 Sep. 1991	Sierra Leone	27 Sep. 1961
Denmark	24 Oct. 1945	Luxembourg	24 Oct. 1945	Singapore[5]	21 Sep. 1965
Djibouti	20 Sep. 1977	Madagascar	20 Sep. 1960	Slovakia[1]	19 Jan. 1993
Dominica	18 Dec. 1978	Malawi	1 Dec. 1964	Slovenia	22 May 1992
Dominican Republic	24 Oct. 1945	Malaysia[5]	17 Sep. 1957	Solomon Islands	19 Sep. 1978
Ecuador	21 Dec. 1945	Maldives	21 Sep. 1965	Somalia	20 Sep. 1960
		Mali	28 Sep. 1960		

MEMBER	DATE OF ADMISSION	MEMBER	DATE OF ADMISSION	MEMBER	DATE OF ADMISSION
South Africa	7 Nov. 1945	Tonga	14 Sep. 1999	Uruguay	18 Dec. 1945
Spain	14 Dec. 1955	Trinidad and Tobago	18 Sep. 1962	Uzbekistan	2 Mar. 1992
Sri Lanka	14 Dec. 1955	Tunisia	12 Nov. 1956	Vanuatu	15 Sep. 1981
Sudan	12 Nov. 1956	Turkey	24 Oct. 1945	Venezuela	15 Nov. 1945
Suriname	4 Dec. 1975	Turkmenistan	2 Mar. 1992	Viet Nam	20 Sep. 1977
Swaziland	24 Sep. 1968	Tuvalu	5 Sep. 2000	Yemen[9]	30 Sep. 1947
Sweden	19 Nov. 1946	Uganda	25 Oct. 1962	Zambia	1 Dec. 1964
Switzerland	10 Sep. 2002	Ukraine	24 Oct. 1945	Zimbabwe	25 Aug. 1980
Syrian Arab Republic[2]	24 Oct. 1945	United Arab Emirates	9 Dec. 1971		
Tajikistan	2 Mar. 1992	United Kingdom of Great Britain and Northern Ireland	24 Oct. 1945		
Thailand	16 Dec. 1946				
The former Yugoslav Republic of Macedonia	8 Apr. 1993	United Republic of Tanzania[8]	14 Dec. 1961		
Timor-Leste	27 Sep. 2002				
Togo	20 Sep. 1960	United States of America	24 Oct. 1945		

[1]Czechoslovakia, which was an original Member of the United Nations from 24 October 1945, split up on 1 January 1993 and was succeeded by the Czech Republic and Slovakia.

[2]Egypt and Syria, both of which became Members of the United Nations on 24 October 1945, joined together—following a plebiscite held in those countries on 21 February 1958—to form the United Arab Republic. On 13 October 1961, Syria, having resumed its status as an independent State, also resumed its separate membership in the United Nations; it changed its name to the Syrian Arab Republic on 14 September 1971. The United Arab Republic continued as a Member of the United Nations and reverted to the name of Egypt on 2 September 1971.

[3]Through accession of the German Democratic Republic to the Federal Republic of Germany on 3 October 1990, the two German States (both of which became United Nations Members on 18 September 1973) united to form one sovereign State. As from that date, the Federal Republic of Germany has acted in the United Nations under the designation Germany.

[4]On 20 January 1965, Indonesia informed the Secretary-General that it had decided to withdraw from the United Nations. By a telegram of 19 September 1966, it notified the Secretary-General of its decision to resume participation in the activities of the United Nations. On 28 September 1966, the General Assembly took note of that decision and the President invited the representatives of Indonesia to take their seats in the Assembly.

[5]On 16 September 1963, Sabah (North Borneo), Sarawak and Singapore joined with the Federation of Malaya (which became a United Nations Member on 17 September 1957) to form Malaysia. On 9 August 1965, Singapore became an independent State and on 21 September 1965 it became a Member of the United Nations.

[6]The Union of Soviet Socialist Republics was an original Member of the United Nations from 24 October 1945. On 24 December 1991, the President of the Russian Federation informed the Secretary-General that the membership of the USSR in all United Nations organs was being continued by the Russian Federation.

[7]Formerly the Federal Republic of Yugoslavia; name changed on 4 February 2003.

[8]Tanganyika was admitted to the United Nations on 14 December 1961, and Zanzibar, on 16 December 1963. Following ratification, on 26 April 1964, of the Articles of Union between Tanganyika and Zanzibar, the two States became represented as a single Member: the United Republic of Tanganyika and Zanzibar; it changed its name to the United Republic of Tanzania on 1 November 1964.

[9]Yemen was admitted to the United Nations on 30 September 1947 and Democratic Yemen on 14 December 1967. On 22 May 1990, the two countries merged and have since been represented as one Member.

Appendix II

Charter of the United Nations and Statute of the International Court of Justice

Charter of the United Nations

NOTE: The Charter of the United Nations was signed on 26 June 1945, in San Francisco, at the conclusion of the United Nations Conference on International Organization, and came into force on 24 October 1945. The Statute of the International Court of Justice is an integral part of the Charter.

Amendments to Articles 23, 27 and 61 of the Charter were adopted by the General Assembly on 17 December 1963 and came into force on 31 August 1965. A further amendment to Article 61 was adopted by the General Assembly on 20 December 1971 and came into force on 24 September 1973. An amendment to Article 109, adopted by the General Assembly on 20 December 1965, came into force on 12 June 1968.

The amendment to Article 23 enlarges the membership of the Security Council from 11 to 15. The amended Article 27 provides that decisions of the Security Council on procedural matters shall be made by an affirmative vote of nine members (formerly seven) and on all other matters by an affirmative vote of nine members (formerly seven), including the concurring votes of the five permanent members of the Security Council.

The amendment to Article 61, which entered into force on 31 August 1965, enlarged the membership of the Economic and Social Council from 18 to 27. The subsequent amendment to that Article, which entered into force on 24 September 1973, further increased the membership of the Council from 27 to 54.

The amendment to Article 109, which relates to the first paragraph of that Article, provides that a General Conference of Member States for the purpose of reviewing the Charter may be held at a date and place to be fixed by a two-thirds vote of the members of the General Assembly and by a vote of any nine members (formerly seven) of the Security Council. Paragraph 3 of Article 109, which deals with the consideration of a possible review conference during the tenth regular session of the General Assembly, has been retained in its original form in its reference to a "vote of any seven members of the Security Council", the paragraph having been acted upon in 1955 by the General Assembly, at its tenth regular session, and by the Security Council.

WE THE PEOPLES
OF THE UNITED NATIONS
DETERMINED

to save succeeding generations from the scourge of war, which twice in our lifetime has brought untold sorrow to mankind, and
to reaffirm faith in fundamental human rights, in the dignity and worth of the human person, in the equal rights of men and women and of nations large and small, and
to establish conditions under which justice and respect for the obligations arising from treaties and other sources of international law can be maintained, and
to promote social progress and better standards of life in larger freedom,

AND FOR THESE ENDS

to practice tolerance and live together in peace with one another as good neighbours, and
to unite our strength to maintain international peace and security, and
to ensure, by the acceptance of principles and the institution of methods, that armed force shall not be used, save in the common interest, and
to employ international machinery for the promotion of the economic and social advancement of all peoples,

HAVE RESOLVED TO
COMBINE OUR EFFORTS TO
ACCOMPLISH THESE AIMS

Accordingly, our respective Governments, through representatives assembled in the city of San Francisco, who have exhibited their full powers found to be in good and due form, have agreed to the present Charter of the United Nations and do hereby establish an international organization to be known as the United Nations.

Chapter I
PURPOSES AND PRINCIPLES

Article 1

The Purposes of the United Nations are:

1. To maintain international peace and security, and to that end: to take effective collective measures for the prevention and removal of threats to the peace, and for the suppression of acts of aggression or other breaches of the peace, and to bring about by peaceful means, and in conformity with the principles of justice and international law, adjustment or settlement of international disputes or situations which might lead to a breach of the peace;

2. To develop friendly relations among nations based on respect for the principle of equal rights and self-determination of peoples, and to take other appropriate measures to strengthen universal peace;

3. To achieve international co-operation in solving international problems of an economic, social, cultural or humanitarian character, and in promoting and encouraging respect for human rights and for fundamental freedoms for all without distinction as to race, sex, language or religion; and

4. To be a centre for harmonizing the actions of nations in the attainment of these common ends.

Article 2

The Organization and its Members, in pursuit of the Purposes stated in Article 1, shall act in accordance with the following Principles:

1. The Organization is based on the principle of the sovereign equality of all its Members.

2. All Members, in order to ensure to all of them the rights and benefits resulting from membership, shall fulfil in good faith the obligations assumed by them in accordance with the present Charter.

3. All Members shall settle their international disputes by peaceful means in such a manner that international peace and security, and justice, are not endangered.

4. All Members shall refrain in their international relations from the threat or use of force against the territorial integrity or political independence of any state, or in any other manner inconsistent with the Purposes of the United Nations.

5. All Members shall give the United Nations every assistance in any action it takes in accordance with the present Charter, and shall refrain from giving assistance to any state against which the United Nations is taking preventive or enforcement action.

6. The Organization shall ensure that states which are not Members of the United Nations act in accordance with these Principles so far as may be necessary for the maintenance of international peace and security.

7. Nothing contained in the present Charter shall authorize the United Nations to intervene in matters which are essentially within the domestic jurisdiction of any state or shall require the Members to submit such matters to settlement under the present Charter; but this principle shall not prejudice the application of enforcement measures under Chapter VII.

Chapter II
MEMBERSHIP

Article 3

The original Members of the United Nations shall be the states which, having participated in the United Nations Conference on International Organization at San Francisco or having previously signed the Declaration by United Nations of 1 January 1942, sign the present Charter and ratify it in accordance with Article 110.

Article 4

1. Membership in the United Nations is open to all other peace-loving states which accept the obligations contained in the present Charter and, in the judgment of the Organization, are able and willing to carry out these obligations.

2. The admission of any such state to membership in the United Nations will be effected by a decision of the General Assembly upon the recommendation of the Security Council.

Article 5

A Member of the United Nations against which preventive or enforcement action has been taken by the Security Council may be suspended from the exercise of the rights and privileges of membership by the General Assembly upon the recommendation of the Security Council. The exercise of these rights and privileges may be restored by the Security Council.

Article 6

A Member of the United Nations which has persistently violated the Principles contained in the present Charter may be expelled from the Organization by the General Assembly upon the recommendation of the Security Council.

Chapter III
ORGANS

Article 7

1. There are established as the principal organs of the United Nations: a General Assembly, a Security Council, an Economic and Social Council, a Trusteeship Council, an International Court of Justice, and a Secretariat.

2. Such subsidiary organs as may be found necessary may be established in accordance with the present Charter.

Article 8

The United Nations shall place no restrictions on the eligibility of men and women to participate in any capacity and under conditions of equality in its principal and subsidiary organs.

Chapter IV
THE GENERAL ASSEMBLY

Composition

Article 9

1. The General Assembly shall consist of all the Members of the United Nations.

2. Each Member shall have not more than five representatives in the General Assembly.

Functions and Powers

Article 10

The General Assembly may discuss any questions or any matters within the scope of the present Charter or relating to the powers and functions of any organs provided for in the present Charter, and, except as provided in Article 12, may make recommendations to the Members of the United Nations or to the Security Council or both on any such questions or matters.

Article 11

1. The General Assembly may consider the general principles of co-operation in the maintenance of international peace and security, including the principles governing disarmament and the regulation of armaments, and may make recommendations with regard to such principles to the Members or to the Security Council or to both.

2. The General Assembly may discuss any questions relating to the maintenance of international peace and security brought before it by any Member of the United Nations, or by the Security Council, or by a state which is not a Member of the United Nations in accordance with Article 35, paragraph 2, and, except as provided in Article 12, may make recommendations with regard to any such questions to the state or states concerned or to the Security Council or to both. Any such question on which action is necessary shall be referred to the Security Council by the General Assembly either before or after discussion.

3. The General Assembly may call the attention of the Security Council to situations which are likely to endanger international peace and security.

4. The powers of the General Assembly set forth in this Article shall not limit the general scope of Article 10.

Article 12

1. While the Security Council is exercising in respect of any dispute or situation the functions assigned to it in the present Charter, the General Assembly shall not make any recommendation with regard to that dispute or situation unless the Security Council so requests.

2. The Secretary-General, with the consent of the Security Council, shall notify the General Assembly at each session of any matters relative to the maintenance of international peace and security which are being dealt with by the Security Council and shall similarly notify the General Assembly, or the Members of the United Nations if the General Assembly is not in session, immediately the Security Council ceases to deal with such matters.

Article 13

1. The General Assembly shall initiate studies and make recommendations for the purpose of:
   a. promoting international co-operation in the political field and encouraging the progressive development of international law and its codification;
   b. promoting international co-operation in the economic, social, cultural, educational and health fields, and assisting in the realization of human rights and fundamental freedoms for all without distinction as to race, sex, language or religion.

2. The further responsibilities, functions and powers of the General Assembly with respect to matters mentioned in paragraph 1 (b) above are set forth in Chapters IX and X.

Article 14

Subject to the provisions of Article 12, the General Assembly may recommend measures for the peaceful adjustment of any situation, regardless of origin, which it deems likely to impair the general welfare or friendly relations among nations, including situations resulting from a violation of the provisions of the present Charter setting forth the Purposes and Principles of the United Nations.

Article 15

1. The General Assembly shall receive and consider annual and special reports from the Security Council; these reports shall include an account of the measures that the Security Council has decided upon or taken to maintain international peace and security.
2. The General Assembly shall receive and consider reports from the other organs of the United Nations.

Article 16

The General Assembly shall perform such functions with respect to the international trusteeship system as are assigned to it under Chapters XII and XIII, including the approval of the trusteeship agreements for areas not designated as strategic.

Article 17

1. The General Assembly shall consider and approve the budget of the Organization.
2. The expenses of the Organization shall be borne by the Members as apportioned by the General Assembly.
3. The General Assembly shall consider and approve any financial and budgetary arrangements with specialized agencies referred to in Article 57 and shall examine the administrative budgets of such specialized agencies with a view to making recommendations to the agencies concerned.

Voting

Article 18

1. Each member of the General Assembly shall have one vote.
2. Decisions of the General Assembly on important questions shall be made by a two-thirds majority of the members present and voting. These questions shall include: recommendations with respect to the maintenance of international peace and security, the election of the non-permanent members of the Security Council, the election of the members of the Economic and Social Council, the election of members of the Trusteeship Council in accordance with paragraph 1 (c) of Article 86, the admission of new Members to the United Nations, the suspension of the rights and privileges of membership, the expulsion of Members, questions relating to the operation of the trusteeship system, and budgetary questions.
3. Decisions on other questions, including the determination of additional categories of questions to be decided by a two-thirds majority, shall be made by a majority of the members present and voting.

Article 19

A Member of the United Nations which is in arrears in the payment of its financial contributions to the Organization shall have no vote in the General Assembly if the amount of its arrears equals or exceeds the amount of the contributions due from it for the preceding two full years. The General Assembly may, nevertheless, permit such a Member to vote if it is satisfied that the failure to pay is due to conditions beyond the control of the Member.

Procedure

Article 20

The General Assembly shall meet in regular annual sessions and in such special sessions as occasion may require. Special sessions shall be convoked by the Secretary-General at the request of the Security Council or of a majority of the Members of the United Nations.

Article 21

The General Assembly shall adopt its own rules of procedure. It shall elect its President for each session.

Article 22

The General Assembly may establish such subsidiary organs as it deems necessary for the performance of its functions.

Chapter V
THE SECURITY COUNCIL

Composition

Article 23[1]

1. The Security Council shall consist of fifteen Members of the United Nations. The Republic of China, France, the Union of Soviet Socialist Republics, the United Kingdom of Great Britain and Northern Ireland and the United States of America shall be permanent members of the Security Council. The General Assembly shall elect ten other Members of the United Nations to be non-permanent members of the Security Council, due regard being specially paid, in the first instance to the contribution of Members of the United Nations to the maintenance of international peace and security and to the other purposes of the Organization, and also to equitable geographical distribution.
2. The non-permanent members of the Security Council shall be elected for a term of two years. In the first election of the non-permanent members after the increase of the membership of the Security Council from eleven to fifteen, two of the four additional members shall be chosen for a term of one year. A retiring member shall not be eligible for immediate re-election.
3. Each member of the Security Council shall have one representative.

Functions and Powers

Article 24

1. In order to ensure prompt and effective action by the United Nations, its Members confer on the Security Council primary responsibility for the maintenance of international peace and security, and agree that in carrying out its duties under this responsibility the Security Council acts on their behalf.
2. In discharging these duties the Security Council shall act in accordance with the Purposes and Principles of the United Nations. The specific powers granted to the Security Council for the discharge of these duties are laid down in Chapters VI, VII, VIII and XII.
3. The Security Council shall submit annual and, when necessary, special reports to the General Assembly for its consideration.

Article 25

The Members of the United Nations agree to accept and carry out the decisions of the Security Council in accordance with the present Charter.

Article 26

In order to promote the establishment and maintenance of international peace and security with the least diversion for armaments of the world's human and economic resources, the Security Council shall be responsible for formulating, with the assistance of the Military Staff Committee referred to in Article

47, plans to be submitted to the Members of the United Nations for the establishment of a system for the regulation of armaments.

Voting

Article 27[2]

1. Each member of the Security Council shall have one vote.
2. Decisions of the Security Council on procedural matters shall be made by an affirmative vote of nine members.
3. Decisions of the Security Council on all other matters shall be made by an affirmative vote of nine members including the concurring votes of the permanent members; provided that, in decisions under Chapter VI, and under paragraph 3 of Article 52, a party to a dispute shall abstain from voting.

Procedure

Article 28

1. The Security Council shall be so organized as to be able to function continuously. Each member of the Security Council shall for this purpose be represented at all times at the seat of the Organization.
2. The Security Council shall hold periodic meetings at which each of its members may, if it so desires, be represented by a member of the government or by some other specially designated representative.
3. The Security Council may hold meetings at such places other than the seat of the Organization as in its judgment will best facilitate its work.

Article 29

The Security Council may establish such subsidiary organs as it deems necessary for the performance of its functions.

Article 30

The Security Council shall adopt its own rules of procedure, including the method of selecting its President.

Article 31

Any Member of the United Nations which is not a member of the Security Council may participate, without vote, in the discussion of any question brought before the Security Council whenever the latter considers that the interests of that Member are specially affected.

Article 32

Any Member of the United Nations which is not a member of the Security Council or any state which is not a Member of the United Nations, if it is a party to a dispute under consideration by the Security Council, shall be invited to participate, without vote, in the discussion relating to the dispute. The Security Council shall lay down such conditions as it deems just for the participation of a state which is not a Member of the United Nations.

Chapter VI
PACIFIC SETTLEMENT OF DISPUTES

Article 33

1. The parties to any dispute, the continuance of which is likely to endanger the maintenance of international peace and security, shall, first of all, seek a solution by negotiation, enquiry, mediation, conciliation, arbitration, judicial settlement, resort to regional agencies or arrangements, or other peaceful means of their own choice.
2. The Security Council shall, when it deems necessary, call upon the parties to settle their dispute by such means.

Article 34

The Security Council may investigate any dispute, or any situation which might lead to international friction or give rise to a dispute, in order to determine whether the continuance of the dispute or situation is likely to endanger the maintenance of international peace and security.

Article 35

1. Any Member of the United Nations may bring any dispute, or any situation of the nature referred to in Article 34, to the attention of the Security Council or of the General Assembly.
2. A state which is not a Member of the United Nations may bring to the attention of the Security Council or of the General Assembly any dispute to which it is a party if it accepts in advance, for the purposes of the dispute, the obligations of pacific settlement provided in the present Charter.
3. The proceedings of the General Assembly in respect of matters brought to its attention under this Article will be subject to the provisions of Articles 11 and 12.

Article 36

1. The Security Council may, at any stage of a dispute of the nature referred to in Article 33 or of a situation of like nature, recommend appropriate procedures or methods of adjustment.
2. The Security Council should take into consideration any procedures for the settlement of the dispute which have already been adopted by the parties.
3. In making recommendations under this Article the Security Council should also take into consideration that legal disputes should as a general rule be referred by the parties to the International Court of Justice in accordance with the provisions of the Statute of the Court.

Article 37

1. Should the parties to a dispute of the nature referred to in Article 33 fail to settle it by the means indicated in that Article, they shall refer it to the Security Council.
2. If the Security Council deems that the continuance of the dispute is in fact likely to endanger the maintenance of international peace and security, it shall decide whether to take action under Article 36 or to recommend such terms of settlement as it may consider appropriate.

Article 38

Without prejudice to the provisions of Articles 33 to 37, the Security Council may, if all the parties to any dispute so request, make recommendations to the parties with a view to a pacific settlement of the dispute.

Chapter VII
ACTION WITH RESPECT TO THREATS TO THE PEACE, BREACHES OF THE PEACE, AND ACTS OF AGGRESSION

Article 39

The Security Council shall determine the existence of any threat to the peace, breach of the peace, or act of aggression and shall make recommendations, or decide what measures shall be taken in accordance with Articles 41 and 42, to maintain or restore international peace and security.

Article 40

In order to prevent an aggravation of the situation, the Security Council may, before making the recommendations or deciding upon the measures provided for in Article 39, call upon the parties concerned to comply with such provisional measures as it deems necessary or desirable. Such provisional measures shall be without prejudice to the rights, claims or position of the parties concerned. The Security Council shall duly take account of failure to comply with such provisional measures.

Article 41

The Security Council may decide what measures not involving the use of armed force are to be employed to give effect to its decisions, and it may call upon the Members of the United Nations to apply such measures. These may include complete or partial interruption of economic relations and of rail, sea, air, postal, telegraphic, radio and other means of communication, and the severance of diplomatic relations.

Article 42

Should the Security Council consider that measures provided for in Article 41 would be inadequate or have proved to be inadequate, it may take such action by air, sea or land forces as may be necessary to maintain or restore international peace and security. Such action may include demonstrations, blockade, and other operations by air, sea, or land forces of Members of the United Nations.

Article 43

1. All Members of the United Nations, in order to contribute to the maintenance of international peace and security, undertake to make available to the Security Council, on its call and in accordance with a special agreement or agreements, armed forces, assistance and facilities, including rights of passage, necessary for the purpose of maintaining international peace and security.
2. Such agreement or agreements shall govern the numbers and types of forces, their degree of readiness and general location, and the nature of the facilities and assistance to be provided.
3. The agreement or agreements shall be negotiated as soon as possible on the initiative of the Security Council. They shall be concluded between the Security Council and Members or between the Security Council and groups of Members and shall be subject to ratification by the signatory states in accordance with their respective constitutional processes.

Article 44

When the Security Council has decided to use force it shall, before calling upon a Member not represented on it to provide armed forces in fulfilment of the obligations assumed under Article 43, invite that Member, if the Member so desires, to participate in the decisions of the Security Council concerning the employment of contingents of that Member's armed forces.

Article 45

In order to enable the United Nations to take urgent military measures, Members shall hold immediately available national air-force contingents for combined international enforcement action. The strength and degree of readiness of these contingents and plans for their combined action shall be determined, within the limits laid down in the special agreement or agreements referred to in Article 43, by the Security Council with the assistance of the Military Staff Committee.

Article 46

Plans for the application of armed force shall be made by the Security Council with the assistance of the Military Staff Committee.

Article 47

1. There shall be established a Military Staff Committee to advise and assist the Security Council on all questions relating to the Security Council's military requirements for the maintenance of international peace and security, the employment and command of forces placed at its disposal, the regulation of armaments, and possible disarmament.
2. The Military Staff Committee shall consist of the Chiefs of Staff of the permanent members of the Security Council or their representatives. Any Member of the United Nations not permanently represented on the Committee shall be invited by the Committee to be associated with it when the efficient discharge of the Committee's responsibilities requires the participation of that Member in its work.
3. The Military Staff Committee shall be responsible under the Security Council for the strategic direction of any armed forces placed at the disposal of the Security Council. Questions relating to the command of such forces shall be worked out subsequently.
4. The Military Staff Committee, with the authorization of the Security Council and after consultation with appropriate regional agencies, may establish regional sub-committees.

Article 48

1. The action required to carry out the decisions of the Security Council for the maintenance of international peace and security shall be taken by all the Members of the United Nations or by some of them, as the Security Council may determine.
2. Such decisions shall be carried out by the Members of the United Nations directly and through their action in the appropriate international agencies of which they are members.

Article 49

The Members of the United Nations shall join in affording mutual assistance in carrying out the measures decided upon by the Security Council.

Article 50

If preventive or enforcement measures against any state are taken by the Security Council, any other state, whether a Member of the United Nations or not, which finds itself confronted with special economic problems arising from the carrying out of those measures shall have the right to consult the Security Council with regard to a solution of those problems.

Article 51

Nothing in the present Charter shall impair the inherent right of individual or collective self-defence if an armed attack occurs against a Member of the United Nations, until the Security Council has taken measures necessary to maintain international peace and security. Measures taken by Members in the exercise of this right of self-defence shall be immediately reported to the Security Council and shall not in any way affect the authority and responsibility of the Security Council under the present Charter to take at any time such action as it deems necessary in order to maintain or restore international peace and security.

Chapter VIII
REGIONAL ARRANGEMENTS

Article 52

1. Nothing in the present Charter precludes the existence of regional arrangements or agencies for dealing with such matters relating to the maintenance of international peace and security as are appropriate for regional action, provided that such arrangements or agencies and their activities are consistent with the Purposes and Principles of the United Nations.
2. The Members of the United Nations entering into such arrangements or constituting such agencies shall make every effort to achieve pacific settlement of local disputes through such regional arrangements or by such regional agencies before referring them to the Security Council.
3. The Security Council shall encourage the development of pacific settlement of local disputes through such regional arrangements or by such regional agencies either on the initiative of the states concerned or by reference from the Security Council.
4. This Article in no way impairs the application of Articles 34 and 35.

Article 53

1. The Security Council shall, where appropriate, utilize such regional arrangements or agencies for enforcement action under its authority. But no enforcement action shall be taken under regional arrangements or by regional agencies

without the authorization of the Security Council, with the exception of measures against any enemy state, as defined in paragraph 2 of this Article, provided for pursuant to Article 107 or in regional arrangements directed against renewal of aggressive policy on the part of any such state, until such time as the Organization may, on request of the Governments concerned, be charged with the responsibility for preventing further aggression by such a state.

2. The term enemy state as used in paragraph 1 of this Article applies to any state which during the Second World War has been an enemy of any signatory of the present Charter.

Article 54

The Security Council shall at all times be kept fully informed of activities undertaken or in contemplation under regional arrangements or by regional agencies for the maintenance of international peace and security.

Chapter IX
INTERNATIONAL ECONOMIC AND SOCIAL CO-OPERATION

Article 55

With a view to the creation of conditions of stability and well-being which are necessary for peaceful and friendly relations among nations based on respect for the principle of equal rights and self-determination of peoples, the United Nations shall promote:
a. higher standards of living, full employment, and conditions of economic and social progress and development;
b. solutions of international economic, social, health, and related problems; and international cultural and educational co-operation; and
c. universal respect for, and observance of, human rights and fundamental freedoms for all without distinction as to race, sex, language, or religion.

Article 56

All Members pledge themselves to take joint and separate action in co-operation with the Organization for the achievement of the purposes set forth in Article 55.

Article 57

1. The various specialized agencies, established by intergovernmental agreement and having wide international responsibilities, as defined in their basic instruments, in economic, social, cultural, educational, health, and related fields, shall be brought into relationship with the United Nations in accordance with the provisions of Article 63.

2. Such agencies thus brought into relationship with the United Nations are hereinafter referred to as specialized agencies.

Article 58

The Organization shall make recommendations for the co-ordination of the policies and activities of the specialized agencies.

Article 59

The Organization shall, where appropriate, initiate negotiations among the states concerned for the creation of any new specialized agencies required for the accomplishment of the purposes set forth in Article 55.

Article 60

Responsibility for the discharge of the functions of the Organization set forth in this Chapter shall be vested in the General Assembly and, under the authority of the General Assembly, in the Economic and Social Council, which shall have for this purpose the powers set forth in Chapter X.

Chapter X
THE ECONOMIC AND SOCIAL COUNCIL

Composition

Article 61[3]

1. The Economic and Social Council shall consist of fifty-four Members of the United Nations elected by the General Assembly.

2. Subject to the provisions of paragraph 3, eighteen members of the Economic and Social Council shall be elected each year for a term of three years. A retiring member shall be eligible for immediate re-election.

3. At the first election after the increase in the membership of the Economic and Social Council from twenty-seven to fifty-four members, in addition to the members elected in place of the nine members whose term of office expires at the end of that year, twenty-seven additional members shall be elected. Of these twenty-seven additional members, the term of office of nine members so elected shall expire at the end of one year, and of nine other members at the end of two years, in accordance with arrangements made by the General Assembly.

4. Each member of the Economic and Social Council shall have one representative.

Functions and Powers

Article 62

1. The Economic and Social Council may make or initiate studies and reports with respect to international economic, social, cultural, educational, health, and related matters and may make recommendations with respect to any such matters to the General Assembly, to the Members of the United Nations, and to the specialized agencies concerned.

2. It may make recommendations for the purpose of promoting respect for, and observance of, human rights and fundamental freedoms for all.

3. It may prepare draft conventions for submission to the General Assembly, with respect to matters falling within its competence.

4. It may call, in accordance with the rules prescribed by the United Nations, international conferences on matters falling within its competence.

Article 63

1. The Economic and Social Council may enter into agreements with any of the agencies referred to in Article 57, defining the terms on which the agency concerned shall be brought into relationship with the United Nations. Such agreements shall be subject to approval by the General Assembly.

2. It may co-ordinate the activities of the specialized agencies through consultation with and recommendations to such agencies and through recommendations to the General Assembly and to the Members of the United Nations.

Article 64

1. The Economic and Social Council may take appropriate steps to obtain regular reports from the specialized agencies. It may make arrangements with the Members of the United Nations and with the specialized agencies to obtain reports on the steps taken to give effect to its own recommendations and to recommendations on matters falling within its competence made by the General Assembly.

2. It may communicate its observations on these reports to the General Assembly.

Article 65

The Economic and Social Council may furnish information to the Security Council and shall assist the Security Council upon its request.

Article 66

1. The Economic and Social Council shall perform such functions as fall within its competence in connexion with the carrying out of the recommendations of the General Assembly.

2. It may, with the approval of the General Assembly, perform services at the request of Members of the United Nations and at the request of specialized agencies.

3. It shall perform such other functions as are specified elsewhere in the present Charter or as may be assigned to it by the General Assembly.

Voting

Article 67

1. Each member of the Economic and Social Council shall have one vote.

2. Decisions of the Economic and Social Council shall be made by a majority of the members present and voting.

Procedure

Article 68

The Economic and Social Council shall set up commissions in economic and social fields and for the promotion of human rights, and such other commissions as may be required for the performance of its functions.

Article 69

The Economic and Social Council shall invite any Member of the United Nations to participate, without vote, in its deliberations on any matter of particular concern to that Member.

Article 70

The Economic and Social Council may make arrangements for representatives of the specialized agencies to participate, without vote, in its deliberations and in those of the commissions established by it, and for its representatives to participate in the deliberations of the specialized agencies.

Article 71

The Economic and Social Council may make suitable arrangements for consultation with non-governmental organizations which are concerned with matters within its competence. Such arrangements may be made with international organizations and, where appropriate, with national organizations after consultation with the Member of the United Nations concerned.

Article 72

1. The Economic and Social Council shall adopt its own rules of procedure, including the method of selecting its President.

2. The Economic and Social Council shall meet as required in accordance with its rules, which shall include provision for the convening of meetings on the request of a majority of its members.

Chapter XI
DECLARATION REGARDING
NON-SELF-GOVERNING TERRITORIES

Article 73

Members of the United Nations which have or assume responsibilities for the administration of territories whose peoples have not yet attained a full measure of self-government recognize the principle that the interests of the inhabitants of these territories are paramount, and accept as a sacred trust the obligation to promote to the utmost, within the system of international peace and security established by the present Charter, the well-being of the inhabitants of these territories and, to this end:

a. to ensure, with due respect for the culture of the peoples concerned, their political, economic, social, and educational advancement, their just treatment, and their protection against abuses;
b. to develop self-government, to take due account of the political aspirations of the peoples, and to assist them in the progressive development of their free political institutions, according to the particular circumstances of each territory and its peoples and their varying stages of advancement;
c. to further international peace and security;
d. to promote constructive measures of development, to encourage research, and to co-operate with one another and, when and where appropriate, with specialized international bodies with a view to the practical achievement of the social, economic, and scientific purposes set forth in this Article; and
e. to transmit regularly to the Secretary-General for information purposes, subject to such limitation as security and constitutional considerations may require, statistical and other information of a technical nature relating to economic, social, and educational conditions in the territories for which they are respectively responsible other than those territories to which Chapters XII and XIII apply.

Article 74

Members of the United Nations also agree that their policy in respect of the territories to which this Chapter applies, no less than in respect of their metropolitan areas, must be based on the general principle of good-neighbourliness, due account being taken of the interests and well-being of the rest of the world, in social, economic, and commercial matters.

Chapter XII
INTERNATIONAL TRUSTEESHIP SYSTEM

Article 75

The United Nations shall establish under its authority an international trusteeship system for the administration and supervision of such territories as may be placed thereunder by subsequent individual agreements. These territories are hereinafter referred to as trust territories.

Article 76

The basic objectives of the trusteeship system, in accordance with the Purposes of the United Nations laid down in Article 1 of the present Charter, shall be:
a. to further international peace and security;
b. to promote the political, economic, social, and educational advancement of the inhabitants of the trust territories, and their progressive development towards self-government or independence as may be appropriate to the particular circumstances of each territory and its peoples and the freely expressed wishes of the peoples concerned, and as may be provided by the terms of each trusteeship agreement;
c. to encourage respect for human rights and for fundamental freedoms for all without distinction as to race, sex, language, or religion, and to encourage recognition of the interdependence of the peoples of the world; and
d. to ensure equal treatment in social, economic, and commercial matters for all Members of the United Nations and their nationals, and also equal treatment for the latter in the administration of justice, without prejudice to the attainment of the foregoing objectives and subject to the provisions of Article 80.

Article 77

1. The trusteeship system shall apply to such territories in the following categories as may be placed thereunder by means of trusteeship agreements:

a. territories now held under mandate;
b. territories which may be detached from enemy states as a result of the Second World War; and
c. territories voluntarily placed under the system by states responsible for their administration.

2. It will be a matter for subsequent agreement as to which territories in the foregoing categories will be brought under the trusteeship system and upon what terms.

Article 78

The trusteeship system shall not apply to territories which have become Members of the United Nations, relationship among which shall be based on respect for the principle of sovereign equality.

Article 79

The terms of trusteeship for each territory to be placed under the trusteeship system, including any alteration or amendment, shall be agreed upon by the states directly concerned, including the mandatory power in the case of territories held under mandate by a Member of the United Nations, and shall be approved as provided for in Articles 83 and 85.

Article 80

1. Except as may be agreed upon in individual trusteeship agreements, made under Articles 77, 79 and 81, placing each territory under the trusteeship system, and until such agreements have been concluded, nothing in this Chapter shall be construed in or of itself to alter in any manner the rights whatsoever of any states or any peoples or the terms of existing international instruments to which Members of the United Nations may respectively be parties.

2. Paragraph 1 of this Article shall not be interpreted as giving grounds for delay or postponement of the negotiation and conclusion of agreements for placing mandated and other territories under the trusteeship system as provided for in Article 77.

Article 81

The trusteeship agreement shall in each case include the terms under which the trust territory will be administered and designate the authority which will exercise the administration of the trust territory. Such authority, hereinafter called the administering authority, may be one or more states or the Organization itself.

Article 82

There may be designated, in any trusteeship agreement, a strategic area or areas which may include part or all of the trust territory to which the agreement applies, without prejudice to any special agreement or agreements made under Article 43.

Article 83

1. All functions of the United Nations relating to strategic areas, including the approval of the terms of the trusteeship agreements and of their alteration or amendment, shall be exercised by the Security Council.

2. The basic objectives set forth in Article 76 shall be applicable to the people of each strategic area.

3. The Security Council shall, subject to the provisions of the trusteeship agreements and without prejudice to security considerations, avail itself of the assistance of the Trusteeship Council to perform those functions of the United Nations under the trusteeship system relating to political, economic, social, and educational matters in the strategic areas.

Article 84

It shall be the duty of the administering authority to ensure that the trust territory shall play its part in the maintenance of international peace and security. To this end the administering authority may make use of volunteer forces, facilities, and assistance from the trust territory in carrying out the obligations towards the Security Council undertaken in this regard by the administering authority, as well as for local defence and the maintenance of law and order within the trust territory.

Article 85

1. The functions of the United Nations with regard to trusteeship agreements for all areas not designated as strategic, including the approval of the terms of the trusteeship agreements and of their alteration or amendment, shall be exercised by the General Assembly.

2. The Trusteeship Council, operating under the authority of the General Assembly, shall assist the General Assembly in carrying out these functions.

Chapter XIII

THE TRUSTEESHIP COUNCIL

Composition

Article 86

1. The Trusteeship Council shall consist of the following Members of the United Nations:
a. those Members administering trust territories;
b. such of those Members mentioned by name in Article 23 as are not administering trust territories; and
c. as many other Members elected for three-year terms by the General Assembly as may be necessary to ensure that the total number of members of the Trusteeship Council is equally divided between those Members of the United Nations which administer trust territories and those which do not.

2. Each member of the Trusteeship Council shall designate one specially qualified person to represent it therein.

Functions and Powers

Article 87

The General Assembly and, under its authority, the Trusteeship Council, in carrying out their functions, may:
a. consider reports submitted by the administering authority;
b. accept petitions and examine them in consultation with the administering authority;
c. provide for periodic visits to the respective trust territories at times agreed upon with the administering authority; and
d. take these and other actions in conformity with the terms of the trusteeship agreements.

Article 88

The Trusteeship Council shall formulate a questionnaire on the political, economic, social, and educational advancement of the inhabitants of each trust territory, and the administering authority for each trust territory within the competence of the General Assembly shall make an annual report to the General Assembly upon the basis of such questionnaire.

Voting

Article 89

1. Each member of the Trusteeship Council shall have one vote.

2. Decisions of the Trusteeship Council shall be made by a majority of the members present and voting.

Procedure

Article 90

1. The Trusteeship Council shall adopt its own rules of procedure, including the method of selecting its President.

2. The Trusteeship Council shall meet as required in accordance with its rules, which shall include provision for the convening of meetings on the request of a majority of its members.

Article 91

The Trusteeship Council shall, when appropriate, avail itself of the assistance of the Economic and Social Council and of the specialized agencies in regard to matters with which they are respectively concerned.

Chapter XIV
THE INTERNATIONAL COURT OF JUSTICE

Article 92

The International Court of Justice shall be the principal judicial organ of the United Nations. It shall function in accordance with the annexed Statute, which is based upon the Statute of the Permanent Court of International Justice and forms an integral part of the present Charter.

Article 93

1. All Members of the United Nations are *ipso facto* parties to the Statute of the International Court of Justice.

2. A state which is not a Member of the United Nations may become a party to the Statute of the International Court of Justice on conditions to be determined in each case by the General Assembly upon the recommendation of the Security Council.

Article 94

1. Each Member of the United Nations undertakes to comply with the decision of the International Court of Justice in any case to which it is a party.

2. If any party to a case fails to perform the obligations incumbent upon it under a judgment rendered by the Court, the other party may have recourse to the Security Council, which may, if it deems necessary, make recommendations or decide upon measures to be taken to give effect to the judgment.

Article 95

Nothing in the present Charter shall prevent Members of the United Nations from entrusting the solution of their differences to other tribunals by virtue of agreements already in existence or which may be concluded in the future.

Article 96

1. The General Assembly or the Security Council may request the International Court of Justice to give an advisory opinion on any legal question.

2. Other organs of the United Nations and specialized agencies, which may at any time be so authorized by the General Assembly, may also request advisory opinions of the Court on legal questions arising within the scope of their activities.

Chapter XV
THE SECRETARIAT

Article 97

The Secretariat shall comprise a Secretary-General and such staff as the Organization may require. The Secretary-General shall be appointed by the General Assembly upon the recommendation of the Security Council. He shall be the chief administrative officer of the Organization.

Article 98

The Secretary-General shall act in that capacity in all meetings of the General Assembly, of the Security Council, of the Economic and Social Council, and of the Trusteeship Council, and shall perform such other functions as are entrusted to him by these organs. The Secretary-General shall make an annual report to the General Assembly on the work of the Organization.

Article 99

The Secretary-General may bring to the attention of the Security Council any matter which in his opinion may threaten the maintenance of international peace and security.

Article 100

1. In the performance of their duties the Secretary-General and the staff shall not seek or receive instructions from any government or from any other authority external to the Organization. They shall refrain from any action which might reflect on their position as international officials responsible only to the Organization.

2. Each Member of the United Nations undertakes to respect the exclusively international character of the responsibilities of the Secretary-General and the staff and not to seek to influence them in the discharge of their responsibilities.

Article 101

1. The staff shall be appointed by the Secretary-General under regulations established by the General Assembly.

2. Appropriate staffs shall be permanently assigned to the Economic and Social Council, the Trusteeship Council, and, as required, to other organs of the United Nations. These staffs shall form a part of the Secretariat.

3. The paramount consideration in the employment of the staff and in the determination of the conditions of service shall be the necessity of securing the highest standards of efficiency, competence, and integrity. Due regard shall be paid to the importance of recruiting the staff on as wide a geographical basis as possible.

Chapter XVI
MISCELLANEOUS PROVISIONS

Article 102

1. Every treaty and every international agreement entered into by any Member of the United Nations after the present Charter comes into force shall as soon as possible be registered with the Secretariat and published by it.

2. No party to any such treaty or international agreement which has not been registered in accordance with the provisions of paragraph 1 of this Article may invoke that treaty or agreement before any organ of the United Nations.

Article 103

In the event of a conflict between the obligations of the Members of the United Nations under the present Charter and their obligations under any other international agreement, their obligations under the present Charter shall prevail.

Article 104

The Organization shall enjoy in the territory of each of its Members such legal capacity as may be necessary for the exercise of its functions and the fulfilment of its purposes.

Article 105

1. The Organization shall enjoy in the territory of each of its Members such privileges and immunities as are necessary for the fulfilment of its purposes.

2. Representatives of the Members of the United Nations and officials of the Organization shall similarly enjoy such privileges and immunities as are necessary for the independent exercise of their functions in connexion with the Organization.

3. The General Assembly may make recommendations with a view to determining the details of the application of paragraphs 1 and 2 of this Article or may propose conventions to the Members of the United Nations for this purpose.

Chapter XVII
TRANSITIONAL SECURITY ARRANGEMENTS

Article 106

Pending the coming into force of such special agreements referred to in Article 43 as in the opinion of the Security Council enable it to begin the exercise of its responsibilities under Article 42, the parties to the Four-Nation Declaration, signed at Moscow, 30 October 1943, and France, shall, in accordance with the provisions of paragraph 5 of that Declaration, consult with one another and as occasion requires with other Members of the United Nations with a view to such joint action on behalf of the Organization as may be necessary for the purpose of maintaining international peace and security.

Article 107

Nothing in the present Charter shall invalidate or preclude action, in relation to any state which during the Second World War has been an enemy of any signatory to the present Charter, taken or authorized as a result of that war by the Governments having responsibility for such action.

Chapter XVIII
AMENDMENTS

Article 108

Amendments to the present Charter shall come into force for all Members of the United Nations when they have been adopted by a vote of two thirds of the members of the General Assembly and ratified in accordance with their respective constitutional processes by two thirds of the Members of the United Nations, including all the permanent members of the Security Council.

Article 109[1]

1. A General Conference of the Members of the United Nations for the purpose of reviewing the present Charter may be held at a date and place to be fixed by a two-thirds vote of the members of the General Assembly and by a vote of any nine members of the Security Council. Each Member of the United Nations shall have one vote in the conference.

2. Any alteration of the present Charter recommended by a two-thirds vote of the conference shall take effect when ratified in accordance with their respective constitutional processes by two thirds of the Members of the United Nations including all the permanent members of the Security Council.

3. If such a conference has not been held before the tenth annual session of the General Assembly following the coming into force of the present Charter, the proposal to call such a conference shall be placed on the agenda of that session of the General Assembly, and the conference shall be held if so decided by a majority vote of the members of the General Assembly and by a vote of any seven members of the Security Council.

Chapter XIX
RATIFICATION AND SIGNATURE

Article 110

1. The present Charter shall be ratified by the signatory states in accordance with their respective constitutional processes.

2. The ratifications shall be deposited with the Government of the United States of America, which shall notify all the signatory states of each deposit as well as the Secretary-General of the Organization when he has been appointed.

3. The present Charter shall come into force upon the deposit of ratifications by the Republic of China, France, the Union of Soviet Socialist Republics, the United Kingdom of Great Britain and Northern Ireland and the United States of America, and by a majority of the other signatory states. A protocol of the ratifications deposited shall thereupon be drawn up by the Government of the United States of America which shall communicate copies thereof to all the signatory states.

4. The states signatory to the present Charter which ratify it after it has come into force will become original Members of the United Nations on the date of the deposit of their respective ratifications.

Article 111

The present Charter, of which the Chinese, French, Russian, English, and Spanish texts are equally authentic, shall remain deposited in the archives of the Government of the United States of America. Duly certified copies thereof shall be transmitted by that Government to the Governments of the other signatory states.

IN FAITH WHEREOF the representatives of the Governments of the United Nations have signed the present Charter.

DONE at the city of San Francisco the twenty-sixth day of June, one thousand nine hundred and forty-five.

---

[1] Amended text of Article 23, which came into force on 31 August 1965.
(The text of Article 23 before it was amended read as follows:
1. The Security Council shall consist of eleven Members of the United Nations. The Republic of China, France, the Union of Soviet Socialist Republics, the United Kingdom of Great Britain and Northern Ireland and the United States of America shall be permanent members of the Security Council. The General Assembly shall elect six other Members of the United Nations to be non-permanent members of the Security Council, due regard being specially paid in the first instance to the contributions of Members of the United Nations to the maintenance of international peace and security and to the other purposes of the Organization, and also to equitable geographical distribution.
2. The non-permanent members of the Security Council shall be elected for a term of two years. In the first election of the non-permanent members, however, three shall be chosen for a term of one year. A retiring member shall not be eligible for immediate re-election.
3. Each member of the Security Council shall have one representative.)

[2] Amended text of Article 27, which came into force on 31 August 1965.
(The text of Article 27 before it was amended read as follows:
1. Each member of the Security Council shall have one vote.
2. Decisions of the Security Council on procedural matters shall be made by an affirmative vote of seven members.
3. Decisions of the Security Council on all other matters shall be made by an affirmative vote of seven members including the concurring votes of the permanent members; provided that, in decisions under Chapter VI, and under paragraph 3 of Article 52, a party to a dispute shall abstain from voting.)

[3] Amended text of Article 61, which came into force on 24 September 1973.
(The text of Article 61 as previously amended on 31 August 1965 read as follows:
1. The Economic and Social Council shall consist of twenty-seven Members of the United Nations elected by the General Assembly.
2. Subject to the provisions of paragraph 3, nine members of the Economic and Social Council shall be elected each year for a term of three years. A retiring member shall be eligible for immediate re-election.
3. At the first election after the increase in the membership of the Economic and Social Council from eighteen to twenty-seven members, in addition to the members elected in place of the six members whose term of office expires at the end of that year, nine

additional members shall be elected. Of these nine additional members, the term of office of three members so elected shall expire at the end of one year, and of three other members at the end of two years, in accordance with arrangements made by the General Assembly.
   4. Each member of the Economic and Social Council shall have one representative.)

[4] Amended text of Article 109, which came into force on 12 June 1968.
  (The text of Article 109 before it was amended read as follows:
   1. A General Conference of the Members of the United Nations for the purpose of reviewing the present Charter may be held at a date and place to be fixed by a two-thirds vote of the members of the General Assembly and by a vote of any seven members of the Security Council. Each Member of the United Nations shall have one vote in the conference.
   2. Any alteration of the present Charter recommended by a two-thirds vote of the conference shall take effect when ratified in accordance with their respective constitutional processes by two thirds of the Members of the United Nations including all the permanent members of the Security Council.
   3. If such a conference has not been held before the tenth annual session of the General Assembly following the coming into force of the present Charter, the proposal to call such a conference shall be placed on the agenda of that session of the General Assembly, and the conference shall be held if so decided by a majority vote of the members of the General Assembly and by a vote of any seven members of the Security Council.)

Statute of the International Court of Justice

Article 1

The International Court of Justice established by the Charter of the United Nations as the principal judicial organ of the United Nations shall be constituted and shall function in accordance with the provisions of the present Statute.

Chapter I
ORGANIZATION OF THE COURT

Article 2

The Court shall be composed of a body of independent judges, elected regardless of their nationality from among persons of high moral character, who possess the qualifications required in their respective countries for appointment to the highest judicial offices, or are jurisconsults of recognized competence in international law.

Article 3

1. The Court shall consist of fifteen members, no two of whom may be nationals of the same state.
2. A person who for the purposes of membership in the Court could be regarded as a national of more than one state shall be deemed to be a national of the one in which he ordinarily exercises civil and political rights.

Article 4

1. The members of the Court shall be elected by the General Assembly and by the Security Council from a list of persons nominated by the national groups in the Permanent Court of Arbitration, in accordance with the following provisions.
2. In the case of Members of the United Nations not represented in the Permanent Court of Arbitration, candidates shall be nominated by national groups appointed for this purpose by their governments under the same conditions as those prescribed for members of the Permanent Court of Arbitration by Article 44 of the Convention of The Hague of 1907 for the pacific settlement of international disputes.
3. The conditions under which a state which is a party to the present Statute but is not a Member of the United Nations may participate in electing the members of the Court shall, in the absence of a special agreement, be laid down by the General Assembly upon recommendation of the Security Council.

Article 5

1. At least three months before the date of the election, the Secretary-General of the United Nations shall address a written request to the members of the Permanent Court of Arbitration belonging to the states which are parties to the present Statute, and to the members of the national groups appointed under Article 4, paragraph 2, inviting them to undertake, within a given time, by national groups, the nomination of persons in a position to accept the duties of a member of the Court.
2. No group may nominate more than four persons, not more than two of whom shall be of their own nationality. In no case may the number of candidates nominated by a group be more than double the number of seats to be filled.

Article 6

Before making these nominations, each national group is recommended to consult its highest court of justice, its legal faculties and schools of law, and its national academies and national sections of international academies devoted to the study of law.

Article 7

1. The Secretary-General shall prepare a list in alphabetical order of all the persons thus nominated. Save as provided in Article 12, paragraph 2, these shall be the only persons eligible.
2. The Secretary-General shall submit this list to the General Assembly and to the Security Council.

Article 8

The General Assembly and the Security Council shall proceed independently of one another to elect the members of the Court.

Article 9

At every election, the electors shall bear in mind not only that the persons to be elected should individually possess the qualifications required, but also that in the body as a whole the representation of the main forms of civilization and of the principal legal systems of the world should be assured.

Article 10

1. Those candidates who obtain an absolute majority of votes in the General Assembly and in the Security Council shall be considered as elected.
2. Any vote of the Security Council, whether for the election of judges or for the appointment of members of the conference envisaged in Article 12, shall be taken without any distinction between permanent and non-permanent members of the Security Council.
3. In the event of more than one national of the same state obtaining an absolute majority of the votes both of the General Assembly and of the Security Council, the eldest of these only shall be considered as elected.

Article 11

If, after the first meeting held for the purpose of the election, one or more seats remain to be filled, a second and, if necessary, a third meeting shall take place.

Article 12

1. If, after the third meeting, one or more seats still remain unfilled, a joint conference consisting of six members, three appointed by the General Assembly and three by the Security Council, may be formed at any time at the request of either the General Assembly or the Security Council, for the purpose of choosing by the vote of an absolute majority one name for each seat still vacant, to submit to the General Assembly and the Security Council for their respective acceptance.

2. If the joint conference is unanimously agreed upon any person who fulfils the required conditions, he may be included in its list, even though he was not included in the list of nominations referred to in Article 7.

3. If the joint conference is satisfied that it will not be successful in procuring an election, those members of the Court who have already been elected shall, within a period to be fixed by the Security Council, proceed to fill the vacant seats by selection from among those candidates who have obtained votes either in the General Assembly or in the Security Council.

4. In the event of an equality of votes among the judges, the eldest judge shall have a casting vote.

Article 13

1. The members of the Court shall be elected for nine years and may be re-elected; provided, however, that of the judges elected at the first election, the terms of five judges shall expire at the end of three years and the terms of five more judges shall expire at the end of six years.

2. The judges whose terms are to expire at the end of the above-mentioned initial periods of three and six years shall be chosen by lot to be drawn by the Secretary-General immediately after the first election has been completed.

3. The members of the Court shall continue to discharge their duties until their places have been filled. Though replaced, they shall finish any cases which they may have begun.

4. In the case of the resignation of a member of the Court, the resignation shall be addressed to the President of the Court for transmission to the Secretary-General. This last notification makes the place vacant.

Article 14

Vacancies shall be filled by the same method as that laid down for the first election, subject to the following provision: the Secretary-General shall, within one month of the occurrence of the vacancy, proceed to issue the invitations provided for in Article 5, and the date of the election shall be fixed by the Security Council.

Article 15

A member of the Court elected to replace a member whose term of office has not expired shall hold office for the remainder of his predecessor's term.

Article 16

1. No member of the Court may exercise any political or administrative function, or engage in any other occupation of a professional nature.

2. Any doubt on this point shall be settled by the decision of the Court.

Article 17

1. No member of the Court may act as agent, counsel, or advocate in any case.

2. No member may participate in the decision of any case in which he has previously taken part as agent, counsel, or advocate for one of the parties, or as a member of a national or international court, or of a commission of enquiry, or in any other capacity.

3. Any doubt on this point shall be settled by the decision of the Court.

Article 18

1. No member of the Court can be dismissed unless, in the unanimous opinion of the other members, he has ceased to fulfil the required conditions.

2. Formal notification thereof shall be made to the Secretary-General by the Registrar.

3. This notification makes the place vacant.

Article 19

The members of the Court, when engaged on the business of the Court, shall enjoy diplomatic privileges and immunities.

Article 20

Every member of the Court shall, before taking up his duties, make a solemn declaration in open court that he will exercise his powers impartially and conscientiously.

Article 21

1. The Court shall elect its President and Vice-President for three years; they may be re-elected.

2. The Court shall appoint its Registrar and may provide for the appointment of such other officers as may be necessary.

Article 22

1. The seat of the Court shall be established at The Hague. This, however, shall not prevent the Court from sitting and exercising its functions elsewhere whenever the Court considers it desirable.

2. The President and the Registrar shall reside at the seat of the Court.

Article 23

1. The Court shall remain permanently in session, except during the judicial vacations, the dates and duration of which shall be fixed by the Court.

2. Members of the Court are entitled to periodic leave, the dates and duration of which shall be fixed by the Court, having in mind the distance between The Hague and the home of each judge.

3. Members of the Court shall be bound, unless they are on leave or prevented from attending by illness or other serious reasons duly explained to the President, to hold themselves permanently at the disposal of the Court.

Article 24

1. If, for some special reason, a member of the Court considers that he should not take part in the decision of a particular case, he shall so inform the President.

2. If the President considers that for some special reason one of the members of the Court should not sit in a particular case, he shall give him notice accordingly.

3. If in any such case the member of the Court and the President disagree, the matter shall be settled by the decision of the Court.

Article 25

1. The full Court shall sit except when it is expressly provided otherwise in the present Statute.

2. Subject to the condition that the number of judges available to constitute the Court is not thereby reduced below eleven, the Rules of the Court may provide for allowing one or more judges, according to circumstances and in rotation, to be dispensed from sitting.

3. A quorum of nine judges shall suffice to constitute the Court.

Article 26

1. The Court may from time to time form one or more chambers, composed of three or more judges as the Court may determine, for dealing with particular categories of cases; for example, labour cases and cases relating to transit and communications.

2. The Court may at any time form a chamber for dealing with a particular case. The number of judges to constitute such a chamber shall be determined by the Court with the approval of the parties.

3. Cases shall be heard and determined by the chambers provided for in this Article if the parties so request.

Article 27

A judgment given by any of the chambers provided for in Articles 26 and 29 shall be considered as rendered by the Court.

Article 28

The chambers provided for in Articles 26 and 29 may, with the consent of the parties, sit and exercise their functions elsewhere than at The Hague.

Article 29

With a view to the speedy dispatch of business, the Court shall form annually a chamber composed of five judges which, at the request of the parties, may hear and determine cases by summary procedure. In addition, two judges shall be selected for the purpose of replacing judges who find it impossible to sit.

Article 30

1. The Court shall frame rules for carrying out its functions. In particular, it shall lay down rules of procedure.

2. The Rules of the Court may provide for assessors to sit with the Court or with any of its chambers, without the right to vote.

Article 31

1. Judges of the nationality of each of the parties shall retain their right to sit in the case before the Court.

2. If the Court includes upon the Bench a judge of the nationality of one of the parties, any other party may choose a person to sit as judge. Such person shall be chosen preferably from among those persons who have been nominated as candidates as provided in Articles 4 and 5.

3. If the Court includes upon the Bench no judge of the nationality of the parties, each of these parties may proceed to choose a judge as provided in paragraph 2 of this Article.

4. The provisions of this Article shall apply to the case of Articles 26 and 29. In such cases, the President shall request one or, if necessary, two of the members of the Court forming the chamber to give place to the members of the Court of the nationality of the parties concerned, and, failing such, or if they are unable to be present, to the judges specially chosen by the parties.

5. Should there be several parties in the same interest, they shall, for the purpose of the preceding provisions, be reckoned as one party only. Any doubt upon this point shall be settled by the decision of the Court.

6. Judges chosen as laid down in paragraphs 2, 3 and 4 of this Article shall fulfil the conditions required by Articles 2, 17 (paragraph 2), 20, and 24 of the present Statute. They shall take part in the decision on terms of complete equality with their colleagues.

Article 32

1. Each member of the Court shall receive an annual salary.
2. The President shall receive a special annual allowance.
3. The Vice-President shall receive a special allowance for every day on which he acts as President.
4. The judges chosen under Article 31, other than members of the Court, shall receive compensation for each day on which they exercise their functions.
5. These salaries, allowances, and compensation shall be fixed by the General Assembly. They may not be decreased during the term of office.
6. The salary of the Registrar shall be fixed by the General Assembly on the proposal of the Court.
7. Regulations made by the General Assembly shall fix the conditions under which retirement pensions may be given to members of the Court and to the Registrar, and the conditions under which members of the Court and the Registrar shall have their travelling expenses refunded.
8. The above salaries, allowances, and compensation shall be free of all taxation.

Article 33

The expenses of the Court shall be borne by the United Nations in such a manner as shall be decided by the General Assembly.

Chapter II
COMPETENCE OF THE COURT

Article 34

1. Only states may be parties in cases before the Court.
2. The Court, subject to and in conformity with its Rules, may request of public international organizations information relevant to cases before it, and shall receive such information presented by such organizations on their own initiative.
3. Whenever the construction of the constituent instrument of a public international organization or of an international convention adopted thereunder is in question in a case before the Court, the Registrar shall so notify the public international organization concerned and shall communicate to it copies of all the written proceedings.

Article 35

1. The Court shall be open to the states parties to the present Statute.
2. The conditions under which the Court shall be open to other states shall, subject to the special provisions contained in treaties in force, be laid down by the Security Council, but in no case shall such conditions place the parties in a position of inequality before the Court.
3. When a state which is not a Member of the United Nations is a party to a case, the Court shall fix the amount which that party is to contribute towards the expenses of the Court. This provision shall not apply if such state is bearing a share of the expenses of the Court.

Article 36

1. The jurisdiction of the Court comprises all cases which the parties refer to it and all matters specially provided for in the Charter of the United Nations or in treaties and conventions in force.

2. The states parties to the present Statute may at any time declare that they recognize as compulsory *ipso facto* and without special agreement, in relation to any other state accepting the same obligation, the jurisdiction of the Court in all legal disputes concerning:

   a. the interpretation of a treaty;
   b. any question of international law;
   c. the existence of any fact which, if established, would constitute a breach of an international obligation;
   d. the nature or extent of the reparation to be made for the breach of an international obligation.

3. The declarations referred to above may be made unconditionally or on condition of reciprocity on the part of several or certain states, or for a certain time.

4. Such declarations shall be deposited with the Secretary-General of the United Nations, who shall transmit copies thereof to the parties to the Statute and to the Registrar of the Court.

5. Declarations made under Article 36 of the Statute of the Permanent Court of International Justice and which are still in force shall be deemed, as between the parties to the present Statute, to be acceptances of the compulsory jurisdiction of the International Court of Justice for the period which they still have to run and in accordance with their terms.

6. In the event of a dispute as to whether the Court has jurisdiction, the matter shall be settled by the decision of the Court.

Article 37

Whenever a treaty or convention in force provides for reference of a matter to a tribunal to have been instituted by the League of Nations, or to the Permanent Court of International Justice, the matter shall, as between the parties to the present Statute, be referred to the International Court of Justice.

Article 38

1. The Court, whose function is to decide in accordance with international law such disputes as are submitted to it, shall apply:
   a. international conventions, whether general or particular, establishing rules expressly recognized by the contesting states;
   b. international custom, as evidence of a general practice accepted as law;
   c. the general principles of law recognized by civilized nations;
   d. subject to the provisions of Article 59, judicial decisions and the teachings of the most highly qualified publicists of the various nations, as subsidiary means for the determination of rules of law.

2. This provision shall not prejudice the power of the Court to decide a case *ex aequo et bono*, if the parties agree thereto.

Chapter III
PROCEDURE

Article 39

1. The official languages of the Court shall be French and English. If the parties agree that the case shall be conducted in French, the judgment shall be delivered in French. If the parties agree that the case shall be conducted in English, the judgment shall be delivered in English.

2. In the absence of an agreement as to which language shall be employed, each party may, in the pleadings, use the language which it prefers; the decision of the Court shall be given in French and English. In this case the Court shall at the same time determine which of the two texts shall be considered as authoritative.

3. The Court shall, at the request of any party, authorize a language other than French or English to be used by that party.

Article 40

1. Cases are brought before the Court, as the case may be, either by the notification of the special agreement or by a written application addressed to the Registrar. In either case the subject of the dispute and the parties shall be indicated.

2. The Registrar shall forthwith communicate the application to all concerned.

3. He shall also notify the Members of the United Nations through the Secretary-General, and also any other states entitled to appear before the Court.

Article 41

1. The Court shall have the power to indicate, if it considers that circumstances so require, any provisional measures which ought to be taken to preserve the respective rights of either party.

2. Pending the final decision, notice of the measures suggested shall forthwith be given to the parties and to the Security Council.

Article 42

1. The parties shall be represented by agents.

2. They may have the assistance of counsel or advocates before the Court.

3. The agents, counsel, and advocates of parties before the Court shall enjoy the privileges and immunities necessary to the independent exercise of their duties.

Article 43

1. The procedure shall consist of two parts: written and oral.

2. The written proceedings shall consist of the communication to the Court and to the parties of memorials, counter-memorials and, if necessary, replies; also all papers and documents in support.

3. These communications shall be made through the Registrar, in the order and within the time fixed by the Court.

4. A certified copy of every document produced by one party shall be communicated to the other party.

5. The oral proceedings shall consist of the hearing by the Court of witnesses, experts, agents, counsel, and advocates.

Article 44

1. For the service of all notices upon persons other than the agents, counsel, and advocates, the Court shall apply direct to the government of the state upon whose territory the notice has to be served.

2. The same provision shall apply whenever steps are to be taken to procure evidence on the spot.

Article 45

The hearing shall be under the control of the President or, if he is unable to preside, of the Vice-President; if neither is able to preside, the senior judge present shall preside.

Article 46

The hearing in Court shall be public, unless the Court shall decide otherwise, or unless the parties demand that the public be not admitted.

Article 47

1. Minutes shall be made at each hearing and signed by the Registrar and the President.

2. These minutes alone shall be authentic.

Article 48

The Court shall make orders for the conduct of the case, shall decide the form and time in which each party must conclude its arguments, and make all arrangements connected with the taking of evidence.

Article 49

The Court may, even before the hearing begins, call upon the agents to produce any document or to supply any explanations. Formal note shall be taken of any refusal.

Article 50

The Court may, at any time, entrust any individual, body, bureau, commission, or other organization that it may select, with the task of carrying out an enquiry or giving an expert opinion.

Article 51

During the hearing any relevant questions are to be put to the witnesses and experts under the conditions laid down by the Court in the rules of procedure referred to in Article 30.

Article 52

After the Court has received the proofs and evidence within the time specified for the purpose, it may refuse to accept any further oral or written evidence that one party may desire to present unless the other side consents.

Article 53

1. Whenever one of the parties does not appear before the Court, or fails to defend its case, the other party may call upon the Court to decide in favour of its claim.

2. The Court must, before doing so, satisfy itself, not only that it has jurisdiction in accordance with Articles 36 and 37, but also that the claim is well founded in fact and law.

Article 54

1. When, subject to the control of the Court, the agents, counsel, and advocates have completed their presentation of the case, the President shall declare the hearing closed.

2. The Court shall withdraw to consider the judgment.
3. The deliberations of the Court shall take place in private and remain secret.

Article 55

1. All questions shall be decided by a majority of the judges present.
2. In the event of an equality of votes, the President or the judge who acts in his place shall have a casting vote.

Article 56

1. The judgment shall state the reasons on which it is based.
2. It shall contain the names of the judges who have taken part in the decision.

Article 57

If the judgment does not represent in whole or in part the unanimous opinion of the judges, any judge shall be entitled to deliver a separate opinion.

Article 58

The judgment shall be signed by the President and by the Registrar. It shall be read in open court, due notice having been given to the agents.

Article 59

The decision of the Court has no binding force except between the parties and in respect of that particular case.

Article 60

The judgment is final and without appeal. In the event of dispute as to the meaning or scope of the judgment, the Court shall construe it upon the request of any party.

Article 61

1. An application for revision of a judgment may be made only when it is based upon the discovery of some fact of such a nature as to be a decisive factor, which fact was, when the judgment was given, unknown to the Court and also the party claiming revision, always provided that such ignorance was not due to negligence.
2. The proceedings for revision shall be opened by a judgment of the Court expressly recording the existence of the new fact, recognizing that it has such a character as to lay the case open to revision, and declaring the application admissible on this ground.
3. The Court may require previous compliance with the terms of the judgment before it admits proceedings in revision.
4. The application for revision must be made at latest within six months of the discovery of the new fact.
5. No application for revision may be made after the lapse of ten years from the date of the judgment.

Article 62

1. Should a state consider that it has an interest of a legal nature which may be affected by the decision in the case, it may submit a request to the Court to be permitted to intervene.
2. It shall be for the Court to decide upon this request.

Article 63

1. Whenever the construction of a convention to which states other than those concerned in the case are parties is in question, the Registrar shall notify all such states forthwith.
2. Every state so notified has the right to intervene in the proceedings; but if it uses this right, the construction given by the judgment will be equally binding upon it.

Article 64

Unless otherwise decided by the Court, each party shall bear its own costs.

Chapter IV
ADVISORY OPINIONS

Article 65

1. The Court may give an advisory opinion on any legal question at the request of whatever body may be authorized by or in accordance with the Charter of the United Nations to make such a request.
2. Questions upon which the advisory opinion of the Court is asked shall be laid before the Court by means of a written request containing an exact statement of the question upon which an opinion is required, and accompanied by all documents likely to throw light upon the question.

Article 66

1. The Registrar shall forthwith give notice of the request for an advisory opinion to all states entitled to appear before the Court.
2. The Registrar shall also, by means of a special and direct communication, notify any state entitled to appear before the Court or international organization considered by the Court, or, should it not be sitting, by the President, as likely to be able to furnish information on the question, that the Court will be prepared to receive, within a time limit to be fixed by the President, written statements, or to hear, at a public sitting to be held for the purpose, oral statements relating to the question.
3. Should any such state entitled to appear before the Court have failed to receive the special communication referred to in paragraph 2 of this Article, such state may express a desire to submit a written statement or to be heard; and the Court will decide.
4. States and organizations having presented written or oral statements or both shall be permitted to comment on the statements made by other states or organizations in the form, to the extent, and within the time limits which the Court, or, should it not be sitting, the President, shall decide in each particular case. Accordingly, the Registrar shall in due time communicate any such written statements to states and organizations having submitted similar statements.

Article 67

The Court shall deliver its advisory opinions in open court, notice having been given to the Secretary-General and to the representatives of Members of the United Nations, of other states and of international organizations immediately concerned.

Article 68

In the exercise of its advisory functions the Court shall further be guided by the provisions of the present Statute which apply in contentious cases to the extent to which it recognizes them to be applicable.

Chapter V
AMENDMENT

Article 69

Amendments to the present Statute shall be effected by the same procedure as is provided by the Charter of the United Nations for amendments to that Charter, subject however to any provisions which the General Assembly upon recommendation of the Security Council may adopt concerning the participation of states which are parties to the present Statute but are not Members of the United Nations.

Article 70

The Court shall have power to propose such amendments to the present Statute as it may deem necessary, through written communications to the Secretary-General, for consideration in conformity with the provisions of Article 69.

Appendix III

Structure of the United Nations

General Assembly

The General Assembly is composed of all the Members of the United Nations.

SESSIONS
Resumed fifty-seventh session: 29 January–15 September 2003.
Fifty-eighth session: 16 September–23 December 2003 (suspended).
Resumed tenth emergency special session: 19 September, 20-21 October and 8 December 2003 (suspended).

OFFICERS
Resumed fifty-seventh session
President: Jan Kavan (Czech Republic).
Vice-Presidents: Austria, Bahrain, Barbados, Chad, China, Ecuador, Egypt, Ethiopia, France, Gambia, Indonesia, Kazakhstan, Mexico, Portugal, Qatar, Russian Federation, Swaziland, Togo, United Kingdom, United States, Viet Nam.

Fifty-eighth and tenth emergency special sessions
President: Julian R. Hunte (Saint Lucia).[1]
Vice-Presidents:[2] Cape Verde, China, Equatorial Guinea, France, Haiti, Honduras, Iran, Luxembourg, Madagascar, Malawi, Morocco, Myanmar, Netherlands, Russian Federation, Senegal, Slovenia, Tajikistan, Turkmenistan, United Kingdom, United States, Yemen.

The Assembly has four types of committees: (1) Main Committees; (2) procedural committees; (3) standing committees; (4) subsidiary and ad hoc bodies. In addition, it convenes conferences to deal with specific subjects.

Main Committees

Six Main Committees have been established as follows:

Disarmament and International Security Committee (First Committee)
Special Political and Decolonization Committee (Fourth Committee)
Economic and Financial Committee (Second Committee)
Social, Humanitarian and Cultural Committee (Third Committee)
Administrative and Budgetary Committee (Fifth Committee)
Legal Committee (Sixth Committee)

The General Assembly may constitute other committees, on which all Members of the United Nations have the right to be represented.

OFFICERS OF THE MAIN COMMITTEES

Resumed fifty-seventh session

Fourth Committee[3]
Chairman: Graham Maitland (South Africa).
Vice-Chairpersons: Mansour Ayyad Sh. A. Al-Otaibi (Kuwait), Margaret Hughes Ferrari (Saint Vincent and the Grenadines), Debra Price (Canada).
Rapporteur: Andrej Droba (Slovakia).

Third Committee[3]
Chairman: Christian Wenaweser (Liechtenstein).
Vice-Chairpersons: Ilham Ibrahim Mohamed Ahmed (Sudan), Loreto Leyton (Chile), Toru Morikawa (Japan).
Rapporteur: Oksana Boiko (Ukraine).

Fifth Committee[3]
Chairman: Murari Raj Sharma (Nepal).
Vice-Chairpersons: Bogdan C. Dragulescu (Romania), Guillermo Kendall (Argentina), Michel Tilemans (Belgium).
Rapporteur: Haile Selassie Getachew (Ethiopia).

Fifty-eighth session[4]

First Committee
Chairman: Jarmo Sareva (Finland).
Vice-Chairmen: Anouar Ben Youssef (Tunisia), Suriya Chindawongse (Thailand), Ionut Suseanu (Romania).
Rapporteur: Miguel Carbo (Ecuador).

Fourth Committee
Chairman: Enrique Loedel (Uruguay).
Vice-Chairmen: Ibrahim Assaf (Lebanon), Isaac C. Lamba (Malawi), Jasna Ognjanovac (Croatia).
Rapporteur: Damian Cole (Ireland).

Second Committee
Chairman: Iftekhar Ahmed Chowdhury (Bangladesh).
Vice-Chairpersons: Ulrika Cronenberg-Mossberg (Sweden), Henri S. Raubenheimer (South Africa), Irena Zubcevic (Croatia).
Rapporteur: José Alberto Briz Gutiérrez (Guatemala).

Third Committee
Chairman: Martin Belinga-Eboutou (Cameroon).
Vice-Chairmen: Michiel Maertens (Belgium), Beatriz Londoño (Colombia), Juraj Priputen (Slovakia).
Rapporteur: Abdullah Eid Salman Al-Sulaiti (Qatar).

Fifth Committee
Chairman: Hynek Kmonícek (Czech Republic).
Vice-Chairmen: Abdelmalek Bouheddou (Algeria), Ronald Elkhuizen (Netherlands), Asdrúbal Pulido León (Venezuela).
Rapporteur: Fouad A. Rajeh (Saudi Arabia).

Sixth Committee
Chairman: Lauro Liboon Baja, Jr. (Philippines).
Vice-Chairmen: Tal Becker (Israel), Allieu Ibrahim Kanu (Sierra Leone), Gaile Anne Ramoutar (Trinidad and Tobago).
Rapporteur: Metod Spacek (Slovakia).

Procedural committees

General Committee
The General Committee consists of the President of the General Assembly, as Chairman, the 21 Vice-Presidents and the Chairmen of the six Main Committees.

Structure of the United Nations

Credentials Committee

The Credentials Committee consists of nine members appointed by the General Assembly on the proposal of the President.

Resumed fifty-seventh session
Argentina, Barbados, Belgium, China, Mali, Namibia, Papua New Guinea, Russian Federation, United States.

Fifty-eighth session[5]
Antigua and Barbuda, Cape Verde, China, Costa Rica, Ethiopia, Fiji, New Zealand, Russian Federation, United States.

Standing committees

The two standing committees consist of experts appointed in their individual capacity for three-year terms.

Advisory Committee on Administrative and Budgetary Questions (ACABQ)

To serve until 31 December 2003: Andrzej T. Abraszewski (Poland); Manlan Narcisse Ahounou (Côte d'Ivoire); Felipe Mabilangan (Philippines); E. Besley Maycock, *Vice-Chairman* (Barbados); C. S. M. Mselle, *Chairman* (United Republic of Tanzania).

To serve until 31 December 2004: Michiel W. H. Crom (Netherlands); Nazareth A. Incera (Costa Rica); Rajat Saha (India); Sun Minqin (China); Nicholas A. Thorne (United Kingdom);[6] Jun Yamazaki (Japan).[7]

To serve until 31 December 2005: Homero Luis Hernandez (Dominican Republic); Vladimir V. Kuznetsov (Russian Federation); Thomas Mazet (Germany); Susan M. McLurg (United States); Mounir Zahran (Egypt).

On 17 December 2003 (dec. 58/405 B), the General Assembly appointed the following for a three-year term beginning on 1 January 2004 to fill the vacancies occurring on 31 December 2003: Andrzej T. Abraszewski (Poland), Manlan Narcisse Ahounou (Côte d'Ivoire), Collen V. Kelapile (Botswana), E. Besley Maycock (Barbados), Murari Raj Sharma (Nepal).

Committee on Contributions

To serve until 31 December 2003: Kenshiro Akimoto (Japan); Petru Dumitriu (Romania); Chinmaya Gharekhan, *Vice-Chairman* (India); Ihor V. Humenny (Ukraine); Gebhard Benjamin Kandanga (Namibia); David A. Leis (United States).

To serve until 31 December 2004: Henry S. Fox (Australia);[8] Bernardo Greiver (Uruguay); Hassan Mohammed Hassan (Nigeria); Eduardo Iglesias (Argentina); Omar Kadiri (Morocco); Eduardo Manuel da Fonseca Fernandes Ramos (Portugal).

To serve until 31 December 2005: Alvaro Gurgel de Alencar Netto (Brazil); Sergei I. Mareyev (Russian Federation); Bernard Meijerman (Netherlands); Hae-yun Park (Republic of Korea); Ugo Sessi, *Chairman* (Italy); Wu Gang (China).

On 17 December 2003 (dec. 58/412), the General Assembly appointed the following for a three-year term beginning on 1 January 2004 to fill the vacancies occurring on 31 December 2003: Kenshiro Akimoto (Japan), Meshal Al-Mansour (Kuwait), Petru Dumitriu (Romania), Haile Selassie Getachew (Ethiopia), Ihor V. Humenny (Ukraine), David A. Leis (United States).

Subsidiary and ad hoc bodies

The following is a list of subsidiary and ad hoc bodies functioning in 2003, including the number of members, dates of meetings/sessions in 2003, document numbers of reports (which generally provide specific information on membership), and relevant decision numbers pertaining to elections. (For other related bodies, see p. 1565.)

Ad Hoc Committee on a Comprehensive and Integral International Convention on Protection and Promotion of the Rights and Dignity of Persons with Disabilities

Session: Second, New York, 16-27 June
Chairman: Luis Gallegos Chiriboga (Ecuador)
Membership: Open to all Member States and observers of the United Nations
Report: A/58/118 & Corr.1

Ad Hoc Committee established by General Assembly resolution 51/210 of 17 December 1996

Session: Seventh, New York, 31 March–2 April
Chairman: Rohan Perera (Sri Lanka)
Membership: Open to all States Members of the United Nations or members of the specialized agencies or of IAEA
Report: A/58/37

Ad Hoc Committee on the Indian Ocean

Meetings: New York, 3 February (organizational), 8 July (session)
Chairman: Chithambaranathan Mahendran (Sri Lanka)
Membership: 43
Report: A/58/29

Ad Hoc Committee on an International Convention against the Reproductive Cloning of Human Beings

Session: Did not meet in 2003
Membership: Open to all States Members of the United Nations or members of the specialized agencies or of IAEA

Ad Hoc Committee on Jurisdictional Immunities of States and Their Property

Session: Second, New York, 24-28 February
Chairman: Gerhard Hafner (Austria)
Membership: Open to all States Members of the United Nations and members of the specialized agencies
Report: A/58/22

Ad Hoc Committee for the Negotiation of a Convention against Corruption

Sessions: Fourth, fifth, sixth and seventh, Vienna, 13-24 January, 10-21 March, 21 July–8 August and 29 September–1 October
Chairman: Héctor Charry Samper (Colombia)
Membership: Open to all States Members of the United Nations or members of the specialized agencies or of IAEA
Report: A/58/422 & Add.1

Ad Hoc Committee on the Scope of Legal Protection under the Convention on the Safety of United Nations and Associated Personnel

Session: Second, New York, 24-28 March
Chairman: Christian Wenaweser (Liechtenstein)
Membership: Open to all States Members of the United Nations or members of the specialized agencies or of IAEA
Report: A/58/52

Advisory Committee on the United Nations Programme of Assistance in the Teaching, Study, Dissemination and Wider Appreciation of International Law

Session: Thirty-eighth, New York, 16 October
Chairman: Thomas Kwesi Quartey (Ghana)
Membership: 25
Report: A/58/446

Board of Auditors

Sessions: Fifty-seventh, New York, 26-27 June; special, Vienna, 19 November
Chairman: François Logerot (France)
Membership: 3
Decision: GA 58/413

Committee on Conferences
Sessions: New York, 22 April (organizational), 8, 10 and 12 September (substantive)
Chairman: Mohammad Tal (Jordan)
Membership: 21
Report: A/58/32
Decisions: GA 57/413 B, 58/409

Committee on the Exercise of the Inalienable Rights of the Palestinian People
Meetings: Throughout the year
Chairman: Papa Louis Fall (Senegal)
Membership: 24
Report: A/58/35

Committee on Information
Session: Twenty-fifth, New York, 28 April–9 May
Chairman: Iftekhar Ahmed Chowdhury (Bangladesh)
Membership: 99 (102 from 9 December)
Report: A/58/21
Decision: GA 58/410

Committee on the Peaceful Uses of Outer Space
Session: Forty-sixth, Vienna, 11-20 June
Chairman: Raimundo González (Chile)
Membership: 65
Report: A/58/20

Committee for Programme and Coordination (CPC)
Sessions: Forty-third, New York, 5 May (organizational), 9 June–3 July and 9 July (substantive)
Chairman: Seyed Morteza Mirmohammad (Iran)
Membership: 34
Report: A/58/16
Decisions: ESC 2003/201 B, GA 57/405 B, 58/408

Committee on Relations with the Host Country
Meetings: New York, 13 February, 21 May, 3 September, 9 and 16 October
Chairman: Sotirios Zackheos (Cyprus)
Membership: 19 (including the United States as host country)
Report: A/58/26

Committee for the United Nations Population Award
Meetings: New York, 26 March, 9 April
Chairman: Jean Claude Alexandre (Haiti)
Membership: 10 (plus 5 honorary members, the Secretary-General and the UNFPA Executive Director)
Report: A/58/151
Decisions: ESC 2003/201 B & E

Disarmament Commission
Sessions: New York, 31 March–17 April (substantive), 6 November (organizational)
Chairman: Mario E. Maiolini (Italy)
Membership: All UN Members
Reports: A/58/42, A/59/42

High-level Committee on the Review of Technical Cooperation among Developing Countries
Sessions: Organizational meeting, New York, 13 May; thirteenth, New York, 27-30 May
President: Boniface Chidyausiku (Zimbabwe)
Membership: All States participating in UNDP
Report: A/58/39

International Civil Service Commission (ICSC)
Sessions: Fifty-sixth, Rome, Italy, 31 March–18 April; fifty-seventh, New York, 14-25 July
Chairman: Mohsen Bel Hadj Amor (Tunisia)
Membership: 15
Report: A/58/30

ADVISORY COMMITTEE ON POST ADJUSTMENT QUESTIONS
Session: Twenty-fifth, New York, 27 January–3 February
Chairman: Eugeniusz Wyzner (Poland)
Membership: 6

International Law Commission
Session: Fifty-fifth, Geneva, 5 May–6 June and 7 July–8 August
Chairman: Enrique Candioti (Argentina)
Membership: 34
Report: A/58/10

Investments Committee
Meetings: New York, 18-19 February, 12-13 May, 19 September, 24 November
Chairman: Emmanuel Noi Omaboe (Ghana)
Membership: 9
Decision: GA 58/414

Joint Advisory Group on the International Trade Centre UNCTAD/WTO
Session: Thirty-sixth, Geneva, 28 April–2 May
Chairman: Faizel Ismail (South Africa)
Membership: Open to all States members of UNCTAD and all members of WTO
Report: ITC/AG(XXXVI)/195

Joint Inspection Unit (JIU)
Chairman: Armando Duque González (Colombia)
Membership: 11
Report: A/59/34
Decision: GA 57/416

Office of the United Nations High Commissioner for Refugees (UNHCR)

EXECUTIVE COMMITTEE OF THE HIGH COMMISSIONER'S PROGRAMME
Session: Fifty-fourth, Geneva, 29 September–3 October
Chairman: Jean-Marc Boulgaris (Switzerland)
Membership: 61
Report: A/58/12/Add.1
Decision: ESC 2003/201 B

High Commissioner: Ruud Lubbers[9]

Panel of External Auditors
Membership: Members of the UN Board of Auditors and the appointed external auditors of the specialized agencies and IAEA

Special Committee on the Charter of the United Nations and on the Strengthening of the Role of the Organization
Meetings: New York, 7-16 April
Chairman: Jagdish Dharamchand Koonjul (Mauritius)
Membership: Open to all States Members of the United Nations
Report: A/58/33

Special Committee to Investigate Israeli Practices Affecting the Human Rights of the Palestinian People and Other Arabs of the Occupied Territories
Meetings: Geneva, 10-12 June; Cairo, Egypt, 14-16 June; Amman, Jordan, 18-20 June; Damascus, Syrian Arab Republic, 21-23 June
Chairperson: C. Mahendran (Sri Lanka)
Membership: 3
Report: A/58/311

Special Committee on Peacekeeping Operations
Meetings: New York, 3-17 March
Chairperson: Arthur C. I. Mbanefo (Nigeria)
Membership: 113
Report: A/57/767

Structure of the United Nations

Special Committee to Select the Winners of the United Nations Human Rights Prize
Meeting: New York, 10 December
Chairman: Julian R. Hunte (Saint Lucia) (President of the General Assembly)
Membership: 5

Special Committee on the Situation with regard to the Implementation of the Declaration on the Granting of Independence to Colonial Countries and Peoples
Session: New York, 12 February and 11 April (first part), 2, 4, 9, 12, 16, 18 and 23 June (second part)
Chairman: Earl Stephen Huntley (Saint Lucia)
Membership: 23 (24 from 9 December)
Report: A/58/23
Decision: GA 58/411 A

United Nations Administrative Tribunal
Sessions: Geneva, 23 June–25 July; New York, 20 October–21 November
President: Julio Barboza (Argentina)
Membership: 7
Report: A/INF/58/7
Decision: GA 58/415

United Nations Capital Development Fund (UNCDF)

EXECUTIVE BOARD
The UNDP/UNFPA Executive Board acts as the Executive Board of the Fund.

Managing Director: Mark Malloch Brown (UNDP Administrator)

United Nations Commission on International Trade Law (UNCITRAL)
Session: Thirty-sixth, Vienna, 30 June–11 July
Chairman: Tore Wiwen-Nilsson (Sweden)
Membership: 36 (60 from 17 November)
Report: A/58/17
Decision: GA 58/407

United Nations Conciliation Commission for Palestine
Membership: 3
Report: A/58/256

United Nations Conference on Trade and Development (UNCTAD)
Membership: Open to all States Members of the United Nations or members of the specialized agencies or of IAEA

Secretary-General of UNCTAD: Rubens Ricupero[10]

TRADE AND DEVELOPMENT BOARD
Sessions: Twentieth special, 27 January; thirty-first executive, 10 March; thirty-second executive, 28 July; fiftieth, 6-17 October; all in Geneva
President: Dimiter Tzantchev (Bulgaria) (twentieth special and thirty-first and thirty-second executive sessions), Sha Zukang (China) (fiftieth session)
Membership: Open to all States members of UNCTAD
Report: A/58/15

SUBSIDIARY ORGANS OF THE TRADE AND DEVELOPMENT BOARD

COMMISSION ON ENTERPRISE,
BUSINESS FACILITATION AND DEVELOPMENT
Session: Seventh, Geneva, 24-27 February
Chairperson: Nathan Irumba (Uganda)
Membership: Open to all States members of UNCTAD
Report: TD/B/EX(31)/5

COMMISSION ON INVESTMENT,
TECHNOLOGY AND RELATED FINANCIAL ISSUES
Session: Seventh, Geneva, 20-24 January
President: Vladimir Malevich (Belarus)
Membership: Open to all States members of UNCTAD
Report: TD/B/EX(31)/3

Intergovernmental Group of Experts on Competition Law and Policy
Session: Fifth, Geneva, 2-4 July
Chairperson: Andreas Mundt (Germany)
Membership: Open to all States members of UNCTAD
Report: TD/B/COM.2/52

Intergovernmental Working Group of Experts on International Standards of Accounting and Reporting
Session: Twentieth, Geneva, 29 September–1 October
Chairperson: Nelson Carvalho (Brazil)
Membership: 34
Report: TD/B/COM.2/58
Decisions: ESC 2003/201 B & E

COMMISSION ON TRADE IN
GOODS AND SERVICES, AND COMMODITIES
Session: Seventh, Geneva, 3-6 February
Chairperson: Toufiq Ali (Bangladesh)
Membership: Open to all States members of UNCTAD
Report: TD/B/EX(31)/4

WORKING PARTY ON THE
MEDIUM-TERM PLAN AND THE PROGRAMME BUDGET
Session: Fortieth, Geneva, 13-17 January (first part) and 21-22 May (second part)
Chairperson: I. Afanassiev (Russian Federation)
Membership: Open to all States members of UNCTAD
Reports: TD/B/EX(31)/2, TD/B/EX(32)/3

United Nations Development Fund for Women (UNIFEM)

CONSULTATIVE COMMITTEE
Session: Forty-third, New York, 18-20 February
Chairperson: Koen Davidse, (Netherlands)
Membership: 5
Decision: GA 58/416

Executive Director of UNIFEM: Noeleen Heyzer

United Nations Environment Programme (UNEP)

GOVERNING COUNCIL
Session: Twenty-second/Global Ministerial Environment Forum, Nairobi, Kenya, 3-7 February
President: Ruhakana Rugunda (Uganda)
Membership: 58
Report: A/58/25
Decision: GA 58/404

Executive Director of UNEP: Klaus Töpfer

United Nations Human Settlements Programme (UN-Habitat)

GOVERNING COUNCIL
Session: Nineteenth, Nairobi, Kenya, 5-9 May
President: Bo Göransson (Sweden)
Membership: 58
Report: A/58/8
Decisions: ESC 2003/201 B & E

Executive Director of UN-Habitat: Anna Kajumulo Tibaijuka

United Nations Institute for Disarmament Research (UNIDIR)

BOARD OF TRUSTEES
Sessions: Fortieth, New York, 5-7 February; forty-first, Geneva, 16-18 July
Chairman: Kostyantyn Gryshchenko (Ukraine)

Membership: 22, plus 1 ex-officio member (Director of UNIDIR)
Report: A/58/316

Director of UNIDIR: Patricia Lewis
Deputy Director: Christophe Carle

United Nations Institute for Training and Research (UNITAR)

BOARD OF TRUSTEES
Session: Forty-first, Geneva, 29 April–1 May
Chairman: Arthur C. I. Mbanefo (Nigeria)
Membership: Not less than 11 and not more than 30, plus 4 ex-officio members

Executive Director of UNITAR: Marcel A. Boisard

United Nations Joint Staff Pension Board
Session: Did not meet in 2003
Membership: 33

United Nations Relief and Works Agency for Palestine Refugees in the Near East (UNRWA)

ADVISORY COMMISSION OF UNRWA
Meeting: Amman, Jordan, 25 September
Chairperson: Koichi Obata (Japan)
Membership: 10
Report: A/58/13 & Corr.1

WORKING GROUP ON THE FINANCING OF UNRWA
Meetings: New York, 10 September, 17 and 20 October
Chairman: Mehmet U. Pamir (Turkey)
Membership: 9
Report: A/58/450

Commissioner-General of UNRWA: Peter Hansen
Deputy Commissioner-General: Karen Koning AbuZayd

United Nations Scientific Committee on the Effects of Atomic Radiation
Session: Fifty-first, Vienna, 27-31 January
Chairperson: Joyce L. Lipsztein (Brazil)
Membership: 21
Report: A/58/46

United Nations Staff Pension Committee
Meeting: New York and Geneva (via videoconference), 30 April
Chairperson: Jean-Michel Jakobowicz (France)
Membership: 12 members and 8 alternates
Decisions: GA 57/411 B & C

United Nations University (UNU)

COUNCIL OF THE UNITED NATIONS UNIVERSITY
Session: Fiftieth, Tokyo, 1-5 December
Chairperson: Elisabeth J. Croll (United Kingdom)
Membership: 24 (plus 3 ex-officio members and the UNU Rector)
Report: A/59/31

Rector of the University: Johannes A. van Ginkel

United Nations Voluntary Fund for Indigenous Populations

BOARD OF TRUSTEES
Session: Sixteenth, Geneva, 31 March–4 April
Chairperson: Victoria Tauli-Corpuz (Philippines)
Membership: 5
Report: E/CN.4/Sub.2/AC.4/2003/12

United Nations Voluntary Fund for Victims of Torture

BOARD OF TRUSTEES
Session: Twenty-second, Geneva, 12-28 May
Chairman: Jaap Walkate (Netherlands)
Membership: 5
Report: A/58/284

United Nations Voluntary Trust Fund on Contemporary Forms of Slavery

BOARD OF TRUSTEES
Session: Eighth, Geneva, 20-24 January
Chairperson: Swami Agnivesh (India)
Membership: 5
Report: A/58/306

Conferences

International Ministerial Conference of Landlocked and Transit Developing Countries and Donor Countries and International Financial and Development Institutions on Transit Transport Cooperation
Session: Almaty, Kazakhstan, 28-29 August
President: Kassymzhomart K. Tokaev (Kazakhstan)
Attendance: 82 States, European Community, ECA, ECE, ESCAP, UNDP, UNCTAD, UN Capital Development Fund, World Bank, IMF and 12 intergovernmental organizations; Palestine (as observer)
Report: A/CONF.202/3

World Summit on the Information Society
Session: Geneva, 10-12 December (first phase)
President: Pascal Couchepin (Switzerland)
Attendance: 175 States, European Community, regional commissions, UN bodies and programmes, regional organizations, specialized agencies, intergovernmental organizations and non-governmental organizations
Report: WSIS-03/GENEVA/9(Rev.1)-E

Security Council

The Security Council consists of 15 Member States of the United Nations, in accordance with the provisions of Article 23 of the United Nations Charter as amended in 1965.

MEMBERS
Permanent members: China, France, Russian Federation, United Kingdom, United States.
Non-permanent members: Angola, Bulgaria, Cameroon, Chile, Germany, Guinea, Mexico, Pakistan, Spain, Syrian Arab Republic.

On 23 October 2003 (dec. 58/403), the General Assembly elected Algeria, Benin, Brazil, the Philippines and Romania for a two-year term beginning on 1 January 2004, to replace Bulgaria, Cameroon, Guinea, Mexico and the Syrian Arab Republic whose terms of office were to expire on 31 December 2003.

PRESIDENT
The presidency of the Council rotates monthly, according to the English alphabetical listing of its member States. The following served as President during 2003:

Structure of the United Nations

Month	Member	Representative
January	France	Jean-Marc de La Sablière
		Dominique Galouzeau de Villepin
February	Germany	Gunter Pleuger
		Joschka Fischer
March	Guinea	Mamady Traoré
		François Lonsény Fall
April	Mexico	Adolfo Aguilar Zinser
		Luis Ernesto Derbez
May	Pakistan	Munir Akram
		Khurshid M. Kasuri
June	Russian Federation	Sergey V. Lavrov
July	Spain	Inocencio F. Arias
		Ana Palacio
August	Syrian Arab Republic	Mikhail Wehbe
September	United Kingdom	Sir Emyr Jones Parry
		Jack Straw
October	United States	John D. Negroponte
November	Angola	Ismael Abraão Gaspar Martins
December	Bulgaria	Stefan Tafrov
		Solomon Passy

Military Staff Committee

The Military Staff Committee consists of the chiefs of staff of the permanent members of the Security Council or their representatives. It meets fortnightly.

Standing committees

Each of the three standing committees of the Security Council is composed of representatives of all Council members:

Committee of Experts (to examine the provisional rules of procedure of the Council and any other matters entrusted to it by the Council)
Committee on the Admission of New Members
Committee on Council Meetings Away from Headquarters

Subsidiary bodies

Counter-Terrorism Committee (CTC)
Chairman: Sir Jeremy Greenstock (United Kingom) (until April), Inocencio F. Arias (Spain) (from 4 April).

United Nations Compensation Commission
Executive Secretary: Rolf Goran Knutsson.

United Nations Monitoring, Verification and Inspection Commission (UNMOVIC)
Executive Chairman: Hans Blix (until 30 June), Demetrius Perricos (Acting) (from 1 July).

Peacekeeping operations

United Nations Truce Supervision Organization (UNTSO)
Chief of Staff: Major General Carl Dodd.

United Nations Military Observer Group in India and Pakistan (UNMOGIP)
Chief Military Observer: Major General Pertti Juhani Puonti.

United Nations Peacekeeping Force in Cyprus (UNFICYP)
Special Adviser to the Secretary-General on Cyprus: Alvaro de Soto.

Acting Special Representative of the Secretary-General and Chief of Mission: Zbigniew Wlosowicz.
Force Commander: Lieutenant General Jin Ha Hwang.

United Nations Disengagement Observer Force (UNDOF)
Force Commander: Major General Bo Wranker (until 12 August), Major General Franciszek Gagor (from 13 August).

United Nations Interim Force in Lebanon (UNIFIL)
Personal Representative of the Secretary-General for Southern Lebanon: Staffan de Mistura.
Force Commander: Major General Lalit Mohan Tewari.

United Nations Iraq-Kuwait Observation Mission (UNIKOM)[11]
Force Commander: Major General Miguel Angel Moreno (until January), Major General Franciszek Gagor (from 17 January).

United Nations Mission for the Referendum in Western Sahara (MINURSO)
Personal Envoy of the Secretary-General: James A. Baker III.
Special Representative of the Secretary-General and Chief of Mission: William Lacy Swing (until 30 June), Alvaro de Soto (from 8 August).
Force Commander: Major General Gyorgy Száraz.

United Nations Observer Mission in Georgia (UNOMIG)
Special Representative of the Secretary-General and Head of Mission: Heidi Tagliavini.
Chief Military Observer: Major General Kazi Ashfaq Ahmed.

United Nations Interim Administration Mission in Kosovo (UNMIK)
Special Representative of the Secretary-General: Harri Holkeri.
Principal Deputy Special Representative: Charles Brayshaw.
Deputy Special Representative for Police and Justice: Jean-Christian Cady.
Deputy Special Representative for Civil Administration: Francesco Bastagli.

United Nations Mission in Sierra Leone (UNAMSIL)
Special Representative of the Secretary-General and Head of Mission: Oluyemi Adeniji (until November), Daudi Ngelautwa Mwakawago (from 1 December).
Deputy Special Representative: Alan Claude Doss.
Force Commander: Lieutenant General Daniel Ishmael Opande (until September), Major General Sajjad Akram (from 1 October).

United Nations Organization Mission in the Democratic Republic of the Congo (MONUC)
Special Envoy of the Secretary-General: Mustapha Niasse.
Special Representative of the Secretary-General and Chief of Mission: Amos Namanga Ngongi (until 30 June), William Lacy Swing (from 1 July).
Deputy Special Representatives: Behrooz Sadry (from 17 February), Lena Sundh.
Force Commander: Major General Mountaga Diallo.

United Nations Mission in Ethiopia and Eritrea (UNMEE)
Special Representative of the Secretary-General: Legwaila Joseph Legwaila.
Deputy Special Representatives: Cheikh Tidiane Gaye, Angela Kane.
Force Commander: Major General Robert Gordon.

United Nations Mission of Support in East Timor (UNMISET)
Special Representative of the Secretary-General and Head of Mission: Kamalesh Sharma.
Deputy Special Representative: Sukehiro Hasegawa.
Force Commander: Major General Tan Huck Gim (until 30 August), Lieutenant General Khairuddin Mat Yusof (from 31 August).
Chief Military Observer: Brigadier General Pedro Rocha Pena Madeira.

United Nations Mission in Côte d'Ivoire (UNMICI)[12]
Special Representative of the Secretary-General and Chief of Mission: Albert Tévoédjré.
Chief Military Liaison Officer: Brigadier General Abdul Hafiz.

United Nations Mission in Liberia (UNMIL)[13]
Special Representative of the Secretary-General and Head of Mission: Jacques Paul Klein.
Deputy Special Representative: Souren Seraydarian.
Force Commander: Lieutenant General Daniel Ishmael Opande.

Political, peace-building and other missions

United Nations Office in Burundi (UNOB)
Special Representative of the Secretary-General and Head of UNOB: Berhanu Dinka.

United Nations Political Office for Somalia (UNPOS)
Representative of the Secretary-General and Head of UNPOS: Winston A. Tubman.

United Nations Peace-building Support Office in Liberia (UNOL)
Representative of the Secretary-General and Head of UNOL: Abou Moussa.

Office of the Special Representative of the Secretary-General for the Great Lakes Region
Special Representative: Ibrahima Fall.

United Nations Political Office in Bougainville (UNPOB)
Head of Office: Noel Sinclair.

United Nations Peace-building Support Office in Guinea-Bissau (UNOGBIS)
Representative of the Secretary-General and Head of UNOGBIS: David Stephen.

Office of the United Nations Special Coordinator for the Middle East (UNSCO)
Special Coordinator for the Middle East Peace Process and Personal Representative of the Secretary-General to the Palestine Liberation Organization and the Palestinian Authority: Terje Roed-Larsen.

United Nations Peace-building Office in the Central African Republic (BONUCA)
Representative of the Secretary-General and Head of BONUCA: General Lamine Cissé.

United Nations Tajikistan Office of Peace-building (UNTOP)
Representative of the Secretary-General: Vladimir Sotirov.

Office of the Special Representative of the Secretary-General for West Africa
Special Representative of the Secretary-General: Ahmedou Ould-Abdallah.

United Nations Assistance Mission in Afghanistan (UNAMA)
Special Representative of the Secretary-General: Lakhdar Brahimi.
Deputy Special Representative for Political Affairs: Jean Arnault.
Deputy Special Representative for Humanitarian Affairs: Nigel Fisher (until June).

United Nations Mission in Angola (UNMA)[14]
Special Representative of the Secretary-General: Ibrahim Gambari.

United Nations Assistance Mission for Iraq (UNAMI)[15]
Head of Mission: Ross Mountain (from 5 December).

Economic and Social Council

The Economic and Social Council consists of 54 Member States of the United Nations, elected by the General Assembly, each for a three-year term, in accordance with the provisions of Article 61 of the United Nations Charter as amended in 1965 and 1973.

MEMBERS

To serve until 31 December 2003: Andorra, Argentina, Brazil, Egypt, Ethiopia, Georgia, Iran, Italy, Nepal, Netherlands, Nigeria, Pakistan, Peru, Republic of Korea, Romania, South Africa, Uganda, United States.

To serve until 31 December 2004: Australia, Bhutan, Burundi, Chile, China, El Salvador, Finland, Ghana, Guatemala, Hungary, India, Libyan Arab Jamahiriya, Qatar, Russian Federation, Sweden, Ukraine, United Kingdom, Zimbabwe.

To serve until 31 December 2005: Azerbaijan, Benin, Congo, Cuba, Ecuador, France, Germany, Greece, Ireland, Jamaica, Japan, Kenya, Malaysia, Mozambique, Nicaragua, Portugal, Saudi Arabia, Senegal.

On 11 November 2003 (dec. 58/406), the General Assembly elected the following for a three-year term beginning on 1 January 2004 to fill the vacancies occurring on 31 December 2003: Armenia, Bangladesh, Belgium, Belize, Canada, Colombia, Indonesia, Italy, Mauritius, Namibia, Nigeria, Panama, Poland, Republic of Korea, Tunisia, United Arab Emirates, United Republic of Tanzania, United States.

By the same decision, the Assembly elected Turkey for the remaining term of office of Portugal, beginning on 1 January 2004.

SESSIONS

Organizational session for 2003: New York, 15, 28, 30 and 31 January.

Resumed organizational session for 2003: New York, 5 and 25 March, 29 April, 1 and 27 May and 24 June.

Special high-level meeting with the Bretton Woods institutions and the World Trade Organization: New York, 14 April.

Substantive session of 2003: Geneva, 30 June–25 July.

Resumed substantive session of 2003: New York, 22 August, 31 October and 19 December.

OFFICERS

President: Gert Rosenthal (Guatemala).
Vice-Presidents: Abdul Mejid Hussein (Ethiopia), Valery P. Kuchinsky (Ukraine), Marjatta Rasi (Finland), Murari Raj Sharma (Nepal).

Subsidiary and other related organs

SUBSIDIARY ORGANS

The Economic and Social Council may, at each session, set up committees or working groups, of the whole or of limited membership, and refer to them any items on the agenda for study and report.

Other subsidiary organs reporting to the Council consist of functional commissions, regional commissions, standing committees, expert bodies and ad hoc bodies.

The inter-agency United Nations System Chief Executives Board for Coordination also reports to the Council.

Structure of the United Nations

Functional commissions

Commission on Crime Prevention and Criminal Justice
Session: Twelfth, Vienna, 13-22 May
Chairman: Peter Poptchev (Bulgaria)
Membership: 40
Report: E/2003/30
Decision: ESC 2003/201 B

Commission on Human Rights
Sessions: Fifty-ninth, Geneva, 20 January and 17 March–25 April
Chairperson: Najat Al-Hajjaji (Libyan Arab Jamahiriya)
Membership: 53
Report: E/2003/23
Decision: ESC 2003/201 B

SUBCOMMISSION ON THE PROMOTION
AND PROTECTION OF HUMAN RIGHTS
Session: Fifty-fifth, Geneva, 28 July–15 August
Chairperson: Halima Warzazi (Morocco)
Membership: 26
Report: E/CN.4/2004/2

Commission on Narcotic Drugs
Session: Forty-sixth, Vienna, 8-17 April and 26-27 November
Chairman: Patricia Olamendi (Mexico)
Membership: 53
Report: E/2003/28/Rev.1
Decision: ESC 2003/201 B

Commission on Population and Development
Session: Thirty-sixth, New York, 31 March–4 April
Chairman: Gediminas Šerkšnys (Lithuania)
Membership: 47
Report: E/2003/25
Decision: ESC 2003/201 B

Commission on Science and Technology for Development
Session: Sixth, Geneva, 5-9 May
Chairperson: Vijaya Kumar (Sri Lanka)
Membership: 33
Report: E/2003/31
Decisions: ESC 2003/201 B & E

Commission for Social Development
Session: Forty-first, New York, 10-21 February
Chairperson: Iftekhar Ahmed Chowdhury (Bangladesh)
Membership: 46
Report: E/2003/26
Decision: ESC 2003/201 B

Commission on the Status of Women
Session: Forty-seventh, New York, 3-14 and 25 March
Chairperson: Othman Jerandi (Tunisia)
Membership: 45
Report: E/2003/27
Decision: ESC 2003/201 B

Commission on Sustainable Development
Session: Eleventh, New York, 27 January and 28 April–9 May
Chairperson: Valli Moosa (South Africa)
Membership: 53
Report: E/2003/29
Decision: ESC 2003/201 B

Statistical Commission
Session: Thirty-fourth, New York, 4-7 March
Chairman: Tamás Mellár (Hungary)
Membership: 24
Report: E/2003/24
Decision: ESC 2003/201 B

United Nations Forum on Forests
Session: Third, Geneva, 26 May–6 June
Chairman: Hossein Moeini Meybodi (Iran)
Membership: Open to all States Members of the United Nations and members of the specialized agencies
Report: E/2003/42

Regional commissions

Economic Commission for Africa (ECA)
Session: Thirty-sixth session of the Commission/Conference of African Ministers of Finance, Planning and Economic Development, Addis Ababa, Ethiopia, 29 May–1 June
Chairman: Trevor Manuel (South Africa)
Membership: 53

Economic Commission for Europe (ECE)
Session: Fifty-eighth, Geneva, 4-6 March
Chairman: Clyde Kull (Estonia)
Membership: 55
Report: E/2003/37

Economic Commission for Latin America and the Caribbean (ECLAC)
Session: Did not meet in 2003
Membership: 41 members, 7 associate members

Economic and Social Commission for Asia and the Pacific (ESCAP)
Session: Fifty-ninth (first phase), Bangkok, Thailand, 24-25 April
Chairperson: Leela Krishnamurthy Ponappa (India)
Membership: 52 members (53 from 18 July), 9 associate members
Report: E/2003/39

Economic and Social Commission for Western Asia (ESCWA)
Session: Twenty-second, Beirut, Lebanon, 14-17 April
Chairman: Mohammad Zeki Abou Amer (Egypt)
Membership: 13
Report: E/2003/41/Rev.1

Standing committees

Committee on Negotiations with Intergovernmental Agencies
Membership: 26
Decisions: ESC 2003/215 A & B

Committee on Non-Governmental Organizations
Sessions: Resumed 2002 session, New York, 8-24 January; 2003 regular session, New York, 5-23 May; resumed 2003 session, New York, 15-19 December
Chairperson: Mihaela Blajan (Romania)
Membership: 19
Reports: E/2003/11, E/2003/32 (Parts I-III) & (Part II)/Corr.1

Committee for Programme and Coordination (CPC)
Sessions: Forty-third, New York, 5 May (organizational), 9 June–3 July and 9 July (substantive)
Chairman: Seyed Morteza Mirmohammad (Iran)
Membership: 34
Report: A/58/16
Decisions: ESC 2003/201 B, GA 57/405 B, 58/408

Expert bodies

Ad Hoc Group of Experts on International Cooperation in Tax Matters
Meeting: Eleventh, Geneva, 15-19 December
Chairman: Antonio Hugo Figueroa (Argentina)
Membership: 25
Report: E/2004/51

Committee for Development Policy
Session: Fifth, New York, 7-11 April
Chairman: Riyokichi Hirono (Japan)

Membership: 24
Report: E/2003/33

Committee on Economic, Social and Cultural Rights
Sessions: Thirtieth and thirty-first, Geneva, 5-23 May and 10-28 November
Chairperson: Virginia Bonoan-Dandan (Philippines)
Membership: 18
Report: E/2004/22

Committee of Experts on Public Administration
Session: Second, New York, 7-11 April
Chairperson: Apolo Nsibambi (Uganda)
Membership: 24
Report: E/2003/44

Committee of Experts on the Transport of Dangerous Goods and on the Globally Harmonized System of Classification and Labelling of Chemicals
Session: Did not meet in 2003
Membership: 52
Decision: ESC 2003/201 D

Permanent Forum on Indigenous Issues
Session: Second, New York, 12-23 May
Chairperson: Ole Henrik Magga (Norway)
Membership: 16
Report: E/2003/43

United Nations Group of Experts on Geographical Names
Session: Did not meet in 2003
Membership: Representatives of the 22 geographical/linguistic divisions of the Group of Experts

United Nations System Chief Executives Board for Coordination (CEB)
Sessions: Paris, 25-26 April; New York, 31 October–1 November
Chairman: The Secretary-General
Membership: Organizations of the UN system
Reports: CEB/2003/1, CEB/2003/2

Other related bodies

International Research and Training Institute for the Advancement of Women (INSTRAW)
BOARD OF TRUSTEES[16]
Session: Did not meet in person in 2003 (only electronically)
Membership: 11
Report: E/2003/59
Decision: ESC 2003/201 E

Joint United Nations Programme on Human Immunodeficiency Virus/Acquired Immunodeficiency Syndrome (UNAIDS)
PROGRAMME COORDINATING BOARD
Meeting: Fourteenth, Geneva, 26-27 June
Chairperson: Brian Chituwo (Zambia)
Membership: 22
Report: UNAIDS/PCB(14)/03.8
Decisions: ESC 2003/201 A-C & E

Executive Director of UNAIDS: Dr. Peter Piot

United Nations Children's Fund (UNICEF)
EXECUTIVE BOARD
Sessions: First and second regular, New York, 13-17 January, 15-19 September; annual, New York, 2-6 and 9 June; extraordinary budgetary, New York, 1-2 December
President: Jenö Staehelin (Switzerland)
Membership: 36
Report: E/2003/34/Rev.1
Decision: ESC 2003/201 B

Executive Director of UNICEF: Carol Bellamy

United Nations Development Programme (UNDP)/ United Nations Population Fund (UNFPA)
EXECUTIVE BOARD
Sessions: First and second regular, New York, 20-23 January, 8-12 September; annual, New York, 6-19 June
President: Roble Olhaye (Djibouti)
Membership: 36
Report: E/2003/35
Decision: ESC 2003/201 B

Administrator of UNDP: Mark Malloch Brown[17]
Associate Administrator: Zéphirin Diabré
Executive Director of UNFPA: Thoraya Obaid

United Nations Interregional Crime and Justice Research Institute (UNICRI)
BOARD OF TRUSTEES
Membership: 7 (plus 4 ex-officio members)
Decision: ESC 2003/234

United Nations Research Institute for Social Development (UNRISD)
BOARD OF DIRECTORS
Session: Forty first, Geneva, 10-11 March
Chairperson: Emma Rothschild (United Kingdom)
Membership: 11 (plus 7 ex-officio members)
Decision: ESC 2003/231

Director of the Institute: Thandika Mkandawire

World Food Programme (WFP)
EXECUTIVE BOARD
Sessions: First, second and third regular, Rome, Italy, 5-7 February, 2-3 June, 20-24 October; annual, Rome, 28-30 May
President: Anthony Beattie (United Kingdom)
Membership: 36
Report: E/2004/36
Decisions: ESC 2003/201 B & E

Executive Director of WFP: James T. Morris

Conference

Sixteenth United Nations Regional Cartographic Conference for Asia and the Pacific
Session: Okinawa, Japan, 14-18 July
President: China
Attendance: 302 representatives and observers from 44 countries, 5 specialized agencies and international scientific organizations and 30 invited speakers
Report: E/2004/57

Trusteeship Council

Article 86 of the United Nations Charter lays down that the Trusteeship Council shall consist of the following:

Members of the United Nations administering Trust Territories;
Permanent members of the Security Council that do not administer Trust Territories;
As many other members elected for a three-year term by the General Assembly as will ensure that the membership of the Council is equally divided between United Nations Members that administer Trust Territories and those that do not.[18]

Members: China, France, Russian Federation, United Kingdom, United States.

International Court of Justice

Judges of the Court

The International Court of Justice consists of 15 Judges elected for nine-year terms by the General Assembly and the Security Council.

The following were the Judges of the Court serving in 2003, listed in the order of precedence:

Judge	Country of nationality	End of term[19]
Shi Jiuyong, *President*	China	2012
Raymond Ranjeva, *Vice-President*	Madagascar	2009
Gilbert Guillaume	France	2009
Abdul G. Koroma	Sierra Leone	2012
Vladlen S. Vereshchetin	Russian Federation	2006
Rosalyn Higgins	United Kingdom	2009
Gonzalo Parra-Aranguren	Venezuela	2009
Pieter H. Kooijmans	Netherlands	2006
Francisco Rezek	Brazil	2006
Awn Shawkat Al-Khasawneh	Jordan	2009
Thomas Buergenthal	United States	2006
Nabil Elaraby	Egypt	2006
Hisashi Owada	Japan	2012
Bruno Simma	Germany	2012
Peter Tomka	Slovakia	2012

Registrar: Philippe Couvreur.
Deputy Registrar: Jean-Jacques Arnaldez.

Chamber of Summary Procedure

Members: Shi Jiuyong (ex officio), Raymond Ranjeva (ex officio), Gonzalo Parra-Aranguren, Awn Shawkat Al-Khasawneh, Thomas Buergenthal.
Substitute members: Nabil Elaraby, Hisashi Owada.

Chamber for Environmental Matters

Members: Shi Jiuyong (ex officio), Raymond Ranjeva (ex officio), Gilbert Guillaume, Pieter H. Kooijmans, Francisco Rezek, Bruno Simma, Peter Tomka.

Parties to the Court's Statute

All Members of the United Nations are ipso facto parties to the Statute of the International Court of Justice.

States accepting the compulsory jurisdiction of the Court

Declarations made by the following States, a number with reservations, accepting the Court's compulsory jurisdiction (or made under the Statute of the Permanent Court of International Justice and deemed to be an acceptance of the jurisdiction of the International Court) were in force at the end of 2003:

Australia, Austria, Barbados, Belgium, Botswana, Bulgaria, Cambodia, Cameroon, Canada, Costa Rica, Côte d'Ivoire, Cyprus, Democratic Republic of the Congo, Denmark, Dominican Republic, Egypt, Estonia, Finland, Gambia, Georgia, Greece, Guinea, Guinea-Bissau, Haiti, Honduras, Hungary, India, Japan, Kenya, Lesotho, Liberia, Liechtenstein, Luxembourg, Madagascar, Malawi, Malta, Mauritius, Mexico, Nauru, Netherlands, New Zealand, Nicaragua, Nigeria, Norway, Pakistan, Panama, Paraguay, Peru,[20] Philippines, Poland, Portugal, Senegal, Serbia and Montenegro, Somalia, Spain, Sudan, Suriname, Swaziland, Sweden, Switzerland, Togo, Uganda, United Kingdom, Uruguay.

United Nations organs and specialized and related agencies authorized to request advisory opinions from the Court

Authorized by the United Nations Charter to request opinions on any legal question: General Assembly, Security Council.

Authorized by the General Assembly in accordance with the Charter to request opinions on legal questions arising within the scope of their activities: Economic and Social Council, Trusteeship Council, Interim Committee of the General Assembly, ILO, FAO, UNESCO, ICAO, WHO, World Bank, IFC, IDA, IMF, ITU, WMO, IMO, WIPO, IFAD, UNIDO, IAEA.

Committees of the Court

BUDGETARY AND ADMINISTRATIVE COMMITTEE
Members: Shi Jiuyong (ex officio) (Chair), Raymond Ranjeva (ex officio), Gilbert Guillaume, Vladlen S. Vereshchetin, Pieter H. Kooijmans, Awn Shawkat Al-Khasawneh.

COMMITTEE ON RELATIONS
Members: Gonzalo Parra-Aranguren (Chair), Francisco Rezek, Awn Shawkat Al-Khasawneh, Hisashi Owada.

COMPUTERIZATION COMMITTEE
Members: Raymond Ranjeva (Chair); open to all interested members of the Court.

LIBRARY COMMITTEE
Members: Abdul G. Koroma (Chair), Pieter H. Kooijmans, Francisco Rezek, Thomas Buergenthal, Peter Tomka.

RULES COMMITTEE
Members: Rosalyn Higgins (Chair), Thomas Buergenthal, Nabil Elaraby, Hisashi Owada, Bruno Simma, Peter Tomka.

Other United Nations–related bodies

The following bodies are not subsidiary to any principal organ of the United Nations but were established by an international treaty instrument or arrangement sponsored by the United Nations and are thus related to the Organization and its work. These bodies, often referred to as "treaty organs", are serviced by the United Nations Secretariat and may be financed in part or wholly from the Organization's regular budget, as authorized by the General Assembly, to which most of them report annually.

Committee on the Elimination of Discrimination against Women (CEDAW)

Sessions: Twenty-eighth, New York, 13-31 January; twenty-ninth, New York, 30 June–18 July
Chairperson: Feride Acar (Turkey)
Membership: 23
Report: A/58/38

Committee on the Elimination of Racial Discrimination (CERD)

Sessions: Sixty-second, Geneva, 3-21 March; sixty-third, Geneva, 4-22 August
Chairman: Ion Diaconu (Romania)
Membership: 18
Report: A/58/18

Committee on the Rights of the Child

Sessions: Thirty-second, thirty-third and thirty-fourth, Geneva, 13-31 January, 19 May–6 June, 15 September–3 October
Chairperson: Jakob Egbert Doek (Netherlands)

Membership: 10
Reports: CRC/C/124, CRC/C/132, CRC/C/133

Committee against Torture

Sessions: Thirtieth, Geneva, 28 April–16 May; thirty-first, Geneva, 10-21 November
Chairman: Peter Burns (Canada)
Membership: 10
Reports: A/58/44, A/59/44

Conference on Disarmament

Meetings: Geneva, 20 January–28 March, 12 May–27 June, 28 July–10 September
President: India, Indonesia, Ireland, Israel, Italy, Japan (successively)
Membership: 61
Report: A/58/27

Human Rights Committee

Sessions: Seventy-seventh, Geneva, 17 March–4 April; seventy-eighth, Geneva, 14 July–8 August; seventy-ninth, Geneva, 20 October–7 November
Chairperson: Abdelfattah Amor (Tunisia)
Membership: 18
Reports: A/58/40, vol. I; A/59/40, vol. I

International Narcotics Control Board (INCB)

Sessions: Seventy-sixth, seventy-seventh and seventy-eighth, Vienna, 3-7 February, 26 May–6 June, 29 October–14 November
President: Philip Onagwele Emafo (Nigeria)
Membership: 13
Report: E/INCB/2003/1 (Sales No. E.04.XI.1)
Decision: ESC 2003/201 E

Principal members of the United Nations Secretariat

(as at 31 December 2003)

Secretariat

The Secretary-General: Kofi A. Annan
Deputy Secretary-General: Louise Fréchette

Executive Office of the Secretary-General

Under-Secretary-General, Chef de Cabinet: S. Iqbal Riza
Under-Secretary-General, Special Adviser to the Secretary-General and Rector of the University for Peace: Maurice Strong
Assistant Secretary-General, Ombudsman: Patricia Durrant

Office of Internal Oversight Services

Under-Secretary-General: Dileep Nair

Office of Legal Affairs

Under-Secretary-General, Legal Counsel: Hans Corell
Assistant Secretary-General: Ralph Zacklin

Department of Political Affairs

Under-Secretary-General: Kieran Prendergast
Under-Secretary-General, Special Adviser on Cyprus: Alvaro de Soto
Assistant Secretaries-General: Tuliameni Kalomoh, Danilo Türk

Department for Disarmament Affairs

Under-Secretary-General: Nobuyasu Abe

Department of Peacekeeping Operations

Under-Secretary-General: Jean-Marie Guéhenno
Assistant Secretaries-General: Hédi Annabi, Jane Holl Lute

Office for the Coordination of Humanitarian Affairs

Under-Secretary-General for Humanitarian Affairs, Emergency Relief Coordinator: Jan Egeland
Deputy Emergency Relief Coordinator: Carolyn McAskie

Department of Economic and Social Affairs

Under-Secretary-General: José Antonio Ocampo
Assistant Secretary-General, Special Adviser on Gender Issues and Advancement of Women: Angela E. V. King
Assistant Secretary-General: Patrizio M. Civili

Department for General Assembly and Conference Management

Under-Secretary-General: Jian Chen

Department of Public Information

Under-Secretary-General for Communications and Public Information: Shashi Tharoor

Department of Management

Under-Secretary-General: Catherine Bertini

OFFICE OF PROGRAMME PLANNING, BUDGET AND ACCOUNTS

Assistant Secretary-General, Controller: Jean-Pierre Halbwachs

OFFICE OF HUMAN RESOURCES MANAGEMENT

Assistant Secretary-General: Rosemary McCreery

OFFICE OF CENTRAL SUPPORT SERVICES

Assistant Secretary-General: Andrew Toh

OFFICE OF THE CAPITAL MASTER PLAN

Assistant Secretary-General, Executive Director: Toshiyuki Niwa

Office of the Iraq Programme

Under-Secretary-General, Executive Director: Benon V. Sevan

Economic Commission for Africa

Under-Secretary-General, Executive Secretary: K. Y. Amoako

Economic Commission for Europe

Under-Secretary-General, Executive Secretary: Brigita Schmögnerová

Economic Commission for Latin America and the Caribbean

Under-Secretary-General, Executive Secretary: José Luis Machinea

Economic and Social Commission for Asia and the Pacific

Under-Secretary-General, Executive Secretary: Kim Hak-Su

Economic and Social Commission for Western Asia

Under-Secretary-General, Executive Secretary: Mervat Tallawy

United Nations Office at Geneva

Under-Secretary-General, Director-General of the United Nations Office at Geneva: Sergei Ordzhonikidze

Office of the United Nations High Commissioner for Human Rights

Assistant Secretary-General, Acting High Commissioner: Bertrand Gangapersaud Ramcharan

United Nations Office at Vienna

Under-Secretary-General, Director-General of the United Nations Office at Vienna and Executive Director of the United Nations Office on Drugs and Crime: Antonio Maria Costa

International Court of Justice Registry
Assistant Secretary-General, Registrar: Philippe Couvreur

Secretariats of subsidiary organs, special representatives and other related bodies

International Trade Centre UNCTAD/WTO
Executive Director: J. Denis Bélisle

Office of the High Representative for the Least Developed Countries, Landlocked Developing Countries and Small Island Developing States
Under-Secretary-General, High Representative: Anwarul Karim Chowdhury

Office of the Special Adviser to the Secretary-General on Africa
Under-Secretary-General, Special Adviser: Mohamed Sahnoun

Office of the Special Adviser to the Secretary-General on Colombia
Under-Secretary-General, Special Adviser: James LeMoyne

Office of the Special Adviser to the Secretary-General for Special Assignments in Africa
Under-Secretary-General, Special Adviser: Ibrahim Gambari

Office of the Special Envoy of the Secretary-General for Myanmar
Under-Secretary-General, Special Envoy: Razali Ismail

Office of the Special Representative of the Secretary-General for Children and Armed Conflict
Under-Secretary-General, Special Representative: Olara A. Otunnu

Office of the Special Representative of the Secretary-General for the Great Lakes Region
Assistant Secretary-General, Special Representative: Ibrahima Fall

Office of the Special Representative of the Secretary-General for West Africa
Under-Secretary-General, Special Representative of the Secretary-General: Ahmedou Ould-Abdallah

Office of the United Nations High Commissioner for Refugees
Under-Secretary-General, High Commissioner: Ruud Lubbers

Office of the United Nations Security Coordinator
Assistant Secretary-General, United Nations Security Coordinator: Tun Myat

Office of the United Nations Special Coordinator for the Middle East
Under-Secretary-General, Special Coordinator for the Middle East Peace Process and Personal Representative of the Secretary-General to the Palestine Liberation Organization and the Palestinian Authority: Terje Roed-Larson

Special Adviser to the Secretary-General on European Issues
Under-Secretary-General, Special Adviser: Jean-Bernard Merimée

Special Adviser to the Secretary-General on Latin American Issues
Under-Secretary-General, Special Adviser: Diego Cordovez

Special Envoy of the Secretary-General for the Commonwealth of Independent States
Under-Secretary-General, Special Envoy: Yuli Vorontsov

Special Envoy of the Secretary-General for Humanitarian Affairs in the Sudan
Under-Secretary-General, Special Envoy: Tom Eric Vraalsen

United Nations Assistance Mission in Afghanistan
Under-Secretary-General, Special Representative of the Secretary-General: Lakhdar Brahimi

Assistant Secretary-General, Deputy Special Representative: Jean Arnault

United Nations Assistance Mission for Iraq
Head of Mission: Ross Mountain

United Nations Children's Fund
Under-Secretary-General, Executive Director: Carol Bellamy
Assistant Secretaries-General, Deputy Executive Directors: Kul Gautam, Katharina Hulshof, Karin Sham Poo

United Nations Compensation Commission
Assistant Secretary-General, Executive Secretary: Rolf Goran Knutsson

United Nations Conference on Trade and Development
Under-Secretary-General, Secretary-General of the Conference: Rubens Ricupero
Assistant Secretary-General, Deputy Secretary-General of the Conference: Carlos Fortin Cabezas

United Nations Development Programme
Administrator: Mark Malloch Brown
Under-Secretary-General, Associate Administrator: Zéphirin Diabré
Assistant Administrator and Director, Bureau for Crisis Prevention and Recovery: Julia V. Taft
Assistant Administrator and Director, Bureau of Management: Jan Mattson
Assistant Administrator and Director, Bureau for Development Policy: Shoji Nishimoto
Assistant Administrator and Regional Director, UNDP Africa: Abdoulie Janneh
Assistant Administrator and Regional Director, UNDP Arab States: Rima Khalaf Hunaidi
Assistant Administrator and Regional Director, UNDP Asia and the Pacific: Hafiz Ahmed Pasha
Assistant Administrator and Regional Director, UNDP Europe and the Commonwealth of Independent States: Kalman Mizsei
Assistant Administrator and Regional Director, UNDP Latin America and the Caribbean: Elena Martinez

United Nations Disengagement Observer Force
Assistant Secretary-General, Force Commander: Major General Franciszek Gagor

United Nations Environment Programme
Under-Secretary-General, Executive Director: Klaus Töpfer
Assistant Secretary-General, Deputy Executive Director: Shafqat S. Kakakhel
Assistant Secretary-General, Executive Secretary: Hamdallah Zedan

United Nations Human Settlements Programme (UN-Habitat)
Under-Secretary-General, Executive Director: Anna Kajumulo Tibaijuka

United Nations Institute for Training and Research
Assistant Secretary-General, Executive Director: Marcel A. Boisard

United Nations Interim Administration Mission in Kosovo
Under-Secretary-General, Special Representative of the Secretary-General: Harri Holkeri
Assistant Secretary-General, Principal Deputy Special Representative: Charles Brayshaw
Assistant Secretaries-General, Deputy Special Representatives: Francesco Bastagli, Jean-Christian Cady

United Nations Interim Force in Lebanon
Assistant Secretary-General, Personal Representative of the Secretary-General for Southern Lebanon: Staffan de Mistura

Assistant Secretary-General, Force Commander: Major General Lalit Mohan Tewari

United Nations Joint Staff Pension Fund
Assistant Secretary-General, Chief Executive Officer: Bernard G. Cochemé

United Nations Military Observer Group in India and Pakistan
Chief Military Observer: Major General Pertti Juhani Puonti

United Nations Mission in Côte d'Ivoire
Special Representative of the Secretary-General and Chief of Mission: Albert Tévoédjré
Chief Military Liaison Officer: Brigadier General Abdul Hafiz

United Nations Mission in Ethiopia and Eritrea
Under-Secretary-General, Special Representative of the Secretary-General: Legwaila Joseph Legwaila
Assistant Secretaries-General, Deputy Special Representatives: Cheikh Tidiane Gaye, Angela Kane
Force Commander: Major General Robert Gordon

United Nations Mission in Liberia
Under-Secretary-General, Special Representative of the Secretary-General and Head of Mission: Jacques Paul Klein
Assistant Secretary-General, Deputy Special Representative: Souren Seraydarian
Assistant Secretary-General, Force Commander: Lieutenant General Daniel Ishmael Opande

United Nations Mission for the Referendum in Western Sahara
Under-Secretary-General, Personal Envoy of the Secretary-General: James A. Baker III
Under-Secretary-General, Special Representative of the Secretary-General and Chief of Mission: Alvaro de Soto
Force Commander: Major General Gyorgy Száraz

United Nations Mission in Sierra Leone
Under-Secretary-General, Special Representative of the Secretary-General and Head of Mission: Daudi Ngelautwa Mwakawago
Assistant Secretary-General, Deputy Special Representative: Alan Claude Doss
Assistant Secretary-General, Force Commander: Major General Sajjad Akram

United Nations Mission of Support in East Timor
Under-Secretary-General, Special Representative of the Secretary-General and Head of Mission: Kamalesh Sharma
Assistant Secretary-General, Deputy Special Representative: Sukehiro Hasegawa
Force Commander: Lieutenant General Khairuddin Mat Yusof
Chief Military Observer: Brigadier General Pedro Rocha Pena Madeira

United Nations Monitoring, Verification and Inspection Commission
Assistant Secretary-General, Acting Executive Chairman: Demetrius Perricos

United Nations Observer Mission in Georgia
Assistant Secretary-General, Special Representative of the Secretary-General and Head of Mission: Heidi Tagliavini
Chief Military Observer: Major General Kazi Ashfaq Ahmed

United Nations Office in Burundi
Assistant Secretary-General, Special Representative of the Secretary-General and Head of Office: Berhanu Dinka

United Nations Office of the Humanitarian Coordinator for Iraq
Assistant Secretary-General, Humanitarian Coordinator: Ramiro Lopes da Silva

United Nations Office for Project Services
Assistant Secretary-General, Executive Director: Nigel Fisher

United Nations Organization Mission in the Democratic Republic of the Congo
Under-Secretary-General, Special Envoy of the Secretary-General: Mustapha Niasse
Under-Secretary-General, Special Representative of the Secretary-General and Chief of Mission: William Lacy Swing
Assistant Secretaries-General, Deputy Special Representatives: Behrooz Sadry, Lena Sundh
Force Commander: Major General Mountaga Diallo

United Nations Peace-building Office in the Central African Republic
Representative of the Secretary-General and Head of Office: General Lamine Cissé

United Nations Peace-building Support Office in Guinea-Bissau
Representative of the Secretary-General and Head of Office: David Stephen

United Nations Peace-building Support Office in Liberia
Representative of the Secretary-General and Head of Office: Abou Moussa

United Nations Peacekeeping Force in Cyprus
Under-Secretary-General, Special Adviser to the Secretary-General on Cyprus: Alvaro de Soto
Assistant Secretary-General, Acting Special Representative of the Secretary-General and Chief of Mission: Zbigniew Wlosowicz
Force Commander: Lieutenant General Jin Ha Hwang

United Nations Political Office in Bougainville
Head of Office: Noel Sinclair

United Nations Political Office for Somalia
Representative of the Secretary-General and Head of Office: Winston A. Tubman

United Nations Population Fund
Under-Secretary-General, Executive Director: Thoraya Obaid
Deputy Executive Director, Management: Imelda Henkin
Deputy Executive Director, Programme: Kunio Waki

United Nations Relief and Works Agency for Palestine Refugees in the Near East
Under-Secretary-General, Commissioner-General: Peter Hansen
Assistant Secretary-General, Deputy Commissioner-General: Karen Koning AbuZayd

United Nations Tajikistan Office of Peace-building
Assistant Secretary-General, Representative of the Secretary-General: Vladimir Sotirov

United Nations Truce Supervision Organization
Assistant Secretary-General, Chief of Staff: Major General Carl Dodd

United Nations University
Under-Secretary-General, Rector: Johannes A. van Ginkel
Director, World Institute for Development Economics Research: Anthony F. Shorrocks

United Nations Verification Mission in Guatemala
Special Representative of the Secretary-General and Chief of Mission: Tom Koenigs

On 31 December 2003, the total number of staff of the United Nations Secretariat with continuous service or expected service of a year or more was 14,815. Of these, 5,373 were in the Professional and higher categories, 865 were experts (200-series Project Personnel staff) and 8,577 were in the General Service and related categories.

[1] Elected on 6 June 2003 (dec. 57/418).
[2] Elected on 6 June 2003 (dec. 57/420).
[3] The only Main Committees to meet at the resumed session.
[4] Chairmen elected by the Committees; announced by the Assembly Acting President on 6 June 2003 (dec. 57/419).
[5] Appointed on 16 September 2003 (dec. 58/401).
[6] Resigned effective 12 November 2003; Richard Moon (United Kingdom) was appointed on 11 November (dec. 58/405 A) to fill the resultant vacancy.
[7] Appointed on 29 January 2003 (dec. 57/406 B) to fill the vacancy created by the resignation of Juichi Takahara (Japan).
[8] Resigned effective 16 October 2003; David Dutton (Australia) was appointed on 17 December (dec. 58/412) to fill the resultant vacancy.
[9] Term extended on 6 October 2003 (dec. 58/402) for a two-year period beginning on 1 January 2004.
[10] Appointment extended on 6 June 2003 (dec. 57/417) for a one-year period, from 15 September 2003 to 14 September 2004.
[11] Mandate ended on 6 October 2003.
[12] Established on 13 May 2003.
[13] Established on 19 September 2003.
[14] Mandate ended on 15 February 2003.
[15] Established on 14 August 2003.
[16] On 24 July 2003 (res. 2003/57), the Economic and Social Council amended the INSTRAW statute and replaced the Board of Trustees with an Executive Board composed of 10 members and 8 ex-officio members.
[17] Appointment extended on 15 April 2003 (dec. 57/415) for a further four-year period beginning on 1 July.
[18] During 2003, no Member of the United Nations was an administering member of the Trusteeship Council, while five permanent members of the Security Council continued as non-administering members.
[19] Term expires on 5 February of the year indicated.
[20] Declaration deposited on 7 July 2003.

Appendix IV
Agendas of United Nations principal organs in 2003

This appendix lists the items on the agendas of the General Assembly, the Security Council and the Economic and Social Council during 2003. For the Assembly, the column headed "Allocation" indicates the assignment of each item to plenary meetings or committees.

Agenda item titles have been shortened by omitting mention of reports, if any, following the subject of the item. Where the subject matter of an item is not apparent from its title, the subject is identified in square brackets; this is not part of the title.

General Assembly
Agenda items considered at the resumed fifty-seventh session
(29 January–15 September 2003)

Item No.	Title	Allocation
2.	Minute of silent prayer or meditation.	Plenary
4.	Election of the President of the General Assembly.	Plenary
6.	Election of the Vice-Presidents of the General Assembly.	Plenary
8.	Adoption of the agenda and organization of work.	Plenary
10.	Report of the Secretary-General on the work of the Organization.	Plenary
16.	Elections to fill vacancies in subsidiary organs and other elections: election of twenty members of the Committee for Programme and Coordination.	Plenary
17.	Appointments to fill vacancies in subsidiary organs and other appointments:	
	(a) Appointment of members of the Advisory Committee on Administrative and Budgetary Questions;	1
	(f) Appointment of a member of the Joint Inspection Unit;	Plenary
	(g) Appointment of members of the Committee on Conferences;	Plenary
	(h) Confirmation of the appointment of the Secretary-General of the United Nations Conference on Trade and Development;	Plenary
	(i) Confirmation of the appointment of the Administrator of the United Nations Development Programme;	Plenary
	(j) Appointment of a member of the United Nations Staff Pension Committee.	1
18.	Election of judges of the International Criminal Tribunal for the Prosecution of Persons Responsible for Genocide and Other Serious Violations of International Humanitarian Law Committed in the Territory of Rwanda and Rwandan Citizens Responsible for Genocide and Other Such Violations Committed in the Territory of Neighbouring States between 1 January and 31 December 1994.	Plenary
27.	The role of diamonds in fuelling conflict.	Plenary
40.	Question of equitable representation on and increase in the membership of the Security Council and related matters.	Plenary
42.	Follow-up to the outcome of the twenty-sixth special session: implementation of the Declaration of Commitment on HIV/AIDS.	Plenary
52.	Strengthening of the United Nations system.	Plenary
53.	Revitalization of the work of the General Assembly.	Plenary
54.	Question of Cyprus.	2
55.	Armed aggression against the Democratic Republic of the Congo.	Plenary
56.	Peace, security and reunification on the Korean peninsula.	Plenary
66.	General and complete disarmament:	
	(i) Convening of the fourth special session of the General Assembly devoted to disarmament.	3
78.	Comprehensive review of the whole question of peacekeeping operations in all their aspects.	4th
86.	Sustainable development and international economic cooperation:	
	(d) High-level dialogue on strengthening international economic cooperation for development through partnership.	4
109.	Human rights questions:	
	(b) Human rights questions, including alternative approaches for improving the effective enjoyment of human rights and fundamental freedoms.	3rd

Item No.	Title	Allocation
110.	Financial reports and audited financial statements, and reports of the Board of Auditors.	5th
111.	Review of the efficiency of the administrative and financial functioning of the United Nations.	5th
112.	Programme budget for the biennium 2002-2003.	5th
114.	Improving the financial situation of the United Nations.	5th
116.	Pattern of conferences.	5th
117.	Scale of assessments for the apportionment of the expenses of the United Nations.	5th
118.	Human resources management.	5th
122.	Report of the Secretary-General on the activities of the Office of Internal Oversight Services.	5th
123.	Administration of justice at the United Nations.	5th
126.	Administrative and budgetary aspects of the financing of the United Nations peacekeeping operations.	5th
127.	Financing of the United Nations peacekeeping forces in the Middle East:	
	(a) United Nations Disengagement Observer Force;	5th
	(b) United Nations Interim Force in Lebanon.	5th
128.	Financing of the United Nations Interim Administration Mission in Kosovo.	5th
129.	Financing of the United Nations Transitional Administration in East Timor and the United Nations Mission of Support in East Timor.	5th
130.	Financing of the United Nations Mission in Ethiopia and Eritrea.	5th
131.	Financing of the United Nations Angola Verification Mission and the United Nations Observer Mission in Angola.	5th
132.	Financing of the activities arising from Security Council resolution 687(1991):	
	(a) United Nations Iraq-Kuwait Observation Mission.	5th [1]
133.	Financing of the United Nations Mission in East Timor.	
134.	Financing of the United Nations Mission in Sierra Leone.	5th
135.	Financing of the United Nations Mission for the Referendum in Western Sahara.	5th
142.	Financing of the United Nations Peacekeeping Force in Cyprus.	5th
143.	Financing of the United Nations Observer Mission in Georgia.	5th
147.	Financing of the United Nations Mission in Bosnia and Herzegovina.	5th
151.	Financing of the United Nations Organization Mission in the Democratic Republic of the Congo.	5th
169.	Global road safety crisis.[5]	Plenary

Agenda of the fifty-eighth session
(first part, 16 September–23 December 2003)

Item No.	Title	Allocation
1.	Opening of the session by the President of the General Assembly.	Plenary
2.	Minute of silent prayer or meditation.	Plenary
3.	Credentials of representatives to the fifty-eighth session of the General Assembly:	
	(a) Appointment of the members of the Credentials Committee;	Plenary
	(b) Report of the Credentials Committee.	Plenary
4.	Election of the President of the General Assembly.	Plenary
5.	Election of the officers of the Main Committees.	1st, 4th, 2nd, 3rd, 5th, 6th
6.	Election of the Vice-Presidents of the General Assembly.	Plenary
7.	Notification by the Secretary-General under Article 12, paragraph 2, of the Charter of the United Nations.	Plenary
8.	Organization of work, adoption of the agenda and allocation of items.	Plenary
9.	General debate.	Plenary
10.	Report of the Secretary-General on the work of the Organization.	Plenary
11.	Report of the Security Council.	Plenary
12.	Report of the Economic and Social Council.	Plenary, 4th, 2nd, 3rd, 5th
13.	Report of the International Court of Justice.	Plenary
14.	Report of the International Atomic Energy Agency.	Plenary
15.	Elections to fill vacancies in principal organs:	
	(a) Election of five non-permanent members of the Security Council;	Plenary
	(b) Election of eighteen members of the Economic and Social Council.	Plenary

Item No.	Title	Allocation
16.	Elections to fill vacancies in subsidiary organs and other elections:	
	(a) Election of forty-three members of the United Nations Commission on International Trade Law;	Plenary
	(b) Election of twenty-nine members of the Governing Council of the United Nations Environment Programme;	Plenary
	(c) Election of seven members of the Committee for Programme and Coordination;	Plenary
	(d) Election of the United Nations High Commissioner for Refugees.	Plenary
17.	Appointments to fill vacancies in subsidiary organs and other appointments:	
	(a) Appointment of members of the Advisory Committee on Administrative and Budgetary Questions;	5th
	(b) Appointment of members of the Committee on Contributions;	5th
	(c) Appointment of a member of the Board of Auditors;	5th
	(d) Confirmation of the appointment of members of the Investments Committee;	5th
	(e) Appointment of members of the United Nations Administrative Tribunal;	5th
	(f) Appointment of the members of the Consultative Committee of the United Nations Development Fund for Women;	Plenary
	(g) Appointment of members of the Committee on Conferences;	Plenary
	(h) Appointment of a member of the Joint Inspection Unit;	Plenary
	(i) Confirmation of the appointment of the Secretary-General of the United Nations Conference on Trade and Development.	Plenary
18.	Admission of new Members to the United Nations.	Plenary
19.	Implementation of the Declaration on the Granting of Independence to Colonial Countries and Peoples.	Plenary, 4th
20.	Support by the United Nations system of the efforts of Governments to promote and consolidate new or restored democracies.	Plenary
21.	The role of diamonds in fuelling conflict.	Plenary
22.	Assistance in mine action.	Plenary
23.	Sport for peace and development:	
	(a) Building a peaceful and better world through sport and the Olympic ideal;	Plenary
	(b) International Year of Sport and Physical Education.	Plenary
24.	Implementation of the resolutions of the United Nations.	Plenary
25.	University for Peace.	Plenary
26.	The situation in Central America: progress in fashioning a region of peace, freedom, democracy and development.	Plenary
27.	Zone of peace and cooperation of the South Atlantic.	Plenary
28.	The situation in Afghanistan and its implications for international peace and security.	Plenary
29.	Necessity of ending the economic, commercial and financial embargo imposed by the United States of America against Cuba.	Plenary
30.	Question of Cyprus.	6
31.	Armed aggression against the Democratic Republic of the Congo.	Plenary
32.	Question of the Falkland Islands (Malvinas).	Plenary, 4th
33.	The situation of democracy and human rights in Haiti.	Plenary
34.	Armed Israeli aggression against the Iraqi nuclear installations and its grave consequences for the established international system concerning the peaceful uses of nuclear energy, the non-proliferation of nuclear weapons and international peace and security.	Plenary
35.	Consequences of the Iraqi occupation of and aggression against Kuwait.	Plenary
36.	Declaration of the Assembly of Heads of State and Government of the Organization of African Unity on the aerial and naval military attack against the Socialist People's Libyan Arab Jamahiriya by the present United States Administration in April 1986.	Plenary
37.	The situation in the Middle East.	Plenary
38.	Question of Palestine.	Plenary
39.	New Partnership for Africa's Development: progress in implementation and international support:	
	(a) New Partnership for Africa's Development: progress in implementation and international support;	Plenary
	(b) Causes of conflict and the promotion of durable peace and sustainable development in Africa.	Plenary
40.	Strengthening of the coordination of humanitarian and disaster relief assistance of the United Nations, including special economic assistance:	
	(a) Strengthening of the coordination of emergency humanitarian assistance of the United Nations;	Plenary
	(b) Special economic assistance to individual countries or regions;	Plenary
	(c) Strengthening of international cooperation and coordination of efforts to study, mitigate and minimize the consequences of the Chernobyl disaster;	Plenary

Item No.	Title	Allocation
	(d) Participation of volunteers, "White Helmets", in the activities of the United Nations in the field of humanitarian relief, rehabilitation and technical cooperation for development;	Plenary
	(e) Assistance to the Palestinian people;	Plenary
	(f) Emergency international assistance for peace, normalcy and reconstruction of war-stricken Afghanistan.	Plenary
41.	Follow-up to the outcome of the special session on children.	Plenary
42.	Follow-up to the United Nations Year for Cultural Heritage.	Plenary
43.	Return or restitution of cultural property to the countries of origin.	Plenary
44.	Culture of peace.	Plenary
45.	Launching of global negotiations on international economic cooperation for development.	Plenary
46.	Towards global partnerships.	Plenary
47.	Follow-up to the outcome of the twenty-sixth special session: implementation of the Declaration of Commitment on HIV/AIDS.	Plenary
48.	Fifty-fifth anniversary of the Universal Declaration of Human Rights.	Plenary
49.	Information and communication technologies for development.	Plenary
50.	Integrated and coordinated implementation of and follow-up to the outcomes of the major United Nations conferences and summits in the economic, social and related fields.	Plenary
51.	2001-2010: Decade to Roll Back Malaria in Developing Countries, Particularly in Africa.	Plenary
52.	Oceans and the law of the sea:	
	(a) Oceans and the law of the sea;	Plenary
	(b) Sustainable fisheries, including through the 1995 Agreement for the Implementation of the Provisions of the United Nations Convention on the Law of the Sea of 10 December 1982 relating to the Conservation and Management of Straddling Fish Stocks and Highly Migratory Fish Stocks, and related instruments.	Plenary
53.	Report of the International Criminal Tribunal for the Prosecution of Persons Responsible for Genocide and Other Serious Violations of International Humanitarian Law Committed in the Territory of Rwanda and Rwandan Citizens Responsible for Genocide and Other Such Violations Committed in the Territory of Neighbouring States between 1 January and 31 December 1994.	Plenary
54.	Report of the International Tribunal for the Prosecution of Persons Responsible for Serious Violations of International Humanitarian Law Committed in the Territory of the Former Yugoslavia since 1991.	Plenary
55.	Revitalization of the work of the General Assembly.	Plenary
56.	Question of equitable representation on and increase in the membership of the Security Council and related matters.	Plenary
57.	United Nations reform: measures and proposals.	Plenary
58.	Restructuring and revitalization of the United Nations in the economic, social and related fields.	Plenary
59.	Strengthening of the United Nations system.	Plenary, 5th
60.	Follow-up to the outcome of the Millennium Summit.	Plenary
61.	Multilingualism.	Plenary
62.	Reduction of military budgets:	
	(a) Reduction of military budgets;	1st
	(b) Objective information on military matters, including transparency of military expenditures.	1st
63.	Verification in all its aspects, including the role of the United Nations in the field of verification.	1st
64.	Implementation of the Declaration of the Indian Ocean as a Zone of Peace.	1st
65.	African Nuclear-Weapon-Free Zone Treaty.	1st
66.	Consolidation of the regime established by the Treaty for the Prohibition of Nuclear Weapons in Latin America and the Caribbean (Treaty of Tlatelolco).	1st
67.	Review of the implementation of the Declaration on the Strengthening of International Security.	1st
68.	Developments in the field of information and telecommunications in the context of international security.	1st
69.	Role of science and technology in the context of international security and disarmament.	1st
70.	Establishment of a nuclear-weapon-free zone in the region of the Middle East.	1st
71.	Conclusion of effective international arrangements to assure non-nuclear-weapon States against the use or threat of use of nuclear weapons.	1st
72.	Prevention of an arms race in outer space.	1st
73.	General and complete disarmament:	
	(a) Notification of nuclear tests;	1st
	(b) Prohibition of the dumping of radioactive wastes;	1st
	(c) Reduction of non-strategic nuclear weapons;	1st

Item No.		Title	Allocation
	(d)	Towards a nuclear-weapon-free world: the need for a new agenda;	1st
	(e)	Convening of the fourth special session of the General Assembly devoted to disarmament;	1st
	(f)	Promotion of multilateralism in the area of disarmament and non-proliferation;	1st
	(g)	Observance of environmental norms in the drafting and implementation of agreements on disarmament and arms control;	1st
	(h)	Relationship between disarmament and development;	1st
	(i)	National legislation on transfer of arms, military equipment and dual-use goods and technology;	1st
	(j)	Bilateral strategic nuclear arms reductions and the new strategic framework;	1st
	(k)	Establishment of a nuclear-weapon-free zone in Central Asia;	1st
	(l)	Assistance to States for curbing the illicit traffic in small arms and collecting them;	1st
	(m)	Missiles;	1st
	(n)	The illicit trade in small arms and light weapons in all its aspects;	1st
	(o)	Nuclear-weapon-free southern hemisphere and adjacent areas;	1st
	(p)	Implementation of the Convention on the Prohibition of the Use, Stockpiling, Production and Transfer of Anti-personnel Mines and on Their Destruction;	1st
	(q)	Transparency in armaments;	1st
	(r)	Regional disarmament;	1st
	(s)	Conventional arms control at the regional and subregional levels;	1st
	(t)	Nuclear disarmament;	1st
	(u)	Consolidation of peace through practical disarmament measures;	1st
	(v)	Implementation of the Convention on the Prohibition of the Development, Production, Stockpiling and Use of Chemical Weapons and on Their Destruction;	1st
	(w)	Measures to prevent terrorists from acquiring weapons of mass destruction;	1st
	(x)	Reducing nuclear danger;	1st
	(y)	Follow-up to the advisory opinion of the International Court of Justice on the *Legality of the Threat or Use of Nuclear Weapons*;	1st
	(z)	United Nations conference to identify ways of eliminating nuclear dangers in the context of nuclear disarmament.	1st
74.		Review and implementation of the Concluding Document of the Twelfth Special Session of the General Assembly:	
	(a)	United Nations regional centres for peace and disarmament;	1st
	(b)	Regional confidence-building measures: activities of the United Nations Standing Advisory Committee on Security Questions in Central Africa;	1st
	(c)	United Nations Regional Centre for Peace, Disarmament and Development in Latin America and the Caribbean;	1st
	(d)	United Nations Regional Centre for Peace and Disarmament in Africa;	1st
	(e)	United Nations Regional Centre for Peace and Disarmament in Asia and the Pacific;	1st
	(f)	Convention on the Prohibition of the Use of Nuclear Weapons.	1st
75.		Review of the implementation of the recommendations and decisions adopted by the General Assembly at its tenth special session:	
	(a)	Advisory Board on Disarmament Matters;	1st
	(b)	United Nations Institute for Disarmament Research;	1st
	(c)	Report of the Disarmament Commission;	1st
	(d)	Report of the Conference on Disarmament.	1st
76.		The risk of nuclear proliferation in the Middle East.	1st
77.		Convention on Prohibitions or Restrictions on the Use of Certain Conventional Weapons Which May Be Deemed to Be Excessively Injurious or to Have Indiscriminate Effects.	1st
78.		Strengthening of security and cooperation in the Mediterranean region.	1st
79.		Comprehensive Nuclear-Test-Ban Treaty.	1st
80.		Convention on the Prohibition of the Development, Production and Stockpiling of Bacteriological (Biological) and Toxin Weapons and on Their Destruction.	1st
81.		Effects of atomic radiation.	4th
82.		International cooperation in the peaceful uses of outer space.	4th
83.		United Nations Relief and Works Agency for Palestine Refugees in the Near East.	4th
84.		Report of the Special Committee to Investigate Israeli Practices Affecting the Human Rights of the Palestinian People and Other Arabs of the Occupied Territories.	4th

Item No.	Title	Allocation
85.	Comprehensive review of the whole question of peacekeeping operations in all their aspects.	4th
86.	Questions relating to information.	4th
87.	Information from Non-Self-Governing Territories transmitted under Article 73 e of the Charter of the United Nations.	4th
88.	Economic and other activities which affect the interests of the peoples of the Non-Self-Governing Territories.	4th
89.	Implementation of the Declaration on the Granting of Independence to Colonial Countries and Peoples by the specialized agencies and the international institutions associated with the United Nations.	4th
90.	Offers by Member States of study and training facilities for inhabitants of Non-Self-Governing Territories.	4th
91.	Macroeconomic policy questions:	
	(a) International trade and development;	2nd
	(b) Science and technology for development;	2nd
	(c) Specific actions related to the particular needs and problems of landlocked developing countries;	2nd
	(d) International financial system and development;	2nd
	(e) External debt crisis and development;	2nd
	(f) Outcome of the International Ministerial Conference of Landlocked and Transit Developing Countries and Donor Countries and International Financial and Development Institutions on Transit Transport Cooperation;	2nd
	(g) Commodities.	2nd
92.	Sectoral policy questions: preventing and combating corrupt practices and transfer of funds of illicit origin and returning such assets to the countries of origin.	2nd
93.	Sustainable development and international economic cooperation:	
	(a) Women in development;	2nd
	(b) Human resources development;	2nd
	(c) International migration and development;	2nd
	(d) Implementation of the Declaration on International Economic Cooperation, in particular the Revitalization of Economic Growth and Development of the Developing Countries, and implementation of the International Development Strategy for the Fourth United Nations Development Decade.	2nd
94.	Environment and sustainable development:	
	(a) Promotion of new and renewable sources of energy, including the implementation of the World Solar Programme 1996-2005;	2nd
	(b) Implementation of the United Nations Convention to Combat Desertification in Those Countries Experiencing Serious Drought and/or Desertification, Particularly in Africa;	2nd
	(c) Convention on Biological Diversity;	2nd
	(d) Further implementation of the Programme of Action for the Sustainable Development of Small Island Developing States;	2nd
	(e) International Strategy for Disaster Reduction;	2nd
95.	Implementation of Agenda 21, the Programme for the Further Implementation of Agenda 21 and the outcomes of the World Summit on Sustainable Development.	2nd
96.	United Nations Decade of Education for Sustainable Development.	2nd
97.	Operational activities for development:	
	(a) Operational activities for development;	2nd
	(b) Economic and technical cooperation among developing countries.	2nd
98.	Implementation of the first United Nations Decade for the Eradication of Poverty (1997-2006).	2nd
99.	Training and research:	
	(a) United Nations Institute for Training and Research;	2nd
	(b) United Nations System Staff College in Turin, Italy.	2nd
100.	Globalization and interdependence.	2nd
101.	Implementation of the outcome of the United Nations Conference on Human Settlements (Habitat II) and of the twenty-fifth special session of the General Assembly.	2nd
102.	Third United Nations Conference on the Least Developed Countries.	2nd
103.	Permanent sovereignty of the Palestinian people in the Occupied Palestinian Territory, including East Jerusalem, and of the Arab population in the occupied Syrian Golan over their natural resources.	2nd
104.	Follow-up to the International Conference on Financing for Development:	
	(a) Follow-up to the International Conference on Financing for Development;	2nd

Item No.	Title	Allocation
	(b) High-level dialogue for the implementation of the outcome of the International Conference on Financing for Development.	Plenary, 2nd
105.	Implementation of the outcome of the World Summit for Social Development and of the twenty-fourth special session of the General Assembly.	3rd
106.	Social development, including questions relating to the world social situation and to youth, ageing, disabled persons and the family.	3rd
107.	Follow-up to the International Year of Older Persons: Second World Assembly on Ageing.	3rd
108.	Crime prevention and criminal justice.	Plenary, 3rd
109.	International drug control.	3rd
110.	Advancement of women.	3rd
111.	Implementation of the outcome of the Fourth World Conference on Women and of the twenty-third special session of the General Assembly, entitled "Women 2000: gender equality, development and peace for the twenty-first century".	3rd
112.	Report of the United Nations High Commissioner for Refugees, questions relating to refugees, returnees and displaced persons and humanitarian questions.	3rd
113.	Promotion and protection of the rights of children.	3rd
114.	Programme of activities of the International Decade of the World's Indigenous People.	3rd
115.	Elimination of racism and racial discrimination:	
	(a) Elimination of racism and racial discrimination;	3rd
	(b) Comprehensive implementation of and follow-up to the Durban Declaration and Programme of Action.	3rd
116.	Right of peoples to self-determination.	3rd
117.	Human rights questions:	
	(a) Implementation of human rights instruments;	3rd
	(b) Human rights questions, including alternative approaches for improving the effective enjoyment of human rights and fundamental freedoms;	3rd
	(c) Human rights situations and reports of special rapporteurs and representatives;	3rd
	(d) Comprehensive implementation of and follow-up to the Vienna Declaration and Programme of Action;	Plenary, 3rd
	(e) Report of the United Nations High Commissioner for Human Rights.	3rd
118.	Financial reports and audited financial statements, and reports of the Board of Auditors:	
	(a) United Nations peacekeeping operations;	5th
	(b) Voluntary funds administered by the United Nations High Commissioner for Refugees.	5th
119.	Review of the efficiency of the administrative and financial functioning of the United Nations.	5th
120.	Programme budget for the biennium 2002-2003.	5th
121.	Proposed programme budget for the biennium 2004-2005.	5th
122.	Programme planning.	5th
123.	Improving the financial situation of the United Nations.	5th
124.	Scale of assessments for the apportionment of the expenses of the United Nations.	5th
125.	Pattern of conferences.	5th
126.	United Nations common system.	5th
127.	Human resources management.	5th
128.	Administration of justice at the United Nations.	5th, 6th
129.	Joint Inspection Unit.	5th
130.	Report of the Secretary-General on the activities of the Office of Internal Oversight Services.	5th
131.	Financing of the International Criminal Tribunal for the Prosecution of Persons Responsible for Genocide and Other Serious Violations of International Humanitarian Law Committed in the Territory of Rwanda and Rwandan Citizens Responsible for Genocide and Other Such Violations Committed in the Territory of Neighbouring States between 1 January and 31 December 1994.	5th
132.	Financing of the International Tribunal for the Prosecution of Persons Responsible for Serious Violations of International Humanitarian Law Committed in the Territory of the Former Yugoslavia since 1991.	5th
133.	Scale of assessments for the apportionment of the expenses of United Nations peacekeeping operations.	5th
134.	Administrative and budgetary aspects of the financing of the United Nations peacekeeping operations.	5th
135.	Financing of the United Nations Angola Verification Mission and the United Nations Observer Mission in Angola.	5th
136.	Financing of the United Nations Mission in Bosnia and Herzegovina.	5th
137.	Financing of the United Nations Peacekeeping Force in Cyprus.	5th

Item No.	Title	Allocation
138.	Financing of the United Nations Organization Mission in the Democratic Republic of the Congo.	5th
139.	Financing of the United Nations Mission in East Timor.	5th
140.	Financing of the United Nations Mission of Support in East Timor.	5th
141.	Financing of the United Nations Mission in Ethiopia and Eritrea.	5th
142.	Financing of the United Nations Observer Mission in Georgia.	5th
143.	Financing of the activities arising from Security Council resolution 687(1991):	
	(a) United Nations Iraq-Kuwait Observation Mission;	5th
	(b) Other activities.	5th
144.	Financing of the United Nations Interim Administration Mission in Kosovo.	5th
145.	Financing of the United Nations peacekeeping forces in the Middle East:	
	(a) United Nations Disengagement Observer Force;	5th
	(b) United Nations Interim Force in Lebanon.	5th
146.	Financing of the United Nations Mission in Sierra Leone.	5th
147.	Financing of the United Nations Mission for the Referendum in Western Sahara.	5th
148.	Progressive development of the principles and norms of international law relating to the new international economic order.	6th
149.	United Nations Programme of Assistance in the Teaching, Study, Dissemination and Wider Appreciation of International Law.	6th
150.	Convention on jurisdictional immunities of States and their property.	6th
151.	Report of the United Nations Commission on International Trade Law on the work of its thirty-sixth session.	6th
152.	Report of the International Law Commission on the work of its fifty-fifth session.	6th
153.	Report of the Committee on Relations with the Host Country.	6th
154.	International Criminal Court.	6th
155.	Report of the Special Committee on the Charter of the United Nations and on the Strengthening of the Role of the Organization.	6th
156.	Measures to eliminate international terrorism.	6th
157.	Scope of legal protection under the Convention on the Safety of United Nations and Associated Personnel.	6th
158.	International convention against the reproductive cloning of human beings.	6th
159.	Observer status for the International Institute for Democracy and Electoral Assistance in the General Assembly.	6th
160.	Global road safety crisis.	Plenary
161.	Financing of the United Nations Mission in Côte d'Ivoire.	5th
162.	Observer status for the Eurasian Economic Community in the General Assembly.	6th
163.	Observer status for the GUUAM in the General Assembly.	6th
164.	Observer status for the East African Community in the General Assembly.	6th
165.	Financing of the United Nations Observer Mission in Liberia.	5th
166.	Admission of the International Criminal Court to membership in the United Nations Joint Staff Pension Fund.	5th

Agenda item considered at the resumed tenth emergency special session
(19 September, 20 and 21 October and 8 December 2003)

Item No.	Title	Allocation
5.	Illegal Israeli actions in Occupied East Jerusalem and the rest of the Occupied Palestinian Territory.	Plenary

Security Council
Agenda items considered during 2003

Item No.[7]	Title
1.	Children and armed conflict.
2.	The situation in the Middle East, including the Palestinian question.

Item No.	Title

3. Threats to international peace and security caused by terrorist acts.
4. Meeting of the Security Council with the troop-contributing countries [to UNOMIG, UNIFIL, MINURSO, UNMEE, UNAMSIL, UNIKOM, UNMISET, MONUC, UNFICYP, UNDOF, MINUCI].
5. High-level meeting of the Security Council: combating terrorism.
6. The situation concerning the Democratic Republic of the Congo.
7. The situation between Iraq and Kuwait.
8. The situation in Liberia.
9. Kimberley Process Certification Scheme [conflict diamonds].
10. The situation in the Middle East.
11. The situation in Georgia.
12. The situation concerning Western Sahara.
13. The situation in Afghanistan.
14. The situation in Côte d'Ivoire.
15. Security Council resolutions 1160(1998), 1199(1998), 1203(1998), 1239(1999) and 1244(1999) [Kosovo].
16. General issues relating to sanctions.
17. The situation in Timor-Leste.
18. The situation in Somalia.
19. The situation between Eritrea and Ethiopia.
20. Proliferation of small arms and light weapons and mercenary activities: threats to peace and security in West Africa.
21. Letter dated 31 March 1998 from the Chargé d'affaires a.i. of the Permanent Mission of Papua New Guinea to the United Nations addressed to the President of the Security Council [implementation of the Agreement on Peace, Security and Development on Bougainville (the Lincoln Agreement)].
22. The situation in Sierra Leone.
23. International Criminal Tribunal for the Prosecution of Persons Responsible for Genocide and Other Serious Violations of International Humanitarian Law Committed in the Territory of Rwanda and Rwandan Citizens Responsible for Genocide and Other Such Violations Committed in the Territory of Neighbouring States between 1 January and 31 December 1994.
24. Africa's food crisis as a threat to peace and security.
25. The situation in Cyprus.
26. The Security Council and regional organizations: facing the new challenges to international peace and security.
27. Wrap-up discussion on the work of the Security Council for the current month [April, May, August].
28. The situation in Burundi.
29. The role of the Security Council in the pacific settlement of disputes.
30. International Tribunal for the Prosecution of Persons Responsible for Serious Violations of International Humanitarian Law Committed in the Territory of the Former Yugoslavia since 1991.
31. Response to the humanitarian situation in Iraq.
32. United Nations peacekeeping.
33. Security Council mission [to Central Africa, 7-16 June 2003; to West Africa, 26 June–5 July 2003; to Afghanistan, 31 October–7 November 2003].
34. The situation in Guinea-Bissau.
35. Protection of civilians in armed conflict.
36. The situation in Bosnia and Herzegovina.
37. Protection of United Nations personnel, associated personnel and humanitarian personnel in conflict zones.
38. Letters dated 20 and 23 December 1991, from France, the United Kingdom of Great Britain and Northern Ireland and the United States of America [violation by the Libyan Arab Jamahiriya of Security Council resolution 748(1992)].
39. Meeting of the Security Council with the potential troop- and civilian police–contributing countries to the proposed United Nations peacekeeping operation in Liberia.
40. Consideration of the draft report of the Security Council to the General Assembly.
41. Justice and the rule of law: the United Nations role.
42. Letter dated 5 October 2003 from the Permanent Representative of the Syrian Arab Republic to the United Nations addressed to the President of the Security Council; letter dated 5 October 2003 from the Permanent Representative of Lebanon to the United Nations addressed to the President of the Security Council [Palestinian suicide bomber in Haifa and Israeli violations of Lebanese and Syrian airspace].
43. Letter dated 2 October 2003 from the Permanent Representative of the Sudan to the United Nations addressed to the President of the Security Council [agreement on security arrangements in the Sudan].
44. Women and peace and security.
45. The importance of mine action for peacekeeping operations.

Item No.	Title

46. The responsibility of the Security Council in the maintenance of international peace and security: HIV/AIDS and international peacekeeping operations.
47. The situation in the Great Lakes region.
48. Central African region.
49. Briefings by Chairmen of Security Council Committees and Working Groups.

Economic and Social Council

Agenda of the organizational and resumed organizational sessions for 2003
(15, 28 30 and 31 January; 5 and 25 March, 29 April, 1 and 27 May and 24 June)

Item No.	Title

1. Election of the Bureau.
2. Adoption of the agenda and other organizational matters.
3. Basic programme of work of the Council.
4. Elections, nominations, confirmations and appointments.

Agenda of the substantive and resumed substantive sessions of 2003
(30 June–25 July; 22 August, 31 October and 19 December)

Item No.	Title

1. Adoption of the agenda and other organizational matters.

   High-level segment

2. Promoting an integrated approach to rural development in developing countries for poverty eradication and sustainable development.

   Operational activities of the United Nations for international development cooperation segment

3. Operational activities of the United Nations for international development cooperation:

   (a) Follow-up to policy recommendations of the General Assembly and the Council;

   (b) Reports of the Executive Boards of the United Nations Development Programme/United Nations Population Fund, the United Nations Children's Fund and the World Food Programme;

   (c) Economic and technical cooperation among developing countries.

   Coordination segment

4. The role of the Economic and Social Council in the integrated and coordinated implementation of the outcomes of and follow-up to major United Nations conferences and summits.

   Humanitarian affairs segment

5. Special economic, humanitarian and disaster relief assistance.

   General segment

6. Implementation of and follow-up to major United Nations conferences and summits:

   (a) Follow-up to the International Conference on Financing for Development;

   (b) Review and coordination of the implementation of the Programme of Action for the Least Developed Countries for the Decade 2001-2010.

7. Coordination, programme and other questions:

   (a) Reports of coordination bodies;

   (b) Proposed programme budget for the biennium 2004-2005;

   (c) Calendar of conferences and meetings in the economic, social and related fields;

   (d) International cooperation in the field of informatics;

   (e) Long-term programme of support for Haiti;

   (f) Mainstreaming a gender perspective into all policies and programmes in the United Nations system;

   (g) Joint United Nations Programme on Human Immunodeficiency Virus/Acquired Immunodeficiency Syndrome (UNAIDS);

   (h) Ad hoc advisory group on African countries emerging from conflict;

   (i) Information and Communication Technologies (ICT) Task Force.

8. Implementation of General Assembly resolutions 50/227 and 52/12 B.

Item No.	Title

9. Implementation of the Declaration on the Granting of Independence to Colonial Countries and Peoples by the specialized agencies and the international institutions associated with the United Nations.
10. Regional cooperation.
11. Economic and social repercussions of the Israeli occupation on the living conditions of the Palestinian people in the occupied Palestinian territory, including Jerusalem, and the Arab population in the occupied Syrian Golan.
12. Non-governmental organizations.
13. Economic and environmental questions:
    (a) Sustainable development;
    (b) Science and technology for development;
    (c) Statistics;
    (d) Human settlements;
    (e) Environment;
    (f) Population and development;
    (g) Public administration and development;
    (h) International cooperation in tax matters;
    (i) United Nations Forum on Forests;
    (j) Assistance to third States affected by the application of sanctions;
    (k) Cartography;
    (l) Transport of dangerous goods;
    (m) Women and development.
14. Social and human rights questions:
    (a) Advancement of women;
    (b) Social development;
    (c) Crime prevention and criminal justice;
    (d) Narcotic drugs;
    (e) United Nations High Commissioner for Refugees;
    (f) Implementation of the Programme of Action for the Third Decade to Combat Racism and Racial Discrimination;
    (g) Human rights;
    (h) Permanent Forum on Indigenous Issues;
    (i) Genetic privacy and non-discrimination.
15. Consideration of the request for conversion of the International Civil Defence Organization, an intergovernmental organization with observer status with the Economic and Social Council, to a specialized agency of the United Nations system.
16. Negotiation of an agreement between the United Nations and the World Tourism Organization to constitute it as a specialized agency of the United Nations system.

[1] Allocated to the Fifth Committee at the first part of the session in 2002 but considered only in plenary meeting at the resumed session.
[2] Not allocated; consideration deferred to the fifty-eighth session.
[3] Allocated to the First Committee at the first part of the session in 2002 but considered only in plenary meeting at the resumed session.
[4] Allocated to the Second Committee at the first part of the session in 2002 but considered only in plenary meeting at the resumed session.
[5] Item added at the resumed session.
[6] On 19 September 2003, the General Assembly adopted the General Committee's recommendation that the item be allocated at an appropriate time during the session.
[7] Numbers indicate the order in which items were taken up in 2003.

Appendix V

United Nations information centres and services

(as at 3 May 2005)

ACCRA. United Nations Information Centre
Gamel Abdul Nassar/Liberia Roads
(P.O. Box GP 2339)
Accra, Ghana
  Serving: Ghana, Sierra Leone

ADDIS ABABA. United Nations Information Service, Economic Commission for Africa
P.O. Box 3001
Addis Ababa, Ethiopia
  Serving: Ethiopia, ECA

ALGIERS. United Nations Information Centre
9a rue Emile Payen, Hydra
(Boîte postale 823, Alger-Gare)
Algiers, Algeria
  Serving: Algeria

ANKARA. United Nations Information Centre
Birlik Mahallesi, 2 Cadde No. 11
06610 Cankaya
(P.K. 407)
Ankara, Turkey
  Serving: Turkey

ANTANANARIVO. United Nations Information Centre
22 rue Rainitovo, Antasahavola
(Boîte postale 1348)
Antananarivo, Madagascar
  Serving: Madagascar

ASUNCION. United Nations Information Centre
Avda. Mariscal López esq. Saraví
Edificio Naciones Unidas
(Casilla de Correo 1107)
Asunción, Paraguay
  Serving: Paraguay

BANGKOK. United Nations Information Service, Economic and Social Commission for Asia and the Pacific
United Nations Building
Rajdamnern Nok Avenue
Bangkok 10200, Thailand
  Serving: Cambodia, Lao People's Democratic Republic, Malaysia, Singapore, Thailand, Viet Nam, ESCAP

BEIRUT. United Nations Information Centre/ United Nations Information Service, Economic and Social Commission for Western Asia
UN House
Riad El-Solh Square
(P.O. Box 11-8575-4656)
Beirut, Lebanon
  Serving: Jordan, Kuwait, Lebanon, Syrian Arab Republic, ESCWA

BOGOTA. United Nations Information Centre
Calle 100 No. 8A-55, Piso 10
Edificio World Trade Center - Torre "C"
(Apartado Aéreo 058964)
Bogotá 2, Colombia
  Serving: Colombia, Ecuador, Venezuela

BRAZZAVILLE. United Nations Information Centre (temporarily inactive)
Avenue Foch, Case Ortf 15
(P.O. Box 13210 or 1018)
Brazzaville, Congo
  Serving: Congo

BRUSSELS. Regional United Nations Information Centre
Résidence Palace
155 rue de la Loi
1040 Brussels, Belgium
  Serving: Belgium, Cyprus, Denmark, Finland, France, Germany, Greece, Holy See, Iceland, Ireland, Italy, Luxembourg, Malta, Netherlands, Norway, Portugal, San Marino, Spain, Sweden, United Kingdom, European Union

BUCHAREST. United Nations Information Centre
c/o UN House
48 A Primaverii Blvd.
Bucharest 011975 1, Romania
  Serving: Romania

BUENOS AIRES. United Nations Information Centre
Junín 1940, 1er piso
1113 Buenos Aires, Argentina
  Serving: Argentina, Uruguay

BUJUMBURA. United Nations Information Centre
117 Avenue de la Révolution
(Boîte postale 2160)
Bujumbura, Burundi
  Serving: Burundi

CAIRO. United Nations Information Centre
1 Osiris Street, Garden City
(P.O. Box 262)
Cairo, Egypt
  Serving: Egypt, Saudi Arabia

COLOMBO. United Nations Information Centre
202/204 Bauddhaloka Mawatha
(P.O. Box 1505, Colombo)
Colombo 7, Sri Lanka
  Serving: Sri Lanka

DAKAR. United Nations Information Centre
Rues de Thann x Dagorne
(Boîte postale 154)
Dakar, Senegal
  Serving: Cape Verde, Côte d'Ivoire, Gambia, Guinea, Guinea-Bissau, Mauritania, Senegal

DAR ES SALAAM. United Nations Information Centre
Morogoro Road/Sokoine Drive
Old Boma Building (ground floor)
(P.O. Box 9224)
Dar es Salaam, United Republic of Tanzania
  Serving: United Republic of Tanzania

DHAKA. United Nations Information Centre
IDB Bhaban (14th floor)
Begum Rokeya Sharani
Sher-e-Bangla Nagar
(G.P.O. Box 3658, Dhaka-1000)
Dhaka-1207, Bangladesh
  Serving: Bangladesh

GENEVA. United Nations Information Service, United Nations Office at Geneva
Palais des Nations
1211 Geneva 10, Switzerland
  Serving: Switzerland

HARARE. United Nations Information Centre
Sanders House (2nd floor)
Cnr. First Street/Jason Moyo Avenue
(P.O. Box 4408)
Harare, Zimbabwe
   Serving: Zimbabwe

ISLAMABAD. United Nations Information Centre
House No. 26, Street 88 G-6/3
(P.O. Box 1107)
Islamabad, Pakistan
   Serving: Pakistan

JAKARTA. United Nations Information Centre
Gedung Surya (14th floor)
Jl. M. H. Thamrin Kavling 9
Jakarta 10350, Indonesia
   Serving: Indonesia

KATHMANDU. United Nations Information Centre
Pulchowk, Patan
(P.O. Box 107, UN House)
Kathmandu, Nepal
   Serving: Nepal

KHARTOUM. United Nations Information Centre
United Nations Compound
Gamma'a Avenue
(P.O. Box 1992)
Khartoum, Sudan
   Serving: Somalia, Sudan

KINSHASA. United Nations Information Centre (temporarily inactive)
Immeuble Losonia
Boulevard du 30 juin
B.P. 7248
Kinshasa 1, Democratic Republic of the Congo
   Serving: Democratic Republic of the Congo

LAGOS. United Nations Information Centre
17 Kingsway Road, Ikoyi
(P.O. Box 1068)
Lagos, Nigeria
   Serving: Nigeria

LA PAZ. United Nations Information Centre
Calle 14 esq. S. Bustamante
Edificio Metrobol II, Calacoto
(Apartado Postal 9072)
La Paz, Bolivia
   Serving: Bolivia

LIMA. United Nations Information Centre
Lord Cochrane 130
San Isidro (L-27)
(P.O. Box 14-0199)
Lima, Peru
   Serving: Peru

LOME. United Nations Information Centre
107 boulevard du 13 janvier
(Boîte postale 911)
Lomé, Togo
   Serving: Benin, Togo

LUSAKA. United Nations Information Centre
Revenue House (ground floor)
Cairo Road (Northend)
(P.O. Box 32905)
Lusaka 10101, Zambia
   Serving: Botswana, Malawi, Swaziland, Zambia

MANAMA. United Nations Information Centre
United Nations House
Bldg. 69, Road 1901
(P.O. Box 26004)
Manama 319, Bahrain
   Serving: Bahrain, Qatar, United Arab Emirates

MANILA. United Nations Information Centre
RCBC Plaza, Yuchengco Tower 30th floor (rooms 30-17 and 30-18)
Sen. Gil Puyat Avenue, corner Ayala Avenue
Makati City, 1229
Metro Manila, Philippines
   Serving: Papua New Guinea, Philippines, Solomon Islands

MASERU. United Nations Information Centre
United Nations Road
UN House
(P.O. Box 301, Maseru 100)
Maseru, Lesotho
   Serving: Lesotho

MEXICO CITY. United Nations Information Centre
Presidente Masaryk 29-2do piso
Col. Chaputelpec Morales
11570 México D.F., Mexico
   Serving: Cuba, Dominican Republic, Mexico

MONROVIA. United Nations Information Centre (temporarily inactive)
UNDP—Simpson Building
P.O. Box 0274
Mamba Point
Monrovia, Liberia
(UNDP Liberia, Grand Central Station, P.O. Box 1608, New York, NY 10163)
   Serving: Liberia

MOSCOW. United Nations Information Centre
4/16 Glazovsky Pereulok
Moscow 121002, Russian Federation
   Serving: Russian Federation

NAIROBI. United Nations Information Centre
United Nations Office
Gigiri
(P.O. Box 30552)
Nairobi, Kenya
   Serving: Kenya, Seychelles, Uganda

NEW DELHI. United Nations Information Centre
55 Lodi Estate
New Delhi 110 003, India
   Serving: Bhutan, India

OUAGADOUGOU. United Nations Information Centre
14 Avenue de la Grande Chancellerie
Secteur no. 4
(Boîte postale 135)
Ouagadougou 01, Burkina Faso
   Serving: Burkina Faso, Chad, Mali, Niger

PANAMA CITY. United Nations Information Centre
Calle Gerardo Ortega y Ave. Samuel Lewis
Banco Central Hispano Building (1st floor)
(P.O. Box 6-9083 El Dorado)
Panama City, Panama
   Serving: Panama

PORT OF SPAIN. United Nations Information Centre
2nd floor, Bretton Hall
16 Victoria Avenue
(P.O. Box 130)
Port of Spain, Trinidad, W.I.
   Serving: Antigua and Barbuda, Bahamas, Barbados, Belize, Dominica, Grenada, Guyana, Jamaica, Netherlands Antilles, Saint Kitts and Nevis, Saint Lucia, Saint Vincent and the Grenadines, Suriname, Trinidad and Tobago

PRAGUE. United Nations Information Centre
nam. Kinskych 6
15000 Prague 5, Czech Republic
   Serving: Czech Republic

PRETORIA. United Nations Information Centre
Metro Park Building
351 Schoeman Street
(P.O. Box 12677)
Pretoria, South Africa
   Serving: South Africa

RABAT. United Nations Information Centre
6 Angle avenue Tarik Ibnou Ziyad et Ruet Roudana
(Boîte postale 601, Casier ONU, Rabat-Chellah)
Rabat, Morocco
   Serving: Morocco

United Nations information centres and services

RIO DE JANEIRO. United Nations Information Centre
Palácio Itamaraty
Av. Marechal Floriano 196
20080-002 Rio de Janeiro RJ, Brazil
  Serving: Brazil

SANA'A. United Nations Information Centre
Street 5, off Al-Bonyia Street
Handlal Zone, beside Handhal Mosque
(P.O. Box 237)
Sana'a, Yemen
  Serving: Yemen

SANTIAGO. United Nations Information Service, Economic Commission for Latin America and the Caribbean
Edificio Naciones Unidas
Avenida Dag Hammarskjöld, Vitacura
(Avenida Dag Hammarskjöld s/n, Vitacura Casilla 179-D)
Santiago, Chile
  Serving: Chile, ECLAC

SYDNEY. United Nations Information Centre
46-48 York Street (5th floor)
(G.P.O. Box 4045, Sydney, N.S.W. 2001)
Sydney, N.S.W. 2000, Australia
  Serving: Australia, Fiji, Kiribati, Nauru, New Zealand, Samoa, Tonga, Tuvalu, Vanuatu

TEHRAN. United Nations Information Centre
No. 39, Shahrzad Blvd.
(P.O. Box 15874-4557, Tehran)
Darous, Iran
  Serving: Iran

TOKYO. United Nations Information Centre
UNU Building (8th floor)
53-70 Jingumae 5-chome, Shibuya-Ku
Tokyo 150-0001, Japan
  Serving: Japan

TRIPOLI. United Nations Information Centre
Khair Aldeen Baybers Street
Hay El-Andalous
(P.O. Box 286)
Tripoli, Libyan Arab Jamahiriya
  Serving: Libyan Arab Jamahiriya

TUNIS. United Nations Information Centre
61 boulevard Bab-Benath
(Boîte postale 863)
Tunis, Tunisia
  Serving: Tunisia

VIENNA. United Nations Information Service, United Nations Office at Vienna
Vienna International Centre
Wagramer Strasse 5
(P.O. Box 500, A-1400 Vienna)
A-1220 Vienna, Austria
  Serving: Austria, Hungary, Slovakia, Slovenia

WARSAW. United Nations Information Centre
A. Niepodleglosci 186
(UN Centre P.O. Box 1, 02-514 Warsaw 12)
00-608 Warszawa, Poland
  Serving: Poland

WASHINGTON, D.C. United Nations Information Centre
1775 K Street, N.W., Suite 400
Washington, D.C. 20006, United States
  Serving: United States

WINDHOEK. United Nations Information Centre
372 Paratus Building
Independence Avenue
(Private Bag 13351)
Windhoek, Namibia
  Serving: Namibia

YANGON. United Nations Information Centre
6 Natmauk Road
Yangon, Myanmar
  Serving: Myanmar

YAOUNDE. United Nations Information Centre
Immeuble Tchinda, Rue 2044, derrière camp SIC TSINGA
(Boîte postale 836)
Yaoundé, Cameroon
  Serving: Cameroon, Central African Republic, Gabon

For more information on UNICs, access the Internet: http://www.un.org/aroundworld/unics

Indexes

USING THE SUBJECT INDEX

To assist the researcher in reading and searching the *Yearbook* index, three typefaces have been employed.

ALL BOLD CAPITAL LETTERS are used for major subject entries, including chapter topics (e.g., **DEVELOPMENT**, **DISARMAMENT**), as well as country names (e.g., **TAJIKISTAN**), region names (e.g., **AFRICA**) and principal UN organs (e.g., **GENERAL ASSEMBLY**).

CAPITAL LETTERS are used to highlight major sub-topics (e.g., POVERTY), territories (e.g., MONTSERRAT), subregions (e.g., CENTRAL AMERICA) and official names of specialized agencies (e.g., UNIVERSAL POSTAL UNION) and regional commissions (e.g., ECONOMIC COMMISSION FOR EUROPE).

Regular body text is used for single entries and cross-reference entries, e.g., armed conflict, mercenaries, terrorism.

1—An asterisk (*) next to a page number indicates the presence of a text (reproduced in full) of General Assembly, Security Council or Economic and Social Council resolutions and decisions, or Security Council presidential statements.

2—Entries, which are heavily cross-referenced, appear under key substantive words, as well as under the first word of official titles.

3—United Nations bodies are listed under major subject entries and alphabetically.

Subject index

Abkhazia, see Georgia
Abuja Declaration and Framework Plan of Action on HIV/AIDS, Tuberculosis and Other Related Infectious Diseases (2001), 1252
Abuja Declaration on Roll Back Malaria (2000), 1251
    Plan of Action, 1252
Advisory Committee on Administrative and Budgetary Questions (ACABQ)
    Habitat, 1079
    International Trade Centre, *975-76
    peacekeeping operations
        financial performance, 82-83
        peacekeeping assets, management of, 94, 95, *96
        personnel matters, *97, 99
        reimbursement issues, *92-93
        resident auditors, 92
    regional economic and social activities, 1001
    UN budget, 1395, 1397, 1414
    UNDP, 903
    UNEP, 1047
AFGHANISTAN, *289-315
    Afghan New Beginnings Programme, 291
    Al-Qaida, 68, 290, 297, 302, 304, 311-15
    arms embargo, 312
    Bonn Agreement (2001), 61, 290-94, 296-97, 301-304, 307-309
    drug control, 291, 292, 294, *296-301, 1277, 1284
    education for girls, 307
    electoral process, 291, 292, 298
    HIV/AIDS, 299
    human rights, 297, 303, 679, 769, 816, *1175-77
    humanitarian assistance, 290-91, 294, 303, *933-36
    International Security Assistance Force (ISAF), 80, 290, 297, 301, 303, *307-11
    judicial issues, 291, 292, 307
    Kabul Declaration on Good-Neighbourly Relations (2002), 302, 303, 308
    Mine Action Centre, 298
    Mine Action Programme, 291
    Partnership for Peace Programme, 292
    reconstruction, 290, 301, 304, *933-36
    refugees, 297, 304, 933-34, 1239
    sanctions, *311-15
    SC mission, *302-11
    security situation, 290-98, *302-307
    Taliban, 68, 290, 297, 302, 304, 308, 311-12, 314-15
    terrorism, 297, 298
    UNAMA, 61, 62, *289-97, 302-303, 307-308, 779
    UN Transitional Assistance Programme for Afghanistan (TAPA), 291, *933-36
    women's rights, 301, 779-80, *1175-77
AFRICA, *102-272, 630, *937-50, 1001-1007
    Ad Hoc Open-ended Working Group on the Causes of Conflict and the Promotion of Durable Peace and Sustainable Development in Africa, *104-107
    African Union, 271-72, see also African Union
    Africa's Orphaned Generations, 1211
    Angola, *269-71, 927
        MONUA, *271
        UNAVEM, *271
        UNMA, 60, 62, 270-71
    Burkina Faso, 930
    Burundi, 108, 113, 128, *145-54, 808-809, 927, *947-48
    Central Africa and Great Lakes region, *107-159, 927
    Central African Economic and Monetary Community, 108, 156-59
    Central African Republic, 108, 110, 155-59, 927
    Chad, 682-83
    Comoros, 272, *951-52
    conflict, countries emerging from, *947-50
        Ad Hoc Advisory Groups
            Burundi, *947-48
            Guinea-Bissau, *948-50
    conflict prevention, 105
    Congo, Republic of the, 928
    Côte d'Ivoire, 161, 162-64, *165-84, 186, 193, 930
    Democratic Republic of the Congo (DRC), 106, 108, *113-45, *809-14, 928, *943-46
        Interim Emergency Multinational Force in Bunia (IEMF), 79, 126, 127, 132, 133
    desertification, 1045, *1053-55
    development, 889
        Tokyo International Conference on African Development (TICAD III), 938, 1002
    disarmament, *573-75
        African Nuclear-Weapon-Free Zone Treaty (1996), *554-55
        Programme for Coordination and Assistance for Security and Development, 161, 203, 573
        regional approaches, *573-75
        Regional Centre for Peace and Disarmament, *587-88
    Djibouti, *946-47
    drug control, 1271-72
    East African Community, *1479-80
    ECA, see Economic Commission for Africa
    economic cooperation, regional, 1001-1007
        development management, 1005-1006
        development policy, 1002-1003
        economic development, 1002-1003
        economic trends, 1002
        food security and sustainable development, 1005
        industrial development, 1004-1005
        information technology, 1003-1004
        transportation and communications, *1004
        women and development, 1006-1007
    economic recovery and development, *937-50
    Economic Report on Africa, 1002
    environment, 1039, 1040-41
    Environmentally Sound Management of Unwanted Stocks of Hazardous Wastes and Their Prevention, First Continental Conference for Africa on, 771
    Eritrea, *230-41, 927
    Ethiopia, *230-41, *961-62
    Ghana, 930

Global Partnership Initiative on Urban Youth Development in, 1078
Great Lakes region, see Central Africa and Great Lakes region
Guinea, 930
Guinea-Bissau, 105, 161, 163-64, *223-29, *948-50
  UNOGBIS, 60, 62, 160, *223-26, 228-29
Horn of Africa, 229-57
human rights, 808-14
humanitarian assistance, 927-33, see also humanitarian assistance
Industrial Development Decade for Africa, Second (1993-2002), 1005
Lesotho, 931
Liberia, 161, 162-64, 171, 174, *184-210, 211-13, *215-20, 683-84, 814, 930-31
Libyan Arab Jamahiriya, *267-69
Madagascar, 272
malaria, *1251-53
  Decade to Roll Back Malaria in Developing Countries, Particularly in Africa (2001-2010), *1251-53
Malawi, *931-32
Mali, 161, 930
Mauritania, 272
Mozambique, 932
New Partnership for Africa's Development (NEPAD), *937-43, 1003, 1036, 1040, 1041, 1068, 1074
North Africa, *257-69
peacekeeping missions, 79-80
political and peace-building missions, 60-61
promotion of peace, *104-107
refugees, *1232-38
Rwanda, 108, 113, 114-16, 117, 124, 133-37, *154-55
Sao Tome and Principe, 110, 272
science and technology, 1065
Sierra Leone, 161, 162-64, 171, 184, 186, 193, *210-23, 684-85, 814, 931
Somalia, *241-56, 685, 814, *928-29
Southern Africa, *269-71, 931
Sudan, 229, 256-57, 814, 929-30
Swaziland, 932-33
trade, 966-67, 974
Uganda, 113, 115, 123, 124, 133-37, 928
UN African Institute for the Prevention of Crime and the Treatment of Offenders, *1124-25
UNFPA, 1090
UN New Agenda for the Development of Africa in the 1990s, 937
West Africa, 159-229
Western Sahara, *257-67, 616, 722
Zambia, 933
Zimbabwe, 814, 933
see also country names; African Union; Economic Commission for Africa; Economic Community of Central African States; Economic Community of West African States; Southern African Development Community
African Union
  African Mission in Burundi (AMIB), *148-49
  Central Organ of the Mechanism for Conflict Prevention, Management and Resolution
    Burundi, 146, *148-49, 150, 809
    Central African Republic, 158
    Comoros, 272
    Côte d'Ivoire, 168
    Iraq, 324
    Liberia, 189-90, 202
    Madagascar, 272
    Mauritania, 272
    Sao Tome and Principe, 272
    Somalia, 246-47
    Sudan, 256
  UN cooperation with, 271-72
AGEING PERSONS, 1218-21
  Economic Commission for Europe Ministerial Conference on Ageing (2002), 1218
  International Plan of Action on Ageing (2002), 1013, 1099, *1218-19
  Plan of Action on Ageing for Asia and the Pacific (1998), 1013
  Shanghai Regional Implementation Strategy, 1013
  women, 1177
  World Assembly on Ageing, Second (2002) follow-up, *1218-21
Agreement on Ceasefire and Cessation of Hostilities (Liberia), 189, 198, 207
agriculture
  Asia and the Pacific, 1012-13
  FAO, 1510-11
  IFAD, 1532
  statistics, 1292
AIDS, see HIV/AIDS
ALGERIA
  Western Sahara, 263, 264
Algiers Peace Agreement (2000, Ethiopia-Eritrea), 230, *232-38
Al-Qaida, 68, 290, 297, 302, 304, 311-15, 325-26, 352
al-Zarqawi, Abu Musab, 325, 328
AMERICAN SAMOA, 605
AMERICAS, *273-87
  Central America, *273-84
  Colombia, *285, 705, 770, 815
  Cuba, 815-16
  Cuba–United States, *285-86
  Declaration on Security in the, 577
  drug control, 1272-75
  El Salvador–Honduras, 286-87
  Guatemala, *278-84
  Haiti, 284-85, 683
  peace and disarmament, *590-91
  refugees, 1238
  terrorism, 275
  see also country names; Caribbean; Central America; Economic Commission for Latin America and the Caribbean; Latin America and the Caribbean; Organization of American States
ANGOLA, *269-71
  human rights, 271
  humanitarian assistance, 270, 271, 927
  internally displaced persons, 270
  Lusaka Protocol (1994), 269, 271

Subject index

political developments, 269-70
refugees, 270
UNAVEM/MONUA, *271
UNMA, 62, 270-71
ANGUILLA, 605
arbitrary detention, 733-34
ARGENTINA
Falkland Islands (Malvinas), 609-10
human rights, 733
armed conflict
children in, 162, 171, 193-94, *788-91, 809, 810-11, 820, 1209
civilians in, *727-33, 810
ARMENIA
Azerbaijan, conflict with, 443-45
arms embargoes
Afghanistan, 312
Liberia, 202-203, 207
Somalia, 242, *250-56
Arta Conference (2000, Somalia), 242, 249
Arusha Agreement on Peace and Reconciliation (2000, Burundi), 108, 145, 147-50, *152-54, 808
ASIA AND THE PACIFIC, *288-396, 1007-15
Afghanistan, *289-315
humanitarian assistance, *933-36
International Security Assistance Force (ISAF), 80, 290, 297, 301, 303, *308-11
Asian-African Subregional Organizations Conference (Bandung), 938
Association of South-East Asian Nations, 555, 575, 912, 1043
Cambodia, *385-91, *679-82, 816
Central Asian Cooperation Organization, 301
DPRK, 61, 391-92, 549, 816-17, 936, 1032
disabilities, persons with, 1013-14
disarmament, 555, 575
drug control, 1275-78
East Timor see Timor-Leste
HIV/AIDS, 1013
human rights, 694, *816-24
India
and Pakistan, 391
UNMOGIP, 80
Indonesia, 378, 380, 936
international trade, 974
Iran, 396, 550, *817-18, 962
Iraq, *315-70
human rights, 316, 356, *818-19
humanitarian assistance, 333-36, 343-45, 347, 353, 365, 818, 915, 936
and Kuwait, *356-70
nuclear verification, 1032
sanctions, 316, *338-41, 361-62
terrorist bombing of UN office in Baghdad, 65, *346-50, 352-53, *1452
UNAMI, 62, *346, 353-55
UNIKOM, 80, 81, 82, 316, 332, *358-60
UNMOVIC, 315-34, 342, 1032
UNSCOM, 317, 331, 342
Korea question, 391-92
Kuwait
and Iraq, *356-70

UNIKOM, 80, 81, 82, 316, 332, *358-60
land transport infrastructure development, 1011
Mekong River Commission, 1014
Myanmar, *819-22
Pakistan
and India, 391
UNMOGIP, 80
Papua New Guinea, 392-95
UNOMB, 392, 394-95
UNPOB, 61-62, 392-95
refugees, 1238-39
Regional Centre for Peace and Disarmament, *588-90
regional cooperation, *1007-15
agriculture and development, 1012-13
communications, 1011
economic trends, 1007-1008
environment and sustainable development, 1012
globalization, 1009-10
infrastructure development, 1011
least developed, landlocked and island developing countries, 1010-11
natural disasters, 1014
policy issues, 1008
poverty reduction, 1008-1009
science and technology, 1011-12
social development, 1013-14
statistics, 1009
technical cooperation, 1011
tourism, 1011
transport and communications, 1011
Republic of Korea, 61, 391-92
Shanghai Cooperation Organization, 298, 342, 575
social development, 1013-14
Solomon Islands, 396
South Pacific, *557-58, 575
States of the Collective Security Treaty Organization, 71, 296, 306
Tajikistan, 396, 937
Timor-Leste, *370-85, 685-86, 916, *953-54, *1015
Turkey, 65, 396
UNFPA, 1090-91
United Arab Emirates, 396
see also country names; Economic and Social Commission for Asia and the Pacific; Economic and Social Commission for Western Asia; Middle East
Association of South-East Asian Nations (ASEAN), 555, 575, 912, 1043
AUSTRALIA
Timor Sea Treaty, 370, 373, 376
AZERBAIJAN
Armenia, conflict with, 443-45
refugees, 444

bacteriological (biological) weapons, *558-60
Convention (1971), 268-69, *559-60
Beijing Declaration and Platform for Action (1995), 778-79, 1006, 1022-23, 1045-46, *1164-67, 1169-70
BELARUS
human rights, 824
BELIZE, 275

BENIN
and Niger (ICJ case), 1305
BERMUDA, 605
bin Laden, Osama, 290, 311, 313, 325
bioethics, 775-76, 1374
Bonn Agreement (2001, Afghanistan), 61, 289-94, 296-97, 301-304, 307-309
BONUCA, see United Nations Peace-building Office in the Central African Republic
BOSNIA AND HERZEGOVINA, *399-411
and Croatia, 409
economic reform and reconstruction, 406-407
General Framework Agreement for Peace in (1995 Peace Agreement)
implementation, *399-409
verification, 576
human rights, 408
human trafficking, 410
International Tribunal for the Former Yugoslavia, cooperation with, 1316
judicial reform, 404-406
media issues, 408-409
military aspects, 410-11
public administration and reform, 407
refugees, 407-408
repossession of property, 407
and Serbia and Montenegro, 409, 1302
Srebrenica massacre (1995), 403-404
Stabilization Force (SFOR), 410-11
UNMIBH, 82, *398-99
International Police Task Force (IPTF), 409
war crimes prosecution, 1316
Bougainville Peace Agreement (2001, Papua New Guinea), 392-95
Brahimi report (2000) (peacekeeping), 71
BRAZIL
human rights, 739-40
Bretton Woods institutions, see International Monetary Fund; World Bank
BRITISH VIRGIN ISLANDS, 605
Brussels Declaration on LDCs (2001), 867, *868-71
BURKINA FASO
humanitarian assistance, 930
BURUNDI, *145-54, *947-48
Ad Hoc Advisory Group on, *947-48
African Mission in (AMIB), *148-50, 153
Arusha Agreement on Peace and Reconciliation (2000), 108, 145, 147-50, *152-54, 808
ceasefire agreement (2002), 146
and DRC, 108, 113, 128
Global Ceasefire Agreement, *151-54
Great Lakes Regional Peace Initiative on, 148, *151-54
HIV/AIDS, 152
human rights, 152, 808-809
humanitarian assistance, 152, 809, 927
Joint Ceasefire Commission, 145-48, 152
Pretoria Protocols, 151
SC mission to, 149-50
security situation, 150-51, 927
transfer of power, *147-49
UNOB, 60, 61, 108, 110, 145, 152

CAMBODIA, *385-91
human rights, *679-82
Khmer Rouge trials, *385-91
UNTAC, 85
CANADA
human rights, 704-705
CARIBBEAN
Caribbean Community, 912
Cuba, *285-86, 815-16
decolonization, 598
drug control, 1272-73
ECLAC activities, 1024
Haiti, 85, 284-85, 683, 816, *952-53
see also country names; Economic Commission for Latin America and the Caribbean; Latin America and the Caribbean
CARTOGRAPHY, 1035
geographic names, standardization of, 1035
UN Regional Cartographic Conference for Asia and the Pacific, 1035
CAYMAN ISLANDS, 605
CEB, see UN System Chief Executives Board for Co-ordination
CEDAW, see Elimination of Discrimination against Women, Committee on the
CENTRAL AFRICA AND GREAT LAKES REGION, *107-59
Declaration of Principles on Good-neighbourly Relations and Cooperation, 112, 113, 133
HIV/AIDS, 110
human rights, 110
humanitarian assistance, 110, 927
international conference, 106, 108, *111-13
Mutual Assistance Pact (2000), 111
Non-Aggression Pact (2001), 111
Protocol on the Council for Peace and Security in Central Africa (2000), 111
refugees, 1232-33
Special Representative of the Secretary-General for the Great Lakes Region, 60, 61, 112
Subregional Centre for Human Rights and Democracy in Central Africa, *693-94
UN Standing Advisory Committee on Security Questions in Central Africa, 108, 111, *573-75, 587
see also country names
Central African Economic and Monetary Community, 108, 110, 158
multinational force, 156, 159
special summit (Brazzaville, Congo), 157
special summit (Libreville, Gabon), 156
transport, 1003
CENTRAL AFRICAN REPUBLIC, 155-59
BONUCA, 60, 62, 155-59
coup d'état, 108, 110, 156, 157
economy, 157
human rights, 157, 159
humanitarian assistance, 927
MINURCA, 155, 159
CENTRAL AMERICA, *273-84
Belize, 275

Canada–Central America Four Free Trade Agreement, 275
Central America Free Trade Agreement, 276
Central American Centre for Coordination of Natural Disaster Prevention, 958
Central American Integration System, 275
  drug control, 1272-73
  ECLAC activities, 1024
  El Salvador, 85, 273, 274, 275, 286-87
    ONUSAL, 85
  Guatemala, 274, 275, 276, *278-84
    MINUGUA, 61, 85, *278-84
  Honduras, 275, 276, 286-87
  human rights, 274
  Mesoamerican Initiative for Sustainable Development, 275
  Nicaragua, 274, 276
  peace-building, 275-76
  Puebla-Panama Plan (2001), 275
  refugees, 1238
  regional security, 274
  sustainable development, 275, *950-51
  see also country names; Economic Commission for Latin America and the Caribbean; Latin America and the Caribbean
Central Emergency Revolving Fund, 922
Central Support Services, Office of, 95, 1386

CHAD
  human rights, 682-83
chemical weapons, 560-61
  Convention (1993), 559, *560-61
  Organization for the Prohibition of, 68, 560-61

CHEMICALS
  Bahia Declaration on Chemical Safety and the Priorities for Action beyond 2000 (2000), 1070
  Committee of Experts on the Transport of Dangerous Goods and on the Globally Harmonized System of Classification and Labelling of Chemicals, 993
  harmful products and waste, protection against, 1069-73
    chemical safety, 1069-71
    cleaner production and sustainable consumption, 1073
    mercury assessment, 1071-72
    persistent organic pollutants, 1045, 1070, 1072
  Inter-Organization Programme for the Sound Management of Chemicals, 1070
  Partnership for Clean Fuels and Vehicles, 1070
  Rotterdam Convention on the Prior Informed Consent Procedure for Certain Hazardous Chemicals and Pesticides in International Trade (1998), 771, 1068-70
  see also pollution
CHILDREN, *780-91, 1202-14
  abducted in Africa, 791
  and armed conflict, 162, 171, 193-94, *788-91, 809, 810-11, 820, 1209-10
  Committee on the Rights of the Child, 667-68, 676, 789
  Convention on the Rights of the Child (1989) and Optional Protocols (2000), 667, 675-76, 737, 770, 1203, 1205-1206, 1231
  GA special session (2002), 1202-1203
  the girl child, 778-79, 1174-75, *1185-87, 1208-1209
  HIV/AIDS, 787, 1174, 1202-1203, 1205-1207, 1209-11
  human rights, *780-91
  Inter-Agency Guiding Principles on Unaccompanied and Separated Children, 1209
  Inter-Agency Standing Committee Task Force on Prevention of Sexual Exploitation, 789
  Inter-Agency Working Group on the Incorporation of Child Protection in United Nations Peacemaking, Peacekeeping and Peace-building Processes, 789
  International Decade for a Culture of Peace and Non-Violence for the Children of the World (2001-2010), *689-91
  labour, 788, 1210
  protection measures, 1209-11
  refugees, *1230-32
  sale of, for prostitution and child pornography, 787-88
  The State of the World's Children 2003, 1203
  Tunza children and youth strategy (UNEP), 1046
  see also United Nations Children's Fund; youth

CHILE
  and European Community (Law of the Sea Tribunal case), 1353
  human rights, 797

CHINA
  economic trends, 863, 1007
  human rights, 770
  trade, 966
CIVIL AND POLITICAL RIGHTS, *720-52
  see also human rights
civilians in armed conflict, *727-33, 810
climate change
  Intergovernmental Panel on, 1056
  International Research Institute for Climate Prediction, 958
  UN Framework Convention on (1992), 896, 1045, *1049-50, 1053, 1056
    Kyoto Protocol (1997), 1049, 1056
  World Climate Change Conference (Moscow), 1056
  World Climate Programme, 1527
  see also environment; pollution; weather; World Meteorological Organization

COLOMBIA
  drug control, 1274-75
  human rights, 705, 770-71, 814-15
  and Nicaragua (ICJ case), 1304-1305
  refugees, 1238
  terrorist attack, 65, *285
commissions, see main part of name
committees, see main part of name
commodities, *977-80
Commonwealth of Independent States (CIS)
  Abkhaz-Georgian peace process, *430-43
  economic trends, 863, 1017

peacekeeping forces of, 430
Regional Conference to Address the Problems of Refugees, Displaced Persons, Other Forms of Involuntary Displacement and Returnees in the Countries of the CIS and Relevant Neighbouring States (1996), *1240-42

COMOROS, 272, *951-52
Framework Agreement for Reconciliation in the (2001), 272

Comprehensive Nuclear-Test-Ban Treaty (CTBT) (1996), 533, *547-48, 577
Preparatory Commission for CTBT Organization, 548

Comprehensive Peace Agreement (Liberia), 160, 185, *192-94, 198, 207, 218
conferences, see main part of title
conflict prevention, *48-57, 630
Ad Hoc Working Group (Africa), 105-106
civil society, role of, 53-54
conflict diamonds
Kimberley Process, *54-57, *202-206, 223
Liberia, *202-207
Sierra Leone, 213, 215, *217-20, 222-23
Global Partnership for the Prevention of Armed Conflict, 53-54
UN-NGO Conflict Prevention Working Group, 54
UN role in, 54-55

CONGO, REPUBLIC OF THE
and France (ICJ case), 1308
humanitarian assistance, 928

Convention on Access to Information, Public Participation in Decision-making and Access to Justice in Environmental Matters (1998), 1018
Convention on Biological Diversity (1992), 775, 1044-45, *1051-53, 1066
Convention on the Control of Transboundary Movements of Hazardous Wastes and their Disposal (1989), 1072
Convention for Cooperation in the Protection and Development of the Marine and Coastal Environment of the West and Central African Region (1981), 1040, 1067-68
Convention for Cooperation in the Protection, Management and Development of the Marine and Coastal Environment of the East African Region (1985), 1040, 1067-68
Convention for Cooperation in the Protection and Sustainable Development of the Marine and Coastal Environment of the North-East Pacific (2002), 1067
Convention on the Elimination of All Forms of Discrimination against Women (1979), 667, *1190-92, 1193
Convention on Environmental Impact Assessment in a Transboundary Context (1991), 1018
Convention on International Interests in Mobile Equipment (2001), 645
Convention on Long-Range Transboundary Air Pollution (1979), 1050-51
Convention on the Physical Protection of Nuclear Material (1979), 580, 1032
Convention on the Prevention and Punishment of the Crime of Genocide (1948), 677, 1302, 1304
Convention on the Prevention and Punishment of Crimes against Internationally Protected Persons, including Diplomatic Agents (1973), 1343
Convention on the Prohibition of the Development, Production and Stockpiling of Bacteriological (Biological) and Toxin Weapons and on Their Destruction (1971), 268-69, *559-60
Convention on the Prohibition of the Development, Production, Stockpiling and Use of Chemical Weapons and on Their Destruction (1993), 559, *560-61
convention on the prohibition of the use of nuclear weapons (proposed), *551-52
Convention on the Prohibition of the Use, Stockpiling, Production and Transfer of Anti-personnel Mines and on Their Destruction (1997), *571-73
Convention on Prohibitions or Restrictions on the Use of Certain Conventional Weapons Which May Be Deemed to Be Excessively Injurious or to Have Indiscriminate Effects (1980), *565-67
Convention on the Protection and Use of Transboundary Watercourses and International Lakes (1992), 1018
Convention on Psychotropic Substances (1971), 1267-68, 1271, 1278
Convention on the Reduction of Statelessness (1961), 1229
Convention on the Rights of the Child (1989) and Optional Protocols (2000), 667, 675-76, 737, 770, 1203, 1205-1206, 1231
Convention for the Safeguarding of the Intangible Cultural Heritage, 1109
Convention on the Safety of United Nations and Associated Personnel (1994), 73, *1340-43
Convention relating to the Status of Refugees (1951) and Protocol (1967), 1226, 1229
Convention relating to the Status of Stateless Persons (1954), 1229
Convention for the Suppression of Terrorist Bombings (1997), 1341
Convention for the Suppression of Unlawful Acts against the Safety of Civil Aviation (1971), 1300
Convention against Torture and Other Cruel, Inhuman or Degrading Treatment or Punishment (1984) and Optional Protocol (2002), 667, 674-75, 741
Convention on the Transboundary Effects of Industrial Accidents (1992), 1018
conventional weapons, *562-73, see also disarmament
conventions, slavery, 776
Cooperative Enforcement Operations Directed at Illegal Trade in Wild Fauna and Flora, Agreement on (1994), 1068
Copenhagen Declaration on Social Development (1995), *1096-99

COSTA RICA, 275
CÔTE D'IVOIRE, 80, 160, 161, 162-64, *165-84
ECOMICI, 172, *180-84
ECOWAS, 80, *165-78, *182-84

Subject index

human rights, 165-66, 172
humanitarian assistance, 171, 930
Kléber arrangements, 170
and Liberia, 184, 186
Linas-Marcoussis Agreement, 163, *166-72, *176-83
MINUCI, 61, 62, 160, *171-84
peacemaking, 166-69
refugees, 171, 174, 184, 193, 1232, 1233
Counter-Terrorism Committee, 63, *66-70, 746, 1123
CRIME PREVENTION AND CRIMINAL JUSTICE, *1116-58
Commission on, 70, *1116-17, 1154, 1155, 1279
corruption, *1126-49
corrupt practices and illegal transfer of funds, *1148-49
UN Convention against, *1126-49
crime prevention programme, *1119-25
crime prevention strategies, *1149-55
International Criminal Police Organization (Interpol), 68, 1279
UN African Institute for Prevention of Crime and the Treatment of Offenders, *1124-25
UN Congress on the Prevention of Crime and the Treatment of Offenders, Seventh (1985), 734; Eighth (1990), 734; Eleventh (2005), 116, *1117-19
UN Convention against Transnational Organized Crime (2000) and Protocols (2000, 2001), 707, 1119, 1123, *1125-26
Conference of parties (2004), 1125
UN Crime Prevention and Criminal Justice Fund, 1119, *1123-24
UN Crime Prevention and Criminal Justice Programme, *1119-24
UN Interregional Crime and Justice Research Institute, 1119, 1123
UN Office on Drugs and Crime (UNODC), 71, 298, 1119, 1123-24, 1149, 1263, *1278-82, 1284, 1286
Centre for International Crime Prevention, 70, *1123-25, 1148, *1149-51
UN standards and norms in, *1155-58
Vienna Declaration on Crime and Justice (2000), 1123
CROATIA
and Bosnia and Herzegovina, 409
and Serbia and Montenegro (ICJ case), 1304
CUBA
host country relations, 1372, 1373
human rights, 815-16
United States embargo against, *285-86
cultural development, *1109-16
Convention for the Safeguarding of the Intangible Cultural Heritage, 1109
cultural diversity, 717
cultural property, return of, *1113-16
Declaration concerning the Intentional Destruction of Cultural Heritage, 1109
Olympic Truce, *1112-13
peace, culture of, *1110-11
sport for development and peace, *1111-13
Universal Declaration on Cultural Diversity (2001), 717
UN Year for Cultural Heritage (2002), *1109-10

Culture of Peace and Non-Violence for the Children of the World, International Decade for (2001-2010), *689-91
CYPRUS, *445-55
Basis for Agreement on a Comprehensive Settlement of the Cyprus Problem (2002), 445, 446-47
good offices mission, *446-51
human rights, 824
Treaty of Accession to the EU, 446, 449, 451
UNFICYP, 80, 82, 445, *450-55

Dar es Salaam agreement (DRC), 122
debt
adverse effects of, 760
Debt Management and Financial Analysis System, 996
developing countries, *983-87
external debt and development, *984-87
Heavily Indebted Poor Countries
Evian Approach, 984
Initiative, 983-84, 989, 1520
Trust Fund, 938
Paris Club, 983-84
WTO Working Group on Trade, Debt and Finance, 984
Decade to Roll Back Malaria in Developing Countries, Particularly in Africa (2001-2010), *1251-53
Declaration on Cities and Other Human Settlements in the New Millennium (2001), 1074-75, 1078
Declaration of Commitment on HIV/AIDS (2001), 807, 1013, *1243-48, 1253
Declaration concerning the Intentional Destruction of Cultural Heritage, 1109
Declaration on the Elimination of All Forms of Intolerance and of Discrimination Based on Religion or Belief (1981), *717-20
Declaration on the Granting of Independence to Colonial Countries and Peoples (1960), *597-604
Declaration of the Indian Ocean as a Zone of Peace (1971), *596-97
Declaration on Measures to Eliminate International Terrorism (1994), 1338
Declaration of Principles on Good-neighbourly Relations and Cooperation (Central Africa and Great Lakes region), 112, 113, 133
Declaration on the Protection of All Persons from Enforced Disappearance (1992), 740
Declaration on the Right to Development (1986), 753
Declaration on the Right and Responsibility of Individuals, Groups and Organs of Society to Promote and Protect Universally Recognized Human Rights and Fundamental Freedoms (1998), *663-67
Declaration on the Rights of Persons Belonging to National or Ethnic, Religious and Linguistic Minorities (1992), 712
DECOLONIZATION, *597-622
Declaration on the Granting of Independence to Colonial Countries and Peoples (1960), *597-604
information on, dissemination, *606-608
International Decade for the Eradication of Colonialism, Second (2001-2010), 598

Caribbean regional seminar, 598
Special Committee, 600, 606, 608
see also Non-Self-Governing Territories; *individual territories*
deforestation, *1057-63
UN Forum on Forests, *1057-63
democracy
electoral process, 59, *736-39
International Conference of New or Restored Democracies, Fifth, *593-95
Ulaanbaatar Declaration and Plan of Action, *593-95
right to, *736-39
support for, *592-94
DEMOCRATIC PEOPLE'S REPUBLIC OF KOREA, 391-92
armistice agreement (1953), 61, 392
human rights, 816-17
humanitarian assistance, 936
IAEA safeguards, 1032, 1506
Treaty on the Non-Proliferation of Nuclear Weapons (1968), 391, 549
DEMOCRATIC REPUBLIC OF THE CONGO, *113-45
and Burundi, 108, 113, 128
child soldiers, 810-11, 1210
conflict prevention and resolution, 106
Dar es Salaam summit and agreement, 122
Drodro, Mambasa and Bunia, events in, *121-27
Gbadolite ceasefire agreement (2002), 114-16
Global and All-Inclusive Agreement on the Transition in the DRC (2002), 108, 113-16, 123, 125, 135, 136
and Guinea (ICJ case), 1302-1303
HIV/AIDS, 117
human rights, 115, *117-20, 121-22, 135, *809-14
humanitarian assistance, 115, 118, 134, 928, *943-46
Interim Emergency Multinational Force (EU), *129-33
internally displaced persons, 117
Katchele, events in, 134
Luanda Agreement (2002), 113, 116, 120
Lusaka Ceasefire Agreement (1999), 108, 113, 120, 124-25
MONUC, 79, 81, 82, *108-109, *113-45, 809, 943
natural resources, exploitation of, *140-45
panel of experts on illegal, *140-45
Pretoria Agreement (2002), 114-16, 120
refugees, 1232-33
and Rwanda, 113, 114-16, 117, 120-24, 133-37
ICJ case, 1305-1306
SC mission, 127-28
transitional government, installation, *129-33
and Uganda, 113, 115, 116, 123, 124, 133-37
ICJ case, 1303
DENMARK
human rights, 797
Department of, *see main part of name*
desertification
UN Convention to Combat Desertification in those Countries Experiencing Serious Drought and/or Desertification, particularly in Africa (1994), 1045, *1053-55

Global Mechanism, 1053
Havana Declaration on the Implementation of the, 1053
DEVELOPING COUNTRIES, *867-78
debt problems, *983-87
economic and technical cooperation among, *910-14, 1011
economic trends, 863-64
finance, *981-83
international trade, 973
island developing countries, *see* small island developing States
landlocked, *see* landlocked developing countries
LDCs, *see* least developed countries
South-South cooperation, 911-14
High-level Conference on, 913
trade, 966
DEVELOPMENT, *831-78, *879-914, *999-1029
Africa
African Development Forum, Fourth, 1005
economic recovery and development, *937-50
New Partnership for Africa's Development (NEPAD), *937-43, 1003, 1036, 1040-41, 1068, 1074
Tokyo International Conference on African Development, 938, 1002
and trade, 966-67
Asia and the Pacific
and agriculture, 1012
and environment and sustainable development, 1012-13
land transport infrastructure development, 988
social development, 1013-14
Commission on Population and, 1085-87
cultural, *1109-16
Declaration on the Right to (1986), 753
Development Account, 905
Development Policy, Committee for, 864-65
disarmament and, *584
economic cooperation, international, *832-38
Europe
sustainable energy development, 1018
and the CIS, 889
trade, industry and enterprise development, 1017
and external debt, *984-87
financing for, *987-90
globalization, *832-35
and human rights, 757-59
goals, UN, progress towards, 837
Human Development Report, 864, *892-93
human resources development, *1158-60
information and communication technologies, *857-60, 1003-1004
International Conference on Financing for (Monterrey Consensus) (2002), 832, 835, 849, 864, 881, 887, *987-90, 1009, 1066, 1074, 1082, 1203
International Conference on Population and (1994), 1005, *1085-89
and international migration, *1086-89
International Year of Microcredit (2005), 848, *853-54

Joint IMF/World Bank Development Committee, 984
Latin America and the Caribbean
  development policy, 1020
  integration of women in development, 1022-23
  population and development, 1022
  social development, 1021-22
Millennium Development Goals (MDGs), 593, 636, 639, 658, 765, 769, 832, 866, 881-82, 890-91, 893-94, 898, 900-901, 938, 996, 1000-1003, 1034, 1081-82, 1089
operational activities, *879-914
through partnership, *835-37
public administration and, *865-67
right to, *752-64
sport for, *1111-13
sustainable, see sustainable development
UN Conference on Environment and Development, Agenda 21 (1992), *838-42
UNDAF, see United Nations Development Assistance Framework
UNDG, see United Nations Development Group
UNDP, see United Nations Development Programme
UN Pledging Conference for Development Activities, 742, 889, 1200
Western Asia
  economic development, 1026
women and, *1177-81
see also country names; economic cooperation, international
diamonds, see conflict diamonds under conflict prevention
diplomatic relations, 1343
  Convention on the Prevention and Punishment of Crimes against Internationally Protected Persons, including Diplomatic Agents (1973), 1343
  Vienna Convention on Consular Relations (1963), 1306, 1343
  Vienna Convention on Diplomatic Relations (1961), 1343
DISABILITIES, PERSONS WITH, 805-806, 1014, *1105-1109
  rights of, 805-806
  Standard Rules on the Equalization of Opportunities for Persons with Disabilities, 806, 1105-1107
  statistics, 1294
  World Programme of Action concerning Disabled Persons (1982), *1105-1107
disappearance of persons, 740-41
DISARMAMENT, *529-91
  Advisory Board on Disarmament Matters, 585-86
  arms limitation and disarmament, *584-85
    bilateral and unilateral measures, *535-47
    multilateral agreements, 532
  bacteriological (biological) weapons, *558-60
    Convention (1971), 268-69, *559-60, 1278
  chemical weapons, 560-61
    Convention (1993), 559, *560-61
    Organization for the Prohibition of, 68, 560-61
  Conference on, 529, *531-35, 568, 581
  conventional weapons, *562-73

anti-personnel mines, Convention (1997), *571-73
excessively injurious, Convention (1980), *565-67
Inter-American Convention against the Illicit Manufacturing of and Trafficking in Firearms, Ammunition, Explosives, and Other Related Materials (1997), 590
practical disarmament, *567-68
small arms, illicit traffic, 111, 161, *562-65, 573, 586, 587
transparency
  in armaments, *568-70
  of military expenditures, *570-71
Treaty on Conventional Armed Forces in Europe (1990), 576
UN register, 568, 585
verification, 571
and development, *584
missiles
  Anti-Ballistic Missile Treaty (1972), *546-47
multilateralism in disarmament and non-proliferation, *581-82
nuclear disarmament, *532-58
  Comprehensive Nuclear-Test-Ban Treaty (CTBT) (1996), 533, *547-48, 577
    Preparatory Commission for CTBT Organization, 548
  Convention on the Physical Protection of Nuclear Material (1979), 580, 1032
  fissile material, *533
  IAEA safeguards, *549-51, 1032-33, 1506-1507
  Middle East, *550-51
  Non-Proliferation of Nuclear Weapons, Treaty on the (1968), 268, 391, 533, 548-49, 1032
  nuclear-weapon-free zones, *554-58
    Africa, *554-55
    Asia, 555
    Central Asia, 555
    Latin America and the Caribbean, *555-56, 590
    Middle East, *556-57
    South-East Asia, 555
    southern hemisphere, *557
    South Pacific, 557
  security assurances, *533-35
nuclear weapons, *535-46
  ICJ advisory opinion on threat or use of, *552-53
  non-strategic, *537
  prohibition of use, *551-52
outer space arms race, prevention of, *582-84
radioactive waste, *553-54
Reduction and Limitation of Strategic Offensive Arms, Treaty on the (START I (1991); START II (1993)), 535
regional centres for peace and disarmament, *586-91
  Africa, *587-88
  Asia and the Pacific, *588-90
  Latin America and the Caribbean, *590-91

regional and other approaches to, *573-79
Strategic Offensive Reductions Treaty (2002), 535, 549
studies, information and training, *585-91
   studies programme, *585
   UN disarmament fellowship, training and advisory services, 586
      UN Disarmament Information Programme, *585-91
   UN Institute for Disarmament Research, 1421
UN role, *529-32
weapons of mass destruction, 535-36
Disarmament Affairs, UN Department for, 529, 567, 576, 585
Disarmament Commission, *529-31, 535, 567
DISASTER RELIEF, *954-64
   Africa, 954-55, *961-62
   Asia and the Pacific, 955, 957, 962, 1014
   Chernobyl aftermath, *961-63
   El Niño, 961-63
   Inter-Agency Task Force for Disaster Reduction, 957-58
   International Conference on Early Warning, Second, 957
   International Consortium on Landslides, 958
   international cooperation, *955-57
   International Strategy for Disaster Reduction, *957-61
   Latin America and the Caribbean, 955
   UN Disaster Assessment and Coordination, 955
   Yokohama Strategy for a Safer World: Guidelines for Natural Disaster Prevention, Preparedness and Mitigation and its Plan of Action (1994), 958
displaced persons
   housing and property restitution, 796
   internally displaced persons, *793-96
      Angola, 270
      DRC, 117
      Guiding Principles on Internal Displacement (1998), 793-94
      Kosovo (Serbia and Montenegro), 423-24
      Liberia, 186
      Somalia, 242, 246
   Palestine, *513-14
   see also refugees; United Nations High Commissioner for Refugees, Office of the

DJIBOUTI
   special economic assistance, *946-47

DRUG ABUSE AND CONTROL, *1262-88
   Action Plan against Illicit Manufacture, Trafficking and Abuse of Amphetamine-type Stimulants and Their Precursors (1998), 1262
   Action Plan for the Implementation of the Declaration on the Guiding Principles of Drug Demand Reduction (1999), 1262, 1283
   Action Plan on International Cooperation on the Eradication of Illicit Drug Crops and on Alternative Development (1998), 1262
   chemical precursors, control of, *1269-70, *1280-81
   Commission on Narcotic Drugs, 1262-63, 1267-68, 1279, *1282-88
   alternative development, *1286-87
   demand reduction, *1282-83
   drug abuse, 1283-84
   illicit cultivation and trafficking, 1284
   regional cooperation, *1287-88
   Convention on Psychotropic Substances (1971), 1267-68, 1271, 1278
   Global Initiative on Primary Prevention of Substance Abuse, 1280
   HIV/AIDS, 1278, 1280, 1283-84
   International Narcotics Control Board, 1267-68, 1270-71, 1273-79
   medical and scientific needs, opiates for, *1268-69
   money-laundering, *1267
   Single Convention on Narcotic Drugs (1961), 1267-68, 1278
      Protocol (1972), 1267-68
   trafficking, see drug trafficking
   UN Convention against Illicit Traffic in Narcotic Drugs and Psychotropic Substances (1988), 1267-68, 1285
   UNDCP, see United Nations International Drug Control Programme
   UN mechanisms, strengthening of, 1288
   UNODC, see United Nations Office on Drugs and Crime
   world drug situation
      Africa, 1271-72
      Americas, 1272-75
      Asia, 1275-78
      Europe, 1278
      Oceania, 1279
drug trafficking, *1284-86
   Afghanistan, 291, 292, 294, *296-301
   assistance to States most affected by, *1284-86
   Conference on Drug Routes from Central Asia to Europe, 298, 1263, 1280
   Guatemala, 280
   UN Convention against Illicit Traffic in Narcotic Drugs and Psychotropic Substances (1988), 1267-68, 1285

EAST TIMOR, see Timor-Leste
ECOFORCE, see ECOWAS Peace Force for Côte d'Ivoire
ECOMICI, see ECOWAS Mission in Côte d'Ivoire
ECOMIL, see ECOWAS Mission in Liberia
ECOMOG, see Monitoring Group of the Economic Community of West African States
ECONOMIC COMMISSION FOR AFRICA (ECA), *1001-1007
   activities, *1002-1006
   Conference of African Ministers of Finance, Planning and Economic Development, *1001-1007
   economic trends, 1002
   MRU countries, assistance to, 164
   NEPAD, 939, 1003
   trade, 1006
ECONOMIC COMMISSION FOR EUROPE (ECE), 1016-20

Subject index

activities, 1017-20
economic trends, 1016-17
Ministerial Conference on Ageing (2002), 1218
Ministerial Conference on the Environment (fifth), 1018-19
operational activities, 1020
statistics, 1019
sustainable development, 839, 1016
ECONOMIC COMMISSION FOR LATIN AMERICA AND THE CARIBBEAN (ECLAC), 275, 1020-24
activities, 1020-24
subregional, 1024
economic trends, 1020
Economic Community of Central African States
UN cooperation with, 109-10, 111
Economic Community of the Great Lakes Countries, 110
Economic Community of West African States (ECOWAS), 160-64
Côte d'Ivoire, 80, *165-78, *182-84
ECOFORCE, 170, 172
ECOMICI, 172, *180-84
ECOMOG, 167
Guinea-Bissau, 224, 227
Liberia, *184-98, 202
ECOMIL, 185, 193, 197, 198
SC, cooperation with, 58
transport, 1003
ECONOMIC COOPERATION, INTERNATIONAL, *831-78
coercive economic measures, *762-64, *837-38
globalization and interdependence, *832-37
international economic relations, *832-62
science and technology, *854-62
sustainable development, *838-48
see also development
Economic Cooperation Organization (ECO)
Ministerial Meeting, 1043
Economic and Monetary Community of Central Africa, 1003
Economic and Social Affairs, UN Department of (DESA), 862-63, 888, 904-905, 944, 948, 966, 977, 980-81, 984, 1001, 1099, 1218, 1383
ECONOMIC AND SOCIAL COMMISSION FOR ASIA AND THE PACIFIC (ESCAP), *1007-16
activities, *1008-15
admission of Timor-Leste, *1015
economic trends, 1007-1008
policy, 1008
programme and organization, 1014
reform, 1014-15
ECONOMIC AND SOCIAL COMMISSION FOR WESTERN ASIA (ESCWA), *1024-29
activities, *1026-29
committee on women, establishment of, *1028
economic and social trends, 1025-26
programme and organization, 1028
UN Arabic language centre, establishment of, *1028
ECONOMIC AND SOCIAL COUNCIL, 1465-66, 1562-64
Advisory Group on Guinea-Bissau, 223, 226
agenda, 1579-80
budget, revised estimates for, 1420

coordination segment, 999
Development Policy, Committee for, 852
functional commissions, 1392
high-level meeting with Bretton Woods institutions and WTO, *987-88
humanitarian affairs segment, 915-16
operational activities segment, *880-89
triennial policy review, 880-81
revitalization, 1391-92
sessions and segments, 1465-66
structure, 1562-64
work programme, 1466
ECONOMIC, SOCIAL AND CULTURAL RIGHTS, *752-807
International Covenant on (1966), 667, *670-73, 717
see also human rights
economic trends, 862-64
Africa, 1002
Asia and the Pacific, 1007-1008
Europe, 1016-17
Latin America and the Caribbean, 1020
Western Asia, 1025-26
ECOWAS Military Observer Group (ECOMOG), 167
ECOWAS Mission in Côte d'Ivoire (ECOMICI), 172, *180-84
ECOWAS Mission in Liberia (ECOMIL), 185, 193, 197, 198
ECOWAS Peace Force for Côte d'Ivoire (ECOFORCE), 170-72
EDUCATION
girls, 1208-1209
right to, 770-71
for sustainable development, *848
UN Decade for Human Rights Education (1995-2004), *686-89
UNESCO, see United Nations Educational, Scientific and Cultural Organization
World Education Forum (2000), 1209
Eldoret Declaration (2002, Somalia), *241-46, 248
Elimination of Discrimination against Women, Committee on the (CEDAW), 667-68, 778, 1181, *1190-92
Elimination of Harmful Traditional Practices, Plan of Action for the (1994), 778
Elimination of Racial Discrimination, Committee on the (CERD), 281, 667-68, 674, *697-98, 716
El Niño, 961
EL SALVADOR, 273, 274, 275, 286-87
and Honduras (ICJ case), 1306
human rights, 274
ONUSAL, 85
ENERGY, *1030-33
Europe, 1018
International Conference for Renewable Energy (2004), 1031
Johannesburg Renewable Energy Coalition, 1018
nuclear, *1032-33, 1505-1507
Sustainable Development, Commission on, *842-48, 1030
Western Asia, 1027
World Commission on Renewable Energy, 1031

World Solar Programme (1996-2005), *1030-32
ENVIRONMENT, *1036-74
Africa, 1040-41
  conventions, 1040, 1067-68
Asia and the Pacific, 1012, 1067
atmosphere, 1042, *1056
desertification, 1045, *1053-55
  International Year of Deserts and Desertification (2006), *1055
disappearance of States for environmental reasons, 771-72
and disarmament agreements, *584-85
emergencies, 1045
Environment Fund, 1047-48
Environmental Management Group, 1038
Environmentally Sound Management of Unwanted Stocks of Hazardous Wastes and Their Prevention, First Continental Conference for Africa on, 771
Europe, 1018-19, 1043
GEO Year Book 2003, 1047
Global Environment Facility, 896, 1031, 1038, 1045-46, 1067
Global Environment Outlook, 1039-40
Global Ministerial Environment Forum, Fourth, *1036-38
governance, international, 1038
harmful products and waste, protection against, 1069-73
human rights concerns, 771-72
International Council for Local Environmental Initiatives, 957
International Year of Ecotourism (2002), 1073-74
Latin America and the Caribbean, 1022
law, 1073
least developed countries, 1042
marine ecosystems, *see* marine resources
Millennium Summit
  ecosystem assessment, 1055-56
  follow-up, 1055-56
Montreal Protocol on Substances that Deplete the Ozone Layer (1987), 896, 1050, 1055
occupied Palestinian and other Arab territories, 1073
Partnership for Clean Fuels and Vehicles, 1070
protection and sustainable development, 772
and refugees, 1230
Rotterdam Convention on the Prior Informed Consent Procedure for Certain Hazardous Chemicals and Pesticides in International Trade (1998), 771, 1068-70
statistics, 1292
and sustainable development, 1042-44
terrestrial ecosystems, *1057-65
  deforestation, *1057-63
  mountain regions, *1063-65
    International Year of Mountains (2002), *1063-65
UN Conference on Environment and Development (1992) (UNCED), 1044
  Agenda 21, *838-42
UNDP, 896

UNEP, *see* United Nations Environment Programme
UN Framework Convention on Climate Change (1992), 896, 1045, *1049-50, 1053, 1056
  Kyoto Protocol (1997), 1049, 1056
UN List of National Parks and Protected Places, 1068
Vienna Convention on the Protection of the Ozone Layer (1985), 1050
Western Asia, 1027
wildlife conservation, *1068-69
World Conservation and Monitoring Centre, 1047, 1068
World Conservation Union, 1046, 1068-69
World Database on Protected Areas, 1068-69
  Consortium, 1046
see also climate change; marine resources; pollution; sustainable development; weather; World Meteorological Organization
ERITREA, *230-41
Algiers Peace Agreement (2000, Ethiopia-Eritrea), 230, *232-38
Boundary Commission, *230-40
human rights, 239
humanitarian assistance, 232, 927
mines, 231-32, 234-35, 237, 239
refugees, 239
UNMEE, 80, 81, *230-41
ETHIOPIA, *230-41
Algiers Peace Agreement (2000, Ethiopia-Eritrea), 230, *232-38
Boundary Commission, *230-40
disaster assistance, 961
human rights, 239
humanitarian assistance, 232
mines, 231-32, 234-35, 237, 239
UNMEE, 80, 81, *230-41
Eurasian Economic Community, *1479
EUROPE AND THE MEDITERRANEAN, *397-456, 1016-20
Armenia, 443-44
Azerbaijan, 443-44
Belarus
  human rights, 824
Bosnia and Herzegovina, *399-411
  implementation of Peace Agreement, 399-409
  International Police Task Force (IPTF), 409
Cyprus, *445-55
  Basis for Agreement on a Compromise Settlement of the Cyprus Problem, 446
  good offices mission, 446-51
  human rights, 824
development, 889
disarmament, *575-77
drug control, 1278
economic trends, 1016-17
energy, 1018
environment, 1018-19
  Ministerial Conference on the Environment for Europe, 1018-19, 1043
Euro-Mediterranean Forum on Disaster Reduction, 958
former Yugoslavia, *398-99

Subject index

FRY, see Serbia and Montenegro
FYROM, 430
Georgia, *430-43
   relations with Russian Federation, 443
   international trade, 974
   refugees, *1239-42
   Regional Forum on Social Aspects and Financing of Industrial Restructuring, 1017
   Russian Federation, 443, 824-25, 937
   security and cooperation in the Mediterranean region, strengthening of, *455-56
   Serbia and Montenegro (formerly FRY), *411-30
   South-Eastern Europe
     stability and development, 456
     Stability Pact (1999), 576
   States of the Collective Security Treaty Organization, 71, 296, 306
   statistics, 1019
   timber, 1017-18
   transport, 1018
   Turkey, *65-66
   see also country names; Economic Commission for Europe; European Union
European Union (EU)
   Barcelona commitments for follow-up to the Monterrey Consensus, 989
   Central African Republic, 159
   Central America, 275
   and Chile (Law of the Sea Tribunal case), 1353
   Cyprus (Treaty of Accession), 446, 449, 451
   DRC, 113
   EU Police Mission in Bosnia and Herzegovina (EUPM), 399, 409-10
   European Commission Joint Research Centre, 958
   Liberia, 190, 198
   Somalia, 243
   West Africa, 160

FALKLAND ISLANDS (MALVINAS), 609-10
FAO, see Food and Agriculture Organization of the United Nations
FEDERAL REPUBLIC OF YUGOSLAVIA (FRY), see Serbia and Montenegro
FINANCE, INTERNATIONAL, *980-93
   financial policy, *980-87
     financial flows, 981
     international financial system, 981-82
   financing for development, *987-90
     International Conference on Financing for Development (Monterrey Consensus) (2002), 832, 835, 849, 864, 881, 887, 1009, 1066, 1074, 1082, 1203
     Barcelona commitment, 989
     follow-up, *987-90
   investment, technology and related financial issues, 990-93
     Commission on, 990-91
     competition law and policy, 991-92
     international standards of accounting and reporting, 992
     taxation, 992-93

UNCTAD, see United Nations Conference on Trade and Development
WTO Working Group on Trade, Debt and Finance, 984
see also International Finance Corporation; International Monetary Fund; World Bank
Financial Regulations of the United Nations, 1429
financing of UN missions, *82-91
   MINUCI, *175
   MINURCA, 159
   MINURSO, *265-67
   MIPONUH, 285
   MONUC, *137-40
   UNAMET, 385
   UNAMIR, 155
   UNAMSIL, *220-22
   UNCRO, 398
   UNFICYP, *453-55
   UNIFIL, *520-22
   UNIKOM, *360-61
   UNLB, *96-97
   UNMEE, *240-41
   UNMIH, 285
   UNMIK, *428-29
   UNMIL, *200-201
   UNMISET, *381-85
   UNMOT, 396
   UNOMIG, *442-43
   UNOMIL, 199
   UNOMUR, 155
   UNPF, 398
   UNPF-HQ, 398
   UNPREDEP, 398
   UNPROFOR, 398
   UNSMIH, 285
   UNTAET, *381-83
   UNTMIH, 285
FINLAND
   human rights, 797-98
FOOD
   Africa, 1005
   FAO, see Food and Agriculture Organization of the United Nations
   food security, 1260-61
   HIV/AIDS and food insecurity, 1250-51
   International Year of Rice (2004), 1260-61
   nutrition, 1261
     UN System Standing Committee on Nutrition, 1261
     UNU activities, 1261
   right to, *766-68
   World Food Programme (WFP), 171, 263, 264, 460, 880-81, 887, 893, 1205, 1223, 1230, 1248, 1259-60
   World Food Summits (1996, 2002), 766, 1260
FOOD AND AGRICULTURE ORGANIZATION OF THE UNITED NATIONS (FAO), 171, 243, 757, 972, 1017, 1068, 1071, 1260, 1510-11
   Committee on World Food Security, 1260
   corporate statistical database of (FAOSTAT), 1289
FORMER YUGOSLAVIA, *398-99
   International Tribunal for the (ICTY), *1310-20

UN operations, *398-99
FORMER YUGOSLAV REPUBLIC OF MACEDONIA, THE (FYROM), 430
　Greece, relations with, 430
　human rights, 663-64
Framework Agreement on Security Arrangements during the Interim Period (2002, Sudan), 257
FRANCE
　Côte d'Ivoire, 165, 166-67
　and Iraq, 325-26, 327, 329-30, 331, 333-34
　New Caledonia, *611-13
　and Republic of the Congo (ICJ case), 1308
Frente Popular para la Liberación de Saguía el-Hamra y de Río de Oro (POLISARIO), *257-65
Gaza Strip, *see under* Middle East
General Agreement on Trade in Services (GATS), 772, 972, 1535-36
GENERAL ASSEMBLY, *1388-91, 1462-65, 1556-60
　agenda, 1463-64, 1570-79
　Committee on Conferences, 1481-85, *1485-89
　credentials, 1463
　Main Committees, 1464, 1556
　Millennium Summit follow-up, *1384-86
　resolutions and decisions, *1464-65
　revitalization, *1388-91
　sessions, organization of, 1462-63
　structure, 1556-60
General Framework Agreement for Peace in Bosnia and Herzegovina (1995 Peace Agreement), *399-410, 576
Geneva Convention, Fourth (1949), 459, *491-92
Geneva International Centre for Humanitarian Demining, 100
genocide
　Convention on the Prevention and Punishment of the Crime of (1948), 677, 1302, 1304
　Rwanda, 108, *154-55
　　International Criminal Tribunal for (ICTR), *1320-29
GEORGIA, *430-43
　Abkhazia, *430-42
　Agreement on a Ceasefire and Separation of Forces (1994, Moscow Agreement), 430, 438
　Basic Principles for the Distribution of Competences between Tbilisi and Sukhumi (2001), *430, 431, 432, 438
　CIS peacekeeping force, 430, 433
　human rights, 441-42, 718
　humanitarian assistance, 437, 439-42
　Russian Federation, relations with, 443
　situation on the ground, 439-41
　UNOMIG, 80, 81, *430-43
GERMANY
　and Iraq, 326, 329-30, 332
GHANA
　humanitarian assistance, 930
GIBRALTAR, *610-11
Global and All-Inclusive Agreement on the Transition in the DRC (2002), 113-16, 123
Global Compact Office (UN), 835
Global Conference on Sustainable Development of Small Island Developing States (1994), 871, 872

Programme of Action, *871-75, 1042-43
Global Environment Facility, 896, 1031, 1038, 1045-46, 1067
Global Environment Outlook, 1039-40
Global Forum on Reinventing Government, 866
　Marrakech Declaration, 866
Global Initiative on Primary Prevention of Substance Abuse, 1280
Global International Waters Assessment (2000), 1041, 1065
Global Programme of Action for the Protection of the Marine Environment from Land-based Activities, 1066
Global Programme against Terrorism (2002), 1123, 1149
global threats and challenges, responding to, *49
globalization
　Asia and the Pacific, 1009-10
　human rights, *757-59
　and interdependence, *832-37
　international trade, 973
　partnership, *835-37
　World Commission on the Social Dimension of, 757, 832
Great Lakes Regional Peace Initiative on Burundi, 148, *151-54
　see also Central Africa and Great Lakes region
GREECE
　Cyprus, 446, 447
　FYROM, relations with, 430
GUAM, 605
GUATEMALA, 273, 274, 275, 276, *278-84
　Agreement on a Firm and Lasting Peace (1996), 275-76, 278
　Agreement on the Implementation, Compliance and Verification Timetable for the Peace Agreement (1997, Timetable Agreement), 278, 280
　and Belize, 275
　Commission to Follow Up the Implementation of the Peace Agreements, 278-81
　drug trafficking, 280
　human rights, 281, 282-83
　MINUGUA, 61, 85, *278-84
GUINEA
　and DRC (ICJ case), 1302-1303
　humanitarian situation, 930
GUINEA-BISSAU, 105, 161, 163-64, *223-29, *948-50
　Ad Hoc Advisory Group on, 223, 226, *948-50
　constitutional and electoral questions, 224, 226
　coup d'état, 227-29
　economic situation, 224
　ECOWAS Mediation and Security Council, 224
　human rights, 225, 226
　UNOGBIS, 60, 62, 160, *223-26, 228-29
GUUAM (Georgia, Ukraine, Uzbekistan, Azerbaijan, Moldova), *1479
GUYANA
　human rights, 703-704

HAITI, 284-85
　human rights, 683, 816

political situation, 285
special economic assistance, *952-53
HEALTH, *1243-59
AIDS, see HIV/AIDS
harmful products and waste, protection against, 1069-73
malaria, *1251-52
medication, access to, *1253-55
road safety, *1257-59
statistics, 1293-94
tobacco control, 1251
Framework Convention on, 1251, 1514
traditional practices affecting the health of women and girls, 778, 1174-75
WHO, see World Health Organization
women, the girl child and HIV/AIDS, 1174
Heavily Indebted Poor Countries Initiative, 983-84, 1520
High-level Panel on Threats, Challenges and Change, *49
HIV/AIDS, 630, 806-807, 938-39, 1002, 1003, 1007, 1159, *1243-51, 1252
Afghanistan, 299
Africa, 110, 117,152, 246, 248-49, 811, 928, 932-33
Africa's Orphaned Generations, 1211
Asia and the Pacific, 299, 1013
children, 787, 1174, 1202-1203, 1205-1207, 1209-11
Declaration of Commitment on (2001), 807, 1013, *1243-48, 1253
drugs, 1278, 1280, 1283-84
food insecurity, 1250-51
Global Fund to Fight AIDS, Tuberculosis and Malaria, 1244, 1248, 1256
Guidelines on HIV/AIDS and Human Rights, 807
IASC Task Force on HIV/AIDS in Emergency Settings, 1223, 1230, 1245
Impact of AIDS, 1094
Inter-Agency Advisory Group on, 1223
Maputo Declaration on Malaria, HIV/AIDS, Tuberculosis and Other Related Infectious Diseases, 1252
peacekeeping operations, 75-76
refugees, 1230
UNAIDS, see Joint United Nations Programme on HIV/AIDS
UNDP, 896-97
UNFPA, 1089
women, 1174, 1193-94
HONDURAS, 274, 275, 276, 286-87
and El Salvador (ICJ case), 1306
and Nicaragua (ICJ case), 1304
HORN OF AFRICA, *229-57
see also country names
Human Development Report, 279, 864, 890-93, 1000
HUMAN RESOURCES
development, *1158-60
Management, Office of Human Resources (UN), 1238, *1439-44, 1447
United Nations Institute for Training and Research (UNITAR), *1160-62, 1369
United Nations University, 1163
University for Peace, 1162-63

HUMAN RIGHTS
advisory services and technical cooperation, *678-86
Africa, *808-14
Angola, 271
Burundi, 152, 808-809
Central Africa and Great Lakes region, 110
Central African Republic, 157, 159
Chad, 682-83
Côte d'Ivoire, 165-66, 172
DRC, 115, 117-18, 121-22, 135, *809-14
Eritrea, 239
Ethiopia, 239
Guinea-Bissau, 225, 226
Liberia, 186, *189-92, 193, 199, 206, 683-84
Morocco, 707
Sierra Leone, 213, 216, 220, 684-85
Somalia, 248, 685
Sudan, 764-65, 814
West Africa, 162, 164
Zimbabwe, 814
Americas, 274
Argentina, 733
Brazil, 739-40
Canada, 704-705
Chile, 797
Colombia, 705, 770, 814-15
Cuba, 815-16
El Salvador, 274
Guatemala, 281, 282-83
Guyana, 703-704
Haiti, 683
Jamaica, 739
Mexico, 797
Peru, 769
Trinidad and Tobago, 703-704
Asia and the Pacific
Afghanistan, 297, 303, 679, 769, *1175-77
Cambodia, *679-82
China, 770
DPRK, 816-17
Iran, 733, 745, *817-18
Iraq, 316, 356, *818-19
Myanmar, *819-22
Thailand, 664-65
Timor-Leste, 375, 380, 685-86, 823
Turkmenistan, *823-24
Yemen, 764
citizenship, regulation by successor States, 716
civil and political rights, 669-70, *720-52
Commission on, 488, *655-57, 667, 696, 1193, 1253
Subcommission on the Promotion and Protection of Human Rights, 656-57, 668, 713-14
Committee on, 667
corruption, 764
Declaration on the Rights and Responsibility of Individuals, Groups and Organs of Society to Promote and Protect Universally Recognized Human Rights and Fundamental Freedoms (1998), *663-67
defenders of, *663-66
democracy, right to, *736-39

democratic and equitable order, 757
development, right to, *752-64
disappearance of persons, 740-41
    Working Group on Enforced or Involuntary Disappearances, 740-41, 811, 824
discrimination based on work and descent, 715
economic, social and cultural rights, *670-73, *752-807
education in, *687-89
education, right to, 770-71
environmental and scientific concerns, 771-72
Europe and the Mediterranean
    Belarus, 824
    Bosnia and Herzegovina, 408
    Cyprus, 824
    Denmark, 797
    Finland, 797-98
    FYROM, 663-64
    Georgia, 441-42, 718
    Norway, 797-98
    Romania, 718
    Russian Federation, 794, 824-25
    Spain, 707, 742
    United Kingdom, 771
food, right to, *766-68
genetic privacy, 775
globalization, *757-59
and good governance, 667
housing, right to, 768-70
and human responsibilities, 666-67
impunity against prosecution, 734
indigenous people, *796-805
instruments, *667-77
    children, 667, 675-76
    civil and political rights, 385, 667-68, 669-70
    discrimination against women, 667
    economic, social and cultural rights, 667, 668, *670-73
    genocide, 677
    migrant workers and their families, 667, *676-77, 707, 716
    racial discrimination, 667, 673-74
    torture, 667, 674-75, 741
    treaty body system, 668
intimidation of individuals cooperating with UN, 694
intolerance, forms of, *710-20
    cultural prejudice, *710-12
    minorities, discrimination against, *712-17
    religious, *717-20
justice, administration of, *725-26
liberalization of trade in services, 759
mercenaries, *722-24
Middle East, *488-92, *721-22, *825-27
    Israeli-occupied territories, 766, 825-27
    Lebanon, *825
    rights of Palestinians, *721-22
migrant workers and their families, 667, *706-10
minorities, *712-17
movement, freedom of, *791-96
    mass exoduses, *791-93

    Recommended Principles and Guidelines on Human Rights and Human Trafficking, 780
    smuggling and trafficking in persons, 780, *1151-53
national institutions, *691-93
non-citizens, 715-16
physical and mental health, right to, *772-75
poverty, extreme, 764-65
promotion of, *655-94
    international cooperation, *661-63
    right to, *663-67
    strengthening, *660-61
protection, *697-807
racism and racial discrimination, *695-710
regional arrangements, *693-94
    Africa, *693-94
    Asia and the Pacific, 694
self-determination, right to, *720-24
slavery and related issues, 776
small arms, 752
terrorism, *745-50
torture and cruel treatment, *741-44
treaties, reservations to, 669
UN Decade for Human Rights Education (1995-2004), *686-89
Universal Declaration of (1948), 669, 713, 816
violations, *808-27
vulnerable groups, *777-807
    children, *780-91
    indigenous people, *796-805
    internally displaced persons, *793-96
    people with HIV/AIDS, 806-807
    persons with disabilities, 805-806
    women, 777-80, *1175-77
weapons of mass destruction, 751-52
women married to foreigners, 716-17
World Conference on (1993), 668, 677-78
World Conference against Racism, Racial Discrimination, Xenophobia and Related Intolerance (2001), 674, *695-98, *798-800
    Durban Declaration and Programme of Action, 696-97
    follow-up, *696-703
World Public Information Campaign on, *695-98
HUMAN SETTLEMENTS, *1074-84
The Challenge of Slums: Global Report on Human Settlements 2003, 1080
Commission on, 1083
Declaration on Cities and Other Human Settlements in the New Millennium (2001), 1074-75, 1078
Europe, 1019
Global Campaign for Secure Tenure, 1080, 1082
Global Campaign for Urban Governance, 1080, 1082
Global Forum of Parliamentarians on Habitat, Fourth, 1074
Global Partnership Initiative on Urban Youth Development in Africa, 1078
Habitat Agenda (1996), 1019, *1075-79
Housing Rights Programme, 1080
Latin America and the Caribbean, 1022

Subject index

occupied Palestinian territories, 1082-83
Rebuilding Iraq—Iraq Reconstruction Plan for Shelter and Urban Development, October 2003, 1081
regional cooperation, 1082-83
UN Conference on Human Settlements (Habitat II) (1996), 1074
UN-Habitat in Iraq, April 2003, 1081
UN Habitat and Human Settlements Foundation, 1074-75, 1079, 1084
  Water and Sanitation Trust Fund, 1074
UN Habitat's Partnership Agreement, 1075
UN Human Settlements Programme (UN-Habitat), 769-70, 801, 888, 939, 958, 1034, 1038, 1040, 1074, *1078-83
  activities, 1080-82
  cooperation with UNEP, 1081
  refugees, 1223
Urban Management Programme, 1080
water and sanitation, 775, 1082
women, role of, 1083
World Urban Forum, 1075, 1079
Humanitarian Affairs, Office for the Coordination of (UN) (OCHA), 171, 955, 957, 1045, 1223
HUMANITARIAN ASSISTANCE, *915-64
  Africa
    Angola, 270, 271, 927
    Burkina Faso, 930
    Burundi, 152, 809, 927
    Central Africa and Great Lakes region, 110, 927
    Central African Republic, 927
    Congo, Republic of the, 928
    Côte d'Ivoire, 171, 930
    DRC, 115, 118, 134, 928
    Eritrea, 232, 927
    Ethiopia, 232
    Ghana, 930
    Guinea, 930
    Lesotho, 931
    Liberia, *186-92, 193, 194, 198-99, 202, 206, 930-31
    Malawi, *931-32
    Mali, 930
    Mozambique, 932
    Sierra Leone, 213, 216, 931
    Somalia, 242, 246, *928-29
    Southern Africa, 931
    Sudan, 929-30
    Swaziland, 932-33
    Uganda, 928
    West Africa, 162, 164, 930
    Zambia, 933
    Zimbabwe, 933
  Asia and the Pacific
    Afghanistan, 290, 291, 294, 303, *933-36
    DPRK, 936
    Indonesia, 936
    Iran, 962
    Iraq, 333-36, 343-45, 347, 353, 365, 818, 915, 936
    Myanmar, 819
    Tajikistan, 937
  consolidated appeals, 922
  coordination of, *915-22

  Europe and the Mediterranean
    Georgia, 437, 439-42
    Russian Federation, 937
  International Search and Rescue Advisory Group, 955
  Middle East, 458-63, 465, 467-69, 483, 488, 497, 499, 503, 505, 836-37
  mine clearance, *see* mines
  personnel, safety of, *921-22
  special economic assistance
    African countries emerging from conflict, *947-90
    African economic recovery and development, *937-51
    Central America, *950-51
    Comoros, *951-52
    Djibouti, *946-47
    DRC, *943-46
    Haiti, *952-53
    Timor-Leste, *953-54
  UNDP, 896
  UNFPA, 1090
  UNIFEM, 1193
  "White Helmets", *922-23

IAEA, *see* International Atomic Energy Agency
IASC, *see* Inter-Agency Standing Committee
ICAO, *see* International Civil Aviation Organization
IMF, *see* International Monetary Fund
impunity for human rights violations, 734
INDIA
  and Pakistan
    Jammu and Kashmir, 80, 391
    UNMOGIP, 80
INDIGENOUS PEOPLE, *796-805
  human rights, *796-805
  International Day of the World's, 801
  International Decade of the World's (1995-2004), 686, *799-803
    UN Voluntary Fund for the, 801
  natural resources, permanent sovereignty over, *805
  Permanent Forum on Indigenous Issues, 798, 801, 803-804
  treaties, agreements and other constructive arrangements, 804-805
  UN Voluntary Fund for Indigenous Populations, 800
  Working Group on Indigenous Populations, *798-800, 803-804
INDONESIA
  humanitarian assistance, 936
  and Timor-Leste, 370, 374, 380
INDUSTRIAL DEVELOPMENT
  Africa, 1004-1005
  Decade for Africa, Second (1993-2002), 1005
  UNIDO, 1533-34
INFORMATION AND COMMUNICATION, *622-39, *857-60
  Committee on Development Information (ECA), 1003-1004

on decolonization, *606-608
Global e-Policy Resource Network, 1003
international security, *639-41
　cyberspace and protection of information infrastructures, 640
　technologies, *857-62, 1003-1004
　　cybersecurity, 640, *861-62
　　Information and Communication Strategy, development of, 859-60, *1492-94
　　Information and Communication Technologies Task Force, 859, 1003
　　World Summit on the Information Society, 641, 745, *857-59, 999, 1003, 1016, 1102, 1183
　UN information systems, 859-60, *1492-95
　　Ad Hoc Open-ended Working Group on Informatics, 1494
　　Communications and Information Technology Service, 95
　　field assets control, 94-95
　　UN system Extranet, 859-60
　UN public information, *622-39
　　Department of Public Information (DPI), *502-503, 585, 606, 622, 630-38
　　　library services, 634-35
　　　reorganization, 630-32, 1383
　　　Strategic Communications Division, 502, 622, 630, 631, 635-38
　　UN Communications Group, 622, 638-39
　　UN information centres (UNICs), 1581-83
　　UN international radio, 632-33
　　UN News Centre, 638
　　web sites, 637-38
　women and the media, *1183-85
　World Public Information Campaign on Human Rights, 686-87
intellectual property rights, 772, 967, 1044
　WIPO, 1530-31
Inter-Agency Advisory Group on AIDS, 1223
Inter-Agency Coordination Group on Mine Action, 924
Inter-Agency Guiding Principles on Unaccompanied and Separated Children, 1209
Inter-Agency Space Debris Coordination Committee, 644-45
Inter-Agency Standing Committee (IASC)
　Task Force on HIV/AIDS in Emergency Settings, 1245
　Task Force on Prevention of Sexual Exploitation, 789
Inter-Agency Task Force for Disaster Reduction, 957-58
Inter-Agency Working Group on the Incorporation of Child Protection in UN Peacemaking, Peacekeeping and Peace-building Processes, 789
Inter-American Convention against the Illicit Manufacturing of and Trafficking in Firearms, Ammunition, Explosives, and Other Related Materials (1997), 590
Intergovernmental Authority on Development (IGAD)
　Somalia, 230, *243-50
　Sudan, 256-57

Interim Emergency Multinational Force in Bunia (DRC), 79
Internal Oversight Services, UN Office of (OIOS), *1386-87
　DPI, 631
　evaluations, proposed, 1430
　human resources management, 1439-40
　international tribunals, 1331
　procurement, 95-96, 1386
　regional commission subprogrammes, 1001
　UNEP, 1047
　UN-Habitat, 1083
　UN Joint Staff Pension Fund, *1458
internally displaced persons, see displaced persons
INTERNATIONAL ATOMIC ENERGY AGENCY (IAEA), 1505-1507
　Agreement on Safeguards, 268
　counter-terrorism, 70, 580
　DPRK, 391, 549
　International Conference on the Safety and Transport of Radioactive Material, 553
　Iran, 550
　Iraq, 319-22, 326-30, 333, 549-50
　Libyan Arab Jamahiriya, 550
　nuclear energy, *1032-33
　nuclear safeguards, *549-51
INTERNATIONAL CIVIL AVIATION ORGANIZATION (ICAO), 1522-23
International Civil Service Commission, *1431-33, 1444-45
International Committee of the Red Cross (ICRC), 230-31, 260, 263, 297, 356-57, 441, 716, 722, 818, 1231
International Conference on Financing for Development (Monterrey Consensus) (2002), *987-90
international conference on the Great Lakes (proposed), *111-13
International Conference of New or Restored Democracies, Fifth, 593-94
International Conference on Population and Development (1994), follow-up, *1085-89
international conferences (UN), follow-up, *1467-74
International Convention on the Elimination of All Forms of Racial Discrimination (1965), 667, 673-74, 696
International Convention on Oil Pollution Preparedness, Response and Cooperation (1990) and Protocol (2000), 1068
International Convention on the Protection of the Rights of All Migrant Workers and Members of Their Families (1990), 667, *676-77, 707, 716, 1172
International Convention against the Recruitment, Use, Financing and Training of Mercenaries (1989), 161, *722-24
International Convention for the Suppression of the Financing of Terrorism (1999), 1341
International Council for Local Environmental Initiatives, 957
INTERNATIONAL COURT OF JUSTICE (ICJ), 1299-1309, 1334
　advisory opinion, Special Rapporteur (1999), 1309

Subject index

Avena and other Mexican nationals (Mexico v. United States), 1306-1308
civil aviation safety convention (1971) (Libyan Arab Jamahiriya v. United Kingdom and United States), 1300
crimes against humanity (Republic of the Congo v. France), 1308
Diallo, Ahmadou Sadio (Guinea v. DRC), 1302-1303
frontier dispute (Benin/Niger), 1305
genocide convention (1948), application of (Bosnia and Herzegovina v. Serbia and Montenegro), 1302
genocide convention (1948) (Croatia v. Serbia and Montenegro), 1304
land, island and maritime frontier dispute (El Salvador v. Honduras), 1306
maritime delimitation (Nicaragua v. Honduras), 1304
nuclear weapons, advisory opinion on threat or use of, *552-53
Occupied Palestinian Territory, wall construction in, 477, *478-82, 1309
oil platforms (Iran v. United States), 1300-1301
Pedra Branca/Pulau Bath Puteh, Middle Rocks and South Ledge, sovereignty over (Malaysia/Singapore), 1308-1309
territorial and maritime dispute (Nicaragua v. Colombia), 1304-1305
Trust Fund to Assist States in the Settlement of Disputes, 1309
UN Charter violation (DRC v. Rwanda), 1305-1306
UN Charter violation (DRC v. Uganda), 1303
International Covenant on Civil and Political Rights (1966) and Optional Protocols (1966, 1989), 385, 667, 669-70, 713, 735, 740, 745
International Covenant on Economic, Social and Cultural Rights (1966), 667, 668, *670-73, 717
International Criminal Court (ICC), 33, *1332-34
Assembly of States, 1298
exception to jurisdiction of, *76-78
Rome Statute (1998), *76-78, 118, 810, 1332
trust fund for LDC participation, 1333
International Criminal Police Organization (Interpol), 68, 1279
International Development Association (IDA), see World Bank
INTERNATIONAL FINANCE CORPORATION (IFC), 888, 1518-19
INTERNATIONAL FUND FOR AGRICULTURAL DEVELOPMENT (IFAD), 888, 1532
International Institute for Democracy and Electoral Assistance, *1479
INTERNATIONAL LABOUR ORGANIZATION (ILO), 1508-1509
Convention on indigenous and tribal peoples (1957), 797
Convention on minimum age for employment (1973), 788
Convention on worst forms of child labour (1999), 788, 1210
globalization, 757, 832

HIV/AIDS, 1247
racial discrimination, 696
refugees, 1223
World Employment Report, 1216
INTERNATIONAL LAW, *1310-62
bioethics law, 1374
Commission, *1334-37
citizenship regulation by successor States, 716
international law, fragmentation of, 1336-37
international liability, 1336
international organizations, responsibility of, 1336
shared natural resources, 1337
unilateral acts of States, 1336
diplomatic relations, 1343
economic law, *1374-79
environmental law, 1073
International Institute for the Unification of Private Law, 645
International Law Seminar, 1369
international State relations and, *1337-43
international terrorism, *1338-40
jurisdictional immunity of States and their property, *1337-38
peacekeeping, *76-78
UN Programme of Assistance in the Teaching, Study, Dissemination and Wider Appreciation of, *1369-71
INTERNATIONAL MARITIME ORGANIZATION (IMO), 1068, 1354, 1529
INTERNATIONAL MONETARY FUND (IMF), 68, 105, 149, 157, 350, 753, 765, 888, 981, 984, 1520-21
International Narcotics Control Board (INCB), 1267-68, 1270-71, 1273-79
International Organization for Migration, 171, 716, 1223
INTERNATIONAL PEACE AND SECURITY, *47-101, *592-97
conflict prevention, *49-57
Declaration on the Strengthening of International Security (1970), 57
Millennium Summit (2000) follow-up, *48-49
peacemaking and peace-building, *57-60
political and peace-building offices, 61-62
regional aspects
Indian Ocean, *596-97
South Atlantic, *595-96
threats to, *63-71
High-level Panel on Threats, Challenges and Change, 49
see also terrorism
International Police Task Force, 409-10
International Research and Training Institute for the Advancement of Women (INSTRAW), *1194-1201, 1462
International Seabed Authority, 1346, 1352-53
International Search and Rescue Advisory Group, 955
International Security Assistance Force (Afghanistan), 80, 290, 297, 301, 303, *307-11
International Strategy for Disaster Reduction, *957-61
INTERNATIONAL TELECOMMUNICATION UNION (ITU), 1525-26
World Summit on the Information Society, *858-59

international trade, see trade
International Trade Centre (ITC), *974-76
INTERNATIONAL TRIBUNALS, *1310-31
    ad litem judges, *1315-16
    conditions of service, *1436-38
    for the Former Yugoslavia (ICTY), 352, 402, 405, 408, 416, *1310-20
        Chambers, 1310-15
            new arrests, surrenders and indictments, 1311-12
            ongoing cases and trials, 1312-15
        completion strategy, 1310, 1316, 1329
        financing, *1317-20
        Prosecutor, Office of the, *1316-17, 1329-31
        Registry, 1317
    functioning, *1329-31
        OIOS report, 1331
    for the Law of the Sea, 1346, 1353
    for Rwanda (ICTR), 811, *1320-29
        Chambers, *1320-25
            election of judges, *1321-25
            new cases, 1320
            ongoing trials, 1320-21
        financing, *1326-29
        Prosecutor, Office of the, 1325
        Registry, 1325-26
International Year of Deserts and Desertification (2006), *1055
International Year of Ecotourism (2002), 1073-74
International Year of the Family (1994), *1103-1105
International Year of Freshwater, 636, 1012, 1033-34, 1041
International Year of Microcredit (2005), 848, *853-54
International Year of Mountains (2002), *1063-65
International Year of Rice (2004), 1260-61
IRAN
    drug control, 1277-78
    human rights, 733, 745, *817-18
    humanitarian issues, 962
    IAEA nuclear safeguards, 550
    refugees, 1239
    and United Arab Emirates, 396
    and United States (ICJ case), 1300-1301
IRAQ, *315-56
    Al-Qaida, 326, 327
    attack on UN headquarters in Baghdad, 65, *346-48, 352, 353, 367, *1452
    Azores meeting (Portugal, Spain, United Kingdom, United States), 332-33, 461
    Coalition Provisional Authority, 337-38, 354-56, 361-62, 368-69
    constitutional timetable, 351
    elections, 343, 345, 351
    environment assessment, 1039-40
    Governing Council, 343, 345-46, 347, 350-56
    human rights, 356, *818-19
    humanitarian needs and assistance, 333-36, 343-45, 347, 353, 365, 818, 915, 936
    Hussein, Saddam, capture of, 355
    IAEA, 319-24, 326, 327, 333, 1032
        Tuwaitha, mission to, 322
        work programme, 320-22
    International Advisory and Monitoring Board, 350, 366-67
    and Kuwait, *356-58, 819
    mass graves, 356
    military conflict and occupation, *333-56
    Nicosia consultations, 354-55
    no-fly zone, 370
    oil-for-food programme, 318, 336, 337, 342, 353, *362-69
    reconstruction, 351, 896, 1081
    Regional Initiative on Iraq, Joint Declaration of the, 323 (Istanbul), 342 (Tehran)
    sanctions, *338-41, 361-62
    security, lack of, 343, 350, 355, 367
    Special Adviser, 336
    Special Representative, 342-46
    UNAMI, 62, *346, 353-55
    UN Compensation Commission, 369-70, 1039
    UNIKOM, 80, 81, 82, 316, 332, *358-60
    UN staff
        attack on (Baghdad headquarters), 65, *346-48, *1452
        downsizing of, 318, *348-50, 352
        Independent Panel on the Safety and Security of UN Personnel in Iraq, 353
    UNMOVIC, 316-34, 342, 1032
        College of Commissioners, 316
    weapons inspections, resumption, 317
    weapons of mass destruction, allegations, 318, 322-33
ISRAEL
    Golan Heights, *485-88, *522-28, 825
        UNDOF, 80, 82, 516, *525-28
    Israeli civilians, attacks against, 461, 462-63, 464, 466-67, 468-69
    Jerusalem, *484-85
    Lebanese detainees, *825
    peace process, *458-96
        Aqaba Peace Summit, 458, 465-67
        Geneva Accord, 482-83
        the Quartet, 462-67, 473-74, 503, 826
        road map, 458-59, 461-66, 468, 470-73, 488
    property rights, *514-15
    territories occupied by, *459-516
        barrier construction, 460, 463, 469, *474-82, 488, 826, 1309
        human rights, *488-92, *721-22, 766-67, 825-27
        humanitarian situation, 458-63, 465, 467-69, 483, 488, 497, 499, 503, 505
        settlements, 462, 467, 469, 471, *492-93, 499
        socio-economic situation, 463, 465, *485-88, 497, 503
        Special Committee on Israeli Practices, 488, *490-91, 522-23, 806, 825
    violence, escalation of, 458-70, 522
    see also Middle East; Palestine

JAMAICA
    human rights, 739
Jammu (and Kashmir), 80, 391

Joint Inspection Unit (JIU), 55, *98-99, 916, 1214, 1288, *1385, 1387-88, 1467, 1494
Joint United Nations Programme on HIV/AIDS (UNAIDS), 76, 888, 1005, 1245, *1247-50, 1280
justice, administration of, *724-36
    arbitrary detention, 733-34
        Working Group on, 816, 824
    capital punishment, 736
    civilians in armed conflict, *727-33, 810
    compensation for victims, 726-27
    forensics, 736
    independence of judicial system, 734-35
    rule of law, 59-60
    state of siege or emergency, 727
justice system, UN Secretariat, 1459-61
    Joint Appeals Board, 1460
    UN Administrative Tribunal, 1460-61

Kabul Declaration on Good-Neighbourly Relations (2002), 302-303, 308
Kashmir (and Jammu), 80, 391
KOSOVO, see Serbia and Montenegro
Kosovo Force (KFOR) (NATO), 426, 429, 1311
KUWAIT
    and Iraq, 316, *356-58, 819
    UNIKOM, 80, 81, 82, 316, 332, *358-60
Kyoto Protocol (1997), *1049-50

labour
    child labour, 788
    ILO, 1508-1509
landlocked developing countries, *875-78
    Asia and the Pacific, 1010-11
    International Ministerial Conference of Landlocked and Transit Developing Countries and Donor Countries and International Financial and Development Institutions on Transit Transport Cooperation, *875-78, 1010, 1023
        Almaty Declaration and Programme of Action, *875-78, 1010, 1023
    Office of the High Representative for the LDCs, Landlocked Developing Countries and Small Island Developing States, 870, 876
LATIN AMERICA AND THE CARIBBEAN, *273-87, 1020-24
    Andean Community, 912
    Argentina, 733
    Belize, 275
    Brazil, 739-40, 787-88
    Chile, 797
    Colombia, 65, *285, 705, 770-71, 814-15
    Conference of Ministers and Heads of Planning of Latin America and the Caribbean, 1021
    Costa Rica, 275
    Cuba, *285-86, 815-16
    development, 889, 1020
    disarmament, *577-79
        regional approaches, *577-79
        regional centre for peace and, *590-91
    Treaty for the Prohibition of Nuclear Weapons in Latin America and the Caribbean (1967), *555-56, 577, 590
    drug control, 1272-75
    economic cooperation, regional, 1020-21
    economic trends, 1020
    El Salvador, 85, 273, 274, 275, 286-87
    Guatemala, 61, 85, 273, 274, 275, 276, *278-84
    Haiti, 85, 284-85, 683, *952-53
    Honduras, 274, 275, 276, 286-87
    human rights, 814-16
    international trade, 974-75
        and integration, 1021
    Jamaica, 739
    Latin American and Caribbean Initiative on Sustainable Development, 1043
    Latin American and Caribbean Institute for Economic and Social Planning, 1021
    Mexico, 797
    natural resources and infrastructure, 1023
    Nicaragua, 274, 275, 276
    Peru, 769
    Preliminary Overview of the Economies of Latin America and the Caribbean, 1020
    refugees, 1238
    Rio Group, 275
    social development and equity, 1021-22
    Social Panorama of Latin America, 1021
    statistics, 1023
    technical cooperation, 1023
    UNFPA programmes, 1091
    women in development, 1022-23
    see also country names; Caribbean; Central America; Economic Commission for Latin America and the Caribbean
LAW OF THE SEA, *1346-62
    Commission on the Limits of the Continental Shelf, 1346, 1354
    Division for Ocean Affairs and the (UN), 1066, 1362
    International Seabed Authority, 1346, 1352-53
    International Tribunal for the, 1346, 1353
    TRAIN-SEA-COAST programme, 1362
    UN Convention on the (1982), *1346-62
        Conservation and Management of Straddling Fish Stocks and Highly Migratory Fish Stocks, Agreement on (1995), *1346-52
        Part XI implementation, 1346
        States Parties to, Meeting of, 1346
    UN Open-ended Informal Consultative Process on Oceans and the, 1065-66, *1354-62
League of Arab States, 58, 201, 245, 328, 331, 336, 461
least developed countries (LDCs), *867-71
    Asia and the Pacific, 1010-11
    Brussels Declaration (2001) and the Programme of Action for LDCs for the Decade 2001-2010, 867, *868-71, 995, 1011, 1042, 1078
    Conference on, Third (2001), 867, 868, *870-71
    Joint ITC/UNCTAD/WTO Integrated Technical Assistance Programme in Selected LDCs and Other African Countries, 974

Least Developed Countries Report, 998
  list of, 867-68
    triennial review, 867-68
  Office of the High Representative for the LDCs, Landlocked Developing Countries and Small Island Developing States, 870, 876
  Office of the Special Coordinator for Africa and the, 104
  technical cooperation, 996
  trust fund for participation in ICC, 1333
  UNCTAD Trust Fund for, 870
LEBANON, *516-22
  human rights, *825
  UNIFIL, 80, 82, *517-22
Legal Affairs, Office of (UN), *see* Secretariat, UN
LESOTHO
  humanitarian assistance, 931
LIBERIA, 160, 161, 162-64, 171, *184-210
  arms embargo, 202-203, 207
  ceasefire agreement, 189-90
  Comprehensive Peace Agreement (Accra), 160, 185, *192-94, 198, 207, 218
  and Côte d'Ivoire, 171, 174, 184, 186, 193
  ECOWAS, *186-98
  human rights, 186, *189-92, 193, 199, 206, 683-84, 814
  humanitarian situation, *186-92, 193, 194, 198-99, 202, 206, 930-31
  internally displaced persons, 186
  International Contact Group on, 188, 192, 198
  multinational force, *190-93
  Panel of Experts (embargo violations), 185
  peace-building, *185-94
  refugees, 1233, *1237-38
  sanctions, *201-10
  and Sierra Leone, 184, 186, 211-13, *215-20
  UNMIL, 61, 81, 160, 185, *194-202
  UNOL, 60-61, 160, 161, 163, 184-85, 187, 194, 202
LIBYAN ARAB JAMAHIRIYA, *267-69
  attack against (1986), 269
  IAEA nuclear safeguards, 550
  Pan Am flight 103, *267-68
  sanctions, *267-68
  and United Kingdom (ICJ case), 1300
  and United States (ICJ case), 1300
  UTA flight 772, *267-68
  weapons of mass destruction, 268-69
Limits of the Continental Shelf, Commission on the, 1346, 1354
Linas-Marcoussis Agreement (Côte d'Ivoire), 163, *166-72, *176-83
Lincoln Agreement (1998, Papua New Guinea), 392
Luanda Agreement (DRC and Uganda), 113, 116, 120
Lusaka Ceasefire Agreement (1999, DRC), 108, 113, 120, 124-25
Lusaka Protocol (1994, Angola), 269, 271

Machakos Protocol (2002, Sudan), 230, 256-57
MADAGASCAR, 272
MALAWI
  humanitarian assistance, *931-32
MALAYSIA
  and Singapore (ICJ case), 1308-1309

and Singapore (Law of the Sea Tribunal case), 1353
MALI, 161, 930
MALVINAS (FALKLAND ISLANDS), 609-10
Mano River Union (MRU), 161, 162, 164, 186, 187, 211
Maputo Declaration on Malaria, HIV/AIDS, Tuberculosis and Other Related Infectious Diseases, 1252
marine resources
  Convention for Cooperation in the Protection and Development of the Marine and Coastal Environment of the West and Central African Region (1981), 1040, 1067-68
  Convention for Cooperation in the Protection, Management and Development of the Marine and Coastal Environment of the East African Region (1985), 1040, 1067-68
  Convention for Cooperation in the Protection and Sustainable Development of the Marine and Coastal Environment of the North-East Pacific (2002), 1067
  coral reefs, 1067
    International Coral Reef Action Network, 1067
    International Coral Reef Initiative, 1067
  global marine assessment, 1355
  Global Meeting of Regional Seas Conventions and Action Plans (Fifth), 1068
  Global Programme of Action for the Protection of the Marine Environment from Land-based Activities, 1066
  Intergovernmental Oceanographic Commission (UNESCO), 1355
  Joint Group of Experts on the Scientific Aspects of Marine Environmental Protection, 1355
  marine ecosystems, 1065-68
  Montreal Declaration on the Protection of the Marine Environment (2001), 1041
  oceans and seas, 1065-68
  Regional Seas Programme, 1067-68
MARITIME ISSUES
  ICJ cases, 1204-1205
  IMO, 1529
  law of the sea, *1346-62
  Review of Maritime Transport 2003, 993
  TRAIN-SEA-COAST programme, 1362
  transport, 993
Marrakech Declaration (public administration), 866
Marrakech Process (sustainable development), 840
MAURITANIA
  coup d'état, 272
Mekong River Commission (natural disasters), 1014
mercenaries, *722-24
  International Convention against the Recruitment, Use, Financing and Training of (1989), 161, *722-24
MEXICO
  drug control, 1273-74
  ECLAC subregional activities, 1024
  human rights, 797
  and United States (ICJ case), 1306-1308
MIDDLE EAST, *457-528
  Aqaba Peace Summit, 465-67

Arab States and development, 889
Geneva Convention, Fourth (1949), 459, *491-92
human rights, *488-92, *721-22
humanitarian situation, 458-63, 465, 467-69, 483, 488, 497, 499, 503, 505, 836-37
Jerusalem, *484-85, 515-16
Lebanon, *516-22
nuclear proliferation, *550-51, *556-57
Occupied Palestinian Territory, *459-516
economic and social situation, *485-88
Israeli settlements in, *492-93
Palestine issues, 496-516
peace process, *458-96
Mitchell report, 464
Quartet initiative, 462-68, 473-74, 503, 826
road map, 458-59, 461-66, 468, 470-73, 488
peacekeeping operations, 80
refugees, 1239
socio-economic situation, 463, 465, *485-88, 497, 503
Special Coordinator for Middle East (UNSCO) and SG Personal Representative, 62, 462-63, 465, 468, 470, 483
Syrian Arab Republic, *522-28
UNDOF, 80, 82, 516, *525-28
UNIFIL, 80, 82, *517-22, 825
UNRWA, *506-16
UNTSO, 80, 516
violence, escalation of, 458-72, 522
see also country names; Palestine
migrant workers
Convention on protection of rights (1990), *676-77, 707, 716, 1172
discrimination, *706-10
women, 778, *1172-74
migration
international and development, *1086-89
International Organization for, 171, 716, 1223
Recommendations on Statistics of International Migration, Revision 1, 1293
see also movement, freedom of
MILLENNIUM SUMMIT OF THE UNITED NATIONS (2000), 887
ecosystem assessment, 1055-56
follow-up, *48-49, 1055-56, *1255-57, 1295, *1384-86
Millennium Declaration, *48-49, 535, 562, 630, 736, 752, 777, 837, 857, 866, 881, 988, 999, 1002, 1019, 1055, 1082
Millennium Development Goals (MDGs), 593, 636, 639, 658, 765, 769, 832, 866, 881-82, 890-91, 893-94, 898, 900-901, 938, 996, 1034, 1081-82, 1089
mines, *923-27
Angola, 271
Eritrea, 231-32, 234-35, 237, 239
Ethiopia, 231-32, 234-35, 237, 239
Geneva International Centre for Humanitarian Demining, 100
Inter-Agency Coordination Group on Mine Action, 924
Mine Action Centre, UN, 298
Mine Action Programme, 291

Mine Action Service (DPKO), 100
peacekeeping mine action, *99-101
Portfolio of Mine-related Projects, 2003, 924
Somalia, 256
UNICEF, 100
minorities, discrimination against, *712-17
anti-Semitism, 703-704
Declaration on the Rights of Persons Belonging to National or Ethnic, Religious and Linguistic Minorities (1992), 712, *714-15
Muslims and Arabs, 703-704
Roma/Gypsies/Sinti/Travellers, 703, 705, 713
United Nations Guide for Minorities, 713
see also racism and racial discrimination
MINUCI, see United Nations Mission in Côte d'Ivoire
MINUGUA, see United Nations Verification Mission in Guatemala
MINURCA, see United Nations Mission in the Central African Republic
MINURSO, see United Nations Mission for the Referendum in Western Sahara
MIPONUH, see United Nations Civilian Police Mission in Haiti
Monitoring Group of the Economic Community of West African States (ECOMOG), 167
Montreal Declaration on the Protection of the Marine Environment (2001), 1041
Montreal Protocol on Substances that Deplete the Ozone Layer (1987), 1050, 1055
MONTSERRAT, 605
MONUA, see United Nations Observer Mission in Angola
MONUC, see United Nations Organization Mission in the Democratic Republic of the Congo
movement, freedom of, *791-96
internally displaced persons, *793-96
mass exoduses, *791-93
Recommended Principles and Guidelines on Human Rights and Human Trafficking (2002), 780
smuggling and trafficking in persons, 780, *1151-53
see also migration
MOZAMBIQUE
humanitarian assistance, 932
MYANMAR
child soldiers, 820
economic and social situation, 820
human rights, *819-22
humanitarian situation, 819

NATURAL RESOURCES, 1033-35
of DRC, *140-45
indigenous people's permanent sovereignty over, *805
Latin America and the Caribbean, 1023
shared, 1337
sustainable development, *842-47
Commission on, 1030
UNDP, 896
water, *1033-35
Western Asia, 1027
NEW CALEDONIA, *611-13

NEW ZEALAND
  Tokelau, *613-16
NICARAGUA, 275, 276
  and Colombia (ICJ case), 1304-1305
  and Honduras (ICJ case), 1304
NIGER
  and Benin (ICJ case), 1305
Non-Governmental Organizations (NGOs), Committee on, 1480-81
Non-Proliferation of Nuclear Weapons, Treaty on the (1968), 268, 391, 533, 548-49, 1032
Non-Self-Governing Territories (NSGTs)
  economic activities affecting, *604-606
  Falkland Islands (Malvinas), 609-10
  Gibraltar, *610-11
  information, dissemination of, *607-608
  island Territories, 605, *616-22
    American Samoa, 605, *619
    Anguilla, 605, *619
    Bermuda, 605, *619
    British Virgin Islands, 605, *620
    Cayman Islands, 605, *620
    Guam, 605, *620-21
    Montserrat, 605, *621
    Pitcairn, *621
    St. Helena, *621
    Turks and Caicos Islands, 605, *621-22
    United States Virgin Islands, 605, *622
  military activities in colonial countries, 604
  New Caledonia, *611-13
  Puerto Rico, 608-609
  study and training for inhabitants, *608
  Tokelau, *613-16
  Western Sahara, *257-67, 616
  see also decolonization
NORTH AFRICA, *257-69
  see also country names
North Atlantic Treaty Organization (NATO)
  Afghanistan, 290, 301, 302, 308-10
  Bosnia and Herzegovina, 399
  counter-terrorism, 70
  Kosovo, 429
  missile defence, 546
  Partnership for Peace, 401-403
  Verification Coordinating Committee, 576
NORWAY
  human rights, 797-98
Nouméa accord (1998, New Caledonia), *611-13
nuclear disarmament, see disarmament
nuclear energy, *1032-33
  Principles Relevant to the Use of Nuclear Power Sources in Outer Space (1992), 645
  Working Group on the Use of Nuclear Power Sources in Outer Space, 644
  see also International Atomic Energy Agency

OCEANIA, 1279
OCEANS AND SEAS, 1065-68, *1346-62
OCHA, see Humanitarian Affairs, Office for the Coordination of
office of, see under main part of name

OHCHR, see United Nations High Commissioner for Human Rights, Office of the
oil
  Iraq, oil-for-food programme, *362-69
  Western Asia, 1025
Olympic Truce, *1112-13
Organisation for Economic Co-operation and Development (OECD) 887-88, 1089, 1289, 1291, 1376
Organization of American States (OAS)
  disarmament, 577
  Guatemala, 280
  human rights, 274
  Inter-American Committee against Terrorism, 275
  SC, cooperation with, 58
Organization of the Islamic Conference (OIC), 391
Organization for the Prohibition of Chemical Weapons, 68, 560-61
Organization for Security and Cooperation in Europe (OSCE)
  Armenia-Azerbaijan conflict (Minsk Group), 443-45
  Bosnia and Herzegovina, 405, 408
  disarmament, 576
  Forum for Security Cooperation, 576
  Georgia, 433
  peacekeeping operations, 101
  SC, cooperation with, 58
OUTER SPACE, *641-50
  arms race in, prevention of, *582-84
  Committee on the Peaceful Uses of, 641-46
  cooperation, international, *646-50
  Integrated Global Observing Strategy Partnership, 644
  Inter-Agency Space Debris Coordination Committee, 644-45
  International Charter on Space and Major Disasters, 643
  Office for Outer Space Affairs (UN), 643-45
  UN Conference on the Exploration and Peaceful Uses of, Third (UNISPACE-III) (1999), *641-44
  United Nations Programme on Space Applications, 642-43
  UN treaties on, 645
  Working Group on the Use of Nuclear Power Sources in, 644

PAKISTAN
  drug control, 1277
  and India
    Jammu and Kashmir, 80, 391
    UNMOGIP, 80
  refugees, 1239
PALESTINE
  assistance to Palestinians, *503-16
  barrier, construction of, 460, 463, 469, *474-82, 488, 826, 1309
  children, *495-96
  civilian deaths, 459, 460-61, 463-64, 468, 469
  Committee on Palestinian Rights, 460-61, 468, 484, 496, *499-501, 825, 1462
  displaced persons, *513-14
  economic and social conditions, *485-88

education, training and scholarships, 515
environment, 1039, 1073
GA emergency special session, *472-73
Geneva Convention, Fourth (1949), *491-92
human rights, *488-92, 766
human settlements/housing, 1082-83
humanitarian assistance, 458-63, 465, 467-69, 483, 488, 497, 499, 503, 505, 836-37
Israeli civilians, attacks against, 459, 461, 463, 464, 466, 467, 469-72, 474
Israeli settlements in, 462, 467, 469, 471, *492-93, 499
Jerusalem, *480-81, *484-85
Occupied Palestinian Territory, *459-516
Palestinian Rights, Division for (UN), *501-502
peace process, *458-99
    Aqaba Peace Summit, 458, 465-67
    Geneva Accord, 482-83
    the Quartet, 462-68, 473-74, 503, 826
    road map, 458-59, 461-66, 468, 470-73, 488
property rights, *514-15
Reform, Task Force on Palestinian, 461-62, 503
refugees, *509-11
self-determination, right to, *721-22
Special Committee on Israeli Practices, 488, *490-91
Special Human Settlements Programme for the Palestinian People, 1083
University of Jerusalem "Al-Quds" (proposed), 515-16
UNRWA, 460, *506-16, 825, 1462
UNTSO, 80, 516
violence, escalation of, 458-72, 522
women, *493-95, 1177
see also Israel; Middle East

PAPUA NEW GUINEA, 392-95
Bougainville Peace Agreement (2001), 392-95
Lincoln Agreement (1998), 392
UNOMB, 392, 394-95
UNPOB, 61-62, 392-95

PEACE-BUILDING, 45-48
Central America, 275-76
electoral assistance, 58-59
justice and the rule of law, *59-60
missions and offices
    in Africa
        Angola, 60, 62, 269-71
        Burundi, 60, 61, 108, 110, 145, 148-49, 152-53
        Central African Republic, 60, 62, 155-59
        Côte d'Ivoire, 61, 62, 160, *171-84
        Great Lakes region, 60, 61, 110-11
        Guinea-Bissau, 60, 62, 160, *223
        Liberia, 60-61, 160, 161, 163, *184, 202
        Somalia, 60, 61, 242-43, 246, 249
        West Africa region, 48, 62, 164-65, 187
    in Americas
        Guatemala, 61, 85, *278-84
    in Asia and the Pacific
        Afghanistan, 61, 62, *289, 292, 294-95
        Iraq, 62, *345, 346-47
        Korean peninsula, 61
        Papua New Guinea, 61-62, 392-95
        Tajikistan, 48, 62, 396

in Middle East
    Special Coordinator/Special Representative, 62
post-conflict efforts in Africa, 105
SC role, *57-58
regional organizations, cooperation with, 58
sport for development and peace, *1111-13

PEACEKEEPING OPERATIONS, *57-99
in Africa
    Côte d'Ivoire, 80, 160, *171-84
    DRC, 79, 81, 82, *113-40
    Eritrea, 81, *230-41
    Ethiopia, 81, 82, *230-41
    Liberia, 81, 160, 185, *194-202
    Sierra Leone, 79, 82, *211-22
    Western Sahara, 79-80, 81, *257-67
in Asia
    India-Pakistan, 80
    Iraq-Kuwait, 80, 81, *358-61
    Timor-Leste, 80, 81, *370-85
comprehensive review, *78-79
cooperation with regional organizations, 101
in Europe and the Mediterranean
    Cyprus, 80, *445-55
    Georgia, 80, 81, *430-43
    Serbia and Montenegro (Kosovo), 80, 81, 82, *411-29
financial and administrative aspects, *82-99
    accounts, *86-88, *89-90, *91-92
    closed missions
        Bosnia and Herzegovina, 398, 399
        liquidation, *85-86
    costs, *90-91
    financing, *82-84
    peacekeeping assets, *94-97
    personnel matters, *97-99
    reimbursement issues, *92-94
    reserve fund, *88-89
    trust funds, 90
and HIV/AIDS, 75-76
Inter-Agency Working Group on the Incorporation of Child Protection in UN Peacemaking, Peace-keeping and Peace-building Processes, 789
international legal system, *76-78
in Middle East
    Israel–Syrian Arab Republic, 80, 82, *522-28
    Lebanon, 80, 82, *516-22, 825
    Palestine, 80, 516
mine action, *99-101
Nobel Peace Prize Memorial Fund, 71
Panel on UN Peace Operations (Brahimi report, 2000), 71
roster of 2003 operations, 80-81
safety and security, 73-74
SC Working Group, 71
strategic deployment stocks, *72-73
troop contributors, consultations with, 73
women and, 74-75
see also country names
Peacekeeping Operations, Department of (UN), 59, 71, 72, 95-96, 99, 174, 230, 371, 410, 1210, 1229
    Criminal Law and Judicial Advisory Unit, 60

information technology systems, 83
Peacekeeping Best Practices Unit, 74
reform, 1383
UN Security Coordinator, cooperation with, 73
Peacekeeping Operations, Special Committee on, 59, 71-72, 73-74, 99-100
Permanent Forum on Indigenous Issues, 798, 803-804
PITCAIRN, *621
Political Affairs, Department of (UN)
　Afghanistan electoral assistance, 291
　decolonization, 606
pollution
　Convention on the Control of Transboundary Movements of Hazardous Wastes and their Disposal (1989), 1072
　　Basel Protocol (1999), 1072
　Convention on Long-Range Transboundary Air Pollution (1979), 1050-51
　　Montreal (1987) Protocol, 1051
　Environmentally Sound Management of Unwanted Stocks of Hazardous Wastes and Their Prevention, First Continental Conference for Africa on (2001), 771
　hazardous wastes, 1072
　International Convention on Oil Pollution Preparedness, Response and Cooperation (1990), 1068
　　Protocol on Preparedness, Response and Cooperation on Pollution Incidents by Hazardous and Noxious Substances (2000), 1068
　mercury assessment, 1071-72
　Partnership for Clean Fuels and Vehicles, 1070
　persistent organic pollutants, 1072
　　Stockholm Convention on (2001), 1045, 1070, 1072
　radioactive waste, *553-54
　Rotterdam Convention on the Prior Informed Consent Procedure for Certain Hazardous Chemicals and Pesticides in International Trade (1998), 771, 1068-70
　toxic waste, 771
　see also climate change; environment; weather
POPULATION, *1085-95
　Commission on Population and Development, 1085-87, 1094
　Demographic Yearbook, 1294
　Impact of AIDS, 1095
　International Conference on Population and Development (1994), *1085-89
　international migration and development, *1086-89
　Population Award, UN, 1093-94
　Population Division (UN), 1086
　State of World Population 2003, 1089
　statistics, 1293
　UNFPA, *see* United Nations Population Fund
　World Fertility Report 2003, 1094
　World Population Prospects: 2002 Revision, 1094
POVERTY
　eradication, 630, *848-54
　　UN Decade for the Eradication of (1997-2006), 686, 765, *848-52
　extreme, and human rights, *764-65

International Year of Microcredit (2005), 848, *853-54
reduction, 893-95
　in Asia and the Pacific, 1008-1009
　poverty reduction strategy papers, 890, 894-95, 938, 984
rural, 852-53
World Solidarity Fund, 852, *889-90, 1041
Pretoria Agreement (2002, DRC and Rwanda), 114-16, 120
Pretoria Protocols (Burundi), 145, 151, 153
Programme of Action to Prevent, Combat and Eradicate the Illicit Trade in Small Arms and Light Weapons in All Its Aspects (2001), 111, 161, *562-65, 573, 586, 587
Programme and Coordination, Committee for (CPC), 939, 1001, 1190
　implementation of Millennium Declaration, 1385
　sanctions, assistance to third States affected by, 1366
　UN budget, 1394, 1399, *1429-30
　women, advancement of, 1190
Programme for Coordination and Assistance for Security and Development (UNDP), 161, 203, 573
Programme Planning, Budget and Accounts, Office of (UN), 90
property
　of displaced persons, 796
　jurisdictional immunity of States and their, *1337-38
　UN premises and properties, *1500-1501
ProVention Consortium, 958
public administration, *865-67
　Committee of Experts on (UN), 865
　Global Forum on Reinventing Government, 866
　Programme in Public Administration and Finance (UN), 865
Public Information, Department of (UN), *502-503, 585, 606, 622, 630-38
PUERTO RICO, 608-609

racism and racial discrimination, *695-710
　Committee on the Elimination of Racial Discrimination (CERD), 281, 667-68, 674, *697-98, 716
　Decade to Combat, Third (1993-2003), 674, 686, 695-96
　　Programme of Action, 695-96
　International Convention on the Elimination of All Forms of Racial Discrimination (1965), 667, 673-74, 696
　World Conference against Racism, Racial Discrimination, Xenophobia and Related Intolerance (2001), 674, *695-98
　　Durban Declaration and Programme of Action, 696-97
　　follow-up, *696-703
　see also human rights; minorities, discrimination against
radiation
　atomic, effects of, *650-51
　Chernobyl accident, 650
　radioactive waste, *553-54, 1506

Joint Convention on the Safety of Spent Fuel Management and on the Safety of Radioactive Waste Management (1997), 553
Safety and Transport of Radioactive Material, International Conference on the, 553
United Nations Scientific Committee on the Effects of Atomic Radiation, *650-51
REFUGEES, *1222-42
Afghanistan, 297, 304, 933-34
Angola, 270
assistance measures, *1230-32
Azerbaijan, 444
Bosnia and Herzegovina, 407-408
children, *1230-32
CIS, *1240-42
Convention on the Reduction of Statelessness (1961), 1229
Convention relating to the Status of Refugees (1951), 1226, 1229
"Convention Plus", 1229-30
Protocol (1967), 1226, 1229
Convention relating to the Status of Stateless Persons (1954), 1229
Côte d'Ivoire, 171, 174, 184
and the environment, 1230
Eritrea, 239
Guinea, 213
and HIV/AIDS, 1230
Liberia, 193, 213
Palestine, *509-11
protection, 1229-30
regional activities
Africa, *1232-38
Americas, 1238
Arab States, 1238
Asia and the Pacific, 1238-39
Europe, *1239-42
sexual exploitation of, in West Africa, *1237-38
Sierra Leone, 216, 217, 220
Somalia, 246, 248
women, 1230
see also displaced persons; United Nations High Commissioner for Refugees, Office of the
REGIONAL ECONOMIC AND SOCIAL ACTIVITIES, *999-1029
see also *specific regional commissions; specific regions*
religious intolerance, *717-20
REPUBLIC OF KOREA
armistice agreement (1953), 61, 392
Rio Declaration on Environment and Development (1992), 1044
road safety, *1257-59
Rome Declaration on Harmonization, 938
Rome Statute of the International Criminal Court (1998), *76-78, 118, 810
Rotterdam Convention on the Prior Informed Consent Procedure for Certain Hazardous Chemicals and Pesticides in International Trade (1998), 771, 1068-70
RUSSIAN FEDERATION
and Georgia, 443

human rights, 824-25
humanitarian assistance, 937
and Iraq, 329-30, 331, 332, 335
Republic of Chechnya, 825
terrorism, 825
RWANDA, *154-55
and DRC, 113, 117, 124, 133-37
and DRC (ICJ case), 1305-1306
International Criminal Tribunal for (ICTR), 811, *1320-29
International Day of Reflection on the Genocide in, 108, *154-55
Pretoria Agreement (2002, with DRC), 114-16, 120
UNAMIR, 155

ST. HELENA, *621
sanctions
Afghanistan (Al-Qaida, Taliban), 290, *311-15
assistance to third States affected by, *1332-35, *1366-69
Iraq, 316, *338-41, 361-62
Liberia, *201-10
Libyan Arab Jamahiriya, *267-68
Sierra Leone, 222-23
Stockholm Process on the Implementation of Targeted Sanctions, 206, 1366
timber, 206, 207
SAO TOME AND PRINCIPE
attempted coup d'état, 272
SCIENCE AND TECHNOLOGY FOR DEVELOPMENT, *854-62
Asia and the Pacific, 1011-12
Asian and Pacific Centre for Transfer of Technology, 1011-12, 1015
biotechnology, 860
Commission on, 853, *854-57
Global Biotechnology Forum, 860
information and communication technologies, *857-60
World Summit on the Information Society, *857-59
Ministerial Council for Managing Science and Technology in Africa, 1005
SECRETARIAT, UN
capital master plan, 1500
commercial activities, *1496-98
conferences and meetings, *1481-92
Department of Public Information, see information and communication
Disarmament Affairs, Department for, 529, 567, 576, 585
Executive Committee on Humanitarian Affairs (ECHA), 916, 1223
General Assembly and Conference Management, Department for, 1383, 1481, 1489
information systems, *1492-95
Legal Affairs, Office of, 1047, 1369
Division for Ocean Affairs and the Law of the Sea, 1066, 1362
Management, Department of, 1383
managerial reform and oversight, *1386-88

Palestinian Rights, Division for, *501-502
Peacekeeping Operations, Department of, 95-96, 99
Political Affairs, Department of, 291, 606
premises and property, 1500-1501
security, *1452-56, 1501
staff, *1431-61
women, status of, *1148-51
Secretary-General
report on work of Organization, 3-44
SECURITY COUNCIL, 1391, 1465
agenda, 1465, 1577-80
budget, revised estimates for, 1420
cooperation with regional organizations, 58
Counter-Terrorism Committee, *66-70, 746, 1123
dispute settlement, role in, *57-58
high-level meeting to combat terrorism, *63-65
membership and related matters, review of, 1391
missions to
Afghanistan, *302-11
Central Africa, *109, 127-28, 149-50
West Africa, *109, 162-65, 189, 197, 218, 228
Repertoire of the Practice of the Security Council, 1363-64
structure, 1560-62
Working Group on Peacekeeping Operations, 71
see also specific topics
Seoul Declaration on Infrastructure Development in Asia and the Pacific, 1011
SERBIA AND MONTENEGRO (formerly FEDERAL REPUBLIC OF YUGOSLAVIA), *411-30
and Bosnia and Herzegovina, 409, ICJ case, 1302
and Croatia (ICJ case), 1304
Kosovo province, *412-30
dialogue between Belgrade and Pristina, *418-19
economic reconstruction and development, 426
education, 424
functioning of democratic institutions, 421-23
future status, 421
judicial system, 424
KFOR (NATO), 426, 429, 1311
language, freedom to use, 424
minorities, 423-25
security situation, 425-26
standards before status benchmarks, *420-21
UNMIK, 80, 81, 398, 411-13, *415-29
relations with UNMIK, 429-30
SFOR (Stabilization Force), 410-11
Shanghai Cooperation Organization, 298, 342, 575
SIERRA LEONE, 160, 161, 162-64, 171, *210-23
Agreement on the Ceasefire and Cessation of Hostilities (2000, Abuja Agreement), 210
diamonds, 213, 215, *217-20, 222-23
human rights, 213, 216, 220, 684-85, 814
humanitarian assistance, 213, 216, 931
and Liberia, 184, 186, 211-13, *215-20
political and security situation, 219
refugees, 193, 213, 216, 217, 220
sanctions, 222-23
UNAMSIL, 79, 81, 82, 160, 161, 162, 190, 202, *211-23

UN Transitional Appeal for Relief and Recovery in, 220
women's rights, 216
SINGAPORE
and Malaysia (ICJ case), 1308-1309
and Malaysia (Law of the Sea Tribunal case), 1353
slavery and related issues, 776
UN Voluntary Trust Fund on Contemporary Forms of Slavery, 778-79
small arms, illicit trade
Inter-American Convention against the Illicit Manufacturing of and Trafficking in Firearms, Ammunition, Explosives, and Other Related Materials (1997), 590
Programme of Action (2001), 111, 161, *562-65, 573, 585, 586
West Africa, *161-62
small island developing States, *871-75
Barbados Programme of Action (1994), 842, *871-75, 1042-43
international review (2004), *871-75
SOCIAL DEVELOPMENT, *1096-1105
Asia and the Pacific, 1013-14
Commission for, 835, 865, 1099, 1214, 1218, 1219-20
cooperation for, *1099-1101
cooperatives in, *1102-1103
Copenhagen Declaration on (1995), 1096
International Year of the Family (1994), *1103-1105
Latin America and the Caribbean, 1021-22
UN Research Institute for, 715, 1099, 1102
Western Asia, 1025-26
World Summit for (1995), *1096-99, 1101, 1220
SOLOMON ISLANDS, 396
SOMALIA, 229, *241-56
arms embargo, 242, *250-56
Arta Conference (2000), 242, 249
Declaration on Cessation of Hostilities and the Structures and Principles of the Somalia National Reconstruction Process (2002, Eldoret Declaration), *241-46, 248
HIV/AIDS, 246, 248-49
human rights, 248, 685, 814
humanitarian assistance, 242, 246, *928-29
Intergovernmental Authority on Development (IGAD), 230, *243-50
internally displaced persons, 242, 246
mines, 256
peace-building, 246
refugees, 246, 248
Somalia National Reconciliation Conference (Mbagathi), 247, *249-53
UNOSOM II, 85
UNPOS, 60, 61, 242-43, 249
SOUTHERN AFRICA, *269-71
humanitarian assistance, 931
see also Angola
Southern Africa Capacity Initiative, 897
Southern African Development Community
disarmament, 573, 587
HIV/AIDS, 897

SPAIN
  Gibraltar, *610-11
  human rights, 707
  and Iraq, 332-33
  Stabilization Force (SFOR), 410-11
States of the Collective Security Treaty Organization, 71, 296, 306
STATISTICS, 1289-96
  capacity-building, 1295
  Committee for the Coordination of Statistical Activities, 1290, 1296
  demographic and social, 1293-94
    health, 1293-94
    population and housing censuses, 1293
  Demographic Yearbook, 1294
  economic, 1290-93
    agriculture, 1292
    Asia and the Pacific, 1009
    Balance of Payments Manual, 1290
    Central Product Classification, 1289, 1294
    environment, 1292
    Europe, 1019
    finance, 1291
    International Comparison Programme, 1289, 1291, 1295
    International Standard Classification of Occupations, 1294-95
    International Standard Industrial Classification, 1289, 1294
    international trade, 1291, 1292
    Intersecretariat Working Group on Price Statistics, 1292
    Latin America and the Caribbean, 1023
    Manual on Statistics of International Trade in Services, 1291
    measuring the new economy, 1292
    Monetary and Financial Statistics Manual, 1290
    national accounts, 1290
    price indices, 1292
  programmes, coordination and integration, 1296
  social, 1294-95
  Statistical Commission, 1019, 1289-96
  Statistics Division (UN), 1009, 1075, 1289-90, 1293-94
Status of Women, Commission on the, 493, 777-78, 1164, 1170-71, 1183, 1190-93, 1220
Stockholm Convention on Persistent Organic Pollutants (2001), 1045, 1070, 1072
Stockholm Process on the Implementation of Targeted Sanctions, 206, 1366
SUDAN, 229, 256-57, 814
  Framework Agreement on Security Arrangements during the Interim Period (2002), 257
  humanitarian assistance, 929-30
  Intergovernmental Authority on Development (IGAD), 256-57
  Machakos Protocol (2002), 230, 256-57
  and Uganda, 257
  Understanding on Cessation of Hostilities (2002), 256
SUSTAINABLE DEVELOPMENT, *821-27, *838-48
  Africa, 1005

  Arab Initiative for, 1043
  Asia and the Pacific, 1012
  Central America, 275, *950-51
  Commission on, 835, *838-48, 871, 1005, 1030, 1037-38, 1051, 1073-74
  consumption and cleaner production, 1073
  education for, UN Decade (2005-2014), *848
  and environment, 772, 1042-44
  environmental law, 1073
  globalization and interdependence, 832
  International Expert Meeting on the 10-Year Framework of Programmes for Sustainable Consumption and Production (Marrakech), 840, 1073
  Johannesburg Declaration on Sustainable Development and Plan for Implementation (2002), 838-39, 881, 957, 993, 1009, 1012
  Latin American and Caribbean Initiative on, 1043
  Marrakech Process, 840
  in mountain regions, *1063-65
  Phnom Penh Regional Platform on Sustainable Development for Asia and the Pacific, 1012
  small island developing States, *871-75, 1042-43
  World Summit on (2002), 636, 641, 643-44, 799, 838, 852, 898, 972, 999, 1010, 1016, 1019
    follow-up, 835, *838-42, 977, 1030, 1042-44
    Partnership for Clean Fuels and Vehicles, 1070
SWAZILAND
  humanitarian assistance, 932-33
SYRIAN ARAB REPUBLIC, *522-28
  Committee on Israeli Practices, 522-23
  Golan Heights, *522-26
  human rights, 522
  UNDOF, 80, 82, 516, *525-28

TAJIKISTAN, 396
  humanitarian assistance, 937
  UNMOT, 396
  UNTOP, 61, 62, 396
Taliban, 68, 290, 297, 302, 304, 308, 311-12, 314-15
TAPA, *see* United Nations Transitional Assistance Programme for Afghanistan
terrorism
  combating, 70, *1149-51
  convention for suppression of nuclear (proposed), *1338-40
  Convention for the Suppression of Terrorist Bombings (1997), 1341
  human rights and, *745-50
  international, *63-71
    Al-Qaida, 68, 290, 297, 302, 304, 311-15, 325-26
    High-level SC meeting, *63-65
    Inter-American Committee against Terrorism, 275
    Inter-American Convention against Terrorism, 275
    measures to eliminate, *66-70, 630, *1338-40
      Commission on Crime Prevention and Criminal Justice, 70
      Counter-Terrorism Committee, 63, *66-70, 746, 1123

Declaration on Measures to Eliminate International Terrorism (1994), 1338
Global Programme against Terrorism (2002), 1123, 1149
IAEA, 68, 70
International Convention for the Suppression of the Financing of (1999), 1341
Organization for the Prohibition of Chemical Weapons, 68, 560-61
States of the Collective Security Treaty Organization, 71, 296, 306
National Laws and Regulations on the Prevention and Suppression of International Terrorism (Part II), 1338
Taliban, 68, 290, 297, 302, 304, 308, 311-12, 314-15
2003 incidents
Afghanistan, 297, 298
Colombia, 65, *285
Iraq, 65, *346-48, 352, 353, *1452
Middle East, 458-70, 522
Russian Federation, 825
Turkey, *65-66, 396
UN Baghdad headquarters, 65, *346-50, *1452
weapons of mass destruction, *579-81
THAILAND
human rights, 664-65
the Former Yugoslav Republic of Macedonia, *see* Former Yugoslav Republic of Macedonia, the
TIMOR-LESTE, *370-85, *1015
economic situation, 377, 379
human rights, 375, 380, 685-86, 823
humanitarian assistance, 916, *953-54
and Indonesia, 370, 374, 380
judicial system, 375, 377-79
police, 372-73, 375-76
resettlement, 378
Timor Sea Treaty (Timor-Leste and Australia), 370, 373-74, 376
UNAMET, 378, 385
UNMISET, 80, 81, 82, *370-85, 953
UNTAET, 82, 371, 376, *381-83
tobacco
Ad Hoc Inter-Agency Task Force on, 1251
WHO Framework Convention on Tobacco Control, 1251
TOKELAU, *613-16
Tokyo International Conference on African Development (TICAD III), 938, 1002
torture and cruel treatment, *741-44
Committee against, 667-68, 675
Convention against Torture and Other Cruel, Inhuman or Degrading Treatment or Punishment (1984) and Optional Protocol (2002), 667, 674-75, 741
UN International Day in Support of Victims of Torture, 742
UN Voluntary Fund for Victims of Torture, 742
tourism
Asia and the Pacific, 1011
International Year of Ecotourism (2002), 1073-74
International Year of Tourism (proposed), 1475
World Tourism Organization (WTO/OMT), *1475-78
TRADE
commodities, *977-80
Common Fund for, 980
meeting of eminent persons on, 977-78
open-ended panel of the GA, *978-79
United Nations Global Compact, 978
GATS, *see* General Agreement on Trade in Services
human rights and liberalization of trade in services, 759
Integrated Framework for Trade-Related Technical Assistance for LDCs, 870
international trade, *965-80
Africa
African Trade Policy Centre, 1006
Building African Capacity for Trade, Programme for, 974
trade performance, 966-67
trade promotion, 1006
arbitration, 1376
Convention on the Recognition and Enforcement of Foreign Arbitral Awards (New York Convention, 1958), 1374, 1376-77
Model Law on International Commercial Arbitration (1985), 1376, 1378
BIOTRADE programme, 972
Commission on Enterprise, Business Facilitation and Development, 976-77
meetings of subsidiary bodies, 977
Commission on Trade in Goods and Services, and Commodities, 972-73
meetings of subsidiary bodies, 972-73
electronic commerce law, 1377-78
Europe, 1017
insolvency law, 1378
interdependence and global economic issues, 973-74
International Trade Centre (ITC), *974-76
Global Trust Fund, 975
Joint Advisory Group, 975
Joint ITC/UNCTAD/WTO Integrated Technical Assistance Programme in Selected LDCs and Other African Countries, 974
Latin America and the Caribbean, 1021
law, *1374-79
Manual on Statistics of International Trade in Services, 1291
multilateral trading system, *967-71
policy, 972-74
privately financed infrastructure projects, *1376-77
Rotterdam Convention on the Prior Informed Consent Procedure for Certain Hazardous Chemicals and Pesticides in International Trade (1998), 771, 1068-70
security interests, 1378-79
statistics, 1291, 1292
trade promotion and facilitation, *974-77
transnational corporations, 761-62

UNCITRAL, see United Nations Commission on International Trade Law
Western Asia, 1025
WTO Ministerial Conference (Fifth, Cancún), 967-68, 972, 1535
WTO Working Group on Trade, Debt and Finance, 984
Trade Policy Review Mechanism, 772
UNCTAD, see United Nations Conference on Trade and Development
see also World Trade Organization
Trade and Development Report, 2003, 863, 965, 973
Trade-Related Aspects of Intellectual Property Rights (TRIPS), Agreement on, 772, 1044
TRAIN-SEA-COAST programme, 1362
transnational corporations, 761-62
TRANSPORT, *993-95
  Africa
    Europe-Africa permanent link, *1004
    Yamoussoukro Declaration (1988), 1006
  Asia and the Pacific, 1011
  dangerous goods, *993-95
  Europe, 1018
  Globally Harmonized System of Classification and Labelling of Chemicals, 993
  law, 1377
  Review of Maritime Transport 2003, 993
  Western Asia, 1026
treaties and agreements
  international organizations, 1344
  multilateral, 1344-45
  registration and publication by UN, 1344-45
  reservations, 669, 1343
  see also main part of name
TRINIDAD AND TOBAGO, 703-704
TURKEY, *65-66, 396
TURKMENISTAN, *823-24
TURKS AND CAICOS ISLANDS, 605
UGANDA
  and DRC, 113, 115, 123, 124, 133-37
  and DRC (ICJ case), 1303
  humanitarian assistance, 928
  Luanda Agreement (DRC), 116, 120
  and Sudan, 257
Ulaanbaatar Declaration and Plan of Action, *593-95
UNAIDS, see Joint United Nations Programme on HIV/AIDS
UNAMA, see United Nations Assistance Mission in Afghanistan
UNAMSIL, see United Nations Mission in Sierra Leone
UNCDF, see United Nations Capital Development Fund
UNCITRAL, see United Nations Commission on International Trade Law
UNCIVPOL, see United Nations Civilian Police
UNCTAD, see United Nations Conference on Trade and Development
UNDAF, see United Nations Development Assistance Framework
UNDCP, see United Nations International Drug Control Programme

UNDG, see United Nations Development Group
UNDOF, see United Nations Disengagement Observer Force
UNDP, see United Nations Development Programme
UNEP, see United Nations Environment Programme
UNFICYP, see United Nations Peacekeeping Force in Cyprus
UNFIP, see United Nations Fund for International Partnerships
UNFPA, see United Nations Population Fund
UNHCR, see United Nations High Commissioner for Refugees, Office of the
UNIDIR, see United Nations Institute for Disarmament Research
UNIDO, see United Nations Industrial Development Organization
UNIFEM, see United Nations Development Fund for Women
UNIFIL, see United Nations Interim Force in Lebanon
UNIKOM, see United Nations Iraq-Kuwait Observation Mission
UNITED ARAB EMIRATES
  and Iran, 396
UNITED KINGDOM
  Falkland Islands (Malvinas), 609-10
  Gibraltar, *610-11
  human rights, 771
  and Iraq, 331, 332-33, 336, 347
  and Libyan Arab Jamahiriya (ICJ case), 1300
UNITED NATIONS
  accounts and auditing, *1428-29
    administrative and budgetary coordination, 1429
  budget, *1393-1422
    2002-2003, *1396-98
    2004-2005, *1399-1422
    Office of Programme Planning, Budget and Accounts, 90
    reforming budgetary planning processes, *1393-96
    unforeseen and extraordinary expenses, *1422
    working capital fund, *1421-22
  Charter, 1541-51
    Special Committee on the Charter of the United Nations and on the Strengthening of the Role of the Organization, *1363-69
  contributions, assessed, *1422-29
  Financial Rules and Regulations of the, 1429
  financial situation, 1393
  financing and programming, *1393-1430
  host country, relations with, *1371-74
  institutional and administrative matters, *1462-1501
    common services, *1495-1500
      commercial activities, *1496-98
      at Geneva, 1496
      outsourcing practices, *1498-99
      UN Postal Administration, 1497-98
      at Vienna, *1495-96
    conferences and meetings, *1481-92
      documentation, 1491-92
      intergovernmental meetings, 1489
      pattern of conferences, *1481-89

regional facilities, 1490-91
services, use of, 1490-91
translation and interpretation, 1492
conversion to UN specialized agency, requests for, *1474-79
cooperation with other organizations
AU, 58, 104, 271-72
Economic Community of Central African States, 58, 109-10, 111
EU, 58
OAS, 58
OSCE, 58
coordination and monitoring, *1466-74
CPC, 1466-67
international conferences, follow-up to, *1467-74
JIU, 1467
CEB, 1466-67
information systems, *1492-95
Galileo system, 95
informatics, international cooperation in, *1494-95
information technology, *1492-94
procedures, review of, *1499
institutional machinery, *1462-66
Economic and Social Council, 1465-66
agenda, 1579-80
functional commissions, 1392
membership and structure, 1562-64
revitalization, 1391-92
sessions and segments, 1465-66
work programme, 1466
General Assembly, *1462-65
agendas, 1463-64, 1570-77
credentials, 1463
membership and structure, 1556-60
resolutions and decisions, 1464
revitalization, *1388-91
sessions, organization of, 1462-63
Security Council, 1465
agenda, 1577-79
membership and related matters, 1391, 1465, 1560-62
structure, 1560-62
membership (UN) roster, 1539-40
observer status, requests for, *1479-80
participation in UN work, requests for, *1480-81
premises and properties, 1500-1501
programme
performance, 1430
planning, *1429-30
reform programme, *1383-88
agenda for change, 1384
general aspects, 1383-84
intergovernmental machinery, *1388-92
Millenium Declaration (2000), implementation, *1384-85
oversight activities, *1386-88
procurement, 1386
strengthening UN system, 1384

Repertoire of the Practice of the Security Council, 1363-64
Repertory of Practice of United Nations Organs, 1363-64
staff, *1431-61
composition, 1446-47
conditions of service, *1431-39
contractual arrangements, 1445
gratis personnel, *1448
human resources management, 1238, *1439-48, 1447
International Civil Service Commission, *1431-33, 1444-45
justice, administration of, *1459-61
mobility, 1445-46
multilingualism, 1451-52
personnel policies, *1439-57
post structure, 1446
principal members, 1566-69
remuneration issues, *1433-39
rules and regulations, 1452
safety and security, *1452-56, 1501
travel-related matters, 1458-59
UN Joint Staff Pension Fund, 1386, *1457-58
UN System Staff College, 1446, *1456-57
women, status of, 1189-90, *1448-51
United Nations African Institute for the Prevention of Crime and the Treatment of Offenders, *1124-25
United Nations Angola Verification Mission (UNAVEM), *271
United Nations Assistance Mission in Afghanistan (UNAMA), 61, 62, *289-97, 302-303, 307-308, 779
United Nations Assistance Mission for Iraq (UNAMI), 62, 315, *346
United Nations Assistance Mission for Rwanda (UNAMIR), 155
United Nations Basic Principles on the Independence of the Judiciary (1985), 734
United Nations Capital Development Fund (UNCDF), 891, 894, 914
United Nations Children's Fund (UNICEF), 1203-14, 1462
Côte d'Ivoire, 171
emergency assistance, 1205
funding, 887-89
Georgia, 440
HIV/AIDS, 1203, 1205, 1206, 1207, 1210-11, 1230, 1248
Inter-Agency Guiding Principles on Unaccompanied and Separated Children, 1209
malaria, 1207, 1251
mine action, 100
operational and administrative matters, 1211-14
programme policies, 1204-1205
programmes, 1205-11
early childhood development, 1206-1207
girls' education, 1208-1209
immunization "plus", 1207-1208
protection from violence, abuse, exploitation and discrimination, 1209-10
regional expenditures, 1205-1206
Somalia, 243

Subject index

The State of the World's Children 2003, 1203
2003 UNICEF Annual Report, 1204
UNAIDS, 1248
water, 1034
see also children; youth
United Nations Civilian Police, 452
United Nations Commission on International Trade Law (UNCITRAL), 1369, *1374-79
  case law on UNCITRAL texts (CLOUT), 1378
  Model Law on International Commercial Arbitration (1985), 1376, 1378
  Model Law on Procurement of Goods, Construction and Services (1994), 1379
  Model Legislative Provisions on Privately Financed Infrastructure Projects, *1376-77
  training and technical assistance, 1379
  Working Group on Electronic Commerce, 1377-78
  Working Group on Insolvency Law, 1378
  Working Group on Security Interests, 1378-79
  Working Group on Transport Law, 1377
United Nations Communications Group, 638-39
United Nations Compensation Commission, 369-70, 1039
United Nations Conciliation Commission for Palestine, 507
United Nations Conference on Environment and Development (1992) (UNCED)
  Agenda 21, *838-42
United Nations Conference on the Exploration and Peaceful Uses of Outer Space, Third (UNISPACE-III) (1999), *641-44
United Nations Conference on LDCs, Third (LDC III) (2001), 867, 868, *870-71
United Nations Conference on the Standardization of Geographical Names, 1035
United Nations Conference on Trade and Development (UNCTAD)
  Africa, 966-67, 995
  commodities, *977-80
  economic trends, 863-64
  EMPRETEC programme, 976
  enterprise, business facilitation and development, 976-77
  financial flows, 981
  funding, 888
  globalization, 757, 973-74
  institutional and organizational questions, 995-98
    medium-term plan and programme budget, 997-98
    technical cooperation, 995-97
  international trade, *966-80
  investment, technology and related financial issues, 990-93
  Israeli-occupied territories, 504, 995
  landlocked countries, 875, 1010
  least developed countries, 870
  multilateral trading system, *968-71
  Trade and Development Board, 968, 973, 977, 995
  trade in goods and services, and commodities, 972-73
  Trust Fund for LDCs, 870
  UNCTAD XI (2004), 870, 991-92, 995, 998

United Nations Congresses on the Prevention of Crime and the Treatment of Offenders, 734 (1985), 734 (1990), 1116, *1117-19 (2005)
United Nations Convention to Combat Desertification in those Countries Experiencing Serious Drought and/or Desertification, particularly in Africa (1994), 1045, *1053-55
  Havana Declaration on the Implementation of the, 1053
United Nations Convention against Corruption, 1119, *1126-49
United Nations Convention against Illicit Traffic in Narcotic Drugs and Psychotropic Substances (1988), 1267-68, 1285
United Nations Convention on the Law of the Sea (1982), *1346-62
United Nations Convention against Transnational Organized Crime (2000) and the Protocols Thereto (2000, 2001), 707, 1119, 1123, *1125-26
  Conference of Parties (2004), 1125
United Nations Crime Prevention and Criminal Justice Fund, 1119, *1123-24
United Nations Crime Prevention and Criminal Justice Programme, *1119-24
United Nations Decade of Education for Sustainable Development (2005-2014), *848
United Nations Decade for the Eradication of Poverty (1997-2006), 686, 765, *848-52
United Nations Decade for Human Rights Education (1995-2004), 686, *687-89
United Nations Development Assistance Framework (UNDAF), 753, 880-82, 886, 890, 901, 939, 1075, 1188, 1203, 1286
United Nations Development Fund for Women (UNIFEM), 243, 494, 770, 777, 882, 891, 899, 1193-94
United Nations Development Group (UNDG), 881, 883, 890, 916, 1205, 1223, 1251, 1260, 1446
United Nations Development Programme (UNDP), 890-904
  Afghanistan, 291, 292
  Africa, 161, 974, 1003
  Audit and Performance Review, Office of, 909-10
  Bosnia and Herzegovina, 407
  Burundi, 809
  Central America, 275, 276
  Côte d'Ivoire, 171
  developing countries, economic and technical cooperation among, 910-11, 912
  environment, 1038, 1041, 1045
  Executive Board (UNDP/UNFPA), 891-93, 906, 1045, 1089
  financing, 902-904
  Georgia, 440
  Habitat, 1080
  HIV/AIDS, 1248
  Human Development Report 2003, 279, 864, 890, 891, 892, 893
  human rights, 655, 714
  mine action, 100
  Palestinian Authority, 503
  Programme for Coordination and Assistance for Security and Development, 161, 203, 573

programme planning and management, 897-902
   Business Plans (2000-2003), 897-98
   funding strategy, 900-902
   monitoring and evaluation, 898-900
   programming arrangements, 898
programme results
   crisis prevention and recovery, 895-96
   democratic governance, 895
   environment and energy, 896
   HIV/AIDS, 896-97
   poverty reduction, 893-95
regional cooperation, 1000
sustainable development, 839
technical cooperation through, 890-904
Timor-Leste, 375
UN Communications Group, 639
UN Volunteers, 910
water resources, 1034
"White Helmets", 922
United Nations Disengagement Observer Force (UNDOF), 80, 82, 516, *525-28
UNITED NATIONS EDUCATIONAL, SCIENTIFIC AND CULTURAL ORGANIZATION (UNESCO), 1512-13
bioethics, 775
Cultural Heritage, United Nations Year for (2002), *1109-10
cultural property, return of, *1113-15
disaster reduction, 957
Education for Sustainable Development, United Nations Decade of (2005-2014), *848
food security and sustainable development, 1005
HIV/AIDS, 1248
human rights, 687, 689, 696, 715
Intergovernmental Oceanographic Commission, 1355
outer space activities, 646
solar energy, 1031
Somalia, 243
water resources, 1033
wildlife conservation, 1068
United Nations Environment Programme (UNEP), *1036-48
accounts and audits, 1047
Africa, 1039, 1040-41
atmosphere, 1042
coordination and cooperation
   business and industry, 1044-45
   civil society, participation of, 1046-47
   environmental emergencies, 1045
   Global Environment Facility, 1645-46
disaster reduction, 957
Environment Fund, 1047-48
Governing Council/Ministerial Environment Forum, *1036-38
monitoring and assessment of global environmental change, 1038-40
policy and advisory services, 1044
post-conflict assessment
   Africa, 1039
   Iraq, 1039
   Occupied Palestinian Territory, 1039
Regional Seas Programme, 1067-68
secretariat, 1047
sustainable development, 839-40, 1642-44
water policy and strategy, 1041-42
see also environment
United Nations Forum on Forests, *1057-63
United Nations Framework Convention on Climate Change (1992), 896, 1045, *1049-50, 1053, 1056
Kyoto Protocol (1997), *1049-50, 1056
United Nations Fund for International Partnerships (UNFIP), 835, 905-906
United Nations Habitat and Human Settlements Foundation, 1074-75, 1079, 1084
United Nations High Commissioner for Human Rights, Office of the (OHCHR), *657-60, 670-71, 678, 686-87, 691
see also human rights
United Nations High Commissioner for Refugees, Office of the (UNHCR), *1222-42
see also refugees
United Nations Human Settlements Programme (UN-Habitat), 769, 770, 801, 888, 939, 958, 1034, 1038, 1040, *1074-84
UNITED NATIONS INDUSTRIAL DEVELOPMENT ORGANIZATION (UNIDO), 939, 1004, 1388, 1533-34
United Nations information centres (UNICs), 502, 622, 631, 635-37, 1581-83
United Nations Institute for Disarmament Research (UNIDIR), 585, 586
subvention, 1421
United Nations Institute for Training and Research (UNITAR), *1160-62, 1369
United Nations Inter-Agency Network on Women and Gender Equality, 882, 1187-88
United Nations Interim Administration Mission in Kosovo (UNMIK), 80, 81, 82, 398, 411-13, *415-29, 1081, 1386
United Nations Interim Force in Lebanon (UNIFIL), 80, 82, *517-22, 825
United Nations International Drug Control Programme (UNDCP), 1248, 1283, 1285, 1288
United Nations Iraq-Kuwait Observation Mission (UNIKOM), 80, 81, 316, 332, *358-60
United Nations Joint Staff Pension Fund, 1386, *1457-58
United Nations Logistics Base (UNLB) at Brindisi, 82, 95, *96-97, 159, 1500
United Nations Military Observer Group in India and Pakistan (UNMOGIP), 80
United Nations Mine Action Centre, 298
United Nations Mission in Angola (UNMA), 60, 62, 269, 270-71
United Nations Mission in Bosnia and Herzegovina (UNMIBH), *398-99
United Nations Mission in the Central African Republic (MINURCA), 155, 159
United Nations Mission in Côte d'Ivoire (MINUCI), 61, 62, 160, *171-84
United Nations Mission in East Timor (UNAMET), 378, 385
United Nations Mission in Ethiopia and Eritrea (UNMEE), 80, 81, *230-41

United Nations Mission in Liberia (UNMIL), 61, 81, 160, 185, *194-202
United Nations Mission of Observers in Tajikistan (UNMOT), 396
United Nations Mission for the Referendum in Western Sahara (MINURSO), 79-80, 81, *258-67
United Nations Mission in Sierra Leone (UNAMSIL), 79, 81, 160, 161, 162, 190, 202, *211-23
United Nations Mission of Support in East Timor (UNMISET), 80, 81, *370-85, 953
United Nations Monitoring, Verification and Inspection Commission (UNMOVIC), 315-34, 342, 1032
  College of Commissioners, 316-19
United Nations Observer Mission in Angola (MONUA), *271
United Nations Observer Mission in Georgia (UNOMIG), 80, 81, *430-43
United Nations Observer Mission in Papua New Guinea (UNOMB), 392, 394-95
United Nations Office in Burundi (UNOB), 60, 61, 108, 110, 145, 152
United Nations Office for the Coordination of Humanitarian Assistance to Afghanistan, 294
United Nations Office on Drugs and Crime (UNODC), 71, 298, 1119, 1149, 1263, 1278-80, 1286
United Nations Office at Nairobi (UNON), 1037, 1047
United Nations Office for Project Services (UNOPS), 891, 906-10
  activities, 906
  audit reports, 909-10
  budget estimates, 908-909
  refugees, 1233
  review, 906-908
United Nations Office at Vienna, *1495-96
United Nations Office for West Africa, 62
United Nations Open-ended Informal Consultative Process on Oceans and the Law of the Sea, 1065-66, *1354-62
United Nations Organization Mission in the Democratic Republic of the Congo (MONUC), 79, 81, *108-109, *113-45, 809, 943
United Nations Partnership Office, 835
United Nations Peace-building Office in the Central African Republic (BONUCA), 60, 62, 155-59
United Nations Peace-building Support Office in Guinea-Bissau (UNOGBIS), 60, 62, 160, *223-26, 228-29
United Nations Peace-building Support Office in Liberia (UNOL), 160, 161, 163, 184-85, 187, 194, 202
United Nations Peace Force (UNPF), 398
United Nations Peace Forces headquarters (UNPF-HQ), 85, 398
United Nations Peacekeeping Force in Cyprus (UNFICYP), 80, 82, 445, *450-55
United Nations Pledging Conference for Development Activities, 742, 889, 1200
United Nations Political Office in Bougainville (Papua New Guinea) (UNPOB), 61-62, 392-95
United Nations Political Office for Somalia (UNPOS), 60, 61, 242-43, 249
United Nations Population Fund (UNFPA), 243, 880-81, 887-89, 1086, 1089-94
  country and intercountry programmes
    Africa, 1090
    Arab States and Europe, 1090
    Asia and the Pacific, 1090-91
    interregional, 1091
    Latin America and the Caribbean, 1091
  Executive Board (UNDP/UNFPA), see United Nations Development Programme
  financial and administrative questions, 1091-93
  HIV/AIDS, 1248
  humanitarian assistance, 1090
  personnel matters, 1093-94
  Technical Advisory Programme, 1093
United Nations Programme of Assistance in the Teaching, Study, Dissemination and Wider Appreciation of International Law, *1369-71
United Nations Programme in Public Administration and Finance, 865
United Nations Register of Conventional Arms, 568, 585
United Nations Relief and Works Agency for Palestine Refugees in the Near East (UNRWA), 460, *506-15, 825, 1462
United Nations Research Institute for Social Development (UNRISD), 715, 1099, 1102
United Nations Scientific Committee on the Effects of Atomic Radiation, *650-51
United Nations Security Coordinator, 73, 1228
United Nations Special Commission (UNSCOM), 317, 331, 342
United Nations Special Coordinator for the Middle East, Office of the, 62
United Nations Standing Advisory Committee on Security Questions in Central Africa, 108, 111, *573-75, 587
United Nations System Chief Executives Board for Coordination (CEB), 55, 832, 840, 916, 938-39, 1000, 1188, 1385, 1429, 1466-67, 1494
  High-level Committee on Management, 859, 1446, 1466
  High-level Committee on Programmes, 840, 1260, 1354, 1385, 1466
United Nations System Staff College, 1446, *1456-57
United Nations Tajikistan Office of Peace-building (UNTOP), 61, 62, 396
United Nations Transitional Administration in East Timor (UNTAET), 82, 371, 376, *381-83
United Nations Transitional Appeal for Relief and Recovery in Sierra Leone (2004), 220
United Nations Transitional Assistance Programme for Afghanistan (TAPA), 291, *933-36
United Nations Truce Supervision Organization (UNTSO), 80, 516
United Nations Trust Fund (Burundi), 153
United Nations University (UNU), 1163, 1261
United Nations Verification Mission in Guatemala (MINUGUA), 61, 85, *278-84
United Nations Voluntary Fund for Indigenous Populations, 800
United Nations Voluntary Fund for the International Decade of the World's Indigenous People, 801

United Nations Voluntary Fund for Victims of Torture, 742
United Nations Voluntary Trust Fund on Contemporary Forms of Slavery, 778-79
United Nations Volunteers, 99, 440, 910, 1223, 1388
United Nations Year for Cultural Heritage (2002), *1109-10
United Nations Year for Violence Prevention (2007), 772
UNITED STATES
    and Cuba, *285-86
    drug control, 1274-75
    as host country, relations with UN, *1371-74, 1462
    human rights, 703
    and Iran (ICJ case), 1300-1301
    and Iraq, 324-25, 327, 331, 332-33, 334, 341, 347
    and Libyan Arab Jamahiriya (ICJ case), 1300
    and Mexico (ICJ case), 1306-1308
    refugees, 1238
UNITED STATES VIRGIN ISLANDS, 605
Universal Declaration on Cultural Diversity (2001), 717
Universal Declaration on the Human Genome and Human Rights (1997), 775
Universal Declaration of Human Rights (1948), 669, 713, 816
UNIVERSAL POSTAL UNION (UPU), 1524
University for Peace, 1162-63
UNLB, see United Nations Logistics Base at Brindisi
UNMA, see United Nations Mission in Angola
UNMEE, see United Nations Mission in Ethiopia and Eritrea
UNMIBH, see United Nations Mission in Bosnia and Herzegovina
UNMIH, see United Nations Mission in Haiti
UNMIK, see United Nations Interim Administration Mission in Kosovo
UNMIL, see United Nations Mission in Liberia
UNMOGIP, see United Nations Military Observer Group in India and Pakistan
UNMOVIC, see United Nations Monitoring, Verification and Inspection Commission
UNOB, see United Nations Office in Burundi
UNODC, see United Nations Office on Drugs and Crime
UNOGBIS, see United Nations Peace-building Support Office in Guinea-Bissau
UNOL, see United Nations Peace-building Support Office in Liberia
UNOMB, see United Nations Observer Mission in Papua New Guinea
UNOMIG, see United Nations Observer Mission in Georgia
UNON, see United Nations Office at Nairobi
UNOPS, see United Nations Office for Project Services
UNOWA, see United Nations Office for West Africa
UNPF, see United Nations Peace Force
UNPF-HQ, see United Nations Peace Forces headquarters
UNPOB, see United Nations Political Office in Bougainville (Papua New Guinea)
UNPOS, see United Nations Political Office for Somalia
UNRWA, see United Nations Relief and Works Agency for Palestine Refugees in the Near East
UNSCO, see United Nations Special Coordinator for the Middle East, Office of the
UNSCOM, see United Nations Special Commission
UNSECOORD, see United Nations Security Coordinator
UNTOP, see United Nations Tajikistan Office of Peace-building
UNTSO, see United Nations Truce Supervision Organization
UNU, see United Nations University
UNV, see United Nations Volunteers

Vienna Convention on Consular Relations (1963), 1306, 1343
Vienna Convention on Diplomatic Relations (1961), 1343
Vienna Convention on the Law of Treaties (1969), 1336
Vienna Convention on the Protection of the Ozone Layer (1985), 1050
    Montreal Protocol on Substances that Deplete the Ozone Layer, 1050, 1055
    Multilateral Fund for Implementation of, 896
Vienna Declaration on Crime and Justice (2000), 1123
Vienna International Centre, 1495

water, *1033-35
    Global International Waters Assessment (2000), 1041, 1065
    International Decade for Action: Water for Life (2005-2015), *1034-35
    International Freshwater Forum, 1034
    International Year of Freshwater, 636, 1012, 1033-34, 1041
    Millennium Task Force on Water and Sanitation, 1041
    water-related technical cooperation, 1035
    water and sanitation, 775, 1082
    Water and Sanitation Trust Fund (UN-Habitat), 1074
    World Water Council, 1033
    World Water Development Report, 1034
    World Water Forum, Third, 1034, 1041
weapons, see disarmament
weather
    El Niño, 961
    WMO, see World Meteorological Organization
    see also climate change; environment
WEST AFRICA, *159-229
    arms moratorium, 203, 573, 587
    humanitarian assistance, 162, 164, 930-31
    human rights, 162, 164
    refugees, sexual exploitation of, *1237-38
    SC mission to, 162-65, 189, 197, 218, 228
    Special Representative for West Africa, Office of the, 162, 164, 165

threats to peace and security, *161-62
UNOWA, 62, 187
see also country names; Economic Community of West African States; Mano River Union
WESTERN ASIA, *1024-29
see also country names; Economic and Social Commission for Western Asia
WESTERN SAHARA, *257-67, 616
MINURSO, 79-80, 81, 82, *258-67
Morocco, *257-65
POLISARIO, *257-65
refugees, 1239
self-determination, right to, 722
wildlife conservation, *1068-69
World Conservation Monitoring Centre, 1047, 1068
World Conservation Union, 1046, 1068-69
World Database on Protected Areas, 1068-69
WOMEN, *1164-1201
in Africa, 1006
DRC, 810-11
Sierra Leone, 216
African Platform for Action (1994), 1006
in Asia
Afghanistan, 301, 779, *1175-77
Akshara Visakha literacy programme (India), 1081
Beijing Declaration and Platform for Action (1995), 778-79, 1006, 1022-23, 1045-46, *1164-67, 1169-70
Commission on the Status of, 493, 777-78, 1164, 1170-71, 1183, 1190-93, 1220
Committee on the Elimination of Discrimination against, 667-68, 778, 1181, *1190-92
Convention on the Elimination of All Forms of Discrimination against (1979), 667, *1190-92, 1193
Optional Protocol (1999), 667, 1190
and development, *1177-81
Division for the Advancement of (UN), 779-80, 1192
Gender Evaluation Report, June 2003, 493, 1081
the girl child, 778-79, 1174, *1185-87, 1208-1209
health
HIV/AIDS, 1174
traditional practices affecting, 778, 1174-75
human rights, 777-80, *1175-77
human settlements, role in, 1083
institutional mechanisms for the advancement of, *1187-89
Inter-Agency Network on Women and Gender Equality (UN), 882, 1187
International Research and Training Institute for the Advancement of, *1194-1201, 1462
in Latin America and the Caribbean, 1022-23
married to foreigners, 716-17
and the media, *1183-85
migrant workers, 778, *1172-74
Office of the Special Adviser on Gender Issues and Advancement of (UN), 1164
older women in society, 1177
in Palestine, *493-95, 1177
peacekeeping operations, 74-75
in power and decision-making, 1167-69

property and housing, right to, 769-70
refugees, 1230
rights of, mainstreaming, 779-80
in rural areas, *1181-83
traffic in women and girls, 75, 780
UN, status in, 1189-90, *1448-51
UNIFEM, see United Nations Development Fund for Women
violence against, 777-78, *1169-72
in Western Asia, *1028-29
World Conference on, Fourth (1995), 778
follow-up, *1164-90
World Assembly on Ageing, Second (2002), *1218-21
WORLD BANK, 1516-17
Africa, 1003
Angola, 270
Central African Republic, 157
children, support to, 1203, 1206, 1210
counter-terrorism, cooperation on, 68
development, 832, 890, 987
operational activities, 882
education, 770
energy, 1031
environment, 1043, 1045
human rights, 714, 765
indigenous people, 799
Iraq, 350
Israeli-occupied territories, 460
Joint IMF/World Bank Development Committee, 981, 984
landlocked developing countries, 876
poverty reduction, 753, 765, 893
Somalia, 243, 248
statistics, 1291
UN, collaboration with, 888
UN/World Bank International Reconstruction Fund Facility for Iraq, 353, 896
World Climate Change Conference, 1056
World Commission on Renewable Energy, 1031
World Commission on the Social Dimension of Globalization, 757, 832
World Conference on Education for All (1990), 1086
World Conference on Human Rights (1993), 677-78
World Conference against Racism, Racial Discrimination, Xenophobia and Related Intolerance (2001), 674, *695-703, 798, 799, 800
Durban Declaration and Programme of Action, *696-703
World Conference on Women, Fourth (1995), 778, *1164-90
World Conservation Monitoring Centre, 1047, 1068
World Conservation Union, 1046, 1068-69
World Database on Protected Areas, 1068-69
World Customs Organization, 68, 876, 1279
World Economic Forum, 939
World Economic Situation and Prospects, 863, 966
World Economic and Social Survey, 2003, 862, 966, 980
World Education Forum (2000), 1209
World Food Programme (WFP), see food
World Food Security, Committee on, 1260
World Food Summits (1996 and 2002), 766, 1260

WORLD HEALTH ORGANIZATION (WHO), 1514-15
- children, 780, 1207
- Côte d'Ivoire, 171
- DPRK, 936
- drug control, 1268
- HIV/AIDS, 1245, 1248
- malaria, 1251
- oversight, external, 1388
- refugees, 1223
- road safety, 1257
- Somalia, 243
- statistics, 1293
- UNICEF/WHO Global Strategy for Infant and Young Child Feeding, 1207
- violence prevention, 772
- WHO Framework Convention on Tobacco Control, 1251

WORLD INTELLECTUAL PROPERTY ORGANIZATION (WIPO), 757, 799, 1003, 1377, 1530-31

WORLD METEOROLOGICAL ORGANIZATION (WMO), 957, 1014, 1056, 1527-28

World Programme of Action concerning Disabled Persons (1982), *1105-1107

World Programme of Action for Youth to the Year 2000 and Beyond (1995), 1214-15

World Public Information Campaign on Human Rights (1988), 686-87

World Public Sector Report, 865

World Solar Programme (1996-2005), *1030-32

World Solidarity Fund (poverty eradication), 852, *889-90, 1041

World Summit on the Information Society, 641, 745, *857-59, 999, 1003, 1016, 1102, 1183

World Summit for Social Development (1995), *1096-99, 1101, 1220

World Summit on Sustainable Development (2002), 636, 641, 643-44, 799, 835, *838-42, 852, 898, 972, 977, 999, 1010, 1016, 1019, 1030, 1042-44

World Tourism Organization (WTO-OMT)
- conversion to specialized agency, *1474-78
- ecotourism, 1074

WORLD TRADE ORGANIZATION (WTO), 967-68, 1535-36
- development
  - financing for, 987
  - and international economic cooperation, 832
- free-trade arrangements, 912
- globalization, 757
- indigenous people, 757, 799
- international trade, 965, 974
- landlocked developing countries, 876
- Ministerial Conference, Fifth (Cancún), 967, 968, 997, 1006, 1021
- Ministerial Conference, Fourth (2001, Doha), 881, 967-68, 972, 978, 987, 992, 1010, 1253
- policy and advisory services, 1044
- pollution control, cooperation on, 1070
- poverty reduction policies, 765
- Working Group on Trade, Debt and Finance, 984

World Urban Forum, 1075, 1079

World Water Forum, Third, 1034

Yokohama Strategy for a Safer World (1994), 958

YOUTH, *1214-18
- employment, *1215-18
- Global Partnership Initiative on Urban Youth Development in Africa, 1078
- Tunza International Youth Conference, First, 1046
- World Programme of Action for Youth to the Year 2000 and Beyond (1995), 1214-15
- *World Youth Report 2003*, 1214-15

ZAMBIA
- humanitarian assistance, 933

ZIMBABWE
- human rights, 814
- humanitarian assistance, 933

Index of resolutions and decisions

Resolution/decision numbers in italics indicate that the text is summarized rather than reprinted in full. (For dates of sessions, refer to Appendix III.)

General Assembly

Fifty-seventh session

Resolution No.	Page
57/4	
Res. C	1427
57/228	
Res. B	385
57/270	
Res. B	1468
57/278	
Res. B	91
57/281	
Res. B	1448
57/283	
Res. B	1481
57/287	
Res. C	1387
57/290	
Res. B	83
57/291	
Res. B	221
57/301	1464
57/302	56
57/303	1385
57/304	1492
57/305	1440
57/306	1237
57/307	1459
57/308	1243
57/309	1257
57/310	1434
57/311	1200
57/312	975
57/313	659
57/314	93
57/315	73
57/316	98
57/317	88
57/318	86
57/319	90
57/320	96
57/321	94
57/322	98
57/323	85
57/324	527
57/325	520
57/326	428
57/327	382
57/328	240
57/329	271
57/330	360
57/331	266
57/332	454
57/333	442
57/334	398
57/335	137
57/336	79
57/337	50
57/338	1452

Decision No.	Page
57/405	
Dec. B	1558, 1563
57/406	
Dec. B	1569
57/411	
Dec. B	1560
Dec. C	1560
57/413	
Dec. B	1558
57/414	
Dec. A	1321
Dec. B	1323
Dec. C	1324
57/415	892, 1569
57/416	1558
57/417	998, 1569
57/418	1569
57/419	1569
57/420	1569
57/503	
Dec. B	1463
57/556	
Dec. B	1386, 1429, 1448, 1458, 1463
57/586	71
57/587	1394, 1463
57/588	88, 94, 95, 99, 1429, 1435, 1436, 1463
57/589	1458
57/590	93
57/591	1391
57/592	530
57/593	989
57/594	989
57/595	1389, 1463
57/596	445, 1463
57/597	137, 1463
57/598	1393, 1463
57/599	385, 1463

Fifty-eighth session

Resolution No.	Page
58/1	
Res. A	1424
Res. B	1424
58/2	978
58/3	1256
58/4	1127
58/5	1111
58/6	1112
58/7	286
58/8	1033
58/9	1258
58/10	596
58/11	689
58/12	1162
58/13	594
58/14	1347
58/15	1103
58/16	49
58/17	1114
58/18	500
58/19	501
58/20	502
58/21	497
58/22	484
58/23	524
58/24	961
58/25	955
58/26	931
58/27	
Res. A	304
Res. B	934
58/28	570
58/29	597
58/30	554
58/31	555
58/32	639
58/33	640
58/34	556
58/35	533
58/36	582
58/37	546
58/38	577
58/39	578
58/40	553
58/41	1390
58/42	569
58/43	578
58/44	581
58/45	584
58/46	552
58/47	536
58/48	580
58/49	557
58/50	537
58/51	538
58/52	561
58/53	572
58/54	568
58/55	576
58/56	541
58/57	533
58/58	563
58/59	543
58/60	590
58/61	587
58/62	589
58/63	586
58/64	551
58/65	574
58/66	531
58/67	530
58/68	550
58/69	566
58/70	455
58/71	547
58/72	559
58/73	1370
58/74	1337
58/75	1374
58/76	1376
58/77	1334

Resolution No.	Page
58/78	1373
58/79	1333
58/80	1367
58/81	1339
58/82	1342
58/83	1479
58/84	1479
58/85	1479
58/86	1480
58/87	1461
58/88	650
58/89	646
58/90	642
58/91	509
58/92	514
58/93	510
58/94	514
58/95	512
58/96	490
58/97	491
58/98	492
58/99	489
58/100	524
58/101	
Res. A	623
Res. B	623
58/102	607
58/103	605
58/104	602
58/105	608
58/106	612
58/107	615
58/108	
Res. A	616
Res. B	619
58/109	264
58/110	606
58/111	598
58/112	868
58/113	504
58/114	919
58/115	928
58/116	946
58/117	950
58/118	922
58/119	963
58/120	951
58/121	953
58/122	1453
58/123	944
58/124	1109
58/125	1463
58/126	1389
58/127	924
58/128	1110
58/129	836
58/130	1097
58/131	1102
58/132	1105
58/133	1217
58/134	1220

GENERAL ASSEMBLY, 58th SESSION (cont.)

Resolution No.	Page	Resolution No.	Page	Resolution No.	Page	Decision No.	Page
58/135	1126	58/197	968	58/259		58/514	316, 1464
58/136	1149	58/198	838	Res. A	139	58/515	571, 1464
58/137	1151	58/199	861	58/260		58/516	57, 1464
58/138	1117	58/200	860	Res. A	384	58/517	545
58/139	1124	58/201	877	58/261		58/518	555, 1464
58/140	1120	58/202	981	Res. A	200	58/519	568, 1464
58/141	1263	58/203	984	58/262	1458	58/520	584
58/142	1167	58/204	978	58/263	1497	58/521	530, 1464
58/143	1173	58/205	1148	58/264	1436	58/522	1375
58/144	1449	58/206	1178	58/265	1435	58/523	1374, 1464
58/145	1191	58/207	1159	58/266	1436	58/524	79
58/146	1181	58/208	1087	58/267		58/525	622
58/147	1170	58/209	1037	Res. A	1397	58/526	611
58/148	1165	58/210	1031	Res. B	1398	58/527	316, 458, 1464
58/149	1234	58/211	1055	58/268	1430	58/528	832, 1464
58/150	1231	58/212	1052	58/269	1395	58/529	1085
58/151	1224	58/213		58/270	1399	58/530	1103
58/152	1227	Res. A	873	58/271		58/531	1117, 1125, 1148
58/153	1226	58/214	958	Res. A	1414	58/532	1190
58/154	1240	58/215	960	Res. B	1416	58/533	1194, 1199
58/155	495	58/216	1063	Res. C	1416	58/534	1245
58/156	1185	58/217	1034	58/272	1417	58/535	674, 698
58/157	781	58/218	840	58/273	1422	58/536	661
58/158	802	58/219	848	58/274	1421	58/537	669, 670, 675, 777
58/159	705	58/220	913	58/275	175	58/538	665, 707, 754, 762
58/160	699	58/221	854	58/276	1499		
58/161	720	58/222	849	58/277	1499	58/539	679, 684, 779, 809, 819, 820, 825
58/162	723	58/223	1161	58/278	1496		
58/163	721	58/224	1456	58/279	1458		
58/164	742	58/225	832	58/280	1499		
58/165	671	58/226	1076	Decision No.	Page	58/540	678
58/166	676	58/227	1079	58/401	1569	58/541	658
58/167	710	58/228	870	58/402	1223, 1569	58/542	1464
58/168	660	58/229	487	58/403	1560	58/543	1466
58/169	792	58/230	989	58/404	1559	58/544	832
58/170	661	58/231	866	58/405		58/545	860
58/171	762	58/232	1475	Dec. A	1569	58/546	858
58/172	754	58/233	941	Dec. B	1557	58/547	878, 1011
58/173	773	58/234	154	58/406	1562	58/548	832
58/174	747	58/235	106	58/407	1559	58/549	837
58/175	692	58/236	1245	58/408	1558, 1563	58/550	1042
58/176	694	58/237	1252	58/409	1558	58/551	1194
58/177	794	58/238	283	58/410	1558	58/552	1094, 1466
58/178	665	58/239	276	58/411		58/553	1464
58/179	1253	58/240	1355	Dec. A	1559	58/554	1062
58/180	737	58/241	564	58/412	1557, 1569	58/555	1093
58/181	688	58/242	1053	58/413	1557	58/556	1466
58/182	714	58/243	1049	58/414	1558	58/557	97, 1500
58/183	725	58/244	1199	58/415	1559	58/558	1238
58/184	718	58/245	790	58/416	1559	58/559	361
58/185	1172	58/246	1108	58/501	1462	58/560	1429
58/186	767	58/247	820	58/502	1462	58/561	1500
58/187	748	58/248	1365	58/503		58/562	638
58/188	662	58/249		Dec. A	1463	58/563	1464
58/189	738	Res. A	1428	58/504	1320	58/564	
58/190	708	58/250	1486	58/505	1310	Dec. A	99, 1386, 1387, 1388, 1444, 1448, 1461, 1464, 1467
58/191	680	58/251	1432	58/506	3		
58/192	750	58/252	1326	58/507	1465		
58/193	758	58/253	1327	58/508	1465	58/565	3, 79, 85, 91, 175, 201, 306, 361, 385, 499, 511, 661, 678, 860, 937, 961, 1110, 1113, 1163, 1203,
58/194	823	58/254	1318	58/509	989		
58/195	817	58/255	1318	58/510	1300		
58/196	811	58/256	91	58/511	610, 1464		
		58/257	98	58/512	269, 1464		
		58/258	97	58/513	1464		

Index of resolutions and decisions

GENERAL ASSEMBLY, 58th SESSION (cont.)

Decision No.	Page
58/565 (cont.)	1245, 1259, 1320, 1329, 1384, 1385, 1390, 1391, 1392, 1396, 1398, 1416, 1427, 1429, 1430, 1462, 1463, 1464, 1465, 1466, 1474, 1489

Tenth emergency special session

Resolution No.	Page
ES-10/12	472
ES-10/13	477
ES-10/14	480

Decision No.	Page
ES-10/22	481

Security Council

Resolution No.	Page
1455(2003)	311
1456(2003)	63
1457(2003)	140
1458(2003)	201
1459(2003)	55
1460(2003)	788
1461(2003)	517
1462(2003)	431
1463(2003)	259
1464(2003)	168
1465(2003)	285
1466(2003)	233
1467(2003)	161
1468(2003)	118
1469(2003)	259
1470(2003)	213
1471(2003)	295
1472(2003)	363
1473(2003)	374
1474(2003)	252
1475(2003)	449
1476(2003)	365
1477(2003)	1323
1478(2003)	203
1479(2003)	173
1480(2003)	377
1481(2003)	1315
1482(2003)	1322
1483(2003)	338
1484(2003)	126
1485(2003)	261
1486(2003)	453
1487(2003)	77
1488(2003)	526
1489(2003)	128
1490(2003)	359
1491(2003)	400
1492(2003)	217
1493(2003)	130
1494(2003)	435
1495(2003)	262

Resolution No.	Page
1496(2003)	519
1497(2003)	190
1498(2003)	177
1499(2003)	142
1500(2003)	346
1501(2003)	132
1502(2003)	921
1503(2003)	1330
1504(2003)	1316
1505(2003)	1325
1506(2003)	268
1507(2003)	237
1508(2003)	218
1509(2003)	194
1510(2003)	310
1511(2003)	348
1512(2003)	1324
1513(2003)	264
1514(2003)	181
1515(2003)	483
1516(2003)	65
1517(2003)	453
1518(2003)	362
1519(2003)	254
1520(2003)	526
1521(2003)	208

Economic and Social Council

Organizational session, 2003

Resolution No.	Page
2003/1	948

Decision No.	Page
2003/201 A	1564
2003/202	1465
2003/203	1466
2003/204	1465
2003/205	999, 1466
2003/206	1465
2003/207	865
2003/208	1480
2003/209	987

First resumed organizational session, 2003

Decision No.	Page
2003/210	915, 1248, 1466
2003/211	880, 1466
2003/212	1480
2003/213	1480
2003/214	992
2003/215 A	1475, 1563

Second resumed organizational session, 2003

Decision No.	Page
2003/201 B	1558, 1559, 1563, 1564
2003/201 C	1564

Decision No.	Page
2003/215 B	1563
2003/216	1480
2003/217	1480
2003/218	802
2003/219	804
2003/220	1271

Third resumed organizational session, 2003

Decision No.	Page
2003/201 D	1564
2003/221	1480
2003/222	1478

Substantive session, 2003

Resolution No.	Page
2003/2	1475
2003/3	883
2003/4	889
2003/5	916
2003/6	1474
2003/7	1015
2003/8	1028
2003/9	1028
2003/10	1103
2003/11	1216
2003/12	1107
2003/13	940
2003/14	1219
2003/15	1100
2003/16	947
2003/17	868
2003/18	1249
2003/19	858
2003/20	1151
2003/21	1125
2003/22	1149
2003/23	1117
2003/24	1123
2003/25	1119
2003/26	1154
2003/27	1069
2003/28	1153
2003/29	1115
2003/30	1155
2003/31	1116
2003/32	1280
2003/33	1283
2003/34	1285
2003/35	1285
2003/36	1267
2003/37	1286
2003/38	1287
2003/39	1269
2003/40	1268
2003/41	1269
2003/42	494
2003/43	1175
2003/44	1183
2003/45	772
2003/46	952
2003/47	987

Resolution No.	Page
2003/48	1494
2003/49	1188
2003/50	947
2003/51	600
2003/52	1004
2003/53	949
2003/54	859
2003/55	871
2003/56	855
2003/57	1195
2003/58	658
2003/59	486
2003/60	865
2003/61	842
2003/62	1075
2003/63	1062
2003/64	994

Decision No.	Page
2003/223	1465
2003/224	1093
2003/225	864, 883, 892, 893, 911, 1035, 1090, 1204, 1259
2003/226	916, 919
2003/227	1260, 1295, 1468, 1474
2003/228	1001, 1015
2003/229	1094
2003/230	1099
2003/231	1564
2003/232	776
2003/233	1117
2003/234	1564
2003/235	1282
2003/236	1271
2003/237	1192
2003/238	825
2003/239	819
2003/240	810
2003/241	808
2003/242	670
2003/243	760
2003/244	766
2003/245	769
2003/246	698
2003/247	733
2003/248	742
2003/249	740
2003/250	735
2003/251	778
2003/252	717
2003/253	802
2003/254	798
2003/255	665
2003/256	746
2003/257	679
2003/258	685
2003/259	684
2003/260	683
2003/261	754
2003/262	818
2003/263	683
2003/264	760

ECONOMIC AND SOCIAL
  COUNCIL, SUBSTANTIVE
  SESSION, 2003 *(cont.)*

Decision No.	Page	Decision No.	Page	Decision No.	Page	Decision No.	Page
		2003/280	868	*2003/297*	1062	*Resumed substantive session, 2003*	
		2003/281	865, 868	*2003/298*	1062		
2003/265	724	*2003/282*	941	*2003/299*	1058		
2003/266	796	*2003/283*	872	*2003/300*	804	Decision No.	Page
2003/267	805	*2003/284*	1290	*2003/301*	804, 1465	2003/201 E	1558, 1559, 1563, 1564, 1566
2003/268	752	*2003/285*	1227	*2003/302*	804		
2003/269	656	*2003/286*	1227	*2003/303*	804		
2003/270	656	*2003/287*	853, 869, 1466	*2003/304*	804	2003/311	947
2003/271	801	*2003/288*	1467	*2003/305*	804	*2003/312*	1480
2003/272	1486	*2003/289*	848	*2003/306*	804	*2003/313*	993
2003/273	504	*2003/290*	853	*2003/307*	804	*2003/314*	1392
2003/274	1001	*2003/291*	857	*2003/308*	1392	*2003/315*	1063
2003/275	1481	*2003/292*	487	*2003/309*	858, 993, 1035, 1037, 1079, 1367	*2003/316*	848
2003/276	1481	*2003/293*	857			*2003/317*	1290
2003/277	1481	*2003/294*	1035	*2003/310*	655, 671, 696, 1103, 1105, 1117, 1223		
2003/278	1481	*2003/295*	848				
2003/279	1481	*2003/296*	848				

Index of 2003 Security Council Presidential Statements

Number	Subject	Date	Page
S/PRST/2003/1	Security Council resolutions 1160(1998), 1199(1998), 1203(1998), 1239(1999) and 1244(1999)	6 February	414
S/PRST/2003/2	The situation in Somalia	12 March	243
S/PRST/2003/3	Threats to international peace and security caused by terrorist acts	4 April	67
S/PRST/2003/4	The situation in Burundi	2 May	148
S/PRST/2003/5	The role of the Security Council in the pacific settlement of disputes	13 May	57
S/PRST/2003/6	The situation concerning the Democratic Republic of the Congo	16 May	123
S/PRST/2003/7	The situation in Afghanistan	17 June	299
S/PRST/2003/8	The situation in Guinea-Bissau	19 June	225
S/PRST/2003/9	The situation in the Middle East	26 June	526
S/PRST/2003/10	The situation between Eritrea and Ethiopia	17 July	235
S/PRST/2003/11	The situation in Côte d'Ivoire	25 July	176
S/PRST/2003/12	Security Council mission	25 July	109
S/PRST/2003/13	Threats to international peace and security caused by terrorist acts	20 August	347
S/PRST/2003/14	The situation in Liberia	27 August	192
S/PRST/2003/15	Justice and the rule of law: the United Nations role	24 September	60
S/PRST/2003/16	Letter dated 2 October 2003 from the Permanent Representative of the Sudan to the United Nations addressed to the President of the Security Council	10 October	257
S/PRST/2003/17	Threats to international peace and security caused by terrorist acts	16 October	69
S/PRST/2003/18	International Criminal Tribunal for Rwanda	27 October	1329
S/PRST/2003/19	The situation in Somalia	11 November	249
S/PRST/2003/20	The situation in Côte d'Ivoire	13 November	181
S/PRST/2003/21	The situation concerning the Democratic Republic of the Congo	19 November	145
S/PRST/2003/22	The importance of mine action for peacekeeping operations	19 November	100
S/PRST/2003/23	The situation in the Great Lakes region	20 November	112
S/PRST/2003/24	The situation between Iraq and Kuwait	20 November	369
S/PRST/2003/25	The situation in Côte d'Ivoire	4 December	183
S/PRST/2003/26	Security Council resolutions 1160(1998), 1199(1998), 1203(1998), 1239(1999) and 1244(1999)	12 December	420
S/PRST/2003/27	Protection of civilians in armed conflict	15 December	727
S/PRST/2003/28	The situation between Iraq and Kuwait	18 December	357
S/PRST/2003/29	The situation in the Middle East	22 December	526
S/PRST/2003/30	The situation in Burundi	22 December	153

How to obtain volumes of the *Yearbook*

Recent volumes of the *Yearbook* may be obtained in many bookstores throughout the world, as well as from United Nations Publications, Room DC2-853, United Nations, New York, N.Y. 10017, or from United Nations Publications, Palais des Nations, CH-1211 Geneva 10, Switzerland.

Older editions are available in microfiche.

Yearbook of the United Nations, 2002
Vol. 56. Sales No. E.04.I.1 $150.

Yearbook of the United Nations, 2001
Vol. 55. Sales No. E.03.I.1 $150.

Yearbook of the United Nations, 2000
Vol. 54. Sales No. E.02.I.1 $150.

Yearbook of the United Nations, 1999
Vol. 53. Sales No. E.01.I.4 $150.

Yearbook of the United Nations, 1998
Vol. 52. Sales No. E.01.I.1 $150.

Yearbook of the United Nations, 1997
Vol. 51. Sales No. E.00.I.1 $150.

Yearbook of the United Nations, 1996
Vol. 50. Sales No. E.97.I.1 $150.

Yearbook of the United Nations, 1995
Vol. 49. Sales No. E.96.I.1 $150.

Yearbook of the United Nations, 1994
Vol. 48. Sales No. E.95.I.1 $150.

Yearbook of the United Nations, 1993
Vol. 47. Sales No. E.94.I.1 $150.

Yearbook of the United Nations, 1992
Vol. 46. Sales No. E.93.I.1 $150.

Yearbook of the United Nations, 1991
Vol. 45. Sales No. E.92.I.1 $115.

Yearbook of the United Nations, 1990
Vol. 44. Sales No. E.98.I.16 $150.

Yearbook of the United Nations, 1989
Vol. 43. Sales No. E.97.I.11 $150.

Yearbook of the United Nations, 1988
Vol. 42. Sales No. E.93.I.100 $150.

Yearbook of the United Nations, 1987
Vol. 41. Sales No. E.91.I.1 $105.

Yearbook of the United Nations, 1986
Vol. 40. Sales No. E.90.I.1 $95.

Yearbook of the United Nations
Special Edition
UN Fiftieth Anniversary
1945-1995
Sales No. E.95.I.50 $95

The first 56 volumes of the *Yearbook of the United Nations* (1946-2002) are now available on CD-ROM in both single-user ($300, Sales No. E.04.I.9) and network ($500, Sales No. E.04.I.8) versions. Special rates are available for individuals and least developed countries. For more information, contact United Nations Publications at the above address.